Florida Rules of Court

Volume III – Local

2019

Mat #42146227

ISBN 978–1–539–20485–5

PREFACE

Designed for use in the office or courtroom, this pamphlet contains selected Florida local rules of court.

WHAT'S NEW

Florida Rules of Court, Volume III – Local, 2019, includes rules and associated material governing practice before the second, fourth, sixth, seventh, ninth, eleventh, thirteenth, fifteenth, seventeenth, eighteenth, and twentieth judicial circuits. It is current with amendments received through February 1, 2019.

CONTACT US

For additional information or research assistance, call the reference attorneys at 1-800-REF-ATTY (1-800-733-2889). Contact our U.S. legal editorial department directly with your questions and suggestions by e-mail at editors.us-legal@tr.com.

Thank you for subscribing to this product. Should you have any questions regarding this product please contact Customer Service at 1-800-328-4880 or by fax at 1-800-340-9378. If you would like to inquire about related publications, or to place an order, please contact us at 1-888-728-7677 or visit us at legalsolutions.thomsonreuters.com.

THE PUBLISHER

March 2019

THOMSON REUTERS PROVIEW™

This title is one of many now available on your tablet as an eBook.

Take your research mobile. Powered by the Thomson Reuters ProView™ app, our eBooks deliver the same trusted content as your print resources, but in a compact, on-the-go format.

ProView eBooks are designed for the way you work. You can add your own notes and highlights to the text, and all of your annotations will transfer electronically to every new edition of your eBook.

You can also instantly verify primary authority with built-in links to WestlawNext® and KeyCite®, so you can be confident that you're accessing the most current and accurate information.

To find out more about ProView eBooks and available discounts, call 1-800-344-5009.

TABLE OF CONTENTS

WEST'S FLORIDA LOCAL RULES AND ADMINISTRATIVE ORDERS

Second Judicial Circuit (Gadsden, Franklin, Jefferson, Leon, Liberty, and Wakulla Counties)

ADMINISTRATIVE ORDERS

Administrative Orders

2018–10. RISK PROTECTION ORDER ASSIGNMENTS AND PROCEDURES

IN THE SECOND JUDICIAL CIRCUIT OF FLORIDA

OFFICE OF THE CHIEF JUDGE

ADMINISTRATIVE ORDER 2018–10

IN RE: RISK PROTECTION ORDER ASSIGNMENTS AND PROCEDURES

WHEREAS, on March 9, 2018, Governor Risk Scott signed into law the "Marjory Stoneman Douglas High School Public Safety Act," which, among other things, created section 790.401, Florida Statutes.

WHEREAS, section 790.401, Florida Statutes, creates a new judicial proceeding where law enforcement can petition the circuit court for a Risk Protection Order to prevent persons who are at high risk of harming themselves or others from possessing or purchasing firearms or ammunition, gives the circuit courts of the state jurisdiction over such risk protection proceedings, and creates specific duties for the Court, it is therefore

ORDERED that in accordance with section 790.401, Florida Statutes, the Second Judicial Circuit hereby establishes, effective upon the signing of this administrative order, the following procedures for all cases in which a party seeks issuance, enforcement, vacation, or extension of a temporary or final Risk Protection Order. Petitions for Risk Protection Orders, Temporary Ex Parte Risk Protection Orders, and compliance hearings, pursuant to section 790.401(7)(f), that come before the Second Judicial Circuit, will be heard as follows:

I. LEON COUNTY ASSIGNMENTS.

A. Requests for Temporary Ex Parte Risk Protection Orders will be heard by the rotating Leon County First Appearance Judge, as assigned by the current administrative order In Re: Circuit and County Judge Assignments.

B. Petitions for Risk Protection Orders will be heard by Leon County Judge Augustus D. Aikens, Jr. in the Probate Division, and will be assigned an "MH" designation by the Clerk.

C. All compliance hearings held pursuant to section 790.401(7)(f), Florida Statutes, will be heard by the rotating Leon County First Appearance Judge, as assigned by the current administrative order In Re: Circuit and County Judge Assignments.

II. FRANKLIN COUNTY, GADSDEN COUNTY, JEFFERSON COUNTY, LIBERTY COUNTY, AND WAKULLA COUNTY ASSIGNMENTS.

A. All cases in which a party seeks issuance, enforcement, vacation, or extension of a temporary or final Risk Protection Order will be heard by the circuit judge assigned to the Probate Division, pursuant to the current administrative order In Re: Circuit and County Judge Assignments.

B. Circuit judges assigned to Franklin, Gadsden, Jefferson, Liberty, and Wakulla Counties shall communicate with the county judge in each county to ensure effective coverage of Risk Protection Order proceedings, in the event that they are unavailable.

III. CIRCUIT–WIDE PROCEDURES. Upon receipt of a petition for a Risk Protection Order, which may be accompanied by a request for a Temporary Ex Parte Risk Protection Order, the Second Judicial Circuit will utilize the following procedures:

A. Temporary Ex Parte Risk Protection Orders.

1. Upon filing of a request for a Temporary Ex Parte Risk Protection Order, a hearing will be heard the day the petition is filed or on the next business day. The hearing may be conducted by telephone. The Court must receive assurances of the identity of the petitioner before conducting a telephonic hearing.

2. Upon finding that there is reasonable cause to believe that the respondent poses a significant danger of causing personal injury to himself or herself or others in the near future by having in his or her custody or control, or by purchasing, possessing, or receiving, a firearm or ammunition, the Court must issue a Temporary Ex Parte Risk Protection Order.

3. A Temporary Ex Parte Risk Protection Order terminates upon the hearing on the Risk Protection Order.

4. If it should become necessary to seek a warrant under section 790.401(7)(d), Florida Statutes, the current procedures for warrants in criminal cases shall be followed.

B. Risk Protection Orders.

1. Upon receipt of a petition, the Court must order a hearing to be held no later than 14 days after receipt of the petition and must issue a notice of hearing to the respondent. The hearing may be conducted by telephone. The Court must receive assurances of the identity of the petitioner before conducting a telephonic hearing.

2. The Clerk of Court shall cause a copy of the notice of hearing and petition to be forwarded on or before the next business day to the appropriate law enforcement agency for service upon the respondent.

3. Upon notice and a hearing, if the Court finds by clear and convincing evidence that the respondent poses a significant danger of causing personal injury to himself or herself or others by having in his or her custody or control, or by purchasing, possessing, or receiving, a firearm or any ammunition, the Court must issue a Risk Protection Order for a period that it deems appropriate, up to and including but not exceeding 12 months.

4. If the Court issues a Risk Protection Order, the Court must inform the respondent that he or she is entitled to request a hearing to vacate the order in the manner provided by section 790.401(6), Florida Statutes. The Court shall provide the respondent with a form to request a hearing to vacate.

5. Upon receipt of the request for a hearing to vacate a Risk Protection Order, the Court shall set a date for a hearing. The hearing must occur no sooner than 14 days and no later than 30 days after the date of service of the request upon the petitioner.

C. Compliance Hearings Pursuant to section 790.401(7)(f), Florida Statutes.

1. Upon the issuance of a Risk Protection Order, including a Temporary Ex Parte Risk Protection Order, the Court shall set a hearing date and require the respondent to appear no later than three business days after the issuance of the order. The Court shall require proof that the respondent has surrendered any firearms or ammunition owned by the respondent in the respondent's custody, control, or possession.

2. The Court may cancel the hearing upon a satisfactory showing that the respondent is in compliance with the order.

D. Miscellaneous Matters.

1. The Clerk of Court shall provide the Sheriff with a copy of any pleading or order required to be served under section 790.401, Florida Statutes.

2. When requested by a law enforcement agency authorized to effect service under section 790.401, Florida Statutes, the Clerk of Court may transmit via email, facsimile, or other electronic transmission permitted under the Florida Rules of Judicial Administration.

3. In order to effectuate service of process under section 790.401, Florida Statutes, a juvenile respondent shall be identified by full name. The Clerk of Court shall independently determine what portions of any pleadings and any documents filed in support of the petition shall be available for public viewing. The Court will strive to balance a juvenile's right to privacy against public safety.

4. The Second Judicial Circuit will require and use the standard petition and order forms prepared by the Office of the State Courts Administrator pursuant to section 790.401(14), Florida Statutes. These forms will be made available on the Clerk of Court website.

DONE and ORDERED in chambers in Tallahassee, Leon County, Florida, this 14th day of June, 2018.

JONATHAN SJOSTROM
Chief Judge

Adopted effective June 14, 2018.

2018-09. SECOND JUDICIAL CIRCUIT ALTERNATIVE DISPUTE RESOLUTION PROGRAM

IN THE SECOND JUDICIAL CIRCUIT OF FLORIDA

OFFICE OF THE CHIEF JUDGE

ADMINISTRATIVE ORDER NO. 2018–09

IN RE: SECOND JUDICIAL CIRCUIT ALTERNATIVE DISPUTE RESOLUTION PROGRAM

WHEREAS, this Court finds mediation and other forms of alternative dispute resolution to be effective tools to reduce litigation, speed resolution, reduce Court workload, maintain litigant privacy, increase finality, and reduce costs; and

WHEREAS, this Court orders mediation and appoints mediators when required by law; and

WHEREAS, rule 1.810(a), Florida Rules of Civil Procedure, requires that the Chief Judge shall maintain a list of qualified persons to serve as arbitrators; and

WHEREAS, Supreme Court of Florida Administrative Order No: AOSC14–64, In Re: Parent Coordinator Application Form and Training Standards, requires "the chief judge or designee(s) ... shall review each application and determine which individuals applying to serve as parent coordinators meet the qualifications ... to be included on a list of qualified parent coordinators for that circuit. Further, each judicial circuit shall establish and maintain a list of parent coordinators from which the court may appoint a qualified parent coordinator;"

WHEREAS, the Florida Legislature has enacted numerous changes to Chapter 44, Florida Statutes, which addresses some or all of the subject matter of these administrative orders and has superseded many provisions thereof; and

WHEREAS, this Court previously entered Administrative Order 06–05 regarding court ordered mediation services and it is outdated or obsolete and must be rescinded to conform to current statutes and procedures; and

NOW, THEREFORE, pursuant to the authority conferred by Rule 2.215, Florida Rules of Judicial Administration, it is **ORDERED** as follows:

1. An Alternative Dispute Resolution (ADR) Unit for the Second Judicial Circuit is hereby re-established by the Court, under the supervision of the Office of Court Administration. The ADR Unit shall be responsible for establishing and executing procedures relating to family, juvenile dependency, Unified Family Court, small claims, and county civil alternative dispute resolution matters which are the responsibility of the Court, except for all referrals made by the Court from a list of Court-appointed mediators or to private mediators. All mediators which conduct Court-ordered mediations shall be certified by the Supreme Court of Florida in the area of certification which is applicable to the type of case being referred.

2. The provisions of Chapters 39, 44, and 61, Florida Statutes, and the applicable provisions of the Florida Rules of Civil Procedure, Florida Rules of Family Law Procedure, and Florida Rules of Juvenile Procedure, and any amendments thereto, as they relate to mediation, are hereby adopted, and incorporated into this Order, and shall become the procedure to be utilized by the ADR Unit, which includes, but is not limited to, setting mediation conferences and establishing the appropriate fee schedule for the Second Judicial Circuit. The fees required by those statutes shall be paid in full by the parties prior to the scheduled mediation session. Failure to pay all mediation fees prior to the mediation session may result in the cancellation of the mediation session and may result in the Court's imposition of sanctions.

3. The Clerks of the Circuit Court for each county shall collect all applicable fees and remit them to the Florida Department of Revenue for deposit into the State Courts Revenue Trust Fund and submit to the Chief Judge, no later than 30 days after the end of each quarter, a report specifying the amount of funds collected during each quarter of the fiscal year as provided by section 44.108, Florida Statutes.

4. All matters pertaining to those divisions set forth in paragraph 1 hereof, which the presiding judges deem appropriate shall be referred to mediation on any contested issue, other than temporary injunctions for domestic and repeat violence, and shall participate in mediation prior to final

hearing or trial. The mediator shall report that mediation is completed prior to final hearing or trial. The presiding judge shall refer all actions described herein to mediation by an order incorporating all requirements of the statutes or rules relating to the division in which the case is pending. All orders of referral shall be standardized within such divisions.

5. Family Law (Excluding Dependency): Parties may request to appear telephonically for the mediation conference by contacting the ADR Unit, at least 10 days prior to the mediation conference so long as the following criteria are met:

a. The litigant resides more than 100 miles from the mediation conference location and the litigant has submitted proof that their permanent and physical residence is more than 100 miles from the mediation conference location; or,

b. The litigant has a verifiable medical reason confirmed by a medical professional that prevents the litigant from being able to physically appear and the litigant has submitted proof from the medical professional to the ADR Unit with the request to appear telephonically; and

c. The litigant must have the ability to receive and send documents via facsimile or email during and at the conclusion of the mediation conference unless a party is incarcerated and then the correctional facility policies shall apply.

6. The Director of the ADR Unit shall manage all alternative dispute resolution functions, be responsible for all alternative dispute resolution revenues and expenses and maintain a list of qualified persons to serve as arbitrators and parent coordinators.

7. The Director of the ADR Unit shall collect and analyze statistical information on all Court-appointed circuit mediations each month, identifying the type and number of cases mediated, and any other relevant data.

8. Nothing contained herein shall abrogate the rights and/or obligations required by any statute.

9. Administrative Order 2006–05 is hereby rescinded.

DONE AND ORDERED, in chambers at Tallahassee, Leon County Florida, this 1st day of Jan. 2018.

JONATHAN SJOSTROM
Chief Judge

Adopted effective June 1, 2018.

2018–07. ADMINISTRATIVE ORDER AUTHORIZING CIRCUIT TWO FIRST STEP, INC., A NON–PROFIT CORPORATION, TO ASSIST IN REHABILITATIVE SERVICES TO DEFENDANTS

IN THE SECOND JUDICIAL CIRCUIT OF FLORIDA

OFFICE OF THE CHIEF JUDGE

ADMINISTRATIVE ORDER 2018–07

IN RE: ADMINISTRATIVE ORDER AUTHORIZING CIRCUIT TWO FIRST STEP, INC., A NON–PROFIT CORPORATION, TO ASSIST IN REHABILITATIVE SERVICES TO DEFENDANTS

WHEREAS, Circuit Two First Step, Inc., a non-profit corporation, has been created and established; and

WHEREAS, the primary purpose of Circuit Two First Step is to assist in the rehabilitation of persons placed on supervised probation within the jurisdiction of the Second Judicial Circuit; and

WHEREAS, Circuit Two First Step will provide offenders serving a period of probation in jurisdiction of the Second Judicial Circuit and may provide such services to offenders recently released from the custody of the Department of Corrections who are not on probation, including but not limited to administration of funds collected pursuant to Section 948.039(2) to supplement the rehabilitative efforts of the Department of Corrections;

NOW, THEREFORE, pursuant to the authority conferred by Florida Rule of Judicial Administration 2.215 and Section 948.039(2), Florida Statutes, it is **ORDERED** as follows:

1. Defendants who are sentenced from the Second Judicial Circuit, including a period of probation under the supervision of the Department of Corrections, shall pay a related cost of $1.00 for each month of the probationary term. The presiding judge shall announce the cost at sentencing *ore tenus*. The initial amount due (the first $36.00 (or less, as applicable)) shall be paid within the first one-hundred eighty (180) days after the beginning of the probationary sentence. Further payments, if any, shall be paid in accordance with a schedule to be established by the probation officer. Failure to pay the amount due shall not result in a violation of probation. Each judge in the Circuit Court of the Second Judicial Circuit shall make the payments set forth above a condition of all orders of probation.

2. Payments collected under this order shall be used for the benefit of offenders under the supervision of the Department of Corrections or who have recently been released from the custody of the Department of Corrections who are not on probation in accordance with the by-laws of Circuit Two First Step, Inc.

3. No payments collected pursuant to this order may be applied to costs of supervision, court costs, fines, or any other court-ordered payments.

DONE AND ORDERED in Tallahassee Leon County, on April 24, 2018.

JONATHAN SJOSTROM
Chief Judge

Adopted effective April 24, 2018.

2018–06. UNIFORM BOND SCHEDULE AND PRETRIAL RELEASE PROCEDURES SECOND JUDICIAL CIRCUIT, FLORIDA

IN THE CIRCUIT COURT OF THE
SECOND JUDICIAL CIRCUIT

OFFICE OF THE CHIEF JUDGE

ADMINISTRATIVE ORDER 2018–06

IN RE: UNIFORM BOND SCHEDULE AND PRETRIAL RELEASE PROCEDURES SECOND JUDICIAL CIRCUIT, FLORIDA

WHEREAS, Fla.R.Cr.P. 3.131 provides that unless charged with a capital offense or an offense punishable by life imprisonment and the proof of guilt is evident or the presumption is great, every person charged with a crime or a violation of a municipal or county ordinance shall be entitled to pretrial release on reasonable conditions. If no conditions of release can reasonably protect the community from risk of physical harm to persons, assure the presence of the accused at trial, or assure the integrity of the judicial process, the accused may be detained; and

WHEREAS, section 903.046, Florida Statutes, provides that the purpose of a bail determination in criminal proceedings is to ensure the appearance of the criminal defendant at subsequent proceedings and to protect the community against unreasonable danger from the criminal defendant; and

WHEREAS, section 903.046, Florida Statutes, also provides that in determining whether to release a defendant on bail or other conditions, and what that bail or those conditions may be, the court shall consider the nature and circumstances of the offense charged; the weight of the evidence against the defendant; the defendant's family ties, length of residence in the community, employment history, financial resources and mental conditions; the defendant's past and present conduct related to criminal history; probability of danger to the community; the source of funds to post bail; and the defendant's legal status; and

WHEREAS, section 903.047, Florida Statutes, also provides conditions of pretrial release; and

WHEREAS, there is a need for continued use of a uniform set of standards to ensure a consistent, objective basis for pretrial release and conditions of release prior to first appearance; it is therefore,

ORDERED THAT:

I. GENERAL PROCEDURES

A. General Authority. Pursuant to this order, there is hereby established a Bond Schedule and Pretrial Release Procedures for the Second Judicial Circuit.

B. Duty to Evaluate.

1. *Booking Officer.* For purposes of this administrative order, the term "booking officer" shall mean the employee of the receiving facility who receives the defendant from the arresting officer. It will be the booking officer's responsibility to gather the following information and provide it to the Pretrial Release Officer:

a. The defendant's identity;

b. The defendant's prior record, including national, state, and local charges;

c. The existence of any pending prosecutions or warrants, and whether the defendant is currently on probation;

d. Whether the arrest is as a fugitive from another state, a warrant from another county, a warrant of the parole commission, a bondsman recommit, or other civil matter such as child support or cash purge cases (as to defendants in this category, no further review needs to be conducted);

e. The defendant's most recent release date from the Department of Corrections, if applicable; and

f. If a defendant is arrested for violating probation or community control, determine whether a "danger to the public" hearing pursuant to section 948.06(4), Florida Statutes, (Jessica Lunsford Act) is required).

g. Whether the defendant is required to register as a sexual offender or a sexual predator.

2. *Leon County Supervised Pretrial Release Program.* An officer of the Leon County Supervised Pretrial Release Program (SPRP) shall be on duty at the Leon County Detention Center every day, twenty-four hours a day. The Pretrial Release Officer shall be responsible for collecting initial information from each defendant for use in determining eligibility for pretrial release, unless the defendant has posted bond under the uniform bond schedule, or unless a bond and the conditions relating thereto, if any, have previously been established by a judge of competent jurisdiction, and those provisions have not been countermanded by this administrative order. The information shall include:

a. Whether the defendant has a verifiable, permanent local address;

b. The extent of the defendant's ties, if any, to the community;

c. The existence of any pending domestic violence injunctions or history of injunctions; and

d. An application/affidavit of indigency for public defender and acknowledgment of statutory public defender application fee.

This information shall be recorded on a pretrial release intake interview form, attached to other pertinent arrest documents, including the probable cause affidavit and the victim statement, if applicable, and provided to the Court at first appearance. The pretrial release interview form is Attachment A.[1] This form may be amended as determined by the Chief Judge without need to amend this order. (Attachment A, Leon County Pretrial Defendant Information form.)

C. Classification. All detainees shall be classified by the booking officer as either eligible for immediate release on monetary bond/release on recognizance or requiring further review. The SPRP officer shall further classify the remaining individuals as first appearance required or eligible for the SPRP and/or monetary release.

In a Leon County case, if a judge sets a bond on a warrant and also indicates that the defendant can be treated as if arrested on view, the booking officer/SPRP shall process the defendant as if arrested on view if the defendant is arrested or detained in Leon County. Defendants arrested outside of Leon County shall only be released pursuant to the bond amount set on the warrant.

D. Other counties. In those counties not having a supervised pretrial release program involved in cases prior to first appearance, the booking officer shall be responsible for all of the above duties.

E. First Appearance Required (FAR).

1. *Offenses Requiring First Appearance.* The following offenses shall require a first appearance unless otherwise specified by the judge issuing the warrant. For purposes of this section, any attempt or conspiracy charge shall be treated the same as the substantive offense.

<u>OFFENSES PUNISHABLE BY LIFE IMPRISONMENT:</u>

All Felony charges classified as Capital Felonies;

All Felony charges classified as Life Felonies;

All Felony charges classified as First Degree Felonies Punishable By Life;

SEX OFFENSES:

Sexual Battery (Section 794.011);

Lewd or Lascivious Offenses (Section 800.04);

CRIMES OF VIOLENCE:

Aggravated Battery (Section 784.045);

Aggravated Assault with Deadly Weapon (Section 784.021);

Any Murder or Attempted Murder including Manslaughter, Driving Under the Influence Manslaughter, and Vehicular Homicide;

Aggravated Stalking (Section 784.048(3));

Stalking (Section 784.048(2));

Domestic Battery (Section 784.03);

Kidnapping (Section 787.01);

False Imprisonment (Section 787.02);

Neglect/Abuse of Elderly (Section 825.102);

Violation of Injunction charges (Sections 741.31 and 784.047);

Violation of Pre-trial Release charges (Section 741.29(6));

ROBBERY:

Home Invasion Robbery (Section 812.135);

Carjacking (Section 812.133);

CRIMES AGAINST CHILDREN:

Sexual Performance By A Child (Section 827.071);

Selling or Buying of Minors (Section 847.0145);

Child Abuse (Section 827.03);

BURGLARY:

Burglary of a Dwelling (Sections 810.02(3)(a) and (b));

Burglary of Occupied Structure (Section 810.02(3)(c));

WEAPONS OFFENSES:

Unlawful Throwing, Placing or Discharging of a Destructive Device or Bomb (Section 790.19);

Possession of a Fire Bomb (Section 806.111);

Possession of Firearm by Convicted Felon (Section 790.23);

WITNESS CRIMES:

Tampering with a Witness (felony) (Section 914.22(1));

Retaliating against a Witness (Section 914.23);

ESCAPE:

Escape (Section 944.40);

Escape from Juvenile Facility (Section 985.721);

MISCELLANEOUS CRIMES:

Aircraft Piracy (Section 860.16);

Trafficking in any controlled substance (Section 893.135);

Arson (Section 806.01);

Failure to Register as a Sex Offender or Sexual Predator (Section 943.0435);

Giving False Name to Officer (Section 837.05)—when defendant's true identity is unknown or seriously questioned;

All Driving Under the Influence charges (Section 316.193) not a first offense; and

All Driving Under the Influence charges (Section 316.193(3)) when personal injury involved.

2. *Other Circumstances Requiring First Appearance Even With Warrant.* Even if a warrant has been issued by a judge setting a specific bond amount, the defendant shall be held for first appearance if arrested under the following circumstances unless the judge issuing the warrant specifically indicated being aware of these circumstances:

a. Any defendant arrested for any felony or a misdemeanor involving actual or threatened violence when the defendant is on felony supervision (probation or community control) or is on bond or pretrial release for a pending felony or violent misdemeanor case;

b. The booking officer has determined pursuant to Section I. B. 1. (f) above that the defendant is charged with violating misdemeanor or felony probation or community control and meets the Jessica Lunsford Act criteria under section 948.06(4), Florida Statutes. First Appearance is required even if the defendant was arrested on a violation of supervision (probation or community control) warrant that would otherwise have allowed release, unless the judge issuing the warrant specifically found that the defendant was not a danger to the public;

c. The defendant is suffering from a mental or emotional illness and it appears that release would endanger the safety of the defendant or others;

d. The pretrial release officer has made a written request that the defendant be held for first appearance stating a bona fide reason for denying bond under the bond schedule. The reason must be limited to the defendant's likelihood of appearance or the safety of the community.

3. *Other Circumstances Requiring First Appearance Unless a Warrant Indicates Otherwise.* Defendants in the following circumstances should be held for first appearance unless there is a warrant issued by a judge of competent jurisdiction setting the terms of release:

a. Any felony offense in which the defendant is alleged to have actually possessed or discharged a firearm;

b. All felony cases in which the defendant has been released from prison within 3 years of the current offense;

c. All violation of probation on view arrests;

d. The arresting officer has made a written request that the defendant be held for first appearance stating a bona fide law enforcement reason supporting the need for a first appearance.

F. Law Enforcement Exception to First Appearance Required. An arresting officer making an on view arrest who determines that the facts and circumstances do not warrant holding a defendant for first appearance may make a written request that the defendant be released. Based on this request, the pretrial release or booking officer may authorize the defendant to be released on SPRP or monetary bond provided the defendant has no other pending charges and no convictions for any misdemeanor involving violence or any felony.

G. Mandatory Conditions. Certain special conditions are mandatory depending on the charge against the defendant. These conditions apply regardless of the nature of the defendant's release, including persons released on monetary bonds or on their own recognizance. These special conditions shall apply in the following circumstances:

1. *Alcohol Offenses.* Alcohol abstinence shall be required in all offenses in which the use of alcohol is an element, including, but not limited to, all charges for driving under the influence, disorderly intoxication and underage drinking.

2. *Criminal Activity.* The defendant shall also refrain from any future criminal activity.

3. *Victim Contact.* As required by section 903.047, Florida Statutes, the defendant shall refrain from having any contact with the victim, directly or indirectly. This shall include the defendant having no contact with the property or premises where the alleged crime took place.

4. *Drug Offenses.* Random urinalysis shall be required for any Defendant charged with a felony violation of Chapter 893, Florida Statutes, who has a prior conviction for a drug offense under chapter 893 (either felony or misdemeanor). In counties having a supervised pretrial release program, these persons will be subject to supervision of the SPRP even though a monetary bond may also be required. The Defendant shall bear all costs of testing and supervision, absent court order to the contrary.

Unless the alleged victim is present at the first appearance and is given an opportunity to be heard, the no-contact condition set forth in 3 above, shall not be deleted or modified except by the judge having trial jurisdiction of the offense. The booking officer will ensure that each defendant sign an acknowledgment of these provisions, witness the document and submit the original document to the court file. The form of acknowledgment is attached to this order.

H. Additional Provisions By Trial Judge. In any case where a defendant has been released pursuant to this administrative order before first appearance, pursuant to notice and hearing the assigned trial judge may impose additional conditions of release to protect the community from risk of physical harm, to assure the presence of the accused at trial, or to assure the integrity of the judicial process.

II. LEON COUNTY SUPERVISED PRETRIAL RELEASE PROGRAM PROCEDURES

A. General Provisions. The SPRP was established to provide an alternative to monetary bail for those Defendants who are likely to appear in court and unlikely to present a danger to the community. Release under the supervision of the SPRP shall be subject to the procedures set forth in subparagraphs B., C. and D.

B. Risk Assessment Review. All persons arrested and admitted to the Leon County Detention Center, charged with a second degree nonviolent felony or lower offense, shall be evaluated using the risk assessment instrument and criteria designated by the Chief Judge, and if the person meets that criteria he or she shall be released on his or her own recognizance with conditions deemed appropriate by the pretrial release director or designee, provided that the other criteria outlined in Section C (Eligibility for Pretrial Release) of the Attached Leon County Pretrial Release Procedures are met. A "violent crime" means any crime which injures or threatens to injure another person.

C. Eligibility for Pretrial Release. The pretrial release officer shall evaluate each Defendant charged with a second degree nonviolent offense or lesser offense using the risk assessment instrument and criteria designated by the Chief Judge to determine eligibility for pretrial release. A Defendant who has made a written request for pretrial release and who has a verified address in the Second Judicial Circuit and meets the risk assessment criteria designated by the Chief Judge shall be eligible for release unless one of the following conditions exist:

1. The Defendant has a history of an escape or an unexcused failure to appear.

2. The Defendant was taken into custody on a warrant that indicates a specific monetary amount, that the Defendant should be held without bond or that the Defendant should be held for first appearance.

3. Pursuant to section I. E. above a first appearance is required.

D. Conditions of Supervised Pretrial Release Program.

1. *General Conditions.* Pretrial release officers have the authority to require a Defendant to meet any of the following conditions of release under the SPRP:

a. Regular contact with the pretrial release officer.

b. No contact with the victim.

c. No return to the property in question.

d. No weapons or firearms.

e. Abstinence from alcohol.

f. Curfew.

g. Surrender of passport.

h. Limitations on residence and travel.

i. Screening for mental illness, drug abuse, or alcohol abuse.

j. Random testing, including urinalysis, for drugs or alcohol.

k. Maintain full-time employment or school.

l. Employment search.

m. Any other condition necessary to ensure community safety.

2. *Violations.* If any Defendant released under the supervision of the pretrial release program violates any of the conditions of release, the officer shall prepare an affidavit and a proposed order to show cause why the Defendant's pretrial release should not be revoked. The affidavit and proposed order to show cause shall be presented to the assigned trial judge. Emergency situations during non-business hours, as determined by the pretrial release officer, shall be presented to any available judge. Any individual arrested under the emergency procedures must be brought before a judge within 24 hours. Otherwise, violations of pretrial release conditions should be promptly presented to the judge having trial jurisdiction over the case. "Emergency situations" shall be defined as circumstances necessary to protect the community from risk of personal injury, to assure the presence of the accused at trial, or to assure the integrity of the judicial process. These procedures shall not be interpreted to extend or limit a law enforcement officer's authority to make a warrantless arrest for violating a condition of release.

III. OTHER COUNTIES—SUPERVISED PRETRIAL RELEASE PROGRAMS

Counties other than Leon County are authorized to develop separate procedures for a supervised pretrial release program as approved by the Chief Circuit Judge in consultation with the judges handling criminal matters in the respective counties.

IV. BOND SCHEDULE

These bond amounts shall apply circuit wide. Absent other specific provision to the contrary set out in this administrative order, a defendant shall be entitled to release upon posting the following specified bond amounts. In Leon County, these bond amounts will apply regardless of the defendant's eligibility for the SPRP. This bond schedule is implemented only for purposes of release of a defendant prior to first appearance. The specific terms of release set for an arrestee at first appearance must be set only after an individualized assessment of the individual arrestee's personal circumstances. The bail amounts listed below have no binding affect at first appearance or thereafter:

Bond should be set at $25,000 on the following charges:
All first degree felonies
Bond should be set at $10,000 on the following charges:
All other second degree felony property crimes
Fleeing and Eluding Law Enforcement Officer (Section 316.1935)
All second degree felony drug charges
Bond should be set at $5,000 on the following charges:
Grand Theft Firearm (Section 812.014(2)(c)5.)
Grand Theft Motor Vehicle (Section 812.014(2)(c)6.)
Dealing In Stolen Property (Section 812.019)
Insurance Fraud (Section 817.234(11)(a))
Driving While License Suspended or Revoked with Injury (Section 322.34(6)(b))
All other third degree felony burglary charges
Criminal Use of Personal Identification (Section 817.568)
Bond should be set at $2,500 on the following charges:
Grand Theft (not otherwise specified herein) (Section 812.014)
Credit Card Fraud (Section 817.481)
Forgery (Section 831.01)
Uttering (Section 831.02)
All third degree felony drug charges
Providing False Information To Officer With Adverse Affect (Section 901.36(2))
Unemployment Compensation Fraud (Section 443.071(1))
Bond should be set at $1,000 on the following charges:
Felony Dumping
Defrauding a Pawnbroker
Public Assistance Fraud $200 or more (Section 414.39(5)(b))
Felony Petit Theft (Section 812.014(3)(c))
Felony Driving While License Suspended or Revoked (Section 322.34(2)(c))
All other third degree felony crimes
Cruelty to Animals (Section 828.12)
Bond should be set at $500 on the following charges:
All other first degree misdemeanors
All first offender misdemeanor Driving Under the Influence charges
Bond should be set at $250 on the following charges, if the defendant does not have a verifiable local address, and release on recognizance (ROR), if the defendant does have a verifiable local address:
All other second degree misdemeanors
All county and city ordinance violations

V. TERMINATION OF OTHER ORDERS/EFFECTIVE DATE

Administrative Orders 2003–8, 2003–10, 2006–02 and the subsequent amendments to those orders are hereby terminated. This order becomes effective immediately.

DONE AND ORDERED in Tallahassee, Leon County, on April 23, 2018.

JONATHAN SJOSTROM
Chief Judge

Adopted effective April 23, 2018.

1 Attachment A not included.

2017–11. UNIFORM PROCEDURES FOR FORFEITURES PURSUANT TO THE FLORIDA CONTRABAND AND FORFEITURE ACT

IN THE SECOND JUDICIAL CIRCUIT OF FLORIDA

OFFICE OF THE CHIEF JUDGE

ADMINISTRATIVE ORDER 2017—11

IN RE: UNIFORM PROCEDURES FOR FORFEITURES PURSUANT TO THE FLORIDA CONTRABAND FORFEITURE ACT

WHEREAS, the Florida Contraband Forfeiture Act sets forth procedural requirements governing the forfeiture of contraband articles. *See* §§ 932.701–932.7062, Florida Statutes; and

WHEREAS, recent statutory changes passed by the Florida Legislature to the Florida Contraband Forfeiture Act necessitate the implementation of these procedures in a uniform manner within the Second Judicial Circuit;

NOW, THEREFORE, in order to provide for the uniform disposition of forfeiture proceedings and ensure consistency amongst all seizing agencies within the Second Judicial Circuit, and pursuant to the authority vested in me as Chief Judge of the Second Judicial Circuit of Florida under Rule 2.215, Florida Rules of Judicial Administration, it is hereby **ORDERED:**

1. In accordance with section 932.704(2), Florida Statutes, of the Florida Contraband Forfeiture Act, all civil forfeiture cases shall be heard by a circuit court judge of the civil division. Such cases shall be assigned to any circuit court civil section judge in the same manner that other civil cases are assigned.

2. Pursuant to section 932.703, Florida Statutes, civil court involvement is required after seizure, but prior to the filing of a complaint. Specifically, section 932.703(2)(a) requires the seizing agency (Seizing Agency) to apply to the circuit court, within ten (10) business days after the date of seizure, for an order determining whether probable cause exists for the seizure of the property. Furthermore, pursuant to the time frames set forth in section 932.703(3)(a), Florida Statutes, which provides the right to an adversarial preliminary hearing, such a hearing may be required prior to the filing of a complaint. Therefore, to ensure that an adequate record of these initial documents is maintained and that a civil case number is available for these filings, the following procedures apply:

I. *Application for an Ex–Parte Order Determining Probable Cause for Seizure*

a. In order to comply with section 932.703(2)(a), Florida Statutes, the Seizing Agency shall, within ten (10) business days after the date of a seizure, submit an Application for an Ex–Parte Order Determining Probable Cause for Seizure (Application), with an accompanying sworn affidavit (Affidavit).

b. Such Application and Affidavit shall be submitted via the Florida Courts e-Filing Portal, and once the e-Filing Portal provides the Seizing Agency with a case number, the Seizing Agency shall promptly send a copy of the Application and Affidavit via e-Courtesy to the assigned judge in compliance with the procedures for emergency matters listed on the assigned judge's webpage.

c. The Application for an Ex–Parte Order Determining Probable Cause for Seizure shall be in substantially the same format as *Attachment A* to this order. The Application shall include a proposed Order Finding Probable Cause for Seizure, substantially the same as *Attachment B* to this order, as well as a proposed Order Denying Probable Cause for Seizure, substantially the same as *Attachment C* to this order.

II. *Notice of Seizure and Right to an Adversarial Preliminary Hearing*

a. Section 932.703(3)(a), Florida Statutes, includes the right to an adversarial preliminary hearing. Pursuant to this statute, the Seizing Agency must provide specific notice of this right. All law enforcement agencies that will be proceeding against contraband in the Second Judicial Circuit shall use the Notice of Seizure customarily utilized by the seizing agency or a Notice of Seizure in substantially the same format as *Attachment D* to this order.

b. The Seizing Agency shall complete a Notice of Seizure containing the name and address of the person(s) who may have an interest in the property and who are known to the Seizing Agency. (Such person(s) to be referred to hereinafter as Claimant.)

c. When any Claimant receiving the notice requests an adversarial preliminary hearing in conformity with the statute, the Seizing Agency is then required to set and notice a hearing. The Seizing Agency shall file both the Noticeof Seizure and the Claimant's request for an adversarial hearing via the e-Filing portal, and shall send copies of both to the assigned judge in compliance with the court's procedures for emergency matters.

III. *Notice of Resolution.* For tracking and administrative purposes, it is necessary for the court to be made aware of the resolution of any seizure proceedings that occur prior to the filing of a complaint. Accordingly, if the Seizing Agency and the Claimant who may have an interest in the seized property reach an agreement concerning the seizure, or otherwise resolve the seizure proceedings, prior to the filing of the complaint, the Seizing Agency shall file a Notice of Resolution (including therein the Order of Dismissal) in substantially the same format as *Attachment E* to this order. The notice shall be filed via the e-Filing Portal and sent to the assigned judge via e-Courtesy to the proposed order library of the judge's e-Courtesy page. Failure to do so in a timely manner may make the Seizing Agency responsible for filing fees.

IV. *Complaint for Forfeiture*

a. In the event the Seizing Agency and the Claimant are unable to reach an agreement concerning the seizure or otherwise resolve the seizure proceedings, the Seizing Agency shall file a complaint for forfeiture (Complaint) within forty-five (45) days after the seizure, which time period may be extended to sixty (60) days for good cause.

b. The Complaint must be filed under the previously assigned case number (as set forth in paragraph I. Application for an Ex-parte Order Determining Probable Cause for Seizure and must, in addition to stating that which is required by sections 932.703(3)(a) and (b), Florida Statutes, as appropriate, describe the property; state the county, place, and date of seizure, and state the name of the law enforcement agency holding the seized property.

c. Additionally, copies of the Order Finding Probable Cause for Seizure and the Affidavit must be provided as attachments to the Complaint.

d. Upon filing the Complaint with attachments and payment of the appropriate filing fee and posting a bond pursuant to section 932.704(4), Florida Statutes, to the Clerk of the Court, the civil forfeiture action will commence.

e. Pursuant to Section 932.704(5)(c), the court shall require any Claimant who desires to contest the forfeiture to file and serve upon the attorney for the Seizing Agency any responsive pleading and affirmative defenses within twenty (20) days after the receipt of the Complaint.

3. Attachments to this Administrative Order may be modified without further changes to this Administrative Order.

4. This Administrative Order becomes effective upon signing.

DONE AND ORDERED in Chambers at Leon County, Florida, this 15th day of November, 2017.

JONATHAN SJOSTROM
Chief Judge

ATTACHMENT A

THE SECOND JUDICIAL CIRCUIT IN AND FOR LEON COUNTY, FLORIDA

CASE NO. ______________________________

CIVIL DIVISION

IN RE: FORFEITURE OF:

(*Description of Property*)

____

APPLICATION FOR AN EX–PARTE ORDER DETERMINING PROBABLE CAUSE FOR SEIZURE

COMES NOW, the Applicant, *(insert agency)*, by and through undersigned counsel, pursuant to section 932.703(2), Florida Statutes, files this Application For An Ex-parte Order Determining Probable Cause For Seizure (Application), and says:

1. On *(date)*, *(insert agency)*, seized for forfeiture *(describe property)* (Property) as more fully set forth in the attached sworn affidavit (Affidavit). This Application is being presented within ten (10) business days of seizing that Property.

2. The requirements specified in section 932.703(1)(a), Florida Statutes, have been satisfied, based on the fact that one of the following facts exist:

_____ The owner of the property was arrested for a criminal offense that forms the basis for determining that the property is a contraband article under section 932.701, Florida Statutes;

_____ The owner of the property cannot be identified after a diligent search or the person in possession of the property denies ownership and the owner of the property cannot be identified by means that are available to the employee or agent of the seizing agency at the time of the seizure;

_____ The owner is a fugitive from justice or is deceased;

_____ An individual who does not own the property was arrested for a criminal offense that forms the basis for determining that the property is a contraband article under section 932.701, Florida Statutes, and the owner of the property had actual knowledge of the criminal activity;

_____ The owner of the property agrees to be a confidential informant as defined in section 914.28, Florida Statutes; or

_____ The property is a monetary instrument.

3. The facts and circumstances surrounding the seizure are contained in the attached Affidavit, which is incorporated as if fully set forth herein.

WHEREFORE, Applicant requests an Order Finding Probable Cause for Seizure pursuant to section 932.703(2), Florida Statutes.

ATTESTATION

I HEREBY ATTEST that a copy of this Application and attached Affidavit have been submitted this ___ day of _________, 20 ___.

____
Signature of Attorney

ATTACHMENT B

THE SECOND JUDICIAL CIRCUIT IN AND FOR LEON COUNTY, FLORIDA

CASE NO. _______________________

CIVIL DIVISION

IN RE: FORFEITURE OF:
(Description of Property)

____

EX–PARTE ORDER FINDING PROBABLE CAUSE FOR SEIZURE

THIS MATTER having come before this Court pursuant to section 932.703(2), Florida Statutes within ten (10) business days of seizure of the above-described property by *(Seizing Agency)*, and the Court having reviewed the sworn affidavit, **FINDS:**

1. The Agency applied for the probable cause determination within ten (10) business days after the date of the seizure.

2. The requirements specified in paragraph (*l*)(a) of section 932.703, Florida Statutes have been satisfied based on the fact that one of the following facts exist:

_____ The owner of the property was arrested for a criminal offense that forms the basis for determining that the property is a contraband article under section 932.701, Florida Statutes;

_____ The owner of the property cannot be identified after a diligent search or the person in possession of the property denies ownership and the owner of the property cannot be identified by means that are available to the employee or agent of the seizing agency at the time of the seizure;

_____ The owner is a fugitive from justice or is deceased;

_____ An individual who does not own the property was arrested for a criminal offense that forms the basis for determining that the property is a contraband article under section 932.701, Florida Statutes, and the owner of the property had actual knowledge of the criminal activity;

_____ The owner of the property agrees to be a confidential informant as defined in section 914.28, Florida Statutes; or

_____ The property is a monetary instrument.

3. Probable cause exists to seize the above-described property under the Florida Contraband Forfeiture Act.

Therefore, the Court having found that the requirements in section 932.703(*l*)(a), Florida Statutes, were satisfied and that probable cause exists for the seizure, it is **ORDERED** that the property shall be held in conformity with the statute until further order of the Court.

DONE and ORDERED in Chambers, in Leon County, Florida, this _____ day of _________, 20 ___.

____
CIRCUIT COURT JUDGE

ATTACHMENT C

THE SECOND JUDICIAL CIRCUIT IN AND FOR LEON COUNTY, FLORIDA

CASE NO. _______________________

CIVIL DIVISION

IN RE: FORFEITURE OF:
(Description of Property)

EX–PARTE ORDER DENYING PROBABLE CAUSE FOR SEIZURE

THIS MATTER having come before this Court pursuant to section 932.703(2), Florida Statutes, upon the Application For An Ex-parte Order Determining Probable Cause For Seizure by *(Seizing Agency)*, and the Court having reviewed the sworn Affidavit, **FINDS:**

_____ The Agency did not apply for the probable cause determination within ten (10) business days after the date of the seizure.

AND/OR

_____ The requirements specified in section 932.703(*l*)(a), Florida Statutes, have not been satisfied.

AND/OR

_____ The Agency has not established probable cause for the seizure based on a review of the attached affidavit.

THEREFORE, it is **ORDERED** that any forfeiture hold, lien, lis pendens, or other civil encumbrance shall be released in conformity with the statute within five (5) days absent further order of the Court.

DONE and ORDERED in Chambers, in Leon County, Florida, this day of __________, 20 ___.

CIRCUIT COURT JUDGE

ATTACHMENT D

NOTICE OF SEIZURE

REPORT NO.: __________ CASE NO.: __________
DATE: (*To be filled in by Clerk of the Court*)
TO: *(Claimant's Name)*
ADDRESS: __________

RE: *(Description of Seized Property)*

This is to advise you that on *(Date)*, *(Seizing Agency)* seized the above-referenced property for a violation of the Florida Contraband Forfeiture Act, sections 932.701–932.7062, Florida Statutes.

YOU ARE HEREBY NOTIFIED that you are entitled by law to request an adversarial preliminary hearing to determine whether there is probable cause to believe the property was used in violation of the Act.

PLEASE NOTE that the adversarial preliminary hearing is not mandatory and you need not request a hearing to later contest the action taken against the property described herein. Each claimant will be given the opportunity to appear in court before final disposition of this matter.

IF YOU DESIRE SUCH A HEARING, you must make a request in writing by certified mail, return receipt requested, to *(Name of Seizing Agency)* at the address listed below, within fifteen (15) days of receiving this Notice. This request must be accompanied by a copy of this Notice. The seizing agency will notify you of the time, date, and place of that hearing.

I HEREBY CERTIFY that I have:

___ provided a copy of this Notice to the person named above, or

___ forwarded a copy of this Notice by certified mail, return receipt requested, to *(person or entity to which Notice was sent)* this ____ day of ________, 20 ___.

Seizing Officer/Person Sending Notice
(Seizing agency)
(Address)
(Person ID/Fla. Bar Number)
(Telephone Number)
(E-mail Address)

I HEREBY CERTIFY that I have:

___ received the foregoing Notice apprising me of my right to post-seizure adversarial hearing.

Claimant

If you are a person with a disability who needs any accommodation in order to participate in this proceeding, you may be entitled, at no cost to you, to the provision of certain assistance. Please contact:

ADA Coordinator
301 South Monroe Street
Tallahassee, FL 32301
850–606–4401

at least 7 days before your scheduled court appearance, or immediately upon receiving this notification if the time before the scheduled appearance is less than 7 days; if you are hearing or voice impaired, call 711.

ATTACHMENT E

THE SECOND JUDICIAL CIRCUIT IN AND FOR LEON COUNTY, FLORIDA

CASE NO. __________

CIVIL DIVISION

IN RE: FORFEITURE OF:
(Description of Property)

NOTICE OF RESOLUTION

(Re: Proceedings Prior to Filing Forfeiture Complaint)

COMES NOW, the *(insert seizing agency)*, by and through undersigned counsel, and gives notice to the Court that:

1. The seizure proceedings concerning *(describe property)* have been resolved in the following manner: __________

2. Accordingly, *(insert agency)* will not be filing a complaint in this matter, and no further action of the Court is necessary.

Attorney Signature Block

ORDER OF DISMISSAL

Based on the foregoing Notice of Resolution, the proceedings regarding the seizure of the aforementioned property having been resolved prior to the filing of a complaint for forfeiture, are hereby dismissed..

DONE AND ORDERED in Chambers at Leon County, Florida, this ___ day of __________ 20 ___.

Circuit Court Judge

Adopted effective November 15, 2017.

2017–09. ORDER GOVERNING INTRODUCTION AND HANDLING OF EVIDENCE CONTAINING HIGH–POTENCY NARCOTICS

IN THE SECOND JUDICIAL CIRCUIT OF FLORIDA

OFFICE OF THE CHIEF JUDGE

ADMINISTRATIVE ORDER 2017—09

IN RE: ORDER GOVERNING INTRODUCTION AND HANDLING OF EVIDENCE CONTAINING HIGH–POTENCY NARCOTICS

WHEREAS, pursuant to Article V, section 2(d) of the Florida Constitution and Section 43.26, Florida Statutes, the chief judge of each judicial circuit is charged with the authority and the power to do everything necessary to promote the prompt and efficient administration of justice; and

WHEREAS, pursuant to the chief judge's constitutional and statutory responsibility for administrative supervision of the courts within the circuit and to create and maintain an organization capable of effecting the efficient, prompt, and proper administration of justice for the citizens of this State, the chief judge is required to exercise direction, See Rules 2.215(b)(2), and (b)(3), Fla. R. Jud. Admin.

WHEREAS, there has been a dramatic increase in the prevalence of high-potency narcotics that are so strong accidental contact or inhalation can be deadly; and

WHEREAS, the health, safety and welfare of those who conduct business within the courthouses of this Circuit, including employees and citizens, are of primary concern to this Court; and

WHEREAS, in an effort to ensure the health and safety of all persons within each courthouse in this Circuit and to prevent any accidental exposure, this Court has recognized that there is a need to establish a procedure for introducing evidence that contains or may contain high-potency narcotics ("HPN Exhibits"); it is therefore

ORDERED, effective immediately, that:

1. HPN Exhibits are those that contain or may contain high-potency narcotics which are highly toxic and may be fatal, including, but not limited to: Fentanyl (Actiq, Fentora, Duragesic, Subsys, Abstral, Lazanda, Ionsys, Onsolis, Duragesic–100, Duragensic–50, Duragensic, Duragensic–75, Sublimaze, Duragensic–25, and Duragensic–12); Carfentanil; Remifentanil; Alfentanil; Sufentanil; and other related high-potency narcotics.

2. In the event any party intends to introduce HPN Exhibits in any court proceeding, the party intending to introduce the evidence must file a notice of possession of an HPN Exhibit at least **five (5) days** prior to the first pretrial conference in a trial case and **ten (10) days** prior to a hearing on a violation of probation.

3. The Court shall conduct a pretrial hearing to determine if the HPN Exhibits can be introduced by admission, statement of fact, photographs, stipulation and/or certificate of analysis. The Court shall not require any party or law enforcement agency to transport or bring the HPN Exhibits to the courthouse for the purpose of the pretrial hearing.

4. If the parties are unable to reach an agreement or stipulation at the pretrial hearing, the deputy clerk(s) present shall promptly notify a manager in the Clerk of Court's Office.

5. In the event the HPN Exhibits are brought into the courthouse for any purpose, including but not limited to trial, the HPN Exhibits shall be double bagged, sealed and clearly labeled. Further, the HPN Exhibits must be handled, labeled and packaged in accordance with additional policies that may be established by federal or local law enforcement, which may be amended from time to time to ensure the safety of all court participants.

6. At the pretrial conference, if the parties are unable to stipulate to alternative presentations of the evidence and an HPN Exhibit is to be introduced into evidence, the Court shall discuss and decide upon the protective gear that may be worn by trial participants, including but not limited to, attorneys, bailiffs, court reporters, clerks and the Court. The Court shall also decide whether the jury may handle the HPN Exhibit and what, if any, protections shall be in place for the benefit of the jurors.

7. The deputy clerk(s) shall promptly notify an evidence clerk manager in the event that HPN Exhibits are marked as exhibits.

8. This order supersedes any provision in any prior administrative order which may be inconsistent and shall remain in effect until further order of the Court.

DONE AND ORDERED at Tallahassee, Florida this 25 day of October, 2017.

JONATHAN SJOSTROM
Chief Judge

Adopted effective October 15, 2017.

2017–02. INTERVIEWS INVOLVING VICTIMS UNDER AGE 16 IN CHILD AND SEXUAL ABUSE CASES

IN THE SECOND JUDICIAL CIRCUIT OF FLORIDA

OFFICE OF THE CHIEF JUDGE

ADMINISTRATIVE ORDER 2017–02

IN RE: INTERVIEWS INVOLVING VICTIMS UNDER AGE 16 IN CHILD AND SEXUAL ABUSE CASES

In accordance with Section 914.16, Florida Statutes (2016), and pursuant to the authority conferred by Rule 2.215, Florida Rules of Judicial Administration, it is **ORDERED** as follows:

1. This order shall apply to the investigation and prosecution of all cases of abuse under Sections 794.011, 800.04, 827.03 or 847.0135(5), Florida Statutes, when the victim is under sixteen (16) years of age or a victim of a violation of Sections 794.011, 800.02, 800.03, or 825.102, Florida Statutes, who is a person with intellectual disability as defined in Section 393.063(21), Florida Statutes, at the time the interviews are sought.

2. For purposes of this order the term "victim" refers to any person who is suspected of or alleged to have been the victim of the above enumerated statutes. The term "interview" is defined as any procedure in which the victim is required or requested to provide a detailed factual account of the circumstances surrounding the allegation of abuse. The term "interview" does not include the following:

A. Information obtained for the purpose of medical or psychological diagnosis or treatment.

B. An initial contact with the victim by law enforcement and/or Florida Department of Children and Families (DCF) to assess the validity of complaint or the need to take protective measures on behalf of the victim.

C. Contacts with DCF legal, victim services, (sexual assault/domestic violence) counselors, guardians ad litem, or assistant state attorneys seeking to carry out responsibilities as designated by statute.

D. Court testimony of the victim.

E. Any initial contact by an agent or employee of the school system.

3. In accord with the foregoing and with the intent of minimizing the negative effects of multiple interviews of victims, such interviews shall be governed by the following:

A. All interviews shall be conducted in a setting and manner designed to minimize the traumatic effects of the interview on the victim.

B. One investigative interview may be conducted for the purposes of criminal delinquency and/or dependency proceedings. All agencies involved in the investigation of the above enumerated statutes including law enforcement, DCF, State Attorney's Office (SAO), Child Protection Team (CPT), shall coordinate their efforts to facilitate this provision, so that only one investigative interview is conducted regardless of whether the investigation is for dependency, delinquency or criminal proceedings, or both. All efforts shall be made to limit the number of persons participating in the interviewing of the child to no more than two. The interview shall be videotaped or recorded whenever possible to insure that other parties have the opportunity to see and hear the victim's statement.

C. A second interview may be conducted by the SAO and/or law enforcement, and may include DCF, victim services (sexual assault/domestic violence), or CPT for the purpose of clarifying and expanding any facts necessary for a determination as to filing of charges or a petition.

D. A third interview may be conducted under the rules governing depositions. Counsel shall notice all parties including the guardian ad litem consistent with the applicable rule of procedure. Any additional discovery depositions will be governed by Rule 3.220, Florida Rules of Criminal Procedure, or Rules 8.060 and 8.245, Florida Rules of Juvenile Procedure.

E. A fourth interview may be conducted by the office of the prosecuting attorney by the SAO or DCF as final preparation for trial.

F. Additional interviews shall be allowed only by order of the court upon motion for good cause shown. Additional interviews shall be limited in scope to assure minimal impact on the victim.

G. Nothing contained in this order shall prevent the trial court from modifying the number, scope or manner of interviews allowed by this order upon motion of any interested party and a showing of good cause of any interested party and a showing of good cause, or from modifying discovery depositions pursuant to the applicable provisions of Civil, Criminal or Juvenile Procedure rules.

DONE and ORDERED in chambers in Tallahassee, Leon County, Florida, this 10th day of March 2017.

JONATHAN SJOSTROM
Chief Judge

Adopted effective March 10, 2017.

2016–05. LEON COUNTY VETERANS TREATMENT COURT PROCEDURES

IN THE SECOND JUDICIAL CIRCUIT OF FLORIDA

OFFICE OF THE CHIEF JUDGE

ADMINISTRATIVE ORDER 2016–05

IN RE: LEON COUNTY VETERANS TREATMENT COURT PROCEDURES

Whereas, the Chief Judge of the Circuit is authorized to establish a Veterans Treatment Court Program by sections 394.47891, 948.08(7), 910.035(5), 948.16 and 948.21 of the Florida Statutes; and

Whereas, the Florida Legislature appropriated recurring state funds to establish a veterans treatment intervention program in Leon County, the Governor signed this legislation into law effective July 1, 2015, and the Leon County Board of County Commissioners agreed to serve as fiscal agent for a veterans court effective July 7, 2015; and

Whereas the Leon County Veterans Treatment Court (VTC) was established in Leon County by Administrative Order 2015–07 in and for the Second Judicial Circuit of Florida with an effective date of November 1, 2015.

It is therefore **ORDERED**:

The following procedures shall apply to the Leon County Veterans Treatment Court.

I. Assignment of VTC Judge by Separate Administrative Order.

The Chief Judge shall assign the VTC Judge by the separate assignment administrative order.

II. Assignment of Misdemeanor Cases to VTC.

A. *Screening of Eligible Veterans and Servicemembers.* Court Administration Staff shall work with the VTC Pretrial

Intervention Officer and the Veterans Justice Outreach Specialist of the Veterans Administration to identify misdemeanor or misdemeanor criminal traffic charged or sentenced defendants who meet eligibility criteria established by sections 394.47891, and 948.16 of the Florida Statutes. As provided by statute, the defendant's participation in VTC must be voluntary. No defendant is eligible for VTC court without the Defendant's agreement to accept all terms and conditions of VTC. No case shall be assigned to VTC until the Veterans Justice Outreach Specialist makes a preliminary eligibility determination.

B. *Delegation of Authority to Assign Misdemeanor Cases Before Trial.* The Chief Judge hereby delegates to the VTC Judge authority to assign, by written order, any eligible misdemeanor charged defendant to the VTC at any time prior to the first pretrial conference.

After the first pretrial conference, no case shall be transferred to VTC without written consent of the regularly assigned judge. If the regularly assigned judge consents, the VTC Judge shall have authority to reassign such case to the VTC by written order.

C. *Delegation of Authority to Assign Misdemeanor Cases After Adjudication.* The Chief Judge hereby delegates to each assigned Leon County Judge authority to assign, by written order, any eligible misdemeanor charged defendant to the VTC after the entry by the defendant of a plea of no contest, plea of guilty, or conviction at trial including for sentencing by the VTC Judge.

D. *Objection to Misdemeanor VTC Assignment.* Should the State wish to contest eligibility of a case for assignment to VTC, the State must file a written motion stating the basis for its objection. The VTC Judge shall have authority to resolve such objections.

III. VTC Misdemeanor Pretrial Case Resolution.

As directed by section 948.16 of the Florida Statutes, at the end of the pretrial intervention period, the court shall consider the recommendation of the treatment program and the recommendation of the state attorney as to disposition of the pending charges.

The court shall determine, by written finding, whether the defendant successfully completed the pretrial intervention program. The parties shall have notice and a fair opportunity to be heard prior to such determination.

If the court finds that the defendant has not successfully completed the pretrial intervention program, the court may order the person to continue in education and treatment or return the charges to the criminal docket for prosecution. The court shall dismiss the charges upon finding that the defendant has successfully completed the pretrial intervention program.

IV. VTC Misdemeanor Post–Adjudicatory Case Resolution.

The VTC Judge shall determine whether the Defendant has adequately completed VTC. All parties shall have notice and a fair opportunity to be heard before such determination.

Upon successful completion of Misdemeanor Post–Adjudicatory Veterans Treatment Court, the VTC Judge may consider withholding adjudication of guilt or early termination of probation by written order. With the consent of the State on the record, the VTC Judge may permit the defendant to withdraw a prior plea of no contest or guilty and administratively dismiss the VTC charges.

Upon unsuccessful completion of Misdemeanor Post–Adjudicatory Veterans Treatment Court, the VTC Judge may order the person to continue in education and treatment, which may include treatment programs offered by licensed service providers or jail-based treatment programs, or return the charges to the criminal docket for prosecution. Prior to such written order, the State and Defendant shall have notice and a fair opportunity to be heard as to the exercise of the Court's discretion.

V. Assignment of Felony Cases to VTC.

A. *Screening of Eligible Veterans and Servicemembers.* Court Administration Staff shall work with the VTC Pretrial Intervention Officer and the Veterans Justice Outreach Specialist of the Veterans Administration to identify felony charged or sentenced defendants who meet eligibility criteria established by sections 394.47891 and 948.08(7)(a) of the Florida Statutes. No case shall be assigned to VTC until the Veterans Justice Outreach Specialist makes a preliminary eligibility determination. As provided by statute, the defendant's participation in VTC must be voluntary. Offenses listed by section 948.06(8)(c) are excluded from assignment to VTC absent written agreement by the State and Defendant and written order approving such agreement by the assigned felony division judge and the VTC Judge.

B. *Delegation of Authority to Assign Felony Cases Before Trial.* The Chief Judge hereby delegates to each judge of the felony division authority to assign, by written order, any eligible felony charged defendant's case to the VTC at any time. The State and Defendant shall have notice and an opportunity to be heard before the issuance of an order assigning any felony case to VTC before trial.

C. *Delegation of Authority to Assign Felony Cases After Adjudication.* The Chief Judge hereby delegates to each judge of the felony division authority to assign, by written order, any eligible felony charged defendant to the VTC after the entry a plea of no contest, plea of guilty, or conviction at trial. The State and Defendant shall have notice and a fair opportunity to be heard before the issuance of an order assigning any felony case to VTC after entry of a plea of guilty or no contest, or after conviction at trial. Each judge of the felony division is delegated authority to assign such cases to the VTC Judge for sentencing after such plea or conviction or to impose completion of VTC as a condition of probation.

The parties may propose a plea agreement specifying VTC as a condition of probation for screened, eligible defendants. If the felony judge accepts a written plea agreement providing for VTC as a condition of probation, the VTC Judge shall have authority to execute a written order assigning all cases subject to such plea agreement to VTC. Any such plea agreement shall designate successful completion of all conditions of VTC as a special condition of probation in addition to any other agreed special conditions of probation.

D. *VTC Felony Pretrial Case Resolution.* As directed by section 948.08(7)(c) of the Florida Statutes, at the end of the pretrial intervention period, the VTC Judge shall consider the recommendation of the treatment program and the recommendation of the State as to disposition of the pending charges.

The VTC Judge shall determine, by written finding, whether the defendant has successfully completed the pretrial intervention program. The parties shall have notice and a fair opportunity to be heard prior to such determination.

If the VTC Judge finds that the defendant has not successfully completed the pretrial intervention program, the VTC Judge may order the person to continue in education and treatment, which may include treatment programs offered by licensed service providers or jail-based treatment programs, or order that the charges revert to normal channels for prosecution.

The VTC Judge shall dismiss the charges upon a finding that the defendant has successfully completed the pretrial intervention program.

E. *VTC Felony Post–Adjudicatory Case Resolution.* The VTC Judge shall determine whether the Defendant has adequately completed VTC.

Upon successful completion of Felony Post–Adjudicatory Veterans Treatment Court, the VTC Judge may consider granting a withhold of adjudication or early termination of probation by written order. With the consent of the State on the record, the VTC Judge may permit the defendant to withdraw a prior plea of no contest or guilty and administratively dismiss the VTC charges.

Upon unsuccessful completion of Felony Post–Adjudicatory Veterans Treatment Court, the VTC Judge shall, by written order, return such cases to the felony criminal division for ordinary prosecution. Prior to such written order, the State and Defendant shall have notice and a fair opportunity to be heard as to the exercise of the Court's discretion.

F. *VTC Conditions, Services and Sanctions.* No case or defendant shall be assigned to VTC unless the Defendant accepts successful completion of VTC conditions as the Defendant's binding, legal responsibility.

VTC conditions shall include waiver of speedy trial for pretrial defendants, attending VTC court dates as directed by the VTC Judge, participating in assessments by the Veterans Administration and such other providers as may be required by the VTC court, attending all scheduled assessment and treatment appointments, refraining from use or possession of illegal substances, submitting to substance abuse testing, and committing no criminal acts.

The VTC Judge shall have authority to designate such other special conditions as the State and Defendant agree or as otherwise ordered by the VTC Judge. Should the Defendant refuse to accept a condition deemed necessary by the VTC Judge, such refusal may be deemed withdrawal of voluntary consent by the Defendant, and therefore, unsuccessful completion of VTC.

All VTC treatment and other services for veterans shall be provided through or under the supervision of the Veterans Administration.

Servicemembers who are eligible for VTC court but excluded from Veterans Administration services shall receive service otherwise available through State, County, local and court administration resources.

The VTC Judge shall have authority to impose sanctions against the Defendant for noncompliance with VTC conditions including imposition of additional assessment and services, community service hours, jail work-camp if otherwise available, up to 10 days of jail time, order to the Department of Corrections for violation of probation processing and sentencing, and unsuccessful completion of VTC referral for ordinary prosecution. The State and Defense shall have notice and an opportunity to be heard before the issuance of an order imposing sanctions.

G. *New Charges During VTC.* The VTC Judge has discretion to determine whether new misdemeanor offenses committed during the period of VTC court supervision shall be referred to VTC court or whether such new offenses shall constitute unsuccessful completion of VTC. The State and Defense shall have notice and an opportunity to be heard before the issuance of an order assigning any new misdemeanor case to VTC or imposing unsuccessful completion sanctions.

Should the Defendant be charged with new felony offenses while assigned to VTC, such new felony offenses shall initially be assigned to the felony division. The assigned felony judge may assign, by written order, any new eligible felony charged defendant to the VTC at any time. The State and Defendant shall have notice and an opportunity to be heard before the issuance of an order assigning any felony case to VTC before trial. The VTC Judge has discretion to determine whether any new felony offense committed during the period of VTC court shall constitute unsuccessful completion of VTC.

VI. Effective Date.

This order shall become effective upon signing.

DONE and ORDERED in chambers in Tallahassee, Leon County, Florida, this 10th day of June 2016.

JONATHAN SJOSTROM
Chief Judge

Adopted effective June 10, 2016.

2016–02. FURLOUGH POLICY

IN THE SECOND JUDICIAL CIRCUIT OF FLORIDA

OFFICE OF THE CHIEF JUDGE

ADMINISTRATIVE ORDER 2016–02

IN RE: FURLOUGH POLICY

Whereas, it is appropriate to establish a uniform policy for the granting of furloughs in the Second Judicial Circuit, it is therefore

ORDERED that:

"Furloughs" as contemplated in this order do not include escorted transportation by law enforcement for medical, dental or psychological reasons.

Furlough applications may be initiated in several different ways:

1. **Defense motion:** All motions for inmate furloughs, both medical and non-medical for both pretrial and sentenced inmates shall adhere to the following procedures:

a. Defense counsel shall notify the Sheriff's designate that they will be seeking a furlough at least thirty-six (36) hours prior to the need for the furlough.

b. In the event that defense counsel cannot notify the Sheriff's Department thirty-six (36) hours prior to the requested furlough time, the Sheriff will make every effort to satisfy the request, but approval will be contingent upon the Sheriff's ability to staff the furlough under the time constraints.

c. Defense counsel shall first contact the Sheriff's designate. Defense counsel shall ascertain whether there is an objection to the furlough, whether the furlough is to be escorted and what the conditions of the furlough are to be. An e-mail should be sent to the Sheriffs designate once first contact (telephone message, e-mail or initial conversation) is made with the Sheriff's staff member. This will allow for planning to begin without regard to any delay in ascertaining court approval.

d. Defense counsel shall contact the Assistant State Attorney and advise of the Sheriff's position. Further, defense counsel shall ascertain the State's position.

e. Defense counsel shall draft a motion outlining all of the particulars. The motion shall set forth the position of the State and Sheriff. It shall state who defense counsel has contacted. The motion shall state whether the furlough is to be escorted, the time of release and the time of return. The motion also shall state that the defendant shall bear the cost of the furlough and that this payment will be paid in advance.

f. The Assistant State Attorney and Sheriff's designate shall be copied in the Certificate of Service of all motions. Likewise, both parties shall be noticed for any hearings that are required.

g. The decision to grant or deny a furlough shall be at the sole decision of the court, after considering input from the Sheriff's Office and the State Attorney's Office.

h. Any order granting a furlough shall be copied to the Office of the State Attorney, the Defense, the applicable detention facility and the Sheriff's designate.

i. If following the issuance of a furlough order, circumstances significantly change which affect the sheriff's ability to carry out the order or bring into question the advisability of carrying out the furlough order and time constraints do not allow review through normal procedures, the sheriff shall directly contact the judge issuing the order, or, if unavailable, the Chief Judge (during business hours) or the duty judge (after hours) for review of the matter.

2. **Informal Inmate Request:** No Sheriff or Sheriff's designate has the authority to grant a furlough based on informal inmate requests absent specific written Court order.

3. **Law Enforcement Request:** Any request by law enforcement to release an inmate for law enforcement purposes should be directed to the responsible Assistant State Attorney. It will be up to the State Attorney's Office to provide the appropriate pleadings to be submitted to the Court for approval. No inmate shall be released for law enforcement purposes absent specific written Court order. No inmate currently sentenced to a term in the state prison can be released for law enforcement purposes.

4. **Sheriff's Authority:** The Court recognizes that the Sheriff has been granted certain authority over inmates sentenced to the county jail by Chapter 951, Florida Statutes. Nothing in this order is intended to interfere with the Sheriff's authority as provided by Chapter 951, Florida Statutes, to allow work release (with Court approval), jail labor teams or gain time.

DONE and ORDERED at Tallahassee, Leon County, Florida this 2nd day of Feb., 2016.

JONATHAN SJOSTROM
Chief Judge

Adopted effective February 2, 2016.

2016–01. QUI TAM CASES UNDER THE FLORIDA FALSE CLAIMS ACT

IN THE SECOND JUDICIAL CIRCUIT OF FLORIDA

OFFICE OF THE CHIEF JUDGE

ADMINISTRATIVE ORDER 2016–01

IN RE: QUI TAM CASES UNDER THE FLORIDA FALSE CLAIMS ACT

WHEREAS, Section 68.083(3), Florida Statutes, provides for the filing of qui tam cases under the Florida False Claims Act only in the Circuit Court of the Second Judicial Circuit, in and for Leon County, Florida; and

WHEREAS, Section 68.083, Florida Statutes, does not provide explicit guidance to the Leon County Clerk of the Circuit Court and Comptroller ("Clerk") as to how to handle the confidentiality of these cases and/or the documents filed in these cases during the time period before the Florida Attorney General's Office notifies the Court of its intervention decision; and

WHEREAS, Section 68.083, Florida Statutes, does refer to the unsealing of the qui tam action in several places as well as the Florida Attorney General Office's ability to request extensions of the seal period (including through in camera submissions) thus indicating that such qui tam cases are initially filed under seal; and

WHEREAS, administrative orders AOSC14–19 and AOSC15–18 from the Florida Supreme Court do not address how the Clerk shall handle the confidentiality of such cases or filings in them; and

WHEREAS, it is necessary for the proper and efficient operation of the civil division to provide for the proper handling of such qui tam cases, it is therefore

ORDERED that:

1. The Clerk will seal the entire case file for 90 days without any need for an initial motion to seal the case file.

2. The Clerk will provide the Florida Attorney General's Office with a searchable report listing all of the sealed qui tam cases through an agency-specific tab on the Clerk's registered user website.

3. In the event the Florida Attorney General's Office does not request a seal extension within 90 days after the case's filing, the Clerk will make the entire case file public unless the Court has previously entered an order sealing all or part of the case file, consistent with Fla. R. Jud. Admin. 2.420.

4. If the Florida Attorney General's Office has filed a timely motion to extend the seal period, the Clerk will keep the entire file sealed pending the Court's ruling on the motion.

5. If the Court enters an order extending the seal period, the Clerk will maintain the confidentiality of the qui tam case file according to the terms of that order.

6. Once the Florida Attorney General's Office has notified the Court of its intervention or dismissal decision within the seal period, the Clerk will promptly make the entire qui tam case file public (without any need for a motion to unseal) unless the Court has previously entered an order sealing all or part of the case file as indicated above in paragraph 5.

DONE and ORDERED in chambers in Tallahassee, Leon County, Florida, this 26th day of January 2016.

JONATHAN SJOSTROM
Chief Judge

Adopted effective January 26, 2016.

2015–07. LEON COUNTY VETERANS TREATMENT COURT

IN THE SECOND JUDICIAL CIRCUIT OF FLORIDA

OFFICE OF THE CHIEF JUDGE

ADMINISTRATIVE ORDER 2015–07

IN RE: LEON COUNTY VETERANS TREATMENT COURT

WHEREAS, most veterans and servicemembers are strengthened by their military service, but for many, their experience has resulted in suffering from "invisible wounds" such as military service-related mental illness, traumatic brain injury, substance abuse disorder, or psychological problems; and

WHEREAS, if left untreated, these "invisible wounds" may directly lead to involvement in the criminal justice system, costing the criminal justice system, the community, the taxpayer, and the veterans or servicemembers themselves; and

WHEREAS, the *T. Patt Maney Veterans' Treatment Act*, section 394.47891, Florida Statutes, and sections 948.08(7)(a), 948.16(2)(a), and 948.21, Florida Statutes, authorizes the chief judge to establish felony and/or misdemeanor pretrial or post-adjudicatory veterans' treatment intervention programs to address the military service-related mental illness, traumatic brain injury, substance abuse disorder, or psychological problems of veterans and servicemembers charged with, or on probation or community control for, criminal offenses; and

WHEREAS, the 2015 Florida Legislature appropriated recurring state funds to establish a felony and/or misdemeanor pretrial or post-adjudicatory veterans treatment intervention program in Leon County, the Governor signed this legislation into law effective July 1, 2015, and the Leon County Board of County Commissioners agreed to serve as fiscal agent for a veterans court effective July 7, 2015; it is therefore

ORDERED that a Veterans Treatment Court (VTC) is established in Leon County in and for the Second Judicial Circuit of Florida, with an effective date of November 1, 2015, Nunc Pro Tunc.

DONE AND ORDERED in Tallahassee, Leon County, Florida this 30th day of November, 2015.

JONATHAN SJOSTROM
Chief Judge

Adopted effective November 1, 2015.

2015–06. CERTIFICATION AND REGULATION OF CIVIL PROCESS SERVERS

IN THE SECOND JUDICIAL CIRCUIT OF FLORIDA

OFFICE OF THE CHIEF JUDGE

ADMINISTRATIVE ORDER NO.: 2015–06

IN RE: CERTIFICATION AND REGULATION OF CIVIL PROCESS SERVERS

WHEREAS, since the inception of Administrative Rule 90–12, In re: Certification of Civil Process Servers, the number of Certified Civil Process Servers in the Circuit has increased ten-fold; and,

WHEREAS, the administrative burden of certification and regulation of Civil Process Servers pursuant to Section 48.25, et seq., Florida Statutes, has increased comparatively to the increase in the number of Certified Civil Process Servers; and,

WHEREAS, the Legislature of the State of Florida clearly intended to supplement service of process by the various sheriffs of Florida counties with an alternate means of service of civil process by Certified Civil Process Servers when it enacted Section 48.25, et seq., Florida Statutes; and,

WHEREAS, if this Court is to continue to exercise its discretionary power to certify and regulate Certified Civil Process Servers pursuant to Section 48.25, et seq., Florida Statutes, the procedures to be followed in the Second Judicial Circuit must be reformed and clarified;

WHEREAS, Administrative Order 2000–07, as amended, 2003–11 and 2010–03, created the Second Judicial Circuit Certified Civil Process Server Review Board which has been operating thereunder since, and the need has arisen for the modification of the procedures and guidelines by which the Second Judicial Circuit Certified Civil Process Server Review Board functions;

IT IS THEREFORE, ORDERED that:

1. Definitions & Authority.

(a) A Certified Civil Process Server means a natural person who has met the requirements for certification provided for in Section 48.29, Florida Statutes and this Administrative Order, and who has been placed on the approved list of certified process servers by the Chief Judge of the Second Judicial Circuit.

(b) A Board means the Second Judicial Circuit Certified Civil Process Server Review Board, as established by this Administrative Order.

(c) *Authority.* Placement of a person's name on the approved list of Certified Civil Process Servers authorizes him or her to serve initial non-enforceable civil process on a person found within the circuit where the process server is certified when a civil action has been filed against such person in the Circuit or County Court in the state. The Chief Judge may certify a civil process server in a specific County or Counties within the Circuit rather than Circuit-wide, in the Chief Judge's discretion and upon request of the applicant.

2. Purpose.

This administrative order is intended to ensure proficiency and professionalism in the service of civil process, in keeping with the public trust and legal importance of proper service of process.

3. Second Judicial Circuit Certified Civil Process Server Review Board.

(a) *Board Composition.* The Second Judicial Circuit Certified Civil Process Server Review Board is hereby created to monitor the certification and conduct of persons certified pursuant to this order and Section 48.25, et seq., Florida Statutes. The Board shall be under the supervisory authority of the Chief Judge of this Circuit. It shall be composed of three (3) Certified Civil Servers, one member of the Florida Bar practicing in this Circuit who regularly employs the services of a Certified Civil Process Server, one representative of a Clerk of Court within this Circuit who is familiar with the service of process, one representative of the law enforcement community in this Circuit who is familiar with the service of process, and one lay person from the general public. All members shall be appointed by the Chief Judge. Service on the Board at the Chief Judge's request shall be a condition of continued certification for the Certified Civil Process Servers.

(b) *Officers; Quorum.* Annually, the Board shall elect one of its members to serve as chair, and one to serve as vice-chair. A majority of the Board shall constitute a quorum.

(c) *Vacancies.* Any vacancy on the Board shall be filled by appointment by the Chief Judge. A person appointed to fill a vacancy shall serve for the remainder of the term of the member being replaced.

(d) *Terms.* The terms of all Board members shall be three (3) years. Board members shall be eligible for reappointment.

(e) *Duties.* The duties of the Board shall include the following:

(1) The Board shall be responsible for the recommendation of certification, receipt and review of complaints regarding Certified Civil Process Servers, issuance of notice of complaints to Certified Civil Process Servers, conduct of hearings, and recommendation of discipline of Certified Civil Process Servers to the Chief Judge of the Circuit.

(2) The Board shall have the authority to adopt rules governing its operating procedures.

(3) The Board may make recommendations to the Chief Judge regarding the amendment of these rules.

(f) *Fees.* Applicants shall pay an application and testing fee of $250.00, payable to "Leon County". The annual renewal fee shall be $150.00, payable to "Leon County", and shall be submitted with the request for renewal of certification as provided in Section 9 hereof. Fees are non-refundable.

(g) *Records.* The Board shall maintain records and minutes of its meetings, hearings, and all other official actions.

(h) *Expenses.* Members of the Board shall serve without compensation.

4. Application for Certification.

All applicants seeking certification shall apply to the Board on the application form attached hereto as attachment Number 1. The application and testing fee must be included with the application.

The Board shall accept applications for certification during normal working hours throughout the year. The Board will act on new applications as provided herein no later than March 15 of the then current year, for certification effective April 1 of that same year. All certifications shall be good for one (1) year, except as set forth in Sections 10 through 14 hereof.

5. Qualification.

Applications must satisfy the following requirements to qualify for certification in this Circuit:

(a) Be at least 18 years of age at the time the Board acts on their pending application as set forth in Section 9 hereof;

(b) Have no mental or legal disability.

(c) Be a permanent resident of this state;

(d) Attest that they have read and become familiar with the statutes, case law and rules governing the service of process;

(e) Take and pass a written examination administered by the Court and approved by the Chief Judge;

(f) Submit to a background investigation, at the applicant's expense, which shall include any criminal record of the applicant as evidenced by a certified copy of such fingerprint based criminal record from the Florida Department of Law Enforcement (Level 2 Background check) or the Federal Bureau of Investigation (NCIC—Identity History Summary Check);

(g) File with the Board a certificate of good conduct certifying:

(1) no record of any pending criminal case against the applicant;

(2) no record of any felony conviction for which civil rights have not been restored;

(3) no record of conviction of the applicant of a misdemeanor involving moral turpitude or dishonesty within the preceding 5 years;

(h) Take an oath of office that he or she will honestly, diligently, and faithfully exercise the duties of a Certified Process Server;

(i) Execute and file with the Board a bond in the amount of $5,000 with a surety bond company authorized to do business in this state for the benefit of any person injured by misfeasance, malfeasance, neglect of duty, or incompetence of the applicant in connection with his or her duties as a process server;

(j) File the forms, attached hereto as attachment number 2, from the Sheriff of each County in the Circuit indicating whether the Sheriff has any objection to the applicant being certified as a Certified Civil Process Server.

6. Examination.

The Court shall develop and administer a written examination to all applicants seeking Certified Civil Process Server certification, to ensure that such applicants possess a satisfactory level of knowledge of the laws and rules regarding the service of process. The contents of the examination shall be subject to the approval of the Chief Judge.

A passing score shall be no less than 80% of the questions answered correctly. The examination shall be administered not less than once each year, at such time and place as may be designated by the Court. Notice of the time and place for the test shall be provided by the Court to all applicants.

No person shall be eligible to sit for the examination until such time as the Board has in its possession the following documents:

a. The completed application referenced in Section 4 hereof;

b. The background investigation required by Section 5(f);

c. The certificate of good conduct required by Section 5(g);

d. The bond required by Section 5(i);

e. The forms from each Sheriff as required by Section 5(j);

f. The application and testing fee required by Section 3(f).

7. Issuance of Certification.

Upon satisfactory completion of the specified prerequisites, the Board shall recommend the applicant to the Chief Judge for entry on the list of Certified Civil Process Servers. If the Chief Judge is satisfied that the conditions have been met, the Chief Judge shall issue an order placing the applicant on the list of Certified Process Servers. The Chief Judge has broad discretion to make determinations considering whether to add an applicant to the list of Certified Process Servers. A copy of the order to the Court administrator and the Clerk of Court for each county shall maintain a list of Certified Process Servers based upon the court orders.

8. Identification Card.

Upon certification as a Certified Civil Process Server, the applicant shall be issued an identification card by the Court in the form prescribed by Section 48.29(5)(b), Florida Statutes. Costs incident to the preparation and issuance of the card shall be paid by the applicant. Each identification card shall be renewable annually upon proof of good standing, current bond, compliance with Section 9 hereof and payment of the renewal fee set out in section 3(f) above.

9. Renewal of Certificate.

(a) *Annual renewal.* Each Certified Civil Process Server shall pay an annual certificate renewal fee, payable to "Leon County", in the amount of $150.00. A certificate shall be suspended automatically upon nonpayment, but shall be reinstated upon application to the Board, accompanied by payment, made within 60 days of the date of suspension. Upon expiration of the 60–day grace period, any request for reinstatement must be made pursuant to sections 4, 5, and 6 of this Order.

(b) In addition to the renewal fee, the Certified Civil Process Server shall be the subject of inquiry to each of the Sheriffs of this Circuit to determine if any has any objections to the certification renewal of the Certified Civil Process Server.

(c) Execute and file with the Board a Renewal Certification on the form attached hereto as attachment number 3.

(d) *Biennial testing.* To assure that Certified Civil Process Servers have maintained adequate knowledge of current laws and rules applicable to service of process, renewal shall require the successful completion of the written examination within two years of the initial certification. A passing score shall be no less than 80% of the questions answered correctly. The renewal examination may be given more frequently and at different locations than the initial application. The Board may require every Certified Civil Process Server to submit to the written examination at any time prior to the renewal of his/her certification.

(e) The Board shall take action as required herein no later than March 15 of the then current year for certification effective April 1 of that same year. All certifications shall be good for one (1) year, except as set forth in Sections 10 through 14 hereof.

10. Prohibited Conduct Generally.

The following conduct is prohibited, and may lead to disciplinary action:

(a) accepting employment in which the Certified Process Server has an interest, or continuing employment after becoming aware of the existence of an interest;

(b) making false statements or misrepresentations regarding other Certified Process Servers in this Circuit to any person with the intent to obtain business as a result of such false statements or misrepresentations;

(c) making false statements or omissions to any person with regard to the Certified Process Server's identity or legal authority in order to effect service of process;

(d) continuation of false or deceptive advertising or other activity intended to generate business after receipt of a cease and desist letter from the Board;

(e) use of threatening or intimidating tactics to obtain client lists or other business records from other Certified Process Servers' offices or from client's offices.

(f) alcohol or drug abuse, physical incapacity, or mental instability, which interferes or is likely to interfere with the performance of the duties of a Certified Civil Process Server;

(g) misrepresentation as to the identity of the party receiving service or the process server who actually delivered the service. (Note that knowingly executing a false return of service is a felony of the third degree);

(h) obtained the certification by fraudulent means;

(i) had his/her certification revoked in another state and/or circuit;

(j) has been the subject of a court order adjudicating the certified civil process server delinquent on his/her child support obligation;

(k) accepting a gratuity, gift or favor that might influence professional judgment;

(*l*) failing to maintain honesty in all professional dealings;

(m) making malicious or intentionally false statements about a colleague;

(n) misrepresenting one's own professional qualifications;

(*o*) submitting fraudulent information on any document in connection with professional activities;

(p) misrepresenting one's own identity in order to avoid service of process;

(q) any other practices which constitute malfeasance, misfeasance, neglect of duty, or incompetence;

(r) having a suspension or revocation of a certified process server's authority to serve process in another circuit.

11. Conduct Warranting Revocation of Certification.

A certificate issued pursuant to these rules may be revoked for any of the following reasons:

(a) conviction of a felony, or of a misdemeanor involving moral turpitude, dishonesty, or false statement;

(b) fraud, dishonesty, or corruption which is related to the functions and duties of a Certified Civil Process Server;

(c) fraud or misrepresentation in obtaining or renewing certification;

(d) nonpayment of renewal fees;

(e) engaging in any of the prohibited activities listed in Subsection 10 above.

12. Disciplinary Procedures.

(a) *Initiation.* Disciplinary proceedings may be initiated before the Board, either by a signed written complaint asserting a violation of these rules, or by the Board, on its own motion.

(b) *Probable Cause; Notification.* If a majority of the Board finds probable cause to believe that a violation of these rules has occurred, it shall send written notice thereof, identifying the rule or rules alleged to have been violated, to the Certified Civil Process Server by certified United States mail directed to the last mailing address on file with the Board. The Board shall further notify the Chief Judge of its finding, who shall have the authority to temporarily suspend the certification of the Certified Civil Process Server pending the outcome of the disciplinary process set forth herein.

(c) *Response.* Within 30 days of the issuance of a finding of probable cause, the Certified Civil Process Server shall file a written response with the Board. If the Certified Civil Process Server does not respond, the violations identified in the finding of probable cause shall be deemed admitted.

(d) *Board Review.* Within 60 days after the filing of the written response to the finding of probable cause or within 60 days following the expiration of the time within which to file a response if none is filed, the Board shall review the complaint, the finding of probable cause, the response (if any), and any other pertinent materials, and decide whether to:

(1) dismiss the proceeding;

(2) issue a proposed disposition; or

(3) set a hearing.

The Board shall promptly send written notice of its decision to the Certified Civil Process Server, by certified United States mail to the last address on file with the Board.

(e) *No Hearing Demanded.* A proposed disposition issued pursuant to subdivision (d)(2) shall become final unless the Certified Civil Process Server demands a hearing within 30 days of the date on which it was issued.

(f) *Timing of Hearing.* Absent good cause, no hearing shall take place less than 30 days, or more than 90 days, from the date of notice pursuant to subdivision (d)(3) or of the Certified Civil Process Server's demand pursuant to subdivision (e).

(g) *Identity of Complainant.* Upon written request filed with the Board after a hearing has been set, the Board shall promptly reveal to the Certified Civil Process Server the identity of the complaining party.

(h) *Legal Representation.* The Certified Civil Process Server may be represented by an attorney at any stage of the proceeding. The Certified Civil Process Server shall be responsible for all of his or her costs and expenses, including attorney fees.

(i) Nothing herein shall limit the power of the Chief Judge to take whatever action he/she deems appropriate pending the conclusion of the Disciplinary Procedures, including but not limited to imposing any of the Disciplinary Dispositions contained herein.

13. Disciplinary Hearings.

(a) *Pre-hearing Discovery.* Pre-hearing discovery shall not be permitted unless expressly authorized by the Board, in response to a written request.

(b) *Rules of Evidence.* Strict rules of evidence shall not apply. The Board may, in its discretion, consider any evidence presented, including affidavits, giving such evidence the weight it deems appropriate.

(c) *Hearings to be Reported.* The Board shall ensure that all hearings are reported.

(d) *Hearing Procedure.* At the hearing, both the Board and the Certified Civil Process Server shall be afforded the opportunity to introduce documents and other relevant evidence, and to elicit sworn testimony.

(e) *Board Deliberations.* Following the presentation of evidence, the Board shall deliberate regarding its decision. Such deliberations shall take place in private.

(f) *Finality of Decision; Rehearing.* Unless the Certified Civil Process Server files a request for rehearing within 10 days of the date he receives the decision, the Board's decision shall be forwarded to the Chief Judge as a recommendation of disposition. If a timely request for rehearing is filed, the decision shall not be forwarded to the Chief Judge until the request has been disposed of by written decision, a copy of which shall be sent to the Certified Civil Process Server by certified United States mail directed to the last mailing address on file with the Board.

14. Disciplinary Dispositions.

(a) *Burden of Proof.* If the Board finds that there is clear and convincing evidence that the Certified Civil Process Server has violated one or more of these rules it shall recommend to the Chief Judge such discipline as it may deem appropriate, consistent with these rules.

(b) *Vote Required; Notification.* All decisions of the Board shall be by majority vote, in writing, and, if adverse to the Certified Civil Process Server, shall contain factual findings supporting the decision. A copy of the decision shall be sent to the Certified Civil Process Server by certified United States mail directed to the last mailing address on file with the Board.

(c) *Sanctions.* Discipline recommended by the Board and imposed by the Chief Judge may consist of one or more of the following:

(1) a reprimand from the Board;

(2) a reprimand from the Chief Judge;

(3) the imposition of costs and expenses incurred by the Board in connection with the proceeding, including investigative costs;

(4) restitution;

(5) requiring that the Certified Civil Process Server certification examination be successfully taken, or retaken;

(6) limiting the geographic scope of practice by county;

(7) suspension of certification not to exceed one (1) year, after which the individual may seek reinstatement of his/her certification as provided in Section 9 hereof, and upon any other conditions the Chief Judge may deem appropriate.

(8) revocation of certification.

(d) If, after reviewing the Board's recommendation and factual findings, the Chief Judge determines that sanctions are appropriate, the Chief Judge shall enter an order imposing sanctions. However, if a reprimand by the Board is the appropriate penalty, the Chief Judge need not enter an order. The Office of the Court Administrator and the Clerk of Court for each County shall update the list of Certified Civil Process Servers with notations or removals based upon the court orders.

15. Confidentiality of Disciplinary Proceedings.

When a disciplinary proceeding is either dismissed or results in a reprimand from the Board, all records of the proceeding shall remain confidential; otherwise, all such records shall become public when the Chief Judge makes a final disposition.

16. Review of Adverse Disciplinary Dispositions.

Within 30 days of a final adverse disciplinary disposition after a hearing, the Certified Civil Process Server may seek review by common law certiorari to the First District Court of Appeal pursuant to Rule 9.100, Florida Rules of Appellate Procedure.

17. Reinstatement.

A Certified Civil Process Server whose certificate has been revoked may apply in writing for reinstatement. Such request shall explain why the applicant believes that he or she should be reinstated, and shall be accompanied by current Sheriffs' Advisory Forms from each Sheriff in the Circuit and a renewal fee of $150.00. Whether to recommend to the Chief Judge for or against such a request shall rest in the sole and absolute discretion of the Board. The Board may recommend such conditions upon reinstatement as it deems appropriate.

18. Effective Date.

This Order shall take effect on December 1, 2015. The provisions of this Order shall apply to all applicants filing applications on or after the effective date hereof, and all renewals sought after the effective date hereof. Current certifications shall remain in effect but shall be renewed under these rules when the current certification expires. Current certifications are subject to the restrictions and disciplinary provisions herein as of December 1, 2015. Administrative Order 2015–05 is **TERMINATED.**

DONE and **ORDERED** this 25th day of November 2015.

JONATHAN SJOSTROM
Chief Judge

Adopted effective December 1, 2015.

2015–04. LEON COUNTY DUTY JUDGE

IN THE SECOND JUDICIAL CIRCUIT OF FLORIDA
OFFICE OF THE CHIEF JUDGE

ADMINISTRATIVE ORDER NO: 2015–04

IN RE: LEON COUNTY DUTY JUDGE

WHEREAS, applications for search warrants and other legal matters of extreme urgency, i.e., matters of life and death or instances of true irreparable harm that require immediate action by a judge, may arise outside the course of normal court business hours in Leon County;

WHEREAS, local law enforcement agencies and other parties have contacted judges of their choice to hear these matters;

WHEREAS, it is appropriate and necessary that the Court create a system to fairly assign this burden and assure access to a judge to consider applications for search warrants and hear other legal matters of extreme urgency outside normal court business hours; and

WHEREAS, pursuant to section 43.19, Florida Statutes, and rule 2.215(b), Florida Rules of Judicial Administration, the Chief Judge is responsible for the administrative supervision of the courts, and has the power and responsibility to promote the prompt and efficient administration of justice in all courts within the circuit; it is therefore

ORDERED that:

1. By separate document, the Chief Judge shall promulgate a Leon County duty judge assignment document so that a judge, hereinafter referred to as the "Leon County duty judge," shall be available as directed in this administrative order to handle applications for search warrants and other emergency matters in Leon County.

2. For purposes of this administrative order, "emergency matters" encompass applications for search warrants and other legal matters of extreme urgency, i.e., matters of life and death or instances of true irreparable harm that require immediate action by a judge. Not included in this definition are matters of extreme urgency when the Leon County Courthouse is open or the irreparable harm will not worsen if addressed during the next normal court business day or at the routine weekend and holiday first appearance hearings held at the Leon County Jail. This order is not intended to replace the responsibility of a judge duly assigned to review domestic and repeat violence injunctions as part of his or her regular assignment during the normal court business day.

3. The Leon County duty judge shall not be responsible for emergency matters in Franklin, Gadsden, Jefferson, Liberty, and Wakulla Counties; those emergency matters will be the responsibility of the local county judge or duly assigned circuit judge.

4. Every judge in the circuit with a Leon County assignment, even part-time assignment, shall be assigned to preside in turn as the Leon County duty judge. The Office of Court Administration for the Second Judicial Circuit will prepare a draft of the Leon County duty judge assignment document for the Chief Judge's review and approval. Once approved, the Leon County duty judge assignment document will be distributed to all assigned judges.

5. Assignment as a Leon County duty judge will coincide, insofar as possible, with the routine weekend and holiday first appearance hearings assigned to each judge. When the routine weekend and holiday first appearance schedule has a non–Leon County assigned judge, then Leon County assigned judges will be scheduled to perform Leon County duty judge duties in as fair a manner as possible, with each having equal assignment over an extended period of time.

6. All Leon County Court Judges are hereby temporarily assigned to serve as Circuit Judges while functioning as the Leon County duty judge and are vested with all and singular the powers and prerogatives conferred by the Constitution and Laws of the State of Florida upon a Circuit Court Judge.

7. Alterations or substitutions in the published Leon County duty judge assignment document must be executed via e-mail between the judges with a copy sent to the Office of Court Administration for the Second Judicial Circuit. Judges may freely assign and re-assign this duty as they see fit, as long as all parties to the reassignment agree and the Office of Court Administration for the Second Judicial Circuit is notified.

8. Local law enforcement or others needing access to the Leon County duty judge will call a single cellular telephone number provided by the Office of Court Administration for the Second Judicial Circuit. The Leon County duty judge cellular telephone will be provided by the Office of Court Administration for the Second Judicial Circuit and given to each Leon County duty judge in turn as their duty period begins.

9. The transfer of responsibility from one Leon County duty judge to the next shall occur at 8:30 a.m. on Tuesday of each week. The Leon County duty judge will receive a cellular telephone and a charger.

10. The Leon County duty judge is responsible to answer this cellular telephone any time other than normal court business days from 7:00 a.m. until 5.00 p.m. This includes answering this cellular telephone on weekends and holidays after the first appearance is completed at the Leon County Jail. The Leon County duty judge will then handle the search warrant or other emergency matters in Leon County. Applications for search warrants and other legal matters of extreme urgency that arise between the times of 7:00 a.m. and until 5:00 p.m. on normal court business days will be handled by the properly assigned judge or procedures, not the Leon County duty judge.

11. If the Leon County duty judge cannot be reached, the party attempting to call the Leon County duty judge should contact the Office of Court Administration for the Second Judicial Circuit, who will likewise attempt to contact the Leon County duty judge, and if unsuccessful, contact the Chief Judge.

12. If the Leon County duty judge determines that the after normal court business hours call was not a matter of extreme urgency, i.e., a matter of life and death or instance of true irreparable harm, they should report this to the Office of Court Administration for the Second Judicial Circuit. The Office of Court Administration for the Second Judicial Circuit will investigate the matter and refer all findings and documents to the Chief Judge, who may or may not act upon this information as the Chief Judge deems appropriate.

13. The provisions of this administrative order shall be complied with effective July 1st, 2015.

14. This administrative order complements Administrative Order 2014–05 and First, Second, Third, and Fourth Amendments thereto, and in no way supersedes Paragraph VIII of said order, especially for emergency matters to be handled during normal court business hours.

DONE AND ORDERED in the Office of the Circuit Judge, this 30th day of June, 2015.

JONATHAN SJOSTROM
Acting–Chief Judge

Adopted effective July 1, 2015.

2014–02. SECOND JUDICIAL CIRCUIT PROFESSIONALISM PANEL—PROCEDURES FOR PROCESSING PROFESSIONALISM COMPLAINTS

IN THE CIRCUIT COURT OF THE
SECOND JUDICIAL CIRCUIT

OFFICE OF THE CHIEF JUDGE

ADMINISTRATIVE ORDER NO. 2014—02

IN RE: SECOND JUDICIAL CIRCUIT PROFESSIONALISM PANEL—PROCEDURES FOR PROCESSING PROFESSIONALISM COMPLAINTS

WHEREAS, the Florida Supreme Court issued its decision In re: Code for Resolving Professionalism Complaints, 116 So. 3d 280 (Fla. 2013) directing the Chief Judge of each circuit to create a local professionalism panel to receive, screen and act upon complaints of unprofessional conduct and resolve those complaints informally, if possible, or refer them to The Florida Bar if necessary, and

WHEREAS, on December 30, 2013, through Second Circuit Administrative Order 2013–09, the Second Judicial Circuit Professionalism Committee was re-constituted as the Second Judicial Circuit Professionalism Panel, and

WHEREAS, the Panel was ordered, within sixty (60) days, to develop and prepare a written procedure for the receipt, screening and resolution of professionalism complaints, and shall have the authority to amend the same from time to time, consistent with the order of The Supreme Court, including requirements for confidentiality.

NOW THEREFORE, in accordance with the order of The Supreme Court of Florida, the Chief Judge's authority under Article V, § 2, Florida Constitution, 2.215 Fla. R. Jud. Admin., and § 43.26, Florida Statutes, it is hereby

ORDERED that the following procedure shall be adopted in the Second Judicial Circuit to process professionalism complaints before the Second Judicial Circuit Professionalism Panel:

I. Standards and Purpose: The purpose of the Local Professionalism Panel is to receive, screen, evaluate and act upon complaints of conduct inconsistent with the "'Standards of Professionalism" as defined in The Supreme Court's opinion, and to resolve those complaints informally, if possible, or refer them to the Attorney Consumer Assistance Program (ACAP) at The Florida Bar depending upon the nature and severity of the complaint.

II. Initiation of a Complaint:

a. The form required for initiation of a complaint shall be made available on the Second Judicial Circuit website.

b. Any person may initiate a professionalism complaint against a member of The Florida Bar through the Professionalism Panel. The Professionalism Panel may also accept referrals sent by ACAP at The Florida Bar.

c. Attorneys are encouraged, prior to referring conduct to the panel, to discuss the situation with the other attorney involved in an effort to reach an amicable resolution consistent with the above-referenced professionalism standards and guidelines.

III. Procedure for Review and Processing Complaints:

a. The Chair of the Professionalism Panel shall create a "Complaint Resolution Sub–Panel" to receive and review any and all professionalism complaints to determine if any action should be taken. The "Complaint Resolution Sub–Panel" shall be comprised of the Chair of the Professionalism Panel or a member of the Professionalism Panel designated by the Chair and two (2) other members of the Professionalism Panel, also designated by the Chair on a per complaint rotating basis.

b. The Complaint Resolution Sub–Panel may decide, by majority, at the initial review of the Complaint that the conduct is too severe to be handled by the Local Professionalism Panel and may determine to refer the Complaint to ACAP at The Florida Bar.

c. If, by majority, the Complaint Resolution Sub–Panel determines that the complaint may be resolved by a telephone consultation with the attorney who is the subject of the complaint, or by an informal meeting, the matter may be resolved informally by such means.

d. In the event the complaint is not resolved by an informal telephone call, and a meeting (formal or informal) is required, the attorney who is the subject of the complaint will be furnished with a letter enclosing a copy of the complaint and providing the subject attorney with an opportunity to submit a written response. The subject attorney shall be advised that participation with the Professionalism Panel is voluntary and intended to avoid further formal action being taken against the subject attorney through The Florida Bar.

e. Any letter sent by the Local Professionalism Panel to a subject attorney requesting that the subject attorney appear before the Local Professionalism Panel shall identify the conduct alleged to be inconsistent with the Standards of Professionalism. The letter shall also advise the subject attorney that the Local Professionalism Panel meeting is a non-disciplinary proceeding. A complete reference to the citations of the Standards of Professionalism shall be included in the letter. The letter shall also advise the subject attorney that if he or she fails to appear before the Local Professionalism Panel without being excused beforehand then the Local Professionalism Panel will proceed with its meeting and decide whether to address the request or refer it to the ACAP at The Florida Bar for resolution.

f. If, by majority, the Complaint Resolution Sub–Panel determines that the complaint presents a serious violation, then the panel will contact the referring party and the attorney who is the subject of the complaint and schedule a formal hearing. At said hearing, each party will have an opportunity to attend and present their positions. The hearing may be conducted with both the referring party and the attorney subject to the complaint present, in a mediation format, or in such other format as the panel deems appropriate.

g. Upon conclusion of a formal hearing, the panel will issue a written decision and submit it to the Chief Judge. Copies will be provided to both the referring party and the attorney who is the subject of the complaint. Among other things, the committee may refer the subject attorney to a professionalism or ethics seminar authorized by The Florida Bar, refer the subject attorney to a mentor, and/or to Florida Lawyers Assistance, Inc., or issue the subject attorney a letter of advice. Failure to follow the recommendations of the Local Professionalism Panel may be a basis for referral to ACAP at The Florida Bar.

h. The Local Professionalism Panel should strive to resolve all referrals within forty-five (45) days of receipt of the request.

IV. Confidentiality: All committee members, referring parties, and subject attorneys will be required to sign statements acknowledging:

a. The Local Professionalism Panel is a voluntary, information program intended to be non-punitive, educational and constructive. The Panel shall not have the authority to impose sanctions or disciplinary measures, but shall serve as an effort to avoid further potential disciplinary proceedings through promoting professionalism. However, failure to comply with the recommendations of the Panel may result in the Complaint being sent to ACAP at The Florida Bar.

b. Should the Local Professionalism Panel choose to process a request, and the referring party and subject attorney agree, information disclosed during the panel process is confidential and may not be disclosed to anyone except other panel members, the referring party, the subject attorney, The Florida Bar, or as otherwise required by law or by rule of court.

V. Records: The Individual Reporting Form for Local Circuit Professionalism Panel, as provided by The Florida Supreme Court, shall be used to make a written record of each complaint and shall include a copy of the complaint, responses (if any), formal decision (if any), and memo outlining the resolution of the complaint.

Said written records will be maintained by the Chair of the Professionalism Panel or a member of the Professionalism Panel designated by the Chair for a period of one hundred and twenty (120) days, and shall be used to compile the information necessary to prepare the Local Circuit Professionalism Panel Quarterly Summary Report to The Florida Supreme Court, as provided by The Florida Supreme Court.

At the conclusion of the one hundred and twenty (120) days, the Individual Reporting Form along with its attachments shall be destroyed. The Chair of the Professionalism Panel or a member of the Professionalism Panel designated by the Chair will maintain program records, in docket form, identifying the complaint file number, the date the complaint was made, the manner in which the complaint was resolved, and the date of the resolution. The records will not include the names of the referring parties or subject attorneys, but will be forwarded and maintained by the Chief Judge in accordance with Rule 2.440, Florida Rules of Judicial Administration.

DONE and ORDERED this 24th day of February, 2014.

CHARLES A. FRANCIS
Chief Judge

Adopted effective February 24, 2014.

2013–09. SECOND JUDICIAL CIRCUIT PROFESSIONALISM PANEL

IN THE CIRCUIT COURT OF THE SECOND JUDICIAL CIRCUIT

OFFICE OF THE CHIEF JUDGE

ADMINISTRATIVE ORDER NO. 2013–09

IN RE: SECOND JUDICIAL CIRCUIT PROFESSIONALISM PANEL

WHEREAS, the bench and bar of the Second Judicial Circuit have historically endeavored to encourage, promote and maintain a high standard of professionalism in the Circuit; and

WHEREAS, the "Tallahassee Bar Association—Code of Professional Courtesy" was endorsed by the judiciary of the Second Judicial Circuit by Administrative Order 90–26; and

WHEREAS, pursuant to the directive of former Chief Justice Gerald Kogan of The Supreme Court of Florida, the Second Judicial Circuit Professionalism Committee was established by Administrative order 2003–12 to assess the status and conditions of professionalism and to encourage and promote professionalism and ethics within the Second Judicial Circuit; and

WHEREAS, in an effort to address professionalism complaints on an informal basis, and to enhance communication, constructive problem solving, respect and courtesy between judges and lawyers of the Second Judicial Circuit, and pursuant to Amended Administrative Order of The Supreme Court of Florida, the Second Judicial Circuit Bench/Bar Committee was formally established by Administrative Order 2003–09 to replace the informal bench/bar committee that had been productively functioning for many years prior to such formal order; and

WHEREAS, The Supreme Court of Florida has issued its opinion entitled "In Re: Code for Resolving Professionalism Complaints" [116 So.3d 280 (Fla. June 6, 2013)] in which the Chief Judge of every Circuit was ordered "to create a Local Professionalism Panel to receive and resolve professionalism complaints informally, if possible."

NOW THEREFORE, in accordance with the order of The Supreme Court of Florida, the Chief Judge's authority under Article V, § 2, Florida Constitution, 2.215, Fla. R. Jud. Admin., and § 43.26, Florida Statutes, it is hereby

ORDERED as follows:

1. The Second Judicial Circuit Professionalism Committee is hereby re-constituted as the Second Judicial Circuit Professionalism Panel ("Panel").

2. The purpose of the Panel is to receive, screen, evaluate and act upon complaints of conduct inconsistent with the "Standards of Professionalism" as defined in The Supreme Court's opinion, and resolve those complaints informally, if possible, or refer them to The Florida Bar if appropriate or necessary, and to perform all duties and responsibilities required by The Supreme Court of Florida in its opinion "In Re: Code for Resolving Professionalism Complaints". In the performance of its duties and responsibilities, the Panel shall not have the authority to discipline attorneys, and shall not have the authority to compel any attorney to appear before it.

3. The Panel shall consist of not less than twenty (20), nor more than forty (40) members selected and appointed from time to time by the Chief Judge. The Chief Judge shall strive to select members who represent a cross-section of the Circuit, with due consideration to such matters as, but not limited to, geographic location, diversity, professional reputation and bar activities. Representatives of bar organizations within the Circuit are encouraged to suggest names of appropriate representatives for future Panel membership. The Chief Judge shall appoint the Chair and Vice–Chair of the Panel.

4. The Chief Judge shall not be a member of the Panel, but may preside over the Panel when deemed by the Chief Judge to be necessary or appropriate.

5. Meetings of the Panel may be called by the Chair, a majority of the Panel members or the Chief Judge. Notice of any Panel meeting shall be given to each Panel member in such a manner as deemed appropriate by the Chair. E-mail or telephonic notice is expressly approved. The notice requirement that notice be given to each member of the Panel shall not be applicable to any meeting of a sub-committee or sub-panel established by the Chair. Notice to the members of the sub-committee or sub-panel shall be sufficient.

6. Those persons listed in Exhibit A [1] attached shall constitute the initial Panel and shall serve at the discretion of the Chief Judge. The membership of the Panel, as it may change from time to time, shall be posted on the Second Judicial Circuit webpage.

7. The Panel shall develop and prepare a written procedure for the receipt, screening and resolution of professionalism complaints, and shall have the authority to amend the same from time to time, consistent with the order of The Supreme Court, including requirements for confidentiality. The written procedures shall be provided to the Chief Judge within sixty (60) days from the date of this order and shall be posted on the Second Judicial Circuit website. Amendments to such procedures as adopted from time to time, and such other matters as the Panel deems appropriate, shall also be posted on the website. Any such procedures shall specifically provide for the use by the Panel of the Individual Reporting Form For Local Circuit Professionalism Panel, attached as Exhibit B, [1]and preparation of the Local Circuit Professionalism Panel Quarterly Summary Report To The Florida Supreme Court, attached as Exhibit C.[1]

8. The Panel shall also assess the status and conditions of professionalism in the Second Judicial Circuit and encourage and develop educational programs and activities to promote the Code of Professionalism in the Circuit. The Panel shall report the results of its assessment, educational and program development and activities in writing to the Chief Judge annually on or before December 1 of each calendar year.

9. The Chair of the Panel shall have the authority to establish such sub-committees and sub-panels of the Panel as deemed necessary or appropriate to fulfill the duties and responsibilities of the Panel, including, but not limited to, a complaint resolution sub-panel(s) and an education and assessment sub-panel(s).

10. The Panel shall meet as is necessary to fulfill its responsibilities, but in no event less than twice annually.

11. Administrative Order 2003–12, as amended is hereby vacated and superceded by this order.

12. This order shall be effective immediately.

Done and Ordered this 30th day of December, 2013.

CHARLES A. FRANCIS
Chief Judge

Adopted effective December 30, 2013.

[1] Exhibits A, B and C not included. Please check 2ndcircuit.leoncountyfl.gov/Professional_directory.php for the current list of Professional Panel members, along with any updated forms needed for the Professionalism Panel.

2013–07. CASE STATUS REPORTING REQUIREMENTS FOR REAL PROPERTY MORTGAGE FORECLOSURE CASES

IN THE SECOND JUDICIAL CIRCUIT OF FLORIDA

OFFICE OF THE CHIEF JUDGE

ADMINISTRATIVE ORDER 2013–07

IN RE: CASE STATUS REPORTING REQUIREMENTS FOR REAL PROPERTY MORTGAGE FORECLOSURE CASES

WHEREAS, the status of a foreclosure case and related definitions have been adopted by the Florida Supreme Court and are published in the Foreclosure Initiative Data Collection Plan promulgated by the Office of the State Courts Administrator; and

WHEREAS, Florida Supreme Court Administrative Order No. AOSC13–15 In Re: Case Status Reporting Requirements for Real Property Mortgage Foreclosure Cases finds it beneficial to require the chief judge of every circuit court to issue an administrative order implementing an effective communication mechanism by which the courts and clerks are notified of case status changes in real property mortgage foreclosure cases in a timely manner, and further requires the chief judge of every circuit court to issue an administrative order providing direction for designating the status of cases as active or inactive, it is therefore

ORDERED that:

1. Foreclosure Initiative Data Collection Plan. The clerks of the courts for the Second Judicial Circuit are directed to comply with the requirements of the Foreclosure Initiative Data Collection Plan as promulgated by the Office of the State Courts Administrator.

2. Notification by Clerk of Change in Case Status. When the clerks of the court become aware of events initiating a change in the status of a case (active or inactive) the clerk shall notify the court for further review.

3. Orders Directing Change of Case Status. When the court becomes aware of events initiating a change in the status of a case or when the clerk notifies the court of events initiating a change in the status of a case, the court shall issue an order directing the change in case status. The attached documents provide sample orders directing the change of status for a case.

4. Effective Date. This order shall be effective immediately.

DONE and ORDERED in Tallahassee, Leon County, Florida, October 24, 2013.

CHARLES A. FRANCIS
Chief Judge

[ATTACHMENT A]

IN THE CIRCUIT COURT OF THE SECOND JUDICIAL CIRCUIT IN AND FOR ________ COUNTY, FLORIDA

Plaintiff

vs. **CASE NO**

Defendant

________/

ORDER PLACING CASE ON INACTIVE STATUS

This cause came before the Court on the motion of ☐ Plaintiff/ ☐ Defendant to place the case on INACTIVE status due to:

☐ Bankruptcy stay, Case No. ___ [BKST]

☐ Case pending resolution of another case, Case No. ___ [CPRC]

☐ Written agreement of the parties [BWAP]

☐ Appeal pending [AP]

☐ Motion to stay or abate due to Department of Justice/Attorney General settlement [DOJ/AG]

☐ Other (a reason must be provided in writing by the presiding judge or designee) [OTH]

____

The Clerk of Court is therefore directed to remove this case from the ACTIVE status, and designate it as an INACTIVE case based on the reason checked above. The parties must move to return the case to active status, with notice to all parties, within 30 days of the termination of grounds for inactive status, and obtain an order of court to return it to active status.

DONE and ORDERED in ________ County, Florida, on this ___ day of ________, 2013.

____
Circuit Judge

[ATTACHMENT B]

IN THE CIRCUIT COURT OF THE SECOND JUDICIAL CIRCUIT IN AND FOR ________ COUNTY, FLORIDA

Plaintiff

vs. CASE NO

Defendant

____________/

ORDER RESTORING CASE TO ACTIVE STATUS

This cause came before the Court on the motion of ☐ Plaintiff/ ☐ Defendant to restore the case to ACTIVE status due to:

☐ Bankruptcy stay having been lifted, Case No. ___ [BKST]

☐ Related case having been resolved or disposed, Case No. ___ [CPRC]

☐ Written agreement of the parties [BWAP]

☐ Appeal disposed [AP]

☐ Department of Justice/Attorney General settlement review has been completed [DOJ/AG]

☐ Other (a reason must be provided in writing by the presiding judge or designee) [OTH]

____

The Clerk of Court is therefore directed to remove this case from the INACTIVE status, and designate it as an ACTIVE case based on the reason checked above.

It is further ORDERED: ____________________

____

____

DONE and ORDERED in ________ County, Florida, on this ___ day of ________, 2013.

____

Circuit Judge

Adopted effective October 24, 2013.

2013–06. COURT INTERPRETER PROGRAM

IN THE SECOND JUDICIAL CIRCUIT,
LEON COUNTY, FLORIDA

OFFICE OF THE CHIEF JUDGE

ADMINISTRATIVE ORDER NO: 2013–06

IN RE: COURT INTERPRETER PROGRAM

WHEREAS, the Florida Supreme Court issued Administrative Order AOSC11–45 in response to the Commission on Trial Court Performance and Accountability's report entitled *Recommendations for the Provision of Court Interpreting Services in Florida's Trial Courts,* containing general recommendations, standards of operation, and best practices; and

WHEREAS, the standards of operation are intended to be mandatory practices that must be implemented. Best practices are suggested practices, intended to improve operations, but are not required, due to local conditions beyond the court's control; and

WHEREAS, one of the mandatory standards of operation is that each circuit shall establish an assignment system for contract court interpreters; it is therefore

ORDERED that these standard operating procedures for the Second Judicial Circuit's Court Interpreter Program are adopted, effective immediately:

1. The Court Interpreter Services Coordinator will schedule and assign all court interpreting events.

2. Interpreters that are recognized by the state to be certified or duly qualified shall be given priority for assignments. Whenever possible, an interpreter certified by the Registry of Interpreters for the Deaf / National Association of the Deaf shall be appointed to provide interpreting services to court participants who are deaf, hard of hearing, late-deafened, or deaf blind. If, after diligent search, a certified or duly qualified interpreter is not available, an interpreter who is otherwise qualified may be appointed if the judge or hearing officer presiding over the proceeding finds that good cause exists for the appointment of an interpreter who is not certified, such as the prevention of burdensome delay, the request or consent of the participant, or other unusual circumstances; and the proposed interpreter is competent to interpret in the proceedings and agrees to do so. The Court Interpreter Services Coordinator shall be contacted in such instance.

3. Remote interpreting shall be used when a live interpreter is not available or when circumstances render it the most feasible option. Remote interpreting includes telephonic and video interpreting. All remote interpreting events shall be reported to the Court Interpreter Services Coordinator.

4. Interpreter services may only be requested by a judge, judicial assistant, trial clerk, or Court Administration. If the services of an interpreter are needed at a hearing, the attorney must so inform the judicial assistant when scheduling the hearing. Counsel must inform the judicial assistant of the need for interpreter services as soon as counsel is made aware of the need. If interpreter services are needed for trial or plea or for a witness who will testify in court, the attorney shall so inform the court at the pre-trial conference.

5. Requests shall be made no less than two (2) business days in advance of the scheduled date for Spanish interpreters, and no less than ten (10) business days in advance of the scheduled date for all other languages. Arrangements will be made for same day requests depending upon the availability of resources.

6. When there is limited availability of interpreters, cases requiring interpreters should be prioritized as follows:

- First appearances, detention hearings and reviews, shelter hearings, and final injunction hearings;
- Felony trials;
- Other felony matters;
- Misdemeanor cases;
- Delinquency cases;
- Dependency cases, except shelter hearings;
- Civil commitment hearings;
- Civil traffic cases;
- Diversion programs operated by the courts; and
- Other civil cases

7. The presiding judge shall call cases involving the use of interpreters before other matters, but shall not be required to interrupt a proceeding that has already begun. Every effort shall be made to minimize the length of time the interpreter must remain in the courtroom.

8. Interpreters for first appearances will receive their assignments on a rotating basis, and be scheduled on a weekly basis for weekdays and a monthly basis for weekends and holidays within each month. Should the assigned interpreter become unavailable, the assigned interpreter shall notify the Court Interpreter Services Coordinator as soon as possible so a replacement can be scheduled. Court Administration will notify all judges, judicial assistants, clerks, and bailiffs of the assigned interpreter each week.

DONE and ORDERED in Tallahassee, Leon County, Florida, on August 21, 2013.

CHARLES A. FRANCIS
Chief Judge

Adopted effective August 21, 2013.

2013–03. FORECLOSURE CASE PROCEDURES

IN THE SECOND JUDICIAL CIRCUIT OF FLORIDA

OFFICE OF THE CHIEF JUDGE

ADMINISTRATIVE ORDER 2013–03
FIRST AMENDMENT

IN RE: FORECLOSURE CASE PROCEDURES

WHEREAS, the Supreme Court of Florida, on June 21, 2013, issued Administrative Order In Re: Final Report and Recommendations of the Foreclosure Initiative Workgroup (AOSC 13–28) in which "each chief judge is hereby directed to establish a case management plan that is consistent with rules 2.215 and 2.545, Florida Rules of Judicial Administration, and that optimizes the respective circuit's utilization of existing and additional resources in the resolution of foreclosure cases"; and

WHEREAS, the circuit has received funding for additional resources to assist in addressing the foreclosure backlog and to continue the statewide Foreclosure and Economic Recovery Program; and

WHEREAS, it is necessary to address new and backlogged foreclosure cases in a manner to provide prompt resolution and disposition of all cases on a priority basis while still ensuring due process to the litigants; and

WHEREAS, pursuant to Article V, section 2(d) of the Florida Constitution, and section 43.26, Florida Statutes, the chief judge of each judicial circuit is charged with the authority and power to do everything necessary to promote the prompt and efficient administration of justice, and rule 2.215(b)(3), Florida Rules of Judicial Administration, mandates the chief judge to "develop an administrative plan for the efficient and proper administration of all courts within the circuit"; and

WHEREAS, rule 2.545, Florida Rules of Judicial Administration, requires that the trial courts "... take charge of all cases at an early stage in the litigation and ... control the progress of the case thereafter until the case is determined ...", which includes "... assuming early and continuous control of the court calendar; ... identifying priority cases;" "... implement such docket control policies as may be necessary to advance priority cases to ensure prompt resolution;" "... develop rational and effective trial setting policies and advancing the trial setting of priority cases, older cases ...";

THEREFORE, pursuant to the directive of the Supreme Court of Florida and the authority vested in me as chief judge, it is **ORDERED:**

1. The dispositions of foreclosure cases filed or re-opened before January 1, 2014, are hereby declared a priority of the 2nd Judicial Circuit and shall be handled by the Backlogged Foreclosure Case Department. Cases filed or re-opened before January 1, 2014, currently set on the assigned judges hearing calendar shall remain set with the assigned judge.

2. There is created a Backlogged Foreclosure Case Department within the Second Judicial Circuit under the administration of the chief judge. Although cases will be scheduled on the backlogged foreclosure case dockets to be handled by a senior judge, they will remain assigned to the civil division judges in the respective counties of the circuit.

3. Senior judges are hereby authorized to preside over backlogged foreclosure case dockets without specific assignment of individual cases. Senior Judge William L. Gary shall have primary responsibility for backlogged foreclosure case dockets, but a specific assignment order shall not be required for any other senior judge or assigned civil division judge to preside over such dockets or otherwise preside over a backlogged foreclosure case.

4. Assigned case managers and administrative assistants under the supervision of Senior Judge Gary, and any staff attorneys assigned to assist him, shall review the case dockets in Franklin, Gadsden, Leon and Wakulla Counties to identify and schedule backlogged foreclosure cases for appropriate hearing dockets in said counties.

5. Due to the low volume of cases in Jefferson and Liberty Counties, the judges assigned in those counties are directed and shall be responsible for reviewing their dockets for backlogged foreclosure cases and managing the same for the prompt and efficient disposition on a high priority basis.

6. All civil division judges in the respective counties responsible for processing new and backlogged foreclosure cases shall expend every effort to work with the program case managers and other assigned personnel, and with each other to facilitate best practices, uniformity, communication and coordination in implementing case management, data collection, and mass scheduling practices utilized in processing all assigned cases and compiling required statistical information as required by the Office of State Courts Administrator.

7. As to any case scheduled on a backlogged foreclosure case docket which may involve issues that appear to require more time than a basic foreclosure action, the presiding judge may conclude that better case management practices suggest such a case would be more appropriately handled by the assigned division judge.

8. The scheduling of all foreclosure hearings by parties, as opposed to those scheduled by court order, in all of the counties of the circuit shall be done directly with the judicial assistants of the assigned circuit judges.

9. All pleadings in real property foreclosure actions are required to be electronically filed in accordance with and except as otherwise provided by Rule 2.525, Florida Rules of Judicial Administration or administrative orders of the Su-

preme Court of Florida. Motions and proposed orders shall not be sent to the court without first confirming that pleadings have been successfully e-filed. Failure to comply with the e-filing requirements may result in the return of the pleadings. Original documents, such as notes and mortgages shall be delivered to the clerk of court, accompanied by a Notice of Filing. Copies of original documents shall be included in the e-filing submission. In the event that there is a lost note, a bond in the face amount of the requested final judgment amount conditioned upon indemnification of the maker(s) of the note for any costs, expenses or damages incurred as the result of the enforcement of the note by any party, and issued by a Florida licensed surety, shall be delivered to the clerk within such time and accompanied by a Notice of Filing. In the case of motions for summary judgment, the originals must be filed before a hearing may be scheduled. In the case of a final evidentiary hearing/non-jury trial, the originals shall be filed at least ten (10) days prior to the scheduled hearing/trial date.

10. No hearing may be scheduled or time reserved for summary judgment, until such time as the motion for summary judgment or motion for final judgment, and all supporting evidence, including, but not limited to the original note, mortgage, and assignment of mortgage where applicable, and all supporting affidavits are properly filed and docketed. A summary judgment or final hearing package shall be transmitted to the judicial assistant of the assigned judge of the case except in the case of those cases scheduled on Judge William L. Gary's backlogged foreclosure case dockets, not less than ten (10) days prior to the hearing. In the case of backlogged foreclosure case dockets, the package should be sent to:

Backlogged Foreclosure Case Department
Attention: Selena Lane
Leon County Courthouse
301 South Monroe Street, Room 301H
Tallahassee, FL 32301

A summary judgment or final judgment packages shall include, but not be limited to:

I. A copy of the filed motion.

II. A copy of the filed Notice of Hearing or order scheduling hearing.

III. A copy of the filed original note, mortgage, assignment(s) of mortgage.

IV. A copy of the filed Affidavit in Support of Summary Judgment or Affidavit of Indebtedness.

V. A copy of the filed Affidavit(s) in Support of Attorney's Fees.

VI. A copy of the Affidavit(s) of Costs.

VII. A proposed Final Judgment or Final Summary Judgment in the form prescribed by Form 1.996(a), Fla. R. Civ. P. No additional language shall be added to the form judgment.

VIII. If applicable, a copy of an Affidavit of Diligent Search and Inquiry in the form prescribed by Form 1.924, Fla. R. Civ. P.

IX. An original Notice of Sale.

X. An original Final Disposition Form.

XI. Sufficient copies and envelopes with sufficient postage attached and addressed to all necessary individuals to be served copies of original orders and notices when entered or issued.

11. NO TELEPHONIC APPEARANCES SHALL BE PERMITTED BY ATTORNEYS, WITNESSES OR PARTIES FOR THE BACKLOGGED FORECLOSURE CASE HEARINGS, AND SHALL NOT BE AUTHORIZED FOR ANY OTHER FORECLOSURE HEARINGS UNLESS EXPRESSLY ORDERED BY THE ASSIGNED JUDGE.

12. Hearings scheduled by order for the backlog foreclosure case dockets may be cancelled or continued only upon the filing of a motion showing good cause, such as actual settlement or resolution of the case, and order of the court. All such motions shall be filed not less than seven (7) days prior to the hearing, except in the event of a bona fide emergency as the same is defined by case law. Any such motions shall be directed to Senior Judge William L. Gary in the Backlog Foreclosure Case Department, and filed with the clerk of the circuit court. A courtesy copy of all motions to cancel or continue shall be submitted to Selena Lane at LaneS@leoncountyfl.gov. No notice of hearing shall be filed or served by any party as to a hearing scheduled by court order.

13. All foreclosure cases other than those scheduled for the backlogged foreclosure case dockets shall also be scheduled through the judicial assistants for the assigned judge in accordance with the instructions and procedures of said judge.

14. Except as provided herein, judicial sales shall be conducted pursuant to section 45.031, Florida Statutes, as the same shall be amended from time to time. The clerk of court shall schedule a sufficient number of judicial sale dates so that sales can be scheduled between 20 and 35 days from the date of the entry of final judgment. Sale dates may be scheduled beyond 35 days only upon order of the court.

15. No foreclosure sale shall be cancelled unless a satisfaction of judgment has been filed, or a court order has been entered cancelling the same, except when a suggestion of bankruptcy is filed in the pending foreclosure action and contains the case name, the bankruptcy case number, and the date upon which the bankruptcy was filed. **The Plaintiff shall have the responsibility to cause the Notice of Sale to be timely published and to timely file the proof of publication.** Failure to publish the Notice of Sale, to provide proof of publication, or failure of Plaintiff's representative to be present at the sale are not grounds for the clerk to cancel the sale.

Failure to pay the clerk's sale fee prior to sale shall not be grounds for cancelling a sale, but a certificate of title shall not be issued unless the clerk's sale fee has been paid.

Any party seeking to cancel or reschedule a sale shall file a motion stating the specific reason why the sale should be cancelled. The motion shall state the number of times the sale has been previously cancelled. The motion shall be filed at least seven (7) business days prior to the sale, and must have any documentation relied upon to justify the cancellation filed with the motion prior to consideration of the motion by the Court.

16. Any party obtaining a judgment or submitting a proposed order on a motion, including pro se parties, shall provide sufficient pre-addressed and stamped envelopes for service, and a copy of the judgment or order for all parties to be served.

17. This order shall supercede and replace Administrative Order 2011–01 which is hereby terminated.

18. All contact and information for the Backlogged Foreclosure Case Department and hearing location information for those dockets shall be posted on the Second Judicial Circuit of Florida Website at: http://2ndcircuit.leoncountyfl.gov.

DONE and ORDERED in Tallahassee, Leon County, Florida, July 3, 2013.

CHARLES A. FRANCIS
Chief Judge

Adopted effective July 3, 2013. Amended effective October 22, 2013; September 3, 2014.

2013–01. DEPARTMENT OF CORRECTIONS REENTRY PROGRAM "THINKING FOR A CHANGE"

IN THE SECOND JUDICIAL CIRCUIT OF FLORIDA

OFFICE OF THE CHIEF JUDGE

ADMINISTRATIVE ORDER 2013–01

IN RE: DEPARTMENT OF CORRECTIONS REENTRY PROGRAM "THINKING FOR A CHANGE"

WHEREAS, The Department of Corrections is utilizing a reentry program entitled Thinking for a Change which program was developed by the National Institute of Corrections. This free program is designed to assist offenders by combining cognitive restructuring theory with cognitive skills theory to create an innovative and integrated curriculum designed to help individuals in the criminal justice system take control of their lives by taking control of their thinking. In the corrections field the targeted behavior is a reduction in reoffending, and cognitive behavioral interventions have been found to be an evidence based practice for achieving this goal. The Department of Corrections is desirous of expanding this program to those individuals who are ordered to perform community service hours as part of a felony sentence.

THEREFORE, pursuant to the authority conferred by Florida Rule of Judicial Administration 2.215, it is **ORDERED** as follows:

1. An offender who is chosen and screened by their probation officer to participate in the Thinking for a Change Program of the Department of Corrections (DOC) will receive credit for court ordered community service for every hour of the program they complete. The offender will be credited with one hour of community service for each hour of the program that they complete.

2. Individuals who have been sentenced to community service as part of a felony case are eligible for consideration. DOC is given discretion to determine if a defendant is an appropriate candidate for the program.

3. If an offender fails to fully complete the program, he or she will be credited only with the hours that they actually attended.

4. DOC is given discretion to terminate an offender's participation in the program if DOC determines that the offender is not making a good faith effort to successfully complete the program. DOC's decision to terminate an offender from the program is final and not subject to appeal to the Court. Failure to complete the program successfully will be considered a violation of probation only if the court has ordered the program as a special condition of supervision.

DONE and ORDERED in Chambers at Tallahassee, Florida, Leon County, Florida, this 18 day of March, 2013.

CHARLES A. FRANCIS
Chief Judge

Adopted effective March 18, 2013.

2012–01. LEON COUNTY JUVENILE DRUG COURT PROGRAM

IN THE SECOND JUDICIAL CIRCUIT OF THE STATE OF FLORIDA

OFFICE OF THE CHIEF JUDGE

ADMINISTRATIVE ORDER 2012–01

IN RE: LEON COUNTY JUVENILE DRUG COURT PROGRAM

WHEREAS, it is the intent of the Florida Legislature as found in section 397.334, Florida Statutes, that "[e]ach county may fund a treatment-based drug court program under which persons in the justice system assessed with a substance abuse problem will be processed in such a manner as to appropriately address the severity of the identified substance abuse problem through treatment services tailored to the individual needs of the participant"; and

WHEREAS, the Chief Judge appointed a Juvenile Drug Court Planning Committee in 1995 to assess the feasibility and need for a Leon County Juvenile Drug Court Program; and

WHEREAS, based upon the recommendation of the Juvenile Drug Court Planning Committee, and funding provided by a Federal Law Enforcement Block Grant Program, the Chief Judge authorized the establishment of a pretrial treatment-based Leon County Juvenile Drug Court Program through Administrative Order 97–03; and

WHEREAS, the Leon County Juvenile Drug Court Program has provided a proven and effective alternative to traditional case disposition in the Second Judicial Circuit; and

WHEREAS, although limited funding is available from the Florida Department of Children and Families to continue the Leon County Juvenile Drug Court Program, additional revenue must be raised from participants to maintain fiscal viability;

IT IS THEREFORE ORDERED THAT:

1. The Leon County Juvenile Drug Court Program (hereinafter Program) is hereby continued for the Family Division of the Second Judicial Circuit in and for Leon County.

2. The participants for this Program shall include substance-involved juvenile delinquency defendants who may also have mental health issues. These participants will not have an extensive juvenile delinquency history and shall include:

a. Juvenile delinquency defendants charged with a drug or alcohol related misdemeanor, felony, or other offenses where the underlying factor is a substance abuse issue;

b. Juvenile delinquency defendants that are physically and mentally stable and agree to participate in the pretrial substance abuse treatment-based Program; and

c. Juvenile delinquency defendants who are not in need of extensive detoxification, emergency medical care, or hospitalization for medical and mental health conditions.

3. Screening of eligible Program participants shall be the responsibility of the Juvenile Assessment Center (JAC), State Attorney's Office, or the Department of Juvenile Justice. Those juveniles screened and deemed appropriate candidates for the Program shall be recommended to the juvenile court at the earliest scheduled court appearance by the JAC case staffing team, or other court party.

4. Juvenile delinquency defendants referred to Program shall be afforded the opportunity to speak with a Public Defender and the Program provider, given an overview of the purpose and requirements for participation in the Program, and asked if they choose to voluntarily participate in the Program. If juvenile delinquency defendant agrees to participate in the program, and there is no objection, they shall be assigned to the Program. Participants are required to sign a Juvenile Drug Court Agreement, which will specify the requirements for successful completion of the Program, which include compliance with all required drug treatment services.

5. Program participants shall be placed on a regularly scheduled juvenile delinquency drug court docket, to occur at least monthly, to ensure monitoring and compliance with the Program. The state attorney, public defender, private attorney, or defendant may request that participation in the Program either continue or cease at these hearings based upon participant success or failure with the Program. If the participant successfully completes the Program, the deferred but pending charge(s) shall be dismissed.

6. Each participant shall be assessed an initial $60.00 fee upon admission into the Program. An additional fee of $20.00 shall be assessed for any positive urinalysis result once a participant has shown that they are testing negative for all substances subsequent to their initial admission into the Program.

7. The order shall be effective immediately, whereupon Administrative Order 97–03 shall be superseded and terminated, and this order shall remain in effect until modified or terminated by subsequent order.

DONE AND ORDERED in Chambers at Tallahassee, Leon County, Florida, this 14th day of February, 2012.

CHARLES A. FRANCIS
Chief Judge

Adopted effective February 14, 2012.

2010–07. COURT REPORTING SERVICES PLAN

IN THE SECOND JUDICIAL CIRCUIT OF FLORIDA

OFFICE OF THE CHIEF JUDGE

ADMINISTRATIVE ORDER 2010–07
FIRST AMENDMENT

IN RE: COURT REPORTING SERVICES PLAN

WHEREAS, the Supreme Court of Florida adopted Florida Rule of Judicial Administration 2.535 (2010) to ensure that court reporting services are provided in an efficient and cost-effective manner consistent with the requirements of state and federal law; and

WHEREAS, in order to provide for the requirements of the Second Judicial Circuit court reporting services

IT IS THEREFORE ORDERED:

I. GENERAL. Court reporting in the Second Judicial Circuit is managed and provided by the Office of Court Administration, Court Reporting Services. Court Reporting Services, supervised by a manager, is responsible for ensuring that proceedings mandated by law to be recorded at public expense are recorded at the highest quality attainable; that accurate transcripts are prepared; that public records requests are responded to appropriately; and that the record is retained and archived as required by law. Court Reporting Services is required to provide their services in all of the counties of the circuit.

As used in this order, the terms "approved court reporter," "approved transcriptionist," "civil court reporter," "court reporting," "electronic record," and "official record" have the same meaning as defined in Florida Rule of Judicial Administration 2.535(a) (2010).

The chief judge of the Second Judicial Circuit, in his or her official capacity, is the owner of all records and electronic recordings made by an official court reporter or quasi-judicial officer in proceedings required to be reported at public expense and proceedings reported for the court's own use. See Florida Rule of Judicial Administration 2.535(d) (2010).

II. COURT REPORTING PROCEDURES WHERE THE COURT DOES NOT PROVIDE A RECORD. The court does not provide court reporting services at public expense for proceedings in the following cases:

circuit civil

county civil

family (Except for proceedings in which the court is required to provide a record at public expense.)

If a party wishes to make a record of a court proceeding for which the court does not provide a record as delineated in this administrative order, it is the responsibility of the party or the party's attorney to secure the services of a "civil court reporter." All costs associated with the court reporter's appearance will be the responsibility of the party requesting the court reporter. This does not preclude the taxation of costs as authorized by law.

III. GRAND JURY PROCEEDINGS. Testimony in grand jury proceedings shall be reported by an approved stenographic or digital court reporter, but shall not be transcribed unless required by order of the court. Whenever the proceedings are being electronically recorded, the digital court reporter will remain in attendance to operate the equipment and ensure that testimony only is recorded. Other parts of grand jury proceedings, including deliberations and voting, shall not be reported. The approved court reporter's work product, including stenographic notes, electronic recordings, and transcripts, shall be filed with the clerk of the court under seal..

IV. COURT REPORTING PROCEDURES IN CAPITAL CASES.. Any proceeding involving the potential or actual imposition of the death penalty, including but not limited to pretrial hearings, sentencing hearings and post-conviction hearings, shall be reported utilizing all measures necessary to expedite the preparation of the transcript, including but not limited to:

1. where available, the use of a certified court-employed stenographic court reporter who has the capacity to provide real-time transcription of the proceedings;

2. if real-time transcription services are not available; the use of a computer-aided transcription qualified court-employed stenographic court reporter;

3. the use of scopists, text editors, alternating court reports or other means to expedite the finalization of the certified transcript; and

4. the imposition of reasonable restrictions on work assignments by employee or contract approved court reporters to ensure that transcript production in capital cases is given a priority.

V. COURT REPORTING PROCEDURES RELATED TO ELECTRONIC RECORDING. All persons entering a courtroom or a hearing room in the Second Judicial Circuit are hereby notified that electronic recording equipment is in use and that anything said in the courtroom or hearing room may be electronically recorded and released upon request.

Court personnel shall provide notice to participants in a courtroom proceeding that electronic recording equipment is in use and that they should safeguard information they do not want recorded. Attorneys shall take all reasonable and available precautions to protect disclosure of confidential communications in the courtroom. Such precautions may include muting microphones or going to a designated location that is inaccessible to the recording equipment. Participants have a duty to protect confidential information. See Florida Rule of Judicial Administration 2.535(5) (2010).

As a general rule, all sidebar conversations are considered part of the record unless the presiding judge indicates otherwise. Extraneous and non-substantive conversations occurring at sidebar (i.e., personal or social banter between the parties or between the parties and the judge) shall not be considered as part of the record. Sidebar conferences that are digitally recorded are generally not capable of being transcribed due to the quality of the recording.

Copies of electronically recorded court proceedings shall be provided upon request. Recordings that take place after July 2009 may be released in their entirety. Recordings of earlier proceedings may be released, subject to review and redaction of any confidential or exempt information. An additional hourly rate for review and redaction is authorized.

VI. COURT REPORTING PROCEDURES BY DIVISION. Court reporting coverage of proceedings recorded at public expense is as follows:

Circuit Criminal

Trials 1st Degree—Stenography

Trials 2nd Degree—Stenography or Digital Recording

Trials 3rd Degree—Stenography or Digital Recording

First Appearance—Digital Recording

Adult Drug Court—Digital Recording

Capital Cases

Trials or Postconviction Proceedings—Stenography (Real time, if available)

All Other Proceedings—Stenography

All Other Circuit Criminal Proceedings

Digital Recording

County Criminal

Trials—Digital Recording

All Other Proceedings—Digital Recording

Family Court

Delinquency—Digital Recording

Juvenile Drug Court—Digital Recording

Dependency—Digital Recording

Termination of Parental Rights (TPR)—Contract stenographer or Digital Recording

Proceedings to Waive Parental Notification of Termination of Pregnancy—Stenography or Digital Recording

Crossover Case (Unified Family Court Cases)—Stenography or Digital Recording

Domestic Violence Injunctions (All Proceedings)

Digital Recording

Baker Act, Marchman Act, Guardianship, and Jimmy Ryce (All Proceedings)

Digital Recording

General Magistrate/Hearing Officer Proceedings

Digital Recording (to be recorded by magistrate/hearing officer)

Proceedings Taking Place Outside of Regular Court Hours

Stenography or Digital Recording

Computer–Aided Real–Time (CART) For Hearing Impaired (ADA)

Stenography (real-time, if available)

VII. PROCEDURES FOR ORDERING WRITTEN TRANSCRIPTS. Any person may request a written transcript of a court proceeding except that proceedings under the Rules of Juvenile Procedure, Baker Act proceedings, or any other statutorily exempt proceeding shall only be provided to those persons authorized by law.

Requests for a written transcript of proceedings should be made in writing, utilizing a Transcript Request Form approved by Court Reporting Services. This form should be submitted to Court Reporting Services, Room 341, Leon County Courthouse, Tallahassee, FL 32301.

Any transcript produced by Court Reporting Services will be filed with the clerk of the circuit court unless the Court orders otherwise or unless a rule of court provides otherwise.

All transcript requests submitted to the court require a deposit in the amount of 50% of the total cost (payable to the State of Florida) before the transcript will be produced; unless the request is accompanied by an order to transcribe. The balance of the cost must be paid prior to receipt of the transcript. A court order is not required to produce a transcript when the requesting party to a case agrees to pay for the transcript at the transcription rates in this order. Rates for production of transcripts will be in accordance with Attachment "A", Schedule of Fees, attached hereto.

Any judge, magistrate, hearing officer or staff attorney may obtain a transcript in rough-draft from an approved real-time court reporter or in its final certified form or a CD of a digital recording by an oral or written request.

Any state attorney, public defender, regional counselor court appointed counsel may obtain a transcript for any court event, including appeals in its final certified form, with an order signed by the presiding judge, at no charge to their offices, due to the July 1, 2004 implementation of the cost sharing agreement for court reporting services. Court Reporting Services shall be copied with the motion and order for transcription. The delivery date will be determined by the current workload.

All transcripts must comply with Florida Rule of Judicial Administration 2.535 (2010).

Appeals require an original and two copies of the transcript, unless otherwise ordered by the court or required by the Clerk of the Court. Standard appeals are due 30 days after "service" of notice of appeal. Most of the time a standard 30–day extension will be granted upon request, if needed. A 60 to 90–day extension may be granted for lengthy trials or an unusually heavy transcript workload. An extension for the amount of time needed must be requested prior to the deadline.

Court Reporting Services is required to transcribe digital and/or audio recordings only when recording equipment is approved, provided, and in the control of Court Reporting Services.

VIII. COURT REPORTING SERVICES FEES. The Chief Judge will issue a separate court reporting services fees schedule and the fee schedule will be posted on the Second Judicial Circuit website at http://2ndcircuit.leoncountyfl.gov/.

IX. PRIOR ORDERS RESCINDED. Administrative Orders 1990–20, 1995–06, (including Addendum), 1996–02, and 2007–03 are rescinded.

DONE and **ORDERED** in Chambers at Tallahassee, e n County, Florida, this 8th day of July, 2010.

CHARLES A. FRANCIS
Chief Judge

ATTACHMENT "A"

SCHEDULE OF FEES

1. Normal Delivery (Within 2 weeks to 30 days)
   $5.00 per page for an original and one copy
   $1.25 per page for each additional copy
2. Expedited Delivery (Within three to five working days)
   $7.50 per page for an original and one copy
   $2.50 per page for each additional copy
3. Rough Draft (Real–Time Stenographer)—An unedited, uncertified transcript (print, disc or e-mail.)
   $5.00 per page.
4. Electronic Record—The following fees are established for providing copies of audio and video recordings of court proceedings:
   $25.00 per audio CD
   $22.50 per hour for review and redaction

Adopted effective July 8, 2010. Amended effective April 6, 2016.

2010–01. APPOINTMENT, POWERS AND DUTIES OF CHILD SUPPORT ENFORCEMENT HEARING OFFICERS OF THE SECOND JUDICIAL CIRCUIT

IN THE SECOND JUDICIAL CIRCUIT
OF THE STATE OF FLORIDA

OFFICE OF THE CHIEF JUDGE

ADMINISTRATIVE ORDER NO 2010–01

IN RE: APPOINTMENT, POWERS AND DUTIES OF CHILD SUPPORT ENFORCEMENT HEARING OFFICERS OF THE SECOND JUDICIAL CIRCUIT

WHEREAS, many matters involving the establishment, enforcement, or modification of child support are brought before the Second Judicial Circuit of Florida; and

WHEREAS, it is necessary to establish procedures for the efficient and speedy resolution of all Title IV–D or non–Title IV–D child support issues; and

WHEREAS, rule 12.491, Florida Family Law Rules of Procedure authorizes the use of child support enforcement hearing officers to hear matters establishing, enforcing, and modifying child support in Title IV–D and non–Title IV–D cases; and

WHEREAS, the Florida State Courts System allocates general magistrates and child support enforcement hearing officers to the Second Judicial Circuit; and

WHEREAS, pursuant to the authority vested in the Chief Judge of the Second Judicial Circuit of Florida under rule 2.215, Florida Rules of Judicial Administration, and all other applicable Rules, it is therefore:

ORDERED, that officers of the court appointed to the Florida State Courts System positions with the class title of administrative magistrate, magistrate, and hearing officer shall have all the powers and duties as provided in rule 12.491, Florida Family Law Rules of Procedure and all other applicable Rules and Statutes; and

Upon the filing of any post-judgment action where the sole issue is the establishment, enforcement, or modification of Title IV–D child support, the action shall be automatically referred to the appropriate Title IV–D support enforcement hearing officer; and

Upon the filing of any post-judgment action where the sole issue is the enforcement or modification of non–Title IV–D child support, the action shall be automatically referred to the appropriate magistrate to sit as a non–Title IV–D support enforcement hearing officer; and

No objections to a referral to a child support enforcement hearing officer pursuant to this section will be entertained by the Court; and

Any party may set the action for hearing before the assigned child support enforcement hearing officer; and

The child support enforcement hearing officer will proceed with the hearings and preparation and filing of a recommended order as provided in rule 12.491, Florida Family Law Rules of Procedure and all other applicable Rules and Statutes; and

Any findings of contempt with a recommendation of immediate incarceration by the child support enforcement hearing officer shall be immediately sent to the assigned circuit judge for entry of an order; and

Administrative Order 2005–04, as amended July 13, 2005, is hereby rescinded.

DONE AND ORDERED in Tallahassee, Leon County, Florida on January 6, 2010.

CHARLES A. FRANCIS
Chief Judge

Adopted effective January 6, 2010.

2009–04. FEES—COSTS FOR PAYMENT OF ATTORNEY'S FEES; PUBLIC DEFENDER APPLICATION FEE

IN THE SECOND JUDICIAL CIRCUIT OF FLORIDA

OFFICE OF THE CHIEF JUDGE

ADMINISTRATIVE ORDER 2009–04

IN RE: FEES—COSTS FOR PAYMENT OF ATTORNEY'S FEES; PUBLIC DEFENDER APPLICATION FEE

WHEREAS, an amendment to section 938.29, Florida Statutes(2008), effective July 1, 2008, mandates that assessments for public defender representation shall be set in all criminal cases at no less than $50.00 per case in misdemeanor and criminal traffic cases, and no less than $100.00 per case when a felony offense is concluded by entry of a guilty or nolo contendere plea or by guilty verdict at trial or hearing, including a proceeding in which the underlying offense is a violation of probation or community control; and

WHEREAS, section 938.29, Florida Statutes, mandates that the sentencing court order costs of defense without regard to the defendant's present ability to pay; and

WHEREAS, section 938.29, Florida Statutes, requires the Clerk of Court to collect and distribute costs of defense in every case; and

WHEREAS, section 27.52(1)(b), Florida Statutes, mandates that a defendant pay a $50.00 Public Defender Application Fee within 7 days of the appointment of the Public Defender and mandates that the Clerk of Court notify the Court if the fee has not been paid at time of sentencing; it is therefore

ORDERED that:

I. Each criminal judgment shall contain an assessment pursuant to section 938.29, Florida Statutes, unless specifically waived by the Court, in the amount of $50.00 in misdemeanor cases and $100.00 in felony cases in all cases in which the defendant received the assistance of the Public Defender's Office or any other court appointed counsel. A similar assessment shall be imposed, unless specifically waived by the Court, in all cases which the defendant has received due process services after being found indigent for costs under section 27.52, Florida Statutes. These assessments shall be made in all original criminal actions as well as violations of probation or community control.

II. A claim for costs higher than $50.00 in misdemeanor cases and $100.00 in felony cases shall be entered at or before sentencing and the defendant shall be given notice of the right to a hearing to contest the claim. The hearing shall be held within 30 days of the date of sentencing.

III. If not previously paid, each criminal judgment shall also include the $50.00 Public Defender application fee if the Defendant applied for the services of the Public Defender and/or the court appointed the Public Defender, unless specifically waived by the court.

IV. The first $50.00 of any fees or costs collected on a case by the Clerk of Court will go toward satisfaction of the Public Defender Application fee, pursuant to section 27.52, Florida Statutes.

V. Administrative Order 2002–09, In Re: Affidavit and Application for Appointment of Public Defender, is hereby rescinded.

DONE and ORDERED in Chambers in Tallahassee, Leon County, Florida, and effective this 11th day of August, 2009.

CHARLES A. FRANCIS
Chief Judge

Adopted effective August 11, 2009.

2008–09. VIOLATION OF PROBATION–BOND ALLOCATION WHEN ONLY ONE CASE BOND IS ORDERED

IN THE SECOND JUDICIAL CIRCUIT OF FLORIDA

OFFICE OF THE CHIEF JUDGE

ADMINISTRATIVE ORDER NO. 2008–09

IN RE: VIOLATION OF PROBATION–BOND ALLOCATION WHEN ONLY ONE CASE BOND IS ORDERED

WHEREAS, the clerk and jail computer systems can be programmed to accept a single case bond on a violation of probation when the case has multiple underlying counts, but only as structured under this order, and

WHEREAS, the clerk, attorneys, defendants, bondsmen, the sheriff, and judges need a uniform default method for timely recording bond in this situation in the absence of a case specific order, and

WHEREAS, the Criminal Justice Coordinating Committee, consisting of stakeholder representatives, recommends this order, it is therefore

ORDERED:

1. A case bond on a violation of probation that involves multiple underlying counts shall be placed on the first active count, in the absence of a case specific order stating otherwise.

2. The remaining active counts shall be ROR (release on own recognizance), effective when probationer posts the bond. This ensures proper jail credit accrues on all counts.

3. A judge may order a different bond structure, but it must be case and count specific. The clerk may rely on this order in lieu of seeking clarification in each instance in which this situation arises. No general directive of a judge may override this administrative order.

DONE AND ORDERED in chambers in Leon County, Florida, this 22nd day of July, 2008.

CHARLES A. FRANCIS
Chief Judge

Adopted effective July 22, 2008.

2008–03. APPOINTED COUNSEL: EXTRAORDINARY RATES

IN THE CIRCUIT COURT IN AND FOR THE SECOND JUDICIAL CIRCUIT

OFFICE OF THE CHIEF JUDGE

ADMINISTRATIVE ORDER NO. 2008–03

IN RE: APPOINTED COUNSEL: EXTRAORDINARY RATES

WHEREAS, section 27.425, Florida Statutes, has been created and mandates certain responsibilities of the Chief Judge regarding services of appointed counsel, and

WHEREAS, section 27.5304, Florida Statutes has been amended to include limitations on compensation of appointed counsel, the Justice Administration Commission's functions, and the court's duties with regard to the reasonableness of all billings for attorney's fees, costs and related expenses, and

WHEREAS, section 27.5304, Florida Statute, provides for payment in excess of the statutory limits for the rare occasions where a case requires extraordinary and unusual effort,

It is therefore **ORDERED** that:

1. Counsel appointed on or after the effective date of the 2007 statutory flat rates seeking compensation that exceeds the limits prescribed in section 27.5304(5), (6), and (7), Florida Statutes and the General Appropriations Act must comply with the requirements of section 27.5304, Florida Statutes before filing a motion requesting an order approving such payment.

2. Any motion requesting a case to be declared extraordinary and unusual for the purpose of securing an order authorizing a fee in excess of the statutory flat rates shall be captioned "Motion to the Chief Judge to Declare Case to Be Extraordinary" and shall be filed with the clerk of court in the county in which the case is pending.

3. Upon the filing of such a motion, the respective Clerk of Court is hereby directed to immediately forward the motion to the Chief Judge for disposition under the provisions of section 27.5304(12), Florida Statutes (2007).

DONE AND ORDERED in Leon County, Florida this 1st day of February, 2008.

CHARLES A. FRANCIS
Chief Judge

Adopted effective February 1, 2008.

Publisher's Note: *Order 2008-03 has been amended by Amendments 1, 3, 4, and 5 (there was no Amendment 2). These amendments have not been incorporated into this order; they do not amend the language of the order itself, instead they designate a particular judge to hear all motions relating to extraordinary fees. As of March 22, 2016, the "Fifth Amendment" named Circuit Judge James C. Hankinson as the designated judge to hear any motions on this issue.*

2007–02. DESTRUCTION OF JUROR NOTES

IN THE CIRCUIT COURT IN AND FOR THE SECOND JUDICIAL CIRCUIT

OFFICE OF THE CHIEF JUDGE

ADMINISTRATIVE ORDER NO. 2007-02

IN RE: DESTRUCTION OF JUROR NOTES

WHEREAS, the Florida Rules of Judicial Administration's Judicial Branch Records Retention Schedule For Administrative Records provides that certain records of the judicial branch may be destroyed after certain periods of time have elapsed; and

WHEREAS, to ensure compliance with the requirements of the Rules of Judicial Administration, in accordance with the authority vested in the Chief Judge by Rule 2.215 (former 2.050), Florida Rules of Judicial Administration, it is

ORDERED that:

A. DEFINITIONS.

1. "Juror notes" as used in this order shall consist of any written notes taken by jurors during civil or criminal trials.

2. "Destroy" as used in this order shall mean physically damaging the documents by shredding, tearing, or otherwise fragmenting so as to obliterate the contents thereof.

B. PROCEDURES. The following procedures shall apply to the discarding of juror notes after issuance of a verdict, or if the trial ends prematurely as a result of a mistrial, plea, or settlement:

1. The bailiff is assigned the duty of collecting and securing the jurors' notes during the trial and shall collect and destroy all jurors' notes immediately after the trial's conclusion, preferably by electronic shredder.

2. If immediate destruction by the preferred method is not feasible, the bailiff shall hold the notes in a secure location until shredding may be commenced.

3. If it is apparent that electronic shredding is not feasible and will not be feasible in the near future, the bailiff shall destroy the notes by hand before disposing of them in the appropriate receptacle.

DONE AND ORDERED in Leon County, this 3rd day of January, 2007.

CHARLES A. FRANCIS
Chief Judge

Adopted effective January 3, 2007.

2006–05. [TERMINATED BY ORDER 2018-09, EFFECTIVE JANUARY 1, 2018.]

2006–02. [TERMINATED BY ORDER 2018-06, EFFECTIVE APRIL 23, 2018.]

2004–07. DUE PROCESS ADMINISTRATION

IN THE SECOND JUDICIAL CIRCUIT OF FLORIDA

OFFICE OF THE CHIEF JUDGE

ADMINISTRATIVE ORDER NO. 2004–07

IN RE: DUE PROCESS ADMINISTRATION

WHEREAS, Sections 27.40(3)(a) and 27.42(2)(c), Florida Statutes, effective July 1, 2004, provide that the Article V Indigent Services Committee shall establish a registry of attorneys in private practice to represent clients in cases requiring court appointment of counsel and develop a schedule of standard fees for court appointed attorneys in various categories of cases; and

WHEREAS, the deadline to establish the registry for appointed counsel is not later than October 1, 2004; and

WHEREAS, provision must be made for compensation and qualifications of appointed counsel prior to the establishment of the registry and/or the processing of a competitive selection process for contracting with individuals to provide appointed counsel services; and

WHEREAS, the Article V Indigent Services Committee did on June 15, 2004, adopt the position that all persons providing appointed counsel services as of June 30, 2004, pursuant to contract with any county within the Second Judicial Circuit, pursuant to an administrative order or order of appointment in effect on June 30, 2004, shall be authorized to continue to provide appointed counsel services on the same terms of compensation as set forth in any such contract, administrative order, or order of appointment; and

WHEREAS, court appointed counsel are entitled to reasonable compensation, White v. Board of County Commissioners, 537 So.2d 1376 (Fla. 1989); Makernson v. Martin County, 491 So.2d 1109 (Fla. 1986), cert. denied, 479 U.S. 1043, 107 S.Ct. 908, 93 L.Ed.2d 857 (1987); Sheppard and White v. City of Jacksonville, 827 So.2d 925 (Fla. 2002); and

WHEREAS, the Justice Administrative Commission (J.A.C.) is now responsible for the payment of appointed counsel; and

WHEREAS, J.A.C. has advised the circuits and persons performing appointed counsel services that it has requested that an administrative order "be entered to authorize continuing the status quo if that is the intent" of the Second Judicial Circuit Indigent Services Committee; and

WHEREAS, in order to provide for the orderly appointment and compensation of court appointed counsel, it is therefore

ORDERED as follows:

1. All persons providing appointed counsel services as of June 30, 2004, pursuant to contract with any county within the Second Judicial Circuit, pursuant to an administrative order of this circuit or pursuant to an order of appointment in any particular case in this circuit, shall be authorized to continue to provide appointed counsel on the same terms of compensation as set forth in any such contract, administrative order, or order of appointment, except that such appointed counsel shall seek payment of compensation from J.A.C.

2. It shall be the responsibility of appointed counsel to comply with the rules and procedures of the Justice Administration Commission to receive compensation.

DONE and **ORDERED** in Chambers at Tallahassee, Florida this 1st day of July, 2004.

CHARLES A. FRANCIS
Chief Judge

Adopted effective July 1, 2004.

2004–04. [RESCINDED BY ORDER 2018-03, EFFECTIVE FEBRUARY 16, 2018.]

2004–01. UNIFIED FAMILY COURT

IN THE SECOND JUDICIAL CIRCUIT OF FLORIDA

OFFICE OF THE CHIEF JUDGE

ADMINISTRATIVE ORDER NO. 2004–01

IN RE: UNIFIED FAMILY COURT

WHEREAS, the Second Judicial Circuit is committed to developing a fully integrated, comprehensive approach to handling all cases involving children and families;[1]

WHEREAS, the Florida Supreme Court has adopted [2] the following guiding principles as a foundation for defining and implementing a model family court;

Children should live in safe and permanent homes;

The needs and best interests of children should be the primary consideration of any family court;

All persons, whether children or adults, should be treated with objectivity, sensitivity, dignity and respect;

Cases involving inter-related family law issues should be consolidated or coordinated to maximize use of court resources to avoid conflicting decisions and to minimize inconvenience to the families;

Family court processes should attempt to address the family's interrelated legal and nonlegal problems, empower families through skills development, assist them to resolve their own disputes, provide access to appropriate services, and offer a variety of dispute resolution forums where the family can resolve problems without additional emotional trauma;

Whenever possible, parties and their attorneys should be empowered to select processes for addressing issues in their cases that are compatible with the family's needs, financial circumstances, and legal requirements;

The court is responsible for managing its cases with due consideration of the needs of the family, the litigants, and the issues presented by the case;

There should be a means of differentiating among cases so that judicial resources are conserved and cases are diverted to non-judicial and quasi-judicial personnel for resolution, when appropriate and consistent with the ends of justice;

Trial courts must coordinate and maximize court resources and establish linkages with community resources;

The court's role in family restructuring is to identify services and craft solutions that are appropriate for long-term stability and that minimize the need for subsequent court action;

Court services should be available to litigants at a reasonable cost and accessible without economic discrimination; and

Courts should have well-trained and highly-motivated judicial and non- judicial personnel.

NOW, THEREFORE, pursuant to the authority vested in me as the Chief Judge of the Second Judicial Circuit, in order to meet the requirements of the Florida Supreme court articulated in In re Report of the Family Court Steering Committee, 794 So. 2d 518 (Fla. 2001), and to better serve the needs of the citizens of the state of Florida, it is hereby ORDERED as follows:

I. JURISDICTION. There is hereby created a Family Division of the Second Judicial Circuit, which shall include the following types of cases:[3]

A. dissolution of marriage:

B. division and distribution of property arising out of a dissolution of marriage;

C. annulment;

D. support unconnected with dissolution of marriage;

E. paternity;

F. child support;

G. URESA/UIFSA;

H. custodial care of and access to children;

I. adoption;

J. name change;

K. declaratory judgment actions related to premarital, marital, or post- marital agreements;

L. civil domestic and repeat violence injunctions;

M. juvenile dependency;

N. termination of parental rights;

O. juvenile delinquency;

P. emancipation of a minor;

Q. CINS/FINS;

R. truancy; and

S. modification and enforcement of orders entered in these cases.

II. ADMINISTRATIVE FAMILY LAW JUDGES. The Chief Judge shall designate for each county of the circuit an administrative judge for the Family Division of that county. The administrative judges shall work together to ensure coordination of cases and utilization of resources. Each Administrative Family Judge will manage the Family Division for his/her county and shall coordinate and develop the overall operation of the Family Division in their respective counties and implementation of the family court concept.

III. ROTATION OF JUDGES. Judges shall be assigned to the Family Division on a rotation determined by the Chief Judge.

Judges who are assigned to the Family Division for the first time or who have not served in the Family Division for two years should receive mandatory training in the fundamentals of family law, domestic violence, juvenile dependency, and juvenile delinquency before assuming the assignment or within 60 days after assuming the assignment.[4]

IV. ESSENTIAL ELEMENTS [5]

A. *CASE MANAGEMENT*. To the extent existing staff and resources can be allocated, the Family Division shall receive case management services and support to enable the family court judge to assess, differentiate, and monitor resources needed for handling cases, to be able to identify all collateral cases affecting the parties involved, and to monitor the movement of cases through the judicial process.

Case management shall include:[6]

1. Initial review and evaluation of cases, including assignment of cases to court divisions or dockets;

2. case monitoring, tracking and coordination; and

3. service referral, coordination, monitoring, and tracking for treatment- based drug programs under section 397.334, Florida Statutes.

B. *SELF HELP*. The Second Judicial circuit shall ensure that Self Help Programs provide litigants with Florida Supreme Court approved forms, instructions, definitions, and procedural information to persons who choose to represent themselves consistent with Rule 12.750, Florida Family Law Rules of Procedure. As part of its intake function, the clerk of the circuit court shall provide ministerial assistance to pro se litigants. Such assistance shall not include the provision of legal advice.[7] The circuit's responsibility for compliance with this directive shall be subject to direction and funding by the Legislature.

C. *DOMESTIC VIOLENCE*. The Administrative Judges of the Family Divisions shall work with other judges within the division, and without, to develop a policy to ensure that cases involving domestic violence are identified and managed in a manner that is organized, timely and sensitive to the special dynamics involved in these cases.[8]

D. *ALTERNATIVE DISPUTE RESOLUTION*. It is the policy of the Second Judicial Circuit to make maximum use of Alternative Dispute Resolution (ADR) in all pending family and dependency cases. Family mediation is mandatory by Administrative Order 92–01 for all contested cases, unless excused by the Court for good cause, and dependency cases are referred to dependency mediation by court order in appropriate cases.

The court, mediation staff, and the case management staff shall screen cases for domestic violence issues to provide for the safety of the participants and the integrity of the mediation process prior to mediation, in accordance with the protocol that has been established for the screening and mediation of those cases. If the court determines that mediation is not appropriate as a result of domestic violence issues, the court may waive mediation.

E. *GUARDIAN AD LITEM*. The judges of the Second Judicial Circuit will coordinate with the Guardian ad Litem program to ensure representation of the best interests of children involved in cases with allegations of abuse, abandonment and neglect.

F. *GENERAL MASTERS/HEARING OFFICERS.* General masters and hearing officers may be utilized to supplement the work of judges within the Family Division when a presiding judge determines that referral of a case is appropriate and consent of the parties is obtained, where required.[9]

G. *SUPERVISED VISITATION.* A list of approved supervised visitation centers is available in the Clerk's office.

H. *PARENTING EDUCATION.* Pursuant to section 61.21, Florida Statutes, all parties to a dissolution of marriage proceeding with minor children or a paternity action which involves issues of parental responsibility shall be required to complete the parent education and family stabilization course prior to the entry of the court's final judgment, unless excused by the Court for good cause.

I. *COUNSELING SERVICES/TREATMENT PROGRAMS.* The Chief Judge of the Second Judicial Circuit, with the advice and assistance of the administrative family law judges in each county, in consultation with the FLAG and pertinent service providers, will develop strategies regarding availability of counseling services and treatment programs to litigants in the Family Division. At a minimum, such strategies shall, to the extent resources are available, ensure the availability of crisis intervention and long-term counseling/treatment programs. Additionally, the strategies shall ensure that compliance is monitored when such services are court-ordered.[10]

J. *SECURITY.* Judges presiding over family matters are aware of the special security issues attendant to family law matters. The Chief Judge and the Administrative Family Law Judges shall collaborate with relevant stakeholders to develop a plan to ensure that adequate and sufficient security personnel and equipment are available to ensure that Family Divisions are safe environments for judges, nonjudicial staff and the public.[11] Domestic violence hearings and any other family hearing or proceeding that the presiding Judge has reason to believe poses special safety concerns shall be held in the courtroom whenever possible.

K. *TECHNOLOGY.* The Judges of the Second Judicial Circuit handling family law matters shall use available technology to access information essential to case management and coordination, to print forms and notices immediately, to generate statistical reports, to provide public and inter-agency access to records and to allow teleconferencing and the appearance of witnesses by electronic means.[12] The Chief Judge and the Trial Court Administrator shall notify judges in each county of the technology available for these enumerated purposes.

V. IDENTIFICATION AND COORDINATION OF RELATED CASES. In order to conserve judicial resources, avoid inconsistent court orders, and eliminate multiple appearances on the same issues, the following procedures and policies will be followed:

A. *IDENTIFICATION OF RELATED CASES.* At the time of filing, parties and/or their attorneys shall be required to complete a "related cases" form and indicate, as appropriate, the existence of any related cases, setting forth, if known, the case number, type, the parties, attorneys, the judge, and the date and description of the last court action.

For purposes of this section, "related cases" shall include all pending and prior family law cases of any type, and all pending cases of any other type, in which one or more of the parties, or their children, have participated.

Before accepting a case for filing in the Family Division, the Clerk shall verify that the related cases form has been completed and, if not, require the filing party/attorney to complete the form. The Clerk shall then conduct a search of available computer data base to verify the information on the related cases form and to correct as appropriate. When it is determined that there are pending related cases in the Family Division, except for Juvenile Delinquency, the newly filed case shall be assigned to the Family Division Judge before whom the related cases are pending.

In addition to the above procedures for identification of related cases, judges, general masters, hearing officers, and other court staff should make inquiry of the parties/attorneys at their first meeting or court appearance, as to the existence of any related cases.

B. *COORDINATION OF RELATED CASES.* Upon discovery of the existence of one or more related cases involving the same parties, or their children, and in which a different judge has been assigned, the judge to whom the newest case has been assigned shall initiate a conference with the other judge(s) to consult and determine how to coordinate the cases, including whether any cases should be reassigned, which proceeding shall take precedence in managing the cases and determining issues, whether one case shall proceed while another is inactive or abated, or how judicial labor should be divided. In making such determinations, the following guideline should be used:

1. Which judge assigned has had the case longest, has been most active and is most familiar with the family and/or its issues.
2. Whether one of the cases is active or closed.
3. Whether there are ongoing financial issues other than child support between the parties.
4. Whether there are ongoing dependency issues which are being addressed by the court as required by law.
5. Whether, and at what stage of the proceedings, a delinquency case has been filed.[13]

When the judges decide it is unnecessary or impractical to assign all of the cases to the same judge, the judges will exchange information so that each judge involved with the family is aware of the other pleadings and the issues being addressed.[14]

VI. FAMILY LAW ADVISORY GROUP[15]**.** The success of a system to handle cases involving children and families in the manner contemplated by the Florida Supreme Court as specified herein is dependent upon effective communication among all stakeholders, both in the judicial system and in the community. The Administrative Judge of the Second Judicial Circuit Family Division shall be the Chair of the Second Judicial Circuit Family Law Advisory Group (FLAG). Membership is determined by the Chief Judge, upon recommendation by the Administrative Judge of the Second Judicial Circuit Family Division, and may include:[16]

Judge(s), Domestic Relations	Judge(s), Dependency
Judge(s), Domestic Violence	Judge(s), Delinquency
Hearing Officer	General Master
Trial Court Administrator	Case Manager

Self Help Center Director	Clerk of Court
Clerk's Office Staff	Mediators
Guardian Ad Litem	Custody Evaluators
Parenting Course Providers	Supervised Visitation Providers
Domestic Violence Advocates/Shelter Staff	Batterers' Intervention Providers
Substance Abuse & Mental Health Providers	Process Servers
Private Attorneys	Public Defenders
State Attorneys	Legal Services/Legal Aid
Department of Revenue	Department of Children & Families
Department of Juvenile Justice	School Board/Dept. of Education
Law Enforcement	Local Government Officials
Community Organizers	Parents and Children (Consumers)
Local Colleges, University Professionals	Parenting Coordinators
Certified Public Accountants	Faith–based Community Programs
Trial Court Technology Officer	

The FLAG shall meet quarterly, or more often upon the call of the Chair. A report on the progress of the group in meeting the goals of the Family Division shall be submitted to the Chief Judge by December 1 of each year.

This Administrative Order shall become effective immediately.

DONE AND ORDERED in Chambers in Leon County, Florida, this 6th day of January, 2004.

CHARLES A. FRANCIS
CHIEF JUDGE

Adopted effective January 6, 2004.

1 In re Report of the Commission on Family Courts, 633 so. 2d 14, 17 (Fla. 1994).

2 See In re Report of the Family Court Steering Committee, 794 So.2d 518, 522 (Fla. 2001).

3 REQUIREMENT: See In re Report of the Family Court Steering Committee, 794 So. 2d 518, 525 (Fla. 2001).

4 REQUIREMENT: See In re Report of the Family Court Steering Committee, 794 So. 2d 518, 532 (Fla. 2001).

5 REQUIREMENT: See In re Report of the Family Court Steering Committee, 794 So. 2d 518 (Fla. 2001) (We wholeheartedly endorse each of these essential elements to the successful function of the model family court.).

6 See Amendments to section 29.004, Florida Statutes, in House Bill 113A, section 40.

7 See Amendments to section 28.215, Florida Statutes, in House Bill 113A, section 27.

8 REQUIREMENT: In re Report of the Family Court Steering Committee, 794 So. 2d 518, 526 (Fla. 2001).

9 SUGGESTION: Report of the Family Court Steering Committee, 2000–2002 Appendix A.

10 REQUIREMENT: See In re Report of the Family Court Steering Committee, 794 So. 2d 518, 526 (Fla. 2001).

11 REQUIREMENT: See In re Report of the Family Court Steering Committee, 794 So. 2d 518, 526 (Fla. 2001).

12 REQUIREMENT: See In re Report of the Family Court Steering Committee, 794 So. 2d 518, 526 (Fla. 2001).

13 SUGGESTION: Administrative Order 00–1, Eleventh Judicial Circuit.

14 SUGGESTION: Administrative Order M2002–04, Fifth Judicial Circuit.

15 REQUIREMENT: See In re Report of the Family Court Steering Committee, 794 So.2d 518, 526 (Fla. 2001) (mandating the establishment of a Family Law Advisory Group in each circuit).

16 Suggested membership approved by the Unified Family Court Subcommittee of the Steering Committee on Families and Children in the Court.

2002–11. FIRST APPEARANCES ON VIOLATIONS OF PROBATION AND VIOLATIONS OF COMMUNITY CONTROL

IN THE SECOND JUDICIAL CIRCUIT OF FLORIDA

CHAMBERS OF THE CHIEF JUDGE

ADMINISTRATIVE ORDER 2002–11

IN RE: FIRST APPEARANCES ON VIOLATIONS OF PROBATION AND VIOLATIONS OF COMMUNITY CONTROL

WHEREAS, Rule 3.131, Florida Rules of Criminal Procedure, provides that "unless charged with a capital offense or an offense punishable by life imprisonment and the proof of guilt is evident or the presumption is great, every person charged with a crime or a violation of municipal or county ordinance shall be entitled to pretrial release on reasonable conditions. If no conditions of release can reasonably protect the community from risk of physical harm to persons, assure the presence of the accused at trial, or assure the integrity of the judicial process, the accused may be detained." And

WHEREAS, a warrant issued in connection with a violation of probation or violation of community control does not a charge a person with a crime or violation of a municipal or county ordinance; and

WHEREAS, when a warrant is issued in connection with an alleged violation of probation or violation of community control the first appearance judge has no authority under Rule 3.313, Florida Rules of Criminal Procedure, to modify a bond or to set a bond in cases where the issuing judge has denied bond; and

WHEREAS, the first appearance judge must limit herself or himself to the appointment of counsel, if required, and to advising the defendant he is being held due to the alleged violation of probation or community control; and

WHEREAS, the only person who may modify a bond or set a bond relating to alleged violation of probation or violation of community control when the issuing judge has denied bond is the judge

A. who imposed the conditions of bail or set the amount of bond;

B. who is the Chief Judge of the circuit in which the defendant is is to appear for a hearing; or

C. who has been assigned to preside over the hearing of the alleged violation of probation or violation of community control.

Accordingly, it is ORDERED that when a warrant is issued in connection with an alleged violation of probation or violation of community control, the first appearance judge shall not modify a bond or set a bond in cases wherein the issuing judge has denied bond unless the first appearance judge is the one who initially set the bond, is the Chief Judge of the circuit in which the defendant is to appear for a hearing, or is the judge assigned to preside over the hearing on the alleged violation of probation or violation of community control.

DONE AND ORDERED in Chambers at Tallahassee, Leon County, Florida, this 14th day of August, 2002.

WILLIAM L. GARY
Chief Judge

Adopted effective August 14, 2002.

2002–05. CONFIDENTIALITY OF JUVENILE RECORDS

IN THE SECOND JUDICIAL CIRCUIT OF FLORIDA
OFFICE OF THE CHIEF JUDGE

ADMINISTRATIVE ORDER 2002–05

IN RE: CONFIDENTIALITY OF JUVENILE RECORDS

WHEREAS, United States armed forces recruiters have requested juvenile delinquency case information from several clerks of court in the Second Judicial Circuit to determine if the juveniles in question qualify for military service; and

WHEREAS, section 985.04(3)(a), Florida Statutes, states that, "... all information obtained under this part in the discharge of official duty by any judge, any employee of the court, any authorized agent of the Department of Juvenile Justice, the Parole Commission, the Department of Corrections, the juvenile justice circuit boards, any law enforcement agent, or any licensed professional or licensed community agency representative participating in the assessment or treatment of a juvenile is confidential ..."; and

WHEREAS, section 985.04(3)(a), Florida Statutes, further states that this confidential information may only be disclosed to, "... the authorized personnel of the court, the Department of Juvenile Justice and its designees, the Department of Corrections, the Parole Commission, law enforcement agents, school superintendents and their designees, or any licensed professional or licensed community agency representative participating in the assessment or treatment of a juvenile, and others entitled under this chapter to receive that information, or upon order of the court"; and

WHEREAS, section 985.04(2), Florida Statutes, states that "... official records required by this part are not open to inspection by the public, but may be inspected only upon order of the court by persons deemed by the court to have a proper interest therein, except that a child and the parents, guardians, or legal custodians of the child and their attorneys, law enforcement agencies, the Department of juvenile justice and its designees, the Parole Commission, and the department of Corrections shall always have the right to inspect and copy any official record pertaining to the child"; and

WHEREAS, rule 2.051(c)(7), Florida Rules of Judicial Administration, states that records of the judicial branch and its agencies shall be confidential if they are, "... made confidential under the Florida and United States Constitutions and Florida and federal law"; and

WHEREAS, section 985.04(3), Florida Statutes, states that, "... All orders of the court entered pursuant to this part must be in writing and signed by the judge ..."; it is therefore,

ORDERED that juvenile records will released only to those authorized by statute and rule, and other requests for release of this information shall be directed to the chief judge. I find that United States armed forces recruiters have a proper interest in juvenile court records. I further find that the definition armed forces recruiter includes personnel employed by the United States Coast Guard as well as those of the traditional four armed forces. However, to balance this proper interest with the privacy rights of the juvenile and their family, I find that consent of both the parent or guardian, and consent of the child, must be evidenced by a notarized release signed by both parties and the military recruiter. The deputy clerk of court shall place the original of the release and a copy of this administrative order in the appropriate case file and subsequently release the requested juvenile information to the armed forces recruiter.

DONE AND ORDERED in Chambers at Tallahassee, Leon County, Florida, this 12th day of March 2002.

William L. Gary
Chief Judge

Adopted effective March 12, 2002.

2001–04. BLOOD OR OTHER BIOLOGICAL SPECIMEN COLLECTION FOR DNA ANALYSIS

IN THE SECOND JUDICIAL CIRCUIT OF FLORIDA

OFFICE OF THE CHIEF JUDGE

ADMINISTRATIVE ORDER 2001–04

IN RE: BLOOD OR OTHER BIOLOGICAL SPECIMEN COLLECTION FOR DNA ANALYSIS

WHEREAS, Subsection 943.325 (3), Florida Statutes (2001) provides that, "The chief judge of each circuit shall, in conjunction with the sheriff or other entity that maintains the county jail, assure implementation of a method to promptly collect required blood specimens or other approved biological specimens and forward the specimens to the Department of Law Enforcement." and

WHEREAS, Subsection 943.325 (1) (a) (1) and (2), Florida Statutes (2001) provides that, "Any person who is convicted or was previously convicted in this state for any offense or attempted offense defined in chapter 794, chapter 800, Section 782.04, Section 784.045, Section 810.02, Section 812.133, or section 812.135 and who is either: still incarcerated or no longer incarcerated yet is within the confines of the legal state boundaries and is on probation, community control, parole, conditional release, control release, or any other court-ordered supervision, shall be required to submit two specimens of blood, or other biological specimens approved by the Department of Law Enforcement, to the Department of Law Enforcement designated testing facility as directed by the department." and

WHEREAS, Subsections 943.325 (10) (a) and 948.03 (11), Florida Statutes (2001) provides for the convicted person to reimburse the appropriate agency for the costs of collecting and transmitting the blood specimens or other approved biological specimens to the Florida Department of Law Enforcement, and

WHEREAS, Subsection 948.03 (5) (a) (8), Florida Statutes (2001) requires certain probationers and community controllees to submit two specimens of blood or other approved biological specimens to the Florida Department of Law Enforcement to be registered with the DNA data bank.

It is **THEREFORE**

ORDERED that:

I. OFFENDERS PLACED ON PROBATION OR COMMUNITY CONTROL

A. Within seven days of sentencing all persons convicted of any offense or attempted offense specified in Subsection 943.325 (1) (a) (1) and (2) shall be required to submit two specimens of blood or other approved biological specimens to the appropriate jail medical provider who in turn shall forward the samples to the Department of Law Enforcement. At the time of sentencing, the sentencing court shall direct the collection of the specimens through the judgment and sentence forms.

B. The local jails shall have the discretion in establishing hours in which the blood or other approved biological specimens may be collected and notify the Department of Corrections/ Department of Juvenile Justice of such hours. In accordance with Subsection 943.325(2), Florida Statutes (2001), the local jails shall have the discretion in establishing the procedures in which the blood or other approved biological specimens are collected.

C. The Department of Corrections/Department of Juvenile Justice shall have the discretion of developing procedures to inform defendants of the required blood draws or collection of other approved biological specimens, as well as the monitoring of whether or not the defendant complies. The Department of Corrections/Department of Juvenile Justice shall prepare a violation of probation affidavit against defendants who fail to appear at the jail to comply with this order within the 7–day period.

D. Unless the convicted person has been declared indigent by the court, the payment for the collecting and transmitting the blood or other approved biological specimens to the Florida Department of Law Enforcement shall be borne by the defendants, in accordance with Subsections 943.325 (10) (a) and (11), Florida Statutes (2001).

E. As provided in Subsection 943.325 (11), Florida Statutes (2001), if the Department of Law Enforcement determines that a convicted person who is required to submit blood or other approved biological specimens has not provided the specimens, the department, a state attorney, or any law enforcement agency may apply to the circuit court for an order that authorizes the taking of the convicted person into custody for the purpose of securing the required specimens. A copy of the motion shall be provided to the counsel of record.

II. OFFENDERS SENTENCED TO COUNTY JAIL

A. While in such custody, all persons convicted of any offense or attempted offense specified in Subsections 943.325 (1) (a) (1) and (2), Florida Statutes (2001) shall be required to submit two specimens of blood or other approved biological specimens to the jail medical provider who in turn shall forward the samples to the Department of Law Enforcement. At the time of sentencing, the sentencing court shall direct the collection of the specimens through the judgement and sentence forms.

B. In accordance with Subsection 943.325(2), Florida Statutes (2001), the local jails shall have the discretion in establishing the procedures in which the blood or other approved biological specimens are collected.

C. Unless the convicted person has been declared indigent by the court, payment for drawing and transmitting the blood or other approved biological specimens to the Florida Department of Law Enforcement may be borne by the defendants, in accordance with Subsection 943.325 (10) (a), Florida Statutes (2001).

D. As provided in Subsection 943.325 (11), Florida Statutes (2001) if the Department of Law Enforcement determines that a convicted person who is required to submit blood or other approved biological specimens has not provided the specimens, the department, a state attorney, or any law enforcement agency may apply to the circuit court for an order that authorizes the taking of the convicted person into custody for the purpose of securing the required specimens.

DONE and ORDERED in chambers at Tallahassee, Leon County, Florida, this 23 day of May 2001.

George S. Reynolds III
Chief Judge

Adopted effective May 23, 2001.

2000–03. INVESTIGATIVE COSTS IN CRIMINAL CASES

IN THE SECOND JUDICIAL CIRCUIT
OF THE STATE OF FLORIDA

CHAMBERS OF THE CHIEF JUDGE

ADMINISTRATIVE ORDER NO 2000–03

IN RE: INVESTIGATIVE COSTS IN CRIMINAL CASES

WHEREAS, Section 938.27 Florida Statutes authorizes sentencing courts to order defendants to pay for the costs of prosecution associated with their cases, and

WHEREAS, costs of prosecution include the investigative costs associated with the case and

WHEREAS, the State Attorney has agreed that the following schedule of costs is fair and reasonable, therefore in consideration of the foregoing, it is

ORDERED that the following guidelines shall apply to the imposition of costs of prosecution in all criminal prosecution in the Second Judicial Circuit **in the event the trial court elects to assess the costs of prosecution.**

A. Circuit Court

1. The minimum cost of prosecution to be assessed in each felony case is $50.00 This cost takes into consideration the time involved in the intake process case preparation (exclusive of pre-trial motion and depositions) and the taking of the plea in court. All law enforcement agencies shall submit a request for reimbursement of investigative costs form (See Example as Attachment A) with each case they are seeking to recover the minimum cost of prosecution.

2. For any amount in excess of the above to be awarded the state shall, at least five (5) business days prior to sentencing unless otherwise provided in a plea agreement, file a Motion to Assess, with the amounts documented therein and furnish a copy to the defense attorney. A proposed order should also be included therewith.

3. Any defendant who objects to the assessment of the investigative costs has the right to request a hearing to

determine the actual investigative costs incurred by the law enforcement agency.

B. County Court

1. The minimum cost of prosecution to be assessed in each misdemeanor and criminal traffic case shall be assessed as follow

a. For a plea at First Appearance, no costs.

b. For a plea entered to a criminal traffic case or to a misdemeanor case subsequent to First Appearance a cost of $25.00 shall be assessed.

c. For a plea entered to an Information prior to trial, a cost of $25.00 shall be assessed.

d. Cases that involve an extraordinary amount of time, motion hearings, depositions or go to trial, shall be handled as set forth in paragraph A 2.

All law enforcement agencies shall submit a request for reimbursement of investigative costs form (See Example as Attachment A) with each case they are seeking to recover the minimum cost of prosecution.

2. Any defendant who objects to the assessment of the investigative costs has the right to request a hearing to determine the actual investigative costs incurred by the law enforcement agency.

IT IS FURTHER ORDERED that all Clerks of the Circuit Court in and for the Second Judicial Circuit of Florida are hereby ordered to receive and disburse payments as reimbursement for investigative costs as may be ordered in criminal cases.

A service charge for the Clerk of the Circuit Court is hereby established in the amount of two dollars ($2.00) per assessment.

Upon receipt of payments or installment payments for reimbursement of investigative costs the Clerk shall, after deducting the service charge of two dollars ($2.00), deposit said payments into the investigative costs account and shall credit the account of each defendant with each payment as received.

The Clerk shall disburse all accumulated payments at the end of each month, to the proper recipient of said reimbursement, along with a specific breakdown of the disbursements.

DONE AND ORDERED in Chambers this 1st day of March, 2000

GEORGE S REYNOLDS III
Chief Judge

[ATTACHMENT "A"]

IN THE COUNTY OR CIRCUIT COURT LEON COUNTY

TALLAHASSEE POLICE DEPARTMENT
REQUEST FOR REIMBURSEMENT
OF INVESTIGATIVE COSTS

Leon County, Florida

____

State of Florida

vs. ______________________

Defendant

____

Agency Case Number

CHARGE(S): ______________________

Pursuant to Florida Statute 938 27 (1997), the TALLAHASSEE POLICE DEPARTMENT respectfully requests reimbursement for the costs Incurred during this investigation Furthermore, it is requested that these costs be included and entered in the judgment rendered against the defendant and direct the Clerk of the Court to collect these costs and dispense the same to the TALLAHASSEE POLICE DEPARTMENT

(*Costs reflect fees Incurred for dispatch, staff/officer labor costs, supervisory review, evidence handling, records processing, lab work, mileage, office supplies, etc as applicable)

The costs are as follows

___ Misdemeanor $25 00 ___ Felony $50 00

___ Extraordinary investigative costs (See attached itemized statement)

____

Who being first duly sworn says that on ___ day of ________, 2000 in Leon County, Florida does swear/affirm that the facts contained herein are true and correct

____________________.

Affiant

Sworn to and subscribed before me this ___ day of ________, 2000

____

Notary Public/Law Enforcement Officer

Adopted effective March 1, 2000.

2000–02. NOTICE TO APPEAR

IN THE SECOND JUDICIAL CIRCUIT OF FLORIDA
OFFICE OF THE CHIEF JUDGE

ADMINISTRATIVE ORDER NO: 2000–02

IN RE: NOTICE TO APPEAR

WHEREAS, the Florida Legislature has created a number of statutes whose violation constitutes a misdemeanor, or a civil infraction, and

WHEREAS, the Florida Administrative Code has created a number of regulations whose violation constitutes a misdemeanor or civil infraction, and

WHEREAS, there is a need for a uniform reporting document that can be used to refer criminal and civil violations of municipal and county ordinances to the Court,

WHEREAS, the Legislature has determined that the adoption of a uniform document for the reporting of non-traffic civil infractions is a local decision, and

WHEREAS, Florida Criminal Rule of Procedure 3 125 requires the Chief Judge to authorize Law Enforcement Agencies in the Second Judicial Circuit to issue, in appropriate cases, a Notice to Appear to persons required to appear before the Court, and

WHEREAS, there is a need for law enforcement officers to be authorized to issue a Notice to Appear that can be used to refer misdemeanor crimes, civil infractions, criminal and civil violations of municipal and county ordinances to the court when the defendant is not arrested or is released on the defendant's own recognizance by a law enforcement officer, and

It is **THEREFORE, ORDERED** that pursuant to Florida Criminal Rule of Procedure 3 125 all Law Enforcement Agencies in the Second Judicial Circuit are authorized to issue a Notice to Appear to refer misdemeanor crimes, civil infractions, criminal and civil violations of municipal and county ordinances to the court when the defendant is not arrested or is released on the defendant's own recognizance by a law enforcement officer

DONE AND ORDERED in Chambers at Tallahassee, Leon County, Florida, this 14 day of January, 2000

GEORGE S REYNOLDS III
Chief Judge

Adopted effective January 14, 2000.

1997–12. LEON COUNTY FELONY DRUG INTERVENTION DIVISION

IN THE SECOND JUDICIAL CIRCUIT
OF THE STATE OF FLORIDA

CHAMBERS OF THE CHIEF JUDGE

ADMINISTRATIVE ORDER NO.: 97–12
FOURTH AMENDMENT

IN RE: LEON COUNTY FELONY DRUG INTERVENTION DIVISION

WHEREAS, for approximately the past four years a Felony Drug Intervention Division has been maintained in Leon County with federal funding support;

WHEREAS, the Florida Department of Corrections, Probation Office, has agreed to assume the supervision and case management of current participants, as well as future participants, effective October 1, 1997, in a community partnership arrangement with Leon County which shall provide certain supplemental funding and personnel assistance; and

WHEREAS, the proposed Leon County Felony Drug Intervention Division will be a joint cooperative effort of the Office of Court Administration, Office of the State Attorney, Public Defender's Office, Leon County Probation Pre–Trial Release Program, Florida Department of Corrections, Clerk of the Court, and the provider of substance abuse treatment; and

WHEREAS, clearly articulated and agreed upon policies with regard to the implementation and operation of the Leon County Felony Drug Intervention Division are required,

IT IS THEREFORE,

ORDERED that:

1. Effective October 1, 1997, supervision of all participants in the Felony Drug Intervention Division shall be the responsibility of the Florida Department of Corrections, Probation and Parole Circuit Office. The Pre–Trial Release Office of the County Probation Division shall be responsible for screening and referral of eligible drug court participants. This program shall be limited to a maximum caseload of 75 participants unless otherwise ordered by the court.

2. Defendants whose offenses occurred on or after October 1, 1997, shall be eligible to participate in such program if they are charged with a second or third degree drug purchase/possession offense under Chapter 893 in accordance with the criteria of Section 948.08(6), Florida Statutes. Participants must not have any pending felony cases or be on active Department of Corrections supervision.

3. Those defendants deemed appropriate for participation in the program will appear before the Felony Drug Intervention Division judge for program orientation at the next scheduled court date to determine the appropriateness for admission into the program.

4. All participants must be Second Circuit residents who have been approved for admission by the Court and Oversight Committee pursuant to Section 910.035, Florida Statutes(Chapter 2001–48).

5. A participant fee of $95.00 per month shall be charged to each participant in the Leon County Felony Intervention Division. Participants may elect to pay the $95.00 fee in partial payments in lieu of a lump sum monthly fee. In accordance with the provisions of section 28.24(26)(b), Florida Statutes, the Leon County Clerk of the Circuit Court may collect $5.00 as an administrative processing charge per month from defendants who make partial payment. The Leon County Clerk of the Circuit Court shall collect all participation fees for deposit in a fund for the operation of the Leon County Felony Drug Intervention Division and provide receipts to each defendant for such fees.

6. Participation in the Felony Drug Intervention Division shall be on a voluntary basis. Eligible defendants electing not to enroll in the program will have their cases transferred to a regular criminal division.

7. Participation in the Felony Drug Intervention Division will be for a minimum period of 12 months and a maximum period of 18 months, unless otherwise ordered by the court. The defendant will receive credit from the day treatment began, even if that date preceded arraignment.

8. Participants must remain drug free for 12 consecutive months and if at any time any participant tests positive for any controlled substance, they will be considered for termination from the treatment program.

9. The cost of supervision fee for the Department of Corrections will be waived in every case until a specific order with respect thereto is entered in such case.

DONE AND ORDERED in Chambers, at Tallahassee, Leon County, Florida, this 25th day of September, 1997.

N. SANDERS SAULS
Chief Judge

Attachment 1
FELONY DRUG INTERVENTION DIVISION FEE SCHEDULE

Category	Income Range	Weekly Fee	Monthly Fee
A	$ 0—$ 4,999	$ 5.00	$ 20.00
B	$ 5,000—$12,499	$10.00	$ 45.00
C	$12,500—$24,999	$20.00	$ 85.00
D	$25,000—$37,499	$30.00	$130.00
E	$37,500—$49,999	$40.00	$175.00
F	$50,000 or more	$50.00	$220.00

Adopted effective October 1, 1997. Amended effective February 23, 1999; October 8, 2001; September 30, 2011; October 1, 2015.

1995–05. PUBLIC GUARDIAN OFFICE

IN THE SECOND JUDICIAL CIRCUIT OF FLORIDA

OFFICE OF THE CHIEF JUDGE

ADMINISTRATIVE ORDER NO 95–05
[FIRST] AMENDMENT

IN RE: Public Guardian Office, Second Judicial Circuit

WHEREAS: The Second Judicial Circuit has implemented a Public Guardianship Program; and

WHEREAS: Florida Statutes, Sections 744.701–744.709 inclusive, sets forth provisions of the "Public Guardianship Act", and

WHEREAS There is a need to develop policies of efficiently implement the provisions of the "Public Guardianship Act" in the Second Judicial Circuit, IT IS THEREFORE

ORDERED that:

The following provisions are hereby enacted to provide policy direction to the Public Guardian in the Second Judicial Circuit:

I. EXEMPTION FROM EDUCATIONAL REQUIREMENTS

A. That Hugh T. Handley, Public Guardian, Second Judicial Circuit of Florida, shall be exempted from the educational requirements pursuant to Florida Law. This exemption is limited solely to cases in which he is appointed guardian in his capacity as Public Guardian. In the event the above-name guardian shall seek appointment to guardianship estates other than as Public Guardian, this Order snail be of no force and effect

B. This exemption shall be comprehensive in nature due to the guardian's extensive experience and education in the administration of guardianship estates The various Clerks of Court are hereby directed to file a copy of this Order in every guardianship estate in which the above referenced guardian currently serves

II. DESIGNATED DEPOSITORY. The Public Guardian of the Second Judicial Circuit is authorized to maintain checking and savings accounts for the deposit and disbursal of wards' funds at depositaries of his selection with the following provisions

A. *Signatures Authorized.*

1. Any check under the sum of $500.00 (Five Hundred and no/100 Dollars), Hugh T. Handley or any person who is an employee of the Public Guardian office and who is designated by the Chief Judge of the Circuit

2. Any check of $500.00 (Five Hundred and no/100 Dollars) up to $1,000.00 (One Thousand and no/100 Dollars), Hugh T Handley only

3. Any check of $1,000.00 (One Thousand and no/100 Dollars) or over, Chief Judge, Second Judicial Circuit, Florida.

4. The authorized signatures as set forth herein may be changed by the Chief Judge of this Circuit or his successor in office by letter to the depository in question

5. No check made payable to any person whose signature is authorized herein snail be honored by the designated depository

III. SURETY BOND. The Public Guardian of the Second Judicial Circuit, shall cause the surety bond currently in full force and effect in the amount of $200,000.00 with surety as prescribed in Section 45.011, Florida Statutes, approved by the Clerk of Leon County, Florida, conditioned on the faithful performance of all duties of said Public Guardian and joint and several in nature and payable to the Governor of the State of Florida and his successors in office, to be decreased to $5,000.00 in compliance with Florida Statutes, Section 744 709 and the memorandum of Roy J. McCaslin, Inspector General of Supreme Court of Florida dated November 5, 1996.

The Public Guardian shall certify monthly to the Chief Judge of the Circuit the total balance of wards' funds over which he exercises control. Any increase and decrease in the amount of the surety bond shall be reported to the Clerk of Leon County, Florida for inclusion with the surety bond on file.

IV. METHOD OF SERVICE. The Public Guardian or his representative may serve all documents required to be served on his ward and capable of being served by mail or hand delivery to be served by delivery of a copy of the document by hand delivery and authorizing the Public Guardian or his representative to retrieve the document for safekeeping in the event the ward cannot or will not respond to the service.

V. PROCEDURES FOR REQUESTING THE APPOINTMENT OF THE PUBLIC GUARDIAN IN INCAPACITY PROCEEDINGS

A. The Public Guardian shall prepare for dissemination a memorandum or letter explaining the contents of this Administrative Order and establishing the Office of the Public Guardian as the source of forms and documents implementing the procedures set forth herein.

B. The Public Guardian shall maintain form petitions to determine incapacity and affidavits approved by the Chief Judge of the Circuit, for distribution to any person wishing to be a petitioner and requesting the appointment of the Public Guardian. The petition to determine incapacity shall include an allegation that the person to be examined is entitled to the services of the Public Guardian and that the appointment of the Public Guardian is requested in the event that the Court finds the person to be incapacitated The affidavit shall be sufficient in form and context for the Court to determine that the person to be examined is indigent within the definition as set forth in Florida Statutes 744.704, that there is no other person to act as guardian and that the petitioner has no monetary interest, either directly or indirectly into the alleged incapacitateds' affairs, and for the Court to ascertain to what extent alternative to guardianship have been explored concerning the person who is thought to be incapacitated The affidavit shall be attached as an exhibit to the Petition.

C. Any person, meeting the requirements of Florida law, who wishes to file a petition for the determination of incapacity of a person alleged to be indigent and requesting the appointment of the Public Guardian may do so by presenting, the petition and affidavit provided for herein, to the Public Guardian

D. The Public Guardian, upon the receipt of a petition to determine incapacity and for the appointment of the Public Guardian together with the affidavit, snail immediately transmit the same to the Probate Judge of the Circuit Court.

E. The Court snail enter such Orders as it deems necessary based upon the petition and accompanying affidavit, defining petitioner's right to proceed in pro per, directing the Public Guardian and providing for the filing and presentation of the petition to the Court

VI. Administrative Order 90–10, IN RE. Public Guardianship Office, Second Judicial Circuit, dated February 9, 1990, as amended is hereby terminated

DONE AND ORDERED in Chambers at the Leon County Courthouse, this 18 day of April, 1995.

PHILIP J PADOVANO
Chief Judge

Adopted effective April 18, 1995. Amended effective February 14, 1997; May 16, 1997.

Publisher's Note: *Amendments 3, 4 and 5, dated May, 16, 1997, August 29, 1997, and June 1, 1998 respectively, have not been included in this order. Those amendments did not amend the text of the order; they gave a temporary extension for filing certain reports. These extensions were through September 30, 1998.*

1994–04. CASH BONDS

IN THE CIRCUIT COURT OF THE SECOND JUDICIAL CIRCUIT, IN AND FOR LEON COUNTY, FLORIDA

ADMINISTRATIVE ORDER NO 94–04

IN RE CASH BONDS

WHEREAS, the First District Court of Appeal decided in Harrell v McMillan, 614 So 2d 1185 (Fla 1st DCA 1993), that trial judges do not have the authority to require a criminal defendant to post a cash bond, and

WHEREAS, the decision of the First District Court of Appeal applies to bail bonds set for probation violators as well as pretrial detainees, and,

WHEREAS, there may be many unserved warrants that were issued before this rule was announced by the court,

It is therefore ORDERED

(1) The sheriffs of each county within the Second Judicial Circuit are directed to treat a cash bond as a surety bond and to allow the defendant to decide whether to post the bond in cash or through a bail bondsman

(2) This order applies to all bonds set in criminal cases including bonds that are set for pretrial detainees and bonds that are set in probation violation cases it does not apply to bonds or writs of attachment set in child support cases or to any other bonds set in civil cases.

(3) This order shall not be construed as a limitation on a trial judge's right to authorize other lawful methods of posting bail or as a limitation on the trial judge's right to impose other conditions or release

DONE AND ORDERED in Chambers, Tallahassee, Leon County, Florida, this 16 day of February, 1994.

PHILIP J. PADOVANO
Circuit Judge

Adopted effective February 16, 1994.

1993–04. LEON COUNTY SCHOOLS JUVENILE DELINQUENCY MENTORING PROGRAM

IN THE SECOND JUDICIAL CIRCUIT OF FLORIDA
OFFICE OF THE CHIEF JUDGE

ADMINISTRATIVE ORDER NO 93–04

IN RE LEON COUNTY SCHOOLS JUVENILE DELINQUENCY MENTORING PROGRAM

WHEREAS, there is currently a need for alternative intervention programs for juvenile delinquents in Leon County, and

WHEREAS, Section 39 0215 (Florida Statutes, 1992) provides local governments the authority to establish and operate programs for the control and rehabilitative treatment of delinquent behavior, and

WHEREAS, the Leon County Schools, in collaboration with the Leon County Circuit Court, has obtained funding to implement and professionally supervise a delinquent mentor program, and

WHEREAS, recent research strongly suggests that the most effective interventions with delinquents involve greater personal contact with, increased supervision of and more individualized and comprehensive services to the juveniles, it is therefore

ORDERED THAT

1. The TIMEOUT juvenile delinquent mentor program is hereby established in Leon County

2. This program shall be administered by the Leon County Schools

3. Beginning April 1, 1993, at the discretion of the Court, juveniles between eight (8) and fourteen (14) years of age for whom adjudication of delinquency is either ordered or withheld on non-violent offenses may be ordered to participate in the program as a condition of community control or JASP administered by the Department of Health and Rehabilitative Services and JASP, respectively

4. Upon receiving such an order, the program supervisor or his/her representative will meet with the juvenile's parent(s) or guardian to encourage their approval and support for their child's participation and will then identify a mentor to be paired with the juvenile and prepare an order that appoints that mentor

5. Volunteer mentors must be at least 18 years old, must be trained to competency in accordance with the curriculum adopted by the Leon County Schools, and must successfully pass criminal history and abuse registry checks

6. An assessment of each referred juvenile's needs must be conducted by the assigned mentor and an individualized program of services be implemented by the mentor, under the supervision of the professional approved by the Leon County Schools

7. These individualized programs shall utilize existing resources in the community and incorporate activities that provide for the development of appropriate social and civic behaviors

8. In the execution of their responsibilities, mentors shall have access to any records maintained by any agency, hospital, organization, school, person or office including the Clerk of this Court, Department of Health and Rehabilitative Services, human service agencies, pediatricians, psychologists, psychiatrists, and police departments that relate to the child, without consent by the child or his/her parents.

9. Upon identification of such a need, mentors shall inform the program supervisor of the need for advocating for the provision or improvement of services for the child and the program supervisor will identify and follow-through with appropriate avenues for advocating for these needs

10. Mentors appointed to juveniles for this program shall maintain any information received from any source as confidential, and will not disclose the same except in reports to the program, the Court and other parties to this cause

DONE AND ORDERED in Chambers at Tallahassee, Leon County, Florida this 1st day of April, 1993

WILLIAM L. GARY
Chief Judge

Adopted effective April 1, 1993.

1992–09. AMERICANS WITH DISABILITY ACT OF 1990

IN THE SECOND JUDICIAL CIRCUIT OF FLORIDA

OFFICE OF THE CHIEF JUDGE

ADMINISTRATIVE ORDER 1992–09
SECOND AMENDMENT

IN RE: AMERICANS WITH DISABILITY ACT OF 1990

WHEREAS, the Americans with Disability Act (ADA) of 1990 requires reasonably accommodations be provided to requesting qualified persons with disabilities in order that they might participate fully in court programs, services, activities, and benefits; and

WHEREAS, it is the intent of the Second Judicial Circuit to facilitate provision of reasonable accommodations when requested by qualified persons with disabilities; and

WHEREAS, Administrative Order 1992–09 In Re: Americans with Disability Act of 1990 orders specific language to be used in all communications noticing court proceedings; and

WHEREAS, Florida Rule of Judicial Administration 2.540 (c), was amended to provide specific language and format of all notices of court proceedings to be held in a public facility and the amended language and format is in conflict with Administrative Order 1992–09 In Re: Americans with Disability Act of 1990; and

WHEREAS, the Second Judicial Circuit has a new telephone system with accompanying new telephone numbers, it is therefore

ORDERED that the order language in Administrative Order 1992–09 is amended as follows to provide a new telephone number: All notices of court proceedings to be held in a public facility, and all process compelling appearance at such proceedings, shall include the following statement in bold face, 14–point Times New Roman or Courier font:

"If you are a person with a disability who needs any accommodation in order to participate in this proceeding, you are entitled, at no cost to you, to the provision of certain assistance. Please contact ADA Coordinator; 301 South Monroe Street, Room 225, Tallahassee, Fl 32301; 850–606–4401 at least 7 days before your scheduled court appearance, or immediately upon receiving this notification if the time before the scheduled appearance is less than 7 days; if you are hearing or voice impaired, call 711."

The revised language regarding the new telephone number in the court notices may begin immediately; however, the revisions to the court notices shall be completed no later than June 30, 2016.

DONE AND ORDERED in Tallahassee, Florida, Leon County, Florida on October 2nd, 2015.

JONATHAN SJOSTROM
Chief Judge

Adopted effective December 17, 1992. Amended effective May 20, 2010; October 2, 2015.

1992–08. [TERMINATED BY ORDER 2017–06, EFFECTIVE JUNE 15, 2017.]

1992–02. GUARDIAN AD LITEM, RIGHT TO BE NOTIFIED OF AND BE PRESENT AT DEPOSITIONS IN CRIMINAL CASES

IN THE CIRCUIT COURT OF THE SECOND JUDICIAL CIRCUIT, IN AND FOR LEON COUNTY FLORIDA

ADMINISTRATIVE ORDER NO. 92–02

IN RE: GUARDIAN AD LITEM, RIGHT TO BE NOTIFIED OF AND BE PRESENT AT DEPOSITIONS IN CRIMINAL CASES.

WHEREAS Section 415.508(1), FLORIDA STATUTES (1991) provides for the appointment of a Guardian Ad Litem to represent the child in any child abuse or child neglect judicial proceeding, whether civil or criminal; and

WHEREAS the proper representation of the child requires his or her Guardian Ad Litem to be notified of and to nave the right to be present not only at the trial, hearings and other proceedings before the Court, but also at depositions of all witnesses; it is therefore:

ORDERED and ADJUDGED as follows:

In any case, civil or criminal, before the Second Judicial Circuit Court, in which a Guardian Ad Litem is appointed to represent a child involved in the case, the Guardian Ad Litem shall be given notice of and have the right to be present at all depositions, as well as trials, hearings, and other proceedings before the Court.

DONE AND ORDERED in Tallahassee, Leon County, Florida this 21st day of September, 1992. Effective September 21, 1992.

WILLIAM L. GARY, CHIEF JUDGE
Second Judicial Circuit

Adopted effective September 21, 1992.

1990–26. TALLAHASSEE BAR ASSOCIATION—CODE OF PROFESSIONAL COURTESY

IN THE SECOND JUDICIAL CIRCUIT IN AND FOR LEON COUNTY, FLORIDA

OFFICE OF THE CHIEF JUDGE

ADMINISTRATIVE ORDER NO: 90–26

RE: TALLAHASSEE BAR ASSOCIATION—CODE OF PROFESSIONAL COURTESY

WHEREAS, the Tallahassee Bar Association has developed a Code of Professional Courtesy and has requested that the Second Circuit endorse this code in an Administrative Order; and

WHEREAS, it is desired that the judiciary give guidance to the local bar associations with regard to their level of professionalism; and

WHEREAS, it will be beneficial for a Code of Professional Courtesy to be enacted for attorneys practicing within the Second Judicial Circuit, it is therefore:

ORDERED THAT:

The following Code of Professional Courtesy is hereby endorsed by the judiciary in the Second Judicial Circuit of Florida. Attorneys practicing in this circuit are encouraged to adhere to this code.

CODE OF PROFESSIONAL COURTESY

1. Attorneys should treat each other, the opposing party, the court and the members of the court staff with courtesy and civility and conduct themselves in a professional manner at all times.

2. Attorneys should, when practical, consult with opposing counsel before scheduling hearings and depositions in a good faith attempt to avoid scheduling conflicts.

3. Notice of cancellations of depositions and hearings should be given to the court and opposing counsel at the earliest possible time.

4. Proposed orders to be submitted to the court should be prepared promptly, and proposed orders on non-routine matters should be submitted to opposing counsel prior to submission to the court.

5. Attorneys should cooperate with each other when there are conflicts and calendar changes are necessary and requested.

6. Except where any material right of the client is involved, counsel should stipulate to matters in order to avoid unnecessary hearings.

7. When scheduling hearings, counsel should attempt to secure sufficient time to allow full presentation and to allow opposing counsel equal time in response.

8. Reasonable extensions of time should be granted to opposing counsel where such extensions will not have a material, adverse effect on the rights of the client. First requests for reasonable extensions of time to respond to litigation deadlines, whether relating to pleadings, discovery or motions, should ordinarily be granted as a matter of courtesy unless time is of the essence.

9. A lawyer should not seek extensions or continuances for the purpose of harassment or prolonging litigation.

10. The timing and manner of service of pleadings or other papers should not be used to the disadvantage of the party receiving the pleadings or other papers. Pleadings or other papers should not be served sufficiently close to a court appearance so as to inhibit the ability of opposing counsel to prepare for that appearance or, where permitted by law, to respond to the pleadings or other papers. Pleadings or other papers should not be served in order to take advantage of an opponent's known absence from the office or at a time or in a manner designed to inconvenience an adversary, such as late on Friday afternoon or the day preceding a secular or religious holiday. Service should be made personally or by facsimile transmission when it is likely that service by mail, even when allowed, will prejudice the opposing party, however, facsimile service shall be in addition to service in a manner required by the rules.

DONE AND ORDERED in chambers in Tallahassee, Leon County, Florida this 10th day of October, 1990.

CHARLES D. MCCLURE
Chief Judge

Adopted effective October 10, 1990.

Fourth Judicial Circuit (Clay, Duval and Nassau Counties)

LOCAL RULES

4. ASSIGNMENT OF CASES IN DUVAL COUNTY.

ADMINISTRATIVE ORDERS

2018–11. ELECTRONIC RECORDING BY THE GENERAL PUBLIC.

2018–07. SEXUAL HARASSMENT POLICY AND PROCEDURES.

2018–05. STANDING FAMILY LAW COURT ORDER IN DISSOLUTION OF MARRIAGE.

2017–09. ALTERNATIVE SANCTIONING PROGRAM.

2017–08 (A2). SERVICE OF PROCESS IN DOMESTIC VIOLENCE CASES.

2017–06. VACATING TITLE IV–D WRITS OF ATTACHMENT.

2016–06 (A1). FLORIDA LEGAL ACCESS GATEWAY PILOT PROGRAM.

2016–03. CREATION OF DIVISION CR–V IN NASSAU COUNTY FOR A VETERANS TREATMENT COURT.

2016–01. IMPOSITION OF MANDATORY ASSESSMENTS IN THE FOURTH JUDICIAL CIRCUIT.

2015–03. COURTHOUSE SECURITY VIDEOTAPING ON DUVAL COUNTY COURTHOUSE GROUNDS.

2015–01. DEFINITION OF "MEDIA" FOR CREDENTIALS AND COVERAGE OF ALL PUBLIC JUDICIAL PROCEEDINGS (EXCEPT THOSE OF EXTRAORDINARY PUBLIC INTEREST).

2014–10 (A1). MINORS SEXTING: SECTION 847.0141, FLORIDA STATUTES (2015).

2014–09. APPEALS FROM COUNTY COURT TO CIRCUIT COURT (IN DUVAL COUNTY ONLY).

2014–07. VACATING OLD WRITS OF ATTACHMENT.

2014–06. [VACATED AND SET ASIDE BY ORDER 2017-11, EFFECTIVE OCTOBER 18, 2017.].

2014–03. MEDIATION IN CIRCUIT CIVIL CASES CLAY AND NASSAU COUNTIES.

2014–01 (A2). ASSESSMENT AND COLLECTION OF DRUG TESTING FEE.

2013–17 (A1). PEACEFUL DEMONSTRATORS: ESTABLISHMENT OF POLICIES AND LOCATION.

2013–16. GUIDELINES FOR CLERK OF COURT TO DESIGNATE FORECLOSURE CASES AS "ACTIVE" AND "INACTIVE".

2013–14. CREATION OF DIVISION CR–V IN DUVAL COUNTY FOR A VETERANS TREATMENT COURT.

2013–13. MEDIATION IN CIRCUIT CIVIL CASES DUVAL COUNTY.

2013–11. CREATION OF DIVISION CR–V IN CLAY COUNTY FOR A VETERANS TREATMENT COURT.

2013–10. CREATION OF DIVISION CR–Y IN CLAY COUNTY FOR AN ADULT DRUG COURT.

2013–09. ESTABLISHMENT OF THE LOCAL PROFESSIONALISM PANEL.

2013–08. MEDIA & TECHNOLOGICAL COVERAGE OF CASES OF EXTRAORDINARY PUBLIC INTEREST.

2013–05. STANDARDS FOR COURT–APPOINTED COUNSEL SERVING ON REGISTRY FOR GUARDIANSHIPS.

2013–01. PROCEDURES FOR QUALIFYING DEAF OR HARD OF HEARING JURORS.

2012–03 (A1). VACATING ADMINISTRATIVE ORDER NO. 2012–03 REGARDING FILING OF DEPOSITIONS IN DUVAL COUNTY.

2012–02. [VACATED AND SET ASIDE BY ORDER 2017-10, EFFECTIVE SEPTEMBER 19, 2017.].

2012–01 (A1). [VACATED AND SET ASIDE BY ORDER 2017-10, EFFECTIVE SEPTEMBER 19, 2017.].

2011–09. RESIDENTIAL HOMESTEAD FORECLOSURE CASES MANDATORY REFERRAL TO MEDIATION—TERMINATION OF PROGRAM.

2011–07. EVIDENTIARY HEARINGS—PROCEDURAL CHANGES FOR MOTIONS TO EXCEED STATUTORY MAXIMUM IN DUE PROCESS AND INDIGENCY–FOR–COST CASES.

2011–06. REASSIGNMENT OF ORIGINAL CASE; SAME NUMBER.

2010–08. JUDICIAL SALES FEE IN ALL FORECLOSURE CASES, CLAY COUNTY.

2010–07. JUDICIAL SALES FEE IN ALL FORECLOSURE CASES, DUVAL COUNTY.

2010–05. ELECTRONIC SIGNATURE OF CLERK ON SUMMONS.

2010–04. APPOINTED COUNSEL AND REGISTRY FOR PETITIONS TO DETERMINE INCAPACITY & GUARDIANSHIPS.

2010–02. WITHDRAWAL OF APPOINTED COUNSEL IN CRIMINAL CASES AFTER DISPOSITION AND PRIOR TO APPEAL.

2010–01 (A1). RESIDENTIAL HOMESTEAD FORECLOSURE CASES MANDATORY REFERRAL TO MEDIATION.

2008–04 (A3). ASSESSMENT AND COLLECTION OF DRUG TESTING FEE FOR DUVAL COUNTY, FLORIDA.

2007–03 (A1). MENTAL HEALTH COURTS.

2007–01. COURT APPOINTED COUNSEL IN DEPENDENCY AND TERMINATION OF PARENTAL RIGHTS PROCEEDINGS.
2006–05. SEALING COURT RECORDS.
2006–03. NOTICE OF RELATED CASES.
2005–03. JIMMY RYCE ACT EXPERT WITNESS FEE COST CONTAINMENT.
2005–02. APPEALS FROM COUNTY COURT AND LOCAL ADMINISTRATIVE AGENCIES; PETITIONS FOR WRITS.
2004–23 (A1). REGISTRY OF CONFLICT COUNSEL.
2004–08 (A1). CONFLICT COUNSEL COMPENSATION AND DUE PROCESS COSTS.
2001–10 (A1). BAKER, MARCHMAN ACT, AND INMATE MENTAL HEALTH HEARINGS.
2001–07 (A5). AUTHORITY OF THE CLERK IN TRAFFIC CASES.
1998–07 (A2). COMPREHENSIVE BAKER ACT PROCEDURES.
1996–10 (A17). ORDER OF REFERRAL TO GENERAL MAGISTRATES AND SUPPORT ENFORCEMENT HEARING OFFICERS.
1995–16 (A5). FAMILY LAW ADMINISTRATIVE POLICIES AND PROCEDURES.
1995–16 (A4). FAMILY LAW FOURTH JUDICIAL CIRCUIT TIMESHARING GUIDELINES (LOCAL AND LONG DISTANCE).
1995–04 (A1). LOCATION OF DEPOSITIONS IN CRIMINAL CASES—DUVAL COUNTY.
1994–02 (A2). CIVIL RIGHTS POLICY STATEMENT AND CIVIL RIGHTS COMPLAINT PROCEDURE.
1993–08 (A4). [DISSOLUTION OF MARRIAGE, PARENTING COURSES].
1993–02 (A3). AMERICANS WITH DISABILITIES ACT OF 1990.
1992–02 (A2). MEDIA & TECHNOLOGICAL COVERAGE OF JUDICIAL PROCEEDINGS.
1992–01 (A6). ADMINISTRATIVE PROVISION FOR FAMILY LAW DIVISION; UNIFIED FAMILY COURT.
1989–09 (A2). PROVIDING THE COURTS WITH ADDRESSED ENVELOPES AND POSTAGE BY ATTORNEYS AND LITIGANTS.
1989–05 (A2). PROCEDURE FOR JUDICIAL WAIVER OF PARENTAL NOTIFICATION OF ABORTION.
1988–21 (A14). SUPERSEDED BY ADMINISTRATIVE ORDER NO. 86–23.
1986–23 (A5). ASSIGNMENT OF CRIMINAL CASES IN CIRCUIT COURT.

Local Rules

RULE 4. ASSIGNMENT OF CASES IN DUVAL COUNTY

(a) Civil Actions. Upon the filing of a civil action the clerk shall assign it to a division in accordance with the confidential automatic schedules of assignments which shall be adopted by the court and delivered to the clerk.

(b) Appeals. Appeals shall be assigned to a division selected by application of the last three digits of the number of the action to the automatic schedule of assignments provided for in subsection (a).

(c) Bond Estreatures. Applications to set aside judgments entered by the clerk pursuant to forfeitures of bail bonds in other courts shall be assigned to a division selected by application of the last three digits of the bond estreature file number to the automatic schedule of assignments provided for in subsection (a).

(d) Criminal Actions. Criminal actions shall be assigned in alphabetical sequence to divisions of the court in the order of the chronological return of indictments.

(e) Reactivated Actions. Actions filed before January 2, 1948, not previously assigned to a division, if reactivated, shall be assigned in alphabetical sequence to divisions of the court in the chronological order of reactivation.

(f) Other Actions. All other actions shall be assigned to divisions of the court in alphabetical sequence according to the schedule maintained by the Presiding Judge.

(g) Reassignment of Actions.

(1) Whenever the judge who presides over the division to which an action is assigned determines that he is disqualified, or that good cause exists for doing so, then such judge, with the consent of another judge, may reassign the action to the division of the consenting judge. An action, including a divorce action, on the same or different grounds, which was formerly assigned to another division, but which was dismissed and thereafter refiled, shall be reassigned to the division in which it was originally pending, by the judge of the division in which it was originally pending.

(2) When two or more actions are pending which may be appropriately tried together, but are assigned to different divisions, the judge of the division to which the case bearing the lower docket number is assigned, upon learning that it is a companion case, shall reassign all other such companion actions to his division.

(3) Copy of any order reassigning an action shall be provided to the judge of any affected division.

(h) Identification of Division. The clerk shall designate on the file cover and progress docket the division to which each action is assigned and upon reassignment shall, change such notations accordingly.

Administrative Orders

2018–11. ELECTRONIC RECORDING BY THE GENERAL PUBLIC

This order is the same as Administrative Order 2018-02.

IN THE CIRCUIT COURT, FOURTH JUDICIAL CIRCUIT, IN AND FOR DUVAL COUNTY, FLORIDA

ADMINISTRATIVE ORDER NO. 2018–11

RE: ELECTRONIC RECORDING BY THE GENERAL PUBLIC

WHEREAS, the Court has the responsibility to preserve the dignity and decorum of the Courthouse, the fair administration of justice and the safety and security of all employees and citizens who enter the Duval County Courthouse;

WHEREAS, within the Duval County Courthouse, a danger to existing security measures occurs when recording by electronic devices captures security features that are in place throughout the Courthouse, sensitive witnesses such as undercover police officers and protected witnesses who are required to appear in court, and jurors or potential jurors who are required to appear in the Courthouse;

WHEREAS, as a result of this danger to existing security measures, it is necessary to prohibit members of the general public from using electronic devices to record within the interior of the Duval County Courthouse absent specific written permission from the Chief Judge of the Fourth Judicial Circuit;

WHEREAS, the United States District Court for the Middle District of Florida has entered General Order 6:13–mc–94–Orl–22 which states that "[n]o one may bring a personal electronic device beyond a courthouse's security checkpoint" but allows for certain exceptions by court order and by judicial discretion, and for employees, jurors and attorneys;

WHEREAS, Rule 2.451(c)(2), Florida Rules of Judicial Administration, states that the "use of electronic devices in a courthouse or court facility is subject at all times to the authority of the chief judge to (A) ensure decorum and prevent distractions; (B) ensure the fair administration of justice; and (C) preserve court security";

NOW THEREFORE, by the authority vested in me as the Chief Judge of the Fourth Judicial Circuit and pursuant to the Florida Rules of Judicial Administration, it is hereby

ORDERED AND ADJUDGED that:

1) Any member of the general public who seeks to electronically record within the interior of the Duval County Courthouse may apply for permission through the Chief Judge of the Fourth Judicial Courthouse using the form attached as Attachment A.

2) Absent written permission from the Chief Judge of the Fourth Judicial Circuit, members of the general public are prohibited from using electronic devices to record within the interior of the Duval County Courthouse. Electronic recording shall include taking photographs, filming, videotaping, audiotaping, broadcasting, and telecasting.

3) Other uses of electronic devices shall continue to be governed by Rule 2.451, Florida Rules of Judicial Administration, and the authority of the Chief Judge pursuant to Rule 2.451(c)(2), Florida Rules of Judicial Administration and Administrative Order No. 2015–1.

4) In the event that a person from the general public who does not have written permission to electronically record from the Chief Judge of the Fourth Judicial Circuit is found to be recording with the interior of the Duval County Courthouse in violation of this Order and that person fails to comply with a request to cease recording, that person shall be escorted out of the Duval County Courthouse and not permitted to return until such time as that person is no longer in possession of any electronic and/or recording devices. If a person is escorted out of the Duval County Courthouse pursuant to this order, that action shall not excuse the person from failing to appear in court as required.

5) This order shall in no way abrogate or amend Administrative Order 2015–1, Administrative Order 2013–08, Second Amended Administrative Order 92–02, or abrogate or amend Rule 2.450 and 2.451, Florida Rules of Judicial Administration.

6) This Administrative Order shall be recorded by the Clerk of Court, in the Official Records of Duval County, in the State of Florida, and shall take effect immediately and remain in full force and effect unless and until otherwise ordered by the Court.

DONE AND ORDERED in Chambers at Jacksonville, Duval County, Florida, this 22nd day of June, 2018.

Mark H. Mahon
Chief Judge

ATTACHMENT A

Request for Permission to Record Electronically in the Duval County Courthouse

Date: ______

Name: ______

Physical address: ______

Email address: ______

Telephone number(s): ______

Date of birth: ______

Driver's license number: ______

Any active or inactive media or similar credentials: ______

Date you would like to record: ______

Specific location you would like to record: ______

Beginning and ending time for when you would like to record: ______________________

____

Purpose for recording within the Duval County Courthouse: ______________________

____

______________________	______________________
Printed name of Requestor	Signature of Requestor

Please submit an original copy of this form no later than 10 business days before the date on which you would like to record to:

Office of the Court Counsel

Duval County Courthouse

501 West Adams Street, Suite 7212

Jacksonville, Florida 32202

2018–07. SEXUAL HARASSMENT POLICY AND PROCEDURES

IN THE CIRCUIT COURT, FOURTH JUDICIAL CIRCUIT, IN AND FOR DUVAL, CLAY AND NASSAU COUNTIES, FLORIDA

ADMINISTRATIVE ORDER NO, 2018–07

RE: SEXUAL HARASSMENT POLICY AND PROCEDURES

WHEREAS, on February 16, 2018, the Supreme Court of Florida issued Administrative Order SC18–6 regarding Sexual Harassment Policy and Procedures for Complaints against Justices and Judges;

WHEREAS, it is the responsibility of this Court to provide a workplace free from all forms of sexual harassment or sexual misconduct;

NOW THEREFORE, by the authority vested in me as the Chief Judge of the Fourth Judicial Circuit and pursuant to the Florida Rules of Judicial Administration, it is hereby

ORDERED AND ADJUDGED that:

1) The Fourth Judicial Circuit hereby adopts and implements the Supreme Court of Florida Administrative Order SC18–6 regarding Sexual Harassment Policy and Procedures for Complaints against Justices and Judges. (AOSC18–6 and the adopted policy and procedures are attached hereto as Attachment A.)

2) The Office of the Trial Court Administrator shall, as soon as practicable, distribute the attached policy to all court personnel of the Fourth Judicial Circuit.

3) This Administrative Order shall be recorded by the Clerk of Court, in the Official Records of Duval, Clay and Nassau Counties, in the State of Florida, and shall take effect immediately and remain in full force and effect unless and until otherwise ordered by this Court,

DONE AND ORDERED in Chambers at Jacksonville, Duval County, Florida, this 4th day of April, 2018.

Mark H. Mahon
Chief Judge

ATTACHMENT A

SEXUAL HARASSMENT POLICY AND PROCEDURES FOR SEXUAL HARASSMENT COMPLAINTS AGAINST JUSTICES AND JUDGES

1. Policy. The chief justice's implementation of this policy is under his or her authority as the administrative officer of the judicial branch and of the supreme court pursuant to rule 2.205(a)(2)(B), Florida Rules of Judicial Administration.

It is the policy of the Florida Supreme Court to foster a workplace free of sexual harassment, or sexual misconduct. Sexual harassment occurs if there are unwelcome sexual advances; unwelcome requests for sexual favors; or unwelcome verbal or physical conduct of a sexual nature from or involving an employee's supervisors, peers, subordinates or other persons in contact with an employee during the course of the conduct of the employee's business when:

1. Submission to such conduct is either explicitly or implicitly a term or condition of employment; or

2. Submission to or rejection of such conduct by an individual is used as the basis for employment decisions affecting such individual or as the basis for any official action; or

3. Such conduct has the purpose or effect of interfering with an individual's work performance or creates a persistently intimidating and hostile environment, as that term is defined in state and federal law.

Sexual misconduct is any behavior of a sexual nature that is committed without consent or by force, intimidation, coercion, or manipulation. Sexual misconduct can occur between strangers or acquaintances, including people involved in an intimate or sexual relationship, and is not necessarily actionable sexual harassment.

The Florida Supreme Court and the entire state court system condemn any sexual harassment or sexual misconduct and advance the position that anyone in contact with the state courts system should feel empowered to bring any such inappropriate activity to the attention of all proper authorities, including and especially the Florida Supreme Court. Anyone authorized to investigate or pursue a complaint of sexual harassment or sexual misconduct hereunder must always maintain an open-door policy that fosters the free expression of any complaint. The chief justice or chief justice's designee has the authority to take any administrative action necessary to protect the complainant from further sexual harassment or sexual misconduct and from retaliation related to a complaint hereunder.

It is the policy of the Florida Supreme Court that all complaints of sexual harassment or sexual misconduct against any justice or judge within the state courts system will be treated seriously and acted upon promptly. The following procedures apply to complaints against justices or judges made by employees of the court system, applicants for employment with the court system, and when applicable attorneys, litigants, or other members of the public. Compliance with these procedures by the chief justice, the chief justice's designee, or a chief judge constitutes a presumption of compliance with the disciplinary responsibilities under Canon 3(D)1 of the Code of Judicial Conduct.

2. Notification. The chief justice may designate any court system officer or employee to be responsible for receiving and documenting complaints of sexual harassment or sexual misconduct against justices of the Supreme Court, judges of the district courts of appeal, or judges of any of the trial courts.

Any employee or applicant for employment with the court system who believes that he or she is the subject of sexual harassment by a justice of the Supreme Court, a judge of any of the district courts of appeal, or a judge of any of the trial courts should submit his or her complaint in writing, or if the person prefers he or she may submit the complaint orally. The complaint may be submitted to any of the following: the chief justice or his or her designee; a local administrator, such as a Trial Court Administrator, human resource manager or Marshal; or the Chief of Human Resources at the Office of the State Courts Administrator (OSCA). If the person receiving the complaint is not the chief justice, the chief justice's designee hereunder, or a chief judge, the person receiving the complaint should forward it to the chief justice,' the chief justice's designee hereunder, or the chief judge of the court in which the subject judge serves for an investigation pursuant to section 4, below. Student interns working for the state courts system who believe they are the subject of sexual harassment may use these complaint procedures, but in all instances, should submit a complaint to their college or university in accordance with school sexual harassment complaint procedures.

If any person has difficulty writing out the complaint and the person requests assistance in reducing the complaint to writing or if the person prefers to submit the complaint orally, the chief justice, local administrator, or OSCA Chief of Human Resources, as appropriate, shall designate a person, who will not be involved in the investigation or adjudication of the complaint, to aid the person in reducing the complaint to writing.

If the chief justice is the subject of a complaint, the employee or applicant should submit the complaint to the inspector general of the Supreme Court, who will refer the complaint to the most senior justice, excluding the chief justice. The justice to whom such a complaint is referred will assume all complaint investigation and resolution duties for which the chief justice otherwise would be responsible, The justice to whom such a complaint is referred also will be responsible for maintaining records pertaining to the complaint.

If an employee or applicant chooses not to file a formal complaint, and any person designated hereunder to receive complaints has actual knowledge or receives information that a substantial likelihood exists that a justice or judge has engaged in sexual harassment or sexual misconduct, the person may inquire into the matter and take appropriate action.

3. Time for Filing Complaints. In order to ensure that Florida Supreme Court complaint procedures can be utilized without risk of precluding the filing of a charge of discrimination with state or federal entities, an employee or applicant should report an incident of sexual harassment within 90 days of the date of occurrence.

4. Investigations. A complaint of sexual harassment or sexual misconduct against a justice or judge will be investigated promptly and thoroughly. If a complaint has been made, the chief justice, the chief justice's designee hereunder, or the chief judge of the court in which the subject judge serves may designate another person to make an initial inquiry into the complaint.

The chief justice, chief justice's designee, or a chief judge of the court in which the subject judge serves will interview the complainant within five days of the submission of the complaint to ascertain relevant facts and circumstances. If the complainant does not divulge names or details of the incident(s), the chief justice or chief justice's designee, or the chief judge of the court in which the subject judge serves will rely upon any information that is available. If another person has been designated to make an initial inquiry into the complaint, the designee will report details of the complaint, including any relevant facts, circumstances, and information, to the chief justice within ten days of the submission of the complaint.

If the chief justice, chief justice's designee, or the chief judge of the court in which the subject judge serves determines the complaint is unfounded or is insufficient to constitute sexual harassment, he or she may decline to pursue any action on the complaint.

If the chief justices, chief justice's designee, or the chief judge of the court in which the subject judge serves determines the complaint is facially sufficient to constitute sexual harassment, the chief justice, chief justice's designee, or the chief judge of the court in which the subject judge serves may appoint an investigating officer or officers to formally investigate the complaint, or may take any other action appropriate under the circumstances.

If the chief justice or chief justice's designee determines the complaint is insufficient to constitute sexual harassment, but nevertheless indicates potential sexual misconduct, the chief justice or chief justice's designee may take any action appropriate to address the circumstances, including but not limited to appointing an investigating officer or officers to formally investigate the complaint.

The chief justice, chief justice's designee, the chief judge of the court in which the subject judge serves, or investigating officer will interview the complainant, the justice or judge implicated, and witnesses, if any, and will review relevant documents. If any investigating officers have been appointed, they will submit a written report to the chief justice, chief justice's designee, or the chief judge of the court in which the subject judge serves within thirty days of the submission of the complaint for formal investigation,

5. Resolution. The chief justice, or pursuant to rule 2.205(a)(2)(D), Florida Rules of Judicial Administration, the other most senior justice if the chief justice is the subject of a complaint, shall determine the course of action for internal resolution of the complaint, and may appoint another person, other than the subject of the complaint, to recommend the course of action for internal resolution.

If the chief justice or chief justice's designee determines the complaint, including any relevant facts, circumstances, and information, is insufficient to constitute sexual harassment, the chief justice, chief justice's designee, or the chief judge of the court in which the subject judge serves may attempt to resolve the complaint informally through mutual conciliation by meeting with the complainant and the subject justice or judge to discuss a method of resolution, including alternative dispute resolution. In attempting to resolve the complaint, the chief justice, chief justice's designee, or the chief judge of the court in which the subject judge serves may counsel or take other appropriate direct action with the justice or judge involved.

If the complaint and investigation reasonably indicate that the subject justice or judge engaged in activity that constitutes sexual harassment, constitutes sexual misconduct, or otherwise raises a substantial question as to a justice's or judge's fitness for office, the chief justice, chief justice's designee, or the chief judge of the court in which the subject judge serves shall refer the complaint and all written documentation pertaining to the complaint to the Judicial Qualifications Commission.

To the extent not otherwise prohibited by statute or rule, a written summary of the resolution will be provided to the complainant within a reasonable time after a determination is made and any action pursuant thereto is taken.

6. Documentation and Confidentiality. All information pertaining to a complaint of sexual harassment must be documented and maintained by the chief justice, chief justice's designee, or the chief judge of the court in which the subject judge serves whichever officer took final action on the resolution of the complaint.

All records made or received by any person pursuant to these complaint procedures are exempt from public disclosure as provided in rule 2.420(c)(3)(A), Florida Rules of Judicial Administration. Such records are exempt from public disclosure for the duration of an initial inquiry, formal investigation and resolution of the complaint, and at all times thereafter, unless the records are forwarded to the Judicial Qualifications Commission.

If records pertaining to a complaint are forwarded to the Judicial Qualifications Commission, such records will be confidential under rule 2.420(c)(3)(A), and rule 23(a), Rules of the Judicial Qualifications Commission, until any format charges against the justice or judge are filed by the Investigative Panel of the Commission with the clerk of the Florida Supreme Court.

Records within the possession of any justice, judge, or court staff and pertaining to a complaint that has been forwarded to the Judicial Qualifications Commission will become public upon formal charges being filed with the clerk of the Florida Supreme Court,

7. Referral to the Judicial Qualifications Commission. The Judicial Qualifications Commission is responsible for investigating all reported instances of judicial misconduct. These procedures do not preclude the referral of a complaint against a justice or judge at any time by any person to the Judicial Qualifications Commission. If a complaint has been referred to the Judicial Qualifications Commission, no further action by the chief justice or chief justice's designee is required.

For anyone wishing to file such a complaint, the Commission's mailing address is P.O. Box 141106, Tallahassee, Florida 32317. The Commission's Executive Director, can be contacted by telephone at 850–488–1581 or by email at contact@floridajqc.com.

8. Referral to the Florida Commission on Human Relations or the United State Equal Employment Opportunity Commission. These procedures do not preclude the filing of a charge of employment discrimination with the Florida Commission on Human Relations or the United States Equal Employment Opportunity Commission.

For anyone wishing to file such a complaint, the Florida Commission on Human Relations (FCHR) is located at: 4075 Esplanade Way Room 110 Tallahassee, FL 32399. The telephone number for the FCHR is: 850–488–7082 or 1–800–342–8170.

The United States Equal Employment Opportunity Commission (EEOC) office with jurisdiction over complaints arising in Florida is the Miami District Office located at 100 SE 2nd Street, Suite 1500, Miami, FL 33131. The telephone number for the EEOC Miami District office is: 1–800–669–4000.

9. Referral to the Chief of Human Resources, Office of the State Courts Administrator. For anyone wishing to file a complaint under this policy, the Chief of Human Resources, OSCA is located at: 500 South Duval Street Tallahassee, Florida 32399–1925. The telephone number is 850–617–4028.

2018–05. STANDING FAMILY LAW COURT ORDER IN DISSOLUTION OF MARRIAGE

IN THE CIRCUIT COURT, FOURTH JUDICIAL CIRCUIT, IN AND FOR DUVAL COUNTY, FLORIDA

ADMINISTRATIVE ORDER NO. 2018–05

RE: USE OF A STANDING FAMILY LAW COURT ORDER IN DISSOLUTION OF MARRIAGE, PATERNITY, SEPARATE MAINTENANCE OR ANNULMENT ACTIONS

WHEREAS, Florida Rule of Judicial Administration 2.215(b)(3) states the Chief Judge "shall, considering available resources, ensure the efficient and proper administration of all courts within [the] circuit";

WHEREAS, the Fourth Judicial Circuit handles family law cases involving dissolution of marriage, paternity, separate maintenance and annulment;

WHEREAS, in dissolution of marriage, paternity, separate maintenance and annulment actions, the circuit seeks to: (1) promote the stability of families engaged in such action; (2) provide guidance to parties in an effort to help parties pattern their behavior and conduct in ways that reduce the negative impact that such proceedings have on the child(ren) and all parties involved; and (3) reduce the number of "emergency" hearings during the beginning stages of dissolution of marriage, paternity and separate maintenance actions, thereby promoting the stability and preserving the resources of the parties and the court;

WHEREAS, this Court finds that it is in the best interest of the parties and any minor child(ren) of the parents in a dissolution of marriage, paternity, separate maintenance or annulment action to adopt and authorize the use of a standing family law order in Duval County, which may be modified as deemed appropriate by the presiding judges in such actions;

NOW THEREFORE, by the authority vested in me as the Chief Judge of the Fourth Judicial Circuit and pursuant to the Florida Rules of Judicial Administration, it is hereby

ORDERED AND ADJUDGED that:

1) The Standing Family Law Court Order (hereinafter referred to as the "Order"), a copy of which is attached hereto, is hereby adopted and authorized for use in dissolution of marriage, paternity, separate maintenance and annulment actions in the Fourth Judicial Circuit, Duval County, Florida, and may be amended from time to time without the filing of an additional administrative order.

2) It shall be the responsibility of the Petitioner and/or counsel for Petitioner to provide the Respondent(s) with a copy of the Order by including it with the petition at the time of service and **file proof** of service of the Order.

3) The Clerk of the Court shall post a copy of the Order on its website to ensure that it is readily available to the Petitioner and/or Petitioner's counsel when the case is filed.

4) Any failure to comply with the Order may result in appropriate sanctions against the offending party, as permitted by Florida law.

5) This Administrative Order shall be recorded by the Clerk of Court, in the Official Records of Duval County, in the State of Florida, and shall take effect immediately and remain in full force and effect unless and until otherwise ordered by the Court.

DONE AND ORDERED in Chambers at Jacksonville, Duval County, Florida, this 6th day of March, 2018.

Mark H. Mahon
Chief Judge

IN THE CIRCUIT COURT, FOURTH JUDICIAL CIRCUIT, IN AND FOR DUVAL COUNTY, FLORIDA

Case No:
Division:

IN RE: THE MATTER OF:

, Petitioner,

And

, Respondent. /

STANDING FAMILY LAW ORDER

The following Standing Court Order shall apply to both parties in an original action for dissolution of marriage, paternity, separate maintenance or annulment. The Order shall be effective with regard to the petitioner upon filing of the petition and with regard to the respondent upon service of the summons and petition or upon waiver and acceptance of service. The following Order shall remain in place during the pendency of the action, unless modified, terminated or amended by further order of the Court upon motion of either of the parties:

It is in the best interests of the parties in dissolution of marriage or paternity action to learn about the problems, duties and responsibilities that may arise during their dissolution of marriage or paternity proceeding. It is also important to act in the best interests of their children and in the cases of dissolution of marriage to preserve their assets and comply with Court orders and applicable Court rules. Therefore, the parties are hereby advised:

IN ALL DISSOLUTION OF MARRIAGE ACTIONS:

DISSIPATION OF ASSETS: Neither party shall sell, transfer, encumber, conceal, assign, damage, remove or in any way dispose of any property, individually or jointly held, nor will any party dissipate or deplete the value of an asset (for example, by adding a mortgage to real estate) without the consent of the other party in writing, or without an order of the court, any property, individually or jointly held by parties, except in the usual course of business or for customary and usual household expenses or for reasonable attorney's fees in connection with this action. Neither party will cancel nor cause to be canceled any utilities, including telephone, electric, or water and sewer which would negatively affect the other party. Any party who violates this provision will be required to render an accounting and may be later sanctioned if found wasting/depleting a marital asset

ADDITIONAL DEBT: Neither party shall incur any unreasonable debts, including but not limited to, further borrowing against any credit line secured by the family residence, further encumbrancing any assets or unreasonable use of credit cards or cash advances against credit or bank cards.

INSURANCE POLICIES: Any insurance policies in effect at the time the petition was filed, shall not be terminated, allowed to lapse, modified, borrowed against, pledged, or otherwise encumbered by either of the parties or at the direction of either party. This includes medical, hospital and/or dental insurance for the other party and/or the minor child(ren). Each party shall maintain the existing life insurance, automobile insurance, homeowner's or renter's insurance policies in full force and effect. Neither party shall change the beneficiaries of any existing life insurance policies. Additionally, each party shall maintain all existing insurance policies in full force and effect, without change of their terms, unless agreed to in writing by both parties. All policy premiums will continue to be paid in full on a timely basis, unless there is an order of the court by the presiding judge or written agreement of the parties to the contrary.

SHARED PARENTAL RESPONSIBILITY: These provisions shall apply unless there is a conflicting Court Order or allegations of domestic violence.

a. If the parents of children live apart during the dissolution proceedings, they shall assist their children in having contact with both parties, consistent with the habits of the family, The contact shall be in person, by telephone, audiovisual communications, and/or in writing.

b. Neither party shall make any disparaging remarks about the other parent or quiz the child(ren) as to the other parent's private life. It is the child(ren)'s right to be spared from experiencing and witnessing any animosity or ill-feeling, if any should occur, between the parents. The minor child(ren) should be encouraged to maintain love, respect and affection for both parents.

c. Neither parent shall conceal the whereabouts of the child(ren) and each parent shall keep the other advised at all times of the residential address and phone numbers where the child(ren) will be residing while with the other parent. Each parent shall notify the other immediately of any emergency pertaining to any child of the parties.

d. Each party shall provide to the other party his or her residence address, work and cellular telephone numbers and e-mail address. Each party shall notify the other party, in writing, of any and all changes in his/her residence address, work and cellular telephone number(s) and e-mail address(es). Such notification shall be done with five (5) days of any such change and shall include the complete new address, telephone number(s) and/or e-mail address(es).

IN ALL DISSOLUTION OF MARRIAGE (WITH DEPENDENT CHILD(REN)) OR PATERNITY ACTIONS:

RELOCATION: Unless there is a prior court order/judgment or agreement signed by both parties to the contrary, neither party shall permanently remove, cause to be removed or. permit the removal of any minor child(ren) of the parties to a location greater than fifty (50) miles from the principal residence of the parent. The intent of the restriction is not to prohibit temporary travel within the State of Florida. Neither party shall apply for any passport or passport services on behalf of any child(ren) without consent of the other parent or an order of the court from the presiding judge.

PARENTING COURSE: Pursuant to the administrative orders issued in the Fourth Judicial Circuit (Duval, Clay, and Nassau Counties) and pursuant to Section 61.21, Florida Statutes, all parties to a dissolution of marriage action with minor child(ren) or to a paternity proceeding shall complete a Parent Education and Family Stabilization Course. This requirement can only be satisfied by completing the Court approved four-hour in-class parenting course. The current approved course information can be obtained from family court service (904) 255–1060. No other course will be accepted without Court approval.

In a dissolution action, the Petitioner must complete the course within forty-five (45) days after the filing of the petition and the other party must complete the course within forty-five days after service of the petition. In a paternity action, the Petitioner must complete the course within forty-five (45) days after filing the petition, and the other party must complete the course within forty-five (45) days after an acknowledgement of paternity by that party, an adjudication of paternity of the party, or an order granting time-sharing to that party.

Non-compliance: If either party does not attend and complete the parenting course, the presiding judge may enter an Order to Show Cause and schedule a hearing date. At the hearing, the non-complying party will be required to demonstrate why he or she has not attended the course. The presiding judge may impose sanctions, including a stay of proceedings or any other sanctions including contempt the presiding judge finds just and permissible under current Florida law.

FINANCIAL DISCLOSURE: In a case involving any financial matters (child support, spousal support, equitable distribution or contempt proceeding regarding support) each party must file a financial affidavit and comply with the mandatory disclosure required by Fla. Fam. L. R. P. 12.285. Income shall be imputed to any party that fails to file a financial affidavit or fails to participate in the proceeding. § 61.30(2)(b) Fla. Stat. The presiding judge may sanction any party who fails, without good cause, to satisfactorily comply with the rules pertaining to the production of financial records and other documents.

JUDICIAL ENFORCEMENT: Failure to comply with the terms of this Order may result in appropriate sanctions against the offending party, as permitted by Florida law.

SERVICE AND APPLICATIONS OF THIS ORDER: The Petitioner or Petitioner's attorney shall serve a copy of this Order with a copy of the petition. This Order shall bind the Petitioner upon the filing of this action and shall become binding on the Respondent upon service of the initial pleading. This Order shall remain in full force and effect until further order of the court. Nothing in this Order shall preclude either party from applying to the Court for further temporary orders. This entire Order shall terminate upon the entry of a Final Judgment or Dismissal of the case.

DONE AND ORDERED in Chamber, Jacksonville, Duval County, Florida this ___ day of ________, 2018.

____

Administrative Judge

2017–09. ALTERNATIVE SANCTIONING PROGRAM

IN THE CIRCUIT COURT, FOURTH JUDICIAL CIRCUIT, IN AND FOR DUVAL COUNTY, FLORIDA

ADMINISTRATIVE ORDER NO. 2017–09

WHEREAS, there is a substantial number of technical violations that do not involve a new arrest or other serious violations; and,

WHEREAS, arresting and incarcerating certain non-violent offenders for minor violations of probation or community control is both expensive and nonproductive; and,

WHEREAS, there is research to support that recidivism may be reduced by utilizing collaborative efforts among the courts, probation and law enforcement to hold the offender accountable and apply swift and certain sanctions for technical violations of probation or community control; and

WHEREAS, an administrative option for processing technical violations will have the potential to offer benefits including:

- Reducing the court docket of probation and community control violation hearings;
- Reducing the workload of prosecutors and defense attorneys involved with many technical violation hearings;
- Reducing law enforcement resources required to serve violation warrants for certain technical violations;
- Reducing jail population for offenders pending violation hearings; and
- Offering the offender an alternative to a violation hearing in court, which will allow the offender to remain engaged in employment, school, and treatment, and allow the offender to take immediate responsibility for their actions and comply with the consequences of those actions.

WHEREAS, § 948.06(1)(h), Florida Statutes, states that the "chief judge of each judicial circuit, in consultation with the state attorney, public defender, and the department, may establish an alternative sanctioning program in which the department, after receiving court approval, may enforce specified sanctions for certain technical violations of supervision."

NOW THEREFORE, by the authority vested in me as the Chief Judge of the Fourth Judicial Circuit and pursuant to

Florida Statutes and the Florida Rules of Judicial Administration, it is

ORDERED:

1. **Alternative Sanctioning Program.** There is created in Duval County, in the Fourth Judicial Circuit, a program that shall be known as the Alternative Sanctioning Program in accordance with § 948.06(1)(h), Florida Statutes. The Alternative Sanctioning Program provides the courts and the Florida Department of Corrections (hereinafter "FDC") an alternative, administrative method of reporting and resolving certain technical violations in lieu of submitting violation of probation affidavits and warrants to the courts.

2.**Eligibility Criteria.** To be eligible for the program, offenders must have been placed on probation or community control under the supervision of the FDC by a judge in Duval County in the Fourth Judicial Circuit, have stable community ties, and have a stable residence in one of the three counties within the Circuit. Offenders who are eligible for the program include probation offenders, drug offenders, and community control supervision offenders. The program only applies to offenders who have committed certain technical violations addressed in the Alternative Sanctioning Program Violation/Sanction Matrix included in section 3 of this order.

The threat an offender poses to public safely is the most important factor in determining eligibility. Offenders with a lengthy or violent criminal history and sex offenders are not eligible to be in the program. Additionally, offenders who have new law violations, are absconders, or have violated a "no contact" condition of supervision are not eligible for the program. No offender who has three or more previous violations is eligible for the program. For further clarification, a technical violation of supervision does not include any new felony offense, misdemeanor offense, or criminal traffic offense committed by an offender, and as such, would not be eligible for the Alternative Sanctioning Program.

3.**Qualifying Technical Violations and Approved Sanctions.** The following matrix lists the specific technical violations that may be addressed through the Alternative Sanctioning Program process for offenders who were sentenced in Duval County in the Fourth Judicial Circuit of Florida. Each technical violation includes a list of sanctions determined and approved by the courts for the probation officer to select from when addressing these technical violations which are based upon the individual offender's circumstances at the time of the violation.

ALTERNATIVE SANCTIONING PROGRAM VIOLATION/SANCTION MATRIX

VIOLATION	APPROVED LIST OF SANCTIONS
Condition (1): Reported late; failed to report as instructed	1. Weekly call in for 6 weeks 2. Daily call in for 30 days 3. Report 2x a month for 60 days
Condition (3): Failed to report changes in residence or employment without first procuring the officer's consent (or notifying immediately if evicted from residence or laid off from job)	1. Twice a month reporting for 3 months 2. Weekly reporting for 6 weeks 3. Participate in 3 sessions with FDC Employment Specialist.
Condition (3): Failed to request permission prior to leaving the county	1. Weekly call in for 6 weeks 2. Twice a month reporting for 60 days 3. Weekly reporting for 6 weeks at discretion of PO.
Condition (6): Found to be associating with person(s) engaged in criminal activity	1. Curfew from 8 pm to 6 am for 90 days (can be modified by PO for treatment or work purposes) 2. 25 hours public service work w/in 30 days 3. Participated in 3 sessions with FDC Employment Specialist
Condition (7): Positive drug test for non-prescribed drugs (first occurrence)	1. Drug evaluation and successfully complete treatment determined necessary 2. Curfew from 8 pm to 6 am for 90 days (can be modified by PO for treatment or work purposes) 3. Increase U/A schedule as per PO for 30 days
Condition (7): Positive drug test for non-prescribed drugs (second occurrence)	1. Increase level of treatment program up to and including residential 2. Curfew from 8 pm to 6 am for 90 days (can be modified by PO for treatment or work purposes) 3. Increase U/A schedule as per PO for 30 days
Condition (8): Failure to maintain employment	1. Weekly reporting with Job Search logs until employed 2. Curfew from 8pm to 6am for 90 days (can be modified by PO for treatment or work purposes) coupled with daily reporting with logs until employed 3. Attend 3 sessions with FDC Employment Specialist
Condition (9): Failure to comply with officer's instructions (depending on nature of instruction and reason for not complying, consequence will vary)	1. Weekly call in for 4 weeks 2. 8 hours Community Service work within 30 days 3. Attend a Life Skills Class as directed by FDC
Condition (10): Failure to pay monthly monetary obligations as required by the Court	1. If unemployed—daily job search 2. If employed—monthly budgeting 3. Participate in 3 sessions with FDC Employment Specialist
Condition (11): Failure to submit to random testing as directed	1. Weekly Reporting by 11 am for 90 days 2. Curfew from 8 pm until 6 am for 90 days (can be modified for treatment of work purposes) 3. Substance Abuse Evaluation and Treatment if determined necessary
Special Condition (1): Failure to attend treatment evaluation or treatment session as scheduled	1. Curfew from 8 pm to 6 am until evaluation is completed 2. Weekly reporting until evaluation is completed 3. Increase U/A schedule as per PO for 30 days
Special Condition (8): Failure to complete community service hours as instructed	1. Daily reporting until community service hours completed and/or current, if unemployed 2. Weekly reporting until community service hours completed and/or current, if employed 3. Complete Victim Awareness Class within 30 days
Special Condition (9): Failure to remain at residence during curfew	1. Weekly reporting for three months

period	2. 30 Community Service Hours within 30 days 3. Electronic Monitoring for 30 days
Community Control Condition (16): Failure to maintain approved schedule—unapproved absence from required location (negligence in getting home late, stopping at store on way home without permission)	1. 10 Hours Community Service work within 30 days 2. 20 Hours Community Service work within 30 days 3. Electronic Monitoring for 30 days

4. Alternative Sanctioning Program Process for Reporting Technical Violations. The probation or community control officer may inform offenders who have committed violations enumerated in Section 3 of this administrative order that they may participate in the Alternative Sanctioning Program for administrative disposition of the violation. No offender is required to participate in the program and may request a formal violation of probation or community control hearing in Circuit Court. The offender's participation in the Alternative Sanctioning Program is voluntary. The offender may elect to waive or discontinue participation in the Alternative Sanctioning Program at any time before the issuance of a court order imposing the recommended sanction. If the offender elects to discontinue participation in the Alternative Sanctioning Program, the offender's prior admission to the technical violation may not be used as evidence in subsequent proceedings pursuant to § 948.06(1)(h)7, Florida Statutes. No sentencing points will be assessed by virtue of entering into the Alternative Sanctioning Program, however points can be assessed if there is a failure to complete the Alternative Sanctioning Program and the offender is, after a hearing, found to have committed the underlying violation that led to the participation in the Alternative Sanctioning Program.

If the offender admits the violation, agrees to accept the administrative sanction(s) recommended by the probation officer, and agrees to waive his/her formal violation hearing, the probation officer will prepare an "Alternative Sanctions Program Technical Violation Notification," which will provide details of the circumstances of the technical violation that occurred and the probation officer's recommended sanction, based upon the sanctions listed in the approved matrix. If the offender agrees to participate in the Alternative Sanctioning Program, he/she will sign the second section of the form entitled "Alternative Sanctioning Program Waiver of Formal VOP/VOCC Hearing, Admission of Violation, and Acceptance of Sanctions," which will be submitted to the Circuit Court once it has been signed and dated by the probation officer.

The Judge shall review the "Alternative Sanctioning Program Technical Violation Notification" and waiver form submitted and, if the Judge agrees that the technical violation should be addressed via the Alternative Sanctioning Program and approves the recommended sanction, the Judge will sign the "Order—Alternative Sanctioning Program." If the Judge does not approve the sanction recommended by the probation officer or does not approve the technical violation being addressed via the Alternative Sanctioning Program, the Judge shall include further instructions on the order.

Upon approval by the Circuit Court, the probation officer will review the sanction with the offender, and inform the offender that failure to complete the imposed sanction as instructed will result in a violation report, affidavit and warrant being submitted to the Circuit Court for the original underlying violation. FDC will provide a copy of the "Alternative Sanctioning Program Technical Violation Notification" and the "Order—Alternative Sanctioning Program" to the Office of the State Attorney for their records. FDC will also notify the listed victim(s) in writing in each case of any sanction imposed by the Circuit Court pursuant to the Alternative Sanctioning Program Violation/Sanction Matrix via the FDC Notification of Offender Status Letter.

At the discretion of FDC, if the offender is deemed to have successfully completed the Alternative Sanctioning Program, the underlying violation of probation will be dismissed with prejudice. Therefore, it will be presumed that the offender successfully completed the Alternative Sanctioning Program, unless an Affidavit is filed for the underlying violation.

5. Administration. The Alternative Sanctioning Program shall be administered by the Fourth Judicial Circuit and the Florida Department of Corrections.

6. Effective Date. This Administrative Order shall be recorded by the Clerk of the Court in the Official Records of Duval County, in the State of Florida, and shall take effect on **September 1, 2017.** This Administrative Order shall remain in full force and effect until further order of this Court.

DONE AND ORDERED at Jacksonville, Duval County, Florida, this 25th day of August, 2017.

MARK H. MAHON
Chief Judge

Adopted effective September 1, 2017.

2017–08 (A2). SERVICE OF PROCESS IN DOMESTIC VIOLENCE CASES

IN THE CIRCUIT COURT, FOURTH JUDICIAL CIRCUIT,
IN AND FOR DUVAL COUNTY, FLORIDA

SECOND AMENDED ADMINISTRATIVE ORDER NO. 2017–08

IN RE: THE JACKSONVILLE SHERIFF'S OFFICE AND MUNICIPAL POLICE DEPARTMENTS AND SERVICE OF PROCESS IN DOMESTIC VIOLENCE, REPEAT VIOLENCE, SEXUAL VIOLENCE, DATING VIOLENCE, STALKING INJUNCTION, AND RISK PROTECTION ORDER CASES

WHEREAS, the Sheriff and Municipal Police Departments have jurisdiction to serve process in all domestic violence, repeat violence, sexual violence, dating violence and stalking injunction cases;

WHEREAS, sections 741.30(8)(a), 784.046(8)(a), and 784.0485(8)(a) of the Florida Statutes provide that the Chief Judge of each circuit, in consultation with the appropriate Sheriff(s), may authorize law enforcement agencies within the Chief Judge's jurisdiction to effect service of injunctions for protection against domestic violence, repeat violence, sexual violence, dating violence and stalking;

WHEREAS, newly enacted section 790.401(5)(a) of the Florida Statutes states that "the chief judge of each circuit, in consultation with the appropriate sheriff, may authorize a law enforcement agency within the jurisdiction to effect service" in risk protection order cases;

WHEREAS, First Amended Administrative Order No. 2017–08 is being amended for the sole purpose of authorizing all Municipal Police Departments within the jurisdiction to effect service pursuant to section 790.401;

NOW THEREFORE, by the authority vested in me as Chief Judge of the Fourth Judicial Circuit pursuant to Florida Rule of Judicial Administration 2.215, it is

ORDERED:

That the Jacksonville Sheriff's Office and all Municipal Police Departments located in Duval County and their individual sworn officers are authorized to effect service of process in lieu of the Sheriff of said County when provided a certified copy of an injunction or other order related to domestic violence, repeat violence, sexual violence, dating violence, or stalking as provided in sections 741.30(8), 784.046(8), and 784.0485(8), Florida Statutes, or related to a risk protection order as provided in section 790.401(5)(a).

That when serving an injunction or other order related to domestic violence, repeat violence, sexual violence, dating violence, stalking, or a risk protection order, law enforcement officers must make personal service upon the respondent and use service and verification procedures consistent with those of the Sheriff, Questions regarding service of process should be directed to the Sheriff's Office with jurisdiction over the residence of the petitioner.

That the Clerk of the Circuit Court must provide a certified copy of any injunction or other order related to domestic violence, repeat violence, sexual violence, dating violence, stalking, or a risk protection order for service by law enforcement or the Sheriff.

That when effecting service of an injunction, risk protection order or other order, the law enforcement officer shall complete the Return of Service/Certificate of Non–Service. The officer shall promptly, or otherwise within 24 hours of service of process, call in and transmit a copy of the Return of Service/Certificate of Non–Service to the Sheriff's Office with jurisdiction over the residence of the petitioner. If attempts at service are unsuccessful, the law enforcement officer attempting service shall promptly call in and electronically transmit the Return of Service/Certificate of Non–Service and include relevant facts to indicate the reason for non-service.

That following receipt of the Return of Service/Certificate of Non–Service, the Sheriff's Office shall promptly file a copy with the Clerk of the Court in accordance with the provisions of Chapter 48, Florida Statutes, or, if not practicable, on the next business day following receipt.

That nothing herein changes the existing policy that primary responsibility for service of process in domestic violence, repeat violence, sexual violence, dating violence, stalking injunction, and risk protection order cases remains with the Jacksonville Sheriff's Office.

That all prior administrative orders addressing the same subject matter are hereby vacated and superseded.

That this Order shall be recorded in the Official Records of Duval County in the State of Florida, and copies furnished to the individuals and entities listed below.

DONE AND ORDERED this 28th day of September 27, 2017, Duval County, Florida.

MARK H. MAHON, CHIEF JUDGE

Adopted effective August 2, 2017. Amended effective August 8, 2017; September 28, 2018.

2017–06. VACATING TITLE IV–D WRITS OF ATTACHMENT

IN THE CIRCUIT COURT, FOURTH JUDICIAL CIRCUIT, IN AND FOR DUVAL, CLAY AND NASSAU COUNTY, FLORIDA

ADMINISTRATIVE ORDER NO. 2017–06

IN RE: VACATING TITLE IV–D WRITS OF ATTACHMENT

WHEREAS, it has come to the attention of the Court that there are a number of outstanding Writs of Attachment issued in excess of three (3) years in Title IV–D Child Support cases.

WHEREAS, these Writs have out-lived their usefulness, are causing needless monitoring and work for the Jacksonville Sheriff's Office, Clay County Sheriff's Office, and the Nassau County Sheriff's Officer (hereafter, "Law Enforcement Agencies"); and should no longer remain in the system.

NOW THEREFORE, by the authority vested in me as the Chief Judge of the Fourth Judicial Circuit and pursuant to the Florida Rules of Judicial Administration, it is hereby

ORDERED AND ADJUDGED that:

1) All Title IV–D Writs of Attachment shall be automatically vacated three (3) years from the date of issue.

2) The named Law Enforcement Agencies are hereby directed to delete all pending Title IV–D Writs affected by this Order from its data banks, and law enforcement is further directed to not execute any of such Writs.

3) This Administrative Order shall be recorded by the Clerk of Court, in the Official Records of Duval County, in the State of Florida, and shall take effect immediately and remain in full force and effect unless and until otherwise ordered by the Court.

DONE AND ORDERED in Chambers at Jacksonville, Duval County, Florida, this 12 day of May, 2017.

MARK H. MAHON
CHIEF JUDGE

2016–06 (A1). FLORIDA LEGAL ACCESS GATEWAY PILOT PROGRAM

IN THE CIRCUIT COURT OF THE FOURTH JUDICIAL CIRCUIT IN AND FOR CLAY COUNTY

AMENDED ADMINISTRATIVE ORDER NO. 2016–06

IN RE: FLORIDA LEGAL ACCESS GATEWAY PILOT PROGRAM

WHEREAS, The Chief Justice of the State of Florida, working with numerous constituent members of the justice system, established the Florida Commission on Access to Civil Justice (FCACJ) by Supreme Court Administrative Order AOSC16–71, with the stated purpose of studying the unmet civil legal needs of disadvantaged, low income and moderate income Floridians; and

WHEREAS, the FCACJ, acting on a temporary basis, established the pilot program of the Florida Legal Access Gateway (FLAG), within the Fourth Judicial Circuit, in Clay County Florida; and

WHEREAS, the purpose of FLAG is to assist Clay County residents in locating information and providing referrals in cases involving Divorces and/or Evictions; and

WHEREAS, providing information regarding FLAG will assist the FCACJ in determining the most effective and efficient mechanisms for the delivery of on-line systems to assist unmet civil legal needs; and

WHEREAS, the original Administrative Order No. 2016–06 required that certain notices be attached in all Summons and Complaint packets to be served in Divorce and Eviction cases filed in Clay County until December 31, 2016, at which time the Order would either be amended or automatically be rescinded;

WHEREAS, in December 2016, the triage pilot project sponsors, together with the project manager, recommended that the pilot be extended until June 30, 2017, to allow for more data to accumulate and to allow for improvement in the evaluation methods. The request for extension was voted upon and approved by both the Florida Justice Technology Center Board and by the Executive Committee of the Florida Bar Foundation Board; and

WHEREAS, accordingly, this Court finds that the original Administrative Order must be amended to extend the time of its application.

NOW, THEREFORE, by the authority vested in me as Chief Judge of the Fourth Judicial Circuit, and pursuant to the Florida Rules of Judicial Administration, it is

IT IS ORDERED that:

A. The Clerk of Court in Clay County shall insert the attached (revised) Exhibit A in all Summons and Complaint packets to be served in Divorce and Eviction cases filed in Clay County **until June 30, 2017**.

B. The original Administrative Order 2016–06 previously entered on November 16, 2016, is hereby rescinded and superseded by this Amended Administrative Order No. 2016–06.

C. This Amended Administrative Order No. 2016–06 shall be recorded by the Clerk of the Court, in the Official Records of Duval County, in the State of Florida.

D. This Amended Administrative Order No. 2016–06 shall take effect immediately and shall remain in full force and effect **until June 30, 2017**, at which time this Order will either be amended or will automatically rescind.

DONE AND ORDERED in Chambers, at Jacksonville, Duval County, Florida, this 16 day of December, 2016.

MARK H. MAHON

CHIEF JUDGE

EXHIBIT A

You are receiving this Notice because you are being served with legal papers concerning either a Divorce or an Eviction matter.

Florida Legal Access Gateway (FLAG) is an online tool to help individuals, like you, find legal help. You can use FLAG to find legal information and resources to assist you with your legal problem. Go to www.clayclerk.com and look for the FLAG logo to begin.

The Florida Commission on Access to Civil Justice established FLAG as a temporary pilot program in Clay County Florida to test how to best connect individuals needing legal help with legal assistance. FLAG is developed jointly by The Florida Bar, The Florida Bar Foundation, the Florida Justice Technology Center, Jacksonville Area Legal Aid, Three Rivers Legal Aid, and the Clay County Clerk's Office.

2016–03. CREATION OF DIVISION CR–V IN NASSAU COUNTY FOR A VETERANS TREATMENT COURT

IN THE CIRCUIT COURT OF THE FOURTH JUDICIAL CIRCUIT, IN AND FOR NASSAU COUNTY, FLORIDA

ADMINISTRATIVE ORDER NO. 2016–3

IN RE: CREATION OF DIVISION CR–V IN NASSAU COUNTY FOR A VETERANS TREATMENT COURT

WHEREAS, a Veterans Treatment Court in Nassau County has been established;

WHEREAS, at this time, there is a need to assign a dedicated Division for the Veterans Treatment Court in Nassau County;

WHEREAS, there is a need for an administrative order creating such division;

THEREFORE, by the authority vested in me as Chief Judge and pursuant to the Florida Rules of Judicial Administration, it is hereby

ORDERED that:

(A) A separate division for a Veterans Treatment Court shall be created in Nassau County, and such Division shall be designated as Division "CR–V".

(B) This Administrative Order shall be recorded by the Clerk of the Court, in the Official Records of Nassau County, in the State of Florida, shall take effect immediately, and shall remain in full force and effect unless and until otherwise ordered by the Court.

DONE AND ORDERED in Chambers, at Jacksonville, Duval County, Florida, this 8th day of July, 2016

MARK A. MAHON

CHIEF JUDGE

2016–01. IMPOSITION OF MANDATORY ASSESSMENTS IN THE FOURTH JUDICIAL CIRCUIT

IN THE CIRCUIT COURT, FOURTH JUDICIAL CIRCUIT IN AND FOR DUVAL, NASSAU, AND CLAY COUNTIES, FLORIDA

ADMINISTRATIVE ORDER NO. 2016–01

RE: IMPOSITION OF MANDATORY ASSESSMENTS IN THE FOURTH JUDICIAL CIRCUIT

WHEREAS, section 28.2457, Florida Statutes, provides for the imposition of mandatory and discretionary court costs, fines, fees, and surcharges ("assessments") in criminal cases; and

WHEREAS, publication of mandatory assessments in the Florida Statutes gives every defendant adequate notice so the Court is not required to orally pronounce these assessments in open court; and

WHEREAS, moreover, the Court must impose mandatory assessments in every judgment against every defendant such that the Court has no discretion to dispense with these assessments, and the defendant's ability to pay is not relevant; and

WHEREAS, the Court cannot impose discretionary assessments, however, before giving a defendant notice and opportunity to be heard; and

WHEREAS, Circuit and county judges in the Fourth Judicial Circuit shall impose assessments uniformly to provide a defendant with a clear and accurate understanding of the assessments imposed and to assist the Clerk of Court ("Clerk") with executing its statutory duties.

NOW THEREFORE, by the authority vested in me as Chief Judge of the Fourth Judicial Circuit and pursuant to the Florida Rules of Judicial Administration and section 43.26, Florida Statutes, it is

ORDERED:

1) All references to the Clerk of Court ("Clerk") shall apply to every Clerk of Court within the Fourth Judicial Circuit, including Duval County, Clay County, and Nassau County.

2) The Court will impose mandatory assessments, except as authorized by law. The parties shall present the Court with the statutory authority for any proposed reduction.

3) Judges are encouraged to impose at least the minimum mandatory assessments. If the Court imposes a lesser amount than statutorily mandated, unless authorized by law, the result is an "under-assessment" in the annual Assessment & Collection Report according to section 28.246, Florida Statutes.

4) Prior to submitting the written judgment and sentence to the presiding judge, the Clerk will include all minimum mandatory assessments in every written judgment and sentence regardless of whether they are announced. If the Court imposes an assessment other than the minimum mandatory, the Court must follow the procedures identified below.

5) If the Court announces a mandated assessment, which is lower than the minimum mandatory, the Clerk, when practical, will inform the Court of the discrepancy before the defendant leaves the courtroom. If the Court intends to impose the lower assessment, the Clerk need only adjust the written judgment and sentence. If the Court's announcement was in error, the Court shall notify the defendant in open court of the accurately imposed assessment.

6) If there is a range in the amount of a mandatory assessment and the Court imposes an assessment greater than the minimum mandatory yet still within the range, the Court must announce the higher assessment and the reason(s) for it.

7) If the Court reduces or suspends a mandatory assessment, as authorized by law, the Court shall announce this on the record. If authorized by law, the reduction or suspension does not result in an under-assessment.

8) If the Court fails to orally pronounce a mandatory assessment, the Clerk shall not record or report the assessment as "waived" without explicit oral pronouncement on the record or written authority from the Court. Likewise, if the Court orally pronounces an amount lower than the mandated assessment, the Clerk shall not record or report the difference as "waived" without explicit oral pronouncement on the record or written authority from the Court. When the Court waives a minimum mandatory assessment, the result is an under-assessment, unless authorized by law.

9) If there is a case with more than one criminal count that has a minimum mandatory assessment, and the Court orally announces a minimum assessment for only one count and is silent as to the remaining counts, the Clerk will record in the Judgment the announced amount as to that count and will also record the minimum mandatory assessment for all remaining counts that have minimum mandatory assessments. If the Court does not specify which count is being assessed, the Clerk will apply the minimum mandatory assessment to the first count and then record in the Judgment the minimum mandatory assessment to each subsequent count. This procedure shall also apply when multiple cases involving the defendant are consolidated and heard concurrently.

10) The Clerk shall forward to the Chief Judge, Trial Court Administrator, State Attorney, Public Defender, and Regional Counsel a copy of the official Annual Assessment and Collections Report. The report shall follow the guidelines as outlined in section 28.246(1), Florida Statutes.

11) This Administrative Order No. 2016–01 shall be recorded by the Clerk of the Court, in the Official Records of Duval County, in the State of Florida, and shall take effect immediately. All terms and conditions set forth herein shall remain in full force and effect unless and until otherwise ordered by the Court.

DONE AND ORDERED in Chambers at Jacksonville, at Duval County, Florida this ___ 23 day of February, 2016.

MARK MAHON

CHIEF JUDGE

2015–03. COURTHOUSE SECURITY VIDEOTAPING ON DUVAL COUNTY COURTHOUSE GROUNDS

IN THE CIRCUIT COURT, FOURTH JUDICIAL CIRCUIT IN AND FOR DUVAL COUNTY, FLORIDA

ADMINISTRATIVE ORDER NO. 2015–3

RE: COURTHOUSE SECURITY VIDEOTAPING ON DUVAL COUNTY COURTHOUSE GROUNDS

WHEREAS, the judiciary has a responsibility to maintain the public confidence in the integrity of the American judicial system; and

WHEREAS, a "courthouse serves . . . to provide a locus in which civil and criminal disputes can be adjudicated" and, while being charged with the responsibility of maintaining proper order and decorum, judges have not only the right, but, "indeed, the duty" to limit the "appearance of favoritism in judicial proceedings" and "appearance of political partiality" according to Huminski v. Corsones, 396 F.3d 53, 91 (2d Cir.2005) (quotations omitted'): see also United States v. Grace, 461 U.S. 171, 103 S.Ct. 1702, 75 L.Ed.2d 736 (1983); and

WHEREAS, recent disturbing activities have occurred on the grounds of the Duval County Courthouse (hereinafter, "the Courthouse") involving videotaping on Courthouse grounds, posing a security threat to the Courthouse and a threat to the integrity of the judicial system; and

WHEREAS, for example, on Friday, May 29, 2015, at approximately 10:20 a.m., an individual videotaped numerous persons, including several people attempting to enter the Courthouse, while shouting out that the Court system and the Judges inside the Courthouse were "corrupt." When officers arrived, the individual stood at the front of the Courthouse, continued to videotape the numerous uniformed law enforcement officers of the Jacksonville Sheriff's Office ("JSO"), yelling that they should be "ashamed" of themselves. He called them "legalized gang members" and "thugs," and even threatened to file an internal affairs complaint because one officer did not immediately provide a name and badge number. People witnessing this encounter appeared to be visibly shaken; in fact, numerous credentialed media representatives left the scene. The individual then turned to them, and yelled that the credentialed media members "continue to ignore the proof" that judges are corrupt, "ignoring corruption is supporting corruption", and that they "should be ashamed of themselves".

The individual then followed the media representatives to the State Attorney's fenced-in parking lot, where he continued to videotape and yell at them. The videotape was later uploaded to YouTube under F–T–G (the last two letters standing for "the government"); and

WHEREAS, this activity created a security threat because it required the time and scarce resources of numerous uniformed JSO officers to leave their posts on Courthouse grounds in order to supervise and monitor the incident. In addition, the individual's actions also publicly denigrated the Court's integrity and core purpose of unbiased and unprejudiced decisions in Duval County as part of the American judicial system; and

WHEREAS, the proper procedure for challenging a court's decision is to file an appeal with the appropriate appellate court. Shouting out on the Courthouse grounds that the Court and judges are "corrupt" during business hours while people are entering the Courthouse is entirely inappropriate and disruptive and is analogous to falsely shouting "fire" in a crowded theater; and

WHEREAS, on Thursday, May 28, 2015, during a fire alarm which went off at approximately 12:05 p.m. (noon) inside the Courthouse, the same individual was holding a sign indicating he was disgruntled about a judge's ruling. The individual was videotaping crowds—including Judges, Judicial Assistants, judicial staff, Clerk's Office staff, and law enforcement personnel—during a mandatory evacuation from certain restricted secure exits of the Courthouse. The video filmed conspicuous signs on each side of the garage door that state "Notice—Secure Area—Authorized Personnel Only." The videotape also depicted judges' and other staff members' vehicles parked in the small secure garage located on the street level (underneath the building) while the garage door was open. In addition, the videotape showed the Security Guard's command center inside the garage, which further compromises the security of the garage and the integrity of the Courthouse security.

The videotape included license plates of some of the judges' vehicles and showed some judges driving out of the secure garage, including their faces and their associated vehicles (make, model, year, and license plates). This disclosure puts the judges in a vulnerable position because the videotape is available on the Internet under the F–T–G label. On this date, the individual was videotaping on Courthouse grounds and the Courthouse perimeter sidewalk on the grounds (not the public sidewalk surrounding the Courthouse grounds) when he again he provoked law enforcement officers, asking in a loud and belligerent tone for the officers' names and badge numbers, all while the officers were preoccupied with controlling the crowds evacuating the building into the building's perimeter sidewalk and directing "everyone to move across the street." While the officers were busy clearing the crowds safely, the individual filmed the secure Courthouse garage, and one officer asked him to "please remove your camera." The individual stated the officer had committed "battery" because she "touched" his "property" and he made repeated and hostile demands to her and to another officer that he see her supervisor. The videotape was later uploaded to YouTube under F–T– G and is available for viewing on the Internet; and

WHEREAS, this activity interfered with the orderly and safe administration of the building, the safety of the public and judicial staff evacuating the building and on the perimeter of the Courthouse and the grounds, and threatened the security of all the judges parking in the secure garage as well as those driving out of the garage; and

WHEREAS, the Courthouse secure garages on Pearl Street and Broad Street, the adjacent State Attorney's fenced-in parking lot, and the Courthouse Sally Port, are all secure areas of the Courthouse grounds. See e.g., Mazzetti v. U.S., 518 F.2d 781 (10th Cir. 1975)(holding local rule prohibiting pictures of prisoners being escorted down a stairway to a bus in a parking lot within the environs of a courthouse was not constitutionally overbroad and was not an improper restraint of First Amendment rights of newspaper photographer who took pictures). Therefore, filming in and around such secure areas jeopardizes the safety of the judges, judicial staff, and personnel of the State Attorney's Office, and compromises the security system in place; and

WHEREAS, pursuant to the Florida Public Records Act, Sections 119.071(4)(d)2.a.(I), c, and d.(I), Florida Statutes, and Rule 2.420, Florida Judicial Administration Rules, expressly adopting confidentiality provisions of Chapter 119 for judicial branch records, certain types of personally identifiable information regarding judges, prosecutors, and other law enforcement officers are exempt from disclosure; and

WHEREAS, courts have "*regularly rejected* the assertion that people who wish to 'propagandize protests or views have a constitutional right to do so whenever and however and wherever they please.'" U.S. v. Grace, 461 U.S. 171, 177–78, 103

S.Ct. 1702, 75 L.Ed.2d 736 (1983) (quoting Adderley v. FL, 385 U.S. 39, 47–48, 87 S.Ct. 242, 17 L.Ed.2d 149 (1966)); and

WHEREAS, public streets, sidewalks and parks have historically been considered to be "public forums" and have been associated with the free exercise of expressive activities for use of assembly, free exchange of certain ideas and speakers. Huminski v. Corsones, 396 F.3d 53, 89–90 (2d Cir.2005); and

WHEREAS, on the other hand, "Courthouses and courthouse grounds (with the exclusion of public sidewalks surrounding the Courthouse grounds) have uniformly been treated as nonpublic forums for purposes of First Amendment analysis." Schmidter v. State, 103 So. 3d 263, 270 (Fla. 5th DCA 2012) (emphasis added), citing U.S. v. Grace, 461 U.S. at 177–79 (holding the Supreme Court building and its grounds other than public sidewalks are not public forums); Huminski, 396 F.3d at 90–91; and

WHEREAS, the Courthouse, including its grounds, is a nonpublic forum and has "not been traditionally held open for the use of the public for expressive activities." Huminski 391 F.3d at 90–91, citing U.S. v. Grace, 461 U.S. at 178; and

WHEREAS, likewise, parking lots adjacent to the Courthouse and the courthouse grounds generally are nonpublic forums. Huminski 391 F.3d at 91. "Other than abutting public streets and sidewalks, the parking lots do not fall within the class of traditional public forums—they are not 'historically associated with the free exercise of expressive activities,' as are 'streets, sidewalks, and parks.'" Id. citing U.S. v. Grace, 461 U.S. at 177; and

WHEREAS, pursuant to Article V, Section 2(d), Florida Constitution, Section 43.26(2)(e), Florida Statutes, and Rule 2.215(b), Florida Rules of Judicial Administration, the chief judge of each judicial circuit is charged with the authority to enter administrative orders along with the power to "do everything necessary to promote the prompt and efficient administration of justice in the courts over which he or she is chief judge" and to regulate the use of all court facilities; and

WHEREAS, "[a]n integral part of any court's duty to administer justice and fairly adjudicate disputes is to ensure that all parties have the opportunity to advance their cause in an atmosphere of safety, decorum, and fairness" In re Mone, 719 A. 2d 626, 632 (N.H. 1998) (citations omitted); and

WHEREAS, it is the court's responsibility "to oversee the operations of the judicial branch for the purposes of maintaining public confidence in the administration of justice" and to "maintain an independent judiciary so that the adjudication of individual controversies is fair and remains uninfluenced by outside forces." Id. at 633 (citations omitted); and

WHEREAS, over 91,600 people use the Courthouse each month, including many citizens who have no choice but to use the facilities in search of justice, in response to a subpoena, or conducting other business, as well as many people who serve the public and work in the judicial system; and

WHEREAS, "court security officers who assist the courts in providing a safe and secure forum for litigants, court staff, witnesses, jurors, and the public" play an integral role and are essential to the court's most fundamental function of administering justice and fairly adjudicating disputes. Id. at 632; and

WHEREAS, "[w]ithout security the public's confidence in the integrity of the judicial system is threatened. The proper administration of justice requires that courts operate in a safe and secure environment". Id. (quoting Bd. of Comm'rs. Weld Co. v. 19th Jud. Dist., 895 P.2d 545, 548–49 (Colo. 1995)); and

WHEREAS, for security purposes, it is in the best interest of the citizens of the Fourth Judicial Circuit, and all visitors to the Courthouse, that security officers are able to devote their resources, focus, and attention on protecting the safety of the persons who use the Courthouse, rather than controlling disturbances created by unreasonable, unprotected speech that (a) is inappropriate when considering its time, place and manner; and (b) forces the public to question the independence and integrity of the judicial system; and

WHEREAS, reasonable restrictions are necessary to ensure the safety of the Courthouse grounds, to protect the security of the Judges, Judicial Assistants, judicial staff, Clerk's Office staff, and law enforcement personnel, and to minimize activities which unreasonably disrupt, interrupt, and interfere with the fair and orderly conduct of the judiciary; and

WHEREAS, reasonable restrictions are necessary to limit expressive conduct, speech, or dissemination of materials, tending to influence individuals as they enter the Courthouse, which serves the reasonable purpose of protecting the actual or perceived integrity of judicial impartiality and independence of the courts in the Duval County Courthouse, a nonpublic forum; and

WHEREAS, any such restriction is being narrowly drawn to achieve that end.

NOW THEREFORE, by the authority vested in me as the Chief Judge of the Fourth Judicial Circuit and pursuant to the Florida Rules of Judicial Administration, it is

ORDERED that:

1. The term "Duval County Courthouse grounds" herein shall apply to the exterior of the Duval County Courthouse at 501 West Adams Street, Jacksonville, Florida, 32202; the lawn area in front of the Courthouse facing Adams Street, perimeter sidewalk leading from Adams Street to the front of the Courthouse, the front steps and the entrance of the Courthouse; the garages on Broad Street, on Pearl Street, and the Sally Port entrance; the adjacent building known as the "State Attorney's Office" which has an overpass bridge leading directly into the Courthouse; all perimeter sidewalks around the Courthouse (on Adams Street, Duval Street, Broad Street and Pearl Street), as well as around the State Attorney's Office building (on Monroe Street, Pearl Street, Julia Street, and Duval Street); and the fenced-in garage of the State Attorney's Office building directly across the street from the judges' garage.

2. The *public* sidewalks along Adams Street; *across* the street from the Duval County Courthouse on Broad Street; and *across* the street from the Duval County Courthouse on Duval Street; are all excluded from the designation of "Duval County Courthouse grounds".

3. Demonstrations or dissemination of materials that degrade or call into question the integrity of the Court or any of its judges (e.g., claiming the Courts, Court personnel or judges are "corrupt", biased, dishonest, partial, or prejudiced), thereby tending to influence individuals appearing before the Courts, including jurors, witnesses, and litigants, shall be prohibited on the Duval County Courthouse grounds.

4. Demonstrations that unreasonably disrupt, disturb, interrupt, or interfere with the impartial and orderly conduct of the judiciary, or that of JSO or other security officers, shall be prohibited on the Duval County Courthouse grounds.

5. The videotaping of secure locations on the Duval County Courthouse grounds, such as the judges' secure parking garages (under the Courthouse at the Pearl Street and Broad Street entrance), the State Attorney's Office garage (on Pearl Street) and the Sally Port, and all security features of the Duval County Courthouse, including non-public entrances to and exits from the Courthouse, shall be prohibited for the protection and security of the judiciary and to avoid breaching the security systems, or revealing the security systems, or security procedures of the Courthouse in place.

6. Any person engaging in the type of expressive conduct as indicated in this Order may be found in criminal contempt of Court.

7. The Jacksonville Sheriff's Office shall give any person on the Courthouse grounds who is violating any provision of this Order a copy of this Order and advise such person of the relevant restrictions herein.

8. In addition, law enforcement personnel shall instruct anyone violating the provisions of this Order to cease and desist immediately.

9. If an individual is observed to engage in conduct that is in violation of this Order after having been provided notice as set forth herein, the Jacksonville Sheriff's Office is hereby DIRECTED to arrest and charge the offending individual with indirect criminal contempt of Court (and any other charges deemed appropriate) and transport such person to the Duval County Jail for identification and processing.

10. Any person who is observed continuing to engage in conduct that is in violation of this Order after having received a copy of the Order and being instructed to cease and desist by law enforcement, may *also* face penalties including injunctive relief, confinement, a monetary fine, or otherwise.

11. This Administrative Order No. 2015–3 shall not prohibit, impede, obstruct, or interfere with credentialed media representatives' ability to use the front Courthouse steps and any exterior areas where the Courthouse has traditionally been used as a backdrop while performing newsgathering, photographing, filming, recording, and broadcasting functions consistent with journalistic practices.

12. Furthermore, such Administrative Order No. 2015–3 shall not, in any way, be construed as superseding or contradicting any of the provisions of the Second Amended Administrative Order No. 2013–17, establishing the policies and location of peaceful demonstrators, which has been previously entered on November 20, 2014.

13. This Administrative Order No. 2015–3 shall be recorded by the Clerk of the Court, in the Official Records of Duval County, in the State of Florida, and shall take effect immediately. All terms and conditions set forth herein shall remain in full force and effect unless and until otherwise ordered by the Court.

DONE AND ORDERED in Chambers at Jacksonville, Duval County, Florida, this 1 day of July, 2015.

MARK H. MAHON

CHIEF JUDGE

2015–01. DEFINITION OF "MEDIA" FOR CREDENTIALS AND COVERAGE OF ALL PUBLIC JUDICIAL PROCEEDINGS (EXCEPT THOSE OF EXTRAORDINARY PUBLIC INTEREST)

IN THE CIRCUIT COURT, FOURTH JUDICIAL CIRCUIT, IN AND FOR DUVAL COUNTY, FLORIDA

ADMINISTRATIVE ORDER NO. 2015–1

RE: DEFINITION OF "MEDIA" FOR CREDENTIALS AND COVERAGE OF ALL PUBLIC JUDICIAL PROCEEDINGS (EXCEPT THOSE OF EXTRAORDINARY PUBLIC INTEREST)

WHEREAS, on April 23, 2013, the Fourth Judicial Circuit entered the Second Amended Administrative Order No. 92–02, which remains in full force and effect and governs media and technological coverage of judicial proceedings in accordance with Rule 2.450, Rules of Judicial Administration; and

WHEREAS, on December 19, 2014, the Fourth Judicial Circuit entered Administrative Order No. 2013–08, which remains in full force and effect and governs media and technological coverage of judicial proceedings in cases of extraordinary public interest; and

WHEREAS, Administrative Order No. 2013–08 regarding cases of extraordinary public interest includes a definition of the "media" to be used by the Media Committee and considered by the Chief Judge in cases of extraordinary public interest when applications are made for credentialing; and

WHEREAS, recent requests have been submitted for permission to videotape proceedings by non-traditional, self-proclaimed newsgathering sources, which has alerted this Circuit as to the absence of any expressly articulated definition for "media" in cases that are not of extraordinary public interest; and

WHEREAS, media coverage of all public judicial proceedings in courtrooms is "subject at all times to the authority of the presiding judge to: (i) control the conduct of proceedings before the court; (ii) ensure decorum and prevent distractions; and (iii) ensure the fair administration of justice in the pending cause," in accordance with certain standards for the technological coverage as set forth by the Florida Supreme Court in Rule 2.450, Rules of Judicial Administration; and

WHEREAS, use of electronic devices by all others (non-media) is also subject to the authority of the presiding judge at all times for the same three reasons, pursuant to Rule 2.451(c)(1), Rules of Judicial Administration; and

WHEREAS, pursuant to Article V, Section 2(d), Florida Constitution, section 43.26, Florida Statutes, and Rule 2.215(b), Florida Rules of Judicial Administration, the Chief Judge of each judicial circuit is charged with the authority and the power to do everything necessary to promote the fair, prompt and efficient administration of justice and the regulation and use of all court facilities, including courtrooms; [1] furthermore, Rules 2.450–2.451, Florida Rules of Judicial Administration govern the use of technology in judicial proceedings and vests the presiding judge with broad authority to control the conduct of proceedings before the court, maintain decorum, prevent distractions, and ensure the safety and security of persons and property; and

WHEREAS, the Court must balance the constitutional right of access with the constitutional right to a fair trial; and

WHEREAS, high profile cases with media coverage require procedures and special accommodations to ensure full access without compromising the right of any litigant to a fair and orderly trial.

NOW THEREFORE, by the authority vested in me as the Chief Judge of the Fourth Judicial Circuit and pursuant to the Florida Rules of Judicial Administration, it is

ORDERED that:

A) The presiding judge has the authority to determine whether the case he or she is presiding over is a case of extraordinary public interest, which would invoke the application of Administrative Order No. 2013–08.

B) A person or entity requesting media credentials, must show proof that it meets the definition of "media" as defined herein. The Court, through Court Administration, will have the discretion to determine whether a person or entity is "media" as defined herein for all cases (except those of extraordinary public interest) as follows:

(1) *Media Defined.* In all cases (except those of extraordinary public interest), "media" is defined as:

(a) traditional print and broadcast communication channels, such as radio and television, newspapers and magazines, through which news and information is disseminated that reach or influence people widely.

(b) the next generation of digital, computerized or networked information and communication technologies not directly associated with traditional print and/or broadcast media entities and defined as:

an online entity which was a previously established, independent site that contains regularly updated original news content above and beyond links, forums, trouble-shooting tips and reader contributions; said content is thoroughly reviewed by an independent editor before publication; has certifiable data demonstrating "unique" and "direct" monthly visits and for which there has been original content generated and published by the applying employee and the entity that has previously covered the judicial branch for the six months immediately prior to requesting a Media Authorization Card.

It is the responsibility of the requesting entity to show proof that it meets the definition of media and it is within the Court's discretion as to whether an entity is media.

C) Media authorization ID cards will be issued at a reasonable cost as set forth by the Court Administration. At all times, these ID cards will remain the property the Court Administration. Furthermore, these ID cards must be displayed at all times while inside the Courthouse. At no time shall any media representative transfer or loan any official ID card or Court-issued media credential to any other person for any reason whatsoever. The transferring or loaning of a media ID card or official Court-issued media credential will result in the revocation of media privileges for the violating media representative and entity.

D) To obtain a media authorization card, an applicant must submit a fully completed Fourth Judicial Circuit of Florida Application for Media Authorization Card, together with all proof requested in the application, as well as any additional information that may be requested by Court Administration.

E) If the person or entity is deemed to be "media" based upon the above definition and the application submitted, then such media shall be governed according to all rules and regulations, including all Fourth Judicial Circuit Administrative Orders and Memoranda issued by the Chief Judge that govern the media, together with the Rules of Judicial Administration; the authority of the presiding judge in all cases; the authority of the Chief Judge in the court facility; and any and all Administrative Orders and Memoranda issued by the Chief Judge governing media that are entered subsequent to this Order.

F) If the person or entity is determined by Court Administration not to be "media", then the individual or organization attempting to use "electronic devices" as an "other" will remain subject to the authority of the presiding judge pursuant to Rule 2.451(c)(1), Florida Rules of Judicial Administration, related to courtrooms as well as subject to the authority of the Chief Judge pursuant to 2.451(c)(2), Florida Rules of Judicial Administration, as to the Court facility.

G) This Administrative Order 2015–1 shall be recorded by the Clerk of the Court, in the Official Records of Duval County, in the State of Florida, shall take effect immediately, and remain in full force and effect unless and until otherwise ordered by the Court.

DONE AND ORDERED in Chambers at Jacksonville, Duval County, Florida, this 5 day of March, 2015.

MARK H. MAHON

CHIEF JUDGE

1 As used herein, the word "courtroom" includes courtrooms, hearing rooms and any other rooms used to conduct court proceedings open to the public, unless specifically stated otherwise.

2014–10 (A1). MINORS SEXTING: SECTION 847.0141, FLORIDA STATUTES (2015)

IN THE CIRCUIT COURT, FOURTH JUDICIAL CIRCUIT, IN AND FOR DUVAL, NASSAU, AND CLAY COUNTY, FLORIDA

FIRST AMENDED ADMINISTRATIVE ORDER NO. 2014–10

RE: MINORS SEXTING: SECTION 847.0141, FLORIDA STATUTES (2015)

WHEREAS, Administrative Order No. 2014–10 was entered on August 21, 2014;

WHEREAS, after Administrative Order No. 2014–10 was entered, section 847.0141, Florida Statutes, was amended, effective July 1, 2015;

WHEREAS, the amendment to section 847.0141, Florida Statutes, has prompted revisions to Administrative Order No. 2014–10 as provided herein;

WHEREAS, as amended, sections 847.0141 (3)(a) and 985.0301(1), Florida Statutes, provide the circuit court with original jurisdiction of proceedings in which a minor is alleged to have committed a delinquent act as well as a noncriminal violation that has been assigned to juvenile court:

WHEREAS, section 847.0141(1), Florida Statutes, remains unchanged as to the statutory violation of the offense of sexting by a minor, i.e., any person under the age of eighteen (18) years, as defined by section 847.001(8) where the minor knowingly:

(a) uses a computer, or any other device capable of electronic data transmission or distribution, to transmit or distribute to another minor any photograph or video of any person which depicts nudity, as defined in section 847.001(9), and is harmful to minors, as defined in section 847.001(6).

(b) possesses a photograph or video of any person that was transmitted or distributed by another minor which depicts nudity, as defined in section 847.001(9), and is harmful to minors, as defined in section 847.001(6);

WHEREAS, section 847.0141(1)(b), Florida Statutes, also remains the same in that a minor is not in violation if the minor did not solicit the photograph or video; took reasonable steps to report the photograph to a legal guardian, school, or law enforcement official; and did not transmit or distribute the photograph or video to a third party;

WHEREAS, as amended, section 847.0141(3)(a), Florida Statutes, provides that a minor who commits the offense of sexting under subsection (1) of section 847.0141, Florida Statutes, commits a noncriminal violation for a first violation, and must sign and accept a citation (as statutorily subscribed and required by subsections 847.0141(3)(a)1.a.–h., Florida Statutes), indicating a promise to appear before the juvenile court or, in lieu of appearing in court, may complete 8 hours of community service work, pay a $60 civil penalty, or participate in a "cyber-safety" program within 30 days after receipt of the citation pursuant to section 847.0141(3)(a), Florida Statutes;

WHEREAS, as amended, subsection 847.0141(3)(a)2., Florida Statutes, provides that if a minor contests a citation for a noncriminal violation for a first violation, and the court determines that the minor committed a noncriminal violation, the Court may order the minor to perform 8 hours of community service, pay a $60 civil penalty, or participate in a cyber-safety program, or any *combination* thereof;

WHEREAS, as amended, subsection 847.0141(3)(a)3., Florida Statutes, provides that a minor who fails to comply with the citation waives the right to contest it, and the Court may impose any of the penalties identified in subparagraph 2. or issue an order to show cause;

WHEREAS, as amended, subsection 847.0141(3)(a)3., Florida Statutes, further provides that where a minor fails to comply with a citation and the Court finds the minor to be in contempt, the Court "may impose additional age-appropriate penalties, which may include issuance of an order to the Department of Highway Safety and Motor Vehicles to withhold issuance of, or suspend the driver license or driving privilege of, the minor for 30 consecutive days;" however, the Court may not impose incarceration;

WHEREAS, as amended, subsection 847.0141(3)(b), Florida Statutes, provides a minor commits a misdemeanor of the first degree for a violation that occurs after the minor has been "found to have committed" a noncriminal violation for sexting or has satisfied the penalty imposed in lieu of a court appearance as provided in paragraph 847.014l(3)(a), punishable as provided in section 775.082 or section 775.083;

WHEREAS, as amended, subsection 847.0141(3)(c), Florida Statutes, provides a minor commits a felony of the third degree for a violation that occurs after the minor has been "found to have committed" a misdemeanor of the first degree for sexting, punishable as provided in section 775.082, section 775.083, or section 775.084;

WHEREAS, pursuant to section 847.0141(5), Florida Statutes, the term "found to have committed" means a "determination of guilt that is the result of a plea or trial, or a finding of delinquency that is the result of a plea or an adjudicatory hearing, regardless of whether adjudication is withheld;"

WHEREAS, because young children may not be aware of the life-long consequences of sexting, which may stigmatize them for the rest of their lives, this Circuit will continue to recognize the value and importance of attending a cyber-safety program; and

WHEREAS, for more than a year, the Fourth Judicial Circuit has successfully established and operated an educational program (now referred to as the cyber-safety program) which has been administered and monitored by Teen Court, and it has had an outstanding record with minors who have received a citation for a noncriminal violation for a first violation of sexting under section 847.0141(1), Florida Statutes.

NOW THEREFORE, by the authority vested in me as the Chief Judge of the Fourth Judicial Circuit and pursuant to the Florida Rules of Judicial Administration, it is

ORDERED that:

In accordance with the amended section 847.0141, Florida Statutes, all alleged violations of sexting cases against minors in the Fourth Judicial Circuit will be processed according to the following procedures:

I. First Violation: Noncriminal

(A) *Fourth Judicial Circuit Cyber–Safety Program.* In the Fourth Judicial Circuit, the cyber-safety program administered and monitored by the Teen Court Program ("Teen Court") has proven to be an extremely valuable educational resource for minors and explains the lifelong ramifications of sexting. Teen Court has an outstanding record with minors who have received a citation for a noncriminal violation for a first violation of sexting under section 847.0141(1), Florida Statutes.

Although it is not mandatory, the cyber-safety program should be the most highly recommended penalty to be completed by a minor who receives a Citation for a noncriminal violation for a first violation of sexting. In extraordinary and unusual circumstances, however, the cyber-safety program may be inappropriate for certain minors or cases.

(B) *Citations—Appearance at Clerk's Office.* Absent extenuating circumstances, all minors who sign and accept a Citation in Duval, Clay, and Nassau Counties, Florida, indicating a promise to appear in Court for a noncriminal violation for a first violation of sexting pursuant to section 847.0141(3)(a), will be referred to the Duval County Clerk's Office.

The minor will need to appear in person with a parent or legal guardian who must have a valid photo identification (ID) at the Duval County Clerk's Office no later than ten (10) calendar days of receiving the Citation in order to enable the minor to comply with the penalty within thirty (30) days of receiving the Citation.

Upon the appearance of the minor and parent or legal guardian (hereinafter, "minor and legal guardian") at the Duval County Clerk's Office, the Clerk will provide the minor and legal guardian: (1) a case number; (2) a copy of sections 847.001 (Definitions) and 847.0141 (Sexting), Florida Statutes; and (3) a written Notice, directing the legal guardian to contact Teen Court within two (2) business days (to allow time for the minor to comply with the statutory requirement of completing the penalties within 30 days after receipt of the Citation). See § 847.0141(3)(a), Fla. Stat. The Notice must have the Case Number and the legal guardian's signature and contact information, including full name, mailing address, home phone number, and alternate phone number—if any. The Clerk will make the Notice available to Teen Court.

(C) *In Lieu of Appearance Before Juvenile Judge*

(1) When a minor's legal guardian contacts Teen Court, a representative will explain that, in lieu of appearing in Court before a Juvenile Judge, the minor and legal guardian may elect to work directly with Teen Court for the minor to complete one of the following three penalties within 30 calendar days after receipt of the Citation, by:

a—participating in the Fourth Judicial Circuit's cyber-safety program administered and monitored by Teen Court;

b— completing 8 hours of community service work; or

c—paying a $60 civil penalty.

For the reasons stated above in subsection I(A), Teen Court should highly recommend participation in the cyber-safety program and refer the minor to either of the other two penalties as an alternative penalty only when otherwise appropriate.

(2) Teen Court will keep a record of the minor's compliance and satisfaction of the penalty imposed in lieu of court appearance.

(a) If the minor timely satisfies the penalty imposed in lieu of court appearance, the Court need not enter an order to make findings that the minor committed a noncriminal violation. If the minor violates section 847.0141 again, after Teen Court's record reflects that the minor has timely satisfied the penalty imposed in lieu of a court appearance, the minor commits a misdemeanor of the first degree, pursuant to section 847.0141(3)(b), Florida Statutes.

(b) On the other hand, if the minor fails to timely satisfy the penalty or if the citation is contested, the matter will be referred to the Juvenile Judge for appropriate action as set forth in detail below.

(D) *Minor Contests Citation: Appearance Before Juvenile Judge.* If the citation is contested, the minor must appear in Court before a Juvenile Delinquency Judge at the next hearing date (which is regularly pre-assigned and set for Sexting cases) for a determination as to whether the minor committed the noncriminal violation. The hearing will be an evidentiary hearing.

(1) Evidentiary Hearing—Written Findings. At the evidentiary hearing, the Juvenile Judge will determine whether the minor committed a noncriminal violation under section 847.0141, Florida Statutes. If the minor did commit such violation, the Court must enter a written order (with a copy to Teen Court), expressly finding the minor has committed the violation. Accordingly, pursuant to section 847.0141(3)(b), should a subsequent violation occur "after the minor has been found to have committed a noncriminal violation for sexting", such findings will serve as a basis for a misdemeanor of the first degree.

(2) Penalties. Once the Court determines a minor (who *contested* the Citation) has committed a noncriminal violation, the Court may:

a—order the minor to participate in the Fourth Judicial Circuit's cyber-safety program administered and monitored by Teen Court (except under extraordinary and unusual circumstances where the Court finds it to be inappropriate);

b—order the minor to perform 8 hours of community service;

c—order the minor to pay a $60 civil penalty; or

d—order any combination thereof.

§ 847.0141(3)(a)2., Fla. Stat.

No deadline is statutorily specified for the completion of penalties when a minor *contests* the Citation (although penalties are statutorily required to be completed within 30 days when a minor accepts a citation). See § 847.0141(3)(a)2., Fla. Stat.; Cf. § 847.0141 (3)(a), Fla. Stat.

(3) Compliance Related to Contested Citation. Teen Court will monitor the minor's progress and full compliance. If the minor provides sufficient, verifiable proof of successful and timely completion of the Court-ordered penalties related to the *contested* Citation, Teen Court's record of the minor's compliance and completion will be recorded and the matter will be closed. If a subsequent violation for sexting occurs, the findings of the noncriminal violation will serve as a basis for a misdemeanor of the first degree pursuant to section 847.0141, Florida Statutes.

(E) *Non-compliance*

(1) Failure to Report to Clerk's Office Within 10 Days—Send Notice to Appear. If the minor, through the minor's legal guardian, fails to report to the Clerk's Office within ten (10) days of receiving the Citation, the Clerk's Office will advise Teen Court, which will make a good faith effort to contact the legal guardian prior to sending the legal guardian a Notice to Appear before Teen Court, indicating a date and time certain to appear. The Notice will explain both the minor and legal guardian must appear before Teen Court to explain the reason for missing the deadline imposed.

(2) Failure to Contact Teen Court Within 2 Days—Send Notice to Appear. If the minor, through the minor's legal guardian, fails to contact Teen Court within two (2) business days of appearing at the Clerk's Office, Teen Court will make a good faith effort to contact the legal guardian prior to sending the legal guardian a Notice to Appear before Teen Court, indicating a date and time certain to appear. The Notice will explain both the minor and legal guardian

must appear before Teen Court to explain the reason for missing the deadline imposed.

(3) Failure to Appear Before Teen Court—Issue Order to Show Cause. If the minor and legal guardian willfully fail to appear after receiving a Notice to Appear before Teen Court, then, "on affidavit of any person having personal knowledge of the facts, the court [Juvenile Judge] may issue and sign an order to show cause" in accordance with 8.150, Florida Rules Juvenile Procedure. See also, § 847.0141(3)(a)3., Fla. Stat., (for failure to comply with Citation). The order to show cause must state the essential facts constituting the contempt charged and require the minor and legal guardian to appear before the court to show cause why the minor should not be held in contempt of court. Id. Such order to show cause will also provide an explanation of the consequences for the minor's willful failure to appear on the date and time specified. In addition, pursuant to Rule 8.150, counsel "must be appointed for all contempt hearings if the [minor] child qualifies for such appointment, or the [minor] child has the right to retain counsel, unless the [minor] child waives counsel in writing as required by rule 8.165."

(4) Failure to Comply with Citation. Where the minor fails to comply with the Citation or has *in*sufficient, verifiable proof of compliance, the minor *waives* the right to contest the Citation pursuant to section 847.0141(3)(a)3., Florida Statutes, **and *either***

(a) the Juvenile Judge may Impose a Penalty by Ordering:

1—the minor to participate in this Circuit's cyber-safety program administered and monitored by Teen Court; or

2—the minor to perform 8 hours of community service; or

3—the minor to pay a $60 civil penalty; or

4—any *combination* thereof;

or

(b) the Juvenile Judge may Issue an Order to Show Cause in accordance with 8.150, Florida Rules Juvenile Procedure, and upon a finding of contempt (for noncompliance with the Citation), the Juvenile Judge may impose *additional* age-appropriate penalties as to the minor's driving privileges, which may include "issuance of an order to the Department of Highway Safety and Motor Vehicles to *withhold* issuance of, or *suspend* the driver license or driving privilege of, the minor for 30 consecutive days." § 847.0141(3)(a)3., Fla. Stat., (emphasis added). The Court, however, may not impose incarceration since this is a noncriminal violation. Id.

In summary, the Florida sexting laws are designed to incentivise the minor to satisfy and complete the penalties in a timely manner and not to repeat a violation for sexting. Noncompliance can lead to increased penalties. A repeat violation leads to criminal charges.

II. Second Violation: Misdemeanor—§ 847.0141(3)(b). A minor commits a misdemeanor of the first degree for a violation that occurs after the minor has satisfied the penalties selected in lieu of a court appearance or after the minor has been "found to have committed" a noncriminal violation for sexting. § 847.0141(3)(b), Fla. Stat. Such misdemeanor case will be referred to the State Attorney's Office. Any petitions filed pursuant to section 847.0141(3)(b), Florida Statutes, will be assigned to the Juvenile Division and heard as a juvenile delinquency case before a Circuit Judge.

III. Subsequent Violation: Felony—§ 847.0141(3)(c). Where a minor commits a felony of the third degree for a violation that occurs after the minor has been "found to have committed" a misdemeanor of the first degree for sexting in violation of section 847.0141, Florida Statutes, the case will be referred to the State Attorney's Office. Any petitions filed pursuant to section 847.0141(3)(c), Florida Statutes, will be assigned to the Juvenile Division and heard as a juvenile delinquency case before a Circuit Judge.

IV. Confidential Records. All juvenile division records and minors sexting records maintained by the Court, Teen Court, and the Office of the Clerk under section 847.0141, Florida Statutes, are confidential and exempt from disclosure to third parties unless an exception under Florida law applies.

V. Record Keeping & Definition of "Found to Have Committed". The Clerk's Office (with the assistance and cooperation of Teen Court) will be responsible for maintaining records on all minors who have been "found to have committed" a noncriminal first violation of sexting pursuant to section 847.0141(3)(a), Florida Statutes, and as defined by section 847.0141(5), Florida Statutes (i.e., a "determination of guilt that is the result of a plea or trial, or a finding of delinquency that is the result of a plea or an adjudicatory hearing, regardless of whether adjudication is withheld"). The Clerk's Office will also track and maintain records on all minors who have been "found to have committed" misdemeanor or felony offenses of sexting.

VI. The Administrative Order No. 2014–10 previously entered on August 21, 2014, and addressing the same subject matter is hereby vacated and superseded.

VII. This First Amended Administrative Order No. 2014–10 shall be recorded by the Clerk of the Court, in the Official Records of Duval County, in the State of Florida, and shall take effect **Monday, March 21, 2016** and remain in full force and effect unless and until otherwise ordered by this Court.

DONE AND ORDERED in Chambers at Jacksonville, Duval County, Florida, this 22ND day of March, 2016.

MARK MAHON

CHIEF JUDGE

2014–09. APPEALS FROM COUNTY COURT TO CIRCUIT COURT (IN DUVAL COUNTY ONLY)

IN THE CIRCUIT COURT, FOURTH JUDICIAL CIRCUIT, IN AND FOR DUVAL COUNTY, FLORIDA

ADMINISTRATIVE ORDER NO. 2014–09

IN RE: APPEALS FROM COUNTY COURT TO CIRCUIT COURT (in Duval County Only)

WHEREAS, this Court has determined that improvements are necessary to the processing, handling, and tracking of both criminal and civil appeals from the County Court to the Circuit Court in Duval County; and

WHEREAS, measures are necessary to insure that Courts promptly resolve all such appeals, and that parties and judges in both the trial court level of the County Court and in the Circuit Court's appellate court level are kept apprised of the status of such appeals; and

WHEREAS, this Court has the inherent authority and responsibility to insure that all appeals reviewed by the Circuit Court are handled in an orderly and timely fashion;

NOW THEREFORE, by the authority vested in me as the Chief Judge of the Fourth Judicial Circuit and pursuant to the Florida Rules of Judicial Administration, it is

ORDERED that:

1. The Appeals Division of the Duval County Clerk of Court for the Fourth Judicial Circuit (hereinafter, "Clerk") will publish an electronic report on a monthly basis (the "Report") to all Circuit and County Court judges, reporting on the status of all pending appeals in their respective division. Such Report will identify and categorize appeals by both the appellate and lower court divisions.

The Report will identify each appeal by Case Style and Case No., and will include:

(a) the date of filing of the Notice of Appeal.

(b) the date of the filing of each brief.

(c) the dale of oral argument, if any;

(d) the date of which the matter becomes "ripe" for rendering of an Opinion (see paragraph 3, *infra*);

(e) the date of which an Opinion has been rendered by the Circuit Court:

(f) the date on which a Mandate has been issued;

(g) the date on which the lower tribunal has placed the matter on its calendar or otherwise resumed jurisdiction following the issuance of a Mandate; and

(h) any other information the Clerk deems appropriate,

2. When the appeal becomes "ripe," the Clerk will send notification by electronic delivery to the assigned Circuit Court Judge (and his Judicial Assistant). Further, the Clerk will send notification by electronic delivery to the County Court Judge (and his Judicial Assistant) from whom the appeal originated upon the Circuit Court's rendering of an Opinion on Appeal.

3. Unless otherwise approved by this Court, Opinions on all appeals shall be rendered by the Circuit Court **within ninety (90)** days of the matter being "ripe." An appeal is determined to be "ripe" on the date of the filing of the reply brief, or the date on which oral argument is concluded, whichever date is later.

4. Mandates shall be filed with the Clerk of Court by the Circuit Court within twenty (20) days following the filing of the Opinion.

5. The lower tribunal (County Court Judge) shall either place the matter on his/her criminal or civil calendar, or otherwise resume jurisdiction following the issuance of a Mandate within **twenty (20) days** of filing the Mandate.

6. The Clerk shall continue to monitor an appeal until the matter has been placed back on the County Court's criminal or civil docket, or until the Clerk has otherwise confirmed that the County Court has resumed jurisdiction of the matter.

7. Any violation of the dictates of this Administrative Order are not intended to affect, and do not affect the validity of any appeal, or the validity of any Opinion or Mandate filed by the Fourth Judicial Circuit.

8. All other Administrative Orders, including Amended Administrative Order 2005–02, that have been previously entered and are still in full force and effect, addressing the same subject matter, shall remain in full force and effect unless any clause appears to be contradictory, in which case, this Administrative Order shall supersede all others.

9. This Administrative Order shall be recorded by the Clerk of the Court, in the Official Records of Duval County, in the State of Florida, and shall take effect immediately and remain in full force and effect unless and until otherwise ordered by the Court.

DONE AND ORDERED in Chambers at Jacksonville, Duval County, Florida, this 2 day of June, 2014

DONALD R. MORAN, JR.
CHIEF JUDGE

2014–07. VACATING OLD WRITS OF ATTACHMENT

IN THE CIRCUIT COURT, FOURTH JUDICIAL CIRCUIT, IN AND FOR DUVAL, CLAY AND NASSAU COUNTIES, FLORIDA

ADMINISTRATIVE ORDER NO. 2014–07

IN RE: VACATING OLD WRITS OF ATTACHMENT

WHEREAS, it has come to the attention of the Court that there are a number of outstanding Writs of Attachment issued in excess of 20 years ago, and

WHEREAS, these Writs have out-lived their usefulness; are causing needless monitoring and work for the Jacksonville Sheriff's Office, Clay County Sheriff's Office, and the Nassau County Sheriff's Office (hereafter, "Law Enforcement Agencies"); and should no longer remain in the system,

NOW THEREFORE, by the authority vested in me as the Chief Judge of the Fourth Judicial Circuit and pursuant to the Florida Rules of Judicial Administration, it is hereby

ORDERED AND ADJUDGED that:

1) All Writs of Attachment (including both general Civil Writs and Child Support Writs) which were issued prior to January 1, 1995 are hereby VACATED, and are no longer in effect. The named Law Enforcement Agencies are hereby directed to delete all pending Writs affected by this Order from its data banks, and law enforcement is further directed to not execute any of such Writs.

2) On or about January 1 of every year hereafter, any Writs of Attachment issued more than 20 calendar years from that date shall at that time be VACATED, and the Law Enforcement Agencies are henceforward directed during the month of January of each year to delete any then-pending Writs affected by this Order from its data banks, and law enforcement is further directed to not execute on any of such Writs. It is the intention of this ORDER that no writs older than 20 years shall be executed,

3) This Administrative Order shall be recorded by the Clerk of the Court, in the Official Records of Duval County, in the State of Florida, and shall take effect immediately and remain in full force and effect unless and until otherwise ordered by the Court

DONE AND ORDERED in Chambers at Jacksonville, Duval County, Florida, this 3 day of June, 2014.

DONALD R. MORAN, JR.
CHIEF JUDGE

2014–06. [VACATED AND SET ASIDE BY ORDER 2017-11, EFFECTIVE OCTOBER 18, 2017.]

2014–03. MEDIATION IN CIRCUIT CIVIL CASES CLAY AND NASSAU COUNTIES

IN THE CIRCUIT COURT, FOURTH JUDICIAL CIRCUIT, IN AND FOR CLAY AND NASSAU COUNTIES

ADMINISTRATIVE ORDER NO. 2014–3

RE: MEDIATION IN CIRCUIT CIVIL CASES CLAY AND NASSAU COUNTIES

WHEREAS, the courts and litigants have been greatly assisted by the mediation process in resolving complex civil cases, and;

WHEREAS, mediation has proven to be effective in reducing the rising costs associated with civil litigation, and;

WHEREAS, the timing of mediation is important to achieving successful results, and;

WHEREAS, mediators in the Fourth Judicial Circuit have been customarily appointed when a case is set for trial without a separate order of referral, and;

WHEREAS, mediators appointed by the Court serve as officers of the Court;

NOW THEREFORE, by the authority vested in me as Chief Judge of the Fourth Judicial Circuit and pursuant to the Florida Rules of Judicial Administration, it is

ORDERED:

1. **Setting Mediation:** The Court will appoint a qualified mediator in accordance with Rule 1.1720(j) of the Florida Rules of Civil Procedure in all circuit court civil mediation cases, except those cases excluded by Rule 1.710(b) and foreclosure cases, in accordance with § 44.302, Florida Statutes, and Rule 1.700, Florida Rules of Civil Procedure, on or before the case is set for trial, unless mediation is determined by the court to be inappropriate or unnecessary. The "Order Setting Case for Jury (or Non–jury) Trial and for Pre–Trial Conference and Requiring Matters to be Completed Prior to Pre–Trial Conference" shall include an order of referral to mediation and appointment of the mediator.

2. **Date, Time, Length, and Location:** The appointed mediator shall be responsible for conferring with counsel (or unrepresented parties) for scheduling the mediation conference. Once the mediation is scheduled, the mediator shall send a Notice of Mediation to the parties confirming the date, time, length, and location of the mediation. The Notice of Mediation shall also include the terms of compensation for the mediator as required by paragraph 7 of this Order. The mediator shall be authorized to resolve scheduling conflicts without further order including rescheduling the mediation conference provided the mediation is concluded before the date of the final pretrial conference.

3. **Service of Mediation Order:** The appointed mediator shall serve a copy of this Administrative Order with the Notice of Mediation.

4. **Attendance:** The personal attendance of all parties or their representatives, counsel for the parties, and insurance representatives is required, unless excused by prior agreement of all parties and/or counsel or by leave of Court. Parties and their representatives shall appear at mediation with complete authority to resolve the matters in dispute without further consultation, as defined in 1.720(b)–(d), Florida Rules of Civil Procedure. A Certification of Authority shall be filed in accordance with 1.720(e), Florida Rules of Civil Procedure.

5. **Notice to Lienholders:** Any party who has knowledge of the existence of a lien, such as worker's compensation lien, medical lien, or other lien with rights of subrogation, shall give the lienholder reasonable notice of the date, time, and place of the mediation conference. Appearance of a lienholder is not mandatory and the absence of a lienholder is not grounds to continue the mediation unless agreed to by the parties or ordered by the Court.

6. **Position Statements:** No fewer than 72 hours prior to the mediation conference, each party shall furnish to the mediator, a copy to all counsel involved, a statement outlining the party's position, the issues involved, and the latest settlement negotiations, and designating the persons who will appear at the mediation conference. Parties and counsel may attach other documents to a position statement. Position statements shall not be filed with the court. Parties are encouraged to review § 44.405, Florida Statutes, regarding the confidentiality of discussions and statements made at mediation.

7. **Terms of Compensation:** The mediator shall fully set forth the terms of her/his requested compensation, including hourly fees, preparation fees (if any), costs, and cancellation or rescheduling fees in the Notice of Mediation required in paragraph 2 of this Order. Any party objecting to the terms of compensation shall file an objection with the court, and serve all parties and the mediator no later than 15 days from the date of service of the Notice of Mediation. Any party making an objection to the terms of compensation shall immediately place the matter on the court's calendar for a hearing. Attorneys shall advise their clients of the mediator's fee structure including hourly fees, preparation fees, cancellation fees, and costs before the commencement of the mediation. Although the obligation to pay mediation fees is that of the client and not the attorney, see Bauer v. Hardy, 651 So. 2d 748 (Fla. 1st DCA 1995), attorneys shall make a diligent effort to ensure the client's payment of the fees.

Unless otherwise ordered by the Court, or mutually agreed to by the parties and the mediator, all mediation charges are to be equally divided between or among the parties. If more than one party is represented by the same counsel, then those parties will be deemed to be "one party" for the purpose of the mediator's charges.

8. Sanctions: Failure to pay mediator's fees and costs may result in the imposition of additional fees, costs, and other sanctions as determined by the Court. Sanctions may include dismissing the case, striking pleadings, entering a default, removing the case from the trial calendar, assessing additional attorney's fees and costs, or imposing any reasonable punishment deemed necessary by the court.

If a party fails to appear at a duly noticed mediation conference without good cause, the court, upon motion or *sua sponte,* may impose sanctions including an award of mediation fees, attorneys' fees, and costs against the party failing to appear.

9. Service of Notice: Service of any notice, pleading, or document required herein shall be made in accordance with Rule 2.516 of the Florida Rules of Judicial Administration.

10. Governing Law: All mediations shall be conducted in accordance with Rules 1.700–1.730 of the Florida Rules of Civil Procedure and Chapter 44 of the Florida Statutes.

11. This Administrative Order supersedes Amended Administrative Order No. 2004–6 and shall be recorded by the Clerk of the Court in the Official Records of Duval County, Florida, and **shall take effect February 1, 2014** in both Clay and Nassau Counties and remain in full force and effect unless and until otherwise ordered by the Court.

ENTERED at Jacksonville, Duval County, Florida, this 22 day of Jan, 2014.

DONALD R. MORAN, JR.
CHIEF JUDGE

2014–01 (A2). ASSESSMENT AND COLLECTION OF DRUG TESTING FEE

IN THE CIRCUIT COURT, FOURTH JUDICIAL CIRCUIT, IN AND FOR CLAY COUNTY, FLORIDA

SECOND AMENDED ADMINISTRATIVE ORDER NO. 2014–01

IN RE: ASSESSMENT AND COLLECTION OF DRUG TESTING FEE FOR CLAY COUNTY, FLORIDA

WHEREAS, it is in the best interest of the citizens of the Fourth Judicial Circuit to insure that the Fourth Judicial Circuit Problem–Solving Court Drug and Alcohol Testing Laboratory be properly maintained; and

WHEREAS, Administrative Order No. 2014–01 entered on January 13, 2014, was amended in the First Amended Administrative Order No. 2014–01 entered on May 3, 2017, for the sole purpose of increasing the drug testing fees in Clay County, Florida. The First Amended Administrative Order No. 2014–01, is amended herein for the sole purpose of correcting the order number in the last sentence of this paragraph. All other remaining portions of the First Administrative Order No. 2014–01 are incorporated herein for the convenience of the reader.

NOW THEREFORE, by the authority vested in me as Chief Judge and pursuant to the Florida Rules of Judicial Administration, it is

ORDERED:

(A) That every individual ordered by the Fourth Judicial Circuit Court, Clay County, Florida (the Court), to complete a drug test shall be required to pay a fee of $30.00, or such reduced amount as deemed appropriate by the Court to ensure the ability to pay, with the exception of individuals found to be indigent upon proper application to the Court;

(B) That individuals found to be indigent upon proper application to the Court shall be exempt from payment of this fee;

(C) That individuals who are ordered for testing shall make payment to the Clay County Clerk of Court, which has agreed to issue a receipt to such individuals as proof of payment, that shall, upon presentation at the Fourth Judicial Circuit Problem–Solving Court Drug and Alcohol Testing Laboratory, enable drug testing to be completed;

(D) That agencies executing a Memorandum of Understanding (MOU) with the Fourth Judicial Circuit Problem–Solving Court Drug and Alcohol Testing Laboratory to perform testing at an agreed upon contracted rate shall, after receipt of an invoice, submit a monthly payment (to the Fourth Judicial Circuit Problem–Solving Court Drug and Alcohol Testing Laboratory made payable to "the Duval County Clerk of Court") along with a copy of the invoice, in accordance with the MOU for tests performed pursuant to a Court order or Child Welfare Case Plan;

(E) That all such payments will be deposited by the Duval County Clerk of Court into the existing Drug Testing Revenue Fund, i.e., GL229387 (F750), as maintained by the Duval County Clerk of Court;

(F) That the Duval County Clerk of Court has agreed to maintain separate accounting records for these funds to ensure proper appropriation of all revenues collected. Upon request from the Court Administration, the Duval County Clerk of Court will establish, and maintain a bank account for receipt of these funds, which shall support any required maintenance fees necessary to operate the account;

(G) That this account shall allow for end of fiscal year cash carryover;

(H) That the fees collected will be deposited by the Clerk of Court into this account, less one dollar ($1.00) per drug testing fee as a service charge to be retained by the Clerk;

(I) That the Chief Judge or his designee shall have authority over these funds for use in maintaining the Fourth Judicial Circuit Problem–Solving Court Drug and Alcohol Testing Laboratory and Problem–Solving Court programs to include drug and alcohol testing lab costs, supplies, lab technicians, ongoing training, and other Problem–Solving Court program expenses as approved at the discretion of the Chief Judge or designee; and that such funds shall only be disbursed by the Duval County Clerk of Court upon request by the Chief Judge or said designee.

(J) That the Second Amended Administrative Order 2008–04 filed on January 13, 2014, concerning Assessment and Collection of Drug Testing Fee for Duval County, Florida shall remain in full force and effect; and

(K) That this First Amended Administrative Order No. 2014–01 shall be recorded by the Clerk of the Court, in the Official Records of Clay and Duval Counties, in the State of Florida, and shall take effect immediately and remain in full force and effect until otherwise ordered by the Court.

DONE AND ORDERED in Chambers at Jacksonville, Duval County, Florida, this 10 day of May, 2017.

MARK H. MAHON
CHIEF JUDGE

2013–17 (A1). PEACEFUL DEMONSTRATORS: ESTABLISHMENT OF POLICIES AND LOCATION

IN THE CIRCUIT COURT, FOURTH JUDICIAL CIRCUIT, IN AND FOR DUVAL COUNTY, FLORIDA

AMENDED ADMINISTRATIVE ORDER NO. 2013–17

RE: PEACEFUL DEMONSTRATORS: ESTABLISHMENT OF POLICIES AND LOCATION

WHEREAS, a recent trial of extraordinary public interest attracted demonstrators who gathered in front of the Courthouse in such a disruptive manner that it has become clear that the original Administrative Order No. 2013–17 needs to be amended to address the use of loudspeakers and an obstruction of the front Courthouse steps; and

WHEREAS, during cases of extraordinary public interest, it is anticipated that the limited seating available in the Courtrooms will most likely restrict the number of people who may attend and participate and will impede the ability of those who wish to demonstrate during the trial; and

WHEREAS, procedures are necessary to ensure the safe and orderly use of the Duval County Courthouse and to minimize activities which unreasonably disrupt, interrupt, and interfere with the fair and orderly conduct of court business, and the orderly and peaceful conduct of court business in a neutral forum free of actual or perceived partiality; and

WHEREAS, pursuant to Article V, Section 2(d), Florida Constitution, and section 43.26, Florida Statutes, the chief judge of each judicial circuit is charged with the authority and the power to do what is deemed necessary to promote the prompt and efficient administration of justice; and

WHEREAS, pursuant to the chief judge's constitutional and statutory responsibility for administrative supervision of the courts within the circuit and to create and maintain an organization capable of affecting the efficient, prompt, and proper administration of justice for the citizens of the State, the chief judge is required to exercise direction. See, Fla.R.Jud.Admin. 2.215(b)(2)–(b)(3); and

WHEREAS, these policies and procedures are set forth to protect the public's safety and to encourage peaceful demonstrations in designated areas on the Courthouse lawn, on Courthouse grounds, which, if otherwise left unrestricted, could lead to interference with the sale ingress and egress of persons appearing in Court to exercise their lawful rights; and

WHEREAS, restriction upon expressive conduct and lawful assembly to express grievances outside of the Courthouse is necessary to serve the State's compelling interest to allow unrestricted access to the Courthouse; and

WHEREAS, any such restriction must be narrowly drawn to achieve that end; and

WHEREAS, such regulation is a proper exercise of the Fourth Judicial Circuit's inherent authority to take supervisory and administrative actions necessary to implement its judicial functions; and

WHEREAS, the authority of the courts to punish for contempt is a longstanding and established power and is inherent in all courts as a necessary power to enable all courts to accomplish the purposes for which they were designed; that is, the orderly trial and decision of causes, the enforcement of public order, the prevention of interferences with their proceedings, and the enforcement of the due respect belonging to them as institutions of the country.

NOW THEREFORE, by the authority vested in me as the Chief Judge of the Fourth Judicial Circuit and pursuant to the Florida Rules of Judicial Administration, it is

ORDERED:

1) Purpose: This Administrative Order specifically designates and restricts the areas and manner in which any person may seek to demonstrate, to engage in oral protest, to display a sign to express an opinion as to any subject in any way (including the use of buttons, materials, and t-shirts or any other attire, depicting photographs, faces, images, or words, etc.), or to otherwise express an opinion on any subject on the grounds of the Duval County Courthouse, 501 West Adams Street, Jacksonville, Florida, 32202 ("Courthouse").

2) Designated Area: The areas that are specifically designated for all expressive, restricted conduct are located on the lawn area in front of the Courthouse, facing Adams Street.

3) JSO Authorized to Separate: In an effort to ensure both public safety and the right of all individuals to be heard, the Jacksonville Sheriff's Office is authorized to separate any demonstrators with conflicting points of view to different parts of the restricted area, using barricades or any means as it deems appropriate, to the following areas:

a) *Group One:* located on the Courthouse lawn, on the East side of the sidewalk that leads into the front Courthouse entrance;

b) *Group Two:* located on the Courthouse lawn, on the West side of the sidewalk that leads into the front Courthouse entrance;

4) Interference and Obstruction Not Permitted:

(a) It shall be a violation of this Order for anyone to use a loud-speaker, bull-horn, or sound system of any type in the vicinity of the Courthouse, which is loud enough to be heard inside the Courthouse, as this results in an obstruction of justice, interferes with the professionalism and administration of justice, and causes a distraction, and therefore, an obstruction to the fairness of ongoing hearings and trials, and is an impediment to the Court's business that is being conducted inside the building;

(b) It shall be a violation of this Order for anyone to (1) protest or (2) stand or remain on the front steps of the Courthouse so as to obstruct the entrance area either while any trial is ongoing or during the Court's hours of operation;

(c) It shall be a violation of this Order for anyone to obstruct the entrance or interfere with the rights of any other person to lawfully enter and leave the Duval County Courthouse. If necessary, at the discretion of the Jacksonville

Sheriffs Office (JSO), the sidewalk leading up to the Courthouse may be barricaded for the safety and protection of Courthouse users.

5) Items Prohibited: The following items are prohibited on the Courthouse lawn and Courthouse steps: a) unattended backpacks, bags, containers or purses of any kind; b) chairs; c) coolers; d) alcoholic beverages; e) tents; f) generators; and g) camping gear. The presence of vendors and the selling of any items are also prohibited on the Courthouse lawn.

6) Violators—Cease and Desist: During cases of extraordinary public interest, the JSO is directed to provide a copy of this Administrative Order to individual(s) engaging in activity that violates this Order, and to advise such individual(s) to cease and desist immediately if they wish to move to—or remain on—the Courthouse lawn in order to demonstrate peacefully.

7) Violators Who Fail to Cease and Desist: Anyone who continues to violate this Administrative Order after receiving a copy of this Order and being instructed to cease and desist by law enforcement, may face indirect civil contempt of court proceedings. If found to be in contempt of court, penalties would include confinement, fines, or both. In addition, nothing precludes JSO's authority to arrest anyone for unlawful conduct.

8) The policies and procedures set forth in this Administrative Order, may be changed from lime to time at the suggestion of the JSO's Incident Management Team Operations Section Chief, who is responsible for managing a peaceful demonstration and protecting the Courthouse users.

9) This Amended Administrative Order shall be recorded by the Clerk of the Court, in the Official Records of Duval County, in the State of Florida, shall take effect immediately, and remain in full force and effect unless and until otherwise ordered by the Court.

DONE AND ORDERED in Chambers at Jacksonville, Duval County, Florida, this 8 day of May, 2014.

DONALD R. MORAN, JR.
CHIEF JUDGE

2013–16. GUIDELINES FOR CLERK OF COURT TO DESIGNATE FORECLOSURE CASES AS "ACTIVE" AND "INACTIVE"

IN THE CIRCUIT COURT, FOURTH JUDICIAL CIRCUIT, IN AND FOR DUVAL COUNTY, FLORIDA

ADMINISTRATIVE ORDER NO. 2013–16

RE: GUIDELINES FOR CLERK OF COURT TO DESIGNATE FORECLOSURE CASES AS "ACTIVE" AND "INACTIVE"

WHEREAS, the Fourth Judicial Circuit has experienced a large volume of mortgage foreclosure cases being filed, which has created a backlog of such pending cases ready to proceed to final disposition in most cases; and

WHEREAS, such pending foreclosure cases have advanced through the Court process at varying degrees of speed depending on the preferences of the Plaintiffs–Lenders for reasons motivated by their own interests; and

WHEREAS, the Fourth Judicial Circuit Court has taken control over said foreclosure cases that have been filed or will be filed in the future, in order to process such suits with all deliberate but reasonable speed, consistent with constitutional due process and the Foreclosure Initiative Data Collection Plan approved by the Florida Supreme Court; and

WHEREAS, the Clerks of Court in Duval, Clay, and Nassau County, have always cooperatively worked together hand in hand with the Court to keep a count of the case-loads in each County, in order to allocate sufficient resources therein to manage the current cases, future anticipated cases filed, and a backlog of such cases, and said resources include, but are not limited to: judges, clerks, technology, docketing procedures, and case managers; and

WHEREAS, in the Court's experience, the foreclosure cases can take on a variety of twists and turns, which require the Court to have readily available a listing of active and inactive cases and to be able to designate any case at any time as active or inactive as a result of some action of a party or the Court; and

WHEREAS, it is the strong opinion of the Court and its Judges that only a Judge be permitted to make a legal conclusion that any case is active or inactive for any stated reason, and that the Clerk of Court refrain from such decisions because they are legal decisions rather than administrative or ministerial decisions; and

WHEREAS, the Court is in a better position to make such conclusions after consultation with counsel for the respective parties to any case;

NOW THEREFORE, by the authority vested in me as the Chief Judge of the Fourth Judicial Circuit and pursuant to the Florida Rules of Judicial Administration, it is

ORDERED that:

1. Any foreclosure action and case shall take on an active status classification immediately upon its filing with the Clerk of Court and shall remain in such classification until Final Judgment is entered in the case, or voluntarily dismissed by Plaintiff, or unless otherwise designated by a Court Order, and only by Court Order. Such designations shall not be the prerogative of the Clerk nor within the Clerk's discretion.

2. Any such foreclosure action and case shall be considered removed from active status immediately upon the entry and docketing of a Final Judgment in the Clerk's records, even though a foreclosure sale is set and yet to be completed at some time subsequent to the entry of the Final Judgment, The Clerk shall also remove from active status any case wherein Notice from Voluntary Dismissal is filed by the Plaintiff.

3. If otherwise appropriate for the case, the Court may, by Court Order, remove and transfer from the active status cases to the inactive status cases when any of the following contingencies may occur;

a. Any party to a foreclosure case has filed for bankruptcy and an order staying the action has been entered or applies;

b. Resolution of a foreclosure case requires the resolution of another significantly related case;

c. An interlocutory or final notice of appeal in the case has been filed with any Florida District Court of Appeals or the Florida Supreme Court;

d. A hold is placed on the case while under the Department of Justice (DOJ) document review, but only when the hold is made mandatory by the DOJ;

e. A judge of the Fourth Judicial Circuit enters an Order for any other reason that classifies an active case to inactive status or classifies inactive status to active status.

4. At any time after the entry of Final Judgment, the Court may from time to time, enter an Order that will seek to vacate that Final Judgment, cancel the sale, discharge the lis pendens, dismiss the case, and return the original documents to the lender. When that occurs, the Clerk may, if necessary to carry out its function and the duties of his office, reactivate the case to active status.

5. At any time and for any good and legal cause or reason, and for the purpose of maintaining an accurate record of all pending cases consistent with fulfilling the intent and purpose of the Foreclosure Initiative Data Collection Plan, the Court may, on its own motion, activate or deactivate a case, and the Clerk shall so impose such classification on that case.

6. A case shall not proceed or transfer from inactive status to active status upon the mere filing of any pleading by a pro se litigant or counsel without first obtaining a Court Order. Any party seeking reactivation shall be informed of a requirement of a Court Order by the Clerk upon attempting to file for reactivation.

7. This Administrative Order shall be recorded by the Clerk of the Court, in the Official Records of Duval County, in the State of Florida, and shall take effect immediately and remain in full force and effect unless and until otherwise ordered by the Court.

DONE AND ORDERED in Chambers at Jacksonville, Duval County, Florida, this 3 day of Dec., 2013.

DONALD R. MORAN, JR.
CHIEF JUDGE

2013–14. CREATION OF DIVISION CR–V IN DUVAL COUNTY FOR A VETERANS TREATMENT COURT

IN THE CIRCUIT COURT OF THE FOURTH JUDICIAL CIRCUIT, IN AND FOR DUVAL COUNTY FLORIDA

ADMINISTRATIVE ORDER NO. 2013–14

IN RE: CREATION OF DIVISION CR–V IN DUVAL COUNTY FOR A VETERANS TREATMENT COURT

WHEREAS, a Veterans Treatment Court in Duval County has been established;

WHEREAS, at this time, there is a need to assign a dedicated Division for the Veterans Treatment Court in Duval County;

WHEREAS, there is a need for an administrative order creating such division;

THEREFORE, by the authority vested in me as Chief Judge and pursuant to the Florida Rules of Judicial Administration, it is hereby

ORDERED that:

(A) A separate division for a Veterans Treatment Court shall be created in Duval County, and such Division shall be designated as Division "CR–V".

(B) This Administrative Order shall be recorded by the Clerk of the Court, in the Official Records of Duval County, in the State of Florida, shall take effect immediately, and shall remain in full force and effect unless and until otherwise ordered by the Court.

DONE AND ORDERED in Chambers at Jacksonville, Duval County, Florida, this 12 day of November, 2013

DONALD R. MORAN, JR
CHIEF JUDGE

2013–13. MEDIATION IN CIRCUIT CIVIL CASES DUVAL COUNTY

IN THE CIRCUIT COURT, FOURTH JUDICIAL CIRCUIT, IN AND FOR DUVAL COUNTY

ADMINISTRATIVE ORDER NO. 2013–13

RE: MEDIATION IN CIRCUIT CIVIL CASES DUVAL COUNTY

WHEREAS, the courts and litigants have been greatly assisted by the mediation process in resolving complex civil cases, and;

WHEREAS, mediation has proven to be effective in reducing the rising costs associated with civil litigation, and;

WHEREAS, the timing of mediation is important to achieving successful results, and;

WHEREAS, mediators in the Fourth Judicial Circuit have been customarily appointed when a case is set for trial without a separate order of referral, and;

WHEREAS, mediators appointed by the Court serve as officers of the Court;

NOW THEREFORE, by the authority vested in me as Chief Judge of the Fourth Judicial Circuit and pursuant to the Florida Rules of Judicial Administration, it is

ORDERED:

1. Setting Mediation: The Court will appoint a qualified mediator in accordance with Rule 1.1720(j) of the Florida Rules of Civil Procedure in all circuit court civil mediation cases, except those cases excluded by Rule 1.710(b) and foreclosure cases, in accordance with § 44.302, Florida Statutes, and Rule 1.700, Florida Rules of Civil Procedure, on or before the case is set for trial, unless mediation is determined by the court to be inappropriate or unnecessary. The "Order Setting Case for Jury (or Non–jury) Trial and for Pre–Trial Conference and Requiring Matters to be Completed Prior to Pre–Trial Conference" shall include an order of referral to mediation and appointment of the mediator.

2. Date, Time, Length, and Location: The appointed mediator shall be responsible for conferring with counsel (or unrepresented parties) for scheduling the mediation conference. Once the mediation is scheduled, the mediator shall send a Notice of Mediation to the parties confirming the date, time, length, and location of the mediation. The Notice of Mediation shall also include the terms of compensation for the mediator as required by paragraph 7 of this Order. The mediator shall be authorized to resolve scheduling conflicts without further order including rescheduling the mediation conference provided the mediation is concluded before the date of the final pretrial conference.

3. Service of Mediation Order: The appointed mediator shall serve a copy of this Administrative Order with the Notice of Mediation.

4. Attendance: The personal attendance of all parties or their representatives, counsel for the parties, and insurance representatives is required, unless excused by prior agreement of all parties and/or counsel or by leave of Court, Parties and their representatives shall appear at mediation with complete authority to resolve the matters in dispute without further consultation, as defined in 1.720(b)–(d), Florida Rules of Civil Procedure. A Certification of Authority shall be filed in accordance with 1.720(e), Florida Rules of Civil Procedure.

5. Notice to Lienholders: Any party who has knowledge of the existence of a lien, such as worker's compensation lien, medical lien, or other lien with rights of subrogation, shall give the lienholder reasonable notice of the date, time, and place of the mediation conference. Appearance of a lienholder is not mandatory and the absence of a lienholder is not grounds to continue the mediation unless agreed to by the parties or ordered by the Court.

6. Position Statements: No fewer than 72 hours prior to the mediation conference, each party shall furnish to the mediator, a copy to all counsel involved, a statement outlining the party's position, the issues involved, and the latest settlement negotiations, and designating the persons who will appear at the mediation conference. Parties and counsel may attach other documents to a position statement. Position statements shall not be filed with the court. Parties are encouraged to review § 44.405, Florida Statutes, regarding the confidentiality of discussions and statements made at mediation.

7. Terms of Compensation: The mediator shall fully set forth the terms of her/his requested compensation, including hourly fees, preparation fees (if any), costs, and cancellation or rescheduling fees in the Notice of Mediation required in paragraph 2 of this Order. Any party objecting to the terms of compensation shall file an objection with the court, and serve all parties and the mediator no later than 15 days from the date of service of the Notice of Mediation, Any party making an objection to the terms of compensation shall immediately place the matter on the court's calendar for a hearing. Attorneys shall advise their clients of the mediator's fee structure including hourly fees, preparation fees, cancellation fees, and costs before the commencement of the mediation. Although the obligation to pay mediation fees is that of the client and not the attorney, see Bauer v. Hardy, 651 So. 2d 748 (Fla. 1st DCA 1995), attorneys shall make a diligent effort to ensure the client's payment of the fees.

Unless otherwise ordered by the Court, or mutually agreed to by the parties and the mediator, all mediation charges are to be equally divided between or among the parties. If more than one party is represented by the same counsel, then those parties will be deemed to be "one party" for the purpose of the mediator's charges.

8. Sanctions: Failure to pay mediator's fees and costs may result in the imposition of additional fees, costs, and other sanctions as determined by the Court. Sanctions may include dismissing the case, striking pleadings, entering a default, removing the case from the trial calendar, assessing additional attorney's fees and costs, or imposing any reasonable punishment deemed necessary by the court.

If a party fails to appear at a duly noticed mediation conference without good cause, the court, upon motion or *sua sponte*, may impose sanctions including an award of mediation fees, attorneys' fees, and costs against the party failing to appear.

9. Service of Notice: Service of any notice, pleading, or document required herein shall be made in accordance with Rule 2.516 of the Florida Rules of Judicial Administration.

10. Governing Law: All mediations shall be conducted in accordance with Rules 1.700–1.730 of the Florida Rules of Civil Procedure and Chapter 44 of the Florida Statutes.

11. This Administrative Order supersedes Amended Administrative Order No. 2004–6 and shall be recorded by the Clerk of the Court in the Official Records of Duval County, Florida, and **shall take effect on January 1, 2014**, and remain in full force and effect unless and until otherwise ordered by the Court.

ENTERED at Jacksonville, Duval County, Florida, this 6 day of December, 2013.

DONALD R. MORAN, JR.
CHIEF JUDGE

2013–11. CREATION OF DIVISION CR–V IN CLAY COUNTY FOR A VETERANS TREATMENT COURT

IN THE CIRCUIT COURT OF THE FOURTH JUDICIAL CIRCUIT, IN AND FOR CLAY COUNTY FLORIDA

ADMINISTRATIVE ORDER NO. 2013–11

IN RE: CREATION OF DIVISION CR–V IN CLAY COUNTY FOR A VETERANS TREATMENT COURT

WHEREAS, a Veterans Treatment Court in Clay County has been established;

WHEREAS, at this time, there is a need to assign a designated division to the Veterans Treatment Court in Clay County;

WHEREAS, there is a need for an administrative order creating such division;

THEREFORE, by the authority vested in me as Chief Judge and pursuant to the Florida Rules of Judicial Administration, it is hereby

ORDERED that:

(A) A separate division for a Veterans Treatment Court shall be created in Clay County, and such Division shall be designated as Division "CR–V".

(B) This Administrative Order shall be recorded by the Clerk of the Court, in the Official Records of Duval County, in the State of Florida, shall take effect October 1, 2013, and shall remain in full force and effect unless and until otherwise ordered by the Court.

DONE AND ORDERED in Chambers at Jacksonville, Duval County, Florida, this 12 day of September, 2013.

DONALD R. MORAN, JR.
CHIEF JUDGE

2013–10. CREATION OF DIVISION CR–Y IN CLAY COUNTY FOR AN ADULT DRUG COURT

IN THE CIRCUIT COURT OF THE FOURTH JUDICIAL CIRCUIT, IN AND FOR CLAY COUNTY FLORIDA

ADMINISTRATIVE ORDER NO. 2013–10

IN RE: CREATION OF DIVISION CR–Y IN CLAY COUNTY FOR AN ADULT DRUG COURT

WHEREAS, an Adult Drug Court has been established in Clay County, Florida, since 2001, but there has not been a designated division assigned to the Adult Drug Court;

WHEREAS, at this time, there is a need to assign a designated division to the Adult Drug Court in Clay County;

WHEREAS, there is a need for an administrative order creating such division;

THEREFORE, by the authority vested in me as Chief Judge and pursuant to the Florida Rules of Judicial Administration, it is hereby

ORDERED that:

(A) A separate Division for an Adult Drug Court in Clay County is hereby created, and such Division shall be designated as Division "CR–Y".

(B) The Clerk of the Circuit Court in and for Clay County shall transfer all active Adult Drug Court cases from the currently assigned Circuit Court Divisions to the Adult Drug Court Division "CR–Y" no later than October 1, 2013.

(C) This Administrative Order shall be recorded by the Clerk of the Court, in the Official Records of Duval County, in the State of Florida, shall take effect October 1, 2013, and shall remain in full force and effect unless and until otherwise ordered by the Court.

DONE AND ORDERED in Chambers at Jacksonville, Duval County, Florida, this 12 day of September, 2013.

DONALD R. MORAN, JR.
CHIEF JUDGE

2013–09. ESTABLISHMENT OF THE LOCAL PROFESSIONALISM PANEL

IN THE CIRCUIT COURT, FOURTH JUDICIAL CIRCUIT, IN AND FOR DUVAL, CLAY AND NASSAU COUNTIES, FLORIDA

ADMINISTRATIVE ORDER NO. 2013–09

RE: ESTABLISHMENT OF THE LOCAL PROFESSIONALISM PANEL

WHEREAS, on June 6, 2013, the Supreme Court of Florida issued its SC13–688, in which it adopted the Code for Resolving Professionalism Complaints and directed the Chief Judge of each circuit in Florida to create a local professionalism panel to receive, screen and act upon complaints of unprofessional conduct and to resolve those complaints informally, if possible, or refer them to The Florida Bar if necessary;

WHEREAS, on April 29, 1998, Chief Justice Gerald Kogan entered an Amended Administrative Order of the Supreme Court of Florida, directing the chief judge of each Circuit in Florida to establish a local bench/bar committee as well as a committee on professionalism with an intended purpose to "enhance communication, constructive problem solving, respect, and courtesy between judges and lawyers" as well as to improve the administration of justice;

WHEREAS, on July 6, 1998, the Fourth Judicial Circuit entered Administrative Order No. 98–9, establishing the joint Professionalism and Bench/Bar Committee;

WHEREAS, in or about 2001, the Professionalism Committee formed the Professionalism Review Program that created a Panel which involved an informal process that would review referrals and, in essence, encourage attorneys to comply with the "Ideals and Standards of Professionalism" promulgated by The Florida Bar and The Jacksonville Bar Association's "Professionalism Guidelines" in an informal, non-punitive, educational and constructive manner;

WHEREAS, for more than a decade, the Professionalism Committee, The Jacksonville Bar Association, and the Fourth Judicial Circuit have worked together to maintain an active Professionalism Committee and to assist in counseling members of the Bar who engage in conduct inconsistent with the Ideals and Standards or with the Professionalism Guidelines;

WHEREAS, in accordance with the Supreme Court of Florida Opinion SC13–688, which was recently issued on June 6, 2013, this Court sets forth new guidelines and procedures for the Professionalism Panel to follow.

NOW THEREFORE, by the authority vested in me as the Chief Judge of the Fourth Judicial Circuit and pursuant to the Florida Rules of Judicial Administration, it is

ORDERED:

A) Establishment of Local Professionalism Panel. The Professionalism Review Program is reconstituted as the "Fourth Judicial Circuit's Local Professionalism Panel" ("Local Professionalism Panel") in accordance with the Supreme Court of Florida Opinion SC13–688.

(1) *Panel Members:* The Local Professionalism Panel shall be composed of the Chairperson (who will contemporaneously serve as the Chairperson of the Professionalism Committee) and up to five (5) members of the Jacksonville Bar Association (JBA), who shall be selected by the Local Professionalism Panel's Chairperson and the President of the JBA with the approval of the Chief Judge, after consultation with the Administrative Judges in the Fourth Judicial Circuit. The Chief Judge may participate as a Local Professionalism Panel member as well.

The Chairperson may designate a substitute from the JBA's Professionalism Committee when necessary.

B) Purpose of Local Professionalism Panel. The purpose of the Local Professionalism Panel is to address attorneys who have conducted themselves in a way that is inconsistent with the standards of professionalism (as set forth in the Oath of Admission to The Florida Bar, The Florida Bar Creed of Professionalism, The Florida Bar "Ideals and Goals of

Professionalism, the Rules Regulating The Florida Bar, the decisions of the Florida Supreme Court, and The Jacksonville Bar Association's "Professionalism Guidelines"—hereinafter, *Ideals and Standards*). The attorneys are to be addressed in an informal, non-punitive, educational and constructive manner.

C) Procedures. The Local Professionalism Panel shall generally follow these procedures:

(1) *Referrals from Judicial Officers or Quasi Judicial Officers:*

(a) When any Judge, Magistrate or Traffic Hearing Officer within the Fourth Judicial Circuit determines that an attorney has engaged in conduct inconsistent with the *Ideals and Standards*, the matter may be referred to the Local Professionalism Panel through the Chief Judge.

(b) Process: The Chairperson of the Local Professionalism Panel may address a letter on behalf of such Panel, to the Respondent attorney, inviting that attorney to meet with the Local Professionalism Panel on a date and time specified.

(2) *Referrals from Attorney & Non–Attorney:*

(a) By an Attorney: If an attorney observes conduct on the part of another attorney that he or she believes, in good faith, is inconsistent with the *Ideals and Standards*, the (Referral) attorney may request that the Local Professionalism Panel consider the matter by completing the Referral Form and submitting it to the Local Professionalism Panel's Chairperson through The JBA.

(b) By a Non–Attorney: If a non-attorney person is directly and adversely affected by conduct on the part of an attorney that is inconsistent with the *Ideals and Standards*, that person may request that the Local Professionalism Panel consider the matter by completing the Referral Form and submitting it to the Local Professionalism Panel's Chairperson through The JBA.

(c) Page Limits for Referral from Attorney & Non–Attorney: The request shall be limited to two (2) pages, exclusive of the exhibits.

(3) *Referrals from The Florida Bar's Attorney Consumer Assistance Program (ACAP).* The Local Professionalism Panel may accept referrals sent by ACAP.

(4) *Process for Referrals from Attorneys, Non–Attorneys and ACAP.* Upon receipt of a referral by an attorney, non-attorney, or ACAP, the Chairperson of the Local Professionalism Panel:

- shall review the request, may consult with the other Local Professionalism Panel members and, if the matter is referred to the Local Professionalism Panel, the Chairperson shall address a letter to the Respondent attorney that:

(a) notifies the Respondent attorney of the referral;

(b) may request a response; and

(c) may invite the Respondent attorney to meet with the Local Professionalism Panel on a date and time specified.

D. General Matters.

(1) *Letters Sent by Local Professionalism Panel:* Any letter sent by the Local Professionalism Panel to a Respondent attorney, requesting that an attorney appear before the Panel, shall identify the conduct alleged to be inconsistent with the *Ideals and Standards.* The letter shall also advise the Respondent attorney that the Local Professionalism Panel meeting is a non-disciplinary proceeding. A complete reference to the citations of the *Ideals and Standards* (provided above) shall be included in the letter.

(2) *Panel Meetings:* The Chairperson alone or the Chairperson together with the Local Professionalism Panel members may meet with the Respondent attorney at the date and time specified in the letter. The purpose of the meeting shall be to discuss with the attorney the conduct and ways the attorney should act in the future, if necessary, to be consistent with the *Ideals and Standards.* The Chairperson may send a letter summarizing the Local Professionalism Panel's discussions to the Respondent attorney.

(3) *Forty–Five (45) Pays to Resolve:* Local Professionalism Panel members should endeavor to resolve all referrals within forty-five (45) days of receipt from The JBA.

(4) *Resolution:* Upon conferring with each other and conducting an investigation, the Local Professionalism Panel members involved may proceed and resolve the issues in the following non-punitive, educational and constructive manner to provide the Respondent with an incentive for self–improvement:

(a) the Chairperson may issue an oral or written decision to the Respondent;

(b) the Local Professionalism Panel, in its discretion, may also refer the Respondent to The Jacksonville Bar Association's Mentorship program or may communicate with an assisting mentor of the Respondent;

(c) the Local Professionalism Panel may refer the Respondent to "The Florida Bar's Ethics School", which is an eight (8) hour ethics course, or any other course(s) deemed appropriate;

(d) the Local Professionalism Panel may advise the Respondent attorney with recommendations that will assist the attorney in the future;

(e) the Local Professionalism Panel, in appropriate circumstances, may refer the Respondent to "Fla, Inc." or other similar, appropriate program(s), for assistance with drug, alcohol and/or emotional problems;

(f) pursuant to Section 2.1 of the Supreme Court Opinion SC13–688, the Local Professionalism Panel has the discretion to direct any referrals to The Florida Bar Attorney Consumer Assistance Program (ACAP) depending upon the nature and severity of the referral; or

(g) the Local Professionalism Panel may form any other such solutions that the Panel may deem as appropriate or necessary.

Depending upon the circumstances involved, Respondent's failure to follow the recommendations of the Local Professionalism Panel may be a basis for its referral to ACAP.

(5) *Confidentiality:* All records regarding referrals to the Local Professionalism Panel will be handled in the same manner as set forth in the Supreme Court Opinion SC13–688 and as outlined in Rule 3–7.1 of *The Rules Regulating the Florida Bar* regarding the confidentiality of disciplinary investigations and proceedings.

(a) Records Retention: All records will be destroyed within thirty (30) days of the conclusion of the process and after the Respondent has completed all of the Local Professionalism Panel's recommendations.

(b) Statement of Confidentiality: all Local Professionalism Panel members, the referring attorney, and the Respondent shall be required to sign a statement acknowledging that:

1. all information disclosed during the Local Professionalism Panel process is confidential and shall not be disclosed to anyone except other Local Professionalism Panel members, the referring attorney, or the Respondent; and

2. the Local Professionalism Panel is a voluntary, informal program which is intended to be non-punitive, educational and constructive; furthermore, participation and successful completion of all recommendations from the Panel shall not result in the imposition of sanctions or discipline.

(6) All other Administrative Orders, including Amended Administrative Order No. 98–12, that have been previously entered, addressing the same subject matter, are hereby vacated and superseded.

(7) This Administrative Order No. 2013–09 shall be recorded by the Clerk of the Court, in the Official Records of Duval County, in the State of Florida, shall take effect immediately, and remain in full force and effect unless and until otherwise ordered by the Court.

DONE AND ORDERED in Chambers at Jacksonville, Duval County, Florida, this 19 day of August, 2013.

DONALD R. MORAN, JR.
CHIEF JUDGE

2013–08. MEDIA & TECHNOLOGICAL COVERAGE OF CASES OF EXTRAORDINARY PUBLIC INTEREST

IN THE CIRCUIT COURT, FOURTH JUDICIAL CIRCUIT IN AND FOR DUVAL, CLAY AND NASSAU COUNTIES, FLORIDA

ADMINISTRATIVE ORDER NO. 2013–08

IN RE: MEDIA & TECHNOLOGICAL COVERAGE OF CASES OF EXTRAORDINARY PUBLIC INTEREST

WHEREAS, pursuant to Rule 2.450, Rules of Judicial Administration, on April 23, 2013, the Fourth Judicial Circuit entered the Second Amended Administrative Order No. 92–02, governing media and technological coverage of judicial proceedings, which remains in full force and effect; and

WHEREAS, the Second Amended Administrative Order No. 92–02, was entered subject to this Court's authority (1) to control the conduct of proceedings before the Court, (2) to ensure decorum and prevent distractions, and (3) to ensure the fair administration of justice in this Court's pending cases, in accordance with certain standards for the technological coverage of judicial proceedings as set forth by the Florida Supreme Court in Rule 2.450, Rules of Judicial Administration; and

WHEREAS, in cases of extraordinary public interest that draw national, and sometimes international, public interest to proceedings, at times certain additional procedures and special accommodations as set forth herein become necessary to ensure the public full access to the Courts without compromising the right of any party to a fair and orderly trial; and

WHEREAS, pursuant to Article V, Section 2(d), Florida Constitution, section 43.26, Florida Statutes, and Rule 2.215(b), Florida Rules of Judicial Administration, the chief judge of each judicial circuit is charged with the authority and the power to do everything necessary to promote the fair, prompt and efficient administration of justice and the regulation and use of all court facilities, including Courtrooms; furthermore, Rule 2.450, Florida Rules of Judicial Administration governs the use of technology in judicial proceedings and vests the presiding judge with broad authority to control the conduct of proceedings before the court, maintain decorum, prevent distractions, and ensure the safety and security of persons and property; and

WHEREAS, a presiding Judge has the authority to determine whether any case is of extraordinary public interest and whether to invoke the procedures set forth in this Order.

NOW THEREFORE, by the authority vested in me as Chief Judge of the Fourth Judicial Circuit and pursuant to the Florida Rules of Judicial Administration, it is

ORDERED that the following policies and procedures will be set forth in this Circuit in cases of extraordinary public interest:

I. GUIDELINES FOR MEDIA COVERAGE OF PUBLIC INTEREST PROCEEDINGS

A. Media Defined. Traditional media such as newspaper, television and radio are relatively easy to identify and define. However, with the advent of the Internet, a new type of media has developed which has not yet been addressed by Court rule or by the Florida Supreme Court. Other Circuits in Florida have successfully defined this "new media," which are primarily Internet-based and not generally directly associated with television, radio or newspaper. The Court hereby adopts this definition and defines the "new media" as follows:

> An online organization that: (1) was a previously established, independent site that contains regularly updated original news content beyond links, forums, troubleshooting tips and reader contributions; (2) provides content that is thoroughly reviewed by an independent editor before publication; and (3) has previously covered the judicial branch for the 6 months immediately prior to the case of extraordinary public interest. Fan sites, web logs and personal web sites do not qualify as "new media."

It is the responsibility of the requesting online organization to show proof that it meets the definition of "new media." In order for members of the "new media" to obtain media credentials, an organization must provide: (1) links to two bylined articles clearly displaying publication title and publication within the past six months of the date of request; (2) either a copy of the current masthead or a business card with the name, title and media outlet's logo or a copy of the online publication's home page and the masthead page with the media's representative's name and title appearing in an editorial capacity or an official letter or assignment from the media outlet; and (3) proof that the judicial branch or the case is being covered for at least the six months previous to the proceeding/trial. Decisions of the Media Committee made pursuant to Section II (A) and (B), and related hereto, shall be presented to the Chief Judge for his consideration,

B. Photo IDs/Media Credentials.

1) Official Court-issued media credentials will be distributed for the Fourth Judicial Circuit to media representatives covering any case of extraordinary public interest. There will be no charge to media representatives for the issuance of this official Court-issued media credential. However, if any media representative requires a replacement of an official Court-issued media credential, the requesting media representative will be required to pay a replacement cost of Ten Dollars ($10.00).

2) All media representatives must display official Court-issued media credentials with photo I.D. at all times while inside the Courthouse. At no time shall any media representative transfer or loan any official Court-issued media credential to any other person for any reason whatsoever. The transferring or loaning of an official Court-issued media credential will result in the revocation of media privileges for the violating media representative for the duration of the trial.

C. Distribution of Information to the Media. All information regarding a case of extraordinary public interest case will be distributed to the media through the Trial Court Administrator/Public Information Officer and will be posted on the Fourth Judicial Circuit's Website.

D. Courtroom Seating and the Media Room.

1) *Media Credential and Seating Pass Required*: Not everyone who wishes to be present during the proceedings may be accommodated in the Courtroom. Specified Courtroom seating will be provided on a limited basis for those possessing a Court-issued credential AND a seating pass. In cases of extraordinary public interest, half of the Courtroom seating will be reserved for reporters and media personnel, except that there will be space specifically reserved to seat family members (or their designees) on the front row on both the right side and the left side of the Courtroom.

2) *Procedure for Assignment of Seats*: Unless otherwise specified by the presiding Judge, seating for media representatives is to be determined by the Court. Media representatives are required to prominently display official Court-issued media credentials at all times while inside the Courtroom. Additional seats, if any, may be made available to the media on a first-come, first-serve basis. Further, one (1) seat will be made available for educational purposes, to be used by students of area or regional law schools.

3) *Jessie–Lynne Kerr Media Room*: In Duval County, the "Jessie–Lynne Kerr–Media Room" ("the Media Room") is located on the second floor of the Courthouse. The Media Room will be open during regular business hours and for extended hours when the court proceedings that are being covered are in session. The Media Room is available to all media representatives with valid press credentials. The Media Room will accommodate monitors and other equipment provided by the media to permit coverage of proceedings by media representatives who are unable to obtain seating in the Courtroom.

E. Prior Arrangements Required. Unless prohibited because of an emergency hearing or otherwise lacking sufficient notice to permit timely compliance herewith, prior arrangements must be made with the Trial Court Administrator and the JSO Courthouse Security Manager (or their designees) at least two (2) business days before the court proceeding for the Courtroom to be made available to the media at a prearranged time, before the proceeding, for the determination and proper location and installation of necessary equipment in accordance with this Administrative Order. Cable lay out and placement, if any, shall be at the direction of the Trial Court Administrator and the Jacksonville Sheriff's Office's Courthouse Security Manager or their designees, and shall not present a safety or security hazard.

F. Equipment and Personnel.

1) Not more than one (1) portable television camera, operated by not more than one (1) camera person, shall be permitted in any court proceeding.

2) Not more than one (1) still photographer, using not more than two (2) still cameras, shall be permitted in any court proceeding.

3) Not more than one (1) audio system for radio broadcast purposes shall be permitted in any court proceeding.

4) Unless prohibited because of an emergency hearing or otherwise lacking sufficient notice to permit timely compliance herewith, any request for additional cameras or other media equipment must be presented to the Chief Judge no later than two (2) business days before the court proceeding intended to be covered by the media.

5) If no technically-suitable audio system exists in the Courtroom, microphones and related wiring essential for media purposes—if any—shall be unobtrusive and shall be located in places designated in advance of any proceeding by the Chief Judge in Duval County or the Administrative Judge in Clay and Nassau Counties in accordance with the "General Terms" in Section III, *infra*.

6) In the event that media equipment of any kind or sort mars or otherwise damages the Courthouse or any of its furnishings, it shall be the sole responsibility of the media organization that caused said damage to pay for the appropriate repair(s) thereof. Further, until such time as the damage is repaired, or acceptable arrangements are made with the Chief Judge for the appropriate and timely repair of the damage, all equipment of the news organization causing the damage will be excluded from all proceedings.

7) Any "pooling" arrangements among the media shall be the sole responsibility of the media. In the absence of advance media agreement on disputed equipment or personnel issues, the presiding Judge shall exclude all equipment belonging to the contesting media representatives from a proceeding. See Section II, *infra*.

8) The pooling camera positioned within the Courtroom shall connect to the media panels located in the rear of the Courtroom to facilitate pooling capabilities for all media outlets not present within the Courtroom. Those media representatives obtaining the pool feed shall do so in the Media Room or other location specified by the Chief Judge. When a live feed of Court proceedings is desired by any media outlet, unless prohibited because of an emergency hearing or otherwise lacking sufficient notice to permit timely compliance herewith, such arrangements must be made through the Trial

Court Administrator and the Jacksonville Sheriff's Office Courthouse Security Manager (or their designees) at least two (2) business days before the court proceeding, in accordance with paragraph I.(E), Prior Arrangements Required, *supra.*[1]

G. Use of Equipment Sound and Light Criteria.

1) *No Coverage While Court in Recess*: As soon as Court ends any proceeding or goes into recess (i.e., whenever Court is not in session), all audio, photographic and electronic equipment (including television cameras, still cameras and microphones), must be turned off immediately and remain off until Court begins session once again.

2) *No Distraction by Sound or Light*: Only television, photographic, audio and electronic equipment that does not produce distracting sound or light shall be used to cover Court proceedings.

3) *Laptops*: Media representatives using laptop computers or any other electronic devices to provide coverage through Internet or social media websites shall ensure such laptop computers or electronic devices do not produce any noise when in use. Silence is required to ensure such coverage does not distract the jury, lawyers, or Courtroom staff from the proceedings. Use of laptop computers in the Courtroom is permitted provided that they operate silently on the lap of the user and do not take up additional seating space. Laptops must operate on battery power. Cabling of extension cords and power supplies is prohibited in the Courtroom.

4) *Duty of Media*: It shall be the affirmative duty of media personnel to ensure that the equipment sought to be used meets the sound and light criteria. A failure to do so shall preclude its use.

5) *No Artificial Lights*: No artificial lighting device of any kind shall be used in connection with the television camera. With the concurrence of (a) the Chief Judge, in consultation with the Jacksonville Sheriff's Office Courthouse Security Manager or his designee in Duval County or (b) the Administrative Judge in Clay and Nassau Counties in accordance with the "General Terms" in Section III, *infra*, modifications and additions may be made in light sources existing in the facility, provided such modifications or additions are installed and maintained without public expense.

H. Location of Equipment and Personnel.

1) *Television Equipment*: Television camera equipment shall be positioned in such location in the Courtroom or at the Courthouse as shall be designated by (a) the Chief Judge, in consultation with the Trial Court Administrator and the Jacksonville Sheriff's Office Courthouse Security Manager or their designee in Duval County or (b) the Administrative Judge in Clay and Nassau Counties in accordance with the "General Terms" on the last page herein. The area designated shall provide reasonable access to coverage. If and when areas remote from the Courthouse that permit reasonable access to coverage are provided, all television cameras and audio equipment shall be positioned only in such areas. Video recording equipment that is not a component part of a television camera shall be located in an area remote from the Courthouse property,

2) *Still Cameras*: A still camera photographer shall position himself or herself in such location in the Courtroom as shall be designated by (a) the Chief Judge, in consultation with the Jacksonville Sheriff's Office Courthouse Security Manager or his designee in Duval County or (b) the Administrative Judge in Clay and Nassau Counties in accordance with the "General Terms" in Section III, *infra.* Once established in a shooting position, the photographer shall not be permitted to move about in order to obtain photographs of Court proceedings.

3) *Portable Systems*: Use of portable signal distribution systems (e.g. portable microwave systems) is prohibited unless prior authorization is obtained from the Court Technology Officer.

I. Media Representatives' Appearance and Movement During Proceedings.

1) *Boundaries*: No person shall enter the well of the Courtroom or place a recording device, of any kind or sort, inside the well or on the well partition of the Courtroom at any time without the express permission of the presiding Judge. Media personnel may not cover "side bar" or "bench" conferences.

2) *Attire*: All media representatives, including reporters, video camera operators, and still photographers, at all times shall be appropriately attired. Long pants and a collared shirt are required for all men. Shirttails must be tucked in at all times while such media representatives are within the Duval County Courthouse. Long pants or a skirt with an appropriate shirt or blouse are required for all women.

3) *Cell Phones and Electronic Photography or Recording Devices*: The use of cell phone cameras or any other photographic or recording electronic device—of any kind or sort—is absolutely prohibited. No media representative at any time for any reason may photograph or record any occurrence in the Courtroom, except by the means provided in I.(H), *supra.* Media are allowed to use their cell phones in the Courtroom only for sending and receiving written, electronic information for business purposes and only if they are used in such a way as not to disrupt or disturb the proceedings. While Court is in session, cell phones shall not be used for telephone calls. All cell phones, pagers, and electronic devices must be turned off or switched to silent mode. The privilege of cell phone use may be revoked at any time if such use becomes disruptive in any way.

4) *No Chewing Gum, Food or Drink*: No chewing gum, food or beverage shall be permitted in the Courtroom.

5) *Set–Up and Removal of Equipment*: News media video, photographic, audio or electronic equipment shall not be placed in, or removed from, the Courtroom except before commencement or after adjournment of proceedings each day, or during a recess.

6) *Equipment Changes*: Television cameras, still cameras and lenses, and all related equipment shall **not** be changed within a Courtroom except during a recess in the proceeding.

7) *No Movement*: All media representatives shall act so as not to call attention to themselves and shall not move about in the Courtroom while proceedings are in session. Microphones or video recording equipment, once positioned, shall not be moved during the pendency of the proceedings. Media personnel should refrain from leaving the Courtroom while Court is in session.

8) *Communication During Session*: Further, media representatives shall at no time endeavor to communicate with any

lawyer, party or Courtroom staff while any Courtroom proceedings are in session.

9) *No Disruption*: Proceedings shall not be disrupted. Visible and audible comments of any kind by anyone during Court proceedings, and provocative or uncivil behavior within the Courthouse at any time will not be tolerated. There shall be no gestures, facial expressions, or the like, suggesting approval or disapproval during the proceedings.

10) *No Distractions*: The Courtrooms and related interior court space in any county Courthouse, including jury rooms and Courthouse hallways, are to be used to conduct judicial proceedings in an efficient and dignified manner. Use of these facilities for distracting, non-judicial purposes, such as a backdrop to a news story, promotion, broadcast or advertisement is inappropriate. Therefore, special access to these areas is prohibited without express permission from the Trial Court Administrator, the Chief Judge, or his designee.

11) *Viewing Outside*: For Court proceedings held outside of the Courthouse, such as jury viewings of the scene of the crime, the media shall comply with the instructions of the presiding Judge and the Jacksonville Sheriff's Office.

12) *Blocking Vehicles, Traffic and Walkways*: Media cabling and equipment cannot block vehicle lanes or walkways at any Courthouse facility. The Trial Court Administrator or the Jacksonville Sheriff's Office should be contacted for special directives that may apply to a specific Court proceeding.

13) *Location of Media Tents, Production Trucks, Trailers, Generators, etc.*: Parking or placing anything on the Courthouse lawn (within the streets that border the Courthouse property) is absolutely prohibited. All vehicles, trucks and media tents must be parked at a location and in a manner designated by the City of Jacksonville.

J. Location of Media Interviews.

1) Should media representatives wish to interview any person, such interview shall be conducted only: (a) in the Media Room; (b) at a location otherwise designated and provided within the Courthouse; or (c) on grounds off the Courthouse property.

2) No interviews will be permitted in the first floor atrium of the Courthouse, or in any hallways, Courtrooms or any other areas on any floor of the Courthouse, unless expressly authorized.

3) To prevent interference with Court proceedings and protect an interested party's rights, no interviews shall be permitted in the presence of the jury or any potential juror. Moreover, no interviews shall be permitted to unreasonably interfere with the safety, security, or movement of persons in any of the areas allowed for interviews.

K. Protecting Confidentiality and Privileged Communication.

1) *Private Conferences*: To protect the attorney-client privilege and the effective right to counsel, there shall be no audio pickup or broadcast of conferences that occur in the Courtroom or elsewhere in the Courthouse between attorneys and their clients, between co-counsel of a client, or between counsel and the presiding Judge held at the bench or at side bar. Media personnel may not cover any side bar conference by any means whatsoever. Further, no person shall enter the well of the Courtroom or place a recording device inside the well of the Courtroom at any time without the express permission of the presiding Judge.

2) *Broadcast Delay*: Delay in broadcasting live feed is the sole responsibility of the media personnel and reporters so as to avoid the sudden, unexpected publication of profanity; repulsive, offensive or gruesome photographs; or unredacted documents that may contain confidential or sensitive information.

3) *Jurors and Potential Jurors*: During the pendency of any matter, jurors and potential jurors shall not be recorded or photographed at any time in any manner. Further, the identity of any juror and potential juror shall not be revealed to the public in any way or by any means whatsoever, or at any time during the trial without prior leave of Court.

In cases of extraordinary public interest, it is especially important to secure the identity of those who are called to be in the *potential* jury pool as well as those who are ultimately chosen to serve as a juror, in order to protect the safety of those citizens. Sometimes these types of cases are lengthy and controversial. All jurors and potential jurors are sometimes required to endure extreme emotional hardships of living in sequestration, apart from families and in fear. Generally, sequestration is a difficult, stressful civil service without the added pressures of an extraordinary case of public interest.

This Circuit will not tolerate any actions from the media placing jurors and potential jurors at risk and in harm's way, or invading any potential juror's privacy in an unnecessary, undue manner. Such conduct, for example, would include, but is not limited to, releasing personal identifying information that was learned about potential jurors during *voir dire*; following jurors and potential jurors to their cars to attempt to obtain their license plate numbers; following jurors and potential jurors to their hotel and contacting them at the hotel; placing surveillance over or among the jurors and potential jurors, from vans, cars, and other extreme means such as helicopters or other aircraft.

Outside pressures, contact, or questions from the media during these types of trials is a serious, unacceptable infringement upon the judicial process, the administration of justice, and every party's right to a fair trial. Therefore, such conduct is strictly prohibited. Endeavoring to contact any juror or potential juror during trial (beginning from the first day of jury selection until the last day that the jury is released from duty) is a serious violation of this Court Order. Interviews of jurors after the jury has been released from service are at the discretion of each juror. Jurors and potential jurors are not allowed to be contacted or approached by anyone, in any way (e.g., by method of handing out flyers containing any content that might influence them) either inside the Courthouse, on Courthouse property within the sidewalks of the Courthouse, or between the Courthouse and the juror's parking garage.

L. Violations. Anyone violating this Order will be subject to contempt proceedings of the Court, and, when appropriate, sanctioned by the Court—including, but not limited to, immediate removal from the Courtroom, prohibition from returning to the Courtroom, and loss of media privileges for the duration of the trial.

II. IMPLEMENTATION OF PROCEDURES

A. Implementation.

1) The Chief Judge, independently, or at the request of the administrative or trial Judge assigned to preside over a case of extraordinary public interest, may instruct Court Administration to implement the procedures set forth in this Administrative Order in any case of extraordinary public interest.

2) Upon implementation of these procedures, the Trial Court Administrator will, as soon as practicable, convene a meeting of interested media representatives for the purpose of creating a media committee to establish protocols for the specific case.

B. Media Committee.

1) A Media Committee shall be organized to attend to issues surrounding the regulation of media representatives and to ensure all media representative's compliance with all Court orders.

2) At the least, the Media Committee, shall consist of one print media representative; one television broadcast media representative; one audio broadcast representative; a representative of the Office of the Clerk of Court; the Trial Court Administrator; the Public Information Officer of the Fourth Judicial Circuit, who will act as a liaison between the Court and the media for the duration of the case; a representative from Court Technology; and the Jacksonville Sheriff's Office Courthouse Security Manager.

3) The committee may select a representative from within the committee to act as a media liaison between the media and the Court for the duration of the case.

4) Any other special need or requested accommodation as it relates to this Order shall be addressed by the Media Committee, the Chief Judge, and the Trial Court Administrator.

III. GENERAL TERMS

A. In cases of extraordinary public interest, nothing in this Administrative Order shall be construed to limit or impair the authority of the presiding Judge, and when warranted, these procedures may be modified to control the conduct of pending proceedings, to ensure the fair administration of justice, and to ensure public safety.

B. Should any questions be raised in Clay or Nassau Counties, they may be determined by the Administrative Judges of those Counties, in the same way that they are authorized to be resolved by the Chief Judge and the Trial Court Administrator through this Administrative Order, in the Duval County Courthouse.

C. The Second Amended Administrative Order 92–02 regarding routine cases of public interest remains in full force and effect.

D. This Administrative Order 2013–08 shall be recorded by the Clerk of the Court, in the Official Records of Duval County, in the State of Florida, and shall take effect immediately and remain in full force and effect unless and until otherwise ordered by this Court.

DONE AND ORDERED at Jacksonville, Duval County, Florida, this 19th day of December, 2013.

DONALD R. MORAN, JR.
CHIEF JUDGE

[1]The Duval County Courthouse originally was designed to include all technological infrastructure necessary to facilitate the pooling of media coverage and connections for live media feeds to the Courtrooms. Such was recommended by the Dan Wiley Report. The Greater Jacksonville Plan paid for, and installed, all necessary fiber-optic cables from all Courtrooms to the IDF rooms, from the IDF rooms to the Media Room, as well as to an outside location near the southeast corner of the Courthouse for live feeds. However, without warning to the Court or consultation with any local media representatives, the funding for the remaining infrastructure (such as receivers, etc.) was cut by the current Mayor's administration of the consolidated government of the City of Jacksonville. Thus, as of the date of this Order, pooling is unavailable. Running equipment cables through Courthouse hallways and elevators is strictly prohibited for safety and security reasons. Accordingly, until such technology is provided, the Chief Judge shall have discretion to arrange for appropriate media coverage of court proceedings, including the number of video cameras permitted within the Courtroom, in consultation with the Trial Court Administrator, the Jacksonville Sheriff's Office Courthouse Security Manager (or their designees), and the presiding Judge.

2013–05. STANDARDS FOR COURT–APPOINTED COUNSEL SERVING ON REGISTRY FOR GUARDIANSHIPS

IN THE CIRCUIT COURT, FOURTH JUDICIAL CIRCUIT, IN AND FOR DUVAL COUNTY, FLORIDA

ADMINISTRATIVE ORDER NO. 2013–5

RE: STANDARDS FOR FOR[1] COURT–APPOINTED COUNSEL SERVING ON REGISTRY FOR GUARDIANSHIPS

WHEREAS, it is important that the alleged incapacitated persons be protected and represented effectively by the most competent court-appointed counsel whose driving forces are the best interest of the alleged incapacitated persons and who are willing and able to attend meaningful, continuing legal education courses that enhance their expertise in guardianship law;

WHEREAS, § 27.40(3)(a)1, Florida Statutes, authorizes the Chief Judge to establish minimum requirements for court-appointed attorneys to meet before being approved for the Registry List;

WHEREAS, many circuits throughout Florida require court-appointed attorneys to meet certain prerequisites for the Registry List in addition to the minimum eight (8) hour guardianship course required by § 744.331, Florida Statutes; and

WHEREAS, by entering this Administrative Order, the Fourth Judicial Circuit is formally implementing new standards for court-appointed attorneys to be approved for the Registry List in order to reflect increased expectations similar to many circuits in Florida in an effort to fully protect the alleged incapacitated persons in this community.

NOW THEREFORE, by the authority vested in me as the Chief Judge of the Fourth Judicial Circuit and pursuant to the Florida Rules of Judicial Administration, it is

ORDERED that:

1. Provided the necessary general statutory prerequisites to be included on the **Registry** List have been met pursuant to § 27.40(3)(a), Florida Statutes (i.e., the certifications and execution of a contract with the Justice Administrative Commission), any attorney who has an LLM degree in Elder Law or is board certified in Elder Law is exempt from the specific Guardianship requirements that are set forth in this Administrative Order and may, therefore, be approved for the Registry List.

2. Also, provided the necessary general statutory prerequisites to be included on the Registry List have been met pursuant to § 27.40(3)(a), Florida Statutes (i.e., the certifications and executions of a contract with the Justice Administrative Commission), a presiding judge may waive the specific Guardianship requirements (that are set forth in this Administrative Order) in order to approve a particular attorney to a specific case (rather than approving the attorney to the entire Registry List).

3. Any attorney seeking to be appointed by the Court for incapacity or guardianship proceedings must have completed at a minimum, the 8 hours of education in Guardianship (specifically, the "Guardianship and Incapacity" CLE course presented by the Fourth Judicial Circuit). § 744.331(2)(d), Fla. Stat. This 8 hour course is available through the Law Library at the Duval County Courthouse. The 8 hour course must be completed within the twelve (12) months preceding the date of the attorney's application for the Fourth Judicial Circuit's Registry List.

4. Any attorney seeking to re-apply at the end of a fiscal year in order to remain on the Registry List as a court-appointed counsel in an incapacity or guardianship proceeding, must have completed a minimum of three (3) CLE hours during the preceding twelve (12) months of service before re-applying.

(a) Acceptable CLE courses shall include guardianship, elder law, advance directives, legislative updates, mental health, capacity and courses of similar nature, but shall not include estate planning, mediation training, family law matters or arbitration training.

(b) Court-appointed counsel must provide proof of the CLE course while re-applying (e.g., certificate of attendance or attach a print out from The Florida Bar).

5. The court-appointed counsel must both live and have the principal office located in the Fourth Judicial Circuit.

6. This Administrative Order shall be recorded by the Clerk of the Court, in the Official Records of Duval County, in the State of Florida, and shall take effect immediately and remain in full force and effect unless and until otherwise ordered by the Court.

DONE AND ORDERED in Chambers at Jacksonville, Duval County, Florida, this 3 day of May, 2013.

DONALD R. MORAN, JR.
CHIEF JUDGE

1 So in original.

2013–01. PROCEDURES FOR QUALIFYING DEAF OR HARD OF HEARING JURORS

IN THE CIRCUIT COURT, FOURTH JUDICIAL CIRCUIT IN AND FOR DUVAL, CLAY AND NASSAU COUNTIES, FLORIDA

ADMINISTRATIVE ORDER NO. 2013–1

RE: PROCEDURES FOR QUALIFYING DEAF OR HARD OF HEARING JURORS

WHEREAS, the Florida Supreme Court enacted Florida Rules of Judicial Administration 2.540, establishing a process for the Courts to provide accommodations to persons with disabilities when needed to access Court services and activities;

WHEREAS, the Americans with Disabilities Act of 1990 ("ADA") requires that the Court's programs, services and activities, to include jury duty, be readily accessible to individuals with disabilities;

WHEREAS, it is the intent of the Fourth Judicial Circuit to include deaf and hard of hearing persons as jurors, when otherwise qualified;

WHEREAS, the following procedures are set forth in an effort to ensure that the combined purpose and spirit of the ADA and § 40.013(5), Florida Statutes, are carried out effectively by the Court whenever a person who is deaf or hard of hearing is both qualified and willing to serve as a juror;

NOW THEREFORE, by the authority vested in me as Chief Judge and pursuant to the Florida Rules of Judicial Administration it is

ORDERED:

A. That the Fourth Judicial Circuit shall adopt the following policy to protect the rights of potential deaf jurors to serve on a jury pursuant to the ADA:

1. Deaf or hard of hearing jurors will not be removed solely based on their disability;

2. The Fourth Judicial Circuit shall give primary consideration to the accommodation requested by a deaf or hard of hearing juror;

3. A deaf or hard of hearing juror shall not be removed prior to voir dire solely due to deafness (unless removal is sought by the juror, or removal is not based on Florida Statute § 40.013(5), but may be removed if another statutory requirement prohibits his or her service), regardless if the recommendation for removal is made by a Bailiff, lawyer or Judge;

4. To ensure compliance with § 40.013 5), Florida Statutes, and to prevent unauthorized dismissal or excuse, all questioning as to a deaf juror's disability, needed accommodations, and all other inquiries as to qualification must be done on the record in consult with the deaf juror;

5. Pursuant to § 40.013(5), Florida Statutes, a Judge may evaluate the individual juror if the Judge believes that the evidence presented in the case requires auditory discrimination or that the timely progression of the trial will be considerably affected by the presence of a juror who is deaf or hearing impaired. Both the evaluation of the juror under these circumstances and the Judge's findings must be put on the record and performed in consult with such juror;

6. When a deaf juror is unable to articulate to the Court which accommodation or auxiliary aid is needed to provide effective communication due to unfamiliarity with either technology or the support services available, the Court shall contact the Circuit Court's ADA Coordinator or the Statewide Court ADA Coordinator for auxiliary aid assistance;

7. If a deaf juror is excused from a venire pool due to deafness after the above outlined policy has been followed, the

deaf juror will be afforded the opportunity to be recycled in the jury pool if such option exists.

B. This Administrative Order shall be in effect immediately and remain in effect full force and effect unless and until otherwise ordered by the Court.

C. This Administrative Order shall be recorded by the Clerk of the Court, in the Official Records of Duval County, in the State of Florida.

DONE AND ORDERED in Chambers at Jacksonville, Duval County, Florida, this 16 day of Jan 2013.

DONALD R. MORAN, JR.
CHIEF JUDGE

2012–03 (A1). VACATING ADMINISTRATIVE ORDER NO. 2012–03 REGARDING FILING OF DEPOSITIONS IN DUVAL COUNTY

IN THE CIRCUIT COURT, FOURTH JUDICIAL CIRCUIT IN AND FOR DUVAL COUNTY, FLORIDA.

AMENDED ADMINISTRATIVE ORDER NO. 2012–03

IN RE: VACATING ADMINISTRATIVE ORDER NO. 2012–03 REGARDING FILING OF DEPOSITIONS IN DUVAL COUNTY

WHEREAS, Administrative Order No. 2012–03 was entered on May 11, 2012, and required parties in all *civil* cases who wished to present deposition evidence at any hearing or trial to bring the original or certified copy to court for the judge's use and to provide a copy to opposing counsel, if needed, and as required by the Florida Rules of Civil Procedure;

WHEREAS, 1.310(f)(3), Florida Rules of Civil Procedure, permits copies of depositions to be filed when the contents must be considered by the Court or ordered by the Court to be filed;

WHEREAS, effective April 1, 2013, electronic filing ("e-filing") in the Court will be mandatory in all civil, probate, small claims, and family law divisions and appeals to the Circuit Courts and on October 1, 2013, it will be mandatory in the criminal law divisions; and

WHEREAS, when e-filing became effective in April 2013, it became necessary for the Court to **vacate the entire** Administrative Order No. 2012–03 in order to allow the Clerk to accept copies of depositions to be filed when the contents must be considered by the Court or Court-ordered to be filed in accordance with Florida Rules Civil Procedure 1.310(f)(3) (e.g., copies of depositions in support of a Motion for Summary Judgment).

NOW THEREFORE, by the authority vested in me as the Chief Judge of the Fourth Judicial Circuit and pursuant to the Florida Rules of Judicial Administration, it is

ORDERED that:

1. Effective immediately, Administrative Order No. 2012–03 shall be **vacated in its entirety** and the Clerk will accept copies of depositions to be e-filed when the contents must be considered by the Court or Court-ordered to be filed in accordance with Florida Rules Civil Procedure 1.310(f)(3) (e.g., copies of depositions in support of a Motion for Summary Judgment).

2. That this Amended Administrative Order shall be recorded by the Clerk of the Court, in the Official Records of Duval County, in the State of Florida, and shall take effect immediately and remain in full force and effect unless and until otherwise ordered by the Court.

DONE AND ORDERED in Chambers at Jacksonville, Duval County, Florida, this 13 day of May, 2013.

DONALD R. MORAN, JR.
CHIEF JUDGE

2012–02. [VACATED AND SET ASIDE BY ORDER 2017-10, EFFECTIVE SEPTEMBER 19, 2017.]

2012–01 (A1). [VACATED AND SET ASIDE BY ORDER 2017-10, EFFECTIVE SEPTEMBER 19, 2017.]

2011–09. RESIDENTIAL HOMESTEAD FORECLOSURE CASES MANDATORY REFERRAL TO MEDIATION—TERMINATION OF PROGRAM

IN THE CIRCUIT COURT, FOURTH JUDICIAL CIRCUIT, IN AND FOR DUVAL, CLAY AND NASSAU COUNTIES, FLORIDA.

ADMINISTRATIVE ORDER NO. 2011–9

IN RE: RESIDENTIAL HOMESTEAD FORECLOSURE CASES MANDATORY REFERRAL TO MEDIATION—TERMINATION OF PROGRAM

WHEREAS, the Florida Supreme Court by its Administrative Order No. AOSC 11–44 signed December 19, 2011 terminated the statewide Managed Mediation Program mandated by AOSC 09–54;

NOW THEREFORE, by the authority vested in me as the Chief Judge of the Fourth Judicial Circuit and for the efficient and proper administration of the Court, pursuant to Rule 2.215 of the Florida Rules of Judicial Administration, it is hereby

ORDERED:

1. That the managed mediation program mandated by Administrative Order No. 2010–1 for the Fourth Judicial Circuit is terminated as to all residential mortgage foreclosure cases filed on or after December 20, 2011. The Program shall remain in full force and effect for all residential mortgage foreclosure cases filed **on or before** December 19, 2011.

2. That this Administrative Order shall be effective Tuesday, December 20, 2011, shall be recorded by the Clerk of Court, in the Official Records of Duval County, State of Florida, and shall remain in full force and effect unless and until otherwise ordered by the Court.

DONE AND ORDERED in Chambers at Jacksonville, Duval County, Florida, this 20 day of December, 2011.

DONALD R. MORAN, JR.
CHIEF JUDGE

2011–07. EVIDENTIARY HEARINGS—PROCEDURAL CHANGES FOR MOTIONS TO EXCEED STATUTORY MAXIMUM IN DUE PROCESS AND INDIGENCY–FOR–COST CASES

IN THE CIRCUIT COURT, FOURTH JUDICIAL CIRCUIT, IN AND FOR DUVAL, CLAY AND NASSAU COUNTIES, FLORIDA

ADMINISTRATIVE ORDER NO. 2011–07

RE: EVIDENTIARY HEARINGS—PROCEDURAL CHANGES FOR MOTIONS TO EXCEED STATUTORY MAXIMUM IN DUE PROCESS AND INDIGENCY–FOR–COST CASES

WHEREAS, due to the economic downturn, the Fourth Judicial Circuit must be more judicious in its discretionary spending and decisions in awarding fees in excess of the statutory maximum allowable by § 27.5304(12)(b), Florida Statutes, every time attorneys request such fees in due process cases and indigent-for-cost cases;

WHEREAS, until now, the trial court judge of each presiding case has been hearing the motions requesting fees in excess of the statutory maximum pursuant to § 27.5304(12), Florida Statutes, and that procedure has resulted in inconsistent rulings and a collective depletion of the Circuit's expense account, making it necessary to implement the new procedures set forth below;

NOW THEREFORE, by the authority vested in me as the Chief Judge of the Fourth Judicial Circuit and pursuant to the Florida Rules of Judicial Administration, it is

ORDERED that:

1) Attorneys filing a motion to exceed the statutory maximum pursuant to section § 27.5304(12)(b), Florida Statutes in any due process court-appointed attorney case or indigent for-cost case pending in the Fourth Judicial Circuit must file the motion with the Chief Judge of this Circuit;

2) In the event that an attorney improperly files a motion to exceed the statutory maximum directly with the trial court Judge, the Judge's Judicial Assistant will forward the motion and its attachments to the Chief Judge. The Chief Judge will also receive a courtesy copy of the motion (without attachments) from the Justice Administrative Commission (JAC), as indicated by the JAC.

3) Once the Chief Judge receives the motion, it will be set for an evidentiary hearing on the Chief Judge's calendar with a notice of hearing copied to the trial court judge.

4) Whenever an attorney requests to exceed the statutory maximum pursuant to section § 27.5304(12)(b), Florida Statutes in any due process court-appointed attorney case and indigent for-cost case, the Chief Judge will hold the statutorily mandated evidentiary hearing to determine whether the case required extraordinary and unusual efforts;

5) The trial court judge may write a letter to the Chief Judge to support or oppose the request for excess fees prior to the hearing based on personal observation and experience of the case as the presiding judge. Such letter will be considered by the Chief Judge, but will not, by itself, be persuasive or binding in any way. Instead, the motion will be determined by the evidentiary hearing, which is based on competent and substantial evidence pursuant to section § 27.5304(12)(b), Florida Statutes.

6) This Administrative Order shall be recorded by the Clerk of the Court, in the Official Records of Duval County, in the State of Florida, and shall take effect immediately and remain in full force and effect unless and until otherwise ordered by this Court.

DONE AND ORDERED in Chambers at Jacksonville, Duval County, Florida, this 18 day of July, 2011.

/s/
DONALD R. MORAN, JR.
CHIEF JUDGE

2011–06. REASSIGNMENT OF ORIGINAL CASE; SAME NUMBER

IN THE CIRCUIT COURT, FOURTH JUDICIAL CIRCUIT, IN AND FOR DUVAL, CLAY AND NASSAU COUNTIES, FLORIDA

ADMINISTRATIVE ORDER NO. 2011–6

RE: LOCAL RULE 4—REASSIGNMENT OF ORIGINAL CASE; SAME NUMBER

WHEREAS, the Local Rules of the Circuit Court of the Fourth Judicial Circuit of Florida were approved by the Florida Supreme Court in 1967;

WHEREAS, at this time, Local Rule 4 is the only Local Rule out of the 23 Local Rules that remains in effect at the Fourth Judicial Circuit;

WHEREAS, Local Rule 4(g)(1) authorizes reassignment of an action if it has been dismissed and later refiled, but the Rule merely indicates that such action must be reassigned to the division in which it was originally pending and does not mention what case number the action should be given at the time of reassignment;

WHEREAS, Local Rule 4(g)(2) also provides that "[w]hen two or more actions are pending which may be appropriately tried together [i.e., consolidated], but are assigned to different divisions, the judge of the division to which the case bearing the lower docket number is assigned . . . shall reassign all other such companion actions to his division;"

WHEREAS, Local Rule 4(g) is silent as to the number that should be assigned to a case if an attorney with several actions pending before various judges with different case numbers (e.g., personal injury cases involving multiple plaintiffs arising out of the same car accident) voluntarily dismisses the lower action and refiles the case. That is, even though the refiled action would be reassigned to the original judge, the question is whether the case should keep the original lower case number rather than be assigned a new number, to prevent an opportunity for strategic judge shopping and consolidation with, in effect—an otherwise—lower case number in another division;

WHEREAS, it is in the best interest of the citizens of the Fourth Judicial Circuit to close this existing loophole in Local Rule 4;

WHEREAS, the Office of the Clerk has indicated that it can assign the original case number to an action that has been voluntarily dismissed and is thereafter refiled and reassigned to the original judge;

NOW THEREFORE, by the authority vested in me as the Chief Judge of the Fourth Judicial Circuit and pursuant to the Florida Rules of Judicial Administration, it is hereby

ORDERED:

1. That as soon as administratively possible, the Clerks of the Court for the Fourth Judicial Circuit will designate the original case number whenever reassigning an action to the division in which it was originally pending where it has been dismissed and later refiled, in accordance with Local Rule 4(g).

3.* That all other amended Administrative Orders No. 98–12 previously entered and addressing the same subject matter are hereby vacated and superseded.

2.* That this Administrative Order shall be recorded by the Clerk of the Court, in the Official Records of Duval County, in the State of Florida, and shall remain in full force and effect unless and until otherwise ordered by the Court.

DONE AND ORDERED in Chambers at Jacksonville, Duval County, Florida, this 20 day of May, 2011.

DONALD R. MORAN, JR.
CHIEF JUDGE

* Numbering as provided in original.

2010–08. JUDICIAL SALES FEE IN ALL FORECLOSURE CASES, CLAY COUNTY

IN THE CIRCUIT COURT, FOURTH JUDICIAL CIRCUIT, IN AND FOR CLAY COUNTY, FLORIDA

ADMINISTRATIVE ORDER NO. 2010–8

RE: JUDICIAL SALES FEE IN ALL FORECLOSURE CASES

WHEREAS, in foreclosure actions, the Office of the Clerk for Clay County has been experiencing substantial difficulty in collecting the judicial sales fees for conducting public sales once final judgments have been entered;

WHEREAS, after final judgment, the plaintiff in a foreclosure action, which is typically the lending institution, more often than not, ultimately purchases the property at the judicial sale;

WHEREAS, it has become necessary to restructure the payment procedures so that the Office of the Clerk can be assured of payment by requiring payment when suit is initially filed;

NOW THEREFORE, by the authority vested in me as the Chief Judge of the Fourth Judicial Circuit and pursuant to the Florida Rules of Judicial Administration, it is

ORDERED:

1. That beginning December 1, 2010, the plaintiff in each and every foreclosure action will be required to pay seventy dollars ($70.00) to the Clerk of Court for Clay County at the time of filing the complaint, as a service charge pursuant to § 45.035(1), Florida Statutes, "for services in making, recording, and certifying the sale and title" which "shall be advanced by the plaintiff before the sale." This seventy dollars ($70.00) service charge may be refunded to the plaintiff if—and only if—the case is voluntarily dismissed prior to the judicial sale.

2. That, should Clay County implement electronic foreclosure sales in the future, then at that time, plaintiffs in each and every foreclosure action will be required to pay an additional seventy dollars ($70.00) to the Clerk of Court for Clay County when filing the complaint, pursuant to § 45.035(3), Florida Statutes, for services in conducting the public sale by electronic means. Such electronic sales costs are statutorily required to be paid by the "winning bidder." Therefore, in the event the winning bidder at the electronic judicial sale is ultimately not the plaintiff, but instead, is a third party purchaser, the Clerk will refund the seventy dollars ($70.00) to the plaintiff within thirty (30) calendar days of the sale.

3. That, unless objections to the public sale are filed with the Court within ten (10) days after filing the certificate of sale pursuant to § 45.031(5), Florida Statutes, the party to whom the certificate of title is issued shall pay the required documentary stamp fees no later than fifteen (15) calendar days from the date the certificate of sale is filed.

4. That beginning December 1, 2010, if a foreclosure sale is incomplete, and the successful third party bidder does not follow through with paying the balance of bid price in full, the 5 % deposit, which the third party bidder has as a credit with the Clerk of Court, shall be forfeited to the Clerk of Court subject to partial distribution to the plaintiff upon application in accordance with Florida law. The plaintiff will be required to file a motion to reschedule the foreclosure sale and simultaneously pay to the Clerk of Court for Clay County: (a) a filing fee in the amount of fifty dollars ($50.00) for reopening the action, as authorized by § 28.241, Florida Statutes; (b) an additional seventy dollars ($70.00) service charge pursuant to § 45.035(1), Florida Statutes, "for services in making, recording, and certifying the sale and title" to be refunded to the plaintiff if the case is voluntarily dismissed; and (c) if, and only if, Clay County implements public sales electronically, then plaintiffs will also have to pay an additional seventy dollars ($70.00) for services in conducting an electronic public sale pursuant to § 45.035(3), Florida Statutes, to be refunded to the plaintiffs within thirty (30) calendar days of the public sale if the "winning bidder" at the electronic judicial sale is ultimately a third party purchaser.

5. That this Administrative Order shall be recorded by the Clerk of the Court in the Official Records of Duval County, in the State of Florida, and shall take effect on December 1, 2010 and remain in full force and effect unless and until otherwise ordered by this Court.

DONE AND ORDERED in Chambers at Jacksonville, Duval County, Florida, this 4 day of Nov, 2010.

DONALD R. MORAN, JR.
CHIEF JUDGE

2010–07. JUDICIAL SALES FEE IN ALL FORECLOSURE CASES, DUVAL COUNTY

IN THE CIRCUIT COURT, FOURTH JUDICIAL CIRCUIT, IN AND FOR DUVAL COUNTY, FLORIDA

ADMINISTRATIVE ORDER NO. 2010–7

RE: JUDICIAL SALES FEE IN ALL FORECLOSURE CASES

WHEREAS, in foreclosure actions, the Office of the Clerk for Duval County has been experiencing substantial difficulty in collecting the judicial sales fees for conducting public sales once final judgments have been entered;

WHEREAS, after final judgment, the plaintiff in a foreclosure action, which is typically the lending institution, more often than not, ultimately purchases the property at the judicial sale;

WHEREAS, it has become necessary to restructure the payment procedures so that the Office of the Clerk can be assured of payment by requiring payment when suit is initially filed;

NOW THEREFORE, by the authority vested in me as the Chief Judge of the Fourth Judicial Circuit and pursuant to the Florida Rules of Judicial Administration, it is

ORDERED:

1. That beginning December 1, 2010, the plaintiff in each and every foreclosure action will be required to pay seventy dollars ($70.00) to the Clerk of Court for Duval County at the time of filing the complaint, as a service charge pursuant to § 45.035(1), Florida Statutes, "for services in making, recording, and certifying the sale and title" which "shall be advanced by the plaintiff before the sale." This seventy dollars ($70.00) service charge may be refunded to the plaintiff if—and only if—the case is dismissed prior to the judicial sale.

2. That beginning December 1, 2010, the plaintiff in each and every foreclosure action will be required to pay an additional seventy dollars ($70.00) to the Clerk of Court for Duval County at the time of filing the complaint, pursuant to § 45.035(3), Florida Statutes, for services in conducting the public sale, which is by electronic means. Such costs are statutorily required to be paid by the "winning bidder." Therefore, if the winning bidder at the judicial sale is ultimately not the plaintiff, but instead, is a third party purchaser, the Clerk shall refund the seventy dollars ($70.00) to the plaintiff within thirty (30) calendar days of the sale.

3. That, unless objections to the public sale are filed with the Court within ten (10) days after filing the certificate of sale pursuant to § 45.031(5), Florida Statutes, the party to whom the certificate of title is issued shall pay the required documentary stamp fees no later than fifteen (15) calendar days from the date the certificate of sale is filed.

4. That beginning December 1, 2010, if a foreclosure sale is incomplete, and the successful third party bidder does not follow through with paying the balance of bid price in full, the 5 % deposit, which the third party bidder has as a credit with the Clerk of Court, shall be forfeited to the Clerk of Court subject to partial distribution to the plaintiff upon application in accordance with Florida law. The plaintiff will be required to file a motion to reschedule the foreclosure sale and simultaneously pay to the Clerk of Court for Duval County: (a) a filing fee in the amount of fifty dollars ($50.00) for reopening the action, as authorized by § 28.241, Florida Statutes; (b) an additional seventy dollars ($70.00) service charge pursuant to § 45.035(1), Florida Statutes, "for services in making, recording, and certifying the sale and title" to be refunded to the plaintiff if the case is voluntarily dismissed; and (c) an additional seventy dollars ($70.00) for services in conducting an electronic public sale pursuant to § 45.035(3), Florida Statutes, to be refunded to the plaintiff within thirty (30) calendar days of the public sale if the "winning bidder" at the judicial sale is ultimately a third party purchaser.

5. That this Administrative Order shall be recorded by the Clerk of the Court, in the Official Records of Duval County, in the State of Florida, and shall take effect on December 1, 2010 and remain in full force and effect unless and until otherwise ordered by this Court.

DONE AND ORDERED in Chambers at Jacksonville, Duval County, Florida, this 27 day of Oct, 2010.

DONALD R. MORAN, JR.
CHIEF JUDGE

2010–05. ELECTRONIC SIGNATURE OF CLERK ON SUMMONS

IN THE CIRCUIT COURT, FOURTH JUDICIAL CIRCUIT, IN AND FOR CLAY COUNTY, FLORIDA

ADMINISTRATIVE ORDER NO. 2010–05

RE: ELECTRONIC SIGNATURE OF CLERK ON SUMMONS

WHEREAS, on July 1, 2009, the Florida Supreme Court entered Administrative Order AOSC09–30, approving updated statewide Standards for Electronic Access to the Court that provides for electronic filing in all Florida state courts;

WHEREAS, the Administrative Order states that the "judicial branch of Florida has long embraced the use of information technologies to increase the effectiveness, efficiency, and accessibility of the courts" (AOSC09–30 at 1);

WHEREAS, the Florida Supreme Court further explains in the Administrative Order, that this "technology can make the process of submitting documents to the court and to other parties simpler, quicker, and less costly [and it] can also reduce the costs incurred by clerks of court for storing and transferring documents" (AOSC09–30 at 2);

WHEREAS, the Florida Supreme Court has approved the electronic filing in the Clay County Clerk of Circuit Court's Office (hereinafter, Clerk) without the necessity of paper follow-up, and, accordingly, the Clerk has implemented electronic filing, effectively rendering it paperless in all Divisions;

WHEREAS, allowing electronic service of process with an electronic signature by a Clerk would improve efficiency in the Clay County Clerk of Circuit Court's Office and would facilitate the processing of cases by the Court;

WHEREAS, the Clay County Clerk of Circuit Court and the Clay County Sheriff's Office have agreed to the terms and conditions for an electronic summons;

NOW THEREFORE, by the authority vested in me as the Chief Judge of the Fourth Judicial Circuit and pursuant to the Florida Rules of Judicial Administration, it is hereby

ORDERED:

1. That in order to improve efficiency in the Clay County Clerk of Circuit Court's Office (hereinafter, Clerk) and in order to facilitate the processing of cases by the Court, the following procedures shall be followed whenever a filer electronically files a Summons upon initial filing of a pleading that requires the responder to appear and answer (i.e., a Complaint, Third Party Complaint, Petitions, Writs, etc.);

2. That, upon receipt of such Summons, the Clerk is authorized to issue the Summons by way of electronic format with an electronic signature, and may electronically send the Summons back to the filer;

3. That the filer is authorized to forward to the Sheriff's Office or process server such electronic Summons and initial filing (i.e., the Complaint, Third Party Complaint, Petitions, etc.), and any other relevant and necessary pleadings (e.g., attached contract, lease, etc.);

4. That the electronic signature on such Summons sent to any county Sheriff's Office or process server shall be treated as the original as long as a service copy is attached thereto;

5. That this Administrative Order does not apply to subpoenas nor to summonses that require a person to appear in Court as a juror or a witness;

6. That this Administrative Order shall take effect in Clay County immediately; and

7. That this Administrative Order shall be recorded by the Clerk of the Court, in the Official Records of Duval County, in the State of Florida, and shall remain in full force and effect unless and until otherwise ordered by this Court.

DONE AND ORDERED in Chambers at Jacksonville, Duval County, Florida, this 17 day of Sept, 2010.

DONALD R. MORAN, JR.
CHIEF JUDGE

2010–04. APPOINTED COUNSEL AND REGISTRY FOR PETITIONS TO DETERMINE INCAPACITY & GUARDIANSHIPS

IN THE CIRCUIT COURT, FOURTH JUDICIAL CIRCUIT, IN AND FOR DUVAL, CLAY AND NASSAU COUNTIES, FLORIDA

ADMINISTRATIVE ORDER NO. 2010–4.

IN RE: APPOINTED COUNSEL AND REGISTRY FOR PETITIONS TO DETERMINE INCAPACITY & GUARDIANSHIPS

WHEREAS, according to Florida Statutes § 744.331(2), when the Court appoints an attorney for an alleged incapacitated person, the Court "must appoint the Office of Criminal Conflict and Civil Regional Counsel [OCCCRC] or a private attorney as prescribed in Florida Statutes § 27.511(6)" and such attorney must be included in the Registry compiled pursuant to Florida Statutes § 27.40;

WHEREAS, pursuant to section § 27.511(6)(c), the Court, in consultation with the Clerk and prior to appointing counsel, will determine, if possible, whether the person entitled to representation is indigent, using the best available evidence, and:

1. if the person is indigent, the Court shall appoint the OCCCRC (or private counsel from the Registry if the OCCCRC is unable to provide representation due to a conflict of interest) and may move to reassign the case to a private attorney if at any time after appointment the OCCCRC determines that the person is not indigent; or

2. if the person is not indigent or if the Court and the Clerk are not able to determine whether the person is indigent at the time of appointment, the Court shall appoint a private attorney, and if at any time after appointment, the private attorney determines that the person is indigent, the attorney may move to reassign the case to the OCCCRC and seek compensation from the Justice Administrative Commission (JAC) in accordance with § 27.511(6)(c)2;

WHEREAS, pursuant to section § 744.331(2)(b), the alleged incapacitated person may substitute an attorney of personal choice for the attorney appointed by the Court.

WHEREAS, Amended Administrative Order 2004–23 was entered to clarify the procedures for maintaining and compiling the Registry for conflict counsel appointed to various Divisions in the Fourth Judicial Circuit except in the determination of incapacity and guardianship cases, which will be addressed herein;

NOW THEREFORE, by the authority vested in me as the Chief Judge of the Fourth Judicial Circuit and pursuant to the Florida Rules of Judicial Administration, it is

ORDERED:

A. Compilation & Maintenance of Registry

1. That the Chief Judge or his designee, shall be responsible for compiling the registry of attorneys ("the Registry"). In compiling the Registry, the Chief Judge or his designee, may consult with the Administrative Judges, other members of the judiciary, and members of the Bar as to the qualifications and suitability of the applicants. The selection, approval, and continuation of an attorney on the Registry is a privilege, not a right, and is dependent not only upon the attorney meeting the requirements for appointment as set forth below, but upon the overall competency of the attorney. The constitutional right, not only to counsel, but to competent counsel, was discussed by the United States Supreme Court in Evitts v. Lucey, 469 U.S. 387, 395 (1985); accord, Gideon v. Wainwright, 372 U.S. 335 (1963).

2. That the Chief Judge or his designee, shall place attorneys on the Registry in accordance with the category of cases in which they are qualified and elect on their application. The categories are listed in the Amended Administrative Order 2004–23. This Administrative Order 2010–04 adds the categories of appointment to represent allegedly incapacitated persons in a determination of incapacity cases and guardianship cases to the list of categories for the Registry.

3. The Office of the Clerks of Court, on behalf of the Chief Judge, will maintain and distribute the Registry, in accordance

with section 27.40, Florida Statutes. The Registry shall be maintained by county and category of case for which the attorney is qualified.

B. Requirements for Placement on Registry

1. To be considered for placement on the Registry, the attorneys shall certify that they have been a member of The Florida Bar in good standing for at least one year, meet any minimum requirements established by general law, this Administrative Order, or other applicable administrative orders of the Fourth Judicial Circuit. The attorneys must also certify that they are available to represent indigent defendants in all cases requiring court appointment of private counsel (within their category of appointment), and are willing to abide by the terms of the Justice Administrative Commission's ("JAC") contract for services.[1] Any attorney who desires to be considered for placement on the Registry, must enter into a contract for services with JAC.

2. Attorneys approved for placement on the Registry shall be responsible for notifying the Chief Judge or his designee, of any of the following:

a. a change of address, telephone number or fax number;

b. a change in categories of cases to which he/she is qualified and willing to be assigned;

c. any disciplinary action taken against him/her by The Florida Bar;

d. that he/she has become inactive or is unavailable for appointment.

3. The experience and other qualifications that each attorney must meet to be considered for, and to maintain placement on, the Registry for various areas of practice chosen are specified on the chart attached to Amended Administrative Order 2004–23, as Attachment "A"[2]

4. Amended Administrative Order 2004–23 and Attachment "A" do not address the qualifications required for an attorney who desires to apply to be court-appointed to cases involving petitions for adjudication of incapacity or guardianship proceedings. Attorneys seeking appointment in such cases shall be required to have completed a minimum of eight (8) hours of education in guardianship pursuant to Florida Statutes § 744.331(2)(d) in addition to being a member of The Florida Bar in good standing for a minimum of one (1) year. The Court may waive the initial training requirement for an attorney who has served as a court-appointed attorney in incapacity proceedings or as an attorney of record for guardians for not less than three (3) years. Fla. Stat. § 744.331(2)(d).

C. Appointment Process and Requirements

Appointment

1. If the Court and the Clerk determine that the person to be represented is indigent, the Court shall appoint the OCCCRC, which will represent the person unless a conflict of interest exists or the person later is determined to be not indigent. Fla. Stat. § 27.511(6)(c)1.

2. If the Court and the Clerk determine that the person is not indigent, or if they are not able to determine whether the person is indigent at the time of appointment, the Court shall appoint a private attorney, and the case may be reassigned if it is later determined that the person is indigent, at which time the private attorney may seek to recover compensation from the JAC according to Florida Statutes § 27.511(6)(c)2.

3. The alleged incapacitated person may be permitted to substitute an attorney for the court-appointed attorney. Fla. Stat. § 744.331(2)(b).

Duties

4. Pursuant to Florida Statutes § 27.40(6), after court appointment, the attorney must immediately file a notice of appearance with the Court, indicating acceptance of the appointment to represent the incapacitated person. The OCCCRC must certify whether it will accept the case or if there is a conflict, and if a conflict exists, private counsel from the Registry will be assigned to the case in accordance with the procedures set forth below.

5. The appointed attorney shall also be appointed as Elisor to serve the Notice of Filing Petition to Determine Incapacity as well as all other pleadings required to be served on the alleged incapacitated person and to file a return of service, showing that the Petition has been served.

6. In addition to serving the Notice of Filing Petition and all other required pleadings at the time of service, the appointed attorney acting as Elisor shall also read the Notice, Petition and all of the pleadings at such time of serving the Notice on the alleged incapacitated person. The purpose of this section is to avoid the expense and to minimize the distress which might be imposed upon the alleged incapacitated person should service otherwise be executed by a process server or a law enforcement officer.

7. Pursuant to Florida Statutes § 27.40(8), and subject to the attorney-client privilege and the work-product privilege, an attorney who withdraws or is removed from representation shall deliver all files, notes, documents, and research to the successor attorney within fifteen (15) days after receiving notice from the successor attorney. The successor attorney shall bear the cost of transmitting all files, notes, documents, and research.

Fees

8. If the Court appoints private counsel for an indigent person in a guardianship case filed under Chapter 744, Florida Statutes, where the OCCCRC is unable to provide representation due to a conflict of interest, the court-appointed counsel will be compensated by the Justice Administrative Commission (JAC). The attorney will be compensated at a flat rate of $400.00 per case for the fiscal year of 2009–2010. This flat fee is subject to change each year, pursuant to Florida Statutes § 27.5304(7) and the General Appropriations Act. (See the JAC website at www.JusticeAdmin.org.) In rare, extraordinary and unusual circumstances, court-appointed counsel may seek compensation that exceeds the statutory limits by following the procedures set forth in Florida Statutes § 27.5304(12).

9. Where the allegedly incapacitated person being represented by court appointed counsel is not indigent, the attorney is "entitled to reasonable fees to be determined by the Court" pursuant to Florida Statutes § 744.331(2), and such fees will be paid in accordance with § 744.108(8).

D. Procedures for Utilizing Registry

1. Pursuant to Florida Statutes §§ 744.331(2)(a) and 27.40(3)(b), the Court shall appoint attorneys in rotating order in the order in which their names appear on the Registry.

2. However, the Court to whom the case is assigned, if good cause exists, may appoint an attorney out of order. Examples of good cause include, but are not limited to, instances where the attorney was previously appointed to represent the client in another case simultaneously pending or filed after the initial representation, or the attorney next in rotation fails to respond in a timely manner. Pursuant to § 27.40(3)(b), should an out of order appointment be necessary, the Court must make a finding of good cause on the record for the appointment. Such finding may be recorded on the open record, in the court file, or by separate written order. Any attorney not appointed in the order in which the attorney's name appears on the list shall remain next in order.

3. Pursuant to § 27.40(7)(a), Florida Statutes, a non registry attorney may be appointed if the Court finds in the order of appointment, that there were no registry attorneys available for representation for that case. A non registry attorney appointed under these circumstances may be compensated under § 27.5304, Florida Statutes.

4. Pursuant to § 27.40(3)(c), Florida Statutes, if the number of attorneys on the Registry in a county or circuit for a particular category of cases is inadequate, the Chief Judge or his designee shall provide to the Clerk of Court the names of at least three private attorneys who have relevant experience. The Clerk of Court shall send an application to each of these attorneys to register for appointment.

E. Removal From Registry

1. An attorney *shall* be removed from the Registry if the attorney:

a. is disbarred or suspended, or surrenders his/her license to practice law in this state;

b. fails to meet the experience or training requirements established herein;

c. submits false or fraudulent billing; or

d. solicits or receives compensation directly from the client for the case(s) to which the attorney has been appointed.

2. An attorney *may* be removed from the Registry if the attorney:

a. unreasonably fails to consult with a client;

b. fails, without cause, to make required court appearances, meet statutory or court-imposed deadlines, or file appropriate motions in a timely manner;

c. fails to zealously represent the interests of a client;

d. engages in misconduct or exhibits a level of incompetence such that the Chief Judge or his designee makes the determination that removal of the attorney from the Registry is necessary for the protection of clients' interests and/or the administration of justice.

3. Pursuant to Florida Statutes § 27.40(9), any interested person may advise the Court of any circumstances affecting the quality of an attorney's representation.

4. This paragraph addresses the procedure for having an attorney considered for removal from the Registry. Any interested person may request, in writing, that an attorney on the Registry be removed for cause. Upon receipt of such request, the Chief Judge or his designee may conduct an investigation, as deemed necessary, to substantiate or refute the basis for the request. The attorney being considered for removal may be requested to respond to such request in writing, in person, or both. The Chief Judge, or other judge appointed by the Chief Judge to preside, may conduct a hearing to receive testimony regarding the request and the attorney's response. Any hearing shall be noticed in accordance with Florida's public meeting laws.

5. Upon a finding of cause, the Chief Judge may suspend the attorney from the Registry, remove the attorney from the Registry, or impose any other sanctions deemed appropriate. The Chief Judge shall provide notice of the decision in writing to the attorney and the person filing the request for removal.

F. Effectiveness of Order

1. This Order is effective immediately and shall remain in effect until further Order of the Court and all the terms and conditions set forth in this Administrative Order shall apply unless otherwise ordered by the Court.

2. This Administrative Order shall be recorded by the Clerk of the Court, in the Official Records of Duval County, in the State of Florida.

DONE AND ORDERED in Chambers at Jacksonville, Duval County, Florida, this 17 day of May, 2010.

DONALD R. MORAN, JR.
CHIEF JUDGE

1 JAC's contract for registry attorneys has a term corresponding with the state's fiscal year commencing on July 1st and ending on June 30. A new contract must be entered into each fiscal year.

2 This Administrative Order does not address the required qualifications for an attorney desiring to handle capital trial and capital appellate cases. Those qualifications are set forth in the Florida Statutes and Florida Rules of Criminal Procedure.

2010–02. WITHDRAWAL OF APPOINTED COUNSEL IN CRIMINAL CASES AFTER DISPOSITION AND PRIOR TO APPEAL

IN THE CIRCUIT COURT, FOURTH JUDICIAL CIRCUIT, IN AND FOR DUVAL, CLAY AND NASSAU COUNTIES, FLORIDA

ADMINISTRATIVE ORDER NO. 2010–02

IN RE: WITHDRAWAL OF APPOINTED COUNSEL IN CRIMINAL CASES AFTER DISPOSITION AND PRIOR TO APPEAL

WHEREAS, § 27.51(1), Florida Statutes, provides that the Public Defender shall represent any person determined to be indigent under § 27.52, Florida Statutes;

WHEREAS, § 27.51(4)(a), Florida Statutes, provides that the Public Defender, Second Judicial Circuit, shall, "after the record on appeal is transmitted to the appellate court," handle all circuit court appeals "on behalf of any public defender within the district comprising the First District Court of Appeal;"

WHEREAS, 9.140, Florida Rules of Appellate Procedure, provides that after judgment and sentence,

(d)(1) The attorney of record for a defendant in a criminal proceeding shall not be relieved of any professional duties, or be permitted to withdraw as defense counsel of record, except with approval of the lower tribunal on good cause shown on written motion, until either the time has expired for filing an authorized notice of appeal and no such notice has been filed by the defendant or the state, or after the following have been completed:

(A) a notice of appeal or cross-appeal has been filed on behalf of the defendant or the state;

(B) a statement of judicial acts to be reviewed has been filed if a transcript will require the expenditure of public funds;

(C) the defendant's directions to the clerk have been filed, if necessary;

(D) designations to the court reporter have been filed for transcripts of those portions of the proceedings necessary to support the issues on appeal or, if transcripts will require the expenditure of public funds for the defendant, of those portions of the proceedings necessary to support the statement of judicial acts to be reviewed; and

(E) in publicly funded defense and state appeals, the lower tribunal has appointed the public defender for the local circuit court, who shall initially remain counsel for the appeal until the record is transmitted to the appellate court . . .;

WHEREAS, the Office of Criminal Conflict and Civil Regional Counsel (OCCCRC), Region One, was created by the Florida Legislature to handle conflict cases in trial cases in which any Public Defender in Region One (First District) certifies conflict and moves to withdraw in the trial court, § 27.511(5)(a)–(d), Florida Statutes, and in appellate cases in which the Public Defender, Second Judicial Circuit (after the record on appeal has been transmitted to the appellate court), files a motion to withdraw in the First District Court of Appeal, certifying conflict consistent with the criteria prescribed in §§ 27.5303, 27.511(5)(e)–(f) and 27.511(8), Florida Statutes;

WHEREAS, under § 27.511, Florida Statutes, and 9.140(d), Florida Rules of Appellate Procedure, once the appeal has been perfected by trial counsel in Region One, the Public Defender in the circuit in which the trial was held initially handles the case only for purposes of transmitting the record on appeal to the First District Court of Appeal and to the Public Defender, Second Judicial Circuit, and of designating the Public Defender, Second Circuit, to handle the appeal once the record has been transmitted to the appellate court;

WHEREAS, the Public Defender, Second Judicial Circuit, handles all indigent appeals for the First District, including cases in which the indigent defendant/appellant was represented at trial by the Public Defender for any judicial circuit in the First District, or by private counsel, or by conflict registry counsel, or by the OCCCRC, pursuant to §§ 27.51(4)(a) and 27.511(8), Florida Statutes;

WHEREAS, it is only after the Office of the Public Defender, Second Judicial Circuit, has determined that a conflict of interest exists preventing it from representing the defendant/appellant on appeal that the OCCCRC is appointed to a case for purposes of appeal, Section 27.511(8), Florida Statutes;

WHEREAS, Florida Rule of Appellate Procedure 9.140(d)(1)(e) provides for appointment of the local Public Defender until the record on appeal has been transmitted to the First District Court of Appeal and the Public Defender for the Second Circuit has been designated;

WHEREAS, if the trial attorney is not allowed to withdraw until all the pleadings required by the rule have been filed and the Public Defender, Fourth Judicial Circuit, has been appointed to handle the case until the record has been transmitted to the First District Court of Appeal in compliance with Rule 9.140(d)(1), the Public Defender, Fourth Circuit, is only required to administratively process the paperwork to its designee, the Public Defender, Second Circuit;

WHEREAS, Rule 9.140 does not compel the local Public Defender to assist trial counsel or to counsel the defendant, and therefore there is no ethical conflict which precludes the Public Defender, Fourth Circuit, from handling a case after the pleadings required by Rule 9.140(d)(1) have been filed until the record on appeal has been transmitted to the First District Court of Appeal and the Public Defender, Second Circuit, has thereafter been designated to handle the appeal, as authorized by statute; and

WHEREAS, the Florida Legislature, in creating the OCCCRC, did not change the system of appointing the Public Defender, Second Judicial Circuit, on all indigent appeals in the First District, nor did the Legislature give the OCCCRC authority to handle appeals except in the limited circumstances after the Public Defender, Second Judicial Circuit, has determined that a conflict of interest exists on appeal.

NOW THEREFORE, by the authority vested in me as Chief Judge and pursuant to the Florida Rules of Judicial Administration, it is

ORDERED:

1. That the presiding judge in any criminal case in the Fourth Judicial Circuit involving an indigent defendant shall not allow trial counsel to withdraw from the case after disposition until either the time has expired for filing an authorized notice of appeal and no such notice has been filed by the defendant or trial counsel has filed all of the pleadings required by 9.140(d)(1)(A)–(D), Florida Rules of Appellate Procedure, and until the Public Defender, Fourth Judicial Circuit, has been appointed to handle the appeal until the record is transmitted to the appellate court, in compliance with Rule 9.140(d)(1)(E).

2. That the presiding judge in any criminal case in the Fourth Judicial Circuit involving an indigent defendant shall not appoint the Office of Criminal Conflict and Civil Regional Counsel for purposes of appeal, except upon orders from the First District Court of Appeal allowing the Public Defender, Second Circuit, to withdraw based upon conflict.

3. That this Administrative Order shall take effect immediately and remain in effect until further Order of the Court, and all terms and conditions set forth herein shall apply in full force and effect unless and until otherwise ordered by this Court.

4. That this Order shall be recorded in the Official Records of Duval County in the State of Florida, and copies furnished by the Clerk of Court in each County.

DONE AND ORDERED in Chambers at Jacksonville, Duval County, Florida, this 24 day of Feb, 2010.

DONALD R. MORAN, JR.
CHIEF JUDGE

2010–01 (A1). RESIDENTIAL HOMESTEAD FORECLOSURE CASES MANDATORY REFERRAL TO MEDIATION

IN THE CIRCUIT COURT, FOURTH JUDICIAL CIRCUIT, IN AND FOR DUVAL, CLAY AND NASSAU COUNTIES, FLORIDA

FIRST AMENDED ADMINISTRATIVE ORDER NO. 2010–1

RE: RESIDENTIAL HOMESTEAD FORECLOSURE CASES MANDATORY REFERRAL TO MEDIATION

WHEREAS, it is in the best interest of the judiciary, the parties involved, the mediators, the Residential Mortgage Foreclosure Mediation (RMFM) Program Manager, and the citizens of the Fourth Judicial Circuit, to establish some reasonable time lines within which the Borrowers must respond to the Program Manager in order to report any intentions of proceeding with the mediation process;

WHEREAS, it has also become necessary to establish accountability for the Borrowers' failure to timely file the "Borrowers' Request to Participate in the RMFM Program," therefore delaying the program schedule so that it is unable to complete credit counseling and the exchange of financial documents with the Plaintiffs as required in order to schedule mediation within 120 days of the date the case is filed;

NOW THEREFORE, by the authority vested in me as the Chief Judge of the Fourth Judicial Circuit and pursuant to the Florida Rules of Judicial Administration, it is

ORDERED:

1. That upon filing a new case, plaintiffs in the Fourth Judicial Circuit shall send a completed Form "A" as revised, amended and attached hereto, and a check in the amount of $400.00 to the Jacksonville Bar Association (hereinafter, the "Program Manager");

2. That within twenty (20) days from the date the Program Manager receives a completed Form A from the Plaintiffs, the Program Manager shall make a diligent, good faith attempt to contact the Borrower and will mail a Packet, including a letter explaining the Residential Mortgage Foreclosure Mediation (RMFM) Program to the Borrower, along with the Borrower's Request to Participate in RMFM Program form, the Borrower's Decline to Participate in RMFM Program form, and a Business Reply envelope for the Borrower's Response.

3. That from the date that the Program Manager mails the Packet to the Borrower, the Borrower shall have twenty-five (25) calendar days, excluding holidays (unless good cause is shown to the Court), within which to submit a response in writing to the Program Manager;

3.a) in its response to the Program Manager, the Borrower may:

(i) submit the Borrower's Request to Participate in RMFM Program form to the Program Manager; or

(ii) submit the Borrower's Decline to Participate in RMFM Program form to the Program Manager.

b) in its response to the Program Manager, if the Borrower timely submits the Borrower's Request to Participate form to the Program Manager, then Mediation must be scheduled within the original one-hundred and twenty (120) days from the date the Program Manager received the completed Form A and the check from the Plaintiffs, unless the Plaintiff fails to timely comply with the financial documentation production requirements contained within Section 6 and 7 of the original Administrative Order No. 2010–1;

c) if the Borrower submits the Borrower's Decline to Participate in RMFM Program form to the Program Manager, fails to respond timely, or ignores the matter, the Program Manager shall file with the Court the Notice of Borrower Nonparticipation with RMFM Program no later than 60 days after the receipt of the completed Form A and check from the Plaintiffs.

4. That if, after submitting the Borrower's Request to Participate in RMFM Program form to the Program Manager, the Borrower then fails to comply with *any* of the requirements of the Mediation process, the Program Manager will forthwith terminate the Mediation process and file with the Court a Notice of Borrower's Nonparticipation;

5. That all of the original Administrative Order No. 2010–1 previously entered and requiring mediation for residential homestead mortgage foreclosure cases is only superseded where it is contrary and inconsistent to the terms provided above; otherwise, it remains in full force and effect; and

6. That this First Amended Administrative Order shall be recorded by the Clerk of the Court, in the Official Records of Duval County, in the State of Florida, and shall take effect immediately and remain in full force and effect unless and until otherwise ordered by the Court.

DONE AND ORDERED in Chambers at Jacksonville, Duval County, Florida, this 13 day of Oct, 2010.

DONALD R. MORAN, JR.
CHIEF JUDGE

Please fill in and file the original with the Clerk of Court

IN THE CIRCUIT COURT IN AND FOR
________ COUNTY, FLORIDA

Case No.:

Plaintiff,

vs.

Defendant(s)

Form "A"

(Certifications Pursuant to Fourth Judicial Circuit Administrative Order 2010–1)

Certificate of Plaintiff's Counsel Regarding Origination of Note and Mortgage

THE UNDERSIGNED, as counsel of record for plaintiff and as an officer of the court, certifies the origination of the note and mortgage sued upon in this action ___ WAS or ___ WAS NOT subject to the provisions of the federal Truth in Lending Act, Regulation Z.

Certificate of Plaintiff's Counsel Regarding Status of Residential Property

THE UNDERSIGNED, as counsel of record for plaintiff and as an officer of the court, certifies the property that is the subject matter of this lawsuit ___ IS or ___ IS NOT a homestead residence. A "homestead residence" means a residential property for which a homestead real estate tax exemption was granted according to the certified rolls of the last assessment by the county property appraiser prior to the filing of the suit to foreclose the mortgage.

If the residential property is a homestead residence, complete both of the following:

Certificate of Plaintiff's Counsel Regarding Pre–Suit Mediation

The following certification ___ DOES or ___ DOES NOT apply to this case: THE UNDERSIGNED, as counsel of record for plaintiff and as an officer of the court, certifies that prior to filing suit a plaintiff's representative with full settlement authority attended and participated in mediation with the borrower, conducted by The Jacksonville Bar Association Fourth Judicial Circuit Residential Mortgage Foreclosure Mediation Program and the mediation resulted in an impasse or a pre-suit settlement agreement was reached but the settlement agreement has been breached. The undersigned further certifies that prior to mediation the borrower received services from a HUD or NFMC approved foreclosure counselor, Borrower's Financial Disclosure for Mediation was provided, and Plaintiff's Disclosure for Mediation was provided.

Certificate of Plaintiffs Counsel Regarding Plaintiff's Representative at Mediation

THE UNDERSIGNED, as counsel of record for plaintiff and as an officer of the court, certifies the following is a list of the persons, one of whom will represent the plaintiff in mediation with full authority to modify the existing loan and mortgage and to settle the foreclosure case, and with authority to sign a settlement agreement on behalf of the plaintiff *(list name, address, phone number, facsimile number, and email address):*

Plaintiff's counsel understands the mediator or the RMFM Program Manager may report to the court who appears at mediation and, if at least one of plaintiff's representatives named above does not appear at mediation, sanctions may be imposed by the court for failure to appear. As required by the Administrative Order, plaintiff's counsel will transmit electronically to the RMFM Program Manager the case number of this action, the contact information regarding the parties, and a copy of this Form A, using the approved web-enable information platform.

Certificate of Borrower's Last Known Address and Occupancy

Borrower Name: ___________

Last Known Mailing Address: ___________

Home Phone Number: ___________

Work Phone Number: ___________

Alternate Phone Number: ___________

Email Address: ___________

An answer of "unknown," "not sure " "not applicable," or other like response will not be accepted.

Is this residence occupied by the borrower? ☐ Yes ☐ No

Borrower's Attorney (if applicable): ___________

Firm Name: ___________

Address: ___________

Phone Number: ___________

If certified property is homestead, please make check payable to The Jacksonville Bar Association—RMFMP in the amount of $400.00

Date: ___________

(Signature of Plaintiff's Counsel)
[Printed name, address, phone number and Fla. Bar No.]

2008–04 (A3). ASSESSMENT AND COLLECTION OF DRUG TESTING FEE FOR DUVAL COUNTY, FLORIDA

IN THE CIRCUIT COURT, FOURTH JUDICIAL CIRCUIT, IN AND FOR DUVAL COUNTY, FLORIDA

THIRD AMENDED ADMINISTRATIVE ORDER NO. 2008–04

IN RE: ASSESSMENT AND COLLECTION OF DRUG TESTING FEE FOR DUVAL COUNTY, FLORIDA

WHEREAS, it is in the best interest of the citizens of the Fourth Judicial Circuit to insure that the Drug Court drug testing laboratory be properly maintained in Duval County, Florida;

WHEREAS, the Second Amended Administrative Order No. 2008–04 is amended herein only to modify paragraph I to clarify the purpose for which the drug testing fees are being used.

NOW THEREFORE, by the authority vested in me as Chief Judge and pursuant to the Florida Rules of Judicial Administration, it is

ORDERED:

(A) That every individual ordered by the Fourth Judicial Circuit Court, Duval County (the Court), to complete a drug test shall be required to pay a fee of $25.00—or such reduced amount as deemed appropriate by the Court to ensure the ability to pay, with the exception of individuals found to be indigent upon proper application to the Court;

(B) That individuals found to be indigent upon proper application to the Court shall be exempt from payment of this fee;

(C) That individuals who are ordered for testing shall make payment to the Duval County Clerk of Court, which has agreed to issue a receipt to such individuals as proof of payment, that shall, upon presentation at the Duval County Drug Court Lab, enable drug testing to be completed;

(D) That agencies executing a Memorandum of Understanding (MOU) with the Duval County Drug Court Lab to perform drug tests at an agreed upon contracted rate shall, after receipt of an invoice, submit a monthly payment (to the Duval County Drug Court Lab made payable to "the Duval County Clerk of Court") along with a copy of the invoice, in accordance with the MOU for tests performed pursuant to a Court order or Child Welfare Case Plan;

(E) That all such payments will be deposited by the Duval County Clerk of Court into the existing Drug Testing Revenue Fund, i.e., GL229387 (F750), as maintained by the Duval County Clerk of Court;

(F) That the Duval County Clerk of Court has agreed to maintain separate accounting records for these funds to ensure proper appropriation of all revenues collected. Upon request from the Court Administration, the Duval County Clerk of Court will establish and maintain a bank account for receipt of these funds, which shall support any required maintenance fees necessary to operate the account;

(G) That this account shall allow for end of fiscal year cash carryover;

(H) That the fees collected will be deposited by the Clerk of Court into this account, less one dollar ($1.00) per drug testing fee as a service charge to be retained by the Clerk;

(I) That the Chief Judge or his designee shall have authority over these funds for use in maintaining the Drug Court Lab and Drug Court programs to include drug lab costs, supplies, lab technicians, ongoing training and other drug court program expenses as approved by the Chief Judge; and that such funds shall only be disbursed by the Duval County Clerk of Court upon request by the Chief Judge or said designee.

(J) That the Administrative Order 2014–01 concerning Assessment and Collection of Drug Testing Fee for Clay County has been entered and remains in full force and effect; and

(K) That this Third Amended Administrative Order 2008–04 shall be recorded by the Clerk of the Court, in the Official Records of Duval County, in the State of Florida, shall take effect immediately and remain in full force and effect unless and until otherwise ordered by the Court.

DONE AND ORDERED in Chambers at Jacksonville, Duval County, Florida, this 12th day of February, 2015.

MARK H. MAHON

CHIEF JUDGE

2007–03 (A1). MENTAL HEALTH COURTS

IN THE CIRCUIT COURT, FOURTH JUDICIAL CIRCUIT IN AND FOR DUVAL AND NASSAU COUNTIES FLORIDA

AMENDED ADMINISTRATIVE ORDER NO. 2007–03

IN RE: MENTAL HEALTH COURTS

WHEREAS, Administrative Order No. 2007–03 created a successful Mental Health Court in Nassau County in 2007; such Court has also been operating successfully in Duval County since 2008;

WHEREAS, a new edition of the diagnostic criteria for an Axis I mental health diagnosis (the Diagnostic and Statistical Manual of Mental Disorders: DSM–V) has been published very recently and evaluators are encouraged to refer to it once it is released and made available;

WHEREAS, this Administrative Order also serves the purpose of simply formalizing into writing the procedures of the Mental Health Court in Duval County, which has been successfully operational since it was established on January 29, 2008;

WHEREAS, the "treatment courts" within the Fourth Judicial Circuit have enhanced the expediency, effectiveness and quality of judicial administration; and

WHEREAS, the rapidly increasing number of criminal cases involving persons with mental illnesses has continued to contribute to congest and overburden the Court dockets; and

WHEREAS, the centralized Mental Health programs have increased the efficiency of the criminal court system in this Circuit;

NOW THEREFORE, by the authority vested in me as the Chief Judge of the Fourth Judicial Circuit and pursuant to the Florida Rules of Judicial Administration, it is

ORDERED that a Mental Health Court shall continue to remain operational as a subdivision within the Circuit Court and County Court Divisions of both Duval and Nassau Counties to adjudicate cases deemed eligible in this Order.

I. ELIGIBILITY

Eligibility for the Mental Health Court includes a review of several factors, which are listed below.

A. CRIMINAL CHARGES:

1. Persons arrested and/or formally charged with misdemeanors, criminal traffic offenses, and/or third degree non-violent felonies (with certain exceptions, such as violent or sexual offenses) may be referred to the Mental Health Court.

2. Persons charged with a second degree non-violent felony may be diverted to Mental Health Court at the discretion of the Office of the State Attorney once the charge is reduced to a lesser included offense.

3. Defendants charged with a violation of county court probation, with consent of the county judge to which the case is assigned.

4. Persons charged with simple battery or domestic battery (e.g., violent crimes), may be admitted with the victim's consent. On an individual case basis, persons charged with domestic violence may be referred and admitted after consultation with the victim.

5. The Mental Health Court, state attorney, and defense attorney will consider the defendant's previous criminal record. The Mental Health Court may refuse entry into the Mental Health Court on an individual case situation based on a history of violence, domestic violence, sexual offenses or other factors.

6. The Mental Health Court, state attorney and defense attorney will also consider whether transfer of all pending cases of a defendant would preclude the acceptance into the Mental Health Court.

B. MENTAL ILLNESS

1. *Permissible Diagnoses*

a. Persons referred to the Mental Health Court must meet the DSM–IV or DSM–V diagnostic criteria for an Axis I mental health diagnosis that is within the categories of Psychotic Disorders, Mood Disorders, or Anxiety Disorders.

b. Co-occurring substance abuse disorders are permissible.

c. A mental health expert, acceptable to the Mental Health Court, must provide the diagnosis.

d. The Diagnostic and Statistical Manual of Mental Disorders, 4th and 5th Editions (DSM–IV and DSM–V) may be used by evaluators to provide diagnoses to the Mental Health Court, but evaluators are encouraged to refer to the DSM–V as that is the Court's preferred diagnostic Manual because it is the most updated source.

2. *Disqualifying Diagnoses*

a. Persons with primary diagnosis of intellectual disability (f.k.a. "mental retardation"), autism, or dementia.

b. Persons with Axis I diagnoses, which are not mental illness diagnoses described in Section B.1.a of the DSM–IV.

C. COMPETENCY, INCOMPETENT TO PROCEED AND NOT GUILTY BY REASONS OF INSANITY CASES

1. Defendants adjudged incompetent to proceed, contesting competency or commitment, or found not guilty by reason of insanity will not participate in the Mental Health Court.

2. Defendants will not be referred to the Mental Health Court for competency determination.

3. Criminal Courts will maintain their authority to enter orders of competency and forensic commitment in cases.

4. Defendants that do not meet the criteria for forensic commitment or are returned from forensic institutions and deemed competent by the referring court may be referred provided they meet other criteria outlined in this Order.

D. EXCEPTIONS

1. The Mental Health Court, with the concurrence of the state attorney, may consider cases that do not meet every stated eligibility criterion.

II. PROCEDURAL MATTERS

A. REFERRALS AND TRANSFERS

1. Defendants may be referred from a variety of sources and some may have cases already pending and in process, while others may be on probation.

2. Referrals may be accepted from Mental Health Court Program staff, First Appearance Court, County and Circuit courts, the jail, a defense attorney, state attorney, mental health agency, probation officers and the Department of Children and Families.

3. The Mental Health Court will establish administrative procedures for referrals, transfers and hearings. Referrals will be pre-screened by the Mental Health Court Monitor.

4. When cases have already been assigned to a Criminal Court and have been deemed appropriate for Mental Health Court, the state attorney shall request the Clerk to transfer the case to Mental Health Court.

B. ADDITIONAL CONDITIONS FOR ENTRY INTO MENTAL HEALTH COURT

1. Defendant must comply with the conditions set forth below, though not all have to be completed immediately upon admission to the Mental Health Court.

a. Voluntarily agree to participate in Mental Health Court;

b. Enter into a Plea Agreement or enter into a Deferred Prosecution Agreement; and

c. Sign a waiver of speedy trial; and

d. Sign a consent for the release of information permitting disclosure of certain confidential information, including prior and current mental health treatment, to the Mental Health Court and other parties; and

e. Agree to and sign a treatment and service plan as part of the Conditional Release or Deferred Prosecution Agreement.

III. CONDITIONS FOR CONTINUATION, SUCCESSFUL COMPLETION, AND DISQUALIFICATION IN MENTAL HEALTH COURT

A. CONDITIONS FOR CONTINUATION

1. Conditions for the defendant's continued participation in the Mental Health Court include, but are not limited to, those listed below. Not all will apply to each case.

a. Comply in good faith effort with provisions of Conditional Release or Deferred Prosecution Agreement.

b. Attend and participate in all appearances before the Mental Health Court.

c. Attend all meetings with Mental Health Court Program staff, defense attorney and other persons designated by the Mental Health Court.

d. Obey all laws and do not commit additional crimes.

2. The Mental Health Court Judge and/or Magistrate will have the authority to impose graduated sanctions for noncompliance, including re-incarceration if appropriate. The Mental Health Court Judge and/or Magistrate may offer various forms of recognition for accomplishments.

B. CONDITIONS FOR SUCCESSFUL COMPLETION OF MENTAL HEALTH COURT

1. In addition to the conditions set forth above, the defendant's participation in the Mental Health Court will end upon

successful completion of his or her treatment and service plan, or upon attainment of substantial progress toward completion of the treatment and service plan.

2. The Mental Health Court may then issue an Order, with the concurrence of the state attorney, dismissing charges, or terminating the violation of probation, and any related criminal case will be closed. The State Attorney's Office may issue a Disposition Notice indicating "Completion of Program" to the Clerk of Court.

C. GENERAL CONDITIONS FOR DISQUALIFICATION AND RETURN TO CRIMINAL COURT

1. The Mental Health Court will have the authority to have defendants re-arrested and to have cases transferred back to the Criminal Division for reasons which include, but are not limited to:

a. Any violation of Section III.A;

b. If a defendant is determined not to meet criteria for mental illness or at any time demands a trial or hearing on a motion to determine legal issues unrelated to mental health;

c. If a defendant has indicated that he or she no longer desires to participate in the Mental Health Court, provided the Judge or Magistrate has the ultimate authority to make the determination as to whether it is in the best interest of the defendant to remain and finish the Mental Health Court treatment and service plan or to be released, disqualified, re-arrested and transferred back to the Criminal Division;

d. If the Court determines that the defendant is no longer sufficiently participating in or benefitting from the Mental Health Court, or that the defendant poses a great threat to public safety;

e. If the defendant is arrested for, or charged with, any new offense, the defendant is no longer eligible for the Mental Health Court without the consent of the Criminal Division, the State Attorney and the defense attorney as to any or all of the defendant's cases.

f. Thereupon, the defendant's right to a speedy trial and formal discovery may be reinstated upon a written demand.

IV. ACCESS TO MENTAL HEALTH COURT RECORDS

The public is entitled to access judicial records. However, patient treatment records are an exception to this rule and are deemed confidential by Florida and/or Federal law and regulations.

V. ADMINISTRATION

FURTHERMORE, IT IS ORDERED that the Honorable Brian J. Davis is hereby designated as the Judge assigned to this treatment court in and for Nassau County, Florida. Magistrate John A. Sampson and Chief Judge Donald R. Moran, Jr. are assigned to this treatment court in and for Duval County, Florida. In that capacity, they will be responsible for administering the Mental Health Court and coordinating the role of the judiciary with the functions of the Department of Children and Family Services, Mental Health Court Program Administration, Nassau County Sheriff's Office, Jacksonville Sheriff's Office, Starting Point Behavioral Health, River Region Human Services, private mental health care providers, Department of Corrections, County Court Probation and other organizations and individuals that may participate on the behalf of the defendants referred to or assigned to the Mental Health Court.

In that Judge Davis, Magistrate John A. Sampson, and Chief Judge Donald R. Moran, Jr. have proven themselves to be learned in the field of mental health and possess a unique understanding with respect to the needs of the mentally ill, and handle such cases accordingly, without compromising the safety of the public, the Office of the State Attorney concurs in these judicial assignments. If, for some reason, Judge Davis or Magistrate Sampson cease to preside over the Mental Health Court, the judicial replacement shall be assigned by the Chief Judge, who may consult with the Office of the State Attorney, the Office of the Public Defender and the criminal defense bar.

IT IS FURTHER ORDERED that all other Administrative Orders, including Administrative Order No. 2007–03, previously entered and addressing the same subject matter and mental health, are hereby vacated and superseded.

IT IS FURTHER ORDERED that this Administrative Order shall be recorded by the Clerk of the Court, in the Official Records of Duval County, in the State of Florida, and shall take effect immediately and remain in full force and effect unless and until otherwise ordered by this Court.

DONE AND ORDERED at Jacksonville, Duval County, Florida this 2 day of July 2013.

DONALD R. MORAN, JR.

CHIEF JUDGE

2007–01. COURT APPOINTED COUNSEL IN DEPENDENCY AND TERMINATION OF PARENTAL RIGHTS PROCEEDINGS

IN THE CIRCUIT COURT, FOURTH JUDICIAL CIRCUIT IN AND FOR DUVAL, CLAY AND NASSAU COUNTIES, FLORIDA

ADMINISTRATIVE ORDER NO. 2007–01

IN RE: COURT APPOINTED COUNSEL IN DEPENDENCY AND TERMINATION OF PARENTAL RIGHTS PROCEEDINGS

WHEREAS, Florida Statutes, Sec. 27.40 directs the Justice Administrative Commission to approve uniform contracts for use in procuring the services of court appointed counsel, which contracts are to be made circuit-specific by the inclusion in Attachment A thereof, of the plan developed in each circuit; and

WHEREAS, the Fourth Judicial Circuit Indigent Services Committee has recognized that this Circuit must be fiscally responsible in approving rates of compensation for court appointed counsel taking into consideration the fiscal policies and limits set by the legislature; and

WHEREAS, the Fourth Judicial Circuit Indigent Services Committee also recognizes that it has a duty to provide indigent parents with competent and qualified counsel;

NOW THEREFORE, by the authority vested in me as the Chief Judge of the Fourth Judicial Circuit and pursuant to the Florida Rules of Judicial Administration, it is

ORDERED that:

1. Effective March 15, 2007, Court appointed counsel for dependency cases in the Fourth Judicial Circuit shall be entitled to compensation pursuant to the following terms and conditions:

a. Dependency cases shall be paid at the rate of One Thousand Dollars ($1,000.00) through the time of appointment until dismissal, protective supervision is closed, the permanency hearing or discharge whichever occurs first.

(1) Counsel shall be entitled to submit a bill for said amount after disposition, dismissal or discharge whichever occurs first.

(2) Unless otherwise discharged by the Court, Counsel, once appointed, shall continue to provide legal representation until protective supervision is closed, or a permanency hearing has been completed.

b. Appointments made after the permanency hearing or protective services have been closed shall be paid at the rate of Five Hundred Dollars ($500.00). In the event a parent requires legal representation at the trial court level after a termination of parental rights hearing, Counsel shall be compensated at the rate of Five Hundred Dollars ($500.00).

(1) A bill may be submitted after the first judicial review after appointment.

(2) Counsel shall continue to represent the parent(s) until protective supervision is closed, permanency hearing or discharged by the Court without any further compensation.

c. Termination of Parental Rights cases shall be paid at the rate of Nine Hundred Dollars ($900.00) per case.

d. Appeals shall be paid at the rate of One Thousand Five Hundred Dollars ($1,500.00).

e. In the event there are any unusual and/or extraordinary circumstances that, in order to provide effective representation, would warrant a fee award in excess of the amounts set forth above, Counsel shall be compensated an additional Five Hundred Dollars ($500.00).

2. Counsel appointed to any case prior to March 15, 2007, shall be paid pursuant to Administrative Order No. 2004–10 executed on September 20, 2004.

3. In the event that Counsel was appointed to a case prior to March 15, 2007 and was subsequently discharged after disposition but prior to the closing of protective supervision, or a permanency hearing, Counsel shall be compensated pursuant to Administrative Order No. 2004–10 executed on September 20, 2004. All other court appointments made on or after March 15, 2007, shall be pursuant to the terms and conditions of representation and compensation set forth above.

4. All other provisions of Administrative Order No. 2004–10 executed on September 20, 2004, not directly in conflict with the provisions of this Order shall remain in full force and effect.

5. That this Administrative Order shall be effective immediately, and remain in full force and effect unless and until otherwise ordered by this Court.

DONE AND ORDERED in Chambers in Jacksonville, Duval County, Florida, this 21 day of March, 2007

DONALD R. MORAN, JR.
CHIEF JUDGE

2006–05. SEALING COURT RECORDS

IN THE CIRCUIT COURT, FOURTH JUDICIAL CIRCUIT IN AND FOR DUVAL, CLAY AND NASSAU COUNTIES, FLORIDA

ADMINISTRATIVE ORDER NO. 2006–05

RE: SEALING COURT RECORDS

WHEREAS, Florida Rules of Judicial Administration 2.051(c)(7) and (8) provide that all "records of the judicial branch shall be confidential" where they are deemed or made to be confidential under the Florida or United States Constitutions; under Florida or federal law; by Florida court rule; by Florida Statutes; by Florida case law; or by the Rules of the Judicial Qualifications Commission. The Florida Supreme Court expressly found that Rule 2.051(c)(8) adopts statutory public records exemptions. State v. Buenoano, 707 So. 2d 714, 718 (Fla. 1998).

WHEREAS, Rule 2.051(c)(9) also sets forth grounds in which the Court may enter an order upon determining that confidentiality of a "court record" is required;

WHEREAS, the Florida Supreme Court has recently suggested that procedures be implemented for sealing court records, so this Court finds it necessary to establish uniform sealing procedures for court records, including progress dockets, court files, particular documents within court files, and the identity of parties in the Fourth Judicial Circuit;

WHEREAS, an effort is being made to provide a uniform method for insuring the confidentiality of court records when such confidentiality is required by law or found warranted by court order to insure that materials are not unintentionally designated as confidential, and to provide a uniform procedure whereby the public can request review of orders to seal;

NOW THEREFORE, pursuant to the authority vested in me as the Chief Judge of the Fourth Judicial Circuit and pursuant to the Rules of Judicial Administration which includes authority to exercise administrative supervision over the courts and to control dockets within the circuit, it is

ORDERED:

That this Administrative Order sets forth procedures that shall be followed for sealing "court records" or portions of court files in the Fourth Circuit Court.

Furthermore, this Administrative Order consists of these four sections:

I. SEALING COURT MATERIALS UNDER RULES 2.051(C)(7) or (8) (PURSUANT TO STATUTES, RULES OR OTHER LEGAL AUTHORITY)

II. SEALING "COURT RECORDS" PURSUANT TO COURT ORDER (BASED ON RULE 2.051(C)(9))

III. PROCEDURES FOR UNSEALING

IV. DEFINITIONS AND APPLICATION

I. SEALING COURT MATERIALS UNDER RULES 2.051(C)(7) or (8) (PURSUANT TO STATUTES, RULES OR OTHER LEGAL AUTHORITY)

A. Sealing a Court File *and* Progress Docket

When both the court file and the progress docket are sealed by operation of law pursuant to a specific statute, rule, or other legal authority, the Clerks of the Circuit and County

Court of Duval, Clay and Nassau Counties are hereby authorized and directed to seal both the court file *and* the progress docket. No court order or public notice shall be required before such sealing may be undertaken. Legal authorities which authorize and require the sealing of both the court file *and* the progress docket include, but are not limited to:

1. Dependency, sections 39.0132(3)–(4), Florida Statutes;

2. Termination of Parental Rights, sections 39.814(3)–(4), Florida Statutes;

3. Adoption, section 63.162(2), Florida Statutes;

4. Surrogacy, section 742.16(9), Florida Statutes;

5. Children and Families in Need of Services, sections 984.06(3)–(4), Florida Statutes; and

6. Delinquency, section 985.05(2), Florida Statutes.

B. Sealing a Court File

When a court file is sealed by operation of law pursuant to a specific statute, rule, or other legal authority, the Clerks of the Circuit and County Court of Duval, Clay and Nassau Counties are hereby authorized and directed to seal such file according to the scope and terms of such legal authority. No court order nor public notice shall be required before such sealing. Legal authorities which authorize and require the sealing of a court file include, but are not limited to, the following:

1. Petitions Regarding Individuals Suspected of Being Infected With or Exposed to a Sexually Transmissible Disease (including petitions for writs of habeas corpus or immediate release), Chapter 384, Florida Statutes;

2. Petitions Regarding Individuals Suspected of Having Tuberculosis (including petitions for immediate release), Chapter 392, Florida Statutes;

3. Waiver of Parental Notification of Termination of Pregnancy, sections 390.01114–.01116 and Florida Juvenile Procedure Rule 8.835;

4. Baker Act (including petitions for writs of habeas corpus filed by individuals held under the act), section 394.4615(1), Florida Statutes;

5. Marchman Act (including petitions for writs of habeas corpus filed by individuals held under the act), section 397.501(7), Florida Statutes;

6. Petitions for Enforcement of an Order of the Department of Health Regarding a Nurse's Fitness to Practice, section 464.018(1)(j), Florida Statutes;

7. Sexual Violence Injunctions, sections 92.56, 119.071(2)(h)(2) and (j)(1), and 784.046, Florida Statutes; and

8. Application for Authorization of Attorney Fee Contract When Filed as a Separate Proceeding Before Suit, Rules Regulating the Florida Bar Rule 4–1.5(f)(4)(B)(ii).

If the Clerks of the Circuit or County Court for Duval, Clay and Nassau Counties receive a request for public access to court files regarding any cases listed in this subsection, the Clerk shall respond as follows:

a. The Clerk shall not release any of the following materials absent a court order authorizing such release in accordance with applicable statutory provisions:

i. clinical records under the Baker Act; or

ii. client records under the Marchman Act.

b. The Clerk may release any other materials only after the Clerk carefully reviews the materials to ensure that any information that reveals the identity of the patient, client, minor or abuse victim, including the names of any family members of such persons, is redacted from the record prior to release.

C. Sealing Document(s) *Within* a Court File

When a document within a court file is sealed by operation of law pursuant to a specific statute, rule, or other legal authority, the Clerks of the Circuit and County Court of Duval, Clay and Nassau Counties are hereby authorized and directed to seal such document according to the scope and terms of such legal authority. No court order nor public notice shall be required before such sealing. Legal authorities which authorize and require the sealing of particular documents include but are not limited to the following:

1. Domestic Violence Petitioner's Request for Confidential Filing of Victim's home and employment address, phone number, personal assets, etc., sections 119.071(2)(j)(1) and 741.30, Florida Statutes, and Florida Family Law Form 12.980(h);

2. Inventory of Personal Representative, section 733.604(1), Florida Statutes;

3. Guardianship Reports, section 744.3701(1), Florida Statutes;

4. Birth Records, section 382.025, Florida Statutes;

5. Clinical Records of Detained Criminal Defendants Found Incompetent to Proceed or Acquitted by Reason of Insanity, section 916.107(8), Florida Statutes;

6. Medical Records, section 456.057(10), Florida Statutes;

7. Psychological and Psychiatric Evaluations, sections 456.057 and 456.059, Florida Statutes;

8. Pre–sentence Reports, Florida Rule of Criminal Procedure 3.712;

9. Notice of Social Security Number, Florida Family Law Form 12.902(j);

10. Application for Authorization of Attorney Fee Contract When Filed Simultaneously with Complaint, Rules Regulating the Florida Bar Rule 4–1.5(f)(4)(B)(ii); and

11. Protected Health Information Under the Health Insurance Portability and Accountability Act of 1996 (HIPAA), Pub. L. No. 104–191, 110 Stat. 1936 (codified as amended in scattered sections of 18, 26, 29 and 42 U.S.C.).

D. Removing a Party's Name from the *Progress Docket*

When the removal of a party's name from the progress docket is dictated under operation of law by a specific statute, rule or other legal authority, the Clerks of the Circuit and County Court of Duval, Clay and Nassau Counties are hereby authorized and directed to remove the name and substitute terminology as follows:

1. For petitions to examine, detain, or compel treatment of individuals suspected of being infected with sexually transmissible diseases or tuberculosis pursuant to Chapters 384 or 392, Florida Statutes, including petitions for habeas corpus or immediate release, by substituting "Subject" for the name of the individual in petitions to examine, detain, or compel treatment; and "Petitioner" for the name of the individual in habeas corpus or immediate release cases;

2. For petitions to waive parental notification of termination of pregnancy filed pursuant to section 390.01116, Florida Statutes, by substituting the initials of the minor or, if a sworn statement of true name and pseudonym is filed, the pseudonym;

3. For petitions alleging a nurse's unfitness to practice filed pursuant to section 464.018(1)(j), Florida Statutes, by substituting "Respondent" for the nurse's name;

4. For petitions seeking a sexual violence injunction pursuant to section 784.046, Florida Statutes, by substituting "Petitioner" for the name of the alleged victim of sexual violence or the parents or legal guardians of a minor who is the alleged victim of sexual violence; and

5. For petitions filed under the Baker or Marchman Acts, including petitions for writs of habeas corpus filed by persons held under these acts, by substituting "Subject" for the name of the patient or client in Baker or Marchman Act cases; and "Petitioner" for the name of the patient or client in habeas corpus cases.

The Clerks of the Circuit and County Court of Duval, Clay and Nassau Counties shall take all reasonable steps necessary to ensure that the docket of the court proceedings on the above-listed cases is available to the public in a manner that does not disclose the identity of the protected party.

E. Other Circumstances for Sealing Based on Legal Authority

1. Paternity Actions

If the Clerks of the Circuit or County Court of Duval, Clay and Nassau Counties receive written notice, accompanied by a copy of a marriage license, that the biological mother in a paternity action has subsequently married the purported father, the Clerk is hereby authorized and directed to seal both the court file and the progress docket in the paternity action pursuant to section 742.091, Florida Statutes. No court order nor public notice shall be required before such sealing may be undertaken.

2. Criminal Investigative Records

The Clerks of the Circuit and County Court of Duval, Clay and Nassau Counties are hereby authorized and directed to seal the following criminal investigative documents, which may be in the possession of the Clerk, and no court order nor public notice shall be required before such sealing may be undertaken:

a. Grand jury notes, stenographers' records, and transcripts, section 905.17, Florida Statutes;

b. Unexecuted search warrants or search warrants and their returns that are part of an ongoing criminal investigation, section 119.071(2)(c)(1), Florida Statutes, Rule of Judicial Administration 2.051(c)(6);

c. Investigative subpoenas, section 119.071(2)(c)(1), Florida Statutes;

d. Records and warrants pertaining to any Indictment or Information until the defendant is in custody or a period of one year has elapsed, Florida Rule of Criminal Procedure 3.140(*l*);

e. Applications for or orders authorizing a wiretap, pen register or trap and trace device, or mobile tracking device, sections 119.071(2)(c)(1), 934.09(8)(c), 934.33, and 934.42, Florida Statutes; and

f. Arrest warrants and supporting affidavits that are unexecuted or a determination is made that execution cannot be made, Rule of Judicial Administration 2.051(c)(6).

II. SEALING "COURT RECORDS" PURSUANT TO COURT ORDER (BASED ON RULE 2.051(C)(9))

A. "Court Records" defined

Rule 2.051(b)(1)(A) defines "court records" as "the contents of the court file, including the progress docket and other similar records generated to document activity in a case, transcripts filed with the clerk, documentary exhibits in the custody of the clerk, and electronic records, videotapes, or stenographic tapes of depositions or other proceedings filed with the clerk, and electronic records, videotapes, or stenographic tapes of court proceedings" (emphasis added).

B. Named Party's Motion to Seal and Notice of Hearing

Motions to seal or make confidential a "court record" filed with the Clerk of the Circuit and County Courts may be granted by the Court provided that:

1. A named party files a motion with the Clerk of Court entitled "Motion to Seal";

2. The named party filing the Motion to Seal also files a pleading entitled "Notice of Hearing on Motion to Seal" and sets the hearing before the judge assigned to the division in which the case is pending; and

3. The Notice of Hearing on Motion to Seal filed by the moving party has provided reasonable notice to the parties, their attorneys, if any, and to the Clerk's Office as to the case number, the names of the parties in the case, and the date, time and location of the scheduled hearing.

C. Grounds for Entry of a Court Order

Any "court record" may be designated as confidential by a court order if it is determined that confidentiality is required for one of the following reasons, as provided by Florida Rule of Judicial Administration 2.051(c)(9)(I)–(vii):

"(i) to prevent a serious and imminent threat to the fair, impartial, and orderly administration of justice;

(ii) to protect trade secrets;

(iii) to protect a compelling governmental interest;

(iv) to obtain evidence to determine legal issues in a case;

(v) to avoid substantial injury to innocent third parties;

(vi) to avoid substantial injury to a party by disclosure of matters protected by a common law or privacy right not generally inherent in the specific type of proceeding sought to be closed; or

(vii) to comply with established public policy set forth in the Florida or United States Constitution or statutes or Florida rules or case law."

See also Barron v. FL Freedom Newspapers, Inc., 531 So.2d 113 (Fla. 1988) (discussing factors to weigh in balancing public and privacy interests); Peyton v. Browning, 541 So.2d 1341 (Fla. 1st DCA 1989) (financial information in dissolution proceedings is protected by Rule 1.611(a)).

D. Requirements for Court Orders

Any order entered by the Court in the Fourth Circuit that declares that a "court record" is to be sealed shall specifically state whether the Court is ordering the sealing of:

-the court file and the progress docket;

-the court file alone;

-particular contents of the file, such as a certain document, exhibit, transcripts filed with the clerk, documentary exhibits in the custody of the clerk, electronic records, videotapes, or stenographic tapes of depositions or other proceedings filed with the clerk, or electronic records, videotapes, or stenographic tapes of court proceedings within the file; or

-the party's name or identifying information of a party from the progress docket and/or documents or contents within.

Furthermore, any order directing that a party's name be removed from the progress docket shall specify the term to be substituted for the party's name as discussed and described in detail above (i.e., a pseudonym such as John Doe; a generic title such as "Petitioner" or the use of the party's initials).

In preparing orders to seal pursuant to Rule 2.051(c)(9), judges may use any order deemed necessary, including one similar to the attached Form "Order Granting/Denying Motion to Seal Pursuant to Florida Rule of Judicial Administration 2.051(c)(9)." See "Attachment A."

E. Clerk's Administrative Responsibilities

The Clerks of the Circuit and County Courts of Duval, Clay, Nassau Counties are hereby authorized and directed to seal materials as follows.

1. If the Order Directs Sealing a *"Court Record"*

If an order directs sealing a "court record" the Clerks of the Circuit and County Courts of Duval, Nassau and Clay Counties shall refer to the "DEFINITIONS" section in this Order to determine all portions of the court file that it must seal. It is important that the progress docket be sealed from any public access system as well.

2. If the Order Directs Sealing a Court File *and* a Party's Identity

The Clerk shall seal the court file and remove the party's name and identity from all parts of the file, including the progress docket, substituting for the party's name a term as directed by the Court; or, if no direction is given, a pseudonym, a general term such as "Petitioner," or the party's initials if the party is not generally identified by initials.

The progress docket shall otherwise remain public; however, the Clerks of the Circuit and County Court of Duval, Clay and Nassau Counties shall take all reasonable steps necessary to ensure that the docket of the court proceedings is made available to the public in a manner that does not disclose the identity of the protected party.

3. If the Order Directs Sealing a Court File but is Silent as to the Progress Docket

The Clerk shall seal the court file only and maintain a public progress docket with no alteration of the parties' names.

F. Posting of Public Notice of Court Order to Seal

Upon the filing of any court order authorizing the sealing of a "court record," the Clerks of the Circuit and County Courts of Duval, Clay and Nassau Counties are hereby authorized and directed to seal the designated record immediately.

In addition, the Clerk will immediately post a notice to the public by posting that the case has been sealed by court order, identifying it by case number only, and posting such notice on the "Public Notice Bulletin Board" located in the Clerk's Office, Room 103 in the Duval County Courthouse, or on the Public Notice Board in the entranceway of the Nassau County Judicial Annex in Yulee, Florida, or in an equally prominent location of the Clerk's Office in Clay County, depending on the county in which the case or court record is maintained. The Clerk should use a form similar to "Attachment B" herein to post the public Notice. Such Notice will be posted for a period of five (5) days from the date the order was filed.

G. Authorization for Fees Assessed to Seal File

When a motion is filed pursuant to Rule of Judicial Administration 2.051(c)(9) to seal a court file, the Clerk of the Circuit Court may assess fees in accordance with section 28.24(25), Florida Statutes, or other statutory authority.

III. PROCEDURES FOR UNSEALING

A. Clerk's Response to Requests for Sealed Record/File

If a member of the public or an entity requests a court file in which the file and progress docket have been sealed or in which a party's identity has been sealed, the Clerks of the Circuit and County Court of Duval, Clay and Nassau Counties are hereby authorized and directed to inform the requesting person or entity that they are unable to confirm or deny the existence of such a file.

B. Unsealing a File that has been Sealed by Court Order

1. Responsibilities of a Movant Requesting to Unseal

When a member of the press or the public seeks access to a sealed court file, sealed progress docket, sealed "court record" or sealed identity of an individual in a case, a written "Motion to Unseal" shall be filed with the Clerk of the Court and a copy of the motion shall be provided to the judge who entered the order sealing the file, record, progress docket or identity of a party. If the judge who entered the order is no longer a judge of the Fourth Judicial Circuit, then a copy of the motion should be provided to the judge in the original judge's division.

If the movant is unable to ascertain the name and address at which to provide notice to the parties, the motion shall reference this Administrative Order and state in prominent or boldface type that the movant requests that a "Notice of Hearing on the Motion to Unseal" be provided to the judge; to the movant; to the parties in the case, and to their attorneys of record, if any.

2. Responsibilities of the Clerk When a Motion to Unseal is Filed

Upon the filing of a Motion to Unseal and written request for a Notice of Hearing, the following will be done:

a. Notice of Hearing: the Clerk of Court will promptly prepare a Notice of Hearing which shall indicate the case number, the date, time and location of the scheduled hearing, and the names of the parties in the case, with the exception that where the identity of any party has been sealed, special care must be made to avoid disclosing any of the sealed names or identifying information anywhere in the Notice of Hearing; and

b. Mailing: the Clerk will promptly send the Notice of Hearing to: the relevant judge; the movant; and the parties of record and their attorneys of record, if any, and respectively to their last known addresses as indicated in the court file, in the most effective and cautious manner so as to attempt to provide notice without inadvertently revealing to the movant or the public the identity or identifying information of any sealed names of parties or any sealed portions of the court file or progress docket.

B.[1] Unsealing by the Clerk of Court for Limited Purpose of Filing

The Clerks of the Circuit and County Court of Duval, Clay and Nassau Counties are hereby authorized to open any court file sealed by operation of law or court order for the purpose of filing documents pertinent to the particular file, as well as for microfilming or imaging files.

The Clerk shall re-seal such files or documents immediately upon completion of the task, with the responsible Clerk's employee annotating the date of the unsealing and re-sealing along with the employee's full name.

C. Unsealing by the Clerk of Court for Purposes of Transmitting Record for Appellate Review

The Clerks of the Circuit and County Court of Duval, Clay and Nassau Counties are hereby authorized to open any file or document sealed by operation of law or court order for the purpose of making a copy of the file or document for transmitting to any appellate tribunal for the purposes of appellate review. When transmitting such copies in the record on appeal, the Clerk shall clearly indicate to the appellate tribunal which documents are under seal in the trial court.

The Clerk shall re-seal such files or documents immediately upon completion of copying, with the responsible Clerk's employee annotating the date of the unsealing and re-sealing along with the employee's full name.

D. Access by Named Parties and the Attorneys of Record in a Sealed File

In all matters except Adoption and Surrogacy cases, notwithstanding the sealing of any court file or portion thereof by operation of law or court order, the Clerks of the Circuit and County Court of Duval, Clay and Nassau Counties are hereby authorized to make all contents of a court file available to adult named parties and their attorneys of record in the sealed file.

The contents and identity of the parties in Adoption and Surrogacy files shall not be made available to any person absent a court order.

IV. DEFINITIONS AND APPLICATION

A. Definitions for purposes of this Administrative Order

1. **"Court Records"** is defined by Rule 2.051(b)(1)(A) defines as "the contents of the court file, including the progress docket and other similar records generated to document activity in a case, transcripts filed with the clerk, documentary exhibits in the custody of the clerk, and electronic records, videotapes, or stenographic tapes of depositions or other proceedings filed with the clerk, and electronic records, videotapes, or stenographic tapes of court proceedings" (emphasis added);

2. **"Court File"** generally means all of the materials within a court file *but not* the progress docket;

3. **"Document"** means a particular item within a court file;

B. Application: Sealing or Expunging Criminal History Records

This Administrative Order does not apply to, nor affect, any of the procedures implemented pursuant Chapter 943, Florida Statutes, and Florida Rule of Criminal Procedure 3.692, for sealing or expunging criminal history records.

C. Application: Other Records Not Intended to be Affected by this Order

The Court does not intend to affect or modify the statutory process or the procedures in place in the Clerk's Office for sealing or expunging criminal history records. The Court also does not intend to address the sealing of particular information within a document. In addition, this Administrative Order is not intended to address the confidentiality of records admitted into evidence as discussed in Sarasota Herald–Tribune v. State, 924 So.2d 8 (Fla. 2d DCA 2006).

DONE AND ORDERED in Chambers, at Jacksonville, Duval County Florida, this 12 day of Oct., 2006.

____
DONALD R. MORAN, Chief Judge

"ATTACHMENT A"

IN THE CIRCUIT COURT OF THE FOURTH JUDICIAL CIRCUIT IN AND FOR DUVAL/CLAY/NASSAU COUNTY, FLORIDA

__________DIVISION

***NOTE: INCLUDE CASE STYLE *ONLY IN CASES* WHERE A DOCUMENT OR DOCUMENTS ALONE HAVE BEEN SEALED.**

IN CASES WHERE A FILE, FILE AND DOCKET, OR A PARTY'S IDENTITY HAS BEEN SEALED, REDACT THE CASE STYLE

______________________ Case No.__________

v

______________________/

ORDER GRANTING/DENYING MOTION TO SEAL PURSUANT TO FLORIDA RULE OF JUDICIAL ADMINISTRATION 2.051(c)(9)

THIS MATTER is before the Court on the Motion of __________ pursuant to Florida Rule of Judicial Administration 2.051(c)(9) for an order sealing the following information relative to this case: [select all that apply]

___ the party's name or identifying information of the party on the progress docket.

___ the party's name or identifying information of the party in the file.

___ particular documents or contents within the court file, specifically ______________________________.

____

___ the entire court file, but not the progress docket.

___ the entire "court record" *including* the progress docket and other similar records generated to document activity in a case, transcripts filed with the clerk, documentary exhibits in the custody of the clerk, and electronic records, videotapes, or stenographic tapes of depositions or other proceedings filed with the clerk, and electronic records, videotapes, or stenographic tapes of court proceedings" (see Rule 2.051, emphasis added);

___ other portions sought to be sealed: ________.

Having fully considered the arguments of the parties, legal authority, and otherwise being fully advised, the Court **DENIES** the Motion because the moving party has failed to carry the burden of proof to establish that confidentiality of the information sought to be sealed is necessary to protect any interest under Rule 2.051(c)(9).

—OR, IF GRANTING, USE NEXT PAGE—

. . . the Court **GRANTS** the Motion as follows:

1. The confidentiality of the information sought to be sealed is required to protect the following interest(s): [select all that apply]

___ a. Preventing a serious and imminent threat to the fair, impartial, and orderly administration of justice, specifically: ________________________________;

___ b. A trade secret;

___ c. A compelling government interest, specifically ________;

___ d. Obtaining evidence to determine the legal issues in a case;

___ e. Avoiding substantial injury to innocent third parties, specifically ________;

___ f. Avoiding substantial injury to a party by the disclosure of matters protected by a common law or privacy right not generally inherent in this type of proceeding, specifically: ________________________________;

___ g. Complying with established public policy set forth in the Florida or United States Constitution or statutes or Florida rules or case law, specifically: ________.

2. The Court further finds that no less restrictive measure is available to protect this/these interest(s), and that the degree, duration and manner of confidentiality ordered herein are no broader than necessary to protect the interest(s). Wherefore, it is hereby

ORDERED that:

A. The Clerk of the Circuit [or County] Court is hereby **DIRECTED TO SEAL** immediately the following materials related to this matter and to keep such materials from public access: [select all that apply]

___ 1. The party's name and identity, and the Clerk of Court shall substitute the following for the party's name: ________. Further, the Clerk shall ensure that the party's name and any and all identifying information of the party (e.g., the party's social security number, address, etc.) is redacted from all public materials in the file and that the final judgment is recorded in a manner that does not reveal the identity of the party, subject to any substitution of a party's name set forth above. However, the progress docket and the file shall otherwise remain available to the public, subject to any substitution of a party's name set forth above.

___ 2. The following documents and materials within the court file: ________________. However, other portions of the file and the progress docket shall otherwise remain available to the public, subject to any substitution of a party's name and redacted identifying information of the party, as set forth above.

___ 3. The entire court file. However, the progress docket shall remain open to the public subject to any substitution of a party's name set forth above.

___ 4. The entire "court record" including the progress docket and other similar records generated to document activity in a case, transcripts filed with the clerk, documentary exhibits in the custody of the clerk, and electronic records, videotapes, or stenographic tapes of depositions or other proceedings filed with the clerk, and electronic records, videotapes, or stenographic tapes of court proceedings" (emphasis added). It is critical that the progress docket is not made available on any public information system.

B. It is further **ORDERED** that any materials sealed pursuant to this Order shall be conditionally disclosed upon the Court's entry of a subsequent order finding that such opening is necessary for purposes of judicial or governmental accountability or First Amendment rights.

C. That any materials sealed pursuant to this Order may otherwise be disclosed only as follows:

1. to any judge of this Circuit for case-related reasons;
2. to the Chief Judge or his or her designee;
3. to adult named parties or their attorneys of record; or
4. by further order of the Court.

D. That the Clerk is hereby directed to post a copy of the attached Notice of Entry of Order Authorizing Sealing for a period of five (5) days to provide public notice, *[choose one of the following descriptions based on the courthouse in which the order is signed]:*

—on the "Public Notice Bulletin Board" located in the Clerk's Office, Room 103 in the Duval County Courthouse or

—on the Public Notice Board in the entranceway of the Nassau County Judicial Annex in Yulee, Florida or

—in an equally prominent location of the Clerk's Office in Clay County, depending on the county in which the case or court record is maintained.

E. That the Clerk is hereby authorized to unseal any materials sealed pursuant to this Order for the purpose of filing, microfilming or imaging files, or transmitting a record to an appellate tribunal. The materials shall be re-sealed immediately upon completion of the filing and in accordance with Administrative Order 2006–05.

DONE AND ORDERED in Chambers, at Duval County, this ___ day of ________, 200 ___.

________ /s/

"ATTACHMENT B"

IN THE CIRCUIT COURT OF THE FOURTH JUDICIAL CIRCUIT IN AND FOR DUVAL/CLAY/NASSAU COUNTY, FLORIDA

________DIVISION

*NOTE: INCLUDE CASE STYLE *ONLY IN CASES* WHERE A DOCUMENT OR DOCUMENTS ALONE HAVE BEEN SEALED.

IN CASES WHERE A FILE, FILE AND DOCKET, OR A PARTY'S IDENTITY HAS BEEN SEALED, REDACT THE CASE STYLE

Case No. ___

NOTICE OF ENTRY OF ORDER AUTHORIZING SEALING

BE ADVISED that on the ___ day of __________, 20 ___, the Court entered an Order in the above-referenced matter authorizing the sealing of court documents pursuant to Florida Rule of Judicial Administration 2.051(c)(9). Any person wishing to contest this Order shall file a motion with the Clerk of the Circuit Court within five (5) days of the date of this notice in accordance with Administrative Order No. 2006–05.

Dated: __________

____
(NAME), Clerk of the Circuit Court)
By: ________________________
Deputy Clerk

1 Lettering as provided in original.

2006–03. NOTICE OF RELATED CASES

IN THE CIRCUIT COURT OF THE FOURTH JUDICIAL CIRCUIT IN AND FOR DUVAL, CLAY, AND NASSAU COUNTIES

ADMINISTRATIVE ORDER NO. 2006–03

IN RE: NOTICE OF RELATED CASES

WHEREAS, Florida Judicial Administration Rule 2.085(d), entitled "Related Cases" has recently been adopted by the Florida Supreme Court, and became effective on January 1, 2006; and

WHEREAS, the Florida Supreme Court has required that every petitioner in a family case shall file with the court a notice of related cases, if related cases are known or reasonably ascertainable; and

WHEREAS, a case is related when: (A) it involves any of the same parties, children or issues and it is pending at the time the party files a family case; (B) it affects the court's jurisdiction to proceed; (C) an order in the related case may conflict with an order on the same issues in the new case; or (D) an order in the new case may conflict with an order in the earlier litigation;

NOW, THEREFORE, having the benefit of the Florida Supreme Court's guidelines recently adopted in Florida Judicial Rule 2.085(d), and by the authority vested in me as the Chief Judge of the Fourth Judicial Circuit and pursuant to the Rules of Judicial Administration, it is

ORDERED:

1. In every family case filed in this circuit where the petitioner knows or can reasonably ascertain the existence of a related case(s), a Notice of Related Cases shall be filed with the initial pleading and all post-judgment pleadings by the filing attorney or the self-represented petitioner.

2. The Notice of Related Cases shall identify the caption and case number(s) of the related case(s), contain a brief statement of the relationship of the actions, and contain a statement addressing whether coordination of related cases will conserve judicial resources and promote an efficient determination of the actions.

3. The notice of related cases shall be served on (a) all parties in the related cases, (b) the presiding judges in all related cases, and (c) the family law administrative judge in the county where the case is filed.

4. The "Notice of Related Cases" form and the "Instruction Sheet for Filing a Notice of Related Cases" attached to this Order are hereby adopted for use in the Fourth Judicial Circuit, until the Florida Supreme Court makes available forms and instructions approved by the Court.

5. The Notice of Related Cases must be filed in the following types of Family Division cases:

a. Dissolution of Marriage;

b. Annulment;

c. Support Unconnected with Dissolution of Marriage;

d. Paternity;

e. Child Support;

f. UIFSA;

g. Custodial Care of and Access to Children;

h. Adoption;

i. Name Change;

j. Declaratory Judgment Actions Related to premarital, marital, or postmarital agreements;

k. Civil Domestic, Repeat Violence, Dating Violence, and Sexual Violence Injunctions;

l. Juvenile Dependency;

m. Termination of Parental Rights;

n. Juvenile Delinquency;

o. Emancipation of a Minor;

p. CINS/FINS;

q. Truancy;

r. Modification and Enforcement of Orders Entered in the above cases.

6. Each party has a continuing duty to inform the Court of any proceeding in this or any other state that could affect the current proceeding.

7. This Order shall take effect immediately, *nunc pro tunc*, and shall remain in effect until further Order of the Court, and all requirements set forth in this Administrative Order shall apply unless otherwise ordered by the Court.

8. This Order shall be recorded in the Official Records of Clay, Duval and Nassau Counties in the State of Florida.

DONE AND ORDERED at Jacksonville, Duval County, Florida, this 17 day of March, 2006, *nunc pro tunc* to January 1, 2006.

____
DONALD R. MORAN, JR.
CHIEF JUDGE

IN THE CIRCUIT COURT OF THE FOURTH JUDICIAL CIRCUIT IN AND FOR ________ COUNTY, FLORIDA

CASE NO.: ________
DIVISION: ________

________________,
Petitioner,
and
________________,
Respondent.
____________________/

NOTICE OF RELATED CASES

Pursuant to Florida Rule of Judicial Administration 2.085(d), the ________________ (Petitioner or Respondent) the following Notice of Related Cases:

1. A related case may be an open or closed civil, criminal, or family case which includes all case types defined in Fla. R. Jud. Admin. 2.085(d). A case is "related" to this family law case if it involves any of the same parties, children, or issues and it is pending at the time the party files a family case; or if it affects the court's jurisdiction to proceed; or if an order in the related case may conflict with an order on the same issues in the new case; or if an order in the new case may conflict with an order in the earlier litigation.

The following cases are related to the instant case:

Related Case No. 1

Case Name(s): ________, Petitioner
________, Respondent
Case No.: ___ Division: ____________
Type of Proceeding: ____________
Court and State: ____________
Date of next hearing: ____________
Date of Court Order/Judgment (if any): ________
Relationship of cases *(select appropriate statement(s))*:
☐ pending case involves same parties, children or issues;
☐ may affect court's jurisdiction;
☐ order in related case may conflict with an order in instant case;
☐ order in instant case may conflict with previous order in related case.
Statement as to the relationship of the cases: ________
____
________________________.

Related Case No. 2

Case Name(s): ________, Petitioner
________, Respondent
Case No.: ___ Division: ____________
Type of Proceeding: ____________
Court and State: ____________
Date of next hearing: ____________
Date of Court Order/Judgment (if any): ________
Relationship of cases *(select appropriate statement(s))*:
☐ pending case involves same parties, children or issues;
☐ may affect court's jurisdiction;
☐ order in related case may conflict with an order in instant case;
☐ order in instant case may conflict with previous order in related case.
Statement as to the relationship of the cases: ________
________________________.

Related Case No. 3

Case Name(s): ________, Petitioner
________, Respondent
Case No.: ___ Division: ____________
Type of Proceeding: ____________
Court and State: ____________
Date of next hearing: ____________
Date of Court Order/Judgment (if any): ________
Relationship of cases *(select appropriate statement(s))*:
☐ pending case involves same parties, children or issues;
☐ may affect court's jurisdiction;
☐ order in related case may conflict with an order in instant case;
☐ order in instant case may conflict with previous order in related case.
Statement as to the relationship of the cases: ________
____
________________________.

{Attach additional pages if other related cases are known or reasonably ascertainable.}

2. Choose one:

☐ I **do not** request coordination of litigation in any of the cases listed above.

☐ I **do** request coordination of litigation in the following cases:
____
____
____

Assignment to one judge or another method of coordination will promote an efficient determination of the actions and will conserve judicial resources for the following reasons:
____
____

____
____
____

Please note that the court on its own accord may decide to coordinate your case for judicial economy and better services for the litigants.

3. I acknowledge that I have a continuing duty to inform the court of any proceedings in this or any other state that could affect the current proceeding.

CERTIFICATE OF SERVICE

I HEREBY CERTIFY that a copy of the foregoing notice was served by (√ one only) ☐ first class mail ☐ fax and mail ☐ hand delivery this ___ day of ________, 200 ___, to the persons listed below:

Party to this case or their attorney:
Name _______________
Address _______________
____
City _______________
State, Zip _______________
Fax Number _______________

Party to related case or their attorney:
Name _______________
Address _______________
____
City _______________
State, Zip _______________
Fax Number _______________

Party to related case or their attorney:
Name _______________
Address _______________
____
City _______________
State, Zip _______________
Fax Number _______________

Presiding Judge in this case:
The Honorable _______________
Address _______________
____
City _______________
State, Zip _______________
Fax Number _______________

Presiding Judge in related case:
The Honorable _______________
Address _______________
____
City _______________
State, Zip _______________
Fax Number _______________

Administrative Judge in County where this case is filed (select one only):

☐ The Honorable David C. Wiggins
Family Division Administrative Judge
for Duval County
Duval County Courthouse
330 East Bay Street
Jacksonville, FL 32202

☐ The Honorable William A. Wilkes
Clay County Administrative Judge
P. O. Drawer 1845
Clay County Courthouse
Green Cove Springs, FL 32043

☐ The Honorable Robert M. Foster
Nassau County Administrative Judge
76347 Veterans Way, Suite 3061
Nassau County Judicial Annex
Yulee, FL 32097

Dated: _______________

____
Signature of Petitioner/Respondent or Attorney for Petitioner/Respondent

Printed Name: _______________
Address: _______________
____
City, State, Zip: _______________
Telephone Number: _______________
Bar No. _______________

Local Form, Notice of Related Cases (03/06)

INSTRUCTION SHEET FOR FILING A NOTICE OF RELATED CASES

Who Is Required to File a Notice of Related Cases

The Florida Rules of Judicial Administration, Rule 2.085(d), **requires all** petitioners in a family case to file a Notice of Related Cases if the petitioner is aware that related cases exist or the petitioner can reasonably discover that related cases exist. The Notice of Related Cases **shall be filed** with the initial pleading by the filing attorney or self-represented petitioner.

What are Related Cases

A case is related when:

- it involves any of the same parties, children or issues and the case is still pending/active at the time a party files a new family case; or
- it affects the court's jurisdiction to proceed; or
- an order in the related case may conflict with an order on the same issues in the new case; or
- an order in the new case may conflict with an order in the earlier litigation.

What Is a Family Case

A family case includes:

- dissolution of marriage
- annulment
- support unconnected with dissolution of marriage
- paternity
- child support
- UIFSA
- custodial care of and access to children
- adoption
- name change
- declaratory judgment actions related to premarital, marital or postmarital agreements
- civil domestic, repeat violence, dating violence, and sexual violence injunctions
- juvenile dependency
- termination of parental rights
- juvenile delinquency
- emancipation of a minor
- CINS/FINS
- truancy
- modification and enforcement of orders entered in the above cases

If the petitioner has or had a case, in any state, that included any of the above-listed issues, that case must be identified as a related case on the Notice of Related Cases,

Service of Notice of Related Cases

The original Notice of Related Cases **shall be** filed with the Clerk of Court in the county where your case is filed. A copy of the Notice of Related Cases **shall** be served on all parties in this case and all related cases, the presiding judges in this case, the division judge(s) in all related cases, and the family law administrative judge in the county (Clay, Duval or Nassau) in this circuit where this case is filed. Keep a copy of the Notice of Related Cases for your records.

Duty To Inform

Each party has a continuing duty to inform the court of any proceedings in this or any other state that could affect the current proceeding.

2005–03. JIMMY RYCE ACT EXPERT WITNESS FEE COST CONTAINMENT

IN THE FOURTH JUDICIAL CIRCUIT IN AND FOR CLAY, DUVAL AND NASSAU COUNTIES, FLORIDA

ADMINISTRATIVE ORDER NO. 2005–03

IN RE: Jimmy Ryce Act Expert Witness Fee Cost Containment

WHEREAS, it is in the best interest of the citizens of the Fourth Judicial circuit to provide for cost containment of expert witness fees in Jimmy Ryce civil commitment proceedings commenced in accordance with Section 394.916, et seq., Florida Statutes;

NOW, THEREFORE, pursuant to the authority vested in me as the Chief Judge of the Fourth Judicial Circuit it is hereby ORDERED as follows:

(A) This Administrative Order applies to Jimmy Ryce civil commitment proceedings commenced in accordance with Section 394.916, et seq., Florida Statutes.

(B) The State Attorney, Public Defender and Conflict Counsel are free to contract with experts of their own choosing. However, unless for good cause shown leave of Court is granted, the following parameters shall govern payment of all experts: (1) No witness fee may exceed $350.00 per hour for any medical, psychiatric or neuro-psychiatric expert; (2) No witness fee may exceed $225.00 per hour for any other type of expert; (3) The total amount paid to a single expert shall not exceed the sum of $5,000.00 excluding travel to and testimony at trial, without leave of court for for good cause shown; (4) Reimbursement of experts for travel time shall be limited to four hours each way; (5) The engaging entity of the expert shall make all air travel and hotel arrangements for the expert and shall secure a state government rate for the same; and (6) Travel expenses for experts shall otherwise be governed by Sections 112.061 and 287.058(1)(b), Florida Statutes. Further, this Administrative Order shall be provided to all experts at the time such expert is retained, and shall be incorporated into any agreement for payment entered into on behalf of the State of Florida by the State Attorney, Public Defender or Conflict Counsel.

(C) Expert witness fee cost containment shall be an issue addressed by all parties in their pretrial stipulations. Accordingly, for every pretrial stipulation filed on behalf of the State by the State Attorney, or on behalf of a defendant by the Public Defender or Conflict Counsel, the party shall include a statement of anticipated cost and expenses associated with the use for trial of any and all expert witnesses whether expected to testify or otherwise, including witness fees, travel expenses, etc. Each party shall further include in their pretrial stipulation a statement of the total amount of expenses incurred prior to the date of the pretrial conference. If the sum of the anticipated expenses and the expenses incurred up to the date of the pretrial conference exceed $5,000.00, the anticipated expenses must be approved at the pretrial conference by the presiding judge.

(D) The initial commitment proceeding commenced pursuant to Section 394.916, et seq., Florida Statutes, and all subsequent annual reviews, shall each be considered different proceedings for purposes of application of this Administrative Order. That is, the cost incurred in the initial commitment proceeding or any prior annual reviews, shall not act to limit the cost which may otherwise be incurred pursuant to this Administrative Order for subsequent annual reviews.

(E) The terms of Amended Administrative Order No. 2003–02 shall remain in full force and effect except as such terms may conflict with the terms of this Administrative Order, in which case the terms of this Administrative Order shall govern.

(F) This Order shall take effect immediately and shall remain in effect until further Order of the Court.

(G) This Administrative Order shall be recorded in the Official Records of Duval, Clay and Nassau Counties in the State of Florida, and certified copies of the same shall be furnished by the Clerks of the Circuit Court for Clay, Duval and Nassau counties to each entity listed below (other than the listed Clerks of the Circuit Court).

DONE and ORDERED in Duval County, Florida, this 31st day of March, 2005.

DONALD R. MORAN, JR.
CHIEF JUDGE

2005–02. APPEALS FROM COUNTY COURT AND LOCAL ADMINISTRATIVE AGENCIES; PETITIONS FOR WRITS

IN THE FOURTH JUDICIAL CIRCUIT IN AND FOR CLAY, DUVAL AND NASSAU COUNTIES, FLORIDA

ADMINISTRATIVE ORDER NO. 2005–02

IN RE: APPEALS FROM COUNTY COURT AND LOCAL ADMINISTRATIVE AGENCIES; PETITIONS FOR WRITS

WHEREAS, Rule 9.030(c)(1) of the Florida Rules of Appellate Procedure requires the circuit courts to review by appeal final orders of lower tribunals as provided by general law; non–final orders of lower tribunals as prescribed by Rule 9.130 of the Florida Rules of Appellate Procedure; and administrative action as provided by general law; and

WHEREAS, Rule 9.030(c)(2) of the Florida Rules of Appellate Procedures states that the certiorari jurisdiction of circuit courts may be sought to review non-final orders of lower tribunals other than as prescribed by Rule 9.130; and

WHEREAS, Rule 9.030(c)(3) of the Florida Rules of Appellate Procedures authorizes circuit courts to issue writs of mandamus, prohibition, quo warranto, common law certiorari, and habeas corpus, and all writs necessary to the complete exercise of the courts' jurisdiction; and

WHEREAS, it is desirable that a mechanism exist by which three judge panels may be constituted for the purpose of reviewing such proceedings; it is, therefore:

ORDERED that the following process governing circuit court responsibilities under the Florida Rules of Appellate Procedure are hereby established:

1. All prior Administrative Orders regarding the appellate responsibilities of the circuit court shall remain in full force and effect, except to the extent inconsistent herewith.

2. It shall be the responsibility of each party to an appellate proceeding, whether represented by counsel or *pro se*, to file an original and four (4) copies of each brief with the Clerk of Court. All briefs should be securely stapled with one staple in the upper left-hand corner.

3. On the Court's own motion, or upon motion of a party, the circuit judge to whom an appeal or petition for writ has been assigned for review, may, wholly at his or her discretion, certify to the Chief Judge the need for review of the appeal or petition for writ by a three judge appellate panel. It is not the intent of this administrative order that every appeal assigned to a given judge be certified for review by a three judge panel. Without setting forth all of the criteria which a judge may consider in certifying the need for a three judge panel, each judge should give great weight to the precedential impact which an appeal's resolution may have on the County Courts within the Circuit.

4. Upon certification of need for a three judge panel, the Clerk of the Court in the county in which the matter is pending shall randomly assign two additional circuit judges, from all of those then serving in the Circuit, to serve on the panel.

5. Where a three judge panel has been constituted, the judge to whom the proceeding was originally assigned shall be the presiding judge of the panel. The presiding judge shall: (a) discharge the administrative duties of the panel, including, but not limited to, mailing of notices of oral argument sessions, as well as scheduling oral argument sessions and panel conferences with other members of the panel; (b) rule on all non-dispositive motions; (c) preside at all sessions and conferences; (d) assign the writing of opinions among the panel members when the presiding judge is in the majority, otherwise such responsibility shall be discharged by the most senior judge in the majority; and (e) ensure the timely disposition of the proceeding.

6. Where a three judge panel has been constituted, every application for an order in connection with appellate proceedings shall be made to the presiding judge. The presiding judge shall have full charge of the proceedings; provided, that upon the absence, failure or inability of the presiding judge to act, any other judge of the panel may be substituted.

7. Where a three judge panel has been constituted, the members of the panel may, at each individual judge's discretion, elect to use separate Staff Attorney's for research assistance.

8. Where a three judge panel has been constituted, whether to grant a request for or otherwise require oral argument shall be wholly within the discretion of the majority of the members of the three judge panel.

9. Where a three judge panel has been constituted, the panel shall meet in conference following oral argument, or in cases where oral argument does not occur, at such time as specified by the presiding judge, at which conference the judges shall confer as to the disposition of the case. Cases shall be decided by the majority of the members on the panel. The panel member assigned to draft a written opinion shall circulate the proposed opinion together with a post draft circulation memorandum on which the remaining panel members shall indicate their concurrence or dissent. See Post Draft Circulation Memorandum attached hereto. All opinions shall be typed, double spaced, and shall follow the format utilized by the district courts of appeal. Following the circulation of the final draft of the majority opinion, as well as any concurring and/or dissenting opinions, the writer of the majority opinion shall combine into one document all opinions. Thereupon, such final document shall be circulated for final approval as the decision of the panel. Thereafter, such decision of the panel shall be filed with the Clerk of the Court, who shall issue the mandate in accordance with Rule 9.340, Fla. R. App. P.

10. This Order shall take effect immediately and shall remain in effect until further Order of the Court.

11. This Administrative Order shall be recorded in the Official Records of Duval, Clay and Nassau Counties in the State of Florida, and certified copies of the same shall be furnished by the Clerks of the Circuit Court for Clay, Duval and Nassau counties to each person listed below that maintains an office within their respective counties.

DONE and ORDERED in Duval County, Florida, this 29th day of March, 2005.

DONALD R. MORAN, JR.
CHIEF JUDGE

POST DRAFT CIRCULATION MEMORANDUM

TO: *Judge* ____________ **(Judge A)**
Judge ____________ **(Judge B)**
FROM: *Judge* ____________ **(Majority Drafter)**
DATE:
RE: *Attached proposed appellate opinion*
CASE NAME: ____________
CASE NO.: ____________

If you plan on concurring specially or dissenting, in whole or in part, please attach your opinion and recirculate until we have all reviewed the other's final drafts of opinions. If you have any short comments please list below.

	Concurs	Concurs specially or in part	Dissents	Dissents in part	With Opinion	Without Opinion
Judge A						
Judge B						

Please check appropriate boxes.
Comments:

2004–23 (A1). REGISTRY OF CONFLICT COUNSEL

IN THE CIRCUIT COURT, FOURTH JUDICIAL CIRCUIT, IN AND FOR DUVAL, CLAY AND NASSAU COUNTIES, FLORIDA

AMENDED ADMINISTRATIVE ORDER NO. 2004–23

IN RE: REGISTRY OF CONFLICT COUNSEL

WHEREAS, in accordance with the terms of section 27.40, Florida Statutes, a Registry of Conflict Counsel for the Fourth Judicial Circuit was created, comprised of attorneys in private practice available for appointment in capital and non-capital criminal cases and certain civil cases, including dependency and termination of parental rights, in which provision is made for court-appointed counsel, but the Office of Criminal Conflict and Civil Regional Counsel is unable to provide representation due to a conflict of interest; and

WHEREAS, section 27.42, Florida Statutes, mandated the creation of an Article V Indigent Services Committee in each circuit, tasked, among other things, with creation and management of the Registry; and

WHEREAS, the Indigent Services Committee has since disbanded, and the responsibilities of the Indigent Services Committee has been delegated to other persons or entities; and

WHEREAS, it has become necessary to amend Administrative Order 2004–23 to update and clarify the guidelines and procedures for compiling a registry of attorneys; and

NOW, THEREFORE, by the authority vested in me as Chief Judge and pursuant to the Florida Rules of Judicial Administration and the applicable Florida Statutes, it is hereby

ORDERED AND ADJUDGED:

A. COMPILATION AND MAINTENANCE OF THE REGISTRY

1. The Chief Judge or his designee, shall be responsible for compiling the registry of attorneys ("the Registry"). In compiling the Registry, the Chief Judge or his designee, may consult with the Administrative Judges, other members of the judiciary, and members of the Bar as to the qualifications and suitability of applicants. The selection, approval, and continuation of an attorney on the Registry is a privilege, not a right, and is dependent not only upon the attorney meeting the requirements for appointment as set forth below, but upon the overall competency of the attorney. The constitutional right, not only to counsel, but competent counsel, was discussed by the United States Supreme Court in Evitts v. Lucey, 469 U.S. 387, 395 (1985):

> As we have made clear, the guarantee of counsel "cannot be satisfied by mere formal appointment," Avery v. Alabama, 308 U.S. 444, 446 (1940). "That a person who happens to be a lawyer is present at trial alongside the accused, however, is not enough to satisfy the constitutional command . . . An accused is entitled to be assisted by an attorney, whether retained or appointed, who plays the role necessary to ensure that the trial is fair." Strickland v. Washington, 466 U.S., at 685; see also McMann v. Richardson, 397 U.S. 759, 771, n. 14 (1970) ("It has long been recognized that the right to counsel is the right to effective assistance of counsel"); Cuyler v. Sullivan, 446 U.S., at 344 . . . Because the right to counsel is so fundamental to a fair trial, the Constitution cannot tolerate trials in which counsel, though present in name, is unable to assist the defendant to obtain a fair decision on the merits.

To appoint incompetent counsel would be tantamount to depriving a defendant of the right to counsel guaranteed by the Sixth Amendment to the Constitution of the United States and the mandate of the Supreme Court of the United States as set forth in Gideon v. Wainwright, 372 U.S. 335 (1963). See French v. State, 161 So. 2d 879, 881 (Fla. 1st DCA 1964).

2. The Chief Judge or his designee, shall place attorneys on the Registry in accordance with the category of cases in which they are qualified and elect to accept on their application. The categories are:

Misdemeanor cases- includes all misdemeanor cases;

Juvenile cases- includes all juvenile cases;

Third degree felony cases- includes all felonies of the third degree and all offenses in lower categories;

Second degree felony cases—includes all felonies of the second degree and all offenses in lower categories;

Life felony cases- includes all offenses punishable by life, capital sexual battery cases, *Jimmy Ryce* cases, and all offenses in lower categories;

Capital cases- includes any first-degree murder case in which the State has not formally waived the death penalty on record;

Criminal appellate cases- includes all non-capital criminal appeals and *Jimmy Ryce* cases;

Dependency cases- includes all dependency cases with the exception of termination of parental rights cases;

Termination of Parental Rights cases- includes all termination of parental rights cases;

Dependency appellate cases- includes all dependency appeals, including appeals of termination of parental rights cases.

3. The Office of the Clerks of Court, on behalf of the Chief Judge, shall maintain and distribute the Registry, in accordance with section 27.40, Florida Statutes. The Registry shall be maintained by county and category of case for which the attorney is qualified. Functional sub-registries shall be maintained in each county and shall be administered by the Chief Judge, the Administrative Judge for the Felony Division in each county, the Administrative Judge for Dependency in each county, or the Court Administrator as deemed appropriate by the Chief Judge.

4. Maintenance of the Registry, in addition to the above, shall also include keeping a log documenting appointments from the Registry.

B. REQUIREMENTS FOR PLACEMENT ON REGISTRY

1. To be considered for placement on the Registry, the attorney shall certify that they meet any minimum requirements established by general law, this Administrative Order, or other applicable administrative orders of the Fourth Judicial Circuit. The attorney must also certify that they are available to represent indigent defendants in all cases requiring court appointment of private counsel (within their category of appointment), and are willing to abide by the terms of the Justice Administrative Commission's ("JAC") contract for services. [1] In addition, any attorney desiring to be considered for placement on the Registry, must enter into a contract for services with JAC.

2. Attorneys approved for placement on the Registry shall be responsible for notifying the Chief Judge or his designee, of any of the following:

a. change of address, telephone number or fax number;

b. change in categories of cases to which he/she is qualified and willing to be assigned;

c. disciplinary action taken against him/her by The Florida Bar;

d. that he/she has become inactive or is unavailable for appointment.

3. The experience and other qualifications that each attorney must meet to be considered for and to maintain placement on the Registry, is specified on the attached chart. (Attachment "A.") [2] The Chief Judge may amend the standards specified on this chart without further amendment to this Administrative Order.

C. POST APPOINTMENT REQUIREMENTS

1. Pursuant to section 27.40(6), Florida Statutes, after court appointment, the attorney must immediately file a notice of appearance with the court indicating acceptance of the appointment to represent the defendant.

2. Pursuant to section 27.40(8), Florida Statutes, and subject to the attorney-client privilege and the work-product privilege, an attorney who withdraws or is removed from representation shall deliver all files, notes, documents, and research to the successor attorney within 15 days after receiving notice from the successor attorney. The successor attorney shall bear the cost of transmitting all files, notes, documents, and research.

D. PROCEDURES FOR UTILIZING REGISTRY

1. Pursuant to section 27.40(3)(b), Florida Statutes, the Court shall appoint attorneys in rotating order in the order in which their names appear on the Registry.

2. However, the court to whom the case is assigned, if good cause exists, may appoint an attorney out of order. Examples of good cause include, but are not limited to, instances where the attorney was previously appointed to represent the client in another case simultaneously pending or filed after the initial representation, or the attorney next in rotation fails to respond in a timely manner. Pursuant to section 27.40(3)(b), should an out of order appointment be necessary, the Court must make a finding of good cause on the record for the appointment. Such finding may be recorded on the open record, in the court file, or by separate written order. Any attorney not appointed in the order in which his or her name appears on the list shall remain next in order.

3. Pursuant to section 27.40(7)(a), Florida Statutes, a non registry attorney may be appointed if the Court finds in the order of appointment, that there were no registry attorneys available for representation for that case. A non registry attorney appointed under these circumstances may be compensated under section 27.5304, Florida Statutes.

4. Pursuant to section 27.40(3)(c), Florida Statutes, if the number of attorneys on the Registry in a county or circuit for a particular category of cases is inadequate, the Chief Judge shall provide to the Clerk of Court the names of at least three private attorneys who have relevant experience. The Clerk of Court shall send an application to each of these attorneys to register for appointment.

E. REMOVAL FROM REGISTRY

1. An attorney *shall* be removed from the Registry if the attorney:

a. is disbarred or suspended, or surrenders his/her license to practice law in this state;

b. fails to meet the experience or training requirements established herein;

c. submits false or fraudulent billing; or

d. solicits or receives compensation directly from the client for the case(s) to which the attorney has been appointed.

2. An attorney *may* be removed from the Registry if the attorney:

a. unreasonably fails to consult with a client;

b. fails, without cause, to make required court appearances, meet statutory or court-imposed deadlines, or file appropriate motions in a timely manner;

c. fails to zealously represent the interests of a client;

d. engages in misconduct or exhibits a level of incompetence such that the Chief Judge makes the determination that removal of the attorney from the Registry is necessary for the protection of clients' interests and/or the administration of justice.

3. Pursuant to section 27.40(9), Florida Statutes, any interested person may advise the Court of any circumstances affecting the quality of an attorney's representation.

4. The procedure for having an attorney considered for removal from the Registry is as follows: Any interested person may request, in writing, that an attorney on the Registry be removed for cause. Upon receipt of such request, the Chief Judge may conduct an investigation, as deemed necessary, to substantiate or refute the basis for the request. The attorney being considered for removal may be requested to respond to such request in writing, in person, or both. The Chief Judge, or other judge appointed by the Chief Judge to preside, may conduct a hearing to receive testimony regarding the request and the attorney's response. Any hearing shall be noticed in accordance with Florida's public meeting laws. Upon a finding of cause, the Chief Judge may suspend the attorney from the Registry, remove the attorney, or impose

any other sanctions deemed appropriate. The Chief Judge shall notify the attorney and the person filing the request for removal, of the decision in writing.

F. This Order is effective immediately and shall remain in effect until further Order of the Court and all the terms and conditions set forth in this Administrative Order shall apply unless otherwise ordered by the Court.

G. This Administrative Order shall be recorded in the Official Records of Duval, Clay and Nassau counties in the State of Florida and certified copies shall be furnished by the Clerks of each Court to each local bar association.

DONE AND ORDERED at Jacksonville, Duval County, Florida, this 5 day of February 2010.

Donald R. Moran, Jr.
CHIEF JUDGE

1 JAC's contract for registry attorneys has a term corresponding with the state's fiscal year commencing on July 1st and ending on June 30. A new contract must be entered into each fiscal year.

2 This Administrative Order does not address the required qualifications for an attorney desiring to handle capital trial and capital appellate cases. Those qualifications are set forth in the Florida Statutes and Florida Rules of Criminal Procedure.

ATTACHMENT "A"

A. NON–CAPITAL CRIMINAL CASES

1. Be a member in good standing of The Florida Bar.

2. Have attended within the previous 12 months prior to application a minimum of ten hours of Florida Bar approved continuing legal education devoted to criminal law. To remain on the Registry, the attorney must attend a minimum of ten hours of Florida Bar approved continuing legal education devoted to criminal law for each 24 month period after placement on the Registry.

3. Meet the following experience requirements:

Misdemeanor cases- member of The Florida Bar for at least one year and have participated in no fewer than two state or federal jury or non-jury trials as first or second chair;

Juvenile cases- a member of The Florida Bar for at least one year, with no fewer than three delinquency dispositions or two state or federal jury or non-jury trials as first or second chair;

Third degree felony cases- a member of The Florida Bar for at least two years, with no fewer than three state or federal jury trials as first or second chair;

Second degree felony cases- a member of The Florida Bar for at least two years, with no fewer than five state or federal jury trials as first or second chair;

Life felonies, capital sexual battery and Jimmy Ryce cases- a member of The Florida Bar for at least five years, with no fewer than ten state or federal jury trials as first or second chair.

B. NON–CAPITAL CRIMINAL APPELLATE CASES (Including Jimmy Ryce cases)

1. Be a member in good standing of The Florida Bar.

2. Have attended within the 12 months prior to application a minimum of ten hours of Florida Bar approved continuing legal education devoted to criminal law. To remain on the Registry, for each 24 month period thereafter, the attorney must attend a minimum of ten hours of Florida Bar approved continuing education devoted to criminal law.

3. Meet the following experience requirements:

(a.) In misdemeanor and third degree felony appeals, have been a member of The Florida Bar for at least two years, and have had experience in the appeal of at least three criminal cases or three state or federal trials as first or second chair.

(b.) In all other non-capital felony appeals and *Jimmy Ryce* cases, have been a member of The Florida Bar for at least three years and have had experience in the appeal of at least five criminal cases or five state or federal trials as first or second chair.

C. DEPENDENCY CASES (Excluding Termination of Parental Rights Cases)

1. Be a member in good standing of The Florida Bar.

2. Have attended at least three hours of continuing legal education at the Dependency Court Improvement Project Conference, or similar training approved by The Florida Bar in the 12 months prior to appointment. To remain on the Registry, the attorney shall obtain at least six hours of such continuing legal education every two years after appointment.

3. Have observed a total of 30 hours of hearings, including six shelter hearings, three contested adjudicatory hearings, and one contested termination of parental rights trial.

D. TERMINATION OF PARENTAL RIGHTS CASES

1. Be a member in good standing of The Florida Bar.

2. Have attended at least three hours of continuing legal education at the Dependency Court Improvement Project Conference, or similar training approved by The Florida Bar in the 12 months prior to appointment. To remain on the Registry, counsel shall obtain at least six hours of continuing legal education within each two years after appointment.

3. Have tried at least ten contested dependency cases and three contested termination of parental rights cases as first or second chair.

E. DEPENDENCY APPELLATE CASES (Including Termination of Parental Rights Cases)

1. Be a member in good standing of The Florida Bar.

2. Have at least three years experience in dependency or appellate law and have been lead counsel in at least three contested dependency trials and three contested termination of parental rights trials.

2004–08 (A1). CONFLICT COUNSEL COMPENSATION AND DUE PROCESS COSTS

IN THE CIRCUIT COURT, FOURTH JUDICIAL CIRCUIT, IN AND FOR DUVAL, CLAY, AND NASSAU COUNTIES, FLORIDA

AMENDED ADMINISTRATIVE ORDER NO. 2004–8

IN RE: CONFLICT COUNSEL COMPENSATION AND DUE PROCESS COSTS

WHEREAS, in 1998, the voters of the State of Florida approved Revision 7 to Article V of the Florida Constitution, effective July 1, 2004, substantially changing the method of, and responsibility for, payment for the services of conflict counsel in the courts of the State of Florida; and

WHEREAS, section 27.42, Florida Statutes, mandated the creation of an Article V Indigent Services Committee in each circuit, tasked, among other things, with the responsibility of recommending compensation rates for court-appointed counsel as well as establishing due process service rates; and

WHEREAS, the Indigent Services Committee has since disbanded, and the Legislature has assumed the responsibility of establishing compensation rates for court-appointed counsel as well as due process service rates for each circuit; and

WHEREAS, the Legislature announced its intent that the flat fees prescribed under section 27.5304 and the General Appropriations Act comprise the full and complete compensation for private-court appointed counsel; and

WHEREAS, section 27.5304, Florida Statutes, prescribes specific conditions, procedures, and amounts for paying compensation to counsel in excess of established limits; and

WHEREAS, section 27.425, Florida Statutes, provides that due process rates will be specified annually in the General Appropriations Act;

NOW THEREFORE, by the authority vested in me as Chief Judge and pursuant to the Florida Rules of Judicial Administration and the applicable Florida Statutes, it is hereby

ORDERED AND ADJUDGED:

A. REGISTRY OF CONFLICT COUNSEL

See Amended Administrative Order No. 2004–23 for information regarding compilation and maintenance of the Registry of conflict counsel, categories of cases to be handled by conflict counsel, qualifications the attorney must meet to be placed on the Registry and appointed to certain types of cases, and how the Registry is utilized.

B. COMPENSATION FOR CONFLICT COUNSEL

1. Private court-appointed counsel shall be compensated by the Justice Administrative Commission ("JAC") as provided in section 27.5304, Florida Statutes, and the General Appropriations Act. The flat fees prescribed in section 27.5304, Florida Statutes, are limitations on compensation. The specific flat fee amounts for compensation shall be established annually in the General Appropriations Act. If the attorney is representing a defendant charged with more than one offense in the same case, the attorney shall be compensated at the rate provided for the most serious offense for which he or she represented the defendant.

2. JAC shall review an intended billing by private court-appointed counsel for attorney's fees based on a flat fee per case for completeness and compliance with contractual and statutory requirements. JAC may approve the intended bill for a flat fee per case for payment without court approval, if the intended billing is correct.

3. An intended billing that seeks compensation for any amount exceeding the flat fee established for a particular type of representation, as prescribed in the General Appropriations Act, shall comply with section 27.5304(12), Florida Statutes.

4. Private court-appointed counsel is entitled to compensation upon final disposition of a case. The attorney shall submit a bill to JAC for attorney's fees, costs, and related expenses within 90 days after the disposition of the case at the lower court level, notwithstanding any appeals. JAC's contract provides that an attorney submitting a bill after 90 days will be penalized pursuant to section 27.5304(4), Florida Statutes.

5. Pursuant to section 27.5304(11)(b), Florida Statutes, if court-appointed counsel is allowed to withdraw from representation prior to the full performance of his or her duties through the completion of the case, and the Court appoints a subsequent attorney, the total compensation for the initial and any and all subsequent attorneys, may not exceed the flat fee established under this section and the General Appropriations Act, except as provided in section 27.5304(12), Florida Statutes.

6. The flat fee rates for capital cases, noncapital, nonlife felony cases, life felony cases, misdemeanor and juvenile cases, criminal appellate cases, dependency proceedings and appeals, termination of parental rights proceedings and appeals, and others, are set forth in section 27.5304(5)–(7), Florida Statutes.[1]

7. The presiding judge retains primary authority and responsibility for determining the reasonableness of all billings for attorney's fees, costs, and related expenses, subject to statutory limitations.

C. DUE PROCESS COSTS (Court–Appointed and Indigent for Costs)

1. General Issues

a. Pursuant to section 27.425, Florida Statutes, the Legislature sets the rates for due process costs annually in the General Appropriations Act.[2]

b. If the rate for a due process service has not been established, JAC, and ultimately the Court, will determine the appropriateness of a rate charged and the total amount of compensation owed according to rates consistent with current practice in this jurisdiction, recommendations from the Article V Indigent Services Advisory Board, or rate guidelines established by further order of this Court.

c. Upon a determination by the Court that a person who has retained counsel is indigent, to the extent that he or she does not have adequate funds to pay the due process costs associated with the representation, retained counsel shall be entitled to recover said due process costs from the State of Florida. The Court's determination of indigency shall be conducted in the same manner as provided by statute for appointment of counsel.

2. Specific Costs

a. **Attorney Expenses**–For dates of appointment on or after July 1, 2007, miscellaneous expenses are no longer permitted, except for mileage reimbursement as provided *infra* in paragraph C.2.j. Thus, JAC will not pay for ordinary miscellaneous expenses including, but not limited to, postage, telephone calls, photocopying, and online research costs. Those costs are incorporated into the flat fee (under the General Appropriations Act) or hourly rate (per s. 27.5304(12),

F.S.). In indigent for costs cases, these expenses are considered office overhead and are not reimbursable due process costs.

An attorney may be reimbursed for costs associated with obtaining documents with limited exceptions. In order to obtain reimbursement, the expense must be supported by a court order, indicating the amount authorized to obtain such documents. JAC does not pay for documents obtained from the Clerk of Court. Under sections 57.081 and 28.345, Florida Statutes, the clerk should not require prepayment to provide copies of court documents to an indigent person or his or her attorney.

b. <u>**Court Reporters**</u>–Conflict counsel shall obtain only court reporter services utilized by the courts, the state attorney, and the public defender in this circuit. All court reporter per diem charges, reporting fees and transcription fees shall not exceed the rate as set forth annually in the General Appropriations Act. It shall not be necessary for counsel to file a motion with the Court to secure the services of a court reporter. Payment shall be made for court reporter services in accordance with JAC contract procedures for payment of due process costs.

c. <u>**Witness Fees**</u>–Conflict counsel shall pay, by check, any applicable witness fees to witnesses subpoenaed for deposition, hearing or trial. The fees paid by conflict counsel are reimbursable.

d. <u>**Transcripts**</u>–Once the matter is set for trial, conflict counsel shall be permitted to order the transcript of any sworn testimony of a Category A witness [3] without a court order. Counsel shall obtain prior court approval, for any other witness transcript or to obtain any transcript before the case is set for trial. The court reporter transcription fees shall not exceed the rate as set forth annually in the General Appropriations Act. Payment shall be made for court reporter transcription services in accordance with JAC contract procedures for payment of due process costs.

e. <u>**Interpreters**</u>–It is contemplated by this Order that the Court will provide interpreters in the courtroom, when necessary. However, in the event that conflict counsel determines that such services of an interpreter are necessary to the representation, he or she shall file a motion with the Court certifying that need in order to obtain an order authorizing an interpreter's services. Thereafter, counsel shall be entitled to obtain services through Court Administration, without further leave of court in accordance with it's contract or contracts for court interpreter services. [4] Payment shall be made for interpreter services in accordance with JAC contract procedures for payment of due process costs.

f. <u>**Investigators and other Paraprofessionals**</u>–Conflict counsel shall be permitted to obtain the services of an investigator or other paraprofessional (such as a paralegal), in an amount not to exceed the rate as set forth annually in the General Appropriations Act, without a court order. Any investigator or other paraprofessional fee over that rate, shall require counsel to file a motion with the Court. Payment shall be made for investigative or other paraprofessional services in accordance with JAC contract procedures for payment of due process costs. For information related to an investigator's ability to bill for mileage, see paragraph C.2.j., *infra.*

g. <u>**Mental Health Professionals**</u>–Conflict counsel shall be permitted to obtain the services of a mental health professional in an amount not to exceed the rate as set forth annually in the General Appropriations Act, without a court order. Any mental health service fee over that rate, shall require counsel to file a motion with the Court. Payment shall be made for mental health professional services in accordance with JAC contract procedures for payment of due process costs.

h. <u>**Other Experts**</u>–Conflict counsel shall file a motion with the Court to obtain authorization to secure the services of any other expert. JAC, and ultimately the Court, will determine the appropriateness of a rate charged in accordance with the procedure set forth *supra,* in paragraph C. 1.b. Payment shall be made for other expert services in accordance with JAC contract procedures for due process costs.

i. <u>**Process Servers**</u>–Conflict counsel shall be permitted to retain the services of a process server without court order. The process server shall be paid in an amount not to exceed the rate as set forth annually in the General Appropriations Act, without a court order. Any process server fee over that rate, shall require counsel to file a motion with the Court, as well as written authorization from the Court.

It should be noted that as a general rule, JAC does not pay for service of process on in-county law enforcement officers. Under section 57.081, Florida Statutes, the sheriff is available to provide service of process without prepayment in cases involving indigent persons. In order to use a private process server to serve in-county law enforcement officers, a specific court order must be provided setting forth the need for use of a private process server. [5]

j. <u>**Travel Expenses**</u>–Conflict counsel shall be entitled to reimbursement for travel expenses associated with the representation, for himself and/or his investigator, only upon prior approval by the Court. Travel expenses shall include transportation, mileage, lodging, meals, and such other expenses as the Court deems reasonably necessary in the performance of constitutional and statutory responsibilities. Rates for travel expenses are set forth in section 112.061, Florida Statutes, the statute addressing travel expenses for all public officers, employees, and authorized persons. JAC, however, has set forth additional requirements related to mileage reimbursement for attorneys and investigators.

For dates of appointment on or after July 1, 2007, counsel may only bill for mileage when the destination is outside of the county or in excess of 50 miles (one-way) from counsel's office. In indigent for costs cases, an attorney may not bill for mileage unless providing services on a *pro bono* basis. Mileage is considered part of overhead and is part of the attorney's fees.

Investigators are only paid for extraordinary mileage, which includes travel between counties or a trip exceeding 50 miles one way within a county. In instances involving multiple destinations within a county, the total mileage for the trip must exceed 100 miles. An out-of-county investigator may not bill for mileage between the investigator's office and the county of the case, unless there is an order authorizing the retention of the out-of-county investigator.

D. NON–DISCLOSURE OF PRIVILEGED MATERIAL

None of the documentation required by this Administrative Order for payment of compensation to conflict counsel or for payment of due process costs, shall be required to contain information which may be subject to a claim of privilege, pursuant to the attorney/client, work product, psychotherapist/patient or any other privilege recognized under Florida law. No due process service provider shall include such information in any application for payment for services rendered to conflict counsel, pursuant to this Administrative Order. In the discretion of the presiding judge, applications for authority to incur due process costs to this Administrative Order may be considered by the Court *ex parte* and under seal. Ake v. Oklahoma, 470 U.S. 68, 82 (1984).

E. This Order is effective immediately and shall remain in effect until further Order of the Court and all the terms and conditions set forth in this Administrative Order shall apply unless otherwise ordered by the Court.

F. This Administrative Order shall be recorded in the Official Records of Duval, Clay, and Nassau Counties in the State of Florida, and certified copies shall be furnished by the Clerks of each Court to each local Bar Association.

DONE AND ORDERED in chambers, at Jacksonville, Duval County, Florida, this 5 day of February, 2010.

Donald R. Moran, Jr.
CHIEF JUDGE

[1] A chart summary of attorney compensation rates may be found on JAC's website,www.justiceadmin.org. The current route to obtaining the information on JAC's website is as follows. Once on the website, click "Court–Appointed Counsel" (to the left of screen). At the top of the next screen is a heading entitled "What's New". Under that heading, click on the last option entitled "COURT–APPOINTED ATTORNEY FLAT RATES BY CASE TYPE & FISCAL YEAR".

[2] As of the date of this Administrative Order, the maximum amount to be paid by JAC for due process services per the General Appropriations Act and section 27.425, Florida Statutes, are the rates approved by the Indigent Services Committee as of June 30, 2007. A chart summary of the Fourth Judicial Circuit's due process rates approved by the Indigent Services Committee as of June 30, 2007 (including some due process rates not discussed within this Order), may be found on JAC's website, www.justiceadmin.org. The current route to obtaining this information on JAC's website is as follows. Once on the website, click "Court–Appointed Counsel" (to the left of screen), and scroll down to a heading entitled "Court–Appointed Payment Packet". Once there, see subheading entitled "DUE PROCESS PAYMENT", and under that subheading are several choices. Go to "Rate Sheet by Circuit", type in 4, and hit enter.

[3] Pursuant to Florida Rule of Criminal Procedure 3.220(b)(1)(A)(i), Category A witnesses shall include (1) eyewitnesses, (2) alibi witnesses and rebuttal to alibi witnesses, (3) witnesses who were present when a recorded or unrecorded statement was taken from or made by the defendant or co-defendant, (4) investigating officers, (5) witnesses known by the prosecutor to have any material information that tends to negate the guilt of the defendant as to any offense charged, (6) child hearsay witnesses, and (7) expert witnesses who have not provided a written report and a curriculum vitae or who are going to testify to test results or give opinions that will have to meet the test set forth in Frye v. United States, 293 F. 1013 (D. C. Cir. 1923).

[4] There was no ISC rate set for court interpreter services in this circuit. See paragraph C.1.b. for the procedure to be followed in such instances. Notwithstanding such procedure, the rates set pursuant to the contract or contracts referenced in paragraph C.2.e., should be viewed as the rates that will presumptively be enforced by the Court absent a compelling objection by JAC.

[5] Under Florida Rule of Criminal Procedure 3.220(h)(5), service of a witness subpoena to a law enforcement officer for depositions is unnecessary; provision of written notice to the appropriate law enforcement official at least five days prior to the date of deposition is sufficient under the Florida Rules of Criminal Procedure.

2001–10 (A1). BAKER, MARCHMAN ACT, AND INMATE MENTAL HEALTH HEARINGS

IN THE CIRCUIT COURT, FOURTH JUDICIAL CIRCUIT, IN AND FOR DUVAL COUNTY, FLORIDA

AMENDED ADMINISTRATIVE ORDER No. 2001–10

IN RE: Baker, Marchman Act, and Inmate Mental Health Hearings;

WHEREAS, the caseload in Duval County is an ever-increasing demand on the Court's resources;

WHEREAS, it appears to be in the best interest of the people of Duval County that the Court dispose of matters before it in the most efficient and expedient way possible;

WHEREAS, the Baker Act at section 394.467(6)(a)(2), Florida Statutes (2015) provides a mechanism by which subject hearings may be delegated to a general magistrate;

WHEREAS, the Marchman Act at section 397.681(1), Florida Statutes (2015) provides a mechanism by which subject hearings may be delegated to a general magistrate;

WHEREAS, section 945.43(3)(a), Florida Statutes (2015) [inmate and mental health] provides a mechanism by which the subject hearings may be delegated to a general magistrate;

NOW THEREFORE, by the authority vested in me as Chief Judge and pursuant to the Florida Rules of Judicial Administration, it is

ORDERED:

(A) Hearings held pursuant to section 394.451 et seq. of the Florida Statutes, otherwise known as the Baker Act, are hereby referred to a general magistrate as authorized by law;

(B) Hearings held pursuant to section 397.301 et seq. of the Florida Statutes, otherwise known as the Marchman Act, are hereby referred to a general magistrate as authorized by law;

(C) Hearings held pursuant to section 945.43(3)(a) et seq. of the Florida Statutes (2015), otherwise known as [inmate and mental health], are hereby referred to a general magistrate;

(D) That the Clerk of Court shall have the authority to reserve and assign a courtroom for this purpose;

(E) That this Order shall take effect immediately and remain in effect until further Order of the Court, and all terms and conditions set forth in this Administrative Order shall apply unless otherwise ordered by the Court.

(F) That this Order shall be recorded in the Official Records of Duval County in the State of Florida, and copies furnished by the Clerk of Court to the Jacksonville Bar Association.

DONE AND ORDERED in Chambers at Jacksonville, Duval County, Florida this 1 day of February, 2016.

MARK H. MAHON
CHIEF JUDGE

2001–07 (A5). AUTHORITY OF THE CLERK IN TRAFFIC CASES

IN THE CIRCUIT COURT, FOURTH JUDICIAL CIRCUIT, IN AND FOR DUVAL COUNTY, FLORIDA

FIFTH AMENDED ADMINISTRATIVE ORDER NO. 2001–7

Re: Authority of the Clerk in Traffic Cases

WHEREAS, the case load in the Duval County Traffic Court is ever increasing, and exists as a constant demand on the Court's time and resources;

WHEREAS, it appears in the best interest of the people of Duval County to ensure that the Court disposes of matters before it in the most efficient and expedient way possible;

WHEREAS, Rule 6.360 of the Florida Traffic Court Rules provides a mechanism for enlargement of the time in which a defendant must appear in Traffic Court;

WHEREAS, Rule 6.480 of the Florida Traffic Court Rules provides a mechanism for enlargement of time in which a defendant must render payment for any penalty imposed pursuant to a traffic citation;

NOW THEREFORE, by the authority vested in me as Chief Judge and pursuant to the Florida Rules of Judicial Administration, it is,

ORDERED as follows:

(A) All defendants shall have thirty (30) calendar days from the date of receipt of the citation in which to schedule a court date or render payment for any penalty imposed. If the defendant has not scheduled a court date, rendered payment in full, or has not entered into a payment plan agreement by the end of the said thirty (30) calendar days, the Clerk of the Court shall commence administrative action for suspension of the defendant's driving license.

(B) The Clerk of the Court shall have the authority to issue continuances in Traffic Court cases, at the request of the defendant, pursuant to the following requirements:

(1) The Clerk of the Court shall advise a defendant requesting a continuance that any defendant who requests and is granted a continuance pursuant to the provisions of this Order shall be considered to have waived any rights to a Court hearing pursuant to Rule 6.325 of the Florida Traffic Rules.

(2) The Clerk of the Court shall issue only two (2) thirty (30) day continuances per defendant. There shall be a notation made of each continuance issued to ensure compliance with this requirement.

(3) The continuance may be issued telephonically. The signature of the defendant shall not be required.

(4) For requests for continuance made before the scheduled court date, the date to which the appearance is continued shall be within thirty (30) days of the originally scheduled appearance.

(5) These provisions for continuances shall not apply to Motions for Rehearing or to the taking of Appeals.

(C) This Order shall take effect immediately and remain in effect until further Order of the Court, and all terms and conditions set forth in this Administrative Order shall apply unless otherwise advised by the Court.

(D) This Order shall be recorded in the Official Records of Duval County in the State of Florida, and copies furnished by the Clerk of Court to the Jacksonville Bar Association.

DONE AND ORDERED at Jacksonville, Duval County Florida, this 2 day of October, 2013.

DONALD R. MORAN, JR.
CHIEF JUDGE

1998–07 (A2). COMPREHENSIVE BAKER ACT PROCEDURES

IN THE CIRCUIT COURT, FOURTH JUDICIAL CIRCUIT, IN AND FOR DUVAL AND NASSAU COUNTIES, FLORIDA

SECOND AMENDED ADMINISTRATIVE ORDER NO. 98–7

IN RE: COMPREHENSIVE BAKER ACT PROCEDURES

WHEREAS, pursuant to section 394.45, et seq., Florida Statutes, a person is subject to involuntary inpatient placement ("Baker Act") for treatment based on the person having a mental illness; and

WHEREAS, the Baker Act case load has increased over recent years, challenging competing judicial resources and changes in technology; and

WHEREAS, the implementation of standardized procedures in Duval County will facilitate the timely scheduling, hearing, and disposition of Petitions for Involuntary Inpatient Placement and Petitions for Writ of Habeas Corpus, pursuant to chapter 394, Florida Statutes; and

WHEREAS, it is the intent of the Fourth Judicial Circuit, in and for Duval County, Florida to comply with the requirements of chapters 394 and 119, Florida Statutes, and with the Rules of Judicial Administration:

NOW THEREFORE, by the authority vested in me as Chief Judge of the Fourth Judicial Circuit and pursuant to the Florida Rules of Judicial Administration,

It is **ORDERED**:

1. **Petition Filings.**

(a) All petitions for involuntary inpatient placement and related documents filed by receiving facility administrators or their designees shall be filed with the Clerk of Circuit Court, Duval County, Florida electronically, unless a facility can demonstrate undue hardship. If a facility does not have electronic filing capabilities and the Court has determined undue hardship, then paper filing is permissible.

(b) All Baker Act petitions and related documents shall be typewritten or if a hand written document, then it shall be legible, except that a Petition for Writ of Habeas Corpus submitted by or on behalf of the patient in his/her own handwriting is permitted and shall be accepted by the Clerk of Court.

(c) The Clerk of Court will provide immediate electronic or telephonic notification to all parties if a document is questioned by the Clerk as to the filing status.

2. **Appointment of Counsel.**

(a) Upon the filing of a Petition for Involuntary Placement of a person or upon the filing of a Petition for Writ of Habeas Corpus under Chapter 394, Florida Statutes (2016), the Office of the Public Defender, Fourth Judicial Circuit, shall be immediately appointed to represent the person.

(b) The Clerk of Court will electronically notify the Office of the Public Defender and the Office of the State Attorney that a petition has been filed and provide each with a copy of the petition and accompanying documents.

(c) The Baker Act receiving facilities shall allow the Office of the Public Defender immediate access to the patient, to any witnesses, and to the patient's complete clinical record; such receiving facilities shall also allow the scanning, copying or photographing of the clinical records as requested by the Office of the Public Defender for the representation of the patient, or the Office of the Public Defender may request copies of any or all of the clinical records.

3. **Notice of Hearings.** Notice of hearings will be provided by the Clerk of Court to all parties, the patient and his or her representative, and guardian or guardian advocate either electronically, or by U.S. Mail or hand delivery, if electronic transmission is unavailable.

4. **Scheduling and Venue.**

(a) The Clerk of Court will set, and the Court shall hold the hearing regarding the involuntary inpatient placement of a patient within five (5) court working days, unless a continuance is granted. Section 394.467(6)(a)1, Fla. Stat. (2016).

(b) If appointment of a guardian advocate is requested for a patient who lacks an alternative substitute decision maker, the receiving facility shall notify all parties and the guardian advocate hearing shall be heard as soon as possible.

(c) Hearings will be conducted at the receiving facility where the patient is being treated unless either party requests a courtroom for this purpose, provided there is reasonable notice and the patient's right to be present has been waived in accordance with Florida Statutes.

(i) Judicial personnel may appear, and the Court may preside, over placement and Habeas hearings by electronic video communication, if such equipment is available, subject to any right of the patient to object and consistent with the patient's best interest.

(ii) Judicial personnel may appear, and the Court may preside, over guardian advocate hearings by electronic or telephonic transmission, if such communication equipment is available, subject to any right of the patient to object and consistent with the patient's best interest.

(d) The receiving facility shall provide a safe and secure area, of sufficient size to conduct a dignified circuit court proceeding without unnecessary noise or other distractions.

(e) Magistrates shall conduct such hearings pursuant to Amended Administrative Order No. 2001–10 unless a party files a written objection or application to the Circuit Court. The patient or his/her attorney may request a courtroom for this purpose. Transportation of the patient to the Courtroom shall be provided by the facility, unless the patient's right to be present has been waived.

5. **Confidentiality of Information.**

(a) The Court finds that it is necessary and appropriate to maintain the confidentiality of records with regard to the person and related family information of persons subject to involuntary inpatient placement under section 394.467, *et seq.* Florida Statutes (2016).

(b) All Baker Act court records, as defined by the Rules of Judicial Administration, including the patient's name, and docket entries, may not be disclosed by the Clerk of Court to the public, and are exempt and confidential under the Rules of Judicial Administration and Chapter 119, Florida Statutes, unless deemed otherwise by Court order.

6. **Habeas Corpus Proceedings.**

(a) When a Petition for a Writ of Habeas Corpus is filed pursuant to section 394.459(8), Florida Statutes (2016), it will be consolidated with, and filed under the same case number as any other Petition for Involuntary Placement regarding the same person and facility to ensure that the same Magistrate or Judge is reviewing both petitions.

(b) In addition to the statutory provisions with regard to a petition for habeas corpus as set forth in section 394.459(8), Florida Statutes (2016), the following procedures will apply:

(i) When a Petition for Writ of Habeas Corpus has been filed and the hearing with regard to the Petition for Involuntary Inpatient Placement has not been previously conducted, the two proceedings may be scheduled on the same day and time, unless the patient needs additional time to call additional witnesses or to obtain an expert witness to testify at the placement hearing, in which case the Petition for Writ of Habeas Corpus shall be heard or reviewed forthwith or by the next available court working day.

(ii) Habeas hearings may be conducted by a Magistrate. If the Magistrate grants a habeas for release, then the ruling will be effective immediately, upon confirmation of a Circuit Court Judge. If a habeas is denied by the Magistrate, then the Respondent may submit the habeas to the domestic violence Circuit Judge on duty for immediate review. Parties may file a written objection to the Magistrate presiding over the habeas hearing and request that the Circuit Judge on rotation duty hear the matter.

(iii) Petitions for a Writ of Habeas Corpus may not require a hearing, and may be ruled on based upon the law if no additional testimony is required.

7. Amended Administrative Order No. 98–7 and Amended Administrative Order No. 85–06 (filed on February 7, 1985), are hereby rescinded and superseded by this Administrative Order.

8. All other Administrative Orders not identified above that have been previously entered addressing Petitions for Involuntary Placement and Petitions for a Writ of Habeas Corpus, shall remain in full force and effect unless any terms or conditions appear to be contradictory, in which case, this Administrative Order shall supersede such Order(s).

9. This Administrative Order shall be recorded by the Clerk of the Court, in the Official Records of Duval County, in the State of Florida, and shall take effect immediately. All terms and conditions set forth herein shall remain in full force and effect unless and until otherwise ordered by the Court.

DONE AND ORDERED in Chambers at Jacksonville, Duval County, Florida, on the 31 day of August, 2016.

MARK H. MAHON
CHIEF JUDGE

1996–10 (A17). ORDER OF REFERRAL TO GENERAL MAGISTRATES AND SUPPORT ENFORCEMENT HEARING OFFICERS

IN THE CIRCUIT COURT OF THE FOURTH JUDICIAL CIRCUIT, IN AND FOR CLAY, DUVAL AND NASSAU COUNTIES, FLORIDA

SEVENTEENTH AMENDED ADMINISTRATIVE ORDER NO. 1996–10

RE: ORDER OF REFERRAL TO GENERAL MAGISTRATES AND SUPPORT ENFORCEMENT HEARING OFFCIERS

WHEREAS, paragraph 1 of the Sixteenth Amended Administrative Order No. 96–10 should be amended to remove the list of specific General Magistrates and/or Support Enforcement Hearing Officers so that further administrative orders do not need to be entered for the sole purpose of amending that list;

WHEREAS, all other portions of Sixteenth Amended Administrative Order No. 96–10 remain the same and are included below for the reader's convenience;

WHEREAS, a large volume of cases are now brought before the Family, Juvenile and Probate Divisions of the Circuit Court;

WHEREAS, the interests of the public and of the litigants require a flexible and speedy resolution of such matters;

WHEREAS, the laws of Florida impose time limitations for the resolution of these matters;

WHEREAS, the Family Division has demonstrated a need for assistance from General Magistrates to comply with the time limitations for conducting proceedings relating to all Family Law matters, pursuant to Rule 12.490, Florida Family Law Rules of Procedure;

WHEREAS, the Family Division has demonstrated a need for assistance from Support Enforcement Hearing Officers to comply with the time limitations for conducting proceedings pursuant to Rule 12.491, Florida Family Law Rules of Procedure, relating to (a) the establishment, enforcement, or modification of child support or (b) the enforcement of any support order for the parent or other person entitled to receive child support in conjunction with an ongoing child support or child support arrearage;

WHEREAS, the Juvenile Division has demonstrated a need for assistance from General Magistrates to comply with the time limitations for conducting proceedings relating to all Juvenile Dependency and Delinquency matters pursuant to Rule 8.257, Florida Rules of Juvenile Procedure, with the exception that a General Magistrate shall not preside over shelter hearings under Rule 8.257(h) and § 39.402, Florida Statutes, or over an adjudicatory hearing under either § 39.507 or § 39.809, Florida Statutes.

WHEREAS, the Probate Division has demonstrated a need for assistance from General Magistrates to comply with the time limitations for conducting proceedings relating to Expedited Judicial Intervention Concerning Medical Treatment Procedures, pursuant to Rule 5.095, Florida Probate Rules, and Chapters 394 and 397, Florida Statutes;

WHEREAS, it is necessary to maintain a record of proceedings conducted before General Magistrates and Support Enforcement Hearing Officers, and electronic recording has proved to be a reliable and economical method of maintaining such a record;

NOW, THEREFORE, by the authority vested in me as the Chief Judge of the Fourth Judicial Circuit of Florida, and pursuant to the Florida Rules of Judicial Administration, Rules 12.490 and 12.491, Florida Family Law Rules of Procedure, Rule 8.257, Florida Rules of Juvenile Procedure, and Rule 5.095, Florida Probate Rules, it is hereby

ORDERED that:

1) All Family Law cases filed *pro se*, all State of Florida Department of Revenue Title IV–D cases, and all cases referred individually by any Circuit Civil Division, shall be referred to a duly designated General Magistrate and/or Support Enforcement Hearing Officer, as named in all current Administrative Orders of the Fourth Judicial Circuit and pursuant to Florida Family Law Rule of Procedure 12.490, Florida Family Law Rule of Procedure 12.491, Florida Rules of Juvenile Procedure 8.257, and Florida Probate Rule 5.095, respectively.

2) The General Magistrate and/or Support Enforcement Hearing Officer shall assign a time and place for proceedings as soon as reasonably possible after the reference is made and give notice to each of the parties involved either directly or by directing counsel to file and serve a notice of hearing.

3) Notice to all parties shall be provided in bold face, 14 point Times New Roman or Courier font, in the following manner in compliance with Florida Rules of Judicial Administration 2.540 and Third Amended Administrative Order No. 1993–02:

a. For all notices compelling appearance at:

i. The Duval County Courthouse; and

ii. The Clay County Courthouse,

the language shall state:

If you are a person with a disability who needs any accommodation in order to participate in this proceeding, you are entitled, at no cost to you, to the provision of certain assistance. Please contact the ADA Coordinator at (904) 255–1695 or crtintrp@coi.net, at least 7 days before your scheduled court appearance, or immediately upon receiving this notification if the time before the scheduled appearance is less than 7 days; if you are hearing or voice impaired, call 711.

b. For all notices compelling appearance at the Nassau County Courthouse, the notice language shall state:

If you are a person with a disability who needs any accommodation in order to participate in this proceeding, you are entitled, at no cost to you, to the provision of certain assistance. Please contact the ADA Coordinator at (904)548–4600 (then press 0) at least 7 days before your scheduled court appearance, or immediately upon receiving this notification if the time before the scheduled appearance is less than 7 days; if you are hearing or voice impaired, call 711.

4) Counties within the State of Florida may have different rules. Parties should consult the Clerk of Court or Family Law Intake Staff relating to this procedure.

5) Administrative Order No. 2014–15, which was vacated and rescinded in its entirety in Sixteenth Amended Administrative Order No. 96–10, will remain vacated and rescinded in its entirety.

6) All other Amended Administrative Orders No. 96–10 previously entered and addressing the same subject matter are hereby vacated and superseded.

7) This Seventeenth Amended Administrative Order No. 96–10 shall be recorded by the Clerk of Court, in the Official Records of Duval County, in the State of Florida, and shall take effect immediately and remain in full force and effect unless and until otherwise ordered by the Court.

DONE AND ORDERED in Chambers at Jacksonville, Duval County, Florida, this 3rd day of October, 2017.

MARK H. MAHON
Chief Judge

1995–16 (A5). FAMILY LAW ADMINISTRATIVE POLICIES AND PROCEDURES

IN THE CIRCUIT COURT, FOURTH JUDICIAL CIRCUIT, IN AND FOR DUVAL, CLAY AND NASSAU COUNTY, FLORIDA

FIFTH AMENDED ADMINISTRATIVE ORDER NO. 1995–16

IN RE: FAMILY LAW ADMINISTRATIVE POLICIES AND PROCEDURES AND PROCEDURES FOR COMPLIANCE WITH SUPREME COURT MANDATED TIME STANDARDS

WHEREAS, on December 1, 1995 the Chief Judge signed into effect Administrative Order No. 95–16, In Re: Family Law Administrative Policies and Procedures and Procedures for Compliance With Supreme Court Mandated Time Standards;

WHEREAS, subsequent amendments to Administrative 95–16 amended Fourth Judicial Guideline Visitation and subsequently created the Fourth Judicial Circuit Timesharing Guidelines (Local and Long Distance) but failed to amend or rescind the remaining administrative policies and procedures which are now outdated;

WHEREAS, the Circuit Judges presently assigned to the Family Division of the Fourth Judicial Circuit have determined that the policies and procedures apart from the Fourth Judicial Timesharing Guidelines, are unnecessary and should be rescinded;

NOW THEREFORE, by the authority vested in me as the Chief Judge of the Fourth Judicial Circuit and pursuant to the Florida Rules of Judicial Administration, it is

ORDERED:

(A) That the Family Law Administrative Policies and Procedures and Procedures For Compliance With The Supreme Court Mandated Time Standards set forth in Administrative Order No. 95–16 filed on December 1, 1995, and set forth in the Amended Administrative Order No. 95–16 filed on March 14, 1996, are hereby vacated and rescinded;

(B) That the Fourth Amended Administrative Order No. 95–16, entitled "In Re: Family Law—Timesharing Guidelines", previously filed on October 5, 2016, shall remain in full force and effect, unless any terms or conditions appear to be contradictory, in which case, this Administrative Order shall supersede such order.

(C) That this Fifth Amended Administrative Order No. 1995–16 shall take effect immediately and remain in full force and effect until further order of this Court, and all terms and conditions set forth in this Order shall apply unless otherwise ordered by this Court.

DONE AND ORDERED at Jacksonville, Duval County, Florida, this 9th day of March, 2017.

MARK H. MAHON
CHIEF JUDGE

1995–16 (A4). FAMILY LAW FOURTH JUDICIAL CIRCUIT TIMESHARING GUIDELINES (LOCAL AND LONG DISTANCE)

IN THE CIRCUIT COURT, FOURTH JUDICIAL CIRCUIT, IN AND FOR DUVAL, CLAY AND NASSAU COUNTIES, FLORIDA

FOURTH AMENDED ADMINISTRATIVE ORDER NO. 95–16

IN RE: FAMILY LAW FOURTH JUDICIAL CIRCUIT TIMESHARING GUIDELINES (LOCAL AND LONG DISTANCE)

WHEREAS, the judges of the Family Law Division of this Circuit, in consultation with members of the Family Law Bar, have deemed it advisable to create timesharing guidelines for use in cases where the parents of a child or children do not reside together; and

WHEREAS, the judges of the Family Law Division and members of the Family Law Bar of this Circuit, after substantial study and consultation, have recommended the adoption of the attached documents, but emphasize that these guidelines are not mandatory, nor binding on any party. The guidelines are adopted for the purpose of assisting the parties in their litigation; and

WHEREAS, the Chief Judge of the Fourth Judicial Circuit of the State of Florida has reviewed the attached timeshare guidelines, and determined that they should be implemented as to matters before the Family Law Division, and pursuant to Rule 2.215, Florida Rules Judicial Administration.

IT IS THEREUPON,

ORDERED AND ADJUDGED:

1. The contents of the attached documents entitled

"FOURTH JUDICIAL CIRCUIT LOCAL TIMESHARING GUIDELINES" and "FOURTH JUDICIAL CIRCUIT COURT LONG DISTANCE TIMESHARING GUIDELINES"

are hereby adopted as guidelines for litigation in the Family Law Division of the Fourth Judicial Circuit.

2. This Fourth Amended Administrative Order No. 95–16 shall take effect immediately, and remain in effect thereafter until further Order of this Court. The Third Amended Administrative Order No. 95–16, entered chronologically out of sequence as a "Third Amended" on October 5, 2016, is hereby rescinded and superseded by this "Fourth Amended" Order.

DONE AND ORDERED in Chambers at Jacksonville, Duval County, Florida, this 5 day of Oct., 2016.

MARK H. MAHON

Chief Judge

FOURTH JUDICIAL CIRCUIT LOCAL TIMESHARING GUIDELINES

NEITHER PARENT SHALL CONCEAL THE WHEREABOUTS OF ANY CHILD(REN) OF THE PARENTS, AND EACH PARENT SHALL KEEP THE OTHER ADVISED AT ALL TIMES OF THE RESIDENTIAL ADDRESS, EMAIL ADDRESS, AND PHONE NUMBERS WHERE THE CHILD(REN) WILL BE STAYING WHILE IN THE PHYSICAL CUSTODY OF EITHER PARENT. EACH PARENT SHALL NOTIFY THE OTHER IMMEDIATELY (NO LATER THAN 3 HOURS) OF ANY EMERGENCY PERTAINING TO ANY CHILD(REN) OF THE PARENTS.

REASONABLE TIMESHARING WITH ANY CHILD(REN) OF THE PARENTS SHALL TAKE PLACE AT SUCH TIME AND PLACE AS THE PARENTS MAY AGREE. IF THE PARENTS CANNOT REACH AN AGREEMENT AS TO DETAILS OF TIMESHARING, THE COURT MAY CONSIDER THESE GUIDELINES IN CRAFTING A TIMESHARING SCHEDULE AFTER TAKING INTO CONSIDERATION THE FACTORS ENUMERATED UNDER APPLICABLE FLORIDA LAW.

Promoting Mutual Respect: These guidelines are predicated upon the premise that the parents will each afford the other the utmost of mutual respect. Each parent shall seek to promote and encourage the love and esteem of the child for the other parent. Neither parent shall intentionally do anything to estrange or alienate the child from the other parent. Neither parent shall make any derogatory remarks about the other parent or the other parent's family in the presence of the child, nor shall either parent allow others to do so. Each parent shall be pleasant and polite in communicating with the other parent.

The child(ren) have a right to spend substantial, quality time with both parents and it is the intent of these Guidelines that the child(ren) spend substantial time with both parents. Each of the parents shall exercise the utmost good faith and shall consent to all reasonable timesharing requests by the other parent. The majority timeshare parent is expected to provide reasonable access to the child(ren) at unscheduled times, if requested, and if to do so does not unreasonably disrupt prior planned activities of the child(ren) or the parent. Therefore, the non-majority timeshare parent is entitled to and shall have the following timesharing with the child(ren):

1. **Weekdays:** One overnight per week from immediately after school/work until the following morning, at which time the child(ren) shall be timely returned to school/daycare or to the other parent by 9:00 a.m., if school is not in session. If the parents cannot agree, the overnight shall be Thursday.

2. **Weekends:**

A. Every other weekend from Friday after school/work until the following Monday morning at which time the child(ren) shall be timely returned to school/daycare.

B. Should the non-majority timeshare parent's regular weekend fall on a three-day weekend which is observed by the child(ren)'s school, and the weekend is a holiday or special occasion not otherwise expressly provided for below, the non-majority timeshare parent shall be entitled to a three-day weekend. In such event, the weekend shall be defined as after school/work the day school recesses for the weekend (Thursday or Friday) through return to school/daycare at the end of the weekend (Monday or Tuesday).

C. As to paragraph 2(A), the majority timeshare parent shall have the alternate weekends.

3. **Holidays:**

A. *Spring Break:* School spring break in even-numbered years from immediately after school/work the day school recesses for the break until the day school resumes when the child(ren) shall be timely returned to school/daycare.

B. *Easter:* Easter weekend in even-numbered years, from after school/work the day school recesses for the weekend until the return to school the day it resumes.

C. *Mother's Day Weekend/Father's Day Weekend:* The child(ren) shall be with the mother on Mother's Day weekend and with the father on Father's Day weekend, and with the other parent the following weekend.

D. *Independence Day:* Independence Day in odd-numbered years from 9:00 a.m. July 4th through 9:00 a.m. July 5th (except it shall be a three-day weekend if July 4th falls on a Friday or Monday).

E. *Thanksgiving Weekend:* Thanksgiving weekend in even-numbered years from immediately after school/work the day school recesses for the holiday until the return to school the day it resumes.

F. *Christmas/Winter Break:*

1. Christmas Holiday. For a parent that celebrates the Christmas holiday, the intent is for the parents to equally divide the number of days the child(ren) have off from school for the holiday, including weather days. The non-majority timeshare parent shall be entitled to the first part of the break in odd-numbered years and the majority parent shall have the first part of the break in even-numbered years. The parent with the first half of the holiday shall have the child(ren) from after school/work the day school recesses for the break until Christmas Day at 2:00 p.m. The parent with the second half of the holiday shall have the child(ren) from 2:00 p.m. on Christmas Day, for a total number of days equal to one-half of the Winter Break, returning the child(ren) at 6:00 p.m. on the last day of his/her part of the break, to the other parent who shall have the remainder of the holiday period until school resumes. The non-majority timeshare parent shall have the second half of the break in even-numbered years and the majority parent shall have the second half of the break in odd-numbered years.

2. Winter Break. For all other parents, the intent is for the parents to equally divide the number of days the child(ren) have off from school for the Winter Break holiday, including weather days. The non-majority timeshare parent shall be entitled to the first part of the break in odd-numbered years and the majority parent shall have the first part of the break in even-numbered years. The parent with the first half of the holiday shall have the child(ren) from after school/work for a total number of days equal to one-half of the Winter Break, returning the children at 6:00 p.m. on the last day of his/her part of the break, to the other parent who shall have the remainder of the holiday period until school resumes.

G. *Birthdays:* Birthdays of the child(ren) in even-numbered years, from after school/work or 9:00 a.m. (if school is not in session) on the birthday until return to school the following morning or 9:00 a.m. (if school is not in session).

H. As to paragraph 3(A) through (E) and (G), the majority timeshare parent shall be entitled to the same time with the child(ren), but in alternate years.

I. Even though several of the above timesharing provisions are related to "school," the non-majority parent shall have the same visitation with children who are not in school.

J. Holidays and special occasions, as provided in paragraphs 3(A) through 3(G), shall have priority over regular weekday and weekend timesharing. In the event the holiday timesharing schedule has the effect of creating three (3) consecutive entire weekends (or in a 50/50 timesharing scenario, three consecutive entire weeks) with one parent, then the third such weekend (or week in a 50/50 timesharing scenario), shall revert to the other parent, after which the regular schedule shall resume. The result will be that each parent will have two weekends in a row (or in a 50/50 timesharing scenario, two weeks in a row) and then return to their alternating schedule.

4. Summer Vacation:

A. The parents shall equally divide the summer break by alternating their timeshare with the child(ren) weekly. Exchanges shall take place on Friday after school/work beginning on the first Friday following the end of school (or if school recesses on a Friday, it shall begin that day) with the non-majority parent having the first full week and the majority timeshare parent having the second full week and alternating weekly thereafter until the Friday before the start of school. (Parents utilizing a 50/50 timesharing schedule during the school year should maintain that same rotation during the summer).

B. Notwithstanding the foregoing, during the summer each parent shall be entitled to reasonable extended out-of-town vacation time of up to two consecutive weeks, uninterrupted by sharing the child with the other parent. The parents shall each notify the other in writing when they elect to take their vacation times with the child(ren) no later than April 1st each year. In the event of a conflict, the Father's vacation time shall have priority in even-numbered years and the Mother's vacation time shall have priority in odd-numbered years.

C. The parent who is not exercising timesharing during a given week shall be entitled to have the child(ren) for dinner from after camp/daycare/work until 8:00 p.m. If the parents cannot agree on a day, it shall be Thursday evening.

D. Each parent shall be responsible for enrolling the child(ren) in and paying for summer camps or, daycare during his/her summer timesharing.

5. Conflicts: Both parents shall endeavor to be punctual in transferring the child(ren). If circumstances prevent either from being punctual, the parents shall communicate and cooperate appropriately.

6. Cancellations: Each parent shall give the other parent at least 24 hours advance notice (or if an emergency occurs, as quickly as possible), if he/she will be unable to exercise weeknight, weekend, Father's Day, Mother's Day, or birthday visitation. As to holidays, there shall be one-week advance notice; as to Christmas and summer, one month advance cancellation notice. Notice as to Christmas and summer vacation shall be in writing.

7. Parent Child(ren) Contact: The parents shall permit the child to have telephone, email, and/or other electronic communication, including audio/visual contact through features such as Skype or Facetime with the other parent, at any reasonable time. If the parents cannot agree on the days and times for such communication, then the child shall be permitted at a minimum to speak with the other parent on Mondays, Wednesdays, and Fridays at 7:30 p.m. EST. Neither parent shall monitor, intercept, interrupt or listen to communications between the child and the other parent absent a Court order authorizing them to do so. If a parent takes away phone privileges from a child as a form of punishment, the child shall still be permitted to have telephone or other such contact with the other parent as set forth herein.

FOURTH JUDICIAL CIRCUIT COURT LONG DISTANCE TIMESHARING GUIDELINES

NEITHER PARENT SHALL CONCEAL THE WHEREABOUTS OF ANY CHILD(REN) OF THE PARENTS, AND EACH PARENT SHALL KEEP THE OTHER ADVISED AT ALL TIMES OF THE RESIDENTIAL ADDRESS, EMAIL ADDRESS, AND PHONE NUMBERS WHERE THE CHILD(REN) WILL BE STAYING WHILE IN THE CUSTODY OF EITHER PARENT. EACH PARENT SHALL NOTIFY THE OTHER IMMEDIATELY (NO LATER THAN 3 HOURS) OF ANY EMERGENCY PERTAINING TO ANY CHILDREN OF THE PARENTS.

"REASONABLE" TIME–SHARING WITH THE CHILD(REN) SHALL TAKE PLACE AT SUCH TIME AND PLACE AS THE PARENTS MAY AGREE. IF THE PARENTS CANNOT REACH AN AGREEMENT AS TO DETAILS OF TIMESHARING, THE COURT MAY CONSIDER THESE GUIDELINES IN CRAFTING A TIMESHARING SCHEDULE, AFTER TAKING INTO CONSIDERATION THE FACTORS ENUMERATED UNDER APPLICABLE FLORIDA LAW, AS APPROPRIATE. THIS TIMESHARING SCHEDULE IS SUGGESTED. AS A GUIDELINE, AS CIRCUMSTANCES MAY VARY SIGNIFICANTLY DUE TO THE DISTANCE BETWEEN THE PARENTS AND THE SPECIFIC LOCATIONS OF THEIR RESPECTIVE RESIDENCES.

Promoting Mutual Respect: These guidelines are predicated upon the premise that the parents will each afford the other the utmost of mutual respect. Each parent shall seek to promote and encourage the love and esteem of the child for the other parent. Neither parent shall intentionally do anything to estrange or alienate the child from the other parent. Neither parent shall make any derogatory remarks about the other parent or the other parent's family in the presence of the child, nor shall either parent allow others to do so. Each parent shall be pleasant and polite in communicating with the other parent.

The child(ren) have a right to spend substantial quality time with both parents and it is the intent of these Guidelines that the child(ren) spend substantial time with both parents. Each of the parents shall exercise the utmost good faith and shall consent to all reasonable timeshare requests by the other parent. Both parents are expected to provide access to the child(ren) at unscheduled times, if requested, and if to do so does not unreasonably disrupt prior planned activities of the child(ren) or the other parent. The parent that lives in excess of 150 miles shall be entitled to and shall have the following timesharing with the child(ren).

1. **Weekends:** The parent who lives in excess of 150 miles may exercise alternate weekend timesharing, as provided in the Fourth Judicial Circuit Local Timesharing Guidelines, in the vicinity of the residence where the child(ren) are the majority of the time. Alternately, the parent that lives in excess of 150 miles shall have weekend timesharing at a location designated by that parent one weekend per month, on any weekend during a month that would encompass a three-day weekend, as well as timesharing in the vicinity of the residence where the child(ren) are the majority of the time, on the alternate weekend. In the event there is no such three-day weekend during a given month, the first full weekend of the month shall be the weekend designated for timesharing, unless otherwise agreed by the parents. Said timesharing shall commence as early as practicable on the day before the holiday or Friday, whichever comes first, and conclude at 5:00 p.m. on Sunday or the day before school resumes, whichever is later.

2. **Holidays:**

A. *Christmas/Winter Break Vacation:* The intent is for the parents to equally divide the number of days the child(ren) have off from school for the Winter Break holiday, including weather days. The parent that lives in excess of 150 miles shall be entitled to the first part of the break in odd-numbered years, from after school/work/daycare on the day school recesses for the holiday, for a total number of days equal to one-half of the Winter Break, returning the child(ren) to the majority timeshare parent at 6:00 p.m. on the last day of his/her part of the break. The parent that lives in excess of 150 miles shall be entitled to the, second part of the break in even-numbered years, picking the child(ren) up at 9:00 a.m. on the day beginning the second half of the break, and returning the child(ren) to the majority parent at 6:00 p.m. on the night before school resumes. In even-numbered years, the majority timeshare parent shall be entitled to the first part of the break as described above and in odd-numbered years shall be entitled to the second part of the break, as described above.

B. *Spring Vacation:* The parent that lives in excess of 150 miles shall have timesharing during the entire spring break every year, commencing on the day school recesses for the break until 6:00 p.m. on the day before school resumes.

C. *Thanksgiving:* The parent that lives in excess of 150 miles shall have time sharing in even-numbered years, from the day school recesses for the holiday until 6:00 p.m. on Sunday immediately following the holiday. In odd-numbered years, the majority timeshare parent shall have the Thanksgiving holiday.

D. *Mother's Day/Father's Day:* Mother's Day and Father's Day shall be spent with the parent being honored by the holiday in question, from the Friday prior to the holiday until 6:00 p.m. on Sunday. The parent that lives in excess of 150 miles shall have timesharing for this holiday in the vicinity of the child(ren)'s residence, unless said timesharing coincides with that parent's summer vacation timesharing.

E. *Birthdays:* The child(ren) shall celebrate their birthday(s) in the home of the majority timeshare parent unless the birthday falls on a regularly scheduled timesharing date with the other parent.

F. *Non–Specified Holidays:* Should the parents recognize a religious holiday not specifically mentioned herein, then the parents shall alternate the holiday. Each parent shall cooperate with the other so that the parent who lives in excess of 150 miles will have the entire holiday in even-numbered years. The parents shall cooperate to work out beginning and ending times for such timesharing. Should only one parent recognize a religious holiday not specifically mentioned herein, then that parent shall be entitled to reasonable timesharing with the child(ren) during that holiday period in every year, with the parents cooperating to work out the beginning and ending times for such holiday timesharing.

3. **Summer Vacation:** The parent that lives in excess of 150 miles shall have summer timesharing with the minor children, commencing 5 days following the end of the school term and ending two weeks prior to the start of the new school term: During said summer vacation timesharing, the parent that usually has the children for the majority of the time during the year shall have timesharing as set forth above. The majority parent's timesharing shall take place in the vicinity of that parent's home.

4. **School Calendars:** School calendars and event calendars shall be provided to the parent who lives in excess of 150 miles by the parent living in the child's school district, immediately upon receipt. The parent living in the child's school district shall also advise the other parent of events not appearing on school calendars as soon as practical after becoming aware of the dates of such events. It is strongly recommended that the parents use OurFamilyWizard.com or TalkingParents.com in order to facilitate the child(ren)'s schedule(s).

5. **Conflicts:** Regular weekend and summer vacation timesharing shall be held in accordance with the schedule set out herein. Should there be any conflict between the regularly scheduled and the holiday timesharing, the holiday timesharing shall control, to–wit: the timesharing set out in paragraphs 2 and 3 takes precedence over the timesharing set out in paragraph 1.

6. **Transportation Costs:** Transportation costs shall be agreed upon by the parents or left to the discretion of the Court. The criteria the Court may consider in allocating transportation costs include, but are not limited to the following:

a) Relative financial positions of the parents;

b) Extent and regularity of timesharing by the parent that lives in excess of 150 miles;

c) Distance;

d) The parent responsible for and the circumstances of the relocation;

e) Any other factor which the Court deems relevant to the particular circumstances of the parents.

7. **Mode of Transportation:** The mode or method of transportation shall be agreed upon by the parents or left to the discretion of the Court. The distance between the parents and the inconvenience and burdens imposed upon the child(ren) shall be considered in determining the mode of transportation.

8. **Waiting Period:** The child(ren) and the parents shall be required to wait a reasonable period of time for the visiting parent to pick up the child(ren) to begin any timesharing. Consideration shall be made for the distance between the various parents and the mode of transportation used to exercise the timesharing, as well as unforeseen delays and flight schedules.

9. **Cancellations:** Cancellation by the parent that lives in excess of 150 miles in any of the aforementioned timesharing shall be made in writing at least 14 days prior to the scheduled commencement of said timesharing.

10. **Parent/Child(ren) Contact:** The parents shall permit the child to have telephone, email, and/or other electronic communication, including audio/visual contact through features such as Skype or Facetime with the other parent, at any reasonable time. If the parents cannot agree on the days and times for such communication, then the child shall be permitted at a minimum to speak with the other parent on Mondays, Wednesdays, and Fridays at 7:30 p.m. EST. Neither parent shall monitor, intercept, interrupt or listen to communications between the child and the other parent absent a Court order authorizing them to do so. If a parent takes away phone privileges from a child as a form of punishment, the child shall still be permitted to have telephone or other such contact with the other parent as set forth herein.

1995–04 (A1). LOCATION OF DEPOSITIONS IN CRIMINAL CASES—DUVAL COUNTY

IN THE CIRCUIT COURT, FOURTH JUDICIAL CIRCUIT, IN AND FOR DUVAL COUNTY, FLORIDA

AMENDED ADMINISTRATIVE ORDER NO. 95–4

RE: LOCATION OF DEPOSITIONS IN CRIMINAL CASES—DUVAL COUNTY

WHEREAS, Rule 3.220(h)(3), of the Florida Rules of Criminal Procedure, provides as follows:

Location of Deposition: Depositions of witnesses residing in the county in which the trial is to take place shall be taken in the building in which the trial shall be held, such other location as is agreed on by the parties, or a location designated by the court.

WHEREAS, it is in the best interest of the judiciary and the Criminal Division practitioners in Duval County to have the location of depositions expressly designated by the Court, except when the parties agree otherwise;

WHEREAS, Administrative Order 95–4 provided that depositions of State witnesses be taken at the Office of the Public Defender located at 25 N. Market Street (unless the State Attorney and defense counsel agreed otherwise) and depositions of defense witnesses in criminal cases be taken in the Courthouse Annex (unless other arrangements were agreed upon between the parties);

WHEREAS, there has been some confusion recently about the appropriate location of depositions for criminal cases since the Duval County Courthouse has changed its location from 330 East Bay Street to 501 West Adams Street, Jacksonville, Florida and the location of the Office of the Public Defender has moved from 25 N. Market Street to 407 N. Laura Street;

WHEREAS, the Office of the Public Defender, which is now located at 407 N. Laura Street, sometimes lacks adequate deposition rooms to facilitate the number of depositions that must be taken;

WHEREAS, certain court programs and departments moved out of the Courthouse Annex located at 220 E. Bay Street and into the new Duval County Courthouse on 501 West Adams Street thereby creating sufficient space in the Courthouse Annex to accommodate criminal depositions in Duval County;

WHEREAS, the new Duval County Courthouse on 501 West Adams Street has deposition rooms and a state-of-the-art security system;

WHEREAS, the Courthouse Annex and new Duval County Courthouse are equipped with armed officers and magnetometers, providing the appropriate security measures necessary to ensure the safety of the individuals involved;

WHEREAS, the proximity of the Courthouse Annex to the Duval County Jail and its security measures makes the Annex conducive as a venue for the taking of depositions of incarcerated witnesses;

WHEREAS, the Courthouse Annex at 220 East Bay Street has the added convenience of ample parking;

NOW THEREFORE, by the authority vested in me as the Chief Judge of the Fourth Judicial Circuit and pursuant to the Florida Rules of Judicial Administration, it is

ORDERED that:

1. Depositions of all State and defense witnesses in criminal cases in which the Public Defender and Regional Conflict Counsel are assigned as counsel will be taken in the Courthouse Annex located at 220 East Bay Street, Jacksonville, Florida, unless the Office of the State Attorney and defense counsel agree to take a deposition at another location.

2. Depositions of all State and defense witnesses in criminal cases in which private counsel serve as defense counsel will be taken in the new Duval County Courthouse at 501 West Adams Street, Jacksonville, Florida, unless the Office of the State Attorney and defense counsel agree to take a deposition at another location.

3. Depositions of all incarcerated witnesses who are being deposed in criminal matters will be taken at the Courthouse Annex located at 220 East Bay Street unless counsel agree to alternative arrangements with appropriate security measures.

4. That Administrative Order 95–4 and any other Administrative Orders previously entered and addressing the same subject matter are hereby vacated and superseded.

5. That this Amended Administrative Order shall be recorded by the Clerk of the Court, in the Official Records of Duval County, in the State of Florida, and shall take effect immediately and remain in full force and effect unless and until otherwise ordered by the Court.

DONE AND ORDERED in Chambers at Jacksonville, Duval County, Florida, this 23 day of July, 2012.

DONALD R. MORAN JR.
CHIEF JUDGE

1994–02 (A2). CIVIL RIGHTS POLICY STATEMENT AND CIVIL RIGHTS COMPLAINT PROCEDURE

IN THE CIRCUIT COURT, FOURTH JUDICIAL CIRCUIT, IN AND FOR DUVAL, CLAY AND NASSAU COUNTIES, FLORIDA

SECOND AMENDED ADMINISTRATIVE ORDER NO. 1994–02

RE: CIVIL RIGHTS POLICY STATEMENT AND CIVIL RIGHTS COMPLAINT PROCEDURE

WHEREAS, the Florida Supreme Court has adopted and incorporated, as part of the State Courts System's Personnel Regulations, the procedures referenced in Administrative Order AOSC12–21 regarding Amendments to the Florida Supreme Court Civil Rights Complaint Procedure;

WHEREAS, the Supreme Court Civil Rights Complaint Procedure attached to Administrative Order AOSC12–21 provides for a procedure by which "complaints of discrimination, by and against officers and employees of the Supreme Court and Office of the State Courts Administrator, because of race, religion, sex, including sexual harassment, national origin, age, disability, marital status or retaliation, may be filed";

WHEREAS, pursuant to instruction from the Florida Supreme Court and the State Courts System, this Court has previously developed and approved procedures for the filing of complaints of discrimination;

WHEREAS, it has come to this Court's attention that First Amended Administrative Order No. 94–2, which was entered by this Court prior to the entry of AOSC12–21, should be updated and amended.

NOW THEREFORE, by the authority vested in me as the Chief Judge of the Fourth Judicial Circuit and pursuant to the Florida Rules of Judicial Administration, it is hereby

ORDERED AND ADJUDGED that:

1) The Fourth Judicial Circuit hereby adopts and implements the Supreme Court of Florida Administrative Order AOSC12–21 in re: Amendments to the Florida Supreme Court Civil Rights Complaint Procedure. (AOSC12–21 and the adopted policy and procedures are attached hereto as Attachment A.)

2) Complaints of discrimination by and against officers and employees of the State of Florida and City of Jacksonville who are personnel employed within the Duval County Courthouse, Clay County Courthouse, and Nassau County Courthouses, because of race, religion, sex, national origin, age, disability, or marital status should be filed using the procedures described herein and in the Fourth Judicial Circuit Civil Rights Policy Statement and the Fourth Judicial Circuit Civil Rights Complaint Procedure. The internal procedures and remedies described herein are not intended to be exclusive, rather, a complaint may be referred to the appropriate outside agency. (The Fourth Judicial Circuit Civil Rights Policy Statement and the Fourth Judicial Circuit Civil Rights Complaint Procedure are attached hereto as Attachment B.)

3) The following positions are hereby appointed as intake officers who shall be responsible for receiving and documenting complaints of discrimination:

a. Trial Court Administrator

b. Director, Office of Judicial Staff Attorneys

c. Judicial Assistant to the Chief Judge

4) A copy of the Supreme Court of Florida AOSC12–21 in re: Amendments to the Florida Supreme Court Civil Rights Complaint Procedure shall be posted and available for review at the following locations:

a. Within the Duval County Courthouse: Main Lobby; Trial Court Administrator's Office; Law Library

b. Nassau County Law Library, Nassau County Courthouse

c. Office of the Administrative Judge, Clay County Courthouse

5) The Office of the Trial Court Administrator shall, as soon as practicable, distribute the attached policy statement and complaint procedure to all court personnel of the Fourth Judicial Circuit.

6) All complaints of sexual harassment will be governed by Administrative Order No. 2018–07 in re: Sexual Harassment Policy and Procedures.

7) All other Administrative Orders under No. 1994–02 previously entered and addressing the same subject matter are hereby vacated and superseded.

8) This Second Amended Administrative Order No. 1994–02 shall be recorded by the Clerk of Court, in the Official Records of Duval, Clay and Nassau Counties, in the State of Florida, and shall take effect immediately and remain in full force and effect unless and until otherwise ordered by the Court.

DONE AND ORDERED in Chambers at Jacksonville, Duval County, Florida, this 29th day of October, 2018.

MARK H. MAHON
CHIEF JUDGE

ATTACHMENT A

Supreme Court of Florida

No. AOSC12–21

IN RE: AMENDMENTS TO THE FLORIDA SUPREME COURT CIVIL RIGHTS COMPLAINT PROCEDURE

ADMINISTRATIVE ORDER

The Florida Supreme Court Civil Rights Complaint Procedure has been updated, clarified and amended to address the confidentiality of complaints of discrimination by and against justices and Supreme Court and Office of the State Courts Administrator employees in accordance with current statutory and court rule requirements. Complaints of sexual harassment against justices are governed by In re: Sexual Harassment Policy and Procedures for Complaints against Justices, AOSC04–07 (March 25, 2004). All other complaints of discrimination by and against justices and employees will be governed by these amended procedures.

The amended procedures are approved and incorporated into the State Courts System Personnel Regulations. They are attached and incorporated into this Administrative Order and will be implemented upon issuance of the Order.

DONE AND ORDERED at Tallahassee, Florida, on June 29, 2012.

Charles T. Canady
Chief Justice

SUPREME COURT CIVIL RIGHTS COMPLAINT PROCEDURE

This procedure was adopted pursuant to Administrative Order In Re: Personnel Rules and Regulations issued by the Chief Justice of the Supreme Court on September 23, 1993 and amended pursuant to In Re: Amendments to the Florida Supreme Court Civil Rights Complaint Procedure, AOSC12–21 (June 29, 2012). The procedure sets forth the steps to be taken to investigate and provide for a prompt and equitable resolution to complaints of discrimination in employment decisions.

Only complaints of discrimination, by and against officers and employees of the Supreme Court and Office of the State Courts Administrator, because of race, religion, sex, Including sexual harassment, national origin, age, disability, marital status or retaliation, may be filed using the procedures described herein. Complaints of sexual harassment against justices must be addressed through the separate procedures outlined in In re: Sexual Harassment Policy and Procedures for Complaints against Justices, AOSC04–07 (March 25, 2004). Complaints of discrimination made under the Americans with Disabilities Act must also be referred to the Court's ADA Coordinator.

A. Intake Officer. The Chief Justice shall appoint an intake officer who will be responsible for receiving and documenting complaints of discrimination by and against officers and employees. The name, office location, and phone number of the intake officer must be posted in a prominent place, along with this complaint procedure.

The Intake Officer for all officers and employees is Karen Samuel, Human Resource Officer. Ms. Samuel may be contacted at (850) 410–0646. Her office is located in Personnel Services, Supreme Court Building.

B. Procedure

1. All complaints of discrimination will be treated seriously and acted upon promptly. Officers or employees will not be retaliated against for exercising their right to file a complaint under this procedure or for assisting or participating in the complaint procedure. Any officer, employee, or applicant for employment, who believes that he or she is a victim of discrimination, should report the matter either orally or in writing, to the intake officer or the employee's supervisor. Complaints of discrimination must be reported within ninety (90) days of the date of the alleged violation. If a complaint of discrimination Is reported to the supervisor, the supervisor must report the complaint to the intake officer within two (2) working days.

2. The intake officer will discuss the allegations of the complaint with the complainant, advise the complainant of the options available under this complaint procedure, and document in writing the option the complainant elects to pursue. The intake officer will interview the officer or employee against whom the complaint is made and report the allegations of the complaint to the Chief Justice within five (5) working days. The Chief Justice may attempt to resolve the complaint informally through mutual conciliation, or may appoint an investigative officer(s) who will investigate the complaint, and report findings of the investigation to the Chief Justice.

3. If mutual conciliation is agreed upon by the complainant and the officer or employee the complaint is against, the Chief Justice or his or her designee will meet with the individuals involved to discuss the nature of the complaint and methods for resolution. The Chief Justice or his or her designee may recommend alternative dispute resolution as a method for resolving the complaint. Alternative dispute resolution may be initiated at any stage of this procedure.

4. Investigations:

a. The investigative officer(s) shall:

1) Interview the complainant concerning the nature and facts of the complaint.

2) Interview the officer or employee the complaint is made against to obtain his or her response to the complaint. The officer or employee the complaint is made against may prepare a written response to the complaint.

3) Interview any witnesses as the investigative officer(s) deems necessary.

4) Prepare and submit a written report to the Chief Justice describing the nature of the complaint and the findings of the investigation.

b. The Chief Justice will determine the validity of the complaint. The Chief Justice may meet with all individuals concerned with a goal toward mutual resolution, dismiss the complaint, authorize appropriate discipline up to and including dismissal, or refer the complaint to the appropriate outside agency. The Chief Justice may meet with the complainant and the officer or employee against whom the complaint is made, either separately or together, and inform them of his or her decision.

C. Confidentiality

1. *Complaints against justices*

All records made or received by the Chief Justice or his or her designee through use of this complaint procedure are exempt from public disclosure under rule 2.420(c)(3)(A), Florida Rules of Judicial Administration. Such records are exempt from public disclosure for the duration of the initial inquiry, internal investigation and resolution of the complaint, and at all times thereafter, unless the records are forwarded to the Judicial Qualifications Commission.

If records pertaining to a complaint of discrimination are forwarded to the Judicial Qualifications Commission, such records will be confidential under rule 2.420(c)(3)(A) and rule 23(a), Rules of the Judicial Qualifications Commission, until any formal charges against the justice are filed by the investigative panel of the commission with the clerk of the Florida Supreme Court.

Records within the possession of the Chief Justice or designee and pertaining to a complaint of discrimination that has been forwarded to the Judicial Qualifications Commission will become public upon formal charges being filed with the clerk of the Florida Supreme Court.

Notes taken by the investigative officer, when used to prepare the investigative report and not circulated to others, are not public record.

2. *Complaints against employees*

All records made or received by the Chief Justice or his or her designee through use of this complaint procedure are exempt from public disclosure until a finding is made relating to probable cause, the investigation of the complaint becomes inactive, or the complaint and related records are made part of the official record of a hearing or court proceeding. Notes taken by the investigative officer, when used to prepare the Investigative report and not circulated to others, are not public record.

D. External Measures

Irrespective of these internal procedures, the complainant retains the right before, during, or after the conclusion of this procedure to seek other remedies as provided by law. The complainant may file a charge with the Equal Employment Opportunity Commission (EEOC) or with the Florida Commission on Human Relations (FCHR). The EEOC may be reached toll free at 1–800–669–4000. The FCHR may be reached at (850) 488–7082. Information about how to file a charge of discrimination with either EEOC or FCHR is posted on the FCHR Internet site at http://fchr.state.fl.us.

Complaints against attorneys may be reported to The Florida Bar at 650 Apalachee Parkway, Tallahassee, Florida 32399–2300. The Florida Bar may be contacted at (850) 561–5600.

E. Records

All complaints of discrimination and their resolution must be documented in writing and maintained by the intake officer. If an investigation takes place, and the investigative officer has submitted a written report to the Chief Justice, the record of any resulting disciplinary action will be maintained in the disciplined employee's personnel file. The investigative report will be maintained by the intake officer.

FOURTH JUDICIAL CIRCUIT

CIVIL RIGHTS POLICY STATEMENT

It is the policy of the Fourth Judicial Circuit to provide a workplace free from any and all forms of illegal discrimination, and to provide equal employment opportunity to every employee and applicant for employment based solely on his or her qualifications to perform the job, and without discrimination on account of race, ethnicity, sex, religion, national origin, disability, marital status, or age, except as provided by law, with respect to recruitment, appointment, training, promotion, retention, separation, or any other employment practice.

In accordance with Title I of the Americans with Disabilities Act of 1990, the Fourth Judicial Circuit will not discriminate in any employment practice against qualified individuals with a disability, individuals regarded as having a disability, or individuals with an association with a person with a known disability. Furthermore, it is the policy of the Fourth Judicial Circuit to provide a reasonable accommodation, if necessary, to all qualified individuals with a disability in order to assure equal opportunity in the application process, to enable a qualified individual with a disability to perform the essential functions of a job, and to enable an employee with a disability to enjoy equal benefits and privileges of employment. A reasonable accommodation will be made, on a case by case basis, if it does not impose an undue hardship on court operations.

It is the policy of the Fourth Judicial Circuit to provide a businesslike environment free from all forms of employee discrimination, including incidents of sexual harassment. Sexual harassment occurs if there are unwelcome sexual advances, unwelcome requests for sexual favors, or unwelcome verbal or physical conduct of a sexual nature from or involving an employee's supervisors, peers, subordinates, or other persons In contact with an employee during the course of the conduct of the employee's business when:

1. Submission to such conduct is made either explicitly or implicitly, a term or condition of an individual's employment; or

2. Submission to or rejection of such conduct by an individual is used as the basis for employment decisions affecting such individual; or

3. Such conduct has the purpose or effect of interfering with an individual's work performance or creating an intimidating, hostile, or offensive work environment.

It Is the policy of the Fourth Judicial Circuit that all complaints of discrimination shall be treated seriously and acted upon promptly In accordance with complaint procedures approved and adopted by the Chief Judge of the Fourth Judicial Circuit.

Failure to comply with this policy may result in discipline up to and including dismissal, and/or referral to appropriate enforcement and disciplinary bodies. No individual shall be discriminated against, harassed, threatened, or intimidated for filing a complaint under these policies. Any individual who knowingly files a false complaint may be subject to discipline up to and including dismissal.

FOURTH JUDICIAL CIRCUIT

CIVIL RIGHTS COMPLAINT PROCEDURE

This procedure is adopted pursuant to Administrative Order En Re: Amendments to the Florida Supreme Court Civil Rights Complaint Procedure issued by the Chief Justice of the Florida Supreme Court on June 29, 2012, and sets forth the steps to be taken to investigate and provide a prompt and equitable resolution to complaints of discrimination.

I. Procedure

1. All complaints of discrimination shall be treated seriously and acted upon promptly. Any individual who believes that he or she is a victim of discrimination should report the matter either orally or in writing to an intake officer or the employee's supervisor within ninety (90) days of the date of the alleged violation. If reported to the supervisor, the supervisor will report the complaint to an intake officer.

2. The intake officer shall interview the individual against whom the complaint is filed and report the details to the Chief Judge within five (5) working days. Complaints of discrimination under the Americans with Disabilities Act shall also be referred to the Court's ADA Coordinator. The Chief Judge may attempt to informally resolve the complaint through mutual conciliation, or appoint an investigative officer(s) who will make an investigation and report to the Chief Judge on the matter.

3. If mutual conciliation is agreed upon by the complainant and the individual against whom the complaint is filed, the Chief Judge, or an appointed representative, will meet with the individuals involved to discuss the nature of the complaint and methods for resolution. The Chief Judge, his or her appointed representative, or the individuals involved may recommend an alternative dispute resolution as a method for resolving the complaint. Alternative dispute resolution may be initiated at any stage of this procedure.

4. If an investigative officer(s) is appointed:

A. The investigative officer(s) shall:

(i) Interview the complainant concerning the nature and facts of the complaint.

(ii) Interview the individual against whom the complaint is filed to obtain his or her understanding of the complaint and perception of the facts of the complaint. The individual against whom the complaint is filed may prepare a written response to the complaint.

(iii) Interview any witnesses as the investigative officer(s) deems necessary

(iv) Prepare and submit a written report to the Chief Judge describing the nature and facts of the complaint.

B. The Chief Judge shall make a determination of the validity of the complaint. The Chief Judge may meet with all individuals concerned with a goal toward mutual resolution, dismissal of the complaint, authorizing the appropriate discipline up to and including dismissal, or referral of the complaint to the appropriate outside agency. The Chief Judge may meet with the complainant and the individual against whom the complaint is filed, either separately or together, and inform them of his or her decision.

II. Confidentiality. Written materials developed through the use of this procedure are confidential pursuant to Rule 2.420, Public Access to and Protection of Judicial Branch Records, Florida Rules of Judicial Administration.

III. Additional Remedies. Irrespective of these internal procedures, the complainant retains the right before, during, or after the proceedings to seek remedy outside the Court's internal procedure as provided by law.

The board of Governors of the Florida Bar, by authority of the Florida Supreme Court, and under its Rules and Regulations, has the jurisdiction to investigate all reported instances of misconduct by members of the Florida Bar. The Florida Bar is located at 651 E. Jefferson Street, Tallahassee, Florida, 32399.

IV. Records. All records of complaints of discrimination and their resolution shall be documented and maintained by the intake officers. If an investigation takes place and the investigative officer has submitted a written report to the Chief Judge, any record of any resulting disciplinary action will be maintained in the disciplined employee's personnel file in case of an employee, or in the Court Administrator's Office in all other cases.

EQUAL EMPLOYMENT OPPORTUNITY

I have received and read a copy of the Fourth Judicial Circuit's Civil Rights Policy Statement and Civil Rights Complaint Procedure. I understand the policy is set forth regarding discrimination, the procedures for resolving civil rights complaints and the consequences of any violation of this policy.

____

Employee's Name

____

Employee's Signature

____

Date

Amended effective April 8, 2003; October 29, 2018.

1993–08 (A4). [DISSOLUTION OF MARRIAGE, PARENTING COURSES]

IN THE CIRCUIT COURT, FOURTH JUDICIAL CIRCUIT, IN AND FOR DUVAL COUNTY, FLORIDA

FOURTH AMENDED ADMINISTRATIVE ORDER NO. 1993–08

WHEREAS, Hope Haven's Children's Clinic and Family Center is a not-for-profit institution that has delivered a quality educational program in satisfaction of section 61.21, Florida Statutes (2016), for over twenty years, with no complaints from the public or the judiciary of the Fourth Judicial Circuit; and

WHEREAS, discretion is vested exclusively in the judiciary to preside over divorce and paternity proceedings, of which the Parent Education and Family Stabilization Course requirement of section 61.21, Florida Statutes, has been a mandatory part for litigants with minor children; and

WHEREAS, this amendment to the Third Amended Administrative Order No. 93–08, is solely for the purpose of addressing the name of the Parent Education and Family Stabilization Course that is required by section 61.21, Florida Statutes, and therefore eliminates the specific name of the class and only refers litigants to Hope Haven's Parent Education and Family Stabilization Course.

NOW THEREFORE, by the authority vested in me as the Chief Judge of the Fourth Judicial Circuit and pursuant to the Florida Rules of Judicial Administration, it is

ORDERED, that the Third Amended Administrative Order No. 93–08 is amended as follows:

(A) That it is in the best interest of the minor children of the Fourth Judicial Circuit that divorcing parents with minor children and parents in a paternity action that involves issues of parental responsibility fulfill the Parent Education and Family Stabilization Course requirement by attending the mandatory course in person, either together or separately, so that both parties may gain the benefit of a group environment that provides for group discussion and interaction with other parents in the same or similar situations, and also provides for case-specific interaction with a live instructor.

(B) That it is important that both parents should be ordered to the same course which would assure consistency in instruction and content rather than have one parent going to one course and the other parent going to another. It has been the judiciary's experience that both parents attending the same course with other parents is most beneficial.

(C) That Hope Have Children's Clinic and Family Center provides to families and children such services as academic assessment, counseling, mental health services, and evaluation services all of which services benefit children and the entire family.

(D) That notwithstanding the provisions of section 61.21, Florida Statutes, as amended, due to the high quality educational programs Hope Haven's Children's Clinic and Family Center has provided, and due to its willingness to accept indigent clients referred by the Court, the Fourth Judicial Circuit in and for Duval County, shall continue with the services of Hope Haven's Children's Clinic and Family Center as the provider for the Parent Education and Family Stabilization Course.

(E) That internet or other distance learning courses are not generally acceptable to the judiciary of the Fourth Judicial Circuit because they do not provide the parents the opportunity to interact with each other, other attendees, and a live course provider, deemed essential by the Fourth Judicial Circuit to comport with the spirit, as well as the letter, of the course requirement.

(F) That any internet or other distance learning courses generally acceptable by entities other than the judiciary of the Fourth Judicial Circuit shall be acceptable to the judiciary of the Fourth Judicial Circuit specifically only in cases of exigent circumstances, such as the permanent relocation of a party out of state, such circumstances to be determined on a case-by-case basis. Parties should receive prior approval from the Court if they request to pursue an alternative course.

(G) That all other Administrative Orders that have been previously entered and are still in full force and effect, addressing the same subject matter, shall remain in full force and effect unless any terms or conditions appear to be contradictory, in which case, this Administrative Order shall supersede such Order(s).

(H) That the Third Amended Administrative Order No. 93–08 previously entered on January 23, 2017, for Duval County is hereby vacated and superseded.

(I) That this Fourth Amended Administrative Order No. 93–08 shall take effect immediately and remain in full force and effect until further order of this Court, and all terms and conditions set forth in this Order shall apply unless otherwise ordered by the Court.

DONE AND ORDERED at Jacksonville, Duval County, Florida, this 16 day of February, 2017.

MARK H. MAHON
CHIEF JUDGE

1993–02 (A3). AMERICANS WITH DISABILITIES ACT OF 1990

IN THE CIRCUIT COURT, FOURTH JUDICIAL CIRCUIT, IN AND FOR DUVAL, CLAY AND NASSAU COUNTIES, FLORIDA

THIRD AMENDED ADMINISTRATIVE ORDER NO. 1993–02

RE: AMERICANS WITH DISABILITIES ACT OF 1990, AS AMENDED ACCOMMODATIONS—REQUESTS AND GRIEVANCE PROCEDURES

WHEREAS, the Americans with Disabilities Act (ADA) of 1990, as amended, requires that the Court's programs, services and activities be readily accessible to individuals with disabilities;

WHEREAS, Administrative Order No. 93–2 was entered on February 8, 1993, with the intent to provide reasonable accommodations where feasible, and to allow ready access to the Court's programs, services and activities to individuals with disabilities;

WHEREAS the first Amended Administrative Order No. 93–2 was entered on March 6, 1997, to revise language used in the notice provision of Administrative Order No. 93–2 regarding all communications that provide notice of court proceedings or activities such as jury summons, court appearances, depositions, etc.;

WHEREAS the Second Amended Administrative Order No. 93–2 was entered on July 6, 2010, to comply with amendments made to Florida Rule of Judicial Administration 2.540 by the Florida Supreme Court;

WHEREAS since the entry of the Second Amended Administrative Order No. 93–2, the Duval County Courthouse has relocated to 501 West Adams Street, thus necessitating a revision to the contact information contained in the Second Amended Administrative Order No. 93–2; and

WHEREAS the Florida Supreme Court in Florida Rule of Judicial Administration 2.540 provides that each court "shall post on its respective website and in each court facility the procedures for obtaining an accommodation as well as the grievance procedure adopted by that court."

NOW THEREFORE, by the authority vested in me as Chief Judge of the Fourth Judicial Circuit and pursuant to the Florida Rules of Judicial Administration, it is

ORDERED:

1. That, in accordance with the Americans with Disabilities Act (ADA) of 1990, as amended, and pursuant to Rule 2.540, the Court's programs, services, and activities are to be readily accessible to all individuals with disabilities who timely request reasonable accommodations; nevertheless, even if a request for ADA accommodations is untimely, the Court, through its ADA Coordinator or designee, will attempt to grant reasonable requests for accommodations if at all possible, to the best of its ability, given the limited resources and time restrictions in light of the minimum advance notice provided.

2. That pursuant to Rule 2.540 "[a]ll notices of court proceedings to be held in a public facility, and all process compelling appearance at such proceedings, shall include the following statement in bold face, 14–point Times New Roman or Courier Font":

a. For all notices at: (i) the Duval County Courthouse; (ii) First Appearance Court in Duval County; and (iii) the Clay County Courthouse, the language shall state: "If you are a person with a disability who needs any accommodation in order to participate in this proceeding, you are entitled, at no cost to you, to the provision of certain assistance. Please contact the ADA Coordinator at (904)255–1695 or crtintrp@coj.net, at least 7 days before your scheduled court appearance, or immediately upon receiving this notification if the time before the schedule appearance is less than 7 days; if you are hearing or voice impaired, call 711."

b. For all notices at either courthouse in Nassau County, the language shall state: "If you are a person with a disability who needs any accommodation in order to participate in this proceeding, you are entitled, at no cost to you, to the provision of certain assistance. Please contact the ADA Coordinator at (904)548–4600 (then press 0) at least 7 days before your scheduled court appearance, or immediately upon receiving this notification if the time before the schedule appearance is less than 7 days; if you are hearing or voice impaired, call 711."

3. That the phone numbers listed above are subject to change.

4. That pursuant to Rule 2.540(c)(2), the Fourth Judicial Circuit will post on its website (currently www.jud4.org) the means for requesting an accommodation as well as the locations in all three counties for obtaining and submitting an ADA Statement of Grievance Form and grievance procedures adopted by the Fourth Judicial Circuit. The website will also post the ADA Accommodation Request Form and the ADA Statement of Grievance Form in a format that has been approved by the Office of the State Courts Administrator.

5. That, to insure that the critical information is disseminated to the public appropriately by Court personnel pursuant to Rule 2.540(c)(2), the Fourth Judicial Circuit will distribute an ADA Information Sheet indicating where to request accommodations and where to obtain an ADA Statement of Grievance Form at each court facility. The ADA Information Sheet will be provided to all judicial assistants, all bailiffs, the receptionist at Court Administration in the Duval County Courthouse, and all appropriate locations in First Appearance Court in Duval County, the Clay County Courthouse, and the Nassau County Courthouses.

6. That pursuant to Rule 2.540(c)(2), the Fourth Judicial Circuit will post signs throughout each court facility that provides court functions in all three counties to clearly indicate the location, phone number, and e-mail address for requesting an accommodation and reporting an ADA grievance.

7. That, pursuant to Rule 2.540(d)(2), "[r]equests for accommodations must include a description of the accommodation sought, along with a statement of the impairment that necessitates the accommodation and the duration that the accommodation is to be provided. The Court, in its discretion, may require the individual with a disability to provide additional information about the impairment. Requests for accommodation shall not include any information regarding the merits of the case."

8. That the Fourth Judicial Circuit will respond to requests for accommodations in accordance with Rule 2.540 and the Americans with Disabilities Act of 1990.

9. That, according to Rule 2.540(e)(2), if the request for an accommodation "is denied or granted only in part, or if an alternative accommodation is granted, the court must respond to the individual with a disability in writing" and provide the reason(s) for the denial in writing. If any part of the request for accommodation is denied, the ADA Coordinator, Court Counsel, a Judicial Staff Attorney, the Court Administrator or a designee of any of the above, must prepare the written response.

10. That, pursuant to Rule 2.540(e)(3), "[i]f the court determines that a person is a qualified person with a disability and an accommodation is needed, a request for accommodation may be denied only when the court determines that the requested accommodation would create an undue financial or administrative burden on the court or would fundamentally alter the nature of the service, program or activity."

11. That all other Administrative Orders, including the Second Amended Administrative Order No. 93–2, addressing the same subject matter are hereby vacated and superseded.

12. This this Third Amended Administrative Order No. 1993–02 shall be recorded by the Clerk of the Court, in the Official Records of Duval County, in the State of Florida, shall take effect immediately, and shall remain in full force and effect until further order of this Court.

DONE AND ORDERED in Chambers at Jacksonville, Duval County, Florida, this 15 day of May, 2017.

MARK H. MAHON
CHIEF JUDGE

1992–02 (A2). MEDIA & TECHNOLOGICAL COVERAGE OF JUDICIAL PROCEEDINGS

IN THE CIRCUIT COURT, FOURTH JUDICIAL CIRCUIT IN AND FOR DUVAL, CLAY AND NASSAU COUNTIES, FLORIDA

SECOND AMENDED ADMINISTRATIVE ORDER NO. 92–02

IN RE: MEDIA & TECHNOLOGICAL COVERAGE OF JUDICIAL PROCEEDINGS

WHEREAS, subject to the authority of the Court (1) to control the conduct of proceedings before the Court, (2) to ensure decorum and prevent distractions, and (3) to ensure the fair administration of justice in the pending cause, all electronic media and still photography coverage of public judicial proceedings shall be allowed in accordance with certain standards for the technological coverage of judicial proceedings as set forth by the Florida Supreme Court in Rule 2.450, Rules of Judicial Administration; and

WHEREAS, the move to the new Duval County Courthouse requires a revision of the First Amended Administrative Order 92–02, entered on April 7, 2011; and

WHEREAS, "the unhindered and untrammeled functioning of our courts is part of the very foundation of our constitutional democracy," Cox v. Louisiana, 379 U.S. 559, 562, 85 S.Ct. 476, 13 L.Ed.2d 487 (1965); and

WHEREAS, the Florida Supreme Court has stated that "[c]ourts have the inherent power "to preserve order and decorum in the courtroom, to protect the rights of the parties and witnesses and generally to further the administration of justice."' Miami Herald Publishing Co. v. Lewis, 426 So.2d 1, 3 (Fla. 1982).

NOW THEREFORE, by the authority vested in me as Chief Judge of the Fourth Judicial Circuit and pursuant to the Florida Rules of Judicial Administration, it is

ORDERED that the following policies and procedures will be set forth in this Circuit:

Jessie–Lynne Kerr Media Room at the Duval County Courthouse

1) The Jessie–Lynne Kerr Media Room ("the Media Room") is located on the second floor of the Courthouse. The Media Room will be open during regular business hours and for extended hours when the court proceedings that are being covered are in session.

2) The Media Room is available to all media representatives with valid press credentials.

3) The Media Room will accommodate monitors and other equipment provided by the media to permit coverage of proceedings by media representatives who are unable to obtain seating in the Courtroom.

Prior Arrangements Required

1) When necessary, the presiding Judge, in consultation with the Jacksonville Sheriff's Office Courthouse Security Manager or his designee, shall designate a specified number and location of seats in the public area of the Courtroom for the following groups: (a) the parties' associates and Court designee(s), (b) the media representatives, and (c) the general public.

2) Unless prohibited because of an emergency hearing or otherwise lacking sufficient notice to permit timely compliance herewith, prior arrangements must be made with the Trial Court Administrator and the Jacksonville Sheriff's Office Courthouse Security Manager (or their designee) at least two (2) business days before the court proceeding for the Courtroom to be made available to the media at a pre-arranged time, before the proceeding, for installation of necessary equipment. Cable lay out and placement, if any, shall be at the direction of the Trial Court Administrator and the Jacksonville Sheriff's Office Courthouse Security Manager or their designee, and shall not present a safety or security hazard.

Equipment and Personnel

1) Not more than one (1) portable television camera, operated by not more than one (1) camera person, shall be permitted in any court proceeding.

2) Not more than one (1) still photographer, using not more than two (2) still cameras, shall be permitted in any court proceeding.

3) Not more than one (1) audio system for radio broadcast purposes shall be permitted in any court proceeding.

4) Unless prohibited because of an emergency hearing or otherwise lacking sufficient notice to permit timely compliance herewith, any request for additional cameras or other media equipment must be presented to the Chief Judge no later than two (2) business days before the court proceeding intended to be covered by the media.

5) If no technically suitable audio system exists in the Courtroom, microphones and related wiring essential for media purposes—if any—shall be unobtrusive and shall be located in places designated in advance of any proceeding by the Chief Judge in Duval County or (b) the Administrative Judge in Clay and Nassau Counties in accordance with paragraph 1 under the "General Terms" on page 8 herein.

6) In the event that media equipment of any kind or sort mars or otherwise damages the Courthouse or any of its furnishings, it shall be the sole responsibility of the media organization that caused said damage to pay for the appropriate repair thereof. Further, until such time as the damage is repaired, or acceptable arrangements are made with the Chief Judge for the appropriate and timely repair of the damage, all equipment of the news organization causing the damage will be excluded from all proceedings.

7) Any "pooling" arrangements among the media shall be the sole responsibility of the media. In the absence of advance media agreement on disputed equipment or personnel issues, the presiding Judge shall exclude all equipment belonging to the contesting media representatives from a proceeding.

8) The pooling camera positioned within the Courtroom shall connect to the media panels located in the rear of the Courtroom to facilitate pooling capabilities for all media outlets not present within the Courtroom. Those media representatives obtaining the pool feed shall do so in the Media Room. When a live feed of Court proceedings is desired by any media outlet, unless prohibited because of an emergency hearing or otherwise lacking sufficient notice to permit timely compliance herewith, such arrangements must be arranged through the Trial Court Administrator and the Jacksonville Sheriff's Office Courthouse Security Manager (or their designee) at least two (2) business days before the court proceeding, in accordance with paragraph 2 of Prior Arrangements Required, page 2, *supra.*[1]

Sound and Light Criteria

1) Only television, photographic, audio and electronic equipment that does not produce distracting sound or light shall be used to cover court proceedings.

2) Media representatives using laptop computers or any other electronic devices to provide coverage through internet or social media websites shall ensure such laptop computers or electronic devices do not produce any noise when in use. Silence is required to ensure such coverage does not distract the jury, lawyers, or courtroom staff from the proceedings.

3) It shall be the affirmative duty of media personnel to ensure that the equipment sought to be used meets the sound and light criteria. A failure to do so shall preclude its use.

4) No artificial lighting device of any kind shall be used in connection with the television camera. With the concurrence of (a) the Chief Judge, in consultation with the Jacksonville Sheriff's Office Courthouse Security Manager or his designee in Duval County or (b) the Administrative Judge in Clay and

Nassau Counties in accordance with paragraph 1 under the "General Terms" on page 8 herein, modifications and additions may be made in light sources existing in the facility, provided such modifications or additions are installed and maintained without public expense.

Location of Equipment and Personnel

1) Television camera equipment shall be positioned in such location in the Courtroom or at the Courthouse as shall be designated by (a) the Chief Judge, in consultation with the Trial Court Administrator and the Jacksonville Sheriff's Office Courthouse Security Manager or their designee in Duval County or (b) the Administrative Judge in Clay and Nassau Counties in accordance with paragraph 1 under the "General Terms" on page 8 herein. The area designated shall provide reasonable access to coverage. If and when areas remote from the Courthouse that permit reasonable access to coverage are provided, all television cameras and audio equipment shall be positioned only in such areas. Video recording equipment that is not a component part of a television camera shall be located in an area remote from the Courthouse.

2) A still camera photographer shall position himself or herself in such location in the Courtroom as shall be designated by (a) the Chief Judge, in consultation with the Jacksonville Sheriff's Office Courthouse Security Manager or his designee in Duval County or (b) the Administrative Judge in Clay and Nassau Counties in accordance with paragraph 1 under the "General Terms" on page 8 herein. Once established in a shooting position, the photographer shall not be permitted to move about in order to obtain photographs of court proceedings.

Media Representatives Appearance and Movement During Proceedings

1) All media representatives, including reporters, video camera operators, and still photographers, at all times shall be appropriately attired. Long pants and a collared shirt are required for all men. Shirttails must be tucked in at all times while such media representatives are within the Duval County Courthouse. Long pants or a skirt with an appropriate shirt or blouse will be required for all women.

2) All cell phones and like devices shall be turned off or placed into silent mode.

3) No chewing gum, food or beverage shall be permitted in the Courtroom.

4) News media video, photographic, audio or electronic equipment shall not be placed in or removed from the Courtroom except before commencement or after adjournment of proceedings each day, or during a recess.

5) Television cameras, still cameras and lenses, and all related equipment shall **not** be changed within a Courtroom except during a recess in the proceeding.

6) All media representatives shall act so as not to call attention to themselves and shall not move about in the Courtroom while proceedings are in session. Microphones or video recording equipment, once positioned, shall not be moved during the pendency of the proceedings.

7) Further, media representatives shall at no time endeavor to communicate with any lawyer, party or courtroom staff while any courtroom proceedings are in session.

Protecting Confidentiality and Privileged Communication

1) To protect the attorney-client privilege and the effective right to counsel, there shall be no audio pickup or broadcast of conferences that occur in the Courtroom or elsewhere in the Courthouse between attorneys and their clients, between co-counsel of a client, or between counsel and the presiding Judge held at the bench.

2) During the pendency of any matter, jurors shall not be recorded or photographed at any time. Further, the identity of any juror shall not be revealed to the public in any way, at any time, or by any means whatsoever, without leave of Court.

Location of Media Interviews

In consultation with the JSO Security, Jacksonville Sheriff's Office, it has been determined to be necessary to the orderly and safe operation of the Courthouse the implementation of the following:

1) Should media representatives wish to interview any person, such interview shall be conducted only: (a) in the Media Room; or (b) within the entrance at the front of the Courthouse, outside of the security magnetometer screening area; or (c) on grounds outside the Courthouse.

2) No interviews will be permitted in the first floor atrium of the Courthouse, or in any hallways, courtrooms or any other areas on any floor of the Courthouse.

General Terms

1) Should any questions be raised in Clay or Nassau Counties, they may be determined by the Administrative Judges of those Counties, in the same way that they are authorized to be resolved by the Chief Judge and Trial Court Administrator through this Administrative Order, in the Duval County Courthouse.

2) The First Amended Administrative Order 92–02 previously entered on this same subject matter is hereby vacated and superseded by this Order.

3) This Second Amended Administrative Order 92–02 shall be recorded by the Clerk of the Court, in the Official Records of Duval County, in the State of Florida, and shall take effect immediately and remain in full force and effect unless and until otherwise ordered by this Court.

DONE AND ORDERED at Jacksonville, Duval County, Florida, this 23 day of April, 2013.

DONALD R. MORAN, JR.

CHIEF JUDGE

[1] The Duval County Courthouse originally was designed to include all technological infrastructure necessary to facilitate the pooling of media coverage and connections for live media feeds to the Courtrooms. Such was recommended by the Dan Wiley Report. The Greater Jacksonville Plan paid for, and installed, all necessary fiberoptic cables from all courtrooms to the IDF rooms, from the IDF rooms to the Media Room, as well as to an outside location near the southeast corner of the Courthouse for live feeds. However, without warning to the Court or consultation with any local media representatives, the funding for the remaining infrastructure (such as receivers, etc.) was cut by the current Mayor's administration of the consolidated government of the City of Jacksonville. Thus, as of the date of this Order pooling is unavailable. Running equipment cables through Courthouse hallways and elevators is strictly prohibited for safety and security reasons. Accordingly, until such technology is provided, the Chief Judge shall have discretion to arrange for appropriate media coverage of court proceedings, including the number of video cameras permitted within the Courtroom, in consultation with the Trial Court Administrator, the Jacksonville

Sheriff's Office Courthouse Security Manager (or their designee), and the presiding Judge.

1992–01 (A6). ADMINISTRATIVE PROVISION FOR FAMILY LAW DIVISION; UNIFIED FAMILY COURT

IN THE CIRCUIT COURT OF THE FOURTH JUDICIAL CIRCUIT IN AND FOR CLAY, DUVAL AND NASSAU, FLORIDA

SIXTH AMENDED ADMINISTRATIVE ORDER NO. 92–1

In re: Administrative Provision for Family Law Division; Unified Family Court

WHEREAS, in response to the Supreme Court of the State of Florida decision In re: Report of the Commission on Family Courts, 588 So. 2d 586 (Fla. 1991), the Chief Judge established in the Fourth Judicial Circuit, in and for Duval County, Florida, a Unified Family Court Division effective January 1, 1993. See Administrative Order No. 92–1, In Re: Administrative Provision for Family Law Division, signed January 9, 1992, by Chief Judge John E. Santora, Jr.

WHEREAS, the Fourth Judicial Circuit has implemented a fully integrated, comprehensive approach to handling all cases involving children and families in the Second Amended Administrative Order 92–1, entered January 26, 2005.[1] An additional Second Amended Administrative Order 92–1 was entered March 5, 2008, and recorded on Official Records Book 14408, Page 882 by Chief Judge Donald R. Moran, Jr. The Fifth Amended Administrative Order 92–1 was entered on October 19, 2015.

WHEREAS, amendments to the administrative order are required to address changes to the Unified Family Court model as espoused in In re: Amendments to Florida Rules of Judicial Administration, 132 So.3d 1114 (Fla. 2014);

WHEREAS, the Florida Supreme Court has adopted the following guiding principles as a foundation for defining and implementing a model family court:[2]

Children should live in safe and permanent homes;

The needs and best interests of children should be the primary consideration of any family court;

All persons, whether children or adults, should be treated with objectivity, sensitivity, dignity and respect;

Cases involving inter-related family law issues should be consolidated or coordinated to maximize use of court resources to avoid conflicting decisions and to minimize inconvenience to the families;

Family court processes should attempt to address the family's interrelated legal and nonlegal problems, empower families through skills development, assist them to resolve their own disputes, provide access to appropriate services, and offer a variety of dispute resolution forums where the family can resolve problems without additional emotional trauma;

Whenever possible, parties and their attorneys should be empowered to select processes for addressing issues in their cases that are compatible with the family's needs, financial circumstances, and legal requirements;

The court is responsible for managing its cases with due consideration of the needs of the family, the litigants, and the issues presented by the case;

There should be a means of differentiating among cases so that judicial resources are conserved and cases are diverted to non-judicial and quasi-judicial personnel for resolution, when appropriate and consistent with the ends of justice;

Trial courts must coordinate and maximize court resources and establish linkages with community resources;

The court's role in family restructuring is to identify services and craft solution that are appropriate for long-term stability and that minimize the need for subsequent court action;

Court services should be available to litigants at a reasonable cost and accessible without economic discrimination; and

Courts should have well-trained and highly-motivated judicial and non-judicial personnel.

NOW, THEREFORE, pursuant to the authority vested in me as the Chief Judge of the Fourth Judicial Circuit, in order to maintain a Unified Family Court that will meet the requirements of the Florida Supreme Court as articulated in In re: Report of the Family Court Steering Committee, 794 So. 2d 518 (Fla. 2001), and In re: Amendments to Florida Rules of Judicial Administration, 132 So. 3d 1114 (Fla. 2014), and to better serve the needs of the citizens of the state of Florida, it is hereby **ORDERED** as follows:

I. The Fifth Amended Administrative Order No. 92–1, entered October 19, 2015, and recorded in the Official Records of Duval County, Florida, in Book 17340, Page 182, is hereby vacated and set aside.

II. Jurisdiction. The Family Court Division and Juvenile Court Division of the Fourth Judicial Circuit shall constitute a Unified Family Court ("UFC"). The UFC shall include, at a minimum, the following types of cases:[3]

A. Dissolution of marriage;

B. Division and distribution of property arising out of a dissolution of marriage;

C. Annulment;

D. Support unconnected with the dissolution of marriage;

E. Paternity;

F. Child support;

G. URESA/UIFSA;

H. Custodial care of and access to children;

I. Adoption authorized in Florida Statutes, Chapter 63;

J. Name change;

K. Declaratory judgment actions related to premarital, marital, or post marital agreements;

L. Civil domestic, dating, sexual, stalking, and repeat violence injunctions;

M. Termination of parental rights as authorized in Florida Statutes, Chapters 39 & 63;

N. Emancipation of a minor;

O. Delayed certificate of birth;

P. Modification and enforcement of orders entered in these cases;

Q. Juvenile Dependency;

R. Juvenile Delinquency;

S. Proceedings for temporary or concurrent custody of minor children by extended family;

T. Truancy; and

U. CINS/FINS.

III. Administrative Family Law Judge. Pursuant to Rule 2.215(b)(5), Rules of Judicial Administration, an administrative judge for the UFC shall be designated to oversee and coordinate the Fourth Judicial Circuit's comprehensive response to children and families in litigation.[4] At the discretion of the Chief Judge, separate administrative judges may be appointed for the Family Division or Juvenile Division. See Amended Administrative Order No. 96–20, In re: Duties of Administrative Family Law Judge, signed December 19, 1996, by Chief Judge Donald R. Moran, Jr.

The Administrative Unified Family Judge will manage the Unified Family Court and be responsible for: [5]

A. Coordinating the circuit's development of the overall plan for implementation of the family court concept;

B. Developing proposed policy, operating procedures, and administrative orders for the implementation of the circuit's plan;

C. Monitoring and reporting progress toward implementation;

D. Coordinating the development of resources that may be required by various courts dealing with family matters, (e.g., guardian ad litem, mediation services, drug referral and treatment, custody evaluations/home studies, parent coordinating services, etc.) and assessing the possible integration of cases regarding involuntary commitments for drug and alcohol dependency or mental health, and as appropriate, guardianships;

E. Developing and facilitating communications with court-related entities on policy with respect to family cases, including but not limited to state attorneys, public defenders, the Department of Children and Families, the Department of Revenue, community social services entities, clerk of courts, and law enforcement agencies; and

F. Developing a means of orienting judges newly assigned to matters affecting children and families to the family court concept for integrating the court's response to cases involving the same family, including directing them to appropriate initial and continuing judicial education offerings and reference material.

Because of the size of the Fourth Judicial Circuit, the court shall also designate an administrative UFC judge of Clay County and Nassau County. The administrative judges shall work together to ensure genuine coordination of cases and a coordinated approach to the overall handling of cases and utilization of resources.

IV. Rotation of Judges. Judges are assigned either to the Family Law Division or Juvenile Division for a term not to exceed two years unless she or he specifically requests to serve for a longer period of time. A rotation schedule shall be established to ensure that no more than one-half of the judges assigned to any UFC division is changed during any one-year assignment period to ensure that UFC judges are experienced in matters relating to children and families [6] and to ensure continuity and consistency can be maintained in the Division. To encourage the retention of judges who are committed to children and families, judges may request additional consecutive terms or permanency in the Family or Juvenile Divisions for consideration by the Chief Judge.[7]

Judges who are assigned to a UFC division for the first time or who have not served in a UFC division for two years should receive mandatory training in the fundamentals of family or juvenile law and domestic violence before assuming the assignment or within sixty (60) days after assuming the assignment, or as soon as such training is available.[8] Such training may be obtained at the College of Advanced Judicial Studies. The Chief Judge will ensure that these judges have this opportunity.

It is the policy of the Fourth Judicial Circuit to ensure that all judges receive proper orientation and are well-prepared to undertake their judicial assignments. Therefore, the administrative judge will designate an experienced UFC judge to function as a mentor to judges entering the division.

V. Essential Elements [9]

A. *Case Management.* The UFC shall receive case management services and support to enable the family and juvenile court judges to assess, differentiate, and monitor the resources needed for handling cases, to be able to identify all collateral cases affecting the parties involved, and to monitor the movement of cases through the judicial process.

Case management shall include:[10]

1. initial review and evaluation of cases, including assignment of cases to court divisions or dockets;
2. case monitoring, tracking and coordination;
3. scheduling of judicial events; and
4. service referral, coordination, monitoring, and tracking of cases for which the Family or Juvenile Division has jurisdiction.

B. *Self Help.* The Fourth Judicial Circuit shall ensure that self-help programs provide litigants with Florida Supreme Court approved forms, instructions, definitions, and procedural information to persons who choose to represent themselves consistent with Rule 12.750, Florida Family Law Rules of Procedure. See Administrative Order 1999–2, In re: Family Self–Help Program, signed January 19, 1999, *nunc pro tunc* to January 1, 1999, by Chief Judge Donald R. Moran, Jr. As part of its intake function, the clerk of the circuit court shall provide ministerial assistance to *pro se* litigants. Such assistance shall not include the provision of legal advice.[11]

C. *Domestic Violence.* The Administrative UFC Judge shall work with other judges within the division to develop a policy to ensure that cases involving domestic violence are identified and managed in a manner that is organized, timely and sensitive to the special dynamics involved in these cases.[12]

D. *Alternative Dispute Resolution.* It is the policy of the Fourth Judicial Circuit to make maximum use of alternative dispute resolution ("ADR") of family matters and issues as authorized by sections 44.102, Florida Statutes, and Florida Family Law Rules of Procedure 12.740 and 12.741. See Amended Administrative Order No. 97–10, In re: Pro Se Referrals to Family Mediation, signed February 11, 1998, by Chief Judge Donald R. Moran, Jr.

The court and any staff member designated by the court to conduct case management should screen cases before a referral to any ADR program is made to ensure that cases with allegations of domestic violence and parties with prior injunctions against domestic violence are identified. The court shall determine whether a referral to ADR is appropriate in light of the domestic violence issues or whether the safety of the parties and the ADR process would be compromised such that a referral to ADR should not be made.

The Fourth Judicial Circuit recognizes that not all litigants have the resources to pay for ADR services and, therefore, such services may be assessed in accordance with the fee schedule established in the Amended Administrative Order No. 98–6 In re: Family Mediation Fees, signed March 20, 2000, by Chief Judge Donald R. Moran, Jr., which provides a sliding scale for the waiver of fees based on litigants' income.

E. *Guardian Ad Litem.* The Fourth Judicial Circuit's Guardian ad Litem Program (GAL) currently provides services only in juvenile dependency cases. The Fourth Judicial Circuit will coordinate with the GAL Program to ensure representation of the best interest of children involved in dependency cases with allegations of abuse, abandonment and neglect. In other family law cases, the Fourth Circuit will appoint qualified persons to serve as guardians when necessary or appropriate. Such persons will either be compensated by the parties when feasible or act as pro bono volunteers.

F. *Magistrates and Child Support Hearing Officers.* General Magistrates and Child Support Hearing Officers may be utilized to supplement the work of judges within a UFC division when a presiding judge determines that referral of a case is appropriate and consent of the parties is obtained.[13] Child Support Hearing Officers may be utilized to supplement the work of judges within the UFC when a presiding judge determines that referral of a case is appropriate. Referrals shall be made in accordance with relevant Rules of Family and Juvenile Procedure, Administrative Order No. 95–17, In re: Reference of Certain Family Law Matters to General Masters, signed December 1, 1995, by Chief Judge Donald R. Moran, Jr., Administrative Order No. 96–5, In re: General Masters, signed January 31, 1996, *nunc pro tunc* to January 1, 1996, by Chief Judge Donald R. Moran, Jr.; Amended Administrative Order No. 96–7, In re: Child Support Hearing Officers, signed April 17, 1998, by Chief Judge Donald R. Moran, Jr.; Sixteenth Amended Administrative Order No. 96–10, In re: Order of Referral to General Magistrates and Support Enforcement Hearing Officers, signed September 30, 2016, Administrative Order 2016–02 signed May 10, 2016, Administrative Order 2017–02 signed February 9, 2017, Administrative Order 2017–04 signed April 3, 2017 by Chief Judge Mark H. Mahon and Third Amended Administrative Order 2004–13, Order of Referral to Child Support Hearing Officer, signed January 31, 2005, by Chief Judge Donald R. Moran, Jr.; and such other similar administrative orders that the Chief Judge enters from time to time.

G. *Custody Evaluation.* When such referrals are made, it is the policy of the Fourth Judicial Circuit to use appropriately credentialed custody evaluators. Judges may order evaluators to conduct court ordered custody evaluations, including interviews of the parties, interviews of children, observation of parent child interactions, background investigations of parties, evaluation of information to report and make recommendations to the court.

H. *Supervised Visitation.* The Family Nurturing Center (formerly known as Family Visitation Center) has been approved by this court to provide supervised visitation and monitored exchange services. See Fourth Judicial Circuit Agreement with Family Visitation Center, signed December 22, 1999, by Chief Judge Donald R. Moran.

Visitation and exchange services from other providers (such as those arranged for by the Department of Children and Families) may be used when approved by the court.

I. *Parenting Education.* Pursuant to Section 61.21, Florida Statutes, all parties to a dissolution of marriage proceeding with minor children or a paternity action that involves issues of parental responsibility shall be required to complete the Parent Education and Family Stabilization Course prior to the entry by the court of a final judgment. Pursuant to Fourth Amended Administrative Order 93–8, entered February 16, 2107, such requirement may only be met by attending such course at Hope Haven Children's Clinic and Family Center. This requirement may generally not be discharged by enrollment in an internet or other such distance learning course without prior Court approval.

J. *Counseling Services/Treatment Programs.* Under the leadership of the Administrative UFC Judge and in consultation with the UFC judges, court staff and community service providers, the Fourth Judicial Circuit will develop strategies to ensure availability of counseling services and treatment programs to litigants in the Family Division. At a minimum, such strategies shall ensure the availability of crisis intervention and long-term counseling/treatment programs. Additionally, the strategies shall ensure that compliance is monitored when such services are court-ordered.[14]

K. *Security.* Judges in the UFC are aware of the special security issues attendant to UFC matters. The Chief Judge and the Administrative Family Law Judge shall collaborate with relevant stakeholders and the Courthouse Security Committee to develop a plan to ensure that adequate and sufficient security personnel and equipment is available to ensure that UFC Divisions are safe environments for judges, non judicial staff and the public.[15]

Due to safety concerns, judges shall hold domestic violence hearings in the courtroom whenever possible. The Chief Judge, the Administrative UFC Judge, and the Sheriff shall develop safety procedures for domestic violence cases that include separating petitioners and respondents before the hearing, monitoring hallways outside the courtroom and providing staggered departure times for the parties when an injunction is entered.

L. *Technology.* The Fourth Judicial Circuit shall use available technology to access information essential to case management and coordination, to print forms and notices immediately, to generate statistical reports, to provide public and inter-agency access to records and to allow teleconferencing and the appearance of witnesses by electronic means.[16]

M. *Parenting Coordinators.* When such referrals are made, it is the policy of the Fourth Judicial Circuit to use appropriately credentialed mental health professionals. Parent coordinators shall be mental health professionals with either a masters or doctorate degree.

VI. Identification and Coordination of Related Cases. The Fourth Judicial Circuit's plan for coordination of cases is based on the coordinated management model adopted by the Florida Supreme Court [17] and is designed to take into account the individual needs and resources within the circuit (and within each county in the circuit). The Circuit will utilize the one family-one judge model in Duval County.

In identifying related cases, the Fourth Circuit recognizes that many family cases involve individuals and issues that are interrelated, but do not involve a family [18] relationship or children. A family judge or case manager will determine if any of the parties or children have pending or closed family cases. If they have pending or closed family cases, the court will decide whether all or some of the cases should be assigned to the same judge or coordinated to conserve judicial resources, avoid inconsistent court orders, and eliminate multiple appearances on the same issue.

A. *Assignment of Crossover Cases.* Any action pending in the Family Law Division, which involves a minor child or party that is then currently the subject of or party to a dependency or termination of parental rights ("TPR") proceeding in the dependency court of the juvenile division, or which involves a child who has ever been found to be dependent within the meaning of Chapter 39, Florida Statutes, shall be transferred by the judge presiding in the Family Law Division to the dependency court of the Juvenile Division for disposition of the entire family law proceeding, unless the dependency court has terminated its jurisdiction over the child. Such proceeding shall remain in the dependency section of the Juvenile Division for purpose of any further actions until such time that the child reaches the age of majority and is not otherwise legally dependent on his or her parents, such as in the case of physical or mental disability. This paragraph shall not be construed, however, to prevent child support hearing officers from hearing any Title IV–D or Title IV–D eligible child support proceedings as otherwise currently heard in this Circuit, notwithstanding that any party or child therein is also involved in a dependency action.

For purpose of this section, "dependency action" means any proceeding brought under Chapter 39, Florida Statutes, whether by petition or otherwise, involving a minor child and specifically includes any case where a dependency judge has addressed the sheltering of a child prior to filing of a dependency action.

Delinquency cases in which the child is also the subject of a dependency case shall be subject to the crossover reassignment rules set forth in the First Amended Administrative Order No. 08–03, In re: Bifurcation of Juvenile Division Delinquency and Dependency Cases.

B. *Domestic Violence Cases.* Each week a circuit judge serving in the Family, Juvenile or Civil Divisions is assigned responsibility for reviewing and acting on all petitions seeking an injunction for protection from domestic, dating or repeat violence. This judge considers only the written petition on an exparte basis in deciding whether to grant temporary injunctive relief.

Each week a different judge serving in the Family, Juvenile, or Civil Divisions is assigned responsibility for conducting evidentiary hearings to consider whether to enter final injunctions for protection. These hearings are conducted in the Duval County Unified Courthouse, 501 West Adams Street, Jacksonville, Florida, 32202. The judge presiding over such hearings shall grant or deny the injunction on the claims raised in the petition for the injunction. In addition to the injunction, the judge may also address any other ancillary claims raised in the petition for injunction, such as claims for child custody and temporary and exclusive use of the marital residence, and any other claims provided for under chapter 741, Florida Statutes. Claims for child support may be referred for hearing to a child support hearing officer and claims for temporary alimony may be referred to a general magistrate. Post–judgment hearings to review a respondent's compliance with court-ordered acts such as substance abuse treatment or batterer's intervention classes may also be referred to a general magistrate.

Motions for rehearing, including motions that address errors in the hearing procedure or sufficiency of the evidence, shall be referred to the judge who conducted the final hearing. All other post-judgment proceedings, such as motions to vacate, modify or enforce injunctions, and motions for contempt, domestic violence cases shall be referred to the juvenile or family law division of the circuit court using the following criteria:

1. if the domestic violence case involves (injunctive relief granted on his or her behalf or custody determination made) a minor child or party who is currently the subject of or party to a dependency or termination of parental rights (TPR) proceeding in the dependency division of the juvenile court, or the case involves a child who has ever been found to be dependent or had the rights of his or her parents terminated under Chapter 39, Florida Statutes, the case shall be transferred to the Juvenile Division that has jurisdiction over the child or parties (but not if the court had previously terminated its jurisdiction over the child);

2. if there is no related dependency proceeding, the domestic violence case shall be transferred to a Family Law Division in which there is either a pending or closed action between the same parties or an action that involves any child also involved in the domestic violence action; and

3. if there are no related cases as defined in subparagraph one or two, the domestic violence case shall be assigned to a Family Law Division on a random basis if additional action is necessary.

C. *Multiple Pending Cases.* Pursuant to Florida Rule of Family Law Procedure 12.003, when multiple related family cases are pending, the related cases must be handled before one judge unless impractical. Upon discovery of two or more cases with substantially the same issues and same parties, the latest filed case shall be closed or consolidated into the first filed of the related actions.

Upon discovery of the existence of other multiple pending related cases, not otherwise subject to the cross-over provisions in Section VI., A or B, should it be impractical for one judge to handle all pending related cases, judges shall confer to determine the best way to address the pending issues in these cases. The judges assigned shall confer to determine how to coordinate the cases, including which division shall take precedence in managing the cases and determining issues, whether one case shall proceed while another is inactive or abated, or how judicial labor should be divided. In making such determinations, the following guidelines should be used except when one case involves the Department of Revenue ("DOR") which shall be handled according to sub-paragraphs 5:

1. Which judge assigned has had the case longest, has been the most active and is most familiar with the family and/or its issues;

2. Whether one of the cases is active or closed;

3. Whether there are ongoing financial issues other than child support between the parties; and

4. Whether there are ongoing dependency issues which are being addressed by the Juvenile Division of the court as required by law.

5. When there is a Department of Revenue **(DOR)** case (including an administrative support order) and a family law case involving the same parents, the cases shall be automatically consolidated into the lower case number and the Clerk of Court shall close the higher case number and no further pleadings shall be accepted in the closed case. The consolidated cases shall remain in the division assigned to the lower numbered case. If the DOR is not included in the case style of the lower numbered case, the style shall be amended to include the DOR as a party.

D. *Coordination Among the Judiciary.* After consultation, if the judges assigned to the cases at issue decide it is impractical to assign all of the related cases to the same judge, the judges will enter appropriate orders expressing such findings and thereafter exchange information so that each judge involved with the family is aware of the other pleadings and the issues being addressed.[19]

VII. Family Law Advisory Group[20]. The success of any UFC is dependent upon effective communication among all stakeholders both in the judicial system and in the community. The Administrative UFC Judge shall oversee the Family Law Advisory Group ("FLAG") for the Fourth Judicial Circuit. Membership may include:[21]

Family Law Division Administrative Judge

Juvenile Division Administrative Judge

Judges, Domestic Relations

Judges, Juvenile

Judges, Domestic Violence

Judges, County

General Counsel or Assistant General Counsel(s), Fourth Judicial Circuit

Hearing Officers

Magistrates

Case Managers

Self Help Center Director

Clerk of Court

Clerk's Office Staff

Supervised Visitation Providers

Domestic Violence Advocates/Shelter Staff

Senior Deputy Court Administrator

State Attorneys

Public Defenders

Criminal Conflict and Civil Regional Conflict Counsel and Staff

Legal Services/Legal Aid Attorneys and Staff

Department of Children and Families

Department of Juvenile Justice

Batterers' Intervention Providers

Office of Guardian ad Litem

Community–Based Care Providers for DCF

Law Enforcement

Community Organizers

Faith–Based–Community Programs

United States Navy Family Services Staff

Attorneys

Bar Association Representatives

Specific details related to establishment of the FLAG and individual membership are addressed in Administrative Order 2001–21.XX. The FLAG shall meet monthly, or more often upon the call of the Chair.

VIII. Clay and Nassau Counties. This Rule (Administrative Order) does not establish a Family Law or Juvenile Division in Clay and Nassau Counties. Clay and Nassau Counties will make every effort to utilize the coordinated management model adopted by the Florida Supreme Court[22], taking into account the individual needs and resources within each county. The essential elements identified by the Family Court Steering Committee will be utilized in Clay and Nassau Counties when available and appropriate.[23] The cross-over provisions of this Rule shall also not apply to Clay and Nassau Counties, but both such counties are encouraged to adopt similar procedure for the consolidation of family law and juvenile actions before the judges serving in such counties.

IX. This Administrative Order shall become effective upon signing and remain in effect until further Order of the Court, and all terms and conditions set forth in this Sixth Amended Administrative Order 92–1 shall apply unless otherwise ordered by the Court.

X. This Sixth Amended Administrative Order No. 92–1 shall be recorded in the Official Records of Duval County in the State of Florida, and Certified Copies of this Order shall be furnished to the Jacksonville Bar Association and the Clerk of Courts in Clay and Nassau Counties for recording in those counties. The Clerks of Court for Clay and Nassau Counties shall provide Certified Copies of this Order to their respective Bar Associations.

ORDERED in Duval County, Florida, this 18th day of May, 2017.

MARK H. MAHON
Chief Judge

1 In re: Report of the Commission on Family Courts, 633 So.2d 14, 17 (Fla. 1994).

2 See In re: Report of the Family Court Steering Committee, 794 So. 2d 518, 522 (Fla. 2001).

3 REQUIREMENT: SeeIn re: Report of the Family Court Steering Committee, 794 So. 2d 518, 525 (Fla. 2001).

4 CONCEPT ENDORSED BY SUPREME COURT: SeeIn re: Report of the Family Court Steering Committee, 794 So. 2d 518, 532 (Fla. 2001) (Although we endorse the principle embodied in these recommendations, we decline to mandate the appointment of [a single] administrative family court judge. Instead, we leave it to each circuit to devise a plan for coordination of cases within the family division to achieve the goals of the model family court.).

5 SeeIn re: Report of the Commission of Family Courts, 633 So. 2d 14, 17–18 (Fla. 1994) (An administrative judge must be appointed in each circuit to be directly responsible for administratively managing the family divisions.).

6 SUGGESTION: Recommendation of the Family Court Steering Committee.

7 SUGGESTION: Administrative Order No. 2001–72, First Judicial Circuit.

8 REQUIREMENT: SeeIn re: Report of the Family Court Steering Committee, 794 So. 2d 518, 532 (Fla. 2001).

9 REQUIREMENT: See In re: Report of the Family Court Steering Committee, 794 So. 2d 518 (Fla. 2001). (We wholeheartedly endorse each of these essential elements to the successful function of the model family court.).

10 See Amendments to section 29.004, Florida Statutes, in House Bill 113A, section 40.

11 See Amendments to section 28.215, Florida Statutes in House Bill 113A, section 27.

12 REQUIREMENT: In re: Report of the Family Court Steering Committee, 794 So. 2d 518, 526 (Fla. 2001).

13 SUGGESTION: Report of the Family Court Steering Committee, 2000–2002 Appendix A.

14 REQUIREMENT: SeeIn re: Report of the Family Court Steering Committee, 794 So. 2d 518, 526 (Fla. 2001).

15 REQUIREMENT: SeeIn re: Report of the Family Court Steering Committee, 794 So. 2d 518, 526 (Fla. 2001).

16 REQUIREMENT: SeeIn re: Report of the Family Court Steering Committee, 794 So. 2d 518, 526 (Fla. 2001).

17 In re: report of the Family Court Steering Committee, 794 So. 2d 518, 528 (Fla. 2001); In re: Amendments to Florida Rules of Judicial Administration, 132 So. 3d 1114 (Fla. 2014).

18 Pursuant to chapter 39 and 985, Florida Statutes, "family"[20] is defined as a collective body of persons, consisting of a child and parent, legal custodian, or adult relative, in which: (a) The persons reside in the same house or living unit; or (b) The parent, legal custodian, or adult relative has a legal responsibility by blood, marriage, or court order to support or care for the child.

19 SUGGESTION: Administrative Order M2002–04, Fifth Judicial Circuit.

20 REQUIREMENT: See In re: Report of the Family Court Steering Committee, 794 SO. 2d 518, 534 (Fla. 2001) (mandating the establishment of a Family Law Advisory Group in each circuit).

21 Suggested membership approved by the Unified Family Court Subcommittee of the Steering Committee on Families and Children in the Court.

22 In re: Report of the Family Court Steering Committee, 794 So. 2d 518, 528 (Fla. 2001).

23 SeeIn re: Report of the Family Court Steering Committee, 794 So. 2d 518, 532 (Fla. 2001).

1989–09 (A2). PROVIDING THE COURTS WITH ADDRESSED ENVELOPES AND POSTAGE BY ATTORNEYS AND LITIGANTS

IN THE CIRCUIT COURT, FOURTH JUDICIAL CIRCUIT IN AND FOR DUVAL COUNTY, FLORIDA

SECOND AMENDED ADMINISTRATIVE ORDER NO. 89–09

IN RE: PROVIDING THE COURTS WITH ADDRESSED ENVELOPES AND POSTAGE BY ATTORNEYS AND LITIGANTS

WHEREAS, this Second Amended Administrative Order No. 89–09 is entered for the sole purpose of changing the cost requirements associated with envelopes and postage in the Family Law Division for *pro se* litigants so that such costs will now apply only to new cases filed and will not be applied to cases filed post-judgment such as re-opened cases;

WHEREAS, for the reader's convenience, all other parts of the prior Amended Administrative Order No. 89–09 is included herein, including the following:

WHEREAS, in March 2009, the Florida Supreme Court required that a Parenting Plan Form similar to Family Law Form 12.995 be used in all cases involving time sharing of minor children, even when time-sharing is not in dispute. In re Amendments to the Florida Supreme Court Approved Family Law Forms, 20 So. 3d 173 (Fla. March 26, 2009);

WHEREAS, the Parenting Plan Form used in the Fourth Judicial Circuit, in Duval County is normally an average of fifteen to seventeen pages long;

WHEREAS, after an evidentiary hearing in the Family Division cases, each *pro se* party is mailed a copy of the Magistrate's Report and Recommendations, a proposed Final Judgment, a Parenting Plan Form, and a proposed Income Deduction Order, amounting to approximately 30 pages, costing the Court additional postage;

WHEREAS, once the Final Judgment is signed, a copy of the Final Judgment, the Parenting Plan, and an Income Deduction Order, amounting to another 25–30 pages, must be mailed to each *pro se* party;

WHEREAS, the cost of postage has increased substantially over the years;

WHEREAS, the increasing expense of envelopes and postage should be placed squarely on the litigants who bring their claims, thereby relieving the taxpayers from the burdensome mailing expenditures;

WHEREAS, although Family Court Services has recently started to require litigants to provide envelopes with postage, it still receives a number of complaints from parties that they have not received a copy of the Final Judgment issued in their case;

WHEREAS, Case Managers in Family Court Services are delayed in scheduling hearings until envelopes with sufficient postage are provided by the parties;

WHEREAS, Magistrates may be delayed in mailing their reports and recommendations to the parties due to insufficient postage;

WHEREAS, the Judges' Final Judgments may not be mailed to the *pro se* litigants unless the proper postage is added;

WHEREAS, improper postage is creating havoc in the efficient administration of justice in the Family Division in Duval County;

WHEREAS, the original portions of the Administrative Order should remain the same;

NOW THEREFORE, by the authority vested in me as the Chief Judge of the Fourth Judicial Circuit and pursuant to the Florida Rules of Judicial Administration, it is

ORDERED:

1. That procedures for envelopes in Duval County for hearings scheduled in Circuit Civil, County Court Civil and Summary Procedures will remain the same as previously provided in Administrative Order No. 89–09, which stated:

the moving party for hearings scheduled in Circuit Civil, County Court Civil and Summary Procedure shall provide to the Judge or his Judicial Assistant sufficient, plain No. 10 envelopes, with appropriate postage affixed, to mail copies of the order or judgment entered to all those entitled to receive same. A plain envelope is required so that the return address of the judge may be affixed. The envelopes shall be pre-addressed, and need not be of bond quality.

2. That if a *pro se* litigant files a new case in the Family Division in Duval County, the litigant must pay $12.00 to the Clerk of Court, Duval County, which will pay for the Court's costs, including envelopes, postage and administrative fees, so that the Clerks can mail the Magistrate's Report and Recommendations, a proposed Final Judgment, a Parenting Plan, the proposed Income Deduction Order, the Final Judgment and the Income Deduction Order to the litigant at the appropriate times during the case.

3. That all other Administrative Orders previously entered, including Amended Administrative Order No. 89–09, addressing the same issues and subject matter, are hereby vacated and superseded by this Second Amended Administrative Order No. 89–09.

4. That this Second Amended Administrative Order No. 89–09 shall be effective on **Wednesday, February 1, 2017**, and shall remain in full force and effect unless and until otherwise ordered by this Court.

5. That this Second Amended Administrative Order No. 89–09 shall be recorded by the Clerk of the Court, in the Official Records of Duval County, in the State of Florida.

DONE AND ORDERED in Chambers at Jacksonville, Duval County, Florida, this 27 day of Jan., 2017.

MARK H. MAHON

CHIEF JUDGE

1989–05 (A2). PROCEDURE FOR JUDICIAL WAIVER OF PARENTAL NOTIFICATION OF ABORTION

IN THE FOURTH JUDICIAL CIRCUIT IN AND FOR CLAY, DUVAL AND NASSAU COUNTIES, FLORIDA

SECOND AMENDED ADMINISTRATIVE ORDER NO. 1989–5

IN RE: Procedure for Judicial Waiver of Parental Notification of Abortion

WHEREAS, the legislature, by passage of 2005 Fla. Laws Ch. 52, created Section 390.01114, Florida Statutes (2005), known as the Parental Notice of Abortion Act, which prohibits the performing or inducement of a termination of pregnancy upon a minor without specified notice, but which provides a mechanism for a judicial waiver of such notice, which became effective July 1, 2005;

WHEREAS, the legislature, by virtue of Section 390.01114(5), Florida Statutes (2005), has requested the Florida Supreme Court to promulgate court rules to ensure that proceedings under the Act are handled in the most expeditious manner, and such rules and proposed forms where issued on an emergency basis in Florida Supreme Court Opinion SC05–950, with such rules and forms being attached hereto as Exhibit "A";

WHEREAS, there is an immediate need for specified local procedures to ensure that proceedings under the Act are handled in the most expeditious manner;

NOW, THEREFORE, pursuant to the authority vested in me as the Chief Judge of the Fourth Judicial Circuit it is hereby **ORDERED** as follows:

(A) This Administrative Order applies to petitions filed pursuant to Section 390.01114, Florida Statutes.

(B) The following procedures shall govern the filing, processing, adjudication, and post-adjudication file management storage of the documents and record of proceedings filed pursuant to Section 390.01114:

(1) **Petitions filed pursuant to Section 390.01114 shall be given precedence over all other pending proceedings.**

(2) Any minor presenting herself to the Office of the Clerk of the Circuit Court, who communicates that she is seeking a judicial waiver of the parental notification requirements of Section 390.01114, shall be provided with a Florida Supreme Court approved standard form for Petition for Judicial Waiver of Parental Notification. Such petition may be filed using a pseudonym consistent with Rule 8.805, Florida Rules of Juvenile Procedure, so long as the minor files a certified copy of the Florida Supreme Court approved standard form for Sworn Statement of True Name and Pseudonym. Any original statement filed shall be kept under seal by the Clerk. At the time the petition is filed, the Minor shall be provided with a certified copy of Form 8.989, Advisory Notice to Minor.

(3) There shall be no filing fee or court costs assessed by the Clerk, pursuant to Section 390.01114(4)(G), against the Petitioner.

(4) Upon accepting the Petition for filing, the Clerk shall enter the exact date and time that the Petition was filed on the face of the first page of the Petition.

(5) The Petition shall be assigned a case number and shall be blindly assigned to a dependency court division.

(6) The Clerk shall immediately thereafter, without delay of any kind, deliver the file to the Judge in the division to whom the case is assigned. If that Judge is not then available, the Clerk will deliver the Petition, in the following order of priority: to any other dependency judge in the County, to any other Unified Family Court Judge in the County, to the Administrative Judge of the Unified Family Court in the County, to any other Circuit Judge assigned to a Civil Division in the County, to the Administrative Judge of the Civil Circuit Division in the County, to any other Circuit Judge in the County, the Duty Judge in the County, or the Chief Judge of the Circuit. Such delivery shall not be accomplished by leaving the file on the desk of the Judge or the Judicial Assistant. (However, if a dependency judge is physically unavailable but can be and is contacted telephonically and the Judge is amenable to conducting the hearing within the statutory time frame, the file may be left with the Judge's designee).

(7) Upon the delivery of the Petition to the Judge who will preside over the action, the Clerk shall obtain from the that Judge's Judicial Assistant a notice of the hearing date, time and place, which shall be within 48 hours of the date and time marked by the Clerk on the face of the first page of the Petition.

(8) The Clerk shall provide notice of the hearing to the minor either directly to the minor, if the minor remains in the Clerk's office while arrangements are made to schedule the hearing, or otherwise through the method elected by the minor as stated in her petition.

(9) The Judicial Assistant for the Judge presiding over the case shall secure the presence of a court reporter for the hearing. At the conclusion of the hearing, the court reporter shall prepare a transcript of the hearing on a non-emergency basis, and provide the original only to the Clerk of the Court for the filing of the Court file.

(10) The Clerk shall provide an assistant clerk to the presiding Judge during the hearing.

(11) Upon completion of the hearing, the Court may either draft or direct the Clerk to draft an order in conformity with the Florida Supreme Court approved forms for either Final Judgment Granting Petition for Judicial Waiver of Parental Notice of Termination of Pregnancy, or Final Order Dismissing Petition for Judicial Waiver of Parental Notice of Termination of Pregnancy. The Court shall then enter such order forthwith and the Clerk shall make such Order a part of the Court file.

(12) If no Order is entered within 48 hours of the date and time marked by the Clerk on the face of the first page of the Petition, the Clerk shall complete a Certificate of Clerk, similar to Exhibit B, certifying that since 48 hours has elapsed since the filing of the Petition and no order has been entered.

(13) Pursuant to Section 390.01116, Florida Statutes, the Clerk shall ensure any information in the record held by the circuit court which could be used to identify the Petitioner will remain confidential and exempt from public disclosure under Section 119.07(1), Florida Statutes, and Section 24, Article I, of the Florida Constitution. Pursuant to Rule 8.835(b), Florida Rules of Juvenile Procedure, "[s]o that the minor shall remain anonymous, the court file shall be sealed unless otherwise ordered by the court."

(14) The Clerk shall timely file all such reports regarding incidence of filings and outcomes of proceedings initiated pursuant to Section 390.01114, as may be requested from time to time by the Chief Judge or the Office of the State Court Administrator.

(C) This Order shall take effect immediately and shall remain in effect until further Order of the Court.

(D) This Administrative Order shall be recorded in the Official Records of Duval, Clay and Nassau Counties in the State of Florida, and certified copies of the same shall be furnished by the Clerks of the Circuit Court for Clay, Duval and Nassau counties to each person listed below (other than the listed Clerks of the Circuit Court) with which has offices in such Clerk's jurisdiction.

DONE AND ORDERED in Duval County, Florida, this 2nd day of Sept., 2005.

____

DONALD R. MORAN, JR.
CHIEF JUDGE

APPENDIX

RULES OF JUVENILE PROCEDURE

PART IV. OTHER PROCEEDINGS

A. [no change]

B. JUDICIAL WAIVER OF PARENTAL NOTICE OF TERMINATION OF PREGNANCY

Rule 8.800. Applicability. These rules apply to proceedings instituted pursuant to section 390.01114, Florida Statutes.

Rule 8.805. Commencement of Proceedings

(a) Petition to Be Filed. Proceedings for a judicial waiver of parental notice of termination of pregnancy shall be commenced by the filing of a petition in any circuit court within the appellate district in which the petitioner resides as provided by section 390.01114(4)(a), Florida Statutes.

(b) Pseudonymous Petitions. Petitions filed under a pseudonym or initials shall be filed simultaneously with a sworn statement containing the minor's true name, date of birth, address and the case number. A certified copy of this Sworn Statement of True Name and Pseudonym shall be given to the minor at the time it is filed. The original sworn statement shall be kept under seal at all times and may only be opened at the minor's request or by court order.

(c) Notice Under Pseudonymous Petitions. So that the minor may receive notice in a safe and secure manner, the minor shall elect to receive notice through the address and phone number of a trusted third person or by personally contacting the clerk's office. If the minor elects to personally contact the clerk's office, she must still provide an address and phone number of a third person through which to receive notice in the event that the court needs to provide notice at a time other than when the minor personally contacts the clerk's office.

(d) Procedures Upon Filing Petition. Upon the filing of a petition, the clerk of the circuit court shall immediately:

(1) open a file and assign a case number;

(2) provide the minor with a certified copy of Form 8.988 Sworn Statement of True Name and Pseudonym;

(3) provide the minor with Form 8.989 Advisory Notice to Minor;

(4) present the petition to the court for scheduling of the hearing and appointment of counsel, if requested; and

(5) provide notice of the hearing to the minor. If it is not possible for the clerk to immediately provide notice at the time the minor files the petition, the clerk shall provide notice through the method elected by the minor in the petition.

(e) Fees and Costs. No filing fees or court costs shall be assessed against any pregnant minor who petitions a court for a waiver of parental notice.

Rule 8.810. Petition. The petition shall include:

(a) the pseudonym or initials of the minor;

(b) the age of the minor;

(c) a statement that the minor is pregnant and notice has not been waived;

(d) a statement that the minor desires to terminate her pregnancy without notice to a parent or legal guardian; and

(e) a short and plain statement of facts to establish any of the following:

(1) The minor is sufficiently mature to decide whether to terminate her pregnancy.

(2) The minor is a victim of child abuse or sexual abuse by one or both of her parents or a guardian.

(3) Notification of a parent or guardian is not in the best interest of the minor.

Rule 8.815. Counsel. As provided by section 390.01114(4)(a), Florida Statutes, the circuit court shall advise the minor that she has a right to court-appointed counsel and shall provide her with counsel upon her request at no cost.

Rule 8.820. Hearing

(a) Hearing by Judge. A judge shall conduct an informal hearing on the petition within the time limits provided by law and these rules. General magistrates and special magistrates shall not hear a petition for a judicial waiver of parental notice of termination of pregnancy.

(b) Evidence. The judge shall hear evidence relating to the emotional development, maturity, intellect, and understanding of the minor, and all other relevant evidence.

(c) Burdens of Proof.

(1) A finding that the minor is sufficiently mature to decide whether to terminate her pregnancy requires proof by clear and convincing evidence.

(2) A finding that the minor is a victim of child abuse or sexual abuse by one or both of her parents or a guardian requires proof by a preponderance of the evidence.

(3) A finding that notification of a parent or guardian is not in the best interest of the minor requires proof by a preponderance of the evidence.

(d) Time Limits. As provided by section 390.01114(4)(b), Florida Statutes:

(1) Cases commenced under this rule take precedence over other pending matters as necessary to ensure that the court can make its ruling and issue written findings of fact and conclusions of law within 48 hours of the filing of the petition.

(2) The 48–hour time limit may be extended at the request of the minor; however, the court remains under an obligation to rule on the petition as soon as practically possible.

(3) If the court fails to rule within the 48–hour period and an extension has not been requested by the minor, the petition shall be deemed granted and an order shall be issued.

(e) Confidentiality of Hearings. Hearings under this part shall be closed to the public and all records thereof shall remain confidential as provided by sections 390.01114(4)(e) and 390.01116, Florida Statutes.

Rule 8.825. Order and Judgment. At the conclusion of the hearing, the court shall issue written and specific findings of fact and conclusions of law in support of its decision and order that a confidential record be maintained.

Rule 8.830. Transcripts. A court that conducts proceedings pursuant to these rules shall provide for a written transcript of all testimony and proceedings as provided by section 390.01114(4)(e), Florida Statutes.

Rule 8.835. Confidentiality of Records

(a) As provided by section 390.01116, Florida Statutes, any information including the petition, documents, transcripts, recordings of cases, and any other information that could be used to identify a minor who has petitioned the court for a judicial waiver of parental notice of termination of pregnancy is confidential and exempt from section 119.07(1), Florida Statutes, and section 24(a), Article I of the State Constitution.

(b) So that the minor shall remain anonymous, the court file shall be sealed unless otherwise ordered by the court.

IN THE CIRCUIT COURT OF THE ______
JUDICIAL CIRCUIT,

IN AND FOR ________ COUNTY, FLORIDA

In the interest of ______________ Case No.: ____
(pseudonym or initials of minor) Division: ____

PETITION FOR JUDICIAL WAIVER OF PARENTAL NOTICE OF TERMINATION OF PREGNANCY

I certify that the following information is true and correct:

(1) The pseudonym or initials of the minor (is/are) __________, and the minor has filed a Sworn Statement of True Name and Pseudonym with the clerk.

(2) The minor is ___ years old.

(3) The minor is pregnant and notice has not been waived.

(4) The minor desires to terminate her pregnancy without notice to a parent or legal guardian for one or more of the following reasons: [check all that apply]

___ a. The minor is sufficiently mature to decide whether to terminate her pregnancy, for the following reason(s):

____

____

____

___ b. The minor is a victim of child abuse or sexual abuse by one or both of her parents or a guardian, for the following reason(s):

____

____

____

___ c. Notification of a parent or guardian is not in the best interest of the minor, for the following reason(s):

____

____

____

(5) The minor requests that the court enter an order authorizing her to consent to the performance or inducement of a termination of pregnancy without notification of a parent or guardian.

(6) The minor requests the appointment of an attorney to represent her in this matter: [check one]

___ yes

___ no

(7) The minor elects the following method or methods for receiving notices of hearings or other court actions in this case:

___ Through a third party whose name is ________ and whose address and phone number for purposes of notice is ________________.

___ The minor will contact the office of the clerk of court at the following phone number ________________.

I understand that by signing this form I am swearing to or affirming the truthfulness of the claims made in this petition and that the punishment for knowingly making a false statement includes fines, imprisonment, or both.

Signature: ________ Date:

(You may sign a name other than your true name, such as Jane Doe or other pseudonym under which your petition is being filed.)

IN THE CIRCUIT COURT OF THE ________ JUDICIAL CIRCUIT,

IN AND FOR ________ COUNTY, FLORIDA

In the interest of ________________ (pseudonym or initials of minor) Case No.: ____ Division: ____

SWORN STATEMENT OF TRUE NAME AND PSEUDONYM

NOTICE TO THE CLERK OF COURT: A CERTIFIED COPY OF THIS DECLARATION WITH THE CASE NUMBER NOTED ON IT SHALL BE GIVEN TO THE MINOR AFTER SHE SIGNS IT.

THE ORIGINAL SHALL IMMEDIATELY BE PLACED IN A SEALED ENVELOPE WHICH SHALL BE FILED UNDER SEAL AND KEPT UNDER SEAL AT ALL TIMES.

(1) My true name is ________________, (print your name)

and my address is ________________. (print your address)

(2) My date of birth is ________________.

(3) I have filed a Petition for Judicial Waiver of Parental Notice of Termination of Pregnancy under the name or initials ________________ on ________. (date)

I understand that by signing this form I am swearing to or affirming the truthfulness of the information herein and that the punishment for knowingly making a false statement includes fines, imprisonment or both.

Dated: ______ Signature: ________________ (You must sign your true name.)

IN THE CIRCUIT COURT OF THE ________ JUDICIAL CIRCUIT,

IN AND FOR ________ COUNTY, FLORIDA

In the interest of ________________ (pseudonym or initials of minor) Case No.: ____ Division: ____

ADVISORY NOTICE TO MINOR

YOU ARE NOTIFIED as follows:

YOUR CASE NUMBER APPEARS AT THE TOP OF THIS FORM. KEEP IT IN A SAFE PLACE. YOU CAN NOT GET INFORMATION FROM THE CLERK WITHOUT YOUR CASE NUMBER.

YOU HAVE BEEN GIVEN A COPY OF THE SWORN STATEMENT YOU SIGNED WITH YOUR TRUE NAME. KEEP IT IN A SAFE PLACE. YOU MAY NEED TO SHOW IT AND THE FINAL JUDGMENT IN YOUR CASE TO YOUR DOCTOR BEFORE TERMINATING YOUR PREGNANCY.

All information in your case is confidential. No papers will be sent to your home, and you will be contacted by this court only through the method you elected in the petition. Your name will not be on your court papers.

If you would like an attorney to help you with your case, the court will appoint one for you at no cost to you. Your attorney will receive notices about your case so he or she can prepare for and attend hearings with you. You may also name someone else you trust to receive notices for you. You can also contact the clerk of court yourself to check on your case.

You have a right to a hearing and a decision on your case within 48 hours of filing your petition unless you or your attorney waives this right or asks for an extension of time. If this time limit is not met you have the right to ask the clerk for a form that will allow your doctor to perform a termination of pregnancy without notifying a parent.

If the court dismisses your petition, you have the right to appeal. You will be given information regarding how to proceed with an appeal, and if you would like an attorney to help you with an appeal, you may request that the court appoint one.

I certify that I have given a copy of this advisory form to the minor.

Dated: ________________

____
Clerk of the Court
________ County Courthouse
________, Florida.

IN THE CIRCUIT COURT OF THE ________ JUDICIAL CIRCUIT, IN AND FOR ________ COUNTY, FLORIDA

In the interest of ________________ (pseudonym or initials of minor) Case No.: ____ Division: ____

FINAL ORDER GRANTING PETITION FOR JUDICIAL WAIVER OF PARENTAL NOTICE OF TERMINATION OF PREGNANCY

THIS CAUSE having come before the court on a petition for judicial waiver of parental notice of termination of pregnancy and the court being otherwise advised in the premises, finds the following:

___ The minor has proven by clear and convincing evidence that she is sufficiently mature to decide whether to terminate her pregnancy, for the following reason(s):

____

____

___

___ The minor has proven by a preponderance of the evidence that she is a victim of child abuse or sexual abuse by one or both of her parents or a guardian, for the following reason(s):

___

___

___

The court, having made a finding under this section, will report the abuse as is required by section 39.201, Florida Statutes.

___ The minor has proven by a preponderance of the evidence that notification of a parent or guardian is not in the best interest of the minor, for the following reason(s):

___

___

THEREFORE, it is ORDERED AND ADJUDGED that:

1. The petition for judicial waiver of parental notice of termination of pregnancy is GRANTED.

2. The minor may consent to the performance or inducement of a termination of pregnancy without notice to a parent or guardian.

3. The clerk shall keep and maintain a confidential record of these proceedings as provided by section 390.01116, Florida Statutes, and shall seal the record.

DONE AND ORDERED in the .... court in and for .... County, Florida, on .... (date) ....

___

.... Judge

IN THE CIRCUIT COURT OF THE ___
JUDICIAL CIRCUIT, IN AND FOR
___ COUNTY, FLORIDA

In the interest of ___ (pseudonym or initials of minor) Case No.: ___ Division: ___

FINAL ORDER DISMISSING PETITION FOR JUDICIAL WAIVER OF PARENTAL NOTICE OF TERMINATION OF PREGNANCY

THIS CAUSE having come before the court on a petition for judicial waiver of parental notice of termination of pregnancy and the court being otherwise advised in the premises, finds the following:

The minor has not proven by sufficient evidence any of the criteria that would permit a judicial waiver of the parental notification requirements of section 390.01114(3), Florida Statutes, for the following reasons:

___

___

___

___

THEREFORE, it is ORDERED AND ADJUDGED that:

1. The petition for judicial waiver of parental notice of termination of pregnancy is DISMISSED.

2. The clerk shall keep and maintain a confidential record of these proceedings as provided by section 390.01116, Florida Statutes, and shall seal the record.

3. The clerk shall immediately provide Form 9.900(a) Notice of Appeal to the minor or petitioner if other than the minor.

DONE AND ORDERED in the .... court in and for .... County, Florida, on .... (date) ....

___

.... Judge

EXHIBIT B

IN THE CIRCUIT COURT OF THE FOURTH
JUDICIAL CIRCUIT, IN AND FOR
DUVAL COUNTY, FLORIDA

IN RE:

___,

Petitioner, A Minor.

CERTIFICATE OF CLERK

I HEREBY CERTIFY that 48 hours have elapsed since the filing of a petition in the above-referenced matter. There has been no request for an extension, and a hearing has not been held within the 48 hour time period.

DATED this ___ day of ___, 200 ___, at ___ o'clock ___.m..

By: ___
Deputy Clerk

1988–21 (A14). SUPERSEDED BY ADMINISTRATIVE ORDER NO. 86–23

1986–23 (A5). ASSIGNMENT OF CRIMINAL CASES IN CIRCUIT COURT

IN THE CIRCUIT COURT, FOURTH JUDICIAL CIRCUIT, IN AND FOR CLAY, NASSAU, AND DUVAL COUNTIES, FLORIDA

FIFTH AMENDED ADMINISTRATIVE ORDER NO. 86–23

IN RE: ASSIGNMENT OF CRIMINAL CASES IN CIRCUIT COURT

The primary purpose of this Order is to set forth in a consolidated manner the current case assignment system for felony cases in this Circuit.

This Order amends and supersedes the Administrative Order of May 14, 1984 entitled Administrative Order and recorded in Volume 5798, Pages 1841 and 1842 of the Official Records Book [No. 84–10]; incorporates the amendments as set forth in the Amended Administrative Order No. 86–23 (Official Records Book, Volume 6270, Page 2079), the Second Amended Administrative Order No. 86–23 (Official Records Book, Volume 6641, Page 502), the Third Amended Administrative Order No. 86–23 (Official Records Book, Volume 6788, Pages 0225 through 0227), the Fourth Amended Administrative Order No. 86–23 (Official Records Book, Volume 17799, Pages 2072 through 2074), the Fourteenth Amended Administrative Order No. 88–21 (Official Records Book, Volume 15523, Pages 23–28), court memoranda, and the practice and policies of the Clerk, State Attorney and Judiciary.

This system has proven workable, eliminates any question of forum shopping and preserves the integrity of the division assignment system.

NOW THEREFORE, by the authority vested in me as the Chief Judge of the Fourth Judicial Circuit and pursuant to the Florida Rules of Judicial Administration, it is

ORDERED as follows:

1. The random assignment of all felony cases shall be initiated through the State Attorney's Office case management software. The State Attorney is designated by Rule and Statute as an Intake Officer for the criminal justice system.

2. Whenever a defendant is arrested and no other felony cases are pending, including pending probation cases existing at the time of case initiation, the case will be randomly assigned to a felony division by the State Attorney's Office case management system.

3. If the defendant has other pending cases, the following reassignment procedures will be utilized:

a. If there is a pending felony case including "probable cause arrest", "at large" or arrest warrant cases, all subsequent cases will be assigned to the division which has the lowest State Attorney case number.

b. When a defendant with felony charges pending is charged with jail related offenses (i.e. Escape, Aiding Escape, Battery in a Detention Facility), the case will be assigned to the division with the pending case. Co-defendants need not be consolidated if charged with these crimes, unless there are no pending cases.

c. If there is a co-defendant, the co-defendant will be assigned to the division which has the lowest State Attorney case number. If there is no pending case, the case should be assigned by the lowest arrest docket number.

4. Probation—Violation: New Cases.

a. When a judge places a defendant on probation and that defendant, while on probation, acquires new felony charges, the case, regardless of the date of offense, shall be assigned to the felony division which placed the defendant on probation; and

b. When co-defendants are involved, each on probation, the new cases will be assigned to the division which has the lowest State Attorney case number on the original felony charge for which the probation was violated.

5. If a defendant is placed in a diversion program by the State Attorney, and the case is thereafter filed, the case will thereafter remain assigned to the original division. If a defendant is rearrested on felony charges while the diversion case is still in diversion status, the new arrest will be assigned to the division with the diversion status.

6. Assignment of "at-large" or "arrest warrant" cases will follow the same procedure as outlined above. "At-large" or "arrest warrant" cases are cases that originate in the State Attorney's Office and not as a probable cause arrest.

7. If an "at-large" or "arrest warrant" case is assigned as a felony, and a probable cause arrest is made based upon the same facts, the probable cause arrest will remain assigned to the original division of the "at-large" or "arrest warrant" case.

8. When an "at-large" felony worthless check case is to be assigned, the case shall be assigned to the division which has the lowest pending State Attorney case number for any of the defendant's prior worthless check cases. In the absence of a prior case, then the case shall follow the random division assignment criteria.

9. If at any time a case has an existing felony division assignment and is dismissed for any reason (i.e., *nolle prosequi*, dismissal, failure to file charges) and is later activated, the case must be reinstated to the original felony division.

10. All homicide cases, as described in Chapter 782, Florida Statutes (which include first degree murder, second degree murder, third degree murder and manslaughter) shall be randomly assigned to a felony division.

11. Homicide cases are not to be transferred unless a co-Defendant charged with the homicide has a lower State Attorney number. Once a homicide case is filed pursuant to the random assignment as described above, all pending cases against the homicide defendant(s) (including probation, diverted or other pending cases, and co-defendants with related cases) shall be transferred to the division to which the homicide case has been assigned.

12. All cases currently assigned to a felony division, including capiases issued prior to January 9, 2017, shall maintain their designated division assignments.

13. All post-conviction and post-judgment matters shall maintain their designated division assignments. Any case in which a defendant's sentence has been reversed on appeal, shall be retried and/or re-sentenced according to the appellate mandate and by the original division to which the case was assigned.

14. All other Administrative Orders addressing the same subject matter that are still in full force and effect and which have not been vacated or superseded, including the Amended Administrative Order No. 86–23, the Second Amended Administrative Order No. 86–23, the Third Amended Administrative Order No. 86–23, and the Fourteenth Amended Administrative Order No. 88–21), shall remain in full force and effect *unless* any terms or conditions appear to be contradictory, in which case, this Administrative Order shall supersede the contradictory portions of such Order(s).

15. The Fourth Amended Administrative Order No. 86–23, which was signed on December 6, 2016, inadvertently indicates that it was entered and signed on the "6th day of *November*" rather than December; therefore, the Fourth Amended Administrative Order is hereby vacated in its entirety and is superseded by this Fifth Amended Administrative Order No. 86–23, with the correct date indicated below.

16. This Administrative Order shall be recorded by the Clerk of the Court, in the Official Records of Duval County, in the State of Florida. All terms and conditions set forth herein shall remain in full force and effect unless and until otherwise ordered by this Court.

DONE AND ORDERED in Chambers at Jacksonville, Duval County, Florida, this 6th day of **December**, 2016 with an **effective date of January 9, 2017**.

MARK H. MAHON, CHIEF JUDGE

Sixth Judicial Circuit (Pasco and Pinellas Counties)

LOCAL RULES

1. Divisions of Court.
2. [Rescinded].
3. Assignment of Cases.
4. [Rescinded].
5. General.
6. Clerks of the Circuit Court.
7. [Rescinded].
8. [Rescinded].

9A. Electronic Jury Selection—Pinellas County.
9B. Electronic Jury Selection—Pasco County.
10. [Reserved].
11. [Rescinded].

ADMINISTRATIVE ORDERS

2019–005. GUARDIANSHIP.
2019–004. MORTGAGE FORECLOSURE PROCEDURES.
2018–068. FISH AND WILDLIFE CONSERVATION COMMISSION VIOLATIONS.
2018–047. ALTERNATIVE SANCTIONS PROGRAM.
2018–042. COURT REPORTING PLAN AND ELECTRONIC RECORDINGS OF COURT PROCEEDINGS.
2018–041. AMERICANS WITH DISABILITIES ACT.
2018–035. INJUNCTIONS FOR PROTECTION AGAINST EXPLOITATION OF VULNERABLE ADULTS.
2018–034. INTERPRETERS FOR NON–ENGLISH SPEAKING PERSONS.
2018–020. UNIFORM BOND SCHEDULE—PINELLAS COUNTY.
2018–019. UNIFORM BOND SCHEDULE—PASCO COUNTY.
2018–013. SEXUAL HARASSMENT POLICY AND DISCRIMINATION POLICY.
2018–008. UNIFIED FAMILY COURT—PINELLAS COUNTY.
2017–072. MOTIONS TO COMPEL DISCOVERY.
2017–064. CONFIDENTIALITY OF COURT RECORDS.
2017–057. CASE FILES IN PINELLAS COUNTY.
2017–039. COURT COSTS, ASSESSMENTS, SURCHARGES, AND FINES.
2017–034. SELECTION AND PAYMENT OF EXPERTS.
2017–033. EXPERT AND PROFESSIONAL FEES.
2017–032. CIVIL TRAFFIC INFRACTION HEARING OFFICER PROGRAM—PINELLAS COUNTY.
2017–027. [RESCINDED BY ORDER 2018-041, EFFECTIVE SEPTEMBER 1, 2018.].
2017–022. [RESCINDED BY ORDER 2018-042, EFFECTIVE AUGUST 14, 2018.].
2017–014. [RESCINDED BY ORDER 2017–034, EFFECTIVE JULY 1, 2017.].
2017–013. [RESCINDED BY ORDER 2017–033, EFFECTIVE JULY 1, 2017.].
2017–007. [RESCINDED BY ORDER 2019–004, EFFECTIVE JANUARY 23, 2019].
2016–077. ELECTRONIC FILING IN PINELLAS COUNTY—AMENDMENT ONE.
2016–058. [RESCINDED BY ORDER 2018-047, EFFECTIVE SEPTEMBER 7, 2018.].
2016–039. UNIFORM PROCEDURES FOR FORFEITURES OF PERSONAL PROPERTY.
2016–038. NOTICE TO CLAIMANTS OF SEIZURE AND FILING REQUIREMENTS.
2016–027. PROCEDURES FOR RETURN OF FIREARMS—PASCO COUNTY.
2016–022. COURT–APPOINTED ATTORNEY STANDARDS & DUE PROCESS COSTS.
2016–020. [RESCINDED BY ORDER 2017–007, EFFECTIVE FEBRUARY 6, 2017.].
2016–018. ELECTRONIC FILING IN PINELLAS COUNTY.
2016–017. [RESCINDED BY ORDER 2016-058, EFFECTIVE SEPTEMBER 9, 2016.].
2016–012. [RESCINDED BY ORDER 2016–017, EFFECTIVE MARCH 23, 2016.].
2016–011. ADULT DRUG COURT EXPANSION—PINELLAS COUNTY.
2016–010. VIOLATIONS OF FELONY PROBATION OR COMMUNITY CONTROL.
2016–006. PROCEDURES FOR RETURN OF FIREARMS—PINELLAS COUNTY.
2015–071. [RESCINDED BY ORDER 2016–080, EFFECTIVE DECEMBER 13, 2016.].
2015–068. [RESCINDED BY ORDER 2017–013, EFFECTIVE FEBRUARY 21, 2017.].
2015–061. PARKING TICKETS.
2015–060. REPORTING OF INDIGENT DETERMINATIONS AND FEE WAIVERS IN CIVIL CASES.
2015–059. [RESCINDED BY ORDER 2018-008, EFFECTIVE FEBRUARY 20, 2018.].
2015–058. [RESCINDED BY ORDER 2018-034, EFFECTIVE JUNE 29, 2018.].
2015–056. MOTIONS DECIDED ON WRITTEN SUBMISSIONS—CIVIL DIVISION.
2015–055. AFTER HOURS PROCEDURES FOR BAKER ACT AND MARCHMAN ACT HEARINGS IN PINELLAS COUNTY.
2015–052. PROFESSIONALISM COMMITTEE AND STANDARDS OF PROFESSIONAL COURTESY.
2015–043. [RESCINDED BY ORDER 2016–020, EFFECTIVE APRIL 1, 2016.].
2015–033. [RESCINDED BY ORDER 2016–022, EFFECTIVE JULY 1, 2016.].
2015–032. [RESCINDED BY ORDER 2016–019, EFFECTIVE APRIL 1, 2016.].
2015–031. HUMAN TRAFFICKING VICTIM RECORD EXPUNCTION.
2015–026. MUNICIPAL POLICE AGENCIES AND SHERIFFS, OR LAW ENFORCEMENT AGENCIES OUTSIDE OF PINELLAS COUNTY, SERVING INJUNCTIONS AGAINST DATING, DOMESTIC, REPEAT, AND SEXUAL VIOLENCE AND STALKING.
2015–017. COURT OPERATIONS IN EMERGENCIES.
2015–012. [RESCINDED BY ORDER 2016-057, EFFECTIVE SEPTEMBER 9, 2016.].

2015–008. E–CIGARETTES.
2015–003. [RESCINDED BY ORDER 2018-029, EFFECTIVE JULY 1, 2018.].
2014–079. [RESCINDED BY ORDER 2016–012, EFFECTIVE MARCH 1, 2016.].
2014–067. [RESCINDED BY ORDER 2019–006, EFFECTIVE JANUARY 23, 2019].
2014–062. [RESCINDED BY ORDER 2018-019, EFFECTIVE APRIL 25, 2018.].
2014–061. [RESCINDED BY ORDER 2018-020, EFFECTIVE APRIL 25, 2018].
2014–047. [RESCINDED BY ORDER 2016–009, EFFECTIVE MARCH 1, 2016.].
2014–043. PROHIBITED CONDUCT TOWARD SUMMONED JURORS.
2014–036. [RESCINDED BY ORDER 2016–022, EFFECTIVE JULY 1, 2016.].
2014–014. BAKER ACT HEARINGS.
2014–012. [RESCINDED BY ORDER 2016–018, EFFECTIVE APRIL 1, 2016.].
2014–011. ELECTRONIC FILING IN THE CRIMINAL DIVISION—PASCO COUNTY.
2013–081. MORTGAGE FORECLOSURE CASE STATUS REPORTING REQUIREMENTS.
2013–072. [RESCINDED BY ORDER 2017–014, EFFECTIVE FEBRUARY 21, 2017.].
2013–064. PRE–TRIAL CONFERENCES.
2013–063. VETERANS TREATMENT COURT.
2013–053. FORECLOSURE CASE STATUS REPORTING AND SERVICE LISTS.
2013–051. [RESCINDED BY ORDER 2017–008, EFFECTIVE FEBRUARY 9, 2017.].
2013–034. PROCEEDINGS TO PROHIBIT PURCHASE OF FIREARMS BY THE MENTALLY ILL.
2013–033. [RESCINDED BY ORDER 2017-039, EFFECTIVE AUGUST 22, 2017.].
2013–028. [RESCINDED BY ORDER 2016–018, EFFECTIVE APRIL 1, 2016.].
2013–027. CONFIDENTIAL INFORMATION CONTAINED IN PROPOSED ORDERS AND PROPOSED JUDGMENTS.
2013–024. [RESCINDED BY ORDER 2017-064, EFFECTIVE NOVEMBER 11, 2017.].
2013–021. [RESCINDED BY ORDER 2016-018, EFFECTIVE APRIL 1, 2016].
2013–017. E–FILING IN COUNTY CIVIL, COUNTY SMALL CLAIMS, CIRCUIT CIVIL, CIRCUIT CIVIL APPELLATE, AND FAMILY LAW DIVISIONS—PASCO COUNTY.
2013–016. [RESCINDED BY ORDER 2016–018, EFFECTIVE APRIL 1, 2016.].
2013–006. [RESCINDED BY ORDER 2016–018, EFFECTIVE APRIL 1, 2016.].
2013–005. [RESCINDED BY ORDER 2017—72, EFFECTIVE DECEMBER 13, 2017].
2013–003. SERVICE OF PLEADINGS AND DOCUMENTS PROBATE AND GUARDIANSHIP.
2012–057. [RESCINDED BY ORDER 2017–022, EFFECTIVE MAY 9, 2017.].
2012–054. AFTER HOURS PROCEDURES FOR DATING, DOMESTIC, REPEAT, AND SEXUAL VIOLENCE AND STALKING INJUNCTIONS.
2012–028. LOCAL ORDINANCE VIOLATIONS FISH AND WILDLIFE CONSERVATION COMMISSION VIOLATIONS UNIFORM FINE SCHEDULE.
2012–027. MOTIONS FOR EXCESS FEES BY COURT APPOINTED ATTORNEYS.
2012–023. [RESCINDED BY ORDER 2017-039, EFFECTIVE AUGUST 22, 2017.].
2011–061. PROCEEDINGS TO WAIVE PARENTAL NOTIFICATION OF TERMINATION OF PREGNANCY.
2011–059. [RESCINDED BY ORDER 2017–022, EFFECTIVE MAY 9, 2017.].
2011–053. [RESCINDED BY ORDER 2016–083, EFFECTIVE DECEMBER 20, 2016.].
2011–006. MEDIATION.
2010–065. [RESCINDED BY ORDER 2017-064, EFFECTIVE NOVEMBER 11, 2017.].
2010–063. [RESCINDED BY ORDER 2018-068, EFFECTIVE DECEMBER 12, 2018].
2010–045. [RESCINDED BY ORDER 2017-027, EFFECTIVE JUNE 7, 2017.].
2009–074. [RESCINDED BY ORDER 2016–011, EFFECTIVE MARCH 1, 2016.].
2009–037. INCAPACITY AND GUARDIANSHIP CASES—APPOINTMENT OF ATTORNEY AND RECOVERY OF COSTS.
2009–036. [RESCINDED BY ORDER 2019–005, EFFECTIVE JANUARY 23, 2019].
2008–076. MEDIA POLICY.
2008–058. INVOLUNTARY COMMITMENT OF SEXUALLY VIOLENT PREDATORS.
2007–081. [RESCINDED BY ORDER 2016–010, EFFECTIVE MARCH 1, 2016.].
2007–080. [RESCINDED BY ORDER 2017–022, EFFECTIVE MAY 9, 2017.].
2007–024. [RESCINDED BY ORDER 2018-068, EFFECTIVE DECEMBER 12, 2018].
2007–001. ADULT DRUG COURT.
2006–097. FIRST APPEARANCE ADVISORY PROCEEDINGS.
2006–070. UNCONTESTED RESIDENTIAL TENANT EVICTIONS.
2006–021. PROCEDURES FOR BOWEN AND SUBSEQUENT REVIEW HEARINGS IN CASES INVOLVING INTRACIRCUIT EXECUTION OF WRIT OF BODILY ATTACHMENT FOR CIVIL CONTEMPT FOR FAILURE TO PAY CHILD SUPPORT.
2006–017. DISCLOSURE OF PROTECTED HEALTH INFORMATION UNDER THE HEALTH INSURANCE PORTABILITY AND ACCOUNTABILITY ACT OF 1996.
2006–006. EN BANC CIRCUIT COURT APPELLATE PROCEDURES.
2005–065. [RESCINDED BY ORDER 2017-074, EFFECTIVE DECEMBER 13, 2017.].
2004–077. [RESCINDED BY ORDER 2018-013, EFFECTIVE MARCH 20, 2018.].
2004–029. [RESCINDED BY ORDER 2019–005, EFFECTIVE JANUARY 23, 2019].
PI–CTY–98–05. [RESCINDED BY ORDER 2017–021, EFFECTIVE APRIL 28, 2017.].
PA/PI–CIR–97–85. [RESCINDED BY ORDER 2019–005, EFFECTIVE JANUARY 23, 2019].

Local Rules

Rule 1. Divisions of Court

(A) Circuit Court. The following shall be the Divisions of the Circuit Court of the Sixth Judicial Circuit:

1. **Appellate Division**

All appeals from the County Courts and designated administrative bodies of Pinellas and Pasco Counties shall be assigned to the Appellate Division in the Circuit Court.

The Appellate Division includes civil appeals and criminal appeals. The judges assigned to the Appellate Division shall sit as three judge panels, and may have separate panels for civil appeals and criminal appeals. Oral argument is in the discretion of the panel and is only granted when the court determines that the issues are so complex or novel that argument would benefit the court.

2. **Civil Division**

All suits, causes, proceedings or actions within the jurisdiction of the Circuit Courts and not herein assigned to another division are assigned to the Civil Division. Cases under section 394.910 et seq, Florida Statutes, involuntary civil commitment of sexually violent predators, (Jimmy Ryce) are assigned to the Civil Division.

3. **Criminal Law Division**

All actions, cases and proceedings within the jurisdiction of the Circuit Court involving the administration of criminal justice are assigned to the Criminal Division.

4. **Family Law Division**

All suits, causes, proceedings or actions relating to dissolution of marriage, child custody, child visitation, grandparent proceedings, annulment, URESA, UIFSA, Title IV–D, child support, alimony, name change, paternity, adoption, domestic, repeat, dating, and sexual violence injunctions, separate maintenance, Chapter 39 and 985, Florida Statutes, and enforcement of domestic or foreign orders or judgments involving these same causes of action, and other proceedings designated by administrative order of the Chief Judge.

An attorney representing a party in a domestic violence or dissolution of marriage case must file a notice with the court informing the court of any dependency or delinquency case involving a child of one of the parties.

The Chief Judge may designate one or more sections in the Family Law Division to serve as a Unified Family Court. The purpose of Unified Family Court is to ensure that children and families involved in multiple court proceedings are assigned to one judge, where possible. Juvenile delinquency and dependency proceedings shall be included within the Unified Family Court Section of the Family Law Division. In addition, related cases from the Family Law Division may be assigned to Unified Family Court as determined by the Unified Family Court section judge.

Contested and uncontested original and post-judgment proceedings may be referred to a general master with the exception of those filed pursuant to Fla. Fam. L.R.P 12.490(c), unless objected to pursuant to Fla. Fam. L.R.P. 12.490.

Original and post-judgment proceedings in which a party is receiving services pursuant to the provisions of Title IV–D of the Social Security Act, 42 U.S.C. § 651, et. seq., and original and post-judgment proceedings dealing solely with child support issues that do not involve a recipient of services pursuant to the provisions of Title IV–D of the Social Security Act shall be assigned to circuit family law sections and may be heard by the child support enforcement hearing officer pursuant to the provisions of Fla. Fam. L.R.P. 12.491, unless heard by a judge.

5. **Probate and Guardianship Division**

All causes, proceedings, matters and actions pertaining to the probate of estates, administration of guardianships, incapacity proceedings, proceedings arising out of Chapter 393, Florida Statutes, the Baker Act, and Marchman Act, the Life–Prolonging Procedures Act, any proceeding arising under the Florida Probate Rules, and the administration of trusts, are assigned to the Probate and Guardianship Division.

(B) Pasco County Court. The following shall be the divisions of the County Court in Pasco County:

1. Civil Division. All suits, causes, proceedings or actions within the jurisdiction of the County Court and not herein assigned to another division are assigned to the Civil Division.

2. Criminal Division. All actions, causes and proceedings within the jurisdiction of the County Court involving the administration of criminal justice and violations of local ordinances are assigned to the Criminal Division.

3. Small Claims Division. All actions, causes and proceedings subject to the Florida Small Claims Rules are assigned to the Small Claims Division.

4. Traffic Division. All actions, causes and proceedings within the jurisdiction of the County Court involving violation of traffic laws are assigned to the Traffic Division.

(C) Pinellas County Court. The following shall be the divisions of the County Court in Pinellas County:

1. Civil Division. All suits, causes, proceedings or actions within the jurisdiction of the County Court and not herein assigned to another division are assigned to the Civil Division. Simplified dissolution of marriage proceedings and uncontested dissolution of marriage proceedings may be heard in the civil division.

2. Criminal Division. All actions, causes and proceedings within the jurisdiction of the County Court involving the administration of criminal justice and violations of local ordinances are assigned to the Criminal Division.

3. Small Claims Division. All actions, causes and proceedings subject to the Florida Small Claims Rules are assigned to the Small Claims Division.

4. Traffic Division. All actions, causes and proceedings within the jurisdiction of the County Court involving violation of traffic laws are assigned to the Traffic Division. If a jury trial is required in a traffic case, the case will be transferred pursuant to administrative order to the Pinellas County Criminal Justice Center.

Rule 2. [Rescinded]

Rule 3. Assignment of Cases

(A) Initial Assignment of Cases

All suits, causes, actions and proceedings shall be assigned to a section in a division on an equal, at random, blind assignment system, except when cases are assigned by administrative order or when a case is assigned by the Chief Judge or his or her designee. The Clerks of the Circuit Court shall assign all cases pursuant to this rule or administrative order of the Chief Judge. When the reference number is discontinued, the Clerk of Court shall include the assigned section number either as the last two digits of the Uniform Case Number or in addition to the Uniform Case Number in all computer systems, court files, and all documents prepared by the Clerk of the Court that include the Uniform Case Number. In complying with this requirement, the Clerk of the Court must ensure that the section number can be used for purposes of data gathering as required by law or directive of the Court.

Any action which was formerly assigned to a specific section in a division shall be assigned to the same section in which it was last pending. Counsel and unrepresented litigants shall be responsible for observation of this rule and cases shall be assigned to the proper section upon discovery of the application of this rule.

(B) Reassignment of Cases

1. Reassignment of companion cases

An attorney representing a party in a case to which there are companion cases shall file a notice of a companion case. The original notice and sufficient copies for filing in each companion case shall be filed with the Clerk and a copy provided to the judge in the section which has been assigned the case bearing the lowest docket number. Said judge may thereupon reassign all such companion cases to the section which has been assigned the case bearing the lowest docket number if the court finds that the companion cases involve common questions of law or fact or the reassignment would result in an efficient administration of justice. The Clerk shall make appropriate notations on the file cover and the progress docket of such reassigned case or cases and thereafter all such companion cases shall be heard, tried, and determined by the judge assigned to the section having the companion case bearing the lowest docket number.

A companion case is

(a) an action filed in the same division involving the same parties or

(b) an action involving at least one party in common and the same transaction or occurrence.

2. Reassignment of cases within a division

A case may be reassigned when the Chief Judge or the Chief Judge's designee determines it is appropriate to do so or when a judge has been recused or disqualified from a case. When a judge has been recused or disqualified from a case, the judge shall direct the Clerk of Court to reassign the case by random, blind rotation in accordance with Local Rule 3(a) unless the case is otherwise reassigned by the Chief Judge. If the judge believes the same circumstances causing his or her disqualification or recusal would exist for other judges in the division or circuit, the judge's Order of Recusal or Disqualification shall direct the case to the Chief Judge for reassignment.

3. Reassignment of cases between divisions

When a motion to consolidate, a motion to transfer, or any similar motion is filed which relates to cases that are in two or more of the Court's divisions, sufficient copies shall be provided for each case and the Clerk shall file the motion in each court file involved. The Chief Judge or the Chief Judge's designee will hear any such motion. A motion to consolidate or transfer cases filed in more than one division of the court shall be granted only when the Chief Judge determines that the efficient administration of justice requires reassignment.

Rule 4. [Rescinded]

Rule 5. General

(A) Cancellation of Proceedings

When a matter is scheduled for hearing and the matter is resolved by agreement or settlement, the party setting the matter for hearing shall notify the court. When a matter is scheduled for trial and the case settles, the plaintiff shall notify the court. Permission of the court must be obtained in order to cancel a trial.

(B) Emergency Matters

All emergency matters arising in any cause pending in any of the Divisions of this Court shall be heard and determined by the assigned judge if available, or if unavailable by the judge designated by the section judge who has agreed to handle such matters during his or her absence, or the emergency duty judge assigned pursuant to administrative order of the Chief Judge.

(C) Affidavit of Good Faith, Motions to Compel

(1) Before filing a motion to compel or a motion for protective order, counsel for the moving party shall confer with counsel for the opposing party in a good faith effort to resolve by agreement the issues raised, and shall file with the Court at the time of the filing of the motion a statement certifying that he or she has so conferred with opposing counsel and that counsel have been unable to resolve the dispute.

(2) Motions to compel discovery shall quote in full each interrogatory, question on deposition, request for admission or request for production to which the motion is addressed and the objection and grounds therefor as stated by the opposing party.

(D) Non–Military Affidavits

(1) Non–Military Affidavits provided for in United States Code 50 App. Section 520 are required in all cases prior to the entry of default by the Clerk of Court.

(2) In the absence of such affidavit, the Clerk shall enter default only upon order of the Court.

Rule 6. Clerks of the Circuit Court

The Clerk of the Circuit Court of each County in this Circuit shall furnish to the Chief Judge and each judge assigned to the County, a list of his or her pending cases at intervals and in such format which shall be designated by the Chief Judge and shall furnish such other reports as may be required.

Rule 7. [Rescinded]

Rule 8. [Rescinded]

Rule 9A. Electronic Jury Selection—Pinellas County

(a) The equipment used in jury selection is the IBM-96-72 with the operating system OS/390, utilized by the Management Information Systems Department of Pinellas County.

(b) The source from which names shall be taken is the Department of Highway Safety and Motor Vehicles database of all persons at least 18 years of age or older, who are citizens of the United States and legal residents of Florida and whose address is in Pinellas County. In every year hereafter, on or before January 1, the Department of Highway Safety and Motor Vehicles will deliver to the Clerk of Circuit Court of Pinellas County a computerized tape of the names of each person at least 18 years of age or older whose name appears in the department database and whose address is Pinellas County. The Clerk of Circuit Court of Pinellas County will protect the tape from further alteration and keep any such tape securely stored in the Management Information Systems Department until such time as jurors have been drawn.

(c) The Clerk of Circuit Court of Pinellas County is designated the official custodian of the computer records of the names to be used in jury selection and shall ensure they are not accessible to anyone other than those directly involved in selection of venires, as herein provided. Functions of the Clerk of Circuit Court may be performed by deputies.

(d) If the entire list of names is not used as the final certified jury list from which venires are selected, then, the Chief Judge, with the aid and assistance of the Clerk of Circuit Court of Pinellas County, shall select enough prospective jurors by lot and at random from the entire list using a user defined COBOL random number generator which generates a seed internally based upon the time of day at which the job starts and utilizes the random program algorithm.

(e) The Clerk of Circuit Court of Pinellas County shall cause jury venires to be selected by the computer system from the Department of Highway Safety and Motor Vehicles database using the method described above in accordance with directions received from the Chief Judge by Administrative Order.

Rule 9B. Electronic Jury Selection—Pasco County

(a) The equipment used in jury selection is an DEC ALPHA 2100 computer located in the secured computer room of the Clerk of the Circuit Court of Pasco County.

(b) The source from which names shall be taken is the Department of Highway Safety and Motor Vehicles database of all persons at least 18 years of age or older, who are citizens of the United States and legal residents of Florida and whose address is in Pasco County. In every year hereafter, on or before January 1, the Department of Highway Safety and Motor Vehicles will deliver to the Clerk of the Circuit Court of Pasco County a computerized tape of the names of each person at least 18 years of age or older whose name appears in the department's database and whose address is in Pasco County. The Clerk of Circuit Court of Pasco County will protect the tape from further alteration and keep such tape secure in the computer room until such time as jurors have been drawn.

(c) The Clerk of Circuit Court of Pasco County is designated the official custodian of the computer tape of the names to be used in jury selection and shall ensure that it is not accessible to anyone other than those directly involved in selection of venires, as herein provided. Functions of the Clerk of Circuit Court of Pasco County may be performed by deputies.

(d) The Chief Judge, with the aid and assistance of the Clerk of Circuit Court of Pasco County shall select sufficient prospective jurors by lot and at random by use of the Department of Highway Safety and Motor Vehicles tape, using the random number generator.

(e) The Clerk of Circuit Court of Pasco County shall cause jury venires to be selected from the final certified jury list programmed into the Pasco County computer in accordance with directions received from the Chief Judge by Administrative Order.

Rule 10. [Reserved]

Rule 11. [Rescinded]

Administrative Orders

2019–005. GUARDIANSHIP

IN THE CIRCUIT COURT, SIXTH JUDICIAL CIRCUIT IN AND FOR PASCO AND PINELLAS COUNTIES, FLORIDA

ADMINISTRATIVE ORDER NO. 2019–005 PA/PI–CIR

RE: GUARDIANSHIP

In order to adequately and effectively protect incapacitated persons placed in guardianships, and to assist the Court with timely review of guardianship accountings, plans, inventories, and background investigations of proposed and appointed guardians, and to clarify guardian education requirements; and

In accordance with Article V, Section 2, Florida Constitution, Rule of Judicial Administration 2.215, and § 43.26, Florida Statutes, it is hereby:

ORDERED:

A. Background Investigations

1. Professional and nonprofessional guardians may be required to submit periodically to credit and criminal background checks. At any time, the Court may require a nonprofessional guardian to undergo additional credit or criminal history background checks.

2. All professional guardians shall comply with the background check requirements of chapter 744, Florida Statutes, and shall submit proof of registration with the Office of Public and Professional Guardians upon filing a Petition for Appointment of Guardian.

3. Along with his or her Petition for Appointment of Guardian, each proposed guardian shall submit for filing an Application for Appointment of Guardian and a Department of Children and Families Release. Professional and non-professional guardians shall pay all fees associated with the application as required by the Florida Statutes.

4. The Clerk of the Circuit Court for Pinellas County and the Clerk of the Circuit Court for Pasco County ("Clerks") shall:

a. Notify the Probate and Guardianship Division when a Petition for Appointment of Guardian is filed.

b. Collect, from each proposed non-professional guardian, the investigation fee necessary to conduct the credit check pursuant to the Florida Statutes.

c. Make the results of any criminal history check conducted by the Federal Bureau of Investigation and the Florida Department of Law Enforcement available to the general magistrate or such other person as directed by the Court.

B. Guardianship and Incapacity Procedures

1. *Determination of Capacity*

a. The court-approved form Application for Appointment of Guardian shall be utilized within the trial courts of the Sixth Judicial Circuit by any petitioner seeking the determination of capacity of an individual located within Pasco or Pinellas County and shall be filed contemporaneously with the Petition to Determine Capacity.

b. Clerks' Duties:

i. Accept the Petition to Determine Capacity, Petition for Appointment of Guardian, and Application for Appointment of Guardian.

ii. Immediately upon receipt of the Petition to Determine Capacity, prepare the Notice to Alleged Incapacitated Person, Order Appointing Examining Committee, and Order Appointing Counsel for the Alleged Incapacitated Person for presentation to the Court. The members of the Examining Committee and the Court Appointed Counsel for the Alleged Incapacitated Person shall be chosen on a rotational basis from the Court approved lists.

iii. Serve by regular or electronic mail a copy of the Petition to Determine Capacity and Petition for Appointment of Guardian and any exhibits upon appointed counsel, members of the examining committee, and all known next of kin of the alleged incapacitated person, and/or such other person as directed by the Court.

iv. Present a copy of the Petition to Determine Capacity, Verified Petition for Appointment of Guardian, Notice and Statement of Rights to the process server for service on the alleged incapacitated person.

v. In addition to monitoring the Return of Service, monitor the completion of the committee's report to ensure that appropriate statutory time frames are met.

vi. Provide a notice to the process server directing the process server to read the petitions and Notice and Statement of Rights to the alleged incapacitated person and to return to the Clerks' Office the Return of Service for filing in the Court file.

2. *Indigent Status.* The Clerk shall inform any petitioner filing for indigent status on behalf of an alleged indigent incapacitated person that he or she is required to complete an Application for Determination of Civil Indigent Status in accordance with section 57.082, Florida Statutes. The application shall be completed using the alleged indigent incapacitated person's information.

3. *Adjudicatory Hearing*

a. The petitioner, petitioner's counsel, the alleged incapacitated person, counsel for the alleged incapacitated person, the proposed guardian, and counsel for the proposed guardian shall attend the adjudicatory hearing. The Court may waive attendance by the alleged incapacitated person, upon request of the alleged incapacitated person's counsel.

b. If requested by the Court, the Clerks may be required to attend adjudicatory hearings and keep court minutes.

4. *Relocation of Ward.* If, after a determination of incapacity, the ward relocates to a different location in the same county, the guardian must file with the court a Notice of Relocation within ten (10) days of the relocation.

C. Implementation of Guardianship Accounting, Plan, and Inventory Forms

1. All accountings, plans, and inventories shall be filed on court-approved forms. Information on obtaining forms and instructions is available on the Court website, www.jud6.org.

2. The Clerks shall:

a. Upon the issuance of Letters of Guardianship, produce a computer- generated Guardianship filing schedule to be distributed with the Letters of Guardianship to the guardian and the counsel for the guardian.

b. Conduct the statutorily required audit of initial, annual, or final guardianship reports pursuant to chapter 744, Florida Statutes, in accordance with the following procedures:

i. Upon completion of the audit of the initial, annual, or final guardianship report, the Clerks shall submit their audit sheet listing any discrepancies to the general magistrate or other such person as directed by the Court.

ii. If discrepancies are identified, prepare and forward to the general magistrate's office, or to such other person as directed by the Court, an Order Disapproving the Initial, Annual, or Final Accounting, Plan, or Inventory ("Order Disapproving") that lists all discrepancies and provides the guardian thirty (30) days to respond.

iii. If a guardian fails to timely file the accounting, plan, or inventory, prepare and forward to the general magistrate's office, or to such other person as directed by the Court, an Order to File Required Documents ("Order to File") that provides the guardian twenty (20) days to comply.

iv. Monitor compliance with the Order Disapproving, the Order to File, and any orders extending the time for compliance with these orders.

v. If the guardian fails to comply with an order listed in subdivision iv., the general magistrate's office or other such person as directed by the Court may ask the Clerks to prepare and forward an Order to Show Cause.

vi. Review the documents filed in accordance with the Order Disapproving or Order to File, and forward the file with the audit sheet to the general magistrate or other such person as directed by the Court.

3. All other audits, including random field audits, shall only be conducted pursuant to Court order.

4. If the documents filed are insufficient, an Order to File or To Show Cause will be issued and a hearing scheduled before the judge. The hearing may only be cancelled or continued by written order of the Court.

5. Motions for extensions of time for filing any required document shall be made in writing prior to the time the document is due. The motion shall disclose whether or not an extension of time has previously been granted for the same or similar filing. The parties shall allege good cause on which the extension is sought and that the time requested is sufficient. No motion for extension of time shall be heard orally. Counsel shall ensure that all interested parties receive adequate notice of all such motions.

D. Disaster Plan. Each initial guardianship plan shall include a Disaster Plan, which sets forth the procedures and plans in place for the ward in the event an evacuation order or other emergency order is issued by federal, state, or local officials. The Disaster Plan shall take into account and reflect how each ward's special needs will be met under the plan in the event the guardian or ward relocates temporarily due to an evacuation order, emergency order, or other emergency situation. The Disaster Plan must be updated if the ward permanently changes residence or if a new guardian is appointed. Information on obtaining forms and instructions related to the disaster plan is available on the Sixth Judicial Circuit Court website, www.jud6.org. If the ward is a minor child residing with his or her parent or other relative who is serving as guardian, that guardian shall be exempt from the requirement of filing a disaster plan.

E. Guardian and Guardian Advocate Training for Incapacity and Guardian Advocate Proceedings

1. *Non–Professional Guardian of Incapacitated Adults Education Requirements*

a. A non-professional person appointed as guardian who is required to comply with the education requirement of section 744.3145, Florida Statutes, shall be considered to have satisfied the education requirements by completing a minimum of eight (8) hours of instruction and training in an approved family member guardian education course.

b. A non-professional guardian education course shall include topics required by section 744.3145(2), Florida Statutes. Any person or organization seeking court approval to act as a provider of a family member guardian education course may submit the curriculum to the Administrative Office of the Courts, Probate Division (Program).

c. Approved courses for basic guardian education:

i. St. Petersburg College, credit course entitled "Legal Guardian Family Training Online", available at the St. Petersburg College website, www.spcollege.edu, or https://spcollege.augusoft.net.

ii. Additional guardianship courses may be approved. Information on additionally approved programs may be received from the Program.

d. Upon completion of a non-professional guardian education course, the guardian shall file a certificate of completion from the course instructor in the guardianship court file.

2. *Professional Guardian Education Requirements.* Each professional guardian shall complete training in accordance with chapter 744, Florida Statutes.

3. *Parent Guardian of a Minor Child Education Requirements*

a. A person who is appointed as guardian of the property of his or her minor child, who is required to comply with the education requirement of section 744.3145(3), Florida Statutes, shall be considered to have satisfied the education requirements by completing a minimum of four (4) hours of instruction and training in an approved guardian of minor child education course. This requirement may be satisfied by completing a St. Petersburg College course entitled "Legal Guardian Family Training Online," available at the St. Petersburg College website, www.spcollege.edu, or https://spcollege.augusoft.net.

b. A guardian of minor child education course shall include topics required in section 744.3145(3), Florida Statutes. Any person or organization seeking court approval to act as a provider of a guardian of minor child education course may submit the curriculum to the Administrative Office of the Courts, Probate Division (Program).

c. Upon completion of a guardian of minor child education course, the guardian shall file a certificate of completion from the course instructor in the guardianship court file.

Administrative Orders No. PA/PI–CIR–97–85, 2004–029 PA/PI–CIR, and 2009–036 PA/PI–CIR, are hereby rescinded.

DONE AND ORDERED in Chambers at St. Petersburg, Pinellas County, Florida this ___ day of January 2019.

ORIGINAL SIGNED ON JANUARY 23, 2019
BY ANTHONY RONDOLINO
CHIEF JUDGE

2019–004. MORTGAGE FORECLOSURE PROCEDURES

IN THE CIRCUIT COURT, SIXTH JUDICIAL CIRCUIT IN AND FOR PASCO AND PINELLAS COUNTIES, FLORIDA

ADMINISTRATIVE ORDER NO. 2019–004 PA/PI–CIR

RE: MORTGAGE FORECLOSURE PROCEDURES UPDATE—JANUARY 2019

Effective June 23, 2018, the Protecting Tenants at Foreclosure Act of 2009 ("the Act") was restored, revising sections 701–703 of the Act as they were on December 30, 2014.

This Administrative Order provides procedures and forms to re-implement the statutory protections and a process to submit an application for a writ of possession to the judge under the Act. **All parties and counsel are hereby noticed of the restoration of the Act, and the requirements in this Order.**

Accordingly, to update the Court's mortgage foreclosure procedures pursuant to the authority of the Chief Judge in Article V, section 2(d), Florida Constitution, Rule of Judicial Administration 2.215, and section 43.26, Florida Statutes, it is

ORDERED:

I. INITIATION OF RESIDENTIAL MORTGAGE FORECLOSURE CASES

1. For each residential mortgage foreclosure case, the Plaintiff/Lender's attorney must:

a. File a verified complaint in accordance with Florida Rules of Civil Procedure 1.110(b) and 1.115, and section 702.015, Fla. Stat. In cases where the original note will be used, a copy must be filed. Because of electronic filing, the Court prefers that the original note be retained for submission at the summary judgment hearing or trial.

b. File with the complaint a **Form A—Plaintiff/Lender's Contact Information** [1]. If the case involves multiple plaintiffs, only one Form A—Plaintiff/Lender's Contact Information must be filed. The Form A—Plaintiff/Lender's Contact Information that must be used is Attachment A to this Administrative Order.

c. File with the complaint a **Form B—Important Notice to Homeowner** [2], which provides notice to the homeowner of mediation alternatives and other resources. Form B—Important Notice to Homeowner, is Attachment B to this Administrative Order. Previous versions of Form B or the Important Notice to Homeowner must not be used.

2. The Clerk shall not issue a summons in a residential mortgage foreclosure case until a Plaintiff/Lender files a verified complaint, a Form A—Plaintiff/Lender's Contact Information, which is Attachment A to this Administrative Order, and a Form B—Important Notice to Homeowner, which is Attachment B to this Administrative Order.

3. For every residential mortgage foreclosure case filed, the process server must note on the return of service that the summons was served with the complaint, Form A—Plaintiff/Lender's Contact Information, which is Attachment A to this Administrative Order, and a Form B—Important Notice to Homeowner, which is Attachment B to this Administrative Order.

II. PROCEDURES APPLICABLE TO ALL MORTGAGE FORECLOSURE CASES

A. Motions for Order to Show Cause for Entry of Final Judgment of Foreclosure pursuant to section 702.10, Florida Statutes

1. *Florida Rule of Civil Procedure Form 1.944(c) Motion.* When a verified complaint in accordance with section 702.015, Fla. Stat., has been filed, section 702.10, Fla. Stat., provides a summary procedure for lienholders to obtain a final judgment of foreclosure. If a lienholder determines that a section 702.10 motion is appropriate, it may file a section 702.10 motion for an order to show cause for entry of final judgment in the format set forth in Florida Rule of Civil Procedure Form 1.944(c). *See In re Amendments to Florida Rules of Civil Procedure*, 153 So. 3d 258, 265–66 (Fla. 2014); Ch. 2013–137, section 8, Laws of Fla.

2. *Florida Rule of Civil Procedure Form 1.944(d) proposed Order To Show Cause.* When filing a section 702.10 motion, the lienholder shall supply the court with a proposed order to show cause for all defendants in the format set forth in Florida Rule of Civil Procedure Form 1.944(d). As required by section 702.10(1)(a)(8), Fla. Stat., attached to the proposed order shall be a proposed updated Form D—Uniform Final Judgment of Foreclosure, which is Attachment D to this Administrative Order. *See* section 702.10(1)(a), Fla. Stat.; *In re Amendments to Florida Rules of Civil Procedure*, 153 So. 3d at 266–67.

3. At the time of filing the section 702.10 motion for an order to show cause, the lienholder is *not* required to file a Form C—Certificate of Compliance with Foreclosure Procedures with the Clerk, which is Attachment C to this Administrative Order.

B. Summary Judgment Hearings

1. *Certificate Filed Prior to Requesting Summary Judgment Hearing Date.* Prior to requesting a summary judgment hearing for a mortgage foreclosure, the attorney of record for the Plaintiff must file an updated **Form C—Certificate of Compliance with Foreclosure Procedures** [3], which is Attachment C to this Administrative Order, with the Clerk. This certifies that the attorney has completed the necessary steps prior to setting the matter for hearing. Only the Form C—Certificate of Compliance with Foreclosure Procedures attached to this Administrative Order may be used.

Previous versions of Form C or the Certificate of Compliance must not be used.

2. *Foreclosure Judgment Packet Prior to Hearing.* In residential and commercial foreclosure cases, unless the presiding judge provides otherwise, the Plaintiff's attorney must deliver a foreclosure judgment package to the presiding judge's office at least five business days prior to the scheduled hearing on a motion for summary judgment. In both residential and commercial foreclosure cases, the Plaintiff's attorney must serve the Defendant's attorney, or if the Defendant is not represented then serve the Defendant, a copy of the foreclosure judgment packet at least five business days prior to a scheduled hearing on a motion for summary judgment. The packet must include:

a. the proposed updated **Form D—Uniform Final Judgment of Foreclosure** [4], which is Attachment D to this Administrative Order (the packet filed with the Court shall include sufficient copies for conforming and stamped, addressed envelopes for all parties);

b. a copy of the Promissory Note (original should be retained for submission at the summary judgment hearing or trial);

c. an affidavit of non-payment with a copy of the payment records upon which the affiant relies;

d. a copy of the Form C—Certificate of Compliance with Foreclosure Procedures, which is Attachment C to this Administrative Order; and

e. a copy of the Notice of Hearing.

Statutory fees must be submitted to the Clerk of the Court and not submitted to the Court with the foreclosure judgment packet.

C. Uniform Judgment of Foreclosure. All proposed final judgments of foreclosure must be in the format of Form D—Uniform Final Judgment of Foreclosure, which is Attachment D to this Administrative Order, unless otherwise specifically approved by the judge entering the final judgment. **Any changes to Form D—Uniform Final Judgment of Foreclosure, which is Attachment D to this Administrative Order, must be brought to the attention of the presiding judge at the final judgment hearing or non-jury trial.**

D. Foreclosure Sales

1. *Notice of Sale.* The Plaintiff is responsible for completing and submitting the Notice of Sale directly to the appropriate newspaper. Notices must be prepared and published in accordance with Florida Statutes, Chapters 45 and 702. Plaintiff's failure to timely publish notice may subject the Plaintiff to sanctions.

2. *Cancelation of Sale.* The sale date set by the judgment can only be canceled and rescheduled by Court order. Any motion or request to cancel this sale must be served on all parties in conformity with Florida Rule of Civil Procedure 1.080(a) and must be set for hearing with proper notice. Claiming this matter is an "emergency" does not avoid this requirement. A violation of any party's due process rights will subject the movant and/or counsel to sanctions. *See Jade Winds v. Citibank,* 63 So. 3d 819 (Fla. 3d DCA 2011). The Court may grant an ex-parte cancellation without hearing, if ALL parties agree.

If a Plaintiff wishes to cancel a sale, a written motion must be filed with the Court in substantial compliance with Florida Rules of Civil Procedure Form 1.996(c). The motion also must state the number of times the Plaintiff has previously requested the cancelation of a sale and must include an affidavit with supporting grounds for the motion. Because of the advent of online sales, publication in a newspaper is not as necessary as it once was. Therefore, the mere failure to publish a notice of sale is not a ground for canceling the sale, and does not impair the clerk's authority to issue a certificate of sale. *See HSBC Bank v. Nixon,* 117 So. 3d 430 (Fla. 4th DCA 2012). Any proposed order prepared to cancel the sale must also include a date to reschedule the sale or provide a blank space for a date to be filled in by the Court or Clerk.

3. *Credit Bids.* Only the judgment owner will be allowed to credit bid. An assignment of the judgment filed with the Clerk prior to the sale will effectively transfer with it the right to credit bid at the sale. Court approval of the assignment is not required.

4. *Certificate of Title.* The filing of a Certificate of Sale by the Clerk gives certain property rights to the highest bidder. In order to assign those rights and have the Certificate of Title issued to a third party, the highest bidder must file a written conveyance made in accordance with section 689.01 or section 692.01, Fla. Stat., governing real estate transfers. Such conveyance must be filed with the Clerk prior to the issuance of the Certificate of Title. Neither the Court nor the Clerk will change a Certificate of Title based upon a conveyance filed after the Certificate of Title has been issued.

E. Bankruptcy. If, prior to the commencement of a foreclosure sale, the Clerk receives a formal Suggestion of Bankruptcy on behalf of a named Defendant in that foreclosure case, the Clerk shall remove the foreclosure sale from the docket without Court order. The Court may order the sale to proceed based upon evidence that there is a valid bankruptcy court order lifting the stay or dismissing the bankruptcy case.

Any interested parties (including the Plaintiff, junior lienholders or third party purchaser) may seek a bankruptcy court order to show there was no valid stay, that the stay was lifted, or to seek other appropriate relief pursuant to 11 U.S.C section 362.

In the event a foreclosure sale proceeds and is later vacated due to a bankruptcy stay, when no formal Suggestion of Bankruptcy was filed in the foreclosure case, the Clerk shall not be required to refund mandatory court registry or sales fees. *See Wilken v. North County Company, Inc.,* 670 So. 2d 181 (Fla. 4th DCA 1976) (holding that a court could determine the party responsible for reimbursing forfeited sales and registry fees upon the invalidation of a foreclosure sale).

F. Clerk of the Circuit Court Responsibilities

1. *Retention of Documents.* All original mortgages and promissory notes in each mortgage foreclosure case are required to be surrendered to the Court, and the Clerk must retain such documents in the court file. The Clerk shall not return any of these instruments to a party absent specific order of the Court. Any other exhibits in the court file may not be released by the Clerk until ninety days after the judgment becomes final.

2. *Certificates of Title.* After the Clerk issues a Certificate of Sale, the Clerk may during the ten day objection period

following the sale, accept a written conveyance made by the highest bidder and issue the Certificate of Title in the name of the grantee provided the conveyance is made in accordance with section 689.01 or section 692.01, Fla. Stat., governing real estate transfers. The Clerk may not issue a Certificate of Title based upon any other attempt to transfer an interest by the winning bidder to another entity. The Clerk may not change a Certificate of Title based upon a conveyance filed after the Certificate of Title is issued.

III. SCHEDULING AND RELATED MATTERS

A. Residential Mortgage Foreclosure Cases. The Court may set the case for trial on its own motion in accordance with Rule of Civil Procedure 1.440.

B. Motions Decided on Written Submissions. There is no rule or law in Florida state or federal court that requires a trial judge to hear oral argument on a pretrial non-evidentiary motion. *See Gaspar, Inc., v. Naples Fed. Sav. & Loan Ass'n,* 546 So. 2d 764 (Fla. 5th DCA 1989). A party is afforded due process on such matters when given an opportunity to present a legal memorandum and then the Court may enter an order based upon submissions without a noticed hearing and oral argument of counsel. *See also Nudel v. Flagstar Bank,* 52 So. 3d 692 (Fla. 4th DCA 2010).

Therefore, all parties are hereby noticed that pretrial non-evidentiary motions may be subject to review and ruling by a judge based only upon the motion along with written argument and any authority timely filed in the action. Each party/counsel filing such a motion shall contemporaneously file with the Clerk and serve opposing party/counsel any additional legal argument the movant wants the Court to consider. The opposing party/counsel shall have ten days after being served to file their argument and legal memorandum with citations of authority in opposition to the relief requested. Following expiration the period allowed for these submissions the Court may at any time rule without further notice or hearing. Interested parties may notify the Court the matter is ripe for decision and request a ruling by letter which should include a simple form order for the judge to indicate whether the specific motion is either granted or denied, along with copies for conforming and stamped addressed envelopes for all parties.

Nothing in this section of the Administrative Order requires a judge to rule without oral argument. Individual judges may prefer hearings on certain pretrial non-evidentiary motions and counsel may consult the judges practice preferences on the website regarding such preferences.

The judicial practice preferences, scheduling information, and location of hearings may be found on the Court's website: www.jud6.org/LegalCommunity/PracticeRequirementsof Judges.html.

C. Commercial Mortgage Foreclosure Cases. Commercial mortgage foreclosure cases are to be scheduled on the assigned section judge's calendar. The judicial practice preferences of each judge, which may contain a judge's individualized procedures for mortgage foreclosure cases, may be found on the Court's website: www.jud6.org/LegalCommunity/PracticeRequirementsofJudges.html.

IV. PROCEDURES APPLICABLE TO WRITS OF POSSESSION

The following provisions apply to motions for a writ of possession arising from the mortgage foreclosure of any residential property.

A. Ex-Parte Writ of Possession—Occupied by Mortgagor

1. In any residential foreclosure case, the new owner/titleholder may, without scheduling a hearing, submit an application to the court for an order directing the clerk to issue a writ of Possession where the property is occupied by the mortgagor in the foreclosure case, or by the child, spouse, or parent of the mortgagor.

2. The titleholder must prepare an application for ex-parte writ of possession, based upon sworn affidavit that the property is occupied by the mortgagor in the foreclosure case, or by the child, spouse, or parent of the mortgagor. This application should be in a form substantially similar to **Form E—Ex-Parte Application and Order for Writ of Possession—Mortgagor** [5], which is Attachment E to this Administrative Order.

3. The original of this application, containing the form order, should be submitted to the assigned judge for review and ruling. If the judge finds the sworn facts support the request, then the order will be granted and filed with the Clerk who shall issue the Writ of Possession, commanding the Sheriff to remove all persons from the property. A copy of the order will be sent to the applicant only if an addressed envelope with postage is provided in the submissions.

B. Writ of Possession—Tenants

1. If the new titleholder does not plan on occupying the premises as a primary residence, a bona fide tenant may continue to occupy the unit until the end of the lease term.

2. If the new titleholder will occupy the premises as a primary residence, the titleholder must file **Form F—Notice to Tenant of Termination** [6], which is Attachment F to this Administrative Order. This notice must certify that the tenants have been provided notice as required by the Protecting Tenants at Foreclosure Act.

3. When a writ of possession is filed, the moving party must contact the judicial assistant for the section judge and set the motion for hearing on the uniform motion calendar, or such other time as may be directed, or the section judge may choose to rule on the motion without a hearing. If a hearing is set, notice of the hearing must be provided to all tenants by the moving party. At the hearing on the motion, the moving party must bring:

a. a copy of the Notice to Tenant of Termination;

b. a copy of the Final Judgment of Foreclosure; and

c. a copy of the Certificate of Title.

C. Motions Seeking a Writ of Possession Based on Other Facts. If the new owner/titleholder seeks a writ of possession but does not use the procedures detailed above, the Court will need to make an evidentiary determination that the occupant is not entitled to the protections of the Act, based on the exclusions under section 702, subsection (b) of the Act, or other facts. This requires the filing of a formal motion and the scheduling of an adversary hearing with notice to the occupant/tenant. At such hearing both sides may present evidence upon which the Court can rule. Prior to filing such a motion, the judicial assistant for judge of the section number on the case must be contacted to obtain a hearing time and date.

D. Issuance of Writ by Clerk. If a Final Judgment of Foreclosure authorizes the Clerk to issue a writ of possession without further action of the Court, the Clerk shall not do so unless the procedures established in this Administrative Order have been followed and the Court has specifically authorized the writ.

Administrative Order 2017–007 PA/PI–CIR is hereby rescinded. The Court may update the attachments to this Administrative Order without an amendment to this Administrative Order.

DONE AND ORDERED in Chambers at St. Petersburg, Pinellas County, Florida, this ___ day of January 2019.

ORIGINAL SIGNED ON JANUARY 23, 2019
BY ANTHONY RONDOLINO
CHIEF JUDGE

1 Attachment A. Form A - Plaintiff/Lender's Contact Information not included. For a current version of this form, please check: http://www.jud6.org/legalcommunity/AdministrativeOrders.html.

2 Attachment B. Form B - Important Notice to Homeowner not included. For a current version of this form, please check: http://www.jud6.org/legalcommunity/AdministrativeOrders.html.

3 Attachment C. Form C - Certificate of Compliance with Foreclosure Procedures not included. For a current version of this form, please check: http://www.jud6.org/legalcommunity/AdministrativeOrders.html.

4 Attachment D. Form D - Uniform Final Judgment of Foreclosure not included. For a current version of this form, please check: http://www.jud6.org/legalcommunity/AdministrativeOrders.html.

5 Attachment E. Form E - Ex-Parte Application and Order for Writ of Possession - Mortgagor not included. For a current version of this form, please check: http://www.jud6.org/legalcommunity/AdministrativeOrders.html.

6 Attachment F. Form F - Notice to Tenant of Termination not included. For a current version of this form, please check: http://www.jud6.org/legalcommunity/AdministrativeOrders.html.

2018–068. FISH AND WILDLIFE CONSERVATION COMMISSION VIOLATIONS

IN THE CIRCUIT COURT, SIXTH JUDICIAL CIRCUIT IN AND FOR PASCO AND PINELLAS COUNTIES, FLORIDA

ADMINISTRATIVE ORDER NO. 2018–068 PI–CTY

RE: LOCAL ORDINANCE VIOLATIONS AND FISH AND WILDLIFE CONSERVATION COMMISSION VIOLATIONS UNIFORM FINE SCHEDULE

In order to provide for the orderly and uniform prosecution of county and municipal ordinance violations in Pinellas County, Florida; to consolidate various administrative orders regarding ordinance violations; and in accordance with the provisions of sections 34.01, 125.69, 379.226, and 379.3311, Florida Statutes, Florida Rules of Criminal Procedure 3.125(j), and Florida Rules of Judicial Administration 2.215 and 2.265; it is

ORDERED:

1. Pinellas County and municipalities located within Pinellas County shall utilize the Pinellas County Ordinance Citation/Notice to Appear form that has been approved by the Chief Judge or his or her designee. The approved Citation/Notice to Appear shall be the official complaint instrument for prosecution of all county and municipal ordinance violations within the jurisdiction of Pinellas County, except for

a. An Indictment or Information

b. Parking Tickets

2. The Citation/Notice to Appear shall be coded and distributed to the Clerk of the Circuit Court, State Attorney, the issuing Agency, the County or Municipal Attorney and Defendant.

3. The Fish and Wildlife Conservation Commission shall issue citations on the required state forms issued to the agency.

4. With the exception of legislatively dictated fine amounts set by the legislative body of a municipality, the County, or the State, the Pinellas County Court Uniform Fine Schedule, including court costs, in Attachment A shall be the sole and exclusive schedule of penalties, including penalties for the uncontested disposition of local ordinance violations, and violations cited by the Fish and Wildlife Conservation Commission without the necessity of court appearance. The Court may authorize a greater or lesser penalty in any individual case.

5. Any person or entity cited for violation of the Fish and Wildlife Conservation Commission may:

a. Elect not to contest the citation. The defendant who elects not to contest the citation may pay the civil penalty, either by mail or phone, through the Clerk of Court website, or in person at the Clerk within thirty (30) calendar days of the date of receiving the citation; or if he or she has posted a bond, forfeit bond by not appearing at the designated time or location.

b. Elect to contest the citation. The defendant electing to contest the citation shall either (1) enter a written plea of not guilty in writing in person or by mail or fax within thirty (30) calendar days of the date of receiving the citation;; or (2) appear in Court for the purpose of entering a plea of not guilty and scheduling a trial on the merits of the alleged violation.

6. Any person or entity cited for violation of a local code or ordinance may:

a. Elect not to contest the citation. The defendant who elects not to contest the citation may plead guilty or no contest by signing the plea waiver form on the citation, and paying the applicable fine in full to the Clerk of Court by mail or phone or in person within thirty (30) calendar days after issuance of the citation, unless the violation requires a mandatory court appearance; or

b. Elect to contest the citation. The defendant electing to contest the citation shall either (1) enter a written plea of not guilty in person, by mail or fax, or through the Clerk of Court website within thirty (30) calendar days after issuance of the citation; or (2) appear in Court for the purpose of entering a plea of not guilty and scheduling a trial on the merits of the alleged violation.

7. If the defendant fails to follow the procedure outlined in paragraphs 5 and 6(a) for electing not to contest the citation, fails to enter a written plea of not guilty, and/or fails to appear for the court appearance date, the presiding judge shall, at the time of the court hearing, take any action that the court deems appropriate. The Court will address any notice issues. The Clerk may assess a fee for the issuance of a summons in accordance with section 28.24, Florida Statutes. The fee for issuance by the Clerk and the cost of service assessed by the Sheriff shall be added to the costs assessed to the defendant.

8. Pinellas County and each municipality therein:

a. May elect to establish by appropriate ordinance, resolution, or rule its own internal policies and procedures governing the issuance and processing of violation citations insofar as the same do not conflict with the provisions of this order; and

b. Shall authorize and designate an official prosecutor who shall be a member of The Florida Bar in good standing and file the name and signature of such person or persons with the Clerk of the Circuit Court for Pinellas County, who shall maintain a register for such purpose. The right to prosecute ordinance violations on behalf of Pinellas County or such various municipalities shall be limited to such official designated and registered prosecutor when the same is required. When the State Attorney's Office has contracted to provide prosecutorial services, any Assistant State Attorney designated by that office may prosecute local ordinance violations.

c. Pursuant to the provisions of Article V, sections 17 and 20 of the Florida Constitution and section 34.13, Florida Statutes, the registered prosecutor shall be responsible for the prosecution of local ordinance violations of the governmental entity that he or she represents from on and after the date upon which he or she has been notified that the case has been placed on the Court's calendar for disposition. The prosecutor shall respond to requests for discovery, summon necessary witnesses for trial, present the case before the Court and perform any other duties necessary for prosecution of the case.

9. The Clerk shall be responsible for calendaring all local ordinance violations. The Clerk shall:

a. Cause county ordinance violations, unless the violation is filed by the Pinellas County Sheriff's Office, to be placed on the Court's calendar for arraignment and trial on Wednesdays.

b. Cause municipal ordinance violations and county ordinance violations filed by the Pinellas County Sheriff's Office to be placed on the Court's calendar for arraignment and trial on Thursdays.

c. Provide notification of the trial date to the designated prosecutor.

10. All summons and notices of trial shall be issued not less than twenty-one (21) days prior to such trial date.

11. Pinellas County and the participating municipalities shall:

a. Reproduce and distribute in booklet form the Instructions for prosecuting Local Ordinance Violations and Uniform Fine Schedule for Pinellas County; and

b. Print the Citation.

12. The court costs and fines schedule in this Administrative Order are effective as of the date this Administrative Order. Attachments to this Administrative Order may be modified without further changes to this Administrative Order.

Administrative Orders 2007–024 and 2010–063 PI–CTY are hereby rescinded.

DONE AND ORDERED in Chambers at St. Petersburg, Pinellas County, Florida this ___ day of December, 2018.

ORIGINAL SIGNED ON DECEMBER 12, 2018
BY ANTHONY RONDOLINO,
CHIEF JUDGE

ATTACHMENT A

UNIFORM FINE SCHEDULE

Please note that the Roman numerals after each entry indicate the class (I–V) in which the violation falls for purposes of assessing the appropriate fine.

ADVERTISING & SIGNS:

HANDBILLS:

Unlawful distribution on private property (IV)

Unlawful distribution in a public place (IV)

Unlawful placing in or upon vehicles (IV)

SIGNS:

Erecting or maintaining a prohibited sign (III)

Erecting or maintaining unsafe signs (IV)

Erecting or maintaining misleading, false or fraudulent signs (IV)

Failure to procure required permit (IV)

AIRPORTS & AIRCRAFT:

Accidents on airport property; failure to report (IV)

Engines; operation during loading or unloading prohibited (II)

Engines; starting engines at prohibited times or places (III)

Flammable liquids; improper storage or protection (III)

Motor vehicles; parking and operation violations (IV)

Obstruction of gates or entrances prohibited (III)

Taxing operations; required and prohibited procedures (II)

ALCOHOLIC BEVERAGES:

Beer and wine; unlawful sale of (I)

Closing hours; doing business in violation (I)

Unlawful consumption on premises (I)

Minors; employment of, sale to, presence on premises prohibited (I)

Packaged liquor; unlawful sale of (I)

Sales near churches or schools prohibited (I)

Sales to habitual drunkards or intoxicated persons prohibited (I)

Nudity in commercial establishment serving alcoholic beverages (I)

Open container violation (IV)

AMBULANCES:

Operation without certificate of need (I)

Emergency and non-emergency failure to comply with rules and regulations (I)

AMUSEMENTS:

Circuses, carnivals, etc.; failure to obtain permits and post bonds (IV)

Failure to obtain required permits (IV)

Hours of operation; conducting business in excess of (IV)

ANIMAL CONTROL & FOWL:

Cruelty to animals and fowl prohibited (I)

Dangerous dog attacking an animal or person (I)

Failure to comply with dangerous dog requirements (II)

Dead animals; improper disposal of (IV)

Public nuisance (III)

Improper confinement of animal in estrus (III)

Interference with animal control officers prohibited (II)

Prohibited animals; unlawful keeping of (IV)

Rabies; improper handling of suspect animals (IV)

Rabies and quarantine violations prohibited (I)

Animal at large (IV)

Licensing violation (III)

Pet dealer violation (III)

Abandonment (II)

Animal left in unattended vehicle (II)

Unlawful tethering of an animal (III)

Neglect (III)

Guard Dog Violation (III)

Bite Incidents ($300.00 minimum fine as per Ord. No. 17–07 Sec. 14–39)

BICYCLES:

Brakes; failure to have minimum required brakes (V)

Carrying articles prohibited (V)

License plates; failure to display (V)

License plates; removing, changing or mutilating prohibited (IV)

Lights; failure to have required lights (V)

Parents' and guardians' responsibility; failure to exercise (IV)

Registration; failure to register bicycle (V)

Registration; unlawful change of (IV)

Sales of bicycles; failure to report (IV)

Serial numbers or identification numbers; offenses involving (IV)

Sidewalks; violation of riding restrictions (V)

BOATS, DOCKS, BEACHES & WATERWAYS:

BEACHES:

Anchoring so as to obstruct beaches and channels prohibited (IV)

Docking watercraft with living facilities; restrictions on (IV)

Glass prohibited on beaches (IV)Littering prohibited (V)

Watercraft; use of within bathing area prohibited (IV)

MARINAS & YACHT BASINS:

Equipment; improper keeping of (IV)

Nets; unlawful use of (IV)

Permit required for sale and soliciting sale of bait (IV)

Reckless operation of watercraft prohibited (II)

Signs on docks, ships and grounds; improper posting of (IV)

Spears or harpoons; unlawful use of (IV)

Trespass on docks or slips prohibited (IV)

Trespass on watercraft prohibited (IV)

SEAWALLS:

Failure to maintain and repair seawall and bulkheads (III)

Failure to comply with minimum standard requirements for the construction of seawalls and bulkheads (III)

WATERWAYS:

Abandoned vessels or watercraft prohibited (IV)

Bathing in boat channels prohibited (IV)

Blocking channels prohibited (II)

Bow riding prohibited (IV)

Careless operation of vessels prohibited (V)

Diving or jumping from bridges or piers prohibited (II)

Dredging operations, prohibited during certain hours (IV)

Fishing; unlawful use of prohibited tackle (V)

Gasoline; improper transportation of (IV)

Hazardous vessels or watercraft prohibited (II)

Piers; unlawful operation of watercraft around (III)

Pumping; unlawful pumping of bilges or disposal of petroleum products (III)

Safety equipment; failure to have proper equipment (V)

Searchlights, horns and whistles; improper use of (V)

Speeds; excessive speed by watercraft prohibited (V)

Swimming and throwing trash; unlawful (V)

Water-ski regulations; violations of (V)

Wharves; improper use of public wharves (IV)

Water and Navigator Control Authority Ordinance (I)

BUILDINGS:

Glass doors; decals or other marking required (IV)

Mailboxes required (IV)

MOVING BUILDINGS:

Designation of moving routes required (III)

Failure to obtain required permit (III)

Failure to satisfy safety requirements (III)

Hours of moving; violation (III)

License; occupational license required all movers (III)

Size of building which may be moved; exceeding maximum (III)

Time within which move is to be made; exceeding allowed time (III)

Numbering doors of non-residential structures required (IV)

Numbering houses required (IV)

POOLS:

Enclosure of swimming pools and fish ponds required (I)

Maintenance of pool equipment and water quality (II)

Prohibited use of property (III)

Salvaged materials; utilization of prohibited (IV)

Water preservation in connection with new developments required (IV)

BUILDING AND CONSTRUCTION SAFETY:

Failure to comply with the requirements for:

Standard Building Code (II)

Standard Plumbing Code (II)

Standard Mechanical Code (II)

Standard Gas Code (II)

National Electric Code (II)

Life Safety 101 (II)

Other local Codes pertaining to repair, construction, improvement, removal, maintenance, or demolition of buildings and property (II)

Failure to comply with any of the above when noncompliance is hazardous to the public (I)

BUSINESS REGULATIONS:

GENERAL:

Failure to obtain all necessary certificates, licenses and permits (II)

Fortune-telling for compensation and similar practices prohibited (III)

Grading and labeling of perishable meats required (III)

Impersonating the consumer division director or an inspector prohibited (III)

Labeling of packages; violations of regulations (III)

Landlords required to disclose profits made from furnishing utilities (III)

Misleading packaging prohibited (III)

Oil; furnace and stove oil to be sold by liquid measure only (III)

Scales for check weighing prepackaged commodities required (III)

Selling, offering for sale or keeping any commodity that has been ordered off sale, marked or tagged prohibited (III)

Operating without a retail tobacco products dealer permit (III)

ADVERTISING STANDARDS:

Advertising where additional purchases are required; violation of regulations (III)

Complete purchase price required to be represented (III)

Misrepresentation of merchandise, services and facilities prohibited (III)

Misrepresentation as to nature of commodity or service prohibited (III)

Misrepresentation of price prohibited (III)

Wholesale; unlawful use of the term (III)

AUCTIONS AND AUCTIONEERS:

Descriptive tags required to be affixed to articles (III)

False bidders and cappers prohibited (II)

False representations as to origin of goods prohibited (III)

Misrepresentation of used articles prohibited (II)

SALES:

Improper conducting of (III)

Prohibited at certain hours and on specified days (III)

Prohibited in public ways (III)

Substitution of articles prohibited (II)

BARBER SHOPS & BEAUTY PARLORS:

Failure to post inspections forms (III)

Reuse or common use of soap, cosmetics and related substances prohibited (III)

Violation of regulations pertaining to cleanliness (III)

CLOSING OUT SALES:

Goods sold required to have been on inventory; replenishment of stock prohibited (III)

Inventory required to be filed (III)

Record of articles sold; failure to file (III)

EMPLOYMENT AGENTS OR AGENCIES:

Accepting fees for specified positions already filled prohibited (II)

Applicants; sending out without bona fide order prohibited (III)

Fees; failure to file and post schedule of fees (III)

Registration fees; violation of restrictions (III)

Fraudulent advertisements prohibited (III)

Records; failure to properly maintain (III)

Refund of expenditures to applicants required (III)

Soliciting termination of employment relationships prohibited (III)

Splitting or sharing fees prohibited (III)

PAWNBROKERS, JUNK & SECONDHAND DEALERS:

Arrangement of stock to facilitate inspection required (III)

Dealing with minors prohibited (III)

Junkyards required to be enclosed (III)

Register of transactions; failure to furnish copies to police (II)

PROMOTERS:

Co-mingling of funds prohibited (I)

Employment of unqualified solicitors prohibited (III)

SOLICITORS:

Character; solicitor required to be of good moral character (III)

Notice of change of address or employment required (III)

Registration required (III)

MISCELLANEOUS OFFENSES NOT ENUMERATED UNDER BUSINESS REGULATION ABOVE: CLASS IV

CONSUMER PROTECTION:

ADULT USE

Unlicensed activity (II)

Unauthorized name change (II)

Failure to maintain required employee records (II)

Failure to provide records upon request (II)

Failure to display license (II)

Failure to update application within 15 days (II)

Operational requirements for establishments (II)

Adult theater requirements (II)

Special cabaret, adult photographic or modeling studios, and adult theaters requirements (II)

Prohibited operations (II)

Allowing employee to engage in prohibited acts (II)

Prohibited advertising (II)

Minors prohibited (II)

Working at unlicensed establishment (II)

Engaging in prohibited activity (II)

Touching of employee by patron (II)

Exceeding occupancy limit of adult booth (II)

Hours of operation (II)

Alteration of license (II)

False statement or false information in applying for license (II)

BINGO:

Unlicensed activity (II)

Failure to display license (II)

Failure to maintain required records (charitable organization) (II)

Failure to establish a separate bank account for bingo proceeds (charitable organization) (II)

Failure to establish a separate bank account for bingo proceeds (lessor) (II)

Failure to provide records upon request (II)

Failure to amend application within 30 days of change (II)

Conduct of bingo (II)

Failure to deposit proceeds within 24 hours (II)

Lease, sublease, assign or rent premises to conduct bingo without a license (II)

Interest by lessor in bingo prohibited (II)

Use of premises (II)

Admission of or participation by minors unlawful (II)

Tampering with notices, etc. (II)

False statements prohibited (II)

Unlawful reproduction or alteration of documents (II)

CHARITABLE SOLICITATIONS:

Failure to obtain the required permit (II)

False statement in connection with a solicitation (II)

Implying county endorsement (II)

Commingling of contributions (II)

Soliciting during pending suspension or revocation (II)

Transfer or assignment of permit (II)

Solicitation to a private residence between 9:00 p.m. and 8:00 a.m. (II)

Failure to possess and exhibit permit and authorization (II)

Concealing identity of organization (II)

Misrepresenting donations as tax deductible (II)

Failure to maintain required records (II)

Failure to surrender permit when required (II)

Failure to provide required records upon request (II)

Unauthorized representation of a charity (II)

Soliciting for individual without depository account (II)

Failure to honor timely request for refund (II)

Improper use of contributions (II)

Use of misleading name (II)

False representation by solicitor (II)

Withholding proceeds from sponsor (II)

Failure to display required information on contribution receptacle (II)

Fail to post human trafficking public awareness sign (II)

LIBRARY MATERIALS:

Overdue library materials (V)

Unreturned library materials (III)

MOVING ORDINANCE:

Failure to provide information required in estimate (II)

Failure to provide estimate (I)

Failure to provide information required in service contract (II)

Failure to provide service contract (I)

Charges in excess of written estimate (I)

Refusal to relinquish household goods (I)

Failure to provide written inventory (II)

Failure to disclose liability coverage (I)

PRESCRIPTION MANAGEMENT:

Operation of unlicensed high prescribing health clinic (I)

Unlawful operation of high prescribing health clinic (I)

Failure to update application within 10 days of any change (I)

TOWING:

Failure to meet prerequisites to towing (II)

Failure to charge correct fee when return of owner prior to tow (drop fee) (II)

Failure to allow consumer access to personal items (II)

Failure to charge proper fees / accept multiple forms of payment (II)

CONTRACTORS:

Advertising; unlawful advertising prohibited (II)

Certificates of competency required (II)

Insurance; contractors required to maintain liability insurance (II)

License; occupational license required (III)

License; display of occupational license required (III)

Signs of vehicles; standards and requirements (III)

Unlawful acts or omissions by contractors (II)

If hazardous to the public (I)

DRUGS & TOXIC SUBSTANCES:

Adulterated or misbranded drugs; sale of prohibited (I)

Advertising drugs; regulations and requirements (I)

Cannabis; possession of preparations containing cannabis prohibited (I)

Handling drugs under unsanitary conditions prohibited (I)

Prescriptions; failure to keep proper files and allow inspection (I)

Sales; unlawful sales of certain drugs and chemicals (I)

Sales; unlawful sales without prescriptions (I)

Use or sale of certain hazardous chemicals prohibited (I)

Withholding from sale articles believed to be in violation required (I)

ENVIRONMENTAL MANAGEMENT:

Burning; open burning prohibited (IV)

Smoke; emission of dense smoke prohibited (III)

Unlawful application of fertilizer (I)

Unlawful distribution (sale or display) of fertilizer (I)

Pollution or damage to air, water, soil, natural resources, or animal plant life (I)

Illicit discharge to the separate storm sewer system, right of way network, or receiving waters (I)

Illicit connection to the separate storm sewer system (I)

Failure to obtain necessary Best Management Practices training certificate, limited certification for urban landscape fertilizer application, or Pinellas County vehicle (II)

EXPLOSIVES AND INFLAMMABLES:

Location; gasoline delivery devices not to be on sidewalks (II)

Storage: installation requirements for aboveground storage tanks (II)

Permit required for bulk storage (II)

Permit required for the storage of explosives (II)

Type, construction and design of storage tanks (II)

FIRE PREVENTION:

Alarms; false alarm reports prohibited (II)

Certificate of occupancy required (II)

Code; violations of Fire Prevention Code prohibited (II)

Heaters; portable oil heaters prohibited (II)

Interference with members of the fire department prohibited (II)

Orders; refusing to obey orders of fire officers (II)

Smoking or carrying of lighted objects in specified places prohibited (II)

FOOD & FOOD HANDLERS:

GENERAL:

Failure to obtain all necessary certificates, licenses and permits (I)

Failure to withhold from sale food believed to be in violation of food regulations (I)

Handling of food under unsanitary conditions prohibited (I)

Ice; sale or distribution when unfit for human consumption prohibited (I)

Impersonating an officer of the health department prohibited (I)

Sale, manufacturing or possessing adulterated or misbranded food prohibited (I)

Sale of meats to which sulphurous acid has been added prohibited (I)

Cleanliness; machinery and fixtures required to be kept clean (I)

Garbage and waste; required to be kept in containers (I)

Peddling of fruits, vegetables, meats and fish; proper protection of food when conveyed through streets required (I)

Refrigeration; sufficient working facilities required; regulations (I)

Re-service of food prohibited (I)

Ventilation; proper ventilation required for all ranges, stoves and ovens (I)

PREMISES:

Construction, maintenance and cleanliness regulation regarding walls, ceilings and floors; violation of regulation (I)

Grease traps and interceptors required and must be properly maintained (I)

Toilet and lavatory facilities, regulations and requirements; violation of (I)

Ventilation, lighting and cleanliness regulations and requirements; violation of (I)

Vermin; premises required to be protected against vermin (I)

Water; ample hot and cold running water required (I)

Failure to submit grease trap and interceptor cleaning or pumping reports (I)

GARBAGE AND REFUSE:

GENERAL:

Burning of garbage or rubbish; incinerators; regulations and requirements (IV)

Permits required for garbage or rubbish burial (IV)

Unlawful accumulations of garbage, refuse, rubbish, junk, debris, or similar noxious material (I)

Unlawful disposal of garbage, refuse or rubbish prohibited (III)

COLLECTORS (PRIVATE):

Area between property lines and curbs to remain clean (IV)

Departures from allowed methods of making collections and routes to travel prohibited (IV)

Insurance; private collectors required to obtain liability insurance (IV)

Permits; failure to obtain required permits (IV)

Time of container placement; violation of (IV)

CONTAINERS:

Adequate containers required; violations of approved specifications (III)

Covers; containers required to be kept tightly covered (IV)

Locations of containers; violation of regulations (IV)

Underground installations prohibited (IV)

Garbage and other refuse required to be stored in containers (III)

HEALTH & SANITATION:

Burials; other than in authorized cemetery prohibited (II)

Mosquitoes; permitting premises to become a breeding place prohibited (II)

RATS:

Affording food or harborage for rats prohibited (II)

Buildings required to be freed of rat harborage (II)

Poultry and stock feed required to be kept in rat proof containers or in rat proof buildings (II)

Removal rat proofing prohibited (II)

HOUSING:

GENERAL:

Abatement of substandard or unsafe buildings required (I)

Placarding dangerous building against habitation required; removal of placards prohibited (I)

Violations of restrictions on furnishing utilities services to substandard dwellings (I)

Improper outdoor storage (I)

MINIMUM STANDARDS:

Failure to meet minimum standard requirements for:

Air and water heating (II)

Cleanliness of dwelling units (III)

Cleanliness of plumbing fixtures (III)

Cleanliness of public area of multiple dwellings (III)

Electric service (I)

Gas service (I)

Light and ventilation (II)

Maintenance (III)

Plumbing systems and equipment (I)

Space, use and location (III)

HOTELS, MOTELS & ROOMING HOUSES:

Failure to meet minimum standard requirements for:

Egress (III)

Light and ventilation (III)

Space, use and occupancy (III)

Toilet and bathing facilities (III)

JUVENILES:

Curfew violations (III)

LAND DEVELOPMENT REGULATIONS:

Drainage regulations violation (I)

Flood damage prevention regulations violation (I)

Floodplain management regulations violation (I)

Site plan regulation; failure to obtain a permit (I)

Site plan regulation; failure to comply with a site plan permit (I)

Stormwater regulations violation (I)

Subdivision regulations violation (I)

Wellfield protection regulations violation (I)

MOBILE HOMES:

Failure to meet minimum standard requirements for:

Air and water heating (II)

Cleanliness of premises (IV)

Construction and maintenance (IV)

Electrical installations (I)

Garbage disposal facilities (IV)

Gas service (I)

Light and ventilation (II)

Plumbing fixtures (I)

Toilet and bathing facilities (III)

Screens required on windows and doors (IV)

MOBILE HOMES & MOBILE HOME PARKS:

Diagram or plat of mobile home park required (IV)

Health and sanitation; minimum requirements must be satisfied (II)

Mobile homes; anchoring and securing of mobile homes required (I)

Mobile homes; blocking of mobile homes required (II)

Location; mobile homes used for dwelling purposes to be located only in mobile home parks (IV)

Parked or stored mobile homes or travel trailers to comply with setback requirements (IV)

Permit required for anchoring and blocking of mobile homes (II)

Permit required for mobile home park operation (IV)

Registration of changes in mobile home park management required (IV)

Registration of mobile home park occupants and keeping of proper records required (IV)

NOISE:

Noise violations (I)

PARKS, RECREATION AND PRESERVES:

Littering prohibited (V)

Performing prohibited acts in parks and preserves (IV)

Performing acts which require special permission without first obtaining such permission (IV)

RAILROADS:

Obstruction of public ways prohibited (I)

Unlawful speed prohibited (I)

SEWERS & SEWAGE DISPOSAL:

Connection to sanitary sewer and abandonment of private sewage disposal facilities required (I)

DISCHARGE:

Harmful, dangerous or nuisance wastes to sewer system prohibited (I)

Untreated sewage or polluted waters to surface or groundwater, or in unsanitary manner prohibited (I)

Unauthorized discharge of waste or septic tank waste to sewer system prohibited (I)

Routing of surface runoff sources or groundwater to sewer system prohibited (I)

PERMITS AND INSPECTIONS:

Permits prior to connection or alteration to sewer system required (I)

Industrial user permit, pretreatment, payment of industrial surcharge, and/or industrial sampling points required (I)

Periodic reports from all federal categorical industrial users required (III)

Inspection before construction or alteration of facilities required (III)

Access for Sewer Department/DER/EPA to property authorized (II)

Septic tanks abandoned and declared hazardous to be rendered inoperative (II)

SHERIFF:

Discharge of Firearms within Pinellas County (I)

SOLID WASTE:

Flow control ordinance violation (I)

Removal of recyclable material from collection centers (III)

Solid waste disposal facility ordinance violation (I)

Unacceptable disposal and removal of hypodermic needles and/or syringes (I)

Unlawful disposal (I)

STREETS & SIDEWALKS:

Debris; leaving building construction debris in public ways prohibited (III)

Illumination; objects in streets required to be illuminated (III)

Mailboxes; maintenance of mailboxes in rights-of-way prohibited (III)

Obstruction of public ways or buildings prohibited (III)

Permit required for building, repairing or removing structures in or on street (III)

Permit required for doing business on streets or sidewalks (III)

Permit required for changing surface area of street (III)

Roadway solicitation ordinance violations (III)

Violations of standards, regulations and requirements pertaining to curbs, sidewalks and public benches (IV)

PARADES:

Parking on parade routes; regulation of required (III)

Permit required for parades (III)

Possession of parade permit required (III)

Public conduct during parades; regulation of (III)

TOURIST DEVELOPMENT:

Tourist development tax ordinance violations (I)

UNLAWFUL VEHICLES:

Inoperative vehicles (III)

Prohibited vehicles (III)

UTILITIES:

Access to premises supplied with water required (IV)

Connections to city water system; violation of regulations (III)

Lines; overhead utility lines within the rights-of-way of interstate highway and other freeways prohibited (IV)

Metering of city gas required (IV)

Meter required prior to connection with city water (IV)

Meter; use of city water without a meter prohibited (III)

Meter; devices preventing the full metering of water prohibited (III)

Sprinkling with city water during daylight hours prohibited under certain circumstances (II)

VEGETATION:

Adhering to upland buffer requirements (I)

Adhering to upland preservation area requirements (I)

Untended growth or excessive accumulation of weeds or other plant material (I)

Failure to remove trees or branches in danger of falling upon a public way or property of another (IV)

Maintaining trees and shrubs in utility easements prohibited (IV)

Maintaining minimum landscape requirements (I)

Minimum height of branches overhanging public ways; failure to comply (IV)

TREES:

Protection of trees during construction activities required (I)

Protection of trees while filling land required (I)

Removal of trees without a permit prohibited (I)

VEHICLES FOR HIRE:

Appearance of taxicabs; required information, color scheme and signs (III)

Failure to obtain and display all required certificates, badges, emblems, permits and licenses (III)

Meters required on all taxicabs (III)

Rates; posting of rates required (III)

Rates; charges to be in accordance with posted tariffs (II)

MISCELLANEOUS ORDINANCE, MARINE PATROL, FISH AND WILDLIFE CONSERVATION COMMISSION, AND NATURAL RESOURCES VIOLATIONS:

All zoning violations not herein specifically provided shall be deemed to be Class III offenses.

All other violations not herein specifically provided shall be deemed to be Class V offenses except that failure to comply with licensure and permit requirements in section 379.354, Florida Statutes, shall be assessed a $50 fine pursuant to section 379.401, Florida Statutes.

Fines may be doubled for a second offense and for each subsequent offense thereafter.

PINELLAS COUNTY UNIFORM FINE SCHEDULE LOCAL COUNTY/CITY ORDINANCE VIOLATIONS

CONTESTED

	FINE	COSTS *	TOTAL
CLASS I	$205.00	$58.00	$263.00
CLASS II	$180.00	$58.00	$238.00
CLASS III	$130.00	$58.00	$188.00
CLASS IV	$105.00	$58.00	$163.00
CLASS V	$ 80.00	$58.00	$138.00

UNCONTESTED

	FINE	COSTS *	TOTAL
CLASS I	$205.00	$13.00	$218.00
CLASS II	$180.00	$13.00	$193.00
CLASS III	$130.00	$13.00	$143.00
CLASS IV	$105.00	$13.00	$118.00
CLASS V	$ 80.00	$13.00	$ 93.00

* COSTS INCLUDE:

$3.00 ADDITIONAL COURT COST CLEARING TRUST FUND, § 938.01, Fla. Stat. (Not assessed in uncontested cases.)

$2.00 CRIMINAL JUSTICE EDUCATION FOR LOCAL GOVERNMENT, § 938.15, Fla. Stat. (Costs shall not be assessed if no court appearance or for cases where adjudication of guilt is withheld.)

$40.00 COST RECOVERY, § 34.045 (1)(b), Fla. Stat. (Assessed against the non-prevailing party when contested.)10.00 FILING FEE RECOVERY, § 34.045 (1)(c), Fla. Stat.

$3.00 TEEN COURT, § 938.19, Fla. Stat. (Section 46–34 Pinellas County Code)

ORDINANCE VIOLATIONS WITH CORRESPONDING FLORIDA STATUTE WRITTEN BY: MARINE PATROL, FISH AND WILDLIFE CONSERVATION COMMISSION AND DEPARTMENT OF ENVIRONMENTAL PROTECTION

	FINE	COSTS **	TOTAL
CLASS I	$200.00	$273.00	$473.00
CLASS II	$175.00	$271.75	$446.75
CLASS III	$125.00	$269.25	$394.25
CLASS IV	$100.00	$268.00	$368.00
CLASS V	$ 75.00	$266.75	$341.75
Licensure and permit violations	$ 50.00	$265.50	$315.50

** COSTS INCLUDE:

$3.00 ADDITIONAL COURT COSTS CLEARING TRUST FUND, § 938.01, Fla. Stat.

$2.00 CRIMINAL JUSTICE EDUCATION FOR LOCAL GOVERNMENT, § 938.15, Fla. Stat. (Costs shall not be assessed if no court appearance or for cases where adjudication of guilt is withheld.)

$50.00 CRIMES COMPENSATION TRUST FUND, § 938.03(1), Fla. Stat.

5% OF FINE SURCHARGE, § 938.04, Fla. Stat.

$60 FINE AND FORFEITURE, § 938.05, Fla. Stat.

$20 CRIME PREVENTION, § 775.083(2), Fla. Stat. (Costs not assessed for cases when adjudication of guilt is withheld).

$20 CRIME STOPPERS, § 938.06, Fla. Stat.

$65 COURT AND JUVENILE PROGRAMS, § 939.185, Fla. Stat.

$40 COST RECOVERY, § 34.045 (1)(b), Fla. Stat.

$10.00 FILING FEE RECOVERY, § 34.045 (1)(c) Fla. Stat.

$3.00 TEEN COURT, § 938.19, Fla. Stat. (Section 46–34 Pinellas County Code)

EXCEPTION: VIOLATIONS OF CHAPTERS 327 OR 328 ARE CLASSIFIED AS NON–CRIMINAL, NON–MOVING OR MOVING VIOLATIONS PAYABLE WITH A CIVIL PENALTY PLUS COSTS.VIOLATIONS OF CHAPTER 379 ARE CLASSIFIED AS LEVEL ONE NON–CRIMINAL VIOLATIONS PAYABLE WITH A CIVIL PENALTY PLUS COSTS. LEVEL TWO VIOLATIONS ARE CLASSIFIED AS MISDEMEANORS.

IN CASES WHERE THE ISSUANCE OF A SUMMONS IS REQUIRED, ADDITIONAL COSTS FOR THE SUMMONS AND SERVICE OF THE SUMMONS SHALL ALSO BE ASSESSED.

ATTACHMENT B

INSTRUCTIONS FOR PROSECUTING LOCAL ORDINANCE VIOLATIONS IN PINELLAS COUNTY

CITATION/NOTICE TO APPEAR

Although the Citation/Notice to Appear serves many purposes, these instructions address only the usage of the form for non-criminal violations. These include ordinance violations and misdemeanors where there is no arrest and the Notice to Appear section is used to cite the civil penalty owed or notify the alleged offender of a required court date and time.

BEFORE BEGINNING PROSECUTION:

Once a Citation/Notice to Appear is issued, it may not be dismissed simply because the cited party complies with the applicable ordinance or corrects a violation. Therefore, if you would be satisfied with compliance or correction, use all proper means short of issuance of a Citation/Notice to Appear to accomplish your purpose.

COMPLETING THE CITATION/NOTICE TO APPEAR:

Fill in every blank on the form. If a blank is not applicable to the particular charge, type "N/A" in the blank. The form may be completed by hand or electronically. The form, and any copies required, may be printed on any medium, including but not limited to NCR paper or thermal paper.

An officer issuing a Citation/Notice to Appear shall inform the defendant that he or she may plead guilty or no contest by signing the plea and waiver on the back of his or her copy of the Citation/Notice to Appear and forwarding it to the Clerk of the Circuit Court at the address indicated, with a check or money order in the amount of the fine. Otherwise, he or she must either file a written plea of not guilty in person or by mail or appear in court on the day and time specified. If a defendant is charged with a violation that requires a mandatory court appearance, the officer shall explain that the defendant *must* appear in court on the day and time specified.

In the event the defendant refuses to accept a copy of the Citation/Notice to Appear or to acknowledge it by signing where defendant's signature is specified, the issuing officer shall note such occurrence on the face of the Citation/Notice to Appear and leave the defendant's copy in his/her presence or post it in a conspicuous location on the premises. The issuing officer shall also note on the face that a copy of the Citation/Notice to Appear was left with the defendant.

When the issuing officer returns an unsigned Citation/Notice to Appear to the appropriate agency, the officer shall sign a certification that he or she left a copy with the defendant or conspicuously posted it. Leaving/posting the Citation/Notice to Appear constitutes sufficient notice to a defendant and the defendant is required to comply. Failure to comply will result in the issuance of a summons.

FILING THE CITATION/NOTICE TO APPEAR:

Within 48 hours after a copy of the Citation/Notice to Appear is given to the defendant, copies of the Notice to Appear for the Clerk and the State Attorney must be sent to the Clerk of the Circuit Court, Criminal Court Records, 14250 49th St. N., Clearwater, FL 33762. In the discretion of the Clerk of the Circuit Court and as technology permits, such copies may be submitted to the Clerk electronically.

If the citation has not been issued by a police officer, the County or Municipal Prosecutor may decline to endorse it. In such a situation, he or she must void the original Citation/Notice to Appear; and if a copy of the Citation/Notice to Appear has been provided to the defendant, the Clerk of the Circuit Court must be advised that the charge has been voided. This can be accomplished by forwarding a copy of the voided Citation/Notice to Appear to the Clerk.

Note, however, that if the citation has been issued by a police officer, then it may not be voided by the County or Municipal Prosecutor but is instead forwarded to the State Attorney for prosecution.

It is recommended that the issuing officer's department and the authorized prosecutor keep an electronic copy of the Citation/Notice to Appear.

PROSECUTING WHERE CITATION/NOTICE TO APPEAR HAS NOT BEEN ISSUED BY A POLICE OFFICER:

When the Clerk's office receives a Citation/Notice to Appear, the Clerk assigns a case number. If it is not voided by the County or Municipal Prosecutor, the Clerk then calendars the case for appearance on the date listed on the Notice. If the defendant has not paid the fine prior to the hearing date and does not appear in Court or enter a written plea of not guilty, the Court shall enter a default judgment against the defendant. The Court will at that time address any notice issues. The Clerk may assess a fee for the issuance of a summons in accordance with section 28.24, Florida Statutes. The fee for issuance by the Clerk and the cost of service assessed by the Sheriff shall be added to the costs assessed to the defendant.

The County or Municipal Prosecutor is responsible for adequately preparing any case that is set for trial, including issuing witness subpoenas and responding to all demands for discovery.

All pre-trial motions shall be heard on the day of trial unless the defendant and the Prosecutor stipulate to the contrary.

Pursuant to Fla. R. Crim. P. 3.111, this Administrative Order shall serve as a written order of no incarceration for all cases governed by it. However, if the Prosecutor requests incarceration as a possible penalty and the court grants this request, such grant must be stated in the record and the court must appoint counsel for the defendant.

Each city or other governmental unit must advise the Clerk's office in Criminal Court Records of the name of its current authorized prosecutor or prosecutors.

FISH AND WILDLIFE CONSERVATION COMMISSION CASES:

All minor violations Class (V)

The Florida Fish and Wildlife Conservation Commission will issue citations on the required state form issued to the agency. Upon issuance, the form must be completed and defendant's signature must be obtained. In addition, the Instructions to Violator Form (sample below) must be completed and a copy attached to the citation given to the defendant if the information is not available on the reverse side of the defendant's copy. The original is to be forwarded to the Clerk of Court, Criminal Court Records. Insert amount of fine (See approved Uniform Fine Schedule) on the Instructions to Violator Form and on upper right corner of Court copy of citation.

Any person cited for a violation by the Florida Fish and Wildlife Conservation Commission may elect to enter a written plea of guilty or no contest and pay a civil penalty, to satisfy a Class V offense without the necessity of a court appearance.

SAMPLE INSTRUCTIONS TO VIOLATOR FORM—FISH AND WILDLIFE

____

VIOLATOR'S NAME DATE

INSTRUCTIONS TO VIOLATOR
YOU MUST, WITHIN THIRTY (30) CALENDAR DAYS OF TODAY'S DATE, DO ONE OF THE FOLLOWING:

1. If you desire to plead guilty or no contest and not appear in Court, you must pay a fine of $ _______ including court costs, either in person or by mail at the address listed below. If you pay the fine you will be deemed to have admitted the civil infraction and you will be adjudicated guilty of the violation. If you desire to pay the fine by mail, you must sign the Plea & Waiver below and enclose it with your citation and payment. Checks or money orders are to be made payable to Clerk of Circuit Court.

Pinellas County Justice Center
Criminal Court Records
14250 49th St. N.
Clearwater, FL 33762

2. If you wish to plead not guilty and appear in court, you must enter a written plea of not guilty either in person or by mail at the Pinellas County Justice Center, Criminal Court Records, 2nd floor, 14250 49th St. N., Clearwater, FL 33762. Forms for Not Guilty Pleas may be obtained there. **FAILURE TO PAY THE FINE IN THE AMOUNT STATED ABOVE WITHIN THIRTY (30) CALENDAR DAYS OR FAILURE TO APPEAR FOR COURT MAY RESULT IN A WARRANT BEING ISSUED FOR YOUR ARREST. ADDITIONAL COSTS MAY ALSO BE ASSESSED.**

3. Violations of law under the jurisdiction of the Fish and Wildlife Conservation Commission may be considered misdemeanors. All convictions will be on record.

I HEREBY CERTIFY that I received a copy of these instructions on the above listed date.

____

VIOLATOR/DEFENDANT'S SIGNATURE

PLEA & WAIVER

I understand the nature of the charge against me; I understand I am waiving my rights to be represented by an attorney, to request a continuance of my hearing and my right to a trial before a judge or a jury.

I plead ______ Guilty ______ No Contest

Defendant ____________________

Date ____________________

Address ____________________

2018–047. ALTERNATIVE SANCTIONS PROGRAM

IN THE CIRCUIT COURT, SIXTH JUDICIAL CIRCUIT IN AND FOR PASCO AND PINELLAS COUNTIES, FLORIDA

ADMINISTRATIVE ORDER NO. 2018–047 PA/PI–CIR

Administrative Order 2016–057 PA/PI–CIR established an Alternative Sanctions Program ("ASP") in Pinellas and Pasco Counties through collaboration between the Sixth Judicial Circuit ("the Court") and the Florida Department of Corrections ("DOC"). To update the criteria for participation in the program, the Administrative Order must be updated.

In accordance with Article V, section 2, Florida Constitution, Rule of Judicial Administration 2.215, and section 43.26, Florida Statutes, it is

ORDERED:

1. The purpose of the ASP is to reduce recidivism and the significant resources expended to prosecute technical violations of probation by creating an administrative option for processing these violations that provides for immediate and court-approved sanctions.

2. Participation in the ASP is limited to offenders who:

a. were sentenced to felony probation in Pasco or Pinellas County;

b. have stable ties to the community;

c. have committed a qualifying technical violation as outlined in the Alternative Sanction Program Violations/Sanction Matrix, which is Attachment A [1] to this Administrative Order; and

d. is not an offender described in paragraph 3 of this Administrative Order.

3. An offender may not participate in the ASP if, in his or her underlying case, the offender:

a. was designated a career offender;

b. was designated a sexual offender or sexual predator;

c. committed any new law violations of probation;

d. is an absconder; or

e. violated a "no contact" condition of supervision.

4. DOC will identify offenders eligible for the ASP through their Correctional Probation Officers ("Probation Officer"). The Probation Officer will inform these offenders of their eligibility.

5. Participating in the ASP is voluntary. An offender must decide whether or not to participate in the ASP prior to the filing of an affidavit of violation of probation. For eligible offenders who decline to participate in the ASP, the affidavit of violation of probation will be filed with the Clerk of the Circuit Court and they will proceed to formal violation of probation proceedings in Circuit Court. For eligible offenders who elect to participate in the ASP, the Technical Violation Notification form, which is part of Attachment B [2] to this Administrative Order, must be completed by the Probation Officer and submitted to the Court. The Probation Officer must use the matrix in Attachment A when completing the Technical Violation Notification form.

6. For any offender who decides to participate in the ASP, the Probation Officer and the offender must complete the "Alternative Sanctions Program Waiver of Formal VOP Hearing, Admission of Violation, and Acceptance of Sanctions" form, which is part of Attachment B to this Administrative Order, and submit it to the Court. By agreeing to proceed in the ASP, the offender waives the right to an evidentiary hearing on the violation of probation, including any determination that the violation was willful and substantial. If the offender chooses to participate in the ASP, the offender must admit the violation, accept the administrative sanction(s) recommended by the Probation Officer, and waive his/her right to a formal violation of probation proceeding in Circuit Court. The offender also must waive his/her right to appeal the sanction(s) imposed under the ASP unless the sanction(s) is/are illegal under State or Federal law.

7. Whether the ASP program is appropriate for a certain technical violation or an eligible offender is within the Court's discretion. While the Probation Officer makes the initial determination of eligibility, judicial approval is required to participate in the ASP. In addition, the sanction(s) selected by the Probation Officer is/are within the Court's discretion. Thus, the judge shall review the Notification and Waiver Form (Attachment B) and, if the judge agrees that the ASP is appropriate for the technical violation and the eligible offender and that the sanction(s) is/are appropriate, the judge will so indicate on an order in the format of the Order on Alternative Sanctions Program form, which is Attachment C [3] to this Administrative Order. If the judge does not agree that the ASP program or the sanction(s) recommended by the Probation Officer is/are appropriate, the judge will so indicate on the order.

8. Upon Court approval, the Probation Officer will instruct the offender on the sanction(s) imposed by the Court and instruct the offender to take actions necessary to ensure the sanction(s) is/are executed immediately. If the offender fails to complete the imposed sanction(s), the Probation Officer must submit a violation report, affidavit, and warrant to the Court.

9. DOC will administer the ASP including compiling statistics, maintaining the necessary documents to demonstrate compliance with any funding requirements, and performing other case management functions as the Court requires.

10. Attachments to this Administrative Order may be modified without further changes to this Administrative Order.

Administrative Order 2016–058 PI–CIR is hereby rescinded.

DONE AND ORDERED in Chambers, at St. Petersburg, Pinellas County, Florida this ___ day of September, 2018.

ORIGINAL SIGNED ON SEPTEMBER 7, 2018
BY ANTHONY RONDOLINO,
CHIEF JUDGE

1 Attachment A not included
2 Attachment B not included
3 Attachment C not included

2018–042. COURT REPORTING PLAN AND ELECTRONIC RECORDINGS OF COURT PROCEEDINGS

IN THE CIRCUIT COURT, SIXTH JUDICIAL CIRCUIT IN AND FOR PASCO AND PINELLAS COUNTIES, FLORIDA

ADMINISTRATIVE ORDER NO. 2018–042 PA/PI–CIR

RE: COURT REPORTING PLAN AND ELECTRONIC RECORDINGS OF COURT PROCEEDINGS

It is necessary to amend the Circuit's court reporting plan based on changes in Court procedure.

Pursuant to the authority of the Chief Judge in Article V, section 2, Florida Constitution, Rule of Judicial Administration 2.215 and 2.535 and sections 29.0195 and 43.26, Florida Statutes, it is

ORDERED:

A. Fundamentals of Court Reporting Plan.

1. *Scope.* The court reporting plan set forth in this Administrative Order delineates procedures to be followed for various proceedings on a circuit-wide basis. In any proceeding in which the type of court reporting equipment or services specified in this Administrative Order are not available, the Administrative Office of the Courts (AOC) may utilize any court-employed court reporter or court equipment, or services with which it has contracted, without further order of the Court except in capital cases. Under emergency or any other exigent circumstances in which contracted services, personnel, or equipment are not available, the AOC may utilize whatever other means of reporting is available under the circumstances, but must notify the Chief Judge of the exigency as soon as possible.

2. *Definitions.* The term "approved court reporter" means a court employee or Sixth Judicial Circuit contractor who performs court reporting services, including transcription, at public expense and who meets the court's certification, training, and other qualifications for court reporting.

The term "approved transcriptionist" means a court employee, Sixth Judicial Circuit contractor, or other individual who performs transcription services for the Sixth Judicial Circuit at public expense and who meets the court's certification, training, and other qualifications for transcribing proceedings.

The term "civil court reporter" means a stenographic court reporter who performs court reporting services in civil proceedings not required to be reported at public expense.

The term "court-employed stenographic court reporter" means an "approved court reporter" who is employed by the court and who meets the court's qualifications to perform stenographic court reporting.

The term "court-employed digital court reporter" means an "approved court reporter" who is employed by the court and who meets the court's qualifications to monitor or transcribe electronic recordings.

The terms "electronic record" or "electronic recording" means the audio, analog, digital, or video record of a court proceeding made using electronic equipment owned or operated by the Sixth Judicial Circuit.

3. *The Record.* For all proceedings in which the Court is required to provide a record, the "official record" is the transcript, which is the written record of court proceedings as produced by an approved court reporter and filed with the Clerk of the Circuit Court. For all other court proceedings, the "official record" is the transcript, which is the written record of court proceedings as produced by a civil court reporter and filed with the Clerk of the Circuit Court. The "official record" does not include CDs, DVDs, tapes, or any other electronic record of a court proceeding nor does it include any transcript of a court proceeding produced by a party or other entity not authorized by this Administrative Order.

Only one "official record" of a court proceeding may be produced. A transcript of a court proceeding that is not produced by an approved court reporter or a civil court reporter is not an official record and may not be used in court proceedings.

4. *Ownership.* The Chief Judge in his or her official capacity is the owner of all records of a court proceeding made by an approved court reporter or quasi-judicial officer. This includes records in paper and electronic format. The Chief Judge retains the right to full and complete access to any unedited notes, paper tapes, electronic files, and recordings used to create an "official record" of a court proceeding.

5. *Officers of the Court.* All approved court reporters, civil court reporters, and approved transcriptionists are officers of the court for all purposes while acting as court reporters in judicial proceedings, or discovery proceedings, or as transcriptionists.

B. Court Reporting Procedures by Court Division.

1. *Circuit Court*

a. Appellate Division. The Court does not provide any court reporting services in Appellate Division matters. However, parties wishing to record oral argument in Appellate Division proceedings may use any civil court reporter in accordance with Section E of this Administrative Order.

b. Civil Division. Parties in Civil Division proceedings where the Court is not required to provide a record may use any civil court reporter in accordance with Section E of this Administrative Order. A court-employed stenographic court reporter shall report all trials in which the Court is required to provide a record, including but not limited to trials under section 394.910 et seq., Florida Statutes. If sufficient court-employed stenographic court reporters are not available, such trials may be reported by any other approved court reporter.

All other Civil Division proceedings in which the Court is required to provide a record, including but not limited to those under section 394.910 et seq., Florida Statutes, shall be reported by an approved court reporter.

c. Criminal Division. Court-employed stenographic court reporters shall report capital proceedings in accordance with Section F of this Administrative Order, and first- and second-degree felony trials. If the Pinellas Criminal Administrative Judge or the Pasco Administrative Judge determines that sufficient court-employed stenographic court reporters are not available to report first- or second-degree felony trials, any other approved court reporter may report such trials. Court-employed digital court reporters shall report all other Criminal Division proceedings. Unless required by law, this paragraph does not apply to depositions.

d. Probate Division. Parties in Probate Division proceedings where the Court is not required to provide a record may use any civil court reporter in accordance with Section E of this Administrative Order. An approved court reporter shall report all proceedings in which the Court is required to provide a record, including but not limited to proceedings pursuant to Chapter 744, Florida Statutes, regarding (1) adjudication of incapacity; (2) appointment of a guardian; (3) modification, termination, or revocation of the adjudication of incapacity; or (4) restoration of capacity, and proceedings pursuant to Chapter 825, Florida Statutes, regarding exploitation of vulnerable adults.

e. Family Division. Parties in proceedings governed by the Florida Family Law Rules of Procedure where the Court is not required to provide a record may use any civil court reporter in accordance with Section E of this Administrative Order. An approved court reporter shall report all proceedings in which the Court is required to provide a record, including but not limited to domestic violence proceedings under section 741.30, Florida Statutes; as well as all dating, sexual, repeat violence, and stalking injunction proceedings under Chapter 784, Florida Statutes.

Court-employed digital court reporters shall report all proceedings under the Florida Rules of Juvenile Procedure, including trials, except that Court-employed stenographic court reporters shall report termination of parental rights trials pursuant to Chapter 39, Florida Statutes, and proceedings to waive parental notification of abortion pursuant to section 390.01114, Florida Statutes. If sufficient court-employed stenographic court reporters are not available, such proceedings shall be reported by any other approved court reporter.

2. *County Court*

a. Civil Division. The Court provides no court reporting services for proceedings in the Civil Division. However, the parties may use any civil court reporter in accordance with Section E of this Administrative Order.

b. Criminal Division. Court-employed digital court reporters shall report all criminal proceedings, including trials.

c. Small Claims Division. The Court provides no court reporting services for proceedings in the Small Claims Division. However, the parties may use any civil court reporter in accordance with Section E of this Administrative Order.

d. Traffic Division

Civil Proceedings: All civil proceedings in the Traffic Division in Pinellas County shall be reported by electronic recording. The Court provides no court reporting services for civil proceedings in the Traffic Division in Pasco County; however, a party may record a civil traffic infraction hearing in accordance with Florida Rule of Traffic Court 6.460(b).

Criminal Proceedings: Court-employed digital court reporters shall report all criminal proceedings in the Traffic Division.

C. Court Reporting Procedures for Hearings Before General magistrates and Hearing Officers. All proceedings before general magistrates and hearing officers shall be reported by electronic recording with the exception of hearings before Civil Traffic Infraction Officers in Pasco County as more fully set forth in Section B(2)d of this Administrative Order.

D. Court Reporting procedures for Hearings Commencing Outside of Regular Court Hours

1. *General Procedures.* The proceedings described in this section will be electronically recorded. If electronic recording is unavailable due to exigent circumstances, the proceeding may be recorded by any other available means, including but not limited to handheld digital voice recorders. The courtroom clerk and bailiff shall ensure that the recording equipment remains on throughout the proceeding.

Regardless of which recording method is used, the date, time, name of the judge or other presiding official, party names, and case number shall be stated at the outset of the recording. If a handheld digital voice recorder is used, the courtroom clerk in attendance shall place the recorder in an envelope and label the envelope with the date of the proceedings and the name of the presiding judge. On the next regular court business day, the courtroom clerk shall deliver the recorder to the digital court reporting department for transfer of the recording to its equipment.

2. *First Appearance Hearings (Advisories) Pursuant to the Florida Rules of Criminal Procedure or Juvenile Procedure.* Advisories commenced on weekends, holidays, or at any other time outside of regular court hours shall be electronically recorded. In Pinellas County, jail personnel shall be responsible for ensuring that the electronic recording equipment is started prior to the commencement of the proceedings. In Pasco County, the AOC shall be responsible for ensuring that electronic recording equipment is set to automatically record proceedings from 8:00 a.m. until 3:00 p.m. on weekends and holidays.

3. *Chapter 39 Shelter Hearings and Proceedings to Waive Parental Notification of Abortion.* Shelter hearings pursuant to Chapter 39, Florida Statutes, and proceedings to waive parental notification of abortion pursuant to section 390.01114, Florida Statutes, which are commenced on weekends, holidays, or any other time outside of regular court hours shall be electronically recorded. In Pinellas County, the AOC shall be responsible for ensuring that the electronic computer recording equipment is started prior to the commencement of the proceedings. In Pasco County, the AOC shall be responsible for ensuring that electronic recording equipment is set to automatically record proceedings from 8:00 a.m. until 3:00 p.m. on weekends and holidays.

4. *Procedures during Emergencies.* Whenever the Sixth Judicial Circuit Administrative Order regarding "Court Operations in Emergencies" is activated, court reporting will be

performed in accordance with that Administrative Order using whatever means may be available under the circumstances.

E. Court Reporting Procedures where the Court does not Provide a Record

1. If a party wishes to make a record of a court proceeding for which the Court does not provide a record as delineated in this Administrative Order, it is the responsibility of the party or the party's attorney to secure the services of a civil court reporter.

2. All notices of hearings for proceedings where the Court does not provide a record must specify whether the party setting a matter for hearing will be securing the services of a court reporter; and, if so, the name and address of the court reporter. All costs associated with the court reporter's appearance will be the responsibility of the party requesting the court reporter. This does not preclude the taxation of costs as authorized by law. See Fla. R. Jud. Admin. 2.535(b).

F. Court Reporting procedures in Capital Cases

1. Any proceeding involving the potential or actual imposition of the death penalty, excluding depositions and including but not limited to pretrial hearings, trials, sentencing hearings, and postconviction hearings, shall be reported by a court-employed stenographic court reporter or a contract stenographic court reporter. Digital court reporting may not be used.

2. When a jury returns a verdict of guilty as charged in a case where the State is seeking the death penalty, the judge should orally instruct the court reporter to immediately begin transcribing the trial as well as any hearings conducted by any judge throughout the pendency of the case.

3. Upon the imposition of the death penalty, the judge should orally instruct the court reporter to immediately begin transcribing the penalty phase of the trial, the Spencer hearing, any other hearings held after the verdict but prior to sentencing, and the actual sentencing hearing.

At the conclusion of a case management conference, Rule of Criminal Procedure 3.850 or 3.851 evidentiary hearing, or any other evidentiary post-conviction hearings in a case in which a death sentence has been imposed, the judge conducting the hearing should orally instruct the court reporter to immediately begin to transcribe the hearing(s).

5. Where immediate transcription instructions in a death penalty proceeding are required by this Administrative Order but are not given, the State Attorney or defense attorney shall move for transcription of the relevant proceedings and prepare an order to transcribe for the signature of the appropriate administrative judge.

6. Any order to transcribe issued pursuant this section shall also be construed as a designation to the court reporter and, unless a different timeframe is ordered by the Court, the transcript of the designated proceeding(s) shall be prepared within thirty (30) days. Court-employed and contract court reporters reporting death penalty proceedings shall use reporting methods, including but not limited to the measures set out in Rule of Judicial Administration 2.535(i)(1)–(4) to ensure that transcripts are prepared expeditiously. However, nothing in this Administrative Order shall be construed to authorize payment for court reporting services beyond the regular contract rates. Payment beyond the regular contract rates may be authorized only by order of the Chief Judge.

7. All appellate transcripts in capital cases will be handled in accordance with Supreme Court Administrative Order No. AOSC 17–27 or any subsequent administrative order of the Supreme Court regarding electronic filing of transcripts in capital cases.

8. Real-time reporting procedures may be used only when specifically authorized by the Chief Judge.

G. Court Reporting Procedures Related to Electronic Recording

1. *Notice to Court Participants and the Public.* All persons entering a courtroom in the Sixth Judicial Circuit are hereby notified that electronic recording equipment is in use and that anything said in the courtroom may be electronically recorded and released upon request. Persons should safeguard information they do not want recorded.

2. *Participant Functions.* In order to ensure an accurate record of proceedings using electronic recording equipment, all participants must comply with the following procedures:

a. All court participants in the courtroom, including Clerks of Court, bailiffs, attorneys, and employees of the Court shall:

i. If unable to easily hear a participant in the proceedings, remind the judge that the participants need to speak with sufficient volume for the system to make an accurate recording,

ii. Have all participants in the courtroom identify themselves for the record.

iii. Not tamper with microphones or electronic recording equipment, and

iv. Immediately notify the Judge when it appears that someone is tampering with or has tampered with the electronic recording equipment.

b. Bailiffs shall:

i. Ensure that no one tampers with microphones or the electronic recording equipment,

ii. Promptly notify the Court of any evidence that the microphones or electronic recording equipment is not functioning properly,

iii. Promptly notify the Court when a microphone at an attorney's table is left muted after a private conversation, and

iv. (iv) Remind participants to speak into the microphone and identify themselves for the record.

c. The courtroom clerk or bailiff shall notify the court-employed digital court reporter by calling the digital court reporting control room when proceedings are about to begin or when they have concluded.

d. The Judge shall:

i. Remind participants to identify themselves and speak into the microphone and answer verbally,

ii. If the judge observes or is otherwise informed that equipment has been tampered with or is malfunctioning, notify the AOC,

iii. If the judge observes participants being careless with equipment, remind participants to protect the court's equipment, and

iv. If unable to easily hear a participant in the proceedings, remind the participants to speak with sufficient volume for the system to make an accurate recording.

e. Attorneys and parties shall:

i. Speak clearly and speak into the microphone,

ii. Not tamper with microphones or electronic recording equipment,

iii. Ensure that microphones are on for all non-private communications,

iv. Ensure that the microphone is muted for private communications, where mutable microphones are provided,

v. Remember that non-verbal communication is not recorded,

vi. Identify themselves for the record, and

vii. Take all reasonable and available precautions to protect disclosure of confidential communications in the courtroom. Such precautions may include muting microphones or going to a designated location that is inaccessible to the recording equipment.

3. *Administrative Office of the Courts Responsibilities*

a. Except for general magistrates and hearing officers, all AOC staff who have access to electronic recording equipment, including but not limited to all "approved court reporters" and Court Technology Office staff, shall execute an oath acknowledging their responsibilities to the Court. New employees shall execute the oath prior to assuming duties.

b. AOC personnel shall operate and maintain equipment so that an accurate recording is made. If the sound quality of a proceeding drops to a level that brings into question the ability to transcribe the proceeding, the judge shall be notified immediately.

c. AOC personnel shall ensure that the electronic recording equipment will reliably provide for recording of the proceeding. Digital recording systems must comply with standards established by the Florida Courts Technology Commission. AOC personnel shall implement procedures for regular testing of digital court reporting systems to ensure proper operation. For proceedings using electronic recording equipment, the AOC shall ensure that the proceeding is recorded to a hard drive and backed up on a server. The data shall be removed from the server and burned to a CD or DVD on a periodic basis.

d. AOC personnel shall maintain the CD or DVD for the period of time prescribed by the Rules of Judicial Administration. AOC personnel shall develop record retention protocols for stenographic paper tape/notes, unedited CAT/real-time text, analog recordings, and digital recordings. Proceedings shall be properly identified, and shall be maintained in a manner that facilitates locating specific court proceedings for purposes of obtaining a transcript. AOC personnel shall comply with storage and retrieval standards for digital recordings as established by the Florida Courts Technology Commission. Storage and retrieval procedures shall ensure timely and secure access to transcripts, analog or digital recordings, and any supporting materials related to the production of the official records. Stenographic court reporter notes shall be maintained under the direction and control of AOC personnel and shall only be available for an "approved court reporter" to transcribe.

e. AOC personnel shall establish a standardized method to tag or index digital recordings and produce a reference document to be provided to and used by all "approved court reporters" and "approved transcriptionists." Proceedings which are exempt from public disclosure shall be indexed as exempt. Proceedings in which there is a significant likelihood that transcripts will be requested must be tagged, including but not limited to proceedings in the Criminal Division of the circuit and county court.

f. AOC personnel shall establish a protocol for producing copies of electronic recordings. The protocol must provide procedures to prevent the release of confidential information, the court's process for ensuring the accuracy of the electronic recording, and certifying the correctness of the recording. The written protocol must at a minimum provide for:

A procedure for attorneys of record, parties to a case, and self-represented litigants to be provided with a copy of an audio recording without that recording being reviewed for confidential information only if the requestor signs a written acknowledgement that confidential information may be contained in the recording, that further dissemination of confidential information contained on the recording is prohibited, and violation of the prohibition may subject the requestor to contempt of court.

AOC shall establish a procedure to review a recording prior to its release to anyone other than an attorney of record, party to a case, or self-represented litigant to ensure that matters protected from public disclosure are kept confidential in accordance with law.

g. "Approved court reporters" and "approved transcriptionists" shall prepare transcripts of proceedings in accordance with protocols and procedures developed by the AOC. Such protocols and procedures shall be in accordance with rules of court and shall include, but not be limited to, standards for addressing off-the-record discussions; sidebar conferences; attorney-client conversations not directed to the Court, confidential information, the process for identifying a need for and obtaining additional transcription services, and certifying the correctness of the transcript prepared.

Priority in the production of transcripts shall be given to capital cases, including capital postconviction cases, juvenile dependency, termination of parental rights, and other cases entitled to priority under Rule of Judicial Administration 2.215(g). If sufficient "court-employed digital court reporters" are not available to prepare transcripts in a timely fashion, the AOC shall arrange for transcription by a "court-employed stenographic court reporter" or "approved transcriptionist" who shall transcribe in accordance with procedures developed by the AOC. The transcript produced by the AOC or "approved transcriptionist" is the official record of the proceeding as more fully detailed in Section A(3) of this Administrative Order.

h. AOC personnel shall prepare and post notices inside and outside of all courtrooms and hearing rooms that electronic recording equipment is in use, that any conversation occurring in the room may be recorded, and that persons should safeguard information they do not want recorded.

i. Any contract entered into for court reporting services must comply with the State Court System Purchasing Directives and comply with contracting requirements as established by the Office of the State Courts Administrator. Contracts for court reporting services must incorporate requirements for expedited transcripts and must specify the consequences for contractors who fail to meet expedited transcript requirements.

4. *Protection of Equipment.* In order to ensure a reliable record of proceedings using electronic recording, microphones and other electronic equipment must be protected. Any willful act that disables or circumvents the proper recording of a proceeding, or any willful destruction of such equipment will be treated as contempt of court and will be enforced in accordance with Rule of Criminal Procedure 3.830 or 3.840.

5. *Access to Control Room.* Access to any electronic recording monitoring location is strictly limited to those court employees whose job functions require access. Access by any other individual is strictly prohibited absent a specific authorization granted by the Chief Judge.

H. Miscellaneous Court Reporting Procedures

1. A court reporter reporting a deposition may report a hearing to have a certified question answered regardless of whether the matter would normally be reported by the Court.

2. Hearings of administrative agencies conducted in court facilities may be reported by the agency's own reporters.

3. The State Attorney, Public Defender, and Regional Counsel shall decide how court reporting services will be provided to their offices. This includes, but is not limited to, depositions noticed by these offices.

I. Procedures for Ordering Written Transcripts

1. Any person may order a written transcript of a court proceeding except that proceedings under the Rules of Juvenile Procedure, Baker Act proceedings, or any other statutorily exempt proceeding shall only be provided to those persons authorized by law.

2. Requests for a written transcript of proceedings should be made in writing utilizing the Transcript Request Form found at www.jud6.org/LegalCommunity/CourtReporters.html. In Pinellas County, this form should be submitted to the Administrative Office of the Courts, 14250 49th Street North, Suite H–2000, Clearwater, Florida 33762, or via email to dcrreporter@jud6.org for proceedings recorded electronically and stenocrcal@jud6.org for proceedings attended by a court-employed stenographic court reporter. In East Pasco County, this form should be submitted to the Administrative Office of the Courts, Court Reporting Department, 38053 Live Oak Avenue, Suite 124, Dade City, Florida 33523, or via email to epreporter@jud6.org. In West Pasco County, this form should be submitted to the Administrative Office of the Courts, Court Reporting Department, 7530 Little Road, Room 201, New Port Richey, Florida 34654, or via email to wpreporter@jud6.org.

3. Any request must include sufficient information necessary to identify the proceeding, including the date of the proceeding, name of the presiding judge, the case name and Uniform Case Number, portion of the proceedings requested, and whether the proceeding was stenographically or electronically reported.

4. Any transcript produced by an approved court reporter will be filed with the Clerk of the Circuit Court unless the Court orders otherwise or unless a rule of court provides otherwise.

5. All transcript requests submitted to the Court require a 50% deposit before the transcript will be produced or the request must be accompanied by a court order to transcribe. The balance must be paid prior to receipt of the transcript. Rates for production of transcripts will be in accordance with separate Administrative Orders establishing rates for court reporting services. Except as otherwise provided, the AOC will not release a transcript until payment has been made in full. All payments must be by check or money order made payable to the State of Florida. Credit and Debit Card payments may be made in person at the Court Reporting office. No refunds will be issued to a person who cancels his or her request.

6. Counsel of record who are members in good standing of The Florida Bar and who also have an account in good standing may order an expedited transcript from the Court without paying a deposit. However, counsel must pay for the entire cost of the transcript prior to receipt. An account is in good standing when counsel has paid for all previously ordered transcripts and CDs.

7. Transcripts requested by the Public Defender or State Attorney shall be billed in accordance with procedures established by the Trial Court Budget Commission. Where a defendant is represented by the Regional Counsel, by the Capital Collateral Regional Counsel, by an attorney appointed from the Registry of the Sixth Judicial Circuit, or by an attorney appointed from the Registry of the Commission on Capital Cases the transcript shall be provided without prepayment. Costs will be paid from the budget of the State Attorney, the Public Defender, the Justice Administrative Commission, or by the Chief Financial Officer as applicable.

8. Prepayment is not required for transcripts requested by the Guardian ad Litem Program or by Pasco or Pinellas Counties. The prepayment requirement may also be waived for other governmental entities by order of the Chief Judge. In the event that a governmental entity does not timely pay for received transcripts or CDs and does not have a cost sharing agreement with the Court, the Chief Judge may reinstate the prepayment requirement without further amendment to this Administrative Order.

J. Procedures for Public Records Requests for Audio Recordings of Court Proceedings

1. Any person may order an audio recording of a court proceeding as detailed below except that proceedings under the Rules of Juvenile Procedure, Baker Act proceedings, and any other statutorily exempt proceeding shall only be provided to those persons statutorily authorized to obtain the record or to those persons who obtain a court order in accordance with the applicable statutory provisions.

2. Requests for an audio recording of proceedings must be made in writing and should be made using the Audio CD Request Form found on the internet at www.jud6.org. In Pinellas County, this form should be submitted to the Administrative Office of the Courts, Suite H–2000, 14250 49th Street

North, Clearwater, Florida 33762, or via email to dcrreporter@jud6.org. In East Pasco County, this form should be submitted to the Administrative Office of the Courts, Court Reporting Department, 38053 Live Oak Avenue, Suite 124, Dade City, Florida 33523, or via email to epreporter@jud6.org. In West Pasco County, this form should be submitted to the Administrative Office of the Courts, Court Reporting Department, 7530 Little Road, Room 201, New Port Richey, Florida 34654, or via email to wpreporter@jud6.org. The request form must include a notice that the CD cannot be used in subsequent court proceedings and inform the requestor of the procedures to obtain a transcript.

3. The request must include sufficient information necessary to identify the proceeding, including the date of the proceeding, name of the presiding judge, the case name, the Uniform Case Number, the portion of the proceedings requested, and must identify whether the requestor is an attorney of record, a party in the case, or a self-represented litigant in the case.

4. Attorneys of record, parties to a case, and self-represented litigants must sign a written acknowledgment that confidential information may be contained on the recording, further dissemination of confidential information on the recording is prohibited, and violation of the prohibition against dissemination may subject the requestor to contempt of court. Upon receipt of the acknowledgement and payment of fees, a copy of the audio recording will be provided to such requestors.

5. Audio recordings of court proceedings requested by all other persons or entities must first be reviewed by AOC personnel to determine whether the audio recording contains confidential or exempt information prior to release of the audio recording. Upon review and redaction of confidential exempt information and payment of fees, a copy of the audio recording will be provided to such requestors.

6. When an audio CD of court proceedings is released, the CD shall include a disclaimer that it is not the official record of court proceedings and that it is not to be used in subsequent court proceedings.

7. The AOC is directed to use its best efforts to provide a CD within 10 business days. Requests for transcripts for use in court proceedings take priority over public records requests for an audio CD. The recording is made for the purpose of preparing transcripts for subsequent court proceedings and giving priority to transcripts will help to avoid costly delays in the processing of cases. However, public records requests must be responded to in a reasonable amount of time.

8. All requests for an audio CD of court proceedings require full payment before the CD will be produced. Payments by check shall be made payable to the State of Florida. No refunds will be issued to a requestor who cancels his or her request.

9. Counsel of record who are members in good standing of The Florida Bar and who also have an account in good standing may order an audio CD without paying a deposit. However, counsel must pay for the entire cost of the CD prior to receipt. An account is in good standing when counsel has paid for all previously ordered transcripts and CDs.

10. Requests for an audio CD from the State Attorney or Public Defender shall be billed in accordance with procedures established by the Trial Court Budget Commission. Requests for audio from the Regional Counsel, the Capital Collateral Regional Counsel, or a court appointed attorney shall be provided without prepayment. Costs will be paid from the budget of the State Attorney, the Public Defender, the Justice Administrative Commission, or by the Chief Financial Officer, as applicable.

11. Prepayment is not required for audio CDs requested by the Guardian ad Litem Program or by Pasco or Pinellas Counties. The prepayment requirement may also be waived for other governmental entities by order of the Chief Judge. In the event that a governmental entity does not timely pay for received transcripts or CDs and does not have a cost sharing agreement with the court, the Chief Judge may reinstate a prepayment requirement without further amendment to this Administrative Order.

K. Court Reporting Fees

1. The fees charged by the AOC for transcription services of proceedings where the Court is required to provide a record will be the calculated actual cost of the service including the cost of recovery. Those fees are set out in Appendix A[1] to this Administrative Order.

2. Fees for providing copies of audio recordings of court proceedings will be charged at the rates set in Appendix A to this Administrative Order. Additional fees will be charged for any request that requires extensive use of staff or technology resources in accordance with Rule of Judicial Administration 2.420. In addition to the cost for a copy of the recording listed in Appendix A, fees will be charged for requests that require AOC staff to listen to the recording and determine whether it contains confidential or exempt information.

3. Nothing in this section or in Appendix A shall affect the contracts entered into between the Court and any court reporter. Further, nothing in this Administrative Order precludes the State Attorney, Public Defender, or Regional Counsel from entering a memorandum of understanding with the Court regarding requests for audio recordings of court proceedings.

4. The Court may amend Appendix A to this Administrative Order to change the rates for transcription services or copies of audio recordings without amending this Administrative Order.

Administrative Orders 2017–022 is hereby rescinded.

DONE AND ORDERED in Chambers at St. Petersburg, Pinellas County, Florida, this ___ day of August, 2018.

ORIGINAL SIGNED ON AUGUST 14, 2018
BY ANTHONY RONDOLINO, CHIEF JUDGE

[1] Appendix A not included.

2018–041. AMERICANS WITH DISABILITIES ACT

IN THE CIRCUIT COURT, SIXTH JUDICIAL CIRCUIT IN AND FOR PASCO AND PINELLAS COUNTIES, FLORIDA

ADMINISTRATIVE ORDER NO. 2018–041 PA/PI–CIR

RE: AMERICANS WITH DISABILITIES ACT

Florida Rule of Judicial Administration 2.540 requires the trial court to establish procedures for obtaining an accommodation under the Americans with Disabilities Act ("Act"). Due to changes in the centralized contact for Pasco County, Administrative Order 2017–027 PA/PI–CIR must be updated.

In accordance with Article V, § 2, Florida Constitution, Rule of Judicial Administration 2.215, and § 43.26, Florida Statutes, it is

ORDERED:

1. The Human Rights Office of Pinellas County continues to be designated as the central contact for requests for accommodation under the Act in Pinellas County. The Human Rights Office, by agreement, provides this service to the constitutional and statutory offices of Pinellas County Government.

2. The Pasco County Human Resources Department is designated as the centralized contact for requests for accommodation under the Act in Pasco County. The Human Resources Department, by agreement, provides this service to the constitutional and statutory offices of Pasco County Government.

3. The central contacts may forward any request for accommodation to the appropriate constitutional officer or statutory offices' ADA Coordinator for response to any accommodation request. For requests for accommodation in a court proceeding, the request should include a description of the accommodation sought, a statement of the impairment that necessitates the accommodation, and the time frame in which the accommodation is needed. The request should not include information about the merits of the case.

4. The Administrative Office of the Court must post on the website for the Sixth Judicial Circuit and in each court facility the procedures for obtaining an accommodation and the grievance procedure.

5. Except as otherwise provided, all notices of court proceedings to be held in a public facility, and all process compelling appearance at such proceedings, shall include the following statement in bold face, 14–point Times New Roman or Courier font:

a. For proceedings before the Courts of Pinellas County:

"If you are a person with a disability who needs any accommodation in order to participate in this proceeding, you are entitled, at no cost to you, to the provision of certain assistance. Please contact the Human Rights Office, 400 S. Ft. Harrison Ave., Ste. 300, Clearwater, FL 33756, (727) 464–4062 (V/TDD) at least 7 days before your scheduled court appearance, or immediately upon receiving this notification if the time before the scheduled appearance is less than 7 days; if you are hearing or voice impaired, call 711."

b. For proceedings before the Courts of Pasco County, effective September 1, 2018:

"If you are a person with a disability who needs any accommodation in order to participate in this proceeding, you are entitled, at no cost to you, to the provision of certain assistance. Please contact either the Pasco County Customer Service Center, 8731 Citizens Drive, New Port Richey, FL 34654, (727) 847–2411 (V) or the Pasco County Risk Management Office, 7536 State Street, New Port Richey, FL 34654, (727) 847–8028 (V) at least 7 days before your scheduled court appearance, or immediately upon receiving this notification if the time before the scheduled appearance is less than 7 days; if you are hearing or voice impaired, call 711."

6. The Clerks of the Circuit Court for Pasco and Pinellas Counties may refuse to issue any document prepared by counsel that does not contain the language required by this Order.

Effective September 1, 2018, Administrative Order No. 2017–027 PA/PI–CIR is hereby rescinded.

DONE AND ORDERED in Chambers at St. Petersburg, Pinellas County, Florida, this ___ day of August, 2018.

ORIGINAL SIGNED ON AUGUST 14, 2018
BY ANTHONY RONDOLINO,
CHIEF JUDGE

2018–035. INJUNCTIONS FOR PROTECTION AGAINST EXPLOITATION OF VULNERABLE ADULTS

IN THE CIRCUIT COURT, SIXTH JUDICIAL CIRCUIT IN AND FOR PASCO AND PINELLAS COUNTIES, FLORIDA

ADMINISTRATIVE ORDER NO. 2018–035 PA/PI–CIR

RE: INJUNCTIONS FOR PROTECTION AGAINST EXPLOITATION OF VULNERABLE ADULTS

The Florida Legislature recently created a new cause of action for an injunction for protection against exploitation of a vulnerable adult, effective July 1, 2018. *See* Ch. 2018–100, Laws of Florida.

In order to establish procedures for injunctions for protection against exploitation of vulnerable adults, and to comply with the newly-enacted statutory requirements set forth in sections 825.101, 825.1035, and 825.1036, Florida Statutes, and

In accordance with Article V, section 2(d), Florida Constitution, Florida Rule of Judicial Administration 2.215, and section 43.26, Florida Statutes,

IT IS ORDERED:

I. CLERK PROCEDURES FOR PETITIONS

A. Intake

1. The Clerk of the Circuit Court ("Clerk") will assist the petitioner in filing Attachment A, Petition for Injunction for Protection Against Exploitation of a Vulnerable Adults ("Petition").

2. If a guardianship petition under chapter 744, Fla. Stat., concerning a vulnerable adult is pending at the time of filing, the petition must be filed in that proceeding pursuant to section 825.1035, Fla. Stat. Otherwise, a petition for injunction for protection against exploitation of a vulnerable adult may only be filed in the circuit in which the vulnerable adult resides.

3. Notwithstanding any other provision of law, the Clerk may not assess an initial filing fee or service charge for Petitions filed pursuant to this Administrative Order ("AO").

4. The Clerk will accept Petitions at the Clearwater Courthouse, the St. Petersburg Judicial Building, the West Pasco Judicial Center, and the Robert D. Sumner Judicial Center.

5. For Petitions filed at the Clearwater Courthouse, the St. Petersburg Judicial Building, or the West Pasco Judicial Center, or the Robert D. Sumner Judicial Center, the Clerk shall present the Petition to the section judge if the section judge is available. When the section judge is unavailable, the Clerk is to provide the temporary injunction as specified in the Pasco County Emergency Duty Schedule, Administrative Order 2018–033 PA–CIR, or the Pinellas County Emergency Duty Schedule, Administrative Order 2017–061 PI–CIR, or subsequent administrative orders.

6. The Clerks will not accept Petitions filed after hours. "After hours" means after 4:00 p.m. or before 8:30 a.m. on a regular work day, or at any time during holiday or weekend day. Petitions filed after hours will be received for filing and date/time stamping by the Clerk, but will be processed on the next working day. Petitioners wishing to file after hours will be informed that they may contact law enforcement or 911 if there is an emergency relating to the Respondent.

B. Assignment of Cases

1. *Pasco County.* Petitions will be assigned based on the U.S. Postal Service Zone Improvement Plan ("ZIP code") of the petitioner in accordance with the procedures for assignment of guardianship cases in Pasco County as specified in Administrative Order PA–CIR–97–21, or subsequent administrative order.

2. *Pinellas County*

a. Petitions will be assigned based on the ZIP code of the petitioner in accordance with the procedures for assignment of probate cases to either section 3 or section 4 in Pinellas County based on ZIP code specified in Administrative Order 2014–030 PI–CIR under 2(a) and (b), or subsequent administrative order.

b. Unless otherwise provided in this AO, Pinellas County cases with an out of county ZIP code, an unknown ZIP code, or a ZIP code not listed in Administrative Order 2014–030 PI–CIR, or subsequent administrative order, are to be assigned in a manner that results in an even distribution of the cases between section 3 and section 4. The Administrative Office of the Courts ("AOC") will review the case distribution at least semi-annually and as needed, adjust the percentage of such cases that are to be assigned to the Clearwater section and the percentage assigned to the St. Petersburg section in order to equalize the workload.

C. Scheduling Calendars

1. Return hearings for section 3 will be scheduled on the section judge's calendar on Wednesdays, or such other days as may be coordinated with the Pinellas County Clerk of Court at the Clearwater Courthouse, Courtroom A, 315 Court Street, Clearwater, Florida 33756.

2. Return hearings for section 4 will be scheduled on the section judge's calendar on Thursdays, or such other days as may be coordinated with the Pinellas County Clerk of Court at the St. Petersburg Judicial Building, Courtroom E, 545 1st Avenue North, St. Petersburg, Florida 33701.

3. Upon at least 30 days' notice to the Pinellas County Clerk of Court by the section 3 or 4 judge, section 3 cases may be scheduled on the section 4 calendar and section 4 cases may be scheduled on the section 3 calendar.

4. Return hearings for sections A, X, I, and J will be scheduled on the section judge's calendar on a date determined by the section judge, at the West Pasco Judicial Center, 7530 Little Road, New Port Richey, Florida 34654.

5. The back-up judge for all proceedings under this AO is the Duty Judge.

6. For Pinellas cases assigned to either the St. Petersburg Judicial Building or the Clearwater Courthouse, the Clerk is to docket cases such that cases are calendared by first assigning a maximum of 5 cases to the 9:30 a.m. calendar and then assigning the remaining cases to the 10:30 a.m. calendar. If the 10:30 a.m. calendar exceeds 5 cases, the additional cases should be assigned to the 1:30 p.m. calendar.

7. When more than one petition for injunction for protection against exploitation is filed with parties in common and a final hearing has not been held on the first petition, the Clerk must calendar such related cases on the same date and at the same time and location.

8. These instructions on calendaring do not restrict the authority of the assigned judge to reset cases on a calendar when service of process has not been obtained. If the calendars are too large for the assigned judge or the duty judge to provide an adequate hearing, the assigned judge may move the hearing to later in the day in his or her sole discretion.

D. Clerk's Duties and Responsibilities

1. The Clerk will provide to the petitioner petition forms for the injunction, any modifications, and forms for the enforcement of any injunction entered. Additionally, the Clerk will provide the petitioner with instructions for the completion of such forms. See section II for service of process.

2. To the extent practicable, the Clerk will ensure the petitioner's privacy while completing the forms.

3. The Clerk will provide the petitioner with two certified copies of the Petition for injunction without charge.

4. The Clerk will provide a copy of the Petition to the guardian of the vulnerable adult in the event the guardian is not the petitioner.

5. If an injunction is entered, the Clerk will provide, without charge, the petitioner with certified copies of the order of injunction, so that the petitioner may effect service upon any person holding property, upon any financial institution holding property or accounts, or upon any financial institution with an open line of credit subject to the freeze.

6. The Clerk will provide petitioners with its informational brochure regarding injunctions for protection against exploitation of a vulnerable adult, published in accordance with section 825.1035, Fla. Stat.

7. The Clerk will provide to the adult protective services program a copy of every Petition filed under this AO and all orders entered on such Petitions.

II. SERVICE

1. Notwithstanding any other provision of law, the Chief Judge, in consultation with the appropriate sheriff, may authorize a law enforcement agency within the circuit to effect service.

2. Petition:

a. When a Petition is filed, but a temporary injunction is not issued, the Clerk will furnish a copy of the Petition, any accompanying affidavits, and the notice of hearing, to the sheriff or a law enforcement agency of the county in which the respondent resides or can be located. The sheriff will then serve these documents upon the respondent as soon as possible on any day of the week and at any time of the day or night.

b. If the petitioner is acting in a representative capacity, the vulnerable adult will be served with a copy of the Petition, financial affidavit, and notice of hearing in the same manner as the respondent.

c. At the request of the sheriff, the Clerk may transmit a certified facsimile or certified, scanned copy of the Petition. The certified facsimile or certified, scanned copy may be served in the same manner as a certified copy.

d. The Clerk will furnish to the sheriff the information pertaining to the respondent's and, when appropriate, the vulnerable adult's, physical description to include the date of birth and location, as required by the Department of Law Enforcement.

e. If a party fails or refuses to acknowledge the receipt of a certified copy of a Petition and notice of hearing while in the Clerk's Office, the Clerk must note on the original Petition that service was effected.

f. If the respondent has been served with the Petition and notice of hearing and has failed to appear at the initial hearing on the temporary injunction, the Clerk may serve any subsequent petition for an injunction seeking an extension of time by certified mail to the respondent, rather than personal service by a law enforcement officer.

3. Temporary Injunction:

a. When a temporary injunction is issued, the Clerk will furnish a copy of the Petition, any accompanying affidavits, and the temporary injunction to the sheriff or a law enforcement agency of the county in which the respondent resides or can be located. The sheriff will then serve these documents upon the respondent as soon as possible on any day of the week and at any time of the day or night.

b. If the petitioner is acting in a representative capacity, the vulnerable adult will be served with a copy of the Petition, financial affidavit, and notice of hearing in the same manner as the respondent.

c. At the request of the sheriff, the Clerk may transmit a certified facsimile or certified, scanned copy of the temporary injunction. The certified facsimile or certified, scanned copy may be served in the same manner as a certified copy.

d. The Clerk will furnish to the sheriff the information pertaining to the respondent's and, when appropriate, the vulnerable adult's, physical description to include the date of birth and location, as required by the Department of Law Enforcement.

e. The Clerk will certify a copy of all orders issued, changed, continued, extended, or vacated subsequent to the original service of the original Petition, notice of hearing, or temporary injunction and deliver the certified copy to the parties at the time of the entry of the order.

f. If a party fails or refuses to acknowledge the receipt of a certified copy of an order at the initial hearing, the Clerk must note on the original Petition that service was effected.

g. If it is not possible to deliver an order directly following the hearing at which it is issued, the Clerk will mail certified copies of such orders to the parties at their respective last known mailing addresses. When an order is served in this manner, the Clerk will notify the sheriff of such service and prepare a written certification to be placed in the court file specifying the time, date, and method of service.

h. If the respondent has been served with the temporary injunction and has failed to appear at the initial hearing on the temporary injunction, the Clerk may serve any subsequent petition for an injunction seeking an extension of time by certified mail to the respondent, rather than personal service by a law enforcement officer.

i. Within 24 hours after the court issues an injunction or changes, continues, extends, or vacates such an injunction, the Clerk must forward certified copy of the order to the sheriff with jurisdiction over the petitioner for service.

j. Within 24 hours after an injunction is terminated or rendered no longer effective by ruling of the court, the Clerk must notify the sheriff receiving original notification of the injunction.

k. Service on a depository or financial institution must be effected by a law enforcement agency as provided in section 655.0201, Fla. Stat.

4. Final Injunction:

a. If it is not possible to deliver a final injunction directly following the hearing at which it is issued, the Clerk will mail certified copies of such orders to the parties at their respective last known mailing addresses. When an order is served in this manner, the Clerk will notify the sheriff of such service and prepare a written certification to be placed in the court file specifying the time, date, and method of service.

b. If a party fails or refuses to acknowledge the receipt of a certified copy of an order at the final hearing, the Clerk must note on the original Petition that service was effected.

c. Within 24 hours after an injunction is terminated or rendered no longer effective by ruling of the court, the Clerk must notify the sheriff receiving original notification of the injunction.

d. Service on a depository or financial institution must be effected by a law enforcement agency as provided in section 655.0201, Fla. Stat.

III. LAW ENFORCEMENT

1. Municipal police departments located in Pinellas and Pasco Counties and their individual sworn officers are authorized to effect service of process instead of the Pinellas or Pasco Sheriff's Office when provided a certified copy of an injunction for protection against exploitation of a vulnerable adult upon arriving at a call for police service.

2. Pasco County—When serving an injunction for protection against exploitation of a vulnerable adult, law enforcement officers must serve it in accordance with Attachment B, Notice

To All Local Law Enforcement Agencies ("Notice"). The Pasco Clerk must attach the Notice to a certified copy of the injunction to be served on the respondent. The Clerk must also provide Attachment C, Return of Service/Certificate of Non-service, when forwarding the injunction for service to law enforcement, including to sheriffs of other Florida counties or to another law enforcement agency, where the respondent resides or can be found. After service of process has been made, the law enforcement officer who served the injunction must immediately file Attachment C, Return of Service/Certificate of Non-service. If attempts at service of process are unsuccessful, the law enforcement officer attempting service must immediately file Attachment C, Return of Service/Certificate of Non-service with the relevant facts that indicate the reason for non-service.

3. Pinellas County—When serving an injunction for protection against exploitation of a vulnerable adult, law enforcement officers must serve it in accordance with Attachment B, Notice. The Pinellas Clerk must attach the Notice to a certified copy of the injunction to be served on the respondent. The Clerk must also provide Attachment C, Return of Service/Certificate of Non-service, when forwarding the injunction for service to law enforcement, including to sheriffs of other Florida counties or to another law enforcement agency, where the respondent resides or can be found. After service of process has been made, the law enforcement officer who served the injunction must immediately file Attachment C, Return of Service/Certificate of Non-service.

4. Service of process authorized by this procedure will give the Court personal jurisdiction over the respondent.

5. Nothing herein changes the existing policy that gives primary responsibility for service of injunctions against exploitation of a vulnerable adult in Pinellas and Pasco Counties to the Pinellas and Pasco County Sheriffs. However, if a municipal police agency receives a call for initial service of an injunction, and the agency believes an immediate harm might occur if the injunction is not served immediately, the agency may elect to serve the injunction. The agency must immediately notify the appropriate Pinellas or Pasco County Sheriff's Office upon serving injunctions under these circumstances.

IV. DUTY JUDGE

1. The duty judge must be available to handle overflow cases and otherwise provide assistance to the assigned judge.

2. The duty judge must maintain sufficient time on his or her calendar on the assigned day so that the duty judge has time to handle return hearings and handle other duty matters.

3. If the duty judge assignment conflicts with any other commitment, the duty judge must make arrangements with a fellow judge to exchange the assignment.

4. Judges assigned to the civil division should not be assigned duty or accept an exchange of duty responsibility during jury trial weeks.

5. The assigned judge is responsible for providing timely notification of the exchange to all persons affected by the exchange.

6. Post-judgment motions will be heard by the assigned section judge.

V. INTERPRETERS

1. The AOC will provide spoken language interpreters as needed for a non-English speaking or limited-English-proficient vulnerable adult, petitioner, and/or respondent in accordance with Fla. R. Jud. Admin. 2.560.

2. Such interpreter will be appointed as specified in Administrative Order 2018–034 PA/PI–CIR, Interpreters for Non–English Speaking Persons, Limited–English Proficient Persons, and Deaf or Hard of Hearing Persons, or subsequent administrative order.

VI. COURT REPORTING

1. All proceedings relating to petitions for injunction for protection against exploitation of a vulnerable adult must be recorded pursuant to section 825.1035, Fla. Stat.

2. Such court reporting will be performed in accordance with the Court Reporting Plan, Administrative Order 2017–022 PA/PI–CIR, or subsequent administrative order.

VII. VIOLATIONS

1. The Clerk will assist the petitioner in filing a petition alleging violation of injunction under this AO. The Clerk will immediately forward such affidavit to the assigned judge's section.

2. The judge will review the affidavit and make a determination of the appropriate action. If the judge determines that the affidavit alleges that a crime has been committed under section 825.1036, Fla. Stat., the Clerk will forward a copy of the affidavit to the appropriate law enforcement agency for investigation.

3. Within 20 days after receipt of the affidavit, the local law enforcement agency will complete its investigation and forward to the state attorney the affidavit and a report containing the agency's findings.

4. When state attorney office receives the report from the local law enforcement agency, the state attorney's office will then determine, within 30 business days, whether its office will file criminal charges, prepare a motion for an order to show cause as to why the respondent should not be held in criminal contempt, prepare both as alternative findings, or file notice that the case remains under investigation or is pending subject to another action.

VIII. ATTACHMENTS

The Court may revise the Attachments to this AO without further amendment to this AO [1].

DONE AND ORDERED in Chambers at St. Petersburg, Pinellas County, Florida, this ___ day of June, 2018.

ORIGINAL SIGNED ON JUNE 29, 2018
BY ANTHONY RONDOLINO,
CHIEF JUDGE

[1] Because the court can amend these attachments without any further amendments, they are not attached. Please visit http://www.jud6.org/legalcommunity/AdministrativeOrders.html for any forms associated with this order.

2018–034. INTERPRETERS FOR NON–ENGLISH SPEAKING PERSONS

IN THE CIRCUIT COURT, SIXTH JUDICIAL CIRCUIT IN AND FOR PASCO AND PINELLAS COUNTIES, FLORIDA

ADMINISTRATIVE ORDER NO. 2018–034 PA/PI–CIR

RE: INTERPRETERS FOR NON–ENGLISH SPEAKING PERSONS, LIMITED ENGLISH PROFICIENT PERSONS, AND DEAF OR HARD OF HEARING PERSONS

Recently, the Supreme Court issued *In Re: Amendments to the Florida Rules of Judicial Administration 2.430, 2.535, 2.560, and 2.565*, No. SC17–1137. The amended rules address when the Court must appoint an interpreter in criminal or juvenile delinquency proceedings and clarify that Rule 2.565 does not require an attorney or self-represented litigant to retain an interpreter when the court is not required to appoint one. To implement these changes, which take effect July 1, 2018, Administrative Order 2015–058 needs to be updated.

Under the authority granted to the Chief Judge by Article V, section 2(d), Florida Constitution, Rule of Judicial Administration 2.215, and § 43.26, Florida Statutes, it is

ORDERED:

I. PROVISION OF SPOKEN LANGUAGE AND SIGN LANGUAGE INTERPRETERS

A. Qualifications of Interpreters

1. Any spoken language interpreter who provides services to the Court must comply with and be bound by the Code of Professional Conduct of the Florida Rules for Certification and Regulation of Spoken Language Court Interpreters (Rule 14). Any sign language interpreter who provides interpreter services to the Court must uphold and adhere to all standards prescribed by the National Association for the Deaf and the Registry of Interpreters for the Deaf (NAD–RID) Code of Professional Conduct. An interpreter must inform the judge, hearing officer, or general magistrate (hereinafter "presiding official") and the Administrative Office of the Courts (AOC) whenever the interpreter believes he or she is out of compliance with an applicable code of conduct.

2. If an interpreter finds that at any time he or she is unable to perform interpreting services satisfactorily, he or she must immediately notify the presiding official. The presiding official will take appropriate action, such as a recess, adjournment, or directing the AOC or the responsible party to provide another qualified interpreter.

B. Court–provided spoken language interpreters: The AOC will provide spoken language interpreters in accordance with Florida Rule of Judicial Administration 2.560. These instances include:

1. *For litigants:* the AOC must provide an interpreter as needed for a non–English speaking or limited–English–proficient litigant in the following types of cases:

a. Circuit and county criminal;

b. Criminal contempt;

c. Parental time-sharing cases in which both parties are unable to pay costs;

d. Dating, domestic, repeat, and sexual violence and stalking injunction return hearings;

e. Delinquency proceeding (including parents and guardians);

f. Dependency proceeding, including termination of parental rights proceedings (including parents and guardians);

g. Petitions for incapacity and other mental health proceedings in which a person may lose the ability to control the decisions about his or her life; and

h. Other proceedings in which a non-English speaking or limited–English–proficient person is a litigant and the Court determines that the litigant's inability to comprehend English deprives the litigant of an understanding of the Court proceedings, *and* a fundamental interest is at stake, *and* no alternative to the appointment of an interpreter exists.

2. *For victims and witnesses:* the AOC must provide non-English speaking or limited–English–proficient victims and witnesses with an interpreter as follows:

a. For victims in juvenile delinquency and criminal cases regardless of whether the victim is a witness; and

b. For non-victim witnesses in juvenile delinquency and criminal cases, and for witnesses in other cases, when directed by the Court in accordance with the Florida Evidence Code.

C. Retention of interpreters by attorneys or self-represented litigants: If appointment of a spoken language interpreter by the Court is not required by this Administrative Order, the attorney or self-represented litigant may retain a spoken language interpreter to assist a non-English speaking or limited English proficient litigant or witness at his or her own expense. However, in these situations, the scheduling services of the AOC's Fiscal Office may be used, and the costs of the interpreter's service may be repaid at the court-contracted rates. Retention of spoken language interpreters by attorneys or self-represented litigants must be in compliance with Rule of Judicial Administration 2.565, including the requirement to give preference to certified and language skilled interpreters.

D. Court provided sign language interpreters: the AOC must facilitate the provision of sign language interpreters for communication between people who are deaf or hard of hearing and people who hear, when required by the Americans with Disabilities Act (ADA) of 1990, 42 U.S.C. § 12101, et. seq., and when required for due process. When sign language interpretation services are required solely by the ADA, the respective County must pay for the services. See § 29.008(1)(f)4, Florida Statutes.

E. Translation of audio and video recordings or written documents: Any party who seeks to introduce or reference an audio or video recording in Court, or to offer written evidence that requires translation into English, must have the item transcribed into English and must provide the translation to the opposing party within a reasonable period of time prior to the Court proceeding. The offering party must provide to the Court at the trial or hearing the transcript of the English translation. The offering party is responsible for such translation and transcription expenses.

F. Preference and priority of assignments for Court-provided interpreters:

1. *When providing a spoken language interpreter*, the AOC will give preference for assignments as described in Rule of Judicial Administration 2.560(e).

2. *When providing a sign language interpreter or other interpreter* to facilitate communication between people who are deaf or hard of hearing and people who hear, the AOC must

first try to provide an interpreter who is currently designated as "Specialist Certified: Legal" by the Registry of Interpreters for the Deaf. If the AOC cannot readily provide a "Specialist Certified: Legal" interpreter, it must then try to provide an interpreter who currently has another certification from RID.

3. If the qualifications of court-contracted interpreters are equal and do not require preference for the assignment of an interpreter in accordance with the direction above, the AOC must ensure that any assignment system for court-contracted interpreters is as fair and balanced as possible.

4. If there are insufficient interpreters for any language required by the Courts on any given day, the AOC will work with the Courts to prioritize the assignments of the available interpreter(s) in accordance with Florida Rule of Judicial Administration 2.550(a) & (b).

G. Requests and cancelations of Court-provided interpreters:

1. When counsel or a pro se litigant requires an interpreter in a case where the interpreter must be provided by the AOC as required by this Order, the counsel or pro se litigant must schedule the request through the AOC's Fiscal Office in the respective County where the services are required. Counsel or the pro se litigant must bring the request to the Court's and the Fiscal Office's attention as soon as possible, preferably at least one week before the scheduled proceeding. Counsel or the pro se litigant must relay any notice of cancellation to the Fiscal Office as soon as possible after he or she knows that an interpreter's services are no longer required.

2. Nothing in this Order prohibits the offices of the Clerk of the Circuit Court, State Attorney, Public Defender, Regional Counsel, or any other agency from utilizing the services of a spoken language interpreter or sign language interpreter of its choosing for out-of-court activities. Any costs incurred for out-of-court activities must be paid by the office utilizing the language interpreter.

H. Recoupment of costs for Court-provided interpreters: The costs incurred by the AOC for providing an interpreter under this Order are subject to cost recovery in accordance with Administrative Order No. 2005–061 or subsequent Administrative Order.

I. Other duties of the Administrative Office of the Courts: In addition to other duties in this Order, in compliance with AOSC11–45, In Re: Court Interpreting Services in Florida's Trial Courts, the AOC will:

1. Periodically review the technology operating in courtrooms to determine the feasibility of establishing remote interpreting capability. If such technology and other resources make it feasible to implement remote interpreting, the AOC will implement remote interpreting as directed by the Chief Judge, including developing and documenting procedures for the appropriate use of remote interpreting.

2. Develop and keep current a Court interpreter page on the Court's Internet page. The Court interpreter page will explain the basic services provided by the Court interpreter program and provide contact information for the Fiscal Offices in Pasco and Pinellas Counties and the ADA Coordinator.

3. Publish information on the Court's Internet page that informs Court participants with disabilities about the rights afforded by the ADA, the federal regulations, and the process for requesting a qualified interpreter or other accommodation under the ADA.

4. Require attendance at trainings sponsored by the Office of State Courts Administrator for individuals involved in the collection and reporting of Uniform Data Reporting System statistics.

II. USE OF INTERPRETERS, PARTICIPANT FUNCTIONS

A. Judges, Hearing Officers, and Magistrates (presiding officials)

1. Prior to the beginning of a proceeding where an interpreter is used, the presiding official will instruct parties and jurors who understand the language being interpreted and who perceive a discrepancy as to the interpretation to bring the issue to the attention of the presiding official.

2. The presiding official will ensure the interpreter is sworn in at the beginning of a proceeding or set of proceedings. See § 90.606, Florida Statutes.

3. When a sign language interpreter is used for a juror who is deaf or hard of hearing, the presiding official will administer an oath of non-involvement, including language stating that the interpreter will not interfere with jury deliberations or reveal the confidences of the jury. See § 90.606, Florida Statutes.

4. As appropriate, the presiding official will inform all parties when an interpreter is being used, particularly when a party or interpreter appears remotely. The presiding official will monitor the proceeding to ensure that the interpretation process flows smoothly and, as needed, instruct the participants to adjust their volume or rate of speech, or refrain from extraneous comments or whispering.

5. Before continuing with any proceeding, the presiding official will ask the litigant, through the interpreter, whether the litigant is confident that the interpreter's skills will ensure adequate and accurate interpretation of the communication of the proceeding, and whether the litigant believes the interpreter is impartial. If either of those answers is "no", the presiding official will take appropriate action.

6. The presiding official will ensure that simultaneous interpretation is used for defendants, respondents, and other litigants who require a spoken language interpreter or a sign language interpreter. The presiding official may allow consecutive interpretation of testimony by a witness who requires a spoken language interpreter or a sign language interpreter.

7. The presiding official will give appropriate jury instructions regarding the use of a court interpreter, including that the interpreter is neutral, impartial, does not represent the interest of any party, and is only present to assist in communication.

8. When an unscheduled need arises and it is in the best interest of the Court to proceed without waiting to obtain another interpreter, a presiding official or his or her designee may directly obtain a telephonic interpreting service such as the Language Line. The presiding official must still comply with Florida Rule of Judicial Administration 2.560 and request the service to provide a designated interpreter in accordance with the preferences described above in section I.F.

B. All Participants—Presiding Officials, Bailiffs, Jurors, Parties and their Counsel, and Interpreters

1. All Court participants must observe the in-court performance of interpreters. When a juror, witness, bailiff, party, or party's counsel observes concerns or has complaints about the in-court performance of an interpreter, that person must report them to the presiding official, immediately if appropriate.

2. Any Court participant may bring concerns about the in-court or out-of-court interpretation performance or other activities of an interpreter to the attention of the Trial Courts Administrator (TCA) or her designee. The TCA or her designee will review such reports and take appropriate action, including but not limited to counseling the interpreter, or refusing the interpreter's service when he or she is provided through a firm. If appropriate, the TCA may cancel the Court's contract with the interpreter.

3. A party who knows or suspects that an interpreter has not been sworn in must bring that to the Court's attention as soon as practicable.

4. All Court participants and the AOC must work toward making the best use of an interpreter's time and availability by ensuring that those cases involving an interpreter are called and brought to the Court's attention as soon as possible.

Administrative Order 2015–058 PA/PI–CIR is hereby rescinded.

DONE AND ORDERED in Chambers at St. Petersburg, Pinellas County, Florida, this ___ day of June, 2018.

ORIGINAL SIGNED ON JUNE 29, 2018
BY ANTHONY RONDOLINO,
CHIEF JUDGE

2018–020. UNIFORM BOND SCHEDULE—PINELLAS COUNTY

IN THE CIRCUIT COURT, SIXTH JUDICIAL CIRCUIT IN AND FOR PASCO AND PINELLAS COUNTIES, FLORIDA

ADMINISTRATIVE ORDER NO. 2018–020 PI–CIR

RE: UNIFORM BOND SCHEDULE—PINELLAS COUNTY

The uniform bond schedule is being amended in Pinellas County in response to § 790.401, Florida Statutes, adopted by the Legislature in Senate Bill 7026, Chapter No. 2018–3, Laws of Florida. This statute creates two new felonies related to the protective orders established by that section. Based on the nature of the new felonies, the Chief Judge has determined that defendants who are charged with these new crimes should have bond set by a judge only. In accordance with Article V, section 2, Florida Constitution, Rule of Judicial Administration 2.215, and § 43.26, Florida Statutes,

IT IS ORDERED:

1. All law enforcement agencies in Pinellas County are urged to use a Notice to Appear (NTA), pursuant to Rule of Criminal Procedure 3.125, where permitted by law.

2. The Sheriff is hereby authorized to release any person on his or her own recognizance (ROR) who is in pre-trial status on a warrant from another jurisdiction and charged with an ordinance violation, misdemeanor, or an offense specified in Attachment A provided:

A. the Sheriff has sent written notice to the other jurisdiction that the inmate will be released pursuant to this Administrative Order if the inmate is not picked up within 72 hours from notification, excluding weekends and holidays,

B. the other jurisdiction has not picked up the inmate in accordance with the notification, and

C. the inmate is not subject to the provisions of § 903.0351, Fla. Stat., or is not otherwise required by law to be held.

3. The Sheriff is hereby authorized to release any person on pre-trial status who is a member of the United States Armed Forces to the custody of MacDill Air Force Base unless the inmate is subject to the provisions of § 903.0351, Fla. Stat., or unless the inmate is otherwise required by law to be held.

4. The following procedures are implemented for setting bond for defendants at those Pinellas Counties receiving facility(ies) housing defendants.

A. *Arresting Officer—Function at Booking Desk*

1. The arresting officer shall complete all information on the complaint affidavit, setting forth the statute number and the degree of the crime for which the defendant is charged, together with a short statement of the facts involved in the alleged crime.

2. The arresting officer shall specifically ask the defendant for his or her current residence address. The arresting officer shall not rely upon any identification furnished by the defendant, unless the defendant is unable to verbally advise the officer of the address. The name and address of the defendant shall be listed on the complaint affidavit.

3. The arresting officer shall leave the bond portion of the complaint affidavit blank, unless the defendant was arrested upon a warrant, in which case the bond set on the warrant shall be entered.

4. For any arrest which has been made based upon probable cause with no warrant involved and where the arresting officer possesses specific reason(s) to believe that a bond, in an amount higher or lower than the amount established pursuant to this Administrative Order should be set, the arresting officer may personally contact a judge and said judge may set a bond outside of the provisions of this Administrative Order. The arresting officer shall enter the amount of bond, as set by the judge, upon the complaint affidavit specifically annotating which judge approved the bond amount.

B. *Booking Officer—Function*

1. For the purposes of this Administrative Order, the term "booking officer" means the employee of the receiving facility who receives the prisoner from the arresting officer.

2. For persons charged with an ordinance violation or a first or second degree misdemeanor, the booking officer may issue a NTA in accordance with Rule of Criminal Procedure 3.125 if the booking officer determines that there is a

likelihood that the accused will appear as directed and the defendant is not otherwise required to be held.

3. The booking officer shall specifically ask the defendant to verify his or her current residence address. The booking officer shall not rely on any address listed on any identification in the possession of the defendant, unless the defendant is unable to verbalize his or her address.

4. If the arrest is based upon a warrant, the booking officer shall confirm that the bond on the warrant has been correctly placed on the complaint affidavit, and, if not, enter the bond amount set out in the warrant.

5. If the defendant is being booked by virtue of an arrest based on probable cause, the booking officer shall enter the bond amount on the complaint affidavit, in the space provided for that purpose.

6. With every defendant, the booking officer shall follow the recommended bond set forth by this Administrative Order for the particular degree of crime charged unless the booking officer determines:

a. that a lower bond or ROR is more appropriate than the recommended bond in which case the booking officer may set the bond down to the lower end of the bond schedule, or

b. that a higher bond is more appropriate than the recommended bond based on the guidelines set forth in this Administrative Order in which case the booking officer may set a higher bond up to the maximum allowable pursuant to this Administrative Order. In order to increase the bond the booking officer must specifically set out, in writing on the complaint affidavit one or more of the aggravating factors enumerated below; or

c. that the arresting officer has contacted a judge pursuant to A.4. above and a judge has authorized a bond different from this Order.

7. Aggravating factors which the booking officer is permitted to consider when an increase in the bond amount is contemplated are:

a. At the time of arrest, the defendant had committed more than one offense.

b. The defendant cannot provide a local address or a permanent place of residence in the Tampa Bay area.

c. The defendant has a prior criminal record.

d. The defendant is on probation, parole, community control or any other form of supervision.

e. There are outstanding warrants or holds for the defendant from this or any other jurisdiction.

f. The arresting officer or booking officer has reason to believe that should the defendant be released, bodily injury may be inflicted upon the alleged victim or another by the defendant.

g. The arresting officer or booking officer has reason to believe that should the defendant be released from custody, the defendant would not return to Court when summoned.

If the booking officer finds aggravating factors (f) or (g), the basis for those aggravating factors should be stated in writing on the complaint advisory affidavit.

C. *Range of Bond—Recommended Amount.* For offenses added to the statutes subsequent to the date of this Order, these ranges of bonds will be used for the new offenses, unless otherwise provided in a subsequent administrative order.

	Category of Crime	Low Bond	High Bond	Recommended Bond
1.	Capital Felony	None	None	None
2.	Life Felony *Exception—See Below	$100,000	None	None
	Life Felony Non-homicide and the defendant is a juvenile	$50,000	None	$150,000
3.	1st Degree Felony (P. B. Life) *Exception—See Below	$50,000	None	$150,000
	Other Exception: 2nd Degree Murder § 782.04(2), (3), Fla. Stat.	$100,000	None	None
4.	1st Degree Felony (other than P. B. Life) *Exception—See Below	$10,000	$100,000	$50,000
5.	2nd Degree Felony *Exception—See Below	$5,000	$20,000	$10,000
	2nd Degree Felony Eligible if specified on Attachment A**	ROR—SUPERVISED	$10,000	$5,000
6.	3rd Degree Felony *Exception—See Below	ROR—SUPERVISED	$10,000	$5,000
	3rd Degree Felony Eligible if specified on Attachment A**	ROR—SUPERVISED	$5,000	$2,000
	Other Exceptions:			
	Any Battery that is a 3rd Degree Felony	$1,000	$5,000	$2,500
	3rd Degree Felony—DUI and BUI offenses, § 316.193 or § 327.35, Fla. Stat.	$2,500	$10,000	$5,000
	3rd Degree Felony—DWLSR offenses, § 322.34, Fla. Stat., where the defendant has 4 or more previous DWLSRs or the defendant's license was previously suspended due to DUI or drug charges.	$2,500	$10,000	$5,000
7.	1st Degree Misdemeanor	ROR—UNSUPERVISED	$500	$150

	*Exception—See Below			
	Other Exceptions:			
	Any Battery that is a 1st Degree Misdemeanor	$250	$1,000	$500
	Any DV-related charge listed in the exceptions below BUT ONLY at or after first appearance	ROR	$5,000	$2,500
	DUI or BUI—Property Damage 1st or **2nd** offense § 316.193(3) (c)1, or § 327.35(3)(c)1, Fla. Stat.	$250	$1,000	$500
	DUI or BUI- Property Damage **3rd** offense § 316.193(3)(c)1, or § 327.35(3)(c)1, Fla. Stat.	$500	$2,500	$1,000
	1st Degree Misdemeanor DWLSR offenses, § 322.34, Fla. Stat., where the defendant has 4 or more previous DWLSRs or the defendant's license was previously suspended due to DUI or drug charges.	$500	$2,500	$1,000
	Failure to Appear (FTA) § 843.15(1)(b), Fla. Stat.	$250	$1,500	$500
	Prostitution offenses, **2nd** and subsequent offense § 796.07, Fla. Stat.	ROR—UNSUPERVISED	$500	$250
8.	**2nd** Degree Misdemeanor	ROR—UNSUPERVISED	$250	ROR—UNSUPERVISED
	*Exception—See Below			
	Other Exception:			
	Disorderly Intoxication § 856.011, Fla. Stat.	ROR—UNSUPERVISED	$250	$100
9.	Criminal Traffic	ROR—UNSUPERVISED	$250	ROR—UNSUPERVISED
	*Exception—See Below			
	Other Exceptions:			
	DUI or BUI- No Property Damage 1st or **2nd** offense § 316.193(2)(a) or § 327.35(2)(a), Fla. Stat.	ROR—UNSUPERVISED	$500	ROR—UNSUPERVISED
	DUI or BUI- No Property Damage **3rd** offense § 316.193(2)(a) or § 327.35(2)(a), Fla. Stat.	$500	$1,000	$750
10.	Municipal Ordinance Violations	ROR—UNSUPERVISED	$250	ROR—UNSUPERVISED

* Exceptions—No Bond:

- For capital crimes the bond is automatically "none."
- The defendant is to be held with no bond until his or her first appearance hearing before the judge for the following:
  - o Leaving the scene of a crash involving death or personal injuries when the defendant has previously been convicted of a violation of § 316.027, § 316.061, § 316.191, or § 316.193, or a felony violation of § 322.34, Fla. Stat.,
  - o Domestic violence as defined by § 741.28, Fla. Stat.,
  - o Non-domestic stalking (§ 784.048, Fla. Stat.),
  - o Any violation of a domestic violence injunction (§ 741.30(9)(b), Fla. Stat.),
  - o Any violation of an injunction for dating, repeat or sexual violence (§ 784.046, Fla. Stat.),
  - o Any violation of an injunction for protection against stalking (§ 784.0487, Fla. Stat.),
  - o Any violation of pretrial release where the original arrest was for an act of domestic violence (§ 741.29(6), Fla. Stat.),
  - o Any arrest where the crime charged is a violation of chapter 874 or alleged to be subject to enhanced punishment under chapter 874,
  - o Any arrest for burglary (§ 810.02, Fla. Stat.) during a state of emergency in the county,
  - o Any arrest for burglary that is reclassified under § 843.22, Fla. Stat., in which a person crosses county lines in an attempt to thwart law enforcement from tracking the stolen items, or
  - o Any arrest under § 790.401(11), Fla. Stat., for making a false statement under oath in a hearing under that section or for purchasing, possessing, or receiving a firearm or ammunition with knowledge that the defendant is prohibited from doing so by an order issued under that section.
- A defendant required to register as a sexual offender under § 943.0435, Fla. Stat., or as a sexual predator under § 775.21, Fla. Stat., is to be held with no bond until his or her first appearance hearing before the judge, unless the defendant's only criminal charge is a misdemeanor offense under Chapter 316.
- For DUI and BUI, pursuant to § 316.193(9) and 327.35(8), Fla. Stat., the defendant is to be held until his or her blood-alcohol level or breath-alcohol level is less than 0.05 or 8 hours have elapsed from the time the he or she was arrested.

THIS SCHEDULE IS FOR LAW ENFORCEMENT. JUDGES MAY USE IT AS A GUIDE AND SET AN APPROPRIATE BOND FOR THE DEFENDANT AT FIRST APPEARANCE BASED UPON THE EVIDENCE PRESENTED.

** Attachment A is a list of eligible second and third degree felonies. [1]

5. The judges who preside over first appearances pursuant to Rule of Criminal Procedure 3.130, (advisories) or bond calendars are encouraged to ROR persons with or without electronic monitoring when the offender is charged with a misdemeanor or an eligible second or third degree felony specified in Attachment A and the judge has determined the defendant is likely to appear for further proceedings before the Court, unless prohibited by § 903.0351, Fla. Stat., or other provisions of law.

6. For misdemeanor offenses which will be charged by an information, the Sheriff is authorized to issue a NTA to any pre-trial defendant whose highest charge is a first degree misdemeanor when such incarcerated pre-trial defendant has not been charged by an information or NTA within (7) days following first appearance, excluding weekends and holidays. The Sheriff shall not release persons pursuant to this paragraph who are charged with crimes of domestic violence as defined by § 741.28, Fla. Stat.; non–domestic stalking (§ 784.048, Fla. Stat.), any violation of a domestic violence injunction (§ 741.30(9)(b), Fla. Stat.), any violation of an injunction for dating, repeat or sexual repeat violence (§ 784.046, Fla. Stat.), any violation of an injunction against stalking (§ 784.0487, Fla. Stat.), or for violation of pretrial release where the original arrest was for an act of domestic violence (§ 741.29(6), Fla. Stat.).

7. The Sheriff shall notify the county criminal administrative judge, the State Attorney, and the Public Defender of any pre-trial misdemeanant defendant who remains in jail for 30 days whose highest charge is a first degree misdemeanor. This notification shall not include those whose misdemeanor charge would constitute a felony violation of probation. The Sheriff shall provide the Public Defender with the information needed for the Public Defender to set these defendants on a bond calendar. If a defendant is pro se or is represented by private counsel, the Sheriff shall provide Court Administration with the information needed for the Court to set the defendant on a bond calendar. The Public Defender and Court Administration shall set such defendants for further review of bond status on the next regularly scheduled bond calendar that will allow for adequate notice to the victim, if any. Defendants who are required by law to be held shall not be included on such calendars.

8. The Sheriff shall notify the criminal administrative judge, the State Attorney, and the Public Defender of any pre-trial defendant who remains in jail for 90 days whose highest charge is a second or third degree felony enumerated on Attachment A. The Sheriff shall provide the Public Defender with the information needed for the Public Defender to set these defendants on a bond calendar. If a defendant is pro se or is represented by private counsel, the Sheriff shall provide Court Administration with the information needed for the Court to set the defendant on a bond calendar. The Public Defender and Court Administration shall set such defendants for further review of bond status on the next regularly scheduled bond calendar that will allow for adequate notice to the victim, if any. Defendants who are required by law to be held shall not be included on such calendars. The bond hearings set pursuant to this paragraph shall be coordinated with the Criminal Administrative Judge to ensure that the number of defendants set on such calendars can be heard.

9. The Public Defender is encouraged to meet with his clients as soon as possible after appointment so that cases can be expedited where appropriate. When the Public Defender and the State Attorney have agreed to a bond reduction or agreed to a plea, and the Public Defender is unable to get that case on a calendar for the change of plea or bond reduction hearing within three (3) business days, the Public Defender shall forthwith provide the case number to the Criminal Administrative Judge.

10. Structured Release of Pre-Trial Detainees. When the population of the jail exceeds 3,300, the Sheriff, after prior consultation with the Chief Judge, may release all inmates who fall within category (A) below. Should this fail to reduce the population to 3,300 or fewer, the Sheriff may release all inmates in each successive category, one category at a time, until the population is reduced to 3,300 or fewer. Persons who are held on a charge of Failure to Appear or held on a capias for Failure to Appear, or who are required by § 903.0351, Fla. Stat., or other provisions of law to be held shall not be released. Persons who are held for crimes of domestic violence as defined by § 741.28, Fla. Stat., non-domestic stalking (§ 784.048, Fla. Stat.), any violation of a domestic violence injunction (§ 741.30(9)(b), Fla. Stat.), any violation of an injunction for dating, repeat, or sexual violence (§ 784.046, Fla. Stat.), any violation of an injunction for protection against stalking (§ 784.0487, Fla. Stat.), or for violation of pretrial release where the original arrest was for an act of domestic violence (§ 741.29(6), Fla. Stat.) and persons held on a violation of probation shall not be released through structured release but may be released through structured review provided in paragraph 11. Persons who are being held on a warrant from another jurisdiction shall not be released pursuant to this paragraph but may be released pursuant to paragraph two or three.

A. all inmates whose highest charge is a local ordinance violation or second degree misdemeanor who have been held in excess of 10 days may be released on unsupervised ROR.

B. all inmates whose highest charge is a local ordinance violation or second degree misdemeanor may be released on unsupervised ROR.

C. all inmates whose highest charge is a first degree misdemeanor who have been held in excess of 30 days may be released on unsupervised ROR.

D. all inmates whose highest charge is a first degree misdemeanor who have been held in excess of 10 days may be released on unsupervised ROR.

E. all inmates whose highest charge is a first degree misdemeanor may be released on unsupervised ROR.

11. Structured Review of Pre-Trial Detainees. If the structured release of pre-trial detainees specified in paragraph 10 has been fully implemented but the population of the jail still exceeds 3,300, the Sheriff shall notify the Criminal Administrative Judge, the State Attorney, and the Public Defender. The Sheriff shall provide the Public Defender with the information needed to set inmates, one category at a time, on a bond calendar. If the defendant is pro se or is represented by private counsel, the Sheriff shall provide Court Administration with the information needed for the Court to set the defendant on a bond calendar. The Public Defender and Court Administration shall set such defendants in category (A) and those in each successive category, one category at a time, on the next bond calendar until the population is reduced to 3,300 or fewer. The defendants shall be set for further review of bond status on the next regularly scheduled bond calendar that will allow for adequate notice to the victim, if any. Persons who are held on a violation of probation shall only be set on such calendars pursuant to subparagraph (A) or subparagraph (J). Persons who are held on a charge of Failure to Appear or held on a capias for Failure to Appear, or who are required by § 903.0351, Fla. Stat. or other provisions of law to be held shall not be included on such bond calendars.

A. all inmates whose highest charge is domestic violence as defined by § 741.28, Fla. Stat., non-domestic stalking (§ 784.048, Fla. Stat.), any violation of a domestic violence injunction (§ 741.30(9)(b), Fla. Stat.), any violation of an injunction for dating, repeat, or sexual violence (§ 784.046, Fla. Stat.), any violation of an injunction for protection against stalking (§ 784.0487, Fla. Stat.), any violation of pretrial release where the original arrest was for an act of domestic violence (§ 741.29(6), Fla. Stat.) or inmates who are held on a misdemeanor violation of probation.

B. all inmates whose highest charge is no more than one 3rd degree felony who have been held over 90 days.

C. all inmates who are charged with no more than one 3rd degree felony who have been held for over 30 days.

D. all inmates who are charged with no more than one 3rd degree felony who have been held for over 10 days.

E. all inmates who are charged with no more than one 3rd degree felony.

F. all inmates who are charged with no more than two 3rd degree felonies who have been held over 90 days.

G. all inmates who are charged with no more than two 3rd degree felonies who have been held for over 30 days.

H. all inmates who are charged with no more than two 3rd degree felonies who have been held for over 10 days.

I. all inmates who are charged with no more than two 3rd degree felonies.

J. all inmates who are charged with violation of probation whose highest charge is a 3rd degree felony.

12. Structured Release of Sentenced Offenders. If the structured release and structured review of pre-trial detainees specified in paragraphs 10 and 11 has been fully implemented but the population of the jail still exceeds 3,300 the Sheriff, after prior consultation with the Chief Judge, may release all inmates who fall within category (A), below. Should this fail to reduce the population to 3,300 or fewer, the Sheriff may release all inmates in each successive category, one category at a time, until the population is reduced to 3,300 or fewer.

A. any sentenced misdemeanant with less than 10 days remaining on his or her sentence may be released by the Sheriff on electronic monitoring or other alternative sentence unless the sentencing court specifically prohibited such release or unless otherwise prohibited by law.

B. any sentenced misdemeanant with less than 30 days remaining on his or her sentence may be released by the Sheriff on electronic monitoring or other alternative unless the sentencing court specifically prohibited such release or unless otherwise prohibited by law.

C. any sentenced misdemeanant may be released by the Sheriff on electronic monitoring or other alternative sentence unless the sentencing court specifically prohibited such release or unless otherwise prohibited by law.

D. any person serving a county jail sentence for the offenses specified in Attachment A with less than 10 days remaining on his or her sentence may be released by the Sheriff on electronic monitoring or other alternative sentence unless the sentencing court specifically prohibited such release or unless otherwise prohibited by law.

E. any person serving a county jail sentence for the offenses specified in Attachment A with less than 30 days remaining on his or her sentence may be released by the Sheriff on electronic monitoring or other alternative sentence unless the sentencing court specifically prohibited such release or unless otherwise prohibited by law.

F. any person serving a county jail sentence for the offenses specified in Attachment A with less than 60 days remaining on his or her sentence may be released by the Sheriff on electronic monitoring or other alternative sentence unless the sentencing court specifically prohibited such release or unless otherwise prohibited by law.

G. any person serving a county jail sentence for the offenses specified in Attachment A may be released by the Sheriff on electronic monitoring or other alternative sentence unless the sentencing court specifically prohibited such release or unless otherwise prohibited by law.

13. Notwithstanding the structured release and structured review provided for in paragraphs 10, 11, and 12, for misdemeanants and felons sentenced to time in the county jail, the Sheriff has and continues to have the authority to place a misdemeanant or felony inmate on electronic monitoring or alternative sentencing program if specifically authorized to do so in the Judgment and Sentence or other specific order of the Court.

14. For purposes of this Administrative Order, alternative sentence programs include but are not limited to electronic monitoring, work release, Parks Program, and any other alternative sentencing program operated by the Sheriff pursuant to law.

15. The State Attorney shall schedule violation of probation or community control hearings on an incarcerated defendant no later than ten (10) calendar days after the arrest of the defendant. The Public Defender shall notify the Criminal Administrative Judge and the Chief Judge if a violation of probation hearing on an incarcerated defendant is not scheduled within this time period.

Administrative Orders 2014–061 is hereby rescinded.

DONE AND ORDERED in Chambers at St. Petersburg, Pinellas County, Florida, this ___ day of April, 2018.

ORIGINAL SIGNED ON APRIL 25, 2018
BY ANTHONY RONDOLINO,
CHIEF JUDGE

1 Attachment A not attached. Please see http://www.jud6.org/legalcommunity/AdministrativeOrders.html for the most up to date list of eligible felonies.

2018–019. UNIFORM BOND SCHEDULE—PASCO COUNTY

IN THE CIRCUIT COURT, SIXTH JUDICIAL CIRCUIT

IN AND FOR PASCO AND PINELLAS COUNTIES, FLORIDA

ADMINISTRATIVE ORDER NO. 2018–019 PA–CIR

RE: UNIFORM BOND SCHEDULE—PASCO COUNTY

The uniform bond schedule is being amended in Pasco County in response to § 790.401, Florida Statutes, adopted by the Legislature in Senate Bill 7026, Chapter No. 2018–3, Laws of Florida. This statute creates two new felonies related to the protective orders established by that section. Based on the nature of the new felonies, the Chief Judge has determined that defendants who are charged with these new crimes should have bond set by a judge only. In accordance with Article V, section 2, Florida Constitution, Rule of Judicial Administration 2.215, and § 43.26, Florida Statutes,

IT IS ORDERED:

1. All law enforcement agencies in Pasco County are urged to use a Notice to Appear (NTA), pursuant to Rule of Criminal Procedure 3.125, where permitted by law.

2. The Sheriff is hereby authorized to release any person on his or her own recognizance (ROR) who is in pre-trial status on a warrant from another jurisdiction and charged with an ordinance violation, misdemeanor, or an offense specified in Attachment A provided:

A. the Sheriff has sent written notice to the other jurisdiction that the inmate will be released pursuant to this Administrative Order if the inmate is not picked up within 72 hours from notification, excluding weekends and holidays,

B. the other jurisdiction has not picked up the inmate in accordance with the notification, and

C. the inmate is not subject to the provisions of § 903.0351, Fla. Stat., or is not otherwise required by law to be held.

3. The Sheriff is hereby authorized to release any person on pre-trial status who is a member of the United States Armed Forces to the custody of MacDill Air Force Base unless the inmate is subject to the provisions of § 903.0351, Fla. Stat., or unless the inmate is otherwise required by law to be held.

4. The following procedures are implemented for setting bond for defendants at those Pasco Counties receiving facilities housing defendants.

A. *Arresting Officer—Function at Booking Desk*

1. The arresting officer shall complete all information on the complaint affidavit, setting forth the statute number and the degree of the crime for which the defendant is charged, together with a short statement of the facts involved in the alleged crime.

2. The arresting officer shall specifically ask the defendant for his or her current residence address. The arresting officer shall not rely upon any identification furnished by the defendant, unless the defendant is unable to verbally advise the officer of the address. The name and address of the defendant shall be listed on the complaint affidavit.

3. The arresting officer shall leave the bond portion of the complaint affidavit blank, unless the defendant was arrested upon a warrant, in which case the bond set on the warrant shall be entered.

4. For any arrest which has been made based upon probable cause with no warrant involved and where the arresting officer possesses specific reason(s) to believe that a bond, in an amount higher or lower than the amount established pursuant to this Administrative Order should be set, the arresting officer may personally contact a judge and said judge may set a bond outside of the provisions of this Administrative Order. The arresting officer shall enter the amount of bond, as set by the judge, upon the complaint affidavit specifically annotating which judge approved the bond amount.

B. *Booking Officer—Function*

1. For the purposes of this Administrative Order, the term "booking officer" means the employee of the receiving facility who receives the prisoner from the arresting officer.

2. For persons charged with an ordinance violation or a first or second degree misdemeanor, the booking officer may issue a NTA in accordance with Rule of Criminal Procedure 3.125 if the booking officer determines that there is a likelihood that the accused will appear as directed and the defendant is not otherwise required to be held.

3. The booking officer shall specifically ask the defendant to verify his or her current residence address. The booking officer shall not rely on any address listed on any identification in the possession of the defendant, unless the defendant is unable to verbalize his or her address.

4. If the arrest is based upon a warrant, the booking officer shall confirm that the bond on the warrant has been correctly placed on the complaint affidavit, and, if not, enter the bond amount set out in the warrant.

5. If the defendant is being booked by virtue of an arrest based on probable cause, the booking officer shall enter the bond amount on the complaint affidavit, in the space provided for that purpose.

6. With every defendant, the booking officer shall follow the recommended bond set forth by this Administrative Order for the particular degree of crime charged unless the booking officer determines:

a. that a lower bond or ROR is more appropriate than the recommended bond in which case the booking officer may set the bond down to the lower end of the bond schedule, or

b. that a higher bond is more appropriate than the recommended bond based on the guidelines set forth in this Administrative Order in which case the booking officer may set a higher bond up to the maximum allowable pursuant to this Administrative Order. In order to increase the bond the booking officer must specifically set out, in writing on the booking advisory sheet one or more of the aggravating factors enumerated below; or

c. that the arresting officer has contacted a judge pursuant to A.4. above and a judge has authorized a bond different from this Order.

7. Aggravating factors which the booking officer is permitted to consider when an increase in the bond amount is contemplated are:

a. At the time of arrest, the defendant had committed more than one offense.

b. The defendant cannot provide a local address or a permanent place of residence in the Tampa Bay area.

c. The defendant has a prior criminal record.

d. The defendant is on probation, parole, community control or any other form of supervision.

e. There are outstanding warrants or holds for the defendant from this or any other jurisdiction.

f. The arresting officer or booking officer has reason to believe that should the defendant be released, bodily injury may be inflicted upon the alleged victim or another by the defendant.

g. The arresting officer or booking officer has reason to believe that should the defendant be released from custody, the defendant would not return to court when summoned.

If the booking officer finds aggravating factors (f) or (g), the basis for those aggravating factors should be stated in writing on the complaint advisory affidavit.

C. *Range of Bond—Recommended Amount.* For offenses added to the statutes subsequent to the date of this Order, these ranges of bonds will be used for the new offenses, unless otherwise provided in a subsequent administrative order.

	Category of Crime	Low Bond	High Bond	Recommended Bond
1.	Capital Felony	None	None	None
2.	Life Felony *Exception—See Below	$100,000	None	None
	Life Felony Non-homicide and the defendant is a juvenile	$50,000	None	$150,000
3.	1st Degree Felony (P. B. Life) *Exception—See Below	$50,000	None	$150,000
	Other Exception: 2nd Degree Murder § 782.04(2), (3), Fla. Stat.	$100,000	None	None
4.	1st Degree Felony (other than P. B. Life) *Exception—See Below	$10,000	$100,000	$50,000
5.	2nd Degree Felony *Exception—See Below	$5,000	$20,000	$10,000
	2nd Degree Felony Eligible if specified on Attachment A**	$1,000	$10,000	$5,000
6.	3rd Degree Felony *Exception—See Below	$1,000	$10,000	$5,000
	3rd Degree Felony Eligible if specified on Attachment A**	$500	$5,000	$2,000
	Other Exceptions:			
	Any Battery that is a 3rd Degree Felony	$1,000	$5,000	$2,500
	3rd Degree Felony—DUI and BUI offenses, § 316.193 or § 327.35, Fla. Stat.	$2,500	$10,000	$5,000
	3rd Degree Felony—DWLSR offenses, § 322.34, Fla. Stat., where the defendant has 4 or more previous DWLSRs or the defendant's license was previously suspended due to DUI or drug charges.	$2,500	$10,000	$5,000
7.	1st Degree Misdemeanor *Exception—See Below	ROR—UNSUPERVISED	$500	$150
	Other Exceptions:			
	Any Battery that is a 1st Degree Misdemeanor	$250	$1,000	$500
	Any DV–related charge listed in the exceptions below BUT ONLY at or after first appearance	ROR	$5,000	$2,500
	DUI or BUI– Property Damage 1st or 2nd offense § 316.193(3)(c)1, or § 327.35(3)(c)1, Fla. Stat.	$250	$1,000	$500
	DUI or BUI– Property Damage 3rd offense § 316.193(3)(c)1, or § 327.35(3)(c)1, Fla. Stat.	$500	$2,500	$1,000
	1st Degree Misdemeanor DWLSR offenses § 322.34, Fla. Stat., where the defendant has 4 or more previous DWLSRs or the defendant's license was previously suspended due to DUI or drug charges.	$500	$2,500	$1,000
	Failure to Appear (FTA) § 843.15(1)(b), Fla. Stat.	$250	$1,500	$500
	Prostitution offenses, 2nd and subsequent offense § 796.07, Fla. Stat.	ROR—UNSUPERVISED	$500	$250

8.	**2nd** Degree Misdemeanor *Exception—See Below	ROR—UNSUPERVISED	$250	ROR—UNSUPERVISED
	Other Exception:			
	Disorderly Intoxication § 856.011, Fla. Stat.	ROR—UNSUPERVISED	$250	$100
9.	Criminal Traffic *Exception—See Below	ROR—UNSUPERVISED	$250	ROR—UNSUPERVISED
	Other Exceptions: DUI or BUI– No Property Damage 1st or **2nd** offense § 316.193(2)(a) or § 327.35(2)(a), Fla. Stat.	ROR—UNSUPERVISED	$500	ROR—UNSUPERVISED
	DUI or BUI– No Property Damage **3rd** offense § 316.193(2)(a) or § 327.35(2)(a), Fla. Stat.	$500	$1,000	$750
10.	Municipal Ordinance Violations	ROR—UNSUPERVISED	$250	ROR—UNSUPERVISED

* Exceptions—No Bond:

- For capital crimes the bond is automatically "none."
- The defendant is to be held with no bond until his or her first appearance hearing before the judge for the following:
  - o Leaving the scene of a crash involving death or personal injuries when the defendant has previously been convicted of a violation of § 316.027, § 316.061, § 316.191, or § 316.193, or a felony violation of § 322.34, Fla. Stat.,
  - o Domestic violence as defined by § 741.28, Fla. Stat.,
  - o Non-domestic stalking (§ 784.048, Fla. Stat.),
  - o Any violation of a domestic violence injunction (§ 741.30(9)(b), Fla. Stat.),
  - o Any violation of an injunction for dating, repeat or sexual violence (§ 784.046, Fla. Stat.),
  - o Any violation of an injunction for protection against stalking (§ 784.0487, Fla. Stat.),
  - o Any violation of pretrial release where the original arrest was for an act of domestic violence (§ 741.29(6), Fla. Stat.),
  - o Any arrest where the crime charged is a violation of chapter 874 or alleged to be subject to enhanced punishment under chapter 874,
  - o Any arrest for burglary (§ 810.02, Fla. Stat.) during a state of emergency in the county,
  - o Any arrest for burglary that is reclassified under § 843.22, Fla. Stat., in which a person crosses county lines in an attempt to thwart law enforcement from tracking the stolen items, or
  - o Any arrest under § 790.401(11), Fla. Stat., for making a false statement under oath in a hearing under that section or for purchasing, possessing, or receiving a firearm or ammunition with knowledge that the defendant is prohibited from doing so by an order issued under that section.
- A defendant required to register as a sexual offender under § 943.0435, Fla. Stat., or as a sexual predator under § 775.21, Fla. Stat., is to be held with no bond until his or her first appearance hearing before the judge, unless the defendant's only criminal charge is a misdemeanor offense under Chapter 316.
- For DUI and BUI, pursuant to § 316.193(9) and 327.35(8), Fla. Stat., the defendant is to be held until his or her blood-alcohol level or breath-alcohol level is less than 0.05 or 8 hours have elapsed from the time the he or she was arrested.

<u>THIS SCHEDULE IS FOR LAW ENFORCEMENT. JUDGES MAY USE IT AS A GUIDE AND SET AN APPROPRIATE BOND FOR THE DEFENDANT AT FIRST APPEARANCE BASED UPON THE EVIDENCE PRESENTED.</u>

** Attachment A is a list of eligible second and third degree felonies. [1]

5. The judges who preside over first appearances pursuant to Rule of Criminal Procedure 3.130, (advisories) or bond calendars are encouraged to ROR persons with or without electronic monitoring when the offender is charged with a misdemeanor or an eligible second or third degree felony specified in Attachment A and the judge has determined the defendant is likely to appear for further proceedings before the Court, unless prohibited by § 903.0351, Fla. Stat. or other provisions of law.

6. For misdemeanor offenses which will be charged by an information, the Sheriff is authorized to issue a NTA to any pre-trial defendant whose highest charge is a first degree misdemeanor when such incarcerated pre-trial defendant has not been charged by an information or NTA within seven (7) days following first appearance, excluding weekends and holidays. The Sheriff shall not release persons pursuant to this paragraph who are charged with crimes of domestic violence as defined by § 741.28, Fla. Stat.; non-domestic stalking (784.048, Fla. Stat.), any violation of a domestic violence injunction (§ 741.30(9)(b), Fla. Stat.), any violation of an injunction for dating, repeat or sexual repeat violence (§ 784.046, Fla. Stat.), any violation of an injunction against stalking (§ 784.0487, Fla. Stat.), or for violation of pretrial release where the original arrest was for an act of domestic violence (§ 741.29(6), Fla. Stat.).

7. The Public Defender is encouraged to meet with his clients as soon as possible after appointment so that cases can be expedited where appropriate. When the Public Defender and the State Attorney have agreed to a bond reduction or agreed to a plea, and the Public Defender is unable to get that case on a calendar for the change of plea or bond reduction hearing within three (3) business days, the Public Defender shall forthwith provide the case number to the Pasco Administrative Judge.

8. Structured Release of Pre–Trial Detainees. When the population of the jail exceeds 1,900, the Sheriff, after prior consultation with the Chief Judge, may release all inmates who fall within category (A) below. Should this fail to reduce the population to 1,900 or fewer, the Sheriff may release all inmates in each successive category, one category at a time, until the population is reduced to 1,900 or fewer. Persons who are held on a charge of Failure to Appear or held on a capias for Failure to Appear, or who are required by § 903.0351, Fla. Stat., or other provisions of law to be held shall not be released. Persons who are held for crimes of domestic violence as defined by § 741.28, Fla. Stat.; non-domestic stalking (§ 784.048, Fla. Stat.), any violation of a domestic violence injunction (§ 741.30(9)(b), Fla. Stat.), any violation of an injunction for dating, repeat or sexual violence (§ 784.046, Fla. Stat.), any violation of an injunction for protection against stalking (§ 784.0487, Fla. Stat.), or for violation of pretrial release where the original arrest was for an act of domestic violence (§ 741.29(6), Fla. Stat.) and persons held on a violation of probation shall not be released through structured release but may be released through structured review provided in paragraph 9. Persons who are being held on a warrant from another jurisdiction shall not be released pursuant to this paragraph but may be released pursuant to paragraph two or three.

A. all inmates whose highest charge is a local ordinance violation may be released on unsupervised ROR.

B. all inmates whose highest charge is a misdemeanor who have been held in excess of 30 days may be released on unsupervised ROR.

C. all inmates whose highest charge is a misdemeanor who have been held in excess of 10 days may be released on unsupervised ROR.

D. all inmates who highest charge is a misdemeanor may be released on unsupervised ROR.

9. Structured Review of Pre–Trial Detainees. If the structured release of pre-trial detainees specified in paragraph 8 has been fully implemented but the population of the jail exceeds 1,900, the Sheriff shall notify the Pasco Administrative Judge, the State Attorney, and the Public Defender. The Sheriff shall provide the Public Defender with the information needed to set inmates, one category at a time, on a bond calendar. If the defendant is pro se or is represented by private counsel, the Sheriff shall provide Court Administration with the information needed for a representative of the court to set the defendant on a bond calendar. The Public Defender and the representative of the court shall set such defendants in category (A) and those in each successive category, one category at a time, on a bond calendar until the population is reduced to 1,900 or fewer. The defendants shall be set for further review of bond status on a bond calendar that will allow for adequate notice to the victim, if any. Persons who are held on a violation of probation shall only be set on such calendars pursuant to subparagraph (A) or subparagraph (J). Persons who are held on a charge of Failure to Appear or held on a capias for Failure to Appear, or who are required by § 903.0351, Fla. Stat., or other provisions of law to be held shall not be included on such bond calendars.

A. all inmates whose highest charge is domestic violence as defined by § 741.28, Fla. Stat.; non-domestic stalking (§ 784.048, Fla. Stat.), any violation of a domestic violence injunction (§ 741.30(9)(b), Fla. Stat.), any violation of an injunction for dating, repeat or sexual violence (§ 784.046, Fla. Stat.), any violation of an injunction for protection against stalking (§ 784.0487, Fla. Stat.), or for violation of pretrial release where the original arrest was for an act of domestic violence (§ 741.29(6), Fla. Stat.), or inmates who are held on a misdemeanor violation of probation.

B. all inmates who are charged with no more than one offense listed in Attachment A who have been held over 90 days.

C. all inmates who are charged with no more than one offense listed in Attachment A who have been held for over 30 days.

D. all inmates who are charged with no more than one offense listed in Attachment A who have been held for over 10 days.

E. all inmates who are charged with no more than one offense listed in Attachment A.

F. all inmates who are charged with no more than two offenses listed in Attachment A who have been held over 90 days.

G. all inmates who are charged with no more than two offenses listed in Attachment A who have been held for over 30 days.

H. all inmates who are charged with no more than two offenses listed in Attachment A who have been held for over 10 days.

I. all inmates who are charged with no more than two offenses listed in Attachment A.

J. all inmates who are charged with felony violation of probation.

10. Structured Release of Sentenced Offenders. If the structured release and structured review of pre-trial detainees specified in paragraphs 8 and 9 has been fully implemented but the population of the jail exceeds 1,900 the Sheriff, after prior consultation with the Chief Judge, may release all inmates who fall within category (A), below. Should this fail to reduce the population to 1,900 or fewer, the Sheriff is hereby authorized to release all inmates in each successive category, one category at a time, until the population is reduced to 1,900 or fewer.

A. any sentenced misdemeanant with less than 10 days remaining on his or her sentence may be released by the Sheriff on electronic monitoring or other alternative sentence unless the sentencing court specifically prohibited such release or unless otherwise prohibited by law.

B. any sentenced misdemeanant with less than 30 days remaining on his or her sentence may be released by the Sheriff on electronic monitoring or other alternative unless the sentencing court specifically prohibited such release or unless otherwise prohibited by law.

C. any sentenced misdemeanant may be released by the Sheriff on electronic monitoring or other alternative sentence unless the sentencing court specifically prohibited such release or unless otherwise prohibited by law.

D. any person serving a county jail sentence for the offenses specified in Attachment A with less than 10 days remaining on his or her sentence may be released by the Sheriff on electronic monitoring or other alternative sentence unless the sentencing court specifically prohibited such release or unless otherwise prohibited by law.

E. any person serving a county jail sentence for the offenses specified in Attachment A with less than 30 days remaining on his or her sentence may be released by the Sheriff on electronic monitoring or other alternative sentence unless the sentencing court specifically prohibited such release or unless otherwise prohibited by law.

F. any person serving a county jail sentence for the offenses specified in Attachment A with less than 60 days remaining on his or her sentence may be released by the Sheriff on electronic monitoring or other alternative sentence unless the sentencing court specifically prohibited such release or unless otherwise prohibited by law.

G. any person serving a county jail sentence for the offenses specified in Attachment A may be released by the Sheriff on electronic monitoring or other alternative sentence unless the sentencing court specifically prohibited such release or unless otherwise prohibited by law.

11. Notwithstanding the structured release and structured review provided for in paragraphs 8, 9, and 10 for misdemeanants and felons sentenced to time in the county jail, the Sheriff has and continues to have the authority to place a misdemeanant or felony inmate on electronic monitoring or other alternative sentencing program if specifically authorized to do so in the Judgment and Sentence or other specific order of the court.

12. For purposes of this Administrative Order, alternative sentence programs include but are not limited to electronic monitoring, work release, and any other alternative sentencing program operated by the Sheriff pursuant to law.

13. The State Attorney shall schedule violation of probation or community control hearings on an incarcerated defendant no later than fourteen (14) calendar days after the arrest of the defendant. The Public Defender shall notify the Pasco Administrative Judge and the Chief Judge if a violation of probation hearing on an incarcerated defendant is not scheduled within this time period.

Administrative Order 2014–62 is hereby rescinded.

DONE AND ORDERED in Chambers at St. Petersburg, Pinellas County, Florida, this ___ day of April, 2018.

ORIGINAL SIGNED ON APRIL 25, 2018
BY ANTHONY RONDOLINO,
CHIEF JUDGE

1 Attachment A not attached. Please see http://www.jud6.org/legalcommunity/AdministrativeOrders.html for the most up to date list of eligible felonies.

2018–013. SEXUAL HARASSMENT POLICY AND DISCRIMINATION POLICY

IN THE CIRCUIT COURT, SIXTH JUDICIAL CIRCUIT IN AND FOR PASCO AND PINELLAS COUNTIES, FLORIDA

ADMINISTRATIVE ORDER NO. 2018–013 PA/PI–CIR

RE: SEXUAL HARASSMENT AND DISCRIMINATION POLICY

The Sixth Judicial Circuit for many years has had a policy of promoting a workplace that is free from discrimination including sexual harassment and has had procedures in place that provide directions for employees to report any alleged occurrences of discrimination or sexual harassment. Florida Supreme Court Administrative Order AOSC18–6 adopted new policies and procedures for complaints against judges for sexual harassment and directed the Chief Judge to adopt those new policies and procedures. Therefore, it is

ORDERED:

1. The Supreme Court's Sexual Harassment Policy and Procedures for Sexual Harassment Complaints Against Justices and Judges is hereby adopted for the Sixth Judicial Circuit. The Policy and Procedures in Appendix A are attached to and made a part of this Order. These procedures supersede and replace the Sixth Judicial Circuit Sexual Harassment Policy and Complaint Procedures Against Judges adopted by Administrative Order No. 2004–077 PA/PI CIR.

2. The Sixth Judicial Circuit Sexual Harassment and Discrimination Policy and Procedures are hereby revised to make them consistent with the Florida Supreme Court policy. The Revised Policy and Procedures in Appendix B are attached to and made a part of this Order. The Revised Policy and Procedures supersede and replace the Policy and Procedures adopted by Administrative Order No. 2004–077 PA/PI–CIR.

3. These policies shall apply to all court personnel of the Sixth Judicial Circuit without regard to position funding source, i.e. county, state, or other payroll classification.

4. The Administrative Office of Courts shall as soon as practicable, distribute these policies to all court personnel of the Sixth Judicial Circuit and obtain signed confirmations of receipt of these policies from all employees, excluding constitutional officer.

Administrative Order 2004–077 PA/PI–CIR is hereby rescinded.

DONE AND ORDERED in Chambers at St. Petersburg, Pinellas County, Florida, this ___ day of March, 2018.

ORIGINAL SIGNED ON MARCH 20, 2018
BY ANTHONY RONDOLINO,
CHIEF JUDGE

APPENDIX A

SEXUAL HARASSMENT POLICY AND PROCEDURES FOR SEXUAL HARASSMENT COMPLAINTS AGAINST JUSTICES AND JUDGES

1. Policy

The chief justice's implementation of this policy is under his or her authority as the administrative officer of the judicial branch and of the supreme court pursuant to rule 2.205(a)(2)(B), Florida Rules of Judicial Administration.

It is the policy of the Florida Supreme Court to foster a workplace free of sexual harassment, or sexual misconduct. Sexual harassment occurs if there are unwelcome sexual advances; unwelcome requests for sexual favors; or unwelcome verbal or physical conduct of a sexual nature from or involving an employee's supervisors, peers, subordinates or other persons in contact with an employee during the course of the conduct of the employee's business when:

1. Submission to such conduct is either explicitly or implicitly a term or condition of employment; or

2. Submission to or rejection of such conduct by an individual is used as the basis for employment decisions affecting such individual or as the basis for any official action; or

3. Such conduct has the purpose or effect of interfering with an individual's work performance or creates a persistently intimidating and hostile environment, as that term is defined in state and federal law.

Sexual misconduct is any behavior of a sexual nature that is committed without consent or by force, intimidation, coercion, or manipulation. Sexual misconduct can occur between strangers or acquaintances, including people involved in an intimate or sexual relationship, and is not necessarily actionable sexual harassment.

The Florida Supreme Court and the entire state court system condemn any sexual harassment or sexual misconduct and advance the position that anyone in contact with the state courts system should feel empowered to bring any such inappropriate activity to the attention of all proper authorities, including and especially the Florida Supreme Court. Anyone authorized to investigate or pursue a complaint of sexual harassment or sexual misconduct hereunder must always maintain an open-door policy that fosters the free expression of any complaint. The chief justice or chief justice's designee has the authority to take any administrative action necessary to protect the complainant from further sexual harassment or sexual misconduct and from retaliation related to a complaint hereunder.

It is the policy of the Florida Supreme Court that all complaints of sexual harassment or sexual misconduct against any justice or judge within the state courts system will be treated seriously and acted upon promptly. The following procedures apply to complaints against justices or judges made by employees of the court system, applicants for employment with the court system, and when applicable attorneys, litigants, or other members of the public. Compliance with these procedures by the chief justice, the chief justice's designee, or a chief judge constitutes a presumption of compliance with the disciplinary responsibilities under Canon 3(D)1 of the Code of Judicial Conduct.

2. <u>Notification</u>

The chief justice may designate any court system officer or employee to be responsible for receiving and documenting complaints of sexual harassment or sexual misconduct against justices of the Supreme Court, judges of the district courts of appeal, or judges of any of the trial courts.

Any employee or applicant for employment with the court system who believes that he or she is the subject of sexual harassment by a justice of the Supreme Court, a judge of any of the district courts of appeal, or a judge of any of the trial courts should submit his or her complaint in writing, or if the person prefers he or she may submit the complaint orally. The complaint may be submitted to any of the following: the chief justice or his or her designee; a local administrator, such as a Trial Court Administrator, human resource manager or Marshal; or the Chief of Human Resources at the Office of the State Courts Administrator (OSCA). If the person receiving the complaint is not the chief justice, the chief justice's designee hereunder, or a chief judge, the person receiving the complaint should forward it to the chief justice, the chief justice's designee hereunder, or the chief judge of the court in which the subject judge serves for an investigation pursuant to section 4, below. Student interns working for the state courts system who believe they are the subject of sexual harassment may use these complaint procedures, but in all instances, should submit a complaint to their college or university in accordance with school sexual harassment complaint procedures.

If any person has difficulty writing out the complaint and the person requests assistance in reducing the complaint to writing or if the person prefers to submit the complaint orally, the chief justice, local administrator, or OSCA Chief of Human Resources, as appropriate, shall designate a person, who will not be involved in the investigation or adjudication of the complaint, to aid the person in reducing the complaint to writing.

If the chief justice is the subject of a complaint, the employee or applicant should submit the complaint to the inspector general of the Supreme Court, who will refer the complaint to the most senior justice, excluding the chief justice. The justice to whom such a complaint is referred will assume all complaint investigation and resolution duties for which the chief justice otherwise would be responsible. The justice to whom such a complaint is referred also will be responsible for maintaining records pertaining to the complaint.

If an employee or applicant chooses not to file a formal complaint, and any person designated hereunder to receive complaints has actual knowledge or receives information that a substantial likelihood exists that a justice or judge has engaged in sexual harassment or sexual misconduct, the person may inquire into the matter and take appropriate action.

3. <u>Time for Filing Complaints</u>

In order to ensure that Florida Supreme Court complaint procedures can be utilized without risk of precluding the filing of a charge of discrimination with state or federal entities, an employee or applicant should report an incident of sexual harassment within 90 days of the date of occurrence.

4. <u>Investigations</u>

A complaint of sexual harassment or sexual misconduct against a justice or judge will be investigated promptly and thoroughly. If a complaint has been made, the chief justice, the chief justice's designee hereunder, or the chief judge of the court in which the subject judge serves may designate another person to make an initial inquiry into the complaint.

The chief justice, chief justice's designee, or a chief judge of the court in which the subject judge serves will interview the complainant within five days of the submission of the complaint to ascertain relevant facts and circumstances. If the complainant does not divulge names or details of the incident(s), the chief justice or chief justice's designee, or the chief judge of the court in which the subject judge serves will rely upon any information that is available. If another person has been designated to make an initial inquiry into the complaint, the designee will report details of the complaint, including any relevant facts, circumstances, and information, to the chief justice within ten days of the submission of the complaint.

If the chief justice, chief justice's designee, or the chief judge of the court in which the subject judge serves determines the complaint is unfounded or is insufficient to constitute sexual harassment, he or she may decline to pursue any action on the complaint.

If the chief justices, chief justice's designee, or the chief judge of the court in which the subject judge serves determines the complaint is facially sufficient to constitute sexual harassment, the chief justice, chief justice's designee, or the chief judge of the court in which the subject judge serves may appoint an investigating officer or officers to formally investigate the complaint, or may take any other action appropriate under the circumstances.

If the chief justice or chief justice's designee determines the complaint is insufficient to constitute sexual harassment, but nevertheless indicates potential sexual misconduct, the chief justice or chief justice's designee may take any action appropriate to address the circumstances, including but not limited to appointing an investigating officer or officers to formally investigate the complaint.

The chief justice, chief justice's designee, the chief judge of the court in which the subject judge serves, or investigating officer will interview the complainant, the justice or judge implicated, and witnesses, if any, and will review relevant documents. If any investigating officers have been appointed, they will submit a written report to the chief justice, chief justice's designee, or the chief judge of the court in which the subject judge serves within thirty days of the submission of the complaint for formal investigation.

5. Resolution

The chief justice, or pursuant to rule 2.205(a)(2)(D), Florida Rules of Judicial Administration, the other most senior justice if the chief justice is the subject of a complaint, shall determine the course of action for internal resolution of the complaint, and may appoint another person, other than the subject of the complaint, to recommend the course of action for internal resolution.

If the chief justice or chief justice's designee determines the complaint, including any relevant facts, circumstances, and information, is insufficient to constitute sexual harassment, the chief justice, chief justice's designee, or the chief judge of the court in which the subject judge serves may attempt to resolve the complaint informally through mutual conciliation by meeting with the complainant and the subject justice or judge to discuss a method of resolution, including alternative dispute resolution. In attempting to resolve the complaint, the chief justice, chief justice's designee, or the chief judge of the court in which the subject judge serves may counsel or take other appropriate direct action with the justice or judge involved.

If the complaint and investigation reasonably indicate that the subject justice or judge engaged in activity that constitutes sexual harassment, constitutes sexual misconduct, or otherwise raises a substantial question as to a justice's or judge's fitness for office, the chief justice, chief justice's designee, or the chief judge of the court in which the subject judge serves shall refer the complaint and all written documentation pertaining to the complaint to the Judicial Qualifications Commission.

To the extent not otherwise prohibited by statute or rule, a written summary of the resolution will be provided to the complainant within a reasonable time after a determination is made and any action pursuant thereto is taken.

6. Documentation and Confidentiality

All information pertaining to a complaint of sexual harassment must be documented and maintained by the chief justice, chief justice's designee, or the chief judge of the court in which the subject judge serves whichever officer took final action on the resolution of the complaint.

All records made or received by any person pursuant to these complaint procedures are exempt from public disclosure as provided in rule 2.420(c)(3)(A), Florida Rules of Judicial Administration. Such records are exempt from public disclosure for the duration of an initial inquiry, formal investigation and resolution of the complaint, and at all times thereafter, unless the records are forwarded to the Judicial Qualifications Commission.

If records pertaining to a complaint are forwarded to the Judicial Qualifications Commission, such records will be confidential under rule 2.420(c)(3)(A), and rule 23(a), Rules of the Judicial Qualifications Commission, until any formal charges against the justice or judge are filed by the Investigative Panel of the Commission with the clerk of the Florida Supreme Court.

Records within the possession of any justice, judge, or court staff and pertaining to a complaint that has been forwarded to the Judicial Qualifications Commission will become public upon formal charges being filed with the clerk of the Florida Supreme Court.

7. Referral to the Judicial Qualifications Commission

The Judicial Qualifications Commission is responsible for investigating all reported instances of judicial misconduct. These procedures do not preclude the referral of a complaint against a justice or judge at any time by any person to the Judicial Qualifications Commission. If a complaint has been referred to the Judicial Qualifications Commission, no further action by the chief justice or chief justice's designee is required.

For anyone wishing to file such a complaint, the Commission's mailing address is P.O. Box 141106, Tallahassee, Florida 32317. The Commission's Executive Director, can be contacted by telephone at 850–488–1581 or by email at contact@floridajqc.com.

8. Referral to the Florida Commission on Human Relations or the United State Equal Employment Opportunity Commission

These procedures do not preclude the filing of a charge of employment discrimination with the Florida Commission on Human Relations or the United States Equal Employment Opportunity Commission.

For anyone wishing to file such a complaint, the Florida Commission on Human Relations (FCHR) is located at: 4075 Esplanade Way Room 110 Tallahassee, FL 32399. The telephone number for the FCHR is: 850–488–7082 or 1–800–342–8170.

The United States Equal Employment Opportunity Commission (EEOC) office with jurisdiction over complaints arising in Florida is the Miami District Office located at 100 SE 2nd Street, Suite 1500, Miami, FL 33131. The telephone number for the EEOC Miami District office is: 1–800–669–4000.

9. Referral to the Chief of Human Resources, Office of the State Courts Administrator

For anyone wishing to file a complaint under this policy, the Chief of Human Resources, OSCA is located at: 500 South Duval Street Tallahassee, Florida 32399–1925. The telephone number is 850–617–4028.

APPENDIX B

SIXTH JUDICIAL CIRCUIT

SEXUAL HARASSMENT AND DISCRIMINATION POLICY AND PROCEDURES REVISED AS OF MARCH X, 2018

It is the policy of the Court to provide all employees of the Sixth Judicial Circuit with a work environment free from sexual harassment or any form of discrimination; including discrimination based on race, color, sex, religion, national origin, disability, marital status, or age; and a work environment free from retaliation against those who oppose or report discrimination or sexual harassment.

Under Title VII of the Civil Rights Act of 1964, no employee, either male or female, shall be subjected to unsolicited and unwelcome sexual overtures, verbal or physical conduct of a sexual nature, or any other verbal or nonverbal conduct that might be construed as sexual in nature. The above described conduct, either by supervisors, co-workers or non-employees will not be tolerated by the Court. Such behavior, whether committed by a supervisor or co-worker, will be considered employee misconduct and will result in appropriate disciplinary or other corrective action. Such conduct by a non-employee will result in appropriate corrective action, which may include contact with the individual's employer.

Sexual harassment is defined as unwelcome sexual advances, requests for sexual favors, and other verbal harassment and violates Title VII when:

1. submission to such conduct is made either explicitly or implicitly a term or condition of an individual's employment,

2. submission to or rejection of such conduct by an individual is used as the basis for employment decisions affecting such individual, or

3. such conduct has the purpose or effect of unreasonably interfering with an individual's work performance or creating an intimidating, hostile, or offensive work environment.

An employee who believes he or she may be the subject of sexual harassment or discrimination should immediately report his or her complaint either orally or in writing in accordance with the procedures set forth below. In any instance in which the complainant believes that the reporting of a complaint to the individual specified below would be futile, the complainant should proceed up the hierarchy to an appropriate level, up to and including the Chief Judge, in order to effectively register a complaint.

A. Complaints Against Co–Employees and Supervisors

Complaints against co-employees should be reported to the complainant's immediate supervisor. If the complainant believes that reporting the conduct of co-employees to the supervisor would be futile, or if the employee has a complaint about the supervisor, the employee should report the conduct to the Human Resources Director. The individual to whom the complaint is made shall immediately report the complaint to the Courts Administrator, who will in turn notify the Chief Judge. The Chief Judge will appoint persons to investigate all complaints against employees. Such persons may include the Court Counsel and the Human Resources Director when appropriate.

After due consideration of all available information, the appointed person(s) shall expeditiously report the nature and facts of the complaint to the Chief Judge. The Chief Judge shall make a determination based upon the complaint and the report and shall take appropriate corrective action. Said action may include employee disciplinary action up to and including dismissal. The Chief Judge shall advise the Courts Administrator of the Court's decision regarding the discrimination or harassment complaint. The Courts Administrator will meet with the complainant and appropriate individuals to advise them of the decision and impose any appropriate disciplinary action.

B. Complaints Against Judges by Employees

Any complaint of sexual harassment or sexual misconduct against a judge, including the Chief Judge, should be reported as provided in the Sexual Harassment Policy and Procedures for Sexual Harassment Complaints Against Justices and Judges, which is located in Appendix A to Administrative Order 2018–013 PA/PI–CIR.

C. Complaints Against the Courts Administrator by Employees

Any complaint against the Courts Administrator shall be brought directly to the attention of the Chief Judge. The Chief Judge shall determine the procedure for addressing the complaint, as specified in section A.

Upon completion of any investigation, the Chief Judge shall make a determination based thereon and shall take appropriate corrective action.

D. Confidentiality and Records

Any investigation of a complaint will be conducted in a professional, confidential, and expeditious manner. Nothing in this policy will guarantee protection from public access other than as provided in Florida or federal law, or court rule.

All records made or received by the Chief Judge or the Chief Judge's designee through use of these complaint procedures are exempt from public disclosure under rules 2.420 (c)(3), and (8), Florida Rules of Judicial Administration. Such records of complaints against employees are exempt until a determination of probable cause is found. Any record of resulting disciplinary action will be maintained in the disciplined employee's personnel file.

E. Protection from Retaliation

In no case will an employee be disciplined or otherwise retaliated against for opposing harassment or discrimination in the workplace by reporting in good faith any violation of this policy. However, any employee who is in receipt of a complaint or has knowledge of a violation and fails to take action by reporting the matter may be subject to disciplinary action ranging from a written reprimand up to and including dismissal. Any employee who knowingly files a false complaint of sexual harassment or other discrimination against another person shall be subject to disciplinary action ranging from a written reprimand up to and including dismissal.

F. Posting

This policy and the administrative order adopting it shall be posted at each courthouse location. This policy shall, further, be distributed as part of all new employee manuals and generally distributed to all judges and court staff on a periodic basis.

SIXTH JUDICIAL CIRCUIT

ACKNOWLEDGEMENT OF RECEIPT OF SEXUAL HARASSMENT AND DISCRIMINATION POLICIES AND PROCEDURES

I have received and read a copy of

(1) the Sexual Harassment Policy and Complaint Procedures Against Judges

(2) the Sixth Judicial Circuit Sexual Harassment and Discrimination Policy and Procedures Revised as of March 20, 2018.

as adopted by Administrative Order 2018–013 PA/PI–CIR. I understand the policy set forth regarding discrimination and sexual harassment, the procedure for reporting and resolving complaints, and the consequences of any violation of this policy.

____

Employee's Name

____

Employee's Signature

____

Date

Human Resources Director, Bill Newton, can be reached by calling (727) 453–7164.

2018–008. UNIFIED FAMILY COURT—PINELLAS COUNTY

IN THE CIRCUIT COURT, SIXTH JUDICIAL CIRCUIT IN AND FOR PASCO AND PINELLAS COUNTIES, FLORIDA

ADMINISTRATIVE ORDER NO. 2018–008 PI–CIR

RE: UNIFIED FAMILY COURT—PINELLAS COUNTY

Unified Family Court in Pinellas County was created in 2001 by Administrative Order No. PI–CIR–2001–29 and consists of sections 1, 2, 5, and 6.

In order to ensure an even distribution of cases in the Pinellas County Unified Family Court sections, postal zone improvement plan (ZIP) codes were realigned in 2005 and 2009 by Administrative Orders 2005–004 PI–CIR and 2009–005 PI–CIR, respectively. In 2015, adoption cases that arise out of Chapter 39 juvenile dependency cases were assigned to the same section as the dependency cases. In order to continue to maintain efficient court operations, it has become necessary to update the Administrative Order assigning cases in Unified Family Court. Therefore,

IT IS ORDERED:

1. Unified Family Court (UFC) shall continue to be comprised of sections 1, 2, 5, and 6.

2. The Clerk of the Circuit Court shall assign the cases described in this Administrative Order using the residential ZIP assignments as follows:

a. Section 1: 33755, 33759, 33761, 33763, 33765, 34660, 34688, 34697, 34677, 34681, 34682, 34683, 34684, 34685, 34688, 34689, 34695, 34697, 34698

b. Section 2: 33756, 33757, 33758, 33764, 33766, 33767, 33770, 33771, 33773, 33774, 33775, 33777, 33778, 33779, 33780, 33781, 33784, 33785, 33786

c. Section 5: 33701, 33702, 33703, 33704, 33705, 33712, 33716, 33760, 33762, 33782

d. Section 6 33706, 33707, 33708, 33709, 33710, 33711, 33713, 33714, 33715, 33744, 33772, 33776

3. New assignments: Every juvenile delinquency case arising from a law enforcement complaint against a minor child, juvenile dependency case, termination of parental rights case (TPR) under Chapter 39, Florida Statutes, action under Chapter 751, Florida Statutes, and action under Chapter 984, Florida Statutes shall be assigned to a UFC section according to the ZIP code of that minor child's most recent residential address. An adoption that emanates from a TPR case under Chapter 39, Florida Statutes, shall be assigned to the UFC section where the juvenile dependency case is pending. An adoption that emanates from a TPR case under Chapter 63, Florida Statutes, shall be assigned to the UFC section where the TPR case is pending. **Previous assignments**: If a minor child has been previously assigned to a section, the Clerk of the Circuit Court shall assign any new juvenile delinquency, dependency, TPR case, case under Chapter 751, Florida Statutes, or case under Chapter 984, Florida Statutes according to the minor child's previously assigned section, even if the minor child has moved to a new residence with a new ZIP code.

4. The Clerk of the Circuit Court shall assign cases with an out of county ZIP code on an equal, at random, blind assignment basis among sections 1, 2, 5, and 6 unless there was a previous case assignment to a Section, in which case the Clerk of Court shall assign the case to the previously assigned Section.

5. The Clerk of the Circuit Court shall assign all co-defendants in a juvenile delinquency case to a UFC section according to their ZIP code as described in paragraph 2. However, should the court determine that it is necessary to reassign one or more co-defendants in order to ensure that all the co-defendants' cases are tried in one section, then the case shall be reassigned by the court.

6. If at any point, for judicial efficiency, it becomes necessary to transfer a case from one section to a different section, then the court on its own motion or on the motion of the state attorney, public defender, regional counsel, court appointed counsel, private counsel for the child, or counsel for the Guardian ad Litem, may request the Clerk's Office to assign all pending cases relating to the child to a single section. Notwithstanding Local Rule 3(B), the motion shall be filed in and heard by the judge of the section in which the older pending case(s) are assigned.

7. The Clerk of the Circuit Court shall continue to assign termination of parental rights cases under Chapter 63, Florida Statutes, and adoption cases under Chapter 63, Florida Statutes (excluding those adoption cases arising from a TPR under Chapter 39, Florida Statutes) on an equal, at random, blind assignment basis among Sections 1, 2, 5, and 6 without regard to the ZIP code.

8. The Clerk of the Circuit Court and the Pinellas County Business Technology Services Department shall take the steps needed to ensure that cases are assigned and reports generated in accordance with this Administrative Order.

9. The Administrative Office of the Courts (AOC) is directed to provide the UFC Administrative Judge with a report, which reflects the number of cases being assigned to each UFC section based upon the ZIP code lists. This report should specifically show how many cases are coming from each individual ZIP code listed in Paragraph 2 above. These reports should be provided to the UFC Administrative Judge on a monthly basis. The AOC shall be responsible for monitoring any significant shifts in the number of cases being assigned to the UFC sections. The AOC shall report to the UFC Administrative Judge any significant shifts in the number of cases being assigned to the judges assigned to UFC.

Administrative Orders 2009–005 PI–CIR and 2015–059 PI–CIR are hereby rescinded.

DONE AND ORDERED in Chambers at St. Petersburg, Pinellas County, Florida this ___ day of February, 2018.

ORIGINAL SIGNED ON FEBRUARY 20, 2018
BY ANTHONY RONDOLINO,
CHIEF JUDGE

2017–072. MOTIONS TO COMPEL DISCOVERY

IN THE CIRCUIT COURT, SIXTH JUDICIAL CIRCUIT IN AND FOR PASCO AND PINELLAS COUNTIES, FLORIDA

ADMINISTRATIVE ORDER NO. 2017–072 PA/PI–CIR

RE: MOTIONS TO COMPEL DISCOVERY

In order to facilitate discovery in cases in the circuit civil division, and in accordance with *Nudel v. Flagstar Bank, FSB*, 52 So. 3d 692 (Fla. 4th DCA 2010), and in accordance with Article V, § 2, Florida Constitution, Rule of Judicial Administration 2.215, and § 43.26, Florida Statutes,

IT IS ORDERED:

1. When a motion to compel discovery is filed in accordance with Rule of Civil Procedure 1.380(a)(2) and the motion alleges

a. a complete failure to respond to or object to discovery, and

b. a request for extension has not been filed, and

c. the motion alleges that counsel has conferred with opposing counsel and has been unable to resolve the dispute, as provided for in Administrative Order 2015–052 and any other subsequent Administrative Orders regarding the Professionalism Committee or Standards of Professional Courtesy,

the court, without hearing, may enter an ex parte order requiring compliance with the original discovery demand. The movant must file the original motion with the Clerk and submit a copy of the motion to compel, a proposed order, and copies of the proposed order along with stamped, addressed envelopes to the Court.

2. The Court may impose sanctions in accordance with Rule of Civil Procedure 1.380(b) if discovery is not completed within ten days from the date of entry of the ex parte order and the proposed order should so provide. A form order on a motion to compel is Attachment A, which may be used.

DONE AND ORDERED in Chambers at St. Petersburg, Pinellas County, Florida this _________ day of December, 2017.

ORIGINAL SIGNED ON DECEMBER 13, 2017
BY ANTHONY RONDOLINO,
CHIEF JUDGE

ATTACHMENT A

IN THE CIRCUIT COURT OF THE SIXTH JUDICIAL CIRCUIT IN AND FOR PASCO/PINELLAS COUNTY, FLORIDA
_________ DIVISION

____
Plaintiff(s),
v.

Case No. ____________
UCN: ____________

____
Defendant(s).
______________________________/

ORDER COMPELLING DISCOVERY

THIS CAUSE is before the Court on ________ Motion to Compel Discovery. Upon consideration, the Court finds that the Motion was filed in accordance with Rule of Civil Procedure 1.380(a)(2) and alleges that:

a. the opposing party has completely failed to respond to or object to discovery, and

b. a request for extension has not been filed, and

c. counsel has conferred with opposing counsel and has been unable to resolve the dispute, as provided for in Administrative Order 2015–052 and any other subsequent Administrative Orders regarding the Professionalism Committee or Standards of Professional Courtesy.

Accordingly, it is hereby

ORDERED AND ADJUDGED that ________ shall comply with the original discovery demand in the above-styled cause no later than ten (10) days from the date of this Order. Failure to comply with this Order may result in Court imposed sanctions in accordance with Rule of Civil Procedure 1.380(b).

DONE AND ORDERED in Chambers, at ________, Pasco/Pinellas County, Florida this ________ day of ______, 20________.

____
Circuit Judge

2017–064. CONFIDENTIALITY OF COURT RECORDS

IN THE CIRCUIT COURT, SIXTH JUDICIAL CIRCUIT IN AND FOR PASCO AND PINELLAS COUNTIES, FLORIDA

ADMINISTRATIVE ORDER NO. 2017–064 PA/PI–CIR

RE: CONFIDENTIALITY OF COURT RECORDS

Florida Rule of Judicial Administration 2.420 regulates public access to and the protection of judicial branch records. In order to assist with the application of this rule, Administrative Orders 2010–065 and 2013–024 were created. These Administrative Orders are now being consolidated and amended to reduce redundancies and reflect recent updates to rule 2.420.

In accordance with the Chief Judge's authority under Article V, section 2, Florida Constitution, Fla. R. Jud. Admin. 2.120(c) and 2.215(e), and section 43.26, Florida Statutes, it is

ORDERED:

I. Directions to parties and affected non–parties

A. *Motion to Determine Confidentiality of Court Records.* To the extent a "Motion to Determine Confidentiality of Court Records" is required under Fla. R. Jud. Admin. 2.420, a form "Motion to Determine Confidentiality of Court Records" is attached as Appendix A. The motion must indicate whether all other parties and affected nonparties, if any, agree with the motion. The motion also must indicate the location of the confidential information in the court file, including, if applicable, the document title and the page and line number where the information is located in the document. One of the form orders attached as Appendixes B–1 and B–2 must accompany the motion.

B. *Motion Requesting Access to Confidential Court Records, Seeking to Vacate an Order Granting a Motion to Determine Confidentiality of Court Records, or Seeking to Unseal Information Designated Confidential by the Clerk.* A copy of any motion that, if granted, would result in access to a confidential court file, confidential document, or confidential information must be provided to the judge who entered the order making the court file, document, or information confidential. If the file, document, or information is maintained as confidential by the Clerk of the Circuit Court without a court order or if the judge who entered the order is no longer a judge of the Sixth Judicial Circuit, then a copy of the motion should be provided to the section judge.

C. *Motion to Determine Confidentiality of Court Records—Special Criminal Records.* A filer who seeks to determine the confidentiality of a plea agreement, substantial assistance agreement, or other court record that reveals the identity of a confidential informant or active criminal investigative information should use a "Motion to Determine Confidentiality of Court Records — Special Criminal Records," which is attached as Appendix C. The motion must indicate if the State, defendant(s), and all affected non-parties agree to the relief requested. The form "Order Granting/Denying Motion to Determine Confidentiality of Court Records—Special Criminal Records" attached as Appendix D must accompany the motion.

D. *Notice.* To the extent notice to affected non-parties is required under Fla. R. Jud. Admin. 2.420, a form "Notice to Affected Non–Party" is attached as Appendix E.

E. *Hearing.* To the extent a hearing is required under Fla. R. Jud. Admin. 2.420, the movant must contact the judicial assistant in the section where the case is assigned so that a hearing can be scheduled in the timeframe set forth by the rule. A form "Notice of Hearing (Confidential records)" that the movant must complete and serve is attached as Appendix F.

II. Directions to clerks of the circuit court

A. *Confidential Cases.* Unless otherwise ordered by the Court, the Clerk of the Circuit Court of Pasco County and the Clerk of the Circuit Court of Pinellas County ("Clerks") are authorized and directed to seal the entire court file and progress docket in the following case types, without requiring any other order of the Court or public notice:

1. Dependency, sections 39.0132(3)–(4), Fla. Stat.; Fla. R. Jud. Admin. 2.420(d)(1)(B)(i).

2. Termination of Parental Rights, sections 39.814(3)–(4), Fla. Stat.; Fla. R. Jud. Admin. 2.420(d)(1)(B)(i).

3. Adoption, section 63.162, Fla. Stat.; Fla. R. Jud. Admin. 2.420(d)(1)(B)(ii).

4. Gestational Surrogacy, section 742.16(9), Fla. Stat.; Fla. R. Jud. Admin. 2.420(d)(1)(B)(xiv).

5. Children and Families in Need of Services, sections 984.06(3)–(4), Fla. Stat.; Fla. R. Jud. Admin. 2.420(d)(1)(B)(xvii).

6. Juvenile Delinquency, sections 985.04(1) and 985.045(2), Fla. Stat.; Fla. R. Jud. Admin. 2.420(d)(1)(B)(xviii).

7. Waiver of Parental Notification of Termination of Pregnancy by Minor, section 390.01116, Fla. Stat.; Fla. R. Jud. Admin. 2.420(d)(1)(B)(vii).

8. Paternity Actions when the Clerks receive written notice, accompanied by a copy of a marriage license, that the biological mother in a paternity action has subsequently married the purported father, section 742.091, Fla. Stat.

9. Marchman Act, section 397.6760, Fla. Stat.; Fla. R. Jud. Admin. 2.420(d)(1)(B)(ix).

B. *Confidential Records.* In addition to the records or information identified in Fla. R. Jud. Admin. 2.420, the Clerks are authorized and directed to maintain the following documents or information as confidential as provided by state or federal law, unless otherwise ordered by the Court, without requiring any other order of the Court or public notice:

1. Psychological and Psychiatric Evaluations, sections 456.057 and 456.059, Fla. Stat.

2. "Notice of Social Security Number," Florida Family Law Form 12.902(j); Fla. R. Jud. Admin. 2.420(d)(1)(B)(iii).

3. Violation of probation reports, section 945.10(1)(b), Fla. Stat.

4. Florida Department of Law Enforcement criminal history records, section 943.054, Fla. Stat.; 28 C.F.R. Part 20.

5. Department of Highway Safety and Motor Vehicles driver history records, section 119.0712(2), Fla. Stat.; the

Driver's Privacy Protection Act (DPPA), 18 U.S.C. § 2721 et seq.

6. A social security number contained in an indictment or information filed by the State Attorney, 42 U.S.C. § 405(c)(2)(C)(viii); Fla. R. Jud. Admin. 2.420(d)(1)(B)(iii).

7. Investigative subpoenas, section 119.071(2)(c)(1), Fla. Stat..

8. Applications for or orders authorizing a wiretap, pen register or trap and trace device, or mobile tracking device, sections 119.071(2)(c)(1), 934.09(8)(c), 934.33, and 934.42, Fla. Stat.

C. *Identifying Information.* When the law, a rule, or a court order requires the Clerk to seal or maintain identifying information as confidential, the Clerks are directed to maintain as confidential the following information for the individual on the specified case, unless otherwise directed by the Court:

1. Name;
2. Alias;
3. Social security number;
4. Address;
5. Date of birth; and
6. Information on the person's tattoos, scars, and birthmarks.

D. *Interpretation of Court Orders.* When the Clerks receive an order directing that a court file, a document, or information contained therein be maintained as confidential, the Clerks are hereby authorized and directed as follows:

1. If a court order directs that a court record be kept confidential, the Clerks shall maintain as confidential both the court file and the progress docket. In the context of the progress docket, the Clerk shall remove the docket from any public access information system. However, unless otherwise indicated herein or by court order, the Clerk shall not treat as confidential the case number, docket number, or any other identifying number of the case that is determined to be confidential.

2. If a court order directs that a court file be kept confidential and is silent regarding the progress docket, the Clerk shall maintain as confidential the court file, but maintain a progress docket with no alteration of the parties' names unless otherwise provided by law, rule, or this Administrative Order.

3. If a court order directs that a court document be kept confidential, the Clerk shall treat only that document as confidential unless otherwise provided by law, rule, or this Administrative Order.

4. If a court order directs that a party's identity is confidential, the Clerks shall take all reasonable steps necessary to ensure that the progress docket is available to the public in a manner that does not disclose the identity of the protected party. This includes substituting the party's name with a pseudonym, a general term such as "Petitioner," or the party's initials if the party is not generally identified by initials.

E. *Access by Parties and Attorneys of Record.* Except as otherwise provided below or except as indicated by the language of a court order, the Clerks are authorized to make any sealed or confidential court file, document, or case information available to adult parties and their attorneys of record in accordance with the Standards for Access to Electronic Court Records and Access Security Matrix. No order of the court is required.

The Clerks are <u>not</u> authorized to make the contents of adoption and surrogacy files, documents, or information available to <u>any</u> person, including adult parties and their attorneys, absent a court order. Section 63.162, Fla. Stat.

The contents of any confidential court file, document, or information in adversarial matters in the probate and guardianship division, whether having been declared adversarial by the Court or adversarial by rule, may be made available to adult parties and their attorneys of record upon request. If a Clerk is unable to determine whether a matter is adversarial, the Clerk may request a determination from the section judge. In all other probate and guardianship matters, the Clerks may make the contents of any sealed or confidential court file, document, or information available only as authorized by law or court order.

F. *Requests for Access by the Public.* If a member of the public or an entity requests a court file by party name and the file and progress docket are sealed or confidential or a party's identity is sealed or confidential, the Clerks are hereby authorized and directed to inform the requesting person or entity that confidentiality laws prohibit the Clerk from confirming or denying the existence of such file or providing the requested records, if any.

III. Directions to judicial assistant. If a motion is filed with the "Confidential Party — Court Service Requested" designation properly displayed, the judicial assistant is responsible for providing service. The judicial assistant shall provide such service so as not to inadvertently reveal the identity of the parties to the movant.

IV. Expunged and sealed records. This Administrative Order does not apply to or affect the procedures in Chapter 943, Fla. Stat., for sealing or expunging criminal history records.

The Court may update the attachments to this Administrative Order without amendment of this Administrative Order.

Administrative Orders 2010–065 PA/PI–CIR and 2013–024 PA/PI–CIR are hereby rescinded.

DONE AND ORDERED in Chambers at St. Petersburg, Pinellas County, Florida, this ___ day of November, 2017.

<u>ORIGINAL SIGNED ON NOVEMBER 7, 2017</u>
<u>BY ANTHONY RONDOLINO,</u>
<u>CHIEF JUDGE</u>

APPENDIX A
IN THE CIRCUIT/COUNTY COURT OF THE SIXTH JUDICIAL CIRCUIT IN AND FOR PASCO/PINELLAS COUNTIES, FLORIDA
________ DIVISION

____
Plaintiff(s),

v. Case No.________
UCN:________

____
Defendant(s).

________________ /

Motion to Determine Confidentiality of Court Records

1. I am a ☐ Plaintiff/Petitioner, ☐ Defendant/Respondent, or ☐ Affected non-party in this case; or ☐ Interested Person.

2. I have given written notice of this motion to all affected non-parties ______________________ [specify names of non–parties], and filed copies of the notice provided. The notice identified this case by docket number; described the confidential information without revealing it; specified the location of the information in the court record; and advised that if the motion is denied by the court then the subject material will not be treated as confidential by the Court or the Clerk.

3. I respectfully request that the Court determine that the following court records or portion of a record are confidential and order the Clerk to seal the records in accordance with ☐ Rule of Judicial Administration 2.420(c)(7)—(c)(8); Rule of Judicial Administration 2.420(c)(9):

_____ particular information within a document (specify the type of information, identify the document title and date, and identify the page and line number where the information is located in the document): ______________

_____ particular documents within the court file (identify the document title and date): ______________.

_____ the entire court file, but not the progress docket.

_____ the entire court file and the progress docket.

_____ the party's name on the progress docket.

[Identify records or portion of a record that you seek to have determined confidential but do not reveal the information to be determined confidential]

4. The Court should determine the record is confidential for the following reasons:

____

____

[Explain why the court should find the record confidential. Do not reveal the information to be determined confidential. If you are an affected non-party or interested person, give your relationship to the parties and how you are affected by the record.]

5. [For Rule 2.420(c)(7) or (c)(8) motions] The legal authority for the Court to determine that the records are confidential is: .

[Provide a court rule, statute, or case law authorizing the Court to determine this type of record is confidential].

6. [For Rule 2.420(c)(9) motions] Confidentiality of the information sought to be sealed is required to protect the following interests: [select all that apply]

_____ a. Prevent serious and imminent threat to the fair, impartial, and orderly administration of justice.

_____ b. Protect trade secrets.

_____ c. Protect a compelling governmental interest.

_____ d. Obtain evidence to determine legal issues in a case.

_____ e. Avoid substantial injury to innocent third parties.

_____ f. Avoid substantial injury to a party by disclosure of matters protected by a common law or privacy right not generally inherent in this type of proceeding, specifically: ________.

_____ g. Complying with established public policy set for in the Florida or U.S. Constitution or statutes or Florida rules or case law, specifically: ______________

7. There is no less restrictive measure available to protect these interests and the degree, duration, and manner of confidentiality sought is no broader than necessary to protect these interests.

8. I have consulted with ______________________ [List all parties and affected non-parties, if any] and they ☐ agree ☐ do not agree with this motion.

9. I certify that this motion is made in good faith and is supported by a sound factual and legal basis.

10. I acknowledge that I may be subject to Court sanctions if this motion is not made in good faith and is not supported by a sound legal or factual basis.

DATED: ______________ [Signature] ______________

Printed name ______________
Address ______________
Phone number ______________
Fax number ______________
Florida Bar No. ______________
Email address ______________

CERTIFICATE OF SERVICE

I certify that the original was filed with the Clerk of the Circuit Court and that a copy of this document was furnished by ( ) Email ( ) U.S. mail ( ) hand delivery or ( ) facsimile to [include all parties and affected non–parties] ______________ on ______________, 20 ______.

____
[Signature]

APPENDIX B–1
IN THE CIRCUIT/COUNTY COURT OF THE SIXTH JUDICIAL CIRCUIT
IN AND FOR PASCO/PINELLAS COUNTIES, FLORIDA
______ DIVISION

____
Plaintiff(s),
v. Case No. ______________
UCN: ______________
____
Defendant(s).

ORDER GRANTING/DENYING MOTION TO DETERMINE CONFIDENTIALITY OF COURT RECORDS IN ACCORDANCE WITH RULE OF JUDICIAL ADMINISTRATION 2.420(c)(7)–(c)(8)

THIS MATTER is before the Court on a Motion to Determine Confidentiality of Court Records filed by ______ pursuant to Florida Rule of Judicial Administration 2.420(c)(7)–(c)(8) for an order sealing the following information relative to this ________ [specify type of case, such as civil action; dissolution of marriage; paternity, etc.] case:

[*select all that apply*]

_____ particular information within a document, specifically: ______________

_____ particular documents within the court file, specifically: ______________

_____ the entire court file, but not the progress docket.

_____ the entire court file and the progress docket.

_____ the party's name on the progress docket.

Affected non-parties were notified of this Motion.

This motion was/was not contested and a hearing was/was not conducted [if conducted, include date].

Having considered the arguments of the parties, legal authority, and otherwise being fully advised, the Court **DENIES** the motion because the moving party has failed to establish that records at issue are made confidential under state or federal law or any other basis under Rule of Judicial Administration 2.420(c)(7)–(c)(8).

— OR —

Having considered the arguments of the parties, legal authority, and otherwise being fully advised, the Court **GRANTS** the motion as follows:

1. The Court finds that the information is made confidential under state or federal law or other basis under Rule of Judicial Administration 2.420(c)(7)–(c)(8): [specify statute, rule, constitution, or case] ________________.

2. The Court further finds that no less restrictive measure is available to protect this/these interest(s), and that the degree, duration and manner of confidentiality ordered herein are no broader than necessary to protect the interest(s).

Wherefore, it is hereby **ORDERED** that:

In accordance with Florida Rule of Judicial Administration 2.420 and the Standards for Access to Electronic Court Records and Access Security Matrix, the Clerk of the Circuit Court is hereby directed to maintain as confidential the following materials related to this matter: [*select all that apply*]

_____1. The following information contained within ______________ [specify pleading]: ______________________ [specify information].

_____2. The following documents within the court file: ______________________. However, the file and progress docket shall otherwise remain available to the public subject to any substitution of a party's name set forth above.

_____3. The entire court file. However, the progress docket may remain open to the public subject to any substitution of a party's name set forth above.

_____4. The entire court file and the progress docket. The progress docket shall not be available on any public information system. However, the case number shall remain public.

_____5. The party's name on the progress docket. On the public progress docket, the Clerk of the Circuit Court shall substitute the following for the party's name: ______________________. Further, the Clerk shall ensure that the party's name is redacted from all public materials in the file and that the final judgment is recorded in a manner that does not reveal the identity of the party. However, the progress docket and the file shall otherwise remain available to the public.

It is further **ORDERED** that the Clerk is not to post this Order because the information is confidential based on federal or state law.

It is further **ORDERED** that the Clerk is hereby authorized to unseal any materials sealed pursuant to this Order for the purpose of filing, microfilming or imaging files, or transmitting a record to an appellate tribunal. The materials shall be resealed immediately upon completion of the filing.

DONE AND ORDERED in Chambers, at [*Courthouse Location*], this ___ day of __________, 20 ___.

APPENDIX B–2

IN THE CIRCUIT/COUNTY COURT OF THE SIXTH JUDICIAL CIRCUIT
IN AND FOR PASCO/PINELLAS COUNTIES, FLORIDA
____________ DIVISION

____

Plaintiff(s),

v. Case No. __________
UCN: __________

____

Defendant(s).

______________________/

ORDER GRANTING/DENYING MOTION TO DETERMINE CONFIDENTIALITY OF COURT RECORDS IN ACCORDANCE WITH RULE OF JUDICIAL ADMINISTRATION 2.420(c)(9)

THIS MATTER is before the Court on a Motion to Determine Confidentiality of Court Records filed by ________________ pursuant to Florida Rule of Judicial Administration 2.420(c)(9) for an order sealing the following information relative to this ________________ [specify type of case, such as civil action; dissolution of marriage; paternity, etc.] case:

[*select all that apply*]

_____ particular information within a document, specifically: __________.

_____ particular documents within the court file, specifically: __________.

_____ the entire court file, but not the progress docket.

_____ the entire court file and the progress docket.

_____ the party's name on the progress docket.

Affected non-parties were notified of this Motion.

This motion was/was not contested and a hearing was/was not conducted [if conducted, include date].

Having considered the arguments of the parties, legal authority, and otherwise being fully advised, the Court **DENIES** the motion because the moving party has failed to establish that confidentiality of the information sought to be sealed is necessary to protect any interest under Rule 2.420(c)(9).

— OR —

Having considered the arguments of the parties, legal authority, and otherwise being fully advised, the Court **GRANTS** the motion as follows:

1. Confidentiality of the [information sought to be sealed] is required in accordance with Rule of Judicial Administration 2.420(c)(9) to protect the following interest(s): [*select all that apply*]

_____ a. Preventing a serious and imminent threat to the fair, impartial, and orderly administration of justice, specifically: ________________.

_____ b. A trade secret.

_____ c. A compelling government interest, specifically ________________.

_____ d. Obtaining evidence to determine the legal issues in a case.

_____ e. Avoiding substantial injury to innocent third parties, specifically __________.

_____ f. Avoiding substantial injury to a party by the disclosure of matters protected by a common law or privacy right not generally inherent in this type of proceeding, specifically ________________.

_____ g. Complying with established public policy set forth in the Florida or U.S. Constitution or statutes or Florida rules or case law, specifically:

____________________.

2. The Court further finds that no less restrictive measure is available to protect this/these interest(s), and that the degree, duration and manner of confidentiality ordered herein are no broader than necessary to protect the interest(s).

Wherefore, it is hereby **ORDERED** that:

In accordance with Florida Rule of Judicial Administration 2.420 and the Standards for Access to Electronic Court Records and Access Security Matrix, the Clerk of the Circuit Court is hereby directed to maintain as confidential the following materials related to this matter: [*select all that apply*]

_____ 1. The following information contained within ____________ [specify pleading]: __________________ [specify information].

_____ 2. The following documents within the court file: __________________. However, the file and progress docket shall otherwise remain available to the public subject to any substitution of a party's name set forth above.

_____ 3. The entire court file. However, the progress docket may remain open to the public subject to any substitution of a party's name set forth above.

_____ 4. The entire court file and the progress docket. The progress docket shall not be available on any public information system. However, the case number shall remain public.

_____ 5. The party's name on the progress docket. On the public progress docket, the Clerk of the Circuit Court shall substitute the following for the party's name: __________________. Further, the Clerk shall ensure that the party's name is redacted from all public materials in the file and that the final judgment is recorded in a manner that does not reveal the identity of the party. However, the progress docket and the file shall otherwise remain available to the public.

It is further **ORDERED** that any materials sealed pursuant to this Order shall be conditionally disclosed upon the entry of a further order by this Court finding that such opening is necessary for purposes of judicial or governmental accountability or First Amendment rights.

It is further **ORDERED** that, within 10 days of the date of this Order, the Clerk shall post a copy of this Order on the bulletin board of [*specify courthouse at which order is being signed*] and the Clerk's website for a period of 30 days to provide public notice.

It is further **ORDERED** that the Clerk is hereby authorized to unseal any materials sealed pursuant to this Order for the purpose of filing, microfilming or imaging files, or transmitting a record to an appellate tribunal. The materials shall be resealed immediately upon completion of the filing.

DONE AND ORDERED in Chambers, at [*Courthouse Location*], this _____ day of ________________, 20 ___.

____________________ /s/

APPENDIX C
IN THE CIRCUIT/COUNTY COURT OF THE SIXTH JUDICIAL CIRCUIT IN AND FOR PASCO/PINELLAS COUNTIES, FLORIDA
__________ DIVISION

____
Plaintiff(s),

v. Case No. __________
UCN: __________

____
Defendant(s).

__________________________ /

DIRECTIONS TO CLERK:

This Motion should be docketed using only the word "Motion."

Motion to Determine Confidentiality of Court Records—Special Criminal Records

[This form to be used only to determine confidentiality of plea agreements, substantial assistance agreements, or other court record that reveals the identity of a confidential informant or active criminal investigative information]

1. This motion is filed by or on behalf of ☐ State of Florida, ☐ Defendant.

2. I respectfully request that the Court determine that the following court records are confidential and order the Clerk to seal the records in accordance with Rule of Judicial Administration 2.420(c)(9):

_______ plea agreement

_______ substantial assistance agreement

_______ documents that reveal the identity of a confidential informant

_______ documents that reveal active criminal investigative information

3. The Court should determine the record is confidential for the following reasons:

____
____.

[Explain why the court should find the record confidential. Do not reveal the information to be determined confidential.]

4. Confidentiality of the information sought to be sealed is required to protect the following interests: [select all that apply]

_______ a. Prevent serious and imminent threat to the fair, impartial, and orderly administration of justice

_______ b. Protect a compelling governmental interest

_______ c. Avoid substantial injury to innocent third parties

_______ d. Complying with established public policy set forth in the Florida or U.S. Constitution or statutes or Florida rules or case law, specifically:

____________________.

5. There is no less restrictive measure available to protect these interests and the degree, duration, and manner of confidentiality sought is no broader than necessary to protect the interests.

6. I have consulted with the ☐ Assistant State Attorney ☐Attorney for Defendant ☐ Defendant and they ☐ agree ☐ do not agree with this motion.

7. I certify that this motion is made in good faith and is supported by a sound factual and legal basis.

8. I acknowledge that I may be subject to Court sanctions if this motion is not made in good faith and is not support by a sound legal or factual basis.

DATED: __________ [Signature]

____

Printed name ________
Address ________
Phone number ________
Fax number ________
Florida Bar No. ________
Email address ________

CERTIFICATE OF SERVICE

I certify that the original was filed with the Clerk of the Circuit Court and that a copy of this document was furnished by ( ) Email ( ) U.S. mail ( ) hand delivery or ( ) facsimile to ______________ on ________, 20 ____.

____

[Signature]

APPENDIX D

IN THE CIRCUIT/COUNTY COURT OF THE SIXTH JUDICIAL CIRCUIT IN AND FOR PASCO/PINELLAS COUNTIES, FLORIDA

________ **DIVISION**

____
Plaintiff(s),

v. Case No. ________
UCN: ________

____
Defendant(s).

______________/

DIRECTIONS TO CLERK:

This Order should be docketed using only the word "Order."

ORDER GRANTING/DENYING MOTION TO DETERMINE CONFIDENTIALITY OF COURT RECORDS—SPECIAL CRIMINAL RECORDS IN ACCORDANCE WITH RULE OF JUDICIAL ADMINISTRATION 2.420(c)(9)

THIS MATTER is before the Court on a Motion to Determine Confidentiality of Court Records filed by ______________ pursuant to Florida Rule of Judicial Administration 2.420(c)(9) in a criminal case for an order sealing:

________ a plea agreement

________ a substantial assistance agreement

________ documents that reveal the identity of a confidential informant

________ documents that reveal active criminal investigative information

This motion was/was not contested and a hearing was/was not conducted [if conducted, include date].

Having considered the arguments of the parties, legal authority, and otherwise being fully advised, the Court **DENIES** the motion because the moving party has failed to establish that confidentiality of the information sought to be sealed is necessary to protect any interest under Rule 2.420(c)(9).

- OR -

Having considered the arguments of the parties, legal authority, and otherwise being fully advised, the Court **GRANTS** the motion as follows:

1. Confidentiality is required in accordance with Rule of Judicial Administration 2.420(c)(9) to protect the following interests: [select all that apply]

________ a. Prevent serious and imminent threat to the fair, impartial, and orderly administration of justice

________ b. Protect a compelling governmental interest

________ c. Avoid substantial injury to innocent third parties

________ d. Complying with established public policy set forth in the Florida or U.S. Constitution or statutes or Florida rules or case law, specifically: ______________.

2. The Court further finds that no less restrictive measure is available to protect this/these interest(s), and that the degree, duration and manner of confidentiality ordered herein are no broader than necessary to protect the interest(s).

Wherefore, it is

ORDERED that the Clerk of the Circuit Court is hereby directed to seal immediately the following materials related to this matter and to keep such materials from public access: [*select all that apply*]

________ a plea agreement

________ a substantial assistance agreement

________ documents that reveal the identity of a confidential informant specifically: ______________

________ documents that reveal active criminal investigative information specifically: ______________

The materials are to remain sealed for ___ days (up to 120 days for original order and up to 60 days for extensions).

It is further **ORDERED** that pursuant to 2.420(f)(3)(D), the Clerk is not to post this Order.

It is further **ORDERED** that any materials sealed pursuant to this Order may otherwise be disclosed only as follows:

1. to any judge of this Circuit for case-related reasons;
2. to the Chief Judge or his or her designee;
3. to the following specific individuals: ________; or
4. by further order of the Court.

It is further **ORDERED** that the Clerk is hereby authorized to unseal any materials sealed pursuant to this Order for the purpose of filing, microfilming or imaging files, electronic verification, or transmitting a record to an appellate tribunal. The materials shall be resealed immediately upon completion of the filing.

DONE AND ORDERED in Chambers, at [*Courthouse Location*], this ____ day of ________, 20 ____.

______________ /s/

APPENDIX E

IN THE CIRCUIT/COUNTY COURT OF THE SIXTH JUDICIAL CIRCUIT IN AND FOR PASCO/PINELLAS COUNTIES, FLORIDA

________ **DIVISION**

____
Plaintiff(s),

v. Case No. ________

UCN: ______

______
Defendant(s).

______ /

Notice to Affected Non–Party

YOU ARE HEREBY NOTIFIED that the attached ☐ Notice of Confidential Information within Court Filing ☐ Motion to Determine Confidentiality of Court Records ☐ Motion to Vacate or Unseal Court Records has been filed with the Court in this case.

The Notice of Confidential Information will result in the information being treated as confidential unless otherwise ordered by the Court.

The Motion seeks to seal/unseal the following type of information: ______

______

______ [describe the confidential information with as much specificity as possible without revealing the confidential information, including specifying the precise location of the information within the court record].

☐ If the Motion to Determine Confidentiality of Court Records is denied these records will not be treated as confidential by the Clerk and the Court.

☐ If the Motion to Vacate or Unseal Court Records is granted these records will no longer be treated by the Clerk and the Court as confidential.

You may file a response with the Clerk of the Circuit Court indicating if you agree or disagree with the motion. You are not required to file a response.

DATED: ______ [Signature] ______

Printed name ______
Address ______
Phone number ______
Fax number ______
Florida Bar No. ______
Email address ______

CERTIFICATE OF SERVICE

I certify that the original was filed with the Clerk of the Circuit Court and that a copy of this document was furnished by ( ) Email ( ) U.S. mail ( ) hand delivery or ( ) facsimile to [include all parties and affected non–parties] ______ on ______, 20 ______.

______
[Signature]

APPENDIX F

Instructions for Notice of Hearing (Confidential Records) Form

When should this form be used?

If you have filed a Motion that you want to be heard by a judge, you need to set a hearing before the **judge** and send notice of the **hearing** to the other party or parties in your case and to any affected non-party.

What should I do first?

To set a hearing date and time, you have to make a good-faith effort to coordinate a mutually convenient date and time for you, the other parties in the case, and the judge. **You should first call the office of the assigned judge and obtain hearing dates and times from his/her assistant.** You should then call the attorney for the other party in your case to determine whether they are available on any of the dates and times given to you by the judge's assistant. The final step is to call the judge's office back to confirm the agreed upon date and time.

Preparing the Notice of Hearing:

After the date and time have been confirmed, you should complete the **Notice of Hearing** form, sign it, make copies of it, and e-mail or U.S. mail a copy to the other party and any affected non-party.

This form should be typed or printed in black ink. After completing this form, you should **E–file** the original with the **clerk of the circuit court** in the county where your case was filed. Make copies first to send to the other party and to keep for your records.

What should I do next?

A copy of this form **must** be e-mailed, U.S. mail, **or** hand delivered to the other party and any affected non-party in your case.

APPENDIX F
IN THE CIRCUIT/COUNTY COURT OF THE SIXTH JUDICIAL CIRCUIT
IN AND FOR PASCO/PINELLAS COUNTIES, FLORIDA
______ DIVISION

______
Plaintiff(s),

v. Case No. ______
UCN: ______

______
Defendant(s).

______ /

Notice of Hearing (Confidential Records) [fill in all blanks]

TO: *{name of other party}* ______

There will be a hearing before Judge *{name}* ______, on *{date}* ______, at *{time}* ______ m., in Room ______ of the Courthouse, located at: *{address}* ______ on the following issues:

☐ Motion to Determine Confidentiality of Court Records

☐ Motion to Determine Confidentiality of Court Records—Special criminal records

☐ Motion to vacate or unseal court records

☐ Other: ______.

If this matter is resolved, the moving party must contact the judge's office to cancel this hearing.

For proceedings before the Courts of Pasco County:

"If you are a person with a disability who needs any accommodation in order to participate in this proceeding, you are entitled, at no cost to you, to the provision of certain assistance. Please contact the Pasco County Human Resources Office, 8731 Citizens Drive, Suite 330, New Port Richey, FL 34654, (727) 847–8103 (V) at least 7 days before your scheduled court appearance, or immediately upon receiving this notification if the time before the

scheduled appearance is less than 7 days; if you are hearing or voice impaired, call 711."

For proceedings before the Courts of Pinellas County:

"If you are a person with a disability who needs any accommodation in order to participate in this proceeding, you are entitled, at no cost to you, to the provision of certain assistance. Please contact the Human Rights Office, 400 S. Ft. Harrison Ave., Ste. 300, Clearwater, FL 33756, (727) 464–4062 (V/TDD) at least 7 days before your scheduled court appearance, or immediately upon receiving this notification if the time before the scheduled appearance is less than 7 days; if you are hearing or voice impaired, call 711."

CERTIFICATE OF SERVICE

I certify that the original was filed with the Clerk of the Circuit Court and that a copy of this document was furnished by ( ) Email ( ) U.S. mail ( ) hand delivery or ( ) facsimile to [include all parties and affected non-parties] ______________________ on ________, 20 _____.

____
Signature of Person Requesting Hearing
Printed name______________
Address______________
Phone number______________
Fax number______________
Florida Bar No.______________
Email address______________

Adopted effective November 11, 2017.

2017–057. CASE FILES IN PINELLAS COUNTY

IN THE CIRCUIT COURT OF THE SIXTH JUDICIAL CIRCUIT IN AND FOR PASCO AND PINELLAS COUNTIES, FLORIDA

ADMINISTRATIVE ORDER NO. 2017–057 PI–CIR

RE: CASE FILES IN PINELLAS COUNTY

In order to achieve a comprehensive electronic documents system, the Court continues to transition to electronic case files. To ensure the integrity and efficient delivery of information to the judiciary, however, the Pinellas County Clerk of the Circuit Court ("Clerk") was required to continue to create and maintain paper case files in Unified Family Court cases and injunction proceedings. The Clerk was also required to provide paper case files or relevant paper documents in specified criminal division proceedings. The Court no longer needs these paper case files or paper documents.

In accordance with Article V, section 2, Florida Constitution, Rules of Judicial Administration 2.215 and 2.525, and section 43.26, Florida Statutes,

IT IS ORDERED:

1. Except as provided below, the Clerk is not required to create or maintain paper case files in new cases. Instead, the Clerk must create, maintain, and make available to the Court electronic case files. In existing cases, the Clerk is not required to maintain the paper case file if it has been fully converted to an electronic case file that is maintained by the Clerk and available to the Court.

2. The Clerk is required to create and maintain paper case files in the following new and existing cases:

a. County to Circuit Criminal Appeals and

b. Cases where the death penalty has been imposed.

The Court will continue to request paper case files for the above cases. The Clerk must deliver the paper case files to the Court within two business days of the request, unless a different time is specified by the Court. The Clerk will continue to deliver paper case files to the courtrooms for scheduled calendars in these cases in accordance with its current practices.

3. In those cases where the case file is electronic, the Clerk is only required to produce a paper case file on specific request of the Court. The Clerk must deliver the paper case files to the Court within two business days of the request, unless a different time is specified by the Court. Such requests will be limited to when paper case files are necessary for the efficient operation of the Court.

4. Given the exigent nature of juvenile and criminal advisory hearings, electronic documents would impede the efficient operation of the Court. Therefore, the Clerk must continue to provide paper copies of charging documents to the Court in accordance with its current practices.

5. In order to facilitate the Court's transition from paper case files to electronic case files, the Clerk is encouraged to convert existing paper case files to electronic case files and make them available to the Court. Documents in electronic case files must be in a searchable PDF format whenever possible.

6. When converting paper case files to electronic case files, the Clerk must convert the entire paper case file to an electronic case file in the following order of priority:

a. Cases in which electronic case files are requested by the Court. Once notified, the Clerk must make the entire case file electronically available within two business days of the request, unless a different time is specified by the Court.

b. Cases where a new pleading requesting or requiring court action is electronically filed

c. Open cases

d. Re–opened cases

e. Closed cases

7. Nothing in this Administrative Order alters the Clerk's responsibility to retain court records as required by Rule of Judicial Administration 2.430 or to maintain original filings in accordance with Administrative Order 2016–018 or subsequent administrative order.

8. The Clerk, upon request, must make the court record available in a format that complies with the Americans with Disabilities Act.

Effective October 1, 2017, Administrative Order 2016–019 PI–CIR is hereby rescinded.

DONE AND ORDERED in Chambers at St. Petersburg, Pinellas County, Florida, this _____ day of September, 2017.

ORIGINAL SIGNED ON SEPTEMBER 25, 2017
BY ANTHONY RONDOLINO,
CHIEF JUDGE

Adopted effective October 1, 2017.

2017–039. COURT COSTS, ASSESSMENTS, SURCHARGES, AND FINES

IN THE CIRCUIT COURT, SIXTH JUDICIAL CIRCUIT IN AND FOR PASCO AND PINELLAS COUNTIES, FLORIDA

ADMINISTRATIVE ORDER 2017–039 PA/PI–CIR

RE: COURT COSTS, ASSESSMENTS, SURCHARGES, AND FINES

In *McNeil v. State*, 215 So. 3d 55 (Fla. 2017), the Florida Supreme Court held that the mandatory costs assessed under §§ 938.08, 938.085, and 938.10, Florida Statutes, are assessed on a per count rather than per case basis. As a result, the attachments to Administrative Orders 2012–023, 2013–033, and 2015–048 must be updated to indicate that these costs must be assessed per count rather than per case. In addition, these three Administrative Orders are being consolidated into one order.

In accordance with Article V, § 2, Florida Constitution, Rule of Judicial Administration 2.215, and § 43.26, Florida Statutes, it is

ORDERED:

1. The Clerks of the Circuit Court are directed to include all statutorily mandated costs, assessments, and surcharges (hereinafter referred to as costs) in all written judgments and sentences submitted to a judge by the Clerk, except as otherwise provided by law as found by the presiding judge. Statutorily mandated costs must be assessed whether or not they are orally announced. *See Reyes v. State*, 655 So. 2d 111, 116 (Fla. 2d DCA 1995).

2. The Clerks are directed to include all statutorily mandated fines in the written judgments and sentences submitted to a judge, regardless of whether the mandatory fine was orally announced by the presiding judge at sentencing. If there is a range in the amount of a mandatory fine to be imposed, the Clerk is directed to include the statutory minimum mandatory amount of the fine in the written judgments and sentences submitted to a judge unless the trial judge imposes a higher fine or, if statutorily authorized, the trial judge reduces or suspends a defendant's fine on the state attorney's motion. *See Angel v. State*, 769 So. 2d 494 (Fla. 4th DCA 2000).

3. Judges of the Sixth Judicial Circuit are encouraged to assess at least the recommended standard assessment, including the discretionary fine as reflected in Attachments A–E. If a defendant does not waive itemization of any discretionary cost or fine, the Court must orally announce those discretionary amounts. See *Reyes v. State*, 655 So. 2d 111, 116 (Fla. 2d DCA 1995). If the Court imposes more than the statutory minimum attorney's fees (currently $100 for a felony, $50.00 for a misdemeanor) and a defendant does not waive his or her right to a hearing on attorneys fees assessed pursuant to § 938.29, Florida Statutes, the Court must allow an opportunity to contest the amount of the attorney's fee. *McMillan v. State*, 8 So.3d 1237 (Fla. 2d DCA 2009).

4. Deputy clerks are to make available to the presiding judge, the recommended standard assessment as reflected in Attachments A–E.*

5. If a judge imposes the standard assessment and does not direct to the contrary, the Clerk is to allocate the standard assessment as reflected in Attachments A–E. The amount assessed shall first be allocated to all mandatory costs and fines applicable in a case. Any amount remaining after assessing mandatory costs and fines shall be allocated as a discretionary fine pursuant to § 775.083(1), Florida Statutes.

6. The Clerks shall prepare an order making the costs and fines imposed in the judgment a lien in favor of the Clerk on behalf of the State of Florida. The judgment lien shall be recorded in the Official Records after it is signed by the Court in accordance with law. The requirement to record a judgment lien does not apply to judgments in delinquency cases where an adjudication of guilt is withheld. The judgment lien is a lien against all property owned by the defendant or property acquired in the future and will accrue interest at the statutory rate. The imposition of a lien shall not replace other collection efforts.

7. For defendants who are placed on probation, the probation agency shall ensure that costs and fines are paid and shall notify the Court of failure to pay in accordance with established practices. If the Court terminates probation and costs and fines are still owing, the Clerks may enter into a payment plan with the defendant and are directed to make every effort to collect all costs, assessments, surcharges, and fines assessed by the Court in accordance with § 28.246, Florida Statutes, including referral to a collections agent.

For defendants who are sentenced to the Department of Corrections or to county jail time, or who receive time served, the Clerks, upon the defendant's release from custody may enter into a payment plan with the defendant and are directed to make every effort to collect all costs, assessments, surcharges, and fines assessed by the Court in accordance with § 28.246, Florida Statutes, including referral to a collections agent.

8. If the Clerks identify systemic obstacles to collection of court costs or fines, the Clerks shall notify the Chief Judge.

9. The Clerks shall provide a collections report to the Chief Judge, Trial Courts Administrator, State Attorney, Public Defender, and Regional Counsel on a monthly basis. The report shall include all Court related collections that are included in the Distribution Schedule of Court Related Filing Fees, Service Charges, Costs, and Fines prepared by the Florida Association of Court Clerks, Inc., identify the authority for the collection of those funds, the amounts collected per month, and the distribution of the amounts collected. The Report shall be in substantially the same format as Attachment F.**

10. The attachments to this Administrative Order may be amended without further amendment to this Administrative Order. A copy of any amended attachments will be provided to the Clerks. Deputy clerks shall reference the most recent version of the relevant attachment when making the standard assessment available to a judge.

Administrative Orders 2012–023 PA/PI–CIR, 2013–033 PA/PI–CIR, and 2015–048 PA/PI–CIR are hereby rescinded.

DONE AND ORDERED in Chambers at Clearwater, Pinellas County, Florida this _____ day of August, 2017.

ORIGINAL SIGNED ON AUGUST 22, 2017
BY ANTHONY RONDOLINO,
CHIEF JUDGE

Adopted effective August 22, 2017.

* Attachments A through F are excluded. Please see http://www.jud6.org for any needed attachments.

** Attachments A through F are excluded. Please see http://www.jud6.org for any needed attachments.

2017–034. SELECTION AND PAYMENT OF EXPERTS

IN THE CIRCUIT COURT, SIXTH JUDICIAL CIRCUIT IN AND FOR PASCO AND PINELLAS COUNTIES, FLORIDA

ADMINISTRATIVE ORDER NO. 2017–034 PA/PI–CIR

RE: SELECTION AND PAYMENT OF EXPERTS

Expert witnesses and other professionals provide a range of services in civil, criminal, juvenile delinquency, juvenile dependency, family, and involuntary civil commitment of sexual predator cases. These services include competency examinations, mental health evaluations, and investigative services. In certain situations, the court system is responsible for the selection and payment of experts.

In order to identify which experts and professional are appointed and paid by the Court as required by § 916.301, and clarified by Florida Supreme Court Administrative Order AOSC17–12, and in accordance with Article V, § 2, Florida Constitution, Rule of Judicial Administration 2.215, and § 43.26, Florida Statutes, it is

ORDERED:

1. When, on written motion of counsel for the defendant, a *pro se* defendant, the State Attorney, or on the court's own motion, the Court orders an adult competency evaluation pursuant to § 916.115(2), Florida Statutes, the Court shall appoint and pay for the experts. Pursuant to AOSC17–12, the Court shall initially appoint only one expert.

2. When the Court orders an adult competency evaluation pursuant to § 916.301, Florida Statutes, for a defendant whose suspected mental condition is intellectual disability or autism, the Court shall appoint the following experts, who shall be paid by the Court:

a. One, or, at the request of any party, two experts selected by the Court to evaluate whether the defendant meets the definition or intellectual disability or autism and, if so, whether the defendant is competent to proceed;

b. A psychologist selected by the Agency for Persons with Disabilities who is licensed or authorized by law to practice in this state, with experience in evaluating persons suspected of having an intellectual disability or autism; and

c. A social service professional selected by the Court, with experience in working with persons who have an intellectual disability or autism.

3. When an expert is appointed by the Court pursuant to § 916.115(2), Florida Statutes, to evaluate the competence of the defendant to proceed and the defense also requests that the defendant be examined for sanity at the time of the offense, the Court will pay for that portion of the expert's fees relating to the evaluation of competency to proceed.

4. When an indigent criminal defendant is represented by a court appointed attorney or is indigent for costs and a request is made in the following circumstances, the defense selects the expert:

a. a confidential examination to determine whether to file a motion pursuant to § 916.301, Florida Statutes;

b. pursuant to Florida Rules of Criminal Procedure 3.216(a) to determine sanity or insanity;

c. for appointment of an expert as an aid for sentencing in accordance with § 921.0026, Florida Statutes, or other mental health defenses in accordance with Florida Rules of Criminal Procedure 3.216(f); or

d. in a capital case where the state has given notice of intent to seek the death penalty and the defense intends to present expert testimony of mental mitigation in accordance with Florida Rules of Criminal Procedure 3.202.

Prior court approval is required for such experts. Payment of experts selected by court appointed attorneys or attorneys for persons determined to be indigent for costs is to be made by the Justice Administrative Commission.

5. When the State Attorney requests an expert pursuant to Florida Rules of Criminal Procedure 3.216(d) to determine sanity or insanity, or in accordance with Florida Rules of Criminal Procedure 3.216(f) on mental health defenses, or in accordance with Florida Rules of Criminal Procedure 3.202(d) following a conviction of capital murder, the State Attorney selects the expert and is responsible for payment.

6. Intellectual Disability as a Bar to Execution:

a. When experts are appointed by the Court pursuant to § 921.137, Florida Statutes, and Florida Rules of Criminal Procedure 3.203(c)(3) to evaluate a defendant or prisoner to determine whether the defendant or prisoner is intellectually disabled and barred from execution, the Court shall select and pay for the experts.

b. When an expert is appointed pursuant to § 921.137, Florida Statutes, on request of the State Attorney under Florida Rules of Criminal Procedure 3.203(c)(2), the State Attorney shall select and pay for the expert.

c. When an expert is otherwise appointed to determine a defendant's or prisoner's intellectual disability as a bar to execution, the Court shall select and pay for the expert(s).

7. Juvenile Evaluations:

a. When an evaluation of a juvenile defendant is ordered pursuant to § 985.19(d), Florida Statutes, to determine if the juvenile defendant is incompetent to proceed due to mental illness, the Court will select and pay for the expert.

b. When an evaluation of a juvenile defendant is ordered pursuant to § 985.19(e), Florida Statutes, to determine if the juvenile defendant is incompetent to proceed due to intellectual disability, the Agency for Persons with Disabilities shall examine the juvenile in accordance with Florida Rule of Juvenile Procedure 8.095.

8. When an independent examination is requested pursuant to § 394.4655 or § 394.467, Florida Statutes, by an indigent respondent in a Baker Act proceeding, the Public Defender shall select and pay for the expert, or if the indigent respondent is represented by court-appointed counsel, the counsel shall select the expert who will be paid by the Justice Administrative Commission for the services. In accordance with § 394.4655(6)(a)2 or § 394.467(6)(a)2, Florida Statutes, the respondent shall pay for the independent expert examination if he or she can afford such examination.

9. When an expert is appointed or reappointed by the Court pursuant to Florida Rules of Criminal Procedure 3.212 to perform a periodic evaluation of a defendant who has been found incompetent to proceed or appointed or reappointed by the Court pursuant to Florida Rules of Criminal Procedure 3.218 after an adjudication of not guilty by reason of insanity, the Court shall select and pay for the expert(s). Provided the same expert is under contract with the Court, for subsequent evaluations the Court will generally reappoint the same expert who performed the last examination of the defendant. However, on the court's own motion or a motion of the State or defense showing good cause, the Court may appoint a new expert by rotation from the list of experts under contract with the Sixth Judicial Circuit.

10. Except when the Court appoints the court psychologist, whenever counsel for the defendant or the State Attorney requests the appointment of an expert to determine competence to proceed or insanity, the Administrative Office of the Courts shall prepare an order for the Court's signature. A form Order Directing Examination For Competence to Proceed is Attachment A to this Administrative Order. A form Order Directing Examination of Defendant's Mental Condition On Motion of Defendant is Attachment B to this Administrative Order. A form Order Directing Examination of Defendant's Mental Condition Upon Motion of the State is Attachment C to this Order. The Order should be prepared and submitted to the Court within five days. The form Orders may be amended without further amendment to this Administrative Order.

11. Except where an expert is reappointed to do an examination or evaluation, the appointment of an expert by the Court will be by rotation from the list of experts under contract with the Sixth Judicial Circuit.

12. Experts appointed by the Court will be entitled to the appropriate compensation determined in Administrative Order Number 2017–033 Re: Expert and Professional Fees, or as provided in any subsequent applicable Administrative Order(s). For an expert to be paid for services rendered, the expert's report and testimony must explicitly address each of the factors and follow the procedures set out in the applicable chapter of the Florida Statutes and in the applicable Florida Rules of Court.

13. Except as otherwise provided herein, experts retained by the Public Defender or the Office of Regional Counsel pursuant to § 29.006, Florida Statutes, or by the State Attorney pursuant to § 29.005, Florida Statutes, shall be selected by the respective offices and paid from the respective budgets of the Public Defender, Regional Counsel, or the State Attorney. An expert retained by court-appointed counsel, by counsel for a defendant who is indigent for costs, or by a pro se defendant who is indigent shall, pursuant to § 29.007, Florida Statutes, be paid by the Justice Administrative Commission; prior court approval is required for experts retained pursuant to § 29.007, Florida Statutes.

14. This Administrative Order does not restrict the ability of the Court to otherwise appoint an expert pursuant to the Family Law Rules of Procedure, Florida Rules of Juvenile Procedure, or other Florida Rules of Court.

This Administrative Order is effective July 1, 2017. Effective July 1, 2017, Administrative Order 2017–014 is hereby rescinded.

DONE AND ORDERED in Chambers at St. Petersburg, Pinellas County, Florida, this ___ day of June, 2017.

ORIGINAL SIGNED ON JUNE 20, 2017
BY ANTHONY RONDOLINO,
CHIEF JUDGE

[Attachment A]

IN THE CIRCUIT COURT FOR THE SIXTH JUDICIAL CIRCUIT
IN AND FOR PASCO/PINELLAS COUNTY, FLORIDA

STATE OF FLORIDA

REF NO: ____________
UCN: ____________

____

VS.

____

____

SPN:

ORDER DIRECTING EXAMINATION FOR COMPETENCE TO PROCEED

THIS CAUSE COMING on to be heard in the above-styled case upon the:

☐ Court's own motion

☐ Motion of the Attorney for the Defendant

☐ Motion of the Pro Se Defendant

☐ Motion of the State

to determine the mental condition of the Defendant regarding competence to proceed. The Court being fully advised, it is hereby

ORDERED:

1. That said motion is granted.

PART I. APPOINTMENT OF EXPERT FOR EXAMINATION OF DEFENDANT; SCHEDULING

2. ☐ The Court appoints Dr. __________, an expert under contract with the Court, to examine the Defendant for purposes of competence to proceed.

☐ Dr. __________, a psychologist selected by the Agency for Persons with Disabilities, is appointed to examine the Defendant for purposes of competence to proceed, and __________, a social service professional under contract with the Court, is appointed to provide a social and developmental history of the Defendant because the Defendant's suspected mental condition is intellectual disability or autism.

As of this date, the Defendant is:

___ Not in Custody. The expert must contact defense counsel for scheduling and must provide defense counsel and the State Attorney advance notice of any scheduled examination of the Defendant.

___ In the [Pasco][Pinellas] County Jail. The expert must notify defense counsel when he or she is available to coordinate examination of the Defendant and must provide defense counsel and the State Attorney advance notice of any scheduled examination of the Defendant.

3. That the Sheriff of [Pasco][Pinellas] County shall permit the above-named expert to enter the [Pasco][Pinellas] County Jail as necessary to conduct the foregoing evaluation of the Defendant upon presentment of this Order.

4. Attorneys for the State and Defendant may be present for the expert's examination.

5. That a copy of the Order serves as authorization for the expert to inspect and copy any discoverable information relating to the Defendant maintained by the Clerk of the Circuit Court, State Attorney's Office, any hospital, doctor, or any health care provider, therapist, psychiatrist, psychologist, counselor, or any mental health provider, or other social or human services agency without the necessity of written consent by Defendant.

6. This cause is scheduled for a hearing on the issue of the Defendant's competence to proceed at ________ on the ___ day of ________, 20 ___.

PART II. EXPERT'S WRITTEN REPORT

ALL REPORTS

7. That the expert must submit to this Court a written report on the Defendant's mental condition or, in the case of a social service professional, social and developmental history, and provide copies to defense counsel and the State Attorney, on or before the ___ day of ________, 20 ___.

All information contained in the motion to determine competence of the Defendant or in any report submitted under this order that relates solely to the issues of competence to proceed, treatment, or commitment of the Defendant, shall be used only in determining the mental competence to proceed, treatment, or commitment of the Defendant. (Fla. R. Crim. P. 3.211(d)).

8. That **all** written reports submitted by an expert must:

(a) identify the specific matters referred for evaluation;

(b) describe the evaluative procedures, techniques, and tests used in the examination and purpose or purposes for each;

(c) state the expert's clinical observations, findings, and opinions on each issue referred for evaluation by the Court; and indicate specifically those issues, if any, on which the expert could not give an opinion; and

(d) identify the sources of information used by the expert and a presentation of the factual basis for the expert's clinical findings and opinions. (Fla. R. Crim. P. 3.211(c)).

REPORTS ON COMPETENCE TO PROCEED: MENTAL ILLNESS

The expert must first determine whether the Defendant has a mental illness. (§ 916.12(2), Fla. Stat). If the expert determines that the Defendant has a mental illness, the expert must then report on the Defendant's competence to proceed. (§ 916.12, Fla. Stat.; Fla. R. Crim. P. 3.211(a)). A defendant is incompetent to proceed if the Defendant does not have sufficient present ability to consult with counsel with a reasonable degree of rational understanding, or if the Defendant has no rational, as well as factual, understanding of proceedings against him or her. (§ 916.12(1), Fla. Stat.).

In considering the issue of competence to proceed, the examining expert must consider and include in his or her report the Defendant's capacity to:

(a) Appreciate the charges or allegations against the Defendant;

(b) Appreciate the range and nature of possible penalties, if applicable, that may be imposed in the proceedings against the Defendant;

(c) Understand the adversary nature of the legal process;

(d) Disclose to counsel facts pertinent to the proceedings at issue;

(e) Manifest appropriate courtroom behavior; and

(f) Testify relevantly. (§ 916.12(3), Fla. Stat.).

The expert must also consider and include in his or her report any other factor deemed relevant by the expert. (§ 916.12(3), Fla. Stat.)

● **Should the expert determine that the Defendant is incompetent to proceed, the expert must also:**

1. **Report on any recommended treatment for the Defendant to attain competence to proceed.** (§ 916.12(4) Fla. Stat.; Fla. R. Crim. P. 3.211(b)).

In considering the issues relating to treatment, the expert must specifically report on:

(a) The mental illness causing the incompetence;

(b) The treatment or treatments appropriate for the mental illness of the Defendant and an explanation of each of the possible treatment alternatives in order of choices;

(c) The availability of acceptable treatment and, if treatment is available in the community, the expert must so state in the report; and

(d) The likelihood of the Defendant attaining competence under the recommended treatment, an assessment of the probable duration of the treatment required to restore competence, and the probability that the Defendant will attain competence to proceed in the foreseeable future. (§ 916.12(4)), Fla. Stat.)

2. **Determine whether the Defendant meets the criteria for involuntary commitment.** (§ 916.13, Fla. Stat.; Fla. R. Crim. P. 3.212(c)).

In evaluating the Defendant to determine whether the Defendant may be involuntarily committed, the appointed expert must determine and report on whether:

(a) The Defendant has a mental illness and because of the mental illness:

i. The Defendant is manifestly incapable of surviving alone or with the help or willing and responsible family or friends, including available alternative services, and without treatment, the Defendant is likely to suffer from neglect or refuse to care for herself or himself and such neglect or refusal poses a real and present threat of substantial harm to the Defendant's well-being; or

ii. There is a substantial likelihood that in the near future the Defendant will inflict serious bodily harm on herself or himself or another person, as evidenced by recent behavior causing, attempting, or threatening such harm;

(b) All available, less restrictive treatment alternatives, including treatment in community residential facilities or community inpatient or outpatient settings, which would offer an opportunity for improvement of the Defendant's condition have been judged to be inappropriate; and

(c) There is a substantial probability that the mental illness causing the Defendant's incompetence will respond to treatment and the Defendant will regain competency to proceed in the reasonably foreseeable future. (§ 916.13(1)(a)–(c), Fla. Stat.).

REPORTS ON COMPETENCE TO PROCEED: INTELLECTUAL DISABILITY OR AUTISM

The expert must first consider whether the Defendant meets the definition of intellectual disability or autism (§ 916.3012(2), Fla. Stat.). If the expert determines that the Defendant has intellectual disability or autism, the expert must then report on the Defendant's competence to proceed. (916.3012, Fla. Stat.) A defendant whose suspected mental condition is intellectual disability or autism is incompetent to proceed if the defendant does not have sufficient present ability to consult with the defendant's lawyer with a reasonable degree of rational understanding or if the defendant has no rational, as well as factual, understanding of the proceedings against him or her. (§ 916.3012(1), Fla. Stat.)

In considering the issue of competence to proceed, the examining expert must consider and include in his or her report the Defendant's capacity to:

(a) Appreciate the charges or allegations against the Defendant;

(b) Appreciate the range and nature of possible penalties, if applicable, that may be imposed in the proceedings against the Defendant;

(c) Understand the adversarial nature of the legal process;

(d) Disclose to counsel facts pertinent to the proceedings at issue;

(e) Manifest appropriate courtroom behavior; and

(f) Testify relevantly. (§ 916.3012(3)(a)–(f), Fla. Stat.).

The expert must also consider in his or her report any other factor deemed relevant by the expert. (§ 916.3012(3), Fla. Stat.)

● **Should the expert determine that the Defendant is incompetent to proceed, the expert must also:**

1. **Report on any recommended training for the Defendant to attain competence to proceed.**

In considering the issues relating to training, the examining expert must specifically report on the following. (§ 916.3012(4), Fla. Stat.).

(a) The intellectual disability or autism causing the incompetence;

(b) The training appropriate for the intellectual disability or autism of the Defendant and an explanation of each of the possible training alternatives in order of choices;

(c) The availability of acceptable training and, if training available in the community, the expert must so state in the report; and

(d) The likelihood of the Defendant's attaining competence under the training recommended, an assessment of the probable duration of the training required to restore competence, and the probability that the defendant will attain competence to proceed in the foreseeable future. (§ 916.3012(4)(a)–(d), Fla. Stat.)

2. **Determine whether the Defendant meets the criteria for involuntary commitment.** (§ 916.302, Fla. Stat.)

In evaluating the Defendant to determine whether the Defendant may be involuntarily committed, the appointed expert must determine whether:

(a) The defendant has intellectual disability or autism;

(b) There is a substantial likelihood that in the near future the Defendant will inflict serious bodily harm on himself or herself or another person, as evidenced by recent behavior causing, attempting, or threatening such harm;

(c) All available, less restrictive alternatives, including services provided in community residential facilities or other community settings, which would offer an opportunity for improvement of the condition have been judged to be inappropriate; and

(d) There is a substantial probability that the intellectual disability or autism causing the Defendant's incompetence will respond to training and the Defendant will regain competence to proceed in the reasonably foreseeable future. (§ 916.302(1)(a)–(d), Fla. Stat.)

PART III. PAYMENT OF EXPERT

The expert will be paid in accordance with the current Administrative Order regarding payment of appointed experts and the terms of his or her contract with the Sixth Judicial Circuit.

The expert must submit his or her appropriate invoice with an attached copy of this Order Directing Examination for Competence to Proceed to:

Court Administration
Administrative Office of the Courts, Fiscal Office
7530 Little Road
New Port Richey, FL 34654

If the expert also examined the Defendant for sanity, then the expert must submit the portion of his or her bill concerning sanity to defense counsel.

DONE AND ORDERED in chambers at ______, [Pasco][Pinellas] County, Florida, this ___ day of ________, 20 ___.

____
CIRCUIT JUDGE

cc:
State Attorney
[Pasco][Pinellas] County Sheriff

__________, Expert
__________, Counsel for the Defendant

[Attachment B]

IN THE CIRCUIT COURT FOR THE SIXTH JUDICIAL CIRCUIT
IN AND FOR PASCO/PINELLAS COUNTY, FLORIDA

STATE OF FLORIDA

REF NO: __________
UCN: __________

vs.

____

SPN:

ORDER DIRECTING EXAMINATION OF DEFENDANT'S MENTAL CONDITION ON MOTION OF DEFENDANT

THIS CAUSE is before the Court upon the:

☐ Motion of the Attorney for the Defendant

☐ Motion of the Pro Se Defendant

to determine the mental condition of the Defendant. The Court being fully advised, it is hereby

ORDERED:

1. That said motion is hereby granted.

PART I. APPOINTMENT OF EXPERT FOR EXAMINATION OF DEFENDANT; SCHEDULING

2. The Court appoints Dr. __________ to examine the Defendant for purposes of:

☐ Confidential Defense Examination to Determine Competence to Proceed

☐ Insanity

☐ Other Mental Health Defenses

☐ Aid for Sentencing

☐ Aid for Sentencing—Capital Case

☐ Intellectual Disability as a Bar to Execution

As of this date, the Defendant is:

___ Not in Custody. The expert should contact defense counsel for scheduling and must provide defense counsel and the State Attorney advance notice of any scheduled examination of the Defendant.

___ In the [Pasco][Pinellas] County Jail. The expert must notify defense counsel when he or she is available to coordinate examination of the Defendant and must provide defense counsel and the State Attorney advance notice of any scheduled examination of the Defendant.

3. The Sheriff of [Pasco][Pinellas] County must permit the above-named expert to enter the [Pasco][Pinellas] County Jail as necessary to conduct the foregoing evaluation of the Defendant upon presentment of this Order.

4. A copy of this Order serves as authorization for the expert to inspect and copy any discoverable information relating to the Defendant maintained by the Clerk of the Court, State Attorney's Office, any hospital, doctor, or any health care provider, therapist, psychiatrist, psychologist, counselor, or any mental health provider, or other social or human services agency without the necessity of written consent by Defendant.

5. This cause is scheduled for a hearing on the issue of __________ at __________ on the ____ day of ________, 20 ___. The expert must submit his or her report to __________ by the ___ day of ________, 20 ___.

PART II. EXPERT'S EXAMINATION AND REPORT

CONFIDENTIAL DEFENSE EXAMINATION TO DETERMINE COMPETENCE TO PROCEED

If the expert is appointed to examine the Defendant for a confidential examination to determine competence to proceed, the expert shall prepare a report in accordance with instructions from defense counsel.

SANITY

If the expert is appointed to examine the Defendant concerning the Defendant's sanity at the time of the alleged offense (M'Naghten Rule) (§ 775.027, Fla. Stat.; Fla. R. Crim. P. 3.216.):

The expert must examine the Defendant to determine whether, at the time of the commission of the acts constituting the alleged offense(s), the Defendant was insane. Insanity is established when:

(a) The Defendant had a mental infirmity, disease, or defect; and

(b) Because of this condition,

1. The Defendant did not know what he or she was doing or its consequences, or

2. Although the Defendant knew what he or she was doing and its consequences, the defendant did not know that what he or she was doing was wrong. (§ 775.027, Fla. Stat.)

The expert is to report only to defense counsel or the pro se Defendant. (Fla. R. Crim. P. 3.216(a)).

OTHER MENTAL HEALTH DEFENSES OR AID FOR SENTENCING

If the expert is appointed to examine the Defendant for mental health defenses or as an aid for sentencing (§ 921.0026, Fla. Stat.; Fla. R. Crim. P. 3.216(f)):

The expert is to examine the Defendant and report to defense counsel or the pro se Defendant on whether the Defendant's mental condition presents any factors that may aid in defense of the Defendant or in sentencing the Defendant. Mitigating circumstances the expert must consider include, but are not limited to, whether:

1. The capacity of the Defendant to appreciate the criminal nature of the conduct or to conform that conduct to the requirements of the law was substantially impaired.

2. The Defendant requires specialized treatment for a mental disorder that is unrelated to substance abuse or addiction or for a physical disability, and the Defendant is amenable to treatment.

3. The Defendant acted under extreme duress or under the domination of another person. (§ 921.0026, Fla. Stat. and 921.0026(2)(j)(k)).

SENTENCING IN A CAPITAL CASE

If the expert is appointed to examine the Defendant (§§ 921.141(6) and 921.142(7), Fla. Stat.; Fla. R. Crim. P. 3.202(b)):

The expert is to examine the Defendant and report to defense counsel or the pro se Defendant regarding statutory or non-statutory mitigating circumstances. Mitigating factors the expert must consider include, but are not limited to, whether:

1. The capital felony was committed while the Defendant was under the influence of extreme mental or emotional disturbance.

2. The Defendant acted under extreme duress or under the substantial domination of another person.

3. The capacity of the Defendant to appreciate the criminality of his or her conduct or to conform his or her conduct to the requirements of the law was substantially impaired.

4. There is the existence of any other factors in the Defendant's background that would mitigate against imposition of the death penalty. (§§ 921.141(6) and 921.142(7), Fla. Stat.)

INTELLECTUAL DISABILITY AS A BAR TO EXECUTION

If the expert is appointed to examine the Defendant concerning intellectual disability as a bar to execution (§ 921.137, Fla. Stat.; Fla. R. Crim. P. 3.203):

The expert must promptly test, evaluate, or examine the Defendant and must submit a written report of any findings to the parties and the Court. Fla. R. Crim. P. 3.203(c)(3). The expert's report must include any findings as to whether the Defendant is intellectually disabled. The term "intellectual disability" or "intellectually disabled" means significantly subaverage general intellectual functioning existing concurrently with deficits in adaptive behavior and manifested during the period from conception to age 18. The term "significantly subaverage general intellectual functioning" means performance that is two or more standard deviations from the mean score on a standardized intelligence test specified in the rules of the Agency for Persons with Disabilities. The term "adaptive behavior" means the effectiveness of degree with which an individual meets the standards of personal independence and social responsibility expected of his or her age, cultural group, and community. § 921.137(1), Fla. Stat.

The expert is to report only to defense counsel or the pro se Defendant.

PART III. PAYMENT OF EXPERT

When defense counsel or the Defendant requests an evaluation of the Defendant to determine the Defendant's sanity, other mental health defenses, or as an aid for sentencing, the requesting party must pay. The expert must submit his or her appropriate invoice and a copy of this Order Directing Examination of Defendant's Mental Condition to:

☐ When requested by the Public Defender:
Public Defender
14250 49th St. North
Clearwater, FL 33762

☐ When requested by Court appointed counsel, counsel for a Defendant
determined indigent for costs, or a pro se Defendant who is indigent for cost:
Justice Administrative Commission
PO BOX 1654
Tallahassee, FL 32302

Payment for evaluations to determine intellectual disability as a bar to execution will be made by the Court. The expert must submit his or her appropriate invoice with an attached copy of this Order Directing Examination of Defendant's Mental Condition to the entity indicated below which is hereby ordered the pay the expert:

Court Administration
Administrative Office of the Courts, Fiscal Office
7530 Little Road
New Port Richey, FL 34654

DONE AND ORDERED in chambers at ________, [Pasco][Pinellas] County, Florida, this ____ day of ________, 20 ____.

____
CIRCUIT JUDGE

cc:
State Attorney
[Pasco][Pinellas] County Sheriff
________, Expert
________, Counsel for the Defendant
________, Entity Ordered to Pay

[Attachment C]

IN THE CIRCUIT COURT FOR THE SIXTH JUDICIAL CIRCUIT
IN AND FOR PASCO/PINELLAS COUNTY, FLORIDA

STATE OF FLORIDA

REF NO: __________
UCN: __________

vs.

____

____
SPN:

ORDER DIRECTING EXAMINATION OF DEFENDANT'S MENTAL CONDITION ON MOTION OF THE STATE

THIS CAUSE is before the Court upon the Motion of the State to determine the mental condition of the Defendant. The Court being fully advised, it is hereby

ORDERED:

1. That said motion is hereby granted.

PART I. APPOINTMENT OF EXPERT FOR EXAMINATION OF DEFENDANT; SCHEDULING

2. The Court appoints Dr. ________ to examine the Defendant for purposes of:

☐ Insanity
☐ Other Mental Health Defenses
☐ Aid for Sentencing
☐ Aid for Sentencing—Capital Case
☐ Intellectual Disability as a Bar to Execution

As of this date, the Defendant is:

___ Not in Custody. The expert should contact defense counsel for scheduling and must provide defense counsel and the State Attorney advance notice of any scheduled examination of the Defendant.

___ In the [Pasco][Pinellas] County Jail. The expert must notify defense counsel when he or she is available to coordinate examination of the Defendant and must provide defense counsel and the State Attorney advance notice of any scheduled examination of the Defendant.

3, The Sheriff of [Pasco][Pinellas] County must permit the above-named expert to enter the [Pasco][Pinellas] County Jail as necessary to conduct the foregoing evaluation of the Defendant upon presentment of this Order.

4. A copy of this Order serves as authorization for the expert to inspect and copy any discoverable information relating to the Defendant maintained by the Clerk of this Court, State Attorney's Office, any hospital, doctor, or any health care provider, therapist, psychiatrist, psychologist, counselor, or any mental health provider, or other social or human services agency without the necessity of written consent by Defendant.

5. This cause is scheduled for a hearing on the issue of _________ at ___ on the ___ day of _________, 20 ___. The expert must submit his or her report to _________ by the ___ day of _________, 20 ___.

PART II. EXPERT'S EXAMINATION AND REPORT

SANITY

If the expert is appointed to examine the Defendant concerning the Defendant's sanity at the time of the alleged offense (M'Naghten Rule) (§ 775.027, Fla. Stat.; Fla. R. Crim. P. 3.216.):

The expert must examine the Defendant to determine whether, at the time of the commission of the acts constituting the alleged offense(s), the Defendant was insane. Insanity is established when:

(a) The Defendant had a mental infirmity, disease, or defect; and

(b) Because of this condition,

1. The Defendant did not know what he or she was doing or its consequences, or

2. Although the Defendant knew what he or she was doing and its consequences, the defendant did not know that what he or she was doing was wrong. (§ 775.027, Fla. Stat.)

When the expert is appointed by the Court on request of the State, attorneys for the State and Defendant may be present at the examination. Fla. R. Crim. P. 3.216(d)).

OTHER MENTAL HEALTH DEFENSES

If the expert is appointed to examine the Defendant on motion of the State (Fla. R. Crim. P. 3.216(f)):

The expert is to examine the Defendant as to the mental health defense raised by the Defendant. Attorneys for the State and Defendant may be present at the examination.

SENTENCING IN A CAPITAL CASE—State request

If the expert is appointed to examine the Defendant on motion of the State (Fla. R. Crim. P. 3.202(d)):

The expert is to examine the Defendant but the examination is to be limited to those mitigating circumstances the Defendant expects to establish through expert testimony. Attorneys for the State and Defendant may be present at the examination.

INTELLECTUAL DISABILITY AS A BAR TO EXECUTION

If the expert is appointed to examine the Defendant concerning intellectual disability as a bar to execution (§ 921.137, Fla. Stat.; Fla. R. Crim. P. 3.203):

The expert must promptly test, evaluate, or examine the Defendant and must submit a written report of any findings to the parties and the court. Fla. R. Crim. P. 3.203(c)(3). The expert's report must include any findings as to whether the Defendant is intellectually disabled. The term "intellectual disability" or "intellectually disabled" means significantly subaverage general intellectual functioning existing concurrently with deficits in adaptive behavior and manifested during the period from conception to age 18. The term "significantly subaverage general intellectual functioning" means performance that is two or more standard deviations from the mean score on a standardized intelligence test specified in the rules of the Agency for Persons with Disabilities. The term "adaptive behavior" means the effectiveness of degree with which an individual meets the standards of personal independence and social responsibility expected of his or her age, cultural group, and community. § 921.137(1), Fla. Stat.

When the expert is appointed by the Court on request of the State, attorneys for the State and Defendant may be present at the examination and the report is to be submitted to the parties and the Court. Fla. R. Crim. P. 3.203(c).

PART III. PAYMENT OF EXPERT

When a request is made for an evaluation of the Defendant to determine the Defendant's sanity or other mental health defenses or when the State Attorney selects the expert under Fla. R. Crim. P. 3.203(c)(2) to determine the State Attorney or the requesting party must pay. The expert must submit his or her appropriate invoice and a copy of this Order Directing Examination of Defendant's Mental Condition to the State Attorney at:

State Attorney
PO BOX 5028
Clearwater, FL 33758–5028

DONE AND ORDERED in chambers at _________, [Pasco][Pinellas] County, Florida, this ___ day of _________, 20 ___.

____
CIRCUIT JUDGE

cc:
State Attorney
[Pasco][Pinellas] County Sheriff
_________, Expert
_________, Counsel for the Defendant
_________, Entity Ordered to Pay

Adopted effective July 1, 2017.

2017–033. EXPERT AND PROFESSIONAL FEES

IN THE CIRCUIT COURT, SIXTH JUDICIAL CIRCUIT IN AND FOR PASCO AND PINELLAS COUNTIES, FLORIDA

ADMINISTRATIVE ORDER NO. 2017–033 PA/PI–CIR

RE: EXPERT AND PROFESSIONAL FEES

Expert witnesses and other professionals provide a range of services in civil, criminal, juvenile delinquency, juvenile dependency, and family cases. These services include competency and capacity examinations, mental health evaluations, and investigative services. In certain circumstances such experts and professionals are paid with state funds through the Office of the State Courts Administrators ("OSCA") or the Justice Administrative Commission ("JAC"). In order to establish fees and rates for experts and professionals paid with state funds that are consistent with Florida Supreme Court Administrative Order AOSC17–12, and

In accordance with Article V, § 2, Florida Constitution, Rule of Judicial Administration 2.215, and § 43.26, Florida Statutes, it is:

ORDERED:

A. Experts Paid With State Funds Through OSCA. The following compensation is authorized unless otherwise provided by court order. Experts examining a defendant located in the Pasco County Jail or located outside the Sixth Judicial Circuit will be paid for mileage and per diem in accordance with Chapter 112, Florida Statutes, in addition to the fees and rates provided below.

1. *Criminal Cases.* When a physician is appointed to determine the competency of a defendant, to determine the sanity of a defendant under stay of execution, to determine the defendant's sanity at the time of sentence, to determine whether a defendant is intellectually disabled and barred from execution, or to examine a defendant who has alleged her pregnancy as a cause for not pronouncing sentence, the physician will be paid a $500.00 flat fee.

When a licensed psychologist or Ph.D. is appointed to determine the competency of a defendant, to determine the sanity of a defendant under stay of execution, or to determine whether a defendant is intellectually disabled and barred from execution, the licensed psychologist or Ph.D. will be paid a $400.00 flat fee.

When a social service professional is appointed to provide a social and developmental history of a defendant, the social service professional will be paid a $175.00 flat fee.

When the same physician, licensed psychologist, or Ph.D. is reappointed to perform a periodic competency evaluation or a follow-up evaluation of a defendant who has been found not guilty by reason of insanity, he or she will be paid a $350.00 flat fee.

These flat fees include payment for reviewing documents, time spent traveling to testify or to see the defendant, testing or examining the defendant, writing the report, consulting with the attorney, and preparing for testimony. Except as provided in paragraph A.3. of this Administrative Order or as provided in a separate court order, no other compensation may be paid pursuant to AOSC17–12.

2. *Juvenile Delinquency Cases.* When a physician is appointed to determine the competency (mental illness) of a defendant, the physician will be paid a $350.00 flat fee.

When a licensed psychologist or Ph.D. is appointed to determine the competency (mental illness) of a defendant, the licensed psychologist or Ph.D. will be paid a $300.00 flat fee.

When the same physician, licensed psychologist, or Ph.D. is reappointed to perform a periodic competency evaluation (mental illness) or a follow-up evaluation of a defendant who has been found not guilty by reason of insanity, he or she will be paid a $250.00 flat fee.

These flat fees include payment for reviewing documents, time spent traveling to testify or to see the defendant, testing or examining the defendant, writing the report, consulting with the attorney, and preparing for testimony. Except as provided in paragraph A.3. of this Administrative Order or as provided in a separate court order, no other compensation may be paid pursuant to AOSC17–12.

3. *Additional Fees In Criminal and Juvenile Delinquency Cases.* Where a physician, licensed psychologist, or Ph.D. is appointed to perform the evaluations described in sections A.1.–A.2., the following amounts may be paid:

Failure of Defendant to appear for evaluation	40% of evaluation fee
In-court time (includes wait time, applies 2–hour cap)	$150.00 per hour

Where a social service professional is appointed to perform the evaluations described in sections A.1.–A.2., the following amounts may be paid:

Failure of Defendant to appear for evaluation	40% of evaluation fee
In-court time (includes wait time, applies 2–hour cap)	$100.00 per hour

4. *Developmental Disabilities Examining Committees and Guardianship Examining Committees.* The following compensation is authorized for appointments to a Guardianship Examining Committee pursuant to § 744.331, Florida Statutes, or a Developmental Disabilities Examining Committee pursuant to § 393.11, Florida Statutes.

When a licensed physician, psychiatrist, or psychologist is appointed, the following amounts will be paid:

Evaluation	$350 flat fee
Failure of ward to appear for evaluation	40% of evaluation fee
In-court testimony (includes wait time, applies 2–hour cap)	$150 per hour
Periodic evaluation or a follow-up evaluation	$250 flat fee
Suggestion of Capacity proceeding	$350 flat fee

For all other professionals appointed, the following amounts will be paid:

Evaluation	$175 flat fee
Failure of ward to appear for evaluation	40% of evaluation fee
In-court testimony (includes wait time, applies 2–hour cap)	$75 per hour
Periodic evaluation or a follow-up evaluation	$125 flat fee

The flat fees include payment for reviewing documents, time spent traveling to testify or to see the ward, testing or examining the ward, writing the report, consulting with the attorney, preparing for testimony, and providing telephonic testimony. Except as provided in this section or provided in a separate court order, no other compensation may be paid pursuant to AOSC17–12.

5. *Payment for Extraordinary Cases.* In extraordinary cases, fees or rates higher than those listed herein may be permitted. Extraordinary cases include, but are not limited to, capital murder cases, first-degree murder cases, and cases that require the expert to expend substantially more time due to their complexity or the circumstances of the case. Any request for higher fees or rates must be directed to the Chief Judge or his or her designee.

B. Experts Paid With State Funds Through JAC. Due process costs under § 29.007, Florida Statutes, include fees and rates for experts and professionals retained by court-appointed counsel, by counsel for a defendant who is indigent for costs, or by a *pro se* defendant who is indigent. These fees and rates are paid with state funds through the JAC. Prior court approval is required for experts or professionals retained pursuant to § 29.007, Florida Statutes. Individuals who are not indigent or indigent for costs are responsible for the payment of their experts.

1. *Baker Act Cases.* The following compensation is authorized for appointments to conduct independent expert examinations in a Baker Act proceeding pursuant to §§ 394.467 and 394.4655, Florida Statutes.

When a physician, Ph.D., or other expert with a doctorate degree is retained to conduct an independent expert examination in a Baker Act proceeding, the following amounts will be paid:

Examination	$300.00 flat fee
In-court testimony	$150.00 per hour

When an expert other than one identified in the preceding paragraph is retained to conduct an independent examination in a Baker Act proceeding, the following amounts will be paid:

Examination	$175.00 flat fee
In-court testimony	$75.00 per hour

These flat fees include payment for reviewing documents, time spent traveling to see the patient, testing or examining the patient, writing the report, consulting with the attorney, and providing telephonic testimony. In addition to the above rates, all experts conducting independent expert examinations in Baker Act proceeding will be paid:

Waiting to testify/testimony preparation	$60.00 per hour
Travel time to and from court to testify	$50.00 per hour

2. *Other Experts and Professionals.* The authorized fees and rates for other experts and professionals paid with state funds through JAC are set forth in the Sixth Circuit Due Process Rate Sheet, which can be found on JAC's website at www.justiceadmin.org/court_app_counsel/formsandrates.aspx. The Sixth Circuit Due Process Rate Sheet is incorporated herein by reference.

This Administrative Order is effective July 1, 2017. The fees and rates in this Administrative Order apply to services provided as a result of appointments on or after July 1, 2017. Services provided as a result of appointments occurring prior to July 1, 2017, may be paid at the fees and rates established under Administrative Order 2017–013 with approval from the Chief Judge or Trial Court Administrator. Effective July 1, 2017, Administrative Order Nos. 2007–017 and 2017–013 are hereby rescinded.

DONE AND ORDERED in Chambers at St. Petersburg, Pinellas County, Florida, this ___ day of June, 2017.

ORIGINAL SIGNED ON JUNE 20, 2017
BY ANTHONY RONDOLINO,
CHIEF JUDGE

Adopted effective July 1, 2017.

2017–032. CIVIL TRAFFIC INFRACTION HEARING OFFICER PROGRAM—PINELLAS COUNTY

IN THE CIRCUIT COURT, SIXTH JUDICIAL CIRCUIT IN AND FOR PASCO AND PINELLAS COUNTIES, FLORIDA

ADMINISTRATIVE ORDER NO. 2017–032 PI–CTY

RE: CIVIL TRAFFIC INFRACTION HEARING OFFICER PROGRAM—PINELLAS COUNTY

In order to update the traffic citation calendars, and address calendaring issues for civil traffic infraction cases in Pinellas County, it is

ORDERED:

1. The Pinellas Clerk of the Circuit Court shall assign non-criminal traffic infraction cases to calendars to be heard at the Criminal Justice Center except as provided herein. Cases currently calendared in accordance with previous administrative orders shall remain as scheduled; however, no new cases shall be set except as provided in this administrative order.

2. Cases shall be set on calendars in accordance with the schedule in Attachment A.[1]

3. Cases may be scheduled so that citations from each law enforcement agency are calendared to minimize the time officers are in court.

4. Additional calendars or modifications to this schedule may be made by the Pinellas County Administrative Judge without modification to this administrative order.

5. The Pinellas Clerk of the Circuit Court shall notify the Pinellas County Administrative Judge when cases cannot be scheduled within thirty (30) days of the defendant's election for a hearing.

6. Requests for continuances of civil traffic infraction cases scheduled at the Criminal Justice Center shall be handled as follows:

a. The Clerk of the Circuit Court shall grant the first continuance requested by a defendant or issuing officer, up until 5:00 p.m. the business day prior to the assigned court date, without prior approval by presiding Judge.

b. Except as provided herein if a second or subsequent continuance is requested, a written motion or request for continuance shall be timely filed with the Clerk of the Circuit Court. The motion or request must state with particularity the reasons for the request for continuance. The motion shall be considered timely if it is filed five (5) business days prior to the scheduled hearing. The Clerk shall direct all motions, including those that are late or non-compliant to the judge at North County Traffic Court or South County Traffic Court, based upon the issuing jurisdiction.

c. In case of an emergency or if the person is unable to file a written motion in accordance with paragraph (b) above, the Clerk of the Circuit Court shall communicate to the party that the presiding civil traffic hearing officer will be advised of the circumstances by the Clerk, and the hearing officer will rule on the request at the scheduled hearing. If granted, a new notice of hearing will be sent to all parties.

d. The attached form Motion for Continuance (Attachment B) shall be used to seek a second or subsequent continuance of a civil traffic infraction hearing.

e. This procedure only applies to civil traffic infraction hearings scheduled for the Criminal Justice Center and does not apply to hearings scheduled at North County Traffic Court or South County Traffic Court.

f. Any matters that arise not provided for by these provisions may be referred to the Pinellas County Administrative Judge.

7. If Law Enforcement discovers that a citation previously issued should be dismissed prior to the scheduled hearing, that request shall be in writing and filed with the clerk. The law enforcement agency's name, officers or deputies' names and badge numbers shall be included in the request for dismissal.

8. If a defendant requests that his or her case be heard by a county judge in accordance with the Florida Rules of Traffic Court 6.630(n), the Pinellas Clerk of the Circuit Court shall calendar the case at a traffic facility.

This Administrative Order is effective July 1, 2017. Effective July 1, 2017, Administrative Order No. 2009–008 PI–CTY is hereby rescinded.

DONE AND ORDERED in Chambers at St. Petersburg, Pinellas County, Florida, this ___ day of June, 2017.

ORIGINAL SIGNED ON JUNE 20, 2017
BY ANTHONY RONDOLINO,
CHIEF JUDGE

[ATTACHMENT B]

IN THE COUNTY COURT, SIXTH JUDICIAL CIRCUIT IN AND FOR PINELLAS COUNTY, FLORIDA

In Re:Citation Number: ________________
Alleged Offender: ________________
(please print legibly)

MOTION FOR SECOND REQUEST TO CONTINUE CIVIL TRAFFIC INFRACTION HEARINGS AT PINELLAS COUNTY JUSTICE CENTER

COMES NOW, *(please print)* ________________, and respectfully requests that this Court continue the civil traffic infraction hearing scheduled for ________ in the above-referenced case to the next available court date and state that:

☐ I am an officer of the ________________ (Law Enforcement Agency & Badge Number); or

☐ I am ________________, the alleged offender in the case. I understand that I have the right to be brought to trial within 180 days from the date I was served with the above-referenced citation. I hereby waive such right. I further understand that if my motion is granted, I may be assessed reasonable costs and fees.

I am unavailable to appear on the calendared date for the following reason(s):

____
____
____

Respectfully submitted this ___ day of ________, ____.

________________________ / ________________
Signature of moving party / Daytime phone

ORDER ON MOTION TO CONTINUE CIVIL TRAFFIC INFRACTION HEARING

The Court having reviewed the above Motion to Continue, the Motion is hereby:

☐ GRANTED
This case is continued to the next available court date. The Clerk of the Circuit Court shall notice all parties of the rescheduled hearing date; or

☐ DENIED
This matter shall be heard as previously scheduled.

DONE AND ORDERED at Pinellas County, Florida, this ___ day of ________, ____.

____
County Court Judge

Adopted effective July 1, 2017.

[1] Attachment A is not included in this order.

2017–027. [RESCINDED BY ORDER 2018-041, EFFECTIVE SEPTEMBER 1, 2018.]

2017–022. [RESCINDED BY ORDER 2018-042, EFFECTIVE AUGUST 14, 2018.]

2017–014. [RESCINDED BY ORDER 2017–034, EFFECTIVE JULY 1, 2017.]

2017–013. [RESCINDED BY ORDER 2017–033, EFFECTIVE JULY 1, 2017.]

2017–007. [RESCINDED BY ORDER 2019–004, EFFECTIVE JANUARY 23, 2019]

2016–077. ELECTRONIC FILING IN PINELLAS COUNTY—AMENDMENT ONE

IN THE CIRCUIT COURT OF THE SIXTH JUDICIAL CIRCUIT IN AND FOR PASCO AND PINELLAS COUNTIES, FLORIDA

ADMINISTRATIVE ORDER NO. 2016–077 PI–CIR

RE: ELECTRONIC FILING IN PINELLAS COUNTY—AMENDMENT ONE

On April 1, 2013, mandatory electronic filing ("e-filing") began in the county civil, county small claims, circuit civil, circuit civil appellate, family law, and probate divisions in accordance with *In Re: Amendments to the Florida Rules of Civil Procedure, et. al., Electronic Filing*, 102 So. 3d 451 (Fla. 2012). On January 1, 2016, mandatory e-filing began in the criminal division. *In re: Electronic Filing of Criminal, Juvenile and Traffic Cases via the Florida Courts E–Filing Portal, AOSC15–7*. Due to implementation concerns, however, e-filing of pleadings and papers was prohibited in Baker Act, Chapter 394, Part I cases. Procedural and technological protocols are now in place to begin e-filing in this case type. Thus, this amendment removes the prohibition on the e-filing of pleadings and papers in Baker Act, Chapter 394, Part I cases.

In order to update and maintain the e-filing procedures in Pinellas County, and in accordance with Article V, section 2, Florida Constitution, Rules of Judicial Administration 2.215 and 2.525, and section 43.26, Florida Statutes, it is

ORDERED:

1. Paragraph 3 is amended to read:

Attorneys must not e-file pleadings and papers in the following types of cases:

f. Proceedings to waive parental notification of abortion; and

g. Criminal appeals from county court to circuit court.

2. Paragraph 13 is amended to read:

Unrepresented litigants are not permitted to e-file pleadings and papers in the following types of cases:

a. Proceedings to waive parental notification of abortion; and

b. Criminal appeals from county court to circuit court.

3. Paragraph 27 is amended to read:

The Clerk will not accept e-filed pleadings and papers in the following types of cases:

f. Proceedings to waive parental notification of abortion; and

g. Criminal appeals from county court to circuit court.

All other provisions of Administrative Order 2016–018 remain in full force and effect.

DONE AND ORDERED in Chambers at St. Petersburg, Pinellas County, Florida, this ________ day of November, 2016.

ORIGINAL SIGNED ON NOVEMBER 15, 2016
BY ANTHONY RONDOLINO, CHIEF JUDGE

2016–058. [RESCINDED BY ORDER 2018-047, EFFECTIVE SEPTEMBER 7, 2018.]

2016–039. UNIFORM PROCEDURES FOR FORFEITURES OF PERSONAL PROPERTY

IN THE CIRCUIT COURT, SIXTH JUDICIAL CIRCUIT IN AND FOR PASCO AND PINELLAS COUNTIES, FLORIDA

ADMINISTRATIVE ORDER NO. 2016–039 PA/PI–CIR

RE: UNIFORM PROCEDURES FOR FORFEITURES OF PERSONAL PROPERTY

The Florida Contraband Forfeiture Act sets forth the procedural requirements governing the forfeiture of contraband articles. *See* §§ 932.701–932.7062, Florida Statutes. Administrative Orders 95–97 and PA–CIR–00–20 were enacted in order to implement these procedures in a uniform manner within the courts of the Sixth Judicial Circuit. Recent statutory changes passed by the Florida Legislature require these procedures to be updated.

In order to provide for the uniform disposition of forfeiture proceedings and ensure consistency amongst all seizing agencies within the Sixth Judicial Circuit, and pursuant to the authority of the Chief Judge in accordance with Article V, section 2, Florida Constitution, Rule of Judicial Administration 2.215, and section 43.26, Florida Statutes, it is therefore

ORDERED:

A. Circuit Civil Forfeiture Proceedings Generally.

1. In accordance with section 932.704(2), Florida Statutes, of the Florida Contraband Forfeiture Act, all civil forfeiture cases shall be heard before a judge of the civil division. In Pinellas County, the Chief Judge (or his/her designee) is hereby designated as the primary Circuit Court Judge of the Civil Division for all forfeiture cases. In Pasco County, the forfeiture cases shall be assigned to any civil section judge in the same manner other circuit civil cases are assigned.

2. Because forfeiture proceedings are civil proceedings, court reporters shall not be provided at county expense. The seizing agency and/or Claimant(s) are responsible for securing the services of and paying the cost of court reporting services.

B. Initial Proceedings Prior to Filing a Complaint. Section 932.703, Florida Statutes, recognizes the fact that after a seizure under the Forfeiture Act prior to filing a civil complaint specific events may occur that require court action. During the 45 day time period between the seizure and the deadline for filing a formal civil action there is a requirement under section 932.703(2)(a), Florida Statutes, that the seizing agency apply to the circuit court for an order determining the existence of probable cause. There is also a requirement under section 932.703(3), Florida Statutes, that the agency provide notice of the right to an adversarial preliminary hearing and that such a hearing may be required prior to filing a complaint. To insure an adequate record of these initial documents is maintained and a civil case number is available for these filings the following procedures apply:

Application for an Ex–Parte Order Finding Probable Cause for Seizure

1. Effective July 1, 2016, to obtain a ruling pursuant to section 932.703(2)(a), Florida Statutes, the seizing agency shall, within 10 business days of the seizure, submit an Application for Seizure Probable Cause Determination with an accompanying affidavit to the court for ex-parte review and ruling. The submission packet must include a proposed Order Finding Probable Cause for Seizure and (as an alternative) a proposed Order Denying Probable Cause for Seizure. The Application for Seizure Probable Cause Determination and the proposed orders shall be substantially the same format as *Attachment A* of this Order. In addition to an original order, copies and envelopes should be included for distribution by the judicial assistant.

2. In Pinellas County, the application shall be to the Chief Judge (or his/her designee). In Pasco County the application shall be to the civil judge assigned by the clerk to the action.

3. If there has not yet been a complaint filed or a circuit civil number issued for the action by the Clerk, the seizing agency shall obtain a case number from the Clerk of Court to be used on these papers prior to submission for ex-parte review.

4. After the assigned Judge has made his/her findings, the judicial assistant will file the original Application and the attached affidavit with the Clerk of Court. The original signed Order (regarding the probable cause determination) will also be filed with the Clerk of Court by the judicial assistant and copies will be mailed to the parties using the return envelopes that were provided by the agency.

Notice of Seizure & Right to Adversary Probable Cause Hearing

1. Section 932.703(3), Florida Statutes, includes a right to an adversary preliminary hearing upon request. Pursuant to this statute a specific notice of this right must be provided. All law enforcement agencies within the Sixth Judicial Circuit shall use a Notice of Seizure in substantially the same format as *Attachment B* of this Order.

2. The seizing agency shall complete a Notice(s) of Seizure containing the name and address of the person(s) who may have an interest in the property and who are known to the seizing agency.

3. When any person receiving the notice requests an adversary hearing in conformity with the statute the seizing agency is then required to set and notice a hearing. The seizing agency shall file both the Notice of Seizure & Right to Adversary Probable Cause Hearing and the responding party's Request for Adversary Hearing with the Clerk of Court.

4. If there has not yet been a formal complaint filed or a civil number issued as a result of a prior ex-parte application for probable cause, the Clerk of Court shall assign a civil case number for the proceedings and maintain the documents in a civil file. In Pinellas County the seizing agency shall schedule the Adversary Preliminary Hearing before the Chief Judge (or his/her designee) to be heard within 10 days of the request or as soon as practicable thereafter. In Pasco County the hearing shall be scheduled before the civil judge assigned to the action by the Clerk of Court.

C. Complaint for Forfeiture and § 932.704(5)(c), Florida Statutes, Administrative Order.

1. All counsel representing seizing agencies seeking forfeiture in the Sixth Judicial Circuit shall use a Complaint for Forfeiture in substantially the same format as *Attachment C* of this Order.

2. Section 932.704(5)(c), Florida Statutes, indicates the court shall require any claimant who desires to contest the forfeiture to file and serve upon the attorney for the seizing agency any responsive pleading and affirmative defenses within 20 days after the receipt of the complaint. To comply with this provision the court has entered Administrative Order 2016–038 *Notice to Claimant of Seizure and Filing Requirements under Florida Statutes Section 932.704(5)(c)* and counsel for the agency shall include a copy of that order with the complaint and summons to be served upon the claimant. This order advising the claimant of the responsive pleading requirements is included as *Attachment D*.

3. Upon filing of the Complaint, affidavit and payment of the appropriate filing fee and posting a bond pursuant to section 932.704(4), Florida Statutes, to the Clerk of the Court shall cause the opening of a circuit civil proceeding which shall be treated in all regards in like manner.

Attachments to this Administrative Order may be modified without further changes to this Administrative Order.

Administrative Orders 95–97 and PA–CIR 00–20 are hereby rescinded.

DONE AND ORDERED in Chambers at St. Petersburg, Pinellas County, Florida this ___ day of June, 2016.

ORIGINAL SIGNED ON JUNE 22, 2016
BY ANTHONY RONDOLINO, CHIEF JUDGE

Attachment A: Ex–Parte Application for Seizure Probable Cause Determination,
Ex–Parte Order Finding Probable Cause for Seizure and
Ex–Parte Order Denying Probable Cause for Seizure

Attachment B: Notice of Seizure

Attachment C: Forfeiture Complaint

Attachment D: Administrative Order 2016–038 re: Notice to Claimants of Seizure and Filing Requirements

IN THE CIRCUIT COURT OF THE SIXTH JUDICIAL CIRCUIT IN AND FOR PASCO AND PINELLAS COUNTIES, FLORIDA [ATTACHMENT A]

IN RE: FORFEITURE OF:

Case No.: __________

(Description of Property)

____________________/

EX–PARTE APPLICATION FOR SEIZURE PROBABLE CAUSE DETERMINATION

COMES NOW the Petitioner, *(insert agency)*, by and through undersigned counsel, pursuant to section 932.703(2), Florida Statutes, and says:

1. On *(date)*, *(insert agency)*, seized for forfeiture *(describe property)* as more fully set forth in the attached Notice of Seizure. This application is being presented within 10 business days of seizing that property.

2. The requirements specified in paragraph (1)(a) of section 932.703, Florida Statutes, have been satisfied based on the fact that one of the following facts exist:

_______ The owner of the property was arrested for a criminal offense that forms the basis for determining that the property is a contraband article under section 932.701, Florida Statutes;

_______ The owner of the property cannot be identified after a diligent search or the person in possession of the property denies ownership and the owner of the property cannot be identified by means that are available to the employee or agent of the seizing agency at the time of the seizure;

_______ The owner is a fugitive from justice or is deceased;

_______ An individual who does not own the property is arrested for a criminal offense that forms the basis for determining that the property is a contraband article under section 932.701, Florida Statutes, and the owner of the property had actual knowledge of the criminal activity;

_______ The owner of the property agrees to be a confidential informant as defined in section 914.28, Florida Statutes; or

_______ The property is a monetary instrument.

3. The facts and circumstances surrounding the seizure are contained in the attached affidavit, which is incorporated as if fully set forth herein.

WHEREFORE, Petitioner requests an Order Finding Probable Cause for Seizure pursuant to section 932.703(2), Florida Statutes.

ATTESTATION

I HEREBY ATTEST that a copy of this Motion and attached affidavit has been submitted to the Judge this ______ day of ________, 20__.

____
Attorney signature block

IN THE CIRCUIT COURT OF THE SIXTH JUDICIAL CIRCUIT IN AND FOR PASCO AND PINELLAS COUNTIES, FLORIDA

IN RE: FORFEITURE OF:

Case No.: __________

(Description of Property)

____________________/

EX–PARTE ORDER FINDING PROBABLE CAUSE FOR SEIZURE

THIS MATTER having come before this Court pursuant to section 932.703(2), Florida Statutes, within 10 business days of seizure of the above-described property by the *(Seizing Law Enforcement Agency)* and the Court having reviewed the sworn affidavit, FINDS:

1. The Agency applied for the probable cause determination within 10 business days after the date of the seizure.

2. The requirements specified in paragraph (1)(a) of section 932.703, Florida Statutes, have been satisfied based on the fact that one of the following facts exist:

_______ The owner of the property was arrested for a criminal offense that forms the basis for determining that the property is a contraband article under section 932.701, Florida Statutes;

_______ The owner of the property cannot be identified after a diligent search or the person in possession of the property denies ownership and the owner of the property cannot be identified by means that are available to the employee or agent of the seizing agency at the time of the seizure;

_______ The owner is a fugitive from justice or is deceased;

_______ An individual who does not own the property is arrested for a criminal offense that forms the basis for determining that the property is a contraband article under section 932.701, Florida Statutes, and the owner of the property had actual knowledge of the criminal activity;

_______ The owner of the property agrees to be a confidential informant as defined in section 914.28, Florida Statutes; or

_______ The property is a monetary instrument.

3. Probable cause exists to seize the above-described property under the Florida Contraband Forfeiture Act.

Therefore the Court having found that the requirements of Florida Statute section 932.703(1)(a) were satisfied and that probable cause exists for the seizure, it is ORDERED that the property shall be held in conformity with the statute until further order of the Court.

DONE AND ORDERED in Chambers, in _________ County, Florida, this ____ day of ____________________, 20__.

____
CIRCUIT COURT JUDGE

Copies to:

Attorney for Petitioner
Claimant

IN THE CIRCUIT COURT OF THE SIXTH JUDICIAL CIRCUIT IN AND FOR PASCO AND PINELLAS COUNTIES, FLORIDA

IN RE: FORFEITURE OF:

Case No.: ___________

(Description of Property)

______________________/

EX-PARTE ORDER DENYING PROBABLE CAUSE FOR SEIZURE

THIS MATTER having come before this Court pursuant to section 932.703(2), Florida Statutes, within 10 business days of seizure of the above-described property by the *(Seizing Law Enforcement Agency)* and the Court having reviewed the sworn affidavit, FINDS:

_______ The Agency did not apply for the probable cause determination within 10 business days after the date of the seizure

AND/OR

_______ The requirements specified in paragraph (1)(a) of section 932.703, Florida Statutes, have not been satisfied.

AND/OR

_______ The Agency has not established probable cause for the seizure based on a review of the attached affidavit.

Therefore the Court having found that the requirements of Florida Statute section 932.703(1) were not satisfied and that probable cause does not exists for the seizure, it is ORDERED that any forfeiture hold, lien, lis pendens, or other civil encumbrance shall be released in conformity with the statute within 5 days.

DONE AND ORDERED in Chambers, in _________ County, Florida, this ____ day of ____________________, 20__.

____
CIRCUIT COURT JUDGE

Copies to:

Attorney for Petitioner
Claimant

NOTICE OF SEIZURE [ATTACHMENT B]

REPORT NO.: ___________ **CASE NO.:** ___________

DATE: ___________ *(To be filled in by Clerk of the Court)*

TO: *(Claimant's Name)*

ADDRESS: ___________

RE: *(Description of Seized Property)*

This is to advise you that on *Date* the *Seizing Agency* seized the above-referenced property for a violation of the Florida Contraband Forfeiture Act, §§ 932.701–932.7062, Florida Statutes.

YOU ARE HEREBY NOTIFIED that you are entitled by law to request an adversarial preliminary hearing to determine whether there is probable cause to believe the property was used in violation of the Act.

PLEASE NOTE that the adversarial preliminary hearing is not mandatory and you need not request a hearing to later contest the action taken against the property described herein. Each claimant will be given the opportunity to appear in court before final disposition of this matter.

IF YOU DESIRE SUCH A HEARING, you must make a request in writing by certified mail, return receipt requested, to *(Name of Seizing Agency)* at the address listed below, within fifteen (15) days of receiving this Notice. This request must be accompanied by a copy of this Notice. The seizing agency will notify you of the time, date, and place of that hearing.

I HEREBY CERTIFY that I have:

_____ provided a copy of this Notice to the person named above, or

_____ forwarded a copy of this Notice by certified mail, return receipt requested, to ____________________ *(person or entity to which Notice was sent)* this ______ day of ____________________, 20__.

____
Seizing Officer/Person Sending Notice

I HEREBY CERTIFY that I have:

_____ received the foregoing Notice apprising me of my right to post-seizure adversarial hearing.

____
Claimant

(Seizing agency)
(Address)
(Person ID/Fla. Bar Number)
(Telephone Number)
(E-mail Address)

If you are a person with a disability who needs any accommodation in order to participate in this proceeding, you are entitled, at no cost to you, to the provision of certain assistance. Please contact the Human Rights Office, 400 S. Ft. Harrison Ave., Suite 300, Clearwater, FL 33756, (727) 464–4062 (V/TDD) at least 7 days before your scheduled court appearance, or immediately upon receiving this notification if the time before the scheduled appearance is less than 7 days; if you are hearing or voice impaired, call 711.

IN THE CIRCUIT COURT, SIXTH JUDICIAL CIRCUIT IN AND FOR PASCO AND PINELLAS COUNTIES, FLORIDA [ATTACHMENT C]

IN RE: FORFEITURE OF:

Case No.: ___________

(Description of Property)

______________________/

COMPLAINT FOR FORFEITURE

COMES NOW Complainant, ______________, for the use and benefit of the ______________, by and through the undersigned attorney, and files this Complaint for Forfeiture under the Florida Contraband Forfeiture Act (the Act), and says:

(1) This is an action for forfeiture pursuant to sections 932.701–932.7062, Florida Statutes; jurisdiction in this Court pursuant to section 932.704, Florida Statutes.

(2) ____________________ is a seizing agency as set forth in section 932.704, Florida Statutes.

(3) A description of the property that is the subject of this action is as follows:

____
(Description of all property)

(4) On or about ______________ *(date property was used in violation of the Act)*, said property was in violation of the Act by virtue of one or more of the following:

a) ____ The property is a contraband article as defined in section 932.701(2)(a), Florida Statutes.

b) ____ The property was used to transport, carry, convey, conceal, or possess a contraband article in violation of section 932.702(1) or (2), Florida Statutes.

c) ____ The property was used to facilitate the transportation, carriage, conveyance, concealment, receipt, possession, purchase, sale, barter, exchange, or giving away of any contraband article, or used as an instrumentality in the commission of or in aiding or abetting in the commission of a felony or violation of the Act, pursuant to sections 932.702(3) and (4), Florida Statutes.

d) ____ The property was acquired by the use of proceeds obtained in violation of the Act in violation of section 932.701 or 932.702(5), Florida Statutes.

e) ____ The property is subject to forfeiture pursuant to: *(This section is for other statutory violations which authorize forfeiture under the Act; e.g., felony littering, VIN–HIN violations, aircraft violations, fleeing in a vessel, etc.)*

(5) On or about ______________ *(date property was actually seized)*, the ______________ *(name of seizing law enforcement agency)* discovered and seized the property described in paragraph 3 above at or near ______________ *(address or location where property was seized)*.

(6) The Complainant has conducted a reasonably diligent search for all persons or entities who may have an interest in the property described in paragraph 3 above by virtue of possession, ownership, registration law, or perfected lien, and who are known to the Complainant as:

(names of persons or entities)

and all others who claim an interest in the following described property: *(describe property)*

(7) Complainant has complied with the Notice requirements of the Act.

(8) Pursuant to 932.703(2)(b), Florida Statutes, on *(date)*, the seizing agency submitted an affidavit setting forth the facts and circumstances upon which the seizure was based and which support the forfeiture of the property and obtained an Order Finding Probable Cause for Seizure.

WHEREFORE, *(Name of Petitioner)*, having provided to the persons or entities listed in Paragraph 6 above, and any other persons or entities who claim an interest in the property described in Paragraph 3 above a copy of the *Notice to Claimant Forfeiture of Personal Property*, and after hearing upon the Complaint for Forfeiture, requests this Court to enter a Final Order of Forfeiture perfecting the right, interest, and title to said property for the use or benefit of the *(name of law enforcement agency)*

____
(Signature of Attorney)
(Name of Attorney)
(Address)
(Telephone Number)

(Person ID/Florida Bar Number
(E-mail Address)

IN THE CIRCUIT COURT, SIXTH JUDICIAL CIRCUIT IN AND FOR PASCO AND PINELLAS COUNTIES, FLORIDA [ATTACHMENT D]

ADMINISTRATIVE ORDER NO. 2016–038 PA/PI–CIR

RE: NOTICE TO CLAIMANTS OF SEIZURE AND FILING REQUIREMENTS UNDER SECTION 932.704(5)(c), FLORIDA STATUTES

The Florida Contraband Forfeiture Act sets forth the procedural requirements governing the forfeiture of contraband articles. *See* §§ 932.701–932.7062, Florida Statutes. Pursuant to section 943.704(5)(c), Florida Statutes, any claimant who desires to contest the forfeiture action shall file and serve upon the attorney representing the seizing agency any responsive pleadings and affirmative defenses. It is therefore

ORDERED:

THAT YOU HAVE BEEN SERVED WITH A FORMAL COMPLAINT AND AS A PERSON WHO CLAIMS AN INTEREST IN THE SEIZED PROPERTY, YOU HAVE TWENTY (20) DAYS FROM SERVICE OF A COPY OF THE COMPLAINT FOR FORFEITURE TO FILE IN THIS COURT ANY RESPONSIVE PLEADING, ANSWER, AND/OR AFFIRMATIVE DEFENSES TO THE COMPLAINT FOR FORFEITURE.

YOU ARE FURTHER COMMANDED TO SERVE A COPY OF SUCH ANSWER OR RESPONSIVE PLEADING WITHIN SAID TIME PERIOD UPON THE ATTORNEY WHO FILED THE COMPLAINT FOR FORFEITURE. FAILURE TO FILE AND SERVE SUCH ANSWER OR PLEADING WITHIN SAID TIME PERIOD SHALL RESULT IN THE ENTRY OF A DEFAULT PURSUANT TO FLORIDA RULE OF CIVIL PROCEDURE 1.500(a), AND A FINAL ORDER OF FORFEITURE.

DONE AND ORDERED in Chambers at St. Petersburg, Pinellas County, Florida this ___ day of June, 2016.

ORIGINAL SIGNED ON JUNE 22, 2016

BY ANTHONY RONDOLINO, CHIEF JUDGE

2016–038. NOTICE TO CLAIMANTS OF SEIZURE AND FILING REQUIREMENTS

IN THE CIRCUIT COURT, SIXTH JUDICIAL CIRCUIT IN AND FOR PASCO AND PINELLAS COUNTIES, FLORIDA

ADMINISTRATIVE ORDER NO. 2016–038 PA/PI–CIR

RE: NOTICE TO CLAIMANTS OF SEIZURE AND FILING REQUIREMENTS UNDER SECTION 932.704(5)(c), FLORIDA STATUTES

The Florida Contraband Forfeiture Act sets forth the procedural requirements governing the forfeiture of contraband articles. *See* §§ 932.701–932.7062, Florida Statutes. Pursuant to section 943.704(5)(c), Florida Statutes, any claimant who desires to contest the forfeiture action shall file and serve upon the attorney representing the seizing agency any responsive pleadings and affirmative defenses. It is therefore

ORDERED:

THAT YOU HAVE BEEN SERVED WITH A FORMAL COMPLAINT AND AS A PERSON WHO CLAIMS AN INTEREST IN THE SEIZED PROPERTY, YOU HAVE TWENTY (20) DAYS FROM SERVICE OF A COPY OF THE COMPLAINT FOR FORFEITURE TO FILE IN THIS COURT ANY RESPONSIVE PLEADING, ANSWER, AND/OR AFFIRMATIVE DEFENSES TO THE COMPLAINT FOR FORFEITURE.

YOU ARE FURTHER COMMANDED TO SERVE A COPY OF SUCH ANSWER OR RESPONSIVE PLEADING WITHIN SAID TIME PERIOD UPON THE ATTORNEY WHO FILED THE COMPLAINT FOR FORFEITURE. FAILURE TO FILE AND SERVE SUCH ANSWER OR PLEADING WITHIN SAID TIME PERIOD SHALL RESULT IN THE ENTRY OF A DEFAULT PURSUANT TO FLORIDA RULE OF CIVIL PROCEDURE 1.500(a), AND A FINAL ORDER OF FORFEITURE.

DONE AND ORDERED in Chambers at St. Petersburg, Pinellas County, Florida this ___ day of June, 2016.

ORIGINAL SIGNED ON JUNE 22, 2016
BY ANTHONY RONDOLINO,CHIEF JUDGE

2016–027. PROCEDURES FOR RETURN OF FIREARMS—PASCO COUNTY

IN THE CIRCUIT COURT OF THE SIXTH JUDICIAL CIRCUIT IN AND FOR PASCO AND PINELLAS COUNTIES, FLORIDA

ADMINISTRATIVE ORDER NO. 2016–027 PA–CIR

IN RE: PROCEDURES FOR RETURN OF FIREARMS—PASCO COUNTY

Section 933.14(3), Florida Statutes, provides that no firearm seized by law enforcement with a search warrant or without a search warrant upon view by an officer of a breach of the peace shall be returned except upon court order. It is necessary for the efficient administration of justice to establish a uniform procedure in Pasco County for determining the appropriateness of ordering the return of firearms taken by law enforcement under section 933.14(3), Florida Statutes, where no arrest was made and no charges were filed.

In order to provide for the timely and uniform disposition of petitions for the return of firearms within Pasco County, and in accordance with Article V, section 2, Florida Constitution, Rule of Judicial Administration 2.215, and section 43.26, Florida Statutes, it is

ORDERED:

1. Any person who seeks the return of a firearm seized by law enforcement under section 933.14(3), Florida Statutes, where no arrest was made and no case was filed must file a Petition for Return of Firearm(s) with the Clerk of Court. The petition must be sworn and must be served on the law enforcement agency in possession of the firearm(s). A form Petition for Return of Firearm(s) is attached to this administrative order as Attachment A.

2. All Petitions for Return of Firearm(s) must specifically identify the firearm(s) and/or ammunition sought to be returned and must further allege that (1) the firearm(s) and/or ammunition is/are the petitioner's personal property; (2) the firearm(s) and/or ammunition is/are not the fruit of criminal activity and was/were not involved in criminal activity; (3) the firearm(s) and/or ammunition is/are not being held as evidence by the relevant law enforcement agency; (4) the petitioner is not prohibited from possessing a firearm under any provision of Florida or federal law, including 18 U.S.C. 922(g)(9); (5) the petitioner has not been convicted of a misdemeanor crime of domestic violence, and has not had adjudication of guilt withheld or the imposition of a sentence suspended on any misdemeanor crime of domestic violence unless 3 years have elapsed since probation or any other conditions set by the relevant court have been fulfilled or expunction has occurred; (6) the petitioner is not prohibited from possessing a firearm and/or ammunition pursuant to the terms of any pretrial release, bond, probation, or any other type of community supervision or court program; (7) the petitioner has not been Baker Acted as a result of this incident or otherwise. If the petitioner has been Baker Acted, the petitioner will provide the Judge with a copy of the documents furnished to the petitioner or the petitioner's representative by the facility, upon or after discharge of the petitioner from the facility, which contain any evaluations, diagnoses, prognoses, recommended course of treatment, and recommended or prescribed medications, and a letter from a licensed mental health professional stating that the person is of sound mind to possess a firearm; (8) the petitioner does not have an active Domestic Violence Injunction or a Repeat Violence Injunction against him/her; (9) the petitioner has not been adjudicated mentally defective as defined by section 790.065(2)(a)4.a., Florida Statutes, or if the petitioner has been adjudicated mentally defective, the petitioner has had his or her capacity restored by a court for at least 5 years from the date of the Petition for Return of Firearm(s); and (10) the petitioner has not been committed to a mental institution as defined in section 790.065(2)(a)4.b., Florida Statutes, or if the petitioner has been committed to a mental institution, the petitioner possesses a certificate from a licensed psychiatrist that he or she has not suffered from a mental disability for at least 5 years since the commitment to a mental institution.

3. The petitioner must attach to the petition a copy of the agency report detailing the circumstances which led to the taking of the firearm(s).

4. All Petitions for Return of Firearm(s) in Pasco County shall be assigned to the Pasco Administrative Judge.

5. The law enforcement agency shall review the Petition for Return of Firearm(s) and attempt to verify the information contained therein and advise the court accordingly.

6. To obtain a hearing on a petition, the petitioner must contact the Pasco Administrative Judge's judicial assistant to be assigned a hearing date. Once assigned a hearing date, the petitioner is responsible for preparing a notice of hearing and serving it on the law enforcement agency in possession of the firearm(s) no less than 14 days prior to the hearing date. The notice shall be hand delivered or sent via certified mail to the law enforcement agency. A form notice of hearing is attached to this administrative order as Attachment B.

7. Should the petitioner and the law enforcement agency stipulate to the return of the firearm(s) without a hearing, a proposed order authorizing the release of the firearm(s) must accompany the stipulation. A form proposed order is attached to this administrative order as Attachment C.

DONE AND ORDERED in Chambers at St. Petersburg, Pinellas County, Florida this ___ day of May, 2016.

ORIGINAL SIGNED ON MAY 10, 2016
BY ANTHONY RONDOLINO
CHIEF JUDGE

Attachment A: Petition for Return of Firearm(s)

Attachment B: Notice of Hearing

Attachment C: Order on Petition for Return of Firearm(s)

IN THE CIRCUIT COURT OF THE SIXTH JUDICIAL CIRCUIT OF THE STATE OF FLORIDA IN AND FOR PASCO COUNTY [ATTACHMENT A]

CRIMINAL DIVISION

________________________________,
Petitioner,

Case Number: _____________

v.

________________________________,
Respondent (Law Enforcement Agency).

PETITION FOR RETURN OF FIREARM(S)

COMES NOW, Petitioner, ____________________, and hereby
(Petitioner's printed name)
requests an order directing Respondent to return his/her firearm(s) and/or ammunition and as grounds would state as follows:

1. On __________, the ____________________ took the following firearm(s)
(Date) (Law enforcement agency)
and/or ammunition:
____
____.
(Specifically identify the firearm(s) and/or ammunition sought to be returned, including the make, model, caliber, and/or gauge of each firearm and the amount and type of ammunition. Attach a separate sheet, if necessary.)
2. I have attached a copy of agency report ________________ from the
(Agency report number)
____________________that describes the circumstances leading to the
(Law enforcement agency)
taking of the above property.
3. The firearm(s) (and, if applicable, ammunition) is/are my personal property. I have included copies of any supporting documentation.
4. The firearm(s) and/ or ammunition is/are not the fruit of criminal activity and was/were not involved in criminal activity.
5. The firearm(s) and/or ammunition is/are not being held as evidence by the law enforcement agency.
6. To the best of my knowledge, ____________________ located at
(Law enforcement agency)
____________________ is in possession of the firearm(s) and/or
(Address of law enforcement agency)
ammunition.
7. I am not prohibited from possessing a firearm and/or ammunition under any provision of Florida or federal law.
8. I have not been convicted of a misdemeanor crime of domestic violence, and I have not had adjudication of guilt withheld or imposition of sentence suspended on any misdemeanor crime of domestic violence unless 3 years have elapsed since probation or any other conditions set by the court have been fulfilled or expunction has occurred.
9. I am not prohibited from possessing a firearm and/or ammunition pursuant to the terms of any pretrial release, bond, probation, or any other type of community supervision or court program.
10. I was/was not (*circle one*) Baker Acted as a result of this incident or otherwise. (Note: If the petitioner has been Baker Acted, the petitioner must provide the Judge with a copy of the documents furnished to the petitioner or the petitioner's representative by the facility, upon or after discharge of the petitioner from the facility, which contain any evaluations, diagnosis, prognoses, recommended course of treatment, and recommended or prescribed medications, and a letter from a licensed mental health professional stating that the person is of sound mind to possess a firearm.)

11. I do not have an active Domestic Violence Injunction or a Repeat Violence Injunction against me.

12. I do not have a Domestic Violence Injunction or a Repeat Violence Injunction pending against me.

13. I have not been adjudicated mentally defective as defined by section 790.065(2)(a)4.a., Florida Statutes, or if I had been adjudicated mentally defective, I have had my capacity restored by a court for at least 5 years from today's date.

14. I have not been committed to a mental institution as defined in section 790.065(2)(a)4.b., Florida Statutes, or if I had been committed to a mental institution, I possess a certificate from a licensed psychiatrist that I have not suffered from a mental disability for at least 5 years since the commitment to a mental institution.

15. My date of birth is: ______________ (Date of birth).

WHEREFORE, Petitioner requests that the Court order Respondent to return the above firearm(s) and/or ammunition to Petitioner.

Under penalties of perjury, I declare that I have read this petition and that the statements in it are true and correct.

Signed this ______ day of ______________, 20 ____

______________________ (Petitioner's signature)

______________________ (Petitioner's printed name)

______________________ (Petitioner's address)

______________________ (Petitioner's city, state, zip code)

______________________ (Petitioner's telephone number)

______________________ (Petitioner's e-mail address, if applicable)

CERTIFICATE OF SERVICE

I hereby certify that a copy of this Petition for Return of Firearm(s) has been furnished to Respondent, ______________________, (Law enforcement agency)

______________________, (Address of law enforcement agency)

by U.S. mail or by hand delivery to the law enforcement agency's front desk on this ______ day of ______________, 20____.

______________________ (Petitioner's signature)

______________________ (Petitioner's printed name)

IN THE CIRCUIT COURT OF THE SIXTH JUDICIAL CIRCUIT OF THE STATE OF FLORIDA IN AND FOR PASCO COUNTY [ATTACHMENT B]

CRIMINAL DIVISION

______________________,
Petitioner,

Case Number: ______________

v.

______________________,
Respondent (Law enforcement agency).

NOTICE OF HEARING

TO: ______________________,
(Name, legal counsel)

____
(Law enforcement agency)

____
(Street address)

____
(City, State, Zip)

YOU ARE HEREBY NOTIFIED that the Petitioner's Petition for Return of Firearm(s) has been scheduled for a hearing before the Honorable ______________, (Judge name) in Courtroom __________ (Courtroom number) at the ______________ (Courthouse name), on the ______ (Day) day of ______________ (Month), 20 ____ (Year), at ____:____ (Time) **a.m. / p.m.** (Circle one) or as soon thereafter as may be heard.

DATED this ______ day of ______________, 20 ____.

Respectfully submitted,

______________________ (Petitioner's signature)

Copies furnished to:

______________________ (Petitioner's printed name)

______________________ (Petitioner's address)

Courtesy copy to Judge

______________________ (Petitioner's city, state, zip code)

______________________ (Law enforcement agency)

______________________ (Petitioner's telephone number)

______________________ (Petitioner's e-mail address, if applicable)

IN THE CIRCUIT COURT OF THE SIXTH JUDICIAL CIRCUIT OF THE STATE OF FLORIDA IN AND FOR PASCO COUNTY [ATTACHMENT C]

CRIMINAL DIVISION

______________________,
Petitioner,

Case Number: ______________

v.

______________________,
Respondent (Law Enforcement Agency).

ORDER ON PETITION FOR RETURN OF FIREARM(S)

THIS CAUSE came before the Court on Petitioner's Petition for Return of Firearm(s). The Court having reviewed the Petition, taken testimony, heard argument, and being otherwise fully advised in the premises, it is:

ORDERED AND ADJUDGED that Petitioner's Petition for Return of Firearm(s) is hereby **GRANTED / DENIED** as to the following firearm(s):

1. ______________________
2. ______________________
3. ______________________
4. ______________________
5. ______________________

DONE AND ORDERED in ______________ County, this ______ day of ______________, 20 ____.

____
Circuit Court Judge

Copies furnished to:
Petitioner
Respondent

2016–022. COURT–APPOINTED ATTORNEY STANDARDS & DUE PROCESS COSTS

IN THE CIRCUIT COURT, SIXTH JUDICIAL CIRCUIT IN AND FOR PASCO AND PINELLAS COUNTIES, FLORIDA

ADMINISTRATIVE ORDER NO. 2016–022 PA/PI–CIR

RE: COURT–APPOINTED ATTORNEY STANDARDS & DUE PROCESS COSTS

Section 27.40, Florida Statutes, requires the Chief Judge to compile and maintain a registry of attorneys available for appointment in specific cases when a conflict of interest arises. The registry is to include qualified and experienced attorneys compiled by county and by category of cases. The registry is provided to the Clerk of the Circuit Court who must maintain the registry and provide to the Court the name of the next attorney for appointment.

In order to provide for the orderly appointment of private counsel and to facilitate the orderly handling of indigent cases, and pursuant to the authority of the Chief Judge in accordance with Article V, section 2, Florida Constitution, Rule of Judicial Administration 2.215, sections 27.40 and 43.26, Florida Statutes, it is

ORDERED:

I. Attorneys

A. *Appointment to the Registry*: An attorney must be on the Sixth Judicial Circuit Registry to receive a court appointment to represent a litigant who is entitled to court-appointed counsel. [1] To be included on the Registry, an attorney must apply during an open or special solicitation. Open solicitations occur periodically; special solicitations occur when the Chief Judge determines that there is a need for additional attorneys on one or more specific Registry lists. To apply, the attorney must certify that he or she meets the qualifications and standards set by law and in this Administrative Order, and must fully complete the applicable Sixth Judicial Circuit application form. In the event there are insufficient Registry attorneys under contract or other exigent circumstances exist as determined by the Chief Judge, the Chief Judge may add an attorney whom he or she determines is qualified to serve.

B. *Registry Standards*: All Registry attorneys must:

1. Be a member in good standing with The Florida Bar.

2. Have and maintain competence to provide representation in the types of cases on the Registry list to which the attorney is assigned.

3. Maintain continuing legal education requirements and any other qualifications specified in Attachment A for his or her assigned Registry list(s).

4. Maintain competency with the utilization of expert witnesses and evidence, including but not limited to, psychiatric and forensic evidence.

5. Enter into and maintain a contract for court-appointed attorney services with the Justice Administrative Commission (JAC).

6. Comply with the JAC requirements for billing.

7. Refrain from soliciting compensation from any person for service on a court-appointed case.

8. Maintain a principal office in Pasco, Pinellas, or Hillsborough County, or a location in Pasco or Pinellas County to meet with clients.

9. Notify the Chief Judge of any formal complaint filed by The Florida Bar; any non-confidential consent agreements entered with The Florida Bar; any finding of ineffective assistance of counsel by a judge or magistrate; any suspension or prohibition on the practice of law; and any suspension or prohibition on accepting court appointments.

10. Refrain from contracting with the Public Defender and Regional Counsel to provide counsel.

11. Notify the Clerk of the Circuit Court and the JAC of any change in his or her status or contact information. An attorney who resigns from the Registry must also notify the Chief Judge.

12. Accept appointments within their Registry list(s) without regard to the type of crime or other proceeding involved.

C. *List–Specific Standards*: In addition to the qualifications stated in Attachment A, the following list-specific standards apply:

1. Guardianship Attorneys: An attorney appointed for a proceeding under Chapter 744, Florida Statutes, may not petition the State for fees if the Court determines that the client is solvent. Instead, the attorney may accept compensation that the Court orders the client to pay. The rate of compensation may be up to $175.00 per hour.

2. Dependency Attorney for Parent: Attorneys serving on a Dependency Attorney for Parent list must appear at any shelter hearings that he or she is scheduled to attend by the Court or the Clerk of the Circuit Court. An attorney who does not appear for a shelter or other hearing as scheduled may not receive appointments or may be removed from the list.

3. Pinellas Attorneys: Each attorney serving in Pinellas County must agree to accept up to three cases in Pasco County per contract period if the attorneys serving in Pasco County are unable to handle a case due to ethical or workload conflict.

4. West Pasco Attorneys: Each attorney serving in West Pasco County must agree to accept up to three cases in East Pasco County per contract period if the attorneys serving in East Pasco County are unable to handle the case due to ethical or workload conflict.

D. *Registry List Qualifications*: Attachment A specifies the names of the Registry lists; their geographic service areas; the types of cases handled by attorneys on each list; and the experience, training, and other qualifications required of attorneys serving on those lists. The Chief Judge may amend the qualifications, geographic service areas, and registry requirements specified in Attachment A without further amendment to this Administrative Order. Attorneys on the Registry have a continuing duty to comply with the qualifications specified in Attachment A and any other standards and qualifications contained in this Administrative Order or established in law. Failure to comply with the standards and qualifications may result in removal of the attorney from all court-appointed lists for three years.

E. *Service*: By accepting an appointment or by continuing to provide representation pursuant to a prior court appointment, an attorney agrees to provide services in accordance with this Administrative Order, any other applicable law or administrative order, and the JAC form contract in effect at the time of appointment. Unless specified otherwise in the attorney's contract with the JAC or prohibited by law, a court-appointed attorney's continued representation of a client after the expiration of the attorney's contract constitutes agreement by the attorney to serve, subject to the fees of his or her prior contract.

F. *Compensation*: Compensation for Registry attorneys representing indigent clients is set at the rates provided in section 27.5304, Florida Statutes, and the General Appropriations Act. Attorneys may also receive reasonable and necessary expenses as provided by statute or under the attorney's contract with the JAC. An attorney whose billing is denied by the JAC, including an attorney seeking additional compensation in an unusual and extraordinary circumstance, must follow the procedures in section 27.5304(12), Florida Statutes, and his or her contract with the JAC; file the appropriate motion; and set the matter for hearing before the Chief Judge or the Chief Judge's designee.

G. *Removal or Suspension*: An attorney's failure to comply with the requirements of this Administrative Order may result in removal of the attorney from all court-appointed lists. The Chief Judge may remove or suspend an attorney from the

Registry with or without notice when there is an indication that the attorney cannot provide competent representation, or there is any apparent failure to comply with this Administrative Order. After notice, such an attorney may respond in writing to the Chief Judge explaining why he or she should not be removed or suspended from the Registry.

An attorney who, after notice of a problem(s) or concern(s) with his or her performance, was removed from a specific list or the entire Registry or who voluntarily removed himself or herself, may reapply for appointment to the Registry as permitted in subparagraph I.A., above, provided that: (1) the attorney applies during a solicitation period that is three years after the effective date of the attorney's removal from the Registry, or after a lesser time specified by the Chief Judge in writing; and (2) the attorney provides satisfactory evidence of remediation.

An attorney removed from the Registry for failure to maintain compliance with his or her CLE requirements, to maintain a contract with the JAC, or to maintain active membership in The Florida Bar may be reinstated if the deficiency is corrected within the time frame allowed by the Chief Judge.

H. *Other Registries*: The Sixth Judicial Circuit Registry does not include attorneys appointed pursuant to section 27.710, Florida Statutes, as an attorney for postconviction capital collateral proceedings.

The Sixth Judicial Circuit Registry also does not include attorneys appointed to represent persons sentenced to death who seek relief through executive clemency. In accordance with section 940.031, Florida Statutes, the Board of Executive Clemency appoints those attorneys from a registry it creates and maintains.

Further, there is no Registry of attorneys for appointment pursuant to 50 U.S.C. section 3931(b)(2) (Servicemembers' Civil Relief Act). The Chief Judge will analyze the type of case involved and use exigent circumstance authority to appoint an appropriately qualified member of The Florida Bar.

II. Clerks of the Circuit Court

The Pinellas Clerk of the Circuit Court and the Pasco Clerk of the Circuit Court (Clerks) will serve as the points of contact for Registry attorneys and maintain the Registry lists provided by the Chief Judge. Until the Clerks establish one database of Registry attorneys, the Clerk of the Circuit Court for Pinellas County will maintain the Registry for all circuit-wide categories.

The Clerks must publish on their website the name and phone number of a point of contact for attorneys to notify them of changes in their phone number, availability, or status.

When requested by the Court, the Public Defender, the Regional Counsel, or a court-appointed attorney, the Clerks must provide the name of the next registry attorney.

As part of maintaining the Registry, the Clerks must report by category and geographic service area the numbers of attorneys on the Registry, the numbers of appointments in each category, and the name of any attorney who notified the Clerk of his or her withdrawal or temporary removal from a Registry list. The Clerks also must report each month to the Chief Judge any issues of concern.

III. Due Process Costs

Due process service rates are set in accordance with section 27.425, Florida Statutes. The JAC maintains the schedule of approved rates for the Sixth Judicial Circuit and posts the schedule on its website at www.justiceadmin.org. Expenditures for due process costs must be pre-approved by the Court. Due process costs not specified on the posted schedule will not be paid unless prior approval is received from the Court or unless the JAC does not object to the expense.

This Administrative Order will be effective July 1, 2016, at which point Administrative Order Nos. 2014–036 PA/PI–CIR and 2015–033 PA/PI–CIR are hereby rescinded.

DONE AND ORDERED in Chambers at St. Petersburg, Pinellas County, Florida, this ___ day of April 2016.

ORIGINAL SIGNED ON APRIL 27, 2016

BY ANTHONY RONDOLINO

CHIEF JUDGE

[1] The Sixth Judicial Circuit Registry does not include attorneys for appointment pursuant to section 27.710, Florida Statutes, (representation in postconviction capital collateral proceedings); or section 940.031, Florida Statutes, (representation in executive clemency proceedings). Attorneys serving on one of those registries must meet any standards or other requirements established by the entity that creates the registry. See paragraph I.H., below.

2016–020. [RESCINDED BY ORDER 2017–007, EFFECTIVE FEBRUARY 6, 2017.]

2016–018. ELECTRONIC FILING IN PINELLAS COUNTY

IN THE CIRCUIT COURT OF THE SIXTH JUDICIAL CIRCUIT IN AND FOR PASCO AND PINELLAS COUNTIES, FLORIDA

ADMINISTRATIVE ORDER NO. 2016–018 PI–CIR

RE: ELECTRONIC FILING IN PINELLAS COUNTY

On April 1, 2013, mandatory electronic filing ("e–filing") began in the county civil, county small claims, circuit civil, circuit civil appellate, family law, and probate divisions in accordance with *In Re: Amendments to the Florida Rules of Civil Procedure, et. al., Electronic Filing*, 102 So. 3d 451 (Fla. 2012). Since that date, court rules and policies have been updated to reflect additional capabilities of the Florida Courts E–filing Portal ("Portal"), including e-mail service ("e–service") and e-filing for self-represented litigants.

The Florida Supreme Court granted an extension of the mandatory electronic filing deadline in the criminal division in Pinellas County until December 31, 2015. *In re: Electronic Filing of Criminal, Juvenile and Traffic Cases via the Florida Courts E–Filing Portal, AOSC15–7*. No further extension of time has been requested for Pinellas County. Accordingly, effective January 1, 2016, e-filing is mandatory in the criminal division in Pinellas County.

In order to update and maintain the e-filing procedures in Pinellas County, and in accordance with Article V, section 2, Florida Constitution, Rules of Judicial Administration 2.215 and 2.525, and section 43.26, Florida Statutes, it is

ORDERED:

DIRECTIONS TO ATTORNEYS

1. Except as otherwise provided in this Administrative Order, attorneys must e-file pleadings and papers in all divisions.

When documents are e-filed, original documents are not to be filed with the Pinellas County Clerk of Court ("Clerk") except as otherwise provided in this Administrative Order.

2. Attorneys must file case-initiating documents in non-electronic form in the following types of cases:

a. County criminal;

b. Circuit criminal;

c. Criminal and civil traffic;

d. Delinquency, including CINS/FINS; and

e. Dependency, including termination of parental rights proceedings.

3. Attorneys must not e-file pleadings and papers in the following types of cases:

f. Proceedings to waive parental notification of abortion;

g. Baker Act, Ch. 394, Part I; and

h. Criminal appeals from county court to circuit court.

4. The following documents may be scanned and electronically filed; however the original must be submitted to the Clerk:

a. Verified and sworn documents (criminal division only);

b. Original paper judgments and sentences;

c. Bonds;

d. Promissory notes;

e. Death certificates;

f. Birth certificates;

g. Certificates of eligibility to seal or expunge;

h. Consents for adoption;

i. Affidavits of nonpaternity;

j. Wills, codicils, and separate writings in estate cases;

k. Wills placed on deposit with the Clerk;

l. Pre-need guardian declarations;

m. Commissions to take oath of witness to will and Certificates of Commissioner;

n. Any other document specifically ordered by the Court; and

o. Any other document required by Florida law to be filed in its original form.

5. Pleadings and papers to be filed with the Court may only be submitted through the Florida Courts E-Filing Portal ("Portal") in accordance with Rule of Judicial Administration 2.525 and the Florida Supreme Court Standards for Electronic Access to the Courts. Attorneys must **not e-mail** the Court or the Clerk with pleadings or papers for filing.

6. Pursuant to Rule of Judicial Administration 2.525, an attorney who has obtained an order from the Court exempting him or herself from e-service requirements in accordance with Rule of Judicial Administration 2.516 is also exempt from e-filing requirements. In order to continue to file hard copies, the attorney must provide the Clerk with a copy of the court order exempting him or herself from e-service along with the hard copy filing.

7. In accordance with Rule of Judicial Administration 2.515, each e-filed document is deemed to have been signed by the attorney submitting the document and must include an electronic signature of such person in the format of "/s", "s/", or "/s/" [NAME], or a reproduction of the attorney's signature. Each document shall also include the attorney's typed name, Florida Bar address, telephone number, primary e-mail address and secondary e-mail addresses, if any, and Florida Bar number.

8. In the event that the Portal is not available due to technical failure of the Portal and an attorney must make a filing that day to meet a deadline, the attorney must attempt to file after 12:00 noon on at least two occasions that are separated by at least one hour. In these circumstances, if the attorney is unsuccessful in having a filing accepted by the Portal, the attorney may, when the Portal is available, file a motion with the Court seeking to have the filing considered timely filed. The Court may, with satisfactory proof, permit the document to be filed nunc pro tunc to the date it was first attempted to be filed electronically.

9. If an attorney has an emergency matter that would normally be presented directly to the section judge or duty judge, the attorney must e-file the emergency matter as provided in this Administrative Order. If the attorney wants the Court to consider the matter on an emergency basis, however, the attorney must contact the section judge or duty judge in accordance with current practices.

10. Attorneys from other jurisdictions who wish to be admitted pro hac vice must obtain a pro hac vice number from The Florida Bar to file through the Portal. Until the attorney receives a pro hac vice number, pleadings must be e-filed by the local Florida attorney designated in the motion. A motion to appear pro hac vice must be filed in each case in which the attorney wishes to appear. The receipt of a pro hac vice number from The Florida Bar for purposes of accessing the Portal does not grant an attorney the right to appear. See http://www.floridabar.org for more information.

DIRECTIONS TO UNREPRESENTED LITIGANTS

11. Unrepresented litigants are **not** required to e-file any pleadings, papers, or documents through the Portal, and the Clerk will continue to accept hard copy filings from such litigants. However, an unrepresented litigant may opt in to e-filing and e-service through the Portal. To do so, the litigant must register a username and password with the Portal at http://www.myfloridacourtaccess.com/.

Unrepresented litigants who choose to e-file documents through the Portal must comply with this Administrative Order and the rules of court governing e-filing. For information on registration, access, and e-filing through the Portal, unrepresented litigants should refer to the Clerk's website at http://www.pinellasclerk.org.

12. Unrepresented litigants may e-file pleadings and papers through the Portal in all divisions unless otherwise provided in this Administrative Order.

13. Unrepresented litigants are not permitted to e-file pleadings and papers in the following cases:

a. Proceedings to waive parental notification of abortion;

b. Baker Act, Ch. 394, Part I; and

c. Criminal appeals from county court to circuit court.

14. The following documents may be scanned and electronically filed; however the original must be submitted to the Clerk:

a. Verified and sworn documents (criminal division only);

b. Original paper judgments and sentences;

c. Bonds;

d. Promissory notes;

e. Death certificates;

f. Birth certificates;

g. Certificates of eligibility to seal or expunge;

h. Consents for adoption;

i. Affidavits of nonpaternity;

j. Wills, codicils, and separate writings in estate cases;

k. Wills placed on deposit with the Clerk;

l. Pre-need guardian declarations;

m. Commissions to take oath of witness to will and Certificates of Commissioner;

n. Any other document specifically ordered by the Court; and

o. Any other document required by Florida law to be filed in its original form.

15. In accordance with Rule of Judicial Administration 2.515, a document e-filed by an unrepresented litigant must include a typographical signature of such person in the format of "/s", "s/", or "/s/" [NAME] or a reproduction of the litigant's signature. The filer must also include his or her address and telephone number, including the area code.

16. In the event that the Portal is not available due to a technical failure, and an unrepresented litigant must make a filing that day to meet a deadline, the litigant should file a hard copy of his or her pleading(s) with the Clerk, regardless of whether the litigant has opted in to e-filing and e-service. If the litigant chooses not to file a hard copy with the Clerk, the litigant assumes the risk that the Court may consider the pleading untimely.

DIRECTIONS TO ALL PORTAL USERS

17. All persons using the Portal to file documents must comply with the Portal's filing requirements. The Portal currently allows filings to be submitted as a Word document or in PDF format. Filers are encouraged to submit filings as a searchable PDF. Each attachment to a pleading or paper should be separated and labeled. Attachments should be included in the same submission as long as the total submission does not exceed the Portal's file size limit.

An attorney filing a pleading or paper that exceeds the Portal's file size limit should divide the pleading or paper in an orderly fashion so that each submission does not exceed the Portal's file size limit. Each submission shall be described as being a portion of the whole pleading or paper (e.g., Part 1 of 5, Part 2 of 5, etc.). Alternatively, the attorney may file the pleading with the Clerk in accordance with Rule of Judicial Administration 2.525(d)(5). When doing so, the attorney should separate each exhibit and denominate it with a title referencing the document to which it relates.

An unrepresented litigant who is unable to meet the requirements of this paragraph should file a paper version of his or her pleading with the Clerk.

18. Each document must be formatted in accordance with the applicable rules of court governing formatting of paper documents.

19. In accordance with Rule of Judicial Administration 2.420, each e-filed document must be reviewed by the filer to determine whether the document contains confidential or exempt information. If the document contains information that is confidential or exempt, the document must be e-filed as a sealed electronic document along with either a notice of confidential filing or motion to determine confidentiality of court record. If the entire court file is maintained as confidential, the filer is not required to file an accompanying notice or motion.

20. With the exception of probate and guardianship cases, proposed orders, proposed judgments, letters, or correspondence directed to a judge may not be e-filed through the Portal, but must be submitted according to the Court's directions. Parties should continue to provide hard copies to the Court, including sufficient copies for conforming, and stamped, addressed envelopes for distribution of orders. Parties should note the Court's requirements for preparing proposed orders and proposed judgments that contain confidential information as detailed in Administrative Order 2013–027 or other subsequent administrative order.

21. A proposed summons should be submitted to the Clerk through the Portal. The Clerk will issue the summons.

22. Documents may be e-filed at any time through the Portal. To be considered filed on a particular date, documents must be e-filed and time stamped at the Portal by 11:59 p.m. local time on that date. The filing date for e-filed documents is the date of receipt by the Portal.

23. E–filing a document does not relieve a party of its evidentiary burden to prove the authenticity of an original document. Filers should maintain original documents, such as affidavits, that may be needed in court hearings unless the original is submitted to the Clerk as provided by this Administrative Order. When original documents are submitted as exhibits at a court hearing, the attorney or unrepresented litigant must notify the Clerk when an original document must be retained as an original.

24. It is the filer's responsibility to serve pleadings and papers in accordance with Rule of Judicial Administration 2.516.

DIRECTIONS TO THE CLERK

25. Except as otherwise provided in this Administrative Order, the Clerk shall receive pleadings and papers e-filed through the Portal in all divisions.

26. The Clerk shall receive case-initiating documents in non-electronic form in the following types of cases:

a. County criminal;

b. Circuit criminal;

c. Criminal and civil traffic;

d. Delinquency, including CINS/FINS; and

e. Dependency, including termination of parental rights proceedings.

27. The Clerk will not accept e-filed pleadings and papers in the following types of cases:

f. Proceedings to waive parental notification of abortion;

g. Baker Act, Ch. 394, Part I; and

h. Criminal appeals from county court to circuit court.

28. The Clerk must continue to receive the following documents in original form:

a. Verified and sworn documents (criminal division only);

b. Original paper judgments and sentences;

c. Bonds;

d. Promissory notes;

e. Death certificates;

f. Birth certificates;

g. Certificates of eligibility to seal or expunge;

h. Consents for adoption;

i. Affidavits of nonpaternity;

j. Wills, codicils, and separate writings in estate cases;

k. Wills placed on deposit with the Clerk;

l. Pre-need guardian declarations;

m. Commissions to take oath of witness to will and Certificates of Commissioner;

n. Any other document specifically ordered by the Court; and

o. Any other document required by Florida law to be filed in its original form.

When original documents are submitted at a hearing, the Clerk must retain the original documents in accordance with existing retention schedules.

29. The Clerk may only receive electronic filings through the Portal or as otherwise provided in this Administrative Order or subsequent administrative order.

The Clerk must receive documents from the Portal in a searchable PDF format, provided that the Portal can transmit documents to the Clerk as a searchable PDF document.

30. The Clerk must accept pleadings and papers that exceed the Portal's file size limit from filers in hard copy format or via electronic storage medium, as provided by Rule of Judicial Administration 2.525(d)(5). Such pleadings and papers must be maintained by the Clerk in a manner that facilitates access to the filing by the Court and the parties. If the pleading or paper is submitted in hard copy format, the Clerk should separate attachments to the pleading or paper, label each attachment, and scan each attachment separately.

31. The Clerk must accept non-electronic pleadings and papers from unrepresented litigants and attorneys who provide a copy of an order exempting them from e-service.

32. The Clerk will scan all pleadings and papers in new and existing cases for unrepresented litigants, attorneys who are exempt from e-service, and as otherwise provided in this Administrative Order.

33. If an attorney who has not provided the Clerk with a copy of a court order exempting him or herself from e-service files hard copy pleadings or papers with the Clerk, the Clerk may reject the pleading or paper. The Clerk must notify the attorney of the rejection and the reason for the rejection. The Clerk shall notify the Court of any attorneys who continue to file hard copy pleadings and papers without a court order.

34. The Clerk and Pinellas County Business Technology Services must comply with all the conditions stated in the e-filing approval letter from the Florida Courts Technology Commission, which is incorporated into this Administrative Order as Attachment A, and all requirements of Rule of Judicial Administration 2.525 and the Florida Supreme Court Standards for Electronic Access to the Courts.

35. Except as provided by Florida rule or law or the Florida Supreme Court Standards for Electronic Access to the Courts, documents and orders prepared by the Clerk or by the Court are not to be e-filed through the Portal.

36. The Clerk shall maintain an information sheet on e-filing for attorneys and unrepresented litigants and post it on the Clerk's website.

Administrative Orders 2013–006 PI–CIR, 2013–016 PI–CIR, 2013–021 PA/PI–CIR, 2013–028 PI–CIR, and 2014–012 PI–CIR are hereby rescinded.

DONE AND ORDERED in Chambers at St. Petersburg, Pinellas County, Florida, this ___ day of April, 2016.

ORIGINAL SIGNED ON APRIL 1, 2016

BY ANTHONY RONDOLINO

CHIEF JUDGE

Attachment A: January 7, 2011 approval letter from the Florida Courts Technology Commission

FLORIDA STATE COURTS TECHNOLOGY

Judge Judith L. Kreeger, Chair

Florida Courts Technology Commission

c/o Office of the State Courts Administrator

500 S. Duval Street, Tallahassee, Florida 32399–1900

January 7, 2011

The Honorable Ken Burke

Pinellas County Clerk of Court

315 Court Street

Clearwater, Florida 33756

RE: request for implementation of electronic filings in all court divisions in Pinellas County, Sixth Judicial Circuit

Dear Mr. Burke:

Supreme Court Opinion No.SC10–241, In re: Amendments to the Florida Rules of Judicial Administration—Rule 2.236 (July 1, 2010) provides that the Florida Courts Technology Commission "evaluate all such applications to determine whether they comply with the technology policies established by the supreme court and the procedures and standards created pursuant to this rule, and approve those applications deemed to be effective and found to be in compliance."

The purpose of this letter is to inform you that on January 6, 2011 the Electronic Filing Committee (EFC) reviewed and recommended approval of your request to implement electronic filing in Pinellas County.

As Chair of the Florida Courts Technology Commission I hereby approve your request to implement electronic filing in all ten court divisions in Pinellas County.

Approval of this electronic initiative is contingent upon compliance with the policy considerations and directives regarding the development and application of new technological standardization and enhancements as set forth by the Supreme Court and is subject to the following terms and conditions, as well as compliance with the chief judge's conditions outlined in his approval letter, dated October 13, 2010. Violation of any of the following conditions shall constitute grounds for revocation of the approval to implement electronic filing in Pinellas County.

a. The Pinellas County Clerk of Court may implement the aforementioned technology procedures in accordance with the approved plan effective on the date of this letter and must adhere to the statewide standards for electronic access to the courts as outlined in In re: Statewide Standards for Electronic Access to the Courts, AOSC09–30 (Fla. July 1, 2009).

b. The Pinellas County Clerk of Court shall ensure that there is no possibility for vendors to release or distribute court data to third parties and that the clerk of court retains the designation as custodian of the court records.

c. The Pinellas County Clerk shall ensure that contract provisions prohibit any vendor from extracting, data mining, or engaging in similar activities with regard to information from original court filings and other court records or any associated databases containing court records in the circuit for commercial or other non-court related uses.

d. The Pinellas County Clerk of Court shall ensure that no fees other than statutorily required fees are assessed or collected by the clerk of court.

e. The Pinellas County Clerk of Court shall ensure that the data is backed up and is recoverable. The clerk of court will ensure that remote data backups are stored in a protected environment a minimum of 50 miles from the primary production location of the court record or at a certified hardened facility, and that the circuit complies with established data backup standards as they are revised and updated.

f. This approval does not constitute an approval of any electronic forms that may be used in this process.

g. The Pinellas County Clerk of Court shall submit monthly progress reports to the court system during the 90–day pilot test. Copies of the monthly progress reports shall be provided to the Chief Judge of the Sixth Judicial Circuit and the State Courts Technology Officer in the Office of the State Courts Administrator.

h. Any attorney, party, or other person who files a document by electronic transmission with the Pinellas County Clerk of Court shall immediately thereafter file the identical document in paper form with an original signature of the attorney, party, or other person if a signature is otherwise required by the Rules of Judicial Administration (hereinafter referred to as the follow-up filing). The follow-up filing of any document that has been previously filed by electronic transmission may be discontinued if, after a 90–day period of accepting electronically filed documents, the Pinellas County Clerk of Court and chief judge certify to the Florida Courts Technology Commission that the electronic filing system is efficient, reliable, and meets the demands of all parties and this Commission has authorized the elimination of the follow-up filing.

i. The Pinellas County Clerk of Court shall abide by In re: Revised Interim Policy on Electronic Release of Court Records, AOSC07–49 (Fla. Sept. 7, 2007).

j. The E–Filing Court Records Portal, developed by the Florida Association of Court Clerks Services Group (FACCSG), has been identified as the statewide e-filing portal. To ensure equal access to electronic filing across the state, the Supreme Court has directed that the Florida Courts Technology Commission make implementation of the statewide system a priority of the judicial branch. All local electronic filing systems must be compatible with the statewide e-filing portal and approval of each of the above electronic filing systems is contingent on the system's compatibility with the statewide portal.

k. At the present time, the Supreme Court is considering enhancements to current electronic filing practices throughout the State. There is a possibility that these enhancements may include the development and application of new business practices and technology standardization. Because these enhancements may occur in the near future, it will be the responsibility of the clerk of court for the respective county to ensure that functionality of the proposed system related to electronic court records will also be made compliant with these new technological enhancements.

l. The Pinellas County Clerk of Court must continue to provide paper to the judiciary until the chief judge authorizes the elimination of paper files. At such time, the Pinellas County Clerk of Court must convert all documents, beginning on the date of Supreme Court or Florida Courts Technology Commission (FCTC) approval, to a searchable document.

m. The Pinellas County Clerk of Court shall continue to accept paper filings at no charge, other than statutorily required fees.

In addition to the foregoing enumerated terms and conditions, the chief judge may, pursuant to the chief judge's constitutional and statutory responsibility for administrative supervision of the courts within the circuit, impose electronic filing system or related requirements by local administrative order that are consistent with the terms and conditions of this approval letter.

Should you have any questions, please do not hesitate to contact my office.

Sincerely,

Judith L. Kreeger

JLK: js

2016–017. [RESCINDED BY ORDER 2016-058, EFFECTIVE SEPTEMBER 9, 2016.]

2016–012. [RESCINDED BY ORDER 2016–017, EFFECTIVE MARCH 23, 2016.]

2016–011. ADULT DRUG COURT EXPANSION— PINELLAS COUNTY

IN THE CIRCUIT COURT, SIXTH JUDICIAL CIRCUIT IN AND FOR PASCO AND PINELLAS COUNTIES, FLORIDA

ADMINISTRATIVE ORDER NO. 2016–011 PI–CIR

RE: ADULT DRUG COURT EXPANSION—PINELLAS COUNTY

Administrative Order 2009–016 PI–CIR was created to identify the defendants to be served by an expanded adult post-adjudicatory drug court and to establish section Z for these cases. In doing so, the Administrative Order made reference to section Q, which has been closed in the interest of judicial efficiency. Thus, Administrative Order 2009–016 must be updated.

In accordance with Article V, section 2, Florida Constitution, Rules of Judicial Administration 2.215, and section 43.26, Florida Statutes,

IT IS ORDERED:

1. Section Z is a post-adjudicatory drug court. The Clerk shall not assign circuit criminal cases on a random basis to section Z as provided in Local Rule three; rather, cases shall be assigned to section Z as further specified in this Administrative Order.

2. The State Attorney's office shall identify those defendants who meet the criteria to be included in the drug court expansion and transferred to section Z. The criteria are listed in Attachment A. The defendant should be identified as soon as possible but by the defendant's first pre-trial. A defendant's case may not be initially assigned by direct information to section Z; rather, the case must first be set for arraignment in a circuit criminal section.

3. When the State Attorney's office has identified a defendant to be transferred to section Z, that office may request the section judge, including the section N judge, to transfer the case to section Z. If the judge determines that the defendant may be suitable for transfer, the judge may authorize the defendant to obtain an evaluation. A defendant who is being considered for section Z must voluntarily and truthfully provide information to aid the Court at each step of the process. The defendant must execute a written consent form with a waiver of confidentiality for the evaluation and treatment in accordance with 42 C.F.R. § 2.31 prior to the evaluation. If the defendant refuses to execute the written consent, the defendant will not be considered for transfer to section Z. The evaluation provides an overall assessment of the defendant's addiction and the resources needed to overcome that addiction. The evaluation will help the Court to determine whether the defendant is an appropriate candidate for section Z. The evaluation must use objective standards and criteria and must be conducted by the licensed, court-approved evaluator. If a section judge authorizes an evaluation, the case should be set on the section judge's calendar for a pre-trial three weeks after the defendant is referred for evaluation.

4. After the evaluation is obtained, the section judge may accept a plea from the defendant, impose a sentence, and transfer the case to section Z for judicial review of drug court treatment. Sanctions imposed by the sentencing judge are within the Court's discretion and include but are not limited to outpatient treatment programs and non-secure residential treatment programs. Other conditions of probation may be ordered, such as random drug testing, a requirement to obtain a G.E.D, or a requirement to participate in transitional housing and related services. Only those defendants who meet the criteria specified in Attachment A, who are approved by the State Attorney, and who are authorized by the section judge, including the section N judge, as appropriate for section Z shall be transferred.

5. Once a defendant is sentenced and the case is transferred to section Z, judicial review of drug court treatment will occur in section Z. The purpose of a judicial review is to assess the defendant's level of participation in treatment, monitor the overall success of treatment, and admonish or encourage the defendant in his or her attempt at rehabilitation. Prior to a judicial review, the judge may hold a case staffing with treatment providers, court staff, Department of Corrections personnel, assistant public defenders, assistant state attorneys, and others selected by the judge.

6. Defendants who successfully complete and graduate from drug court may receive a reduced probationary period. The section Z judge will review a defendant's successful completion of the assigned treatment and make the ultimate decision whether a defendant may graduate from drug court.

7. Staff in the Administrative Office of the Courts will facilitate the process by which a defendant is evaluated; coordinate the procedure by which the written evaluation is furnished to the State Attorney's office, defense counsel, and judge; assist the Court in managing its caseload; compile statistics; prepare the cases scheduled on the section Z calendar; schedule initial appointments with treatment providers; and perform other case management functions for the Court as required.

8. The sanctions imposed by the section Z judge for violating probation due to a failed or suspect substance abuse test are within the Court's discretion. The judge may continue probation, may revoke probation and order a new term of probation, may impose a term of incarceration in either the county jail or Department of Corrections, as provided by the Criminal Punishment Code, or impose any other sanction authorized by law. A violation of probation due to any reason other than a failed or suspect substance abuse test may result in the case being transferred back to the original section judge for hearing the violation of probation.

9. No more than 300 defendants may be in section Z at any one time unless the judge assigned to section Z specifically authorizes that number to be exceeded. The Administrative Office of the Courts shall notify the State Attorney when section Z does not have the capacity for additional defendants.

10. Attachments to this Administrative Order may be modified without further changes to this Administrative Order.

Administrative Order 2009–074 PI–CIR is hereby rescinded.

DONE AND ORDERED in Chambers, at St. Petersburg, Pinellas County, Florida this __________ day of March, 2016.

ORIGINAL SIGNED ON MARCH 1, 2016
BY ANTHONY RONDOLINO, CHIEF JUDGE

Section Z Criteria

ATTACHMENT A

Criminal Section/Section N ⇩ **Section Z** *(section 948.01)*	The Court may place a Defendant into the drug court program in section Z as a condition to probation or community control if the Defendant: ☐ Committed an offense on or after July 1, 2009 ☐ Sentence points on the Criminal Punishment Code score sheet are not more than 52 points ☐ Is a nonviolent offender, meaning: o A third-degree felony violation under chapter 810, Fla. Stat. (burglary or trespass), or o Any other felony offense that is not a forcible felony as defined in section 776.08, Fla. Stat. ☐ Is amenable to substance abuse treatment ☐ Is otherwise qualified under section 397.334(3), Fla. Stat.
Criminal Section (Violation of Probation or Community Control) ⇩ **Div. Z** *(section 948.06)*	The Court may order a Defendant to complete the drug court program in section Z if: ☐ The Court finds or the Defendant admits a violation of probation or community control ☐ The violation was due <u>only</u> to a failed or suspect substance abuse test ☐ Sentence points are not more than 52 points (*including* points for the violation) ☐ The underlying offense is a nonviolent felony, meaning: o A third-degree felony violation under chapter 810, Fla. Stat. (burglary or trespass), or o Any other felony offense that is not a forcible felony as defined in section 776.08, Fla. Stat. ☐ The Defendant is amenable to substance abuse treatment ☐ The Defendant agrees to participate after explanation of the program ☐ The Defendant otherwise qualifies under section 397.334(3), Fla. Stat.

section 397.334(3)--**Entry into any post-adjudicatory treatment-based drug court program, as a condition of probation or community control (pursuant to sections 948.01, 948.06, 948.20), must be based on the sentencing court's assessment of the Defendant's**:

☐ Criminal history
☐ Substance abuse screening outcome
☐ Amenability to the services of the program
☐ Total sentence points
☐ Recommendation of the State Attorney and victim (if any)
☐ Agreement to enter the program

Sixth Circuit Administrative Order 2016-011 - Attachment A

2016–010. VIOLATIONS OF FELONY PROBATION OR COMMUNITY CONTROL

IN THE CIRCUIT COURT, SIXTH JUDICIAL CIRCUIT IN AND FOR PASCO AND PINELLAS COUNTIES, FLORIDA

ADMINISTRATIVE ORDER NO. 2016–010 PA/PI–CIR

RE: VIOLATIONS OF FELONY PROBATION OR COMMUNITY CONTROL

Administrative Order 2007–081 PA/PI–CIR was enacted to specify the types of violations of probation that are to be reported by a technical violation letter or Notice to Appear in accordance with section 948.06, Florida Statutes, and to direct that these violations be submitted to the judge assigned to section Q or the assigned section judge. It has become necessary in the interests of judicial efficiency to close section Q, and these procedures must be updated.

In order to ensure that technical notification letters and Notices to Appear are to be submitted to the assigned section judge, and in accordance with Article V, section 2, Florida Constitution, Rule of Judicial Administration 2.215, and section 43.26, Florida Statutes,

IT IS ORDERED:

1. The Department of Corrections ("DOC") may report alleged violations of probation or community control by a technical notification letter or by affidavit and a Notice to Appear when the offender:

a. failed to report to the probation officer as directed,

b. failed to be truthful to the probation officer,

c. failed to follow instructions of the probation officer,

d. failed to obtain permission prior to moving from an approved residence,

e. failed to obtain permission prior to leaving approved employment,

f. failed to comply with the terms of curfew,

g. failed to obtain permission prior to leaving the county,

h. failed to make restitution payments,

i. failed to pay court costs under a payment plan,

j. failed to perform required community service, or

k. committed an ordinance violation.

2. The DOC may report alleged violations of probation or community control by submitting an affidavit and proposed Notice to Appear when the offender:

a. has positive results of a drug screen, or

b. has committed a second degree misdemeanor.

3. A technical notification letter or affidavit and Notice to Appear is to be submitted to the assigned section judge.

For a technical notification letter, if the judge agrees that the alleged violation does not require action by the court, the technical notification letter shall be forwarded to the Clerk of the Circuit Court for filing in the court file. If the judge determines that the alleged violation requires court review, then the judge shall return the letter to the DOC with a directive to promptly submit an affidavit so that the court may either issue a Notice to Appear or a warrant.

If an affidavit and proposed Notice to Appear is submitted but the judge determines that the alleged violation requires arrest of the offender, the judge shall return the Notice to Appear to the DOC with a directive to promptly submit a warrant.

4. The DOC shall report all other alleged violations of probation or community control by submitting an affidavit and warrant. The affidavit and warrant is to be submitted to the assigned section judge.

5. When the DOC submits an affidavit regarding a person alleged to have violated probation or community control the DOC shall:

a. Indicate whether the DOC seeks a warrant for the arrest of the offender or is requesting the Court to issue a Notice to Appear.

b. Indicate whether the offender has ever been convicted of committing or is currently alleged to have committed a qualifying offense as defined in section 948.06, Florida Statutes.

6. If the DOC requests a Notice to Appear, the DOC may also request that the date of the hearing be set after the next scheduled appointment with the offender. When the Court signs a Notice to Appear, the Court shall set a date for a hearing on the violation. The DOC is to provide notice to the offender. The attached form Notice to Appear in Attachment A may be used.

When a Notice to Appear is to be issued, the DOC shall submit an original and four (4) copies to the Court. The Court shall sign the original and provide the original to the Clerk, two copies to the DOC, one copy to the State Attorney, and one copy to the Public Defender.

7. If the DOC is unable to provide notice to an offender of the hearing date, the DOC shall prepare a warrant for the offender's arrest.

8. Attachments to this Administrative Order may be modified without further changes to this Administrative Order.

Administrative Order 2007–081 PA/PI–CIR is hereby rescinded.

DONE AND ORDERED in Chambers, at St. Petersburg, Pinellas County, Florida this ________ day of March, 2016.

ORIGINAL SIGNED ON MARCH 1, 2016
BY ANTHONY RONDOLINO, CHIEF JUDGE% tr

Attachment A: Notice to Appear

IN THE CIRCUIT COURT OF THE SIXTH JUDICIAL CIRCUIT OF THE STATE OF FLORIDA IN AND FOR PASCO COUNTY
CRIMINAL DIVISION

STATE OF FLORIDA

v. Case No.: ________ WS

________, Defendant Division: ________

SPN: ________

DOC #: ________

N__ A__

You are hereby ordered to appear to respond to charges that you violated probation. You are ordered to appear at the West Pasco Judicial Center, 7530 Little Road, Courtroom ____, New Port Richey, Florida on ________, 20 __ at ____ am / pm.

Failure to appear for the above-referenced hearing will result in a warrant being issued for your arrest for an alleged violation of probation.

TO BE COMPLETED BY THE DEPARTMENT OF CORRECTIONS:
Date: ________
The above offender is not a Violent Felony Offender of Special Concern.

____
Probation Officers Signature

________ ________
Date Judge's Signature

If you are a person with a disability who needs any accommodation in order to participate in this proceeding, you are entitled, at no cost to you, to the provision of certain assistance. Please contact the Public Information Dept., Pasco County Government Center, 7530 Little Road, New Port Richey, FL 34654; (727) 847–8110 (V) for proceedings in New Port Richey; (352) 521–4274, ext. 8110 (V) for proceedings in Dade City at least 7 days before your scheduled court appearance, or immediately upon receiving this notification if the time before the scheduled appearance is less than 7 days; if you are hearing or voice impaired, call 711.

Distribution: Original: Clerk • First & Second Copy: DOC • Third Copy: State Attorney • Fourth Copy: Public Defender

IN THE CIRCUIT COURT OF THE SIXTH JUDICIAL CIRCUIT OF THE STATE OF FLORIDA IN AND FOR PASCO COUNTY
CRIMINAL DIVISION

STATE OF FLORIDA

v. Case No.: ________ ES

________, Defendant Division: ________

SPN: ________

DOC #: ________

N__ A__

You are hereby ordered to appear to respond to charges that you violated probation. You are ordered to appear at the Robert D. Sumner Judicial Center, 38053 Live Oak Avenue, Courtroom _____, Dade City, Florida on _________, 20___ at _____ am/pm.

Failure to appear for the above-referenced hearing will result in a warrant being issued for your arrest for an alleged violation of probation.

TO BE COMPLETED BY THE DEPARTMENT OF CORRECTIONS:
Date: ________
The above offender is not a Violent Felony Offender of Special Concern.

____
Probation Officers Signature

________________ ________________
Date Judge's Signature

If you are a person with a disability who needs any accommodation in order to participate in this proceeding, you are entitled, at no cost to you, to the provision of certain assistance. Please contact the Public Information Dept., Pasco County Government Center, 7530 Little Road, New Port Richey, FL 34654; (727) 847–8110 (V) for proceedings in New Port Richey; (352) 521–4274, ext. 8110 (V) for proceedings in Dade City at least 7 days before your scheduled court appearance, or immediately upon receiving this notification if the time before the scheduled appearance is less than 7 days; if you are hearing or voice impaired, call 711.
Distribution: Original: Clerk • First & Second Copy: DOC • Third Copy: State Attorney • Fourth Copy: Public Defender

IN THE CIRCUIT COURT OF THE SIXTH JUDICIAL CIRCUIT OF THE STATE OF FLORIDA IN AND FOR PINELLAS COUNTY
CRIMINAL DIVISION

STATE OF FLORIDA

v. Case No.: ____________

______________, Defendant Division: ____________

PID: ____________

DOC #: ____________

N___ A___

You are hereby ordered to appear to respond to charges that you violated probation. You are ordered to appear at the Pinellas County Justice Center at 14250 49th Street North, Courtroom, Clearwater _____, Florida, on _________, 20 ___ at _____ am / pm.

Failure to appear for the above-referenced hearing will result in a warrant being issued for your arrest for an alleged violation of probation.

TO BE COMPLETED BY THE DEPARTMENT OF CORRECTIONS:
Date: ________
The above offender is not a Violent Felony Offender of Special Concern.

____
Probation Officers Signature

________________ ________________
Date Judge's Signature

If you are a person with a disability who needs any accommodation in order to participate in this proceeding, you are entitled, at no cost to you, to the provision of certain assistance. Please contact the Human Rights Office, 400 S. Ft. Harrison Ave., Suite 300, Clearwater, FL 33756, (727) 464–4062 (V/TDD) at least 7 days before your scheduled court appearance, or immediately upon receiving this notification if the time before the scheduled appearance is less than 7 days; if you are hearing or voice impaired, call 711.
Distribution: Original: Clerk • First & Second Copy: DOC • Third Copy: State Attorney • Fourth Copy: Public Defender

Sixth Circuit Administrative Order 2016–010—Attachment A

2016–006. PROCEDURES FOR RETURN OF FIREARMS—PINELLAS COUNTY

IN THE CIRCUIT COURT OF THE SIXTH JUDICIAL CIRCUIT IN AND FOR PASCO AND PINELLAS COUNTIES, FLORIDA

ADMINISTRATIVE ORDER NO. 2016–006 PI–CIR

RE: PROCEDURES FOR RETURN OF FIREARMS—PINELLAS COUNTY

Section 933.14(3), Florida Statutes, provides that no firearm seized by law enforcement with a search warrant or without a search warrant upon view by an officer of a breach of the peace shall be returned except upon court order. It is necessary for the efficient administration of justice to establish a uniform procedure in Pinellas County for determining the appropriateness of ordering the return of firearms taken by law enforcement under section 933.14(3), Florida Statutes, where no arrest was made and no charges were filed.

In order to provide for the timely and uniform disposition of petitions for the return of firearms within Pinellas County, and in accordance with Article V, section 2, Florida Constitution, Rule of Judicial Administration 2.215, and section 43.26, Florida Statutes, it is

ORDERED:

1. Any person who seeks the return of a firearm seized by law enforcement under section 933.14(3), Florida Statutes, where no arrest was made and no case was filed must file a Petition for Return of Firearm(s) with the Clerk of Court. The petition must be sworn and must be served on the law enforcement agency in possession of the firearm(s). A form Petition for Return of Firearm(s) is attached to this administrative order as Attachment A.

2. All Petitions for Return of Firearm(s) must specifically identify the firearm(s) and/or ammunition sought to be returned and must further allege that (1) the firearm(s) and/or ammunition is/are the petitioner's personal property; (2) the firearm(s) and/or ammunition is/are not the fruit of criminal activity and was/were not involved in criminal activity; (3) the firearm(s) and/or ammunition is/are not being held as evidence by the relevant law enforcement agency; (4) the petitioner is not prohibited from possessing a firearm under any provision of Florida or federal law, including 18 U.S.C. 922(g)(9); (5) the petitioner has not been convicted of a misdemeanor crime of domestic violence, and has not had adjudication of guilt withheld or the imposition of a sentence suspended on any misdemeanor crime of domestic violence unless 3 years have elapsed since probation or any other conditions set by the relevant court have been fulfilled or expunction has occurred; (6) the petitioner is not prohibited from possessing a firearm and/or ammunition pursuant to the terms of any pretrial release, bond, probation, or any other type of community supervision or court program; (7) the petitioner has not been Baker Acted as a result of this incident or otherwise. If the petitioner has been Baker Acted, the petitioner will provide the Judge with a copy of the documents furnished to the petitioner or the petitioner's representative by the facility, upon or after discharge of the petitioner from the facility, which contain any evaluations, diagnoses, prognoses, recommended course of treatment, and recommended or prescribed medications; (8) the petitioner does not have an active Domestic Violence Injunction or a Repeat Violence Injunction against him/her; (9) the petitioner has not been adjudicated mentally defective as defined by section 790.065(2)(a)4.a., Florida Statutes, or if the petitioner has been adjudicated mentally defective, the petitioner has had his or her capacity restored by a court for at least 5 years from the date of the Petition for Return of Firearm(s); and (10) the petitioner has not been committed to a mental institution as defined in section 790.065(2)(a)4.b., Florida Statutes, or if the petitioner has been committed to a mental institution, the petitioner possesses a certificate from a licensed psychiatrist that he or she has not suffered from a mental disability for at least 5 years since the commitment to a mental institution.

3. The petitioner must attach to the petition a copy of the agency report detailing the circumstances which led to the taking of the firearm(s).

4. All Petitions for Return of Firearm(s) in Pinellas County shall be assigned to Division J.

5. To obtain a hearing on a petition, the petitioner must contact the Division J judicial assistant to be assigned a hearing date. Once assigned a hearing date, the petitioner is responsible for preparing a notice of hearing and serving it on the law enforcement agency in possession of the firearm(s) no less than 14 days prior to the hearing date. The notice shall be hand delivered or sent via certified mail to the law enforcement agency. A form notice of hearing is attached to this administrative order as Attachment B.

6. Should the petitioner and the law enforcement agency stipulate to the return of the firearm(s) without a hearing, a proposed order authorizing the release of the firearm(s) must accompany the stipulation. A form proposed order is attached to this administrative order as Attachment C.

DONE AND ORDERED in Chambers at St. Petersburg, Pinellas County, Florida this ___ day of February, 2016.

ORIGINAL SIGNED ON FEBRUARY 18, 2016
BY ANTHONY RONDOLINO, CHIEF JUDGE

Attachment A: Petition for Return of Firearm(s)

Attachment B: Notice of Hearing

Attachment C: Order on Petition for Return of Firearm(s)

IN THE CIRCUIT COURT OF THE SIXTH JUDICIAL CIRCUIT OF THE STATE OF FLORIDA IN AND FOR PINELLAS COUNTY CRIMINAL DIVISION [ATTACHMENT A]

______________________________,
Petitioner,

Case Number: ____________

v.

______________________________,
Respondent (Law Enforcement Agency).

PETITION FOR RETURN OF FIREARM(S)

COMES NOW, Petitioner, ______________________, and hereby
(Petitioner's printed name)
requests an order directing Respondent to return his/her firearm(s) and/or ammunition and as grounds would state as follows:

1. On ________, the ____________________ took the following firearm(s)
(Date) (Law enforcement agency)
and/or ammunition:
____
(Specifically identify the firearm(s) and/or ammunition sought to be returned, including the make, model, caliber, and/or gauge of each firearm and the amount and type of ammunition. Attach a separate sheet, if necessary.)
2. I have attached a copy of agency report ____________ from the
(Agency report number)
____________________ that describes the circumstances leading to the
(Law enforcement agency)
taking of the above property.
3. The firearm(s) (and, if applicable, ammunition) is/are my personal property. I have included copies of any supporting documentation.
4. The firearm(s) and/ or ammunition is/are not the fruit of criminal activity and was/were not involved in criminal activity.
5. The firearm(s) and/or ammunition is/are not being held as evidence by the law enforcement agency.
6. To the best of my knowledge, ____________________ located at
(Law enforcement agency)
____________________ is in possession of the firearm(s) and/or
(Address of law enforcement agency)
ammunition.
7. I am not prohibited from possessing a firearm and/or ammunition under any provision of Florida or federal law.
8. I have not been convicted of a misdemeanor crime of domestic violence, and I have not had adjudication of guilt withheld or imposition of sentence suspended on any misdemeanor crime of domestic violence unless 3 years have elapsed since probation or any other conditions set by the court have been fulfilled or expunction has occurred.
9. I am not prohibited from possessing a firearm and/or ammunition pursuant to the terms of any pretrial release, bond, probation, or any other type of community supervision or court program.
10. I was/was not *(circle one)* Baker Acted as a result of this incident or otherwise. (Note: If the petitioner has been Baker Acted, the petitioner must provide the Judge with a copy of the documents furnished to the petitioner or the petitioner's representative by the facility, upon or after discharge of the petitioner from the facility, which contain any evaluations, diagnosis, prognoses, recommended course of treatment, and recommended or prescribed medications.)
11. I do not have an active Domestic Violence Injunction or a Repeat Violence Injunction against me.
12. I do not have a Domestic Violence Injunction or a Repeat Violence Injunction pending against me.
13. I have not been adjudicated mentally defective as defined by section 790.065(2)(a)4.a., Florida Statutes, or if I had been adjudicated mentally defective, I have had my capacity restored by a court for at least 5 years from today's date.
14. I have not been committed to a mental institution as defined in section 790.065(2)(a)4.b., Florida Statutes, or if I had been committed to a mental institution, I possess a certificate from a licensed psychiatrist that I have not suffered from a mental disability for at least 5 years since the commitment to a mental institution.
15. My date of birth is: ____________________.
(Date of birth).

WHEREFORE, Petitioner requests that the Court order Respondent to return the above firearm(s) and/or ammunition to Petitioner.

Under penalties of perjury, I declare that I have read this petition and that the statements in it are true and correct.

Signed this ______ day of ____________, 20____.

____
(Petitioner's signature)

____
(Petitioner's printed name)

____
(Petitioner's address)

____
(Petitioner's city, state, zip code)

____
(Petitioner's telephone number)

____
(Petitioner's e-mail address, if applicable)

CERTIFICATE OF SERVICE

I hereby certify that a copy of this Petition for Return of Firearm(s) has been furnished to Respondent, ______________________________,
(Law enforcement agency)
____,
(Address of law enforcement agency)
by U.S. mail or by hand delivery to the law enforcement agency's front desk on this ______ day of ____________, 20____.

____
(Petitioner's signature)

____
(Petitioner's printed name)

IN THE CIRCUIT COURT OF THE SIXTH JUDICIAL CIRCUIT OF THE STATE OF FLORIDA IN AND FOR PINELLAS AND PASCO COUNTIES CRIMINAL DIVISION [ATTACHMENT B]

______________________________,
Petitioner,

Case Number: ____________

v.

______________________________,
Respondent (Law enforcement agency).

NOTICE OF HEARING

TO: ______________________________
(Name, legal counsel)

____
(Law enforcement agency)
____
(Street address)
____
(City, State, Zip)

YOU ARE HEREBY NOTIFIED that the Petitioner's Petition for Return of Firearm(s) has been scheduled for a hearing before the Honorable ________, (Judge name) in Courtroom ________ (Courtroom number) at the ________ (Courthouse name), on the ______day (Day) of ________ (Month), 20 ____ (Year), at ____:______ (Time) **a.m. / p.m.** (Circle one) or as soon thereafter as may be heard.

DATED this ________ day of ____________, 20 ____.
Respectfully submitted,

____
(Petitioner's signature)

Copies furnished to:
____
(Petitioner's printed name)
____
(Petitioner's address)

Courtesy copy to Judge
____
(Petitioner's city, state, zip code)

____
(Law enforcement agency)
____
(Petitioner's telephone number)
____
(Petitioner's e-mail address, if applicable)

IN THE CIRCUIT COURT OF THE SIXTH JUDICIAL CIRCUIT OF THE STATE OF FLORIDA IN AND FOR PINELLAS COUNTY CRIMINAL DIVISION [ATTACHMENT C]

______________________,
Petitioner,

Case Number: ____________

v.

______________________,
Respondent (Law Enforcement Agency).

ORDER ON PETITION FOR RETURN OF FIREARM(S)

THIS CAUSE came before the Court on Petitioner's Petition for Return of Firearm(s). The Court having reviewed the Petition, taken testimony, heard argument, and being otherwise fully advised in the premises, it is:

ORDERED AND ADJUDGED that Petitioner's Petition for Return of Firearm(s) is hereby **GRANTED / DENIED** as to the following firearm(s):

1. ______________________
2. ______________________
3. ______________________
4. ______________________
5. ______________________

DONE AND ORDERED in ____________, ____________ County, this ________ day of ________, 20 ____.

____
Circuit Court Judge

Copies furnished to:
Petitioner
Respondent

2015–071. [RESCINDED BY ORDER 2016–080, EFFECTIVE DECEMBER 13, 2016.]

2015–068. [RESCINDED BY ORDER 2017–013, EFFECTIVE FEBRUARY 21, 2017.]

2015–061. PARKING TICKETS

IN THE CIRCUIT COURT, SIXTH JUDICIAL CIRCUIT IN AND FOR PASCO AND PINELLAS COUNTIES, FLORIDA

ADMINISTRATIVE ORDER NO. 2015–061 PI–CTY

RE: PARKING TICKETS

In Administrative Order No. 90–19, this Circuit established procedures for the uniform enforcement of parking tickets in Pinellas County. The current process of issuing warrants when a person fails to pay or fails to appear has not had the desired enforcement effect and many parking tickets continue to go unpaid. Accordingly, the Court now finds it necessary to update the procedures.

In accordance with Article V, § 2, Florida Constitution, Florida Rule of Judicial Administration 2.215, and §§ 43.26 and 28.246(6), Florida Statutes, it is therefore

ORDERED:

A. Parking Ticket Citations.

1. Parking tickets issued by any authorized agency or authority within Pinellas County must substantially conform in detail to the Approved Form Parking Ticket, which is Attachment A to this Administrative Order. However, a Uniform Traffic Citation may be issued for handicap parking violations under § 316.1955, Fla. Stat. (2014).

2. Every parking ticket must conspicuously bear the words "DO NOT SEND CASH," in **boldface** type or red print. Envelopes provided for submission of payment by U.S. mail must be of sufficient paperweight and printing style so as to prevent viewing of the contents through the envelope.

3. The issuing officer must complete the parking ticket entering the charged violation and fine amount in accordance with State law, or municipal or county ordinance. All fines must be within State statutory maximum limits.

4. Any parking ticket not paid within the time specified on the ticket will become payable at the higher of the fine amount of the charged ordinance violation or at the maximum State statutory amount. A certified copy of any municipal or county ordinance effecting a change in the fine amount of any parking violation must be recorded with the Pinellas Clerk of the Circuit Court (Clerk) prior to assessment and enforcement of the new fine amounts.

B. Post–Citation Procedures.

1. Allowing for mail time as provided in Florida Rule of Judicial Administration 2.514, fifteen days after the issuance date of any parking citation, the Clerk will send a warning notice to the registered owner of the offending vehicle advising the owner that unless the fine is paid within ten days of the date of the notice a court summons will be issued.

2. A registered owner may seek cancelation of a parking ticket based upon the theft, care, custody, or control of the offending vehicle by another at the time of the parking violation by filing a sworn affidavit with the Court. The registered owner must execute the Affidavit in a form substantially similar to Attachment B to this Administrative Order and include the name, address, and driver license number of the individual who had the care, custody, or control of the offending vehicle at the time of the parking violation or the name of the law enforcement agency to which the vehicle's theft was reported along with a report number and report date. In the event the registered owner did not report the vehicle as stolen and is unable to name an individual who had care, custody, or control of the offending vehicle at the time of the parking violation, the Clerk will calendar the case for hearing by a Civil Traffic Infraction Hearing Officer or for hearing as otherwise directed by the Court.

3. A registered owner may plead "not guilty" to any alleged parking violation, and the Clerk will calendar the case for hearing by a Civil Traffic Infraction Hearing Officer or for hearing as otherwise directed by the Court. The Clerk will

issue a notice of hearing directing the owner to appear in Court at a given date and hour.

4. The Clerk will issue a summons if: the fine has not been paid within the time allowed; a not guilty plea has not been received within that time; or the registered owner has filed an affidavit seeking cancelation of the parking ticket based on another's care, custody, or control of the offending vehicle at the time of the parking violation. The summons will direct the registered owner; or as applicable, the person having care, custody, or control of the offending vehicle at the time of the alleged parking violation, to appear in Court at a given date and hour unless the person makes full payment of the delinquent fine beforehand.

C. Collections.

1. The Clerk will send parking ticket violations to collections for the delinquent amount plus a collection fee of 40% if the person who receives a notice or summons in accordance with subparagraphs B.2, 3. or 4. of this Administrative Order:

a. fails to appear in Court and then does not pay the assessed fine within 90 days; or

b. appears in Court but then fails to pay any fine assessed within 90 days or other date set by the Court.

2. The Clerk will send all existing parking ticket violations that have not been paid for 90 days or more and are less than 24 months old to collections for the delinquent amount plus a collection fee of 40%.

D. Clerk's Records.

1. The Clerk will record as dismissed any existing parking ticket violation that has remained outstanding on the Clerk's records for a period of 24 months or longer from the date of this Administrative Order. The Clerk will withdraw and cancel any warrant issued solely for the failure to pay a parking ticket violation.

2. In accordance with any enacted Pinellas County Ordinance and § 316.1967(6), Fla. Stat., any time the Clerk's records indicate three or more delinquent parking violations or any delinquent violations of the handicap parking laws or ordinances, against any given tag, the Clerk will transmit the tag number of the registered owner to the Department of Highway Safety and Motor Vehicles.

3. The Clerk will record as dismissed any parking violation issued to a vehicle with an out-of-state license tag or a tag in which the registered owner cannot be ascertained, if the violation remains unpaid for a period of 180 days from the date of the warning notice.

Administrative Orders 90–19 and 2006–010 PI–CTY are hereby rescinded.

DONE AND ORDERED in Chambers at St. Petersburg, Pinellas County, Florida, this __________ day of November, 2015.

ORIGINAL SIGNED ON NOVEMBER 4, 2015
BY ANTHONY RONDOLINO,
CHIEF JUDGE

Attachment A: Approved Form Parking Ticket

Attachment B: Care, Custody, or Control Affidavit

TICKET NUMBER
PARKING CITATION

DATE ______________ TIME ______________ AM/PM

MAKE OF VEHICLE ______________ TAG YEAR ______________

TAG NO. ______________ STATE ______________

METER NO. ______________ OFFICER ______________

LOCATION ______________

YOU HAVE BEEN CHARGED WITH THE PARKING ORDINANCE MARKED BELOW:

1. ______ OVERTIME PARKING
   ______ METERED ______ UNMETERED
2. ______ IMPROPER PARKING TO WIT: ______________
3. ______ DOUBLE PARKING
4. ______ NO PARKING ZONE TO WIT: ______________
5. ______ MOTOR RUNNING - NO ATTENDANT
6. ______ KEYS IN IGNITION
7. ______ DISABLED PERMIT ONLY
8. ______ OTHER TO WIT ______________

NOTES: ______________

IMPORTANT - *PLEASE READ CAREFULLY*

A. IF PAID AFTER 15 DAYS $ ______ B. IF PAID WITHIN 15 DAYS $ ______

1. THIS IS A NON-CRIMINAL VIOLATION;
2. REGISTERED VEHICLE OWNERS ARE RESPONSIBLE FOR PAYMENT OF THE FINE UNLESS THE TICKET IS CANCELLED BASED UPON OWNER FURNISHING ADMISSIBLE EVIDENCE OF THE NAME OF THE PERSON WHO HAD CARE, CUSTODY, OR CONTROL OF THE VEHICLE AT THE TIME THE TICKET WAS ISSUED;
3. PERSONS WHO FEEL THEY ARE NOT GUILTY OF THE VIOLATION CHARGED MAY ELECT TO APPEAR BEFORE A COURT OFFICIAL. ADDITIONAL CIVIL PENALTIES AND COURT COSTS MAY BE ASSESSED IF FOUND GUILTY OF THIS VIOLATION;
4. **WARNING:** FAILURE TO EITHER PAY FINE, PLEAD NOT GUILTY, OR RESPOND TO COURT NOTICES MAY RESULT IN A WARRANT FOR THE VEHICLE OWNERS ARREST AND MAY RESULT IN DENIAL OF THE VEHICLE TAG RENEWAL.

DO NOT SEND CASH

NAME OF MUNICIPALITY

ATTACHMENT B

PINELLAS COUNTY

______________ TRAFFIC DEPARTMENT

AFFIDAVIT

____
(Name of Registered Owner of Vehicle)

____
(Parking Ticket Number)

IN THE COUNTY COURT,
IN AND FOR PINELLAS COUNTY, FLORIDA

Before me, personally appeared, ______________, who, having been duly sworn, deposes and says:

1) I am employed by ______________,
(Name of Company)
located at ______________,
(Address: Street, City, State and Zip Code)
My position with the company is that of ______________
(Title of Position)

2) At the time of the alleged violation on the ___ day of ______, 20 ___, the vehicle with tag number ________, issued by the State of ____ was in the custody or car 1 of the individual whose complete name and address is listed as:
____
____
____
and whose driver license number is ______________.

3) The Rental Agreement (a copy of which is attached) states that the vehicle listed above was rented on the ___ day of ______, 20 ___, at ______.M. and returned the ___ day of ______, 20 ___, at ______.M.

4) At the time of the alleged violation on the ___ day of ______, 20 ___, the vehicle with tag number ________, issued by the State of ____, was reported stolen to ______________,
(Name of Law Enforcement Agency)
Offense # ______________.

____
Signature of Affiant

Sworn to and subscribed before me this ____ day of ________, 20 ____. *(SEAL)*

____

Deputy Clerk, County Court or Notary Public

[1] So in original.

2015–060. REPORTING OF INDIGENT DETERMINATIONS AND FEE WAIVERS IN CIVIL CASES

IN THE CIRCUIT COURT, SIXTH JUDICIAL CIRCUIT IN AND FOR PASCO AND PINELLAS COUNTIES, FLORIDA

ADMINISTRATIVE ORDER NO. 2015–060 PA/PI–CIR

RE: REPORTING OF INDIGENT DETERMINATIONS AND FEE WAIVERS IN CIVIL CASES

Filing fees are important revenues of the State of Florida and its State Court System. The fees, which are set in statute, help fund the courts and their clerks and enable them to perform their required court-related functions. Filing fees also help apportion the costs of the judicial system onto those who directly use those services. Therefore, where case filing fees and costs are due, it is important to collect and track the collection of all of the fees required by Florida law.

In accordance with Article V, section 2, Florida Constitution, Rule of Judicial Administration 2.215, and § 43.26, Florida Statutes, it is

ORDERED:

1. The Pasco Clerk of the Circuit Court and Pinellas Clerk of the Circuit Court (the Clerk) shall review applications for indigent status in civil cases and make an initial determination of indigence for purposes of waiver of a filing fee or deferring prepayment of a cost under section 57.082, Florida Statutes.

2. When the Clerk makes an initial determination that the applicant is not indigent, the applicant may request court review of that determination in accordance with Administrative Order 2005–040 or subsequent administrative order.

3. The Clerk shall report yearly (July 1—June 30) and otherwise as requested by the Chief Judge and the Trial Courts Administrator the cases, sorted by division, where a party has sought waiver of filing fees or deferral of costs under section 57.082, Florida Statutes. This report shall be substantially in the format of Attachment A and include the following:

a. The cases where a person applied for a determination of indigent status for purposes of waiving filing fees, deferral of costs, or both in a civil case, including simplified civil cases where both parties are required to apply;

b. Indication of the Clerk's initial determination of indigence, either "indigent" or "not indigent";

c. Where the Clerk initially determined that the applicant was "not indigent," indication of whether the applicant sought further review by the Court;

d. The court's finding on review of the above circumstances, either "indigent" or "not indigent"; and

e. The value of any filing fees waived or costs deferred, which includes the total number of occurrences; sorted by division, and reported as a combined total value.

Administrative Order 2014–022 PA/PI–CIR is hereby rescinded.

DONE AND ORDERED in Chambers at St. Petersburg, Pinellas County, Florida on this ________ day of November 2015.

ORIGINAL SIGNED ON NOVEMBER 4, 2015
BY ANTHONY RONDOLINO,
CHIEF JUDGE

Attachment A

Yearly Report on Waiver of Filing Fees or Costs Deferred in Civil Cases

(YEAR)	APPLIED FOR WAIVER OF CIVIL FILING FEES/ DEFERRED COSTS	INITIAL DETERMINATION OF INDIGENCE BY CLERK	PETITIONED FOR REVIEW	COURT'S DETERMINATION	VALUE OF WAIVED FILING FEES
Family Total					$
Case no.					$
(list all)					
Civil Total					$
Case no.					$
(list all)					
Probate Total					$
Case no.					$
(list all)					
Total for (YEAR)					$

Sixth Circuit Administrative Order 2015-060 - Attachment A

2015–059. [RESCINDED BY ORDER 2018-008, EFFECTIVE FEBRUARY 20, 2018.]

2015–058. [RESCINDED BY ORDER 2018-034, EFFECTIVE JUNE 29, 2018.]

2015–056. MOTIONS DECIDED ON WRITTEN SUBMISSIONS—CIVIL DIVISION

IN THE CIRCUIT COURT, SIXTH JUDICIAL CIRCUIT IN AND FOR PASCO AND PINELLAS COUNTIES, FLORIDA

ADMINISTRATIVE ORDER NO. 2015–056 PA/PI–CIR

RE: MOTIONS DECIDED ON WRITTEN SUBMISSIONS—CIVIL DIVISION

There is no rule or law in Florida state or federal court that requires a trial judge to hear oral argument on a pretrial non-evidentiary motion. *See Gaspar, Inc., v. Naples Fed. Sav. & Loan Ass'n, 546 So.2d 764 (Fla. 5th DCA 1989).* A party is afforded due process on such matters when given an opportunity to present a legal memorandum and then Court may enter an order based upon submissions without a noticed hearing and oral argument of counsel. *See also Nudel v. Flagstar Bank*, 42 So.3d 692 (Fla. 4th DCA 2010).

In an effort to maximize judicial efficiency through standardized procedures for handling pretrial non-evidentiary motions, and in accordance with Article V, section 2, Florida Constitution, Rule of Judicial Administration 2.215, and § 43.26, Florida Statutes, it is

ORDERED:

All parties are hereby noticed that pretrial non-evidentiary motions may be subject to review and ruling by a judge based only upon the motion along with written argument and any authority timely filed in the action. Each party/counsel filing such a motion shall contemporaneously file with the Clerks of the Circuit Court and serve opposing party/counsel any additional legal argument the movant wants the Court to consider. The opposing party/counsel shall have ten days after being served to file their argument and legal memorandum with citations of authority in opposition to the relief requested. Following expiration the period allowed for these submissions, the Court may at any time rule without further notice or hearing. Interested parties may notify the Court the matter is ripe for decision and request a ruling by letter which should include a simple form order for the judge to indicate whether the specific motion is either granted or denied, along with copies for conforming and stamped addressed envelopes for all parties.

In circumstances where a motion was filed before this Administrative Order and neither the movant nor the opposing side has yet scheduled the motion for a hearing, the opportunity to orally argue the motion is deemed waived. If the parties want the Court to consider argument they must now file written submissions in the form of legal memorandum on such pending motions in these cases within thirty days of this order. Thereafter, the Court may rule without further notice or hearing.

Nothing in this Administrative Order requires a judge to rule without oral argument. Individual judges may prefer hearings on certain pretrial non-evidentiary motions and counsel may consult the judges practice preferences on the website regarding such preferences.

The judicial practice preferences, scheduling information, and location of hearings for Senior Judges who hear civil cases may be found on the Court's website: http://www.jud6.org/LegalCommunity/PracticeRequirementsofJudges.html.

DONE AND ORDERED in Chambers at St. Petersburg, Pinellas County, Florida this ________ day of October, 2015.

ORIGINAL SIGNED ON OCTOBER 23, 2015
BY ANTHONY RONDOLINO, CHIEF JUDGE

2015–055. AFTER HOURS PROCEDURES FOR BAKER ACT AND MARCHMAN ACT HEARINGS IN PINELLAS COUNTY

IN THE CIRCUIT COURT, SIXTH JUDICIAL CIRCUIT IN AND FOR PASCO AND PINELLAS COUNTIES, FLORIDA

ADMINISTRATIVE ORDER NO. 2015–055 PI–CIR

RE: AFTER HOURS PROCEDURES FOR BAKER ACT AND MARCHMAN ACT HEARINGS IN PINELLAS COUNTY

In order to improve the processing of petitions filed under Chapters 394 (Baker Act) and 397 (Marchman Act), Florida Statutes, the regular hours for filing these petitions in Pinellas County must be modified. When litigants arrive at the Courthouse after 4:00 p.m. seeking to file these petitions, it usually results in overtime expenditures for the Clerk of the Circuit Court and increases operating costs for the county because staff must remain after 5:00 p.m. to process the paperwork. After consulting with the Clerk, it was agreed that the best way to address this budgetary concern was to utilize the after hours procedures beginning at 4:00 p.m. on regular work days. Accordingly, it is

ORDERED:

Effective immediately, the following after hours procedures for filing petitions for involuntary examination or involuntary placement under the Baker Act (Chapter 394, Florida Statutes) and for involuntary assessment and stabilization or involuntary treatment under the Marchman Act, (Chapter 397, Florida Statutes) are implemented:

1. After hours means after 4:00 p.m. or before 8:00 a.m. on a regular work day, or at anytime during a holiday or weekend day.

2. Baker Act petitions for involuntary examination or for involuntary placement and Marchman Act petitions for involuntary assessment and stabilization will be received for filing and date/time stamping by the Clerk of Court but will not be processed after hours. After hours filings will be processed on the next working day.

3. Petitioners wishing to file afterhours shall be informed of the following;

a. Their petition will be processed the following work day.

b. Petitioner may contact law enforcement or call 911 in the event of an emergency relating to the respondent.

DONE AND ORDERED in Chambers at St. Petersburg, Pinellas County, Florida, this ___ day of October 2015.

ORIGINAL SIGNED ON OCTOBER 8, 2015
BY ANTHONY RONDOLINO, CHIEF JUDGE

2015–052. PROFESSIONALISM COMMITTEE AND STANDARDS OF PROFESSIONAL COURTESY

IN THE CIRCUIT COURT, SIXTH JUDICIAL CIRCUIT IN AND FOR PASCO AND PINELLAS COUNTIES, FLORIDA

ADMINISTRATIVE ORDER NO. 2015–052 PA/PI–CIR

RE: PROFESSIONALISM COMMITTEE AND STANDARDS OF PROFESSIONAL COURTESY

On or about January 9, 1998, then Chief Justice Gerald Kogan of the Florida Supreme Court requested that the Chief Judge of each judicial circuit appoint a Circuit Committee on Professionalism. The Committee was charged with the overall responsibility of initialing and coordinating professionalism activities within the circuit and to assist the Commission on Professionalism.

On or about January 14, 1998, the Sixth Judicial Circuit Professionalism Committee was established. The Bench and

Bar of the Sixth Judicial Circuit have historically maintained a high level of professionalism. That high standard was reflected in the Sixth Circuit Standards of Professional Courtesy and the Professional Implementation Procedures (PIP) Committee, first adopted in Administrative Order 99–46. Since that time the Circuit has had a PIP Committee designed to address complaints about professionalism problems on an informal basis. The commitment to high standards of professionalism in this Circuit was reaffirmed in Administrative Orders 2007–006, 2008–077, 2009–066, 2011–002, 2013–046, and 2013–075.

The Florida Supreme Court adopted a Code for Resolving Professionalism Complaints. *In Re: Code for Resolving Professionalism Complaints*, 116 So.3d 280 (Fla. 2013). The Court required each Chief Judge to establish a Local Professionalism Panel to receive and resolve professionalism complaints informally. The Sixth Circuit has had a PIP Committee to receive and resolve professionalism complaints informally. The Professional Implementation Procedures Committee shall be renamed the Local Professionalism Panel (LPP).

Administrative Order 2013–046 was adopted, directing the Professionalism Committee to review the new Code and make recommended changes to the Sixth Circuit procedures to comply with the Code. After review of the Code, Standards of Professional Courtesy is amended in order to bring the Sixth Circuit and its procedures into compliance as reflected in Attachment A.

In accordance with the Chief Judge's authority under Article V, section 2, Florida Constitution, Rule of Judicial Administration 2.215, and section 43.26, Florida Statutes, it is hereby

ORDERED:

1. The Sixth Judicial Circuit Professionalism Committee ("Committee") will continue to operate in the Sixth Judicial Circuit ("Circuit").

2. The Chief Judge of the Circuit will continue to serve as the Chair of the Committee.

3. The following appointments to the Committee are continued:

a. Pasco Administrative Judge

b. Pasco and Pinellas Appellate Division Administrative Judge

c. Pasco and Pinellas Family Law Division (including Unified Family Court) Administrative Judge

d. Pasco County Court Administrative Judge

e. Pinellas Civil Division Administrative Judge

f. Pinellas County Court Administrative Judge

g. Pinellas Criminal Division Administrative Judge

h. Pinellas Probate and Guardianship Division Administrative Judge

i. State Attorney for the Sixth Judicial Circuit

j. Public Defender for the Sixth Judicial Circuit

k. Criminal Conflict and Civil Regional Counsel, Second District

l. President of the Clearwater Bar Association, or his or her designee

m. President of the St. Petersburg Bar Association, or his or her designee

n. President of the Tampa Bay Chapter of the American Board of Trial Advocates (ABOTA), or his or her designee

o. President of the West Pasco Bar Association, or his or her designee

p. President of the Young Lawyers Division, Clearwater Bar Association, or his or her designee

q. President of the Young Lawyers Section, St. Petersburg Bar Association, or his or her designee

r. President of the Young Lawyers Division, West Pasco Bar Association, or his or her designee

s. Dean of Stetson University College of Law, or his or her designee

t. Such others named by the Chief Judge of the Circuit.

4. The Committee will:

a. meet quarterly to discuss the status of professionalism and professionalism activities in the Circuit and issue a quarterly report to Justice Lewis;

b. issue an annual report each January to the Chair of the Supreme Court Commission on Professionalism;

c. on a periodic basis, offer Continuing Legal Education courses on professionalism; and

d. continue to designate a subcommittee to function as the LPP Committee.

5. The Standards of Professional Courtesy and Implementation Procedures, which are Attachment A to this Administrative Order, are amended and adopted to comply with the Code for Resolving Professionalism Complaints.

Administrative Order 2013–075 PA/PI–CIR is hereby rescinded.

DONE AND ORDERED in Chambers at St. Petersburg, Pinellas County, Florida, this ___ day of September 2015.

ORIGINAL SIGNED ON SEPTEMBER 30, 2015

BY ANTHONY RONDOLINO, CHIEF JUDGE

ATTACHMENT A: The Standards of Professional Courtesy and Implementation Procedures

STANDARDS OF PROFESSIONAL COURTESY FOR THE SIXTH JUDICIAL CIRCUIT

Although not every lawyer will agree with every standard, these standards reflect an effort to continue decency and courtesy in our professional lives without intruding unreasonably on each lawyer's choice of style or tactic. Some of the guidelines may not apply in criminal proceedings, or where a specific judge has a different rule.

A. GENERAL

1. We will treat parties, counsel, witnesses, jurors and prospective jurors, court personnel and judges with courtesy, in writing and orally. We will avoid undignified or discourteous conduct. We will avoid disparaging personal remarks or acrimony toward opposing counsel.

2. We will not show marked attention or unusual informality to any judge, except if outside of court and supported by a personal relationship. We will avoid anything calculated to

gain, or having the appearance of gaining, special consideration or favor from a judge.

3. We will adhere strictly to all express promises to and agreements with opposing counsel, whether oral or in writing. We will adhere in good faith to all agreements implied by the circumstance or by local custom.

4. We will not knowingly misstate, misrepresent, distort, or exaggerate any fact, opinion, or legal authority to anyone. We will not mislead by inaction or silence. Further, if it occurs unintentionally and is later discovered, we will disclose or otherwise correct it.

5. We will not demean opposing counsel in the course of litigation unless relevant to the issues of the case.

B. SCHEDULING, CONTINUANCES, AND EXTENSIONS OF TIME

1. We will communicate with opposing counsel to schedule depositions, hearings, and other proceedings, at times mutually convenient for all interested persons.

2. We will provide opposing counsel and other affected persons reasonable notice of all proceedings except upon agreement of counsel when expedited scheduling is necessary. We will immediately notify opposing counsel of any hearing time reserved.

3. We will request enough time for hearings and adjudicative proceedings to permit full and fair presentation of the matter and to permit response by opposing counsel. When scheduling depositions, we will schedule enough time to permit the conclusion of the deposition, including examination by all parties, without adjournment.

4. We will call potential scheduling problems to the attention of those affected, including the court, as soon as they become apparent. We will avoid last minute cancellations.

5. We will make request for changes only when necessary. We will not request rescheduling, cancellations, extension or postponements solely for the purpose of delay or obtaining unfair advantage.

6. We will cooperate with opposing counsel when conflicts and calendar changes are necessary and requested.

7. We will grant reasonable requests for scheduling, rescheduling, cancellations, extensions, and postponements that do not prejudice our client's opportunity for full, fair and prompt consideration and adjudication of the client's claim or defense.

8. First requests for reasonable extensions of time to respond to litigation deadlines relating to pleadings, discovery, or motions, should be granted as a matter of courtesy unless time is of the essence or other circumstances require otherwise.

9. We will resolve subsequent requests by balancing the need for expedition against the deference we should give to opposing counsel's schedule of professional and personal engagements, the reasonableness of the length of extension requested, opposing counsel's willingness to grant reciprocal extensions, the time needed for the task, and whether it is likely a court would grant the extension.

10. We will not attach unfair or extraneous conditions to extensions. We will impose conditions required to preserve rights that an extension might jeopardize. We may seek reciprocal scheduling concessions. When granting an extension, we will not try to preclude an opponent's substantive rights.

C. SERVICE OF PAPERS

1. The timing and manner of service should not be used to the disadvantage of the party receiving the papers. This includes the use of facsimile transmissions and any additional expedited means of communication approved by the court.

2. We will not serve papers to take advantage of opposing counsel's known absence from the office or at a time or in a manner designed to inconvenience an opponent, such as late on Friday afternoon or the day preceding a secular or religious holiday.

3. We will not serve papers, including briefs and memoranda, so close to a court appearance that the ability of opposing counsel to prepare for that appearance or, where permitted, to respond, is inhibited.

4. Service should be made personally or by facsimile transmission when it is likely that service by mail, even when allowed, will prejudice the opposing party.

D. WRITTEN SUBMISSIONS TO A COURT

1. In written briefs or memoranda, we will not rely on facts that are not properly part of the record. We may, however, present historical, economic or sociological data if the data appears in or is derived from generally available sources.

E. COMMUNICATIONS WITH ADVERSARIES

1. We will not write letters to ascribe to our opponent a position he or she has not taken or to create "a record" of events that have not occurred.

2. We will use letters intended only to make a record sparingly and only when necessary under all the circumstances.

3. We will not send letters between counsel to judges unless specifically permitted or invited by the court.

F. DISCOVERY

1. We will use discovery only when necessary to ascertain information, to perpetuate testimony, or to obtain documents or things necessary for the prosecution or defense of an action. We will never use discovery as a means of harassment or to impose an inordinate burden or expense.

2. We will file motions for protective orders as soon as possible and notice them for hearing as soon as practicable. Absent an agreement or court order a deposition may not be properly canceled due to a pending motion.

3. Prior to filing a motion to compel or for protective order, we will confer with opposing counsel in a good faith effort to resolve the issues raised. We will file with the motion a statement certifying that we have complied and been unable to resolve the dispute.

4. Motions to compel shall quote in full each interrogatory, question on deposition, request for admission or request for production to which the motion is addressed and the objection and grounds stated by opposing counsel.

DEPOSITIONS

5. In scheduling depositions, we will make reasonable attempts to accommodate the schedule of the deponent, but not at the expense of our client's rights.

6. We will not inquire into a deponent's personal affairs or question a deponent's integrity unless the inquiry is relevant to the subject matter of the deposition.

7. We will refrain from repetitive and argumentative questions and those asked solely for purposes of harassment.

8. We will limit objections to those that are well founded and necessary to protect a client's interest. Most objections are preserved and must be interposed only when the form of a question is defective or privileged information is sought.

9. While a question is pending, we will not, through objections or otherwise, coach the deponent or suggest answers.

10. We will not direct a deponent to refuse to answer questions unless they seek privileged information, are manifestly irrelevant, are calculated to harass, or are not calculated to lead to admissible evidence.

11. We will not make self-serving speeches during depositions.

12. We will not engage in any conduct during a deposition that would not be allowed in the presence of a judicial officer.

DOCUMENT DEMANDS

13. In responding to document demands, we will not strain to interpret the request in an artificially restrictive manner in order to avoid disclosure.

14. We will withhold documents on the grounds of privilege only where appropriate.

15. We will not produce documents in a disorganized or unintelligible fashion, or in a way calculated to hide or obscure the existence of particular documents.

16. We will not delay document production to prevent opposing counsel from inspecting documents prior to depositions or for any other tactical reason.

INTERROGATORIES

17. We will avoid "gamesmanship" in answering interrogatories.

18. Objections must be based on good faith belief in their merit. We will not make objections in order to withhold relevant information. If an interrogatory is objectionable only in part, we will answer the unobjectionable portion.

G. MOTION PRACTICE

1. We will make every reasonable effort to resolve the issue before setting a motion for hearing.

2. We will not force opposing counsel to make motions we do not intend to oppose unless circumstances require or the client requires.

3. After a hearing, we will make a good faith effort to quickly agree or disagree upon a proposed order and submit the result to the court. Unless otherwise instructed by the court, or agreed to by counsel, all proposed orders shall be provided to other counsel for approval or comment prior to submission to the court. We will not submit controverted orders to the court with a copy to opposing counsel for "objections within ___ days". Courts prefer to know that the order is either agreed upon or opposed.

4. We will not use post-hearing submissions of proposed orders as a guise to reargue the merits of the matter.

H. EX PARTE COMMUNICATIONS WITH THE COURT AND OTHERS

1. We will avoid ex parte communications on the substance of a pending case with a judge before whom the case is pending.

2. If an ex parte application or communication is permitted, we will make diligent efforts to notify the opposing party or a lawyer known or likely to represent the opposing party before making the application or communication. We will make reasonable efforts to accommodate the schedule of the lawyer so that the opposing party will be represented. We will make the application or communication only if there is a bona fide emergency whereby the client will be seriously prejudiced by a failure to make the application or communication on regular notice.

3. We will notify opposing counsel of all oral or written communications with the court or other tribunal, except those involving only scheduling. We will provide simultaneously to opposing counsel copies of all submissions to the court by substantially the same method of delivery by which they are provided to the court.

I. SETTLEMENT AND ALTERNATE DISPUTE RESOLUTION

1. Unless there are strong and overriding issues of principle, we will raise and explore the issue of settlement as soon as enough is known to make settlement discussions meaningful.

2. We will not falsely hold out the possibility of settlement to adjourn discovery or delay trial.

3. We will consider whether the client's interest could be adequately served and the controversy more expeditiously and economically disposed of by arbitration, mediation or other forms of alternative dispute resolution.

J. TRIAL CONDUCT AND COURTROOM DECORUM

1. When a matter is noted for trial on a court calendar, it may be removed only with the permission of the judge.

2. We will conduct examination of jurors and witnesses from a suitable distance. We will not crowd or lean over the witness or jury. We will avoid blocking opposing counsel's view of the witness during interrogation.

3. We will address all public remarks to the court, not to opposing counsel. We will address objections, requests and observations to the court.

4. We will request permission before approaching the bench. We will submit all documents to opposing counsel for examination prior to submission to the court.

5. We will have the clerk pre-mark potential exhibits.

6. We will admonish all persons at counsel table that gestures, facial expressions, audible comments, or the like, as manifestations of approval or disapproval during the testimony of witnesses, or at any other time, are absolutely prohibited.

7. During trials and evidentiary hearings, we will notify the court and opposing counsel of the number of witnesses and duration of testimony anticipated to be called that day and the following day (include depositions to be read). We will cooperate in sharing with opposing counsel all visual-aid equipment.

8. We will not mark on or alter exhibits, charges, graphs, and diagrams without opposing counsel's permission or leave of court.

9. We will accede to reasonable requests for waivers of potential formalities if the client's interests are not adversely affected.

10. In civil cases, we will stipulate all facts and principles of law which are not in dispute.

K. TRANSACTIONAL PRACTICE

1. We will draft letters of intent, memorializations of oral agreements, and written contracts reflecting agreements in concept, so that they fairly reflect the agreement of the parties.

2. We will point out to opposing counsel that changes have been made from one draft to another. If requested, we will identify those changes.

PROFESSIONALISM IMPLEMENTATION PROCEDURES

A. TERMINOLOGY

1. Initiator: The complaining party

2. Contact Attorney: The person who accepts referrals from various organizations, practitioners or the Initiator

3. Intermediary: The member of the Professionalism Committee who the Contact Attorney calls to handle the complaint

4. Concerned Party: The attorney or judge whose behavior is the subject of the complaint

B. LOCAL PROFESSIONALISM PANEL

The goal of the Local Professionalism Panel (LPP) is to handle complaints about professionalism problems in an informal and confidential manner, functioning almost as a mediation process without the formality of actually bringing the parties into contact with each other. These procedures are meant to address unprofessional conduct. Unprofessional conduct means substantial or repeated violations of the *Oath of Admission to The Florida Bar, The Florida Bar Creed of Professionalism, The Florida Bar Professionalism Expectations, The Rules Regulating The Florida Bar*, or the decisions of The Florida Supreme Court. It also means violation of these Standards of Professional Courtesy or the Code of Judicial Conduct.

The LPP will handle complaints of alleged unprofessional conduct in a confidential and informal manner on two levels, which will be through a Contact Attorney and an Intermediary. The LPP will initially consist of all members of the Professionalism Committee, who will also function as Intermediaries. Twelve members of the LPP shall function as Contact Attorneys, divided between Pinellas County and Pasco County. The number of Contact Attorneys and the membership of the LPP may be changed from time to time as deemed necessary by the Chief Judge. Recommendations for appointment to the LPP may be received from local bar associations, other professional organizations, judges, and practitioners. The Chair of the LPP shall be appointed by the Chief Judge.

The LPP is the "Local Professionalism Panel" as defined by Rule 1.5 of the Code for Resolving Professionalism Complaints (*In re Code for Resolving Professionalism Complaints*, No. SC13–688 (June 6, 2013)). Professionalism complaints may be initiated directly through LPP or through the Attorney Consumer Assistance and Intake Program (ACAP) of The Florida Bar, as prescribed by Rule 2.1 of the Code for Resolving Professionalism Complaints.

C. PROCEDURES

1. The Initiator is referred from various organizations, practitioners, or makes contact on his or her own with one of the Contact Attorneys.

2. The Contact Attorney, without making any judgments concerning the complaint, shall contact an Intermediary and describe the complaint. When contacting an Intermediary the Contact Attorney shall take into account the geographic location, area of practice and the position (Judge or Attorney) of the Concerned Party.

3. The Intermediary has the discretion to:

i. Contact the Concerned Party and discuss the complaint and secure a resolution.

ii. Consult with any other Intermediary on how to handle the complaint.

iii. Decide there is no unprofessional conduct or insufficient information upon which to act.

iv. Go outside the LPP to request that a Senior Judge, a sitting Judge, or a respected attorney contact the Concerned Party to secure a resolution.

v. Refer the complaint to the ACAP of The Florida Bar pursuant to the Code for Resolving Professionalism Complaints.

4. Once the matter has been informally resolved, a determination made that there is no violation, there is insufficient information upon which to act, or the matter has been referred to the ACAP, the Intermediary shall contact the Initiator to explain the resolution.

5. Confidentiality:

i. Except as provided herein, confidentiality shall be required throughout the process and there shall be no discussions of the matter beyond the Initiator, Contact Attorney, Intermediary, the Concerned Party, or any person engaged pursuant to paragraph 3.iv above.

ii. The confidentiality rule in paragraph 5.i shall apply to complaints handled by the LPP. If a complaint is referred to the ACAP, Rule 3.5 of the Code for Resolving Professionalism Complaints shall superseded paragraph 5.i.

D. LPP MEETINGS AND REPORTS

The LPP shall meet from time to time to discuss the types of situations that have arisen and their resolutions, to discuss possible modifications in procedure or structure of the process.

2015–043. [RESCINDED BY ORDER 2016–020, EFFECTIVE APRIL 1, 2016.]

2015–033. [RESCINDED BY ORDER 2016–022, EFFECTIVE JULY 1, 2016.]

2015–032. [RESCINDED BY ORDER 2016–019, EFFECTIVE APRIL 1, 2016.]

2015–031. HUMAN TRAFFICKING VICTIM RECORD EXPUNCTION

IN THE CIRCUIT COURT, SIXTH JUDICIAL CIRCUIT IN AND FOR PASCO AND PINELLAS COUNTIES, FLORIDA

ADMINISTRATIVE ORDER NO. 2015–031 PA/PI–CIR

RE: HUMAN TRAFFICKING VICTIM RECORD EXPUNCTION

Section 943.0583, Florida Statutes, provides for the expunction of a criminal history record for certain offenses committed while a person was a victim of human trafficking. Pursuant to amendments effective October 1, 2015, that section provides that any court in the circuit in which the petitioner was arrested has the discretion to order the expunction of the criminal history record, so long as the Court has jurisdiction over the class of offense or offenses sought to be expunged.

In order to provide for the expedient and consistent handling of petitions for human trafficking victim expunction, and in accordance with Article V, § 2, Florida Constitution, Rule of Judicial Administration 2.215, and section 43.26, Florida Statutes, it is:

ORDERED:

1. In Pinellas County, Section J shall continue to be the section for matters involving petitions for expunction of criminal history records, which shall include human trafficking victim petitions for expunction, in accordance with Administrative Order 2007–051.

2. In Pasco County, all petitions for human trafficking victim expunction of criminal history records shall be heard by the Pasco Administrative Judge.

All other terms and conditions of Administrative Order 2007–051 and 2014–047 remain in full force and effect.

DONE AND ORDERED in Chambers, at St. Petersburg, Pinellas County, Florida, this ___ day of June, 2015.

ORIGINAL SIGNED ON JUNE 26, 2015
BY ANTHONY RONDOLINO, ACTING CHIEF JUDGE

2015–026. MUNICIPAL POLICE AGENCIES AND SHERIFFS, OR LAW ENFORCEMENT AGENCIES OUTSIDE OF PINELLAS COUNTY, SERVING INJUNCTIONS AGAINST DATING, DOMESTIC, REPEAT, AND SEXUAL VIOLENCE AND STALKING

IN THE CIRCUIT COURT, SIXTH JUDICIAL CIRCUIT IN AND FOR PASCO AND PINELLAS COUNTIES, FLORIDA

ADMINISTRATIVE ORDER NO. 2015–026 PI–CIR

RE: MUNICIPAL POLICE AGENCIES AND SHERIFFS, OR LAW ENFORCEMENT AGENCIES OUTSIDE OF PINELLAS COUNTY, SERVING INJUNCTIONS AGAINST DATING, DOMESTIC, REPEAT, AND SEXUAL VIOLENCE AND STALKING

The Sheriff has jurisdiction to serve process in all dating, domestic, repeat, and sexual violence and stalking injunction cases. Sections 741.30(8)(a)(1), 784.046(8)(a)(1), and 784.0485(8)(a)(1), Florida Statutes, provide that the Chief Judge, in consultation with the Sheriff, may authorize a law enforcement agency within the Chief Judge's jurisdiction to effectuate this type of service.

In 1996, the Chief Judge, after consultation with the Pinellas County Sheriff, authorized certain municipal police departments to effect service of process during a call for municipal police services when the petitioner had a certified copy of the injunction. Administrative Order 2000–37 authorized all municipal police departments located in Pinellas County to serve a domestic violence injunction or a repeat violence injunction when provided a certified copy of the injunction by the petitioner upon arriving at a call for police service. Administrative Order 2012–055 authorized all municipal police departments located in Pinellas County to serve injunctions against dating, domestic, repeat, and sexual violence and stalking when provided a certified copy of the injunction by the petitioner upon arriving at a call for police service.

A number of respondents live or are found outside of Pinellas County and are served by the sheriff or law enforcement agency of that locality. Accordingly, the Court finds it necessary to update the Return of Service procedures to ensure that the appropriate sheriff or law enforcement agency receives all the required paperwork.

In accordance with Article V, § 2, Florida Constitution, Florida Rule of Judicial Administration 2.215, and § 43.26 Florida Statutes, it is therefore

ORDERED:

1. Municipal police departments located in Pinellas County and their individual sworn officers are hereby authorized to effect service of process in lieu of the Pinellas County Sheriff's Department when provided a certified copy of an injunction against dating, domestic, repeat, or sexual violence, or stalking by the petitioner upon arriving at a call for police service.

2. When serving an injunction against dating, domestic, repeat, or sexual violence, or stalking, law enforcement officers must serve it in accordance with Attachment A—Notice To All Local Law Enforcement Agencies (Notice). The Pinellas Clerk of the Circuit Court (Clerk) must attach the Notice to a certified copy of the injunction to be served on the respondent. The Clerk must also provide Attachment B—Return of Service/Certificate of Non-service, when forwarding the injunction for service to law enforcement, including to sheriffs of other Florida counties or to another law enforcement agency, where the respondent resides or can be found.

3. After service of process has been made, the law enforcement officer who served the injunction must immediately file the Return of Service/Certificate of Non-service, Attachment B, in accordance with the provisions of Chapter 48, Florida Statutes. If attempts at service of process are unsuccessful, the law enforcement officer attempting service must immediately file the attached Return of Service/Certificate of Non-service with the relevant facts that indicate the reason for non-service.

4. Service of process authorized by this Administrative Order will give the Court personal jurisdiction over the respondent.

5. Nothing herein changes the existing policy that gives primary responsibility for service of dating, domestic, repeat, and sexual violence, and stalking injunctions in Pinellas County to the Pinellas County Sheriff. However, if a municipal police agency receives a call for initial service of an injunction, and the agency believes an immediate harm might occur if the injunction is not served immediately, the agency may elect to serve the injunction. The agency must immediately notify the Pinellas County Sheriff's Office upon serving injunctions under these circumstances.

6. The Court may revise the Attachments to this Administrative Order without further amendment to this Administrative Order.

Administrative Order 2012–055 PI–CIR is hereby rescinded.

DONE AND ORDERED in Chambers at Clearwater, Pinellas County, Florida, this ___ day of May, 2015.

ORIGINAL SIGNED ON MAY 12, 2015 BY J. THOMAS MCGRADY, CHIEF JUDGE

Attachment A: Notice to All Local Law Enforcement Agencies
Attachment B: Return of Service/Certificate of Non-service

NOTICE TO ALL LAW ENFORCEMENT AGENCIES

The injunction should be read aloud to the respondent. Injunctions must be personally served on the respondent. They cannot be served on any other person. Any questions on service should be referred to the Pinellas County Sheriff's Office, Fugitive Section (727–582–6192). Once service has been made pursuant to Section 741.30(8)(a)(1), 784.046(8)(a)(1), or 784.0485(8)(a)(1), Florida Statutes, this service information form must be completed and faxed to the Pinellas County Sheriff's Office, Fugitive Section (727–582–6142). The agency serving the injunction must complete a Return of Service form and forward it to the Pinellas County Clerk of the Circuit Court's Office, 315 Court Street, Clearwater, FL 33756.

SERVICE INFORMATION

Served on: ______________________________
(Name of Respondent)

Race: ______________ Sex: ______ Date of birth: ______________

Date served: ______________ Time served: ______________

Address where served: ______________________________

____

Served by: ______________________________
(Name of Officer)

Agency: ______________________________

IN THE CIRCUIT COURT OF THE SIXTH JUDICIAL CIRCUIT IN AND FOR PINELLAS COUNTY, FLORIDA

______________________________, PETITIONER,

Vs.

______________________________, RESPONDENT.

Case No.: ______________
UCN: ______________

Return of Service

SERVE TO: ______________ RESPONDENT

Address: ______________ Street Address

______________ City, State, Zip

Type of Process: (Mark **ALL** that Apply)

- ☐ Temporary Injunction (type) ______________
- ☐ Final Injunction (type) ______________
- ☐ Firearms Affidavit (Respondent's Sworn Statement of Possession of Firearms/Ammunition)
- ☐ Order to Attend Batterer's Intervention Program
- ☐ Order to Appear at Mandatory Compliance Hearing
- ☐ Other ______________

I received this process on ________ Month ________ Day, 20 ____ Year, and served it on ______________ Name of Respondent /Defendant

at ______________ Address ______________ City, State, Zip

in ______________ County at ________ Time a.m. / p.m., on ________ Month ________ Day ,20________ Year, by delivering to the above-named person a certified copy of the Order entered in the above-styled cause with the date and hour of service endorsed thereon by me.

☐ Respondent refuses to surrender his / her firearms and ammunition.
☐ Respondent stated he/she has no firearms and ammunition.
☐ Respondent surrendered his/her firearms and ammunition. ______________________
☐ Respondent was identified by his/her. ______________________
☐ Additional Comments: ______________________

Respondent stated that his/her current residential address is ______________________
Address City, State, Zip

☐ **NON–SERVICE:** For the reason that after diligent search and inquiry, ______________________
Name of Respondent/Defendant

could not be found or ______________________
Reason

________ ________ ,20____.
Month Day Year

Served by:

Law Enforcement Agency ______________
City or County of ______________
State of ______________

____
Signature of Officer Serving Process Badge / ID #

____
Print Name

2015–017. COURT OPERATIONS IN EMERGENCIES

IN THE CIRCUIT COURT, SIXTH JUDICIAL CIRCUIT IN AND FOR PASCO AND PINELLAS COUNTIES, FLORIDA

ADMINISTRATIVE ORDER NO. 2015–017 PA/PI–CIR

RE: COURT OPERATIONS IN EMERGENCIES

In order for the Court, Pasco County, and Pinellas County to carry out their respective functions efficiently during an emergency in a manner that minimizes disruptions and conserves taxpayer dollars, it is important that each cooperate with the other. Administrative Order 2005–042 PA/PI–CIR as amended by Administrative Orders 2006–038 PA/PI–CIR and 2012–056 PA/PI–CIR, set forth the policies and procedures of the Sixth Judicial Circuit regarding court operations in emergencies. It is necessary to consolidate and update these policies and procedures.

Pasco County and Pinellas County are required to provide facilities for the trial courts. *See* Art. V, section 14, Fla. Const.; section 29.008, Fla. Stat. The County Administrators have the power to supervise the care and custody of county property. *See* section 125.74, Fla. Stat. Pasco County and Pinellas County are required to have emergency operations plans and "establish, as necessary, a primary and one or more secondary emergency operating centers to provide continuity of government" during emergencies. *See* section 252.38(3), Fla. Stat.

The Chief Judge is responsible for the administrative supervision of the courts in the circuit and has the power to regulate the use of courtrooms and do everything necessary to promote the prompt and efficient administration of justice. *See* Art. V, section 2, Fla. Const.; section 43.26, Fla. Stat.; Fla. R. Jud. Admin. 2.215.

The State Attorney, the Public Defender, the Clerks of the Circuit Court (Clerks), and the Sheriffs each play an important role in court operations in an emergency and the cooperation of each constitutional officer is important to ensure continued operations of the Court. The Sheriffs are required to provide for security for the Court. *See* section 30.15, Fla. Stat.

The Court recognizes that some emergencies will arise with prior warning, while others will not. Some emergencies will result in only minor disruptions to court operations and other emergencies may be catastrophic resulting in loss of one or more court facilities for extended periods. This Order is intended to address these various situations to the extent practicable under the circumstances.

The Court desires to cooperate with each county and with the affected constitutional officers in the event of an emergency and establish procedures to ensure the continued operations of the Sixth Judicial Circuit in the event of an emergency.

In accordance with Article V, Section 2, Florida Constitution, Rule of Judicial Administration 2.215, and section 43.26, Florida Statutes, it is

ORDERED:

1. When an emergency situation or threat of emergency arises that requires closure of the courts, this Administrative Order shall be activated by order of the Chief Judge and regular court operations shall cease within the affected county or counties within the Sixth Judicial Circuit. An emergency or threat of emergency may arise from any weapon (e.g., biological, germ, explosive device, technological, or any similar weapon), natural disaster (e.g., fire, flood, hurricane, tornado, thunderstorms, or other natural disasters), or other emergencies (e.g., civil unrest, nuclear, or hazardous conditions). When this Administrative Order is activated, it shall take precedence over all other administrative orders in conflict with it.

2. When regular court operations cease, the following shall occur:

A. All court dockets, hearings, trials, and proceedings of any kind, including foreclosure sales are cancelled except for crucial functions.

B. All court files will either be returned to the Clerk(s) or secured in a room without windows.

C. The Chief Judge will request that the Chief Justice suspend deadlines pursuant to Rule of Judicial Administration 2.205.

3. When regular court operations cease, crucial functions shall continue as specified below. Crucial functions shall continue to the extent possible except that no judge, court personnel, or other persons necessary to conduct these crucial functions shall be endangered in order to continue crucial functions. Crucial functions include:

A. First appearance hearings pursuant to Rules of Criminal Procedure 3.130.

B. Detention hearings pursuant to § 985.255, Fla. Stat.

C. Shelter and arraignment hearings pursuant to §§ 39.402 and 39.506, Fla. Stat.

D. Ex parte injunctions for dating violence, domestic violence, repeat violence, sexual violence, or stalking pursuant to sections 26.20, 741.30, 784.046, and 784.0485, Fla. Stat.

E. Issuance of warrants or authorization for wiretaps.

F. Any other emergency matter such as involuntary examination orders pursuant to § 394.463, Fla. Stat., emergency medical treatment pursuant to Florida Probate Rule 5.900, or other emergencies requiring immediate action by the Court to prevent harm to persons or property. Emergency matters are not subject to easy definition. As such, the judge must determine if the law or totality of the circumstances require immediate action. In the event the judge decides the matter is not an emergency, he or she will require the matter to be set before the assigned section judge on the regular calendar after regular court operations resume.

G. Other time sensitive matters as determined by the judge.

4. Hearing time for crucial functions will be scheduled at a time and place established by the Chief Judge and to the extent possible will be scheduled at the regular time for Advisories. In addition to the scheduled time, ex parte relief for crucial functions may be requested from the Emergency Response Team Judge. When an emergency condition is anticipated, the Chief Judge may determine that hearings for crucial functions may be conducted prior to the regularly scheduled time for Advisories.

A. In Pasco County, crucial functions may be scheduled at the:

1. Pasco County Jail at 20101 Central Blvd., Land O'Lakes,

2. Robert D. Sumner Judicial Center at 38053 Live Oak Ave., Dade City, or

3. West Pasco Judicial Center at 7530 Little Rd., New Port Richey,

in that order of preference with the specific location to be determined by the Pasco Administrative Judge in consultation with the Chief Judge based upon conditions at the time.

B. In Pinellas County, crucial functions may be scheduled at the:

1. Pinellas County Justice Center at 14250 49th St. North, Clearwater,

2. Pinellas County Jail at 14400 49th St. North, Clearwater,

3. Clearwater Courthouse at 315 Court St., Clearwater, or

4. St. Petersburg Judicial Building at 545 1st Ave. North, St. Petersburg,

in that order of preference with the specific location to be determined by the Chief Judge based upon conditions at the time.

In the event none of these facilities are available or cannot be reasonably accessed to conduct crucial functions, the Chief Judge may suspend crucial functions, or may, after consultation with the County Administrator or his or her designee, designate any other county owned or county leased facility that can be accessed for the purpose of conducting crucial functions, or may determine that crucial functions in Pasco County should be conducted in Pinellas County or the crucial functions in Pinellas County should be conducted in Pasco County.

5. The Chief Judge may activate Emergency Response Teams as necessary depending upon the circumstances. When activated, the following individuals shall lead the Emergency Response Teams:

Team A—Pinellas Criminal Administrative Judge

Team B—Pasco County Court Administrative Judge

Team C—Chief Judge

Team D—Pasco Administrative Judge

Team E—Pinellas County Court Administrative Judge

Each of the foregoing administrative judges may designate another judge who has agreed to serve in that capacity. The name of the designated judge must be provided to the Chief Judge in writing to relieve the foregoing administrative judges from this responsibility. The Chief Judge may name a judge as his or her designee to serve as team leader for Emergency Response Team C. The designee has the responsibilities specified in this Order for a judge on the Emergency Response Team but does not have any other responsibilities of the Chief Judge or Acting Chief Judge specified in this Order.

Each Emergency Response Team shall consist of:

A. The administrative judge,

B. An assistant state attorney, and if the State Attorney determines it is necessary, an investigator for the state attorney and one support staff for the state attorney,

C. An assistant public defender, and if the Public Defender determines it is necessary, an investigator for the Public Defender and one support staff for the Public Defender,

Two deputy clerks of court,

E. Three bailiffs,

F. A court reporter, and

G. If the administrative judge determines it is necessary, court technology staff, and one additional court staff.

The applicable public official shall designate the specific individuals for the teams. Teams A, C, and E will be staffed by Pinellas County. Teams B and D will be staffed by Pasco County. If during a specific emergency a team member is not available, the applicable public official shall designate an alternative team member for that emergency.

Once this Administrative Order is activated, the administrative judge, the deputy clerks of court, the assistant state attorney, and the assistant public defender for Team A are responsible for conducting crucial functions in Pinellas County prior to and during the emergency and the administrative judge, the deputy clerks of court, the assistant state attorney, and the assistant public defender for Team B are responsible for conducting crucial functions in Pasco County prior to and during the emergency. Crucial functions prior to and during an emergency may be limited or suspended at any time if the Administrative Judge or Chief Judge determines that it is not reasonable to continue crucial functions.

All teams may be activated to conduct crucial functions following an emergency to the extent that the team members are reasonably available. Following the emergency, the Emergency Response Team Judge may handle crucial functions and any other court business that is properly before the Court.

6. Once this Administrative Order is activated, the Trial Courts Administrator shall, to the extent possible under emergency conditions:

A. Notify all judges and court personnel by email that this Emergency Order has been activated.

B. Notify the following entities by email that this Emergency Order has been activated: the Clerks, State Attorney, Public Defender, Sheriffs, the Department of Juvenile Justice, and the Department of Children and Families, the Emergency Management Director for Pasco County, the Emergency Management Director for Pinellas County, and the Director of Justice Coordination in Pinellas County. Each entity shall provide the Trial Courts Administrator with the name and email address of the person to receive notification that this Emergency Order has been activated.

C. Establish a voice mail system at the main line for the Administrative Office of the Courts (727–464–4470) advising the public of the state of emergency and the suspension of regular court proceedings and advising lawyers and litigants how to have crucial matters heard.

D. Issue a press release to media outlets and post notice on the Court's website advising the public of the state of emergency and the suspension of regular court proceedings.

E. Activate the telephone tree for judges, judicial assistants, and court staff if necessary under the circumstances.

7. Once this Administrative Order is activated, judges, judicial assistants, and court staff should call the voice mail system at the Administrative Office of the Courts at 727–464–4470 or 727–582–7511 or an alternate number provided or check the Court's website at www.jud6.org to obtain information about the status of court operations. In the event the Trial Courts Administrator is aware that the voice mail system is inaccessible but phone service is still available, the telephone tree will be activated. The telephone tree is a notification system that has three parts:

A. The Chief Judge will notify the administrative judges who in turn notify the judges in their division. All judges notify their judicial assistant.

B. The Trial Courts Administrator will notify senior court staff, who in turn notify supervisors, who in turn notify all employees.

C. The Court Counsel will notify the senior staff attorneys, who in turn notify staff attorneys and other employees.

If a judge, judicial assistant, or court staff has not been able to access the voice mail system and has not been contacted about the status of court operations, the reverse of the telephone tree should be used. Administrative judges are to contact the Chief Judge, judges are to contact their administrative judge, judicial assistants are to contact their judge, and court staff are to contact their supervisor to obtain information. In the event that phone service is disrupted or the website cannot be accessed, media reports should be reviewed to obtain information about the status of court operations.

8. Judges are encouraged to provide a phone number to the Trial Courts Administrator to be used if the telephone tree is activated during an emergency. If a judge decides not to provide an emergency phone number, the judge shall inform the Trial Courts Administrator and the judge will not be included in any notifications using the telephone tree. Judicial assistants are encouraged to provide a phone number to their judge so that if the telephone tree is activated, the judge can notify the judicial assistant about the status of court operations.

9. All court personnel are required to:

A. Provide a telephone number to their supervisor where they can be reached during an emergency,

B. Once this Administrative Order is activated, remain in contact with the Court by contacting the voice mail call in system or their supervisor, and

C. In the event of loss of telephone service, monitor media reports for information on the status of court operations and information about when and where to report to work.

In addition, court reporters, court technology staff, and other court staff may be assigned to an Emergency Response Team or may be required to perform functions prior to, during, and after an emergency.

10. Once this Administrative Order is activated, the Clerk(s), State Attorney, Public Defender, Sheriffs, the Department of Juvenile Justice, and the Department of Children and Families, shall call the voice mail system at the Administrative Office of the Courts at 727–464–4470 or an alternate number provided to each entity to obtain information about the status of court operations. In the event the voice mail system is inaccessible, the above entities are to contact the Chief Judge or Trial Courts Administrator through phone or radio service to obtain information about the status of court operations. In the event that phone service and radio service is disrupted, media reports should be reviewed to obtain information about the status of court operations. Other entities such as the Department of Corrections, the Salvation Army, Domestic Violence shelters, the Emergency Management Director for Pasco County, the Emergency Management Director for Pinellas County, and the Director of Justice Coordination in Pinellas County are encouraged to call the voice mail system to obtain information about the status of court operations.

11. The Public Defender will:

A. Provide the Trial Courts Administrator with the name and email information for the person to receive notification that this Administrative Order has been activated.

B. Once this Administrative Order is activated, periodically call the voice mail system at 727–464–4470 in the Administrative Office of the Courts to determine the status of court proceedings. If the voice mail system is not accessible, contact the Trial Courts Administrator for information on the status of court operations.

C. Designate staff for the Emergency Response Teams so that crucial functions can be performed.

D. Communicate with the Chief Judge regarding any issues affecting the ability of the Public Defender's Office to perform crucial functions during an emergency.

12. The State Attorney will:

A. Provide the Trial Courts Administrator with the name and email information for the person to receive notification that this Administrative Order has been activated.

B. Once this Administrative Order is activated, periodically call the voice mail system at 727–464–4470 in the Administrative Office of the Courts to determine the status of court proceedings. If the voice mail system is not accessible, contact the Trial Courts Administrator for information on the status of court operations.

C. Designate staff for the Emergency Response Teams so that crucial functions can be performed.

D. Communicate with the Chief Judge regarding any issues affecting the ability of the State Attorney's Office to perform crucial functions during an emergency.

13. The Clerks of the Circuit Court will:

A. Provide the Trial Courts Administrator with the name and email information for the person to receive notification that this Administrative Order has been activated.

B. Provide sufficient staff to maintain regular services to the Court until regular court operations cease.

C. Once this Administrative Order is activated, periodically call the voice mail system at 727–464–4470 in the Administrative Office of the Courts to determine the status of court proceedings. If the voice mail system is not accessible, contact the Chief Judge for information on the status of court operations.

D. Designate deputy clerks necessary for Emergency Response Teams and sufficient means to manually take minutes and otherwise document court proceedings.

E. Communicate with the Chief Judge regarding any issues affecting the ability of the Clerks to perform crucial functions during an emergency.

When regular court operations cease, the Clerk(s) are encouraged to also cease regular court operations. If the Clerk(s) continue regular operations when regular court operations have ceased, the Clerk(s) shall bring all emergency matters that are filed to the attention of the Emergency Response Team Judge in a manner directed by the judge.

14. The Sheriffs will:

A. Provide the Trial Courts Administrator with the name and email information for the person to receive notification that this Administrative Order has been activated.

B. Designate bailiffs to provide security for Emergency Response Teams.

C. Once this Administrative Order is activated, periodically call the voice mail system at 727–464–4470 in the Administrative Office of the Courts to determine the status of court proceedings. If the voice mail system is not accessible, contact the Chief Judge for information on the status of court operations.

D. Provide transportation for the Clerk(s), Public Defender, State Attorney, emergency judge, court reporter, and others determined necessary by the Emergency Response Team Judge to the facility designated for crucial functions upon request of the Emergency Response Team Judge or Chief Judge if conditions require such transportation in order to conduct crucial functions.

E. When this Administrative Order is activated, the Sheriffs are authorized:

1. To relocate any person in the custody of the Sheriff to an alternative jail or prison facility or other secure facility within the State of Florida.

2. To assign a deferred reporting date to all persons who are scheduled to report to the jail, including those who are scheduled for weekend jail time.

F. When this Administrative Order is activated and when mandatory evacuation is ordered by the Board of County Commissioners, the Sheriff or the Sheriff's designee may in his or her sole discretion relocate or release, on their own recognizance, those persons listed below who are housed in those sections of the jail for which mandatory evacuation has been directed. Should release, rather than relocation of the inmates be necessary, the Sheriff shall release inmates on the following stages:

1. Work release inmates including those who are electronically monitored and those who are not electronically monitored. Those who are electronically monitored should continue to be electronically monitored as conditions permit.

2. County court sentenced misdemeanants as determined by the Sheriff.

3. Non–sentenced misdemeanants as determined by the Sheriff.

4. Non–violent felons as determined by the Sheriff.

If the Pasco County Sheriff determines that additional inmates should be released, the Sheriff will consult with the Pasco Administrative Judge or the Chief Judge and advise him or her of the facts and circumstances making the release of additional inmates necessary for the safety and security of the inmates and the detention and corrections staff. If the Pinellas County Sheriff determines that additional inmates should be released, the Sheriff will consult with the Pinellas Criminal Administrative Judge or the Chief Judge and advise him or her of the facts and circumstances making the release of additional inmates necessary for the safety and security of the inmates and the detention and corrections staff. Should the designated judge find the release of inmates necessary and appropriate under the particular facts and circumstances described to him or her by the Sheriff or the Sheriff's designee, the designated judge may order the release of the following inmates:

5. Inmates whose sentence will be completed within 7 days following release.

6. Other inmates designated by the Pasco Administrative Judge for Pasco County, the Pinellas Criminal Administrative Judge for Pinellas County, or the Chief Judge for either county.

G. Should the Sheriff determine that an emergency situation, other than when the Board of County Commissioners has ordered mandatory evacuation, requires the release of inmates, the Sheriff will consult with the Chief Judge and advise him or her of the facts and circumstances which make release of inmates necessary for the safety and security of the inmates and the detention and corrections staff. Should the Chief Judge find the release of inmates necessary and appropriate under the particular facts and circumstances described to him by the Sheriff or the Sheriff's designee, the Chief Judge may order the release of inmates in the following stages:

1. Work release inmates including those who are electronically monitored and those who are not electronically monitored. Those who are electronically monitored should continue to be electronically monitored as conditions permit.

2. County court sentenced misdemeanants as determined by the Sheriff.

3. Non–sentenced misdemeanants as determined by the Sheriff.

4. Non–violent felons as determined by the Sheriff.

5. Inmates whose sentence will be completed within 7 days following release.

6. Other inmates designated by the Chief Judge.

The Sheriff must provide all persons who are released pursuant to paragraph F. or G. a date and time to return to the jail for completion of his or her sentence following the emergency, except that inmates who are released by specific approval of the Pasco Administrative Judge in Pasco County, the Pinellas Criminal Administrative Judge in Pinellas County, or the Chief Judge pursuant to paragraph F.5 or G.5 because his or her sentence will be completed within 7 days following release will be deemed to have completed his or her sentence and are not required to return to jail.

Inmates who are released pursuant to paragraph F. or G. and who return as provided herein above shall be given one day's credit against his or her sentence for each day or portion thereof during such time as the inmate was released. Inmates who fail to timely return shall not be given credit against his or her sentence for any time released pursuant to this Order. A warrant shall be issued for the arrest for any inmate who fails or refuses to report as provided herein and such warrants shall be presented to the Pasco Administrative Judge or Pinellas Criminal Administrative Judge. Inmates who fail to appear will be subject to court sanctions, possible contempt, and may be charged with additional criminal violations. When the Sheriff provides a date and time for the inmate to return, the Sheriff shall also provide notice of these consequences for failure to return.

Release of a defendant pursuant to paragraph F. or G. is solely to address the emergency circumstances and is not pretrial release. Such release does not change the bond status of the defendant when released or upon the return of the defendant to jail.

Within 15 days following the release of any inmate pursuant to paragraph F. or G., the Sheriff shall provide a report to the Chief Judge on the number of inmates released and the Status of those inmates.

15. Pasco and Pinellas Counties will:

A. Provide and maintain the facilities designated for crucial functions in the county by maintaining electricity, sewer, water, telephone, computer networks, computer mainframe, and other essential services to the building during an emergency to the extent it is safe to do so and within the control of the county.

B. Provide communication equipment for the Chief Judge, Pasco Administrative Judge, Pasco County Court Administrative Judge, Pinellas Criminal Administrative Judge, the Trial Courts Administrator, the Court Counsel, and four additional court personnel designated by the Chief Judge. Such communications equipment must function between counties and be designed to function during an emergency.

C. Assist the Chief Judge in identifying alternative county properties where court functions may be conducted during or after an emergency if the designated courthouses are not available.

D. After an emergency condition has ceased, quickly inspect court facilities. The inspection shall be done in conjunction with court staff and a joint report provided to the Chief Judge regarding the status of court facilities.

E. In the event the Chief Judge determines, after consultation with the County Administrator or his or her designee, that the condition of a facility prevents regular court operations from being resumed, immediately identify an alternative facility where regular court operations can resume.

16. When this Administrative Order is activated, local law enforcement agencies shall issue a notice to appear for all local ordinance violations and all first or second-degree misdemeanors unless otherwise required by law to arrest a person.

17. When this Administrative Order is activated, the bond schedule shall be modified so that all persons charged with a local ordinance violation or persons charged with a misdemeanor shall be released on the defendant's own recognizance (ROR) except as follows:

A. The bond schedule is not modified for those defendants charged with failure to appear in violation of § 843.15, Fla. Stat., stalking in violation of § 784.048, Fla. Stat., or any domestic violence offense as defined in § 741.28, Fla. Stat.

B. Those defendants charged with a non-felony DUI in violation of § 316.193, Florida Statutes, or a non-felony BUI in violation of § 327.35, Fla. Stat. must be retained until the statutory criteria are met. Once the criteria are met, the defendants shall be released on ROR.

18. In the event of the death of the Chief Judge or any other emergency that prevents the Chief Judge from carrying out his or her duties or from appointing an Acting Chief Judge, the powers and duties of the Chief Judge shall be discharged by the following Acting Chief Judge in the order of succession specified:

A. The senior most Circuit Judge with the longest service as a judge, including service as a county judge;

B. The senior most former Chief Judge;

C. The Pinellas Criminal Administrative Judge;

D. The Pasco Administrative Judge.

The Acting Chief Judge shall serve until the Chief Judge is able to carry out his or her duties. If the event permanently deprives the Chief Judge of the ability to carry out the duties of Chief Judge, the Acting Chief Judge will hold that position until the Chief Justice or the Chief Justice's designee appoints a successor Chief Judge or the Judges of the Circuit elect a successor, whichever comes first.

19. In the event a catastrophic event prevents activation of this Administrative Order and communications are disrupted, the Emergency Response Teams will meet in Pasco County at the West Pasco Judicial Center, 7530 Little Road, New Port Richey or in Pinellas County at the Pinellas County Justice Center, 14250 49th Street North, Clearwater, at noon, 48 hours after the cessation of the emergency.

20. Once this Administrative Order is activated, regular court operations shall resume only to the degree and manner designated by the Chief Judge or the Acting Chief Judge.

21. For proceedings that were cancelled during the emergency, the following procedure shall apply to rescheduling of hearings. If the parties scheduled the hearing or the proceeding was set upon request of a party, it is the responsibility of the parties to reschedule the hearing provided that the Court may sua sponte reschedule the matter. Proceedings such as traffic court and domestic violence proceedings that are scheduled by the Court will be rescheduled by the Clerk(s) on order of the Court.

Administrative Orders 2005–042 PA/PI–CIR, 2006–038 PA/PI–CIR, and 2012–056 PA/PI–CIR are hereby rescinded.

DONE AND ORDERED in Chambers at Clearwater, Pinellas County, Florida, this ___ day of March, 2015.

ORIGINAL SIGNED ON MARCH 27, 2015
BY J. THOMAS MCGRADY,
CHIEF JUDGE

2015–012. [RESCINDED BY ORDER 2016-057, EFFECTIVE SEPTEMBER 9, 2016.]

2015–008. E-CIGARETTES

IN THE CIRCUIT COURT, SIXTH JUDICIAL CIRCUIT IN AND FOR PASCO AND PINELLAS COUNTIES, FLORIDA

ADMINISTRATIVE ORDER NO. 2015–008 PA/PI–CIR

RE: E-CIGARETTES

The use of electronic cigarettes, also known as e-cigarettes, and other nicotine dispensing devices is increasing in public spaces. These battery-powered devices allow users to inhale vaporized nicotine, flavor, and other chemicals, without fire, smoke, ash, or carbon dioxide. While the devices do not create secondhand "smoke," they do emit aerosols that may contain toxic metals or chemicals, which may be harmful to persons nearby.

In order to maintain the health, safety, and well-being of the officers, employees, and visitors in each of the Circuit's courthouses, and to the extent e-cigarettes are not explicitly proscribed by the Florida Clean Indoor Air Act, it is necessary to prohibit the use of these products within the courthouses of this Circuit.

In accordance with Article V, section 2, Florida Constitution, Rule of Judicial Administration 2.215, and § 43.26, Florida Statutes, it is

ORDERED:

1. For purposes of this Administrative Order, an "electronic cigarette" is any product that employs a battery, chemical, or mechanical means to produce an aerosol from any substance containing nicotine or other product or chemical, including but not limited to an electronic cigar, electronic cigarillo, electronic pipe, vaporizer, vape pen, or other similar device or product.

2. Any and all use of an electronic cigarette is prohibited within the courthouses of the Sixth Judicial Circuit, including use of an electronic cigarette to dispense chemicals or substances that do not contain nicotine. Affected areas include but are not limited to courtrooms, hearing rooms, judicial chambers, hallways, cafeterias, offices of court staff, witness rooms, juror assembly rooms, jury deliberation rooms, the offices of the Clerk of the Circuit Court, the offices of the State Attorney, the offices of the Public Defender, and areas utilized by the Sheriff's Offices, including adjacent restrooms, break rooms, conference rooms, and reception areas.

3. Any and all use of an electronic cigarette is prohibited within 50 feet of all entrances to the courthouses of the Sixth Judicial Circuit. Notwithstanding this provision, e-cigarettes may be used in an area outside of the courthouse that the County has designated for smoking.

DONE AND ORDERED in Chambers at Clearwater, Pinellas County, Florida this __________ day of February, 2015.

ORIGINAL SIGNED ON FEBRUARY 24, 2015
BY J. THOMAS MCGRADY,
CHIEF JUDGE

2015–003. [RESCINDED BY ORDER 2018-029, EFFECTIVE JULY 1, 2018.]

2014–079. [RESCINDED BY ORDER 2016–012, EFFECTIVE MARCH 1, 2016.]

2014–067. [RESCINDED BY ORDER 2019–006, EFFECTIVE JANUARY 23, 2019]

2014–062. [RESCINDED BY ORDER 2018-019, EFFECTIVE APRIL 25, 2018.]

2014–061. [RESCINDED BY ORDER 2018-020, EFFECTIVE APRIL 25, 2018]

2014–047. [RESCINDED BY ORDER 2016–009, EFFECTIVE MARCH 1, 2016.]

2014–043. PROHIBITED CONDUCT TOWARD SUMMONED JURORS

IN THE CIRCUIT COURT, SIXTH JUDICIAL CIRCUIT IN AND FOR PINELLAS AND PASCO COUNTIES, FLORIDA

ADMINISTRATIVE ORDER NO. 2014–043 PA/PI–CIR

RE: PROHIBITED CONDUCT TOWARD SUMMONED JURORS

The Chief Judge has the authority and power to do everything necessary to promote the prompt and efficient administration of justice, in accordance with Article V, section 2(d), Florida Constitution and section 43.26, Florida Statutes.

The Chief Judge is also to ensure the safe and orderly transaction of court business and use of court facilities, and to minimize activities which unreasonably disrupt, interrupt, or interfere with the fair and orderly conduct of jury trials, and the orderly and peaceable conduct of court business in a neutral forum free of actual or perceived partiality. *See* Rule of Judicial Administration 2.215.

Citizens who come to the courthouse to perform their civic duty in response to a summons for jury duty should not be subject to intimidation, harassment, or attempts to influence their jury service or prospective jury service.

Oral expressive conduct and the dissemination of leaflets and other materials containing written information tending to influence summoned jurors as they enter any courthouse complex may be in violation of section 918.12, Florida Statutes. Such occurrences severely impact the court's ability to efficiently, promptly, and properly administer of justice.

Restriction upon oral expressive conduct and the dissemination of leaflets and other materials containing written information tending to influence summoned jurors as they enter the courthouse is necessary to serve the State's compelling interest in protecting the integrity of the jury system.

Such regulation is a proper exercise of the Court's inherent authority to take supervisory and administrative actions necessary to implement its judicial functions.

The Court finds that explicit regulation of conduct and materials that tend to influence summoned jurors is necessary and is the least restrictive means to effectuate the proper administration of justice.

The powers of courts to punish for contempt is of immemorial antiquity, and is inherent in all courts as a necessary power in order to enable courts to accomplish the purposes for which they were designed; that is, the orderly trial and decision of causes, the enforcement of public order, the prevention of interferences with their proceedings, and the enforcement of the due respect belonging to them as institutions of the government.

In accordance with Article V, section 2, Florida Constitution, Rule of Judicial Administration 2.215, and section 43.26, Florida Statutes, it is

ORDERED:

1. The dissemination of all leaflets and other materials to summoned jurors containing written or pictorial information tending to influence summoned jurors, as well as communicating or attempting to communicate with a summoned juror for the purpose of displaying a sign, or engaging in oral protest, education or counseling with information tending to influence summoned jurors on any matter, question, cause, or proceeding which may be pending, or which may by law be brought before him or her as a juror, is prohibited on the courthouse complex grounds in Pasco and Pinellas Counties.

2. For purposes of this Administrative Order, the term "courthouse complex grounds" includes the following locations as also indicated on the attached maps.

a. *Pinellas County.* The **Pinellas County Justice Center** complex grounds, which includes the courthouse courtyard, courthouse parking lots and parking garage, all other grounds surrounding the courthouse from the intersection of 49th Street North and 144th Avenue North, to the intersection of 49th Street North and 140th Avenue to the most westward side of 140th Avenue and the courthouse parking garage continuing along the westward side of the County Justice Center to the Pinellas County Jail entrance, from the Pinellas County Jail entrance to the intersection of 49th Street North and 144th Avenue North, but excluding the private property at the intersection of 49th Street North and 140th Avenue. The public sidewalks that comprise the boundaries of this designated perimeter are excluded from this designation of the courthouse complex grounds. See Attachment A [1].

The **Clearwater Courthouse and the Clearwater Historical Courthouse** complex grounds, which includes, the courthouse courtyard, courthouse parking lots, and all other grounds surrounding the courthouse, from the intersection of South Ft. Harrison Avenue and Court Street to the intersection of Court Street and Bay Avenue, to the intersection of Bay Avenue and State Road 60 (also known as Chestnut Street), to the intersection of State Road 60 and South Ft. Harrison Avenue to the intersection of South Ft. Harrison Avenue and Court Street. Also included in the courthouse complex grounds are the metered parking lot located on Court Street and the east side of Osceola Avenue and the metered parking lot on Oak Avenue between Court Street and Chestnut Street. The public sidewalks that comprise the boundaries of this designated perimeter are excluded from this designation of the courthouse complex grounds. See Attachment B [2].

The **St. Petersburg Judicial Building** and the **501 Building** complex grounds, which includes, the courthouse courtyard, courthouse parking lot, and all other grounds surrounding the courthouses, from the intersection of Mirror Lake Drive North and 5th Street North, to the intersection of 5th Street North and 1st Avenue North, to the intersection of 1st Avenue North and 6th Street North, to the intersection of 6th Street North and Mirror Lake Drive North, to the intersection of Mirror Lake Drive North and 5th Street North. The public sidewalks that comprise the boundaries of these designated perimeters are excluded from this designation of the courthouse complex grounds. See Attachment C [3].

b. *Pasco County.* The **West Pasco Judicial Center** complex grounds, which includes the adjacent courthouse parking lot, the courthouse courtyard, and all other grounds surrounding the courthouse, from the intersection of Little Road and Government Drive, to the intersection of Government Drive and Citizens Drive, to the intersection of Citizen Drive (running North–South) and Citizen Drive (running West–East), to the intersection of Citizen Drive and Little Road, to the intersection of Little Road and Government Drive. The public sidewalks that comprise the boundaries of this designated perimeter are excluded from this designation of the courthouse complex grounds. See Attachment D [4].

The **Robert D. Sumner Judicial Center** complex grounds, which includes the adjacent courthouse parking lot, the courthouse courtyard, and all other grounds surrounding the courthouse, from the intersection of Robinson Avenue and 5th Street, continuing on the dirt road extension of Robinson

Avenue to the intersection with Lakeland Road/US 301 (aka Old Lakeland Highway), to the intersection of Lakeland Road/US 301 and Meridian Avenue to the intersection of Meridian Avenue and 5th Street to the intersection of 5th Street and Robinson Avenue. The public sidewalks that comprise the boundaries of this designated perimeter are excluded from this designation of the courthouse complex grounds. See Attachment E [5].

3. Regardless of whether the conduct at issue occurs on the courthouse complex grounds, any person who influences the judgment or decision of any grand or petit juror on any matter, question, cause, or proceeding which may be pending, or which may by law be brought, before him or her as such juror, with intent to obstruct the administration of justice, may be in violation of section 918.12, Fla. Stat.

4. Anyone engaging in the type of expressive conduct prohibited by this Order may be in violation of section 918.12, Florida Statutes, may be subject to criminal trespass as provided in section 810.09, Florida Statutes, and may be subject to contempt of court.

5. The Pinellas County Sheriff's Office and the Pasco County Sheriff's Office shall give a copy of this Order to anyone who is violating the provisions of this Order within the courthouse complex grounds, as described in this Order, and shall advise such person of the restrictions on expressive conduct contained within this Order. Further, law enforcement shall instruct anyone violating the provisions of this Order to cease and desist immediately.

6. When law enforcement observes anyone continuing to engage in such conduct as prohibited by this Order after such person has received a copy of this Order and has been instructed to cease and desist by law enforcement, law enforcement shall notify the Chief Judge and facility coordinator of such violations. Such persons may be charged with civil or criminal contempt of court. If a person is found to be in contempt of court, penalties include confinement, fine, or both.

DONE AND ORDERED in Chambers at Clearwater, Pinellas County, Florida, this ___ day of July, 2014.

ORIGINAL SIGNED ON JULY 15, 2014
BY J. THOMAS MCGRADY,
CHIEF JUDGE

1 Attachment not included.
2 Attachment not included.
3 Attachment not included.
4 Attachment not included.
5 Attachment not included.

2014–036. [RESCINDED BY ORDER 2016–022, EFFECTIVE JULY 1, 2016.]

2014–014. BAKER ACT HEARINGS

IN THE CIRCUIT COURT, SIXTH JUDICIAL CIRCUIT

IN AND FOR PASCO AND PINELLAS COUNTIES, FLORIDA

ADMINISTRATIVE ORDER NO. 2014–014 PA–CIR

RE: BAKER ACT HEARINGS

Pasco County currently has two facilities for receiving involuntary patients under the Baker Act, §§ 394.451–394.47891, Florida Statutes. This Court has been notified that two new facilities in Pasco County will soon be receiving involuntary patients. The offices of both the State Attorney and the Public Defender have informed the Court that they do not have the resources necessary to attend Baker Act hearings at all four facilities. Therefore, the Court finds it necessary to designate the facilities where Baker Act hearings will be scheduled and set forth procedures for conducting such hearings.

In accordance with Article V, section 2, Florida Constitution, Rules of Judicial Administration 2.215 and 2.514, and § 43.26, Florida Statutes, it is

ORDERED:

I. Definitions. For purposes of this Administrative Order, the following terms have the following meanings:

A. *Receiving Facility.* A "receiving facility" means any public or private facility designated by the Department of Children and Families to receive and hold involuntary patients under emergency conditions for psychiatric evaluation and to provide short-term treatment. The term does not include a county jail.

B. *Host Facility.* A "host facility" means a receiving facility which has been designated by this Court to serve as a facility at which Baker Act Hearings shall be conducted.

C. *Transporting Facility.* A "transporting facility" means a receiving facility which has not been designated to serve as a facility at which Baker Act hearings shall be conducted, and that therefore is required to transport its patients to a host facility for Baker Act hearings.

II. Designations.

A. *Host Facilities.* The Medical Center of Trinity—West Pasco Campus and Morton Plant North Bay Hospital are hereby designated as host facilities.

B. *Transporting Facilities.* The Harbor Behavioral Health Care Institute and North Tampa Behavioral Health are hereby designated as transporting facilities.

III. Responsibilities.

A. *Transporting Facilities*

1. Transportation

Each transporting facility shall provide for:

a. The safe transport of patients and a paper copy of their clinical records to the designated host facility for Baker Act hearings. All patients of the Harbor Behavioral Health Care Institute shall be transported to The Medical Center of Trinity—West Pasco Campus for Baker Act hearings. All patients of North Tampa Behavioral Health shall be transported to Morton Plant North Bay Hospital for Baker Act hearings.

b. Arrival of the patient at the host facility at least 15 minutes prior to the scheduled start time of the patient's Baker Act hearing.

c. The assignment of at least one clinical attendant to travel with the patient or patients to and from the Baker Act hearing. The transporting facility shall ensure that the clinical attendant is adequately trained to fulfill this duty.

d. Regardless of the outcome of the hearing, the safe transport of the patient back to the transporting facility at the conclusion of all hearings involving patients of the transporting facility.

2. Assessment and Notification. If, on the day of the hearing, the patient either refuses transport or the attending physician of the transporting facility assesses that the patient is clinically unstable for transport,

a. The attending physician shall document on the Baker Act Transportation Stability Assessment Form (Assessment Form), which is Attachment A, the patient's refusal or the specific risks assessed by him or her on the morning of the hearing and sign the form. The attending physician shall also be available by phone or in person to discuss his or her findings with the Public Defender or patient's counsel and the General Magistrate.

b. The transporting facility's Baker Act coordinator or designee shall contact the Office of the Public Defender or patient's counsel of record by phone as soon as possible. The Baker Act coordinator or designee shall also assure that the completed Assessment Form is hand-delivered to the General Magistrate prior to the scheduled start of the patient's hearing.

B. *Host Facility.* Each host facility shall:

1. Provide a safe and secure area in which patients from the transporting facility may wait until their hearings are called.

2. Provide a room of adequate size and decorum, with sufficient dignity to elicit the customary respect given to court proceedings, in which the General Magistrate may conduct Baker Act hearings. This area shall display an American flag and the flag of the State of Florida.

C. *General Magistrate.* Each General Magistrate conducting Baker Act hearings shall:

1. Display at all hearings a nameplate bearing his or her title and the seal of the Sixth Judicial Circuit.

2. In the event a General Magistrate receives an Assessment Form from a transporting facility stating that the patient has refused transport or is clinically unstable for transport, enter the form into evidence as part of the court proceedings/file. The General Magistrate shall then ask the Public Defender or the patient's counsel whether he or she wishes to proceed without the patient present or request a continuance.

D. *Clerk of the Circuit Court.* The Clerk of the Circuit Court shall:

1. As soon as possible but no later than 3:00 p.m. on the day before a scheduled hearing, notify the Baker Act coordinator or designee of each transporting facility of the patients from that facility who are on the court's docket and the time of their hearings.

2. Schedule the hearings of patients of The Harbor Behavioral Health Care Institute at The Medical Center of Trinity—West Pasco Campus; and the hearings of patients of North Tampa Behavioral Health at Morton Plant North Bay Hospital.

3. Place the cases of those patients from transporting facilities first on the hearing docket, ahead of the cases of patients from the host facility.

A Schedule for Baker Act hearings at host facilities is attached hereto as Attachment B. The Pasco Probate Administrative Judge is hereby given the authority to change this schedule at any time as warranted by the interests of justice.

DONE AND ORDERED in Chambers at Clearwater, Pinellas County, Florida this ___ day of February 2014.

ORIGINAL SIGNED ON FEBRUARY 27, 2014
BY J. THOMAS MCGRADY,
CHIEF JUDGE

Attachment A: Baker Act Transportation Stability Assessment Form

Attachment B: Pasco County Baker Act Hearing Schedule

BAKER ACT TRANSPORTATION STABILITY ASSESSMENT FORM

Patient Name ______________________ Date ______________

☐ The patient ***REFUSES*** transportation

The above names patient has been assessed by me on this date and in my professional opinion and with reasonable certainty is ***NOT*** stable for transportation for the following reason(s):

☐ The patient is currently and actively suicidal (i.e. searching for methods of self-harm within the confines of the unit).
As evidenced by: ______________________

☐ Has made real and specific actions or threats to harm staff or others.
As evidenced by: ______________________

☐ Has poorly controlled agitation, aggression or severe behavioral disturbance.
As evidenced by: ______________________

☐ Is deemed medically unstable.
As evidenced by: ______________________

☐ Transportation will exacerbate his/her condition and subsequently necessitate medication and restraint that would not otherwise be administered.
As evidenced by: ______________________

Attending Physician Signature ______________________ Date ______________

Printed Name ______________________

PASCO COUNTY BAKER ACT HEARING SCHEDULE

Sunday	Monday	Tuesday	Wednesday	Thursday	Friday	Saturday
			8:30 AM Hearings @ The Medical Center of Trinity-West Pasco Campus for: • The Medical Center of Trinity • Harbor Behavioral Health Care Institute	**9:00 AM Hearings @ Morton Plant North Bay Hospital for:** • Morton Plant North Bay Hospital • North Tampa Behavioral Health		

2014–012. [RESCINDED BY ORDER 2016–018, EFFECTIVE APRIL 1, 2016.]

2014–011. ELECTRONIC FILING IN THE CRIMINAL DIVISION—PASCO COUNTY

IN THE CIRCUIT COURT OF THE SIXTH JUDICIAL CIRCUIT IN AND FOR PASCO AND PINELLAS COUNTIES, FLORIDA

ADMINISTRATIVE ORDER NO. 2014–011 PA–CIR

RE: ELECTRONIC FILING IN THE CRIMINAL DIVISION—PASCO COUNTY

The Pasco Clerk of the Circuit Court, ("Clerk"), has informed the Chief Judge that it would like to begin voluntary electronic filing in the criminal, traffic, and juvenile case types. The new case maintenance system, CLERICUS, has not yet been fully implemented in these case types. For this reason, and at the request of the Court, the State Attorney's Office, and the Public Defender's Office of the Sixth Judicial Circuit, the Florida Supreme Court granted an additional extension of the mandatory electronic filing and electronic service deadline in these cases types until July 1, 2014. *In re: Electronic Filing of Criminal, Juvenile and Traffic Cases via the Florida Courts E–Filing Portal, AOSC14–01*. The Florida Supreme Court, however, permitted immediate voluntary electronic filing in these case types when the Clerk announces readiness. The Clerk has indicated its readiness to accept electronic filings in criminal, traffic, delinquency, and dependency cases and assures this Court that it has sufficient resources to begin voluntary electronic filing in these cases and to timely implement CLERICUS.

In order to implement voluntary electronic filing in these case types in Pasco County, and in accordance with Article V, § 2, Florida Constitution, Rules of Judicial Administration 2.215 and 2.525, and section 43.26, Florida Statutes, it is

ORDERED:

DIRECTIONS TO ATTORNEYS

1. Except as otherwise provided in this Administrative Order, effective immediately, attorneys may, with the exception of case initiating documents, electronically file pleadings and papers in Pasco County in the following cases:

a. County Criminal;

b. Criminal and Civil Traffic;

c. Circuit Criminal;

d. Delinquency, including CINS/FINS; and

e. Dependency, including Termination of Parental Rights.

Attorneys are not permitted to electronically file pleadings and papers in new and existing cases in Pasco County in the following cases:

f. Proceedings to Waive Parental Notification of Abortion;

g. Baker Act, Chapter 394, Part I;

h. Involuntary Commitment of Sexually Violent Predators, Ch. 394, Part V; and

i. Criminal Appeals from County Court to Circuit Court.

Original documents are not to be filed when the filing has been made electronically, except as otherwise provided in this Administrative Order.

2. The following documents may be scanned and electronically filed; however the original must be submitted to the Clerk:

a. Verified and sworn documents,

b. Original paper judgments and sentences,

c. Death certificates,

d. Birth certificates,

e. Certificates of Eligibility for Expungements,

f. Consents for adoption,

g. Affidavits of Nonpaternity,

h. Any other document specifically ordered by the Court, and

i. Any other document required by Florida law to be filed in its original form.

3. In order for an attorney to electronically file in accordance with this Administrative Order, the attorney must register with the E–Filing Portal at https://www.myflcourtaccess.com/ and submit pleadings and papers through the E–Filing

Portal. Attorneys must **not e-mail** the Court or the Clerk with pleadings or papers for filing. Pleadings and papers to be filed with the Court may only be submitted through the E–Filing Portal. Once assigned a user name and password from the E–Filing Portal, it is the responsibility of the attorney to safeguard his or her username and password to prevent unauthorized filings. Any electronic filings received via the attorney's username are presumed to have been submitted by the attorney. Law Firm Administrator Accounts may not be used for electronic filing on behalf of individual attorney members of the firm.

4. Attorneys must comply with all filing requirements of the E–Filing Portal. Currently the E–Filing Portal allows filings to be submitted in a Word, Word Perfect, or PDF format. For filings made in Pasco County, attorneys are encouraged to submit filings as a searchable PDF. Attorneys should separate attachments to a pleading or paper, and label each attachment. Attachments should be included in the same submission as long as the total submission does not exceed 25 MB. If a pleading or paper exceeds 25 MB, the attorney should divide the pleading or paper in an orderly fashion so that each submission does not exceed 25 MB. If the attorney is unable to divide the pleading or paper so that it does not exceed 25 MB, the attorney may submit the pleading or paper to the Clerk and is not required to electronically file such pleading or paper.

5. Each document must be formatted in accordance with the applicable rules of court governing formatting of paper documents.

6. In accordance with Rule of Judicial Administration 2.420, each electronically filed document must be reviewed by the attorney submitting the document to determine whether the document contains confidential or exempt information. If the document contains information that is confidential or exempt, the document must be electronically filed as a sealed electronic document along with either a notice of confidential filing or motion to determine confidentiality of court record.

7. In accordance with Rule of Judicial Administration 2.515, each electronically filed document is deemed to have been signed by the attorney submitting the document and must include an electronic signature of such person in the format of /s, s/, or /s/ John Doe or a reproduction of the attorney's signature. Each document shall also include the attorney's typed name, Florida Bar address, telephone number, primary e-mail address and secondary e-mail addresses, if any, and Florida Bar number.

8. Proposed orders, proposed judgments, letters, or correspondence directed to a judge may not be electronically filed through the E–Filing Portal but must be submitted according to the Court's directions. Attorneys should continue to provide hard copies to the Court, including sufficient copies for conforming, and stamped, addressed envelopes for distribution of orders.

9. Documents may be electronically filed at any time through the E–Filing Portal. Documents must be electronically filed and time stamped at the E–Filing Portal by 11:59 p.m. local time in order to be considered filed that date. The filing date for electronically filed documents is the date of receipt by the E–Filing Portal.

10. In the event that the E–Filing Portal is not available due to technical failure of the E–Filing Portal and an attorney must make a filing that day to meet a deadline, the attorney must attempt to file after 12:00 noon on at least two occasions that are separated by at least one hour. In these circumstances, if the attorney is unsuccessful in having a filing accepted by the E–Filing Portal, the attorney may, when the E–Filing Portal is available, file a motion with the Court seeking to have the filing considered timely filed. The Court may, with satisfactory proof, permit the document to be filed nunc pro tunc to the date it was first attempted to be filed electronically.

11. Electronically filing a document does not relieve a party of its evidentiary burden to prove the authenticity of an original document. Attorneys should maintain original documents, such as affidavits, that may be needed in court hearings unless the original is submitted as provided in paragraph two. When original documents are submitted as exhibits at a court hearing, the attorney must indicate on the document or notify the Clerk in writing when an original document must be retained as an original.

12. Until mandatory electronic filing begins in Criminal and Civil Traffic, County Criminal, and Circuit Criminal, attorneys choosing to electronically file must serve the electronically filed document by delivering or mailing a hard copy of the document. Attorneys choosing to electronically file in Delinquency, including CINS/FINS, and Dependency, including Termination of Parental Rights, must comply with Rule of Judicial Administration 2.516. Except as otherwise provided in this Administrative Order, hard copies of electronically filed documents are not to be filed with the Clerk.

13. If an attorney has an emergency matter that would normally be presented directly to the section judge or duty judge, the attorney may electronically file the emergency matter as provided in this Administrative Order. If the attorney wants the Court to consider the matter on an emergency basis, however, the attorney must contact the section judge or duty judge in accordance with current practices.

14. Attorneys from other jurisdictions who wish to be admitted pro hac vice must obtain a pro hac vice number from The Florida Bar to file through the E–Filing Portal. Until the attorney receives a pro hac vice number, pleadings must be electronically filed by the local Florida attorney designated in the motion. A motion to appear pro hac vice must be filed in each case in which the attorney wishes to appear and the receipt of a pro hac vice number from The Florida Bar for purposes of accessing the E–Filing Portal does not grant an attorney the right to appear. See http://www.floridabar.org for more information.

DIRECTIONS TO OTHER FILERS

15. Unrepresented litigants must file pleadings and papers in hard copy with the Clerk until the E–Filing Portal allows access to such filers.

DIRECTIONS TO THE CLERK

16. Except as otherwise provided in this Administrative Order, effective immediately, the Clerk may, with the exception of case initiating documents, receive pleadings and papers electronically filed through the E–Filing Portal in the following cases:

a. County Criminal;

b. Criminal and Civil Traffic;

c. Circuit Criminal;

d. Delinquency, including CINS/FINS; and

e. Dependency, including Termination of Parental Rights.

The Clerk will not accept pleadings and papers in new and existing cases in the follow [1] cases:

f. Proceedings to Waive Parental Notification of Abortion;

g. Baker Act, Chapter 394, Part I;

h. Involuntary Commitment of Sexually Violent Predators, Ch. 394, Part V; and

i. Criminal Appeals from County Court to Circuit Court.

17. The Clerk may only receive electronic filings through the E–Filing Portal or as otherwise provided in this Administrative Order.

18. The Clerk must receive documents from the E–Filing Portal in a searchable PDF format.

19. The Clerk must continue to receive the following documents in original form:

a. Verified and sworn documents,

b. Original paper judgments and sentences,

c. Death certificates,

d. Birth certificates,

e. Certificates of Eligibility for Expungements,

f. Consents for adoption,

g. Affidavits of Nonpaternity,

h. Any other document specifically ordered by the Court, and

i. Any other document required by Florida law to be filed in its original form.

When original documents are submitted at a hearing the Clerk must retain the original documents in accordance with existing retention schedules.

20. If a filer is unable to separate a pleading or paper so that it does not exceed 25 MB, the Clerk must accept such pleadings and papers in hard copy. Such pleadings and papers must be scanned by the Clerk in a manner that facilitates access to the filing by the Court and parties. The Clerk should separate attachments to a pleading or paper, label each attachment, and scan each attachment separately.

21. In accordance with Standard 4.1 of the Florida Supreme Court Standards for Electronic Access to the Courts (Jan. 2013 update, version 8.0), the Clerk must continue to maintain existing hard copy court files and create hard copy files in accordance with its current practices or when requested for use by the Court.

22. Until further order of the Court, the Clerk will continue to deliver hard copy court files to the courtrooms for scheduled calendars in accordance with its current practices. In addition, the Court may order hard copy court files through TrakMan for County Criminal; Criminal and Civil Traffic; Circuit Criminal; Delinquency, including CINS/FINS; and Dependency, including Termination of Parental Rights. The hard copy court files ordered by the Court must continue to be delivered within 48 hours of the request unless sooner requested by the Court. As soon as mandatory electronic filing in the criminal divisions is successfully implemented, the equipment and software needed by the Court are available, users have been instructed in its operation, court processes are modified to accommodate electronic court files, and the Clerk is able to convert court records to searchable PDF the Court intends to amend this Administrative Order to discontinue this requirement for hard copy court files.

23. The Clerk must provide public access to court records either from the hard copy court file or from terminals in the Clerk's offices and must do so in accordance with limitations on electronic access to court records as provided in AOSC07–49 or subsequent order. The Clerk must ensure that information that is exempt from public disclosure is not disclosed through public terminals in the Clerk's office or through any other public access.

24. The Clerk must make the court record available in a manner that complies with the Americans with Disabilities Act.

25. The Clerk must comply with all the conditions stated in the electronic filing approval letter from the Florida Courts Technology Commission, which is incorporated into this Administrative Order as Attachment A, and all requirements of Rule of Judicial Administration 2.525, Supreme Court Administrative Order AOSC09–30, *In Re: Statewide Standards for Electronic Access to the Courts*, including updated Standards for Electronic Access to the Courts, Supreme Court Administrative Order AOSC10–32, *In Re: Interim Policy on Electronic Appellate Court Records*, Supreme Court Administrative Order AOSC013–12, *In Re: Electronic Filing in the State Courts System via the Florida Courts E-filing Portal.*

26. Documents and orders prepared by the Clerk or by the Court are not to be electronically filed through the E–Filing Portal.

27. The Clerk shall prepare an information sheet on electronic filing for attorneys and for unrepresented litigants and post it on the Clerk's website.

OTHER MATTERS

28. Electronic filing in the probate division will continue as provided in Administrative Order 2005–065 as modified by Supreme Court Administrative Order AOSC07–23. Electronic filing in county civil, county small claims, circuit civil, circuit civil appeals, and family law (excluding dependency) will continue as provided in Administrative Orders 2013–017 and 2013–029.

Administrative Order 2013–071 PA/PI–CIR is hereby rescinded for Pasco County.

DONE AND ORDERED in Chambers, Clearwater, Pinellas County, Florida this ___ day of February 2014.

ORIGINAL SIGNED ON FEBRUARY 13, 2014
BY J. THOMAS MCGRADY,
CHIEF JUDGE

Attachment A: March 28, 2013 approval letter from Florida Courts Technology Commission

Judge Lisa Taylor Munyon, Chair

Florida Courts Technology Commission

c/o Office of the State Courts Administrator

500 S. Duval Street, Tallahassee, Florida 32399–1900

March 28, 2013

The Honorable Paula S. O'Neil
Pasco County Clerk of Court
Pasco County Courthouse
7530 Little Road, Suite 220
New Port Richey, Florida 34654

RE: request for implementation of electronic filings in remaining court (Circuit Civil, County Civil, and Family Law) divisions in Pasco County, Sixth Judicial Circuit

Dear Dr. O'Neil:

Supreme Court Opinion No.SC10–241, In re: Amendments to the Florida Rules of Judicial Administration—Rule 2.236 (July 1, 2010) provides that the Florida Courts Technology Commission "evaluate all such applications to determine whether they comply with the technology policies established by the Supreme Court and the procedures and standards created pursuant to this rule, and approve those applications deemed to be effective and found to be in compliance."

The purpose of this letter is to inform you that on April 27, 2005 the Electronic Filing Committee (EFC) reviewed and recommended approval of your request to implement electronic filing in Pasco County in the probate division which was granted by the Supreme Count via AOSC05–15.

As Chair of the Florida Courts Technology Commission I hereby approve your request to implement electronic filing in the Circuit Civil, County Civil and Family Law divisions in Pasco County.

Approval of this electronic initiative is contingent upon compliance with the policy considerations and directives regarding the development and application of new technological standardization and enhancements as set forth by the Supreme Court and is subject to the following terms and conditions. Violation of any of the following conditions shall constitute grounds for revocation of the approval to implement electronic filing in Pasco County.

a. The Pasco County Clerk of Court may implement the aforementioned technology procedures in accordance with the approved plan effective on the date of this letter and must adhere to the statewide standards for electronic access to the courts as outlined in In re: Statewide Standards for Electronic Access to the Courts, AOSC09–30 (Fla. July 1, 2009).

b. The Pasco County Clerk of Court shall ensure that there is no possibility for vendors to release or distribute court data to third parties and that the clerk of court retains the designation as custodian of the court records.

c. The Pasco County Clerk of Court shall ensure that contract provisions prohibit any vendor from extracting, data mining, or engaging in similar activities with regard to information from original court filings and other court records or any associated databases containing court records in the circuit for commercial or other non-court related uses.

d. The Pasco County Clerk of Court shall ensure that no fees other than statutorily required fees are assessed or collected by the clerk of court.

e. The Pasco County Clerk of Court shall ensure that the data is backed up and is recoverable. The clerk of court will ensure that remote data backups are stored in a protected environment a minimum of 50 miles from the primary production location of the court record or at a certified hardened facility, and that the circuit complies with established data backup standards as they are revised and updated.

f. This approval does not constitute an approval of any electronic forms that may be used in this process.

g. The Pasco County Clerk of Court shall submit monthly progress reports to the court system during the 90–day pilot test. Copies of the monthly progress reports shall be provided to the Chief Judge of the Sixth Judicial Circuit and the State Courts Technology Officer in the Office of the State Courts Administrator.

h. The Pasco County Clerk of Court shall abide by In re: Revised Interim Policy on Electronic Release of Court Records, AOSC07–49 (Fla. Sept. 7, 2007).

i. The E–Filing Court Records Portal, developed by the Florida Association of Court Clerks Services Group (FACCSG), has been identified as the statewide e-filing portal. To ensure equal access to electronic filing across the state, the Supreme Court has directed that the Florida Courts Technology Commission make implementation of the statewide system a priority of the judicial branch. All local electronic filing systems must be compatible with the statewide e-filing portal and approval of each of the above electronic filing systems is contingent on the system's compatibility with the statewide portal. The Pasco County Clerk of Court must now migrate to the statewide e-filing portal.

j. The Pasco County Clerk of Court must continue to provide paper to the judiciary until the chief judge authorizes the elimination of paper files. At such time, the Pasco County Clerk of Court must convert all documents, beginning on the date of Supreme Court or Florida Courts Technology Commission (FCTC) approval, to a searchable electronic document.

k. The Pasco County Clerk of Court shall continue to accept paper filings at no charge, other than statutorily required fees until such time as the Supreme Court may require electronic filing.

In addition to the foregoing enumerated terms and conditions, the chief judge may, pursuant to his constitutional and statutory responsibility for administrative supervision of the courts within the circuit, imposed additional conditions that must be adhered by to implement an electronic filing system.

1. Pasco County will comply with the E–Access Standards in accordance with Supreme Court Administrative Order AOSC 09–30. The Florida Courts Technology Commission last amended the Standards January 2013, version 8.0, and you must comply with this or any future revisions to the E–Access Standards.

2. Pasco County will follow any implementation schedule developed by the Florida Courts Technology Commission and coordinate implementation with the Chief Judge.

3. Pasco County will continue to assemble and deliver paper case files and documents until authorized by the Chief Judge to discontinue paper files.

4. The electronic file to be provided to the Court must meet or exceed the capabilities and ease of use currently

provided by paper case files, for both in and out of court processing and use. Documents in an electronic court file must be provided to the Court as a searchable PDF.

5. The Court must be provided and approve in advance any business process that impacts Court operations.

6. Pasco County will provide the Court with direct unrestricted access to the Pasco County court data, images and documents.

Should you have any questions, please do not hesitate to contact my office.

Sincerely,

Lisa T. Munyon
Circuit Judge

1 So in original.

2013–081. MORTGAGE FORECLOSURE CASE STATUS REPORTING REQUIREMENTS

IN THE CIRCUIT COURT, SIXTH JUDICIAL CIRCUIT IN AND FOR PASCO AND PINELLAS COUNTIES, FLORIDA

ADMINISTRATIVE ORDER NO. 2013–081 PA/PI–CIR

RE: MORTGAGE FORECLOSURE CASE STATUS REPORTING REQUIREMENTS

The Foreclosure Initiative Data Collection Plan promulgated by the Office of the State Courts Administrator provides new reporting requirements and definitions for the status of a foreclosure case. The Supreme Court recently adopted Administrative Order AOSC13–51, which requires use of those definitions. That Administrative Order also requires each chief judge to issue an administrative order establishing a mechanism that enables judges to provide explicit direction to each clerk of court's office regarding the status of a foreclosure case for statistical reporting purposes.

In accordance with AOSC13–51 and Article V, section 2, Florida Constitution, Rule of Judicial Administration 2.215, and section 43.26, Florida Statutes, it is hereby

ORDERED:

1. The Pasco Clerk of the Circuit Court and the Pinellas Clerk of the Circuit Court (Clerks) are directed to comply with the Foreclosure Initiative Data Collection Plan and use the definitions and coding in that Plan as provided in AOSC13–51.

2. Whenever the following events occur in a mortgage foreclosure case, the Clerks are to record the case as inactive for reporting purposes:

a. A notice of a pending federal bankruptcy proceeding is filed in the case,

b. The Court has entered an order granting a motion to stay or abate,

c. A notice of appeal is filed,

d. The case is consolidated with a lower case number, or

e. An order is issued by the Court directing the Clerk to treat the case as inactive. The Court may direct the Clerk to treat the case as inactive when:

i. Resolution of the foreclosure case requires resolution of a related case,

ii. There are on-going settlement negotiations, or there is an agreement of the parties,

iii. The Department of Justice or the Attorney General are conducting a document review, or

iv. Any other basis that is consistent with the definition of an inactive case.

When the events stated in (a) —(d) occur, the Clerk is to record the case as inactive without further order of the Court.

3. Whenever the following events occur in a mortgage foreclosure case, the Clerks are to reinstate the case as active for reporting purposes:

a. A federal bankruptcy court has lifted the bankruptcy stay and a copy of that order is filed with the Clerk,

b. A motion is filed,

c. A notice of hearing is filed, or

d. An order is issued by the Court directing the Clerk to treat the case as active.

When the events stated in (a) —(c) occur, the Clerk is to record the case as active without further order of the Court.

4. Parties to a mortgage foreclosure case are directed to notify the Clerk as soon as an event occurs that would change the status of a case.

5. The form order in Attachment A is available for judges when the judge determines that the case should be reported as inactive or if a matter specified in 2(a) —(d) occurs and the Clerk has not already placed the case on inactive status.

The form order in Attachment B is available for judges when the judge determines that a case should be reported as active or if a matter specified in 3(a) —(c) occurs and the Clerk has not already placed the case on active status.

DONE AND ORDERED in Chambers at Clearwater, Pinellas County, Florida, this ___ day of December 2013.

ORIGINAL SIGNED ON DECEMBER 10, 2013
BY J. THOMAS MCGRADY,
CHIEF JUDGE

Attachment A: Form Order Placing Case on Inactive Status
Attachment B: Form Order Placing Case on Active Status

IN THE CIRCUIT COURT OF THE SIXTH JUDICIAL CIRCUIT IN AND FOR PASCO/PINELLAS COUNTIES, FLORIDA
CIVIL DIVISION

______________,
PLAINTIFF(S), REF. NO:
UCC NO.:

vs.

______________,
DEFENDANT(S).

______________/

ORDER PLACING CASE ON INACTIVE STATUS FOR STATISTICAL REPORTING PURPOSES

1. This case came before the Court on its own motion.

2. The following event(s) has occurred in this case which require it to be reported as INACTIVE for statistical reporting purposes:

☐ Resolution of this case requires resolution of, Case No. ________.

☐ There are on-going settlement negotiations or there is an agreement of the parties.

☐ The Department of Justice or Attorney General are conducting a document review.

☐ Other ________.

3. The following event(s) occurred in this case and the Clerk has not reported the case as INACTIVE for statistical reporting purposes:

☐ A notice of a pending federal bankruptcy proceeding was filed.

☐ The Court has entered an order granting a motion to stay or abate.

☐ A notice of appeal was filed.

☐ The case was consolidated with Case No. ________.

THEREFORE IT IS ORDERED:

The Clerk of the Circuit Court is directed to remove this case from **ACTIVE** status, and designate it as an **INACTIVE** case for statistical reporting purposes only. This Order does not preclude a party from reactivating the case by filing any pleading authorized by the Rules of Civil Procedure. This Order does not authorize the Clerk to charge an additional fee.

DONE and **ORDERED** in ________ County, Florida, this ___ day of ________ 20 ___.

____
Circuit Judge

IN THE CIRCUIT COURT OF THE SIXTH JUDICIAL CIRCUIT IN AND FOR PASCO/PINELLAS COUNTIES, FLORIDA CIVIL DIVISION

________________,
PLAINTIFF(S), REF. NO:
vs. UCC NO.:

________________,
DEFENDANT(S).
________________/

ORDER RETURNING CASE TO ACTIVE STATUS FOR STATISTICAL REPORTING PURPOSES

1. This case came before the Court on its own motion.

2. The Court finds that this case should be reported as ACTIVE because: ________.

3. The following event(s) has occurred in this case and the Clerk has not reported the case as ACTIVE for statistical reporting purposes:

☐ A federal bankruptcy court has lifted the bankruptcy stay and a copy of that order was filed with the Clerk.

☐ A motion was filed.

☐ A notice of hearing was filed.

THEREFORE IT IS ORDERED:

The Clerk of the Circuit Court is directed to remove this case from **INACTIVE** status, and designate it as an **ACTIVE** case for statistical reporting purposes only. This Order does not authorize the Clerk to charge an additional fee.

DONE and **ORDERED** in ________ County, Florida, this ___ day of ________ 20 ___.

____
Circuit Judge

2013–072. [RESCINDED BY ORDER 2017–014, EFFECTIVE FEBRUARY 21, 2017.]

2013–064. PRE–TRIAL CONFERENCES

IN THE CIRCUIT COURT, SIXTH JUDICIAL CIRCUIT IN AND FOR PASCO AND PINELLAS COUNTIES, FLORIDA

ADMINISTRATIVE ORDER NO. 2013–064 PA/PI–CIR

RE: PRE–TRIAL CONFERENCES

Rule 1.200(c) of the Florida Rules of Civil Procedure requires that orders setting pre-trial conferences be uniform throughout the territorial jurisdiction of the Court.

A committee of Judges in the Sixth Judicial Circuit, chaired by Circuit Judge Stan Mills, has undertaken a review of the existing pre-trial conference orders to update and improve these orders. The committee sought input from local Bar Associations including the Clearwater Bar Association, the St. Petersburg Bar Association, and the West Pasco Bar Association. A Joint Bar Committee was formed that provided valuable input. The final recommendation adopted in this Administrative Order represents significant effort by the Bench and Bar, and is a substantial change from the existing procedures.

In order to update the uniform pre-trial conference orders and in accordance with Article V, section 2, of the Florida Constitution, Rule of Judicial Administration 2.215, and § 43.26, Florida Statutes, it is

ORDERED:

Effective November 1, 2013, the attached Orders and Procedures shall be utilized in setting pre-trial conferences within the Sixth Judicial Circuit Court. These Orders and Procedures may not be changed unless a majority of the judges assigned to the civil divisions in Pasco and Pinellas Counties have agreed to the changes. All changes must be uniform and adopted by administrative order of the Chief Judge.

Administrative Order PA/PI–CIR–98–49 is rescinded November 1, 2013.

DONE AND ORDERED in Chambers at Clearwater, Pinellas County, Florida, this ___ day of October, 2013.

ORIGINAL SIGNED ON OCTOBER 3, 2013
BY J. THOMAS MCGRADY
CHIEF JUDGE

Attachments:

Order Setting Jury Trial and Pre–Trial Conference

Notice Regarding Scheduling of Expert Witnesses for Trial Testimony to be Served with Trial Subpoena

Uniform Pre–Trial Conference Order (Jury Trial)

IN THE CIRCUIT COURT FOR THE SIXTH JUDICIAL CIRCUIT IN AND FOR PASCO/PINELLAS COUNTY, FLORIDA

CIVIL DIVISION

Case No. ____________

Plaintiff(s),

vs.

Defendant(s).

ORDER SETTING JURY TRIAL AND PRE–TRIAL CONFERENCE

Pre-trial Date and time:
Jury Trial Date and time:
*Note paragraph 15 regarding any conflicts with this trial date.

Judge:
Location:____________

I hereby certify that a copy of this Order has been furnished by U.S. Mail [or other approved delivery method] this ___ day of ________, 20 ___, to:

____

Judicial Assistant

THIS CAUSE being at issue and the Court being otherwise fully advised in the premises, it is hereby

ORDERED AND ADJUDGED as follows:

PRE–TRIAL CONFERENCE

1. A pre-trial conference shall be held as noticed on the preceding cover page.

JURY TRIAL

2. A jury trial shall be held as noticed on the preceding cover page.

WITNESS AND EXHIBIT DISCLOSURE

3. At least 60 days before the pre-trial conference, counsel for all parties, and any unrepresented party, shall serve opposing counsel and any unrepresented party and **file directly** with the clerk:

a) a list of the names and addresses of all lay and expert witnesses who are expected to testify at trial, whether for substantive, corroborative, impeachment or rebuttal purposes.

b) In addition to names and addresses of each expert retained to formulate an expert opinion, the parties shall provide:

1. the subject matter about which the expert is expected to testify;

2. the substance of the facts and opinions about which the expert is expected to testify;

3. a summary of the grounds for each opinion;

4. a copy of any written reports issued by the expert regarding this case; and

5. a copy of the expert's curriculum vitae.

c) a list of all exhibits which are expected to be admitted at trial whether for substantive, demonstrative, corroborative, impeachment or rebuttal purposes.

4. At least 45 days before the pre-trial conference, counsel for all parties, and any pro se party, may serve a list of additional witnesses and exhibits as described above.

5. Witnesses and exhibits which are not listed as described above may provide testimony or be admitted at trial only upon stipulation of all parties or as allowed by order of the court **at or before** the pre-trial conference.

6. At least 60 days before the pre-trial conference, counsel for each defendant shall serve a list of the names and addresses of all non-parties (Fabre defendants) defendant intends to request the Court to include on the verdict form.

COMPLETION OF DISCOVERY

7. All depositions and discovery, including all examinations of persons conducted pursuant to Fla. R. Civ. P. 1.360, must be completed at least 45 days prior to the pre-trial conference or, **if agreed to by all parties**, up to the date of the Pre–Trial Conference. All reports of any examination conducted pursuant to Fla.R.Civ.P.1.360 shall be served no later than 30 days prior to the pre-trial conference. Depositions and discovery after the pre-trial conference shall be permitted only as allowed by order of the court. However, the deposition of any examiner pursuant to Fla. R. Civ. P. 1.360 shall be allowed without order of court any time within 30 days of service of their report and more than 10 days prior to the date trial is scheduled to commence. Any discovery requiring a response from the adverse party must be served in time for the response to be due prior to the deadline date established herein. Unavailability of hearing times on motions prior to the Pre–Trial Conference shall not be grounds for extension of deadlines or continuation of the Pre–Trial Conference or Trial, absent exceptional circumstances, as determined by the court.

8. At the deposition of any expert witness taken within the time periods set forth in this order and in answering any interrogatories concerning expert witnesses which were served by the party submitting such interrogatories within 45 days of the pre-trial conference, all expert witnesses shall provide, and all parties shall provide (1) complete information regarding the witness' qualifications as an expert; (2) the subject matter upon which the expert witness is expected to testify; (3) the substance of the facts and opinions to which the expert witness is expected to testify; and (4) a summary of the grounds for each opinion. If the expert is not prepared to fully testify regarding such matters at a deposition scheduled within 45 days of the pre-trial or if a party does not provide complete information regarding such matters in answering interrogatories served within 45 days of the pre-trial conference, the court will consider excluding the testimony of the expert at trial or, in the alternative, limit the testimony of the expert to those matters revealed at any such deposition or in answers to any such interrogatories. Pursuant to Fla. R. Civ. P. 1.280(b)(4)(C), the party seeking this discovery shall pay experts a reasonable fee for the time spent in responding to discovery and pay the responding party a fair part of the fees and expenses reasonably incurred by the responding party in obtaining facts and opinions from the expert, such payment to be made after an expert deposition or service of expert interrogatory answers. Objections made at expert witness depositions taken pursuant to this paragraph **must** be resolved by agreement or by properly bringing them before the court in such a manner as to not result in delay of the trial and, in any event, before the date the trial is to begin. Failure to comply with this paragraph may result in removal of the case from the trial calendar or such other sanctions as may appear appropriate. While the court is prohibited from appointing a general or special master/magistrate without the consent of the parties, the parties should feel free to agree upon a master/magistrate to resolve such objections, if hearing time before the court is not available. Any such master/magistrate shall be governed by Rule 1.490, Fla.R.Civ.P. Care must be taken to allow sufficient time for compliance with the time periods set forth in the rule.

9. Deposition Designations. Except as set forth in paragraph 7 above, no later than 5 days prior to the Pre–Trial Conference, each party shall serve designations of depositions (video or otherwise) each party intends to offer as testimony in their case-in-chief. No later than 3 days prior to the Pre–Trial Conference, each opposing party shall serve counter designations to portions of depositions designated, together with objections to the depositions, or portions thereof, originally designated. No later than the Pre–Trial Conference, each party shall serve their objections to counter designations served by an opposing party. All such objections **must** be resolved prior to the first day of trial or will be considered waived. Video depositions to be shown at trial must be appropriately edited **prior to trial.** Failure to comply with this paragraph may result in removal from the trial calendar or such other sanctions as may appear appropriate.

MOTIONS

10. All motions, including motions in limine, shall be filed and served at least 3 days prior to the pre-trial conference and, unless good cause exists why the motions were not heard previously, such motions **must** be heard prior to the first day of trial. All motions to continue or motions to allow deposition after the pre-trial conference based on witness unavailability must be served prior to the pre-trial conference, unless good cause exists for such failure. All motions in limine must relate to specific evidence to be adduced at trial. The court will not hear or consider "boiler-plate" motions in limine. Examples of "boiler-plate" motions in limine are motions seeking the exclusion of "golden rule" arguments in closing, motions seeking to prevent counsel from expressing personal beliefs, etc. The court will assume that all trial counsel are aware of the rules of evidence. All *Frye/Daubert* motions shall be heard prior to the Pre–Trial Conference. Any party seeking to exclude evidence under a *Frye/Daubert* analysis shall file a motion identifying the specific basis for the *Frye/Daubert* challenge. All *Frye/Daubert* motions not scheduled and heard before the Pre–Trial Conference will be considered waived, absent exceptional circumstances.

TRIAL WITNESSES

11. The parties shall, **prior to the pre-trial conference,** contact each witness they will call at trial to determine their availability to appear at trial.

12. A copy of the Notice titled "Notice Regarding Scheduling of Experts for Trial Testimony" attached hereto **shall be provided to any expert witness subpoenaed as an expert witness for trial, no later than 10 days prior to trial.**

PRE–TRIAL CONFERENCE

13. Prior to the pre-trial conference, the attorneys and pro se parties are directed to meet together by agreement instigated by counsel for the Plaintiff, and draft one proposed pre-trial conference order (using the form attached) that shall be submitted **directly** to the court (submit original and a copy for each party) at least **3 days** prior to the pre-trial conference. In the event the parties are unable to agree on any matter in the pre-trial conference order, they shall leave the matter blank and the court will resolve the dispute at the pre-trial conference. The parties shall also discuss the possibility of settlement, stipulate to as many facts and issues as possible, examine all exhibits and demonstrative aids (including any to be used in opening statement, unless they are completely unaltered enlargements or compilations of items already disclosed in discovery, in which case, they may be exchanged the morning the trial is to begin), review all video depositions and complete all other matters which may expedite both the Pre–Trial Conference and the Trial of this case. **This meeting is mandatory and cannot be waived by agreement of the parties.**

14. The court will consider all matters as may be appropriate as set forth in Fla. R. Civ. P. 1.200.

15. At the pre-trial conference, each pro se litigant will appear and each represented party will be represented by lead trial counsel or at least one of the attorneys who will participate in the trial and is authorized to make binding decisions. Any attorney or party having conflicts with the trial date set forth above must provide the court and opposing counsel/party with written notification of such conflict (including, at a minimum, the court, case number and the date any conflicting trial was set), as soon as practicable but, in no event later than the pre-trial conference. **The court and opposing counsel shall be provided written notification immediately in the event any such conflicts are resolved.**

16. At the pre-trial conference, counsel and pro se litigants shall be prepared to negotiate settlement. Counsel shall have full authority to make stipulations and to settle the case or have available by telephone, or in person, a party or representative who does have full authority to make stipulations and to settle the case.

17. Any request for a "view" must be made at the pre-trial conference and included in the pre-trial order.

18. Any claim for statutory preference or advancement on the trial calendar not previously made **must** be made immediately and **must** be clearly stated and discussed at the pre-trial conference. Failure to comply with this paragraph may be considered a waiver of any such claim.

MEETING PRIOR TO TRIAL

19. The attorneys for the parties and all pro se litigants are directed to meet at least 5 days before the commencement of trial, to:

a) mark all exhibits for identification and prepare a chronological exhibit list for use of clerk and court at trial (actual exhibits and documentation evidence shall be available for inspection at this time);

b) admit or not admit items as evidence and list specific objections, if any;

c) stipulate as to any matter of fact and/or law about which there is no issue, to avoid unnecessary proof;

d) review all depositions which are to be offered for any purpose other than impeachment, to resolve objections to the portions to be offered in evidence;

e) discuss the possibility of settlement;

f) submit an itemized statement of special damages plaintiff expects to prove;

g) discuss and complete any other matters which may simplify the issues or aid in the speedy disposition of this action, its pre-trial conference and trial.

20. At the meeting prior to commencement of trial, each party will be represented by one of the attorneys who will participate in the trial and all pro se litigants. Such attorney or individual shall be vested with full authority to make all inspections, stipulations, agreements and admissions as described above.

21. Additional Exhibits, Witnesses or Objections. At trial, the parties shall be strictly limited to exhibits and witnesses disclosed and objections reserved on the schedules attached to the Pre–Trial Order, absent agreement specifically stated in the Pre–Trial Order or order of the Court, upon good cause shown. Failure to reserve objections will constitute a waiver. A party desiring to use an exhibit or witness not disclosed when counsel conferred pursuant to paragraphs 13 and 19 of this order shall immediately furnish the Court and opposing counsel with a complete description of the exhibit or with the witness' name and address, the expected subject matter of the witness' testimony and the reason for the late discovery of the witness or exhibit. Use of the exhibit or witness may be allowed by the Court for good cause shown or to prevent manifest injustice.

22. Unique Questions of Law. Prior to the Pre–Trial Conference, counsel for the parties are directed to exchange and simultaneously submit to the Court appropriate memoranda, with citations of legal authority, in support of any unique legal questions which may reasonably be expected to arise during the course of the trial.

JURY INSTRUCTIONS

23. No later than 3 days before the Pre–Trial Conference, the Plaintiff shall provide to the Court a complete set of proposed jury instructions and verdict form(s), with a copy to opposing counsel and any pro se litigant. The Defendant(s) shall provide only special instructions or those standard instructions not included in the proposal submitted by Plaintiff, together with any specific objections to the instructions submitted by Plaintiff and shall do so no later than the date of the Pre–Trial Conference. All instructions submitted to the Court shall be by email or by disc or flash-drive and shall be in Microsoft Word format. All instructions shall be in a form suitable for submission to the jury and, in the case of standard instructions, shall bear the number and title assigned in the standard instructions approved by the Florida Supreme Court. The jury instructions electronically submitted to the Court are for purposes of permitting the Court to provide the jury with written instructions for their use during deliberations and should be "clean", i.e., they should make no reference to the party submitting the instructions or citations to supporting authority. These requirements are completely separate from anything the parties intend to submit to the Clerk for purposes of any appellate record. This paragraph shall not foreclose the right of each party to seek to modify instructions up to and including the instruction conference at the close of evidence.

TRIAL

24. Counsel for the parties shall be required to bring blank notepads and advertising-free pens to trial for the jury to take notes. Jurors will be permitted to submit questions for consideration by the Court and Counsel after the completion of each witness' examination by the parties.

25. The parties shall be prepared to discuss the time required for voir dire at the pre-trial conference, keeping in mind that voir dire is for selection of a fair and impartial jury, not for argument or "conditioning" the jurors. The parties should attempt to agree on a reasonable time for voir dire, however, it must be understood that the Court will have the final decision on the length of voir dire.

26. The parties shall be prepared to discuss the time required for opening statements at the pre-trial conference. The parties should attempt to agree on a reasonable time for opening statement, however, it must be understood that the Court will have the final decision on the length of opening statements.

27. The parties shall be prepared to discuss the time required for closing arguments at the pre-trial conference. The parties should attempt to agree on a reasonable time for closing arguments, however, it must be understood that the Court will have the final decision on the length of closing arguments.

NOTICE OF SETTLEMENT

28. Counsel and pro se litigants shall immediately provide **written** notification to the court in the event of settlement, and promptly submit a stipulation for an order of dismissal and a final disposition form. Written notification shall include fax transmission and email sent to the Court, with copies to all counsel. Failure to provide **written** notification of settlement to the court may result in sanctions against parties and/or counsel, including, but not limited to, fines equal to the expense incurred in summoning a jury, when a trial is not conducted.

29. All provisions of this order that require compliance by counsel are likewise applicable to any party appearing pro se.

SANCTIONS

30. Failure to comply with the requirements of this Order shall subject counsel and pro se litigants to such sanctions as the court shall determine just and proper under the circumstances. Such sanctions may include, but are not limited to, striking of pleadings, dismissal of case and monetary sanctions.

31. PLEASE REVIEW THIS ORDER TO SEE THAT IT HAS BEEN SENT TO ALL PROPER PARTIES/COUNSEL, AT PROPER ADDRESSES. FAILURE TO IMMEDIATELY NOTIFY THE COURT OF ANY ERRORS MAY RESULT IN REMOVAL FROM THE TRIAL CALENDAR, ALONG WITH POSSIBLE SANCTIONS.

DONE AND ORDERED in Chambers, at __________, ___ County, Florida, this ___ day of ________, 20 ___.

____

Circuit/County Judge

IN THE CIRCUIT COURT FOR THE SIXTH JUDICIAL CIRCUIT IN AND FOR PASCO/PINELLAS COUNTY, FLORIDA

CIVIL DIVISION

NOTICE REGARDING SCHEDULING OF EXPERT WITNESSES FOR TRIAL TESTIMONY TO BE SERVED WITH TRIAL SUBPOENA

Many different cases are set for civil jury trial by the Court on the same day at the same time. Usually all cases are scheduled to begin at 9:00 a.m. on Monday mornings. Consequently, the lawyer requesting your testimony at trial in this case will not know when during a one or two week trial period your testimony will be needed. It is for this reason that experts are subpoenaed for the trial period and a definite time for your testimony is rarely able to be set in advance. The expert is, therefore, placed on “standby” or “alert” status. The lawyer will periodically keep you advised as to the progress of the trial so that you will have as much advance notice as possible, hopefully resulting in a minimal disruption to your routine schedule. If you have been subpoenaed for trial and it is subsequently determined that your testimony will not be needed, the lawyer will notify you as soon as that determination has been made. If you are going to be unavailable during the trial period, you should immediately notify the lawyer subpoenaing you so that lawyer may take action he or she deems appropriate.

IN THE CIRCUIT COURT FOR THE SIXTH JUDICIAL CIRCUIT IN AND FOR PASCO/PINELLAS COUNTY, FLORIDA

CIVIL DIVISION

________________,
Plaintiff(s), Case No.:
UCN:

vs.

________________,
Defendant(s).

____________________ /

UNIFORM PRE–TRIAL CONFERENCE ORDER (JURY TRIAL)

On this date, the parties to this action and/or their respective attorneys appeared before the court at a Pre-trial Conference, pursuant to Rule 1.200, Florida Rules of Civil Procedure. The following action was taken:

APPEARING FOR PLAINTIFF(S):

APPEARING FOR DEFENDANT(S):

1. CONCISE AND NEUTRAL STATEMENT OF THE CASE:

2. ISSUES:

3. ADMISSIONS:

4. STIPULATIONS AND WAIVERS:

(Yes or No)

a) Less than 6 jurors if one becomes incapacitated. ____

b) Use of expert testimony at any time during trial as a result of unavailability at other time. ____

c) Waive technicians for imaging studies identified in discovery to date. ____

d) Waive records custodians for documents produced in discovery to date. This is **not** the equivalent of a stipulation to the admissibility of the documents in question. ____

e) Copies of ordinances or foreign laws. ____

f) Other: ____

5. PLEADINGS:

A list of pleadings upon which the case will be tried, including the date of filing for each.

6. REMAINING MATTERS:

A list of all remaining matters that require action by the Court, including the dates of filing for any motions:

7. PARTIES AND WITNESSES:

a) Special needs:

b) Interpreter:

c) Limitations on the number of witnesses (e.g. expert witnesses, before and after witnesses, etc.):

8. A LIST OF SPECIAL DAMAGES CLAIMED IS ATTACHED.

9. JURY PREEMPTORY CHALLENGES PER LITIGANT:

10. ESTIMATED LENGTH OF THE CASE IN CHIEF FOR EACH LITIGANT AND THE ENTIRE TRIAL, INCLUDING VOIR DIRE:

11. MAXIMUM NUMBER OF TRIAL DAYS, EXCLUDING JURY SELECTION: ________.

12. SETTLEMENT POSSIBILITIES:

13. THE __________ IS RESPONSIBLE FOR ATTENDANCE OF THE COURT REPORTER.

14. ADDITIONAL MATTERS:

15. THE PARTIES WILL COMPLY WITH THE UNIFORM ORDER SETTING TRIAL AND PRE–TRIAL CONFERENCE SPECIFICALLY REGARDING MEETING PRIOR TO TRIAL AND ACTIONS TO BE TAKEN ON THE FIRST DAY OF TRIAL.

16. FAILURE TO COMPLY WITH THE REQUIREMENTS OF THIS ORDER WILL SUBJECT THE PARTY AND/OR COUNSEL TO APPROPRIATE SANCTIONS.

DONE AND ORDERED in Chambers, at ________, ________ County, Florida, this ___ day of ________, 201 ___.

____
Circuit/County Judge

2013–063. VETERANS TREATMENT COURT

IN THE CIRCUIT COURT, SIXTH JUDICIAL CIRCUIT IN AND FOR PASCO AND PINELLAS COUNTIES, FLORIDA

ADMINISTRATIVE ORDER NO. 2013–063 PA/PI–CIR

RE: VETERANS TREATMENT COURT

The Florida Legislature has appropriated non-recurring general revenue funds to the Sixth Judicial Circuit for the purpose of creating pretrial felony or misdemeanor veterans' treatment intervention programs in accordance with sections 948.08 and 948.16, Florida Statutes. See Ch. 2013–40, Line Item 3203. In addition, Pinellas County has received a grant from the Substance Abuse and Mental Health Services Administration to establish a Veterans Treatment Court.

In order to create a Veterans Treatment Court docket in Pasco and Pinellas Counties and identify the defendants to be served, and in accordance with Article V, section 2, of the Florida Constitution, Rule of Judicial Administration 2.215, and § 43.26, Florida Statutes, it is

ORDERED:

1. The purpose of Veterans Treatment Court, ("VTC"), is to comprehensively address, through collaboration between the court system, treatment providers, and the United States Department of Veterans Affairs, the service-related mental health and substance abuse issues of certain veterans and members of the United States Armed Forces who are charged with criminal offenses. The goal is to reduce recidivism through treatment.

2. The Clerk of the Circuit Court for Pasco County (Pasco Clerk) is directed to create a new docket in sections 30 and 31 of the Criminal Division. The Clerk of the Circuit Court for Pinellas County (Pinellas Clerk) is directed to create a new docket in section N of the Criminal Division. The Clerks shall not assign criminal cases on a random basis to these sections as provided in Local Rule 3, rather cases shall be assigned as further specified in this Administrative Order.

3. The State Attorney's Office (State Attorney) will accept and review applications for VTC. The State Attorney shall identify those applicants who meet the eligibility criteria for either Criteria Set One or for Criteria Set Two. The eligibility criteria are listed in Attachment A. In making the initial determination of eligibility, the State Attorney will consider, among other things, the facts of the case, the input of the victim, the defendant's criminal record, and the defendant's relevant service records. If a defense attorney desires to have a case heard in VTC, he or she must submit an application to the State Attorney. Regardless of eligibility for VTC, the State Attorney will refer all applicants for VTC to the appropriate Veterans Administration Judicial Outreach Coordinator.

4. Cases of eligible defendants may be initially filed in VTC by the State Attorney or may be transferred to VTC from another criminal section upon written notification by the State Attorney to the Administrative Office of the Courts. Cases may be transferred to VTC pre-plea or post-plea, however, post-plea cases may only be transferred if funds other than those appropriated in Ch. 2013–40, Line Item 3203, are used.

5. While the State Attorney makes the initial determination of eligibility, judicial approval is required to participate in VTC. If the Court decides that a case will not remain on the VTC calendar, the State Attorney and the defense attorney shall be notified. If the case was initially filed in VTC, the applicable Clerk shall transfer the case to another criminal section within the county in accordance with Local Rule 3. If the case was transferred to VTC from another criminal section, the applicable Clerk shall transfer the case back to that section.

6. The Circuit Court Judges assigned to VTC will handle both misdemeanor and felony cases. Pursuant to Administrative Order 2013–060, and subsequent administrative orders, the assigned Circuit Court Judge may proceed as an acting County Court Judge to hear misdemeanor cases in VTC.

7. Participating in VTC is voluntary. At any point, a defendant may elect not to have his or her case heard in VTC. Upon such an election, the applicable Clerk shall transfer the defendant's case to another criminal section within the county in accordance with Local Rule 3, or, if the defendant's case was transferred to VTC from another criminal section, the applicable Clerk shall transfer the case back to that section.

8. By agreeing to have his or her case heard in VTC, the defendant waives the right to a speedy trial. The defendant also agrees that no depositions will be taken, trial dates scheduled, or substantive pre-trial motions heard. If a pretrial motion must be heard, the case shall be transferred to a regular criminal section.

9. Each defendant only has one opportunity to have his or her case heard in VTC. If a defendant is charged with a new offense and has already had a prior case heard and resolved in VTC, the case cannot be scheduled on the VTC calendar without specific approval from the State Attorney.

10. A defendant who applies or participates in VTC must voluntarily and truthfully provide information to aid VTC at each step of the process. To participate in VTC, the defendant must submit to a mental health and substance abuse assessment. This assessment will evaluate the defendant's mental health and substance abuse issues and the resources needed for proper treatment. The assessment will help determine the defendant's eligibility for VTC and assist the Court in fashioning an appropriate sentence. The mental health and substance abuse assessment must use objective standards and criteria and must be conducted by the Court's licensed contract provider.

11. Prior to submitting to the mental health and substance abuse assessment, the defendant must execute a written consent form with a waiver of confidentiality as outlined in 42 C.F.R § 2.31 for records made confidential under 42 U.S.C.S. 290dd–2, Fla. Stat. § 397.501, and Fla. Stat. § 394.4615. If the defendant refuses to execute the written consent or provide any other information necessary for VTC, the defendant's case shall not be filed in or transferred to VTC. To the extent already filed in or transferred to VTC, the applicable Clerk shall transfer the case to another criminal section within the county in accordance with Local Rule 3 or shall transfer it to the section from which it was transferred, respectively.

12. In Pasco County, no more than 75 persons may be in VTC at any one time. The Administrative Office of the Courts shall notify the State Attorney when VTC does not have the capacity for additional defendants. If there are 75 persons in Pasco County VTC and the State Attorney identifies additional persons who are eligible for VTC, the State Attorney may request that the Chief Judge authorize additional persons for VTC. The Chief Judge may authorize additional persons if resources permit.

13. In Pinellas County, no more than 150 persons may be in VTC at any one time. The Administrative Office of the Courts shall notify the State Attorney when VTC does not have the capacity for additional defendants. If there are 150 persons in Pinellas County VTC and the State Attorney identifies additional persons who are eligible for VTC, the State Attorney may request that the Chief Judge authorize additional persons for VTC. The Chief Judge may authorize additional persons if resources permit.

14. The sanctions imposed in VTC are within the Court's discretion, and include but are not limited to outpatient treatment programs, non-secure residential treatment programs, and intensive, secure, long-term residential treatment programs. Other conditions of probation may be ordered, such as anger management, Batterer's Intervention Program or other domestic violence counseling, random drug testing, a requirement to obtain a G.E.D, or a requirement to participate in transitional housing and related services.

15. The sanctions imposed in VTC for violating probation are within the Court's discretion. The judge may continue probation, may revoke probation and order a new term of probation, may impose a term of incarceration in either the county jail or Department of Corrections, as provided by the Criminal Punishment Code, or impose any other sanction authorized by law.

16. Every defendant participating in VTC must periodically return to court for a judicial review. The purpose of a judicial review is to assess the defendant's level of participation in treatment, monitor the overall success of treatment, and admonish or encourage the defendant in his or her attempt at rehabilitation. Prior to a judicial review, the judge may hold a case staffing with treatment providers, Court staff, probation personnel, the defendant's counsel, assistant state attorneys, and others selected by the judge.

17. Defendants who entered VTC pre-plea and who successfully complete and graduate from VTC may have their charges dismissed. Defendants who entered VTC post-plea and who successfully complete and graduate from VTC may have an adjudication of guilt withheld or receive a reduced probationary period. The VTC judge will review a defendant's successful completion of the assigned treatment and make the ultimate decision of whether a defendant may graduate from VTC.

18. The Administrative Office of the Courts will facilitate the process by which a defendant is assessed; coordinate the procedure by which the written assessment is furnished to the State Attorney, defense counsel, and judge; assist the court in managing its caseload; compile statistics; maintain the necessary documents to demonstrate compliance with any funding requirements, prepare the cases scheduled on the VTC calendar; schedule initial appointments with treatment providers; and perform other case management functions for the court as required.

DONE AND ORDERED in Chambers at Clearwater, Pinellas County, Florida, this ___ day of October, 2013.

ORIGINAL SIGNED ON OCTOBER 1, 2013
BY J. THOMAS MCGRADY
CHIEF JUDGE

ATTACHMENT A

Eligibility Criteria for Veterans Treatment Court

Criteria Set One

The following criteria apply if funds appropriated in Ch. 2013–40, Line Item 3203 are used to fund the veteran's treatment intervention program:

1. The defendant is a veteran as defined by section 1.01, Florida Statute, or servicemember, as defined by section 250.01, Florida Statute;

2. The defendant suffers from a military service-related mental illness, traumatic brain injury, substance abuse disorder, or psychological problem;

3. The charge or charges are misdemeanors or felonies, other than a felony listed in 948.06(8)(c);

4. The defendant has not entered a plea or been adjudicated on the charge or charges prior to entry into the section that includes VTC; and

5. The defendant has not previously participated in VTC, unless this criterion is specifically waived by the State Attorney's Office.

Criteria Set Two

The following criteria apply if funds other than those appropriated in Ch. 2013–40, Line Item 3203 are used to fund the veteran's treatment intervention program:

1. The defendant has served or is serving in the United States Armed Forces, as defined in 10 U.S.C. § 101(a)(4);

2. The defendant suffers from a military service-related mental illness, traumatic brain injury, substance abuse disorder, or psychological problem;

3. The charge or charges are misdemeanors or third-degree felonies; and

4. The defendant has not previously participated in VTC, unless this criterion is specifically waived by the State Attorney's Office.

2013–053. FORECLOSURE CASE STATUS REPORTING AND SERVICE LISTS

IN THE CIRCUIT COURT, SIXTH JUDICIAL CIRCUIT IN AND FOR PASCO AND PINELLAS COUNTIES, FLORIDA

ADMINISTRATIVE ORDER NO. 2013–053 PI–CIR

RE: FORECLOSURE CASE STATUS REPORTING AND SERVICE LISTS

Through Administrative Order No. 2013–036 PI–CIR, the Chief Judge directed the implementation of circuit civil section 33 to help manage the backlog of residential mortgage foreclosure cases in Pinellas County. Since then, the Pinellas Clerk has reassigned all open commercial foreclosure cases, homestead residential foreclosure cases, and non-homestead residential foreclosure cases filed in Pinellas County prior to January 1, 2013, to section 33. Clarifying case status and properly identifying service lists for providing proper notice to parties in pending residential foreclosure cases will further improve the handling of those cases in section 33.

Therefore, in accordance with Article V, section 2, Florida Constitution, Rules of Judicial Administration 2.215, and § 43.26, Florida Statutes, it is

ORDERED:

1. Plaintiff's counsel for each pending residential mortgage foreclosure case filed in Pinellas County before December 31, 2011, except as provided in paragraph 2 below, must provide the Court with the following.

a. An accurate and fully executed Plaintiff's Foreclosure Case Status Form, which is Attachment A to this Administrative Order. All parties listed on the Complaint must be addressed in the Foreclosure Case Status Form.

b. A current, accurate service list for ALL parties, including Plaintiff's counsel, Defense counsel, and pro se Defendants as appropriate, with mail and e-mail addresses;

c. Pre–addressed, postage paid standard business size mailing envelopes for the entire Service List with the case number referenced on the face of the envelopes;

For this Administrative Order, a "pending" case is one in which a final judgment has not been entered, or one with a vacated previously entered final judgment.

2. The requirements of this Administrative Order are not applicable to plaintiffs that are an Association governed by Chapters 718, 719, 720, or 723, Florida Statutes.

3. The Plaintiff's counsel must provide the Court with the documents and envelopes specified in paragraph 1 within the applicable timeline as follows:

a. The deadline for receipt for cases filed in 2008 or earlier is September 30, 2013

b. The deadline for receipt for cases filed in 2009 is December 2, 2013

c. The deadline for receipt for cases filed in 2010 is April 30, 2014

d. The deadline for receipt for cases filed in 2011 is September 30, 2014

4. The Plaintiff's counsel shall deliver the required documents and envelopes to: Foreclosure Case Managers, 545 1st Avenue North, Room 103, St. Petersburg, FL 33701. Early submissions are encouraged and accepted. Please do not hold these items until the deadline. Partial timely deliveries are encouraged.

5. For each applicable case, Plaintiff must also file with the Pinellas Clerk a notice of compliance with this Administrative Order with copies of the Foreclosure Case Status Form and the Service List.

6. Nothing in this Administrative Order precludes a party from scheduling appropriate cases for hearings. Plaintiffs are encouraged to visit the Court's website at www.jud6.org for the latest information about foreclosure case scheduling procedures. Failure to comply with this Administrative Order may result in the imposition of sanctions, including contempt of court or dismissal of the action.

DONE AND ORDERED in Chambers at Clearwater, Pinellas County, Florida this ___ day of September 2013.

ORIGINAL SIGNED ON SEPTEMBER 4, 2013
BY J. THOMAS MCGRADY,
CHIEF JUDGE

Attachment A: Plaintiff's Foreclosure Case Status Form

IN THE CIRCUIT COURT FOR THE SIXTH JUDICIAL CIRCUIT IN AND FOR PINELLAS COUNTY, FLORIDA CIVIL DIVISION

Plaintiff(s),

v. **REF #:**
UCN:

Defendant(s).
____________________/

PLAINTIFF'S FORECLOSURE CASE STATUS FORM

1. **Outstanding Motion to Dismiss?** Yes or No. **Currently set?** Yes or No. If "yes" date of hearing __________
2. **Outstanding Motion for Default filed?** Yes or No. If "yes", when filed __________
3. **Is this case at issue?** (See Fla.R.Civ.P. 1.440(a)) Yes or No. __________
4. **Amount of time needed for trial:** __________

NAME OF DEFENDANT(S) (Every defendant MUST be listed)	DATE AND METHOD OF SERVICE (Personal, Publication, or Substitute)	STATUS OF DEFENDANT(S) (Dropped, Default entered, Represented, or filed Pro Se Answer)	AFFIRMATIVE DEFENSES FILED ["yes or no". If "yes", include when.]	REPLY TO AFFIRMATIVE DEFENSES ["yes or no". If "yes", include when.]

5. ___ (initial) **I have attached a service list for ALL parties.**

As counsel of record for the Plaintiff/Lender and as an officer of the court, I declare that I have read the foregoing Foreclosure Case Status Form and that the facts stated in it are true.

DATED: ______________ ______________

(Attorney Signature)
Attorney Name:
Attorney for Plaintiff/Lender(s):
Address:
Direct Telephone Number:
Fax Number:
Florida Bar No.:

2013–051. [RESCINDED BY ORDER 2017–008, EFFECTIVE FEBRUARY 9, 2017.]

2013–034. PROCEEDINGS TO PROHIBIT PURCHASE OF FIREARMS BY THE MENTALLY ILL

IN THE CIRCUIT COURT, SIXTH JUDICIAL CIRCUIT IN AND FOR PASCO AND PINELLAS COUNTIES, FLORIDA

ADMINISTRATIVE ORDER NO. 2013–034 PA/PI–CIR

RE: PROCEEDINGS TO PROHIBIT PURCHASE OF FIREARMS BY THE MENTALLY ILL

The Legislature has enacted HB 1355, which became Ch. 2013–249, Laws of Fla. This bill, entitled "An act relating to the purchase of firearms by mentally ill persons," establishes a procedure so that certain persons voluntarily admitted for mental health treatment will be prohibited from purchasing a firearm. This Act does not change existing procedures to report involuntary admissions and the resulting prohibition on such persons purchasing a firearm. The Act does create a new matter to be brought before the Court for persons voluntarily admitted with time limits established by law. Accordingly, new procedures need to be established in the Sixth Judicial Circuit.

As specified in the Act, within 24 hours of a qualifying patient's agreement to a voluntary admission to a mental institution, the administrator of the receiving or treatment facility must file with the Clerk of the Circuit Court (Clerk):

a. The examining physician's finding that the person is an imminent danger to himself/herself or others, including a description of the person's behavior that led to the finding;

b. The examining physician's certification that if the patient did not agree to voluntary treatment that a petition for involuntary outpatient or inpatient treatment would have been filed under § 394.463(2)(i)4, Fla. Stat., or a petition for involuntary treatment was filed and the patient subsequently agreed to voluntary treatment prior to a court hearing on the petition;

c. Written notice of the examining physician's finding and certification that the patient received prior to agreeing to voluntary treatment, which contained a statement that the patient would be prohibited from purchasing a firearm and would not be eligible to apply for or retain a concealed weapon or firearm license under § 790.06, Fla. Stat.; and

d. The patient's written acknowledgment that he/she understands the above described findings.

The Act also requires the Clerk to transmit the filing to the Court within 24 hours and to transmit the Court's order to the Florida Department of Law Enforcement within 24 hours of receipt of the order.

The Act does not specify a method of computing these 24 hour time periods. Rule of Judicial Administration 2.514, provides that when a statute does not specify a method of computing time, time is computed as specified in the Rule. Rule 2.514(2)(c) provides that when the period is stated in hours, and when a time period would end on a Saturday, Sunday, or legal holiday, or during any period of time extended through an order of the Chief Justice, the period continues to run until the same time on the next day that is not a Saturday, Sunday, or legal holiday and does not fall within any period of time extended through an order of the Chief Justice.

In accordance with Article V, section 2, Florida Constitution, Rules of Judicial Administration 2.215 and 2.514, and § 43.26, Florida Statutes, it is

ORDERED:

1. The Clerks of the Circuit Court (Clerks) are directed to comply with the statutory time periods as computed in accordance with Rule of Judicial Administration 2.514. The Clerk is not required to perform any duties required under the Act on weekends, holidays, or during periods of time extended by the Chief Justice.

2. When the Clerk of the Circuit Court receives a filing to exclude a voluntarily admitted patient from purchasing a firearm, the Clerk must, within 24 hours of receipt of the filing, present the filings to the Court. The 24–hour period shall be computed as provided in Rule of Judicial Administration 2.514(a)(2).

a. In Pinellas County, the filings must be provided to the Magistrate's office in the Probate and Guardianship Division who will review the matter with the Probate Administrative Judge or another probate judge. If a probate judge is unavailable, the Magistrate's office will submit it to the duty judge.

b. In Pasco County, the filings must be provided to the Probate Judge. If the Probate Judge is unavailable, the filings must be submitted to the civil judge assigned to section G. If neither the probate judge nor the judge assigned to section G is available, the filings must be submitted to the duty judge.

3. The judge reviewing the matter may use Attachment A, Confidential Ex Parte Order Directing Entry of Record in FDLE's Database of Persons Prohibited From Purchasing Firearms or Attachment B, Confidential Ex Parte Interim Order Requiring Further Documentation On Voluntary Commitment.

4. In the event the Clerk has not received an order from the Court within 24 hours after submission of the filings to the judge(s) as described above, the Clerk is directed to forthwith notify the Chief Judge by telephone or e-mail. The 24–hour period shall be computed as provided in Rule of Judicial Administration 2.514(a)(2).

5. If the Court orders that the record be submitted to the Florida Department of Law Enforcement, the Clerk must submit it to the FDLE within 24 hours of receipt of the order from the Court. The 24–hour period shall be computed as provided in Rule of Judicial Administration 2.514(a)(2).

6. The Clerks of Pasco County and Pinellas County are directed to

a. Develop a new case type or docket code for these submissions,

b. Track the number of submissions made under this Act, and

c. Report any problems with these procedures to the Chief Judge.

7. Nothing in this Administrative Order modifies the procedures for reporting involuntary admissions to mental institutions and the resulting prohibition on purchasing firearms by such persons.

DONE AND ORDERED in Chambers at Clearwater, Pinellas County, Florida this ___ day of July, 2013.

ORIGINAL SIGNED ON JULY 1, 2013
BY J. THOMAS MCGRADY,
CHIEF JUDGE

IN THE CIRCUIT COURT, SIXTH JUDICIAL CIRCUIT IN AND FOR PASCO/PINELLAS COUNTY, FLORIDA PROBATE DIVISION

IN RE: [NAME]
[ADDRESS]

UCN:
REF #:

CONFIDENTIAL EX PARTE ORDER DIRECTING ENTRY OF RECORD IN FDLE'S DATABASE OF PERSONS PROHIBITED FROM PURCHASING FIREARMS

THIS CAUSE came before the Court on [date] to determine if [name] may be prohibited from purchasing a firearm because of his/her voluntary admission to a mental institution for outpatient or inpatient treatment after an involuntary examination under section 394.463, Florida Statutes.

The Court, having reviewed the following records:

___ The examining physician's finding that the person is an imminent danger to himself/herself or others;

___ The examining physician's certification that:

___ if the person did not agree to voluntary treatment that a petition for involuntary outpatient or inpatient treatment would have been filed under section 394.463(2)(i)4, OR

___ a petition for involuntary treatment was filed and the person subsequently agreed to voluntary treatment prior to a court hearing on the petition;

___ The written notice of the examining physician's finding and certification that the person received prior to agreeing to voluntary treatment, and which contained a statement that he/she would be prohibited from purchasing a firearm and would not be eligible to apply for or retain a concealed weapon or firearm license under section 790.06; and

___ [Name]'s written acknowledgment that he/she understands the above-described finding, certification and notice;

FINDS the record supports the classification of [name] as an imminent danger to himself/herself or others and hereby **ORDERS** that such record be submitted to the Florida Department of Law Enforcement in accord with Section 790.065, Florida Statutes. The Clerk of Court is **DIRECTED** to forward the record and this Order to the Florida Department of Law Enforcement within 24 hours of the entry of this Order.

DONE AND ORDERED in Chambers, at ________, ________ County, Florida, this ___ day of ________, 2013, at ___: ___ am/pm.

____
CIRCUIT JUDGE

IN THE CIRCUIT COURT, SIXTH JUDICIAL CIRCUIT IN AND FOR PASCO/PINELLAS COUNTY, FLORIDA PROBATE DIVISION

IN RE: [NAME]
[ADDRESS]

UCN:
REF #:

CONFIDENTIAL EX PARTE INTERIM ORDER REQUIRING FURTHER DOCUMENTATION ON VOLUNTARY COMMITMENT

THIS CAUSE came before the Court on [date] to determine if [name] may be prohibited from purchasing a firearm because of his/her voluntary admission to a mental institution for outpatient or inpatient treatment after an involuntary examination under section 394.463, Florida Statutes.

The Court, having reviewed the submitted documentation, **FINDS** as follows:

___ The examining physician's finding that the person is an imminent danger to himself/herself or others is missing;

___ The examining physician's finding that the person is an imminent danger to himself/herself or others lacks a description of the person's behavior that resulted in such a finding and must be supplemented;

___ The examining physician's certification that if the person did not agree to voluntary treatment that a petition for involuntary outpatient or inpatient treatment would have been filed under section 394.463(2)(i)4, Florida Statutes, OR a petition for involuntary treatment was filed and the person subsequently agreed to voluntary treatment prior to a court hearing on the petition is missing;

___ The written notice of the examining physician's finding and certification that the person received prior to agreeing to voluntary treatment, and which contained a statement that the person would be prohibited from purchasing a firearm and would not be eligible to apply for or retain a concealed weapon or firearm license under section 790.06 is missing;

___ [Name]'s written acknowledgment that he/she understands the above-described finding, certification and notice is missing;

___ [Name]'s written acknowledgment that he/she understands the above-described finding, certification, and notice contains the notation that the acknowledgment was refused;

___ Other: ______________________.

Based on the incomplete record presented to the Court by the examining physician, the Court cannot at this time find that [name]'s voluntary commitment procedure met the requirements of Section 790.065, Florida Statutes, so as to require that he/she be prohibited from purchasing a firearm or that his/her name be added to the FDLE's Mental Competency (MECOM) database. It is therefore

ORDERED that the examining physician file with this Court adequate documentation of this voluntary commitment procedure within 3 days. The Court reserves jurisdiction to enter further orders in this matter. It is further

ORDERED that a failure to timely file the documentation requested will result in:

• A dismissal of the matter with prejudice, without further order of this Court,

• The person's record will not be submitted to the FDLE database, and

• The person will not be precluded from purchasing a firearm because of a voluntary admission to a mental institution.

DONE AND ORDERED in Chambers, at ________, ________ County, Florida, this ___ day of ________, 2013, at ___ : ___ am/pm.

____

CIRCUIT JUDGE

2013–033. [RESCINDED BY ORDER 2017-039, EFFECTIVE AUGUST 22, 2017.]

2013–028. [RESCINDED BY ORDER 2016–018, EFFECTIVE APRIL 1, 2016.]

2013–027. CONFIDENTIAL INFORMATION CONTAINED IN PROPOSED ORDERS AND PROPOSED JUDGMENTS

IN THE CIRCUIT COURT OF THE SIXTH JUDICIAL CIRCUIT IN AND FOR PASCO AND PINELLAS COUNTIES, FLORIDA

ADMINISTRATIVE ORDER NO. 2013–027 PA/PI–CIR

RE: CONFIDENTIAL INFORMATION CONTAINED IN PROPOSED ORDERS AND PROPOSED JUDGMENTS

The Florida Supreme Court adopted amendments to Rule of Judicial Administration 2.420 effective May 1, 2013. *In re: Amendments to Florida Rule of Judicial Administration 2.420,* No. SC11–2466 (Fla. 2013). Specifically, subdivision (d)(5) was created, which requires the Court to take certain actions when filing an order or other document that contains confidential information.

In order to comply with subdivision (d)(5) of the rule, and in accordance with Article V, § 2, Florida Constitution, Rules of Judicial Administration 2.215 and 2.525, and section 43.26, Florida Statutes,

IT IS ORDERED:

1. Proposed orders and proposed judgments, whether submitted on a party's own initiative or as directed by the Court, must comply with Florida Rule of Judicial Administration 2.420. Attorneys submitting proposed orders or proposed judgments to the Court should determine whether they contain confidential information as defined in Florida Rule of Judicial Administration 2.420. Appendix A to this Administrative Order lists confidential information commonly found in court documents.

2. Except when the entire court file is maintained as confidential, if the proposed order or proposed judgment contains any confidential information, the attorney should add the word "confidential" to the title of the document and provide the Court with a redacted version of the document that omits the confidential information.

DONE AND ORDERED in Chambers, Clearwater, Pinellas County, Florida this ___ day of June 2013.

ORIGINAL SIGNED ON JUNE 24, 2013
BY J. THOMAS MCGRADY,
CHIEF JUDGE

APPENDIX A [1]

Confidential Information Commonly Found In Court Documents

Sensitive Financial Information

• Social Security, bank account, charge, debit, and credit card numbers [§ 119.0714(1)(i)–(j), (2)(a)–(e), Fla. Stat.]

• Estate inventories and accountings [§ 733.604(1), Fla. Stat.]

• Trade Secrets and proprietary confidential business information [§§ 570.544(7), 815.045, Fla. Stat.]

Certain Medical, Mental Health, and Substance Abuse Information

• Patient records in hospitals, nursing homes, or hospices [§§ 395.3025, 400.022(1)(m), and 400.611(3), Fla. Stat.]

• Certain medical records and certain psychological and psychiatric evaluations [§§ 456.057 and .059, Fla. Stat.]

• Protected health information under HIPPA [Pub. L. No. 104–191, 110 Stat. 1936]

• Birth records and portions of death and fetal death records [§§ 382.008(6) and 382.025(1), Fla. Stat.]

• HIV test results and the identity of any person upon whom an HIV test has been performed [§ 381.004(3)(e), Fla. Stat.]

• Records, including test results, held by the Department of Health or its authorized representatives relating to sexually transmissible diseases [§ 384.29, Fla. Stat.]

• Records disclosing the identity of persons subject to tuberculosis proceedings and records held by the DOH or its authorized representatives relating to known or suspected cases of tuberculosis or exposure to tuberculosis [§§ 392.545 and 392.65, Fla. Stat.]

• Information that can be used to identify a minor petitioning for a waiver of parental notice when seeking to terminate pregnancy [§§ 390.01114–16, Fla. Stat.]

• Clinical records under the Baker Act [§§ 394.4615(1) and (7), Fla. Stat.]

• Clinical records of criminal defendants found incompetent to proceed or acquitted by reason of insanity [§ 916.107(8), Fla. Stat.]

• Records of substance abuse service providers that pertain to the identity, diagnosis, and prognosis of and service provision to individuals [§ 397.501(7), Fla. Stat.]

Certain Sensitive Criminal Records

• Identity, home or employment phone number, home or employment address, or personal assets of crime victims in documents *received* by an agency [§ 119.07(2)(j)(1), Fla. Stat.]

• Criminal intelligence of investigation information that reveals the personal assets of a crime victim, if those assets were not involved in the crime [§ 119.071 (2)(i), Fla. Stat.]

• The victim's contact information or asset information in a domestic violence, aggravated stalking, harassment, aggravated battery, sexual battery, or child abuse action on request of the victim [§§ 741.30(3)(b) and 119.071(2)(j)(1), Fla. Stat.]

• Certain records and information regarding victims of child abuse or sexual offenses [§§ 39.202(1), 92.56, 119.071(2)(h), 119.0714(1)(h), and 415.107(1), Fla. Stat.]

• Certain information in a sexual violence or domestic abuse injunction [§§ 92.56, 119.071(2)(h)(2), (j)(1), and 784.046, Fla. Stat.]

• Records of abuse, neglect, or exploitation of a vulnerable adult [§ 415.107, Fla. Stat.]

• Active criminal investigative or intelligence material [§ 119.071(2)(c)1.]

• Certain information relating to criminal investigation, including but not limited to confessions, surveillance techniques, and information revealing confidential informants or undercover personnel [§§ 119.071(2)(d)–(f) and 119.0714, Fla. Stat.]

• Copies of arrest and search warrants and supporting affidavits retained by judges, clerks, or other court personnel until execution of said warrants or until a determination is made by law enforcement authorities that execution cannot be made [Rule of Judicial Administration 2.420(c)(6) and § 119.071(2)(c)(1), Fla. Stat.]

• Investigative subpoenas [§ 119.071(2)(c)(1), Fla. Stat.]

• Indictments or Informations and records relating thereto until the defendant is in custody or a period of one year has elapsed [Rule of Criminal Procedure 3.140(1)]

• Wiretap, pen register or trap and trace device or mobile tracking applications and orders [§§ 934.09(8)(c), 934.33, 934.42, 119.071(2)(c)(1) Fla. Stat.]

• Confidential information held by the Department of Corrections, including violation of probation reports [§ 945.10(1), Fla. Stat.]

• Complete presentence investigation reports [Fla. R. Crim. P. 3.712.]

• Criminal history records from federal systems or other states [§ 943.053(2), Fla. Stat.]

Certain Sensitive Family or Juvenile Information

• Chapter 39 records relating to dependency matters, termination of parental rights, guardians ad litem, child abuse, neglect, and abandonment [§§ 39.0132(3), 39.0132(4)(a), Fla. Stat.]

• Adoption records [§ 63.162, Fla. Stat.]

• Gestational surrogacy records [§ 742.16(9), Fla. Stat.]

• Guardianship reports, orders appointing court monitors, and orders relating to findings of no probable cause in guardianship cases [§§ 744.1076, 744.3701, Fla. Stat.]

• Records acquired by courts and law enforcement regarding family services for children [§§ 984.06(3)–(4), Fla. Stat.]

• Juvenile delinquency records [§§ 985.04(1), 985.045(2), Fla. Stat.]

• Child Support cases from county child support enforcement agencies and child support IV–D cases [§§ 61.1827 and 409.2579, Fla. Stat.]

• Paternity if parents subsequently marry [§ 742.091, Fla. Stat.]

Motor Vehicle Records

• Personal information, including driver's license numbers, contained in a motor vehicle record [§ 119.0712(2)(b), Fla. Stat.]

Confidential Information That May Be Found In Court Documents

Court and Attorney Work Product

• Records from the court's decision making process (memorandums, drafts, notes, etc.) [Rule of Judicial Administration 2.420(c)(1)]

• Attorney work product [§ 119.071(1)(d), Fla. Stat.]

• Petition to approve a contingency contract and related proceedings and documents [Rules Regulating the Florida Bar 4–1.5(f)(4)(B)(ii).]

Mediation/Settlement Information

• Written communications or materials from certain mediation proceeding [§§ 44.102(3) and 61.183, Fla. Stat.]

• Citizen dispute settlement center records [§ 44.201(5), Fla. Stat.]

Certain Complaints

• Complaints alleging misconduct against judges until probable cause is established or complaints filed with the Judicial Qualification Commission [Rule of Judicial Administration 2.420(c)(3)(A) and Art. V, Section 12(a), Fla. Const.]

• Complaints against entities or individuals licensed or regulated by the courts until a finding of probable cause or no probable cause is established [Rule of Judicial Administration 2.420 (c)(3)(B)]

Certain Records Relating to Juries

• Certain grand jury records [§§ 905.17 and 905.28(1), Fla. Stat.]

• Civil juror notes [§ 40.50(2), Fla. Stat.]

[1]Appendix A is only a reference guide. The statutes identified herein should be consulted to determine whether information is confidential. Further, Appendix A is not an exhaustive list of confidential information and there may be court rules or orders that impact whether information is confidential.

2013–024. [RESCINDED BY ORDER 2017-064, EFFECTIVE NOVEMBER 11, 2017.]

2013–021. [RESCINDED BY ORDER 2016-018, EFFECTIVE APRIL 1, 2016]

2013–017. E–FILING IN COUNTY CIVIL, COUNTY SMALL CLAIMS, CIRCUIT CIVIL, CIRCUIT CIVIL APPELLATE, AND FAMILY LAW DIVISIONS—PASCO COUNTY

IN THE CIRCUIT COURT OF THE SIXTH JUDICIAL CIRCUIT IN AND FOR PASCO AND PINELLAS COUNTIES, FLORIDA

ADMINISTRATIVE ORDER NO. 2013–017 PA–CIR

RE: E–FILING IN COUNTY CIVIL, COUNTY SMALL CLAIMS, CIRCUIT CIVIL, CIRCUIT CIVIL APPELLATE, AND FAMILY LAW DIVISIONS—PASCO COUNTY

The Pasco Clerk of the Circuit Court (Clerk) has informed the Chief Judge that the Clerk is ready for electronic filing in the county civil, county small claims, circuit civil, circuit civil appellate, and family law divisions. While there has not been a test period using CLERICUS in Pasco County, this system has been tested in other counties. The Supreme Court has mandated e-filing as of April 1, 2013, in these divisions unless the Clerk seeks a waiver or in certain other limited circumstances. *In re Amendments to the Florida Rules of Civil Procedure, et al,—Electronic Filing,* 102 So. 3d 451 (Fla. 2012).

E-filing is only one step in managing electronic court records and electronic court processes. The Court anticipates that it will obtain and use the Judicial Application Workflow System (JAWS), a product developed in the Thirteenth Judicial Circuit. The Court must proceed carefully to ensure that the transition to electronic court records and electronic court processes does not have a negative impact on the operations of the Court or the public's access to the Court and its records. Until the Court has obtained and implemented a system in the various court divisions to conduct its work efficiently and effectively using electronic records, it will continue conducting court business in the customary manner with paper files.

In order to implement electronic filing in these divisions in Pasco County, and in accordance with Article V, § 2, Florida Constitution, Rules of Judicial Administration 2.215 and 2.525, and section 43.26, Florida Statutes,

IT IS ORDERED:

DIRECTIONS TO ATTORNEYS

1. Effective April 1, 2013, attorneys must electronically file pleadings and papers in new and existing cases in Pasco County through the Florida Courts E–Filing Portal in the following divisions, except as otherwise provided in this Administrative Order:

a. county civil,

b. county small claims,

c. circuit civil,

d. circuit civil appellate, and

e. family law (excluding dependency cases).

Original documents are not to be filed when the filing has been made electronically, except as otherwise provided in this Administrative Order.

2. The following documents may be scanned and e-filed; however the original must be submitted to the Pasco Clerk of the Circuit Court: [Paragraph 2 amended by Administrative Order 2013-017, effective June 25, 2013]

a. Affidavits

b. Bonds

c. Certificates of Title

d. Death certificates

e. Deeds

f. Mortgages

g. Notices of Action

h. Promissory Notes

i. Wills

j. Writs

k. Consents for adoption

l. Affidavits of Nonpaternity

m. Any other document specifically ordered by the Court

n. Any other document required by Florida law to be filed in its original form.

3. In order for an attorney to e-file in accordance with this Administrative Order, the attorney must register with the Florida Courts E–Filing Portal at https://www.myflcourtaccess.com/ and submit pleadings and papers through the E–Filing Portal. Attorneys must **not e-mail** the Court or the Clerk with pleadings or papers for filing. Pleadings and papers to be filed with the Court may only be submitted through the E–Filing Portal. Once assigned a user name and password from the E–Filing Portal, it is the responsibility of the attorney to safeguard his or her username and password to prevent unauthorized filings. Any electronic filings received via the attorney's username are presumed to have been submitted by the attorney. Law Firm Administrator Accounts may not be used for e-filing on behalf of individual attorney members of the firm.

4. Attorneys must comply with all filing requirements of the E–Filing Portal. Currently the E–Filing Portal allows filings to be submitted as a Word document or in PDF format. For filings made in Pasco County, attorneys are encouraged to submit filings as a searchable PDF. Attorneys should separate attachments to a pleading or paper, and label each attachment. Attachments should be included in the same submission as long as the total submission does not exceed 25 MB. If a pleading or paper exceeds 25 MB, the attorney should divide the pleading or paper in an orderly fashion so that each submission does not exceed 25 MB. If the attorney is unable to divide the pleading or paper so that it does not exceed 25 MB, the attorney may submit the pleading or paper to the Clerk and is not required to e-file such pleading or paper.

5. Each document must be formatted in accordance with the applicable rules of court governing formatting of paper documents.

6. In accordance with Rule of Judicial Administration 2.420, each electronically filed document must be reviewed by the attorney submitting the document to determine whether the document contains confidential or exempt information. If the document contains information that is confidential or exempt, the document must be electronically filed as a sealed electronic document along with either a notice of confidential filing or motion to determine confidentiality of court record.

7. In accordance with Rule of Judicial Administration 2.515, each electronically filed document is deemed to have been signed by the attorney submitting the document and must include a typographical signature of such person in the format of /s, s/, or /s/ John Doe or a reproduction of the attorney's signature. Each document shall also include the attorney's typed name, Florida Bar address, telephone number, primary e-mail address and secondary e-mail addresses, if any, and Florida Bar number.

8. Proposed orders, proposed judgments, letters, or correspondence directed to a judge may not be electronically filed through the E-Filing Portal but must be submitted according to the Court's directions. Other than new requirements for preparing proposed orders and proposed judgments that contain confidential information as detailed in Administrative Order 2013-027, the procedure for submitting proposed orders and proposed final judgments to the Court is not changing at this time. Attorneys should continue to provide hard copies to the Court, including sufficient copies for conforming, and stamped, addressed envelopes for distribution of orders. [Paragraph amended by Administrative Order 2013-017, effective June 25, 2013]

9. An original and two copies of a proposed summons should be submitted in paper form to the Clerk. The proposed summons should include the case number received when the case was e-filed. The $10.00 summons fee should continue to be submitted directly to the Clerk. If the issued summons will not be picked up, stamped, addressed envelopes for return of the summons must also be submitted.

10. Documents may be electronically filed at any time through the E–Filing Portal. Documents must be electronically filed and time stamped at the E–Filing Portal by 11:59 p.m. local time in order to be considered filed that date. The filing date for e-filed documents is the date of receipt by the E–Filing Portal.

11. In the event that the E–Filing Portal is not available due to technical failure of the E–Filing Portal and an attorney must make a filing that day to meet a deadline, the attorney must attempt to file after 12:00 noon on at least two occasions that are separated by at least one hour. In these circumstances, if the attorney is unsuccessful in having a filing accepted by the E–Filing Portal, the attorney may, when the E–Filing Portal is available, file a motion with the Court seeking to have the filing considered timely filed. The Court may, with satisfactory proof, permit the document to be filed nunc pro tunc to the date it was first attempted to be filed electronically.

12. An attorney who has obtained an order from the Court exempting him or herself from e-service requirements in accordance with Rule of Judicial Administration 2.516 is also exempt from e-filing requirements. In order to continue to file hard copies, the attorney must provide a copy of the court order exempting him or herself from e-service along with the hard copy filing.

13. E-filing a document does not relieve a party of its evidentiary burden to prove the authenticity of an original document. Attorneys should maintain original documents that may be needed in court hearings unless the original is submitted as provided in paragraph two. When original documents are submitted as exhibits at a court hearing, the attorney must indicate on the document or notify the Clerk in writing when an original document must be retained as an original.

14. E-filing through the E–Filing Portal does not relieve an attorney of his or her responsibility to serve pleadings and papers in accordance with the requirements of Rule of Judicial Administration 2.516.

15. If an attorney has an emergency matter that would normally be presented directly to the section judge or duty judge, the attorney must e-file the emergency matter as provided in this Administrative Order. If the attorney wants the Court to consider the matter on an emergency basis, the attorney must contact the section judge or duty judge in accordance with current practices.

16. Attorneys from other jurisdictions who wish to be admitted pro hac vice must obtain a pro hac vice number from The Florida Bar to file through the E–Filing Portal. Until the attorney receives a pro hac vice number, pleadings must be e-filed by the local Florida attorney designated in your motion. A motion to appear pro hac vice must be filed in each case in which the attorney wishes to appear and the receipt of a pro hac vice number from The Florida Bar for purposes of accessing the E–Filing Portal does not grant an attorney the right to appear. See http://www.floridabar.org for more information.

DIRECTIONS TO OTHER FILERS

17. Unrepresented litigants must file pleadings and papers in hard copy with the Clerk until the E–Filing Portal allows access to such filers.

DIRECTIONS TO THE CLERK

18. The Clerk may receive pleadings and papers electronically filed through the Florida Court's E–Filing Portal in new and existing cases in the following divisions, except as otherwise provided in this Administrative Order:

a. county civil,

b. county small claims,

c. circuit civil,

d. circuit civil appellate, and

e. family law (excluding dependency cases).

The Clerk must receive documents from the E–Filing Portal in a searchable PDF format, provided the E–Filing Portal can transmit the documents to the Clerk as a searchable PDF.

19. The Clerk may only receive electronic filings through the Florida Court's E–Filing Portal or as otherwise provided in this Administrative Order.

20. Except as otherwise provided in this Administrative Order, the Clerk may only receive non-electronic pleadings and papers from:

a. Unrepresented litigants.

b. Attorneys who are exempt from e-service who provide a copy of an order exempting them from e-service.

21. The Clerk must continue to receive the following documents in original form: [Paragraph 21 amended by Administrative Order 2013-017, effective June 25, 2013]

a. Affidavits

b. Bonds

c. Certificates of Title

d. Death certificates

e. Deeds

f. Mortgages

g. Notices of Action

h. Promissory Notes

i. Wills

j. Writs

k. Consents for adoption

l. Affidavit of Nonpaternity

m. Any other document specifically ordered by the Court

n. Any other document required by Florida law to be filed in its original form

When original documents are submitted at a hearing the Clerk must retain the original documents in accordance with existing retention schedules.

22. If a filer is unable to separate a pleading or paper so that it does not exceed 25 MB, the Clerk must accept such pleadings and papers in hard copy. Such pleadings and papers must be scanned by the Clerk in a manner that facilitates access to the filing by the Court and parties. The Clerk should separate attachments to a pleading or paper, label each attachment, and scan each attachment separately.

23. The Clerk will scan all pleadings and papers in new and existing cases for unrepresented litigants, attorneys who are exempt from e-service, and as otherwise provided in this Administrative Order.

24. In accordance with Standard 4.1 of the Florida Supreme Court Standards for Electronic Access to the Courts (Jan. 2013 update, version 8.0) the Clerk must continue to maintain existing hard copy court files and create hard copy files when requested for the use by the Court. The Court will continue to order hard copy court files through TrakMan and the hard copy court file must continue to be delivered within 48 hours of the request unless sooner requested by the Court. The Court anticipates that it will transition to electronic court files on dates to be established by the Court.

25. After the transition to electronic court files for each division, the Clerk must provide the electronic court file to the Court, with each document in a searchable format. The Court will continue to order court files and instead of delivering the hard copy file, the Clerk must make the entire file available in CLERICUS within 48 hours of the request, unless sooner requested by the Court or unless a longer time is authorized by the Court.

26. The Clerk must provide public access to court records either from the hard copy court file or from terminals in the Clerk's offices and must do so in accordance with limitations on electronic access to court records as provided in AOSC07–49 or subsequent order. The Clerk must ensure that information that is exempt from public disclosure is not disclosed through public terminals in the Clerk's office or through any other public access.

27. The Clerk must make the court record available in a format that complies with the Americans with Disabilities Act.

28. The Clerk must comply with all the conditions stated in the e-filing approval letter from the Florida Courts Technology Commission, dated March 28, 2013, which is incorporated into this Administrative Order as Attachment A, and all requirements of Rule of Judicial Administration 2.525, Supreme Court Administrative Order AOSC09–30, *In Re: Statewide Standards for Electronic Access to the Courts,* including updated Standards for Electronic Access to the Courts.

29. Documents and orders prepared by the Clerk or by the Court are not to be electronically filed through the E–Filing Portal.

30. The Clerk shall prepare an information sheet on electronic filing for attorneys and for unrepresented litigants and post it on the Clerk's website.

OTHER MATTERS

31. E-filing in the probate division will continue as provided in Administrative Order 2005–065 as modified by Supreme Court Administrative Order AOSC07–23.

DONE AND ORDERED in Chambers, Clearwater, Pinellas County, Florida this ___ day of March 2013.

ORIGINAL SIGNED ON MARCH 28, 2013

BY J. THOMAS MCGRADY,
CHIEF JUDGE

Attachment A: March 28, 2013 approval letter from Florida Courts Technology Commission

Judge Lisa Taylor Munyon, Chair Florida Courts Technology Commission c/o Office of the State Courts Administrator 500 S. Duval Street, Tallahassee, Florida 32399–1900

March 28, 2013

The Honorable Paula S. O'Neil
Pasco County Clerk of Court
Pasco County Courthouse
7530 Little Road, Suite 220
New Port Richey, Florida 34654

RE: request for implementation of electronic filings in remaining court (Circuit Civil, County Civil, and Family Law) divisions in Pasco County, Sixth Judicial Circuit

Dear Ms. Brown:

Supreme Court Opinion No.SC10–241, In re: Amendments to the Florida Rules of Judicial Administration—Rule 2.236 (July 1, 2010) provides that the Florida Courts Technology Commission "evaluate all such applications to determine whether they comply with the technology policies established by the Supreme Court and the procedures and standards created pursuant to this rule, and approve those applications deemed to be effective and found to be in compliance."

The purpose of this letter is to inform you that on April 27, 2005 the Electronic Filing Committee (EFC) reviewed and recommended approval of your request to implement electronic filing in Pasco County in the probate division which was granted by the Supreme Count via AOSC05–15.

As Chair of the Florida Courts Technology Commission I hereby approve your request to implement electronic filing in the Circuit Civil, County Civil and Family Law divisions in Pasco County.

Approval of this electronic initiative is contingent upon compliance with the policy considerations and directives regarding the development and application of new technological standardization and enhancements as set forth by the Supreme Court and is subject to the following terms and conditions. Violation of any of the following conditions shall constitute grounds for revocation of the approval to implement electronic filing in Pasco County.

a. The Pasco County Clerk of Court may implement the aforementioned technology procedures in accordance with the approved plan effective on the date of this letter and must adhere to the statewide standards for electronic access to the courts as outlined in In re: Statewide Standards for Electronic Access to the Courts, AOSC09–30 (Fla. July 1, 2009).

b. The Pasco County Clerk of Court shall ensure that there is no possibility for vendors to release or distribute court data to third parties and that the clerk of court retains the designation as custodian of the court records.

c. The Pasco County Clerk of Court shall ensure that contract provisions prohibit any vendor from extracting, data mining, or engaging in similar activities with regard to information from original court filings and other court records or any associated databases containing court records in the circuit for commercial or other non-court related uses.

d. The Pasco County Clerk of Court shall ensure that no fees other than statutorily required fees are assessed or collected by the clerk of court.

e. The Pasco County Clerk of Court shall ensure that the data is backed up and is recoverable. The clerk of court will ensure that remote data backups are stored in a protected environment a minimum of 50 miles from the primary production location of the court record or at a certified hardened facility, and that the circuit complies with established data backup standards as they are revised and updated.

f. This approval does not constitute an approval of any electronic forms that may be used in this process.

g. The Pasco County Clerk of Court shall submit monthly progress reports to the court system during the 90–day pilot test. Copies of the monthly progress reports shall be provided to the Chief Judge of the Sixth Judicial Circuit and the State Courts Technology Officer in the Office of the State Courts Administrator.

h. The Pasco County Clerk of Court shall abide by In re: Revised Interim Policy on Electronic Release of Court Records, AOSC07–49 (Fla. Sept. 7, 2007).

i. The E–Filing Court Records Portal, developed by the Florida Association of Court Clerks Services Group (FACCSG), has been identified as the statewide e-filing portal. To ensure equal access to electronic filing across the state, the Supreme Court has directed that the Florida Courts Technology Commission make implementation of the statewide system a priority of the judicial branch. All local electronic filing systems must be compatible with the statewide e-filing portal and approval of each of the above electronic filing systems is contingent on the system's compatibility with the statewide portal. The Pasco County Clerk of Court must now migrate to the statewide e-filing portal.

j. The Pasco County Clerk of Court must continue to provide paper to the judiciary until the chief judge authorizes the elimination of paper files. At such time, the Pasco County Clerk of Court must convert all documents, beginning on the date of Supreme Court or Florida Courts Technology Commission (FCTC) approval, to a searchable electronic document.

k. The Pasco County Clerk of Court shall continue to accept paper filings at no charge, other than statutorily required fees until such time as the Supreme Court may require electronic filing.

In addition to the foregoing enumerated terms and conditions, the chief judge may, pursuant to his constitutional and statutory responsibility for administrative supervision of the courts within the circuit, imposed additional conditions that must be adhered by to implement an electronic filing system.

1. Pasco County will comply with the E–Access Standards in accordance with Supreme Court Administrative Order AOSC 09–30. The Florida Courts Technology Commission last amended the Standards January 2013, version 8.0, and you must comply with this or any future revisions to the E–Access Standards.

2. Pasco County will follow any implementation schedule developed by the Florida Courts Technology Commission and coordinate implementation with the Chief Judge.

3. Pasco County will continue to assemble and deliver paper case files and documents until authorized by the Chief Judge to discontinue paper files.

4. The electronic file to be provided to the Court must meet or exceed the capabilities and ease of use currently provided by paper case files, for both in and out of court processing and use. Documents in an electronic court file must be provided to the Court as a searchable PDF.

5. The Court must be provided and approve in advance any business process that impacts Court operations.

6. Pasco County will provide the Court with direct unrestricted access to the Pasco County court data, images and documents.

Should you have any questions, please do not hesitate to contact my office.

Sincerely,
Lisa T. Munyon
Circuit Judge

2013–016. [RESCINDED BY ORDER 2016–018, EFFECTIVE APRIL 1, 2016.]

2013–006. [RESCINDED BY ORDER 2016–018, EFFECTIVE APRIL 1, 2016.]

2013–005. [RESCINDED BY ORDER 2017—72, EFFECTIVE DECEMBER 13, 2017]

2013–003. SERVICE OF PLEADINGS AND DOCUMENTS PROBATE AND GUARDIANSHIP

IN THE CIRCUIT COURT, SIXTH JUDICIAL CIRCUIT IN AND FOR PASCO AND PINELLAS COUNTIES, FLORIDA

ADMINISTRATIVE ORDER NO. 2013–003 PA–CIR

RE: SERVICE OF PLEADINGS AND DOCUMENTS PROBATE AND GUARDIANSHIP

Effective September 1, 2012, Florida Rule of Judicial Administration 2.516 requires that unless the court orders otherwise, generally all pleadings and documents in civil, probate, small claims, and family law matters must be filed electronically and served upon the other parties via email. *In re: Amendments to the Florida Rules of Judicial Administration*, No. SC10–2101 (Fla. Oct. 18, 2012) (effective *nunc pro tunc* September 1, 2012).

For several years, all filings in the probate of estates, the administration of guardianships, and incapacity proceedings in Pasco County have been submitted electronically to the Pasco County Clerk of Court via LexisNexis® File and Serve®. This system also allows attorneys to set up electronic service of process.

The LexisNexis® File and Serve® system has functioned successfully, and the probate attorneys and the Pasco County Clerk of Court are accustomed to using this system. Thus, the Court finds this an appropriate situation in which to order electronic filing and service by means other than that provided in Florida Rule of Judicial Administration 2.516.

Therefore, under the authority granted the Chief Judge in Article V, section 2(d), of the Florida Constitution, section 43.26, Florida Statutes, Rule of Judicial Administration 2.215, and Rules of Judicial Administration 2.516(a),

IT IS ORDERED:

1. Any attorney using the Pasco County LexisNexis® File and Serve® system is hereby exempt from the electronic filing and service requirements of Florida Rule of Judicial Administration 2.516 because the LexisNexis® File and Serve® system provides for electronic filing and service.

2. Where electronic service is not permitted, attorneys shall follow the service requirements of Florida Rule of Judicial Administration 2.516, Florida Probate Rule 5.040, or any other applicable rule or statute.

DONE AND ORDERED in Chambers at Clearwater, Pinellas County, Florida, this ________ day of January 2013.

ORIGINAL SIGNED JANUARY 15, 2013

BY J. THOMAS MCGRADY, CHIEF JUDGE

2012–057. [RESCINDED BY ORDER 2017–022, EFFECTIVE MAY 9, 2017.]

2012–054. AFTER HOURS PROCEDURES FOR DATING, DOMESTIC, REPEAT, AND SEXUAL VIOLENCE AND STALKING INJUNCTIONS

IN THE CIRCUIT COURT, SIXTH JUDICIAL CIRCUIT IN AND FOR PASCO AND PINELLAS COUNTIES, FLORIDA

ADMINISTRATIVE ORDER NO. 2012–054 PA/PI–CIR

RE: AFTER HOURS PROCEDURES FOR DATING, DOMESTIC, REPEAT, AND SEXUAL VIOLENCE AND STALKING INJUNCTIONS

In Administrative Order 2007–033, the Chief Judge modified the after hours procedure for obtaining a temporary injunction for protection in dating, domestic, repeat, and sexual violence cases. Section 26.20, Florida Statutes, provides that at least one judge must be available after hours including weekdays after hours, Saturdays, Sundays, and holidays, to review ex parte motions for temporary injunctions in domestic violence cases. Circumstances may also require the issuance of an ex parte temporary injunction in dating, sexual or repeat violence cases after hours.

The Legislature passed HB 1099, creating a cause of action for a civil injunction for protection against stalking. See Ch. 2012–153, Laws of Fla. The procedure for a person seeking a temporary injunction for protection needs to be modified to include stalking.

In both Pasco and Pinellas County, the responsibilities of the Clerks of the Circuit Court and the Sheriffs should be specified to ensure that injunctions for protection can be issued after hours. Further, it is important to provide information to the public on how to access the duty judge for these purposes.

In accordance with Article V, section 2, Florida Constitution, Rule of Judicial Administration 2.215, and section 43.26, Florida Statutes,

IT IS ORDERED:

1. The Pasco and Pinellas Clerks of the Circuit Court and the Pasco and Pinellas Sheriffs must follow these procedures to ensure that injunctions for protection can be issued after hours. After hours means after 4:00 p.m. or before 8:00 a.m. on a regular work day, or at any time on a weekend or holiday.

2. When a person has reasonable cause to believe that he or she is the victim of dating, domestic, repeat, or sexual violence, or stalking in accordance with the provisions of section 741.30, section 784.046, or section 784.0485, Florida Statutes, and desires to seek an injunction for protection after hours, a person may contact the following:

EAST PASCO COUNTY Dade City	WEST PASCO COUNTY Hudson	NORTH PINELLAS COUNTY Clearwater	SOUTH PINELLAS COUNTY St. Petersburg
Sunrise of Pasco County, Inc.	Salvation Army Domestic Violence	THE HAVEN	C.A.S.A. (Community Action Stops Abuse)

352–521–3120 727–856–5797 727–442–4128 727–895–4912

If a program is unable to locate safe shelter for the litigant and the litigant's children, or if the litigant chooses not to go to a shelter, the staff at the facility will call a deputy clerk who will meet the litigant at the Sheriff's Office. In Pasco County, the litigant will meet the deputy clerk at a location selected by the deputy clerk based upon the location of the parties which will be either: the Sheriff's Office, 8700 Citizen Dr., New Port Richey, the Pasco County Detention Center, located at 20101 Central Blvd. in Land O' Lakes, or the Sheriff's Office in Dade City (if the Dade City office has deputies on site). In Pinellas County the litigant will meet the deputy clerk at Sheriff's Administration, 10750 Ulmerton Road, Largo.

3. When law enforcement is contacted by an individual seeking an injunction for protection against dating, domestic, repeat, or sexual violence, or stalking after hours, a law enforcement officer, in accordance with section 741.29, Florida Statutes, shall refer the litigant to the closest shelter listed in paragraph two. If the litigant chooses not to go to a shelter, the individual may speak with shelter personnel who will call a deputy clerk. The deputy clerk will meet the litigant at the Sheriff's Office. In Pasco County, the litigant will meet the deputy clerk at a location selected by the deputy clerk based upon the location of the parties which will be the Sheriff's Office, 8700 Citizen Dr., New Port Richey, the Pasco County Detention Center, located at 20101 Central Blvd. in Land O' Lakes, or the Sheriff's Office in Dade City (if the Dade City office has deputies on site). In Pinellas County the litigant will meet the deputy clerk at Sheriff's Administration, 10750 Ulmerton Road, Largo.

4. The Sheriffs of Pasco and Pinellas County shall provide a location within the facilities specified in this order for a deputy clerk to meet with a litigant in order to complete a petition for an injunction for protection. The Sheriffs shall also make a facsimile machine available for the deputy clerk to send and receive a facsimile.

5. The Clerks of the Circuit Court in Pasco and Pinellas County shall make the names and contact information for deputy clerks available to shelters in their respective counties. When contacted by a shelter, a deputy clerk shall go to the Sheriff's Office and assist a litigant with a petition for an injunction for protection. The deputy clerk shall contact the duty judge and follow the instructions of the duty judge to transmit the petition to the judge.

6. In addition to the procedures specified in this Administrative Order, a petition for an injunction for protection may be submitted to the judge at advisories on weekends or holidays.

7. The duty judge shall review a petition either by having the deputy clerk transmit the petition by facsimile or by other electronic means or by traveling to the Sheriff's office and reviewing the petition in person. The duty judge shall report any problems with the after hour procedures to the Chief Judge.

Administrative Orders 2007–033 PA/PI–CIR and 2008–083 PI–CIR are hereby rescinded.

DONE AND ORDERED in Chambers at Clearwater, Pinellas County, Florida, this ___ day of November 2012.

ORIGINAL SIGNED ON NOVEMBER 14, 2012
BY J. THOMAS MCGRADY,
CHIEF JUDGE

2012–028. LOCAL ORDINANCE VIOLATIONS FISH AND WILDLIFE CONSERVATION COMMISSION VIOLATIONS UNIFORM FINE SCHEDULE

IN THE CIRCUIT COURT, SIXTH JUDICIAL CIRCUIT IN AND FOR PASCO AND PINELLAS COUNTIES, FLORIDA

ADMINISTRATIVE ORDER NO. 2012–028 PA–CTY

RE: LOCAL ORDINANCE VIOLATIONS FISH AND WILDLIFE CONSERVATION COMMISSION VIOLATIONS UNIFORM FINE SCHEDULE

In order to provide for the orderly and uniform prosecution of county and municipal ordinance violations in Pasco County, Florida; and in accordance with Article V, section 2(d), Florida Constitution, Rules of Judicial Administration 2.215 and 2.265, Rule of Criminal Procedure 3.125, and sections 34.01, 43.26, 125.69, 379.3311 and 379.407, Florida Statutes; it is

ORDERED:

1. Pasco County and municipalities located within Pasco County shall utilize the Pasco County Ordinance Citation/Notice to Appear form that has been approved by the Pasco Administrative Judge or his or her designee. The approved Citation/Notice to Appear shall be the official complaint instrument for prosecution of all county and municipal ordinance violations within the jurisdiction of Pasco County, except for

a. An Indictment or Information

b. Parking Tickets

2. The Citation/Notice to Appear shall be printed on NCR paper, which shall be coded and distributed to the Clerk of the Circuit Court, the issuing Agency, the County or Municipal Attorney and Defendant.

3. The Fish and Wildlife Conservation Commission shall issue citations on the required state forms issued to the agency.

4. Attachment A is the Pasco County Court Uniform Fine Schedule, including court costs. Except for legislatively dictated fine amounts set by the legislative body of a municipality, the County or the State, it is the sole and exclusive schedule of penalties that can be paid without the necessity of a court appearance. It applies to penalties for the uncontested disposition of local ordinance violations, and violations cited by the Fish and Wildlife Conservation Commission. The Court may authorize a greater or lesser penalty in any individual case.

5. Any person or entity cited for violation of the Fish and Wildlife Conservation Commission may:

a. Elect not to contest the citation. The defendant who elects not to contest the citation may pay the civil penalty, either in mail or in person at the Clerk of the Circuit Court within thirty (30) calendar days of the date of receiving the citation; or if he or she has posted a bond, forfeit bond by not appearing at the designated time or location.

b. Elect to contest the citation. The defendant electing to contest the citation shall either (1) enter a written plea of not guilty in writing in person or by mail; or (2) appear in Court for the purpose of entering a plea of not guilty and scheduling a trial on the merits of the alleged violation.

6. Any person or entity cited for violation of a local code or ordinance may:

a. Elect not to contest the citation. The defendant who elects not to contest the citation may plead guilty or no contest by signing the plea waiver form on the citation, and paying the applicable fine in full to the Clerk of the Circuit Court by mail or in person within thirty (30) calendar days after issuance of the citation, unless the violation requires a mandatory court appearance; or

b. Elect to contest the citation. The defendant electing to contest the citation shall either (1) enter a written plea of not guilty in writing in person or by mail; or (2) appear in Court for the purpose of entering a plea of not guilty and scheduling a trial on the merits of the alleged violation.

7. If the defendant electing to contest the citation fails to enter a written plea of not guilty or fails to appear for the court appearance date, the presiding judge shall at that time issue a capias for the arrest of the defendant for noncompliance with instructions on the citation, dismiss the case or take any other action that the Court deems appropriate. However, a capias will not be issued in those cases where the defendant has refused to sign the Notice to Appear or when the Notice to Appear has been posted at the property of the defendant. In such cases, if the defendant does not appear the Court will direct the Clerk of the Circuit Court to issue a Summons for a subsequent date and the Clerk shall arrange for service of the Summons on the defendant by personal service. The Clerk may assess a fee for the issuance of the summons in accordance with section 28.24, Florida Statutes. The fee for issuance by the Clerk and the cost of service assessed by the Sheriff shall be added to the costs assessed to the defendant.

8. Consistent with applicable state statutes and rules, which shall prevail in the event of a conflict, Attachment B, Instructions for Prosecuting Local Ordinance Violations and Flow Chart shall govern the issuance and prosecution of local ordinance violations in the Pasco County Court. In addition, Pasco County and each municipality therein:

a. May elect to establish by appropriate ordinance, resolution or rule its own internal policies and procedures governing the issuance and processing of violation citations insofar as the same do not conflict with the provisions of this order.

b. Shall authorize and designate an official prosecutor who shall be a member of The Florida Bar in good standing and file the name and signature of such person or persons with the Clerk of the Circuit Court for Pasco County who shall maintain a register for such purpose. The right to prosecute ordinance violations on behalf of Pasco County or such various municipalities shall be limited to such official designated and registered prosecutor when the same is required.

c. In accordance with Article V, section 17, Florida Constitution, and section 34.13, Florida Statutes, the registered prosecutor shall be responsible for the prosecution of local ordinance violations of the governmental entity that he or she represents from on and after the date upon which he or she has been notified that the case has been placed on the Court's calendar for disposition. The prosecutor shall respond to requests for discovery, summon necessary witnesses for trial, present the case before the Court and perform any other duties necessary for prosecution of the case.

9. The Pasco County Attorney shall be responsible for calendaring all local ordinance violations. The County Attorney shall:

a. Cause local ordinance violations to be placed on the Court's calendar for simultaneous plea and trial.

b. Transmit a copy of the Citation, together with the notification of trial date to the designated prosecutor.

10. All summons and notices of trial shall be for the purpose of pleas and trial and shall be issued not less than twenty-one (21) days prior to such trial date. In a Fish and Wildlife Conservation Commission violation, the Clerk of the Circuit Court is responsible for summoning any witnesses. In local ordinance violation cases, the prosecuting attorney is responsible for summoning its witnesses.

11. In accordance with Rule of Criminal Procedure 3.111, this Administrative Order serves as a written order of no incarceration for all cases governed by it. However, if the prosecuting attorney requests incarceration as a possible penalty and the Court grants this request, such must be stated on the record and the court will appoint counsel for an indigent defendant.

12. Pasco County and the participating municipalities shall:

a. Reproduce and distribute in booklet form the Instructions for prosecuting Local Ordinance Violations and Uniform Fine Schedule to Pasco County.

b. Assure that the approved Citation is printed.

Administrative Orders 2003–027 PA–CTY and 2005–036 PA–CTY are hereby rescinded.

DONE AND ORDERED in Chambers at Clearwater, Pinellas County, Florida this ___ day of August 2012.

ORIGINAL SIGNED ON AUGUST 17, 2012
BY J. THOMAS MCGRADY,
CHIEF JUDGE

ATTACHMENT A

UNIFORM FINE SCHEDULE

ADVERTISING & SIGNS:

Erecting or maintaining sign in waterway (IV)

Erecting or maintaining a prohibited sign (IV)

Distributing commercial circulars, handbills (I)

Handbills, distribution generally (V)

Handbills, distribution in public places (V)

Handbills, in or on automobiles or other vehicles (V)

Handbills, on vacant premises (V)

Handbills, distributing where requested not to do so or posted by signs (V)

Violations of adult sign requirements (I)

All other violations of sign requirements (IV)

Failure to renew annual billboard permit (I)
All other billboard violations (VI)

ALCOHOLIC BEVERAGES:

Unlawful sale of beer and wine (I)
Doing business in violation of closing hours (I)
Premises to be closed during certain hours (I)
Hours of sale (I)
Persons permitted on the premises after closing (V)
Indecent exposure at commercial establishment (VI)
Possession, consumption of alcoholic beverages on public property (IV)

AMUSEMENTS AND ENTERTAINMENT:

Failure to obtain required permits for outdoor festival (VI)
Failure to follow permit conditions (VI)
Failure to post bond (VI)
Failure to obtain and/or maintain insurance (VI)
Finances; performers; fees; county indemnity from damages; bonds (VI)

ANIMAL CONTROL & FOWL:

Interference with Animal Control Officer (I)
Cruelty to Animals (I)
Humane Treatment (I)
Abandonment (I)
Disposal of Dead Animals (I)
Animals in parks and on beaches (II)
Vicious or aggressive animals (I)
Dangerous dogs (I)
Ownership of wild animals (IV)
Rabies vaccination of dogs and cats (III)
Rabies vaccination of other animal species (IV)
Reporting animal bites (IV)
Surrender of animal for quarantine or destruction (I)
Killing or removal of rabid animal from county prohibited (I)
Surrender of carcass of rabid animal (I)
Failure to obtain license tags for cats and dogs (III)
Running at large prohibited; Impounding of dogs and pot-bellied pigs (IV)
Dogs, pot-bellied pigs and other animals constituting a nuisance prohibited (III)
Sterilization of cats and dogs upon adoption (III)
Kennel maintenance and inspection (II)
Health requirements when transported or offered for sale (II)
Registration (III)
Records required for selling dogs (III)
City designated bird sanctuary (I)
Keeping livestock, fowl regulated (I)
Sanitary conditions (V)
Limitation on number of cats and dogs in households (V)

BOATS & WATERWAYS:

Reckless or careless operation of vessel (V)
Excessive speed by vessel (V)
Speed limits (II)
Violation of water-skiing regulations (V)
Age of operations violation (V)
Violation of traffic rules (V)
Junked, wrecked, abandoned, or derelict property (IV)
Obstruction of watercourse (II)
Violation of speed limits (II)
Blocking of waterways (II)
Water skies and aquaplanes (V)
Sailboats and rowboats (V)
Adoption of state safety law (V)
Traffic rules (V)
License and operational compliance (V)
U.S. Coast Guard regulations (V)
Restricted areas (V)
Airboats prohibited on certain lakes (V)
Improper mooring (V)
Hours for running engines in residential districts (V)
Wake control; designation of "no wake" areas (V)
Authority to board and impound vessel (V)
Muffling and noise devices (V)
Vessels to observe health and conduct rules (V)
Cleanliness of docks (V)
Penalties (V)
Bathing and swimming in certain lakes (V)

BUSINESS REGULATIONS:

Collection vehicles and equipment (V)
Curbside Recycling Service (V)
Garage sales, permit required (V)

ADULT USE REGULATIONS:

General requirements (V)
Sale or consumption of alcoholic beverages on the premises (V)
Operation of adult use without valid adult use license (V)
Prohibited adult use operations (V)
Allowing employee to engage in prohibited acts (V)
Advertising prohibited activity (V)
Minors prohibited (V)
Working at establishment which does not have valid adult entertainment (V)
Records for employees (V)
Engaging in prohibited activity (V)
Touching of employee by person (V)
Exceeding occupancy limit of adult booth (V)
Use of restrooms or dressing room (V)
Hours of operation (V)
Alteration of license permit (V)

False statement or false information in applying for license (V)

Alcoholic beverages (V)

CONSUMER PROTECTION:

CABLE COMMUNICATONS:[1]

Franchise required (VI)

ELECTIONS:

Violations (V)

EMERGENCY SERVICES:

Certificate of public convenience and necessity required (VI)

Failure to maintain liability insurance (I)

FIRE PREVENTION AND PROTECTION:

Certificate of occupancy required (II)

Failure to maintain hydrant (VI)

GARBAGE AND REFUSE:

Burying or burning garbage, trash, vegetation (I)

Depositing garbage and trash in city (III)

Motor vehicles for collection of garbage or trash (I)

Hauling of certain garbage prohibited (I)

Placement of waste for collection (I)

Duties of collector, customer (I)

Collection hours and days (I)

Penalty (I)

HEALTH AND SANITATION:

Storage of garbage and refuse (III)

Unlawful accumulation (I)

Accumulation of certain materials under certain conditions (I)

Stormwater discharges to the MS4 and U. S. waters (V)

Stormwater discharges from industrial activities and construction sites (V)

Control of pollutant contributions from interconnected MS4's (V)

Control of non-stormwater discharges (V)

Reporting illicit discharges or illicit connections (V)

Control of illicit discharges or illicit connections (V)

OFFENSES AND MISCELLANEOUS PROVISIONS:

Excessive noise levels prohibited (I)

Unlawful creation of noise at night (I)

Unnecessary noises prohibited (I)

Street name and numbering—compliance required; display of numbers required (VI)

Damaging or removing city property (V)

PEDDLERS AND SOLICITORS:

Failure to obtain the required permit (I)

Failure to display permit (V)

Home solicitation sales (I)

Unlawful acts (V)

Effect of no soliciting signs (V)

Charitable roadway solicitation—permit, requirements, prohibitions (I)

Charitable roadway solicitation—additional requirements and prohibitions (V)

Solicitation of funds from persons in motor vehicles in certain locations (I)

PRIVATE COLLECTORS:

Collection vehicles and equipment (V)

Curbside Recycling Service (V)

TITLE LOANS:

All violations (VI)

LAND DEVELOPMENT REGULATIONS:

CONSTRUCTION AND DEMOLITION DEBRIS DISPOSAL:

Failure to obtain required facility permit (VI)

Failure to comply with conditions of permit approval (VI)

Failure to provide or maintain required financial responsibility (VI)

Disposal of non-construction and demolition debris (VI)

Failure to file annual report (VII)

Failure to pay required fees (VII)

DEVELOPMENT:

Failure to obtain a permit (VI)

Failure to follow permit conditions (VI)

MINING:

Failure to obtain required permit (VI)

Failure to comply with conditions of permit approval (VI)

Failure to provide or maintain required financial responsibility (VI)

Failure to pay required fees (VII)

Failure to follow permit conditions (VI)

RIGHT–OF–WAY USE PERMIT:

Failure to obtain required permit (III)

Failure to restore property (VII)

SHORT–TERM RENTALS:

Failure to register (I)

Failure to comply with requirements of operation—all violations (IV)

SIGNS:

Failure to obtain required permit (II)

SUPPLEMENTAL REGULATIONS:

Failure to protect uncontrolled access to swimming pools (VII)

Failure to properly park or store trailers, recreational vehicles and recreational equipment on private property (III)

Obstruction of clear-sight triangle requirements –Corner lot roadway obstruction (II)

General storage of trash and junk (III)

Temporary use permit required for tents, carnivals, revivals, etc. (II)

Violations of temporary use permit (II)

Violations relating to junkyards (VII)

Junkyards, motor vehicle wrecking yards—fence required (VI)

Junkyards, Motor vehicle wrecking yards—maintenance (VI)

Improper fence installation on waterfront property (III)

Violations related to fences and walls (III)

Improper parking of trucks, truck tractors, and certain commercial vehicles in certain residential districts (III)

TREE REMOVAL AND PROTECTION:

Failure to obtain required permit (VI)

Failure to post permit (V)

Failure to perform permit conditions (VI)

All other violations (VII)

WASTE DISPOSAL AND LAND SPREADING:

Failure to obtain required permit (VI)

Failure to comply with conditions of permit approval (VI)

Violations of general prohibitions (VI)

ZONING:

Unauthorized uses in a zoning district (II)

Alteration, extension, expansion, change or restoration of a nonconforming use without proper approvals or beyond allowed limits (VI)

MINORS:

Prohibited in public places, second violation (IV)

Responsibility of parents, penalty for violation, second violation (IV)

Curfew (IV)

NATURAL RESOURCES:

Irrigation during restricted days (V)

Unnecessary washing or cleaning of streets, driveways, sidewalks, or other impervious areas (V)

PARKS & RECREATIONS:

PARK RULES VIOLATIONS:

Littering prohibited (V)

Performing prohibited acts in parks (V)

Performing acts which require special permission without first obtaining such permission (IV)

Removal from parks upon request of authorized personnel (V)

Interference with county officers and employees (V)

Meetings and group activities prohibited (IV)

Tampering with park property (V)

Tampering with natural objects (V)

Tampering with plants (V)

Climbing on park property (V)

Responsibility for children (V)

Picnicking, not in designated areas (V)

Fires, igniting not in designated areas (V)

Animals, molesting, harming, etc. (V)

Swimming, not in designated areas (V)

Beach shelters, erecting, maintaining (V)

Washing in swimming areas (V)

Watercraft, operating not in designated areas (V)

Fishing, where swimming and bathing permitted (V)

Commercial fishing (V)

Hunting; weapons (IV)

Firearms, possession and discharge without authorization (IV)

Fireworks, possession, exploding, discharge without authorization (IV)

Camping, not in designated areas (V)

Alcoholic beverages (IV)

Peddling, prohibited (IV)

Posting handbills, advertising (IV)

Polluting waters (V)

Refuse, trash disposal (V)

Closing times for Sims Park and all other city parks (V)

Vending within city parks (V)

PARK TRAFFIC:

Interfering with traffic (V)

Authority to direct traffic, compliance required (V)

Manner of Operation (V)

Speed limits (V)

Restricted areas (V)

Parking on roadway (V)

Parking in designated areas (V)

Bicycles (V)

ROAD AND BRIDGES:

Commercial use of public rights-of-way prohibited (VI)

Numbering of buildings required (VI)

SOLID WASTE:

Dumping on right-of-way or public property prohibited (I)

Unlawful disposal of solid waste prohibited (I)

Dumping on private or public property prohibited; accumulation of solid waste on private property prohibited (I)

Flow control (I)

Collection vehicles and equipment (V)

Curbside recycling service (V)

Unlawful acts (I)

TAXATION:

Failure to obtain required permit (III)

Failure to display license (III)

Term of license, delinquency (III)

Application for, issuance and display of license (III)

TRAFFIC AND VEHICLES:

Identification of commercial vehicles required (III)

Trucks and commercial vehicles on certain streets (V)

Permit required for moving oversized or overweight loads (VII)

Storage of abandoned motor vehicles prohibited (III)

Obstructing mufflers (V)

Storage of abandoned, junked, dismantled vehicles on property prohibited (III)

Notice of removal of certain motor vehicles (III)

Removal of certain motor vehicles (III)

Violation; penalty (III)

Overnight parking of certain trucks in residential areas (III)

UTILITIES:

Access to premises supplied with water required (IV)

Connections to county water system; violation of regulations (III)

Meter required prior to connection with county (III)

Unauthorized discharge to county sewer system prohibited (VI)

Required water conservation measures (V)

MISCELLANEOUS ORDINANCE AND WILDLIFE CONSERVATION COMMISSION VIOLATIONS:

All zoning violations not herein specifically provided shall be deemed to be Class III offenses.

All violations not herein specifically provided shall be deemed to be Class IV offenses.

Fines shall be doubled for a second offense and for each subsequent offense thereafter.

PASCO COUNTY UNIFORM FINE SCHEDULE

LOCAL COUNTY/CITY ORDINANCE VIOLATIONS

CONTESTED

	FINE	COSTS*	TOTAL
CLASS I	$155.00	$ 58.00	$213.00
CLASS II	$130.00	$ 58.00	$188.00
CLASS III	$ 80.00	$ 58.00	$138.00
CLASS IV	$ 55.00	$ 58.00	$113.00
CLASS V	$ 30.00	$ 58.00	$ 88.00
CLASS VI	$500.00	$ 58.00	$558.00
CLASS VII	$250.00	$ 58.00	$308.00

UNCONTESTED

	FINE	COSTS*	TOTAL
CLASS I	$155.00	$ 13.00	$168.00
CLASS II	$130.00	$ 13.00	$143.00
CLASS III	$ 80.00	$ 13.00	$ 93.00
CLASS IV	$ 55.00	$ 13.00	$ 68.00
CLASS V	$ 30.00	$ 13.00	$43.00
CLASS VI	$500.00	$ 13.00	$513.00
CLASS VII	$250.00	$ 13.00	$263.00

*COSTS INCLUDE:
$3.00 ADDITIONAL COURT COSTS CLEARING TRUST FUND, 938.01, Fla. Stat.
$2.00 CRIMINAL JUSTICE EDUCATION FOR LOCAL GOVERNMENT, 938.15, Fla. Stat.
(Costs shall not be assessed if no court appearance or for cases where adjudication of guilt is withheld).
$40 COST RECOVERY, § 34.045 (1)(b), Fla. Stat.
$10 FILING FEE RECOVERY, § 34.045 (1)(c) Fla. Stat. (effective 7/1/05).
$3.00 TEEN COURT, §938.19, Fla. Stat. (effective 7/1/05). Pasco County Code, Section 34-8.

ORDINANCE VIOLATIONS WITH CORRESPONDING FLORIDA STATUTE
WRITTEN BY: FISH AND WILDLIFE CONSERVATION COMMISSION

	FINE	COSTS**	TOTAL
CLASS I	$150.00	$270.50	$420.50
CLASS II	$125.00	$269.25	$394.25
CLASS III	$ 75.00	$266.75	$341.75
CLASS IV	$ 50.00	$265.50	$315.50
CLASS V	$ 25.00	$264.25	$289.25
Licensure and permit violations	$ 50.00	$265.50	$315.50

**COSTS INCLUDE:
$3.00 ADDITIONAL COURT COSTS CLEARING TRUST FUND, 938.01, Fla. Stat.
$2.00 CRIMINAL JUSTICE EDUCATION FOR LOCAL GOVERNMENT, 938.15, Fla. Stat.
(Costs shall not be assessed if no court appearance or for cases where adjudication of guilt is withheld).
$50.00 CRIMES COMPENSATION TRUST FUND, 938.03(1), Fla. Stat.
5% OF FINE SURCHARGE, 938.04, Fla. Stat.
$50 FINE AND FORFEITURE, 938.05, Fla. Stat.
$20 CRIME PREVENTION, 775.083(2), Fla. Stat. (Costs not assessed for cases when adjudication of guilt is withheld)
$20 CRIME STOPPERS, 938.06, Fla. Stat.
$65 COURT AND JUVENILE PROGRAMS, 939.185, Fla. Stat.
$40 COST RECOVERY, § 34.045 (1)(b), Fla. Stat.
$10 FILING FEE RECOVERY, § 34.045 (1)(c) Fla. Stat. (effective 7/1/05).
$3.00 TEEN COURT, §938.19, Fla. Stat. (effective 7/1/05). Pasco County Code, Section 34-8.

EXCEPTION: VIOLATIONS OF THE FOLLOWING STATUTES ARE NON-CRIMINAL INFRACTIONS PAYABLE WITH A $50.00 FINE WITHIN THIRTY (30) CALENDAR DAYS. ANY PERSON FAILING TO PAY THE CIVIL PENALTY OR FAILING TO APPEAR, HAVING ELECTED TO APPEAR OR BEING REQUIRED TO APPEAR, IS GUILTY OF A MISDEMEANOR OF THE SECOND DEGREE. NON-CRIMINAL INFRACTIONS: Sections 327.73, 370.0605(1)(a), 370.0605(1)(b), 370.1111(1)(a), 370.14(10)(a), 372.57, 372.83, 372.988, Fla. Stat.

ATTACHMENT B

INSTRUCTIONS FOR PROSECUTING LOCAL ORDINANCE VIOLATIONS IN PASCO COUNTY

Before Beginning Prosecution [2]

The issuance of a Citation/Notice to Appear with the intent to dismiss upon compliance or correction is not permitted. Use all proper means short of issuance of a Citation/Notice to Appear to accomplish these purposes.

Completing the Citation

The Citation/Notice to Appear is on NCR paper and does not require carbon paper. However, in filling in the blanks you must type or print firmly enough to show on all copies.

Fill in every blank on the form. If it is not applicable to the particular charge, write "N/A" in the blank.

CITATION/NOTICE TO APPEAR:

Although the Citation/Notice to Appear serves many purposes, these instructions address only the usage of the form for non-criminal violations. These include ordinance violations and misdemeanors where there is no arrest and the Notice to Appear section is to cite a civil penalty owed or notify the alleged offender of a required court date and time.

• BEFORE BEGINNING PROSECUTION:

Once a Citation/Notice to Appear is issued, it may not be dismissed simply because the cited party complies with the applicable ordinance or corrects a violation. Therefore, if you would be satisfied with compliance or correction, use all proper means short of the issuance of a Citation/Notice to Appear to accomplish these purposes.

• COMPLETING THE CITATION:

The Citation/Notice to Appear is on NCR paper. However, in filling in the blanks, you must type or print firmly enough to show on all copies.

Fill in every blank on the form except the case number. If it is not applicable to your particular charge, then write N/A in the blank.

The certificate is certifying the signature of the law enforcement officer or complainant, not the signature of the defendant. This can be accomplished when the Citation/Notice to Appear is delivered to the agency.

An officer issuing a Citation/Notice to Appear shall inform the defendant that he or she may plead guilty or no contest by signing the plea and waiver on the back of his or her copy of the Citation/Notice to Appear and forwarding it to the Clerk of the Circuit Court at the address indicated, with a cashier's-check or money order in the amount of the fine. Otherwise, he or she must either file a written plea of not guilty in person or by mail, or appear in court on the day and time specified. If the defendant is charged with a violation that requires a mandatory court appearance, the officer shall explain that the defendant *must* appear in court on the day and time specified.

In the event the defendant refuses to accept his/her copy of the Citation/Notice to Appear or to acknowledge it by signing where defendant's signature is specified, the issuing officer shall note such occurrence on the face of the Citation/Notice to Appear and leave the defendant's copy in his or her presence or post it in a conspicuous location on the premises. The issuing officer shall also note on the face that a copy of the Citation/Notice to Appear was left with the defendant.

When the issuing officer returns an unsigned Citation/Notice to Appear to the appropriate agency, the officer shall sign a certification that he or she left a copy with the defendant or conspicuously posted it. The leaving/posting of the Citation/Notice to Appear constitutes sufficient notice to a defendant and the defendant is required to comply. However, failure to comply will result in the issuance of a summons rather than a capias.

• FILING THE CITATION/NOTICE TO APPEAR:

Within 48 hours after a copy of the Citation/Notice to Appear is given to the defendant, the Clerk and County or Municipal Attorney's copies of the Notice to Appear must be sent to the Clerk of the Circuit Court, Traffic Violations Bureau, at the West Pasco Judicial Center, 7530 Little Road, New Port Richey, FL 34654 or at the Robert D. Sumner Judicial Center, 38053 Live Oak Avenue, Dade City, FL 33525 or, placed in your agency's pick-up location for the Clerk's courier.

Your prosecutor must acknowledge the original Citation/Notice to Appear in the area provided for such acknowledgment. If your prosecutor declines to do so, then he or she must write "void" across the original Citation/Notice to Appear. If a copy of the Citation/Notice to Appear has been provided to the defendant, the Clerk of the Circuit Court must be advised that the charge has been voided. This can be accomplished by forwarding a copy of the Citation/Notice to Appear to the Clerk. Note, however, that if the citation has been issued by a police officer, then it may not be voided.

The additional copy of the Citation/Notice to Appear may be retained by the agency. It is recommended that the issuing officer's department and the authorized prosecutor keep a copy of the Citation/Notice to Appear.

• PROSECUTING WHERE CITATION/NOTICE TO APPEAR HAS NOT BEEN ISSUED BY A POLICE OFFICER (PLEASE REFER TO FLOWCHART):

When the Citation/Notice to Appear is received in the Clerk's office, it is entered in the computer and assigned a case number. If it is not voided by the County or Municipal Prosecutor, the County Attorney will calendar the case for appearance on the date you have listed on the Notice. If the defendant has not paid the fine prior to the hearing date and does not appear in Court or enter a written plea of not guilty, a capias may be issued for the arrest of the defendant. However, a capias will not be issued in those cases where the defendant has refused to sign the Notice to Appear acknowledging receipt of a copy or when the Notice to Appear has been posted at the property of the defendant. In such cases, if the defendant does not appear the Court will direct the Clerk of the Circuit Court to issue a summons for a subsequent date and the Clerk shall arrange for personal service of the summons. The Clerk may assess a fee for the issuance of the summons in accordance with section 28.24, Florida Statutes. The fee for issuance by the Clerk and the cost of service assessed by the Sheriff shall be added to the costs assessed to the defendant.

The County or Municipal Prosecutor is responsible for adequately preparing the case for trial, including issuance of witness subpoenas and responding to all demands for discovery.

All pre-trial motions shall be heard on the day of trial unless the defendant and the Prosecutor stipulate to the contrary.

The original court files will be kept in the Clerk's office, Traffic Violations Bureau.

Each city or other governmental unit must advise the Clerk's office in the Traffic Violations Bureau of the name of its current authorized prosecutor or prosecutors.

FISH AND WILDLIFE CONSERVATION COMMISSION CASES:

All minor violations Class (IV)

The Florida Fish and Wildlife Conservation Commission will issue citations on the required state form issued to the agency. Upon issuance, the form must be completed and defendant's signature must be obtained. In addition, the Instructions to Violator form (sample below) must be completed and a copy attached to the citation given to the defendant if the information is not available on the reverse side of the defendant's copy. The original is to be forwarded to the Clerk of Court, Traffic Violations Bureau. Insert amount of fine on the Instructions to Violator form and on upper right corner of Court copy of citation.

Any person cited for a violation by the Florida Fish and Wildlife Conservation Commission may elect to enter a written plea of guilty or no contest and pay a civil penalty, to satisfy a class IV offense without the necessity of a court appearance.

SAMPLE INSTRUCTIONS TO VIOLATOR FORM — FISH AND WILDLIFE

VIOLATOR'S NAME ______________ DATE ______________

INSTRUCTIONS TO VIOLATOR
YOU MUST, WITHIN THIRTY (30) DAYS OF TODAY'S DATE, DO ONE OF THE FOLLOWING:

1. If you desire to plead guilty or no contest and not appear in court, you must pay a fine of $______ including court costs, either in person or by mail at one of the addresses listed below. If you pay the fine you will be deemed to have admitted the civil infraction and you will be adjudicated guilty of the violation. If you desire to pay the fine by mail, you must sign the Plea & Waiver below and enclose it with your citation and payment. Cashiers checks or money orders are to be made payable to Clerk of Circuit Court. Personal checks will be accepted only in person with proper identification.

( ) Clerk of Court
West Pasco Judicial Center
7530 Little Road
New Port Richey, FL 34656-0338

OR

( ) Clerk of Court, Room 207
Robert D. Sumner Judicial Center
38053 Live Oak Avenue
Dade City, FL 33525-3894

2. If you wish to plead not guilty and appear in court, you must enter a written plea of not guilty either in person or by mail at the West Pasco Judicial Center, 7530 Little Road, New Port Richey, FL 34654 or the Robert D. Sumner Judicial Center, 38053 Live Oak Avenue, Dade City, FL 33525. Forms for Not Guilty Pleas may be obtained at either location.

FAILURE TO PAY THE FINE IN THE AMOUNT STATED ABOVE WITHIN THIRTY (30) DAYS OR FAILURE TO APPEAR FOR COURT MAY RESULT IN A WARRANT BEING ISSUED FOR YOUR ARREST. ADDITIONAL COSTS MAY ALSO BE ASSESSED.

3. Violations of law under the jurisdiction of the Fish and Wildlife Conservation Commission may be considered misdemeanors. All convictions will be on record.

I HEREBY CERTIFY that I received a copy of these instructions on the above listed date.

____
VIOLATOR'S/DEFENDANT'S SIGNATURE

PLEA & WAIVER

I understand the nature of the charge against me; I understand I am waiving my rights to be represented by an attorney, to request a continuance of my hearing and my right to a trial before a judge or a jury.

I plead ______ Guilty ______ No Contest

Defendant ______________________________

Date ______________________________

Address ______________________________

____

MOST IMPORTANT--DATE FOR MANDATORY COURT APPEARANCE--

At the time any type of citation is written, schedule the hearing at one of the locations listed below on the first available date not less than 30 days from the date of the citation in accordance with the calendar provided by the Court.

West Pasco Judicial Center, 7530 Little Road, New Port Richey, Florida, County Courtroom

OR

Robert D. Sumner Judicial Center, 38053 Live Oak Ave., Dade City, Florida, County Courtroom

Since court schedules are subject to change, please refer to recent memoranda and directives for valid court dates.

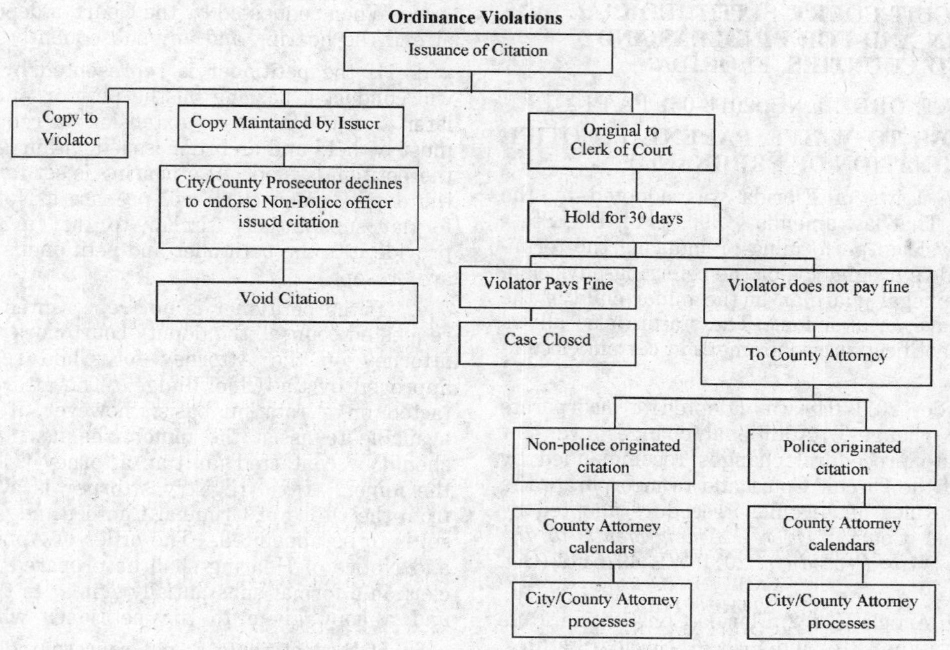

1 So in original.

2 For a copy of the Pasco County Complaint Affidavit and Notice to Defendant Form, please contact the Pasco County Sheriff's Office at (727) 847–5878.

2012–027. MOTIONS FOR EXCESS FEES BY COURT APPOINTED ATTORNEYS

IN THE CIRCUIT COURT, SIXTH JUDICIAL CIRCUIT IN AND FOR PASCO AND PINELLAS COUNTIES, FLORIDA

ADMINISTRATIVE ORDER 2012–027 PA/PI–CIR

RE: MOTIONS FOR EXCESS FEES BY COURT APPOINTED ATTORNEYS

Chapter 2012–123, section 4, Laws of Florida, amended section 27.5304, Florida Statutes, to provide for the Chief Judge or a single designee in Pasco County and Pinellas County to hear motions made by court appointed attorneys for additional compensation in cases requiring extraordinary and unusual effort. *See*, section 27.5304(12), Florida Statutes. In order to provide for the designation of the judge who, in addition to the Chief Judge, may hear such motions in Pasco and Pinellas Counties; and

In accordance with Article V, section 2, Florida Constitution, Rule of Judicial Administration 2.215, and section 43.26, Florida Statutes,

IT IS ORDERED:

1. A court appointed attorney in any type of case in Pasco or Pinellas County, who seeks additional compensation for extraordinary and unusual effort, must follow the procedures prescribed in section 27.5304(1), Florida Statutes. If an evidentiary hearing is required, the attorney must set the matter for hearing by the Chief Judge or other designated judge hearing the Pinellas Criminal Section J calendar at the Criminal Justice Center, Clearwater, Florida.

2. This Administrative Order controls to the extent that it may conflict with Administrative Order 2007–051 PI–CIR.

DONE AND ORDERED in Chambers, at Clearwater, Pinellas County, Florida, this ___ day of August 2012.

ORIGINAL SIGNED ON AUGUST 9, 2012
BY J. THOMAS MCGRADY,
CHIEF JUDGE

2012–023. [RESCINDED BY ORDER 2017-039, EFFECTIVE AUGUST 22, 2017.]

2011–061. PROCEEDINGS TO WAIVE PARENTAL NOTIFICATION OF TERMINATION OF PREGNANCY

IN THE CIRCUIT COURT, SIXTH JUDICIAL CIRCUIT IN AND FOR PINELLAS AND PASCO COUNTIES, FLORIDA

ADMINISTRATIVE ORDER NO. 2011–061 PA/PI–CIR

RE: PROCEEDINGS TO WAIVE PARENTAL NOTIFICATION OF TERMINATION OF PREGNANCY

Chapter 2011–227, Laws of Florida was adopted by the Florida legislature. That law amends § 390.01114, Fla. Stat., which requires a physician performing or inducing the termination of a minor child's pregnancy, or the referring-physician, to notify a parent or legal guardian of the minor child of the child's decision to have an abortion. The statute also allows for a waiver of that notification requirement in certain circumstances.

Administrative Order 2011–048 was adopted to incorporate the 2011 legislative changes. Additional changes are now needed to incorporate procedural changes recommended by the Pinellas Clerk of the Circuit Court and to incorporate the amendments to the Rules of Juvenile Procedure adopted by the Florida Supreme Court. *In re: Amendments to the Florida Rules of Juvenile Procedure*, 2011 WL 4975440 (Oct. 20, 2011).

In accordance with Article V, § 2, Florida Constitution, Rule of Judicial Administration 2.215, and § 43.26, Florida Statutes, it is

ORDERED:

1. Petitions filed pursuant to § 390.01114, Fla. Stat., that are filed in Pinellas County shall be filed with the Clerk of the Circuit Court at the Criminal Justice Center, Juvenile Department, 14250 49th St. N., Clearwater, FL which is where the Unified Family Court judges are located. Those petitions that are filed in Pasco County may be filed at either courthouse and should be filed with the Clerk of the Circuit Court, Juvenile Counter.

2. In Pinellas County, such petitions shall be assigned to a Unified Family Court section using an equal, at random, blind assignment system and assigned a DP case number. In Pasco County the petition shall be assigned to the dependency section at the courthouse where the petition is filed and assigned a DP case number. A new case number shall be assigned and a separate court file maintained, regardless of any pending cases involving the petitioner.

3. When the petition is filed in Pinellas County, the Clerk of the Circuit Court shall take the following actions:

a. Immediately contact the judge to whom the petition is assigned by phoning the judge's judicial assistant who will notify the judge that a petition has been filed. If the judicial assistant or the assigned judge cannot be contacted, the Clerk shall contact and notify any other Unified Family Court judge using an equal, at random, blind system, that a petition has been filed.

b. The deputy clerk will place the court file in the designated judge's bin and the judicial assistant will provide the file to the judge. The petitioner, and petitioner's attorney, if any, shall be advised by the deputy clerk to proceed to judicial reception to obtain access to the judge's chamber or to the location designated by the judge for a hearing pursuant to paragraph c, d, or e below.

c. When requested by the Court, a deputy court clerk must attend the hearing and any subsequently scheduled hearings.

d. If the petitioner **is** represented by counsel, the judge will conduct a hearing on the petition or set a hearing for a later time. Unless an extension is requested, the hearing must be held and an order issued within 3 business days after the petition is filed. If a hearing is set for a subsequent time, the deputy court clerk will prepare a Notice of Hearing in a format substantially similar to that in Attachment A and provide it to the petitioner and petitioner's attorney while they are present.

e. If the petitioner **is not** represented by counsel and has requested counsel, the deputy court clerk will contact the next attorney on the Attorney for Child registry of attorneys approved by the Chief Judge. The attorneys should be contacted on a rotation basis; however, if an attorney is not available to assist the minor, the next attorney on the list should be contacted until an attorney is located to represent the minor. If no registry attorney is available, an attorney from the Office of Criminal Conflict and Civil Regional Counsel is to be appointed. The order of Appointment of Counsel and Notice of Hearing shall be prepared by the deputy court clerk in a format substantially similar to that in Attachment B and a copy given to the petitioner while she is present.

f. If the petitioner is not represented by counsel and has not requested counsel in the petition, the Court will conduct a hearing to advise the petitioner that she has a right to court-appointed counsel at no cost to her. After inquiry, the Court may appoint counsel if requested by the petitioner or as the circumstances require.

i. If the petitioner requests counsel or the Court otherwise determines that counsel should be appointed, the deputy court clerk will follow the procedures in subparagraph e, above.

ii. If the petitioner does not request counsel and the Court does not otherwise determine that counsel should be appointed, the Court will conduct a hearing on the petition or set a hearing for a later time. Unless an extension is requested, the hearing must be held and an order issued within 3 business days after the petition is filed. If a hearing is set for a subsequent time, the deputy court clerk will prepare a notice of hearing and provide it to the petitioner while she is present.

4. When the petition is filed in Pasco County, the Clerk of the Circuit Court shall take the following actions:

a. Immediately contact the judge to whom the petition is assigned and obtain a date and time for the hearing. If the dependency judge is not available, the judge handling shelter hearings shall handle the matter. If the dependency judge and the judge handling shelter hearings are not available to schedule the hearing and issue an order within 3 business days, the Clerk shall contact the duty judge who shall handle the matter.

b. If the minor is not represented by counsel, contact the next attorney on the Attorney for Child registry of attorneys approved by the Chief Judge. The attorneys should be contacted on a rotation basis, however, if an attorney is not immediately available to assist the minor, the next attorney on the list should be contacted until an attorney is located to represent the minor. If no registry attorney is available, an attorney from the Office of Criminal Conflict and Civil Regional Counsel is to be appointed.

c. Prepare an order of Appointment of Counsel and Notice of Hearing for the judge's signature using the form in Attachment B or if the minor already has counsel, a Notice of Hearing using the form in Attachment A.

d. Provide a copy of the order of Appointment of Counsel and Notice of Hearing to the minor before the minor leaves the Clerk's office.

e. Provide a copy of the order of Appointment of Counsel and Notice of Hearing to the minor's attorney.

5. If the petitioner leaves prior to obtaining notification of the date and time of the hearing, the deputy court clerk shall provide notice to the minor in the manner requested in the petition.

6. The judicial assistant for the judge handling the petition is to:

a. Obtain the file and deliver it to the judge.

b. Request an in-court clerk for the hearing.

c. Request that the Stenographic Court Reporting Department provide a court reporter, except that in New Port Richey, the contract court reporters should be notified. A court reporter is required for all proceedings held pursuant to § 390.01114, Fla. Stat., including any hearing on appointment of counsel.

d. Notify the bailiff.

7. Judges are encouraged to hold such hearings at a place and time that will provide the maximum privacy to the minor, ensure that unauthorized persons are not in the courtroom, that unauthorized persons cannot see or hear the proceedings, and to otherwise recognize the sensitive nature of these proceedings.

8. In Pinellas County, if none of the Unified Family Court judges are available to schedule the hearing and issue an order within 3 business days, the Clerk shall contact the duty judge who shall handle the matter. In Pasco County, if the dependency judge and the judge handling shelter hearings are not available to schedule the hearing and issue the order within 3 business days, the Clerk shall contact the duty judge.

9. If the Court fails to rule within 3 business days after the petition is filed, the minor may petition the Chief Judge for a hearing by filing with the Clerk of the Circuit Court an Emergency Request for the Chief Judge. The Emergency Request should be filed at the juvenile counter and Attachment C may be used for this purpose. Upon receiving an Emergency Request, the deputy clerk shall immediately contact the office of the Chief Judge, or if the Chief Judge is not available, the duty judge. As appropriate in the circumstances, the procedures in this Order for the initial proceeding will be followed. If a hearing has not already been conducted, a hearing must be scheduled within 48 hours of receipt of the petition and an order issued within 24 hours of the hearing. If the Clerk is unable to reach the Chief Judge and the matter is directed to the duty judge, the Clerk shall also promptly notify the Chief Judge.

10. Any records generated by the Clerks of the Circuit Court shall use the initials of the minor or, if a sworn statement of true name and pseudonym is filed, the pseudonym.

11. If an appeal of the order dismissing a petition for judicial waiver of parental notice of termination of pregnancy is filed, the Clerk shall prepare and transmit the record as described in Rule 9.200(d) within two days from the filing of the notice to appeal.

Administrative Order 2011–048 is hereby rescinded.

DONE AND ORDERED in Chambers at Clearwater, Pinellas County, Florida, this ___ day of December, 2011.

ORIGINAL SIGNED on December 6, 2011
BY J. THOMAS MCGRADY,
CHIEF JUDGE

Attachment A

IN THE CIRCUIT COURT OF THE SIXTH JUDICIAL CIRCUIT IN AND FOR PASCO/PINELLAS COUNTIES, FLORIDA

IN THE INTEREST(S) OF:

Ref No: ________ DPANO
________________ UCN: ____________
Petitioner, a minor

Notice of Hearing

The hearing in this proceeding shall be held at ________
(Time)
on ____________, 20 ___ at ______________________.
(month/day) Courthouse / Courtroom #

DONE AND ORDERED in Chambers at Pasco/Pinellas County, Florida, this ___ day of ________ 20 ___.

____
CIRCUIT JUDGE

Attachment B

IN THE CIRCUIT COURT OF THE SIXTH JUDICIAL CIRCUIT IN AND FOR PASCO/PINELLAS COUNTIES, FLORIDA

IN THE INTEREST(S) OF:

Ref No: ________ DPANO
________________ UCN: ____________
Petitioner, a minor

APPOINTMENT OF COUNSEL AND NOTICE OF HEARING

Attorney ____________ is hereby appointed to represent the minor in this proceeding. The minor shall contact the attorney prior to the hearing on this matter, at ____________.
(Telephone No)

The hearing in this proceeding shall be held at ______ (Time) on ________, 20 __ at ____________.
(month/day) Courthouse / Courtroom #

DONE AND ORDERED in Chambers at Pasco/Pinellas County, Florida, this ___ day of ________ 20 __.

____
CIRCUIT JUDGE

Attachment C

IN THE CIRCUIT COURT OF THE SIXTH JUDICIAL CIRCUIT IN AND FOR PASCO/PINELLAS COUNTIES, FLORIDA

IN THE INTEREST(S) OF:

______________________ Ref No: ________ DPANO
UCN: ____________

[use pseudonym or initials if a sworn statement of true name is filed]
Petitioner, a minor

EMERGENCY REQUEST FOR CHIEF JUDGE TO REQUIRE A HEARING ON A PETITION FOR JUDICIAL WAIVER OF NOTICE

I hereby petition the Chief Judge for an order directing a hearing and ruling on my petition for judicial wavier [1] of notice in accordance with the statutory time periods.

In support of this petition, I state:

1. The Petitioner/Petitioner's Attorney filed a Petition on ________ in this case.
[date]

2. The third business day from the date of filing the petition was ________ The statutory time period in
[date]
§ 390.01114, Fla. Stat., has expired.

3. I have not requested an extension of time for the hearing to be conducted or a ruling to be made.

4. ☐ A hearing has been held on the Petition, but no ruling has been made within the statutory time period.
☐ A hearing has not been held on the Petition and no ruling has been made.

Submitted this ___ day of ________, 20 ___ at ________ A.M/ P.M.

____
Petitioner or Petitioner's Attorney Signature
[Petitioner should use pseudonym or initials if a sworn statement of true name is filed]
Print name of attorney if any ____________
Address ____________
Phone number ____________
Florida Bar No. ____________

[1] So in original.

2011–059. [RESCINDED BY ORDER 2017–022, EFFECTIVE MAY 9, 2017.]

2011–053. [RESCINDED BY ORDER 2016–083, EFFECTIVE DECEMBER 20, 2016.]

2011–006. MEDIATION

IN THE CIRCUIT COURT, SIXTH JUDICIAL CIRCUIT IN AND FOR PASCO AND PINELLAS COUNTIES, FLORIDA

ADMINISTRATIVE ORDER NO. 2011–006 PA/PI–CIR

RE: MEDIATION

The Sixth Judicial Circuit has provided for mediation services at least since small claims pretrial mediation services began in Pasco County in 1985 and in Pinellas County in 1986. The Court has several administrative orders governing different types of mediation, which the Court has amended and which need amendment again.

Therefore, in order to continue the existing Sixth Judicial Circuit mediation programs and provide for their efficient conduct, in accordance with Article V, section 2, Florida Constitution; Rule of Judicial Administration 2.215; section 43.26, Florida Statutes; and Florida Supreme Court Administrative Order AOSC09–19, it is hereby

ORDERED:

A. Administration of the Sixth Judicial Circuit Arbitration and Mediation Program. The Trial Courts Administrator is directed to provide a Program of court-provided mediation in accordance with this Administrative Order for juvenile dependency cases, small claims pretrial matters, county civil cases, and family law cases. The Program will perform such duties as assigned by the Chief Judge. The administrative judges and associate administrative judges may also assign duties to the Program that are consistent with this Order, as it relates to cases referred to mediation within their respective divisions.

The presiding judge may order parties to mediation in circuit civil cases. The Program may provide services for such cases as authorized by this Administrative Order. The Trial Courts Administrator will not provide a program of court-provided mediation for circuit civil cases. When ordered, the parties will conduct such mediation in accordance with the order of referral, and will directly pay the mediator for his or her service. In mediation of other circuit civil cases, if the parties select the mediator, the mediator will be compensated at the rate agreed to by the mediator and the parties. If the Program selects the mediator by rotation, the mediator will be compensated at the rate of not more than $200.00 per hour.

"Court-provided mediation" as described in this Administrative Order refers to mediation conducted by a certified mediator who is under contract with and paid by the Court. Fees may be assessed for court-provided mediation in accordance with section 44.108, Florida Statutes, and this Administrative Order. [Section A was amended by Administrative Order 2015-016, effective April 1, 2015.]

B. Mediation Program Responsibilities. The Program responsibilities mean the duties assigned in this Order to the Alternative Dispute Resolution Manager and staff in Pinellas County and the Diversion Programs Manager and staff in

Pasco County. In support of mediation within the Sixth Judicial Circuit, on a continuing basis the Program will:

1. Provide administrative support to the Court in accordance with the Rules of Civil Procedure; Rules for Certified and Court–Appointed Mediators; Family Law Rules of Procedure; Rules of Juvenile Procedure; Florida Supreme Court Administrative Order AOSC09–19; and Chapter 44, Florida Statutes;

2. Establish scheduling policies for court-ordered mediation proceedings;

3. Promulgate the necessary forms for the administration of the Program, including form Orders of Referral for use by the Court in referring cases to mediation;

4. Maintain a list of mediators who are certified by the Florida Supreme Court and who are willing to serve the Court in such capacity in this Circuit;

5. Manage cases referred to mediation;

6. Maintain required statistical information;

7. Perform other functions as described in this and other applicable administrative orders, and such other duties as may be assigned to the Program; and

8. For each case referred to court-provided mediation, assign in rotation a mediator who is under contract with the Court. For non-court-provided mediation, the Program will also assign a contracted mediator in rotation when the parties do not timely select their own mediator in accordance with Family Law Rule of Procedure 12.741(b)(6)(A) or Rule of Civil Procedure 1.720(f)(1).

C. Conduct of Mediation

1. All Mediation:

a. Mediation must be conducted in accordance with the applicable Rule of Procedure, the Florida Rules For Certified and Court–Appointed Mediators 10.200, *et seq.*, Chapter 44, Florida Statutes, the order of referral, and instructions of the Program regarding the mediation process. The presiding judge will hear all matters regarding mediation, including all motions.

b. In each case of court-provided mediation, the mediator must be under contract with the Court. The mediator must also be certified in accordance with Rule 10, the Florida Rules for Certified and Court–Appointed Mediators, within his or her area of appointment. Contracted mediators are paid in accordance with the terms and rates specified in the contract with the Court. The mediator may accept only the compensation provided by the terms of the contract.

c. Parties may opt-out of court-provided mediation. In that case, the parties must still comply with the order of referral and will pay the mediator's fee directly to the mediator.

d. On motion or request of a party or on its own motion, a judge will not refer any case to mediation if it finds there has been a history of domestic violence that would compromise the mediation process, or for other good cause shown.

f. Failure to appear at a duly noticed mediation conference without good cause shown may result, on motion, in the imposition of sanctions including an award of mediator and attorney fees and other costs against the party failing to appear.

g. When mediation fees are due for court-provided mediation in accordance with this Administrative Order and section 44.108, Florida Statutes, the Clerk of Circuit Court for Pasco County and the Clerk of Circuit Court for Pinellas County must collect those fees from the parties in addition to any filing fees required by section 44.108, Florida Statutes. The Clerk must not collect fees from a person who is determined indigent by the presiding judge, from a person who was determined indigent by the Clerk in the current proceeding, or a person who was determined indigent in another proceeding in the Sixth Judicial Circuit within the previous six months. Any party may pay any other party's mediation fee. A mediation fee collected from any party is refundable only when the presiding judge vacates the order of referral, or when the Clerk accepts payment in excess of the mediation fee provided in this Order.

2. Juvenile Dependency Mediation: When ordered by a judge, parties must participate in mediation of any juvenile dependency matter arising under Chapter 39, Florida Statutes. On order of referral to mediation, the Program will assign a Certified Dependency Mediator to conduct the mediation. Fees are not to be assessed for dependency mediation.

3. Small Claims Pretrial Mediation: When ordered by a judge or by a small claims hearing officer, parties must participate in court-provided mediation for the mediation of any matter referred by the judge or hearing officer. At the direction of the County Administrative Judge, the Program will assign Certified County Mediators to small claims pretrial calendars to conduct these mediations. Fees are not to be assessed for small claims mediation.

4. County Civil Mediation:

a. When ordered by a judge, parties must participate in mediation of county civil cases.

b. Court-provided mediation will be available in county civil cases when referred by the presiding judge and the judge has determined that a party lacks the ability to pay the mediator's fee. On order of referral to mediation, the Program will assign a Certified County Mediator to conduct the mediation. Each party who will participate in court-provided county civil mediation will pay a fee of $60.00 per mediation session to the Clerk of Circuit Court. Parties who are eligible for court-provided mediation may opt to obtain private mediation, in which case the mediation fee will not be assessed. A husband and wife who are either both defendants or both plaintiffs in a suit are one "party" for purposes of the mediation fee. Fees are not to be assessed for eviction cases.

c. In each case referred to court-provided mediation, the Program will monitor payments of mediation fees, scheduling, and completion of mediation.

i. When the parties in a suit have been determined eligible for court-provided mediation and at least one party is either indigent or has paid the required fee, the Program will issue a "Notice of Mediation Conference" informing the parties of the scheduled mediation conference. A non-indigent party who has not paid his or her required mediation fee by the time of a mediation conference will, prior to beginning the mediation conference, execute a form agreement to pay the fee. The mediator will file the form with the report of mediation. Such forms will be supplied to all mediators under contract with the Court.

ii. When the parties have not paid the mediation fees within 20 days of the order of referral, the Program will issue a "Notice to Comply with Court–Provided Mediation" to the parties, which advises the parties to pay the fee within 10 days of the date of the Notice. If the mediation fees are not paid by at least one of the parties within that 10 days and neither party has been found indigent, the parties are deemed ineligible for court-provided mediation. At that time, the Program will select a mediator by rotation from the Program's list of Certified County Court mediators. The parties will then compensate the mediator as if the parties had privately retained the mediator.

d. Parties eligible for court-provided mediation who opt for private mediation and parties who are not eligible for court-provided mediation will select and retain their own mediator and hold a mediation conference in accordance with the order of referral. In such cases, the parties must compensate the mediator at the rate agreed to by the mediator and the parties. If the parties do not select their own mediator in accordance with Rule of Civil Procedure 1.720(f)(1) within 10 days of the order of referral, the Program will select a mediator by rotation, who the parties will then compensate as if the parties had privately retained the mediator. Whether the parties or the Program selects the mediator, in the absence of a written agreement providing for the mediator's compensation, the parties will pay the mediator at the rate of not more than $150.00 per hour.

e. In Pinellas County the presiding judge may refer certain county civil cases for court-provided mediation by a Certified County Mediator on a day that the Court provides small claims pretrial mediation services. The presiding judge may only refer parties to this mediation after determining that the parties lack the ability to pay the mediator's fee. On order of referral, the parties must pay and the Clerk must collect the $60.00 fee per party per mediation session that is prescribed for other cases referred to court-provided county civil mediation. The Program will assign the parties to a mediator who is performing small claims pretrial mediation on the same day. Such mediation will be conducted in accordance with the order of referral and in accordance with the direction of the Pinellas County Administrative Judge.

f. A "session" for court-provided mediation is one scheduled mediation. The mediator must obtain the written consent of all parties to continue mediation beyond the initial session. Such consent must contain a statement from the parties that they understand an additional mediation fee must be paid by each non-indigent party to the Clerk of the Circuit Court pursuant to section 44.108, Florida Statutes. If the mediator reports an impasse between the parties or recommends another conference, any subsequent mediation conference is another "session" and will require the parties to pay their respective fees prior to mediation.

g. After a case is referred to mediation, counsel of record and pro se litigants must prepare and present any appropriate judgment, order, or notice of dismissal or stipulation of the parties in accordance with the mediated settlement.

5. **Family Mediation:**

a. When ordered by the presiding judge, or when automatically referred to mediation in accordance with this Administrative Order, parties must participate in mediation of family cases.

b. Court–provided mediation will be available in family cases when referred by the presiding judge or automatically referred by this Administrative Order, and the parties combined gross income is less than $100,000. Parties in family cases whose combined gross income is $100,000 or more are not eligible for court-provided mediation, but may still be ordered to mediation, either by the presiding judge or by automatic referral. To determine eligibility for court-provided family mediation and the appropriate amount that each party must pay, each party must submit a current Florida Family Law Financial Affidavit (Family Law Forms 12.902 (b) or 12.902 (c)), an Affidavit of Income for Purposes of Establishing Mediation Fees, or a Financial Affidavit to the Program within ten (10) days of the order of referral. All of the forms may be obtained online at www.jud6.org. A party determined indigent in the present case or in another case in the Sixth Judicial Circuit within the last six months may rely on that determination by notice through letter and a copy of that determination to the Program and other parties.

c. The Program will issue a "Notice of Referral to Mediation" to the parties when court-ordered mediation has not been assigned to a mediator within 20 days of the order of referral. The written Notice will inform the parties that within 10 days of the date of the Notice, each must:

(i) file financial information with the Program to determine eligibility for court-provided mediation, and if eligible, provide the Program with evidence of payment of his or her applicable fee;

(ii) file financial information with the Program to determine eligibility for court-provided mediation and, if not eligible, agree on and select a privately retained mediator and schedule a mediation conference; or

(iii) agree on and select a privately retained mediator and schedule a mediation conference.

If one party has filed financial information with the Program that indicates he or she may be eligible for court-provided mediation, but the other party has not completed any of the above actions within 10 days of the date of the written Notice of Referral to Mediation, the Program will inform the presiding judge of the other party's failure to cooperate. The presiding judge may set the case for a show-cause hearing or take other action as the presiding judge determines appropriate to facilitate resolution of the case. If no party completes any of the actions in this subparagraph within 10 days of the date of the Notice of Referral to Mediation, the parties will be deemed ineligible for court-provided mediation. At that time, the Program will select a mediator by rotation from the Program's list of Certified Family mediators. The parties will then compensate the mediator as if the parties had privately retained the mediator.

d. Each party who will participate in court-provided family mediation will pay the following mediation fees:

i. $120.00 per person per session in family mediation when the parties' combined gross income is $50,000 or more, but less than $100,000 per year; or

ii. $60.00 per person per session in family mediation when the parties' combined gross income is less than $50,000 per year. Parties who are eligible for court-provided mediation may opt to obtain private mediation, in which case the mediation fees above will not be assessed.

e. In each case referred to court-provided mediation, the Program will monitor payments of mediation fees, scheduling, and completion of mediation.

i. When the parties in a suit have been determined eligible for court-provided mediation and at least one party has paid the required fee or been found indigent, the Program will issue a "Notice of Mediation Conference" informing the parties of the scheduled mediation conference. A non-indigent party who has not paid his or her required mediation fee by the time of a mediation conference will, prior to beginning the mediation conference, execute a form agreement to pay the fee. The mediator will file the form with the report of mediation. The Program will supply such forms to all mediators under contract with the Court.

ii. When parties who are eligible for court-provided mediation have not paid the mediation fees within 20 days of that determination, the Program will issue a "Notice to Comply with Court–Provided Mediation" to the parties, which advises the parties to pay the fee within 10 days of the date of the Notice. If the mediation fees are not paid by at least one of the parties within 10 days, the parties are deemed ineligible for court-provided mediation. At that time, the Program will select a mediator by rotation from the Program's list of Certified Family mediators. The parties will then compensate the mediator as if the parties had privately retained the mediator.

f. Parties eligible for court-provided mediation who opt for private mediation and parties who are not eligible for court-provided mediation will select and retain their own mediator and hold a mediation conference in accordance with the order of referral. In such cases, the parties must compensate the mediator at the rate agreed to by the mediator and the parties. If the parties do not select their own mediator in accordance with Family Law Rule of Procedure 12.741(b)(6)(A) within 10 days of the order of referral, the Program will select a mediator by rotation, who the parties will then compensate as if the parties had privately retained the mediator. Whether the parties or the Program selects the mediator, in the absence of a written agreement providing for the mediator's compensation, the parties will pay the mediator at the rate of not more than $150.00 per hour.

g. Automatic referral of family law cases in Pinellas County:

i. In all St. Petersburg and Clearwater family law sections, except as provided herein, all post judgment matters and temporary support matters are automatically referred to mediation. Cases excluded from automatic referral to mediation are those where the Department of Revenue is a party, and any case seeking contempt for failure to pay court-ordered or stipulated child support, or court-ordered or stipulated alimony.

ii. This Administrative Order serves as the Order of Referral for family cases automatically referred to mediation, as if an Order of Referral was entered in each individual case.

iii. Notwithstanding the mediation mandated by this Order, each judge retains the discretion to waive the mandates herein on a case-by-case basis, including those cases where on motion or request of a party or on its own motion, the presiding judge finds that there has been a history of domestic violence that would compromise the mediation process.

h. A "session" for court-provided mediation is one scheduled mediation. The mediator must obtain the written consent of all parties to continue mediation beyond the initial session. Such consent must contain a statement from the parties that they understand an additional mediation fee must be paid by each nonindigent party to the Clerk of the Circuit Court pursuant to section 44.108, Florida Statutes. If the mediator reports an impasse between the parties or recommends another conference, any subsequent mediation conference is another "session" and will require the parties to pay their respective fees prior to mediation.

i. After a case is referred to mediation, counsel of record and pro se litigants must prepare and present any appropriate judgment, order, or notice of dismissal or stipulation of the parties in accordance with the mediated settlement.

Administrative Order 2005–005 PA/PI–CIR "Civil and Family Mediation"; Administrative Order 2005–032 PA/PI–CIR "Juvenile Dependency Mediation Appointment & Compensation"; Administrative Order 2006–062 PI–CIR "Automatic Referral to Family Mediation"; Administrative Order 2007–030 PA/PI–CIR "Mediation Program"; and Administrative Order 2008–034 PA/PI–CIR "Family Mediation—Additional Changes" are hereby rescinded.

Administrative Order 2005–030 PA/PI–CIR "Small Claims Pretrial Hearings and Mediation" is amended to reflect that the rate of compensation for small claims pretrial mediators is set by contract with the Court; the rate of compensation is no longer set by Administrative Order. All other terms and conditions of Administrative Order 2005–030 remain in full force and effect.

DONE AND ORDERED in Chambers at Clearwater, Pinellas County, Florida, this ___ day of March, 2011.

ORIGINAL SIGNED March 1, 2011
BY J. THOMAS MCGRADY,
CHIEF JUDGE

2010–065. [RESCINDED BY ORDER 2017-064, EFFECTIVE NOVEMBER 11, 2017.]

2010–063. [RESCINDED BY ORDER 2018-068, EFFECTIVE DECEMBER 12, 2018]

2010–045. [RESCINDED BY ORDER 2017-027, EFFECTIVE JUNE 7, 2017.]

2009–074. [RESCINDED BY ORDER 2016–011, EFFECTIVE MARCH 1, 2016.]

2009–037. INCAPACITY AND GUARDIANSHIP CASES—APPOINTMENT OF ATTORNEY AND RECOVERY OF COSTS

IN THE CIRCUIT COURT, SIXTH JUDICIAL CIRCUIT IN AND FOR PASCO AND PINELLAS COUNTIES, FLORIDA

ADMINISTRATIVE ORDER NO. 2009–037 PA/PI–CIR

RE: INCAPACITY AND GUARDIANSHIP CASES—APPOINTMENT OF ATTORNEY AND RECOVERY OF COSTS

Effective July 1, 2009, Chapter 2009–61, Laws of Florida, amends § 57.081, Florida Statutes, to waive payment of filing fees in a guardianship case when the Court or the Clerk has found the alleged incapacitated person indigent. To implement those statutory amendments, the Circuit's procedures for the recovery of fees and costs in guardianship cases need updating.

The Clerks of the Circuit Court, the Sixth Judicial Circuit on behalf of the State of Florida, and the Justice Administrative Commission on behalf of the State of Florida incur various costs when a petition to determine incapacity is filed under Chapter 744, Florida Statutes.[1] The filing fees for the petition to determine capacity and the petition for appointment of guardian are to be paid to the Clerk of the Circuit Court (Clerk). The Sixth Judicial Circuit will expend funds for the guardianship examining committee. The members of the guardianship examining committee are under contract with the Court and, in cases involving an indigent ward, are paid through funds appropriated by the Florida Legislature to the state courts system.

An attorney must be appointed for the alleged incapacitated person. See § 744.331(2)(b), Florida Statutes. Section 27.511(6)(c), Florida Statutes requires the Court, in consultation with the Clerk to determine, if possible, whether the alleged incapacitated person is indigent.[2] If the alleged incapacitated person is indigent, the Office of Criminal Conflict and Civil Regional Counsel (Regional Counsel) is to be appointed. If the alleged incapacitated person is not indigent, or if it is not possible to determine whether the alleged incapacitated person is indigent, counsel from the Registry of attorneys approved by the Chief Judge is to be appointed. If the Regional Counsel is appointed and it is later determined that the alleged incapacitated person is not indigent, the Regional Counsel must move to withdraw and request appointment of an attorney from the Registry. If an attorney is appointed from the Registry and it is later determined that the alleged incapacitated person is indigent, the Registry attorney must move to withdraw and request appointment of the Regional Counsel. The transfer of representation will likely be disruptive to the alleged incapacitated person and may delay needed services for the alleged incapacitated person.

Whether the Regional Counsel or a private attorney is appointed, the State of Florida Justice Administrative Commission will expend funds for an attorney to represent the alleged incapacitated person if the person is determined indigent or is found not to be incapacitated.

In order to update procedures for determining whether an alleged incapacitated person is indigent, to minimize disruption to the alleged incapacitated person by withdrawals by attorneys appointed to represent the alleged incapacitated person, and to continue procedures for the recovery of costs that have been incurred by the Clerk, the Sixth Judicial Circuit on behalf of the State of Florida, and the Justice Administrative Commission on behalf of the State of Florida,

IT IS ORDERED:

1. When a petition to determine incapacity and for the appointment of a guardian is filed, the Clerk shall prepare an order appointing an attorney from the Registry provided to the Clerk by the Chief Judge, unless the petition is filed by the Public Guardian and the filing meets the requirements of paragraph two.

2. When a petition to determine incapacity and for the appointment of a guardian is filed by the Public Guardian and the Public Guardian requests waiver of the filing fee because the alleged incapacitated person is known by that office to be indigent, the Clerk shall prepare an order appointing the Regional Counsel.

3. When a suggestion of capacity is filed and the ward is known to have assets based upon a previous inventory, or if an inventory has not yet been filed, the Clerk shall prepare an order appointing an attorney from the Registry provided to the Clerk by the Chief Judge.

4. When a suggestion of capacity is filed and the ward is known to be indigent based upon a previous inventory, the Clerk shall prepare an order appointing the Regional Counsel.

5. When payment of filing fees is deferred due to the possible indigence of the alleged incapacitated person, the Clerk may file a statement of claim in the guardianship case. The claim form shall be substantially similar to Attachment A. The claim shall be accompanied by a proposed order requiring payment. The order shall be in a form substantially similar to Attachment B.

6. When the Court appoints a guardianship examining committee or other expert to examine the ward, including a physician appointed pursuant to § 744.464, Florida Statutes, and the State of Florida Sixth Judicial Circuit pays such costs, the Clerk shall file a statement of claim on behalf of the State of Florida Sixth Judicial Circuit. The statement of claim shall be substantially similar to Attachment A. The claim shall be accompanied by a proposed order requiring payment.

7. When the State of Florida Justice Administrative Commission has paid for the costs for the Regional Counsel or for a court appointed attorney, the court appointed attorney or the Regional Counsel may file a statement of claim on behalf of the State of Florida Justice Administrative Commission. The value of the fees for the Regional Counsel shall be the amount set forth in the General Appropriations Act, unless otherwise set by the court. The statement of claim shall be substantially similar to the Attachment C and shall be accompanied by a proposed order requiring payment.

8. If the alleged incapacitated person is found by the court not to be incapacitated and the Court finds that the petition was filed in bad faith, the Court may direct the Petitioner to pay filing fees to the Clerk, to pay the examining committee fees to the State of Florida Sixth Judicial Circuit, and attorneys fees to the State of Florida Justice Administrative Commission.

9. If the alleged incapacitated person is found to be incapacitated by the court and the ward is determined by the court, either at the time of the guardianship hearing or the filing of the inventory, to have sufficient assets, the filing fees, the fees for the guardianship examining committee, and the attorney's fees will be paid by the guardian from the assets of the ward.

10. If the alleged incapacitated person is found to be incapacitated by the court and the ward is determined not indigent, but still found by the court at the time of the inventory not to have sufficient assets to pay the claims for the filing fee, guardianship examining committee, and the attorneys fees, and such fees are paid by the State of Florida, the court will defer payment of the claims by the guardian until the ward has sufficient assets to pay the claims.

11. When the Clerk incurs additional costs as specifically provided for in Chapter 744, the Clerk may file a statement of claim for those costs in the guardianship case. Whenever the Clerk files a statement of claim, the Clerk shall prepare a proposed order. The Order shall be substantially similar to Attachment B.

12. If assets are later discovered or accumulated in the guardianship estate, the guardian may, without further order of the Court, pay claims from the Clerk, the State of Florida Sixth Judicial Circuit, and the Justice Administrative Commission. All checks submitted for such payments by the guardian shall include the case number on the check. Unless the judge in an individual case orders a different priority, payments shall be made in the following order of priority:

a. Filing fees. Checks should be made payable to Clerk of the Circuit Court. In Pasco County, checks should be forwarded to:

Clerk of the Circuit Court

Attention: Guardianship Section

P.O. Drawer 338

New Port Richey, FL 34654

In Pinellas County, checks should be forwarded to:

Clerk of the Circuit Court

Attention: Probate Court Records, Room 106

315 Court Street

Clearwater, FL 33756

b. Guardianship examining committee fees or fees for other expert appointed by the Court to examine the ward, including a physician appointed pursuant to § 744.464, Florida Statutes. Checks should be made payable to the State of Florida, Sixth Judicial Circuit.

In Pasco County, checks should be forwarded to:

Clerk of the Circuit Court

Attention: Guardianship Section

P.O. Drawer 338

New Port Richey, FL 34654

The Clerk will docket receipt of payment and forward it to the Administrative Office of the Courts in New Port Richey.

In Pinellas County, checks should be forwarded to:

Fiscal Office

Administrative Office of the Courts

14250 49th Street North

Clearwater, FL 33762

c. Additional statutory fees including any audit fees assessed by the Clerk. Checks should be made payable to the Clerk of the Circuit Court and forwarded to the address listed in paragraph a.

d. Costs for the Regional Counsel or the court appointed attorney. Checks should be made payable to the State of Florida, Justice Administrative Commission and forwarded to:

Justice Administrative Commission

P.O. Box 1654

Tallahassee, FL 32302

13. The Clerk, the Administrative Office of the Courts for the Sixth Judicial Circuit, and the Justice Administrative Commission shall file a notice of receipt of payment in the guardianship case whenever payment is made by the guardian.

14. The Clerk, when conducting the annual accounting, shall review whether any claims for the filing fee, other fees for the Clerk, guardianship examining committee or other expert fees, or attorneys fees are outstanding and include such information with the accounting.

15. The Chief Judge may update or make other amendments to the attachments of this Administrative Order without further amendment to this Administrative Order.

Administrative Order 2007–103 PA/PI–CIR and Administrative Order 2008–005 PA/PI–CIR are hereby rescinded.

DONE AND ORDERED in Chambers at Clearwater, Pinellas County, Florida this day 30 of June 2009.

____

Robert J. Morris, Jr., Chief Judge

1 Guardian Advocate proceedings filed pursuant to section 393.12, Florida Statutes, are governed by Chapter 744 and accordingly the provisions in this Administrative Order apply to such proceedings.

2 Governor Crist noted in his letter of June 19, 2007, to the Secretary of State regarding this legislation (SB 1088), that the determination of indigent status cannot be accurately made prior to the filing of an inventory by the guardian.

Attachment A

IN THE CIRCUIT COURT OF THE SIXTH JUDICIAL CIRCUIT IN AND FOR PASCO/PINELLAS COUNTY, FLORIDA

PROBATE DIVISION

IN RE: THE GUARDIANSHIP OF CASE NO.: _______
UCN: _______

____

Incapacitated

STATEMENT OF CLAIM

COMES NOW the Clerk of the Circuit Court of Pasco/Pinellas County, on behalf of the State of Florida, and herewith files its claim for reimbursement of amounts advanced said guardianship by the State of Florida pursuant to § 744.331 or § 744.464, Florida Statutes, and in support thereof states as follows:

1. The following fees were expended in the above-captioned guardianship case:

FEES EXPENDED

Filing Fees and Costs (Make check payable to Clerk of the Circuit Court)	$_______

Examining Committee Fees (Make check payable to The State of Florida, Sixth Judicial Circuit)	$________
Physician Fees	$________
(Make check payable to The State of Florida, Sixth Judicial Circuit)	
TOTAL AMOUNT OF CLAIM	$________

2. These fees and costs have been incurred as a result of the proceedings to determine capacity of the above-mentioned individual, in guardianship case number ________.

3. Pursuant to § 57.081, Florida Statutes, the filing fees in a guardianship case are waived if the ward is indigent and has obtained a certification of indigence under § 27.52 or § 57.082, Florida Statutes. However, when the ward is found not indigent, the Clerk of the Circuit Court is entitled to file a claim for reimbursement of filing fees waived that were deferred while awaiting determination of the ward's indigent-status. Pursuant to § 744.105, Florida Statutes, costs may be awarded in guardianship proceedings.

4. Pursuant to § 744.331, Florida Statutes, fees for the examining committee of an indigent individual in a guardianship proceeding shall be paid by the State of Florida. After payment of examining committee fees, pursuant to § 744.331(7)(b), Florida Statutes, the State of Florida is entitled to file a claim against the guardianship to recover those fees paid by the State on behalf of the indigent person.

5. Pursuant to § 744.464, Florida Statutes, the Court shall appoint a physician to examine the incapacitated individual when a suggestion of capacity is filed. When the incapacitated person is indigent, the cost of the physician is paid by the State of Florida and the State is entitled to file a claim against the guardianship to recover those fees paid by the State on behalf of the indigent person.

6. The Clerk of the Circuit Court of Pasco/Pinellas County, on behalf of the Clerk and the State of Florida, hereby requests this Court enter an order requiring immediate reimbursement of said fees from, or upon discovery of, any assets, income, or property of the ward or of this guardianship estate.

7. In addition, the Clerk of the Circuit Court of Pasco/Pinellas County, on behalf of the State of Florida, expects the State of Florida to make future expenditures on the estate. Accordingly, the Clerk requests that this Court consider this as a claim for future fees and costs to be reimbursed and that the Court retain jurisdiction of this claim.

WHEREFORE, the Clerk of the Circuit Court of Pasco/Pinellas County, on behalf of the Clerk and on behalf of the State of Florida, Sixth Judicial Circuit, requests that this Court consider this as a claim for the amounts set forth above to secure repayment of the respective claims and requests such other and further relief to which it may be entitled.

DATED this ___ day of ________, 20 ___.

CLERK OF THE CIRCUIT
COURT OF PASCO/PINELLAS
COUNTY, FLORIDA

By: ____________________
DEPUTY CLERK

Attachment B

IN THE CIRCUIT COURT, SIXTH JUDICIAL CIRCUIT IN AND FOR PASCO/PINELLAS COUNTY, FLORIDA

PROBATE DIVISION

IN RE: THE GUARDIANSHIP OF CASE NO.: ______
UCN: ________

____
Incapacitated

ORDER REQUIRING PAYMENT OF FILING FEES AND COSTS

THIS CAUSE coming on to be heard on the motion of the Clerk of the Circuit Court and the Court having reviewed the file and being otherwise fully advised in the premises, the Court finds that filing fees and costs were previously deferred by the Clerk of the Circuit Court of Pasco/Pinellas County in the above-captioned guardianship after it was alleged that the ward was indigent. Pursuant to §§ 27.52 and 744.105, Florida Statutes, the Clerk of the Circuit Court has a right to recover these filing fees and costs in the event assets, income, or property are identified as part of the guardianship estate. Therefore, it is

ORDERED AND ADJUDGED that, in the event sufficient funds are identified as part of the guardianship estate, the guardian shall be required to pay the Clerk of the Circuit Court of Pasco/Pinellas County for the filing fees and costs deferred in the guardianship.

DONE AND ORDERED in Chambers at ________, Pasco/Pinellas County, Florida, this ___ day of ________, 20 ___.

____
CIRCUIT COURT JUDGE

Attachment C

IN THE CIRCUIT COURT OF THE SIXTH JUDICIAL CIRCUIT IN AND FOR PASCO/PINELLAS COUNTY, FLORIDA

PROBATE DIVISION

IN RE: THE GUARDIANSHIP OF CASE NO.: ______
UCN: ________

____
Incapacitated

STATEMENT OF CLAIM

COMES NOW________, the attorney appointed by the Court to represent the incapacitated person named above, on behalf of the State of Florida Justice Administrative Commission, and herewith files a claim for reimbursement of amounts advanced said guardianship by the State of Florida pursuant to § 744.331 or § 744.464, Florida Statutes, and in support thereof states as follows:

1. The following fees and costs were expended in the above-captioned guardianship case:

FEES EXPENDED

Attorney Fees and Costs $________
(Make check payable to State of Florida, Justice Administrative Commission)

TOTAL AMOUNT OF CLAIM $________

2. These fees and costs have been incurred as a result of the proceedings to determine capacity of the above-captioned individual, in guardianship case number ________.

3. Pursuant to §§ 27.511 and 744.331, Florida Statutes, fees for the regional counsel or for a private attorney appointed to represent an individual in a guardianship proceeding may be paid by the State of Florida in certain circumstances. After payment of such attorney fees, pursuant to § 744.331(7)(b), Florida Statutes, the State of Florida is entitled to file a claim against the guardianship to recover those fees paid by the State on behalf of the ward or alleged incapacitated person.

4. Pursuant to § 744.464, Florida Statutes, when an objection to the suggestion of capacity is filed or when the medical examination suggests that a full restoration of rights is not appropriate, the Court shall appoint the regional counsel or a private attorney to represent the ward if the ward does not have an attorney. Fees for the regional counsel or for a private attorney appointed to represent an individual in a guardianship proceeding may be paid by the State of Florida in certain circumstances.

5. Therefore, ________, the attorney appointed to represent the ward or alleged incapacitated person in the above-captioned guardianship case, on behalf of the State of Florida, Justice Administrative Commission, hereby requests this Court enter an order requiring immediate reimbursement of said fees from, or upon discovery of, any assets, income, or property of the ward or of this guardianship estate.

WHEREFORE,________, the attorney for the above-captioned incapacitated person, on behalf of the State of Florida, Justice Administrative Commission, requests that this Court consider this as a claim for the amount set forth above to secure repayment of the claim and requests such other and further relief to which it may be entitled.

DATED this ___ day of ________, 20 ___.

BY: ________________
ATTORNEY FOR THE INCAPACITATED WARD

2009–036. [RESCINDED BY ORDER 2019–005, EFFECTIVE JANUARY 23, 2019]

2008–076. MEDIA POLICY

IN THE CIRCUIT COURT, SIXTH JUDICIAL CIRCUIT IN AND FOR PASCO AND PINELLAS COUNTIES, FLORIDA

ADMINISTRATIVE ORDER NO. 2008–076 PA/PI–CIR

RE: MEDIA POLICY

Florida Rule of Judicial Administration 2.450 governs the use of technology in judicial proceedings. Rule 2.450 vests the presiding judge with broad authority to control the conduct of proceedings before the court, ensure decorum and prevent distractions, and ensure the fair administration of justice. Rule 2.450 also vests the chief judge with broad authority to determine the location and placement of audio systems, microphones, television cameras and equipment, still camera photographers and equipment, light sources, and related technological devices in courtrooms and courthouses. The Rules of Judicial Administration can be accessed on The Florida Bar's webpage at http://www.floridabar.org/.

Recent technological advancements in consumer electronics, coupled with the installation of wireless technology in many courthouses, now make it more difficult for the presiding judge and court security to ensure that people attending court proceedings are not recording or broadcasting the court proceedings without the court's approval. Any non-approved recording or broadcasting of court proceedings violates Florida Rule of Judicial Administration 2.450.

In order to ensure that professional journalists continue to have appropriate access to court proceedings, to ensure that members of The Florida Bar continue to have the ability to operate approved technological devices, to prevent disruptions to court proceedings, to prevent non-approved audio or visual recordings, to ensure safety and security in the hallways and other areas of ingress and egress in the courthouses, and to assist court security in the uniform enforcement of issues related to Florida Rule of Judicial Administration 2.450, it is hereby

ORDERED:

1. **Definitions.**

a. "Professional journalist" is defined as a person regularly engaged in collecting, photographing, recording, writing, editing, reporting, or publishing news, for gain or livelihood, who obtained the information sought while working as a salaried employee of, or independent contractor for, a newspaper, news journal, news agency, press association, wire service, radio or television station, network, or news magazine.

b. "News" is defined as information of public concern relating to local, statewide, national, or worldwide issues or events.

2. No device capable of taking pictures or capturing sound may be operated inside any room in which a judicial proceeding is taking place or immediately prior to a scheduled judicial proceeding without prior approval of the presiding judge. Such devices include, but are not limited to, cell phones, cameras, digital voice recorders, tape recorders, laptops, personal digital assistants, or similar technological devices. A person who operates a non-approved device will have the device confiscated by court security and such person may be issued a trespass warning or may be held in contempt of court or both.

3. In order to ensure security and the orderly administration of justice, persons seeking prior approval to operate a device capable of taking pictures or capturing sound shall do the following:

a. A person not meeting the definition of "professional journalist" shall present his or her request to the Public

Information Officer (PIO) of the Sixth Judicial Circuit as far in advance of the scheduled proceeding as circumstances permit. The PIO shall communicate all requests made under this provision to the presiding judge. The PIO will then inform the requester whether or not the presiding judge has approved the request.

b. A person meeting the definition of "professional journalist" may present his or her request to the presiding judge or to the Public Information Officer (PIO) of the Sixth Judicial Circuit as far in advance of the scheduled proceeding as circumstances permit.

4. Members of The Florida Bar appearing before the court shall be allowed to operate technological devices to the extent customarily allowed by the presiding judge.

5. Nothing in this Administrative Order shall be construed to limit or impair a presiding judge's authority to grant, deny, or otherwise respond to a request by a person to operate a device capable of taking pictures or capturing sound in a room used for a judicial proceeding.

6. Nothing in this Administrative Order shall be construed to limit or impair a presiding judge's authority to exclude any items from the courtroom in order to ensure safety or the orderly administration of justice.

7. No person may conduct photography or audio or visual recording in any area of the courthouse that is primarily used for ingress to or egress from the interior rooms in the courthouse. Such rooms include, but not limited to, courtrooms, chambers, conference rooms, offices, and the secure areas adjacent to the courthouse entrances. A person who conducts photography or audio or visual recording in any area of the courthouse that is primarily used for ingress to or egress from the interior rooms in the courthouse will have the device confiscated by court security and such person may be issued a trespass warning or may be held in contempt of court or both.

8. Designated places to conduct interviews may be provided by the court on a case-by-case basis as circumstances permit. Requests to conduct interviews in a courthouse area should be submitted to the Public Information Officer (PIO) of the Sixth Judicial Circuit as far in advance of the desired date as circumstances permit.

9. The Sheriff of Pasco County and the Sheriff of Pinellas County shall enforce this Administrative Order by confiscating devices that are being used in violation of paragraph 2 or paragraph 7 above. The Sheriff does not need to confiscate all devices capable of taking pictures or capturing sound that are simply brought into courthouses or rooms used for judicial proceedings. Rather such devices shall be confiscated when:

a. the device is being operated without prior approval from the presiding judge in a room where a judicial proceeding is taking place; or

b. the device is being operated to conduct photography or audio or visual recording in an area of the courthouse that is primarily used for ingress to or egress from the interior rooms in the courthouse.

10. The Chief Judge may delegate his or her authority under Florida Rule of Judicial Administration 2.450 to determine the location and placement of audio systems, microphones, television cameras and equipment, still camera photographers and equipment, light sources, and related technological devices to the presiding judge in order to accomplish the orderly administration of justice.

Administrative Order PA/PI–CIR–99–77 is hereby rescinded.

DONE AND ORDERED in Chambers at Clearwater, Pinellas County, Florida on this 1 day of November 2008.

Robert J. Morris, Jr.
Chief Judge

2008–058. INVOLUNTARY COMMITMENT OF SEXUALLY VIOLENT PREDATORS

IN THE CIRCUIT COURT, SIXTH JUDICIAL CIRCUIT IN AND FOR PASCO AND PINELLAS COUNTIES, FLORIDA

ADMINISTRATIVE ORDER NO. 2008–058 PI–CIR

RE: INVOLUNTARY COMMITMENT OF SEXUALLY VIOLENT PREDATORS

In order to consolidate the handling of proceedings for the Involuntary Civil Commitment of Sexually Violent Predators, section 394.910 et seq., Florida Statutes, (Jimmy Ryce Act) in Pinellas County, it is

ORDERED:

1. Section 60 is continued as a section within the Civil Division of the Circuit Court, in and for Pinellas County Florida.

2. The State Attorney may request an order seeking return of a respondent for a determination of counsel and a determination of indigence prior to filing a petition for the Involuntary Civil Commitment of a Sexually Violent Predator, pursuant to section 394.910, et seq., Florida Statutes. The request shall be made to the judge assigned to section 60.

3. When the Clerk of the Circuit Court receives a petition for the Involuntary Civil Commitment of a Sexually Violent Predator pursuant to section 394.910 et seq., Florida Statutes, the Clerk shall assign the case to section 60.

4. Section 60 will handle all pre-trial, trial, and annual review proceedings for these cases.

5. Petitions for attorney's fees shall be in accordance with Administrative Order 2004–028 PA/PI–CIR or subsequent order regarding attorney's fees and where court approval is required shall be directed to the judge assigned to section 60. Petitions for approval of fees for experts shall also be directed to the judge assigned to section 60.

This Administrative Order shall take effect January 1, 2009, at which time Administrative Order 2006–084 PI–CIR is hereby rescinded.

DONE AND ORDERED in Chambers at Clearwater, Pinellas County, Florida, this 10th day of September 2008.

Robert J. Morris, Jr., Chief Judge

2007–081. [RESCINDED BY ORDER 2016–010, EFFECTIVE MARCH 1, 2016.]

2007–080. [RESCINDED BY ORDER 2017–022, EFFECTIVE MAY 9, 2017.]

2007–024. [RESCINDED BY ORDER 2018-068, EFFECTIVE DECEMBER 12, 2018]

2007–001. ADULT DRUG COURT

IN THE CIRCUIT COURT, SIXTH JUDICIAL CIRCUIT IN AND FOR PASCO AND PINELLAS COUNTIES, FLORIDA

ADMINISTRATIVE ORDER NO. 2007–001 PA/PI–CIR

RE: ADULT DRUG COURT

Section N of the circuit criminal division in Pinellas County was first created by Administrative Order PI–CIR–00–02 as a regular criminal section in the criminal division. Section N began operating as an adult drug court as contemplated by section 397.334, Florida Statutes, effective January 16, 2001. See Administrative Order 2004–102 PI–CIR.

Adult drug court in Pinellas County has had a beneficial impact in Pinellas County. See Pinellas County Adult Drug Court Annual Report 2005. Pasco County has appropriated funds for drug treatment and the Florida Legislature has provided for an additional circuit judge and court staff so that it is now possible to establish an adult drug court in Pasco County. Accordingly, it is:

ORDERED:

1. The purpose of drug court is to reduce recidivism by emphasizing treatment and rehabilitation as an alternative to incarceration, while also requiring offender accountability. The goal of drug court is to provide the defendant with the resources and skills necessary to overcome addiction so that the defendant may become a productive member of society.

2. The State Attorney's Office has provided for pre-trial intervention for certain drug offenders in Pinellas County pursuant to section 948.08, Florida Statutes, and intends to provide pre-trial diversion for certain drug offenders in Pasco County. Subject to applicable law, defendants who successfully complete the pre-trial diversion program and graduate from the program will have their charges dismissed. The provisions of this Administrative Order do not apply to pre-trial diversion defendants.

3. The Clerk of the Circuit Court in Pasco County shall not assign circuit Criminal cases to section 30 or 31 on a random basis and the Clerk of the Circuit Court in Pinellas County shall not assign Circuit criminal cases on a random basis to section N. Cases shall be assigned to sections 30 and 31 in Pasco County and to section N in Pinellas County accordance with this Administrative Order. Pasco County sections 30 and 31 and Pinellas County section N are hereinafter referred to as the drug court sections.

4. The State Attorney's Office is to identify which cases are to be heard in drug court. The State Attorney's Office may use whatever procedures it deems appropriate to identify those cases to be heard in drug court. The cases may either be initially assigned by direct information to the drug court section by the State Attorney's Office or be transferred from another criminal section to a drug court section upon written notification by the State Attorney's Office to the Administrative Office of the Courts. In Pasco County, no more than 260 defendants (both pretrial diversion and post plea) may be in adult drug court at any one time. The Administrative Office of the Courts shall notify the State Attorney when drug court does not have the capacity for additional defendants.

5. If the defense attorney desires to have a case heard in drug court, he or she must make a request to transfer, which must be processed and approved by the State Attorney's Office.

6. The drug court judge retains the ultimate responsibility for determining that a case assigned to drug court by the State Attorney is appropriate for drug court. While the State Attorney's Office makes the decision whether a case will be filed in or transferred to a drug court section, the judge assigned to a drug court section retains the authority to decide that a case will not remain in that section. If the judge decides that a case will not remain in the drug court section, the State Attorney's Office and the defense attorney shall be notified and the case shall be transferred back to the regular criminal section from which it was transferred. If a case has been initially assigned to a drug court section, the case shall be assigned to another criminal section in accordance with local rule 3.

7. A defendant may voluntarily elect not to have his or her case heard in drug court. Upon a defendant electing not to have his or her case heard in drug court, the case shall be transferred back to the regular criminal section from which it was transferred. If a case has been initially assigned to a drug court section, the case shall be assigned to another criminal section in accordance with local rule 3.

8. Each defendant has only one opportunity to have his or her case heard in drug court. If a defendant is charged with a new offense and has already had a prior case heard and resolved in drug court, the new case will be heard in a regular circuit felony division absent specific approval by the State Attorney's Office.

9. By agreeing to have his or her case heard in drug court, the defendant agrees that no depositions will be taken, trial dates scheduled, or substantive pre-trial motions heard. If a pretrial motion must be heard, the case shall be transferred back to the regular criminal section from which it was transferred. If a case has been initially assigned to a drug court section, the case shall be assigned to another criminal section in accordance with local rule 3.

10. A defendant whose case has been assigned to drug court must voluntarily and truthfully provide information to aid the court at each step in the process. As a condition of having his or her case heard in drug court, the defendant must execute a written consent form with a waiver of confidentiality as to treatment in accordance with 42 C.F.R. § 2.31, prior to disposition of the case. If the defendant refuses to execute the written consent, the case shall be transferred back to the regular criminal section from which it was transferred. If a case has been initially assigned to a drug court section, the case shall be assigned to another criminal section in accordance with local rule 3.

11. Before a plea is tendered or a defendant can be sentenced in drug court, the defendant must submit to an initial

substance abuse evaluation. The evaluation should occur within 21 days of arraignment or within such other time as may be ordered by the court. The evaluation provides an overall assessment of the defendant's addiction and the resources needed to overcome that addiction. The provider who administers the evaluation must use objective standards and criteria and must be licensed by the Department of Children and Families. The written evaluation is the primary document consulted by the trial judge in fashioning an appropriate sentence.

12. Staff in the Administrative Office of the Courts facilitate the process by which a defendant is evaluated; coordinate the procedure by which the written evaluation is furnished to the state, defense counsel, and the trial judge; assist the court in managing its caseload; compile statistics; prepare the cases scheduled on the calendar; schedule initial appointments with treatment providers; and perform other case management functions for the courts as required.

13. The sanctions imposed in drug court are within the court's discretion and include but are not limited to outpatient treatment programs, non-secure residential treatment programs, and intensive, secure, long-term residential treatment programs. Treatment providers must be licensed by the Department of Children and Families for the type of treatment provided. Some providers are funded by Pasco County or Pinellas County and are selected through a request for proposal process. Other providers are funded and selected by the Department of Corrections. Drug court probation is the initial sanction typically imposed. As a condition of drug court probation, a defendant will typically be sentenced to the least intensive treatment program necessary for rehabilitation. Other conditions of probation may be ordered, such as random drug testing or obtaining a G.E.D.

14. The sanctions imposed for a violation of probation are within the trial judge's discretion. The trial judge may continue probation, may revoke probation and order a new term of probation, may impose a term of incarceration in either the county jail or Department of Corrections, as provided by the Criminal Punishment Code, or impose any other sanction authorized by law.

15. Every defendant sentenced in drug court must periodically return to court for a judicial review. The purpose of a judicial review is to assess the defendant's level of participation in treatment, monitor the overall success of treatment, and admonish or encourage the defendant in his or her attempt at rehabilitation. Prior to a judicial review, the judge may hold a case staffing with treatment providers, court staff, Department of Corrections personnel, assistant public defenders, assistant state attorneys, and others selected by the judge.

16. Defendants who successfully complete and graduate from adult drug court may have an adjudication of guilt withheld or receive a reduced probationary period.

17. The trial judge will review a defendant's successful completion of the assigned treatment. The trial judge will make the ultimate decision as to whether a defendant may graduate from drug court.

This Administrative Order shall take effect January 16, 2007, at which time Administrative Order 2004–102 is rescinded.

DONE AND ORDERED in Chambers at St. Petersburg, Pinellas County, Florida, this 2d day of January, 2007.

David A. Demers, Chief Judge

2006–097. FIRST APPEARANCE ADVISORY PROCEEDINGS

IN THE CIRCUIT COURT, SIXTH JUDICIAL CIRCUIT IN AND FOR PASCO AND PINELLAS COUNTIES, FLORIDA

ADMINISTRATIVE ORDER NO. 2006–097 PA/PI CIR

RE: FIRST APPEARANCE ADVISORY PROCEEDINGS

A first appearance affords an arrested person the opportunity to be advised of his or her constitutional rights, as well as the opportunity to be advised of the charges against him or her. Rule of Criminal Procedure 3.130(a). At the beginning of each first appearance (advisories), the presiding Circuit Judge or County Judge provides an initial advisement to all the arrested persons. That initial advisement states that the arrested person is not required to say anything; that anything said by the arrested person may be used against him or her; that if unrepresented, the arrested person has a right to counsel, and that counsel will be provided if the arrested person is financially unable to afford counsel; and that the arrested person has a right to communicate with counsel, family, or friends, and will be provided reasonable means to do so. Rule of Criminal Procedure 3.130(b).

In an effort to maximize judicial efficiency and standardize the advisement process, a prerecorded statement of the initial advisement will be played to accomplish the same advisement of rights that has heretofore been done in person. The prerecorded advisement will increase judicial efficiency by reducing the need for judges to deliver the advisement in person without restricting the inmate's ability to communicate with the Court when his or her case is called.

Pursuant to Rule of Judicial Administration 2.215 (2006), the Chief Judge has the authority to adopt administrative orders necessary to ensure the efficient operation of the court system. Accordingly, it is hereby

ORDERED:

1. When all inmates scheduled for advisories are assembled, and the reporting or electronic recording of the proceeding has been started, Sheriff's personnel shall play a prerecorded advisement of rights provided by the Court.

2. Sheriff's personnel shall activate the recording equipment and shall then play the prerecorded advisement so that the prerecorded advisement is recorded as part of the record of the advisory proceeding. When the presiding judge first appears, the Sheriff's personnel present shall notify the presiding judge that the prerecorded advisement was played before inmates present for advisories and that to the best of their knowledge the recording equipment was operating during the playing of the prerecorded advisement.

3. The provisions of this Administrative Order shall take effect November 15, 2006.

DONE AND ORDERED in Chambers at St. Petersburg, Pinellas County, Florida this 14th day of November 2006.

David A. Demers, Chief Judge

2006–070. UNCONTESTED RESIDENTIAL TENANT EVICTIONS

IN THE CIRCUIT COURT, SIXTH JUDICIAL CIRCUIT IN AND FOR PASCO AND PINELLAS COUNTIES, FLORIDA

ADMINISTRATIVE ORDER NO. 2006–070 PI–CTY

RE: UNCONTESTED RESIDENTIAL TENANT EVICTIONS

The procedures for uncontested residential tenant evictions in Pinellas County need to be clarified and updated.

Nonlawyer property managers are authorized to complete, sign and file complaints for eviction and motions for default as well as to obtain final judgments and writs of possession. In re Nonlawyer Preparation of and Representation of Landlord in Uncontested Residential Evictions, 627 So. 2d 485 (Fla. 1993). In order to ensure consistency in the handling of such proceedings and define the limited scope of such proceedings, it is hereby

ORDERED:

1. In order for a property manager to file a complaint on behalf of a landlord for uncontested residential eviction, the property manager must attach to the complaint the landlord's written authorization for the property manager to act on the landlord's behalf. This authorization must be limited to the completion, signing, and filing of the pleadings necessary to evict a tenant for the nonpayment of rent.

2. Any authorization attempting to permit a property manager to serve as a plaintiff in an eviction action or to seek recovery of past rent due is invalid.

3. Any complaint filed by a property manager must be brought by and styled with the landlord as the plaintiff and signed by the property manager as "property manager for the plaintiff."

4. A residential tenant eviction shall be deemed contested if a hearing is required. Once a residential tenant action becomes contested, the landlord must either represent himself or herself or be represented by an attorney.

5. A "property manager" means a natural person or corporation retained by either an individual or corporate landlord to be responsible for the rental and management of the subject residential property on a day-to-day basis. Such day-to-day responsibility is evidenced by, but is not limited to, renting of units, maintenance of the rental property, and collection of rent.

6. The Clerk of the Circuit Court shall make available an instruction sheet consistent with this Administrative Order.

7. The Clerk of the Circuit Court has prepared a package of forms for use in residential eviction proceedings which the Clerk shall make available upon payment of the applicable fee.

8. In the event a petition is filed that does not comply with the above requirements, the Clerk shall immediately forward the matter to the assigned section judge.

Administrative Order No. 95–10 is hereby rescinded.

DONE AND ORDERED in Chambers at St. Petersburg, Pinellas County, Florida, this 25th day of August, 2006.

DAVID A. DEMERS, Chief Judge

2006–021. PROCEDURES FOR BOWEN AND SUBSEQUENT REVIEW HEARINGS IN CASES INVOLVING INTRACIRCUIT EXECUTION OF WRIT OF BODILY ATTACHMENT FOR CIVIL CONTEMPT FOR FAILURE TO PAY CHILD SUPPORT

IN THE CIRCUIT COURT, SIXTH JUDICIAL CIRCUIT IN AND FOR PASCO AND PINELLAS COUNTIES, FLORIDA

ADMINISTRATIVE ORDER NO. 2006–021 PA/PI–CIR

RE: PROCEDURES FOR BOWEN AND SUBSEQUENT REVIEW HEARINGS IN CASES INVOLVING INTRA-CIRCUIT EXECUTION OF WRIT OF BODILY ATTACHMENT FOR CIVIL CONTEMPT FOR FAILURE TO PAY CHILD SUPPORT

Pursuant to section 38.22, Florida Statutes, and Florida Family Law Rule of Procedure 12.615, a circuit court may find a person in civil contempt for failure to pay child support and may issue a writ of bodily attachment of the contemnor. This writ may be served by law enforcement personnel outside of the county where the writ originated. Because the Sixth Judicial Circuit is comprised of both Pasco and Pinellas counties, circumstances may arise where a writ of bodily attachment has been issued in one county within the Sixth Judicial Circuit and is subsequently served in the other county within the Sixth Judicial Circuit.

Pursuant to Florida Family Law Rule of Procedure 12.615, and Bowen v. Bowen, 471 So. 2d 1274 (Fla. 1985), a hearing to determine whether the contemnor has the present ability to comply with the purge provisions of the contempt order must be held within 48 hours of contemnor's arrest on a writ of bodily attachment for civil contempt due to failure to pay child support. (This hearing shall hereinafter be referred to as a "Bowen hearing.")

Pursuant to Florida Family Law Rule of Procedure 12.615(f), at any time after a contemnor is incarcerated for failure to pay child support, upon the motion of the contemnor or any other party or upon the court's own motion, the court may review the contemnor's present ability to comply with the purge conditions, may review the duration of incarceration, and may modify any of its prior orders.

In order to ensure that the contemnor's due process rights are met, that the Bowen hearing is held within 48 hours as required, that any subsequent review hearings are held expeditiously, and that no hearing is delayed due to transportation of the contemnor between Pasco and Pinellas counties, the Sixth Judicial Circuit has determined that it is appropriate to establish procedures that will apply when a writ of bodily attachment for failure to pay child support was issued in one county within the Sixth Judicial Circuit, but the contemnor is arrested and incarcerated in the other county within the Sixth Judicial Circuit.

IT IS THEREFORE ORDERED:

1. If a person is arrested due to a writ of bodily attachment for civil contempt for failure to pay child support, the Sheriff's Department of the county where the contemnor was arrested shall schedule a Bowen hearing to take place within 48 hours after arrest and shall:

a. Arrange the Bowen hearing to take place via videoconference from the jail, before a child support hearing officer of the county where the contemnor was arrested and is being held or before the weekend or holiday advisory judge of that county.

This hearing shall be scheduled for the next available time, but not later than 48 hours after arrest, either on the regular in-custody calendar of the child support hearing officer of the county where the contemnor was arrested or on the weekend or holiday advisory judge's calendar of that county.

If, for some reason, neither a hearing officer nor a weekend or holiday advisory judge is available to handle the Bowen hearing within 48 hours of contemnor's arrest, the Sheriff shall contact the Administrative Office of the Courts in the county in which the contemnor was arrested for assistance in scheduling the hearing before a judge within 48 hours of arrest.

b. Prior to the Bowen hearing, provide via facsimile transmission a copy of the recommended order/writ of bodily attachment to the child support hearing officer or to the weekend or holiday advisory judge who will be presiding over the Bowen hearing.

2. The Clerk of the Circuit Court in Pasco County and the Clerk of the Circuit Court in Pinellas County shall establish procedures by which the child support hearing officers and weekend and holiday advisory judges in each county shall have access via computer to the contemnor's child support payment history from the county where the writ of bodily attachment was issued.

3. If the matter comes before the weekend or holiday advisory judge in the county where the contemnor was arrested, and that judge determines that there is sufficient time remaining for the matter to be reset before a child support hearing officer in that county prior to expiration of the 48 hour period, then the judge, in his or her discretion, may order the matter to be reset on the calendar of the hearing officer in the county of arrest, at the time normally scheduled for hearings involving a party in custody of law enforcement. If, however, the matter cannot be heard by the child support hearing officer within 48 hours after the contemnor was arrested, then the weekend or holiday advisory judge shall hold the Bowen hearing.

4. If, at the Bowen hearing, a finding is made that the contemnor has the present ability to comply with the purge provisions, and thus he or she is ordered to remain incarcerated, but the contemnor has not yet been transported from the county where the he or she was arrested to the county where the writ of bodily attachment was issued, and the contemnor subsequently requests another review of his or her current ability to comply with the purge provisions, as set forth in Florida Family Law Rule of Procedure 12.615(f), then the review hearing shall be scheduled to be held via videoconference at the next available time on the in-custody calendar of a child support hearing officer in the county where the contemnor is currently incarcerated.

5. When a Bowen hearing is held before a child support hearing officer in the county where the contemnor was arrested and is being held, the hearing officer's recommended order shall be presented for signature to any judge of the Family Division (including Unified Family Court if applicable) in the county where the Bowen hearing was conducted. [Added pursuant to Administrative Order 2006-048 PA/PI-CIR, dated July 5, 2006]

DONE AND ORDERED in Chambers at St. Petersburg, Pinellas County, Florida, this 24th day of March 2006.

David A. Demers, Chief Judge

2006–017. DISCLOSURE OF PROTECTED HEALTH INFORMATION UNDER THE HEALTH INSURANCE PORTABILITY AND ACCOUNTABILITY ACT OF 1996

IN THE CIRCUIT COURT, SIXTH JUDICIAL CIRCUIT IN AND FOR PASCO AND PINELLAS COUNTIES, FLORIDA

ADMINISTRATIVE ORDER NO. 2006–017 PA/PI–CIR

RE: DISCLOSURE OF PROTECTED HEALTH INFORMATION UNDER THE HEALTH INSURANCE PORTABILITY AND ACCOUNTABILITY ACT OF 1996

The federal Health Insurance Portability and Accountability Act of 1996 (HIPPA), Pub. L. No. 104–191, 110 Stat. 1936 (codified as amended in scattered sections of 18, 26, 29 and 42 U.S.C.) authorizes an entity covered by federal regulations to disclose protected health information in response to a subpoena, discovery requests, or other lawful process under certain circumstances see 45 C.F.R. parts 160–164; and

A qualified protective order is a court order or stipulation by the parties to litigation that prohibits the parties from using or disclosing protected health information for any purpose other than the litigation and requires the information to be returned or destroyed at the conclusion of the litigation; and

The many requests the Court receives for such orders make it desirable to have a form qualified protective order and order to disclose protective health information available to the litigants and the Bar and it is desirable to update the existing form order; it is therefore

ORDERED:

1. The form HIPPA Qualified Protective Order and Order to Disclose Protected Health Information, attached hereto as Exhibit "A," is made available for use in the Sixth Judicial Circuit. Any deviation from this form should be brought to the court's attention by the party seeking the order.

2. This administrative order does not limit the discretion of the trial judge to enter other appropriate orders in matters before the Court.

3. Where a party who obtains protected health information from a covered entity by subpoena, other discovery, or in response to a qualified protective order, and the party files such information with the Court, the party shall identify such information to the Clerk of the Circuit Court for sealing. A separate order sealing the records is not required. Discovery shall only be filed with the Court in accordance with the Florida Rules of Procedure.

4. Any party who obtains protected health information from a covered entity where such information is admitted into evidence shall identify such information to the Court and the Clerk of the Circuit Court for a determination by the Court at that time whether the evidence will be sealed.

5. The Clerk of the Circuit Court shall retain protected health information identified by the parties in the court file or received into evidence by the Court in accordance with Rule of Judicial Administration 2.051 and shall destroy such records in accordance with Rule of Judicial Administration 2.075 and applicable federal regulations.

Administrative Order 2003–014 PA/PI–CIR is hereby rescinded in its entirety.

DONE AND ORDERED in Chambers at St. Petersburg, Pinellas County, Florida, this 14th day of March 2006.

____
David A. Demers, Chief Judge

IN THE CIRCUIT COURT OF THE SIXTH JUDICIAL CIRCUIT IN AND FOR __________ COUNTY, FLORIDA

CIVIL DIVISION

____
____
________________________,

Plaintiff(s), CASE NO. __________
UCN ____________

vs.

____
____
________________________,

Defendant(s).

ORDER ON DEFENDANT(S)' MOTION FOR A HIPAA QUALIFIED PROTECTIVE ORDER AND ORDER TO DISCLOSE PROTECTED HEALTH INFORMATION

This matter is before the Court on the motion of Defendant(s), __________, for a Qualified Protective Order and Order to Disclose Protected Health Information pursuant to the federal Health Insurance Portability and Accountability Act of 1996 (HIPAA), Pub. L. No. 104–191, 110 Stat. 1936 (codified as amended in scattered sections of 18, 26, 29 and 42 U.S.C.). The Court having considered the argument of counsel, legal authority, and being otherwise fully advised, it is

ORDERED AND ADJUDGED as follows:

1. Defendant(s)' motion is **GRANTED.**

Qualified Protective Order

2. In accordance with and as defined by the regulations promulgated under HIPAA, specifically 45 C.F.R. section 164.512(e)(1)(ii)(B) and (v), the Court hereby enters a HIPAA Qualified Protective Order (QPO). Pursuant to this QPO, all parties to this lawsuit are:

a) prohibited from using or disclosing protected heath[1] information (PHI) for any purpose other than the litigation of the above-styled lawsuit; and

b) required to destroy all copies of the PHI or to return them to the disclosing entity at the conclusion of the above-styled lawsuit.

3. For purposes of this QPO, "conclusion" is understood to include the time for any records retention requirement and statute of limitations applicable to a party or a party's counsel. "Litigation" is understood to include all appellate proceedings or the expiration of time to commence such appellate proceedings without appeal.

4. Based upon this QPO and commencing immediately from the date of this QPO, all persons, including but not limited to physicians and other medical providers,

a) shall comply with any and all subpoenas for records without deposition pursuant to Florida Rule of Civil Procedure 1.351 to which no objection has been timely filed as well as other subpoenas served upon them at any future time in the course of this litigation; and

b) are authorized and ordered to use or disclose PHI in response to said subpoenas.

Authorization and Order to Disclose PHI in the Course of Discovery and Judicial Proceedings (Order to Disclose)

5. Additionally, pursuant to 45 C.F.R. section 164.512(e)(1)(i) and for purposes of HIPAA compliance, and without waiver of any right to the prepayment of costs or any other appropriate objection or privilege that may be timely asserted, the attorneys, employees, agents, or designees of each party or each party's legal counsel in this case, and all duly noticed persons, are expressly and specifically **AUTHORIZED** and **ORDERED** to:

a) respond to valid Interrogatories served pursuant to the Florida Rules of Civil Procedure in the above-styled matter seeking PHI;

b) respond to valid Requests for Production served pursuant to the Florida Rules of Civil Procedure in the above-styled matter seeking PHI;

c) respond to valid and timely Requests for Copies or Requests for Production from Non–Parties served pursuant to the Florida Rules of Civil Procedure in the above-styled matter for production of documents and things without deposition concerning PHI; and

d) respond to each of a party's own experts who request, either orally or in writing, PHI for the purposes of reviewing the above-styled matter in whole or in part, regardless of whether the expert is a consulting or trial expert or is considered retained for compensation or not retained,

by disclosing and providing such requested PHI.

6. Additionally, pursuant to 45 C.F.R. section 164.512(e)(1)(i) and for purposes of HIPAA compliance, without waiver of any right to the prepayment of costs or any other appropriate objection or privilege that may be timely asserted, each deponent duly noticed for deposition in the above-styled litigation, including but not limited to a party, a fact witness, a records custodian, an expert, or a healthcare provider of any type, is expressly and specifically **AUTHORIZED** and **ORDERED** to use or to disclose to the attorneys, agents, employees, and designees of each party or each party's legal counsel in this case the PHI of a party that is responsive

to deposition questions or a valid subpoena duces tecum at such duly-noticed deposition in the above-styled litigation.

7. Additionally, pursuant to 45 C.F.R. section 164.512(e)(1)(i) and for purposes of HIPAA compliance, without waiver of any right to the prepayment of costs or any other appropriate objection or privilege that may be timely asserted, all witnesses duly appearing at, or subpoenaed for, any judicial proceeding related to this litigation, including but not limited to trial, are specifically and expressly **AUTHORIZED** and **ORDERED** to use and disclose the PHI of a party in any form at such judicial proceeding.

8. In compliance with both HIPAA and any applicable state law not preempted by HIPAA, the authorizations and orders set forth in paragraphs 5, 6, and 7 of this Order to Disclose expressly include PHI concerning psychological and mental heath [2] records, disability status and records, substance abuse and treatment history, and HIV status, as well as records concerning other sexually transmitted diseases if so requested.

9. The commands of the Court in paragraphs 5, 6 and 7 of this Order to Disclose are a separate authorization for use or disclosure of PHI in addition to, and potentially inclusive of, the use and disclosures authorized under paragraph 2 of the QPI.

10. Violation of paragraphs 5, 6, or 7 of the Order to Disclose may subject the non-compliant party, or that party's counsel, to sanctions, including but not limited to the costs and attorney's fees attributable to such non-compliance, the striking of evidence or testimony, or the striking of the party's claims or defenses.

11. Pursuant to 45 C.F.R. section 164.512(e)(1)(i) and for purposes of HIPAA compliance, without waiver of any right to the prepayment of costs or any other appropriate objection or privilege that may be timely asserted, any person or entity authorized or ordered above to use or disclose PHI is expressly and specifically **AUTHORIZED** and **ORDERED** to do so with, to, or before any court reporter service, videographer service, translation service, photocopy service, document management service, records management service, graphics service, or other such litigation service, designated by a party or a party's legal counsel in this case. The protections and requirements of paragraph 2 of the QPI apply to such service providers. Each party or the party's legal counsel is charged with obtaining advance consent of such service to comply with this paragraph. Upon such consent, the service provider will be deemed to have voluntarily submitted to this Court's jurisdiction during the pendency of the above-styled matter for purposes of enforcement of this paragraph, including but not limited to the imposition of such sanctions as may be appropriate for any non-compliance.

12. Except for business associate agreements (as defined by HIPAA) entered into by a party or a party's legal counsel for purposes of satisfying the requirements of paragraph 11 of the Order to Disclose, the uses and disclosures of PHI authorized under the Order to Disclose are separate from, and not to be deemed subject to, any business associate agreement that has been or will be executed by any party, any party's legal counsel, or any disclosing person or entity. No use or disclosure made pursuant to the Order to Disclose shall be deemed to require the execution of a business associate agreement (as defined by HIPAA). The intent of the Order to Disclose is that such business associate agreements, including any requirement for such agreements under the HIPAA regulations, should be construed as inapplicable to uses and disclosures under this Order and as limited only to uses and disclosures of PHI outside of the Order to Disclose.

13. Unless a motion for enforcement of the Order to Disclose has been filed in this case and remains pending at the time, the Order to Disclose shall expire upon the conclusion of the litigation as defined in paragraph 3.

14. Nothing in the Order to Disclose or QPI shall permit the counsel for any party, other than the party representing the patient, to engage in ex parte communications with the healthcare provider, except for those communications necessary for compliance with any subpoena duces tecum.

15. This QPI and Order to Disclose are self-executing and effective upon entry.

16. A copy of this QPI and Order to Disclose shall be valid as an original.

DONE AND ORDERED in Chambers, at _________, _________ County, Florida, on this ___ day of _________, 2 ___.

____

Circuit Judge

[1] So in original.

[2] So in original.

2006-006. EN BANC CIRCUIT COURT APPELLATE PROCEDURES

IN THE CIRCUIT COURT, SIXTH JUDICIAL CIRCUIT IN AND FOR PASCO AND PINELLAS COUNTIES, FLORIDA

ADMINISTRATIVE ORDER NO. 2006-006 PA/PI-CIR

RE: EN BANC CIRCUIT COURT APPELLATE PROCEDURES

While infrequent, there are times when two Sixth Judicial Circuit appellate panels reach conflicting decisions under similar facts. This may lead to uncertainty at the county court level on how to proceed on a particular point of law. In the absence of procedures to resolve conflicts among such decisions, the county court must make its independent decision. See State v. Lopez, 633 So.2d 1150, 1151 (Fla. 5th DCA 1994).

The purpose of this Administrative Order is to establish procedures to resolve a conflict within the appellate division of the Circuit Court, so that the appellate court provides uniformity in its decisions.

In order to promote uniformity in appellate decisions, to enhance judicial efficiency involving appeals to the Circuit Court, and pursuant to Rule of Judicial Administration 2.050, it is hereby

ORDERED:

(a) En Banc Proceedings on the Court's own Initiative

1. A majority of the circuit appellate court three-judge panel participating in an assigned appeal may order that a proceeding before the court be determined en banc.

2. En banc hearings shall not be ordered unless the case is of exceptional importance or unless necessary to maintain uniformity in the court's decisions.

3. If a determination is made that an appeal will be heard en banc, the three-judge panel shall enter the appropriate order informing the parties of such action. A party shall have 15 days from the entry of the order to file and serve a request for oral argument pursuant to the Florida Rule of Appellate Procedure 9.320. The court, on its own initiative, may require the parties to present oral argument, may limit the issues to be heard, and may require the filing of additional briefs.

4. A circuit appellate court en banc shall consist of those appellate panel judges within the subject area to which the case is assigned, either civil or criminal, in both Pinellas and Pasco counties.

5. The en banc decision shall be by a majority of the appellate judges actually participating and voting on the case. It is anticipated that all appellate panel judges within the subject area, either civil or criminal, will participate and vote on the case, unless otherwise recused or unless there is a conflict between a civil and criminal case under similar facts which would warrant the participation of all appellate panel judges. In the event of a tie vote, the decision of the appellate three-judge panel to which the case was assigned shall stand as the decision of the court.

6. Hearings en banc may be ordered only by the circuit appellate court on its own motion. A party may not request an en banc hearing. A motion seeking the hearing shall be stricken.

7. An order for an appeal to be heard en banc may be entered at any time up until the issuance of the mandate by the Clerk of Court.

(b) Rehearings En Banc on the Court's own Initiative or on Motion of a Party

1. Rehearings en banc may be ordered by the circuit appellate court on its own motion, in the same manner as set forth in (a) 1, within 15 days from entry of the final order. Additionally, a party has the option of filing a motion for rehearing en banc; however, such motion must be filed and served in conjunction with a timely filed motion for rehearing pursuant to the Florida Rule of Appellate Procedure 9.330, within 15 days from entry of the final order.

2. A party may move for an en banc rehearing solely on the grounds that the case is of exceptional importance or that such consideration is necessary to maintain uniformity in the court's decisions. A response may be filed and served within 10 days of service of the motion.

3. A rehearing en banc is an extraordinary proceeding. If filed by an attorney, the motion shall contain either or both of the following statements:

> I express a belief, based on a reasoned and studied professional judgment, that the panel decision is of exceptional importance.
>
> **Or**
>
> I express a belief, based on a reasoned and studied professional judgment, that the panel decision is contrary to the following decision(s) of this court and that a consideration by the full court is necessary to maintain uniformity of decisions in this court (citing specifically the case or cases).

/s/ ______________________

____

Attorney for ______________________
(name of party)

____
(address and phone number)
Florida Bar No. ______________

This requirement does not apply to an unrepresented party.

4. A majority of the circuit appellate court three-judge panel that participated in the final order shall determine if rehearing en banc is to be granted and shall enter the appropriate order. A party shall have 15 days from the entry of the order granting rehearing en banc to file and serve a request for oral argument pursuant to the Florida Rule of Appellate Procedure 9.320. The court, on its own initiative, may require the parties to present oral argument, may limit the issues to be reheard, and may require the filing of additional briefs.

5. If rehearing en banc is granted, the rehearing en banc panel shall be comprised as set forth in (a) 4. The final decision on rehearing en banc shall be entered by the court in the same manner as set forth in (a) 5.

6. The provisions of (b) 2 and (b) 3 apply only to final orders entered by a single three-judge panel. If the final order is entered by an en banc panel, then a motion for rehearing must be filed pursuant to the Florida Rule of Appellate Procedure 9.330, and need not contain the statements set forth in (b) 3. When considering a motion for rehearing of an en banc final order, a majority of the en banc panel that participated in the appeal will determine if the motion for rehearing will be granted and proceed in accordance with this Administrative Order.

DONE AND ORDERED in Chambers at St. Petersburg, Pinellas County, Florida this 24th day of January 2006.

____
David A. Demers, Chief Judge

2005–065. [RESCINDED BY ORDER 2017-074, EFFECTIVE DECEMBER 13, 2017.]

2004–077. [RESCINDED BY ORDER 2018-013, EFFECTIVE MARCH 20, 2018.]

2004–029. [RESCINDED BY ORDER 2019–005, EFFECTIVE JANUARY 23, 2019]

PI–CTY–98–05. [RESCINDED BY ORDER 2017–021, EFFECTIVE APRIL 28, 2017.]

PA/PI–CIR–97–85. [RESCINDED BY ORDER 2019–005, EFFECTIVE JANUARY 23, 2019]

Seventh Judicial Circuit (Flagler, Putnam, St. Johns and Volusia Counties)

ADMINISTRATIVE ORDERS

CIVIL ORDERS

CV–2000–001–SC. CODIFICATION OF ADMINISTRATIVE ORDERS IN THE CIRCUIT CIVIL DIVISION.

CV–2003–002–SC. CIVIL PRETRIAL PROCEDURES.

CV–2000–003–SC. NOTICE OF ISSUE AND REQUEST TO DOCKET.

CV–2004–004–SC (A). MOTIONS TO COMPEL DISCOVERY IN CIVIL ACTIONS.

CV–2006–005–SC. FILING FEE FOR PETITIONS FOR 90–DAY EXTENSION IN ACTIONS FOR PERSONAL INJURY OR WRONGFUL DEATH ARISING OUT OF MEDICAL NEGLIGENCE.

CV–2009–006–SC. PROCEDURES FOR INDIGENCY DETERMINATION IN CERTAIN CIVIL CASES.

CV–2000–007–SC. ADDRESSES AND SOCIAL SECURITY NUMBERS OF PARTIES ON FINAL JUDGMENTS.

CV–2019–008–SC. INFORMATION RETURNS REPORTING.

CV–2003–009–SC. FILING OF DEPOSITION TRANSCRIPTS.

CV–2017–010–VL. ESTABLISHING WESTERN, EASTERN AND SOUTHERN CIVIL DIVISIONS OF THE CIRCUIT AND COUNTY COURT.

CV–2000–011–VL. EMINENT DOMAIN CASES.

CV–2016–012–SC. ELECTRONIC SALE OF PROPERTIES IN FORECLOSURE CASES.

CV–2015–013–SC. CONSENT TO DISMISSAL AND CLOSURE FOR LACK OF PROSECUTION IN EVICTION CASES SEEKING POSSESSION ONLY.

CV–2013–014–SC. CASE STATUS REPORTING REQUIREMENTS FOR REAL PROPERTY MORTGAGE FORECLOSURE CASES.

CV–2014–015–SC. FORECLOSURE TRIAL EXHIBITS.

CV–2010–016–SC. WRITS OF POSSESSION IN RESIDENTIAL MORTGAGE FORECLOSURE CASES.

CV–2017–017–SC. APPOINTMENT OF ADMINISTRATIVE CIVIL DIVISION JUDGE.

CV–2008–018–SC. COUNTY COURT CIVIL MEDIATION.

CV–2009–019–SC. NON–BINDING ARBITRATION.

CV–2006–020–VL. NEGLECTED OR MISTREATED ANIMALS.

CV–2009–021–SJ. IN THE CIRCUIT COURT OF FLORIDA, SEVENTH JUDICIAL CIRCUIT IN AND FOR ST. JOHNS COUNTY.

CRIMINAL ORDERS

CR–2017–001–SC. CODIFICATION OF ADMINISTRATIVE ORDERS IN THE CRIMINAL DIVISION.

CR–2017–002–SC. BAIL SCHEDULE FOR FLAGLER, PUTNAM, ST. JOHNS AND VOLUSIA COUNTIES.

CR–2019–003–SC. Misdemeanor Payable Fish and Wildlife Offenses / Notices to Appear.

CR–2017–004–SC. MODIFICATION OF BONDS BY FIRST APPEARANCE JUDGES.

CR–2017–005–SC. MISDEMEANOR PAYABLE OFFENSES/NOTICES TO APPEAR.

CR–2017–006–SC. CRITERIA/PROCEDURES FOR NOTICES TO APPEAR ISSUED BY JAIL PERSONNEL.

CR–2017–007–SC. REFUNDS OF SURETY/CASH BONDS.

CR–2017–008–SC. APPLICATION OF CASH DEPOSIT TO FINES AND COSTS.

CR–2017–009–VL. FIRST APPEARANCES/JAIL ARRAIGNMENTS/AND OTHER RELATED PROCEEDINGS.

CR–2017–010–VL. JUDICIAL INQUIRY SYSTEM—FIRST APPEARANCES.

CR–2017–011–FG/PT/SJ. CRIMINAL COURT PROCEEDINGS BY AUDIO–VISUAL DEVICE.

CR–2017–012–SC. ADOPTION OF SA 7–07 CHARGING AFFIDAVIT.

CR–2017–013–SC. PROCESSING OF ARREST, COMPLAINT AND NOTICE TO APPEAR PAPERWORK (ADULT).

CR–2017–014–VL. BLIND FILING OF NON–INDICTMENT FELONY CASES.

CR–2017–015–VL. BLIND FILING OF FELONY INDICTMENTS.

CR–2017–016–SC. COMPANION INFRACTIONS TO CRIMINAL CHARGES.

CR–2017–017–VL. EXTRADITION INFORMATION ON WARRANTS/CAPIASES.

CR–2017–018–SC. CORRECTION OF SCRIVENERS' ERRORS ON WARRANTS.

PROBATE/GUARDIANSHIP ORDERS

PB–2004–019–SC (A). MOTIONS TO COMPEL DISCOVERY IN PROBATE ACTIONS (AMENDED).

PB–2016–020–SC. RATES OF COMPENSATION FOR EXAMINING COMMITTEE IN INDIGENT CASES.

PB–2007–021–SC. INCAPACITY PETITIONER SERVING AS GUARDIAN.

PB–2009–022–SC. IN THE CIRCUIT COURT OF FLORIDA, SEVENTH JUDICIAL CIRCUIT IN AND FOR FLAGLER, PUTNAM, ST. JOHNS AND VOLUSIA COUNTIES.

FAMILY/JUVENILE ORDERS

FM–2002–001–SC. CODIFICATION OF ADMINISTRATIVE ORDERS IN THE FAMILY DIVISION.

FM–2007–002–SC. FAMILY LAW DIVISION.

FM–2012–003–VL. ESTABLISHING WESTERN, EASTERN AND SOUTHERN FAMILY DIVISIONS OF THE CIRCUIT COURT.

FM–2011–004–SC. APPOINTMENT OF ADMINISTRATIVE FAMILY LAW JUDGE.

FM–2003–005–SC. APPOINTMENT OF FAMILY LAW ADVISORY GROUP.

FM–2004–006–SC (A). MOTIONS TO COMPEL DISCOVERY IN FAMILY LAW ACTIONS.

FM–2009–007–SC. PROCEDURES FOR INDIGENCY DETERMINATION IN CERTAIN FAMILY LAW CASES.

FM–2015–008–SC. FAMILY SELF–HELP PROGRAM.

FM–2018–009–SC. UNITED FAMILY COURTS.

FM–2002–010–SC. APPROVAL OF LOCAL FAMILY LAW FORMS.

FM–2002–011–SC. INJUNCTION FOR PROTECTION FORMS.

FM–2002–012–SC. CROSS ASSIGNMENT/INJUNCTIONS FOR PROTECTION.

FM–2010–013–VL. PROCEDURE FOR ISSUANCE OF EMERGENCY INJUNCTIONS FOR PROTECTION AGAINST DOMESTIC VIOLENCE.

FM–2010–014–SC. SERVICE OF DOMESTIC, REPEAT, SEXUAL & DATING VIOLENCE INJUNCTIONS FOR PROTECTION BY MUNICIPAL LAW ENFORCEMENT AGENCIES.

FM–2004–015–SC (A). ASSIGNMENT OF INJUNCTIONS FOR PROTECTION/DOMESTIC RELATIONS / JUVENILE DEPENDENCIES.

FM–2013–016–SC. PARENT EDUCATION AND FAMILY STABILIZATION COURSE IN FAMILY LAW CASES.

FM–2005–017–SC. PARENT EDUCATION AND FAMILY STABILIZATION COURSE PROVIDERS.

FM–2015–018–SJ. CHILD EDUCATION COURSE IN DISSOLUTION CASES.

FM–2002–019–SC. SUPERVISED VISITATION PROGRAMS.

FM–2012–020–SC. CHILD SUPPORT ENFORCEMENT HEARING OFFICERS.

FM–2012–021–SC. GENERAL MAGISTRATES.

FM–2004–022–SC. GENERAL MAGISTRATES' REPORTS.

FM–2004–023–SC. ELECTRONIC REPORTING OF GENERAL MAGISTRATE AND CHILD SUPPORT ENFORCEMENT HEARINGS.

FM–2006–024–SC (A). SUPPORT INFORMATION SHEETS (AMENDED).

FM–2002–025–SC. CHILD SUPPORT AND PURGE PAYMENTS.

FM–2002–026–SC. RESTITUTION PAYMENTS BY CLERKS OF COURT IN JUVENILE CASES.

FM–2012–027–SC. FAMILY MEDIATION.

FM–2002–028–VL. ELECTRONIC ACCESS TO SCHOOL INFORMATION.

FM–2014–029–SC. POST–INCARCERATION CHILD SUPPORT REVIEWS.

FM–2015–030–SC. BATTERERS' INTERVENTION PROGRAM PROVIDERS.

FM–2015–031–SC. DISTRIBUTION OF SHELTER PETITIONS.

FM–2018–032–VL. EAST–VOLUSIA UNITED FAMILY COURT.

FM–2002–033–SC. ELECTRONIC RECORDING OF DOMESTIC VIOLENCE INJUNCTION HEARINGS.

FM–2015–034–SC. ASSIGNMENT ORDER FOR SHELTER HEARINGS.

FM–2008–035–SC. SUSPENSION OF FAMILY CUSTODY INVESTIGATION PROGRAM.

FM–2007–036–VL. WEST–VOLUSIA UNIFIED FAMILY COURT.

FM–2011–037–SC. JUDICIAL WAIVERS OF PARENTAL NOTICE OF ABORTION.

FM–2006–038–SC. DIRECT CHILD SUPPORT/ALIMONY PAYMENTS.

FM–2006–039–SC. SUPPORT INSTALLMENT PAYMENTS.

FM–2018–040–SC. STANDING FAMILY COURT ORDER.

FM–2018–041–SC. TIMESHARING SCHEDULES/GUIDELINES.

FM–2007–042–SC. WITHDRAWAL OF TRIAL COUNSEL IN DEPENDENCY, TERMINATION OF PARENTAL RIGHTS AND CHILDREN/FAMILIES IN NEED OF SERVICES PROCEEDINGS.

FM–2010–043–SC. NOTICES TO APPEAR ISSUED BY ARRESTING OFFICERS IN JUVENILE CASES.

FM–2008–044–VL. ESTABLISHMENT OF CHILD SUPPORT IN JUVENILE DEPENDENCY CASES.

FM–2009–045–SC. AFFIDAVIT OF CONTINUING CHILD SUPPORT.

FM–2015–046–SC. PARENTING COORDINATORS.

FM–2018–047–SC. COLLABORATIVE LAW PROCESS.

Administrative Orders

Civil Orders

CV–2000–001–SC. CODIFICATION OF ADMINISTRATIVE ORDERS IN THE CIRCUIT CIVIL DIVISION

IN THE CIRCUIT COURT OF FLORIDA, SEVENTH JUDICIAL CIRCUIT IN AND FOR FLAGLER, PUTNAM, ST. JOHNS AND VOLUSIA COUNTIES

REF: CV–2000–01–SC

Re: Codification of Administrative Orders in the Circuit Civil Division

WHEREAS, it has been made known to the undersigned that the codification of Circuit Civil Administrative Orders in the Seventh Judicial Circuit is necessary for the efficient and proper administration of justice,

NOW, THEREFORE, I, ROBERT K. ROUSE, JR., Chief Judge of the Seventh Judicial Circuit, hereby order the codification of all Administrative Orders in the Circuit Civil Division of the Seventh Judicial Circuit.

IT IS FURTHER ORDERED that said administrative orders shall be numbered for reference in the following manner:

Subject—Year—Numerical Order—Circuit / County
[i.e., CV–2000–001–SC (Seventh Circuit)]
[CV–2000–001–VL (Volusia County)]

IT IS FURTHER ORDERED that all administrative orders related to the administration of Circuit Civil matters issued prior to the date of this order are hereby rescinded.

TO BE RECORDED IN FLAGLER, PUTNAM, ST. JOHNS AND VOLUSIA COUNTIES.

DONE AND ORDERED at Daytona Beach, Volusia County, Florida, this 3rd day of August, 2000.

ROBERT K. ROUSE, JR.
CHIEF JUDGE

Adopted effective August 3, 2000.

CV–2003–002–SC. CIVIL PRETRIAL PROCEDURES

IN THE CIRCUIT COURT OF FLORIDA, SEVENTH JUDICIAL CIRCUIT IN AND FOR FLAGLER, PUTNAM, ST. JOHNS AND VOLUSIA COUNTIES

REF: CV 2003–002 SC (Rescinds CV–2000–002–SC)

RE: Civil Pretrial Procedures

WHEREAS, it has been made known to the undersigned that the establishment of Uniform Pretrial Procedures in Civil Actions in the Seventh Judicial Circuit and the creation of appropriate form orders related to such procedures is necessary for the efficient and proper administration of justice, and

WHEREAS, the Circuit Judges in the Seventh Judicial Circuit have approved the use of such procedures and orders throughout the Seventh Judicial Circuit,

NOW THEREFORE, I, ROBERT K. ROUSE, JR., Chief Judge of the Seventh Judicial Circuit, hereby approve and authorize the use of the attached Uniform Pretrial Procedures in Civil Actions and related orders throughout the Seventh Judicial Circuit.

IT IS FURTHER ORDERED that Administrative Order # CV–2000–002–SC is hereby rescinded.

TO BE RECORDED in Flagler, Putnam, St. Johns and Volusia Counties.

DONE AND ORDERED in DeLand, Volusia County, Florida, this 4th day of June, 2003.

ROBERT K. ROUSE, JR.
CHIEF JUDGE

UNIFORM PRETRIAL PROCEDURES
IN CIVIL ACTIONS

BY ORDER OF THE COURT, each party and all counsel shall comply with the following Uniform Pretrial Procedures in Civil Actions:

1. **REFERRAL TO MEDIATION; DEADLINE.**

(a) Unless this matter has been previously mediated or is excluded from mediation by Fla.R.Civ.P. 1.710(b), this case is hereby referred to mediation in accordance with Fla.R.Civ.P. 1.700.et seq. Plaintiff's counsel (or Defendant's counsel, if Plaintiff is unrepresented), shall submit a mutually agreeable mediation order to the Court at least seventy-five (75) days prior to docket sounding. If the parties are unable to agree on a mediator and a place and time for mediation, counsel shall promptly notify the Court.

(b) **Mediation shall be completed and the mediation report filed with the Court prior to docket sounding. The requirement to mediate this case cannot be waived by agreement of the parties.**

2. **WITNESS LISTS.**

(a) **EXPERT WITNESSES.** No less than seventy-five (75) days before docket sounding, each party seeking affirmative relief will file with the Court and serve on all other parties a notice containing the names, addresses and telephone numbers of each expert witness whom the noticing party in good faith expects to call as a witness at trial. No later than sixty (60) days before docket sounding, each party not seeking affirmative relief shall file with the Court and serve on all other parties a notice containing the names, addresses and telephone numbers of each expert witness whom the noticing party in good faith expects to call as a witness at trial. For each expert witness listed, the noticing party shall designate his/her area of expertise (i.e. "accident reconstruction", "economist", "treating orthopedic physician" etc.).

(b) **NON–EXPERT WITNESSES.** No less than sixty (60) days prior to docket sounding, each party will file with the Court and serve on all other parties a notice containing the names and addresses of each non-expert witness whom the noticing party in good faith expects to call as a witness at trial.

(c) A party may amend or supplement his/her witness list without leave of Court at any time until the deadline for the filing of witness lists set forth in paragraphs 2(a) and (b) above. If a witness list is amended or supplemented, it shall be restated in full.

(d) Absent good cause, no witness shall be permitted to testify unless the party calling that witness has complied with this Order.

(e) All expert witnesses must be ready to testify and be reasonably available for deposition no less than thirty (30) days before docket sounding.

(f) The Court may, on its own motion or on the motion of any party, limit the number of experts or other witnesses permitted to testify at trial.

3. **DISCOVERY.**

(a) Except as otherwise provided herein or agreed to by the parties in writing, discovery shall remain open until ten (10) days prior to the trial date.

(b) No interrogatories, requests to produce or requests for admissions shall be served later than forty-five (45) days prior to the trial date. Exceptions shall be permitted only by written stipulation of the parties or by Court order.

4. **CONTINUANCES.** Motions for continuance must be in writing and specifically set forth: (a) the reason for the requested continuance; (b) if any party objects to the requested continuance and; (c) when it is anticipated the case will be ready for trial. The rule requires that the party (not just the attorney) requesting the continuance should sign the motion or stipulation. Fla. R. Jud. Admin. 2.085(c). If the requested continuance is based on the unavailability of a witness, the Court must be advised of when it is believed the witness will be available. The inability to require the attendance of a witness at trial shall not be the basis for continuance of the trial unless a witness subpoena was issued and served on the witness (or was attempted to be served on the witness) at least ten (10) days prior to the trial date.

5. **PRETRIAL MOTIONS.**

(a) **DEADLINES FOR MOTIONS.** Motions filed within thirty (30) days of the trial date will not be considered if predicated on matters the movant knew or should have known with the exercise of reasonable diligence at least thirty (30) days prior to the trial date. Because of busy court calendars, hearing time may not be available to consider motions filed close to the deadline. The inability of a party to obtain hearing time will generally not constitute grounds for a continuance of the trial.

(b) **MOTIONS GENERALLY.** The failure of a party to call up for hearing any timely filed motion at least ten (10) days prior to the trial date may constitute a waiver thereof unless the grounds therefor did not exist or the party was not aware of the grounds for the motion(s) prior to the filing of such motion(s) after the exercise of reasonable diligence.

(c) **CERTIFICATE OF GOOD FAITH.** Before any motion is filed, the moving party shall contact the opposing party and attempt, in good faith, to amicably resolve the issues raised by the motion(s). Each motion shall contain a certificate of the movant's attorney if represented (or the moving party if unrepresented) certifying his/her compliance with this requirement. This provision does not apply to motions for summary judgment or other case dispositive motions.

(d) ***FRYE*** **TEST HEARINGS.** Any challenge to the admissibility of evidence at trial asserted to be "novel scientific evidence" in accordance with the principals set forth in Frye v. United States, 293 Fed. 1013 (D.C. Cir. 1923), must be raised by a motion in limine filed at least thirty (30) days prior to the trial date. See, Hadden v. State, 690 So.2d 573 (Fla. 1997); Ramirez v. State, 651 So.2d 1164 (Fla. 1995); Flanagan v. State, 625 So.2d 827 (Fla. 1993). Failure to meet either deadline without just cause shall be deemed a waiver.

6. **COURT REPORTER.** The parties shall coordinate the scheduling of a court reporter if a reporter is desired.

7. **SETTLEMENT.** If this case is settled or is dismissed prior to the trial date, the parties shall promptly notify the Court by telephone and confirm the settlement or dismissal in writing. **A notice of voluntary dismissal or joint motion to dismiss shall be submitted to the Court within thirty (30) days after the Court is first advised of the settlement.**

8. **PRETRIAL MEETING OF ATTORNEYS AND UNREPRESENTED PARTIES.**

(a) **MANDATORY PRETRIAL MEETING.** No later than ten (10) days prior to docket sounding (or ten (10) days prior to the pretrial conference, if one is scheduled), trial counsel and all unrepresented parties shall meet together. Attendance at this meeting (in person or by telephone) is mandatory. Plaintiff's attorney (or if Plaintiff is unrepresented, Defendant's attorney) shall arrange a mutually agreeable time, date and place for this meeting. If the parties are unable to agree, counsel shall promptly notify the Court in writing and the Court will then set the time, date and place for the meeting.

At the pretrial meeting, the attorneys and unrepresented parties shall:

(1) Discuss and attempt to settle the case.

(2) Produce, examine and initial every evidentiary exhibit intended to be offered at trial; agree on those which can be admitted as joint exhibits, those which can be admitted without objection, and identify those to which objections will be made and the grounds for each objection, and note this on a separate copy of each party's exhibit list. Objections not reserved or grounds not noted on the annotated exhibit lists will be deemed waived at trial. The annotated copies of the exhibit lists will be attached to and made a part of the joint pretrial statement required by paragraph 8(b) of this Order. **Any listed exhibit not objected to will be admitted into evidence.**

(3) Review the witness lists and note on a separate copy which witnesses and depositions the parties in good faith anticipate will actually be used at trial. The annotated

copies of the witness lists will be attached to the joint pretrial statement required by paragraph 8(b) of this Order.

(4) Discuss and stipulate as to those facts which do not require proof at trial.

(5) Discuss, clarify and frame all factual issues to be tried.

(6) Identify all significant issues of law, procedure or evidence to be decided by the Court prior to or during trial.

(7) Agree upon and draft a concise but complete statement of the case to be read by the Court to the jury at the beginning of the case, if a jury trial.

(8) Attempt to agree upon the number of peremptory challenges, if a jury trial.

(9) Discuss and attempt to agree upon any other matters which will lead to a more orderly trial (e.g., copies in lieu of originals, witnesses out of turn, how depositions will be presented, the treatment of collateral source set-offs, the need to call records custodians, etc.)

(b) **JOINT PRETRIAL STATEMENT.** Following the meeting required by paragraph 8(a), Plaintiff's attorney (or Defendant's attorney, if Plaintiff is unrepresented) shall prepare and present to opposing counsel and all unrepresented parties a proposed joint pretrial statement. The statement shall be signed by all attorneys and unrepresented parties. The original shall be filed with the Clerk and one copy shall be mailed or delivered to the Judge no later than docket sounding; provided, however, that if the Court schedules a pretrial conference, the joint pretrial statement shall be provided to the Court at or before the pretrial conference. To the extent the parties differ as to how portions of the pretrial statement should read, the differing views should be set forth in the statement.

The pretrial statement shall contain the following items in the following format:

(1) A statement of the case to be read to the jury, if a jury trial.

(2) A statement of facts which are admitted and which of those admitted facts may be read in evidence at trial as a stipulation of the parties.

(3) A list of issues raised by the pleadings that are abandoned.

(4) A list of the issues of fact to be tried (framed as they would be set forth in an interrogatory verdict).

(5) A list of significant issues of law, procedure or evidence to be determined by the Court prior to or during trial.

(6) An itemized list of special damages that each party claiming special damages expects to prove.

(7) The annotated copy of each party's list of exhibits showing objections required by paragraph 8(a)(2) of this Order.

(8) The annotated copy of each party's witness list required by paragraph 8(a)(3) of this Order.

(9) The number of peremptory challenges agreed upon or requested, if no agreement is reached, if a jury trial.

(10) A current estimate of the number of days required for trial and the time requested for opening statements.

(11) Any other agreed matters.

9. **JURY INSTRUCTIONS.** If this case is scheduled for a jury trial, no later than the beginning of trial, each party shall submit to the Court an original and one copy of that party's proposed jury instructions and verdict form. Each jury instruction shall be on a separate page; shall contain citations of supporting authorities, if any; shall designate the party submitting the instruction; and shall be numbered in sequence. Counsel shall confer prior to trial and attempt to agree on the jury instructions and verdict form. This paragraph shall not foreclose the right of each party to modify proposed instructions up to and including the charge conference at the close of evidence.

10. **INCONSISTENCY WITH CASE MANAGEMENT ORDER.** If any provision of this order is inconsistent with any case management order entered in this case, the case management order will govern.

11. **MARKING EXHIBITS BEFORE TRIAL.** Each party shall, a reasonable time prior to trial, meet with the Judge's Court Clerk and assist the Clerk in marking all exhibits for identification in the manner directed by the Clerk.

12. **EXTENSION OF TIME LIMITS.** No extension of deadlines or compliance dates established by this Order is permitted if the extension or modification would cause a continuance of the trial or would prevent the completion of mediation prior to docket sounding. Any extension or modification agreed to shall be by written stipulation signed by all parties to this action and filed with the Court. Any other extension of the deadlines or compliance dates established herein or modifications of this Order requires Court approval.

13. **STANDARDS OF CONDUCT.** Conduct that may be characterized as uncivil, abusive, hostile or obstructive impedes the fundamental goal of resolving cases fairly and efficiently and will not be tolerated. Such conduct tends to delay and deny justice. Accordingly, in addition to the standards imposed on all attorneys by the Florida Code of Professional Responsibility, the following standards will apply to all attorneys and parties to this action:

(a) All attorneys, parties and witnesses will be treated in a civil and courteous manner, not only in court, but at depositions and in all written and oral communications.

(b) No attorney or party will abuse or indulge in offensive conduct directed to other attorneys, parties or witnesses. Counsel and all parties shall abstain from disparaging personal remarks or acrimony towards other attorneys, parties or witnesses. Adverse witnesses and parties will be treated with fair consideration.

(c) Absent good cause, no attorney or party shall attribute bad motives or improper conduct to opposing counsel or any adverse party or bring the legal profession into disrepute by unfounded accusations of impropriety.

(d) All attorneys and parties shall make good faith efforts to resolve by agreement any objections to matters contained in pleadings, discovery requests or objections.

(e) No attorney or unrepresented party shall time the filing or service of motions or pleadings in any way that unfairly limits the other party's opportunity to respond and will consult with each other regarding scheduling matters in a good faith effort to avoid scheduling conflicts.

(f) All attorneys and parties shall make all reasonable efforts to expedite this litigation.

(g) Counsel shall strictly abide by Fla. Bar Code Prof. Resp. Rule 4.3–6 regarding trial publicity.

(h) Before hearings are scheduled, or if that is not feasible, immediately thereafter, counsel and all unrepresented parties will attempt to verify the availability of necessary participants and witnesses so that the Court can be notified of any foreseeable problems.

(i) Nothing in this Order supersedes or detracts from the Code of Professional Responsibility or alters existing standards of conduct. Counsel and all parties shall comply with the Court Conduct Handbook on Gender Equality in the Courts.

14. **SANCTIONS.** The unexcused failure of counsel or any party to comply with the requirements of this Order will subject the offending counsel or party to appropriate sanctions which may include, but are not limited to contempt, dismissal, default, the striking of pleadings, claims or defenses, the exclusion of evidence or witnesses, the assessment of fees or costs, or such other sanctions as may be appropriate.

ATTENTION: PERSONS WITH DISABILITIES

In accordance with the Americans With Disabilities Act, persons with disabilities needing a special accommodation to participate in this proceeding should contact the individual or agency sending the notice not later than seven (7) days prior to the proceeding at the address given on the notice. Telephone: (904) 257–6096. **For hearing impaired individuals:** Telecommunications Device for the Deaf (TDD): 1–800–955–8771 or Florida Relay Service: 1–800–955–8770.

THIS IS NOT A COURT INFORMATION LINE.

COMPLIANCE TIMES UNDER UNIFORM PRETRIAL PROCEDURES IN CIVIL ACTIONS

A.	Submission of agreed mediation order	75 days before docket sounding
B.	Disclosure of expert witnesses	75 days before docket sounding for parties seeking affirmative relief; 60 days before docket sounding for parties not seeking affirmative relief
C.	Disclosure of non–expert witnesses	60 days before docket sounding
D.	Cut-off for Interrogatories, requests to produce and requests for admission	45 days before trial date
E.	Cut-off for filing of pretrial motions	30 days before trial date
F.	Issuance and service of trial subpoenas, if to be grounds for continuance	10 days before trial date
G.	Discovery cut-off (except see D above)	10 days before trial date
H.	Hearing cut-off	10 days before trial date
I.	Pretrial meeting	10 days before docket sounding or 10 days before pretrial conference, whichever occurs first
J.	Mediation completed and report filed	any time prior to docket sounding
K.	Pretrial statement delivered to Court	at docket sounding or at the pretrial conference, whichever occurs first
L.	Jury instructions filed with Clerk and delivered to Court	beginning of trial

IN THE CIRCUIT COURT, SEVENTH JUDICIAL CIRCUIT, IN AND FOR VOLUSIA COUNTY, FLORIDA

CASE NO.:
DIVISION:

Plaintiff(s),

vs.

Defendant(s).
____________________/

ORDER SETTING JURY TRIAL AND DIRECTING PRE-TRIAL PROCEDURE

It appearing that this case is at issue and can be set for trial, and it is ORDERED as follows:

1. **TRIAL DATE AND DOCKET SOUNDING.** This case is set for jury trial during the ___ (___) week period commencing __________, **200 ___, at ___ a.m.,** in Courtroom No. ___, ________, ________, ________, Florida. The first day of the trial period is hereinafter referred to as the "trial date". **Docket sounding** (calendar call) will be held in **Courtroom ___, ________ on ________, 200 ___ at ___ a.m./p.m. Appearance at docket sounding by counsel and all unrepresented parties is mandatory. Failure to attend docket sounding may result in the dismissal of this action, the entry of a default or other appropriate sanctions. NO MOTIONS WILL BE HEARD AT DOCKET SOUNDING.**

2. **PRETRIAL CONFERENCE.** No pretrial conference will be scheduled unless requested in writing at least forty-five (45) days prior to the trial date. Please provide a copy of your request for a pretrial conference to the Judge's Judicial Assistant so that one can be scheduled.

3. **UNIFORM PRETRIAL PROCEDURE.** The attached Uniform Pretrial Procedures in Civil Action is incorporated herein and shall govern all further proceedings.

4. **FAMILIARITY WITH THIS ORDER.** Counsel and all unrepresented parties shall read this Order and the attached Uniform Pretrial Procedures in Civil Actions, be familiar with its contents and comply with the requirements of both. Material non-compliance with this Order or the Uniform Pretrial Procedures in Civil Actions by counsel or any party will

subject the offending counsel or parties to appropriate sanctions which may include, but are not limited to, contempt, dismissal, default, the striking of pleadings, claims or defenses, the exclusion of evidence or witnesses, the assessment of fees or costs, or such other sanctions as may be appropriate.

DONE AND ORDERED in Chambers at ______, ______ County, Florida, this ___ day of ______, 200 ___.

______
CIRCUIT JUDGE

Copies to:

IN THE CIRCUIT COURT, SEVENTH JUDICIAL CIRCUIT, IN AND FOR VOLUSIA COUNTY, FLORIDA

CASE NO.:
DIVISION:

Plaintiff(s),

vs.

Defendant(s),
______/

ORDER SETTING JURY TRIAL AND PRETRIAL CONFERENCE AND DIRECTING PRE-TRIAL PROCEDURE

It appearing that this case is at issue and can be set for trial, it is ORDERED as follows:

1. **TRIAL DATE AND DOCKET SOUNDING.** This case is set for jury trial during the ___ (___) **week** period commencing ______, **200** ___ **at** ___ **a.m./p.m.,** in Courtroom No. ___, ______, ______, Florida. The first day of the trial period is hereinafter referred to as the "trial date". Docket sounding (calendar call) will be held in Courtroom ___, ______, on ______, **200** ___ **at** ___ **a.m./p.m. Appearance at docket sounding by counsel and all unrepresented parties is mandatory. Failure to attend docket sounding may result in the dismissal of this action, the entry of a default or other appropriate sanctions. NO MOTIONS WILL BE HEARD AT DOCKET SOUNDING.**

2. **PRETRIAL CONFERENCE.** On ______, **200** ___ **at** ___, **a.m./p.m.,** the Court will hold a pretrial conference in Room ___, ______, ___, ______, Florida, pursuant to the provisions of Rule 1.200(b), Florida Rules of Civil Procedure. Attendance at the pretrial conference by the attorney, if any, who will try the case and all unrepresented parties is mandatory. (___ minutes reserved)

3. **UNIFORM PRE-TRIAL PROCEDURE.** The attached Uniform Pretrial Procedures in Civil Actions is incorporated herein and shall govern all further proceedings.

4. **FAMILIARITY WITH THIS ORDER.** Counsel and all unrepresented parties shall read this Order and the attached Uniform Pretrial Procedures in Civil Actions, be familiar with its contents and comply with the requirements of both. Material non-compliance with this Order or the Uniform Pretrial Procedures in Civil Actions by counsel or any party will subject the offending counsel or parties to appropriate sanctions which may include, but are not limited to, contempt, dismissal, default, the striking of pleadings, claims or defenses, the exclusion of evidence or witnesses, the assessment of fees or costs, or such other sanctions as may be appropriate.

DONE AND ORDERED at ______, ______ County, Florida, this ___ day of ______, 200 ___.

______
Circuit Judge

Copies to:

IN THE CIRCUIT COURT, SEVENTH JUDICIAL CIRCUIT, IN AND FOR VOLUSIA COUNTY, FLORIDA

CASE NO.:
DIVISION:

Plaintiff(s),

vs.

Defendant(s).
______/

ORDER SETTING NON-JURY TRIAL AND DIRECTING PRE-TRIAL PROCEDURE

It appearing that this case is at issue and can be set for trial, it is ORDERED as follows:

1. **TRIAL DATE AND DOCKET SOUNDING.** This case is set for non-jury trial during the ___ (___) **week** period commencing ______, **200** ___ **at** ___ **a.m./p.m.,** in Courtroom No. ___, ______, ______, ______, Florida. The first date of the trial period is hereinafter referred to as the "trial date". Docket sounding (calendar call) will be held in Courtroom ___, ______ on ______, **200** ___ **at** ___ **a.m./p.m. Appearance at docket sounding by counsel and all unrepresented parties in mandatory. Failure to attend docket sounding may result in the dismissal of this action, the entry of a default or other appropriate sanctions. NO MOTIONS WILL BE HEARD AT DOCKET SOUNDING. NO CONTINUANCE WILL BE GRANTED AT DOCKET SOUNDING.**

2. **PRETRIAL CONFERENCE.** No pretrial conference will be scheduled unless requested in writing at least forty-five (45) days prior to the trial date. Please provide a copy of your request for a pretrial conference to the Judge's Judicial Assistant so that one can be scheduled.

3. **UNIFORM PRE-TRIAL PROCEDURE.** The attached Uniform Pretrial Procedures in Civil Actions is incorporated herein and shall govern all further proceedings.

4. **FAMILIARITY WITH THIS ORDER.** Counsel and all unrepresented parties shall read this Order and the attached Uniform Pretrial Procedures in Civil Actions, be familiar with its contents and comply with the requirements of both. Material non-compliance with this Order or the Uniform Pretrial Procedures in Civil Actions by counsel or any party will subject the offending counsel or parties to appropriate sanctions which may include, but are not limited to, contempt, dismissal, default, the striking of pleadings, claims or defenses, the exclusion of evidence or witnesses, the assessment of fees or costs, or such other sanctions as may be appropriate.

DONE AND ORDERED at ________, ________ County, Florida this ___ day of ________, 200 ___.

____
Circuit Judge

Copies to:

IN THE CIRCUIT COURT, SEVENTH JUDICIAL CIRCUIT, IN AND FOR VOLUSIA COUNTY, FLORIDA

CASE NO:
DIVISION:

Plaintiff(s),

vs.

Defendant(s).
______________/

ORDER SETTING NON-JURY TRIAL AND PRETRIAL CONFERENCE AND DIRECTING PRE-TRIAL PROCEDURE

It appearing that this case is at issue and can be set for trial, it is ORDERED as follows:

1. **TRIAL DATE AND DOCKET SOUNDING.** This case is set for non-jury trial during the ___ (___) **week period** commencing ________, **2001** at ___ a.m./p.m., in Courtroom No. ___, ________, ________, ________, Florida. The first day of the trial period is hereinafter referred to as the "trial date". **Docket sounding** (calendar call) will be held in Courtroom ___, ________, on ________, **200 ___ at a.m./p.m. Appearance at docket sounding by counsel and all unrepresented parties is mandatory. Failure to attend docket sounding may result in the dismissal of this action, the entry of a default or other appropriate sanctions. NO MOTIONS WILL BE HEARD AT DOCKET SOUNDING.**

2. **PRETRIAL CONFERENCE.** On ________, **2001 at ___ a.m./p.m.**, the Court will hold a pretrial conference in Room ___, ________, ________, ________, Florida, pursuant to the provisions of Rule 1.200(b), Florida Rules of Civil Procedure. Attendance at the pretrial conference by the attorney, if any, who will try the case and all unrepresented parties is mandatory. (___ minutes reserved)

3. **UNIFORM PRETRIAL PROCEDURE.** The attached Uniform Pretrial Procedures in Civil Actions is incorporated herein and shall govern all further proceedings.

4. **FAMILIARITY WITH THIS ORDER.** Counsel and all unrepresented parties shall read this Order and the attached Uniform Pretrial Procedures in Civil Actions, be familiar with its contents and comply with the requirements of both. Material non-compliance with this Order or the Uniform Pretrial Procedures in Civil Actions by counsel or any party will subject the offending counsel or parties to appropriate sanctions which may include, but are not limited to, contempt, dismissal, default, the striking of pleadings, claims or defenses, the exclusion of evidence or witnesses, the assessment of fees or costs, or such other sanctions as may be appropriate.

DONE AND ORDERED at ________, ________ County, Florida, this ___ day of ________, 200 ___.

____
Circuit Judge

Copies to:

Amended effective June 4, 2003.

CV–2000–003–SC. NOTICE OF ISSUE AND REQUEST TO DOCKET

IN THE CIRCUIT COURT OF FLORIDA, SEVENTH JUDICIAL CIRCUIT IN AND FOR FLAGLER, PUTNAM, ST. JOHNS AND VOLUSIA COUNTIES

REF: CV 2000–003 SC

RE: NOTICE OF ISSUE AND REQUEST TO DOCKET

WHEREAS, the efficient and proper operation of the Civil and Family Law divisions of the Seventh Judicial Circuit Court requires the entry of an administrative order governing Notices of Issue and Requests to Docket;

NOW, THEREFORE, I, ROBERT K. ROUSE, JR., Chief Judge of the Seventh Judicial Circuit of Florida, hereby order as follows:

1. When a party files a Notice of Issue and Request to Docket with the Clerk of Court pursuant to Rule 1.440, Florida Rules of Civil Procedure, or Rule 12.440, Florida Family Law Rules, said party shall include stamped-addressed envelopes in sufficient quantities to permit distribution of conformed copies of the Court's subsequent order to all parties.

2. Upon receipt of said Notice of Issue and Request to Docket, the Clerk of Court shall forward the court file, together with any envelopes which have been received, to the assigned judge for his/her consideration.

TO BE RECORDED in Flagler, Putnam, St. Johns and Volusia Counties

DONE AND ORDERED at Daytona Beach, Volusia County, Florida, this 3rd day of August, 2000.

ROBERT K. ROUSE, JR.
CHIEF JUDGE

Adopted effective August 3, 2000.

CV–2004–004–SC (A). MOTIONS TO COMPEL DISCOVERY IN CIVIL ACTIONS

IN THE CIRCUIT COURT OF FLORIDA, SEVENTH JUDICIAL CIRCUIT IN AND FOR FLAGLER, PUTNAM, ST. JOHNS AND VOLUSIA COUNTIES

REF: CV 2004–004 SC (A) (Rescinds CV–2004–004–SC)

RE: MOTIONS TO COMPEL DISCOVERY IN CIVIL ACTIONS (Amended)

WHEREAS, the undersigned has determined that the issuance of an Administrative Order governing motions to compel discovery in civil actions is necessary for the efficient and proper administration of justice in the Seventh Judicial Circuit;

NOW THEREFORE, I, JULIANNE PIGGOTTE, Chief Judge of the Seventh Judicial Circuit of Florida, hereby order that no motion to compel discovery in any civil action may be **filed** in the Seventh Judicial Circuit unless the moving party has complied with the following procedures:

1. The moving party must notify the opposing party, **in writing**, of the **specific** nature of the deficiencies of his/her discovery response and the specific actions necessary to cure said asserted deficiencies. Said written notice must provide 10 days, plus mailing time, for the opposing party to cure said asserted deficiencies, or such shorter time as may be required by the Court.

2. Upon failure to resolve the issue within the time mentioned in # 1 above, the moving party may then file a motion to compel discovery and request that a hearing be set. A copy of the written notice of deficiency, and any response thereto, must be attached to the motion. Once set, the hearing may not be cancelled by either party without the Court's consent.

3. When a motion to compel discovery alleges a complete failure to respond or object to discovery, and where there has been no request for extension, an ex-parte order may be entered by the Court requiring compliance with the original discovery demand within 10 days of the signing of the order. The moving party must submit a proposed order and self-addressed, stamped envelopes for the Court's use.

4. If the opposing party fails to respond to a proper discovery request, or responds in a manner deemed by the Court to be in bad faith, a presumption in favor of sanctions against the offending party shall arise. Said sanctions may include, but are not limited to, attorneys' fees and costs. Bad faith in propounding improper or unreasonable discovery requests may be sanctioned in a like manner.

IT IS FURTHER ORDERED that Administrative Order # CV-2004-004-SC is hereby rescinded.

TO BE RECORDED in Flagler, Putnam, St. Johns and Volusia counties.

DONE AND ORDERED in Daytona Beach, Volusia County, Florida this 29th day of March, 2004.

JULIANNE PIGGOTTE
CHIEF JUDGE

Amended effective March 29, 2004.

CV-2006-005-SC. FILING FEE FOR PETITIONS FOR 90-DAY EXTENSION IN ACTIONS FOR PERSONAL INJURY OR WRONGFUL DEATH ARISING OUT OF MEDICAL NEGLIGENCE

IN THE CIRCUIT COURT OF FLORIDA, SEVENTH JUDICIAL CIRCUIT IN AND FOR FLAGLER, PUTNAM, ST. JOHNS AND VOLUSIA COUNTIES

CV—2006-005-SC (Rescinds CV-2000-005-SC)

RE: Filing Fee For Petitions for 90-Day Extension In Actions For Personal Injury Or Wrongful Death Arising Out Of Medical Negligence

WHEREAS, Section 766.104(2), Florida Statutes, provides that a filing fee be paid to the Clerk of the Circuit Court for petitions for an automatic 90-day extension of the statute of limitations to allow reasonable investigation in actions for personal injury or wrongful death arising out of medical negligence,

NOW THEREFORE, I, WILLIAM A. PARSONS., Chief Judge of the Seventh Judicial Circuit, hereby establish a $37.50 filing fee in such actions, payable to the Clerk of the Circuit Court in the county in which the underlying cause of action is to be filed. This shall not be deemed to revive a cause of action on which the statute of limitations has run.

IT IS FURTHER ORDERED that Administrative Order # CV-2000-005-SC is hereby rescinded.

TO BE RECORDED in Flagler, Putnam, St. Johns and Volusia Counties.

DONE AND ORDERED at Daytona Beach, Volusia County, Florida, this 17th day of February, 2006.

WILLIAM A. PARSONS
CHIEF JUDGE

Amended effective February 17, 2006.

CV-2009-006-SC. PROCEDURES FOR INDIGENCY DETERMINATION IN CERTAIN CIVIL CASES

IN THE CIRCUIT COURT OF FLORIDA, SEVENTH JUDICIAL CIRCUIT IN AND FOR FLAGLER, PUTNAM, ST. JOHNS AND VOLUSIA COUNTIES

RE: Procedures for Indigency Determination in Certain Civil Cases

REF: CV-2009-006-SC (Rescinds CV-2006-006-SC)

WHEREAS, §§ 57.081 and 57.085, Florida Statutes, provide that certain indigent persons in judicial proceedings (the "Litigant") are entitled to receive certain services of the Courts, Sheriffs and Clerks of Court on Flagler, Putnam, St. Johns and Volusia Counties (the "Clerk") without the payment or prepayment of costs, and

WHEREAS, 57.082, Florida Statutes, requires the Clerk to determine if a non-prisoner litigant is indigent based upon information provided in an Application for Determination of Indigent Status, and

WHEREAS, 57.085, Florida Statutes sets forth additional requirements for prisoners as defined by subsection (1) who wish to file civil court actions as indigents, and

WHEREAS, detailed financial information is necessary to properly evaluate applications for indigent status.

NOW THEREFORE, I, J. DAVID WALSH, Chief Judge of the Seventh Judicial Circuit of Florida, hereby order as follows:

1. Application/Affidavit for Determination of Indigent Status

a) Non-Prisoner Litigants

Any party to or intervenor in any civil case, excluding matters filed pursuant to § 741.30 or § 784.046, Florida Statutes, who wish to proceed as an indigent in order to receive certain Court, Sheriff and Clerk services without the payment or prepayment of costs shall, prior to obtaining a Clerk's certificate of indigency, file a fully completed Application for Determination of Indigent Status. The application required to be filed by non-prisoner litigants pursuant to §§ 57.081 and 57.082, Florida Statutes, is attached as Exhibit A.

b) Prisoner Litigants

A "prisoner" {see § 57.085(1), Florida Statutes} who wishes to proceed as an indigent in order to receive certain Court, Sheriff and Clerk services without prepayment must file a fully completed affidavit. The affidavit required to be filed by prisoner litigants pursuant to § 57.085(2), Florida Statutes, is attached as Exhibit B.

In addition, pursuant to § 57.085(7), Florida Statutes, if a prisoner litigant has been determined indigent twice in the preceding 3 years, said prisoner litigant may not be determined indigent to pursue a new suit without first obtaining leave of court. Therefore, any prisoner litigant who wishes to proceed as an indigent in order to receive certain Court, Sheriff and Clerk services without prepayment must, prior to obtaining a clerk's certificate of indigency, file a fully completed Affidavit of Prior Litigation attached as Exhibit C.

2. The Clerk is directed to stamp or otherwise indicate on the court case file that a person involved with the case is seeking indigent status.

3. The Clerk is directed to provide litigants seeking indigent status with blank copies of the appropriate application/affidavit in substantially the same forms as Exhibits A, B and/or C and must inform said litigants that the application(s)/affidavit(s) must be fully completed and filed with the Clerk before his/her office makes a determination of indigency.

4. If the Clerk, based upon the application filed, determines a non-prisoner litigant to be indigent, the Clerk will immediately file the certificate of indigency in the court case file.

5. In the following instances, the Clerk is directed to forward the court case file to the assigned judge for the judge's consideration:

a) The Clerk determines a prisoner litigant to be indigent;

b) If the Clerk determines a litigant not to be indigent and the litigant files a petition seeking review of the clerk's determination.

6. In the event the Clerk is unable to make an indigency determination based on a litigant's application, the Clerk may seek assistance / guidance from the assigned judge.

7. Judicial Consideration

a) Non–Prisoner Litigants

The assigned judge will promptly review the application to determine if the litigant is indigent. The judge may set the issue of the litigant's indigency for hearing upon notice to the litigant or may rule on the litigant's indigency status based on the information provided in the application. The litigant has the burden of proving indigency. When the file is sent to the judge, the Clerk is directed to prepare and also send an order in substantially the same form as attached Exhibit D.

b) Prisoner Litigants

Pursuant to § 57.085(7), Florida Statutes, if a prisoner litigant has been determined indigent twice in the preceding 3 years, the prisoner litigant may not be determined indigent to pursue a new suit without first obtaining leave of court. Therefore, the assigned judge will promptly review the Affidavit of Prior Litigation by Prisoner to determine if the prisoner litigant requires leave of court to be determined indigent. When the file is sent to the judge, the Clerk is directed to prepare and also send an order in substantially the same form as attached Exhibit E.

If the judge determines that the prisoner litigant qualifies under § 57.085(7), or grants the prisoner litigant leave to proceed, the assigned judge will promptly review the affidavit to determine if the litigant is indigent. The judge may set the issue of the litigant's indigency for hearing upon notice to the litigant or may rule on the litigant's indigency status based on the information provided in the affidavit. The litigant has the burden of proving indigency. When the file is sent to the judge, the Clerk is directed to prepare and also send an order in substantially the same form as attached Exhibit F.

In addition, before an indigent prisoner may intervene in, initiate, or continue any judicial proceeding, the Court must review the prisoner's claim to determine whether it is legally sufficient to state a cause of action for which the court has jurisdiction and may grant relief {see § 57.085(6), (8), Florida Statutes}. When the file is sent to the judge, the Clerk is directed to prepare and also send an order in substantially the same form as attached Exhibit G. All or part of an indigent prisoner's claim must be dismissed if one or more of the enumerated criteria contained in said order is met.

8. If a litigant fails to file a fully completed application/affidavit, or if the judge determines that the litigant is not indigent based on the information provided in the application/affidavit and that a hearing on the indigency issue is not necessary, the judge will issue an order declaring that the person has not adequately demonstrated indigency and will revoke the Clerk's certificate of indigency. If payment of all appropriate fees is not made to the Clerk for disbursement to the appropriate agencies within fourteen (14) days after the issues of the revocation order, the cause will automatically be dismissed without prejudice. These time limits may be extended at the discretion of the assigned judge.

9. Indigent litigants are only entitled to those services enumerated in § 57.081, Florida Statutes, without prepayment. Any other service requested by the litigant must be paid for at the standard rate.

10. In the event multiple parties to a case seek indigent status, each party must complete the appropriate application/affidavit and each party must fully comply with all requirements of this Administrative Order.

11. If a litigant who has been determined indigent prevails in the action, costs will be taxed in his/her favor as provided by law, and when collected, will first be applied to pay costs which otherwise would have been required and which have not been paid. The Clerk will make note for the judge of the costs to be taxed before final hearing, for inclusion in the Order or Judgment in favor of the indigent litigant.

12. When possible, the Clerk is directed to notify the judge at the time he/she reviews the litigant's indigency status as to other pending actions in which said litigant sought indigent status and the determinations reached in such other actions.

13. Administrative Order CV–2006–006–SC is hereby rescinded.

TO BE RECORDED in Flagler, Putnam, St. Johns and Volusia counties.

DONE AND ORDERED in Daytona Beach, Volusia County, Florida this 21st day of July 2009.

Judge J. David Walsh
Chief Judge

EXHIBIT A

IN THE CIRCUIT/COUNTY COURT OF THE SEVENTH JUDICIAL CIRCUIT

IN AND FOR ______ COUNTY, FLORIDA

CASE NO.
DIVISION

______________________,
Plaintiff/Petitioner
or In the Interest of

vs.

______________________.
Defendant/Respondent

APPLICATION FOR DETERMINATION OF CIVIL INDIGENT STATUS

Notice to Applicant: If you do not qualify for civil indigency and you cannot afford to pay the filing fee, you must enroll in the Clerk's Office payment plan and pay a one-time administrative fee of $25.00.

1. **I have ______ dependents.** (Do not include children not living at home and do not include a working spouse or yourself.)

2. **I have a take-home income of $** ______ paid ( ) weekly ( ) bi- weekly ( ) semi-monthly ( ) monthly ( ) yearly. (Take home income equals salary, wages, bonuses, commissions, allowances, overtime, tips and similar payments, minus deductions required by law and other court ordered support payments.)

3. **I have $ ______ in other income** paid ( ) weekly ( ) bi-weekly ( ) semi-monthly ( ) monthly ( ) yearly. (Circle "Yes" and fill in the amount if you have this kind of income, otherwise circle "No")

Social Security benefits	Yes $____	No
Unemployment compensation	Yes $____	No
Union funds	Yes $____	No
Workers compensation	Yes $____	No
Retirement/pensions	Yes $____	No
Trusts or gifts	Yes $____	No
Veteran's benefits	Yes $____	No
Child Support or other regular support from family members/spouse	Yes $____	No
Rental income	Yes $____	No
Dividends or interests	Yes $____	No
Other kinds of income not on the list	Yes $____	No

4. **I have other assets.** (Circle "Yes" and fill in the value of the property, otherwise circle "No".)

Cash	Yes $____	No
Bank account(s)	Yes $____	No
Certificates of deposit or money market account	Yes $____	No
*Equity in Boats and other tangible property	Yes $____	No
Savings	Yes $____	No
Stocks and bonds	Yes $____	No
*Equity in Real estate (excluding homestead)	Yes $____	No
*Equity in Motor vehicles	Yes $____	No

5. **I have total amount of liabilities and debts in the amount of $** ______________________.

6. **I have a private lawyer in this case– Yes No**

A person who knowingly provides false information to the clerk or the court in seeking a determination of indigent status under F.S. 57.082 commits a misdemeanor of the first degree, punishable as provided in s.775.082 or s.775.083. **I attest that the information I have provided on this application is true and accurate to the best of my knowledge.**

Signed this ___ day of ______, 20___.

____
Signature of Applicant for Indigent Status
Print Full Legal Name ______

____
Date of Birth

____
Drivers License or ID Number

Address, P O Address, Street, City, State, Zip Code

Note: If applicant is determined by the clerk to be Not Indigent, you may seek judicial review by filing a petition to review.

CLERK'S DETERMINATION

Based on the information in this Application, I have determined the applicant to be ______ **Indigent** ______ **Not indigent**, according to 57. 082, F.S.

Dated this ___ day of ______, 20___.

By ______________________
Deputy Clerk

This form was completed with the assistance of ______ Clerk/Deputy Clerk/Other.

EXHIBIT B

IN THE CIRCUIT/COUNTY COURT OF THE SEVENTH JUDICIAL CIRCUIT

IN AND FOR ______ COUNTY, FLORIDA

CASE NO.
DIVISION

______________________,
Plaintiff(s)/Petitioner(s)/ Appellant(s),

vs

AFFIDAVIT FOR DETERMINATION OF INDIGENT STATUS BY PRISONER PURSUANT TO F.S. 57.085

____
Defendant(s)/Respondent(s)/ Appellee(s).

1. **I have a take-home income of $** ______ paid ( ) weekly ( ) bi- weekly ( ) semi-monthly ( ) monthly ( ) yearly. (Take home income equals salary, wages, bonuses, commissions, allowances, overtime, tips and similar payments, minus deductions required by law and other court ordered support payments.)

2. **I have $ ___ in other income** paid ( ) weekly ( ) bi-weekly ( ) semi-monthly ( ) monthly ( ) yearly. (Circle "Yes" and fill in the amount if you have this kind of income, otherwise circle "No")

Social Security benefits	Yes $____	No
Unemployment compensation	Yes $____	No
Union funds	Yes $____	No
Workers compensation	Yes $____	No
Retirement/pensions	Yes $____	No
Trusts or gifts	Yes $____	No
Veteran's benefits	Yes $____	No
Child Support or other regular support from family members/spouse	Yes $____	No
Rental income	Yes $____	No
Dividends or interests	Yes $____	No
Other kinds of income not on the list	Yes $____	No

3. **I have the following real estate:**

____________ Value $________
____________ Value $________
____________ Value $________
____________ Value $________

4. **I have tangible and intangible property worth more than $100:**

Stocks and Bonds	Yes $____	No
Other ________	Yes $____	No
Automobile	Yes $____	No
Other ________	Yes $____	No

5. **I have other assets.** (Circle "Yes" and fill in the value of the property, otherwise circle "No".)

Cash	Yes $____	No
Bank account(s)	Yes $____	No
Savings	Yes $____	No
Money Market account	Yes $____	No

6. **I have ___ dependents.** (Do not include children not living at home and do not include a working spouse or yourself.)

Age	Name

7. **I owe the following creditors:** (mortgage or rent payments, credit cards, etc.) If more space is required, use back of form.

Creditors Name	Amount Owed
	$
	$
	$
	$
	$
	$
	$
	$
	$

Prisoner's Monthly Expenses	
	$
	$
	$
	$
	$

8. During the past three years, have you been permitted two or more times to proceed without prepayment of court costs or fees in Florida or federal courts or adjudicatory forums, or to intervene in actions in these courts or adjudicatory forums without prepayment of court costs or fees, pursuant to sections 57.081 or 57.085, Florida Statutes, or 28 U.S.C. § 1915? Yes ( ) No ( )

If your answer is yes, list below all suits, actions, claims, proceedings, or appeals that you have brought or intervened in during the past five years in any court or adjudicatory forum.

Name of Court	Case Number	Nature of Action	Disposition

(If necessary, attach additional pages that reflect the required information.)

____

I have attached to this affidavit a photocopy of the trust account records for my prison account for the preceding six (6) months or for the length of my incarceration, whichever period is shorter.

I am presently unable to pay court costs and fees. Under penalties of perjury, I swear or affirm that all statements in this affidavit are true and complete.

______________ Inmate # ________ Date of Birth ________
Print Full Legal Name

Name of Institution: ______________________

Address, PO Address, Street, City, State, Zip Code

____

Dated: ______________________

____
Signature of Petitioner

Sworn to and subscribed before me this ___ day of ________, 20 ___, by the affiant, ________, who is personally known to me or produced ________ as identification.

____
Signature of Notary Public or Correctional Officer
Print, Type or Stamp Commissioned Name of Notary Public
Commission Expires: ______________
Commission #: ______________

DETERMINATION OF INDIGENT STATUS

Based on the information in the petitioner's Affidavit for Indigent Status, I have determined that the petitioner ___ **Is Indigent** ___ **Is Not indigent**, according to Federal Poverty Guidelines. If the petitioner disagrees with the clerk's determination, they may file a written request for Judicial Review to determine their indigency status. The request must be filed within fourteen (14) days from the date of this determination or the case will be closed.

Dated this ___ day of ________, 20___.

Copy provided to prisoner by mail by ________ (initials of clerk).

CLERK OF THE CIRCUIT COURT
By ______________________
Deputy Clerk

EXHIBIT C

IN THE CIRCUIT/COUNTY COURT OF THE SEVENTH JUDICIAL CIRCUIT

IN AND FOR ________ COUNTY, FLORIDA

CASE NO.
DIVISION

____

Plaintiff(s)/Petitioner(s)/ Appellant(s),

vs

AFFIDAVIT OF PRIOR LITIGATION BY PRISONER PURSUANT TO F.S. 57.085(7)

____

Defendant(s)/Respondent(s)/ Appellee(s).

I ________ (*full legal name*), state the following in support of my application to defer the prepayment of court costs and fees in the above matter pursuant to Section 57.085(7), Florida Statutes:

1. I have been convicted of a crime and am currently incarcerated for that crime or I am being held in custody pending extradition or sentencing.

2. (*Check one)*

___ I am an intervener in the above-styled judicial proceeding.

___ I initiated the above-styled judicial proceeding.

3. I am a pro se litigant and am not represented by an attorney.

4. I certify that I have neither been paid nor promised to pay anyone for services on my behalf in connection with this judicial proceeding.

5. I am presently unable to pay court costs and fees otherwise payable by law to the court, clerk and sheriff for their services. Therefore, I am applying for a deferral of prepayment of costs and fees pursuant to Section 57.085, Florida Statutes

6. I have previously been adjudicated indigent under Section 57.085, Florida Statutes (prisoner indigence). Yes ( ) No ( )

7. I have previously been adjudicated indigent under Section 57.081, Florida Statutes (civil indigence). Yes ( ) No ( )

8. I have previously been adjudicated indigent under 28 U.S.C. 1915 by a federal court. Yes ( ) No ( )

If you answered "yes" to questions 6, 7, or 8, list below *all* suits, actions, claims, proceedings, or appeals, including dates, which you brought or in which you intervened in any court or other adjudicatory forum within the past five years.

____

____

____

____

____

____

9. As I have been adjudicated indigent twice in the preceding three years, pursuant to § 57.085(7), Florida Statutes, I am requesting leave of the court to proceed as an indigent prisoner litigant pursuant to § 57.085(7). As the referenced statute requires, I have provided a complete listing of cases, please see #8 above, and I have attached a copy of each complaint, petition, or other document purporting to commence a lawsuit and a record of disposition of the proceeding. Yes ( ) No ( )

10. Attached and incorporated into this Affidavit is a photocopy of my trust account records for my prison account for the preceding six (6) months or for the length of my incarceration, whichever period is shorter.

I am presently unable to pay court costs and fees. Under penalties of perjury, I swear or affirm that all statements in this affidavit are true and complete.

Print Full Legal Name ______________________

Inmate # ________ Date of Birth ________

Name of Institution: ______________________

Address, ______________________

Dated: ______________________

____
Signature of Petitioner

Sworn to and subscribed before me this ___ day of ________, 20___, by the affiant, ________, who is personally known to me or produced ________ as identification.

____

Signature of Notary Public or Correctional Officer

Print, Type or Stamp Commissioned Name of Notary Public

Commission Expires: ______________________

Commission #: ______________________

EXHIBIT D

IN THE CIRCUIT/COUNTY COURT OF THE SEVENTH JUDICIAL CIRCUIT
IN AND FOR ________ COUNTY, FLORIDA

______________________,

CASE NO.
DIVISION

vs.

______________________,

ORDER ON APPLICATION FOR INDIGENT STATUS

THIS MATTER is before the Court on the referral of the application of for indigent status pursuant to § 57.081 and § 57.082, Florida Statutes by the Clerk of Court. Having reviewed the court file, the Court finds that:

(1) ___ The petitioner is indigent and is entitled to proceed without prepayment of the costs associated with those services set forth in 57.081 and 57.082, Florida Statutes. If the litigant prevails in this action, all costs shall be taxed in his/her favor, when collected, shall be applied to pay costs which otherwise would have been received and which have not previously been paid.

(2) ___ Based on the information furnished, the petitioner has not adequately proven indigency. The litigant shall pay the appropriate filing fees and sheriff's service charges to the Clerk of the Court or enter into a payment plan with the Clerk of Court within 14 days of this order, or this action shall be dismissed without prejudice and without further order of the Court.

(3) ___ Based on the information provided to this Court, the Court cannot determine the litigant's indigency status. Ac-

cordingly, the Court shall hold a hearing on the litigant's indigency status on ________, at ___ am/pm in ___, Florida. The litigant shall bring with him/her all relevant financial information to substantiate his/her claim of indigency as more fully set forth in the litigant's application for indigency.

(4) ___ The petitioner is indigent and entitled to proceed without costs for services provided through the Family Law/Dependency Mediation Program.

DONE AND ORDERED in ________, ________ County, Florida this ___ day of ________, 20 ________.

____
CIRCUIT/COUNTY COURT JUDGE

Copies furnished to:

EXHIBIT E

IN THE CIRCUIT/COUNTY COURT OF THE SEVENTH JUDICIAL CIRCUIT

IN AND FOR ________ COUNTY, FLORIDA

________________, **CASE NO.**
DIVISION

vs.

________________,

ORDER ON PRIOR INDIGENCE DETERMINATIONS PURSUANT TO F.S. 57.085(7)

THIS MATTER is before the Court pursuant to the requirements of § 57.085(7) and § 57.082, Florida Statutes. Accordingly, the court finds and orders as follows:

(1) ___ The prisoner litigant **has not** at least twice in the preceding three years been adjudicated indigent for purposes of prepayment of court costs and fees. Therefore, it is appropriate for the court to proceed and determine if the prisoner litigant is indigent.

(2) ___ The prisoner litigant **has** at least twice in the preceding three years been adjudicated indigent for purposes of prepayment of court costs and fees, and **has not** attached a complete listing of each suit, action, claim, proceeding or appeal brought by or intervened in by the inmate in any court in the preceding five years and/or **has not** attached a copy of each complaint, petition, or other document purporting to commence a lawsuit and a record of disposition of the proceeding. Based upon the prisoner litigant's failure to attach said listings and pleadings, the court is unable to grant leave to find the prisoner litigant indigent. The prisoner litigant shall pay the appropriate filing fees and Sheriff's service charges to the Clerk of the Court within fourteen (14) days of the date of this Order, or this action shall be dismissed without prejudice and without further order of the Court.

(3) ___ The prisoner litigant **has** at least twice in the preceding three years been adjudicated indigent for purposes of prepayment of court costs and fees, and **has** attached a complete listing of each suit, action, claim, proceeding or appeal brought by or intervened in by the inmate in any court in the preceding five years and **has** attached a copy of each complaint, petition, or other document purporting to commence a lawsuit and a record of disposition of the proceeding. The court considers this a valid request for leave of court to determine if the prisoner litigant is indigent for the purposes of the above-styled proceedings. Upon review of the submitted documents the court GRANTS (________) DENIES (________) the prisoner litigant's request to proceed. If the request is GRANTED it is appropriate for the court to proceed and determine if the prisoner litigant is indigent.

If denied, state reason(s) below:

____

____

____

DONE AND ORDERED in ________, ________ County, Florida this ___ day of ________, 20 ________.

____
CIRCUIT/COUNTY COURT JUDGE

Copies furnished to:

EXHIBIT F

IN THE CIRCUIT/COUNTY COURT OF THE SEVENTH JUDICIAL CIRCUIT

IN AND FOR ________ COUNTY, FLORIDA

________________, **CASE NO.**
DIVISION

vs.

________________,

ORDER ON APPLICATION FOR INDIGENT STATUS OF PRISONER LITIGANT

THIS MATTER is before the Court on the referral of the application of ________ (prisoner litigant) for indigent status pursuant to § 57.085, Florida Statutes by the Clerk of Court. Having reviewed the court file, the Court finds that:

(1) ___ Based upon the information furnished the **prisoner litigant** has not adequately proven indigency. The prisoner litigant shall pay the appropriate filing fees and Sheriff's service charges to the Clerk of Court within fourteen (14) days of the date of this Order, or this action shall be dismissed without prejudice and without further order of the Court.

(2) ___ The prisoner litigant is indigent and is:

________ entitled to proceed without the **initial prepayment** of the costs associated with those services set forth in § 57.081, Florida Statutes.

________ able to pay part of the court costs and fees associated with this action before issuance of the initial process in this action. The prisoner litigant is hereby ordered to make an **initial partial payment** toward those court costs and fees pursuant to § 57.085(4), Florida Statutes within twenty (20) days of the date of this Order. Until such payment is made, no process shall issue.

Pursuant to § 57.085(5), Florida Statutes, the prisoner litigant is hereby ordered to make monthly payments until such time as the costs and fees associated with this action totaling $ ___ are paid in full. The Court reserves jurisdiction to assess and require the payment of additional fees and costs if any are incurred.

The Florida Department of Corrections or local detention facility shall place a lien on the inmate's prison trust account for the full amount of the court costs and fees associated with this action and shall withdraw the prisoner litigant's monthly payment, pursuant to § 57.085(5), and forward the monthly payment to the Clerk of the Circuit Court at the following address:

____

until such time as the costs and fees associated with this action are paid in full.

The Clerk of this Court shall provide a certified copy of this Order to the Superintendent of the Correctional Facility, at ________ so that the Florida Department of Corrections or local detention facility can comply with paragraph(s) 1 and/or 2 this Order.

(3) ___ Based on the information provided to this Court, the Court cannot determine the litigant's indigency status. Accordingly, the Court shall hold a hearing on the litigant's indigency status on ________, at ___ a.m./p.m. in ________, Florida. The litigant shall bring with him/her all relevant financial information to substantiate his/her claim of indigency as more fully set forth in the litigant's financial affidavit.

DONE AND ORDERED in ________, ________ County, Florida this ___ day of, ________, 20 ________.

____
CIRCUIT/COUNTY COURT
JUDGE

Copies furnished to:

EXHIBIT G

IN THE CIRCUIT/COUNTY COURT OF THE SEVENTH JUDICIAL CIRCUIT

IN AND FOR ________ COUNTY, FLORIDA

________________, **CASE NO.**
DIVISION

vs.

________________,

ORDER DISMISSING PRISONER LITIGATION

THIS MATTER came before the Court on the Plaintiff/Petitioner's ________, and the Court, having considered the petition/complaint and court file, and being otherwise fully advised in the premises, hereby finds as follows:

(1) ___ the petition/complaint fails to state any claim for which relief may be granted and has no arguable basis in law or fact.

(2) ___ the claim(s) raised in the petition/complaint is/are substantially similar to previously litigated claim(s) involving the same parties or arising from the same operative facts as the subject claim(s).

(3) ___ the petition/complaint seeks monetary relief from respondents/defendants who are immune from suit.

(4) ___ the plaintiff/petitioner's claim of indigency was false or misleading.

(5) ___ this Court is without the requisite jurisdiction to entertain the prisoner's petition for writ of mandamus or habeas corpus because the prisoner is not incarcerated within this judicial circuit.

(6) ___ this Court is without the requisite jurisdiction to entertain the prisoner's petition for writ of mandamus because the prisoner has failed to allege or demonstrate in his petition that he has exhausted the two-step administrative grievance procedure provided for in Rules 33–29.006 and 33–29.007, Florida Administrative Code (1993).

(7) ___ the petition for writ of habeas corpus fails to allege or demonstrate that the petitioner is entitled to immediate release.

(8) ___ the petition/complaint was frivolously filed and the prisoner shall, in accordance with Section 944.279, Florida Statutes (1996), be subject to a forfeiture of earned and unearned gain time as a penalty for instituting this frivolous proceeding in this Court.

(9) ___ the plaintiff/petitioner failed to pay court costs and fees assessed by prior Court order despite having the ability to pay.

(10) ___ the plaintiff/petitioner's claim has little likelihood of success on its merits.

(11) ___ the allegations of fact in the complaint/petition claim are fanciful or not credible.

(12) ___ the complaint/petition seeks relief for mental or emotional injury where there has been no related allegation of a physical injury.

(13) ___ the complaint/petition is frivolous, malicious, or reasonably appears to be intended to harass one or more named defendants.

(14) ___ Other ______________________________

____

Accordingly, it is, ORDERED AND ADJUDGED that:

___ the Plaintiff/Petitioner's ________, is hereby DISMISSED with prejudice; and

___ the Clerk of Court's Office in and for ________ County, Florida is hereby directed to provide a certified copy of this order to the Superintendent of so that disciplinary action may be instituted against the Plaintiff/Petitioner, DC # ___), in accordance with Section 944.28(2)(a), Florida Statutes.

DONE AND ORDERED in ________, ________ County, Florida this ___ day of ________, 20 ________.

____
CIRCUIT/COUNTY COURT
JUDGE

Copies furnished to:

Amended effective July 21, 2009.

CV–2000–007–SC. ADDRESSES AND SOCIAL SECURITY NUMBERS OF PARTIES ON FINAL JUDGMENTS

IN THE CIRCUIT COURT OF FLORIDA, SEVENTH JUDICIAL CIRCUIT IN AND FOR FLAGLER, PUTNAM, ST. JOHNS AND VOLUSIA COUNTIES

CV 2000–007 SC

RE: Addresses And Social Security Numbers Of Parties On Final Judgments

WHEREAS, it has been made known to the undersigned that the efficient and proper administration of justice and the processing of Circuit Civil and County Civil matters requires the inclusion of the addresses and social security numbers of each party on Final Judgments as required in Section 55.01(2), Florida Statutes;

NOW THEREFORE, I, ROBERT K. ROUSE, JR., Chief Judge of the Seventh Judicial Circuit, hereby order as follows:

1. When a party submits a proposed Final Judgment to the Clerk of the Court or to the Judge for signature, the Final Judgment shall contain the address and the social security number, if known to the prevailing party, of each person against whom judgment is rendered.

TO BE RECORDED in Flagler, Putnam, St. Johns and Volusia Counties.

DONE AND ORDERED at Daytona Beach, Volusia County, Florida, this 3rd day of August, 2000.

ROBERT K. ROUSE, JR.
CHIEF JUDGE

Adopted effective August 3, 2000.

CV–2019–008–SC. INFORMATION RETURNS REPORTING

IN THE CIRCUIT COURT OF FLORIDA, SEVENTH JUDICIAL CIRCUIT IN AND FOR FLAGLER, PUTNAM, ST. JOHNS AND VOLUSIA COUNTIES

RE: Information Returns Reporting (Form 1099) By Clerks Of Court, Seventh Judicial Circuit

REF: CV–2019–008–SC

(Rescinds CV–2000–008–SC)

WHEREAS, the Clerks of Court are responsible for filing information returns (Form 1099) with the Internal Revenue Service for interest collected and paid on Judgments, and

WHEREAS, an appropriate procedure is necessary to acquire requisite information for purposes of completing information returns (Form 1099),

NOW THEREFORE, I, RAUL A. ZAMBRANO, Chief Judge of the Seventh Judicial Circuit, hereby order that parties/litigants applying for payment of monies from Judgments are to provide the Clerk of Court with a valid Social Security or Tax ID number.

TO BE RECORDED in Flagler, Putnam, St. Johns and Volusia counties.

DONE AND ORDERED at Daytona Beach, Volusia County, Florida, this 10th day of January 2019.

RAUL A. ZAMBRANO
CHIEF JUDGE

Adopted effective August 3, 2000. Amended effective January 10, 2019.

CV–2003–009–SC. FILING OF DEPOSITION TRANSCRIPTS

IN THE CIRCUIT COURT OF FLORIDA, SEVENTH JUDICIAL CIRCUIT IN AND FOR FLAGLER, PUTNAM, ST. JOHNS AND VOLUSIA COUNTIES

REF: CV–2003–009–SC (Rescinds CV–2000–009–SC)

RE: FILING OF DEPOSITION TRANSCRIPTS

WHEREAS, pursuant to Rule 1.310(f)(3), Florida Rules of Civil Procedure, (see also Rule 12.020, Florida Family Law Rules of Procedure), deposition transcripts are to be filed with the Clerk only when the contents of the deposition must be considered by the Court in a matter pending before the Court (i.e., a scheduled hearing on a motion for summary judgment), and

WHEREAS, the undersigned has been advised that deposition transcripts are being filed with the Clerks of the Seventh Judicial Circuit in cases where no hearing or other matter is scheduled or pending before the Court and,

WHEREAS, the undersigned has also been advised that deposition transcripts are being filed with the Clerks of the Seventh Judicial Circuit in cases where a hearing is scheduled, but the date of said hearing is more than 30 days from the date the transcripts are filed, and

WHEREAS, limited storage space exists within the court facilities of the Seventh Judicial Circuit wherein the Clerks may reasonably and properly store and maintain deposition transcripts;

NOW THEREFORE, I, Julianne Piggotte, Chief Judge of the Seventh Judicial Circuit, hereby order that a deposition transcript shall only be filed in a civil (including family, juvenile and probate) case if the hearing, or trial to which it relates, is scheduled to take place within 30 days of the date the transcript is filed.

IT IS FURTHER ORDERED that in accordance with Rule 1.310(f)(3), Florida Rules of Civil Procedure, any deposition transcript submitted for filing in a civil case must be accompanied by a Notice of Filing of Deposition Transcript. Said Notice must contain a certification that the deposition is being filed for the purpose of being considered by the Court in a matter pending before the Court. Furthermore, the certification must specifically identify the matter to be considered by the Court, as well as the date and time of the hearing or other such proceeding.

IT IS FURTHER ORDERED that the Clerks of Court of the Seventh Judicial Circuit shall refuse to accept for filing, and/or return, deposition transcripts in cases where no hearings are scheduled, or where hearings, or trials to which they relate, are scheduled more than 30 days from the date the transcripts are submitted for filing. The Clerks shall also refuse to accept for filing, and/or return, deposition transcripts which are not accompanied by a Notice of Filing of Deposition Transcript containing the certification as described above.

IT IS FURTHER ORDERED that Administrative Order # CV–2000–009–SC is hereby rescinded.

TO BE RECORDED in Flagler, Putnam, St. Johns and Volusia counties.

DONE AND ORDERED in Daytona Beach, Volusia County, Florida this 12th day of August 2003.

JULIANNE PIGGOTTE
CHIEF JUDGE

Amended effective August 12, 2003.

CV–2017–010–VL. ESTABLISHING WESTERN, EASTERN AND SOUTHERN CIVIL DIVISIONS OF THE CIRCUIT AND COUNTY COURT

IN THE CIRCUIT COURT OF FLORIDA,
SEVENTH JUDICIAL CIRCUIT IN
AND FOR VOLUSIA COUNTY

IN THE CIRCUIT COURT OF FLORIDA,
SEVENTH JUDICIAL CIRCUIT IN
AND FOR VOLUSIA COUNTY

RE: Establishing Western, Eastern and Southern Civil Divisions of the Circuit and County Court

REF: CV–2017–010–VL (Rescinds CV–2008–010–VL)

WHEREAS, it has been made known to the undersigned that the efficient and proper administration of justice and the processing of Civil cases in the Circuit and County Courts in Volusia County requires the establishment of Western, Eastern, and Southern divisions of these courts;

NOW THEREFORE, I, TERENCE R. PERKINS, Chief Judge of the Seventh Judicial Circuit of Florida, hereby order and adjudge as follows:

1. Western Civil Divisions of the Circuit and County Courts in Volusia County are established, to which at least one judge of these respective courts may be assigned, and in which those cases arising in the divisions as ordered by the Chief Judge and as defined in #4 below are to be filed.

2. Eastern Civil Divisions of the Circuit and County Courts in Volusia County are established, to which at least one judge of these respective courts may be assigned, and in which those cases arising in the divisions as ordered by the Chief Judge and as defined in #5 below are to be filed.

3. Southern Civil Divisions of the Circuit and County Courts in Volusia County are established, to which at least one judge of these respective courts may be assigned, and in which those cases arising in the divisions as ordered by the Chief Judge and as defined in #6 below are to be filed.

4. The Western Civil Divisions consist of those portions of Volusia County contained within zip codes 32102, 32105, 32130, 32180, 32190, 32706, 32713, 32720, 32721, 32722, 32723, 32724, 32725, 32728, 32738, 32739, 32744, 32753, 32763 and 32774.

5. The Eastern Civil Divisions consist of those portions of Volusia County contained within zip codes 32110, 32114, 32115, 32116, 32117, 32118, 32119, 32120, 32121, 32122, 32123, 32124, 32125, 32126, 32127, 32128, 32129, 32136, 32173, 32174, 32175, 32176 and 32198.

6. The Southern Civil Divisions consist of those portions of Volusia County contained within zip codes 32132, 32141, 32168, 32169, 32170, 32754, 32759 and 32764.

IT IS FURTHER ORDERED that cases are to be assigned to the respective geographic Civil divisions based on the following criteria:

1. One Defendant / Respondent

a. Defendant's / Respondent's residence / address

b. Where cause of action arose

c. Location of property in litigation.

2. Multiple Defendants / Respondents

a. Where cause of action arose

b. Location of property in litigation

In the event the Clerk of Court's office is unable to determine the proper geographic division assignment in a case due to the absence of a zip code on the civil cover sheet, the case may be assigned using the city of the defendant's/respondent's residence/address, where the cause of action arose, or the location of the property in litigation. Additional direction/guidance concerning the assignment of cases to divisions may be provided by separate administrative order. If any further uncertainty or ambiguity concerning the assignment of a case to a geographical division exists, the matter should be referred to the Court Administrator's office for resolution by the Chief Judge {see Kruckenberg v. Powell, 422 So. 2d 994 (Fla. 5 DCA 1982)}.

IT IS FURTHER ORDERED that Administrative Orders CV–2008–010–VL is hereby rescinded.

TO BE RECORDED in Volusia County, Florida.

DONE AND ORDERED in Daytona Beach, Volusia County, Florida this 1st day of May 2017.

TERENCE R. PERKINS
Chief Judge

Amended effective January 1, 2009; May 2, 2017.

CV–2000–011–VL. EMINENT DOMAIN CASES

IN THE CIRCUIT COURT OF FLORIDA,
SEVENTH JUDICIAL CIRCUIT IN
AND FOR VOLUSIA COUNTY

CV 2000–011 VL

RE: EMINENT DOMAIN CASES

WHEREAS, it has been made known to the undersigned that the efficient and proper administration of justice in Volusia County requires each parcel in eminent domain proceedings to be individually accounted for in the Circuit Court, therefore requiring files for each parcel,

NOW THEREFORE, I, ROBERT K. ROUSE, JR., Chief Judge of the Seventh Judicial Circuit of Florida, hereby order as follows:

1) When a party files any pleading in an eminent domain case in Volusia County other than the initial Complaint, Lis Pendens, Order of Taking, Order Regulating Pleadings, Summonses or other paper common to all parcel(s), the pleading(s) or paper must contain the appropriate parcel number under the case number caption.

a) The Clerk of the Circuit Court in Volusia County will maintain a master docket for each case. Each parcel will have a separate court file and court docket sheet. All orders, pleadings, motions and other papers will, when filed and docketed, be placed in the appropriate parcel file.

b) All orders, pleadings, motions and other papers will bear the initial case style. Documents intended to apply only to particular parcel(s) will indicate in their caption the parcel number(s) to which they apply and sufficient copies shall be provided to the Clerk of Court to allow the filing and docketing of each relevant paper in each parcel file.

c) If a party fails to supply sufficient copies of a paper for each parcel, the Clerk of Court shall file the paper, but shall contact the party and request sufficient copies for filing in each parcel file.

TO BE RECORDED in Volusia County, Florida.

DONE AND ORDERED at Daytona Beach, Volusia County, Florida, this 3rd day of August, 2000.

ROBERT K. ROUSE, JR.
CHIEF JUDGE

Adopted effective August 3, 2000.

CV–2016–012–SC. ELECTRONIC SALE OF PROPERTIES IN FORECLOSURE CASES

IN THE CIRCUIT COURT OF FLORIDA, SEVENTH JUDICIAL CIRCUIT IN AND FOR FLAGLER, PUTNAM AND VOLUSIA COUNTIES

RE: ELECTRONIC SALE OF PROPERTIES IN FORECLOSURE CASES

REF: CV–2016–012–SC

(Rescinds CV–2016–012–FG/PT/VL)

WHEREAS, pursuant to § 45.031(10), Florida Statutes, the Clerk of Court is authorized to conduct the sale of real or personal property under an order or judgment by electronic means, and

WHEREAS, the Volusia County Clerk of Court has been conducting on-line foreclosure auctions, in lieu of on-site auctions, since May 2013 at www.volusia.realforeclose.com, and

WHEREAS, the Putnam County Clerk of Court has been conducting on-line foreclosure auctions, in lieu of on-site auctions, since June 2015 at www.putnam.realforeclose.com;

WHEREAS, the Flagler County and the St. Johns County Clerks of Court would like to begin conducting on-line foreclosure auctions in lieu of on-site auctions beginning July 1, 2016 at www.flagler.realforeclose.com;

NOW THEREFORE, I, TERENCE R. PERKINS, Chief Judge of the Seventh Judicial Circuit of Florida, hereby order as follows:

1. Effective July 1, 2016, the Clerks of Court in Flagler, Putnam, St. Johns and Volusia counties are currently authorized to conduct on-line auctions of real property, in lieu of on-site auctions, notwithstanding the location provisions which may be included in the final judgments or court orders.

2. The Clerks are responsible for informing the public and for the training of all interested parties in the on-line sale process.

3. Upon reasonable request, the Clerks will make provisions for registered bidders lacking proper equipment to participate in on-line auctions.

4. In accordance with §§ 45.031(2) and 702.035, Florida Statutes, plaintiffs, or plaintiffs' attorneys, are responsible for preparing and submitting Notices of Sale to appropriate newspapers for publishing.

a) Original Notices of Sale are to be filed in the court file and copies sent to newspapers for publishing.

b) Plaintiffs, or plaintiffs' attorneys, are responsible for instructing newspapers to promptly file original Proofs of Publication together with Affidavits of Proof with the Clerks. Failure to file items mentioned herein does not obligate the Clerks to cancel or otherwise delay sales.

5. A written motion substantially similar to Form 1.996(b), Florida Rules of Civil Procedure, must be filed in the event a plaintiff, or plaintiff's attorney, wishes to cancel and reschedule a sale. Furthermore, the motion must state the number of previous requests for cancellation of sale filed by the plaintiff in the case. Absent the Court issuing an Order to Cancel the Sale, or a Notice/Suggestion of Bankruptcy as to a named defendant being filed prior to the scheduled sale date/time, the sale will proceed as scheduled. Any order issued by a judge of the US Bankruptcy Court that restricts the Clerks from conducting a sale shall be filed by the plaintiff, or plaintiff's attorney. Such must be as a separate filing and not as an attachment or exhibit.

6. A $70 service charge must be advanced by the plaintiff prior to the sale (see § 45.031(1), Florida Statutes). If not paid in advance, the service charge will be assessed and deducted from the plaintiff's funds on deposit with the on-line auction service on the day of the sale.

7. Those interested in participating in online auctions must register with the Clerks or Realauction by establishing a bidder account containing sufficient funds to cover the cost of a deposit equaling five percent of the final bid and payment of a $70 electronic sale service charge (see § 45.035(3), Florida Statutes). The $70 electronic sale service charge must be paid by the winning bidder and may not be covered by the plaintiff's judgment credit amount.

8. The plaintiff, or plaintiff's attorney, must provide a legible, recordable proposed Final Judgment. The Clerks may require resubmission of a proposed Final Judgment if it is illegible for recording purposes.

9. Unless stated otherwise in the Final Judgment of Foreclosure, timeshare interests in property will be sold as individual units and will require the payment of service charges referenced in sections 6 and 7 above for each unit sold.

10. Administrative Order CV–2015–012–FG/PT/VL is hereby rescinded effective July 1, 2016.

TO BE RECORDED in Flagler, Putnam, St. Johns and Volusia counties.

DONE AND ORDERED in Daytona Beach, Volusia County, Florida this 15th day of June 2016.

TERENCE R. PERKINS
CHIEF JUDGE

Amended effective July 1, 2016.

CV–2015–013–SC. CONSENT TO DISMISSAL AND CLOSURE FOR LACK OF PROSECUTION IN EVICTION CASES SEEKING POSSESSION ONLY

IN THE CIRCUIT COURT OF FLORIDA, SEVENTH JUDICIAL CIRCUIT IN AND FOR FLAGLER, PUTNAM, ST. JOHNS AND VOLUSIA COUNTIES

RE: Consent to Dismissal and Closure for Lack of Prosecution in Eviction Cases Seeking Possession Only

REF: CV–2015–013–SC

WHEREAS, pursuant to Rule 2.545, Florida Rules of Judicial Administration, ligation should be concluded as soon as reasonably and justly possible to do so, and

WHEREAS, Rule 1.420(e), Florida Rules of Civil Procedure, provides for the dismissal of actions for failure to prosecute where no record activity has taken place in 10 months, and

WHEREAS, eviction cases in which plaintiffs (landlords) are only seeking possession of subject premises, unlike other County Civil cases, are often resolved within thirty (30) days of filing, and

WHEREAS, in many instances the issue of possession in eviction cases is resolved by defendants (tenants) vacating premises upon service of process, and

WHEREAS, time and resources could be saved if, at the time of filing, plaintiffs (landlords) were afforded an opportunity to voluntarily agree to dismiss/close their case after a certain period of inactivity;

NOW THEREFORE, I, TERENCE R. PERKINS, Chief Judge of the Seventh Judicial Circuit, hereby order that effective May 1, 2015, the Clerks of Court in Flagler, Putnam, St. Johns and Volusia counties (Clerks) shall include a *Consent to Case Closure after 90 days of Inactivity* form (attached and incorporated herein as Exhibit A) in the eviction forms package and as the Clerks otherwise deem appropriate.

Upon receipt of a completed *Consent to Case Closure after 90 days of Inactivity* form from a plaintiff (landlord), Clerks are to notify the assigned judge after 90 days of inactivity have elapsed, whereupon the judge may consider entering an order of dismissal/case closure similar to the attached *Order of Dismissal and Closure of Case* (attached and incorporated herein as Exhibit B).

TO BE RECORDED in Flagler, Putnam, St. Johns and Volusia counties.

DONE AND ORDERED in Daytona Beach, Volusia County, Florida this 2nd day of April 2015.

TERENCE R. PERKINS
CHIEF JUDGE

Amended effective May 1, 2015.

CV-2013-014-SC. CASE STATUS REPORTING REQUIREMENTS FOR REAL PROPERTY MORTGAGE FORECLOSURE CASES

IN THE CIRCUIT COURT OF FLORIDA, SEVENTH JUDICIAL CIRCUIT IN AND FOR FLAGLER, PUTNAM, ST. JOHNS AND VOLUSIA COUNTIES

RE: CASE STATUS REPORTING REQUIREMENTS FOR REAL PROPERTY MORTGAGE FORECLOSURE CASES

REF: CV-2013-014-SC

WHEREAS, the Florida Supreme Court has adopted definitions related to the status of a foreclosure case that are published in the Foreclosure Initiative Data Collection Plan promulgated by the Office of the State Courts Administrator, and

WHEREAS, the Florida Supreme Court requires the chief judge of every circuit to issue an administrative order implementing an effective communication mechanism by which the courts and clerks are notified of case status changes in a timely manner. Furthermore, each chief judge is required to issue an administrative order providing explicit direction for designating the status of cases as active or inactive. (See AOSC13-51 In Re: Case Status Reporting Requirements for Real Property Mortgage Foreclosure Cases);

NOW THEREFORE, I TERENCE R. PERKINS, Chief Judge of the Seventh Judicial Circuit, hereby order as follows:

1. The Clerks of Court of the counties of Flagler, Putnam, St. Johns & Volusia (Clerks) shall comply with the requirements of the Foreclosure Initiative Data Collection Plan promulgated by the Office of the State Courts Administrator.

2. The Clerks shall notify presiding judges if they become aware of events that may initiate a change in the status of a case (active or inactive) and await further direction.

3. Upon being made aware of events that may initiate a change in the status of a case, the presiding judge should review the matter and if appropriate, issue an order changing the status of the case (see attached form orders).

4. Nothing in this order prohibits judges from entering orders changing the status of cases on their own accord, without being made aware of a qualifying event by a clerk.

TO BE RECORDED in Flagler, Putnam, St. Johns and Volusia counties.

DONE AND ORDERED in Daytona Beach, Volusia County, Florida this 6th day of November 2013.

TERENCE R. PERKINS
CHIEF JUDGE

Adopted effective November 6, 2013.

CV-2014-015-SC. FORECLOSURE TRIAL EXHIBITS

IN THE CIRCUIT COURT OF FLORIDA, SEVENTH JUDICIAL CIRCUIT IN AND FOR FLAGLER, PUTNAM, ST. JOHNS AND VOLUSIA COUNTIES

RE: FORECLOSURE TRIAL EXHIBITS

REF: CV 2014-015-SC

WHEREAS, Rule 2.430(f), Florida Rules of Judicial Administration, provides that all exhibits, except exhibits in criminal proceedings, shall be retained by the clerk until 90 days after a judgment has become final, and any party or attorney of record may ask the clerk to return exhibits upon receiving 30 days' notice of the clerk's intent to destroy or dispose of the exhibit, and

WHEREAS, original promissory notes and mortgages are routinely filed as exhibits in foreclosure trials, and these original documents may need to be preserved in the event they are canceled subsequent to the entry of a judgment or the parties renegotiate the loan;

NOW THEREFORE, I, TERENCE R. PERKINS, Chief Judge of the Seventh Judicial Circuit, hereby hereby[1] order that:

1. Original notes and mortgages filed as exhibits in foreclosure cases will be kept in the court file and retained by the clerk in accordance with the Rule 2.430(c), Florida Rules of Judicial Administration.

2. Parties who wish to have the original note or mortgage returned to them must seek a court order for the return of those documents.

TO BE RECORDED in Flagler, Putnam, St. Johns and Volusia Counties.

DONE AND ORDERED in Daytona Beach, Volusia County, Florida this 26th day of February, 2014.

Judge Terence R. Perkins
Chief Judge

Adopted effective February 26, 2014.

[1] So in original.

CV–2010–016–SC. WRITS OF POSSESSION IN RESIDENTIAL MORTGAGE FORECLOSURE CASES

IN THE CIRCUIT COURT OF FLORIDA, SEVENTH JUDICIAL CIRCUIT IN AND FOR FLAGLER, PUTNAM, ST. JOHNS AND VOLUSIA COUNTIES

RE: WRITS OF POSSESSION IN RESIDENTIAL MORTGAGE FORECLOSURE CASES

REF: CV–2010–016–SC (Rescinds CV–2002–016–VL)

WHEREAS, the Federal Protecting Tenants at Foreclosure Act (Public Law 111–22, Division A, Title VII) became law on May 20, 2009, and

WHEREAS, it has come to the attention of the undersigned that some may not be aware of the provisions of the Act;

NOW THEREFORE, I, J. DAVID WALSH, Chief Judge of the Seventh Judicial Circuit, hereby order that effective April 1, 2010, persons filing motions for Writs of Possession in residential mortgage foreclosure proceedings in the counties of the Seventh Judicial Circuit of Florida must include the following certification in said motions:

- I HEREBY CERTIFY that there are no tenants in possession of the subject property, or, if there are, that such tenants have been provided with requisite notice pursuant to the Federal Protecting Tenants at Foreclosure Act, and this motion does not seek an order that violates any tenant's right to continued occupancy under the Act.

TO BE RECORDED in Flagler, Putnam, St. Johns & Volusia counties.

DONE AND ORDERED in Daytona Beach, Volusia County, Florida this 26th day of March 2010.

Judge J. David Walsh
Chief Judge

Amended effective March 26, 2010.

CV–2017–017–SC. APPOINTMENT OF ADMINISTRATIVE CIVIL DIVISION JUDGE

IN THE CIRCUIT COURT OF FLORIDA, SEVENTH JUDICIAL CIRCUIT IN AND FOR FLAGLER, PUTNAM, ST. JOHNS AND VOLUSIA COUNTIES

RE: APPOINTMENT OF ADMINISTRATIVE CIVIL DIVISION JUDGE

Re: CV–2017–017–SC

(Rescinds CV–2015–017–SC)

WHEREAS, chief judges are authorized to appoint administrative judges pursuant to Rule 2.050(b)(5), Florida Rules of Judicial Administration, and

WHEREAS, the undersigned has determined that the appointment of an administrative judge for the civil division is in the best interest of the Seventh Judicial Circuit;

NOW THEREFORE, I, RAUL A. ZAMBRANO, Chief Judge of the Seventh Judicial Circuit of Florida, hereby appoint the Honorable J. Michael Traynor as Administrative Judge of the Civil Division in the Seventh Judicial Circuit. The duties of the Administrative Judge of the Civil Division include, but are not limited to, the following:

1. Coordinating and overseeing the operation and administration of the civil division;

2. Developing proposed policies, operating procedures, and administrative orders related to the operation of the civil division;

3. Coordinating the development of resources that may be required to effectively handle civil matters by the judges in the civil division;

4. Developing and facilitating communications with appropriate entities concerning the operation of the civil division;

5. Assisting with the training and orientation of judges newly assigned to the civil division; and

6. Performing other related duties as may be assigned by the Chief Judge of the Seventh Judicial Circuit.

IT IS FURTHER ORDERED that Administrative Order # CV–2015–017–SC is hereby rescinded.

TO BE RECORDED in Flagler, Putnam, St. Johns and Volusia counties.

DONE AND ORDERED in Daytona Beach, Volusia County, Florida this 9th day of October 2017.

RAUL A. ZAMBRANO
Chief Judge

Amended effective March 13, 2015; October 9, 2017.

CV–2008–018–SC. COUNTY COURT CIVIL MEDIATION

IN THE CIRCUIT COURT OF FLORIDA, SEVENTH JUDICIAL CIRCUIT IN AND FOR FLAGLER, PUTNAM, ST. JOHNS AND VOLUSIA COUNTIES

RE: COUNTY COURT CIVIL MEDIATION

REF: CV–2008–018–SC (Rescinds CV–2004–018–SC (A))

WHEREAS, pursuant to § 44.108, Florida Statutes, mediation should be accessible to all parties, regardless of financial status, and

WHEREAS, pursuant to Florida Rules of Civil Procedure and Florida Small Claims Rules, mediation may be used in county court civil proceedings, and

WHEREAS, the use of mediation in county court civil proceedings has been deemed necessary by the judges of the Seventh Judicial Circuit;

NOW THEREFORE, I, J. DAVID WALSH, Chief Judge of the Seventh Judicial Circuit of Florida, hereby order that effective July 1, 2008, mediation in county court civil proceedings in Flagler, Putnam, St. Johns and Volusia counties take place in accordance with the following:

1. County Court judges may refer parties in county court civil cases to private mediators or to the Seventh Judicial Circuit's contracted County Mediation Program. When referring a case to the Circuit's program, an Order of Referral in a format substantially similar to that attached hereto as Exhibit A must be used.

2. Indigent parties and parties in small claims and eviction cases referred to the Circuit's County Mediation Program shall not be required to pay fees for mediation services.

3. Other parties referred to the Circuit's County Mediation Program shall be required to pay mediation fees to the Clerk of Court in the amount of $60.00 per person, per mediation session.

TO BE RECORDED in Flagler, Putnam, St. Johns and Volusia counties.

DONE AND ORDERED in Daytona Beach, Volusia County, Florida this 18th day of June 2008.

Judge J. David Walsh
Chief Judge

Amended effective June 18, 2008.

CV–2009–019–SC. NON–BINDING ARBITRATION

IN THE CIRCUIT COURT OF FLORIDA, SEVENTH JUDICIAL CIRCUIT IN AND FOR FLAGLER, PUTNAM, ST. JOHNS AND VOLUSIA COUNTIES

RE: NON–BINDING ARBITRATION

REF: CV–2009–019–SC (Rescinds CV–2008–019–SC)

WHEREAS, the use of non-binding arbitration to aid in the resolution of civil disputes is authorized pursuant to § 44.103, Florida Statutes, and

WHEREAS, rules governing arbitration are contained in Rules 1.700, 1.800, 1.810 and 1.820, Florida Rules of Civil Procedure, and

WHEREAS, rules governing individuals serving as arbitrators are contained in Rules 11.010 and 11.020, Florida Rules for Court–Appointed Arbitrators, and

WHEREAS, the circuit judges of the Seventh Judicial Circuit have endorsed the use of non-binding arbitration in circuit civil, family law, and probate/guardianship/trust actions;

NOW THEREFORE, I, J. DAVID WALSH, Chief Judge of the Seventh Judicial Circuit, hereby order that the following procedures apply to the operation of the non-binding arbitration program in the Seventh Judicial Circuit:

1. Pursuant to Rule 1.810(a), Florida Rules of Civil Procedure, the Court Administrator's Office shall maintain a list of individuals who are qualified to serve as arbitrators and who express interest in serving as arbitrators.

2. In cases referred to non-binding arbitration, the presiding judge will appoint an arbitrator from the Court's list. In the alternative, the parties may mutually agree upon the selection of an arbitrator from the Court's list.

3. Except for those types of cases precluded by rule (see Rule 1.800, Florida Rules of Civil Procedure), the presiding judge may refer any circuit civil, family law, or probate/guardianship/trust action to non-binding arbitration. When referring a case to non-binding arbitration, an Order of Referral in a format substantially similar to that attached hereto as Attachment A must be used.

4. Arbitrators will be compensated at the rate of $225 per hour (see Rule 1.810(b), Florida Rules of Civil Procedure); said compensation to be borne equally by the parties. The parties shall pay the arbitrator his/her fee for two hours at least 10 days prior to the commencement of the arbitration hearing. If a previously scheduled arbitration hearing is cancelled due to resolution of the case within 10 days of the scheduled hearing, the arbitrator will be entitled to retain the aforementioned fee. If an arbitration hearing is conducted outside the county of residence/business of the arbitrator, the arbitrator will be entitled to compensation for his/her travel time at the rate of $75 per hour, plus mileage reimbursement at the State rate. If the time necessary to complete the arbitration process exceeds two hours, or if the arbitrator incurs travel expenses, the parties shall pay the arbitrator the balance of his/her fees/expenses upon request.

5. Arbitration hearings must be conducted in accordance with applicable statutes, rules and laws. Arbitrators will set the date, time and place of arbitration hearings using a standard Notice of Court–Ordered, Non–Binding Arbitration. Arbitration hearings may **not** be conducted in Court facilities. Fees associated with procuring space to conduct arbitration hearings may be charged to the parties.

6. Arbitrators must supply summary statistical information to the Court Administrator's Office in a manner and format prescribed by the Court.

IT IS FURTHER ORDERED that Administrative Order # CV–2008–019–SC is hereby rescinded.

TO BE RECORDED in Flagler, Putnam, St. Johns and Volusia counties.

DONE AND ORDERED in Daytona Beach, Volusia County, Florida this 22nd day of May 2009.

Judge J. David Walsh
Chief Judge

Amended effective May 22, 2009.

CV–2006–020–VL. NEGLECTED OR MISTREATED ANIMALS

IN THE CIRCUIT COURT OF FLORIDA, SEVENTH JUDICIAL CIRCUIT IN AND FOR FLAGLER, PUTNAM, ST. JOHNS AND VOLUSIA COUNTIES

RE: NEGLECTED OR MISTREATED ANIMALS

CV–2006–020–VL

(Rescinds G–89–005)

WHEREAS, § 828.03, Florida Statutes, provides for the custody and disposition of neglected or mistreated animals, and

WHEREAS, § 828.073, Florida Statutes, provides for the means for removal of neglected or mistreated animals from their present custody, or made the subject of an order to provide care, and

WHEREAS, § 828.073, Florida Statutes, provides for a county court civil judge to preside over such proceedings, and

WHEREAS, § 828.073, Florida Statutes, provides that no filing fee shall be charged for the filing of a petition and the service of the papers, and

WHEREAS, the establishment of a uniform method for resolving issues related to the custody and disposition of neglected or mistreated animals is necessary;

NOW THEREFORE, I, WILLIAM A. PARSONS, Chief Judge of the Seventh Judicial Circuit of Florida, hereby order that the following procedures and related forms shall be used in cases concerning the custody and disposition of neglected or mistreated animals in Volusia County:

1. The person taking custody of any such neglected or mistreated animal must file an original and duplicate copies of a petition for hearing in the office of the Clerk of the Court, Civil Division, setting forth the petitioner's name, agency, address and telephone number as well as a description of the animal, the date and place of seizure, the name and address of the animal's owner or custodian, a description of the neglect or cruel treatment causing the seizure and the place where the animal is being kept.

2. The clerk may not charge for receiving and filing such a petition. The clerk will create a file, assign it to a county judge in the same manner as other civil cases, and promptly transmit the file to the assigned judge.

3. The judge will prepare a notice of hearing and forward it to the clerk for filing. The clerk will forward copies of the notice to the petitioner.

4. It is the petitioner's responsibility to transmit proper papers to the Sheriff of Volusia County, Florida for service upon the animal's owner or custodian not less than five days before the hearing. The Sheriff will make his/her return upon the certified copy of the notice of hearing as in other cases and promptly file with the Civil Division of the office of the Clerk of the Court. The Sheriff may not charge for serving said notice.

5. Witness subpoenas are to be issued and served as in other civil cases without charge.

6. A hearing must be conducted as in other civil cases, and upon its conclusion, the judge will make findings of fact and enter an order as required by § 828.073, Florida Statutes.

7. The petition, notice of hearing and order should be in formats substantially similar to those attached hereto as exhibits A, B & C.

IT IS FURTHER ORDERED that County Court Administrative Order G–89–005 is hereby rescinded.

TO BE RECORDED in Volusia County, Florida.

DONE AND ORDERED in Daytona Beach, Volusia County, Florida this 1st day of December 2006.

WILLIAM A. PARSONS
CHIEF JUDGE

Exhibit A

IN THE COUNTY COURT IN AND FOR

VOLUSIA COUNTY, FLORIDA

CASE NO.

DIVISION

In re:

A NEGLECTED OR MISTREATED ANIMAL,

PETITION FOR HEARING

The undersigned, a law enforcement officer or agent duly appointed pursuant to § 828.03, Florida Statutes, has taken custody of a neglected or mistreated animal(s) in Volusia County and hereby petitions the County Court for Volusia County, Florida to conduct a hearing to determine whether the alleged owner is able to provide adequately for the animal(s) and is fit to have custody of the animal(s), pursuant to the provisions of § 828.073, Florida Statutes. The animal(s) and particulars of seizure are:

Description of animal(s): ____________

Date of seizure: ____________

Place of seizure: ____________

Name and address of owner or custodian: ____________

____

Description of neglect or cruel treatment: ____________

____

____

____

Present location of animal: ____________

Date of this petition: ____________

____

____

Signature, name, agency, address and telephone number of Petitioner

Exhibit B

IN THE COUNTY COURT IN AND FOR

VOLUSIA COUNTY, FLORIDA

CASE NO.
DIVISION:

In re:

A NEGLECTED OR MISTREATED ANIMAL,

NOTICE OF HEARING

TO: ____________

____

____

You will please take notice that the undersigned county judge will conduct a hearing pursuant to § 828.073, Florida Statutes, at ___ o'clock ___ m. on ________ located at:

____

to determine whether you, as the alleged owner(s) or custodian(s) of the animal(s) described in the petition attached hereto, are able to provide adequately for the animal(s) and are fit to have custody of the animal(s).

Petitioner shall have this notice and copy of the petition served upon the alleged owner or custodian by the sheriff of Volusia County not less than five days prior to the hearing.

Failure of the alleged owner or custodian to attend the hearing may result in the forfeiture or destruction of the animal(s) and the entry of judgment against him/her for the care of the animal(s).

Dated this ___ day of ________, ____.

____
County Court Judge

Copy to Petitioner

Exhibit C

IN THE COUNTY COURT IN AND FOR

VOLUSIA COUNTY, FLORIDA

In re:	CASE NO.
	DIVISION:
A NEGLECTED OR MISTREATED	
ANIMAL,	ORDER PURSUANT TO § 828.073(4), FLORIDA
STATUTES	

The court, having heard and considered the testimony and evidence presented, finds and orders as follows:

( ) The owner is able to provide adequately for and have custody of the animal(s) described in these proceedings and in the petitioner's possession. Said animals(s) shall be claimed and removed by the owner within 7 days from the date of this order.

( ) The owner of the animal(s) described in these proceeding is unable or unfit to adequately provide for the animal(s) described in these proceedings and shall have no further custody of the animal(s). The animal(s) shall:

( ) be sold at public auction, the proceeds to be disbursed as provided in § 828.073(7), Florida Statutes, and if not bid upon, shall be remanded to the custody of the petitioner, to be disposed of as petitioner sees fit, or

( ) be destroyed, or

( ) be remanded directly to the custody of petitioner, to be disposed of as petitioner sees fit.

( ) Petitioner shall recover from the owner the cost of care of the animal(s) described in these proceedings while in the petitioner's custody the sum of $ ________, for which let execution issue.

DONE AND ORDERED in ________, Volusia County, Florida this ___ day of ________, ____.

____
County Court Judge

cc:
Owner
Petitioner

Amended effective December 1, 2006.

CV–2009–021–SJ. IN THE CIRCUIT COURT OF FLORIDA, SEVENTH JUDICIAL CIRCUIT IN AND FOR ST. JOHNS COUNTY

IN THE CIRCUIT COURT OF FLORIDA, SEVENTH JUDICIAL CIRCUIT IN AND FOR ST. JOHNS COUNTY

RE: SERVICE OF CIVIL PROCESS

REF: CV–2009–021–SJ

WHEREAS, pursuant to § 48.021, Florida Statutes, a Sheriff may appoint "special process servers" to serve initial non-enforceable civil process in his/her county, and

WHEREAS, the Sheriff of St. Johns County, Florida has advised the Court of his intention to create a "Special Process Server" program in St. Johns County;

NOW THEREFORE, I, J. DAVID WALSH, Chief Judge of the Seventh Judicial Circuit of Florida, hereby endorse the St. Johns County Sheriff's plan to establish a Special Process Server* program as outlined in § 48.021, Florida Statutes, and authorize the Sheriff to appoint special process servers to serve initial non-enforceable civil process in St. Johns County, Florida effective June 1, 2009.

***NOTE:** The establishment of the special process server program described above may obviate the need for motions to appoint individuals to serve process pursuant to Rule 1.070(b), Florida Rules of Civil Procedure. As a result, judges in St. Johns County, Florida may rightfully deny such motions.

TO BE RECORDED in St. Johns County, Florida.

DONE AND ORDERED in Daytona Beach, Volusia County, Florida this 17th day of April 2009.

Judge J. David Walsh
Chief Judge

Adopted effective April 17, 2009.

Criminal Orders

CR–2017–001–SC. CODIFICATION OF ADMINISTRATIVE ORDERS IN THE CRIMINAL DIVISION

IN THE CIRCUIT COURT OF FLORIDA, SEVENTH JUDICIAL CIRCUIT IN AND FOR FLAGLER, PUTNAM, ST. JOHNS AND VOLUSIA COUNTIES

RE: Codification of Administrative Orders in the Criminal Division

REF: CR–2017–001–SC

WHEREAS, it has been made known to the undersigned that the codification of Criminal administrative orders in the Seventh Judicial Circuit is necessary for the efficient and proper administration of justice,

NOW THEREFORE, I, TERENCE R. PERKINS, Chief Judge of the Seventh Judicial Circuit of Florida, hereby order the codification of all administrative orders in the Criminal Division of the Seventh Judicial Circuit.

IT IS FURTHER ORDERED that said administrative orders be numbered for reference in the following manner:

Subject—Year—Numerical Order—Circuit/County

[i.e., CR 2017–001–SC (Seventh Circuit)]

[–FG (Flagler County)]

[–PT (Putnam County)]

[–SJ (St. Johns County)]

[–VL (Volusia County)]

IT IS FURTHER ORDERED that all administrative orders related to the administration of Criminal matters issued prior to the date of this order are hereby rescinded.

TO BE RECORDED in Flagler, Putnam, St. Johns and Volusia counties.

DONE AND ORDERED in Daytona Beach, Volusia County, Florida this 30th day of June 2017.

TERENCE R. PERKINS

CHIEF JUDGE

Adopted effective June 30, 2017.

CR–2017–002–SC. BAIL SCHEDULE FOR FLAGLER, PUTNAM, ST. JOHNS AND VOLUSIA COUNTIES

IN THE CIRCUIT COURT OF FLORIDA, SEVENTH JUDICIAL CIRCUIT IN AND FOR FLAGLER, PUTNAM, ST. JOHNS AND VOLUSIA COUNTIES

RE: Bail Schedule for Flagler, Putnam, St. Johns and Volusia counties

REF: CR–2017–002–SC

WHEREAS, the right to reasonable bail in certain circumstances is an essential part of the criminal justice system, and

WHEREAS, a bail schedule enables bail to be set in a uniform manner before First Appearance for certain alleged offenders arrested without a warrant, and

WHEREAS, a bail schedule is necessary to ensure uniformity and equality of treatment to alleged offenders who may be entitled to release prior to First Appearance before a judge,

NOW THEREFORE, I, TERENCE R. PERKINS, Chief Judge of the Seventh Judicial Circuit of Florida, hereby order as follows:

ADOPTION OF BAIL SCHEDULE: Except in cases where bail has previously been set or denied (as, in a warrant), the Bail Schedule set forth in this order and by attachment incorporated by reference is established with respect to release of alleged offenders prior to First Appearance and thereafter unless modified in accordance with the Florida Rules of Criminal Procedure on a case-by-case basis, or in accordance with exceptions specifically set forth in this order.

This bail schedule is for use in setting bail in Flagler, Putnam, St. Johns and Volusia counties before First Appearance, and is not intended to and does not in any manner bind judges conducting First Appearance hearings or bond hearings. Judges setting bail as a condition of release may set such bail in any reasonable amounts in accordance with the factors set forth in the Florida Rules of Criminal Procedure and Florida Statutes.

WARRANTS: Bail prior to first appearance for persons arrested on a violation of probation warrant, a failure to appear warrant, or an arrest warrant, shall be as provided for in the warrant, but if the warrant is silent as to bail amount, the bail shall be as provided in this order.

EXTRADITION CASES: Bail amounts set by judges in extradition cases must be in conformity with §§ 941.15 and 941.16, Florida Statutes.

SPECIAL CONDITION OF RELEASE—PROBATION/COMMUNITY CONTROL: Any person arrested in Flagler, Putnam, St. Johns or Volusia counties who, on the date of arrest, is on probation or community control with supervision by the Florida Department of Corrections shall, as an additional condition of release, report to the DOC probation office before the close of business on the first business day following release, and comply with all terms and conditions of his/her probation/community control order. Any such arrested person shall not be released until instructed of this special condition by a booking officer/jail official.

SPECIAL CONDITION OF RELEASE—VIOLENT OFFENDERS AND SEXUAL OFFENDERS: Any person arrested for an offense involving an allegation of violence to another person or for any sexual offense shall, as an additional condition of release, be prohibited from having direct or indirect contact with any person listed as a victim in the arrest report, unless otherwise determined by a judge. Any such arrested person shall not be released until instructed of this special condition by a booking officer/jail official.

TEMPORARY DETENTION: If, in the opinion of the arresting officer or booking officer, further violence or additional violations of law are likely to imminently result if an arrested person is released in accordance with the bail schedule herein adopted, so that no release on bail can reasonably protect the community from risk of physical harm to person, or assure the presence of the arrested person at trial, an Assistant State Attorney may be notified, and said Assistant State Attorney may contact a judge for authority to detain the alleged offender in custody until First Appearance.

BAIL BEFORE CONVICTION; CONDITION OF UNDERTAKING: If a person is admitted to bail for appearance for a preliminary hearing, or on a charge that a judge is empowered to try, the condition of the undertaking shall be that the person will appear for such hearing, or to answer the charge, and will submit to the orders and processes of the judge trying the same, and will not depart without leave.

If a person is admitted to bail after being held to answer by a judge, or after an indictment or information on which the person is to be tried has been filed, the condition of the undertaking shall be that the person will appear to answer the charges before the court in which he or she may be prosecuted and submit to the orders and processes of the Court, and will not depart without leave.

EFFECT OF FILING NOTICE OF NO INFORMATION OR NOLLE PROSEQUI: If a person arrested for any offense(s) occurring within Flagler, Putnam, St. Johns or Volusia counties is admitted to bail but has not yet been released from custody, and the State Attorney files a notice of

No Information or Nolle Prosequi with respect to all charges arising out of a single arrest, jail officials shall, without further order of Court, release the person from custody as to the charges named.

As to the named charges and person, all bail undertaking, not defaulted, shall be canceled, all sureties on undefaulted bail shall be exonerated and all release on recognizance obligations shall be discharged without further order of Court. A bench warrant or capias which may be outstanding and is yet unserved upon a named individual for a specified charge shall also be canceled upon the filing of a No Information or Nolle Prosequi, without further order of Court.

IT IS FURTHER ORDERED that all previous administrative orders that provide for the setting of bail or bond before First Appearance in Flagler, Putnam, St. Johns and/or Volusia counties are hereby rescinded.

TO BE RECORDED in Flagler, Putnam, St. Johns and Volusia counties, Florida.

DONE AND ORDERED in Daytona Beach, Volusia County, Florida, this 30th day of June 2017.

TERENCE R. PERKINS
CHIEF JUDGE

[Attachment]

BAIL SCHEDULE—FLAGLER, PUTNAM, ST. JOHNS & VOLUSIA COUNTIES

OFFENSES FOR WHICH NO BAIL IS TO BE GRANTED AND NO RELEASE PERMITTED BEFORE FIRST APPEARANCE:

- **Capital felony**
- **Life felony**
- **First degree felony which may be punishable by life imprisonment**
- **Escape—F.S. 944.40**
- **Domestic Violence—any offense defined in F.S. 741.28(2)**
- **Aggravated Stalking—F.S. 784.048(3)**
- **Burglary committed during declared state of emergency—F.S. 810.02**
- **Violation of domestic or repeat violence injunction when the alleged violation involves violence or attempt to commit violent act or stalking**
- **Any felony, if the person arrested is on pre-trial release (including bail, ROR, etc.), pre-sentence release, or probation/community control, and is arrested on probable cause**
- **RICO Act violation—F.S. 895.03**
- **Offenses not otherwise mentioned below.**

OFFENSE		BAIL
Drug Trafficking		
	Min. mandatory 25 years	$500,000
	Min. mandatory 15 years	$150,000
	Min. mandatory 7 years	$ 50,000
	Min. mandatory 3 years	$ 25,000
1st degree Felony:		
	Non–Violent	$15,000
2nd degree Felony:		
	Non–Violent	$ 5,000
3rd degree Felony:		
	Non–Violent	$ 2,500
1st degree Misdemeanor		
	Non–Violent	NTA / $500
2nd degree Misdemeanor		
		NTA / $500

• Any offense not involving physical harm or actual threat of physical harm to another person is a "non-violent" offense. Any offense involving physical harm to another person, or having as one of its elements assault or threat of violence, or involving the use or threatened use of a deadly weapon, is a "violent" offense. Burglary of a dwelling is considered a "violent" offense.

OFFENSE		BAIL
DUI		
	1st offense	$1,000*
	If prior DUI conviction(s) within 5 years, or, with bodily injury	$2,500*

*Release must also comply with F.S. 316.193(9)

OFFENSE		BAIL
Leaving scene of accident		
	Misdemeanor	NTA / $500
	Felony (injuries)	$2,500
	Felony (death)	$5,000
Reckless Driving		
	No accident	NTA / $500
	Accident	NTA / $1,000
Driving with suspended/revoked license		
	Driving with suspended/revoked license	NTA / $500
	1 prior conviction	NTA / $1,000
	2 or more prior convictions	$2,000
Willful failure to comply with LEO/FD		
		NTA / $500

Other criminal traffic violations (Ch. 320 & 322, F.S.)		
		NTA / $200
Municipal ordinance violations		
	As suggested by municipality or	NTA / $200

• This bail schedule pertains to release of alleged offenders **prior to First Appearance,** when a judge has not previously established conditions of release (for example, in an arrest warrant). The First Appearance judge may increase or decrease/eliminate the amount of bail and set other conditions of release, pursuant to Rule 3.131(a), Fla.R.Crim.P., and other applicable rules and statutes.

• Rules 3.125(b) and (c) provide that arresting officers and booking officers may issue **notices to appear** in certain circumstances where the arrest is for a misdemeanor of the first or second degree. Such notices to appear may be issued in accordance with the rule when "NTA" appears on this schedule.

• § 903.046(2)(d), F.S. provides that a defendant who **failed to appear** shall not be eligible for release on recognizance, and shall be subject to a monetary undertaking of $2,000 or twice the original bond, whichever is greater. However, this does not apply if the defendant proves circumstances beyond his/her control resulted in the failure to appear.

Adopted effective June 30, 2017.

CR–2019–003–SC. Misdemeanor Payable Fish and Wildlife Offenses / Notices to Appear

IN THE CIRCUIT COURT OF FLORIDA, SEVENTH JUDICIAL CIRCUIT

IN AND FOR FLAGLER, PUTNAM, ST. JOHNS AND VOLUSIA COUNTIES

RE: Misdemeanor Payable Fish and Wildlife Offenses / Notices to Appear

REF: CR–2019–003–SC

(Rescinds CR–2017–003–SC and O–99–104)

WHEREAS, it has been made known to the undersigned that the prompt and efficient administration of justice requires revisions to the administrative order on this subject;

NOW THEREFORE, I, RAUL A. ZAMBRANO, Chief Judge of the Seventh Judicial Circuit of Florida, hereby order that violations of the Florida state statutes listed below do **not** require court appearances and are therefore deemed to be payable offenses. (Note: This Order applies to violations alleged to have been committed by adults in the counties of Flagler, Putnam, St. Johns and/or Volusia). Payable amounts are to be as reflected herein.

Offenses	Statutory Citations	Payable Amounts	
		Flagler / St. Johns / Volusia	Putnam
Misdemeanor violations of fish and wildlife laws or administrative rules that constitute level two violations per § 379.401, and which are punishable under § 379.401(2)(b)1, but not violations which are punishable under § 379.401(2)(b)2, 3 or 4	§ 379.401(2)(a)1–14, 20 or 21, F.S.	$273	$270
Misdemeanor violations of fish and wildlife laws or administrative rules that constitute level three violations per § 379.401(3)(a)1, 7 or 8, and which are punishable under § 379.401(3)(b)1, but not violations which are punishable under § 379.401(3)(b)2 or 3	§ 379.401(3)(a)1, 7 or 8, F.S.	$273	$270
Misdemeanor violations of State Park laws which are punishable under § 258.008(3)	§ 258.008(3)(a)–(e), F.S.	$273	$270

Included in each of these payable amounts are costs of prosecution in the amount of $50.00 (see § 938.27, F.S.).

IT IS FURTHER ORDERED that in accordance with Rule 3.125, Florida Rules of Criminal Procedure, alleged violators of the above-listed offenses are eligible for releases on Notices to Appear. If the payable amount listed on a Notice to Appear differs from the payable amount listed above, the lesser amount controls. Notices to Appear issued by law enforcement agencies are to be forwarded to the appropriate Clerk of Court's office within 72 hours of issuance.

IT IS FURTHER ORDERED that alleged violators who fail to pay the monetary penalty or request a court date within 30 days of the date the notice/citation was issued, are to be set for arraignment before a County Court judge.

IT IS FURTHER ORDERED that upon receipt of payment(s), the Clerks of Court shall enter pleas of nolo contendre in cases affected by this Order and shall withhold adjudications of guilt, withdraw any capias issued, and close the cases.

IT IS FURTHER ORDERED that this Order does **not** apply to cases in which alleged violators are arrested and booked into jail. If an alleged violator is arrested and booked into jail for violating one of the above-listed offenses, bond is to be set in accordance with the bond schedule in effect at the time of the arrest, and the alleged violator scheduled for a First Appearance. If bond is posted prior to First Appearance, the alleged violator is to be set for an arraignment.

IT IS FURTHER ORDERED that administrative orders CR–2017–003–SC and O–99–104 are hereby rescinded.

TO BE RECORDED in Flagler, Putnam, St. Johns and Volusia counties.

DONE AND ORDERED in Daytona Beach, Volusia County, Florida this 10th day of January 2019.

RAUL A. ZAMBRANO
CHIEF JUDGE

Adopted effective June 30, 2017. Amended effective January 10, 2019.

CR–2017–004–SC. MODIFICATION OF BONDS BY FIRST APPEARANCE JUDGES

IN THE CIRCUIT COURT OF FLORIDA, SEVENTH JUDICIAL CIRCUIT IN AND FOR FLAGLER, PUTNAM, ST. JOHNS AND VOLUSIA COUNTIES

RE: Modification of Bonds by First Appearance Judges

REF: CR–2017–004–SC

WHEREAS, pursuant to Rule 3.131(b)(2), Florida Rules of Criminal Procedure, the judge presiding at a defendant's First Appearance shall consider all available relevant factors to determine what form of release is necessary to assure the defendant's appearance, and

WHEREAS, an administrative order which limited judges presiding at First Appearance hearings from modifying bonds in certain circumstances had previously been adopted, and

WHEREAS, the Florida Supreme Court in *State v. Norris* (768 So. 2d 1070) held that a defendant is entitled to an independent bail determination in front of the First Appearance judge after a consideration of all relevant factors;

NOW THEREFORE, I, TERENCE R. PERKINS, Chief Judge of the Seventh Judicial Circuit of Florida, hereby order that judges presiding at First Appearance hearings are to consider all relevant factors available to him/her in determining appropriate forms/conditions of release.

TO BE RECORDED in Flagler, Putnam, St. Johns and Volusia counties.

DONE AND ORDERED in Daytona Beach, Volusia County, Florida, this 30th day of June 2017.

TERENCE R. PERKINS

CHIEF JUDGE

Adopted effective June 30, 2017.

CR–2017–005–SC. MISDEMEANOR PAYABLE OFFENSES/NOTICES TO APPEAR

IN THE CIRCUIT COURT OF FLORIDA, SEVENTH JUDICIAL CIRCUIT IN AND FOR FLAGLER, PUTNAM, ST. JOHNS AND VOLUSIA COUNTIES

RE: Misdemeanor Payable Offenses/Notices to Appear

REF: CR–2017–005–SC

WHEREAS, it has been made known to the undersigned that the prompt and efficient administration of justice requires revisions to the administrative order on this subject;

NOW THEREFORE, I, TERENCE R. PERKINS, Chief Judge of the Seventh Judicial Circuit of Florida, hereby order that violations of the state statutes listed below do **not** require court appearances and are therefore deemed to be payable offenses. (Note: This Order applies to violations alleged to have been committed by adults in the counties of Flagler, Putnam, St. Johns and/or Volusia). Payable amounts shall be as reflected herein.

Offenses	Statutory Citations	Payable Amounts	
		Flagler, St. Johns & Volusia	Putnam
Unlawful Sale/Use of Fireworks	§ 791.02(1), F.S.	$273.00	$270.00
Trespassing	§ 810.08(1) / (2)(a)&(b), F.S.	$273.00	$270.00
	§ 810.09(1) / (2)(a)&(b), F.S.		
Obstruction by Disguise	§ 843.03, F.S.	$273.00	$270.00
Altering Date of Birth On Driver's License or ID	§ 322.212(5)(b), F.S.	$273.00	$270.00
Unlawful Use of Another's Driver's License	§ 322.32(3), F.S.	$273.00	$270.00
Unlawful Use of an ID	§ 322.051(6), F.S	$273.00	$270.00
Disorderly Conduct	§ 877.03, F.S.	$273.00	$270.00
Disorderly Intoxication	§ 856.011, F.S.	$288.00	$285.00
Possession of Alcohol under 21	§ 562.111, F.S.	$288.00	$285.00
Misrepresenting Age to Obtain Alcohol	§ 562.11(2), F.S	$288.00	$285.00

Included in each of these payable amounts are costs of prosecution in the amount of $50.00 (see § 938.27, F.S.).

IT IS FURTHER ORDERED that in accordance with Rule 3.125, Florida Rules of Criminal Procedure, alleged violators of the above-listed offenses are eligible for releases on Notices to Appear. If the payable amount listed on a Notice to Appear differs from the payable amount listed above, the lesser amount controls. Notices to Appear issued by law enforcement agencies are to be forwarded to the appropriate Clerk of Court's office within 72 hours of issuance.

IT IS FURTHER ORDERED that alleged violators who fail to pay the monetary penalty or request a court date, within 30 days of the date the notice/citation was issued, are to be set for arraignment before a County Court judge.

IT IS FURTHER ORDERED that upon receipt of payment(s), the Clerks of Court shall enter pleas of nolo contendre in cases affected by this Order and shall withhold adjudications of guilt, withdraw any capias issued, and close the cases.

IT IS FURTHER ORDERED that this Order does **not** apply to cases in which alleged violators are arrested and booked into jail. If an alleged violator is arrested and booked into jail for violating one of the above-listed offenses, bond is to be set in accordance with the bond schedule in effect at the time of the arrest, and the alleged violator scheduled for a First Appearance. If bond is posted prior to First Appearance, the alleged violator is to be set for an arraignment.

TO BE RECORDED in Flagler, Putnam, St. Johns and Volusia counties.

DONE AND ORDERED in Daytona Beach, Volusia County, Florida this 30th day of June 2017.

TERENCE R. PERKINS

CHIEF JUDGE

Adopted effective June 30, 2017.

CR–2017–006–SC. CRITERIA/PROCEDURES FOR NOTICES TO APPEAR ISSUED BY JAIL PERSONNEL

IN THE CIRCUIT COURT OF FLORIDA, SEVENTH JUDICIAL CIRCUIT IN AND FOR FLAGLER, PUTNAM, ST. JOHNS COUNTY AND VOLUSIA COUNTIES

RE: Criteria/Procedures for Notices to Appear Issued by Jail Personnel

REF: CR–2017–006–SC

WHEREAS, the prompt and efficient administration of justice requires the establishment of procedures governing the issuance of Notices to Appear within the counties of the Seventh Judicial Circuit, and

WHEREAS, Rule 3.125(j), Florida Rules of Criminal Procedure, authorizes the chief judge to establish procedures governing the exercise of authority to issue Notices to Appear;

NOW THEREFORE, I, TERENCE R. PERKINS, Chief Judge of the Seventh Judicial Circuit of Florida, hereby order that authorized jail personnel in Flagler, Putnam, St. Johns and Volusia counties may issue Notices to Appear to arrestees who meet the following criteria:

1. Arrestee was arrested for a violation of a municipal or county ordinance, or a non-violent criminal misdemeanor (excluding DUI), triable in the county of arrest; and

2. Arrestee has established community ties as evidenced by one or more of the following: (a) stable residence in an identifiable community within the United States for at least 3 continuous months; (b) well established family ties in the resident community; (c) steady employment in an identifiable community within the United States for at least 2 continuous months; (d) current enrollment as a student at a college, university, trade school, or high school in the resident community; and

3. Arrestee has no prior history of felony convictions (*) for the past 24 months, no prior history of misdemeanor (non-traffic) convictions (*) for the past 6 months, no open/pending criminal charges; is not currently on probation/community control; and

4. Arrestee has no record of willful failures to appear for court appearances in cases other than the case at issue for the past 36 months.

*(*) A criminal history report that shows an arrest without a corresponding disposition is **not** considered a conviction for purposes of this Order.*

Upon verification that an arrestee meets the aforementioned criteria, the Booking Unit may release the arrestee unconditionally on his/her own recognizance through issuance of a Notice to Appear. Said Notice to Appear must substantially comply with the format set forth in Rule 3.125(*l*), Florida Rules of Criminal Procedure. Prior to releasing the arrestee, the Booking Unit must verify the arrestee's mailing address. The Clerk of Court shall use this address to mail proper notice of the date, time and location of the arrestee's next court appearance.

An arrestee who does not meet the aforementioned criteria, and who has not posted bail prior to his/her scheduled First Appearance hearing, shall appear before a judge for a First Appearance hearing.

TO BE RECORDED in Flagler, Putnam, St. Johns and Volusia counties, Florida.

DONE AND ORDERED in Daytona Beach, Volusia County, Florida this 30th day of June 2017.

TERENCE R. PERKINS

CHIEF JUDGE

Adopted effective June 30, 2017.

CR–2017–007–SC. REFUNDS OF SURETY/CASH BONDS

IN THE CIRCUIT COURT OF FLORIDA, SEVENTH JUDICIAL CIRCUIT IN AND FOR FLAGLER, PUTNAM, ST. JOHNS AND VOLUSIA COUNTIES

RE: Refunds of Surety/Cash Bonds

REF: CR–2017–007–SC

WHEREAS, surety and/or cash bail bonds may be executed to secure the pretrial release of an arrestee pursuant to Rule 3.131(b)(1) & (h), Florida Rules of Criminal Procedure, and

WHEREAS, court rulings regarding the obligations of sureties/depositors when criminal charges are subsequently changed, recast, or supplemented have been issued which require further determinations be made, and

WHEREAS, the undersigned has been advised of the necessity to issue an Administrative Order on this subject for the prompt and efficient administration of justice in the Seventh Judicial Circuit;

NOW THEREFORE, I, TERENCE R. PERKINS, Chief Judge of the Seventh Judicial Circuit of Florida, hereby order that the release of a bail bond to a depositor and/or the discharge of a surety shall occur only after all criminal charges related to the instant offense have been disposed of, when judgment on forfeiture is paid, upon the filing of a PTI/DPA by the State Attorney, upon further order of the court, or upon the surrender of the defendant to an appropriate law enforcement agency or correctional facility as permitted by law. Individuals seeking the release of a bail bond or the discharge of a surety absent the occurrence of the above-referenced actions shall file an appropriate motion with the court.

TO BE RECORDED in Flagler, Putnam, St. Johns and Volusia counties.

DONE AND ORDERED in Daytona Beach, Volusia County, Florida, this 30th day of June 2017.

TERENCE R. PERKINS

CHIEF JUDGE

Adopted effective June 30, 2017.

CR–2017–008–SC. APPLICATION OF CASH DEPOSIT TO FINES AND COSTS

IN THE CIRCUIT COURT OF FLORIDA, SEVENTH JUDICIAL CIRCUIT IN AND FOR FLAGLER, PUTNAM, ST. JOHNS AND VOLUSIA COUNTIES

RE: Application of Cash Deposit to Fines and Costs

REF: CR–2017–008–SC

WHEREAS, § 939.17, Florida Statutes, directs the Clerk of Court, under the direction of the Court, to apply money deposited by or on behalf of a defendant upon a judgment for the payment of a fine and costs, toward the satisfaction of such fine and costs and return the remainder to the depositor, and

WHEREAS, the Florida Attorney General's Office has issued Advisory Legal Opinion #97–24 regarding this subject;

NOW THEREFORE, I, TERENCE R. PERKINS, Chief Judge of the Seventh Judicial Circuit of Florida, hereby order the Clerks of Court in Flagler, Putnam, St. Johns and Volusia counties to apply money deposited by or on behalf of a defendant upon a judgment for the payment of fines and costs, toward the satisfaction of such fines and costs, and to return the remainder to the depositor.

TO BE RECORDED in Flagler, Putnam, St. Johns and Volusia counties.

DONE AND ORDERED in Daytona Beach, Volusia County, Florida, this 30th day of June 2017.

TERENCE R. PERKINS

CHIEF JUDGE

Adopted effective June 30, 2017.

CR–2017–009–VL. FIRST APPEARANCES/JAIL ARRAIGNMENTS/AND OTHER RELATED PROCEEDINGS

IN THE CIRCUIT COURT OF FLORIDA,
SEVENTH JUDICIAL CIRCUIT IN
AND FOR VOLUSIA COUNTY

RE: First Appearances/Jail Arraignments/And Other Related Proceedings

REF: CR–2017–009–VL

WHEREAS, it has been determined that procedural changes regarding the scheduling of First Appearances, Jail Arraignments, and related proceedings are necessary;

NOW THEREFORE, I, TERENCE R. PERKINS, Chief Judge of the Seventh Judicial Circuit of Florida, hereby order that First Appearances and Jail Arraignments are to be scheduled as follows:

1. Non-holiday weekday First Appearance hearings will commence at 1:30 p.m. at the Volusia County Branch Jail.

2. Weekend and holiday First Appearance hearings will commence at 8:30 a.m. at the Volusia County Branch Jail.

3. Jail Arraignment hearings will be conducted on non-holiday weekdays only and will commence immediately following First Appearance hearings.

4. The non-holiday weekday Jail Arraignment docket will consist of cases wherein at least one misdemeanor offense or ordinance violation (excluding assault, domestic violence assault, battery, domestic violence battery, stalking and violation of injunction for protection) is open and pending against an arrestee who remains in custody at least three (3) calendar days after a First Appearance hearing. Said arraignments will be conducted on all non-holiday weekdays.

5. The maximum number of arrestees set on a weekday Jail Arraignment docket will be 35. When the number of arrestees eligible for a Jail Arraignment docket exceeds 35, hearings will be set according to the date and time of the arrestees' booking (earliest date and time first). Subsequent eligible arrestees (those in excess of 35) will be placed on the next Jail Arraignment docket.

6. Waiver of Extradition hearings will be conducted at the Volusia County Branch Jail on non-holiday weekdays only and will commence at the discretion of the presiding judge.

7. Juvenile Detention hearings will be conducted at the Volusia County Branch Jail on weekends and holidays. On rare occasions, with the concurrence of the judge presiding at First Appearances, non-holiday weekday Detention hearings may also be conducted at the Volusia County Branch Jail.

8. Juvenile Dependency Shelter hearings will be conducted at the Volusia County Branch Jail on weekends and holidays. On rare occasions, with the concurrence of the judge presiding at First Appearances, non-holiday weekday Shelter hearings may also be conducted at the Volusia County Branch Jail.

IT IS FURTHER ORDERED that in cases where a First Appearance hearing is conducted in which an arrestee is accused of committing at least one misdemeanor assault, domestic violence assault, battery, domestic violence battery, stalking and/or violation of injunction for protection offense, and said arrestee remains in custody, an arraignment hearing will be scheduled before the assigned judge no less than ten (10), but no more than sixteen (16), calendar days after said arrestee's First Appearance hearing. Said arraignments will be conducted at a location determined by the assigned judge.

TO BE RECORDED in Volusia County, Florida.

DONE AND ORDERED in Daytona Beach, Volusia County, Florida this 30th day of June 2017.

TERENCE R. PERKINS

CHIEF JUDGE

Adopted effective June 30, 2017.

CR–2017–010–VL. JUDICIAL INQUIRY SYSTEM—FIRST APPEARANCES

IN THE CIRCUIT COURT OF FLORIDA,
SEVENTH JUDICIAL CIRCUIT IN
AND FOR VOLUSIA COUNTY

RE: Judicial Inquiry System—First Appearances

REF: CR–2017–010–VL

WHEREAS, the availability of background information concerning individuals scheduled to appear in Court is necessary for the prompt and efficient administration of justice in Volusia County, and

WHEREAS, the Office of the State Courts Administrator has developed the Judicial Inquiry System (JIS) to enable users to obtain background information concerning individuals scheduled to appear in Court, and

WHEREAS, having this information available will aid in the expeditious processing of certain cases;

NOW THEREFORE, I, TERENCE R. PERKINS, Chief Judge of the Seventh Judicial Circuit of Florida, hereby order that the Judicial Inquiry System (JIS) be made available to prosecution and defense counsel for purposes of obtaining background information concerning individuals scheduled to appear at first appearance hearings in Volusia County.

IT IS FURTHER ORDERED that Volusia County Pretrial Services personnel are relieved of the responsibility of providing background information (including criminal histories) concerning individuals scheduled to appear at first appearance hearings in Volusia County to prosecution and defense counsel.

IT IS FURTHER ORDERED, that until further notice, Volusia County Pretrial Services personnel shall provide the First Appearance Judge with background information concerning individuals scheduled to appear at first appearance hearings in Volusia County utilizing the Judicial Inquiry System (JIS).

TO BE RECORDED in Volusia County, Florida.

DONE AND ORDERED in Daytona Beach, Volusia County, Florida this 30th day of June 2017.

TERENCE R. PERKINS

CHIEF JUDGE

Adopted effective June 30, 2017.

CR–2017–011–FG/PT/SJ. CRIMINAL COURT PROCEEDINGS BY AUDIO–VISUAL DEVICE

IN THE CIRCUIT COURT OF FLORIDA, SEVENTH JUDICIAL CIRCUIT IN AND FOR FLAGLER, PUTNAM AND ST. JOHNS COUNTIES

RE: Criminal Court Proceedings by Audio–Visual Device

REF: CR–2017–011–FG/PT/SJ

WHEREAS, Rules 3.130 and 3.160, Florida Rules of Criminal Procedure, authorize the use of audio-visual technology to conduct certain proceedings, and

WHEREAS, equipment has been purchased and installed in Flagler, Putnam and St. Johns counties for these purposes, and

WHEREAS, it has been determined that the use of such equipment/technology enhances public safety and reduces inmate transportation costs;

NOW THEREFORE, I, TERENCE R. PERKINS, Chief Judge of the Seventh Judicial Circuit of Florida, hereby order that when authorized by the Florida Rules of Criminal Procedure, court proceedings may be conducted using audio-visual devices/technology in Flagler, Putnam and St. Johns counties.

IT IS FURTHER ORDERED that the use of the aforementioned equipment/technology is at the discretion of the presiding judge and its use is not required.

TO BE RECORDED in Flagler, Putnam and St. Johns counties.

DONE AND ORDERED in Daytona Beach, Volusia County, Florida this 30th day of June 2017.

TERENCE R. PERKINS

CHIEF JUDGE

Adopted effective June 30, 2017.

CR–2017–012–SC. ADOPTION OF SA 7–07 CHARGING AFFIDAVIT

IN THE CIRCUIT COURT OF FLORIDA, SEVENTH JUDICIAL CIRCUIT IN AND FOR FLAGLER, PUTNAM, ST. JOHNS AND VOLUSIA COUNTIES

RE: Adoption of SA 7–07 Charging Affidavit

REF: CR–2017–012–SC

WHEREAS, it has been made known to the undersigned that law enforcement agencies are required to capture certain information on all persons charged with criminal offenses and report said information to the Florida Department of Law Enforcement, and

WHEREAS, the State Attorney's Office and Law Enforcement agencies within the Seventh Judicial Circuit have developed a form for that purpose (SA 7–07);

NOW THEREFORE, I, TERENCE R. PERKINS, Chief Judge of the Seventh Judicial Circuit of Florida, hereby order all law enforcement agencies throughout the Seventh Judicial Circuit to utilize forms which substantially comply with the SA 7–07 for purposes of capturing and reporting relevant information.

IT IS FURTHER ORDERED that the State Attorney's Office will provide training to all affected parties regarding the use of the revised forms.

TO BE RECORDED in Flagler, Putnam, St. Johns and Volusia counties.

DONE and ORDERED in Daytona Beach, Volusia County, Florida, this 30th day of June 2017.

TERENCE R. PERKINS

CHIEF JUDGE

Adopted effective June 30, 2017.

CR–2017–013–SC. PROCESSING OF ARREST, COMPLAINT AND NOTICE TO APPEAR PAPERWORK (ADULT)

IN THE CIRCUIT COURT OF FLORIDA, SEVENTH JUDICIAL CIRCUIT IN AND FOR FLAGLER, PUTNAM, ST. JOHNS AND VOLUSIA COUNTIES

RE: Processing of Arrest, Complaint and Notice to Appear Paperwork (Adult)

REF: CR–2017–013–SC

WHEREAS, it has come to the attention of the undersigned that the prompt and efficient administration of justice in the Seventh Judicial Circuit, requires the issuance of an Administrative Order regarding the delivery and processing of paperwork related to arrests, complaints and Notices to Appear in adult cases;

NOW THEREFORE, I, TERENCE R. PERKINS, Chief Judge of the Seventh Judicial Circuit, hereby order as follows:

1. All paperwork related to **arrests,** including related traffic citations, in cases involving adults in Flagler, Putnam, St. Johns and Volusia counties is to be delivered to the appropriate county jail by the arresting agency. Jail officials are then to promptly forward the paperwork to the appropriate Clerk of Court's office.

2. All paperwork related to **complaints** in cases involving adults in Flagler, Putnam, St. Johns and Volusia counties is to be delivered promptly to either the State Attorney's office or the appropriate municipal prosecutor's office by the arresting agency.

3. All paperwork related to **Notices to Appear issued by arresting agencies**, including related traffic citations, in cases involving adults in Flagler, Putnam, St. Johns and Volusia counties is to be delivered promptly to the appropriate Clerk of Court's office. The Clerk's Office is then to promptly forward relevant copies to the State Attorney's office or the appropriate municipal prosecutor's office. **Notices to Appear issued by county jail personnel** are to be processed pursuant to paragraph #1.

4. The State Attorney's office, or the appropriate municipal prosecutor's office, is to review all **complaint** paperwork upon receipt and file the originals of said paperwork with the Clerk of Court's office when they elect to file:

a) an information

b) a complaint affidavit, accompanied by a Notice of Intent to Prosecute

c) a no-information

d) a request for warrant

e) a Deferred Prosecution Agreement

f) a Pretrial Intervention Order.

5. The Clerk of Court is not to set complaint affidavits issued by arresting agencies for arraignment until the State Attorney or municipal prosecutor has made a filing decision pursuant to paragraph #4 above. If a warrant is issued, an arraignment is not to be set until the warrant is served.

6. The assignment of case numbers and the assignment of cases to judicial divisions are the responsibility of the Clerk of Court.

IT IS FURTHER ORDERED that this Order does not apply to paperwork related to delinquent acts by juveniles. Paperwork related to delinquent acts by juveniles is to be processed pursuant to Chapter 985, Florida Statutes, or other relevant provisions as required by law.

TO BE RECORDED in Flagler, Putnam, St. Johns and Volusia counties.

DONE AND ORDERED in Daytona Beach, Volusia County, Florida, this 30th day of June 2017.

TERENCE R. PERKINS

CHIEF JUDGE

Adopted effective June 30, 2017.

CR–2017–014–VL. BLIND FILING OF NON–INDICTMENT FELONY CASES

IN THE CIRCUIT COURT OF FLORIDA, SEVENTH JUDICIAL CIRCUIT IN AND FOR VOLUSIA COUNTY

RE: Blind Filing of Non–Indictment Felony Cases

REF: CR–2017–014–VL

WHEREAS, an automated blind filing system to assign non-indictment felony cases to Circuit Court felony divisions is necessary;

NOW THEREFORE, I, TERENCE R. PERKINS, Chief Judge of the Seventh Judicial Circuit of Florida, hereby order that the Clerk of Circuit Court in Volusia County institute an automated blind filing system to assign non-indictment felony cases to selected divisions in Volusia County in accordance with the terms of this Order.

IT IS FURTHER ORDERED that the following criteria (listed in priority order) are to be followed when assigning cases to divisions:

1. (Open Cases)

If a new case is filed in which the defendant in said case already has an open, pending case in a division, said newly filed case is to be assigned to the division to which the "open" case is assigned.

2. (Co–Defendants)

If a new case or cases involving more than one defendant are filed, said newly filed cases involving all defendants are to be assigned to the same division.

3. (Closed Cases)

If a defendant is currently on probation, is participating in a pretrial diversion program, or is committed to a state hospital, a newly filed case involving the same defendant is to be assigned to the division to which the "closed" case is assigned.

4. (Location of Offense)

If a new case is filed in which criteria 1—3 are not applicable, said newly filed case is to be assigned to a division based on the geographic location of the offense. Administrative Orders governing geographic assignments and the distribution of cases among divisions are to be followed.

5. (Reopened Cases)

If a previously disposed case is reopened, said case is to be assigned to the same division in which the previously disposed case was assigned. If said division cannot be reasonably ascertained, said case is to be assigned to a division utilizing criteria 1–4.

IT IS FURTHER ORDERED that after the initial assignment of a case to a division pursuant to the above referenced criteria is accomplished, any subsequent assignment or reassignment of the case to a different division is not to occur absent a court order.

TO BE RECORDED in Volusia County, Florida.

DONE AND ORDERED in Daytona Beach, Volusia County, Florida, this 30th day of June 2017.

TERENCE R. PERKINS

CHIEF JUDGE

Adopted effective June 30, 2017.

CR–2017–015–VL. BLIND FILING OF FELONY INDICTMENTS

IN THE CIRCUIT COURT OF FLORIDA, SEVENTH JUDICIAL CIRCUIT IN AND FOR VOLUSIA COUNTY

RE: Blind Filing of Felony Indictments

REF: CR–2017–015–VL

WHEREAS, an automated blind filing system to assign felony indictments to Circuit Court felony divisions is necessary;

NOW THEREFORE, I, TERENCE R. PERKINS, Chief Judge of the Seventh Judicial Circuit of Florida, hereby order that the Clerk of Circuit Court in Volusia County institute an automated blind filing system to assign felony indictments to selected divisions in Volusia County in accordance with the terms of this Order.

IT IS FURTHER ORDERED that said system must ensure an equitable distribution of felony indictments among all felony divisions. Felony indictment assignments to divisions are to be tracked using "indictment assignment counters." When a felony indictment is filed and ready to be assigned to a division, said system is to review the "indictment assignment counters" and assign the indictment to the division with the lowest number of indictments assigned. If 2 or more divisions' "indictment assignment counters" are equal, the system should randomly select the division. In the event a felony indictment involves co-defendants, all such related cases are to be assigned to the same felony division, with said division receiving credit for multiple assignments. In the event the Chief Judge reassigns a felony indictment to another division, the "indictment assignment counters" of the affected divisions should be updated accordingly. Felony indictments are to be assigned without regard to the geographic location of the alleged offense within Volusia County. The Clerk of Court's office shall generate and distribute a report on a quarterly basis listing the felony indictments assigned to each division during the quarter and a cumulative total of each division's "indictment assignment counters". The Clerk of Court's office and Court Administrator's office shall confer to periodically reset each division's "indictment assignment counters" to 0 (zero).

TO BE RECORDED in Volusia County, Florida.

DONE AND ORDERED in Daytona Beach, Volusia County, Florida this 30th day of June 2017.

TERENCE R. PERKINS

CHIEF JUDGE

Adopted effective June 30, 2017.

CR–2017–016–SC. COMPANION INFRACTIONS TO CRIMINAL CHARGES

IN THE CIRCUIT COURT OF FLORIDA, SEVENTH JUDICIAL CIRCUIT IN AND FOR FLAGLER, PUTNAM, ST. JOHNS AND VOLUSIA COUNTIES

RE: Companion Infractions to Criminal Charges

REF: CR–2017–016–SC

WHEREAS, it has been made known to the undersigned that the prompt and efficient administration of justice would be best served by having civil infractions that accompany criminal charges to be heard by the judge to which the criminal case is assigned;

NOW THEREFORE, I, TERENCE R. PERKINS, Chief Judge of the Seventh Judicial Circuit of Florida, hereby order that all civil infractions that accompany criminal charges are to remain with the criminal charges and be disposed of by the judge to which the criminal case is assigned.

TO BE RECORDED in Flagler, Putnam, St. Johns and Volusia counties, Florida.

DONE AND ORDERED at Daytona Beach, Volusia County, Florida, this 30th day of June 2017.

TERENCE R. PERKINS

CHIEF JUDGE

Adopted effective June 30, 2017.

CR–2017–017–VL. EXTRADITION INFORMATION ON WARRANTS/CAPIASES

IN THE CIRCUIT COURT OF FLORIDA, SEVENTH JUDICIAL CIRCUIT IN AND FOR VOLUSIA COUNTY

RE: Extradition Information on Warrants/Capiases

REF: CR–2017–017–VL

WHEREAS, it has been made known to the undersigned that the inclusion of extradition information on warrants and capiases is necessary in order for the Volusia County Sheriff's Office to properly carry out its assigned duties;

NOW THEREFORE, I, TERENCE R. PERKINS, Chief Judge of the Seventh Judicial Circuit of Florida, hereby order that warrants and capiases issued by Circuit and County Court Judges of the Seventh Judicial Circuit, Volusia County, be clearly marked with appropriate extradition information.

IT IS FURTHER ORDERED that in the absence of clearly marked extradition information, the Volusia County Sheriff's office may presume that the following applicable default provisions apply to warrants and/or capiases issued:

- Felony release on recognizance (ROR) warrants and/or capiases have "Florida Only—FCIC" applicability.
- All other felony warrants and/or capiases have "Nationwide—NCIC" applicability.
- First-degree misdemeanor warrants and/or capiases have "Volusia and Surrounding Counties" applicability. For purposes of this Order, "Surrounding Counties" is defined as the counties of Brevard, Flagler, Lake, Marion, Orange, Putnam, Seminole and St. Johns.
- Second-degree misdemeanor and ordinance violation warrants and/or capiases have "Volusia Only" applicability.

IT IS FURTHER ORDERED that the above referenced default provisions will apply only in cases when warrants and/or capiases do not contain clearly marked extradition information. Said default provisions may be overridden by the issuing judge.

IT IS FURTHER ORDERED that absent the appearance of an expiration date on the face of a misdemeanor warrant and/or capias, said warrant and/or capias will automatically expire two years after its issuance.

TO BE RECORDED in Volusia County, Florida.

DONE AND ORDERED in Daytona Beach, Volusia County, Florida this 30th day of June 2017.

TERENCE R. PERKINS

CHIEF JUDGE

Adopted effective June 30, 2017.

CR–2017–018–SC. CORRECTION OF SCRIVENERS' ERRORS ON WARRANTS

IN THE CIRCUIT COURT OF FLORIDA, SEVENTH JUDICIAL CIRCUIT IN AND FOR FLAGLER, PUTNAM, ST. JOHNS AND VOLUSIA COUNTIES

RE: Correction of Scriveners' Errors on Warrants

REF: CR–2017–018–SC

WHEREAS, it has been made known to the undersigned that issuance of an administrative order authorizing the Warrants Divisions of the respective Sheriffs' Offices to correct obvious scriveners' errors on warrants is i n the best interest of the Seventh Judicial Circuit Court;

NOW THEREFORE, I, TERENCE R. PERKINS, Chief Judge of the Seventh Judicial Circuit of Florida, hereby order that in instances where it is readily ascertainable that a scrivener's error exists on the face of a warrant issued by a judge of the Seventh Judicial Circuit of Florida, personnel within Warrants Divisions of the respective Sheriffs' Offices of counties within the Seventh Judicial Circuit of Florida are hereby authorized to correct said errors. Examples of said errors include, but are not limited to, obvious typographical errors or simple transpositions of numbers.

IT IS FURTHER ORDERED that in instances where the existence of a scrivener's error is not readily ascertainable, or where a more substantial correction is necessary, the warrant is to be returned to the issuing judge for further action.

TO BE RECORDED in Flagler, Putnam, St. Johns and Volusia counties.

DONE AND ORDERED in Daytona Beach, Volusia County, Florida this 30th day of June 2017.

TERENCE R. PERKINS

CHIEF JUDGE

Adopted effective June 30, 2017.

CR–2017–019–SC. EXPIRATION DATES FOR MISDEMEANOR WARRANTS

IN THE CIRCUIT COURT OF FLORIDA, SEVENTH JUDICIAL CIRCUIT IN AND FOR FLAGLER, PUTNAM, ST. JOHNS AND VOLUSIA COUNTIES

RE: Expiration Dates for Misdemeanor Warrants

REF: CR–2017–019–SC

WHEREAS, it has been made known to the undersigned that the prompt and efficient administration of justice would be best served by the establishment of a policy setting expiration dates for misdemeanor warrants where said warrants do not include expiration dates on their faces;

NOW THEREFORE, I, TERENCE R. PERKINS, Chief Judge of the Seventh Judicial Circuit of Florida, hereby order that all misdemeanor warrants in Flagler, Putnam, St. Johns and Volusia counties, including, but not limited to, warrants issued as a result of a violation of probation, (including instances where a capias has been served on a violation of probation and the defendant subsequently fails to appear), shall automatically expire two (2) years from date of issuance, absent some other expiration date on the face of said warrants.

In regards to the misdemeanor violation of probation warrants affected by this Order, **IT IS FURTHER ORDERED** that any monies paid by defendants toward the satisfaction of monetary penalties imposed be remitted by the supervising misdemeanor probation agency to the Clerk of Court, who is to disburse said monies in accordance with applicable statutory provisions and other established policies. Efforts to collect any unpaid balances are to be undertaken (including referring the debt to a collection agency) and/or said unpaid balances are to be converted to final judgments for costs. Said warrants are to be dismissed and probation terminated unsuccessfully.

In regards to other misdemeanor warrants affected by this Order, **IT IS FURTHER ORDERED** that said warrants are to be dismissed and the underlying charges are to be dismissed without prejudice.

TO BE RECORDED in Flagler, Putnam, St. Johns and Volusia counties.

DONE AND ORDERED in Daytona Beach, Volusia County, Florida this 30th day of June 2017.

TERENCE R. PERKINS

CHIEF JUDGE

Adopted effective June 30, 2017.

CR–2017–020–SC. DISMISSAL OF MISDEMEANOR CASES

IN THE CIRCUIT COURT OF FLORIDA, SEVENTH JUDICIAL CIRCUIT IN AND FOR FLAGLER, PUTNAM, ST. JOHNS AND VOLUSIA COUNTIES

RE: Dismissal of Misdemeanor Cases

REF: CR–2017–020–SC

WHEREAS, misdemeanor criminal division dockets throughout the circuit are comprised of numerous cases that are older than 6 years, and

WHEREAS, it has been made known to the undersigned that the prompt and efficient administration of justice in the Seventh Judicial Circuit would be best served by the establishment of a policy setting dismissal dates for misdemeanor cases that remain on dockets for more than 6 years, and

WHEREAS, a separate administrative order creates by default a 2–year expiration date for warrants in misdemeanor cases;

NOW THEREFORE, I, TERENCE R. PERKINS, Chief Judge of the Seventh Judicial Circuit of Florida, hereby order that all pending misdemeanor cases in Flagler, Putnam, St. Johns and Volusia counties shall automatically be dismissed 6 years from the date of the last Court action, absent a specific directive to the contrary in individual cases by the presiding judge. This dismissal includes pending violations of probation, cases where warrants have expired, and cases where no warrants were issued, but D–6 suspensions were issued. Any pending violations of probation are to be terminated unsuccessfully. Any pending D–6 suspensions are to be released without costs. Any unpaid monetary obligations owed by defendants in affected cases are to be referred to collection agencies and/or converted to civil judgments.

TO BE RECORDED in Flagler, Putnam, St. Johns and Volusia counties.

DONE AND ORDERED in Daytona Beach, Volusia County, Florida, this 30th day of June 2017.

TERENCE R. PERKINS

CHIEF JUDGE

Adopted effective June 30, 2017.

CR–2017–021–SC. BLANKET NOTICE TO PARTICIPATE IN DISCOVERY

IN THE CIRCUIT COURT OF FLORIDA, SEVENTH JUDICIAL CIRCUIT IN AND FOR FLAGLER, PUTNAM, ST. JOHNS AND VOLUSIA COUNTIES

RE: Blanket Notice to Participate in Discovery

REF: CR–2017–021–SC

WHEREAS, the State Attorney and the Public Defender of the Seventh Judicial Circuit both recognize that the institution of a Blanket Demand for Discovery, pursuant to Florida Rule of Criminal Procedure 3.220 and Florida Rule of Juvenile Procedure 8.060 in all criminal and juvenile cases filed in the Circuit and County Courts of the Seventh Judicial Circuit, will allow for a more efficient handling of cases without prejudicing the defense or the State, and

WHEREAS, the Public Defender has made such a Blanket Demand, the original of which is attached hereto, and

WHEREAS, the State Attorney has agreed to accept this Blanket Demand for Discovery which obligates the State Attorney to comply with the applicable provisions of Florida Rule of Criminal Procedure 3.220 within fifteen (15) days of the appointment of the Office of the Public Defender, and Florida Rule of Juvenile Procedure 8.060 within five (5) days of the appointment of the Office of the Public Defender, and

WHEREAS, the Public Defender has agreed to accept the Blanket Demand as a full and complete demand for reciprocal discovery pursuant to Florida Rule of Criminal Procedure 3.220 and Florida Rule of Juvenile Procedure 8.060.

NOW THEREFORE, I, TERENCE R. PERKINS, Chief Judge of the Seventh Judicial Circuit of Florida, hereby order as follows:

1. For purposes of discovery pursuant to Florida Rule of Criminal Procedure 3.220 and Florida Rule of Juvenile Procedure 8.060 the Blanket Demand for Discovery attached hereto is deemed to be filed in each Circuit Court criminal and juvenile delinquency case and County Court criminal case filed in the Seventh Judicial Circuit at the time of the appointment of the Office of the Public Defender as defense counsel.

2. Said demand is to be treated as a full and complete demand for all discovery permitted by the State or defense pursuant to the above-cited rules.

3. This order remains in effect until further order of the Chief Judge.

TO BE RECORDED in Flagler, Putnam, St. Johns and Volusia counties.

DONE AND ORDERED in Daytona Beach, Volusia County, Florida this 30th day of June 2017.

TERENCE R. PERKINS

CHIEF JUDGE

[ATTACHMENT]

IN THE CIRCUIT AND COUNTY COURTS OF FLORIDA, CRIMINAL AND JUVENILE DIVISIONS, SEVENTH JUDICIAL CIRCUIT, IN AND FOR FLAGLER, PUTNAM, ST. JOHNS AND VOLUSIA COUNTIES

IN RE: BLANKET NOTICE OF DEMAND FOR DISCOVERY

TO: HONORABLE R. J. LARIZZA
STATE ATTORNEY
SEVENTH JUDICIAL CIRCUIT

Pursuant to Florida Rule of Criminal Procedure 3.220, and Florida Rule of Juvenile Procedure 8.060, I hereby give formal notice of intent to participate in discovery in all Circuit and County Court Criminal Division misdemeanor, felony and juvenile cases filed wherein the Defendant has been adjudged indigent and the Office of the Public Defender has been appointed as Defendant's counsel. I acknowledge that this notice incurs the reciprocal responsibility to provide your office with information required by these rules. In the event that discovery is not desired in any particular case, written notice to that effect will be provided to your office prior to acceptance of any discovery materials. This blanket notice is made effective January 15, 2009, and will remain in effect until and unless it is revoked in writing and delivered to you by myself, or my successor in office.

DATED this 6th day of January, 2009.

JAMES S. PURDY
PUBLIC DEFENDER
SEVENTH JUDICIAL CIRCUIT
FLORIDA BAR NUMBER: 0261696

Adopted effective June 30, 2017.

CR–2017–022–SC. LIMITS ON INTERVIEWS OF UNDERAGE OR INTELLECTUALLY DISABLED VICTIMS OF ABUSE

IN THE CIRCUIT COURT OF FLORIDA, SEVENTH JUDICIAL CIRCUIT IN AND FOR FLAGLER, PUTNAM, ST. JOHNS AND VOLUSIA COUNTIES

RE: Limits on Interviews of Underage or Intellectually Disabled Victims of Abuse

REF: CR–2017–022–SC

WHEREAS, § 914.16, Florida Statutes, requires the chief judge of each circuit, after consultation with appropriate officials, to provide for limits on the number of interviews that victims of certain crimes who are under the age of sixteen, or who are mentally retarded, must submit to for law enforcement or discovery purposes;

NOW THEREFORE, I, TERENCE R. PERKINS, Chief Judge of the Seventh Judicial Circuit, hereby order and direct as follows:

1. All law enforcement agencies within the Seventh Judicial Circuit (Flagler, Putnam, St. Johns and Volusia counties) shall, whenever possible, coordinate and consolidate the initial interviews of victims of violations of §§ 794.011, 800.04, 827.03, or 847.0135(5), Florida Statutes, who is under the age of sixteen, or victims of violations of §§ 794.011, 800.02, 800.03, or 825.102, Florida Statutes, who are mentally retarded, and whenever possible, shall record said interviews by audio and/or video;

2. All subsequent interviews are limited to a maximum of two, unless permission is granted by the presiding judge for good cause shown, and all subsequent interviews shall be recorded by audio and/or video;

3. The Department of Children and Families, other child protective agencies and their respective employees, agents, or contract providers, shall limit their interviews of said victims to a maximum of three, without further court order, and shall record said interviews by audio and/or video;

4. Discovery depositions shall be coordinated by all interested parties, where there are pending juvenile, civil, or criminal cases involving the same victim, in order to prevent repetition through multiple depositions; and

5. Nothing in this order limits a judge in a specific case from considering further limitations upon application of any interested party pursuant to the provisions of §§ 92.53, 92.54 and 92.55, Florida Statutes.

TO BE RECORDED in Flagler, Putnam, St. Johns and Volusia counties.

DONE AND ORDERED in Daytona Beach, Volusia County, Florida this 30th day of June 2017.

TERENCE R. PERKINS

CHIEF JUDGE

Adopted effective June 30, 2017.

CR–2017–023–SC. CONVENING OF GRAND JURIES

IN THE CIRCUIT COURT OF FLORIDA, SEVENTH JUDICIAL CIRCUIT IN AND FOR FLAGLER, PUTNAM, ST. JOHNS AND VOLUSIA COUNTIES

RE: Convening of Grand Juries

REF: 2017–023–SC

WHEREAS, Chapter 2013–25, Laws of Florida, repeals several statutes related to "terms of court," but also imposes a requirement that chief judges "regularly order the convening of the grand jury for a term of 6 months";

NOW THEREFORE, I, TERENCE R. PERKINS, Chief Judge of the Seventh Judicial Circuit of Florida, hereby order that pursuant to § 905.01(3), Florida Statutes, grand juries in the counties of the Seventh Judicial Circuit are to be convened in accordance with the following schedule:

Spring Terms

Flagler County—first Monday in April

Putnam County—second Monday in April

St. Johns County—third Monday in April

Volusia County—fourth Monday in April

Fall Terms

Flagler County—first Monday in October

Putnam County—second Monday in October

St. Johns County—third Monday in October

Volusia County—fourth Monday in October

TO BE RECORDED in Flagler, Putnam, St. Johns and Volusia counties.

DONE AND ORDERED in Daytona Beach, Volusia County, Florida this 30th day of June 2017.

TERENCE R. PERKINS

CHIEF JUDGE

Adopted effective June 30, 2017.

CR–2017–024–SC. SETTING GENERAL PRIORITIES FOR DISBURSEMENT OF RESTITUTION, COURT COSTS, FINES AND FEES

IN THE CIRCUIT COURT OF FLORIDA, SEVENTH JUDICIAL CIRCUIT IN AND FOR FLAGLER, PUTNAM, ST. JOHNS AND VOLUSIA COUNTIES

RE: Setting General Priorities for Disbursement of Restitution, Court Costs, Fines and Fees

REF: CR–2017–024–SC

WHEREAS, the establishment of priorities for the disbursement of restitution, court costs, fines and fees through the Department of Corrections, Probation and Parole, as well as all County misdemeanor probation service providers, is necessary for the efficient and proper administration of justice;

NOW THEREFORE, I, TERENCE R. PERKINS, Chief Judge of the Seventh Judicial Circuit of Florida, hereby order that in the absence of any specific order by the sentencing judge, all probation entities shall disburse money paid by probationers in accordance with the following priorities:

1. Restitution;
2. Unpaid Public Defender Application Fee—Indigent Criminal Defense Trust Fund (§ 27.52(1)(c), F.S.)
3. Crimes Compensation Trust Fund (§ 938.03, F.S.);
4. Remaining court costs, fines, fees and other costs ordered by the Court.

In the event payments are received from probationers in cases in which restitution has not yet been determined, the supervising probation agencies are authorized to disburse said payments in accordance with priorities #2—#4 above, pending the issuance of restitution orders.

TO BE RECORDED in Flagler, Putnam, St. Johns and Volusia counties.

DONE AND ORDERED in Daytona Beach, Volusia County, Florida this 30th day of June 2017.

TERENCE R. PERKINS

CHIEF JUDGE

Adopted effective June 30, 2017.

CR–2017–025–SC. DISHONORED PAYMENTS TO FINE AND FORFEITURE FUND

IN THE CIRCUIT COURT OF FLORIDA, SEVENTH JUDICIAL CIRCUIT IN AND FOR FLAGLER, PUTNAM, ST. JOHNS AND VOLUSIA COUNTIES

RE: Dishonored Payments to Fine and Forfeiture Fund

REF: CR–2017–025–SC

WHEREAS, the Clerks of Court are statutorily required to accept checks, drafts and other forms of payment for civil traffic citations, criminal fines and costs, and

WHEREAS, such payments are sometimes dishonored by financial institutions after receipt due to insufficient funds, stop payment orders, or other such reasons, and

WHEREAS, the effect of such actions by financial institutions is non-payment of the civil penalty, fine, or cost, and

WHEREAS, although the Clerks of Court secure information required pursuant to Ch. 832, Florida Statutes, payments so dishonored may or may not be recoverable, and the time elapsed between actions taken by financial institutions and recovery of payments may be lengthy;

NOW THEREFORE, I, TERENCE R. PERKINS, Chief Judge of the Seventh Judicial Circuit of Florida, hereby order that the Clerks of Court in and for Flagler, Putnam, St. Johns and Volusia counties are authorized to classify payments made to their Fine and Forfeiture fund which have been dishonored by financial institutions as "Non-payment of Penalty, Fine or Cost." Upon receipt of such a notice from a financial institution, the Clerks are authorized to reverse the corresponding payment and to take appropriate actions as if the payment in question had never been tendered.

IT IS FURTHER ORDERED that upon a reversal such as that mentioned above, the Clerks of Court are not precluded from attempting other forms of recovery as outlined in Ch. 832, Florida Statutes.

TO BE RECORDED in Flagler, Putnam, St. Johns and Volusia counties.

DONE AND ORDERED in Daytona Beach, Volusia County, FL this 30th day of June 2017.

TERENCE R. PERKINS

CHIEF JUDGE

Adopted effective June 30, 2017.

CR–2017–026–SC. UNCLAIMED RESTITUTION COLLECTED BY PROBATION SUPERVISION ENTITIES

IN THE CIRCUIT COURT OF FLORIDA, SEVENTH JUDICIAL CIRCUIT IN AND FOR FLAGLER, PUTNAM, ST. JOHNS AND VOLUSIA COUNTIES

RE: Unclaimed Restitution Collected by Probation Supervision Entities

REF: CR–2017–026–SC

WHEREAS, defendants placed under the supervision of probation entities are often required to pay restitution to victims as a condition of probation, and

WHEREAS, in some instances, victims to whom restitution is owed cannot be located and/or restitution collected goes unclaimed;

NOW THEREFORE, I, TERENCE R. PERKINS, Chief Judge of the seventh Judicial Circuit of Florida, hereby order that pursuant to § 945.31(3), Florida Statutes, probation entities in the Seventh Judicial Circuit shall remit unclaimed restitution payments to the General Revenue Fund of the State of Florida.

TO BE RECORDED in Flagler, Putnam, St. Johns and Volusia counties.

DONE AND ORDERED in Daytona Beach, Volusia County, Florida this 30th day of June 2017.

TERENCE R. PERKINS

CHIEF JUDGE

Adopted effective June 30, 2017.

CR–2018–027-SC. STANDING FAMILY COURT ORDER

IN THE CIRCUIT COURT OF FLORIDA, SEVENTH JUDICIAL CIRCUIT IN AND FOR FLAGLER, PUTNAM, ST. JOHNS AND VOLUSIA COUNTIES

RE: Cost of Supervision Fee for Misdemeanor Probation

REF: CR–2018–027–SC

(Rescinds CR–2017–027–SC)

WHEREAS, pursuant to § 948.09(1)(b), Florida Statutes, persons placed on misdemeanor probation are required to contribute not less than $40 per month to the entity providing probation supervision, and

WHEREAS, the undersigned has determined that an increase to the standard monthly cost of supervision amount is warranted;

NOW THEREFORE, I, RAUL A. ZAMBRANO, Chief Judge of the Seventh Judicial Circuit of Florida, hereby order the standard cost of supervision fee for individuals placed on misdemeanor probation in Flagler, Putnam, St. Johns and Volusia counties on or after July 2, 2018 to be $50 per month.

TO BE RECORDED in Flagler, Putnam, St. Johns and Volusia counties.

DONE AND ORDERED in Daytona Beach, Volusia County, Florida this 8th day of May 2018.

RAUL A. ZAMBRANO
Chief Judge

Adopted effective June 30, 2017. Amended effective May 8, 2018.

CR–2017–028–SC. COST OF SUPERVISION FEES FOR FELONY PROBATION

IN THE CIRCUIT COURT OF FLORIDA, SEVENTH JUDICIAL CIRCUIT IN AND FOR FLAGLER, PUTNAM, ST. JOHNS AND VOLUSIA COUNTIES

RE: Cost of Supervision Fees for Felony Probation

REF: CR–2017–028–SC

WHEREAS, pursuant to § 948.09, Florida Statutes, persons placed on probation, drug offender probation, community control, or other similar programs, must, as a condition of supervision, pay the Department of Corrections a total sum of money not to exceed the actual per diem cost of said supervision;

NOW THEREFORE, I, TERENCE R. PERKINS, Chief Judge of the Seventh Judicial Circuit of Florida, hereby order that in the absence of any specific amount set by the sentencing judge, cost of supervision fees ordered as a condition of supervision, shall be set at $50.00 per month. Payment of said cost of supervision fees may be waived by the sentencing judge if he/she is of the opinion that the defendant does not possess the ability to pay said fees.

IT IS FURTHER ORDERED that if a defendant fails to pay court ordered fees, fines, or costs, and the supervising officer believes he/she possesses the ability to pay said fees, fines, or costs, the supervising officer shall report said failure to pay to the Court in a timely fashion. Regardless of a defendant's ability to pay, if he/she fails to pay cost of supervision fees, or court ordered costs other than restitution, the supervising officer shall report said failure to pay to the Court no later than 120 days prior to the expiration of the defendant's term of supervision. In either event, reports alleging a defendant's failure to pay fees, fines, or costs, must be accompanied by information related to the defendant's ability to pay.

IT IS FURTHER ORDERED that regardless of a defendant's ability to pay, if he/she fails to pay restitution, the supervising officer shall immediately report said failure to pay to the Court.

TO BE RECORDED in Flagler, Putnam, St. Johns and Volusia counties.

DONE AND ORDERED in Daytona Beach, Volusia County, Florida this 30th day of June 2017.

TERENCE R. PERKINS

CHIEF JUDGE

Adopted effective June 30, 2017.

CR–2017–029–SC. SCHEDULING OF FELONY VIOLATION OF PROBATION/COMMUNITY CONTROL CASES

IN THE CIRCUIT COURT OF FLORIDA, SEVENTH JUDICIAL CIRCUIT IN AND FOR FLAGLER, PUTNAM, ST. JOHNS AND VOLUSIA COUNTIES

RE: Scheduling of Felony Violation of Probation/Community Control Cases

REF: CR–2017–029–SC

WHEREAS, it has been determined that cases in which it is alleged that offenders have violated conditions of felony probation/community control must be dealt with in an expeditious fashion, and

WHEREAS, pursuant to Rule 2.215(b)(8), Florida Rules of Judicial Administration, the chief judge is responsible for monitoring the jail population, and

WHEREAS, the undersigned has conferred with affected judges regarding this matter;

NOW THEREFORE, I, TERENCE R. PERKINS, Chief Judge of the Seventh Judicial Circuit of Florida, hereby order that in instances where an offender is arrested for allegedly violating conditions of his/her felony probation/community control, and said offender remains incarcerated following his/her first appearance hearing, the Clerk of Court's office shall schedule the offender for an arraignment on the violation of probation/community control case before the assigned circuit judge **no later than 10 days** from the date of the offender's first appearance hearing.

IT IS FURTHER ORDERED that in instances where an offender's violation of felony probation/community control case is not disposed of at an arraignment proceeding referenced above, absent extenuating circumstances, the Clerk of Court's office shall schedule the offender for a hearing on the violation of felony probation/community control case before the assigned circuit judge **no later than 28 days** from the date of the offender's arraignment.

TO BE RECORDED in Flagler, Putnam, St. Johns and Volusia counties.

DONE AND ORDERED in Daytona Beach, Volusia County, Florida this 30th day of June 2017.

TERENCE R. PERKINS

CHIEF JUDGE

Adopted effective June 30, 2017.

CR–2017–030–SC. CRIMINAL (FELONY) ALTERNATIVE VOP SANCTIONS PROGRAM

IN THE CIRCUIT COURT OF FLORIDA, SEVENTH JUDICIAL CIRCUIT IN AND FOR FLAGLER, PUTNAM, ST. JOHNS AND VOLUSIA COUNTIES

RE: Criminal (Felony) Alternative VOP Sanctions Program

REF: CR–2017–030–SC

WHEREAS, many technical violations of probation or community control do not involve new arrests or other serious violations, and

WHEREAS, arresting and incarcerating certain non-violent offenders for minor violations of probation or community control is expensive and often unproductive, and

WHEREAS, holding offenders accountable by applying swift and certain sanctions for technical violations of probation or community control can reduce recidivism is supported by research, and

WHEREAS, potential benefits of administratively processing certain technical violations include:

- fewer probation and community control violation hearings,
- fewer law enforcement resources required to serve violation warrants for certain technical violations,
- a reduction in the number of offenders awaiting violation hearings while in jail, and
- offering offenders an alternative to a violation hearing in court, allowing offenders to remain engaged in employment, school, treatment, etc., and providing offenders with an opportunity to take immediate responsibility for their actions and consequences of those actions;

NOW THEREFORE, I, TERENCE R. PERKINS, Chief Judge of the Seventh Judicial Circuit of Florida, hereby order the establishment of a Felony Alternative V.O.P. Sanctions program in the Seventh Judicial Circuit effective July 1, 2015. The following provisions apply:

1. Eligibility. In order to be eligible for the program, offenders must have been placed on probation or community control under the supervision of the Department of Corrections by a judge in Flagler, Putnam, St. Johns, or Volusia counties; have stable community ties; and have a stable residence in the county where sentenced. Offenders who are eligible for the program include probation offenders (including drug offenders) and community control supervision offenders. The program applies only to offenders who have committed certain technical violations addressed in the Alternative Sanctions Program Violation/Sanction Matrix included in this order. The threat an offender poses to public safety is an important factor in determining eligibility. Offenders with lengthy or violent criminal backgrounds (including sex offenders) are not eligible for the program. Additionally, offenders who are charged with new law violations, have absconded, or have violated a "no contact" condition of supervision are not eligible for the program. Offenders with three or more previous violations are not eligible for the program.

2. Qualifying Technical Violations and Approved Sanctions. The following matrix lists the specific technical violations that may be addressed through the Alternative Sanctions process for offenders who were sentenced in Flagler, Putnam, St. Johns, or Volusia counties. Each technical violation includes a list of sanctions determined and approved by the court for the probation officer to select from when reporting these technical violations, based on an individual offender's circumstances at the time of the violation.

ALTERNATIVE SANCTIONS PROGRAM VIOLATION/SANCTION MATRIX

VIOLATION	APPROVED LIST OF SANCTIONS
Condition (1): Reported late; failed to report as instructed	1. Weekly call-in for 6 weeks 2. Daily call-in for 30 days 3. Report 2 times per month for 60 days
Condition (3): Failed to report changes in residence or employment without first procuring the officer's consent (or notifying immediately if evicted from residence or laid off from job)	1. Weekly call-in for 6 weeks 2. Report 2 times per month for 90 days 3. Weekly reporting for 6 weeks
Condition (3): Failed to request permission prior to leaving the county	1. Weekly call-in for 6 weeks 2. Report 2 times per month for 60 days 3. Weekly reporting for 6 weeks
Condition (6): Found to be associating with person(s) engaged in criminal activity	1. Curfew from 8:00 p.m. to 6:00 a.m. for 90 days (can be modified by probation officer ["PO"] for treatment or work purposes). 2. Weekly call-in for 6 weeks 3. 25 hours of community service work
Condition (7): Positive drug test for non-prescribed drugs (first occurrence)	1. Drug evaluation and successful completion of treatment deemed necessary 2. Increased level of treatment program up to and including residential 3. Curfew from 8:00 p.m. to 6:00 a.m. for 90 days (can be modified by PO for treatment or work purposes).
Condition (7): Positive drug test for non-prescribed drugs (second occurrence)	1. Drug evaluation and successful completion of treatment deemed necessary 2. Increased level of treatment program up to and including residential 3. Curfew from 8:00 p.m. to 6:00 a.m. for 90 days (can be modified by PO for treatment or work purposes).
Condition (8): Failure to maintain employment	1. Weekly reporting with job search logs until employed 2. Daily reporting with job search logs until employed 3. Curfew from 8:00 p.m. to 6:00 a.m. for 90 days (can be modified by PO for treatment or work purposes).
Condition (9): Failure to answer inquiries truthfully (depending on nature of question, response, and reason for being untruthful, consequence will vary)	1. Weekly call-in for 4 weeks 2. 8 hours of community service work
Condition (10): Failure to pay monthly monetary obligations as stipulated by the Court.	1. If unemployed, daily job search. 2. If employed, monthly budgeting. 3. Weekly call in until monetary obligations are current.
Condition (11): Failure to submit to random testing as directed	1. Weekly reporting by 11 a.m. 2. Reporting 3 times per week by 11 a.m. 3. Drug evaluation and successful completion of treatment deemed necessary 4. Curfew from 8:00 p.m. to 6:00 a.m. for 90 days (can be modified by PO for treatment or work purposes).
Special Condition (1): Failure to attend treatment evaluation or treatment session as scheduled	1. Daily call-in until evaluation completed 2. Weekly reporting until evaluation completed 3. Curfew from 8:00 p.m. to 6:00 a.m. until evaluation completed (can be modified by PO for treatment or work purposes).
Special Condition (8): Failure to complete community service hours as instructed	1. Daily reporting until community service hours completed/current, if unemployed 2. Weekly reporting until community service hours completed/current, if employed
Special Condition (9): Failure to remain at residence during curfew period	1. Weekly reporting for 3 months 2. GPS Electronic Monitoring for 30 days.
Community Control Condition (16): Failure to maintain approved schedule—unapproved absence from required location (negligence in getting home late, stopping at store on way home without permission, etc.)	1. 10 hours Community Service Work 2. GPS Electronic Monitoring for 30 days.

3. Alternative Sanctions Program Process

A. The probation or community control officer shall inform offenders who have committed violations enumerated above that they may participate in the Alternative Sanctions Program for administrative disposition of the violation. No offender is required to participate in the Alternative Sanctions Program and may opt for a formal violation of probation or community control proceeding.

B. If the offender admits the violation, agrees to accept the administrative sanction(s) recommended by the probation officer, and agrees to waive a formal violation hearing to modify his/her sentence, the probation officer will prepare an "Alternative Sanctions Program Technical Violation Notification", which will provide details of the circumstances of the technical violation that occurred and the probation officer's recommended sanction, based on the sanctions listed in the approved matrix. If the offender agrees to participate in the Alternative Sanctions Program, he/she will sign the second section of the form entitled "Alternative Sanctions Program Waiver of Formal VOP/VOCC Hearing, Admission of Violation, and Acceptance of Sanctions," which will be submitted to the court once the probation officer signs and dates the form.

C. The "Alternative Sanctions Program Technical Violation Notification" and waiver form will be submitted to a judge for review. If the judge agrees that the technical violation should be addressed via the Alternative Sanctions Program and agrees with the recommended sanction, he/she will sign an "Order—Alternative Sanctions Program." If the judge does not agree with the particular sanction recommended by the officer or does not agree that the technical violation should be addressed via the Alternative Sanctions Program, he/she will provide further direction.

D. Upon court approval, the probation officer will instruct the offender on the sanction imposed by the court and instruct the offender to take actions necessary to ensure the sanction is fulfilled promptly. Failure to complete the imposed sanction as instructed will result in a violation report, affidavit and warrant being submitted to the court.

E. Participation in the Alternative Sanctions Program is not considered a conviction for a violation of probation or community control (not a scoreable violation) for purposes of Section VI of the Criminal Punishment Code Scoresheet.

TO BE RECORDED in Flagler, Putnam, St. Johns and Volusia counties.

DONE AND ORDERED in Daytona Beach, Volusia County, Florida this 30th day of June 2017.

TERENCE R. PERKINS

CHIEF JUDGE

Adopted effective June 30, 2017.

CR–2017–031–SC. NOTIFICATION OF TECHNICAL VIOLATIONS OF PROBATION BY DEPARTMENT OF CORRECTIONS, PROBATION AND PAROLE

IN THE CIRCUIT COURT OF FLORIDA, SEVENTH JUDICIAL CIRCUIT IN AND FOR FLAGLER, PUTNAM, ST. JOHNS AND VOLUSIA COUNTIES

RE: Notification of Technical Violations of Probation by Department of Corrections, Probation and Parole

REF: CR–2017–031–SC

WHEREAS, the Florida Department of Corrections, Probation and Parole, prepares and submits Probation Violation Reports when notifying judges of alleged technical violations of probation, and

WHEREAS, the preparation of Notification of Technical Violation letters has been determined to be a more efficient utilization of limited resources;

NOW THEREFORE, I, TERENCE R. PERKINS, Chief Judge of the Seventh Judicial Circuit of Florida, hereby order that absent specific orders by sentencing judges to the contrary, the Florida Department of Corrections, Probation and Parole, may submit Notification of Technical Violation letters in lieu of formal Probation Violation Reports when advising judges of alleged technical violations of probation.

TO BE RECORDED in Flagler, Putnam, St. Johns and Volusia counties.

DONE AND ORDERED in Daytona Beach, Volusia County, Florida this 30th day of June 2017.

TERENCE R. PERKINS

CHIEF JUDGE

Adopted effective June 30, 2017.

CR–2017–032–SC. APPROVED OFFENDER LEAVE AND FURLOUGH FOR COMMUNITY CONTROLLEES IN INPATIENT TREATMENT

IN THE CIRCUIT COURT OF FLORIDA, SEVENTH JUDICIAL CIRCUIT IN AND FOR FLAGLER, PUTNAM, ST. JOHNS AND VOLUSIA COUNTIES

RE: Approved Offender Leave and Furlough for Community Controllees in Inpatient Treatment

REF: CR–2017–032–SC

WHEREAS, it is the goal of approved offender leaves, furloughs and recreational/leisure activities to motivate offenders toward self-improvement, to gradually re-integrate offenders back into the community, to strengthen family ties, to accustom offenders to self-reliance, and to expose offenders to beneficial programs and experiences;

NOW THEREFORE, I, TERENCE R. PERKINS, Chief Judge of the Seventh Judicial Circuit of Florida, hereby order that persons on Community Control Supervision who are undergoing inpatient treatment, may be allowed to attend and participate in approved offender leaves, furloughs and recreational/leisure activities, as approved by the Florida Department of Corrections, in compliance with the Non-secure Treatment Program Manual, unless specifically prohibited by order of the sentencing judge.

TO BE RECORDED in Flagler, Putnam, St. Johns and Volusia counties.

DONE AND ORDERED in Daytona Beach, Volusia County, Florida this 30th day of June 2017.

TERENCE R. PERKINS

CHIEF JUDGE

Adopted effective June 30, 2017.

CR–2017–033–SC. CONFISCATION AND DISPOSAL OF WILDLIFE, FRESHWATER AND SALTWATER PRODUCTS EVIDENCE

IN THE CIRCUIT COURT OF FLORIDA, SEVENTH JUDICIAL CIRCUIT IN AND FOR FLAGLER, PUTNAM, ST. JOHNS AND VOLUSIA COUNTIES

RE: Confiscation and Disposal of Wildlife, Freshwater and Saltwater Products Evidence

REF: CR–2017–033–SC

WHEREAS, it has been determined that procedures to process petitions and orders for the disposal of wildlife, freshwater and/or saltwater products seized during lawful arrests pursuant to chapter 379, Florida Statutes, would be beneficial;

NOW THEREFORE, I, TERENCE R. PERKINS, Chief Judge of the Seventh Judicial Circuit of Florida, hereby order that in Flagler, Putnam, St. Johns and Volusia counties, law enforcement officers who confiscate perishable fish and/or game products incidental to arrests pursuant to Chapter 379, Florida Statutes, may dispose of such evidence in accordance with the following procedures:

1. In order to determine the fair value of confiscated fish and/or game products, unless otherwise determined by a judge, three (3) bids must be obtained and the value set at the highest price obtainable. Once fair value has been established, the defendant shall be afforded an opportunity to post a bond or cash deposit in like amount, payable to the Fish and Wildlife Conservation Commission, to be held in escrow. The defendant will then have 24 hours to transport the confiscated products out of state for sale or other disposition. If the defendant fails to post the required monetary amount, or submits a written waiver of his/her right to do so, the confiscated products will be sold to the highest bidder. Proceeds are to be made payable to the Fish and Wildlife Conservation

Commission and held in escrow pending resolution of court proceedings.

2. In the event confiscated fish and/or game products are undersized, taken during closed seasons, and/or cannot be lawfully sold in Florida, the law enforcement officer is to so indicate on the complaint affidavit. The law enforcement officer may then deliver said confiscated products to any charitable or governmental entity for use in feeding the indigent, sheltered and/or incarcerated, and is to properly receipt said transaction. The officer may retain a representative sample of the confiscated products for discover/evidentiary purposes until court proceedings are concluded.

3. In the event confiscated saltwater products are inedible or otherwise unsuitable for human consumption, the law enforcement officer, after first retaining a representative sample for discovery/evidentiary purposes, may release said products back into the water/wild, destroy them, or use them for investigative/educational/scientific purposes.

4. In all such instances, law enforcement officers are to prepare appropriate documentation detailing the manner of disposal of confiscated fish and/or game products and submit said documentation, along with complaint affidavits and other related information, to the State Attorney's office.

5. If corresponding court proceedings result in a conviction, the Fish and Wildlife Conservation Commission shall deposit funds held in escrow into the Marine Resources Conservation Trust Fund. Such deposits shall constitute confiscation.

6. If corresponding court proceedings result in an acquittal, the Fish and Wildlife Conservation Commission shall return funds held in escrow to the defendant.

TO BE RECORDED in Flagler, Putnam, St. Johns and Volusia counties.

DONE AND ORDERED in Daytona Beach, Volusia County, Florida this 30th day of June 2017.

TERENCE R. PERKINS

CHIEF JUDGE

Adopted effective June 30, 2017.

CR–2017–034–SC. FORFEITURE OF ILLEGAL SEINES, NETS, TRAPS OR OTHER FISHING DEVICES/EQUIPMENT

IN THE CIRCUIT COURT OF FLORIDA, SEVENTH JUDICIAL CIRCUIT IN AND FOR FLAGLER, PUTNAM, ST. JOHNS AND VOLUSIA COUNTIES

RE: Forfeiture of Illegal Seines, Nets, Traps or Other Fishing Devices/Equipment

REF: CR–2017–034–SC

WHEREAS, Article X, Section 16, Florida Constitution, enacts limitations on marine net fishing in Florida waters, and

WHEREAS, § 379.337, Florida Statutes, sets forth procedures for the confiscation, seizure and forfeiture of illegal fishing gear;

NOW THEREFORE, I, TERENCE R. PERKINS, Chief Judge of the Seventh Judicial Circuit of Florida, hereby order that in Flagler, Putnam, St. Johns and Volusia counties, where it is alleged that an illegal seine, net, trap or other fishing devices/equipment is found and taken into custody, and the owner thereof is not known to the officer finding the same, this Order shall serve as the order forfeiting said item to the Florida Fish & Wildlife Conservation Commission referenced in § 379.337(3), Florida Statutes.

IT IS FURTHER ORDERED that property forfeited pursuant to this Order must be destroyed or disposed of in accordance with the provisions of § 379.337(4), Florida Statutes.

TO BE RECORDED in Flagler, Putnam, St. Johns and Volusia counties.

DONE AND ORDERED in Daytona Beach, Volusia County, Florida this 30th day of June 2017.

TERENCE R. PERKINS

CHIEF JUDGE

Adopted effective June 30, 2017.

CR–2017–035–SC. IMPOUNDMENT/IMMOBILIZATION OF VEHICLES AND VESSELS

IN THE CIRCUIT COURT OF FLORIDA, SEVENTH JUDICIAL CIRCUIT IN AND FOR FLAGLER, PUTNAM, ST. JOHNS AND VOLUSIA COUNTIES

RE: Impoundment/Immobilization of Vehicles and Vessels

REF: CR–2017–035–SC

WHEREAS, pursuant to § 316.193(6), Florida Statutes, the impoundment/immobilization of vehicles used in driving under the influence (DUI) cases are ordered by the Court, and

WHEREAS, pursuant to § 327.35(6), Florida Statutes, the impoundment/immobilization of vessels used in boating under the influence (BUI) cases are ordered by the Court, and

WHEREAS, the misdemeanor probation providers in Flagler, Putnam, St. Johns and Volusia counties have assumed the responsibility for impounding/immobilizing said vehicles and vessels, and

WHEREAS, the County Court judges have authorized the misdemeanor probation provider to perform said impoundment/immobilization duties;

NOW THEREFORE, I, TERENCE R. PERKINS, Chief Judge of the Seventh Judicial Circuit of Florida, hereby order that the misdemeanor probation providers in Flagler, Putnam, St. Johns and Volusia counties shall be responsible for the impoundment/immobilization of vehicles and vessels ordered by the Court pursuant to §§ 316.193(6) and 327.35(6), Florida Statutes.

IT IS FURTHER ORDERED that all orders received by the Sheriffs of Flagler, Putnam, St. Johns and Volusia counties for the impoundment/immobilization of vehicles and vessels located in their respective counties, from outside jurisdictions, shall be delivered promptly to the misdemeanor probation providers in their respective counties for proper execution and action.

TO BE RECORDED in Flagler, Putnam, St. Johns and Volusia counties.

DONE AND ORDERED in Daytona Beach, Volusia County, Florida, this 30th day of June 2017.

TERENCE R. PERKINS

CHIEF JUDGE

Adopted effective June 30, 2017.

CR–2017–036–FG. FLAGLER COUNTY ADULT DRUG COURT

IN THE CIRCUIT COURT OF FLORIDA, SEVENTH JUDICIAL CIRCUIT IN AND FOR FLAGLER COUNTY

RE: Flagler County Adult Drug Court

REF: CR–2017–036–FG

WHEREAS, a Drug Court Task Force previously recommended that an adult drug court program be established in Flagler County, and

WHEREAS, the Task Force's recommendation led to the establishment of an Adult Drug Court in Flagler County in 2006;

NOW THEREFORE, I, TERENCE R. PERKINS, Chief Judge of the Seventh Judicial Circuit of Florida, hereby reaffirm the establishment of the Flagler County Adult Drug Court division and program, to which certain drug-related criminal cases in Circuit Court may be referred/assigned.

IT IS FURTHER ORDERED that a circuit judge will be assigned to the Flagler County Adult Drug Court division and that it will be designated as Division 24 for assignment purposes. Upon receipt of appropriate orders of the Court, the Flagler County Clerk of Court shall assign/transfer designated cases to Division 24 (Adult Drug Court).

IT IS FURTHER ORDERED that defendants participating in the Flagler County Adult Drug Court program will be supervised mutually by Drug Court staff and Florida Department of Corrections staff.

IT IS FURTHER ORDERED that the Drug Court judge shall convene a Drug Court Advisory Committee, comprised of relevant stakeholders and other interested parties, to advise and assist the Drug Court judge and Chief Judge in the operation of the Flagler County Adult Drug Court program. The Drug Court judge shall serve as chair of the advisory committee.

TO BE RECORDED in Flagler County, Florida.

DONE AND ORDERED in Daytona Beach, Volusia County, Florida, this 30th day of June 2017.

TERENCE R. PERKINS

CHIEF JUDGE

Adopted effective June 30, 2017.

CR–2017–037–PT. PUTNAM COUNTY ADULT DRUG COURT

IN THE CIRCUIT COURT OF FLORIDA, SEVENTH JUDICIAL CIRCUIT IN AND FOR PUTNAM COUNTY

RE: Putnam County Adult Drug Court

REF: CR–2017–037–PT

WHEREAS, a Drug Court Task Force previously recommended that an adult drug court program be established in Putnam County, and

WHEREAS, the Task Force's recommendation led to the establishment of an Adult Drug Court in Putnam County in 2002;

NOW THEREFORE, I, TERENCE R. PERKINS, Chief Judge of the Seventh Judicial Circuit, hereby reaffirm the establishment of the Putnam County Adult Drug Court division and program, to which certain drug-related criminal cases in Circuit Court may be referred/assigned.

IT IS FURTHER ORDERED that a circuit judge will be assigned to the Putnam County Adult Drug Court division and that it will be designated as Division 25 for assignment purposes. Upon receipt of appropriate orders of the Court, the Putnam County Clerk of Court shall assign/transfer designated cases to Division 25 (Adult Drug Court).

IT IS FURTHER ORDERED that defendants participating in the Putnam County Adult Drug Court program will be supervised mutually by Drug Court staff and Florida Department of Corrections staff.

IT IS FURTHER ORDERED that the Drug Court judge shall convene a Drug Court Advisory Committee, comprised of relevant stakeholders and other interested parties, to advise and assist the Drug Court judge and Chief Judge in the operation of the Putnam County Adult Drug Court program. The Drug Court judge shall serve as chair of the advisory committee.

TO BE RECORDED in Putnam County, Florida.

DONE AND ORDERED in Daytona Beach, Volusia County, Florida, this 30th day of June 2017.

TERENCE R. PERKINS

CHIEF JUDGE

Adopted effective June 30, 2017.

CR–2017–038–SJ. ST. JOHNS COUNTY ADULT DRUG COURT

IN THE CIRCUIT COURT OF FLORIDA, SEVENTH JUDICIAL CIRCUIT IN AND FOR ST. JOHNS COUNTY

RE: St. Johns County Adult Drug Court

REF: CR–2017–038–SJ

WHEREAS, a Drug Court Task Force previously recommended that an adult drug court program be established in St. Johns County, and

WHEREAS, the Task Force's recommendation led to the establishment of an Adult Drug Court in St. Johns County in 2002;

NOW THEREFORE, I, TERENCE R. PERKINS, Chief Judge of the Seventh Judicial Circuit of Florida, hereby reaffirm the establishment of the St. Johns County Adult Drug Court division and program, to which certain drug-related criminal cases in circuit court may be referred/assigned.

IT IS FURTHER ORDERED that a Circuit Judge will be assigned to the St. Johns County Adult Drug Court division and that it will be designated as Division 26 for assignment purposes. Upon receipt of appropriate orders of the Court, the St. Johns County Clerk of Court shall assign/transfer designated cases to Division 26 (Adult Drug Court).

IT IS FURTHER ORDERED that defendants participating in the St. Johns County Adult Drug Court program will be supervised mutually by Drug Court staff and Florida Department of Corrections staff.

IT IS FURTHER ORDERED that the Drug Court judge shall convene a Drug Court Advisory Committee, comprised of relevant stakeholders and other interested parties, to advise and assist the Drug Court judge and the Chief Judge in the operation of the St. Johns County Adult Drug Court program. The Drug Court judge shall serve as chair of the advisory committee.

TO BE RECORDED in St. Johns County, Florida.

DONE AND ORDERED in Daytona Beach, Volusia County, Florida, this 30th day of June 2017.

TERENCE R. PERKINS

CHIEF JUDGE

Adopted effective June 30, 2017.

CR–2017–039–VL. VOLUSIA COUNTY ADULT DRUG COURT

IN THE CIRCUIT COURT OF FLORIDA, SEVENTH JUDICIAL CIRCUIT IN AND FOR VOLUSIA COUNTY

RE: Volusia County Adult Drug Court

REF: CR–2017–039–VL

WHEREAS, a Drug Court Task Force previously recommended that an adult drug court program be established in Volusia County, and

WHEREAS, the Task Force's recommendation led to the establishment of an Adult Drug Court in Volusia County in 1997;

NOW THEREFORE, I, TERENCE R. PERKINS, Chief Judge of the Seventh Judicial Circuit, hereby reaffirm the establishment of the Volusia County Adult Drug Court division and program, to which certain drug-related criminal cases in circuit court may be referred/assigned.

IT IS FURTHER ORDERED that a Circuit Judge will be assigned to the Volusia County Adult Drug Court division and that it will be designated as Divisions 21 and 22 for assignment purposes. Upon receipt of appropriate orders of the Court, the Volusia County Clerk of Court will assign designated cases to Divisions 21 and 22 (East Volusia Adult Drug Court and West Volusia Adult Drug Court).

IT IS FURTHER ORDERED that defendants participating in the Volusia County Adult Drug Court program will be supervised mutually by Drug Court staff and Florida Department of Corrections staff.

IT IS FURTHER ORDERED that the Drug Court judge shall convene a Drug Court Advisory Committee, comprised of relevant stakeholders and other interested parties, to advise and assist the Drug Court judge and Chief Judge in the operation of the Volusia County Adult Drug Court program. The Drug Court judge shall serve as chair of the advisory committee.

TO BE RECORDED in Volusia County, Florida.

DONE and ORDERED in Daytona Beach, Volusia County, Florida this 30th day of June 2017.

TERENCE R. PERKINS

CHIEF JUDGE

Adopted effective June 30, 2017.

CR–2017–040–VL. VOLUSIA COUNTY MISDEMEANOR DUI COURT

IN THE CIRCUIT COURT OF FLORIDA, SEVENTH JUDICIAL CIRCUIT IN AND FOR VOLUSIA COUNTY

RE: Volusia County Misdemeanor DUI Court

REF: CR–2017–040–VL

WHEREAS, a DUI Treatment Court Task Force previously recommended the establishment of a Misdemeanor DUI Court in Volusia County, and

WHEREAS, the Task Force's recommendation led to the establishment of a Misdemeanor DUI Court in Volusia County in 2012;

NOW THEREFORE, I, TERENCE R. PERKINS, Chief Judge of the Seventh Judicial Circuit of Florida, hereby reaffirm the establishment of a Volusia County Misdemeanor DUI Court division and program, to which certain driving under the influence cases may be referred/assigned.

IT IS FURTHER ORDERED that a Volusia County Court Judge be assigned to the Volusia County Misdemeanor DUI Court division and that said division be designated as Division 87 for assignment purposes. Upon receipt of appropriate orders of the Court, the Volusia County Clerk of Court shall assign/transfer cases so designated to Division 87 (Misdemeanor DUI Court).

IT IS FURTHER ORDERED that the DUI Court judge shall convene a DUI Court Advisory Committee, comprised of relevant stakeholders and other interested parties, to advise and assist the DUI Court judge and Chief Judge in the operation of the Volusia County Misdemeanor DUI Court program. The DUI Court judge shall serve as chair of the advisory committee.

TO BE RECORDED in Volusia County, Florida.

DONE AND ORDERED in Daytona Beach, Volusia County, Florida this 30th day of June 2017.

TERENCE R. PERKINS

CHIEF JUDGE

Adopted effective June 30, 2017.

CR–2017–041–SJ. ST. JOHNS COUNTY VETERANS TREATMENT COURT

IN THE CIRCUIT COURT OF FLORIDA, SEVENTH JUDICIAL CIRCUIT IN AND FOR ST. JOHNS COUNTY

RE: St. Johns County Veterans Treatment Court

REF: CR–2017–041–SJ

WHEREAS, §§ 948.08(7) and 948.16(2), Florida Statutes, provide for the establishment of Veterans Treatment Court programs; and

WHEREAS, Veterans Treatment Courts help provide for the needs of justice-involved veterans suffering from military-related mental illnesses, traumatic brain injuries, substance abuse disorders, and/or psychological problems; and

WHEREAS, there is a recognized need for a Veterans Treatment Court program in St. Johns County;

NOW THEREFORE, I, TERENCE R. PERKINS, Chief Judge of the Seventh Judicial Circuit of Florida, hereby order the establishment of a St. Johns County Veterans Treatment Court division and program to which certain criminal cases involving military veterans meeting program eligibility criteria may be referred/assigned;

IT IS FURTHER ORDERED that a judge of the Seventh Judicial Circuit will be assigned to the St. Johns County Veterans Treatment Court division and that it will be designated as Division 27 for assignment purposes. Upon receipt of appropriate orders of the Court, the St. Johns County Clerk of Court shall assign/transfer designated cases to Division 27 (Veterans Court).

IT IS FURTHER ORDERED that the Veterans Court judge shall convene a Veterans Court Advisory Committee, comprised of relevant stakeholders and other interested parties, to advise and assist the Veterans Court Judge and Chief Judge in the operation of the St. Johns County Veterans Treatment Court program. The Veterans Court judge shall serve as chair of the advisory committee.

TO BE RECORDED in St. Johns County, Florida.

DONE AND ORDERED in Daytona Beach, Volusia County, Florida, this 30th day of June 2017.

TERENCE R. PERKINS

CHIEF JUDGE

Adopted effective June 30, 2017.

CR–2017–042–SC. DETERMINATION OF INDIGENCE IN FELONY, MISDEMEANOR AND JUVENILE DELINQUENCY CASES

IN THE CIRCUIT COURT OF FLORIDA, SEVENTH JUDICIAL CIRCUIT IN AND FOR FLAGLER, PUTNAM, ST. JOHNS AND VOLUSIA COUNTIES

RE: Determination of Indigence in Felony, Misdemeanor and Juvenile Delinquency Cases

REF: CR–2017–042–SC

WHEREAS, the Florida Legislature has placed the responsibility for determining indigence in felony, misdemeanor and juvenile delinquency cases with the Clerks of Court;

NOW THEREFORE, I, TERENCE R. PERKINS, Chief Judge of the Seventh Judicial Circuit of Florida, hereby order that indigence determinations in felony, misdemeanor and juvenile delinquency cases shall be made by the Clerks of Court in accordance with § 27.52, Florida Statutes.

IT IS FURTHER ORDERED that pursuant to § 27.52(1), F.S., judges may make preliminary indigence determinations pending further review by Clerks of Court and may appoint counsel on an interim basis. Interim judicial appointments of the Public Defender issued at First Appearance hearings, Juvenile Detention hearings, or any other court proceeding, remain in effect until the Public Defender is relieved. The filing of a Notice of Appearance by a private attorney in a case in which the Public Defender was previously appointed is sufficient evidence of said relief.

TO BE RECORDED in Flagler, Putnam, St. Johns and Volusia counties.

DONE AND ORDERED in Daytona Beach, Volusia County, Florida this 30th day of June 2017.

TERENCE R. PERKINS

CHIEF JUDGE

Adopted effective June 30, 2017.

CR–2017–043–SC. RATES OF COMPENSATION FOR COURT–APPOINTED ATTORNEYS

IN THE CIRCUIT COURT OF FLORIDA, SEVENTH JUDICIAL CIRCUIT IN AND FOR FLAGLER, ST. JOHNS, PUTNAM AND VOLUSIA COUNTIES

RE: Rates of Compensation for Court–Appointed Attorneys

REF: CR–2017–043–SC

WHEREAS, Florida Statutes require counsel be appointed to represent individuals in certain proceedings before the Court, and

WHEREAS, rates of compensation for court-appointed attorneys are contained in § 27.5304, Florida Statutes, and the General Appropriations Act;

NOW THEREFORE, I, TERENCE R. PERKINS, Chief Judge of the Seventh Judicial Circuit of Florida, hereby order that in cases in which private attorneys are appointed by the Court to represent indigent parties, the following provisions apply:

1. Attorneys are required to enter into appropriate contracts with the Justice Administrative Commission and will be compensated by the Justice Administrative Commission as outlined in § 27.5304, Florida Statutes, and the General Appropriations Act.

2. Attorneys appointed prior to July 1, 2012, or on or after July 1, 2014, may seek compensation in excess of the legislatively established fees by following the procedure set forth in § 27.5304(12)(a), Florida Statutes. Attorneys appointed between July 1, 2012 and July 1, 2014 all indicated a willingness to accept the prescribed flat fees as full payment, except for RICO and capital/death penalty cases and related appeals. Attorneys appointed between July 1, 2012 and July 1, 2014 in RICO and capital/death penalty cases, including appeals of said cases, may seek compensation in excess of established fees by following the statutory procedure.

3. Pursuant to § 27.5304(12)(b), the undersigned chief judge hereby designates Judge Leah R. Case to conduct all required evidentiary hearings in cases arising in the Seventh Judicial Circuit in which attorneys seek compensation in excess of the statutorily established fees. Motions for compensation in excess of the statutorily established fees are to be filed with the Chief Judge. Hearings on said motions will be conducted by Judge Case.

4. Attorneys are required to render legal services to his/her client from the time he/she is appointed through conclusion of the case. Attorneys will remain attorneys of record until the Court terminates jurisdiction, or until otherwise relieved from further representation by the presiding judge.

5. Attorneys are deemed to be independent contractors and are wholly responsible for the manner in which he/she performs legal services. Attorneys also assume responsibility for the acts of his/her employees as they relate to the provision of services included herein.

TO BE RECORDED in Flagler, Putnam, St. Johns and Volusia counties.

DONE AND ORDERED in Daytona Beach, Volusia County, Florida this 30th day of June 2017.

TERENCE R. PERKINS

CHIEF JUDGE

Adopted effective June 30, 2017.

CR–2017–044–SC. INDIGENT FOR COSTS DETERMINATIONS

IN THE CIRCUIT COURT OF FLORIDA, SEVENTH JUDICIAL CIRCUIT IN AND FOR FLAGLER, ST. JOHNS, PUTNAM AND VOLUSIA COUNTIES

RE: Indigent for Costs Determinations

REF: CR–2017–044–SC

WHEREAS, under certain circumstances, privately retained counsel may seek to have their clients declared indigent for purposes of having state government pay for the provision of certain due process services, and

WHEREAS, it has been determined that the establishment of a standard procedure for the consideration and disposition of these claims is in the best interest of the Seventh Judicial Circuit;

NOW THEREFORE, I, TERENCE R. PERKINS, Chief Judge of the Seventh Judicial Circuit of Florida, hereby establish the following procedure for the consideration and disposition of "indigent for costs" requests from privately retained counsel:

1. Counsel seeking to have a client declared "indigent for costs" must file a written motion and obtain hearing time from the presiding judge. The motion must contain the following information:

a. Clarification as to whether the legal services provided by counsel are pro bono, paid by the client, or paid by a third party.

b. If paid by the client or third party, the amount and justification for said fee.

c. If claim is based on fee being paid by a third party due to the client's indigence, proof that the client has completed an Indigency Affidavit and been declared indigent by the Clerk of Court's office pursuant to § 27.52, Florida Statutes.

d. If claim is based on insufficiency of client-paid fee to procure due process services, a completed Indigency Affidavit.

e. Specific due process services to be obtained, justification for said services, and costs for said services.

f. Certification that copies were provided to the State Attorney, Justice Administrative Commission, and other attorneys/parties of record.

2. Upon consideration of the motion and argument(s) of counsel, the Court's resultant order should include:

a. A statement that counsel is providing legal services to the defendant and that services are either provided pro bono or are being paid by the defendant or a third party.

b. Whether or not the defendant is deemed to be "indigent for costs."

c. If "indigent," the type and amount of due process costs approved and a statement requiring counsel to abide by the schedule of costs and fees for due process providers specified annually by the Florida Legislature in the General Appropriations Act when procuring due process services.

d. If "indigent," a statement that counsel is required to enter into an appropriate contract with the Justice Administrative Commission and that approved due process costs will be paid by the Justice Administrative Commission.

e. Certification that copies were provided to defense counsel, State Attorney, Justice Administrative Commission, and other attorneys/parties of record.

TO BE RECORDED in Flagler, Putnam, St. Johns and Volusia counties.

DONE AND ORDERED in Daytona Beach, Volusia County, Florida this 30th day of June 2017.

TERENCE R. PERKINS

CHIEF JUDGE

Adopted effective June 30, 2017.

CR–2017–045–SC. LIMITED DISCLOSURE OF SEALED OR EXPUNGED CRIMINAL RECORDS

IN THE CIRCUIT COURT OF FLORIDA, SEVENTH JUDICIAL CIRCUIT IN AND FOR FLAGLER, PUTNAM, ST. JOHNS AND VOLUSIA COUNTIES

RE: Limited Disclosure of Sealed or Expunged Criminal Records

REF: CR–2017–045–SC

WHEREAS, it has come to the attention of the undersigned that the examination of sealed or expunged court files is warranted in certain instances, and

WHEREAS, permission to examine said files has been requested by the United States Department of Defense, and

WHEREAS, obtaining information from said files for national security purposes is warranted;

NOW THEREFORE, I, TERENCE R. PERKINS, Chief Judge of the Seventh Judicial Circuit of Florida, hereby order the Clerks of Court in Flagler, Putnam, St. Johns and Volusia counties to allow authorized representatives of the United States Department of Defense to examine sealed or expunged court files upon presentation of proper departmental identification and a signed Authorization for Release of Information form in substantially the form set forth in Attachment A. A copy of such form shall be retained by the Clerk.

IT IS FURTHER ORDERED that the provisions of this order pertain only to cases wherein the entire court file has been sealed or expunged. In the event specific portions of the files have been sealed, a separate court order from the presiding judge or Chief Judge is necessary to unseal the contents of said file.

IT IS FURTHER ORDERED that upon completion of the examination of the file and/or its contents, the Clerk of Court shall reseal any information which was unsealed for purposes of said examination.

TO BE RECORDED in Flagler, Putnam, St. Johns and Volusia counties.

DONE AND ORDERED in Daytona Beach, Volusia County, Florida, this 30th day of June 2017.

TERENCE R. PERKINS

CHIEF JUDGE

Adopted effective June 30, 2017.

CR–2017–046–SC. RECORDING OF JUDGMENTS IN CRIMINAL CASES

IN THE CIRCUIT COURT OF FLORIDA, SEVENTH JUDICIAL CIRCUIT IN AND FOR FLAGLER, PUTNAM, ST. JOHNS AND VOLUSIA COUNTIES

RE: Recording of Judgments in Criminal Cases

REF: CR–2017–046–SC

WHEREAS, pursuant to § 28.246(4), Florida Statutes, the clerk of court must accept partial payments for court-imposed monetary penalties in accordance with the terms of established payment plans, and

WHEREAS, while § 939.185(1)(d), Florida Statutes, requires the clerk of court to record a certified copy of court orders imposing costs pursuant to § 939.185(1)(a), the statute makes no mention of a time frame related to the recording of said orders, and

WHEREAS, the judges of the Seventh Judicial Circuit Court have agreed that individuals who enter into payment plans with the clerks' offices and/or are given time to pay monetary obligations by the court pursuant to court order, should be afforded an opportunity to comply with said plans/orders prior to having certified copies of their judgments recorded;

NOW THEREFORE, I, TERENCE R. PERKINS, Chief Judge of the Seventh Judicial Circuit, hereby order that pursuant to § 939.185(1)(d), Florida Statutes, the clerks of court shall cause certified copies of criminal cost judgments to be recorded when defendants fail to satisfy their payment obligations as established by payment plans with the clerks or court orders. The recording of such certified copies shall not occur in instances where defendants have satisfied their payment obligations by the date(s) agreed upon in payment plans with the clerks or set forth in court orders.

TO BE RECORDED in Flagler, Putnam, St. Johns and Volusia counties.

DONE AND ORDERED in Daytona Beach, Volusia County, Florida this 30th day of June 2017.

TERENCE R. PERKINS

CHIEF JUDGE

Adopted effective June 30, 2017.

CR–2017–047–SC. FILING OF DEPOSITION TRANSCRIPTS IN CRIMINAL CASES

IN THE CIRCUIT COURT OF FLORIDA, SEVENTH JUDICIAL CIRCUIT IN AND FOR FLAGLER, ST. JOHNS, PUTNAM AND VOLUSIA COUNTIES

RE: Filing of Deposition Transcripts in Criminal Cases

REF: CR–2017–047–SC

WHEREAS, pursuant to Rule 3.190(i)(5), Florida Rules of Criminal Procedure, rules governing the filing of deposition transcripts in civil actions shall apply in criminal cases, and

WHEREAS, pursuant to Rule 1.310(f)(3), Florida Rules of Civil Procedure, deposition transcripts shall be filed with the Clerk only when the contents of the deposition must be considered by the Court in a matter pending before the Court, and

WHEREAS, limited storage space exists within the court facilities of the Seventh Judicial Circuit wherein the Clerks may reasonably and properly store and maintain deposition transcripts;

NOW THEREFORE, I, TERENCE R. PERKINS, Chief Judge of the Seventh Judicial Circuit of Florida, hereby order that original deposition transcripts in criminal cases shall be forwarded to the requesting party upon completion. It is the receiving party's responsibility to file the transcript with the Clerk if/when it is appropriate to do so.

IT IS FURTHER ORDERED that a deposition transcript shall only be filed in a criminal case if the hearing, or trial to which it relates, is scheduled to take place within 30 days of the date the transcript is filed. Pursuant to Rule 1.310(f)(3), Florida Rules of Civil Procedure, any deposition transcript submitted for filing must be accompanied by a Notice of Filing of Deposition Transcript. Said Notice must contain a certification that the deposition transcript is being filed for the purpose of being considered by the Court, in a matter pending before the Court. Furthermore, the certification must specifically identify the matter to be considered by the Court, as well as the date and time of the hearing or other such proceeding.

IT IS FURTHER ORDERED that the Clerks of Court of the Seventh Judicial Circuit shall refuse to accept for filing, and/or return, deposition transcripts in cases where no hearings are scheduled, or where hearings, or trials to which they relate, are scheduled more than 30 days from the date the transcripts are submitted for filing. The Clerks shall also refuse to accept for filing, and/or return, deposition transcripts which are not accompanied by a Notice of Filing of Deposition Transcript containing the certification as described above.

TO BE RECORDED in Flagler, Putnam, St. Johns and Volusia counties.

DONE AND ORDERED in Daytona Beach, Volusia County, Florida this 30th day of June 2017.

TERENCE R. PERKINS

CHIEF JUDGE

Adopted effective June 30, 2017.

CR–2018–048–VL. FIRST APPEARANCE DOCKET

IN THE CIRCUIT COURT OF FLORIDA, SEVENTH JUDICIAL CIRCUIT IN AND FOR VOLUSIA COUNTY

RE: First Appearance Docket

REF: CR–2018–048–VL

WHEREAS, judges conduct first appearance proceedings every day of the year, and

WHEREAS, a review of first appearance dockets has revealed that individuals routinely appear on dockets who have already had a first appearance hearing and/or are not legally required to have one, and

WHEREAS, the amount of time devoted to first appearance hearings has risen to a level whereby the undersigned finds it necessary to limit first appearance dockets by removing certain cases from it;

NOW THEREFORE, I, RAUL A. ZAMBRANO, Chief Judge of the Seventh Judicial Circuit of Florida, hereby order that effective December 3, 2018, individuals incarcerated solely for the following reasons are to no longer be placed on First Appearance dockets, provided that is the only reason for his/her incarceration:

1. **Bond surrenders**—Cases in which a defendant has previously been released from incarceration by virtue of a surety bond subsequent to first appearance, and the bondsman decides to curtail the contractual relationship and "surrenders" the defendant to the jail. Unless the judge to whom the case is assigned has entered an order revoking the defendant's release, the bond amount originally set upon the defendant's arrest, or at first appearance following arrest, is to be reinstated.

2. **Bond revocations**—Cases in which a defendant has previously been released from incarceration by virtue of posting a bond or through any other means, and the judge to whom the case is assigned enters an order revoking the defendant's release.

3. **Parole Violators**—Cases in which a defendant is awaiting a hearing on a violation of parole or other form of release from state prison.

4. **Contempt of Court hearings for Baker or Marchman Acts**—Cases in which an individual is incarcerated on a civil contempt of court warrant pursuant to Chapters 394 and 397, Florida Statutes. In these instances, upon such an individual's entry into the jail, booking personnel are to promptly notify Clerk of Court personnel, who are to then schedule the case for hearing before the judge to whom the case is assigned. The affected individual is to be transported forthwith to the judge to whom the case is assigned for a hearing on the civil contempt of court.

5. **Treatment court sanction warrants**—Cases in which a defendant/participant in a treatment court program (Drug Court, DUI Court, Veterans' Court) has received a short jail sentence as a sanction, provided that the length of incarceration is clearly stated on the warrant and language such as "COURT SANCTION: NO FIRST APPEARANCE NECESSARY" appears on the warrant. In instances in which a treatment court defendant has absconded from supervision and is booked into jail on a "NO BOND" warrant, booking personnel are to promptly notify Clerk of Court personnel, who are to then schedule the case for hearing before the judge to whom the case is assigned. The defendant is to be transported forthwith to the judge to whom the case is assigned for a hearing on the warrant.

6. **Writs of Bodily Attachment**—Cases in which an individual is incarcerated on a civil contempt of court warrant for failure to pay child support pursuant to Rule 12.615, Florida Family Law Rules of Procedure. In instances in which an individual is booked into jail on a warrant issued by a judge in a Volusia County case, booking personnel are to promptly notify Clerk of Court personnel, who are to then schedule the case for a hearing before a magistrate, hearing officer, or judge within 48 hours. If the individual does not post the cash bond purge amount prior to his/her hearing, he/she is to be transported forthwith for a hearing on the civil contempt of court warrant.

In instances in which an individual is booked into jail on a warrant issued by a judge in a case outside of Volusia County, booking personnel are to promptly notify personnel in the originating county of the execution of the warrant. If the individual has no outstanding local charges, or, after the local charges have been resolved, the individual is to be released on his/her own recognizance without further order of the Court if the originating county does not appear to retrieve the individual within 48 hours of being notified.

TO BE RECORDED in Volusia County, Florida.

DONE AND ORDERED in DeLand, Volusia County, Florida this 6th day of October 2018.

RAUL A. ZAMBRANO
CHIEF JUDGE

Adopted effective December 3, 2018.

Probate/Guardianship Orders

PB–2000–001–SC. CODIFICATION OF ADMINISTRATIVE ORDERS IN THE PROBATE/ GUARDIANSHIP/MENTAL HEALTH DIVISION

IN THE CIRCUIT COURT OF FLORIDA, SEVENTH JUDICIAL CIRCUIT IN AND FOR FLAGLER, PUTNAM, ST. JOHNS AND VOLUSIA COUNTIES

PB–2000–001–SC

RE: Codification of Administrative Orders in the Probate/Guardianship/ Mental Health Division

WHEREAS, it has been made known to the undersigned that the codification of Probate/Guardianship/Mental Health Administrative Orders in the Seventh Judicial Circuit is necessary for the efficient and proper administration of justice,

NOW, THEREFORE, I, ROBERT K. ROUSE, JR. Chief Judge of the Seventh Judicial Circuit, hereby order the codification of all Administrative Orders in the Probate/ Guardianship/Mental Health Division of the Seventh Judicial Circuit.

IT IS FURTHER ORDERED that said administrative orders shall be numbered for reference in the following manner:

Subject—Year—Numerical Order—Circuit/County
[i.e. PB-2000-001-SC (Seventh Circuit)]
[PB-2000-001-VL (Volusia County)]

IT IS FURTHER ORDERED that all administrative orders related to the administration of Probate/Guardianship/Mental Health matters issued prior to the date of this order are hereby rescinded.

TO BE RECORDED in Flagler, Putnam, St. Johns and Volusia Counties.

DONE AND ORDERED at Daytona Beach, Volusia County, Florida this 4th day of October, 2000.

ROBERT K. ROUSE, JR.
CHIEF JUDGE

Adopted effective October 4, 2000.

PB-2000-002-SC. ASSIGNMENT OF COMPANION CASES IN GUARDIANSHIP MATTERS

IN THE CIRCUIT COURT OF FLORIDA, SEVENTH JUDICIAL CIRCUIT IN AND FOR FLAGLER, PUTNAM, ST. JOHNS AND VOLUSIA COUNTIES

PB 2000-002 SC

RE: Assignment Of Companion Cases In Guardianship Matters

WHEREAS, it has been made known to the undersigned that the efficient and proper administration of justice requires the issuance of an Administrative Order regarding the assignment of companion cases in guardianship matters;

NOW THEREFORE, I, ROBERT K. ROUSE, JR. Chief Judge of the Seventh Judicial Circuit, hereby order the Clerks of Court in the Counties of Flagler, Putnam, St. Johns, and Volusia to assign companion cases in guardianship matters involving spouses, children and siblings to the division to which the original guardianship case is assigned. The Clerks of Court in the respective counties are further ordered to track said assignments to ensure an equal number of case assignments to those divisions designated to handle guardianship matters.

TO BE RECORDED in Flagler, Putnam, St. Johns and Volusia Counties.

DONE AND ORDERED at Daytona Beach, Volusia County, Florida this 4TH day of October, 2000.

ROBERT K. ROUSE, JR.
CHIEF JUDGE

Adopted effective October 4, 2000.

PB-2005-003-SC. INITIAL GUARDIANSHIP PLAN PHYSICIAN'S REPORT

IN THE CIRCUIT COURT OF FLORIDA, SEVENTH JUDICIAL CIRCUIT IN AND FOR FLAGLER, PUTNAM, ST. JOHNS AND VOLUSIA COUNTIES

PB 2005-003 SC (Rescinds PB-2000-003-SC)

RE: INITIAL GUARDIANSHIP PLAN PHYSICIAN'S REPORT

WHEREAS, § 744.363 (1)(e), Florida Statutes, requires physical and mental examinations necessary to determine the ward's medical and mental health treatment needs be included in initial guardianship plans, and

WHEREAS, the judges of the Seventh Judicial Circuit Court have determined that a physician's report should accompany the initial guardianship plan for purposes of determining the physical/medical status of the prospective ward;

NOW, THEREFORE, I, WILLIAM A. PARSONS, Chief Judge of the Seventh Judicial Circuit of Florida, hereby order that except in cases wherein guardianship of the property of a minor is sought, all initial guardianship plans filed in the Seventh Judicial Circuit shall be accompanied by a physician's report to aid the court in determining the physical/medical status of the prospective ward.

IT IS FURTHER ORDERED that Administrative Order # PB-2000-003-SC is hereby rescinded.

Nothing in this Order shall prohibit judges from waiving the requirements of this Order in individual cases.

TO BE RECORDED in Flagler, Putnam, St. Johns and Volusia Counties.

DONE AND ORDERED in Daytona Beach, Volusia County, FL this 30th day of September 2005.

WILLIAM A. PARSONS
CHIEF JUDGE

Amended effective September 30, 2005.

PB-2000-005-SC. RECORDING DEATH CERTIFICATES

IN THE CIRCUIT COURT OF FLORIDA, SEVENTH JUDICIAL CIRCUIT IN AND FOR FLAGLER, PUTNAM, ST. JOHNS AND VOLUSIA COUNTIES

PB 2000-005 SC

RE: RECORDING DEATH CERTIFICATES

WHEREAS, pursuant to Section 382.008(6), Florida Statutes, the cause of death section of all death and fetal death records is confidential and exempt from the provisions of § 119.07(1), Florida Statutes, except under limited circumstances, and

WHEREAS, Attorney General's opinion 92-24, dated March 20, 1992, addressed to the attorney for the Clerk of the Circuit Court of Polk County states "Absent statutory authority or judicial direction, the clerk of court may not accept and record death certificates into the official public records", and

WHEREAS, the practice of recording a certified copy of a death certificate has long been utilized in Florida for both probate and real property matters; in particular, the recording of a certified copy of the death certificate of the deceased title holder has been recognized as the method for terminating a life estate in real property, vesting title in a surviving spouse to real property held as tenants by the entireties or vesting title to real property in the co-owners of real property held as joint tenants with rights of survivorship;

NOW THEREFORE, I, ROBERT K. ROUSE, JR., Chief Judge of the Seventh Judicial Circuit, hereby order that the Clerks of the Circuit Court of the Seventh Judicial Circuit are hereby authorized and directed to record certified copies of death certificates which are presented for recordation. If the certified copy of the death certificate contains information deemed confidential under § 382.008, Florida Statutes, the filing party or clerk shall conceal the cause-of-death section of the death certification prior to its recordation with a slip of paper stating "This section is deleted per F. S. 382.008".

The Clerks of Court may refuse to record a certified copy of a death certificate if the information deemed confidential by § 382.008, Florida Statutes, is not covered and concealed as required herein.

TO BE RECORDED in Flagler, Putnam, St. Johns and Volusia Counties.

DONE AND ORDERED at Daytona Beach, Volusia County, Florida this 4th day of October, 2000.

ROBERT K. ROUSE, JR.
CHIEF JUDGE

Adopted effective October 4, 2000.

PB–2011–006–SC. GUARDIANSHIP EDUCATION REQUIREMENTS

IN THE CIRCUIT COURT OF FLORIDA, SEVENTH JUDICIAL CIRCUIT IN AND FOR FLAGLER, PUTNAM, ST. JOHNS AND VOLUSIA COUNTIES

RE: GUARDIANSHIP EDUCATION REQUIREMENTS

REF: PB–2011–006–SC (Rescinds PB–2000–006–SC)

WHEREAS, § 744.3145(2), Florida Statutes, requires individuals appointed by the court to serve as guardians (except parents serving as guardians of the property of their minor children) to receive at least 8 hours of instruction and training, and

WHEREAS, § 744.3145(3), Florida Statutes, requires individuals appointed by the court to serve as guardians of the property of their minor children to receive at least 4 hours of instruction and training, and

WHEREAS, § 744.3145(4), Florida Statutes, requires the aforementioned instruction and training to be completed through a course approved by the Chief Judge of the circuit court and taught by a court-approved organization;

NOW THEREFORE, I, WILLIAM A. PARSONS, Chief Judge of the Seventh Judicial Circuit of Florida, hereby order that courses provided and taught by the following organizations are approved for use in the Seventh Judicial Circuit:

- Daytona State College
Institute for Health Services
P.O. Box 2811
1200 W. International Speedway Blvd.
Daytona Beach, FL 32120–2811
(386) 506–3522

- Cathedral Foundation of Jacksonville
4250 Lakeside Drive, Suite 300
Jacksonville, FL 32210
(904) 807–1252

IT IS FURTHER ORDERED that the provisions of this Order do not apply to professional guardians.

IT IS FURTHER ORDERED that Administrative Order PB–2000–006–SC is hereby rescinded.

TO BE RECORDED in Flagler, Putnam, St. Johns and Volusia counties.

DONE AND ORDERED in Daytona Beach, Volusia County, Florida this 19th day of September 2011.

Judge William A. Parsons
CHIEF JUDGE

Amended effective September 19, 2011.

PB–2016–007–SC. PROFESSIONAL GUARDIANSHIP EDUCATION

RE: PROFESSIONAL GUARDIANSHIP EDUCATION

REF: PB–2016–007–SC

Rescinds PB–2011–07–SC

WHEREAS,"Professional Guardian" is defined in § 744.102(17), Florida Statutes, and

WHEREAS, § 744.2003(3), Florida Statutes, requires professional guardians to receive a minimum of 40 hours of initial instruction and training and a minimum of 16 hours of continuing education every 2 years thereafter, and

WHEREAS, the aforementioned education and training must be completed through courses approved or offered by the Office of Public and Professional Guardians,

WHEREAS, § 744.2003(6), Florida Statutes, requires professional guardians to demonstrate their competency by taking and passing an examination approved by the Department of Elderly Affairs, and

WHEREAS, § 744.2003(8), Florida Statutes, requires that the Department of Elderly Affairs waive the aforementioned examination requirement provided certain criteria are met;

NOW THEREFORE, I, TERENCE R. PERKINS, Chief Judge of the Seventh Judicial Circuit of Florida, hereby order that pursuant to § 744.2003(9), Florida Statutes, judges may not appoint individuals to serve as professional guardians who have not met the requirements of this Order and §§ 744.2002 & 744.2003, Florida Statutes.

TO BE RECORDED in Flagler, Putnam, St. Johns and Volusia counties.

DONE AND ORDERED at Daytona Beach, Volusia County, Florida this 30th day of September 2016.

TERENCE R. PERKINS
CHIEF JUDGE

Amended effective September 30, 2016.

PB–2016–008–SC. GUARDIANSHIP BLANKET BONDS

RE: GUARDIANSHIP BLANKET BONDS

REF: PB–2016–008–SC

Rescinds PB–2000–08–SC

WHEREAS, it has been made known to the undersigned that pursuant to § 744.2003(2), Florida Statutes, blanket fiduciary bonds must be filed by professional guardians with the Clerks of the Circuit Court, in the respective counties of the Seventh Judicial Circuit, and

WHEREAS, the court has been advised that the Clerks of Court in the Seventh Judicial Circuit have means to file, document and inform the Court of guardians who have met legal requirements and filed said blanket fiduciary bonds;

NOW THEREFORE, I, TERENCE R. PERKINS, Chief Judge of the Seventh Judicial Circuit of Florida, hereby order as follows:

1. All professional guardians in the Seventh Judicial Circuit shall file an original blanket fiduciary bond with the Clerk of Court in the county in which the guardian's primary place of business is held.

2. A certified copy of said bond, signed by the Clerk of Court of the county in which the guardian's primary place of business is located, shall be filed by professional guardians with all other Clerk's offices in counties wherein the guardian conducts business.

3. Annually, each professional guardian shall provide evidence that said bond remains in full force and effect.

4. The Clerks of Court shall request a blanket fiduciary bond or certified copy of a blanket fiduciary bond to be filed from any guardian who is appointed to represent more than two wards to who he/she is not related.

TO BE RECORDED in Flagler, Putnam, St. Johns and Volusia counties.

DONE AND ORDERED at Daytona Beach, Volusia County, Florida this 30th day of September 2016.

TERENCE R. PERKINS
CHIEF JUDGE

Amended effective September 30, 2016.

PB–2000–009–SC. PROFESSIONAL GUARDIAN CREDIT REPORTS

IN THE CIRCUIT COURT OF FLORIDA, SEVENTH JUDICIAL CIRCUIT IN AND FOR FLAGLER, PUTNAM, ST. JOHNS AND VOLUSIA COUNTIES

PB–2000–009–SC

RE: PROFESSIONAL GUARDIAN CREDIT REPORTS

WHEREAS, pursuant to § 744.3135, Florida Statutes, professional guardians are required to submit to an investigation of his/her credit history, and

WHEREAS, the Court must consider the results of said investigations when appointing guardians, and

WHEREAS, the results of said investigations are filed with the Clerks' Offices and are therefore open to public inspection, and

WHEREAS, certain information contained in said investigations, primarily, credit card numbers and other account numbers, should not be open to public inspection;

NOW THEREFORE, I, Robert K. Rouse, Jr., Chief Judge of the Seventh Judicial Circuit of Florida, after consultation with the circuit judges of the Seventh Judicial Circuit, hereby order that the Clerks of Court of the counties of Flagler, Putnam, St. Johns and Volusia are directed to redact credit card numbers and other account numbers contained in credit investigation reports filed pursuant to § 744.3135, Florida Statutes.

TO BE RECORDED in Flagler, Putnam, St. Johns and Volusia Counties, FL.

DONE AND ORDERED in Daytona Beach, Volusia County, FL this 4th day of October, 2000.

ROBERT K. ROUSE, JR.
CHIEF JUDGE

Adopted effective October 4, 2000.

PB–2017–010–SC. GUARDIAN ADVOCATE TRAINING—BAKER ACT/MARCHMAN ACT

IN THE CIRCUIT COURT OF FLORIDA, SEVENTH JUDICIAL CIRCUIT IN AND FOR FLAGLER, PUTNAM, ST. JOHNS AND VOLUSIA COUNTIES

RE: Guardian Advocate Training—Baker Act/Marchman Act

REF: PB–2017–010–SC

(Rescinds PB–2011–010–SC)

WHEREAS, pursuant to §§ 394.4598(4) and 397.6978(4), Florida Statutes, individuals appointed to serve as guardian advocates must attend a training course approved by the court prior to exercising authority, and

WHEREAS, the Department of Children and Families is responsible for developing the referenced training courses for prospective guardian advocates, and

WHEREAS, such training courses must be approved by the Chief Judge and taught by a court-approved organization;

NOW, THEREFORE, I, RAUL A. ZAMBRANO, Chief Judge of the Seventh Judicial Circuit, hereby order as follows:

1. The on-line training courses developed by the Department of Children and Families, in conjunction with the Florida Certification Board (FCB) (see http://fcbonlineed.mrooms3.net) are hereby approved for use in the Seventh Judicial Circuit. The Seventh Judicial Circuit will also recognize courses approved by other judicial circuits and taught by organizations authorized by other judicial circuits.

2. It is the responsibility of each guardian advocate to ensure that he/she receives a Certificate of Completion upon achieving a passing grade on the training course examination. Said certificate must be made available to the Court upon request.

IT IS FURTHER ORDERED that Administrative Order PB–2011–010–SC is hereby rescinded.

TO BE RECORDED in Flagler, Putnam, St. Johns and Volusia Counties.

DONE AND ORDERED at Daytona Beach, Volusia County, Florida this 4th day of October, 2000.[1]

RAUL A. ZAMBRANO
CHIEF JUDGE

Amended effective September 19, 2011; August 29, 2017.

[1] Should read: August 29, 2017

PB–2011–011–SC. SEALING CONFIDENTIAL PORTIONS OF COURT FILES IN BAKER ACT PROCEEDINGS

IN THE CIRCUIT COURT OF FLORIDA, SEVENTH JUDICIAL CIRCUIT IN AND FOR FLAGLER, PUTNAM, ST. JOHNS AND VOLUSIA COUNTIES

RE: Sealing Confidential Portions Of Court Files In Baker Act Proceedings

REF: PB–2011–011–SC (Rescinds PB–2000–011–SC)

WHEREAS, § 394.4615, Florida Statutes, provides that a clinical record of a patient treated pursuant to the Baker Act is confidential and exempt from the provisions of § 119.07(1), Florida Statutes relating to public records, and

WHEREAS, § 394.455(3), Florida Statutes, defines "clinical record" as all parts of the record required to be maintained and includes all medical records, progress notes, charts, and admission and discharge data, and all other information recorded by a facility which pertains to the patient's hospitalization and treatment, and

WHEREAS, § 394.467(2), Florida Statutes, provides that a patient may be retained by a receiving facility or involuntarily placed in a treatment facility upon the recommendation of the administrator of the receiving facility where the patient has been examined and after adherence to the notice and hearing procedures provided for in § 394.4599, Florida Statutes, and

WHEREAS, such recommendations must be supported by the opinion of a psychiatrist and the second opinion of a clinical psychologist or another psychiatrist that the criteria for involuntary placement are met, and

WHEREAS, these recommendations are part of the patient's clinical record and become part of the court file, and

WHEREAS, during hearings required for involuntary placement, the clerk routinely transcribes portions of the testimony, including information contained in the clinical record, on the hearing sheets which are made part of the court file, and

WHEREAS, hearings required for involuntary placement, including information contained in the clinical record, are reported/recorded and sometimes transcribed, and

WHEREAS, § 394.467(6)(a)2, Florida Statutes, provides that reports of any independent experts who examine the patient shall be confidential;

NOW, THEREFORE, I, WILLIAM A. PARSONS, Chief Judge of the Seventh Judicial Circuit, hereby order as follows:

1. The Clerk of Court shall seal the following portions of a court file in a Baker Act proceeding:

A. The clinical record or chart of the patient, or any portion thereof which is made a part of the court file;

B. The report of any expert examiner appointed by the Court to examine the patient, or of any expert who examines the patient at the patient's request;

C. The clerk's notes with respect to any hearing regarding the involuntary placement of the patient or matters pertaining thereto;

D. Any transcript or portion of any transcript of proceedings which is contained in the court file.

2. Unless specifically ordered to do so, the Clerk of Court shall **not** seal the ex parte order for involuntary examination or any subsequent order, including but not limited to, orders requiring involuntary placement of a patient in a receiving or treatment facility and order for discharge from involuntary treatment.

3. Any clerk or court administration employee or contractor who records/reports any hearing held pursuant to the Baker Act shall treat verbatim records of the proceedings as confidential and shall only disclose or provide transcripts, recordings or notes of the proceedings to the patient, the patient's guardian, the patient's attorney, or upon order of the Court

IT IS FURTHER ORDERED that Administrative Order PB–2000–011–SC is hereby rescinded.

TO BE RECORDED in Flagler, Putnam, St. Johns and Volusia counties.

DONE AND ORDERED in Daytona Beach, Volusia County, FL this 19th day of September 2011.

Judge William A. Parsons
CHIEF JUDGE

Amended effective September 19, 2011.

PB–2000–012–SC. APPOINTMENT OF PUBLIC DEFENDER IN BAKER ACT PROCEEDINGS

IN THE CIRCUIT COURT OF FLORIDA, SEVENTH JUDICIAL CIRCUIT IN AND FOR FLAGLER, PUTNAM, ST. JOHNS AND VOLUSIA COUNTIES

PB 2000–012 SC

RE: Appointment of Public Defender in Baker Act Proceedings

WHEREAS, § 394.467(4), Florida Statutes, requires the appointment of the public defender to represent a person who is the subject of a petition for involuntary placement within one (1) working day after the filing of the petition, unless the person is otherwise represented by counsel, and

WHEREAS, it has been determined that the issuance of an administrative order covering all such cases would be more efficient than issuing individual orders of appointment in each applicable case,

NOW THEREFORE, I, ROBERT K. ROUSE, JR., Chief Judge of the Seventh Judicial Circuit, hereby order the appointment of the Public Defender of the Seventh Judicial Circuit of Florida to represent persons who are the subjects of petitions for involuntary placement filed in the Seventh Judicial Circuit pursuant to § 349.467(4), Florida Statutes. The Public Defender shall not be appointed in those cases where the subjects are represented by private counsel. The Clerk of Court shall notify the Public Defender of all cases in which the office is appointed pursuant to the terms of this order.

TO BE RECORDED in Flagler, Putnam, St. Johns and Volusia Counties.

DONE AND ORDERED at Daytona Beach, Volusia County, Florida this 4th day of October, 2000.

ROBERT K. ROUSE, JR.
CHIEF JUDGE

Adopted effective October 4, 2000.

PB–2000–013–SC. CROSS ASSIGNMENT/BAKER ACTS

IN THE CIRCUIT COURT OF FLORIDA, SEVENTH JUDICIAL CIRCUIT IN AND FOR FLAGLER, PUTNAM, ST. JOHNS AND VOLUSIA COUNTIES

PB–2000–013–SC

RE: CROSS ASSIGNMENT/BAKER ACTS

WHEREAS, § 394.455, (7) Florida Statutes, defines "court" as circuit court, and

WHEREAS, County Court judges in the Seventh Judicial Circuit may be called upon to preside at hearings or issue orders related to Ch. 394 (Part I), Florida Statutes, otherwise known as the Baker Act, and

WHEREAS, it has been made known to the undersigned that the efficient and proper administration of justice regarding Baker Acts requires the temporary assignment of County Court judges in the Seventh Judicial Circuit to Circuit Court jurisdiction;

NOW THEREFORE, I, ROBERT K. ROUSE, JR., Chief Judge of the Seventh Judicial Circuit hereby order that all County Court judges of the Seventh Judicial Circuit are temporarily assigned to Circuit Court jurisdiction for purposes of handling matters related to the Baker Act. The County Court judges herein assigned to Circuit Court are hereby vested with all and singular the powers and prerogatives conferred by the State of Florida upon a judge of the Court to which they are assigned.

TO BE RECORDED in Flagler, Putnam, St. Johns and Volusia Counties.

DONE AND ORDERED in Daytona Beach, Volusia County, Florida, this 4th day of October, 2000.

ROBERT K. ROUSE, JR.
CHIEF JUDGE

Adopted effective October 4, 2000.

PB–2000–014–VL. PROBATE FILES

IN THE CIRCUIT COURT OF FLORIDA, SEVENTH JUDICIAL CIRCUIT IN AND FOR VOLUSIA COUNTY

PB 2000–014 VL

RE: PROBATE FILES

WHEREAS, the Supreme Court of Florida has adopted Rule 2.085, Florida Rules of Judicial Administration, setting case time standards and requiring the trial courts to take charge of all cases in order to monitor and control the pace of litigation, and

WHEREAS, it appears from the court records that there are estate files in Volusia County which have not been concluded within the time standards as set forth in Rule 2.085, Florida Rules of Judicial Administration and

WHEREAS, the duties and responsibilities of the Clerk of the Circuit Court are not clearly defined with regard to monitoring these files and keeping judges informed as to which cases exceed the time standards,

NOW, THEREFORE, I, ROBERT K. ROUSE, JR, Chief Judge of the Seventh Judicial Circuit, hereby direct the clerk as follows:

1. The Office of the Clerk of the Circuit Court of Volusia County, shall review all estate files to determine if these cases have been concluded within the case time standards. In performing the review, if the clerk finds that a case has not been concluded within the time standards, the attached "ORDER TO FILE DOCUMENTS" shall be submitted to the assigned judge for his/her consideration.

2. If the personal representative or attorney fail to comply with the ORDER TO FILE DOCUMENTS, the clerk shall forward the attached "ORDER TO SHOW CAUSE" to the assigned judge for his/her consideration.

3. Nothing in this order requires any judge to use the forms submitted by the clerk or prevents any judge from entering such other orders as may be appropriate.

TO BE RECORDED in Volusia County, Florida.

DONE AND ORDERED at Daytona Beach, Volusia County, Florida this 4th day of October, 2000.

ROBERT K. ROUSE, JR.
CHIEF JUDGE

IN THE CIRCUIT COURT, SEVENTH JUDICIAL CIRCUIT IN AND FOR VOLUSIA COUNTY, FLORIDA, PROBATE DIVISION

RE: Estate of
, Deceased

File No:
Division:

TO:

ORDER TO FILE DOCUMENTS

THIS CAUSE came before the Court on its own motion and the Court finding from an examination of the file and records that this file exceeds the time standards for closing, it is therefore,

ORDERED AND ADJUDGED that ___, the personal representative and ___, the attorney of record, are hereby required to IMMEDIATELY FILE the documents necessary to close this estate or submit a petition and proposed order extending time stating with particularity the status of the estate, why it is not ready to be closed, and when it will be ready to close, within 30 days of this order.

Failure to file these documents within the thirty (30) days specified may result in an ORDER TO SHOW CAUSE why the Court should not remove the personal representative or impose appropriate sanctions against the personal representative or attorney, or both.

DONE AND ORDERED in chambers at, Florida this ___ day of ________, 2001.

tmp

____
Circuit Judge

I HEREBY CERTIFY that a copy of this Order has been furnished by U. S. Mail to the parties listed on this ___ day of _________, 2001.

DIANE M. MATOUSEK
Clerk of Circuit Court
By: _________
Deputy Clerk

19-0367-9204

IN THE CIRCUIT COURT, SEVENTH JUDICIAL CIRCUIT IN AND FOR VOLUSIA COUNTY, FLORIDA, PROBATE DIVISION

IN RE: Estate of CASE NO:
DIVISION:

TO:

ORDER TO SHOW CAUSE

THIS CAUSE came before the Court on its own motion and the Court finding from an examination of the file that this matter has been pending beyond the time permitted by F.S. 733.901(1), and the time standards set forth in Fla. Rules of Judicial Administration 2.085, and that the Court has ordered the filing of all documents necessary to close this estate and that a Petition Extending Time to Close this Estate has not been granted by this Court, or the time granted in the extension has now run, it is therefore,

ORDERED AND ADJUDGED that, the personal representative and attorney of record, are hereby required to appear before this court in chambers, at the following date, time and location:

DATE: TIME:
LOCATION:

and show cause why this court should not remove the personal representative for failure to file required documents.

This hearing may not be canceled or continued without order of this Court or the entry of an Order of Discharge.

DONE AND ORDERED in chambers at DeLand, Florida this ___ day of _________, 2001.

tmp

____
Circuit Judge

I HEREBY CERTIFY that a copy of this Order has been furnished by U.S. Mail to the parties listed on this ___ day of _________, 2001.

DIANE M. MATOUSEK
Clerk of Circuit Court
By: _________
Deputy Clerk

ATTENTION PERSONS WITH DISABILITIES—If you are a person with a disability who needs any accommodation in order to participate in this proceeding, you are entitled, at no cost to you, to the provision of certain assistance. Please contact **Court Administration, at Suite 201, Courthouse Annex, 125 E. Orange Avenue, Daytona Beach, FL 32114; Telephone: 904-257-6096** within two (2) working days of your receipt of this Order to Show Cause. **If you are hearing or voice impaired, call 1-800-955-8771. THIS IS NOT A COURT INFORMATION LINE.**

Adopted effective October 4, 2000.

PB-2005-015-SC. FORMS FOR BAKER ACT PROCEEDINGS

IN THE CIRCUIT COURT OF FLORIDA, SEVENTH JUDICIAL CIRCUIT IN AND FOR FLAGLER, PUTNAM, ST. JOHNS AND VOLUSIA COUNTIES

PB-2005-015-SC (Rescinds PB-2000-015-VL)

RE: FORMS FOR BAKER ACT PROCEEDINGS

WHEREAS, it has been made known to the undersigned that the adoption of standardized forms for Baker Act proceedings is in the best interest of the Seventh Judicial Circuit, and

WHEREAS, the standardized forms for Baker Act proceedings have recently been revised;

NOW THEREFORE, I, JULIANNE PIGGOTTE, Chief Judge of the Seventh Judicial Circuit of Florida, hereby order the adoption and use of the forms attached hereto for Baker Act proceedings in the Seventh Judicial Circuit of Florida until further order.

IT IS FURTHER ORDERED that Administrative Order # PB-2000-015-VL is hereby rescinded.

Nothing in this Order shall prohibit judges from modifying or deviating from the attached "form" orders in individual cases, or as circumstances warrant.

TO BE RECORDED in Flagler, Putnam, St. Johns and Volusia counties.

DONE AND ORDERED in Daytona Beach, Volusia County, Florida this 17th day of March 2005

Judge Julianne Piggotte
CHIEF JUDGE

IN THE CIRCUIT COURT OF FLORIDA, SEVENTH JUDICIAL CIRCUIT IN AND FOR FLAGLER, PUTNAM, ST. JOHNS AND VOLUSIA COUNTIES

IN RE:

_________/

ORDER FOR DISCHARGE OF PATIENT FROM INVOLUNTARY TREATMENT

THIS MATTER was heard pursuant to Chapter 394, Florida Statutes, on the issue of whether the above-named person should be involuntarily placed or retained in a mental health treatment or receiving facility for involuntary treatment for mental illness, and the Court being fully advised in the premises, finds as follows:

1. The petition for involuntary placement was previously filed in this cause and hearing was conducted.

2. The above-named person is presently located in the County of ________.

3. The above-named person does not meet the criteria for involuntary placement as set forth in Section 394.467(1), Florida Statutes. This finding is determined from the evidence presented, including the testimony of ______________.

On the basis of the above findings, it is, hereby

ORDERED that the above-named person be discharged this date from any involuntary detention or involuntary treatment for mental illness pursuant to Chapter 394, Florida Statutes.

DONE AND ORDERED in ________ County, Florida, this ___ day of ________, 20 ___.

________________	________________
Printed Name of Circuit Court Judge	Signature of Circuit Court Judge

IN THE CIRCUIT COURT, SEVENTH JUDICIAL CIRCUIT, IN AND FOR ________ COUNTY, FLORIDA

CASE NO.:

IN RE:

________________/

ORDER FOR INVOLUNTARY PLACEMENT/RETENTION, AND SCHEDULING REHEARING

THIS MATTER came to be heard pursuant to Chapter 394, Florida Statutes, on the issue of whether the above-named person should be involuntarily placed in a mental health treatment or receiving facility, and the Court being advised in the premises, finds as follows:

1. The petition for involuntary placement was filed in this cause on ________, 20 ___. Written notice of the filing of the petition was given as required by Section 394.4599.

2. The above-named person is presently located in the County of ________.

3. The above-named person was represented at the hearing by privately retained counsel or by the public defender.

4. The above-named person presently meets the criteria for involuntary placement as set forth in Section 394.467(1), Florida Statutes. This finding is determined from clear and convincing evidence, including the testimony of ______. The nature and extent of the mental illness is specified as follows:

____

____

____

____

5. The above-named person is in need of continued treatment or services from the facility where the patient now resides; said person may, in the near future, require treatment in a different facility, or no longer meet criteria for involuntary placement.

6. All available treatment alternatives which are less restrictive than that ordered hereinbelow have been judged to be inappropriate.

Whereupon, it is

ORDERED as follows:

1. The above-named person shall be involuntarily retained at the facility wherein said person is presently located and residing.

2. If said person has not been discharged by the administrator of the said facility or transferred to voluntary status, then rehearing and reconsideration of this matter will take place and is scheduled on ________, 20 ___.

DONE AND ORDERED in ________ County, Florida this ___ day of ________, 20 ___.

____

Circuit Court Judge

IN THE CIRCUIT COURT, SEVENTH JUDICIAL CIRCUIT IN AND FOR ________ COUNTY, FLORIDA

IN RE: ____________ CASE NO.: ____________

________________/

Order for Involuntary Inpatient Placement

This matter came to be heard pursuant to the Petition for Involuntary Placement filed herein on the issue of whether the above-named person should be involuntarily placed in a mental health treatment or receiving facility, and the Court being fully advised in the premises, finds by clear and convincing evidence as follows:

1. The above-named person has been represented by counsel; said person appeared at the hearing, or said presence at the hearing was waived, without objection of said person's counsel.

2. Said person meets the following criteria for involuntary placement pursuant to s.394.467(1), F.S.:

(a) He or she is mentally ill and because of his or her mental illness:

(1) has refused voluntary placement for treatment after sufficient and conscientious explanation and disclosure of the purpose of placement for treatment; or

(2) is unable to determine for himself or herself whether placement is necessary, **AND**

(b) Either

(1) He or she is manifestly incapable of surviving alone or with the help of willing and responsible family or friends, including available alternative services, and, without treatment, is likely to suffer from neglect or refuse to care for himself or herself, and such neglect or refusal poses a real and present threat of substantial harm to his or her well-being; or

(2) There is substantial likelihood that in the near future he or she will inflict serious bodily harm on himself or herself or another person, as evidenced by recent behavior causing, attempting, or threatening such harm; and

(c) All available less restrictive treatment alternatives which would offer an opportunity for improvement of his or her condition have been judged to be inappropriate.

3. The nature and extent of the above-named person's mental illness is as follows: ______________________

4. The Court considered testimony and evidence regarding the patient's competence to consent to treatment. The patient was found to be ________ competent, ________ incompetent to consent to treatment. If found to be incompetent, a guardian advocate is appointed by separate order.

Whereupon, it is

ORDERED that the above-named person be placed in a designated mental health receiving or treatment facility on an involuntary basis for a period not to exceed 6 months from the date of this order, or until discharged by the administrator or transferred to voluntary status.

DONE AND ORDERED in ________ County, Florida, this ___ day of ________, 20 ___.

______________________	______________________
Printed Name of Circuit Court Judge	Signature of Circuit Court Judge

This order must accompany patient to the treatment facility.

IN THE CIRCUIT COURT OF THE SEVENTH JUDICIAL CIRCUIT IN AND FOR ________ COUNTY, FLORIDA

IN RE: ____________ CASE NO.: ____________

______________/

ORDER FOR INVOLUNTARY OUTPATIENT PLACEMENT OR CONTINUED INVOLUNTARY OUTPATIENT PLACEMENT

This matter came to be heard pursuant to s.394.4655, F.S., and on ________ Petition for Involuntary Outpatient Placement or, ________ Petition for Continued Involuntary Outpatient Placement, and the Court being fully advised in the premises, finds by clear and convincing evidence as follows:

1. The above-named person has been represented by counsel; said person ________ appeared at the hearing, or ________ presence at the hearing was waived, without objection of said person's counsel.

2. The above-named person meets the following criteria for involuntary outpatient placement pursuant to s.394.4655(1), F.S.: the person is 18 years of age or older; has a mental illness; is unlikely to survive safely in the community without supervision, based on a clinical determination; and, has a history of lack of compliance with treatment for a mental illness.

3. The above-named person has: (not applicable to **continued** involuntary outpatient placement)

________ A. At least twice within the immediately preceding 36 months been involuntarily admitted to a receiving or treatment facility as defined in s.394.455, or has received mental health services in a forensic or correctional facility; **or**

________ B. Engaged in one or more acts of serious violent behavior toward self or others, or attempts at serious bodily harm to self or others, within the preceding 36 months.

4. The above-named person is, as result of mental illness, unlikely to voluntarily participate in the recommended treatment plan and has refused voluntary placement for treatment after sufficient and conscientious explanation and disclosure of the purpose of placement for treatment, or is unable to determine whether placement is necessary.

5. The above-named person's treatment history and current behavior mandates the conclusion that the person is in need of involuntary outpatient placement in order to prevent a relapse or deterioration that would be likely to result in serious bodily harm to the person or others, or a substantial harm to his or her well-being through neglect or refusal to care for self as set forth in s.394.463 (1), F.S.

6. It is likely that the above-named person will benefit from involuntary outpatient placement. All available less restrictive treatment alternatives which would offer an opportunity for improvement of said person's condition are inappropriate.

7. The treatment plan which is attached hereto specifies the nature and extent of the above-named person's mental illness and specifies the outpatient treatment to be provided. The treatment plan contains a certification to the court that sufficient services for improvement and stabilization are currently available, funded, and that the service provider agrees to provide those services.

8. The services described in the treatment plan are clinically appropriate. This finding is supported by evidence presented, including the testimony of ____________.

9. The Court considered testimony and evidence regarding the above-named person's competence to consent to treatment. The person is found to be ________ competent, ________ incompetent to consent to treatment. If found to be incompetent, a guardian advocate is appointed by separate order.

10. If the petition was referred to and heard by a Magistrate, the Magistrate's Report and Recommendation are attached, incorporated by reference, and adopted by the Court.

Whereupon, IT IS ORDERED that the above-named person be treated as an outpatient in accordance with the treatment plan attached hereto, for a period not to exceed 6 months from the date of this order, or until discharged by the administrator or transferred to voluntary status.

DONE AND ORDERED in ________ County, Florida, this ___ day of ________, 20 ___.

______________________	______________________
Printed Name of Circuit Court Judge	Signature of Circuit Court Judge

IN THE CIRCUIT COURT OF THE SEVENTH JUDICIAL CIRCUIT IN AND FOR ________ COUNTY, FLORIDA

IN RE: ____________ CASE NO.: ____________

______________/

Order Appointing Guardian Advocate

This matter came to be heard on the issue of whether the above-named person should be adjudicated incompetent to consent to treatment, and the Court finds by clear and convincing evidence as follows:

1. Said person has been represented by counsel.

2. Said person is not presently adjudicated incapacitated with a duly appointed guardian with authority to consent to treatment.

3. Said person meets the definition for being incompetent to consent to treatment pursuant to Section 394.455(15), Florida Statutes. The court has considered testimony and other evidence regarding said person's competence to consent to treatment and based on such testimony and evidence has concluded that said person is not competent to consent to treatment.

On the basis of these findings, it is

ORDERED:

1. That the above-named person presently within the county, is incompetent to consent to treatment because his/her judgment is so affected by mental illness that he/she lacks the capacity to make a well-reasoned, willful, and knowing decision concerning his or her medical and/or mental health treatment.

2. ________, whose relationship to the patient is:

___ Health Care Surrogate ___ Person's Spouse ___ Person's Adult Child

___ Person's Parent ___ Person's Adult Next of Kin ___ Person's Adult Friend

___ Adult trained and willing to serve

and who has agreed to serve as guardian advocate, is appointed as guardian advocate, to act on the above-named person's behalf to give express and informed consent, refuse consent, or revoke consent for ________ mental health treatment ________ medical treatment.

3. The guardian advocate:

a. Will obtain from the facility sufficient information in order to decide whether to give express and informed consent to the treatment, including information that the treatment is essential to the care of the 7, and that the treatment does not present an unreasonable risk of serious, hazardous, or irreversible side effects.

b. Has agreed to meet and talk to the person and the person's physician in person, and by telephone if not, before giving consent to treatment.

c. Has completed or will undergo and complete a training course approved by this Court prior to exercising this authority, unless waived by this Court.

d. Will be provided access to the appropriate clinical records of the person.

4. The guardian advocate may not consent to abortion, sterilization, electroconvulsive treatment, psychosurgery, or experimental treatments except upon express Court approval by separate order after further hearing.

This appointment as guardian advocate shall terminate upon the discharge of the person from the receiving or treatment facility or the transfer of the person to voluntary status, or an order of the court restoring the person's competence.

DONE AND ORDERED in ________ County, Florida, this ___ day of ________, 20___.

________________________ ________________________

Printed Name of Circuit Court Judge — Signature of Circuit Court Judge

cc: ___ Above–named Person ___ Guardian Advocate ___ Representative ___ Facility Administrator

IN THE CIRCUIT COURT OF THE SEVENTH JUDICIAL CIRCUIT IN AND FOR ________ COUNTY, FLORIDA

IN RE: ________ CASE NO.: ________

________/

Order Authorizing Guardian Advocate to Consent to Extraordinary Treatment

This matter came to be heard on the issue of whether ________, guardian advocate for the above-named person who is involuntarily placed, should be given express court approval for extraordinary treatment. Upon the evidence presented, the Court finds as follows:

1. The guardian advocate was appointed for the above-named person by order previously entered in this cause after an earlier hearing.

2. The person has been represented by counsel.

3. The treatment or procedure approved herein is essential to the care of the person and the treatment does not present an unreasonable risk of serious, hazardous, or irreversible side effects.

On the basis of these findings, it is

ORDERED that the above-named guardian advocate for the above-named person, presently within the county, is authorized to provide consent for: ________

ORDERED in ________ County, Florida, this ___ day of ________, 20___.

____

Printed Name of Circuit Court Judge — Signature of Circuit Court Judge

Individual	Date Copy Provided (mm/dd/yyyy)	Time Copy Provided	Initial of Who Provided Copy
Patient		am pm	
Guardian Advocate		am pm	
Facility Administrator		am pm	

IN THE CIRCUIT COURT, SEVENTH JUDICIAL CIRCUIT IN AND FOR ________ COUNTY, FLORIDA

IN RE: ________ **CASE NO.:** ________

________/

ORDER FOR EVALUATION FOR INVOLUNTARY OUTPATIENT PLACEMENT

THIS MATTER came to be heard on ________, pursuant to s. 394.467, F.S., on petition for involuntary inpatient placement of the above-named person, and the court being advised in the premises, finds as follows:

1. The above-named person does not meet the criteria for involuntary inpatient placement in a mental health treatment or receiving facility.

2. The above-named person is 18 years of age or older, has a mental illness, and has a history of lack of compliance with treatment for mental illness.

3. The above-named person is unlikely to survive safely in the community without supervision; this finding is support by

testimony of ________________ as to his/her clinical determination.

4. The above-named person has:

A. At least twice within the preceding 36 months been involuntarily admitted to a receiving or treatment facility as defined in s.394.455, or received mental health services in a forensic or correctional facility, **or**

B. Engaged in or attempted to engage in one or more acts of serious violent behavior toward self or others within the preceding 36 months.

5. The above-named person is, as a result of mental illness, unlikely to voluntarily participate in recommended treatment and has either refused voluntary placement for recommended treatment after sufficient and conscientious explanation and disclosure of the purpose of placement, or is unable to determine whether placement is necessary.

6. In view of the person's treatment history and current behavior, the person is in need of involuntary outpatient placement in order to prevent a relapse or deterioration that would be likely to result in serious bodily harm to the person or others, or a substantial harm to the person's well-being through neglect or refusal to care for self as set forth in s. 394.463(1);

7. It is likely that the person will benefit from involuntary outpatient placement. All available less restrictive alternatives that would offer an opportunity for improvement of his or her condition are either inappropriate or unavailable.

Whereupon, IT IS ORDERED

1. That the above-named person be discharged this date from any involuntary **inpatient** placement and treatment for mental illness.

2. That the above-named person shall be evaluated by __________ located at ________________ for involuntary **outpatient** placement within ___ days of the date of this hearing.

DONE AND ORDERED in Chambers in ________ County, Florida, this ___ day of ________, 20 ___.

____________________	____________________
Printed Name of Circuit Court Judge	Circuit Court Judge

IN THE CIRCUIT COURT, SEVENTH JUDICIAL CIRCUIT IN AND FOR ________ COUNTY, FLORIDA

IN RE: **CASE NO.:**

____________________/

ORDER FOR DISCHARGE FROM INVOLUNTARY INPATIENT TREATMENT AND FOR INVOLUNTARY OUTPATIENT PLACEMENT

THIS MATTER came to be heard pursuant to s. 394.467, F.S., on petition for involuntary placement of the above-named person for treatment as an inpatient, and the court being advised in the premises, finds as follows:

1. The above-named person does not meet the criteria for involuntary inpatient placement in a mental health treatment or receiving facility.

2. The above-named person waived notice of the filing of a petition for involuntary placement for treatment as an outpatient, and notice of hearing on said petition. The petition seeking involuntary outpatient treatment, with attached treatment plan, has been filed in the record of this action.

3. The above-named person is 18 years of age or older, has a mental illness, and has a history of lack of compliance with treatment for mental illness.

4. The above-named person is unlikely to survive safely in the community without supervision; this finding is supported by testimony of ________________ as to his/her clinical determination.

5. The above-named person has:

___ A. At least twice within the preceding 36 months been involuntarily admitted to a receiving or treatment facility as defined in s.394.455, or received mental health services in a forensic or correctional facility, or

___ B. Engaged in or attempted to engage in one or more acts of serious violent behavior toward self or others within the preceding 36 months.

6. The above-named person is, as a result of mental illness, unlikely to voluntarily participate in recommended treatment and has either refused voluntary placement for recommended treatment after sufficient and conscientious explanation and disclosure of the purpose of placement, or is unable to determine whether placement is necessary.

7. In view of the person's treatment history and current behavior, the person is in need of involuntary outpatient placement in order to prevent a relapse or deterioration that would be likely to result in serious bodily harm to the person or others, or a substantial harm to the person's well-being through neglect or refusal to care for self as set forth in s. 394.463(1);

8. It is likely that the person will benefit from involuntary outpatient placement. All available less restrictive alternatives that would offer an opportunity for improvement of his or her condition are either inappropriate or unavailable.

Whereupon, IT IS ORDERED

1. That the above-named person be discharged this date from any involuntary inpatient placement and inpatient treatment for mental illness.

2. That the above-named person be treated as an outpatient in accordance with the treatment plan attached hereto, for a period __________ not to exceed 6 months from the date of this order, or __________, or until discharged by the administrator or transferred to voluntary status.

DONE AND ORDERED in Chambers at ________ County, Florida, this ___ day of ________, 20 ___.

____________________	____________________
Printed Name of Circuit Court Judge	Signature of Circuit Court Judge

IN THE CIRCUIT COURT, SEVENTH JUDICIAL CIRCUIT IN AND FOR ________ COUNTY, FLORIDA

IN RE: ____________ CASE NO.: ____________

____________________/

Order Requiring Involuntary Assessment and Stabilization for Substance Abuse and for Baker Act Discharge of Person

THIS MATTER came to be heard pursuant to Section.394.467, F.S., on the issue of whether the above-named person should be involuntarily placed in a mental health receiving or treatment facility, and the court having considered testimony and evidence and having heard the argument of counsel, has concluded as follows

1. The above-named person does not meet the criteria for involuntary placement in a treatment facility pursuant to the provisions of Chapter 394, Florida Statutes

2. There is a good faith reason to believe that the above-named person is substance abuse impaired, and, because of such impairment, has lost the power of self-control with respect to substance abuse, and

___ has inflicted, or threatened or attempted to inflict, or unless admitted to involuntary treatment for substance abuse is likely to inflict physical harm on himself or herself or another.

___ is in need of substance abuse services, and, by reason of substance abuse impairment, has such impaired judgment that said person is incapable of appreciating his or her need for such services and of making a rational decision in regard thereto.

3. The above-named person should be admitted to a hospital or to a licensed detoxification facility or addictions receiving facility for involuntary assessment and, if necessary, stabilization, pursuant to Section. 394.467(6) and Section.397.6811, Florida Statutes.

4. The admission ordered herein below is the least restrictive appropriate alternative for the assessment and stabilization of the above-named person who may be substance abuse impaired.

Whereupon, it is

ORDERED

___ That the above-named person shall be discharged this date from any involuntary detention or treatment for mental illness pursuant to Chapter 394, Florida Statutes.

___ That the above-named person shall be admitted on __________ for a period not to exceed 5 days to ____________________ for substance abuse involuntary assessment and, if necessary, stabilization.

___ shall take the above-named person into custody and deliver said person to the licensed service provider specified above, or, if none is specified, to the nearest appropriate licensed service provider for involuntary assessment.

___ The Public Defender is discharged as counsel for the above-name person.

DONE AND ORDERED in __________ County, Florida, this ___ day of __________, 20 ___.

____________________	____________________
Printed Name of Circuit Court Judge	Signature of Circuit Court Judge

IN THE CIRCUIT COURT OF THE SEVENTH JUDICIAL CIRCUIT IN AND FOR __________ COUNTY, FLORIDA

IN RE: CASE NO.:

____________________/

ORDER APPOINTING INDEPENDENT EXPERT EXAMINER

THIS MATTER came to be heard pursuant to Section 394.467(6), Florida Statutes, in which the above-named person seeks the services of a court appointed independent expert, and it being determined by the Court that said person is unable to afford the services of such independent expert, it is, therefore

ORDERED as follows:

1. __________, act as an independent expert to examine the patient for the purpose of determining whether the patient meets the criteria for involuntary placement pursuant to Section 394.467, Florida Statutes.

2. That said person to be examined is presently in __________ and that an examination by said independent expert shall be conducted and results provided to the attorney of record prior to the hearing on involuntary placement, presently scheduled for the ___ day of __________, 20 ___.

3. Said independent expert's report shall be confidential and not discoverable, unless said expert is to be called as a witness for the patient at the hearing. A COPY SHALL BE SENT ONLY TO THE ATTORNEY for the above-named person.

4. Said independent expert shall be compensated by the Office of the Public Defender, in such reasonable amount as established by the Office of the Public Defender.

DONE AND ORDERED in __________ County, Florida, this ___ day of __________, 20 ___.

____________________	
Typed or Printed Name of Circuit Court Judge	Signature of Circuit Court Judge

IN THE CIRCUIT COURT OF THE SEVENTH JUDICIAL CIRCUIT IN AND FOR __________ COUNTY, FLORIDA

IN RE: CASE NO.:

____________________/

Ex Parte Order for Involuntary Examination

THIS MATTER having been considered by the Court pursuant to section 394.463(2)(a)1, Florida Statutes, and the Court having received sworn testimony, finds that the above-named person, presently within the county, appears to meeting the following criteria for involuntary examination:

1. There is reason to believe the above-named person has a mental illness as defined in Section 394.455(18), F.S., and because of this mental illness said person:

___ (a) has refused voluntary examination after conscientious explanation and disclosure of the purpose of the examination; **or**

___ (b) is unable to determine for himself/herself whether examination is necessary, **AND**

2. Either (Check a or b)

___ (a) Without care or treatment the above-named person is likely to suffer from neglect or refuse to care for himself/herself, and such neglect or refusal poses a real and present threat of substantial harm to his or her well-being and it is not apparent that such harm may be avoided through the help of willing family members or friends or the provision of other services; **OR**

___ (b) There is substantial likelihood that without care or treatment the above-named person will cause serious bodily harm to ___ himself or herself or ___ another person in the near future, as evidence by recent behavior.

One or more Petitions or Affidavits Seeking Order Requiring Involuntary Examination (CF–MH 3002 or equivalent) on which the above conclusion is based is attached.

3. Additional information, if any, upon which this order is based is as follows: ___________

____

Therefore, it is

ORDERED

That a law enforcement officer, or designated agent of the Court take the above-named person into custody and deliver or arrange for the delivery of said person to the **nearest** receiving facility for involuntary examination, and that this order and petition be made part of said person's clinical record. A law enforcement officer or agent may serve and execute this order on any day of the week, at any time of the day or night. A law enforcement officer or agent may use such reasonable physical force as is necessary to gain entry to the premises, and any dwellings, buildings, or other structures located on the premises, and to take custody of the person who is the subject of this ex parte order.

This order expires in _____ days. If no time limit is specified in this order, the order shall be valid for seven (7) days after the date that the order was signed.

ORDERED in __________ County, Florida, this ___ day of ________, 20 ___.

______________________	______________________
Typed or Printed Name of Circuit Court Judge	Signature of Circuit Court Judge

IN THE CIRCUIT COURT, SEVENTH JUDICIAL CIRCUIT IN AND FOR ________ COUNTY, FLORIDA

IN RE: ____________ CASE NO.: __________

____________/

Ex Parte Order Denying Involuntary Examination

This court, having reviewed the sworn petition for involuntary examination, finds that the above named person does not appear to meet the statutory criteria for involuntary examination. Whereupon,

IT IS ADJUDGED that the petition for involuntary examination is hereby denied.

DONE AND ORDERED in Chambers in ________ County, Florida, this ___ day of ________, 20 ___.

______________________	______________________
Printed Name of Circuit Court Judge	Signature of Circuit Court Judge

IN THE CIRCUIT COURT, SEVENTH JUDICIAL CIRCUIT IN AND FOR ________ COUNTY, FLORIDA

IN RE: ____________ CASE NO.: __________

____________/

ORDER FOR INVOLUNTARY EXAMINATION

Pursuant to Section 394.463, Florida Statutes, this Court, having received sworn testimony and/or personally observed the above-named person, states that the above-named person, presently within the county:

1. Appears to meet the following criteria for involuntary examination:

A. There is reason to believe the above-named person is mentally ill, and because of this mental illness said person is unable to determine for himself/herself whether examination is necessary AND

B. Either (Check (1) or (2))

___ (1) without care or treatment the above-named person is likely to suffer from neglect or refuse to care for himself/herself, and such neglect or refusal poses a real and present threat of substantial harm to his or her well-being and it is not apparent that such harm may be avoided through the help of willing family members or friends or the provision of other services; **OR**

___ (2) there is substantial likelihood that without care or treatment the above-named person will cause serious bodily harm to himself or herself or another person in the near future, as evidenced by recent behavior.

(applicable only if initialed by judge)

___ 2. Is presently committed to the custody of the Department of Corrections of the County of ________, Florida should not be permitted to be at liberty, and should be returned to the custody of the Department of Corrections upon discharge from any receiving or treatment facility.

____

Therefore, it is

ORDERED:

___ 1. That a law enforcement officer, or designated agent of the Court take the above-named person into custody and deliver or arrange for the delivery of said person to the nearest receiving facility for involuntary examination pursuant to Chapter 394, and that this order be made part of said person's clinical record. Said law enforcement officer or agent may use such reasonable physical force as is necessary to take custody of and to deliver the person who is subject of this order.

(applicable only if initialed by judge)

___ 2. At such time as it appears that it is appropriate that the above-named person be discharged from involuntary examination and treatment pursuant to Chapter 394, F.S., the facility shall, before any discharge, give reasonable notice to the undersigned judge, to the Department of Corrections, and to the Sheriff of ________ County, and shall discharge said person only to the custody of the Department or the Sheriff.

ORDERED THIS ___ day of ________, 20 ___.

______________________	______________________
Printed Name of Circuit Court Judge	Signature of Circuit Court Judge

IN THE CIRCUIT COURT, SEVENTH JUDICIAL CIRCUIT IN AND FOR ________ COUNTY, FLORIDA

IN RE: ____________ CASE NO.: ____________

____________/

ORDER FOR INVOLUNTARY EXAMINATION OF CHILD

Pursuant to Sections 394.463, 985.224, and Chapter 39, Florida Statutes, this Court, having received sworn testimony and/or personally observed the above-named person, a minor child, states that the above-named person, presently within the county

1. Appears to meet the following criteria for involuntary examination:

A. There is reason to believe the above-named person is mentally ill, and because of this mental illness said person is unable to determine for himself/herself whether examination is necessary AND

B. Either (Check (1) or (2))

___ (1) without care or treatment the above-named person is likely to suffer from neglect or refuse to care for himself/herself, and such neglect or refusal poses a real and present threat of substantial harm to his or her well-being and it is not apparent that such harm may be avoided through the help of willing family members or friends or the provision of other services: OR

___ (2) there is substantial likelihood that without care or treatment the above-named person will cause serious bodily harm to himself or herself or another person in the near future, as evidenced by recent behavior.

applicable only if initialed by judge)

___ 2. Is presently committed to the custody of the Department of Juvenile Justice of the State of Florida, should not be permitted to be at liberty, and should be returned to the custody of the Department of Juvenile Justice upon discharge from any receiving or treatment facility.

___ 3. Is presently subject to a shelter order or has been placed into foster care pursuant to court order.

Therefore, it is

ORDERED:

___ 1. That a law enforcement officer, or designated agent of the Court take the above-named person into custody and deliver or arrange for the delivery of said person to Halifax Behavioral Services, 841 Jimmy Ann Drive, Daytona Beach, Florida, a receiving facility, or, if not available, to Halifax Medical Center, for involuntary examination pursuant to Chapter 394, and that this order be made part of said person's clinical record. Said law enforcement officer or agent may use such reasonable physical force as is necessary to take custody of and to deliver the person who is the subject of this order.

(applicable only if initialed by judge)

___ 2. At such time as it appears that it is appropriate that the above-named person be discharged from involuntary examination and treatment pursuant to Chapter 394, F.S., the facility shall, before any discharge, give reasonable notice to the undersigned judge, to the Department of Juvenile Justice, and to the Sheriff of ________ County, and shall discharge said person only to the custody of the Department which shall provide secure transportation immediately upon such notification.

___ 3. At such time as it appears that it is appropriate that the above-named person be discharged from involuntary examination and treatment pursuant to Chapter 394, F.S., the facility shall, before any discharge, give reasonable notice to the undersigned judge, to the Department of Children and Families, and shall discharge said person only to the custody of the Department of Children and Families, which shall provide secure transportation immediately upon such notification.

ORDERED THIS ___ day of ________, 20 ___.

____________	____________
Printed Name of Circuit Court Judge	Signature of Circuit Court Judge

IN THE CIRCUIT COURT, SEVENTH JUDICIAL CIRCUIT IN AND FOR ________ COUNTY, FLORIDA

IN RE: ____________ CASE NO.: ____________

____________/

ORDER DISMISSING ACTION — BAKER ACT

THIS CAUSE having come before the Court on a Petition for Involuntary Placement, pursuant to Chapter 394, Florida Statutes, and the Court being fully advised in the premises, finds and orders as follows:

1. ____________

2. This action should be dismissed.

Whereupon, it is

ORDERED that the above described Petition, and this action, be and the same are DISMISSED.

DONE AND ORDERED in ________ County, Florida, this ___ day of ________, 20 ___.

____________	____________
Printed Name of Circuit Court Judge	Signature of Circuit Court Judge

IN THE CIRCUIT COURT, SEVENTH JUDICIAL CIRCUIT IN AND FOR ________ COUNTY, FLORIDA

IN RE: ____________ CASE NO.: ____________

____________/

WRIT OF HABEAS CORPUS AND ORDER TO SHOW CAUSE (ORDER SCHEDULING HEARING)

THIS MATTER came to be considered by the court on the Petition for Writ of Habeas Corpus filed by or on behalf of the above-named person on ________, ___. The said petition seeks release from actual and involuntary restraint and custody. The court has reviewed the petition, which appears to make a prima facie showing that the above-named person has been unlawfully deprived of liberty without probable cause. Whereupon,

IT IS ORDERED that the administrator of the facility in which the above-named person is detained is directed to bring the above-named person before the court on the ___ day of ________, ___, at ___ (am)(pm), at the Baker Act hearing held at the ________, ________, ________, Florida, to show cause why the petition should not be granted.

DONE AND ORDERED in Chambers, in ________ County, Florida, this ___ day of ________, 20___.

________________ ________________
Printed Name of Circuit Court Judge   Signature of Circuit Court Judge

IN THE CIRCUIT COURT, SEVENTH JUDICIAL CIRCUIT IN AND FOR ________ COUNTY, FLORIDA

IN RE: ________ CASE NO.: ________
________/

ORDER DISMISSING PETITION FOR WRIT OF HABEAS CORPUS

THIS MATTER came to be considered by the court on the Petition for Writ of Habeas Corpus filed by or on behalf of the above-named person on ________, 20___. The court has carefully reviewed the petition, and has concluded that the petition fails to show that the above-named person has been unlawfully deprived of liberty without probable cause. Whereupon,

IT IS ADJUDGED that the Petition for Writ of Habeas Corpus is DISMISSED.

DONE AND ORDERED in Chambers, in ________ County, Florida this ___ day of ________, 20___

________________ ________________
Printed Name of Circuit Court Judge   Signature of Circuit Court Judge

IN THE CIRCUIT COURT, SEVENTH JUDICIAL CIRCUIT IN AND FOR ________ COUNTY, FLORIDA

IN RE: ________ CASE NO.: ________
________/

ORDER DENYING PETITION FOR WRIT OF HABEAS CORPUS AND REMANDING TO CUSTODY

THIS CAUSE came to be heard on the Petition for Writ of Habeas Corpus filed by or on behalf of the above-named person. On the evidence presented,

IT IS ADJUDGED that the above-named person is not unlawfully detained, and that the Petition for Writ of Habeas Corpus is hereby DENIED. Petitioner is, therefore, remanded to the custody of the administrator of the facility where the above-named person is presently detained.

DONE AND ORDERED in Chamber in ________ County, Florida, this ___ day of ________, 20___.

________________ ________________
Printed Name of Circuit Court Judge   Signature of Circuit Court Judge

Amended effective March 17, 2005.

PB–2005–016–SC. FORMS FOR MARCHMAN ACT PROCEEDINGS

IN THE CIRCUIT COURT OF FLORIDA, SEVENTH JUDICIAL CIRCUIT IN AND FOR FLAGLER, PUTNAM, ST. JOHNS AND VOLUSIA COUNTIES

PB–2005–016 SC (Rescinds PB–2002–018–VL)

RE: FORMS FOR MARCHMAN ACT PROCEEDINGS

WHEREAS, it has been made known to the undersigned that the adoption of standardized forms for Marchman Act proceedings is in the best interest of the Seventh Judicial Circuit, and

WHEREAS, the standardized forms for Marchman Act proceedings have recently been revised;

NOW THEREFORE, I, JULIANNE PIGGOTTE, Chief Judge of the Seventh Judicial Circuit of Florida, hereby order the adoption and use of the forms attached hereto for Marchman Act proceedings in the Seventh Judicial Circuit of Florida until further order.

IT IS FURTHER ORDERED that Administrative Order # PB–2002–018–VL is hereby rescinded.

Nothing in this Order shall prohibit judges from modifying or deviating from the attached "form" orders in individual cases, or as circumstances warrant.

TO BE RECORDED in Flagler, Putnam, St. Johns and Volusia counties.

DONE AND ORDERED in Daytona Beach, Volusia County, Florida this 17th day of March 2005.

JULIANNE PIGGOTTE
CHIEF JUDGE

IN THE CIRCUIT COURT, SEVENTH JUDICIAL CIRCUIT IN AND FOR ________ COUNTY, FLORIDA

IN RE: ________ CASE NO.: ________
________/

Ex Parte Order for Involuntary Assessment and/or Stabilization—Marchman Act for Adult

THIS MATTER having been considered by the Court, pursuant to Sections 397.6811 and 397.6815, Florida Statutes, and upon a sworn petition for involuntary assessment and/or stabilization, the Court finds as follows:

1. A sworn petition has been filed with the clerk of the circuit court in the county where the above-named person is located. The petition was executed by the above-named person's relative, guardian, a "private practitioner" as defined (including physician), the director or director's designee of a licensed service provider, or three adults with personal knowledge of the above named person's impairment and condition.

2. The above-named person meets the criteria for involuntary admission, because there is good faith reason to believe that said person is substance abuse impaired, and, because of such impairment, has lost the power of self control with respect to substance abuse; and either

___ (a) has inflicted, threatened or attempted to inflict, or unless admitted is likely to inflict physical harm on himself/herself or another **or**

___ (b) is in need of substance abuse services, and, by reason of substance abuse impairment, is incapable of appreciating the need for such services and of making a rational decision in regard thereto.

Whereupon, it is

ORDERED

That the Sheriff of ________ County or other law enforcement officer shall take the above-named person into custody and deliver or arrange for the delivery of said person to ________, or, if for reasons provided in s.397.6751 (including but not limited to client's behavior being beyond safe management capability), the treatment provider cannot admit the client to its facility, then to the nearest appropriate licensed receiving facility (including hospitals), for the purpose of stabilization and/or involuntary assessment of an adult pursuant to the provisions of Florida Statutes Chapter 397. If a petition for treatment is thereafter timely initiated and filed, the above-named person may be detained at said facility until further order of Court. Said law enforcement officer or agent may serve and execute this order on any day of the week, at any time of the day or night, and may use such reasonable physical force as is necessary to gain entry to the premises, and any dwellings, buildings, or other structures located on the premises, and to take custody of the person who is the subject of this ex parte order.

This order is in full effect and force for a period not to exceed 5 days from the date of entry.

ORDERED in ________ County, Florida this ___ day of ________, 20 ___.

________________________ ________________________

Printed Name of Circuit Court Judge Signature of Circuit Court Judge

IN THE CIRCUIT COURT, SEVENTH JUDICIAL CIRCUIT IN AND FOR ________ COUNTY, FLORIDA

IN RE: ____________ CASE NO.: ____________

____________/

Ex Parte Order for Involuntary Assessment and/or Stabilization—Marchman Act for Adolescent

THIS MATTER having been considered by the Court, pursuant to Sections 397.6811 and 397.6815, Florida Statutes, and upon a sworn petition for the stabilization and/or involuntary assessment of an adolescent, the Court finds as follows:

1. A sworn petition has been filed with the clerk of the circuit court in the county where the above-named person is located. The petition was executed by the above-named person's parent, legal guardian, legal custodian, or a licensed service provider.

2. The above-named person meets the criteria for involuntary admission, because there is good faith reason to believe that said person is substance abuse impaired, and, because of such impairment, has lost the power of self-control with respect to substance abuse; and either

___ (a) Has inflicted, threatened or attempted to inflict, or unless admitted is likely to inflict physical harm on himself/herself or another OR

___ (b) is in need of substance abuse services, and, by reason of substance abuse impairment, is incapable of appreciating the need for such services and of making a rational decision in regard thereto.

Whereupon, it is ORDERED

That the Sheriff of ________ County, or other law enforcement officer, shall take the above-named person into custody and deliver said person to ________________, Florida. Upon receiving medical clearance at this facility, the facility will make arrangements for transfer to ________________ or another appropriate provider, or, if for reasons provided in s. 397.6751 (including but not limited to client's behavior being beyond safe management capability), the treatment provider cannot admit the client to its facility, then to the nearest appropriate licensed receiving facility (including hospitals), for the purpose of stabilization and/or involuntary assessment of an adolescent pursuant to the provisions of Florida Statutes Chapter 397. Said law enforcement officer or agent may serve and execute this order on any day of the week, at any time of the day or night, and may use such reasonable physical force as is necessary to gain entry to the premises, and any dwellings, buildings, or other structures located on the premises, and to take custody of the person who is the subject of this ex parte order.

This order is in full effect and force for a period not to exceed 5 days from the date of entry.

ORDERED in ________ County, Florida this ___ day of ________, 20 ___.

________________________ ________________________

Printed Name of Circuit Court Judge Signature of Circuit Court Judge

IN THE CIRCUIT COURT, SEVENTH JUDICIAL CIRCUIT, IN AND FOR ________ COUNTY, FLORIDA

IN RE: ____________ CASE NO.: ____________

____________/

Order To Appear at Hearing, and Denying Ex Parte Assessment/Stabilization (Marchman Act)

THIS MATTER came to be considered pursuant to sections 397.6811, 397.6814 and 397.6815, Florida Statutes, upon a petition for ex parte order authorizing the involuntary assessment and/or stabilization of the above-named person. The Court, having considered the petition, finds as follows

1. An ex parte order directing a law enforcement officer to take the above-named person into custody and deliver said person to the nearest appropriate licensed service provider should not be entered at this time, because:

___ The petition does not demonstrate that the above-named person meets the criteria for involuntary admission set forth in section 397.675, Florida Statutes.

___ The petition is not shown to have been executed by a relative, guardian, "private practitioner" as defined (including physician or licensed psychologist), the director or director's designee of a licensed service provider, or three adults with personal knowledge of the person's situation.

___ Other, ________________________________

Whereupon,

It is ORDERED that:

___ No ex parte order requiring stabilization and/or assessment shall be entered at this time; any request for such order is DENIED.

___ Hearing will be scheduled and will be conducted within 10 days hereof.

___ Hearing on this matter, and specifically on the issue of whether the above-named person should be stabilized and/or assessed, shall be conducted at ___ a.m./p.m., on _________ at _________________, Florida.

___ A copy of the petition and this order shall be provided to the above-named person and his/her attorney, if known. The above-named person shall be summoned to appear and is hereby ORDERED TO APPEAR at said hearing. A copy of this order shall be served on the petitioner(s), and the above-named person's spouse or guardian, if known, and the parent(s) if the above-named person is a minor.

ORDERED in _________ County, Florida, this ___ day of ________, 20___.

______________________	______________________
Printed Name of Circuit Court Judge	Signature of Circuit Court Judge

FAILURE TO APPEAR AT THE SCHEDULED HEARING WILL RESULT IN ACTION BY THE COURT WHICH MAY INCLUDE A CONTEMPT PROCEEDING RESULTING IN INCARCERATION AND OTHER SANCTIONS.

IN THE CIRCUIT COURT, SEVENTH JUDICIAL CIRCUIT, IN AND FOR _________ COUNTY, FLORIDA

IN RE: _____________ CASE NO.: _____________

_________________/

Order for Involuntary Assessment and /or Stabilization—Marchman Act

THIS CAUSE came to be heard by the Court pursuant to Chapter 397, Florida Statutes, upon a petition for court-ordered involuntary assessment and/or stabilization. The Court, being fully advised in the premises, finds as follows:

1. The petition was executed by a relative, guardian, "private practitioner" as defined (including physician), the director or director's designee of a licensed service provider, or three adults with personal knowledge of the above-named person's impairment and condition.

2. The above-named person, having been duly and properly summoned, did appear at the hearing.

___ Said person was represented by counsel **[or]**

___ The appointment of counsel was not deemed appropriate, or was waived.

3. The above-named person meets the criteria for involuntary admission for assessment and/or stabilization pursuant to section 397.675, and 397.6811, Florida Statutes.:

There is good faith reason to believe that the person is substance abuse impaired, and, because of such impairment, has lost the power of self-control with respect to substance abuse; and either

___ (a) has inflicted, threatened or attempted to inflict, or unless admitted is likely to inflict physical harm on himself/herself or another, **or**

___ (b) is in need of substance abuse services and, by reason of substance abuse impairment, is incapable of appreciating the need for such services and of making a rational decision in regard thereto.

4. The nature and extent of the alleged or existing substance use/abuse is briefly summarized as follows: _________

5. Less restrictive alternatives with respect to stabilization and/or assessment than are ordered herein below have been considered and are judged to be inappropriate.

Whereupon, it is

ORDERED

___ The above-named person shall appear and undergo an assessment and/or stabilization at _________ on _________, or, if for reasons provided in s.397.6751 (including but not limited to client's behavior being beyond safe management capability) the treatment provider cannot admit the client to its facility, then at the nearest appropriate licensed receiving facility (including hospitals), for involuntary assessment and/or stabilization for a period not to exceed 5 days.

___ The Sheriff of _________ County, or other law enforcement officer, shall take the above-named person into custody and shall immediately deliver him/her to _________, or, if for reasons provided in s.397.6751 (including but not limited to client's behavior being beyond safe management capability) the treatment provider cannot admit the client to its facility, then to the nearest appropriate licensed receiving facility (including hospitals), for involuntary assessment and/or stabilization for a period of up to 5 days. This section of the order shall expire in 7 days.

ORDERED in _________ County, Florida this ___ day of ________, 20___.

______________________	______________________
Printed Name of Circuit Court Judge	Signature of Circuit Court Judge

FAILURE TO COMPLY WITH THIS ORDER WILL RESULT IN CONSIDERATION AND ACTION BY THE CIRCUIT COURT, WHICH MAY INCLUDE A CONTEMPT PROCEEDING. CONTEMPT OF COURT MAY RESULT IN INCARCERATION, A FINE, AND OTHER SANCTIONS.

IN THE CIRCUIT COURT, SEVENTH JUDICIAL CIRCUIT, IN AND FOR _________ COUNTY, FLORIDA

IN RE: _____________ CASE NO.: _____________

_________________/

Order for Involuntary Treatment—Marchman Act

THIS CAUSE came to be heard by the Court, pursuant to Chapter 397, Florida Statutes, upon a petition for court-ordered involuntary treatment for substance abuse. The Court, being fully advised in the premises, finds as follows:

1. The petition was executed by a relative, guardian, "private practitioner" as defined (including physician), the director or director's designee of a licensed service provider, or three adults with personal knowledge of the above-named person's impairment and condition.

2. The above-named person, having been duly and properly summoned, did appear at the hearing.

___ Said person was represented by counsel **[or]**

___ The appointment of counsel was not deemed appropriate, or was waived.

3. The above-named person meets the criteria for involuntary treatment for substance abuse, in that there is clear and convincing evidence that the above-named person is substance abuse impaired, and because of such impairment has lost the power of self-control with respect to substance abuse, and either

1. Has inflicted or is likely to inflict physical harm on himself/herself or others unless involuntarily treated; or

2. The refusal to voluntarily receive treatment is based on judgment so impaired by reason of substance abuse that the above-named person is incapable of appreciating the need for care and treatment and of making a rational decision regarding that need.

4. The nature and extent of the substance use/abuse is briefly summarized as follows: ____________.

IT IS ORDERED

1. The above-named person will enter into, participate in, and successfully complete the ____________

2. The above-named person will not use alcohol and will not use drugs unless prescribed by a physician.

3. This Order shall be effective for 60 days from the date hereof.

4. ____________________________________

____

____

DONE AND ORDERED in ________ County, Florida this ___ day of ________, 20 ___.

____________	____________
Printed Name of Circuit Court Judge	Signature of Circuit Court Judge

FAILURE TO COMPLY WITH THIS ORDER WILL RESULT IN CONSIDERATION AND ACTION BY THE CIRCUIT COURT, WHICH MAY INCLUDE A CONTEMPT PROCEEDING. CONTEMPT OF COURT MAY RESULT IN INCARCERATION, A FINE, AND OTHER SANCTIONS.

IN THE CIRCUIT COURT, SEVENTH JUDICIAL CIRCUIT IN AND FOR ________ COUNTY, FLORIDA

IN RE: ____________ CASE NO.: ____________

____________/

Notice of Completion of Assessment and Filing of Petition for Involuntary Treatment (Marchman Act)

________, a licensed service provider as defined in Chapter 397, Florida Statutes, gives notice to this court that the above-named respondent has undergone an assessment, as that term is defined in Chapter 397, by a qualified professional. Notice is further given that a petition for involuntary treatment has been filed with respect to the above-named respondent, and said petition was filed in accordance with provisions of Section 397.693, Florida Statutes. The results of the assessment have been filed with the petition for involuntary treatment.

____________	____________
(Date)	(Signature)
	____________
	(Printed/Typed Name and Title)

ORDER DISMISSING ACTION FOR INVOLUNTARY ASSESSMENT

THIS MATTER came to be heard on the court's own motion, upon receipt by this court of the above notice. The court has concluded that the petition seeking a court-ordered assessment is now moot, and this action should therefore be dismissed. Whereupon,

IT IS ADJUDGED that this action is DISMISSED. The action seeking court-ordered treatment remains pending.

DONE AND ORDERED in Chambers in ________ County, Florida, this ___ day of ________, 20 ___.

____________	____________
Printed Name of Circuit Court Judge	Signature of Circuit Court Judge

**This order does not dismiss the petition and any action seeking court-ordered involuntary treatment. That action, and any hearing scheduled in that action, remains pending.

Copies to:
Petitioner(s)
Respondent
Service Provider

IN THE CIRCUIT COURT, SEVENTH JUDICIAL CIRCUIT, IN AND FOR ________ COUNTY, FLORIDA

IN RE: ____________ CASE NO.: ____________

____________/

Order Dismissing Action—Marchman Act

THIS CAUSE having come before the Court on a Petition for Involuntary Assessment and Stabilization, and/or a Petition for Involuntary Treatment for Substance Abuse, pursuant to Chapter 397, Florida Statutes, and the Court being fully advised in the premises, finds and orders as follows:

1. ____________________________________

____

____

2. This action should be dismissed.

Whereupon, it is

ORDERED that the above-described Petition, and this action, be and the same are DISMISSED.

DONE AND ORDERED in ________ County, Florida this ___ day of ________, 20 ___.

____________	____________
Printed Name of Circuit Court Judge	Signature of Circuit Court Judge

IN THE CIRCUIT COURT, SEVENTH JUDICIAL CIRCUIT, IN AND FOR ________ COUNTY, FLORIDA

IN RE: ___________ CASE NO.: ________

___________/

ORDER TO SHOW CAUSE (Marchman Act)

This matter coming before the Court on evidence presented in an affidavit signed by ________ (copy attached hereto), that respondent has failed to:

___ abide by the Order for Involuntary Treatment–Marchman Act signed by the Honorable ________ on the ___ day of ________, 20 ___.

___ [other] ________.

Whereupon, it is **ORDERED** that Respondent, ________ is summoned and required to appear before the Court at ________ on the date and time indicated below, where you may show cause, if any, why you should not be found in Indirect Criminal Contempt of Court. At said hearing the need for treatment may also be considered. Respondent may appear with counsel; if Respondent does not appear with counsel, a lawyer will be provided at the time of hearing to represent Respondent.

DATE AND TIME OF HEARING: ________

IF YOU FAIL TO APPEAR AS HEREIN COMMANDED, A WARRANT MAY BE ISSUED FOR YOUR ARREST.

DONE AND ORDERED in ________ County, Florida, this ___ day of ________, 20 ___.

______________	______________
Printed Name of Circuit Court Judge	Signature of Circuit Court Judge

IN THE CIRCUIT COURT, SEVENTH JUDICIAL CIRCUIT, IN AND FOR ________ COUNTY, FLORIDA

IN RE: ___________ CASE NO.: ________

___________/

ORDER TO SHOW CAUSE (Marchman Act—Failure to Attend Hearing)

This matter coming before the Court on the failure of Respondent to appear at the scheduled hearing on ________, 20 ___, at ________, after having been served with an order requiring Respondent to appear. Whereupon,

It is **ORDERED** that Respondent, ________ is summoned and required to appear before the Court at ________ on the date and time indicated below, where you may show cause, if any, why you should not be found in Indirect Criminal Contempt of Court. At said hearing the need for treatment may also be considered. Respondent may appear with counsel; if Respondent does not appear with counsel, a lawyer will be provided at the time of hearing to represent Respondent.

DATE AND TIME OF HEARING: ________

IF YOU FAIL TO APPEAR AS HEREIN COMMANDED, A WARRANT MAY BE ISSUED FOR YOUR ARREST.

DONE AND ORDERED in ________ County, Florida, this ___ day of ________, 20 ___.

______________	______________
Printed Name of Circuit Court Judge	Signature of Circuit Court Judge

IN THE CIRCUIT COURT, SEVENTH JUDICIAL CIRCUIT, IN AND FOR ________ COUNTY, FLORIDA

IN RE: ___________ CASE NO.: ________

___________/

ORDER TO SHOW CAUSE, DETAIN, TRANSPORT (Indirect Contempt—Marchman Act)

This matter coming before the Court on evidence presented in an affidavit signed by ________ (copy attached hereto), that respondent has failed to:

___ abide by the Order for Involuntary Treatment–Marchman Act signed by the Honorable ________ on the ___ day of ________, 20 ___.

___ [other] ____

____.

It appears to the Court that the Respondent may be in need of substance abuse treatment and will not seek such treatment on his/her own volition. Whereupon,

It is ORDERED that the Sheriff of ________ County and all singular Law Enforcement Officials in the County of ________ and the State of Florida are hereby directed to APPREHEND the said Respondent and TRANSPORT him/her to the ________ ________, ________, ________, Florida, where Respondent is to be DETAINED. A hearing will be scheduled so that Respondent may show cause to the Court why Respondent should not be found in INDIRECT CONTEMPT OF COURT. This hearing will be scheduled by the Clerk of the Circuit Court, who should be notified of Respondent's detention as soon as practicable.

DONE AND ORDERED in ________ County, Florida, this ___ day of ________, 20 ___.

______________	______________
Printed Name of Circuit Court Judge	Signature of Circuit Court Judge

IN THE CIRCUIT COURT, SEVENTH JUDICIAL CIRCUIT IN AND FOR ________ COUNTY, FLORIDA

IN RE: ___________ CASE NO.: ________

___________/

JUDGMENT OF CONTEMPT (Indirect Criminal Contempt—Marchman Act)

THIS CAUSE came to be heard by the Court pursuant to an Order to Show Cause entered ________ 20 ___. The above-named Respondent was represented by counsel. Upon evidence received, the above-named person is found to have willfully violated the Order dated ________ 20 ___, in that:

___ she/he failed to appear for and successfully complete treatment/ assessment for substance abuse as ordered by this Court.

____

____

Whereupon, it is ORDERED that:

___ the above-named person is hereby ADJUDICATED GUILTY of indirect criminal contempt.

___ adjudication of guilt is withheld.

SENTENCE

The above-named person, being personally before this Court, accompanied by counsel, and the court having given said person an opportunity to show cause why said person should not be sentenced as provided by law, and no cause being shown,

It Is The Sentence Of The Court That:

___ The above-named person is hereby committed to the custody of the Department of Corrections of __________ County, Florida for a term of __________.

___ Said SENTENCE SUSPENDED for a period of ___ days, subject to the above-named person fully complying with all the orders of the Court.

___ It is further ordered that the above-named person shall be allowed a total of ___ days of credit for time incarcerated before imposition of this sentence.

DONE AND ORDERED in __________ County, Florida this ___ day of __________, 20___.

Printed Name of Circuit Court Judge	Signature of Circuit Court Judge

Amended effective March 17, 2005.

PB–2011–017–VL. ELECTRONIC RECORDING OF BAKER ACT, MARCHMAN ACT AND ADULT PROTECTIVE SERVICES ACT HEARINGS

IN THE CIRCUIT COURT OF FLORIDA, SEVENTH JUDICIAL CIRCUIT IN AND FOR VOLUSIA COUNTY

RE: Electronic Recording of Baker Act, Marchman Act and Adult Protective Services Act Hearings

REF: PB–2011–017–VL (Rescinds PB–2003–017–VL)

WHEREAS, Baker Act (§ 394.451, FL. Stat.), Marchman Act (§ 397.301, FL. Stat.) and Adult Protective Services Act (§ 415.101, FL. Stat.) hearings are required to be reported at public expense, and

WHEREAS, the Seventh Judicial Circuit has elected to make a record in these proceedings by electronic means as provided by Rule 2.535(h)(4), Florida Rules of Judicial Administration;

NOW THEREFORE, I, WILLIAM A. PARSONS, Chief Judge of the Seventh Judicial Circuit of Florida, hereby order as follows:

1. Baker Act, Marchman Act and Adult Protective Services Act hearings are to be electronically recorded.

2. The electronic recording equipment is to be operated in such a manner as to ensure the production of an accurate, understandable record.

3. Personnel operating recording equipment shall maintain logs of all proceedings recorded during each court session. The logs and corresponding recordings shall be properly identified and safely stored. Retention of these records shall be in accordance with Rule 2.430(e), Florida Rules of Judicial Administration.

4. Parties may obtain copies of recordings for a fee set by the Chief Judge.

5. In the event a party would like to obtain a transcript of a proceeding, he/she must purchase a copy of the recording and make independent arrangements for its transcription with a certified court reporter or transcriber.

IT IS FURTHER ORDERED that Administrative Order PB–2003–017–VL is hereby rescinded.

TO BE RECORDED in Volusia County, FL.

DONE AND ORDERED in Daytona Beach, Volusia County, Florida this 19th day of September 2011.

Judge William A. Parsons
CHIEF JUDGE

Amended effective September 19, 2011.

PB–2016–018–SC. GUARDIANSHIP EXAMINING COMMITTEES

RE: Guardianship Examining Committees

REF: PB–2016–018–SC

Rescinds PB–2008–18–SC

WHEREAS, § 744.331(3)(d), Florida Statutes, requires individuals serving as members of guardianship examining committees to complete a minimum of four (4) hours of initial training and two (2) hours of continuing education every 2 years thereafter, and

WHEREAS, said training, developed under the supervision of the Office of Public and Professional Guardians, is available to individuals in the Seventh Judicial Circuit, and

WHEREAS, § 744.331(3)(c), Florida Statutes, requires the chief judge to prepare a list of individuals qualified to serve as members of guardianship examining committees;

NOW THEREFORE, I, TERENCE R. PERKINS, Chief Judge of the Seventh Judicial Circuit of Florida, hereby order that those individuals whose names appear on the list attached hereto as "Exhibit A"[1] are qualified to serve as members of guardianship examining committees in the Seventh Judicial Circuit.

IT IS FURTHER ORDERED that in-person, video, internet and all other examining committee training and education courses that meet statutory criteria are hereby approved and accepted in the Seventh Judicial Circuit.

TO BE RECORDED in Flagler, Putnam, St. Johns and Volusia counties.

DONE AND ORDERED in Daytona Beach, Volusia County, FL this 30th day of September 2016.

TERENCE R. PERKINS
CHIEF JUDGE

Amended effective September 30, 2016.

1 Attachment not included.

PB–2004–019–SC (A). MOTIONS TO COMPEL DISCOVERY IN PROBATE ACTIONS (AMENDED)

IN THE CIRCUIT COURT OF FLORIDA, SEVENTH JUDICIAL CIRCUIT IN AND FOR FLAGLER, PUTNAM, ST. JOHNS AND VOLUSIA COUNTIES

REF: PB 2004–019 SC (A) (Rescinds) PB 2004–019 SC

RE: MOTIONS TO COMPEL DISCOVERY IN PROBATE ACTIONS (Amended)

WHEREAS, the undersigned has determined that the issuance of an Administrative Order governing motions to compel discovery in probate / guardianship actions is necessary for the efficient and proper administration of justice in the Seventh Judicial Circuit;

NOW THEREFORE, I, JULIANNE PIGGOTTE, Chief Judge of the Seventh Judicial Circuit of Florida, hereby order that no motion to compel discovery in any probate / guardianship action may be **filed** in the Seventh Judicial Circuit unless the moving party has complied with the following procedures:

1. The moving party must notify the opposing party, **in writing**, of the **specific** nature of the deficiencies of his/her discovery response and the specific actions necessary to cure said asserted deficiencies. Said written notice must provide 10 days, plus mailing time, for the opposing party to cure said asserted deficiencies, or such shorter time as may be required by the Court.

2. Upon failure to resolve the issue within the time mentioned in # 1 above, the moving party may then file a motion to compel discovery and request that a hearing be set. A copy of the written notice of deficiency, and any response thereto, must be attached to the motion. Once set, the hearing may not be cancelled by either party without the Court's consent.

3. When a motion to compel discovery alleges a complete failure to respond or object to discovery, and where there has been no request for extension, an ex-parte order may be entered by the Court requiring compliance with the original discovery demand within 10 days of the signing of the order. The moving party must submit a proposed order and self-addressed, stamped envelopes for the Court's use.

4. If the opposing party fails to respond to a proper discovery request, or responds in a manner deemed by the Court to be in bad faith, a presumption in favor of sanctions against the offending party shall arise. Said sanctions may include, but are not limited to, attorneys' fees and costs. Bad faith in propounding improper or unreasonable discovery requests may be sanctioned in a like manner.

IT IS FURTHER ORDERED that Administrative Order # PB–2004–019–SC is hereby rescinded.

TO BE RECORDED in Flagler, Putnam, St. Johns and Volusia counties.

DONE AND ORDERED in Daytona Beach, Volusia County, Florida this 29th day of March, 2004.

JULIANNE PIGGOTTE
CHIEF JUDGE

Amended effective March 29, 2004.

PB–2016–020–SC. RATES OF COMPENSATION FOR EXAMINING COMMITTEE IN INDIGENT CASES

IN THE CIRCUIT COURT OF FLORIDA, SEVENTH JUDICIAL CIRCUIT IN AND FOR FLAGLER, PUTNAM, ST. JOHNS AND VOLUSIA COUNTIES

RE: Rates of Compensation for Examining Committee in Indigent Cases

REF:. PB–2016–020–SC

WHEREAS, it has been determined that the issuance of an Administrative Order establishing rates of compensation for members of examining committees appointed in indigent cases pursuant to §§ 393.11(5) and 744.331(3), Florida Statutes, is necessary for the efficient and proper administration of justice in the Seventh Judicial Circuit, and

WHEREAS, pursuant to §§ 393.11(5)(g) and 744.331(7), the Court is responsible for determining reasonable fees to be paid to members of examining committees, and

WHEREAS, the existing rates were established several years ago and it has been recommended that the rates of compensation for members of examining committees in indigent cases be reviewed;

NOW THEREFORE, I, TERENCE R. PERKINS, Chief Judge of the Seventh Judicial Circuit of Florida, hereby order that members of examining committees appointed on or after July 1, 2016 in indigent cases pursuant to §§ 393.11(5) and 744.331(3), Florida Statutes, or in cases where good faith petitions are dismissed (§ 744.331(7)), shall be entitled to compensation in accordance with the following:

Committee Member	Rate of Compensation
Psychiatrist, Psychologist, or other Physician	Not to Exceed $300 per exam
Other Qualified Person	Not to Exceed $150 per exam.

IT IS FURTHER ORDERED that in cases in which the Clerk of Court's office has determined the ward or person to be examined to be indigent, or in cases in which a good faith petition is dismissed, the judge should issue a "compensation order" that includes the names of the committee members, the rate of compensation to which each member is entitled, that the Court is responsible for payment of said compensation, and that invoices should be sent to the Court Administrator's office for payment.

IT IS FURTHER ORDERED that in cases subject to this Order, examining committee members must submit **original** invoices to the Court Administrator's office in order to be compensated. Said invoices **must** include the committee member's name, mailing address, social security # or tax ID #, and signature and date in blue ink. Said invoices **must** also include the court case number, the name of the person examined, the date of the examination, and the amount of compensation sought. A copy of the judge's Order Appointing Examining Committee in the instant case **must** accompany the invoice.

IT IS FURTHER ORDERED that Administrative Order PB–2005–020–SC is hereby rescinded effective July 1, 2016.

TO BE RECORDED in Flagler, Putnam, St. Johns and Volusia counties.

DONE AND ORDERED in Daytona Beach, Volusia County, Florida this 20th day of May 2016.

TERENCE R. PERKINS
Chief Judge

Adopted effective January 20, 2005. Amended effective July 1, 2016.

PB–2007–021–SC. INCAPACITY PETITIONER SERVING AS GUARDIAN

IN THE CIRCUIT COURT OF FLORIDA, SEVENTH JUDICIAL CIRCUIT IN AND FOR FLAGLER, PUTNAM, ST. JOHNS AND VOLUSIA COUNTIES

RE: Incapacity Petitioner Serving as Guardian

REF: PB–2007–021–SC

WHEREAS, it has been made known to the undersigned that the prompt and expeditious administration of justice requires that the guardianship division of the circuit court take all appropriate steps to expeditiously consider all incapacity and guardianship petitions, and to protect the rights of alleged incapacitated persons in cases filed pursuant to chapter 744, Florida Statutes, and

WHEREAS, petitioners in incapacity and guardianship cases commonly file both incapacity and guardianship petitions and seek to be appointed guardian; often, such petitioners are immediate family members of the alleged incapacitated person, but many alleged incapacitated persons have no family or other interested persons willing to file such pleadings or to serve as guardian, and without willing petitioners, persons in need of guardianship services would remain neglected and vulnerable, and

WHEREAS, Chapter 744, Florida Statutes, contains numerous specific provisions that provide the circuit court with the duty and authority to protect the rights of alleged incapacitated persons; *to wit*, section 744.331(2) provides that each alleged incapacitated person must have an attorney independent of the petitioner or any other interested party; and section 744.309(3) prohibits the court from appointing a guardian who has a professional or business relationship with the alleged incapacitated person unless the court determines that any potential conflict of interest is insubstantial and that the appointment would be in the best interest of the ward; and section 744.446 lists conflicts of interest and prohibited activities, but does not include in its prohibitions the appointment of the person or entity that filed the initial incapacity and guardianship pleadings.

NOW THEREFORE, I, J. DAVID WALSH, Chief Judge of the Seventh Judicial Circuit of Florida, hereby find that nothing in chapter 744, Florida Statutes, prohibits the court from appointing a person, entity or the Public Guardian as established under section 744.703 because that person, entity or Public Guardian filed the incapacity or guardianship petition; further, the function of filing both a petition to determine incapacity and a petition to appoint the petitioner as guardian, standing alone, does not create a substantial conflict of interest as described in section 744.309(3), Florida Statutes, but that the guardianship court and the attorney for the alleged incapacitated person should examine each petition to determine if any further conflict exists, disqualifying the petitioner. If no further conflict exists, the guardianship court should proceed to consider the petition.

IT IS FURTHER ORDERED that nothing in this order is intended to limit the court's discretion in appointing guardians or to alter the court's duty to faithfully and uniformly apply all guardianship statues [1] and rules.

TO BE RECORDED in Flagler, Putnam, St. Johns & Volusia counties.

DONE AND ORDERED in Daytona Beach, Volusia County, Florida this 6 day of August 2007.

J. DAVID WALSH
CHIEF JUDGE

Adopted effective August 6, 2007.

[1] So in original.

PB–2009–022–SC. IN THE CIRCUIT COURT OF FLORIDA, SEVENTH JUDICIAL CIRCUIT IN AND FOR FLAGLER, PUTNAM, ST. JOHNS AND VOLUSIA COUNTIES

IN THE CIRCUIT COURT OF FLORIDA, SEVENTH JUDICIAL CIRCUIT IN AND FOR FLAGLER, PUTNAM, ST. JOHNS AND VOLUSIA COUNTIES

RE: Adversary Case Style on Probate Pleadings

REF: PB–2009–022–SC

WHEREAS, the probate and guardianship division of the circuit court must take all appropriate steps to protect the rights of persons interested in adversary probate or guardianship cases filed pursuant to chapters 731, 732, 733, 734, 735, and 744, Florida Statutes (2009), and the Florida Probate Rules, and

WHEREAS, Rule 5.025, Florida Probate Rules, declares that the following proceedings shall be adversary, unless otherwise ordered by the court: proceedings to remove a personal representative, surcharge a personal representative, remove a guardian, surcharge a guardian, probate a lost or destroyed will or later discovered will, determine beneficiaries, construe a will, cancel a devise, partition property for the purposes of distribution, determine pretermitted share, determine amount of elective share and contribution, and for revocation of probate of a will, proceedings declared to be adversary by an interested person, and proceedings determined to be adversary by the court; and

WHEREAS, the adversary case style, described in Fla. Prob. R. 5.025(d), is required on all pleadings named in Fla. Prob. R. 5.025(a), (b), and (c), and

WHEREAS, when adversary pleadings are filed, the court follows adversary rules of procedure, which differ from non-adversary rules of procedure; the presiding judge must apply strict rules of ethics to communications with counsel in such proceedings; and the Committee Notes to Fla. Prob. R. 5.025 recognize that the adversary case style is necessary and useful to facilitate the clerk's and the court's ability to segregate such adversary proceedings from the main court file;

NOW THEREFORE, I, J. DAVID WALSH, Chief Judge of the Seventh Judicial Circuit of Florida, hereby find that pleadings declared to be adversary by Rule 5.025, Florida Probate Rules, that do not contain the adversary case style described in Fla. Prob. R. 5.025(d) are not authorized by law and shall be returned by the clerk of court to the pleader, or the pleader's attorney, un-filed. This applies to all pleadings in adversary proceedings, whether initial or subsequent.

IT IS FURTHER ORDERED that nothing in this order limits the authority of the court to declare proceedings to be non-adversary pursuant to Fla. Prob. R. 5.025(a).

TO BE RECORDED in Flagler, Putnam, St. Johns, and Volusia Counties, Florida.

DONE AND ORDERED in Daytona Beach, Volusia County, Florida this 22nd day of May 2009.

Judge J. David Walsh
Chief Judge

Adopted effective May 22, 2009.

Family/Juvenile Orders

FM–2002–001–SC. CODIFICATION OF ADMINISTRATIVE ORDERS IN THE FAMILY DIVISION

IN THE CIRCUIT COURT OF FLORIDA, SEVENTH JUDICIAL CIRCUIT IN AND FOR FLAGLER, PUTNAM, ST. JOHNS AND VOLUSIA COUNTIES

REF: FM–2002–001–SC

RE: CODIFICATION OF ADMINISTRATIVE ORDERS IN THE FAMILY DIVISION

WHEREAS, it has been made known to the undersigned that the codification of Family Administrative Orders in the Seventh Judicial Circuit is necessary for the efficient and proper administration of justice,

NOW, THEREFORE, I, ROBERT K. ROUSE, JR., Chief Judge of the Seventh Judicial Circuit of Florida, hereby order the codification of all Administrative Orders in the Family Division of the Seventh Judicial Circuit.

IT IS FURTHER ORDERED that said administrative orders shall be numbered for reference in the following manner:

Subject—Year—Numerical Order — Circuit / County
[i.e., FM–2002–001–SC (Seventh Circuit)]
[FM–2002–001–FG (Flagler County)]
[FM–2002–001–PT (Putnam County)]
[FM–2002–001–SJ (St. Johns County)]
[FM–2002–001–VL (Volusia County)]

IT IS FURTHER ORDERED that all administrative orders related to the administration of Family matters issued prior to the date of this order are hereby rescinded.

TO BE RECORDED in Flagler, Putnam, St. Johns and Volusia counties.

DONE AND ORDERED in Daytona Beach, Volusia County, Florida this 15th day of July, 2002.

ROBERT K. ROUSE, JR.
CHIEF JUDGE

Adopted effective July 15, 2002.

FM–2007–002–SC. FAMILY LAW DIVISION

IN THE CIRCUIT COURT OF FLORIDA, SEVENTH JUDICIAL CIRCUIT IN AND FOR FLAGLER, PUTNAM, ST. JOHNS AND VOLUSIA COUNTIES

RE: FAMILY LAW DIVISION

REF: FM–2007–002–SC
(Rescinds FM–2005–002–SC)

WHEREAS, the Supreme Court of Florida has encouraged the establishment of Family Law Divisions in each judicial circuit (see In Re: Report of the Family Court Steering Committee, 794 So2d 518), and

WHEREAS, a Family Law Division has previously been established in the Seventh Judicial Circuit, and

WHEREAS, the undersigned has determined that changes to the composition of the Family Law Division are necessary;

NOW THEREFORE, I, WILLIAM A. PARSONS, Chief Judge of the Seventh Judicial Circuit of Florida, hereby order that effective July 2, 2007, the Family Law Division in the Seventh Judicial Circuit shall operate in accordance with the following:

1. **Jurisdiction**

The following categories of cases fall under the jurisdiction of the Family Law Division:

- Simplified Dissolution of Marriage
- Dissolution of Marriage
- Separate Maintenance
- Annulment
- Injunction for Protection Against Domestic Violence
- Injunction for Protection Against Repeat / Dating / Sexual Violence
- Name Change
- Paternity
- Adoption
- Pre–Adoption Termination of Parental Rights
- Custody
- Temporary Custody by Extended Family
- Child Support
- UIFSA
- Declaratory Judgment related to premarital, marital, or post-marital agreements
- Juvenile Delinquency
- Truancy
- Juvenile Dependency
- Juvenile Emancipation
- Children/Families in Need of Services (CINS/FINS)
- Termination of Parental Rights (TPR) (Dependency)
- Waiver of Parental Notice of Abortion

2. **Judicial Resources**

The assignment of judicial divisions to the Family Law Division is left to the sole discretion of the Chief Judge. Said assignments are based on caseload, available judicial resources, and other related factors. The assignment of judges to judicial divisions within the Family Law Division is also left to the sole discretion of the Chief Judge. The Chief Judge may consider such factors as individual desire, subject matter experience, seniority, geography, and other related factors. In addition, the Chief Judge may appoint a Family Law Division judge to serve as Administrative Family Law Judge to oversee the administration of the Family Law Division.

3. Quasi-Judicial Resources

Pursuant to Administrative Order, the Chief Justice of the Supreme Court of Florida has authorized the Seventh Judicial Circuit to utilize child support enforcement hearing officers to assist in the resolution of cases in the Family Law Division. The Seventh Judicial Circuit has also utilized the services of general magistrates to assist in the resolution of cases in the Family Law Division. The assignment of general magistrates and child support enforcement hearing officers is left to the sole discretion of the Chief Judge. Said assignments are based on caseload, available judicial resources, funding availability, and other related factors. The types of matters to be heard by general magistrates and child support enforcement hearing officers are determined by the Chief Judge, consistent with applicable rules of procedure. General magistrates serve at the pleasure of the Chief Judge. Child support enforcement hearing officers serve at the pleasure of the Chief Judge and a majority of the circuit judges in the circuit. General magistrates and child support enforcement hearing officers report to and are supervised by the Court Administrator or his/her designee.

4. Supplemental Resources

The use of supplemental resources to assist in the resolution of cases in the Family Law Division is left to the sole discretion of the Chief Judge. Caseload, funding availability, resource availability, and other related factors are considered when making decisions related to the use of supplemental resources. Examples of such supplemental resources include, but are not limited to, mediators, case managers, self-help programs, custody evaluators, supervised visitation, monitored exchange, batterers intervention monitoring and law clerks.

IT IS FURTHER ORDERED that the assignment of judges to divisions, the assignment of divisions to the Family Law Division and the assignment of cases to divisions are governed by separate administrative orders issued by the Chief Judge of the Seventh Judicial Circuit.

IT IS FURTHER ORDERED that Administrative Order FM-2005-002-SC is hereby rescinded effective July 2, 2007.

TO BE RECORDED in Flagler, Putnam, St. Johns and Volusia counties.

DONE AND ORDERED in Daytona Beach, Volusia County, Florida this 7th day of June 2007.

WILLIAM A. PARSONS
CHIEF JUDGE

Amended effective July 2, 2007.

FM-2012-003-VL. ESTABLISHING WESTERN, EASTERN AND SOUTHERN FAMILY DIVISIONS OF THE CIRCUIT COURT

IN THE CIRCUIT COURT OF FLORIDA, SEVENTH JUDICIAL CIRCUIT IN AND FOR VOLUSIA COUNTY

RE: ESTABLISHING WESTERN, EASTERN AND SOUTHERN FAMILY DIVISIONS OF THE CIRCUIT COURT

REF: FM-2012-003-VL (Rescinds FM-2011-003-VL)

WHEREAS, it has been made known to the undersigned that the efficient and proper administration of justice and the processing of Family cases in the Circuit Court in Volusia County requires the establishment of Western, Eastern, and Southern divisions of this court;

NOW THEREFORE, I, WILLIAM A. PARSONS, Chief Judge of the Seventh Judicial Circuit of Florida, hereby order as follows:

1. A Western Family Division of the Circuit Court in Volusia County is established, to which at least one judge of this court may be assigned, and in which those cases arising in the division as ordered by the Chief Judge and as defined in #4 below are to be filed.

2. An Eastern Family Division of the Circuit Court in Volusia County is established, to which at least one judge of this court may be assigned, and in which those cases arising in the division as ordered by the Chief Judge and as defined in #5 below are to be filed.

3. A Southern Family Division of the Circuit Court in Volusia County is established, to which at least one judge of this court may be assigned, and in which those cases arising in the division as ordered by the Chief Judge and as defined in #6 below are to be filed.

4. The Western Family Division consists of those portions of Volusia County contained within zip codes 32102, 32105, 32130, 32180, 32190, 32706, 32713, 32720, 32721, 32722, 32723, 32724, 32725, 32728, 32738, 32739, 32744 32753, 32763 and 32774.

5. The Eastern Family Division consists of those portions of Volusia County contained within zip codes 32110, 32114, 32115, 32116, 32117, 32118, 32119, 32124, 32120, 32121, 32122, 32123, 32124, 32125, 32126, 32127, 32128, 32129, 32136, 32173, 32174, 32175, 32176 and 32198.

6. The Southern Family Division consists of those portions of Volusia County contained within zip codes 32132, 32141, 32168, 32169, 32170, 32754, 32759 and 32764.

IT IS FURTHER ORDERED that cases are to be assigned to the respective geographic Family divisions based on the following criteria:

1. Defendant's / Respondent's residence / address
2. Petitioner's residence / address.

In the event the Clerk of Court's office is unable to determine the proper geographic division assignment in a case due to the absence of a zip code on the civil cover sheet, the case may be assigned using the city of the defendant's/respondent's residence/address, or the city of the petitioner's residence/address. In cases in which neither party resides in Volusia County, the

Clerk's office is to assign said cases to judges in the Western Family Division. Additional direction/guidance concerning the assignment of cases to divisions may be provided by separate administrative order. If any further uncertainty or ambiguity concerning the assignment of a case to a geographical division exists, the matter should be referred to the Court Administrator's office for resolution by the Chief Judge {see Kruckenberg v. Powell, 422 So. 2d 994 (Fla. 5 DCA 1982)}.

IT IS FURTHER ORDERED that Administrative Order FM–2011–003–VL is hereby rescinded.

TO BE RECORDED in Volusia County, Florida.

DONE AND ORDERED in Daytona Beach, Volusia County, Florida this 19th day of January 2012.

WILLIAM A. PARSONS
CHIEF JUDGE

Amended effective January 19, 2012.

FM–2011–004–SC. APPOINTMENT OF ADMINISTRATIVE FAMILY LAW JUDGE

IN THE CIRCUIT COURT OF FLORIDA, SEVENTH JUDICIAL CIRCUIT IN AND FOR FLAGLER, PUTNAM, ST. JOHNS AND VOLUSIA COUNTIES

RE: APPOINTMENT OF ADMINISTRATIVE FAMILY LAW JUDGE

REF: FM–2011–004–SC (Rescinds FM–2007–004–SC (A))

WHEREAS, a chief judge is authorized to appoint administrative judges pursuant to Rule 2.215(b)(5), Florida Rules of Judicial Administration, and

WHEREAS, the undersigned has determined that the appointment of an administrative judge for the family division is in the best interest of the Seventh Judicial Circuit;

NOW THEREFORE, I, WILLIAM A. PARSONS, Chief Judge of the Seventh Judicial Circuit of Florida, hereby appoint the **Honorable John M. Alexander** as Administrative Judge of the Family Division in the Seventh Judicial Circuit. The Family Division includes domestic relations, juvenile delinquency, juvenile dependency, and other related case types. The duties of the Administrative Judge of the Family Division include, but are not limited to, the following:

1. Chairing a circuit-wide Family Law Advisory Group (the circuit-wide Family Law Advisory Group must meet at least twice per year);

2. Chairing a circuit-wide Juvenile Dependency Court Planning Committee for purposes of establishing Model Dependency Courts in those counties interested in pursuing such an endeavor;

3. Encouraging judges assigned to the family division to conduct periodic meetings with stakeholders in their respective counties;

4. Developing proposed policies for the Chief Judge's consideration related to the operation of the family division;

5. Making recommendations concerning the need for and use of resources that may be required to effectively adjudicate family matters by the judges in the family division;

6. Assisting with the training and orientation of judges newly assigned to the family division; and

7. Performing other related duties as may be assigned by the Chief Judge.

IT IS FURTHER ORDERED that Administrative Order # FM–2007–004–SC (A) is hereby rescinded.

TO BE RECORDED in Flagler, Putnam, St. Johns and Volusia counties.

DONE AND ORDERED in Daytona Beach, Volusia County, Florida this 22nd day of September 2011.

Judge William A. Parsons
CHIEF JUDGE

Amended effective September 22, 2011.

FM–2003–005–SC. APPOINTMENT OF FAMILY LAW ADVISORY GROUP

IN THE CIRCUIT COURT OF FLORIDA, SEVENTH JUDICIAL CIRCUIT IN AND FOR FLAGLER, PUTNAM, ST. JOHNS AND VOLUSIA COUNTIES

REF: FM–2003–005–SC (Rescinds FM–2002–005–SC)

RE: APPOINTMENT OF FAMILY LAW ADVISORY GROUP

WHEREAS, the Court believes that the perspective of stakeholders with an interest in the family court system will assist the Court designing a more effective and efficient family court system, and

WHEREAS, the Florida Supreme Court has recommended that each circuit create a family law advisory group to support and advise the family court;

NOW, THEREFORE, I, JULIANNE PIGGOTTE, Chief Judge of the Seventh Judicial Circuit of Florida, hereby appoint the following to membership on the Seventh Judicial Circuit's Family Law Advisory Group (FLAG):

Administrative Family Law Judge, Chair

Circuit Court Judges, Family Division

Clerks of Court, or designee(s)

Court Administrator, or designee

Sr Deputy Court Administrator, Family Court Svcs

Court Administration staff designee(s)

Flagler County Bar Association designee

Putnam County Bar Association designee

St. Johns County Bar Association designee

Volusia County Bar Association designee

Department of Children and Families designee

Department of Juvenile Justice designee

Department of Revenue designee

Family/Dependency mediator

Legal Aid services provider(s)

The FLAG will meet at the discretion of the chair. The FLAG'S primary purpose is to provide an open forum to discuss improvements to the family court system within the Seventh Judicial Circuit and to facilitate communication with family court stakeholders.

Nothing in this Order prohibits the formation of FLAG subcommittees in each county of the circuit to address county specific issues.

IT IS FURTHER ORDERED that Administrative Order # FM-2002-005-SC is hereby rescinded.

TO BE RECORDED in Flagler, Putnam, St. Johns and Volusia counties, Florida.

DONE AND ORDERED in Daytona Beach, Volusia County, Florida, this 30th day of October, 2003.

JULIANNE PIGGOTTE
CHIEF JUDGE

Amended effective October 30, 2003.

FM-2004-006-SC (A). MOTIONS TO COMPEL DISCOVERY IN FAMILY LAW ACTIONS

IN THE CIRCUIT COURT OF FLORIDA, SEVENTH JUDICIAL CIRCUIT IN AND FOR FLAGLER, PUTNAM, ST. JOHNS AND VOLUSIA COUNTIES

RE: MOTIONS TO COMPEL DISCOVERY IN FAMILY LAW ACTIONS (Amended)

REF: FM-2004-006-SC (A) (Rescinds FM-2002-006-SC)

WHEREAS, the undersigned has determined that the issuance of an Administrative Order governing motions to compel discovery in family law actions is necessary for the efficient and proper administration of justice in the Seventh Judicial Circuit;

NOW THEREFORE, I, JULIANNE PIGGOTTE, Chief Judge of the Seventh Judicial Circuit of Florida, hereby order that no motion to compel discovery in any family law action may be **filed** in the Seventh Judicial Circuit unless the moving party has complied with the following procedures:

1. The moving party must notify the opposing party, **in writing**, of the **specific** nature of the deficiencies of his/her discovery response and the specific actions necessary to cure said asserted deficiencies. Said written notice must provide 10 days, plus mailing time, for the opposing party to cure said asserted deficiencies, or such shorter time as may be required by the Court.

2. Upon failure to resolve the issue within the time mentioned in # 1 above, the moving party may then file a motion to compel discovery and request that a hearing be set. A copy of the written notice of deficiency, and any response thereto, must be attached to the motion. Once set, the hearing may not be cancelled by either party without the Court's consent.

3. When a motion to compel discovery alleges a complete failure to respond or object to discovery, and where there has been no request for extension, an ex-parte order may be entered by the Court requiring compliance with the original discovery demand within 10 days of the signing of the order. The moving party must submit a proposed order and self-addressed, stamped envelopes for the Court's use.

4. If the opposing party fails to respond to a proper discovery request, or responds in a manner deemed by the Court to be in bad faith, a presumption in favor of sanctions against the offending party shall arise. Said sanctions may include, but are not limited to, attorneys' fees and costs. Bad faith in propounding improper or unreasonable discovery requests may be sanctioned in a like manner.

IT IS FURTHER ORDERED that Administrative Order # FM-2002-006-SC is hereby rescinded.

TO BE RECORDED in Flagler, Putnam, St. Johns and Volusia counties.

DONE AND ORDERED in Daytona Beach, Volusia County, Florida this 29th day of March, 2004.

Judge Julianne Piggotte
CHIEF JUDGE

Amended effective March 29, 2004.

FM-2009-007-SC. PROCEDURES FOR INDIGENCY DETERMINATION IN CERTAIN FAMILY LAW CASES

IN THE CIRCUIT COURT OF FLORIDA, SEVENTH JUDICIAL CIRCUIT IN AND FOR FLAGLER, PUTNAM, ST. JOHNS AND VOLUSIA COUNTIES

RE: Procedures for Indigency Determination in Certain Family Law Cases

REF: FM-2009-007-SC

(Rescinds FM-2006-007-SC)

WHEREAS, §§ 57.081 and 57.085, Florida Statutes, provide that certain indigent persons in judicial proceedings (the "Litigant") are entitled to receive certain services of the Courts, Sheriffs and Clerks of Court on Flagler, Putnam, St. Johns and Volusia Counties (the "Clerk") without the payment or prepayment of costs, and

WHEREAS, 57.082, Florida Statutes, requires the Clerk to determine if a non-prisoner litigant is indigent based upon information provided in an Application for Determination of Indigent Status, and

WHEREAS, 57.085, Florida Statutes sets forth additional requirements for prisoners as defined by subsection (1) who wish to file civil court actions as indigents, and

WHEREAS, detailed financial information is necessary to properly evaluate applications for indigent status.

NOW THEREFORE, I, J. DAVID WALSH, Chief Judge of the Seventh Judicial Circuit of Florida, hereby order as follows:

1. Application/Affidavit for Determination of Indigent Status

a) <u>Non-Prisoner Litigants</u>

Any party to or intervenor in any family law case, excluding matters filed pursuant to § 741.30 or § 784.046, Florida Statutes, who wish to proceed as an indigent in order to receive certain Court, Sheriff and Clerk services without the payment or prepayment of costs shall, prior to obtaining a Clerk's certificate of indigency, file a fully completed Application for Determination of Indigent Status. The application required to be filed by non-prisoner litigants pursuant to §§ 57.081 and 57.082, Florida Statutes, is attached as <u>Exhibit A</u>.

b) <u>Prisoner Litigants</u>

A "prisoner" {see § 57.085(1), Florida Statutes} who wishes to proceed as an indigent in order to receive certain Court, Sheriff and Clerk services without prepayment must file a fully completed affidavit. The affidavit required to be filed by prisoner litigants pursuant to § 57.085(2), Florida Statutes, is attached as Exhibit B.

In addition, pursuant to § 57.085(7), Florida Statutes, if a prisoner litigant has been determined indigent twice in the preceding 3 years, said prisoner litigant may not be determined indigent to pursue a new suit without first obtaining leave of court. Therefore, any prisoner litigant who wishes to proceed as an indigent in order to receive certain Court, Sheriff and Clerk services without prepayment must, prior to obtaining a clerk's certificate of indigency, file a fully completed Affidavit of Prior Litigation attached as Exhibit C.

2. The Clerk is directed to stamp or otherwise indicate on the court case file that a person involved with the case is seeking indigent status.

3. The Clerk is directed to provide litigants seeking indigent status with blank copies of the appropriate application/affidavit in substantially the same forms as Exhibits A, B and/or C and must inform said litigants that the application(s)/affidavit(s) must be fully completed and filed with the Clerk before his/her office makes a determination of indigency.

4. If the Clerk, based upon the application filed, determines a non-prisoner litigant to be indigent, the Clerk will immediately file the certificate of indigency in the court case file.

5. In the following instances, the Clerk is directed to forward the court case file to the assigned judge for the judge's consideration:

a) The Clerk determines a prisoner litigant to be indigent;

b) If the Clerk determines a litigant not to be indigent and the litigant files a petition seeking review of the clerk's determination.

6. In the event the Clerk is unable to make an indigency determination based on a litigant's application, the Clerk may seek assistance / guidance from the assigned judge.

7. Judicial Consideration

a) Non–Prisoner Litigants

The assigned judge will promptly review the application to determine if the litigant is indigent. The judge may set the issue of the litigant's indigency for hearing upon notice to the litigant or may rule on the litigant's indigency status based on the information provided in the application. The litigant has the burden of proving indigency. When the file is sent to the judge, the Clerk is directed to prepare and also send an order in substantially the same form as attached Exhibit D.

b) Prisoner Litigants

Pursuant to § 57.085(7), Florida Statutes, if a prisoner litigant has been determined indigent twice in the preceding 3 years, the prisoner litigant may not be determined indigent to pursue a new suit without first obtaining leave of court. Therefore, the assigned judge will promptly review the Affidavit of Prior Litigation by Prisoner to determine if the prisoner litigant requires leave of court to be determined indigent. When the file is sent to the judge, the Clerk is directed to prepare and also send an order in substantially the same form as attached Exhibit E.

If the judge determines that the prisoner litigant qualifies under § 57.085(7), or grants the prisoner litigant leave to proceed, the assigned judge will promptly review the affidavit to determine if the litigant is indigent. The judge may set the issue of the litigant's indigency for hearing upon notice to the litigant or may rule on the litigant's indigency status based on the information provided in the affidavit. The litigant has the burden of proving indigency. When the file is sent to the judge, the Clerk is directed to prepare and also send an order in substantially the same form as attached Exhibit F.

In addition, before an indigent prisoner may intervene in, initiate, or continue any judicial proceeding, the Court must review the prisoner's claim to determine whether it is legally sufficient to state a cause of action for which the court has jurisdiction and may grant relief {see § 57.085(6), (8), Florida Statutes}. When the file is sent to the judge, the Clerk is directed to prepare and also send an order in substantially the same form as attached Exhibit G. All or part of an indigent prisoner's claim must be dismissed if one or more of the enumerated criteria contained in said order is met.

8. If a litigant fails to file a fully completed application/affidavit, or if the judge determines that the litigant is not indigent based on the information provided in the application/affidavit and that a hearing on the indigency issue is not necessary, the judge will issue an order declaring that the person has not adequately demonstrated indigency and will revoke the Clerk's certificate of indigency. If payment of all appropriate fees is not made to the Clerk for disbursement to the appropriate agencies within fourteen (14) days after the issues of the revocation order, the cause will automatically be dismissed without prejudice. These time limits may be extended at the discretion of the assigned judge.

9. Indigent litigants are only entitled to those services enumerated in § 57.081, Florida Statutes, without prepayment. Any other service requested by the litigant must be paid for at the standard rate.

10. In the event multiple parties to a case seek indigent status, each party must complete the appropriate application/affidavit and each party must fully comply with all requirements of this Administrative Order.

11. When possible, the Clerk is directed to notify the judge at the time he/she reviews the litigant's indigency status as to other pending actions in which said litigant sought indigent status and the determinations reached in such other actions.

12. Administrative Order FM–2006–007–SC is hereby rescinded.

TO BE RECORDED in Flagler, Putnam, St. Johns and Volusia counties.

DONE AND ORDERED in Daytona Beach, Volusia County, Florida this 21st day of July 2009.

Judge J. David Walsh
Chief Judge

EXHIBIT A

IN THE CIRCUIT/COUNTY COURT OF THE SEVENTH JUDICIAL CIRCUIT

IN AND FOR ________ COUNTY, FLORIDA

CASE NO.
DIVISION

____________________,
Plaintiff/Petitioner or In the Interest of

vs.

____________________.
Defendant/Respondent

APPLICATION FOR DETERMINATION OF INDIGENT STATUS

Notice to Applicant: If you do not qualify for civil indigency and you cannot afford to pay the filine [1] fee, you must enroll in the Clerk's Office payment plan and pay a one-time administrative fee of $25.00.

1. **I have ________ dependents.** (Do not include children not living at home and do not include a working spouse or yourself.)

2. **I have a take-home income of $ ___** paid ( ) weekly ( ) bi-weekly ( ) semi-monthly ( ) monthly ( ) yearly.
(Take home income equals salary, wages, bonuses, commissions, allowances, overtime, tips and similar payments, minus deductions required by law and other court ordered support payments.)

3. **I have $ ___** in other income paid ( ) weekly ( ) bi- weekly ( ) semi-monthly ( ) monthly ( ) yearly. (Circle "Yes" and fill in the amount if you have this kind of income, otherwise circle "No")

Social Security benefits	Yes $_____	No
Unemployment compensation	Yes $_____	No
Union funds	Yes $_____	No
Workers compensation	Yes $_____	No
Retirement/pensions	Yes $_____	No
Trusts or gifts	Yes $_____	No
Veteran's benefits	Yes $_____	No
Child Support or other regular support from family members/spouse	Yes $_____	No
Rental income	Yes $_____	No
Dividends or interests	Yes $_____	No
Other kinds of income not on the list	Yes $_____	No

4. **I have other assets.** (Circle "Yes" and fill in the value of the property, otherwise circle "No".)

Cash	Yes $_____	No
Bank account(s)	Yes $_____	No
Certificates of deposit or money market account	Yes $_____	No
*Equity in Boats and other tangible property	Yes $_____	No
Savings	Yes $_____	No
Stocks and bonds	Yes $_____	No
*Equity in Real estate (excluding homestead)	Yes $_____	No
*Equity in Motor vehicles	Yes $_____	No

5. **I have total amount of liabilities and debts in the amount of $ ____________.**

6. **I have a private lawyer in this case** **Yes** **No**

A person who knowingly provides false information to the clerk or the court in seeking a determination of indigent status under F.S. 57.082 commits a misdemeanor of the first degree, punishable as provided in s.775.082 or s.775.083. **I attest that the information I have provided on this application is true and accurate to the best of my knowledge.**

Signed this __ day of ___, 20 __.

____
Signature of Applicant for Indigent Status

____
Date of Birth

Print Full Legal Name____________

____
Drivers License or ID Number

____
Address, P O Address, Street, City, State, Zip Code

Note: If applicant is determined by the clerk to be Not Indigent, you may seek judicial review by filing a petition to review.

CLERK'S DETERMINATION

Based on the information in this Application, I have determined the applicant to be ______ Indigent ________ Not indigent, according to 57.082, F.S.

Dated this ___ day of _________, 20 ___.

By ____________________
Deputy Clerk

This form was completed with the assistance of ________ Clerk/Deputy Clerk/Other.

EXHIBIT B

IN THE CIRCUIT/COUNTY COURT OF THE SEVENTH JUDICIAL CIRCUIT

IN AND FOR ________ COUNTY, FLORIDA

CASE NO.
DIVISION

____
Plaintiff(s)/Petitioner(s)/ Appellant(s),

vs

____
Defendant(s)/Respondent(s)/ Appellee(s).

AFFIDAVIT FOR DETERMINATION OF INDIGENT STATUS BY PRISONER PURSUANT TO F.S. 57.085

1. **I have a take-home income of $ ___** paid ( ) weekly ( ) bi-weekly ( ) semi-monthly ( ) monthly ( ) yearly.
(Take home income equals salary, wages, bonuses, commissions, allowances, overtime, tips and similar payments, minus deductions required by law and other court ordered support payments.)

2. **I have $_________ in other income** paid ( ) weekly ( ) bi-weekly ( ) semi-monthly ( ) monthly ( ) yearly.
(Circle "Yes" and fill in the amount if you have this kind of income, otherwise circle "No")

Social Security benefits	Yes $_____	No
Unemployment compensation	Yes $_____	No
Union funds	Yes $_____	No
Workers compensation	Yes $_____	No
Retirement/pensions	Yes $_____	No
Trusts or gifts	Yes $_____	No
Veteran's benefits	Yes $_____	No
Child Support or other regular support from family members/spouse	Yes $_____	No
Rental income	Yes $_____	No
Dividends or interests	Yes $_____	No
Other kinds of income not on the list	Yes $_____	No

3. **I have the following real estate:**

____________________	Value $________
____________________	Value $________
____________________	Value $________

____________________ Value $______

4. **I have tangible and intangible property worth more than $100:**

Stocks and Bonds	Yes $____	No
Other____________	Yes $____	No
Automobile	Yes $____	No
Other____________	Yes $____	No

5. **I have other assets.** (Circle "Yes" and fill in the value of the property, otherwise circle "No".)

Cash	Yes $____	No
Bank account(s)	Yes $____	No
Savings	Yes $____	No
Money Market account	Yes $____	No

6. **I have ____ dependents.** (Do not include children not living at home and do not include a working spouse or yourself.)

Age	Name

7. **I owe the following creditors:** (mortgage or rent payments, credit cards, etc.) If more space is required, use back of form.

Creditors Name	Amount Owed
	$
	$
	$
	$
	$
	$
	$
	$

Prisoner's Monthly Expenses	
	$
	$
	$
	$

8. During the past three years, have you been permitted two or more times to proceed without prepayment of court costs or fees in Florida or federal courts or adjudicatory forums, or to intervene in actions in these courts or adjudicatory forums without prepayment of court costs or fees, pursuant to sections 57.081 or 57.085, Florida Statutes, or 28 U.S.C. § 1915? Yes ( ) No ( )

If your answer is yes, list below all suits, actions, claims, proceedings, or appeals that you have brought or intervened in during the past five years in any court or adjudicatory forum.

Name of Court	Case Number	Nature of Action	Disposition

(If necessary, attach additional pages that reflect the required information.)

____

____

I have attached to this affidavit a photocopy of the trust account records for my prison account for the preceding six (6) months or for the length of my incarceration, whichever period is shorter.

I am presently unable to pay court costs and fees. Under penalties of perjury, I swear or affirm that all statements in this affidavit are true and complete.

____________ Inmate # ______ Date of Birth ______

Print Full Legal Name

Name of Institution: ____________

Address, PO Address, Street, City, State, Zip Code

____

Dated: __________

Signature of Petitioner

Sworn to and subscribed before me this ___ day of ______, 20 ___, by the affiant, ______, who is personally known to me or produced ______ as identification.

Signature of Notary Public or Correctional Officer

Print, Type or Stamp Commissioned Name of Notary Public

Commission Expires: __________

Commission #: __________

DETERMINATION OF INDIGENT STATUS

Based on the information in the petitioner's Affidavit for Indigent Status, I have determined that the petitioner ______ **Is Indigent** ______ **Is Not indigent**, according to Federal Poverty Guidelines. If the petitioner disagrees with the clerk's determination, they may file a written request for Judicial Review to determine their indigency status. The request must be filed within fourteen (14) days from the date of this determination or the case will be closed.

Dated this ____ day of ______, 20__.

Copy provided to prisoner by mail by ______ (initials of clerk).

CLERK OF THE CIRCUIT COURT
By ____________
Deputy Clerk

EXHIBIT C

IN THE CIRCUIT/COUNTY COURT OF THE SEVENTH JUDICIAL CIRCUIT

IN AND FOR ____________
COUNTY, FLORIDA

CASE NO.
DIVISION

____

Plaintiff(s)/Petitioner(s)/ Appellant(s),

vs

AFFIDAVIT OF PRIOR LITIGATION BY PRISONER PURSUANT TO F.S. 57.085(7)

____

Defendant(s)/Respondent(s)/ Appellee(s).

I ________ (*full legal name*), state the following in support of my application to defer the prepayment of court costs and fees in the above matter pursuant to Section 57.085(7), Florida Statutes:

1. I have been convicted of a crime and am currently incarcerated for that crime or I am being held in custody pending extradition or sentencing.

2. (*Check one*)

___ I am an intervener in the above-styled judicial proceeding.

___ I initiated the above-styled judicial proceeding.

3. I am a pro se litigant and am not represented by an attorney.

4. I certify that I have neither been paid nor promised to pay anyone for services on my behalf in connection with this judicial proceeding.

5. I am presently unable to pay court costs and fees otherwise payable by law to the court, clerk and sheriff for their services. Therefore, I am applying for a deferral of prepayment of costs and fees pursuant to Section 57.085, Florida Statutes

6. I have previously been adjudicated indigent under Section 57.085, Florida Statutes (prisoner indigence). Yes ( ) No ( )

7. I have previously been adjudicated indigent under Section 57.081, Florida Statutes (civil indigence). Yes ( ) No ( )

8. I have previously been adjudicated indigent under 28 U.S.C. 1915 by a federal court. Yes ( ) No ( )

If you answered "yes" to questions 6, 7, or 8, list below *all* suits, actions, claims, proceedings, or appeals, including dates, which you brought or in which you intervened in any court or other adjudicatory forum within the past five years.

____

____

____

____

____

____

9. As I have been adjudicated indigent twice in the preceding three years, pursuant to § 57.085(7), Florida Statutes, I am requesting leave of the court to proceed as an indigent prisoner litigant pursuant to § 57.085(7). As the referenced statute requires, I have provided a complete listing of cases, please see #8 above, and I have attached a copy of each complaint, petition, or other document purporting to commence a lawsuit and a record of disposition of the proceeding. Yes ( ) No ( )

10. Attached and incorporated into this Affidavit is a photocopy of my trust account records for my prison account for the preceding six (6) months or for the length of my incarceration, whichever period is shorter.

I am presently unable to pay court costs and fees. Under penalties of perjury, I swear or affirm that all statements in this affidavit are true and complete.

Print Full Legal Name ________________

Inmate # __________ Date of Birth ________

Name of Institution: ____________________

Address,____________________________

Dated: ____________ __________________

Signature of Petitioner

Sworn to and subscribed before me this ___ day of ________, 20 ___, by the affiant, ________, who is personally known to me or produced ________ as identification.

____

Signature of Notary Public or Correctional Officer

Print, Type or Stamp Commissioned Name of Notary Public

Commission Expires: ____________

Commission #: ____________

EXHIBIT D

IN THE CIRCUIT/COUNTY COURT OF THE SEVENTH JUDICIAL CIRCUIT

IN AND FOR ________ COUNTY, FLORIDA

____________________, **CASE NO.**

DIVISION

vs.

____________________,

ORDER ON APPLICATION FOR INDIGENT STATUS

THIS MATTER is before the Court on the referral of the application of for indigent status pursuant to 57.081 and 57.082, Florida Statutes by the Clerk of the Court. Having reviewed the court file, the Court finds that:

(1) ___ The petitioner is indigent and is entitled to proceed without prepayment of the costs associated with those services set forth in 57.081 and 57.082, Florida Statutes. If the litigant prevails in this action, all costs shall be taxed in his/her favor, when collected, shall be applied to pay costs which otherwise would have been received and which have not previously been paid.

(2) ___ Based on the information furnished, the petitioner has not adequately proven indigency. The litigant shall pay the appropriate filing fees and Sheriff's service charges to the Clerk of the Court or enter into a payment plan with the Clerk of the Court within 14 days of this order or this action shall be dismissed without prejudice and without further order of the Court.

(3) ___ Based on the information provided to this Court, the Court cannot determine the litigant's indigency status. Accordingly, the Court shall hold a hearing on the litigant's indigency status on ________, at ___ am/pm in ________, Florida. The litigant shall bring with him/her all relevant financial information to substantiate his/her claim of indigency as more fully set forth in the litigant's application for indigency

(4) ___ The petitioner is indigent and entitled to proceed without costs for services provided through the Family Law/Dependency Mediation Program.

DONE AND ORDERED in ________, ________ County, Florida this ___ day of ________, 20___.

____
CIRCUIT/COUNTY COURT
JUDGE

EXHIBIT E

IN THE CIRCUIT/COUNTY COURT OF THE SEVENTH JUDICIAL CIRCUIT

IN AND FOR ________ COUNTY, FLORIDA

____________________, CASE NO.
DIVISION
vs.

____________________,

ORDER ON PRIOR INDIGENCE DETERMINATIONS PURSUANT TO F.S. 57.085(7)

THIS MATTER is before the Court pursuant to the requirements of § 57.085(7) and § 57.082, Florida Statutes. Accordingly, the court finds and orders as follows:

(1) ___ The prisoner litigant **has not** at least twice in the preceding three years been adjudicated indigent for purposes of prepayment of court costs and fees. Therefore, it is appropriate for the court to proceed and determine if the prisoner litigant is indigent.

(2) ___ The prisoner litigant **has** at least twice in the preceding three years been adjudicated indigent for purposes of prepayment of court costs and fees, and **has not** attached a complete listing of each suit, action, claim, proceeding or appeal brought by or intervened in by the inmate in any court in the preceding five years and/or **has not** attached a copy of each complaint, petition, or other document purporting to commence a lawsuit and a record of disposition of the proceeding. Based upon the prisoner litigant's failure to attach said listings and pleadings, the court is unable to grant leave to find the prisoner litigant indigent. The prisoner litigant shall pay the appropriate filing fees and Sheriff's service charges to the Clerk of the Court within fourteen (14) days of the date of this Order, or this action shall be dismissed without prejudice and without further order of the Court.

(3) ___ The prisoner litigant **has** at least twice in the preceding three years been adjudicated indigent for purposes of prepayment of court costs and fees, and **has** attached a complete listing of each suit, action, claim, proceeding or appeal brought by or intervened in by the inmate in any court in the preceding five years and **has** attached a copy of each complaint, petition, or other document purporting to commence a lawsuit and a record of disposition of the proceeding. The court considers this a valid request for leave of court to determine if the prisoner litigant is indigent for the purposes of the above-styled proceedings. Upon review of the submitted documents the court GRANTS (________) DENIES (________) the prisoner litigant's request to proceed. If the request is GRANTED it is appropriate for the court to proceed and determine if the prisoner litigant is indigent.

If denied, state reason(s) below:

____

____

____

DONE AND ORDERED in ________, ________ County, Florida this ___ day of ________, 20___.

____
CIRCUIT/COUNTY COURT
JUDGE

EXHIBIT F

IN THE CIRCUIT/COUNTY COURT OF THE SEVENTH JUDICIAL CIRCUIT

IN AND FOR ________ COUNTY, FLORIDA

____________________, CASE NO.
DIVISION
vs.

____________________.

ORDER ON APPLICATION FOR INDIGENT STATUS OF PRISONER LITIGANT

THIS MATTER is before the Court on the referral of the application of ________ (prisoner litigant) for indigent status pursuant to § 57.085, Florida Statutes by the Clerk of Court. Having reviewed the court file, the Court finds that:

(1) ___ Based upon the information furnished the **prisoner litigant** has not adequately proven indigency. The prisoner litigant shall pay the appropriate filing fees and Sheriff's service charges to the Clerk of Court within fourteen (14) days of the date of this Order, or this action shall be dismissed without prejudice and without further order of the Court.

(2) ___ The prisoner litigant is indigent and is:

___ entitled to proceed without the **initial prepayment** of the costs associated with those services set forth in § 57.081, Florida Statutes.

___ able to pay part of the court costs and fees associated with this action before issuance of the initial process in this action. The prisoner litigant is hereby ordered to make an **initial partial payment** toward those court costs and fees pursuant to § 57.085(4), Florida Statutes within twenty (20) days of the date of this Order. Until such payment is made, no process shall issue.

Pursuant to § 57.085(5), Florida Statutes, the prisoner litigant is hereby ordered to make monthly payments until such time as the costs and fees associated with this action totaling $ ___ are paid in full. The Court reserves jurisdiction to assess and require the payment of additional fees and costs if any are incurred.

The Florida Department of Corrections or local detention facility shall place a lien on the inmate's prison trust account for the full amount of the court costs and fees associated with this action and shall withdraw the prisoner litigant's monthly payment, pursuant to § 57.085(5), and forward the monthly payment to the Clerk of the Circuit Court at the following address:

________ until such time as the costs and fees associated with this action are paid in full.

The Clerk of this Court shall provide a certified copy of this Order to the Superintendent of the Correctional Facility, at ________ so that the Florida Department of Corrections or local detention facility can comply with paragraph(s) 1 and/or 2 this Order.

(3) ___ Based on the information provided to this Court, the Court cannot determine the litigant's indigency status. Accordingly, the Court shall hold a hearing on the litigant's indigency status on ________, at ___ a.m./p.m. in ________, Florida. The litigant shall bring with him/her all relevant financial information to substantiate his/her claim of indigency as more fully set forth in the litigant's financial affidavit.

DONE AND ORDERED in ________, ________ County, Florida this ___ day of, ________, 20___.

____

CIRCUIT/COUNTY COURT JUDGE

EXHIBIT G

IN THE CIRCUIT/COUNTY COURT OF THE SEVENTH JUDICIAL CIRCUIT

IN AND FOR ________ COUNTY, FLORIDA

CASE NO.
DIVISION

________________,

vs.

________________.

ORDER DISMISSING PRISONER LITIGATION

THIS MATTER came before the Court on the Plaintiff/Petitioner's ________, and the Court, having considered the petition/complaint and court file, and being otherwise fully advised in the premises, hereby finds as follows:

(1) ___ the petition/complaint fails to state any claim for which relief may be granted and has no arguable basis in law or fact.

(2) ___ the claim(s) raised in the petition/complaint is/are substantially similar to previously litigated claim(s) involving the same parties or arising from the same operative facts as the subject claim(s).

(3) ___ the petition/complaint seeks monetary relief from respondents/defendants who are immune from suit.

(4) ___ the plaintiff/petitioner's claim of indigency was false or misleading.

(5) ___ this Court is without the requisite jurisdiction to entertain the prisoner's petition for writ of mandamus or habeas corpus because the prisoner is not incarcerated within this judicial circuit.

(6) ___ this Court is without the requisite jurisdiction to entertain the prisoner's petition for writ of mandamus because the prisoner has failed to allege or demonstrate in his petition that he has exhausted the two-step administrative grievance procedure provided for in Rules 33–29.006 and 33–29.007, Florida Administrative Code (1993).

(7) ___ the petition for writ of habeas corpus fails to allege or demonstrate that the petitioner is entitled to immediate release.

(8) ___ the petition/complaint was frivolously filed and the prisoner shall, in accordance with Section 944.279, Florida Statutes (1996), be subject to a forfeiture of earned and unearned gain time as a penalty for instituting this frivolous proceeding in this Court.

(9) ___ the plaintiff/petitioner failed to pay court costs and fees assessed by prior Court order despite having the ability to pay.

(10) ___ the plaintiff/petitioner's claim has little likelihood of success on its merits.

(11) ___ the allegations of fact in the complaint/petition claim are fanciful or not credible.

(12) ___ the petition/complaint seeks relief for mental or emotional injury where there has been no related allegation of a physical injury.

(13) ___ the petition/complaint is frivolous, malicious, or reasonably appears to be intended to harass one or more named defendants.

(14) ___ Other ________________________

Accordingly, it is, ORDERED AND ADJUDGED that:

___ the Plaintiff/Petitioner's ________, is hereby DISMISSED with prejudice; and

___ the Clerk of Court's Office in and for ________ County, Florida is hereby directed to provide a certified copy of this order to the Superintendent of so that disciplinary action may be instituted against the Plaintiff/Petitioner, DC # ___), in accordance with Section 944.28(2)(a), Florida Statutes (1996).

DONE AND ORDERED in ________, ________ County, Florida this ___ day of ________, 20___.

____

CIRCUIT/COUNTY COURT JUDGE

Amended effective July 21, 2009.

1 So in original.

FM–2015–008–SC. FAMILY SELF–HELP PROGRAM

IN THE CIRCUIT COURT OF FLORIDA, SEVENTH JUDICIAL CIRCUIT IN AND FOR FLAGLER, PUTNAM, ST. JOHNS AND VOLUSIA COUNTIES

RE: FAMILY SELF–HELP PROGRAM

REF: FM–2015–008–SC

Rescinds (FM–2002–008–SC)

WHEREAS, Rule 12.750, Florida Family Law Rules of Procedure, authorizes chief judges to establish and operate self-help programs under the auspices of the court to facilitate access to family courts, and

WHEREAS, statistics show that a large percentage of family law case filings involve at least one self represented litigant, and

WHEREAS, the undersigned believes that to the extent possible, the Seventh Judicial Circuit Court should take steps to ensure that it is accessible, convenient, understandable and affordable to the citizens of the circuit;

NOW THEREFORE, I, TERENCE R. PERKINS, Chief Judge of the Seventh Judicial Circuit of Florida, authorize the Court Administrator's office to operate a Family Self–Help Program for purposes of assisting self represented litigants to achieve fair and efficient resolutions to their family law cases.

IT IS FURTHER ORDERED as follows:

1. The Self–Help Program described herein operates under the auspices of the court in Flagler, Putnam and Volusia counties.

2. "Family Law cases" include those categories of cases enumerated in this court's administrative order establishing a Family Law Division.

3. Services provided by program staff comports with those outlined in Rule 12.750(c), Florida Family Law Rules of Procedure.

4. Program services are made available to all self represented litigants in family law cases, regardless of income, unless otherwise provided by law.

5. A disclaimer entitled "Notice of Limitation of Services Provided" (see Rule 12.750(h), Florida Family Law Rules of Procedure) is posted in each Self–Help Program office.

6. Administrative order FM–2002–008–SC is hereby rescinded effective October 1, 2015.

Nothing in this Order shall be construed to limit or restrict services provided to family law litigants by Clerks of Court or other agencies.

TO BE RECORDED in Flagler, Putnam, St. Johns and Volusia counties.

DONE AND ORDERED in Daytona Beach, Volusia County, Florida, this 27th day of August 2015.

TERENCE R. PERKINS
CHIEF JUDGE

Amended effective August 27, 2015.

FM–2018–009–SC. UNITED FAMILY COURTS

IN THE CIRCUIT COURT OF FLORIDA, SEVENTH JUDICIAL CIRCUIT IN AND FOR FLAGLER, PUTNAM, ST. JOHNS AND VOLUSIA COUNTIES

RE: UNITED FAMILY COURTS

REF: FM–2018–009–SC

WHEREAS, the Florida Supreme Court has encouraged judicial circuits to establish Unified Family Courts as a way to more efficiently and effectively address the needs of families with multiple related Family Law court cases, and

WHEREAS, the judges and various other stakeholders throughout the Seventh Judicial Circuit are also supportive of Unified Family Courts and have worked diligently to bring the UFC concept to fruition in all counties of the circuit;

NOW THEREFORE, I, RAUL A. ZAMBRANO, Chief Judge of the Seventh Judicial Circuit Court of Florida, hereby order that Unified Family Courts be formally established in Flagler, Putnam, St. Johns and Volusia counties to hear such matters involving related Family Law cases as may be assigned.

IT IS FURTHER ORDERED that topics such as definitions, case assignments/reassignments, division designations, and judicial rotations will be the subjects of separate administrative orders. In summary, when a Family Law case is filed, the Clerk's office will ascertain if an active Family Law case involving the same family exists. If such an active related Family Law case exists, the newly filed case is to be assigned to the same judicial division. Family Case Management staff will assist the Clerks' offices with the identification of related cases and the assignment/reassignment thereof. Additional issues that may arise are to be coordinated and mutually agreed upon by the affected judges.

IT IS FURTHER ORDERED that the Clerks' offices are to make provisions within their respective case maintenance systems to "link" related Family Law cases.

TO BE RECORDED in Flagler, Putnam, St. Johns and Volusia Counties.

DONE AND ORDERED in DeLand, Volusia County, Florida, this 2nd day of August 2018.

RAUL A. ZAMBRANO
CHIEF JUDGE

Adopted effective August 2, 2018.

FM–2002–010–SC. APPROVAL OF LOCAL FAMILY LAW FORMS

IN THE CIRCUIT COURT OF FLORIDA, SEVENTH JUDICIAL CIRCUIT IN AND FOR FLAGLER, PUTNAM, ST. JOHNS AND VOLUSIA COUNTIES

RE: APPROVAL OF LOCAL FAMILY LAW FORMS

REF: FM–2002–010–SC

WHEREAS, the Supreme Court of Florida adopted Rule 12.750, Florida Family Law Rules of Procedure, which authorizes chief judges to approve in writing forms in substantial compliance with and not inconsistent with the Supreme Court approved forms, and

WHEREAS, such forms, which include local requirements, have been drafted and reviewed by the Family Law judges, and

WHEREAS, the undersigned has been advised of the necessity to approve such forms for use throughout the circuit;

NOW, THEREFORE, I, ROBERT K. ROUSE JR., Chief Judge of the Seventh Judicial Circuit of Florida, hereby approve the forms listed in Attachment A, attached hereto, for use within the Seventh Judicial Circuit.

IT IS FURTHER ORDERED that forms may be added to, or deleted from, the list of approved forms, upon approval of the Family Law judges, without benefit of a revised Administrative Order. In the event the list of approved forms is amended, the Court Administrator's office shall update said list and circulate it to interested parties, including those designated by Rule 12.750, Florida Family Law Rules of Procedure.

TO BE RECORDED in Flagler, Putnam, St. Johns and Volusia counties.

DONE AND ORDERED in Daytona Beach, Volusia County, Florida, this 15th day of July, 2002.

Judge Robert K. Rouse, Jr.
Chief Judge

Adopted effective July 15, 2002.

FM–2002–011–SC. INJUNCTION FOR PROTECTION FORMS

IN THE CIRCUIT COURT OF FLORIDA, SEVENTH JUDICIAL CIRCUIT IN AND FOR FLAGLER, PUTNAM, ST. JOHNS AND VOLUSIA COUNTIES

RE: INJUNCTION FOR PROTECTION FORMS

REF: FM–2002–011–SC

WHEREAS, the undersigned has determined that the entry of an administrative order regarding the use of standardized forms in Injunction for Protection proceedings in the Seventh Judicial Circuit is necessary for the efficient and proper administration of justice;

NOW THEREFORE, I, ROBERT K. ROUSE, JR., Chief Judge of the Seventh Judicial Circuit of Florida, hereby order that pursuant to Rule 12.610(c)(2)(A), Florida Family Law Rules of Procedure, forms approved by the Supreme Court of Florida shall be used in temporary and permanent injunction for protection proceedings (see chapters 741 and 784, Florida Statutes) in the Seventh Judicial Circuit.

TO BE RECORDED in Flagler, Putnam, St. Johns and Volusia counties.

DONE AND ORDERED in Daytona Beach, Volusia County, Florida this 15th day of July, 2002.

Judge Robert K. Rouse, Jr.
Chief Judge

Adopted effective July 15, 2002.

FM–2002–012–SC. CROSS ASSIGNMENT/INJUNCTIONS FOR PROTECTION

IN THE CIRCUIT COURT OF FLORIDA, SEVENTH JUDICIAL CIRCUIT IN AND FOR FLAGLER, PUTNAM, ST. JOHNS AND VOLUSIA COUNTIES

REF: FM–2002–012–SC

RE: **CROSS ASSIGNMENT/INJUNCTIONS FOR PROTECTION**

WHEREAS, it has been made known to the undersigned that the efficient and proper administration of justice regarding issuance of Temporary Injunctions for Protection in the Seventh Judicial Circuit requires the temporary assignment of County Court judges to Circuit Court jurisdiction;

NOW, THEREFORE, I, ROBERT K. ROUSE, JR., Chief Judge of the Seventh Judicial Circuit of Florida, hereby order that all County Court judges of the Seventh Judicial Circuit are temporarily assigned to Circuit Court jurisdiction for purposes of issuing Temporary Injunctions for Protection pursuant to §§ 741.30 and 784.046, Florida Statutes. The County Court judges herein assigned to Circuit Court are hereby vested with all and singular the powers and prerogatives conferred by the State of Florida upon a judge of the Court to which they are assigned.

TO BE RECORDED in Flagler, Putnam, St. Johns and Volusia counties.

DONE AND ORDERED in Daytona Beach, Volusia County, Florida, this 15th day of July, 2002.

ROBERT K. ROUSE, JR.
CHIEF JUDGE

Adopted effective July 15, 2002.

FM–2010–013–VL. PROCEDURE FOR ISSUANCE OF EMERGENCY INJUNCTIONS FOR PROTECTION AGAINST DOMESTIC VIOLENCE

IN THE CIRCUIT COURT OF FLORIDA, SEVENTH JUDICIAL CIRCUIT IN AND FOR VOLUSIA COUNTY

RE: PROCEDURE FOR ISSUANCE OF EMERGENCY INJUNCTIONS FOR PROTECTION AGAINST DOMESTIC VIOLENCE

REF: FM–2010–013–VL

(Rescinds FM–2003–013–VL)

WHEREAS, §§ 741.29, 741.2901, 741.2902, 741.30 and 741.31, Florida Statutes, mandate certain procedures related to domestic violence, and

WHEREAS, § 26.20, Florida Statutes, requires a judge to be available on weekends, holidays, and after hours on weekdays, to consider ex parte motions for temporary injunctions in domestic violence cases;

NOW THEREFORE, I, J. DAVID WALSH, Chief Judge of the Seventh Judicial Circuit of Florida, hereby establish the following procedure for issuance of **emergency** Injunctions for Protection against Domestic Violence in Volusia County:

1. When responding to domestic violence complaints, law enforcement officers shall provide victims with written materials concerning Injunctions for Protection against Domestic Violence. Said materials should include, at a minimum: instructions for seeking an Injunction for Protection during normal business hours; instructions for seeking an Injunction for Protection on weekends and holidays at First Appearance Court; and instructions for seeking an **emergency** Injunction for Protection on weekends, holidays, and after hours on weekdays. The Volusia County Clerk of Court's office shall provide law enforcement agencies with suggested language for said written materials, which may include more than the above-stated minimum. If a defendant is arrested and booked into the Volusia County Branch Jail as a result of domestic violence, the associated victim may seek an Injunction for Protection at a Volusia County court facility during normal business hours or at the Branch Jail on weekends and holidays.

2. If, after following procedures established by the Clerk's office, a victim elects to pursue issuance of an **emergency** Injunction for Protection, he/she must contact a Clerk employee who will make arrangements to meet the victim at the Branch Jail or some other designated location. The victim must make his/her own arrangements for transportation to the Branch Jail or other designated location.

3. The Clerk employee will assist the victim in the proper completion of a Petition for Injunction for Protection against Domestic Violence and other related paperwork.

4. Upon completion of all paperwork, the Clerk employee will contact the Duty Judge by telephone, and inform the Duty

Judge of the information contained in the Petition for Injunction for Protection against Domestic Violence.

5. If the Duty Judge determines that sufficient grounds for issuance of an **emergency** temporary Injunction for Protection against Domestic Violence do **not** exist, he/she will verbally instruct the Clerk employee to complete an appropriate denial order and advise the victim of that decision. The Clerk employee shall prepare a denial order in accordance with the Duty Judge's verbal instructions, review it with the Duty Judge, date it, affix the Duty Judge's conformed signature to it, certify that it is a conformed copy of the original order, and provide a copy to the victim. At the next available opportunity, the Duty Judge will affix his/her original signature to the original order and "nunc pro tunc" said order to the date of its oral issuance. Said "nunc pro tunc" order shall be filed in the appropriate court file. The failure of the Duty Judge to sign the original order will not affect the validity of the order.

6. If the Duty Judge determines that sufficient grounds for issuance of an **emergency** temporary Injunction for Protection against Domestic Violence exist, the Duty Judge will select one of the following methods for its issuance:

a) **Telephone:** The Duty Judge will verbally instruct the Clerk employee to issue an appropriate order granting the temporary Injunction for Protection against Domestic Violence and advise the victim of that decision. The Clerk employee shall prepare an appropriate order granting the petition in accordance with the Duty Judge's verbal instructions, review it with the Duty Judge, date it, affix the Duty Judge's conformed signature to it, certify that it is a conformed copy of the original order, provide a copy to the victim, and fax a copy to the Warrants Division of the Volusia County Sheriff's office for service. At the next available opportunity, the Duty Judge will affix his/her original signature to the original order and "nunc pro tunc" said order to the date of its oral issuance. Said "nunc pro tunc" order shall be filed in the appropriate court file. The failure of the Duty Judge to sign the original order will not affect the validity of the order.

b) **Facsimile:** The Duty Judge will instruct the Clerk employee to complete portions of an appropriate temporary Injunction for Protection against Domestic Violence. The Clerk employee shall then fax the proposed order granting the petition to the Duty Judge for consideration, completion and signature. The Duty Judge will fax the completed order back to the Clerk employee who will certify that it is a copy of the original order, provide a copy to the victim, and fax a copy to the Warrants Division of the Volusia County Sheriff's office for service. At the next available opportunity, the original, signed order shall be filed in the appropriate court file.

c) **In Person:** The Duty Judge will instruct the Clerk employee to complete portions of an appropriate temporary Injunction for Protection against Domestic Violence. The Clerk employee will then contact the Volusia County Sheriff's office, which shall transport the proposed order granting the petition to the Duty Judge for consideration, completion and signature. The Sheriff's office will then return the original, signed order to the Clerk employee who shall provide a certified copy to the victim and fax a copy to the Warrants Division of the Volusia County Sheriff's office for service. The original, signed order shall be filed in the appropriate court file.

7. The Volusia County Sheriff is herewith authorized and empowered to accept a certified copy of a conformed, signed Injunction for Protection against Domestic Violence for service of process.

8. Hearings on **emergency** temporary Injunctions for Protection against Domestic Violence shall be scheduled before assigned judges within 15 days of dates of issuance.

IT IS FURTHER ORDERED that the Court Administrator's office shall prepare a notebook containing appropriate forms, orders, and other relevant materials for use by the Duty Judge.

IT IS FURTHER ORDERED that Administrative Order FM–2003–013–VL is hereby rescinded effective February 1, 2010

This Order takes effect February 1, 2010.

TO BE RECORDED in Volusia County, Florida

DONE AND ORDERED in Daytona Beach, Volusia County, Florida this 28th day of January 2010.

Judge J. David Walsh
Chief Judge

Amended effective February 1, 2010.

FM–2010–014–SC. SERVICE OF DOMESTIC, REPEAT, SEXUAL & DATING VIOLENCE INJUNCTIONS FOR PROTECTION BY MUNICIPAL LAW ENFORCEMENT AGENCIES

IN THE CIRCUIT COURT OF FLORIDA, SEVENTH JUDICIAL CIRCUIT IN AND FOR FLAGLER, PUTNAM, ST. JOHNS AND VOLUSIA COUNTIES

RE: SERVICE OF DOMESTIC, REPEAT, SEXUAL & DATING VIOLENCE INJUNCTIONS FOR PROTECTION BY MUNICIPAL LAW ENFORCEMENT AGENCIES

REF: FM–2010–014–SC

(Rescinds FM–2002–014–SC)

WHEREAS, §§ 741.30(8)(a)1 and 784.046(8)(a)1, Florida Statutes, provide that the chief judge of each judicial circuit, in consultation with appropriate sheriffs, may authorize law enforcement agencies within his/her judicial circuit to effect service of injunctions for protection against domestic violence, repeat violence, sexual violence and dating violence, and

WHEREAS, the undersigned chief judge has consulted with the Sheriffs' offices in Flagler, Putnam, St. Johns and Volusia counties concerning this matter;

NOW THEREFORE, I, J. DAVID WALSH, Chief Judge of the Seventh Judicial Circuit of Florida, hereby order that the Sheriffs' departments of Flagler, Putnam, St. Johns and Volusia counties shall be the primary entities responsible for the service of domestic violence, repeat violence, sexual violence and dating violence injunctions for protection issued by the judges of the Seventh Judicial Circuit against respondents located in their respective jurisdictions.

IT IS FURTHER ORDERED that when presented with a serviceable copy of an injunction for protection against domestic violence, repeat violence, sexual violence or dating violence, law enforcement officers with municipal police departments within Flagler, Putnam, St. Johns and Volusia counties are authorized to effect service of process on respondents located in their respective jurisdictions. Law enforcement officers with municipal police departments serving injunctions pursuant to this Order shall use service and verification procedures consistent with those of the Sheriff's office of the county in which they are located.

IT IS FURTHER ORDERED that Administrative Order FM–2002–014–SC is hereby rescinded.

TO BE RECORDED in Flagler, Putnam, St. Johns and Volusia counties.

DONE AND ORDERED in Daytona Beach, Volusia County, Florida this 28th day of January 2010.

Judge J. David Walsh
Chief Judge

Amended effective January 28, 2010.

FM–2004–015–SC (A). ASSIGNMENT OF INJUNCTIONS FOR PROTECTION/DOMESTIC RELATIONS / JUVENILE DEPENDENCIES

IN THE CIRCUIT COURT OF FLORIDA, SEVENTH JUDICIAL CIRCUIT IN AND FOR FLAGLER, PUTNAM, ST. JOHNS AND VOLUSIA COUNTIES

RE: ASSIGNMENT OF INJUNCTIONS FOR PROTECTION/DOMESTIC RELATIONS / JUVENILE DEPENDENCIES

REF: FM–2004–015–SC (A) (Rescinds FM–2004–015–SC)

WHEREAS, it has been made known to the undersigned that the efficient and proper administration of justice requires that a procedure be developed to assign Injunctions for Protection and Domestic Relations cases (Simplified Dissolution of Marriage, Dissolution of Marriage, Separate Maintenance, Annulment, Domestic Violence Injunctions, Custody, Child Support, UIFSA) involving the same parties to the same judicial division, and

WHEREAS, it has also been made known to the undersigned that a procedure must be developed to assign Injunctions for Protection and Juvenile Dependency cases involving the same parties to the same judicial division;

NOW THEREFORE, I, JULIANNE PIGGOTTE, Chief Judge of the Seventh Judicial Circuit of Florida, hereby order that upon the filing of an Injunction for Protection, the Clerk of Court's Office shall ascertain if a Domestic Relations case or a Juvenile Dependency case involving the same parties exists. If so, the Clerk's Office shall assign the Injunction for Protection to the judicial division to which the Domestic Relations case or the Juvenile Dependency case is assigned. In the event that both a Domestic Relations case and a Juvenile Dependency case involving the same parties exist, the Clerk's Office shall assign the Injunction for Protection to the judicial division to which the Juvenile Dependency case is assigned.

IT IS FURTHER ORDERED that upon the filing of a Domestic Relations case or a Juvenile Dependency case, the Clerk of Court's Office shall ascertain if an Injunction for Protection involving the same parties exists. If so, the Clerk's Office shall assign the Domestic Relations case or Juvenile Dependency case to the judicial division to which the Injunction for Protection is assigned, provided Domestic Relations cases or Juvenile Dependency cases are normally assigned to said judicial division. If said judicial division is **not** normally assigned to handle Domestic Relations cases or Juvenile Dependency cases, the Clerk's Office shall assign the Domestic Relations case or Juvenile Dependency case to a judicial division normally assigned to handle such cases and shall administratively reassign/transfer the Injunction for Protection to said judicial division.

IT IS FURTHER ORDERED that upon the filing of a Domestic Relations case, the Clerk of Court's Office shall ascertain if a Juvenile Dependency case involving the same parties exists. If so, the Clerk's Office shall assign the Domestic Relations case to a judicial division normally assigned to handle such cases and shall promptly notify each of the affected judicial divisions of the existence of said cases. Conversely, upon the filing of a Juvenile Dependency case, the Clerk of Court's Office shall ascertain if a Domestic Relations case involving the same parties exists. If so, the Clerk's Office shall assign the Juvenile Dependency case to a judicial division normally assigned to handle such cases and shall promptly notify each of the affected judicial divisions of the existence of said cases.

IT IS FURTHER ORDERED that Administrative Order # FM–2004–015–SC is hereby rescinded.

TO BE RECORDED in Flagler, Putnam, St. Johns and Volusia counties.

DONE AND ORDERED in Daytona Beach, Volusia County, Florida this 5th day of August, 2004

Judge Julianne Piggotte
CHIEF JUDGE

Amended effective August 5, 2004.

FM–2013–016–SC. PARENT EDUCATION AND FAMILY STABILIZATION COURSE IN FAMILY LAW CASES

IN THE CIRCUIT COURT OF FLORIDA, SEVENTH JUDICIAL CIRCUIT IN AND FOR FLAGLER, PUTNAM, ST. JOHNS AND VOLUSIA COUNTIES

RE: PARENT EDUCATION AND FAMILY STABILIZATION COURSE IN FAMILY LAW CASES

REF: FM–2013–016–SC (Rescinds FM–2012–016–SC)

WHEREAS, the Court believes that the perspectives of minor children should be considered by all parties in Family Law cases and that participation in an appropriate program will help parties foster stronger, more stable relationships with their children, and

WHEREAS, it has been made known to the undersigned that the efficient and proper adjudication of Family Law cases involving parents with minor children necessitates the establishment of certain guidelines regarding these programs;

NOW, THEREFORE, I, TERENCE R. PERKINS, Chief Judge of the Seventh Judicial Circuit of Florida, hereby order as follows:

1. Pursuant to § 61.21(4), Florida Statutes, all parties to a dissolution of marriage proceeding with minor children, or a paternity action which involves issues of parental responsibility, shall attend and successfully complete a Parent Education and Family Stabilization course approved by the Department of Children and Family Services in accordance with § 61.21(2), Florida Statutes. The course(s) shall be designed to assist parents with children's issues as they make transitions during and after a divorce or separation.

2. In Family Law cases involving issues of shared parental responsibilities and/or timesharing of minor children, both parties shall attend and successfully complete a Parent Education and Family Stabilization course prior to the entry of a final judgment. Parties who have previously completed a parenting education course and have filed a Certificate of Completion are exempt from this requirement.

3. In cases affected by this order, the Clerk of Court shall advise the Petitioner and/or Petitioner's attorney of the requirements of this order by providing him/her with a copy, in either physical or electronic format, of instructions and information on how to access a list of providers when the case is filed. The Clerk shall document the provision of these materials to the Petitioner and/or Petitioner's attorney, and the method by which they were provided, in the appropriate case file. It is the responsibility of the Petitioner and/or Petitioner's attorney to provide the Respondent with a copy of the instructions and information on how to access a list of providers by including such with the petition at time of service. In cases where the Clerk of Court forwards the petition to the Sheriff for service, a copy of the instructions and information on how to access a list of providers must be included. The Court Administrator's office will provide the Clerk with the aforementioned instructions and information.

4. In dissolution of marriage cases, the Petitioner shall enroll in a program of his/her choosing within twenty (20) days after filing the petition and shall complete said program within forty-five (45) days after filing. The Respondent shall enroll in a program of his/her choosing within twenty (20) days after service of the petition and shall complete said program within forty-five (45) days after service. Parties shall complete the chosen program(s) before participating in court-ordered mediation, or before the scheduled trial date, whichever is sooner. Upon successful completion of the chosen program(s), each party shall file a Certificate of Completion, supplied by the program provider, with the Clerk of Court, who shall file said Certificate in the appropriate case file.

5. In paternity actions, the Petitioner shall enroll in a program of his/her choosing within twenty (20) days after filing the petition and shall complete said program within forty-five (45) days after filing. The respondent shall enroll in a program of his/her choosing and shall complete said program within forty-five (45) days after an acknowledgement of paternity by him/her, an adjudication of paternity as to him/her, or issuance of an order granting visitation to, or support from, him/her. Upon successful completion of the chosen program(s), each party shall file a Certificate of Completion, supplied by the program provider, with the Clerk of Court, who shall file said Certificate in the appropriate case file.

6. Each party ordered to attend shall pay the cost of attending the program. The cost of the program shall be set by the program provider, but shall be based on each party's ability to pay, as determined by the program provider.

7. Parties many attend any Parent Education and Family Stabilization course approved by the Department of Children and Family Services.

8. Nothing in this order requires parties to attend an approved Parent Education and Family Stabilization course together.

9. Nothing in this order prohibits judges from referring parties to Parent Education and Family Stabilization courses in cases not subject to this order.

10. Nothing in this order prohibits judges from waiving the requirements of this order upon presentation of a proper motion in individual cases.

11. Failure to comply with the terms of this order may result in appropriate sanctions against the offending party.

IT IS FURTHER ORDERED that Administrative Order # FM–2012–016–SC is hereby rescinded.

TO BE RECORDED in Flagler, Putnam, St. Johns and Volusia counties.

DONE AND ORDERED in Daytona Beach, Volusia County, Florida, this 25th day of September 2013.

TERENCE R. PERKINS
CHIEF JUDGE

Amended effective September 25, 2013.

FM–2005–017–SC. PARENT EDUCATION AND FAMILY STABILIZATION COURSE PROVIDERS

IN THE CIRCUIT COURT OF FLORIDA, SEVENTH JUDICIAL CIRCUIT IN AND FOR FLAGLER, PUTNAM, ST. JOHNS AND VOLUSIA COUNTIES

REF: FM–2005–017–SC

Rescinds (FM–2003–017–SC)

RE: PARENT EDUCATION AND FAMILY STABILIZATION COURSE PROVIDERS

WHEREAS, pursuant to § 61.21, Florida Statutes, litigants in certain family law proceedings are required to attend an approved Parent Education and Family Stabilization course, and

WHEREAS, pursuant to § 61.21 (2), Florida Statutes, the responsibility for approving Parent Education and Family Stabilization courses and providers rests with the Department of Children and Family Services;

NOW THEREFORE, I, JULIANNE PIGGOTTE, Chief Judge of the Seventh Judicial Circuit of Florida, hereby order that Parent Education and Family Stabilization course providers must seek approval from the Department of Children and Family Services in order to provide educational services mandated by § 61.21, Florida Statutes.

IT IS FURTHER ORDERED that pursuant to § 61.21 (3)(a), Florida Statutes, the Department of Children and Family Services shall supply the Seventh Judicial Circuit Court Administrator's Office with a list of approved programs and providers in the circuit.

IT IS FURTHER ORDERED that Administrative Order # FM–2003–017–SC is hereby rescinded.

TO BE RECORDED in Flagler, Putnam, St. Johns and Volusia counties.

DONE AND ORDERED in Daytona Beach, Volusia County, FL this 30th day of June, 2005.

JULIANNE PIGGOTTE
CHIEF JUDGE

Amended effective June 30, 2005.

FM-2015-018-SJ. CHILD EDUCATION COURSE IN DISSOLUTION CASES

IN THE CIRCUIT COURT OF FLORIDA, SEVENTH JUDICIAL CIRCUIT IN AND FOR ST. JOHNS COUNTY

RE: CHILD EDUCATION COURSE IN DISSOLUTION CASES

REF: FM-2015-018-SJ

(Rescinds FM-2002-018-SJ)

WHEREAS, the Supreme Court of Florida issued an opinion on May 3, 2001, In re: Report of the Family Court Steering Committee (Case No. SC00-1410), and

WHEREAS, the Florida Supreme Court's opinion indicates that Family Courts should strive to meet the needs of families and children involved in the court system by offering appropriate services and linkages to community service providers, and

WHEREAS, this Court believes that it would be in the best interest of children of divorcing parents to attend an educational program designed to assist children in coping with divorce;

NOW, THEREFORE, I, Terence R. Perkins, Chief Judge of the Seventh Judicial Circuit of Florida, hereby order as follows:

1. All children, between the ages of six and seventeen, whose parents have filed a Petition for Dissolution of Marriage in St. Johns County, Florida, may be ordered to attend a course designed to assist the children of parents involved in dissolution proceedings. Classes must be a minimum of two hours in length and geared toward assisting children with issues related to their parents' divorce.

2. Parents of minor children shall make arrangements to ensure that their children attend said course, if so ordered.

3. The course provider shall set the cost of the program, but no party shall be refused due to their inability to pay.

4. Costs shall initially be borne by the custodial parent, unless otherwise ordered by the court. The court may thereafter order costs to be redistributed.

5. Upon completion of the course, the course provider shall forward Certificates of Completion to the Clerk of Court's office for inclusion in case files.

6. Nothing in this Order prohibits judges from ordering attendance at a Child Education Course in cases not subject to this Order.

7. Nothing in this Order prohibits judges from waiving the requirements of this Order upon presentation of a proper motion in individual cases.

8. Failure to comply with the terms of this Order may result in appropriate sanctions against the offending party.

TO BE RECORDED in St. Johns County, Florida.

DONE AND ORDERED in Daytona Beach, Volusia County, Florida, this 2nd day of April 2015.

TERENCE R. PERKINS
CHIEF JUDGE

Amended effective April 2, 2015.

FM-2002-019-SC. SUPERVISED VISITATION PROGRAMS

IN THE CIRCUIT COURT OF FLORIDA, SEVENTH JUDICIAL CIRCUIT IN AND FOR FLAGLER, PUTNAM, ST. JOHNS AND VOLUSIA COUNTIES

RE: SUPERVISED VISITATION PROGRAMS

REF: FM-2002-019-SC

WHEREAS, the Supreme Court of Florida entered an Administrative Order dated November 18, 1999, adopting minimum standards for supervised visitation programs and directing the chief judge of each circuit to enter into an agreement with supervised visitation centers willing to comply with the minimum standards, and

WHEREAS, the undersigned believes that supervised visitation programs are an element of a model family court and an important resource to family law judges, and

WHEREAS, supervised visitation centers are opening throughout the Seventh Judicial Circuit;

NOW, THEREFORE, I, **ROBERT K. ROUSE, JR.,** Chief Judge of the Seventh Judicial Circuit of Florida, hereby order as follows:

1. Any supervised visitation program operating in the Seventh Judicial Circuit, that wishes to receive cases pursuant to court order, shall comply with standards adopted by the Florida Supreme Court by Administrative Order, dated November 19, 1999.

2. Prior to accepting cases pursuant to court order, said visitation program(s) shall enter into an agreement with the Chief Judge of the Seventh Judicial Circuit.

3. Judges who refer cases to a supervised visitation program shall utilize only the services of those programs which have entered into an agreement pursuant to paragraph # 2 above.

4. The Court Administrator's Office shall maintain a list of supervised visitation programs in the Seventh Judicial Circuit who comply with the terms of this Order. Said list shall be updated periodically and circulated to interested parties.

TO BE RECORDED in Flagler, Putnam, St. Johns and Volusia counties.

DONE AND ORDERED in Daytona Beach, Volusia County, Florida, this 15th day of July, 2002.

Judge Robert K. Rouse, Jr.
Chief Judge

Adopted effective July 15, 2002.

FM-2012-020-SC. CHILD SUPPORT ENFORCEMENT HEARING OFFICERS

IN THE CIRCUIT COURT OF FLORIDA, SEVENTH JUDICIAL CIRCUIT IN AND FOR FLAGLER, PUTNAM, ST. JOHNS AND VOLUSIA COUNTIES

RE: CHILD SUPPORT ENFORCEMENT HEARING OFFICERS

REF: FM–2012–020–SC (Rescinds FM–2009–020–SC)

WHEREAS, pursuant to Rule 12.491, Florida Family Law Rules of Procedure, circuits may utilize Child Support Enforcement Hearing Officers if approval for such has been granted by the Chief Justice of the Florida Supreme Court, and

WHEREAS, pursuant to administrative orders issued by the Florida Supreme Court, the Seventh Judicial Circuit is authorized to utilize Child Support Enforcement Hearing Officers in both Title IV–D and non IV–D proceedings;

NOW THEREFORE, I, William A. Parsons, Chief Judge of the Seventh Judicial Circuit of Florida, hereby order that Child Support Enforcement Hearing Officers may be utilized in proceedings related to the establishment, enforcement (including contempt), or modification of child support filed in Flagler, Putnam, St. Johns and Volusia counties.

IT IS FURTHER ORDERED that the Clerks of the Court shall refer causes of action or other proceedings for the establishment, enforcement or modification of child support to a Child Support Enforcement Hearing Officer within the circuit. Alternatively, judges may also refer matters related to the establishment, enforcement or modification of child support to a Child Support Enforcement Hearing Officer when child support is the sole subject of the initiating filing, or when a temporary child support issue must be addressed prior to a final hearing before a judge.

IT IS FURTHER ORDERED as follows:

1. A Child Support Enforcement Hearing Officer's duties may include:

a. conducting hearings for the establishment, enforcement (including contempt), or modification of child support wherein the party seeking support is receiving services pursuant to Title IV–D of the Social Security Act;

b. conducting hearings to modify or enforce a support order that was previously entered as a result of a permanent injunction wherein the party seeking support is receiving services pursuant to Title IV–D of the Social Security Act;

c. conducting hearings in non–Title IV–D cases;

d. conducting hearings to modify or enforce a support order that was previously entered as a result of a permanent injunction;

e. performing such other duties as may be assigned by the Chief Judge pursuant to Rule 12.491, Florida Family Law Rules of Procedure.

2. A Child Support Hearing Officer appointed for the singular purpose of providing services pursuant to Title IV–D of the Social Security Act is permitted to provide the aforementioned duties in Title–IV–D cases only.

3. A Child Support Enforcement Hearing Officer's duties may **not** include conducting hearings on issues included in injunctions for protection against domestic violence other than those outlined above (see Rule 12.610(c)(1)C, Florida Family Law Rules of Procedure).

4. The general powers and duties of a child support enforcement hearing officer are those specified in Rule 12.491(e), Florida Family Law Rules of Procedure.

5. A Child Support Enforcement Hearing Officer is deemed to be an employee of the Seventh Judicial Circuit Court and functions under the direction of the Chief Judge and Court Administrator, or their designees.

IT IS FURTHER ORDERED that the appointment of individuals to serve as Child Support Hearing Officers shall be accomplished by separate administrative order.

IT IS FURTHER ORDERED that administrative order FM–2009–020–SC is hereby rescinded.

TO BE RECORDED in Flagler, Putnam, St. Johns and Volusia counties.

DONE AND ORDERED in Daytona Beach, Volusia County, Florida this 1st day of August 2012.

Judge William A. Parsons
CHIEF JUDGE

Amended effective August 1, 2012.

FM–2012–021–SC. GENERAL MAGISTRATES

IN THE CIRCUIT COURT OF FLORIDA, SEVENTH JUDICIAL CIRCUIT IN AND FOR LAGLER, PUTNAM, ST. JOHNS AND VOLUSIA COUNTIES

RE: GENERAL MAGISTRATES

REF: FM– 2012–021–SC (Rescinds FM–2007–021–SC)

WHEREAS, pursuant to Rule 12.490(a), Florida Family Law Rules of Procedure, and Rule 8.257(a), Florida Rules of Juvenile Procedure, circuits may utilize General Magistrates, and

WHEREAS, the use of General Magistrates has been deemed necessary by the judges of the Seventh Judicial Circuit;

NOW THEREFORE, I, WILLIAM A. PARSONS, Chief Judge of the Seventh Judicial Circuit of Florida, hereby order that General Magistrates may be utilized in domestic relations (Family Law) and Juvenile Dependency proceedings filed in Flagler, Putnam, St. Johns and Volusia counties.

IT IS FURTHER ORDERED as follows:

1. A General Magistrate's duties may include:

a. conducting temporary and post-judgment hearings in domestic relations (Family Law) cases ("Post-judgment" issues are defined as those issues that arise from cases that have been previously closed by an order or judgment that provides resolution to the last or all matters raised in the filing that initiated the case);

b. conducting case management conferences pursuant to Rule 12.200, Florida Family Law Rules of Procedure;

c. conducting hearings in simplified and uncontested dissolution of marriage cases;

d. conducting hearings in name change proceedings;

e. conducting post-disposition Judicial Reviews, pretrial hearings and other related proceedings in juvenile dependency cases;

f. performing such other duties as may be assigned by the Chief Judge pursuant to Rule 12.490, Florida Family Law Rules of Procedure, or Rule 8.257, Florida Rules of Juvenile Procedure.

2. A General Magistrate's duties may **not** include conducting hearings in domestic, repeat, dating, or sexual violence cases, other than those outlined above (see Rule 12.490 (c), Florida Family Law Rules of Procedure), or conducting Permanency hearings in juvenile dependency cases.

3. A General Magistrates is deemed to be an employee of the Seventh Judicial Circuit Court and functions under the direction of the Chief Judge and Court Administrator, or their designees.

IT IS FURTHER ORDERED that the appointment of individuals to serve as General Magistrates shall be accomplished by separate administrative order.

IT IS FURTHER ORDERED that administrative order FM–2007–021–SC is hereby rescinded.

TO BE RECORDED in Flagler, Putnam, St. Johns and Volusia counties.

DONE AND ORDERED in Daytona Beach, Volusia County, Florida this 1st day of August 2012.

Judge William A. Parsons
Chief Judge

Amended effective August 1, 2012.

FM–2004–022–SC. GENERAL MAGISTRATES' REPORTS

IN THE CIRCUIT COURT OF FLORIDA, SEVENTH JUDICIAL CIRCUIT IN AND FOR FLAGLER, PUTNAM, ST. JOHNS AND VOLUSIA COUNTIES

REF: FM–2004–022–SC

(Rescinds FM–2002–022–SC)

RE: **GENERAL MAGISTRATES' REPORTS**

WHEREAS, Rule 12.490(f) Florida Family Law Rules of Procedure, provides, in part:

The magistrate shall file the report and serve copies on the parties. The parties may serve exceptions to the report within ten (10) days from the time it is served on them. If no exceptions are filed within that period, the court shall take appropriate action on the report. If exceptions are filed, they shall be heard on reasonable notice by either party, or the court.

NOW THEREFORE, I, JULIANNE PIGGOTTE, Chief Judge of the Seventh Judicial Circuit of Florida, hereby direct the General Magistrates to file their reports with the Clerks of the Circuit Court upon completion and serve copies on the parties. Copies of said reports are to be maintained in the General Magistrates' Offices in a tickler calendar system.

Any party filing an exception to this report shall copy the General Magistrate. The report and exceptions shall immediately be forwarded to the judge in whose division the case is assigned for hearing.

If no exceptions are served within ten (10) days, the report is to be forwarded to the judge in whose division the case is assigned, to take appropriate action on the report.

IT IS FURTHER ORDERED that Administrative Order # FM–2002–022–SC is hereby rescinded.

TO BE RECORDED in Volusia County, Florida.

DONE AND ORDERED at Daytona Beach, Volusia County, Florida, this 14th day of October,

JULIANNE PIGGOTTE.
CHIEF JUDGE

Amended effective October 14, 2004.

FM–2004–023–SC. ELECTRONIC REPORTING OF GENERAL MAGISTRATE AND CHILD SUPPORT ENFORCEMENT HEARINGS

IN THE CIRCUIT COURT OF FLORIDA, SEVENTH JUDICIAL CIRCUIT IN AND FOR FLAGLER, PUTNAM, ST. JOHNS AND VOLUSIA COUNTIES

REF: FM–2004–023–SC

(Rescinds FM–2003–023–SC)

RE: ELECTRONIC REPORTING OF GENERAL MAGISTRATE AND CHILD SUPPORT ENFORCEMENT HEARINGS

WHEREAS, the Seventh Judicial Circuit utilizes General Magistrates and Child Support Enforcement Hearing Officers pursuant to Rules 12.490 and 12.491, Florida Family Law Rules of Procedure, and

WHEREAS, the Seventh Judicial Circuit has elected to make a record in these proceedings by electronic means as provided by Rule 2.070(g)(3), Florida Rules of Judicial Administration;

NOW THEREFORE, I, JULIANNE PIGGOTTE, Chief Judge of the Seventh Judicial Circuit of Florida, hereby order as follows:

1. Electronic recording equipment shall be used for the purpose of recording such proceedings conducted by General Magistrates and Child Support Enforcement Hearing Officers which are required to be reported.

2. The electronic recording equipment shall be operated by the General Magistrates and Child Support Enforcement Hearing Officers, or other qualified personnel, in such a manner as to ensure the production of an accurate, understandable record.

3. The General Magistrates, Child Support Enforcement Hearing Officers, or other qualified personnel, shall maintain logs of all proceedings recorded during each court session. The logs and corresponding recordings shall be properly identified and safely stored in locations designated by the respective Clerks of Court. Such logs and recordings less than six (6) months old may be stored in the General Magistrate/Child Support Enforcement Hearing Officer's office to allow for duplication, when necessary. Destruction of these records shall be in accordance with Rule 2.075 (f), Florida Rules of Judicial Administration.

4. Parties may obtain copies of recordings for a fee set by the Chief Judge.

5. In the event a party would like to obtain a transcript of a proceeding, he/she must purchase a copy of the recording and make independent arrangements for its transcriptions with a certified court reporter or transcriber.

6. In the event the Court requires a transcript of a proceeding, a copy of the recording shall be made and forwarded

to the Official Court Reporter in the appropriate county for transcription.

IT IS FURTHER ORDERED that Administrative Order # FM–2003–023–SC is hereby rescinded.

TO BE RECORDED in Flagler, Putnam, St. Johns and Volusia counties.

DONE AND ORDERED in Daytona Beach, Volusia County, Florida, this 14th day of October, 2004.

JULIANNE PIGGOTTE
CHIEF JUDGE

Amended effective October 14, 2004.

FM–2006–024–SC (A). SUPPORT INFORMATION SHEETS (AMENDED)

IN THE CIRCUIT COURT OF FLORIDA, SEVENTH JUDICIAL CIRCUIT IN AND FOR FLAGLER, PUTNAM, ST. JOHNS AND VOLUSIA COUNTIES

REF: FM–2006–024–SC (A)
(Rescinds FM–2006–024–SC)

RE: SUPPORT INFORMATION SHEETS (Amended)

WHEREAS, pursuant to Chapter 61, Florida Statutes, certain pertinent information is required to be included in all judgments related to child support and/or alimony, and

WHEREAS, the inclusion of this information is necessary for the efficient operation of the respective Clerks of Court offices in the Seventh Judicial Circuit;

NOW THEREFORE, I, WILLIAM A. PARSONS, Chief Judge of the Seventh Judicial Circuit, hereby order that a completed Support Information Sheet be filed with and made part of every Final Judgment, Modification of Final Judgment, and/or Post Judgment Decree regarding child support and/or alimony issued in the Seventh Judicial Circuit. The Support Information Sheet must be in a format substantially similar to that attached hereto as Attachment A.

IT IS FURTHER ORDERED that Administrative Order # FM–2006–024–SC is hereby rescinded.

TO BE RECORDED in Flagler, Putnam, St. Johns and Volusia counties.

DONE AND ORDERED in Daytona Beach, Volusia County, Florida this 21st day of April 2006.

WILLIAM A. PARSONS
CHIEF JUDGE

IN THE CIRCUIT COURT, SEVENTH JUDICIAL CIRCUIT IN AND FOR ________ COUNTY, FLORIDA

Case No. ___

Division _________

____

Petitioner,

and

____

Respondent.

SUPPORT INFORMATION SHEET

For Child Support or Alimony—Pursuant to Florida Statutes, Chapter 61

INFORMATION REQUIRED FOR EACH ORDER

Names of Minor(s)	Birth Date	Social Security Number

	PARTY OBLIGATED TO PAY	PARTY ENTITLED TO RECEIVE
Name		
Address		
Mailing Address (If different)		
Telephone Number		
Date of Birth		
Social Security Number		
Driver's License Number		
Current Employer		
Employer Address		
Employer Telephone Number		

Amended effective April 21, 2006.

FM–2002–025–SC. CHILD SUPPORT AND PURGE PAYMENTS

IN THE CIRCUIT COURT OF FLORIDA, SEVENTH JUDICIAL CIRCUIT IN AND FOR FLAGLER, PUTNAM, ST. JOHNS AND VOLUSIA COUNTIES

RE: CHILD SUPPORT AND PURGE PAYMENTS

REF: FM–2002–025–SC

WHEREAS, it has been made know to the undersigned that checks received by the Clerk of Circuit Court for payment of child support and/or purges are occasionally returned and deemed worthless;

NOW THEREFORE, I ROBERT K. ROUSE, JR., Chief Judge of the Seventh Judicial Circuit of Florida, hereby order as follows:

1. Clerks of Court in the Seventh Judicial Circuit are authorized to refuse personal checks for ongoing child support payments, and for purge payments tendered by a party other than the payor, unless the payor's name is reflected on the face of the check. This shall not be construed to prevent acceptance of checks tendered by a business as the result of an Income Deduction Order.

2. Pursuant to § 61.18 (5), Florida Statutes, the Clerks of Court in the Seventh Judicial Circuit are authorized to refuse any payment except cash, cashier's check, or money order, from a payor if any previously accepted check has been deemed worthless.

3. Clerks of Court in the Seventh Judicial Circuit are authorized to retain any subsequent payment(s) received from a payor to recover monies disbursed to the corresponding payee prior to notification from a banking institution that a check received was worthless.

TO BE RECORDED in Flagler, Putnam, St Johns and Volusia counties.

DONE AND ORDERED in Daytona Beach, Volusia County, Florida this 15th day of July, 2002.

Judge Robert K. Rouse, Jr.
Chief Judge

Adopted effective July 15, 2002.

FM–2002–026–SC. RESTITUTION PAYMENTS BY CLERKS OF COURT IN JUVENILE CASES

IN THE CIRCUIT COURT OF FLORIDA, SEVENTH JUDICIAL CIRCUIT IN AND FOR FLAGLER, PUTNAM, ST. JOHNS AND VOLUSIA COUNTIES

RE: RESTITUTION PAYMENTS BY CLERKS OF COURT IN JUVENILE CASES

REF: FM–2002–026–SC

WHEREAS, juvenile defendants in the Seventh Judicial Circuit are often required to pay restitution to victims, and

WHEREAS, the undersigned has been advised that victims to whom restitution should be paid cannot be located in some instances;

NOW, THEREFORE, I, **ROBERT K. ROUSE, JR.,** Chief Judge of the Seventh Judicial Circuit of Florida, hereby order that Clerks of Court in the Seventh Judicial Circuit, after making diligent efforts to locate victims, and failing to locate same, shall collect court ordered restitution payments and disburse same to the Crimes Compensation Trust Fund.

TO BE RECORDED in Flagler, Putnam, St. Johns and Volusia counties.

DONE AND ORDERED in Daytona Beach, Volusia County, Florida, this 15th day of July, 2002.

Judge Robert K. Rouse, Jr.
Chief Judge

Adopted effective July 15, 2002.

FM–2012–027–SC. FAMILY MEDIATION

IN THE CIRCUIT COURT OF FLORIDA, SEVENTH JUDICIAL CIRCUIT IN AND FOR FLAGLER, PUTNAM, ST. JOHNS AND VOLUSIA COUNTIES

RE: FAMILY MEDIATION

REF: FM–2012–027–SC (Rescinds FM–2011–027–SC)

WHEREAS, pursuant to § 44.108, Florida Statutes, mediation should be accessible to all parties, and

WHEREAS, pursuant to Rule 12.740, Florida Family Law Rules of Procedure, mediation may be utilized in family law matters, and

WHEREAS, the use of certified mediators in family law cases has been deemed necessary by the judges of the Seventh Judicial Circuit;

NOW THEREFORE, I, WILLIAM A. PARSONS, Chief Judge of the Seventh Judicial Circuit of Florida, hereby order that certified mediators shall be utilized in family law cases in Flagler, Putnam, St. Johns and Volusia counties in accordance with the following:

1. Judges may refer appropriate family law cases in which the combined incomes of the parties do not exceed $100,000 per year to the Seventh Judicial Circuit Court's Family Mediation Program. When referring cases to the court's program, Orders of Referral in formats substantially similar to those attached hereto as Exhibit A (Volusia County) and Exhibit B (Flagler, Putnam and St Johns counties) must be used. Payment of fees must be determined prior to referring a case to the mediation program. If an Order of Referral lacks requisite payment information, the mediator is directed to return the case to the referring judge for determination of the appropriate fee before proceeding.

2. Parties in Family Law cases who are referred to the court's Family Mediation Program are required to pay fees to the Clerk of Court in accordance with the following schedule:

(a) One-hundred twenty dollars ($120) per person, per scheduled family mediation session, when the parties' combined incomes are greater than $50,000, but less than $100,000 per year;

(b) Sixty dollars ($60) per person, per scheduled family mediation session, when the parties' combined incomes are $50,000 or less per year;

(c) No mediation fees are to be assessed against parties determined to be indigent.

3. Parties in Family Law cases with combined incomes of $100,000 or more per year are not eligible for the court's Family Mediation Program and must therefore be referred to private mediators.

IT IS FURTHER ORDERED that Administrative Order FM–20011–027–SC is hereby rescinded.

TO BE RECORDED in Flagler, Putnam, St. Johns and Volusia counties.

DONE AND ORDERED in Daytona Beach, Volusia County, Florida this 9th day of January 2012.

Judge William A. Parsons
Chief Judge

Amended effective January 9, 2012.

FM–2002–028–VL. ELECTRONIC ACCESS TO SCHOOL INFORMATION

IN THE CIRCUIT COURT OF FLORIDA, SEVENTH JUDICIAL CIRCUIT IN AND FOR VOLUSIA COUNTIES

REF: FM–2002–028–VL

RE: ELECTRONIC ACCESS TO SCHOOL INFORMATION

WHEREAS, the exchange of information between the school system of Volusia County and the Juvenile Divisions of the Circuit Court is necessary, and

WHEREAS, the legislative intent for the juvenile justice system as stated in § 985.02(1)(f), Florida Statutes, includes equal opportunity and access to quality and effective education which will meet the needs of the individual child, and

WHEREAS, § 984.151, Florida Statutes, invests the court with authority over habitual truants and assumes information sharing between the courts and the schools, and

WHEREAS, the delinquency case management system emphasizes multi- disciplinary assessments, including attendance, behavioral, curriculum, grade, psychological, special services and other school record information, beginning at the intake stage, and continuing throughout all stages of the court proceedings; and

WHEREAS, Chapter 39, Florida Statutes, requires the court to consider psychological, medical and educational records in dependency hearings, and

WHEREAS, the timely and accurate exchange of information is in the best interest of the child and family, especially in early intervention and in prevention of further problems, and can best be achieved by the court's electronic access to school records,

NOW THEREFORE, I, ROBERT K. ROUSE, JR., Chief Judge of the Seventh Judicial Circuit of Florida, hereby order and direct the Superintendent of Schools, Volusia County, and appropriate school personnel, to provide, upon request of the Juvenile Divisions of the court, information from individual school records, including grades, curriculum, attendance, discipline referrals, psychological reports, special education services and records, diagnosis and placement, and enrollment history, without consent of the child/parent, when such information is required by the court for proper use in court proceedings. These records may be accessed electronically to facilitate timely and efficient use thereof.

TO BE RECORDED in Volusia County, Florida.

DONE AND ORDERED in Daytona Beach, Volusia County, Florida, this 15th day of July, 2002.

ROBERT K. ROUSE, JR.
CHIEF JUDGE

Adopted effective July 15, 2002.

FM-2014-029-SC. POST-INCARCERATION CHILD SUPPORT REVIEWS

IN THE CIRCUIT COURT OF FLORIDA, SEVENTH JUDICIAL CIRCUIT IN AND FOR FLAGLER, PUTNAM, ST. JOHNS AND VOLUSIA COUNTIES

RE: POST-INCARCERATION CHILD SUPPORT REVIEWS

REF: FM-2014-029-SC

WHEREAS, Rule 12.615(e), Florida Family Law Rules of Procedure, requires that upon incarceration, contemnors must be brought before the court within 48 hours for a determination of whether they continue to have the present ability to pay the purges previously established, and

WHEREAS, it has been suggested to the undersigned that contemnors who are arrested pursuant to writs of bodily attachment should be brought before judges presiding at First Appearance hearings in order to comply with the provisions of the above-referenced rule;

NOW THEREFORE, I, TERENCE R. PERKINS, Chief Judge of the Seventh Judicial Circuit of Florida, hereby order that persons arrested and incarcerated pursuant to writs of bodily attachment issued in child support matters by judges or child support enforcement hearing officers are to be brought before judges presiding at First Appearance hearings promptly (no later than 48 hours after booking) for independent determinations as to whether they continue to have the present ability to pay the purge amounts previously established. Nothing in this Order prohibits judges from granting such relief as may be appropriate.

TO BE RECORDED in Flagler, Putnam, St. Johns and Volusia counties.

DONE AND ORDERED in Daytona Beach, Volusia County, Florida this 9th day of January 2014.

TERENCE R. PERKINS
CHIEF JUDGE

Adopted effective January 9, 2014.

FM-2015-030-SC. BATTERERS' INTERVENTION PROGRAM PROVIDERS

IN THE CIRCUIT COURT OF FLORIDA, SEVENTH JUDICIAL CIRCUIT IN AND FOR FLAGLER, PUTNAM, ST. JOHNS AND VOLUSIA COUNTIES

RE: BATTERERS' INTERVENTION PROGRAM PROVIDERS

REF: FM-2015-030-SC

WHEREAS, it has been suggested that standardized programming be made available in the justice system to protect domestic violence victims and their children and to hold the perpetrators of domestic violence accountable for their acts, and

WHEREAS, pursuant to Florida Statutes, requirements for the provision of batterers' intervention programs have been established, and

WHEREAS, the court, or any entity designated by the court, must provide respondents ordered to attend a batterers' intervention program with a list of available program providers;

NOW THEREFORE, I, TERENCE R. PERKINS, Chief Judge of the Seventh Judicial Circuit of Florida, hereby designate the Court Administrator's Office of the Seventh Judicial Circuit as the entity responsible for maintaining a list of batterers' intervention program providers who meet the requirements of § 741.325, Florida Statutes, for use by the court. Inclusion on or removal from the list is at the sole discretion of the Chief Judge or his designee.

IT IS FURTHER ORDERED that individuals who wish to be considered for inclusion on the above-referenced batterers' intervention program provider list must complete the attached batterers' intervention program provider application and submit it to: Court Administration, 125 E. Orange Avenue; Room 201, Daytona Beach, FL 32114. Any batterers' intervention program provider included on the list must submit an Affidavit of Compliance, a copy of which is attached hereto, to Court Administration by June 30th each year. Failure to update necessary information or provide the Affidavit of Compliance, as required, will result in removal from the list of batterers' intervention program providers.

TO BE RECORDED in Flagler, Putnam, St. Johns and Volusia counties.

DONE AND ORDERED in Datona [1] Beach, Volusia County, Florida, this 27th day of April 2015.

TERENCE R. PERKINS
CHIEF JUDGE

Adopted effective April 27, 2015.

[1] So in original.

FM-2015-031-SC. DISTRIBUTION OF SHELTER PETITIONS

IN THE CIRCUIT COURT OF FLORIDA, SEVENTH JUDICIAL CIRCUIT IN AND FOR FLAGLER, PUTNAM, ST. JOHNS AND VOLUSIA COUNTIES

RE: DISTRIBUTION OF SHELTER PETITIONS

REF: FM-2015-031-SC

WHEREAS, pursuant to § 39.001(1)(c), Florida Statutes, the child protection system is intended to reflect a partnership between the Department of Children and Families, the Court, other agencies, law enforcement, service providers, and local communities, and

WHEREAS, pursuant to § 39.402(14)(e), Florida Statutes, dependency proceedings are intended to be completed in a timely fashion;

NOW THEREFORE, I, TERENCE R. PERKINS, Chief Judge of the Seventh Judicial Circuit of Florida, hereby order as follows:

1. This Order pertains to all cases in which a Shelter Petition is filed in the Seventh Judicial Circuit and is effective at the time of filing of such petitions.

2. In every case in which the Department of Children and Families (DCF) files a Shelter Petition pursuant to § 39.402(6), Fla.Stat., the Guardian ad Litem program for the Seventh Circuit is provisionally appointed for shelter hearings (see § 39.402(8)(c)(1), Fla. Stat.). In addition, the Office of Criminal Conflict and Civil Regional Counsel for the Fifth District and attorneys on the Court's court-appointed dependency attorney registry are provisionally appointed for the purpose of representing parents at shelter hearings (see § 39.402(8)(c)(2), Fla.Stat.). The appointment of the Guardian ad Litem program and attorneys for parents for proceedings subsequent to shelter proceedings shall be made by separate order of a presiding judge.

3. Upon finalizing a Shelter Petition, DCF, or its designee, is to immediately provide the petition to authorized court personnel, the attorneys appointed pursuant to this order, and the Guardian ad Litem program.

4. Any person receiving a Shelter Petition must keep it and the information contained therein confidential and may not disclose it to anyone other than those authorized to receive it (see § 39.202, Fla.Stat.). Failure to comply with the terms of this Order may be punishable by contempt of court. Any party seeking to modify the terms of this Order in a specific case must submit a written motion and schedule same for hearing before the presiding judge.

TO BE RECORDED in Flagler, Putnam, St. Johns and Volusia counties.

DONE AND ORDERED in Datona[1] Beach, Volusia County, Florida, this 27th day of May 2015.

TERENCE R. PERKINS
CHIEF JUDGE

Adopted effective May 27, 2015.

[1] So in original.

FM–2018–032–VL. EAST–VOLUSIA UNITED FAMILY COURT

IN THE CIRCUIT COURT OF FLORIDA, SEVENTH JUDICIAL CIRCUIT IN AND FOR VOLUSIA COUNTY

RE: EAST–VOLUSIA UNITED FAMILY COURT

REF: FM–2018–032–VL

WHEREAS, the Florida Supreme Court has encouraged judicial circuits to establish Unified Family Courts as a way to more efficiently and effectively address the needs of families with multiple related Family Law court cases, and

WHEREAS, a Unified Family Court was previously established in west–Volusia County, and

WHEREAS, the judges and various other stakeholders have concluded that a Unified Family Court should be established in east–Volusia County;

NOW THEREFORE, I, RAUL A. ZAMBRANO, Chief Judge of the Seventh Judicial Circuit Court of Florida, hereby order that a Unified Family Court be established in east–Volusia County effective September 1, 2018 to hear such matters involving related Family Law cases as may be assigned.

IT IS FURTHER ORDERED that when a case defined by administrative order as under the jurisdiction of Family Law is initiated, the Clerk of Court's office shall ascertain if an active Dependency / Termination of Parental Rights case involving the same family exists in east–Volusia County. If so, said Family Law case shall be assigned to the judicial division to which the related Dependency/TPR case is assigned. In addition, when a Dependency/TPR case is initiated in east–Volusia County, the Clerk's office shall assign said case to a judicial division in accordance with other case assignment directives, but shall also ascertain if an active Family Law case involving the same family exists. If such an active related Family Law case exists, it shall be reassigned to the judicial division to which the related Dependency/TPR case is assigned. Family Case Management staff shall assist the Clerk's office with the identification of related cases and the assignment/reassignment thereof as specified herein. Any additional reassignments of related Family Law/Dependency/TPR cases to the east–Volusia Unified Family Court divisions must be coordinated and mutually agreed upon by the affected judges.

IT IS FURTHER ORDERED that the Clerk's office shall link any related cases as specified herein in its case management system.

IT IS FURTHER ORDERED that in addition to being designated as the judicial divisions to which juvenile cases are assigned, Divisions 37 and 38 shall also be designated as the east–Volusia Unified Family Court divisions for assignment purposes.

TO BE RECORDED in Volusia County.

DONE AND ORDERED in DeLand, Volusia County, Florida, this 2nd day of August 2018.

RAUL A. ZAMBRANO
CHIEF JUDGE

Adopted effective August 2, 2018.

FM–2002–033–SC. ELECTRONIC RECORDING OF DOMESTIC VIOLENCE INJUNCTION HEARINGS

IN THE CIRCUIT COURT OF FLORIDA, SEVENTH JUDICIAL CIRCUIT IN AND FOR FLAGLER, PUTNAM, ST. JOHNS AND VOLUSIA COUNTIES

REF: FM–2002–033—SC

RE: ELECTRONIC RECORDING OF DOMESTIC VIOLENCE INJUNCTION HEARINGS

WHEREAS, pursuant to sec. 741.30(6)(h), Florida Statutes, domestic violence injunction hearings must be recorded, and

WHEREAS, the Seventh Judicial Circuit has elected to make a record in these proceedings by electronic means, as provided by Rule 2.070(g)(3), Florida Rules of Judicial Administration;

NOW THEREFORE, I, ROBERT K. ROUSE, JR., Chief Judge of the Seventh Judicial Circuit of Florida, hereby order as follows:

1. Electronic recording equipment shall be used for the purpose of recording such domestic violence injunction hearings that are required to be recorded.

2. The electronic recording equipment shall be operated by Deputy Clerks of Court, or other qualified personnel, in such a manner as to ensure the production of an accurate, understandable record.

3. The Deputy Clerks of Court, or other qualified personnel, shall maintain logs of all proceedings recorded during each

court session. The logs and the corresponding recordings shall be properly identified and safely stored in locations designated by the respective Clerks of Court. Destruction of these records shall be in accordance with Rule 2.075(f), Florida Rules of Judicial Administration.

4. Parties may obtain copies of recordings for a fee set by the Chief Judge.

5. In the event a party would like to obtain a transcript of a proceeding, he/she must purchase a copy of the recording and make independent arrangements for its transcription with a certified court reporter or transcriber.

6. In the event the Court requires a transcript of a proceeding, the Clerk of Court shall make a copy of the recording and forward it to the Official Court Reporter in the appropriate county for transcription.

TO BE RECORDED in Flagler, Putnam, St. Johns and Volusia counties.

DONE AND ORDERED in Daytona Beach, Volusia County, Florida, this 26th day of December, 2002.

ROBERT K. ROUSE, JR.
CHIEF JUDGE

Adopted effective December 26, 2002.

FM–2015–034–SC. ASSIGNMENT ORDER FOR SHELTER HEARINGS

IN THE CIRCUIT COURT OF FLORIDA, SEVENTH JUDICIAL CIRCUIT IN AND FOR FLAGLER, PUTNAM, ST. JOHNS AND VOLUSIA COUNTIES

RE: ASSIGNMENT ORDER FOR SHELTER HEARINGS

REF: FM–2015–034–SC

(Rescinds FM–2013–034–VL)

WHEREAS, it has been made known to the undersigned that the efficient administration of justice would be best served by authorizing all judges of the Family Law Division to conduct juvenile shelter hearings on an as needed basis;

NOW THEREFORE, I, TERENCE R. PERKINS, Chief Judge of the Seventh Judicial Circuit of Florida, hereby authorize all judges of the Family Law divisions in the Seventh Judicial Circuit, as well as those judges previously assigned to juvenile dependency dockets, to conduct juvenile shelter hearings throughout the circuit on an as needed basis.

IT IS FURTHER ORDERED that shelter hearings conducted by those judges mentioned above need not be reviewed as set forth in § 39.402(12), Florida Statutes and Rule 8.305(b)(14), Florida Rules of Juvenile Procedure.

TO BE RECORDED in Flagler, Putnam, St. Johns & Volusia counties.

DONE AND ORDERED in Daytona Beach, Volusia County, Florida this 4th day of March 2015.

TERENCE R. PERKINS
CHIEF JUDGE

Amended effective March 4, 2015.

FM–2008–035–SC. SUSPENSION OF FAMILY CUSTODY INVESTIGATION PROGRAM

IN THE CIRCUIT COURT OF FLORIDA, SEVENTH JUDICIAL CIRCUIT

IN AND FOR FLAGLER, PUTNAM, ST. JOHNS AND VOLUSIA COUNTIES

RE: Suspension of Family Custody Investigation Program

REF: FM–2008–035–SC (Rescinds FM–2007–035–SC)

WHEREAS, the Seventh Judicial Circuit Court allocates a portion of its state budget to operate a Family Custody Investigation Program, and

WHEREAS, Florida's economic situation is such that the Court must reduce its budgetary expenditures;

NOW THEREFORE, I, J. DAVID WALSH Chief Judge of the Seventh Judicial Circuit of Florida, hereby order the suspension of the Seventh Judicial Circuit's Family Custody Investigation Program, effective March 1, 2008. This suspension will remain in effect until further order of the Chief Judge.

IT IS FURTHER ORDERED that Administrative Order # FM–2007–035–SC is hereby rescinded effective March 1, 2008.

TO BE RECORDED in Flagler, Putnam, St. Johns and Volusia counties.

DONE AND ORDERED in Daytona Beach, Volusia County, Florida this 25th day of February 2008.

Judge J. David Walsh
Chief Judge

Amended effective February 25, 2008.

FM–2007–036–VL. WEST–VOLUSIA UNIFIED FAMILY COURT

IN THE CIRCUIT COURT OF FLORIDA, SEVENTH JUDICIAL CIRCUIT IN AND FOR VOLUSIA COUNTY

RE: WEST–VOLUSIA UNIFIED FAMILY COURT

REF: FM–2007–036–VL

(Rescinds FM–2005–036–VL)

WHEREAS, the Florida Supreme Court has encouraged judicial circuits to establish Unified Family Courts as a way to more efficiently and effectively address the needs of families with multiple related Family Law court cases, and

WHEREAS, Administrative Order **FM–2005–036–VL** established a Unified Family pilot project in west–Volusia County, and

WHEREAS, following one year of operation, the Unified Family Court Steering Committee recommended the formal establishment of the Unified Family Court in west–Volusia County;

NOW THEREFORE, I, WILLIAM A. PARSONS, Chief Judge of the Seventh Judicial Circuit of Florida, hereby order that a Unified Family Court be established in west–Volusia County to hear such matters involving related Family Law cases as may be assigned.

IT IS FURTHER ORDERED that when a case defined by administrative order as under the jurisdiction of Family Law is initiated, the Clerk of Court's office shall ascertain if an active Dependency/Termination of Parental Rights case involving the same family exists in west–Volusia County. If so, said Family Law case shall be assigned to the west–Volusia Unified Family Court division. The related Dependency/TPR case may then also be reassigned to the west–Volusia Unified Family Court division. In addition, when a Dependency/Termination of Parental Rights case is initiated in west–Volusia County, the Clerk of Court's office shall ascertain if an active Family Law case involving the same family exists. If so, said Dependency/TPR case shall be assigned to the west–Volusia Unified Family Court division. The related Family Law case may then also be reassigned to the Unified Family Court division. Any additional reassignments of related Family Law/Dependency/TPR cases to the west–Volusia Unified Family Court division must be coordinated and mutually agreed upon by the affected judges.

IT IS FURTHER ORDERED that the Unified Family Court division shall continue to be designated as Division 15 for assignment purposes.

IT IS FURTHER ORDERED that Administrative Order FM–2005–036–VL be rescinded

TO BE RECORDED in Volusia County, Florida.

DONE AND ORDERED in Daytona Beach, Volusia County, Florida, this 7th day of May 2007.

WILLIAM A. PARSONS
CHIEF JUDGE

Amended effective May 7, 2007.

FM–2011–037–SC. JUDICIAL WAIVERS OF PARENTAL NOTICE OF ABORTION

IN THE CIRCUIT COURT OF FLORIDA, SEVENTH JUDICIAL CIRCUIT IN AND FOR FLAGLER, PUTNAM, ST. JOHNS AND VOLUSIA COUNTIES

RE: JUDICIAL WAIVERS OF PARENTAL NOTICE OF ABORTION

REF: FM–2011–037–SC (Rescinds FM–2007–037–SC)

WHEREAS, § 390.01114, Florida Statutes, the *Parental Notice of Abortion Act*, requires physicians performing procedures which terminate pregnancies of minors in certain circumstances to give notice to the parents of said minors, and

WHEREAS, § 390.01114(4)(a), Florida Statutes, permits a minor to petition any circuit court in which the minor resides for a waiver of the notice requirements and permits said minor to participate in proceedings on her own behalf, and

WHEREAS, pursuant to Administrative Order, Judicial Waivers of Parental Notice of Abortion cases have been assigned to the Family Law division, and

WHEREAS, it has come to the attention of the undersigned that a more specific assignment of said cases to judges presiding in juvenile dependency matters should be made and that a procedure must therefore also be established that addresses the handling of such cases in the event a dependency judge is not available, and

WHEREAS, a case involving a minor petitioning the court for Judicial Waiver of Parental Notice of Abortion is time sensitive and must be given precedence. Pursuant to § 390.01114(4)(b), Florida Statutes, absent a request by the minor to extend the time, the Court shall rule and issue written findings within 3 business days after the petition is filed.

NOW THEREFORE, I, WILLIAM A. PARSONS, Chief Judge of the Seventh Judicial Circuit of Florida, hereby order that upon the filing of a Petition for Judicial Waiver of Parental Notice of Abortion in any county within the Seventh Judicial Circuit, such filing shall be delivered immediately to a judge assigned to hear juvenile dependency matters within the county for his/her review and scheduled for hearing within 3 business days of filing.

IT IS FURTHER ORDERED, that in the event a juvenile dependency judge is not available to review and/or hear such matter within 3 business days, the matter shall be delivered to a different judge in the Family Law division within the county for his/her review and/or hearing within 3 business days.

IT IS FURTHER ORDERED, that the Court Administrator's office, shall prepare a reference guide containing relevant statutory authorities and forms, along with other related literature, to facilitate prompt and expeditious rulings and promote consistency throughout the circuit.

IT IS FURTHER ORDERED that Administrative Order FM–2007–037–SC is hereby rescinded.

TO BE RECORDED, in Flagler, Putnam, St. Johns and Volusia counties.

DONE AND ORDERED in Daytona Beach, Volusia County, Florida this 15th day of December 2011.

Judge William A. Parsons
Chief Judge

Amended effective December 15, 2011.

FM–2006–038–SC. DIRECT CHILD SUPPORT/ALIMONY PAYMENTS

IN THE CIRCUIT COURT OF FLORIDA, SEVENTH JUDICIAL CIRCUIT IN AND FOR VOLUSIA COUNTY

REF: FM–2006–038–SC

RE: DIRECT CHILD SUPPORT/ALIMONY PAYMENTS

WHEREAS, § 61.13(1)(d), Fla. Stat. (2005), requires that all child support orders entered on or after January 1, 1985, direct that child support payments be made through the depository in the county where the court is located, and

WHEREAS, there are instances where child support or alimony has, contrary to an existing Court order, been paid directly to the recipient rather than through the local depository, and

WHEREAS, the obligor wishes to be credited for the direct payment of support and the recipient is willing to sign a notarized affidavit attesting that the payments were received directly, and

WHEREAS, this procedure is desirable for judicial expediency and to allow the local depository to give credit where there is sufficient proof that payment has been made;

NOW THEREFORE, I, WILLIAM A. PARSONS, Chief Judge of the Seventh Judicial Circuit of Florida, hereby order that unless a payment order expressly prohibits or authorizes direct payments, the Clerks of Court in Flagler, Putnam, St. Johns & Volusia counties, serving as the local depositories, may accept, one time per case, a notarized affidavit stating that payment (s) have been received directly by the recipient. Upon receipt of such affidavit, Clerks may then credit the obligor's account for the direct support payments. If expressly prohibited, credit for direct payment will not be given. An affidavit of direct payment must include a statement by the parties acknowledging that future payments must be made through the depository and that no further credit for direct payments will be allowed without modification of the original support order. The aforementioned affidavit must be in a format substantially similar to that attached hereto as Attachment A.

IT IS FURTHER ORDERED that an affidavit attesting to a direct payment must include the notarized signature of the support recipient. Absent said notarized signature, the Clerk of Court shall refuse to credit the obligor's account with the direct payment.

Nothing in this Order shall be construed to limit a judge's ability to authorize/approve direct payments in individual cases.

TO BE RECORDED in Flagler, Putnam, St. Johns & Volusia counties.

DONE AND ORDERED in Daytona Beach, Volusia County, Florida this 30th day of March 2006.

WILLIAM A. PARSONS
CHIEF JUDGE

Attachment A

IN THE CIRCUIT COURT OF THE SEVENTH JUDICIAL CIRCUIT, IN AND FOR FLAGLER, PUTNAM, ST. JOHNS & VOLUSIA COUNTIES, FLORIDA

CASE NO.:

____
Petitioner

and

____
Respondent

AFFIDAVIT OF DIRECT SUPPORT PAYMENT

I, the undersigned recipient, hereby attest that support payments in the above-referenced case in the amount of $ ___ have been paid directly to me.

Under penalty of perjury, I declare that I have read the foregoing affidavit and that the facts stated in it are true.

______________________ ______________________
Recipient's Signature Printed Name

The foregoing instrument was acknowledged before me this ___ day of ________, ___ by ________ who is personally known to me or has produced ________ as identification.

Notary Public__________ Printed Name ________

Commission# __________ Seal

We, the undersigned parties, hereby acknowledge that all future support payments must be made through the Clerk of the Circuit Court, Child Support Division, and that no additional direct payments will be recognized or credited to the support account in this case without further order of the court.

______________ ____ ______________ ____
Recipient's Signature **Date** **Obligor's Signature** **Date**

______________ ______________
Printed Name **Printed Name**

Adopted effective March 30, 2006.

FM–2006–039–SC. SUPPORT INSTALLMENT PAYMENTS

IN THE CIRCUIT COURT OF FLORIDA, SEVENTH JUDICIAL CIRCUIT IN AND FOR VOLUSIA COUNTY

REF: FM–2006–039–SC

RE: SUPPORT INSTALLMENT PAYMENTS

WHEREAS, in most instances, support payments are made through the Clerks of Court as the local support depositories, and

WHEREAS, in some instances, obligors' pay periods differ from the installment payment periods specified in the Court's orders, and

WHEREAS, when pay periods and installment payment periods differ, the reconciliation process undertaken by the local support depositories becomes more difficult;

NOW THEREFORE, I, WILLIAM A. PARSONS, Chief Judge of the Seventh Judicial Circuit of Florida, hereby order that the Clerks of Court in Flagler, Putnam, St. Johns & Volusia counties, serving as the local support depositories, are authorized to change the frequency of installment payments ordered to be paid through the support depository to make said payments consistent with obligors' pay periods.

This is an administrative procedure only and does not authorize the Clerks to change the total amount of support ordered.

TO BE RECORDED in Flagler, Putnam, St. Johns & Volusia counties.

DONE AND ORDERED in Daytona Beach, Volusia County, Florida this 30th day of March 2006.

WILLIAM A. PARSONS
CHIEF JUDGE

Adopted effective March 30, 2006.

FM–2018–040-SC. STANDING FAMILY COURT ORDER

IN THE CIRCUIT COURT OF FLORIDA, SEVENTH JUDICIAL CIRCUIT IN AND FOR FLAGLER, PUTNAM, ST. JOHNS AND VOLUSIA COUNTIES

RE: STANDING FAMILY LAW COURT ORDER

REF: FM–2018–040–SC

(Rescinds FM–2013–040–SC)

WHEREAS, it has been made known to the undersigned that the establishment of a standing family law court order dealing with the parties' responsibilities in dissolution of marriage, paternity and/or support actions is necessary for the efficient and proper administration of justice,

NOW, THEREFORE, I, RAUL A. ZAMBRANO, Chief Judge of the Seventh Judicial Circuit of Florida, hereby order as follows:

1. A Standing Family Law Court Order, in substantially the same format as Exhibit A attached hereto, is to be issued in dissolution of marriage, paternity and/or support actions.

2. In cases affected by this order, the Clerk of Court is to advise the Petitioner and/or Petitioner's attorney of the requirements of this order by providing him/her with a copy, in either physical or electronic format, of the "Standing Family Law Court Order" when the case is filed. The Clerk's provision of the order and the method by which it was provided, is to be noted in the appropriate case file. It is the responsibility of the Petitioner and/or Petitioner's attorney to provide the Respondent with a copy of the "Standing Family Law Court Order by including it with the petition at time of service. In cases where the Clerk of Court forwards the petition to the Sheriff for service, a copy of the Standing Family Law Court Order is to be included with the service packet. Upon request, the Court Administrator's office will provide the Clerk with copies of the Standing Family Law Court Order for distribution.

3. Nothing in this order prohibits judges from issuing similar orders in other types of Family Law actions or providing service of the Standing Family Law Court Order in some other manner as they deem appropriate.

4. Failure to comply with the terms of the Standing Family Law Court Order may result in appropriate sanctions against the offending party.

IT IS FURTHER ORDERED that Administrative Order # FM–2013–040–SC is hereby rescinded.

TO BE RECORDED in Flagler, Putnam, St. Johns and Volusia counties.

DONE AND ORDERED in Daytona Beach, Volusia County, Florida, this 7th day of June 2018.

RAUL A. ZAMBRANO
Chief Judge

Amended effective September 25, 2013; June 7, 2018.

FM–2018–041-SC. TIMESHARING SCHEDULES/GUIDELINES

IN THE CIRCUIT COURT OF FLORIDA, SEVENTH JUDICIAL CIRCUIT IN AND FOR FLAGLER, PUTNAM AND VOLUSIA COUNTIES

RE: TIMESHARING SCHEDULES/GUIDELINES

REF: FM–2018–041–FG/PT/VL

(Rescinds: FM–2010–041–SC)

WHEREAS, pursuant to § 61.13, Florida Statutes, it is the public policy of Florida to assure that minor children have frequent and continuing contact with both parents after the parents separate or the marriage of the parties is dissolved and to encourage parents to share the rights and responsibilities and joys of childrearing, and

WHEREAS, pursuant to § 61.13, Florida Statutes, parental responsibility for minor children must be shared by both parents unless the court finds that shared parental responsibility would be detrimental to the children, and

WHEREAS, it has been made known to the undersigned that the efficient and proper administration of justice requires that timesharing schedules/guidelines be developed to assist parties in structuring timesharing arrangements that best meet the needs of their children and themselves;

NOW THEREFORE, I, RAUL A. ZAMBRANO, Chief Judge of the Seventh Judicial Circuit of Florida, hereby adopt the attached Timesharing Schedules/Guidelines for use in Flagler, Putnam and Volusia counties to assist parties in structuring timesharing arrangements that best meet the needs of their children and themselves. Terms of this Order should not be construed as to require the use of the attached timesharing schedules/guidelines in individual cases.

IT IS FURTHER ORDERED that Administrative Order FM–2010–041–SC is hereby rescinded.

TO BE RECORDED in Flagler, Putnam and Volusia counties.

DONE AND ORDERED in DeLand, Volusia County, Florida this 8th day of June 2018.

RAUL A. ZAMBRANO
Chief Judge

Amended effective July 2, 2010; June 8, 2018.

FM–2007–042–SC. WITHDRAWAL OF TRIAL COUNSEL IN DEPENDENCY, TERMINATION OF PARENTAL RIGHTS AND CHILDREN/FAMILIES IN NEED OF SERVICES PROCEEDINGS

IN THE CIRCUIT COURT OF FLORIDA, SEVENTH JUDICIAL CIRCUIT IN AND FOR FLAGLER, PUTNAM, ST. JOHNS AND VOLUSIA COUNTIES

RE: Withdrawal of Trial Counsel in Dependency, Termination of Parental Rights and Children/Families in Need of Services Proceedings

REF: FM–2007–042–SC

WHEREAS, § 39.815(1), Florida Statutes, directs District Courts of Appeal to give appeals from orders terminating parental rights priority in docketing and to render decisions on such appeals as expeditiously as possible, and

WHEREAS, Rule 9.146(g), Florida Rules of Appellate Procedure, directs courts to give priority to appeals in juvenile dependency, termination of parental rights and Children/Families in Need of Services proceedings, and

WHEREAS, the assistance of trial courts has been sought to aid in the expeditious resolution of appeals in juvenile dependency, termination of parental rights and Children/Families in Need of Services proceedings;

NOW THEREFORE, I, WILLIAM A. PARSONS, Chief Judge of the Seventh Judicial Circuit of Florida, hereby order that in juvenile dependency, termination of parental rights and Children/Families in Need of Services proceedings, in which appeals are contemplated and/or being pursued, trial counsel for parties may not be permitted to withdraw as counsel of record until the following activities have been completed:

• A notice of appeal has been filed;

• Directions to the clerk have been filed;

• Designations to the court reporter have been filed for transcripts of those portions of the proceedings necessary to support the issues on appeal; and

• A motion to have the requisite proceedings transcribed has been filed (see Rules 8.255(g) & 8.625(f), Florida Rules of Juvenile Procedure).

TO BE RECORDED in Flagler, Putnam, St. Johns & Volusia counties.

DONE AND ORDERED in Daytona Beach, Volusia County, Florida this 17th day of April 2007.

WILLIAM A. PARSONS
CHIEF JUDGE

Adopted effective April 17, 2007.

FM–2010–043–SC. NOTICES TO APPEAR ISSUED BY ARRESTING OFFICERS IN JUVENILE CASES

IN THE CIRCUIT COURT OF FLORIDA, SEVENTH JUDICIAL CIRCUIT IN AND FOR FLAGLER, PUTNAM, ST. JOHNS AND VOLUSIA COUNTIES

RE: NOTICES TO APPEAR ISSUED BY ARRESTING OFFICERS IN JUVENILE CASES

REF: FM–2010–043–SC (Rescinds FM–2008–043–SC (A))

WHEREAS, the prompt and efficient administration of justice in the Seventh Judicial Circuit requires the establishment of procedures governing the issuance of Notices to Appear by law enforcement officers for initial hearings in juvenile delinquency cases after arrest, and

WHEREAS, Rule 8.045(b), Florida Rules of Juvenile Procedure, authorizes law enforcement officers to issue Notices to Appear for initial hearings in juvenile delinquency cases after arrest provided certain criteria are met, and

WHEREAS, the use of Notices to Appear will assist the Court in conducting said initial hearings in a timely fashion and will afford the State Attorney an opportunity to screen cases for possible dismissal, or diversion, or filing of a petition, and/or allow early assessment of the youth for substance abuse and/or mental health treatment needs;

NOW THEREFORE, I, J. DAVID WALSH, Chief Judge of the Seventh Judicial Circuit of Florida, hereby order that the following procedures be utilized by law enforcement officers when considering the release of a youth on a Notice to Appear upon arrest:

1. The arresting law enforcement officer having custody of the youth is to either:

a. Call the Juvenile Screening Center or Call Center (at a designated phone # to be provided by DJJ) and advise the screening official of the delinquency offense(s) for which the youth has been arrested, and/or any court orders, warrants, capias, or teletypes pursuant to which the youth has been arrested, and request the screening official to conduct a prescreen on the youth to determine eligibility for release; or

b. Send by e-mail or fax to the Juvenile Screening Center or Call Center (to a designated e-mail address or fax # provided by DJJ) copies of the arrest report of the delinquency offense(s) for which the youth has been arrested, and/or copies of any court orders, warrants, capias, or teletypes pursuant to which the youth has been arrested, along with a written request that the screening official conduct a pre-screen on the youth to determine eligibility for release.

2. Upon screening the youth, the DJJ screening official is to inform the law enforcement officer (by phone, fax, or e-mail) of the screening decision (release, release w/ home detention, or secure detention).

3. If the screening official determines that the youth qualifies for release, or release w/home detention, said screening official is to provide the law enforcement officer with the date, time and location for the youth's initial court hearing.

4. The law enforcement officer is to use this information to prepare a Notice to Appear (by inserting the date, time and location of the initial hearing in the designated section of the form) and have a parent (or responsible adult) and the youth sign the agreement to appear in the designated section. The law enforcement officer is then to release the youth directly to a parent (or responsible adult) and provide the youth and parent (or responsible adult) with copies of the completed Notice to Appear. Said Notice to Appear must be in a format substantially similar to that set forth in Form 8.930, Florida Rules of Juvenile Procedure. In addition, if the youth is to be released w/ home detention, the law enforcement officer is to inform the youth of the required Home Detention status pending the initial hearing.

5. If the screening official determines that the youth does not qualify for release and is to be securely detained, the law enforcement officer is to deliver the youth to the designated Juvenile Detention Center. Youth must be medically cleared (if necessary) before being transported to the Detention Center.

6. Immediately following the release of a youth on a Notice to Appear, the law enforcement officer is to send by e-mail or fax to the Clerk of Court (to a designated e-mail address or fax # provided by the Clerk of Court) the arrest report and completed Notice to Appear.

IT IS FURTHER ORDERED that administrative order FM–2008–043–SC (A) is hereby rescinded.

TO BE RECORDED in Flagler, Putnam, St. Johns & Volusia counties.

DONE AND ORDERED in Daytona Beach, Volusia County, Florida this 26th day of March 2010.

Judge J. David Walsh
CHIEF JUDGE

Amended effective October 17, 2008; March 26, 2010.

FM–2008–044–VL. ESTABLISHMENT OF CHILD SUPPORT IN JUVENILE DEPENDENCY CASES

IN THE CIRCUIT COURT OF FLORIDA, SEVENTH JUDICIAL CIRCUIT IN AND FOR VOLUSIA COUNTY

RE: ESTABLISHMENT OF CHILD SUPPORT IN JUVENILE DEPENDENCY CASES REF: FM–2008–044–VL (Rescinds W–2008–001)

WHEREAS, one of the principles outlined *In re: Report of Family Court Steering Committee*, 794 So.2d 518 (Fla. 2001) is consideration of child support matters by judges hearing related juvenile dependency actions to avoid conflicting orders and multiple court appearances by the parties, as well as to increase efficiency and wisely utilize court resources, and

WHEREAS, the pilot project established by Administrative Order W–2008–001 to experiment with utilizing the "Best Practices Model for Child Support in Dependency Cases" proved to be successful, efficient and beneficial in dealing with child support and promoting the best interest of children involved in juvenile dependency cases;

NOW THEREFORE, I, J. DAVID WALSH, Chief Judge of the Seventh Judicial Circuit of Florida, hereby order that the "Best Practices Model for Child Support in Dependency Cases" be utilized in juvenile dependency cases assigned to Divisions 05, 15 and 38 in Volusia County effective January 1, 2009.

IT IS FURTHER ORDERED that effective January 1, 2009 the Clerk of Court's office is directed to assign Orders of Child Support, where child support is initiated within Volusia County juvenile dependency cases as follows:

- All Orders of Child Support initiated within east-Volusia juvenile dependency cases are to be assigned to Division 38. Said child support cases should continue to receive separate Family Law case numbers. Any pre-existing, active, related child support cases may be re-assigned to Division 38 at the discretion of the Juvenile Dependency Judge or the assigned Domestic Relations Judge. Upon conclusion of the juvenile dependency case, where termination of jurisdiction occurs, any related child support case previously assigned / re-assigned to Division 38 pursuant to this section, shall be re-assigned to an appropriate Domestic Relations division pursuant to the criteria established in the current assignment order for Family Law cases for any further action.

- All Orders of Child Support initiated within west-Volusia juvenile dependency cases are to be assigned to Division 15 (Unified Family Court) pursuant to existing UFC assignment procedures. Said child support cases should continue to receive separate Family Law case numbers. Any pre-existing, active, related child support cases may be re-assigned to Division 15 at the discretion of the Juvenile Dependency Judge/Unified Family Court Judge or the assigned Domestic Relations Judge. Upon conclusion of the juvenile dependency case, where termination of jurisdiction occurs, any related child support case assigned / re-assigned to Division 15 pursuant to this section shall remain assigned to Division 15, recognizing the "best interests" Unified Family Court principle.

IT IS FURTHER ORDERED that Administrative Order W–2008–001 is hereby rescinded effective January 1, 2009.

TO BE RECORDED in Volusia County, Florida.

DONE AND ORDERED in Daytona Beach, Volusia County, Florida this 3rd day of December 2008.

Judge J. David Walsh
Chief Judge

Amended effective December 3, 2008.

FM–2009–045–SC. AFFIDAVIT OF CONTINUING CHILD SUPPORT

IN THE CIRCUIT COURT OF FLORIDA, SEVENTH JUDICIAL CIRCUIT IN AND FOR FLAGLER, PUTNAM, ST. JOHNS AND VOLUSIA COUNTIES

RE: AFFIDAVIT OF CONTINUING CHILD SUPPORT

REF: FM–2009–045–SC

WHEREAS, unless otherwise provided in a child support order, clerks of court acting as local depositories normally terminate the assessment of child support upon the youngest child reaching the age of majority (18), and

WHEREAS, there are instances where a child support order provides that the support obligation continues beyond a child's 18th birthday if the child remains in high school or equivalent institution, as outlined in § 743. 07(2), Florida Statutes, and

WHEREAS, some parties may wish to continue the support assessment according to the terms of the child support order without seeking a judicial determination that the school continuation condition has been met, and

WHEREAS, in order for a local depository to continue the assessment in such cases, sufficient information must be provided indicating that the child will remain in school beyond his/her 18th birthday;

NOW THEREFORE, I, J. DAVID WALSH, Chief Judge of the Seventh Judicial Circuit of Florida, hereby order that if a child support order provides that the support obligation is to extend beyond the minor's 18th birthday if that child remains in high school or equivalent schooling, one or both parties may execute an affidavit of continuing support. Said affidavit must include the anticipated graduation date from the school of attendance, and state that the school continuation condition has been met. If only one party executes such an affidavit, official documentation of the child's anticipated graduation date from the school of attendance must be included. Upon completion of the affidavit along with documentation from the school of attendance and submission to the clerk of court as local depository, the clerk will continue or reinstate the child support assessment according to the terms of the current support order. The aforementioned affidavit must be in a format substantially similar to that attached hereto as Attachment A.

IT IS FURTHER ORDERED that an affidavit of continuing support must include the notarized signature of one or both parties, and if only one party executes the affidavit he/she must certify that a copy was provided to the other party (or mailed to the other party's last known address).

Nothing in this Order shall be construed to limit a judge's ability to determine, modify or eliminate the conditions for continuation of child support or to modify prior orders.

TO BE RECORDED in Flagler, Putnam, St. Johns & Volusia counties.

DONE AND ORDERED in Daytona Beach, Volusia County, Florida this 22nd day of May 2009.

Judge J. David Walsh
Chief Judge

Attachment A

IN THE CIRCUIT COURT, SEVENTH JUDICIAL CIRCUIT, IN AND FOR ______ COUNTY, FLORIDA

______ Case No.:

Petitioner

vs.

______

Respondent

AFFIDAVIT OF CONTINUING CHILD SUPPORT

The Affiant(s), after being duly sworn, say(s):

I/We, the undersigned, hereby attest that the current child support order in the above-styled case provides that upon certain conditions child support will continue beyond the emancipation date (18th birthday) for the following child: ______ Date of Birth ______

I/We, the undersigned, hereby acknowledge that the conditions for the continuing assessment of support have been met and that the child support obligation for the above named child should continue beyond the 18th birthday of the child.

I/We further acknowledge that the Clerk of the Circuit Court will continue to assess child support until the anticipated graduation date of ______, but in no event beyond 19 years of age. (If only one parent signs this Affidavit, documentation from the school of attendance stating the child's anticipated graduation date must be provided with this Affidavit in order to terminate the child support obligation based upon that date).

Under penalty of perjury, I declare that I have read the foregoing Affidavit and that the facts stated in it are true. **I certify that a copy of this Affidavit and any attachments have been provided to the other party.**

______ Recipient's Signature	______ Obligor's Signature
______ Printed Name	______ Printed Name
The foregoing instrument was acknowledged before me this ___ day of ______, ___, by ______ who is personally known to me or has produced ______ as identification.	The foregoing instrument was acknowledged before me this ___ day of ______, ___, by ______ who is personally known to me or has produced ______ as identification.
Notary Public ______ Print Name	Notary Public ______ Print Name
Signature ______	Signature ______
Commission# ______	Commission# ______

Adopted effective May 22, 2009.

FM-2015-046-SC. PARENTING COORDINATORS

IN THE CIRCUIT COURT OF FLORIDA, SEVENTH JUDICIAL CIRCUIT IN AND FOR FLAGLER, PUTNAM, ST. JOHNS AND VOLUSIA COUNTIES

RE: PARENTING COORDINATORS

REF: FM-2015-046-SC

(Rescinds FM-2011-046-SC)

WHEREAS, parenting coordination is recognized as a viable method of dispute resolution in the family law arena, and

WHEREAS, Florida Supreme Court Administrative Order AOSC14-64 bestows administrative responsibility for establishment and management of parenting coordinator rosters on the chief judges of the judicial circuits or their designees;

NOW THEREFORE, I, TERENCE R. PERKINS, Chief Judge of the Seventh Judicial Circuit, hereby designate the Court Administrator's Office of the Seventh Judicial Circuit to perform administrative tasks associated with the establishment and management of a roster of qualified parenting coordinators for the circuit.

IT IS FURTHER ORDERED that individuals who wish to be considered for inclusion on the roster of qualified parenting coordinators must complete and submit a uniform statewide parenting coordination application and all required documents to: Court Administration, 125 E. Orange Ave., Rm. 201, Daytona Beach, FL 32114. Individuals included on the roster must update information contained in their applications, if necessary, by providing written notice of any changes to Court Administration within 30 days of said changes. Furthermore, individuals included on the roster must submit an Affidavit of Compliance, a copy of which is attached hereto, to Court Administration by June 30th each year. Failure to update necessary information or provide an Affidavit of Compliance, as required, will result in removal from the roster of qualified parenting coordinators.

TO BE RECORDED in Flagler, Putnam, St. Johns and Volusia counties.

DONE AND ORDERED in Daytona Beach, Volusia County, Florida this 16th day of February 2015.

TERENCE R. PERKINS
CHIEF JUDGE

Amended effective February 16, 2015.

FM-2018-047-SC. COLLABORATIVE LAW PROCESS

IN THE CIRCUIT COURT OF FLORIDA, SEVENTH JUDICIAL CIRCUIT IN AND FOR FLAGLER, PUTNAM, ST. JOHNS AND VOLUSIA COUNTIES

RE: Collaborative Law Process

REF: FM-2018-047-SC

WHEREAS, pursuant to § 61.55, Florida Statutes, the expressed policy of the State of Florida is to encourage the peaceful resolution of disputes and the early resolution of pending litigation through a voluntary settlement process. The collaborative law process is a unique non-adversarial process that preserves a working relationship between the parties and reduces the emotional and financial toll of litigation, and

WHEREAS, if the parties are in agreement, the Seventh Judicial Circuit Court supports their use of the collaborative law process model in lieu of the traditional adversarial litigation process to resolve their family law disputes;

NOW, THEREFORE, I, RAUL A. ZAMBRANO, Chief Judge of the Seventh Judicial Circuit of Florida, hereby order as follows:

1. Judges assigned to Family Law divisions are encouraged to support parties' use of the collaborative law process model set forth in §§ 61.55–61.58, Florida Statutes.

2. If they so elect, parties may proceed with collaborative process dispute resolution before or after any of the proceedings set forth under § 61.56(5), Florida Statutes, have been initiated. If such a proceeding has been initiated, the parties are to notify the Court of their intention to proceed under the Collaborative Law Process Act by filing a Notice of Intent to Proceed Under the Collaborative Law Process Act. Once the notice is filed, the proceedings before the Court will abate until the Collaborative Process has terminated as set forth in § 61.57, Florida Statutes.

3. Parties and designated professionals who wish to engage in collaborative conflict resolution must contractually commit to such and may not seek Court intervention to decide any issues between the parties except as specifically set forth herein.

4. In the event the collaborative process ends without a full agreement having been reached, the parties are to file an appropriate notice with the Court. The matter will thereafter proceed as required under the Rules of Court.

5. Proceedings conducted under the collaborative process are confidential. If an agreement is reached, the parties must file such documents with the Court as are necessary for a judge to render a Final Judgment. The parties may be required to present the underlying documents to a judge for review and approval, but are not required to file said documents in the Court file. A judge may also seek to review the parties' financial affidavits, Collaborative Marital Settlement Agreement, and Parenting Plan in order to approve the Final Judgment, but may not require it absent the agreement by the parties.

6. If the parties agree that any temporary or partial agreements that may have been reached during the process survive the termination of the collaborative process, judges are to ratify said agreements if requested to do so.

TO BE RECORDED in Flagler, Putnam, St. Johns and Volusia counties.

DONE AND ORDERED in DeLand, Volusia County, Florida, this 7th day of September 2018.

RAUL A. ZAMBRANO
CHIEF JUDGE

Adopted effective September 7, 2018.

FM–2015–048–SC. DIVISION ASSIGNMENT OF SEXTING CASES

IN THE CIRCUIT COURT OF FLORIDA, SEVENTH JUDICIAL CIRCUIT IN AND FOR FLAGLER, PUTNAM, ST. JOHNS AND VOLUSIA COUNTIES

RE: Division Assignment of Sexting Cases

REF: FM–2015–048–SC (Rescinds P–2013–228)

WHEREAS, it has been made known to the undersigned that the prompt and expeditious administration of justice requires that direction be given to the clerks of court concerning the assignment of sexting cases (§ 847.0141, Florida Statutes);

NOW THEREFORE, I, TERENCE R. PERKINS, Chief Judge of the Seventh Judicial Circuit of Florida, hereby order that first-time violations of § 847.0141(1), Florida Statutes (sexting cases), are designated as noncriminal violations and are to be heard by circuit judges assigned to hear juvenile delinquency matters (see § 985.0301(1)(b), Florida Statutes.)

IT IS FURTHER ORDERED that that[1] alleged first-time violators may elect to perform 8 hours of community service, pay a $60 civil penalty, or participate in a cyber-safety program in lieu of appearing in court (see § 847.0141(3)(a), Florida Statutes). Alleged violators who fail to submit proof of performance of community service hours, payment of the civil penalty, or participation in a cyber-safety program within 30 days of the date the citation was issued are to be scheduled for a court date before the assigned judge.

IT IS FURTHER ORDERED that administrative order P–2013–228 is rescinded.

TO BE RECORDED in Flagler, Putnam, St. Johns and Volusia counties.

DONE AND ORDERED in Daytona Beach, Volusia County, Florida this 20th day of August 2015.

TERENCE R. PERKINS
CHIEF JUDGE

Amended effective August 20, 2015.

[1] So in original.

FM–2010–049–SC. ASSIGNMENT OF TRAFFIC CASES INVOLVING JUVENILES

IN THE CIRCUIT COURT OF FLORIDA, SEVENTH JUDICIAL CIRCUIT IN AND FOR FLAGLER, PUTNAM, ST. JOHNS AND VOLUSIA COUNTIES

RE: ASSIGNMENT OF TRAFFIC CASES INVOLVING JUVENILES

REF: FM–2010–049–SC (Rescinds H–88–23)

WHEREAS, the prompt and efficient administration of justice in the Seventh Judicial Circuit requires the establishment of procedures governing the assignment of traffic cases involving juveniles, and

WHEREAS, the Fifth District Court of Appeal has provided some guidance concerning the proper assignment of juvenile traffic cases in *State v. W.W. (a child), 16 So.3d 305;*

NOW THEREFORE, I, J. DAVID WALSH, Chief Judge of the Seventh Judicial Circuit of Florida, hereby order that traffic cases involving juveniles be assigned to circuit and county court judicial divisions by the clerks of court in accordance with the following:

1. In instances where a juvenile is alleged to have committed a misdemeanor criminal traffic offense only, said traffic case is to be assigned to a County Court judge hearing such matters.

2. In instances where a juvenile is alleged to have committed a civil traffic infraction only, said infraction is to be assigned to a County Court judge hearing such matters.

3. In instances where a juvenile is alleged to have committed a misdemeanor criminal traffic offense arising out of the

same episode as a delinquent act (felony or misdemeanor), said traffic offense is to be assigned to a Circuit judge hearing juvenile delinquency matters.

4. In instances where a juvenile is alleged to have committed a civil traffic infraction arising out of the same episode as a delinquent act (felony or misdemeanor), said traffic infraction is to be assigned to a Circuit judge hearing juvenile delinquency matters.

IT IS FURTHER ORDERED that administrative order H–88–23 is hereby rescinded.

TO BE RECORDED in Flagler, Putnam, St. Johns & Volusia counties.

DONE AND ORDERED in Daytona Beach, Volusia County, Florida this 20th day of September 2010.

J. DAVID WALSH

Amended effective September 20, 2010.

Ninth Judicial Circuit (Orange and Osceola Counties)

UNIFORM ADMINISTRATIVE POLICIES AND PROCEDURES

BUSINESS COURT PROCEDURES

UNIFORM POLICIES AND PROCEDURES OF THE DOMESTIC DIVISION

ADMINISTRATIVE ORDERS

2017–03. MENTAL HEALTH COURT, NINTH JUDICIAL CIRCUIT.
2016–22. CHILDREN IN NEED OF SERVICES/FAMILIES IN NEED OF SERVICES PROCEEDINGS, ORANGE COUNTY.
2016–20. [VACATED BY ORDER 2017-21, EFFECTIVE DECEMBER 8, 2017.].
2016–11. PROCEDURES FOR THE APPOINTMENT OF CERTIFIED LEGAL INTERNS.
2016–07. VETERANS COURT.
2016–02–01. "SEXTING" PURSUANT TO SECTION 847.0141, FLORIDA STATUTES, NINTH JUDICIAL CIRCUIT.
2015–10–02. APPELLATE PROCESS, NINTH JUDICIAL CIRCUIT.
2015–09. [VACATED BY ADMINISTRATIVE ORDER NO. 2016–20, EFFECTIVE OCTOBER 13, 2016].
2015–06. EARLY CHILDHOOD COURT.
2015–02. GOVERNING BLOOD TEST SCREENING FOR CERTAIN DISEASES TRANSMITTED THROUGH A SIGNIFICANT EXPOSURE.
2014–27. CERTIFIED PROCESS SERVER PROGRAM, NINTH JUDICIAL CIRCUIT.
2014–26. CERTIFIED THERAPY DOG PROGRAM (K–9th CIRCUIT PROGRAM), ORANGE COUNTY.
2014–19. NINTH JUDICIAL CIRCUIT COURT DOMESTIC COURT GUIDELINES.
2014–09–01. [VACATED BY ORDER 2017-10, EFFECTIVE OCTOBER 2, 2017.].
2014–07–01. NINTH JUDICIAL CIRCUIT COURT LOCAL PROFESSIONALISM PANEL.
2014–04–01. CELLULAR TELEPHONES AND OTHER PORTABLE ELECTRONIC DEVICES IN COURTROOMS, ORANGE AND OSCEOLA COUNTIES.
2014–03–01. DOMESTIC VIOLENCE INJUNCTIONS.
2013–28. CASE REPORTING REQUIREMENTS FOR REAL PROPERTY MORTGAGE FORECLOSURE CASES.
2013–21. JUVENILE DEPENDENCY DRUG COURT PROGRAM, ORANGE COUNTY.
2013–20–02. JUVENILE DELINQUENCY DRUG COURT PROGRAM.
2013–04. RELEASE OF SELECTED INDIVIDUALS INTO ORANGE COUNTY CORRECTIONS DEPARTMENT HOME CONFINEMENT PROGRAM.
2012–07–01. [VACATED BY ORDER 2018-020, EFFECTIVE JULY 12, 2018.].
2012–06–03. RESIDENTIAL FORECLOSURE MEDIATION PROCEDURES, ORANGE COUNTY.
2012–03. NINTH JUDICIAL CIRCUIT COURT CIRCUIT CIVIL COURT GUIDELINES.
2012–02. [VACATED BY ADMINISTRATIVE ORDER NO. 2016–09, EFFECTIVE JUNE 2, 2016].
2010–27. TEMPORARY ORDER FOR PATERNITY ACTIONS, ORANGE & OSCEOLA COUNTIES.
2008–06. [VACATED BY ORDER 2018-10, EFFECTIVE APRIL 12, 2018.].
2008–01–02. THE NINTH JUDICIAL CIRCUIT COURT INTERPRETER POLICY.
2007–04–01. [VACATED BY ORDER 2018-07, EFFECTIVE MARCH 27, 2018.].
2006–16. [VACATED BY ADMINISTRATIVE ORDER NO. 2016–24, EFFECTIVE AUGUST 18, 2016].
2006–09. [VACATED BY ADMINISTRATIVE ORDER NO. 2016–24, EFFECTIVE AUGUST 18, 2016].
2006–05. [VACATED BY ADMINISTRATIVE ORDER NO. 2016–24, EFFECTIVE AUGUST 18, 2016].
2005–16–08. UNIFIED FAMILY COURT AND THE ASSIGNMENT AND SCHEDULING OF DOMESTIC RELATIONS AND JUVENILE CASES, OSCEOLA COUNTY.
2004–06. [VACATED BY ADMINISTRATIVE ORDER NO. 2016–24, EFFECTIVE AUGUST 18, 2016].
2004–05–04. STANDING TEMPORARY ORDER FOR DISSOLUTION OF MARRIAGE ACTIONS.
2003–18–01. [VACATED BY ADMINISTRATIVE ORDER NO. 2016–24, EFFECTIVE AUGUST 18, 2016].
2003–07–02. THE NINTH JUDICIAL CIRCUIT COURTROOM DECORUM POLICY.
2003–04–04. [VACATED BY ORDER 2018-07, EFFECTIVE MARCH 27, 2018.].
2001–19–04. [VACATED BY ORDER 2018-07, EFFECTIVE MARCH 27, 2018.].
2000–18–06. [VACATED BY ORDER 2018-07, EFFECTIVE MARCH 27, 2018.].
2000–08–01. [VACATED AND SET ASIDE BY ORDER 2017-03, EFFECTIVE MARCH 28, 2017.].
2000–04–02. [VACATED BY ORDER 2018-07, EFFECTIVE MARCH 27, 2018.].
07–99–47–1. [VACATED BY ADMINISTRATIVE ORDER NO. 2016–24, EFFECTIVE AUGUST 18, 2016].
07–98–48–03. MOVEMENT OF SELECTED INMATES INTO COMMUNITY CORRECTIONS PROGRAMS, OSCEOLA COUNTY.
07–98–47–17. PRETRIAL RELEASE, PRETRIAL DETENTION, AND FIRST APPEARANCE PROCEEDINGS IN OSCEOLA COUNTY.
07–98–37–01. MANDATORY EDUCATIONAL PROGRAMS FOR ALL PARTIES IN DISSOLUTION ACTIONS WHICH INCLUDE MINOR CHILDREN.
07–96–19–03. MEDIA.
07–96–12. [VACATED BY ADMINISTRATIVE ORDER NO. 2016-24, EFFECTIVE AUGUST 18, 2016].
07–96–06. [VACATED BY ADMINISTRATIVE ORDER NO. 2016–24, EFFECTIVE AUGUST 18, 2016].
07–94–53. [VACATED AND SET ASIDE BY ORDER 2017-08, EFFECTIVE AUGUST 16, 2017.].
07–93–58–07. MOVEMENT OF SELECTED INMATES INTO COMMUNITY CORRECTIONS PROGRAMS, ORANGE COUNTY.
07–93–43–02. STANDARDS AND PROCEDURES FOR THE PROTECTION OF MINORS.
07–92–17. [VACATED BY ADMINISTRATIVE ORDER NO. 2016–24, EFFECTIVE AUGUST 18, 2016].

Uniform Administrative Policies and Procedures
Revised November 2006

SECTION 1. EFFECTIVE DATE; SCOPE; PURPOSE.

(A) These administrative policies and procedures are in effect and apply to all cases filed in the Civil Division.

(B) The purpose of these administrative policies and procedures is to supplement the Florida Rules of Civil Procedure and Judicial Administration, and applicable statutory and case law. In some instances, they track existing administrative orders and statutes. They are intended to furnish all system users with a guide to the administrative policies and procedures of the Civil Division of the Circuit Court of Orange County, Florida.

SECTION 2. ORGANIZATION OF THE DIVISION; PRESIDING JUDGES; SUPPORT STAFF.

(A) Division 2 is the General Civil Division is presently comprised of six (6) subdivisions which are designated as follows:

Division 33
Division 34
Division 35
Division 37
Division 39
Division 40

(B) The Complex Business Litigation Court is presently comprised of two (2) subdivisions which are designated as follows:

Division 32
Division 43

(1) Business Court was established pursuant to Administrative Order 2003–17–1 and is governed under Administrative Order 2003–17–3.

(2) The procedures for Business Court are established in Administrative Order 2004–03.

(C) Each division is presided over by a Circuit Judge who is assigned to that division by the Chief Judge. The names, business addresses and telephone numbers of the currently assigned presiding Judges can be obtained on the Court's web site www.ninja9.org.

(C)[1] Each Judge has a Judicial Assistant. The names of the current Judicial Assistants can be obtained on the Court's web site www.ninja9.org.

(D) The Civil Division has one Magistrate assigned to hear matters referred by the Judge. The Magistrate generally hears all discovery matters and motions to dismiss but can hear other matters that are agreed upon by the Judge and the parties. Once a referral Order is signed by the Judge, if agreed upon, the parties shall sign a consent to use of the Magistrate. The hearing shall be scheduled with the Magistrate using the Judicial Automated Calendaring System. After the hearing, the Magistrate shall issue a report on the hearing. The parties have ten (10) days to file an exception to the hearing. If no exception is filed within ten (10) days, the Magistrate's assistant shall forward an order to the Judge to approve the report. If an exception is filed, the Magistrate's assistant shall forward the exception along with a copy of the report to the Judge for review and action. If a hearing is set on the exception, the hearing is only on the exception filed, not on the motion itself.

(E) Each Judge is assigned a Trial Clerk by the Clerk's office. The address of the Trial Clerk's office is 425 North Orange Avenue, Orlando, Florida 32801, telephone 407/836–2055.

(F) Each Judge is assigned a Court Deputy by the Sheriff's Office. The address and telephone number of the Court Deputy's office is 425 North Orange Avenue, Orlando, Florida 32801, telephone 407/836–6060.

(G) The court does not employ in-house court reporters for civil cases. A party desiring that the proceedings be recorded must hire a court reporter at that party's initial expense. The cost of court reporter per diem and transcripts may be taxed at the conclusion of the case as prescribed by law. Court reporters when taking a deposition in a pending case, a hearing or trial are considered officers of the court and are governed by the provisions of Florida Rules of Judicial Administration 2.070(b), (e), (f) and (h), and 2.075(e). The Court does not allow court reporters during ex parte unless permission is obtained from the presiding Judge.

[1] So in original.

SECTION 3. ADMINISTRATIVE JUDGE; ALTERNATE JUDGES; DUTY JUDGE.

(A) Administrative Judge. One of the presiding Judges of the division is appointed Administrative Judge by the Chief Judge to serve at his pleasure. Unless specifically reserved, the Administrative Judge has all of the powers of the Chief Judge with respect to cases assigned to the Civil Division.

The Administrative Judge shall be responsible for generally overseeing the operation and functioning of the Civil Division.

(B) Alternate Judge. Each Judge of the Civil Division has an assigned alternate Judge. A list of the Judges and their alternates is maintained in the Court Administrator's office. This list may also be obtained on the Court's web site under Administrative Orders. In the event the assigned Judge is absent or otherwise unable to take action in the case, time-sensitive and emergency matters will be handled during business hours by his or her alternate, or, if the alternate is not available, by a Judge designated by the Administrative Judge or the Chief Judge. The alternate Judge may, but is not required to, hear routine matters not of a true time-sensitive or emergency nature.

(C) Duty Judge. There is a duty Judge on duty after hours and on weekends and holidays on a continuous basis. True emergency matters arising on weekends, holidays or after business hours which can not await hearing during regular business hours should be referred to the duty Judge. The duty Judge must be contacted through the Orange County Sheriff's Communications Section, telephone 407/836–3980.

SECTION 4. ASSIGNMENT, REASSIGNMENT AND TRANSFER OF CASES.

(A) Initial Assignment.

(1) All new cases filed in the Civil Division will be assigned to the Civil Judges by the Clerk by use of a random electronic data assignment system.

(2) The docket, file folder and initial pleading shall have the case number and division number affixed to it by the Clerk. A copy of the Clerk's receipt for the filing fee or original insolvency papers showing the division number will be placed in the file.

(B) Reassignment of Cases.

(1) After Recusal or Disqualification. After entry of an order of disqualification on a motion of a party or an order of recusal on his or her own motion, the Judge will forward the file with the order attached to the Administrative Judge. The Administrative Judge will sign and file the order and serve copies on the affected Judges, counsel of record and unrepresented parties.

(2) Related Cases. When there are two or more cases assigned to different divisions which might be more efficiently handled by the same Judge, such related cases should be brought to the attention of the Judge with the lower case number by a motion to transfer. After the hearing, if the Judge believes that the higher numbered case should be transferred, he or she will contact the Judge to whom the case is assigned to determine if the latter agrees. If there is agreement, the Administrative Judge will enter an order transferring the case. If there is a disagreement, the matter will be referred to the Administrative Judge who, after examining the files and consulting both Judges, will determine whether to transfer the case.

(3) Refiled Cases. Whenever a case is terminated by voluntary dismissal, dismissal for lack of prosecution or involuntary dismissal without prejudice, and is refiled without substantial change in claims or parties, the attorney refiling the case should notify the Administrative Judge who will reassign the new case to the same division to which the prior case was assigned. If this procedure is not followed, counsel for the opposing party shall notify the Administrative Judge.

(4) Reassignment to Complex Business Litigation Court. If a case is filed and qualifies for Complex Business Litigation Court pursuant to Administrative Order 2003–17–3 but is not filed directly into Complex Business Litigation Court, the file may be reassigned by the Administrative Judge either by request of the assigned Judge or by Motion of a party. If contested, the Motion must be set for hearing before the Administrative Judge during ex parte. If the parties agree that the case should be reassigned, the parties may file a Stipulated Motion and send a copy to the Administrative Judge for review along with a proposed order. The order must include language that requires the parties to bring all pending motions into compliance with the Complex Business Litigation Court rules.

(5) By Chief Judge Or Administrative Judge For Any Reason. The Chief Judge or Administrative Judge may reassign any case for any good and sufficient reason.

(C) Transfer Of Cases To Or From Other Courts.

(1) To Another Circuit Court. Where an order has been entered transferring a case from this court to another Florida circuit court on grounds of improper venue or forum non conveniens, the party designated in the order to pay the transfer costs shall within thirty (30) days of the date of the order deliver to the Clerk of this court the filing fee for the other court to accompany the file being sent to the other court.

(2) Transfer To Or From Orange County Court. Whenever this court or the county court finds the other court has subject matter jurisdiction, the assigned Judge shall enter an order transferring the case to the other court and specifying which party shall pay the filing fee for the court to which the case is transferred. When the case and filing fee has been received, the Clerk shall assign the case to a Judge as if it was a newly filed case. If a counterclaim or cross-claim is filed in a county court case which exceeds the subject matter of that court, upon transfer the Circuit Judge will sit as a County Judge to hear any other claims of which the county court has exclusive jurisdiction.

SECTION 5. COURT FILES AND RECORDS.

Pursuant to Florida Statute 28.13 and Florida Rule of Judicial Administration 2.050, the following procedures apply to court files.

(A) The Clerk is required by statute to keep all papers filed in the Clerk's office with utmost care and security.

(B) No person, other than a Judge or the Clerk or a Deputy Clerk shall insert, delete, destroy or make an entry on any paper filed with the Clerk or the file folder in which it is placed unless authorized by a Judge to do so.

(C) Removal, Maintenance and Return of Files.

(1) See Administrative Order 07–98–02 for procedures for removal of court files.

(D) Violations of Removal Procedures. The Clerk is authorized to suspend or revoke removal privileges for violation of paragraphs (B) and (C) and shall report all violations of paragraph (B) and any failure to return a file to the Judge to which the case is assigned.

SECTION 6. APPEARANCE, SUBSTITUTION AND WITHDRAWAL OF ATTORNEYS.

(A) Every appearance of an attorney either by filing a paper or by oral announcement at the commencement of a hearing or trial shall be considered a general appearance, except that a limited special appearance may be made for the purpose of filing a motion to dismiss for lack of jurisdiction over the person, or from insufficiency of process or insufficiency of service of process.

(B) Appearance of attorneys from other states (pro hac vice), appearance of additional counsel, substitution and withdrawal of attorneys are governed by the Florida Rule of Judicial Administration 2.060 and strict adherence to those procedures is required.

(C) Every Order of Withdrawal as counsel of record must contain an address for service of papers upon and telephone number for the client.

SECTION 7. UNREPRESENTED (PRO SE) PARTIES.

(A) Every party to a legal proceeding has the right to appear and prosecute a claim or maintain a defense without being represented by an attorney. There are three exceptions where a party must be represented by an attorney.

(1) Corporations and limited liability companies must be represented by an attorney and may not represent themselves through non-lawyer employees, officers, directors or shareholders, even where such non-lawyer person is the sole shareholder. The only exception is that a corporate landlord may bring an action through its non-lawyer managing agent to evict a tenant for nonpayment of rent.

(2) A guardian of a minor or incompetent must be represented by an attorney unless the guardian is an attorney.

(3) A personal representative of a decedent's estate must be represented by an attorney, unless the personal representative is an attorney or unless the personal representative is the sole person to receive assets from the estate.

(B) The court strongly urges that every party retain an attorney to represent them. However, if a party entitled to represent himself or herself chooses not to retain an attorney, he or she is hereby advised:

(1) Neither the Judge nor his or her Judicial Assistant nor employees of the Clerk's office will give an unrepresented party legal advice.

(2) The unrepresented party will be governed by the same rules of law, procedure, and evidence that attorneys are required to follow.

(3) There is a full service law library available to unrepresented parties at no cost located on the fourth floor, Orange County Public Library, 101 East Central Avenue, Orlando, Florida.

(4) An unrepresented party may not communicate privately with the Judge either by letter, telephone, in person or otherwise. Copies of legal papers or other written materials should not be sent to the Judge unless specifically requested by the Judge or required by these administrative procedures. Any unrequested or non-required papers or materials sent to a Judge may not be read but may be returned to the sender or placed unread into the court file.

(5) An unrepresented party must file his or her papers with the Clerk and send copies to other attorneys or unrepresented parties. All such papers must be typed double-spaced on plain white 8 ½ × 11 paper, with the name of the case and case number at the top and the party's mailing address, telephone number and FAX number, if any, below his or her signature at the end of the paper. Such unrepresented party must immediately notify the Clerk and all other counsel or parties of record in writing of any change in mailing address or telephone or FAX number. Failure to promptly notify of change of address could result in a dismissal or default entered against such party.

SECTION 8. INDIGENT PARTIES

(A) Original Proceedings In Circuit Court. A party claiming financial inability who desires to have certain Clerk's and Sheriff's fees and cost waived will complete and file an affidavit on a form provided by the Clerk. If the affidavit is sufficient, the Clerk will issue and file a written certificate and provide copies of the certificate to the insolvent party. If the Clerk deems the affidavit insufficient, the party may file a motion to have the assigned Judge determine whether the affidavit is sufficient for a waiver of costs and fees. Only a party to a legal action which is presently pending and undisposed of is entitled to a certificate waiving costs and fees. If a party is represented by an attorney the attorney shall make a written certificate as required by Florida Statute 57.018 (1).

(B) Appeal From County Court to Circuit Court Or From Circuit Court to District Court of Appeal. A party claiming financial inability who desires to have Clerk's fees and costs waived in connection with an appeal from Orange County Court to the Civil Division of this court or from the Civil Division of this court to an appellate court must file a motion accompanied by affidavit and serve copies on the opposing parties. If no written objection is filed by an opposing party within five (5) days of the filling and service of the motion and affidavit, the movant must then promptly present a proposed order to the presiding Judge either at ex parte hour or by mail. If a written objection is to be filed, the objecting party must obtain hearing time within not less than four (4) nor more than seven (7) working days and file and serve notice of hearing simultaneously with the objection.

SECTION 9. ASSISTANCE FOR DISABLED PERSONS.

Attorneys, parties, witnesses, jurors and other persons with speech, hearing, sight impairments or other physical disabilities who need special accommodation to participate in legal proceeding should contact the Court Administrator's Office, Room 2130, 425 North Orange Avenue, Orlando, Florida, 32801, telephone 407/836–2303, not later than two (2) days prior to the proceedings. If hearing or voice impaired, contact (TDD) 1–800–955–8771.

SECTION 10. HEARINGS.

(A) Regularly Scheduled Hearings.

(1) Each attorney shall utilize the courts web page, www.ninja9.org under Judicial Automated Calendaring System, for available hearing time and the Judge's schedule before telephoning the Judicial Assistant.

(2) The hearing will be scheduled with the Judge's Judicial Assistant. Written or fax notice must be received in opposing counsel's office at least four (4) working days before the hearing.

(3) Moving counsel must present a proposed order with space for ruling left blank at the conclusion of the hearing and must serve conformed copies on all other counsel and unrepresented parties.

(B) Ex Parte Matters. Ex parte matters are heard by all civil divisions. Times and availability can be located on www.ninja9.org under Judicial Automated Calendaring System. Contested matters generally will not be heard during this time unless the Judge's approval has been obtained in advance through his or her Judicial Assistant. Counsel should check out the court file from the Clerk's office and return it after the matter has been heard unless the Judge wishes to retain the file. If the Judge is unavailable, simple matters requiring no explanation by counsel may be left together with the file with the Judge's Judicial Assistant for later consideration by the Judge. An order should be brought to the hearing for the Judge to sign.

(C) Uniform Motion Calendar.

(1) Contact the Judge's office to ascertain whether short matters are heard by the specific division.

(2) Types of motions suitable for hearing on the motion calendar are simple motions to dismiss complaints with only one or two counts, to strike one or two affirmative defenses, for more definite statement, to amend pleadings, to compel discovery, for protective order, objections to IME, etc. Complex motions, motions requiring testimony or motions for summary judgment (except uncontested mortgage foreclosures), or more than two motions to be heard at one time should not be scheduled on this calendar and will not be heard by the Court.

(D) Other Motion Hearings. All other motions should be specially set through the Judge's Judicial Assistant for a date and time certain. Requests for hearing time in excess of one (1) hour will require special permission of the Judge obtained through the Judicial Assistant or by personal appearance of counsel at ex parte time.

(E) Telephone Appearances. Counsel or unrepresented parties may arrange through the Judge's Judicial Assistant to appear by telephone at a scheduled time and date certain hearing. The published practices and procedures of the individual Judge should be reviewed or if not available, the Judge should be contacted to determine the policy on telephonic appearances. If two or more attorneys are to appear by telephone, one of them should arrange to connect the other attorney or attorneys on a conference call.

(F) Hearings On Motions For Rehearing, Reconsideration or New Trial. Motions for rehearing, reconsideration or new trial will not be set for hearing unless the Judge so directs. Counsel filing such a motion should simultaneously send a chambers copy directly to the Judge with a cover letter requesting a hearing if one is desired. The Judge will then either rule upon the motion without a hearing and serve copies of his or her order on all parties or have his or her Judicial Assistant contact moving counsel and to obtain hearing time to be noticed by moving counsel.

SECTION 11. MOTION PRACTICE GENERALLY.

(A) Form of Motions.

(1) Every written motion shall cite the particular rule or statute and/or leading case upon which the motion is based.

(2) Fla.R.Civ.P. 1.140(b) relating to motions to dismiss requires that the "grounds ... and the substantial matters of law to be argued shall be stated specifically and with particularity."

(3) Fla.R.Civ.P. 1.510(c) relating to motions for summary judgment requires that "the motion shall state with particularity the grounds upon which it is based and the substantial matters of law to be argued." To comply with this rule, every such motion must contain (a) a concise, non-argumentative statement of all material facts as to which movant contends there are no genuine issues for trial and (b) a brief statement of the legal proposition(s) relied upon.

(B) Chambers Copies of Memorandums, Etc. Legal memorandums in support of or opposition to motions are optional. But if filed, counsel must furnish the Judge with chambers copies of the memorandum and highlighted copies of primary legal authorities cited therein. As an alternative to a memorandum, a list of primary legal authorities with highlighted copies attached may be submitted. Chambers copies and authority lists must be under cover letter referencing the case style and number and stating the date and time of the hearing. Counsel who serves a memorandum or authority list first should also include a copy of the motion, any papers to which it is addressed, and the response, if any. In order for the Judge to properly review a submission in advance, it must be received in the Judge's office at least three (3) working days before the hearing.

(C) Obtaining Hearing Times.

(1) If the motion is one which might be resolved by stipulation or agreed order, moving counsel must explore that possibility with opposing counsel before reserving hearing time.

(2) If at all possible, hearing time for complex motions or several motions to be heard at one time should be cleared with all affected counsel so as to avoid calendar conflicts.

(3) If hearing time cannot be coordinated with opposing counsel, attorneys shall appear at ex parte to resolve the issue.

(D) Notices of Hearing.

(1) Every notice must specify the motions to be heard. A notice calling up "all pending motions" is insufficient.

(2) Additional motions should not be "piggy-backed" by cross-notice unless counsel first confirms with opposing counsel and the Judge's Judicial Assistant that there can be sufficient additional time reserved in which to hear them.

(E) Canceling Hearings. Only the attorney who noticed a hearing may cancel it.

If a hearing becomes unnecessary after it has been noticed, the Judge's Judicial Assistant and all other counsel must be notified immediately and effectively that the hearing is canceled.

SECTION 12. ORDERS AND JUDGMENTS.

(A) Who Is To Prepare.

(1) Proposed orders and judgments will be prepared by the prevailing attorney unless the Judge designates some other attorney or states that he or she will prepare the order or judgment.

(2) When submitting proposed orders or judgments, counsel shall also include sufficient copies and self address stamped envelopes for all parties.

(B) Requirements For Orders.

(1) All orders will be on 8 ½ × 11 plain white paper (not lined paper or letterhead paper) and be double spaced.

(2) The order must contain a title indicating what matter the order pertains to, e.g., "Order On Defendant Smith's Motion To Dismiss."

(3) The preamble of the order should include the date of the hearing and what motions were heard.

(4) The adjudication portion of the order should state what relief is ordered. Simply stating that "the motion is granted" without more is insufficient.

(5) The order should indicate the specific time period of any act ordered to be done and should state whether the time period runs from the date of the hearing or the date the order is signed or some other specified date.

(6) The order should contain a full certificate of service with the complete names and addresses of the attorneys and unrepresented parties to be served. Merely showing "copies to" is insufficient.

(7) If an order of dismissal is final (i.e., it disposes of the entire case) the title should contain the word "Final." When the order is not final but leaves other counts or claims against other defendants pending, it should so state in a separate paragraph.

(8) When submitting stipulations, orders shall be by separate order, not attached to the stipulation.

(C) Requirements For Judgements.

(1) Every judgment will indicate whether it is a "Final Judgment" (i.e., the judgment disposes of the entire case) or "Partial Final Judgment," and if the latter, it should specify in a separate paragraph what other counts or claims against other parties remain pending.

(2) All judgments should contain the address and the social security number of the judgment debtor, if known.

(3) All judgments which award accrued interest or prejudgment interest must be accompanied by a writing showing in detail how the amount of interest was computed.

(4) All judgments must contain a certificate of service showing the names and addresses of all attorneys and unrepresented parties to be served.

(5) Copies of default judgments must be mailed by the Judge's Judicial Assistant to the parties against whom the judgment is entered if the address is known.

(D) How Presented.

(1) Counsel preparing the Final Judgment or order should draft and circulate copies within two (2) working days of the ruling or jury verdict.

(2) If counsel preparing the Final Judgment or order gets approval as to form of the order from all counsel, the original with copies and envelopes should be sent directly to the Judge with a cover letter stating all counsel agree to the form of the order or judgment. If other counsel objects to the form or cannot be reached for approval, counsel preparing the judgment or order shall notice a motion for entry of the order or judgment. If objecting counsel does not furnish the Judge prior to or at the hearing with a proposed judgment or order version with copies under cover letter stating the reasons for the objection, all objections will be deemed waived. Orders and judgments should not be submitted to the Judge to hold waiting for an objection.

(3) Unsigned orders or judgments should not be sent to the Clerk's office for transmission to the Judge.

SECTION 13. GENERAL DISCOVERY GUIDELINES.

(A) General Principles. Counsel should be guided by courtesy, candor and common sense and conform to the Florida Rules of Civil Procedure and any applicable orders. In particular, counsel should have in mind the broad scope of discovery allowed by the Civil Rules of Procedure. **Direct and informal communication between counsel is encouraged to facilitate discovery and resolve disputes.**

(B) Timeliness. The time limit specified in the rules and applicable orders must be observed. If additional time is needed, an extension must be sought before the time limit expires by stipulation, or failing that, by motion and order.

(C) Filing of Motions. Interrogatories and answers thereto, copies of documents produced in response to a request and depositions are not be filed with the Clerk unless they are needed for a hearing or trial.

(D) Discovery Motions. Before requesting hearing time on a Motion to Compel or for Protective Order, the moving attorney must contact the opposing attorney and attempt to resolve the dispute or narrow the issues to be decided. If a hearing is set, the notice of hearing must contain or be accompanied by a certificate of the noticing attorney that reasonable efforts have been made to contact opposing counsel and failed; or that counsel have conferred, failed to resolve all issues; and that a hearing is necessary. A copy of the certificate will be handed to the Judge at the beginning of the hearing.

SECTION 14. DEPOSITION GUIDELINES.

(A) Scheduling. If the time for taking a deposition cannot be coordinated with other counsel in advance, at least ten (10) working days notice should be given. Note that it is often less expensive to bring the witness to the deposition (and for the parties to share the expense) than for the lawyers to travel.

Likewise, a telephone deposition of a secondary witness will save expense.

(B) Questioning. Questions should be brief, clear and simple. Each question should deal with only a single point. Argumentative or unnecessary embarrassing questions are out of order. The purpose of a deposition is not to harass or intimidate, but simply to make a clear and unambiguous record of what the witness' testimony would be at trial or to locate other witnesses or admissible evidence.

(C) Documents And Exhibits. Normally, a witness should be shown a document or exhibit and given a reasonable opportunity to examine it before being questioned about it.

(D) Objections. Objections to the conduct of counsel or other persons present should be noted on the record. Objection to the form of a question should state the specific grounds, i.e., leading, compound, etc., but the question should be answered unless the examiner rephrases the question. In the absence of a good faith claim of privilege, violation of a protective order, or other appropriate ground, instruction not to answer are rarely justified and may lead to sanctions. Speaking objections and frequent recesses or other tactics to coach a deponent are improper and may also be cause for sanctions. If counsel believes that a motion to terminate or limit the examination would be warranted, the deposition should be recessed and counsel should promptly initiate a telephone conference call to the presiding Judge to attempt to resolve the problem or obtain a ruling, or, if the assigned Judge is unavailable, promptly file a motion and set a hearing.

(E) Multiple Depositions of Same Witness.

Generally, a witness or party should be deposed only once in a given case. All counsel of record should be given notice of the deposition and an opportunity to examine. Counsel who fail to attend or fail to examine a witness after notice shall be deemed to have waived their right to depose the witness. A second deposition may be taken of a witness only upon stipulation of counsel or court order, and if allowed will generally be limited to new matters occurring after the first deposition.

SECTION 15. ALTERNATIVE DISPUTE RESOLUTION.

It is the policy of the Civil Division Judges to maximize the use of alternative dispute resolution procedures. Except where prohibited by statute, mediation will be ordered in all cases where jury trial is requested and in selected cases which are to be tried non-jury. Also, selected cases will be referred for court-annexed non-binding arbitration through the Orange County Bar Association Arbitration Service. Counsel may move to dispense with or defer mediation or arbitration or move to modify the referral order for good cause. (See form mediation order in Appendix hereto.)

SECTION 16. SETTING CASES FOR TRIAL.

When a party files with the Clerk a Notice for Trial pursuant to Fla.R.Civ.P. 1.440, there shall be included therewith a sufficient number of stamped addressed envelopes for all counsel and unrepresented parties of record. The Clerk will staple the envelopes to the inside of the case file folder, then forward the file to the assigned Judge's Judicial Assistant for preparation of the order setting the case for trial. The notice must correctly indicate whether the case is to be tried by jury or non-jury and estimate the total number of days or hours needed for the trial.

SECTION 17. SETTLEMENTS.

(A) Immediate Notice. Counsel will <u>**immediately**</u> notify the Judge's Judicial Assistant by telephone of the settlement of any case scheduled for trial so they can be removed from the trial docket.

(B) Settlement of Cases Involving Minors or Incompetents.

(1) Court approval of settlement is required where (a) the gross settlement of a minor's claim for the minor's own injury exceeds $15,000; (b) in a wrongful death case where there are multiple claims including a claim on behalf of a minor survivor or (c) in a case where there are multiple claims including a claim by a minor for permanent injury to a parent; or (d) where the minor is one of several plaintiffs or defendants and only equitable relief is to be granted.

(2) A legal guardianship shall be required when the amount of the net settlement exceeds $15,000, pursuant to section 744.387, Florida Statutes. In any case which the gross settlement for the claim of the minor exceeds $15,000, the court may, prior to the approval of the settlement, appoint a guardian ad litem to represent the minor's interests, pursuant to section 744.301(4)(a). After the guardianship is established and the attorney's trust account is in receipt of the funds, the Probate Division Judge shall then direct further disbursement of the minor's funds from the attorney's trust account to the guardianship

(3) A guardian ad litem must be appointed to represent a minor and protect the minor's interests where the gross settlement exceeds $25,000, pursuant to section 744.301 (4)(a).

(4) If there is no case pending, the petition for approval of settlement shall be filed in the Probate, Guardianship and Mental Health Division (Division 01). If there is a personal injury or wrongful death case pending in a Civil Division, the petition for approval of the settlement (and for apportionment) shall be filed in that pending case.

(5) If a guardian has been appointed, petition for approval of settlement of the claim will be filed in the pending civil case, or, if no civil case is pending, in the guardianship case.

(C) Settlements by Governmental Agencies. Florida Statute 69.081, known as the "Sunshine in Litigation" law, requires that a governmental agency which settles a tort claim for an amount in excess of $5,000 shall provide notice in accordance with Chapter 50 or have the settlement approved by a court. As a matter of policy, the Civil Division Judges will approve governmental agency settlements of tort claims of minors but will decline to entertain any petitions to approve settlements with adults and will require that the governmental agency utilize the notice provision.

(D) Written Stipulations With Default Judgment Provisions. There are certain cases in which the parties enter into a written stipulation which provides for one party to make periodic payments of money and in default, that a judgment be entered against that party. In such cases, the Judge will enter a Final Order of Dismissal with prejudice but retaining jurisdiction to enforce the stipulation. (See form order in

Appendix hereto.) Counsel should deliver to the assigned Judge an executed copy of the stipulation, the order with copies and pre-addressed envelopes. All stipulations will be deemed to provide that reasonable notice shall be given to the defaulting party of any application for default judgment. The application for default judgment may be noticed for ex parte time, but if contested, the matter will be reset for hearing at a later time.

SECTION 18. PROMPT CLOSURE OF CASES.

When a case had been finally disposed of by Final Judgment, Final Order of Dismissal or Notice of Voluntary Dismissal, counsel for prevailing party or counsel preparing settlement papers **must** promptly file with the Clerk **Final Disposition Form 1.998** (found in the forms appended to the Florida Rules of Civil Procedure). The form may accompany the proposed final order of Final Judgment and the Judge will send it to the Clerk for filing along with the signed Final Order or Final Judgment.

SECTION 19. REMOVALS TO FEDERAL COURT.

Whenever a petition has been filed to remove a case from a Civil Division to federal District Court, the Clerk will remove the case from the Judge's active case list. If there is a remand of the case back to this court, counsel who sought the removal will notify the assigned Judge by letter and the Clerk will reinstate the case on the Judge's active case list upon the filing of a copy of the remand order. If, however, the case is finally disposed of in federal court, including all pendent claims, counsel who sought the removal will file with the Clerk of this Court a copy of the Final Order or judgment of the federal district court together with Final Disposition Form 1.998 and the clerk will close the case.

SECTION 20. JUDICIAL SALES.

Unless the order or judgment providing for a judicial sale specifies otherwise, the sale will be conducted pursuant to Florida Statute 45.031 and the following additional procedures.

(A) The time of sale shall be scheduled at 11:00 a.m. on the day of the week assigned to the division for sales and may be continued until no later than 2:00 p.m. at the discretion of the Clerk for the purpose of allowing bidders to produce payment. Sales for time share cases shall be scheduled for 11:00 a.m. on Wednesday.

(B) The highest bidder shall identify himself or herself by individual name, and, if in a representative capacity, the name of the corporation, partnership or individuals (s) represented.

(C) Payment shall be made in cash, bank cashier's check, or practicing attorney's trust account check. Personal checks and fiduciary's trust account checks cannot be accepted.

(D) At the conclusion of the sale the successful high bidder shall post with the clerk a deposit equal to five percent of the final bid or $1,000, whichever is less. If the balance of the bid is not paid by 2:00 p.m., the clerk shall readvertise the sale and pay all costs of the sale from the deposit and apply any remaining funds from the deposit towards the judgment.

(E) A party obtaining an order of sale may move the court for an order requiring the deposit at the sale to be greater than five percent of the final bid or $1,000 upon a showing of good cause.

SECTION 21. ENFORCEMENT OF POST JUDGMENT DISCOVERY.

Upon the filing of a verified motion by a judgment creditor that a judgment debtor has wholly failed to respond to interrogatories, a request to produce documents and/or notice of taking deposition in aid of execution, the court will issue an ex parte order compelling the judgment debtor to furnish such discovery or attend a deposition by or on a certain date, or, upon failure to do so, to appear before the court on a date and time certain and show cause why the judgment debtor should not be held in contempt. (See form order in Appendix hereto). The order with copy of interrogatories or request to produce attached must be personally served upon the judgment debtor if he or she is an individual. If after personal service the individual judgment debtor fails to make the ordered discovery or attend the ordered deposition and fails to appear at the show cause hearing, the judgment creditor may present ex parte an affidavit to that effect and a proposed order of arrest for civil contempt. The order may contain a provision for bail. When the judgment debtor is taken into custody, the judgment creditor's attorney will be notified by the Judge's Judicial Assistant of the time of the contempt hearing. The attorney must bring a court reporter to the hearing.

SECTION 22. PROCEDURES FOR APPEAL FROM COUNTY TO THE CIVIL COURT

The administrative procedures for appeals from County Court to the Civil Division are set forth in a separate publication entitled "County Court Appeal Procedures," which appears in the Appendix hereto.

SECTION 23. PROFESSIONALISM.

As a matter of policy, the Civil Division Judges endorse the Ninth Judicial Circuit Courtroom Decorum Policy and the concepts contained in the "Orange County Bar Association Standards of Professional Courtesy" dated November 13, 1990 and the Guidelines for Professional Conduct prepared by the Trial Lawyers Section of the Florida Bar and approved by the Florida Conference of Circuit Judges in September 1995. All attorneys are urged to familiarize themselves and their office staff with these standards and to adhere to them. (A copy of these Standards appears in the Appendix hereto.)

APPENDIX

FORM 1 Order of Referral to Mediation

FORM 2 Final Order of Dismissal With Prejudice

FORM 3 Order to Comply with Post–Judgment Discovery or Show Cause

Amended Local Rule #6 on County Court Appeal Procedures

Administrative Order 07–98–02 regarding removal of court files

Ninth Judicial Circuit Courtroom Decorum Policy

Orange County Bar Association Standards of Professionalism, Professional Courtesy, and Courtroom Decorum

IN THE CIRCUIT COURT OF THE
NINTH JUDICIAL CIRCUIT, IN AND
FOR ORANGE COUNTY, FLORIDA.

CASE NO.
DIVISION

( ) CASE SET FOR TRIAL

Plaintiff,

vs. ( ) CASE NOT SET FOR TRIAL

Defendant /

ORDER OF REFERRAL TO MEDIATION

It appearing to the Court that this case is appropriate for Mediation, it is

ORDERED as follows:

1. This case is hereby referred to Mediation pursuant to Chapter 44, Florida Statutes and Florida Rules of Civil Procedure 1.700 et seq.

2. The Court appoints ________, whose address is ________ and whose telephone number is ___, as the court's Mediator to assist the parties in attempting to reach a mutually acceptable settlement of the issues in this case.

3. A Mediation conference shall be held on ________, the ___ day of ________, 200 ___, at ___ a.m./p.m. at ________, ________, Florida.

(or)

A Mediation conference shall be held at such time and place as the parties may agree but not later than the cut-off date in the Order setting this case for trial.

4. Counsel and all parties are hereby ordered to appear at the Mediation conference and any subsequent or follow-up Mediation conferences as may be set by the Mediator, until Mediation has been successfully concluded or has been terminated by the Mediator. A corporate party will send a management representative. If a party is insured, a representative of the insurance company must attend. If the attending insurance representative does not have authority to settle up to the limit of Plaintiff's current demand or the policy limits, whichever is lower, the insurance company will have a person who does have such authority on telephone stand-by during all sessions. If the defendant is a self-insured public officer or entity, the risk manager or a risk committee member or other person designated by the risk committee must attend all sessions and be prepared to commit to a tentative settlement to be recommended to the risk management committee and thence to the public officer or entity for approval.

5. Not later than ten (10) days prior to the first mediation conference, each party will provide the Mediator with a brief written summary of the facts and issues and include therein the name of the attorney and party as well as the insurance or risk management representative who will attend. Copies of the written summary need not be served on opposing parties or filed with the Court.

6. If it becomes impossible for an attorney, party, or insurance or risk management representative to attend either the initial or a subsequent conference, such person shall immediately advise plaintiff's attorney, who will then coordinate rescheduling of the conference and confirm the same in writing.

7. The Mediator shall be compensated at the rate of $ ___ per hour. Each party shall pay a pro-rata share of the total compensation unless otherwise agreed between them. Each party must pay their share of the Mediator's compensation within thirty (30) days of receipt of the Mediator's statement.

8. If the Mediator and the parties desire to use one of the Court's mediation rooms, contact the Court's judicial assistant, in advance, to reserve a date and time for the use of the room.

9. Failure to comply, in good faith, with the statute, rules or any provision of this Order should be reported immediately to the Court by the Mediator, and such non-compliance will subject the offending attorney or party to appropriate sanctions.

Orlando, Florida this ___ day of ________, 200 ___.

CIRCUIT JUDGE

IN THE CIRCUIT COURT OF THE
NINTH JUDICIAL CIRCUIT, IN AND
FOR ORANGE COUNTY, FLORIDA.

CASE NO.
DIVISION

Plaintiff,

vs.

Defendant /

FINAL ORDER OF DISMISSAL WITH PREJUDICE

(Written Stipulation for Settlement)

The parties have filed a written stipulation for settlement with the Court. The Court has reviewed the file, reviewed the stipulation and counsel have approved the entry of this order. It is, based upon the stipulation,

ORDERED that:

1. The stipulation is approved and incorporated by reference into this order.

2. This cause is dismissed with prejudice.

3. The Court reserves jurisdiction to enforce the stipulation.

Orlando, Florida this ___ day of ________, 200 ___.

CIRCUIT JUDGE

(CERTIFICATE OF SERVICE)

IN THE CIRCUIT COURT OF THE
NINTH JUDICIAL CIRCUIT, IN AND
FOR ORANGE COUNTY, FLORIDA.

CASE NO.
DIVISION

Plaintiff,

vs.

Defendant

_______________ /

ORDER TO COMPLY WITH POST–JUDGMENT DISCOVERY OR SHOW CAUSE

This cause came on to be heard on this date on _________'s motion to compel post-judgment discovery. It appears that _________ failed to (appear for deposition) (answer written interrogatories) (respond to a request to produce documents). It is therefore

ORDERED as follows:

1. _________ will appear for deposition at the office of _________, attorney, located at _________, _________, Florida, on the ___ day of _________, 200 ___, at ___ a.m./p.m., and bring with him/her the following documents:

OR

_________ will answer the interrogatories in writing, have the answers notarized, and deliver the written notarized answers to the office of the _________'s attorney whose name, address and telephone number appears on the copy of the interrogatories, not later than the ___ day of _________, 200 ___ at ___ a.m./p.m. A copy of the interrogatories is attached to this Order.

OR

_________ will produce at the office of the _________'s attorney located at _________, _________, Florida, _________ on the ___ day of _________, 200 ___ at ___ a.m./p.m. the documents specified in the request to produce and allow the attorney or a member of his/her staff to inspect and copy the documents. A copy of the request to produce is attached to this Order.

2. If _________ fails to comply with paragraph (1) above, he/she is hereby ORDERED to appear before the undersigned Judge in Room ___, Orange County Courthouse, 425 N. Orange Avenue, Orlando, FL 32801 on the ___ day of _________, 200 ___, at ___ a.m./p.m. and show cause why he/she should not be punished for contempt of court.

Orlando, Florida, this ___ day of _________, 200 ___.

____

CIRCUIT JUDGE

AMENDED LOCAL RULE #6 ON COUNTY COURT APPEAL PROCEDURES [VACATED AND SUPERSEDED BY ADMINISTRATIVE ORDER NO. 2015-10-01]

ADMINISTRATIVE ORDER 07–98–02 REGARDING REMOVAL OF COURT FILES

IN THE CIRCUIT COURT OF THE NINTH JUDICIAL CIRCUIT, IN AND FOR ORANGE AND OSCEOLA COUNTIES, FLORIDA

ADMINISTRATIVE ORDER NO. 07–98–02

SECOND AMENDED ADMINISTRATIVE ORDER CONCERNING REMOVAL OF COURT FILES FROM OFFICES OF CLERK OF THE CIRCUIT AND COUNTY COURTS

WHEREAS, pursuant to rule 2.050 and rule 2.072, Florida Rules of Judicial Administration, the following procedures for the removal of court files from the offices of the Clerk of Circuit and County courts are hereby established; and

WHEREAS, rule 2.072, Florida Rules of Judicial Administration, prohibits the removal of court records from the clerk's office by any person other than judges and authorized court employees, except by order of the Chief Judge upon a showing of good cause. According to the Florida Supreme Court, a chief judge has the authority to enter general administrative orders to allow the removal of court files for particular purposes. In re: Florida Rule of Judicial Administration 2.072, No. 87,058 (Fla. June 27, 1996);

NOW, THEREFORE, I, Belvin Perry, Jr., pursuant to the authority vested in me as Chief Judge of the Ninth Judicial Circuit of Florida under rule 2.050 and rule 2.072 of the Florida Rules of Judicial Administration hereby order the following:

1. No person other than judges and authorized court employees may remove court records from the offices of the Clerk of the Circuit and County Courts except as may be allowed by this Administrative Order or by order of the Chief Judge or presiding judge upon a showing of good cause.

2. Any judge may allow, by specific court order, the removal of a court file upon a showing by the person requesting the removal of the court file that the removal is necessary. Persons requesting to remove a court file must submit to the Court a motion and proposed order which states the reasons for the need to remove the court file. Such motion and proposed order should substantially comply with the forms attached to this Administrative Order.

3. Any court file removed from the Clerk's office in Orange County or Osceola County pursuant to a court order or this Administrative Order must remain in Orange County or Osceola County unless the judge grants special permission for its removal to another county. Persons who request that a court file be mailed must submit the request in writing to the presiding judge. Should the presiding judge order a court file to be mailed, the file must be sent and returned by registered mail, return receipt requested, and insured for an amount to be determined by the presiding judge, at the expense of the party designated by the presiding judge.

4. Unless the judge orders otherwise, all court files must be returned to the Clerk's office by the third business day. However, the Clerk or a deputy clerk may, at any time, require that the court file be returned immediately if requested by the Clerk or by a judge.

5. In order to remove a file from the Clerk's office, a person duly authorized to do so must sign a receipt furnished by the Clerk. The Clerk may allow the file to be removed without obtaining a signature if the person's signature is on file in the Clerk's office on a properly executed signature card captioned "authorization for removal of case files from the offices of the Clerk of the Circuit and County Courts".

6. The Clerk is required by Section 28.13, Florida Statutes, to keep all papers filed in the Clerk's office with the utmost care and security. No person, other than a judge or the Clerk or a judicial assistant under the direction of the judge, may insert, delete, destroy, or make an entry on any paper filed with the Clerk or the file folder in which it is placed unless authorized by a judge to do so.

7. Any court file removed by an authorized person must be maintained with the utmost of care and returned intact with the papers in proper sequence. No file may be released to a third party or sent to a commercial printer or copy center for copying purposes. If an authorized person removes a court file and leaves it with a judge, the authorized person is responsible for notifying the Clerk to check out the file to the judge.

8. The Clerk is authorized to suspend or revoke removal privileges for violations of the above stated provisions. The Clerk shall report all violations of these procedures, including the failure to timely return a file, to the Chief Judge or to the Administrative Judge of the division in which the case is assigned.

9. Nothing herein is intended to allow the removal of evidence from the custody of the Clerk without leave of court.

10. Nothing herein is intended to allow the removal of court records that are confidential from the custody of the Clerk without leave of court.

11. Nothing herein is intended to allow removal of court records from the custody of the clerk without leave of court when the records pertain to cases filed within the Criminal Justice Division, the Juvenile Division, the Probate Division, or the Criminal Justice or Traffic subdivisions of the County Court Division.

12. **Judges and Court Personnel:**

It is specifically intended by the undersigned that nothing in this order shall prevent the removal of any court file from any Clerk's office by the judges, judicial assistants, judicial staff attorneys (law clerks) and the Court Administrator or his or her staff when necessary in the performance of their duties. It is implicit in Court Administration's administrative assistance to the Chief Judge that the staff perform on behalf of, and as directed by, the Chief Judge.

All court personnel when forwarding a court file to a person who is authorized to remove the court file pursuant to a court order or this Administrative Order shall ensure that the Clerk's office is notified as to whom the court file has been forwarded. Should a judge or the judge's staff wish to forward a court file to authorized persons outside of the judge's division, the judge or the judge's staff shall return the court file to the Clerk's office with written instructions to the Clerk to forward the court file to those persons. All court personnel are prohibited from forwarding a court file to a person who is not authorized to remove court files.

13. **The Florida Department of Professional Regulation:**

The Florida Department of Professional Regulation is hereby authorized to remove **closed civil court files** for a period of seventy-two (72) hours. Said Department may remove **open civil court files** for forty-eight (48) hours by written authorization to the Clerk from the assigned Judge or the Chief Judge. The Department may make copies of the documents in the court file for its use, but shall not, in so doing, take apart any deposition transcripts or other bound documents and shall comply with the procedures stated in paragraphs 3. through 10. of this Administrative Order. The authorization provided to the Department of Professional Regulation is limited to removal of **civil court files** and does not extend to court files pertaining to cases filed within the Criminal Justice Division, the Juvenile Division, the Probate Division or the Criminal Justice or Traffic subdivisions of the County Court Division.

14. **Attorneys of Record:**

In any proceeding within the **General Civil Division**, the **Domestic Relations Division**, or the **general civil subdivisions of the County Court Division**, an attorney of record or other authorized person may remove a court file for the limited purposes of delivery to the judge for matters including, but not limited to, ex parte hearings. The court file may not be removed from the courthouse and must be returned to the Clerk's office immediately following the conclusion of the proceeding.

As stated in paragraph 2. of this Administrative Order, attorneys of record who request to remove a court file from the courthouse must submit a motion and proposed order to the Court stating the reasons for the need to remove the court file. Such motion and proposed order must substantially comply with the forms attached to this Administrative Order.

Furthermore, should a court order be granted allowing the removal of the court file, the attorney must comply with the procedures stated above in paragraphs 3. through 10. of this Administrative Order.

15. **Legal Aid Society:**

The Legal Aid Society of the Orange County Bar Association is responsible for the initial clearing of all cases referred to private attorneys through the Orange County Bar Association's Pro Bono Program. For cases in which there is ongoing litigation, it is necessary that the court files be removed by the Legal Aid Society's staff in order to review the cases to determine whether the cases warrant representation by the Legal Aid Society and pro bono attorneys. Therefore, for court files pertaining to **Domestic, Circuit Civil or County Civil matters** in which the Legal Aid Society contemplates the filing of an appearance, the Legal Aid Society's staff is authorized to remove court files in accordance with the procedures as stated above in paragraphs 3. through 10. of this Administrative Order.

16. **Child Support Enforcement:**

The Florida Department of Revenue, Child Support Enforcement and its agents in the enforcement of child support in the Title IV–D cases are authorized to remove court files for the purpose of review in order to file appropriate subsequent pleadings and must comply with the procedures stated above in paragraphs 3. through 10. of this Administrative Order.

17. **Juvenile Division:**

The Clerk shall keep all official records prescribed in section 39.045, Florida Statutes, separate from other records of the Circuit Court. These records shall not be open to inspection by the public. No record shall be inspected except upon order of the Court permitting inspection by persons deemed by the Judge to have a proper interest therein. However, a child and the parents or legal custodians of the child and their attorneys shall always have the right to inspect and copy any official record pertaining to the child. Furthermore, other persons who are designated within the statute may inspect and copy court files by Court order. Liaison personnel employed with the Department of Juvenile Justice and the Department of Health and Rehabilitative Services are authorized to remove court files for the purpose of bringing the court files to and from the judges' chambers, hearing rooms, courtrooms and the Clerk's office. However, these persons shall not remove court files from the courthouse.

Administrative Order No. 07–96–40 titled "Order Regarding Research by the Florida Juvenile Justice Advisory Board Concerning Transfers of Juveniles for Prosecution as Adults" allows the Juvenile Justice Advisory Board professional staff and the staff's authorized agents access to Juvenile Division court files for the limited purpose of completing research concerning the transfers of juveniles for prosecution as adults. When removing court files, these persons must comply with the provisions in Administrative Order No. 07–96–40 and the procedures and limitations as stated above in paragraphs 3. through 10. of this Administrative Order.

18. **Mediators:**

Mediators, who are appointed by the Court to conduct mediations at the Court for both county civil cases and domestic cases are authorized to remove court files for the limited purpose of bringing the court files to and from the mediations. The Clerk shall maintain a list of these mediators' names and upon removing the court files, the mediators shall present to the Clerk proper identification for such removal. The court files shall not be removed from the courthouse by the mediators except upon written order from the Court.

19. **Court Reporters:**

Court Reporters, except those who are employees of the Ninth Judicial Circuit, must have a written order from the Court to remove court files.

20. **Pro Se Litigant (i.e. a party to a lawsuit who is proceeding without an attorney):**

Pro Se litigants must have a written order from the presiding judge or the Administrative Judge of a specific division to remove court files; and the removal of court files shall only be for the limited purpose of bringing the court file to the presiding judge for a pending court proceeding or for bringing the court file to a mediator for a scheduled mediation, or for bringing the court file to a hearing officer for a hearing. Under no circumstances shall pro se litigants be authorized to remove court files from the courthouse.

21. **Effective Date:**

This Administrative Order shall become effective immediately. Administrative Order No. 07–96–57 is vacated and set aside.

DONE AND ORDERED at Orlando, Florida, this 11th day of August, 1998.

/s/ Belvin Perry, Jr.
Belvin Perry, Jr.
Chief Judge

Copies to:

All Circuit & County Judges, Ninth Judicial Circuit
State Attorney's Office, Ninth Judicial Circuit
Public Defender's Office, Ninth Judicial Circuit
General Counsel, Orange County Sheriff's Office
Orange County Corrections
Orange County Bar Association
Bar Briefs, Orange County Bar Association
Paul C. Perkins Bar Association
Hispanic Bar Association
Clerk of Courts, Orange County
Orange County Law Library
Clerk of Courts, Osceola County
The Osceola County Bar Association
The Osceola County Law Library
The Osceola County Sheriff's Office
Office of the Statewide Prosecutor
Central Florida Criminal Defense Attorneys Association
Legal Aid Society of the Orange County Bar Association
Executive Director of The Florida Bar
Official Records, Orange County Comptroller

Administrative Order No. 07–98–02

FORM 1.

IN THE CIRCUIT/COUNTY COURT
OF THE NINTH JUDICIAL CIRCUIT,
IN AND FOR ORANGE/OSCEOLA
COUNTY, FLORIDA

Case No. ________
Division No. ________

________,

Plaintiff,

vs.

________,

Defendant.
________/

MOTION TO REMOVE COURT FILE

COMES NOW, ________, and moves this Court to allow the removal of the court file in case number _____ from the court facility and as grounds would show:

1. The removal of the court file from the court facility is necessary because (state reasons/purposes for the necessity of removing the court file).

2. Should the Court grant this Motion, Movant and Movant's duly authorized representatives, including, but not limited to, employees and associates, shall comply with the procedures stated in this Court's Order and in Administrative Order 07–98–02.

WHEREFORE, Movant respectfully requests this Honorable Court grant this Motion to allow Movant to remove said court file from the court facility for the purposes stated above.

DATED this ___ day of ___, 19 ___.

____
Person's printed name and signature, address, telephone number (if an attorney, state Florida Bar #)

CERTIFICATE OF SERVICE

I HEREBY CERTIFY that a true and correct copy of the foregoing has been furnished to the following persons by United States mail this ___ day of _____, 199___: (list persons' names)

____
Person's printed name and signature

FORM 2.
IN THE CIRCUIT/COUNTY COURT
OF THE NINTH JUDICIAL CIRCUIT,
IN AND FOR ORANGE/OSCEOLA
COUNTY, FLORIDA

Case No. ____________
Division No. ________

______________________,

Plaintiff,

vs.

______________________,

Defendant.
______________________/

ORDER ON MOTION FOR REMOVAL OF COURT FILE

THIS CAUSE having come before me upon the Motion for Removal of Court File, and the Court having reviewed said Motion and being fully advised in the premises, it is hereby

ORDERED AND ADJUDGED:

1. Motion is granted/denied.

2. The Clerk of Court is ordered to allow __________, Movant and Movant's duly authorized representatives to remove the court file from the court facility for the purposes of (list purposes).

3. Movant and Movant's duly authorized representatives, including, but not limited to, employees and associates, shall comply with the procedures stated in Administrative Order No. 07–98–02 governing the removal of court files. Failure of Movant and Movant's duly authorized representatives to comply with said procedures shall constitute a violation of this Order and Administrative Order No. 07–98–02 and the Clerk is authorized to suspend or revoke removal privileges for such violation.

4. Movant and Movant's duly authorized representatives shall keep the court file with the utmost care and security. Movant and Movant's duly authorized representatives shall not insert, delete, destroy, or make an entry on any paper or the file folder itself in the court file and shall return the court file intact. Movant and Movant's duly authorized representatives shall not release the court file to any third party, or firm, nor shall the court file be given to any commercial printer or copy center for copying purposes.

5. Movant or Movant's duly authorized representative shall return the court file to the Clerk's office within three (3) days (or earlier should the Court or Clerk deem necessary) from the date the court file is checked out to Movant or to Movant's duly authorized representative by the Clerk.

DONE AND ORDERED at Orlando/Kissimmee, Florida this ___ day of _____, 19___.

____
Circuit/County Judge

CERTIFICATE OF SERVICE

I HEREBY CERTIFY that a true and correct copy of the foregoing has been furnished to the following persons by United States Mail this ___ day of _____, 19___: (list persons' names)

____
Judicial Assistant

NINTH JUDICIAL CIRCUIT COURTROOM DECORUM POLICY

The purpose of this policy is to state certain basic principles concerning courtroom behavior and decorum. When appearing in this Court, unless excused by the presiding Judge, all counsel (including all persons at counsel table) shall abide by the following:

1. Stand when Court is opened, recessed or adjourned. Stand when addressing, or being addressed by the Court. Stand when the jury enters or retires from the courtroom. When making opening statements, closing arguments or examining witnesses, do not approach either the jury or the witness without the Court's permission. Remain at the lectern unless using exhibits or charts.

2. Address all remarks to the Court, not to opposing counsel or the opposing party.

3. Avoid disparaging personal remarks or acrimony toward opposing counsel and remain wholly detached from any ill feeling between the litigants or witnesses.

4. Refer to all persons, including witnesses, other counsel and the parties by their surnames and not by their first or given names unless the permission of the Court is sought in advance.

5. Only one attorney for each party shall examine, or cross examine each witness. The attorney stating objections, if any, during direct examination, shall be the attorney recognized for cross examination.

6. Counsel should request permission before approaching the bench. Any documents counsel wishes to have the Court examine should be handed to the clerk. Any paper or exhibit not previously marked for identification should first be handed to the clerk to be marked before it is tendered to a witness for his examination; and any exhibit offered in evidence should, at the time of such offer, be handed to opposing counsel.

7. No exhibit, whether marked for identification or not, shall be held in any manner, or placed in any position in the courtroom, that would allow the trier of fact to see the exhibit unless it has been admitted into evidence and permission to publish the exhibit to the jury has been obtained from the Court.

8. In making objections counsel should state only the legal grounds for the objection and should withhold all further comment or argument unless elaboration is requested by the Court.

9. When examining a witness, counsel shall not repeat or echo the answer given by the witness.

10. Offers of, or requests for, a stipulation should be made privately, not within the hearing of the trier of fact.

11. In opening statements and in arguments to the trier of fact, counsel shall not express personal knowledge or opinions concerning any matter in issue.

12. Counsel shall admonish all persons at the counsel table who make gestures, facial expressions, audible comments, or the like, as manifestations of approval or disapproval during the testimony of witnesses, or at any other time. This behavior is strictly prohibited.

13. All parties, attorneys and witnesses should refrain from interrupting or talking over one another.

14. Counsel shall refrain from attempting to make a reargument after the Judge has ruled.

15. Counsel shall complete resolution negotiations and advise clients of their settlement options in advance of court hearings.

16. No tobacco use in any form is permitted. No bottles, beverage containers, paper cups or edibles are allowed in the courtroom, except as permitted by the Court. No gum chewing is permitted.

17. Cell phones and pagers should be turned off or in a vibrate mode. Computers should be used with audio off.

18. All counsel shall provide a copy of this policy to clients prior to coming to court.

19. Pursuant to Family Law Rule of Procedure 12.407, no children are allowed in the courtroom, waiting area or adjacent hallway without prior approval of the court, unless the child(ren) is a party to the action.

OCBA Standards of Professionalism

Orange County Bar Association Standards of Professionalism,Professional Courtesy and Courtroom Decorum

Preamble

The practice of law is largely an adversarial process and Attorneys are ethically bound to zealously represent and advocate in their clients' interest.

Lawyers are officers of the court and they are responsible to the judiciary for the propriety of their professional activities. Within that context, the legal profession has been granted powers of self-regulation which help maintain the legal profession's independence from undue government domination by the legislative and executive branches. Supervision by an independent judiciary, and conformity with the rules the judiciary adopts for the profession, assures both the independence and the responsibility of the legal profession.

In addition to Attorneys' professional responsibilities prescribed by substantive and procedural law, Attorneys are also guided by personal conscience and the approbation of professional peers;

In Orange County, Florida, there have developed certain community standards of legal professionalism, professional courtesy, and courtroom decorum previously acknowledged and recognized through the adoption in 1990 of the Orange County Bar Association Standards of Professional Courtesy and in 2003 through entry of Administrative Order 2003–07 establishing the Orange County Courtroom Decorum Policy;

Attorneys should strive to attain certain ideals of professionalism and demonstrate a minimum level of professional courtesy necessary to lend dignity to the practice of law in our community and instill public confidence in the justice system.

In order to promote and perpetuate the long tradition of professionalism among and between members of the Orange County Bar Association and the bench and to assist in the efficient administration of justice, the following Standards of Professionalism, Professional Courtesy and Courtroom Decorum, "Standards", are hereby adopted.

Introduction

The Standards set forth herein are those expected of Attorneys practicing in the Courts of the Ninth Judicial Circuit in and for Orange County. While not meant to be exhaustive, the Standards also set a tone or guide for conduct that might not be specifically covered by these Standards. The overriding principles promoted by the Standards are communication and civility between counsel, as well as cooperation with the Courts and other participants in the justice system.

The Standards have been codified with the hope that their dissemination will educate new Attorneys and others who may be unfamiliar with the Orange County legal community's expectations regarding legal professionalism, professional courtesy, and courtroom decorum. They have received the approval of the Executive Council of the Orange County Bar Association. They have also been approved by the Judges of the Ninth Judicial Circuit. These standards should be read consistently with the Ideals and Goals of Professionalism adopted by the Board of Governors of The Florida Bar in 1990 and the Conference of Circuit Judges and County Court Judges and Trial Lawyers Section of the Florida Bar Guidelines for Professional Conduct, (2008 Edition).

I. Discovery, Litigation Practice, and Scheduling

1. Attorneys shall refrain from discovery requests not reasonably related to the matter at issue. Attorneys shall not use discovery for the purpose of harassing, embarrassing, causing needless duplication of effort, or causing the adversary to incur unnecessary expenses.

2. Attorneys shall not propound or object to discovery for the purpose of causing undue delay, needless vexation or obtaining unfair advantage.

3. Attorneys shall ensure that responses to reasonable discovery requests are timely, complete, and consistent with the obvious intent of the request. Attorneys shall not, and must counsel their clients not to produce documents in a way calculated to hide or obscure the existence of documents.

4. Attorneys shall, whenever appropriate, discuss and coordinate discovery planning with counsel for each party to the action. (e.g., counsel should cooperate in scheduling and coordinating depositions after requested documents pertaining to the deponent have been disclosed.)

5. When setting hearings, conferences, and depositions, Attorneys shall not schedule any matter without first making a good faith effort to coordinate the date and time with counsel for each party to the action. Depositions and hearings shall only be set, with less than one week's notice, by agreement of counsel or when a genuine emergency exists. When scheduling hearings Attorneys shall reserve sufficient time to permit a complete presentation by counsel for all parties.

6. Upon receiving a scheduling inquiry concerning a proposed time for a hearing, deposition, meeting, or other proceeding, Attorneys shall promptly agree to the proposal or offer a counter suggestion that is as close in time as is reasonably possible. When scheduling changes are absolutely necessary and requested due to professional or family commitments or emergencies, Attorneys shall cooperate with each other in agreeing to calendar changes when rescheduling will not have a material adverse effect on the rights of the client.

7. Reasonable extensions of time should be granted where such extensions will not have a material adverse effect on the rights of the client or result in undue delay (e.g., permitting a deadline for a response to discovery to be extended or not objecting to a first-time motion for extension of time in which to file an appellate brief or reply etc.).

II. Conduct toward the Court, Attorneys, and Other Participants

1. Attorneys shall refrain from disrespectful and disruptive behavior towards the Court and likewise refrain from rude and offensive behavior towards opposing counsel, parties, and witnesses.

2. Attorneys shall abide by the spirit and letter of all rulings of the Court and instruct their clients to do the same.

3. Attorneys shall be, and shall impress upon their clients and witnesses the need to be, courteous and respectful towards the Court, opposing counsel, parties, and witnesses.

4. Attorneys shall make an effort to explain to non-party witnesses the purpose of their required attendance at depositions, hearings, or trials. Absent compelling circumstances, Attorneys shall give adequate notice to non-party witnesses before the scheduling of their depositions and make a reasonable effort when possible to provide advance notice of a subpoena for a deposition, hearing, or trial. Attorneys shall, when possible, accommodate the schedules of non-party witnesses when scheduling their appearance and promptly notify them of any cancellations.

5. Attorneys shall act and speak civilly to courtroom deputies, clerks, court reporters, judicial assistants, and other court personnel and recognize that they are an integral part of the judicial system. Attorneys shall be selective in inquiries posed to judicial assistants to avoid wasting their time. Attorneys shall endeavor to be knowledgeable about the Court administrative orders, local rules, and each Judge's published or posted practices and procedures.

6. Attorney shall endeavor to operate under these Standards when dealing with unrepresented litigants.

III. Candor and Fairness to the Court, Counsel, and Others

1. In all matters litigation or not, Attorneys shall not knowingly misstate, misrepresent, or distort any fact or legal authority to the Court or to counsel for any party to the action. Further, if this occurs unintentionally and is later discovered, it shall immediately be disclosed or otherwise corrected.

2. Attorneys shall notify opposing counsel of all oral or written communications with the Court or other tribunal, except those involving only scheduling matters. Attorneys shall simultaneously provide to counsel for each party to the action by substantially similar mode of delivery, copies of any submissions, correspondence, memoranda or [1] law, case law, etc. to the Court (e.g., if a memorandum of law is hand-delivered to the Court, a copy shall simultaneously either be hand-delivered or faxed to each party). If the Court requests the parties to submit a proposed order, written closing argument, or statement of a party's legal position, unless otherwise specified by the Court, the submission shall be in the form of a pleading, memoranda, or proposed order and not in the form of a letter.

3. Attorneys shall draft proposed orders promptly, and the orders shall fairly and adequately represent the ruling of the Court. Attorneys shall promptly provide, either orally or in writing, proposed orders to counsel for each party to the action for approval. Any objections to entry of the proposed order shall promptly be communicated. The drafting Attorney shall clearly advise the Court as to whether or not the proposed order has been approved by opposing counsel.

4. In drafting agreements and other documents, Attorneys shall use their knowledge, training, skill, and integrity to ensure that the agreements and documents fairly reflect the true intent of the parties. Where revisions are made to an agreement or other document, Attorneys shall point out or otherwise highlight any such additions, deletions, or modifications to counsel for each party to the action.

IV. Efficient Administration of Justice

1. Attorneys shall not use the Court system for the primary purpose of harassing, embarrassing, causing needless duplication of effort, or causing an adversary to incur unnecessary expenses.

2. Attorneys shall endeavor to stipulate to all facts and legal authority not reasonably in dispute.

3. Attorneys shall encourage principled negotiations and efficient resolution of disputes on their merits.

4. Attorneys shall make a good faith effort to contact counsel for each party to the action prior to filing and upon receiving a motion to determine, first, whether the matter can be resolved without the necessity of Court hearing, or second, whether there are any matters raised to which all parties can stipulate. Adequate communication between Attorneys may alleviate the need for filing a motion and may allow entry of an agreed upon order in lieu of hearing. Adequate communication may further serve to narrow the issues that need to be litigated and reduce the amount of hearing time necessary to resolve a matter.

5. Attorneys shall promptly notify the Court or other tribunal of any resolution between parties that renders a scheduled Court appearance unnecessary or otherwise moot.

6. Attorneys shall notify counsel for each party to the action and the Court of a scheduling conflict and make efforts to ensure that others impacted by a scheduling conflict are notified as soon as it becomes apparent. Further, Attorneys shall cooperate with one another regarding all reasonable rescheduling requests that do not prejudice their clients or unduly delay a proceeding.

V. Courtroom Decorum

1. When appearing in Court, unless excused by the presiding Judge, it is expected that the Attorneys shall stand when Court is opened, recessed, or adjourned; when addressing, or being addressed by the Court; and when the jury enters or retires from the courtroom.

2. When making opening statements, closing arguments, or examining witnesses, Attorneys shall not approach either the

jury or the witness without the Court's permission. Attorneys shall remain at the lectern unless using exhibits or charts.

3. Attorneys shall address all remarks to the Court and not to opposing counsel or the opposing party.

4. Attorneys shall avoid making disparaging personal remarks or showing acrimony toward opposing counsel and remain detached from any ill feeling between the litigants or witnesses.

5. Attorneys shall refer to all persons (including witnesses, other counsel, and the parties) by their surnames and not by their first or given names unless the permission of the Court is sought in advance.

6. Unless the court grants permission, only one Attorney for each party shall conduct the direct examination or cross examination each witness. The Attorney stating objections, if any, during direct examination, shall be the Attorney recognized for cross examination.

7. Attorneys shall request permission before approaching the bench. Any documents counsel wishes to have the Court examine should be handed to the clerk. Any paper or exhibit not previously marked for identification should first be handed to the clerk to be marked before it is tendered to a witness during examination. Any exhibit offered in evidence should, at the time of such offer, be handed to opposing counsel.

8. Attorneys shall not hold or place in any position in the courtroom that would allow the jury to see, any exhibit, whether marked for identification or not, unless the exhibit has been admitted into evidence and permission to publish the exhibit to the jury has been obtained from the Court.

9. In making objections, Attorneys shall state only the legal grounds for the objection, withholding all further comment or argument unless elaboration is requested by the Court. In examining witnesses, Attorneys questions should not be echoing the witness's response.

10. Attorneys shall make all offers of settlement or requests for a stipulation privately and not within the hearing of the jury.

11. In opening statements and in arguments to the jury, Attorneys shall not express personal knowledge or opinions concerning any matter in issue.

12. It is inappropriate for any person present in Court to make gestures, facial expressions, a nodding or shaking of the head, outbursts, audible comments or the like manifesting approval or disapproval of witness testimony or whatever else is occurring during Court proceedings. Attorneys certainly shall not engage in this type of conduct and shall instruct their clients not to engage in this type of behavior. Attorneys shall further endeavor to inform those observers appearing supportively for their client or witness not to engage in this type of behavior. This behavior is strictly prohibited.

13. Attorneys shall refrain from making re-argument after the Court has ruled.

14. Attorneys shall ensure that their clients are adequately informed of any settlement proposals.

15. Attorneys shall cooperate with counsel for each party to the action during trials and evidentiary hearings by disclosing the identities of all witnesses reasonably expected to be called and the length of time needed to present their entire case. Attorneys should cooperate with a request to call a witness out of turn when the circumstances justify it, unless a client's material rights would be adversely affected.

16. In the courtroom, Attorneys shall not use tobacco in any form, chew gum, or bring bottles, beverage containers, paper cups, or edibles, except as permitted by the Court.

17. Attorneys shall turn off or place in silent mode all cell phones and pagers. Attorneys shall further turn off or mute the audio of any computers brought into or used in Court, unless specifically permitted by the Court as part of the proceedings.

Committee notes:

Section I. 3. Producing requested discovery documents in the middle of one of several boxes of unindexed, unorganized materials with no clue or annotation may be obstructionist or vexatious. Any misleading response obscuring the existence of discoverable material, of course, should as well be deterred. It would be in the interest of professionalism to deter both the "needle in the haystack" document production <u>and</u> a response to discovery calculated to mislead.

Section III. 1. See *Boca Burger, Inc v. Forum*, 912 So.2d 561 (Fla. 2005).

[1] So in original. Probably should be "of".

Business Court Procedures

SECTION 1. PHILOSOPHY, SCOPE AND GOALS

1.1—Citation to Procedures. These Business Court Procedures shall be known and cited as the Business Court Procedures. They may also be referred to in abbreviated form as "BCP" or "Business Court Procedures," e.g., this section may be cited as "BCP 1.1."

1.2—Purpose and Scope. The Business Court Procedures are designed to facilitate the proceedings of cases in the Business Court Subdivision of the Civil Division of the Ninth Judicial Circuit Court of Florida ("Business Court"). The Business Court Procedures shall apply to all actions in the Business Court.

1.3—Goals. The Business Court Procedures are intended to provide better access to court information for litigants, counsel and the public; increase the efficiency and understanding of court personnel, counsel and witnesses; decrease costs for litigants and others involved in the court system; and facilitate the efficient and effective presentation of evidence in the courtroom. The Business Court Procedures shall be construed and enforced to avoid technical delay, encourage civility, permit just and prompt determination of all proceedings and promote the efficient administration of justice.

1.4—Professionalism. The Business Court directs the reader's attention to BCP 14 of the Business Court Procedures concerning decorum and professionalism standards for the Business Court. The Business Court expects the highest level of professionalism and full compliance with BCP 14 from practitioners and their clients.

1.5—Integration with Other Rules. The Business Court Procedures are intended to supplement, not supplant, the rules adopted by the Supreme Court of Florida. Should any conflict be deemed to exist between the Business Court Procedures and the rules adopted by the Supreme Court of Florida, then the rules adopted by the Supreme Court of Florida shall control.

Amended effective November 4, 2016.

SECTION 2. CASE FILING, ASSIGNMENT, TRACKING AND IDENTIFICATION

2.1—Cases Subject to the Business Court. The principles set out in Amended Administrative Order 2003–17–07 which is located on the Business Court Website at http://www.ninthcircuit.org/about/divisions/civil–circuit–courts/complex–business–litigation–court shall govern the assignment of cases to the Business Court.

2.2—Case Identification Numbers. On assignment of any matter to the Business Court, the matter shall retain the civil action number assigned to it by the Clerk of Courts.

Amended effective November 4, 2016; January 1, 2018.

SECTION 3. VIDEOCONFERENCING AND TELEPHONE APPEARANCES

3.1—Videoconference by Agreement. By mutual agreement, counsel may arrange for any proceeding or conference to be held by videoconference by coordinating a schedule for such hearing that is convenient with the Business Court. All counsel and other participants shall be subject to the same rules of procedure and decorum as if all participants were present in the courtroom.

3.2—Responsibility for Videoconferencing Facilities. The parties and/or counsel wishing to attend by videoconference are responsible for obtaining all communications facilities and arranging all details as may be required to connect and interface with the videoconferencing equipment available to the Business Court. The Business Court will endeavor to make reasonable technical assistance available to the parties and/or counsel, but all responsibility for planning and executing all technical considerations required to successfully hold a videoconference shall remain solely with the parties and/or counsel wishing to attend by videoconference.

3.3—Allocation of Videoconferencing Costs. In the absence of a contrary agreement among the parties, the parties and/or counsel participating by videoconference shall bear their own costs of participating via this method.

3.4—Court Reporter. Where any proceeding is held by videoconference, the court reporter transcribing such proceeding will be present in the same room as the judge presiding over the proceeding.

3.5—Exchange of Exhibits and Evidence to be Used in Videoconference Hearing. Any exhibits or evidence to be used in a videoconference hearing must be provided to opposing counsel and to the court three business days prior to the hearing. All exhibits or evidence so provided shall bear exhibit tags marked with the case name, case number, identity of the propounding party and an identification number. Any objections to any exhibit or evidence must be provided to the court in writing at least one day in advance of the hearing and reference the appropriate exhibit tags.

3.6—Telephone Appearances. Parties and/or counsel may appear by telephone when allowed by the court. No prior authorization for telephone appearances is necessary for the court's regularly scheduled Short Matters and Ex Parte times. The court has only one telephone line into each courtroom, so all parties and/or counsel who wish to attend any matter telephonically have the responsibility for arranging a conference call to the courtroom at the time set for the hearing. The responsibility for planning and executing all technical considerations to appear telephonically shall remain solely with the parties and/or counsel wishing to appear telephonically **and conference line log in information shall be included on the notice of hearing**. The procedures for appearing telephonically can be found by selecting the applicable Subdivision under Policies and Procedures on the Complex Business Litigation Court page at http://www.ninthcircuit.org/about/divisions/civil/complex–business–litigation–court.shtml.

Amended effective November 4, 2016; January 1, 2018.

SECTION 4. CALENDARING, APPEARANCES AND SETTLEMENT

4.1—Preparation of Calendar. The calendar for the Business Court shall be prepared under the supervision of the Business Court Judge(s) and published on the Complex Business Litigation Court page on the website for the Ninth Judicial Circuit Court of Florida.

4.2—Appearances. An attorney who is notified to appear for any proceeding before the Business Court must, consistent with ethical requirements, appear or have a partner, associate or another attorney familiar with the case appear.

4.3—Notification of Settlement. When any cause pending in the Business Court is settled, all attorneys or unrepresented parties of record must notify the assigned Business Court Judge or the Business Court Judge's designee within twenty-four (24) hours of the settlement and must advise the court of the party who will prepare and present the judgment, dismissal or stipulation of dismissal and when such filings will be presented. The court will not abate cases for extended time periods to facilitate settlement.

Amended effective November 4, 2016.

SECTION 5. MOTION PRACTICE

5.1—Form. All motions, unless made orally during a hearing or a trial, shall be accompanied by a memorandum of law, except as provided in BCP 5.12. Any memorandum of law shall be filed in support of one motion only and **the motion and memorandum shall not exceed twenty-five (25) pages in length, in total. For the purposes of calculating the page limits, the signature block, certificate of service, certificate of good faith conference and case caption are excluded.** Each motion shall be filed separately containing its own supporting memorandum of law. Motions that are inextricably intertwined and either substantively related or in the alternative may be filed together.

5.2—Content of Motions. All motions shall: (1) state with particularity the grounds for the motion; (2) cite any statute or rule of procedure relied upon; and (3) state the relief sought. Factual statements in a motion for summary judgment shall be supported by specific citations to the supporting documents. The parties shall not raise issues at the hearing on the motion that were not addressed in the motion and memoranda in support of and in opposition to the motion. The practice of offering previously undisclosed cases to the court at the hearing is specifically disallowed.

5.3—Certificate of Good Faith Conference. Before filing any motion in the Business Court, the moving party shall confer with counsel for the opposing party in a good faith effort to resolve the issues raised by the motion, and shall file with the motion a statement certifying that the moving party has conferred with opposing counsel and that counsel have been unable to agree on the resolution of the motion.

a. The term "confer," as used herein, requires a substantive conversation between counsel ***in person or by telephone*** in a good faith effort to resolve the motion without court action and does not envision an exchange of ultimatums by email, fax or letter. Counsel who merely attempt to confer have not conferred. Counsel must respond promptly to inquiries and communications from opposing counsel. The court will sua sponte deny motions that fail to include an appropriate and complete Certificate of Good Faith conference under this section.

b. The Certificate of Good Faith Conference shall set forth the date of the conference, the names of the participating attorneys and the specific results achieved. It shall be the responsibility of counsel for the movant to arrange for the conference.

c. No conference, and therefore no Certificate of Good Faith Conference, is required in motions for injunctive relief without notice, for judgment on the pleadings, for summary judgment or to permit maintenance of a class action.

d. A party alleging that a pleading fails to state a cause of action shall confer with counsel for the opposing party before moving to dismiss and, upon request of the other party, will stipulate to an order permitting the filing of a curative amended pleading in lieu of filing a motion to dismiss.

5.4—Motions Decided on Papers and Memoranda. Motions shall be considered and decided by the court on the pleadings, admissible evidence, the court file and memoranda, without hearing or oral argument, unless otherwise ordered by the court. Any party seeking oral argument shall file a separate motion setting forth the reasons oral argument should be granted and shall send a proposed order granting oral argument to the court with service copies and stamped envelopes. A party who believes a matter requires an evidentiary hearing must file a motion for oral argument. Motions for oral argument must contain a separate Certificate of Good Faith Conference under BCP 5.3, and must set forth the length of time needed for oral argument.

If the court grants oral argument on any motion, it shall either order the parties to coordinate a hearing or give the parties at least five (5) business days' notice of the date and place of oral argument. The court, for good cause shown, may shorten the five (5) days' notice period. All papers relating to the issues to be argued at the hearing shall be delivered to opposing counsel and the court at least five (5) business days before the hearing. Service and receipt of the papers less than five (5) business days before the hearing is presumptively unreasonable and may result in the hearing being cancelled by the court.

5.5—Motions for Summary Judgment and for Partial Summary Judgment. Motions for summary judgment and for partial summary judgment shall be considered and decided by the court on the affidavits, answers to interrogatories, admissions, depositions and other materials as would be admissible in evidence ("summary judgment evidence") and, if a hearing is not waived, based on arguments at the summary judgment hearing.

The court will hold a hearing if the right to a hearing is not waived in the Case Management Report under BCP 6.3. In the event of a hearing, the court will also consider any additional summary judgment evidence filed in accordance with the provisions of Florida Rule of Civil Procedure 1.510(c). In order to obtain a hearing, the moving party shall (but either party may) schedule a hearing on the motion immediately after filing the motion. The parties shall also comply with the provisions of BCP 5.14 on submission of proposed orders.

In the event the hearing referenced in Florida Rule of Civil Procedure 1.510(c) is waived by the parties in the Case Management Report, the motion for summary judgment or a motion for partial summary judgment shall be decided by the court based on the summary judgment evidence in the court file. In order to obtain a ruling from the court, the moving party shall (but either party may) provide notice to the court that the motion for summary judgment or for partial summary judgment is fully briefed by filing a Notice of Fully Briefed Motion pursuant to BCP 5.14 which shall advise the court that the right to a hearing is waived. The form and content of the notice of fully briefed motion is available at the Business Court page on the court's website at http://www.ninthcircuit.org/about/divisions/civil–circuit–courts/complex–business–litigation–court The parties shall also comply with the provisions of BCP 5.14 on submission of orders.

5.6—Delivery of Materials for Oral Argument. Parties shall deliver copies of materials to the court in preparation for oral argument at least five (5) business days prior to a hearing. Materials may include, but not be limited to, copies of the motion, response and reply and cases cited therein with exhibits which will be referenced in the oral argument. If such materials exceed fifty (50) pages in total, then the parties shall deliver the materials only on a USB drive. Parties must insure that the electronic copy of the materials is indexed and that the index contains a hyperlink to the document/exhibit/case indexed. For an example of this format, see http://www.ninthcircuit.org/sites/default/files/Example–of–electronic–courtesy–copy.pdf.

5.7—Response to Motion and Memoranda. The party opposing a motion shall file a memorandum in opposition within twenty (20) days after service of the motion or within thirty (30) days of service if the motion is for summary judgment. The response memorandum shall clearly identify the title and date of filing of the motion to which it responds. Memoranda in opposition shall not exceed twenty-five (25) pages in length. If supporting documents are not then available, a party may move for an extension of time to file a response. For good cause appearing therefore, a party may be required by the court to file any response and supporting documents, including a memorandum, within such shorter period of time as the court may specify.

5.8—Reply Memorandum. The moving party may file a reply memorandum within ten (10) days of service of the memorandum in opposition to the motion. A reply memorandum is limited to discussion of matters raised in the memorandum in opposition and shall not exceed ten (10) pages in length. The reply memorandum must clearly identify the titles and dates of filing of the original motion and the response memorandum.

5.9—Extension of Time for Filing Supporting Documents and Memoranda. Upon proper motion accompanied by a proposed order and in addition to the relief available under BCP 5.7, the court may enter an order, specifying the time within which supporting documents and memoranda may be filed, if it is shown that such documents are not available or cannot be filed contemporaneously with the motion or response. The time allowed to an opposing party for filing a response shall not run during any such extension.

5.10—Font and Spacing Requirements. All motions and memoranda shall be double-spaced and in Times New Roman 14–point font or Courier New 12–point font. Page margins shall not be less than 1 inch.

5.11—Suggestion of Subsequently Decided Authority. A suggestion of controlling or persuasive authority that was decided after the filing of the last memorandum may be filed at any time prior to the court's ruling and shall contain only the citation to the authority relied upon, if published, or a copy of the authority if it is unpublished, and shall not contain argument.

5.12—Motions Not Requiring Memoranda. Memoranda are not required by either the moving party or the opposing party, unless otherwise directed by the court, with respect to the following motions:

a. discovery motions, if the parties have agreed to have the matter heard by a general magistrate (discovery motions to be heard by the presiding Business Court Judge must be fully briefed unless excused from this requirement by the presiding Business Court Judge);

b. extensions of time for the performance of an act required or allowed to be done, provided that the request is made before the expiration of the period originally prescribed or extended by previous orders;

c. to continue a pretrial conference, hearing or the trial of an action;

d. to add or substitute parties;

e. to amend the pleadings;

f. to file supplemental pleadings;

g. to appoint a next friend or guardian ad litem;

h. to stay proceedings to enforce judgment;

i. for pro hac vice admission of counsel who are not members of The Florida Bar;

j. relief from the page limitations imposed by the Business Court Procedures; and

k. request for oral argument.

The above motions must state good cause therefore and cite any applicable rule, statute or other authority justifying the relief sought. If the motion is agreed upon by all parties, then these motions must be accompanied by a cover letter indicating that opposing counsel has reviewed and approved the proposed order and a proposed order, together with copies for all parties and stamped, addressed envelopes. If the motion is contested and can be heard in 20 minutes or less without the taking of evidence, then the moving party may set the motion for hearing at the court's short matter hearing time.

5.13—Failure to File and Serve Motion Materials. The failure to file a memorandum in opposition or reply within the time specified in this section shall constitute a waiver of the right thereafter to file such memorandum in opposition or reply, except upon a showing of excusable neglect. A motion unaccompanied by a required memorandum may, in the discretion of the court, be summarily denied. Failure to timely file a memorandum in opposition to a motion may result in the pending motion being considered and decided as an uncontested motion.

5.14—Submission of Orders. When a motion is fully briefed, either by the filing of a memorandum in opposition and reply or by virtue of the time passing for the filing of those pleadings, the moving party shall prepare and file a Notice of Fully Briefed Motion. The form and content of the Notice of Fully Briefed Motion is available on the Business Court page of the court's website at http://www.ninthcircuit.org/about/divisions/civil/complex–business–litigation–court.shtml. The Notice of Fully Briefed Motion, the checklist for the Notice of Fully Briefed Motion and a proposed order shall be sent to the court when the motion is fully briefed and ready for the court to rule upon it. The order must also be emailed to the court in accordance with Notice of Changes found on the Complex Business Litigation Court section of the court's website at http://www.ninthcircuit.org/about/divisions/civil/complex–business–litigation–court.shtml. No agreed order will be entered unless the party proffering such an order represents to the court in writing that he or she has provided copies to the opposing parties in advance, and they have no objection to the form of the order. When sending to the court a proposed order entering a final judgment of default, a party must contemporaneously provide the court with sufficient information establishing that the motion for entry of a final judgment by default should be granted. If the court has directed that a party prepare a proposed order following a hearing on the motion, the party preparing the order must provide a copy of the proposed order to opposing counsel. The court will not accept "dueling orders" unless specifically requested by the court. If an agreement among the parties cannot be reached on a proposed order, the parties must convene a hearing at the court's short matter hearing time to address any objections to the proposed order.

5.15—Short Matters and Ex Parte. The court will hear ex parte matters and short matters (contested hearings of 20 minutes or less where no testimony or evidence is required) on a schedule to be published on the court's website at http://apps.ninthcircuit.org/jacsatt/availableslotframe.asp. [To find information for Subdivision 43, you must use the Select Calendar feature and then by selecting the down arrow to go to the respective divisions.]

5.16—Determination of Motions through Oral Argument without Briefs. The parties may present motions and the court may resolve disputes regarding the matters described in BCP 5.12 through the use of an expedited oral argument procedure, if such procedure is agreed upon by all parties with an interest in the outcome of the motion who are also present for the oral argument. Applicable motions are those that are limited to matters which can be argued and determined in twenty minutes or less and may be heard on the court's short matters docket, which requires coordination with counsel, but not the reservation of a specific time through the judicial assistant. The dates and times of short matters hearings will be posted on the Complex Business Litigation Court section at the court's website at http://apps.ninthcircuit.org/jacsatt/availableslotframe.asp. [To find information for Subdivision 43, you must use the Select Calendar feature and then by selecting the down arrow to go to the respective Subdivision.]

5.17—Motions to Compel and for Protective Order. Any party seeking to compel discovery or to obtain a protective order with respect to discovery must identify the specific portion of the material that is directly relevant and ensure that it is filed as an attachment to the application for relief. **Filing the entire discovery response is discouraged.**

5.18—Motions to File Under Seal. Whether documents filed in a case may be filed under seal is a separate issue from whether the parties may agree that produced documents are confidential. Motions to file under seal are disfavored. The court will permit the parties to file documents under seal only upon a finding of extraordinary circumstances and particularized need. A party seeking to file a document under seal must file an appropriate motion in accordance with Florida Rule of Judicial Administration 2.420(d), together with a proposed order thereon. The motion, whether granted or denied, will remain in the public record.

5.19—Emergency Motions. The court may consider and determine emergency motions at any time. Counsel should be aware that the designation "emergency" may cause a judge to abandon other pending matters in order to immediately address the emergency. The court will sanction any counsel or party who designates a motion as an emergency under circumstances that are not true emergencies. It is not an emergency when counsel has delayed discovery until the end of the discovery period.

Amended effective November 4, 2016; January 1, 2018.

SECTION 6. CASE MANAGEMENT NOTICE, MEETING, REPORT, CONFERENCE AND ORDER

6.1—Notice of Hearing and Order on Case Management Conference. Within thirty (30) days of filing or transfer of a case to the Business Court, the court will issue an Order Setting Case Management Conference (the "Case Management Notice"). Counsel for Plaintiff(s) shall immediately thereafter serve a copy of the Case Management Notice on all Defendants. Defendant(s) shall immediately serve a copy of the Case Management Notice on all Third–Party Defendants.

6.2—Case Management Meeting. Regardless of the pendency of any undecided motions, Lead Trial Counsel shall meet no less than thirty (30) days in advance of the Case Management Conference and address the following subjects, along with other appropriate topics, including those set forth in Florida Rule of Civil Procedure 1.200(a), some of which subjects and topics will be incorporated into a Case Management Order prepared by the court:

a. Pleadings issues, service of process, venue, joinder of additional parties, theories of liability, damages claimed and applicable defenses;

b. The identity and number of any motions to dismiss or other preliminary or pre-discovery motions that have been filed and the time period in which they shall be filed, briefed and argued;

c. A discovery plan and schedule including the length of the discovery period, the number of fact and expert depositions to be permitted and, as appropriate, the length and sequence of such depositions;

d. Anticipated areas of expert testimony, timing for identification of experts, responses to expert discovery and exchange of expert reports;

e. An estimate of the volume of documents and computerized information likely to be the subject of discovery from parties and nonparties and whether there are technological means that may render document discovery more manageable at an acceptable cost;

f. The advisability of using special master(s) for fact finding, mediation, discovery disputes or such other matters as the parties may agree upon;

g. The time period after the close of discovery within which post-discovery dispositive motions shall be filed, briefed and argued and a tentative schedule for such activities;

h. The possibility of settlement and the timing of Alternative Dispute Resolution, including the selection of a mediator or arbitrator(s);

i. Whether or not a party desires to use technologically advanced methods of presentation or court-reporting and, to the extent this is the case, a determination of the following:

(1) Fairness issues, including but not necessarily limited to use of such capabilities by some but not all parties and by parties whose resources permit or require variations in the use of such capabilities;

(2) Issues related to compatibility of court and party facilities and equipment;

(3) Issues related to the use of demonstrative exhibits and any balancing of relevance and potential prejudice that may need to occur in connection with such exhibits;

(4) The feasibility of sharing the technology resources or platforms amongst all parties so as to minimize disruption at trial; and

(5) Such other issues related to the use of the court's and parties' special technological facilities as may be raised by any party, the court or the court's technological advisor, given the nature of the case and the resources of the parties.

j. A good faith estimate by each party based upon consultation among the parties of the costs and attorneys' fees each party is likely to incur in pursuing the litigation through trial court adjudication;

k. A preliminary listing of the principal disputed legal and factual issues;

l. A preliminary listing of any legal principle and facts that are not in dispute;

m. Any law other than Florida law which applies to the issues in the case;

n. A good faith estimate by each party of the length of time to try the case;

o. Whether a demand for jury trial has been made;

p. The track to which the case will be assigned. The Business Court typically employs the following management tracks: Business Expedited (Target Trial Date within 13 months of filing of complaint); Business Standard (Target Trial Date within 18 months of filing of complaint); and Business Complex (Target Trial Date within two years of filing of complaint); and

q. Such other matters as the court may assign to the parties for their consideration.

6.3—Joint Case Management Report.

a. No less than ten (10) days in advance of the Case Management Conference, the parties shall file the Joint Case Management Report addressing the matters described above. All counsel and parties are responsible for filing a Joint Case Management Report in full compliance with the Business Court Procedures. Contemporaneous with filing the Joint Case Management Report, counsel for Plaintiff(s) shall deliver via US Mail or hand delivery a copy of the report to the court. Counsel for Plaintiff(s) shall have the responsibility to coordinate the meeting between the parties and the filing of the Joint Case Management Report. If a non-lawyer Plaintiff is proceeding pro se, counsel for Defendant(s) shall coordinate compliance and service of the copy to the court. If counsel is unable to coordinate such compliance, counsel shall timely notify the court by written motion or request for a status conference.

b. In the Joint Case Management Report, Lead Trial Counsel for each party shall certify that the party (if an individual) or an authorized representative of the party (if an entity) will attend the Case Management Conference in person, unless the court has entered an order excusing compliance with this requirement. In the certificate, Lead Trial Counsel for any entity party shall provide the name and title of the representative who will attend the Case Management Conference and shall certify that the representative has authority to make appropriate decisions regarding such issues listed in BCP 6.2 above as are pertinent to the case or on which there are material differences of opinion. If the court has entered an order permitting the attendance of a party or authorized representative by telephone, videoconference, or other means, Lead Trial Counsel shall certify that the party or authorized representative shall attend the Case Management Conference in the manner permitted by the court's order.

6.4—Case Management Conference. The attendance in person by Lead Trial Counsel for all parties is mandatory. All parties and representatives of any entity parties with the authority described in BCP 6.3(b) must attend the Case Management Conference in person unless excused by the court upon a timely motion and order thereon. A motion for relief from the personal attendance requirement must be filed before the deadline for filing the Joint Case Management Report as set forth in BCP 6.3(a), unless the basis for the request could not reasonably have been anticipated at that time. At the Case Management Conference, the court will hear the views of counsel on such issues listed in BCP 6.2 above as are pertinent to the case or on which there are material differences of opinion. If Lead Trial Counsel, a party, or a representative of an entity party with the authority described in BCP 6.3(b) fails to attend the Case Management Conference in person or in such other manner as is permitted by order of the court, the court may impose appropriate sanctions on the noncomplying party, attorney, or both.

6.5—Case Management Order. Following the Case Management Conference, the court will issue a Case Management Order. The provisions of the Case Management Order may not be deviated from without notice, an opportunity to be heard, a showing of good cause and entry of an order by the court. The Case Management Order may also specify a schedule of status conferences, when necessary, to assess the functioning of the Case Management Order, assess the progress of the case and enter such further revisions to the Case Management Order as the court may deem necessary or appropriate.

Amended effective November 4, 2016; January 1, 2018.

SECTION 7. DISCOVERY

7.1—Presumptive Limits On Discovery Procedures. Presumptively, subject to stipulation of the parties and order of the court for good cause shown, each party is limited to the following:

a. Fifty (50) interrogatories (including sub-parts);

b. Fifty (50) requests for admission on each opposing party;

c. Twelve (12) depositions (not including depositions of testifying experts) taken by Plaintiff(s), twelve (12) depositions taken by Defendant(s), and twelve (12) depositions taken by the Third–Party Defendant(s), regardless of the number of separate parties designated as Plaintiffs, Defendants, and Third–Party Defendants.

The parties may agree by stipulation on other limits on discovery within the context of the limits and deadlines established by the Business Court Procedures and the court's Case Management Order, but the parties may not alter the limitations provided by the Business Court Procedures without leave of court.

7.2—Depositions. The court expects counsel to conduct discovery in good faith and to cooperate and be courteous in all phases of the discovery process. Depositions shall be conducted in accordance with the following guidelines:

a. Counsel shall make reasonable attempts to coordinate the scheduling of depositions, including non-party depositions. If counsel is unsuccessful in coordinating the scheduling of a deposition after reasonable efforts, counsel may notice the deposition for a date and time at least ten (10) business days in the future.

b. Counsel shall not direct or request that a witness not answer a question, unless counsel has objected to the question on the ground that the answer is protected by privilege or a limitation on evidence directed by the court.

c. Counsel shall not make objections or statements that might suggest an answer to a witness. Counsel's statements when making objections should be succinct, stating the basis of the objection and nothing more.

d. Counsel and their clients shall not engage in private, off-the-record conferences during the client's deposition, except for the purpose of deciding whether to assert a privilege.

e. Deposing counsel shall provide to the witness's counsel a copy of all documents shown to the witness during the deposition. The copies shall be provided either before the deposition begins or contemporaneously with the showing of each document to the witness. The witness and the witness's counsel do not have the right to discuss documents privately before the witness answers questions about the documents.

f. When the deponent or any party demands that the deposition be read and signed, the failure of the deponent to read and sign the deposition within thirty days from the date the transcript becomes available to the deponent shall be deemed to ratify the entire deposition.

g. The court will entertain telephonic hearings regarding issues raised during depositions then in progress.

7.3—Electronic Discovery. Upon agreement by the parties and stipulated order or by order of the court, mediators or special masters may be utilized to facilitate the resolution of disputes related to electronically stored information.

7.4—General or Special Magistrates. The court may, at any time, on its own motion or on the motion of any party, appoint a general or special magistrate in any given case pending in the Business Court in accordance with Florida Rule of Civil Procedure 1.490. Unless otherwise ordered, the parties shall bear equally the cost of proceeding before a special magistrate, and such fees may be taxed as costs.

7.5—No Filing of Discovery Materials. Depositions and deposition notices, notices of serving interrogatories, interrogatories, requests for documents, requests for admission and answers and responses thereto shall not be filed unless the court so orders or unless the parties will rely on such documents in a pretrial proceeding. **For depositions, the filing of excerpts as opposed to the entire depositions is encouraged.** All discovery materials **filed with the court** must be served on other counsel or parties. The party taking a deposition or obtaining any material through discovery (including through third-party discovery) is responsible for the preservation and delivery of such material to the court when needed or ordered in the form specified by the court.

7.6—Discovery with Respect to Expert Witnesses. Discovery with respect to experts must be conducted within the discovery period established by the Case Management Order. In complying with the obligation to exchange reports relating to experts, the parties shall disclose all opinions to be expressed and the basis and reasons therefor; the data or other information considered by the witness in forming the opinions; any exhibits to be used as a summary of or support for the opinions; the qualifications of the witness, including a list of publications authored by the witness within the preceding ten years; the compensation to be paid for the study and testimony; and a listing of any other cases in which the witness has testified as an expert at trial or by deposition or affidavit within the preceding four years. Each party offering an expert witness shall provide three alternative dates for the deposition of the expert in the following thirty (30) days.

7.7—Completion of Discovery. The requirement that discovery be completed within a specified time mandates that adequate provisions must be made for interrogatories and requests for admission to be answered, for documents to be produced and for depositions to be held within the discovery period. The court does not anticipate entertaining motions relating to discovery conducted after the close of the discovery period as set forth in the court's Case Management Order.

7.8—Extension of the Discovery Period or Request for Additional Discovery. Motions seeking an extension of the discovery period or permission to take more discovery than is permitted under the Case Management Order must be presented prior to the expiration of the time within which discovery is required to be completed. Such motions must set forth good cause justifying the additional time or additional discovery and will only be granted upon such a showing of good cause and that the parties have diligently pursued discovery. The court usually will only permit additional depositions upon a showing of exceptionally good cause.

7.9—Trial Preparation After the Close of Discovery. Ordinarily, the deposition of a material witness not subject to subpoena should be taken during discovery. However, the deposition of a material witness who agrees to appear for trial, but later becomes unavailable or refuses to attend, may be taken at any time prior to or during trial.

7.10—Confidentiality Agreements. The parties may reach their own agreement regarding the designation of materials as confidential. There is no need for the court to endorse the confidentiality agreement. The court discourages unnecessary stipulated motions for protective orders. The court will enforce signed confidentiality agreements. Each confidentiality agreement shall provide or shall be deemed to provide that no party shall file documents under seal without having first obtained an order granting leave of court to file documents under seal based upon a showing of particularized need.

Amended effective November 4, 2016.

SECTION 8. ALTERNATIVE DISPUTE RESOLUTION

8.1—Alternative Dispute Resolution Mandatory in All Cases. Alternative Dispute Resolution ("ADR") is a valued tool in the resolution of litigated matters. An appropriate mechanism for ADR shall be discussed by the court and counsel at the Case Management Conference. The Case Management Order shall order the parties to a specific ADR process, to be conducted either by a court-assigned or an agreed-upon facilitator and shall establish a deadline for its completion.

8.2—Non-Binding Arbitration. The parties may agree to submit to non-binding arbitration or it may be ordered upon motion of any party. The rules governing arbitration shall be selected by the parties or failing agreement, the court will order use of all or a part of the arbitration rules common to the Ninth Judicial Circuit of Florida, the American Arbitration Association or other available rules.

8.3—Mediation. The following rules shall apply to all mediations conducted in cases pending in the Business Court:

a. *Case Summaries*—Not less than ten (10) business days prior to the mediation conference, each party shall deliver to the mediator a written summary of the facts and issues of the case.

b. *Identification of Business Representative*—As part of the written summary, counsel for each entity shall state the name and general job description of the authorized representative who will *attend and participate with full authority to settle* on behalf of the entity.

c. *Attendance Requirements and Sanctions—Lead* Trial Counsel and each party including, in the case of an entity, an authorized representative, and in the case of an insurance company, the insurance company representative as set forth in Florida Rule of Civil Procedure 1.720(b)(3) with full authority to settle, *shall* attend and participate in the mediation conference. In the case of an insurance company, the term "full authority to settle" means authority to settle up to the amount of the party's last demand or the policy limits, whichever is less, without further consultation. The court will impose sanctions upon Lead Trial Counsel and parties who do not attend and participate in good faith in the mediation conference.

d. *Authority to Declare Impasse*—Participants shall be prepared to spend as much time as may be necessary to settle the case. No participant may force the early conclusion of mediation because of travel plans or other engagements. Only the mediator may declare an impasse or end the mediation.

e. *Rate of Compensation*—The mediator shall be compensated at an hourly rate stipulated by the parties in advance of mediation. Upon motion of the prevailing party, the party's share may be taxed as costs in this action.

f. *Settlement and Report of Mediator*—A settlement agreement reached between the parties shall be reduced to writing and signed by the parties and their attorneys in the presence of the mediator. Within ten business days of the conclusion of the mediation conference, the mediator shall file and serve a written mediation report stating whether all required parties were present, whether the case settled and whether the mediator was forced to declare an impasse.

Amended effective November 4, 2016.

SECTION 9. JOINT FINAL PRETRIAL STATEMENT

9.1—Meeting and Preparation of Joint Final Pretrial Statement. On or before the date established in the Case Management Order, Lead Trial Counsel for all parties and any unrepresented parties shall meet together in person for the purpose of preparing a Joint Final Pretrial Statement that strictly conforms to the requirements of this section. The case must be fully ready for trial when the Joint Final Pretrial Statement is filed. Lead Trial Counsel for all parties, or the parties themselves if unrepresented, shall sign the Joint Final Pretrial Statement. The court will strike pretrial statements that are unilateral, incompletely executed or otherwise incomplete. Inadequate stipulations of fact and law will be stricken. Sanctions may be imposed for failure to comply with this section, including the striking of pleadings. At the conclusion of the final pretrial conference, all pleadings are deemed to merge into the Joint Final Pretrial Statement, which will control the course of the trial.

9.2—Contents of Joint Final Pretrial Statement. The Joint Final Pretrial Statement Shall contain the following:

a. *Stipulated Facts*—The Parties shall stipulate to as many facts and issues as possible. To assist the court, the parties shall make an active and substantial effort to stipulate at length and in detail as to agreed facts and law, and to limit, narrow and simplify the issues of fact and law that remain contested.

b. *Exhibit List*—An exhibit list containing a description of all exhibits to be introduced at trial and in compliance with the approved form located on the Business Court website at http://www.ninthcircuit.org/research/court–forms/complex–litigation, must be filed with the Joint Final Pretrial Statement. Each party shall maintain a list of exhibits on USB drive to allow a final list of exhibits to be provided to the Clerk of Court at the close of the evidence. Unlisted exhibits will not be received into evidence at trial, except by order of the court in the furtherance of justice. The Joint Final Pretrial Statement must attach each party's exhibit list on the approved form listing each *specific* objection ("all objections reserved" does *not* suffice) to each numbered exhibit that remains after full discussion and stipulation. Objections not made—or not made with specificity—are waived.

c. *Witness List*—The parties and counsel shall prepare a witness list designating in good faith which witnesses will likely be called and which witnesses may be called if necessary. Absent good cause, the court will not permit testimony from unlisted witnesses at trial over objection. This restriction does not apply to rebuttal witnesses. Records custodians may be listed, but will not likely be called at trial, except in the event that authenticity or foundation is contested. Notwithstanding the Business Court Procedures regarding videoconferencing, for good cause shown in compelling circumstances the court may permit presentation of testimony in open court by contemporaneous transmission from a different location.

d. *Depositions*—The court encourages stipulations of fact to avoid calling unnecessary witnesses. Where a stipulation will not suffice, the court permits the use of videotaped depositions at trial. At the required meeting, counsel and unrepresented parties shall agree upon and specify in writing in the Joint Final Pretrial Statement the pages and lines of each deposition (except where used solely for impeachment) to be published to the trier of fact. The parties shall include in the Joint Final Pretrial Statement a page-and-line description of any testimony that remains in dispute after an active and substantial effort at resolution, together with argument and authority for each party's position. The parties shall prepare for submission and consideration at the final pretrial conference or trial edited and marked copies of any depositions or deposition excerpts which are to be offered into evidence, including edited videotaped depositions. Designation of an entire deposition will not be permitted except on a showing of necessity.

e. *Joint Jury Instructions and Verdict Form*—In cases to be tried before a jury, counsel shall attach to the Joint Final Pretrial Statement a copy and an original set of jointly-proposed jury instructions, together with a single jointly-proposed jury verdict form. The parties should be considerate of their juries, and therefore should submit short, concise verdict forms. The court prefers pattern jury instructions approved by the Supreme Court of Florida. A party may include at the appropriate place in the single set of jointly-proposed jury instructions a contested charge, so designated with the name of the requesting party and bearing at the bottom a citation of authority for its inclusion, together with a summary of the opposing party's objection. The parties shall submit a USB drive in Word format containing the single set of jury instructions and verdict form with the Joint Final Pretrial Statement.

9.3—Coordination of Joint Final Pretrial Statement. All counsel and parties are responsible for filing a Joint Final Pretrial Statement in full compliance with the Business Court Procedures at least ten (10) days prior to the pretrial conference. Counsel for Plaintiff(s) shall have the *primary* responsibility to coordinate the meeting of Lead Trial Counsel and unrepresented parties and the filing of a Joint Final Pretrial Statement and related material. If a non-lawyer Plaintiff is proceeding pro se, then counsel for Defendant(s) shall coordinate compliance.

If counsel is unable to coordinate such compliance, counsel shall timely notify the court by written motion or request for a status conference.

Amended effective November 4, 2016.

SECTION 10. TRIAL MEMORANDA AND OTHER MATERIALS

10.1—Trial Memoranda. In the case of a non-jury trial, no later than ten (10) days before the first day of the trial period for which the trial is scheduled, the parties shall file and serve Trial Memoranda with proposed findings of fact and conclusions of law, together with a USB drive in Word format. In the case of a jury trial, no later than ten (10) days before the first day of the trial period for which the trial is scheduled, the parties may file and serve Trial Memoranda, together with a USB drive.

10.2—Motions in Limine. Motions in limine may be filed for the purpose of seeking an advance ruling on the admissibility of specific evidence at trial. **The court typically does not consider motions in limine for bench trials.** Each motion in limine must attach, or specify in detail, the document, item or statement at issue. The court may strike as superfluous any motion in limine requesting a broad order that a rule of evidence, procedure or professional conduct should be followed at trial. Motions in limine shall not be used as a procedural vehicle to circumvent the passing of the deadline to file dispositive motions.

Amended effective November 4, 2016.

SECTION 11. FINAL PRETRIAL CONFERENCE

11.1—Mandatory Attendance. Lead Trial Counsel and local counsel for each party, together with any unrepresented party, *must* attend the final pretrial conference in person unless previously excused by the court.

11.2—Substance of Final Pretrial Conference. At the final pretrial conference, all counsel and parties must be prepared and authorized to address the following matters: the formulation and simplification of the issues; the elimination of frivolous claims or defenses; admitting facts and documents to avoid unnecessary proof; stipulating to the authenticity of documents; obtaining advance rulings from the court on the admissibility of evidence; settlement and the use of special procedures to assist in resolving the dispute; disposing of pending motions; establishing a reasonable limit on the time allowed for presenting evidence and argument; and such other matters as may facilitate the just, speedy and inexpensive disposition of the actions.

Amended effective November 4, 2016.

SECTION 12. SANCTIONS

12.1—Grounds. The court may impose sanctions on any party (including any unrepresented party) or any attorney: 1) who fails to coordinate and attend the meeting of counsel to prepare the Joint Case Management Report referenced in BCP 6.3 or refuses to sign or file the Joint Case Management Report; 2) who fails to attend the Case Management Conference; 3) who fails to attend and to actively participate in the meeting to prepare the Joint Final Pretrial Statement or refuses to sign or file the Joint Final Pretrial Statement; 4) who fails to attend the final pretrial conference, or who is substantially unprepared to participate; 5) who fails to attend the mediation and actively participate in good faith, who attends the mediation without full authority to negotiate a settlement or who is substantially unprepared to participate in the mediation; or 6) who otherwise fails to comply with the Business Court Procedures or law. Sanctions may include, without limitation, any, some or all of the following: an award of reasonable attorneys' fees and costs, the striking of pleadings, the entry of default, the dismissal of the case or a finding of contempt of court.

12.2—Notice of Noncompliance. If a filing does not comply on its face with the formatting, certification, page limit, timeliness, or other requirements of the Business Court Procedures, any party may file a Notice of Noncompliance. The Notice of Noncompliance shall be limited to identifying the filing and the facial defect(s) at issue and shall not contain argument or raise factual disputes. The party filing the Notice of Noncompliance shall send copies of the Notice of Noncompliance and the filing to which it relates to the Subdivision email address: div43copies@ocnjcc.org for Subdivision 43. In response to a Notice of Noncompliance or acting *sua sponte*, the court may in its sole discretion strike the noncompliant filing or impose other sanctions. The filing of a Notice of Noncompliance shall not toll any response time or suspend any other obligation unless the court orders otherwise.

Amended effective November 4, 2016; January 1, 2018.

SECTION 13. TRIAL

13.1—Examination of Witnesses. When several attorneys are retained by the same party, the examination or cross-examination of each witness for such party shall be conducted by one attorney, but the examining attorney may change with each successive witness or, with leave of the court, during a prolonged examination of a single witness. The examination of witnesses is limited to direct, cross and re-direct. Parties seeking further examination shall request a bench conference to discuss the reasons therefore, and, upon the articulation of good cause, may be allowed further examination.

13.2—Objections. Speaking objections are not permitted. A party interposing an objection shall state the legal basis for the objection only. No response from the interrogating party will be permitted unless requested by the court.

13.3—Trial Date. Trial shall commence on the date established by the court, normally through the Case Management Order or amendments thereto, or in such other manner as the court shall deem appropriate.

13.4—Continuances. The court will consider a request to continue a trial date only if the request is signed by both the party and counsel for the party.

Amended effective November 4, 2016.

SECTION 14. COURTROOM DECORUM AND PROFESSIONALISM

14.1—Communications and Position. Counsel are at all times to conduct themselves with dignity and propriety. All statements and communications to the court shall be clearly and audibly made from a standing position behind the counsel table or the podium. Counsel shall not approach the bench except upon the permission or request of the court. Abusive language, offensive personal references, colloquies between opposing counsel and disrespectful references to opposing counsel are all strictly prohibited. Witnesses and parties must be treated with fairness and due consideration. The examination of witnesses and jurors shall be conducted from behind the podium, except as otherwise permitted by the court. Counsel may only approach a witness with the court's permission and for the purpose of presenting, inquiring about or examining that witness with respect to an exhibit, document or diagram. Except in extraordinary circumstances, and then only with leave of court and permission of the witness, all witnesses shall be addressed by honorific and surname (*e.g.*, Mrs. Smith, Reverend Jones, Dr. Adams), rather than by first names.

14.2—Professional Demeanor. The conduct of the lawyers before the court and with other lawyers should be characterized by consideration, candor and fairness. Counsel shall not knowingly misrepresent the contents of documents or other exhibits, the testimony of a witness, the language or argument of opposing counsel or the language of a decision or other authority; nor shall counsel offer evidence known to be inadmissible. In an argument addressed to the court, remarks or statements may not be interjected to improperly influence or mislead the jury.

14.3—Professionalism. The Court expects all who practicing before it to practice with professionalism and the Court would prefer that professionalism disputes be resolved outside of the Courtroom. On June 6, 2013, the Supreme Court of Florida adopted SC13–688 which includes a Code for Resolving Professionalism Complaints. In the Ninth Judicial Circuit, Administrative Order No. 2014–07–A established the Ninth Judicial Circuit Court Local Professionalism Panel (the "Professionalism Panel") to receive, screen, evaluate and act upon such reasonable complaints of unprofessional conduct as may be referred to the Professionalism Panel. Such complaints are reviewed and evaluated in the context of the standards of professionalism set forth in the Oath of Admission to the Florida Bar, The Florida Bar Creed of Professionalism, The Florida Bar Ideals and Goals of Professionalism, the Rules Regulating the Florida Bar, the decisions and administrative directives of the Florida Supreme Court, the professional standards of the Osceola County Bar Association and the Orange County Bar Association's Professionalism Guidelines. The Professionalism Panel will seek to resolve complaints informally if possible, and, if necessary and appropriate, refer such complaints to the Florida Bar. Proceedings before the Professionalism Panel will remain confidential.

Amended effective November 4, 2016.

SECTION 15. JURY INSTRUCTIONS

15.1—Jury Instruction Conference. At the close of the evidence (or at such earlier time as the judge may direct) in every jury trial, the judge shall conduct a conference on instructions with the parties. Such conference shall be out of the presence of the jury and shall be held for the purpose of discussing the proposed instructions.

15.2—Objections to Instructions. The parties shall have an opportunity to request any additional instructions or to object to any of those instructions proposed by the judge. Any such requests, objections and rulings of the court thereon shall be placed on the record. At the conclusion of the charge and before the jury begins its deliberations (and out of the hearing, or upon request, out of the presence of the jury), the parties shall be given an opportunity to object on the record to any portion of the charge as given, or omission therefrom, stating with particularity the objection and grounds therefor.

Amended effective November 4, 2016.

SECTION 16. WEBSITE AND PUBLICATION

16.1—Website. The Business Court shall maintain a website for ready access to members of the bar and public. The website shall be located at the uniform resource locator http://

www.ninthcircuit.org/about/divisions/civil–circuit–courts/complex–business–litigation–court The website will store for ready retrieval basic information about the Business Court, including but not limited to these Business Court Procedures and the procedure for Complex Business Case designation. In addition, the website will store, in the sole discretion of the Business Court Judge:

a. the court's docket;
b. papers filed with the court;
c. motions filed with the court;
d. briefs filed with the court; and
e. the opinions of the court.

Amended effective November 4, 2016.

Uniform Policies and Procedures of the Domestic Division

SECTION 1. EFFECTIVE DATE; SCOPE; PURPOSE

(A) As a matter of policy, the Domestic Division Judges shall enforce the policies and procedures contained herein, as adopted on the 1st day of November, 2014.

(B) These policies and procedures are effective upon adoption and apply to all cases filed in the Domestic Division.

(C) The purpose of these policies and procedures is to supplement the Florida Rules of Civil Procedure, the Family Laws of Procedure, and the Rules of Judicial Administration, as well as the applicable statutory and case law. In some instances, they track existing administrative orders and statutes. They are intended to furnish all system users with a guide to the administrative policies and procedures of the Domestic Division of the Circuit Court of Orange County, Florida.

SECTION 2. ADMINISTRATIVE JUDGE; ALTERNATE JUDGES; DUTY JUDGE

(A) Administrative Judge. One of the presiding Judges of the division is appointed Administrative Judge by the Chief Judge to serve at his or her pleasure. The Administrative Judge shall be responsible for generally overseeing the operation and functioning of the Domestic Division.

(B) Alternate Judge. Each Judge of the Domestic Division has an assigned alternate Judge. This list may be obtained on the Court's website under Administrator's Orders, at http://www.ninthcircuit.org/research/admin–orders. In the event the assigned Judge is absent or otherwise unable to take action in the case, time-sensitive and emergency matters will be handled during business hours by his or her alternate, or, if the alternate is not available, by a Judge designated by the Administrative Judge or the Chief Judge. The alternate Judge may, but is not required, hear routine matters not of a true time-sensitive or emergency nature.

SECTION 3. APPEARANCE, SUBSTITUTION AND WITHDRAWAL OF ATTORNEYS

(A) Appearance of attorneys from other states (pro hac vice), appearance of additional counsel, substitution and withdrawal of attorneys are governed by the Florida Rules of Judicial Administration 2.505 and 2.510 and strict adherence to those procedures is required.

(B) Every Order of Withdrawal as counsel of record must contain an address for service of papers upon, and telephone number for, the client.

SECTION 4. UNREPRESENTED (PRO SE) PARTIES

(A) Every party to a legal proceeding has the right to appear and prosecute a claim or maintain a defense without being represented by an attorney. There are three exceptions where a party must be represented by an attorney:

(1) Corporations and limited liability companies must be represented by an attorney and may not represent themselves through non-lawyer employees, officers, directors or shareholders, even where such non-lawyer person is the sole shareholder. The only exception is that a corporate landlord may bring an action through its non-lawyer managing agent to evict a tenant for nonpayment of rent.

(2) A guardian of a minor or incompetent must be represented by an attorney unless the guardian is an attorney.

(3) A personal representative of a decedent's estate must be represented by an attorney, unless the personal representative is an attorney or unless the personal representative is the sole person to receive assets from the estate.

(B) The court strongly urges that every party retain an attorney to represent them. However, if a party entitled to represent himself or herself chooses not to retain an attorney, he or she is hereby advised:

(1) Neither the Judge nor his or her Judicial Assistant nor employees of the Clerk's office will give an unrepresented party legal advice.

(2) The unrepresented party will be governed by the same rules of law, procedure, and evidence that attorneys are required to follow.

(3) There is a court resource center available to unrepresented parties at no cost located in Room 365, of the Orange County Courthouse.

(4) No party may communicate privately with the Judge either by letter, telephone, e-mail, in person or otherwise. Copies of legal papers or other written materials should not be sent to the Judge unless specifically requested by the Judge or required by these administrative procedures. Any unrequested or non-required papers or materials sent to a Judge may not be read but may be returned to the sender or placed unread into the court file.

(5) An unrepresented party must file his or her papers with the Clerk and send copies to other attorneys or unrepresented parties. All such papers must be on Florida Supreme Court Approved Forms; available on the Florida Courts' website at www.flcourts.org and at the following specific link http://www.flcourts.org/resources–and–services/family–courts/family–law–self–help–information/family–law–forms.stml, with the name of the case and case number at the top and the party's mailing address, telephone number, fax number, if any, and e-mail address, if any, below his or her signature at the end of the paper. Such unrepresented party must immediately notify the Clerk and all other counsel or parties of record in writing or any change in mailing address or telephone or FAX number. Failure to promptly notify of a change of address could result in a dismissal or default entered against such party.

SECTION 5. INDIGENT PARTIES

(A) Original Proceedings in Circuit Court. A party claiming financial inability who desires to have certain Clerk's and Sheriff's fees and cost waived will complete and file an affidavit on a form provided by the Clerk. If the affidavit is sufficient, the Clerk will issue and file written certificate and provide copies of the certificate to the insolvent party. If the Clerk deems the affidavit insufficient, the party may file a motion to have the assigned Judge determine whether the affidavit is sufficient for a waiver of costs and fees. Only a party to a legal action which is presently pending and undisposed of is entitled to a certificate waiving costs and fees. If a party is represented by an attorney the attorney shall make a written certificate as required by Florida Statute 57.018(1).

(B) Appeal from Circuit Court to District Court of Appeal. A party claiming financial inability who desires to have Clerk's fees and costs waived in connection with an appeal from the Domestic Division to an appellate court must file a motion accompanied by affidavit and serve copies on the opposing parties. If no written objection is filed by an opposing party within five (5) days of the filing and service of the motion and affidavit, the movant must then promptly present a proposed order to the presiding Judge either at ex parte or by mail. If a written objection is to be filed, the objecting party must obtain hearing time within not less than four (4) nor more than seven (7) working days and file and serve notice of hearing simultaneously with the objection.

SECTION 6. ASSISTANCE FOR DISABLED PERSONS

If you are a person with a disability who needs any accommodation in order to participate in a proceeding, you are entitled, at no cost to you, to the provision of certain assistance. Please contact the ADA Coordinator, Human Resources, Orange County Courthouse, 425 N. Orange Avenue, Suite 510, Orlando, Florida, (407) 836–2303, at least 7 days before your scheduled court appearance, or immediately upon receiving this notification if the time before the scheduled appearance is less than 7 days; if you are hearing or voice impaired, call 711.

SECTION 7. HEARINGS

(A) Regularly Scheduled Hearings.

(1) Moving counsel must present a proposed order with space for ruling left blank at the conclusion of the hearing and must serve conformed copies on all other counsel and unrepresented parties.

(B) Ex Parte Matters. Ex parte and short matters are heard by all Domestic Subdivisions. Time and availability can be located at http://www.ninthcircuit.org/ under Judicial Automated Calendaring System. Contested matters requiring evidence generally will not be heard during this time unless the Judge's approval has been obtained in advance through his or her Judicial Assistant. Counsel should check out the court file from the Clerk's office and return it after the matter has been heard unless the Judge wishes to retain the file. An order should be brought to the hearing for the Judge to sign.

(C) Short Matters.

(1) Contact the Judge's office to ascertain whether short matters are heard by the specific division.

(2) There is no testimony permitted at short matters. Contested matters are permitted only if the issue can be heard in five (5) minutes or less.

(D) Other Motion Hearings. All other motions should be specially set through the Judge's Judicial Assistant for a date and time certain. Requests for hearing time in excess of one (1) hour will require special permission of the Judge obtained through the Judicial Assistant or by personal appearance of counsel at ex parte time.

(E) Hearings on Motions for Rehearing, Reconsideration or New Trial. Motions for rehearing, reconsideration or new trial will not be set for hearing unless the Judge so directs. Counsel filing such a motion should simultaneously send a chambers copy directly to the Judge with a cover letter requesting a hearing if one is desired. The Judge will then either rule upon the motion without a hearing and serve copies of his or her order on all parties or have his or her Judicial Assistant contact moving counsel and to obtain hearing time to be noticed by moving counsel.

SECTION 8. MOTION PRACTICE GENERALLY

(A) Form of Motions. Every written motion shall cite the particular rule or statute and/or leading case upon which the motion is based.

(B) Copies of Memorandums, Etc. Legal memorandums in support of or opposition to motions are optional. If filed, counsel must furnish the Judge and opposing counsel with copies of the memorandum and highlighted copies of primary legal authorities cited therein. As an alternative to a memorandum, a list of primary legal authorities with highlighted copies attached may be submitted. Chambers copies and authority lists must be under cover letter referencing the case style and number and stating the date and time of the hearing. Counsel who serves a memorandum or authority list first should also include a copy of the motion, any papers to which it is addressed, and the response, if any. In order for the Judge to properly review a submission in advance, it must be received in the Judge's office at least three (3) working days before the hearing.

(C) Obtaining Hearing Times. Counsel shall comply with Administrative Order No. 2014–19, Paragraph 6.

(D) Notices of Hearing.

(1) Every notice must specify the motions to be heard. A notice calling up "all pending motions" is insufficient.

(2) Additional motions should not be "piggy-backed" by cross-notice unless counsel first confirms with opposing counsel and the Judge's Judicial Assistant that there can be sufficient additional time reserved in which to hear them.

(E) Canceling Hearings. Only the attorney who noticed a hearing may cancel it.

If a hearing becomes unnecessary after it has been noticed, the Judge's Judicial Assistant and all other counsel must be notified <u>immediately</u> and <u>effectively</u> that the hearing is canceled.

SECTION 9. ORDERS AND JUDGMENTS

(A) Who Is To Prepare.

(1) Proposed orders and judgments will be prepared by the prevailing attorney unless the Judge designates some other attorney or states that he or she will prepare the order or judgment.

(2) When submitting proposed orders or judgments, counsel shall also include sufficient copies and self-addressed stamped envelopes for all parties and their counsel.

(B) Requirements for Orders.

(1) All orders will be on 8 ½ × 11 plain white paper (not lined paper or letterhead paper) and be double spaced.

(2) The order must contain a title indicating what matter the order pertains to, e.g., "Order On Wife's Motion To Dismiss."

(3) The preamble of the order should include the date of the hearing and what motions were heard.

(4) The adjudication portion of the order should state what relief is ordered. Simply stating that "the motion is granted" without more is insufficient.

(5) The order should indicate the specific time period of any act ordered to be done and should state whether the time period runs from the date of the hearing or the date the order is signed or some other specified date.

(6) The order should contain a full certificate of service with the complete names and addresses of the attorneys and unrepresented parties to be served. Merely showing "copies to" is insufficient.

(7) When submitting stipulations, orders shall be by separate order, not attached to the stipulation.

C. Requirements for Judgments.

(1) Every judgment will indicate whether it is a "Final Judgment" (i.e., the judgment disposes of the entire case) or "Partial Final Judgment," and if the latter, it should specify in a separate paragraph what other counts or claims against other parties remain pending.

(2) All judgments must contain a certificate of service showing the names and addresses of all attorneys and unrepresented parties to be served.

(3) Copies of default judgments must be mailed by the Judge's Judicial Assistant to the parties against whom the judgment is entered if the address is known.

SECTION 10. GENERAL DISCOVERY GUIDELINES

(A) General Principles. Counsel should be guided by courtesy, candor and commonsense and conform to the Family and Florida Rules of Civil Procedure and any applicable orders. In particular, counsel should have in mind the broad scope of discovery allowed by the Rules of Procedure. **Direct and informal communication between counsel is encouraged to facilitate discovery and resolve disputes.**

(B) Timeliness. The time limit specified in the rules and applicable orders must be observed. If additional time is needed, an extension must be sought before the time limit expires by stipulation, or failing that, by motion and order.

(C) Filing of Motions. Interrogatories and answers thereto, copies of documents produced in response to a request, and depositions are not to be filed with the Clerk unless they are needed for a hearing or trial.

SECTION 11. DEPOSITION GUIDELINES

(A) Scheduling. If the time for taking a deposition cannot be coordinated with other counsel in advance, at least thirty (30) days' notice should be given. Note that it is often less expensive to bring the witness to the deposition (and for the parties to share the expense) than for the lawyers to travel. Likewise, a telephone deposition of a secondary witness will save expense.

(B) Questioning. Questions should be brief, clear and simple. Each question should deal with only a single point. Argumentative or unnecessary embarrassing questions are out of order. The purpose of a deposition is not to harass or intimidate, but simply to make a clear and unambiguous record of what the witness' testimony would be at trial or to locate other witnesses or admissible evidence.

(C) Documents and Exhibits. Normally, a witness should be shown a document or exhibit and given a reasonable opportunity to examine it before being questioned about it.

(D) Objections. Objections to the conduct of counsel or other persons present should be noted on the record. Objection to the form of a question should state the specific grounds, i.e., leading, compound, etc., but the question should be answered unless the examiner rephrases the question. In the absence of a good faith claim of privilege, violation of a protective order, or other appropriate ground, instruction not to answer are rarely justified and may lead to sanctions. Speaking objections and frequent recesses or other tactics to coach a deponent are improper and may also be cause for sanctions. If counsel believes that a motion to terminate or limit the examination would be warranted, the deposition should be recessed and counsel should promptly initiate a telephone conference call to the presiding Judge to attempt to resolve the problem or obtain a ruling, or, if the assigned Judge is unavailable, promptly file a motion and set a hearing.

SECTION 12. ALTERNATE DISPUTE RESOLUTION, MEDIATION

Mediation will be ordered in all cases. Counsel may only dispense with mediation by court order.

SECTION 13. SETTING CASES FOR TRIAL

Counsel shall send a copy of the Notice for Trial to the Judicial Assistant, along with self-addressed stamped envelopes for all unrepresented parties and counsel and a completed Form 50. The notice must indicate an estimate the total number of days or hours needed for the trial.

SECTION 14. SETTLEMENTS

Counsel will <u>**immediately**</u> notify the Judge's Judicial Assistant by telephone and/or email of the settlement of any case scheduled for trial or hearing so it can be removed from the docket.

Administrative Orders

2018–25. MENTAL COMPETENCE TO PROCEED

IN THE CIRCUIT COURT OF THE NINTH JUDICIAL CIRCUIT, IN AND FOR ORANGE AND OSCEOLA COUNTIES, FLORIDA

ADMINISTRATIVE ORDER NO. 2018–25

ADMINISTRATIVE ORDER GOVERNING MENTAL COMPETENCE TO PROCEED

WHEREAS, pursuant to Article V, Section 2(d) of the Florida Constitution and section 43.26, Florida Statutes, the chief judge of each judicial circuit is charged with the authority and the power to do everything necessary to promote the prompt and efficient administration of justice; and

WHEREAS, to create and maintain an organization capable of effecting the efficient, prompt, and proper administration of justice for the citizens of this State, the chief judge is required to exercise direction, *see* Fla. R. Jud. Admin. 2.215(b)(2), (b)(3); and

WHEREAS, standardized procedures and manners of communication between the parties and the court best serve the interests of those that come before the court, preserve valuable judicial resources and prevent confusion and delay; and

WHEREAS, in order to provide effective coordination and in the interest of promoting judicial economy, the prompt and efficient administration of justice and in service to the citizens of the Ninth Circuit;

NOW, THEREFORE, I, Frederick J. Lauten, in order to facilitate the efficient operation of the administration of justice, and pursuant to the authority vested in me as Chief Judge of the Ninth Judicial Circuit of Florida under Florida Rule of Judicial Administration 2.215, hereby order the following, **effective January 1, 2019,** to continue until further order and superseding any provisions in prior Administrative Orders which may be inconsistent:

1. A fully completed Notice of Related Cases, in the form attached hereto as "Attachment A," must be filed with a Motion to Declare a Defendant Incompetent to Proceed to Trial by the filing attorney or self-represented defendant in each of the related cases that are currently open and pending with the court and served on all other parties in each of the related cases. A defendant must file supplemental notices as related cases become known or reasonably ascertainable. The Notice of Related Cases shall contain a list of all pending cases in which the defendant is named, the case number and assigned subdivision of each case.

2. Upon the filing of a Motion to Declare a Defendant Incompetent to Proceed to Trial in circuit or county court, all pending circuit and county court cases shall be stayed pending a determination of competency by the circuit court holding the lowest open case number. If there are no pending circuit court cases, the competency determination shall occur in the county case having the lowest open case number. Upon issuance of a stay order, the trial courts handling the related cases shall set a status hearing no later than 90 days from the issuance of the stay.

3. The parties shall apprise the evaluating experts of all open cases involving the defendant. All reports generated by experts relative to the motion to establish competency shall be filed under seal in all cases related to the defendant.

4. Upon entry of an order on the motion to establish competency, the Clerk of Court is directed to file copies of such orders in all cases listed on the Notice of Related Cases.

5. Once a finding is made as to the defendant's competency in a circuit court proceeding in which the Motion to Declare Defendant Incompetent was filed, the other courts in which a defendant has a pending case shall set a review hearing with notice to the state and defense on the status of competency. At the hearing, or upon proper notice, each court may adopt any findings related to defendant's competency, lift the stay order, or—if applicable—supplement or modify the terms of the defendant's conditional release

DONE AND ORDERED at Orlando, Florida, this 12th day of December, 2018.

Frederick J. Lauten
Chief Judge

"Attachment A"

IN THE CIRCUIT COURT OF THE NINTH JUDICIAL CIRCUIT IN AND FOR ORANGE COUNTY

Plaintiff(s),

Case No.: ____________

vs. Division: ____________

Defendant(s).

____________________ /

NOTICE OF RELATED CASES

Defendant submits this Notice of Related Cases pursuant to Ninth Judicial Circuit Court Administrative Order No. 2018–25, as may be amended.

RELATED CASE NO 1.

Name of the other case: ____________
Case Number: ____________ Subdivision: ____________
Judge: ____________
Date of filing: ____________

RELATED CASE NO 2.

Name of the other case: ____________
Case Number: ____________ Subdivision: ____________
Judge: ____________
Date of filing: ____________

RELATED CASE NO 3.

Name of the other case: ____________
Case Number: ____________ Subdivision: ____________
Judge: ____________
Date of filing: ____________

RELATED CASE NO 4.

Name of the other case: ____________
Case Number: ____________ Subdivision: ____________
Judge: ____________

Date of filing: ____________

____

ACKNOWLEDGEMENT

The Defendant acknowledges a continuing duty to inform the court of any cases in this or any other state that could affect the current proceeding.

Date

Signature of Defendant/Attorney for Defendant
Print Name:
Address:
City, State, Zip:
Telephone Number:
Fax Number:
E-mail address:
Florida Bar Number:

CERTIFICATE OF SERVICE

I HEREBY CERTIFY that I delivered a copy of this Notice of Related Cases to:

Signature of Defendant/Attorney for Defendant
Print Name:
Address:
City, State, Zip:
Telephone Number:
Fax Number:
E-mail address:
Florida Bar Number:

2018–24. ORDER ESTABLISHING A FELONY PRE–TRIAL INTERVENTION PROGRAM

IN THE CIRCUIT COURT OF THE NINTH JUDICIAL CIRCUIT, IN AND FOR ORANGE AND OSECOLA COUNTIES, FLORIDA

ADMINISTRATIVE ORDER NO. 2018–24

ORDER ESTABLISHING A FELONY PRE–TRIAL INTERVENTION PROGRAM

WHEREAS, pursuant to Article V, Section 2(d) of the Florida Constitution and section 43.26, Florida Statutes, the chief judge of each judicial circuit is charged with the authority and the power to do everything necessary to promote the prompt and efficient administration of justice; and

WHEREAS, section 948.08(6)(a), Florida Statutes, and the inherent authority of the Ninth Judicial Circuit allows for the establishment of a Pre–Trial Substance Abuse Education and Treatment Intervention Program for felonies; and

WHEREAS, the interests of justice will be served by establishing a consistent fair process whereby qualified defendants can be afforded an opportunity to participate in a Pre–Trial Intervention Program; and

WHEREAS, the proper implementation of a Pre–Trial Intervention Program will provide a valuable alternative to prosecution in appropriate cases and will provide a substantial benefit to the criminal justice system and the community as a whole for defendants who are identified as having substance abuse disorders, meet the requirements for the Program, and qualify pursuant to Florida Statutes;

NOW, THEREFORE, I, Frederick J. Lauten, in order to facilitate the efficient operation of the administration of justice, and pursuant to the authority vested in me as Chief Judge of the Ninth Judicial Circuit of Florida under Florida Rule of Judicial Administration 2.215, hereby order that, **effective immediately** unless otherwise provided herein, to continue until further order, and superseding any provisions in prior Administrative Orders which may be inconsistent:

A. Pre–Trial Substance Abuse Education and Treatment Intervention Program for Felonies

1. Any person charged with a nonviolent felony defined as a third degree felony violation of chapter 810 or any other felony offense that is not a forcible felony as defined in section 776.08, Florida Statutes, and is identified as having a substance abuse problem or is charged with a felony of the second or third degree for purchase or possession of a controlled substance under chapter 893, prostitution, tampering with evidence, solicitation for purchase of a controlled substance, or obtaining a prescription by fraud; who has not been charged with a crime involving violence, including, but not limited to, murder, sexual battery, robbery, carjacking, home-invasion robbery, or any other crime involving violence; and who has not previously been convicted of a felony is eligible for voluntary admission into a pretrial substance abuse education and treatment intervention program for a period of not less than one (1) year in duration, upon motion of either party or the court's own motion, except:

a. If a defendant was previously offered admission to a pretrial substance abuse education and treatment intervention program at any time prior to trial and the defendant rejected that offer on the record, then the court or the state attorney may deny the defendant's admission to such a program.

b. If the state attorney believes that the facts and circumstances of the case suggest the defendant's involvement in the dealing and selling of controlled substances, the court shall hold a preadmission hearing. If the state attorney establishes, by a preponderance of the evidence at such hearing, that the defendant was involved in the dealing or selling of controlled substances, the court shall deny the defendant's admission into a pretrial intervention program.

2. While enrolled in the pretrial intervention program, the participant will be supervised by the Department of Corrections and must pay all supervision fees.

3. While enrolled in the pretrial intervention program, the participant must complete a substance abuse assessment and any recommended treatment at the defendant's own expense.

4. The defendant must complete a substance abuse assessment and subsequent treatment from a provider approved by the Department of Corrections.

5. The court may order the defendant to complete additional requirements.

6. The court will hold periodic hearings, no less than every ninety (90) days, to ensure the defendant's continued compliance with the requirements of the Pre-trial Intervention Program.

7. The court shall use the uniform "Order Granting Defendant's Motion for Pre–Trial Substance Abuse Education and Treatment Intervention Program and Setting Status Hearing" attached hereto as "Attachment A" for Orange County and "Attachment B" for Osceola County when authorizing participation in the Pre-trial Intervention Program.

8. At the end of the pretrial intervention period, the court shall consider the recommendation of the state attorney as to disposition of the pending charges. The court shall determine,

by written finding, whether the defendant has successfully completed the Pre-trial Intervention Program.

9. If the court finds that the defendant has not successfully completed the Pre-trial Intervention Program, the court may order the defendant to continue in education and treatment, which may include substance abuse treatment programs offered by licensed service providers as defined in section 397.311, Florida Statutes, or jail-based treatment programs, or order that the charges revert to normal channels for prosecution.

10. The court shall dismiss the charges upon a finding that the defendant has successfully completed the Pre-trial Intervention Program.

11. Administrative Order 2009–19–01 is vacated and set aside except to the extent that it has been incorporated and/or amended herein. Vacating an Administrative Order that vacates a prior Order does not revive the prior Order.

DONE AND ORDERED at Orlando, Florida, this 24th day of September, 2018.

Frederick J. Lauten
Chief Judge

"Attachment A"

IN THE CIRCUIT COURT, NINTH JUDICIAL CIRCUIT, CRIMINAL JUSTICE DIVISION, IN AND FOR ORANGE COUNTY, FLORIDA

CASE NO:
DIVISION:

STATE OF FLORIDA
Plaintiff,

v.

Defendant.

______________________/

ORDER GRANTING DEFENDANT'S MOTION FOR PRE–TRIAL SUBSTANCE ABUSE EDUCATION AND TREATMENT INTERVENTION PROGRAM AND SETTING STATUS HEARINGS

THIS CAUSE having come before the Court and the Court having been fully advised in the premises, it is hereby

ORDERED that the Defendant's Motion for Pre–Trial Substance Abuse Education and Treatment Intervention Program is GRANTED. It is further,

ORDERED, pursuant to F.S. 948.08(6), that the Defendant enter into the Pre–Trial Substance Abuse Education and Treatment Intervention Program (the Program). Defendant is to comply with the following conditions:

1. This Court places Defendant into the Program for ___ years and ___ months. (Minimum of 1 year pursuant to F.S. 948.08(6)(a).)

2. Pursuant to F.S. 948.08(1), the Department of Corrections will supervise Defendant while in the Program.

3. The Department of Corrections will report on the Defendant's progress in the Program to the Court. The Department will provide these reports to the Court at least three business days before each Program status date.

4. Defendant must report to the probation office, located at 29 Coburn Avenue, Orlando, FL, 32805, Phone: (407) 245–0701, within 48 hours.

5. Defendant will report to the probation office as directed by the officer, but not less than monthly. Not later than the fifth day of each month, unless otherwise directed, Defendant will make a full and truthful report to the officer on the form provided for that purpose.

6. Defendant will pay the State of Florida the amount of $20.00 per month, toward cost of supervision, in accordance with F.S. 948.09(1)(a)2, unless otherwise exempted in compliance with Florida Statutes.

7. Defendant will promptly and truthfully answer all inquiries directed by the court or the officer, and allow the officer to visit in Defendant's home and will comply with all instructions the officer may give.

8. Defendant will remain in a specified place. Defendant will not change residence or employment or leave the county of residence without first procuring the consent of the officer.

9. Defendant will not possess, carry or own any firearms. Defendant will not possess, carry, or own any weapons without first procuring the consent of the officer.

10. Defendant shall refrain from violation of any federal, state or local law. A Court's finding of probable cause to arrest, while in the Program, subjects Defendant to revocation of the Program at the discretion of the Court.

11. Defendant will not associate with any person engaged in any criminal activity.

12. Defendant will maintain full time employment or attend school/vocational school full time or a combination of school/work during the term of the Program, unless excused by the Court or supervising officer. Employment shall be verified by paycheck stubs. The officer ___ **shall** ___ **shall not** notify the employer of the supervision and the offense or offenses for which the defendant is in the Program.

13. Defendant will abstain entirely from the use of alcohol and/or illegal drugs and will not associate with anyone who is illegally using drugs or consuming alcohol.

14. Defendant must undergo a drug and alcohol evaluation and, if treatment is deemed necessary. Defendant must successfully complete the treatment and be responsible for the payment of any costs incurred while receiving said evaluation and treatment.

15. Defendant will submit to random testing as directed by the officer or the professional staff of the treatment center where Defendant is receiving treatment to determine the presence or use of alcohol or controlled substances. Random testing shall be no less than monthly. Defendant will be required to pay for drug testing.

Check all that apply of paragraphs 16 through 22.

___ 16. Defendant must complete ___ hours of community service through the Alternative Community Service program or other non-profit agency approved by the officer.

___ 17. Defendant will have no contact (direct or indirect) with the victim or the victim's family during the period of the Program.

___ 18. Defendant will pay restitution, court costs, and/or fees in accordance with special conditions imposed or in accordance with the attached orders.

___ 19. Defendant will have no contact with co–defendant(s).

For cases charged pursuant to F.S. 796.07(4)(b):

___ 20. Defendant will attend an HIV/AIDS Awareness Program consisting of a class of not less than two (2) hours or more than four (4) hours in length, the costs for which will be paid by Defendant.

___ 21. Defendant must take an HIV/STD test.

___ 22. Defendant must not return to the prostitution mapping zone.

___ 23. ______________________________

24. Any violation of this Order, as determined by this Court, subjects Defendant to revocation from the Program or other sanctions as authorized by law, at the discretion of the Court.

25. Defendant is released on their own recognizance as to this case only.

Pre–Trial Intervention status hearings are set as follows:

____

The hearings will be conducted in Courtroom ___, Orange County Courthouse, 425 N. Orange Avenue, Orlando, Florida 32801. **Defendant must be present at each of these hearings.**

DONE and ORDERED this ___ day of ________, 20 ___.

____

Circuit Judge

If you are a person with a disability who needs any accommodation in order to participate in this proceeding, you are entitled, at no cost to you, to the provision of certain assistance. Please contact the ADA Coordinator, Human Resources, Orange County Courthouse, 425 N. Orange Avenue, Suite 510, Orlando, Florida, (407) 836–2303, at least 7 days before your scheduled court appearance, or immediately upon receiving this notification if the time before the scheduled appearance is less than 7 days; if you are hearing or voice impaired, call 711.

"Attachment B"

IN THE CIRCUIT COURT, NINTH JUDICIAL CIRCUIT, CRIMINAL JUSTICE DVISION, IN AND FOR OSCEOLA COUNTY, FLORIDA

CASE NO:
DIVISION:

STATE OF FLORIDA
Plaintiff,

v.

Defendant.
________________/

ORDER GRANTING DEFENDANT'S MOTION FOR PRE–TRIAL SUBSTANCE ABUSE EDUCATION AND TREATMENT INTERVENTION PROGRAM AND SETTING STATUS HEARINGS

THIS CAUSE having come before the Court and the Court having been fully advised in the premises, it is hereby

ORDERED that the Defendant's Motion for Pre–Trial Substance Abuse Education and Treatment Intervention Program is GRANTED. It is further,

ORDERED, pursuant to F.S. 948.08(6), that the Defendant enter into the Pre–Trial Substance Abuse Education and Treatment Intervention Program (the Program). Defendant is to comply with the following conditions:

1. This Court places Defendant into the Program for ___ years and ___ months. (Minimum of 1 year pursuant to F.S. 948.08(6)(a).)

2. Pursuant to F.S. 948.08(1), the Department of Corrections will supervise Defendant while in the Program.

3. The Department of Corrections will report on the Defendant's progress in the Program to the Court. The Department will provide these reports to the Court at least three business days before each Program status date.

4. Defendant must report to the probation office, located at 1605 N. John Young Parkway, Kissimmee, FL, 34741, Phone: (407) 846–5215, within 48 hours.

5. Defendant will report to the probation office as directed by the officer, but not less than monthly. Not later than the fifth day of each month, unless otherwise directed, Defendant will make a full and truthful report to the officer on the form provided for that purpose.

6. Defendant will pay the State of Florida the amount of $20.00 per month, toward cost of supervision, in accordance with F.S. 948.09(1)(a)2, unless otherwise exempted in compliance with Florida Statutes.

7. Defendant will promptly and truthfully answer all inquiries directed by the court or the officer, and allow the officer to visit in Defendant's home and will comply with all instructions the officer may give.

8. Defendant will remain in a specified place. Defendant will not change residence or employment or leave the county of residence without first procuring the consent of the officer.

9. Defendant will not possess, carry or own any firearms. Defendant will not possess, carry, or own any weapons without first procuring the consent of the officer.

10. Defendant shall refrain from violation of any federal, state or local law. A Court's finding of probable cause to arrest, while in the Program, subjects Defendant to revocation of the Program at the discretion of the Court.

11. Defendant will not associate with any person engaged in any criminal activity.

12. Defendant will maintain full time employment or attend school/vocational school full time or a combination of school/work during the term of the Program, unless excused by the Court or supervising officer. Employment shall be verified by paycheck stubs. The officer ___ **shall** ___ **shall not** notify the employer of the supervision and the offense or offenses for which the defendant is in the Program.

13. Defendant will abstain entirely from the use of alcohol and/or illegal drugs and will not associate with anyone who is illegally using drugs or consuming alcohol.

14. Defendant must undergo a drug and alcohol evaluation and, if treatment is deemed necessary. Defendant must successfully complete the treatment and be responsible for the payment of any costs incurred while receiving said evaluation and treatment.

15. Defendant will submit to random testing as directed by the officer or the professional staff of the treatment center where Defendant is receiving treatment to determine the presence or use of alcohol or controlled substances. Random testing shall be no less than monthly. Defendant will be required to pay for drug testing.

Check all that apply of paragraphs 16 through 22.

___ 16. Defendant must complete ___ hours of community service through the Alternative Community Service program or other non-profit agency approved by the officer.

___ 17. Defendant will have no contact (direct or indirect) with the victim or the victim's family during the period of the Program.

___ 18. Defendant will pay restitution, court costs, and/or fees in accordance with special conditions imposed or in accordance with the attached orders.

___ 19. Defendant will have no contact with co-defendant(s).

For cases charged pursuant to F.S. 796.07(4)(b):

___ 20. Defendant will attend an HIV/AIDS Awareness Program consisting of a class of not less than two (2) hours or more than four (4) hours in length, the costs for which will be paid by Defendant.

___ 21. Defendant must take an HIV/STD test.

___ 22. Defendant must not return to the prostitution mapping zone.

23. ______________________________

24. Any violation of this order, as determined by this Court, subjects Defendant to revocation from the Program or other sanctions as authorized by law, at the discretion of the Court.

25. Defendant is released on their own recognizance as to this case only.

26. Pre–Trial Intervention status hearings are set as follows:

____

The hearings will be conducted in Courtroom ________, Osceola County Courthouse, 2 Courthouse Square, Kissimmee, Florida 34741. **Defendant must be present at each of these hearings.**

DONE and ORDERED this ___ day of ________, 20 ___.

____

Circuit Judge

If you are a person with a disability who needs any accommodation in order to participate in this proceeding, you are entitled, at no cost to you, to the provision of certain assistance. Please contact the ADA Coordinator, Human Resources, Osceola County Courthouse, 2 Courthouse Square, Kissimmee, Florida, (407) 742–2417, at least 7 days before your scheduled court appearance, or immediately upon receiving this notification if the time before the scheduled appearance is less than 7 days; if you are hearing or voice impaired, call 711.

2018–07. ADULT DRUG COURT PROGRAMS

IN THE CIRCUIT COURT OF THE NINTH JUDICIAL CIRCUIT, IN AND FOR ORANGE AND OSCEOLA COUNTIES, FLORIDA

ADMINISTRATIVE ORDER NO. 2018–07

ADMINISTRATIVE ORDER GOVERNING THE ADULT DRUG COURT PROGRAMS

WHEREAS, section 948.08(6)(a), Florida Statutes, and the inherent authority of the Ninth Judicial Circuit allows for the establishment of a Pre–Trial Substance Abuse Education and Treatment Intervention Program; and

WHEREAS, section 397.334, Florida Statutes, and the inherent authority of the Ninth Judicial Circuit allows for the establishment of Treatment-based Drug Court Programs to include Pretrial Treatment Based Drug Court Programs authorized by section 948.08(6)(a), Florida Statutes and Post-adjudicatory Treatment–Based Drug Court Programs as a condition of probation or community control pursuant to sections 948.01, 948.06 and 948.20, Florida Statutes; and

WHEREAS, the proper implementation of an Adult Drug Court Program will provide a valuable alternative to prosecution in appropriate cases; and

WHEREAS, Adult Drug Court will provide a substantial benefit to the criminal justice system and the community as a whole for defendants who are identified as having substance abuse disorders, meet the requirements for the Adult Drug Court Program, and qualify pursuant to section 397.334, Florida Statutes, as well as section(s) 948.01 or 948.06 or 948.08 or 948.20, Florida Statutes;

NOW, THEREFORE, I, Frederick J. Lauten, in order to facilitate the efficient operation of the administration of justice, and pursuant to the authority vested in me as Chief Judge of the Ninth Judicial Circuit of Florida under Florida Rule of Judicial Administration 2.215, hereby order that, **effective immediately** unless otherwise provided herein, to continue until further order, and superseding any provisions in prior Administrative Orders which may be inconsistent:

1. **Eligible Offenses and Defendants:**

a. Offenses eligible for referral to the Drug Court Program (Program) are any misdemeanor, third degree felonies of chapter 810, Florida Statutes, or any other felony offense that is not a forcible felony as defined in section 776.08, Florida Statutes.

b. Violation of probation cases which are eligible for inclusion in the Program are those cases where the defendant has violated any technical term of probation or has committed a new criminal offense as stated above.

c. Defendants must reside in either Orange or Osceola County, must participate in the Program in the county in which they reside, must suffer from a substance abuse disorder and, in Orange County, score High Risk and/or High Need on the Drug Court Program Office assessment. Exceptions may be made in Orange County as it relates to Risk on a case by case basis.

2. Ineligible Offenses and Defendants:

a. Ineligible offenses for referral to the Program as cases where the defendant has violated probation by the commission of a forcible felony offense as defined in section 776.08, Florida Statutes.

b. Ineligible defendants are those persons who score more than 60 points on a score sheet for the violation of probation or for the newly committed criminal offense, or defendants who have been previously ejected from the Program, or are currently on parole, or who are currently on felony probation for ineligible offense(s).

3. The procedure for placement of eligible defendants into Drug Court is as follows:

a. Entry into the Adult Drug Court Program is voluntary.

b. The referral of a defendant into Drug Court may be made by any of the criminal trial divisions with no plea taken, and may be made by defense counsel, the State Attorney's Office, the Court, the Drug Court Office, the Pretrial Services Unit of the Orange or Osceola County Department of Corrections, or any other interested party.

c. As part of the referral, the referring person/agency shall initiate the issuance of a Drug Court Referral Form (hereinafter referred to as "Referral Form") and shall submit the Referral Form to the Drug Court Office or, in Orange County, place the Referral Form in any Drug Court Basket in any criminal courtroom for screening and assessment.

d. All necessary information regarding the defendant shall be provided on the Referral Form.

e. Screening and assessment shall include a determination of eligibility of the offense, eligibility of the defendant's criminal history, severity of substance abuse problem and any current funding body's additional inclusion or exclusion criteria for program participation.

f. If the Drug Court Office approves the Referral Form, the Drug Court Office shall forward the Referral Form to the Treatment Provider for assessment of suitability of the defendant for participation in Drug Court if required by the Program.

g. At the same time the Drug Court Office will send the original Referral Form to the State Attorney's Office. Upon receipt of the Referral Form, the State Attorney's Office shall determine whether or not the defendant is eligible, shall indicate this information on the Referral Form, and shall forward the Referral Form back to the Drug Court Office. The Drug Court Office will then forward the completed Referral Form to the Clerk of Court's Office for placement of the case on the Drug Court Contract Signing docket.

h. Prior to the contract signing, the defendant may enter treatment and begin random urinalysis testing. The defendant's progress as to the treatment and random urinalysis testing shall be reported to the Problem Solving Court Judge prior to the defendant being ordered into Drug Court.

i. At the Drug Court Contract Signing, if the defendant elects to participate in Drug Court and was approved for a post-adjudicatory track, the defendant shall enter a plea to the charges and shall sign the Drug Court Agreement. If the Problem Solving Court Judge agrees that Drug Court is appropriate for the defendant, he/she shall sentence the defendant to a term of no less than three years of probation on a felony case, or an appropriate term on a misdemeanor case, with a special condition of "the successful completion of Drug Court according to the terms of the Drug Court Agreement." All other standard and any other special conditions as needed shall be imposed.

j. At the Drug Court Contract Signing if the defendant elects to participate in Drug Court and was approved for the diversion track by the State Attorney, the defendant shall sign the Drug Court Agreement and waive speedy trial.

k. At contract signing, if the defendant elects not to participate in Drug Court or if the Problem Solving Court Judge determines that the defendant is not appropriate for Drug Court, then the case shall be returned to the original trial subdivision.

l. If a diversion drug court participant choses to opt out of drug court at any time, the case may be re-assigned to the subdivision where the case was originally assigned at the Problem Solving Court Judge's discretion.

m. A copy of the completed Referral Form shall be forwarded by the Drug Court Office, to the assigned trial judge, to defense counsel, and to the State Attorney's Office.

n. Post-plea defendants shall be supervised by the Florida Department of Corrections, Orange County Probation, or Osceola County Probation. Defendants shall pay all costs of supervision.

o. Case management shall be provided by the Treatment Provider or Program staff.

p. Should a post-plea defendant be ejected from Drug Court as a result of a program violation, the Florida Department of Corrections or Orange or Osceola County Probation shall initiate an affidavit of violation of probation and shall submit the affidavit to the Problem Solving Court Judge. Nothing herein shall prohibit the Florida Department of Corrections from filing a violation of probation for any failure of the defendant to comply with conditions of probation. If the Problem Solving Court Judge determines that there is a legal basis to do so, he/she shall issue a warrant for violation of probation. Upon arrest on the violation of probation warrant, the Problem Solving Court Judge shall resolve the violation of probation proceeding via a plea or hearing and impose a sentence if appropriate. The Court shall not reinstate or resentence the defendant to Drug Court as part of the disposition of the violation of probation.

q. Should a diversion defendant be ejected from drug court because of a program violation, the case may be re-assigned to the subdivision where the case was originally assigned at the Problem Solving Court Judge's discretion.

r. Should a post-plea defendant successfully complete Drug Court and comply with all other special and standard conditions of probation (including restitution) the Court shall give due consideration to the early termination of probation.

s. Should a diversion defendant successfully complete Drug Court, the State Attorney shall file a nolle prosequi.

4. Defendants participating in the Orange County Adult Drug Court Program shall pay a fee of $900.00 dollars to the Orange County Drug Court Program. This fee must be paid to the Orange County Clerk of Court. The Orange County Clerk of Court shall retain $15.00 from each $900.00 fee for processing costs. The remainder of those fees, pursuant to an agreement with the Orange County Clerk of Court, shall be remitted by the Orange County Clerk to the Orange County Drug Abuse Trust Fund (Source Revenue # 4599, a designated account for Drug Court funding goals and objectives) established by the Board of County Commissioners, Orange County. Defendant may apply for a fee reduction with the Orange County Drug Court Program Office.

5. Defendants participating in the Osceola County Adult Drug Court Program shall pay a fee of $1,525.00. This amount includes $1,080.00 for drug testing, $420.00 for treatment services and a $25.00 initial services fee to the Osceola County Clerk of Court. All defendants exceeding twelve months in the Program shall pay $120.00 per month ($90.00 drug testing and $35 treatment costs) until graduation or discharge from the Program.

6. Administrative Order Nos. 2000–04–02, 2000–18–06, 2001–19–04, 2003–04–04, and 2007–04–02 are vacated and set aside except to the extent that each has been incorporated and/or amended herein. Vacating an Administrative Order that vacates a prior Order does not revive the prior Order.

DONE AND ORDERED at Orlando, Florida, this 27th day of March, 2018.

Frederick J. Lauten
Chief Judge

2018–04. SEXUAL HARASSMENT POLICY AND COMPLAINT PROCEDURES AGAINST JUDGES

IN THE CIRCUIT COURT OF THE NINTH JUDICIAL CIRCUIT, IN AND FOR ORANGE AND OSCEOLA COUNTIES, FLORIDA

ADMINISTRATIVE ORDER NO. 2018–04

ADMINISTRATIVE ORDER ADOPTING SEXUAL HARASSMENT POLICY AND COMPLAINT PROCEDURES AGAINST JUDGES

WHEREAS, pursuant to Article V, section 2(d) of the Florida Constitution and section 43.26, Florida Statutes, the chief judge of each judicial circuit is charged with the authority and the power to do everything necessary to promote the prompt and efficient administration of justice; and

WHEREAS, pursuant to the chief judge's constitutional and statutory responsibility for administrative supervision of the courts within the circuit and to create and maintain an organization capable of effecting the efficient, prompt, and proper administration of justice for the citizens of this State, the chief judge is required to exercise direction, *see* Fla. R. Jud. Admin. 2.215(b)(2), (b)(3); and

WHEREAS, the creation and implementation of uniform procedures for court personnel and others to report any alleged occurrence(s) of sexual harassment is necessary to fulfill the Ninth Judicial Circuit's longstanding policy to make the workplace free of sexual harassment; and

WHEREAS, on February 16, 2018, the chief justice entered Administrative Order No. SC18–6, approving the Sexual Harassment Policy and Procedures for Complaints against Judges as the uniform policy and procedures for circuit courts and directing chief judges of the district courts of appeal and chief judges of the circuit courts to adopt and implement the policy and procedures in their respective courts. The policy and procedures approved replace and supersede the policies and procedures adopted in In re: Sexual Harassment Policy and Procedures for Complaints Against Justices, Fla. Admin. Order No. AOSC04–07 (March 25, 2004), and In re: Sexual Harassment Policy and Procedures for Complaints Against Trial Court Judges, Fla. Admin. Order No. AOSC04–08 (March 25, 2004);

NOW, THEREFORE, I, Frederick J. Lauten, in order to facilitate the efficient operation of the administration of justice, and pursuant to the authority vested in me as Chief Judge of the Ninth Judicial Circuit of Florida under Florida Rule of Judicial Administration 2.215, hereby order that, **effective immediately** unless otherwise provided herein, to continue until further order, and superseding any provisions in prior Administrative Orders which may be inconsistent:

1. The Ninth Judicial Circuit Sexual Harassment Policy and Complaint Procedures for Complaints Against Judges, attached hereto as Attachment "A" and incorporated herein, is hereby adopted and shall be implemented immediately in the Ninth Judicial Circuit.

DONE AND ORDERED at Orlando, Florida, this 7th day of March, 2018.

Frederick J. Lauten
Chief Judge

Attachment "A"

SEXUAL HARASSMENT POLICY AND PROCEDURES FOR SEXUAL HARASSMENT COMPLAINTS AGAINST JUDGES

1. Policy. It is the policy of the Ninth Judicial Circuit to foster a workplace free of sexual harassment or sexual misconduct. Sexual harassment occurs if there are unwelcome sexual advances; unwelcome requests for sexual favors; or unwelcome verbal or physical conduct of a sexual nature from or involving an employee's supervisors, peers, subordinates or other persons in contact with an employee during the course of the conduct of the employee's business when:

A. Submission to such conduct is either explicitly or implicitly a term or condition of employment; or

B. Submission to or rejection of such conduct by an individual is used as the basis for employment decisions affecting such individual or as the basis for any official actions; or

C. Such conduct has the purpose or effect of interfering with an individual's work performance or creates a persistently intimidating and hostile environment, as that term is defined in state and federal law.

Sexual misconduct is any behavior of a sexual nature that is committed without consent or by force, intimidation, coercion, or manipulation. Sexual misconduct can occur between strangers or acquaintances, including people involved in an intimate or sexual relationship, and is not necessarily actionable sexual harassment.

The Florida Supreme Court and the entire state court system condemn any sexual harassment or sexual misconduct and advance the position that anyone in contact with the state courts system should feel empowered to bring any such inappropriate activity to the attention of all proper authorities, including and especially the Florida Supreme Court. Anyone authorized to investigate or pursue a complaint of sexual harassment or sexual misconduct hereunder must always maintain an open-door policy that fosters the free expression of any complaint. The chief judge or chief judge's designee has the authority to take any administrative action necessary to protect the complainant from further sexual harassment or sexual misconduct and from retaliation related to a complaint hereunder.

It is the policy of the Ninth Judicial Circuit that complaints of sexual harassment or sexual misconduct against any judge within the state courts system will be treated seriously and acted upon promptly. The following procedures apply to complaints against judges made by employees of the court system, applicants for employment with the court system, and when applicable attorneys, litigants, or other members of the public. Compliance with these procedures by the chief judge, or the chief judge's designee, constitutes a presumption of compliance with the disciplinary responsibilities under Canon 3(D)1 of the Code of Judicial Conduct.

2. Notification. The chief judge may designate any person, including a non-judge, to be responsible for receiving and documenting complaints of sexual harassment against judges.

Any employee or applicant for employment with the court who believes that he or she is the subject of sexual harassment by a county court judge or a circuit court judge should report his or her complaint in writing, or if the person prefers he or she may submit the complaint orally. The complaint may be submitted to any of the following: the chief justice or his or her designee; a local administrator, such as a Trial Court Administrator, human resource manager or Marshal; or the Chief of Human Resources at the Office of the State Courts Administrator (OSCA). If the person receiving the complaint is not the chief justice, the chief justice's designee, or a chief judge, the person receiving the complaint should forward it to the chief justice, the chief justice's designee, or the chief judge of the court in which the subject judge serves for an investigation pursuant to section 4, below. Student interns working for the state courts system who believe they are the subject of sexual harassment may use these complaint procedures, but in all instances, should submit a complaint to their college or university in accordance with school sexual harassment complaint procedures.

If any person has difficulty writing out the complaint and the person requests assistance in reducing the complaint to writing or if the person prefers to submit the complaint orally, the chief justice, local administrator, or OSCA Chief of Human Resources, as appropriate, shall designate a person, who will not be involved in the investigation or adjudication of the complaint, to aid the person in reducing the complaint to writing.

If the chief judge is the subject of a complaint, the employee or applicant should report the complaint to the court administrator who will refer such complaint to the most senior judge in the Ninth Judicial Circuit. The judge to whom such a complaint is referred will assume all complaint investigation and resolution duties as provided for in these procedures. The judge to whom such a complaint is referred will also be responsible for maintaining any records pertaining to the complaint.

If an employee or applicant chooses not to file a formal complaint, and any person designated hereunder to receive complaints has actual knowledge or receives information that a substantial likelihood exists that a judge has engaged in sexual harassment or sexual misconduct, the person may inquire into the matter and take appropriate action.

3. Time for Filing Complaints. In order to ensure that the Ninth Judicial Circuit complaint procedures can be utilized without risk of precluding the filing of a charge of discrimination with state or federal entities, an employee or applicant should report an incident of sexual harassment within 90 days of the date of occurrence.

4. Investigation. A complaint of sexual harassment or sexual misconduct against a judge will be investigated promptly and thoroughly. If a complaint has been made to the chief judge or the chief judge's designee, he or she may designate another person to make an initial inquiry into the complaint.

The chief judge or the chief judge's designee will interview the complainant within five days of the submission of the complaint to ascertain relevant facts and circumstances. If the complainant does not divulge names or details of the incident(s), the chief judge or the chief judge's designee will rely upon information that is available, to the extent possible. If another person has been designated to make an initial inquiry into the complaint, such designee will report details of the complaint to the chief judge within ten days of the submission of the complaint.

If the chief judge or the chief judge's designee determines the complaint is unfounded or is insufficient to constitute sexual harassment, he or she may decline to pursue any action on the complaint.

If the chief judge or the chief judge's designee determines the complaint is facially sufficient to constitute sexual harassment, the chief judge or the chief judge's designee may appoint an investigating officer or officers to formally investigate the complaint, or may take any other action appropriate under the circumstances.

If the chief judge or the chief judge's designee determines the complaint is insufficient to constitute sexual harassment, but nevertheless indicates potential sexual misconduct, the chief judge or the chief judge's designee may take any action appropriate to address the circumstances, including but not limited to appointing an investigating officer or officers to formally investigate the complaint.

The chief judge, the chief judge's designee, or investigating officer will interview the complainant, the judge implicated, and witnesses, if any, and will review relevant documents. If any investigating officers have been appointed, they will submit a written report to the chief judge or the chief judge's designee within thirty days of the submission of the complaint for formal investigation.

5. Resolution. The chief judge, or pursuant to rule 2.215(c)(4), Florida Rules of Judicial Administration, the other most senior judge if the chief judge is the subject of a complaint, shall determine the course of action for internal resolution of the complaint, and may appoint another person, other than the subject of the complaint, to recommend the course of action for internal resolution.

If the chief judge or the chief judge's designee determines the complaint, including any relevant facts, circumstances, and information, is insufficient to constitute sexual harassment, the chief judge or the chief judge's designee may attempt to resolve the complaint informally through mutual conciliation by meeting with the complainant and the subject judge to discuss a method of resolution, including alternative dispute resolution. In attempting to resolve the complaint, the chief judge or the chief judge's designee may counsel or take other appropriate direct action with the judge involved.

If the complaint and investigation reasonably indicate that the subject judge engaged in activity that constitutes sexual harassment, constitutes sexual misconduct, or otherwise raises a substantial question as to a judge's fitness for office, the chief judge or the chief judge's designee shall refer the complaint and all written documentation pertaining to the complaint to the Judicial Qualifications Commission.

To the extent not otherwise prohibited by statute or rule, a written summary of the resolution will be provided to the complainant within a reasonable time after a determination is made and any action pursuant thereto is taken.

6. Documentation and Confidentiality. All information pertaining to a complaint of sexual harassment must be documented and maintained by the chief judge or the chief judge's designee of the court in which the subject judge serves whichever officer took final action on the resolution of the complaint.

All records made or received by the chief judge or the chief judge's designee through use of these complaint procedures are exempt from public disclosure under rule 2.051(c)(3)(A), Florida Rules of Judicial Administration. Such records are exempt for the duration of an initial inquiry, formal investigation and resolution of the complaint, and at all times thereafter, unless the records are forwarded to the Judicial Qualifications Commission.

All records made or received by any person pursuant to these complaint procedures are exempt from public disclosure as provided in rule 2.420(c)(3)(A), Florida Rules of Judicial Administration. Such records are exempt from public disclosure for the duration of an initial inquiry, formal investigation and resolution of the complaint, and at all times thereafter, unless the records are forwarded to the Judicial Qualifications Commission.

If records pertaining to a complaint are forwarded to the Judicial Qualifications Commission, such records will be confidential under rule 2.420(c)(3)(A), and rule 23(a), Rules of the Judicial Qualifications Commission, until any formal charges against the judge are filed by the Investigative Panel of the Commission with the clerk of the Florida Supreme Court.

Records within the possession of any justice, judge, or court staff and pertaining to a complaint that has been forwarded to the Judicial Qualifications Commission will become public upon formal charges being filed with the clerk of the Florida Supreme Court.

7. Referral to the Judicial Qualifications Commission. The Judicial Qualifications Commission is responsible for investigating all reported instances of judicial misconduct. These procedures do not preclude the referral of a complaint against a judge at any time by any person to the Judicial Qualifications Commission. If a complaint has been referred to the Judicial Qualifications Commission, no further action by the chief judge or chief judge's designee is required.

For anyone wishing to file such a complaint, the Commission's mailing address is P.O. Box 141106, Tallahassee, Florida 32317. The Commission's Executive Director can be contacted by telephone at 850–488–1581 or by email at contact@floridajqc.com.

8. Referral to the Florida Commission on Human Relations or the United States Equal Employment Opportunity Commission. These procedures do not preclude the filing of a charge of employment discrimination with the Florida Commission on Human Relations or the United States Equal Employment Opportunity Commission.

For anyone wishing to file such a complaint, the Florida Commission on Human Relations (FCHR) is located at: 4075 Esplanade Way Room 110 Tallahassee, FL 32399. The telephone number for the FCHR is: 850–488–7082 or 1–800–342–8170.

The United States Equal Employment Opportunity Commission (EEOC) office with jurisdiction over complaints arising in Florida is the Miami District Office located at 100 SE 2nd Street, Suite 1500, Miami, FL 33131. The telephone number for the EEOC Miami District office is: 1–800–669–4000.

9. Referral to the Chief of Human Resources, Office of the State Courts Administrator. For anyone wishing to file a complaint under this policy, the Chief of Human Resources, OSCA is located at: 500 South Duval Street Tallahassee, Florida 32399–1925. The telephone number is 850–617–4028.

2018–03. ALTERNATIVE SANCTIONS PROGRAM

IN THE CIRCUIT COURT OF THE NINTH JUDICIAL CIRCUIT, IN AND FOR ORANGE AND OSCEOLA COUNTIES, FLORIDA

ADMINISTRATIVE ORDER NO. 2018–03

ORDER GOVERNING ALTERNATIVE SANCTIONS PROGRAM

WHEREAS, pursuant to Article V, section 2(d) of the Florida Constitution and section 43.26, Florida Statutes, the chief judge of each judicial circuit is charged with the authority and the power to do everything necessary to promote the prompt and efficient administration of justice; and

WHEREAS, pursuant to the chief judge's constitutional and statutory responsibility for administrative supervision of the courts within the circuit and to create and maintain an organization capable of effecting the efficient, prompt, and proper administration of justice for the citizens of this State, the chief judge is required to exercise direction, *see* Fla. R. Jud. Admin. 2.215(b)(2), (b)(3); and

WHEREAS, there are a substantial number of technical violations that do not involve a new arrest or other serious violations; and

WHEREAS, arresting and incarcerating certain non-violent offenders for minor violations of probation or community control is both expensive and nonproductive; and

WHEREAS, there is research to support that recidivism may be reduced by utilizing collaborative efforts among the courts, probation and law enforcement to hold the offender accountable and apply swift and certain sanctions for technical violations of probation or community control; and

WHEREAS, an administrative option for processing technical violations will have the potential to offer benefits including:

- Reducing the court docket of probation and community control violation hearings;
- Reducing the workload of prosecutors and defense attorneys involved with many technical violation hearings;
- Reducing law enforcement resources required to serve violation warrants for certain technical violations;
- Reducing jail population for offenders pending violation hearings; and
- Offering the offender an alternative to a violation hearing in court, which will allow the offender to remain engaged in employment, school, treatment, etc. and allow the offender to take immediate responsibility for their actions and comply with the consequences of those actions; and

WHEREAS, the Florida Legislature recognizes the value of an alternative sanctioning program for technical violations of probation and community control and has authorized trial court chief judges, in consultation with the state attorney, public defender, and the Department of Corrections to establish a local alternative sanctioning program. Ch. 2016–100, § 1, Laws of Fla.;

NOW, THEREFORE, I, Frederick J. Lauten, in order to facilitate the efficient operation of the administration of justice, and pursuant to the authority vested in me as Chief Judge of the Ninth Judicial Circuit of Florida under Florida Rule of Judicial Administration 2.215, hereby order the following, **effective immediately**, to continue until further order and superseding any provisions in prior Administrative Orders which may be inconsistent:

1. **ALTERNATIVE SANCTIONING PROGRAM.** There is created in the Ninth Judicial Circuit a program that shall be known as the Alternative Sanctioning Program in accordance with section 948.06(1)(h), Florida Statutes. The Alternative Sanctioning Program provides the court and the Florida Department of Corrections (FDC) an alternative, administrative method of reporting and resolving certain technical violations in lieu of submitting violation of probation affidavits and warrants to the court.

2. **ELIGIBILITY CRITERIA.** To be eligible for the program, offenders must have been placed on probation or community control under the supervision of the Department of Corrections by a judge in the Ninth Judicial Circuit, have stable community ties, and have a stable residence in either Orange or Osceola County, Florida. Offenders who are eligible for the program include probation offenders, drug offenders, and community control supervision offenders. The program only applies to offenders who have committed certain technical violations addressed in the Alternative Sanctioning Program Violation/Sanction Matrix included in section (3) of this Order. The threat an offender poses to public safety is the most important factor in determining eligibility. Offenders with a lengthy or violent criminal history and sex offenders, are not eligible to be in the program. Additionally, offenders who have new law violations, are absconders, or have violated a "no contact" condition of supervision are not eligible for the program. No offender who has three or more previous violations is eligible for the program.

3. **QUALIFYING TECHNICAL VIOLATIONS AND APPROVED SANCTIONS.** The following matrix lists the specific technical violations that may be addressed through the Alternative Sanctioning Program process for offenders who were sentenced in the Ninth Judicial Circuit. Each technical violation includes a list of sanctions determined and approved by the court for the probation officer to select from when reporting these technical violations, based on the individual offender's circumstances at the time of the violation.

ALTERNATIVE SANCTIONING PROGRAM VIOLATION/SANCTION MATRIX

VIOLATION	APPROVED LIST OF SANCTIONS
Condition (1): Reported late; failed to report as instructed.	1. Weekly call in for 6 weeks. 2. Twice a month reporting for 3 months. 3. Weekly reporting for 6 weeks. 4. Attend a Lifeskills/Career Readiness class as directed by DOC. 5. Thinking for Change program through DOC. 6. Participate in 3 sessions with DOC Employment Specialist.
Condition (3): Failed to report changes in residence or employment without first procuring the officer's consent (or notifying immediately if evicted from residence or laid off from job).	1. Weekly call in for 6 weeks. 2. Twice a month reporting for 3 months. 3. Weekly reporting for 6 weeks. 4. Attend a Lifeskills class as directed by DOC. 5. Thinking for Change program through DOC. 6. Participate in 3 sessions with DOC Employment Specialist.

Condition (3): Failed to request permission prior to leaving the county.	1. Weekly call in for 6 weeks. 2. Twice a month reporting for 60 days. 3. Weekly reporting for 6 weeks at discretion of PO.
Condition (6): Found to be associating with person(s) engaged in criminal activity.	1. Curfew from 8 p.m. to 6 a.m. for 90 days (can be modified by PO for treatment or work purposes). 2. Weekly call in for 6 weeks. 3. 25 hours public service work. 4. Thinking for Change class through DOC. 5. Attend a Lifeskills/Career Readiness class as directed by DOC. 6. Attend the GED program if deemed appropriate through PO. 7. Participate in 3 sessions with DOC Employment Specialist.
Condition (7): Positive drug test for non-prescribed drugs (first occurrence).	1. Drug evaluation and successfully complete treatment determined necessary. 2. Increase level of treatment program up to and including residential. 3. Curfew from 8 p.m. to 6 a.m. for 90 days (can be modified by PO for treatment or work purposes). 4. Thinking for Change class through DOC. 5. Attend a Lifeskills/Career Readiness class as directed by DOC. 6. Attend 90 days NA/AA meetings.
Condition (7): Positive drug test for non-prescribed drugs (second occurrence).	1. Drug evaluation and successfully complete treatment determined necessary. 2. Increase level of treatment program up to and including residential. 3. Curfew from 8 p.m. to 6 a.m. for 90 days (can be modified by PO for treatment or work purposes). 4. Thinking for Change class through DOC. 5. Attend a Lifeskills/Career Readiness class as directed by DOC. 6. Attend 90 days NA/AA meetings.
Condition (8): Failure to maintain employment.	1. Weekly reporting with Job Search logs until employed. 2. Daily reporting with job search logs until employed. 3. Curfew from 8 p.m. to 6 a.m. for 90 days (can be modified by PO for treatment or work purposes). 4. Attend 3 sessions with the DOC Employment Specialist. 5. Thinking for Change class through DOC. 6. Participation in the GED program through DOC. 7. Attend a Lifeskills/Career Readiness class as directed by DOC.
Condition (9): Failure to answer inquiries truthfully (depending on nature of question, response, and reason for being untruthful, consequence will vary).	1. Weekly call-in for 4 weeks. 2. 8 hours of community service work.

Condition (9): Failure to comply with officer's instructions (depending on nature of instruction and reason for not complying, consequence will vary).	1. Weekly call in for 4 weeks. 2. 8 hours Community service work. 3. Thinking for Change class through DOC. 4. Attend a Lifeskills/Career Readiness class as directed by DOC. 5. If employment related, participate in three sessions with DOC Employment Specialist.
Condition (10): Failure to pay restitution or court costs.	1. If unemployed-daily job search. 2. If employed-monthly budgeting. 3. Curfew from 8 p.m. to 6 a.m. (can be modified by PO for treatment or work purposes). 4. Weekly call in until monetary obligations are current. 5. Extend probation to auto term upon completion of all conditions. 6. Attend Lifeskills/Career Readiness class as directed by DOC. 7. Attend and participate in three sessions with DOC Employment Specialist.
Condition (11): Failure to submit to random testing as directed.	1. Weekly reporting by 11 am. 2. Reporting 3 times per week by 11 am. 3. Curfew from 8 p.m. until 6 a.m. for 90 days (can be modified by PO for treatment or work purposes). 4. Attend Lifeskills/Career Readiness class as directed by DOC. 5. Substance abuse evaluation and treatment determined necessary. 6. Thinking for Change class through DOC. 7. Attend 90 NA/AA meetings.
Special Condition (1): Failure to attend treatment evaluation or treatment session as scheduled.	1. Curfew from 8 p.m. to 6 a.m. until evaluation is completed. 2. Weekly reporting until evaluation is completed. 3. Daily call in until evaluation is completed. 4. Thinking for Change class through DOC.
Special Condition (8): Failure to complete community service hours as instructed.	1. Weekly reporting until community service hours completed/current, if employed. 2. Enrollment in Thinking for Change class through DOC.
Special Condition (9): Failure to remain at residence during curfew period.	1. Weekly reporting for three months. 2. Electronic Monitoring for 30 days.
Community Control Condition (16): Failure to maintain approved schedule – unapproved absence from required location (negligence in getting home late, stopping at store on way home without permission).	1. Electronic Monitoring for 30 days. 2. 10 Hours Community Service work. 3. 20 Hours Community Service work. 4. Thinking for Change class through DOC. 5. Attend Lifeskills/Career Readiness class as directed by DOC.

4. ALTERNATIVE SANCTIONING PROGRAM PROCESS.

A. The probation or community control officer may inform offenders who have committed violations enumerated in section 3 of this Order that they may participate in the Alternative Sanctioning Program for administrative disposition of the violation. No offender is required to participate in the Alternative Sanctioning Program and may instead opt for a formal violation of probation or community control proceeding in Circuit Court. The offender's participation in the Alternative Sanctioning Program is voluntary. The offender may elect to waive or discontinue participation in the Alternative Sanctioning Program at any time before the issuance of a court order imposing the recommended sanction. If the offender elects to discontinue participation in the Alternative Sanctioning Program, the offender's prior admission to the technical violation may not be used as evidence in subsequent proceedings.

B. If the offender admits the violation, agrees to accept the administrative sanction recommended by the probation officer, and agrees to waive all their rights associated with a formal violation hearing to modify their sentence, the probation officer will prepare an "Alternative Sanctioning Program Technical Violation Notification and Offender's Waiver of Formal VOP/VOCC Hearing, Admission of Violation and Acceptance of Sanctions" (DC3–2027) form, which will provide details of the circumstances of the technical violation that occurred and the probation officer's recommended sanction, based on the sanctions listed in the approved matrix. Offenders agreeing to participate in the Alternative Sanctioning Program agree to waive the right to:

1. Be represented by legal counsel,

2. Require the state to prove their guilt before a neutral and detached hearing body,

3. Subpoena witnesses and present to a judge evidence in their defense.

4. Confront and cross-examine witnesses, and

5. Receive a written statement from a fact finder as to the evidence relied on and the reasons for the sanctions imposed.

If the offender agrees to participate in the Alternative Sanctioning Program, they will sign the second section of the DC3–2027 form titled "Offender's Waiver of Formal VOP/VOCC Hearing, Admission of Violation, and Acceptance of Sanctions," which will be submitted to the court once the probation officer and supervisor signs and dates the form.

C. The judge shall review the "Alternative Sanctioning Program Technical Violation Notification and Offender's Waiver of Formal VOP/VOCC Hearing, Admission of Violation and Acceptance of Sanctions" (DC3–2027) form submitted and, if the judge agrees that the technical violation should be addressed via the Alternative Sanctioning Program and agrees with the recommended sanction, the judge will sign the "Order—Alternative Sanctions Program." If the judge does not agree with the particular sanction recommended by the officer or does not agree that the technical violation should be addressed via the Alternative Sanctioning Program, the judge shall reflect further instructions on the order.

D. Upon court approval the probation officer will instruct the offender on the sanction imposed by the court and instruct the offender to take actions necessary to ensure the sanction is executed immediately. Failure to complete the imposed sanction as instructed will result in a violation report, affidavit and warrant being submitted to the court.

5. **ADMINISTRATION.** The Alternative Sanctioning Program shall be administered by the Ninth Judicial Circuit and the Florida Department of Corrections.

DONE AND ORDERED at Orlando, Florida, this 12th day of February, 2018.

Frederick J. Lauten
Chief Judge

2018–02. FIRST STEP, INC. OF THE NINTH JUDICIAL CIRCUIT, A NON–PROFIT CORPORATION

IN THE CIRCUIT COURT OF THE NINTH JUDICIAL CIRCUIT, IN AND FOR ORANGE AND OSCEOLA COUNTIES, FLORIDA

ADMINISTRATIVE ORDER NO. 2018–02

ADMINISTRATIVE ORDER REGARDING FIRST STEP, INC. OF THE NINTH JUDICIAL CIRCUIT, A NON–PROFIT CORPORATION

WHEREAS, pursuant to Article V, section 2(d) of the Florida Constitution and section 43.26, Florida Statutes, the chief judge of each judicial circuit is charged with the authority and the power to do everything necessary to promote the prompt and efficient administration of justice; and

WHEREAS, pursuant to the chief judge's constitutional and statutory responsibility for administrative supervision of the courts within the circuit and to create and maintain an organization capable of effecting the efficient, prompt, and proper administration of justice for the citizens of this State, the chief judge is required to exercise direction, *see* Fla. R. Jud. Admin. 2.215(b)(2), (b)(3); and

WHEREAS, First Step, Inc., a non-profit corporation, has been created and established in the Ninth Judicial Circuit; and

WHEREAS, the primary purpose of such corporation is to assist in the rehabilitation of persons placed on supervised probation within the jurisdiction of the Ninth Judicial Circuit by providing to such persons ancillary services such as, but not limited to, employment, counseling, education, training, and related services, assistance and opportunities; and

WHEREAS, section 948.039(2), Florida Statutes, provides that court determined conditions of probation or community control may include that the offender or probationer in community control "[p]ay not more than $1 per month during the term of probation or community control to a nonprofit organization established for the sole purpose of supplementing the rehabilitative efforts of the Department of Corrections;" and

WHEREAS, section 948.039, Florida Statutes, mandates that trial courts impose special conditions of probation by oral pronouncement and written order. Such special conditions include requirements that the offender "[p]ay not more than $1 per month during the term of probation or community control to a nonprofit organization established for the sole purpose of supplementing the rehabilitative efforts of the Department of Corrections;" and

WHEREAS, in *Velez–Pizzini v. State*, 58 So. 3d 278 (Fla. 5th DCA 2011), the Fifth District Court of Appeal found that First Step of the Fifth Judicial Circuit, Inc. is not only a program as contemplated by section 948.039, Florida Statutes, but also that the costs associated with the program may only be imposed if orally pronounced;

NOW, THEREFORE, I, Frederick J. Lauten, in order to facilitate the efficient operation of the administration of justice, and pursuant to the authority vested in me as Chief Judge of the Ninth Judicial Circuit of Florida under Florida Rule of Judicial Administration 2.215, hereby order that, **effective immediately** unless otherwise provided herein, to continue until further order, and superseding any provisions in prior Administrative Orders which may be inconsistent:

1. Each defendant within the Ninth Judicial Circuit sentenced to a term of probation or community control supervision with the Department of Corrections may be ordered to pay the sum of one dollar ($1.00) per month for each month of supervision. The amount due, up to the first $36.00, shall be paid within ninety (90) days after the beginning of the probationary sentence. Further payments, if any, shall be paid in accordance with a schedule to be established by the probation officer, if the offender agrees, or by the court.

2. If the court determines any special terms and conditions of probation or community control, the court shall impose the special terms and conditions by oral pronouncement at sentencing and include the terms and conditions in the written sentencing order.

3. Monies collected pursuant to this Order shall be used for the benefit of those individuals under the supervision of the Department of Corrections, or recently released from the custody of the Department of Corrections, as set forth in the bylaws of First Step Corporation of the Ninth Judicial Circuit. First Step shall also provide assistance to offenders released from the Department of Corrections, who are not on probation or community control, but who return to the Ninth Judicial Circuit.

4. No monies collected pursuant to this Order shall be used for costs of supervision, court costs, fines, or any other court ordered payments, including Collections Court.

DONE AND ORDERED at Orlando, Florida, this 5th day of February, 2018.

Frederick J. Lauten
Chief Judge

2017–22. APPOINTMENT AND PAYMENT OF COURT APPOINTED MENTAL HEALTH EXPERTS

IN THE CIRCUIT COURT OF THE NINTH JUDICIAL CIRCUIT, IN AND FOR ORANGE AND OSCEOLA COUNTIES, FLORIDA

ADMINISTRATIVE ORDER NO. 2017–22

ADMINISTRATIVE ORDER GOVERNING APPOINTMENT AND PAYMENT OF COURT APPOINTED MENTAL HEALTH EXPERTS

Pursuant to Administrative Order AOSC17–12 issued by the Supreme Court of Florida, each Circuit is directed to implement a statewide rate structure for the payment of specific categories of expert witnesses and to adopt general standards and best practices, if possible, to encourage uniformity across the state.

THEREFORE, IT IS ORDERED:

1. General Provisions:

a. *Types of Evaluations:* This Order governs appointment of experts who are paid by the Court. Generally, Court paid evaluations include:

1. Criminal competency (§ 916.115, Fla. Stat.)

2. Criminal competency—intellectual disabilities or autism (§ 916.301, Fla. Stat.)

3. Juvenile competency (§ 985.19, Fla. Stat.)

4. Juvenile competency—intellectual disabilities or autism (§ 985.19, Fla. Stat.)

5. Guardianship examining committees (§ 744.331, Fla. Stat.)

6. Developmental Disability Examining Committees (§ 393.11, Fla. Stat.)

7. Criminal Case—Determination of Intellectual Disability as a Bar to Execution (Fla. R. Crim. P. 3.203)

8. Extraordinary evaluations not dealing with competency and not listed above.

b. *Evaluations/Services For Which Court Will Not Pay:* The Court does not pay for sanity evaluations or competency restoration services. The Court does not pay experts who are privately retained by the State Attorney, Public Defender, Office of Criminal Conflict and Civil Regional Counsel, conflict counsel, private counsel, or any other person or entity. If a court order designating experts to examine a defendant for sanity purposes is required for payment purposes, the order must be separate from any order appointing experts for competency evaluations. The Court does not pay for an expert's time for a deposition or conference with the attorneys. The Court does not pay fees to an expert who is an employee of a government agency; that expert will be paid by his/her employer.

c. *Standard Orders Required:* In cases involving a competency evaluation, except guardianship cases, the moving party must prepare the proposed order appointing the expert(s) and must use the appropriate standardized competency order posted on the Circuit's website. The standardized orders are: Form A—criminal cases; Form B—criminal cases in which a defendant is alleged to be incompetent due to intellectual disabilities or autism; Form C—juvenile cases; Form D—juvenile cases in which a child is alleged to have intellectual disabilities or autism; Form E—appointment of a second expert in criminal competency—requesting party pays for expert. **In all certificates of service, the expert(s) and Court Administration's Expert Witness Payments Department must be included. To send the order by email, use: ctadhw1@ocnjcc.org. To send a copy of the order by mail, send to: Court Administration, Expert Witness Payments, Suite 2130, 425 North Orange Avenue, Orlando, Florida 32801.**

d. *Non-Standard Orders:* On those infrequent occasions in which the standard payment rate is insufficient or there is a need for a type of evaluation not specifically encompassed in this Administrative Order, an order appointing an expert who is to be paid by the Court, must include the payment amount and an explanation why it is necessary to exceed the standard fee. The presiding Judge must first obtain approval from the Administrative Judge or the Chief Judge to pay more than the standard fee. The order must specifically state that the evaluation/services and the amount were preapproved by either the Administrative Judge or the Chief Judge. **In all certificates of service, the expert(s) and Court Administration's Expert Witness Payments Department must be included. To send the order by email, use: ctadhw1@ocnjcc.org. To send a copy of the order by mail, send to: Court Administration, Expert Witness Payments, Suite 2130, 425 North Orange Avenue, Orlando, Florida 32801.**

e. *Expert Witness Registries:*

1. The Judge must select the expert(s) from the Circuit's expert witness registry unless paragraph 2 below is applicable. The Circuit will maintain a registry of expert witnesses on its website for each type of evaluation. Expert witness's curriculum vitae will be kept on file with Court Administration.

2. If an appropriate expert witness is not available in this Circuit, then, if possible, an expert must be selected from another Circuit's registry. If the person to be examined is located outside the areas where this Circuit's experts are located, then the Judge must use an expert from the registry of the Circuit in which the person resides. In these situations, the Court will pay the standard rate established by the Circuit in which the expert is located. The appointment order must specifically state that rate. For example, if a defendant is incarcerated in a correctional facility located in the Eighth Circuit and cannot be brought to the Ninth Circuit for evaluation, an expert from the Eighth Circuit's registry must be appointed. These procedures must be

preapproved by the Administrative Judge or the Chief Judge and the order of appointment must state that the appointment and fee were preapproved by either the Administrative Judge or the Chief Judge. In all orders under this section, the **certificates of service must include the expert(s) and Court Administration's Expert Witness Payments Department. To send the order by email, use: ctadhw1@ocnjcc.org. To send a copy of the order by mail, send to: Court Administration, Expert Witness Payments, Suite 2130, 425 North Orange Avenue, Orlando, Florida 32801.**

f. *Fees When Multiple Cases Involved:* All fees are based on per person and not per case. For example, if a defendant has three different cases and an expert is appointed to evaluate the defendant in all three cases, the expert will be paid a single fee and not three separate fees. The Judges must attempt to appoint the same expert across multiple cases and attempt to use an evaluation in another case if relatively close in time to the current case. If a subsequent evaluation is required for any reason, whenever possible the Judge should appoint an expert who previously evaluated the person.

g. *Flat Fee Payments and Reports:* All flat fee payments for evaluations include travel time, review of all documents, preparation time, actual evaluation, preparation of the written report, and the timely submission of a written report to the Court.

h. *Committee:* A committee, whose members will be appointed by the Chief Judge, will be created to address complaints and grievances regarding experts on the Court's registry. The committee chair and members will be posted on the Circuit's Expert Witness webpage, along with the procedures necessary to intake and process any complaints or grievances.

2. Criminal Competency (No Suggestion of Intellectual Disability or Autism) (Section 916.115, Florida Statutes):

a. *Only one expert may be initially appointed.*

1. Initial Finding—Defendant is Competent: If the expert determines the defendant is competent to stand trial and either party requests a second opinion, **the requesting party must pay for the second expert**. If the second expert determines the defendant is incompetent to proceed, the Judge may either hold a hearing to determine competency based on the two experts' opinions, or the Judge may select a third expert who will be paid by the Court. Any no shows or follow-up evaluations involving the second expert must be paid by the requesting party.

2. Initial Finding—Defendant is Incompetent: If the expert determines the defendant is incompetent to stand trial, and a party disputes the expert's findings, the Judge will either reject the dispute and act accordingly, or may select a second expert. If the second expert determines the defendant is competent to proceed, the Judge may either hold a hearing to determine competency based on the two experts' opinions, or the Judge may select a third expert. These experts will be paid by the Court.

b. In order for an expert to be paid for services rendered, the expert must file a written report with the Judge that explicitly addresses each of the factors listed in the order of appointment.

c. Experts appointed under this provision must be either a Florida licensed psychiatrist, psychologist, or physician, satisfactorily complete the approved training as an expert by the Department of Children and Family Services, have a least five years of experience in this area of expertise, and maintain a business office in Orange, Osceola, Lake, Brevard, Seminole, or Polk Counties.

d. The Court customarily does not pay experts for their time while testifying. In those rare instances when the Judge specifically orders the expert to testify, and preapproval is obtained from the Administrative Judge or the Chief Judge, the Court will pay for the expert's time while testifying; however, for payment purposes, the Judge must enter an order directing the expert to testify indicating it is the Court's intent the expert testify. This order must be preapproved by the Administrative Judge or Chief Judge. Payment for testimony is limited to a two hour maximum and includes travel time, preparation time, waiting to testify, and the actual testimony. The expert must attach a copy of the order to the invoice.

e. *Payment Rates:*

Initial Evaluation	$400.00
Follow-up Evaluations—Same defendant/Same expert	$200.00
No Show (40% of the evaluation rate—only two no shows allowed per defendant)	$160.00/$80.00
In–Court Testimony (in rare cases required by Judge)	$150.00 per hour
—2 hour maximum including wait time	

3. Criminal Competency—Suggestion of Intellectual Disability or Autism (Section 916.301, Florida Statutes):

a. The Court should appoint one, or at the request of any party, two experts from the appropriate Circuit registry and appoint the Agency for Persons with Disabilities which will then select a qualified psychologist.

b. In order for an expert to be paid for services rendered, the expert must file a written report with the Judge that explicitly addresses each of the factors listed in the order of appointment.

c. Experts appointed under this provision must be either a Florida licensed psychiatrist, psychologist, or physician, qualified by the Agency for Persons with Disabilities to perform evaluations of persons with intellectual disabilities and autism, have a least five years of experience in this area of expertise, and maintain a business office in Orange, Osceola, Lake, Brevard, Seminole or Polk Counties.

d. The Court customarily does not pay experts for their time while testifying. In those rare instances when the Judge specifically orders the expert to testify, and preapproval is obtained from the Administrative Judge or the Chief Judge, the Court will pay for the expert's time while testifying; however, for payment purposes, the Judge must enter an order directing the expert to testify indicating it is the Court's intent the expert testify. This order must be preapproved by the Administrative Judge or Chief Judge. Payment for testimony is limited to a two hour maximum and includes travel time, preparation time, waiting to testify, and the actual testimony. The expert must attach a copy of the order to the invoice.

e. *Payment Rates:*

Initial Evaluation	$750.00
All Follow-up Evaluations—Same defendant/Same expert	$200.00
No Show (only two no shows paid per defendant)	$140.00
In–Court Testimony (in rare cases required by Judge)	$150.00 per hour
—2 hour maximum including wait time	

4. Juvenile Competency (No Suggestion of Intellectual Disability or Autism) (Section 985.19, Florida Statutes):

a. The Court should appoint at least two but no more than three experts from the appropriate registry. Judges are encouraged to initially appoint only two experts.

b. In order for an expert to be paid for services rendered, the expert must file a written report with the Judge that explicitly addresses each of the factors listed in the order of appointment.

c. Experts appointed under this provision must be either a Florida licensed psychiatrist, psychologist, or physician, satisfactorily complete the approved training as an expert by the Department of Children and Family Services, have a least five years of experience in this area of expertise, and maintain a business office in Orange, Osceola, Lake, Brevard, Seminole or Polk Counties.

d. The Court customarily does not pay experts for their time while testifying. In those rare instances when the Judge specifically orders the expert to testify, and preapproval is obtained from the Administrative Judge or the Chief Judge, the Court will pay for the expert's time while testifying; however, for payment purposes, the Judge must enter an order directing the expert to testify indicating it is the Court's intent the expert testify. This order must be preapproved by the Administrative Judge or Chief Judge. Payment for testimony is limited to a two hour maximum and includes travel time, preparation time, waiting to testify, and the actual testimony. The expert must attach a copy of the order to the invoice.

e. *Payment Rates:*

Initial Evaluation	$350.00
All Follow-up Evaluations—Same juvenile/Same expert	$200.00
No Show (40% of the evaluation rate—only two no shows allowed per juvenile)	$140.00/$80.00
In–Court Testimony (in rare cases required by Judge)	$150.00 per hour
—2 hour maximum including wait time	

5. Juvenile Competency—Suggestion of Intellectual Disability or Autism (Section 985.19, Florida Statutes):

a. The Court should appoint the Agency for Persons with Disabilities to examine the child.

b. In order for an expert to be paid for services rendered, the expert must file a written report with the Judge that explicitly addresses each of the factors listed in the order of appointment.

c. The Court customarily does not pay experts for their time while testifying. In those rare instances when the Judge specifically orders the expert to testify, and preapproval is obtained from the Administrative Judge or the Chief Judge, the Court will pay for the expert's time while testifying; however, for payment purposes, the Judge must enter an order directing the expert to testify indicating it is the Court's intent the expert testify. This order must be preapproved by the Administrative Judge or Chief Judge. Payment for testimony is limited to a two hour maximum and includes travel time, preparation time, waiting to testify, and the actual testimony. The expert must attach a copy of the order to the invoice.

d. *Payment Rates:*

Initial Evaluation	$750.00
All Follow-up Evaluations—Same juvenile/Same expert	$200.00
No Show (only two no shows paid per juvenile)	$140.00
In–Court Testimony (in rare cases required by Judge)	$150.00 per hour
—2 hour maximum including wait time	

6. Guardianship Examining Committee (Section 744.331, Florida Statutes):

a. The Court will pay the Examining Committee members only if the Ward is indigent as determined by the Court.

b. Three members are to be appointed by the Court but selected by the Clerk of Court from the appropriate list maintained on the Court's website. One must be a psychiatrist or a physician while the other two must be either a psychologist, gerontologist, psychiatrist, physician, registered nurse, nurse practitioner, licensed social worker, person with an advanced degree in gerontology from an accredited college or university, or other person who by knowledge, skill, experience, training, or education, may, in the Court's discretion, advise the Court in the form of an expert opinion. The members must also have at least five years of experience in area of expertise, four hours of initial training and two hours of continuing education during each 2–year period after the initial training. Initial training may be waived by the Chief Judge. A member must maintain either a business office or residence in Orange, Osceola, Lake, Brevard, Seminole or Polk Counties.

c. In order for an expert to be paid for services rendered, the expert must file a written report with the Judge.

d. *Payment Rates:*

M.D., D.O., Ph.D	$300.00
ARNP, RN, MSW, LPN, LCSW, Lay Person	$120.00

7. Developmental Disability Examining Committee (Section 393.11, Florida Statutes):

a. Experts appointed for this Committee must have expertise in the diagnosis, evaluation, and treatment of persons who have intellectual disabilities or autism.

b. The Committee must include at least one licensed and qualified physician, one licensed and qualified psychologist, and one qualified professional who, at a minimum, has a master's degree in social work, special education, or vocational rehabilitation counseling.

c. In order for an expert to be paid for services rendered, the expert must file a written report with the Judge that explicitly addresses each of the factors listed in the order of appointment.

d. Experts must have at least five years of experience in area of expertise and must maintain a business office or residence in Orange, Osceola, Lake, Brevard, Seminole or Polk Counties.

e. *Payment Rates:*

M.D., D.O., Ph.D	$300.00
ARNP, RN, MSW, LPN, LCSW, Lay Person	$200.00

8. Criminal Cases—Determination of Intellectual Disability as a Bar to Execution (Rule 3.203 of the Florida Rules of Criminal Procedure):

a. Experts appointed under this provision must be a Florida licensed psychiatrist, psychologist, or physician, qualified by the Agency for Persons with Disabilities to perform evaluations of persons with intellectual disabilities and autism, and have at least 5 years of experience in this area of expertise.

b. In order for an expert to be paid for services rendered, the expert must file a written report with the Judge that explicitly addresses each of the factors listed in the order of appointment unless specifically waived by the Judge.

c. The Court customarily does not pay experts for their time while testifying. In those rare instances when the Judge specifically orders the expert to testify, and preapproval is obtained from the Administrative Judge or the Chief Judge, the Court will pay for the expert's time while testifying; however, for payment purposes, the Judge must enter an order directing the expert to testify indicating it is the Court's intent the expert testify. This order must be preapproved by the Administrative Judge or Chief Judge. Payment for testimony is limited to a two hour maximum and includes travel time, preparation time, waiting to testify, and the actual testimony. The expert must attach a copy of the order to the invoice.

d. *Payment Rates:*

Evaluation	$750.00
Travel time, if necessary, to and from Florida State Prison or Union Correctional Institution	$50.00 per hour maximum of 6 hours
In-Court Testimony (in rare cases required by Judge)	$150.00 per hour
—2 hour maximum including wait time	

9. Extraordinary Evaluations (Not Competency) Including Capital Murder and First-Degree Murder Cases Not Listed Above:

a. Mental health experts required for evaluations not addressed above will be paid at the rate of $160.00 per hour up to a maximum of five (5) hours for services including preparation, evaluation, and submission of a timely written report. All orders for evaluations under this paragraph must be preapproved by the Administrative Judge. The order appointing an expert under this provision must state that preapproval was obtained from the Administrative Judge and specifically state what services the expert is to perform.

b. In order for an expert to be paid for services rendered, the expert must file a written report with the Judge that explicitly addresses each of the factors listed in the order of appointment.

c. The Court customarily does not pay experts for their time while testifying. In those rare instances when the Judge specifically orders the expert to testify, and preapproval is obtained from the Administrative Judge or the Chief Judge, the Court will pay for the expert's time while testifying; however, for payment purposes, the Judge must enter an order directing the expert to testify indicating it is the Court's intent the expert testify. This order must be preapproved by the Administrative Judge or Chief Judge. Payment for testimony is limited to a two hour maximum and includes travel time, preparation time, waiting to testify, and the actual testimony. The expert must attach a copy of the order to the invoice.

10. Expert's Invoices: Experts must abide by the *Billing Manual for Experts Seeking Compensation From The Court* issued by Court Administration and by any contract they sign. The *Billing Manual* will be maintained on the Court's website. Experts must submit a Uniform Invoice for Expert Witness Services as developed by the Office of the State Courts Administrator, along with a copy of the appointment order. The order must state with specificity the amount to be paid to the expert. If the invoice is for services not paid by a standard flat fee, the invoice must be descriptive and include identifying details with enough information for a meaningful audit by Court Administration. The expert must specifically identify the names of tests, examinations, evaluations, documents reviewed, and must itemize the time spent performing each task. Generic descriptions are insufficient.

All invoices must be submitted within thirty days after the completion of the services provided or compensation may be denied. Invoices must be submitted to Court Administration, Expert Witness Payments, Suite 2130, 425 North Orange Avenue, Orlando, Florida, 32801.

11. Previous Administrative Orders Superseded: Any provisions in other active Administrative Orders that may be inconsistent with this Administrative Order are superseded and this Administrative Order shall control.

12. Effective Date: This Administrative Order is effective October 1, 2017. New payment rates and new procedures apply only to orders entered on or after October 1, 2017.

DONE AND ORDERED at Orlando, Florida, this 15th day of September, 2017.

Frederick J. Lauten
Chief Judge

2017-20. [VACATED BY ORDER 2018-26, EFFECTIVE NOVEMBER 15, 2018]

2017-10-01. AMENDED ORDER GOVERNING UNIFIED FAMILY COURT, ORANGE COUNTY

ADMINISTRATIVE ORDER NO. 2017-10-01

IN THE CIRCUIT COURT OF THE NINTH JUDICIAL CIRCUIT, IN AND FOR ORANGE COUNTY, FLORIDA

UNIFIED FAMILY COURT, ORANGE COUNTY

WHEREAS, pursuant to Article V, section 2(d) of the Florida Constitution and section 43.26, Florida Statutes, the chief judge of each judicial circuit is charged with the authority and the power to do everything necessary to promote the prompt and efficient administration of justice; and

WHEREAS, pursuant to the chief judge's constitutional and statutory responsibility for administrative supervision of the courts within the circuit and to create and maintain an organization capable of effecting the efficient, prompt, and proper administration of justice for the citizens of this State, the chief judge is required to exercise direction, *see* Fla. R. Jud. Admin. 2.215(b)(2), (b)(3); and

WHEREAS, the Florida Supreme Court, in *In re Report of the Family Court Steering Committee*, 794 So. 2d 518 (Fla. 2001), endorsed the guiding principles and characteristics of the model family court developed by the Family Court Steering Committee and reaffirmed its goal of the creation of a fully integrated, comprehensive approach to handling all cases involving children and families; and

WHEREAS, the Florida Supreme Court, in *In re Amendments to the Florida Rules of Judicial Administration and In re Florida Family Law Rules of Procedure*, 132 So. 3d 1114 (Fla. 2014), adopted proposed amendments of the Steering Committee providing for case management of open related family cases through the filing of a Notice of Related Cases, for all related family cases involving the same family and/or children to be handled before one judge ("one family, one judge"), for a more formal manner of coordination of related cases and hearings, and for the access and review of related family files by the judiciary and parties; and

WHEREAS, the Ninth Judicial Circuit Court supports the goal of ensuring that cases involving families and children are managed in an efficient manner that serves the best interests of the parties; and

WHEREAS, the policies and procedures outlined herein are meant to provide the greatest degree of flexibility to effectuate efficient and proper procedures for the Ninth Judicial Circuit Court, consequently, this Court shall continue to periodically review and revise family court procedure and process in an effort to achieve the ultimate goal of creating a fully integrated, comprehensive and coordinated approach to handling all cases involving families and children as fully as possible given limitations and abilities;

NOW, THEREFORE, I, Frederick J. Lauten, in order to facilitate the efficient operation of the administration of justice, and pursuant to the authority vested in me as Chief Judge of the Ninth Judicial Circuit of Florida under Florida Rule of Judicial Administration 2.215, hereby order the following, **effective immediately**, to continue until further order and superseding any provisions in prior Administrative Orders which may be inconsistent:

I. Related Cases.

A. Pursuant to Florida Rule of Judicial Administration 2.545(d)(1)(A)—(D), a family case is related when:

1. it involves any of the same parties, children, or issues and it is pending at the time the party files a family case; or

2. it affects the court's jurisdiction to proceed; or

3. an order in the related case may conflict with an order on the same issues in the new case; or

4. an order in the new case may conflict with an order in the earlier litigation.

For purposes of this Administrative Order, a Related Case is defined as two or more cases pending in the Domestic Relations and/or Domestic Violence Divisions which involve any of the same parties, children, or fact issues. Related Cases involving the same family will be handled before one judge so that the cases will be coordinated, heard, and determined in a manner that will minimize the number of times and places that a family has to appear in court and will minimize the possibility of conflicting determinations in related cases.

B. The following types of Related Cases are included in the Unified Family Court Division:

1) dissolution of marriage

2) division and distribution of property arising out of a dissolution of marriage

3) annulment

4) support unconnected with dissolution of marriage

5) paternity, including, but not limited to, disestablishment of paternity

6) child support

7) Uniform Reciprocal Enforcement of Support Act/ Uniform Interstate Family Support Act (URESA/UIFSA)

8) custodial care of and access to children, including, but not limited to, temporary or concurrent custody of minor children by extended family

9) adoption

10) name change

11) declaratory judgment actions related to premarital, marital, or post marital agreements

12) civil domestic, repeat, dating, stalking and sexual violence injunctions

13) relocation of minor children

14) modification and enforcement of orders entered in these cases

C. For purposes of this Administrative Order, a Magnet Case is the domestic case that determines to which subdivision all Related Cases will be assigned.

1. If there is an active final civil domestic injunction of any length issued, or an active temporary civil domestic injunction six (6) months or longer in duration issued, all Related Cases must be assigned to the domestic violence subdivision to which the injunction is assigned.

2. If there is either an inactive civil domestic injunction of any length or an inactive temporary civil domestic injunction that was issued for six (6) months or longer in duration then, for a period of one (1) year after the termination of the injunction, all Related Cases must be assigned to the domestic violence subdivision to which the injunction is assigned.

3. If there is no civil domestic injunction, then the case which has had record activity within the past year will be the Magnet Case and will determine to which subdivision the Related Cases will be assigned.

4. A Department of Revenue case will not be a Magnet Case.

II. Identification—Related Cases will be identified by.

A. *Notice of Related Cases.* In accordance with Florida Rule of Judicial Administration 2.545(d)(4), a fully completed Notice of Related Cases, in the form attached hereto as "Attachment A," must be filed with the initial pleading by the filing attorney or self-represented petitioner in each of the Related Cases that are currently open and pending with the court and served on all other parties in each of the Related Cases. Parties may file joint notices. To the extent that any issues of confidentiality apply, all legal requirements must be observed, including any requirements as set forth in Florida Rule of Judicial Administration 2.420. Parties must file supplemental notices as Related Cases become known or reasonably ascertainable.

B. *Notice of Social Security Number.* In each case listed in section I. B. above, the parties must file a Notice of Social Security Number, Florida Supreme Court Approved Family Law Form 12.902(j). The Petitioner must file the Notice of Social Security Number with the initial pleading and serve it on all parties. A Respondent must file the Notice of Social Security Number within thirty (30) days of service of the original action or the re-opened case and serve it on all parties. Parties may file a joint notice. The information in this Notice will assist the Family Court Case Management (FCCM) Department and the Clerk of Court in identifying Related Cases upon the filing of a new case or one reopened post-judgment.

C. The FCCM Department and each Clerk of Court for the Ninth Judicial Circuit is responsible for identifying Related Cases upon the filing of a new case or one reopened post-judgment when provided with notice or court order. Each Clerk of Court is charged with the responsibility to identify overlap between related family cases and notify the FCCM Department who must complete a thorough review of the matter and related issues and prepare an Order of Reassignment and forward to the Family Court Division Administrative Judge for signature.

D. Upon identification, each Clerk's Office must enter Related Cases into the Related Case and Case Cross Reference fields in Odyssey, and link all Related Cases together in the system. Family Law Rule of Procedure 12.004(b) defines a related family case as another pending or closed family case, as that term is defined in Rule of Judicial Administration 2.545(d).

III. Reassignment/Transfer Timeframes.

A. To advance the purposes of Unified Family Court, a case may be reassigned by the appropriate Administrative Judge or designee.

B. Until such time as a Related Case is officially transferred to the subdivision where the Magnet Case is assigned, the designated subdivision judge will continue to hear all matters in that case to ensure compliance with all state and federal statutes, rules, and regulations.

C. If the transfer of a case occurs in error, the case will be reassigned/transferred back to the appropriate subdivision.

IV. Resources.

A. Pursuant to Family Law Rule of Procedure 12.006, each Clerk of Court for the Ninth Judicial Circuit will ensure that copies of court orders are filed in related family cases involving the same parties. The Clerk must record all relevant case numbers on the orders and a separate copy must be placed in each related case file.

B. A judge hearing a family case is authorized, pursuant to Family Law Rule of Procedure 12.004(a), to access and review the files of any related case, including but not limited to the types of Related Cases listed in section I. B. of this Administrative Order as well as juvenile dependency, termination of parental rights, juvenile delinquency, emancipation of a minor, Children in Need of Services/ Families in Need of Services (CINS/FINS) and truancy cases, whether pending or closed.

C. Each Clerk of Court for the Ninth Judicial Circuit is directed to link related family cases, including but not limited to the types of Related Cases listed in section I. B. of this Administrative Order as well as juvenile dependency, termination of parental rights, juvenile delinquency, emancipation of a minor, Children in Need of Services/ Families in Need of Services (CINS/FINS) and truancy cases in their respective case maintenance systems to advance the implementation of this rule.

V. Interdivisional Cooperation.

A. In order to advance the purposes and goals of Unified Family Court, Family Court Division and Juvenile Division Judges must consult and coordinate with each other so no inconsistent rulings are entered, to ensure certainty for families appearing in the courts, and to minimize the number of appearances families must make in court.

B. All Divisions in the Ninth Judicial Circuit must work cooperatively together to ensure that multiple judicial determinations concerning a single family do not conflict with one another.

VI. Periodic Evaluation of Unified Family Court.

A. The Family Court Division will be evaluated by the Chief Judge, or his/her designee(s), to determine its effectiveness in implementing this Circuit's goal of addressing family law matters in a comprehensive, coordinated manner.

VII. Vacating Administrative Order.

A. This Order takes precedence over all conflicting provisions contained in any prior administrative orders. All conflicting provisions in any prior administrative order are hereby vacated while the remainder of any such administrative order will remain in full force and effect.

B. Administrative Orders 2014–09–01, 2000–2–2 and 2017–10 are vacated and set aside except to the extent that each has been incorporated and/or amended herein. Vacating an Administrative Order that vacates a prior Order does not revive the prior Order.

DONE AND ORDERED at Orlando, Florida, this 5th day of February, 2018.

Frederick J. Lauten
Chief Judge

Attachment "A"

NINTH JUDICIAL CIRCUIT COURT FOR ORANGE AND OSCEOLA COUNTIES, FLORIDA

UNIFIED FAMILY COURT DIVISION

INSTRUCTIONS FOR FILING NOTICE OF RELATED CASES

When should this form be used?

Florida Rule of Judicial Administration 2.545(d) requires the **petitioner** in a **family law case** to file with the court a **Notice of Related Cases**. The Notice of Related Cases form is used to provide the required notice to the court. The Notice of

Related Cases is required even if the case is uncontested and/or even if there are no related cases. The Notice of Related Cases must be filed with the initial pleading and served on the other parties in the **related cases**.

What is a family law case?

A family law case is any case in the circuit that is assigned to the family law division. Family Court is comprised of many different case types as listed in the Rules of Judicial Administration, Rule 2.454. See list below.

Family law cases include:

- UIFSA
- truancy
- adoption
- paternity
- annulment
- CINS/FINS
- child support
- name change
- juvenile dependency
- juvenile delinquency
- dissolution of marriage
- emancipation of a minor
- termination of parental rights
- temporary custody by extended family
- custodial care of and access to children
- support unconnected with dissolution of marriage
- modification and enforcement of orders entered in these cases
- declaratory judgment actions related to premarital, marital, or post-marital agreements, and
- civil domestic violence, repeat violence, dating violence, and sexual violence injunctions.

What is a related case?

A case is "related" to the family law case if it involves any of the same parties, children, or issues and it is pending at the time the party files a family case. A related case may be a separate open or closed civil, criminal, guardianship, domestic violence, juvenile delinquency, juvenile dependency, or domestic relations case. A case is considered related if the case:

- involves any of the same parties, children, or issues and it is pending at the time the party files a family case; or
- affects the court's jurisdiction to proceed; or
- an order in the related case may conflict with an order on the same issues in the new case; or
- an order in the new case may conflict with an order in the earlier case.

What should I do next?

Before you complete the required Notice of Related Cases form you must make a reasonable effort to determine if any related cases exist from your own records/recollection and from public records that may be available in the clerk's office or by web search.

The parties involved in the case have a continuing duty to inform the court of any proceedings in this or any other state that could affect the current proceedings.

The Notice of Related Cases form should be typed or printed in black ink. After completing the form, you should file the original with the Clerk of the Circuit Court in the county where your case is filed and keep a copy for your records. A copy of this form must be mailed, e-mailed or hand-delivered to any other party in your case and must be in accordance with Florida Rule of Judicial Administration 2.516.

Special Notes:

Please note that when completing the Notice of Related Cases Form you will need to provide your address: **However, if you fear that disclosing your address would put you in danger because you are the victim of sexual battery, aggravated child abuse, stalking, aggravated stalking, harassment, aggravated battery, or domestic violence, you should write "Confidential" where your address is requested and file a Supreme Court Approved Family Law Form 12.980(h), Request for Confidential Filing of Address, along with your Notice of Related Cases Form.**

For additional information:

You should read the "General Information for Self–Represented Litigants" found at the beginning of the Family Law Forms in the Florida Rules of Court, Family Law Rules, http://www.flcourts.org. Also, you may read the instructions for Florida Supreme Court Approved Family Law Form 12.980(h). You may also refer to Florida Rule of Judicial Administration 2.545(d) and 2.516.

IN THE CIRCUIT COURT OF THE NINTH JUDICIAL CIRCUIT IN AND FOR ORANGE AND OSCEOLA COUNTIES

IN RE: CASE NO.: ______
DIVISION: ______

______,
Petitioner,
And
______,
Respondent.

NOTICE OF RELATED CASES

Petitioner submits this Notice of Related Cases as required by Florida Rule of Judicial Administration 2.545(d). A related case may be an open or closed civil, criminal, guardianship, domestic violence, juvenile delinquency, juvenile dependency, or domestic relations case. A case is "related" to this family law case if it involves any of the same parties, children, or issues and it is pending at the time the party files a family case; if it affects the court's jurisdiction to proceed; if an order in the related case may conflict with an order on the same issues in the new case; or if an order in the new case may conflict with an order in the earlier litigation.

I. OTHER CASES INVOLVING THE PARTIES/CHILDREN: [check one only]

☐ To the best of my knowledge, I hereby certify that there are no "other cases" involving any of the above named parties or their child(ren).

☐ The following are the related cases involving any of the above named parties or their child(ren). Attach additional pages if necessary.

RELATED CASES OF ANY OF THE ABOVE PARTIES OR THEIR CHILD(REN)

RELATED CASE NO 1.

Name of the other case: ______
(Example: Jane Doe v. John Doe; In the Interest of:; State v. John Doe, etc.,)

Type of Case: ______
(Please refer to "What is a Family Law Case?" and/or "What is a related Case?" on the instructions for reference/guidance)

Case Number: ______ Judge: ______

Where was it filed? ______ Date of filing: ______

Is the Case: __ Over (closed) __ Still going on (open)

RELATED CASE NO 2.

Name of the other case: ______
(Example: Jane Doe v. John Doe; In the Interest of:; State v. John Doe, etc.,)

Type of Case: ______
(Please refer to "What is a Family Law Case?" and/or "What is a related Case?" on the instructions for reference/guidance)

Case Number: ______ Judge: ______

Where was it filed? ______ Date of filing: ______

Is the Case: __ Over (closed) __ Still going on (open)

RELATED CASE NO 3.

Name of the other case: ______
(Example: Jane Doe v. John Doe; In the Interest of:; State v. John Doe, etc.,)

Type of Case: ______
(Please refer to "What is a Family Law Case?" and/or "What is a related Case?" on the instructions for reference/guidance)

Case Number: ______ Judge: ______

Where was it filed? ______ Date of filing: ______

Is the Case: __ Over (closed) __ Still going on (open)

RELATED CASE NO 4.

Name of the other case: ______
(Example: Jane Doe v. John Doe; In the Interest of:; State v. John Doe, etc.,)

Type of Case: ______
(Please refer to "What is a Family Law Case?" and/or "What is a related Case?" on the instructions for reference/guidance)

Case Number: ______ Judge: ______

Where was it filed? ______ Date of filing: ______

Is the Case: __ Over (closed) __ Still going on (open)

II. **RELATIONSHIP BETWEEN CASES [check *all* that apply]**

☐ pending case(s) involves same parties, children, or issues;
☐ may affect court's jurisdiction;
☐ order in related case(s) may conflict with an order in this case;
☐ order in the case(s) may conflict with previous order in related case.

III. **COORDINATION OF CASES [check only *one*]**

☐ I **do not** request coordination of litigation in any of the cases listed above.
☐ I **do** request coordination of the following cases:
______
______

and request that the cases listed in Section III: [check ***all*** that apply]
☐ Be assigned to one judge.
☐ Coordination of existing cases will conserve judicial resources and promote an efficient determination of these cases because: ______
______

IV. **ACKNOWLEDGEMENT**

The Petitioner acknowledges a continuing duty to inform the court of any cases in this or any other state that could affect the current proceeding.

______ ______
Date Signature or Petitioner/Attorney for Petitioner

Print Name: ______
Address: ______
City, State, Zip: ______
Telephone Number: ______
Fax Number: ______
E-mail address: ______
Florida Bar Number: ______

CERTIFICATE OF SERVICE

I HEREBY CERTIFY that I delivered a copy of this Notice of Related Cases to the County Sheriff's Department or a certified process server for service on the Respondent, and [**check all used**] ( ) e-mailed ( ) mailed ( )hand delivered, a copy to {name} ______, who is a party on the related case, {name} ______, who is the attorney for the Respondent on the related case on {date} ______.

______
Signature of Petitioner/Attorney for Petitioner
Print Name: ______
Address: ______
City, State, Zip: ______
Telephone Number: ______
Fax Number: ______
E-mail address: ______
Florida Bar Number: ______

2017–08. PRO SE LITIGANTS IN THE DOMESTIC RELATIONS DIVISION, ORANGE COUNTY

IN THE CIRCUIT COURT OF THE NINTH JUDICIAL CIRCUIT, IN AND FOR ORANGE COUNTY, FLORIDA

ADMINISTRATIVE ORDER NO. 2017–08

ORDER GOVERNING PROCEDURES FOR PRO SE LITIGANTS IN THE DOMESTIC RELATIONS DIVISION, ORANGE COUNTY

WHEREAS, pursuant to Article V, section 2(d) of the Florida Constitution and section 43.26, Florida Statutes, the chief judge of each judicial circuit is charged with the authority and the power to do everything necessary to promote the prompt and efficient administration of justice; and

WHEREAS, pursuant to the chief judge's constitutional and statutory responsibility for administrative supervision of the courts within the circuit and to create and maintain an organization capable of effecting the efficient, prompt, and proper administration of justice for the citizens of this State, the chief judge is required to exercise direction, *see* Fla. R. Jud. Admin. 2.215(b)(2), (b)(3); and

WHEREAS, the Circuit Court in Orange County is concerned with the effective and proper administration of domestic relations cases filed by pro se litigants in the Domestic Relations Division; and

WHEREAS, it has been determined that a Family Court Case Management (FCCM) Department is necessary to assist pro se litigants who file domestic relations cases in the Domestic Relations Division; and

WHEREAS, such assistance by the FCCM Department will expedite domestic relations cases filed by pro se litigants, thereby providing greater convenience to these pro se litigants;

NOW, THEREFORE, I, Frederick J. Lauten, in order to facilitate the efficient operation of the administration of justice, and pursuant to the authority vested in me as Chief Judge of the Ninth Judicial Circuit of Florida under Florida Rule of Judicial Administration 2.215, hereby order the following, **effective immediately for all pro se litigants who file a dissolution of marriage, name change, paternity, or temporary/concurrent custody by extended family member case,**

to continue until further order and superseding any provisions in prior Administrative Orders which may be inconsistent:

The following procedures are adopted for all pro se litigants filing a dissolution of marriage case, a name change case, a paternity case, or a temporary/concurrent custody by extended family member case in the Domestic Relations Division.

1. **Registering with FCCM:**

a. Prior to filing a dissolution of marriage, name change, paternity, or temporary/concurrent custody by an extended family member case in the Domestic Relations Division, all pro se litigants must register with the FCCM Department located in room 330. All registered cases must be stamped by a FCCM Department case manager prior to filing with the Clerk of Court.

b. A thorough review will be conducted by the FCCM Department to ensure accuracy and completeness of all required documents. Pursuant to this Administrative Order, family court case managers are permitted to notarize accurate and thorough Florida Supreme Court Approved Family Law forms, and "approved forms" under Florida Family Law Rule of Procedure 12.750(b)(5).

c. The FCCM Department will provide limited assistance to pro se litigants within the bounds of Florida Family Law Rule of Procedure 12.750.

2. **Scheduling of Uncontested Final Hearings:**

a. All final hearings for uncontested dissolution of marriage, name change, paternity, or temporary/concurrent custody by extended family member cases in the Domestic Relations Division, for which both litigants, or at minimum the petitioner is representing himself/herself, will be coordinated by the FCCM Department case managers.

b. Upon belief by the pro se litigant that the case is ready to be set for final hearing, the pro se litigant must notify their assigned FCCM Department case manager. Upon such notification, the case manager will review the court file prior to scheduling the final hearing.

c. All required documents must be filed with the Clerk of Court, Domestic Relations Division before any hearing will be scheduled.

3. **Referring to Mediation:**

a. All contested dissolution of marriage, paternity, and temporary/concurrent custody by extended family cases in which all litigants are representing themselves and their disagreement involves distribution of property, alimony, and/or primary parental responsibility, or visitation and/or support of the minor child(ren), must be referred to the court-annexed Dispute Resolution Services family mediation prior to setting a final hearing or trial.

b. The parties may not be referred to mediation if there is a history of domestic violence except by court order.

4. **Vacating Administrative Order:**

a. Administrative Order 07–94–53 is vacated and set aside except to the extent that it has been incorporated and/or amended herein. Vacating an Administrative Order that vacates a prior Order does not revive the prior Order.

DONE AND ORDERED at Orlando, Florida, this 16th day of August, 2017.

Frederick J. Lauten
Chief Judge

2017–07–01. PROBABLE CAUSE AFFIDAVITS

IN THE CIRCUIT COURT OF THE NINTH JUDICIAL CIRCUIT, IN AND FOR ORANGE AND OSCEOLA COUNTIES, FLORIDA

ADMINISTRATIVE ORDER NO. 2017–07–01

AMENDED ADMINISTRATIVE ORDER GOVERNING PROBABLE CAUSE AFFIDAVITS

WHEREAS, pursuant to Article V, Section 2(d) of the Florida Constitution and section 43.26, Florida Statutes, the chief judge of each judicial circuit is charged with the authority and the power to do everything necessary to promote the prompt and efficient administration of justice; and

WHEREAS, judges sign arrest warrants as part of their responsibilities; and

WHEREAS, judges rely upon the facts mentioned in the affidavit of probable cause when presented with arrest warrants from law enforcement agencies; and

WHEREAS, the Court, the State of Florida, and counsel for the defense need access to the probable cause affidavit at first appearance in order to determine if probable cause exists to detain the defendant and to determine appropriate conditions of release; and

WHEREAS, access to the probable cause affidavits for arrest warrants at first appearance has proven difficult; and

WHEREAS, the Court and the parties to first appearance need access to the probable cause affidavit in order to perform essential responsibilities;

NOW, THEREFORE, I, Frederick J. Lauten, in order to facilitate the efficient operation of the administration of justice, and pursuant to the authority vested in me as Chief Judge of the Ninth Judicial Circuit of Florida under Florida Rule of Judicial Administration 2.215, hereby order that, **effective immediately** unless otherwise provided herein, to continue until further order, and superseding any provisions in prior Administrative Orders which may be inconsistent:

1. All law enforcement agencies must file with the Clerk of the Court the affidavit of probable cause with the signed arrest warrant.

2. The Clerk of Court shall event the affidavit of probable cause as a confidential document immediately upon receipt.

3. The Clerk of Court shall seal the affidavit of probable cause until no longer confidential as defined by the Florida Statutes and the Florida Rules of Court.

Administrative Order 2017–07 is vacated and set aside except to the extent that it has been incorporated and/or amended herein. Vacating an Administrative Order that vacates a prior Order does not revive the prior Order.

DONE AND ORDERED at Orlando, Florida, this 13th day of October, 2017.

Frederick J. Lauten
Chief Judge

2017–06. INTRODUCTION OF EVIDENCE CONTAINING HIGH–POTENCY NARCOTICS, NINTH JUDICIAL CIRCUIT

IN THE CIRCUIT COURT OF THE NINTH JUDICIAL CIRCUIT, IN AND FOR ORANGE AND OSCEOLA COUNTIES, FLORIDA

ADMINISTRATIVE ORDER NO. 2017–06

ORDER GOVERNING INTRODUCTION OF EVIDENCE CONTAINING HIGH–POTENCY NARCOTICS, NINTH JUDICIAL CIRCUIT

WHEREAS, pursuant to Article V, section 2(d) of the Florida Constitution and section 43.26, Florida Statutes, the chief judge of each judicial circuit is charged with the authority and the power to do everything necessary to promote the prompt and efficient administration of justice; and

WHEREAS, pursuant to the chief judge's constitutional and statutory responsibility for administrative supervision of the courts within the circuit and to create and maintain an organization capable of effecting the efficient, prompt, and proper administration of justice for the citizens of this State, the chief judge is required to exercise direction, *see* Fla. R. Jud. Admin. 2.215(b)(2), (b)(3); and

WHEREAS, there has been a steady increase in the amount of opioid-related arrests; and

WHEREAS, there has been a dramatic increase in the prevalence of high-potency narcotics that are so strong accidental contact or inhalation can be deadly; and

WHEREAS, the health, safety and welfare of those who conduct business within the courthouses of this Circuit, including employees and citizens, are of primary concern to this Court; and

WHEREAS, in an effort to ensure the health and safety of all persons within each courthouse in this Circuit and to prevent any accidental exposure, this Court has recognized that there is a need to establish a procedure for introducing evidence that contains or may contain high-potency narcotics ("HPN Exhibits");

NOW, THEREFORE, I, Frederick J. Lauten, in order to facilitate the efficient operation of the administration of justice, and pursuant to the authority vested in me as Chief Judge of the Ninth Judicial Circuit of Florida under Florida Rule of Judicial Administration 2.215, hereby order the following, **effective immediately**, to continue until further order and superseding any provisions in prior Administrative Orders which may be inconsistent:

1. HPN Exhibits are those that contain or may contain high-potency narcotics which are highly toxic and may be fatal, including, but not limited to: Fentanyl (Actiq, Fentora, Duragesic, Subsys, Abstral, Lazanda, Ionsys, Onsolis, Duragesic–100, Duragensic–50, Duragensic, Duragensic–75, Sublimaze, Duragensic–25, and Duragensic–12); Carfentanil; Remifentanil; Alfentanil; Sufentanil; and other related high-potency narcotics.

2. In the event any party intends to introduce HPN Exhibits in any court proceeding, the party intending to introduce the evidence must file a notice of its possession of an HPN Exhibit at least five (5) days prior to the pretrial conference in a trial case and ten (10) days prior to a hearing on a violation of probation.

3. The court shall conduct a pre-trial hearing to determine if the HPN Exhibits can be introduced by admission, statement of fact, photographs, stipulation and/or certificate of analysis. The court shall not require any party or law enforcement agency to transport or bring the HPN Exhibits to the courthouse for the purpose of the pretrial hearing.

4. If the parties are unable to reach an agreement or stipulation at the pretrial hearing, the trial clerk(s) shall promptly notify a manager in the trial clerks' division of the clerk of the circuit court.

5. In the event that HPN Exhibits are brought into the courthouse for any purpose, including but not limited to trial, the HPN Exhibits shall be double bagged, sealed and clearly labeled. Further, the HPN Exhibits must be handled, labeled and packaged in accordance with additional policies that may be established by federal or local law enforcement, which may be amended from time to time to ensure the safety of all court participants.

6. At the pretrial conference, if the parties are unable to stipulate to alternative presentations of the evidence and an HPN Exhibit is to be introduced into evidence, the court shall discuss and decide upon the protective gear that may be worn by trial participants, including but not limited to, attorneys, court deputies, court reporters, trial clerks and the court. The court shall also decide whether the jury may handle the HPN Exhibit and what, if any, protections shall be in place for the benefit of the jurors.

7. The trial clerk(s) shall promptly notify an evidence clerk manager in the event that HPN Exhibits are marked as exhibits.

DONE AND ORDERED at Orlando, Florida, this 10th day of August, 2017.

Frederick J. Lauten
Chief Judge

2017–04–01. NINTH JUDICIAL CIRCUIT COURT COUNTY CIVIL GUIDELINES, ORANGE COUNTY

ADMINISTRATIVE ORDER NO. 2017–04–01

IN THE CIRCUIT COURT OF THE NINTH JUDICIAL CIRCUIT, IN AND FOR ORANGE COUNTY, FLORIDA

AMENDED ADMINISTRATIVE ORDER ESTABLISHING NINTH JUDICIAL CIRCUIT COURT COUNTY CIVIL COURT GUIDELINES, ORANGE COUNTY

WHEREAS, pursuant to Article V, Section 2(d) of the Florida Constitution and section 43.26, Florida Statutes, the chief judge of each judicial circuit is charged with the authority and the power to do everything necessary to promote the prompt and efficient administration of justice; and

WHEREAS, to create and maintain an organization capable of effecting the efficient, prompt, and proper administration of justice for the citizens of this State, the chief judge is required to exercise direction, *see* Fla. R. Jud. Admin. 2.215(b)(2), (b)(3); and

WHEREAS, standardized procedures and manners of communication between the parties and the court best serve the interests of those that come before the court, preserve valuable judicial resources and prevent confusion and delay; and

WHEREAS, in order to provide effective coordination and in the interest of promoting judicial economy, the prompt and efficient administration of justice and in service to the citizens of the Ninth Circuit;

NOW, THEREFORE, I, Frederick J. Lauten, in order to facilitate the efficient operation of the administration of justice, and pursuant to the authority vested in me as Chief Judge of the Ninth Judicial Circuit of Florida under Florida Rule of Judicial Administration 2.215, hereby order the following, **effective immediately**, to continue until further order and superseding any provisions in prior Administrative Orders which may be inconsistent:

1. A mandatory meet and confer process is hereby established, as set forth below, for all motions to be **set for hearing** in the county civil division and to occur **before** scheduling the hearing except for the following motions: injunctive relief without notice; judgment on the pleadings; summary judgment or any hearings where a pro se litigant is involved.

Counsel with full authority to resolve the matter shall confer before scheduling the hearing on the motion to attempt to resolve or otherwise narrow the issues raised in the motion, and include a Certificate of Compliance (attached hereto as "Exhibit A") that the conference has occurred in the Notice of Hearing filed with the Court. It shall be the responsibility of counsel who schedules the hearing to arrange the conference.

The term "confer" requires a substantive conversation in person or by telephone in a good faith effort to resolve the motion without the need to schedule a hearing, and does not envision an exchange of ultimatums by fax, email or letter. Counsel who merely attempt to confer have not conferred for purposes of this Order.

Counsel must respond promptly to inquiries and communications from opposing counsel who notices the hearing and is attempting to schedule the conference. If counsel who notices the hearing is unable to reach opposing counsel to conduct the conference after three (3) good faith attempts, counsel who notices the hearing must identify in the Certificate of Compliance the dates and times of the efforts made to contact opposing counsel. Counsel shall include in the Notice of Hearing the Certificate of Compliance certifying that the meet and confer occurred (or did not occur and setting out the good faith attempts to schedule the conference) and identifying the date of the conference, the names of the participating attorneys, and the specific results obtained.

Counsel who notices the hearing shall ensure that the court and the court's judicial assistant are aware of any narrowing of the issues or other resolution because of the conference.

2. Counsel is required to provide the court (and opposing counsel) with courtesy copies of any memoranda, case law or any other materials on which counsel may rely at a scheduled hearing at least three (3) court days before the scheduled hearing.

3. A party seeking to schedule hearing time shall check the Judicial Automated Calendaring System via the Ninth Judicial Circuit Court website for available time slots. The party shall then follow the procedures by the court for that particular division.

4. In the event that a party seeks to cancel a previously scheduled hearing, the party must email the judge's judicial assistant and file a notice of cancellation.

5. Administrative Order 2017–04 is vacated and set aside except to the extent that it has been incorporated and/or amended herein. Vacating an Administrative Order that vacates a prior Order does not revive the prior Order.

DONE AND ORDERED at Orlando, Florida, this 27th day of March, 2018.

Frederick J. Lauten
Chief Judge

"Exhibit A"

First Option

CERTIFICATE OF COMPLIANCE

I HEREBY CERTIFY that (name of lawyer) in my firm, with full authority to resolve this matter, had a substantive conversation in person or by telephone with opposing counsel (name) on (specific date) in a good faith effort to resolve this motion before the motion was noticed for hearing and (specific results obtained).

/S/ ________

Counsel for the party who noticed the matter for hearing.

Second Option

CERTIFICATE OF COMPLIANCE

I HEREBY CERTIFY that a lawyer (name of lawyer) in my firm with full authority to resolve this matter attempted in good faith to contact opposing counsel (name of lawyer) in person or by telephone on:

1. (Date) at (Time);
2. (Date) at (Time); and
3. (Date) at (Time);

to discuss resolution of this motion without a hearing and the lawyer in my firm was unable to speak with opposing counsel.

/S/ ________

Counsel for the party who noticed the matter for hearing.

2017–03. MENTAL HEALTH COURT, NINTH JUDICIAL CIRCUIT

IN THE CIRCUIT COURT OF THE NINTH JUDICIAL CIRCUIT, IN AND FOR ORANGE AND OSCEOLA COUNTIES, FLORIDA

ADMINISTRATIVE ORDER NO. 2017–03

ORDER GOVERNING MENTAL HEALTH COURT, NINTH JUDICIAL CIRCUIT

WHEREAS, pursuant to Article V, section 2(d) of the Florida Constitution and section 43.26, Florida Statutes, the chief judge of each judicial circuit is charged with the authority and the power to do everything necessary to promote the prompt and efficient administration of justice; and

WHEREAS, pursuant to the chief judge's constitutional and statutory responsibility for administrative supervision of the courts within the circuit and to create and maintain an organization capable of effecting the efficient, prompt, and proper administration of justice for the citizens of this State, the chief judge is required to exercise direction, *see* Fla. R. Jud. Admin. 2.215(b)(2), (b)(3); and

WHEREAS, this Circuit has recognized that the creation of problem solving courts has enhanced the expediency, effectiveness and quality of judicial administration; and

WHEREAS, it is essential that a strategy be implemented in view of the unique nature of mental health conditions, to isolate and focus upon individuals arrested for non-violent misdemeanor and felony offenses who have untreated mental health conditions, and the need for appropriate treatment; and

WHEREAS, there is a recognized need for the Court to expedite those with mental health conditions through the criminal justice system into the most appropriate treatment environment while ensuring community protection and safety for all citizens; and

WHEREAS, it is necessary that this Circuit utilize available community resources and support, to establish an individualized judicial process that will, where appropriate, tailor treatment rather than punishment for the defendants with mental health conditions; and

WHEREAS, the proper implementation of a mental health court program authorized by section 394.47892, Florida Statutes, would provide a valuable alternative to traditional prosecution in appropriate cases;

NOW, THEREFORE, I, Frederick J. Lauten, in order to facilitate the efficient operation of the administration of justice, and pursuant to the authority vested in me as Chief Judge of the Ninth Judicial Circuit of Florida under Florida Rule of Judicial Administration 2.215, hereby order the following, **effective immediately**, to continue until further order and superseding any provisions in prior Administrative Orders which may be inconsistent:

A. Mental Health Court Programs hereinafter referred to as "MHC" were approved and are currently operating in both Orange and Osceola counties.

B. MHC is a non-adversarial team approach to case processing designed to address the unique needs of criminal justice involved individuals with mental health conditions by providing appropriate treatment services.

C. The team may consist of the following entities depending on the county in which the court resides: Judge, Prosecutor, Defense Attorney, Orange County Corrections Health Services (CHS) staff, Orange and Osceola County Corrections and Pretrial Services, Forensic Social Worker, Mental Health Specialist, Community Corrections Division (CCD) Supervising Officer, Florida Department of Corrections and the Problem Solving Court (PSC) program office (Program Office).

D. Potential MHC participants may be identified and referred to MHC at any time in the judicial process. The referral of a defendant to MHC may be made by any of the judicial divisions with no plea taken, and may be made by Defense Counsel, the State Attorney's Office, the Court, the Program Office, Mental Health Pre–Trial Release (MHPTR), Corrections Health Services staff (CHS) or any other interested party.

E. No participant will be contacted, assessed, pre-screened or screened by PSC staff for MHC without the prior approval of the participant's defense attorney. Participation in MHC is voluntary. In order to participate, the defendant must waive their right to a speedy trial prior to being court ordered in to MHC. If speedy trial has not been waived prior to a defendant's initial status review date in MHC, execution of a MHC agreement shall serve as a waiver of speedy trial.

F. To initiate the referral, the referring entity must complete a MHC referral form and submit the referral form to the Program Office.

G. After receipt of a referral form, the Program Office shall confirm with defense counsel that they would like the case considered for MHC if the referral came from another interested party. The Program Office shall screen referrals for program eligibility based on the criteria set forth in this Administrative Order.

H. Each individual will be provided with a treatment plan by a qualified professional as defined in section 394.455(38), Florida Statutes, or Mental Health Counselor as defined by section 394.455(26), Florida Statutes, or MHC team member licensed under sections 491.005 and 491.006, Florida Statutes, a Clinical Social Worker as defined in section 394.455(7), Florida Statutes, or Forensic Social Worker prior to admission in to MHC.

a. Individuals with co-occurring disorders may require a period of detoxification and stabilization prior to discussing a treatment plan and/or referral to the MHC.

b. The treatment plan will include:

i. Treatment options (Mental Health Pretrial Release—MH–PTR; Florida Assertive Community Treatment—FACT; Clinical Case Management—CCM; other licensed community based treatment programs)

ii. Assigned Clinical Case Manager and/or PSC Case Manager

iii. Housing Arrangements

iv. Appointments for Assessment, if required

v. Treatment follow-up schedule and medications.

vi. Discharge plan that would go into effect upon the offender's completion of MHC.

c. MHPTR staff (if the defendant is on MHPTR supervision), the Forensic Social Worker, Supervising Probation Officer and Program Office staff will be required to give information to the team at all status hearings concerning the defendant's adherence to the MHC treatment plan.

I. After screening, the referral package shall be forwarded to the State Attorney's office to include the referral form, documentation from a mental health professional that the defendant suffers from a mental illness as defined in section 394.455(28), Florida Statutes, and a copy of the proposed treatment plan.

a. For the purposes of this Administrative Order, a "mental health professional" may include a qualified professional as defined in section 394.455(38), Florida Statutes, a Clinical Social Worker as defined in section 394.455(7), Florida Statutes, a Mental Health Counselor as defined by 394.455(26), Florida Statutes, or a MHC team member licensed under sections 491.005 and 491.006, Florida Statutes, who is appropriately licensed to make a determination of the existence of a mental illness.

J. Upon receipt of the referral package, the State Attorney's office shall determine whether the defendant is eligible to participate in MHC, shall indicate this information on the referral form, and shall forward the referral form back to the Program Office.

a. The State Attorney's office has sole discretion on approvals for the diversion track of MHC.

b. If a referral is denied for the MHC program by the State Attorney's office for any track other than diversion, the defense attorney may file a motion for reconsideration directly to the MHC judge with proper notice to the assigned MHC Prosecutor and the matter will be placed on the next MHC docket for final determination of appropriateness for participation in the post-adjudicatory track of the MHC program.

K. The Program Office will forward the final completed referral form to the Clerk of Court's office to have the case placed on the next MHC docket for the defendant to sign their participation agreement and be court ordered into the MHC program by the MHC judge. A copy of the final completed referral form shall also be forwarded to the assigned trial judge, defense counsel and the State Attorney's Office.

L. At the defendant's first court date, if the defendant is approved for the diversion track of the MHC program, the defendant shall sign the MHC agreement as agreed to by the State and be entered into the MHC program. If the defendant is approved for the post adjudicatory track of the MHC program, the defendant shall enter a plea and shall sign the MHC agreement and be entered into the MHC program as a condition of probation or community control pursuant to section 948.01(8)(a), Florida Statutes. At that time, MHPTR may be removed by the judge as a condition of release.

M. Only defendants ordered to participate in MHC as a condition of probation will be supervised by County or State Probation. These defendants will be required to pay all County or State Probation drug testing and supervision fees unless waived by the supervising department.

N. If the defendant in any track elects not to participate in MHC at their first MHC date, then the case shall be returned to the original trial subdivision.

O. The defendant may be unsuccessfully discharged from MHC and returned to normal channels for prosecution for failure to comply with the treatment plan or orders of the court.

P. MHC shall hear cases involving defendants arrested for misdemeanors or felonies who:

a. Suffer from a mental illness as defined in section 394.455(28), Florida Statutes, as documented by a qualified professional as defined in section 394.455(38), Florida Statutes, Clinical Social Worker as defined in section 394.455(7), Florida Statutes or Mental Health Counselor as defined by section 394.455(26), Florida Statutes, or MHC team member licensed under sections 491.005 and 491.006, Florida Statutes;

b. Are amenable to mental health treatment (including taking prescribed medications);

c. Have documented access to housing, medication and follow-up care in the community either through MHPTR or a provider in the community that must be adequately documented prior to admission in to MHC in a treatment plan.

d. Are willing and able to sign the MHC participation agreement;

e. Do not have any current charges or prior convictions of any forcible felonies as defined by section 776.08, Florida Statutes, except aggravated assault;

f. Have waived speedy trial;

g. Reside in Orange or Osceola county (some exceptions for other counties that are contiguous to the Ninth Judicial Circuit); and qualify for one of the tracks of MHC.

Q. The State Attorney has absolute and sole discretion over admittance to the diversion track of the MHC program. The offender must meet the following qualifications to be considered for the diversion track of the MHC program:

a. The defendant volunteers for admission in to the MHC program;

b. The defendant has never been convicted of a felony; and the defendant is charged with: a misdemeanor; or a non-violent felony that includes a third degree felony violation of chapter 810 or any other felony offense that is not a forcible felony as defined in section 776.08, Florida Statutes; or resisting officer with violence under section 843.01, Florida Statutes, if the law enforcement officer and state attorney consent to the defendant's participation; or battery on a law enforcement officer under section 784.07, Florida Statutes, if the law enforcement officer and state attorney consent to the defendant's participation; or aggravated assault, if the victim and state attorney consent to the defendant's participation.

i. Upon successful completion of the MHC program diversion track the State Attorney shall issue a nolle prosequi on the case. If the defendant does not successfully complete the diversion track, the court may order that the charges revert to normal channels for prosecution or the matter may be resolved on the MHC docket based on the recommendation of the State Attorney.

ii. The offender must meet the following qualifications for the post adjudicatory track of the MHC program:

1. The defendant qualifies for the program pursuant to section 948.01(8)(a) or 948.06, Florida Statutes: the offense is a non-violent felony (a third degree felony under chapter 810 or any other felony offense that is not a forcible felony as defined in section 776.08, Florida Statutes.

2. Defendants charged with resisting an officer with violence under section 843.01, Florida Statutes, battery on a law enforcement officer under section 784.07, Florida Statutes, or aggravated assault may participate in the post-adjudicatory track of the MHC program if the court so orders after the victim is given his or her right to provide testimony or written statement to the court as provided in section 921.143, Florida Statutes; and

3. The defendant is otherwise qualified under section 394.47892(4), Florida Statutes.

4. Entry into a post-adjudicatory MHC program as a condition of probation must be based upon the MHC's assessment of the defendant's criminal history, mental health screening outcome, amenability to the services of the program, and total sentence points; the recommendation of the state attorney and the victim, if any; and the defendant's agreement to enter the program.

5. A defendant who is sentenced to a post-adjudicatory MHC program who, while a MHC program participant, is the subject of a violation of probation or community control under section 948.06, Florida Statutes, shall have the violation heard by the judge presiding over the MHC program. After a hearing on, or admission of the violation, the judge shall dispose of any such violation as he or she deems appropriate.

iii. All misdemeanors will remain in MHC for a minimum of 6 months. All felonies will remain in MHC for a minimum of 12 months.

Administrative Order 2000–08–02 is vacated and set aside and has been incorporated and/or amended herein. The provisions of Administrative Order 2003–39–24 relating only to Section II, E and Attachment F are vacated. Vacating an Administrative Order that vacates a prior Order does not revive the prior Order.

DONE AND ORDERED at Orlando, Florida, this 28th day of March, 2017.

Frederick J. Lauten
Chief Judge

2016–22. CHILDREN IN NEED OF SERVICES/FAMILIES IN NEED OF SERVICES PROCEEDINGS, ORANGE COUNTY

IN THE CIRCUIT COURT OF THE NINTH JUDICIAL CIRCUIT, IN AND FOR ORANGE COUNTY, FLORIDA

ADMINISTRATIVE ORDER NO. 2016–22

ADMINISTRATIVE ORDER GOVERNING CHILDREN IN NEED OF SERVICES/FAMILIES IN NEED OF SERVICES PROCEEDINGS, ORANGE COUNTY

WHEREAS, Chapter 984 of the Florida Statutes provides help to families and children who need services to improve the behaviors on the part of the child, help the family to move beyond crisis and prevent further problems. The Florida Department of Juvenile Justice (DJJ) funds and supports these programs to keep kids out of serious trouble; and

WHEREAS, Children In Need of Services (CINS)/Families In Need of Services (FINS) is an adjudication status for a child or a family for whom there is no pending investigation into an allegation or suspicion of abuse, neglect, or abandonment; no pending referral alleging the child is delinquent; or no current supervision by the Department of Juvenile Justice or the Department of Children and Family Services for an adjudication of dependency or delinquency. A family in need of services is not an adjudicated status; and

WHEREAS, section 984.04(6), Florida Statutes, and Florida Rule of Juvenile Procedure 8.625(h) provides authority for the appointment of general or special magistrates to hear issues involved in CINS/FINS proceedings;

NOW, THEREFORE, I, Frederick J. Lauten, pursuant to the authority vested in me as Chief Judge of the Ninth Judicial Circuit of Florida, under Florida Rule of Judicial Administration 2.215, hereby order the following, effective **immediately**, unless otherwise provided herein, superseding any provisions in prior Administrative Orders which may be inconsistent, and to continue until further order of this Court:

1. **General Provisions.** Pursuant to section 984.04(6), Florida Statutes, and Florida Rule of Juvenile Procedure 8.625(h) the general magistrate assigned to the Juvenile Division shall preside over CINS/FINS hearings.

2. **Case Assignment.** All cases shall be assigned to **Subdivision 07–4.** The Judge in that subdivision shall be responsible for the CINS/FINS cases. Cases shall be filed with the Clerk of Court's Office in the Juvenile Division.

DONE AND ORDERED at Orlando, Florida, this 13th day of July, 2016.

Frederick J. Lauten
Chief Judge

2016–20. [VACATED BY ORDER 2017-21, EFFECTIVE DECEMBER 8, 2017.]

2016–11. PROCEDURES FOR THE APPOINTMENT OF CERTIFIED LEGAL INTERNS

IN THE CIRCUIT COURT OF THE NINTH JUDICIAL CIRCUIT, IN AND FOR ORANGE COUNTY, FLORIDA

ADMINISTRATIVE ORDER NO. 2016–11

ADMINISTRATIVE ORDER GOVERNING PROCEDURES FOR THE APPOINTMENT OF CERTIFIED LEGAL INTERNS UNDER THE FLORIDA AGRICULTURAL AND MECHANICAL UNIVERSITY (FAMU) COLLEGE OF LAW CRIMINAL DEFENSE CLINIC IN COUNTY CRIMINAL COURT, ORANGE COUNTY

WHEREAS, pursuant to Article V, Section 2(d) of the Florida Constitution and section 43.26, Florida Statutes, the chief judge of each judicial circuit is charged with the authority and the power to do everything necessary to promote the prompt and efficient administration of justice; and

WHEREAS, pursuant to the chief judge's constitutional and statutory responsibility for administrative supervision of the courts within the circuit and to create and maintain an organization capable of effecting the efficient, prompt, and proper administration of justice for the citizens of this State, the chief judge is required to exercise direction, *see* Fla. R. Jud. Admin. 2.215(b)(2), (b)(3); and

WHEREAS, FAMU College of Law provides among its clinical offerings a criminal defense clinic (hereinafter referred to as "FAMU Criminal Clinic") through which legal interns certified through the Florida Supreme Court and under the supervision of a licensed attorney can participate on a pro bono basis as advocates for indigent defendants in appropriate misdemeanor cases; and

WHEREAS, pursuant to letter dated November 6, 2015, FAMU Criminal Clinic has been approved as a legal aid organization by the Florida Supreme Court to represent indigent persons in appropriate cases;

NOW, THEREFORE, I, Frederick J. Lauten, pursuant to the authority vested in me as Chief Judge of the Ninth Judicial Circuit of Florida, under Florida Rule of Judicial Administration 2.215, hereby order the following, effective **immediately**, to continue until further order and superseding any provisions in prior Administrative Orders which may be inconsistent:

1. In the County Criminal Subdivisions, the Judges may appoint FAMU Criminal Clinic in lieu of the Public Defender to represent, on a pro bono basis, indigent defendants in appropriate county criminal cases. However, no court appointment shall be made to any Driving Under the Influence case or any domestic related battery or criminal case. The County Court shall advise defendants who seek court appointed counsel of the option to be represented by the Public Defender or alternatively the FAMU Criminal Clinic. If the FAMU Criminal Clinic is appointed, the lien for payment of attorney's fees pursuant to section 938.29, Florida Statutes, shall not be imposed.

2. Upon presentation of a copy of the order of appointment and proper identification by FAMU Criminal Clinic staff and legal interns, the Clerk of Court shall provide access to FAMU Criminal Clinic to court files relating to cases where FAMU Criminal Clinic is appointed. FAMU Criminal Clinic shall comply with the Florida Statutes, Florida Rules of Criminal Procedure and all Ninth Judicial Circuit Court Administrative Orders, including strict compliance with the procedures established in Administrative Order No. 07–98–02, or subsequent Administrative Order, concerning the removal of court files from the offices of the Clerk of Court.

3. The clinical instructors must be active members of The Florida Bar and, under whose supervision an eligible law student does any of the things permitted by chapter 11 of the Rules Regulating the Florida Bar, shall:

(a) be a lawyer whose service as a supervising lawyer for this program is approved by the dean of the law school in which the law student is enrolled and who is a member of The Florida Bar in good standing;

(b) be a lawyer employed by a state attorney, public defender, an approved legal aid organization, a state officer, or a governmental entity enumerated in rule 11–1.2(d);

(c) assume personal professional responsibility for the student's guidance in any work undertaken and for supervising the quality of the student's work; and

(d) assist the student in the student's preparation to the extent the supervising lawyer considers it necessary.

R. Regulating Fla. Bar 11–1.7.

DONE AND ORDERED at Orlando, Florida, this 2nd day of June, 2016.

Frederick J. Lauten

Chief Judge

2016–07. VETERANS COURT

IN THE CIRCUIT COURT OF THE NINTH JUDICIAL CIRCUIT, IN AND FOR ORANGE AND OSCEOLA COUNTIES, FLORIDA

ADMINISTRATIVE ORDER NO. 2016–07

ORDER GOVERNING VETERANS COURT

WHEREAS, pursuant to Article V, section 2(d) of the Florida Constitution and section 43.26, Florida Statutes, the chief judge of each judicial circuit is charged with the authority and the power to do everything necessary to promote the prompt and efficient administration of justice; and

WHEREAS, pursuant to the chief judge's constitutional and statutory responsibility for administrative supervision of the courts within the circuit and to create and maintain an organization capable of effecting the efficient, prompt, and proper administration of justice for the citizens of this State, the chief judge is required to exercise direction, *see* Fla. R. Jud. Admin. 2.215(b)(2), (b)(3); and

WHEREAS, section 394.47891, Florida Statutes, provides authority for the establishment of military and service members court programs; and

WHEREAS, the purpose of Veterans Court is to reduce recidivism by emphasizing treatment and rehabilitation as an alternative to incarcerations, while also requiring offender accountability and increasing public safety; and

WHEREAS, this specialized division will enable consideration of the unique nature of the issues related to veterans, the need for appropriate treatment in an environment conducive to wellness, as well as the continuing necessity to ensure the protection of the public. Veterans Court authorizes a judge to expeditiously and efficiently divert veterans with service-related issues into available veteran treatment programs without compromising the safety of the public;

NOW, THEREFORE, I, Frederick J. Lauten, pursuant to the authority vested in me as Chief Judge of the Ninth Judicial Circuit of Florida, under Florida Rule of Judicial Administration 2.215, hereby order the following, effective **immediately**, to continue until further order and superseding any provisions in prior Administrative Orders which may be inconsistent:

A. The Ninth Judicial Circuit shall develop and implement a Veterans Treatment Court Program (VTC) to facilitate the provision of services to veterans involved in the criminal justice system. Qualified participants are veterans who, either by pre-trial diversion, plea, or verdict are charged or convicted of a misdemeanor or felony criminal offense other than a felony listed in section 948.06(8)(c), Florida Statutes, and who suffer from a military-related mental illness, traumatic brain injury, substance abuse disorder, or psychological issue.

B. The referral of a defendant into VTC may be made by any of the criminal trial divisions with no plea taken, and may be made by defense counsel, the State Attorney's Office, the Court, the Veterans Court Program Office (Program office), or any other interested party.

C. As part of the referral, the referring person/agency must complete and submit a Veterans Court referral packet to the Program Office to initiate the referral approval process.

D. Participation in VTC is voluntary and in order to participate, the defendant must waive their right to a speedy trial prior to entering the VTC.

E. Upon receipt of a completed referral packet, the Program Office will send all eligible and completed packets the State Attorney's Office for determination of track and to the Veterans Administration for confirmation of military service and benefits qualification.

F. Upon receipt of the referral packet, the State Attorney's Office shall determine whether or not the defendant is eligible for a specific track of the VTC, shall indicate this information on the referral packet, and shall forward the Referral Packet back to the Program Office.

G. The Program Office will then forward the completed Referral packet with a VTC initial status date to the Clerk of Court's Office for placement of the case on the next VTC docket.

H. The Program Office will also notify the referring subdivision's judicial assistant, clerk, and attorneys that the case has been approved for VTC and that it may be removed from the referring subdivision's docket.

I. At the initial status hearing in VTC, if the defendant desires to enter VTC, a signed Veterans Court Agreement outlining all of the requirements for participation and successful completion will be entered on the case. At the initial status hearing, the defendant will be ordered to enter and successfully complete the VTC program. If the defendant is entering VTC on the post-plea condition of probation track, then the Unified Problem Solving Court Judge will sentence the defendant to an appropriate term of probation with VTC as a special condition.

J. Once the defendant signs the Agreement and enters VTC, the case will remain assigned by the clerk's office to VTC for status purposes.

K. Defendants accepted into VTC will attend court hearings as ordered by the Unified Problem Solving Court Judge. The defendant shall participate in ongoing assessments, treatment and discharge planning until VTC graduation. The minimum length of stay in VTC is six (6) months for misdemeanors and twelve (12) months for felonies, up to the statutory maximum. The minimum length of stay in VTC may be modified for diversion cases at the discretion of the State Attorney or, in the case of post-plea condition of probation cases, the Unified Problem Solving Court Judge. If a defendant fails to successfully complete VTC, the case may be returned to the original subdivision for further prosecution.

L. In diversion cases where the defendants have been rejected from participating in VTC, or cases where the defendant has chosen to opt out of VTC, the case may be reassigned back to the subdivision where the case was originally assigned or resolved in VTC.

M. In diversion cases where the defendant has successfully completed VTC, the State Attorney shall file a nolle prosequi.

N. In probation cases, should the defendant be ejected from VTC as a result of a VTC violation, the Florida Department of Corrections or the respective county probation office shall initiate an affidavit of violation of probation and shall submit the affidavit to the Problem Solving Court Judge. Nothing herein shall prohibit the Florida Department of Corrections or the respective county probation office from filing a violation of probation for any failure of the defendant to comply with conditions of probation. If the Problem Solving Court Judge determines that there is a legal basis to do so, he/she shall issue a warrant for violation of probation. Upon arrest on the violation of probation warrant, the Problem Solving Court Judge shall resolve the violation of probation proceeding via a plea or hearing and impose a sentence if appropriate.

O. In probation cases where the defendant has complied with all other special and standard conditions of probation (including restitution) the Court shall give due consideration to the early termination of probation.

DONE AND ORDERED at Orlando, Florida, this 17th day of May, 2016.

Frederick J. Lauten
Chief Judge

2016–02–01. "SEXTING" PURSUANT TO SECTION 847.0141, FLORIDA STATUTES, NINTH JUDICIAL CIRCUIT

IN THE CIRCUIT COURT OF THE NINTH JUDICIAL CIRCUIT, IN AND FOR ORANGE AND OSCEOLA COUNTIES, FLORIDA

ADMINISTRATIVE ORDER NO. 2016–02–01

AMENDED ORDER GOVERNING "SEXTING" PURSUANT TO SECTION 847.0141, FLORIDA STATUTES, NINTH JUDICIAL CIRCUIT

WHEREAS, pursuant to Article V, section 2(d) of the Florida Constitution and section 43.26, Florida Statutes, the chief judge of each judicial circuit is charged with the authority and the power to do everything necessary to promote the prompt and efficient administration of justice; and

WHEREAS, pursuant to the chief judge's constitutional and statutory responsibility for administrative supervision of the courts within the circuit and to create and maintain an organization capable of effecting the efficient, prompt, and proper administration of justice for the citizens of this State, the chief judge is required to exercise direction, *see* Fla. R. Jud. Admin. 2.215(b)(2), (b)(3); and

WHEREAS, to provide for the efficient processing of sexting offense cases pursuant to section 847.0141, Florida Statutes;

NOW, THEREFORE, I, Frederick J. Lauten, in order to facilitate the efficient operation of the administration of justice, and pursuant to the authority vested in me as Chief Judge of the Ninth Judicial Circuit of Florida under Florida Rule of Judicial Administration 2.215, hereby order the following, **effective immediately,** to continue until further order and superseding any provisions in prior Administrative Orders which may be inconsistent:

1. First-time violations of section 847.0141, Florida Statutes, are designated as non-criminal violations that are to be heard by the Circuit Judges assigned to hear juvenile delinquency matters. *See* § 985.0301(1)(b), Fla. Stat. (2015).

2. First-time violators must sign and accept a citation indicating a promise to appear before the Juvenile Court.

3. Pursuant to section 847.0141(3)(a)1., Florida Statutes, the citation must contain all of the following:

a. The date and time of issuance.

b. The name and address of the minor to whom the citation is issued.

c. A thumbprint of the minor to whom the citation is issued.

d. Identification of the noncriminal violation and the time it was committed.

e. The facts constituting reasonable cause.

f. The specific section of law violated.

g. The name and authority of the citing officer.

h. The procedures that the minor must follow to contest the citation, perform the required community service, pay the civil penalty, or participate in a cyber-safety program.

Additionally, the citation must contain a statement that the first-time violator will receive a notice of hearing from the Clerk of Court.

4. The citation is filed with the Clerk of Court who shall assign the citation a noncriminal infraction number, assign the citation to a division, and set a court date for 45 days from the date of the offense.

5. The Clerk of Court shall send a notice of hearing to the alleged first-time violator advising that in lieu of appearing in Court, pursuant to section 847.0141(3)(a), Florida Statutes, first-time violators may complete 8 hours community service work, pay a $60.00 civil penalty and applicable court costs, or participate in a cyber-safety program if such a program is locally available. The first-time violator must satisfy any penalty, and provide proof of such to the Clerk of Court within 30 days after receipt of the citation.

If one of the three sanctions is completed, proof given and confirmed by the Clerk of Court, in conjunction with the Alternative Sanctions Program Office, within 30 days of the offense, the hearing date will be cancelled and the Clerk of Court will mail notice of the cancellation of the hearing to the first-time violator. The notice shall further advise that failure to complete one of the three sanctions within 30 days after receipt of the citation will require the first-time violator's appearance in Court on the scheduled arraignment date.

Administrative Order 2016–02 is vacated and set aside and has been incorporated and/or amended herein. Vacating an Administrative Order that vacates a prior Order does not revive the prior Order.

DONE AND ORDERED at Orlando, Florida, this 6th day of July, 2016.

Frederick J. Lauten

Chief Judge

2015–10–02. APPELLATE PROCESS, NINTH JUDICIAL CIRCUIT

IN THE CIRCUIT COURT OF THE NINTH JUDICIAL CIRCUIT, IN AND FOR ORANGE AND OSCEOLA COUNTIES, FLORIDA

ADMINISTRATIVE ORDER NO. 2015–10–02

AMENDED ORDER GOVERNING APPELLATE PROCESS, NINTH JUDICIAL CIRCUIT

WHEREAS, pursuant to Article V, section 2(d) of the Florida Constitution and section 43.26, Florida Statutes, the chief judge of each judicial circuit is charged with the authority and the power to do everything necessary to promote the prompt and efficient administration of justice; and

WHEREAS, pursuant to the chief judge's constitutional and statutory responsibility for administrative supervision of the courts within the circuit and to create and maintain an organization capable of effecting the efficient, prompt, and proper administration of justice for the citizens of this State, the chief judge is required to exercise direction, *see* Fla. R. Jud. Admin. 2.215(b)(2), (b)(3); and

WHEREAS, the Circuit Court is charged with the responsibility of hearing and ruling on appeals and petitions for extraordinary writs from County Court and local administrative bodies;

NOW, THEREFORE, I, Frederick J. Lauten, in order to facilitate the efficient operation of the administration of justice, and pursuant to the authority vested in me as Chief Judge of the Ninth Judicial Circuit of Florida under Florida Rule of Judicial Administration 2.215, hereby order that, **effective immediately** unless otherwise provided herein, to continue until further order, and superseding any provisions in prior Administrative Orders which may be inconsistent.

In an effort to promote uniformity of appellate decisions and to avoid intra–Circuit conflict if possible, and in order to enhance judicial efficiency involving appeals to the Circuit Court, the following procedures are established concerning appeals to the Circuit Court and certain writs arising from the County Court and from administrative agencies:

I. THE APPELLATE COURT

A. Panels

1. All appeals from the County Courts of Orange and Osceola Counties, all petitions for writ of certiorari which seek review of a quasi-judicial decision of any public body, city or county commission or council, administrative board or agency, or decision of the County Courts, all writs of prohibition and mandamus directed to the County Courts or Judges thereof, or to any public body or agency in exercise of its quasi-judicial function, shall be resolved by an appellate panel consisting of three Circuit Judges. In specific detail:

a. All appeals invoking the appellate jurisdiction of the Circuit Court, pursuant to Florida Rule of Appellate Procedure 9.030(c).

b. All petitions for extraordinary writs which are filed pursuant to Florida Rule of Appellate Procedure 9.030(c) and which seek review of a lower tribunal ruling, except those qualifying Writs of Habeas Corpus and other Emergency Writs that are ruled upon by the Presiding Judge.

c. Actions filed pursuant to Florida Rule of Civil Procedure 1.630 **shall not** be heard by an appellate panel consisting of three Circuit Judges.

2. Every Circuit Judge, except as determined by the Chief Judge, shall be assigned to a panel by the Chief Judge and will remain on the panel for one calendar year. Prior to January of each year, the Chief Judge or the Chief Judge's designee

will reassign each Judge to a new panel. The Chief Judge shall also ensure that the panels comply with the time guidelines contained herein. The Circuit Appellate Court Clerks shall randomly assign cases to the appellate panels on a rotating basis. Cases assigned to the panel will remain with that particular panel until the case is concluded, even if resolution occurs after the Judges are assigned to new panels. Cases may be reassigned on an as needed basis by the Administrative Judge of the Appellate Division.

3. Each year, the Chief Judge will determine the number of appellate panels and will assign the Judges to a panel. This determination will be made with every effort to assign all Judges to an appellate panel. The Chief Judge will not be assigned to a panel but shall remain available for substitute service on an as needed basis.

4. Every panel shall have a Presiding Judge. Each individual panel member will sit in turn as the Presiding Judge. Once the assignments are made, the first Judge listed for each panel shall be the Presiding Judge for the period of January through April. The second Judge listed shall be the Presiding Judge for May through August and finally, the third Judge shall be the Presiding Judge for September through December, unless otherwise agreed amongst themselves.

5. The Presiding Judge shall hear all motions filed in every appeal assigned to the panel. This includes whether oral argument should be granted. If oral argument is granted, the Presiding Judge shall coordinate scheduling of the oral argument with the remaining panel members. If a Judge is unable to attend the oral argument, that Judge must obtain a substitute Judge who shall then be responsible for that panel member's case. Any Judge who obtains a substitute shall notify the other panel members and ensure that the Substitute Judge receives the documents filed in the case prior to oral argument.

6. Each Judge is ultimately responsible for every appeal filed during the time he or she is Presiding Judge. The determinative date for assignment to a particular panel is the day the Notice of Appeal is filed with the Clerk of the Circuit Court.

7. When a Judge assigned to an appellate panel is absent, is disqualified in an action, or is otherwise unable to perform the duties regarding the appellate cases to which that Judge is assigned, then the Administrative Judge of the Appellate Division shall reassign another Judge to serve on the panel for the case. If the Judge who is unable to serve was the presiding Judge of the panel, then the newly assigned Judge will become the presiding Judge of the panel.

B. Oral Argument

1. If oral argument is scheduled on a case, the documents filed in the appellate case file shall be reviewed by the Presiding Judge prior to oral argument. The Presiding Judge shall give the initial presentation to the remaining panel members at the panel conference.

2. If oral argument is held, the panel will immediately thereafter conference in order to decide the appeal. No per curiam reversals are permitted. The proposed opinion will be circulated simultaneously to the other panel members for consideration. Any Judge may write a concurring or dissenting opinion which must also be circulated prior to the filing of the majority opinion.

C. En Banc

1. A hearing en banc may be ordered only by a majority of the Presiding Judges, so designated based upon the specific administrative order which governs the panel assignment of the particular appeal. A party may not request an en banc hearing. A motion seeking an en banc hearing shall be stricken. The same Judges who were Presiding Judges at the time the decision was made to determine the issue en banc, shall constitute the en banc panel. En banc hearings and rehearings shall not be ordered unless the case is of exceptional importance or unless necessary to maintain uniformity within the Circuit. The en banc decision shall be by the majority of the en banc panel. In the event of a tie vote, the panel decision shall stand as the decision of the Court. If there is no panel decision, a tie vote will affirm the lower court decision.

2. A rehearing en banc is an extraordinary proceeding. A rehearing en banc may be ordered by the Court on its own motion or on motion of a party. Within the time prescribed by rule 9.330, Florida Rules of Appellate Procedure, a party may move for an en banc rehearing solely on the grounds that the case or issue is of exceptional importance or that such consideration is necessary to maintain uniformity in the court's decisions. A motion based on any other ground shall be stricken. A response may be served within ten (10) days of service of the motion.

A vote will not be taken on a motion for rehearing en banc unless requested by a Judge. Judges who did not sit on the panel are under no obligation to consider the motion unless a vote is requested. A motion for rehearing en banc shall be disposed of by order. If rehearing en banc is granted, the Court may limit the issues to be reheard, require the filing of additional briefs, and may require additional argument.

II. THE CLERK OF COURT

A. Acknowledgment

1. The Clerk will send an Acknowledgment of Filing the appeal to the Presiding Judge, all counsel of record and all pro se parties, substantially in the form attached hereto as "Exhibit A," for Orange County and "Exhibit "B," for Osceola County indicating the panel and panel members to which the case is assigned, date filed and appellate case number.[1]

2. The Acknowledgment will contain a notification that all documents are to be filed with Clerk's Office, not with Presiding Judge.

3. A Notice to Attorneys and Parties, in a form substantially similar to "Exhibit C" attached hereto, will be available on the Court's website.

B. Filing Fee

1. If an appeal is filed without either the filing fee or an application for determination of indigent status finding appellate indigent, the Court may enter an "Order to Comply with Appellate Rules or Show Cause Why Sanctions Should Not Be Imposed" within the time as determined by the Court after the Notice of Appeal has been filed.

2. If a response to an Order to Show Cause is filed, the Clerk will immediately notify the Presiding Judge of the response for review.

3. If a response is not filed, the filing fee is not paid or an application for determination of indigent status finding appellant indigent is not submitted within the time as directed by the Court, the Court may enter a "Final Order Dismissing Appeal Pursuant to Rule 9.410."

C. Record on Appeal

1. If the appellant fails to pay the lower court for preparation of Record on Appeal, such record will not be filed with the appellate court Clerk but will be retained by the lower court Clerk until payment is made.

2. If time has expired for filing of the Record on Appeal, the Court may enter an "Order to Comply with Appellate Rules or Show Cause Why Sanctions Should Not Be Imposed."

3. If a response to the Order to Show Cause is filed, the Clerk will immediately notify the Presiding Judge of the response for review. If a response or the Record on Appeal has not been filed within the time directed by the Court, the Court may enter a "Final Order Dismissing Appeal Pursuant to Rule 9.410."

D. Motions. The Clerk will notify the Presiding Judge of the motion within five (5) days after filing of a motion.

E. Briefs

1. All briefs shall be filed with the Clerk of Court.

2. If the initial brief is not filed within the time set forth in the Florida Rules of Appellate Procedure, the Court may enter an "Order to Comply with Appellate Rules or Show Cause Why Sanctions Should Not Be Imposed."

3. If a response to an Order to Show Cause is filed, the Clerk will immediately notify the Presiding Judge of the response for review. If a response or initial brief is not filed within the time directed by the Court, the Court may enter a "Final Order of Dismissal Pursuant to Rule 9.410."

4. If an answer brief is not filed within twenty-five (25) days of filing the Initial Brief, the Court may enter an "Order to Comply with Appellate Rules or Show Cause Why Sanctions Should Not Be Imposed."

F. Final Decision. When an appeal has been perfected for decision (i.e., all briefs have been filed or the time for filing briefs has expired), the Clerk will notify the appropriate Panel for decision. The Clerk will prepare and issue a mandate fifteen (15) days from date of final order unless the order states mandate to be issued forthwith. If motion for rehearing or clarification is filed, the Clerk will notify the Panel five (5) days after the motion is filed.

G. Voluntary Dismissal. When a voluntary dismissal or joint stipulation of dismissal is filed in the Clerk's Office, the Court will enter a "Final Order Dismissing Appeal."

H. Returning Court Orders to Clerk's Office. After entry of an order at any stage of the appellate process, the Judicial Assistant will send out all necessary copies and immediately e-file or forward the original order to the Clerk's Office to be filed.

Administrative Orders 2005–17 and 2015–10–01 are vacated and set aside except to the extent that each has been incorporated and/or amended herein. Vacating an Administrative Order that vacates a prior Order does not revive the prior Order.

DONE AND ORDERED at Orlando, Florida, this 23rd day of August, 2018.

Frederick J. Lauten
Chief Judge

"Exhibit C"

NINTH JUDICIAL CIRCUIT COURT—
APPELLATE DIVISION

NOTICE TO ATTORNEYS & PARTIES

RE: COUNTY COURT APPEALS, PETITIONS FOR WRIT OF CERTIORARI AND APPEALS FROM LOCAL ADMINISTRATIVE ACTION

The following rules of the Ninth Judicial Circuit Court should be followed by all attorneys and parties filing appeals to the Circuit Court from County Court, both civil and criminal, appeals from local administrative action, and Petitions for Writ of Certiorari filed pursuant to Rule 9.100.

PLEASE READ THESE RULES TO ENSURE YOUR APPEAL WILL PROCEED IN A TIMELY FASHION AND TO AVOID DISMISSAL OF YOUR APPEAL FOR FAILURE TO FOLLOW THESE RULES.

THE FLORIDA RULES OF APPELLATE PROCEDURE APPLY TO ALL APPEALS AND ORIGINAL PROCEEDINGS.

A. Appeal of County Court Judgments and Administrative Orders

1. The Notice of Appeal shall be filed with payment of the appropriate filing fees. For appeals of local government decisions, the Notice of Appeal must also be filed with the local government's clerk. *See* Florida Rule of Appellate Procedure 9.110(c).

2. Persons seeking indigent status must comply with Florida Rule of Appellate Procedure 9.430.

3. The Notice of Appeal must be served on all parties or their attorneys. *See* Florida Rule of Appellate Procedure 9.420(c).

4. The date of rendition of the order must be indicated on the Notice of Appeal. *See* Florida Rule of Appellate Procedure 9.020(i).

5. The Notice of Appeal shall contain the names of all parties to the appeal whether it is an appeal of a final or non-final order.

6. For record preparation, please comply with Florida Rules of Appellate Procedure 9.200. Please be sure to pay the Clerk for the cost of any record preparation. Otherwise, your appeal may be subject to dismissal. For appeals of administrative action, it is the Appellant's responsibility to ensure that the local government clerk prepares the record and sends it to the Clerk of Court.

7. If no transcript of the lower courts proceedings exist, you may file a statement of the evidence, which is your best recollection of the proceedings, with the lower court, and serve a copy on all parties or their attorneys, who may serve objections or proposed amendments to it within 10 days of

service. The lower court must approve the statement of the evidence before it is filed in this Court. It is the Appellant's responsibility to obtain this approval. *See* Florida Rule of Appellate Procedure 9.200(b).

8. In civil cases, the Appellant must file with the Notice of Appeal: (1) the Final Order/Judgment/or Order of Final Administrative Action being appealed; AND (2) any subsequent order on a Motion for Retrial or Rehearing.

9. Please advise the Court in writing as soon as possible of any other cases pending before this Court involving related issues of which you have personal knowledge.

B. Petitions for Writ of Certiorari (non-final orders, zoning and land use orders, and other quasi-judicial local government action)

1. The Petition and the Appendix shall be filed together with payment of the appropriate filing fee. *See* Florida Rule of Appellate Procedure 9.100(g) for the required contents of the Petition.

2. Persons seeking indigent status must comply with Florida Rule of Appellate Procedure 9.430.

3. The Petition shall be served on all parties or their attorneys and shall contain a certificate of service and certificate of compliance.

4. The Petitioner must include in the Appendix a conformed copy of: (1) the Final Order/Judgment/or Order of Final Administrative Action being appealed; AND (2) any subsequent order on a Motion for Retrial or Rehearing.

5. Please advise the Court in writing as soon as possible of any other cases pending before this Court involving related issues of which you have personal knowledge.

C. Motions

1. Please file motions with the Clerk of Court. Please do not file or send courtesy copies unless requested. Any record material necessary for resolution of the motion should be attached to the motion as an Appendix. *See* Florida Rule of Appellate Procedure 9.300(a) for required content of and procedure for motions.

2. Motions shall contain a certificate of service showing service on all parties or their attorneys. Motions must also contain express representations (except on motions where a party seeks disposition of all or part of another party's appeal) that opposing counsel has been contacted and will or will not stipulate to the relief requested.

3. Responses to motions shall be served within 10 days after service of the motion. No reply will be considered unless specifically authorized by the Court. Any unauthorized reply will be stricken without consideration. *See* Fla. R. App. P. 9.300.

4. Request for Oral Argument should be filed as a separate document in compliance with Florida Rule of Appellate Procedure 9.320. Oral argument, if granted, will generally be limited to 10 minutes per side. If there are multiple parties to a side, then the parties must determine among themselves how to split the 10 minutes per side among them. Oral Argument will be granted by the Court only in those cases where it is genuinely believed necessary for disposition of the cause.

5. Excessive and unnecessary motion practice is discouraged and may result in the imposition of sanctions under Florida Rule of Appellate Procedure 9.410. *See Dubowitz v. Century Village East., Inc.*, 381 So. 2d 252 (Fla. 4th DCA 1979).

D. Briefs

1. All briefs shall be filed with the Clerk of Court. *See* Florida Rule of Appellate Procedure 9.210 for required contents of and procedure for briefs. Please do not file or send courtesy copies unless requested.

2. An initial brief must be served within 70 days of filing the notice of appeal, except in criminal cases. *See* Florida Rule of Appellate Procedure 9.110(f). For criminal cases, the initial brief must be served within 30 days of service of the record. *See* Florida Rule of Appellate Procedure 9.140(g). Except for post-conviction appeals, your appeal can be dismissed if you fail to file an initial brief.

3. For post-conviction appeals where no evidentiary hearing was held, the initial brief, if any, must be filed within 30 days of filing the notice of appeal.

4. An answer brief must be served within 20 days of service of the initial brief, and any reply brief must be served within 20 days of service of the answer brief.

5. All briefs shall include a certificate of service showing service of the brief on the opposing parties or their attorneys, as well as a certificate of compliance pursuant to Florida Rule of Appellate Procedure 9.210(a)(2).

6. Failure to cite to the record for facts stated in the brief, in compliance with Florida Rule of Appellate Procedure 9.210, may result in the brief being stricken.

7. A party's brief should contain all relevant authority published prior to submission of the brief. A Notice of Supplemental Authority should cite only to newly discovered cases (copy of the opinion should be attached to the Notice) with a clear designation of the point on appeal to which the authority is pertinent. Argument is not permitted in the Notice of Supplemental Authority.

8. If not filed electronically, all briefs shall be securely stapled with one staple in the upper left-hand corner and without brief covers. No onion skin or similar quality copies will be accepted.

E. Extensions of Time

1. In expedited cases, no motions for extensions of time will be granted.

2. Requests for extension of time should be filed in compliance with Florida Rule of Appellate Procedure 9.300(a). No motion for extension of time will be granted that does not contain a certificate that opposing counsel has been contacted, and the position opposing counsel takes on the extension. A motion for extension of time served after the time for serving the brief or response has expired will not be granted absent a showing of good cause.

3. In lieu of an agreed motion for extension of time to file a brief, the Court will accept a notice from a party that the parties have agreed to a specific extension of time. This notice shall state that the parties have agreed on the extension, how long the agreement entails, and when the new due date will be. Agreed notices for extension of time will be accepted for a total of 90 days for an initial or answer brief and 60 days for a reply brief. The notice need not be signed

by both parties. No order will issue from the Court. This procedure shall apply to criminal and civil appeals, but it shall not apply to any expedited or emergency appeals. A notice of agreed extension of time filed after the time for serving the brief or response has expired will be stricken absent a showing of good cause.

F. Other Information

1. To ensure you receive copies of all motions, orders, and opinions, **FILE A NOTICE OF CHANGE OF ADDRESS WHEN YOU MOVE.** It is not the Court's responsibility to track down your new address.

2. Requests for the status of the matter pending before the Court should be directed to the Clerk of Court either at the Orange County Clerk of Courts at (407) 836–2000 or the Osceola County Clerk of Courts at (407) 742–3500, depending upon which Clerk's Office you filed. Please be advised that the Clerk can only tell you what has or has not been filed into the Appeal case file. You should not ask the Clerk legal questions because they are not trained or licensed to give legal advice.

1 Exhibits A and B are not included.

2015–09. [VACATED BY ADMINISTRATIVE ORDER NO. 2016–20, EFFECTIVE OCTOBER 13, 2016]

2015–06. EARLY CHILDHOOD COURT

IN THE CIRCUIT COURT OF THE NINTH JUDICIAL CIRCUIT, IN AND FOR ORANGE COUNTY, FLORIDA

ADMINISTRATIVE ORDER NO. 2015–06

ORDER GOVERNING EARLY CHILDHOOD COURT

WHEREAS, pursuant to Article V, section 2(d) of the Florida Constitution and section 43.26, Florida Statutes, the chief judge of each judicial circuit is charged with the authority and the power to do everything necessary to promote the prompt and efficient administration of justice; and

WHEREAS, pursuant to the chief judge's constitutional and statutory responsibility for administrative supervision of the courts within the circuit and to create and maintain an organization capable of effecting the efficient, prompt, and proper administration of justice for the citizens of this State, the chief judge is required to exercise direction, *see* Fla. R. Jud. Admin. 2.215(b)(2), (b)(3); and

WHEREAS, the purpose of Early Childhood Court is to increase the likelihood of reunification of families and permanency for children through targeted treatment interventions and close judicial supervision; and

WHEREAS, this specialized division will enable consideration of the unique nature of the issues related to young children in the dependency system, the need for appropriate treatment in an environment conducive to wellness, as well as the continuing necessity to ensure the protection of the child;

NOW, THEREFORE, I, Frederick J. Lauten, in order to facilitate the efficient operation of the administration of justice, and pursuant to the authority vested in me as Chief Judge of the Ninth Judicial Circuit of Florida under Florida Rule of Judicial Administration 2.215, hereby order the following, **effective immediately**, and to continue until further order:

1. The Ninth Judicial Circuit Early Childhood Court Program for Orange County ("Program") is hereby established.

2. Eligibility Criteria: Families where children have been sheltered as a result of an allegation of abuse, abandonment, neglect, violence or substance abuse. Children must be less than five (5) years of age at the time of referral to the Program and be placed by the Department of Children and Families in Orange County. Parents who have perpetrated an egregious act of violence against the child or committed violent or sexual criminal offenses may be ineligible for participation at the sole discretion of the Early Childhood Court judge.

3. Referral Process: A referral form must be completed and submitted to the Early Childhood Court Coordinator (Coordinator). The parent(s) must schedule and complete a screening with the Coordinator.

4. Participation: The Program will provide participating families with additional services through its community partnerships to help parents complete case plans with the Department of Children and Families while addressing the unique needs of young children involved in Dependency cases. As part of the Program the families will engage in treatment for substance abuse and/or mental health issues as well as life skills and parenting classes as ordered. Assessment and treatment will be made available to the parents and children.

5. Early Childhood Court will be in session one (1) day, biweekly, as directed by the Early Childhood Court judge. Cases will be staffed and reviewed on a bi-weekly basis until the family completes the Program. The dependency case will continue to be reviewed in Early Childhood Court according to state mandates to ascertain compliance with the case plan.

DONE AND ORDERED at Orlando, Florida, this 11th day of August, 2015.

Frederick J. Lauten
Chief Judge

2015–02. GOVERNING BLOOD TEST SCREENING FOR CERTAIN DISEASES TRANSMITTED THROUGH A SIGNIFICANT EXPOSURE

IN THE CIRCUIT COURT OF THE NINTH JUDICIAL CIRCUIT, IN AND FOR ORANGE AND OSCEOLA COUNTIES, FLORIDA

ADMINISTRATIVE ORDER NO. 2015–02

ORDER GOVERNING BLOOD TEST SCREENING FOR CERTAIN DISEASES TRANSMITTED THROUGH A SIGNIFICANT EXPOSURE AND ALLOWING FOR THE LIMITED DISCLOSURE OF TEST RESULTS

WHEREAS, pursuant to Article V, section 2(d) of the Florida Constitution and section 43.26, Florida Statutes, the chief judge of each judicial circuit is charged with the authority and the power to do everything necessary to promote the prompt and efficient administration of justice; and

WHEREAS, pursuant to the chief judge's constitutional and statutory responsibility for administrative supervision of the courts within the circuit and to create and maintain an organization capable of effecting the efficient, prompt, and proper administration of justice for the citizens of this State, the chief judge is required to exercise direction, *see* Fla. R. Jud. Admin. 2.215(b)(2), (b)(3); and

WHEREAS, Florida law authorizes an officer as defined in section 943.10(14), Florida Statutes; support personnel as defined in section 943.10(11), Florida Statutes, who are employed by the Department of Law Enforcement, including, but not limited to, any crime scene analysts, forensic technologists, or crime lab analysts; firefighter as defined in section 633.102, Florida Statutes; or ambulance driver, paramedic, or emergency medical technician, as defined in section 401.23, Florida Statutes, acting within the scope of employment, or the employer of such individual, who comes into contact with a person in such a way that significant exposure of bodily fluids, as defined in section 381.004, Florida Statutes, has occurred, to request that the person be screened for sexually transmittable diseases that can be transmitted through a significant exposure pursuant to section 384.287, Florida Statutes; and

WHEREAS, if the person will not voluntarily submit to screening, the officer, support personnel of the Department of Law Enforcement, firefighter, ambulance driver, paramedic, or emergency medical technician, or the employer of any of the employees described above, acting on behalf of the employee, may seek a court order directing that the person who is the source of the significant exposure to bodily fluids, to submit to the screening of said person's blood pursuant to section 384.287, Florida Statutes; and

WHEREAS, early determination and disclosure of the screening results to appropriate medical personnel and the person(s) who has been exposed is a critical factor in the diagnosis and treatment of the exposed person; is necessary to prevent unnecessary mental anguish; and, is in the best interests of public health, safety and welfare; and

WHEREAS, due to the time, location and circumstances surrounding the occurrence of a significant exposure, it often can be difficult for the exposed person or his/her employer to obtain the required court order in a timely fashion so as to facilitate prompt testing and disclosure as intended by the Legislature, the Court finds that this Administrative Order is necessary in order to prevent unnecessary delay and aid in the early diagnosis and treatment of the exposed person(s); and

WHEREAS, this Administrative Order is further designed to harmonize the competing interests of the due process rights and expectation of privacy of individuals carrying one or more infectious pathogens, with society's special need to protect persons who may otherwise come into contact with such persons by virtue of the nature of their employment, thus allowing immediate testing and disclosure of the individual's blood test results in the least intrusive way by means of this Administrative Order, within the parameters of the case law, legislative intent, and statutory authority;

NOW, THEREFORE, I, Frederick J. Lauten, in order to facilitate the efficient operation of the administration of justice, and pursuant to the authority vested in me as Chief Judge of the Ninth Judicial Circuit of Florida under Florida Rule of Judicial Administration 2.215, hereby order the following, **effective immediately**, and to continue until further order:

1. This Administrative Order shall be deemed to take effect as an Order authorizing prompt blood testing and disclosure of blood test results under the parameters set forth below.

2. Whenever an officer, as defined in section 943.10(14), Florida Statutes; support personnel as defined in section 943.10(11), Florida Statutes, who is employed by the Department of Law Enforcement, including, but not limited to, any crime scene analysts, forensic technologists, or crime lab analysts; firefighter as defined in section 633.102, Florida Statutes; or ambulance driver, paramedic, or emergency medical technician, as defined in section 401.23, Florida Statutes, acting within the scope of his or her employment, comes into contact with a person in such a way that causes significant exposure to bodily fluids, as defined in section 381.004, Florida Statutes, and thereafter, said individual will not voluntarily submit to screening, then the officer, support personnel of the Department of Law Enforcement, firefighter, ambulance driver, paramedic, or emergency medical technician, or the employer of any of the employees described above, acting on behalf of their employee, may, upon receipt of a sworn statement by a physician, licensed under Chapter 458 or Chapter 459 attesting that a significant exposure has occurred and that in the physician's medical judgment, the screening is medically necessary to determine the course of treatment for the exposed person, utilize this Administrative Order as a standing order:

(a) directing the person who is the source of the significant exposure to submit to immediate screening; and

(b) providing for the prompt disclosure of the results of any such screening to the person who is the source of the significant exposure, to the person subjected to the significant exposure, to the physicians of the persons screened, and to the employer of the person subjected to the significant exposure, if necessary for the filing of a Worker's Compensation claim or any other disability claim based on the significant exposure pursuant to section 384.287, Florida Statutes.

3. The sworn statement by a physician, licensed under Chapter 458 or Chapter 459 attesting that a significant exposure has occurred and that in the physician's medical judgment, the screening is medically necessary to determine the course of treatment for the exposed person must be filed with the Clerk of the Court within twenty-four (24) hours after testing has occurred.

4. All screenings performed pursuant to this Administrative Order must be conducted by the Department of Health or the Department's authorized representative or by licensed medical personnel at a licensed facility designated by the attesting physician. The cost of the screening shall be borne by the employer.

5. In order to use the provisions of this Administrative Order, the person subjected to the significant exposure must also be screened for the same sexually transmittable diseases.

6. A person who receives the results of a test pursuant to this Administrative Order, which results disclose human immunodeficiency virus infection and are otherwise confidential pursuant to law, shall maintain the confidentiality of the information received and the identity of the person tested as required by section 381.004, Florida Statutes. Violation of this confidentiality may constitute a misdemeanor of the first degree, punishable as provided in section 775.082 or 775.083, Florida Statutes.

DONE AND ORDERED at Orlando, Florida, this 23rd day of June, 2015.

Frederick J. Lauten
Chief Judge

2014–27. CERTIFIED PROCESS SERVER PROGRAM, NINTH JUDICIAL CIRCUIT

ADMINISTRATIVE ORDER NO. 2014–27

IN THE CIRCUIT COURT OF THE NINTH JUDICIAL CIRCUIT, IN AND FOR ORANGE AND OSCEOLA COUNTIES, FLORIDA

ORDER GOVERNING CERTIFIED PROCESS SERVER PROGRAM, NINTH JUDICIAL CIRCUIT

WHEREAS, pursuant to Article V, section 2(d) of the Florida Constitution and section 43.26, Florida Statutes, the chief judge of each judicial circuit is charged with the authority and the power to do everything necessary to promote the prompt and efficient administration of justice; and

WHEREAS, pursuant to the chief judge's constitutional and statutory responsibility for administrative supervision of the courts within the circuit and to create and maintain an organization capable of effecting the efficient, prompt, and proper administration of justice for the citizens of this State, the chief judge is required to exercise direction, *see* Fla. R. Jud. Admin. 2.215(b)(2), (b)(3); and

WHEREAS, sections 48.25 through 48.31, Florida Statutes, the Florida Certified Process Server Act ("Process Server Act"), expressly vests in the chief judge the authority to establish an approved list of Certified Process Servers who have met the requirements for certification under the Process Server Act and the requirements set forth by the Ninth Judicial Circuit of Florida; and

WHEREAS, the Sheriff of Orange County has discontinued, effective December 31, 2014, the special process server program created by the Sheriff under the provisions of section 48.021, Florida Statutes, and will not renew any appointments that lapse prior to said date; and

WHEREAS, the Sheriff of Osceola County will discontinue, effective December 31, 2014, the special process server program created by the Sheriff under the provisions of section 48.021, Florida Statutes; and

WHEREAS, due to the actions of the Sheriff of Orange County, and to prevent the lapse of appointments of a group of specially appointed process servers for Orange County, Emergency Administrative Order No. 2014–23, was issued September 29, 2014; and

WHEREAS, Emergency Administrative Order No. 2014–23 is temporary in nature, effective only until December 31, 2014, unless amended or superseded earlier by another administrative order, and shall not be construed as limiting or directing this Administrative Order in any manner; and

WHEREAS, section 48.27, Florida Statutes, authorizes the chief judge to establish said list of Certified Process Servers as an alternative means for the service of initial non-enforceable civil process, criminal witness subpoenas, and criminal summonses; and

WHEREAS, the undersigned Chief Judge has determined that establishing an approved list of Certified Process Servers for Orange and Osceola County would serve the interest of justice and judicial economy, preserve judicial resources, assist the bar in discharging the duties and obligations to clients, and benefit the citizens of Orange and Osceola County; and

WHEREAS, it is necessary for the Chief Judge to establish an administrative process for renewal, review, approval, certification and regulation of individuals meeting the necessary requirements to be certified as a process server empowered to serve process including initial non-enforceable civil process as provided by the Florida Statutes and this Administrative Order throughout the Ninth Judicial Circuit;

NOW, THEREFORE, I, Frederick J. Lauten, pursuant to the authority vested in me as Chief Judge of the Ninth Judicial Circuit of Florida under Florida Rule of Judicial Administration 2.215, do hereby order that the following standards, requirements and procedures shall be established for individuals to be eligible for inclusion on the approved list of Certified Process Servers for the Ninth Judicial Circuit, **effective immediately**, and to continue until further order:

I. DEFINITIONS:

A. The *Act* shall mean the Florida Certified Process Server Act, sections 48.25 through 48.31, Florida Statutes.

B. The *Designee* shall mean one or more members of court administration staff, as assigned to assist with the ministerial operational aspects of the Certified Process Server Program and shall be referred to herein in the gender neutral plural ("its").

C. The *Committee* shall mean the group of natural persons appointed by the Chief Judge.

D. The *Panel* is a group composed of three Committee members.

E. The *Program* is the process for certification of process servers as provided by the Act and this Administrative Order to allow them to serve process in both Orange and Osceola County as authorized by section 48.27, Florida Statutes.

F. *Certified Process Server* or *CPS* means a natural person who has met the requirements for certification pursuant to the Act, as well as those established by this Administrative Order, and who has been approved and placed on the Certified Process Server List.

G. The *Certified Process Server List* or *CPSL* shall mean the list of CPS maintained by Court Administration, and published by and available from Court Administration, the Orange County Clerk of Court, or the Osceola County Clerk of Court.

H. A *New Applicant* is a natural person applying for certification as provided in section 48.29, Florida Statutes, under the Program established by this Administrative Order.

I. A *Renewal Applicant* is a natural person who has already been certified as a process server as provided in section 48.29, Florida Statutes, under the Program established by this Administrative Order.

J. The *CPS Identification Card* shall mean the identification card to be issued by the Designee as required by section 48.29(5)(b), Florida Statutes. The CPS Identification Card is the property of the Ninth Judicial Circuit and must be immediately surrendered upon request of the Chief Judge or the Designee. The CPS Identification Card shall be valid for one (1) year from the date of issuance. It is the responsibility of the Applicant to safeguard the CPS Identification Card issued pursuant to the guidelines contained herein. There is a $20.00 replacement fee if the CPS Identification Card is lost or stolen.

II. PURPOSE. The purpose of this Administrative Order is to establish a Program for the certification of process servers in the Ninth Judicial Circuit, for both Orange County and Osceola County, Florida, and to authorize them to serve process, as established by section 48.27, Florida Statutes, throughout the Ninth Judicial Circuit.

III. MAINTENANCE OF THE CERTIFIED PROCESS SERVER LIST. The Designee shall maintain a CPSL of process servers meeting the requirements of the Act and this Administrative Order. The CPSL may be amended at any time. The Designee and both the Orange County Clerk of Court and the Osceola County Clerk of Court shall make the CPSL available on the Court and respective Clerk's webpage and upon request.

IV. THE DESIGNEE:

A. The Designee shall supervise the operation of the Program, recommend certification or removal of process servers from the CPSL, review any allegation of noncompliance and recommend disciplinary action relating to CPS, and perform such other responsibilities as assigned.

B. The Designee, subject to approval by the Chief Judge, may adopt rules and regulations to implement and carry out the provisions of the Act, this Administrative Order or any part thereof, or any subsequent administrative order relating to the certification of process servers in the Ninth Judicial Circuit.

C. The Designee shall maintain records and minutes of any meetings, hearings, and all other official actions.

D. The name and contact information to reach the Designee is:

Helene Welch Court Operations Consultant Phone: (407) 836–0471 Email: ctadhw1@ocnjcc.org

V. THE COMMITTEE:

A. The Chief Judge may appoint a group of natural persons to investigate and recommend process servers for inclusion in the CPSL, review allegations of non-compliance and recommend disciplinary action against CPS, recommend changes to the Program, or perform such other tasks as are established by this Administrative Order or delegated by the Chief Judge.

B. The Chief Judge shall make all appointments to the Committee. Each appointee shall serve at the Chief Judge's pleasure and discretion.

C. All Committee members shall serve without compensation or reimbursement of expenses.

D. The Chief Judge shall determine the size and composition of the Committee, but said Committee shall have at minimum:

1. One person certified as a process server pursuant to the provisions of this Administrative Order;

2. Two persons designated by the Orange County Bar Association (OCBA) with one of the two from the OCBA's Paralegal Section;

3. One person designated by the Osceola County Bar Association;

4. One person designated by the Sheriff of Orange County;

5. One person designated by the Sheriff of Osceola County;

5[1]. One person designated by the Orange County Clerk of Courts;

6. One person designated by the Osceola County Clerk of Courts; and

7. One person designated by the Chief Judge from the Ninth Judicial Circuit Court Administration.

E. The Chief Judge, in his discretion, may divide the Committee into Panels to investigate and recommend process servers for inclusion in the CPSL, review allegations of non-compliance and recommend disciplinary action against CPS, or perform such other tasks as are established by this Administrative Order or delegated by the Chief Judge.

F. Subject to approval by the Chief Judge, the Committee, Panel, or Panels may prescribe rules and regulations, norms and codes of conduct, and other requirements regarding the investigation and recommendation for inclusion of process servers in the CPSL, the review of allegations of non-compliance and recommendations of disciplinary action against CPS, and the performance of such other tasks as are delegated to the Committee, Panel, or Panels by the Chief Judge.

VI. CERTIFICATION OF PROCESS SERVERS. Any natural person seeking certification as a CPS shall be at least eighteen years of age, be a permanent resident of the State of Florida, have no mental or legal disability, and meet the requirements of the Act and this Administrative Order.

VII. APPLICATION FOR CERTIFICATION OF PROCESS SERVERS:

A. New Applicants:

1. The Applicant must submit an application, along with a non-refundable application fee via personal check, cashier's check, or money order made payable to the State of Florida in the amount of $300.00, to the Designee. See Exhibit "A" to this Administrative Order for the initial CPS application.

2. The Applicant shall submit to a background investigation which shall include a review of the applicant's criminal record, if any exists. The Applicant shall present to the Designee a Criminal History Check from the Florida Department of Law Enforcement.

3. The Applicant shall obtain and file with the Application a Certificate of Good Conduct certifying that there is no record of: (a) any pending criminal case against the Applicant; (b) any felony conviction of Applicant for which civil rights have not been restored; or (c) any conviction of the Applicant for a misdemeanor involving moral turpitude or dishonesty

within the preceding five years. See Exhibit "C" to this Administrative Order.

4. Persons who have completed an application and satisfied the requirements set forth herein shall submit to a written examination testing the Applicant's knowledge of the laws and rules regarding the service of process. A passing examination grade is hereby fixed at eighty percent (80%) out of a possible score of one hundred percent (100%). The content, frequency and location of the examination shall be approved by the Chief Judge or his Designee. Examinations administered by any vendor accepted, approved, or certified by: (i) the Criminal Justice Standards & Training Commission of Florida to present seminars and courses for career advancement credit for Florida Sheriffs, (ii) any Florida Judicial Circuit, or (iii) any Florida Sheriff shall meet the requirements of this Administrative Order. The written examination must be taken within eleven (11) months prior to the day the application is submitted.

5. Applicants must file with the Designee evidence of a performance bond in the amount of $5,000.00 with a surety company authorized to do business within the State of Florida, which bond must be maintained at all times during the certification period and renewable annually. Each time the performance bond is renewed, Applicant must file proof of the renewal with the Designee. See Exhibit "D" to this Administrative Order.

6. An Applicant who successfully completes the application process shall take an oath that he or she will honestly, diligently, and faithfully exercise the duties of a Certified Process Server.

7. Upon meeting the requirements of paragraphs "VII. A.1, 2, 3, 4, 5 and 6" of this Administrative Order, the Designee shall issue a CPS Identification Card, as required by section 48.29(5)(b), Florida Statutes. The CPS Identification Card shall be valid for one (1) year from the date of issuance and must be renewed annually before its expiration. It is the responsibility of the Applicant to safeguard the CPS Identification Card issued pursuant to the guidelines contained herein. There is a $20.00 replacement fee if the CPS Identification Card is lost or stolen.

8. An Applicant who completes the requirements of the Act and this Administrative Order shall be placed on the CPSL, and shall be authorized to serve initial non-enforceable civil process as authorized by section 48.27, Florida Statutes, in the Ninth Judicial Circuit.

B. Renewal Applicants:

1. The Applicant must submit a renewal application, along with a non-refundable renewal application fee via personal check, cashier's check, or money order made payable to the State of Florida in the amount of $250.00, to the Designee. See Exhibit "B" to this Administrative Order for the renewal CPS application.

2. The Applicant shall submit to a background investigation which shall include a review of the applicant's criminal record, if any exists. The Applicant shall present to the Designee a Criminal History Check from the Florida Department of Law Enforcement.

3. The Applicant shall obtain and file with the Application a Certificate of Good Conduct certifying that there is no record of: (a) any pending criminal case against the Applicant; (b) any felony conviction of Applicant for which civil rights have not been restored; or (c) any conviction of the Applicant for a misdemeanor involving moral turpitude or dishonesty within the preceding five years. See Exhibit "C" to this Administrative Order.

4. Persons who have completed a renewal application and satisfied the requirements set forth shall submit to a written renewal examination testing the Applicant's knowledge of the laws and rules regarding the service of process. A passing examination grade is hereby fixed at eighty percent (80%) out of a possible score of one hundred percent (100%). The content, frequency and location of the examination shall be approved by the Chief Judge or his Designee. Examinations administered by any vendor accepted, approved, or certified by (i) the Criminal Justice Standards & Training Commission of Florida to present seminars and courses for career advancement credit for Florida Sheriffs, (ii) any Florida Judicial Circuit, or (iii) any Florida Sheriff shall meet the requirements of this Administrative Order. The written renewal examination must be taken within eleven (11) months prior to the day the renewal application is submitted.

5. Renewal Applicants must file with the Designee evidence of a performance bond in the amount of $5,000.00 with a surety company authorized to do business within the State of Florida, which bond must be maintained at all times during the certification period and renewable annually. Each time the performance bond is renewed, Applicant must file proof of the renewal with the Designee. See Exhibit "D" to this Administrative Order.

6. A Renewal Applicant who successfully complete the application process shall take an oath that he or she will honestly, diligently, and faithfully exercise the duties of a certified process server.

7. Upon meeting the requirements of paragraphs "VII. B.1, 2, 3, 4, 5 and 6" of this Administrative Order, the Designee shall issue a CPS Identification Card, as required by section 48.29(5)(b) of the Florida Statutes. The CPS Identification Card shall be valid for one (1) year from the date of issuance and must be renewed annually before its expiration. It is the responsibility of the Applicant to safeguard the CPS Identification Card issued pursuant to the guidelines contained herein. There is a $20.00 replacement fee if the CPS Identification Card is lost or stolen.

8. A Renewal Applicant who completes the requirements of the Act and this Administrative Order shall be placed on the CPSL, and shall be authorized to serve initial non-enforceable civil process as authorized by section 48.27, Florida Statutes, in the Ninth Judicial Circuit.

VIII. APPLICATION FEE. As provided by section 48.29(2), Florida Statutes, the Designee may charge a reasonable fee for processing an application filed pursuant to the Act and this Administrative Order. The Chief Judge must approve the fee amount prior to implementation. The amount may be changed by the Chief Judge at any time and without notice but any changes will apply only to applications filed with the Designee after the effective date of the change.

IX. CPS'S DUTIES AND CODE OF CONDUCT:

A. Servers on the CPSL shall comply and keep current with all applicable rules, regulations, administrative orders and statutes (to include Florida and other Federal, foreign or domestic jurisdictions) pertaining to service of process.

B. Servers on the CPSL shall serve only non-enforceable process.

C. While serving process, Servers on the CPSL shall present their CPS Identification Card upon request.

D. Servers on the CPSL shall charge a reasonable fee for the service of process. There is no minimum or maximum amount that must be charged.

E. Although Servers on the CPSL are not employees, agents, officers, or representatives of the Ninth Judicial Circuit, its Judges or employees, the Clerks, the State of Florida, Orange County, Osceola County, or any municipality and any of its divisions, agencies, or departments, because Servers on the CPSL by virtue of their power and identification give the appearance that they represent the Ninth Judicial Circuit when serving process, they shall:

1. be competent, courteous, professional, properly groomed and appropriately attired,

2. portray a professional appearance to general public, and

3. refrain from any act, or statement that would impugn the Judiciary or Court Administration.

F. Servers on the CPSL shall conduct themselves professionally and with dignity while on or in the premises of the Courthouses. Conduct with the Judges, Deputies, Deputy Clerks, and other employees of the Judiciary, Designee, or of the Clerks shall be respectful at all times.

G. Servers on the CPSL shall serve process in a timely manner.

H. Servers on the CPSL shall not serve process in any cause of action in which they have an interest.

I. Servers on the CPSL are required to type, legibly write, stamp, or by other printed methods, record the information required by section 48.21, Florida Statutes, plus insert the title "Certified Process Server" and their CPS Identification Card number on the original and all copies of process. The return of process shall be notarized.

J. Any lawsuits brought against a server on the CPSL due to his or her actions as a Certified Process Server in any jurisdiction, foreign or domestic, shall be reported immediately to the Designee.

K. Servers must immediately notify the Designee if the Server is arrested for any crime, including criminal traffic offenses, or is given a criminal Notice to Appear.

L. Servers on the CPSL must report any change in home or work address or telephone number to the Designee within five (5) calendar days of the change.

M. Servers on the CPSL must comply with any request made by the Chief Judge, the Committee or the Designee within five (5) calendar days of the day of the request.

N. Servers on the CPSL shall truthfully answer all questions and inquiries from the Chief Judge, the Designee, the Committee or a Panel.

O. If any server on the CPSL has his or her appointment or certification suspended or revoked in another county or judicial circuit in Florida, or in any other Federal, domestic or foreign jurisdiction, his or her Ninth Judicial Circuit certification shall also be suspended or revoked.

P. No server on the CPSL shall serve process or subcontract with a natural person or business entity whose authority to serve process has been suspended or revoked in the Ninth Judicial Circuit, in any other county or judicial circuit in Florida, or in any other Federal, domestic or foreign jurisdiction.

Q. Servers on the CPSL shall comply with all administrative orders, rules, regulations and statutes pertaining to the service and return of service of process at all times.

R. Servers on the CPSL shall immediately report to the Designee any disciplinary complaint or charges brought or filed against such Server due to the Server's actions as a process server in any jurisdiction, foreign or domestic, in any county or judicial circuit in Florida, or with any Florida Sheriff.

S. All Servers on the CPSL, as a condition of their appointments, must agree if requested by the Chief Judge to serve on the Committee or a Panel without compensation or reimbursement of expenses. Refusal shall constitute by itself sufficient reason for removal from the CPSL.

X. DISCIPLINE:

A. Any server on the CPSL may be removed from the CPSL for good cause. Good cause shall include malfeasance, misfeasance, neglect of duty or incompetence in connection with the duties of a Certified Process Server, violation of any of the provisions of this Administrative Order, section 48.31, Florida Statutes, or of any applicable rules, regulations, administrative orders and statutes (to include Florida and other Federal, foreign or domestic jurisdictions) pertaining to service of process.

B. Any person aggrieved by the actions of a CPS may file a complaint with the Designee. If a Committee or a Panel has been appointed by the Chief Judge, the Designee shall refer the complaint to said Committee or Panel for investigation and recommendation.

C. If no Committee or Panel has been appointed by the Chief Judge, the Designee shall investigate and review the complaint. After a hearing in which the Certified Process Server has an opportunity to be heard and present evidence, the Designee, shall forward its findings and recommendations to the Chief Judge. The Designee can request the Chief Judge issue subpoenas to compel the attendance of witnesses.

D. If a Committee or a Panel is appointed by the Chief Judge, the Committee or Panel shall investigate and review the complaint. After a hearing in which the Certified Process Server has an opportunity to be heard and present evidence, the Committee or Panel shall forward its findings and recommendations to the Designee. The Designee shall forward the Committee or Panel report to the Chief Judge for review, ultimate decision, and imposition of sanctions. The sanctions may include admonishment or suspension or revocation of certification. The Committee or Panel can request the Chief Judge to issue subpoenas to compel the attendance of witnesses.

E. A complaint shall remain in the CPS's file for a period of five (5) years. The CPS's file shall be a public record.

F. The standard of proof in disciplinary proceedings shall be preponderance of the evidence.

G. Nothing herein shall limit the power of the Chief Judge or any other Judge in Florida or in any other Federal, foreign or domestic jurisdiction to take whatever action he or she deems appropriate without the necessity of referral to the Designee, the Committee, or a Panel

H. The decision of the Chief Judge is final.

XI. NO WAIVER OF IMMUNITY. No provision of this Administrative Order is intended to waive, in whole or in part, judicial, sovereign, or other immunity held by the Courts of this Circuit as either a body or as an individual.

XII. NO AGENCY RELATIONSHIP ESTABLISHED:

A. Servers on the CPSL are not employees, agents, officers or representatives of the Ninth Judicial Circuit, its Judges or employees, the Orange County Clerk of Court, the Osceola County Clerk of Court, the State of Florida, Orange County, Osceola County or any municipality and any if[2] its divisions, agencies or departments. Said Servers are independent contractors hired by third parties to serve process within the Ninth Judicial Circuit.

B. Servers on the CPSL are not under the supervision, direction or control of the Ninth Judicial Circuit, its Judges or employees, the Orange County Clerk of Court, the Osceola County Clerk of Court, the State of Florida, Orange County, Osceola County or any municipality and any of its divisions, agencies or departments. Said Servers are independent contractors hired by third parties to serve process within Orange County or Osceola County, Florida.

XIII. MISCELLANEOUS:

A. The Chief Judge may amend or expand the provisions or coverage of this Administrative Order at any time and without notice.

B. The Chief Judge may issue other or further administrative orders as he or she, in his or her discretion, may deem necessary.

XIV. APPLICABILITY:

A. This Administrative Order shall not apply to the Sheriffs of Orange or Osceola County or any of their divisions or departments.

B. This Administrative Order shall only apply to those natural persons seeking to serve process as a CPS in the Ninth Judicial Circuit Court.

C. Emergency Administrative Order No. 2014–23 is temporary in nature, effective only until December 31, 2014, unless amended or superseded earlier by another administrative order, and shall not be construed as limiting or directing this Administrative Order in any manner. Further, this Administrative Order does not amend or supersede Emergency Administrative Order No. 2014–23. Additionally, those individuals named Grandfathered Special Process Servers, pursuant to Emergency Administrative Order No. 2014–23, must apply to be a CPS pursuant to this Administrative Order should they wish to continue serving process in Orange or Osceola County beyond December 31, 2014.

Administrative Order No. 07–87–10 and No. 07–91–05 are hereby vacated and set aside, effective December 31, 2014, and have been incorporated and/or amended herein.

DONE AND ORDERED at Orlando, Florida, this 18th day of November, 2014.

Frederick J. Lauten
Chief Judge

EXHIBIT "A"

INITIAL CERTIFIED PROCESS SERVER APPLICATION

NINTH JUDICIAL CIRCUIT

PERSONAL DATA

NAME ____
Last First Initial

ADDRESS ____
Number and Street City State Zip

MAILING ADDRESS ____________________________________
P.O. Box City State Zip

TELEPHONE ____

Request posting of mailing address and business phone number on the certified process server web page. Yes ____________ No ____________

SOCIAL SECURITY NUMBER ____________________________

CITIZENSHIP _______________________________________

IF ALIEN, check which type of work authorization you have:

__________ Alien Registration Form I–151

__________ Refugee Status Form I–94

File Number of Form __________

If NATURALIZED, record the following forms of identification:

Naturalization Certificate Number __________

U.S. Passport Number __________

Voter's Registration Number __________

ARE YOU 18 OR MORE YEARS OLD? __________

DATE OF BIRTH __________

DO YOU HAVE ANY MENTAL OR LEGAL LIABILITIES: __________

If so, please list them __________

ARE YOU A PERMANENT FLORIDA RESIDENT: __________

HAVE YOU EVER BEEN A MEMBER OF THE U.S. ARMED SERVICES:

Yes __________ No __________

Type of discharge: HONORABLE __________ GENERAL __________

OTHER __________

If other, please explain __________

RESIDENCY DATA

PLEASE LIST YOUR RESIDENCES FOR THE PAST FIVE YEARS IN RE-
VERSE
CHRONOLOGICAL ORDER.

____
Number & Street City State Zip

____
Number & Street City State Zip

____
Number & Street City State Zip

____
Number & Street City State Zip

____
Number & Street City State Zip

EDUCATION

PLEASE LIST THE SCHOOLS WHICH YOU ATTENDED IN CHRONOLOGICAL ORDER BEGINNING WITH HIGH SCHOOL.

School Level Name

Number & Street City Zip

Dates Attended Graduate Y/N Major Degree

School Level Name

Number & Street City Zip

Dates Attended Graduate Y/N Major Degree

School Level Name

Number & Street City Zip

Dates Attended Graduate Y/N Major Degree

EMPLOYMENT DATA

PLEASE LIST YOUR THREE MOST RECENT EMPLOYERS IN REVERSE CHRONOLOGICAL ORDER

Employer

Number & Street City Zip

Dates Employed Position

Employer

Number & Street City Zip

Employer

Number & Street City Zip

Dates Employed Position

IF YOU HAVE EVER WORKED AS A PROCESS SERVER BEFORE, PLEASE ANSWER THE FOLLOWING QUESTIONS:

When and where did you work as a process server?

While working as a process server, were any lawsuits or disciplinary complaint or charge brought or filed against you as a server in any

jurisdiction, foreign or domestic, in any Florida County, Florida Circuit or Florida Sheriff shall be (even if they resolved amicably)?
Circle one: Yes No

If yes, please answer the following.

When and where was the action filed?

____

Please explain the details of the action—why were you charged and what was the disposition?

____

____

Please attach to this application copies of all of the documents relevant to the legal action or
disciplinary action, including the complaint and disposition.

Were you ever terminated from your position as a process server, or have you ever had your
appointment as a process server revoked?
Circle one: Yes No

If yes, please answer the following.

When and where were you terminated?

____

Why were you terminated?

____

____

If there were any documents involved in the termination, such as a formal termination letter, please attach copies to this application.

OCCUPATIONAL/PROFESSIONAL LICENSES OR CERTIFICATES

____

TYPE NUMBER

____

DATE OBTAINED RENEWAL DATE

DRIVER'S OR CHAUFFEUR'S LICENSE

Type______________________________________

Number____________________________________

State______________________________________

Expiration _________________________________

BACKGROUND INFORMATION:

PERSONAL DATA

CITIZENSHIP ______________________________

DATE OF BIRTH ______________________________

PLACE OF BIRTH ______________________________

RACE ____________________ HEIGHT __________
WEIGHT __________

HAIR COLOR ____________________ EYE COLOR __________

DO YOU HAVE ANY IDENTIFYING MARKS: ______ IF SO, PLEASE LIST THE TYPE OF MARK AND ITS LOCATION

____

CRIMINAL HISTORY

PLEASE LIST ANY OFFENSE FOR WHICH YOU HAVE BEEN CONVICTED, OR ANY CHARGE AGAINST YOU CURRENTLY.

____
Offense County State Date

____
Offense County State Date

____
Offense County State Date

____
Offense County State Date

____
Offense County State Date

Under the provisions of section 92.525, Florida Statutes, **under penalties of perjury**, I declare that I have read the foregoing document and that the facts stated in it are true. I further understand that any misinformation supplied herein shall result in an immediate forfeiture of any opportunity to become or remain a certified process server in the Ninth Judicial Circuit.

______________________________ ______________________________
Signature Date

EXHIBIT "B"

CERTIFIED PROCESS SERVER RENEWAL APPLICATION NINTH JUDICIAL CIRCUIT

DATE ______________________________

LAST NAME __________ FIRST NAME __________ MI ___

HOME ADDRESS ______________________________

STATE __________ ZIP CODE __________ HOME PHONE

____

SS# __________ WEIGHT ___ COLOR EYES ___ HAIR COLOR ______________________________

BUSINESS NAME ______________________________

BUSINESS ADDRESS ______________________________

STATE __________ ZIP CODE __________ SUPERVISOR

____

BUSINESS PHONE __________ CELL # __________

HAVE YOU EVER BEEN ARRESTED? ___ IF YES, CHARGE AND DATE ______________________________

____

Attach statement with details and disposition of arrest(s)

LIST ALL COUNTIES IN WHICH YOU ARE CERTIFIED OR SPECIALLY APPOINTED TO SERVE PROCESS AND THE DATE YOUR CERTIFICATION OR APPOINTMENT EXPIRES:

____

____

Under the provisions of Section 92.525, Florida Statutes, **under penalties of perjury**, I declare that I have read the foregoing document and that the facts stated in it are true. I further understand that any misinformation supplied herein shall result in an immediate forfeiture of any opportunity to become or remain a certified process server in the Ninth Judicial Circuit.

____________________ ____________________

Signature Date

DO NOT WRITE BELOW THIS LINE— FOR OFFICE USE ONLY

ID# ________ ISSUED ________ RENEWAL DATE __

LAST TRAINING ______________________________

EXHIBIT "C"

CERTIFICATE OF GOOD CONDUCT

I, ________________, certify that as of the date of this Certificate, I have:

1. No pending criminal case against me.
2. No record of any felony conviction.
3. No record of a misdemeanor involving moral turpitude or dishonesty within the past five (5) years.

____

Applicant/Appointee's signature

____

Address

____

City, State, and Zip Code

____

Date

STATE OF FLORIDA COUNTY OF ORANGE

The foregoing instrument was acknowledge before me this ___ day of ________ 20 __ by ________ who is personally known { } or produced identification { } Type of Identification ________ and who did take an oath.

____

Notary Public

EXHIBIT "D"

PROCESS SERVER'S BOND

Bond No. ________________________________

KNOW ALL MEN BY THESE PRESENTS:

That we, ________, as Principal, and ________, a corporation duly licensed for the purpose of making, guaranteeing or becoming a sole surety upon bonds, or undertakings, required by the laws of the State of Florida, as Surety, are held and firmly bound unto the State of Florida, Ninth Judicial Circuit, in the sum of $5,000, lawful money of the United States of America, for the payment whereof well and truly to be made, we bind ourselves, our heirs, executors, successors and assigns, jointly and severally, firmly by these presents.

THE CONDITION OF THE FOREGOING OBLIGATION IS SUCH, THAT

WHEREAS, if the above bounded Principal shall well, truly and faithfully comply with the provisions of statutes in the State of Florida, then this obligation shall be null and void, otherwise to remain in full force and effect.

The Surety hereunder may relieve itself from liability to the extent and in the manner set forth in the provisions of the statutes governing the termination by the surety of liability under the bond provided; however, that in no event shall it be relieved from liability as respects transactions occurring before the date of termination.

If the Surety shall so elect this bond may be canceled by giving 30 days written notice to Obligee.

This bond shall be in effect from ________ and expires on ________.

Signed and sealed this ________ day of ________, ________.

________________	________________
Principal (print or type name)	Name of Surety
By: ________________	________________
Signature of Principal	Attorney in Fact
	________________
	Address of Surety
	________________
	________________

1 Numbering as provided in original.

2 So in original.

2014–26. CERTIFIED THERAPY DOG PROGRAM (K–9th CIRCUIT PROGRAM), ORANGE COUNTY

IN THE CIRCUIT COURT OF THE NINTH JUDICIAL CIRCUIT, IN AND FOR ORANGE COUNTY, FLORIDA

ADMINISTRATIVE ORDER NO. 2014–26

ADMINISTRATIVE ORDER ESTABLISHING A CERTIFIED THERAPY DOG PROGRAM (K–9th CIRCUIT PROGRAM), ORANGE COUNTY

WHEREAS, pursuant to Article V, section 2(d) of the Florida Constitution and section 43.26, Florida Statutes, the chief judge of each judicial circuit is charged with the authority and the power to do everything necessary to promote the prompt and efficient administration of justice; and

WHEREAS, pursuant to the chief judge's constitutional and statutory responsibility for administrative supervision of the courts within the circuit and to create and maintain an organization capable of effecting the efficient, prompt, and proper administration of justice for the citizens of this State, the chief judge is required to exercise direction, *see* Fla. R. Jud. Admin. 2.215(b)(2), (b)(3); and

WHEREAS, section 92.55(4), Florida Statutes, enables the court to establish conditions it finds just and appropriate when taking the testimony of a child, including the use of a service or therapy animal that has been evaluated and registered according to national standards, in any proceeding involving a sexual offense; and

WHEREAS, the use of therapy dogs to assist the victim witness may be appropriate in other traumatic proceedings including family court or dependency and Termination of Parental Rights proceedings; and

WHEREAS, witnesses, including children and victims, are sometimes required to wait for an extended period of time before testifying in court; and

WHEREAS, it is necessary to provide specific guidelines for the presence and conduct of animal therapy teams within and/or on the premises of a Courthouse Facility of the Ninth Judicial Circuit;

NOW, THEREFORE, I, Frederick J. Lauten, pursuant to the authority vested in me as Chief Judge of the Ninth Judicial Circuit of Florida under Florida Rule of Judicial Administration 2.215, do hereby order that the following standards, requirements and procedures shall be established for the Therapy Dog Program, hereinafter referred to as the "K–9th Circuit Program," **effective immediately** and to continue until further order:

1. If the Office of the State Attorney, the Office of the Public Defender, the Department of Children and Families, the Guardian Ad Litem, or private retained counsel determine that the presence and use of a therapy dog may aid in the testimony of a child/victim/witness at hearing, trial or deposition, that agency or individual may contact an approved therapy dog provider [1] to determine availability of a therapy team and use of one of their therapy dogs.

2. Prior to the trial or hearing date, a timely motion requesting approval for the use of an animal therapy team must be filed and a hearing scheduled with notice to all interested parties.

3. The moving party is solely and exclusively responsible to facilitate all communication with the dog handler regarding the date and time and location of any and all court events and case related events, including informing the dog handler of any changes in date and/or time of the scheduled trial/hearing. This includes not only events occurring at a Courthouse Facility, but also any off-site interactions with the dog handler.

4. The therapy dog team is permitted on the premises of and inside the Juvenile Courthouse Facility and/or the Orange County Courthouse Facility for all scheduled court events as well as case related events scheduled by another agency. It is the responsibility of the moving party, and an absolute requirement, to ensure that an appropriate third party/representative is present at all times with the therapy dog team while aiding in the testimony of a child/victim/witness in a Courthouse Facility. [2] An appropriate third party/representative of the moving party is one who has no personal interest in the case; for example, a Guardian Ad Litem volunteer or a State Attorney Victim Advocate may serve as a third party/representative. At no time shall the dog and its handler be permitted to be alone with any child/victim/witness without the presence of the third party/representative of the moving party.

5. If the motion is granted the Presiding Judge may enter any orders deemed appropriate for proper procedures, conduct and use of the dog in their courtroom.

6. The approved provider shall:

a. Ensure that handlers and dogs have completed any and all therapy training and have passed a nationally recognized skills and aptitude test and evaluation by an organization that certifies the team as appropriate to provide animal assisted therapy.

b. Ensure that all handlers/dogs adhere to all policies of their individual certifying organizations and remain current on their certifications.

c. Ensure that the dogs have been examined by a Florida veterinarian to ensure good health within the past year and all immunizations, including rabies vaccination, is current.

d. Ensure that every dog is properly registered/licensed in the State of Florida.

e. Carry a minimum of one million dollars ($1,000,000) in liability insurance with a rider that includes therapy dogs on the premises of the Juvenile Courthouse Facility and/or the Orange County Courthouse Facility and naming Orange County as a named insurer.

f. Provide a copy of the insurance liability insurance rider page to Orange County's Risk Management Office.

g. Ensure that all dogs will be leashed at all times with the handler in control of the dog and the leash.

h. Advise handlers to refrain from any and all overt displays of emotion during all court proceedings.

i. Ensure that handlers will adhere to their certifying organization's policies regarding grooming and zoonotic disease/parasite control in attempts to reduce allergens and/or parasites.

j. Ensure that handlers will inquire if there are any known allergies or concerns prior to entering an enclosed space, including elevators.

k. Ensure that handlers are responsible for arriving early enough to exercise the dog to avoid any elimination issues. All dogs must be trained not to eliminate indoors. Outdoor elimination must be cleaned up by the handler using proper disposal methods to control odors, etc.

l. Ensure that any incidents are immediately reported to the Presiding Judge and the Office of the Chief Judge. Reportable incidents include injuries to a person or an animal; situations with a high potential that an injury could have occurred either to a person or an animal, even though no one was hurt at the time; situations with a perception of an accident or injury, and damages to property, including animal elimination in the courthouse facility. The incident report form is available on the Circuit's website at http://www.ninthcircuit.org/.

m. Ensure that all handlers have passed a background check to serve as a court volunteer. The information contained therein and specific findings are confidential and the approved provider will be advised in writing only as to whether the specific individual handler is approved or not approved to provide services to the Ninth Judicial Circuit.

n. Ensure that all handlers will immediately report to Court Administration any incident that may change the status of their background check, including but not limited to any arrest, conviction or other incident involving law enforcement.

o. Ensure that handlers will maintain the confidentiality of all information including, but not limited to, information pertaining to the individuals testifying and their families, whether written or verbal, received through the scope of interaction with the individual testifying. Handlers will sign an oath of confidentiality, available on the Circuit's website at http://www.ninthcircuit.org/.

p. Ensure that all handlers have received, acknowledged and endorsed an Acknowledgement of Terms and Conditions Sheet available on the Circuit's website at http://www.ninthcircuit.org/.

q. Ensure that every therapy dog handler shall carry with and produce their certifying organization identification card, an identification card bearing their association or employment with the approved provider, and their court-issued volunteer identification card and shall produce same upon request by any court official. Additionally, all therapy dogs shall identify themselves by wearing a dog therapy vest or other identifying garment.

7. All approved therapy dog providers and their contact information shall be listed on the Ninth Judicial Circuit website at www.ninthcircuit.org. Any organization seeking approval to be added as an approved provider must submit the following information to Court Administration:

a. A written request for approval;

b. Company information including years established, present services provided, number of dogs available, present certification as set forth in Paragraph 6(a) and (b) of this Order, availability of handlers to provide proper services, and any other information which demonstrates the ability to comply with the terms and conditions of this Order; and

c. Proof of proper insurance as set forth in paragraph 6(e) of this Order.

The Chief Judge shall determine, in his or her sole discretion, whether an organization is an approved provider for the Ninth Judicial Circuit.

DONE AND ORDERED at Orlando, Florida, this 27th day of October, 2014.

Frederick J. Lauten
Chief Judge

1A list of approved therapy dog providers shall be listed on the Ninth Circuit's website located at www.ninthcircuit.org.

2The "third party" is not a judicial officer or court administration staff. It is inappropriate for the court or court staff to actively participate or interact with the therapy dog in any capacity because the K–9th Circuit Program is a support mechanism for victims/witnesses. *See Florida Code of Judicial Conduct*, Canon 3 C(2); Canon 3 B(5); Cannon 3 B(7); and Cannon 3 B(9).

2014–19. NINTH JUDICIAL CIRCUIT COURT DOMESTIC COURT GUIDELINES

ADMINISTRATIVE ORDER NO. 2014–19

IN THE CIRCUIT COURT OF THE NINTH JUDICIAL CIRCUIT, IN AND FOR ORANGE AND OSCEOLA COUNTIES, FLORIDA

ADMINISTRATIVE ORDER ESTABLISHING NINTH JUDICIAL CIRCUIT COURT DOMESTIC COURT GUIDELINES

WHEREAS, pursuant to Article V, Section 2(d) of the Florida Constitution and section 43.26, Florida Statutes, the chief judge of each judicial circuit is charged with the authority and the power to do everything necessary to promote the prompt and efficient administration of justice; and

WHEREAS, to create and maintain an organization capable of effecting the efficient, prompt, and proper administration of justice for the citizens of this State, the chief judge is required to exercise direction, *see* Fla. R. Jud. Admin. 2.215(b)(2), (b)(3); and

WHEREAS, standardized procedures and manners of communication between the parties and the court best serve the interests of those that come before the court, preserve valuable judicial resources and prevent confusion and delay; and

WHEREAS, the Ninth Judicial Circuit Family Law Commission (Commission) was tasked with, and did submit to the Court, recommendations for accomplishing standardized procedures for the Domestic Divisions of the Ninth Judicial Circuit Court; and

WHEREAS, in order to provide effective coordination and in the interest of promoting judicial economy, the prompt and efficient administration of justice and in service to the citizens of the Ninth Circuit;

NOW, THEREFORE, I, Belvin Perry, Jr., in order to facilitate the efficient operation of the administration of justice, and pursuant to the authority vested in me as Chief Judge of the Ninth Judicial Circuit of Florida under Florida Rule of Judicial Administration 2.215, hereby order that, **effective immediately** and to continue until further order:

1. If an *ex parte* or short matter is to start late or be covered by a different division, without prior notice, attorneys and litigants shall be made aware through the posting of a note on the hearing room door.

2. In the interest of judicial economy and promotion of the prompt and efficient administration of justice, all circuit civil judges shall start *ex parte*, short matter and regular hearings on time, or as soon as practicable, and all judges shall strictly enforce allotted hearing time between attorneys except for good cause shown.

3. In the event that a party seeks to cancel a hearing that has been previously scheduled with the Court, the party must immediately notify the judge's judicial assistant and file a notice of cancellation with a copy to the judicial assistant as soon as it is cancelled. If the judicial assistant requests confirmation via an e-mail correspondence, the party shall comply.

4. A mandatory meet and confer process is hereby established, as set forth below, for all motions to be ***set for hearing*** in the domestic division and must occur ***before*** scheduling the hearing, except for the following motions: injunctive relief without notice; judgment on the pleadings; or summary judgment.

> Counsel with full authority to resolve the matter shall confer ***before*** scheduling the hearing on the motion to attempt to resolve or otherwise narrow the issues raised in the motion, and include a Certificate of Compliance (attached hereto as "Exhibit A") that the conference has occurred in the Notice of Hearing filed with the court. It shall be the responsibility of counsel who schedules the hearing to arrange the conference.
>
> The term "confer" requires a substantive conversation in person or by telephone in a good faith effort to resolve the

motion without the need to schedule a hearing, and does not envision an exchange of ultimatums by fax, e-mail or letter. Counsel who merely attempt to confer have not conferred for purposes of this Order.

Counsel must respond promptly to inquiries and communications from opposing counsel who notices the hearing and is attempting to schedule the conference. If counsel who notices the hearing is unable to reach opposing counsel to conduct the conference after three (3) good faith attempts, counsel who notices the hearing must identify in the Certificate of Compliance the dates and times of the efforts made to contact opposing counsel.

Counsel shall include in the Notice of Hearing the Certificate of Compliance certifying that the meet and confer occurred (or did not occur and setting out the good faith attempts to schedule the conference) and identifying the date of the conference, the names of the participating attorneys, and the specific results obtained.

Counsel who notices the hearing shall ensure that the court and the court's judicial assistant are aware of any narrowing of the issues or other resolution as a result of the conference.

5. Counsel is required to provide the court (and opposing counsel) with courtesy copies of any memoranda, case law or any other materials on which counsel may rely at a scheduled hearing at least three (3) court days before the scheduled hearing.

6. A party seeking to schedule hearing time shall check the Judicial Automated Calendaring System (JACS) via the Ninth Judicial Circuit website (http://www.ninthcircuit.org/) for available time slots. Once a hearing time is agreed to, the party seeking to set the hearing shall then send an e-mail correspondence to the judicial assistant to confirm the hearing time. This may be done by phone if allowed by the judicial assistant. The opposing party may not refuse to cooperate with setting the hearing just because they object to the hearing being set. The party seeking to set the hearing must give the opposing party at least three (3) proposed specific dates and times for the hearing by e-mail. If the opposing party does not respond to requests for availability within two (2) business days by either picking one of the proposed dates or by providing alternative dates and times within seven (7) days of the originally proposed dates, the party seeking to schedule the hearing may go ahead set the hearing. However, the hearing must be noticed for a time at least fifteen (15) days from the date the notice is served and must certify the party made a good effort to coordinate the hearing with the opposing party. The hearing will go forward as noticed unless the opposing party files its objection to the hearing detailing the conflict with the case style, number and presiding judge within 48 hours of the date the notice is served. The opposing party must set the hearing on its objection at short matters to occur within ten (10) days of the date the notice of hearing was first served. The Court will use Fla. R. Jud. Admin 2.550 as a guide in resolving conflicts. Mediations and depositions shall not take priority over Court appearances. Conflicts due to vacations are discretionary with the Court. The requirement to cooperate in coordinating mediation shall apply in the same manner.

7. All communications from a party to scheduling hearings shall be by e-mail correspondence copying the opposing party, unless the judicial assistant allows communication by phone or specifies otherwise. If the judicial assistant requests a follow-up or confirmation e-mail correspondence, the party shall comply. When communicating with the judicial assistant by e-mail correspondence the case name, number and attorney name must be included.

8. As the court system continues to move toward a paperless system, and as technology related to electronic filing, scheduling of hearing time and other related matters continues to become available, judges, judicial assistants and parties appearing before the court are strongly encouraged to utilize said technology when feasible. Where court technologies as contemplated by this Order become the standard, use of such technologies will be required without need for amendment of this Order.

DONE AND ORDERED at Orlando, Florida, this 5th day of August, 2014.

Belvin Perry, Jr.
Chief Judge

"Exhibit A"

First Option

CERTIFICATE OF COMPLIANCE

I HEREBY CERTIFY that a lawyer in my firm with full authority to resolve this matter had a substantive conversation in person or by telephone with opposing counsel in a good faith effort to resolve this motion before the motion was noticed for hearing but the parties were unable to reach an agreement.

/S/ ____________________
Counsel for the party who noticed the matter for hearing.

Second Option

CERTIFICATE OF COMPLIANCE

I HEREBY CERTIFY that a lawyer in my firm with full authority to resolve this matter attempted in good faith to contact opposing counsel in person or by telephone on:

1. (Date) at (Time) ;
2. (Date) at (Time) ; and
3. (Date) at (Time) ;

, to discuss resolution of this motion without a hearing and the lawyer in my firm was unable to speak with opposing counsel.

/S/ ____________________
Counsel for the party who noticed the matter for hearing.

2014–09–01. [VACATED BY ORDER 2017-10, EFFECTIVE OCTOBER 2, 2017.]

2014–07–01. NINTH JUDICIAL CIRCUIT COURT LOCAL PROFESSIONALISM PANEL

ADMINISTRATIVE ORDER NO. 2014–07–01

IN THE CIRCUIT COURT OF THE NINTH JUDICIAL CIRCUIT, IN AND FOR ORANGE AND OSCEOLA COUNTIES, FLORIDA

AMENDED ADMINISTRATIVE ORDER ESTABLISHING THE NINTH JUDICIAL CIRCUIT COURT LOCAL PROFESSIONALISM PANEL

WHEREAS, pursuant to Article V, Section 2(d) of the Florida Constitution and section 43.26, Florida Statutes, the chief judge of each judicial circuit is charged with the authority and the power to do everything necessary to promote the prompt and efficient administration of justice; and

WHEREAS, to create and maintain an organization capable of effecting the efficient, prompt, and proper administration of justice for the citizens of this State, the chief judge is required to exercise direction, *see* Fla. R. Jud. Admin. 2.215(b)(2), (b)(3); and

WHEREAS, the Supreme Court of Florida issued Administrative Order No. SC13–688, on June 6, 2013, in which it adopted the Code for Resolving Professionalism Complaints and directed the Chief Judge of each circuit in Florida to create a local professionalism panel to receive, screen and act upon complaints of unprofessional conduct and to resolve those complaints informally, if possible, or refer them to The Florida Bar if necessary; and

WHEREAS, in accordance with AOSC13–688, this Order establishes the Ninth Judicial Circuit Professionalism Panel and sets forth guidelines, policies and procedures for the Professionalism Panel;

NOW, THEREFORE, I, Frederick J. Lauten, in order to facilitate the efficient operation of the administration of justice, to foster the highest standards of professionalism throughout the Ninth Judicial Circuit, and pursuant to the authority vested in me as Chief Judge of the Ninth Judicial Circuit of Florida under Florida Rule of Judicial Administration 2.215, hereby order, **effective immediately,** to continue until further order and superseding any provisions in prior Administrative Orders which may be inconsistent, and in accordance with AOSC13–688, that the Ninth Judicial Circuit Court Local Professionalism Panel and governing guidelines, policies and procedures are established under the following:

1. Establishment of Local Professionalism Panel.

A. The Ninth Judicial Circuit Local Professionalism Panel ("Local Professionalism Panel") is hereby established in accordance with AOSC13–688.

B. *Panel Members.* The Local Professionalism Panel shall be composed of the Chairperson, to be appointed by the Chief Judge, with a Vice–Chairman and all subsequent Chairpersons to be elected by the Local Professionalism Panel, and further comprised of the following members: one (1) member from the Central Florida Association for Women Lawyers; one (1) member from the Paul C. Perkins Bar Association; one (1) member from the Hispanic Bar Association of Central Florida; one (1) member from the American Board of Trial Advocates; one (1) member from the Orange County Bar Association Young Lawyers Division; one (1) member from the George C. Young Inns of Court; one (1) member from the Central Florida Family Law American Inn of Court; two (2) members from the Osceola County Bar Association; one (1) member from the Greater Orlando Asian American Bar Association; three (3) members from the Orange County Bar Association Professionalism Committee; and three (3) at-large members to be appointed by the Chief Judge. All members must meet the approval of the Chief Judge, who may consult with the Administrative Judges in the Ninth Judicial Circuit. The Chief Judge may participate as a Local Professionalism Panel member at his or her discretion.

C. The Panel Members' term limits, subject to the discretion of the Chief Judge are as follows: six (6) Panel Members' terms will be one year; six (6) Panel Members' terms will be two years; and six (6) Panel Members' terms will be three years. Unless ordered otherwise by the Chief Judge the maximum amount of time any Panel Member may serve on the Local Professionalism Panel is six years.

D. The Local Professionalism Panel will screen and work to resolve individual referrals and cases in rotating groups of three (3) Panel Members to be selected by the Chairperson.

2. Purpose of Local Professionalism Panel. The purpose of the Local Professionalism Panel is to receive, screen, evaluate and act upon such reasonable complaints of unprofessional conduct as may be referred to the Panel asserting improper behavior of attorneys who may have conducted themselves in contravention or disregard of the standards of professionalism as set forth in the Oath of Admission to The Florida Bar, The Florida Bar Creed of Professionalism, The Florida Bar Ideals and Goals of Professionalism, the Rules Regulating The Florida Bar, the decisions and administrative directives of the Florida Supreme Court, professional standards of the Osceola County Bar Association and the Orange County Bar Association's Professionalism Guidelines—all of which are hereinafter referred to collectively as "*Ideals and Standards*," and resolve those complaints informally, if possible, or refer the complaints to The Florida Bar, if appropriate or necessary. The conduct of the attorneys who are the subject of such complaints shall be reviewed and addressed in a prompt, informal, respectful, non-punitive, educational and constructive manner, as may be appropriate.

3. Procedures. The Local Professionalism Panel shall generally follow these procedures:

A. *Referrals from Judicial Officers or Quasi Judicial Officers.*

i. When any Judicial Officer or Quasi Judicial Officer within the Ninth Judicial Circuit determines in good faith that an attorney has engaged in conduct inconsistent with the *Ideals and Standards*, the matter may be referred to the Local Professionalism Panel by completing the Referral Form, attached hereto as "Exhibit A" and submitting it to the Chief Judge of the Ninth Judicial Circuit for referral to the Panel.

ii. Process: The Chairperson of the Local Professionalism Panel may address a letter on behalf of such Panel to the Respondent Attorney inviting that attorney to meet with a designated three-person subgroup of the Local Professionalism Panel on a date and time specified to review, discuss, and endeavor to resolve the matter.

B. *Referrals from Attorneys and Non–Attorneys.*

i. By an Attorney: If an attorney observes conduct on the part of another attorney that he or she believes, in good faith, is inconsistent with the applicable *Ideals and Stan-*

dards, the referring attorney may request the Local Professionalism Panel consider the matter by completing the Referral Form and submitting it to the Chief Judge of the Ninth Judicial Circuit for referral to the Panel.

ii. By a Non–Attorney: If a non-attorney person is directly and adversely affected by conduct of an attorney that is inconsistent with the applicable *Ideals and Standards*, that person may request that the Local Professionalism Panel consider the matter by completing the Referral Form and submitting it to the Chief Judge of the Ninth Judicial Circuit for referral to the Panel.

iii. Page Limits for Referral from Attorney and Non–Attorney: The Complaint shall be completed on the form attached hereto as "Exhibit A" and limited to two (2) pages, exclusive of the exhibits.

C. *Referrals from the Florida Bar's Attorney Consumer Assistance Program (ACAP).* The Local Professionalism Panel may accept referrals from ACAP through the office of the Chief Judge of the Ninth Judicial Circuit.

D. *Processing Referrals from Attorneys, Non–Attorneys and ACAP.* Upon receipt of a referral by an attorney, non-attorney, or ACAP, the Chairperson of the Local Professionalism Panel shall review the request, may consult with the other Local Professionalism Panel members and, if the matter is accepted for review by the Local Professionalism Panel, the Chairperson shall address a letter by e-mail and hard copy, certified mail, to the Respondent Attorney that:

i. notifies the Respondent Attorney of the referral;

ii. may request a response; and

iii. may invite the Respondent Attorney to meet in person with a designated three-person subgroup of the Local Professionalism Panel on a date and time specified.

4. General Matters.

A. *Letters Sent by Local Professionalism Panel.* Any correspondence sent by the Local Professionalism Panel to a Respondent Attorney requesting that the Respondent Attorney appear before the Panel shall identify in general terms the conduct alleged to be inconsistent with or in disregard of the *Ideals and Standards*. The correspondence shall also advise the Respondent Attorney that the Local Professionalism Panel meeting is a non-disciplinary proceeding. The request may also include general references to the *Ideals and Standards* alleged to have been breached. The letter shall also advise the Respondent Attorney that if he or she fails to appear before the Local Professionalism Panel without being excused beforehand then the Local Professionalism Panel will proceed with its meeting and decide whether to address the request or refer it to ACAP for resolution.

B. *Panel Meetings.* The Chairperson and the Local Professionalism Panel members may meet with the Respondent Attorney at the date and time specified in the letter. The purpose of the meeting is to discuss with the Respondent Attorney the conduct alleged to be inconsistent with the *Ideal and Standards* and attempt to resolve the alleged inconsistent conduct or behavior. The Chairperson may send a letter summarizing the Local Professionalism Panel's discussions and suggestions to the Respondent Attorney.

If the Respondent Attorney fails to appear for the meeting, the Local Professionalism Panel members present shall discuss the conduct or behavior alleged to be inconsistent with the *Ideals and Standards*, and may summarize the Local Professionalism Panel's discussions by letter to the Respondent Attorney. Consistent with the provisions of paragraph 4.A of this Order, the Local Professionalism Panel may consider the Respondent Attorney's failure to appear in determining whether referral of the matter to ACAP is appropriate.

C. *Forty–Five (45) Days to Resolve.* The Local Professionalism Panel should strive to resolve all referrals within forty-five (45) days of receipt of the referral.

D. *Resolution.* Upon conferring with each other and conducting an appropriate review and investigation, the Local Professionalism Panel members may resolve the issues in any one or more of the following non-punitive, educational and constructive ways to provide the Respondent Attorney with proper incentives for professional-improvement:

i. The Chairperson may issue an oral or written decision to the Respondent Attorney;

ii. The Local Professionalism Panel, in its discretion, may refer the Respondent Attorney to the Orange County Bar Association's Mentorship program or may communicate with an assisting mentor of the Respondent Attorney;

iii. The Local Professionalism Panel may refer the Respondent Attorney to "The Florida Bar's Ethics School," which is an eight (8) hour ethics course, and/or any other course(s) deemed appropriate;

iv. The Local Professionalism Panel may provide the Respondent Attorney with specific recommendations or guidelines that will assist the attorney in the future;

v. The Local Professionalism Panel, in appropriate circumstances, may refer the Respondent Attorney to "Florida Lawyers Assistance," or other similar, appropriate program(s), for assistance with drug, alcohol and/or emotional problems;

vi. Pursuant to Section 2.1 of AOSC13–688, the Local Professionalism Panel has the discretion to direct any referrals to ACAP, depending upon the nature and severity of the referral or in the event the Respondent Attorney fails or refuses to meet with the Panel upon proper request; or

vii. The Local Professionalism Panel may recommend any other solution it deems to be appropriate or necessary.

Depending upon the circumstances, Respondent's failure to follow the recommendations of the Local Professionalism Panel may be a basis for referral to ACAP.

E. *Confidentiality.* All records regarding referrals to the Local Professionalism Panel shall be handled in the manner set forth in AOSC13–688 and as outlined in Rule 3–7.1, The Rules Regulating the Florida Bar, regarding the confidentiality of disciplinary investigations and proceedings.

F. *Indemnity.* All members of the Local Professionalism Panel acting within the scope of their duties under this Order shall be entitled to protections and immunities to the same extent and under the same privileges accorded mediators and arbitrators pursuant to sections 44.106 and 44.107, Florida Statutes.

Administrative Order 2014–07 is vacated and set aside and has been incorporated and/or amended herein. Vacating an

Administrative Order that vacates a prior Order does not revive the prior Order.

DONE AND ORDERED at Orlando, Florida, this 18th day of August, 2016.

Frederick J. Lauten
Chief Judge

"Exhibit A"

NINTH JUDICIAL CIRCUIT PROFESSIONALISM PANEL

COMPLAINT REFERRAL FORM

Please submit the completed form, together with any supporting documents by hand delivery or U.S. Mail to Chief Judge, Ninth Judicial Circuit, Orange County Courthouse, 425 N. Orange Avenue, Orlando, Florida 32801.

Your name: ______________________

Address: ______________________

Telephone Number: ______________________

Lawyer's Name: ______________________

Address: ______________________

Telephone Number: ______________________

COMPLAINT

Complaints cannot be made against a firm. You must name an individual lawyer or lawyers. Please describe your connection to the lawyer and state in no more than 2 pages what the lawyer did or failed to do that you feel was unprofessional. You may also attach copies of any documents that would help explain or support your complaint:

____

____

____

____

____

____

____

____

____

____

Signature

____

Date

2014–04–01. CELLULAR TELEPHONES AND OTHER PORTABLE ELECTRONIC DEVICES IN COURTROOMS, ORANGE AND OSCEOLA COUNTIES

IN THE CIRCUIT COURT OF THE NINTH JUDICIAL CIRCUIT, IN AND FOR ORANGE AND OSCEOLA COUNTIES, FLORIDA

ADMINISTRATIVE ORDER NO. 2014–04–01

AMENDED ADMINISTRATIVE ORDER GOVERNING CELLULAR TELEPHONES AND OTHER PORTABLE ELECTRONIC DEVICES IN COURTROOMS [1], ORANGE AND OSCEOLA COUNTIES

WHEREAS, under Article V, section 2(d) of the Florida Constitution and section 43.26, Florida Statutes, the chief judge of each judicial circuit is charged with the authority and the power to do everything necessary to promote the prompt and efficient administration of justice; and

WHEREAS, under the chief judge's constitutional and statutory responsibility for administrative supervision of the courts within the circuit and to create and maintain an organization capable of effecting the efficient, prompt, and proper administration of justice for the citizens of this State, the chief judge must exercise direction, *see* Fla. R. Jud. Admin. 2.215(b)(2), (b)(3); and

WHEREAS, to ensure the safe and orderly use of court facilities, and to minimize activities which disrupt the fair, orderly and peaceable conduct of court business, provisions regarding protocol, decorum, and using electronic devices in the courtroom are necessary, and

WHEREAS, such regulation is within the Court's inherent authority to take supervisory and administrative actions necessary to implement its judicial functions; and

WHEREAS, the Court's longstanding commitment to making courts open to the public and accessible to the media is of the utmost importance in fashioning such regulation; and

WHEREAS, the proper decorum required in a proceeding must be maintained but the Court recognizes the increasing use of mobile devices for business purposes and the trend towards "paperless" offices. Therefore, the overall purpose of this Order is to secure litigants' rights to a fair and impartial proceeding while providing the public, attorneys, and media access to the proceedings.

FINDINGS OF FACT

After much consideration, discussion and thoughtful analysis of all facets of this complex issue, and receiving a great deal of input from various interested persons, the Court finds:

1. The Court has seen a consistent increase in the public's and media's use of devices such as cell phones to take video and still photographs during court proceedings. These activities routinely disrupt courtroom proceedings, cause safety concerns and reduce the solemnity and dignity necessary for such proceedings. Due to the prevalent and pervasive nature of all such portable technologies, Judges and courtroom personnel are constantly being pulled from their primary duties to engage in technology management functions seriously impacting court functions.

2. Standards must be established to balance the use of portable electronic devices with the competing needs and desires of the Court, Judges, media, litigants, defendants, attorneys, and the general public during court proceedings.

3. Media coverage of judicial proceedings is "[s]ubject at all times to the authority of the presiding judge to: (i) control the conduct of proceedings before the court; (ii) ensure decorum and prevent distractions; and (iii) ensure the fair administration of justice in the pending cause." Fla. R. Jud. Admin. 2.450(a).

4. The Court must balance the constitutional right to a fair trial with the constitutional right to a free press.

5. The standards must contain safeguards to ensure media coverage and public attendance at court proceedings does not detract from or degrade those proceedings, impair or interrupt the Court's orderly procedures, or otherwise interfere with a fair trial.

6. The increasing use of ever more sophisticated portable electronic equipment has proven to be a tremendous burden and distraction for courtroom deputies continually removed from their primary duty of providing security to instead manage the usage of portable electronic equipment by attendees of court proceedings. Court deputies cannot quickly ascertain what type of device is being utilized, for what purpose is it being used, and who may be allowed to use such technology. The more involved courtroom security becomes in managing technology as opposed to managing security, the more perilous the safety and security of all those who enter the courthouse becomes. This issue is directly alleviated by banning types of usage of certain devices from court proceedings and requiring uniform, court-issued media authorization cards.

7. It is within the Court's discretion whether to permit the use of laptop computers, cell phones, or similar devices during a court proceeding. Traditionally, all portable electronic devices have been banned from the courtroom and there is no court rule that specifically allows the use of laptop computers or similar devices in a courtroom. Court–issued media authorization cards are the most effective and least burdensome method available to allow court security to instantly identify some of those persons (who are usually not known to court security) who may utilize specified equipment without unduly interfering with their primary duty of providing security.

NOW THEREFORE, I, Frederick J. Lauten, to facilitate the efficient administration of justice, under the authority vested in me as Chief Judge of the Ninth Judicial Circuit of Florida under Florida Rule of Judicial Administration 2.215, order the following, **effective January 1, 2015**:

CELL PHONES

1. **Public**—Members of the public may not use or display cellular telephones in any courtroom. All cellular phones must be turned off or placed in mute or vibrate mode and shall not be used, viewed or otherwise displayed while in any courtroom.

2. **Attorneys**—With the permission of the presiding Judge, attorneys, including those who are not the attorney of record, may utilize cellular telephones for texting, organizational functions, research and writing functions, and other data transmission functions. Cellular telephones and other similar devices cannot be used to record or send photographs, video, or audio. All cellular phones must be placed in either mute or vibrate mode. All Bluetooth and similar wireless devices must be turned off, removed from the wearer and secured out of sight.

3. **Media**—Members of the media, who have obtained a media authorization card as provided in Administrative Order No. 07–96–19–02, and which card is visible, may utilize cellular telephones for texting, organizational functions, research and writing functions, and other data transmission functions. Cellular telephones and other similar devices cannot be used to record or send photographs, video, or audio. All cellular phones must be placed in either mute or vibrate mode. All Bluetooth and similar wireless devices must be turned off, removed from the wearer and secured out of sight.

4. **Court Employees & Certain Contractual Vendors**—Certain court employees and certain contractual vendors such as interpreters, court reporters, and court technology personnel, may use cellular phones for texting, organizational functions, research and writing functions, and other data transmission functions. All cellular phones must be placed in either mute or vibrate mode. In rare instances, with the permission of the presiding Judge, a court employee may use a cellular phone to make or receive telephone calls while in the courtroom.

LAPTOP COMPUTERS, SIMILAR DEVICES AND OTHER PORTABLE ELECTRONIC DEVICES [2]

5. **Public**—Use of laptop computers and other portable electronic devices is prohibited.

6. **Attorneys and Litigants Representing Themselves**—Attorneys and litigants representing themselves may use a computer when their case is in session and they are actively participating in the proceeding. Attorneys may use electronic devices to conduct research, check calendars, check or send emails and perform other related tasks when seated in the well of the courtroom or during lengthy calendar calls while awaiting their cases to be called when they are in an area designated by the presiding Judge for attorneys. No computer or other electronic device can be used to record or send photographs, video, or audio. The transmission of materials on a computer to other peripheral devices also in use during the proceeding, and specifically in advancement of the proceeding, is permissible. For example, the transmission and display of a power point presentation is allowable.

7. **Media**—

a. Media representatives may use laptop computers or similar devices provided the devices operate silently on the user's lap and do not require additional seating space. Media representatives must obtain a media authorization card, as provided in Administrative Order No. 07–96–19–02, to use a laptop computer within a courtroom. No laptop computer shall be used to record or send photographs, video, or audio. Use of a laptop computer is solely to record and transmit text data. Only laptop computers or similar devices with virtual or silent keyboards are permitted and they must operate on battery power. Cabling of extension cords and power supplies is prohibited. Other devices equipped with virtual keyboards such as tablets (i.e. iPads and similar devices) may be utilized for text recording and transmission. A presiding Judge may exclude laptop computers or similar devices or other portable electronic devices from the courtroom.

b. While using a laptop computer or similar device, court-issued media authorization cards must be visible while in the court proceeding. The rules and procedures governing court-issued media authorization cards are contained within Administrative Order No. 07–96–19–02.

c. The operation of any permitted devices in a courtroom must be in a manner that does not disturb or disrupt the proceedings or distract the participants.

d. Media representatives attending any court proceeding and using a laptop computer or similar device shall generally sit in the row of seating at the back of the courtroom to lessen the distraction to others. If no seating is available on the back row of the gallery, such as during voir dire, media shall use the back row of the jury box when using a laptop computer or similar device.

GENERAL PROVISIONS

8. Nothing in this Order is intended to apply to persons who require electronic devices (or services requiring the use of electronic devices) under the Americans with Disabilities Act except that electronic devices cannot be used to take photographs, video or audio during a proceeding unless specifically approved by the presiding Judge.

9. Court Deputies shall instruct anyone violating this Order to stop. Violating this Order may result in seizure or forfeiture of the cell phone or other electronic device. If Court Deputies remove any device from a person, it shall be at the presiding judge's direction and under this Order. If the conduct continues, the presiding Judge can direct the person be removed from the courtroom. Anyone violating this Order may face contempt proceedings and/or other sanctions. Media representatives violating this Order may also be banned from future use of portable electronic devices during court proceedings and may lose their media authorization cards.

DONE AND ORDERED at Orlando, Florida, this 15th day of December, 2014.

Frederick J. Lauten
Chief Judge

[1] As used herein, the word "courtroom" includes courtrooms, hearing rooms and any other places used to conduct court proceedings, unless specifically stated otherwise.

[2] As used herein, the phrase "laptop computers or similar devices" includes traditional laptop computers, as well as tablets, iPads and all other similar devices, unless specifically stated otherwise..

2014–03–01. DOMESTIC VIOLENCE INJUNCTIONS

ADMINISTRATIVE ORDER NO. 2014–03–01

IN THE CIRCUIT COURT OF THE NINTH JUDICIAL CIRCUIT, IN AND FOR ORANGE AND OSCEOLA COUNTIES, FLORIDA

AMENDED ORDER GOVERNING DOMESTIC VIOLENCE INJUNCTIONS

WHEREAS, pursuant to Article V, section 2(d) of the Florida Constitution and section 43.26, Florida Statutes, the chief judge of each judicial circuit is charged with the authority and the power to do everything necessary to promote the prompt and efficient administration of justice; and

WHEREAS, pursuant to the chief judge's constitutional and statutory responsibility for administrative supervision of the courts within the circuit and to create and maintain an organization capable of effecting the efficient, prompt, and proper administration of justice for the citizens of this State, the chief judge is required to exercise direction, *see* Fla. R. Jud. Admin. 2.215(b)(2), (b)(3); and

WHEREAS, the clerks of court provide court-related functions which are essential to the orderly operation of the judicial branch and are required by section 28.13, Florida Statutes, to keep all papers filed in the clerk's office with the utmost care and security; and

WHEREAS, the protection of persons who are victims of domestic violence is a primary goal of the Ninth Judicial Circuit Court; and

WHEREAS, integral to protecting persons who are victims of domestic violence is providing a safe and secure method of navigating the process of seeking an injunction for protection; and

WHEREAS, the Court is aware of instances of attorneys and media contacting respondents in cases where a petitioner has filed for an injunction for protection before the respondent is served thereby creating a potentially volatile situation; and

WHEREAS, after consultation with the clerks of court and the judges who handle domestic violence matters each day, the Court finds that it is essential to protect all information related to a Petition for Injunction for Protection as confidential until such time as the court has issued an order and the respondent has been served with the petition; and

WHEREAS, in order to prevent a serious and imminent threat to the fair, impartial and orderly administration of justice, temporary confidentiality is required;

NOW, THEREFORE, I, Frederick J. Lauten, in order to facilitate the efficient operation of the administration of justice, and pursuant to the authority vested in me as Chief Judge of the Ninth Judicial Circuit of Florida under Florida Rule of Judicial Administration 2.215, hereby order the following, **effective immediately**, to continue until further order and superseding any provisions in prior Administrative Orders which may be inconsistent:

1. Pursuant to Florida Rule of Judicial Administration 2.420(c)(9)(A), this Court finds that confidentiality is required to:

(i) prevent a serious and imminent threat to the fair, impartial, and orderly administration of justice;

(ii) avoid substantial injury to innocent third parties;

(iii) avoid substantial injury to a party by disclosure of matters protected by a common law or privacy right not generally inherent in the specific type of proceeding sought to be closed;

(iv) comply with established public policy set forth in the Florida or United States Constitution or statutes or Florida rules or case law.

Further, this Court finds that degree, duration, and manner of confidentiality as contemplated by this Order is no broader than necessary to protect the interests set forth above and no less restrictive measures are available to protect the interests set forth in this Order.

2. The Orange County Clerk of Court and the Osceola County Clerk of Court are directed to temporarily seal as confidential any Petition for Injunction for Protection under sections 741.30, 784.046, or 784.0485, Florida Statutes, until such time as the court has reviewed the Petition and either grants the Petition and the Respondent is served, denies the Petition, the Petition is voluntarily dismissed, or any other action occurs which concludes the case.

3. Once the order granting the Petition issues and the Respondent is served, or the court denies the Petition, the Orange County Clerk of Court and the Osceola County Clerk of Court are directed to make the Petition for Injunction for Protection which was temporarily confidential, public record unless some other confidentiality provision also applies.

Administrative Order 2014–03 is vacated and set aside except to the extent that it has been incorporated and/or amended herein. Vacating an Administrative Order that vacates a prior Order does not revive the prior Order.

DONE AND ORDERED at Orlando, Florida, this 5th day of February, 2018.

Frederick J. Lauten
Chief Judge

2013–28. CASE REPORTING REQUIREMENTS FOR REAL PROPERTY MORTGAGE FORECLOSURE CASES

IN THE CIRCUIT COURT OF THE NINTH JUDICIAL CIRCUIT, IN AND FOR ORANGE AND OSCEOLA COUNTIES, FLORIDA

ADMINISTRATIVE ORDER NO. 2013–28

ORDER GOVERNING CASE REPORTING REQUIREMENTS FOR REAL PROPERTY MORTGAGE FORECLOSURE CASES

WHEREAS, pursuant to Article V, section 2(d) of the Florida Constitution and section 43.26, Florida Statutes, the chief judge of each judicial circuit is charged with the authority and the power to do everything necessary to promote the prompt and efficient administration of justice; and

WHEREAS, pursuant to the chief judge's constitutional and statutory responsibility for administrative supervision of the courts within the circuit and to create and maintain an organization capable of effecting the efficient, prompt, and proper administration of justice for the citizens of this State, the chief judge is required to exercise direction, *see* Fla. R. Jud. Admin. 2.215(b)(2), (b)(3); and

WHEREAS, pursuant to the Supreme Court of Florida Administrative Order No. AOSC13–51, entered October 16, 2013, each chief judge of every circuit court is required to issue an administrative order establishing a mechanism that enables judges and magistrates to provide explicit direction to each clerk of court's office with regard to designating a change in the status of a mortgage foreclosure case; and

WHEREAS, the purpose of this Order is to implement an effective communications mechanism by which the courts and clerks are notified of case status changes in a timely manner; and

WHEREAS, this mechanism will facilitate the communication of cases known to the circuit to change status from ACTIVE to INACTIVE or INACTIVE to ACTIVE to the clerk of courts who can report that status to the Office of State Courts Administrator as indicated in this Order and to the circuit judges who can act on this information; and

WHEREAS, in many instances, the events initiating a change in the status of a case may become known to either the judge and magistrate or the clerk's office, but not always both; and

WHEREAS, it is necessary for the clerk of court's office to notify the judge or magistrate when events occur that change the status of a foreclosure case; and

WHEREAS, status change reason codes are an integral part of case age reporting as envisioned by Florida Rule of Judicial Administration 2.225(a)(2); and

WHEREAS, the timely and accurate submission of meaningful case status data is considered an essential component of the Foreclosure Initiative;

NOW, THEREFORE, I, Belvin Perry, Jr., pursuant to the authority vested in me as Chief Judge of the Ninth Judicial Circuit of Florida under Florida Rule of Judicial Administration 2.215, do hereby order as follows, **effective immediately**, and to continue until further order:

I. DEFINITIONS

Filing event: A filing event occurs when an action is brought before the court as the result of a petition, pleading, complaint or any other recordable action (those happenings relating to court activity that would appear on a court docket or otherwise require the making of an historical record by the clerk of courts in their official capacity) sufficient to begin a case. This definition includes the filing of any document or action recorded with the court authorized to initiate a case. The initiation of a case by whatever means is referred to as a filing event.

Open case: A case that has one or more issues outstanding that require active resolution by the court.

Disposition event: A disposition event has occurred when a case is closed for court activity as a result of judicial decision, order or other recordable action that provides resolution, by the court, on the issues raised by and subsequent to the filing event.

Closed case: A case that has had all issues raised by and subsequent to the filing event resolved and no further action of the court is required. This definition of closure does not indicate that the clerk of courts or other agencies have completed all of their required activity with regards to the case, only that the court has rendered judgment on the matters of the case and will take no further action (excluding planned review or scheduled future action).

Reopen event: A reopen event occurs when a motion, pleading or other recordable action occurs on a case that requires additional court activity after a disposition event has closed the case for court activity. Note that a reopen event involves at least one action and that additional post-judgment actions may occur before the case is reclosed.

Reclosure event: A reclosure event occurs when the last (or only) post-judgment action has been resolved by judicial decision, order or other recordable action, thereby completing court proceedings on the issues raised by and since the reopen event occurred.

II. SIX STATUSES IN WHICH A CASE CAN BE PLACED AS THE CASE MOVES FROM INITIATION TO RESOLUTION

Active—A case is considered in an active status when the court is engaged in activity directly related to the resolution of the specific matters and issues associated with the case.

Inactive—A case is considered in an inactive status when court activity on that case is suspended pending resolution of an issue external to the court or that does not directly involve the court in resolving that issue; for example, awaiting the results of an appeal or the disposition of a related case. A case placed in an inactive status is not closed and does not need to be reopened when the case returns to active status, regardless of the length of time involved.

Closed—A case is considered to be closed, or disposed, (that is, in a closed status) for court activity on the date of the judicial decision, order or other recordable action that provides resolution to the last (or all) of the matters brought before the court as a consequence of the filing event that initiated the case. The court, then, has no further action to take on the case.

Reopened Active—A case will be considered to be in a reopened status (either active or inactive), from the date that the first post-judgment motion/pleading is filed or other action occurs that reopens a case for court activity (i.e. the reopen event) until the date of the last judicial decision/order resolving all overlapping court proceedings (i.e. the reopen closure event). Each period in which a case is reported as in a reopened status may involve one or more overlapping post-judgment actions. A case is considered to be in a reopened active status when one or more post-judgment actions are pending and the court is actively engaged in their resolution.

Reopened Inactive—A case is considered to be in a reopened inactive status if the activity on all outstanding post-judgment actions is held in abeyance pending resolution of some issue external to the court or that does not directly involve the court in resolving that issue. In this circumstance, the court is not actively working to resolve the matter(s).

Reclosed—A case that has had one or more post-judgment actions will be considered closed, or disposed, (that is, in a reclosed status) for court activity on the date of the judicial decision, order or other recordable action that provides resolution to the last (or all) of the matters brought before the court since the reopen event occurred. The court, then, has no further action to take on the case.

III. PROCEDURE

1. A case transitions from INACTIVE to ACTIVE when any event occurs which enables the court to take further action on the case. The filing of a motion or the scheduling of a hearing or case conference requesting the court to take further action would be examples of events that move a case from INACTIVE to ACTIVE status, regardless of the existence of the six (6) recognized reasons [1] which may move a case from ACTIVE to INACTIVE status, or conversely from INACTIVE to ACTIVE, *unless* that requested action must also be on hold until the reason for inactivity is resolved.

2. A status change will occur as of the document stamp date of the document directing the status change.

3. It is incumbent on each clerk of court to enter the status change of any case so that judges, magistrates, case managers, and judicial assistants are apprised of the proper status of each case within their purview.

4. For case age reporting purposes, a case on INACTIVE status should not be considered pending until it becomes ACTIVE by order of the presiding judge.

5. Both parties must notify the clerk of courts as soon as an event occurs that would change the status of a case, such as when a bankruptcy is filed or an agreement is reached.

6. The uniform form orders attached hereto shall be the only orders utilized to move a case from ACTIVE to INACTIVE status, or conversely from INACTIVE to ACTIVE status.

DONE AND ORDERED at Orlando, Florida, this 21st day of November, 2013.

Belvin Perry, Jr.
Chief Judge

IN THE CIRCUIT COURT OF THE NINTH JUDICIAL CIRCUIT, IN AND FOR ORANGE AND OSCEOLA COUNTIES, FLORIDA

____
Plaintiff **CIRCUIT CIVIL DIVISION:** __________

vs.

____
Defendant CASE NO.: ____________

ORDER PLACING CASE ON INACTIVE STATUS DUE TO:

This case came before the Court, and the Court directs the Clerk to place the case on **INACTIVE** status due to:

☐ Bankruptcy stay, Case No. ___ **[BKST]**

☐ Case pending resolution of another case, Case No. ___ **[CPRC]**

☐ Written agreement of the parties **[BWAP]**

☐ Appeal pending **[AP]**

☐ Motion to stay or abate due to Department of Justice/Attorney General settlement **[DOJ/AG]**

☐ Other (a reason must be provided in writing by the presiding judge or designee) **[OTH]**

____

The Clerk of Court is therefore directed to remove this case from the **ACTIVE** status, and designate it as an **INACTIVE** case category based on the reason checked above. The parties must return the case to active status by motion, with notice to all parties, within 30 days of the termination of grounds for inactive status, and seeking an order of court returning it to active status.

DONE and **ORDERED** in ________ County, Florida, this ___ day of ________ 20 ___.

____
Presiding Judge

CERTIFICATE OF SERVICE

I hereby certify a true and correct copy of the foregoing was furnished by U.S. mail this ___ day of ________, ______, to the below parties.

____
Judicial Assistant

IN THE CIRCUIT COURT OF THE NINTH JUDICIAL CIRCUIT, IN AND FOR ORANGE AND OSCEOLA COUNTIES, FLORIDA

______
Plaintiff **CIRCUIT CIVIL DIVISION:** ________

vs.

______
Defendant **CASE NO.:** ________

ORDER PLACING CASE ON ACTIVE STATUS DUE TO:

This case came before the Court, and the Court has been advised that the Plaintiff/Defendant have/has moved to place the case on **ACTIVE** status due to:

☐ Plaintiff/defendant stipulates that the bankruptcy stay has been lifted, Case No. ________ **[BKST LFT]**

☐ Plaintiff/defendant stipulates that related case has been disposed, Case No. ________ **[CPRC DISP]**

☐ Written agreement of the parties **[BWAP]**

☐ Plaintiff/defendant stipulates that pending appeal has been disposed **[AP DISP]**

☐ Plaintiff/defendant stipulates that Department of Justice/Attorney General review is complete **[DOJ/AG DISP]**

☐ Other (a reason must be provided in writing by the presiding judge or designee) **[OTH DISP]**

____

The Clerk of Court is therefore directed to remove this case from the **INACTIVE** status, and designate it as an **ACTIVE** case category based on the reason checked above.

DONE and **ORDERED** in ________ County, Florida, this ___ day of ________ 20 ___.

____
Presiding Judge

CERTIFICATE OF SERVICE

I hereby certify a true and correct copy of the foregoing was furnished by U.S. mail this ___ day of ________, ______, to the below parties.

____
Judicial Assistant

[1] The six recognized reasons as of the effective date of this Order are: (1) A stay of bankruptcy; (2) Resolution of foreclosure case requires a resolution of a related case; (3) On-going settlement negotiations or agreement by both parties; (4) Foreclosure case is on hold pending appeal; (5) A hold is placed on case due to Department of Justice or Attorney General Review; (6) When directed by the presiding judge consistent with the definitions of an inactive case as defined herein.

2013–21. JUVENILE DEPENDENCY DRUG COURT PROGRAM, ORANGE COUNTY

IN THE CIRCUIT COURT OF THE NINTH JUDICIAL CIRCUIT, IN AND FOR ORANGE COUNTY, FLORIDA

ADMINISTRATIVE ORDER NO. 2013–21

ADMINISTRATIVE ORDER GOVERNING THE JUVENILE DEPENDENCY DRUG COURT PROGRAM, ORANGE COUNTY

WHEREAS, pursuant to Article V, Section 2(d) of the Florida Constitution and section 43.26, Florida Statutes, the chief judge of each judicial circuit is charged with the authority and the power to do everything necessary to promote the prompt and efficient administration of justice; and

WHEREAS, issues of abuse, abandonment and neglect of children involved in dependency actions and termination of parental rights proceedings are often related to an underlying substance addiction of one or both parents; and

WHEREAS, the Ninth Judicial Circuit, in partnership with the Department of Children and Families, has determined that the implementation of a dependency drug court program will assist parents whose children have been adjudicated dependent and who may have their parental rights terminated as a result of their addiction; and

WHEREAS, a dependency drug court program can provide intensive drug treatment for parents who have substance abuse problems and give these parents an opportunity to overcome their addiction so that they will be able to maintain or regain a parental relationship with their children;

NOW, THEREFORE, I, Belvin Perry, Jr., pursuant to the authority vested in me as Chief Judge of the Ninth Judicial Circuit of Florida under Florida Rule of Judicial Administration 2.215 hereby order the following, **effective immediately** and to continue until further order:

1. The Ninth Judicial Circuit Dependency Drug Court Program for Orange County ("Program") is hereby established.

2. The criteria for participation are:

a. A petition for dependency regarding the parent's child or children has been filed in Orange County; or

b. A non-shelter petition case referred by the Department of Children and Families (Department); and

c. The parent has a history of substance abuse; and

d. The parent is a resident of Orange County.

3. When the Department or an attorney associated with the case suspects a parent may have a substance abuse problem, the Department or attorney may ask the judge at the shelter hearing to order the parent to undergo a Dependency Drug Court screening and follow the recommendations of the Program and treatment provider. The judge may also order a screening at his or her own discretion.

4. A community based care agency case manager or the Department may refer a parent to the Program if the case plan is mediated and includes a referral to the Program for a screening and instructions for the parent to follow the recommendations of the Program and treatment provider.

5. At the screening, the Juvenile Drug Court Program Office (Program Office) will determine if the parent qualifies for the Program. If a parent qualifies for the Program then the screening documents will be sent to the treatment provider for assessment. If the parent is deemed appropriate by the Orange County Dependency Drug Court team based on the screening and assessment, the parent will be court ordered to participate in the Program.

6. In the event that the parent does not meet the criteria for entering the Program, or fails to comply with the Program after entry and is discharged, the Department will review the case to determine if a termination of parental rights proceeding should be initiated.

7. The Program will consist of a multi-phase treatment model of services, to include intensive outpatient counseling, case management and random urinalysis testing. The Orange County Dependency Drug Court team shall consist of the Dependency Drug Court judge, the Drug Court Manager, the Drug Court Coordinator, the Child Welfare Legal Services attorney, the Case Manager for the community based care agency assigned to the case and the treatment provider. The team shall conduct staffings prior to each dependency drug court session to review the status of current cases.

8. The dependency case will continue to be reviewed in dependency court according to state mandates to ascertain compliance with the case plan.

9. Dependency Drug Court will be in session one day bi-weekly as directed by the Dependency Drug Court judge. Cases will be reviewed on a bi-weekly basis until the parent completes the Program. During phases three and four, cases will be reviewed on a monthly basis, or as determined by the judge.

10. The treatment provider has a valid interest in having partial access to the dependency court file of a child whose parent is a current participant for the purpose of assisting that parent in complying with the case plan. The treatment provider is therefore authorized to attend hearings and have electronic access to the docket and events of the specified court files pursuant to section 39.0132(3), Florida Statutes. Pursuant to section 39.0132(4), Florida Statutes, the treatment provider shall not disclose any information obtained from that access to persons other than those authorized by that section.

DONE AND ORDERED at Orlando, Florida, this 27th day of August, 2013.

Belvin Perry, Jr.
Chief Judge

2013–20–02. JUVENILE DELINQUENCY DRUG COURT PROGRAM

IN THE CIRCUIT COURT OF THE NINTH JUDICIAL CIRCUIT, IN AND FOR ORANGE AND OSCEOLA COUNTIES, FLORIDA

ADMINISTRATIVE ORDER NO. 2013–20–02

AMENDED ADMINISTRATIVE ORDER GOVERNING THE JUVENILE DELINQUENCY DRUG COURT PROGRAM

WHEREAS, pursuant to Article V, Section 2(d) of the Florida Constitution and section 43.26, Florida Statutes, the chief judge of each judicial circuit is charged with the authority and the power to do everything necessary to promote the prompt and efficient administration of justice; and

WHEREAS, pursuant to the chief judge's constitutional and statutory responsibility for administrative supervision of the courts within the circuit and to create and maintain an organization capable of effecting the efficient, prompt, and proper administration of justice for the citizens of this State, the chief judge is required to exercise direction, *see* Fla. R. Jud. Admin. 2.215(b)(2), (b)(3); and

WHEREAS, drug and drug related cases have a considerable impact on the juvenile justice system; and

WHEREAS, there is strong community support for providing these services as well as support from the State Attorney, Public Defender, Department of Juvenile Justice and local law enforcement; and

WHEREAS, the Ninth Judicial Circuit, in partnership with other agencies, determined that a juvenile delinquency drug court was feasible and practicable;

NOW, THEREFORE, I, Frederick J. Lauten, pursuant to the authority vested in me as Chief Judge of the Ninth Judicial Circuit of Florida, under Florida Rule of Judicial Administration 2.215, hereby order the following, **effective immediately**, to continue until further order and superseding any provisions in prior Administrative Orders which may be inconsistent:

1. The criteria for participation are:

a. Must be a resident of either Orange County or Osceola County,

b. Must be at least 14 years of age by referral date and able to successfully complete the Juvenile Delinquency Drug Court Program (Program) before turning 19 years of age,

c. Must be physically and mentally capable to complete the Program and understand its requirements.

2. Offenses or charges eligible for referral to the Program include: possession of drugs and/or paraphernalia, misdemeanor cases and violation of probation cases where drug use may be suspected or where the defendant had a positive drug screen, and, any other offenses deemed appropriate by the Unified Problem Solving Court Judge. In cases that do not include a drug charge, suspicion that the defendant has a substance abuse problem and is in need of treatment is sufficient for referral to the Program.

3. Offenses or charges that are ineligible for referral to the Program include weapons offenses or charges, intent to sell or distribute offenses or charges (unless the State Attorney's Office enters a Petition for Delinquency with a memo to the court file referring the case to the pre-trial diversion track), sexual battery offenses or charges or those whose current offense or charge is likely to merit commitment of direct file charges.

4. The State Attorney's Office determines which cases are eligible for the Juvenile Delinquency Drug Court Diversion Track and refers those cases to the Program for screening, assessment and admittance. Cases that are deemed eligible are accepted into the Program and the juvenile begins treatment as soon as possible. Upon successful completion of the Program, the juvenile's case is non-filed. Cases that are deemed ineligible during the screening and assessment process by Program staff are returned to the State Attorney's Office within thirty (30) days of that determination for routine case processing.

5. Any Juvenile Court Judge may order a case to be referred to the Program for screening, assessment and admittance into the Pretrial Intervention Track. Upon completion of the screening and assessment of the case, the Program staff will notify the referring Judge as to suitability for the Program. If deemed eligible, that juvenile is accepted into the Program and begins treatment as soon as possible. Upon successful completion of the Program, the juvenile's case is nolle prossed. Cases that are deemed ineligible during the screening and assessment process by Program staff are returned to the referring division within thirty (30) days of that determination for routine case processing.

6. Any Juvenile Court Judge may refer a case to the Probation Track if that Judge orders at disposition of the case that the juvenile be screened by the Program Office and follow the recommendations of the Program Office and treatment provider.

Upon completion of the screening and assessment of the case, the Program staff will notify the referring Judge as to suitability for the Program. If deemed eligible, the juvenile is accepted into the Program and begins treatment as soon as possible. Completion of the Program may result in early termination of probation. Cases that are deemed ineligible during the screening and assessment process will be returned to the referring Division within thirty (30) days of that determination for routine case processing.

7. Before a juvenile begins any track of the Program the juvenile and the parent or legal guardian must complete the Program contract and associated paperwork. Failure to complete the required paperwork in a timely manner will result in referral back to the State Attorney's Office or division of origination.

Administrative Order No. 2013–20–01 is vacated and set aside and has been incorporated and/or amended herein. Vacating an Administrative Order that vacates a prior Order does not revive the prior Order.

DONE AND ORDERED at Orlando, Florida, this 4th day of April, 2016.

Frederick J. Lauten
Chief Judge

2013–04. RELEASE OF SELECTED INDIVIDUALS INTO ORANGE COUNTY CORRECTIONS DEPARTMENT HOME CONFINEMENT PROGRAM

IN THE CIRCUIT COURT OF THE NINTH JUDICIAL CIRCUIT IN AND FOR ORANGE COUNTY, FLORIDA

ADMINISTRATIVE ORDER NO. 2013–04

ORDER GOVERNING RELEASE OF SELECTED INDIVIDUALS INTO ORANGE COUNTY CORRECTIONS DEPARTMENT HOME CONFINEMENT PROGRAM WHERE ARREST WARRANT ALLOWS FOR RELEASE ON BOND AND HOME CONFINEMENT

WHEREAS, pursuant to Article V, section 2(d) of the Florida Constitution and section 43.26, Florida Statutes, the chief judge of each judicial circuit is charged with the authority and the power to do everything necessary to promote the prompt and efficient administration of justice; and

WHEREAS, pursuant to the chief judge's constitutional and statutory responsibility for administrative supervision of the courts within the circuit and to create and maintain an organization capable of effecting the efficient, prompt, and proper administration of justice for the citizens of this State, the chief judge is required to exercise direction, *see* Fla. R. Jud. Admin. 2.215(b)(2), (b)(3);

NOW, THEREFORE, I, Belvin Perry, Jr., pursuant to the authority vested in me as Chief Judge of the Ninth Judicial Circuit of Florida under Florida Rule of Judicial Administration 2.215, do hereby order as follows, **effective immediately**, in all matters involving the release of selected individuals into the Orange County Corrections Department Home Confinement Program:

All individuals arrested on a warrant for a felony offense which allows for release on a bond and home confinement must be brought before the initial appearance judge before release. No one shall be released automatically by the Orange County Corrections Department before an initial appearance.

DONE AND ORDERED at Orlando, Florida, this 1st day of March, 2013.

Belvin Perry, Jr.
Chief Judge

2012–07–01. [VACATED BY ORDER 2018-020, EFFECTIVE JULY 12, 2018.]

2012–06–03. RESIDENTIAL FORECLOSURE MEDIATION PROCEDURES, ORANGE COUNTY

IN THE CIRCUIT COURT OF THE NINTH JUDICIAL CIRCUIT, IN AND FOR ORANGE COUNTY, FLORIDA

ADMINISTRATIVE ORDER NO. 2012–06–03

AMENDED ADMINISTRATIVE ORDER GOVERNING RESIDENTIAL FORECLOSURE MEDIATION PROCEDURES, ORANGE COUNTY

For all referenced Exhibits found in this administrative order, please refer to https://www.ninthcircuit.org for the most current version of these forms.

WHEREAS, pursuant to Article V, section 2(d) of the Florida Constitution, and section 43.26, Florida Statutes, the Chief Judge of each judicial circuit is charged with the authority and power to do everything necessary to promote the prompt and efficient administration of justice, and rule

2.215(b)(3), Florida Rules of Judicial Administration, mandates the Chief Judge to "develop an administrative plan for the efficient and proper administration of all courts within the circuit;" and

WHEREAS, rule 2.545 of the Rules of Judicial Administration requires that the trial courts "...take charge of all cases at an early stage in the litigation and...control the progress of the case thereafter until the case is determined...", which includes "...identifying cases subject to alternative dispute resolution processes;" and

WHEREAS, a statewide managed mediation program for residential mortgage foreclosure cases was established in 2009 by In re: Final Report and Recommendations on Residential Mortgage Foreclosure Cases, AOSC09–54, (Dec. 28, 2009); and

WHEREAS, program requirements were clarified in 2010 by In re: Guidance Concerning Managed Mediation Programs for Residential Mortgage Foreclosure Cases, AOSC10–57, (Nov. 5, 2010); and

WHEREAS, the Supreme Court of Florida has reviewed the reports on the program and determined it cannot justify continuation of the program; and

WHEREAS, pursuant to In re: Managed Mediation Program for Residential Mortgage Foreclosure Cases, AOSC11–44, (Dec. 19, 2011), the statewide managed mediation program was terminated upon issuance of said Order; and

WHEREAS, in order to address the immediate effective date of Administrative Order AOSC11–44, the Court issued Administrative Order 2012–02 on January 20, 2012. That Administrative Order terminated the managed residential foreclosure mediation program and provided that a further order on mediation foreclosure cases would be forthcoming after the Court considered all possible options and measures the Court deems necessary and appropriate. Administrative Order 2012–02 also provided that parties could continue to file a Motion to Participate in Circuit Civil Mediation in accordance with section 44.102, Florida Statutes, and Florida Rules of Civil Procedure 1.700–1.730 and nothing in that Order prohibits judges from referring residential mortgage foreclosure cases or homeowner association foreclosure cases to mediation on a case-by-case basis; and

WHEREAS, residential mortgage foreclosure case filings and homeowner association foreclosure case filings have increased substantially in recent years and the backlog of pending foreclosure cases in the Ninth Circuit is significant. Mediation is an alternative means of resolving disputes and can be helpful in resolving foreclosure cases. It provides a forum for the parties to resolve their own dispute. Resolving foreclosure cases through mediation can help to prevent more serious increases in the backlog of cases and is consistent with the Court's responsibility to take charge of cases at an early stage of the litigation. Mediation also provides a more efficient use of limited judicial resources in an overburdened court system and state and county budget constraints have limited the ability of the courts in the Ninth Judicial Circuit to manage these cases in a timely manner; and

WHEREAS, Chapter 44, Florida Statutes, and rules 1.700–1.750, Florida Rules of Civil Procedure, provide a framework for court-ordered mediation of civil actions, except those matters expressly excluded by rule 1.710(b), which does not exclude residential foreclosure actions; and

WHEREAS, the Orange County Bar Association is an is an independent, not for profit corporation that was selected as the Foreclosure Program Manager for the Ninth Judicial Circuit's managed mediation program required by Supreme Court Administrative Order AOSC09–54. That selection was made after thorough and diligent consideration of all factors involved. The Orange County Bar Association has proven experience with the Court, has demonstrated expertise with a managed mediation program, and has effectively managed a large number of mediation referrals. The exchange of information between the Plaintiff and Defendant is an important prerequisite to successful mediation of a mortgage foreclosure case or homestead homeowner association foreclosure.

The process that was developed by the Orange County Bar Association to allow for exchange of information between the Plaintiff and Defendant is critical to the success of a managed mediation program. Because of the Orange County Bar Association's proven capabilities and expertise, the continued availability of its services, and the compatibility of existing services with the program manager services provided for in this Order, the Court is continuing with the Orange County Bar Association to assist in the processing of foreclosure cases that are referred to mediation; and

WHEREAS, this Court hosted a summit in which Lenders, Plaintiff attorney firms, consumer advocate representatives and other interested parties discussed the benefits and concerns of a managed foreclosure mediation program. Positive and constructive feedback was received and has been considered by this Court in formulating a local managed foreclosure mediation program; and

WHEREAS, mediation of certain homestead residential mortgage foreclosure actions or homestead homeowner association foreclosure actions **prior to the matter being set for final hearing** will facilitate the laudable goals of communication, facilitation, problem-solving between the parties with the emphasis on self-determination, the parties' needs and interests, procedural flexibility, full disclosure, fairness, and confidentiality. Referring these cases to mediation will also facilitate and provide a more efficient use of limited judicial and clerk resources in a court system that is already overburdened;

NOW, THEREFORE, I, Frederick J. Lauten, in order to facilitate the efficient operation of the administration of justice, and pursuant to the authority vested in me as Chief Judge of the Ninth Judicial Circuit of Florida under Florida Rule of Judicial Administration 2.215, hereby order the following, **effective immediately**, to continue until further order and superseding any provisions in prior Administrative Orders which may be inconsistent:

Effective Date

1. This Administrative Order shall apply to all residential homestead foreclosure cases filed beginning 12:01 a.m. on April 23, 2012, until further notice from the Chief Judge.

Certain other foreclosure cases may be referred to mediation as contemplated by this Administrative Order, at the discretion of the presiding judge as specified in paragraph 2 below.

Scope

2. Residential Foreclosures. This Administrative Order shall apply to (1) all residential mortgage foreclosure actions filed in Orange County in which the origination of the note and mortgage sued upon was subject to the provisions of the Federal Truth in Lending Act, Regulation Z; and (2) all residential lien foreclosures in which the plaintiff is a homeowner association, community association, or condominium association. However, compliance with this Order varies depending on whether the property secured by the mortgage or encumbered by the residential lien is a homestead residence.

The parties to the foreclosure action shall comply with the conditions and requirements imposed by this Order. If the foreclosure action is a mandatory referral to the Residential Foreclosure Mediation Program pursuant to this Order, it is not necessary to file a Request for Mediation with the court.

Upon the effective date of this Order, as specified in paragraph 1, all newly filed mortgage foreclosure actions filed against a homestead residence or residential lien foreclosure actions filed against a homestead residence in which the plaintiff is a homeowner association, community association, or condominium association shall be referred to the Orange County Residential Foreclosure Mediation Program (RFMP) unless the plaintiff and defendant agree in writing otherwise.

In actions to foreclose on a homestead residence, the plaintiff and defendant shall attend at least one mediation session, unless:

(a) the plaintiff and defendant agree in writing not to participate in the RFMP Program; or

(b) the Program Manager files a Notice of Defendant Non–Participation.

Upon the original effective date of this Order, all newly filed residential foreclosure actions involving property that is not a homestead residence shall comply with the requirements of filing a Form A as required by paragraph 6 below.

At the discretion of the presiding judge, compliance with this Order may also be required:

(a) for homestead residential foreclosure actions filed prior to the effective date of this Order, including those actions filed during the period of time between the cessation of the prior residential foreclosure mediation program and the effective date of this Order;

(b) for foreclosure actions involving non-homestead residences; and

(c) any other residential foreclosure action the presiding judge deems appropriate.

A party requesting that the case be sent to mediation with the RFMP Program at the discretion of the presiding judge shall make the request in the format of Exhibit 3 attached.

The following cases will automatically be removed from participating in the RFMP Program by the Program Manager:

(a) cases where there is no living defendant to mediate;

(b) cases where mail from Program Manager is returned indicating the property is vacant or mail is undeliverable;

(c) cases where the defendant has an automatic stay with the Bankruptcy Court; and

(d) cases where at least one note signer/title holder does not agree to participate in mediation.

When a case is deemed ineligible for mediation due to one of the above specified reasons, the Program Manager shall file a Notice of Non–Participation with the Court and serve copies of such Notice to all parties. The Notice of Non–Participation will indicate the reason that the case is being removed from the RFMP Program.

If the plaintiff certifies in Form A that the property is **NOT** a homestead residence, the matter may proceed to a final hearing, summary judgment, or default final judgment in accordance with the rules of civil procedure without any further requirement to attend mediation, unless otherwise ordered by the presiding judge.

3. Referral to Mediation. This Order constitutes a formal referral to mediation pursuant to the Florida Rules of Civil Procedure in actions involving a foreclosure of a homestead residence. The plaintiff and defendant are deemed to have stipulated to mediation by a mediator assigned by the Program Manager unless pursuant to rule 1.720(f), Florida Rules of Civil Procedure, the plaintiff and defendant file a written stipulation choosing not to participate in the RFMP Program. Referral to the RFMP Program is for administration and management of the mediation process and assignment of a Florida Supreme Court certified circuit civil mediator who has been trained in mediating residential foreclosure actions and who has agreed to be on the panel of available certified circuit civil mediators. Mediation through the RFMP Program shall be conducted in accordance with Florida Rules of Civil Procedure and Florida Rules for Certified and Court–Appointed Mediators.

4. Compliance Prior to Judgment. The parties must comply with this Order and the mediation process must be completed ***before*** the plaintiff applies for default judgment, a summary judgment hearing, or a final hearing in an action to foreclose a mortgage or lien on a homestead residence unless a Notice of Non–Participation is filed by the Program Manager.

5. Delivery of Notice of RFMP Program with Summons. After the effective date of this Order, in all actions to foreclose a mortgage or lien on residential property the plaintiff shall attach to the summons to be served on each defendant a notice regarding managed mediation for homestead residences in the format of Exhibit 2, in both English and Spanish, attached.

The clerk of court shall provide a daily list of each homestead foreclosure filing, with the case number, to the Program Manager.

Procedure

6. Responsibilities of Plaintiff's Counsel. When suit is filed, counsel for the plaintiff must file a completed Form A with the clerk of court. If the property is a homestead residence, all certifications in Form A must be filled out completely. Within one (1) business day after Form A is filed with the clerk of court, counsel for plaintiff shall also mail a copy of Form A to the Program Manager and include contact information for all note signer/title holders. The contact information must include at a minimum the last known mailing address and phone number for each note signer/title holder.

Within five (5) days after Form A is filed with the clerk of court, counsel for the plaintiff shall send a check or money order made payable to the Orange County Bar Association, 880 North Orange Avenue, Orlando, Florida 32801 in the amount of $100.00. PLAINTIFF SHALL ATTACH A PHOTOCOPY OF FORM A TO THE CHECK AND PROVIDE THE NOTE SIGNER/TITLE HOLDER'S CONTACT INFORMATION INCLUDING THE PROPERTY ADDRESS AND LAST KNOWN TELEPHONE NUMBER. The check must match the information provided on Form A and the court case number must be included on the check. NO PERSONAL CHECKS WILL BE ACCEPTED.

Counsel for the plaintiff shall also send all defendants, at defendant's last known mailing address, a copy of the complaint, a copy of the summons and a copy of Exhibit 2 of this Order, Notice of RFMP Program to be Served with Summons, in both English and Spanish, via U.S. Mail within forty-eight (48) hours of filing the complaint.

As different payment options become available, the Program Manager may change payment acceptance terms without the necessity of amending this Administrative Order.

In Form A, plaintiff's counsel must affirmatively certify whether the origination of the note and mortgage sued upon was subject to the provisions of the Federal Truth in Lending Act, Regulation Z or is a homeowner association, community association, or condominium association. In Form A, plaintiff's counsel must also affirmatively certify whether the property is a homestead residence. Plaintiff's counsel is not permitted to respond to the certification with "unknown," "unsure," "not applicable," or similar nonresponsive statements.

Plaintiff's counsel may designate more than one plaintiff's representative. At least one of the plaintiff's representatives designated in Form A must attend any mediation session scheduled pursuant to this Order.

Form A may be amended to change the designated plaintiff's representative, and the amended Form A must be filed with the court no later than five (5) days prior to the mediation session. All amended Forms A must be transmitted to the Program Manager via a secure dedicated e-mail address no later than one (1) business day after being filed with the clerk of court.

Within five (5) business days of the complaint filing date, or date of the court order referring the case to the RFMP Program, (see Exhibit 7), [1] the plaintiff must submit Form A, provide the defendant's contact information and pay the Program Manager the $100.00 payment. If the plaintiff fails to comply with this deadline, they will incur a $50.00 penalty fee. If within ten (10) business days of the complaint filing date, or date of the Court Order Referring Case to the RFMP Program, the case is still not in compliance and the penalty fee has not been paid, the Program Manager may submit a proposed Order to Show Cause to the Court.

In the event of plaintiff non-compliance, the timeline shall begin from the date of plaintiff's full compliance. Full compliance shall consist of: completed Form A, payment of fees, court/clerk case number and contact information as specified in paragraph 6 of this Order.

7. Responsibilities of Defendant. Upon the Program Manager receiving the Form A copy, the $100.00 payment and plaintiff counsel has provided all required information for the case to the Program Manager, the Program Manager shall begin efforts to contact the defendant to explain the RFMP Program to the defendant and the requirements that the defendant must comply with to obtain a mediation. The Program Manager shall also ascertain whether the defendant wants to participate in the RFMP Program.

The defendant must do the following prior to mediation being scheduled:

(a) pay the Program Manager $250.00 for Mediation Program Fees within the forty (40) day defendant contact period; and

(b) provide to the Program Manager the List of Defendant Documents requested by plaintiff's counsel within fifty-five (55) days from the date eligible; and

(c) schedule mediation with the Program Manager within fifty-five (55) days from the date eligible. [2]

The List of Defendant Documents crafted for each individual case needed for scheduling mediation will be provided to the Program Manager by counsel for plaintiff. The plaintiff creates the List of Defendant Documents needed for mediation for each individual case based upon whatever workout option the parties are pursuing. When the Program Manager receives all of the documents on the List from defendant, the Program Manager shall transmit the documents to counsel for plaintiff via e-mail. The deadline for scheduling mediation is tolled by any additional days it may take for plaintiff counsel to provide the List of Defendant Documents requested by the plaintiff and payment of the $150.00 fee by the plaintiff to the Program Manager. The Program Manager is not responsible or liable for the accuracy of defendant's financial information.

8. Information to be Provided to the Program Manager. All information to be provided to the Program Manager to advance the mediation process, such as Form A, List of Defendant's Documents, as well as the case number of the action and contact information for the note signer/title holders, should be submitted via a secure dedicated e-mail address or by mail. Please refer to the Orange County Bar Association's website for further information. http://www.orangecountybar.org.

9. Non-participation by Defendant. If the defendant does not want participate in the RFMP Program, or if the defendant fails or refuses to cooperate with the Program Manager, or if the Program Manager is unable to contact the defendant, or the case is a matter subject to removal for one of the stated ineligibility categories described fully in Paragraph 2, the Program Manager shall file a Notice of Non–Participation in the format of Exhibit 4 attached. The Notice of Non–Participation shall be filed after the forty (40) day defendant contact period has expired, or as soon as the Program Manager has been notified that defendant affirmatively opts out of the RFMP Program, or as soon as possible when a case has been deemed ineligible for the RFMP Program due to meeting one of the stated ineligibility categories described in Paragraph 2. A copy of the Notice of Non–Participation shall be served on the parties by the Program Manager.

10. Encouragement to Seek Foreclosure Counseling. The Program Manager shall be responsible for encouraging the defendant to seek foreclosure counseling prior to scheduling mediation.

11. Referrals for Legal Representation. In actions referred to the RFMP Program, the Program Manager shall advise any defendant who is not represented by an attorney that the defendant has the right to consult with an attorney at any time during the mediation process and the right to bring an attorney to the mediation session. The Program Manager shall also advise the defendant that the defendant may apply for a volunteer pro bono attorney in programs run by lawyer referral, legal services, and legal aid programs as may exist within this Circuit.

If the defendant applies to one of those agencies and is coupled with a legal services attorney or a volunteer pro bono attorney, the attorney shall file a notice of appearance with the clerk of the court and provide a copy to the attorney for the plaintiff and the Program Manager. The appearance may be limited to representation only to assist the defendant with mediation but, if a defendant secures the services of an attorney, counsel of record must attend the mediation. If any defendant retains a private attorney, the attorney must file a notice of appearance and provide the Program Manager with a copy of such notice of appearance as the Program Manager is not a party to the case and does not automatically receive such notifications otherwise.

12. Scheduling Mediation. The plaintiff's representative, plaintiff's counsel, and the defendant are all required to comply with the time limitations imposed by this Order and attend a mediation session as scheduled by the Program Manager.

Within fifty-five (55) days after suit is filed, the Program Manager shall schedule a mediation session.

The mediation session shall be scheduled for a date and time convenient to the plaintiff's representative, the defendant, and counsel for the plaintiff and the defendant, using a mediator from the panel of Florida Supreme Court certified circuit civil mediators who have been specially trained to mediate residential foreclosure disputes. Mediation sessions will be held at a suitable location(s) within this Circuit obtained by the Program Manager for mediation. Mediation shall be completed within the time requirements established by rule 1.710(a), Florida Rules of Civil Procedure.

Once the date, time, and place of the mediation session have been scheduled by the Program Manager, the Program Manager shall promptly file with the clerk of court and serve on all parties a Notice of Mediation.

Absent good cause, as determined by the court, mediation must be completed within one hundred (100) days after suit is filed. If mediation fails to be completed within 100 days after suit is filed, and the court makes a determination that such failure is attributable to either party, and that party is unable to show good cause as to why mediation could not be completed within the specified time frame, the court may dismiss the action without prejudice, or impose such other sanctions as the court deems appropriate.

13. Attendance at Mediation. The following persons are required to be physically present at the mediation session: (a) the defendant; (b) the defendant's counsel of record, if any; (c) the plaintiff's lawyer; and (d) the plaintiff's representative with full authority to settle as designated in the most recently filed Form A. Full authority to settle shall include the ability to negotiate and agree to both retention and disposition options, which shall include but is not limited to: authority to approve loan modifications; consent to defendant refinancing; reduction of principal; short sale; deed-in-lieu of foreclosure; consent to judgment; and consent to other workout options.

However, the plaintiff's representative may appear at mediation through the use of communication equipment, if plaintiff files and serves at least five (5) days prior to the mediation a notice in the format of Exhibit 5 attached advising that the plaintiff's representative will be attending through the use of communication equipment and designating the person who has full authority to sign any settlement agreement reached. Plaintiff's counsel may be designated as the person with full authority to sign the settlement agreement.

At the time that the mediation is scheduled to physically commence, but prior to the commencement of the mediation conference, and prior to any discussion of the case in the presence of the mediator, the Program Manager or designee shall take a written roll consisting of the signature and printed name of each party present. That written roll is a determination of the presence of: (a) the defendant; (b) the defendant's counsel of record, if any; (c) the plaintiff's lawyer; and (d) the plaintiff's representative with full authority to settle.

Determination of plaintiff's representative's full authority to settle shall be verified through completion of a certificate affirming said representative has full authority to settle. The Program Manager shall provide a Certificate of Authority document at the mediation for execution by plaintiff counsel in consultation with the plaintiff representative appearing via phone or in person in the format of Exhibit 8 attached.

If either the plaintiff's counsel acting on behalf of plaintiff's representative appearing via phone or plaintiff's representative appearing in person cannot sign the Certificate of Authority document ensuring that the plaintiff representative has: (1) full settlement authority to negotiate a settlement with the defendant(s) without further consultation, and (2) has fully reviewed all documents provided by Program Manager for the case to the plaintiff's legal counsel then Program Manager must not allow the mediation to begin and reschedule the mediation at plaintiff's expense in the amount of $150.00. If cancellation and rescheduling of the mediation is required under this section, then no Mediation Report shall be filed as no mediation has taken place.

If the Program Manager, or designee, determines that the plaintiff's representative present does not have full authority to settle, it shall be reported on the written roll that the plaintiff's representative did not appear with full settlement authority as required by this Order. If a party appears via telephonic means, that should be notated by the Program Manager, or designee, or the mediator on the written roll. The written roll and execution of the Certificate of Authority document with the Program Manager, or designee, is not a mediation communication.

THE RIGHT TO APPEAR THROUGH THE USE OF COMMUNICATION EQUIPMENT WILL BE TERMINATED AS TO ANY AND ALL PLAINTIFFS WHO FAIL TO SECURE PARTICIPATION BY A REPRESENTATIVE WITH FULL AUTHORITY TO NEGOTIATE FOR ANY MEDIATION THAT IS UTILIZING APPEARANCE VIA COMMUNICATION EQUIPMENT.

The authorization by this Order for the plaintiff's representative to appear through the use of communication equipment is pursuant to rule 1.720(b), Florida Rules of Civil Procedure (court order may alter physical appearance requirement), and in recognition of the emergency situation created by the massive number of residential foreclosure cases being filed in this Circuit and the impracticality of requiring physical attendance of a plaintiff's representative at every mediation. Additional reasons for authorizing appearance through the use of communication equipment for foreclosure mediation include a number of protective factors that do not exist in other civil cases, namely the administration of the program by a program manager and required disclosure of information prior to mediation. The implementation of this Order shall not create any expectation that appearance through the use of communication equipment will be authorized in other civil cases.

If the plaintiff's representative attends mediation through the use of communication equipment, the person authorized by the plaintiff to sign a settlement agreement must be physically present at mediation. If the plaintiff's representative attends mediation through the use of communication equipment, the plaintiff's representative must remain on the communication equipment at all times during the entire mediation session. If the plaintiff's representative attending via communication equipment does not participate in the mediation for the entire time of the mediation once he or she has been reached, the Program Manager may report the mediation as a no show mediation as to the plaintiff representative's attendance and the failure to fully participate shall be grounds to impose sanctions against the plaintiff including requiring the physical appearance of the plaintiff's representative at a second mediation, taxation of the costs of a second mediation to the plaintiff, and dismissal of the action.

Junior lienholders may appear at mediation by a representative with full settlement authority. If a junior lienholder is a governmental entity comprised of an elected body, such junior lienholder may appear at mediation by a representative who has authority to recommend settlement to the governing body. Counsel for any junior lienholder may also attend the mediation. The participants physically attending mediation may consult on the telephone during the mediation with other persons as long as such consultation does not violate the provisions of sections 44.401–406, Florida Statutes.

14. Failure to Appear at Mediation. If either the plaintiff's representative designated in the most recently filed Form A or the defendant fails to appear at a properly noticed mediation and the mediation does not occur, or when a mediation results in a no agreement, the Mediation Report shall notify the presiding judge regarding who appeared at mediation without making further comment as to the reasons for a no agreement. The Program Manager shall attach a copy of the written roll as described in paragraph 13 of this Order to the Mediation Report.

If the defendant fails to appear, or if the mediation results in a no agreement with all required parties present, and if the defendant has been lawfully served with a copy of the complaint, and if the time for filing a responsive pleading has passed, the matter may proceed to a final hearing, summary judgment, or default final judgment in accordance with the rules of civil procedure without any further requirement to attend mediation.

If plaintiff's counsel or the plaintiff's representative fails to appear, the court may dismiss the action without prejudice, order plaintiff's counsel or the plaintiff's representative(s) to appear at mediation, or impose such other sanctions as the court deems appropriate including, but not limited to, attorney's fees and costs if the defendant is represented by an attorney. If the defendant or defendant's counsel of record fails to appear, the court may impose such other sanctions as the court deems appropriate, including, but not limited to, attorney's fees and costs.

15. Written Settlement Agreement; Mediation Report. If a partial or final agreement is reached, it shall be reduced to writing and signed by the parties and their counsel, if any. Pursuant to rule 1.730(b), Florida Rules of Civil Procedure, if a partial or full settlement agreement is reached, the mediator shall report the existence of the signed or transcribed agreement to the court without comment. If the parties do not reach an agreement as to any matter as a result of mediation, the mediator shall report the lack of an agreement to the court without comment or recommendation. In the case of a no agreement, the report shall advise the court who attended the mediation, and a copy of Form A or any amended Form A shall be attached to the report for the court to determine if at least one of the plaintiff's representative named in Form A appeared for mediation. The mediator's report to the court shall be in the format of Exhibit 6 attached. Each mediation report shall be completed and reported to the Program Manager, or designee, immediately after each mediation session. The Program Manager, or designee, shall then file each mediation report with the clerk of court.

16. Mediation Communications. All mediation communications occurring as a result of this Order, including information provided to the Program Manager that is not filed with the court shall be confidential and inadmissible in any subsequent legal proceeding pursuant to Chapter 44, Florida Statutes, the Florida Rules of Civil Procedure, and the Florida Rules for Certified and Court–Appointed Mediators, unless otherwise provided for by law.

17. Failure to Comply with Administrative Order. In all residential foreclosure actions, if a notice for trial, motion for default final judgment, or motion for summary judgment is filed with the clerk of court, no action will be taken by the court to set a final hearing or enter a summary or default final judgment until the requirements of this Order have been met. In cases involving a homestead residence, the presiding judge shall require that copies of either: 1) the most recently filed Form A and the Mediation Report, or 2) the most recently filed Form A and the Notice of Defendant's Non–Participation be sent to the presiding judge by the plaintiff or plaintiff's counsel prior to setting a final hearing or delivered with the packet requesting a summary or default final judgment.

The failure of a party to fully comply with the provisions of this Order may result in the imposition of any sanctions available to the court, including dismissal of the cause of action without further notice.

Summary of RFMP Program Timelines

18. RFMP Program Timelines. The following timelines shall be followed:

SUIT IS FILED	FORM A FILED WITH COMPLAINT EXHIBIT 2, IN BOTH ENGLISH AND SPANISH, ATTACHED TO SUMMONS
WITHIN 1 BUSINESS DAY AFTER SUIT IS FILED	FORM A TRANSMITTED TO PROGRAM MANAGER BY PLAINTIFF'S COUNSEL
WITHIN 48 HOURS AFTER SUIT IS FILED	PLAINTIFF'S COUNSEL SHALL SEND DEFENDANT VIA U.S. MAIL, AT DEFENDANT'S LAST KNOWN MAILING ADDRESS: A COPY OF THE COMPLAINT, A COPY OF THE SUMMONS, AND A COPY OF EXHIBIT 2, IN BOTH ENGLISH AND SPANISH
WITHIN 5 DAYS AFTER SUIT IS FILED OR CASE REFERRED TO RFMP BY COURT ORDER	FORM A AND $100.00 PAYMENT SUBMITTED TO PROGRAM MANAGER AND CONTACT INFORMATION AND PHONE NUMBER FOR ALL NOTE SIGNER/TITLE HOLDERS SUBMITTED TO PROGRAM MANAGER BY PLAINTIFF'S COUNSEL ($50.00 LATE FEE APPLIES IF NON–COMPLIANT)
WITHIN 40 DAYS AFTER DATE ELIGIBLE*	DEFENDANT MUST CONTACT PROGRAM MANAGER AND PAY $250.00 MEDIATION FEE
WITHIN 40 DAYS AFTER DATE ELIGIBLE*	PROGRAM MANAGER WILL CONTACT PLAINTIFF'S COUNSEL TO OBTAIN LIST OF DOCUMENTS REQUESTED BY PLAINTIFF AND $150.00 PAYMENT ONLY AFTER THE DEFENDANT HAS PAID THEIR PORTION OF THE MEDIATION FEE ($250.00)
WITHIN 55 DAYS AFTER DATE ELIGIBLE*	DEFENDANT MUST SUBMIT LIST OF DOCUMENTS REQUESTED BY PLAINTIFF TO PROGRAM MANAGER
WITHIN 55 DAYS AFTER DATE ELIGIBLE*	MEDIATION SESSION MUST BE SCHEDULED
AT LEAST 5 DAYS PRIOR TO MEDIATION	ANY AMENDED FORM A DESIGNATION OF THE PLAINTIFF'S REPRESENTATIVE MUST BE FILED WITH CLERK
1 DAY PRIOR TO MEDIATION	ANY AMENDED FORM A DESIGNATION OF THE PLAINTIFF'S REPRESENTATIVE MUST BE TRANSMITTED TO PROGRAM MANAGER
WITHIN 100 DAYS AFTER DATE ELIGIBLE*	MEDIATION IS COMPLETED
WITHIN 10 DAYS AFTER MEDIATION	MEDIATION REPORT FILED WITH THE CLERK BY PROGRAM MANAGER

*Date Eligible = plaintiff's counsel submits Form A, defendant contact information and $100.00 payment is received by the Program Manager.

19. Reinstatement Procedures. In the event of reinstatement to the RFMP Program, defendant is responsible for paying their share of the program fees ($250.00) within five (5) days of the reinstatement date. After the defendant pays their share of the fees, the case timeline will be tolled by the number of additional days until Program Manager receives both the $150.00 payment and List of Defendant Documents crafted for each individual case from the plaintiff. After a case is reinstated, defendant has twenty (20) days to send Program Manager the List of Defendant Documents as requested by plaintiff and to schedule mediation. The defendant has fifty (50) days from the date of reinstatement to complete mediation. The Program Manager may file a Notice of Non–Participation if defendant fails to comply with these deadlines. When a case is reinstated by agreement of the parties, the Program Manager may file a Notice of Withdrawal of Non–Participation.

In the event of reinstatement, the following timelines shall be followed:

SUMMARY OF RFMP TIMELINES FOR REINSTATED CASES

WITHIN 5 DAYS AFTER REINSTATEMENT DATE*	DEFENDANT SHALL PAY $250.00 PROGRAM FEE
WITHIN 5 DAYS AFTER REINSTATEMENT AND PAYMENT OF $250.00 BY THE DEFENDANT	PROGRAM MANAGER WILL CONTACT PLAINTIFF'S COUNSEL TO OBTAIN LIST OF DOCUMENTS REQUESTED BY PLAINTIFF AND $150.00 PAYMENT ONLY AFTER THE DEFENDANT HAS PAID THEIR PORTION OF THE MEDIATION FEE ($250.00)
WITHIN 20 DAYS OF REINSTATEMENT DATE*	DEFENDANT SHALL PROVIDE LIST OF DOCUMENTS REQUESTED BY PLAINTIFF TO PROGRAM MANAGER AND SCHEDULE DATE FOR MEDIATION WITH PROGRAM MANAGER
WITHIN 50 DAYS OF REINSTATEMENT DATE*	MEDIATION MUST OCCUR

*Reinstatement Date = date of plaintiff consent to reinstate or receipt of reinstatement order by the Program Manager.

RFMP Program Fees

20. RFMP Program Fees. The fee structure for the RFMP Program is based on the assumption that a successful mediation can be accomplished with one mediation session. Accordingly, pursuant to rule 1.720(k), Florida Rules of Civil Procedure, the reasonable program fees for the managed mediation, the mediator's fee, and administration of the managed mediation program, is a total of no more than $500.00 payable as follows:

1) $100.00 paid by plaintiff to the Program Manager within five (5) days after filing Form A with the clerk of court for program fees of the RFMP Program, including outreach to the defendant and case screening fees; and

2) $250.00 paid by defendant to the Program Manager within the defendant contact time period for RFMP Program fees; and

3) $150.00 paid by plaintiff to the Program Manager only after defendant has paid their share of program fees.

The first $100.00 payment by plaintiff must be sent to the Program Manager within five (5) days after filing Form A with the clerk of court. A photocopy of Form A must accompany payment, and the information on the payment must match the information recorded on Form A. Payment shall be in the form of check or money order made payable to the Orange County Bar Association, 880 North Orange Avenue, Orlando, Florida 32801. No personal checks will be accepted. The court case number must be recorded on the check.

If the case is not resolved through the mediation process, the presiding judge may tax the program fees as a cost or apply it as a set off in the final judgment of foreclosure.

If mediation is scheduled and the defendant announces an intention not to participate further in the RFMP Program prior to the mediation session, or the defendant fails to provide the requested documents and/or schedule mediation within the timelines provided, or if the case settles and the Program Manager has notice of the settlement at least one (1) business day prior to the mediation session, the parties shall be entitled to a refund of the Program Fees allocated for the mediation session. In this case, each party will be refunded $75.00 for mediator fees.

The total fees include the mediator's fees and costs and the cost to the Program Manager for administration of the managed mediation program which includes but is not limited to providing neutral meeting and caucus space, scheduling, telephone lines and instruments, infrastructure to support a secure dedicated e-mail address or other secure system for information.

In order to cancel and/or reschedule mediation, all parties must consent to the change and notify the Program Manager. If a mediation session is cancelled the same day the mediation was scheduled to occur, the parties will not be refunded the portion of the fee set aside for payment to the mediator. If all parties agree to reschedule the mediation the same day mediation was scheduled to occur, the parties will not be refunded the mediation fee. If all parties agree to reschedule the mediation the same day mediation was scheduled to occur, the parties must pay an additional mediator fee, unless the reschedule is due to a medical emergency for a party. Mediators will be paid for same day cancellations by a party unless the cancellation is due to a medical emergency for a party. If mediation is cancelled prior to the date that mediation was scheduled to occur, both parties will receive a refund of $75.00 for the mediator fee. In the event of an adjournment, all parties must agree to adjourn and pay the additional mediator fee but the parties will not have to pay any additional program fees.

If a case is settled prior to mediation, plaintiff's counsel must provide the Program Manager a copy of the dismissal order. Upon receipt of the dismissal order, Program Manager shall refund each party the amount of $75.00 for the mediator fee.

Program Manager to Monitor Compliance and Satisfaction

21. Monitoring Compliance Concerning Certain Provisions of This Order, Satisfaction with RFMP Program, and Program Operation. The Program Manager shall be responsible for monitoring whether Form A has been filed in all residential foreclosure actions that commence after the effective date of this Order and whether the RFMP Program fees have been paid if the residence is a homestead residence. The Program Manager shall send compliance reports to the Chief Judge or the Chief Judge's designee in the format requested by the Chief Judge. The reports shall be monthly or quarterly as determined by the Chief Judge.

The Program Manager may assist with enforcing compliance with this Order upon filing a written motion pursuant to rule 1.100(b), Florida Rules of Civil Procedure, stating with particularity the grounds therefore and the relief or order sought. Example orders are attached as Exhibit 7. The Program Manager shall also provide the Chief Judge with periodic reports as to whether plaintiffs and defendants are satisfied with the RFMP Program. The Program Manager shall also provide the Chief Judge with reports containing statistical information about the status of cases in the RFMP Program and RFMP Program finances in the format and with the frequency requested by the Chief Judge. The reports shall be upon request of the Chief Judge or Chief Judge's designee.

The Program Manager shall also implement a reporting system to collect data on the number of cases referred to the Program and whether the cases settled, adjourned, or ended in no agreement. Further, the Program Manager shall track the percentage of cases referred to the Program that result in the Program Manager successfully contacting defendant; the percentage of scheduled mediations failing to go forward because plaintiff's representative did not appear; the percentage of scheduled mediations failing to go forward because the defendant did not appear; and the percentage of mediations resulting in partial or complete agreements compared to those resulting in no agreement.

22. Designation of Plaintiff Liaisons with RFMP Program. Any plaintiff who has filed five (5) or more foreclosure actions in the Ninth Judicial Circuit while this Order is in effect shall appoint two RFMP Program liaisons, one of whom shall be a lawyer and the other a representative of the entity servicing the plaintiff's mortgages, if any, and, if none, a representative of the plaintiff. Plaintiff's counsel shall provide written notice of the name, phone number (including extension), e-mail, and mailing address of both liaisons to the Chief Judge and the Program Manager within thirty (30) days after the effective date of this Order, and on the first Monday of each February thereafter while this Order is in effect.

The liaisons shall be informed of the requirements of this Order and shall be capable of answering questions concerning the administrative status of pending cases and the party's internal procedures relating to the processing of foreclosure cases, and be readily accessible to discuss administrative and logistical issues affecting the progress of the plaintiff's cases through the RFMP Program. Plaintiff's counsel shall promptly inform the Chief Judge and the Program Manager of any changes in designation of the liaisons and the contact information of the liaisons. The liaisons shall act as the Court's point of contact in the event the plaintiff fails to comply with this Order on multiple occasions and there is a need to communicate with the plaintiff concerning administrative matters of mutual interest.

List of Participating Mediators and Rotation of Mediators

23. List of Participating Mediators and Rotation of Mediators. The Program Manager shall post on its website the list of Florida Supreme Court certified mediators it will use to implement the RFMP Program and will state in writing the criteria, subject to approval by the Chief Judge, the Program will use in selecting mediators. The Program Manager shall also state in writing the procedure, subject to the approval by the Chief Judge, the program will use to rotate the appointment of mediators. The RFMP Program shall require the use of mediators who have been trained to mediate foreclosure cases, reflecting the diversity of the community in which it operates. Assignment of mediators shall be on a rotation basis that fairly spreads work throughout the pool of mediators working in the RFMP Program, unless the parties mutually agree, in writing, on a specific mediator or the case requires a particular skill on the part of the mediator.

In an effort to maintain the performance and quality of the RFMP Program, it shall be in the Chief Judge's discretion to remove any mediator from rotation, in consultation with the Program Manager, should circumstances arise which warrant the removal of the mediator from the RFMP Program list of mediators.

Program Manager

24. Program Manager. The Orange County Bar Association, an independent, nonpartisan, nonprofit organization is hereby retained as Program Manager of the Orange County RFMP Program. The Orange County Bar Association has ably demonstrated its ability to assist the Court with managing the large number of residential mortgage foreclosure actions that have been filed in Orange County.

25. Administrative Order 2012–06–02 is vacated and set aside except to the extent that it has been incorporated and/or amended herein. Vacating an Administrative Order that vacates a prior Order does not revive the prior Order.

DONE AND ORDERED at Orlando, Florida, this 12th day of April, 2018.

Frederick J. Lauten
Chief Judge

[1] Cases that are initiated by referral to the Program by Court Order will follow the same timeline as cases subject to mandatory referral to this Program pursuant to this Administrative Order.

[2] Date Eligible is the date that the Program Manager is in receipt of the following: plaintiff's counsel has provided Form A to the Program Manager, plaintiff's counsel has provided defendant contact information including property address, phone number and email (if available) for all note signer/title holders, and full payment of $100.00 for program fees by plaintiff.

2012–03. NINTH JUDICIAL CIRCUIT COURT CIRCUIT CIVIL COURT GUIDELINES

ADMINISTRATIVE ORDER NO. 2012–03

IN THE CIRCUIT COURT OF THE NINTH JUDICIAL CIRCUIT, IN AND FOR ORANGE AND OSCEOLA COUNTIES, FLORIDA

ADMINISTRATIVE ORDER ESTABLISHING NINTH JUDICIAL CIRCUIT COURT CIRCUIT CIVIL COURT GUIDELINES

WHEREAS, pursuant to Article V, Section 2(d) of the Florida Constitution and section 43.26, Florida Statutes, the chief judge of each judicial circuit is charged with the authority and the power to do everything necessary to promote the prompt and efficient administration of justice; and

WHEREAS, to create and maintain an organization capable of effecting the efficient, prompt, and proper administration of justice for the citizens of this State, the chief judge is required to exercise direction, *see* Fla. R. Jud. Admin. 2.215(b)(2), (b)(3); and

WHEREAS, standardized procedures and manners of communication between the parties and the court best serve the interests of those that come before the court, preserve valuable judicial resources and prevent confusion and delay; and

WHEREAS, the Ninth Judicial Circuit Civil Courts Commission (Commission) was tasked with, and did submit to the Court, recommendations for accomplishing standardized procedures for the Circuit Civil Division of the Ninth Judicial Circuit Court; and

WHEREAS, the Court expresses its sincere appreciation to the Commission and its Chair for 2010–11, Mr. David King, Esq., for their dedication and commitment in undertaking this daunting task and reaching agreement on the recommendations; and

WHEREAS, in order to provide effective coordination and in the interest of promoting judicial economy, the prompt and efficient administration of justice and in service to the citizens of the Ninth Circuit;

NOW, THEREFORE, I, Belvin Perry, Jr., in order to facilitate the efficient operation of the administration of justice, and pursuant to the authority vested in me as Chief Judge of the Ninth Judicial Circuit of Florida under Florida Rule of Judicial Administration 2.215, hereby order that, **effective immediately** and to continue until further order:

1. Orange County only: During non-trial weeks, each circuit civil division shall schedule one hour to hear both *ex parte* and short matters at 8:30 a.m. Monday through Thursday. During times when the judge is scheduled to be out of the office, notice shall be posted on the Judicial Automated Calendaring System. *Ex parte* matters shall be heard first whenever possible. For purposes of this Order, an *ex parte* matter is defined as a purely uncontested matter and a short matter is defined as a contested matter that requires less than ten (10) minutes of the court's time.

2. Orange County only: During trial weeks, each circuit civil division in trial shall either arrange for coverage for *ex parte* and short matters by another division not in trial or shall schedule a minimum of thirty (30) minutes to hear both *ex parte* and short matters at 8:30 a. m. Monday through Thursday. During times when the judge is scheduled to be out of the office, notice shall be posted on the Judicial Automated Calendaring System. *Ex parte* matters shall be heard first whenever possible. In the event foreclosure cases return to the general civil divisions, the time allotted for *ex parte* and short matters will expand to one hour. For purposes of this Order, an *ex parte* matter is defined as a purely uncontested matter and a short matter is defined as a contested matter that requires less than ten (10) minutes of the court's time.

3. If an *ex parte* or short matter is to start late or be covered by a different division, without prior notice, attorneys and litigants shall be made aware through the posting of a note on the hearing room door.

4. In the interest of judicial economy and promotion of the prompt and efficient administration of justice, all circuit civil judges shall start *ex parte*, short matter and regular hearings on time and all judges shall strictly enforce allotted hearing time between attorneys.

5. In the event that a party seeks to cancel a previously scheduled hearing, the party must telephone the judge's judicial assistant and file a notice of cancellation. If the judicial assistant requests confirmation via an e-mail correspondence, the party shall comply.

6. A mandatory meet and confer process is hereby established, as set forth below, for all motions to be ***set for hearing*** in the circuit civil division and to occur ***before*** scheduling the hearing except for the following motions: injunctive relief without notice; judgment on the pleadings; summary judgment; or to permit maintenance of a class action.

Counsel with full authority to resolve the matter shall confer ***before*** scheduling the hearing on the motion to attempt to resolve or otherwise narrow the issues raised in the motion, and include a Certificate of Compliance (attached hereto as "Exhibit A") that the conference has occurred in the Notice of Hearing filed with the court. It shall be the responsibility of counsel who schedules the hearing to arrange the conference.

The term "confer" requires a substantive conversation in person or by telephone in a good faith effort to resolve the motion without the need to schedule a hearing, and does not envision an exchange of ultimatums by fax, e-mail or letter. Counsel who merely attempt to confer have not conferred for purposes of this Order.

Counsel must respond promptly to inquiries and communications from opposing counsel who notices the hearing and is attempting to schedule the conference. If counsel who notices the hearing is unable to reach opposing counsel to conduct the conference after three (3) good faith attempts, counsel who notices the hearing must identify in the Certificate of Compliance the dates and times of the efforts made to contact opposing counsel.

Counsel shall include in the Notice of Hearing the Certificate of Compliance certifying that the meet and confer occurred (or did not occur and setting out the good faith attempts to schedule the conference) and identifying the date of the conference, the names of the participating attorneys, and the specific results obtained.

Counsel who notices the hearing shall ensure that the court and the court's judicial assistant are aware of any narrowing of the issues or other resolution as a result of the conference.

7. Counsel is required to provide the court (and opposing counsel) with courtesy copies of any memoranda, case law or any other materials on which counsel may rely at a scheduled hearing at least three (3) court days before the scheduled hearing.

8. A party seeking to schedule hearing time shall check the Judicial Automated Calendaring System (JACS) via the Ninth Judicial Circuit Court website (http://www.ninthcircuit.org/) for available time slots. The party shall then either call or send an e-mail correspondence to the judicial assistant to confirm the hearing time.

9. All communications from a party, other than those relating solely to scheduling hearing time, with a judicial assistant for any given matter before the court shall be by telephone. If the judicial assistant requests a follow-up or confirmation e-mail correspondence, the party shall comply.

10. As the court system continues to move toward a paperless system, and as technology related to electronic filing, scheduling of hearing time and other related matters continues to become available, judges, judicial assistants and parties appearing before the court are strongly encouraged to utilize said technology when feasible. Where court technologies as contemplated by this Order become the standard, use of such technologies will be required without need for amendment of this Order.

DONE AND ORDERED at Orlando, Florida, this 12th day of April, 2012.

Belvin Perry, Jr.
Chief Judge

"Exhibit A"

First Option

CERTIFICATE OF COMPLIANCE

I HEREBY CERTIFY that a lawyer in my firm with full authority to resolve this matter had a substantive conversation in person or by telephone with opposing counsel in a good faith effort to resolve this motion before the motion was noticed for hearing but the parties were unable to reach an agreement.

/S/ ____________________
Counsel for the party who noticed the matter for hearing.

Second Option

CERTIFICATE OF COMPLIANCE

I HEREBY CERTIFY that a lawyer in my firm with full authority to resolve this matter attempted in good faith to contact opposing counsel in person or by telephone on:

1. (Date) at (Time) ;
2. (Date) at (Time) ; and
3. (Date) at (Time) ;

to discuss resolution of this motion without a hearing and the lawyer in my firm was unable to speak with opposing counsel.

/S/ ____________________
Counsel for the party who noticed the matter for hearing.

2012–02. [VACATED BY ADMINISTRATIVE ORDER NO. 2016–09, EFFECTIVE JUNE 2, 2016]

2010–27. TEMPORARY ORDER FOR PATERNITY ACTIONS, ORANGE & OSCEOLA COUNTIES

ADMINISTRATIVE ORDER NO. 2010–27

IN THE CIRCUIT COURT OF THE NINTH JUDICIAL CIRCUIT, IN AND FOR ORANGE & OSCEOLA COUNTIES, FLORIDA

ORDER IMPLEMENTING A STANDING TEMPORARY ORDER FOR PATERNITY ACTIONS, ORANGE & OSCEOLA COUNTIES

WHEREAS, to promote the stability of parties and their children through a paternity action; and

WHEREAS, to provide guidance to parties in paternity actions to help parties pattern their behavior in ways that will reduce conflict and improve the lives of the children; and

WHEREAS, to reduce the negative impact that paternity actions have on children and the parties involved; and

WHEREAS, to reduce the number of "emergency" hearings during the beginning stages of paternity actions thereby promoting stability and preserving resources of the parties and the Court; and

WHEREAS, it is in the best interests of the parties and children, or child as the case may be, that parents in a paternity case learn about the problems, duties, and responsibilities of litigation and co-parenting, and that the parties comply with Court rules; and

WHEREAS, the Judges assigned to the Domestic Relations Division have developed, with the assistance of the Family Law Bar, a standing temporary order to be utilized in paternity cases in an effort to achieve the above stated goals;

NOW THEREFORE, I, Belvin Perry, Jr., in order to facilitate the efficient administration of justice, and pursuant to the authority vested in me as Chief Judge of the Ninth Judicial Circuit of Florida under Florida Rule of Judicial Administration 2.215, hereby order the following, **effective immediately**, and to continue until further order:

1. Service, Application, and Term of this Order.

a. This Standing Temporary Order for Paternity Actions shall be utilized and complied with immediately upon the filing of contested paternity actions in Orange and Osceola Counties, except in cases initiated by the Department of Revenue or where there is a written agreement by the parties to the contrary before or after this order takes effect. In cases filed by the Department of Revenue, any petition requesting a determination of parental responsibility and time-sharing must be filed under a new and separate case number in which the Department of Revenue is not a party.

b. Except in cases initiated by the Department of Revenue, the Clerk of Court shall docket and provide a copy of this Standing Temporary Order to the Petitioner or to the Petitioner's counsel at the time the Petitioner files the Petition for Paternity or a Petition requesting the Court to establish parental responsibility and time-sharing if paternity has previously been established by a Court.

c. In addition, the Petitioner shall deliver a copy of this Standing Temporary Order to the process server to be served on the Respondent with the Petition for Paternity or other petition requesting the Court to establish parental responsibility and time-sharing.

d. This Order is binding on the Petitioner upon the filing of this action and on the Respondent upon service of this Order.

e. This Order shall not supercede or modify any existing domestic violence injunction or other order by a court having jurisdiction over the parties or minor children concerning these matters.

f. This Order shall remain in full force and effect until further order of the Court such as the entry of a final judgment, a dismissal of this cause, or until the entry of a subsequent temporary order, whichever shall occur first. This Order does not preclude a Judge from modifying or amending this Order in individual cases where the Judge deems necessary. Any part of this order not changed by a subsequent order shall remain in effect.

2. Contact with Both Parents: Shared Parenting.

a. Pursuant to section 742.031(2), Florida Statutes, if a judgment of paternity contains only a child support award and no parenting plan or time-sharing schedule, the parent receiving the child support has sole parental responsibility and time-sharing until further order of the Court. If a paternity judgment does not establish child support, the mother is presumed to have sole parental responsibility and time-sharing until further order of the Court.

b. If the petition or counter-petition asks the Court to establish contact between the children and other parent, the Court must consider the request after it has determined the paternity of the child. It is the law that, unless the Court makes a specific ruling that it would be detrimental to the children, the Court shall order shared parental responsibility, contact with both parents is in the children's best interests, and children are entitled to frequent and continuing contact with both parents when the parents live separately. In establishing the parenting plan and time-sharing schedule, the Court will analyze the factors set forth in section 61.13(3), Florida Statutes.

c. Further, the parent who wants to have the majority of the time-sharing with the children has an affirmative obligation to encourage and nurture a relationship between the children and the other parent. A parent who unreasonably restricts access of the children to the other parent and does not encourage a relationship between the children and the other parent, for no valid reason, perhaps should have less time-sharing with the children. Such a parent is not acting in the children's best interests and is not following the law.

d. Once paternity has been established, the Court orders "shared parenting" of the children by the parents. This means that wherever the children are living from time to time, the parents must confer with each other and agree upon all MAJOR parenting decisions. Therefore, both parents must participate in all parenting decisions and immediately work out their own time sharing schedules. If the parents cannot agree on any issue, then the Court will decide.

e. While not specifically ordered by the Court at this time, the attached Shared Parenting Guidelines and the parents respect for them shall be considered by the Court in future child related matters, such as the determination of the parenting plan and time-sharing schedule with the children.

f. Once the Court enters a parenting plan and time-sharing schedule, the parties must abide the Court's Order regardless of whether child support is paid. If a party fails to abide by a Court Order, the other party may seek enforcement of the Order by filing a motion with the Clerk of the Court.

3. Parenting Class Required. Pursuant to section 61.21, Florida Statutes, and Amended Administrative Order No. 07–98–37–01, all parties to a paternity action that involves issues of parental responsibility must attend and complete The Parent Education and Family Stabilization Course prior to entry by the Court of a final judgment. Completion of the course is mandatory in all cases, contested or uncontested. Therefore, even if the parties have settled, they must both attend the course.

All parties required to complete a parenting course under this section shall begin the course as expeditiously as possible. Unless excused by the court for good cause, the Petitioner must complete the course within 45 days after filing the petition, and any other party must complete the course within 45 days after an acknowledgment of paternity by that party, an adjudication of paternity of that party, or an order granting visitation to or support from that party. Each party to a paternity action shall file a certificate of completion of the course with the court prior to the entry of the final judgment. Failure to comply with this Order may result in the Court's dismissal of the action, striking of pleadings, and/or other appropriate sanctions.

4. **No Relocation of Children.** Neither party shall change the residence of the children from the school zone in which the children's home is currently located without the written agreement of both parties or an order of this Court. Neither party may change a child's assigned school zone nor change the day care arrangement without the written agreement of both parties or an order of this Court.

5. **Child Support.** In general, the law requires child support to be paid from the date the parties separated, which is nearly always a date before the petition was filed. Therefore, to avoid building up an arrearage in child support, the parent with whom the children are not residing a majority of the time must make voluntary payments of child support to the other parent with whom the children spent a majority of the time prior to the entry of an order requiring payment of support. Waiting for an order can be very expensive because child support can be ordered from the date that the parties stopped living together in the same household with the children but no more than two (2) years before the paternity action was filed. If child support is paid in excess of that required by the statute, the paying parent may ask for a refund. Child support will be determined by the child support guidelines, pursuant section 61.30, Florida Statutes. Therefore, it is in both parties' best interests to determine the correct amount of child support quickly and begin paying promptly. Once child support is ordered, the Order must be followed regardless of whether the paying parent has visitation with the children and regardless of whether the other parent is denying timesharing. If a party fails to abide by a Court Order, the other party may seek enforcement of the Order by filing a motion with the Clerk of the Court.

6. **Conduct of the Parties During the Case; Sanctions.** Any unwanted physical contact between the parents is a crime and is vigorously prosecuted. Failure to obey this Order may result in restraining orders and contempt proceedings. Contempt of Court is punishable by a sentence in the county jail.

7. **Personal and Business Records/Insurance.** Neither party may, directly or indirectly conceal from the other or destroy any family records, business records, or any records of income, debt, or other obligations. Any insurance policies covering the minor children in effect at the time the petition for paternity was filed may not be terminated, allowed to lapse, concealed, modified, borrowed against, pledged or otherwise encumbered by either of the parties or at the direction of either party. All insurance policies covering the minor children may not be changed, except by written agreement signed by the parties or order of the Court. The parties shall continue to pay all premiums on a timely basis unless there is a written consent by both parties or an order of the Court.

8. **Sanctions for Failure to Comply with Court Rules.** If a party fails to comply with the rules requiring the production of financial records and other documents, or fails to answer interrogatories or attend a deposition, or otherwise fails to comply with the rules requiring disclosure or discovery, that party will be sanctioned by an order the Court, which may include a monetary payment to the other party.

9. **Mediation.** Mediation is encouraged early in the proceedings and **prior** to noticing the case for trial and on temporary matters, prior to scheduling a temporary hearing. Several mediation conferences should be held in all cases when required and in order to accomplish a result that both parties fully understand and with which they are both comfortable.

10. **Communication.** The attorneys and parties shall communicate with each other in a civil and courteous manner. Attorneys shall make a good faith effort to communicate **personally** with each other by telephone or in person if a problem exists before filing a motion. The attorneys, appointed experts and the parties shall be courteous and respectful of everyone in the process. Both parties and attorneys shall share documentary information in such a manner as to avoid duplication of work. When setting hearings, conferences, and depositions, an attorney may not schedule any matter without first making a good faith effort to coordinate the date and time with opposing counsel's office and certifying on the notice of hearing that a good faith effort has been made with opposing counsel to resolve the issues of the motion.

11. **Forms.** Individuals who are not represented by counsel may obtain forms that have been approved by the Florida Supreme Court by accessing the Court's website at www.ninthcircuit.org. Once at the website, click the "self help" tab on the right of the page, then look for "court forms". A link to the Florida Supreme Court family court forms website is also provided under this tab. The forms are available without charge.

DONE AND ORDERED on this 3rd day of November, 2010.

Belvin Perry, Jr.
Chief Judge

SHARED PARENTING GUIDELINES

The safety, financial security and well-being of the children involved in this case are the Court's primary concern. Parents should follow these guidelines:

It is the law, except in certain rare circumstances, that both parents will share parental responsibility for all minor children involved in this case. The law requires parents to share the children's time and to participate together in making all important decisions concerning the children. The law expects parents to put aside their feelings and cooperate on all decisions involving the children. Therefore, parents must recognize the following:

Children have a right to a loving, open and continuing relationship with *both parents*. They have the right to express love, affection and respect for one parent in the presence of the other parent.

Neither parent may alienate a child's affection for the other parent.

Parents must separate any bad feelings for one another from their duties as parents. Their duty is to share the children's time and share in making parenting decisions. Children must be free to draw their own conclusions about each parent, without the prejudicial influences of the other parent.

Children have the right to *never* hear a parent, or a relative or friend of a parent, run down or degrade the other parent.

Children have the right to be free from guilt because the parents have decided to separate. They are entitled to honest answers to questions about changes taking place in family makeup.

Parents should *never* be so preoccupied with their own problems that they fail to meet the children's needs. Separation of the parents usually has a worse impact on the children than on the parents, a fact both parents should never forget.

Each parent should openly, honestly, respectfully and regularly communicate with the other parent to avoid misunderstandings. They should never argue about the children in front of them.

Parents should discuss *all* differences regarding their separation and financial issues between them and parenting decisions out of the presence of the child. Both parents should always try to present a united front in handling any problems with the children.

Generally, children have the right to regular and continuing contact with both parents. Parents should arrange all time-sharing and exchanges together and not through the child. The child should never be the messenger between the parents.

Time-sharing plans should be kept and *never cancelled* unless absolutely necessary. If plans change, children should be given an explanation, preferably in advance and by the parent causing the cancellation.

Common courtesies (politeness, promptness, readiness, calling to notify if one is going to be late) should always be observed when picking up and dropping off children. These times can be very stressful on children, so it is imperative that parents always behave as responsible adults.

Between visits, children should be encouraged to contact the absent parent by letter and phone, frequently and continuously.

Parent/child access and child support, while they may be emotionally connected, are ***separate and distinct*** under the law. Accordingly, a child's right of access to his or her parent is not contingent upon the payment of child support.

A child should ***never*** be the delivery person for support payments.

Both parents are entitled to participate in and attend all special activities in which their children are engaged, such as religious activities, school programs, sports events and other extra-curricular activities and programs.

2008–06. [VACATED BY ORDER 2018-10, EFFECTIVE APRIL 12, 2018.]

2008–01–02. THE NINTH JUDICIAL CIRCUIT COURT INTERPRETER POLICY

ADMINISTRATIVE ORDER NO. 2008–01–02

IN THE CIRCUIT COURT OF THE NINTH JUDICIAL CIRCUIT, IN AND FOR ORANGE AND OSCEOLA COUNTIES, FLORIDA

AMENDED ADMINISTRATIVE ORDER ESTABLISHING THE NINTH JUDICIAL CIRCUIT COURT INTERPRETER POLICY

WHEREAS, pursuant to Article V, section 2(d) of the Florida Constitution and section 43.26, Florida Statutes, the chief judge of each judicial circuit is charged with the authority and the power to do everything necessary to promote the prompt and efficient administration of justice; and

WHEREAS, pursuant to the chief judge's constitutional and statutory responsibility for administrative supervision of the courts within the circuit and to create and maintain an organization capable of effecting the efficient, prompt, and proper administration of justice for the citizens of this State, the chief judge is required to exercise direction, *see* Fla. R. Jud. Admin. 2.215(b)(2), (b)(3); and

WHEREAS, qualified foreign language and sign language interpreters for limited English proficient (LEP) persons are ordered by the court, as mandated by sections 90.606 and 90.6063, Florida Statutes, and under the provisions of the Americans with Disability Act, for all courts. Furthermore, those persons who require the assistance of a foreign language interpreter sometimes require the assistance of an interpreter of languages of limited diffusion, also referred to as minority languages, exotic languages, or rare languages (LLD); and

WHEREAS, an LLD may generally be defined as a language used in a country by a group which is significantly smaller in number than the rest of the population and spoken by a relatively small number of people. For purposes of this Order, in an effort to maintain the smooth and efficient operation of the Court and safeguard limited financial resources, an LLD shall include all languages other than Spanish and Creole; and

WHEREAS, the Court Interpreter Department employs full-time staff interpreters. The court also contracts with freelance interpreters for all other languages and for Spanish, on occasion, when staff is unable to cover the demand for services; and

WHEREAS, Interpreter Services are provided to the Criminal Divisions of the Circuit, County, and Juvenile Court, as well as Domestic Violence Injunction and child support proceedings; and

WHEREAS, due to the expenses associated with engaging a qualified interpreter of LLDs and making provisions for other intensive coverage trials and proceedings, such as but not limited to: travel arrangements, the standard cancellation policy that binds the Circuit to pay an interpreter whenever hired and the trial does not go forward, and the requirement that all trials must have the assistance of two interpreters due to the fatigue factor which affects accuracy; and

WHEREAS, due to a shortage of certified interpreters, the Ninth Judicial Circuit has created and utilizes virtual remote interpreting; and

WHEREAS, in an effort to ensure the effective administration of justice, and in an effort to safeguard taxpayer funds, it is necessary that a policy be established to provide certain basic principles concerning court interpreters in the Ninth Judicial Circuit;

NOW, THEREFORE, I, Frederick J. Lauten, in order to facilitate the efficient operation of the administration of justice, and pursuant to the authority vested in me as Chief Judge of the Ninth Judicial Circuit of Florida under Florida Rule of Judicial Administration 2.215, hereby order that that all judges, judicial assistants, trial clerks, and attorneys appearing in this Court, as well as Court Administration, shall abide by the following, **effective immediately** and to continue until further order:

1. Scope of Coverage: Staff interpreters are assigned to the primary courthouses in Orange and Osceola Counties. Staff interpreters, as well as freelance interpreters, will provide their services remotely whenever possible, but, if necessary, interpreters will travel to branch courthouses (Juvenile, Jail, Apopka, Ocoee & Winter Park) for language interpretation. Interpreter services shall be utilized for individuals appearing before the court in Criminal Divisions of the Circuit, County, and Juvenile Court, as well as Domestic Violence Injunction proceedings. Interpreter services are also provided for LEP parents or LEP guardians of a minor who is directly involved in a juvenile court proceeding. Spoken language interpreter services shall not be used to cover mediations, depositions, or for persons summoned for jury service.

2. Requesting Interpreters for Proceedings: If the services of an interpreter are needed at a court proceeding, the attorney, or opposing counsel, must so inform the judicial assistant when scheduling the proceeding or as soon as the need for interpreter services is identified. The request should specify whether one or multiple interpreters are needed. The judicial assistant must submit the requesting form to the Court Interpreter Department via email: Interpreter@ocnjcc.org. Trial clerks or court staff should make same day requests by telephone at 407–836–2399, which shall be covered whenever possible, depending on interpreter availability.

3. Requesting Interpreters for Trials: As a best practice, two interpreters should be assigned for jury trials. Trials requiring interpreter services shall be coordinated with the Court Interpreter Office no less than **two (2) business days** in advance from the scheduled date for Spanish interpreters, no less than **ten (10) business days** in advance of the scheduled date for Creole, Portuguese and American Sign Language interpreters, and no less than **thirty (30) days** for all other languages (LLDs).

4. Special Requirements for LLD Cases: Due to the enormous costs involved with hiring interpreters for these matters, cases requiring LLD interpreters, as defined herein, shall comply with the following procedures:

a. The Defendant's Attorney must certify that he has met with the defendant and shall notify the court within **forty-five (45) days** of filing a Notice of Appearance that the case requires an LLD interpreter to move forward with the case.

b. Within **thirty (30) days** of receiving notification of the need for an LLD interpreter, the court will hold a status conference, with the defendant present, to establish a case management schedule and to determine whether the case will be resolved by plea or set for trial.

c. Judges, prior to ordering the services of an interpreter for trial, shall set a status conference to determine whether all the appropriate steps have been taken to resolve the case by plea or other means.

5. Prioritizing Interpreter Services: The presiding judge shall call cases involving the use of interpreters before other matters, but shall not be required to interrupt a proceeding that has already begun. **Interpreters shall move to their next assignment if the presiding judge does not utilize the interpreter's services within fifteen (15) minutes of their arrival, or the conclusion of the immediate case before the court, whichever occurs first**. The Court Interpreter Department will be notified when the interpreter is to return to the courtroom if the case for which their services were requested is not ready to be heard. When interpreters are requested for a general trial call, only one interpreter shall be present to assist with possible pleas or negotiations. Every effort shall be made to minimize the length of time the interpreter must remain in any courtroom.

6. Prioritizing Coverage of Trials: When interpreter services are needed to assist in more trials than the Interpreter Department has personnel to cover, cases will be given priority in the following order: (1) capital cases; (2) cases in which speedy trial has not been waived and the end of the speedy trial time period is most quickly approaching; and (3) by the severity of the offense. In the event of a conflict concerning the severity of the offense, the chief judge or his designee shall decide which case will be given precedence. Cases for which interpreter services were not available on the preceding day will be given priority the following day, if possible.

7. Interpreter Assistance to Attorneys and Pro Se Litigants:

a. Court interpreters shall not be required to sit in the jury box with a defendant and shall not accompany an attorney into a holding cell to conduct "in-custody" client interviews, except where a unique circumstance occurs which requires the court to proceed to a holding cell to advise a defendant of certain consequences of his actions where a defendant refuses to leave a holding cell.

b. The interpreter may assist an attorney with conducting a brief "in-custody" client exchange, such as updating or conveying an offer, within the courtroom. This shall only occur under unique circumstances as the presiding judge may deem necessary.

8. Translating Documents and Interpreting Audio/Video Recordings: Interpreters may sight translate brief court documents during a court proceeding, but shall not explain court documents, procedures, or otherwise communicate with litigants outside of the court proceeding. If foreign language audio or video recordings are to be used as evidence in a trial or hearing, the party offering the tape shall transcribe and translate the recording into English at their own expense, or as provided for indigent criminal defendants, and shall provide in advance a copy of the recording, foreign language transcript, and transcript of the English translation to opposing counsel and the court. The court interpreter shall not interpret audio or video recordings during court proceedings.

9. Contracting Freelance Interpreters: Court Administration will seek the services of a freelance interpreter if a staff interpreter is unavailable to cover the assignment. The manager of the Court Interpreter Department must approve all individual or agency contracts. Federal or State certified interpreters will have right of first refusal on any assignment over otherwise qualified interpreters. Every effort must be made to obtain the most qualified interpreter for each court proceeding.

10. Weekend/Holiday Coverage: Interpreter services will be available for initial appearance and other proceedings during weekends and holidays. Spanish interpreters are always present during weekend and holiday sessions. If the need for an interpreter for a language other than Spanish, including American Sign Language, were to arise during the weekend, the trial clerk may request that the staff interpreter present during the proceeding attempt to call a freelance interpreter to cover the assignment. In the event the Spanish interpreter covering that weekend is not a staff interpreter, the clerk is directed to contact the department coordinator at 407–982–0890 for assistance.

11. Sign Language Interpreting: A person requiring the need for a sign language interpreter should call the Court's ADA number at 407–836–2303 at least **five (5) days** before the date services are needed. Sign language interpreters are provided for all court proceedings or court programs, including for civil cases, jury service, and mediation.

12. Remote Interpreting: Staff and freelance interpreters shall provide their services remotely whenever possible.

13. Telephonic Phone Interpreting: The use of telephonic phone interpreting companies, such as LanguageLine Solutions, shall only be used for last-minute proceedings for languages other than Spanish.

14. Miscellaneous: The use of headsets and wireless microphones shall be used in all venues wherever possible. Judges may not conduct group pleas.

Administrative Order No. 2008–01–02 is hereby vacated and set aside and has been incorporated and/or amended herein.

DONE AND ORDERED at Orlando, Florida, this 17th day of September, 2015.

Frederick J. Lauten

Chief Judge

2007–04–01. [VACATED BY ORDER 2018-07, EFFECTIVE MARCH 27, 2018.]

2006–16. [VACATED BY ADMINISTRATIVE ORDER NO. 2016–24, EFFECTIVE AUGUST 18, 2016]

2006–09. [VACATED BY ADMINISTRATIVE ORDER NO. 2016–24, EFFECTIVE AUGUST 18, 2016]

2006–05. [VACATED BY ADMINISTRATIVE ORDER NO. 2016–24, EFFECTIVE AUGUST 18, 2016]

2005–16–08. UNIFIED FAMILY COURT AND THE ASSIGNMENT AND SCHEDULING OF DOMESTIC RELATIONS AND JUVENILE CASES, OSCEOLA COUNTY

ADMINISTRATIVE ORDER NO. 2005–16–08

IN THE CIRCUIT COURT OF THE NINTH JUDICIAL CIRCUIT, IN AND FOR OSCEOLA COUNTY, FLORIDA

AMENDED ORDER GOVERNING UNIFIED FAMILY COURT AND THE ASSIGNMENT AND SCHEDULING OF DOMESTIC RELATIONS AND JUVENILE CASES, OSCEOLA COUNTY

WHEREAS, it is not unusual for parties in domestic relations and juvenile cases to have multiple cases pending in the Domestic Relations and Juvenile Divisions of the Circuit Court that are assigned to different subdivisions; and

WHEREAS, for purposes of judicial economy, it is frequently requested that these cases be reassigned to a single judge for purposes of case disposition; and

WHEREAS, in the process of establishing a Unified Family Court in Osceola County, the expenditure of substantial legal and judicial labor has been necessitated by the preparation, filing, and processing of motions and orders to accomplish reassignment in the past, which could be avoided through the authority of an administrative order to permit such cases to be automatically reassigned by the Clerk of Court; and

WHEREAS, in an effort to achieve the ultimate goal of creating a fully integrated comprehensive approach to handling all cases involving families and children as fully as possible given current limitations and abilities, each unified family court subdivision judge shall maintain a detailed schedule which shall be provided to and followed by the Clerk;

NOW, THEREFORE, I, Frederick J. Lauten, pursuant to the authority vested in me as Chief Judge of the Ninth Judicial Circuit, pursuant to Florida Rule of Judicial Administration 2.215, order the following, effective immediately, unless otherwise provided herein, and to continue until further order:

1. For purposes of this Administrative Order, the following definitions apply:

a. A **"related case"** shall be defined as any pending Unified Family Court domestic relations, domestic violence, or juvenile case in which the parties or children are the same as the parties or children appearing in the newly filed domestic relations, domestic violence, or juvenile case.

b. A **"pending domestic relations case"** shall be defined as any open domestic relations case in which no final judgment has been entered or, where a domestic relations case has been finalized but later re-opened by motion or supplemental petition, any re-opened domestic relations case where the court has not entered a final order or supplemental final judgment.

c. A **"pending domestic violence case"** shall be defined as any open domestic violence case in which no final judgment has been entered or, where a domestic violence case has been finalized but later re-opened by motion or supplemental petition, any re-opened domestic violence case where the court has not entered a final order or supplemental final judgment.

d. A "**pending juvenile dependency case**" shall be defined as any juvenile dependency case where neither the Dependency Court's supervision nor jurisdiction has been terminated.

e. A "**pending juvenile delinquency case**" shall be defined as any open juvenile delinquency case in which no final disposition has been entered.

2. The Clerk of Court shall determine if any "related" cases exist before assigning or reassigning domestic relations, domestic violence, or juvenile cases to any subdivision of the Unified Family Court. To assist with this process, the Department of Children and Family Services, litigants appearing pro-se, and attorneys are required to file a "Notice of Related Cases" at the same time a new case, supplemental petition, motion requesting a case be re-opened, etc., is filed with the court. All pleadings filed with the court shall include the dates of birth of all children required to be named in the caption of those pleadings and shall be accompanied by a completed coversheet provided by the Clerk of Court. Cases will be assigned to a division only upon receipt of the completed coversheet.

3. With the exception of cases identified in paragraph 1 above, the Clerk of Court shall automatically assign/reassign cases within the Unified Family Court as follows:

a. *Domestic Relations Cases:* The Clerk of Court shall assign all new domestic relations cases that end with an odd case number to Subdivision 40–C, except that where a new domestic relations case is "related" to a pending juvenile dependency case, the new domestic relations case shall be assigned to Subdivision 41–C.

The Clerk of Court shall assign all new domestic relations cases that end with an even case number to Subdivision 30–C, except that where a new domestic relations case is "related" to a pending juvenile dependency case, the new domestic relations case shall be assigned to Subdivision 41–C.

b. *Juvenile Dependency Cases:* The Clerk of Court shall assign/reassign all juvenile dependency cases to Subdivision 41–C. Additionally, if a new juvenile dependency case is filed that has a "related" pending domestic relations case, the new juvenile dependency case shall be assigned to Subdivision 41–C and the "related" domestic relations case shall be reassigned to Subdivision 41–C.

c. *Domestic Violence and Repeat/Sexual/Dating Violence/Stalking Injunction Cases:* All new domestic violence injunction cases and all new repeat/sexual/dating violence/stalking injunction cases shall be assigned on a three-week rotating basis to the subdivision (either Subdivision 30–C, 40–C or 41–C) scheduled to accept such assignments during the week that the new domestic violence or repeat/sexual/dating violence/stalking injunction case is filed. Each domestic violence or repeat/sexual/dating violence/stalking injunction case shall then remain with the judge who signed the temporary injunction or notice of hearing until entry of a final judgment on the domestic violence or repeat/sexual/dating violence/stalking injunction.

After entry of a final judgment on the domestic violence or repeat/sexual/dating violence/stalking injunction, only domestic violence or repeat/sexual/dating violence/stalking injunction cases with a "related" domestic relations case or juvenile dependency case shall be assigned/reassigned to the subdivision assigned the "related" domestic relations or juvenile dependency case.

All repeat/sexual/dating violence/stalking injunction cases that have been extended to future dates shall be heard by the original subdivision (either Subdivision 30–C, 40–C or 41–C) during the week that the extended repeat/sexual/dating violence/stalking is ready to be heard.

d. *Juvenile Delinquency Cases:* The Clerk of Court shall reassign all juvenile delinquency cases that end with an odd case number from Subdivision 30–C and 41–C to Subdivision 40–C. The Clerk of Court shall assign all new juvenile delinquency cases that end with an odd case number to Subdivision 40–C.

The Clerk of Court shall reassign all juvenile delinquency cases that end with an even case number from Subdivisions 40–C and 41–C to Subdivision 30–C. The Clerk of Court shall assign all new juvenile delinquency cases that end with an even case number to Subdivision 30–C.

Where there is an open juvenile delinquency case, any new case filed on the same defendant shall be assigned to the division with the pending juvenile delinquency case. If there is no pending juvenile delinquency case, all new juvenile delinquency cases, regardless of whether the defendant is a repeat offender, shall be assigned to Subdivision 30–C where the case ends with an even case number or 40–C where the case ends with an odd case number.

In the event there is a child with multiple charges and cases that have been opened at the same time, the lowest case number will steer assignment of other cases for the child. The same shall apply to co-defendant cases that are opened at the same time with the lowest case number steering assignment(s).

e. *Juvenile Drug Court Cases:* In an effort to conform with best practices models wherever practicable, and the Ten Key Components of Drug Court Programs as defined by the Nation Association of Drug Court Professionals, all juvenile drug court cases shall be heard every other week beginning with the week of January 12, 2015, and pursuant to the detailed schedule, as maintained by each unified family court subdivision judge and provided to and followed by the Clerk. The Clerk of Court shall assign/reassign all juvenile drug court cases pursuant to the detailed scheduled as provided by each unified family court subdivision judge.

4. Notwithstanding the foregoing, no case shall be reassigned from a subdivision of the Unified Family Court in the following circumstances:

a. Where assignment to a subdivision was the result of an order of recusal; or

b. Where a judge has specifically requested that a case remain within his or her presently assigned subdivision.

5. In an effort to achieve the ultimate goal of creating a fully integrated comprehensive approach to handling all cases involving families and children as fully as possible given current limitations and abilities, each unified family court subdivision judge shall maintain a detailed schedule which shall be provided to and followed by the Clerk.

6. Immediately upon signing and distribution of this Order, all dependency cases that have court dates in January 2015, and beyond must be reset by the Clerk's office to conform with the approved schedule for Subdivision 41–C. Amended notices and/or order rescheduling matters must be prepared and sent out by the Clerk's office.

7. Immediately upon signing and distribution of this Order, any juvenile delinquency matters that may have been extended into January 2015, and beyond must be rescheduled by the Clerk's office to conform with the schedules established for Subdivisions 30–C and 40–C and based upon the even/odd case number assignment established herein. Amended notices and/or orders rescheduling matters must be prepared and sent out by the Clerk's office.

8. Additionally, and immediately upon signing and distribution of this Order, the Clerk of Court shall compile a master list of reassigned cases, by name and by case number, and shall post this list in a conspicuous location for public viewing. It is the duty of the attorneys in each case to determine if any of his/her cases have been reassigned.

9. The Clerk of Court shall place an Identifier in their database by those cases that have been identified as a "related" case.

10. As previously directed by Administrative Order No. 2014–21, Order Governing Case Assignment Method, Osceola County, the Clerk of Court shall continue to assign all cases in all divisions by division number only so as to prevent confusion and inefficiencies when a judge is assigned to another division.

11. This Order does not preclude any Judge being given an assignment by the Chief Judge of the Ninth Judicial Circuit Court for the proper administration of justice.

12. Administrative Order 2005–16–07 is vacated and set aside.

DONE AND ORDERED at Orlando, Florida, this 12th day of January, 2015.

Frederick J. Lauten
Chief Judge

2004–06. [VACATED BY ADMINISTRATIVE ORDER NO. 2016–24, EFFECTIVE AUGUST 18, 2016]

2004–05–04. STANDING TEMPORARY ORDER FOR DISSOLUTION OF MARRIAGE ACTIONS.

Read the attached order carefully. It applies to you and you will be responsible for complying with the order.

Highlights

ADMINISTRATIVE ORDER NO. 2004–05–04

IN THE CIRCUIT COURT OF THE NINTH JUDICIAL CIRCUIT, IN AND FOR ORANGE & OSCEOLA COUNTIES, FLORIDA

AMENDED ORDER IMPLEMENTING A STANDING TEMPORARY ORDER FOR DISSOLUTION OF MARRIAGE ACTIONS WITH OR WITHOUT MINOR CHILDREN, ORANGE & OSCEOLA COUNTIES

WHEREAS, to promote the stability of families going through a divorce; and

WHEREAS, to provide guidance to parties in dissolution of marriage actions to help parties pattern their behavior in ways that will reduce conflict and make the divorce work for the family; and

WHEREAS, to reduce the negative impact that dissolution of marriage actions have on children and the parties involved; and

WHEREAS, to reduce the number of "emergency" hearings during the beginning stages of dissolution of marriage actions thereby promoting stability and preserving resources of the parties and the Court; and

WHEREAS, it is in the best interests of the parties and children, or child as the case may be, that parents in a divorce case learn about the problems, duties, and responsibilities of litigation and parenting after separation and divorce, and that the parties preserve their assets and comply with Court rules; and

WHEREAS, the Judges assigned to the Domestic Relations Division have developed, with the assistance of the Family Law bar, a standing temporary order to be utilized in dissolution of marriage cases in an effort to achieve the above stated goals;

NOW THEREFORE, I, Belvin Perry, Jr., in order to facilitate the efficient administration of justice, and pursuant to the authority vested in me as Chief Judge of the Ninth Judicial Circuit of Florida under Florida Rule of Judicial Administration 2.215, hereby order the following, **effective immediately,** and to continue until further order:

1. Service, Application, and Term of this Order.

a. This Standing Temporary Order for Dissolution of Marriage Action With or Without Minor Children shall be utilized and complied with immediately upon the filing of contested dissolution of marriage actions in Orange and Osceola Counties, except in cases where there is a written agreement by the parties to the contrary before or after this order takes effect.

b. The Clerk of Court shall docket and provide a copy of this Standing Temporary Order to the Petitioner or to the Petitioner's counsel at the time the Petitioner files the Petition for Dissolution of Marriage.

c. In addition, the Petitioner shall deliver a copy of this Standing Temporary Order to the process server to be served on the Respondent with the Petition for Dissolution of Marriage.

d. This Order is binding on the Petitioner upon the filing of this action and on the Respondent upon service of this Order.

e. This Order shall not supercede or modify any existing domestic violence injunction or other order by a court having jurisdiction over the parties or minor children concerning these matters.

f. This Order shall remain in full force and effect until further order of the court such as the entry of a final judgment, a dismissal of this cause, or until the entry of a subsequent temporary order, whichever shall occur first. This Order is without prejudice and does not preclude a Judge from modifying or amending this Order in individual cases as the Judge sees fit. Any part of this Order not changed by a subsequent order shall remain in effect.

2. Contact with Both Parents: Shared Parenting.

a. It is the law that, unless the Court makes a specific ruling that it would be detrimental to the children, the Court shall order shared parental responsibility, contact with both parents is in the children's best interests, and children are entitled to frequent and continuing contact with both parents when the parents separate or divorce. In establishing the parenting plan and time sharing schedule, the Court will analyze the factors set forth in section 61.13(3), Florida Statutes. However, until a court order is entered each party is entitled to the same rights to timesharing with the children.

b. Further, a parent who wants to have the majority of the time-sharing with the children has an affirmative obligation to encourage and nurture a relationship between the children and the other parent. A parent who unreasonably restricts access of the children to the other parent and does not encourage a relationship between the children and the other parent, for no valid reason, perhaps should have less time-sharing with the children. Such a parent is not acting in the children's best interests and is not following the law.

c. The Court hereby orders "shared parenting" of the children by the parents. This means that wherever the children are living from time to time, the parents must confer with each other and agree upon all MAJOR parenting decisions. Therefore, both parents must participate in all major parenting decisions and shall immediately work out their own time sharing schedules, with each party having substantial overnight timesharing on a regular basis. If the parents cannot agree on any issue, then the Court will decide.

d. The attached shared parenting guidelines and the parents respect for and compliance with them shall be considered by the Court in future child related matters, such as the determination of the parenting plan and time-sharing schedule with the children.

3. Parenting Class Required. Pursuant to section 61.21, Florida Statutes, and Amended Administrative Order No. 07–98–37–01, all parties to a dissolution of marriage proceeding with minor children must attend and complete The Parent Education and Family Stabilization Course prior to entry by the Court of a final judgment. Completion of the course is mandatory in all cases, contested or uncontested, where the parents have minor children. Therefore, even if the parties have settled, they must both attend the course.

All parties required to complete a parenting course under this section shall begin the course as expeditiously as possible. Unless excused by the court for good cause, the Petitioner must complete the course within 45 days after the filing of the petition, and all other parties must complete the course within 45 days after service of the petition. Each party to a dissolution action shall file a certificate of completion of the course with the court prior to the entry of the final judgment. Failure to comply with this Order may result in the Court's dismissal of the action, striking of pleadings, and/or other appropriate sanctions.

4. No Relocation of Children or Foreign Travel. Neither party shall change the residence of the children from the school zone in which the children's home is currently located without the written agreement of both parties or an order of this Court. Neither party may change a child's assigned school zone nor change the day care arrangement without the written agreement of both parties or an order of this Court. Neither party shall allow the children to travel outside the country without written agreement of the parties or Court order.

5. Child Support. In general, the law requires child support to be paid from the date the parties separated, which is nearly always a date before the petition was filed. Therefore, to avoid building up an arrearage in child support, the parent with a support obligation according to the guidelines must make voluntary payments of child support to the other parent prior to the entry of an order requiring payment of support. Waiting for an order can be very expensive because child support can be ordered from the date of separation. If child support is paid in excess of that required by the statute, the paying parent may ask for a credit. Child support will be determined by the child support guidelines, pursuant section 61.30, Florida Statutes. Therefore, it is in both parties' best interests to determine the correct amount of child support quickly and begin paying promptly.

6. Conduct of the Parties During the Case; Sanctions. Any unwanted physical contact between a husband and a wife is a crime and is vigorously prosecuted. Food, shelter, utilities, transportation and necessary medical expenses shall continue to be paid as they were during the intact marriage until further order of the Court or written agreement of the parties. Failure to obey this provision and/or any other part of this Order may result in injunction orders and/or contempt proceedings. Contempt of Court is punishable by a sentence in the county jail.

7. Disposition of Assets; Accounting. Neither party may conceal, damage, or dispose of any asset, whether marital or non-marital, and neither party may dissipate the value of an asset, for example, by adding a mortgage to real estate or by failing to take care of any asset. Neither party may dispose of any asset other than in the customary conduct of business and personal affairs. The parties may spend their incomes in the ordinary course of their personal and family affairs. Neither party may conceal, hoard or waste jointly owned funds, whether in the form of cash, bank accounts or other liquid assets, except funds may be spent for the necessities of life. The use of funds or income after separation must be accounted for and justified as reasonable and necessary for the necessities of the party or to preserve marital assets or pay marital debts. Both parties are accountable for all money or property in their possession during the marriage and after separation. Attorney's fees and costs are necessities and must be accounted for.

Nothing herein prohibits the Court from allocating attorney's fees and costs paid out of marital funds to either party in equitable distribution as allowed by law.

8. Personal and Business Records/Insurance. Neither party may, directly or indirectly conceal from the other or destroy any family records, business records, or any records of income, debt, or other obligations. Any insurance policies in effect at the time the petition for dissolution was filed may not be terminated, allowed to lapse, concealed, modified, borrowed against, pledged or otherwise encumbered by either of the parties or at the direction of either party. All insurance policies of any kind may not be changed, except by written agreement signed by the parties or order of the Court. The parties shall continue to pay all premiums on a timely basis unless there is a written consent by both parties or an order of the Court.

9. Additional Debt. Neither party will incur additional debt which would bind the other party, pledge, encumber and/or mortgage any assets, except by written consent of the parties, order of this Court or as provided herein. The parties are urged to temporarily stop using joint credit cards. This does not prohibit use of joint credit for absolute necessities but only as a last resort. No joint credit cards may be cancelled or modified absent agreement of the parties or court order. Any party using a joint credit card after separation must be prepared to justify all charges as reasonable and necessary for necessities.

10. Sanctions for Failure to Comply with Court Rules and this Order. If a party fails to comply with the rules requiring the production of financial records and other documents, or fails to answer interrogatories or attend a deposition, or otherwise fails to comply with the rules requiring disclosure or discovery, or if a party fails to comply with the terms of this Order, that party will be sanctioned by an order the Court, which may include a monetary payment to the other party.

11. Mediation. Mediation is encouraged early in the proceedings and **prior** to noticing the case for trial and on temporary matters, prior to scheduling a temporary hearing. Several mediation conferences should be held in all cases when required and in order to accomplish a result that both parties fully understand and with which they are both comfortable.

12. Communication with Opposing Party, Court Policies and Procedures. The attorneys and parties shall communicate with each other in a civil and courteous manner. Attorneys shall make a good faith effort to communicate **personally** with each other by telephone or in person if a problem exists before filing a motion. The attorneys, appointed experts, and the parties shall be courteous and respectful of everyone in the process. Both parties and attorneys shall share documentary information in such a manner as to avoid duplication of work. When setting hearings, conferences, and depositions, an attorney may not schedule any matter without first making a good faith effort to coordinate the date and time with opposing counsel's office and certifying on the notice of hearing that a good faith effort has been made with opposing counsel to resolve the issues of the motion.

The parties and their attorneys shall comply with Ninth Judicial Circuit Court Administrative Order No. 2014–19 (as may be amended), Establishing Domestic Court Guidelines and Administrative Order No. 2003–07–01 (as may be amended), Establishing the Ninth Judicial Circuit Courtroom Decorum Policy. Additionally parties and attorneys shall comply with the Uniform Policies and Procedures for the Domestic Division of the Circuit Court, Orange County.

13. Forms. Individuals who are not represented by counsel may obtain forms that have been approved by the Florida Supreme Court by accessing the Court's website at www.ninthcircuit.org. Once at the website, click the "self help" tab on the right of the page, then look for "court forms". A link to the Florida Supreme Court family court forms website is also provided under this tab. The forms are available without charge.

Administrative Order 2004–05–03 is vacated and set aside and has been incorporated and/or amended herein.

DONE AND ORDERED on this 5th day of August, 2014.

Belvin Perry, Jr.
Chief Judge

SHARED PARENTING GUIDELINES

The safety, financial security and well-being of the children involved in this case are the Court's primary concern. Parents should follow these guidelines:

It is the law, except in certain rare circumstances, that both parents will share parental responsibility for all minor children involved in this case. The law requires parents to share the children's time and to participate together in making all important decisions concerning the children. The law expects parents to put aside their feelings and cooperate on all decisions involving the children. Therefore, parents must recognize the following:

Children have a right to a loving, open and continuing relationship with *both parents*. They have the right to express love, affection and respect for one parent in the presence of the other parent.

Neither parent may alienate a child's affection for the other parent.

Parents must separate any bad feelings for one another from their duties as parents. Their duty is to share the children's time and share in making parenting decisions. Children must be free to draw their own conclusions about each parent, without the prejudicial influences of the other parent.

Children have the right to *never* hear a parent, or a relative or friend of a parent, run down or degrade the other parent.

Children have the right to be free from guilt because the parents have decided to separate. They are entitled to honest answers to questions about changes taking place in family makeup.

Parents should *never* be so preoccupied with their own problems that they fail to meet the children's needs. Separation of the parents usually has a worse impact on the children than on the parents, a fact both parents should never forget.

Each parent should openly, honestly, respectfully and regularly communicate with the other parent to avoid misunderstandings. They should never argue about the children in front of them.

Parents should discuss all differences regarding their separation and financial issues between them and parenting decisions out of the presence of the child. Both parents should always try to present a united front in handling any problems with the children.

Generally, children have the right to regular and continuing contact with both parents. Parents should arrange all time-sharing and exchanges together and not through the child. The child should never be the messenger between the parents.

Time-sharing plans should be kept and *never cancelled* unless absolutely necessary. If plans change, children should be given an explanation, preferably in advance and by the parent causing the cancellation.

Common courtesies (politeness, promptness, readiness, calling to notify if one is going to be late) should always be observed when picking up and dropping off children. These times can be very stressful on children, so it is imperative that parents always behave as responsible adults.

Between visits, children should be encouraged to contact the absent parent by letter and phone, frequently and continuously.

Parent/child access and child support, while they may be emotionally connected, are ***separate and distinct*** under the law. Accordingly, a child's right of access to his or her parent is not contingent upon the payment of child support.

A child should ***never*** be the delivery person for support payments.

Both parents are entitled to participate in and attend all special activities in which their children are engaged, such as religious activities, school programs, sports events and other extra-curricular activities and programs.

[1] Publisher's Note: Page numbers correspond to the numbering in the original order copy.

2003–18–01. [VACATED BY ADMINISTRATIVE ORDER NO. 2016–24, EFFECTIVE AUGUST 18, 2016]

2003–07–02. THE NINTH JUDICIAL CIRCUIT COURTROOM DECORUM POLICY

IN THE CIRCUIT COURT OF THE NINTH JUDICIAL CIRCUIT, IN AND FOR ORANGE AND OSCEOLA COUNTIES, FLORIDA

ADMINISTRATIVE ORDER NO. 2003–07–02

AMENDED ADMINISTRATIVE ORDER ESTABLISHING THE NINTH JUDICIAL CIRCUIT COURTROOM DECORUM POLICY

WHEREAS, pursuant to Article V, Section 2(d) of the Florida Constitution and section 43.26, Florida Statutes, the chief judge of each judicial circuit is charged with the authority and the power to do everything necessary to promote the prompt and efficient administration of justice; and

WHEREAS, to create and maintain an organization capable of effecting the efficient, prompt, and proper administration of justice for the citizens of this State, the chief judge is required to exercise direction, *see* Fla. R. Jud. Admin. 2.215(b)(2), (b)(3); and

WHEREAS, in an effort to ensure the effective and orderly administration of justice, it is necessary that a policy be established to provide certain basic principles concerning courtroom behavior and decorum in the Ninth Judicial Circuit;

NOW, THEREFORE, I, Frederick J. Lauten, in order to facilitate the efficient operation of the administration of justice, to foster the highest standards of professionalism throughout the Ninth Judicial Circuit, and pursuant to the authority vested in me as Chief Judge of the Ninth Judicial Circuit of Florida under Florida Rule of Judicial Administration 2.215, hereby order, **effective immediately,** to continue until further order, that all counsel (including all persons at the counsel table) when appearing in this Court, unless excused by the presiding Judge, shall abide by the following:

1. Stand when Court is opened, recessed or adjourned. Stand when addressing, or being addressed by the Court. Stand when the jury enters or retires from the courtroom. When making opening statements, closing arguments or examining witnesses, do not approach either the jury or the witness without the Court's permission. Remain at the lectern unless using exhibits or charts.

2. Address all remarks to the Court, not to opposing counsel or the opposing party.

3. Avoid disparaging personal remarks or acrimony toward opposing counsel and remain wholly detached from any ill feeling between the litigants or witnesses.

4. Refer to all persons, including witnesses, other counsel and the parties by their surnames and not by their first or given names unless the permission of the Court is sought in advance.

5. Only one attorney for each party shall examine, or cross examine each witness. The attorney stating objections, if any, during direct examination, shall be the attorney recognized for cross examination.

6. Counsel should request permission before approaching the bench. Any documents counsel wishes to have the Court examine should be handed to the clerk. Any paper or exhibit not previously marked for identification should first be handed to the clerk to be marked before it is tendered to a witness for his examination; and any exhibit offered in evidence should, at the time of such offer, be handed to opposing counsel.

7. No exhibit, whether marked for identification or not, shall be held in any manner, or placed in any position in the courtroom, that would allow the trier of fact to see the exhibit unless it has been admitted into evidence and permission to publish the exhibit to the jury has been obtained from the Court.

8. In making objections, counsel should state only the legal grounds for the objection and should withhold all further comment or argument unless elaboration is requested by the Court.

9. When examining a witness, counsel shall not repeat or echo the answer given by the witness.

10. Offers of, or request for, a stipulation should be made privately, not within the hearing of the trier of fact.

11. In opening statements and in arguments to the trier of fact, counsel shall not express personal knowledge or opinions concerning any matter in issue.

12. Counsel shall admonish all persons at the counsel table who make gestures, facial expressions, audible comments, or the like, as manifestations of approval or disapproval during the testimony of witnesses, or at any other time. This behavior is strictly prohibited.

13. All parties, attorneys and witnesses should refrain from interrupting or talking over one another.

14. Counsel shall refrain from attempting to make a re-argument after the Judge has ruled.

15. Counsel shall complete resolution negotiations and advise clients of their settlement options in advance of court hearings.

16. No tobacco use in any form is permitted. No bottles, beverage containers, paper cups or edibles are allowed in the courtroom, except as permitted by the Court. No gum chewing is permitted.

17. Cell phones and pagers should be turned off or in a vibrate mode. Computers should be used with audio off.

18. All counsel should provide a copy of this policy to clients prior to coming to court.

Administrative Order No. 2003–07–01 is vacated and set aside and has been incorporated and/or amended herein.

DONE AND ORDERED at Orlando, Florida, this 11th day of September, 2014.

Frederick J. Lauten
Chief Judge

2003–04–04. [VACATED BY ORDER 2018-07, EFFECTIVE MARCH 27, 2018.]

2001–19–04. [VACATED BY ORDER 2018-07, EFFECTIVE MARCH 27, 2018.]

2000–18–06. [VACATED BY ORDER 2018-07, EFFECTIVE MARCH 27, 2018.]

2000–08–01. [VACATED AND SET ASIDE BY ORDER 2017-03, EFFECTIVE MARCH 28, 2017.]

2000–04–02. [VACATED BY ORDER 2018-07, EFFECTIVE MARCH 27, 2018.]

07–99–47–1. [VACATED BY ADMINISTRATIVE ORDER NO. 2016–24, EFFECTIVE AUGUST 18, 2016]

07–98–48–03. MOVEMENT OF SELECTED INMATES INTO COMMUNITY CORRECTIONS PROGRAMS, OSCEOLA COUNTY

IN THE CIRCUIT COURT OF THE NINTH JUDICIAL CIRCUIT, IN AND FOR OSCEOLA COUNTY, FLORIDA

ADMINISTRATIVE ORDER NO. 07–98–48–03

AMENDED ORDER GOVERNING THE MOVEMENT OF SELECTED INMATES INTO COMMUNITY CORRECTIONS PROGRAMS, OSCEOLA COUNTY

WHEREAS, there is a need to allow the Osceola County Corrections Department to place selected inmates, described below, into certain community corrections programs administered by the Department without seeking further judicial intervention in the case;

NOW, THEREFORE, I, Belvin Perry, Jr., pursuant to the authority vested in me as Chief Judge of the Ninth Judicial Circuit of Florida under Florida Rule of Judicial Administration 2.215, do hereby order that the following procedures and standards are amended as follows, **effective immediately**, in all matters involving the movement of selected inmates into community corrections programs of the Osceola County Corrections Department:

I. GENERAL PROVISIONS. Those offenders, who after proper and thorough review, are determined to meet the eligibility requirements listed below and for whom written approval is obtained from the sentencing judge, may be placed in the community corrections programs specified in this Order when space becomes available. Approval must be granted within sixty (60) days from the date of sentence for Home Confinement or Day Reporting unless the jail sentence is a condition of probation, then placement into Home Confinement or Day Reporting may be granted at any time.

Offenders sentenced to the Osceola County Department of Corrections will serve the prescribed sentence at the Osceola County Corrections Facility as a fully incarcerated inmate until such time as there is space available in the Work Release Center Program. If, when sentencing an offender or issuing an arrest warrant based upon an alleged violation of probation, the judge either "recommends" work release or indicates "no objection" to work release, the offender may immediately be placed at the Work Release Center, without first serving any part of the specified sentence, so long as he or she otherwise meets the criteria below, as determined by the Osceola County Corrections Department.

Osceola County Department of Corrections is hereby authorized to place Work Release participants enrolled in the Osceola County Work Release Program into the Home Confinement Program upon obtaining prior written approval from the sentencing judge(s). Program placement will be solely based upon the criteria established by the Department of Corrections. Any resident given the opportunity to participate in the Home Confinement Program must have a suitable residence, an active unrestricted phone line within said residence, have met the placement criteria established for placement into the Osceola County Work Release Program and agree to the terms and conditions of the Home Confinement Program. Any violation of the Home Confinement Program will result in notification to the sentencing judge and disciplinary action being taken against the participant up to and including possible return to the Osceola County Jail to complete the balance of his/her sentence.

Any judge of the Circuit or County Court may prevent the release of any offender whom the judge feels should not be released into one of the Community Corrections programs described in this Order, by so indicating on the sentencing document.

If the Osceola County Jail finds that an offender does not qualify pursuant to the criteria established in this Order, after being so ordered by the presiding judge, the jail must notify the presiding judge, in writing (including the offender's prior convictions and case numbers and any other pertinent information), with a detailed explanation of the reasons the offender does not qualify. The jail shall also copy the administrative judge for that division and the Chief Judge. Said notification may be sent via e-mail, read receipt, with copy to the court file.

NO OFFENDER WILL BE ACCEPTED INTO ANY PROGRAM AS CONTEMPLATED BY THIS ORDER IF THE OSCEOLA COUNTY JAIL FINDS THAT THE OFFENDER DOES NOT QUALIFY PURSUANT TO THE CRITERIA CONTAINED HEREIN.

II. OFFENSE CRITERIA:

A. Offenders may be eligible for Community Corrections programs when sentenced for the following:

1. Misdemeanors
2. Traffic Offenses
3. Second Degree Felonies
4. Third Degree Felonies
5. Battery, only in domestic violence cases in which the victim agrees to the Release.

B. Offenders shall be ineligible for Community Corrections programs when sentenced for the following:

1. Any offense of a violent nature (excluding the Domestic Battery exception listed under A. of this Order);
2. Any offense involving the abuse of children;
3. Any offense involving the use of a firearm, or any type of deadly Weapon in the commission of a crime;
4. Any offense involving a lewd act in the presence of a minor;
5. Any homicide;
6. Any robbery;
7. Any sexual battery;
8. Any trafficking in Controlled Substances;
9. Any Criminal or Civil contempt of Court (excluding civil contempt in child support cases and writs of attachment for Collection Court)
10. Arson

C. Offenders may be eligible for Community Corrections Programs if the prior record satisfies the following requirements:

1. Offender has not been convicted in the last seven (7) years of a felony offense involving violence, the use of a weapon, or any offense involving the abuse of children.

2. Offender has not been convicted of more than two (2) non-violent felony offense in the last three (3) years, excluding the instant offense.

3. Offender has not been designated as a sexual predator pursuant to section 775.21(5), Florida Statutes, or required to register as a sexual offender pursuant to section 943.0435, Florida Statutes.

D. Offenders will be ineligible for placement in Community Corrections programs when the offender has a hold from any other jurisdiction unless the jurisdiction has specified it will not pick up or extradite. Offenders serving a sentence for additional charges which do not meet the program requirements will not be accepted. Inmates with a current protection order (injunction for protection) will be accepted if they meet all other criteria and the injunction was issued two (2) or more years previously; the current charge is not domestic violence; and there have been no arrests for violation of the injunction within the past two (2) years.

III. HEALTH CRITERIA:

A. Offenders with a serious medical condition, requiring frequent care, will not be eligible for participation in the Community Corrections programs as detailed in this Order.

B. Offenders who are identified as acutely psychotic, severely mentally retarded, currently suicidal, or otherwise unable to cope with the program structure or understand the program conditions, will not be eligible for the Community Corrections programs, as detailed in this Order.

IV. OTHER CRITERIA:

A. Other criteria which may be used as a determining factor of eligibility include:

1. Place and length of residence in the community;
2. Family ties in the community;
3. Employment record;
4. Escape risk;
5. Any such other fact or consideration which may pose a risk to the community;

B. No inmate will be placed in a Community Corrections program without prior written approval from the sentencing judge(s).

V. PROGRAMS INCLUDED. The programs at Osceola County Corrections Department which may accept offenders under the terms of this Order include the Work Release Center, Home Confinement and Day Reporting.

VI. DRUG COURT PARTICIPANTS. Drug Court participants may be placed in the Community Corrections programs specified in this Order without having served any part of a jail sentence.

VII. REVOCATIONS. Offenders who fail to comply with the conditions of the program in which they have been placed are subject to be returned to the jail to serve the balance of the sentence originally imposed. The Community Corrections Department must hold an administrative hearing, by disinterested parties, to determine whether an offender has violated the conditions of the program prior to returning the offender to jail, but is not required to seek an arrest warrant or capias to return the offender to jail.

VIII. ESCAPE. In those cases in which the offender cannot be located to return for an administrative hearing, the Community Corrections Department will seek a capias or warrant for the offender's arrest and will report the matter to the appropriate law enforcement agency for criminal prosecution for escape.

Administrative Order 07–98–48–02 is vacated and set aside and has been incorporated and/or amended herein.

DONE AND ORDERED at Orlando, Florida, this 2nd day of April, 2013.

Belvin Perry, Jr.
Chief Judge

07–98–47–17. PRETRIAL RELEASE, PRETRIAL DETENTION, AND FIRST APPEARANCE PROCEEDINGS IN OSCEOLA COUNTY

IN THE CIRCUIT COURT OF THE NINTH JUDICIAL CIRCUIT, IN AND FOR OSCEOLA COUNTY, FLORIDA

ADMINISTRATIVE ORDER NO. 07–98–47–17

AMENDED ORDER GOVERNING PRETRIAL RELEASE, PRETRIAL DETENTION, AND FIRST APPEARANCE PROCEEDINGS IN OSCEOLA COUNTY

WHEREAS, this Order is to govern the administrative procedures needed to implement the laws of Florida and the Florida Rules of Criminal Procedure relating to pretrial release, detention of criminal defendants, and first/initial appearance proceedings (hereinafter referred to as "first appearance"); and

WHEREAS, this Order represents an effort to provide the most efficient, cost effective, and fair management of these matters consistent with applicable law and court rules; and

WHEREAS, this Order is the result of the cooperative and continuing efforts of representatives of various organizations which play a critical part in the criminal justice process, together with the recommendations contained in the report by the Jail Oversight Commission;

NOW, THEREFORE, I, Frederick J. Lauten, pursuant to the authority vested in me as Chief Judge of the Ninth Judicial Circuit of Florida under Florida Rule of Judicial Administration 2.215, do hereby order that the following procedures are amended as follows, effective **immediately**, unless otherwise provided herein:

I. Judge Assignment to Hear Pretrial Matters. First appearance shall be performed by each judge assigned to Osceola County on a rotating basis. When the courthouse is closed, the emergency duty judge shall conduct the first appearance. All pretrial matters not heard at the first appearance shall be scheduled before the judge to whom the case is assigned, including bond hearings and modifications of release conditions.

In accordance with law, applications to set or modify bail are to be heard "promptly." This Order contemplates a hearing will be held as soon as possible, but with due regard for the notice provisions of the Florida Rules of Criminal Procedure and any other factor properly considered to allow the parties to have a fair opportunity to present their case at the hearing. If a judge is not able to hold a hearing on a motion to set or modify bail within three (3) business days, the movant may seek a hearing before that judge's alternate or the Chief Judge. The three-day period does not commence until filing of the motion and actual notice has been provided.

II. Establishment and Availability of Release Programs. No person arrested for a capital crime, a felony punishable by life, a first degree felony punishable by up to life, or for any lewd or lascivious exhibition, lewd or lascivious molestation, lewd or lascivious battery, or other sexual act involving a minor, or for any failure of a person deemed to be a sexual predator to follow registration, reporting, and/or employment restrictions, pursuant to chapters 775 and 943 of the Florida Statutes, or for burglary of a structure or dwelling during a natural disaster/act of God, acts of terrorism, or war (i.e., looting during a state of emergency) shall be eligible for release under this section. These persons are to be held until first appearance, at which time the first appearance judge will decide conditions of release, if any. Any motion for bail or bond regarding defendants with the above outstanding charges, with the exception of burglary of a structure or dwelling during a natural disaster/act of God, acts of terrorism, or war (i.e., looting during a state of emergency), shall include the following information: attachment copy of charging affidavit and any other supporting documents; addresses and phone numbers of defendant; address and phone numbers of defendant's employers; and any aliases of defendant. A copy of such motion shall be forwarded to the Department of Corrections at their designated office. A Form Order designed to assist the Court in making a bail determination is attached hereto as Attachment D.

Osceola County Jail personnel shall immediately contact the Court Administration 24 hour help line at (407) 836–0522 upon the booking of an individual who appears to need a sign language interpreter. Court Administration will make arrangements to provide the services of a sign language interpreter for initial appearance.

A. Notice to Appear or Release on Own Recognizance (ROR).

1. When a person is arrested for a misdemeanor of the first or second degree, a criminal traffic offense, or a violation of a municipal or county ordinance, except for charges relating to prostitution, domestic battery/domestic violence, violation of domestic battery injunctions, fleeing or attempting to elude a law enforcement officer, or driving under the influence, the accused shall be released at the scene of the arrest through the issuance of a Notice to Appear, except in those cases requiring mandatory booking pursuant to section two of this Order below. In any case where persons are not booked into jail, the Notice to Appear form must include information stating the type of identification provided by the person arrested and right and left thumb prints of the person arrested. The arresting officer shall have the discretion, however, to book the accused person into the county jail if the officer determines that any of the following factors exist:

a. The subject of the arrest is known by the arresting officer to be a habitual offender;

b. The alleged crime is one of a violent nature or one which indicates a reckless disregard for the safety of others;

c. The nature of the accused person is clearly violent or disorderly;

d. The arresting officer has reason to believe that the accused person will repeat the offense if not detained;

e. The accused person has no valid, verifiable address;

f. The accused person does not reside in Osceola County or a bordering county;

g. The arresting officer has reason to believe that the accused person meets the criteria for the Baker Act, or the Marchman Act, or is a substance abuser, or suffers from a mental illness.

2. The accused person shall be booked into the county jail if any of the following circumstances exist:

a. The accused person failed to sufficiently identify himself or herself or supply the necessary information for completion of the Notice to Appear or traffic citation;

b. The accused person refused to sign the Notice to Appear;

c. The arresting officer has reason to believe that the continued liberty of the accused person constitutes an unreasonable risk of bodily injury to others;

d. The accused person has no ties with the jurisdiction sufficient to assure the accused's appearance at court or there is substantial risk that the accused will refuse to respond to the notice or citation;

e. The arresting officer has a reasonable belief the accused person may be wanted in any jurisdiction;

f. The arresting officer has a reasonable belief that the accused person has previously failed to respond to a notice or summons or has violated the conditions of any pretrial release program; or

g. The accused person is arrested for prostitution or a prostitution related offense, including violations of probation involving prostitution mapping zone.

3. If a person accused of a misdemeanor, criminal traffic offense, or violation of city or county ordinance is brought to the jail because the person failed to sufficiently identify himself or herself or supply the information necessary for completion of the Notice to Appear, or because it appeared to the arresting officer that the accused person had previously failed to respond to a notice or summons or had violated the conditions of any pretrial release program, Osceola County Corrections staff shall begin a preliminary investigation to determine if the accused person is a likely candidate for release on his/her own recognizance. The investigation shall include the following facts:

a. The accused person provides residence information and currently resides in Osceola, Orange, Seminole, Brevard, Lake, Polk, Indian River or Okeechobee County;

b. The accused person provides the name, address and phone number of an emergency contact;

c. The accused person provides current employment or student information or is a homemaker, retired or disabled;

d. The accused person is not exhibiting mental illness or behavior indicating he/she may cause harm to himself/herself or another.

4. After the accused person is booked and positively identified through AFIS, the Osceola County Corrections staff shall make a final determination after reviewing the following information:

The accused person's local, state and national criminal history is reviewed for prior convictions and failures to appear. To be eligible for ROR the accused person must meet the criteria established by the Corrections Department.

5. Pursuant to above paragraph 3 and 4 of this subsection, once it is determined that the accused person is likely to appear as directed, the accused person shall be released upon the issuance of a ROR pursuant to Florida Rule of Criminal Procedure 3.125(c).

6. Any accused person booked into the Osceola County Jail on a worthless check warrant may be released on his or her own recognizance once the Osceola County Corrections staff determines the accused person is likely to appear based on the criteria set out in the above paragraphs 3, 4, and 5 of this Order.

7. Any accused person who is released on his or her own recognizance pursuant to this Order, shall receive a notice substantially stating the following:

"You are being released pursuant to administrative order because you have met the criteria for release. You have supplied an address to which all future court process will be sent. As a condition of your release, you must refrain from criminal activity of any kind and you must refrain from any contact with the alleged victim of the crime which you have been charged except through pretrial discovery if stipulated by all parties or if ordered by the Judge on a showing of good cause pursuant to Florida Rule of Criminal Procedure 3.220(h)(7). If you violate these conditions or fail to appear for any of your court dates, your recognizance status will be revoked and you may remain in jail or be required to post a substantial bond until your charges have been disposed." You must notify the Clerk of Court if your address has been changed within 24 hours from the date the address has changed.

8. *Extradition and Out-of-County Warrants.*

a. When an inmate of the Osceola County Jail has had all local charges cleared and is detained solely and exclusively on a warrant from another jurisdiction, the Corrections staff shall immediately teletype to the other agency that the inmate must be picked up by a date and time certain or he/she will be released from jail on ROR or bond, unless the agency requests an extension for good cause shown. The same procedure shall be followed by the Sheriff's Extradition Deputy for out-of-state fugitives where the inmate has waived extradition or has been ordered surrendered after habeas corpus proceedings have been completed and Notice of Appeal was not filed or the appeal was dismissed or affirmed.

b. The time periods shall not include Saturdays, Sundays, and holidays, and shall be as follows:

(1) Inmates held for contiguous Florida counties, e.g.: Orange, Polk, Lake, Okeechobee, Indian River, and Brevard—24 hours from Initial Appearance; with no local charges;

(2) Inmates held for all other Florida counties—72 hours from Initial Appearance with no local charges;

(3) Inmates held for other states—30 days from date of notification;

c. The telephone contact and teletype message from the Correctional Release Specialist or the Sheriff's Extradition Deputy shall provide a date and time certain for pickup.

d. If the time deadline passes without the pickup agency requesting an extension for good cause, the Corrections staff or the Sheriff's Extradition Deputy, as the case may be, will notify the Clerk of Court within 24 hours from the next business day to apply to the Judge conducting Initial Appearance hearings or to the weekend duty Judge for a written order of ROR or setting bond. If the inmate is held on a Florida warrant, the ROR order shall direct that he/she report to the proper court on a date and time certain; if the bond is set or reduced, the order shall direct that the inmate report to the court "when notified." If the inmate is held on an out-of-state charge, the order for ROR or setting bond shall direct that the inmate appear before the judge conducting fugitive hearings when notified. The Corrections staff or the Sheriff's Extradition Deputy shall immediately notify the pickup agency contact person by teletype that this action was taken, and shall mail a copy of the order to the contact person.

9. The State Attorney or his designee has the authority to release pre-trial detainees without the approval of the court. Such authority shall extend only to those prisoners whom the State Attorney has determined shall not be prosecuted for the instant charged offense. The State Attorney's office may initiate such an order of release by notifying the Osceola County Department of Corrections by telephone, and thereafter filing a written Notice of Release with the Chief Judge, the Clerk, and the Osceola County Department of Corrections within one (1) day of the pre-trial detainee's release.

10. Nothing contained herein shall abrogate pretrial release, reduction of bond or other procedures established by Florida Law or Rule.

11. After an accused person has been booked into the Osceola County Department of Corrections and the arresting agency determines that an error occurred and the accused should be released, then Osceola County Department of Corrections will release the accused provided as follows: (1) that the accused person has been properly identified; (2) the accused person does not have any outstanding warrants or writs which would hold the accused on another matter; (3) the arresting agency files with Osceola County Department of Corrections an affidavit requesting release which includes an explanation of the alleged error.

B. Procedures for Notices to Appear. This section is in lieu of physical arrest and /or release on own recognizance after booking, for County or municipal ordinance violations, and first or second degree misdemeanors, except those related to traffic, when committed by persons over the age of 17 years.

A COURT APPEARANCE IS MANDATORY FOR ALL NOTICES TO APPEAR THAT COULD RESULT IN A CRIMINAL CHARGE.

In any case where persons are not booked into jail, the Notice to Appear form must include information stating the type of identification provided by the person arrested and right and left thumb prints of the person arrested.

1. *Issuance and Intake Processing.*

a. Before releasing a violator on a Notice to Appear, arresting officers will apply the criteria set forth in paragraphs (b) and (c) of Florida Rule of Criminal Procedure 3.125.

b. Before releasing a violator on ROR, Correctional staff will apply the criteria set for Section A, paragraphs 3, 4, and 5.

c. When a Notice to Appear is to be issued the following will be done by the arresting officer:

(1) Prepare an original and three copies of the Notice to Appear;

(2) Give one copy to the arrestee after he has agreed to respond to the Notice to Appear and has signed the other three copies;

(3) Retain one copy, signed by arrestee, for his agency record;

(4) Forward the original and one copy, signed by the arrestee and sworn to by the arresting officer before a Notary Public or deputy clerk, to the appropriate division of the Clerk's office,—as defined elsewhere in this Order;

(5) Prepare copies of Schedule of Witnesses and Evidence, retaining one copy and delivering the original and one copy to the appropriate division of the Clerk's Office in which the Notice to Appear is filed. (When no witnesses are known, the Schedule should be submitted showing "No Witnesses".);

(6) Provide in the Notice to Appear and/or the ROR for a court appearance on the date and at a time agreed upon by the State Attorney and the Judges of the County Court of Osceola County at the Osceola County Courthouse, 2 Courthouse Square, Kissimmee, FL 34741;

(7) Upon issuance of Notices to Appear, the Notices to Appear and any accompanying paperwork shall be delivered to the Clerk of the Court at the geographically designated court facility;

d. When Notices to Appear are received by the Clerk's office, the following will be done:

(1) Upon receipt of a charge on Notice to Appear, retain the original of each Notice to Appear and Schedule of Witnesses and Evidence and send one copy of each to the prosecuting authority;

(2) Schedule for arraignment and assign to a Judge, who will handle all proceedings after arraignment;

(3) Receive payment of all fines and costs resulting from Notices to Appear.

2. *Failure to Appear.* When a person signs a written Notice to Appear in the case at issue and fails to respond, a warrant of arrest shall be issued pursuant to Rule 3.121, Florida Rules of Criminal Procedure or a capias pursuant to Rule 3.730, Florida Rules of Criminal Procedure and that the minimum bond on either a capias or a warrant is set in the amount of $2,000.00 as required by section 903.046(d), Florida Statutes.

3. *Venue.*

a. All Notices to Appear issued in Osceola County will be returnable to the County Court of Osceola County in the Osceola County Courthouse, Kissimmee.

4. The individual county and municipalities shall promulgate internal rules/policies as to which ordinances shall be subject to these procedures as stated in the above paragraphs.

5. Functions, duties and authority delegated to the Clerk's office shall be as follows:

a. Receive and process all Notices to Appear issued for offenses committed within the geographical area of jurisdiction of the court served, as prescribed in section II of this Order.

b. Receive, receipt for, account for and distribute in accordance with section 34.191, Florida Statutes, and other applicable statutes, once sentenced by the Court, all fines and court costs assessed upon conviction or plea of guilty of offenses charged under Notices to Appear issued pursuant to Rule 3.125, Fla. R. Crim. P.

c. Accept an appearance and plea of "Not Guilty", in writing, in person or by an attorney, to a charge of committing a first or second degree misdemeanor offense, or a county or municipal ordinance violation, when a Notice to Appear was issued and have the case assigned for trial at a future date.

d. Receive motions for new hearings or in arrest of judgment pursuant to Florida Rules of Criminal Procedure, within prescribed time limits and notify the defendant or his counsel of the time scheduled for a hearing.

e. Maintain records of all cases processed, numbering and reporting for identification and statistical purposes, separately from cases disposed of in open court.

f. Issue a capias, pursuant to Rule 3.750, Fla. R. Crim. P., for the arrest of any resident of this State, or any nonresident upon whom process may be served in this State, who fails to respond to a Notice to Appear lawfully served upon such person. The capias shall be directed to all law enforcement officers, state, county or municipal, in the State, and may be executed in any county in this State.

g. Notify the arresting agency of the disposition of the case.

h. Any additional duties or responsibilities as may be delegated by the Chief Judge of the Ninth Judicial Circuit.

C. Osceola County Pretrial Release Program (PTR).

A. It is the policy of this State that persons committing serious criminal offenses, posing a threat to the safety of the community or the integrity of the judicial process, or failing to appear at trial be detained upon arrest. However, persons found to meet specified criteria shall be released under certain conditions until proceedings are concluded and adjudication has been determined. The policy of pretrial detention and release will assure the detention of those persons posing a threat to society; while reducing the costs for incarceration by releasing, until trial, those persons not considered a danger to the community who meet certain criteria.

Unless a judge specifically orders otherwise, a person arrested for a non-violent misdemeanor of the first or second degree, a criminal traffic offense, or a violation of a municipal or county ordinance, except for charges relating to domestic violence shall be released into the Osceola County Pretrial Release Program before Initial Appearance provided that:

1. Pursuant to section 907.041(3)(b), Florida Statutes, the Osceola County Pretrial Release Program certifies to the court that it has investigated or otherwise verified:

a. The circumstances of the accused person's family, employment, character, mental condition and length of residence in the community;

b. The accused person's record of convictions, of appearances at court proceedings, or flight to avoid prosecution, or failure to appear at court proceedings; and

c. Other facts necessary to assist the court in its determination of the indigence of the accused person and whether she or he should be released under the supervision of the service.

d. The accused person must reside in or own real property in the State of Florida.

2. In addition, the accused person must meet the following qualifications:

a. The accused person does not have any current charges related to domestic violence or violation of domestic battery injunctions or any prior conviction for murder, attempted murder, sex crimes, home invasion, crimes against children, carjacking, or any other capital or life felonies;

b. The accused person must have a risk assessment score * of moderate or below;

c. The accused person is not currently on bail (monetary or nonmonetary), or probation or parole, or other legal constraint;

d. The accused person has not exhibited mental illness or behavior indicating he/she might cause harm to himself/herself or another.

B. Pursuant to Florida Rule of Criminal Procedure 3.131, unless a person is charged with a capital offense or an offense punishable by life imprisonment and the proof of guilt is evident or the presumption of guilt is great, that person is entitled to pretrial release on reasonable conditions. If no condition of release can reasonably protect the community from risk of harm, assure the accused presence at trial, or assure the integrity of the judicial process, the accused may be detained. It is also the intent of the Legislature to create a presumption in favor of release on nonmonetary conditions for any person who is granted pretrial release unless such person is charged with a dangerous crime as defined in section 907.041(4), Florida Statutes.

Any accused person may be released into the Pretrial Release Program after Initial Appearance, with a judicial order, provided that:

1. Pursuant to section 907.041(3)(b), Florida Statutes, the Osceola County Pretrial Release Program certifies to the court that it has investigated or otherwise verified:

a. The circumstances of the accused person's family, employment, character, mental condition and length of residence in the community;

b. The accused person's record of convictions, of appearances at court proceedings, or flight to avoid prosecution, or failure to appear at court proceedings; and

c. Other facts necessary to assist the court in its determination of the indigence of the accused person and whether she or he should be released under the supervision of the service.

2. Based upon a criminal history investigation, the accused person must meet the following qualifications:

a. The accused person does not have any current charges of murder, attempted murder, sex crimes, home invasion, robbery, crimes against children, or any other capital or life felonies;

b. The accused person is not currently on bail (monetary or nonmonetary), probation or parole, or other legal constraint;

c. The accused person has not exhibited mental illness or behavior indicating he/she might cause harm to himself/herself or another.

3. Pursuant to section 903.0351, Florida Statutes, in the instance of an alleged violation of felony probation or community control, bail or any other form of pretrial release shall not be granted prior to the resolution of the probation-violation hearing or the community-control violation hearing to:

a. a violent felony offender of special concern as defined in section 948.06, Florida Statutes;

b. a person who is on felony probation or community control for any offense committed on or after March 12, 2007, and who is arrested for a qualifying offense as defined in section 948.06(8)(c); or

c. a person who is on felony probation or community control and has previously been found by a court to be a habitual violent felony offender as defined in section 775.084(1)(b), a three-time violent felony offender as defined in section 775.084(1)(c), or a sexual predator under section 775.21, and who is arrested for committing a qualifying offense as defined in section 948.06(8)(c) on or after March 12, 2007.

However, section II.C.B.3 of this Order shall not apply where the alleged violation of felony probation or community control is based solely on the probationer or offender's failure to pay costs or fines or make restitution payments.

No accused person will be released to the Pretrial Release Program who does not qualify regardless of any other condition set in conjunction therewith. If an accused person is ordered to PTR or Bond with PTR and it is determined that the accused does not meet the criteria for acceptance into the Program, the jail must notify the judge who ordered the PTR or Bond with PTR and the accused must then be brought before the assigned judge to set new terms of release.

The Osceola County Corrections Department conducts routine assessments of the jail population. If the Chief of Corrections or his/her designee determines that an inmate incarcerated for a non-violent misdemeanor of the first or second degree, a criminal traffic offense, or a violation of a municipal or county ordinance, except for charges relating to domestic violence, qualifies for release based on established criteria as outlined in Section C (A, 1 & 2), then that inmate shall be released into the Pretrial Release Program.

Release under this Program shall include a condition that the person comply with all orders of the court, appear at all court hearings, refrain from any criminal activity, refrain from contact with any alleged victims, and any other condition specifically ordered by the court. All Program participants will be supervised according to their pretrial risk assessment score. If a person released under this Program violates any condition of release or is arrested for a crime for which probable cause has been found by a judge, the Program shall apply to the judge assigned to have his/her release revoked and have a warrant issued.

D. Osceola County Mental Health Pretrial Release (MH/PTR). Any accused person may be released into the Osceola County Mental Health Pretrial Release Program after first appearance provided that:

1. The Osceola County Mental Health Pretrial Release Program certifies at first appearance to the court that it has investigated or otherwise verified that the accused person is currently suffering symptoms from a severe and persistent mental illness under the current Diagnostic and Statistical Manual of Mental Disorders, and provides to the court a preliminary treatment plan to meet the individual's needs and that the arrestee is an Osceola County Resident or the individual can access the appropriate treatment services in an adjacent county;

AND THAT,

2. The accused person must meet the following qualifications:

a. The accused person does not have any current charges for driving under the influence or have current charges or a prior conviction for murder, attempted murder, sex crimes, home invasion, robbery, crimes against children, aggravated battery, or any other capital life felonies;

b. The accused person is not currently on bail (monetary or non-monetary) or other legal constrain;

c. The accused person has not exhibited mental illness or behavior indicating he/she might cause harm to himself/herself or another;

d. If the accused is on community control, probation or parole, approval must be granted by the officer supervising the accused person;

e. Any accused person with an active domestic violence injunction/protection order, or currently charged with domestic violence must have victim input;

f. An arrestee shall not be released without the judge's authority under this program if any law enforcement officer or the State Attorney has communicated his/her objection release under this program;

Release under this Program shall include a condition that the person comply with all orders of the court, appear at all court hearings, refrain from any criminal activity, refrain from contact with any alleged victims, and any other condition specifically ordered by the court. If a person meets the guidelines for participation in the Mental Health Pretrial Release Program, he/she may be required to obtain a mental health evaluation through the designated provider and participate in all treatment including taking prescribed medication. If a person released under this Program violates any condition of release or is arrested for a crime for which probable cause has been found by a judge, the Program shall apply to the judge assigned to have his/her release revoked and have a warrant issued.

It is anticipated that occasionally accused persons who do not meet the requirements of this Order may, due to other circumstances, appear to be acceptable candidates for participation in the Mental Health Pretrial Release Program. In those cases, specific orders allowing the release from jail will be sought from the first appearance judge or if charges have been filed, the assigned judge.

3. *Criteria for the Extension of the Limits of Confinement for the Purposes of Mental Health Evaluation and Treatment.*

a. Accused persons who meet the following conditions may be transferred to a Baker Act receiving facility until such time as the Baker Act receiving facility staff determines that the offender may be safely returned to the custody of the jail:

Accused persons who are charged with misdemeanors, traffic cases, and second and third degree felonies will be considered eligible for the extension of limits of confinement, as established in this Order. However, accused persons whose instant offense is a felony sex offense, or involves the use of a deadly weapon will not be granted an extension of the limits of confinement under the terms of this Order. Specifically, the following crimes will not be accepted under the terms of this Order:

(1) Criminal Justice Criteria:

Any Homicide
Any Sexual Battery
Any Offense involving the use of a deadly weapon
Any Lewd and Lascivious Act

(2) Mental Health Criteria: Accused person meets criteria for involuntary examination as defined in section 394.463(1), Florida Statutes, as determined by a physician, psychologist licensed pursuant to chapter 490, Florida Statutes, a psychiatric nurse or licensed clinical social worker.

(3) Appointment of the Public Defender: In actions for involuntary placement under chapter 394, section 394.467, Florida Statutes, where a person is subject to involuntary placement, the Public Defender shall be automatically appointed to represent such persons. This Administrative Order shall provide the authority for appointments of the Public Defender in lieu of the issuance of a Court order in each case.

E. Violent Felony Offenders of Special Concern. Persons arrested for new law violations who have been identified as a violent felony offender of special concern pursuant to the Anti–Murder Act, sections 903.0351, 948.06, and 948.064, Florida Statutes, but have not yet been arrested for a violation of probation, shall be placed on a five (5) day administrative hold. Osceola County Corrections shall immediately notify the Department of Corrections of the new arrest so that the Department of Corrections can take the appropriate action.

F. Bail Schedule. The bail bond schedule, attached hereto as Attachments A 1, A 2, & A 3, is for use in setting bail in Orange and Osceola Counties prior to first appearance, and is not intended to and does not in any manner bind judges conducting first appearance hearings or bond hearings. Judges setting bail as a condition of release may set such bail in any reasonable amount in accordance with the factors set forth in Florida Rule of Criminal Procedure 3.131(b)(3) and section 903.046, Florida Statutes.

Unless a judge has ordered the defendant held without bail or has previously set bail, a defendant may be released from jail before first appearance if he/she posts the bail set forth in this section and otherwise meets the conditions of this section. In addition to the posting of the monetary bail, the person's release conditions shall include an obligation to comply with all court orders, to appear at all court hearings, to refrain from any criminal activity, and to refrain from any contact with the alleged victim. Double the stated amount of the following bail schedule will be required of persons who do not reside in Florida.

Pursuant to Florida Rule of Criminal Procedure 3.131, as amended, unless a person is charged with a capital offense or an offense punishable by life imprisonment and the proof of guilt is evident or the presumption of guilt is great, that person is entitled to pretrial release on reasonable conditions. If no condition of release can reasonably protect the community from risk of harm, assure the accused's presence at trial, or assure the integrity of the judicial process, the accused may be detained. An arrestee shall not be released without the judge's authority if any law enforcement officer or the State Attorney has communicated his or her objection to release under monetary release conditions.

Pursuant to section 903.047, Florida Statutes, as amended, a separate bail amount shall be set for each charge, with the exception of warrants issued prior to October 1, 2006. Bail on those warrants shall be governed by the amount set in the warrant. Where multiple charges have been filed, the bond amount on the highest offense will continue to be set according to the bond schedule attached hereto as **"Attachment A 1"** [1] for felonies, **"Attachment A 2"** [2] for nontraffic misdemeanors and ordinance violations, and **"Attachment A 3"** [3]for criminal traffic misdemeanors. The bond amount for additional subsequent charges shall be set as follows:

Felony, Life, PBL	No Bond
Felony, 1st degree	Set by Bond Schedule
Felony, 2nd degree	$ 150.00
Felony, 3rd degree	$ 150.00
Misdemeanor, non-traffic	$ 100.00
Misdemeanor, traffic	$ 100.00

However, an exception arises where there are multiple deaths. Each criminal offense that results in a death shall be set according to the bond schedule attached hereto as **"Attachment A 1"**.

1. For felonies not appearing on the bond schedule attached hereto as **"Attachment A 1,"** the following bond amounts shall apply:

Felony, 1st degree	$ 5,000.00 to $10,000.00
Felony, 2nd degree	$ 2,500.00 to $ 5,000.00
Felony, 3rd degree	$ 1,000.00 to $ 2,500.00
All Other First Degree Felony Drug Offenses	$10,000.00 to $50,000.00

Where multiple charges have been filed, the bond amount on the highest offense will continue to be set according to the bond schedule attached hereto as **"Attachment A 1"** for felonies, **"Attachment A 2"** for non-traffic misdemeanors and ordinance violations, and **"Attachment A 3"** for criminal traffic misdemeanors. The bond amount for additional subsequent charges shall be set as follows:

Felony, Life, PBL	No Bond
Felony, 1st degree	Set by Bond Schedule
Felony, 2nd degree	$ 150.00
Felony, 3rd degree	$ 150.00
Misdemeanor, non–traffic	$ 100.00
Misdemeanor, traffic	$ 100.00

However, an exception arises where there are multiple deaths. Each criminal offense that results in a death shall be set according to the bond schedule attached hereto as **"Attachment A 1"**.

A person arrested for a capital crime, a felony punishable by life, a first degree felony punishable by up to life, or for any lewd or lascivious exhibition, lewd or lascivious molestation, lewd or lascivious battery, or other sexual act involving a minor, or for any failure of a person deemed to be a sexual predator to follow registration, reporting, and/or employment restrictions, pursuant to chapters 775 and 943 of the Florida Statutes, or for burglary of a structure or dwelling during a natural disaster/act of God, acts of terrorism, or war (i.e., looting during a state of emergency) shall not be eligible for release under this section. These persons are to be held until first appearance, at which time the first appearance judge will decide conditions of release, if any. Any motion for bail or bond regarding defendants with the above outstanding charges, with the exception of burglary of a structure or dwelling during a natural disaster/act of God, acts of terrorism, or war (i.e., looting during a state of emergency), shall include the following information: attachment copy of charging affidavit and any other supporting documents; addresses and phone numbers of defendant; address and phone numbers of defendant's employers; and any aliases of defendant. A copy of such motion shall be forwarded to the Department of Corrections at their designated office. A Form Order designed to assist the Court in making a bail determination is attached hereto as Attachment D.

2. For traffic and non-traffic misdemeanors and ordinance violations not appearing on the bond schedules attached hereto as **"Attachment A 2"** or **"Attachment A 3,"** the following bond amounts shall apply:

Misdemeanor, 1st degree	$250.00 to $500.00
Misdemeanor, 2nd degree	$150.00 to $250.00
Ordinance Violation	$150.00 to $250.00

Where multiple charges have been filed, the bond amount on the highest offense will continue to be set according to the bond schedule attached hereto as **"Attachment A 1"** for felonies, **"Attachment A 2"** for non-traffic misdemeanors and ordinance violations, and **"Attachment A 3"** for criminal traffic misdemeanors. The bond amount for additional subsequent charges shall be set as follows:

Felony, Life, PBL	No Bond
Felony, 1st degree	Set by Bond Schedule
Felony, 2nd degree	$ 150.00
Felony, 3rd degree	$ 150.00
Misdemeanor, non-traffic	$ 100.00
Misdemeanor, traffic	$ 100.00

However, an exception arises where there are multiple deaths. Each criminal offense that results in a death shall be set according to the bond schedule attached hereto as **"Attachment A 1"**.

3. *Bond When Charges are Modified and Defendant is Still in Custody.* If the charge(s) filed by the State Attorney are more numerous, as compared to the offense(s) that were before the court when the bond was last set, the Osceola County Department of Corrections shall release the defendant on the additional charge(s) on his or her own recognizance, unless application for modification of the conditions of release has been made by either party and granted by a court of competent jurisdiction. If the charge(s) filed by the State Attorney are higher or lower in degree than the offenses that were before the court when the bond was last set, the bond shall remain the same as that last set, unless application for modification of the conditions of release has been made by either party and granted by a court in its sound discretion. Additionally, the court may adjust the bond if deemed appropriate or proportional.

The total amount of each original bond remains in effect, regardless of any change in charge(s) filed, until otherwise ordered by the court sua sponte or pursuant to a motion to conform bond to charges as filed.

4. *Disqualifications From Pre–First Appearances Release by Bail Schedule.* The following persons shall not be eligible for release under this section:

a. Any person currently free on monetary or non-monetary release for an offense if the offense for which they are currently free on monetary or non-monetary release occurred prior to the offense at issue. (i.e., a person free on release conditions for Offense A is eligible for pre-first appearance release on Offense B if Offense B occurred prior to Offense A, but not if Offense B occurred after Offense A.) This shall also apply to failure to appear where a bond is set;

b. Any person whose identity has not been clearly ascertained;

c. Any person whose arrest affidavit contains a statement of ineligibility by the arresting officer made with the specific approval of his/her supervisor. The arresting officer shall also state the reason for disqualification on the charging or arrest affidavit;

d. Any person who refuses to provide a blood sample after a request by a law enforcement officer, as authorized by section 796.08, Florida Statutes, may not be released prior to first appearance.

G. Home Confinement Program (HC). It is the policy of this State that persons committing serious criminal offenses, posing a threat to the safety of the community or the integrity of the judicial process, or failing to appear at trial be detained upon arrest. However, persons found to meet specified criteria shall be released under certain conditions until proceedings are concluded and adjudication has been determined. The policy of pretrial detention and release will assure the detention of those persons posing a threat to society while reducing the costs for incarceration by releasing, until trial, those persons not considered a danger to the community who meet certain criteria. The Home Confinement Program provides the judiciary another alternative to incarceration for pretrial detainees awaiting trial. In addition to a court order, the accused person must meet the following qualifications:

1. Home Confinement can only be supervised utilizing GPS equipment which has a radio frequency component. This requires all persons who are accepted into the Home Confinement Program to wear a GPS monitoring device. This condition cannot be waived;

2. The accused person must live in an approved residence within Orange or Osceola Counties, (some areas of Polk County are also considered);

3. If home confinement is ordered as a condition of bond, the bond must be paid prior to releasing the accused person;

4. The accused person must have a standard land line phone with basic phone service with no added features and toll free access. Cell phone service is not sufficient;

5. The accused person cannot have any holds for any other criminal matters;

6. The accused person is not serving a jail sentence for another charge;

7. It is recommended that the accused person have a risk assessment score of Moderate or High for participation in the Home Confinement Program. Low and Low Moderate risk defendants have a higher rate of success without this level of supervision.

8. The accused person does not have any current charges of murder, attempted murder, sex crimes, home invasion, robbery, crimes against children, or any other capital life felonies.

Only persons who meet the criteria established herein and are referred by the court to the Home Confinement Program will be accepted. Random substance abuse testing is completed to ensure the accused person's sobriety. The accused person's movement is restricted to essential travel only (essential travel is to be limited to employment, educational programs, court ordered conditions, or medical or lawyer appointments). If a person released under this Program violates any condition of release or is arrested for a crime for which probable cause has been found by a judge, the Program shall apply to the judge assigned to have his/her release revoked and have a warrant issued.

If an accused person is ordered to the Home Confinement Program and it is determined that the accused does not meet the criteria for acceptance into the Home Confinement Program, the jail must notify the judge who ordered the home confinement. The accused must then be brought before the assigned judge to set new terms of release.

If and when the Home Confinement Program reaches capacity as determined by the Osceola County Chief of Corrections in consultation with the Chief Judge, the Chief of Corrections shall have the authority to refuse admittance of anyone into the Program until such time as space becomes available.

III. Establishment of Persons to Be Presented for First Appearance Hearings and Procedures for First Appearance Hearings.

A. Persons to be Presented for First Appearance Hearings. Florida Rule of Criminal Procedure 3.130(a) requires that every person arrested on a criminal charge who is still in custody 24 hours after arrest must be taken before a judge for a first appearance hearing unless such person was previously arrested and released from custody on that same charge.

Persons who fall into the following categories, and only those persons, will be presented for first appearance hearings in Osceola County.

1. Arrest without warrant;

2. Arrest under an "at large" capias;

3. Initial arrest under an "at large" arrest warrant;

4. Arrest under a Failure to Appear (FTA) warrant where the person was never arrested but served with a summons and failed to appear for arraignment, or summons which was issued was never served;

5. Persons arrested via a charging affidavit for violating the special condition of probation requiring that the defendant not return to the "prostitution mapping zone" must appear at the Initial Appearance proceedings and at such proceedings the judge may set a bond of the defendant's release;

6. Persons arrested via a charging affidavit for on view violation of probation conditions by officer;

7. Persons arrested on violation of probation or violation of community control warrants.

8. Persons arrested on collection court writs.

9. Persons arrested who have not been released on monetary conditions and are certified eligible, pursuant to section 907.041(3)(b), Florida Statutes, to be released into the Osceola County Pretrial Release Program.

10. Persons turned in by bail bond agent (TIBB) prior to arraignment.

11. Persons whose ROR release was revoked prior to arraignment.

B. Persons No Longer to be Presented at First Appearance Hearings are:

1. Persons arrested on civil writs;

2. Persons turned in by bail bond agent (TIBB) after arraignment;

3. Persons who prison control release (PCR) or ROR release was revoked;

4. Persons who ROR release was revoked after arraignment;

5. Persons arrested on a contempt of court warrant;

C. If there is any doubt as to whether an arrested person should be presented for a first appearance hearing, that doubt should be resolved in favor of the defendant appearing at the first appearance.

D. Operational Procedures for First Appearances Held in Osceola County. There will be one session for first appearance hearings in Osceola County, Florida, at 1:30 p.m., Monday through Friday, except on holidays and weekends. The time frames may be changed upon twenty-four hours notice, as a result of experience, collection court, in-jail arraignments and bond hearings.

IV. Returnable Dates and Locations.

A. Felonies. Persons arrested for felony offenses and released from jail prior to arraignment are to report to the Osceola County Courthouse, 2 Courthouse Square, Kissimmee, FL 34741, for arraignment when notified by the Clerk of the Court.

B. Misdemeanors.

1. *Misdemeanors.* Persons arrested for misdemeanor offenses which will be heard in the Osceola County Courthouse and who were released prior to arraignment, will be ordered to report before a judge of the appropriate division of County Court of Osceola County, to the courthouse upon dates and at locations set from time to time by the Administrative Judge of the County Court of Osceola County or his/her designee.

C. Traffic Offenses.

1. *Traffic Offenders Returnable to the Courthouse.* Persons arrested for traffic offenses which will be heard in the Osceola County Courthouse and who were released prior to arraignment, will be ordered to report before a judge of the appropriate division of County Court of Osceola County, to the

courthouse upon dates and at locations set from time to time by the Administrative Judge of the County Court of Osceola County or his/her designee.

D. Persons released from custody after having appeared for arraignment in any court shall report on whatever date was scheduled at arraignment.

E. Emergency Procedures if Fiber Network System Not Operational. If a problem occurs with the system, the trial clerk will call the emergency technician using the pager number provided. The technician will call to determine the extent of the problem and approximate time to repair. In the event the system cannot be repaired in a reasonable time, the presiding Judge and Court Personnel may travel to the Osceola County Jail Facility Courtroom to conduct first appearance proceedings live, or as directed by the Chief Administrative Judge.

F. How to Contact Involved Individuals. See contact list attached hereto as "Attachment B."

V. Consolidation and/or Transfer Regarding Felony Cases, Misdemeanor Cases, and Traffic Cases.

The Chief Judge shall have authority to reassign and assign cases among the various divisions of the Circuit and County Courts and their subdivisions, as well as between the County and Circuit Courts of the Ninth Judicial Circuit as may be appropriate. (07–85–21).

Under the authority vested in the Chief Judge pursuant to Rule 2.215(b)(5) of the Florida Rules of Judicial Administration, various administrative orders and directives of the Chief Judge may be entered regarding the authority of the administrative judges to reassign cases. (07–85–21 with changes). A pending case is defined as one in which an information has been filed and the defendant has not been tried or sentenced.

A. Felony Cases. No other judge other than the Chief Judge, the administrative judges and the assigned initial appearance judge as authorized by the Chief Judge from time to time shall have any authority to reassign any felony cases. If any judge, other than the Chief Judge, his designated administrative judges or his designated initial appearance judge, has or shall reassign any felony case such reassignment shall be null and void and of no force and effect. Any such felony case so reassigned by any other judge shall not be considered reassigned and the Clerk shall not so reassign the case. (07–85–21 with changes).

1. Felonies cases for the same defendant which are assigned to various felony divisions shall be reassigned to the division with the lowest case number without the approval of the Chief Judge or the Administrative Judge of the felony divisions.

2. Individuals who are on felony probation, shall have new law violations reassigned to the division with the felony probation pending, without the approval of the Chief Judge or the Administrative Judge of the felony divisions.

3. Before an information is filed, felony cases involving co-defendants shall have the co-defendants cases transferred to the division with the lower case number without the approval of the Chief Judge or the Administrative Judge of the felony divisions. (07–97–52, par. 3 is vacated).

4. New cases involving the defendant and another defendant(s) are not to be reassigned by virtue of this Order.

5. In the rare event that cases involving co-defendants, filed in a single information, are assigned to more than one division (i.e., co-defendant A is assigned to division 10 and co-defendant B is assigned to division 12), the Clerk of Court shall assign that single case to the division to which co-defendant A is assigned.

B. Misdemeanor / Traffic Cases.

1. When both criminal traffic and criminal misdemeanor cases arising out of the same criminal episode are pending for the same defendant, counsel for the State, counsel for the defendant, or the defendant may file in the case a Request for Administrative Transfer or request in open court that a transfer occur and the Clerk of Court is hereby directed to transfer the case(s) pending in the criminal misdemeanor case to the Division with the criminal traffic case, without the necessity of further court order.

2. When both criminal traffic and criminal misdemeanor cases are pending, but the cases are not related other than the same defendant is charged in each case, then either the State or the Defendant may file in the cause a Request for Administrative Transfer or request in open court that a transfer occur and the Clerk of Court is hereby directed to transfer the case(s) pending to the Division which has the case where the earliest date of offense occurred.

3. When a defendant has more than one criminal traffic case pending, but the cases are not related except that the same defendant is charged in each case, then either the State or the defendant may file in the case a Request for Administrative Transfer and the Clerk of Court is hereby directed to transfer the case(s) pending to the Division which has the case where the earliest date of offense occurred.

4. When a defendant has either criminal misdemeanor or criminal traffic case(s) pending and there are also non-criminal traffic infractions arising out of the same episode, then either the State or the defendant may file in the cause a Request for Administrative Transfer or request in open court that a transfer occur and the Clerk of Court is hereby directed to transfer the non-criminal traffic infractions to the Division assigned the criminal misdemeanor or criminal traffic case, without the necessity of further court order.

5. In no event shall misdemeanor/traffic cases transfer or be consolidated if they are in capias status.

C. Miscellaneous matters relating to transfers/consolidations regarding felony, misdemeanor and traffic cases:

1. Nothing in this Order is meant or intended to require or preclude the filing of Motions or Orders that may call for the transfer, reassignment or consolidation of other cases as the circumstances of such other may require. (07–97–52, par 4 included).

2. The attorney representing the State of Florida or the attorney of record for the defendant may file a Motion for Transfer and shall provide the motion and proposed Order to the court. The private attorneys moving for transfer must provide addressed, stamped envelopes along with the proposed order. The motion, order, and envelopes shall be provided to the administrative judge of the criminal division. No judge other than the Chief Judge, or the administrative judges as authorized by the Chief Judge from time to time, shall have the authority to reassign any felony cases.

3. Upon the filing of an information charging a defendant with a crime other than is charged in the arrest affidavit, the State Attorney shall determine if the new crime charged is within the jurisdiction of the same court. If the new crime charged is not within the jurisdiction of the court to whom the case was originally assigned, the State Attorney shall deliver a signed Motion to Transfer to the Clerk of the Court to whom the case was originally assigned, reciting the ground for the transfer and advising the Clerk of the Court to whom the case should be transferred. In the Motion to Transfer, the State Attorney may direct the Clerk to dismiss a capias and to issue a summons directing the defendant to appear to answer the new charge. Upon receipt of the motion, the Clerk shall, by authority of this Administrative Order, transfer the case file to the Clerk of the Court to whom the transfer has been requested. (07–89–05, incorporated).

VI. Establishment of Procedures to Effect Florida Rule of Criminal Procedure 3.134.

A. Hearings addressing violations of the 33–day rule shall be heard by the judge to whom the case is assigned.

B. Defense counsel and pro se defendants shall file with the Clerk's Office Motions for Release and Notices of Hearings addressing violation of the 33–day rule by 12:00 p.m. on the business day before the scheduled hearing and shall simultaneously forward via the most expeditious means possible, including e-mail, copies of the Motions and Notices to all interested persons, including the judicial assistant for the judge who is to preside over the hearing, the persons with the State Attorney's Office and the Osceola County Sheriff's Office. See contact list attached hereto as "Attachment C."

C. Immediately upon receipt of the Notice of Hearing and if possible by 12:00 p.m. on the business day before the scheduled hearing, the judicial assistant for the judge who is to preside over the hearing shall forward via the most expeditious means possible, including e-mail, copies of the Notices to the persons with the State Attorney's Office and the persons with the Clerk of Court's Office: See contact list attached hereto as "Attachment C."

D. Should defense counsel or pro se defendants file on a Friday, Motions and Notices for a hearing to be scheduled for the following business day, defense counsel and pro se defendants shall forward copies of the Motion and Notice of Hearing, in the same manner as stated in paragraph C to the judicial assistant for the judge scheduled to hear video arraignments for that business day.

VII. Vacating/Incorporation of Related Administrative Orders and Review Provision.

A. The following Administrative Orders are vacated and set aside and have been incorporated and/or amended herein: 07–92–16, 07–97–04–1, 07–98–46–1, 07–98–47–2, 07–98–47–3, 07–98–47–4, 07–98–47–5, 07–98–47–6, 07–98–47–7, 07–98–47–8, 07–98–47–9, 07–98–47–10, 07–98–47–11, 07–98–47–12, 07–98–47–13, 07–98–47–14, 07–98–47–15, 07–98–47–16, 07–98–50, 7–99–39, 2002–07, and 2003–26–2.

B. Administrative Order No. 2003–19–01 addressing involuntary placement proceedings in the Mental Health Division are also incorporated herein, but shall also remain in effect for post first appearance proceedings.

DONE AND ORDERED at Orlando, Florida, this 28th day of April, 2016.

Frederick J. Lauten
Chief Judge

1 Attachment A not included.
2 Attachment B not included.
3 Attachment C not included.

07–98–37–01. MANDATORY EDUCATIONAL PROGRAMS FOR ALL PARTIES IN DISSOLUTION ACTIONS WHICH INCLUDE MINOR CHILDREN

ADMINISTRATIVE ORDER NO: 07–98–37–01

IN THE CIRCUIT COURT OF THE NINTH JUDICIAL CIRCUIT, IN AND FOR ORANGE & OSCEOLA COUNTIES, FLORIDA

AMENDED ADMINISTRATIVE ORDER PERTAINING TO MANDATORY EDUCATIONAL PROGRAMS FOR ALL PARTIES IN DISSOLUTION ACTIONS WHICH INCLUDE MINOR CHILDREN OR PATERNITY ACTIONS INVOLVING ISSUES OF PARENTAL RESPONSIBILITY IN ORANGE AND OSCEOLA COUNTIES

WHEREAS, pursuant to Section 61.21, Florida Statutes, parenting courses are mandated for all parties in dissolution of marriage proceedings which involve minor children or paternity actions which involve issues of parental responsibility;

NOW, THEREFORE, I, Belvin Perry, Jr., pursuant to the authority vested in me as Chief Judge of the Ninth Judicial Circuit of Florida, under Rule 2.215, Florida Rules of Judicial Administration, and section 61.21, Florida Statutes, do hereby order that effective immediately, Administrative Order No. 07–98–37 is vacated and set aside and this Administrative Order shall supersede said Administrative Order.

IT IS HEREBY ORDERED that:

A. Provisions for Proceedings in Orange County and Osceola County:

1. Mandatory attendance at an educational program known generally as The Parent Education and Family Stabilization Course is established as a required policy in the Ninth Judicial Circuit for all parties in dissolution actions which include minor children or paternity actions involving issues of parental responsibility.

2. In all said actions all parties required to complete said parenting course shall begin the course as expeditiously as possible. For dissolution of marriage actions, unless excused by the court for good cause, the petitioner must complete the course within 45 days after the filing of the petition, and all other parties must complete the course within 45 days after service of the petition. For paternity actions, unless excused by the court for good cause, the petitioner must complete the course within 45 days after filing the petition, and any other party must complete the course within 45 days after an acknowledgment of paternity by that party, an adjudication of paternity of that party, or an order granting visitation to or support from that party. Each party to a dissolution or

paternity action shall file proof of compliance with the Clerk of Court prior to the entry of the final judgment.

3. No divorce or paternity judgments involving issues of parental responsibility shall be granted in this Circuit, subject to the exceptions set forth herein, without proof of such compliance being received from the parties.

4. The Court shall reserve the right to waive or modify the educational program requirement upon good cause shown, in writing; but such waivers shall not be liberally provided. Certificates of completion from out of state providers may be accepted by the Court.

5. The Department of Children and Family Services shall approve the parenting course which shall be a course of a minimum of four (4) hours designed to educate, train, and assist divorcing parents in regard to the consequences of divorce on parents and children. The Department of Children and Family Services shall provide the Circuit with a list of approved course providers and sites at which The Parent Education and Family Stabilization course may be completed.

6. The Clerk of the Circuit Court shall make such list available to the parties so they may attend the course of their choice. It shall be the responsibility of the Clerk of the Circuit Court to appropriately docket the court records to show completion of the program upon receipt of the certificate of completion from each parent.

7. All parties to whom this requirement applies shall be responsible for enrolling in and completing such educational course, and for paying the required fee.

8. Upon completion of any Court approved educational program, all parties to whom this requirement applies shall be responsible for providing a certificate of completion to the Clerk of the Circuit Court. Failure to comply with this Order may result in the Court's dismissal of the action, striking of pleadings, and/or other appropriate sanctions.

DONE AND ORDERED at Orlando, Florida this 31st day of July, 2007.

Belvin Perry, Jr.
Chief Judge

07–96–19–03. MEDIA

IN THE CIRCUIT COURT OF THE NINTH JUDICIAL CIRCUIT, IN AND FOR ORANGE AND OSCEOLA COUNTIES, FLORIDA

ADMINISTRATIVE ORDER NO. 07–96–19–03

AMENDED ADMINISTRATIVE ORDER GOVERNING MEDIA

WHEREAS, pursuant to Article V, Section 2(d) of the Florida Constitution and section 43.26, Florida Statutes, the chief judge of each judicial circuit is charged with the authority and the power to do everything necessary to promote the prompt and efficient administration of justice; and

WHEREAS, the Florida Supreme Court has promulgated rules entitled "Technological Coverage of Judicial Proceedings;" and

WHEREAS, media coverage of public judicial proceedings is "[s]ubject at all times to the authority of the presiding judge to: (i) control the conduct of proceedings before the court; (ii) ensure decorum and prevent distractions; and (iii) ensure the fair administration of justice in the pending cause," Fla. R. Jud. Admin. 2.450(a); and

WHEREAS, the Court must balance the constitutional right to a free press with the constitutional right to a fair trial; and

WHEREAS, special interest/high visibility proceedings require procedures and special accommodations to ensure full access without compromising the right of any litigant to a fair and orderly trial; and

WHEREAS, the standards must contain certain safeguards to ensure media coverage will not detract from or degrade court proceedings, impair or interrupt the orderly procedures of the Court, or otherwise interfere with a fair trial; and

WHEREAS, the lack of a uniform, state-wide definition for media that has kept pace with the dramatic and rapidly evolving use of new technologies, forums and mediums for gathering and disseminating information and news to the public has posed significant challenges. Traditional media such as newspaper, television and radio are relatively easy to identify and define. However, with the advent of the Internet, a new type of media not directly associated with television, radio or newspaper has developed which has not yet been addressed by court rule or by the Florida Supreme Court; and

WHEREAS, it is within the Court's discretion whether to permit the use of laptop computers or similar devices during a court proceeding. There is no court rule or statute specifically allowing laptop computers or similar devices in a courtroom.[1] Therefore, the media must be required to display a court-issued media authorization card for the privilege of using equipment that is not generally allowed otherwise. These court-issued media authorization cards are the most effective and least burdensome method available to allow court security to instantly identify those who may utilize certain specified equipment without unduly interfering with their primary duty of providing security; and

WHEREAS, the presiding judge has the authority to determine whether the case he or she is presiding over is a special interest/high profile case and to determine whether to invoke the special interest/high profile case procedures established by this Order;

NOW, THEREFORE, I, Frederick J. Lauten, in order to facilitate the efficient operation of the administration of justice, and pursuant to the authority vested in me as Chief Judge of the Ninth Judicial Circuit of Florida under Florida Rule of Judicial Administration 2.215, hereby order that, **effective immediately** unless otherwise provided herein, to continue until further order, and superseding any provisions in prior Administrative Orders which may be inconsistent:

I. GENERAL PROVISIONS APPLICABLE TO ALL MEDIA FOR ALL PROCEEDINGS:

Definition of Media and Media Authorization Cards

(a) Media Defined. For purposes of this Order, "media" is defined as: 1) traditional print and broadcast communication channels, such as radio and television, newspapers, and magazines, through which news and information is disseminated that reach or influence people widely, and 2) the next generation of digital, computerized or networked information and communication technologies, not directly associated with traditional print and/or broadcast media entities and defined as:

> An online entity which was a previously established, independent site that contains regularly updated original news content above and beyond links, forums, troubleshooting tips and reader contributions; said content is thoroughly reviewed by an independent editor before publication; has a readership of more than 1,000 hits per month; and has previously covered the judicial branch for the six (6) months immediately prior to requesting authorization cards. Fan sites, web logs or blogs and portable websites do not qualify as media.

The requesting media entity must show proof it meets the definition of media. The Court, via Court Administration, will determine whether an entity is media. To obtain media authorization cards,[2] those media entities meeting the definition as set forth in section I(a)2 above must submit the following, as well as any additional information which may be requested:

1. Links to two bylined articles clearly displaying publication title and published within the past six (6) months of the date of request; and

2. Either a copy of the current masthead or business card with the name, title and media entity's logo or a copy of the online publication homepage and the masthead page with the media representative's name and title appearing in an editorial capacity or an official letter of assignment from the media entity; and

3. Proof the judicial branch or the case at issue has been covered for at least the six months prior to the date of request.

(b) Credentials and Media Authorization Card. All media representatives must exhibit media credentials and a court-issued media authorization card while utilizing any permitted device, including pool camera while in a courtroom. If a media representative loses his or her authorization card, he or she must immediately notify Court Administration. There is a $20.00 fee to replace lost authorization cards. Authorization cards cannot be transferred to others. Loaning another individual an authorization card will result in the loss of that authorization card and all media privileges to use electronic devices. There is a limit of ten (10) authorization cards per each media agency at no cost. Additional authorization cards may be purchased for $20.00 each.

Application must be made to Court Administration to receive media authorization cards. Media authorization cards are valid through the end of the two (2) year renewal period. Additional information regarding application procedure, renewal guidelines and other rules and requirements may be found on the Ninth Judicial Circuit Court's website.

Media authorization cards must be surrendered at the direction of the presiding judge, Court Administration, the Orange County Sheriff's Office, the Osceola County Sheriff's Office, or at the end of the two (2) year renewal period.

Conduct

(c) All media representatives must read this Administrative Order and Florida Rule of Judicial Administration 2.450 governing technological coverage of judicial proceedings, as well as all Administrative Orders governing cellular telephones and other portable electronic devices in courtrooms.

(d) All media representatives must exhibit proper courtroom decorum and dress professionally at all times. There is no eating, drinking or gum chewing in court proceedings.

(e) As outlined in Rule 2.450, only one video recording device and operator, one still camera and operator, and one audio recording device and operator are permitted to cover a court proceeding unless additional equipment is authorized by the presiding judge. Additional video recording devices, including those not turned on or recording, must remain outside the courtroom. Credentialed media may use cell phones pursuant to Administrative Order 2014–04–01, as may be amended, but not to record audio or video of any proceedings. Use of an "on-board" microphone is prohibited by anyone, including the pool camera. Use of laptop computers in the courtroom is permitted as provided by separate Administrative Order. Cabling of extension cords and power supplies is prohibited in the courtroom, except by the pool camera. All media representatives may view open proceedings provided there is available seating. Unless otherwise specified by the presiding judge, seating for media representatives is on a first-come basis.

(f) Media access to a courtroom is granted at the time the deputy opens the courtroom to the public. All media equipment is subject to search at any time. All set-up and breakdown of cameras and recording devices must be done when court is not in session or during breaks. Media may not set-up once a proceeding has begun. Video cameras must be operated from a tripod. Cameras and recording devices must operate silently and not produce distracting light. Photographers must position themselves near the courtroom media panel unless otherwise designated by the judge. Still photographers shall not shoot video, unless no other video camera is present. When recording video, still photographers must coordinate with other media to share pool video footage, photographs, and other recordings. Media representatives shall not engage in any movement or discussions that attract undue attention.

(g) For court proceedings held outside of the courthouse, such as jury viewings of the scene of the crime, the media shall comply with the instructions of the presiding judge, Court Administration, and the Orange or Osceola County Sheriffs' Offices.

(h) Assignment of a video and/or still pool camera is the sole responsibility of the media. The video pool camera operator must provide BNC and XLR cables to feed signal into the courtroom media panel to serve as a pool camera. The pool operator must contact the AV Department at the number listed on the panel, regardless of whether any other media entity is present at the courthouse facilities, to coordinate routing of the signal to other media. The pool camera operator must also visibly display a court-issued media authorization card while present in any courtroom. All pool audio is provided by the courtroom microphones and requires an XLR cable to plug into the media panel. Placement or use of additional microphones is prohibited without prior approval of the presiding judge and Court Administration. Additional camera lighting is also prohibited in the courtroom.

(i) Still photographers serving as the pool must coordinate with other media to share pool video footage, photographs, and other recordings.

(j) Use of portable signal distribution systems (e.g. portable microwave systems, streaming devices, etc.) are prohibited within the courthouse facility without advance notice to the Chief Judge and Court Administration. Direct live streaming is strictly prohibited from any courtroom. All streaming signals must be sourced through the media pedestal or from the designated media room. Additionally, all audio must be sourced from the medial panel audio. Use of "streaming backpacks" or the streaming feature of any camera within a courtroom is strictly prohibited.

Contact Court Administration via email at ctadkl1@ocnjcc.org or ctadjs1@ocnjcc.org to coordinate notice of live streaming requests twenty-four (24) hours prior to the court event.

(k) Media representatives may not cover "side bar" or "bench" conferences. There shall be no recording or broadcast of conferences that occur in court between attorneys and their clients, between co-counsel, or between counsel and the presiding judge held at the bench. Interviews of jurors after their release from service is at the individual juror's discretion.

(*l*) So as not to interfere with court proceedings or with a litigant's rights, no interviews shall be permitted in the presence of a juror or prospective jurors. No interviews are permitted within any courthouse facility which unreasonably interferes with the safety, security, or movement of persons in any courtroom, doorway, hallway, and other areas of any courthouse facility, or which disrupts any court proceeding. Additionally, media representatives shall not station themselves or their equipment in public areas of the courthouse in any manner that unreasonably interferes with the safety, security, or movement of persons or which is disruptive to any court proceeding to be determined on a case-by-case basis at the discretion of Court Administration or the Sheriff's Department. Further, when court is not in session, media may not film in courtrooms without prior permission from Court Administration.

(m) A media room (room #230 in the Orange County Courthouse and room #1905 of the Osceola County Courthouse) is available to credentialed media representatives during regular business hours. Use of this room and its distribution feeds is on a first-come basis. Media representatives are expected to utilize this room for professional business only.

(n) At the Orange County Courthouse, a media pedestal for connection to "live trucks" is available at the courtyard semicircle located adjacent to Orange Avenue. Media vehicles may only park in the lane closest to the courthouse. Vehicles parked in the lane farthest from the courthouse, on sidewalks, or along Orange Avenue are subject to being towed. At the Osceola County Courthouse, a media pedestal is provided off Patrick Street with parking available in the public parking spaces on Patrick Street. At the Orange County Booking and Release Center, a pedestal is located in the parking lot outside the main entrance with limited parking available. At the Thomas S. Kirk Juvenile Justice Center no media pedestal is available. Media representatives interested in covering proceedings at this facility must arrange among themselves to share pool video footage, photographs, and audio recordings. Media cabling and equipment cannot cross or block vehicle lanes or walkways at any courthouse facility. Please note, in those courtrooms at the Orange County Courthouse that do not have the necessary feed, interested media must share pool video, footage, photographs, and audio recording when covering proceedings held in such locations.

(*o*) Media representatives wishing to utilize the Court's infrastructure in Orange County to send/receive audio and video signals must contact Court Administration's Audio/Visual Department at least twenty-four (24) hours prior to the court event to ensure timely routing of signal. Requests for signal routing should be made to 407–836–0522. Media representatives should leave their name, contact number, and the requested signal path on the automated system, which will then page the on-call engineer to fill the request. In Osceola County signal routing requests may be made by calling 407–742–2488 twenty-four (24) hours prior to the scheduled court event. Media representatives are strongly encouraged to also contact Court Administration via email at: ctadkl1@ocnjcc.org to ensure a smooth facilitation of their needs twenty-four (24) hours prior to the scheduled court event.

(p) No media member is allowed to use his or her media credentials in any proceeding in which he or she is a party or in which he or she has a personal interest such as a relative's proceeding. No member of the media is allowed to video, record, photograph, or in any way report any proceeding in which he or she is a party or in which he or she has a personal interest such as a relative's proceeding. No person, including members of the media, is allowed to hire, retain or otherwise engage a company, person or other entity qualifying as media to video, record, photograph, or in any way report any proceeding in which he or she is a party or in which he or she has a personal interest such as a relative's proceeding.

II. ADDITIONAL PROCEDURES FOR SPECIAL INTEREST/HIGH PROFILE PROCEEDINGS:

(a) The Chief Judge may instruct Court Administration to implement the Special Interest/High Profile Procedures set forth in this Administrative Order.

(b) Upon implementation of these procedures, Court Administration will, as soon as practicable, convene a meeting of interested media representatives for the purpose of creating a media committee to establish protocols for the specific case.

(c) The committee shall consist of at least one print media representative, one television broadcast media representative, and one audio broadcast representative, as well as a member of Court Administration. Additionally, representatives from facilities, court operations, the Clerk of Court's Office, the Court Audio/Visual Department, and local law enforcement may be asked to sit on the committee as deemed necessary.

(d) The duties of the media committee shall include: Selection of a media representative to act as a liaison between the media and the Court for the duration of the case; designation of the pool camera positions in accordance with Florida Rule of Judicial Administration 2.450; evaluation of parking needs and availability and, if necessary, facilitate a lottery system for media parking; evaluation of available courtroom seating and, if necessary, facilitate a lottery system for media seating in the courtroom; determination of a process for dissemination of information to include timely access to examine and photograph submitted evidence; coordinate notices for live streaming; and identification of other special needs regarding media credentials, access through courthouse security, staging of equipment, additional power requirements, and any other issue.

(e) At all times, the procedures set forth in this Administrative Order are subject to the authority of the presiding judge who may modify these procedures to control the conduct of pending proceedings, ensure the fair administration of justice, or ensure public safety.

Administrative Order 07–96–19–02 is vacated and set aside except to the extent that it has been incorporated and/or amended herein. Vacating an Administrative Order that vacates a prior Order does not revive the prior Order.

DONE AND ORDERED at Orlando, Florida, this 26th day of November, 2018.

Frederick J. Lauten
Chief Judge

1 As used herein, the word "courtroom" includes courtrooms, hearing rooms and any other rooms used to conduct court proceedings, unless specifically stated otherwise.

2 A limited number of temporary media authorization cards may be available on a case-by-case basis.

07–96–12. [VACATED BY ADMINISTRATIVE ORDER NO. 2016-24, EFFECTIVE AUGUST 18, 2016]

07–96–06. [VACATED BY ADMINISTRATIVE ORDER NO. 2016–24, EFFECTIVE AUGUST 18, 2016]

07–94–53. [VACATED AND SET ASIDE BY ORDER 2017-08, EFFECTIVE AUGUST 16, 2017.]

07–93–58–07. MOVEMENT OF SELECTED INMATES INTO COMMUNITY CORRECTIONS PROGRAMS, ORANGE COUNTY

IN THE CIRCUIT COURT OF THE NINTH JUDICIAL CIRCUIT IN AND FOR ORANGE COUNTY, FLORIDA

ADMINISTRATIVE ORDER NO. 07–93–58–07

AMENDED ORDER GOVERNING THE MOVEMENT OF SELECTED INMATES INTO COMMUNITY CORRECTIONS PROGRAMS, ORANGE COUNTY

WHEREAS, there is a need to allow the Orange County Corrections Department to place selected inmates, described below, into certain community corrections programs administered by the Department without seeking further judicial intervention in the case;

NOW, THEREFORE, I, Belvin Perry, Jr., pursuant to the authority vested in me as Chief Judge of the Ninth Judicial Circuit of Florida under Florida Rule of Judicial Administration 2.215, do hereby order that the following procedures and standards are amended as follows, **effective immediately**, in all matters involving the movement of selected inmates into community corrections programs of the Orange County Corrections Department:

I. GENERAL PROVISIONS:

Offenders who meet the criteria below, and who have served one-third or thirty (30) days, whichever is less, of the specified jail sentence, may be placed in the community corrections programs specified in this Order. If, when sentencing an offender or issuing an arrest warrant based upon an alleged violation of probation, any judge either "recommends" work release or indicates "no objection" to work release, then the offender may immediately be placed at the Work Release Center (without first serving any part of the specified sentence), so long as he or she otherwise meets the criteria below, at the reasonable discretion of the Orange County Corrections Department.

Any judge of the Circuit or County Court may prevent the release of any offender whom the judge feels should not be released into any community corrections program described in this Order by so indicating on the sentencing document.

If the Orange County Jail finds that an offender does not qualify pursuant to the criteria established in this Order, after being so ordered by the presiding judge, the jail must notify the presiding judge, in writing (including the offender's prior convictions and case numbers and any other pertinent information), with a detailed explanation of the reasons the offender does not qualify. The jail shall also copy the administrative judge for that division and the Chief Judge. Said notification may be sent via e-mail, read receipt, with copy to the court file.

NO OFFENDER WILL BE ACCEPTED INTO ANY PROGRAM AS CONTEMPLATED BY THIS ORDER IF THE ORANGE COUNTY JAIL FINDS THAT THE OFFENDER DOES NOT QUALIFY PURSUANT TO THE CRITERIA CONTAINED HEREIN.

II. OFFENSE CRITERIA:

A. Offense: Offenders who are sentenced for misdemeanors, traffic offenses, and second and third degree felonies will be considered eligible for participation in the Corrections Department programs, as established in this Order. However, offenders whose instant offense is of a violent nature (with the exception of battery in domestic violence cases in which the victim agrees to the release), involves the abuse of children, involves a felony sex offense, or involves the use of a deadly weapon in the commission of a crime, will not be eligible for an extension of the limits of confinement under the terms of this Order, regardless of whether adjudication was withheld. Specifically, the following crimes will not be accepted under the terms of this Order:

Any Homicide
Any Robbery
Any Sexual Battery
Any Child Abuse/Neglect
Any Offense of Lewd Act in the Presence of a Minor
Any Trafficking in Controlled Substances
Any Offense involving the use of a deadly weapon
Any Criminal or Civil Contempt of Court (excluding civil contempt in child support cases and writs of attachment for Collections Court) Arson
Any Offense of Extortion with an Element of Threat or Coercion

B. Prior Record:

1. Offender has not been convicted in the last eight (8) years of a felony offense involving violence, the use of a weapon, any felony sex offense, or any offense involving the abuse of children.

2. Offender has not been convicted of more than three (3) non-violent felony offenses in the last five (5) years, excluding the instant offense.

3. Offender has not been designated as a sexual predator pursuant to Section 775.21(5), Florida Statutes, or required to register as a sexual offender pursuant to Section 943.0435, Florida Statutes.

III. HEALTH CRITERIA:

A. **Physical Condition:** Offenders with a serious medical condition, requiring frequent care will not be eligible for participation in any Corrections program, as detailed in this Order.

B. Offenders who are identified as acutely psychotic, severely mentally retarded, currently suicidal, or otherwise unable to cope with the program structure or understand the program conditions, will not be eligible for any Corrections program, as detailed in this Order.

IV. OTHER CRITERIA:

No inmate wanted by another jurisdiction will be accepted into a program unless that jurisdiction has specified that they will not pick-up or extradite. Inmates serving a sentence for additional charges that do not meet the program requirements will not be accepted. Inmates with a current protection order (injunction for protection) will be accepted if they meet all other criteria and the injunction was issued three (3) or more years previously; the current charge is not domestic violence; and there have been no arrests of violation of injunction or domestic violence within the past three (3) years. Additionally, any inmate who poses a security hazard for reasons including, but not limited to, disciplinary confinement or confirmed gang membership may not be accepted into a program.

V. PROGRAMS INCLUDED:

The only program included in the Corrections Department which may accept offenders under the terms of this Order is the Work Release Center.

VI. DRUG COURT PARTICIPANTS:

Drug Court participants may be placed in any Corrections program specified in this Order without having served any part of a jail sentence.

VII. REVOCATIONS:

Offenders who fail to comply with the conditions of the program in which they have been placed are subject to be returned to the jail to serve the balance of the sentence originally imposed. The Orange County Corrections Department must hold an administrative hearing to determine whether an offender has violated the conditions of the program, but is not required to seek an arrest warrant or capias to return the offender to jail in the case of a violation of program conditions.

VIII. ESCAPE:

In those cases in which the offender cannot be located to return for an administrative hearing, the Orange County Corrections Department will seek a capias or warrant for the offender's arrest. In so doing, the Work Release Center will formally advance the capias or warrant within 24 hours of the inmate's failure to return.

Administrative Order No. 07–93–58–06 is vacated and set aside and has been incorporated and/or amended herein.

DONE AND ORDERED at Orlando, Florida, this 2nd day of April, 2013.

Belvin Perry, Jr.
Chief Judge

07–93–43–02. STANDARDS AND PROCEDURES FOR THE PROTECTION OF MINORS

IN THE CIRCUIT COURT OF THE NINTH JUDICIAL CIRCUIT, IN AND FOR ORANGE AND OSCEOLA COUNTIES, FLORIDA

ADMINISTRATIVE ORDER NO. 07–93–43–02

AMENDED ADMINISTRATIVE ORDER RE: STANDARDS AND PROCEDURES FOR THE PROTECTION OF MINORS IN THE SETTLEMENT OF PERSONAL INJURY, WRONGFUL DEATH AND MEDICAL MALPRACTICE LAWSUITS AND CLAIMS

WHEREAS, there is a need to establish uniform standards and procedures for the protection of minors in the settlement of personal injury, wrongful death and medical malpractice lawsuits wherein minors are among the claimants; and in settlements which have not involved the filing of a lawsuit;

NOW, THEREFORE, I, Belvin Perry, Jr., pursuant to the authority vested in me as Chief Judge of the Ninth Judicial Circuit of Florida under Florida Rule of Judicial Administration 2.050, do hereby order that the following procedures and standards are hereby adopted in all matters involving the settlement of personal injury, wrongful death and medical malpractice lawsuits ("filed action") or claims not the subject of a lawsuit ("unfiled actions") arising wherein one or more minors are involved:

Part I

Petitions for Approval of a Settlement of a Minor shall be filed in a pending action in the **Civil Division** or independently in the **Probate Division** when no pending action exists in the Civil Division, pursuant to **Florida Probate Rule 5.636 & the Uniform Administrative Policies and Procedures of the Civil Division**. If a **Legal Guardianship** preexists the filing of the **Petition for Approval of Settlement of a Minor,** and the Petition was filed in a pending action within the Civil Division, the Civil Division judge may transfer the Petition to the division where the Legal Guardianship exists.

Part II

A. **When the amount involved in the claim on behalf of the minor does not exceed $15,000.00,** the natural guardian or guardians may settle and consummate a settlement of a minor without court approval, pursuant to section 744.301(2), Florida Statutes. However, if a party requests court approval, and the amount involved is $15,000 or less, then the **Probate Division** shall have jurisdiction to authorize disbursements, determine the need for a depository, or take any necessary action to protect the minor's interests. The Court shall consider the appropriateness of requiring the natural guardian or guardians to establish a designated financial institution/depository to receive the minor's funds, pursuant to section 69.031, Florida Statutes.

B. When the gross settlement for the claim of the minor exceeds $15,000.00 but is less than $25,000.00, then a **Guardian Ad Litem** may be appointed, pursuant to **section 744.301(4)(a), Florida Statutes.** Counsel for the natural guardian(s) should determine if the Civil Division Judge before which the case is pending chooses to have a Guardian Ad Litem appointed to represent the minor's interests and if so, the Court will appoint a Guardian Ad Litem to represent the minor's interest.

C. In a case where the amount of the gross settlement involving the minor equals or exceeds $25,000.00, a **Guardian Ad Litem shall** be appointed, pursuant to section **744.301(4)(a), Florida Statutes.** The Guardian Ad Litem shall represent the interest of the minor or minors with respect to the petition and shall file a report, pursuant to Florida Probate Rule 5.636(f).

D. If a Legal Guardianship preexists the filing of the Petition for Approval of Settlement of a Minor and the judge finds that the existing **Legal Guardian** has no potential adverse interest to the minor, the Court need not appoint a Guardian Ad Litem to represent the minor's interest, unless the Court determines the appointment is otherwise necessary, pursuant to **section 744.301(4)(a), Florida Statutes**. The Court may require the **Legal Guardian** to file the same report that is required of a guardian ad litem, pursuant to Florida Probate Rule 5.636(f).

Part III

A. If the net settlement to the minor exceeds $15,000.00, said order shall require the establishment of **a legal guardianship** and the appointment of **a Guardian of the Property** to receive the minor's settlement share, pursuant to **section 744.387, Florida Statutes.** After the guardianship is established and the attorney's trust account is in receipt of the funds, the **Probate Division Judge** shall then direct further disbursement of the minor's funds from the attorney's trust account to the guardianship.

B. The Civil Division Judge may consider the appropriateness of waiving the establishment of **a legal guardianship** for settlements when recommended by the Guardian Ad Litem and when:

(a) a structured settlement or binding annuity is requested by the natural guardians and the structured settlement is recommended by the Guardian Ad Litem or

(b) the net proceeds are to be deposited in a financial institution/depository pursuant to section 69.031, Florida Statutes, and subject to release only upon order of the court. A receipt from the depository is to be filed with the court.

Counsel should be prepared to demonstrate to the Court why waiving a **legal guardianship** would be in the best interest of the minor.

C. Upon entry of the order appointing a Guardian of the Property and directing payment of the settlement proceeds to the guardianship, the responsibilities of the **Guardian Ad Litem** shall be considered completed. Upon petition served on all interested persons, the Civil Division Judge shall enter an order discharging the **Guardian Ad Litem.**

Part IV

Upon approval of the settlement amount and the apportionment thereof, the Civil Division Judge shall enter an appropriate order which shall authorize the payment of the gross settlement proceeds into an interest-bearing trust account under the control and supervision of the attorney for the Plaintiff with directions as to its disbursement.

Part V

A. Matters to be considered in determining if settlement is in the best interest of the minor:

1. Liability aspects;
2. Damages–evaluation;
3. Insurance coverage and/or individual assets;
4. Apportionment among the beneficiaries—section 768.25, Florida Statutes;
5. Attorney fees and costs—reasonableness—Nixon v. Bryson, 488 So. 2d 607 (Fla. 3d DCA 1986);
6. Consider if future withdrawals from depository would be handled by attorney without charge where no guardianship exists;
7. Relevant statutes and rules to consider: **Florida Statutes, sections 744.301, 744.387, 69.031, 768.23,** and **768.25,** and **Florida Probate Rules 5.636** and **5.555.**

This Administrative Order amends Administrative Order No. 07–93–43–1 and is effective immediately.

DONE AND ORDERED at Orlando, Florida, this 18th day of August, 2005.

Belvin Perry, Jr.
Chief Judge

07–92–17. [VACATED BY ADMINISTRATIVE ORDER NO. 2016–24, EFFECTIVE AUGUST 18, 2016]

07–91–40–01. OPERATING POLICY FOR THE ACCEPTANCE OF JUVENILES BY JAIL FACILITIES

ADMINISTRATIVE ORDER NO. 07–91–40–01

IN THE CIRCUIT COURT OF THE NINTH JUDICIAL CIRCUIT, IN AND FOR ORANGE AND OSCEOLA COUNTIES, FLORIDA

AMENDED ORDER ON OPERATING POLICY FOR THE ACCEPTANCE OF JUVENILES BY JAIL FACILITIES CONSISTENT WITH THE FEDERAL JUVENILE JUSTICE AND DELINQUENCY PREVENTION ACT OF 1974 AND FLORIDA STATUTES, CHAPTER 985

WHEREAS, The Federal Juvenile Justice Delinquency Prevention (JJDP) Act of 1974, as amended [42 U.S.C. 5601, et. seq.], was adopted by the U.S. Congress in order to establish a comprehensive nationwide program of juvenile delinquency prevention, offender rehabilitation and juvenile justice improvements; and

WHEREAS, States which receive JJDP funds are required to comply with the mandates contained in the JJDP Act of which Florida receives the benefits of the Federal JJDP Program; and

WHEREAS, The State's continued funding in this area is contingent upon compliance with this Act;

NOW, THEREFORE, I, Belvin Perry, Jr., pursuant to the authority vested in me as Chief Judge of the Ninth Judicial Circuit of Florida under Florida Rule of Judicial Administration 2.215, do hereby order that the following procedures, which originally became effective on June 10, 1992, in order to effectuate orderly and efficient compliance with Federal and State Law, for the acceptance of juveniles into the Orange and Osceola County Jails, are amended as follows, effective immediately, unless otherwise provided herein:

A juvenile who has not been transferred to the adult system by felony direct file or waiver, grand jury indictment, or has not been found to have previously committed an offense as an adult and received adult sanctions, may be held in temporary custody for a period not to exceed six hours in a secure booking area of the jail for the purpose of awaiting release, fingerprinting and/or photographing the juvenile, or awaiting appropriate transport to the Department of Juvenile Justice pursuant to section 985.115(3), Florida Statutes. Juvenile misdemeanant offenders transferred for criminal prosecution pursuant to section 985.565, Florida Statutes, shall not be detained or held in the Orange or Osceola County Jail for more than six hours. Unless a juvenile is wanted in another jurisdiction for prosecution as an adult, or is convicted of a traffic offense involving death or personal injury, a juvenile shall not be placed in the Orange or Osceola County Jail unless one of the following documents is present:

Indicted Juvenile. The Arrest and Booking Report shall be accompanied by the grand jury indictment.

Waived Juvenile. The Arrest and Booking Report shall be accompanied by a copy of the transfer order certifying that the juvenile has been transferred on felony charges for prosecution as an adult.

Direct Filed Juvenile. The Arrest and Booking Report Shall be accompanied by a certificate of filing of direct information on felony charges by the State Attorney.

Previously Adjudicated Juvenile. Any juvenile who has previously been found to have committed an offense as an adult, on either felony or misdemeanor charges, and the court imposed adult sanctions, may be treated as an adult on any subsequent arrest. The arrest and booking report should reflect the date of the prior adult court disposition and sanctions. This date must be verified by jail staff or authorized court designee at the earliest opportunity.

Juvenile Contempt Citations. Juveniles cited with contempt of court shall be detained pursuant to the court order. All juveniles charged with contempt of court are entitled to bond as set by the court. Juveniles found by the court to be in contempt of court shall be detained pursuant to the order of the court.

When a minor is taken into custody for a criminal traffic offense or a driver license violation, law enforcement is required to make every reasonable effort to notify the minor's parents, guardian or responsible adult relative of the action taken. After making every reasonable effort to give notice and release the juvenile within the six-hour requirement, the arresting officer shall follow the provisions of section 316.635(3), Florida Statutes, in effecting the release of the juvenile within the six-hour period. This can include: The issuance of a notice to appear and subsequent release of the minor with a court date to a parent, guardian, responsible adult relative or other responsible adult within six hours; The issuance of a notice to appear and subsequent release of the minor through a bond process; The issuance of a notice to appear and delivery of the minor to an appropriate substance abuse treatment or rehabilitation facility or refer the juvenile to an appropriate medical facility. If the juvenile cannot be delivered to such a facility, the arresting officer may deliver the juvenile to an appropriate intake office of the Department of Juvenile Justice which shall take custody of the juvenile and make any appropriate referrals; or, if the violation constitutes a felony, and the minor cannot be released on bail, transport or deliver the juvenile to an appropriate Department of Juvenile Justice intake office. The Department shall assume custody. A minor shall not be imprisoned for a traffic offense in an adult jail except upon conviction of an offense involving death or personal injury.

I FURTHER DIRECT that juveniles arrested on capias for traffic offenses who are not issued a notice to appear; not released to their parents; not transferred to the Department of Juvenile Justice; or not bonded out, be released pursuant to the six-hour requirement of the Juvenile Justice Delinquency Prevention Act and Florida Statutes.

Administrative Order 07–91–40 is vacated and set aside and has been incorporated and/or amended herein.

DONE AND ORDERED in Chambers at Orlando, Orange County, Florida, this 30th day of March, 2007.

Belvin Perry, Jr.
Chief Judge

07–84–06–01. LIMITS ON INTERVIEWS OF CHILD AND SEXUAL ABUSE VICTIMS UNDER SIXTEEN YEARS OF AGE OR PERSONS WITH MENTAL RETARDATION

ADMINISTRATIVE ORDER NO. 07–84–06–01

IN THE CIRCUIT COURT OF THE NINTH JUDICIAL CIRCUIT, IN AND FOR ORANGE AND OSCEOLA COUNTIES, FLORIDA

AMENDED ADMINISTRATIVE ORDER GOVERNING LIMITS ON INTERVIEWS OF CHILD AND SEXUAL ABUSE VICTIMS UNDER SIXTEEN YEARS OF AGE OR PERSONS WITH MENTAL RETARDATION

WHEREAS, pursuant to Article V, Section 2(d) of the Florida Constitution and section 43.26, Florida Statutes, the chief judge of each judicial circuit is charged with the authority and the power to do everything necessary to promote the prompt and efficient administration of justice; and

WHEREAS, the Florida Legislature originally enacted section 914.16, Florida Statutes, effective October 1, 1984; and

WHEREAS, section 914.16, Florida Statutes, reads as follows:

> The chief judge of each judicial circuit, after consultation with the state attorney and the public defender for the judicial circuit, the appropriate chief law enforcement officer, and any other person deemed appropriate by the chief judge, shall provide by order reasonable limits on the number of interviews that a victim of a violation of s. 794.011, s. 800.04, s. 827.03, or s. 847.0135(5) who is under 16 years of age or a victim of a violation of s. 794.011, s. 800.02, s. 800.03, or s. 825.102 who is a person with mental retardation as defined in s. 393.063 must submit to for law enforcement or discovery purposes. The order shall, to the extent possible, protect the victim from the psychological damage of repeated interrogations while preserving the rights of the public, the victim, and the person charged with the violation.

WHEREAS, it is necessary to promote the continued implementation of the provisions of section 914.16, Florida Statutes, to protect child abuse and sexual abuse victims under age sixteen, as first considered and realized by Administrative Order 07-84-06 effective October 1, 1984; and

WHEREAS, I, Belvin Perry, Jr., Chief Judge of the Ninth Judicial Circuit of Florida, pursuant to section 914.16, Florida Statutes, met and consulted with the appropriate parties in order access the current state and feasibility of limits on interviews of child abuse and sexual abuse victims under age sixteen or persons with mental retardation previously formulated and contained in Administrative Order 07-84-06;

NOW, THEREFORE, I, Belvin Perry, Jr., in order to continue the limits and standards as established in Administrative Order 07-84-06 in accordance with section 914.16, Florida Statutes, and pursuant to the authority vested in me as Chief Judge of the Ninth Judicial Circuit of Florida under Florida Rule of Judicial Administration 2.215, hereby order that, effective immediately:

1. All law enforcement agencies in the Ninth Judicial Circuit of Florida shall whenever possible coordinate and consolidate the initial and subsequent interviews of an alleged victim of a violation of sections 794.011, 800.04, 827.03, or 847.0135(5), Florida Statutes, who is under sixteen years of age, or a victim of a violation of sections 794.011, 800.02, 800.03, or 825.102, Florida Statutes, who is a person with mental retardation as defined in section 393.063, Florida Statutes.

2. In order to carry out the intent of section 914.16, Florida Statutes, Orange and Osceola Counties have established Children's Advocacy Centers which coordinate and cooperate in the response and investigation of victim interviews covered by section 914.16, Florida Statutes. Each county has also established a Sexual Assault Response Team, which includes the Children's Advocacy Centers as partner agencies. The Sexual Assault Response Teams have established protocols that require, to the extent possible, that only one interview be conducted of victims during the investigative stage of the case.

3. Whenever possible initial examinations and interviews of such child abuse or sexual abuse victims shall be preserved by audio-visual equipment in order to prevent repetition through multiple interviews.

4. Courts of appropriate jurisdiction may consider further limitations upon application of any interested party.

5. Matters concerning defense discovery depositions shall be handled on a case by case basis by the court having jurisdiction of the case.

6. Whenever possible, where there are pending juvenile, civil or criminal cases which arise from the same incident of sexual or child abuse, discovery depositions shall be coordinated by all interested parties.

This Order shall remain in effect until further order of the Court. Administrative Order 07-84-06 is vacated and set aside and has been incorporated and/or amended herein.

DONE AND ORDERED at Orlando, Florida, this 11th day of July, 2008.

Belvin Perry, Jr.
Chief Judge

07-79-02. [VACATED BY ADMINISTRATIVE ORDER NO. 2016-24, EFFECTIVE AUGUST 18, 2016]

07-76-32. [VACATED BY ADMINISTRATIVE ORDER NO. 2016-24, EFFECTIVE AUGUST 18, 2016]

Eleventh Judicial Circuit (Miami–Dade County)

LOCAL RULES

ADMINISTRATIVE ORDERS

CIRCUIT COURT CIVIL

CIRCUIT COURT CRIMINAL

CIVIL TRAFFIC INFRACTION HEARING OFFICERS

COUNTY COURT CIVIL

04–05. RE–ESTABLISHMENT AND JURISDICTION OF COUNTY COURT DISTRICTS.

COURT ADMINISTRATION

18–02. ALTERNATIVE SANCTIONS PROGRAM.

18–01. CREATION OF SECTION PMH 06 IN THE PROBATE DIVISION OF THE ELEVENTH JUDICIAL CIRCUIT OF FLORIDA.

17–11. REAFFIRMATION OF THE CREATION OF COMPLEX BUSINESS LITIGATION IN THE CIRCUIT CIVIL DIVISION OF THE ELEVENTH JUDICIAL CIRCUIT OF FLORIDA.

17–02. ESTABLISHING CERTAIN FILING AND OTHER PROCEDURES IN THE CIRCUIT APPELLATE DIVISION, TO INCLUDE EMAIL SERVICE OF COURT DOCUMENTS AND E–FILING BY REGISTERED USERS OF FLORIDA COURTS E–FILING PORTAL.

16–14. ESTABLISHMENT OF VETERANS TREATMENT COURT.

16–12. [RESCINDED BY ORDER 17-11, EFFECTIVE JANUARY 2, 2018].

16–11. CERTIFICATION AND REGULATION OF CERTIFIED CIVIL PROCESS SERVERS WITHIN THE ELEVENTH JUDICIAL CIRCUIT.

16–07. COMPENSATION OF COURT APPOINTED COUNSEL AND CASE RELATED EXPENSES IN CASES INVOLVING THE INVOLUNTARY CIVIL COMMITMENT OF SEXUALLY VIOLENT PREDATORS.

16–04. ESTABLISHMENT OF PROCEDURES FOR TRANSFERRING RELATED CASES FROM THE COUNTY COURT CIVIL DIVISION TO THE CIRCUIT COURT CIVIL DIVISION.

16–03. REASSIGNMENT/TRANSFER OF RELATED CASES IN THE JUVENILE, DOMESTIC RELATIONS AND DOMESTIC VIOLENCE DIVISIONS TO THE UNIFIED FAMILY COURT DIVISION.

16–02. REAFFIRMATION OF UNIFIED FAMILY COURT PLAN AND ESTABLISHMENT OF PROCEDURES FOR UNIFIED FAMILY COURT DIVISION IN THE ELEVENTH JUDICIAL CIRCUIT OF FLORIDA.

14–12. RE–ESTABLISHMENT OF PROCEDURE FOR APPOINTMENT OF COUNSEL IN CRIMINAL AND CIVIL PROCEEDINGS.

14–03. PROCEDURES TO PROHIBIT THE PURCHASE OF FIREARMS AND ELIGIBILITY TO APPLY FOR OR RETAIN A CONCEALED WEAPON OR FIREARMS LICENSE BY MENTALLY ILL PERSONS.

14–02. USE OF ELECTRONIC DEVICES IN THE COURTROOM AND COURT FACILITIES.

13–03 (A1). AMENDING DISPOSITION OF TOBACCO CASES.

13–03. DISPOSITION OF TOBACCO CASES.

13–01 (A1). [1] CREATION OF THE INTERNATIONAL COMMERCIAL ARBITRATION COURT IN THE CIRCUIT CIVIL DIVISION OF THE ELEVENTH JUDICIAL CIRCUIT OF FLORIDA AND PROCEDURES FOR THE ASSIGNMENT AND REASSIGNMENT OF CASES TO THE INTERNATIONAL COMMERCIAL ARBITRATION SECTION.

13–01. ESTABLISHMENT OF SECURITY BY-PASS PROGRAM FOR ATTORNEYS AT RICHARD E. GERSTEIN JUSTICE BUILDING.

12–01. TERMINATION OF MANDATORY RESIDENTIAL MORTGAGE FORECLOSURE MEDIATION PROGRAM; DESIGNATION OF OASIS ALLIANCE CORPORATION AS MEDIATION PROVIDER.

11–08. APPLICATION FEE FOR COURT–APPOINTED COUNSEL IN CIVIL PROCEEDINGS.

10–10. PROCEDURES AND CRITERIA FOR SEALING COURT RECORDS.

10–01 (A1). AMERICANS WITH DISABILITY ACT OF 1990–DESIGNATION OF ADA COORDINATOR, RE–ESTABLISHING NOTICE AND REQUEST FOR REASONABLE ACCOMMODATIONS REQUIREMENTS AND RE–ADOPTION OF GRIEVANCE PROCEDURE.

09–17. FORFEITURE/DISPOSAL OF ILLEGALLY TAKEN FISH AND WILDLIFE.

09–13 (A1). ENLARGEMENT AND EXPANSION OF THE CURRENT PILOT PROJECT FOR ELECTRONIC SUBMISSIONS OF COURTESY COPIES FOR UNIFORM MOTION CALENDAR AND REQUESTS FOR SPECIAL SET HEARINGS, EMERGENCY MOTIONS, AND PROPOSED ORDERS.

09–04 (A1). CLARIFICATION RE FEES—COSTS OF DEFENSE; APPLICATION FEE FOR COURT APPOINTED COUNSEL.

09–04. FEES—COSTS OF DEFENSE; APPLICATION FEE FOR COURT APPOINTED COUNSEL.

09–03. ABOLISHMENT OF SECTION 02 AND ESTABLISHING SECTION 05 OF THE PROBATE DIVISION OF THE ELEVENTH JUDICIAL CIRCUIT OF FLORIDA AND THE REASSIGNMENT OF CASES CURRENTLY IN SECTION 02 TO SECTION 05.

08–19. ELIMINATION OF SECTION 02 IN THE COUNTY COURT CIVIL DIVISION AND REASSIGNMENT OF CASES IN SECTION 02 TO SECTIONS 03 AND 04 IN SAID DIVISION.

08–18. RE–ESTABLISHMENT OF STANDARDS AND PROCEDURES FOR THE PROTECTION OF MINORS IN THE SETTLEMENT OF PERSONAL INJURY, WRONGFUL DEATH AND MEDICAL MALPRACTICE LAWSUITS AND CLAIMS.

08–14. REASSIGNMENT AND CONSOLIDATION OF PUBLIC DEFENDER'S MOTIONS TO APPOINT OTHER COUN-

SEL IN UNAPPOINTED NONCAPITAL FELONY CASES.

07–07. ESTABLISHING PROCEDURES, REVISING ORDER, CREATING AND MAINTAINING QUALIFIED ARBITRATORS AND RE–ESTABLISHING COMPENSATION FOR COURT APPOINTED ARBITRATORS.

07–04. PROCEDURES FOR APPOINTMENT OF APPELLATE COUNSEL IN DEPENDENCY APPEALS.

07–03. IMPLEMENTATION OF THE COMPLEX BUSINESS LITIGATION COURT PROCEDURES.

07–02 (A1). SUPPLEMENTAL PROCEDURES FOR SPECIAL INTEREST/HIGH VISIBILITY PROCEEDINGS AT RICHARD E. GERSTEIN JUSTICE BUILDING.

07–02. PROCEDURES FOR SPECIAL INTEREST/HIGH VISIBILITY PROCEEDINGS AT RICHARD E. GERSTEIN JUSTICE BUILDING.

06–41. ORDER REVISING CIVIL COVER SHEET.

06–40. CREATION OF SECTION 40 ("COMPLEX BUSINESS LITIGATION SECTION") IN THE GENERAL JURISDICTION DIVISION OF THE ELEVENTH JUDICIAL CIRCUIT OF FLORIDA.

06–09. EX PARTE MOTIONS TO COMPEL DISCOVERY IN CIVIL ACTIONS.

05–08 (A2). EXPANSION OF JUVENILE DRUG COURT.

05–08. EXPANSION OF JUVENILE DRUG COURT.

04–41. AUTHORIZATION FOR CLERK'S PARTIAL PAYMENT PROGRAM FOR FEES, SERVICE CHARGES, COSTS AND FINES.

03–02 (A1). ASBESTOS LITIGATION ELECTRONIC SERVICE PROGRAM.

03–02. ASBESTOS LITIGATION ELECTRONIC SERVICE PROGRAM.

03–01. [RESCINDED BY ADMINISTRATIVE ORDER NO. 16–07, EFFECTIVE MAY 4, 2016].

02–14 (A2). [RESCINDED BY ADMINISTRATIVE ORDER NO. 16–02, EFFECTIVE FEBRUARY 17, 2016].

2–14–01 (A1). ELEVENTH JUDICIAL CIRCUIT PROFESSIONALISM AND CIVILITY COMMITTEE AND LOCAL PROFESSIONALISM PANEL.

DOMESTIC VIOLENCE

13–07. PROCEDURES FOR THE ASSIGNMENT OF CRIMINAL CASES WITHIN THE DOMESTIC VIOLENCE DIVISION OF THE ELEVENTH JUDICIAL CIRCUIT OF FLORIDA.

08–01 (A1). AUTHORIZATION FOR CONTINUATION OF CIVIL/DOMESTIC VIOLENCE OVERFLOW BACK–UP SECTION.

FAMILY

15–04. ESTABLISHMENT OF REGISTRY FOR APPOINTMENT OF PROFESSIONAL GUARDIAN(S) IN PROBATE PROCEEDINGS IN THE ELEVENTH JUDICIAL CIRCUIT OF FLORIDA; DESIGNATION AND AUTHORIZATION OF CLERK OF THE COURTS TO OPERATE THE PROFESSIONAL GUARDIANSHIP REGISTRY.

15–03. AUTHORIZING THE SELF–HELP PROGRAM TO ESTABLISH AND IMPLEMENT CRITERIA FOR A COST SCHEDULE FOR FAMILY COURT SELF–HELP FORMS PACKET FOR THE ELEVENTH JUDICIAL CIRCUIT OF FLORIDA.

14–13. ADOPTION OF AND AUTHORIZATION TO UTILIZE STATUS QUO TEMPORARY DOMESTIC RELATIONS ORDER, WITH OR WITHOUT MINOR CHILDREN, IN THE ELEVENTH JUDICIAL CIRCUIT OF FLORIDA.

14–05. REQUIREMENT TO COMPLETE A PARENTING EDUCATION AND FAMILY STABILIZATION COURSE.

14–04. CESSATION OF CIRCUIT CERTIFIED CHILD EDUCATION AND CONSULTATION PROGRAM IN DISSOLUTION CASES INVOLVING MINORS.

14–01. REAFFIRMATION OF THE FAMILY MEDIATION UNIT OF THE CIRCUIT COURT.

09–15 (A1). AMENDING PARENTING COORDINATION IN FAMILY LAW CASES.

09–15. PARENTING COORDINATION IN FAMILY LAW CASES.

07–08. AUTHORIZING THE COLLABORATIVE PROCESS DISPUTE RESOLUTION MODEL IN THE ELEVENTH JUDICIAL CIRCUIT OF FLORIDA.

02–03. [RESCINDED BY ADMINISTRATIVE ORDER NO. 16–02, EFFECTIVE FEBRUARY 17, 2016].

GENERAL MAGISTRATE/SUPPORT HEARING

02–15–05. ESTABLISHMENT OF AND APPOINTMENT TO THE PART–TIME CHILD SUPPORT ENFORCEMENT HEARING OFFICER SELECTION COMMITTEE FOR THE ELEVENTH JUDICIAL CIRCUIT OF FLORIDA.

JUVENILE

14–08. APPOINTING FOSTER CARE REVIEW, INC., TO CONTINUE TO ADMINISTER THE ELEVENTH JUDICIAL CIRCUIT'S CITIZEN REVIEW PANEL PROGRAM; RE–ESTABLISHING PROCEDURES FOR SUCH PROGRAM.

05–08 (A1). EXPANSION OF JUVENILE DRUG COURT.

02–15–06. ASSIGNMENT OF CASES INVOLVING CHILDREN KNOWN OR SUSPECTED OF BEING VICTIMS OF HUMAN TRAFFICKING IN THE DEPENDENCY SECTION OF THE JUVENILE DIVISION.

MEDIATION ARBITRATION

10–09. INFORMATION TO BE SUPPLIED IN FILING CERTAIN PETITIONS IN THE OFFICE OF THE CLERK OF COURTS REGARDING FAMILY MEDIATION.

09–10. ESTABLISHMENT OF PROCEDURES FOR MEDIATION IN COUNTY COURT CIVIL DIVISION.

09–01. DISMISSAL OF TRAFFIC CITATIONS ISSUED FOR FAILURE TO PAY TOLLS.

Local Rules

R–1–3. GENERAL JURISDICTION DIVISION

The General Jurisdiction Division of the Circuit Court is hereby established and will be responsible for the disposition of the following matters within the jurisdiction of the Circuit Court:

1. Bond Validation: All matters relating to validity of bonds of state and local governments and agencies, including notice; elections, validation requirements and marketability; industrial development bonds.

2. Contracts & Indebtedness: All contract actions and all actions relating to promissory notes and other debts, including those arising from sale of goods; uniform commercial code litigation.

3. Eminent Domain: All matters relating to taking of private property for public use, including inverse condemnation, by state agencies, political subdivisions and public service corporations.

4. Landlord & Tenant: All matters relating to landlords' liens, distress proceedings, defaults, sales of distrained property, and common law actions for damages connected with landlord and tenant.

5. Mortgage Foreclosure: All matters relating to the involvement of legal and equitable liens against real property including mechanics' and materialmen's liens, including foreclosures and sales.

6. Automobile Negligence: All matters relating to liability suits for damages sustained as the result of automobile-connected death, automobile- connected personal injury, or automobile-connected damage to property; includes insurance-related suits and claims as well as third party litigation arising out of automobile-connected negligence; includes claims for statutory relief on account of injury or death.

7. All Other Negligence: All matters relating to all forms of liability suit involving negligence-related death; injury or damage to property or property interests; including claims for statutory relief on account of death or injury.

8. Real Property: All matters relating to possession, title and boundaries to real property, including purchase, partition, quieting title and removing encumbrances, sales, reformation, rescissions and cancellations and ejectment actions.

9. Replevin, Statutory Liens and Chattel Foreclosures: All matters relating to enforcement of statutory liens on chattels, chattel mortgage acts and foreclosures and replevin actions.

10. Tax Litigation: All matters relating to assessment and levy of taxes and tolls on all kinds of property and property interests, including real, personal, tangible and intangible property.

11. Other Complaints: All other civil complaints not listed above, or when subject matter cannot be determined, and not expressly assigned to another Division of the Circuit Court.

12. Other Petitions: All other equitable matters and petitions not listed above, or when subject matter cannot be determined, and not expressly assigned to another Division of the Circuit Court.

13. Bond Estreatures.

14. Such other related matters as may be assigned or reassigned by the Chief Judge.

R–1–7. FAMILY DIVISION

The Family Division of the Circuit Court is hereby established and will be responsible for the disposition of the following matters

1. Such matters as apply to families and/or a child, including adoption, separate maintenance, paternity, custody and support, dissolution of marriage, delinquency and dependency,

2. Such other family type matters as may be assigned or reassigned by the Chief Judge. NOTE By Administrative Order of the Chief Judge (No. 80–23–A1), entered in (Case No. 80–1), the Family Division Of the Circuit Court was divided into two Departments, Family Juvenile and Family Civil. By Administrative Orders No. 80–23–A1 entered in Case No. 80–1, the Family Civil Department was attached to the General Jurisdiction Division for administrative control.

R–1–9. PROBATE DIVISION

The Probate Division of the Circuit Court is hereby established and will be responsible for the disposition of the following proceedings:

1. The administration of decedents' estates.

2. Guardianships of minors and adult incompetents.

3. Approval of settlement of claims of minors in personal injury actions where action has not been filed in General Jurisdiction.

4. Petitions for determination of competency.

5. Involuntary hospitalization under the Baker Act.

6. Involuntary hospitalization for alcoholics and drug addicts.

7. Civil actions filed in General Jurisdiction involving the estate of decedents and incompetents formerly cognizable in

equity may be transferred from General Jurisdiction for trial in the Probate Division of the Circuit Court before the Judge to whom the estate or guardianship proceeding is assigned.

8. Such other related matters as may be assigned or reassigned by the Chief Judge.

R–1–11. CIVIL DIVISION OF THE COUNTY COURT

The Civil Division of the County Court is hereby established and will be responsible for the disposition of the following matters:

Actions in which the matter in controversy does not exceed the sum of Twenty–Five Hundred Dollars ($2500.00), exclusive of interest, cost and attorney's fees.

Landlord and tenant cases involving claims in amounts which are within the jurisdiction and limitations of the County Court.

Proceedings relating to the right of possession of real property and to the forcible or unlawful detention of lands and tenements, except as provided in Section 26.012, Florida Statutes.

Such other related matters as may be assigned or reassigned by the Chief Judge.

NOTE: The jurisdiction of the County Court to hear Civil actions was increased to $5,000 by Ch. 80–165, Laws of Florida (1980).

R–2–1. CRIMINAL DIVISION OF THE CIRCUIT COURT

The Criminal Division of the Circuit Court is hereby established and will be responsible for the disposition of the following matters:

All felonies and all misdemeanors arising out of the same circumstances as a felony which is also charged.

Such other related matters as may be assigned or reassigned by the Chief Judge.

R–2–7. CRIMINAL DIVISION OF THE COUNTY COURT

The Criminal Division of the County Court is hereby established and will be responsible for the disposition of the following matters:

1. Misdemeanor cases not cognizable by the Circuit Court.
2. Violations of municipal or county ordinances.
3. Traffic infractions and offenses.
4. Such other related matters as may be assigned or reassigned by the Chief Judge.

R–2–11. CRIMINAL DIVISION, DRIVER IMPROVEMENT SCHOOLS

The following Driver Improvement Schools are approved by the Chief Judge of this Circuit:

A. Defensive Driving Course given by the Dade County School Board.

B. Student Traffic Safety Council.

C. D.U.I. Countermeasures of Dade County, Inc.

R–3–1. APPELLATE DIVISION OF CIRCUIT COURT

The Appellate Division of the Circuit Court is hereby established and will be responsible for the disposition of the following matters:

Appeals from the County Court, Dade County.

Petitions for writ of certiorari which seek review of a decision of any public body, city or county commission or council, administrative board or agency, or the County Court.

The cases referred to in paragraphs numbered I and 2 will be captioned as in the "Appellate Division" of the Circuit Court and will be filed with the Clerk for the Appellate Division to be located in the Metropolitan Justice Building or Dade County Courthouse as designated by the Chief Judge from time to time. Such cases will be consecutively numbered.

The cases referred to in paragraphs numbered I and 2 will be heard on their merits by three-judge panels of the Appellate Division, which panels will be determined by random selection among all the judges assigned to the division. Matters preliminary to final determination of such cases will be determined in accordance with rules of the Appellate Division to be hereinafter promulgated by the Chief Judge or Administrative Judge of the Appellate Division.

Such other related matters as may be assigned or reassigned by the Chief Judge.

NOTE: This Local Rule was approved by the Supreme Court of Florida on December 14, 1982. It amended the Local Rule previously approved.

R–4–1. ALTERNATE METHOD OF JURY SELECTION FOR PETIT JURY IN THE CIRCUIT AND COUNTY COURTS, MIAMI–DADE COUNTY GRAND JURY AND STATEWIDE GRAND JURY BY USE OF COMPUTER PURSUANT TO F.S. 40.225

THE ELEVENTH JUDICIAL CIRCUIT MIAMI–DADE COUNTY, FLORIDA

ALTERNATE METHOD OF JURY SELECTION FOR PETIT JURY IN THE CIRCUIT AND COUNTY COURTS, MIAMI–DADE COUNTY GRAND JURY AND STATEWIDE GRAND JURY BY USE OF COMPUTER PURSUANT TO F.S. 40.225

Please refer to Supreme Court Of Florida No. AOSC08–25 In Re: Juror Selection Plan: Miami–Dade County

WHEREAS, the present method of selecting jurors can be expedited without additional expense or loss of the sanctity of random selection by the use of the electronic computer available for use by Miami–Dade County; and

WHEREAS, the source of such selection is from the list provided by the Department of Highway Safety and Motor Vehicles which is in computer compatible form and under the custody and control of the Clerk of the Circuit Court of Miami–Dade County, Florida;

IT IS THEREFORE RESOLVED that the Rules of the Eleventh Judicial Circuit for procedure in all courts of Miami–Dade County in which jury trials are held shall be amended to include this additional Rule adopting the following alternative plan for the selection of persons for petit jury, grand jury and statewide grand jury service by use of computer pursuant to F.S. 40.225:

1. **Equipment:** The equipment used in jury selection is an I.B.M. Z Series #2084 computer located in the secured computer room of the Office of Computer Services and Information Systems of Miami–Dade County.

2. **Alternative Method of Selecting Venire:**

a. The source from which names shall be taken is the list provided by the Department of Highway Safety and Motor Vehicles.

b. The Clerk of the Circuit Court is designated the official custodian of the computer records of the lists to be used in jury selection and shall ensure they are not accessible to anyone other than those directly involved in selection of venires, as herein provided. Functions of the Clerk of the Circuit Court may be performed by his deputies.

c. If the entire list provided by the Department of Highway Safety and Motor Vehicles is not used as the final certified jury list from which venires are selected, then the Chief Judge or his designated representative, with the aid and assistance of the Clerk of the Circuit Court, shall select enough prospective jurors for the year by lot and at random from the entire list of registered voters using the method described in Attachment A.

d. The Clerk of the Circuit Court shall cause jury venires to be selected from the final certified jury list programmed into the Miami–Dade County computer using the method described in Attachment A in accordance with directions received from the Chief Judge or his designated representative.

ATTACHMENT A The Universal Random Number Generator

The following narrative describes the basic procedures for writing the Universal Random Number Generator in any software language.

The following looping procedures generates a table of 97 random numbers. The 97 numbers are created using a routine that calculates a 1 or 0, 24 times thus creating a 24 bit fraction. The procedures for this part of the generator are as follows:

All numbers in this process are real except for the integer starting seed values.

Choose starting seed values for I, J, and K to be a integer between 1 and 178 and L between 0 and 168.

Initialize S = 0

Initialize T = .5

Do the following 24 times to create the first number in the 97 number table:

Multiply I times J and divide by 179.

Multiply the remainder by K and divide by 179. Let M = the remainder.

Let I = J, J = K, K = M

Multiply 53 times L, add I, divide by 169.

Let L = remainder

Multiply L times M and divide by 64. If the remainder is greater or equal to 32 then S = S + T else S = S.

T = .5 times T (This places the 1 or 0 in the proper bit location).

S = the first 24 bit number after completing above process 24 times.

Return to the step that initializes S to 0 and continue until the table of 97 numbers is complete.

After completing the table,

Set C = 362436/16777216

Set CD = 7654321/16777216

Set CM = 16777213/16777216

The second part of the generator uses the 97 number table. Each location in the table (array) must be able to be specified. The following process completes the function of generating a random number:

Both X and Y are pointers.

Set X to be the 97th place in the table.

Set Y to be the 33rd place in the table.

Let UNI = The random number in the X location minus the random number in the Y location.

If UNI is less than zero, then UNI = UNI + I else UNI = UNI.

Replace the random numbers in the X location with the computed UNI.

Let X = X–1

If X = 0, then X = 97

Let Y = Y–1

If Y = 0, then Y = 97

Let C = C–CD (C and CD are defined above)

If C is less than zero, then C = C + CM else C = C

Let UNI = UNI = C

If UNI is less than zero, UNI = UNI + 1 else UNI = UNI.

Once the 97 number table is set up, the above routine is looped through for each call for a random number. UNI will be a random number between 0 and 1. To select a person from a list, the list must be numbered in a sequential order from 1 to the size of the list. The UNI is then multiplied times the size of the list and one is added to this result to obtain the randomly selected prospective juror. The four seed values, I, J, K, and L should be stored in a table for each selection purpose and the same combination should not be used for the year.

STATE OF FLORIDA

COUNTY OF MIAMI–DADE

R–09/29/94. DOMESTIC VIOLENCE DIVISIONS OF CIRCUIT & COUNTY COURTS

The Domestic Violence Division of the Circuit and County Courts is hereby established and will be responsible for the disposition of the following matters:

1. Petitions for Temporary and Permanent Injunctions for Protection arising under Chapter 741 (Domestic Violence), Florida Statutes, and enforcement thereof as provided by Law;

2. Petitions for Temporary and Permanent Injunctions for Protection arising under Chapter 784 (Repeat Violence), Florida Statutes, and enforcement thereof as provided by Law;

3. All misdemeanor cases involving domestic and repeat violence and criminal violations of injunctions;

4. Such other related matters as may be assigned or reassigned by the Chief Judge;

5. This Local Rule may be rescinded by the Chief Judge with the concurrence of the majority of the Circuit and County Court Judges without further order of the Supreme Court.

Respectfully submitted this 21st day of July, 1994.

NOTE: This Local Rule was approved by the Supreme Court of Florida on September 29, 1994.

R-03-11-1997. LOCAL RULE TO ESTABLISH PROCEDURES FOR PRO SE PARTIES IN THE FAMILY DIVISION OF CIRCUIT COURT

Pro Se parties in dissolution of marriage, name change, paternity, custody and post-judgment modification cases in the Family Division of the Circuit Court shall observe the following procedures, unless waived by the Administrative or Associate Administrative Judge, Family Division, for good cause shown:

1. Pro Se parties shall acquire and utilize the Eleventh Judicial Circuit forms packet or forms substantially in compliance therewith, which are available, at a cost not to exceed Thirty Five ($35.00) Dollars, from the Clerk's Office;

2. Pro Se parties shall register with and receive information and instructions on relevant Family Court rules and procedures, referrals to social service agencies, and other appropriate assistance which is available from the Circuit's Family Court Self Help Program;

3. At the time of filing their pleadings and papers with the Court, Pro Se parties shall have those pleadings and papers reviewed as to form by Family Court Self Help Program; and

4. All Pro Se parties shall obtain a final hearing date from the Family Court Self Help Program.

The above procedures shall apply to a Pro Se party who seeks to file or files a dissolution of marriage, name change, paternity, custody or post-judgment modification case in the Family Division of the Circuit Court subsequent to the date the Supreme Court approves this Local Rule.

A waiver request filed under this Local Rule shall be considered an emergency ex parte motion pursuant to Rule 12.741(b)(1), Family Law Rules of Procedure, and shall be disposed of expeditiously in order to avoid any inconvenience to the requesting party.

This Local Rule may be rescinded by the Chief Judge with the concurrence of the majority of the Circuit and County Court Judges without further order of the Supreme Court.

Approved by the Supreme Court March 11, 1997.

Administrative Orders

Circuit Court Civil

15–02. ESTABLISHMENT OF SECTION 35 IN THE CIRCUIT CIVIL DIVISION OF THE ELEVENTH JUDICIAL CIRCUIT OF FLORIDA

THE ELEVENTH JUDICIAL CIRCUIT MIAMI–DADE COUNTY, FLORIDA

CASE NO. 15–1 (Court Administration)

ADMINISTRATIVE ORDER NO. 15–02

IN RE: ESTABLISHMENT OF SECTION 35 IN THE CIRCUIT CIVIL DIVISION OF THE ELEVENTH JUDICIAL CIRCUIT OF FLORIDA

WHEREAS, due to the volume of new cases continually filed and pending in Section 40 in the Circuit Civil Division of the Eleventh Judicial Circuit of Florida ("Division"), to include complex business litigation cases and foreclosure cases, it has been determined that the establishment of another section within the Division is necessary in furtherance of judicial economy and administrative efficiency; and

WHEREAS, upon the establishment of a new section, the Clerk of the Courts will transfer all of the pending foreclosure cases in Section 40 to the new section;

NOW, THEREFORE, pursuant to the authority vested in me as Chief Judge of the Eleventh Judicial Circuit of Florida, under Rule 2.215 of the Florida Rules of Judicial Administration, it is hereby **ORDERED:**

1. The Clerk of the Court is hereby authorized and directed to immediately take whatever steps are necessary to establish Section 35 in the Circuit Civil Division of the Eleventh Judicial Circuit of Florida. In any event, Section 35 shall be established no later than close of business on Friday, March 20, 2015.

2. Upon the establishment of Section 35, the Clerk will transfer all of the pending foreclosure cases in Section 40 to Section 35.

3. Due to the establishment of Section 35, the Clerk shall notify all attorneys of record in any pending foreclosure matters assigned to Section 40, that such matters have been reassigned to Section 35.

This Administrative Order shall take effect immediately and shall remain in effect until further order of the Court.

DONE AND ORDERED in Chambers at Miami–Dade County, Florida, this 18th day of March, 2015.

JENNIFER BAILEY, ACTING CHIEF JUDGE
ELEVENTH JUDICIAL CIRCUIT OF FLORIDA

15–01. ESTABLISHMENT OF SECTION 34 IN THE CIRCUIT CIVIL DIVISION OF THE ELEVENTH JUDICIAL CIRCUIT OF FLORIDA

THE ELEVENTH JUDICIAL CIRCUIT MIAMI–DADE COUNTY, FLORIDA

CASE NO. 15–1 (Court Administration)

ADMINISTRATIVE ORDER NO. 15–01

IN RE: ESTABLISHMENT OF SECTION 34 IN THE CIRCUIT CIVIL DIVISION OF THE ELEVENTH JUDICIAL CIRCUIT OF FLORIDA

WHEREAS, due to the volume of new cases continually filed and pending in Section 42 in the Circuit Civil Division of the Eleventh Judicial Circuit of Florida ("Division"), to include asbestos cases and cases generally associated with the Division, it has been determined that the establishment of another section within the Division is necessary in furtherance of judicial economy and administrative efficiency; and

WHEREAS, upon the establishment of a new section, the Clerk of the Courts will transfer all of the pending cases in Section 42 that are generally associated with the Division to the new section, excluding the asbestos cases;

NOW, THEREFORE, pursuant to the authority vested in me as Chief Judge of the Eleventh Judicial Circuit of Florida, under Rule 2.215 of the Florida Rules of Judicial Administration, it is hereby **ORDERED:**

1. The Clerk of the Court is hereby authorized and directed to immediately take whatever steps are necessary to establish Section 34 in the Circuit Civil Division of the Eleventh Judicial Circuit of Florida. In any event, Section 34 shall be established no later than close of business on Friday, March 20, 2015.

2. Upon the establishment of Section 34, the Clerk will transfer all of the pending cases in Section 42 that are generally associated with the Division, excluding the asbestos cases, to Section 34.

3. Due to the establishment of Section 34, the Clerk shall notify all attorneys of record in any pending matters assigned to Section 42, that are generally associated with the Division, excluding asbestos cases, that such matters have been reassigned to Section 34.

This Administrative Order shall take effect immediately and shall remain in effect until further order of the Court.

DONE AND ORDERED in Chambers at Miami–Dade County, Florida, this 17th day of March, 2015.

JENNIFER BAILEY, ACTING CHIEF JUDGE
ELEVENTH JUDICIAL CIRCUIT OF FLORIDA

14–14. [RESCINDED BY ADMINISTRATIVE ORDER NO. 16–12, JANUARY 2, 2017]

14–10. ESTABLISHING PROCEDURES FOR FILING AND RETRIEVING ORIGINAL NOTES IN CONNECTION WITH FORECLOSURE CASES

THE ELEVENTH JUDICIAL CIRCUIT MIAMI–DADE COUNTY, FLORIDA

CASE NO. 14–1 (Court Administration)

ADMINISTRATIVE ORDER NO. 14–10

IN RE: ESTABLISHING PROCEDURES FOR FILING AND RETRIEVING ORIGINAL NOTES IN CONNECTION WITH FORECLOSURE CASES

WHEREAS, the Eleventh Judicial Circuit is in the process of transitioning to digital court filing; and

WHEREAS, many foreclosure cases wherein plaintiffs elected to voluntarily dismiss such cases have been re-filed; and

WHEREAS, consequently, in order to assure the availability of the original paper promissory notes ("Original Notes"), it has been deemed necessary to establish the procedures for filing and retrieving Original Notes;

NOW, THEREFORE, pursuant to the authority vested in me as Chief Judge of the Eleventh Judicial Circuit of Florida, under Rule 2.215, Florida Rules of Judicial Administration, it is hereby **ORDERED** that parties in foreclosure cases shall comply with the following procedures:

1. In any currently pending foreclosure case, Plaintiff's counsel must immediately locate the Original Note. If the Original Note was filed in a court file, in either the current proceeding or in a previously filed and dismissed proceeding, Plaintiff's counsel shall execute the attached form and request the return of the Original Note by the Clerk of Courts. This obligation shall continue to operate prospectively for ail future foreclosure cases.

2. Counsel shall not file Original Notes through the Clerk of the Courts. Original Notes must be tendered to the Court at trial or at summary judgment hearings.

3. The Clerk of the Courts shall return Original Notes pursuant to the requesting form in the following manner:

a. The requesting law firm must provide a correct copy of the Original Note to be substituted for the Original Note with the requesting form.

b. An individual lawyer must sign for receipt of the Original Note from the Clerk of the Courts and bar numbers shall be listed on the receipt.

c. A copy of the request and the signed receipt shall be scanned and filed into the court file by the Clerk of the Courts.

d. No court order shall be required to secure the return of the Original Note under this procedure. Plaintiff's counsel should not submit Orders Directing Return of the Original Note to division judges.

4. The requirement to retrieve Original Notes shall not apply to cases upon which a Final Judgment has been entered and sale has occurred.

5. If a Final Judgment is vacated by subsequent court order, Plaintiff's counsel shall take immediate steps to request the return of the Original Note pursuant to this procedure.

6. Plaintiffs and their attorneys are cautioned to attend to the well-established and long standing policies codified in Rule 2.430, Florida Rules of Judicial Administration, which provide for a five (5) year record retention period from the date of the original Final Order.

7. There is no procedure to screen or remove any documents from files that are subject to disposal under these procedures. It is the responsibility of parties and their lawyers to secure their documents, most importantly, Original Notes which may be the subject of re-filed litigation, pursuant to this Administrative Order prior to the scheduled disposition of the file.

This Administrative Order shall take effect on May 14, 2014 and shall remain in effect until further order of the Court.

DONE AND ORDERED in Chambers at Miami–Dade County, Florida, this 14th day of May, 2014,

BERTILA SOTO, CHIEF JUDGE
ELEVENTH JUDICIAL CIRCUIT OF FLORIDA

REQUEST FOR ORIGINAL NOTE:

Current Case No. ______

The Original Note was previously filed in: ______

___ **Prior Case No.** ______

___ **Current File:** ______

___ **Date of previous filing:** ______

The Note is requested:

___ to be in Court at ______ (location) on ______ (date set/time).

___ to be released to Plaintiff's firm.

Requesting law firm: ______

Requesting attorney: ______ **Bar No.** ______

Contact info: Email address: ______

Telephone No.: ______

Receipt upon delivery of note:

______

______

______

This form may be hand-delivered to the court clerk, or clerk supervisor Dorian Mathis in the clerk's office, (305)349–7413

14–09. ESTABLISHING NOTICE OF RELATED PROBATE CASES FILING REQUIREMENT; AUTHORIZING AND DIRECTING CLERK OF THE COURTS TO TRANSFER RELATED CASES TO PROBATE SECTION WITH THE OLDER DOCKET NUMBER

THE ELEVENTH JUDICIAL CIRCUIT MIAMI–DADE COUNTY, FLORIDA

CASE NO. 14–1 (Court Administration)

ADMINISTRATIVE ORDER NO. 14–09

IN RE: ESTABLISHING NOTICE OF RELATED PROBATE CASES FILING REQUIREMENT; AUTHORIZING AND DIRECTING CLERK OF THE COURTS TO TRANSFER RELATED CASES TO PROBATE SECTION WITH THE OLDER DOCKET NUMBER

WHEREAS, in an effort to conserve judicial resources and promote an efficient determination of actions in the Probate Division, whenever a probate case is filed with the Clerk of the Courts, it has been determined that a notice of related cases form must accompany such filing; and

WHEREAS, it was further determined that such related cases should be assigned to one judge;

NOW, THEREFORE, pursuant to the authority vested in me as Chief Judge of the Eleventh Judicial Circuit of Florida, under Rule 2.215, Florida Rules of Judicial Administration, it is hereby **ORDERED** that the following procedures shall be followed when filing a case in the Probate Division:

1. The attached Notice of Related Probate Cases must accompany the initial pleading by the filing attorney or self-represented party.

2. Each party shall have a continuing duty to inform the court of any related proceedings and must therefore submit separate or joint supplemental notices as related cases become known or reasonably ascertainable.

3. Whenever it appears to a party that two or more pending cases present common or fairly similar issues of fact and that assignment to one judge will significantly promote the efficient administration of justice, conserve judicial resources, avoid inconsistent results, or prevent multiple court appearances by the same parties on the same issues, the party must file a Notice of Related Probate Cases and may request coordination of the litigation.

4. The Notice of Related Probate Cases shall be served on all parties in the related cases and e-filed.

5. Unless otherwise ordered by the Administrative Judge of the Probate Division, the Clerk of the Courts, upon receipt and review of a Notice of Related Probate Cases, is hereby authorized and directed to automatically transfer any and all related probate cases to the Probate Section with the earlier-filed probate case, as referenced by the Clerk's docket number.

6. The Clerk of the Courts shall continuously conduct a random inventory search for lower case docket numbers to determine whether the later-filed cases should be transferred to the Probate Section with the earlier-case file. If so determined, the Clerk shall transfer the related probate cases to the Probate Section with the earlier-filed probate case, as referenced by the Clerk's docket number.

This Administrative Order shall become effective immediately upon execution and shall remain in effect until further order of the Court.

DONE AND ORDERED in Chambers at Miami–Dade County, Florida, this 9th day of July, 2014.

BERTILA SOTO, CHIEF JUDGE

ELEVENTH JUDICIAL CIRCUIT OF FLORIDA

IN THE CIRCUIT COURT OF THE ELEVENTH JUDICIAL CIRCUIT IN AND FOR MIAMI–DADE COUNTY, FLORIDA

PROBATE DIVISION CASE NO.: ____ SECTION: ____
IN RE: ________________/

NOTICE OF RELATED PROBATE CASES

1. (Petitioner) / (Respondent) submits this Notice of Related Probate Cases as required by Administrative Order 14–09. A related probate law case may be an open or closed Estate, Trust, Guardianship, Determination of Incapacity, or Restoration of Rights. A case is "related" when:

a. It involves any of the same parties, family members to include children, beneficiaries, parties of interest, or issues, and it is pending at the time the party files a probate case;

b. It arises from the same or substantially identical transactions, happenings, or events, or involves determining the same or substantially identical legal questions;

c. It affects the court's jurisdiction to proceed; or

d. An order from the earlier case may conflict with an order on the same issues in this one, and vice versa.

2. There is/are [check **one** only]:

___ No related cases for this filing.

___ The following related case(s) (add additional pages if necessary): ____________

RELATED CASE NO. 1

Case Name: ____________
Case Number: ____________
Division: ____________
Petitioner: ____________
Respondent: ____________
Type of Proceeding [Check all that Apply]: ___ Estate ___ Guardianship ___ Trust ___ Incapacity Determination ___ Restoration of Rights

RELATED CASE NO. 2

Case Name: ____________
Case Number: ____________
Division: ____________
Petitioner: ____________
Respondent: ____________
Type of Proceeding [Check all that Apply]: ___ Estate ___ Guardianship ___ Trust ___ Incapacity Determination ___ Restoration of Rights

RELATED CASE NO. 3

Case Name: ____________
Case Number: ____________
Division: ____________
Petitioner: ____________

Respondent: ____________

Type of Proceeding [Check all that Apply]: ___ Estate ___ Guardianship ___ Trust ___ Incapacity Determination ___ Restoration of Rights

CERTIFICATE OF SERVICE

I CERTIFY that I delivered a copy of this Notice of Related Cases to the ________ County Sheriff's Department or a certified process server for service on the **(Petitioner)** / **(Respondent)**, and [**check all used**] ___ e-mailed, ___ mailed, ___ hand delivered, a copy to {*name*} ________, a party to the related case, on {*date*} ________.

Dated: ____________

____
Attorney's Signature
Printed Name: ________
Bar Number: ________
Address: ________
City, State, Zip: ________
Telephone Number: ________
Fax Number: ________
E-mail Address(es): ________

14–07 (A1). CLARIFICATION OF PROBATE–RELATED AND NON–PROBATE–RELATED TRUST CASES

THE ELEVENTH JUDICIAL CIRCUIT MIAMI–DADE COUNTY, FLORIDA

CASE NO. 14–1
(Court Administration)

ADMINISTRATIVE ORDER NO. 14–07 A1
(Superseding and Clarifying AO 14–07)

IN RE: CLARIFICATION OF PROBATE–RELATED AND NON–PROBATE–RELATED TRUST CASES

WHEREAS, subsequent to the issuance of Administrative Order No. 14–07 it was deemed necessary to further clarify within the Circuit Civil and Probate Divisions the status of proceedings concerning trusts; and

WHEREAS, accordingly, this Administrative Order seeks to provide such clarification;

NOW, THEREFORE, pursuant to the authority vested in me as Chief Judge of the Eleventh Judicial Circuit of Florida, under Rule 2.215 of the Florida Rules of Judicial Administration, it is hereby ORDERED that:

1. The following proceedings shall be deemed Probate-related and shall be commenced as follows:

a. *Chapter 736 Proceedings.* Any proceeding arising under or governed by Chapter 736, Florida Statutes (except trust registration) shall constitute an original proceeding and shall be filed with the Clerk of the Probate Division of the Circuit Court and payment of the filing fee prescribed by law for the filing of a civil action.

All assignments will be made by section in accordance with the blind filing system and the applicable Rules of Civil Procedure.

When a proceeding emanates from an estate subject to probate in the Probate Division, it may be assigned by the Administrative Judge of that Division to the Judge who presided over the original estate proceeding or by the Clerk of the Courts based upon the lower case number as authorized by Administrative Order No. 14–09.

b. *Equitable Claims against an Estate.* Suits involving the personal representative of the estate of a decedent or ward that were wholly cognizable in equity according to former chancery practice shall be commenced as an original proceeding by filing a complaint with the Clerk of the Probate Division and payment of the filing fee prescribed for the filing of a civil action.

After commencement of the suit, it shall be assigned by the Clerk as a companion case to the Probate Judge responsible for the estate or guardianship proceeding from which it emanated.

Any claim, improvidently filed, in another Division shall, upon application of the parties to the Administrative Judge of the Circuit Civil Division be transferred to the Probate Judge responsible for the estate or guardianship pending. Such equitable claim shall include by way of illustration rather than limitation, property claimed as being held by the decedent or ward as trustee or in some other fiduciary capacity; or suits involving rescission, cancellation, reformation and specific performance of antenuptial or postnuptial agreements, land sale contracts or other instruments or transactions.

2. The following proceedings shall not be deemed Probate related cases and shall be commenced as follows:

Creditors' and Personal Representatives' Claims. All claims of creditors against the estate of a decedent or ward and all claims of a personal representative or guardian (not within the purview of paragraph 1b above) shall be commenced in a court of competent jurisdiction as an independent action and litigated to judgment there.

3. Administrative Order No. 14–07 is hereby superseded by this Administrative Order and held for naught.

This Administrative Order shall take effect immediately upon execution, and shall remain in effect until further order of the Court.

DONE and **ORDERED** in Chambers at Miami–Dade County, Florida, this 9 day of August, 2014.

HONORABLE BERTILA SOTO,
CHIEF JUDGE
ELEVENTH JUDICIAL CIRCUIT
OF FLORIDA

Amended effective July 9, 2014.

13–08. CREATION OF THE INTERNATIONAL COMMERCIAL ARBITRATION COURT, A SUBSECTION OF SECTION 40 ("COMPLEX BUSINESS LITIGATION SECTION") IN THE CIRCUIT CIVIL DIVISION OF THE ELEVENTH JUDICIAL CIRCUIT OF FLORIDA AND

PROCEDURES FOR THE ASSIGNMENT AND REASSIGNMENT OF CASES TO THIS SUBSECTION [1]

THE ELEVENTH JUDICIAL CIRCUIT MIAMI–DADE COUNTY, FLORIDA

CASE NO. 13–1 (Court Administration)

ADMINISTRATIVE ORDER NO. 13–08
(Companion AO to AO No. 11–04)

IN RE: CREATION OF THE INTERNATIONAL COMMERCIAL ARBITRATION COURT, A SUBSECTION OF SECTION 40 ("COMPLEX BUSINESS LITIGATION SECTION") IN THE CIRCUIT CIVIL DIVISION OF THE ELEVENTH JUDICIAL CIRCUIT OF FLORIDA AND PROCEDURES FOR THE ASSIGNMENT AND REASSIGNMENT OF CASES TO THIS SUBSECTION

WHEREAS, Miami, Florida has become one of the leading venues in the Americas within which to conduct international commercial arbitration proceedings; and

WHEREAS, international commercial arbitration is a specialized area of law; and

WHEREAS, designating particular trained judges to hear all international commercial arbitration matters will foster greater judicial expertise and understanding of this area of the law, will lead to more uniformity in legal decisions, and help establish a consistent body of case law; and

WHEREAS, in 2006, pursuant to Administrative Order No. 06–40, the Eleventh Circuit previously identified the need for experienced, trained judicial adjudication in commercial cases by establishing the Complex Business Litigation Section (Section 40), which was reaffirmed pursuant to Administrative Order No. 11–04, entered by this Court on May 19, 2011, and which section has significant experience in handling complicated business disputes;

NOW, THEREFORE, pursuant to the authority vested in me as Chief Judge of the Eleventh Judicial Circuit of Florida, under Rule 2.215, Judicial Administration Rules, it is hereby **ORDERED**:

1. An International Commercial Arbitration ("ICA") Subsection is created within Section 40, the Complex Business Litigation Section ("ICA Subsection").

2. The ICA Subsection shall handle all ICA cases and shall consist of judges who have experience in handling complex commercial matters and who receive specific judicial education in the handling of international commercial arbitration ("ICA Judges"). The Chief Judge (or designee) shall specify the training requirements and no judge shall be assigned to ICA cases without having previously completed the educational requirement.

3. ICA cases shall be assigned to Section 40, and then referred to ICA Judges for handling. Only ICA Judges shall serve as emergency alternates in ICA cases, notwithstanding other alternate assignments within the Circuit Civil Division. ICA Judges shall, for SRS purposes, be designated as referral judges for purposes of reporting case handling statistics. The reporting mechanism may be amended as needed by the Administrative Judge (or designee) of the Circuit Civil Division.

4. The Chief Judge shall assign judges to the ICA subsection of the Complex Business Litigation section as are sufficient and appropriate to meet ICA case load demand.

It is further **ORDERED** that the following procedures shall be followed as to the assignment and reassignment of cases with respect to the Complex Business Litigation Section:

Section 1. General Information.

a. All cases which involve International Commercial Arbitration shall be assigned to Section 40, the Complex Business Litigation Division. Attorneys filing ICA cases shall designate these cases as CBL cases on the Civil Cover Sheet, pursuant to Form 1.999, Florida Rules of Civil Procedure as modified by the Eleventh Judicial Circuit.

b. A separate notice (form) shall be filed with the complaint by the filing attorney indicating that the case being filed appears to arise under the Florida International Commercial Arbitration Act (Chapter 684, Florida Statutes; or under the Federal Arbitration Act, 9 U.S.C. § 1 et seq., except matters arising out of a relationship which is entirely between citizens of the United States, unless that relationship involves property located abroad, envisages performance or enforcement abroad, or has some other reasonable relation with one or more foreign states; and all cases reassigned to the ICA Subsection by the Administrative Judge (or designee) of the Circuit Civil Division. For the purpose of this order, a corporation is a citizen of the United States if it is incorporated or has its principal place of business in the United States.

c. Cases designated as subject to ICA shall be assigned to the ICA subsection by the Administrative Judge (or designee) of the Circuit Civil Division.

Section 2. Cases Not Subject to the International Commercial Arbitration Subsection.

Matters which do not arise under the Florida International Commercial Arbitration Act or under the Federal Arbitration Act shall not be assigned to the ICA Subsection, unless the case meets the definition of related case as arising out of the same transaction or occurrence as those matters properly heard before the ICA Subsection.

Section 3. Assignment of Cases in and out of the International Commercial Arbitration Subsection.

a. Judges assigned to the Circuit Civil Division and litigants who have cases filed in the Circuit Civil Division may submit a request to the Administrative Judge (or designee) of the Circuit Civil Division to assign/transfer a pending case that meets the criteria of the ICA Subsection.

b. If any party disagrees with the assignment or lack of assignment of a case to the ICA Subsection, then that party may submit a request for reconsideration to the Administrative Judge (or designee) of the Circuit Civil Division for re-evaluation and/or case re-assignment.

c. The Administrative Judge (or designee) of the Circuit Civil Division shall resolve controversies which may arise concerning the assignment/transfer of any case to or from the ICA Subsection. If there is an issue as whether a matter is subject to arbitration, that controversy shall be assigned to the ICA Subsection for determination.

Section 4. Complex Business Litigation Section Procedures.

Matters assigned to the ICA Subsection are not subject to the Complex Business Litigation Section Procedures for the Eleventh Judicial Circuit except as otherwise ordered by the judge assigned to the case, except that all filings in the ICA Subsection shall follow the directions of CBL with regard to efiling, ecourtesy, and cbl@jud11.flcourts.org, which may be found on the CBL webpage.

This Order shall take effect immediately upon execution and shall remain in effect until further order of the Court.

DONE AND ORDERED in Chambers at Miami–Dade County, Florida this 3rd of December, 2013.

BERTILA SOTO, CHIEF JUDGE
ELEVENTH JUDICIAL CIRCUIT

[1] See order 1–13–1 A for the amendment relating to the creation of the international commercial arbitration court.

13–06. ESTABLISHING CASE STATUS REQUIREMENTS FOR REAL PROPERTY MORTGAGE FORECLOSURE CASES

THE ELEVENTH JUDICIAL CIRCUIT MIAMI–DADE COUNTY, FLORIDA

CASE NO. 13–1 (Court Administration)

ADMINISTRATIVE ORDER NO. 13–06

IN RE: ESTABLISHING CASE STATUS REQUIREMENTS FOR REAL PROPERTY MORTGAGE FORECLOSURE CASES

WHEREAS, the status of a foreclosure case and related definitions have been adopted by the Florida Supreme Court and are published in the "FY 2013–14 Foreclosure Initiative Data Collection Plan" promulgated by the Office of the State Courts Administrator; and

WHEREAS, as set forth in Florida Supreme Court Administrative Order No. AOSC13–51 In Re: Case Status Reporting Requirements for Real Property Mortgage Foreclosure Cases ("AOSC13–51"), the Supreme Court found it beneficial to require the Chief Judge of every circuit court to issue an administrative order implementing an effective communication mechanism by which the courts and clerks are notified of case status changes in real property mortgage foreclosure cases in a timely manner; and

WHEREAS, AOSC13–51 further requires the Chief Judge of every circuit to include in such administrative order, direction for designating the status of cases as active or inactive;

NOW, THEREFORE, pursuant to the authority vested in me as Chief Judge of the Eleventh Judicial Circuit of Florida, it is hereby **ORDERED**:

1. The Clerk of Courts ("Clerk") shall prepare and submit to the Chief Judge and the Trial Court Administrator, a written procedure by December 15, 2013 as to how they are collecting and reporting to the Office of the State Courts Administrator ("OSCA") each of the Foreclosure Initiative Data Elements ("Data Element(s)") as outlined in the "FY 2013–14 Foreclosure Initiative Data Collection Plan" ("Data Collection Plan").

2. The Clerk shall provide the required information to OSCA on each Data Element required by the Data Collection Plan and shall simultaneously report same, by Data Element, to the Chief Judge and Trial Court Administrator.

3. The Clerk shall be responsible for monitoring data accuracy submitted to OSCA and complying with the Data Collection Plan.

4. The Clerk shall amend any inaccuracies identified in data reported to OSCA and within thirty (30) days of identifying inaccuracies, any amended reports submitted to OSCA shall be provided simultaneously to the Chief Judge and Trial Court Administrator with an explanation of said amendment.

5. The Circuit Civil Division and Foreclosure Initiative (collectively the "Court") shall assist in the implementation of the reporting mechanism by notifying the Clerk as soon as an event occurs that would change the status of a case from active to inactive status or vice versa. Such event(s) shall be specified on the Order Placing Case On Active Status or Order Placing Case On Inactive Status. *See*, attached sample Orders, which may be periodically revised as deemed appropriate.

6. When the Court becomes aware of any event that changes the status of a case, the Court shall issue one of the aforementioned Orders directing the Clerk to assign the appropriate case status, which the Clerk shall execute upon receipt.

7. When the Clerk becomes aware of events initiating a change in the status of a case, the Clerk shall immediately notify the Court for further review. Thereafter, upon such review, the procedure set forth in paragraph 6 hereinabove shall be followed.

This Administrative Order shall take effect immediately and shall remain in effect until further order of the Court.

DONE AND ORDERED in Chambers at Miami–Dade County, Florida, this 26th day of November, 2013.

BERTILA SOTO, CHIEF JUDGE
ELEVENTH JUDICIAL CIRCUIT
OF FLORIDA

OPCA

IN THE CIRCUIT COURT OF THE ELEVENTH JUDICIAL CIRCUIT IN AND FOR MIAMI–DADE COUNTY, FLORIDA

____
Plaintiff,

vs.

____
Defendant

CIRCUIT CIVIL DIVISION

UNIFORM CASE NO.: ____________

ORDER PLACING CASE ON ACTIVE STATUS

This case came before the Court, and the Court has been advised that the Plaintiff/ Defendant have/has moved to place the case on ACTIVE status due to:

☐ Plaintiff/defendant stipulates that the bankruptcy stay has been lifted, Case No. ____________

☐ Plaintiff/defendant stipulates that related case has been disposed, Case No. ____________

☐ By written agreement of the parties

☐ Plaintiff/defendant stipulates that pending appeal has been disposed

☐ Plaintiff/defendant stipulates that Department of Justice/Attorney General review is complete

☐ Other (a reason must be provided in writing by the presiding judge or designee)

DONE and **ORDERED** in Miami–Dade County, Florida, this ___ day of ___ 20 ___.

Presiding Judge or Magistrate

IN THE CIRCUIT COURT OF THE ELEVENTH JUDICIAL CIRCUIT IN AND FOR MIAMI–DADE COUNTY, FLORIDA

Plaintiff,

vs.

Defendant

CIRCUIT CIVIL DIVISION

UNIFORM CASE NO.:

ORDER PLACING CASE ON INACTIVE STATUS

This case came before the Court, and the Court has been advised that the Plaintiff/ Defendant have/has moved to place the case on INACTIVE status due to:

- ☐ Bankruptcy stay, Case No. ___ **[BKST]**
- ☐ Case pending resolution of another case, Case No. ___ **[CPRC]**
- ☐ Written agreement of the parties **[WAGT]**
- ☐ Appeal pending **[APLP]**
- ☐ Motion to stay or abate due to Department of Justice/Attorney General settlement **[DJAD]**
- ☐ Other (a reason must be provided in writing by the presiding judge or designee) **[OTHR]**

The Clerk of Court is therefore directed to remove this case from the **ACTIVE** status, and designate it as an **INACTIVE** case category based on the reason checked above. The parties must return the case to active status by motion, with notice to all parties, within 30 days of the termination of grounds for inactive status, and seeking an order of court returning it to active status.

DONE and **ORDERED** in Miami–Dade County, Florida, this ___ day of ___ 20 ___.

Presiding Judge or Magistrate

11–07. DISSOLUTION OF SECTION 50; ESTABLISHMENT OF JUDICIAL SECTIONS 58 AND 59; REASSIGNMENT OF PENDING CASES IN SECTION 50 TO CERTAIN SECTIONS, IN THE CIRCUIT CIVIL DIVISION OF THE ELEVENTH JUDICIAL CIRCUIT OF FLORIDA

THE ELEVENTH JUDICIAL CIRCUIT MIAMI–DADE COUNTY, FLORIDA

CASE NO. 11–1 (Court Administration)

ADMINISTRATIVE ORDER NO. 11–07

IN RE: DISSOLUTION OF SECTION 50; ESTABLISHMENT OF JUDICIAL SECTIONS 58 AND 59; REASSIGNMENT OF PENDING CASES IN SECTION 50 TO CERTAIN SECTIONS, IN THE CIRCUIT CIVIL DIVISION OF THE ELEVENTH JUDICIAL CIRCUIT OF FLORIDA

WHEREAS, pursuant to Administrative Order No. 10–06, Section 50 of the Circuit Civil Division of the Eleventh Judicial Circuit of Florida ("Section 50") was specifically established in an effort to eliminate the backlog of foreclosure cases in civil areas, under the non-recurring State funded Foreclosure and Economic Recovery Program ("FERP"); and

WHEREAS, funding for the FERP will be discontinued after June 30, 2011; and

WHEREAS, upon the defunding of the FERP, and in the interest of judicial administration, it is necessary to establish and implement a protocol to effectively manage aged residential mortgage foreclosure cases in Section 50 due to the loss of the FERP funding; and

WHEREAS, while the majority of the Section 50 foreclosure cases have been disposed of, the disposition of those cases in Section 50 pending upon the defunding of FERP on June 30, 2011 ("Pending Cases"), must be handled in a fair and efficient manner; and

WHEREAS, it has been determined that a fair and efficient manner for handling the Pending Cases would be to equitably reassign such cases to four judicial sections in the Circuit Civil Division; and

WHEREAS, a portion of the Pending Cases will be reassigned to judicial Sections 40 and 42, to which Judge Gill Freeman and Judge Joseph P. Farina, respectively, are currently assigned; and

WHEREAS, the remaining Pending Cases will be reassigned to the two (2) herein established judicial sections, to which Judge Michael Genden and Judge Ellen Leesfield, respectively, shall be assigned;

NOW, THEREFORE, pursuant to the authority vested in me as Chief Judge of the Eleventh Judicial Circuit of Florida, under Rule 2.215, under the Florida Rules of Judicial Administration, it is hereby **ORDERED:**

1. **DISSOLUTION**. Section 50 of the Circuit Civil Division of the Circuit Civil Division shall be dissolved at the close of business on Thursday, June 30, 2011.

2. **ESTABLISHMENT**. Sections 58 and 59 shall be established on Friday, July 1, 2011, to which Judge Michael Genden and Judge Ellen Leesfield, respectively, shall be assigned.

3. **CASE REASSIGNMENT**. Commencing Friday, July 1, 2011, the Clerk of the Courts is hereby directed and authorized to reassign all of the Pending Cases to the following judicial sections, in a manner historically used by the Clerk to ensure that such sections are equitably populated:

	JUDICIAL SECTION NUMBER	ASSIGNED JUDGE
A.	40	Judge Gill Freeman
B.	42	Judge Joseph P. Farina
C.	58	Judge Michael Genden
D.	59	Judge Ellen Leesfield

4. **NOTICE OF CASE REASSIGNMENT**. On or about July 1, 2011, the Clerk of the Courts shall provide notice that the Pending Cases have been reassigned to one of the aforementioned judicial sections.

DONE AND ORDERED in Chambers at Miami–Dade County, Florida, this 19th day of May, 2011.

JOEL H. BROWN, CHIEF JUDGE
ELEVENTH JUDICIAL CIRCUIT
OF FLORIDA

09–09 (A1). AMENDING ADMINISTRATIVE ORDER AND FINAL JUDGMENT OF FORECLOSURE FORM

THE ELEVENTH JUDICIAL CIRCUIT MIAMI–DADE COUNTY, FLORIDA

CASE NO. 09-1 (Court Administration)

ADMINISTRATIVE ORDER NO. 09–09 A1 (Amending AO No. 09–09)

IN RE: AMENDING ADMINISTRATIVE ORDER AND FINAL JUDGMENT OF FORECLOSURE FORM

WHEREAS, pursuant to Administrative Order No. 09–09, certain residential mortgage foreclosure documents were ordered to be submitted in a form as authorized by the Court; and

WHEREAS, one such form was the Final Judgment of Foreclosure; and

WHEREAS, pursuant to Section 45.031(10), Florida Statutes, the Clerk of the Courts is statutorily authorized to conduct the sale of real or personal property under an order or judgment by electronic means; and

WHEREAS, the Final Judgment of Foreclosure must reflect such authorization; and

WHEREAS, the "Protecting Tenants At Foreclosure Act of 2009", enacted by the U.S. Congress, prescribes certain procedures to be followed in foreclosure actions involving tenant occupied residential properties wherein the originating lender loans were made by Fannie Mae, Ginnie Mae, or a financial institution insured by the Federal Government; and

WHEREAS, such Act should be referenced in Administrative Order No. 09–09 and in the Final Judgment of Foreclosure;

NOW, THEREFORE, pursuant to the authority vested in me as Chief Judge of the Eleventh Judicial Circuit of Florida, under Rule 2.215, of the Florida Rules of Judicial Administration, it is hereby **ORDERED**:

1. Paragraph 5 of Administrative Order is hereby revised to read as follows:

"**Writs of Possession**. The courts shall not issue writs of possession in foreclosure actions involving homestead or non-homestead residential properties without evidence that all parties involved in such action have been properly served, notice of hearing has bee provided and a hearing is held before the court. Further, the issuance of writs of possession is subject to the provisions of the Protecting Tenant At Foreclosure Act of 2009." (Emphasis added)

2. Administrative Order No. 09–09 is amended to reflect the revisions to the Final Judgment of Foreclosure that provide for the electronic sale of real property in the form attached hereto.

3. Except as herein amended, Administrative Order No. 09–09 shall remain in full force and effect.

This Order shall take effect immediately and shall remain in full force and effect until further order of the Court.

DONE AND ORDERED in Chambers at Miami–Dade, Florida, this ___ day of November, 2009.

____

JOEL H. BROWN, CHIEF JUDGE
ELEVENTH JUDICIAL CIRCUIT OF FLORIDA

ATTACHMENT

IN THE CIRCUIT COURT OF THE ELEVENTH JUDICIAL CIRCUIT IN AND FOR MIAMI–DADE COUNTY, FLORIDA

GENERAL JURISDICTION DIVISION

CASE NO.:

Plaintiff,

vs.

Defendant(s).

____

FINAL JUDGMENT OF FORECLOSURE

(Pursuant to Administrative Order 09–09)

THIS ACTION was heard before the Court on Plaintiff's Motion for Summary Final Judgment on ______________, 20 ______. On the evidence presented, **IT IS ORDERED AND ADJUDGED that:**

1. The Plaintiff's Motion for Summary Judgment is GRANTED. Service of process has been duly and regularly obtained over Defendants: ______________________________
______________________________.

2. **Amounts Due**. There is due and owing to the Plaintiff the following:

Principal due on the note secured by the mortgage foreclosed:	$______
Interest on the note and mortgage from ____ to ____	$______
Per diem interest at ______ % from ____ to ____	$______
Title search expenses	$______
Taxes for the year of ______	$______
Insurance premiums	$______
Court Costs:	
Filing fee	$______
Service of Process at $ ______ per defendant	$______
Publication for ______	$______
SUBTOTAL	$______
Additional Costs:	
______	$______
______	$______
______	$______
SUBTOTAL	$______
Attorney fees based upon ___ hours at $ ___ per hour	$______
Less: Undisbursed escrow funds	$______
Less: Unearned insurance premiums	$______
GRAND TOTAL	$______

3. **Interest**. The grand total amount referenced in Paragraph 2 shall bear interest from this date forward at the prevailing legal rate of interest.

4. **Lien on Property**. Plaintiff, whose address is ______________________________, holds a lien for the grand total sum

specified in Paragraph 2 herein. The lien of the plaintiff is superior in dignity to any right, title, interest or claim of the defendants and all persons, corporations, or other entities claiming by, through, or under the defendants or any of them and the property will be sold free and clear of all claims of the defendants, with the exception of any assessments that are superior pursuant to Florida Statutes, Section 718.116. The plaintiff's lien encumbers the subject property located in Miami Dade County, Florida and described as:

(LEGAL DESCRIPTION)

Property address: ______________________

5. **Sale of Property**. If the grand total amount with interest at the rate described in Paragraph 3 and all costs accrued subsequent to this judgment are not paid, the Clerk of the Court shall sell the subject property at public sale on __________, 20 ___, to the highest bidder for cash, except as prescribed in Paragraph 6, at:

[ ] Room 908, 140 West Flagler Street, Miami, Florida at 11:00 a.m.

[ ] www.miamidade.realforeclose.com, the Clerk's website for on-line auctions at 9:00 a.m.

after having first given notice as required by Section 45.031, Florida Statutes.

6. **Costs.** Plaintiff shall advance all subsequent costs of this action and shall be reimbursed for them by the Clerk if plaintiff is not the purchaser of the property for sale. If plaintiff is the purchaser, the Clerk shall credit plaintiff's bid with the total sum with interest and costs accruing subsequent to this judgment, or such part of it, as is necessary to pay the bid in full. The Clerk shall receive the service charge imposed in Section 45.031, Florida Statutes, for services in making, recording, and certifying the sale and title that shall be assessed as costs.

7. **Right of Redemption.** On filing of the Certificate of Sale, defendant's right of redemption as proscribed by Florida Statutes, Section 45.0315 shall be terminated.

8. **Distribution of Proceeds.** On filing the Certificate of Title, the Clerk shall distribute the proceeds of the sale, so far as they are sufficient, by paying: first, all of the plaintiff's costs; second, documentary stamps affixed to the Certificate; third, plaintiff's attorneys' fees; fourth, the total sum due to the plaintiff, less the items paid, plus interest at the rate prescribed in paragraph 2 from this date to the date of the sale. During the sixty (60) days after the Clerk issues the certificate of disbursements, the Clerk shall hold the surplus pending further Order of this Court.

9. **Right of Possession.** Upon filing of the Certificate of Title, defendant and all persons claiming under or against defendant since the filing of the Notice of Lis Pendens shall be foreclosed of all estate or claim in the property and the purchaser at sale shall be let into possession of the property, subject to the provisions of the "Protecting Tenant At Foreclosure Act of 2009."

10. **Attorney Fees.** The Court finds, based upon the affidavits presented and upon inquiry of counsel for the plaintiff, that ___ hours were reasonably expended by plaintiff's counsel and that an hourly rate of $ __________ is appropriate. PLAINTIFF'S COUNSEL REPRESENTS THAT THE ATTORNEY FEE AWARDED DOES NOT EXCEED ITS CONTRACT FEE WITH THE PLAINTIFF. The Court finds that there are no reduction or enhancement factors for consideration by the Court pursuant to *Florida Patient's Compensation Fund v. Rowe*, 472 So.2d 1145 (Fla. 1985).

11. **NOTICE PURSUANT TO AMENDMENT TO SECTION, 45.031, FLA. ST. (2006)**

IF THIS PROPERTY IS SOLD AT PUBLIC AUCTION, THERE MAY BE ADDITIONAL MONEY FROM THE SALE AFTER PAYMENT OF PERSONS WHO ARE ENTITLED TO BE PAID FROM THE SALE PROCEEDS PURSUANT TO THE FINAL JUDGMENT.

IF YOU ARE A SUBORDINATE LIEN HOLDER CLAIMING A RIGHT TO FUNDS REMAINING AFTER THE SALE, YOU MUST FILE A CLAIM WITH THE CLERK NO LATER THAN SIXTY (60) DAYS AFTER THE SALE. IF YOU FAIL TO FILE A CLAIM, YOU WILL NOT BE ENTITLED TO ANY REMAINING FUNDS.

IF YOU ARE THE PROPERTY OWNER, YOU MAY CLAIM THESE FUNDS YOURSELF. YOU ARE NOT REQUIRED TO HAVE A LAWYER OR ANY OTHER REPRESENTATION AND YOU DO NOT HAVE TO ASSIGN YOUR RIGHTS TO ANYONE ELSE IN ORDER FOR YOU TO CLAIM ANY MONEY TO WHICH YOU ARE ENTITLED. PLEASE CHECK WITH THE CLERK OF THE COURT, 140 WEST FLAGLER STREET, ROOM 908, MIAMI, FLORIDA (TELEPHONE: (305) 375–5943), WITHIN (10) DAYS AFTER THE SALE TO SEE IF THERE IS ADDITIONAL MONEY FROM THE FORECLOSURE SALE THAT THE CLERK HAS IN THE REGISTRY OF THE COURT.

IF YOU DECIDE TO SELL YOUR HOME OR HIRE SOMEONE TO HELP YOU CLAIM THE ADDITIONAL MONEY, YOU SHOULD READ VERY CAREFULLY ALL PAPERS YOU ARE REQUIRED TO SIGN, ASK SOMEONE ELSE, PREFERABLY AN ATTORNEY WHO IS NOT RELATED TO THE PERSON OFFERING TO HELP YOU, TO MAKE SURE THAT YOU UNDERSTAND WHAT YOU ARE SIGNING AND THAT YOU ARE NOT TRANSFERRING YOUR PROPERTY OR THE EQUITY IN YOUR PROPERTY WITHOUT THE PROPER INFORMATION. IF YOU CANNOT AFFORD TO PAY AN ATTORNEY, YOU MAY CONTACT THE LEGAL AID SOCIETY AT THE DADE COUNTY BAR ASSOCIATION, 123 N.W. FIRST AVENUE, SUITE 214, MIAMI, FLORIDA, (TELEPHONE: (305) 579–5733), TO SEE IF YOU QUALIFY FINANCIALLY FOR THEIR SERVICES. IF THEY CANNOT ASSIST YOU, THEY MAY BE ABLE TO REFER YOU TO A LOCAL BAR REFERRAL AGENCY OR SUGGEST OTHER OPTIONS. IF YOU CHOOSE TO CONTACT THE DADE COUNTY BAR ASSOCIATION LEGAL AID SOCIETY, YOU SHOULD DO SO AS SOON AS POSSIBLE AFTER RECEIPT OF THIS NOTICE.

12. **Jurisdiction.** The Court retains jurisdiction of this action to enter further orders that are proper, including, without limitation, writs of possession and deficiency judgments.

DONE AND ORDERED in Chambers in Miami Dade County, Florida, this ___ day of __________, 20 ___.

Circuit Judge

09–09. REVISIONS TO UNIFORM FINAL JUDGMENT OF FORECLOSURE FORM, ADOPTION OF OTHER FORECLOSURE FORMS, AND ESTABLISHMENT OF OTHER FORECLOSURE PROCEDURES

THE ELEVENTH JUDICIAL CIRCUIT MIAMI–DADE COUNTY, FLORIDA

CASE NO. 09–1 (Court Administration)

ADMINISTRATIVE ORDER NO. 09–09 (Rescinding AO 06–02 and AO 06–02 A1)

IN RE: REVISIONS TO UNIFORM FINAL JUDGMENT OF FORECLOSURE FORM, ADOPTION OF OTHER FORECLOSURE FORMS, AND ESTABLISHMENT OF OTHER FORECLOSURE PROCEDURES

WHEREAS, as acknowledged in Administrative Order No. 06–02, and as amended by Administrative Order No. 06–02 A1, it had become common practice for attorneys to submit Final Judgments of Foreclosure containing various terms and provisions not included in Form 1.996 of the Florida Rules of Civil Procedure; and

WHEREAS, pursuant to said Administrative Orders, in an effort to promote uniformity and ease of review in examining these proposed Final Judgments, a specific format for such Final Judgments was prescribed; and

WHEREAS, on July 1, 2006, amended statutory requirements regarding mortgage foreclosure procedures became effective and were accordingly incorporated in the Final Judgments of Foreclosure; and

WHEREAS, pursuant to Administrative Order No. 09–08, the 11th Circuit Homestead Access to Mediation Program ("CHAMP") was established for the case management of residential foreclosure cases filed on or after May 1, 2009 in this Circuit through the implementation of mandatory mediation of mortgage foreclosure actions involving homestead properties; and

WHEREAS, in compliance with AO No. 09–08, certain forms have to be revised or created to include, (i) Civil Cover Sheet, (ii) Plaintiff's Certification of Settlement Authority, (iii) Plaintiff's Certification of Residential Mortgage Foreclosure Case Status and (iv) Final Judgment of Foreclosure; and

WHEREAS, with regard to actions involving condominium and homeowner's association fee foreclosures, private investor mortgage foreclosures, foreclosures of non-homestead properties, construction lien foreclosures, and homestead foreclosure actions filed prior to May 1, 2009, while CHAMP is unavailable for the parties, mediation procedures as set forth in Rule 1.720(f), Florida Rules of Civil Procedure, will continue to be available; and

WHEREAS, other foreclosure procedures governing the issuance of writs of possession for homestead and non-homestead residential properties need to be established;

NOW, THEREFORE, pursuant to the authority vested in me as Chief Judge of the Eleventh Judicial Circuit of Florida, under Rule 2.215 of the Florida Rules of Judicial Administration, it is hereby **ORDERED:**

1. **Residential Mortgage Foreclosure Documents**. The following documents shall be submitted in the form attached hereto:

A. Civil Cover Sheet

B. Plaintiff's Certification of Settlement Authority

C. Plaintiff's Certification of Residential Mortgage Foreclosure Case Status

D. Final Judgment of Foreclosure

2. **Reformation and/or lost notes**. With regard to those foreclosure matters wherein the circumstances require the court to address reformation and/or lost note(s) issues, if properly pleaded in the Complaint and proved in the Motion for Final Summary Judgment of Foreclosure, the Final Judgment of Foreclosure may address such issues. With regard to lost notes, the language to be included in the Final Judgment must be written in bold print and stated as follows:

"The Court finds that the Plaintiff has reestablished the terms of the lost note and its right to enforce the instrument as required by Section 673. 3091, Florida Statutes. Plaintiff shall hold the Defendant maker of the note harmless and shall indemnify them from any loss they may incur by reason of a claim by any other person to enforce the lost note. Since adequate protection is provided as required by Section 673.3091, Florida Statutes, judgment is hereby entered in favor of the Plaintiff as to its request to enforce the lost note."

With regard to reformation, attorneys may propose the language to be included in bold print in the Final Judgment, for the court's consideration.

3. **Supplemental Orders**. As provided in the Final Judgment of Foreclosure (attached hereto), the court shall retain jurisdiction to enter further orders for additional relief that are proper, including, without limitation, writs of possession (as hereinafter stated) and deficiency judgments. Any such additional relief sought to be included as part of the Final Judgment of Foreclosure may be allowed if within the court's jurisdiction, and properly pleaded. If such relief is granted, it must be entered as a Supplemental Order to the Final Judgment of Foreclosure.

4. **Mediation for Other Homestead and Non-homestead Properties**. In accordance with Administrative Order No. 09–08, only foreclosure actions against homestead properties filed on or after May 1, 2009 are eligible for the 11th Circuit Homestead Access to Mediation Program ("CHAMP").

Condominium and homeowner's association fee foreclosures, private investor mortgage foreclosures, foreclosures of non-homestead properties, construction lien foreclosures, and homestead foreclosure actions filed prior to May 1, 2009, **are not eligible for CHAMP**. Such foreclosures will continue to follow the mediation procedures set forth in Rule 1.720(f), Florida Rules of Civil Procedure.

5. **Writs of Possession**. The court shall not issue writs of possession in foreclosure actions involving homestead or non-homestead residential properties without evidence that all parties involved in such action have been properly served,

notice of hearing has been provided and a hearing is held before the court.

Administrative Order No. 06–02 and Administrative Order No. 06–02 A1 are hereby rescinded in their entirety and shall be held for naught.

This Administrative Order shall take effect immediately and shall remain in effect until further order of the Court.

DONE AND ORDERED in Chambers at Miami–Dade, Florida, this ___ day of May, 2009.

JOSEPH P. FARINA, CHIEF JUDGE
ELEVENTH JUDICIAL CIRCUIT OF FLORIDA

ATTACHMENT A

☐IN THE CIRCUIT COURT OF THE ELEVENTH JUDICIAL CIRCUIT IN AND FOR MIAMI–DADE COUNTY, FLORIDA
☐IN THE COUNTY COURT IN AND FOR MIAMI–DADE COUNTY, FLORIDA

DIVISION **CASE NUMBER**
☐CIVIL
☐DISTRICTS
☐FAMILY
☐OTHER

CIVIL COVER SHEET

PLAINTIFF **VS. DEFENDANT** **CLOCK IN**

The civil cover sheet and the information contained here does not replace the filing and service of pleadings or other papers as required by law. This form is required by the Clerk of Court for the purpose of reporting judicial workload data pursuant to Florida Statute 25.075. See instructions and definitions on reverse of this form.

TYPE OF CASE (Place an 'x' in one box only)

Domestic Relations	Torts	Other Civil
☐Simplified dissolution	☐ Professional Malpractice	☐ Contracts ☐Condominium
☐Dissolution of Marriage	☐ Products liability	☐Real property
☐Support—IV–D	☐ Auto negligence	☐ Mortgage foreclosure ☐Commercial
☐Support—Non IV–D	☐ Other negligence	☐Residential
☐UIFSA—IV–D		☐ Homestead ☐Non–Homestead
☐UIFSA—Non IV–D		☐Eminent Domain
☐Domestic Violence		☐ Challenge to proposed Constitutional Amendment
☐Other domestic relations		☐ Other

DATE:

Is Jury Trial Demanded in Complaint? ☐Yes☐No

COMPLEX BUSINESS COURT

This action is appropriate for assignment to Complex Business Court as delineated in the attached addendum pursuant to Administrative Order. ☐Yes☐No

Signature of Attorney for party initiating action: ___ Print Name: ___

Address ___

Telephone ___

JUDGE:

INSTRUCTIONS FOR ATTORNEYS COMPLETING CIVIL COVER SHEET

I. Class Style. Enter the name of the court, the appropriate case number assigned at the time of filing of the original complaint or petition, the name of the judge assigned (if applicable) and the name (last, first, middle initial) of plaintiff(s) and defendant(s).

II. Type of Case. Place an "X" in the appropriate box. If the cause fits more than one type of case, select the most definitive. Definitions of the cases are provided below.

(A) **Simplified Dissolution of Marriage**—Petitions for the termination of marriage pursuant to Fla.C.Civ.P.1.1611(C).

(B) **Dissolution of Marriage**—Petitions for the termination of marriage other than simplified dissolution.

(C) **Support—IV–D**—all matters relating to child or spousal support in which an application for assistance has been filed under Title IV–D, Social Security Act; except for such matters relating to dissolution of marriage petitions (F.S. 409.2564, 409.2571 and 490.2597), paternity, or UIFSA.

(D) **Support—Non IV–D**—all matters relating to child or spousal support in which an application for assistance has been filed under Title IV–D, Social Security act.

(E) **UIFSA—IV–D**—all matters relating to Chapter 88, Florida Statutes, in which an application for assistance has not been filed under Title IV–D, Social Security Act.

(F) **UIFSA—Non IV–D**—all matters relating to Chapter 88, Florida Statutes, in which an application for assistance has not been filed under Title IV–D, Social Security Act.

(G) **Domestic Violence**—all matters relating to injunctions for protection against domestic violence pursuant to F.S. 741.30.

(H) **Domestic Relations**—all matters involving adoption, paternity, change of name, child custody, separate maintenance, annulment, or other matters not included in categories (A) through (G).

(I) **Auto Negligence**—all matters arising out of a party's allegedly negligent operation of a motor vehicle.

(J) **Professional Malpractice**—all professional malpractice lawsuits.

(K) **Products Liability**—all matters involving injury to person or property allegedly resulting from the manufacture or sale of a defective product or from a failure to warn.

(L) **Other Negligence**—all actions sounding in negligence, including statutory claims for relief on account of death or injury, not included in categories (I), (J), and (K).

(M) **Condominium**—all civil lawsuits pursuant to Chapter 718, Florida Statutes, where a condominium association is a party in the lawsuit.

(N) **Eminent Domain**—all matters relating to the taking of private property for public use, including inverse condemnation by state agencies, political subdivisions and public service corporations.

(O) **Real Property/Mortgage Foreclosure**—all matters relating to the possession, title and boundaries of real property including: homestead and non-homestead residential foreclosures, commercial foreclosures and foreclosures associated with condominium associations and condominium units.

(P) **Contracts and Indebtedness**—all contract actions relating to promissory notes and other debts, including those arising from the sale of goods. Excludes contract disputes involving condominium associations.

(Q) **Change to proposed constitutional amendment**—a challenge to a legislatively initiated proposed constitutional amendment. Excludes challenges to citizen-initiated proposed constitutional amendments, because the Florida Supreme Court has direct jurisdiction of such challenges.

(R) **Other Civil**—all civil matters not included in categories (A) through (Q).

III. Is Jury Trial Demanded in Complaint? Check the appropriate box to indicate whether or not a jury is being demanded in the complaint.

IV. Complex Business Court—Check the appropriate box to indicate whether or not this case is to be assigned to the Complex Business Court.

DATE AND ATTORNEY SIGNATURE. Date and sign the civil cover sheet.

ATTACHMENT B

IN THE CIRCUIT COURT OF THE ELEVENTH JUDICIAL CIRCUIT IN AND FOR MIAMI–DADE COUNTY, FLORIDA

GENERAL JURISDICTION DIVISION

CASE NO.:

Plaintiff,

vs.

Defendant(s).

____

PLAINTIFF'S CERTIFICATION OF SETTLEMENT AUTHORITY

The undersigned counsel, on behalf of Plaintiff/Lender, does hereby file its certification of settlement authority and states as follows:

1. Plaintiff/Lender's representative in this matter is ________ ("Representative").

2. During the course of these proceedings, Representative shall either appear in person or telephonically at ________ (Toll free number).

I HEREBY CERTIFY that the undersigned has spoken with the Plaintiff/Lender's Representative and confirmed that the Representative has full and complete settlement authority to enter into a binding agreement this ___ day of ________, 200 ___.

Signature: ______________________
Printed name: ______________________
Bar Number: ______________________
Address: ______________________
Telephone No.: ______________________

ATTACHMENT C

IN THE CIRCUIT COURT OF THE ELEVENTH JUDICIAL CIRCUIT IN AND FOR MIAMI–DADE COUNTY, FLORIDA

GENERAL JURISDICTION DIVISION

CASE NO.:

Plaintiff,

vs.

Defendant(s).

____

PLAINTIFF'S CERTIFICATION OF RESIDENTIAL MORTGAGE FORECLOSURE CASE STATUS

The undersigned attorney hereby certifies that the information provided herein is true and correct:

DEFENDANTS	SERVED	DROPPED	ANSWER	DEFAULT

Confirm courtesy copies were mailed to defendants and indicate dates:

________ Motion for Summary Judgment.
________ Notice of Hearing on Summary Judgment.
________ Affidavit of Indebtedness.
________ Affidavit of Costs.
________ Affidavit of Attorney Fees.
________ Affidavit as to Reasonableness of Attorney Fees.

Confirm compliance and indicate dates:

________ Original note and mortgage, and assignment, if applicable, provided to the Court.
________ Affidavit of lost note filed.
________ Case under CHAMP program, compliance attached.

Undersigned counsel further certifies, under penalty of perjury, that in accordance with Administrative Order No. 09–08:

a. The Summary Final Judgment of Foreclosure submitted is the court-approved form, without any alterations or additions; and

b. That the amounts in the final judgment are accurate and correspond with the affidavits filed herein.

______________________ ______________________
Date Signature of Attorney

ATTACHMENT D

IN THE CIRCUIT COURT OF THE ELEVENTH JUDICIAL CIRCUIT IN AND FOR MIAMI–DADE COUNTY, FLORIDA

GENERAL JURISDICTION DIVISION

CASE NO.:

Plaintiff,

vs.

Defendant(s).

____

FINAL JUDGMENT OF FORECLOSURE

(Pursuant to Administrative Order 09–09)

THIS ACTION was heard before the Court on Plaintiff's Motion for Summary Final Judgment on ________, 200 ___. On the evidence presented, **IT IS ORDERED AND ADJUDGED** that:

1. The Plaintiff's Motion for Summary Judgment is **GRANTED**. Service of process has been duly and regularly obtained over Defendants: ________.

2. **Amounts Due.** There is due and owing to the Plaintiff the following:

Principal due on the note secured by the mortgage foreclosed:	$________
Interest on the note and mortgage from ________ to ________	$________
Per diem interest at ________ % from ________ to ________	$________
Title search expenses	$________
Taxes for the year of ________	$________
Insurance premiums	$________
Court Costs:	
Filing fee	$________
Service of Process at $ ________ per defendant	$________
Publication for ________	$________
SUBTOTAL	$________
Additional Costs:	
________	$________
________	$________
SUBTOTAL	$________
Attorney fees based upon ___ hours at $ ________ per hour	$________
Less: Undisbursed escrow funds	$________
Less: Unearned insurance premiums	$________
GRAND TOTAL	$________

3. **Interest.** The grand total amount referenced in Paragraph 2 shall bear interest from this date forward at the prevailing legal rate of interest.

4. **Lien on Property.** Plaintiff, whose address is ________________, holds a lien for the grand total sum specified in Paragraph 2 herein. The lien of the plaintiff is superior in dignity to any right, title, interest or claim of the defendants and all persons, corporations, or other entities claiming by, through, or under the defendants or any of them and the property will be sold free and clear of all claims of the defendants, with the exception of any assessments that are superior pursuant to Florida Statutes, Section 718.116. The plaintiff's lien encumbers the subject property located in Miami Dade County, Florida and described as:

(LEGAL DESCRIPTION)

Property address: ________

5. **Sale of property.** If the grand total amount with interest at the rate described in Paragraph 3 and all costs accrued subsequent to this judgment are not paid, the Clerk of the Court shall sell the subject property at public sale on ________, 200 ___, at 11:00 A.M. to the highest bidder for cash, except as prescribed in Paragraph 6, at Room 908, 140 West Flagler Street, Miami, Florida after having first given notice as required by Section 45.031, Florida Statutes.

6. **Costs.** Plaintiff shall advance all subsequent costs of this action and shall be reimbursed for them by the Clerk if plaintiff is not the purchaser of the property for sale. If plaintiff is the purchaser, the Clerk shall credit plaintiff's bid with the total sum with interest and costs accruing subsequent to this judgment, or such part of it, as is necessary to pay the bid in full. The Clerk shall receive the service charge imposed in Section 45.031, Florida Statutes, for services in making, recording, and certifying the sale and title that shall be assessed as costs.

7. **Right of Redemption.** On filing of the Certificate of Sale, defendant's right of redemption as proscribed by Florida Statutes, Section 45.0315 shall be terminated.

8. **Distribution of Proceeds.** On filing the Certificate of Title, the Clerk shall distribute the proceeds of the sale, so far as they are sufficient, by paying: first, all of the plaintiff's costs; second, documentary stamps affixed to the Certificate; third, plaintiff's attorneys' fees; fourth, the total sum due to the plaintiff, less the items paid, plus interest at the rate prescribed in paragraph 2 from this date to the date of the sale. During the sixty (60) days after the Clerk issues the certificate of disbursements, the Clerk shall hold the surplus pending further Order of this Court.

9. **Right of Possession.** Upon filing of the Certificate of Title, defendant and all persons claiming under or against defendant since the filing of the Notice of Lis Pendens shall be foreclosed of all estate or claim in the property and the purchaser at sale shall be let into possession of the property.

10. **Attorney Fees.** The Court finds, based upon the affidavits presented and upon inquiry of counsel for the plaintiff, that ________ hours were reasonably expended by plaintiff's counsel and that an hourly rate of $ ________ is appropriate. PLAINTIFF'S COUNSEL REPRESENTS THAT THE ATTORNEY FEE AWARDED DOES NOT EXCEED ITS CONTRACT FEE WITH THE PLAINTIFF. The Court finds that there are no reduction or enhancement factors for consideration by the Court pursuant to *Florida Patient's Compensation Fund v. Rowe*, 472 So.2d 1145 (Fla. 1985).

11. **NOTICE PURSUANT TO AMENDMENT TO SECTION, 45.031, FLA. ST. (2006)**

IF THIS PROPERTY IS SOLD AT PUBLIC AUCTION, THERE MAY BE ADDITIONAL MONEY FROM THE SALE AFTER PAYMENT OF PERSONS WHO ARE ENTITLED TO BE PAID FROM THE SALE PROCEEDS PURSUANT TO THE FINAL JUDGMENT.

IF YOU ARE A SUBORDINATE LIEN HOLDER CLAIMING A RIGHT TO FUNDS REMAINING AFTER THE SALE, YOU MUST FILE A CLAIM WITH THE CLERK NO LATER THAN SIXTY (60) DAYS AFTER THE SALE. IF YOU FAIL TO FILE A CLAIM, YOU WILL NOT BE ENTITLED TO ANY REMAINING FUNDS.

IF YOU ARE THE PROPERTY OWNER, YOU MAY CLAIM THESE FUNDS YOURSELF. YOU ARE NOT REQUIRED TO HAVE A LAWYER OR ANY OTHER REPRESENTATION AND YOU DO NOT HAVE TO ASSIGN YOUR RIGHTS TO ANYONE ELSE IN ORDER FOR YOU TO CLAIM ANY MONEY TO WHICH YOU ARE ENTITLED. PLEASE CHECK WITH THE CLERK OF THE COURT, 140 WEST FLAGLER STREET, ROOM 908, MIAMI, FLORIDA (TELEPHONE: (305) 375–5943), WITHIN (10) DAYS AFTER THE SALE TO SEE IF THERE IS ADDITIONAL MONEY FROM THE FORECLOSURE SALE THAT THE CLERK HAS IN THE REGISTRY OF THE COURT.

IF YOU DECIDE TO SELL YOUR HOME OR HIRE SOMEONE TO HELP YOU CLAIM THE ADDITIONAL MONEY, YOU SHOULD READ VERY CAREFULLY ALL PAPERS YOU ARE REQUIRED TO SIGN, ASK SOMEONE ELSE, PREFERABLY AN ATTORNEY WHO IS NOT RELATED TO THE PERSON OFFERING TO HELP YOU, TO MAKE SURE THAT YOU UNDERSTAND WHAT YOU ARE SIGNING AND THAT YOU ARE NOT TRANSFERRING YOUR PROPERTY OR THE EQUITY IN YOUR PROPERTY WITHOUT THE PROPER INFORMATION. IF YOU CANNOT AFFORD TO PAY AN ATTORNEY, YOU MAY CONTACT THE LEGAL AID SOCIETY AT THE DADE COUNTY BAR ASSOCIATION, 123 N.W. FIRST AVENUE, SUITE 214, MIAMI, FLORIDA, (TELEPHONE: (305) 579–5733), TO SEE IF YOU QUALIFY FINANCIALLY FOR THEIR SERVICES. IF THEY CANNOT ASSIST YOU, THEY MAY BE ABLE TO REFER YOU TO A LOCAL BAR REFERRAL AGENCY OR SUGGEST OTHER OPTIONS. IF YOU CHOOSE TO CONTACT THE DADE COUNTY BAR ASSOCIATION LEGAL AID SOCIETY, YOU SHOULD DO SO AS SOON AS POSSIBLE AFTER RECEIPT OF THIS NOTICE.

12. **Jurisdiction.** The Court retains jurisdiction of this action to enter further orders that are proper, including, without limitation, writs of possession and deficiency judgments.

DONE AND ORDERED in Chambers in Miami Dade County, Florida, this ___ day of __________, 200___.

____
Circuit Judge

03–01 (A1). [RESCINDED BY ADMINISTRATIVE ORDER NO. 16–07, EFFECTIVE MAY 4, 2016]

Circuit Court Criminal

15–06. HOUSE ARREST AND ELECTRONIC MONITORING PROGRAMS

THE ELEVENTH JUDICIAL CIRCUIT OF FLORIDA

CASE NO. 15–01 (Court Administration)

ADMINISTRATIVE ORDER NO. 15–06

IN RE: HOUSE ARREST AND ELECTRONIC MONITORING PROGRAMS

WHEREAS, pursuant to Fla. R. Crim. P 3.131(b)(C), in setting terms and conditions of pretrial release, a court may consider "placement of restrictions on the travel, association, or place of abode of the defendant;" and

WHEREAS, pursuant to Fla. R. Crim. P. 3.131(b)(1)(D), such placement may be in the custody of a designated person or organization agreeing to supervise the defendant; and

WHEREAS, Section 907.041(3)(b), Florida Statutes authorizes release of defendants to a pretrial release service; and

WHEREAS, Section 907.043(2)(b), Florida Statutes further defines a pretrial release program as one that includes electronic monitoring; and

WHEREAS, consistent with the aforementioned Florida Rules of Criminal Procedure and the Statutes, a court may admit a defendant to the Monitored Release Program ("House Arrest") operated by the Miami–Dade Corrections and Rehabilitation Department ("the Department") as set forth in Miami–Dade County Administrative Order 4–116; and

WHEREAS, a defendant admitted to House Arrest is in the custody of, but not housed by, the Department; rather, the defendant is permitted to reside at his/her own residence, under certain conditions, to include, wearing a GPS monitor at all times and submitting to visits and inspections by House Arrest officers;

NOW, THEREFORE, pursuant to the authority vested in me as Chief Judge of the Eleventh Judicial Circuit of Florida under Rule 2.215, Florida Rules of Judicial Administration, it is hereby **ORDERED** that defendants shall be released to House Arrest under the following conditions:

1. The Department is entitled to recoup from a defendant a reasonable portion of the cost of House Arrest, as provided in Section 951.033, Florida Statutes.

2. It is the responsibility of the court, and not of the Department, to determine the material conditions of the defendant's House Arrest, such as whether, and upon what terms, the defendant may leave home; whether the defendant is subject to drug testing; whether there are geographical locations that the defendant cannot enter for any reason, etc.

3. A defendant admitted to House Arrest is permitted to leave his/her residence as is reasonably necessary for work; school; care of children; medical services; attorney visits; court attendance; and religious services. The court may restrict a defendant from leaving his/her residence for any of these purposes only upon stating the grounds justifying such restriction.

4. Upon violation of any condition of House Arrest, the Department shall take a defendant into the secure custody of the jail pending further order of the court. The Department need not obtain a warrant or court order before returning the defendant into secure custody. The Department shall promptly advise the court that the defendant is in custody and the nature of the violation(s).

5. If the Department determines that the defendant, for any reason, poses a risk of danger to the community, it may take the defendant into the secure custody of the jail pending further order of the court. The Department need not obtain a warrant or court order before returning the defendant into secure custody. The Department shall promptly advise the court that the defendant is in custody and the reason(s) why the Department removed him/her from the House Arrest program.

6. Admission to House Arrest is solely for the benefit of the defendant. The Department is not responsible for any medical or other expenses of the defendant while on House Arrest.

This Administrative Order shall take effect immediately and shall remain in effect until further order of the Court.

DONE AND ORDERED in Chambers, in Miami–Dade County, Florida, this 17th day of June, 2015.

BERTILA SOTO, CHIEF JUDGE
ELEVENTH JUDICIAL CIRCUIT
OF FLORIDA

06–01. ESTABLISHMENT OF REPEAT OFFENDER COURT SECTIONS

THE ELEVENTH JUDICIAL CIRCUIT MIAMI–DADE COUNTY, FLORIDA

CASE NO. 06–1 (Court Administration)

ADMINISTRATIVE ORDER NO. 06–01 (Rescinding Administrative Order No. 05–06)

IN RE: ESTABLISHMENT OF REPEAT OFFENDER COURT SECTIONS

WHEREAS, pursuant to Section 775.0841, Florida Statutes, the Legislature has determined that a substantial and disproportionate number of serious crimes are committed in Florida by a relatively small group of multiple and repeat felony offenders; and

WHEREAS, as set forth in Section 775.0841, Florida Statutes, the Legislature has concluded that priority should be given to the prosecution of career criminals, and the Legislature supports increased efforts by the State to investigate and prosecute career criminals; and

WHEREAS, local rules, under the umbrella of Article V, Section 20(c)(10) of the Florida Constitution, create divisions or subdivisions within the circuit courts, this Administrative Order, pursuant to Florida Rules of Judicial Administration 2.050 and consistent with prior rulings of the Florida Supreme Court, has the express and exclusive objective of facilitating and advancing the efficient administration of justice in the Miami–Dade Circuit Criminal Courts; and

WHEREAS, consistent with Florida Supreme Court holdings, this Order merely creates sections of the circuit court's criminal division, a matter within the broad administrative authority of this circuit's Chief Judge; and

WHEREAS, the designation of specialized sections, within the criminal division, to hear cases limited to prison releasee reoffenders and/or habitual violent felony offenders and/or violent career criminals promotes the efficiency of judicial administration;

NOW, THEREFORE, pursuant to the authority vested in me as Chief Judge of the Eleventh Judicial Circuit of Florida under Rule 2.050 of the Florida Rules of Judicial Administration, it is hereby **ORDERED** that:

I. ESTABLISHMENT OF REPEAT OFFENDER COURT SECTIONS

Section "70" and Section "71" are hereby established as Repeat Offender Court sections of the circuit court's criminal division to hear cases limited to prison releasee reoffenders and/or habitual violent felony offenders and/or violent career criminals.

II. RANDOM ASSIGNMENT

All cases pending on or filed after January 23, 2006, in which the State Attorney files a Designation or list indicating that at least one of the defendants meets the following criteria, shall be randomly assigned to sections "70" and "71" in the criminal division of the circuit court.

III. CRITERIA FOR ASSIGNMENT

In the initial operational stages of the Repeat Offender Court section, only life or first degree felonies under the following statutory criteria, will be assigned to these sections. Cases involving any homicide, and cases where the only qualifying offense is one pursuant to Florida Statute 893, however, will not be assigned to the sections in the initial operational stages. After periodic review by the Chief Judge, other felonies in accordance with Florida Statutes may also be assigned to the sections. The Office of the State Attorney and the Office of the Public Defender will be notified one month prior to the commencement of assignment of other felonies to the sections.

A. *VIOLENT CAREER CRIMINAL*

Violent career criminal criteria shall be in accordance with Fla. Stat. 775.084(1)(d) and (e), as amended from time to time, and which presently provide as follows:

(d)1. The defendant has previously been convicted as an adult three or more times for an offense in this state or other qualified offense that is:

a. Any forcible felony, as described in s. 776.08;

b. Aggravated stalking, as described in s. 784.048(3) and (4);

c. Aggravated child abuse, as described in s. 827.03(2);

d. Aggravated abuse of an elderly person or disabled adult, as described in s. 825.102(2);

e. Lewd or lascivious battery, lewd or lascivious molestation, lewd or lascivious conduct, or lewd or lascivious exhibition, as described in s. 800.04;

f. Escape, as described in s. 944.40; or

g. A felony violation of chapter 790 involving the use or possession of a firearm.

2. The defendant has been incarcerated in a state prison or a federal prison.

3. The primary felony offense for which the defendant is to be sentenced is a felony enumerated in subparagraph 1. and was committed on or after October 1, 1995, and:

a. While the defendant was serving a prison sentence or other sentence, or court-ordered or lawfully imposed supervision that is imposed as a result of a prior conviction for an enumerated felony; or

b. Within 5 years after the conviction of the last prior enumerated felony, or within 5 years after the defendant's release from a prison sentence, probation, community control, control release, conditional release, parole, or court-ordered or lawfully imposed supervision or other sentence that is imposed as a result of a prior conviction for an enumerated felony, whichever is later.

4. The defendant has not received a pardon for any felony or other qualified offense that is necessary for the operation of this paragraph.

5. A conviction of a felony or other qualified offense necessary to the operation of this paragraph has not been set aside in any post-conviction proceeding.

(e) "Qualified offense" means any offense, substantially similar in elements and penalties to an offense in this state, which is in violation of a law of any other jurisdiction, whether that of another state, the District of Columbia, the United States or any possession or territory thereof, or any foreign jurisdiction, that was punishable under the law of such jurisdiction at the time of its commission by the defendant by death or imprisonment exceeding 1 year.

B. *HABITUAL VIOLENT FELONY OFFENDER*

Habitual Violent Felony Offender criteria shall be in accordance with Fla. Stat. 775.084(1)(b), as may be amended from time to time, and which presently provides as follows:

1. The defendant has previously been convicted of a felony or an attempt or conspiracy to commit a felony and one or more of such convictions was for:

a. Arson;

b. Sexual battery;

c. Robbery;

d. Kidnapping;

e. Aggravated child abuse;

f. Aggravated abuse of an elderly person or disabled adult;

g. Aggravated assault with a deadly weapon;

h. Murder;

i. Manslaughter;

j. Aggravated manslaughter of an elderly person or disabled adult;

k. Aggravated manslaughter of a child;

l. Unlawful throwing, placing, or discharging of a destructive device or bomb;

m. Armed burglary;

n. Aggravated battery; or

o. Aggravated stalking.

2. The felony for which the defendant is to be sentenced was committed:

a. While the defendant was serving a prison sentence or other sentence, or court-ordered or lawfully imposed supervision that is imposed as a result of a prior conviction for an enumerated felony; or

b. Within 5 years of the date of the conviction of the last prior enumerated felony, or within 5 years of the defendant's release from a prison sentence, probation, community control, control release, conditional release, parole, or court-ordered or lawfully imposed supervision or other sentence that is imposed as a result of a prior conviction for an enumerated felony, whichever is later.

3. The defendant has not received a pardon on the ground of innocence for any crime that is necessary for the operation of this paragraph.

4. A conviction of a crime necessary to the operation of this paragraph has not been set aside in any post-conviction proceeding.

C. *PRISON RELEASEE REOFFENDER*

Prison Releasee Reoffender criteria shall be in accordance with Fla. Stat. 775.082(9)(a), as may be amended from time to time, and which presently provides:

1. Any defendant who commits, or attempts to commit:

a. Treason;

b. Murder;

c. Manslaughter;

d. Sexual battery;

e. Carjacking;

f. Home–invasion robbery;

g. Robbery;

h. Arson;

i. Kidnapping;

j. Aggravated assault with a deadly weapon;

k. Aggravated battery;

l. Aggravated stalking;

m. Aircraft piracy;

n. Unlawful throwing, placing, or discharging of a destructive device or bomb;

o. Any felony that involves the use or threat of physical force or violence against an individual;

p. Armed burglary;

q. Burglary of a dwelling or burglary of an occupied structure; or

r. Any felony violation of s. 790.07, s. 800.04, s. 827.03, or s. 827.071;

within 3 years after being released from a state correctional facility operated by the Department of Corrections or a private vendor or within 3 years after being released from a correctional institution of another state, the District of Columbia, the United States, any possession or territory of the United States, or any foreign jurisdiction, following incarceration for an offense for which the sentence is punishable by more than 1 year in this state.

2. Prison releasee reoffender also means any defendant who commits or attempts to commit any offense listed in sub-subparagraphs (a)1.a.–r. while the defendant was serving a prison sentence or on escape status from a state correctional facility operated by the Department of Corrections or a private vendor or while the defendant was on escape status from a correctional institution of another state, the District of Columbia, the United States, any possession or territory of the United States, or any foreign jurisdiction, following incarceration for an offense for which the sentence is punishable by more than 1 year in this state.

IV. PENDING CASES

A. On or before January 23, 2006, a list of all pending cases in which the State Attorney is seeking transfer for one or more of the defendants therein, based on the criteria in paragraph III above, shall be filed with the Clerk. Co–defendants that would not otherwise be eligible for the section may seek severance after the transfer, pursuant to Fla. R. Crim. P. 3.152, and in compliance with Fla. R. Crim. P. 3.220. The court will consider the fact that the co-defendant would not otherwise be eligible for the section in determining whether to grant the severance.

B. Upon receipt of the State Attorney's list, the Clerk shall transfer and randomly assign the pending cases to section "70" or "71".

V. CASES FILED AFTER JANUARY 23, 2006

A. In cases filed on or after January 23, 2006, the State Attorney, prior to or at the defendant's arraignment, may file a Designation indicating the State's intent to seek enhanced or mandatory sentences and its good faith belief that at least one defendant in a specified case meets the criteria set forth in paragraph III above. Upon timely receipt of the State's Designation, the Clerk shall transfer and randomly assign the case to section "70" or "71". The State Attorney may establish its good faith belief that a defendant meets the criteria by attaching to the Designation a printout of the defendant's qualifying criminal convictions. Co–defendants that would not otherwise be eligible for the section may seek severance after the transfer, pursuant to Fla. R. Crim. P. 3.152, and in compliance with Fla. R. Crim. P. 3.220. The court will consider the fact that the co-defendant would not otherwise be eligible for the section in determining whether to grant the severance.

B. Cases filed on or after January 23, 2006 shall be transferred to section "70" or "71," subsequent to a defendant's arraignment, when the State Attorney files a Designation indicating the State's intent to seek mandatory or enhanced sentences and its good faith belief that at least one defendant in a specified case meets the criteria set forth in paragraph III. The State Attorney may establish its good faith belief that a defendant meets the criteria by attaching to the Designation a printout of the defendant's qualifying criminal convictions. If, however, the case was filed and pending in another section for more than sixty (60) days prior to the filing of the Designation, then the case shall remain in the original section.

C. Cases shall be transferred out of section "70" and "71" and randomly assigned upon timely motion by the defense or the state when it is shown by the movant that no defendant meets the criteria set forth in Paragraph III above.

VI. MULTIPLE CASES

If a defendant in a case assigned to section "70" or "71" has one or more felony cases pending in another section, the pending case(s) shall be transferred to section "70" or "71", without the necessity of any Motion or Order.

VII. POST–JUDGMENT MATTERS

All post-judgment matters, e.g., reversals of sentence or judgment, motions for post-conviction relief, Writs of Habeas Corpus, etc., resulting from cases assigned to a section "70" or "71" judge prior to the effective date of this order shall continue to be handled by that section "70" or "71" judge.

VIII. VIOLATION OF PROBATION

If a defendant in a case assigned to section "70" or "71" has one or more violations of probation or community control cases pending in another section, the pending case(s) shall be transferred to section "70" or "71" without the necessity of any Motion or Order.

Furthermore, Administrative Order No. 05–06 is hereby rescinded in its entirety and held for naught.

This Order shall take effect as of January 23, 2006 and shall remain in effect until further order of the Court.

DONE AND ORDERED in Chambers at Miami–Dade, Florida, this ___ day of January, 2006.

JOSEPH P. FARINA, CHIEF JUDGE
ELEVENTH JUDICIAL CIRCUIT OF FLORIDA

04–42. THE AMENDMENT AND RESCISSION OF ADMINISTRATIVE ORDERS AFFECTED BY THE ARTICLE V INDIGENT SERVICES COMMITTEE'S ATTACHMENT "A" EXECUTED ON SEPTEMBER 29, 2004

IN THE ELEVENTH JUDICIAL CIRCUIT OF FLORIDA IN AND FOR MIAMI–DADE COUNTY, FLORIDA

CASE NO. 04–1 (Court Administration)

ADMINISTRATIVE ORDER NO. 04–42

IN RE: THE AMENDMENT AND RESCISSION OF ADMINISTRATIVE ORDERS AFFECTED BY THE ARTICLE V INDIGENT SERVICES COMMITTEE'S ATTACHMENT "A" EXECUTED ON SEPTEMBER 29, 2004

WHEREAS, pursuant to Rule of Judicial Administration 2.050, the Chief Judge of the Eleventh Judicial Circuit has the authority to adopt administrative orders necessary to ensure the operation of the Eleventh Judicial Circuit ("Court"); and

WHEREAS, effective July 1, 2004, Section 27.42, Florida Statutes (2004) provided for the establishment of an Article V Indigent Services Committee in each judicial circuit; and

WHEREAS, Administrative Order 04–07 established the Eleventh Judicial Circuit's Article V Indigent Services Committee ("ISC"); and

WHEREAS, effective July 1, 2004, the State of Florida, Justice Administrative Commission ("JAC") assumed responsibility, within statutory limits, for the payment of fees for court appointed counsel for indigent parties and the cost of due process services; and

WHEREAS, the Court, through Administrative Orders 04–09, 04–10, and 04–11, continued the established rates of compensation for court appointed counsel for indigent parties and the cost of due process services in effect on June 30, 2004 for the interim period from July 1, 2004 through September 30, 2004 so that the ISC had time to adopt new rates of compensation; and

WHEREAS, the ISC approved and adopted Administrative Orders 04–09, 04–10, and 04–11 at its meeting on July 8, 2004; and

WHEREAS, on September 29, 2004, the ISC approved and executed an Attachment "A" for this Circuit which continued the Registries of court appointed counsel in effect on September 30, 2004 and established new rates of compensation for and policies and procedures associated with court appointed counsel for indigent parties and the cost of due process services as of October 1, 2004; and

WHEREAS, the interim period referred to in Administrative Orders 04–09, 04–10, and 04–11 ended on September 30, 2004 and on or after October 1, 2004, each JAC contract with court appointed counsel in this Circuit incorporates Attachment "A," it is necessary that the Court acknowledge that Attachment "A" establishes and implements new rates of compensation for and policies and procedures associated with court appointed counsel for indigent parties and the cost of due process services for all work performed and services provided on or after October 1, 2004; and

WHEREAS, with Attachment "A" effective as of October 1, 2004, it is necessary to clarify the validity and applicability of the following Administrative Orders as of October 1, 2004 as there are invoices for fees for court appointed counsel and due process costs, which have been submitted or which will be submitted to Miami–Dade County, Florida or the State of Florida for work performed and services provided on or before September 30, 2004 and which are subject to the following Administrative Orders:

a. Administrative Order 89–29, entered in Case No. 89–1, In Re: Establishment of Additional Standard Fee Guidelines Relative to Compensation for Services Rendered in Criminal Case–Related Matters.

b. Administrative Order 89–29–A1, entered in Case No. 89–1, In Re: Amendment to Administrative Order No. 89–29; Establishment of Additional Standard Fee Guidelines Relative to Compensation for Services Rendered in Criminal Case–Related Matters;

c. Administrative Order 92–38, entered in Case No. 92–1, In Re: Special Assistant Public Defenders, Method of Appointment, Compensation;

d. Administrative Order 92–38–A1, entered in Case No. 94–1, In Re: Amendment to Administrative Order No. 92–38; Special Assistant Public Defenders Method of Appointment, Compensation;

e. Administrative Order 92–38–A2, entered in Case No. 97–1, In Re: Amendment to Administrative Order No. 92–38; Special Assistant Public Defenders Method of Appointment, Compensation—Capital Cases

f. Administrative Order 92–38–A3, entered in Case No. 97–1, In Re: Amendment to Administrative Order No. 92–38; 92–38–A1; 92–38–A2; Conflict Attorneys Method of Appointment, Compensation—Capital Cases;

g. Administrative Order 92–38–A4, entered in Case No. 99–1, In Re: Amendment to Administrative Order No. 92–38 and 92–38–A2; Compensation for Conflict Attorneys Appointed in Appeals of Capital Cases;

h. Administrative Order 94–27, entered in Case No. 94–1, In Re: Method of Appointment and Compensation of Court Appointed Attorneys in Dependency and Termination of Parental Rights Cases;

i. Administrative Order 94–27–A1, entered in Case No. 94–1, In Re: Amendment to Administrative Order 94–27;

j. Administrative Order 95–11, entered in Case No. 95–1, In Re: Establishment of Procedures for the Compensation of Expert Witnesses Engaged to Render Services in Criminal Cases Where a Defendant is Indigent;

k. Administrative Order 97–08, entered in Case No. 97–1, In Re: Guardian Advocate Compensation;

l. Administrative Order 99–07, entered in Case No. 99–1, Reissued to Reflect Change in Number, also Administrative Order No. 92–38–A4; In Re: Amendment to Administrative Order No. 92–38 and 92–38–A2; Compensation for Conflict Attorneys Appointed in Appeals of Capital Cases;

m. Administrative Order 99–08, entered in Case No. 99–1, Reissued to Reflect Change in Number, In Re: Amendment to Administrative Order No. 92–38 and 92–38–A2; Compensation for Conflict Attorneys Appointed in Appeals of Capital Cases;

n. Administrative Order 99–12, entered in Case No. 99–1, In Re: Procedures for Appointment of Attorneys in the Probate Division of the Eleventh Judicial Circuit;

o. Administrative Order 99–12–A1, entered in Case No. 99–1, In Re: Amendment to Administrative Order 99–12; Procedures for Appointment of Attorneys in the Probate Division of the Eleventh Judicial Circuit;

p. Administrative Order 01–04, entered in Case No. 01–1, In Re: Compensation for Mental Health Examinations Performed in Probate and Guardianship Division (Rescinds Order No. 96–23);

q. Administrative Order 02–08, entered in Case No. 02–1, In Re: Revised Fee Schedule for Probate Attorneys and Guardian Advocates;

r. Administrative Order 04–09, entered in Case No. 04–1, In Re: The Appointment and Compensation for Court Appointed Attorneys in Criminal Cases for the Interim Period of July 1, 2004 through September 30, 2004;

s. Administrative Order 04–10, entered in Case No. 04–1, In Re: The Appointment and Compensation for Court Appointed Attorneys in Dependency and Termination of Parental Rights Cases for the Interim Period of July 1, 2004 through September 30, 2004;

t. Administrative Order 04–11, entered in Case No. 04–1, In Re: The Appointment and Compensation for Court Appointed Attorneys in Other Civil Cases for the Interim Period of July 1, 2004 through September 30, 2004; and

WHEREAS, it is necessary to amend the terms "Special Assistant Public Defender," "SAPD," "Conflict Attorney," and "Wheel" as they appear in certain Administrative Orders; and

WHEREAS, it is necessary to continue in effect after September 30, 2004 certain policies and procedures regarding court appointed counsel for the benefit of the Administrative Office of the Courts ("AOC") until the ISC can approve new policies and procedures;

NOW, THEREFORE, pursuant to the authority vested in me as Chief Judge of the Eleventh Judicial Circuit of Florida, it is hereby **ORDERED** that:

1. After September 30, 2004, court appointed counsel, experts, and due process service providers will continue to use the policies and procedures and rates of compensation in effect on September 30, 2004 pursuant to either a JAC contract, a statute, an agreement, or an Administrative Order, whether or not the Administrative Order is rescinded as of October 1, 2004, for billing either Miami–Dade County, Florida or the State of Florida for any and all work performed, services provided, or costs incurred by them on or before September 30, 2004, but subject to Miami–Dade County, Florida and the State of Florida honoring their requests for payment.

2. To the extent that an Administrative Order listed hereinafter continues in effect and for such time that it remains in effect, wherever the terms "Special Assistant Public Defender," "SAPD," or "Conflict Attorney" appear, they are amended to read as "court appointed counsel."

3. To the extent that an Administrative Order listed hereinafter continues in effect and for such time that it remains in effect, wherever the term "Wheel" appears, it is amended to read as "Registry."

4. The Criminal Division of the AOC Division shall continue to operate the Criminal and Delinquency Registry.

5. The Juvenile Division of the AOC shall continue to operate the Dependency and Termination of Parental Rights Registry.

6. The Probate and Guardianship Division of the AOC shall continue to operate the Probate and Guardianship Registry.

7. Attachment "A," which is effective October 1, 2004, supercedes, replaces, and/or amends the following Administrative Orders and the following Administrative Orders are hereby rescinded and held for naught as to any and all work performed by court appointed counsel for indigent parties and services provided by due process service providers on or after October 1, 2004:

a. Administrative Order 89–29, entered in Case No. 89–1, In Re: Establishment of Additional Standard Fee Guidelines Relative to Compensation for Services Rendered in Criminal Case–Related Matters.

b. Administrative Order 89–29–A1, entered in Case No. 89–1, In Re: Amendment to Administrative Order No. 89–29; Establishment of Additional Standard Fee Guidelines Relative to Compensation for Services Rendered in Criminal Case–Related Matters;

c. Administrative Order 92–38, entered in Case No. 92–1, In Re: Special Assistant Public Defenders, Method of Appointment, Compensation;

d. Administrative Order 92–38–A1, entered in Case No. 94–1, In Re: Amendment to Administrative Order No. 92–38; Special Assistant Public Defenders Method of Appointment, Compensation;

e. Administrative Order 92–38–A2, entered in Case No. 97–1, In Re: Amendment to Administrative Order No. 92–38; Special Assistant Public Defenders Method of Appointment, Compensation—Capital Cases

f. Administrative Order 92–38–A3, entered in Case No. 97–1, In Re: Amendment to Administrative Orders No. 92–38; 92–38–A1; 92–38–A2; Conflict Attorneys Method of Appointment, Compensation—Capital Cases;

g. Administrative Order 92–38–A4, entered in Case No. 99–1, In Re: Amendment to Administrative Order No. 92–38 and 92–38–A2; Compensation for Conflict Attorneys Appointed in Appeals of Capital Cases;

h. Administrative Order 94–27, entered in Case No. 94–1, In Re: Method of Appointment and Compensation of Court Appointed Attorneys in Dependency and Termination of Parental Rights Cases;

i. Administrative Order 94–27–A1, entered in Case No. 94–1, In Re: Amendment to Administrative Order 94–27;

j. Administrative Order 95–11, entered in Case No. 95–1, In Re: Establishment of Procedures for the Compensation of Expert Witnesses Engaged to Render Services in Criminal Cases Where a Defendant is Indigent;

k. Administrative Order 97–08, entered in Case No. 97–1, In Re: Guardian Advocate Compensation;

l. Administrative Order 99–07, entered in Case No. 99–1, Reissued to Reflect Change in Number, also Administrative Order No. 92–38–A4; In Re: Amendment to Administrative Order No. 92–38 and 92–38–A2; Compensation for Conflict Attorneys Appointed in Appeals of Capital Cases;

m. Administrative Order 99–08, entered in Case No. 99–1, Reissued to Reflect Change in Number, In Re: Amendment to Administrative Order No. 92–38 and 92–38–A2; Compensation for Conflict Attorneys Appointed in Appeals of Capital Cases;

n. Administrative Order 01–04, entered in Case No. 01–1, In Re: Compensation for Mental Health Examinations Performed in Probate and Guardianship Division (Rescinds Order No. 96–23);

o. Administrative Order 02–08, entered in Case No. 02–1, In Re: Revised Fee Schedule for Probate Attorneys and Guardian Advocates;

p. Administrative Order 04–09, entered in Case No. 04–1, In Re: The Appointment and Compensation for Court Appointed Attorneys in Criminal Cases for the Interim Period of July 1, 2004 through September 30, 2004;

q. Administrative Order 04–10, entered in Case No. 04–1, In Re: The Appointment and Compensation for Court Appointed Attorneys in Dependency and Termination of Parental Rights Cases for the Interim Period of July 1, 2004 through September 30, 2004;

r. Administrative Order 04–11, entered in Case No. 04–1, In Re: The Appointment and Compensation for Court Appointed Attorneys in Other Civil Cases.

8. The following Administrative Orders only pertain in part to court appointed counsel for an indigent party pursuant to the ISC's Attachment "A" and to the extent that Attachment "A," which is effective October 1, 2004, is applicable and supercedes, replaces, and/or amends the following Administrative Orders, the following Administrative Orders are hereby rescinded and held for naught as to any work performed by court appointed counsel for indigent parties and services provided by due process service providers on or after October 1, 2004:

a. Administrative Order 99–12, entered in Case No. 99–1, In Re: Procedures for Appointment of Attorneys in the Probate Division of the Eleventh Judicial Circuit;

b. Administrative Order 99–12–A1, entered in Case No. 99–1, In Re: Amendment to Administrative Order 99–12; Procedures for Appointment of Attorneys in the Probate Division of the Eleventh Judicial Circuit.

9. As to any portion of Administrative Orders 99–12–A1 and 99–12 to which Attachment "A" or the ISC is not applicable, the Orders remain in effect until further order of the Court.

10. There is no guarantee of payment for an attorney on any case involving a court appointment pursuant to Administrative Orders 99–12–A1 and 99–12.

11. This Administrative Order shall take effect on October 1, 2004 and shall remain in effect until further order of the Court.

12. The Clerk is directed to file a copy of this Administrative Order in Case No. 04–1, 02–1, 01–1, 99–1, 97–1, 95–1, 94–1, 92–1, and 89–1.

DONE AND ORDERED in Chambers at Miami, Miami-Dade County, Florida, this ___ day of October, 2004.

____

JOSEPH P. FARINA, CHIEF JUDGE
ELEVENTH JUDICIAL CIRCUIT OF FLORIDA

04–39. ESTABLISHMENT OF PROCEDURES FOR CONSIDERATION AND DISPOSITION OF REQUESTS FOR DEFENDANTS TO BE DECLARED INDIGENT FOR DUE PROCESS COSTS ONLY

THE ELEVENTH JUDICIAL CIRCUIT MIAMI-DADE COUNTY, FLORIDA

CASE NO. 04–1 (Court Administration)

ADMINISTRATIVE ORDER NO. 04–39

IN RE: ESTABLISHMENT OF PROCEDURES FOR CONSIDERATION AND DISPOSITION OF REQUESTS FOR DEFENDANTS TO BE DECLARED INDIGENT FOR DUE PROCESS COSTS ONLY

____

WHEREAS, there are certain circumstances wherein privately retained counsel request that the court declare their clients indigent for due process costs only; and

WHEREAS, it has been determined that under such circumstances counsel must provide sufficient written information for the court's consideration;

NOW, THEREFORE, pursuant to the authority vested in me as Chief Judge of the Eleventh Judicial Circuit of Florida, it is hereby ORDERED that the following procedures are established for the court's consideration and disposition of requests from privately retained counsel for a declaration that their clients are indigent for costs only:

1. Privately retained counsel must submit a written motion to be heard on calendar (not ex-parte) that includes the following information:

a. Clarification as to whether the legal services are being provided pro-bono or being paid for by the client or a third party (without disclosing the name of the third party).
b. If the legal services are being paid for by the client or a third party, the amount of attorney's fee.
c. The justification for such fee.
d. Specific due process services to be obtained.
e. The costs for such services.
f. The justification for the cost for these services.
g. An indigency affidavit utilizing the form approved by the Florida Supreme Court. (Attached hereto as Attachment "A")
h. Certification that copies of motion were provided to all attorneys of record, including State Attorney, Justice Administrative Commission, and the Administrative Office of the Courts.

2. Upon hearing argument of counsel, the court's order must include:

a. Whether or not the defendant is indigent for due process costs only.
b. That the privately retained counsel is providing legal services pro-bono or that the legal fees are being paid for by the defendant or a third party (without disclosing the name of the third party).
c. Specific amount of due process costs approved.
d. That counsel must utilize due process providers approved by the Eleventh Judicial Circuit's Indigent Services Committee at the approved rates.
e. Copies furnished to all attorneys of record, including State Attorney, Justice Administrative Commission, Administrative Office of the Courts, and Court File.

This Order shall take effect immediately and shall remain in effect until further order of the Court.

DONE AND ORDERED in Chambers at Miami–Dade, Florida, this ___ day of ________, 2004.

____

JOSEPH P. FARINA, CHIEF JUDGE
ELEVENTH JUDICIAL CIRCUIT OF FLORIDA

ATTACHMENT "A"

IN THE CIRCUIT/COUNTY COURT OF THE ______ JUDICIAL CIRCUIT IN AND FOR ______ COUNTY, FLORIDA

STATE OF FLORIDA vs. / IN THE INTEREST OF:

CASE NO. ____

____
Defendant / Minor Child(ren)

AFFIDAVIT OF INDIGENT STATUS

Notice to Applicant: The provision of a public defender/court–appointed lawyer is not free. A judgment and lien may be imposed against all real or personal property you own to pay for legal and other services provided on your behalf (or on behalf of the person for whom you are making this application). If the $40.00 application fee is not paid to the Clerk of the Court within 7 days, it will be added to any costs that may be assessed against you at the conclusion of this case. If you are a parent/guardian making this affidavit on behalf of a minor child or tax-dependent adult, the information contained in this affidavit must include your income and assets.

1. **I have ___ dependents.** (*Do not include children not living at home and do not include working spouses.*)

2. **I have take-home income of $ ______** paid ( ) weekly ( ) bi-weekly ( ) semi-monthly ( ) monthly (*Take–home income equals salary, wages, bonuses, commissions, allowances, overtime, tips and similar payments minus deductions required by law and other court-ordered payments.*)

3. **I have $ ______ in other annual income:** *(Circle "Yes" and fill in the amount if you have this kind of income or circle "No" if you do not have this kind of income)*

Social Security benefits	Yes $ ___	No
Unemployment compensation	Yes $ ___	No
Union funds	Yes $ ___	No
Workers' compensation	Yes $ ___	No
Retirement/pensions	Yes $ ___	No
Trusts or gifts	Yes $ ___	No
Veterans' benefits	Yes $ ___	No
Other regular support from family members/spouse	Yes $ ___	No
Rental income	Yes $ ___	No
Dividends or interest	Yes $ ___	No
Other kinds of income not on the list	Yes $ ___	No

4. **I have $ ___ in other assets.** *(Circle "Yes" and fill in the value of the property or circle "No" if you do not have this kind of property.)*

Cash	Yes $ ___	No
Savings	Yes $ ___	No
Bank account(s)	Yes $ ___	No
Stocks and bonds	Yes $ ___	No
Certificates of deposit or money market accounts	Yes $ ___	No
Real estate (your ownership interest)	Yes $ ___	No
Boat(s) or aircraft (your ownership interest)	Yes $ ___	No
Motor vehicle(s) (your ownership interest)	Yes $ ___	No
Life Insurance (cash value)	Yes $ ___	No
Other valuable tangible property (like jewelry, coin collections, etc.)	Yes $ ___	No

5. **I receive:** *(Circle "Yes" or "No")*

Temp. Assistance for Needy Families–Cash Assistance	Yes	No
Poverty-related veterans' benefits	Yes	No
Supplemental Security Income (SSI)	Yes	No

6. **I have been released on bail in the amount of $5,000 or more in this case** .... Yes No

7. **I have a private lawyer in this case** .... Yes No

8. I expect to get or receive something of value at a later date (Like a tax refund, payments from lawsuits, accrued vacation leave, a bonus, or inheritance)... Yes $ ___ No

**(*Elect and complete either the notarized oath or the written declaration below pursuant to section 92.525, Florida Statutes*)

NOTARIZED OATH

I, ______ (*full legal name*), being first duly sworn, state under oath and under penalty of perjury that the facts stated in the foregoing affidavit are true.

____
Signature of Applicant for Indigent Status Date Signed

PRINT Full Legal Name ______________

Address ______________

Driver's License # or ID # ______________

Date of Birth ______________

Telephone ______________

WRITTEN DECLARATION

Under penalties of perjury, I declare that the facts stated in the foregoing affidavit are true.

____
Signature of Applicant for Indigent Status Date Signed

PRINT Full Legal Name ______________

Address ______________

Driver's License # or ID # ______________

Date of Birth ______________

Telephone ______________

**(*If a clerk or deputy clerk helped you fill out this form, he or she must fill out the blank below.*)

This form was completed with the assistance of ______, Clerk/Deputy Clerk.

DETERMINATION OF INDIGENT STATUS

Based on the information in this Affidavit, I have determined that the applicant is ( ) Indigent ( ) Not Indigent pursuant to section 27.52, F.S.

______________________________ 20 ___
,Clerk of Court by Deputy Clerk Date

Civil Traffic Infraction Hearing Officers

08–04. ESTABLISHMENT OF PROCEDURES FOR PRE–TRIAL CONFERENCES IN CIVIL TRAFFIC INFRACTION CASES

THE ELEVENTH JUDICIAL CIRCUIT MIAMI–DADE COUNTY, FLORIDA

CASE NO. 08–1 (Court Administration)

ADMINISTRATIVE ORDER NO. 08–04
(Rescinds AO No. 99–15)

IN RE: ESTABLISHMENT OF PROCEDURES FOR PRE–TRIAL CONFERENCES IN CIVIL TRAFFIC INFRACTION CASES

WHEREAS, pursuant to Administrative Order No. 99–15, entered on May 24, 1999, this Circuit, based upon the recommendation of an Ad Hoc Committee chaired by the Honorable Steve Leifman, initiated a pilot program featuring a Pre–Trial Conference procedure for civil traffic infraction cases where a request for trial is filed ("Pilot Program"); and

WHEREAS, the Pilot Program was very effective as a method of reducing the backlog of such cases;

NOW THEREFORE, pursuant to the authority vested in me as Chief Judge of the Eleventh Judicial Circuit of Florida, the following procedures are hereby established to be implemented throughout this Circuit for civil traffic cases where a request for trial is filed:

1. Except as otherwise provided herein, a Pre–Trial Conference shall be conducted in traffic infraction cases where trials have been duly requested.

2. The Pre–Trial Conference Program shall exclude civil traffic infraction cases involving a personal injury or death; cases involving a civil traffic infraction issued in conjunction with a criminal traffic offense; civil traffic infraction cases which have prior trial settings; and toll violations issued by Miami–Dade Expressway Authority (MDX) and SunPass agencies.

3. For continuance/reset requests, the appropriate judicial officer shall review each continuance request, and cases in which continuances are granted shall be reset for Pre–Trial Conferences.

4. Pre–Trial motions—All motions relating to defects in the Charging Document shall be made at the Pre–Trial Conference, or they are waived. Once waived, no such matter shall be revisited. All motions relating to irregularities or informalities in the charging Document, or factual disputes, may be denied without prejudice and noted on the file, but may be raised again only during a trial of the case.

5. Failure to Appear—If a defendant, or his or her attorney, fails to appear at a Pre–Trial Conference scheduled pursuant to this Administrative Order, the Court shall enter a D6, suspension of license, pursuant to § 318.15(1), Florida Statutes.

6. Notice of Appearance—Prior to representation of any defendant in a traffic infraction case, a notice of appearance shall be filed by the responsible attorney with the Clerk of Courts.

7. On the effective date of this Administrative Order, the Clerk of the Court is hereby directed to begin scheduling Pre–Trial Conferences.

This Administrative Order shall become effective immediately upon execution and shall remain in effect until further order of the Court.

Administrative Order No. 99–15 in Case No. 99–1 (Court Administration) is hereby rescinded in its entirety and shall be held for naught.

DONE AND ORDERED in Chambers at Miami–Dade, Florida, this ___ day of __________, 2008.

____
JOSEPH P. FARINA
CHIEF JUDGE
ELEVENTH JUDICIAL CIRCUIT OF FLORIDA

County Court Civil

09–06. CREATION OF SECTION 06 IN THE COUNTY COURT CIVIL DIVISION IN AND FOR MIAMI–DADE COUNTY

THE ELEVENTH JUDICIAL CIRCUIT MIAMI–DADE COUNTY, FLORIDA

CASE NO. 09–1 (Court Administration)

ADMINISTRATIVE ORDER NO. 09–06

IN RE: CREATION OF SECTION 06 IN THE COUNTY COURT CIVIL DIVISION IN AND FOR MIAMI–DADE COUNTY

WHEREAS, notwithstanding the efforts of the Judges in the Civil Division of the County Court to reduce the number of pending cases in each of their respective judicial sections, such cases continue to increase; and

WHEREAS, the Court has determined that in the interest of effecting the prompt disposition of cases, an additional judicial section must be created in the Civil Division of the County Court;

NOW, THEREFORE, pursuant to the authority vested in me as Chief Judge of the Eleventh Judicial Circuit of Florida under Rule 2.050, Florida Rules of Judicial Administration, it is hereby **ORDERED**:

1. Effective immediately on even date herewith, Section 06 to be located at the North Dade Justice Center Court (Location 23) is hereby created in the Civil Division of the County Court, and thereafter immediately populated with new and pending cases.

2. Notwithstanding Section 06 being populated with cases as set forth in Paragraph hereinabove, the Judge assigned to

this Section will commence presiding over matters on or about April 13, 2009.

3. Cases shall be assigned and/or reassigned to this Section at the direction of the Administrative Judge of the Civil Division of the County Court. Whenever possible and practicable, the assignment and/or reassignment of such cases shall be accomplished under the blind filing system historically utilized in making such assignments and reassignments, or any similar method which will result in such cases being filed equally among all of the sections of the Civil Division of the County Court in an unpredictable manner.

4. Any inequities in caseload distribution among the sections of the Civil Division of the County Court will be adjusted by the Administrative Judge.

5. The Clerk of the Court shall notify in writing all attorneys of record as to the assignment or reassignment of their pending case in the Family Division.

6. No cases shall be retained or heard by a judge when reassigned to another section, except as follows:

a. Motions for rehearing or new trial;

b. Motions to vacate final judgments, including summary judgments;

c. Completion of hearing or trial after judge has commenced taking testimony in the case;

d. Disposition of cases tried;

e. Good cause

This Administrative Order shall become effective upon execution and shall remain in effect until further order of the Court.

DONE AND ORDERED in Chambers at Miami–Dade, Florida, this ___ day of March, 2009.

JOSEPH P. FARINA, CHIEF JUDGE
ELEVENTH JUDICIAL CIRCUIT OF FLORIDA

06–39. CREATION OF SECTION 05 IN THE COUNTY COURT CIVIL DIVISION IN AND FOR MIAMI–DADE COUNTY

THE ELEVENTH JUDICIAL CIRCUIT MIAMI–DADE COUNTY, FLORIDA

CASE NO. 06–1 (Court Administration)

ADMINISTRATIVE ORDER NO. 06–39

IN RE: CREATION OF SECTION 05 IN THE COUNTY COURT CIVIL DIVISION IN AND FOR MIAMI-DADE COUNTY

WHEREAS, notwithstanding the efforts of the Judges in the Civil Division of the County Court to reduce the number of pending cases in each of their respective judicial sections, such cases continue to increase; and

WHEREAS, the Court has determined that in the interest of effecting the prompt disposition of cases, an additional judicial section must be created in the Civil Division of the County Court;

NOW, THEREFORE, pursuant to the authority vested in me as Chief Judge of the Eleventh Judicial Circuit of Florida under Rule 2.050, Florida Rules of Judicial Administration, it is hereby **ORDERED**:

1. Effective December 12, 2006, Section 05 to be located at the North Dade Justice Center Court (Location 23) is hereby created in the Civil Division of the County Court, and thereafter immediately populated with new and pending cases.

2. Notwithstanding Section 05 being populated with cases as set forth in Paragraph hereinabove, the Judge assigned to this Section will commence presiding over matters on or about January 16, 2007.

3. Cases shall be assigned and/or reassigned to this Section at the direction of the Administrative Judge of the Civil Division of the County Court. Whenever possible and practicable, the assignment and/or reassignment of such cases shall be accomplished under the blind filing system historically utilized in making such assignments and reassignments, or any similar method which will result in such cases being filed equally among all of the sections of the Civil Division of the County Court in an unpredictable manner.

4. Any inequities in caseload distribution among the sections of the Civil Division of the County Court will be adjusted by the Administrative Judge.

5. The Clerk of the Court shall notify in writing all attorneys of record as to the assignment or reassignment of their pending case in the Family Division.

6. No cases shall be retained or heard by a judge when reassigned to another section, except as follows:

a. Motions for rehearing or new trial;

b. Motions to vacate final judgments, including summary judgments;

c. Completion of hearing or trial after judge has commenced taking testimony in the case;

d. Disposition of cases tried;

e. Good cause

This Administrative Order shall become effective on December 12, 2006, nunc pro tunc.

DONE AND ORDERED in Chambers at Miami–Dade, Florida, this ___ day of January, 2007.

JOSEPH P. FARINA
CHIEF JUDGE
ELEVENTH JUDICIAL CIRCUIT OF FLORIDA

06–38. CREATION OF SECTION 04 IN THE COUNTY COURT CIVIL DIVISION IN AND FOR MIAMI–DADE COUNTY

THE ELEVENTH JUDICIAL CIRCUIT MIAMI–DADE COUNTY, FLORIDA

CASE NO. 06–1 (Court Administration)

ADMINISTRATIVE ORDER NO. 06–38

IN RE: CREATION OF SECTION 04 IN THE COUNTY COURT CIVIL DIVISION IN AND FOR MIAMI–DADE COUNTY

WHEREAS, notwithstanding the efforts of the Judges in the Civil Division of the County Court to reduce the number of pending cases in each of their respective judicial sections, such cases continue to increase; and

WHEREAS, the Court has determined that in the interest of effecting the prompt disposition of cases, an additional judicial section must be created in the Civil Division of the County Court;

NOW, THEREFORE, pursuant to the authority vested in me as Chief Judge of the Eleventh Judicial Circuit of Florida under Rule 2.050, Florida Rules of Judicial Administration, it is hereby **ORDERED**:

1. Effective December 26, 2006, Section 04 to be located at the Coral Gables Branch Court (Location 25) is hereby created in the Civil Division of the County Court, and thereafter immediately populated with new and pending cases.

2. Notwithstanding Section 04 being populated with cases as set forth in Paragraph hereinabove, the Judge assigned to this Section will commence presiding over matters on or about January 16, 2007.

3. Cases shall be assigned and/or reassigned to this Section at the direction of the Administrative Judge of the Civil Division of the County Court. Whenever possible and practicable, the assignment and/or reassignment of such cases shall be accomplished under the blind filing system historically utilized in making such assignments and reassignments, or any similar method which will result in such cases being filed equally among all of the sections of the Civil Division of the County Court in an unpredictable manner.

4. Any inequities in caseload distribution among the sections of the Civil Division of the County Court will be adjusted by the Administrative Judge.

5. The Clerk of the Court shall notify in writing all attorneys of record as to the assignment or reassignment of their pending case in the Family Division.

6. No cases shall be retained or heard by a judge when reassigned to another section, except as follows:

a. Motions for rehearing or new trial;

b. Motions to vacate final judgments, including summary judgments;

c. Completion of hearing or trial after judge has commenced taking testimony in the case;

d. Disposition of cases tried;

e. Good cause

This Administrative Order shall become effective on December 26, 2006, nunc pro tunc.

DONE AND ORDERED in Chambers at Miami–Dade, Florida, this ___ day of January, 2007.

JOSEPH P. FARINA
CHIEF JUDGE
ELEVENTH JUDICIAL CIRCUIT
OF FLORIDA

04–05. RE–ESTABLISHMENT AND JURISDICTION OF COUNTY COURT DISTRICTS

THE ELEVENTH JUDICIAL CIRCUIT MIAMI–DADE COUNTY, FLORIDA

CASE NO. 04–1 (Court Administration)

ADMINISTRATIVE ORDER NO. 04–05

(Rescinding Administrative Order No. 97–19, Administrative Order No. 97–19 A1 and Administrative Order No. 2–07)

IN RE: RE–ESTABLISHMENT AND JURISDICTION OF COUNTY COURT DISTRICTS

WHEREAS, pursuant to Administrative Order No. 97–19, as amended by Administrative Order No. 97–19–A1 (collectively the "Administrative Order"), the Court deemed it necessary, for the prompt and efficient filing and assignment of cases in the various, previously established County Court Districts ("Districts"), to relocate some of the court facilities in the Districts and define the jurisdiction of such Districts in a more precise and objective manner; and

WHEREAS, in view of the changes which have occurred within the Districts since the enactment of the Administrative Order, the Court has determined that it is once again necessary to re-establish and define the jurisdiction of the respective Districts;

NOW, THEREFORE, pursuant to the authority vested in me as Chief Judge of the Eleventh Judicial Circuit of Florida, it is hereby **ORDERED**:

1. Location of County Court Districts.

The location of the County Court Districts shall be the following:

- Central District (05), located at the Dade County Courthouse, 73 West Flagler Street, Miami (civil actions), and the Richard E. Gerstein Justice Building, 1351 Northwest 12th Street, Miami (criminal, traffic offenses and infractions);

- North Central (Caleb) District (20), located at the Joseph Caleb Community Center, 5400 Northwest 22nd Avenue, Miami provides limited services by the Clerk of the Court. All pending matters, designated for section (20), filed prior to January 1, 2004, will be re-assigned amongst the six (6) judicial sections at the Dade County Courthouse. Pending cases filed after January 1, 2004, will be designated (21) for handling at the Northwest District;

- Northwest District (21), located at 11 East 6th Street, Hialeah;

- North District (23), located at 15555 Biscayne Boulevard, Miami;

- East District (24), located at 1130 Washington Avenue, Miami Beach;

- South Central District (25), located at 3100 Ponce de Leon Boulevard, Coral Gables; and

- South District (26), located at the South Dade Government Center, 10710 Southwest 211th Street, Miami.

2. Boundaries of County Court Districts.

Each of the following County Court Districts shall consist of the geographic areas located within the zip codes as indicated below:

Central District (05)

33109 33122 33125 33126 33127 33128
33129 33130 33131 33132 33133 33135
33136 33137 33142 33145 33147 33149
33150 33166 33172 33174 33182 33184
33192 33194

North Central District (20)

(Limited services; use zip code to determine the District in which to file cases.)

Northwest District (21)

33010 33012 33013 33014 33016 33018
33178

North District (23)

33015 33054 33055 33056 33138 33160
33161 33162 33167 33168 33169 33179
33180 33181

East District (24)

33139 33140 33141 33154

South Central District (25)

33134 33143 33144 33146 33155 33165
33173

South District (26)

33030 33031 33032 33033 33034 33035
33039 33156 33157 33158 33170 33175
33176 33177 33183 33185 33186 33187
33189 33190 33193 33196

3. **Filing in County Court Districts**

(a) **Mandatory Filing**:

All actions for recovery of possession of property under Chapters 82 and 83 of the Florida Statutes; all actions for damages under Chapter 82 of the Florida Statutes and actions for the recovery of rent or rent security deposits in which the demand involved does not exceed Fifteen Thousand Dollars ($15,000.00), exclusive of costs, interest and attorney's fees, shall be filed in the District in which the real property is located.

(b) **Optional Filing**:

Except as provided under subparagraph 3(a) above, the venue for filing all other actions at law of a civil nature in which the demand or value of property involved does not exceed Fifteen Thousand Dollars ($15,000.00), exclusive of costs, interest and attorney's fees, shall be controlled and determined, at the option of the plaintiff, by Sections 47.011, 47.021, 47.041, 47.051 and 47.061 of the Florida Statutes

4. **Traffic and Penal Cases.**

Traffic and penal cases may be assigned for trial at any County Court facility, or any other facility, for the convenience of parties, witnesses and police officers.

5. **Landlord/Tenant Cases.**

Landlord/tenant cases should be filed in the District with the zip code that corresponds with the zip code for the property.

6. **Jury Trials.**

Jury trials in civil, criminal and traffic offenses may be assigned to and heard at any County Court facility.

7. **North Central (Caleb) Branch Court Annex.**

The window in the public service counter at the Dade County Courthouse to accept only those cases that would ordinarily be filed at the North Central Branch Court, as designated by Administrative Order No. 2–07, is hereby closed.

Administrative Order No. 97–19, as amended by Administrative Order No. 97–19–A1, entered in Case No. 97–1 (Court Administration) and Administrative Order No. 2–07, entered in Case No. 02–1 (Court Administration), are hereby rescinded in their entirety and held for naught.

This Order shall become effective on July 6, 2004 and shall remain in effect until further order of the Court.

DONE AND ORDERED in Chambers at Miami–Dade, Florida, this ___ day of June, 2004.

____
JOSEPH P. FARINA, CHIEF JUDGE
ELEVENTH JUDICIAL CIRCUIT OF FLORIDA

Court Administration

18–02. ALTERNATIVE SANCTIONS PROGRAM

THE ELEVENTH JUDICIAL CIRCUIT MIAMI–DADE COUNTY, FLORIDA

CASE NO. 18–1 (Court Administration)

ADMINISTRATIVE ORDER NO. 18–02I

IN RE: ALTERNATIVE SANCTIONS PROGRAM

WHEREAS, the Florida legislature in Chapter 2016–100, Laws of Florida, amended section 948.06, Florida Statutes; and

WHEREAS, section 948.06, Florida Statutes authorizes the Chief Judge of each judicial circuit to establish an alternative sanctioning program; and

WHEREAS, there are many technical violations of probation or community control that do not involve a new arrest or other serious violations; and

WHEREAS, arresting and incarcerating certain non-violent offenders for minor violations of probation or community control is expensive and nonproductive; and

WHEREAS, research supports that recidivism may be reduced by utilizing collaborative efforts among the courts, probation and law enforcement to hold offenders accountable and apply swift and certain sanctions for technical violations of probation or community control; and

WHEREAS, an administrative option for processing certain technical violations has the potential to offer benefits including reducing court dockets for probation and community control violation hearings, reducing the workload of prosecutors and defense attorneys involved in technical violation hearings, reducing law enforcement time required to serve violation warrants for certain technical violations, and reducing jail population for offenders waiting for technical violation hearings;

NOW, THEREFORE, pursuant to the authority vested in me as Chief Judge of the Eleventh Judicial Circuit of Florida under Rule 2.215 of the Florida Rules of Judicial Administration, it is hereby **ORDERED**:

1. The Alternative Sanctions Program is hereby created in the Eleventh Judicial Circuit, Miami–Dade County.

2. Eligibility. The program is available to any person who is on probation, drug offender probation, or community control, under the supervision of the Department of Corrections, has stable community ties, and has a stable residence in Florida.

a. The program is only available to offenders who have committed a technical violation identified in the Alternative Sanctions Program Violation/Sanctions Matrix.

b. The following offenders are ineligible for the program:

- Offenders with three or more prior felony convictions or three previous probation violations in the same case.
- Offenders who are designated sex offenders.
- Offenders who qualify as Violent Felony Offenders of Special Concern pursuant to Florida Statutes section 948.06(8)(c), unless the trial judge at the time of imposing the term of probation designated the offender for the program.
- Offenders who are charged with new law violations, are absconders, or have violated a "no contact" condition of supervision are not eligible for the program.

3. Qualifying Technical Violations and Approved Sanctions. The following matrix lists the specific technical violations that may be addressed through the Alternative Sanctions Program process for offenders who were sentenced in Miami–Dade County, Florida. Each technical violation includes a list of sanctions determined and approved by the court for the probation officer to select from when reporting these technical violations, based on the individual's offender's circumstances at the time of the violation.

ALTERNATIVE SANCTIONS PROGRAM VIOLATION/SANCTION MATRIX

VIOLATION	APPROVED LIST OF SANCTIONS
Condition (1): Reported late; failed to report as instructed	• Verbal counseling. • Report 2 times a month for 60 days. • Weekly reporting for 45 days. • Additional 10 hours of community service.
Condition (2): Failed to pay Cost of Supervision (COS)	• Waive arrearage for costs of supervision (if offender has no ability to pay). • Waive costs of supervision (if offender has no ability to pay). • Set up a payment plan (if offender has ability to pay)
Condition (3): Failed to report changes in residence or employment without first procuring the officer's consent (or notifying immediately if evicted from residence or laid off from job) *****Inapplicable if Offender is on Community Control*****	• Verbal counseling. • Report 2 times a month for 60 days. • Weekly reporting for 45 days. • Additional 10 hours of community service.
Condition (3): Failed to request permission prior to leaving the county *****Inapplicable if Offender is on Community Control*****	• Verbal counseling. • Report 2 times a month for 60 days. • Weekly reporting for 45 days. • Additional 10 hours of community service.
Condition (6): Found to be associating with person(s) engaged in criminal activity *****Inapplicable if Offender is on Community Control*****	• Verbal counseling. • Report 2 times a month for 60 days. • Weekly reporting for 45 days. • Additional 10 hours of community service.
Condition (8): Failure to maintain employment	• Referral to employment assistance agencies. • Weekly reporting with 20 job search log entries until employed. • Daily reporting with 5 job search log entries until employed.
Condition (9): Failure to answer inquiries truthfully (depending on nature of question, response, and reason	• Verbal counseling. • Report 2 times a month for 60 days. • Weekly reporting for 45 days.

for being untruthful, consequence will vary)	• Additional 10 hours of community service.
Condition (9): Failure to comply with officer's instructions (depending on nature of instruction and reason for not complying, consequence will vary) *****Inapplicable if Offender is on Community Control*****	• Verbal counseling. • Report 2 times a month for 60 days. • Weekly reporting for 45 days. • Additional 10 hours of community service.
Condition (10): Failure to pay restitution	• Extend probation (will auto terminate upon completion of all conditions). This sanction requires filing of Affidavit of Violation, and victim should be notified and allowed to come to hearing if requested. • Referral to employment assistance agencies (if unemployed).
Condition (11): Failure to submit to random testing as directed	• Verbal counseling. • Drug use evaluation and require treatment as necessary. • Modify to drug offender probation. • Increase level of treatment program up to and including residential. • AA/NA 1x per week for 60 days. • Curfew from 8pm to 6am for 30 days (can be modified by probation officer for treatment/work purposes). • Additional 10 hours of community service.
Special Condition (1): Failure to attend treatment evaluation or treatment session as scheduled	1. Verbal counseling. 2. Additional 10 hours of community service. 3. Weekly reporting until offender in compliance.

Special Condition (8): Failure to complete community service hours as instructed	1. Verbal counseling. 2. Additional 10 hours of community service. 3. Weekly reporting until offender in compliance.
Special Condition (9): Failure to remain at residence during curfew period	1. Verbal counseling. 2. Report 2 times a month for 60 days. 3. Weekly reporting for 45 days. 4. Electronic monitoring for up to 90 days. 5. Additional 10 hours of community service.

4. Alternative Sanctions Process.

a. The probation officer shall inform offenders who have committed a qualifying violation that they may participate in the Alternative Sanctions Program for administrative disposition of the violation. No offender is required to participate in the Alternative Sanctions Program and may opt for a formal violation of proceeding in the Criminal Division of the Circuit Court in Miami–Dade County, Florida.

b. If the offender admits the violation, agrees to accept the alternative sanction(s) recommended by the probation officer, and agrees to waive his/her formal violation hearing to modify his/her sentence, the probation officer will prepare an "Alternative Sanctions Program Technical Violation Notification" (Attachment A), which will provide details of the circumstances of the technical violation that occurred and the probation officer's recommended sanction(s), based on the sanctions listed in the Alternative Sanctions Program Violation/Sanction Matrix. If the offender agrees to participate in the Alternative Sanctions Program, he/she will sign the section of the form titled "Offender's Waiver of Formal Violation of Probation Hearing, Admission of Violation, and Acceptance of Sanctions." (Attachment A) Once the form is signed and dated by the offender, the probation officer, and the officer's supervisor, the form will be submitted to the Court.

c. The judge shall review the submitted "Alternative Sanctions Program Technical Violation Notification" form. If the judge agrees that the technical violation should be addressed via the Alternative Sanctions Program and agrees with the recommended sanction(s), the judge will sign the "Order on Alternative Sanctions Program" (Attachment B). If the judge does not agree with the particular sanction(s) recommended by the officer or does not agree that the technical violation should be addressed via the Alternative Sanctions Program, the judge shall reflect further instructions on the order.

d. Upon court approval, the probation officer will instruct the offender on the sanction(s) imposed by the court and instruct the offender to take actions necessary to ensure the sanction is executed immediately. Failure to complete the imposed sanction as instructed will result in a violation report, affidavit and warrant being submitted to the court citing the original condition that was violated.

e. Participation in the Alternative Sanctions Program is not considered a conviction for a violation of probation or community control (not a scoreable violation) for purposes of Section VI of the Criminal Punishment Scoresheet.

f. The Clerk of Court shall collaborate with the Administrative Office of the Courts to create a unique docket code to track each Alternative Sanctions Order entered for statistical reporting purposes.

5. Administration. The Alternative Sanctions Program shall be administered by the Miami–Dade County Circuit Court and the Florida Department of Corrections.

This Administrative Order shall take effect immediately upon execution and shall remain in effect until further order of the Court. Upon execution of this Administrative Order, The Alternative Sanctions Program shall apply to all pending and future cases before the Circuit Court in Miami–Dade County.

DONE AND ORDERED in Chambers at Miami–Dade County, Florida, this 5th day of March, 2018.

BERTILA SOTO, CHIEF JUDGE

ELEVENTH JUDICIAL CIRCUIT OF FLORIDA

18–01. CREATION OF SECTION PMH 06 IN THE PROBATE DIVISION OF THE ELEVENTH JUDICIAL CIRCUIT OF FLORIDA

THE ELEVENTH JUDICIAL CIRCUIT MIAMI–DADE COUNTY, FLORIDA

CASE NO. 18–1 (Court Administration)

ADMINISTRATIVE ORDER NO. 18–01

IN RE: CREATION OF SECTION PMH 06 IN THE PROBATE DIVISION OF THE ELEVENTH JUDICIAL CIRCUIT OF FLORIDA

WHEREAS, notwithstanding the efforts of the Judges in the Probate Division to reduce the number of pending cases in each of their respective judicial sections, such cases continue to increase; and

WHEREAS, the Court has determined that in the interest of effecting the prompt disposition of cases, one (1) additional judicial section must be created in the Probate Division;

NOW, THEREFORE, pursuant to the authority vested in me as Chief Judge of the Eleventh Judicial Circuit of Florida under Rule 2.215, Florida Rules of Judicial Administration, it is hereby **ORDERED**:

1. Section PMH 06 is established in the Probate Division.

2. Newly filed cases shall be randomly assigned by the Clerk of Court pursuant to a blind filing system.

3. As to existing cases, twenty percent of the following types of cases shall be randomly and blindly selected from each of the other Sections and transferred by the Clerk of Court to Section PMH 06:

a. closed mental health cases concerning determinations of competency;

b. closed estate cases; and

c. pending cases

4. Any inequities in caseload distribution among the sections of the Probate Division will be adjusted by the Administrative Judge.

5. If all parties in a case desire the original judge to retain a case, counsel shall submit a joint motion to the original judge giving reasons for retention. If the judge agrees to retain the case, an order will be entered by the Administrative Judge, or designee, transferring the case back to the original judge, without the necessity of a hearing.

6. In addition, cases may also be transferred in accordance with previous existing Administrative Orders and Administrative Memoranda, including Administrative Order No. 14–09.

7. All trials and hearings of reassigned cases presently scheduled on or after the effective date of this Administrative Order must be confirmed with the new judge or reset as necessary.

This Administrative Order shall be effective January 18, 2018, *nunc pro tunc.*

DONE AND ORDERED in Chambers at Miami–Dade, Florida, this 12th day of February, 2018.

BERTILA SOTO, CHIEF JUDGE

ELEVENTH JUDICIAL CIRCUIT OF FLORIDA

17–11. REAFFIRMATION OF THE CREATION OF COMPLEX BUSINESS LITIGATION IN THE CIRCUIT CIVIL DIVISION OF THE ELEVENTH JUDICIAL CIRCUIT OF FLORIDA

THE ELEVENTH JUDICIAL CIRCUIT MIAMI–DADE COUNTY, FLORIDA

CASE NO. 17–1

ADMINISTRATIVE ORDER NO. 17–11

(Rescinding AO No. 16–12)

IN RE: REAFFIRMATION OF THE CREATION OF COMPLEX BUSINESS LITIGATION IN THE CIRCUIT CIVIL DIVISION OF THE ELEVENTH JUDICIAL CIRCUIT OF FLORIDA; RE–DESIGNATION OF CBL SECTIONS; AND MODIFICATION OF PROCEDURES FOR THE ASSIGNMENT AND REASSIGNMENT OF CASES TO CBL SECTIONS

WHEREAS, Section 40 was created and dedicated as the Complex Business Litigation Section ("CBL") within the General Jurisdiction (n/k/a the Circuit Civil Division) of this Circuit (hereinafter referred to as "Section 40"); and

WHEREAS, pursuant to subsequent Administrative Orders entered by this Court, Section 40 was reaffirmed and certain procedures were modified for assignment and reassignment of cases to this section; and

WHEREAS, since its creation, the Court has continued to study and consider the nature and volume of complex business litigation cases filed in the Complex Business Litigation Section; and

WHEREAS, pursuant to Administrative Order No. 16–12, entered by this court October 27, 2016, this Circuit implemented three significant changes as a pilot project, to include (1) increasing the number of judges (from one to three full time judges, with the Administrative Judge of the Circuit Civil Division serving part time on a limited caseload), exclusively assigned to hear the Circuit's complex business litigation as defined by Administrative Order No. 16–12, (2) certain causes of action as defined by action code on the civil case cover sheet were assigned to the Complex Business Litigation sections on a mandatory basis, and (3) the required minimum amount in controversy to be assigned to one of the CBL sections was increased to Seven Hundred Fifty Thousand Dollars ($750,000.00); and

WHEREAS, the pilot project having concluded, and based upon the Court's analysis of the current complex business litigation caseload in the Circuit Civil Division, it has been determined that the previously established procedures for the assignment and reassignment of cases to CBL must be modified to promote the efficient handling of this caseload; and

NOW, THEREFORE, pursuant to the authority vested in me as Chief Judge of the Eleventh Judicial Circuit of Florida under Rule 2.215, Florida Rules of Judicial Administration, it is hereby **ORDERED** that the creation of complex business litigation sections ("CBL") is reaffirmed and will continue within the Circuit Civil Division of this Court ("Division").

It is further **ORDERED** that the following procedures shall be followed as to the assignment and reassignment of cases with respect to CBL:

Section 1.

(a) *Closure of Section 40 and reassignment /transfer of CBL Caseload.* The CBL section of the Division (Section 40) shall be closed as of January 1, 2018, and cases assigned to Section 40 shall be reassigned and transferred to Sections 43 and 44, exclusively assigned to hear complex business litigation matters as defined below. The CBL Judges will serve as a "back-up" judge to each other, if the need arises. Further, in the event a CBL Judge is unable to preside over a CBL case due to recusal or disqualification, such case will be reassigned to the other CBL Judge.

(b) *Closure of Section 35 and reassignment /transfer of Foreclosure Caseload.* The Foreclosure section of the Division (Section 35) shall be closed as of January 1, 2018, and cases assigned to Section 35 shall be reassigned and transferred to Sections 20 and 58.

(c) *CBL Caseload and Foreclosure Caseload Distribution.*

i. The existing and closed caseload in Section 40 shall be redistributed and reassigned to Sections 43 and 44.

ii. The existing and closed caseload in Section 35 shall be reassigned to Sections 20 and 58.

iii. New CBL cases filed on and after the effective date of this Administrative Order (January 2, 2018) shall be distributed amongst the two CBL Sections by utilizing the current blind-filing system or variation thereof.

iv. The Section 03 Judge shall continue to preside over the current complex business litigation cases involving a specific set of similar construction defect claims and all additional newly-filed construction defect claims on related issues. In addition, Section 03 may preside over the other specifically designated matters or when called upon by Section judges to assist.

v. The Administrative Judge, in consultation with the CBL Judges, is hereby authorized to temporarily suspend the transfer of any complex business litigation case to the CBL Sections based on the number and complexity of the cases in the CBL Sections. The Administrative Judge shall notify the Associate Administrative Judge and other section Judges in the Division whenever a temporary suspension of transfers is imposed and lifted.

(d) *Caseload Coverage During Trial.* Each CBL Judge will be expected to try his/her own cases, regardless of its anticipated duration. However, if a particular trial is protracted, thereby potentially delaying the timely disposition of other CBL cases, the other CBL Judge may provide caseload coverage for the subject judge during the duration of the trial.

Section 2. General Information.

A. *Definition of Complex Business Litigation.* Rule 1.201(a), Florida Rules of Civil Procedure, provides the definition of complex litigation. In furtherance thereto, for purposes of the CBL Sections, a "complex business case" is defined as one involving complex legal and case management issues requiring extensive judicial management in order to expedite the case, to promote effective decision making by the Court, counsel and parties, and to keep costs reasonable.

B. *CBL Designations.* The Clerk shall assign to the CBL Sections all newly filed cases that have been identified as subject to mandatory filing to CBL as hereinafter designated. Recognizing that cases may be subject to multiple action codes, but only one action code will be accepted by the Clerk/Portal, Counsel are advised to carefully and thoughtfully prepare their civil cover sheets to identify action codes that are appropriate for assignment to CBL.

C. *Final CBL Determination.* The Administrative Judge (or designee) shall ultimately determine whether an action meets a substantial number of the criteria in order to qualify for assignment to the CBL, or will otherwise place an undue burden on a regular Circuit Civil section due to the complexity and extended time management issues involved. Those cases which meet the definition of complex business litigation, or qualifying in the interests of judicial economy and the overall administration of justice, will be assigned to the CBL.

Section 3. Cases Subject to Mandatory Assignment to the Complex Business Litigation Sections Pursuant to Action Code. Cases which are filed under the following action codes are subject to mandatory assignment to the CBL Sections, subject to confirmation of amount in controversy is in the amount of or greater than Seven Hundred Fifty Thousand Dollars ($750,000.00), exclusive of interest, costs and attorney's fee:

A. *003–Breach of Contracts and indebtedness.* If parties are filing a breach of contract action, they must file a complaint which sets forth the required amount in controversy as opposed to simply pleading "in excess of Fifteen Thousand Dollars ($15,000.00).

B. *Negligence–Other*

i. 097–Business Governance

ii. 098–Business Torts

C. *101 –Construction Defect Professional Malpractice*

i. 094–Malpractice–Business

ii. 096–Malpractice–Other Professional

D. *Other*

i. 121–Business Transactions

ii. 124–Corporate Trust

iii. 129–Shareholder Derivative Action

iv. 130–Securities Litigation

v. 131–Trade Secrets

E. *Assignment for the Benefit of Creditors*

Section 4. Discretionary Case Assignment to the Complex Business Litigation Sections. The principles set forth below shall guide the parties and the Court in the assignment and reassignment of cases to the CBL Sections, if such cases meet the minimum amount in controversy of Seven Hundred Fifty Thousand Dollars ($750,000.00) and may result in:

A. Numerous pre-trial motions raising difficult or novel legal issues, or legal issues inextricably intertwined and time consuming;

B. Management of large numbers of separately represented parties on main actions, cross claims, counterclaims, third party claims;

C. Management of large amounts of documents, both paper and electronic, during the pendency of the matter and at trial;

D. Protracted trial;

E. Management of large numbers of expert witnesses;

F. Multiple claims resulting in consolidation of numerous individual actions;

G. Potential of significant impact on the parties' business, whether from a monetary or corporate governance standpoint;

H. A high degree of case management, including the handling of discovery disputes and motion practice;

I. Due to the complexity of the case, the services of a Special or General Magistrate would be beneficial.

Section 5. Assignment of Cases in and out of CBL Sections

A. Parties who wish to be assigned to CBL must either identify their case upon filing as a mandatory case or file a Motion to Transfer to CBL at time of filing if their case is subject to discretionary review for assignment. Defendants who wish to seek assignment to CBL must file a Motion to Transfer within fifteen (15) days of their first filing in the case.

B. The Administrative Judge (or designee) shall resolve any controversy which may arise concerning the assignment/transfer of any case to or from a CBL Section.

Section 6. Cases not subject to CBL Sections. The following types of matters shall not be assigned to the Complex Business Litigation Section absent special circumstances:

A. A matter involving occupational health or safety;

B. An environmental claim which does not involve the sale or disposition of a business or insurance coverage dispute;

C. A matter in eminent domain;

D. An administrative agency, tax, zoning, or other appeal;

E. A matter required by statute or other law to be heard in some other Court or Court Division;

F. A case that is appropriately transferred out of a CBL Section;

G. Tobacco litigation;

H. Business foreclosures; and

I. Chinese Drywall related cases.

Section 7. Complex Business Litigation Section Procedures. In furtherance of Rules 1.200 and 1.201, Florida Rules of Civil Procedure, and this Administrative Order, the Complex Business Litigation Procedures for the Eleventh Judicial Circuit, will be revised and published on the Circuit's website, and will be available for review on each CBL Section web page.

Administrative Order No. 16–12, entered on October 27, 2016, is hereby rescinded in its entirety and held for naught.

This Order shall take effect on January 2, 2018 and shall remain in effect until further order of the Court.

DONE AND ORDERED in Chambers at Miami–Dade County, Florida this 12 day of December, 2017.

Bertila Soto, Chief Judge
Eleventh Judicial Circuit of Florida

17–02. ESTABLISHING CERTAIN FILING AND OTHER PROCEDURES IN THE CIRCUIT APPELLATE DIVISION, TO INCLUDE EMAIL SERVICE OF COURT DOCUMENTS AND E-FILING BY REGISTERED USERS OF FLORIDA COURTS E–FILING PORTAL

THE ELEVENTH JUDICIAL CIRCUIT MIAMI–DADE COUNTY, FLORIDA

CASE NO. 17–1

ADMINISTRATIVE ORDER NO. 17–02

IN RE: ESTABLISHING CERTAIN FILING AND OTHER PROCEDURES IN THE CIRCUIT APPELLATE DIVISION, TO INCLUDE EMAIL SERVICE OF COURT DOCUMENTS AND E–FILING BY REGISTERED USERS OF FLORIDA COURTS E–FILING PORTAL; ELECTRONIC FILING OF APPELLATE RECORDS; ELECTRONIC FILING OF APPENDICES; AGREED EXTENSIONS OF TIME FOR FILING BRIEFS; UTILIZATION OF COURT REPORTERS; AND ELECTRONIC MEDIA AND STILL PHOTOGRAPHY COVERAGE

WHEREAS, Local Rule R–3–1 created the Appellate Division of the Eleventh Judicial Circuit of Florida (Appellate Division) and therein prescribed that three-judge panels hear all appellate cases; and

WHEREAS, pursuant to Administrative Order No. 82–22, certain writs (i.e., prohibition, mandamus and habeas corpus) are not to be heard by the Appellate Division; rather such writs should be filed as an original action in the respective Circuit Court Division corresponding to the respective County Court Division; and

WHEREAS, the Appellate Division seeks to adopt various procedures which are currently in use in the Third District Court of Appeal; and

WHEREAS, accordingly, this Administrative Order hereby establishes procedures which will streamline the grant of extensions to time; provides guidance for litigants who wish to bring court reporters to Circuit Appellate oral arguments; prescribes that the guidelines for electronic media and still photography coverage of proceedings in the Appellate Division shall be in accordance with existing, Florida Rules of Appellate Procedure, Florida Rules of Judicial Administration and Administrative Orders; provides procedures in the Appellate Division for email service of court documents and e-filing by registered users of the Florida Courts E–Filing Portal; and provides procedures for the e-filing of appellate records and appendices in the Appellate Division; and

WHEREAS, the Florida Supreme Court promulgated certain standards of conduct and technology for public judicial proceedings;

NOW, THEREFORE, pursuant to the authority vested in me as Chief Judge of the Eleventh Judicial Circuit of Florida by Rule 2.215, Florida Rules of Judicial Administration, it is hereby **ORDERED** as follows:

A. Email Service of Court Documents and E–Filing by Registered Users of the Florida Courts E–Filing Portal

(1) Electronic Filing on the Florida Court's E–Filing Portal (Portal) shall be as prescribed by the Portal for all other divisions of the Court and in accordance with this Circuit's Administrative Order No 17–02. It is the responsibility of the filer to safeguard his or her username and password to prevent unauthorized filings. Any electronic filings received via the filer's username are presumed to have been submitted by the filer. Submission of a document to the Portal by a registered attorney will constitute a notice of appearance in the case by that attorney if an appearance in the case has not previously been made.

(2) In accordance with Florida Rule of Judicial Administration 2.515, all documents filed with the Court must contain the name of the attorney of record, along with the current Florida Bar number, address, telephone number, including area code, primary email address and secondary email address, if any. Documents filed electronically with the Court shall not contain an original signature. The filer should sign the document using "/s" followed by the filer's name, which signifies that the filer has read the document and confirms the filer's intent that the filing be accepted by the Court. The filer agrees that submitting the document for electronic filing creates the same

good faith obligations as the original signature creates on a paper document.

(3) Documents are required to contain a certificate of service, pursuant to Florida Rule of Appellate Procedure 9.420 in the form prescribed by Florida Rule of Judicial Administration 2.516(f), as amended. Thus, if a document is served on the opposing side by email or some other electronic means, the certificate of service must state the electronic means used as well as the date of service. Electronic filings which do not contain a certificate of service may be rejected.

(4) The date of filing of an electronic document shall be the date it is electronically received by the Court up to 11:59 p.m., Eastern Time, on that date. Any filing on or after midnight will be deemed to have been filed the next business day. Filings on a weekend, holiday or any day the Court is closed will be deemed to have been filed on the next business day. Filers should leave a sufficient top margin on the first page to accommodate the Court's time/date stamp. Filers must submit documents so that they are properly oriented to be read without needing to be rotated. After a document has been electronically filed through the Portal, confirmation will be automatically emailed to the filer at the filer's registered email address confirming receipt by the Court.

(5) Any document filed by an attorney or a pro se party must have all confidential material redacted. Only the redacted document should be filed. See Florida Rules of Judicial Administration 2.420 and 2.425.

(6) Failure to comply with this Administrative Order may result in the filing being stricken and the case being dismissed or the filing begin stricken and submission of the case to the Court without the benefit of the filing. If, for any reason, a party is unable to comply with this Administrative Order, counsel must file a motion as a separate document with the paper original brief or document setting forth the reasons counsel cannot comply and requesting a hardship exception.

B. Electronic Filing of Appellate Records

(7) Effective October 6, 2017, the County Court Divisions in Miami–Dade County, in lieu of paper records, shall prepare and submit records on appeal to the Appellate Division electronically. Paper copies of the record must be served on the parties as specified by the Florida Rules of Appellate Procedure unless the parties agree to accept an electronic copy or until electronic copies are required to be served on the parties by Florida Rule of Judicial Administration 2.516.

(8) The submission of records on appeal electronically must be made in Adobe portable document format (pdf) and in accordance with this Court's procedures for filing electronic records through the Court's FTP server. The record must be properly indexed and bookmarked or hyperlinked and fully searchable. The electronic record shall be compiled in the format specified by Florida Rule of Appellate Procedure 9.200 and shall include an index, a copy of the lower court, lower tribunal, or state agency progress docket and a certification page containing a scanned or electronic copy of the Clerk of the Courts ("Clerk") certification. The Clerk's certification should contain the Clerk's name, address, phone number and email address. The Clerk shall redact the document in compliance with Florida Rule of Judicial Administration 2.420(d), and the documents contained in the record on appeal shall be the redacted version. A party may file a motion in the Appellate Division for the inclusion of the unredacted version of a document in the record on appeal, respecting the confidentiality of such documents as required under Florida Rule of Judicial Administration 2.420. With the exception of sealed or confidential records, all volumes of the record on appeal being submitted to the Court electronically must be included in the same document, except as limited by the FTP server.

Electronic records must be complete and readable. Lower tribunal, lower court and state agency clerks may be required to re-send an electronic record if it is missing pages, missing volumes, is not properly indexed or hyperlinked or if portions of the record are unreadable.

(9) The standard naming conventions which must be used are:

YYYY–123456–AP–01 or YYYY–123456–AC–01

(a) Multiple Volume Record. If a multiple volume record requires more than one pdf document, each pdf shall be consecutively numbered by placing a numeral after the word "record" in the name.

(b) Supplemental Record. Subsequently filed volumes of supplemental record must be transmitted as separate documents using the naming convention. Additional supplemental records should be numbered consecutively.

(c) Confidential and Sealed Records. Confidential and sealed records must be submitted in pdf document separate from any other portion of the record also being electronically filed with the Court. Sealed or confidential records should be combined and submitted as a separate pdf file and named using the naming convention.

(10) If a record on appeal contains transcripts, those should be electronically filed with record on appeal and not as a separate pdf file.

(11) A copy of the index to all volumes of the record must be contained at the beginning of the record. Summary records shall also be indexed and bookmarked or hyperlinked and sent separately from the Notice of Appeal. Electronic records containing known confidential information must be marked on the cover page and, if possible, the specific documents containing the confidential information should be marked on the index to the record. Transmittal letters are not permitted to be filed electronically or in paper with the record on appeal.

(12) The date of filing an electronic record shall be the date it is actually received by the Court up to 11:59 p.m., Eastern Time, on that date. Any record e-filed at or after midnight will be deemed to have been filed on the next business day. Electronic filings made on a weekend, a holiday or any other day the Court is closed will be deemed to be filed on the next business day.

(13) Paper exhibits (including photographs) should be indexed, scanned, and transmitted electronically. To be viewable electronically, pictures should be scanned in color, if possible, or, if not, then in grayscale. If a party wishes to request that the actual exhibits or physical evidence be sent to the Court with the record on appeal, that party shall file a motion specifically addressing the need for the Court to receive the designated exhibits and justify why the filing of the physical evidence or exhibits is necessary.

C. Electronic Filing of Appendices

(14) Effective as of the effective date of this Administrative Order any appendix filed electronically with the Court shall comply with this Administrative Order.

(15) The electronic submission of an appendix with a petition, brief, motion, response or reply must be made in Adobe portable document format (pdf) and in accordance with this Court's procedures for electronic filing. The appendix must be properly indexed and either bookmarked or hyperlinked and fully searchable. All appendices shall be in compliance with Florida Rules of Judicial Administration 2.420 and 2.425. Filers may be required to resend an electronic appendix if it is missing pages, missing volumes, is not properly indexed, bookmarked or hyperlinked, or if portions of the record are unreadable.

(16) The electronically filed index and appendix shall be filed as one document but shall be filed separately from the petition, brief, motion, response or reply.

D. Agreed Extensions of Time for Filing Briefs

(17) Effective immediately, a party who has obtained the agreement of opposing counsel to a specific extension of time for the filing of an initial, answer or reply brief may file a notice of an extension of time in lieu of a motion seeking an extension of time, pursuant to Florida Rule of Appellate Procedure 9.300(a). The notice shall be in substantially the form prescribed below:

The undersigned (Appellant/Appellee) or counsel for (Appellant/Appellee) has agreed with (Appellant/Appellee) or counsel for (Appellant/Appellee) that the time for serving (Appellant/Appellee's) (initial, answer or reply brief) may be extended for _________ days to (date).

(18) An agreed notice of extension of time will be accepted for an aggregate total of 120 days for an initial or answer brief and 30 days for a reply brief. The notice must be signed by the party filing it but need not be signed by the other parties. No order will issue from the Court upon receipt of the notice.

(19) Any extensions in the aggregate beyond 120 days for initial or answer briefs and 30 days for reply briefs, whether agreed upon or not, must be made by motion to the Court.

E. Court Reporters

(20) A party who desires to bring a court reporter to an oral argument must seek permission from the Court by motion at least ten days before the date of the oral argument. The Presiding Judge of the panel which will hear the oral argument shall grant or deny the motion in his or her discretion.

F. Electronic media and still photography coverage.

(21) Electronic media and still photography coverage of public proceedings in the Appellate Division shall be allowed in accordance with the standards of conduct and technology promulgated by the Supreme Court of Florida, and effectuated pursuant to Florida Rule of Judicial Administration 2.450 and this Court's Administrative Order Nos.: 00–05, 07–02, 07–02 A1 and 08–11.

G. Effective Date. This Administrative Order shall take effective immediately upon execution unless as otherwise specifically provided in certain provisions herein and shall remain in effect until further order of the Court.

DONE AND ORDERED in Chambers at Miami–Dade County, Florida, this 1st day of August, 2017.

BERTILA SOTO, CHIEF JUDGE
ELEVENTH JUDICIAL CIRCUIT
OF FLORIDA

16–14. ESTABLISHMENT OF VETERANS TREATMENT COURT

IN THE CIRCUIT COURT OF THE ELEVENTH JUDICIAL CIRCUIT IN AND FOR MIAMI DADE COUNTY

CASE NO. 16–1

(Court Administration)

ADMINISTRATIVE ORDER NO. 16–14

IN RE: ESTABLISHMENT OF VETERANS TREATMENT COURT

WHEREAS, a significant number of veterans who were exposed to prolonged combat resulting in physical injuries, post-traumatic stress disorder or traumatic brain injury, that result in mental health conditions and substance abuse disorders; and

WHEREAS, such conditions sometimes make it difficult for veterans to reintegrate to civilian life, and sometimes lead to behaviors resulting in arrest; and

WHEREAS, the United States Department of Veterans Affairs (Department) is able to assist the court with the provision of services for veterans eligible to receive benefits from the Department who are arrested for municipal ordinance violations, misdemeanors, and felonies; and

WHEREAS, the services provided by the Department will provide meaningful treatment for veterans that as anticipated will reduce recidivism and improve public safety; and

WHEREAS, pursuant to Rule 2.215(b)(3), Judicial Administration Rules, the Chief Judge shall "considering available resources, ensure the efficient and proper administration of all courts within [this] Circuit;" and

WHEREAS, accordingly, it has been determined the establishment of a Veterans Treatment Court ("VTC") in this Circuit would provide a means to divert eligible veteran participants from the traditional criminal justice system and provide them support and rehabilitation through comprehensive substance abuse and/or mental health treatment, education, vocational programs; and community resource referrals for housing, childcare, and transportation, all while being judicially monitored; and

WHEREAS, towards that end, the Circuit, and its justice and community partners applied for and received a grant from the U.S. Department of Justice in the amount of Three Hundred Fifty Thousand Dollars ($350,000) to support the establishment of the VTC; and

WHEREAS, additional funding in the amount of Seventy-five Thousand Dollars ($75,000) was provided by the Board of County Commissioners through its Military Affairs Board to supplement the cost of establishing the VTC; and

WHEREAS, the VTC is made up of an extensive collaboration of dedicated partners, including criminal justice, federal veterans' agencies, and local community veterans' organizations; and

WHEREAS, the target population for the VTC includes military veterans ("Veterans") and service members ("Service Members") who have been charged with felony non-violent criminal offenses that may or may not have accompanying misdemeanor offense(s) and who are identified with substance dependency and/or serious mental health issues; and

WHEREAS, the VTC as an immediate and highly structured judicial intervention process will require the successful completion of the treatment program in lieu of probation or incarceration; and

WHEREAS, the VTC will maintain strict compliance with all applicable state and federal laws, and specifically the Florida Criminal Laws and Rules, and Section 394.47891, Florida Statutes; and

WHEREAS, The Department has agreed to provide the Circuit with a Veterans Justice Outreach (VJO) Coordinator, on a regular basis, to be housed at the Dade County Jail, to effectuate the early identification of Veterans and Service Members who may be eligible for the VTC, to attend VTC proceedings, and to develop individualized treatment plans for each eligible Veteran or Service Member in an effort to alleviate the problems that resulted in the Veteran's or Service Member's arrest; and

WHEREAS, South Florida Behavioral Health Network, Inc. (SFBHN), a network system of care is able to assist the VTC with the provisions of service for Veterans and Service Members who may not otherwise be eligible for services from the Department, with its goal being to develop, implement and refine a coordinated system of behavioral health care that is anticipated to enhance treatment and recovery services for those at risk of or who are suffering from mental health and substance abuse problems, which will further reduce recidivism and improve public safety; and

WHEREAS, in addition to SFBHN, various community treatment providers have agreed to collaborate with the VTC to enhance the services provided to Veterans; and

WHEREAS, the Circuit will establish a volunteer mentor program, as more specifically described hereinafter;

NOW, THEREFORE, pursuant to the authority vested in me as Chief Judge of the Eleventh Judicial Circuit of Florida, under Rule 2.215, Rules of Judicial Administration, it is hereby **ORDERED:**

(1) General Provisions.

(a) *Establishment.* The Veterans Treatment Court Program ("VTC") is established for county and circuit criminal cases, effective January 19, 2017.

(b) *Presiding Judge.* A judge assigned to the Criminal Division shall preside over the VTC, with the exclusive authority to establish the calendar for VTC hearings ("VTC Judge").

(c) *Eligibility Criteria.* In order to be transferred to the VTC, an individual must:

i. Be a Veteran or Service Member who was arrested for a non-violent felony offense that may or may not have an accompanying misdemeanor offense (hereinafter referred to as "Defendant"). At the time of booking at a jail or first appearance, an attempt shall be made by the VJO Coordinator to determine if the Defendant is a Veteran or Service Member. If the Defendant is identified as a Veteran or Service Member, the VJO Coordinator will determine eligibility for services from the Department.

ii. Suffer from a military-related mental illness, traumatic brain injury, substance abuse disorder, or psychological problem.

iii. Be eligible for a pretrial intervention program as prescribed in Section 948.08, Florida Statutes.

iv. Have sufficient time to consult with counsel, voluntarily agree to enter into the VTC, waive the right to a speedy trial, and review the proposed coordinated strategy while in a pretrial intervention program.

(d) *Transfer Procedures.* In order for a defendant to be transferred to the VTC:

i. The originally assigned judge in the Circuit Criminal Division ("Division Judge") may recommend during court proceedings the transfer of the Defendant to the VTC.

ii. Based upon such recommendation, the Defendant will be assessed to determine if he/she meets the Eligibility Criteria set forth in paragraph (c)ii hereinabove.

iii. If the assessment determines the Defendant meets the criteria, along with input from the Division Judge, State Attorney, and Defense Counsel, the VTC Judge will make the final determination as to whether the Defendant is to be transferred to the VTC.

iv. If the transfer is authorized by the VTC Judge, the defendant will be required to execute the VTC Participation Agreement.

v. Notwithstanding the above mentioned Transfer Procedures, for good cause shown, the VTC Judge shall have the discretion to authorize the transfer of a Veteran or Service Member into the VTC who does not meet all of the Eligibility Criteria.

(e) *VTC Section Designation.* The Clerk of the Court is hereby authorized and designated to establish Section 57 in the Circuit Criminal Division for VTC cases and effectuate any and all requisite changes in CJIS regarding Section 57. Accordingly, after transfer, VTC cases will be designated as being in Section 57.

(f) *Volunteer Mentor Program.* The Circuit will establish a volunteer mentor program comprised of specially trained volunteers to guide and support the Veterans and Service Members through the judicial process and to assist them with their treatment plan(s) and other services available from the Department and community treatment providers.

(g) *Services for Ineligible defendants.* Those identified Veterans or Service Members who may not be eligible for services from the Department, will be screened and assessed by Circuit personnel to determine what services may be provided by collaborating community treatment providers.

(h) *Termination from VTC.* If a Defendant is terminated from the VTC for any reason, the case shall be transferred to the originally assigned division judge for further proceedings.

(i) *Number of Participants.* The number of Defendants who are eligible for the VTC may be limited subject to continued authorization for the VTC and funding availability.

(2) VTC Policies and Procedures.

(a) *Adoption of Policy and Procedure Manual.* The Miami–Dade County Veterans Treatment Court Policy and Procedure Manual as proposed in April, 2016, incorporated by reference herein, is hereby adopted.

(b) *Amendments.* Any amendments to the Policy and Procedure Manual may be implemented without the necessity of an Administrative Order.

DONE AND ORDERED in Chambers at Miami, Dade County, Florida on this 16th day of December, 2016.

BERTILA SOTO, CHIEF JUDGE

ELEVENTH JUDICIAL CIRCUIT OF FLORIDA

16–12. [RESCINDED BY ORDER 17-11, EFFECTIVE JANUARY 2, 2018]

16–11. CERTIFICATION AND REGULATION OF CERTIFIED CIVIL PROCESS SERVERS WITHIN THE ELEVENTH JUDICIAL CIRCUIT

THE ELEVENTH JUDICIAL CIRCUIT MIAMI–DADE COUNTY, FLORIDA

CASE NO. 16–1

(Court Administration)

(Rescinding AO Nos. 94–18 and 09–12)

ADMINISTRATIVE ORDER NO. 16–11

IN RE: CERTIFICATION AND REGULATION OF CERTIFIED CIVIL PROCESS SERVERS WITHIN THE ELEVENTH JUDICIAL CIRCUIT

WHEREAS, Rule 2.215 of the Rules of Judicial Administration places responsibility in the Chief Judge for the development of an administrative plan for the efficient and proper administration of all courts within the Circuit; and

WHEREAS, the Florida Certified Process Server Act, Florida Statutes §§ 48.25 through 48.31 ("Process Server Act"), expressly vests in the Chief Judge the authority to establish an approved list of process servers who have met the requirements for certification under the Process Server Act and the requirements set forth by the Eleventh Judicial Circuit of Florida; and

WHEREAS, the Legislature has provided in Chapter 48 a method of certification of process servers and has authorized the chief judge of each circuit to establish a list of such certified process servers who may serve process in that circuit; and

WHEREAS, § 48.29(6), Fla. Stat., provides that returns of service shall be made by certified process servers on a form which has been reviewed and approved by the court; and

WHEREAS, § 92.525, Fla. Stat., establishes alternate methods for verification of documents; and

WHEREAS, § 48.27, Fla. Stat., provides that certain standards and requirements as prescribed under the Process Server Act were established for the designation of certified process servers to be eligible to be included on an approved list for the Eleventh Judicial Circuit of Florida to serve initial non-enforceable civil process; and

WHEREAS, accordingly, this Administrative Order serves to amend and reestablish the standards and requirements governing certified process servers within the Eleventh Judicial Circuit;

NOW, THEREFORE, pursuant to the authority vested in me as Chief Judge of the Eleventh Judicial Circuit of Florida, under Rule 2.215, Rules of Judicial Administration, the following standards and requirements governing certified process servers within the Eleventh Judicial Circuit are hereby reestablished:

A. Standards and Requirements:

1. Individuals seeking certification must submit an application with a reasonable processing fee, as set forth in the current Information Sheet for Applicants issued by the Administrative Office of the Courts ("AOC"), and must fulfill the following requirements:

(a) The applicant shall be a permanent resident of the State of Florida, shall be at least eighteen (18) years of age, and must have no mental or legal disability.

(b) The applicant shall submit to a background investigation which shall include a review of the applicant's criminal record, if any exists.

(c) The applicant shall obtain and file with the application a certificate of good conduct which specifies all of the following:

(1) There is no pending criminal case against the applicant.

(2) There is no record of any felony conviction of the applicant.

(3) There is no record of a conviction of the applicant for a misdemeanor involving moral turpitude or dishonesty within the past five (5) years.

(d) Persons who have completed an application and satisfied the requirements set forth in paragraphs 1(a)–(c) shall submit to a written examination testing the applicant's knowledge of the laws and rules regarding the service of process. A passing examination grade is hereby fixed at eighty percent (80%) out of a possible score of one hundred percent (100%).. The content, frequency and location of the examination shall be approved by the Chief Judge or Chief Judge's designee.

(e) An applicant shall execute a performance bond with a surety company authorized within Miami–Dade County in the amount of Five Thousand Dollars ($5,000.00) as provided in § 48.29(3)(g), Fla. Stat. Such bond shall be approved by the Clerk of the Courts prior to presentation to the AOC and shall be renewable on an annual basis.

(f) An applicant who successfully completes the written examination shall take an oath that he or she will honestly, diligently, and faithfully exercise the duties of a certified process server.

(g) An applicant who completes the requirements set forth in Chapter 48 and set forth in this Administrative Order shall be eligible to be placed on the approved list of process servers to serve initial non-enforceable civil process as may be authorized in § 48.27, Fla. Stat.

2. The identification card issued to each certified process server shall be renewed annually, upon proof of good standing, completion of re-certification course, and current bond. At the time of renewal, a reasonable renewal fee set by the Chief Judge shall be due from each process server.

3. Certified process servers approved for the Eleventh Judicial Circuit shall comply with all rules and statutes pertaining to service of process and will be expected to keep up to date with any new provisions within said rules and statutes.

4. A certified process server on the approved List of Certified Process Servers eligible to serve process within the Eleventh Judicial Circuit may be removed from the List for good cause. Good cause shall include, but shall not be limited to, malfeasance, misfeasance, neglect of duty, or incompetence in connection with the duties of a certified process server. Furthermore,

(a) Any person aggrieved by the actions of a Certified Process Server may file a complaint with the Process Server Review Board of the Eleventh Judicial Circuit.

(b) The Board shall review the complaint and, after affording the process server an opportunity to be heard, shall forward its recommendations to the Chief Judge or the Chief Judge's designee for consideration. If the Chief Judge has named a designee, the Chief Judge's designee shall forward their approval or disapproval of the recommendation to the Chief Judge. Any substantiated complaint shall remain on file for a period of five (5) years.

(c) Nothing herein shall limit the power of the Chief Judge to take whatever action deemed appropriate without the necessity of referral to the Process Server Review Board.

B. Verified Return of Service Form.

1. A return of service form provided by a certified Process Server that is captioned "Verified Return of Process" and which contains the following information shall be authorized for use in this Circuit:

(a) The court, case number, and caption of the case.

(b) The date and time when process was received by the Certified Process Server.

(c) The date and time when service was made.

(d) The specific manner of execution (section of statute, if applicable).

(e) The name of the person on whom service was made.

(f) If a person was served in a representative capacity, the position occupied by the person.

(g) The signature of the certified process server.

(h) The printed name and identification number of the certified process server.

(i) A statement that the person serving process is a certified process server in good standing in the judicial circuit in which the process was served and that the Certified Process Server is disinterested in the process being served.

2. Verification of the Return of Service shall be accomplished by either of the methods prescribed in § 92.525, Fla. Stat.:

(a) An oath before a notary that, by personal knowledge, the facts and matters contained within the Verified Return of Service are true and correct; or

(b) A signed declaration containing the following language: "Under penalty of perjury, I declare that I have read the foregoing Verified Return of Service and that the facts stated are true."

3. A Verified Return of Service, to be valid, need not refer to any particular Administrative Order nor to any order or blanket appointment.

4. A Verified Return of Service which contains information in addition to those items mentioned above shall not be invalidated on that basis.

C. Maintenance of List of Approved Certified Process Servers: The Administrative Office of the Courts and the Clerk of the Courts are hereby authorized and directed to maintain and update the List of Approved Certified Process Servers.

D. Process Server Review Board.

1. *Board Composition.* The Board will be composed of a chair, co-chair(s), member-at-large, certified civil process server, board secretary, and coordinator. All are voting members except for the board secretary and the coordinator. All members of the Board shall be appointed by the Chief Judge.

2. *Quorum.* A quorum consists of three voting members.

3. *Vacancies.* Any vacancy on the Board shall be filled by appointment by the Chief Judge. The person appointed shall serve the remainder of the vacant term.

4. *Terms.* The Board will serve for a minimum of a two-year term beginning on April 1 of the new term calendar year.

This Administrative Order shall become effective immediately upon execution and shall remain in full force and effect until further order of the Court. Administrative Order Nos. 94–18 and 09–12 are hereby rescinded in their entirety and held for naught.

DONE AND ORDERED in Chambers at Miami–Dade County, Florida, this 21st day of September, 2016.

BERTILA SOTO, CHIEF JUDGE

ELEVENTH JUDICIAL CIRCUIT OF FLORIDA

16–07. COMPENSATION OF COURT APPOINTED COUNSEL AND CASE RELATED EXPENSES IN CASES INVOLVING THE INVOLUNTARY CIVIL COMMITMENT OF SEXUALLY VIOLENT PREDATORS

THE ELEVENTH JUDICIAL CIRCUIT MIAMI–DADE COUNTY, FLORIDA

CASE NO. 16–01

(Court Administration)

ADMINISTRATIVE ORDER NO. 16–07

(Rescinding Administrative Orders Nos. 03–01, 03–01–A1, and 04–08)

IN RE: COMPENSATION OF COURT APPOINTED COUNSEL AND CASE RELATED EXPENSES IN CASES INVOLVING THE INVOLUNTARY CIVIL COMMITMENT OF SEXUALLY VIOLENT PREDATORS

WHEREAS, pursuant to section 394.916(3), Florida Statutes, the legislature has determined that in adversarial civil commitment proceedings for sexually violent predators (commonly referred to as the Jimmy Ryce Act), the person subject to such proceedings is entitled to the assistance of counsel, and, if the person is indigent, the court shall appoint the public defender or, if a conflict exists, other counsel ("court appointed counsel") to assist the person; and

WHEREAS, pursuant to the Laws of Florida, the legislature provided for specific appropriation funds for attorney fees and case-related expenses associated with prosecuting and defending sexual predator civil commitment cases; and

WHEREAS, Administrative Order No. 03–01, *In re: Establishment of Guidelines for Compensation of Professional Services and Conflict Counsel in Jimmy Ryce Civil Commitment Cases* established guidelines for court appointed counsel and professional service expenses; and

WHEREAS, Administrative Order No. 03–01 A1, *Amendment of Administrative Order 03–01; In re: Establishment of Guidelines for Compensation of Professional Services and Court Appointed Counsel in Jimmy Ryce Civil Commitment Cases,* established guidelines for attorneys approved by the Indigent Services Committee in accordance with section 27.42, Florida Statutes; and

WHEREAS, section 27.42, Florida Statutes, has been repealed by Chapter 2007–62, section 30, Laws of Florida; and

WHEREAS, Administrative Order No. 04–08, *In re: The Appointment and Compensation for Court Appointed Attorneys in Jimmy Ryce Civil Commitment Cases for the Interim Period of July 1, 2004 through September 30, 2004,* was entered for an interim period to remain in effect until further order of the Court; and

WHEREAS, the interim period delineated in Administrative No. 04–08 has lapsed and no longer needs to remain in effect; and

WHEREAS, the legislature has provided that a court-appointed attorney must enter into a contract for services with the Justice Administrative Commission to be included on the court's registry in accordance with section 27.40, Florida Statutes; and

WHEREAS, the Justice Administrative Commission oversees the compensation of court-appointed attorneys handling the involuntary civil commitment proceedings for sexually violent predators;

NOW, THEREFORE, pursuant to the authority vested in me as Chief Judge of the Eleventh Judicial Circuit of Florida under Rule 2.215, Florida Rules of Judicial Administration, it is hereby **ORDERED** that:

1. Prior to being included on the Circuit's registry, accepting and defending sexual predator civil commitment cases (commonly referred to as "Jimmy Ryce Civil Commitment Cases"), Court-appointed counsel shall satisfy this Circuit's registry requirements.

2. In addition to satisfying the Circuit's registry requirements, Court-appointed counsel shall satisfy any requirements of the Justice Administrative Commission to obtain attorney fees and case related expenses associated with prosecuting and defending the sexual predator civil commitment cases in accordance with Florida statutes and rules.

This Administrative Order shall take effect immediately upon execution and shall remain in effect until further order of the Court. Administrative Orders Nos. 03–01, 03–01–A1, and 04–08, and any amendments thereto, are hereby rescinded and held for naught.

DONE AND ORDERED in Chambers at Miami–Dade County, Florida, this 4th day of May, 2016.

BERTILA SOTO, CHIEF JUDGE
ELEVENTH JUDICIAL CIRCUIT OF FLORIDA

16–04. ESTABLISHMENT OF PROCEDURES FOR TRANSFERRING RELATED CASES FROM THE COUNTY COURT CIVIL DIVISION TO THE CIRCUIT COURT CIVIL DIVISION

THE ELEVENTH JUDICIAL CIRCUIT MIAMI-DADE COUNTY, FLORIDA

CASE NO. 16–1 (Court Administration)

ADMINISTRATIVE ORDER NO. 16–04

IN RE: ESTABLISHMENT OF PROCEDURES FOR TRANSFERRING RELATED CASES FROM THE COUNTY COURT CIVIL DIVISION TO THE CIRCUIT COURT CIVIL DIVISION

WHEREAS, occasionally, open, related cases appear in county and circuit civil court and the parties prefer that a single judge resolve both cases (hereinafter referred to as "Related Case(s)"); and

WHEREAS, while having the same judge for the Related Cases may be best for judicial efficiency, there is no legal authority to transfer a case within the exclusive jurisdiction of the county court to the circuit court, or vice versa, and then consolidate those cases together; and

WHEREAS, however, it is permissible to have the same judge preside over the Related Cases by temporarily designating the circuit civil court judge to serve as an acting county civil court judge or to temporarily designate the county civil court judge to serve as a circuit civil court judge; and

WHEREAS, although such temporary designations would not consolidate the Related Cases in the same court, the same judge would be authorized to preside over both cases; and

WHEREAS, pursuant to long established case law and Rule 2.215(b)(4), Florida Rules of Judicial Administration, the undersigned is authorized to assign any judge to temporary service for which the judge is qualified in any court in the same circuit; and

WHEREAS, accordingly, semi-annually, the undersigned executes Administrative Orders to effectuate such temporary assignments whereby circuit court judges are temporarily assigned to act in the capacity of a county court judge and likewise county court judges are temporarily assigned to act in the capacity of a circuit court judge; and

WHEREAS, it was determined that it would be preferable for a circuit civil court judge to preside over the Related Cases; and

WHEREAS, in addition to such authority vested in circuit court judges and county court judges under the Administrative Orders it was deemed appropriate to establish procedures for transferring Related Cases from the county court civil division (hereinafter referred to as "county civil court") to the circuit court civil division (hereinafter referred to as "circuit civil court") under certain circumstances;

NOW, THEREFORE, pursuant to the authority vested in me as Chief Judge of the Eleventh Judicial Circuit of Florida, under Rule 2.215, Florida Rules of Judicial Administration, the following procedures are hereby established for transferring Related Cases from the county civil court to the circuit civil court where there is no jurisdictional or other legal basis for the transfer:

1. **Agreed Motions to Transfer.** Where the jurisdiction is properly within the county civil court and there is no jurisdictional or other legal basis in which to transfer a case from county civil court to circuit civil court; but, there is a Related Case in circuit civil court and the parties are in agreement, the following procedure for transfer shall be followed:

a. The parties shall submit a Joint Motion to Transfer along with an Agreed Order to the Administrative Judge of the Circuit Civil Division who has the discretion to either sign the Agreed Order or set a hearing regarding the motion.

b. The style of the case including the parties and case number of the Related Case in the circuit civil court case shall be referenced in the Agreed Order.

c. Once an Agreed Order is signed by the Administrative Judge of the Circuit Court Civil Division, the county civil court case will be assigned to the circuit civil court judge that has the Related Case.

2. **Contested Motions to Transfer.** Where the jurisdiction is properly within the county civil court and there is no jurisdictional or legal basis in which to transfer a case from county civil court to circuit civil court; but, there is a Related Case in the circuit civil court and the parties are not in agreement regarding the transfer, the following procedure for transfer shall be followed:

a. A Motion to Transfer shall be filed and scheduled before the county court civil judge assigned to the county court civil case who shall hear the arguments of the parties. Thereafter, the county court civil judge shall forward a recommendation to the Administrative Judge of the Circuit Court Civil Division to either grant or deny the Motion to Transfer (i.e., Order Recommending Approval of Transfer or Order Recommending Denial of Transfer), which shall contain the circuit civil court case style, including the parties and the case number in the Related Case.

b. Thereafter, the Administrative Judge of the Circuit Court Civil Division shall have the discretion to (i) enter an order Granting the Transfer ("Transfer Order") based on the Order Recommending Approval of Transfer, (ii) enter an order Denying the Transfer based on the Order Recommending Denial of Transfer, or (iii) hold a hearing on the Motion to Transfer before entering an order.

c. If the Administrative Judge of the Circuit Court Civil Division signs a Transfer Order, the county civil court case will be assigned to the circuit civil court judge that has the Related Case.

d. Pursuant to Paragraph 2b hereinabove, if after hearing the argument of the parties who do not agree with the transfer and the transfer is not approved, the Administrative Judge of the Circuit Court Civil Division shall refer the county civil court case back to the Administrative Judge of the County Court Civil Division for reassignment of said case back to the original county civil court judge.

3. **Objection to Transfer Order.** If an order is entered by the Administrative Judge of the Circuit Court Civil Division transferring the county civil court case to the circuit civil court judge presiding over the Related Case as provided under Paragraphs 1 (c) or 2(c) herein, the parties in the circuit civil court case shall have thirty (30) days from the date of the Transfer Order to file an objection to said Order with the circuit civil court judge. Within twenty (20) days, the circuit civil court judge shall notify the Administrative Judge of the Circuit Civil Division of the objection so that the county civil court case is referred back to the Administrative Judge of the County Court Civil Division as prescribed in paragraph 2(d) hereinabove.

4. In the aforementioned Order(s) allowing the transfer of the Related Case, the Administrative Judge of the Circuit Court Civil Division shall reference the Administrative Order authorizing circuit civil court judges to act as county civil court judges in effect at the time of the transfer.

5. The Related Cases shall not be consolidated and shall retain their original case styles and case numbers, but would be heard and disposed of by the same circuit civil court judge if the transfer is completed.

DONE AND ORDERED in Chambers at Miami–Dade County, Florida, this 29th day of February, 2016.

BERTILA SOTO, CHIEF JUDGE
ELEVENTH JUDICIAL CIRCUIT OF FLORIDA

16–03. REASSIGNMENT/TRANSFER OF RELATED CASES IN THE JUVENILE, DOMESTIC RELATIONS AND DOMESTIC VIOLENCE DIVISIONS TO THE UNIFIED FAMILY COURT DIVISION

THE ELEVENTH JUDICIAL CIRCUIT MIAMI–DADE COUNTY, FLORIDA

CASE NO. 16–1

(Court Administration)

ADMINISTRATIVE ORDER NO. 16–03

(Companion to AO No. 16–02)

IN RE: REASSIGNMENT/TRANSFER OF RELATED CASES IN THE JUVENILE, DOMESTIC RELATIONS AND DOMESTIC VIOLENCE DIVISIONS TO THE UNIFIED FAMILY COURT DIVISION

WHEREAS, pursuant to Rule 2.215, Florida Rules of Judicial Administration, the Chief Judge is authorized to exercise administrative supervision over all courts within the judicial circuit in the exercise of judicial powers and over the judges and officers of the court; and

WHEREAS, in the exercise of such judicial powers, the Chief Judge may adopt administrative orders to effectuate the efficient and proper administration of all courts within the circuit and to effect the prompt disposition of cases; and

WHEREAS, the Florida Supreme Court, in *In re Report of the Family Court Steering Committee,* 794 So. 2d 518 (Fla. 2001), endorsed the guiding principles and characteristics of the model family court developed by the Family Court Steering Committee and reaffirmed its goal of the creation of a fully integrated, comprehensive approach to handling all cases involving children and families; and

WHEREAS, the Florida Supreme Court, in *In re Amendments to the Florida Rules of Judicial Administration and In re Florida Family Law Rules of Procedure,* 132 So. 3d 1114 (Fla. 2014), adopted proposed amendments of the Steering Committee providing for case management of open related family cases through the filing of a Notice of Related Cases, for all related family cases involving the same family and/or children to be handled before one judge ("one family, one judge"), for a more formal manner of coordination of related cases and hearings, and for the access and review of related family files by the judiciary and parties; and

WHEREAS, in order to achieve the goals of the model family court endorsed by the Florida Supreme Court in *In re Report of the Family Court Steering Committee,* 794 So. 2d 518 (Fla. 2001), and *In re Amendments to the Florida Rules of Judicial Administration and In re Florida Family Law Rules of Procedure,* 132 So. 3d 1114 (Fla. 2014), the Eleventh Judicial Circuit's Unified Family Court Division will continue to be comprised of related cases from the Juvenile, Domestic Relations and Domestic Violence Divisions of the Court; and

WHEREAS, the undersigned Chief Judge finds it necessary to reassign/transfer such Related Cases to Unified Family Court Division to effectuate the prompt disposition of these cases and control the court's dockets;

NOW THEREFORE, pursuant to authority vested in me as Chief Judge of the Eleventh Judicial Circuit of Florida, it is hereby **ORDERED:**

1. Upon identification as defined in Administrative Order No. 16–02 Related Cases in the Juvenile, Domestic Relations, and Domestic Violence Divisions shall be reassigned/transferred to the Unified Family Court Division of the Eleventh Judicial Circuit Court. The Clerk's Office shall enter Related Cases into the Related Case and Case Cross Reference fields in Odyssey, and link all related cases together in the system.

2. Upon such identification of the Related Cases, the Clerk of Court is hereby directed to reflect the reassignment/transfer of the Related Cases in the official court records to the Unified Family Court Division. Cases shall be randomly assigned to the Unified Family Court Division by the Clerk of Court pursuant to a blind filing system.

3. All cases in the Complex Litigation Section (formerly known as Complex Litigation Division) of the Unified Family Court Division, Section 48, will be reassigned/transferred as follows:

a. All open cases currently assigned to the Complex Litigation Section of the Unified Family Court (Section 48), shall be reassigned/transferred by the Clerk of Court from Section 48 to Section 201, and depending upon open related case types, transferred and docketed in D201 and/or J201 and/or FC201.

b. All closed cases currently assigned to the Complex Litigation Section of the Unified Family Court Division will remain in Section 48. Upon any activity, the reassignment/transfer of such cases is as follows:

i) All Section 48 cases that were closed on or before December 31, 2014 shall be blind filed by the Clerk of Court to Unified Family Court Division and transferred and docketed to the appropriate Unified Family Court Section, (specifically, D201, D202 and D203; and/or J201, J202 and J203; and/or FC201, FC202 and FC203), as may be amended, if necessary.

ii) All Section 48 cases that were closed on or after January 1, 2015 shall be reassigned/transferred by the Clerk of Court to Section 201, and depending upon open related case types, transferred and docketed in D201 and/or J201 and/or FC201.

DONE AND ORDERED in Chambers at Miami–Dade County, Florida this 17th day of February, 2016.

BERTILA SOTO, CHIEF JUDGE
ELEVENTH JUDICIAL CIRCUIT OF FLORIDA

16–02. REAFFIRMATION OF UNIFIED FAMILY COURT PLAN AND ESTABLISHMENT OF PROCEDURES FOR UNIFIED FAMILY COURT DIVISION IN THE ELEVENTH JUDICIAL CIRCUIT OF FLORIDA

THE ELEVENTH JUDICIAL CIRCUIT MIAMI–DADE COUNTY, FLORIDA

CASE NO. 16–1

(Court Administration)

ADMINISTRATIVE ORDER NO. 16–02

(Rescinding Administrative Order Nos. 02–03, 02–14, 02–14–A1, 02–14–A2, 03–15, and 10–08)

(Companion to AO No. 16–03)

IN RE: REAFFIRMATION OF UNIFIED FAMILY COURT PLAN AND ESTABLISHMENT OF PROCEDURES FOR UNIFIED FAMILY COURT DIVISION IN THE ELEVENTH JUDICIAL CIRCUIT OF FLORIDA

WHEREAS, the Florida Supreme Court, in *In re Report of the Commission of Family Courts,* 588 So. 2d. 586 (Fla. 1991), directed each judicial circuit to develop a local rule establishing a Family Court, or a means to coordinate family law matters that affect one family if the circuit or part thereof is of such limited size that it is unable to administratively justify such a court; and

WHEREAS, the Florida Supreme Court in *In re Report of the Commission on Family Courts,* 633 So. 2d 14 (Fla. 1994) provisionally approved the local rules and administrative orders submitted by the respective circuits giving the opportunity to review and revise the plans in accordance with this opinion in the context of local rule requirements; and

WHEREAS, the Florida Supreme Court, in *In re Report of the Commission of Family Courts,* 646 So.2d 178 (Fla. 1994) approved such Administrative Orders and Local Rules submitted by the circuits; and

WHEREAS, the Florida Supreme Court, in *In re Report of the Family Court Steering Committee,* 794 So. 2d 518 (Fla. 2001), endorsed the guiding principles and characteristics of the model family court developed by the Family Court Steering Committee and reaffirmed its goal of the creation of a fully integrated, comprehensive approach to handling all cases involving children and families; and

WHEREAS, the Florida Supreme Court, in *In re Amendments to the Florida Rules of Judicial Administration and In re Florida Family Law Rules of Procedure,* 132 So. 3d 1114 (Fla. 2014), adopted proposed amendments of the Steering Committee providing for case management of open related family cases through the filing of a Notice of Related Cases, for all related family cases involving the same family and/or children to be handled before one judge ("one family, one judge"), for a more formal manner of coordination of related cases and hearings, and for the access and review of related family files by the judiciary and parties; and

WHEREAS, pursuant to Administrative Order No. 01–16, dated October 19, 2001, the Unified Family Court for the Eleventh Judicial Circuit of Florida was established to provide a comprehensive, coordinated approach to addressing family law matters; and

WHEREAS, pursuant to Administrative Order 03–15, the Unified Family Court Plan was reaffirmed and the Complex Litigation Section (formerly known as Complex Litigation Division) was established to implement the Unified Family Court in the Eleventh Judicial Circuit of Florida to provide a comprehensive, coordinated approach to addressing family law matters, thereby rescinding Administrative Order 01–16; and

WHEREAS, the policies and procedures outlined in Administrative Order 03–15 were meant to be elastic so as to provide the greatest degree of flexibility and allow for fine-tuning to the extent necessary to effectuate efficient and proper procedures for the Eleventh Judicial Circuit Court and thus subject to change at any time; and

NOW, THEREFORE, pursuant to the authority vested in me as Chief Judge of the Eleventh Judicial Circuit of Florida under Rule 2.215 of the Florida Rules of Judicial Administration, it is hereby ordered that:

I. UNIFIED FAMILY COURT DIVISION STRUCTURE AND JURISDICTION

A. The following types of Related Cases are included in the Unified Family Court Division:

1. dissolution of marriage
2. division and distribution of property arising out of a dissolution of marriage
3. annulment
4. support unconnected with dissolution of marriage
5. paternity, including, but not limited to, disestablishment of paternity
6. child support
7. Uniform Reciprocal Enforcement of Support Act/ Uniform Interstate Family Support Act (URESA/UIFSA)
8. custodial care of and access to children, including, but not limited to, relocation and temporary or concurrent custody of minor children by extended family
9. adoption
10. name change
11. declaratory judgment actions related to premarital, marital, or post marital agreements
12. civil domestic, repeat, dating, stalking and sexual violence injunctions
13. juvenile dependency
14. termination of parental rights
15. juvenile delinquency
16. emancipation of a minor
17. Children in Need of Services/ Families in Need of Services (CINS/FINS)
18. truancy
19. modification and enforcement of orders entered in these cases

B. For the purposes of this Administrative Order, the Division traditionally referred to as the Family Division in this Circuit will be referred to as the Domestic Relations Division.

II. ADMINISTRATION/JUDICIAL ASSIGNMENTS

A. In order to achieve the goals of the model family court endorsed by the Florida Supreme Court in *In re Report of the Family Court Steering Committee,* 794 So. 2d 518 (Fla. 2001), and *In re Amendments to the Florida Rules of Judicial Administration and In re Florida Family Law Rules of Procedure,* 132 So. 2d 1114 (Fla. 2014), the Eleventh Judicial Circuit's Unified Family Court Division will continue to be comprised of Related Cases from the Juvenile, Domestic Violence, and Domestic Relations Divisions of the Court.

B. All Administrative Orders pertaining to the Juvenile, Domestic Violence, and Domestic Relations Divisions will be effective, if applicable, to the cases assigned to the Unified Family Court Division.

C. The Chief Judge of this Circuit or the designated Administrative Judge of the Unified Family Court Division will manage and be responsible for:

1. Ensuring that the Circuit's policy, operating procedures, and administrative orders for implementation of the Unified Family Court Division are followed;
2. Periodically evaluating the progress of the Unified Family Court Division;
3. Coordinating the development of resources that may be required by various courts dealing with family matters, (e.g., guardian ad litem, mediation services, drug referral and treatment, home studies, etc.) and assessing the possible integration of cases regarding involuntary commitments for drug and alcohol, dependency or mental health, and as appropriate, guardianships;
4. Continuing the development and facilitation of communications with court-related entities on policy with respect to

family cases, including but not limited to state attorneys, public defenders, the Department of Children and Families, the Department of Revenue, the Department of Juvenile Justice, community social services entities, Clerk of Courts, and law enforcement agencies; and

5. Developing a means of orienting Judges newly assigned to matters affecting children and families to the family court concept for integrating the Eleventh Judicial Circuit Court's response to cases involving the same family, including directing them to appropriate initial and continuing judicial education offerings and reference materials.

D. The Chief Judge shall appoint Judges to serve in the Unified Family Court Division located at the Miami–Dade County Children's Courthouse, or another designated location.

E. All Judges who are assigned to the Unified Family Court Division for the first time and who have not served a minimum of two years in the Juvenile, Domestic Relations, and Domestic Violence Divisions respectively, must receive mandatory training before assuming the assignment, or preferably within 60 days after assuming the assignment, in accordance with course availability. This training shall consist of the fundamentals of family law, domestic violence, juvenile dependency, juvenile delinquency and child development of both healthy and maltreated children. The training includes, but is not limited to, fundamentals at Phase II of Judicial College, and the 16 hour domestic violence training provided by the Office of the State Courts Administrator, or other state or nationally accredited domestic violence course.

F. All judges assigned to the Unified Family Court Division shall be designated as Juvenile, Domestic Relations and Domestic Violence judges for the purposes of hearing all matters addressed in the Unified Family Court Division.

III. ESSENTIAL ELEMENTS

The following elements are essential or fundamental to the Unified Family Court Division as enumerated in *In re Report of the Family Court Steering Committee*, 794 So. 2d 518 (Fla. 2001):

A. Case Management. Supervising, coordinating, directing, and overseeing the process and progress of a case.

B. Self–Help Programs. Providing intake, screening, and procedural guidance to self-represented litigants in family law cases.

C. Domestic Violence. Ensuring that cases involving domestic violence are identified and managed in a manner that is organized, in compliance with all statutory time frames, and sensitive to the special dynamics involved in these cases.

D. Alternative Dispute Resolution (ADR). Offering alternatives to reduce the trauma of traditional adversarial litigation process, unless otherwise prohibited by law.

E. Guardian ad Litem. Utilizing guardians ad litem in all family cases involving abused, abandoned or neglected children, and children at risk of harm to the extent such services are available.

F. General Magistrates/Hearing Officers. Using quasi-judicial officers to expedite hearings and expand judicial resources.

G. Custody Evaluation. Providing the court with evaluative information in proceedings involving custody disputes.

H. Supervised Visitation. Promoting the utilization of qualified programs for supervised visitation and/or monitored exchange.

I. Education Programs for Parents. Utilizing education programs for parents involved in family law proceedings.

J. Counseling Services/Treatment Programs. Assuring the availability of crisis intervention and long-term counseling/treatment programs and ensuring that compliance is monitored when such services are court ordered.

K. Security. Providing adequate and sufficient security personnel and equipment to ensure that family divisions are safe environments for judges, non-judicial staff, and the public.

L. Technology. Providing computer hardware, systems, and training to access information essential to case management and coordination, to print forms and notices immediately, and to generate statistical reports, to provide public and interagency access to records, and to allow teleconferencing and appearance of witnesses by electronic means.

IV. OPERATIONAL PROTOCOL, COORDINATION AND TRANSFER OF RELATED CASES

A. Operational Protocol. The operational protocol for handling Related Cases will be followed as established by the Clerk of Court and Administrative Office of the Courts (AOC), in conjunction with those protocols established by the Juvenile, Domestic Relations, and Domestic Violence Divisions. However, all protocols of the respective Divisions are subject to revision and modification to effectuate efficient procedures and to ensure that the mandates of the Florida Supreme Court are being followed by this Circuit.

1. *Definition.* A **Related Case** is defined as two or more cases pending in the Juvenile, Domestic Relations, and/or Domestic Violence Divisions which involve any of the same parties, children, or issues. Related Cases involving the same family shall be handled before one judge in order that they shall be coordinated, heard and determined in a manner that will minimize the number of times and places that a family has to appear in court and will minimize the possibility of conflicting determinations of the same or Related Case.

2. *Identification.* Related Cases will be identified by:

a. Notice of Related Cases. In accordance with Florida Rule of Judicial Administration 2.545(d)(4), a fully completed Notice of Related Cases shall be filed with the initial pleading by the filing attorney or self-represented petitioner in each of the Related Cases that are currently open and pending with the court and served on all other parties in each of the Related Cases. Parties may file joint notices. To the extent that any issues of confidentiality apply, all legal requirements shall be observed, including any requirements as set forth in Florida Rule of Judicial Administration 2.420. Parties shall file supplemental notices as Related Cases become known or reasonably ascertainable.

b. The AOC Unified Family Court Division, in conjunction with the Clerk of Court, shall be responsible for identifying Related Cases upon the filing of a new case or one reopened post-judgment when provided with notice or court order. Upon identification, the Clerk's Office shall enter Related Cases into the Related Case and Case Cross Reference fields in Odyssey, and link all Related Cases together in the system.

c. Judges and court staff, including, but not limited to, the Family Court Self Help Program.

d. System and agency partners.

3. *Notification.* The AOC Unified Family Court Division shall be notified of these Related Cases by any of the methods indicated above in IV.A.2.a–d and will take the appropriate actions as delineated in Section IV.B. of this Administrative Order.

4. *Reassignment/Transfer Timeframes.* Until such time as a Related Case is officially transferred by the Clerk of Court to the Unified Family Court Division, the designated division judge shall continue to hear all matters in that case to ensure compliance with all state and federal statutes, rules, and regulations.

5. *Reassignment/Transfer Order.* A Reassignment/Transfer Order shall be issued only by the Unified Family Court Administrative Judge in instances where Related Cases have not been blind filed into the Unified Family Court Division or assigned pursuant to a Standing Order of Reassignment/Transfer.

6. *Reassignment/Transfer Errors.* If the transfer of a case is conducted in error, upon clarification of no open Related Cases, the case shall be reassigned/transferred to the appropriate division. If a reassignment/transfer order was entered in error, the order shall be vacated and the case shall be reassigned/assigned to the appropriate division.

7. *Resources.* In order to avoid duplication and maximize the efficient use of resources, all reports, evaluations, memoranda and orders pertaining to Related Cases shall be made accessible to the Unified Family Court Judge assigned to such cases, and to all counsel and the parties for purposes of hearings, dispositions and resolution of the matters before the Unified Family Court. To the extent that any issues of confidentiality may apply, all legal requirements shall be observed.

8. *Closed Cases/Post–Judgment Matters.* When all Unified Family Court issues have been resolved, the matter will be closed and remain in the Unified Family Court Division. Any Related Cases that are reopened which are part of the Unified Family Court matter will remain in the Unified Family Court Division through case disposition and for all post-judgment activity.

9. *Subsequent Related Case Filings.* Any subsequent Related Case filings involving the same parties, children, or issues shall be assigned by the Clerk of Court to the same Unified Family Court section, to be handled through case disposition, including when any Related Cases open post-judgment.

B. Related Case Type Categories. Generally, the operational protocol will be as follows:

1. *Domestic Relations /Juvenile Cases.* The following types of cases shall be specifically assigned as follows:

a. Dependency/TPR case filed where there is an open Domestic Relations case or a Domestic Relations case filed where there is an open Dependency/TPR case. All Related Cases will be filed in or transferred to the Unified Family Court Division before an assigned Unified Family Court Judge.

b. Dependency/TPR case filed where there is a closed Domestic Relations case. The AOC Unified Family Court Division will facilitate providing the Related Domestic Relations Case information to the Juvenile Dependency Judge, as needed. The Juvenile Dependency Judge shall confer with the Domestic Relations Judge, as applicable.

c. Domestic Relations case filed where there is a closed Dependency/TPR case. The AOC Unified Family Court Division will facilitate providing the Related Dependency/TPR Case information to the Domestic Relations Judge, as needed. The Domestic Relations Judge shall confer with the Juvenile Dependency Judge, as applicable.

d. Juvenile Delinquency case filed where there is an open Domestic Relations case or a Domestic Relations case is filed where there is an open Juvenile Delinquency case. All Related Cases will be filed in or transferred to the Unified Family Court Division before an assigned Unified Family Court Judge.

e. Juvenile Delinquency case filed where there is a closed Domestic Relations case. The AOC Unified Family Court Division will facilitate providing the Related Domestic Relations Case information to the Juvenile Delinquency Judge, as needed. The Juvenile Delinquency Judge shall confer with the Domestic Relations Judge, as applicable.

f. Domestic Relations case filed where there is a closed Juvenile Delinquency case. The AOC Unified Family Court Division will facilitate providing the Related Delinquency Case information to the Domestic Relations Judge, as needed. The Domestic Relations Judge shall confer with the Juvenile Delinquency Judge, as applicable.

g. Open Dependency/TPR case where there is a related, open Adoption case filed in the Juvenile Division. The Adoption case shall be set for hearing before the assigned Juvenile Dependency Judge, to be handled together with the Related Dependency/TPR Case through case disposition and for all post-judgment matters.

2. *Related Domestic Relations/Domestic Violence Injunction Cases.* The following types of cases shall be specifically assigned as follows:

a. Petition for Injunction filed where there is an open Domestic Relations case (pre or post-judgment) or Domestic Relations case filed where there is an open Injunction for Protection case. The Injunction for Protection case shall be filed in or transferred to the Unified Family Court Division and set for final hearing before an assigned Unified Family Court Judge. The Domestic Relations case shall be transferred to the Unified Family Court Judge, to be handled together with the Related Injunction Case through case disposition and for all post-judgment matters, including when the Domestic Relations case is open post-judgment.

b. Petition for Injunction filed where there is a closed Domestic Relations case. The case shall be set for final hearing in the Domestic Violence Division.

c. Domestic Relations case filed subsequent to entry of Temporary Injunction but prior to entry of Permanent Injunction. The Domestic Relations case shall be filed in or transferred to the Unified Family Court Division. The Injunction case shall be transferred to and set for final hearing before the Unified Family Court Judge in accordance with reasonable time constraints, to be handled together through case disposition and for all post-judgment matters, including when the Domestic Relations case is open post-judgment.

d. Motions for Modification/Extension/Vacating of Permanent Injunction filed where there is an open Domestic Relations case (pre or post-judgment). The Injunction case shall be set for hearing before the assigned Domestic Relations Judge, to be handled together with the Related Domestic Relations Case through case disposition and for all post-judgment matters.

e. Open Domestic Relations case where there is a related, closed Injunction for Protection case. The Related Injunction Case may be transferred to the assigned Domestic Relations Judge for purposes of modifying the injunction provisions to comport with orders entered in the Domestic Relations case which involve the same parties, children, or issues.

3. *Related Juvenile Dependency/Delinquency Cases.* In order to create administrative coordination between the delinquency and dependency courts, where a juvenile has case(s) in both jurisdictions of the Juvenile Court Division, and to ensure that multiple determinations concerning a juvenile are complementary to, and do not conflict with one another, consistent with the one family, one judge model, these case types will be assigned and handled as follows:

Juvenile Dependency/TPR case filed where there is an open Juvenile Delinquency case or a Juvenile Delinquency case is filed where there is an open Juvenile Dependency/TPR case. Both Related Cases shall be filed in or transferred to the Unified Family Court Division on a case-by-case basis, to be heard before an assigned Unified Family Court Judge, and handled together through case disposition and for all post-judgment matters.

4. *Related Domestic Violence Injunction / Juvenile Dependency/TPR Cases.* This section shall apply to those cases wherein a matter is pending only in the Domestic Violence and Juvenile Dependency Division. This section **does not** apply to those cases wherein a case is also pending in the Domestic Relations Division. The following types of cases shall be specifically assigned as follows:

a. Petition for Injunction for Protection filed where there is an open Juvenile Dependency/TPR/Chapter 39 Injunction case or Juvenile Dependency/TPR/Chapter 39 Injunction case filed where there is an open Injunction for Protection case. The Injunction for Protection case shall be filed in or transferred to the Unified Family Court Division and set for final hearing before an assigned Unified Family Court Judge in accordance with reasonable time constraints. The Dependency/TPR/Chapter 39 Injunction case shall be transferred to that Unified Family Court Judge, to be handled together with the Related Injunction for Protection Case through case disposition and for all post-judgment matters, including when the Dependency/TPR/Chapter 39 Injunction case reopens post-judgment.

b. Petition for Injunction for Protection filed, except a Chapter 39 Injunction, where there is a closed Juvenile Dependency/TPR case. The case shall be set for final hearing in the Domestic Violence Division.

c. Juvenile Dependency case filed subsequent to entry of Temporary Injunction but prior to entry of Permanent Injunction. The Juvenile Dependency case shall be filed in or transferred to the Unified Family Court Division. The Injunction case shall be transferred to and set for final hearing before the Unified Family Court Judge in accordance with reasonable time constraints, to be handled together through case disposition and for all post-judgment matters, including when the Domestic Relations case is open post-judgment.

d. Motions for Modification / Extension / Vacating of Permanent Injunction filed where there is an open Juvenile Dependency/TPR case. The Injunction case shall be set for hearing before the assigned Juvenile Dependency Judge, to be handled together with the Related Dependency/TPR Case through case disposition and for all post-judgment matters.

e. Open Dependency / TPR case where there is a related, closed Injunction for Protection case. The Related Injunction Case may be transferred to the assigned Juvenile Dependency Judge for purposes of modifying the injunction provisions to comport with orders entered in the Dependency/TPR case which involve the same parties and children.

V. INTERDIVISIONAL COOPERATION

All divisions in the Eleventh Judicial Circuit shall work cooperatively together to ensure that multiple judicial determination concerning a single family do not conflict with one another.

VI. PERIODIC EVALUATION OF UNIFIED FAMILY COURT

The Unified Family Court Division shall be evaluated by the Chief Judge, or his/her designee(s), to determine its effectiveness in implementing this Circuit's goal of addressing family law matters in a comprehensive, coordinated manner. Such evaluation may consist of, but not be limited to: (i) a review and analysis of statistical data provided by the AOC Unified Family Court Division Director, in conjunction with Court Information Technology Services (CITeS) detailing the amount and types of Related Cases handled during the quarter and (ii) anecdotal documentation of Related Cases provided by participants in the cases (i.e., judiciary, attorneys, litigants, etc.).

This Order, along with Companion Administrative Order No. 16–03 shall take effect upon execution and shall remain in effect until further order of this Court. Administrative Order Nos. 02–03, 02–14, 02–14–A1, 02–14–A2, 03–15, and 10–08, and any amendments thereto, are hereby rescinded and held for naught. The Clerk of the Court is hereby directed to file a copy of this Administrative Order in Case No. 16–1 (Court Administration).

DONE and ORDERED in Chambers at Miami-Dade County, Florida, this 17th day of February, 2016.

BERTILA SOTO, CHIEF JUDGE
ELEVENTH JUDICIAL CIRCUIT OF FLORIDA

14–12. RE-ESTABLISHMENT OF PROCEDURE FOR APPOINTMENT OF COUNSEL IN CRIMINAL AND CIVIL PROCEEDINGS

THE ELEVENTH JUDICIAL CIRCUIT MIAMI–DADE COUNTY, FLORIDA

CASE NO. 14–1 (Court Administration)

ADMINISTRATIVE ORDER NO. 14–12 (Rescinds AO Nos. 12–02, including amendments 12–02 (A–1) and 12–02 (A2))

IN RE: RE–ESTABLISHMENT OF PROCEDURE FOR APPOINTMENT OF COUNSEL IN CRIMINAL AND CIVIL PROCEEDINGS

WHEREAS, the Chief Judge of the Eleventh Judicial Circuit, pursuant to Rule 2.215, Florida Rule of Judicial Administration, has the authority to adopt administrative orders necessary to ensure the operation of the Eleventh Judicial Circuit ("Court"); and

WHEREAS, Section 27.40, Florida Statutes, sets forth the duties and responsibilities of the Chief Judge in establishing a registry of attorneys for appointment to represent persons in those cases in which the Office of Criminal Conflict and Civil Regional Counsel is unable to provide representation due to a conflict of interest, and providing same to the Clerk of Courts; and

WHEREAS, Chapter 2014–49, Laws of Florida, effective July 1, 2014, amends Section 27.40, Florida Statutes, and eliminates the limited registry for private counsel willing to waive compensation in excess of the flat fee prescribed in Section 27.5304, Florida Statutes, notwithstanding the provisions of Section 27.5304 (12), Florida Statutes;

NOW, THEREFORE, pursuant to the authority vested in me as Chief Judge of the Eleventh Judicial Circuit of Florida, it is hereby **ORDERED:**

1. **APPOINTMENT TO REGISTRY.** The selection, approval, and continuation of a private attorney on the registry is dependent upon qualifications, training, and other factors as determined by the Chief Judge by and through the Eleventh Judicial Circuit Court Screening Committees, as established pursuant to Administrative Order No. 1–12–03, for the criminal and juvenile delinquency registry, juvenile dependency and termination of parental rights registry, and probate and guardianship registry. The number of appointments an attorney receives is subject to the number of cases filed, the number of cases for which the Office of Public Defender (Public Defender) or Office of Criminal Conflict and Civil Regional Counsel (Regional Counsel) cannot provide representation, and the number of attorneys on the registry. Attorneys shall be responsible for entering into any and all Agreements required by the Justice Administrative Commission (JAC). The Chief Judge will advise the JAC and Clerk of Courts (Clerk) of the attorneys to be added to or removed for cause from the registry.

3.[1] **REGISTRY APPLICATIONS.** An attorney must complete an application for each of the respective division's registries. The respective division's registry applications with corresponding instructions and requirements may be found on the Eleventh Judicial Circuit Court website located at www.jud.11.flcourts.org under the "Court Appointed Counsel" link.

4. **SELECTION OF ATTORNEY FROM THE REGISTRY.** When requested by the Court, the Clerk of Circuit Court must provide the name of the next registry attorney.

5. **REMOVAL FROM THE REGISTRY.**

(A) An attorney may be removed from active status from the registry if he or she:

i. resigns from the registry. Upon resignation, the attorney shall immediately send such notice as required by the JAC. The notice shall state if the attorney is resigning from all categories to which the attorney is entitled to receive appointments or only some categories to which the attorney is entitled to receive appointments. A copy of the notice of resignation shall be provided by the attorney to the Chief Judge, Screening Committee, and Clerk and shall be relied upon, at the time of receipt, that the attorney will be removed from the registry as set forth in the notice. If an attorney later decides that he or she wants to be reinstated to the registry, the attorney must follow the policies and procedures of the respective Screening Committee to be considered by the Screening Committee and approved by the Chief Judge.

ii. fails to comply with terms of contract with JAC.

iii. fails to notify the Chief Judge, Screening Committee, Clerk, and JAC of any change in status. The removal may be temporary until such time as the attorney notifies the Chief Judge, Screening Committee, Clerk, and JAC, or may be permanent, in the discretion of the Chief Judge, based upon the nature of the change of status.

iv. fails to maintain a valid e-mail address for communication with the Chief Judge, Screening Committee, Clerk, and JAC.

v. fails to enter into any and all agreement(s) and addendums to agreement(s) as required by JAC on or before the last weekday of August for each fiscal year the attorney is eligible for inclusion on the registry.

vi. fails to enter into any and all other agreement(s) and addendums to agreement(s) as required by JAC within 30 days of a request by the JAC.

vii. has his or her contract terminated by JAC.

viii. terminates his or her contract with JAC.

ix. reassigns or subcontracts a case to another attorney.

x. has circumstances that have effected his or her quality of representation, as ultimately determined by the Chief Judge after the procedures set forth below in paragraph 7, "Complaints," have been followed. Such circumstances include, but are not limited to, matters set forth in Section 27.40(9).

(B) If an attorney is disbarred, suspended, has surrendered his or her license, or is not a member in good standing with The Florida Bar, the attorney must promptly notify the Chief Judge in writing. The Chief Judge has the authority to remove an attorney from the registry who is disbarred, suspended, surrendered his or her license, or not in good standing with The Florida Bar even if the attorney fails to provide notice. An attorney removed for any reason set forth in this paragraph, upon reinstatement to The Florida Bar, will be required to file a new application to be considered by the Screening Committee and approved by the Chief Judge for reinstatement to the registry.

(C) At any time an attorney is removed from the registry and later reinstated, the attorney will be placed at the bottom of the list for rotation for the category for which the attorney is eligible to receive appointments.

6. **APPOINTMENT OF NON–REGISTRY ATTORNEY.**

(A) A Non–Registry attorney may be appointed if:

i. no attorneys are on the registry for a category of cases requiring appointment of counsel; or

ii. all attorneys on the registry for a category of cases have withdrawn or declined the appointment of the case; or

iii. all attorneys on the registry for a category are precluded by statute or rule of court from accepting any additional appointments.

(B) When appointing a non-registry attorney, the presiding judge shall set forth in the order of appointment that the Public Defender and Regional Counsel are unable to represent the individual and one of the reasons from paragraph 6 (A).

(C) The attorney appointed shall be ordered to execute any and all Agreements required by the JAC to be compensated and for payment of due process expenses.

7. COMPLAINTS. Complaints by any interested party shall be in writing and addressed and delivered to the Chief Judge, with a copy to the respective division's Administrative Judge and Screening Committee Chair. Upon receipt of a complaint, the Screening Committee shall hold a public meeting where the subject attorney shall have the opportunity to be present and heard on the matter. After the meeting, the Screening Committee shall give written recommendations to the Chief Judge. The Chief Judge shall make the final decision as to what action, if any, should be taken regarding the attorney's status on the registry. Written notification of any action taken by the Chief Judge shall be provided to the subject attorney, the respective division's Administrative Judge and Screening Committee, the Clerk of Court, and the Justice Administrative Commission.

8. REFERENCES. Any and all references to the Chief Judge, Clerk, Administrative Judge, judge, general magistrate, Public Defender, or Regional Counsel shall be deemed to include his or her designee.

Administrative Order No.12–02, entered in Case No. 12–1, Including amendments 12–02 (A–1) and 12–02 (A2), are hereby rescinded, effective June 30, 2014, in its entirety and held for naught.

This Administrative Order shall become effective July 1, 2014, nunc pro tunc, and shall remain in effect further order of the Court.

DONE AND ORDERED in Chambers at Miami–Dade County, Florida, this 2nd day of July, 2014.

BERTILA SOTO
CHIEF JUDGE
ELEVENTH JUDICIAL CIRCUIT
OF FLORIDA

1 So in original.

14–03. PROCEDURES TO PROHIBIT THE PURCHASE OF FIREARMS AND ELIGIBILITY TO APPLY FOR OR RETAIN A CONCEALED WEAPON OR FIREARMS LICENSE BY MENTALLY ILL PERSONS

IN THE CIRCUIT COURT OF THE ELEVENTH JUDICIAL CIRCUIT IN AND FOR MIAMI–DADE COUNTY, FLORIDA

CASE NO. 14–01 (Court Administration)

ADMINISTRATIVE ORDER NO. 14–03

IN RE: PROCEDURES TO PROHIBIT THE PURCHASE OF FIREARMS AND ELIGIBILITY TO APPLY FOR OR RETAIN A CONCEALED WEAPON OR FIREARMS LICENSE BY MENTALLY ILL PERSONS

WHEREAS, the Legislature has enacted House Bill 1355, which became Chapter 2013–249, Laws of Florida, effective July 1, 2013; and

WHEREAS, this bill, entitled "[A]n act relating to the purchase of firearms by mentally ill persons," amends Section 790.065(2)(a), Florida Statutes and provides conditions under which a person who has been transferred to voluntary status at a mental institution for treatment and who has been found to be imminently dangerous will be prohibited from purchasing a firearm and would not be eligible to apply for or retain a concealed weapon or firearms license under Section 790.06, Florida Statutes ("Act"); and

WHEREAS, this Act does not change existing procedures for reporting involuntary placement and the resulting prohibition on such persons purchasing a firearm; however, the Act does create a new matter to be brought before the Court for persons transferred to voluntary status with time limits established by law; and

WHEREAS, accordingly, new procedures need to be implemented in the Eleventh Judicial Circuit to comply with the new law; and

WHEREAS, the House Bill 1355 Implementation Workgroup ("Workgroup") was established by the Florida Department of Law Enforcement ("FDLE") to assist in implementing the new law; and

WHEREAS, the Workgroup developed process workflows and sample forms to clarify the process, attached hereto as Attachments "A" through "I", which are incorporated by reference herein;[1]

NOW, THEREFORE, in accordance with the Act, and pursuant to the authority vested in me as Chief Judge of the Eleventh Judicial Circuit under Rule 2.215 of the Rules of Judicial Administration, the following procedures are hereby established:

I. Within 24 hours after a qualifying person's agreement to a voluntary admission at a mental institution, the administrator of the receiving or treatment facility must file with the Clerk of Court (Clerk):

a. The examining physician's finding that the person is an imminent danger to himself or herself or others, to include, but not limited to, a description of the person's behavior that led to the finding;

b. The examining physician's certification that if the person did not agree to voluntary treatment that a petition for involuntary outpatient or inpatient treatment would have been filed under Section 394.463(2)(i)4, Florida Statutes, or a petition for involuntary treatment was filed and the person subsequently agreed to voluntary treatment prior to a court hearing on the petition. (See Attachment F, Finding and Certification by an Examining Physician of Person's Imminent Dangerousness);

c. Written notice of the examining physician's finding and certification that the person received prior to agreeing to voluntary treatment, which contained a statement that the person would be prohibited from purchasing a firearm and would not be eligible to apply for or retain a concealed weapon or firearms license under Section 790.06, Florida Statutes; and

d. The person's written acknowledgment that he/she understands the above-described findings. (See Attachment G, Patient's Notice and Acknowledgment, Purchase of Firearms and Application for or Retention of a Concealed Weapon or Firearms License, and Attachment H, Application for Voluntary Admission of an Adult).

II. If applicable, the administrator of the receiving or treatment facility may file with the Clerk Attachment I, Notification to the Court of Withdrawal of Petition For Hearing on Involuntary Inpatient or Involuntary Outpatient Placement.

III. Any forms filed with the Court should be completed in their entirety and submitted with Attachment E, Cover Sheet, Confidential Information, which contains a checklist of the forms being filed with the Clerk.

IV. The Clerk is required to transmit the filing to the Court within 24 hours. Further, the Clerk shall transmit the Court's order, which directs the entry of the record in the FDLE database, to the FDLE within 24 hours of receipt of the order.

V. While the Act does not specify a method of computing these 24 hour time periods, Rule of Judicial Administration 2.514 provides that when a statute does not specify a method of computing time, time is computed as specified in the Rule. Accordingly, Rule 2.514(2)(c) provides that when the period is stated in hours, and when a time period would end on a Saturday, Sunday, or legal holiday, or during any period of time extended through an order of the Chief Justice, the period continues to run until the same time on the next day that is not a Saturday, Sunday, or legal holiday and does not fall within any period of time extended through an order of the Chief Justice.

FURTHER, the Clerk of the Courts is hereby ordered and directed to:

1. Comply with the statutory time periods as computed in accordance with Rule of Judicial Administration 2.541. The Clerk is not required to perform any duties required under the Act on weekends, holidays, or during periods of time extended by the Chief Justice.

2. Upon receipt of a filing to exclude a voluntarily admitted person from purchasing a firearm and being eligible to apply for a concealed weapon or firearms license, the Clerk, pursuant to Section 790.065, Florida Statutes, must present the filings to the Court within 24 hours of receipt of the filing. The 24 hour period shall be computed as provided in Rule of Judicial Administration 2.514(a)(2). The filings must be provided by the Clerk to the General Magistrate, or Circuit Court Judge if the General Magistrate is not available, in the Probate and Guardianship Division, who will review the matter.

3. Upon reviewing the matter, use the following:

(i) Attachment "J", Confidential Ex Parte Order Directing Entry of Record in FDLE's Database of Persons Prohibited from Purchasing Firearms and Ineligible to Apply for or Retain a Concealed Weapon or Firearms License; or

(ii) Attachment "K", Confidential Ex Parte Interim Order Requiring Further Documentation Regarding Firearm Prohibition and Ineligibility to Apply for or Retain a Concealed Weapon or Firearms License; or

(iii) Attachment "L", Confidential Ex Parte Order Not Directing Entry of Record in FDLE's Database of Persons Prohibited from Purchasing Firearms and Ineligible to Apply for or Retain a Concealed Weapon or Firearms License.

4. In the event the Clerk has not received an order from the Court within 72 hours after submission of the filings to the Court as described above, the Clerk shall notify the Administrative Judge of the Probate Division by telephone and e-mail. The 72 hour period shall be computed as provided in the Rule of Judicial Administration 2.514(a)(2).

5. If the Court orders that the record be submitted to the FDLE, the Clerk must submit the record to the FDLE within 24 hours of receipt of the order from the Court. The 24 hour period shall be computed as provided in Rule of Judicial Administration 2.514(a)(2).

6. To effectuate the requirements enumerated under the Act, the Clerk shall perform the following:

a. Create a new case type and/or docket code for these submissions.

b. Track the number of submissions made under this Act.

c. Report any problems with these procedures to the Administrative Judge of the Probate Division.

This Administrative Order shall take effect immediately upon execution, and shall remain in effect until further order of the Court.

DONE AND ORDERED in Chambers at Miami–Dade County, Florida, this 18th day of March, 2014.

BERTILA SOTO, CHIEF JUDGE
ELEVENTH JUDICIAL CIRCUIT
OF FLORIDA

1 Attachments A through D not included.

Cover Sheet

Confidential Information

Submission to Clerk of Court of Statutorily Required Documents for Review by Judge or Magistrate Regarding Purchase of Firearms or Applying / Retaining Concealed Weapon or Firearms License By Persons who have a Mental Illness and are Deemed Imminently Dangerous

Attached are the following forms regarding the determination that an individual in this receiving or treatment facility has been found to be an imminent danger to self or others:

☐ Findings and Certification by an examining Physician that the individual is in an imminent danger to self or others

☐ Notice to and Acknowledgement by Person (patient)

☐ Application for Voluntary Admission

☐ Withdrawal of Petition for Involuntary Placement (if applicable)

________________ ____________ ____________

Signature of Administrator or Designee | Date | Time

Printed Name of Administrator or Designee | Name of Receiving or Treatment Facility

Printed Name of Patient ________ Gender ________

Date of Birth ________ Race ________

Social Security Number: ________

See s. 394.463(2)(i)4, 790.06 and 790.065 Florida Statutes

Confidential Information

Revised 10/8/13

Attachment E

Finding and Certification by an Examining Physician Of Person's Imminent Dangerousness

I, ________, a physician licensed pursuant to chapter 458 or 459, Florida Statutes, examined ________, a patient in ________ (name of receiving or treatment facility) on ________ (date) at ____ a.m./p.m.

I determined that this individual is an imminent danger to self or others based on the following:

____

____

____

____

____

Please Check One

☐ I certify that if the person had not agreed to voluntary treatment, a petition for involuntary outpatient or inpatient treatment would have been filed.

☐ I certify that a petition was filed and the person subsequently agreed to voluntary treatment prior to a court hearing on the petition.

☐ Not Applicable.

I have found that this person has the capacity to make well-reasoned, willful, and knowing decisions concerning his or her medical or mental health treatment and therefore is competent to transfer to voluntary status and to consent to treatment.

Signature of Examining Physician | Date | Time

Printed Name of Examining Physician | License Number

Printed Name of Patient: ________ Gender: ________

Date of Birth: ________ Race: ________

Social Security Number: ________

See s. 790.06 and 790.065 Florida Statutes

Confidential information

Revised 11/4/13

Attachment F

Patient's Notice and Acknowledgment

Purchase of Firearms and Application for or Retention of a Concealed Weapon or Firearms License

I, ________________ do hereby
(Full printed name of person whose admission is being requested)
confirm that I have received written notice of the finding and certification from an examining physician advising that if I do not agree to voluntary admission, a petition for involuntary outpatient or inpatient treatment will be filed under s. 394.463(2)(i)4, or the examining physician certified that a petition was filed and I have subsequently agreed to voluntary treatment prior to a court hearing on the petition. I further acknowledge that I understand that the doctor who examined me believes I am an imminent danger to myself or to others. I understand that if I do not agree to voluntary treatment, a petition will be filed in court to require me to receive involuntary treatment. I understand that if that petition is filed, I have the right to contest it. I understand that by agreeing to voluntary treatment in either of these situations, I may be prohibited from purchasing firearms and from applying for, or retaining, a concealed weapons or firearms license until I apply for, and receive, relief from that restriction under Florida law.

Signature of Competent Adult | Printed Name | Date | Time

Signature of Witness | Printed Name | Date | Time

Printed Name of Patient: ________ Gender: ________

Date of Birth: ________ Race: ________

Social Security Number: ________

See s. 394.463(2)(i)4, 790.06 and 790.065, Florida Statutes

Confidential information

Revised 10/8/13

Attachment G

Application for Voluntary Admission of an Adult

(Receiving Facility)

I, ______________ do hereby apply for admission to
Full printed name of person whose admission is being requested

____
Fill in name of facility

for observation, diagnosis, care, and treatment of a mental illness, and I certify that the information given on this application is true and correct to the best of my knowledge and belief.

I am making this application for voluntary admission after sufficient explanation and disclosure to make a knowing and willful decision without any element of force, fraud, deceit, duress, or other form of constraint or coercion. The reason for my admission to this facility is:

____

____

____

I am a competent adult with the capacity to make well-reasoned, willful, and knowing decisions concerning my medical or mental health treatment. I do not have a guardian, guardian advocate, or currently have a health care surrogate/proxy making health care decisions for me.

I ☐ have ☐ have not provided a copy of advance directive(s).

If so, the advance directives include my:
☐ Living Will
☐ Health Care Surrogate,
☐ Mental Health Care Surrogate,
☐ Other as specified:

I have been provided with a written explanation of my rights as a person on voluntary status and they have been fully explained to me. 1 understand that this facility is authorized by law to detain me without my consent for up to 24 hours after I make a request for discharge; unless a petition for involuntary inpatient placement or Involuntary outpatient placement is filed with the Court within two (2) court working days of my request for discharge in which case I may be held pending a hearing on the petition.

I understand that I may be billed for the cost of my treatment.

______________ ______ ______ am pm
Signature of Competent Adult — Date — Time

__________ __________ ______ ______ am pm
Printed Name of Witness — Signature of Witness — Date — Time

____

No notice of this admission is to be made without the consent of the person except in case of an emergency. The use of this form for a voluntary admission requires that a "Certification of Person's Competence to Provide Express and Informed Consent" be completed within 24 hours and if the form is used for a transfer of a person from involuntary to voluntary status, the "Certification" must be completed prior to the "Application". The "Application" and "Certification" must be placed in the person's clinical record.

See s. 394.455(9), 394.459, 394.4625, Florida Statutes
CF–MH 3040, Feb 05 (obsoletes previous editions) (Recommended Form) — BAKER ACT

Attachment H

IN THE CIRCUIT COURT OF THE ________ JUDICIAL CIRCUIT
IN AND FOR ________, COUNTY, FLORIDA

IN RE: ______________ CASE NO.: ________

Notification to Court of Withdrawal of Petition For Hearing on Involuntary Inpatient or Involuntary Outpatient Placement

YOU ARE HEREBY INFORMED THAT______________
Name of Person

at______________________________,
Facility Name and Address

☐ has made application by express and informed consent for voluntary admission, due to an improvement in his/her condition.
☐ was discharged on ________ to ________ Date — Destination (If known)
☐ was transferred on ________ to ________ Date — Destination (If known)
☐ was converted to Marchman Act on ________ Date
☐ Other (specify): ______________

Please withdraw my Petition for:
☐ involuntary Outpatient Placement ☐ Involuntary Inpatient Placement ☐ Continued Involuntary Outpatient Placement

The respondent has ☐ or has not ☐ been determined to be an Imminent danger to self or others,
If yes, the record of the finding, certification, notice, and written acknowledgement is attached to this Notification filed on Date: ________. The Petition for Adjudication of Incompetence to Consent to Treatment and Appointment of a Guardian Advocate, if any, is also being withdrawn.

______________ ________ ________
Signature of Administrator or Designee — Date — Time

____
Printed Name of Administrator or Designee

cc: ☐ Clerk of the Court (Probate Division) ☐ Person ☐ Guardian
☐ Assistant State Attorney ☐ Representative ☐ Person's Attorney

When a petition for involuntary placement is withdrawn, the court, state attorney, public defender or other attorney for the person, and guardian or representative must be notified by telephone within one business day of the decision, unless such decision is made within 24 hours prior to the hearing. In such cases, the notification must be made immediately.

____

Printed Name of Patient: ___ Gender: ________

Date of Birth: ________ Race: ________

Social Security Number: ________

Confidential Information

Revised 10/8/13

Attachment I

IN THE CIRCUIT COURT OF THE ELEVENTH JUDICIAL CIRCUIT IN AND FOR MIAMI–DADE COUNTY, FLORIDA

PROBATE DIVISION:

CASE NUMBER:

IN RE:

________/

ORDER OF COURT

Confidential Ex Parte Order Directing Entry of Record in FDLE'S DataBase of Persons Prohibited from Purchasing Firearms and Ineligible to Apply for or Retain a Concealed Weapon or Firearms License

This Cause came before the Court on [________ (*date*)], upon the filing of a record by [________ (*name of receiving facility*)] on [________ (*date*)] to determine if [________ (*person*)] may be prohibited from purchasing a firearm and would not be eligible to apply for or retain a concealed weapon or firearms license under Section 790.06, Fla. Stat., because of his/her transfer to voluntary status at a mental institution for outpatient or inpatient treatment after an involuntary examination under section 394.463, Florida Statutes.

The Court, having reviewed the following records:

___ The examining physician's finding that the person is an imminent danger to himself/herself or others; and

___ The examining physician's certification that:

___ if the person did not agree to voluntary treatment that a petition for involuntary outpatient or inpatient treatment would have been filed under section 394.463(2)(i)4; or

___ a petition for involuntary treatment was filed and the person subsequently agreed to voluntary treatment prior to a court hearing on the petition; and

___ The written notice of the examining physician's finding and certification that the person received prior to agreeing to voluntary treatment, and which contained a statement that he/she would be prohibited from purchasing a firearm and would be ineligible to apply for or retain a concealed weapon or firearms license under section 790.06; and

___ The above-named person's written acknowledgment that he/she understands the above-described finding, certification and notice;

FINDS the record supports the classification of [________ (*person*)] as an imminent danger to himself/herself or others and hereby **ORDERS** that such record be submitted by the Clerk to the Florida Department of Law Enforcement in accordance with Section 790.065, Florida Statutes. The Clerk of Court is **DIRECTED** to forward the record and this Order to the Florida Department of Law Enforcement within 24 hours of the entry of this Order.

DONE and **ORDERED** in Chambers this ___ day of ________, 20 ___, Miami–Dade County, Florida.

____

☐ **GENERAL MAGISTRATE**
☐ **CIRCUIT COURT JUDGE**

Copies furnished to:

☐ Receiving/Treatment Facility Administrator;
☐ [________ (*above-named person*)]*
☐ SAO
☐ PDO/above-named person's Counsel.

* *The Receiving/Treatment Facility is to print the above-named person's copy and provide it to the person at the facility*

Eleventh Judicial Circuit Administrative Order 2014–Attachment J

IN THE CIRCUIT COURT OF THE ELEVENTH JUDICIAL CIRCUIT IN AND FOR MIAMI–DADE COUNTY, FLORIDA

IN RE:

PROBATE DIVISION:

________/ CASE NUMBER:

ORDER OF COURT

Confidential Ex Parte Interim Order Requiring Further Documentation Regarding Firearm Prohibition and Ineligibility to Apply for or Retain a Concealed Weapon or Firearms License

This Cause came before the Court on [________ (*date*)], upon the filing of a record, by [________ (*name of receiving facility*)] on [________ (*date*)] to determine if [________ (*person*)] may be prohibited from purchasing a firearm and would not be eligible to apply for or retain a concealed weapon or firearms license under Section 790.06, Fla. Stat., because of his/her transfer to voluntary status at a mental institution for outpatient or inpatient treatment after an involuntary examination under section 394.463, Florida Statutes.

The Court, having reviewed the submitted documentation, **FINDS** as follows:

___ The examining physician's finding that the person is an imminent danger to himself/herself or others is missing or incomplete; and/or

___ The examining physician's finding that the person is an imminent danger to himself/herself or others lacks a description of the person's behavior that resulted in such a finding and must be supplemented; and/or

___ The examining physician's certification that if the person did not agree to voluntary treatment that a petition for involuntary outpatient or inpatient treatment would have been filed under section 394.463(2)(i)4, OR a petition for involuntary treatment was filed and the person subsequently agreed to voluntary treatment prior to a court hearing on the petition is incomplete or inadequate because:

___ The written notice of the examining physician's finding and certification that the person received prior to agreeing to voluntary treatment, and which contained a statement that he/she would be prohibited from purchasing a firearm and would not be eligible to apply for or retain a concealed weapon or firearm license under section 790.06 is missing or incomplete; and/or

___ The above-named person's written acknowledgment that he/she understands the above-described finding, certification and notice is missing or incomplete; and/or

___ The above-named person's written acknowledgment that he/she understands the above-described finding, certification and notice contains the notation that the acknowledgment was refused; and/or

___ Other: ______________________________

Based upon the above findings of fact, it is hereby ORDERED:

1. That the above-named person's voluntary commitment procedure has not met the requirements of Section 790.065, Florida Statutes, so as to require that he/she be prohibited from purchasing a firearm and ineligible to apply for or retain a concealed weapon or firearms license.

2. That the examining physician's file with this Court adequate documentation of the voluntary commitment procedure within three (3) court working days.

3. That the Court reserve jurisdiction to enter further orders in this matter.

4. That failure to timely file the documentation requested will result in:

a. A dismissal of the matter without further order of this court; and

b. The person's record will not be submitted to the FDLE database; and

c. The person will not be precluded from purchasing a firearm or being eligible to apply for a concealed weapon or firearms license because of a transfer to voluntary status at a mental institution.

DONE and **ORDERED** in Chambers this ___ day of ________, 20 ___, Miami–Dade County, Florida.

____

☐ **GENERAL MAGISTRATE**
☐ **CIRCUIT COURT JUDGE**

Copies furnished to:

☐ Receiving/Treatment Facility Administrator;

☐ [________ (*above-named person*)] *

☐ SAO

☐ PDO/above-named person's Counsel

* *The Receiving/Treatment Facility is to print the above-named person's copy and provide it to the person at the facility*

Eleventh Judicial Circuit Administrative
Order 2014–Attachment K

IN THE CIRCUIT COURT OF THE ELEVENTH JUDICIAL CIRCUIT IN AND FOR MIAMI—DADE COUNTY, FLORIDA

PROBATE DIVISION:

CASE NUMBER:

IN RE:

__________/

ORDER OF COURT

Confidential Ex Parte Order Directing that No Entry of Record be made in FDLE'S DataBase of Persons Prohibited from Purchasing Firearms and Ineligible to Apply for or Retain a Concealed Weapon or Firearms License

This Cause came before the Court on [________ (*date*)], upon the filing of a record by [________ (*name of receiving facility*)] on [________ (*date*)] to determine if [________ (*person*)] may be prohibited from purchasing a firearm and would not be eligible to apply for or retain a concealed weapon or firearms license under Section 790.06, Fla. Stat., because of his/her transfer to voluntary status at a mental institution for outpatient or inpatient treatment after an involuntary examination under section 394.463, Florida Statutes.

The Court, having reviewed the following records:

___ The examining physician's finding that the person is an imminent danger to himself/herself or others; and

___ The examining physician's certification that:

___ if the person did not agree to voluntary treatment that a petition for involuntary outpatient or inpatient treatment would have been filed under section 394.463(2)(i)4, or

___ a petition for involuntary treatment was filed and the person subsequently agreed to voluntary treatment prior to a court hearing on the petition; and

___ The written notice of the examining physician's finding and certification that the person received prior to agreeing to voluntary treatment, and which contained a statement that he/she would be prohibited from purchasing a firearm and would be ineligible to apply for or retain a concealed weapon or firearms license under section 790.06; and

___ The above-named person's written acknowledgment that he/she understands the above-described finding, certification and notice;

FINDS the record does **NOT** support the classification of the above-named person as an imminent danger to himself/herself or others and hereby **ORDERS** that No Entry of such record be submitted by the Clerk to the Florida Department of Law Enforcement's database in accordance with Section 790.065, Florida Statutes.

DONE and **ORDERED** in Chambers this ___ day of, ________, 20 ___, Miami–Dade County, Florida.

____

☐ **GENERAL MAGISTRATE**
☐ **CIRCUIT COURT JUDGE**

Copies furnished to:

☐ Receiving/Treatment Facility Administrator;

☐ [________ (*above-named person*)]*

☐ SAO

☐ PDO/above-named person's Counsel

** The Receiving/Treatment Facility is to print the above-named person's copy and provide it to the person at the facility*

Eleventh Judicial Circuit Administrative
Order 2014–Attachment L

14–02. USE OF ELECTRONIC DEVICES IN THE COURTROOM AND COURT FACILITIES

THE ELEVENTH JUDICIAL CIRCUIT MIAMI-DADE COUNTY, FLORIDA

CASE NO. 14–1

(Court Administration)

ADMINISTRATIVE ORDER NO. 14–02

(Rescinding AO No. 01–15 and AO No. 90–27)

IN RE: USE OF ELECTRONIC DEVICES IN THE COURTROOM AND COURT FACILITIES

WHEREAS, the Supreme Court of Florida promulgated standards of conduct and technology, codified in the Rules of Judicial Administration (Rules), subject at all times to the authority of the presiding judge to: (i) control the proceedings before the court; (ii) ensure decorum and prevent distractions; and (iii) ensure the fair administration of justice in the pending cause; and

WHEREAS, Rule 2.450, Florida Rules of Judicial Administration (Rule 2.450), entitled "Technological Coverage of Judicial Proceedings," governs the use of technology by the media or professional journalist in judicial proceedings; and

WHEREAS, pursuant to Supreme Court of Florida Order No. SC12–764, the Supreme Court adopted new Rule 2.451, Florida Rules of Judicial Administration (Rule 2.451), entitled "Use of Electronic Devices," governing the use of electronic devices by jurors and other non-media courtroom and court facility attendees, which became effective on October 1, 2013; and

WHEREAS, in addition to the mandatory and discretionary guidelines set forth in Rule 2.450 and Rule 2.451, it has been determined that due to the necessary usage of electronic devices by certain individuals, including media attendees, involved in or attending court proceedings in order to perform their professional obligations or to record such proceedings for further legal proceedings, guidelines should be established for such usage; and

WHEREAS, as prescribed by such Rules, the use of electronic devices in a courthouse or court facility is subject at all times to the authority of the chief judge to: (i) ensure decorum and prevent distractions; (ii) ensure the fair administration of justice; and (iii) preserve court security; and

NOW, THEREFORE, pursuant to the authority vested in me as Chief Judge of the Eleventh Judicial Circuit of Florida, under Rule 2.215, Florida Rules of Judicial Administration, it is hereby **ORDERED**:

1. Incorporation of Rules 2.450 and 2.451, Florida Rules of Judicial Administration. Rules 2.450 and 2.451, Florida Rules of Judicial Administration ("Rules") are hereby incorporated as if fully set forth herein.

2. Applicability. The Rules and this Administrative Order are applicable to all court proceedings presided over by judicial and quasi-judicial officers and the use of electronic devices in court facilities.

3. Definitions. For purposes of this Administrative Order, the following definitions are hereby adopted:

a. *Electronic Devices.* An electronic device is any device capable of making or transmitting still or moving photographs, video recordings, or images of any kind; any device capable of creating, transmitting, or receiving text or data; and any device capable of receiving, transmitting, or recording sound. Electronic devices include, without limitation film cameras, digital cameras, video cameras, any other type of camera, cellular telephones, tape recorders, digital voice recorders, any other type of audio recorders, laptop computers, personal digital assistants, or other similar technological devices with the ability to make or transmit video recordings, audio recordings, images, text, or data.

b. *Media or Professional Journalist.* A person regularly engaged in collecting, photographing, recording, writing, editing, reporting, or publishing news, for gain or livelihood, who obtained the information sought while working as a salaried employee of, or independent contractor for, a newspaper, news journal, news agency, press association, wire service, radio or television station, network, or news magazine.

c. *New Media.* An online organization which was a previously established, independent site that contains regularly updated original news content above and beyond links, forums, troubleshooting tips and reader contributions, said content being thoroughly reviewed by an independent editor before publication. Fan sites, web logs and personal web sites do not qualify as "new media."

d. *News.* Information of public concern relating to local, statewide, national, or worldwide issues or events.

e. *Presiding Judge.* The judicial officer or quasi-judicial officer who hears and/or decides legal matters in a court proceeding.

f. *Court Proceeding.* Any procedural means wherein the business of the court is conducted.

g. *Quasi–judicial Officers.* Persons who, pursuant to State law or court rules, perform judicial functions under the direction or supervision of a judge, to include, General Magistrates, Special Magistrates, Child Support Hearing Officers, and Civil Traffic Hearing Officers.

4. Limitations re use of Electronic Devices During Court Proceedings. Subject at all times to the authority and prior approval of the Presiding Judge:

a. Electronic devices may not be used by anyone for photography or videography unless they have prior approval from the Presiding Judge. Such devices include, but are not limited to cell phones, cameras, digital voice recorders or similar technical devices.

b. Media, court staff, state attorneys, public defenders, attorneys, police officers on duty, and members of the public should be allowed to use certain electronic devices (i.e., cellphones, pagers) for sending and receiving written information only (i.e., email, text messages, instant messages). All cell phones, pagers, and electronic recording devices must be turned off or switched to silent or vibrate mode. The privilege of cellphone or pager use may be revoked at any time by the Presiding Judge if such use becomes disruptive in any way.

c. In addition to laptops or tablets with virtual, silent keyboards, laptops or tablets with regular keyboards should be allowed so long as they do not create distracting noise. The Presiding Judge shall have the exclusive authority to determine whether the sound from the laptop or tablet is distracting. Power for these devices will not be provided in the courtroom.

5. Limitations re use of Electronic Devices in Court Facilities. Subject at all times to the authority and prior approval of the Chief Judge or the Chief Judge's designees (specifically, Administrative Judges and Associate Administrative Judges in their respective court facilities), electronic devices may not be used by anyone for photography or videography in the hallways and common areas of court facilities. Such devices include, but are not limited to cell phones, cameras, digital voice recorders or similar technical devices.

6. Audio–only recorders. Subject at all times to the authority and prior approval of the Presiding Judge, audio-only recorders (i.e., tape recorders or micro-cassette recorders) may be used by the following individuals:

a. *Professional Journalists*—Professional journalists using audio recorders as a supplement to their written notes as a memory aid, and so they can accurately quote statements made in open court proceedings.

b. *Traffic Court Litigants*–Individuals who appear before Civil Traffic Hearing Officers who require a recording of the proceeding in order to pursue redress from an appellate tribunal.

c. *Court Reporters*–individuals engaged to provide court reporting services using audio recorders as a supplement to their stenographic or digital notes as a memory aid, and so they can accurately quote statements made in open court proceedings.

7. Media Access. Professional journalists will have access to the media room and certain other areas in the court house or court facility designated as media areas, will be allowed to use designated media seating in a courtroom, and will be allowed to use electronic devices in the courtroom if authorized by the Presiding Judge.

Persons who do not meet the definition of "professional journalist" may contact the Court's Public Information Officer (PIO) to obtain approval to use the media room and designated media areas, request inclusion in the designated media setting in a courtroom, and to obtain permission to use certain electronic devices in the courtroom if authorized by the Presiding Judge. If any access is granted to such persons, they must follow all the requirements of the Rule 2.450 and this Administrative Order as if they were a professional journalist.

8. Media Identification. Professional journalists must display identifying credentials to gain access to media rooms, designated media areas, and to obtain other media privileges. Such identification may either be court-issued or employer-issued identification. Lost court-issued credentials should be immediately reported to the PIO.

9. Media rooms/areas. Certain rooms and areas of the courthouse may be designated by the chief judge, or the chief judge's designee, as media areas on an ongoing or case-by-case basis. These areas are available on a first come, first served basis and are accessible only to professional journalists who display identifying credentials or who have been approved by the PIO.

The designated media rooms or areas will have video feed from the pool video cameras in the courtroom. The use of laptops, cell phones, and other electronic devices is permitted in these designated media rooms and media areas. Electrical outlets in these rooms and areas may be used, but, any multi-plug devices or extension cords will be subject to safety inspections by building management personnel in the court houses or court facilities.

The Eleventh Circuit is not responsible or liable for laptops, cameras, cell phones, other equipment, or personal property left unattended in the courtrooms, court facilities, media rooms or media areas.

Persons using the media rooms or media areas are prohibited from physically (via actual physical network cable) connecting to the Circuit's network or from using the Circuit's equipment. However, a free public wireless network (Wi–Fi) is available to the public at most courthouses, though speed of transmission on these wireless networks is not guaranteed and can degrade if too many users are connected. Accordingly, members of the media are encouraged to bring their own wireless network cards to ensure reliable and fast data transmission for their professional news gathering purposes.

10. Violations and Enforcement. Anyone violating the Rules or this Administrative Order will be subject to the discipline of the Court, including, but not limited to, the Court's contempt authority, immediate removal from the courtroom or court facility, prohibition from returning to the courtroom or court facility, and if a professional journalist, loss of media privileges.

Additionally, Court Liaison Officers or Bailiffs shall enforce this Administrative Order by confiscating electronic devices that are being used in violation of this Administrative Order. Such devices shall be returned to the violator at the conclusion of the proceeding or at the close of business, as applicable.

The Court Liaison Officers or Bailiffs do not need to confiscate all devices capable of taking pictures or capturing sound that are simply brought into courthouses or court facilities to be used for judicial proceedings. Rather such devices shall be confiscated when:

a. The device is being operated without prior approval from the Presiding Judge in a courtroom where a judicial proceeding is taking place; or

b. The device is being operated to conduct photography or audio or visual recording without the prior approval of the Chief Judge or his/her designee in the hallways or common areas or an area of the courthouse or court facility that is primarily used for ingress to or egress from the interior rooms in the courthouse or court facility.

11. Delegation of Authority. The Chief Judge may designate his or her authority under the Rules to the Presiding Judge in a judicial proceeding or the Administrative Judges and Associate Administrative Judges regarding court facilities, in order to accomplish the orderly administration of justice.

Administrative Order No. 01–15 and Administrative Order No. 90–27 are hereby rescinded in their entirety and held for naught.

This Administrative Order shall be effective immediately upon execution, and shall remain in effective until further order of the Court.

DONE AND ORDERED in Chambers at Miami–Dade County, Florida, this 8th day of January, 2014.

BERTILA SOTO, CHIEF JUDGE
ELEVENTH JUDICIAL CIRCUIT
OF FLORIDA

13–03 (A1). AMENDING DISPOSITION OF TOBACCO CASES

THE ELEVENTH JUDICIAL CIRCUIT MIAMI–DADE COUNTY, FLORIDA

CASE NO. 13–1 (Court Administration)

ADMINISTRATIVE ORDER NO. 13–03
A1 (Amending AO No. 13–03)

IN RE: AMENDING DISPOSITION OF TOBACCO CASES

WHEREAS, pursuant to Administrative Order No. 13–03, entered on July 9, 2013, the undersigned determined that after one (1) year of the effective date of the Administrative Order, pending tobacco cases in the Eleventh Judicial Circuit will either be dismissed for "lack of prosecution" (commonly referred to as "fwopped") or remain open and adjudicated in the manner prescribed by the Rules of Civil Procedure; and

WHEREAS, notwithstanding the Administrative Order's specific historical litigation references to *Engle v. Liggett Group, Inc., et al,* 95 So. 2d 1246 (Fla. 2006) and its progeny, the Circuit's disposition of such pending tobacco cases, as set forth in the Administrative Order, is applicable to other tobacco cases, to include the cases encompassed in *Broin vs. Philip Morris Companies* (Case No. 91–49738 CA 01), *Holley vs. Philip Morris Incorporated, et al* (Case No.: 99–28502 CA 20), and *Jett vs. Philip Morris* (Case No. 00–01680 CA 22) and the related flight attendant cases (collectively the "Flight Attendant Tobacco Cases");

NOW, THEREFORE, pursuant to the authority vested in me as Chief Judge of the Eleventh Judicial Circuit of Florida, under Rule 2.215, Judicial Administration Rules, it is hereby **ORDERED**:

1. Administrative Order No. 13–03 is hereby amended to specifically clarify that the manner in which the Circuit will dispose of all pending tobacco cases, as set forth therein, is applicable to the multiple tobacco cases encompassed in *Broin v. Philip Morris Companies, Holley vs. Philip Morris Incorporated, et al, Jett vs. Philip Morris,* the Flight Attendant Cases, and any and all cases derivative therefrom.

2. Except as specifically amended herein, all terms and conditions of Administrative Order No. 13–03 remain in full force and effect.

This Administrative Order is effective as of July 9, 2013, nunc pro tunc.

DONE AND ORDERED in Chambers at Miami–Dade County, Florida, this 12th day of July, 2013.

BERTILA SOTO, CHIEF JUDGE
ELEVENTH JUDICIAL CIRCUIT
OF FLORIDA

13–03. DISPOSITION OF TOBACCO CASES

THE ELEVENTH JUDICIAL CIRCUIT MIAMI–DADE COUNTY, FLORIDA

CASE NO. 13–1 (Court Administration)

ADMINISTRATIVE ORDER NO. 13–03

IN RE: DISPOSITION OF TOBACCO CASES

WHEREAS, the tobacco class action lawsuit in *Engle v. Liggett Group, Inc., et al.,* 95 So. 2d 1246 (Fla. 2006), was brought by "citizens and residents, and their survivors who suffered, presently suffer or who have died from diseases and medical conditions caused by their addiction to cigarettes that contain nicotine;" and

WHEREAS, the *Engle* lawsuit was divided into three phases, to wit: (a) in Phase I, the jury adjudicated common issues of liability and causation for all class members and the entitlement of the class to punitive damages, (b) in Phase II, the same jury determined the individual class representatives' entitlement to and amount of compensatory damages, and determined a lump sum punitive damages award to be assessed in favor of the class as a whole, and (c) in Phase III, new juries were to decide the individual liability and compensatory damages claims for each class member; and

WHEREAS, however, subsequent to Phase II, the Florida Supreme Court decertified the class; but, it held, inter alia, that former *Engle* plaintiffs could bring actions within one (1) year of its decision, and that certain *Engle* Phase I findings would have *res judicata* effect in the individual actions; and

WHEREAS, during the pendency of the *Engle* appeals, administrative memoranda and procedures were adopted in this Circuit regarding individual tobacco cases ("Tobacco Cases") that allowed such cases to remain open and not be dismissed either under a "nfe" (no further effort) order or for "lop" (lack of prosecution); and

WHEREAS, a significant number of Tobacco Cases were individually filed in the Eleventh Judicial Circuit, most of which have not been brought to trial and still remain open as pending matters, yet there has been little or no case activity in connection therewith, presumably due to certain outstanding issues on appeal; and

WHEREAS, in *Phillip Morris USA, Inc. v. Douglas,* 110 So. 3d 419 (Fla. 2013), the Supreme Court of Florida holdings settled issues that were common amongst the *Engle* litigants, to include, inter alia (1) common class action liability findings had res judicata effect on individual class plaintiffs' individual damages actions; (2) giving res judicata effect to common class liability findings did not constitute an arbitrary deprivation of tobacco companies' property; (3) res judicata, rather than issue preclusion, applied to individual class action plaintiffs' damages claims; and (4) judgment in *Engle* Phase I class action trial was a final judgment, for purposes of res judicata effect; and

WHEREAS, given the longevity of the pending Tobacco Cases, and in view of the *Douglas* holdings, it has been determined that the remaining issues in the Tobacco Cases will be adjudicated in the manner prescribed by the Rules of Civil Procedure; and

WHEREAS, it has been furthered determined that the aforementioned administrative memoranda and procedures will be of no force and effect with the execution of this Administrative Order;

NOW, THEREFORE, pursuant to the authority vested in me as Chief Judge of the Eleventh Judicial Circuit of Florida, under Rule 2.215, Judicial Administration Rules, it is hereby **ORDERED**:

1. After one (1) year of the effective date of this Administrative Order, those pending Tobacco Cases in the Eleventh Judicial Circuit will either be dismissed for "lack of prosecution" (commonly referred to as "fwopped") or remain open and adjudicated in the manner prescribed by the Rules of Civil Procedure.

2. Any administrative memoranda or procedures in conflict with this Administrative Order are held for naught and are of no force and effect.

This Administrative Order shall be effective immediately upon execution.

DONE AND ORDERED in Chambers at Miami–Dade County, Florida, this 9th day of July, 2013.

BERTILA SOTO, CHIEF JUDGE
ELEVENTH JUDICIAL CIRCUIT
OF FLORIDA

13–01 (A1).[1] CREATION OF THE INTERNATIONAL COMMERCIAL ARBITRATION COURT IN THE CIRCUIT CIVIL DIVISION OF THE ELEVENTH JUDICIAL CIRCUIT OF FLORIDA AND PROCEDURES FOR THE ASSIGNMENT AND REASSIGNMENT OF CASES TO THE INTERNATIONAL COMMERCIAL ARBITRATION SECTION

THE ELEVENTH JUDICIAL CIRCUIT MIAMI–DADE COUNTY, FLORIDA

CASE NO. 16–1 (Court Administration)

ADMINISTRATIVE ORDER NO. 13–1A
(Amending AO No. 13–1)

IN RE: AMENDING AO NO. 13–1 IN RE: CREATION OF THE INTERNATIONAL COMMERCIAL ARBITRATION COURT IN THE CIRCUIT CIVIL DIVISION OF THE ELEVENTH JUDICIAL CIRCUIT OF FLORIDA AND PROCEDURES FOR THE ASSIGNMENT AND REASSIGNMENT OF CASES TO THE INTERNATIONAL COMMERCIAL ARBITRATION SECTION

WHEREAS, Miami, Florida has become one of the leading venues in the Americas within which to conduct international commercial arbitration proceedings; and

WHEREAS, international commercial arbitration is a specialized area of law; and

WHEREAS, designating particular trained judges to hear all international commercial arbitration matters will foster greater judicial expertise and understanding of this area of the law, will lead to more uniformity in legal decisions, and help establish a consistent body of case law; and

WHEREAS, in 2006, pursuant to Administrative Order No. 06–40, the Eleventh Circuit previously identified the need for experienced, trained judicial adjudication in commercial cases by establishing the Complex Business Litigation Section (Section 40), which was reaffirmed pursuant to Administrative Order No. 11–04, entered by this Court on May 19, 2011, and which section has significant experience in handling complicated business disputes; and

WHEREAS, an International Commercial Arbitration ("ICA") Subsection was created within Section 40, the Complex Business Litigation Section ("ICA Subsection"); and

WHEREAS, the volume of cases assigned to the Complex Business Litigation Section has greatly increased;

NOW, THEREFORE, pursuant to the authority vested in me as Acting Chief Judge of the Eleventh Judicial Circuit of Florida, under Rule 2.215, Rules of Judicial Administration, it is hereby **ORDERED:**

1. The International Commercial Arbitration Subsection originally created within the Complex Business Litigation Section (Section 40), shall henceforth be comprised of independent sections within the Circuit Civil Division.

2. The Clerk of the Courts is hereby authorized and directed to create such sections within forty-five days of the date of this Administrative Order ("ICA Sections").

3. All cases involving International Commercial Arbitration as designated on the Civil Cover Sheet or identified by the pleadings filed shall be assigned to the one of the ICA Sections.

4. The ICA Sections shall handle all ICA cases and shall consist of judges who have experience in handling complex commercial matters and who receive special judicial education in the handling of international commercial arbitration("ICA Judges").

5. The Chief Judge (or designee) shall specify the training requirements and no judge shall be assigned to ICA cases without having previously completed the educational requirement.

6. Only ICA Judges shall serve as emergency alternates in ICA cases, notwithstanding other alternate assignments within the Circuit Civil Division.

7. The Chief Judge shall assign judges to the ICA Sections as are sufficient and appropriate to meet ICA case load demand.

8. The following trained judges are assigned to handle ICA cases, and will be assigned to specific ICA Sections:

a. Honorable Jose M. Rodriguez (who will serve as the ICA Administrative Judge);

b. Honorable Lisa S. Walsh;

c. Honorable John W. Thornton, Jr.; and

d. Honorable Jennifer D. Bailey.

9. ICA cases shall be blind-filed into the ICA Sections and may be reassigned based on urgency, workload, or as justice requires by the ICA Administrative Judge to ICA Judges in Section 40 (Judge Thornton) and Section 03 (Judge Bailey.

It is further **ORDERED** that the following procedures shall be followed in ICA cases:

Section 1. General Information.

a. Attorneys filing ICA cases shall designate these cases as ICA cases on the Civil Cover Sheet, pursuant to Form 1.999, Florida Rules of Civil Procedure as modified by the Eleventh Judicial Circuit.

b. A separate notice (form) shall be filed with the complaint by the filing attorney indicating that the case being filed pursuant to jurisdiction under the Florida International Commercial Arbitration Act (Chapter 584, Florida Statutes; or under the Federal Arbitration Act, 9 U.S.C § 1 et seq., as it governs international commercial relationships).

c. Domestic arbitration matters which do not involve international commercial arbitration or relationships shall not be filed in ICA nor assigned to an ICA Section.

Section 2. Cases Not Subject to the International Commercial Arbitration Sections.

a. Matters which do not arise under the Florida International Commercial Arbitration Act or under the Federal Arbitration Act shall not be assigned to an ICA Section, unless the case meets the definition of related case as arising out of the same transaction or occurrence as those matters properly heard before an ICA Section.

Section 3. Assignment of Cases in and out of ICA Sections.

a. Judges assigned to the general Circuit Civil Division and litigants who have cases filed in the general Circuit Civil Division should submit a motion to the Administrative Judge (or designee) of the Circuit Civil Division to assign/transfer a pending case that meeting the criteria as an ICA case.

b. If any party disagrees with the assignment or lack of assignment of a case to an ICA Section, then that party may submit a motion for reconsideration to the Administrative Judge (or designee) of the Circuit Civil Division for re-evaluation and/or case re-assignment.

c. The Administrative Judge (or designee) of the Circuit Civil Division shall resolve controversies which may arise concerning the assignment/transfer of any case to or from an ICA Section.

d. If there is an issue as to whether a matter is subject to arbitration, that controversy shall be assigned to an ICA Section for determination.

e. Matters assigned to an ICA Section are not subject to the Complex Business Litigation Section Procedures for the Eleventh Judicial Circuit.

f. All filings in an ICA Section shall follow the Florida Rules of Civil Procedure unless other procedural rules are determined to apply by the presiding judge in the case, and shall the ecourtesy and filing requirements of the respective ICA Judge as listed on their judicial webpage.

Except as amended herein, all other provisions set forth in Administrative Order No. 13–1 remain in full force and effect.

This Order shall take effect on January 2, 2017 and shall remain in effect until further order of the Court.

DONE AND ORDERED in Chambers at Miami–Dade County, Florida, this 14th day of November, 2016.

BERTILA SOTO, CHIEF JUDGE

ELEVENTH JUDICIAL CIRCUIT OF FLORIDA

[1] **Publisher's Note:** The court likely was referring to past administrative order 13–08, and intended to amend 13–08, not 13–1. Please see administrative order 13–08 for additional information on the creation of the international commercial arbitration court.

13–01. ESTABLISHMENT OF SECURITY BY-PASS PROGRAM FOR ATTORNEYS AT RICHARD E. GERSTEIN JUSTICE BUILDING

THE ELEVENTH JUDICIAL CIRCUIT MIAMI–DADE COUNTY, FLORIDA

CASE NO. 13–1 (Court Administration)

ADMINISTRATIVE ORDER NO. 13–01

IN RE: ESTABLISHMENT OF SECURITY BY–PASS PROGRAM FOR ATTORNEYS AT RICHARD E. GERSTEIN JUSTICE BUILDING

WHEREAS, jurors, litigants, witnesses, and other interested persons in the general public (hereinafter collectively referred to as the "General Public") attending court proceedings at the Richard E. Gerstein Justice Building ("REG"), who entered REG through three (3) magnetometers in the main entrance, located on NW 12th Street, and one (1) magnetometer in the north entrance on NW 13th Street, created long lines that often resulted in their inability to timely attend court proceedings or they were adversely impacted by inclement weather; and

WHEREAS, on or about March 1, 2012, in an effort to ameliorate the consequences of the long lines and in furtherance of the administration of justice, particularly regarding the timely and appropriate disposition of cases, the Security By-Pass Pilot Program was implemented whereby active members of The Florida Bar were allowed to by-pass the public screening check points at the REG Building, including the designated attorney lane located in the rear entrance of REG on NW 13th Street ("Designated Attorney Entrance"), subject to certain criteria and procedures; and

WHEREAS, on or about September 4, 2012, as a component of the Security By-Pass Pilot Program, the General Public was allowed to enter REG through the rear entrance through the Designated Attorney Entrance; and

WHEREAS, since its inception to the present date, as a result of the Security By-Pass Pilot Program, the problems associated with the long lines at REG have been significantly minimized; and

WHEREAS, pursuant to Rule 2.215(b)(3), Judicial Administration Rules, the chief judge shall develop an administrative plan that, inter alia, is capable of effecting the prompt disposition of cases; and

WHEREAS, the undersigned has determined that it is in the best interest of the Eleventh Judicial Circuit that the Security By-Pass Pilot Program continue as the Security By-Pass Program for Attorneys at the REG;

NOW, THEREFORE, pursuant to the authority vested in me as Chief Judge of the Eleventh Judicial Circuit of Florida, under Rule 2.215, Judicial Administration Rules, it is hereby **ORDERED**:

1. **Effective Date:** The Security By-Pass Program is hereby authorized and established as of the effective date of this Administrative Order as set forth herein below.

2. **Criteria and Procedures:** The Administrative Office of the Courts ("AOC") will establish and implement the criteria and procedures for the Security By-Pass Program, to include the following:

a. Active members of The Florida Bar ("Member(s)" will by-pass the public screening check points at the Richard E. Gerstein Justice Building, provided the Member's Application ("Application") is approved by the AOC and the Member's criminal background check conducted by the AOC is satisfactory.

b. Upon the approval of the Application and the criminal background clearance, Members shall be issued a Security Access Identification Badge ("Badge") by the AOC to be produced upon entering REG. Failure to produce the Badge will require the Member to be subject to security screening.

c. Members will be randomly screened at the security check points to determine if they are in possession of weapons. Should there be a discovery of a weapon, the Member's privilege to by-pass security may be suspended or revoked.

d. Jurors, litigants, witnesses, and other interested persons in the general public, in addition to entering through the main entrance at REG, will continue to be allowed to enter through the rear entrance of the REG located on NW 13th Street, formerly designated exclusively for entry by attorneys.

3. Active members of The Florida Bar who have received the Badge before the effective date of this Administrative Order will be allowed to use such Badge until it expires.

This Administrative Order shall take effect immediately upon execution hereof and shall remain in effect until further order of the Court.

DONE AND ORDERED in Chambers at Miami–Dade County, Florida, this 3rd day of April, 2013.

BERTILA SOTO, CHIEF JUDGE
ELEVENTH JUDICIAL CIRCUIT
OF FLORIDA

12–01. TERMINATION OF MANDATORY RESIDENTIAL MORTGAGE FORECLOSURE MEDIATION PROGRAM; DESIGNATION OF OASIS ALLIANCE CORPORATION AS MEDIATION PROVIDER

THE ELEVENTH JUDICIAL CIRCUIT MIAMI–DADE COUNTY, FLORIDA

CASE NO. 12–1 (Court Administration)

ADMINISTRATIVE ORDER NO. 12–01
(Rescinding AO No. 11–09)

IN RE: TERMINATION OF MANDATORY RESIDENTIAL MORTGAGE FORECLOSURE MEDIATION PROGRAM; DESIGNATION OF OASIS ALLIANCE CORPORATION AS MEDIATION PROVIDER

WHEREAS, pursuant to Florida Supreme Court Administrative Order SC 09–54, In RE: Final Report and Recommendation on Residential Mortgage Foreclosure Cases ("AOSC 09–54"), the Florida Supreme Court determined that mediation programs for homestead residential mortgage foreclosure actions should be mandatory throughout the state; and

WHEREAS, pursuant to AOSC 09–54, the Florida Supreme Court recommended the creation of a Residential Mortgage Foreclosure Mediation Program ("RMFM Program") in each circuit; and

WHEREAS, AOSC 09–54 further recommended that the judicial circuits engage an organization to serve as Program Manager for their respective RMFM Programs; and

WHEREAS, based, in part, on AOSC 09–54, the Eleventh Judicial Circuit of Florida ("11th Circuit") by and through Administrative Order No. 11–09 ("AO 11–09"), created a RMFM Program and as a result of a competitive selection process, designated Oasis Alliance Corporation ("Oasis"), as the Program Manager for its RMFM Program, effective July 1, 2011; and

WHEREAS, pursuant to Florida Supreme Court Administrative Order SC 11–44, the statewide managed mediation program was terminated effective December 19, 2011; and

WHEREAS, AOSC 11–44 further provided that cases already referred to and pending in an RMFM Program on or before December 19, 2011 will remain in the program through the completion of mediation; and

WHEREAS, as additionally stated in AOSC 11–44, circuit chief judges are vested under article V, section 2(d), Florida Constitution, with responsibility for the administrative supervision of their circuits, and Section 43.26, Florida Statutes, authorizes chief judges "to do everything necessary to promote the prompt and efficient administration of justice"; and

WHEREAS, pursuant to such authority, upon the termination of the statewide managed mediation program, in order for the Court to determine the appropriate measures to adopt or employ as permitted by statute or court rule to manage pending and new residential mortgage foreclosure cases, including referral of cases to mediation on a case-by-case basis pursuant to Section 44.102, Florida Statutes, and Florida Rule of Civil Procedure 1.700(a), the Court suspended the 11th Circuit RMFM Program as to cases filed on or after December 20, 2011, until further order of the Court; and

WHEREAS, after due consideration, it has been determined that it is in the best interest of the Court to terminate the RMFM Program as authorized pursuant to AO 11–09; and

WHEREAS, notwithstanding such termination, in view of the inordinate number of mortgage foreclosure cases pending and anticipated to be filed in the 11th Circuit; it has been further determined that mediation is an alternative means of resolving disputes and can be helpful in resolving mortgage foreclosure cases; and

WHEREAS, due to limited statutory authority, financial and personnel resources, the 11th Circuit is unable to internally provide mediation services to the extent needed for mortgage foreclosure cases; and

WHEREAS, in addition to the afore referenced authority, Rule 2.215, Judicial Administration Rules, requires the chief judge to develop an administrative plan for the efficient and proper administration of all courts within that circuit, wherein, inter alia, the prompt disposition of cases shall be effectuated; and

WHEREAS, in view of the immediacy of the need to continue managed mediation in the short term until a more long term plan is developed in the 11th Circuit to address the continuing mortgage foreclosure crisis, inasmuch as Oasis has demonstrated the expertise to manage the mediation of the volume of mortgage foreclosure cases in the 11th Circuit, in the interest of judicial economy and efficiency, it is prudent to engage Oasis to continue to provide certain managed mediation services as a mediation provider ("Oasis") until June 30, 2012; and

WHEREAS, such services may include, but are not limited to, maintaining a master list of certified foreclosure mediators and assigning cases referred to Oasis to said certified foreclosure mediators on a rotating basis; and

WHEREAS, accordingly, this Administrative Order is being issued, in the best interest of the 11th Circuit, to encourage parties to mortgage foreclosure cases and judges in the 11th Circuit's civil division to refer such cases to Oasis;

NOW, THEREFORE, pursuant to the authority vested in me as Chief Judge of the Eleventh Judicial Circuit of Florida, under Rule 2.215, of the Florida Rules of Judicial Administration, it is hereby **ORDERED:**

1. The 11th Circuit RMFM Program, herein suspended for cases filed after December 19, 2011, *nunc pro tunc*, is terminated as of the effective date of this Administrative Order.

2. Administrative Order 11–09, requiring mandatory mediation in all homestead residential mortgage foreclosure cases and referring all such cases to Oasis, as Program Manager, is rescinded as to new cases filed on or after December 20, 2011.

3. Cases filed on or before December 19, 2011, shall remain in the RMFM Program through the completion of mediation, and are subject to the provisions of AO 11–09.

4. Oasis is hereby designated as the mediation provider for the 11th Circuit, until June 30, 2012, to provide and manage the mediation of mortgage foreclosure cases, as set forth in the "Order of Referral to Foreclosure Mediation" hereinafter referenced in paragraph 5c.

5. As of the effective date of this Administrative Order, the following procedures shall be followed for the mediation of mortgage foreclosure cases:

a. After service of the complaint, either party may request in writing to the presiding judge, that such case be referred to mediation ("Request for Mediation"). Upon receipt of the Request for Mediation, the presiding judge may evaluate and determine, on a case by case basis, whether the case should be referred to mediation pursuant to Section 44.102, Florida Statutes and Florida Rule of Civil Procedure.

b. Alternatively, if neither party requests that such case be referred to mediation, the presiding judge may evaluate and determine, on a case by case basis, whether the case should be referred to mediation pursuant to Section 44.102, Florida Statutes and Florida Rule of Civil Procedure 1.700(a).

c. If the presiding judge determines that such case should be referred to mediation, the judge may enter an "Order of Referral to Foreclosure Mediation." For the purposes of uniformity, attached hereto is a recommended Order of Referral to Foreclosure Mediation, which may be amended from time to time without the necessity of amending this Administrative Order.

6. Only Supreme Court certified circuit civil mediators who are specially trained in mortgage foreclosure cases may be designated to provide mediation services for the 11th Circuit. Further, if a certified foreclosure mediator is agreed upon by the parties or designated by the presiding judge to mediate the mortgage foreclosure case, said certified foreclosure mediator should facilitate the electronic exchange of pertinent documents prior to the commencement of mediation.

7. Mediation services provided by Oasis shall not exceed the rate of Two Hundred Fifty Dollars ($250.00) per hour, with a two (2) hour minimum.

This Administrative Order shall take effect immediately and remain in full force and effect until further order of the Court.

DONE AND ORDERED in Chambers at Miami–Dade County, Florida, this 27th day of January, 2012.

JOEL H. BROWN, CHIEF JUDGE
ELEVENTH JUDICIAL CIRCUIT OF FLORIDA

ATTACHMENT

IN THE CIRCUIT COURT OF THE ELEVENTH JUDICIAL CIRCUIT IN AND FOR MIAMI DADE COUNTY, FLORIDA

CIRCUIT CIVIL DIVISION CASE NO.

PENDING HEARING DATES:

SUMMARY JUDGMENT: ____________
TRIAL DATE SET FOR: ____________

Plaintiff(s),

vs.

Defendant(s).

ORDER OF REFERRAL TO FORECLOSURE MEDIATION

Pursuant to Chapter 44 of the Florida Statutes, Rules 1.700–1.750 Fla. R. Civ. P. (2011), the above styled cause is hereby referred to mediation:

(1) Within fifteen (15) days (ten days plus an additional five days for mailing) of this Order of Referral the parties may mutually agree upon the designation of a certified foreclosure mediator of their choice ("Mediator"). If the parties mutually agree on a Mediator, other than Oasis Alliance, Corp. ("Oasis"), the plaintiff shall, within the time period set forth hereinabove, file with the Clerk of the Court, and serve upon the parties, with an electronic copy to Oasis via its web-enabled information platform, a "Notice of Stipulation of Mediator" which shall identify the name, address, and telephone number of the mediator agreed upon, said Mediator shall be deemed designated without further order of the Court; or

(2) If the parties are unable to mutually agree upon the designation of a certified foreclosure mediator within fifteen (15) days (ten days plus an additional five days for mailing) of the entry of this Order of Referral,

Oasis, as a mediation provider, is hereby appointed to provide mediation services for this action, without further order of the Court ("Oasis Referral").

(3) If Oasis is mutually agreed to by the parties as the mediation provider in accordance with paragraph (1) or designated as the mediation provider in accordance with paragraph (2) above:

a) the plaintiff counsel shall electronically submit to Oasis through the Oasis web-enabled information platform, a fully completed mediation contact form, which shall include the parties contact information, including name, address, telephone number, and email address for each party to the action, and their respective counsel ("Contact Form"). A copy of the Contact Form is attached hereto as Exhibit "A" and available on the Oasis website at www.foreclosureoasis.org.

b) Plaintiff counsel shall have twenty (20) days from the date of this Order to electronically submit the Contact Form to Oasis via its web-enabled information platform.

(4) Within thirty (30) days of the filing of the "Notice of Stipulation of Mediator" or Oasis' electronic receipt of the Contact Form, the Defendant/Borrower:

a) Shall be encouraged by the Mediator or Oasis to meet with an approved mortgage foreclosure counselor, by providing a list of HUD certified foreclosure counselors;

b) If Defendant/Borrower is seeking a loan modification, the Defendant/Borrower must complete Borrower's Financial Disclosure for Loan Modification referenced as Exhibit A. Borrower must provide said Financial Disclosure to the Mediator or Oasis for transmittal to the Plaintiff and assessment of the Borrower's financial condition; and

c) If Defendant/Borrower is pursuing alternative workout options, such as a short sale or a deed in lieu of foreclosure, Exhibits B and C, as applicable, must be provided to Mediator or Oasis for transmittal to Plaintiff.

The financial documents referenced in subsections b) and c) must be provided thirty (30) days prior to mediation to the Mediator or Oasis for transmittal to the Plaintiff and used during the mediation. These documents may be found on the 11th Circuit's website located at www.jud11.flcourts.org.

No later than twenty (20) days **PRIOR** to the mediation, Plaintiff must advise the Defendant and the Mediator or Oasis of any additional documents required or missing.

(5) Within twenty (20) days of the designation of the Mediator or Oasis, Defendant may request the Plaintiff to provide the following document to be provided thirty (30) days prior to mediation:

a) Documentary evidence that the Plaintiff is the owner and holder in due course of the note and mortgage sued upon;

b) A history showing the application of all payments by the Borrower during the life of the loan;

c) A statement of the Plaintiff's position on the present net value of the mortgage loan;

d) The most current appraisal of the subject property available to the Plaintiff.

Failure by either party to provide or review the required documents, as required, shall be considered a non-appearance and shall be reported by the opposing party to the Court.

All information to be provided to the Mediator or Oasis to advance the mediation process, such as Borrower's Financial Disclosure for Mediation, Plaintiff's Disclosure for Mediation, as well as the case number of the action and contact information for the parties, shall be submitted electronically via a secure dedicated e-mail address or in a web-enabled information platform with XML data elements.

(6) The appearance of counsel, and each party or representative of each party with authority to enter into a full and complete compromise and settlement, without further consultation, is mandatory. Live appearance by the parties is required unless otherwise ordered by the Court.

(7) Mediation services provided by Oasis, which services include maintaining a web-enabled information platform, the coordination of the collection and exchange of financial documents, coordinating and scheduling the mediation, providing mediation facilities, assignment of a mediator and other related administrative tasks associated with the mediation conference (collectively "Oasis Mediation Services"), shall not exceed the rate of Two Hundred Fifty Dollars ($250.00) per hour, with a two (2) hour minimum ("Mediation Fees"), to be either:

[check as applicable]

___ (a) divided equally between the parties;

___ (b) split between the parties as follows: __________; or

___ (c) to be fully paid by the Plaintiff; or

___ (d) to be fully paid by the Borrower.

This minimum two (2) hour Mediation Fee shall be paid by the responsible party(ies) as indicated above directly to Oasis within twenty (20) days of the date of this Order, and the balance of the Mediation Fee, if any, shall be paid at the conclusion of the Conference. Counsel for the respective parties is responsible for financial arrangements with their clients and timely payment of Mediation Fees.

(8) If at any time one or both of the parties after commencement of the Oasis Mediation Services (i) fails to timely complete the necessary financial document exchange (ii) fails to make themselves available for mediation in a timely manner, or (iii) cancels a mediation conference at least three (3) days prior to the previously scheduled mediation conference date and refuses to reschedule the conference for any reason whatsoever, Oasis shall retain Two Hundred Fifty Dollars ($250.00) of the Mediation Fee as payment for the Mediation Services previously rendered.

(9) Written notice to Oasis of any change or cancellation of the scheduled mediation conference must be given at least three (3) days prior to said conference ("Timely Cancellation Notice"). Failure to provide a Timely Cancellation Notice shall result in Oasis retaining the full Mediation Fee. If the parties desire to reschedule cancelled mediation which did not have a Timely Cancellation Notice, then the party and/or parties responsible for cancelling the original mediation shall pay an additional two (2) hour minimum fee ("Mediation Rescheduling Fee") to Oasis for the rescheduled mediation, unless the Court orders otherwise for exceptional circumstances beyond the parties' control or Oasis agrees to waive same. The Mediation Rescheduling Fee shall be paid by the responsible party and/or parties within ten (10) days of the date of the filing of the Amended Notice of Mediation by Oasis.

(10) The designated Mediator (including Mediators assigned by Oasis), must be Supreme Court certified circuit civil mediators who are specially trained in mortgage foreclosure cases and are ordered and directed to proceed with mediation in accordance with the Rules of Civil Procedure, which mediation shall be held prior to commencement of the trial period. If any of the parties fails to comply with the obligations set forth herein to ensure that mediation is accomplished expeditiously, the Court may, on its own Motion or on Motion of any party, dismiss the case, strike pleadings, enter default, remove the case from the summary judgment or trial calendar, or impose any other sanctions that it may deem appropriate under the circumstances.

(11) Within ten (10) days of the completed mediation conference, the designated Mediator (including Mediators assigned by Oasis) must complete and file a Mediator Report with the Clerk of Court for Miami–Dade County using the form attached hereto as Exhibit "E".

DONE AND ORDERED in Chambers at Miami–Dade County, Florida, this ___ day of __________, 20 ___.

______________________, CIRCUIT COURT JUDGE

"If you are a person with a disability who needs any accommodation in order to participate in this proceeding, you are entitled, at no cost to you, to the provision of certain assistance. Please contact the Eleventh Judicial Circuit Court's ADA Coordinator, Lawson E. Thomas Courthouse Center, 175 N.W. 1st Ave., Suite 2702, Miami, FL 33128, Telephone (305) 349–7175; TDD (305) 349–7174, Fax (305) 349–7355 at least 7 days before your scheduled court appearance, or immediately upon receiving this notification if the time before the scheduled appearance is less than 7 days; if you are hearing or voice impaired, call 711."

EXHIBIT A

[Please complete this form online through the Oasis Alliance, Corp. web-enabled information platform at www.foreclosureoasis.org and file original with the Clerk of Court]

IN THE CIRCUIT COURT FOR THE ELEVENTH JUDICIAL CIRCUIT
IN AND FOR MIAMI-DADE COUNTY, FLORIDA

[Name of Plaintiff]

Plaintiff, Case No.:

vs.

[Names of Defendant(s)]

Defendant(s)

Contact Form

(Certification Pursuant to Eleventh Judicial Circuit Administrative Order No.12-01)

Certificate of Plaintiff's Counsel Regarding Contact Information of the Parties

THE UNDERSIGNED, as counsel of record for Plaintiff and as an officer of the court, certifies the following contact information (name, address, telephone number and e-mail address (if e-mail address is known)) for the Plaintiff, Defendant and their respective counsel (if applicable):

Plaintiff Representative

Name:

Address:

Telephone:

E-Mail:

Defendant

Name:

Address:

Telephone:

E-Mail:

Plaintiff Counsel

Name:

Address:

Telephone:

E-Mail:

Defendant Counsel (if applicable)

Name:

Address:

Telephone:

E-Mail:

As required by Administrative Order 12-01, Plaintiff's counsel will transmit this form electronically to Oasis Alliance, Corp. as the designated mediator for this action, using the approved web-enable information platform at www.foreclosureoasis.org.

Date:

____

[Signature of Plaintiff's Counsel]
[Printed name, address, phone number and Fla. Bar No.]

EXHIBIT B

BORROWER'S FINANCIAL DISCLOSURE FOR MEDIATION
(LOAN MODIFICATION)

FORECLOSURE MEDIATION FINANCIAL WORKSHEET	
Case No.:	
v.	
Plaintiff's Name	First Defendant's Name

SECTION 1: PERSONAL INFORMATION			
Borrower's Name		Co-Borrower's Name	
Social Security Number	Date of Birth (mm/dd/yyyy)	Social Security Number	Date of Birth (mm/dd/yyyy)
☐ Married	☐ Civil Union/ Domestic Partner	☐ Married	☐ Civil Union/ Domestic Partner
☐ Separated	☐ Unmarried (single, divorced, widowed)	☐ Separated	☐ Unmarried (single, divorced, widowed)
Dependents (Not listed by Co-Borrower)		Dependents (Not listed by Borrower)	
Present Address (Street, City, State, Zip)		Present Address (Street, City, State, Zip)	

SECTION 2: EMPLOYMENT INFORMATION			
Employer	☐ Self Employed	Employer	☐ Self Employed
Position/Title	Date of Employment	Position/Title	Date of Employment
Second Employer		Second Employer	
Position/Title	Date of Employment	Position/Title	Date of Employment
	Borrower	**Co-Borrower**	**Total**
Gross Salary/Wages			
Net Salary/Wages			
Unemployment Income			
Child Support/Alimony			
Disability Income			
Rental Income			
Other Income			
Total (do not include Gross income)			

SECTION 3: EXPENSE AND LIABILITIES		
	Monthly Payments	**Balance Due**
First Mortgage		
Second Mortgage		
Other Liens/Rents		
Homeowners' Association Dues		
Hazard Insurance		
Real Estate Taxes		
Child Care		
Health Insurance		
Medical Charges		
Credit Card/Installment Loan		
Credit Card/Installment Loan		
Credit Card/Installment Loan		
Automobile Loan 1		
Automobile Loan 2		
Auto/Gasoline/Insurance		
Food/Spending Money		
Water/Sewer/Utilities		
Phone/Cell Phone		
Other		
Total		

SECTION 4: ASSETS

	Estimated Value
Personal Residence	
Real Property	
Personal Property	
Automobile 1	
Automobile 2	
Checking Accounts	
Saving Accounts	
IRA/401K/Keogh Accounts	
Stock/Bonds/CDs	
Cash Value of Life Insurance	
Other	
Total	

Reason for Delinquency/Inability to Satisfy Mortgage Obligation:

☐ Reduction in income ☐ Medical issues ☐ Death of family member

☐ Poor budget management skills ☐ Increase in expenses ☐ Business venture failed

☐ Loss of Income ☐ Divorce/separation ☐ Increase in loan payment

☐ Other: ______________________________

SECTION 4: ASSETS CON'T

Further Explanation:

I/We obtained a mortgage loan(s) secured by the above-described property.

I/We have described my/our present financial condition and reason for default and have attached required documentation.

I/We consent to the release of this financial worksheet and attachments to the mediator and the Plaintiff or Plaintiff's servicing company by way of the Plaintiff's attorney.

By signing below, I/we certify the information provided is true and correct to the best of my/our knowledge.

______________________	____________	________
Signature of Borrower	SSN	Date
______________________	____________	________
Signature of Co-Borrower	SSN	Date

Please attach the following:

✓ Last federal tax return filed

✓ Proof of income (e.g. one or two current pay stubs)

✓ Past two (2) bank statements

✓ If self-employed, attach a copy of the past six month's profit and loss statement

This is an attempt to collect a debt and any information obtained will be used for that purpose.

Fannie Mae Hardship Form 1021

Home Affordable Modification Program Hardship Affidavit

Borrower Name (first, middle, last):____
Date of Birth:____
Co-Borrower Name (first, middle, last):______________________________________
Date of Birth:____
Property Street Address:____
Property City, State, Zip:____
Servicer:____
Loan Number:____

In order to qualify for ________________________'s ("Servicer") offer to enter into an agreement to modify my loan, I/we am/are submitting this form to the Servicer and indicating by my/our checkmarks the one or more events that contribute to my/our difficulty making payments on my/our mortgage loan:

My income has been reduced or lost. For example: unemployment, underemployment, reduced job hours, reduced pay, or a decline in self-employed business earnings. I have provided details below under "Explanation."

Borrower: Yes ____ No ____ Co-Borrower: Yes ____ No ____

My household financial circumstances have changed. For example: death in family, serious or chronic illness, permanent or short-term disability, increased family responsibilities (adoption or birth of a child, taking care of elderly relatives or other family members). I have provided details below under "Explanation."

Borrower: Yes ____ No ____ Co-Borrower: Yes ____ No ____

My expenses have increased. For example: monthly mortgage payment has increased or will increase, high medical and health-care costs, uninsured losses (such as those due to fires or natural disasters), unexpectedly high utility bills, increased real property taxes. I have provided details below under "Explanation."

Borrower: Yes ____ No ____ Co-Borrower: Yes ____ No ____

My cash reserves are insufficient to maintain the payment on my mortgage load and cover basic living expenses at the same time. Cash reserves include assets such as cash, savings, money market funds, marketable stocks or bonds (excluding retirement accounts). Cash reserves do not include assets that serve as an emergency fund (generally equal to three times my monthly debt payments). I have provided details below under "Explanation."

Borrower: Yes ____ No ____ Co-Borrower: Yes ____ No ____

My monthly debt payments are excessive, and I am overextended with my creditors. I may have used credit cards, home equity loans or other credit to make my monthly mortgage payments. I have provided details below under "Explanation."

Borrower: Yes ____ No ____ Co-Borrower: Yes ____ No ____

There are other reasons I/we cannot make our mortgage payments. I have provided details below under "Explanation."

INFORMATION FOR GOVERNMENT MONITORING PURPOSES

The following information is requested by the federal government in order to monitor compliance with federal statutes that prohibit discrimination in housing. You are not required to furnish this information, but are encouraged to do so. The law provides that a lender or servicer may not discriminate either on the basis of this information, or on whether you choose to furnish it. If you furnish the information, please provide both ethnicity and race. For race, you may check more than one designation. If you do not furnish ethnicity, race, or sex, the lender or servicer is required to note the information on the basis of visual observation or surname if you have made this request for a loan modification in person. If you do not wish to furnish the information, please check the box below.

BORROWER:
Ethnicity:
____ Hispanic/Latino
____ Not Hispanic/Latino

Race:
____ American Indian/Alaska Native
____ Asian
____ Black/African American
____ Native Hawaiian/Other Pacific Islander
____ White

____ I do not wish to furnish this information

CO-BORROWER:
Ethnicity:
____ Hispanic/Latino
____ Not Hispanic/Latino

Race:
____ American Indian/Alaska Native
____ Asian
____ Black/African American
____ Native Hawaiian/Other Pacific Islander
____ White

____ I do not wish to furnish this information

TO BE COMPLETED BY INTERVIEWER

Interviewer's Name:______________________________
[Print or Type]

Name of Interviewer's Employer:______________________________

Address of Interviewer's Employer:______________________________

Face-to-face interview

Interviewer's Signature:____________________ Date:__________

Address:______________________________

Telephone Number:______________________________
[Include Area Code]

Internet Address:______________________________

BORROWER/CO-BORROWER ACKNOWLEDGEMENT

1. Under penalty of perjury, I/we certify that all of the information in this affidavit is truthful and the event(s) identified above has/have contributed to my/our need to modify the terms of my/our mortgage loan.

2. I/we understand and acknowledge the Servicer may investigate the accuracy of my/our statements, may require me/us to provide supporting documentation, and that knowingly submitting false information may violate Federal law.

3. I/we understand the Servicer will pull a current credit report on all Borrowers obligated on the Note.

4. I/we understand that if I/we have intentionally defaulted on my/our existing mortgage, engaged in fraud or misrepresented any fact(s) in connection with this Hardship Affidavit, or if I/we do not provide all of the required documentation, the Servicer may cancel the Agreement and may pursue foreclosure on my/our home.

5. I/we certify that my/our property is owner-occupied and I/we have not received a condemnation notice.

6. I/we certify that I/we am/are willing to commit to credit counseling if it is determined that my/our financial hardship is related to excessive debt.

7. I/we certify that I/we am/are willing to provide all requested documents and respond to all Servicer communication in a timely manner. I/we understand that time is of the essence.

8. I/we understand that the Servicer will use this information to evaluate my/our eligibility for a loan modification or other workout, but the Servicer is not obligated to offer me/us assistance based solely on the representations in this affidavit.

9. I/we authorize and consent to Servicer disclosing to the U.S. Department of Treasury or other government agency, Fannie Mae and/or Freddie Mac any information provided by me/us or retained by Servicer in connection with the Home Affordable Modification Program.

______________________	________	______________________	________
Borrower Signature	Date	Co-Borrower Signature	Date

Borrower	Co-Borrower
E-mail Address:____________________	E-mail Address:____________________
Cell Phone No.:____________________	Cell Phone No.:____________________
Home Phone No.:____________________	Home Phone No.:____________________
Work Phone No.:____________________	Work Phone No.:____________________
Social Security No.:________-____-______	Social Security No.:________-____-______

EXPLANATION:

(Provide any further explanation of the hardship making it difficult for you to pay on your mortgage.)

EXHIBIT C

BORROWER'S FINANCIAL DISCLOSURE FOR MEDIATION (SHORT SALE)

In addition to Exhibit A, the Financial Disclosure for Mediation, the following information must be provided to the mediation manager for transmittal to the Plaintiff:

- Signed purchase contract for the homestead residence;
- Listing agreement for sale of the homestead residence;
- Preliminary HUD–1;
- Written permission from the Borrower authorizing the Plaintiff or any agent of the Plaintiff to speak with the real estate agent about the Borrower's loan.

Borrowers should be reminded that the sale MUST be an arm's length transaction, and the property cannot be sold to anyone with close personal or business ties to the Borrower.

EXHIBIT D

BORROWER'S FINANCIAL DISCLOSURE FOR MEDIATION (DEED IN LIEU OF FORECLOSURE)

In addition to the Borrower's submission of FANNIE MAE HARDSHIP FORM 1021 in Exhibit A above, the following information must be submitted by Plaintiff:

- Current title search for the homestead residence.

EXHIBIT E

IN THE CIRCUIT COURT FOR THE ELEVENTH JUDICIAL CIRCUIT
IN AND FOR MIAMI-DADE COUNTY, FLORIDA

Plaintiff(s), Case No(s).:

vs.

Defendant(s).

MEDIATION REPORT

Pursuant to the Court's Order, a Mediation Conference was conducted by *[name of mediator]*, Certified Circuit Civil Mediator, on *[date]*.

1. The following were present:

   a) The Plaintiff's Representative, *[name]*, and Plaintiff's attorney, *[name]*.

   b) The Defendant[s], *[name(s)]*, and his/her/their attorney[s], *[name(s)]*.

2. The result of the Mediation Conference is as follows *(Mediator selects only one)*:

   ___ A signed **SETTLEMENT AGREEMENT** was reached during this Conference.

   ___ The parties have reached a total **IMPASSE**.

   ___ The parties have agreed to **ADJOURN** the mediation to *[date]*.

   ___ Mediation has been **TERMINATED**.

[Certificate of Service]

11–08. APPLICATION FEE FOR COURT-APPOINTED COUNSEL IN CIVIL PROCEEDINGS

THE ELEVENTH JUDICIAL CIRCUIT MIAMI-DADE COUNTY, FLORIDA

CASE NO. 11–1

(Court Administration)

ADMINISTRATIVE ORDER

NO. 11–08

(Rescinding AO No. 09–07)

IN RE: APPLICATION FEE FOR COURT-APPOINTED COUNSEL IN CIVIL PROCEEDINGS

WHEREAS, Section 57.082, Fla. Stat., effective July 1, 2010, requires a person seeking appointment of an attorney in a civil case eligible for court-appointed counsel, or seeking relief from payment of fees and costs under section 57.081, Fla. Stat., based upon an inability to pay, to apply to the clerk of court for a determination of civil indigent status; and

WHEREAS, Section 57.082(1)(d), Fla. Stat., mandates that a person seeking appointment of an attorney in a proceeding under Chapter 39, Fla. Stat., at shelter hearings or during the adjudicatory process, during the judicial review process, upon the filing of a petition to terminate parental rights, or upon the filing of any appeal, or if the person seeks appointment of an attorney in a reopened proceeding, for which an indigent person is eligible for court-appointed representation must pay a $50 application to the clerk for each application filed, and that the application fee be paid within seven (7) days of submitting the application; and

WHEREAS Section 57.082(1)(d), Fla. Stat., requires the court to enter an order requiring payment if the applicant has not paid the fee within seven (7) days, and the clerk pursues collection under Section 28.246, Fla. Stat.; and

WHEREAS Section 57.082(1)(d), Fla. Stat., requires the clerk of court to transfer monthly all application fees collected to the Department of Revenue for deposit into the Indigent Civil Defense Trust Fund; and

WHEREAS Section 57.082(1)(d), Fla. Stat., requires a person who cannot pay the application fee to be enrolled in a payment plan by the clerk under Section 28.246, Fla. Stat.; and

WHEREAS Section 28.246(3), Fla. Stat., mandates that court costs, fines and other dispositional assessments be enforced by order of the court, collected by the clerks of circuit and county courts, and disbursed in accordance with authorizations and procedures as established by general law;

NOW, THEREFORE, pursuant to the authority vested in me as Chief Judge, under Rule 2.215, Florida Rules of Judicial Administration, it is hereby **ORDERED**:

1. The court shall include in each order in which a person has filed an application seeking a determination of civil indigent status for the appointment of counsel in a proceeding under Chapter 39, Fla. Stat., for which an indigent person is eligible for court-appointed representation, an assessment of a $50 application fee pursuant to Section 57.082(1)(d), Fla. Stat., to be paid to the clerk for each application filed, and shall further require the person to enroll in an agreed upon payment plan pursuant to Section 28.246, Fla. Stat.

2. If the person pays the application fee within seven (7) days of the date of said order, the person's agreed upon payment plan shall not take effect. If the person fails to make payment within seven (7) days of the date of said order, the person's agreed upon payment plan shall take effect and be self-executing.

3. The Clerk of Courts shall collect all application fees and transfer such fees to the Department of Revenue for deposit into the Indigent Civil Defense Trust Fund pursuant to Section 57.082, Fla. Stat.

This Administrative Order hereby rescinds Administrative Order No. 09–07, Case No. 09–1, entered on March 13, 2009.

DONE AND ORDERED in Chambers at Miami–Dade County, Florida, this ____ day of June, 2011.

JOEL H. BROWN, CHIEF JUDGE
ELEVENTH JUDICIAL CIRCUIT OF FLORIDA

10–10. PROCEDURES AND CRITERIA FOR SEALING COURT RECORDS

THE ELEVENTH JUDICIAL CIRCUIT MIAMI-DADE COUNTY, FLORIDA

CASE NO. 10–1 (Court Administration)

ADMINISTRATIVE ORDER NO. 10–10

(Rescinding and superseding Administrative Order No. 06–36, as amended)

IN RE: PROCEDURES AND CRITERIA FOR SEALING COURT RECORDS

WHEREAS, pursuant to Administrative Order No. 06–36 and Administrative Order 06–36 A1, this court established the procedures and criteria for sealing court records; and

WHEREAS, subsequent to the effective dates of said Administrative Orders, the Florida Supreme Court renumbered the Florida Rules of Judicial Administration. *In re Amendments to Fla. R. of Jud. Admin.—Reorganization of the Rules,* 939 So. 2d 966 (Fla. 2006); and

WHEREAS, Rule 2.050 of the Florida Rules of Judicial Administration has been renumbered as Rule 2.215; and

WHEREAS, Rule 2.051 of the Florida Rules of Judicial Administration has been renumbered as Rule 2.420; and

WHEREAS, subsequent to the effective dates of said Administrative Orders, the Florida Supreme Court amended Rule 2.420, Florida Rules of Judicial Administration. *In re Amendments to Fla. R. of Jud. Admin. 2.420 and the Fla. R. of App. P.*, 31 So. 3d 756 (Fla. 2010);

NOW, THEREFORE, pursuant to the authority vested in me as Chief Judge of the Eleventh Judicial Circuit, under Rule 2.215 of the Florida Rules of Judicial Administration to exercise administrative supervision over the courts within the circuit and to control dockets; and in order to provide a uniform method for insuring the confidentiality of court records when such confidentiality is required by law or found warranted by court order, insure that materials are not unintentionally designated as confidential, and provide a procedure whereby the public can request review of orders to seal, it is hereby **ORDERED:**

1. All requests and orders regarding sealing trial court records shall strictly comply with Rule 2.420 of the Florida Rules of Judicial Administration and the attached sample orders.

2. The Clerk of the Courts for the Eleventh Judicial Circuit of Florida ("Clerk") shall designate and maintain the confidentiality of any information within a court record that is described in subdivision (d)(1)(A) or (d)(1)(B) of Rule 2.420 of the Florida Rules of Judicial Administration.

A. *Subdivision (d)(1)(A) of Rule 2.420.* The following information shall be maintained as confidential:

(1) Trial and appellate court memoranda, drafts of opinions and orders, court conference records, notes, and other written materials of a similar nature prepared by judges or court staff acting on behalf of or at the direction of the court as part of the court's judicial decision-making process utilized in disposing of cases and controversies before Florida courts unless filed as a part of the court record;

(2) Memoranda or advisory opinions that relate to the administration of the court and that require confidentiality to protect a compelling governmental interest, including, but not limited to, maintaining court security, facilitating a criminal investigation, or protecting public safety, which cannot be adequately protected by less restrictive measures. The degree, duration, and manner of confidentiality imposed shall be no broader than necessary to protect the compelling governmental interest involved, and a finding shall be made that no less restrictive measures are available to protect this interest. The decision that confidentiality is required with respect to such administrative memorandum or written advisory opinion shall be made by the chief judge;

(3)(A) Complaints alleging misconduct against judges until probable cause is established;

(B) Complaints alleging misconduct against other entities or individuals licensed or regulated by the courts, until a finding of probable cause or no probable cause is established, unless otherwise provided. Such finding should be made within the time limit set by law or rule. If no time limit is set, the finding should be made within a reasonable period of time;

(4) Periodic evaluations implemented solely to assist judges in improving their performance, all information gathered to form the bases for the evaluations, and the results generated therefrom;

(5) Only the names and qualifications of persons applying to serve or serving as unpaid volunteers to assist the court, at the court's request and direction, shall be accessible to the public. All other information contained in the applications by and evaluations of persons applying to serve or serving as unpaid volunteers shall be confidential unless made public by court order based upon a showing of materiality in a pending court proceeding or upon a showing of good cause; and

(6) Copies of arrest and search warrants and supporting affidavits retained by judges, clerks, or other court personnel until execution of said warrants or until a determination is made by law enforcement authorities that execution cannot be made.

B. *Subdivision (d)(1)(B)(i)–(xix) of Rule 2.420.* The following information shall be maintained as confidential:

(1) Chapter 39 records relating to dependency matters, termination of parental rights, guardians ad litem, child abuse, neglect, and abandonment. § 39.0132(3), Fla. Stat.

(2) Adoption records. § 63.162, Fla. Stat.

(3) Social Security, bank account, charge, debit, and credit card numbers in court records. § 119.0714(1)(i)–(j), (2)(a)–(e), Fla. Stat. (Unless redaction is requested pursuant to 119.0714(2), this information is exempt only as of January 1, 2011.)

(4) HIV test results and patient identity within those test results. § 381.004(3)(e), Fla. Stat.

(5) Sexually transmitted diseases—test results and identity within the test results when provided by the Department of Health or the department's authorized representative. § 384.29, Fla. Stat.

(6) Birth and death certificates, including court-issued delayed birth certificates and fetal death certificates. §§ 382.008(6), 382.025(1)(a), Fla. Stat.

(7) Identifying information in a petition by a minor for waiver of parental notice when seeking to terminate pregnancy. § 390.01116, Fla. Stat.

(8) Identifying information in clinical mental health records under the Baker Act. § 394.4615(7), Fla. Stat.

(9) Records of substance abuse service providers which pertain to the identity, diagnosis, and prognosis of and service provision to individuals who have received services from substance abuse service providers. § 397.501(7), Fla. Stat.

(10) Identifying information in clinical records of detained criminal defendants found incompetent to proceed or acquitted by reason of insanity. § 916.107(8), Fla. Stat.

(11) Estate inventories and accountings. § 733.604(1), Fla. Stat.

(12) The victim's address in a domestic violence action on petitioner's request. § 741.30(3)(b), Fla. Stat.

(13) Information identifying victims of sexual offenses, including child sexual abuse. §§ 119.071(2)(h), 119.0714(1)(h), Fla. Stat.

(14) Gestational surrogacy records. § 742.16(9), Fla. Stat.

(15) Guardianship reports and orders appointing court monitors in guardianship cases. §§ 744.1076, 744.3701, Fla. Stat.

(16) Grand jury records. Ch. 905, Fla. Stat.

(17) Information acquired by courts and law enforcement regarding family services for children. § 984.06(3)–(4), Fla. Stat.

(18) Juvenile delinquency records. §§ 985.04(1), 985.045(2), Fla. Stat.

(19) Information disclosing the identity of persons subject to tuberculosis proceedings and records of the Department of Health in suspected tuberculosis cases. §§ 392.545, 392.65, Fla. Stat.

C. Except as provided by court order, information subject to Rule 2.420(c)(7) or Rule 2.420(c)(8) of the Florida Rules of Judicial Administration is currently confidential or exempt from section 119.07, Florida Statutes, and article I, section 24(a) of the Florida Constitution.

3. **Notice of Confidential Information within Court Filing.**

A. Any person filing any document containing confidential information shall at the time of filing, file with the Clerk a "Notice of Confidential Information within Court Filing." A form "Notice of Confidential Information within Court Filing" is attached to this Administrative Order. See Attachment "A."

B. The clerk of court shall review filings identified by filers as containing confidential information to determine whether the purported confidential information is facially subject to confidentiality under the identified provision in Rule 2.420(d)(1)(B) of the Florida Rules of Judicial Administration.

C. If the clerk determines that filed information is not subject to confidentiality under the identified provision, the clerk shall notify the person who filed the document in writing within 5 days of the filing and thereafter shall maintain the information as confidential for 10 days from the day such notice is served.

D. The information shall not be held as confidential for more than 10 days, unless the filer has filed a motion pursuant to Rule 2.420(d)(3) of the Florida Rules of Judicial Administration.

4. **Motion to Determine Confidentiality of Court Records.** A person filing information that he or she believes in good faith to be confidential but is not described in Rule 2.420(d)(1) of the Florida Rules of Judicial Administration shall file a "Motion to Determine Confidentiality of Court Records."

A. The Motion to Determine Confidentiality of Court Records must:

(1) identify the particular court records or a portion of a **record that the movant seeks to have determined as** confidential with as much specificity as possible without revealing the information subject to the confidentiality determination;

(2) specify the bases for determining that such court records are confidential;

(3) set forth the specific legal authority and any applicable legal standards for determining such court records to be confidential; and

(4) must include a signed certification by the party or the attorney for the party making the request that the motion is made in good faith and is supported by a sound factual and legal basis.

B. Any information that is subject to a "Motion to Determine Confidentiality of Court Records" must be treated as confidential by the clerk pending the court's ruling on the motion.

C. Notwithstanding any of the foregoing, the court may not determine that the case number, docket number, or other number used by the clerk's office to identify the case file is confidential.

D. Except when a motion filed under Rule 2.420(e)(1) of the Florida Rules of Judicial Administration represents that all parties agree to all of the relief requested, the court must, as soon as practicable but no later than 30 days after the filing of a motion under this subdivision, hold a hearing before ruling on the motion.

E. Pursuant to Rule 2.420(e)(2) of the Florida Rules of Judicial Administration, the hearing must be an open proceeding but any person may request that the court conduct all or part of the hearing in camera to protect the interests outlined in Rule 2.420(c) of the Florida Rules of Judicial Administration.

F. The moving party shall be responsible for ensuring that a complete record of any hearing held pursuant to this subdivision be created, either by use of a court reporter or by any recording device that is provided as a matter of right by the court.

G. The court may in its discretion require public notice of the hearing on the "Motion to Determine Confidentiality of Court Records" or other public notice as the court deems appropriate.

H. The court must issue a ruling on the "Motion to Determine Confidentiality of Court Records" within 30 days of the hearing.

I. An Order granting in whole or in part a "Motion to Determine Confidentiality of Court Records" filed under Rule 2.420(e) of the Florida Rules of Judicial Administration must state the following with as much specificity as possible without revealing the information subject to the confidentiality determination:

(1) the type of case in which the order is being entered;

(2) the particular grounds under Rule 2.420(c) of the Florida Rules of Judicial Administration for determining the information to be confidential;

(3) whether any party's name is determined to be confidential and, if so, the particular pseudonym or other term to be substituted for the party's name;

(4) whether the progress docket or similar records generated to document activity in the case are determined to be confidential;

(5) the particular information that is determined to be confidential;

(6) identification of persons who are permitted to view the confidential information;

(7) that the court finds that:

(i) the degree, duration, and manner of confidentiality ordered by the court are no broader than necessary to protect the interests set forth in Rule 2.420(c) of the Florida Rules of Judicial Administration;

(ii) no less restrictive measures are available to protect the interests set forth in Rule 2.420(c) of the Florida Rules of Judicial Administration;

(iii) the clerk of the court is directed to publish the order in accordance with Rule 2.420(e)(4) of the Florida Rules of Judicial Administration.

J. *Clerk's posting of entry of an order granting in whole or in part a Motion to Determine Confidentiality.* Except as provided by law or court rule, notice must be given of any order granting in whole or in part a motion made under Rule 2.420(e)(1) of the Florida Rules of Judicial Administration in the following manner:

(1) Within 10 days following the entry of the order, the clerk of court must post a copy of the order on the clerk's website and in a prominent public location in the courthouse;

(2) The order must remain posted in both locations for no less than 30 days.

(3) This subdivision shall not apply to orders determining that court records are confidential under Rule 2.420(c)(7) or Rule 2.420(c)(8) of the Florida Rules of Judicial Administration.

K. *Nonparty's request to vacate all or part of an order granting in whole or part a Motion to Determine Confidentiality of Court Records.*

(1) A nonparty may request the court to:

(a) vacate all or part of an order issued under Rule 2.420(e) of the Florida Rules of Judicial Administration or

(b) order the unsealing of records designated as confidential under Rule 2.420(d) of the Florida Rules of Judicial Administration.

(2) A nonparty shall comply with the provisions delineated in Rule 2.420(e)(5) of the Florida Rules of Judicial Administration.

(3) The request:

(a) must be made by a written motion filed in that court;

(b) must state with as much specificity as possible the bases of the request; and

(c) must set forth the specific legal authority and any applicable legal standards supporting the request.

(4) The movant must serve all parties and all affected nonparties with a copy of the motion.

(5) Confidential Party—Court Service Requested. If the subject order determines that the names or addresses of one or more parties are confidential, the movant must state prominently in the caption of the motion "Confidential Party–Court Service Requested." The Court shall be responsible for providing a copy of the motion to all parties and all affected non-parties in such a way as not to reveal the confidential information to the movant.

(6) The court must, as soon as practicable but no later than 30 days after the filing of a motion under this subdivision, hold a hearing on the motion.

(7) In accordance with Rule 2.420(e)(5) of the Florida Rules of Judicial Administration, the court may in its discretion hold a hearing on the motion regardless of whether any motion filed under this subdivision is agreed to by the parties.

(8) Hearing. In accordance with Rule 2.420(e)(5) of the Florida Rules of Judicial Administration, the hearing must be an open proceeding, except that any person may request that the court conduct all or part of the hearing in camera to protect the interests set forth in Rule 2.420(c) of the Florida Rules of Judicial Administration.

(9) The court must issue a ruling on the motion within 30 days of the hearing.

(10) The movant shall be responsible for ensuring that a complete record of any hearing held pursuant to this subdivision be created, either by use of a court reporter or by any recording device that is provided as a matter of right by the court.

L. *Sanctions.* After notice and an opportunity to respond, the court may impose sanctions against any party or non-party and/or their attorney, if:

(1) the court determines that a designation made under Rule 2.420(d) or a motion made under Rule 2.420(d)(3) or 2.420(e) of the Florida Rules of Judicial Administration was not made in good faith and was not supported by a sound legal or factual basis, or

(2) a document is filed in violation of Rule 2.420(d)(2) or Rule 2.420(d)(3) of the Florida Rules of Judicial Administration.

5. Motion to Determine Confidentiality of Court Records in Criminal Cases.

A. The procedural requirements delineated in Rule 2.420(f) of the Florida Rules of Judicial Administration shall be followed.

B. Rule 2.420(e) shall apply to any motion by the state or a defendant to determine the confidentiality of trial court records under Rule 2.420(c), except as provided by Rule 2.420(f)(3) of the Florida Rules of Judicial Administration.

C. *Rule 2.420(f)(3) of the Florida Rules of Judicial Administration.*

(1) In accordance with Rule 2.420(f)(3), a written motion captioned "Motion to Determine Confidentiality of Court Records" may be made to determine whether a court record that pertains to a plea agreement, substantial assistance agreement, or other court record that reveals the identity of a confidential informant or active criminal investigative information is confidential:

(a) to prevent a serious and imminent threat to the fair, impartial, and orderly administration of justice; Fla. R. Jud. Admin. 2.420(c)(9)(A)(i);

(b) to protect a compelling governmental interest; Fla. R. Jud. Admin. 2.420(c)(9)(A)(iii);

(c) to avoid substantial injury to innocent third parties; Fla. R. Jud. Admin. 2.420(c)(9)(A)(v); or

(d) to comply with established public policy set forth in the Florida or United States Constitution or statutes or Florida rules or case law. Fla. R. Jud. Admin. 2.420(c)(9)(A)(vii).

(2) Any motion made under Rule 2.420(f)(3) must be treated as confidential and indicated on the docket by generic title only, pending a ruling on the motion or further order of the court.

(3) Information that is the subject of such motion must be treated as confidential by the clerk pending the court's ruling on the motion. Filings containing the information

must be indicated on the docket in a manner that does not reveal the confidential nature of the information.

(4) Any motion made under this provision shall also comply with the specific requirements as outlined in Rule 2.420(f)(3)(B).

(5) Time for sealing of court records under Rule 2.420(f)(3).

(a) No order entered under this subdivision may authorize or approve the sealing of court records for any period longer than is necessary to achieve the objective of the motion, and in no event longer than 120 days.

(b) Extensions of an order issued hereunder may be granted for 60–day periods, but each such extension may be ordered only upon the filing of another motion in accordance with the procedures set forth under Rule 2.420(f).

(c) In the event of an appeal or review of a matter in which an order is entered under this subdivision, the lower tribunal shall retain jurisdiction to consider motions to extend orders issued hereunder during the course of the appeal or review proceeding.

(6) The clerk of the court shall comply with the provisions delineated in Rule 2.420(f)(3)(D).

6. Request to Determine Confidentiality of Appellate Court Records in Noncriminal Cases.

A. The guidelines to file a motion to determine the confidentiality of appellate court records shall be followed as provided for in Rule 2.420(g)(1)–(9) of the Florida Rules of Judicial Administration.

B. A motion to determine the confidentiality of appellate court records in noncriminal cases under Rule 2.420(c) must be filed in the appellate court and must be in compliance with the guidelines set forth in Rule 2.420(e)(1) of the Florida Rules of Judicial Administration.

C. A motion may be made with respect to a record that was presented or presentable to a lower tribunal, but no determination concerning confidentiality was made by the lower tribunal, or a record presented to an appellate court in an original proceeding.

D. Any order granting in whole or in part a motion filed under Rule 2.420(g)(1) must be in compliance with the guidelines set forth in Rule 2.420(e)(3)(A)–(H) of the Florida Rules of Judicial Administration.

E. Any order requiring the sealing of an appellate court record operates to also make those same records confidential in the lower tribunal during the pendency of the appellate proceeding.

F. *Clerk's posting of an order granting a motion under Rule 2.420(g)(1).* Except as provided by law, within 10 days following the entry of an order granting a motion under Rule 2.420(g)(1), the clerk of the appellate court must post a copy of the order on the clerk's website and provide a copy of the order to the clerk of the lower tribunal, with directions that the clerk is to seal the records identified in the order. The order must remain posted for no less than 30 days.

G. *Nonparty's request to vacate all or part of an order issued under Rule 2.420(g)(3) or unsealing of records designated as confidential under Rule 2.420(d) of the Florida Rules of Judicial Administration.*

(1) The request:

(a) must be made by a written motion filed in that court;

(b) must state with as much specificity as possible the bases of the request; and

(c) must set forth the specific legal authority and any applicable legal standards supporting the request.

(2) The movant must serve all parties and all affected nonparties with a copy of the motion.

(3) Confidential Party—Court Service Requested. If the subject order determines that the names or addresses of one or more parties are confidential, the movant must state prominently in the caption of the motion "Confidential Party–Court Service Requested." The Court shall be responsible for providing a copy of the motion to all parties and all affected non-parties in such a way as not to reveal the confidential information to the movant when the motion states "Confidential Party—Court Service Requested."

(4) A response to a motion may be served within 10 days of service of the motion.

H. In accordance with Rule 2.420(g)(6) of the Florida Rules of Judicial Administration, a party seeking to have an appellate record sealed has the responsibility:

(1) to ensure that the clerk of the lower tribunal is alerted to the issuance of the order sealing the records; and

(2) to ensure that the clerk takes appropriate steps to seal the records in the lower tribunal.

I. *Sanctions.* If the court determines that a designation made under Rule 2.420(d) or a motion made under Rule 2.420(g)(1) of the Florida Rules of Judicial Administration was not made in good faith and was not supported by a sound legal or factual basis, the court may impose sanctions on the movant after notice and an opportunity to respond.

J. *Records of a lower tribunal determined to be confidential by that tribunal.*

(1) The records must be treated as confidential during any review proceedings;

(2) If the information has been determined to be confidential under Rule 2.420, the clerk of the lower tribunal shall so indicate in the index transmitted to the appellate court; and

(3) If the information was determined to be confidential in an order, the clerk's index must identify such order by date or docket number.

(4) Rule 2.420(g) of the Florida Rules of Judicial Administration does not preclude review by an appellate court, under Florida Rule of Appellate Procedure 9.100(d), or affect the standard of review by an appellate court, of an order by a lower tribunal determining a record to be confidential.

7. Denial of Access request for Administrative Records.

A. Requests for access to administrative records shall comply with the provisions outlined in Rule 2.420(h) of the Florida Rules of Judicial Administration.

B. The phrase "Administrative records" is defined in section 11 of this Administrative Order.

8. Procedure to request access to records under Rule 2.420.

A. Requests and responses to requests for access to records shall comply with the provisions outlined in Rule 2.420(i) of the Florida Rules of Judicial Administration.

B. Requests and responses to requests for access to records shall be in a reasonable manner.

C. Request for access to records shall:

(1) be in writing;

(2) be directed to the custodian; and

(3) provide sufficient specificity to enable the custodian to identify the requested records.

D. "Custodian" is defined in section 11 of this Administrative Order.

E. *Fees for copies of records.* Fees for copies of records in all entities in the judicial branch of government, except for copies of court records, shall be the same as those provided in section 119.07, Florida Statutes (2001).

9. A form "Order Granting/Denying Motion to Determine Confidentiality of Court Records" accompanies this Administrative Order. See Attachment "B."

10. A form "Notice of Entry of Order Authorizing Sealing" accompanies this Administrative Order. See Attachment "C."

11. Definitions. In accordance with Rule 2.420(b) of the Florida Rules of Judicial Administration and for the purposes of this Administrative Order, the following terms are defined as follows:

A. "Administrative records," are records, other than Court records, made or received pursuant to court rule, law, or ordinance, or in connection with the transaction of official business by any judicial branch entity.

B. "Affected non-party" means any non-party identified by name in a court record that contains confidential information pertaining to that non-party.

C. "Court records" means the contents of the court file, including the progress docket and other similar records generated to document activity in a case, transcripts filed with the clerk, documentary exhibits in the custody of the clerk, and electronic records, videotapes, or stenographic tapes of depositions or other proceedings filed with the clerk, and electronic records, videotapes, or stenographic tapes of court proceedings.

D. "Confidential," as applied to information contained within a record of the judicial branch, means that such information is exempt from the public right of access under article I, section 24(a) of the Florida Constitution and may be released only to the persons or organizations designated by law, statute, or court order. As applied to information contained within a court record, the term "exempt" means that such information is confidential. Confidential information includes information that is confidential under Rule 2.420 of the Florida Rules of Judicial Administration or under a court order entered pursuant to Rule 2.420. To the extent reasonably practicable, restriction of access to confidential information shall be implemented in a manner that does not restrict access to any portion of the record that is not confidential.

E. "Custodian" of all administrative records of any court is the chief justice or chief judge of that court, except that each judge is the custodian of all records that are solely within the possession and control of that judge. As to all other records, the custodian is the official charged with the responsibility of maintaining the office having the care, keeping, and supervision of such records. All references to "custodian" mean the custodian or the custodian's designee.

Administrative Order No. 06–36 and Administrative Order No. 06–36 A1 are hereby rescinded in their entirety and held for naught.

This Administrative Order shall take effect immediately and shall remain in effect until further order of the Court.

DONE AND ORDERED in Chambers at Miami–Dade, Florida, this 15th day of November, 2010.

JOEL H. BROWN, CHIEF JUDGE
ELEVENTH JUDICIAL CIRCUIT
OF FLORIDA

ATTACHMENT A IN THE CIRCUIT COURT OF THE ELEVENTH JUDICIAL CIRCUIT IN AND FOR MIAMI–DADE COUNTY, FLORIDA

OR

IN THE COUNTY COURT IN AND FOR MIAMI–DADE COUNTY, FLORIDA

________ DIVISION

CASE NO: ________________

SECTION NO: ________________

____

v.

____

NOTICE OF CONFIDENTIAL INFORMATION WITHIN COURT FILING

Pursuant to Florida Rule of Judicial Administration 2.420(d)(2), the filer of a court record at the time of filing shall indicate whether any confidential information is included within the document being filed; identify the confidentiality provision that applies to the identified information; and identify the precise location of the confidential information within the document being filed.

Title/Type of Document(s): ________________

Indicate the applicable confidentiality provision(s) below from Rule 2.420(d)(1)(B), by specifying the location within the document on the space provided:

___ Chapter 39 records relating to dependency matters, termination of parental rights, guardians ad litem, child abuse, neglect, and abandonment. § 39.0132(3), Fla. Stat. (If the document is filed within a Chapter 39 case, this form is not required.)

____ Adoption records. § 63.162, Fla. Stat. (If the document is filed within a Chapter 63 adoption case, this form is not required.)

____ Social Security, bank account, charge, debit, and credit card numbers in court records. § 119.0714(1)(i)–(j), (2)(a)–(e), Fla. Stat. (Unless redaction is requested pursuant to § 119.0714(2), this information is exempt only as of January 1, 2011.)

____ HIV test results and patient identity within the HIV test results. § 381.004(3)(e), Fla. Stat.

____ Sexually transmitted diseases—test results and identity within the test results when provided by the Department of Health or the department's authorized representative. § 384.29, Fla. Stat.

____ Birth and death certificates, including court-issued delayed birth certificates and fetal death certificates. §§ 382.008(6), 382.025(1)(a), Fla. Stat.

____ Identifying information in petition by minor for waiver of parental notice when seeking to terminate pregnancy. § 390.01116, Fla. Stat. (If the document is filed within a Ch. 390 waiver of parental notice case, this form is not required.)

____ Identifying information in clinical mental health records under the Baker Act. § 394.4615(7), Fla. Stat.

____ Records of substance abuse service providers which pertain to the identity, diagnosis, and prognosis of and service provision to individuals who have received services from substance abuse service providers. § 397.501(7), Fla. Stat.

____ Identifying information in clinical records of detained criminal defendants found incompetent to proceed or acquitted by reason of insanity. § 916.107(8), Fla. Stat.

____ Estate inventories and accountings. § 733.604(1), Fla. Stat.

____ Victim's address in domestic violence action on petitioner's request. § 741.30(3)(b), Fla. Stat.

____ Information identifying victims of sexual offenses, including child sexual abuse. §§ 119.071(2)(h), 119.0714(1)(h), Fla. Stat.

____ Gestational surrogacy records. § 742.16(9), Fla. Stat.

____ Guardianship reports and orders appointing court monitors in guardianship cases. §§ 744.1076, 744.3701, Fla. Stat.

____ Grand jury records. Ch. 905, Fla. Stat. (If the document is filed in a Ch. 905 grand jury proceeding, this form is not required.)

____ Information acquired by courts and law enforcement regarding family services for children. § 984.06(3)–(4), Fla. Stat. (If the document is filed in a Ch. 984 family services for children case, this form is not required.)

____ Juvenile delinquency records. §§ 985.04(1), 985.045(2), Fla. Stat. (If the document is filed in a Ch. 985 juvenile delinquency case, this form is not required.)

____ Information disclosing the identity of persons subject to tuberculosis proceedings and records of the Department of Health in suspected tuberculosis cases. §§ 392.545, 392.65, Fla. Stat.

Submitted and filed this ____ day of ________, 20 ____.

____
/s/

CERTIFICATE OF SERVICE

I HEREBY CERTIFY that a copy of the foregoing was furnished by U.S. mail/ personal service to: ________, on ________, 20 ____.

____
Attorney
Address
Phone
Florida Bar No.

Note: The clerk of court shall review filings identified as containing confidential information to determine whether the information is facially subject to confidentiality under the identified provision. The clerk shall notify the filer in writing within 5 days if the clerk determines that the information is NOT subject to confidentiality, and the records shall not be held as confidential for more than 10 days, unless a motion is filed pursuant to subdivision (d)(3) of the Rule. Fla. R. Jud. Admin. 2.420(d)(2).

ATTACHMENT B IN THE CIRCUIT COURT OF THE ELEVENTH JUDICIAL CIRCUIT IN AND FOR MIAMI–DADE COUNTY, FLORIDA

OR

IN THE COUNTY COURT IN AND FOR MIAMI–DADE COUNTY, FLORIDA

________ DIVISION

CASE NO: ______________________

SECTION NO: ______________________

____

v.

____

ORDER GRANTING/DENYING MOTION TO SEAL PURSUANT TO FLORIDA RULE OF JUDICIAL ADMINISTRATION 2.420(c)(9)

THIS MATTER is before the Court on the motion of ________ pursuant to Florida Rule of Judicial Administration 2.420(c)(9) for an order sealing the following information relative to this case: [*select all that apply*]

____ the party's name on the progress docket.

____ particular documents within the court file, specifically ______________________
____

____ the entire court file, but not the progress docket.

____ the entire court file and the progress docket.

Having considered the arguments of the parties, legal authority, and otherwise being fully advised, the Court **DENIES** the motion because the moving party has failed to establish that confidentiality of the information sought to be sealed is necessary to protect any interest under Rule 2.420(c)(9).

—OR—

the Court **GRANTS** the motion as follows:

1. Confidentiality of the [information sought to be sealed] is required to protect the following interest(s): [*select all that apply*]

____ a. Preventing a serious and imminent threat to the fair, impartial, and orderly administration of justice, specifically: ________________.

____ b. A trade secret.

____ c. A compelling government interest, specifically: ________________.

____ d. Obtaining evidence to determine the legal issues in a case.

____ e. Avoiding substantial injury to innocent third parties, specifically: ________________.

____ f. Avoiding substantial injury to a party by the disclosure of matters protected by a common law or privacy right not generally inherent in this type of proceeding, specifically: ________________.

____ g. Complying with established public policy set forth in the Florida or United States Constitution or statutes or Florida rules or case law, specifically: ________________;

2. The Court further finds that no less restrictive measure is available to protect this/these interest(s), and that the degree, duration and manner of confidentiality ordered herein are no broader than necessary to protect the interest(s).

Wherefore, it is hereby **ORDERED** that:

The Clerk of the Circuit Court is hereby directed to seal immediately the following materials related to this matter and to keep such materials from public access: [*select all that apply*]

____ 1. The party's name on the progress docket. On the public progress docket, the Clerk of the Circuit Court shall substitute the following for the party's name: __________. Further, the Clerk shall ensure that the party's name is redacted from all public materials in the file and that the final judgment is recorded in a manner that does not reveal the identity of the party. However, the progress docket and the file shall otherwise remain available to the public.

____ 2. The following documents within the court file: __________. However, the file and progress docket shall otherwise remain available to the public subject to any substitution of a party's name set forth above.

____ 3. The entire court file. However, the progress docket shall remain open to the public subject to any substitution of a party's name set forth above.

____ 4. The entire court file and the progress docket. The progress docket shall not be available on any public information system.

It is further **ORDERED** that any materials sealed pursuant to this Order shall be conditionally disclosed upon the entry of a further order by this Court finding that such opening is necessary for purposes of judicial or governmental accountability or First Amendment rights.

It is further **ORDERED** that any materials sealed pursuant to this Order may otherwise be disclosed only as follows:

1. to any judge of this Circuit for case-related reasons;
2. to the Chief Judge or his or her designee;
3. to adult parties or their attorneys of record; or
4. by further order of the Court.

It is further **ORDERED** that the Clerk is hereby directed to post a copy of the attached Notice of Entry of Order Authorizing Sealing on the Clerk's and Court's websites and in a prominent location in the courthouse for a period *not less than thirty* (30) days and to affix a copy of the Order on the outside of the court record.

It is further **ORDERED** that the Clerk is hereby authorized to unseal any materials sealed pursuant to this Order for the purpose of filing, microfilming or imaging files, or transmitting a record to an appellate tribunal. The materials shall be resealed immediately upon completion of the filing.

DONE AND ORDERED in Chambers, at Miami–Dade County, Florida, this ___ day of ________, 20 ___.

____

/s/

ATTACHMENT C IN THE CIRCUIT COURT OF THE ELEVENTH JUDICIAL CIRCUIT IN AND FOR MIAMI–DADE COUNTY, FLORIDA

OR

IN THE COUNTY COURT IN AND FOR MIAMI–DADE COUNTY, FLORIDA

________ DIVISION

CASE NO: ____________________

SECTION NO: ____________________

____

v.

____

NOTE: INCLUDE CASE STYLE ONLY IN CASES WHERE A DOCUMENT OR DOCUMENTS ALONE HAVE BEEN SEALED. IN CASES WHERE A FILE, FILE AND DOCKET, OR A PARTY'S IDENTITY HAS BEEN SEALED, REDACT THE CASE STYLE.

NOTICE OF ENTRY OF ORDER AUTHORIZING SEALING

BE ADVISED that on the ___ day of ________, 20 ___, the Court entered an Order in the above-referenced matter authorizing the sealing of court documents pursuant to Florida Rule of Judicial Administration 2.420(c)(9).

Dated: ____________ ____________

Harvey Ruvin, Clerk of the Courts

By: ____________

Deputy Clerk

10–01 (A1). AMERICANS WITH DISABILITY ACT OF 1990–DESIGNATION OF ADA COORDINATOR, RE–ESTABLISHING NOTICE AND REQUEST FOR REASONABLE ACCOMMODATIONS REQUIREMENTS AND RE–ADOPTION OF GRIEVANCE PROCEDURE

THE ELEVENTH JUDICIAL CIRCUIT MIAMI–DADE COUNTY, FLORIDA

CASE NO. 10–1 (Court Administration)

ADMINISTRATIVE ORDER NO. 10–01 (Rescinding Administrative Order No. 98–19)

IN RE: AMERICANS WITH DISABILITY ACT OF 1990–DESIGNATION OF ADA COORDINATOR, RE–ESTABLISHING NOTICE AND REQUEST FOR REASONABLE ACCOMMODATIONS REQUIREMENTS AND RE–ADOPTION OF GRIEVANCE PROCEDURE

WHEREAS,the Americans with Disabilities Act of 1990 ("ADA") requires that upon request, reasonable accommodations be provided to qualified persons with disabilities in order that they might participate fully, equitably and fairly in court proceedings, programs, services, activities and benefits; and

WHEREAS, it is the intent of the Eleventh Judicial Circuit to facilitate provisions for reasonable accommodations when requested by qualified persons with disabilities; and

WHEREAS, Rule 2.540, Florida Rules of Judicial Administration, sets forth language that shall be on all communications noticing court proceedings; and

WHEREAS, Title II of the ADA ("Title II") requires that a grievance procedure be implemented for each public entity with 50 or more employees; and

WHEREAS, the ADA requires such public entity to designate a responsible person to carry out its responsibilities by ensuring the prompt and equitable resolution of complaints alleging noncompliance or complaints alleging any actions that would be prohibited under Title II;

NOW, THEREFORE,pursuant to the authority vested in me as Chief Judge of the Eleventh Judicial Circuit of Florida under Rule 2.215, Florida Rules of Judicial Administration, it is hereby **ORDERED**:

1. **Designation of Responsible Person.** In accordance with the American with Disabilities Act of 1990, there shall be an employee of the Eleventh Judicial Circuit designated to serve as the ADA Coordinator for the Circuit. The ADA Coordinator for this Circuit shall be Maria E. Mihaic, until further order of the Court.

2.Notice to Persons with Disabilities. **All notices of court proceedings to be held in a public facility, and all process compelling appearance at such proceedings, shall include the following statement in bold face, 14–point Times New Roman or Courier font:**

If you are a person with a disability who needs any accommodation in order to participate in this proceeding, you are entitled, at no cost to you, to the provision of certain assistance. Please contact Maria E. Mihaic, the Eleventh Judicial Circuit's ADA Coordinator at Lawson E. Thomas Courthouse Center, 175 NW 1st Avenue, Suite 2702, Miami, Florida 33128; Telephone (305) 349–7175; TDD (305) 349–7174; or via Fax at (305) 349–7355, at least seven (7) days before your scheduled court appearance, or immediately upon receiving this notification if the time before the scheduled appearance is less than seven (7) days; if you are hearing or voice impaired, call 711."

3. **Other Requests for Reasonable Accommodations.** In addition to participation in a court proceeding, should a person with a disability who needs a reasonable accommodation wish to participate in any court program, service, activity or benefit, such person must contact the ADA Coordinator in the manner set forth in paragraph 2 herein within two (2) working days of the program, service, activity or benefit.

4. **Re-adoption of Internal Grievance Procedure.** The Americans with Disabilities Act of 1990 Designation of Responsible Person and Internal Grievance Procedure for the Eleventh Judicial Circuit, attached hereto as Attachment "A" is hereby re-adopted and shall remain in full force and effect until further order of the Court.

5. Administrative Order No. 98–19 is hereby rescinded in its entirety and held for naught.

This Administrative Order shall take effect upon execution and shall remain in full force and effect until further order of the Court.

DONE AND ORDEREDin Chambers at Miami–Dade, Florida, this 27th day of January, 2010.

JOEL H. BROWN, CHIEF JUDGE ELEVENTH JUDICIAL CIRCUIT OF FLORIDA

ATTACHMENT

Americans with Disabilities Act of 1990

Designation of Responsible Person and Internal Grievance Procedure for the Eleventh Judicial Circuit

I. Authority

Federal regulations implementing the Americans with Disabilities Act of 1990 (ADA) requires public entities with 50 or more employees to designate a responsible employee and adopt grievance procedures providing for prompt and equitable resolution of complaints alleging noncompliance or complaints alleging any actions that would be prohibited under Title II of the ADA. (28 C.F.R. § 35.107)

II. Intent and Purpose

It is the intent of the Eleventh Judicial Circuit to fully comply with the ADA and to assure equity, fairness, and full participation in the judicial system for persons with disabilities.

The purpose of this procedure is to establish a mechanism for resolving complaints without requiring the complainant to resort to federal complaint procedures. However, complainants would not be required to exhaust this grievance procedure before they could file a complaint at the federal level.

It is the intent of the Eleventh Judicial Circuit that complainants be consulted and advised, and that communications be maintained, at each step of the grievance process. It is further the intent of the Eleventh Judicial Circuit to engage alternative dispute resolution techniques whenever necessary, and at any point in the grievance process.

III. Definitions

A. *Americans with Disabilities Act (ADA)*—Public Law 101–336, the Americans with Disabilities Act of 1990, which prohibits discrimination on the basis of disability.

B. *ADA Coordinator*—Same as "*Responsible Employee.*"

C. *Disability or Persons with Disabilities*—With respect to an individual, a physical or mental impairment that substantially limits one or more of the major life activities of such individual; a record of such impairment; or being regarded as having such an impairment as defined in Public Law 101–336 and 28 C.F.R. § 35.104.

D. *Grievance*—A formal complaint made by a person, or on behalf of a person, alleging that he or she has been subjected to unlawful discrimination, or inaccessibility to facilities, programs, services, benefits, or activities on the basis of a disability.

E. *Office of the General Counsel*—An operational division of the Office of the State Courts Administrator, Supreme Court of Florida, Tallahassee.

F. *Office of the State Courts Administrator (OSCA)*—The administrative office of the Supreme Court of Florida, Tallahassee, which serves as the liaison between the Supreme Court and other court entities and other branches of government.

G. *Responsible Employee*—An employee designated to coordinate a public entity's efforts to comply with and carry out its responsibilities under Title II of the ADA. These responsibilities include any investigation and/or follow through of any complaint alleging noncompliance or alleging any actions that would be prohibited by Title II of the ADA.

H. *State Courts System*—All Florida courts at both appellate and trial levels.

I. *Title II*—The second section of the ADA that prohibits discrimination on the basis of disability in state and local government services.

IV. Designation of Responsible Person

The ADA coordinator for the Eleventh Judicial Circuit is:

Maria E. Mihaic
ADA Coordinator
Administrative Office of the Courts
Lawson E. Thomas Courthouse Center
175 NW First Ave., Suite 2702
(305)349–7351
E-mail: ADA@jud11.flcourts.org

V. Grievances

A complaint shall contain the following minimum information:

A. Name, address, and telephone number of the complainant on whose behalf the complaint is being made.

B. The court facility in which the violation is alleged to have occurred.

C. A complete statement of the grievance and the facts upon which it is based.

D. The desired remedy or solution requested.

E. The names of any witnesses who can provide supportive or relative information.

VI. Procedure for Grievances Relating to the Eleventh Judicial Circuit

A. Filing

1. Complaints must be filed with the ADA coordinator no later than one hundred eighty (180) days from the date of the alleged discrimination.

2. The filing deadline may be extended upon a show of good cause.

B. Assessment and Determination of Team Members

1. The ADA coordinator will determine which function(s) of the court is at issue: facilities, programs, services, benefits, or activities.

2. The ADA coordinator will notify the chief judge and the court administrator of the complaint.

3. A team consisting of the ADA coordinator, the administrator(s), and a member of the Office of the General Counsel shall address the complaint. Individual(s) who are charged in the complaint with alleged discriminatory conduct shall not be a member of the team.

C. Fact Finding

1. The team, or a member of the team, will review the complaint with the complainant.

2. The team, or a member of the team, will interview witnesses who can provide supportive or relative information and complete the fact finding.

D. Test of Legal Sufficiency

1. The team member representing the Office of the General Counsel will determine the legal sufficiency of the complaint.

E. Action

1. If a complaint is legally deficient, the complaint shall immediately be brought to closure.

2. If a complaint is legally sufficient, the team will establish a course of action to resolve the complaint.

3. To the extent necessary, the court will make reasonable modifications to its programs, services, benefits, and activities to ensure future compliance with the ADA.

4. The court may invoke the course of action described in the regulations implementing the ADA (28 C.F.R. § 35.164) when modifications would result in a fundamental alteration in the nature of a service, program, or activity or in undue financial and administrative burdens.

F. Closure, Notification, and Records Retention

1. The ADA coordinator shall communicate the results of the investigation and the chosen course of action to the complainant not later than thirty (30) working days from the date the complaint was filed.

2. A record of the grievance shall be maintained for three (3) years; the record shall be located with the Office of the General Counsel.

Adopted in January, 1993

Modified in January 2009 to ensure electronic accessibility and to reflect current contact information.

Americans with Disabilities Act of 1990

Statement of Grievance

Name of Individual Making the Complaint ____________

Address ____________

City ____________

State ____________

Zip ____________

Day Telephone ____________

Evening Telephone ____________

Complete the following section if the complaint is being filed by a person other than the individual making the complaint:

Complaint Filed By ____________

Title (if appropriate) ____________

Firm (if appropriate) ____________

Address ____________

City ____________

State ____________

Zip ____________

Day Telephone ____________

Evening Telephone ____________

This section is for court use only:

*Date Filed*____________ *Time Filed*____________

*Complaint Taken By*____________

Staff Person's Name

Complainant's Last Name ____________

1. Name the court or court facility in which the violation is alleged to have occurred

____

2. Describe what happened that led to the decision to file this complaint. (If necessary, use an additional page to complete the statement.)

____

Complainant's Last Name ____________

3. State the desired remedy or the solution requested

____

4. List those witnesses who can provide information that supports or is relevant to your complaint:

Witness ____________

Address ____________

City ____________

State ____________

Zip ____________

Day Telephone ____________

Evening Telephone ____________

Witness ____________

Address ____________

City ____________

State ____________

Zip ____________

Day Telephone ____________

Evening Telephone ____________

Order 1-10-10 adopted January 27, 2010. Amended with Order 10-01 A1, effective April 4, 2012.

09–17. FORFEITURE/DISPOSAL OF ILLEGALLY TAKEN FISH AND WILDLIFE

THE ELEVENTH JUDICIAL CIRCUIT MIAMI–DADE COUNTY, FLORIDA

CASE NO. 09–1 (Court Administration)

ADMINISTRATIVE ORDER NO. 09–17
(Rescinding AO No. 01–06)

IN RE: FORFEITURE/DISPOSAL OF ILLEGALLY TAKEN FISH AND WILDLIFE

WHEREAS, the law enforcement officers (hereinafter referred to as "Officers") of the Florida Fish and Wildlife Conservation Commission (FWC), [1] are charged with enforcing all laws, rules, and regulations relating to wildlife, freshwater fish, and saltwater fish; and

WHEREAS, in the course of carrying out their duties, the Officers must occasionally seize living and dead illegally taken wildlife, freshwater fish, and saltwater fish (hereinafter, collectively called "contraband"); and

WHEREAS, it is more consistent with the Officers' mission if they are able to return living contraband to its natural habitat; and

WHEREAS, it is more economical, practical, and desirable to promptly dispose of dead contraband instead of storing it during the pendency of prosecutions; and

WHEREAS, § 379.338 (1), Fla. Stat., [2] permits, in accordance with a court order if the court so orders, the forfeiture and disposal of such contraband by the investigating law enforcement agency, prior to conviction; and

WHEREAS, § 379.3381, Fla. Stat., [3] permits a properly authenticated photograph to be substituted for any contraband seized by Officers and for the photographs to be admitted into evidence to the same extent that the contraband itself would be admissible;

NOW, THEREFORE, pursuant to the authority vested in me as Chief Judge of the Eleventh Judicial Circuit of Florida, under Rule 2.215 of the Florida Rules of Judicial Administration, it is hereby **ORDERED**:

1. DEFINITIONS

(a) "Authentication" means a law enforcement officer that meets the requirements of § 379.3381, Fla. Stat., as amended from time to time.

(b) "Contraband" means all illegal or illegally taken wildlife, freshwater fish, and saltwater fish.

(c) "Statutory authority" means the provisions of Chapter 379 of the Florida Statutes and the rules of the Florida Administrative Code made by the Fish and Wildlife Conservation Commission pursuant to that Chapter, as same may be amended from time to time.

2. APPLICATION

(a) When an arrest is made pursuant to statutory authority and contraband is seized, the law enforcement agency that seized the contraband is authorized to dispose of it, immediately or as soon as practicable, in accordance with § 379.338, Fla. Stat. and the rules of the Florida Administrative Code made by the Fish and Wildlife Conservation Commission pursuant to Chapter 379, as amended from time to time, and paragraph (b) below.

(b) All photographs of contraband must be authenticated as required by § 379.3381, Fla. Stat., as amended from time to time, and this Administrative Order, and after authentication, the photographs shall be filed with the law enforcement agency or the court as soon as practicable.

Administrative Order No. 01–06 is hereby rescinded in its entirety and held for naught.

This Order shall take effect immediately and shall remain in effect until further order of the Court.

DONE AND ORDERED in Chambers at Miami–Dade, Florida, this ___ day of November, 2009.

JOEL H. BROWN, CHIEF JUDGE
ELEVENTH JUDICIAL CIRCUIT OF FLORIDA

[1] Although reference is made to FWC Officers because they are the law enforcement personnel most likely to be involved in seizures of living or dead wildlife, freshwater fish, and saltwater fish, the provisions of this order are equally applicable to any certified law enforcement officer and law enforcement agency.

[2] Section 379.338 (1). Confiscation and disposition of illegally taken wildlife, freshwater fish, and saltwater fish.

All wildlife, freshwater fish, and saltwater fish seized under the authority of this chapter, any other chapter, or rules of the commission shall, upon conviction of the offender or sooner in accordance with a court order if the court so orders, be forfeited to the investigating law enforcement agency. The law enforcement agency may elect to retain the wildlife, freshwater fish, or saltwater fish for the agency's official use; transfer it to another unit of state or local government for official use; donate it to a charitable organization; sell it at a public sale pursuant to s. 705.103; or destroy the wildlife, freshwater fish, or saltwater fish if none of the other options is practicable or if the wildlife, freshwater fish, or saltwater fish is unwholesome or otherwise not of appreciable value. All illegally possessed live wildlife, freshwater fish, and saltwater fish that are properly documented as evidence as provided in s. 379.3381 may be returned to the habitat unharmed. Any unclaimed wildlife, freshwater fish, or saltwater fish shall be retained by the investigating law enforcement agency and disposed of in accordance with this subsection.

[3] Section 379.3381. Photographic evidence of illegally taken wildlife, freshwater fish, and saltwater fish. In any prosecution for a violation of this chapter, any other chapter, or rules of the commission, a photograph of illegally taken wildlife, freshwater fish, or saltwater fish may be deemed competent evidence of such property and may be admissible in the prosecution to the same extent as if such wildlife, freshwater fish, or saltwater fish were introduced as evidence. Such photograph shall bear a written description of the wildlife, freshwater fish, or saltwater fish alleged to have been illegally taken, the name of the violator, the location where the alleged illegal taking occurred, the name of the investigating law enforcement officer, the date the photograph was taken, and the name of the photographer. Such writing shall be made under oath by the investigating law enforcement officer, and the photograph shall be identified by the signature of the photographer.

09–13 (A1). ENLARGEMENT AND EXPANSION OF THE CURRENT PILOT PROJECT FOR ELECTRONIC SUBMISSIONS OF COURTESY COPIES FOR UNIFORM MOTION CALENDAR AND REQUESTS FOR SPECIAL SET HEARINGS, EMERGENCY MOTIONS, AND PROPOSED ORDERS

THE ELEVENTH JUDICIAL CIRCUIT MIAMI–DADE COUNTY, FLORIDA

CASE NO. 10–1 (Court Administration)

ADMINISTRATIVE ORDER NO. 09–13–A1 (Amending and Superseding AO No. 09–13)

IN RE: ENLARGEMENT AND EXPANSION OF THE CURRENT PILOT PROJECT FOR ELECTRONIC SUBMISSIONS OF COURTESY COPIES FOR UNIFORM MOTION CALENDAR AND REQUESTS FOR SPECIAL SET HEARINGS, EMERGENCY MOTIONS, AND PROPOSED ORDERS

WHEREAS, pursuant to Administrative Order No. 09–13, in an effort to enhance the efficiency of judicial review of motions, exhibits, submitted case law and other hearing specific documents of motion calendar and special set hearings (collectively "Motions") by reducing the quantity of paper work involved in such review in the General Jurisdiction Division (n/k/a and hereinafter referred to as "Circuit Civil Division") of the Circuit Court in the Eleventh Judicial Circuit ("Court"), a pilot project ("Pilot Project"), using Windows SharePoint Services created by Microsoft ("SharePoint") was established in Section CA 15 of the Circuit Civil Division, under the auspices of the Honorable Israel Reyes, Associate Administrative Judge, Circuit Civil Division (hereinafter "Judge Reyes"); and

WHEREAS, the Pilot Project required courtesy copies of the Motions to be electronically transmitted by attorneys to the Court; and

WHEREAS, so as to further determine the effectiveness of SharePoint and begin to expand the Pilot Project to other sections of the Circuit Civil Division, Judge Reyes has volunteered to continue with the implementation of its usage within Section CA 15 of the Circuit Civil Division; and

WHEREAS, based upon the overall success of the Pilot Project as evidenced by the effective participation of attorneys and pro se parties, Judge Reyes' positive assessment, and suggestions from attorneys as to how to enhance the effectiveness of the Pilot Project, it has been determined that the Pilot Project should be enlarged and expanded, with certain procedures and protocol further clarified, to include, inter alia that, preferably, courtesy copies of documents are also electronically transmitted by and to opposing counsel and pro se parties and in accordance with Rule 2.525(d)(2), Florida Rules of Judicial Administration, the Rules of Civil Procedure, and other applicable rules of the Court;

NOW, THEREFORE, pursuant to the authority vested in me as Chief Judge of the Eleventh Judicial Circuit of Florida, under Rule 2.215 of the Rules of Judicial Administration, it is hereby **ORDERED**:

1. **Enlargement.** The Pilot Project requiring the electronic submission of courtesy copies of Motions, is hereby enlarged to include proposed orders (collectively "Motions and Proposed Orders"), utilizing SharePoint, in Section CA 15 of the Circuit Civil Division of the Circuit Court in the Eleventh Judicial Circuit ("Pilot Project").

2. **Effective Date.** The Pilot Project which commenced on Monday, September 28, 2009 and continued for approximately six months is hereby expanded and enlarged to continue until further order of the Court.

3. **Participants.** With the exception of pro se litigants who are unable to electronically furnish the subject items, all attorneys of record shall be required to follow the protocol set forth in paragraph 4 herein below. Pro se litigants who are unable to electronically furnish the subject documents may continue to follow the same procedures regarding submission of courtesy copies for Uniform Motion Calendar, Requests for Special Set Hearings, Emergency Motions and Proposed Orders that were in effect prior to the effective date of Administrative Order No. 09–13.

4. **Protocol.** The following protocol shall be followed for the electronic submission of Motions and Proposed Orders. However, Motions and Proposed Orders for Summary Judgment in residential mortgage foreclosure cases, Motions for Writs of Possession, and Motions to Cancel Sale must be set pursuant to this Circuit's Foreclosure Master Calendar procedures, which may be found at www.jud11.flcourts.org/fmc.htm

a. *For all Documents.* All submitted documents shall be titled with the Court Case Number and the name/type of document using the following format: two digit year followed by a hyphen with the sequential case number (e.g., 09–1; 91–12; 08–123; 07–1234; or 09–12345). Do not use zeros after the hyphen to fill in the sequential case number. For example:

- 10–776 Defendant's Motion to Compel;
- 99–23 Order Granting Plaintiff's Motion for Continuance;
- 09–5768 Memorandum of Law in Support of Plaintiff's Motion for Sanctions;
- 07–4 Affidavit of James Smith
- 02–444 Defendant's Emergency Motion to Stay Proceedings
- 08–3235 Caselaw *Metcalfe v. Lee*

b. *Uniform Motion Calendar.*

i. Each party may set only one five minute motion per case. Multiple motions must be specially set or set on different motion calendars (one five minute motion per party per case), so as not to encroach on the time the Court is allotting for other litigants/attorneys. Consequently, the parties are advised to use good faith efforts to resolve the issues set forth in the motion **prior** to the setting of a motion; coordinate the date and time of the hearing; and confirm that the hearing shall require no more than five minutes (if the hearing will require more than 5 minutes, then it must be a Special Set Hearing).

In addition to providing proper service pursuant to Rule 1.080(b), Florida Rules of Civil Procedure, courtesy copies of the Motion and Memorandum of Law for the Uniform Motion Calendar (e.g., Notice of Hearing, Motions, Exhibits, submitted case law, and other hearing specific documents) must be electronically attached to an email using either Microsoft Word or WordPerfect format (not as a PDF document) and sent via email to:

(a) The Court at CA15MotionCalendar@jud11.flcourts.org;

(b) Opposing counsel at their fax number as provided to The Florida Bar (see www.FloridaBar.org and then click on "Find a Lawyer") or any other fax number provided on a Pleading, Motion to Quash Service, Motion to Dismiss Complaint or Notice of Appearance, whichever is most recent; and

(c) Pro se parties at their last known fax number or any other fax number provided on a Pleading, Motion to

Quash Service, Motion to Dismiss Complaint or Notice of Appearance, whichever is most recent.

ii. If a scheduling attorney or a scheduling pro se party does not have a fax number, then a courtesy copy of Motions and Proposed orders must be sent as an attachment to the service of process required pursuant to Rule 1.080(b), Florida Rules of Civil Procedure.

iii. The subject line of the email must contain only the numeric motion calendar hearing date using the following format: mm/dd/yy (two digit month forward slash; two digit day forward slash; two digit year). For example: 06/15/10

iv. The above referenced email address for the Court is to be exclusively utilized to electronically submit the Motions for the Uniform Motion Calendar. The Court will not respond to any emails sent to the above address nor is the email to contain any explanations, arguments, or messages to the Court.

v. Hyperlinks in the attachments, (not in the body of the email) are encouraged just as are submissions in Microsoft Word format. Electronic versions submitted in WordPerfect will be converted by the Court to Microsoft Word and there is no guarantee that the document will be converted without error.

vi. The Court does not require courtesy copies of Final Summary Judgments of Foreclosure.

vii. Should any scheduled hearing become unnecessary or have to be cancelled, the scheduling attorney or scheduling pro se party shall immediately, but, not later than by Noon on the business day prior to the hearing date and time, send an email to CA15MotionCalendar@jud11.flcourts.org regarding the cancellation of the Motion Calendar hearing with an electronically attached Notice of Cancellation formatted in the same manner (using Microsoft Word or Word Perfect) as the email that scheduled the Motion Calendar hearing and in the same manner as the Motions and Notices. Example of attached file name: 09–13423 Notice of Cancellation.

viii. The subject line of the email, and not the file name, must contain only the numeric Motion Calendar hearing date that is being cancelled using the following format: mm/dd/yy (two digit month forward slash; two digit day forward slash; two digit year). For example: 06/15/10

ix. Failure of an attorney or pro se party to appear for a scheduled hearing (other than for lack of due process, emergency, or Court scheduling conflict) may result in sanctions being imposed against the non-appearing attorney or non-appearing pro se party.

x. A sample email is appended to the Order as Attachment "A".[1]

c. *Special Set Hearing.*

i. In addition to providing proper service pursuant to Rule 1.080(b), Florida Rules of Civil Procedure, a request for the Special Set Hearing (available for download at www.jud11.flcourts.org at Judge Reyes' webpage) and a courtesy copy of the Motion(s) must be attached electronically to an email using either Microsoft Word or Wordperfect formats (not as a PDF document) and sent via email to:

(a) The Court at CA15SpecialSets@jud11.flcourts.org;

(b) Opposing counsel at their fax number as provided to The Florida Bar (see www.FloridaBar.org and then click on "Find a Lawyer") or any other fax number provided on a Pleading, Motion to Quash Service, Motion to Dismiss Complaint or Notice of Appearance, whichever is most recent; and

(c) Pro se parties at their last known fax number or any other fax number provided on a Pleading, Motion to Quash Service, Motion to Dismiss Complaint or Notice of Appearance, whichever is most recent.

ii. If a scheduling attorney or a scheduling pro se party does not have a fax number, then a courtesy copy of the documents for the Special Set Hearing must be sent as attachment to the service of process required pursuant to Rule 1.080(b), Florida Rules of Civil Procedure.

iii. The subject line of the email must contain only the Court Case Number using the following format: two digit year followed by a hyphen with the sequential case number. Do not use zeros after the hyphen to fill in the sequential case number (e.g., 09–1; 91–12; 08–123; 07–1234; or 09–12345).

iv. The above referenced Court email address is to be exclusively utilized to electronically submit the courtesy copy of the special set motion along with the request for the Special Set Hearing. The Court will not respond to any emails sent to the above address nor is the email to contain any explanations, arguments, or messages to the Court.

v. Upon receipt of the above items, the judicial assistant or the Court will provide instructions to the moving party.

vi. No parties are permitted to unilaterally set additional special set motions for hearing during the above time period without prior approval of the Court.

vii. To be considered by the Court, responses to all motions, *except* Motions for Summary Judgments that are Special Set, along with supporting documents and evidence, if any, must be served by mail at least seven (7) business/working days prior to the day of the hearing, to the attorneys and pro se parties, with courtesy copies also sent to:

(a) The Court at CA15SpecialSets@jud11.flcourts.org;

(b) Opposing counsel at their fax number as provided to The Florida Bar (see www.FloridaBar.org and then click on "Find a Lawyer") or any other fax number provided on a Pleading, Motion to Quash Service, Motion to Dismiss Complaint or Notice of Appearance, whichever is most recent; and

(c) Pro se parties at their last known fax number or any other fax number provided on a Pleading, Motion to Quash Service, Motion to Dismiss Complaint or Notice of Appearance, whichever is most recent.

viii. To be considered by the Court, responses to Motions for Summary Judgments that are Special Set, along with supporting documents and evidence, if any, must be served by mail at least five (5) days prior to the day of the hearing, or hand-delivered prior to the Special Set Hearing, but no later than two (2) business days before 5:00 p.m. to the attorneys and pro se parties, with courtesy copies also sent to:

(a) The Court at CA15SpecialSets@jud11.flcourts.org;

(b) Opposing counsel at their fax number as provided to The Florida Bar (see www.FloridaBar.org and then click on "Find a Lawyer") or any other fax number provided on a Pleading, Motion to Quash Service, Motion to Dismiss Complaint or Notice of Appearance, whichever is most recent; and

(c) Pro se parties at their last known fax number or any other fax number provided on a Pleading, Motion to Quash Service, Motion to Dismiss Complaint or Notice of Appearance, whichever is most recent.

ix. Should any scheduled hearing become unnecessary or has to be cancelled, the scheduling attorney or scheduling pro se party shall immediately, but, not later than by Noon on the business day prior to the hearing date and time, send an email to CA15SpecialSets@jud11.flcourts.org regarding the cancellation of the Special Set hearing with an electronically attached Notice of Cancellation formatted in the same manner (using Microsoft Word or WordPerfect) as the email that scheduled the Special Set hearing and in the same manner as the Motions and Notices. Example of attached file name: 09–13423 Notice of Cancellation.

x. The subject line of the email must contain only the Court Case Number using the following format: two digit year followed by a hyphen with the sequential case number. Do not use zeros after the hyphen to fill in the sequential case number (e.g., 09–1; 91–12; 08–123; 07–1234; or 09–12345).

xi. Failure of an attorney or pro se party to appear for a scheduled hearing (other than for lack of due process, emergency, or Court scheduling conflict) may result in sanctions being imposed against the non-appearing attorney or non-appearing pro se party.

xii. A sample email is appended to this Order as Attachment "B".[2]

d. *Emergency Motions*.

i. A courtesy copy of the Emergency Motion(s) must be emailed to CA15EmergencyMotions@jud11.flcourts.org

ii. The subject line of the email must contain only the Court Case Number using the following format: two digit year followed by a hyphen with the sequential case number. Do not use zeros after the hyphen to fill in the sequential case number (e.g., 09–1; 91–12; 08–123; 07–1234; or 07–1234).

iii. The above referenced email address is to be exclusively utilized to electronically submit the courtesy copy of the Emergency Motion. The Court will not respond to any emails sent to the above address nor is the email to contain any explanations, arguments, or messages to the Court.

iv. Upon receipt of the above items, the judicial assistant will contact the parties to advise as to how the Court will proceed upon review of the Emergency Motion.

v. A sample email is appended to this Order as Attachment "C".[3]

e. *Proposed Orders*.

i. Any Proposed Order must be emailed to CA15ProposedOrders@jud11.flcourts.org along with the applicable Motion. The cover letter and any exhibits or other supporting documentation may be submitted as a PDF or scanned. But the Order and Motion must be sent in Word or WordPerfect format.

ii. The above referenced email address is to be exclusively utilized to electronically submit the courtesy copy of the Proposed Order. The Court will not respond to any emails sent to the above address nor is the email to contain any explanations, arguments, or messages to the Court.

iii. The subject line of the email must contain only the Court Case Number using the following format: two digit year followed by a hyphen with the sequential case number. Do not use zeros after the hyphen to fill in the sequential case number (e.g., 09–1; 91–12; 08–123; 07–1234; or 09–12345).

iv. On the bottom portion of the Order, list the name and fax number of every recipient entitled to a copy of the Order using the following format: Bracket followed by FAX: and then the first and last name of the recipient followed by @area code and the telephone number ending with a bracket. For example:

a. **[First Name Last Name @(305)-xxx-xxxx]**

b. **[First Name Last Name @1–954-xxx-xxxx]**

Any telephone number with an area code other than 305 must be preceded by a one.

By following the above format, the Court can cut and paste the recipient information onto an email and immediately fax the signed order back to the recipients using Microsoft Outlook. This will avoid the need for the recipients to furnish envelopes and stamps and will reduce costs.

If a recipient does not have a fax number, then the moving party will be responsible for furnishing the Order to that recipient and file proof of service with the Clerk of Courts.

v. Upon receipt of the above items, the Court will review the Proposed Order and forward the results to the movant.

vi. A sample email is appended to this Order as Attachment "D".[4]

5. Additional Information. Step by step guides containing detailed instructions on how to submit the above documents can be found at www.jud11.flcourts.org on Judge Reyes' webpage and thereafter clicking on the link titled "Calendar Information."

6. Judicial Discretion. It shall be within the discretion of the Court to waive the requirements set forth herein or to impose sanctions for failure to comply with such requirements.

7. Compliance with Rules. All notice and time provisions of the Florida Rules of Civil Procedure and this Circuit's local rules and Administrative Orders, as applicable, must continue to be followed.

This Administrative Order amends and supersedes Administrative Order No. 09–13. This Administrative Order shall take effect immediately upon execution and shall remain in full force and effect until further order of the Court.

DONE AND ORDERED in Chambers at Miami–Dade County, Florida, this 28th day of June, 2010.

JOEL H. BROWN, CHIEF JUDGE

ELEVENTH JUDICIAL CIRCUIT
OF FLORIDA

[1] For a copy of Attachment A, please see: http://www.jud11.flcourts.org/
[2] For a copy of Attachment B, please see: http://www.jud11.flcourts.org/
[3] For a copy of Attachment C, please see: http://www.jud11.flcourts.org/
[4] For a copy of Attachment D, please see: http://www.jud11.flcourts.org/

09–04 (A1). CLARIFICATION RE FEES—COSTS OF DEFENSE; APPLICATION FEE FOR COURT APPOINTED COUNSEL

THE ELEVENTH JUDICIAL CIRCUIT MIAMI-DADE COUNTY, FLORIDA

CASE NO. 09–1 (Court Administration)

ADMINISTRATIVE ORDER NO. 09–04 A1 (Amends AO. No. 09–04)

IN RE: CLARIFICATION RE FEES—COSTS OF DEFENSE; APPLICATION FEE FOR COURT APPOINTED COUNSEL

WHEREAS, pursuant to Administrative Order No. 09–04, the Court set forth the manner in which the Eleventh Judicial Circuit would comply with Section 938.29, Florida Statutes, in connection with the assessment, collection, and disposition of the application fees mandated to be paid by a defendant convicted of a criminal act or in violation of probation or community control, and who has received the assistance of the public defender's office, a special assistant public defender, the office of criminal conflict and civil regional counsel, a private conflict attorney, or who has received due process services after being found indigent for costs under Section 27.525, Florida Statutes and attorney's fees and costs; and

WHEREAS, in order to clarify to whom such application fees are to be distributed, it was determined that Administrative Order No. 09–04 should be amended accordingly;

NOW, THEREFORE, pursuant to the authority vested in me as Chief Judge of the Eleventh Judicial Circuit of Florida, under Rule 2.215 of the Florida Rules of Judicial Administration, it is hereby **ORDERED** that Administrative Order No. 09–04 is amended in the following particulars:

1. Paragraph 3 of Administrative Order No. 09–04 is amended to read as follows:

"The first $50.00 of any fees and costs collected on a case by the Clerk of the Court will go toward satisfaction of the Application Fee, and said fee must be collected and transferred monthly by the Clerk to the Department of Revenue for deposit in the Indigent Criminal Defense Trust Fund administered by the Florida Justice Administrative Commission to be used for the purposes of indigent criminal defense as appropriated by the Legislature to the public defender or the office of criminal conflict and civil regional counsel in accordance with Section 27.525. Fla.Stat."

2. Except as amended herein, Administrative Order No. 09–04 shall remain in full force and effect.

This Order shall take effect immediately upon execution and shall remain in full force and effect until further order of the Court.

DONE AND ORDERED in Chambers at Miami–Dade, Florida, this ___ day of February, 2009.

JOSEPH P. FARINA, CHIEF JUDGE
ELEVENTH JUDICIAL CIRCUIT OF FLORIDA

09–04. FEES—COSTS OF DEFENSE; APPLICATION FEE FOR COURT APPOINTED COUNSEL

THE ELEVENTH JUDICIAL CIRCUIT MIAMI-DADE COUNTY, FLORIDA

CASE NO. 09–1 (Court Administration)

ADMINISTRATIVE ORDER NO. 09–04 (Rescinds AO No. 97–05)

IN RE: FEES—COSTS OF DEFENSE; APPLICATION FEE FOR COURT APPOINTED COUNSEL

WHEREAS, Section 938.29, Fla. Stat., effective July 1, 2008, mandates that a defendant convicted of a criminal act or in violation of probation or community control, and who has received the assistance of the public defender's office, a special assistant public defender, the office of criminal conflict and civil regional counsel, a private conflict attorney, or who has received due process services after being found indigent for costs under Section 27.52, Fla. Stat., shall be liable for payment of the assessed application fee under Section 27.52 and attorney's fees and costs; and

WHEREAS, an amendment to Section 938.29, Fla. Stat., mandates that attorney's fees and costs shall be set in all cases at no less than $50.00 per case when a misdemeanor or criminal traffic offense is charged and no less than $100.00 per case when a felony offense is charged, including a proceeding in which the underlying offense is a violation of probation or community control; and

WHEREAS, Section 938.29, Fla. Stat., requires that the court shall impose the attorney's fees and costs notwithstanding the defendant's present ability to pay; and

WHEREAS, Section 938.29, Fla. Stat., mandates that the clerk of court enforce, satisfy, compromise, settle, subordinate, release, or otherwise dispose of any debt or lien imposed under this section; and

WHEREAS, Section 27.52(1)(b), Fla. Stat., requires an applicant to pay a $50.00 fee to the clerk for each application for court-appointed counsel filed, and that the application fee be paid within 7 days of submitting the application; and

WHEREAS, Section 27.52(1)(b), Fla. Stat., mandates that the clerk of court notify the court if the application fee has not been paid prior to the disposition of the case;

NOW, THEREFORE, pursuant to the authority vested in me as Chief Judge of the Eleventh Judicial Circuit of Florida, under Rule 2.215 of the Florida Rules of Judicial Administration, it is hereby **ORDERED**:

1. The court shall include in each judgment in which the convicted person received the assistance of the Eleventh Judicial Circuit's Office of the Public Defender, a special assistant

public defender, the office of criminal conflict and civil regional counsel, or a private conflict attorney, or who has received due process services after being found indigent for costs under Section 27.52, Fla. Stat., an assessment of no less than $50.00 in misdemeanor cases and $100.00 in felony cases, including original actions and violations of probation or community control.

2. The Clerk of the Courts shall notify the court prior to the disposition of the case if the defendant has not paid the $50.00 application fee, and, if not paid, the court shall assess the application fee as part of the sentence or as a condition of probation; or assess the application fee pursuant to Section 938.29, Fla. Stat.

3. The first $50.00 of any fees and costs collected on a case by the Clerk of Courts will go toward satisfaction of the application fee, and said fee must be collected and transferred to the Indigent Criminal Defense Trust Fund administered by the Florida Justice Administrative Commission ("Commission") for the benefit of this Circuit's Office of the Public Defender in accordance with Section 27.525, Fla. Stat.

Administrative Order No. 97–05, entered in Case No. 97–01, is hereby rescinded in its entirety and held for naught.

This Order shall take effect immediately upon execution and shall remain in full force and effect until further order of the Court.

DONE AND ORDERED in Chambers at Miami–Dade, Florida, this ___ day of February, 2009.

JOSEPH P. FARINA, CHIEF JUDGE
ELEVENTH JUDICIAL CIRCUIT OF FLORIDA

09–03. ABOLISHMENT OF SECTION 02 AND ESTABLISHING SECTION 05 OF THE PROBATE DIVISION OF THE ELEVENTH JUDICIAL CIRCUIT OF FLORIDA AND THE REASSIGNMENT OF CASES CURRENTLY IN SECTION 02 TO SECTION 05

THE ELEVENTH JUDICIAL CIRCUIT MIAMI-DADE COUNTY, FLORIDA

CASE NO. 09–1 (Court Administration)

ADMINISTRATIVE ORDER NO. 09–03
(Rescinding AO No. 08–16)

IN RE: ABOLISHMENT OF SECTION 02 AND ESTABLISHING SECTION 05 OF THE PROBATE DIVISION OF THE ELEVENTH JUDICIAL CIRCUIT OF FLORIDA AND THE REASSIGNMENT OF CASES CURRENTLY IN SECTION 02 TO SECTION 05

WHEREAS, pursuant to Administrative Order No. 08–16 (AO No. 08–16), entered on September 29, 2008, Section 02 was abolished and Section 05 was established within the Probate Division of the Eleventh Judicial Circuit of Florida; and

WHEREAS, AO No. 08–16 categorized all cases to be reassigned from Section 02 to Section 05 as Civil Probate (CP) cases; however, the Probate Division also handles Guardianship (GD) and Mental Health (MH) cases; and

WHEREAS, it was determined that rather than distinguishing the three types of cases individually, the newly established section would be referred to as Section 05, thereby encompassing all such cases;

NOW, THEREFORE, PURSUANT TO the authority vested in me as Chief Judge of the Eleventh Judicial Circuit of Florida, under Rule 2.215 of the Florida Rules of Judicial Administration, it is hereby **ORDERED:**

1. Section 02 of the Probate Division of the Eleventh Judicial Circuit of Florida is hereby abolished and Section 05 is hereby established in said Division, effective as of the close of business on Monday, January 26, 2009.

2. Due to the closure of Section 02 and the establishment of Section 05, the Clerk of the Court is hereby directed to:

a. Allow Section 05 to receive all case assignment types associated with the Probate Division heretofore assigned to Section 02.

b. At the close of business on Monday, January 26, 2009, reassign all open cases in Section 02 to Section 05.

c. At the close of business on Monday, January 26, 2009, reassign all closed cases in the active database under Section 02 to Section 05.

d. Immediately notify all attorneys of record in any pending matter assigned to Section 02 as to the abolishment of Section 02 and the establishment of Section 05 in the Probate Division.

Administrative Order No. 08–16, entered on September 29, 2008 is hereby rescinded in its entirety and held for naught.

DONE AND ORDERED in Chambers at Miami–Dade, Florida, this ___ day of January, 2009.

JOSEPH P. FARINA, CHIEF JUDGE
ELEVENTH JUDICIAL CIRCUIT OF FLORIDA

08–19. ELIMINATION OF SECTION 02 IN THE COUNTY COURT CIVIL DIVISION AND REASSIGNMENT OF CASES IN SECTION 02 TO SECTIONS 03 AND 04 IN SAID DIVISION

THE ELEVENTH JUDICIAL CIRCUIT MIAMI-DADE COUNTY, FLORIDA

CASE NO. 08–1 (Court Administration)

ADMINISTRATIVE ORDER NO. 08–19

IN RE: ELIMINATION OF SECTION 02 IN THE COUNTY COURT CIVIL DIVISION AND REASSIGNMENT OF CASES IN SECTION 02 TO SECTIONS 03 AND 04 IN SAID DIVISION

WHEREAS, it was determined that Section 02 in the County Court Civil Division, located at the South Dade Justice Center should be eliminated; and

WHEREAS, upon such elimination, cases presently pending in Section 02 should be equitably reassigned to Sections 03 and 04 in said Division;

NOW, THEREFORE, pursuant to the authority vested in me as Chief Judge of the Eleventh Judicial Circuit of Florida, under Rule 2.215, Florida Rules of Judicial Administration, it is hereby **ORDERED:**

1. Effective, Monday, November 3, 2008, Section 02 in the County Court Civil Division, located at the South Dade Justice Center, shall be eliminated.

2. Upon such elimination, pending cases in said Section shall be equitably reassigned to the remaining two County Court Civil Sections as follows:

a. SP cases should be equally reassigned to Sections 03 and 04.

b. CC cases should be equally reassigned to Sections 03 and 04.

3. Any inequities in caseload distribution among Sections 03 and 04 will be adjusted by the Administrative Judge of the County Court Civil Division.

4. No cases shall be retained or heard by the original judge upon reassignment to either Section 03 or 04, except as follows:

a. Motions for rehearing or new trial;

b. Motions to vacate final judgments, including summary judgments;

c. Completion of hearing or trial after judge has commenced taking testimony in the case;

d. Disposition of cases tried; and/or

e. Good cause.

5. If all parties in a case desire the original judge to retain a case, the parties shall submit a joint motion to the original judge stating specific reasons for retention of the case. If the judge agrees to retain the case, an order will be entered by the Administrative Judge of the County Court Civil Division, or designee, transferring the case back to the original judge, without the necessity of a hearing. In all other situations, a case shall be placed on a regularly scheduled transfer calendar before the Administrative Judge of the County Court Civil Division.

6. The Clerk of the Courts shall immediately notify all attorneys of record as to the elimination of Section 02 and the reassignment of any pending cases therein.

This Order shall take effect on Monday, November 3, 2008 and shall remain in effect until further order of the Court.

DONE AND ORDERED in Chambers at Miami–Dade, Florida, this ___ day of _________, 2008.

____

JOSEPH P. FARINA, CHIEF JUDGE
ELEVENTH JUDICIAL CIRCUIT OF FLORIDA

08–18. RE–ESTABLISHMENT OF STANDARDS AND PROCEDURES FOR THE PROTECTION OF MINORS IN THE SETTLEMENT OF PERSONAL INJURY, WRONGFUL DEATH AND MEDICAL MALPRACTICE LAWSUITS AND CLAIMS

THE ELEVENTH JUDICIAL CIRCUIT MIAMI–DADE COUNTY, FLORIDA

CASE NO. 08–1 (Court Administration)

ADMINISTRATIVE ORDER NO. 08–18 (Rescinding AO No. 06–04 and AO No. 08–05)

IN RE: RE–ESTABLISHMENT OF STANDARDS AND PROCEDURES FOR THE PROTECTION OF MINORS IN THE SETTLEMENT OF PERSONAL INJURY, WRONGFUL DEATH AND MEDICAL MALPRACTICE LAWSUITS AND CLAIMS

WHEREAS, in view of certain recent statutory amendments, there is a need to re-establish uniform standards and procedures for the protection of minors in the settlement of personal injury, wrongful death and medical malpractice lawsuits; and

WHEREAS, in the event that there is a pending civil action in the General Jurisdiction Division of the Circuit Court, the petition for approval of a minor's settlement should be filed in the pending civil action; or if there is no civil action pending in the General Jurisdiction Division, the petition for approval of settlement should be filed in the Probate Division of the Circuit Court. *See* committee notes to Fla. Prob. R. 5.636;

NOW, THEREFORE, pursuant to the authority vested in me as Chief Judge of the Eleventh Judicial Circuit of Florida under Florida Rule of Judicial Administration 2.215, the following procedures and standards are hereby re-established and adopted in all matters involving the settlement of personal injury, wrongful death and medical malpractice lawsuits ("filed action") or claims that are not the subject of a lawsuit ("unfiled actions"), arising wherein one or more minors are involved:

Part I Where Petition for Approval is filed.

1. Petitions for Approval of a Settlement of a Minor shall be filed in a pending action in the General Jurisdiction Division; or, in the absence thereof, the Petition for Approval of Settlement of a Minor ("Petition") shall be filed in the Probate Division of the Circuit Court. If a Legal Guardianship preexists, the filing of the Petition, and said Petition is filed in a pending action of within the General Jurisdiction Division, the General Jurisdiction Division Judge may transfer the Petition to the Probate Division. Motions to transfer a guardianship to another jurisdiction shall be made in the Probate Division.

2. The Guardian Ad Litem shall represent the interest of all plaintiffs under the age of 18 years with respect to the Petition and he/she shall file a written report with respect to the Petition and he/she shall file a written report with respect to the proposed apportionment of the settlement proceeds, and with respect to the determination of attorney's fees and costs and the apportionment thereof. Said written report shall be served on all interested parties. The Order approving the Petition may also award costs to the Guardian Ad Litem. The Guardian Ad Litem should serve on a pro bono publico basis, unless the Court determines that the matter is unusually time consuming or complex, or the Court finds that other extraordinary circumstances warrant a fee being allowed. If a fee is to be awarded, the Court may consider the reasonably anticipat-

ed remaining services to be performed by the Guardian Ad Litem. The Guardian Ad Litem shall be given an opportunity to testify at the hearing or telephonically at the discretion of the Court.

Part II Re: Court approval and appointment of the Guardian Ad Litems.

1. The court may appoint a Guardian Ad Litem to represent the minor's interest before approving a settlement of a minor's portion of the claim in any case in which a minor has a claim for personal injury, property damage, wrongful death, or other cause of action in which the gross settlement of the claims exceeds $15,000.00. *See* § 744.3025(1)(a), Fla. Stat. (2006).

2. The court shall appoint a Guardian Ad Litem to represent the minor's interest before approving a settlement of the minor's claim in any case in which the gross settlement involving a minor equals or exceeds $50,000.00. *See* § 744.3025(1)(b), Fla. Stat. (2006).

3. The appointment of the Guardian Ad Litem must be without the necessity of bond or notice. *See* § 744.3025(1)(c), Fla. Stat. (2006).

4. The duty of the Guardian Ad Litem is to protect the minor's interests as described in the Florida Probate Rules. *See* § 744.3025(1)(d), Fla. Stat. (2006), Fla. Prob. R. 5.636.

5. A court need not appoint a Guardian Ad Litem for the minor if a guardian of the minor has previously been appointed and that guardian has no potential adverse interest to the minor. A court may appoint a Guardian Ad Litem if the court believes a Guardian Ad Litem is necessary to protect the interests of the minor or the court determines that representation of the minor's interest is otherwise inadequate. *See* § 744.3025(1)(e), Fla. Stat. (2006), Fla. Prob. R. 5.636(d).

6. Unless waived, the court shall award reasonable fees and costs to the Guardian Ad Litem to be paid out of the gross proceeds of the settlement. *See* § 744.3025(2), Fla. Stat. (2006).

7. A proposed settlement is deemed to exceed $50,000.00 if the gross amount payable exceeds $50,000.00, without reduction to reflect present value or fees and costs. *See* Fla. Prob. R. 5.636(e).

8. A Guardian Ad Litem appointed with respect to a proposed settlement affecting the interests of a minor shall, not later than 5 days prior to the hearing on a petition for order authorizing settlement, file and serve a report indicating the Guardian Ad Litem's determination regarding whether the proposed settlement will be in the best interest of the minor. *See* Fla. Prob. R. 5.636(f) for details of what the report must contain.

Part III Re: Disbursement of settlement proceeds and Legal Guardianship.

1. Upon approval of the petition for settlement of the minor's claim including attorney's fees and costs the Judge before whom the civil action is pending in the General Jurisdiction Division shall enter an appropriate order which shall authorize the payment of the gross settlement proceeds into an interest-bearing trust account under the control and supervision of the attorney for the Plaintiff. Said order shall authorize such attorney to disburse to all plaintiffs, other than the minor(s) plaintiff(s) who are subject of a guardianship proceeding, the settlement proceeds which have been apportioned to such persons, and shall further authorize the disbursement of the approved attorney's fees and costs attributable to the minor's settlement. However, as to any net settlement proceeds which will be used to fund a tax-free structured settlement for the benefit of the minor, upon agreement of the parties, said proceeds may be held by the Defendant pending the funding of the structured settlement and a court order approving such. (See attached form order) The attorney's fees spent for the opening of the guardianship shall be included as a general rule in the attorney's fees in the personal injury case. When there is minimum compensation to the attorney in the personal injury case, then the Court may exercise its discretion and award additional attorney's fees.

2. If the net settlement to the minor exceeds $15,000.00, the settlement may be approved by the General Jurisdiction Judge, subject to the establishment of a legal guardianship in the Probate Division and the appointment of a Guardian of the Property to receive the minor's net settlement share, pursuant to § 744.387, Florida Statutes (2002). (See attached form order). No settlement after an action has been commenced by or on behalf of a ward shall be effective unless approved by the court having jurisdiction of the action. § 744.387(3)(a), Fla. Stat. (2002).

3. After the guardianship is established by the Probate Division Judge and the attorney's trust account is in receipt of the minor's net settlement share of the settlement, the Probate Division Judge shall have the sole discretion to direct further disbursements of the minor's funds from the attorney's trust account to an appropriate financial institution/depository; whether disbursements are structured settlements, special needs trust, or the like. Disbursements are only to be made pursuant to a court disbursement order. Copies of the signed closing statement, Guardian Ad Litem's report, and the Final Order from the General Jurisdiction Division shall be served on all interested persons. Any costs involved with the purchase of an annuity shall be included in the closing statement.

4. Copies of the Guardian Ad Litem's report, the closing statement, and final order of the General Jurisdiction Judge, and any other orders of disbursement, shall be promptly filed in the Probate guardianship file. After an order designating a restricted depository is entered by the Court, and after an order authorizing disbursement into a restricted depository is entered by the Court, the original depository receipt of assets shall be promptly filed into the Probate Division file. *See generally* § 69.031, Fla. Stat. (1967).

5. Upon entry of the order appointing a Guardian of the Property and directing payment of the minor's net settlement proceeds into the restricted depository or for the purchase of the annuity, the responsibilities of the Guardian Ad Litem shall be considered completed. Upon petition served on all interested persons, the General Jurisdiction Division Judge or Probate Division Judge shall enter an order discharging the Guardian Ad Litem.

This Administrative Order shall take effective immediately upon execution. Administrative Order No. 06–04 and Administrative Order No. 08–05 are hereby rescinded in their entirety and held for naught.

DONE AND ORDERED in Chambers at Miami–Dade, Florida, this ___ day of __________, 2008.

JOSEPH P. FARINA, CHIEF JUDGE
ELEVENTH JUDICIAL CIRCUIT OF FLORIDA

08–14. REASSIGNMENT AND CONSOLIDATION OF PUBLIC DEFENDER'S MOTIONS TO APPOINT OTHER COUNSEL IN UNAPPOINTED NONCAPITAL FELONY CASES

THE ELEVENTH JUDICIAL CIRCUIT MIAMI–DADE COUNTY, FLORIDA

CASE NO. 08–1 (Court Administration)

ADMINISTRATIVE ORDER NO. 08–14

IN RE: REASSIGNMENT AND CONSOLIDATION OF PUBLIC DEFENDER'S MOTIONS TO APPOINT OTHER COUNSEL IN UNAPPOINTED NONCAPITAL FELONY CASES

WHEREAS, pursuant to Rule 2.215, Rules of Judicial Administration, the Chief Judge is authorized to exercise administrative supervision over all courts within the judicial circuit in the exercise of judicial powers and over the judges and officers of the courts; and

WHEREAS, in the exercise of such judicial powers, the Chief Judge may adopt administrative orders to effectuate the efficient and proper administration of all courts within the circuit and to effect the prompt disposition of cases; and

WHEREAS, on June 24, 2008, the Honorable Bennett H. Brummer, Public Defender for the Eleventh Judicial Circuit of Florida, filed identical motions seeking to have the court appoint other counsel in unappointed noncapital felony cases, due to the Public Defender's alleged conflicts of interest with pending and future cases, with identical appendices in the following actions: *State of Florida v. Munoz*, Case No. F08–2314 (Judge John Thornton); *State of Florida v. McIntyre*, Case No. F08–5820 (Judge Bertila Soto); and *State of Florida v. Andujar*, Case No. F08–5109 (Judge Ellen Leesfield); and

WHEREAS, the undersigned Chief Judge finds it necessary to reassign and consolidate such motions under one section of the Circuit Court Criminal Division to effectuate the prompt disposition of these motions and to control the court's dockets;

NOW, THEREFORE, pursuant to authority vested in me as Chief Judge of the Eleventh Judicial Circuit of Florida, it is hereby **ORDERED:**

1. The Public Defender's motions to appoint other counsel in unappointed noncapital felony cases due to conflict of interest filed in *State of Florida v. Munoz*, Case No. F08–2314 (Judge John Thornton), *State of Florida v. McIntyre*, Case No. F08–5820 (Judge Bertila Soto), and *State of Florida v. Andujar*, Case No. F08–5109 (Judge Ellen Leesfield) are hereby reassigned and consolidated under Section CF 61 of the Circuit Court Criminal Division, before the Honorable Stanford Blake, Administrative Judge, Circuit Court Criminal Division.

2. The Clerk of the Court is hereby directed to appropriately reflect the reassignment and consolidation of the motions in the official court records and upon request from Judge Blake to forward to him any and all documents filed in connection with said motions.

3. It is further ordered that all similar or identical motions filed by the Public Defender in future unappointed noncapital felony cases be reassigned and consolidated before Judge Blake.

This Order shall become effective immediately upon signing, and shall remain in effect until further order of the Court.

DONE AND ORDERED in Chambers at Miami–Dade, Florida, this ___ day of _________, 2008.

JOSEPH P. FARINA, CHIEF JUDGE
ELEVENTH JUDICIAL CIRCUIT OF FLORIDA

07–07. ESTABLISHING PROCEDURES, REVISING ORDER, CREATING AND MAINTAINING QUALIFIED ARBITRATORS AND RE–ESTABLISHING COMPENSATION FOR COURT APPOINTED ARBITRATORS

THE ELEVENTH JUDICIAL CIRCUIT MIAMI–DADE COUNTY, FLORIDA

CASE NO. 07–1 (Court Administration)

ADMINISTRATIVE ORDER NO. 07–07 (Rescinding AO 5–03 and AO 5–03 A1)

IN RE: ESTABLISHING PROCEDURES, REVISING ORDER, CREATING AND MAINTAINING QUALIFIED ARBITRATORS AND RE–ESTABLISHING COMPENSATION FOR COURT APPOINTED ARBITRATORS

WHEREAS, pursuant to Fla. R. Civ. P. 1.810 and 1.820, the Chief Judge of this Circuit, or his designee, has the authority and responsibility for establishing procedures for determining the time and the place of arbitration hearings and for establishing other procedures for the expeditious and orderly operation of such hearings; and

WHEREAS, section 44.103, Fla. Stat. (2007), concerning court-ordered, nonbinding arbitration, has been amended by the Florida Legislature thereby necessitating revisions to certain procedures and the order of referral followed in connection with court appointed arbitrators for this Circuit; and

WHEREAS, pursuant to Administrative Order No. 05–03, as amended, the Court established procedures for creating and maintaining the "Circuit's List of Qualified Arbitrator's" and established a reasonable rate of compensation for such arbitrators; and

WHEREAS, this Order consolidates all such procedures and the rate of compensation;

NOW, THEREFORE, pursuant to the authority vested in me as Chief Judge of the Eleventh Judicial Circuit of Florida, it is hereby **ORDERED** that the following are hereby established as the procedures, order, and rate of compensation to be followed in connection with court appointed arbitrators:

1. Notice of Non–Binding Arbitration Hearing Procedures (Attached hereto as Attachment "A" and incorporated as if fully set forth herein)

2. Order of Referral to Non–Binding Arbitration (Attached hereto as Attachment "B" and incorporated as if fully set forth herein)

3. Official List of Qualified Arbitrators for the Eleventh Judicial Circuit (Attached hereto as Attachment "C" and incorporated as if fully set forth herein)[2] Said list, to be made available to all judges of the Circuit, is comprised of qualified persons, who are certified as arbitrators by the State of Florida and have agreed to serve as arbitrators for the Circuit. Pursuant to the Fla. R. Civ. P. 1.810(a), the List may be revised or updated as the need arises by the Director of the Arbitration/Mediation Division of the Circuit, as the Chief Judge's designee.

4. Compensation–The compensation of arbitrators selected by the Court from the list of qualified arbitrators shall be at the rate of One Hundred Fifty Dollars ($150.00) per hour. Such compensation shall be initially borne proportionally by each side unless otherwise agreed to by the parties or ordered by the Court. This cost may be taxed at the conclusion of the case pursuant to law.

This Administrative Order shall take effect on October 1, 2007, and shall remain in effect until further order of the Court. Administrative Order No. 5–03, entered on June 7, 2005 and Administrative Order No. 05–03 A1, entered on July 22, 2005, shall be rescinded in their entirety and held for naught on the effective date of this Order.

DONE AND ORDERED in Chambers at Miami–Dade, Florida, this ___ day of October, 2007.

____

JOSEPH P. FARINA
CHIEF JUDGE
ELEVENTH JUDICIAL CIRCUIT
OF FLORIDA

ATTACHMENT "A"

NOTICE OF NON–BINDING ARBITRATION HEARING PROCEDURES

PLEASE READ CAREFULLY

AUTHORITY

A judge may refer any contested civil action filed in a circuit or county court to non-binding arbitration § 44.103, Fla. Stat.

DESCRIPTION

Non-binding arbitration is a quasi-judicial proceeding conducted in an informal setting. The presentation of testimony and evidence shall be kept to a minimum, and most matters are to be presented through the statements and argument of counsel. The arbitrator is a finder of fact and applier of law. The arbitrator functions as judge and jury. The arbitrator's decision is not binding if the parties subsequently choose to seek a trial. *See* § 44.103 Fla. Stat. and Fla. R. Civ. P. 1.820(b).

DESIGNATION OF ARBITRATOR[S]

Arbitrators designated by the Court shall be selected from the list of certified arbitrators maintained by the Chief Judge or his designee pursuant to Fla. R. Civ. P. 1.810, and Administrative Order No. 07–07 Arbitrators shall comply with all ethical requirements set forth in the Florida Rules for Court Appointed Arbitrators.

COMMENCEMENT

The initial arbitration hearing shall be held within sixty (60) days of the signed referral order. Fla. R. Civ. P. 1.700(a). It is the responsibility of the chief arbitrator [1] to notify the parties in writing of the date, time, and place of all conferences and/or hearings unless the Order of Referral specifies the date, time and place. Fla. R. Civl. P. 1.700(a)(2).

POWER OF ARBITRATORS

An arbitrator, or the chief arbitrator of a panel, shall have authority to commence and adjourn the arbitration hearing, and carry out other such duties as are prescribed by § 44.103(4), Fla. Stat. The chief arbitrator shall not have authority to hold any person in contempt or in any way impose sanctions against any person. Fla. R. Civ. P. 1.820(a).

Any party to the arbitration may petition the court in the underlying action, for good cause shown, to authorize the arbitrator to issue subpoenas for the attendance of witnesses and for the production of books, records, documents, and other evidence at the arbitration and may petition the court for orders compelling such attendance and production at the arbitration. Subpoenas shall be served and shall be enforceable in the manner provided by law. See § 44.103(4), Fla. Stat.

CONDUCT OF HEARING

The arbitration hearing shall be conducted informally. Presentation of testimony shall be kept to a minimum, and matters shall be presented to the arbitrator primarily through the statements and arguments of counsel. Fla. R. Civ. P. 1.820(c). Also, a brief summary of the issues and facts shall be submitted to each arbitrator at least one (1) week before the arbitration hearing.

Individual parties or authorized representatives of corporate parties shall personally attend the arbitration hearing unless excused in advance by the chief arbitrator for good cause shown. Failure to appear without having been excused by the chief arbitrator or by the Court may result in the arbitrator rendering a decision based upon the evidence presented by parties in attendance.

COMPLETION

Arbitration shall be completed within thirty (30) days of the first arbitration hearing unless extended by order of the court on motion of the chief arbitrator or of a party. No extension of time shall be for a period exceeding sixty (60) days from the date of the first arbitration hearing. Fla. R. Civ. P. 1.820(g)(1).

DECISION AND TRIAL DE NOVO

At the conclusion of the presentation, the arbitrators[s] shall retire to consider and discuss the testimony and render a decision. The decision shall be reduced to writing and submitted to the parties within ten (10) days. Fla. R. Civ. P. 1.820(g)(3). The parties then shall have twenty (20) days from the date of service of the decision to move for trial. Fla. R. Civ. P. 1.820(h). If no such motion is made, the arbitration decision shall be final and shall be referred to the presiding judge who shall enter any orders or judgments as may be required to carry out the terms of the decision. Counsel is responsible for preparing and submitting any proposed orders or judgments for this purpose. Fla. R. Civ. P. 1.820(h).

Upon motion made by either party within 30 days after entry of judgment, the court may assess costs against the party requesting a trial de novo, including arbitration costs, court costs, reasonable attorney's fees, and other reasonable costs such as investigation expenses and expenses for expert or other testimony which were incurred after the arbitration hearing and continuing through the trial of the case in accordance with the guidelines for taxation of costs as adopted by the Supreme Court.

If a party in non-binding arbitration is not satisfied with the award and seeks a trial, as allowed, the party does so at the peril of having to pay all arbitration costs, court costs, attorneys' fees, investigation expenses for expert testimony or evidence, and other "reasonable costs" if the ultimate decision is not "more favorable than the arbitration decision." Specifically, if a plaintiff or petitioner requests a trial de novo after arbitration and obtains a judgment at trial which is at least Twenty-five (25) percent less than the arbitration award, then costs and attorney's fees shall be set off against the award. In addition, when the costs and attorney's fees total more than the amount of the judgment, the court shall enter judgment for the defendant against the plaintiff for the amount of the costs and attorney's fees, less the amount of the award to the plaintiff. Similarly, a defendant who files for a trial de novo may be liable for the plaintiffs' attorney's fees and costs if the judgment entered against the defendant is at least Twenty-five (25) percent more than the arbitration award. See, § 44.103(6), Fla. Stat.

1 In the case of a panel, one of the arbitrators shall be appointed as the chief arbitrator. Where there is only one arbitrator, that person shall be the chief arbitrator. Fla. R. Civ. P. 1.810. *See also* Fla. Arb. 11.010.

ATTACHMENT "B"

IN THE CIRCUIT COURT FOR THE 11TH JUDICIAL CIRCUIT IN AND FOR MIAMI–DADE COUNTY, FLORIDA

GENERAL JURISDICTION DIVISION

CASE NO.:

Plaintiff,

vs.

Defendant.

____________________________ /

ORDER OF REFERRAL TO NON-BINDING ARBITRATION

THIS COURT has reviewed its docket and the case file in this matter and has determined that this cause is appropriate for non-binding arbitration. Accordingly, pursuant to § 44.103, Florida Statutes, Fla. R. Civ. P. 1.700, 1.800, 1.1810 and 1.820 and upon this Court's own motion, and/or upon motion or stipulation of the parties, it is **ORDERED** as follows:

1. This case is referred to non-binding arbitration on all issues, including attorney's fees and costs.

2. Within fifteen (15) days after service of the "Order of Referral to Non-Binding Arbitration," the parties may agree upon the designation of one (1) or a panel of three (3) qualified arbitrators. If the parties are able to agree upon the designation of an arbitrator or a panel of arbitrators, the plaintiff or petitioner shall, within the time period set forth above, file with the Clerk of the Court, and with the arbitrator(s) contingently designated in paragraph three (3) below, a "Notice of Stipulation of Arbitrator(s)" which shall identify the name, address and the telephone number of the arbitrator or arbitrators agreed upon.

3. In the event the parties are unable to agree upon the designation of one or more qualified arbitrators within the period specified in paragraph two (2) of this Order and fail to timely file the "Notice of Stipulation of Arbitrator(s)," the Court designates and appoints __________, whose address is __________ and phone number is (___) __________ to serve as arbitrator in the case.

4. Court ordered non-binding arbitration shall be conducted in an informal manner. The presentation of testimony and evidence shall be kept to a minimum, and most matters are to be presented through the statements and argument of counsel.

5. Upon motion for good cause, the parties may petition the court to stay proceedings, pending arbitration.

6. The compensation of arbitrators selected by the Court from the list of qualified arbitrators shall be at the rate of One Hundred Fifty Dollars ($150.00) per hour. The cost shall be initially borne proportionally by each side unless otherwise agreed to by the parties or ordered by the Court. The cost may be taxed at the conclusion of the case pursuant to law.

7. Further, if a plaintiff or petitioner moves for a trial de novo after arbitration and obtains a judgment at trial which is at least Twenty-five (25) percent less than the arbitration award, then costs and attorney's fees shall be set off against the award. In addition, when the costs and attorney's fees total more than the amount of the judgment, the court shall enter judgment for the defendant against the plaintiff for the amount of the costs and attorney's fees, less the amount of the award to the plaintiff. Similarly, a defendant or respondent who moves for a trial de novo may be liable for the plaintiffs' attorney's fees and costs if the judgment entered against the defendant is at least Twenty-five (25) percent more than the arbitration award.

8. The procedures attached hereto, entitled "Notice of Non-binding Arbitration Hearing Procedures," are hereby incorporated into this Order and made a part hereof and shall be complied with by all persons subject to this Order.

DONE AND ORDERED at Miami–Dade County, Florida this ___ day of __________, 200 ___.

____

Circuit Court Judge

2 Attachment C not included, please see the 11th circuit's website for an up to date list of Qualified Arbitrators.

07–04. PROCEDURES FOR APPOINTMENT OF APPELLATE COUNSEL IN DEPENDENCY APPEALS

THE ELEVENTH JUDICIAL CIRCUIT MIAMI–DADE COUNTY, FLORIDA

CASE NO. 07–1 (Court Administration)

ADMINISTRATIVE ORDER NO. 07–04

IN RE: PROCEDURES FOR APPOINTMENT OF APPELLATE COUNSEL IN DEPENDENCY APPEALS

WHEREAS, the Eleventh Judicial Circuit and for Miami-Dade County, Florida recognizes the necessity to assure expeditious dependency appellate proceedings; and

WHEREAS, some of the delays in prosecuting dependency appeals result from confusion in the appointment of appellate counsel, the preparation of the record and transcripts; and

WHEREAS, clarification of the appointment of appellate counsel process in dependency cases is needed;

NOW, THEREFORE, pursuant to the authority vested in me as Chief Judge of the Eleventh Judicial Circuit of Florida, this Circuit hereby establishes the following procedures which shall be followed in the appointment of appellate counsel for dependency appeals:

1. When trial counsel receives the written final judgment rendered by the trial court and the client informs counsel that he/she wants to appeal the final judgment, trial counsel shall prepare a motion for appointment of appellate counsel.

2. The motion for appointment of appellate counsel shall be submitted to the division judge *ex parte* and shall include the following:

a. A copy of the Notice of Appeal, filed by the trial counsel;

b. A copy of the designations to the court reporter, including all trial dates;

c. Attestation that the attorney has spoken to the parent and affirmed that the parent wishes to appeal the order;

d. An order allowing payment of transcripts; and

e. A current affidavit of financial indigence.

3. The above-listed documents will be submitted to the case coordinator for the termination of parental rights back-up division ("case coordinator"), who will place the motion for appointment of appellate counsel and accompanying documents in front of the division judge within forty-eight (48) hours of receipt.

4. When the appointment has been signed by the division judge, the case coordinator shall place the order of appointment in the appointed lawyer's court house mail box and telephone the lawyer to inform him or her of the appointment.

5. Appellate counsel shall, upon receipt of the appointment, immediately file a substitution of counsel with the Third District Court of Appeal. *See, Interest of P.G.,* No. 2D06–1264, slip op. at 7–8 (Fla. 2nd, Nov. 17, 2006).

This Order shall take effect on March 1, 2007 and shall remain in effect until further order of the Court.

DONE AND ORDERED in Miami–Dade County this ___ day of February, 2007.

____

JOSEPH P. FARINA
CHIEF JUDGE
ELEVENTH JUDICIAL CIRCUIT
OF FLORIDA

ATTESTATION OF DESIRE TO SEEK APPEAL

IN THE INTEREST OF: Case No.:

____

Name of Child, Date of Birth

______________________/

I, ________, have conferred with the mother/father in the above-captioned case and hereby attest that he/she wishes to pursue an appeal of the final judgment adjudicating dependency/terminating parental rights (circle one).

____

Date

07–03. IMPLEMENTATION OF THE COMPLEX BUSINESS LITIGATION COURT PROCEDURES

THE ELEVENTH JUDICIAL CIRCUIT MIAMI–DADE COUNTY, FLORIDA

CASE NO. 07–1 (Court Administration)

ADMINISTRATIVE ORDER NO. 07–03

IN RE: IMPLEMENTATION OF THE COMPLEX BUSINESS LITIGATION COURT PROCEDURES

WHEREAS, pursuant to Administrative Order No. 06–40, the Complex Business Litigation Section was created within the General Jurisdiction Division of the Eleventh Judicial Circuit of Florida; and

WHEREAS, pursuant to such creation, the implementation of procedures is necessary to provide for efficient and effective processing of all actions in the Complex Business Litigation Section; and

WHEREAS, the Complex Business Litigation Section Procedures are designed to facilitate the pretrial and trial of cases by the Complex Business Litigation Section; and

WHEREAS, the Complex Business Litigation Section Procedures are intended to provide better access to court information for litigants, counsel, and the public; increase the efficiency and understanding of court personnel, counsel, and witnesses; decrease costs for litigants and others involved in the court system; and facilitate the efficient and effective presentation of evidence in the courtroom; and

WHEREAS, the Complex Business Litigation Section Procedures shall be construed and enforced to avoid technical delay, encourage civility, permit just and prompt determination of all proceedings, and promote the efficient administration of justice;

NOW, THEREFORE, pursuant to the authority vested in me as Chief Judge of the Eleventh Judicial Circuit of Florida under Florida Rule of Judicial Administration 2.050, it is hereby **ORDERED** that the Complex Business Litigation Section Court Procedures, attached hereto as Attachment "A", shall be adhered to by all litigants, counsel, and other applicable persons/entities involved in actions in the Complex Business Litigation Section within the General Jurisdiction Division of the Eleventh Judicial Circuit of Florida.

This Order shall take effect immediately and shall remain in effect until further order of the Court.

DONE AND ORDERED at Miami–Dade County, Florida, this ___ day of ________, 2007.

Joseph P. Farina
Chief Judge
Eleventh Judicial Circuit of Florida

ATTACHMENT "A"

COMPLEX BUSINESS LITIGATION SECTION PROCEDURES FOR THE ELEVENTH JUDICIAL CIRCUIT COURT, IN AND FOR MIAMI–DADE COUNTY, FLORIDA

SECTION 1—TITLE, SCOPE AND PURPOSE

1.1—Title: These Procedures shall be known and cited as the Complex Business Litigation Section Procedures. They may also be referred to in abbreviated form as "CLP".

1.2—Scope: The Complex Litigation Procedures shall apply to all actions in the Complex Business Litigation Section of the Civil Division of the Eleventh Judicial Circuit Court of Florida (also referred to herein as the "Complex Business Litigation Section"), except to the extent that, in any particular action, they are superseded by an order of the presiding Circuit Judge.

1.3—Purpose: The Complex Litigation Procedures are designed to facilitate the proceedings of cases by the Eleventh Judicial Circuit Complex Business Litigation Section; to promote the transmission and access to case information by the Court, litigants, counsel, and the public; and to facilitate the efficient and effective presentation of evidence in the courtroom. These Procedures shall be construed and enforced to avoid technical delay, encourage civility, permit just and prompt determination of all proceedings, and promote the efficient administration of justice.

1.4—Integration with Other Rules: These Procedures are intended to supplement, not supplant, the rules adopted by the Supreme Court of Florida. If any conflict exists between the Complex Litigation Procedures and the rules, then the rules shall control.

SECTION 2—CASE FILING, ASSIGNMENT, TRACKING, AND IDENTIFICATION

2.1—Cases Subject to Complex Business Litigation Section: The principles set out in Amended Administrative Order 2006–40 shall govern the assignment of cases to the Complex Business Litigation Section.

2.2—Case Identification Numbers: On assignment of any matter to the Complex Business Litigation Section, the action shall retain the civil action number assigned to it by the Clerk of Courts.

SECTION 3—CALENDARING, APPEARANCES, AND SETTLEMENT

3.1—Preparation of Calendar: The calendar for the Complex Business Litigation Section shall be prepared under the supervision of the Complex Business Litigation Section Judge and published in accordance with the administrative orders of the Court.

3.2—Appearances: An attorney who is notified to appear for any proceeding before the Court, must, consistent with ethical requirements, appear or have a partner, associate, or another attorney familiar with the case present.

3.3—Notification of Settlement: When any cause pending in the Complex Business Litigation Section is settled, all attorneys or unrepresented parties of record shall notify the Complex Business Litigation Section Judge within two (2) business days of the settlement and shall advise the Court of the party who will prepare and present the judgment, dismissal, or stipulation of dismissal and the date when such filings will be delivered to the Court.

SECTION 4—MOTION PRACTICE

4.1—Form of Motions, Responses, Replies: All motions, unless made orally during a hearing or a trial, shall be accompanied by a memorandum of law, except for the motions listed in CLP § 4.8. The memorandum of law shall not exceed twenty (20) pages in length. Each party opposing a motion shall serve an opposing memorandum of law not later than ten (10) days after service of the motion as computed in the Fla. R. Civ. P. 1.090. The opposing memorandum shall not exceed twenty (20) pages in length. Failure to comply with this rule may be deemed sufficient cause for granting the motion by default. The moving party may, within five (5) days after service of an opposing memorandum of law, serve a reply memorandum in support of the motion, which shall be strictly limited to rebuttal of matters raised in the memorandum in opposition without re-argument of matters covered in the moving party's initial memorandum of law. The reply memorandum shall not exceed ten (10) pages in length. These page limitations shall not be exceeded without permission of this Court.

4.2—Content of Motions: All motions shall state with particularity the grounds therefore, cite any statute or rule of procedure relied and shall set forth the relief sought. Factual statements in a motion for summary judgment shall be supported by specific citations to the supporting documents. The parties shall not raise issues at the hearing on the motion that were not addressed in the motion and memoranda in support of and in opposition to the motion. The practice of offering previously undisclosed cases to the Court at the hearing is specifically discouraged. Newly decided authority may be considered in compliance with CLP § 4.7.

4.3—Certificate of Good Faith Conference: Before filing any discovery motion or any other motion identified in CLP § 4.8, the moving party **shall** confer with counsel for the opposing party in a good faith effort to resolve the issues raised by the motion and **shall** file with the motion a statement consistent with subparagraph b certifying that the moving party has conferred with opposing counsel and that counsel have been unable to agree on the resolution of the motion (the "Certificate"). No conference and therefore no certificate is required in motions for injunctive relief without notice.

a. The term "confer," as used herein, requires a substantive conversation in person or by telephone in a good faith effort to resolve the motion without court action and does not envision a written exchange of ultimatums. Counsel who merely attempt to confer have not conferred. Counsel **shall** respond promptly to inquiries and communications from opposing counsel. The Court may sua sponte deny motions that fail to include an appropriate and complete Certificate under this section.

b. The Certificate shall set forth the date of the conference, the names of the participating attorneys, and the specific results achieved. It shall be the responsibility of counsel for the moving party to arrange for the conference.

c. Before filing a motion to dismiss, the moving party shall confer with the opposing party, explaining the bases for the prospective motion. If the opposing party agrees with the prospective motion to dismiss and requests to file a curative pleading, the moving party shall stipulate to the filing of a curative pleading in lieu of filing a motion to dismiss.

4.4—Motions May Be Decided on Papers and Memoranda: Unless otherwise ordered by the Court, non-dispositive motions and those found in CLP § 4.8 shall be considered and decided by the Court on the pleadings, admissible evidence, the court file, and memoranda, without hearing or oral argument. Any party seeking oral argument shall file a request setting forth the reasons oral argument would be of assistance to the Court. If the Court grants oral argument on any motion, it shall give the parties at least five (5) business days' notice of the date and place of oral argument. The Court, for good cause shown, may shorten the five (5) day notice period. All papers relating to the issues to be argued at the hearing set with ten (10) day or more prior notice shall be delivered to opposing counsel and the Court at least five (5) business days before the hearing. Service and receipt of the papers less than five (5) business days before the hearing is presumptively unreasonable.

4.5—Motions for Summary Judgment: Motions for summary judgment shall comply with CLP § 4.1 and attach a concise statement of the material facts which the moving party contends are undisputed. The summary judgment motion shall reference pleadings, depositions, answers to interrogatories, answers to admissions, and affidavits, all of which shall be filed with the Court simultaneously with the filing of the motion for summary judgment, unless previously filed with the Court for another purpose. The papers opposing a motion for summary judgment shall comply with CLP § 4.1 and attach a single concise statement of the disputed material facts as to which it is contended that there exists a genuine issue to be tried, which shall reference pleadings, depositions, answers to interrogatories, answers to admissions, and affidavits on file with the Court. No statement of facts shall exceed ten (10) pages in length, absent permission of the Court.

4.6—Font and Spacing Requirements: All motions and memoranda shall be double-spaced on 8.5″ × 11″ paper with a 1″ margin and in Times New Roman or Arial with a minimum 12-point font.

4.7—Suggestion of Subsequently Decided Authority: A suggestion of controlling or persuasive authority that was decided after the filing of the last memorandum may be filed at any time prior to the Court's ruling and shall contain only the citation to the authority relied upon, if published, or a copy of the authority if it is unpublished, and shall not contain argument.

4.8—Motions Not Requiring Memoranda: Memoranda of law are not required by either the movant or the opposing party, unless otherwise directed by the Court, with respect to the following motions:

a. discovery motions (except as provided in CLP § 4.12);

b. extensions of time for the performance of an act required or allowed to be done, provided that the request is made before the expiration of the period originally prescribed or extended by previous orders;

c. to continue a pre-trial conference, hearing, or the trial of an action;

d. to add or substitute parties;

e. to amend the pleadings;

f. to file supplemental pleadings;

g. to appoint a next friend or guardian ad litem;

h. for pro hac vice admission of counsel who are not members of The Florida Bar;

i. relief from the page limitations imposed by these Procedures; and

j. request for oral argument.

The above motions shall state good cause therefor and cite any applicable rule, statute or other authority justifying the relief sought. These motions shall be accompanied by proposed orders.

4.9—Failure to File and Serve Motion Materials: Except upon a showing a good cause, the failure to file a memorandum within the time specified in CLP § 4.1 shall constitute a waiver of the right thereafter to file such memorandum. A motion unaccompanied by a required memorandum may, in the discretion of the Court, be summarily rejected or denied. Failure to timely file a memorandum in opposition to a motion may result in the pending motion being considered and decided as an uncontested motion.

4.10—Preparation and Submission of Proposed Orders: All motions identified in CLP §§ 4.8 and 4.12 shall be accompanied by a proposed order. The Court may direct parties to submit proposed orders in electronic and/or paper format. Each motion shall be accompanied by postage pre-paid envelopes addressed to all counsel or record and pro se parties. If, after ruling, the Court directs a party to submit an order, the Court will not enter the order submitted unless the submitting party represents that he or she has provided the order to each opposing party and there are no objections to the form of the order. If an agreement cannot be reached, the objecting party shall submit a brief statement of the objections without rearguing the Court's ruling and if available, a transcript of the proceeding may be submitted in conjunction with any proposed order or objection.

4.11—Determination of Motions On Oral Argument Without Briefs: The parties may present motions and the Court may resolve disputes regarding the matters described in CLP § 4.8 through the use of an expedited limited hearing. Applicable motions are those that are limited to matters which can be argued and determined in ten (10) minutes or less, and may be heard on the Court's Motion Calendar docket.

4.12—Motions to Compel and for Protective Order: All motions to compel compliance with discovery or for protective order from discovery shall comply with the following:

a. Except for motions grounded upon complete failure to respond to the discovery sought to be compelled or upon assertion of general or blanket objections to discovery, motions to compel discovery in accordance with Fla. R. Civ. P. 1.310, 1.320, 1.340, 1.350, 1.351, and 1.370 shall set forth each separate interrogatory question, request for production, request for admission, subpoena request, or deposition question, followed by: (i) the specific item to be compelled; (ii) the specific objections; (iii) the grounds assigned for the objection (if not apparent from the objection); and (iv) the reasons assigned as supporting the motion as it relates that specific item. The party shall write this information in immediate succession (e.g., specific request for production, objection, grounds for the objection, reasons to support motion; next request for production, objection, grounds for the objection, reasons to support motion; and so on) to enable the Court to rule separately on each individual item in the motion.

b. Except for motions for an order to protect a party or other person from whom discovery is sought from having to respond to an entire set of written discovery, from having to appear at a deposition, or from having to comply with an entire subpoena for production or inspection, motions for protective order under Florida Rule of Civil Procedure 1.280(c) shall, for each separate interrogatory question, request for production, request for admission, subpoena request, or deposition question, followed by: (i) the specific item of discovery; (ii) the type of protection the party requests; and (iii) the reasons supporting the protection. The party shall write this information in immediate succession (e.g., specific request for protection, protection sought for that request for production, reasons to support protection, next request for production, protection sought for that request for production, reasons to support protection, and so on) to enable the Court to rule separately on each individual item in the motion.

4.13—Motions to File Under Seal: Whether documents filed in a case may be filed under seal is a separate issue from whether the parties may agree that produced documents are confidential. Motions to file under seal are disfavored particularly when the portions of the document which the Court should consider may be submitted in redacted form in lieu of a sealed filing. A party seeking to file a document under seal must first file a motion to file under seal. The motion will be addressed in the same manner as a motion to file under seal in any other proceeding in the Civil Division of the Eleventh Judicial Circuit Court of Florida and consistent with A.O. 06–36. The motion, whether granted or denied, will remain in the public record.

4.14—Emergency Motions, Injunctions, Motions to Appoint Receiver: The Court may consider and determine emergency motions, including motions seeking injunctive relief or the appointment of a receiver at any time. Counsel should be aware that the designation of a motion as an "emergency" requires that counsel be immediately available for setting of an expedited hearing at the earliest available time on the Court's calendar. The Court may sanction any counsel or party who designates a motion as an emergency under circumstances that are not true emergencies, or who designates a motion as an emergency and then, due to a scheduling conflict, fails to appear for the hearing on the motion at the earliest available time the judge has to address the emergency motion.

SECTION 5—MANDATORY CASE MANAGEMENT CONFERENCE

5.1—Notice of Hearing and Order on Case Management Conference: Within thirty (30) days of filing or transfer of an action to the Complex Business Litigation Section, the Court will issue and serve a Notice of Hearing and Order on Case Management Conference (the "Notice"). Plaintiff's counsel shall immediately thereafter serve a copy of the Notice on all Defendants. Defendants shall immediately serve a copy of the Notice on all Third Party Defendants.

5.2—Case Management Meeting: Regardless of the pendency of any undecided motions, thirty (30) days prior to the Case Management Conference ("CMC"), lead trial counsel shall meet to discuss the following subjects,

a. Issues related to the pleading, whether a demand for jury trial has been made, service of process, venue, joinder of additional parties, theories of liability, damages claimed and applicable defenses;

b. The identity and number of any motions to dismiss or other preliminary or pre-discovery motions that have been filed or the time period within which such motions shall be filed, briefed and argued;

c. A discovery plan and schedule including the length of the discovery period, the number of fact witnesses and witnesses' depositions to be permitted and, as appropriate, the length and sequence of such depositions;

d. Anticipated areas of expert witness testimony, timing for identification of experts witnesses, responses to expert witnesses discovery and exchange of expert witness reports;

e. An estimate of the volume of documents and computerized information likely to be the subject of discovery from parties and nonparties and whether there are technological means that may render document discovery more manageable at an acceptable cost;

f. The advisability of using the general magistrate or a special magistrate for fact finding, mediation, discovery disputes or such other matters as the parties may agree upon;

g. The time period after the close of discovery within which post-discovery dispositive motions shall be filed, briefed and argued and a tentative schedule for such motions;

h. The possibility of settlement and the timing of Alternative Dispute Resolution, including the selection of a mediator or arbitrator(s);

i. Whether or not a party desires to use technologically advanced methods of presentation or court reporting and, to the extent this is the case, a determination of the following:

1. Fairness issues, including but not necessarily limited to use of such capabilities by some but not all parties and by parties whose resources permit or require variations in the use of such capabilities;

2. Issues related to compatibility of court and party facilities and equipment;

3. Issues related to the use of demonstrative exhibits and any balancing of relevance and potential prejudice that may need to occur in connection with such exhibits;

4. The feasibility of sharing the technology resources or platforms among all parties so as to minimize disruption at trial; and

5. Such other issues related to the use of the Court's and parties' special technological facilities as may be raised by any party, the Court or the Court's technological advisor, given the nature of the case and the resources of the parties.

j. A good faith estimate by each party based upon consultation among the parties of the costs each party is likely to incur in pursuing the litigation through trial court adjudication;

k. A preliminary listing of the disputed legal principles and material facts at issue;

l. A preliminary listing of any legal principle and facts that are not in dispute;

m. A good faith estimate by each party of the length of time to try the case; and

n. Such other matters as the Court may assign to the parties for their consideration.

5.3—Joint Case Management Report: No less than ten (10) days in advance of the CMC, the Parties shall file the Joint Case Management Report addressing the matters described above and shall provide the Court, but not file with the clerk, a diskette, CD or e-mail attachment containing the Joint Case Management Report. All counsel and parties are responsible for filing a Joint Case Management Report in full compliance with these Procedures. Plaintiff's counsel shall have the primary responsibility to coordinate the meeting between the parties and the filing of the Joint Case Management Report. If a non-lawyer plaintiff is proceeding pro se, defense counsel shall coordinate compliance. If counsel is unable to coordinate such compliance, counsel shall timely notify the Court by written motion and request for a status conference.

5.4—Case Management Conference: The attendance by lead trial counsel and a party representative for each party is mandatory. The Court will hear the views of counsel on such issues listed in CLP § 6.2 above as are pertinent to the case or on which there are material differences of opinion.

5.5—Case Management Order. Following the CMC, the Court will issue a Case Management Order. The provisions of the Case Management Order may not be deviated from without notice, an opportunity to be heard, a showing of good cause and entry of an order by the Court.

The Case Management Order may also specify a schedule of status conferences, when necessary, to assess the functioning of the Case Management Order, assess the progress of the case, and enter such further revisions to the Case Management Order as the Court may deem necessary or appropriate.

SECTION 6—DISCOVERY

6.1—No Filing of Discovery Materials. Depositions and deposition notices, notices of serving interrogatories, interrogatories, requests for documents, requests for admission, and answers and responses thereto shall not be filed unless the Court so orders or unless the parties will rely on such discovery documents for a pending matter before the Court. Absent an order permitting the filing of the discovery material, at the time of filing any discovery material counsel shall file a separate written certification that counsel believes in good faith that it is necessary for the Court to consider the discovery material for a pending matter, which shall identify the pending matter with particularity. All discovery materials relating to a motion for summary judgment (i.e., summary judgment evidence) shall be filed simultaneously with the motion for summary judgment and not beforehand, unless previously filed for another purpose. The party taking a deposition or obtaining any material through discovery (including through third party discovery) is responsible for the preservation and delivery of such material to the Court when needed or ordered in the form specified by the Court.

6.2—Discovery with Respect to Expert Witnesses: Discovery with respect to experts must be conducted within the discovery period established by the Case Management Order. In complying with the obligation to exchange reports relating to experts, the parties shall disclose the information identified in Florida Rule of Civil Procedure 1.280(a)(4)(A). Each party offering an expert witness shall provide three alternative dates for the deposition of the expert.

6.3—Completion of Discovery: The requirement that discovery be completed within a specified time mandates that adequate provisions must be made for interrogatories and requests for admission to be answered, for documents to be produced, and for depositions to be held within the discovery period.

6.4—Extension of the Discovery Period or Request for Additional Discovery: Motions seeking an extension of the discovery period or permission to take more discovery than is permitted under the Case Management Order shall be presented prior to the expiration of the time within which discovery is required to be completed. Such motions must set forth good cause justifying the additional time or additional discovery and will only be granted upon such a showing of good cause and that the parties have diligently pursued discovery.

6.5—Confidentiality Agreements: The parties may reach their own agreement regarding the designation of materials as confidential. There is no requirement that the Court endorse the confidentiality agreement in advance. The parties may submit an agreed confidentiality order. On the motion of any party, the Court will enforce the parties' signed confidentiality agreement against any other signing party, and may exercise its contempt powers against the signing party or the signing party's counsel, provided that the Court makes a specific finding that the confidentiality agreement is reasonable and consistent with the public interest. Each confidentiality agreement shall provide or shall be deemed to provide that no party shall file documents under seal without having first obtained an order granting leave of Court to file documents under seal based upon a showing of particularized need.

6.6—General Magistrate and Special Magistrates: The Court may, at any time, on its own motion or on the motion of any party, refer a pending matter or matters to a general magistrate or may appoint a special magistrate in any given case pending in the Business Litigation Section Court in accordance with Fla. R. Civ. P. 1.490. Unless otherwise directed, the parties shall equally share the cost of proceeding before a special magistrate, although such fees may ultimately be taxed as costs.

SECTION 7—VIDEOCONFERENCING

7.1—By Agreement. By mutual agreement of all parties, counsel may arrange for any proceeding or conference may be held by videoconference. All counsel and other participants shall be subject to the same rules of procedure and decorum as if participants were present in the courtroom.

7.2—Responsibility for Videoconferencing: The parties are responsible for obtaining all communications facilities and arranging all details as may be required to connect and interface with the videoconferencing equipment, if any, already available to the Complex Business Litigation Section. The Court will endeavor to make reasonable technical assistance available to the parties, but all responsibility for planning and executing all technical considerations required to successfully hold a videoconference shall remain solely with the parties.

7.3—Allocation of Videoconferencing Costs: In the absence of a contrary directive of the Court or agreement among the parties, the parties participating by videoconference shall bear their own costs of participating via this method.

7.4—Court Reporter: The court reporter transcribing any videoconference proceeding shall be present in the same room as the presiding judge.

7.5—Exchange of Exhibits and Evidence to Be Used in Videoconference Hearing. Absent good cause shown, any evidence to be offered at a videoconference hearing shall be provided to opposing counsel and to the Court five (5) business days prior to the date of the hearing, and shall bear an exhibit label and identification number. Objections to any evidence which is provided five (5) business days before the hearing shall be submitted to the Court at least two (2) business days before the hearing and reference the appropriate exhibit tags.

SECTION 8—ALTERNATIVE DISPUTE RESOLUTION

8.1—Alternative Dispute Resolution Mandatory in All Cases: Alternative Dispute Resolution ("ADR") is a valued tool in the resolution of litigated matters. An appropriate mechanism for ADR shall be discussed by the Court and counsel at the Case Management Conference. The Case Management Order shall order the parties to a specific ADR process, to be conducted either by a Court-assigned or an agreed-upon facilitator and shall establish a deadline for its completion.

8.2—Mediation:

a. Confidential Case Summaries. Not less than five (5) business days prior to the mediation conference, each party shall deliver to the mediator a confidential written summary of the facts and issues of the case.

b. Identification of Business Representative. As part of the written summary, counsel for each corporate party shall state the name and general job description of the employee or agent who will attend and participate with full authority to settle on behalf of the business entity.

c. Attendance Requirements and Sanctions. Lead trial counsel and each party (including, in the case of a business party, a business representative, and in the case of an insurance company, the insurance company representative as set forth in Florida Rule of Civil Procedure 1.720(b)(3)) with full authority to settle **shall** attend and participate in the mediation conference. In the case of an insurance company, the term "full authority to settle" means authority to settle up to the amount of the party's last demand or the policy limits, whichever is less, without further consultation. The Court may impose sanctions upon lead trial counsel and parties who do not attend and participate in good faith in the mediation conference.

d. Authority to Declare Impasse. Participants shall be prepared to spend as much time as may be reasonably necessary to settle the case. No participant may force the early conclusion of mediation because of travel plans or other engagements. Only the mediator may declare an impasse or end the mediation.

e. Rate of Compensation. The mediator shall be compensated at an hourly rate stipulated by the parties in advance of mediation.

f. Settlement and Report of Mediator. A settlement agreement reached between the parties shall be reduced to writing and signed by the parties and their attorneys in the presence of the mediator. Within five (5) business days of the conclusion of the mediation conference, the mediator shall file and serve a written mediation report stating whether all required parties were present, whether the case settled, and whether the mediator was forced to declare an impasse.

8.3—Non-Binding Arbitration: The parties may agree or the Court may order non-binding arbitration or it may be ordered upon motion of any party. Non–binding arbitration shall be pursuant to Florida Rule of Civil Procedure 1.820. The rules governing the arbitration shall be selected by the parties or failing agreement, the Court will order use of all or a part of the arbitration rules common to the Eleventh Judicial Circuit, the American Arbitration Association, or other available rules.

SECTION 9—JOINT FINAL PRETRIAL STATEMENT

9.1—Meeting and Preparation of Joint Final Pretrial Statement: The case must be fully ready for trial when the Joint Final Pretrial Statement is filed. Lead trial counsel for all parties, or the parties themselves if unrepresented, shall sign the Joint Final Pretrial Statement. The Court may strike pretrial statements that are unilateral, incompletely executed, or otherwise incomplete. Inadequate stipulations of fact and law may be stricken. Sanctions may be imposed for failure to comply with this section, including attorneys fees and/or the striking of pleadings.

9.2—Contents of Joint Final Pretrial Statement:

a. Jury Selection.

1. Preemptory Strikes. Subject to the limitations imposed by Florida Rule of Civil Procedure 1.431(d), in cases involving multiple parties, the parties shall stipulate to the number of peremptory challenges to be exercised by each side.

2. Proposed Voir Dire Questionnaire. If a party wants to use a special written questionnaire for jurors to complete prior to voir dire, the proposed questionnaire shall be attached to the Joint Final Pretrial Statement and included in the discussions leading to the preparation of the Final Joint Pretrial Statement. The questionnaire shall not exceed three (3) pages, including space for the juror responses, and shall comply with the requirements of CLP § 5.12.

b. Stipulated Facts. The Parties shall stipulate to as many facts and issues as possible. To assist the Court, the parties shall make an active and substantial effort to stipulate at length and in detail as to agreed facts and law, and to limit, narrow and simplify the issues of fact and law that remain contested.

c. Exhibit List. An exhibit list containing a description of all exhibits to be introduced at trial and in compliance with the approved form approved by the Court shall be filed with the Joint Final Pretrial Statement. Each party shall maintain a list of exhibits on disk or CD to allow a final list of exhibits to be provided to the Clerk of Court at the close of the evidence. Unlisted exhibits will not be received into evidence at trial, except by order of the Court in the furtherance of justice. The Joint Final Pretrial Statement must attach each party's exhibit list on the approved form listing each specific objection ("all objections reserved" does not suffice) to each numbered exhibit that remains after full discussion and stipulation. Objections not made, including objections not made with specificity are waived. Counsel for each party shall prepare an exhibit notebook for the Court and one for each other party.

d. Witness List. The parties and counsel shall prepare a witness list designating in good faith which witnesses will likely be called and which witnesses may be called if necessary. Absent good cause, the Court will not permit testimony from unlisted witnesses at trial over objection. This restriction does not apply to rebuttal witnesses. Records custodians may be listed, but will not likely be called at trial, except in the event that authenticity or foundation is contested. Notwithstanding the Complex Litigation Procedures regarding videoconferencing, for good cause shown in compelling circumstances the Court may permit presentation of testimony in open court by contemporaneous transmission from a different location.

e. Depositions. The Court encourages stipulations of fact to avoid calling unnecessary witnesses. Where a stipulation will not suffice, the Court permits the use of reading deposition transcripts as well as videotaped depositions at trial. At the required meeting, counsel and unrepresented parties **shall** agree upon and specify in writing in the Joint Final Pretrial Statement the pages and lines of each deposition (except where used solely for impeachment) to be published to the trier of fact. The parties shall include in the Joint Final Pretrial Statement a page-and-line description of any testimony that remains in dispute after an active and substantial effort at resolution, together with argument and authority for each party's position. The parties **shall** prepare for submission and consideration at the final pretrial conference or trial edited and marked copies of any depositions or deposition excerpts which are to be offered into evidence, including edited videotaped depositions. Designation of an entire deposition will not be permitted except on a showing of necessity.

f. Joint Jury Instructions, Verdict Form. In cases to be tried before a jury, counsel shall attach to the Joint Final Pretrial Statement a copy and an original set of jointly-proposed jury instructions, together with a single jointly-proposed jury verdict form. The parties should be considerate of their juries, and therefore should submit short, concise verdict forms. The Court prefers pattern jury instructions approved by the Supreme Court of Florida. A party may include at the appropriate place in the single set of jointly-proposed jury instructions a contested charge, so designated with the name of the requesting party and bearing at the bottom a citation of authority for its inclusion, together with a summary of the opposing party's objection. The parties shall submit a computer diskette or CD containing the single set of jury instructions and verdict form with the Joint Final Pretrial Statement.

g. Juror Notebooks. If the parties agree, the jury may have notebooks to aid them in the hearing and deliberation of the case. The parties shall stipulate to the notebook contents and one notebook for each juror (including alternates), the judge, and each opposing party shall be prepared and brought to trial. The notebooks shall be identical in every respect and shall contain only those exhibits that the parties intend to use at trial. The proposed contents to be placed in the notebooks **shall** be provided to all other parties prior to the Final Pretrial Conference. Any disagreements about the content of a notebook shall be resolved at the Final Pretrial Conference.

9.3—Coordination of Joint Final Pretrial Statement: All counsel and parties are responsible for filing a Joint Final Pretrial Statement in full compliance with these Procedures. Plaintiff's counsel shall have the **primary** responsibility to coordinate the meeting of lead trial counsel and unrepresented parties and the filing of a Joint Final Pretrial Statement and related material. If a non-lawyer plaintiff is proceeding pro se, then defense counsel shall coordinate compliance. If counsel is unable to coordinate such compliance, counsel shall timely notify the Court by written motion and request for a status conference.

SECTION 10—TRIAL MEMORANDA AND OTHER MATERIALS

10.1—Trial Memoranda: In the case of a non-jury trial, no later than ten (10) days before the first day of the trial period for which the trial is scheduled, the parties shall file and serve Trial Memoranda with proposed findings of fact and conclusions of law, together with a computer diskette or CD. In the case of a jury trial, no later than ten (10) days before the first day of the trial period for which the trial is scheduled, the parties may file and serve Trial Memoranda, together with a computer diskette or CD.

SECTION 11—FINAL PRETRIAL CONFERENCE

11.1—Mandatory Attendance: Lead trial counsel and local counsel for each party, together with any unrepresented party, **shall** attend the final pretrial conference in person unless previously excused by the Court.

11.2—Substance of Final Pretrial Conference. At the final pretrial conference, all counsel and parties must be prepared and authorized to address the following matters: the formulation and simplification of the issues; the elimination of frivolous claims or defenses; admitting facts and documents to avoid unnecessary proof; stipulating to the authenticity of documents; obtaining advance rulings from the Court on the admissibility of evidence; settlement and the use of special procedures to assist in resolving the dispute; disposing of pending motions; establishing a reasonable limit on the time allowed for presenting evidence and argument; and such other matters as may facilitate the just, speedy, and inexpensive disposition of the actions.

07–02 (A1). SUPPLEMENTAL PROCEDURES FOR SPECIAL INTEREST/HIGH VISIBILITY PROCEEDINGS AT RICHARD E. GERSTEIN JUSTICE BUILDING

THE ELEVENTH JUDICIAL CIRCUIT MIAMI–DADE COUNTY, FLORIDA

CASE NO. 07–1 (Court Administration)

ADMINISTRATIVE ORDER NO. 07–02 A–1 (Supplementing AO No. 07–02)

IN RE: SUPPLEMENTAL PROCEDURES FOR SPECIAL INTEREST/HIGH VISIBILITY PROCEEDINGS AT RICHARD E. GERSTEIN JUSTICE BUILDING

WHEREAS, pursuant to Administrative Order No. 7–02, entered on January 12, 2007, this Court established procedures to be implemented for special interest/high profile proceedings scheduled to be heard at the RICHARD E. GERSTEIN JUSTICE BUILDING, located at 1351 N.W. 12th Street, Miami, Florida; and

WHEREAS, inasmuch as jurors in such proceedings must be assured of the ability to go about their daily business without being identified or accosted by individuals in the community who may recognize their names or faces from media coverage of the proceedings, reasonable steps need to be taken to restrict the release of identifying information of the jurors; and

WHEREAS, every court has supervisory powers over its own records and transcripts;

NOW, THEREFORE, pursuant to the authority vested in me as Chief Judge of the Eleventh Judicial Circuit of Florida, Administrative Order No. 07–02 is hereby supplemented to set forth the restrictions regarding juror identification which shall remain in effect until the conclusion of the special interest/high visibility proceedings, unless otherwise provided by order of the court, as follows:

1. The clerk of the court shall not release to any person the names, addresses, or any other identifying information concerning **prospective or seated jurors.**

2. Trial Counsel for the State of Florida and the Defendant(s) are hereby exempted from the above provision and shall be given full access to potential juror information. Trial Counsel may use such information to investigate for the purposes of the voir dire process, but shall not reveal this information to anyone who is not a party to this action or a member of the trial counsel's litigation team.

3. On jury selection days, **prospective jurors** will be assigned numbers. In open court, the presiding Judge, trial counsel, the courtroom clerk, and personnel in the jury division of the Clerk's office, shall refer to the **prospective jurors (and eventually seated jurors)** only by their respective numbers. At no time shall anyone in open court reference a prospective or seated juror by name or reveal juror-identifying information, such as home addresses.

4. The faces of **prospective and sitting jurors** shall not be photographed, videotaped, drawn or in any manner revealed from voir dire through the conclusion of the trial.

Except as herein supplemented, Administrative Order No. 7–02 remains in full force and effective.

DONE AND ORDERED in Chambers at Miami–Dade, Florida, this ___ day of _________, 2007.

____
JOSEPH P. FARINA
CHIEF JUDGE
ELEVENTH JUDICIAL CIRCUIT OF FLORIDA

07–02. PROCEDURES FOR SPECIAL INTEREST/HIGH VISIBILITY PROCEEDINGS AT RICHARD E. GERSTEIN JUSTICE BUILDING

THE ELEVENTH JUDICIAL CIRCUIT MIAMI–DADE COUNTY, FLORIDA

CASE NO. 07–1 (Court Administration)

ADMINISTRATIVE ORDER NO. 07–02

IN RE: PROCEDURES FOR SPECIAL INTEREST/HIGH VISIBILITY PROCEEDINGS AT RICHARD E. GERSTEIN JUSTICE BUILDING

WHEREAS, the Supreme Court of Florida, in Rule 2.450 Florida Rules of Judicial Administration, has promulgated standards of conduct and technology for electronic media and still photography coverage of public judicial proceedings; and

WHEREAS, any media coverage of public judicial proceedings is subject at all times to the authority of the presiding judge to: (i) control the conduct of proceedings before the court; (ii) ensure decorum and prevent distractions; and (iii) ensure the fair administration of justice in the pending cause; and

WHEREAS, special interest/high visibility proceedings require procedures and special accommodations to ensure full access without compromising the right of any litigant to a fair and orderly trial; and

NOW, THEREFORE, pursuant to the authority vested in me as Chief Judge of the Eleventh Judicial Circuit of Florida, I hereby establish the following procedures to be implemented for special interest/high profile proceedings scheduled to be heard at the **RICHARD E. GERSTEIN JUSTICE BUILDING**, located at 1351 N.W. 12th Street, Miami, Florida:

1. The undersigned Chief Judge, independently, or at the request of the administrative or trial judge assigned to preside over a proceeding of great public interest, may instruct the Court Public Information Officer ("PIO") to implement the procedures set forth within this Administrative Order.

2. Upon implementation of this Order, the Court PIO shall as soon as practicable convene a meeting of interested media representatives for the purpose of establishing a media committee which will establish media protocols for the specific case. The Court PIO will continue to act as liaison between the Court and the media for the duration of the case.

3. The media committee shall consist of at least one representative from the video broadcast, audio broadcast and print media, as well as the Court PIO, the Court Operations Director, the Administrative Judge or his designee, and the Clerk of Court or his designee. Other media representatives or Court personnel may also be included when necessary.

4. The duties of the media committee shall include: designating pool coverage and camera locations in accordance with Rule 2.450, Fla. R. Jud. Adm.; recommending to the administrative judge suitable interview and press conference areas; assisting with the allocation of court-issued press credentials and courtroom seating assignments; overseeing the dissemination of information and providing a clearinghouse for media/court issues arising during the case; equipping the media room(s); working with the court to accommodate other special needs of the media; and setting up a final meeting of media personnel a few days prior to the commencement of the proceedings to explain procedures and instructions.

5. A media room will be designated within close proximity to the special interest proceeding. The media room, under the supervision of the Court PIO or Court Operations Director, will be open during normal working hours to all media representatives with court-issued credentials. The room will accommodate monitors and other equipment provided by the media committee to permit coverage of the proceedings by media representatives who are unable to obtain seating in the courtroom.

6. No more than one manned video camera, one remote-controlled video camera, and one still photography camera will be allowed in the courtroom, except as may be otherwise authorized by the Chief Judge or his designee. Locations for these cameras will be coordinated in advance with the Court PIO.

7. So as not to interfere with court proceedings or with a litigant or interested party's rights, no interviews are permitted within or immediately outside the courtroom at any time. Media personnel shall ensure that no hallways, exits or emergency exits are blocked by media equipment and/or media personnel. Due to public access issues and life safety concerns, any interviews to be conducted immediately outside the

Richard E. Gerstein Justice Building shall be held in the areas designated for that purpose.

8. For trials held in courtrooms of the Richard E. Gerstein Justice Building, the areas both inside and outside the courtrooms will be monitored by Court Liaison Officers of the Miami–Dade Police Department. All persons entering the courtroom areas must pass through a metal detector and conform to such other appropriate security measures as is deemed appropriate by the Miami–Dade Police Department. Such measures may include requiring photo identification from any person who wishes to enter a courtroom.

9. All persons, including media personnel, shall recognize and comply with the order of any judge regarding the order and control of persons in courthouse facility hallways, corridors, courtrooms, and judicial chambers.

10. Satellite trucks and other media vehicles will be parked in an area designated by Court Administration so as not to interfere with normal traffic and parking regulations. Court Administration will work with the appropriate authorities for parking decisions and determinations. Any unauthorized vehicle parked in a reserved space will result in the vehicle being towed.

11. At the close of each day during the trial or proceeding, there will be an opportunity for the defense counsel, plaintiff's counsel, state attorney, or their respective representatives, to answer questions from the media. Whether they avail themselves of this opportunity is solely at their discretion and convenience. An area to conduct such interviews will be determined on a case by case basis and as needed after the undersigned Chief Judge has conferred with the administrative judge, trial judge, PIO and other such interested parties. An order from the Chief Judge, or his designee, containing and outlining such designations and instructions will be distributed accordingly.

12. In responding to such media questions, as prescribed in Fla. Bar Rule 4–3.6, counsel shall not make an extrajudicial statement that a reasonable person would expect to be disseminated by means of public communication if counsel knows or reasonably should know that it will have a substantial likelihood of materially prejudicing an adjudicative proceeding due to its creation of an imminent and substantial detrimental effect on that proceeding.

13. No communication shall ever be permitted between the media and the jury or any alternate juror while in the jury box, courtroom, in the jury deliberation room, during recess, entering, or exiting the courthouse. This includes the time period for when the jurors are having their meals, or if sequestered, at any lodging facility. Any ban on juror interviews will expire at the conclusion of the jurors' participation in the trial.

14. No disruptions, interference, outbursts, public demonstrations, loud or intrusive noises or distractions shall be permitted in the courtroom or its immediate surroundings. Anyone who fails to maintain decorum may be removed from the courtroom and/or banned from the courtroom for the duration of the trial.

15. All public, press and media activities within, outside of, and around the Courthouse must be in conformance with all city and county ordinances and state and federal laws and statutes. Court staff and county staff will accommodate the media and the general public to fullest extent possible within the guidelines of this Order and Rule 2.450.

16. Violation of this Order could result in the suspension of an individual, or the media organization they represent, from the courthouse for the duration of the trial or proceeding, or in the arrest of, or charge of contempt of court, or a combination thereof, whichever may be deemed appropriate.

This Order shall be effective immediately upon the date it is signed, and shall remain in effect until vacated, amended, or supplemented.

DONE AND ORDERED in Chambers at Miami–Dade, Florida, this ___ day of January, 2007.

____

JOSEPH P. FARINA
CHIEF JUDGE
ELEVENTH JUDICIAL CIRCUIT
OF FLORIDA

06–41. ORDER REVISING CIVIL COVER SHEET

THE ELEVENTH JUDICIAL CIRCUIT MIAMI–DADE COUNTY, FLORIDA

CASE NO. 06–1 (Court Administration)

ADMINISTRATIVE ORDER NO. 06–41

IN RE: ORDER REVISING CIVIL COVER SHEET

WHEREAS, pursuant to the creation of the Complex Business Litigation Section within the General Jurisdiction Division of the Eleventh Judicial Circuit in Miami–Dade County, the Civil Cover Sheet used when filing a cause of action needs to be revised to effectively reflect the creation of Complex Business Litigation Section; and

WHEREAS, the revised Civil Cover Sheet is designed to better process newly filed civil cases to its appropriate Division, including the Complex Business Litigation Section; and

WHEREAS, the revised Civil Cover Sheet shall be used to avoid technical delay, permit just and prompt processing of actions filed, and promote the efficient administration of justice;

NOW, THEREFORE, pursuant to the authority vested in me as Chief Judge of the Eleventh Judicial Circuit of Florida under Florida Rule of Judicial Administration 2.050, it is hereby **ORDERED** that the Civil Cover Sheet shall be revised as follows:

1. The revised Civil Cover Sheet, reflecting the creation of the Complex Business Litigation Section, shall include an additional line and box where the party or attorney signing the Civil Cover Sheet must designate whether the action is appropriate for assignment to the Complex Business Litigation Section.

2. Such Civil Cover Sheet, a sample of which is attached to this Order as Attachment A, is hereby required to be filed with all initial filings that meet the Complex Business Litigation Section criteria as set forth in Administrative Order No. 06–40 and are filed on or after the effective date of this Order.

3. The filing party or attorney shall indicate on the Civil Cover Sheet the applicable type or types of action that qualify

the case for assignment to the Complex Business Litigation Section.

4. A copy of the Civil Cover Sheet shall be served on all parties.

This Order shall take effect on January 8, 2007.

DONE AND ORDERED in Chambers at Miami–Dade, Florida, this ___ day of November, 2006.

JOSEPH P. FARINA, CHIEF JUDGE
ELEVENTH JUDICIAL CIRCUIT OF FLORIDA

ATTACHMENT A

☐ IN THE CIRCUIT COURT OF THE ELEVENTH JUDICIAL CIRCUIT IN AND FOR MIAMI-DADE COUNTY, FLORIDA
☐ IN THE COUNTY COURT IN AND FOR MIAMI-DADE COUNTY, FLORIDA

DIVISION ☐ CIVIL ☐ DISTRICTS ☐ FAMILY ☐ OTHER	CIVIL COVER SHEET	CASE NUMBER
PLAINTIFF	VS. DEFENDANT	CLOCK IN

The civil cover sheet and the information contained here does not replace the filing and service of pleadings or other papers as required by law. This form is required by the Clerk of Court for the purpose of reporting judicial workload data pursuant to Florida Statute 25.075. See instructions and definitions on reverse of this form.

TYPE OF CASE (Place an 'x' in one box only)

Domestic Relations	Torts	Other Civil
☐ Simplified dissolution	☐ Professional Malpractice	☐ Contracts
☐ Dissolution of Marriage	☐ Products liability	☐ Condominium
☐ Support - IV-D	☐ Auto negligence	☐ Real property/Mortgage foreclosure
☐ Support - Non IV-D	☐ Other negligence	☐ Eminent domain
☐ UIFSA - IV-D		☐ Challenge to propsed Constitutional Amendment
☐ UIFSA - Non IV-D		☐ Other
☐ Domestic Violence		
☐ Other domestic relations		

Is Jury Trial Demanded in Complaint ? ☐ Yes ☐ No

DATE:

COMPLEX BUSINESS COURT

This action is appropriate for assignment to Complex Business Court as delineated in the attached addendum pursuant to Administrative Order. ☐ Yes ☐ No

Signature of Attorney for party initiating action:

JUDGE:

CLK/CT 96 Rev. 10/06 Clerk's web address: www.miami-dadeclerk.com

INSTRUCTIONS FOR ATTORNEYS COMPLETING CIVIL COVER SHEET

I. Class Style. Enter the name of the court, the appropriate case number assigned at the time of filing of the original complaint or petition, the name of the judge assigned (if applicable) and the name (last, first, middle initial) of plaintiff(s) and defendant(s).

II. Type of Case. Place an "X" in the appropriate box. If the cause fits more than one type of case, select the most definitive. Definitions of the cases are provided below.

(A) Simplified Dissolution of Marriage—Petitions for the termination of marriage pursuant to Fla.C.Civ.P.1.1511(C).

(B) Dissolution of Marriage—Petitions for the termination of marriage other than simplified dissolution.

(C) Support—IV–D—all matters relating to child or spousal support in which an application for assistance has been filed under Title IV–D, Social Security Act; except for such matters relating to dissolution of marriage petitions (F.S. 409.2584, 409.2571 and 490.2597), paternity, or UIFSA.

(D) Support—Non IV–D—all matters relating to child or spousal support in which an application for assistance has been filed under Title IV–D, Social Security act.

(E) UIFSA—IV–D—all matters relating to Chapter 88, Florida Statutes, in which an application for assistance has not been filed under Title IV–D, Social Security Act.

(F) UIFSA—Non IV–D—all matters relating to Chapter 88, Florida Statutes, in which an application for assistance has not been filed under Title IV–D, Social Security Act.

(G) Domestic Violence—all matters relating to injunctions for protection against domestic violence pursuant to F.S. 741.30.

(F [1]) Domestic Relations—all matters involving adoption, paternity, change of name, child custody, separate maintenance, annulment, or other matters not included in categories (A) through (G).

(I) Auto Negligence—all matters arising out of a party's allegedly negligent operation of a motor vehicle.

(J) Professional Malpractice—all professional malpractice lawsuits.

(K) Products Liability—all matters involving injury to person or property allegedly resulting from the manufacture or sale of a defective product or from a failure to warn.

(L) Other Negligence—all actions sounding in negligence, including statutory claims for relief on account of death or injury, not included in categories (I), (J), and (K).

(M) Condominium—all civil lawsuits pursuant to Chapter 716, Florida Statutes, where a condominium association is a party in the lawsuit.

(N) Eminent Domain—all matters relating to the taking of private property for public use, including inverse condemnation by state agencies, political subdivisions and public service corporations.

(O) Real Property/Mortgage Foreclosure—all matters relating to the possession, title and boundaries of real property. All matters involving foreclosures and sales, including foreclosures associated with condominium associations and condominium units.

(P) Contracts and indebtedness—all contract actions relating to promissory notes and other debts, including those arising from the sale of goods. Excludes contract disputes involving condominium associations.

(Q) Change to proposed constitutional amendment—a challenge to a legislatively initiated proposed constitutional amendment. Excludes challenges to citizen-initiated proposed constitutional amendments, because the Florida Supreme Court has direct jurisdiction of such challenges.

(R) Other Civil—all civil matters not included in categories (A) through (Q).

III. Is Jury Trial Demanded in Complaint? Check the appropriate box to indicate whether or not a jury is being demanded in the complaint.

IV. Complex Business Court—Check the appropriate box to indicate whether or not this case is to be assigned to the Complex Business Court.

DATE AND ATTORNEY SIGNATURE. Date and sign the civil cover sheet.

[1] Lettering as provided in original.

06–40. CREATION OF SECTION 40 ("COMPLEX BUSINESS LITIGATION SECTION") IN THE GENERAL JURISDICTION DIVISION OF THE ELEVENTH JUDICIAL CIRCUIT OF FLORIDA

THE ELEVENTH JUDICIAL CIRCUIT MIAMI–DADE COUNTY, FLORIDA

CASE NO. 06–1 (Court Administration)

ADMINISTRATIVE ORDER NO. 06–40

IN RE: CREATION OF SECTION 40 ("COMPLEX BUSINESS LITIGATION SECTION") IN THE GENERAL JURISDICTION DIVISION OF THE ELEVENTH JUDICIAL CIRCUIT OF FLORIDA

WHEREAS, the Circuit and County Courts in Miami–Dade County are organized into divisions for more efficient case and records management; and

WHEREAS, caseloads in each division are identified by numbered sections to facilitate the exchange of caseloads when changes of division assignment occur; and

WHEREAS, the Court has carefully studied and considered the creation of a complex business litigation section, including analyzing the business litigation section operating in the Ninth Judicial Circuit and similar courts in other jurisdictions throughout the country and the reports and evaluations of those divisions by legal commentators and experts and has received input from a cross section of the legal community; and

WHEREAS, the nature and volume of business litigation cases filed in the General Jurisdiction Division of this Court warrant the creation of another section designated to handle complex business litigation cases;

NOW, THEREFORE, pursuant to the authority vested in me as Chief Judge of the Eleventh Judicial Circuit of Florida under Rule 2.050, Florida Rules of Judicial Administration, it is hereby **ORDERED** that Section 40 is hereby created and dedicated as the Complex Business Litigation Section, within the General Jurisdiction Division of this Court.

It is further **ORDERED** that the following procedures shall be followed as to the assignment and reassignment of cases with respect to Section 40:

Section 1. The Clerk of the Court shall assign to Section 40 all newly filed cases that appear to meet the criteria established in this Administrative Order as designated on the Civil Cover Sheet by the filing attorney or party; and all cases reassigned to the Complex Business Litigation Section by the Administrative Judge (or designee).

Section 2. Cases Subject to the Complex Business Litigation Section.

The principles set forth below shall guide the parties and the Court in the assignment and reassignment of cases to the Complex Business Litigation Section. Notwithstanding anything to the contrary in any prior general Administrative Order of Court procedure, all jury, non-jury, injunction and class action cases shall be assigned to the Complex Business Litigation Section, if they are among the following types of actions:

a) Any of the following where the matter in controversy exceeds the amount of Seventy-five Thousand Dollars ($75,000.00), exclusive of interest, costs and attorney's fees:

i. A breach of contract action, including a claim involving an employment agreement (except a claim primarily based upon allegations of discrimination) or a partnership, shareholder, joint venture or other business arrangement;

ii. An action asserting a business tort, such as a claim for breach of fiduciary duty, fraud, misrepresentation, unfair competition and the like;

iii. An action based on a statutory or common law violation where the breach or violation is alleged to arise out of a business dealing;

iv. An action asserting a claim arising under the U.C.C., including a claim involving the sale of goods or services by or to a business enterprise;

v. An action involving the purchase, sale or restructuring of a business or the purchase or sale of the stock, assets or liabilities of a business;

vi. An action relating to a surety bond;

vii. An action arising from a franchisee/franchisor relationship and associated liabilities;

viii. An insurance coverage dispute, bad faith suit, or third party indemnity action against an insurer arising under a policy issued to a business, such as a claim arising under a commercial general liability policy or commercial property policy;

ix. An action under the Uniform Fraudulent Transfer Act (except proceedings supplementary in a case assigned to another Division).

x. An action under the Florida Deceptive and Unfair Trade Practices Act;

xi. A construction defect case not primarily based upon a claim of personal injury;

xii. A case that is appropriately transferred to the Complex Business Litigation Section pursuant to Section 4 below; and

b) Any of the following without regard to the amount in controversy:

i. An action relating to trade secrets or a non-compete agreements;

ii. An action involving the dissolution of a business entity or an assignment for the benefit of creditors;

iii. An action asserting an intellectual property claim;

iv. An actions involving securities or asserting a claim under a state or other securities law;

v. An action under a state or other antitrust law;

vi. A shareholder derivative action or other action relating to director and officer liability or a corporate governance issue.

Section 3. Cases Not Subject to the Complex Business Litigation Section.

The following types of matters shall not be assigned to the Complex Business Litigation Section absent special circumstances:

a) A matter involving occupational health or safety;

b) An environmental claim which does not involve the sale or disposition of a business or coverage dispute addressed in paragraph 2(a)(viii) above;

c) A matter in eminent domain;

d) An employment law case, other than the type described in paragraphs 2(a)(i) and 2(b)(i) above;

e) An administrative agency, tax, zoning, or other appeal;

f) A matter required by statute or other law to be heard in some other Court or Court Division;

g) A case that is appropriately transferred out of the Complex Business Litigation Section pursuant to section 4 below.

Section 4. Assignment of Cases In and out of the Business Litigation Section.

a) Cases filed on or after January 1, 2007 that otherwise meet the criteria for transfer to the Complex Business Litigation Section shall not be transferred if a trial date has been set within three months from the date of this Order.

b) Judges assigned to the General Jurisdiction Division and/or litigants who have cases filed in the General Jurisdiction Division may submit a request to the Administrative Judge (or designee) of the General Jurisdiction Division to assign/transfer a pending case that meets the criteria of the Complex Business Litigation Section to Section 40.

c). If any party disagrees with the assignment or lack of assignment of a case to the Complex Business Litigation Section, then that party may submit a request to the Administrative Judge (or designee) of the General Jurisdiction Division for re-evaluation and/or case re-assignment.

d). The Administrative Judge of the General Jurisdiction Division (or designee) shall resolve controversies which may arise concerning the assignment/transfer of any case to or from the Complex Business Litigation Section.

This Order shall take effect on January 8, 2007.

DONE AND ORDERED in Chambers at Miami–Dade, Florida this ___ day of November, 2006.

____

Joseph P. Farina, Chief Judge
Eleventh Judicial Circuit of Florida

JOSEPH P. FARINA, CHIEF JUDGE
ELEVENTH JUDICIAL CIRCUIT OF FLORIDA

06–09. EX PARTE MOTIONS TO COMPEL DISCOVERY IN CIVIL ACTIONS

THE ELEVENTH JUDICIAL CIRCUIT MIAMI–DADE COUNTY, FLORIDA

CASE NO. 06–1 (Court Administration)

ADMINISTRATIVE ORDER NO. 06–09

IN RE: EX PARTE MOTIONS TO COMPEL DISCOVERY IN CIVIL ACTIONS

WHEREAS, Rule 1.380 of the Florida Rules of Civil Procedure prescribes the method for applying for an order compelling discovery; and

WHEREAS, pursuant to Waters v. American General Corporation, 770 So. 2d 1275 (Fla. 4th DCA 2000), an ex parte order compelling discovery may be entered only when the motion to compel alleges a complete failure to respond or object to discovery, and there has been no request for extension of time;

NOW, THEREFORE, pursuant to the authority vested in me as Chief Judge of the Eleventh Judicial Circuit of Florida under Rule 2.050 of the Florida Rules of Judicial Administration, in light of the ever-increasing case load, in order to efficiently and expeditiously conduct the court's business, the following procedures governing ex parte motions to compel discovery in civil actions are hereby promulgated:

1. A motion to compel discovery ex parte in a civil action may be submitted to the Court if the moving party has complied with the following procedures:

a. The moving party must serve the motion on the opposing party at least seven (7) days prior to the submission of the order to the Court.

b. The motion must include the following:

i. the nature of the discovery and the date upon which the discovery was propounded and due;

ii. that there has been a complete failure to respond or object to discovery, and the non-moving party has failed to request an extension of time to respond to discovery; and

iii. that the moving party has otherwise complied with Fla. R. Civ. P. 1.380(a)(2), certifying that he has conferred, or attempted to confer, with the person or party failing to make the discovery in an effort to secure the information or material without court action.

2. In the event that the non-moving party fails to provide the requested discovery, fails to object to discovery, or fails to request an extension of time to respond to the discovery within seven (7) days of service of the motion, the moving party may submit an ex parte order to the court.

3. In entering the ex parte order, the court may direct that the non-moving party comply with the outstanding discovery request within ten (10) days or such other time, within the discretion of the Court. The court may also, in its discretion, order that the non-moving party pay costs and/or attorney's fees, if appropriate.

This Order shall take effect immediately upon execution and shall remain in effect until further order of the Court.

DONE AND ORDERED in Chambers at Miami–Dade, Florida, this ___ day of June, 2006.

05–08 (A2). EXPANSION OF JUVENILE DRUG COURT

THE ELEVENTH JUDICIAL CIRCUIT MIAMI–DADE COUNTY, FLORIDA

CASE NO. 10–1 (Court Administration)

ADMINISTRATIVE ORDER NO. 05–08–A2 (Amending AO No. 05–08, as amended by AO No. 5–08 A1)

IN RE: EXPANSION OF JUVENILE DRUG COURT

WHEREAS, in view of the success of the Juvenile Drug Court in the Eleventh Judicial Circuit of Florida for eligible post-adjudication drug cases in Miami–Dade County, pursuant to Administrative Order No. 05–08–A1, entered on May 16, 2005 with an effective date of January 1, 2006, Juvenile Drug Court was to be expanded to include eligible pre-adjudication drug cases in an effort to reduce recidivism by emphasizing treatment and rehabilitation as an alternative to incarceration, while also requiring offender accountability; and

WHEREAS, notwithstanding the entry of AO No. 05–08 A1, such expansion was not effectuated pending clarification of certain eligibility criteria and other matters; and

WHEREAS, the State Attorney's Office, in collaboration with the Office of the Public Defender and Regional Counsel (collectively, "Defense Counsel"), have agreed that the procedures set forth herein address their concerns;

NOW, THEREFORE, pursuant to the authority vested in me as Chief Judge of the Eleventh Judicial Circuit of Florida, under Rule 2.215 of the Florida Rules of Judicial Administration, it is hereby ORDERED that Administrative Order No. 05–08, as amended by Administrative Order No. 5–08 A1, is further amended as hereinafter set forth:

A. Eligible Pre–Adjudication Cases.

1. Pursuant to Section 985.345, Fla. Stat. (2007), a juvenile who is charged by petition under Chapter 893, Fla. Stat., with a felony of the second or third degree for purchase or possession of a controlled substance, tampering with evidence; solicitation for purchase of a controlled substance; or obtaining a prescription by fraud, and who has not previously been adjudicated for a felony is eligible for voluntary admission into a delinquency pretrial substance abuse education and treatment intervention program, including a treatment-based drug court program established pursuant to s. 397.334, approved by the chief judge or alternative sanctions coordinator of the circuit to the extent that funded programs are available, for a period based on the program requirements and the treatment services are suitable for the offender, upon motion of either party or the court's own motion.

2. Additionally, if the State Attorney believes that the facts and circumstances of the case suggest the youth's involvement in the dealing and selling of controlled substances, the court shall hold a preadmission hearing after a petition has been filed, and within 35 days of the initial sounding on the petition, but prior to the day of the adjudicatory hearing. If the State

Attorney establishes by a preponderance of the evidence at such hearing that the youth was involved in the dealing and selling of controlled substances, the youth is ineligible and the court shall deny the youth's admission into Juvenile Drug Court.

B. Ineligible Pre–Adjudication Cases.

The following offenses are ineligible and do not meet the criteria for preadjudication participation in Juvenile Drug Court:

1. Additional felony charges;

2. Sale of, possession with intent to sell a controlled substance;

3. Firearm charges;

4. Pending crimes of violence, on a separate count contained in the same petition, without victim consent to enter program;

5. Concurrent misdemeanor charge in same petition involving restitution. However, such charge will not make a child ineligible as long as the victim and child/parent/guardian agree on the amount and the child/parent/guardian has the ability to pay restitution within period of drug court; and

6. Youths who were previously referred to any diversion program on the same case are presumptively not eligible for pre-adjudicatory Juvenile Drug Court. The Court shall determine the eligibility upon review of facts and circumstances of the case.

C. Acceptance: Pre–Adjudicatory Drug Court.

After a petition has been filed, and within 35 days of the initial sounding on the petition, but prior to the day of the adjudicatory hearing, and after the Staffing Team determines a juvenile is eligible to participate in Juvenile Drug Court, the Defense Counsel then meets with his/her client to discuss whether or not the juvenile wishes to participate in Juvenile Drug Court. If the juvenile wishes to participate, the case is referred to the Juvenile Drug Court Judge for acceptance into the Juvenile Drug Court.

D. Pre and Post Adjudication Process.

1. Placement Procedure: The procedure for placement of eligible defendants into Juvenile Drug Court is as follows:

a. Referral: A referral can be made to Juvenile Drug Court by Judges, Defense Counsels, Assistant State Attorneys, Juvenile Probation Officers, and others.

b. Screening: Most of the Juvenile Drug Court participants are initially screened by the Juvenile Assessment Center ("JAC"). If the JAC, or other service provider, after testing the juvenile, determines that the juvenile has a substance abuse problem, the JAC will classify the juvenile as mild, moderate or severe drug abuser.

c. Eligibility Determination: After a juvenile is found to be a drug abuser by the JAC or other service provider, then the staffing team consisting of members from the Administrative Office of the Courts, Defense Counsels, the Office of the State Attorney, the Department of Juvenile Justice, Miami–Dade Public School System, and various treatment providers (collectively, "Staffing Team"), will meet once a week to screen new filings to determine Juvenile Drug Court eligibility.

d. Acceptance: After the Staffing Team determines a juvenile is eligible to participate in Juvenile Drug Court, the Defense Counsel then meets with his/her client to discuss whether or not the juvenile wishes to participate in Juvenile Drug Court. If the juvenile wishes to participate, the case is referred to the Juvenile Drug Court Judge for acceptance into the Juvenile Drug Court.

i. Acceptance for Post–Adjudicatory Drug Court. After a petition has been filed, but prior to disposition, and after the Staffing Team determines a juvenile is eligible to participate in Juvenile Drug Court, the Defense Counsel then meets with his/her client to discuss whether or not the juvenile wishes to participate in Juvenile Drug Court. If the juvenile wishes to participate, the case is referred to the Juvenile Drug Court Judge for acceptance into the Juvenile Drug Court.

ii. Acceptance for Pre–Adjudicatory Drug Court: Please refer to paragraph C hereinabove.

2. Once the juvenile is accepted into Juvenile Drug Court, the juvenile is monitored by the Staffing Team on a weekly basis. If the Staffing Team determines that Juvenile Drug Court is no longer a viable option for the juvenile or the juvenile drops out of Juvenile Drug Court, the Juvenile Drug Court Judge will refer the case back to the original delinquency division.

3. As provided in Section 985.345 (3), Fla. Stat., at the end of the delinquency pretrial intervention period, the court shall consider recommendation of the state attorney and the program administrator as to disposition of the pending charges. The court shall determine, by written findings, whether the child has successfully completed the delinquency pretrial intervention program. Not withstanding the coordinated strategy developed by a drug court team pursuant to s. 397.334 (3), if the court finds that the child has not successfully completed the delinquency pretrial intervention program, the court may order the child to continue in an education, treatment, or urine monitoring program if resources and funding are available or order that the charges revert to normal channels for prosecution. The court may dismiss the charges upon a finding that the child has successfully completed the delinquency pretrial intervention program.

E. Non-eligible Post-Adjudication Cases.

Youths who have been charged with the following offenses will not be eligible for post-adjudicatory drug court:

1. Firearm offenses;

2. Sale of drug offenses including possession with intent to sell a controlled substance;

3. Violent offenses except with SAO approval;

4. Sexual battery offenses;

5. Those whose current offense is likely to merit commitment or direct file charges;

6. Those who live outside of Juvenile Drug Court boundaries;

7. Youths who are 18 years or older;

8. Youths with severe mental illness, retardation, or other severe disabilities that would likely result in the inability to successfully complete the drug court conditions;

9. Youths who meet the criteria for long term residential services; and

10. If the State Attorney believes that the facts and circumstances of the case suggest the youth's involvement in the dealing and selling of controlled substances, the court shall hold a preadmission hearing. If the State Attorney establishes by a preponderance of the evidence at such hearing that the youth was involved in the dealing and selling of controlled substances, the youth is ineligible and the court shall deny the youth's admission into Juvenile Drug Court.

Except as amended herein, Administrative Order No. 05–08, as amended by Administrative Order No. 05–08–A1 remains in full force and effect.

This Order shall take effect upon execution and shall remain in effect until further order of the Court

DONE AND ORDERED in Chambers at Miami–Dade County, Florida, this 18th day of May, 2010.

JOEL H. BROWN, CHIEF JUDGE
ELEVENTH JUDICIAL CIRCUIT
OF FLORIDA

05–08. EXPANSION OF JUVENILE DRUG COURT

THE ELEVENTH JUDICIAL CIRCUIT MIAMI–DADE COUNTY, FLORIDA

CASE NO. 05–1 (Court Administration)

ADMINISTRATIVE ORDER NO. 05–08[1]

IN RE: EXPANSION OF JUVENILE DRUG COURT

WHEREAS, the Miami–Dade County Juvenile Drug Court of the Eleventh Judicial Circuit ("Juvenile Drug Court") was established as a mechanism to increase the participation of juveniles in community-based substance abuse intervention and treatment services, who were arrested and identified as having a substance abuse problem; and

WHEREAS, Juvenile Drug Court was founded on the premise that arrest and court involvement provides an ideal opportunity for the juvenile justice system and treatment providers to work together to intervene in adolescent delinquent and substance abusing behaviors; and

WHEREAS, the goal of the Juvenile Drug Court is to reduce juvenile recidivism rates by providing offenders with the tools and community support to assist them in curbing the substance abusing behavior that may be putting them at risk of delinquent behavior; and

WHEREAS, the Juvenile Drug Court is designed to be a multi-faceted collaborative effort between the Judiciary, the Office of the State Attorney, the Office of the Public Defender, the Administrative Office of the Courts, the Department of Children and Families, the Department of Juvenile Justice, Department of Human Services, Miami–Dade County Police Department, Miami–Dade County Public Schools, and community treatment providers; and

WHEREAS, the Juvenile Drug Court is intended to provide comprehensive assessment, referrals and linkages to community services, ongoing case management, family intervention, and consistent judicial monitoring of the offender's progress based on a structured reward and consequence system; and

WHEREAS, the Juvenile Drug Court is intended to serve Miami–Dade County residents, between the ages of 13 and 17, who have been arrested and identified as having a moderate to severe drug abuse problem; and

WHEREAS, pursuant to the success of the Juvenile Drug Court currently in effect in this Circuit for eligible post-adjudication drug cases in Miami–Dade County, expansion of the Juvenile Drug Court to include eligible pre-adjudication drug cases will provide a substantial benefit to the criminal justice system and the community as a whole in that it will reduce recidivism by emphasizing treatment and rehabilitation as an alternative to incarceration, while also requiring offender accountability;

NOW, THEREFORE, pursuant to the authority vested in me as Chief Judge of the Eleventh Judicial Circuit of Florida, under Rule 2.050 of the Florida Rules of Judicial Administration, it is hereby **ORDERED** that:

1. Effective January 1, 2006, the Juvenile Drug Court, currently in effect in the Eleventh Judicial Circuit for eligible post-adjudication drug cases will expand to provide for the inclusion of eligible pre-adjudication drug cases.

2. **Eligible Offenses**: Pursuant to Section 985.306, Fla. Stat. (1998), a juvenile who is charged by petition under Chapter 893, Fla. Stat., with a felony of the second or third degree for purchase or possession of a controlled substance, and who has not previously been adjudicated for a felony nor been admitted to a delinquency pretrial intervention program under Section 985.306(1)(a), Fla. Stat., is eligible for admission into a delinquency pretrial substance abuse program.

3. **Non–eligible Offenses**: Youth who have been charged with the following offenses will not be eligible:

a. gun offenses (i.e., possession of a firearm);

b. sale of drug offenses (i.e., intent to sell);

c. violent offenses (i.e., aggravated assault; aggravated battery; assault charges (misdemeanor or felony); strong arm robbery (unless victim approval is given for misdemeanor and felony battery charges only);

d. sexual battery offenses;

e. those whose current offense is likely to merit commitment or direct file charges;

f. those who live outside of Juvenile Drug Court boundaries;

g. youths who are 18 years of age or older;

h. youths with severe mental illness, retardation, or other severe disabilities that would likely result in the inability to successfully complete the drug court conditions; and

i. youths who meet the criteria for long term residential services.

Additionally, if the State Attorney believes that the facts and circumstances of the case suggest the youth's involvement in the dealing and selling of controlled substances, the court shall hold a preliminary hearing. If the State Attorney establishes by a preponderance of the evidence at such hearing that the youth was involved in the dealing and selling of controlled substances, the youth is ineligible and the court shall deny the youth's admission into Juvenile Drug Court.

4. **Placement Procedure**: The procedure for placement of eligible defendants into Juvenile Drug Court is as follows:

a. **Referral**: A referral can be made to Juvenile Drug Court by Judges, Assistant Public Defenders, Assistant State Attorneys, Juvenile Probation Officers, and others.

b. **Screening**: Most of the Juvenile Drug Court participants are initially screened by the Juvenile Assessment Center ("JAC"). If the JAC, or other service provider, after testing the juvenile, determines that the juvenile has a substance abuse problem, the JAC will classify the juvenile as mild, moderate or severe drug abuser.

c. **Eligibility Determination**: After a juvenile is found to be a drug abuser by the JAC or other service provider, then the staffing team consisting of members form the Administrative Office of the Courts, the Office of the Public Defender, the Office of the State Attorney, the Department of Juvenile Justice, Miami–Dade Public School System, and various treatment providers (collectively, "Staffing Team"), will meet once a week to screen new filings to determine Juvenile Drug Court eligibility.

d. **Acceptance**: After a petition has been filed, but prior to adjudication and after the Staffing Team determines a juvenile is eligible to participate in Juvenile Drug Court, the Assistant Public Defender then meets with his/her client to discuss whether or not the juvenile wishes to participate in Juvenile Drug Court. If the juvenile wishes to participate, the case is referred to the Juvenile Drug Court Judge for acceptance into the Juvenile Drug Court.

5. Once the juvenile is accepted into Juvenile Drug Court, the juvenile is monitored by the Staffing Team on a weekly basis. If the Staffing Team determines that Juvenile Drug Court is no longer a viable option for the juvenile or the juvenile drops out of Juvenile Drug Court, the Juvenile Drug Court Judge will refer the case back to the original delinquency division.

6. As provided in Section 985.306 (1)(b)(2), Fla. Stat., the court shall determine, by written finding, whether the youth has successfully completed the delinquency pretrial intervention program and may dismiss the charges upon finding that the youth has successfully completed the delinquency pretrial intervention program.

This Order shall take effect as of January 1, 2006 and shall remain in effect until further order of the Court.

DONE AND ORDERED in Chambers at Miami–Dade, Florida, this ___ day of ________, 2005.

JOSEPH P. FARINA, CHIEF JUDGE
ELEVENTH JUDICIAL CIRCUIT OF FLORIDA

[1] Amended by AO 1–05–08 A1, Juvenile, and AO 1–05–08–A2, Court Administration.

04–41. AUTHORIZATION FOR CLERK'S PARTIAL PAYMENT PROGRAM FOR FEES, SERVICE CHARGES, COSTS AND FINES

THE ELEVENTH JUDICIAL CIRCUIT MIAMI–DADE COUNTY, FLORIDA

CASE NO. 04–1 (Court Administration)

ADMINISTRATIVE ORDER NO. 04–41

IN RE: AUTHORIZATION FOR CLERK'S PARTIAL PAYMENT PROGRAM FOR FEES, SERVICE CHARGES, COSTS AND FINES

WHEREAS, section 21 of chapter 2004–265, Laws of Florida, amended section 28.246, Florida Statutes, regarding payment of court-related fees, service charges, costs and fines; and

WHEREAS, section 28.246, Florida Statutes (2004) authorizes the clerk of the circuit court to accept partial payments for court-related fees, service charges, costs and fines if a determination is made as to an individual's inability to make payments in full; and

WHEREAS, the Clerk of the Courts for the Eleventh Judicial Circuit ("Clerk") is willing to make an initial determination regarding an individual's inability to make payments in full and allow such individuals to be enrolled in the Clerk's periodic payment program without a formal court hearing; and

WHEREAS, it is necessary for the efficient and proper administration of justice in this Circuit to authorize such a periodic payment program;

NOW, THEREFORE, pursuant to the authority vested in me as Chief Judge of the Eleventh Judicial Circuit of Florida, it is hereby ORDERED:

1. Any individual seeking to defer payment of court-related fees, service charges, costs, or fines shall be enrolled by the Clerk in a payment program, with periodic payment amounts corresponding to the individual's ability to pay, if the Clerk makes an initial determination that such individual is unable to make full payment. For purposes of this Order, a determination that an individual is unable to make full payment of court-related fees, service charges, costs or fines will be termed a "partial payment determination."

2. If the Clerk cannot make a partial payment determination, such partial payment determination will be made by the judge assigned to the division in which the individual's case is pending or was last heard. Any judge making a partial payment determination shall order the individual to enroll in the Clerk's periodic payment program pursuant to section 28.246, Florida Statutes (2004).

This Order shall take effect July 1, 2004, nunc pro tunc.

DONE AND ORDERED in Chambers at Miami–Dade, Florida, this ___ day of ________, 2004.

JOSEPH P. FARINA, CHIEF JUDGE
ELEVENTH JUDICIAL CIRCUIT OF FLORIDA

03–02 (A1). ASBESTOS LITIGATION ELECTRONIC SERVICE PROGRAM

THE ELEVENTH JUDICIAL CIRCUIT MIAMI–DADE COUNTY, FLORIDA

CASE NO. 03–1 (Court Administration)

ADMINISTRATIVE ORDER NO. 03–02–A1 (amending AO 03–02 dated March 7, 2003)

IN RE: ASBESTOS LITIGATION ELECTRONIC SERVICE PROGRAM

WHEREAS, the court entered Administrative Order No. 03–02 on March 7, 2003 authorizing the Asbestos Litigation Electronic Service Program (hereinafter, "Program"), pursuant to which a copy of all motions, memoranda of law, declarations, orders, responses, discovery demands, notices of hearings, or other documents filed in asbestos cases shall be served electronically through the Verilaw System; and

WHEREAS, pursuant to Administrative Order No. 03–02, the Program shall not become effective until the court has issued an order notifying all parties of an activation date, after which a copy of all documents filed in asbestos cases shall be served electronically through the Verilaw System;

THEREFORE, PURSUANT to the authority vested in me as Chief Judge of the Eleventh Judicial Circuit of Florida, it is **ORDERED** that:

1. The activation date, upon which the Asbestos Litigation Electronic Service Program shall become effective, shall be Tuesday, May 27, 2003. Accordingly, a copy of all documents filed in asbestos cases on or after that date shall be served electronically through the Verilaw System.

2. No party or court personnel shall electronically serve an order or other paper on behalf of the court until the court has issued an order notifying all parties that service of orders and other papers by the court shall be made via the Verilaw System.

All provisions of Administrative Order No. 03–02 shall remain in full force and effect.

DONE AND ORDERED in Chambers at Miami–Dade, Florida, this 22 day of May, 2003.

JOSEPH P. FARINA, CHIEF JUDGE
ELEVENTH JUDICIAL CIRCUIT OF FLORIDA

ASBESTOS LITIGATION ELECTRONIC SERVICE PROGRAM

I. GENERAL PROVISIONS

A. Scope of the Program Except as expressly provided herein, or as expressly authorized by the court, all motions, memoranda of law, declarations, orders, responses, discovery demands, notice of hearings, or other documents filed in asbestos cases shall be served electronically through the Verilaw System. Any exhibits or attachments, including proposed court orders, shall be electronically served along with the pertinent document. All initial complaints must be served via traditional process of service in accordance with Florida Rules of Civil Procedure and applicable Florida law. All electronic service of documents via the Verilaw System shall be done in addition to conventional filing with the clerk of court.

B. Definitions The following terms in this Order shall be defined or described as follows:

1. Conventional Service— service of documents, other than the initial complaint, by mail, hand-delivery, or fax service in accordance with Florida Rules of Court and applicable Florida laws;
2. Electronic Service— an electronic transmission containing a hyperlink to an original document, other than the initial complaint, to designated registered users via the Verilaw System;
3. Master Docket— a docket with all orders and documents to correlate with the All Asbestos Cases docket, case number 91–80000;
4. Registered User— court personnel and counsels of record or their designees within their law firms. Each registered user will receive a user name and password to access the Verilaw System. Court personnel are special registered users that can access the Verilaw System, but cannot be electronically served by other registered users;
5. Verilaw System— a web site specifically created by Verilaw Technologies, Inc. for the electronic service, delivery, and storage of documents in asbestos cases litigated in Dade County, Florida. The web site will contain a Master Docket and individual dockets for each asbestos case.

C. Effect of Electronic Service Electronic service shall be considered to substitute conventional service for registered users.

D. Conventional Filing and Service

1. *Conventional Filing*: Electronic service via the Verilaw System shall be conducted in addition to conventional filing of the documents with the clerk of court. The clerk's filing record will be the only determination of whether a document has been properly filed.
2. *Conventional Service*: Electronic service between registered users satisfies all service requirements and no additional conventional service is necessary.
3. All parties must serve the initial complaint by traditional process of service in accordance with the Florida Rules of Civil Procedure and applicable Florida laws.

E. Appearance of Document(s) All parties must adhere to the Florida Rules of Civil Procedure and Florida laws in the drafting of all documents in asbestos cases. Documents that are electronically served must be exact copies of the document filed with the clerk with the exception of technological changes as discussed below.

1. Word-processing documents transferred to the Verilaw System will not contain visual representations of the filing attorneys' original signatures. On word-

processing documents that parties submit, parties shall, in place of a signature and where the signature would normally appear, place "Original Signature on File with the Court." The original documents filed in the court's record must have original signatures.

2. All Documents Filed Under Seal

a. If any part of a document to be served is under seal, the party serving the document shall serve electronically only the portion that is not under seal with appropriate indication of the portion that has been conventionally filed under seal with the court reflected in the electronically served portion of the document. The portion of the document under seal shall be filed with the clerk of court in paper form.

b. If the sealed portion(s) of the document is so substantial that the balance of the document is essentially unintelligible or the entire document is under seal, the entire document may be filed in paper form with the clerk of court and no electronic service of the document is required. However, a notice of filing under seal in paper form shall be served electronically.

3. A party serving exhibits that are real objects or otherwise not readily susceptible to electronic service and/or viewing shall electronically serve a notice of filing detailing the exhibit served and the alternate manner of service.

F. Electronic Service of Orders and Other Papers by the Court. Florida Rules of Judicial Administration 2.090 requires that the court receive the approval of the Florida Supreme Court to electronically serve orders and other papers by the court. Such approval is currently pending.

1. Pending Approval No party or court personnel shall electronically serve an order or other paper by the court. Verilaw has agreed that registered users may post orders and other papers by the court on the Verilaw system at no cost. However, all parties must continue to serve via conventional service all orders and other papers by the court until notified otherwise.

2. Subject to Approval If the Verilaw System is approved for electronic service of orders and other papers by the court, the court shall issue an order notifying all parties that service of orders and other papers by the court shall be made via the Verilaw System after an activation date provided in the order. The order shall outline the specific procedure for electronic service of the orders and other papers by the court.

At no time should the posting and/or electronic service of documents by the court substitute for conventional filing of court orders.

II. VERILAW SYSTEM

A. General Verilaw Technologies, Inc. (hereinafter, "Verilaw") personnel will perform all administrative functions for the Verilaw System. The Verilaw System will be privately funded by the parties as discussed below. The Verilaw System will have docket, on-line event calendar, and bulletin board features.

B. Docket Verilaw shall make available to the court and parties in asbestos cases a web site for electronic service, delivery, and storage of documents. Registered users, except for court personnel, shall receive a notice of service via e-mail of documents served. A registered user may personally change its user's information by contacting a Verilaw representative. Any additions or deletions to the registered users' list must be submitted to Verilaw.

C. On-line Event Calendar As part of the web site, Verilaw shall provide a calendaring feature in the Master Docket and for each individual asbestos case. All depositions, motions, status conferences, and hearings shall be noticed by the parties in the respective case calendar. The system shall notify the registered users of the applicable case by e-mail of the date, time, location, and type of events noticed.

1. No party in an action shall notice a deposition without first contacting all counsels of record in the case to clear available times. All parties shall cooperate to facilitate the discovery process, avoid conflicts, and to keep court intervention in discovery disputes to a minimum.

2. Parties setting motion matters shall communicate with the court regarding hearing date and time. Thereafter, all documents related thereto shall be filed and served consistent with the procedures in this order. The moving party shall then make certain that the matter is properly noticed in the applicable case calendar with the date, time, location, and type of event.

3. The court may use the calendar system to schedule any hearing or conference.

D. Bulletin Board As part of the web site, Verilaw shall establish for each individual asbestos case, as well as for the Master Docket, an electronic Bulletin Board to facilitate communication between and amongst counsels. Verilaw shall provide a plaintiffs' Bulletin Board and a defendants' Bulletin Board that will be accessible only by relevant plaintiffs' counsels or defense counsels, as applicable.

III. ELECTRONIC SERVICE PROCEDURES

A. Verilaw System Access Access to the Verilaw System will be limited to registered users only. There will be no public access to the Verilaw System.

1. All firms litigating in asbestos cases shall become registered users of the Verilaw System no later than fourteen (14) days after entry of this Order. All firms shall pay an initial set up fee of $350 per firm to register. The check should be made out to "Verilaw Technologies, Inc." and sent to 400 East Lancaster Avenue, Suite 300, Wayne, Pennsylvania 19087, c/o Dade County Asbestos Litigation. Verilaw requires specific data from each law firm to make the system operational. Verilaw will collect this data electronically. Within seven (7) days of the date of this Order, Verilaw will contact all law firms with instructions on how to submit the necessary data. If Verilaw does not contact a firm, the firm should contact Chris Huff, a Verilaw representative, at (610) 688–1926(X3603).

2. When the Verilaw System has been designed and implemented for registered users, the court will issue an order notifying all parties that electronic service shall be via the Verilaw System after an activation date provided in the order.
3. New firms that become counsel of record in any present asbestos case or file new asbestos cases in Dade County, after the effective date of this order, shall become registered users of the Verilaw System no later than fourteen (14) days after initiation of the lawsuit as a plaintiff or no later than fourteen (14) days after service of the complaint as a defendant.

B. Procedure for Electronic Service

1. On the same day that a document is conventionally filed pursuant to the Florida Rules of Civil Procedure and applicable Florida laws, an exact copy of that document shall be sent to Verilaw for service by one of the following methods: (1) electronic transfer or downloading of the document via the Internet onto the Verilaw System; (2) fax transmission to Verilaw; or (3) hard copy via overnight mail to Verilaw. All documents electronically served via the Verilaw system shall be clearly titled as to identify the document and the party on whose behalf such document is being submitted.
2. Each time a registered user serves a document via the Verilaw System, the firm is charged 50 ¢ per firm on the service list for the asbestos case indicated, subject to a $12 minimum. The transaction fee will not vary based on the number of pages transmitted (subject to the exception of a lower fee for certain 1–2 page documents). There is no additional fee for exhibits and attachments submitted with a document. However, there is an additional 30 ¢ per page handling charge for faxed or mailed documents. It is the responsibility of the firm to insure that it maintains its debit account with Verilaw to effectuate service based on these charges.
3. Verilaw will convert all documents into Adobe Portable Document format and make them available to parties on the Verilaw System. Verilaw will post all documents on the Verilaw System according to the following timetable:
   a. Electronic documents will be posted on the Verilaw System within one (1) hour of receipt of such documents from a registered user;
   b. Faxed documents will be posted on the Verilaw System within six (6) business hours of receipt from a registered user; and
   c. Mailed hard copy documents will be posted on the Verilaw System within twenty-four (24) hours of receipt of the overnight mail package.
4. There are two options to receive notice of the service of a new document posted on the Verilaw System. Within one hour of posting of the document on the Verilaw System, Verilaw shall send an e-mail to all registered users, except for court personnel, notifying them of the new document. Alternatively, Verilaw provides a daily digest notification option, which aggregates all the e-mails distributed in one day into a single e-mail. The e-mail or digest shall contain a hypertext link(s) to the document(s) location(s) on the Verilaw System.

C. Timeliness of Electronic Service Verilaw shall date and time stamp (electronically or otherwise) each document served. Unless a conventionally filed document is rejected by the clerk, Verilaw's date and time stamp shall constitute the date and time of service of the document. Any document received by Verilaw after 8:00 p.m. Eastern Time on a day the court is open for business or received on a day the court is closed for business shall be deemed as have been served on the next court day that is not a Saturday, Sunday, or legal holiday. Parties must adhere to all filing and service deadline requirements in the Florida Rules of Civil Procedure and applicable Florida laws and must adjust its electronic service to satisfy these rules and laws.

D. Use of the Verilaw System The Verilaw System shall contain an index of all documents served in the asbestos cases, which will be searchable and sortable according to methods that provide useful access to the documents. All documents on the system will be identified by (1) the name of the filing party; (2) the name of the filing law firm (3) the precise title of the document; and (4) the case-specific court docket number(s) to which the document applies.

IV. MISCELLANEOUS PROVISIONS

A. Court Costs There will be no cost to the court to utilize the Verilaw System.

B. Courtesy Copy The court will not receive electronic notice of electronically served documents. Therefore, parties must insure that the court receives a courtesy copy in its chambers of all documents necessary for the court's response.

C. Verilaw System Training It is the responsibility of each firm to insure that its attorney and staff are properly trained in the use of the Verilaw System.

D. Verilaw System or User Errors Verilaw shall designate a Verilaw representative to provide technical support for the web site to all parties and the court.

DONE AND ORDERED in Chambers in Miami–Dade County, Florida, this ____ day of ____________, 2003.

JOSEPH P. FARINA, CHIEF JUDGE
ELEVENTH JUDICIAL CIRCUIT COURT

03–02. ASBESTOS LITIGATION ELECTRONIC SERVICE PROGRAM

THE ELEVENTH JUDICIAL CIRCUIT MIAMI–DADE COUNTY, FLORIDA

CASE NO. 03–1 (Court Administration)

ADMINISTRATIVE ORDER NO. 03–02

IN RE: ASBESTOS LITIGATION ELECTRONIC SERVICE PROGRAM

WHEREAS, technology is considered by this Circuit as a valuable tool in the ongoing effort to serve the community and the legal system in the most efficient manner possible; and

WHEREAS, the court has the authority to order alternative means of service pursuant to Florida Rules of Civil Procedure 1.080 and it believes that an electronic service system would be a just and reasonable manner of service for the parties in the asbestos litigation cases;

NOW THEREFORE, pursuant to the authority vested in me as Chief Judge of the Eleventh Judicial Circuit Court of Florida, it is

ORDERED that:

1. The Asbestos Litigation Electronic Service Program (hereinafter, " Program") is hereby authorized as a program to be conducted, in addition to conventional filing with the court clerk, in all cases specific to asbestos (hereinafter, "asbestos cases"). Program participation is mandatory for all asbestos firms in all asbestos cases litigated in Dade County, commenced before or after the effective date of this order.
2. This Order shall take effect immediately and remain in effect until otherwise directed to cease participating in the Program by the Chief Judge of the Eleventh Judicial Circuit Court of Florida, and all the terms and conditions set forth in this Order shall apply unless otherwise ordered by the court.

03–01. [RESCINDED BY ADMINISTRATIVE ORDER NO. 16–07, EFFECTIVE MAY 4, 2016]

02–14 (A2). [RESCINDED BY ADMINISTRATIVE ORDER NO. 16–02, EFFECTIVE FEBRUARY 17, 2016]

2–14–01 (A1). ELEVENTH JUDICIAL CIRCUIT PROFESSIONALISM AND CIVILITY COMMITTEE AND LOCAL PROFESSIONALISM PANEL

THE ELEVENTH JUDICIAL CIRCUIT MIAMI–DADE COUNTY, FLORIDA

CASE NO. 14–02 (Court Administration)

ADMINISTRATIVE ORDER NO. 14–01 A1 (Rescinding and superseding Administrative Order No. 14–01, as amended)

IN RE: ELEVENTH JUDICIAL CIRCUIT PROFESSIONALISM AND CIVILITY COMMITTEE AND LOCAL PROFESSIONALISM PANEL

WHEREAS, the Supreme Court of Florida previously mandated that the Chief Judge of each judicial circuit establish a Circuit Committee on Professionalism; and

WHEREAS, pursuant to the Supreme Court of Florida's Administrative Order *In re: Commission on Professionalism*, dated June 11, 1998, each Chief Judge was directed to maintain in continuous operation a Circuit Committee on Professionalism; and

WHEREAS, thereafter, the Eleventh Judicial Circuit Professionalism and Civility Committee was established; and

WHEREAS, on June 6, 2013 the Supreme Court of Florida adopted *In re: Code for Resolving Professionalism Complaints*, that mandates that the Chief Judge of each judicial circuit create a Local Professionalism Panel to receive and resolve professionalism complaints informally;

NOW, THEREFORE, pursuant to the authority vested in me as the Chief Judge of the Eleventh Judicial Circuit of Florida, under Rule 2.215, of the Florida Rules of Judicial Administration, it is hereby **ORDERED:**

1. The Eleventh Judicial Circuit Professionalism and Civility Committee ("Committee") will continue to operate in the Eleventh Judicial Circuit ("Circuit").

a. In accordance with the Supreme Court of Florida's Administrative Order *In re: Commission on Professionalism*, the Chief Judge of the Circuit will serve as the Chair of the Committee.

b. The Committee shall be comprised of the following members:

i. Judiciary:

1. The Chief Judge of the Eleventh Judicial Circuit
2. Third District Court of Appeal Judge
3. Circuit Civil Division Judge
4. Circuit Criminal Division Judge
5. Circuit Family Division Judge
6. Circuit Probate Division Judge
7. Circuit Juvenile Division Judge
8. County Civil Division Judge
9. County Criminal Division Judge
10. County Domestic Violence Division Judge

ii. Attorneys:

1. State Attorney for Miami–Dade County or designee
2. Public Defender for Miami–Dade County or designee
3. Regional Counsel for the Third District or designee
4. Any other lawyer appointed by the Chief Judge that practices within the Eleventh Judicial Circuit and has demonstrated adherence to the professional standards of conduct set forth in the *Oath of Admission to the Florida Bar, The Florida Bar Creed of Professionalism, The Florida Bar Ideals and Goals of Professionalism, The Rules Regulating The Florida Bar*, the *Standards of Professional Courtesy and Civility for South Florida*, and the decisions of The Florida Supreme Court relating to professionalism.

c. Members of the Committee shall serve for a term of two (2) years.

d. The function and purpose of the Committee is to assess the status of professionalism among attorneys and to promote adherence to the professional standards of conduct set forth in the *Oath of Admission to the Florida Bar, The Florida Bar Creed of Professionalism, The Florida Bar Ideals and Goals of Professionalism, The Rules Regulating The Florida Bar*, the *Standards of Professional Courtesy and Civility for South Florida*, and the decisions of The Florida Supreme Court relating to professionalism and ethics within the Circuit.

e. The Committee shall discuss, monitor and/or coordinate professionalism activities within the Circuit, and may take action deemed appropriate by the Committee in furtherance of promoting and encouraging professionalism within the legal community.

f. The Committee shall meet quarterly, or on a schedule otherwise established by the Committee.

g. Each January, the Committee shall submit to the Chair of the Commission on Professionalism, an annual report on the status of professionalism and professionalism activities within the Circuit.

h. The Committee shall report to the Chief Judge.

2. Local Professionalism Panels are hereby established and charged with receiving, screening, and acting upon complaints of unprofessional conduct pursuant to *In re: Code for Resolving Professionalism Complaints*, 116 So. 3d 280 (Fla. 2013). The Panels shall begin receiving, screening and resolving complaints on September 1, 2014. Further,

a. In accordance with the Code for Resolving Professionalism Complaints, the Circuit hereby adopts and hereby incorporates as if fully set forth herein: the *Oath of Admission to the Florida Bar, The Florida Bar Creed of Professionalism, The Florida Bar Ideals and Goals of Professionalism* (Exhibit A), *The Rules Regulating The Florida Bar*, the *Standards of Professional Courtesy and Civility for South Florida* (Exhibit A), and the decisions of The Florida Supreme Court relating to professionalism, collectively referred to as the *Standards of Professionalism and Civility* ("*Standards*").

b. The Local Professionalism Panel ("Panel") will consist of respected attorneys in the community who will informally resolve complaints against attorneys practicing in the Circuit, in accordance with the procedures set forth in Exhibit B.

c. If deemed appropriate, the Panel may refer complaints to The Florida Bar.

Administrative Order No. 14–01 is hereby rescinded and superseded by this Administrative Order and held for naught.

This Administrative Order shall take effect immediately upon execution and shall remain in effect until further order of the Court.

DONE AND ORDERED in Chambers at Miami–Dade County, Florida, this 18th day of July, 2014.

BERTILA SOTO, CHIEF JUDGE
ELEVENTH JUDICIAL CIRCUIT
OF FLORIDA

Exhibit A

Eleventh Judicial Circuit Standards of Professionalism and Civility

The Eleventh Judicial Circuit adopts and hereby incorporates as if fully set forth herein: the *Oath of Admission to the Florida Bar, The Florida Bar Creed of Professionalism, The Rules Regulating The Florida Bar*, the decisions of The Florida Supreme Court relating to professionalism, *The Florida Bar Ideals and Goals of Professionalism*, the *Standards of Professional Courtesy and Civility for South Florida*, collectively referred to as the *Standards of Professionalism and Civility* ("*Standards*"). Attorneys practicing within the Eleventh Circuit shall govern themselves according to these *Standards*.

The Florida Bar Ideals and Goals of Professionalism

1. Commitment to Equal Justice Under Law and the Public Good.

Ideal:

A Florida lawyer should, in both professional and personal conduct, recognize that a license to practice law is a privilege which gives the lawyer a special position of trust, power and influence in our society. This privilege brings corresponding duties, for which the lawyer is accountable to the public, namely, to use that position and power in an honest and fair manner which respects the dignity of others, promotes the public good, and protects our system of equal justice under the law.

Goals:

1.1 A lawyer should at all times avoid the appearance of impropriety.

1.2 A lawyer should counsel and encourage other lawyers to abide by these ideals of professionalism.

1.3 A lawyer should at all times promote in the general public an understanding of the role of the legal profession in our system of equal justice under law.

1.4 A lawyer should encourage and support only those judicial candidates who by skill, knowledge, experience, integrity, temperament and commitment to public service are qualified to hold such positions.

1.5 When considering whether to advertise and what methods of advertising to use, a lawyer's first goal should be to promote and protect public confidence in a just and fair legal system founded on the rule of law.

1.6 Upon being employed by a new client, a lawyer should discuss fee and cost arrangements at the outset of the representation, and promptly confirm those arrangements in writing.

1.7 In any representation in which the fee arrangement is other than a contingent percentage-of-recovery fee or a fixed, flat-sum fee or in which the representation is anticipated to be of more than brief duration, a lawyer should bill clients on a regular, frequent interim basis.

1.8 When a fee dispute arises that cannot be amicably resolved, a lawyer should endeavor to refer the dispute to the appropriate fee arbitration panel.

2. Adherence to a Fundamental Sense of Honor, Integrity, and Fair Play.

Ideal:

A lawyer should at all times be guided by a fundamental sense of honor, integrity, and fair play, and should counsel his or her client to do likewise.

Goals:

2.1 A lawyer should not impose arbitrary or unreasonable deadlines for action by others.

2.2 A lawyer should not make scheduling decisions with the motive of limiting opposing counsel's opportunity to prepare or respond.

2.3 A lawyer should not unreasonably oppose an adversary's application for an order or an adversary's request to insert a term or provision in a document.

2.4 A lawyer should never permit nonlawyer support personnel to communicate with a judge or judicial officer on any matters pending before the judge or officer or with other court personnel except on scheduling and other ministerial matters.

2.5 A lawyer should notify opposing counsel of all communications with the court or other tribunal, except those involving only scheduling or clerical matters.

2.6 When submitting any written communication to a court or other tribunal, a lawyer should provide opposing counsel with a copy of the document contemporaneously, and sufficiently in advance of any related hearing to assure both the court and opposing counsel have a reasonable opportunity to review it beforehand.

2.7 A lawyer should promptly comply with requests to prepare proposed orders.

2.8 When scheduling hearings and other adjudicative proceedings, a lawyer should request an amount of time that is truly calculated to permit full and fair presentation of the matter to be adjudicated and to permit equal response by the lawyer's adversary.

2.9 A lawyer should immediately notify all counsel of any hearing time that the lawyer has reserved with the court or tribunal.

2.10 When there has been pre-trial disclosure of trial witnesses, a lawyer should make a reasonable, good-faith effort to identify those witnesses whom the lawyer believes are reasonably likely to be called to testify.

2.11 During trials and evidentiary hearings the lawyers should mutually agree to disclose the identities, and duration of witnesses anticipated to be called that day and the following day, including depositions to be read, and should cooperate in sharing with opposing counsel all visual-aid equipment.

2.12 When there has been pre-trial disclosure of trial exhibits, a lawyer should make a reasonable good-faith effort to identify those exhibits that the lawyer believes will be proffered into evidence.

2.13 A lawyer should not mark on or alter exhibits, charts, graphs, and diagrams without opposing counsel's permission or leave of court.

2.14 A lawyer should abstain from conduct calculated to detract or divert the factfinder's attention from the relevant facts or otherwise cause it to reach a decision on an impermissible basis.

3. Honesty and Candor.

Ideal:

A lawyer's word should be his or her bond. The lawyer should not knowingly misstate, distort, or improperly exaggerate any fact or opinion and should not improperly permit the lawyer's silence or inaction to mislead anyone.

Goals:

3.1 In drafting a proposed letter of intent, the memorialization of an oral agreement or a written contract reflecting an agreement reached in concept, a lawyer should draft a document that fairly reflects the agreement of the parties.

3.2 In drafting documents, a lawyer should point out to opposing counsel all changes that the lawyer makes or causes to be made from one draft to another.

3.3 A lawyer should not withhold information from a client to serve the lawyer's own interest or convenience.

4. Fair and Efficient Administration of Justice.

Ideal:

A lawyer should always conduct himself or herself to assure the just, speedy, and inexpensive determination of every action and resolution of every controversy.

Goals:

4.1 A lawyer should endeavor to achieve the client's lawful objectives as economically and expeditiously as possible.

4.2 A lawyer should counsel the client concerning the benefits of mediation, arbitration, and other alternative methods of resolving disputes.

4.3 A lawyer should counsel the client to consider and explore settlement in good faith.

4.4 A lawyer should accede to reasonable requests for waivers of procedural formalities when the client's legitimate interests are not adversely affected.

4.5 A lawyer should not invoke a rule for the purpose of creating undue delay.

4.6 A lawyer should never use discovery for the purpose of harassing or improperly burdening an adversary or causing the adversary to incur unnecessary expense.

4.7 A lawyer should frame reasonable discovery requests tailored to the matter at hand.

4.8 A lawyer should assure that responses to proper requests for discovery are timely and complete and are consistent with the obvious intent of the request.

4.9 In civil cases, a lawyer should stipulate all facts and principles of law which are not in dispute, and should promptly respond to requests for stipulations of fact or law.

4.10 After consulting with the client, a lawyer should voluntarily withdraw claims [and] defenses when it becomes apparent that they are without merit, are superfluous or merely cumulative.

4.11 A lawyer should appear at a hearing before a court or other tribunal fully prepared to submit the matter at issue to the court or tribunal for adjudication.

4.12 A lawyer should not use the post-hearing submission of proposed orders as a guise to argue or reargue the merits of the matter to be determined.

4.13 A lawyer should not request rescheduling, cancellations, extensions, and postponements without legitimate reasons and never solely for the purpose of delay or obtaining unfair advantage.

5. Courtesy.

Ideal:

A lawyer should treat all persons with courtesy and respect and at all times abstain from rude, disruptive and disrespectful behavior. The lawyer should encourage the lawyer's clients and support personnel to do likewise even when confronted with rude, disruptive and disrespectful behavior.

6. Respect for the Time and Commitments of Others.

Ideal:

A lawyer should respect the time and commitments of others.

Goals:

6.1 Before scheduling a hearing on any motion or discovery objection, a lawyer should endeavor to resolve or narrow the issue at hand.

6.2 In scheduling depositions upon oral examination, a lawyer should allow enough time to permit the conclusion of the deposition, including examination by all parties, without adjournment.

6.3 Unless circumstances compel more expedited scheduling, a lawyer should endeavor to provide litigants, witnesses, and other affected persons or parties with ample advance notice of hearings, depositions, meetings, and other proceedings, and whenever practical, schedule such activities at times that are convenient to all interested persons.

6.4 A lawyer should accede to all reasonable requests for scheduling, rescheduling, cancellations, extensions, and postponements that do not prejudice the client's opportunity for full, fair and prompt consideration and adjudication of the client's claim or defense.

6.5 Upon receiving an inquiry concerning a proposed time for a hearing, deposition, meeting, or other proceeding, a lawyer should promptly agree to the proposal or offer a counter suggestion.

6.6 A lawyer should call potential scheduling conflicts or problems to the attention of those affected, including the court or tribunal, as soon as they become apparent to the lawyer.

6.7 A lawyer should avoid last-minute cancellations of hearings, depositions, meetings, and other proceedings.

6.8 A lawyer should promptly notify the court or tribunal of any resolution by the parties that renders a scheduled court appearance unnecessary.

6.9 A lawyer should be punctual in attending all court appearances, depositions, meetings, conferences, and other proceedings.

6.10 A lawyer should respond promptly to inquiries and communications from clients and others.

7. Independence of Judgment.

Ideal:

A lawyer should exercise independent judgment and should not be governed by a client's ill will or deceit.

Goals:

7.1 A lawyer should counsel the client or prospective client, even with respect to a meritorious claim or defense, concerning the public and private burdens of pursuing the claim as compared with the benefits to be achieved.

7.2 A lawyer should at all times provide the client with objective evaluations and advise without purposefully understating or overstating achievable results or otherwise creating unrealistic expectations.

7.3 A lawyer should not permit the client's ill will toward an adversary, witness, or tribunal to become that of the lawyer's.

7.4 A lawyer should counsel the client against the use of tactics designed: (a) to hinder or improperly delay the process involved; or (b) to embarrass, harass, intimidate, improperly burden, or oppress an adversary, party or any other person and should withdraw from representation if the client insists on such tactics.

7.5 In contractual and business negotiations, a lawyer should counsel the client concerning what is reasonable and customary under the circumstances.

Standards of Professional Courtesy and Civility for South Florida

Preamble

Attorneys are often retained to represent their clients in disputes or transactions. The practice of law is often an adversarial process. Attorneys are ethically bound to zealously represent and advocate in their clients' best interests. Nonetheless, certain standards of professional courtesy exist that must be observed in the courtroom, the board room, or any other setting in which an attorney is present.

The following standards of professional courtesy describe the conduct expected of attorneys practicing before courts and other tribunals in South Florida, including Broward, Indian River, Martin, Miami–Dade, Monroe, Okeechobee, Palm Beach, and St. Lucie counties. These standards are not meant to be exhaustive, but instead to set a tone or guide for conduct not specifically covered by these standards. The overriding principles promoted by these standards are good-faith, civil and respectful communication between counsel and similar cooperation with judges, arbitrators, mediators, clerks, court staff, witnesses and non-parties.

These standards have been codified with the intent that their dissemination will educate and remind attorneys and their clients that attorneys practicing in South Florida are expected to behave professionally and civilly at all times. In 1990, the Board of Governors of The Florida Bar adopted the Ideals and Goals of Professionalism. In 2011, the Florida Supreme Court amended its oath of attorney admission ("Oath of Attorney Admission") to require that attorneys taking the oath pledge to opposing parties and counsel "fairness, integrity, and civility, not only in court, but also in all written and oral communications." In 2013, the Florida Supreme Court issued an opinion entitled *In re: Code for Resolving Professionalism Complaints* (SC13–688) that requires each judicial circuit in Florida to create a local professionalism panel to hear grievances for professionalism and civility violations. These standards below should be read together with the Ideals and Goals of Professionalism, the Oath of Attorney Admission, and the Florida Supreme Court's opinion aimed at improving attorneys' professionalism and civility.

I. Scheduling.

1. Attorneys should endeavor to provide opposing counsel and pro se litigants (collectively, "opposing counsel"), parties, witnesses, and other affected persons, sufficient notice of depositions, hearings and other proceedings, except upon agreement of counsel, in an emergency, or in other circumstances compelling more expedited scheduling. As a general rule, actual notice should be given that is no less than five (5) business days for in-state depositions, ten (10) business days for out-of-state depositions and five (5) business days for hearings.

2. Attorneys should communicate with opposing counsel prior to scheduling depositions, hearings and other proceed-

ings, so as to schedule them at times that are mutually convenient for all interested persons. Further, sufficient time should be reserved to permit a complete presentation by counsel for all parties. Upon receiving an inquiry concerning a proposed time for a hearing, deposition, meeting or other proceeding, a lawyer should promptly agree to the proposal or offer a counter suggestion that is as close in time as is reasonably available, and attorneys should cooperate with each other when conflicts and calendar changes are reasonably necessary. Only after making a reasonable effort to confer with opposing counsel should attorneys unilaterally schedule depositions, hearings or other matters.

3. Attorneys should notify opposing counsel, the court or other tribunal, and others affected, of scheduling conflicts as soon as they become apparent. Further, attorneys should cooperate with one another regarding all reasonable rescheduling requests that do not prejudice their clients or unduly delay a proceeding and promptly offer reasonable alternative dates to reschedule a matter.

4. Attorneys should promptly notify the court or other tribunal of any resolution between parties that renders a scheduled court appearance unnecessary or otherwise moot.

5. Attorneys should grant reasonable requests by opposing counsel for extensions of time within which to respond to pleadings, discovery and other matters when such an extension will not prejudice their client or unduly delay a proceeding.

6. Attorneys should cooperate with opposing counsel during trials and evidentiary hearings by disclosing with reasonable advance notice the identities of all witnesses reasonably expected to be called and the length of time needed to present the attorney's client's case, except when a client's material rights would be adversely affected. The attorneys also should cooperate with the calling of witnesses out of turn when the circumstances justify it.

II. Discovery.

1. Attorneys should pursue discovery requests that are reasonably related to the matter at issue. Attorneys should not use discovery for the purpose of harassing, embarrassing or causing the adversary to incur unnecessary expenses.

2. Attorneys should not use discovery for the purpose of causing undue delay or obtaining unfair advantage.

3. Attorneys should ensure that responses to reasonable discovery requests are timely, organized, complete and consistent with the obvious intent of the request. Attorneys should not produce documents in a way calculated to hide or obscure the existence of documents. A response to a request to produce should refer to each of the items in the request and the responsive documents should be produced as they correspond to each request or as they are kept in the usual course of business.

III. Conduct Directed to Opposing Counsel, the Court/Tribunal, and Other Participants in the Proceedings.

1. As it brings dishonor to the legal profession, attorneys should refrain from criticizing or denigrating opposing counsel, the court/tribunal and their staff, the parties, and witnesses before clients, the public, and the media.

2. Attorneys should be, and should impress upon their clients and witnesses the need to be, courteous and respectful and not rude or disruptive with the court/tribunal, opposing counsel, parties and witnesses.

3. Attorneys should make an effort to explain to witnesses the purpose of their required attendance at depositions, hearings or trials. Absent compelling circumstances, attorneys should give adequate notice to non-party witnesses before the scheduling of their depositions, advance notice of a subpoena for a deposition, hearing or trial. Attorneys further should attempt to accommodate the schedules of witnesses when resetting their appearance and promptly notify them of any cancellations.

4. Attorneys should respect and abide by the spirit and letter of all rulings of the court and advise their clients to do the same.

5. Attorneys and their staff should a) act and speak civilly and respectfully to courtroom deputies and bailiffs, clerks, court reporters, judicial assistants and law clerks; b) be selective in inquiries posed to judicial assistants as their time and resources are limited; and c) familiarize themselves with the court's administrative orders, local rules and each judge's published standing orders, practices and procedures.

IV. Candor to the Court/Tribunal and Opposing Counsel.

1. Attorneys should not knowingly misstate, misrepresent, or distort any fact or legal authority to the court, tribunal or opposing counsel and shall not mislead by inaction or silence. Further, if this occurs unintentionally and is later discovered, the attorney immediately should disclose and correct the error. Attorneys, likewise, should affirmatively notify the court or tribunal of controlling legal authority that is contrary to their client's legal position.

2. Attorneys immediately should notify opposing counsel of all oral or written communications with the court or other tribunal, except those involving only scheduling or administrative matters.

3. Copies of any submissions to the court or other tribunal (such as e-mails, correspondence, motions, pleadings, memoranda or law, legal authorities, exhibits, transcripts, etc.), should be simultaneously provided to opposing counsel by e-mail or delivery of an electronic or hard copy. For example, if a memorandum of law is hand-delivered to the court, a copy should be simultaneously e-mailed or hand-delivered to opposing counsel.

4. Attorneys should submit factual or legal argument to a court in a motion or memorandum of law and not in the form of an e-mail or letter. Tribunals other than courts, however, may permit more informal means than a motion or memorandum of law for the submission of factual or legal argument.

5. Attorneys should draft proposed orders promptly after a hearing or decision and the orders should fairly and adequately represent the ruling of the court or tribunal. Attorneys should promptly provide, either orally or in writing, proposed orders to opposing counsel for approval. In response, opposing counsel should communicate promptly any objections to the drafting attorney. The drafting attorney then should promptly submit a copy of the proposed order to the court or other tribunal and state whether opposing counsel agrees or objects to the form of the order.

6. Attorneys should draft agreements and other documents promptly after the discussions or agreement so as to fairly reflect the true intent of the parties. Where revisions are made to an agreement or other document, attorneys should point out, redline or otherwise highlight any such additions, deletions or modifications for opposing counsel.

V. Efficient Administration.

1. Attorneys should refrain from actions intended primarily to harass or embarrass and should refrain from actions which cause unnecessary expense or delay.

2. Attorneys should, whenever possible, prior to filing or upon receiving a motion, contact opposing counsel to determine if the matter can be resolved in whole or in part. This may alleviate the need for filing the motion or allow submission of an agreed order in lieu of a hearing.

3. Attorneys should, whenever appropriate, discuss discovery planning. Attorneys should also endeavor to stipulate to all facts and legal authority not reasonably in dispute.

4. Attorneys should encourage principled negotiations and efficient resolution of disputes on their merits.

EXHIBIT B

ELEVENTH JUDICIAL CIRCUIT PROCEDURAL RULES GOVERNING LOCAL PROFESSIONALISM PANELS

I. Standards and Purpose. Pursuant to *In re: Code for Resolving Professionalism Complaints*, 116 So. 3d 280 (Fla. 2013), the purpose of the Local Professionalism Panel ("Panel") is to receive, screen, and act upon complaints of unprofessional conduct and resolve those complaints informally, if possible, or refer to The Florida Bar, if deemed appropriate.

The Panel may discuss complaints, if appropriate, with the attorney alleged to have engaged in unprofessional conduct ("Respondent Attorney") and address conduct inconsistent with the *Standards of Professionalism and Civility* ("*Standards*") in an informal, non-punitive, and educational manner. *See* Exhibit A. The Panel shall have no authority to discipline any attorney or to compel any attorney to appear before the Panel. The Panel may counsel attorneys if it determines such counseling will further the goals of the *Standards*.

II. Panel Membership.

a. The Panel shall be composed of attorneys practicing within the Eleventh Judicial Circuit and who have demonstrated adherence to the professional standards of conduct set forth in the *Oath of Admission to the Florida Bar, The Florida Bar Creed of Professionalism, The Florida Bar Ideals and Goals of Professionalism, The Rules Regulating The Florida Bar*, and the decisions of The Florida Supreme Court relating to professionalism.

b. The Panel members shall be nominated by the Professionalism and Civility Committee ("Committee"), and appointed by the Chief Judge of the Eleventh Judicial Circuit.

c. In nominating attorneys for the Panel, the Committee shall consider the following factors:

i. Length of time in practice

ii. Board certification

iii. Trial experience

iv. Reputation

v. Leadership in voluntary bars or other areas of the community

d. Once selected, Panel members shall serve for two-year terms. Commencing September 1, 2014, two Panels consisting of three (3) members each, shall be assigned to receive, screen and resolve complaints on a rotating quarterly basis.

III. Initiation of a Complaint by a Person.

a. Any person may initiate a professionalism complaint against an attorney practicing in the Eleventh Judicial Circuit by submitting an electronic Complaint form on the Circuit's website (www.jud11.flcourts.org) [1] or by mailing a Complaint form to (Exhibit C) to:

Eleventh Judicial Circuit of Florida
ATTN: Professionalism Panel
Lawson E. Thomas Courthouse Center, Room 3016
175 Northwest 1st Avenue
Miami, Florida 33128

b. Absent extenuating circumstances, such a complaint shall be filed within fifteen (15) days of the conduct complained of, or within fifteen (15) days of the conclusion of the trial in which the conduct occurred.

c. The complaint shall be limited to five (5) pages, including exhibits.

d. Upon receipt, the Panel will review the complaint and make a determination as to whether a hearing is warranted. If necessary, the Panel may request additional written clarification from the complaining party. If the alleged misconduct is minor and appears to be an isolated incident, the Panel will not notify the Respondent Attorney that a complaint was filed and the Panel will take no further action.

e. If a complaint is referred to the Panel, the Panel may conduct an investigation, request a response from the Respondent Attorney, or invite the Respondent Attorney to appear before the Panel to address the complaint on a date and time specified.

IV. Initiation of a Complaint by The Florida Bar's Attorney Consumer Assistance Program (ACAP).

a. The Panel may accept referrals from ACAP.

b. The Panel shall review the referral, notify the Respondent Attorney of the referral, and determine whether the matter justifies review. If necessary, the Panel may request a response from the Respondent Attorney and invite the attorney to meet with the Panel on a date and time specified.

V. Investigation and Hearing.

a. The Professionalism Panel shall endeavor to resolve all referrals within forty-five (45) days of receipt of the complaint or referral.

b. At a reasonable time before any final findings are made by the Panel, the Respondent Attorney shall be advised of the conduct that is being investigated and the *Standards* that may have been violated. Any letter(s) sent to the Respondent Attorney by the Panel, shall advise the Respondent Attorney that the hearing is not a disciplinary proceeding.

c. The Respondent Attorney may be accompanied by counsel. The respondent shall be provided with all materials considered by the Panel and shall be given an opportunity to make a written statement, sworn or unsworn, explaining, refuting, or admitting the alleged unprofessional conduct.

d. The Respondent Attorney may record the hearing before the Panel at his or her own cost.

VI. Remedial Action.

a. If the Panel determines that the Respondent Attorney's conduct is inconsistent with the *Standards*, it may take remedial action including but not limited to the following:

i. Counsel the Respondent Attorney about the behavior and take no further action;

ii. Refer the Respondent Attorney to the Eleventh Judicial Circuit's Mentoring Program;

iii. Refer the Respondent Attorney to ACAP;

iv. Refer the Respondent Attorney to one of The Florida Bar's Practice and Professionalism Enhancement Programs, such as: The Florida Bar's Ethics School, Professionalism Workshops, Law Office Management Assistance Service (LOMAS), Anger Management Classes, etc.; and/or

v. Impose other remedies the Panel deems appropriate.

b. If the Respondent Attorney is referred to the Mentoring Program or for other remedial assistance, and the Respondent Attorney does not comply with the referral within thirty (30) days, the Committee may refer the Respondent Attorney to ACAP.

c. If the Respondent Attorney fails to appear at the hearing, the Panel shall discuss the alleged conduct inconsistent with the *Standards* and may summarize the Panel's findings by letter to the Respondent Attorney. The Panel may consider the Respondent Attorney's failure to appear in determining whether referral to ACAP is appropriate.

VII. Confidentiality.

a. The Committee and Panel shall maintain the confidentiality of the proceedings governed by these rules.

b. The Administrative Office of the Courts shall maintain the confidentiality of documents and records in its possession and control as required by applicable law in accordance with the requirements of Fla. R. Jud. Admin 2.420 and Rule 3–7.1 of the Rules Regulating the Florida Bar.

c. All findings by the Panel shall be published on the Eleventh Judicial Circuit website. However, the names of the parties shall remain confidential.

d. At the inception of the proceedings governed by these rules, all Panel members, the Complainant, and the Respondent Attorney shall be required to sign a statement acknowledging that:

i. All information disclosed during the Panel process is confidential and shall not be disclosed to anyone except other Panel members, the Complainant, or the Respondent Attorney, except in instances where the Panel publishes its findings as described in subsection c; and

ii. The Panel is a voluntary, informal program intended to be non-punitive, educational, and constructive; furthermore, participation and successful completion of all recommendations from the Panel shall not result in the imposition of sanctions or discipline.

(Exhibit C)

LOCAL PROFESSIONALISM PANEL COMPLAINT FORM

PART ONE: COMPLAINANT INFORMATION

Your Name: ______
Organization: ______
Street Address: ______
City, State, Zip Code: ______
Telephone: ______
E–mail: ______
Florida Bar Number: ______

Client ___ Member of public ___ Lawyer ___ Judge ___

Does this complaint pertain to a matter currently in litigation? Yes ___ No ___

PART TWO: RESPONDENT ATTORNEY INFORMATION

Attorney's Name: ______
Organization: ______
Street Address: ______
City, State, Zip Code: ______
Telephone: ______
E–mail: ______
Florida Bar Number: ______

PART THREE: FACTS/ALLEGATIONS

Nature of Incident

___ Appearance of impropriety	___ Honesty, integrity, candor
___ Unprofessional conduct	___ Unfair play, dilatory tactics
___ Uncivil, unruly	___ Used profanity/obscene gestures
___ Rude, discourteous, disruptive, disrespectful	___ Bullying or badgering
___ Offensive personality	___ Disorganized or unprepared
___ Abusive	___ Other:

***Standards* Implicated (Refer to Exhibit A)** ______

______

Incident date(s): ______

______

The specific incident or incidents I am complaining about are (attach additional sheets as necessary): ______

PART FOUR: WITNESSES
The witnesses in support of my allegations are (include name, address, and telephone number for each witness):

PART FIVE: SIGNATURE:
Under penalties of perjury, I declare that the foregoing facts are true, correct and complete.

Print Name

Signature

Date

[1]Upon submission of an electronic Complaint form, the Complainant must print and sign the Complaint form and mail the original Complaint to the Panel. If the signed Complaint is not received following the electronic submission, the Panel will not accept the Complaint. Signature photocopies will not be accepted.

Domestic Violence

13–07. PROCEDURES FOR THE ASSIGNMENT OF CRIMINAL CASES WITHIN THE DOMESTIC VIOLENCE DIVISION OF THE ELEVENTH JUDICIAL CIRCUIT OF FLORIDA

THE ELEVENTH JUDICIAL CIRCUIT MIAMI–DADE COUNTY, FLORIDA

CASE NO. 13–1 (Court Administration)

ADMINISTRATIVE ORDER NO. 13–07

IN RE: PROCEDURES FOR THE ASSIGNMENT OF CRIMINAL CASES WITHIN THE DOMESTIC VIOLENCE DIVISION OF THE ELEVENTH JUDICIAL CIRCUIT OF FLORIDA

WHEREAS, pursuant to Local Rule R–09/29/94 ("Local Rule"), the Domestic Violence Division of the Circuit and County Courts in the Eleventh Judicial Circuit was established ("DV Division"), to, inter alia, be responsible for the disposition of certain matters in connection with domestic, dating, sexual, stalking, and repeat violence arising under Chapter 741, Florida Statutes and Chapter 784, Florida Statutes, respectively; and

WHEREAS, the Local Rule also entrusts the DV Division with jurisdiction over all misdemeanor cases involving domestic, dating, sexual, stalking and repeat violence and criminal violations of injunctions;

NOW, THEREFORE, pursuant to the authority vested in me as Chief Judge of the Eleventh Judicial Circuit of Florida, under Rule 2.215, Florida Rules of Judicial Administration, it is hereby **ORDERED:**

The Judges assigned to the Domestic Violence Criminal Division shall hear the following criminal misdemeanor matters:

1. Criminal Contempt and Violation of Injunctions Chargers: All charges of criminal contempt of injunctions and all violations of injunctions for protection pursuant to Chapter 741, Florida Statutes or Chapter 784, Florida Statutes, will be heard by the designated Domestic Violence Division Judge. Such charges include all misdemeanor injunction violation cases involving domestic, dating, repeat violence or stalking injunction violations. All criminal violations of injunctions filed in the Branch Courts shall be transferred to the Domestic Violence Criminal Division.

2. Misdemeanor Charges: All other misdemeanor criminal cases involving family or household members as defined in Chapter 741, Florida Statutes, and current or former intimate/dating partners, shall be filed in the Domestic Violence Criminal Division.

This Administrative Order shall be effective upon execution and shall remain in effect until further order of the Court.

DONE AND ORDERED in Chambers at Miami–Dade County, Florida, this 3rd day of December, 2013.

BERTILA SOTO, CHIEF JUDGE
ELEVENTH JUDICIAL CIRCUIT OF FLORIDA

08–01 (A1). AUTHORIZATION FOR CONTINUATION OF CIVIL/DOMESTIC VIOLENCE OVERFLOW BACK–UP SECTION

THE ELEVENTH JUDICIAL CIRCUIT MIAMI–DADE COUNTY, FLORIDA

CASE NO. 08–1 (Court Administration)

ADMINISTRATIVE ORDER NO. 08–01
A1 (Amending AO No. 08–01)

IN RE: AUTHORIZATION FOR CONTINUATION OF CIVIL/DOMESTIC VIOLENCE OVERFLOW BACK–UP SECTION

WHEREAS, pursuant to Administrative Order No. 08–01, entered on January 15, 2008, the Court determined that in the interest of reducing the number of pending cases and effecting the prompt disposition of such cases in the Civil Division and the Domestic Violence Division of the County Court, it was necessary to create the County Civil/Domestic Violence Overflow Back-up Section ("Back-up Section"); and

WHEREAS, the Back-up Section was created as a pilot project for one (1) year for the period covering February 4, 2008 through February 3, 2009 ("Pilot Project"); and

WHEREAS, notwithstanding the significant reduction in the number of pending cases and their prompt disposition as a result of the Back-up Section, it has been determined that the Pilot Project should be continued in order to sustain its effectiveness;

NOW, THEREFORE, pursuant to the authority vested in me as Chief Judge of the Eleventh Judicial Circuit of Florida under Rule 2.215, Florida Rules of Judicial Administration, it is hereby **ORDERED**:

1. The County Civil/Domestic Violence Overflow Back-up Section as a pilot project is to continue beyond February 3, 2009 and will remain as such until further order of the Court.

2. Except as modified herein, all other provisions of Administrative Order No. 08–01 remain in full force and effect.

This Order shall take effect upon execution and shall remain in effect until further order of the Court.

DONE AND ORDERED in Chambers at Miami–Dade, Florida, this ___ day of November, 2008.

JOSEPH P. FARINA, CHIEF JUDGE
ELEVENTH JUDICIAL CIRCUIT OF FLORIDA

Family

15–04. ESTABLISHMENT OF REGISTRY FOR APPOINTMENT OF PROFESSIONAL GUARDIAN(S) IN PROBATE PROCEEDINGS IN THE ELEVENTH JUDICIAL CIRCUIT OF FLORIDA; DESIGNATION AND AUTHORIZATION OF CLERK OF THE COURTS TO OPERATE THE PROFESSIONAL GUARDIANSHIP REGISTRY

THE ELEVENTH JUDICIAL CIRCUIT MIAMI–DADE COUNTY, FLORIDA

CASE NO. 15–1 (Court Administration)

ADMINISTRATIVE ORDER NO. 15–04

IN RE: ESTABLISHMENT OF REGISTRY FOR APPOINTMENT OF PROFESSIONAL GUARDIAN(S) IN PROBATE PROCEEDINGS IN THE ELEVENTH JUDICIAL CIRCUIT OF FLORIDA; DESIGNATION AND AUTHORIZATION OF CLERK OF THE COURTS TO OPERATE THE PROFESSIONAL GUARDIANSHIP REGISTRY

WHEREAS, Chapter 744, Florida Statutes, authorizes court appointment of professional guardians ("Professional Guardians"), subject to the considerations set forth in Section 744.312, Florida Statutes; and

WHEREAS, such Professional Guardians are usually appointed to serve as legal guardians of a ward ("Ward") under those rare circumstances where no qualified family member or friend of the Ward is able to accept the appointment and the Ward is not indigent and therefore cannot qualify for the state-funded Public Guardianship Program; and

WHEREAS, periodically, the Judges in the Probate Division of the Eleventh Judicial Circuit ("Probate Division") appoint Professional Guardians; and

WHEREAS, the Office of the Statewide Guardian in the Department of Elder Affairs, through the Clerks Guardianship Auditing Department, provides the Probate Division with a current list of professional guardians, who are also listed on the Department of Elder Affairs website ("Statewide Guardianship List"); and

WHEREAS, each Judge in the Probate Division ("Probate Judge") has the discretion to appoint a Professional Guardian from the Statewide Guardianship List as the need arises; and

WHEREAS, while the Statewide Guardianship List is a comprehensive list of Professional Guardians, in addition to the minimum requirements to be included thereon, it includes individuals who are full time employees of various entities and have not sought appointments from the Probate Division, or they live outside of the South Florida area; thereby, limiting the number of Professional Guardians who can be appointed by the Probate Judges; and

WHEREAS, given such limitation and to avoid any appearance of impropriety regarding the repetitive appointment of Professional Guardians, it was determined that the establishment of the Professional Guardianship Registry ("PGR") for the Probate Division will provide all qualified Professional Guardians in Miami–Dade County, an equal opportunity to be appointed by the Probate Judges;

NOW, THEREFORE, pursuant to the authority vested in me as Chief Judge of the Eleventh Judicial Circuit of Florida, under Rule 2.215, Florida Rules of Judicial Administration, it is hereby **ORDERED:**

1. **Establishment of Professional Guardianship Registry.** The Professional Guardianship Registry ("PGR") is hereby established in the Eleventh Judicial Circuit of Florida to provide guardianship services to individuals who are not indigent and therefore do not qualify for the state-funded Public Guardianship Program.

2. **Eligibility Requirements.** In order to be included on the PGR, Professional Guardians must have met the minimum requirements to be included on the Statewide Guardianship List, completed the Professional Guardianship Program Application for the Eleventh Judicial Circuit, and recommended for such inclusion by the Probate Judges, subject to the approval of the Administrative Judge of the Probate Division, pursuant to a competitive selection process.

3. **Competitive Selection Process and Bi–Annual Review.** The Probate Division shall conduct a competitive selection process to select the Professional Guardians to be included on the PGR. After the initial competitive selection process and the creation of the PGR, from time to time, but at least

every two years thereafter, the Probate Judges shall review the PGR to determine if the PGR should be modified.[1]

4. **Designation and Authorization of Clerk of the Courts to Operate the PGR.** The Clerk of the Courts is hereby designated and authorized to operate the PGR in the manner set forth below:

a. The PGR shall be populated with the Professional Guardians who met the Eligibility Requirements set forth in paragraph 2.

b. If at any time, the Clerk is notified in writing, either by letter or email, by the Statewide Public Guardianship Office that a Professional Guardian on the PGR is no longer in compliance with the minimum requirements to be included on the Statewide Guardianship List, or by the Administrative Judge of the Probate Division that a Professional Guardian is not in compliance with any judicial requirements, the Clerk shall immediately remove the Professional Guardian from the PGR and notify the Administrative Judge of the Probate Division of such removal. Upon the receipt of a notice that the Professional Guardian is in compliance, the Professional Guardian shall be eligible for reinstatement, but placed at the bottom of the PGR, if the Administrative Judge of the Probate Division authorizes the reinstatement.

c. Upon receipt of the written request with the case number (sent via facsimile or electronic mail), from a Probate Judge or designee for the name of a Professional Guardian, the Clerk will select the next name on the PGR and forward same to the Probate Judge or designee.

d. Once the Professional Guardian accepts the appointment, the Probate Judge or designee will so advise the Clerk via facsimile or electronic mail. However, if the selected Professional Guardian does not accept the appointment, upon being so advised by the Probate Judge or designee via facsimile or electronic mail, the Clerk will place the name of said Professional Guardian at the bottom of the PGR and select another name for the case.

This Administrative Order shall take effect immediately upon execution and shall remain in effect until further order of the Court.

DONE AND ORDERED in Chambers at Miami–Dade County, Florida, this 23rd day of March, 2015.

BERTILA SOTO, CHIEF JUDGE
ELEVENTH JUDICIAL CIRCUIT OF FLORIDA

[1] It is hereby acknowledged that the initial competitive selection process commenced on November 19, 2014 and culminated on January 14, 2015 with the Probate Judges approving eleven (11) Professional Guardians to be on the Professional Guardianship Registry. The names of such Professional Guardians shall be listed alphabetically on the PGR.

15–03. AUTHORIZING THE SELF–HELP PROGRAM TO ESTABLISH AND IMPLEMENT CRITERIA FOR A COST SCHEDULE FOR FAMILY COURT SELF–HELP FORMS PACKET FOR THE ELEVENTH JUDICIAL CIRCUIT OF FLORIDA

THE ELEVENTH JUDICIAL CIRCUIT MIAMI–DADE COUNTY, FLORIDA

CASE NO. 15–1 (Court Administration)

ADMINISTRATIVE ORDER NO. 15–03

IN RE: AUTHORIZING THE SELF–HELP PROGRAM TO ESTABLISH AND IMPLEMENT CRITERIA FOR A COST SCHEDULE FOR FAMILY COURT SELF–HELP FORMS PACKET FOR THE ELEVENTH JUDICIAL CIRCUIT OF FLORIDA

WHEREAS, pursuant to Rule 12.750, Family Law Rules, it was established that in order to assist self-represented litigants to achieve fair and efficient resolution of their family law case, self-help personnel may provide certain services to such litigants; and

WHEREAS, Rule 12.750 further provided that self-help programs may require self-represented litigants to pay the cost of services provided for thereunder; and

WHEREAS, pursuant to Administrative Order No. 08–09, it was determined that Sixty-five Dollars ($65.00) was established as the amount to be charged for the Circuit's Forms Packet and Forms, along with the provision of quality services by the Circuit's Self–Help Program personnel; and

WHEREAS, AO 08–09 also provided that the charges for indigents were to be substantially reduced or waived; and

WHEREAS, it has also been determined that other self-represented parties, while not necessarily indigent, given their financial circumstances, should also be eligible for reduced or waived charges; and

WHEREAS, in order to determine the amount of charges, if any, to be paid by all self-represented parties, it has been recommended that the Circuit establish criteria for the Self–Help Program personnel to make such determination; and

WHEREAS, notwithstanding such criteria and its utilization by the Self–Help Program personnel to determination charges, it is further recommended that a party may still submit an Affidavit Requesting Waiver of Cost of the Family Court Self–Help Packet for consideration by the presiding judge in the matter;

NOW, THEREFORE, pursuant to the authority vested in me as Chief Judge of the Eleventh Judicial Circuit of Florida, under Rule 2.215, Florida Rules of Judicial Administration, it is hereby **ORDERED**:

1. The Self Help Program shall establish and implement criteria to be utilized by the Self–Help Program personnel to determine the amount of charges, if any, to be paid by all self-represented parties for the Family Court Self–Help Packet in the Eleventh Judicial Circuit, as may be modified from time to time.

2. Notwithstanding such determination, a self-represented party may still submit an Affidavit Requesting Waiver of Cost of the Family Court Self–Help Packet for consideration by the presiding judge in the matter.

This Administrative Order shall become effective immediately upon execution, and shall remain in effect until further order of the Court.

DONE AND ORDERED in Chambers at Miami–Dade County, Florida, this 20th day of March, 2015.

BERTILA SOTO, CHIEF JUDGE
ELEVENTH JUDICIAL CIRCUIT
OF FLORIDA

14–13. ADOPTION OF AND AUTHORIZATION TO UTILIZE STATUS QUO TEMPORARY DOMESTIC RELATIONS ORDER, WITH OR WITHOUT MINOR CHILDREN, IN THE ELEVENTH JUDICIAL CIRCUIT OF FLORIDA

THE ELEVENTH JUDICIAL CIRCUIT MIAMI–DADE COUNTY, FLORIDA

CASE NO. 14–1 (Court Administration)

ADMINISTRATIVE ORDER NO. 14–13

IN RE: ADOPTION OF AND AUTHORIZATION TO UTILIZE STATUS QUO TEMPORARY DOMESTIC RELATIONS ORDER, WITH OR WITHOUT MINOR CHILDREN, IN THE ELEVENTH JUDICIAL CIRCUIT OF FLORIDA

WHEREAS, to promote the stability of families going through a divorce or in paternity actions; and

WHEREAS, to provide guidance to parties in a dissolution of marriage or paternity action to help parties pattern their behavior in ways that reduce the negative impact that such proceedings have on the children and the parties involved; and

WHEREAS, to reduce the number of "emergency" hearings during the beginning stages of dissolution of marriage and paternity actions, thereby promoting stability and preserving resources of the parties and the court; and

WHEREAS, it is in the best interest of the parties and children or child, as the case may be, that parents in a divorce or paternity case learn about the problems, duties, and responsibilities of litigation and parenting after separation and divorce, and that the parties preserve their assets and comply with court rules; and

WHEREAS, the judges assigned to the Family Division of the Eleventh Judicial Circuit, with the assistance of the Family Law Bar, developed a status quo temporary order (hereinafter "Order") to be utilized in dissolution of marriage and paternity actions, in an effort to achieve the hereinabove stated goals; and

WHEREAS, the undersigned finds that it is in the best interest of the parties and any minor children of the parents in dissolution of marriage and paternity actions to adopt and authorize the use of the Order in this Circuit, as may be modified as deemed appropriate by the presiding judges in such actions;

NOW, THEREFORE, pursuant to the authority vested in me as Chief Judge of the Eleventh Judicial Circuit of Florida, under Rule 2.215, Florida Rules of Judicial Administration, it is hereby **ORDERED**:

1. The Status Quo Temporary Domestic Relations Order, With or Without Minor Children (hereinafter referred to as "Order"), attached hereto as Exhibit "A" is hereby adopted and authorized for use in dissolution of marriage and paternity actions in the Eleventh Judicial Circuit of Florida, as may be generally amended from time to time. The terms and conditions of said Order may be modified, terminated, or amended as deemed appropriate by the presiding judges in such actions.

2. It is the responsibility of the Petitioner and/or Petitioner's counsel to provide the Respondent with a copy of the Order by including it with the petition at time of service.

3. The Clerk of Court is hereby directed to post a copy of the Order on its website so that it is readily available to the Petitioner and/or Petitioner's counsel when the case is filed.

4. Failure to comply with the Order may result in appropriate sanctions against the offending party.

This Administrative Order shall take effect immediately upon execution and shall remain in effect until further order of the Court.

DONE AND ORDERED in Chambers at Miami–Dade County, Florida, on this 6th day of August, 2014.

BERTILA SOTO, CHIEF JUDGE
ELEVENTH JUDICIAL CIRCUIT
OF FLORIDA

14–05. REQUIREMENT TO COMPLETE A PARENTING EDUCATION AND FAMILY STABILIZATION COURSE

THE ELEVENTH JUDICIAL CIRCUIT MIAMI–DADE COUNTY, FLORIDA

CASE NO. 14–1 (Court Administration)

ADMINISTRATIVE ORDER NO. 14–05
(Rescinding AO No. 98–04)

IN RE: REQUIREMENT TO COMPLETE A PARENTING EDUCATION AND FAMILY STABILIZATION COURSE

WHEREAS, pursuant to Administrative Order No. 98–04 ("AO 98–04"), certain standards were established within the Eleventh Judicial Circuit for parties to attend a parenting course prior to obtaining a Final Judgment or Post–Judgment Final Order in any proceeding involving a dissolution of marriage matter with minor children or a modification of a final judgment action involving parental responsibilities, custody, or visitation; and

WHEREAS, since the enactment of AO 98–04, it has been determined that the Circuit's requirement for parties to attend a Parent Education and Family Stabilization Course ("Parenting Course") shall be revised to comply with section 61.21, Florida Statutes; and

WHEREAS, section 61.21, Florida Statutes, designates the Department of Children and Family Services to approve a Parenting Course for parents to attend who are separating or divorcing;

NOW, THEREFORE, pursuant to the authority vested in me as Chief Judge of the Eleventh Judicial Circuit of Florida, under Rule 2.215 of Judicial Administration, it is hereby **ORDERED**:

1. All parties to a dissolution of marriage proceeding with minor children or a paternity action that involves issues of parental responsibility shall be required to complete the parenting course prior to the entry of a final judgment by the Court.

2. All parties to a modification of a final judgment involving a parenting plan or a time-sharing schedule may be required to complete a Parenting Course prior to the entry of an order modifying the final judgment.

3. In accordance with section 61.21, Florida Statutes, course providers offering a Parenting Course may charge a fee to each party attending the course.

4. All parties are required to begin a Parenting Course as expeditiously as possible, specifically:

(a) *Dissolution of Marriage Actions With Minor Children.*

(1) Unless excused by the Court, the Petitioner must complete the course within 45 days after the filing of the petition.

(2) All other parties must complete the course within 45 days after service of the petition.

(b) *Paternity Actions.*

(1) Unless excused by the Court, the Petitioner must complete the course within 45 days after the filing of the petition.

(2) Any other party must complete the course within 45 days after an acknowledgment of paternity by the party, an adjudication of paternity of the party, or an order granting time-sharing to or support from the party.

5. Prior to the entry of the final judgment, all parties are required to file proof of compliance of completion of the Parenting Course with the Clerk of the Court.

6. The Court may excuse a party from attending the Parenting Course, or from completing the Parenting Course within the required time, for good cause shown.

7. The Court may hold any parent who fails to attend a required Parenting Course in contempt, or that parent may be denied shared parental responsibility or time-sharing, or otherwise sanctioned as the Court deems appropriate.

8. The Court may, without motion of either party, prohibit the parties from taking the Parenting Course together, if there is a history of domestic violence between the parties.

Administrative Order No. 98–04 is hereby rescinded in its entirety and shall be held for naught.

This Administrative Order shall become effective immediately upon execution.

DONE AND ORDERED in Chambers at Miami–Dade County, Florida, this 14th day of March, 2014.

BERTILA SOTO, CHIEF JUDGE
ELEVENTH JUDICIAL CIRCUIT OF FLORIDA

14–04. CESSATION OF CIRCUIT CERTIFIED CHILD EDUCATION AND CONSULTATION PROGRAM IN DISSOLUTION CASES INVOLVING MINORS

THE ELEVENTH JUDICIAL CIRCUIT MIAMI–DADE COUNTY, FLORIDA

CASE NO. 14–1 (Court Administration)

ADMINISTRATIVE ORDER NO. 14–04
(Rescinding AO No.98–03)

IN RE: CESSATION OF CIRCUIT CERTIFIED CHILD EDUCATION AND CONSULTATION PROGRAM IN DISSOLUTION CASES INVOLVING MINORS

WHEREAS, the Eleventh Judicial Circuit Court of Florida, by and through Administrative Order 98–03 ("AO 98–03") required children, between the ages of six and seventeen, whose parents were before the court on a petition for dissolution of marriage, custody modification, or determination of paternity, to complete a Circuit certified education program or an alternative court approved program; and

WHEREAS, it has been determined that the Administrative Office of the Courts ("AOC") no longer provides a list of Circuit certified child education and consultation programs or alternate court approved programs for use by the Family Division of the Circuit Court; and

WHEREAS, the AOC no longer approves the fees for Circuit certified child education and consultation programs or alternate court approved programs;

NOW, THEREFORE, pursuant to the authority vested in me as Chief Judge of the Eleventh Judicial Circuit of Florida, under Rule 2.215 Rules of Judicial Administration, it is hereby **ORDERED**:

Administrative Order No. 98–03 is rescinded in its entirety and shall be held for naught.

This Administrative Order shall become effective immediately upon execution.

DONE AND ORDERED in Chambers at Miami–Dade County, Florida, this 17th day of March, 2014.

BERTILA SOTO, CHIEF JUDGE
ELEVENTH JUDICIAL CIRCUIT OF FLORIDA

14–01. REAFFIRMATION OF THE FAMILY MEDIATION UNIT OF THE CIRCUIT COURT

THE ELEVENTH JUDICIAL CIRCUIT MIAMI–DADE COUNTY, FLORIDA

CASE NO. 14–1 (Court Administration)

ADMINISTRATIVE ORDER NO. 14–01
(Amending AO No. 93–54)

IN RE: REAFFIRMATION OF THE FAMILY MEDIATION UNIT OF THE CIRCUIT COURT

WHEREAS, the Chief Judge of the Eleventh Judicial Circuit of Florida, pursuant to Rule 2.215 of Florida Rule of Judicial Administration, has the authority to adopt administrative orders necessary to ensure the operation of the Eleventh Judicial Circuit of Florida; and

WHEREAS, as acknowledged in Administrative Order No. 93–54, the Family Mediation Unit of the Eleventh Judicial Circuit was created as the Conciliation Unit to serve the needs of the Family Division of the Circuit Court;

NOW, THEREFORE, in accordance with the authority vested in the Chief Judge of the Eleventh Judicial Circuit of Florida, it is hereby **ORDERED**:

1. Paragraph 2 of Administrative Order No. 93–54, is hereby amended in the following particulars:

"2. If the parties' income statutorily permits them to receive court-provided mediation services, they shall be eligible to receive the services of the Mediation Division within the Eleventh Judicial Circuit. Payment for the mediation session must be made in advance. Fees for court-ordered mediation sessions will be assessed and collected in accordance with section 44.108, Florida Statutes."

2. Except as amended herein, Administrative Order No. 93–54, executed on August 12, 1993, remains in full force and effect.

This Administrative Order shall take effect immediately and shall remain in effect until further order of the Court.

DONE and ORDERED in Chambers at Miami–Dade, Florida, this 14th day of March, 2014.

BERTILA SOTO, CHIEF JUDGE
ELEVENTH JUDICIAL CIRCUIT
OF FLORIDA

09–15 (A1). AMENDING PARENTING COORDINATION IN FAMILY LAW CASES

THE ELEVENTH JUDICIAL CIRCUIT MIAMI-DADE COUNTY, FLORIDA

CASE NO. 14–1 (Court Administration)

ADMINISTRATIVE ORDER NO. 09–15
A1 (Amending AO No.09–15)

IN RE: AMENDING PARENTING COORDINATION IN FAMILY LAW CASES

WHEREAS, pursuant to Administrative Order No. 09–15, entered on October 1, 2009, this Circuit established certain procedures for the proper administration of parenting coordination in family law cases; and

WHEREAS, subsequent to the effective date of Administrative Order 09–15, the Florida Supreme Court adopted amendments to the Florida Family Law Rules of Procedure and New Rules for Qualified and Court–Appointed Parenting Coordinators. *In re Amendments to the Florida Family Law Rules of Procedure; New Rules for Qualified and Court Appointed Parenting Coordinators*, 142 So.3d 831 (2014); and

WHEREAS, pursuant to such Amendments, the Florida Supreme Court, inter alia, requires that each judicial circuit establish a process for parenting coordinator qualification;

NOW, THEREFORE, pursuant to the authority vested in me as Chief Judge of the Eleventh Judicial Circuit of Florida, under Rule 2.215 of the Florida Rules of Judicial Administration, it is hereby **ORDERED**:

1. The provisions set forth in section 61.125, Florida Statutes, shall be followed in this Circuit regarding parenting coordination.

2. The following forms, attached hereto, are hereby adopted and shall be used in carrying out the provisions of section 61.125, Florida Statutes:

a. Attachment "A"—Order of Referral to Parenting Coordinator.

b. Attachment "B"—Response by Parenting Coordinator.

c. Attachment "C"—Parenting Coordinator Report of an Emergency.

d. Attachment "D"—Parenting Coordinator Request for Status Conference.

e. Attachment "E"—Report of General Magistrate on Motion for Referral to Parenting Coordinator.

3. Except as herein amended, Administrative Order No. 09–15 shall remain in full force and effect.

This Order shall take effect immediately and shall remain in effect until further order of the Court.

DONE AND ORDERED in Chambers at Miami–Dade, Florida, this 6th day of October, 2014.

BERTILA SOTO, CHIEF JUDGE
ELEVENTH JUDICIAL CIRCUIT
OF FLORIDA

ATTACHMENT "A"

IN THE CIRCUIT COURT OF THE 11TH JUDICIAL CIRCUIT IN AND FOR DADE COUNTY, FLORIDA

Petitioner,

and

DIVISION:
CASE NUMBER:
SECTION:

Respondent.
____________________/

ORDER OF REFERRAL TO PARENTING COORDINATOR

The Court considered the ☐ motion of the court, ☐ joint motion of the parties, ☐ motion of a party, reviewed the court file, considered the testimony presented. Based on this information, the court FINDS that:

A. **Appropriateness of Process.** This matter is appropriate for parenting coordination and it is in the best interest of the child(ren).

B. **Parenting Coordination Process.** Parenting coordination is a child-focused alternative dispute resolution process whereby a parenting coordinator assists the parties in creating or implementing their parenting plan by facilitating the resolution of disputes, providing education and making recommendations to the parties; and, with the prior consent of the parties and approval of the court, making limited decisions within the scope of this order of referral.

C. **Parenting Coordinator.** A parenting coordinator is an impartial third person whose role is to assist the parties in successfully creating or implementing a parenting plan.

D. **Selection of Parenting Coordinator.** Family Court Services will provide the parties' referral to a parenting coordinator and will report to the court the parenting coordinator selected and agreed upon by the parties or selected through Family Court Services as per Family Law Rules of Procedure

12.742(b) and 11th Judicial Circuit Administrative Order 09–15 A1.

E. **History of Domestic Violence.** Based upon testimony and evidence presented and a review of related court records, the court has determined:

☐ There is no history of domestic violence.

☐ There has been a history of domestic violence, and:

☐ Each party has had an opportunity to consult with an attorney or domestic violence advocate before this court has accepted the parties' consent.

☐ Each party has consented to this referral and the consent has been given freely and voluntarily.

It is therefore, **ORDERED**:

1. **Parenting Coordinator.** The parties are referred to parenting coordination for an initial period of ________ months (not to exceed two years).

The parties are ordered to contact Family Court Services within (5) working days from the date of this order at: Lawson E. Thomas Courthouse Center, 175 NW 1st Avenue, Suite 1503, Miami, Florida 33128, tel: 305–349–5508, fax: 305–349–5634. The parties will notify Family Court services that they have agreed to a specific parenting coordinator or Family Court Services will designate a qualified parenting coordinator for the parties.

a. The parenting coordinator shall file a response to this Order within 30 days accepting or declining the appointment. The response to the appointment must be in substantial compliance with Form 12.984(b).

b. The parties or their attorneys must provide to the parenting coordinator copies of all pleadings and orders related to domestic violence and any other pleadings and orders requested by the parenting coordinator related to parenting coordination.

2. **Meetings.** Unless prohibited herein as a domestic violence safeguard or by another court order, the parenting coordinator may meet with the parties and/or child(dren) together or separately, in person or by any electronic means. The parenting coordinator shall determine the schedule for subsequent appointments.

3. **Domestic Violence Safeguards.** The parties shall adhere to all provisions of any injunction for protection or conditions of bail, probation, or a sentence arising from criminal proceedings. In addition to any safety measures the parenting coordinator deems necessary, the following domestic violence safeguards must be implemented:

[Choose all that apply]

☐ None are necessary.

☐ No joint meetings.

☐ No direct negotiations.

☐ No direct communications.

☐ Other: ______________________________

4. **Role, Responsibility, and Authority of Parenting Coordinator.** The parenting coordinator shall have the following role, responsibility, and authority:

a. Assisting the parties in creating and implementing a parenting plan;

b. Facilitating the resolution of disputes regarding the creation or implementation of the Parenting Plan;

c. Recommending to parties strategies for creating or implementing the Parenting Plan. Such recommendations may include that one or both parents avail themselves of accessible and appropriate community resources, including, but not limited to, random drug screens, parenting classes, and individual psychotherapy and/or family counseling, if there is a history or evidence that such referrals are appropriate;

d. Recommending to the parents changes to the Parenting Plan;

e. Educating the parties to effectively:

i. Parent in a manner that minimizes conflicts;

ii. Communicate and negotiate with each other and their child(ren);

iii. Develop and apply appropriate parenting skills;

iv. Understand principles of child development and issues facing child(ren) when their parents no longer live together;

v. Disengage from the other parent when engagement leads to conflicts and non-cooperation;

vi. Identify the sources of their conflict with each other and work individually and/or jointly to minimize conflict and lessen its deleterious effects on the child(ren); and,

vii. Allow the child(ren) to grow up free from the threat of being caught in the middle of their parents' disputes.

f. Facilitating the ability of both parents to maintain ongoing relationships with their children.

g. Reporting or communicating with the court concerning non-confidential matters as provided in paragraph 7 of this order. In the event the parenting coordinator is unable to adequately perform the duties in accordance with the court's direction, the parenting coordinator shall file a written request for a status conference and the court shall set a timely status hearing. The request for status conference must be in substantial compliance with Florida Family Law Rules of Procedure Form 12.984(d). A report to the court of an emergency pursuant to section 61.125(8), Florida Statutes, must be in substantial compliance with Florida Family Law Rules of Procedure Form 12.984(c).

h. Communicating with the parties and their child(ren), separately or together, in person, by telephone or electronic means, unless otherwise prohibited by court order or applicable law.

5. **Scope of Authority.** The parenting coordinator shall make limited decisions within the scope of this order of referral. Limited decision making authority shall include, but may not be limited to: ________

6. **Fees and Costs for Parenting Coordination.** [Choose all that apply]

a. ___ The parties have consented to this referral to parenting coordination.

___ This order is without the consent of the parties, but the court has determined that the parties have the financial ability to pay the parenting coordination fees and costs.

b. The court allocates payment of fees and costs for parenting coordination as follows:

☐ % shall be paid by the Father.

☐ % shall be paid by the Mother.

☐ No fees as Family Court Services to provide parenting coordination

☐ Other: ______________________________

c. If a party causes the parenting coordinator to expend an unreasonable and unnecessary amount of time, that party may be held solely responsible for payment of the parenting coordinator's fees and costs for such time expended, and the court reserves jurisdiction to reallocate the payment of fees and costs in that event. Failure to pay the parenting coordinator's fees and costs in a timely manner may subject the party to sanctions for contempt of court.

d. The parenting coordinator shall not proceed until he/she is satisfied with the terms and conditions of payment for his/her services. Further, the parenting coordinator shall not perform nor continue to perform the parenting coordination services in this case unless all of his/her fees and costs are paid by the parties as ordered, and, in the event of nonpayment, the parenting coordinator shall file a Request for Status Conference, and the court will address the issue of nonpayment of fees and costs.

7. **Confidentiality.** All communications made by, between, or among the parties and the parenting coordinator during parenting coordination sessions are confidential. The parenting coordinator and each party may not testify or offer evidence about communications made by a party or the parenting coordinator during the parenting coordination sessions, except if:

a. It is necessary to identify, authenticate, confirm, or deny a written agreement entered into by the parties during parenting coordination;

b. The testimony or evidence is necessary to identify an issue for resolution by the court without otherwise disclosing communications made by any party or the parenting coordinator;

c. The testimony or evidence is limited to the subject of a party's compliance with the order of referral to parenting coordination, orders for psychological evaluation, counseling ordered by the court or recommended by a health care provider, or for substance abuse testing or treatment;

d. The parenting coordinator reports that the case is no longer appropriate for parenting coordination;

e. The parenting coordinator reports that he or she is unable or unwilling to continue to serve and that a successor parenting coordinator should be appointed;

f. The testimony or evidence is necessary pursuant to s. 61.125(5)(b) or s. 61.125(8), Florida Statutes;

g. The parenting coordinator is not qualified to address or resolve certain issues in the case and a more qualified coordinator should be appointed;

h. The parties agree that the testimony or evidence be permitted; or

i. The testimony or evidence is necessary to protect any person from future acts that would constitute domestic violence under Chapter 741, Florida Statutes; child abuse, neglect, or abandonment under Chapter 39, Florida Statutes; or abuse, neglect, or exploitation of an elderly or disabled adult under Chapter 825, Florida Statutes.

8. **Agreement on Nonconfidentiality.** The parties can agree to waive confidentiality of a specific communication or all communications. The waiver must be in writing, signed by the parties and their respective counsel. The waiver shall be filed with the court and a copy served on the parenting coordinator. Either party may revoke his or her waiver of confidentiality by providing written notice signed by the party. The revocation shall be filed with the court and a copy served on the other party and the parenting coordinator.

9. **Withdrawal Procedure.** With Court approval, the parenting coordinator may withdraw from the role of parenting coordinator. The parenting coordinator shall apply directly to the Court with a request to be discharged, and shall provide notice to the parties and their counsel of their request to withdrawal. Either party may seek to terminate the parenting coordinator's services by filing a motion with the Court. The parenting coordinator's services may not be terminated by either of the parties (or at the request of both parties) without order of this court.

11.[1] **Stipulation.** Any written stipulation of parties to utilize the parenting coordination process filed with this court is incorporated into this Order.

10.[2] **Reservation of Jurisdiction.** This Court specifically reserves jurisdiction to enforce and/or modify the terms and conditions of this Order.

DONE AND ORDERED in Miami–Dade County, Florida, on this ___ day of ________, 201__.

____

Circuit Judge

Copies to:

Name of Party:

Counsel for Party

Address of Counsel

Name of Party:

Counsel for Party

Address of Counsel

Guardian ad Litem

Address of GAL

If you are a person with a disability who needs any accommodation in order to participate in this proceeding, you are entitled, at no cost to you, to the provision of certain assistance. Please contact the Eleventh Judicial Circuit Court's ADA Coordinator, Lawson E. Thomas Courthouse Center, 175 NW 1st Ave., Suite 2702, Miami, FL 33128, Telephone (305) 349–7175; TDD (305) 349–7174, Fax (305) 349–7355 at least 7 days before your scheduled court appearance, or immediately upon receiving this notification if the time before the scheduled appearance is less than 7 days; if you are hearing or voice impaired, call 711.

"ATTACHMENT "B"

IN THE CIRCUIT COURT OF THE 11TH JUDICIAL CIRCUIT IN AND FOR DADE COUNTY, FLORIDA

Petitioner,

and FAMILY DIVISION
CASE NUMBER:
SECTION:

Respondent.
_______________/

RESPONSE BY PARENTING COORDINATOR

I, {*name*} ________, notify the Court and affirm the following:

1. Acceptance [check one only]

☐ I accept the appointment as parenting coordinator.

☐ I decline the appointment as parenting coordinator.

2. Qualifications [check **one** only]

☐ I meet the qualifications in section 61.125(4), Florida Statutes.

☐ I do not meet the qualifications in section 61.125(4), Florida Statutes. However, the parties have chosen me by mutual consent and I believe I can perform the services of a parenting coordinator because:

____

____

____

3. I am not aware of any conflict, circumstance, or reason that renders me unable to serve as the parenting coordinator in this matter and I will immediately inform the court and the parties if such arises.

4. I understand my role, responsibility, and authority under the Order of Referral to Parenting Coordinator, Florida Family Law Rules of Procedure Form 12.984(a); and section 61.125, Florida Statutes; Florida Family Law Rule of Procedures 12.742; and Rules for Qualified and Court Appointed Parenting Coordinators.

I hereby affirm the truth of the statements in this acceptance and understand that if I make any false representations in this acceptance, I am subject to sanctions by the Court.

Date ________ ______________________________
Signature of Parenting Coordinator
Printed Name: ______________
Address: ______________
City, State, Zip: ______________
Telephone Number: ______________
E–mail: ______________
Professional License # (if applicable) __
Professional Certification # (if applicable) ______________

Copies to:

________ Presiding Judge

________ Petitioner

________ Attorney for Petitioner

________ Respondent

________ Attorney for Respondent

________ Other:______________________

IF A NONLAWYER HELPED YOU FILL OUT THIS FORM, HE/SHE MUST FILL IN THE BLANKS BELOW:

[fill in **all** blanks] This form was completed with the assistance of:
{*name of individual*} ________,
{*name of business*),
{*address*} ________,
{*city*} ________, {*state*} ________, {*telephone number*}.

ATTACHMENT "C"

IN THE CIRCUIT COURT OF THE 11TH JUDICIAL CIRCUIT IN AND FOR DADE COUNTY, FLORIDA

Petitioner,

and DIVISION:
CASE NUMBER:
SECTION:

Respondent.
_______________/

PARENTING COORDINATOR REPORT OF AN EMERGENCY

The undersigned parenting coordinator reports an emergency to the court:

1. ________ With notice to the parties. A party has obtained a final order or injunction of protection against domestic violence or has been arrested for an act of domestic violence as provided under chapter 741, F.S.

2. ________ Without notice to the parties pursuant to section 61.125 (8)(a), Florida Statutes, because: (choose all that apply)

a. ________ There is a reasonable cause to suspect that a child will suffer or is suffering abuse, neglect, or abandonment as provided under chapter 39, Florida Statutes.

b. ________ There is a reasonable cause to suspect a vulnerable adult has or is being abused, neglected, or exploited as provided under chapter 415, Florida Statutes.

c. ________ A party, or someone acting on a party's behalf, is expected to wrongfully remove or is wrongfully removing the child from the jurisdiction of the court without prior approval or compliance with the requirements of section 61.13001, Florida Statutes.

3. Describe the emergency:

____

____

____

VERIFICATION BY PARENTING COORDINATOR

I, ________ (name of parenting coordinator) do hereby swear or affirm that the facts contained in this Parenting Coordinator Report of an emergency are true and correct to the best of my knowledge and belief.

Date ________ ______________________________
Signature of Parenting Coordinator
Printed Name: ______________
Address: ______________
City, State, Zip: ______________
Telephone Number: ______________
E–mail: ______________
Professional License # (if applicable) __
Professional Certification # (if applicable) ______________

STATE OF FLORIDA
COUNTY OF ______________________

Sworn to or affirmed and signed before me on ________ by ________.

____
NOTARY PUBLIC or DEPUTY CLERK

____
[Print, type, or stamp commissioned name of notary or deputy clerk.]

___ Personally known
___ Produced identification
Type of identification produced ______________

Copies to:
________ Presiding Judge
________ Petitioner
________ Attorney for Petitioner
________ Respondent
________ Attorney for Respondent
________ Other:______________

IF A NONLAWYER HELPED YOU FILL OUT THIS FORM, HE/SHE MUST FILL IN THE BLANKS BELOW:
[fill in all blanks] This form was completed with the assistance of:

{*name of individual*} ________,
{*name of business*} ________,
{*address*} ________,
{*city*} ________, {*state*} ________, {*telephone number*} ________.

ATTACHMENT "D"

IN THE CIRCUIT COURT OF THE 11TH JUDICIAL CIRCUIT IN AND FOR DADE COUNTY, FLORIDA

Petitioner,

and

Respondent.
______________/

DIVISION:
CASE NUMBER:
SECTION:

PARENTING COORDINATOR REQUEST FOR STATUS CONFERENCE

The undersigned Parenting Coordinator requests a status conference in this case: (choose all that apply)

1. ___ To request direction from the court concerning: ________ ______________________ ________.

2. ___ To request resolution by the court regarding: ________ ______________________ ________.

3. ___ To report ☐ petitioner's ☐ respondent's noncompliance with the Order of Referral to Parenting Coordinator, orders for psychological evaluation, counseling ordered by the court or recommended by a health care provider, or for substance abuse testing or treatment.

4. ___ To report that the case is no longer appropriate for parenting coordination.

5. ___ To report that the undersigned parenting coordinator is not qualified to address or resolve certain issues in this case and a more qualified successor parenting coordinator should be appointed.

6. ___ The undersigned parenting coordinator is unable or unwilling to continue to serve and a successor parenting coordinator should be appointed.

WHEREFORE, the undersigned Parenting Coordinator requests that a Status Conference be set by the Court.

Date ________ ______________________
Signature of Parenting Coordinator
Printed Name: ______________
Address: ______________
City, State, Zip: ______________
Telephone Number: ______________
E-mail: ______________
Professional License # (if applicable) ___
Professional Certification # (if applicable) ______________

Copies to:
________ Presiding Judge
________ Petitioner
________ Attorney for Petitioner
________ Respondent
________ Attorney for Respondent
________ Other:______________

IF A NONLAWYER HELPED YOU FILL OUT THIS FORM, HE/SHE MUST FILL IN THE BLANKS BELOW:
[fill in all blanks] This form was completed with the assistance of:

{*name of individual*} ________,
{*name of business*} ________,
{*address*} ________,
{*city*}, {*state*}, ________, {*telephone number*} ________.

ATTACHMENT "E"

IN THE CIRCUIT COURT OF THE 11TH JUDICIAL CIRCUIT IN AND FOR DADE COUNTY, FLORIDA

Petitioner,

and

Respondent.
______________/

DIVISION:
CASE NUMBER:
SECTION:

REPORT OF GENERAL MAGISTRATE ON MOTION FOR REFERRAL TO PARENTING COORDINATOR

The above cause came before the undersigned General Magistrate on this ___ day of ________, upon the ☐ joint motion of the parties, ☐ motion of a party, having considered Rule 12.472, Florida Family Law Rules of Procedure, and the General Magistrate, having considered the evidence presented and after being otherwise advised in the premises, FINDS, CONCLUDES AND RECOMMENDS **THAT:**

A. **Appropriateness of Process.** This matter is appropriate for parenting coordination and it is in the best interest of the child(ren).

B. **Parenting Coordination Process.** Parenting coordination is a child-focused alternative dispute resolution process whereby a parenting coordinator assists the parties in creating or implementing their parenting plan by facilitating the resolution of disputes, providing education and making recommendations to the parties; and, with the prior consent of the parties and approval of the court, making limited decisions within the scope of this order of referral.

C. **Parenting Coordinator.** A parenting coordinator is an impartial third person whose role is to assist the parties in successfully creating or implementing a parenting plan.

D. **Selection of Parenting Coordinator.** Family Court Services will provide the parties' referral to a parenting coordinator and will report to the court the parenting coordinator selected and agreed upon by the parties or selected through Family Court Services as per Family Law Rules of Procedure 12.742(b) and 11th Judicial Circuit Administrative Order 09–15 A1.

E. **History of Domestic Violence.** Based upon testimony and evidence presented and a review of related court records, the court has determined:

☐ There is no history of domestic violence.

☐ There has been a history of domestic violence, and:

☐ Each party has had an opportunity to consult with an attorney or domestic violence advocate before this court has accepted the parties' consent.

☐ Each party has consented to this referral and the consent has been given freely and voluntarily.

It is therefore, **ORDERED:**

1. **Parenting Coordinator.** The parties are referred to parenting coordination for an initial period of ___ months (not to exceed two years).

The parties are ordered to contact Family Court Services within (5) working days from the date of this order at: Lawson E. Thomas Courthouse Center, 175 NW 1 st Avenue, Suite 1503, Miami, Florida 33128, tel: 305–349–5508, fax: 305–349–5634. The parties will notify Family Court services that they have agreed to a specific parenting coordinator or Family Court Services will designate a qualified parenting coordinator for the parties.

a. The parenting coordinator shall file a response to this Order within 30 days accepting or declining the appointment. The response to the appointment must be in substantial compliance with Form 12.984(b).

b. The parties or their attorneys must provide to the parenting coordinator copies of all pleadings and orders related to domestic violence and any other pleadings and orders requested by the parenting coordinator related to parenting coordination.

2. **Meetings.** Unless prohibited herein as a domestic violence safeguard or by another court order, the parenting coordinator may meet with the parties and/or child(dren) together or separately, in person or by any electronic means. The parenting coordinator shall determine the schedule for subsequent appointments.

3. **Domestic Violence Safeguards.** The parties shall adhere to all provisions of any injunction for protection or conditions of bail, probation, or a sentence arising from criminal proceedings. In addition to any safety measures the parenting coordinator deems necessary, the following domestic violence safeguards must be implemented:

[Choose all that apply]

☐ None are necessary.

☐ D No joint meetings.

☐ No direct negotiations.

☐ No direct communications.

☐ Other:

4. **Role, Responsibility, and Authority of Parenting Coordinator.** The parenting coordinator shall have the following role, responsibility, and authority:

a. Assisting the parties in creating and implementing a parenting plan;

b. Facilitating the resolution of disputes regarding the creation or implementation of the Parenting Plan;

c. Recommending to parties strategies for creating or implementing the Parenting Plan. Such recommendations may include that one or both parents avail themselves of accessible and appropriate community resources, including, but not limited to, random drug screens, parenting classes, and individual psychotherapy and/or family counseling, if there is a history or evidence that such referrals are appropriate;

d. Recommending to the parents changes to the Parenting Plan;

e. Educating the parties to effectively:

i. Parent in a manner that minimizes conflicts;

ii. Communicate and negotiate with each other and their child(ren);

iii. Develop and apply appropriate parenting skills;

iv. Understand principles of child development and issues facing child(ren) when their parents no longer live together;

v. Disengage from the other parent when engagement leads to conflicts and non-cooperation;

vi. Identify the sources of their conflict with each other and work individually and/or jointly to minimize conflict and lessen its deleterious effects on the child(ren); and,

vii. Allow the child(ren) to grow up free from the threat of being caught in the middle of their parents' disputes.

f. Facilitating the ability of both parents to maintain ongoing relationships with their children.

g. Reporting or communicating with the court concerning non-confidential matters as provided in paragraph 7 of this order. In the event the parenting coordinator is unable to adequately perform the duties in accordance with the court's direction, the parenting coordinator shall file a written request for a status conference and the court shall set a timely status hearing. The request for status conference must be in substantial compliance with Florida Family Law Rules of Procedure Form 12.984(d). A report to the court of an emergency pursuant to section 61.125(8), Florida Statutes, must be in substantial compliance with Florida Family Law Rules of Procedure Form 12.984(c).

h. Communicating with the parties and their child(ren), separately or together, in person, by telephone or electronic means, unless otherwise prohibited by court order or applicable law.

5. **Scope of Authority.** The parenting coordinator shall make limited decisions within the scope of this order of referral. Limited decision making authority shall include, but may not be limited to: __________.

6. **Fees and Costs for Parenting Coordination.** [Choose all that apply]

a. ___ The parties have consented to this referral to parenting coordination.

___ This order is without the consent of the parties, but the court has determined that the parties have the financial ability to pay the parenting coordination fees and costs.

b. The court allocates payment of fees and costs for parenting coordination as follows:

☐ % shall be paid by the Father.

☐ % shall be paid by the Mother.

☐ No fees as Family Court Services to provide parenting coordination

☐ Other: ______________________________

c. If a party causes the parenting coordinator to expend an unreasonable and unnecessary amount of time, that party may be held solely responsible for payment of the parenting coordinator's fees and costs for such time expended, and the court reserves jurisdiction to reallocate the payment of fees and costs in that event. Failure to pay the parenting coordinator's fees and costs in a timely manner may subject the party to sanctions for contempt of court.

d. The parenting coordinator shall not proceed until he/she is satisfied with the terms and conditions of payment for his/her services. Further, the parenting coordinator shall not perform nor continue to perform the parenting coordination services in this case unless all of his/her fees and costs are paid by the parties as ordered, and, in the event of nonpayment, the parenting coordinator shall file a Request for Status Conference, and the court will address the issue of nonpayment of fees and costs.

7. **Confidentiality.** All communications made by, between, or among the parties and the parenting coordinator during parenting coordination sessions are confidential. The parenting coordinator and each party may not testify or offer evidence about communications made by a party or the parenting coordinator during the parenting coordination sessions, except if:

a. It is necessary to identify, authenticate, confirm, or deny a written agreement entered into by the parties during parenting coordination;

b. The testimony or evidence is necessary to identify an issue for resolution by the court without otherwise disclosing communications made by any party or the parenting coordinator;

c. The testimony or evidence is limited to the subject of a party's compliance with the order of referral to parenting coordination, orders for psychological evaluation, counseling ordered by the court or recommended by a health care provider, or for substance abuse testing or treatment;

d. The parenting coordinator reports that the case is no longer appropriate for parenting coordination;

e. The parenting coordinator reports that he or she is unable or unwilling to continue to serve and that a successor parenting coordinator should be appointed;

f. The testimony or evidence is necessary pursuant to s. 61.125 (5)(b) or s.61.125(8), Florida Statutes;

g. The parenting coordinator is not qualified to address or resolve certain issues in the case and a more qualified coordinator should be appointed;

h. The parties agree that the testimony or evidence be permitted; or

i. The testimony or evidence is necessary to protect any person from future acts that would constitute domestic violence under Chapter 741, Florida Statutes; child abuse, neglect, or abandonment under Chapter 39, Florida Statutes; or abuse, neglect, or exploitation of an elderly or disabled adult under Chapter 825, Florida Statutes.

8. **Agreement on Nonconfidentiality.** The parties can agree to waive confidentiality of a specific communication or all communications. The waiver must be in writing, signed by the parties and their respective counsel. The waiver shall be filed with the court and a copy served on the parenting coordinator. Either party may revoke his or her waiver of confidentiality by providing written notice signed by the party. The revocation shall be filed with the court and a copy served on the other party and the parenting coordinator.

9. **Withdrawal Procedure.** With Court approval, the parenting coordinator may withdraw from the role of parenting coordinator. The parenting coordinator shall apply directly to the Court with a request to be discharged, and shall provide notice to the parties and their counsel of their request to withdrawal. Either party may seek to terminate the parenting coordinator's services by filing a motion with the Court. The parenting coordinator's services may not be terminated by either of the parties (or at the request of both parties) without order of this court.

11.[1] **Stipulation.** Any written stipulation of parties to utilize the parenting coordination process filed with this court is incorporated into this Order.

10.[2] **Reservation of Jurisdiction.** This Court specifically reserves jurisdiction to enforce and/or modify the terms and conditions of this Order.

WHEREFORE, the undersigned General Magistrate files this Report with the Office of the Clerk of the Court and recommends the entry of an order approving this Report.

Dated Miami–Dade County, Florida, on this ___ day of __________, 20 ___.

____

General Magistrate

Copies to:
Name of Party:
Counsel for Party
Address of Counsel
Name of Party:
Counsel for Party
Address of Counsel
Guardian ad Litem
Address of GAL

If you are a person with a disability who needs any accommodation in order to participate in this proceeding, you are entitled, at no cost to you, to the provision of certain assistance. Please contact the Eleventh Judicial Circuit Court's ADA Coordinator, Lawson E. Thomas Courthouse Center, 175 NW 1st Ave., Suite 2702, Miami, FL 33128, Telephone (305) 349–7175; TDD (305) 349–7174, Fax (305) 349–7355 at least 7 days before your scheduled court appearance, or immediately upon receiving this notification if the time before the scheduled appearance is less than 7 days; if you are hearing or voice impaired, call 711.

1 Numbering as provided in original.
2 Numbering as provided in original.

09–15. PARENTING COORDINATION IN FAMILY LAW CASES

THE ELEVENTH JUDICIAL CIRCUIT MIAMI–DADE COUNTY, FLORIDA

CASE NO. 09–1 (Court Administration)

ADMINISTRATIVE ORDER NO. 09–15

(Rescinding AO No. 06–03 and amendments thereto)

IN RE: PARENTING COORDINATION IN FAMILY LAW CASES

WHEREAS, children caught in the middle of high parental conflict are more likely to be harmed; and

WHEREAS, it is the public policy of the State of Florida to assure that each minor child has frequent and continuing contact with both parents after the parents separate or the marriage of the parties is dissolved and to encourage parents to share the rights, responsibilities, and joys of childrearing; and

WHEREAS, the Florida Supreme Court adopted a guiding principle encouraging a family court process to "empower families through skills development, assist them to resolve their own disputes, provide access to appropriate services, and offer a variety of dispute resolution forums where the family can resolve problems without additional emotional trauma," as set forth in *In re Report of the Family Court Steering Committee (Family Courts IV)*, 794 So. 2d 518, 522 (Fla. 2001); and

WHEREAS, parenting coordination is a process whereby an impartial third person, called a parenting coordinator, helps the parties implement their parenting plan by facilitating the resolution of disputes between parents and/or legal guardians, providing education, making recommendations to the parties and, with the prior approval of the parties and the court, making decisions within the scope of the court order of appointment; and

WHEREAS, the use of parenting coordinators promotes the best interests of minor children and their parents in high conflict cases by reducing the duration and severity of parental conflict, thereby protecting children from the harmful effects of such conflict; and

WHEREAS, in that parenting coordination provide a form of alternative dispute resolution that enhances the purposes of Chapter 61, Florida Statutes, the legislature enacted Section 61.125, Florida Statutes, to establish the procedures for the proper administration of parenting coordination within the State of Florida, thereby obviating the need for the adoption of separate provisions for this Circuit; and

WHEREAS, Section 61.125, Florida Statutes, became effective on October 1, 2009; and

WHEREAS, this Circuit has developed certain forms that are relevant to this Circuit that will assist with the effectuation of the provisions set forth in Section 61.125, Florida Statutes;

NOW, THEREFORE, pursuant to the authority vested in me as Chief Judge of the Eleventh Judicial Circuit of Florida, under Rule 2.215, of the Florida Rules of Judicial Administration, it is hereby **ORDERED**:

1. The provisions set forth Section 61.125, Florida Statutes, shall be followed in this Circuit regarding parenting coordination.

2. The following forms, attached hereto, are hereby adopted and shall be used in carrying out the provisions of Section 61.125, Florida Statutes:

a. Report Of General Magistrate On Motion For Referral To Parenting Coordinator.

b. Order Of Referral To Parenting Coordinator.

Further, Administrative Order No. 06–03, and all amendments thereto, are hereby rescinded in their entirety and held for naught.

This Administrative Order shall be effective as of October 1, 2009, nunc pro tunc, and shall remain in effect until further order of the Court.

DONE AND ORDERED in Chambers at Miami–Dade, Florida, this ___ day of October, 2009.

JOEL H. BROWN, CHIEF JUDGE
ELEVENTH JUDICIAL CIRCUIT
OF FLORIDA

ATTACHMENT

IN THE CIRCUIT COURT OF THE 11TH JUDICIAL CIRCUIT IN AND FOR DADE COUNTY, FLORIDA

FAMILY DIVISION

CASE NO.:

Petitioner,

and

Respondent.

_____________________________/

ORDER OF REFERRAL TO PARENTING COORDINATOR

The Court considered the ☐ motion of the court, ☐ joint motion of the parties, ☐ Motion of a party, reviewed the court file, considered the testimony presented. Based on this information, the court FINDS that:

A. **Appropriateness of Process.** This matter is appropriate for parenting coordination and it is in the best interest of the child(ren).

B. **Parenting Coordination Process.** Parenting coordination is a child-focused alternative dispute resolution process whereby a parenting coordinator assists the parties in creating or implementing their parenting plan by facilitating the resolution of disputes, providing education and making recommendations to the parties; and, with the prior consent of the parties and approval of the court, making limited decisions within the scope of this order of referral.

C. **Parenting Coordinator.** A parenting coordinator is an impartial third person whose role is to assist the parties in successfully creating or implementing a parenting plan.

D. **Selection of Parenting Coordinator.** The parties are to contact Family Court Services within (5) working days from the date of this order at: Lawson E. Thomas Courthouse Center, 175 N.W. 1st Avenue, Suite 1503, Miami, Florida 33128, tel: 305–349–5508, fax: 305–349–5634. The parties may agree to a specific parenting coordinator or Family Court Services will designate a qualified parenting coordinator for the parties. Family Court Services will inform the court of the parenting coordinator designated.

E. **History of Domestic Violence.** Based upon testimony and evidence presented and a review of related court records, the court has determined:

☐There is no history of domestic violence.

☐There has been a history of domestic violence, and:

☐Each party has had an opportunity to consult with an attorney or domestic violence advocate before this court has accepted the parties' consent.

☐Each party has consented to this referral and the consent has been given freely and voluntarily.

It is therefore, **ORDERED**:

1. **Parenting Coordinator.** The parties are referred to parenting coordination for an initial period of ___ months (not to exceed two years):

a. The parenting coordinator shall file a response to this Order within 30 days accepting or declining the appointment. The response to the appointment must be in substantial compliance with Form 12.984.

b. The parties or their attorneys must provide to the parenting coordinator copies of all pleadings and orders related to domestic violence and any other pleadings and orders requested by the parenting coordinator related to parenting coordination.

2. **Meetings.** Unless prohibited herein as a domestic violence safeguard or by another court order, the parenting coordinator may meet with the parties and/or child(dren) together or separately, in person or by any electronic means.

3. **Domestic Violence Safeguards.** The parties shall adhere to all provisions of any injunction for protection or conditions of bail, probation, or a sentence arising from criminal proceedings. In addition to any safety measures the parenting coordinator deems necessary, the following domestic violence safeguards must be implemented:

☐None are necessary.

☐No joint meetings.

☐No direct negotiations.

☐No direct communications.

☐Other: ____________________________

4. **Role, Responsibility, and Authority of Parenting Coordinator.** The parenting coordinator shall have the following role, responsibility, and authority:

a. Assisting the parties in creating and implementing a parenting plan;

b. Facilitating the resolution of disputes regarding the creation or implementation of the Parenting Plan;

c. Recommending to parties strategies for creating or implementing the Parenting Plan. Such recommendations may include that one or both parents avail themselves of accessible and appropriate community resources, including, but not limited to, random drug screens, parenting classes, and individual psychotherapy and/or family counseling, if there is a history or evidence that such referrals are appropriate;

d. Recommending to the parents changes to the Parenting Plan;

e. Educating the parties to effectively:

i. Parent in a manner that minimizes conflicts;

ii. Communicate and negotiate with each other and their child(ren);

iii. Develop and apply appropriate parenting skills;

iv. Understand principles of child development and issues facing child(ren) when their parents no longer live together;

v. Disengage from the other parent when engagement leads to conflicts and non-cooperation;

vi. Identify the sources of their conflict with each other and work individually and/or jointly to minimize conflict and lessen its deleterious effects on the child(ren); and,

vii Allow the child(ren) to grow up free from the threat of being caught in the middle of their parents' disputes.

f. Facilitating the ability of both parents to maintain ongoing relationships with their children.

g. Reporting or communicating with the court concerning non-confidential matters as provided in paragraph 6 of this order;

h. Communicating with the parties and their child(ren), separately or together, in person or by telephone, unless otherwise prohibited by court order or applicable law. The parenting coordinator shall determine the schedule for subsequent appointments;

i. Providing information to health care providers for the parents and the children, and to any third parties, when the parenting coordinator deems it is reasonably necessary.

5. **Scope of Authority.** The parenting coordinator shall make limited decisions within the scope of this order of referral. Limited decision making authority shall include, but may not be limited to:

____

____

6. **Fees and Costs for Parenting Coordination.**

a. ☐ The parties have consented to this referral to parenting coordination and have agreed that they have the present ability to pay parenting coordination fees.

☐The parties have consented to this referral to parenting coordination and the Court finds that: ___ petitioner ___ respondent ___ both parties has/have the present financial ability to pay parenting coordination fees.

☐This order is without the consent of the parties and the court has determined that: ___ petitioner ___ respondent ___ both parties has/have the financial ability to pay the parenting coordination fees and costs.

☐This order is with or without the consent of the parties, the court has found both parties to be indigent based upon the factors in Section 57.082, Florida Statutes, and Family Court Services will provide parenting coordination.

b. The court allocates payment of fees and costs for parenting coordination as follows:

___% shall be paid by the Father.

___% shall be paid by the Mother.

___% No fees as Family court Services to provide parenting coordination

Other: ______________________________

c. If a party has caused the parenting coordinator to expend an unreasonable and unnecessary amount of time, the Court may later determine that party will be solely responsible for payment of the parenting coordinator's fees and costs for such time expended or that the party shall reimburse the other party for the parenting coordinator's fees and costs paid by the other party for such time expended. Failure to pay the parenting coordinator's fees and costs in a timely manner may subject the party to sanctions for contempt of court.

d. The parenting coordinator shall not proceed until he/she is satisfied with the terms and conditions of payment for his/her services. Further, the parenting coordinator shall not perform nor continue to perform the parenting coordination services in this case unless all of his/her fees and costs are paid by the parties as ordered, and, in the event of nonpayment, the parenting coordinator shall file a Request for Status Conference, and the court will address the issue of nonpayment of fees and costs.

7. **Confidentiality.** All communications made by, between, or among the parties and the parenting coordinator during parenting coordination sessions are confidential. The parenting coordinator and each party may not testify or offer evidence about communications made by a party or the parenting coordinator during the parenting coordination sessions, except if:

a. It is necessary to identify, authenticate, confirm, or deny a written agreement entered into by the parties during parenting coordination;

b. The testimony or evidence is necessary to identify an issue for resolution by the court without otherwise disclosing communications made by any party or the parenting coordinator;

c. The testimony or evidence is limited to the subject of a party's compliance with the order of referral to parenting coordination, orders for psychological evaluation, counseling ordered by the court or recommended by a health care provider, or for substance abuse testing or treatment;

d. The parenting coordinator is reporting that the case is no longer appropriate for parenting coordination;

e. The parenting coordinator is reporting that he or she is unable or unwilling to continue to serve and that a successor parenting coordinator should be appointed;

f. The testimony or evidence is necessary pursuant to s. 61.125(5)(b) or s. 61.125(8), Florida Statutes;

g. The parenting coordinator is not qualified to address or resolve certain issues in the case and a more qualified coordinator should be appointed;

h. The parties agree that the testimony or evidence be permitted; or

i. The testimony or evidence is necessary to protect any person from future acts that would constitute domestic violence under Chapter 741, Florida Statutes; child abuse, neglect, or abandonment under Chapter 39, Florida Statutes; or abuse, neglect, or exploitation of an elderly or disabled adult under Chapter 825, Florida Statutes.

8. **Agreement on Nonconfidentiality.** The parties can agree to waive confidentiality of a specific communication or all communications. The waiver must be in writing, signed by the parties and their respective counsel. The waiver shall be filed with the court and a copy served on the parenting coordinator. Either party may revoke his or her waiver of confidentiality by providing written notice signed by the party. The revocation shall be filed with the court and a copy served on the other party and the parenting coordinator.

9. **Withdrawal Procedure.** With Court approval, the parenting coordinator may withdraw from the role of parenting coordinator. The parenting coordinator shall apply directly to the Court with a request to be discharged, and shall provide notice to the parties and their counsel of their request to withdrawal. Either party may seek to terminate the parenting coordinator's services by filing a motion with the Court. The parenting coordinator's services may not be terminated by either of the parties (or at the request of both parties) without order of this court.

10. **Reservation of Jurisdiction.** This Court specifically reserves jurisdiction to enforce and/or modify the terms and conditions of this Order.

DONE AND ORDERED in __________ County, Florida, on this ___ day of __________, 2009.

____

, Circuit Judge

ATTACHMENT

IN THE CIRCUIT COURT OF THE 11TH JUDICIAL CIRCUIT IN AND FOR DADE COUNTY, FLORIDA

FAMILY DIVISION
CASE NO.:

Petitioner,

and

Respondent.

________________________/

REPORT OF GENERAL MAGISTRATE ON MOTION FOR REFERRAL TO PARENTING COORDINATOR

The above cause came before the undersigned General Magistrate on this day of _________, ___, upon the ☐ joint motion of the parties ☐ motion of a party, pursuant to Rule 12.490, Florida Family Law Rules of Procedure, and the General Magistrate, having considered the evidence presented and after being otherwise advised in the premises, **FINDS, CONCLUDES AND RECOMMENDS** that:

A. **Appropriateness of Process.** This matter is appropriate for parenting coordination and it is in the best interest of the child(ren).

B. **Parenting Coordination Process.** Parenting coordination is a child-focused alternative dispute resolution process whereby a parenting coordinator assists the parties in creating or implementing their parenting plan by facilitating the resolution of disputes, providing education and making recommendations to the parties; and, with the prior consent of the parties and approval of the court, making limited decisions within the scope of this order of referral.

C. **Parenting Coordinator.** A parenting coordinator is an impartial third person whose role is to assist the parties in successfully creating or implementing a parenting plan.

D. **Selection of Parenting Coordinator.** The parties are to contact Family Court Services within (5) working days from the date of this order at: Lawson E. Thomas Courthouse Center, 175 N.W. 1st Avenue, Suite 1503, Miami, Florida 33128, tel: 305–349–5508, fax: 305–349–5634. The parties may agree to a specific parenting coordinator or Family Court Services will designate a qualified parenting coordinator for the parties. Family Court Services will inform the court of the parenting coordinator designated.

E. **History of Domestic Violence.** Based upon testimony and evidence presented and a review of related court records, the court has determined:

☐There is no history of domestic violence.

☐There has been a history of domestic violence, and:

☐Each party has had an opportunity to consult with an attorney or domestic violence advocate before this court has accepted the parties' consent.

☐Each party has consented to this referral and the consent has been given freely and voluntarily.

Therefore:

1. **Parenting Coordinator.** The parties are referred to parenting coordination for an initial period of ___ months (not to exceed two years):

a. The parenting coordinator shall file a response to this Order within 30 days accepting or declining the appointment. The response to the appointment must be in substantial compliance with Form 12.984.

b. The parties or their attorneys must provide to the parenting coordinator copies of all pleadings and orders related to domestic violence and any other pleadings and orders requested by the parenting coordinator related to parenting coordination.

2. **Meetings.** Unless prohibited herein as a domestic violence safeguard or by another court order, the parenting coordinator may meet with the parties and/or child(dren) together or separately, in person or by any electronic means.

3. **Domestic Violence Safeguards.** The parties shall adhere to all provisions of any injunction for protection or conditions of bail, probation, or a sentence arising from criminal proceedings. In addition to any safety measures the parenting coordinator deems necessary, the following domestic violence safeguards must be implemented:

☐None are necessary.

☐No joint meetings.

☐No direct negotiations.

☐No direct communications.

☐Other: __________________________________

4. **Role, Responsibility, and Authority of Parenting Coordinator.** The parenting coordinator shall have the following role, responsibility, and authority:

a. Assisting the parties in creating and implementing a parenting plan;

b. Facilitating the resolution of disputes regarding the creation or implementation of the Parenting Plan;

c. Recommending to parties strategies for creating or implementing the Parenting Plan. Such recommendations may include that one or both parents avail themselves of accessible and appropriate community resources, including, but not limited to, random drug screens, parenting classes, and individual psychotherapy and/or family counseling, if there is a history or evidence that such referrals are appropriate;

d. Recommending to the parents changes to the Parenting Plan;

e. Educating the parties to effectively:

i. Parent in a manner that minimizes conflicts;

ii. Communicate and negotiate with each other and their child(ren);

iii. Develop and apply appropriate parenting skills;

iv. Understand principles of child development and issues facing child(ren) when their parents no longer live together;

v. Disengage from the other parent when engagement leads to conflicts and non-cooperation;

vi. Identify the sources of their conflict with each other and work individually and/or jointly to minimize conflict and lessen its deleterious effects on the child(ren); and,

vii. Allow the child(ren) to grow up free from the threat of being caught in the middle of their parents' disputes.

f. Facilitating the ability of both parents to maintain ongoing relationships with their children.

g. Reporting or communicating with the court concerning non-confidential matters as provided in paragraph 6 of this order;

h. Communicating with the parties and their child(ren), separately or together, in person or by telephone, unless otherwise prohibited by court order or applicable law. The parenting coordinator shall determine the schedule for subsequent appointments;

i. Providing information to health care providers for the parents and the children, and to any third parties, when the parenting coordinator deems it is reasonably necessary.

5. **Scope of Authority.** The parenting coordinator shall make limited decisions within the scope of this order of referral. Limited decision making authority shall include, but may not be limited to:

____

____

6. **Fees and Costs for Parenting Coordination.**

a. ☐ The parties have consented to this referral to parenting coordination and have agreed that they have the present ability to pay parenting coordination fees.

☐The parties have consented to this referral to parenting coordination and the Court finds that: ___ petitioner ___ respondent ___ both parties has/have the present financial ability to pay parenting coordination fees.

☐This order is without the consent of the parties and the court has determined that: ___ petitioner ___ respondent ___ both parties has/have the financial ability to pay the parenting coordination fees and costs.

☐This order is with or without the consent of the parties, the court has found both parties to be indigent based upon the factors in Section 57.082, Florida Statutes, and Family Court Services will provide parenting coordination.

b. The court allocates payment of fees and costs for parenting coordination as follows:

___% shall be paid by the Father.

___% shall be paid by the Mother.

___No fees as Family Court Services to provide parenting coordination

Other: ______________________________

c. If a party has caused the parenting coordinator to expend an unreasonable and unnecessary amount of time, the Court may later determine that party will be solely responsible for payment of the parenting coordinator's fees and costs for such time expended or that the party shall reimburse the other party for the parenting coordinator's fees and costs paid by the other party for such time expended. Failure to pay the parenting coordinator's fees and costs in a timely manner may subject the party to sanctions for contempt of court.

d. The parenting coordinator shall not proceed until he/she is satisfied with the terms and conditions of payment for his/her services. Further, the parenting coordinator shall not perform nor continue to perform the parenting coordination services in this case unless all of his/her fees and costs are paid by the parties as ordered, and, in the event of nonpayment, the parenting coordinator shall file a Request for Status Conference, and the court will address the issue of nonpayment of fees and costs.

7. **Confidentiality.** All communications made by, between, or among the parties and the parenting coordinator during parenting coordination sessions are confidential. The parenting coordinator and each party may not testify or offer evidence about communications made by a party or the parenting coordinator during the parenting coordination sessions, except if:

a. It is necessary to identify, authenticate, confirm, or deny a written agreement entered into by the parties during parenting coordination;

b. The testimony or evidence is necessary to identify an issue for resolution by the court without otherwise disclosing communications made by any party or the parenting coordinator;

c. The testimony or evidence is limited to the subject of a party's compliance with the order of referral to parenting coordination, orders for psychological evaluation, counseling ordered by the court or recommended by a health care provider, or for substance abuse testing or treatment;

d. The parenting coordinator is reporting that the case is no longer appropriate for parenting coordination;

e. The parenting coordinator is reporting that he or she is unable or unwilling to continue to serve and that a successor parenting coordinator should be appointed;

f. The testimony or evidence is necessary pursuant to s. 61.125(5)(b) or s. 61.125(8), Florida Statutes;

g. The parenting coordinator is not qualified to address or resolve certain issues in the case and a more qualified coordinator should be appointed;

h. The parties agree that the testimony or evidence be permitted; or

i. The testimony or evidence is necessary to protect any person from future acts that would constitute domestic violence under Chapter 741, Florida Statutes; child abuse, neglect, or abandonment under Chapter 39, Florida Statutes; or abuse, neglect, or exploitation of an elderly or disabled adult under Chapter 825, Florida Statutes.

8. **Agreement on Nonconfidentiality.** The parties can agree to waive confidentiality of a specific communication or all communications. The waiver must be in writing, signed by the parties and their respective counsel. The waiver shall be filed with the court and a copy served on the parenting coordinator. Either party may revoke his or her waiver of confidentiality by providing written notice signed by the party. The revocation shall be filed with the court and a copy served on the other party and the parenting coordinator.

9. **Withdrawal Procedure.** With Court approval, the parenting coordinator may withdraw from the role of parenting coordinator. The parenting coordinator shall apply directly to the Court with a request to be discharged, and shall provide notice to the parties and their counsel of their request to withdrawal. Either party may seek to terminate the parenting coordinator's services by filing a motion with the Court.

The parenting coordinator's services may not be terminated by either of the parties (or at the request of both parties) without order of this court.

10. **Reservation of Jurisdiction.** The Court shall have specific reserved jurisdiction to enforce and/or modify the terms and conditions of the Order on this Report.

WHEREFORE, the undersigned General Magistrate files this Report with the Office of the Clerk of the Court and recommends the entry of an order approving this Report.

Dated at Miami–Dade County, Florida on this ___ day of ________, 20 ___.

____
, General Magistrate

07–08. AUTHORIZING THE COLLABORATIVE PROCESS DISPUTE RESOLUTION MODEL IN THE ELEVENTH JUDICIAL CIRCUIT OF FLORIDA

THE ELEVENTH JUDICIAL CIRCUIT MIAMI–DADE COUNTY, FLORIDA

CASE NO. 07–1 (Court Administration)

ADMINISTRATIVE ORDER NO. 07–08

IN RE: AUTHORIZING THE COLLABORATIVE PROCESS DISPUTE RESOLUTION MODEL IN THE ELEVENTH JUDICIAL CIRCUIT OF FLORIDA

WHEREAS, the courts of the Eleventh Judicial Circuit in and for Miami–Dade County believe that the collaborative process dispute resolution model is a suitable alternative to full scale adversarial litigation in cases involving family law cases should the parties so agree; and

WHEREAS, beginning in the 1990's the Collaborative Process Dispute Resolution Model has been adopted in several states both by common law and by statute; and

WHEREAS, in Florida, the creation of family law divisions and necessary support services in the 1990's and the adoption of the Model Family Court in 2001 reflected the recognition by the Supreme Court and legislature that families in conflict needed a forum that does not wreak havoc or prohibit the restructuring of family relationships; and

WHEREAS, the Supreme Court recognized that family cases needed "a system that provided non-adversarial alternatives and flexibility of alternatives; a system that preserved rather than destroyed family relationships; . . . and a system that facilitated the process chosen by parties." In re Report of Family Court Steering Committee, 794 So.2d 518, 523 (Fla. 2001); and

WHEREAS, the Supreme Court's acceptance of recommendations for a model family court was consistent with the principles of collaborative practice because the collaborative process empowers parties to make their own decisions guided and assisted by counsel in a setting outside of the court;

NOW THEREFORE, pursuant to the authority vested in the Chief Judge by Rule 2.050 of the Florida Rules of Judicial Administration and Section 43.26 Florida Statutes, it is **ORDERED** that:

1. The Collaborative Process Dispute Resolution Model (hereinafter "Collaborative Process"), is authorized in the Eleventh Judicial Circuit of Florida to resolve dissolution of marriage and other family matters and all attendant issues therein according to the following definitions and specifications herein.

2. The Collaborative Process is confidential and utilizes interest based negotiation to resolve disputes through structured assistance of collaboratively trained professionals, including, but not limited to lawyers, mental health and financial professionals.

3. If the parties and professionals desire to engage the Collaborative Process, they shall enter into a contractual commitment to negotiate a settlement without using the court system to decide any issues of the parties. A copy of the contractual commitment, "the Participation Agreement", which incorporates the "Declaration of Principles", is attached hereto and made a part hereof as a Composite Attachment.

4. The Collaborative Process commences before any pleading is filed with the court. Upon the Collaborative Process concluding successfully in dissolution of marriage, an executed Agreement is filed with a Joint Petition for Dissolution of Marriage and Answer signed by both parties and counsel. In other family law matters, the resulting executed agreement is filed with an appropriate document. Thereafter, the matter is set with the court, if necessary.

5. The parties will agree to make a full and candid exchange of information so that a proper resolution of the case can occur, which will include a full disclosure of the nature and extent of all assets and liabilities, income of the parties and all relevant information concerning the parties' children. Any material change in the information provided must be promptly updated. No formal discovery procedures will be used requiring a court order.

6. The parties agree to maintain the confidentiality of any oral or written communications relating to the subject matter of the Collaborative Process, their counsel or other participants in the Collaborative Process, unless the parties otherwise mutually agree in writing.

7. Fees and expenses: Counsel and other retained professionals are entitled to be paid for their services. The parties agree to pay them as part of their contract. If appropriate, one party may be asked to pay all or a disproportionate share of the fees when the assets, liabilities and income of the parties are compared. The determination of fees is also subject to the Collaborative Process

8. If the Collaborative Process breaks down due to bad faith demonstrated by either party or either party seeking to litigate, counsel for the parties must withdraw.

9. Upon a breakdown of the Collaborative Process, all engaged professionals are disqualified from testifying as witnesses, expert or otherwise, regarding the case and their writings are inadmissible in any judicial proceedings unless the parties otherwise mutually agree in writing.

10. The responsibility of collaborative professionals are as follows:

A. The neutral mental health professional may:

1) Afford the children a voice in the process.

2) Work with the parties to do the following:

i. Prioritize parties' concerns.

ii. Help develop conflict resolution skills.

iii. Develop co-parenting skills.

iv. Enhance communication skills.

v. Reduce misunderstandings.

vi. Assist in focusing on working toward resolution.

B. The neutral financial professional is available to both parties and will assist in the following activities.

1) Provide each party with necessary financial planning regarding the division of the assets, liabilities and support, both child and spousal.

2) Provide analysis of the nature and composition of specific marital assets (e.g. retirement, capital gain consideration, tax implication, etc.).

3) Take responsibility for neutrally gathering all relevant financial information.

4) Assist development for and understanding of any valuation processes.

5) Assist with estate planning issues.

C. The lawyers advise, counsel and guide their respective clients through the process. They analyze choices and consequences, considering the costs and benefits of the negotiation choices, facilitate negotiation and create written agreements.

11. During the Collaborative Process the court will not adjudicate any dispute between the parties. If an executed Marital Settlement Agreement is reached, counsel will ask the court to approve the Settlement Agreement.

12. During the Collaborative Process, the parties may, from time to time, resolve temporary issues in an executed writing. In the event the Collaborative Process breaks down, the parties agree to abide by the terms of the temporary written agreements and these agreements shall be ratified by court order once litigation ensues.

This Order shall become effective immediately upon execution and shall remain in effect until further order of the court.

DONE AND ORDERED in Chambers at Miami–Dade, Florida, this ___ day of October, 2007.

____

JOSEPH P. FARINA
CHIEF JUDGE
ELEVENTH JUDICIAL CIRCUIT OF FLORIDA

COMPOSITE ATTACHMENT

COLLABORATIVE LAW PARTICIPATION AGREEMENT DISSOLUTION OF MARRIAGE WITH CHILDREN

PURPOSE

The WIFE/HUSBAND, __________, and her/his attorney, __________, and the HUSBAND/WIFE, __________, and his/her attorney, __________, have chosen to use the principles of Collaborative Law to settle the issues arising from the dissolution of their marriage. The primary goal of Collaborative Law is to settle in a non-adversarial manner, the issues of the parties' separation and dissolution of their marriage. The parties have retained Collaborative Lawyers to assist them in reaching this goal.

COMMUNICATION

The parties intend to effectively communicate with each other to efficiently and economically settle the dissolution of their marriage. Written and verbal communications will be respectful and constructive and will not make accusations or claims not based in fact.

It is agreed that communication during settlement meetings will be focused on the economic and parenting issues in the dissolution and the constructive resolution of those issues. The parties and their lawyers understand that the costs for settlement meetings are substantial and require everyone's cooperation to make the best possible use of available resources. To achieve this goal, the parties agree not to engage in unnecessary discussions of past events.

To maintain an objective and constructive settlement process, the parties agree to discuss settlement of their dissolution issues only in the settlement conference setting. All discussions in the conferences are confidential between the parties and their counsel. Discussions outside of the conference setting must be agreed to by the parties **and** their lawyers. Settlement issues will not be discussed in the presence of the parties' children, nor at unannounced times by telephone calls or appearances at the other party's residence.

The parties acknowledge that inappropriate communications regarding their dissolution can be harmful to their children. Communication with the children regarding these issues will occur only if it is appropriate and done by mutual agreement or with the advice of a child specialist. The parties specifically agree that their child/children will not be included in any discussion regarding the dissolution except as described in this agreement.

EXPERTS

When appropriate and needed, the parties will use neutral experts for purposes of valuation, cash flow analysis, parenting issues and any other issue which requires expert advice and/or recommendations. The parties will agree in advance as to how the costs of the third party expert will be paid. Any experts used in the collaborative process shall not be used in any litigation that may occur if the process terminates unless the parties otherwise mutually agree in writing. New consultants will be permitted to review the work product and reports of prior consultants to facilitate the transition for the parties, and shall be inadmissible as evidence unless the parties otherwise mutually agree in writing.

INFORMATION

The parties and their lawyers agree to deal with each other in good faith to promptly provide all necessary and reasonable information requested. No formal discovery procedures will be used unless specifically agreed to in advance by the parties.

The parties acknowledge that by using informal discovery, they are giving up certain investigative procedures and methods that would be available to them in the litigation process. They give up these measures with the specific understanding that both parties make full financial disclosure of all assets, income, liabilities and other information necessary for an equitable settlement. Participation in the collaborative process, and the settlement reached, is based upon the assumption that both parties have acted in good faith and have provided complete and accurate information to the best of their ability. The parties shall be required to sign a sworn statement making full and fair disclosure of their income, assets and liabilities in accordance with Florida Law. Additionally, both parties have a continuing duty to supplement the disclosure made, including, but not limited to an amended sworn financial statement.

ENFORCEABILITY OF AGREEMENTS

In the event that either party requires a temporary agreement for any purpose, the agreement will be put in writing and signed by the parties and their lawyers. If either party withdraws from the collaborative process, the written agreement shall be presented to the Court as a basis for an Order, which the Court shall make retroactive to the date of the written agreement. Similarly, once a final agreement is signed, if a party should refuse to honor it, the final agreement may be presented to the Court in any subsequent action.

LEGAL PROCESS

Court Proceedings: Unless otherwise agreed, prior to reaching final agreement on all issues, no Summons and Petition will be served or filed, nor will any other motion or document be prepared or filed which would initiate court intervention. When the parties have reached a final agreement, a Joint Petition for Dissolution of Marriage will be filed by the parties with both parties executing a Joint Answer. Both parties may appear with counsel at the uncontested final hearing at which time they will request that the Court enter the Final Judgment of Dissolution of Marriage. This is the only time an appearance in Court is required.

Withdrawal from Collaborative Law Process: If a party decides to withdraw from the collaborative process, prompt written notice will be given to the other party through his or her lawyer which terminates the process and both attorneys' representation. Abuse of the collaborative process as set forth in the Declaration of Principles of Collaborative Law, incorporated herein, shall also terminate the process and both attorneys' representation. Upon withdrawal from the collaborative process there will be a thirty (30) day waiting period (unless there is an emergency) before any court hearing, to permit both parties to retain lawyers and make an orderly transition as it is mandatory that both collaborative lawyers withdraw upon the breakdown of the collaborative process. All temporary agreements will remain in full force and effect during this period. The intent of this provision is to avoid surprise and prejudice to the rights of the other party. It is therefore mutually agreed that either party may bring this provision to the attention of the Court in requesting a postponement of a hearing.

RIGHTS AND OBLIGATIONS PENDING SETTLEMENT

Although the parties have agreed to work outside the judicial system, consistent with Florida Law, the parties agree that:

(1) NEITHER PARTY WILL DISPOSE OF ANY ASSETS EXCEPT

(i) FOR THE NECESSARY, CUSTOMARY GENERATION OF INCOME OR PRESERVATION OF ASSETS, OR

(ii) OTHERWISE AGREED TO IN WRITING BY THE PARTIES; AND

(2) NEITHER PARTY MAY HARASS THE OTHER PARTY; AND

(3) ALL CURRENTLY AVAILABLE INSURANCE COVERAGE MUST BE MAINTAINED AND CONTINUED. NEITHER PARTY SHALL BORROW AGAINST, CANCEL, TRANSFER, DISPOSE OF OR CHANGE BENEFICIARIES OF ANY INSURANCE OR OTHER COVERAGE INCLUDING LIFE, HEALTH, AUTOMOBILE AND DISABILITY HELD FOR THE BENEFIT OF THE PARTIES; AND

(4) NEITHER PARTY WILL, WITHOUT WRITTEN PERMISSION OF THE OTHER PARTY, INCUR ANY DEBTS OR LIABILITIES FOR WHICH THE OTHER PARTY MAY BE HELD RESPONSIBLE; AND

(5) VIOLATION OF ANY OF THESE PROVISIONS MAY TERMINATE THE COLLABORATIVE PROCESS.

ACKNOWLEDGMENT

Both parties and their lawyers acknowledge that they have read this Agreement, understand its terms and conditions, and agree to abide by them. The parties understand that by agreeing to this alternative method of resolving their dissolution issues, they are giving up certain rights, including the right to formal discovery, formal court hearings, and other procedures provided by the adversarial legal system. The parties have chosen the collaborative process to reduce emotional and financial costs, and to generate a final agreement that addresses their concerns. They agree to work in good faith to achieve these goals and further acknowledge the incorporation of the Declaration of Principles of Collaborative Law attached hereto.

____________________	____________________
Wife	Husband
____________________	____________________
Attorney for Wife	Attorney for Husband
____________________	____________________
Florida Bar No.	Florida Bar No.
____________________	____________________
Date	Date

COMPOSITE ATTACHMENT

COLLABORATIVE LAW PARTICIPATION AGREEMENT DISSOLUTION WITHOUT CHILDREN

PURPOSE

The WIFE/HUSBAND, __________, and her/his attorney, __________, and the HUSBAND/WIFE, __________, and his/her attorney, __________, have chosen to use the principles of Collaborative Law to settle the issues arising from the dissolution of their marriage. The primary goal of Collaborative Law is to settle in a non-adversarial manner, the issues of the parties' separation and dissolution of their marriage. The parties have retained Collaborative Lawyers to assist them in reaching this goal.

COMMUNICATION

The parties intend to effectively communicate with each other to efficiently and economically settle the dissolution of their marriage. Written and verbal communications will be respectful and constructive and will not make accusations or claims not based in fact.

It is agreed that communication during settlement meetings will be focused on the economic issues in the dissolution and the constructive resolution of those issues. The parties and their lawyers understand that the costs for settlement meetings are substantial and require everyone's cooperation to make the best possible use of available resources. To achieve this goal, the parties agree not to engage in unnecessary discussions of past events.

To maintain an objective and constructive settlement process, the parties agree to discuss settlement of their dissolution issues only in the settlement conference setting. All discussions in the conferences are confidential between the parties and their counsel. Discussions outside of the conference setting must be agreed to by the parties **and** their lawyers.

EXPERTS

When appropriate and needed, the parties will use neutral experts for purposes of valuation, cash flow analysis, psychological issues and any other issue which requires expert advice and/or recommendations. The parties will agree in advance as to how the costs of the third party expert will be paid. Any experts used in the collaborative process shall not be used in any litigation that may occur unless the parties otherwise mutually agree in writing. New consultants will be permitted to review the work product and reports of prior consultants to facilitate the transition for the parties, and shall be inadmissible in evidence unless the parties otherwise mutually agree in writing.

INFORMATION

The parties and their lawyers agree to deal with each other in good faith to promptly provide all necessary and reasonable information requested. No formal discovery procedures will be used unless specifically agreed to in advance by the parties.

The parties acknowledge that by using informal discovery, they are giving up certain investigative procedures and methods that would be available to them in the litigation process. They give up these measures with the specific understanding that both parties make full financial disclosure of all assets, income, liabilities and other information necessary for an equitable settlement. Participation in the collaborative process, and the settlement reached, is based upon the assumption that both parties have acted in good faith and have provided complete and accurate information to the best of their ability. The parties will be required to sign a sworn statement making full and fair disclosure of their income, assets and liabilities in accordance with Florida Law. Additionally, both parties have a continuing duty to supplement the disclosure made, including, but not limited to an amended sworn financial statement.

ENFORCEABILITY OF AGREEMENTS

In the event that either party requires a temporary agreement for any purpose, the agreement will be put in writing and signed by the parties and their lawyers. If either party withdraws from the collaborative process, the written agreement shall be presented to the Court as a basis for an Order, which the Court shall make retroactive to the date of the written agreement. Similarly, once a final agreement is signed, if a party should refuse to honor it, the final agreement may be presented to the Court in any subsequent action.

LEGAL PROCESS

Court Proceedings: Unless otherwise agreed, prior to reaching final agreement on all issues, no Summons and Petition will be served or filed, nor will any other motion or document be prepared or filed which would initiate court intervention. When the parties have reached a final agreement, a Joint Petition for Dissolution of Marriage will be filed by the parties with both parties executing a joint Answer. Both parties may appear with counsel at an uncontested final hearing at which time they will request the Court enter the Final Judgment for Dissolution of Marriage. This is the only time an appearance in Court is required.

Withdrawal from Collaborative Law Process: If a party decides to withdraw from the collaborative process, prompt written notice will be given to the other party through his or her lawyer which terminates the process and both attorneys' representation. Abuse of the collaborative process as set forth in the Declaration of Principles of Collaborative Law, incorporated herein, shall also terminate the process and both attorneys' representation. Upon withdrawal from the collaborative process there will be a thirty (30) day waiting period (unless there is an emergency) before any court hearing, to permit both parties to retain lawyers and make an orderly transition as it is mandatory that both collaborative lawyers withdraw upon the breakdown of the collaborative process. All temporary agreements will remain in full force and effect during this period. The intent of this provision is to avoid surprise and prejudice to the rights of the other party. It is therefore mutually agreed that either party may bring this provision to the attention of the Court in requesting a postponement of a hearing.

RIGHTS AND OBLIGATIONS PENDING SETTLEMENT

Although the parties have agreed to work outside the judicial system, consistent with Florida Law, the parties agree that:

(1) NEITHER PARTY WILL DISPOSE OF ANY ASSETS EXCEPT

(i) FOR THE NECESSARY, CUSTOMARY GENERATION OF INCOME OR PRESERVATION OF ASSETS, OR

(ii) OTHERWISE AGREED TO IN WRITING BY THE PARTIES, AND;

(2) NEITHER PARTY MAY HARASS THE OTHER PARTY; AND

(3) ALL CURRENTLY AVAILABLE INSURANCE COVERAGE MUST BE MAINTAINED AND CONTINUED. NEITHER PARTY SHALL BORROW AGAINST, CANCEL, TRANSFER, DISPOSE OF OR CHANGE BENEFICIARIES OF ANY INSURANCE OR OTHER COVERAGE INCLUDING LIFE, HEALTH, AUTOMOBILE AND DISABILITY HELD FOR THE BENEFIT OF THE PARTIES; AND

(4) NEITHER PARTY WILL INCUR, WITHOUT WRITTEN PERMISSION OF THE OTHER PARTY, ANY DEBTS OR LIABILITIES FOR WHICH THE OTHER PARTY SHALL BE HELD RESPONSIBLE; AND

(5) VIOLATION OF ANY OF THESE PROVISIONS MAY TERMINATE THE COLLABORATIVE PROCESS.

ACKNOWLEDGMENT

Both parties and their lawyers acknowledge that they have read this Agreement, understand its terms and conditions, and agree to abide by them. The parties understand that by agreeing to this alternative method of resolving their dissolution issues, they are giving up certain rights, including the right to formal discovery, formal court hearings, and other procedures provided by the adversarial legal system. The parties have chosen the collaborative process to reduce emotional and financial costs, and to generate a final agreement that addresses their concerns. They agree to work in good faith to achieve these goals and further acknowledge the incorporation of the Declaration of Principles of Collaborative Law attached hereto.

______________________	______________________
Wife	Husband
______________________	______________________
Attorney for Wife	Attorney for Husband
______________________	______________________
Florida Bar No.	Florida Bar No.
______________________	______________________
Date	Date

COMPOSITE ATTACHMENT

DECLARATION OF PRINCIPLES OF COLLABORATIVE LAW WITH CHILDREN

I. THE COLLABORATIVE LAW PROCESS

Collaborative Law is a cooperative, confidential voluntary conflict resolution vehicle for parties going through a separation, dissolution or other family law matter.

The participants, which include both the attorneys and the parties, acknowledge that the essence of "Collaborative Law" is the shared belief that it is in the best interest of parties and their families in Family Law matters to commit themselves to avoiding adversarial proceedings, particularly litigation, and instead to work together to create shared solutions to the issues presented by the parties.

The goal of Collaborative Law is to minimize, if not eliminate, the negative economic, social and emotional consequences of litigation to families.

Choosing Collaborative Law requires a commitment to resolving differences justly and equitably.

II. NO COURT OR OTHER INTERVENTION

Collaborative Law requires a commitment to settling the issues involved without court intervention.

Participants must agree to give full, honest and open disclosure of all information, whether requested or not. Participants must agree to engage in informal discussions and conferences to settle all issues.

III. CAUTIONS

There is no guarantee that the process will be successful in resolving a dispute.

The Collaborative process cannot eliminate concerns about the disharmony, distrust and irreconcilable differences which have led to the current conflict.

Although the participants are committed to reaching a shared solution, each party is still expected to identify and assert his or her respective interest and the parties' respective attorneys will help each of them do so.

IV. PARTICIPATION WITH INTEGRITY

Participants must commit to protecting the privacy, respect and dignity of all involved, including parties, attorneys and consultants.

Each participant must commit to maintaining a high standard of integrity, specifically; participants shall not take advantage of the other participants, or of the miscalculations or inadvertent mistakes of others, but shall identify and correct them.

V. EXPERTS AND CONSULTANTS

Sometimes the input of outside experts such as accountants, appraisers, therapists and mediators might be needed to assist the participants in reaching creative and informed solutions. If any such experts are needed, they will be retained jointly. All such experts and other consultants retained in the Collaborative process shall be directed to work in a cooperative effort to resolve issues.

In the event that the Collaborative Law process terminates, all consultants will be disqualified as witnesses and their work product will be inadmissible as evidence unless the parties otherwise mutually agree in writing, the parties mutually agree otherwise in writing. However, new consultants will be permitted to review the work product and reports of prior consultants to facilitate the transition for the parties.

VI. CHILDREN'S ISSUES

In resolving issues about sharing the enjoyment of and responsibility for children, the parents, attorneys and therapists shall make every effort to reach amicable solutions that promote the children's best interests.

Parents will act quickly to resolve differences related to the children and to promote a caring, loving and involved relationship between the children and both parents.

Every effort will be made to insulate children from involvement in the parents' disputes.

Parents will attend "Children of Divorcing Parents" and the children will attend "Kids In Divorce Succeeding". In a county where said programs are not available, a similar parent-child divorce education program shall be attended by the parties.

VII. NEGOTIATION IN GOOD FAITH

The process, even with full and honest disclosure, will involve vigorous good faith negotiation.

Each participant will be expected to take a reasoned position in all disputes. Where such positions differ, each participant will use his or her best efforts to create proposals that meet the fundamental needs of both parties and if necessary to compromise to reach a settlement of all issues.

Although participants may discuss the likely outcome of a litigated result, none will use threats of abandoning the collaborative process or of litigation as a way of forcing settlement.

VIII. ATTORNEYS' ROLE–ATTORNEYS' FEES AND COSTS

The attorneys' role is to provide an organized framework that will make it easier for the parties to reach an agreement on each issue. The attorneys will help the parties communicate with each other, identify issues, ask questions, make observations, suggest options, help them express needs, goals and feelings, check the workability of proposed solutions and prepare and file all written paperwork for the court. The attorneys and the parties shall work together to reach a solution which serves the needs of both parties.

The Collaborative process requires payment to each attorney. The parties will make funds available for this purpose.

Each attorney is independent from the other attorneys in the Collaborative Family Lawyers Institute, and has been retained by only one party in the collaborative process.

IX. ABUSE OF THE COLLABORATIVE PROCESS

A Collaborative Law attorney will withdraw from a case as soon as possible upon learning that his or her client has withheld or misrepresented information or otherwise acted so as to undermine or take unfair advantage of the Collaborative Law process. Examples of such violations of the process are: the secret disposition of marital, quasi-marital or separate property, failing to disclose the existence or the true nature of assets and/or obligations, failure to participate in the spirit of the Collaborative process, abusing the minor children of the parties or planning to flee the jurisdiction of the court with the children.

X. DISQUALIFICATION BY COURT INTERVENTION

An attorney's representation in the Collaborative process is limited to that process. No attorney representing a party in the Collaborative process can ever represent that party in court in a proceeding against the other spouse. In the event a court filing is unavoidable, both attorneys are disqualified from representing either client and will assist their respective clients in the transition process.

COMPOSITE ATTACHMENT

DECLARATION OF PRINCIPLES OF COLLABORATIVE LAW WITHOUT CHILDREN

I. THE COLLABORATIVE LAW PROCESS

Collaborative Law is a cooperative, confidential voluntary conflict resolution vehicle for parties going through a separation, dissolution or other family law matter.

The participants, which include both the attorneys and the parties, acknowledge that the essence of "Collaborative Law" is the shared belief that it is in the best interest of parties and their families in Family Law matters to commit themselves to avoiding adversarial proceedings, particularly litigation, and instead to work together to create shared solutions to the issues presented by the parties.

The goal of Collaborative Law is to minimize, if not eliminate, the negative economic, social and emotional consequences of litigation to families.

Choosing Collaborative Law requires a commitment to resolving differences justly and equitably.

II. NO COURT OR OTHER INTERVENTION

Collaborative Law requires a commitment to settling the issues involved without court intervention.

Participants must agree to give full, honest and open disclosure of all information, whether requested or not. Participants must agree to engage in informal discussions and conferences to settle all issues.

III. CAUTIONS

There is no guarantee that the process will be successful in resolving a dispute.

The Collaborative process cannot eliminate concerns about the disharmony, distrust and irreconcilable differences which have led to the current conflict.

Although the participants are committed to reaching a shared solution, each party is still expected to identify and assert his or her respective interest and the parties' respective attorneys will help each of them do so.

IV. PARTICIPATION WITH INTEGRITY

Participants must commit to protecting the privacy, respect and dignity of all involved, including parties, attorneys and consultants.

Each participant must commit to maintaining a high standard of integrity, specifically; participants shall not take advantage of the other participants, or of the miscalculations or inadvertent mistakes of others, but shall identify and correct them.

V. EXPERTS AND CONSULTANTS

Sometimes the input of outside experts such as accountants, appraisers, therapists and mediators might be needed to assist the participants in reaching creative and informed solutions. If any such experts are needed, they will be retained jointly. All such experts and other consultants retained in the Collaborative process shall be directed to work in a cooperative effort to resolve issues.

In the event that the Collaborative Law process terminates, all consultants will be disqualified as witnesses and their work product will be inadmissible as evidence, unless the parties otherwise mutually agree in writing. However, new consultants will be permitted to review the work product and reports of prior consultants to facilitate the transition for the parties.

VI. NEGOTIATION IN GOOD FAITH

The process, even with full and honest disclosure, will involve vigorous good faith negotiation.

Each participant will be expected to take a reasoned position in all disputes. Where such positions differ, each participant will use his or her best efforts to create proposals that meet the fundamental needs of both parties and if necessary to compromise to reach a settlement of all issues.

Although participants may discuss the likely outcome of a litigated result, none will use threats of abandoning the collaborative process or of litigation as a way of forcing settlement.

VII. ATTORNEYS' ROLE—ATTORNEYS' FEES AND COSTS

The attorney's role is to provide an organized framework that will make it easier for the parties to reach an agreement on each issue. The attorneys will help the parties communicate with each other, identify issues, ask questions, make observations, suggest options, help them express needs, goals and feelings, check the workability of proposed solutions and prepare and file all written paperwork for the court. The attorneys and the parties shall work together to reach a solution which serves the needs of both parties.

The Collaborative process requires payment to each attorney. The parties will make funds available for this purpose.

Each attorney is independent from the other attorneys in the Collaborative Family Lawyers Institute, and has been retained by only one party in the collaborative process.

VIII. ABUSE OF THE COLLABORATIVE PROCESS

A Collaborative Law attorney will withdraw from a case as soon as possible upon learning that his or her client has withheld or misrepresented information or otherwise acted so as to undermine or take unfair advantage of the Collaborative Law process. Examples of such violations of the process are: the secret disposition of marital, quasi-marital or separate property, failing to disclose the existence or the true nature of assets and/or obligations or failure to participate in the spirit of the Collaborative process.

IX. DISQUALIFICATION BY COURT INTERVENTION

An attorney's representation in the Collaborative process is limited to that process. No attorney representing a party in the Collaborative process can ever represent that party in court in a proceeding against the other spouse. In the event a court filing is unavoidable, both attorneys are disqualified from representing either client and will assist their respective clients in the transition process.

02–03. [RESCINDED BY ADMINISTRATIVE ORDER NO. 16–02, EFFECTIVE FEBRUARY 17, 2016]

General Magistrate/Support Hearing

02–15–05. ESTABLISHMENT OF AND APPOINTMENT TO THE PART–TIME CHILD SUPPORT ENFORCEMENT HEARING OFFICER SELECTION COMMITTEE FOR THE ELEVENTH JUDICIAL CIRCUIT OF FLORIDA

THE ELEVENTH JUDICIAL CIRCUIT MIAMI–DADE COUNTY, FLORIDA

CASE NO. 15–2 (Court Administration)

ADMINISTRATIVE ORDER NO. 15–05

IN RE: ESTABLISHMENT OF AND APPOINTMENT TO THE PART–TIME CHILD SUPPORT ENFORCEMENT HEARING OFFICER SELECTION COMMITTEE FOR THE ELEVENTH JUDICIAL CIRCUIT OF FLORIDA

WHEREAS, the Eleventh Judicial Circuit accepted applications for the position of Part–Time Child Support Enforcement Hearing Officer ("Hearing Officer") through December 5, 2014; and

WHEREAS, the Hearing Officer will be providing highly responsible professional legal work, calendaring and conducting hearings before a circuit court and making rulings on Title IV–D support matters in the Circuit's Family Division; and

WHEREAS, the Hearing Officer shall be selected by the undersigned; and

WHEREAS, in order to assist in the selection of the Hearing Officer, the undersigned deemed it appropriate to establish a selection committee to be comprised of Family Division Judges, General Magistrates and representatives from various voluntary bar associations;

NOW, THEREFORE, pursuant to the authority vested in me as Chief Judge of the Eleventh Judicial Circuit of Florida, under Rule 2.215, Florida Rules of Judicial Administration, it is hereby **ORDERED**:

1. **Establishment and Purpose:** The Part–Time Child Support Enforcement Hearing Officer Selection Committee for the Eleventh Judicial Circuit ("Selection Committee") is hereby established to assist the undersigned in the selection of the Hearing Officer.

2. **Selection Committee Members.** The following individuals are hereby appointed to serve as the Selection Committee, to include Administrative Judge Scott Bernstein, who shall serve as the chairperson:

a. Associate Administrative Judge Stanford Blake,

b. Administrative General Magistrate Carlos Fernandez,

c. General Magistrate Karl Brown,

d. General Magistrate Melissa Tenenbaum,

e. Fritznie Abigail Jarbath, Esquire, President, Haitian Bar Association,

f. Leigh–Ann Amanda Buchanan, Esquire, President, Wilkie D. Ferguson, Jr. Bar Association,

g. Lisa Lehner, Esquire, Representative, Florida Association for Women Lawyers,

h. Herman Joseph Russomanno, III, Esquire, President, Dade County Bar Association,

i. Manny Crespo, Esquire, President, Cuban American Bar Association),

j. Patrick Vilar, Esquire, President, The First Family Law American Inn of Court, and

k. Cecilia Armenteros, Esquire, Representative, Gay and Lesbian Lawyers Association.

3. **Selection Committee Responsibilities.** The Selection Committee will be responsible for screening, interviewing and making recommendations to the undersigned regarding the selection of individuals qualified to serve as Hearing Officer.

4. **Administrative Staff Support.** The Administrative Office of the Courts will provide supportive services to the Selection Committee, as needed.

5. **Legal Assistance.** The Office of the General Counsel will provide legal assistance to the Selection Committee, as needed.

This Administrative Order shall take effect immediately upon execution.

DONE AND ORDERED in Chambers at Miami–Dade County, Florida, this 3rd day of February, 2015.

BERTILA SOTO, CHIEF JUDGE
ELEVENTH JUDICIAL CIRCUIT
OF FLORIDA

Juvenile

14–08. APPOINTING FOSTER CARE REVIEW, INC., TO CONTINUE TO ADMINISTER THE ELEVENTH JUDICIAL CIRCUIT'S CITIZEN REVIEW PANEL PROGRAM; RE–ESTABLISHING PROCEDURES FOR SUCH PROGRAM

THE ELEVENTH JUDICIAL CIRCUIT MIAMI–DADE COUNTY, FLORIDA

CASE NO. 14–1

ADMINISTRATIVE ORDER NO. 14–08 (Rescinding AO 91–15)

IN RE: APPOINTING FOSTER CARE REVIEW, INC., TO CONTINUE TO ADMINISTER THE ELEVENTH JUDICIAL CIRCUIT'S CITIZEN REVIEW PANEL PROGRAM; REESTABLISHING PROCEDURES FOR SUCH PROGRAM

WHEREAS, pursuant to Florida Statutes 39.701 and 39.702, Citizen Review Panels are permitted to conduct judicial reviews in dependency cases upon judicial referral; and

WHEREAS, pursuant to Florida Statute 39.702(2), Citizen Review Panels in Florida must be administered by a non-profit organization; and

WHEREAS, Administrative Order 91–15, issued by this court on June 25, 1991, authorized Foster Care Review, Inc., a non-profit organization operating in Florida, to administer the Citizen Review Panel Program in the Eleventh Judicial Circuit and Foster Care Review has continually done so since that time; and

WHEREAS, the Juvenile Division of the Eleventh Judicial Circuit and child welfare system stakeholders support the referral of cases to the Citizen Review Panel Program operated by Foster Care Review; and

WHEREAS, the Administrative Office of the Courts has responsibility for the efficient handling of dependency cases and supporting the effective operation of the Citizen Review Panel Program;

NOW, THEREFORE, I, BERTILA SOTO, pursuant to the authority vested in me as Chief Judge of the Eleventh Judicial Circuit, it is hereby **ORDERED:**

1. **Authorization to Administer Citizen Review Panel.** Foster Care Review, Inc. is hereby authorized to continue to administer the Citizen Review Panel Program for the Eleventh Judicial Circuit in accordance with this Administrative Order, applicable laws and the Florida Rules of Juvenile Procedure.

2. **Administration of the Citizen Review Panel Program.** The Citizen Review Panel Program shall be administered in accordance with the requirements delineated in Section 39.702(5), Florida Statute, as specifically set forth below:

a. In collaboration with the Department of Children and Families ("Department") develop policies to assure that citizen review panels comply with all applicable state and federal laws.

b. Establish policies for the recruitment, selection, retention, and terms of volunteer panel members. Final selection of citizen review panel members shall, to the extent possible, reflect the multicultural composition of the community which they serve. A criminal background check and personal reference check shall be conducted on each citizen review panel member prior to the member serving on a citizen review panel.

c. In collaboration with the Department, develop, implement, and maintain a training program for citizen review volunteers and provide training for each panel member prior to that member serving on a review panel. Such training may include, but shall not be limited to, instruction on dependency laws, departmental policies, and judicial procedures.

d. Ensure that all citizen review panel members have read, understood, and signed an oath of confidentiality relating to written or verbal information provided to the panel members for review hearings.

e. Establish policies to avoid actual or perceived conflicts of interest by panel members during the review process and to ensure accurate, fair reviews of each child dependency case.

f. Establish policies to ensure ongoing communication with the Department and the court.

g. Establish policies to ensure adequate communication with the parent, the foster parent or legal custodian, the guardian ad litem, and any other person deemed appropriate.

h. Establish procedures that encourage attendance and participation of interested persons and parties, including the parents, foster parents, or legal custodian with whom the child is placed, at citizen review hearings.

i. Coordinate with existing citizen review panels to ensure consistency of operating procedures, data collection, analysis, and report generation.

j. Make recommendations as necessary to the court concerning attendance of essential persons at the review and other issues pertinent to an effective review process.

k. Ensure consistent methods of identifying barriers to the permanent placement of the child and delineation of findings and recommendations to the court.

l. Submit an annual report to the Chief Judge by January 15th of each year.

3. Citizen Review Panel Program Volunteers:

a. Foster Care Review will recruit, train and supervise volunteer members of the Citizen Review Panel volunteer members and develop volunteer policies and standards in accordance with Florida statute and best practices for volunteer management.

b. Citizen Review Panel members shall serve without compensation.

c. Pursuant to Section 786.1355, Florida Statute, a member or agent of a Citizen Review Panel acting in good faith is not liable for damages as a result of any review or recommendation with regard to a dependency matter unless such member or agent exhibits wanton and willful disregard of human rights, safety, or property.

4. Citizen Review Panel Referral and Review: Citizen Review Panel Hearings shall be conducted in accordance with all applicable Florida Statutes, Rules of Juvenile Rules of Procedure [1], and federal law, as follows:

a. The Citizen Review Panel will conduct judicial reviews of children referred by the Juvenile Division.

b. The court shall select the cases appropriate for referral to the Citizen Review Panel.

c. The Clerk of the Court shall schedule reviews before the Citizen Review Panel in coordination with Foster Care Review and the court.

d. Seventy-two (72) hours prior to the Citizen Review Panel's hearing, a Judicial Review Social Study Report (JRSSR) and attachments required pursuant to Fla. Stat. s. 39.701(b) must be filed by the Agency with the court and distributed to all parties and Foster Care Review, Inc.

e. Foster Care Review may set a post–Judicial Review hearing before the court if the Citizen Review Panel: (1) finds the agency in non-compliance with its obligations as specified in the written case plan; (2) has serious concerns that were identified during the panel's hearing; or (3) if the panel is recommending extending the permanency goal of reunification beyond 12 months from the date of removal.

f. The Citizen Review Panel may not conduct more than two consecutive reviews without the child and the parties coming before the court for a judicial review.

g. In accordance with Rule 8.255, Florida Rules of Juvenile Procedure, the child and the parents or the caregivers of the child may be examined separately and apart from each other.

h. The Citizen Review Panel shall submit its written findings and recommendations report to the presiding judge within 10 days of its review hearing.

5. Special Considerations. Effective January 1, 2014, Section 39.625(18), Florida Statute permits young adults age 18–21 who were formerly in foster care to remain in licensed care under the jurisdiction of the court and in the care of the department. The court maintains jurisdiction over these young adults and is required to review their status every 6 months and to conduct a permanency hearing at least annually. The court may refer eligible young adults who opt into the extended foster care program to the Citizen Review Panel for regular reviews. The Office of the Clerk, Foster Care Review, agencies and the court shall work together to establish an effective referral process.

Administrative Order No. 91–15 is hereby rescinded in its entirety and held for naught.

This Administrative Order shall take effect immediately upon execution and shall remain in effect until further order of the Court.

DONE AND ORDERED in Chambers at Miami–Dade County, Florida this 6th day of May, 2014.

Honorable Bertila Soto, Chief Judge
Eleventh Judicial Circuit of Florida

[1] So in original.

05–08 (A1). EXPANSION OF JUVENILE DRUG COURT

THE ELEVENTH JUDICIAL CIRCUIT MIAMI–DADE COUNTY, FLORIDA

CASE NO. 06–1 (Court Administration)

ADMINISTRATIVE ORDER NO. 05–08–A1 (Amending AO No. 05–08)[1]

IN RE: EXPANSION OF JUVENILE DRUG COURT

WHEREAS, pursuant to Administrative Order No. 05–08, in view of the success of the Juvenile Drug Court in the Eleven Judicial Circuit of Florida for eligible post-adjudication drug cases in Miami–Dade County, Juvenile Drug Court was expanded to include eligible pre-adjudication drug cases in an effort to reduce recidivism by emphasizing treatment and rehabilitation as an alternative to incarceration, while also requiring offender accountability; and

WHEREAS, to further clarify the eligibility criteria for participation in Juvenile Drug Court, it was recommended that the Administrative Order be amended to (a) add to eligible offenses "has no additional felony charges, firearm charges or violent offenses" and (b) to distinguish that eligible offenses are for pre-adjudication cases and non-eligible offenses are for post-adjudication cases;

NOW, THEREFORE, based on the aforementioned recommendations, pursuant to the authority vested in me as Chief Judge of the Eleventh Judicial Circuit of Florida, under Rule 2.050 of the Florida Rules of Judicial Administration, it is hereby **ORDERED** that Administrative Order No. 05–08 is accordingly amended:

1. Effective January 1, 2006, the Juvenile Drug Court, currently in effect in the Eleventh Judicial Circuit for eligible post-adjudication drug cases will expand to provide for the inclusion of eligible pre-adjudication drug cases.

2. **Eligible Offenses (Pre–adjudication cases)**: Pursuant to Section 985.306, Fla. Stat. (1998), a juvenile who is charged by petition under Chapter 893, Fla. Stat., with a felony of the second or third degree for purchase or possession of a controlled substance, and has no additional felony charges, firearm charges or violent offenses, and who has not previously been adjudicated for a felony nor been admitted to a delinquency pretrial intervention program under Section 985.306(1)(a), Fla. Stat., is eligible for admission into a delinquency pretrial substance abuse program.

3. **Non–eligible Offenses (Post–adjudication cases)**: Youth who have been charged with the following offenses will not be eligible:

a. gun offenses (i.e., possession of a firearm);

b. sale of drug offenses (i.e., intent to sell);

c. violent offenses (i.e., aggravated assault; aggravated battery; assault charges (misdemeanor or felony); strong arm robbery (unless victim approval is given for misdemeanor and felony battery charges only);

d. sexual battery offenses;

e. those whose current offense is likely to merit commitment or direct file charges;

f. those who live outside of Juvenile Drug Court boundaries;

g. youths who are 18 years of age or older;

h. youths with severe mental illness, retardation, or other severe disabilities that would likely result in the inability to successfully complete the drug court conditions; and

i. youths who meet the criteria for long term residential services.

Additionally, if the State Attorney believes that the facts and circumstances of the case suggest the youth's involvement in the dealing and selling of controlled substances, the court shall hold a preliminary hearing. If the State Attorney establishes by a preponderance of the evidence at such hearing that the youth was involved in the dealing and selling of controlled substances, the youth is ineligible and the court shall deny the youth's admission into Juvenile Drug Court.

4. **Placement Procedure**: The procedure for placement of eligible defendants into Juvenile Drug Court is as follows:

a. **Referral**: A referral can be made to Juvenile Drug Court by Judges, Assistant Public Defenders, Assistant State Attorneys, Juvenile Probation Officers, and others.

b. **Screening**: Most of the Juvenile Drug Court participants are initially screened by the Juvenile Assessment Center ("JAC"). If the JAC, or other service provider, after testing the juvenile, determines that the juvenile has a substance abuse problem, the JAC will classify the juvenile as mild, moderate or severe drug abuser.

c. **Eligibility Determination**: After a juvenile is found to be a drug abuser by the JAC or other service provider, then the staffing team consisting of members form the Administrative Office of the Courts, the Office of the Public Defender, the Office of the State Attorney, the Department of Juvenile Justice, Miami–Dade Public School System, and various treatment providers (collectively, "Staffing Team"), will meet once a week to screen new filings to determine Juvenile Drug Court eligibility.

d. **Acceptance**: After a petition has been filed, but prior to adjudication and after the Staffing Team determines a juvenile is eligible to participate in Juvenile Drug Court, the Assistant Public Defender then meets with his/her client to discuss whether or not the juvenile wishes to participate in Juvenile Drug Court. If the juvenile wishes to participate, the case is referred to the Juvenile Drug Court Judge for acceptance into the Juvenile Drug Court.

5. Once the juvenile is accepted into Juvenile Drug Court, the juvenile is monitored by the Staffing Team on a weekly basis. If the Staffing Team determines that Juvenile Drug Court is no longer a viable option for the juvenile or the juvenile drops out of Juvenile Drug Court, the Juvenile Drug Court Judge will refer the case back to the original delinquency division.

6. As provided in Section 985.306 (1)(b)(2), Fla. Stat., the court shall determine, by written finding, whether the youth has successfully completed the delinquency pretrial intervention program and may dismiss the charges upon finding that the youth has successfully completed the delinquency pretrial intervention program.

Except as amended herein, Administrative Order No. 05–08 remains in full force and effect.

This Order shall take effect upon execution and shall remain in effect until further order of the Court.

DONE AND ORDERED in Chambers at Miami–Dade, Florida, this ___ day of __________, 2005.

JOSEPH P. FARINA, CHIEF JUDGE
ELEVENTH JUDICIAL CIRCUIT OF FLORIDA

[1] Amended by AO 1–05–08–A2, Court Administration.

02–15–06. ASSIGNMENT OF CASES INVOLVING CHILDREN KNOWN OR SUSPECTED OF BEING VICTIMS OF HUMAN TRAFFICKING IN THE DEPENDENCY SECTION OF THE JUVENILE DIVISION

THE ELEVENTH JUDICIAL CIRCUIT MIAMI–DADE COUNTY, FLORIDA

CASE NO. 15–2 (Court Administration)

ADMINISTRATIVE ORDER NO. 15–06

IN RE: ASSIGNMENT OF CASES INVOLVING CHILDREN KNOWN OR SUSPECTED OF BEING VICTIMS OF HUMAN TRAFFICKING IN THE DEPENDENCY SECTION OF THE JUVENILE DIVISION

WHEREAS, Rule 2.215, Florida Rules of Judicial Administration, grants the Chief Judge the authority to adopt administrative orders necessary to ensure the operation of the court system; and

WHEREAS, it has been determined, that in the interest of judicial economy, the Chief Judge finds it necessary to establish procedures for the expeditious and efficient resolution of cases involving children known or suspected of being a victim of human trafficking ("Human Trafficking Cases"), as provided in section 787.706, Florida Statutes; and

WHEREAS, specialized training and expertise of the judiciary is required in order to appropriately handle Human Trafficking Cases; and

WHEREAS, the Honorable Maria Sampedro–Iglesia has received such training and has the expertise;

NOW, THEREFORE, pursuant to the authority vested in me as Chief Judge of the Eleventh Judicial Circuit of Florida, under Rule 2.215, Florida Rules of Judicial Administration, it is hereby **ORDERED**:

1. All cases involving children known or suspected of being a victim of human trafficking, initially filed in the dependency section of the Juvenile Division and unrelated to any other cases in the Eleventh Judicial Circuit, shall be assigned and, if necessary, transferred by the Clerk of Court to the Honorable Maria Sampedro–Iglesia.

2. In the event Judge Sampedro–Iglesia is unavailable, the Administrative Judge of the Juvenile Division shall determine who shall handle the Human Trafficking Case(s) in her stead.

3. If related cases are identified in other divisions of the Circuit after the assignment or transfer of the Human Trafficking Cases to Judge Sampedro–Iglesia, the disposition of such cases shall be governed by the procedures established for handling crossover related cases in the Circuit, as applicable.

This Order shall become effective immediately upon signing, and shall remain in effect until further order of the Court.

DONE AND ORDERED in Chambers at Miami–Dade, Florida, this 5th day of March, 2015.

BERTILA SOTO, CHIEF JUDGE
ELEVENTH JUDICIAL CIRCUIT
OF FLORIDA

Mediation Arbitration

10–09. INFORMATION TO BE SUPPLIED IN FILING CERTAIN PETITIONS IN THE OFFICE OF THE CLERK OF COURTS REGARDING FAMILY MEDIATION

THE ELEVENTH JUDICIAL CIRCUIT MIAMI–DADE COUNTY, FLORIDA

CASE NO. 10–1 (Court Administration)

ADMINISTRATIVE ORDER NO. 10–09

(Rescinding and Superseding AO No. 06–35)

IN RE: INFORMATION TO BE SUPPLIED IN FILING CERTAIN PETITIONS IN THE OFFICE OF THE CLERK OF COURTS REGARDING FAMILY MEDIATION

WHEREAS, pursuant to Administrative Order No. 06–35, this Court adopted certain provisions to expedite the functions of the Family Mediation Unit and the Office of the Clerk of Courts, by requiring attorneys representing parties and pro se parties to append to all Petitions filed in the Family Division, an Information Sheet containing identifying information of the Petitioner, Respondent, and all minor children if any;

WHEREAS, the data required on the Information Sheet is generally not confidential under provisions of Rule 2.420 of the Florida Rules of Judicial Administration; and

WHEREAS, subsequent to the effective date of Administrative Order 06–35, Rule 2.420 of the Florida Rules of Judicial Administration was amended which requires the clerk of the court to designate and maintain the confidentiality of information contained within a court record;

NOW, THEREFORE, pursuant to the authority vested in me as Chief Judge of the Eleventh Judicial Circuit of Florida, under Rule 2.215 Rules of Judicial Administration, it is hereby **ORDERED**:

1. Any party or party's attorney filing the following Petitions with the Office of the Clerk of Courts is required to append to the Petition an Information Sheet containing, as far as known, the names, addresses, phone numbers, date(s) of birth, of the Petitioner, Respondent, and all minor children, if any:

(a) Dissolution Petitions

(b) Paternity Petitions

(c) Annulments

(d) Petitions for Support

(e) Petitions for Custody

(f) Adoptions

(g) Name Changes

(h) Termination of Parental Rights

(i) All other Petitions filed in the Family Division

2. Social security numbers are designated exempt under Rule 2.420(d)(1)(B)(iii) of the Florida Rules of Judicial Administration as of January 1, 2011.

3. Prior to January 1, 2011, redaction may be requested pursuant to section 119.0714(2), Florida Statutes.

4. If the filing party requests that certain data required on the Information Sheet remain confidential under Rule 2.420 of the Florida Rules of Judicial Administration, or under any applicable State or federal law, the filing party shall complete the Information Sheet without such data. However, the filing party shall also provide to the Office of the Clerk of the Courts a sealed envelope containing the data. The filing party shall, simultaneously with filing the Petition, the incomplete Information Sheet, and the sealed envelope, file a "Notice of Confidential Information within Court Filing" pursuant to Rule 2.420(d) of the Florida Rules of Judicial Administration with the Court for a determination as to whether the data contained in the sealed envelope should be considered confidential, and sealed, pursuant to Rule 12.280(d), Fla. R. Fam. P. Upon making such determination, the information set forth in the sealed envelope shall be accorded such treatment by the Clerk as the Court determines.

5. Definitions. For purposes of this Administrative Order:

A. The term "confidential" as applied to information contained within a record of the judicial branch, means that such information is exempt from the public right of access under article I, section 24(a) of the Florida Constitution and may be released only to the persons or organizations designated by law, statute, or court order.

B. The term "exempt" means that such information is confidential.

Administrative Order No. 06–35 is hereby rescinded in its entirety and held for naught.

This Order shall take effect immediately and shall remain in effect until further order of the Court.

DONE AND ORDERED in Chambers at Miami–Dade, Florida, this 15th day of November, 2010.

JOEL H. BROWN, CHIEF JUDGE
ELEVENTH JUDICIAL CIRCUIT
OF FLORIDA

09–10. ESTABLISHMENT OF PROCEDURES FOR MEDIATION IN COUNTY COURT CIVIL DIVISION

THE ELEVENTH JUDICIAL CIRCUIT MIAMI–DADE COUNTY, FLORIDA

CASE NO. 09–1 (Court Administration)

ADMINISTRATIVE ORDER NO. 09–10

IN RE: ESTABLISHMENT OF PROCEDURES FOR MEDIATION IN COUNTY COURT CIVIL DIVISION

WHEREAS, mediation is a pre-trial resource which may be used to resolve a dispute prior to trial; however, mediation is not a substitute for trial; and

WHEREAS, due to the current economic climate, the court's mediation resources have been significantly constrained, resulting in the need to implement and strictly adhere to procedures that will maximize such resources, while maintaining the level of productivity and effectiveness of mediation in the County Court Civil Division;

NOW, THEREFORE, pursuant to the authority vested in me as Chief Judge of the Eleventh Judicial Circuit of Florida, under Rule 2.215 of the Florida Rules of Judicial Administration, it is hereby **ORDERED** that the following procedures are established for utilizing mediation services in the County Court Civil Division, in and for Miami–Dade County, Florida:

1. Cases shall only be referred to mediation by the judge and only if:

a. All motions to dismiss have been resolved;

b. There is no possibility of a counterclaim; and

c. The parties before the court have full authority to settle the matter.

2. The County Court Mediation Division will only schedule mediations for judges at the Dade County Courthouse for "SP" or "CC" cases that have been referred to mediation and have been noticed for trial. All other matters referred to mediation, including branch court mediations, are to be scheduled by a judge's judicial assistant.

3. At the commencement of the pre-trial session, the judge should announce that mediation is a voluntary process to assist litigants in resolving the pending dispute. It should be stressed that mediators are licensed professionals and that mediation is confidential and voluntary. If one party objects to mediation, the case should not be referred.

4. In accordance with the requirements of a non-adversarial process through impartial dispute resolution, the County Court mediation staff shall not be present during any pre-trial conference where the court refers the action to in-house mediation. In the Branch Courts, mediators will be available in designated mediation rooms; in the Dade County Courthouse, the mediators will remain in the lobby adjacent to courtroom 6–4.

5. The bailiff, clerk, or judge's designee shall take the parties and the file to mediation. On resolved small claims cases, the mediator will present the executed stipulation and file to the judicial staff or clerk for the judge's signature and the judicial staff or clerk shall provide the parties/attorneys with conformed copies in court. It is a judicial responsibility that all stipulations, orders or dismissal, and final judgments are signed by the close of the session.

6. On resolved landlord/tenant cases simultaneously set with the pre-trial session, the mediator will present the executed stipulation and court file to the judicial staff or clerk for the judge's signature and the judicial staff or clerk will provide conformed copies to the litigants/attorneys. If a judge prefers to execute closing documents on landlord/tenant cases <u>outside</u> the pre-trial session, the mediator is to take the file with the executed stipulation to the judge's office for signature. The judicial staff shall conform and distribute the stipulation and order of dismissal or final judgment to the parties.

7. On cases which have been <u>specially set</u> for mediation and have been resolved, the mediator will take the file and the stipulation/order of dismissal to the judge's office for signature and distribution by the judicial staff.

8. If the case is referred to mediation and the mediator reasonably concludes the participants are unable or unwilling to meaningfully participate in the process or that an agreement is unlikely, the mediator shall suspend the session. The mediator shall file a written report evidencing the impasse without comment or recommendation and without personal appearance before the judge. This report should be delivered to the judge's chambers with the court file and left with the judicial staff for further judicial action (e.g., setting case management conference or trial).

9. After an impasse is declared, including any landlord tenant action, the case shall not be sent back to mediation unless the court enters an order specifically stating the rea-

sons for the re-referral, including the change in circumstances (e.g., new evidence, new parties, or new attorney) and there is an agreement by the parties for further mediation.

10. If an agreement is reached, the mediator shall reduce the agreement to a written stipulation to be signed by the parties or designated authority and the mediator and delivered to the judge's chambers for execution. The mediator shall file a Memo of Disposition as to the existence of the signed agreement without comment or personal appearance.

11. In that telephone mediations present difficulties that may make the success of mediation less likely, landlord/tenant matters, in particular, are not to be mediated telephonically. In other matters, telephone mediations should be used infrequently and on a case by case basis. Accordingly, if a telephonic mediation is authorized, the court must specify in writing the circumstances necessitating the telephonic mediation; however, under no circumstance shall there be telephonic mediations where more than one party is on the telephone.

12. Once the parties and attorneys (if applicable) appear for trial, the case must be tried rather than sent to mediation.

This Order shall take effect immediately and shall remain in full force and effect until further order of the Court.

DONE AND ORDERED in Chambers at Miami–Dade, Florida, this ___ day of _________, 2009.

JOSEPH P. FARINA, CHIEF JUDGE
ELEVENTH JUDICIAL CIRCUIT OF FLORIDA

09–01. DISMISSAL OF TRAFFIC CITATIONS ISSUED FOR FAILURE TO PAY TOLLS

THE ELEVENTH JUDICIAL CIRCUIT MIAMI–DADE COUNTY, FLORIDA

CASE NO. 09–1 (Court Administration)

ADMINISTRATIVE ORDER NO. 09–01 (Rescinding AO No. 00–13 and AO No. 00–13 A1)

IN RE: DISMISSAL OF TRAFFIC CITATIONS ISSUED FOR FAILURE TO PAY TOLLS

WHEREAS, Section 316.1001(c), Florida Statutes, provides that when an owner of a motor vehicle is issued a citation for failure to pay a toll, but the owner is not the alleged violator, the owner may file an affidavit establishing the identity of the person who had the care, custody or control of the motor vehicle at the time of the violation; and

WHEREAS, a more efficient utilization of both judicial and Clerk of the Court resources can be achieved by establishing a procedure for the administrative disposition of such citations;

NOW, THEREFORE, pursuant to the authority vested in me as Chief Judge of the Eleventh Judicial Circuit of Florida, under Rule 2.215, Florida Rules of Judicial Administration, it is hereby ordered that:

1. If a toll violation citation is filed against an owner of a vehicle who alleges that the vehicle was stolen prior to the time of the alleged violation, and files an affidavit attesting to the theft with the police report documenting the theft attached, the Clerk of Court shall dismiss the citation.

2. If a toll violation citation is filed and a person other than the individual cited for the violation admits to committing the violation and wishes to pay the civil penalty, the Clerk of Court shall provide an Affidavit Acknowledging Responsibility for the person to complete and submit, accepting responsibility for the violation. If payment of the penalty is remitted at that time, the Clerk of Court shall amend the citation to reflect the name, address, driver license number and date of birth of the actual violator.

3. If the Toll Enforcement Authority files a Request for Dismissal with the Clerk of the Court for a citation issued in error, the Clerk of the Court shall dismiss the citation.

Administrative Order No. 00–13 and Administrative Order No. 00–13 A1 are hereby rescinded in their entirety and held for naught.

This Administrative Order shall be effective upon signing.

DONE AND ORDEREDin Chambers at Miami–Dade, Florida, this ___ day of January, 2009.

JOSEPH P. FARINA, CHIEF JUDGE
ELEVENTH JUDICIAL CIRCUIT OF FLORIDA

06–35. INFORMATION TO BE SUPPLIED IN FILING CERTAIN PETITIONS IN THE OFFICE OF THE CLERK OF COURTS REGARDING FAMILY MEDIATION

THE ELEVENTH JUDICIAL CIRCUIT MIAMI–DADE COUNTY, FLORIDA

CASE NO. 06–1 (Court Administration)

ADMINISTRATIVE ORDER NO. 06–35 (Rescinds AO No. 97–13)

IN RE: INFORMATION TO BE SUPPLIED IN FILING CERTAIN PETITIONS IN THE OFFICE OF THE CLERK OF COURTS REGARDING FAMILY MEDIATION

WHEREAS, pursuant to Administrative Order No. 97–13, in an effort to expedite the function of the Family Mediation Unit and the Office of the Clerk of Courts, the Court ordered attorneys representing parties and pro se parties to append to all Dissolution of Marriage Petitions, an Information Sheet containing, as far as known, the names, addresses, dates of birth and security numbers of both Petitioner and Respondent, and of the minor children involved, if any; and

WHEREAS, in addition to the Dissolution Petitions, there are other Petitions that are filed with the Office of the Clerk of Courts that are referred to Family Mediation from which information should be obtained; and

WHEREAS, the data required on the Information Sheet is generally not confidential under provisions of Rule 2.051, Fla. R. Jud. Admin.;

NOW, THEREFORE, pursuant to the authority vested in me as Chief Judge of the Eleventh Judicial Circuit of Florida, it is hereby **ORDERED**:

1. Any party or party's attorney filing the following Petitions with the Office of the Clerk of Courts is required to append to the Petition an Information Sheet containing, as far as known, the names, addresses, phone numbers, dates of birth and social security numbers of the Petitioner, Respondent, and all minor children, if any.

a. Dissolution Petitions

b. Paternity Petitions

c. Annulments

d. Petitions for Support

e. Petitions for Custody

f. Adoptions

g. Name Changes

h. Termination of Parental Rights

i. All other Petitions filed in the Family Division

2. Such information will be for the use of the Family Mediation Unit and Office of the Clerk of Courts.

3. If the filing party request that certain data required on the Information Sheet remain confidential under Rule 2.051, Fla. R. Jud. Admin., or under any applicable State or federal law, the filing party shall complete the Information Sheet without such data. However, the filing party shall also provide to the Office of the Clerk of the Courts a sealed envelope containing the data. The filing party shall, simultaneously with filing the Petition, the incomplete Information Sheet, and the sealed envelope, file a written request of the Court for a determination as to whether the data contained in the sealed envelope should be considered confidential, and sealed, pursuant to Rule 12.280(d), Fla. R. Fam. P. Upon making such determination, the information set forth in the sealed envelope shall be accorded such treatment by the Clerk as the Court determines.

Administrative Order No. 97–13, entered on July 15, 1997, is hereby rescinded in its entirety and held for naught.

This Order shall take effect immediately and shall remain in effect until further order of the Court.

DONE AND ORDERED in Chambers at Miami–Dade, Florida, this ___ day of ________, 2006.

JOSEPH P. FARINA, CHIEF JUDGE
ELEVENTH JUDICIAL CIRCUIT OF FLORIDA

05–03 (A1). CLARIFICATION OF AMOUNT OF COMPENSATION TO BE PAID TO COURT APPOINTED ARBITRATORS

THE ELEVENTH JUDICIAL CIRCUIT MIAMI–DADE COUNTY, FLORIDA

CASE NO. 05–1 (Court Administration)

ADMINISTRATIVE ORDER NO. 05–03 A1 (Amends AO No. 05–03)

IN RE: CLARIFICATION OF AMOUNT OF COMPENSATION TO BE PAID TO COURT APPOINTED ARBITRATORS

WHEREAS, pursuant to Administrative Order No. 05–03, this Court established procedures for creating and maintaining the "Circuit's List of Qualified Arbitrator's" and established a reasonable rate of compensation for such arbitrators; and

WHEREAS, it has been determined that there is a need to clarify that the established hourly rate of One Hundred Fifty Dollars ($150.00) to be paid to court appointed arbitrators is not subject to negotiation;

NOW, THEREFORE, pursuant to the authority vested in me as Chief Judge of the Eleventh Judicial Circuit of Florida, it is hereby **ORDERED** that Administrative Order No. 05–03 is amended in the following particulars:

"3. The compensation of arbitrators selected by the Court from the list of qualified arbitrators shall be at the rate of One Hundred Fifty Dollars ($150.00) per hour. The cost shall be initially borne proportionally by each side unless otherwise agreed to by the parties or ordered by the Court. This cost may be taxed at the conclusion of the case pursuant to law."

Except as amended herein, all other provisions of Administrative Order No. 05–03 remain in full force and effect.

This Order shall take effect immediately upon execution and shall remain in effect until further order of the Court.

DONE AND ORDERED in Chambers at Miami–Dade, Florida, this ___ day of ________, 2005.

JOSEPH P. FARINA, CHIEF JUDGE
ELEVENTH JUDICIAL CIRCUIT OF FLORIDA

Unified Family Court

16–06. ASSIGNMENT OF CASES INVOLVING CHILDREN KNOWN OR SUSPECTED OF BEING VICTIMS OF HUMAN TRAFFICKING IN THE UNIFIED FAMILY COURT DIVISION

THE ELEVENTH JUDICIAL CIRCUIT MIAMI–DADE COUNTY, FLORIDA

CASE NO. 16–1

(Court Administration)

ADMINISTRATIVE ORDER NO. 16–06

(Companion to AO NO. 16–02)

IN RE: ASSIGNMENT OF CASES INVOLVING CHILDREN KNOWN OR SUSPECTED OF BEING VICTIMS OF HUMAN TRAFFICKING IN THE UNIFIED FAMILY COURT DIVISION

WHEREAS, the Florida Supreme Court in *In re Report of the Family Court Steering Committee,* 794 So. 2d 518 (Fla. 2001), endorsed the guiding principles and characteristics of the model family court developed by the Family Court Steering Committee and reaffirmed its goal of the creation of a fully integrated, comprehensive approach to handling all cases involving children and families; and

WHEREAS, pursuant to Administrative Order No. 16–02, the Unified Family Court Plan was reaffirmed and procedures were established to implement the Unified Family Court Division in the Eleventh Judicial Circuit of Florida to provide a comprehensive, coordinated approach to addressing family law matters; and

WHEREAS, it has been determined, that in the interest of judicial economy, the Chief Judge finds it necessary to establish procedures for expeditious and efficient resolution of cases involving children known or suspected of being a victim of human trafficking as defined in section 787.06(2)(d), Florida Statutes ("Human Trafficking cases"); and

WHEREAS, specialized training and expertise of the judiciary is required in order to appropriately handle Human Trafficking cases; and

WHEREAS, the policies and procedures outlined in Administrative Order 16–02 were meant to be elastic so as to provide the greatest degree of flexibility and allow for fine-tuning to the extent necessary to effectuate efficient and proper procedures for the Court and thus subject to change at any time; and

NOW, THEREFORE, pursuant to the authority vested in me as Chief Judge of the Eleventh Judicial Circuit of Florida under Rule 2.215, Florida Rules of Judicial Administration, it is hereby **ORDERED** that:

I. ESTABLISHMENT OF OPERATIONAL PROTOCOL

The following operational protocol is hereby established for cases involving children known or suspected of being a victim of human trafficking when Related Cases are identified:

A. Identification. Human Trafficking Cases will be identified by:

i. *Notice of Related Cases.* In accordance with Florida Rule of Judicial Administration 2.545(d), a fully completed Notice of Related Cases shall be filed with the initial pleading by the filing attorney or self-represented petitioner in each of the Related Cases that are currently open and pending with the court and served on all other parties in each of the Related Cases. Parties may file joint notices. To the extent that any issues of confidentiality apply, all legal requirements shall be observed, including any requirements as set forth in Florida Rule of Judicial Administration 2.420. Parties shall file supplemental notices as Related Cases become known or reasonably ascertainable.

ii. The AOC Juvenile Division, in conjunction with the Clerk of Court, shall be responsible for identifying Related Cases upon the filing of a new case or one reopened post-judgment when provided with notice or a court order. Upon identification, the Clerk's Office shall enter Related Cases into the Related Case and Case Cross Reference fields in Odyssey, and link all related cases together in the system.

iii. Judges and court staff, including, but not limited to, Family Self- Help Program

iv. System and agency partners

B. Notification. The AOC Juvenile Division shall be notified of these Related Cases by any of the methods indicated above.

C. Assignment of Cases. The following Juvenile Division Human Trafficking Cases shall be specifically assigned in the following manner:

1. *Open Dependency/TPR case designated as Human Trafficking where there is a related, open Juvenile Delinquency, Domestic Relations, or Injunction for Protection Case.* Related cases shall be filed in or transferred to the Human Trafficking Section of the Unified Family Court Division. The related cases shall be heard before a designated judge to handle all Human Trafficking cases in the circuit, who will serve as a specially sitting Unified Family Court Judge for purposes of handling these related cases through case disposition and for all post-judgment matters.

2. *Open Delinquency case designated as Human Trafficking where there is a related, open Juvenile Dependency/TPR, Domestic Relations, or Injunction for Protection Case.* Related cases shall be filed in or transferred to the Human Trafficking Section of the Unified Family Court Division. The related cases shall be heard before a designated judge to handle all Human Trafficking cases in the circuit, who will serve as a specially sitting Unified Family Court Judge for purposes of handling these related cases through case disposition and for all post-judgment matters.

D. Training. In addition to the requirements for judges assigned to the Unified Family Court Division set forth in Administrative Order No. 16–02, any judge assigned to the Human Trafficking court, either as the primary judge or as the back-up judge, will have six (6) months from the date of the assignment to complete at least an eight (8) hour course given by the National Judicial Institute on Domestic Child Sex Trafficking or a comparable course approved by the Administrative Judge of the Juvenile Division.

E. In the event the Honorable Maria Sampedro–Iglesia is unavailable, the Administrative Judge of the Unified Family Court Division shall determine who shall handle the Unified Family Court Human Trafficking Case(s) in her stead.

II. INTERDIVISIONAL COOPERATION

All divisions in the Eleventh Judicial Circuit shall work cooperatively together to ensure that multiple judicial determination concerning a single family do not conflict with one another.

This Administrative Order is a companion to Administrative Order No. 16–02.

This Administrative Order shall take effect immediately upon execution and shall remain in effect until further order of the Court.

DONE AND ORDERED in Chambers at Miami–Dade County, Florida, this 28th day of April, 2016.

BERTILA SOTO, CHIEF JUDGE
ELEVENTH JUDICIAL CIRCUIT OF FLORIDA

10–08. [RESCINDED BY ADMINISTRATIVE ORDER NO. 16–02, EFFECTIVE FEBRUARY 17, 2016]

03–15. [RESCINDED BY ADMINISTRATIVE ORDER NO. 16–02, EFFECTIVE FEBRUARY 17, 2016]

Thirteenth Judicial Circuit (Hillsborough County)

Local Rules

Local Rule 1. CIRCUIT COURT DIVISIONS

IN THE THIRTEENTH JUDICIAL CIRCUIT COURT FOR HILLSBOROUGH COUNTY, FLORIDA

LOCAL RULE 1

CIRCUIT COURT DIVISIONS

In accordance with article V, section 7, Florida Constitution and section 43.30, Florida Statutes, the following four major subject matter divisions are hereby reestablished for the administrative management of court proceedings in the Thirteenth Judicial Circuit.

A. Circuit Civil Division. All suits, actions, proceedings, or matters within the jurisdiction of the circuit court and not assigned to other subject matter divisions are assigned to the Circuit Civil Division.

B. Circuit Criminal Division. All actions, cases, and proceedings involving the administration of criminal justice within the jurisdiction of the circuit court are assigned to the Circuit Criminal Division. All habeas corpus actions are to be filed in the Circuit Criminal Division except for the following:

- Habeas corpus petitions involving custody of minors are to be filed in the Unified Family Court Division; and
- Habeas corpus petitions related to any matter filed in the Probate, Guardianship, Mental Health and Trust Division are to be filed in the Probate, Guardianship, Mental Health and Trust Division.

C. Probate, Guardianship, Mental Health and Trust Division. All causes, proceedings, matters, and actions arising under the following provisions of the Florida Statutes are assigned to the Probate, Guardianship, Mental Health and Trust Division: chapter 384 (the Control of Sexually Transmissible Disease Act); chapter 392 (the Tuberculosis Control Act); chapter 393 (developmental disabilities); Part I of Chapter 394 (the Florida Mental Health Act or the Baker Act); 397 (Hal S. Marchman Alcohol and Other Drug Services Act); chapter 415 (the Adult Protective Services Act); chapters 731–735 (Florida Probate Code); chapter 736 (Florida Trust Code); chapter 744 (guardianship); chapter 747 (conservatorship); and chapter 765 (health care advance directives). Any subsequent provision of Florida law relating to the settlement of estates of decedents and minors, the granting of letters testamentary, guardianship, involuntary hospitalization, and the determination of incompetency other than in criminal justice matters are assigned to the Probate, Guardianship, Mental Health and Trust Division. All petitions under Florida Probate Rule 5.900 (expedited judicial intervention concerning medical treatment procedures) are also assigned to the Probate, Guardianship, Mental Health and Trust Division.

D. Unified Family Court Division. In accordance with *In re: Amendments to the Florida Rules of Judicial Administration and In re: Amendments to the Florida Family Law Rules of Procedure,* 132 So. 3d 1114 (Fla. 2014), and its predecessor cases[1], all related family cases must be handled before one judge unless impractical. To implement the unified family court concept envisioned by the Florida Supreme Court, the following proceedings and actions are assigned to the Unified Family Court Division: dissolution of marriage; annulment; support unconnected with dissolution of marriage; paternity; child support; Uniform Interstate Family Support Act; custodial care of and access to children; proceedings for temporary or concurrent custody of minor children by extended family; adoption; name change; declaratory judgment actions related to premarital, marital, or postmarital agreements; civil domestic violence, repeat violence, dating violence, stalking, and sexual violence injunctions; juvenile dependency; termination of parental rights; juvenile delinquency; emancipation of a minor; Children in Need of Services / Families in Need of Services; truancy; and modification and enforcement of orders entered in these cases.

E. Subdivisions. In accordance with *Mann v. Chief Judge of the Thirteenth Judicial Circuit*, 696 So. 2d 1184 (Fla. 1997) and *Physicians Healthcare Plans, Inc. v. Pfeifler*, 846 So. 2d 1129 (Fla. 2003), the chief judge is empowered, through the issuance of administrative orders, to establish subdivisions within any of the subject matter divisions approved by this local rule.

CERTIFICATE

I certify that prior to submission of revised Local Rule 1 to the Florida Supreme Court, the requirements of Florida Rule of Judicial Administration 2.215(e)(1) have been satisfied. The Thirteenth Judicial Circuit hereby requests approval of Local Rule 1 by the Florida Supreme Court.

DATED this 5th day of January, 2015.

Ronald N. Ficarrotta, Chief Judge

[Editor's Note: Amended Local Rule No. 1 was approved by the Supreme Court of Florida on April 1, 2015.]

[1] *In re: Report of the Commission on Family Courts (Family Courts I)*, 588 So. 2d 586 (Fla. 1991); *In re: Report of the Commission on Family Courts (Family Courts II)*, 633 So. 2d 14 (Fla. 1994); *In re: Report of the Commission on Family Courts (Family Courts III)*, 646 So. 2d 178 (Fla. 1994); *In re: Report of the Family Court Steering Committee (Family Courts IV)*, 794 So. 2d 518 (Fla. 2001).

Local Rule 2. COUNTY COURT DIVISIONS

IN THE THIRTEENTH JUDICIAL CIRCUIT COURT FOR HILLSBOROUGH COUNTY, FLORIDA

LOCAL RULE 2

COUNTY COURT DIVISIONS

In accordance with article V, section 7, Florida Constitution and section 43.30, Florida Statutes, the following three subject matter divisions are hereby reestablished for the administrative management of court proceedings in the Hillsborough County Court of the Thirteenth Judicial Circuit.

A. County Civil Division. All suits, actions, proceedings, or matters within the jurisdiction of the county court and not assigned to other subject matter divisions are assigned to the County Civil Division.

B. County Criminal Division. All actions, cases, and proceedings involving the administration of criminal justice within the jurisdiction of the county court are assigned to the County Criminal Division.

C. Traffic Division. Except for enhanced penalties and other proceedings solely within the jurisdiction of the circuit court, all proceedings arising under the following chapters of the Florida Statutes are assigned to the Traffic Division: 316 (state uniform traffic control); 317 (off-highway vehicle titling); 318 (disposition of traffic infractions); 320 (motor vehicle licenses); 322 (driver licenses); and 338 (limited access and toll facilities). Matters assigned to the Traffic Division may be civil in nature or criminal in nature.

D. Subdivisions. In accordance with *Mann v. Chief Judge of the Thirteenth Judicial Circuit*, 696 So. 2d 1184 (Fla. 1997) *and Physicians Healthcare Plans, Inc. v. Pfeifler*, 846 So. 2d 1129 (Fla. 2003), the chief judge is empowered, through the issuance of administrative orders, to establish subdivisions within any of the subject matter divisions approved by this local rule.

CERTIFICATE

I certify that prior to submission of revised Local Rule 2 to the Florida Supreme Court, the requirements of Florida Rule of Judicial Administration 2.215(e)(1) have been satisfied. The Thirteenth Judicial Circuit hereby requests approval of Local Rule 2 by the Florida Supreme Court.

DATED this 5th day of January, 2015.

Ronald N. Ficarrotta, Chief Judge

[Editor's Note: Amended Local Rule No. 2 was approved by the Supreme Court of Florida on April 1, 2015.]

Local Rule 3. BUSINESS COURT PROCEDURE

THIRTEENTH JUDICIAL CIRCUIT HILLSBOROUGH COUNTY, FLORIDA

LOCAL RULE 3

BUSINESS COURT PROCEDURE

In accordance with Rule 2.215(e), Florida Rules of Judicial Administration, the following local rule of procedure applies only to cases in the Business Court, Circuit Civil Division "L" in the Thirteenth Judicial Circuit of Florida, as established by Administrative Order S–2013–021 (the "governing administrative order") and its predecessors. It supersedes and rescinds the document titled Complex Business Procedures, last revised May 2014.

3.1. Effective Date. This local rule becomes effective only if approved by the Florida Supreme Court following proposal by the majority of judges in the circuit and a recommendation by the local rules advisory committee. Rule 2.215(e)(1). Under subdivision (E), the local rule becomes effective on the date specified by the Court, Pending such approval, these rules are to be considered guidelines that litigants should follow.

3.2. Interpretation. This rule facilitates application of and supplies omissions in the Florida Rules of Civil Procedure due to a local condition as specified in Rule 2.120(b)(1). Specifically, the Thirteenth Judicial Circuit is one of a minority of circuits that have specialized business courts. Business Court cases are facilitated by rules which, for example, require filing of legal memoranda with motions and filing of written oppositions to motions, providing for decisions without hearing when appropriate, and providing clear expectations for case management. The provisions of this rule are not to be interpreted to conflict with any rules or administrative orders adopted by the Florida Supreme Court, or with any administrative order of the chief judge of the circuit; any of which would control over these provisions.

3.3. Citation. The provisions of this rule may be cited as "Thirteenth Circuit Local Rule 3.x," or for brevity, "Rule 3.x."

3.4. Filing. The governing administrative order specifies classes of "mandatory" cases which must be assigned to Business Court. A plaintiff filing a mandatory case must complete and electronically file, along with the complaint, the form entitled "Civil Cover Sheet and Addendum for Business Court Case" located at: http://www.fliud13.org/Forms.aspx. The Clerk will then assign the case to Business Court Division "L."

3.5. Transfer—Discretionary Cases. If a party believes a case pending in a Circuit Civil Division meets some or all of the Business Court discretionary transfer criteria set forth under the governing administrative order, the party may file a motion to transfer the case to Business Court in the Circuit Civil Division in which the case is pending. A Circuit Civil Division judge may also initiate a transfer if he or she believes the case is appropriate for Business Court. The Circuit Civil Division judge will then recommend in writing, either via an order recommending referral or informal memorandum to the file, to the Business Court judge that transfer occur. The Business Court judge will then make a determination and, if he or she finds transfer appropriate, the Business Court judge will enter the order of transfer.

3.6. Notification of Settlement. When any cause pending in Business Court is settled, all attorneys or unrepresented parties of record must notify the Business Court judge or the judge's designee within 24 hours of the settlement and must advise the court of the party who will prepare and present the judgment, dismissal or stipulation of dismissal and when such filings will be presented.

3.7. Motions—Certificate of Good Faith Conference. Before filing any motion, the moving party must confer in person or telephonically with counsel for the opposing party in a good faith effort to resolve the issues raised by the motion and must file with the motion a statement certifying that the moving party has conferred with opposing counsel and that counsel have been unable to agree on the resolution of the motion, Counsel must respond promptly to efforts by opposing counsel who wish to confer to resolve motions prior their filing. Prior to filing a motion to dismiss for failure to state a cause of action, counsel must notify opposing counsel in writing of the intention to file a motion to dismiss and must identify the reason(s) counsel will allege that the complaint fails to state a cause of action. If requested, counsel will stipulate to the filing of an amended complaint in lieu of filing the motion. No conference is required prior to the filing of a motion for injunctive relief without notice, for summary judgment, or to permit maintenance of a class action.

3.8. Motions—Memorandum in Support and Memorandum in Opposition. All substantive motions must be accompanied by a memorandum of law, which must not exceed 25 pages in length. A memorandum in opposition may be filed within 10 days thereafter and must not exceed 25 pages in length. A reply memorandum may be filed within 5 days following the filing of a memorandum in opposition, which must not exceed 5 pages in length and must address only those matters raised in the memoranda in opposition. With respect to memorandums in opposition to summary judgment, however, the timeframe is extended to 20 days, and with respect to replies thereto, the timeframe is extended to 10 days. Memorandum may be supplemented by time lines, charts, diagrams, visual aids, or exhibits.

3.9. Motions—Exceptions to Memoranda Requirements. Memoranda of law are not required for motions; (a) to extend time; (b) to continue; (c) to amend the pleadings or substitute parties; (d) for pro hac vice admission; (e) for relief from page limitations imposed by these rules; or (f) for discovery motions. In the event memoranda of law are filed, they should meet the page limitations set forth above.

3.10. Motions—Setting Hearing. Promptly after filing a motion, if the motion is contested and the hearing is not waived, the moving party must initiate the scheduling of a hearing. The parties must confer and, if possible, set the motion for hearing at a mutually agreeable time at least 5 business days after the time has expired for the filing of a reply memorandum. If the parties are unable to agree on a hearing date, they must promptly advise the court and the court will set the hearing. A motion requiring a hearing under this subdivision may be deemed abandoned and denied without prejudice if a notice of hearing on the motion is not filed within 45 days of its filing.

3.11. Motions—Waiver of Hearing. The court will decide a contested motion only after hearing unless:

(a) The parties waive a hearing, by filing a waiver with a copy e-mailed to chambers, but the court may nonetheless request the parties to schedule a hearing if the court finds oral argument would be helpful; or

(b) The court determines that extraordinary circumstances justify a decision without a hearing, in which case any party may request a hearing upon a motion for reconsideration.

3.12. Case Management—Conference. Within 60 days following the service of a complaint in the Business Court Division or within 30 days following the transfer of a case to the Business Court Division, counsel for the respective parties must meet in person or telephonically to prepare and thereafter file a Case Management Report. The parties must cooperate in the scheduling of a case management conference, following which plaintiff's counsel must coordinate, schedule, and notice a case management conference at a time reasonably convenient to the parties.

3.13. Case Management—Meeting and Report. The parties must meet in person or by telephone to discuss and prepare a Case Management Report, which must be submitted to the court no later than 5 days before fee case management conference, The parties' Case Management Report must address those matters set forth in rules 1.200(a) and 1.201 of the Florida Rules of Civil Procedure as well as the following:

(a) A summary of the claims and defenses of the parties and whether a jury trial has been demanded;

(b) A discovery schedule including, an estimate of the number of facts witnesses to be deposed, the number and expertise of experts to be deposed, and whether the parties anticipate any problems in doing so;

(c) Anticipated areas of expert testimony, timing for identification of experts, and responses to expert discovery;

(d) The necessity for a protective order to facilitate discovery;

(e) The time period after the close of discovery within which dispositive motions must be filed, briefed and argued and a tentative schedule for such activities;

(f) The timing of Alternative Dispute Resolution, including the selection of a mediator or arbitrator(s);

(g) Proposals for the formulation and simplification of issues, including the elimination of frivolous claims or defenses;

(h) A preliminary listing of the principal disputed legal and factual issues;

(i) A preliminary listing of any legal principles and facts that are not in dispute;

(j) A good faith, preliminary estimate by each party of the length of time to try the case, along with a statement of when the parties anticipate being ready for trial;

(k) Any issues known or anticipated discovery issues;

(*l*) The extent to which the parties anticipate or would prefer amendments or additions to the court's Uniform Trial Order and, if so, the reasons therefor;

(m) Such other matters as the parties may suggest that would facilitate the orderly, economical and expeditious management of the litigation by the court or the parties.

3.14. Case Management—Attendance. The attendance by lead trial counsel for each party is mandatory.

3.15. Case Management—Order. Following the case management conference, the parties will submit to the court a proposed Case Management Order. The Case Management Order may also specify a schedule of status conferences, when necessary, to assess the functioning of the Case Management Order, assess the progress of the case, and enter such further revisions to the Case Management Order as the court may deem necessary or appropriate.

3.16. Discovery—Guidelines. With respect to the conduct of discovery generally, in addition to the applicable rules of procedure and professional conduct, counsel are encouraged to consult the latest edition of the HANDBOOK ON DISCOVERY PRACTICE issued by the Joint Committee of The Trial Lawyers Section of the Florida Bar and Conferences of the Circuit and County Court Judges. The Handbook can be found on the website of the Trial Lawyers Section of The Florida Bar (http://www.flatls.org/).

3.17. Discovery—Experts. Discovery with respect to experts must be conducted within the discovery period established by the Case Management Order. At least 30 days before the deposition of any expert (or, if no deposition is required, within the time set by the court), the party who retained the expert must produce an expert report which discloses, at a minimum, the expert's opinions and the bases and facts underlying such opinions; the data or other information considered by the witness in forming the opinions; any exhibits to be used as a summary of or support for the opinions; the qualifications of the witness, including a list of publications authored by the witness within the preceding ten years; the compensation paid for the expert's work and expected costs for his or her testimony; and a listing of any other cases in which the witness has testified as an expert at trial or by deposition or affidavit within the preceding four years.

3.18. Discovery—Extension of Time or Request for Additional Discovery. Motions seeking an extension of the discovery period must be presented prior to the expiration of the time within which discovery is required to be completed. Such motions must set forth good cause justifying the additional time or additional discovery and will only be granted upon a showing of good cause.

3.19. Confidentiality Agreements. The parties may reach their own agreement regarding the designation of materials as confidential. The parties may submit a stipulated motion and proposed order incorporating the agreed upon confidentiality agreement. A party must not file documents under seal without having first obtained an order granting leave of court to file documents under seal based upon a showing of particularized need in accordance with Florida law.

3.20. Mediation. The parties in all cases assigned to Business Court must be ordered to attend mediation to be conducted by a mediator who the parties agree upon or who the court assigns.

3.21. Non–Binding and Voluntary Binding Arbitration. Non-binding and voluntary binding arbitration are governed by Florida Statutes, Florida Rules of Civil Procedure, and the Thirteenth Judicial Circuit Non–Binding Arbitration administrative order, as amended from time to time.

3.22. Pretrial—Meeting and Preparation of Joint Final Pretrial Statement. On or before the date established in the

Case Management Order, lead trial counsel for all parties and any self-represented parties must meet together in person for the purpose of preparing a Joint Final Pretrial Statement that is in substantial compliance with the Uniform Pretrial Conference Order applicable to civil cases in this circuit and strictly conforms to the requirements of this section. The case must be fully ready for trial when the Joint Final Pretrial Statement is filed. Lead trial counsel for all parties, or the parties themselves if unrepresented, must sign the Joint Final Pretrial Statement. The court will strike pretrial statements that are unilateral, incompletely executed, or otherwise incomplete. Inadequate stipulations of fact and law will be stricken. Sanctions may be imposed for failure to comply with this section, including the striking of pleadings, At the conclusion of the final pretrial conference, all pleadings are deemed to merge into the Joint Final Pretrial Statement, which will control the course of the trial.

3.23. Pretrial—Coordination of Joint Final Pretrial Statement. All counsel and parties are responsible for filing a Joint Final Pretrial Statement in full compliance with these Procedures. Plaintiff's counsel has the *primary* responsibility for coordinating the meeting of lead trial counsel and self-represented parties and the filing of a Joint Final Pretrial Statement and related material. If a non-lawyer plaintiff is self-represented, then defense counsel must coordinate compliance. If counsel is unable to coordinate such compliance, counsel must timely notify the court by written motion or request for a status conference.

3.24. Pretrial—Mandatory Attendance. Lead trial counsel and local counsel for each party, together with all parties, *must* attend the final pretrial conference in person unless previously excused by the court.

3.25. Pretrial—Substance of Final Pretrial Conference. At the final pretrial conference, all counsel and parties must be prepared and authorized to address the following matters: the formulation and simplification of the issues; the elimination of frivolous claims or defenses; admitting facts and documents to avoid unnecessary proof; stipulating to the authenticity of documents; obtaining advance rulings from the court on the admissibility of evidence; settlement and the use of special procedures to assist in resolving the dispute; disposing of pending motions; establishing a reasonable limit on the time allowed for presenting evidence and argument; and such other matters as may facilitate the just, speedy, and inexpensive disposition of the actions.

3.26. Pretrial—Sanctions. The court may impose sanctions on any party or attorney who; (a) fails to attend and to actively participate in the meeting to prepare the Joint Final Pretrial Statement or refuses to sign or file the Joint Final Pretrial Statement; or (b) fails to attend the final pretrial conference or is substantially unprepared to participate.

3.27. Website. The presiding judge of the Business Court Division will maintain a website for ready access to members of the Bar and the public. The website is located at the uniform resource locator (URL): http://www.fliud13.org/businesscourt.aspx. The website will store for ready retrieval basic information about the Business Court Division, including but not limited to, these Procedures and the procedure for Business Court Division case designation.

Administrative Orders

Court Operations

S–2019–003. PROFESSIONALISM COMMITTEE

IN THE THIRTEENTH JUDICIAL CIRCUIT HILLSBOROUGH COUNTY, FLORIDA

ADMINISTRATIVE ORDER S–2019–003 (Supersedes Administrative Order S–2015–056)

PROFESSIONALISM COMMITTEE

The current professionalism movement in Florida traces its formal beginning to a Florida Bar task force created in 1989 which generated a report that lawyers' professionalism was in a state of "steep decline." In 1996, The Florida Bar requested that the Florida Supreme Court create a Commission on Professionalism with the overarching objective of increasing the professionalism aspirations of all lawyers in Florida and ensuring that the practice of law remains a high calling with lawyers invested not only in the service of individual clients but also service to the public good as well.

In accordance with an administrative order issued by the chief justice of the Florida Supreme Court in 1998, the chief judge of each circuit was directed to create and maintain in continuous operation a circuit Committee on Professionalism. The Thirteenth Judicial Circuit has since created and maintained its Circuit Committee on Professionalism. In 2013, in response to surveys of both lawyers and judges reporting that professionalism is one of the most significant problems that negatively impacts the practice of law in Florida today, the Florida Supreme Court directed the chief judge of every circuit to develop a Local Professionalism Panel to receive, screen, and act upon complaints of unprofessional conduct to informally resolve complaints, if possible. The chief judge may designate the Circuit Committee on Professionalism as the Local Professionalism Panel. *In Re: Code for Resolving Professionalism Complaints*, 116 So.3d 280 (Fla. 2013), as amended by *In Re: Amendments to the Code for Resolving Professionalism Complaints*, 174 So.3d 995 (Fla. 2015).

It is necessary to amend some of the assignments regarding the Thirteenth Judicial Circuit Professionalism Committee. By the power vested in the chief judge under article V, section 2(d), Florida Constitution; section 43.26, Florida Statutes; and Florida Rule of Judicial Administration 2.215(b)(2), it is ORDERED:

1. Professionalism Committee. The Thirteenth Judicial Circuit Professionalism Committee (Committee) will initiate and coordinate professionalism activities in Hillsborough County. The Committee will also be responsible for overseeing and training a subcommittee designated as the Local Professionalism Panel (LPP).

2. Committee Leadership and Structure. The Chief Judge will appoint the Executive Chair of the Committee. In consultation with the President of the Hillsborough County Bar Association and Executive Chair of the Committee, the Chief Judge will appoint the LPP Subcommittee Co–Chairs, the Professionalism CLE and Events Subcommittee Chair, and the Professionalism Promotion Subcommittee Chair. The Executive Chair is authorized to create and maintain additional subcommittees necessary to affect this administrative order and to appoint Chairs of such committees. The Executive Chair of the Committee, with approval of the Chief Judge and consultation of subcommittee Chairs, will appoint the members of all subcommittees.

A. *Committee Chair and Executive Chair.* The Honorable Chief Judge Ronald N. Ficarrotta will serve as the Chair of the Committee. As Chair, the chief judge may at any time make decisions that pertain to the Committee as Chair, including reconsidering any decision of the Executive Chair. The Honorable Cheryl Thomas is appointed Executive Chair of the Committee.

B. *Professionalism CLE and Events Subcommittee Chair.* The Professionalism CLE and Events Subcommittee Chair will be responsible for ensuring the Thirteenth Circuit provides sufficient professionalism training opportunities and recognition events for lawyers and judges. Caroline Johnson–Levine is appointed Professionalism CLE and Events Subcommittee Chair.

C. *Professionalism Promotion Subcommittee Chair.* The Professionalism Promotion Subcommittee Chair will be responsible for ensuring the activities of the Committee are made known to the local bar and practicing attorneys within the Thirteenth Judicial Circuit through local legal organizations' publications, such as the Hillsborough County Bar Association *Lawyer* magazine, and other marketing and media outlets. Joan Boles is appointed Professionalism Promotion Subcommittee Chair.

D. *Professionalism Committee Award Subcommittee Chair.* The Professionalism Committee Award Subcommittee Chair will be responsible for accepting nominations for the Professionalism Award which has been established to annually recognize both a public sector attorney and a private sector attorney who have consistently demonstrated honesty, integrity, fairness, courtesy, and an abiding sense of responsibility to comply with the standards and rules of professionalism in the practice of law. The Honorable Frances M. Perrone is appointed Professionalism Committee Award Subcommittee Chair.

E. *Medical–Legal Professionalism Code Subcommittee Chair.* The Medical–Legal Professionalism Code Subcommittee Chair will be responsible for coordinating updates to the established guidelines for responsible, respectful and ethical interaction between lawyers and physicians and their patients in cases pending before the court. The Honorable Gregory P. Holder is appointed Medical–Legal Professionalism Code Subcommittee Chair.

F. *LPP Subcommittee Co–Chairs.* LPP Subcommittee Co–Chairs will be responsible for oversight and management of the LPP as provided in section 5 of this administrative order. William Kalish and Anthony D. Martino are appointed LPP Subcommittee Co–Chairs.

G. *LPP Members.* The Executive Chair of the Committee will ensure there are a sufficient number of members on the LPP to efficiently and effectively address professionalism complaints within the Thirteenth Judicial Circuit in accordance with the Florida Supreme Court's opinion *In Re: Code for Resolving Professionalism Complaints*, 116 So.3d 280 (Fla. 2013), as amended by *In Re: Amendments to the Code for Resolving Professionalism Complaints*, 174 So.3d 995 (Fla. 2015). All judges appointed to the Committee will serve on the LPP. LPP Members must be members in good standing of the Hillsborough County Bar Association and the Florida Bar, not have been reprimanded or disciplined by the Florida Bar, have been in practice at least ten years and have attained the highest respect of their peers and the judiciary for their professionalism and quality of practice.

H. *LPP Training Coordinator.* David A. Rowland is appointed LPP Training Coordinator and will be responsible for training all LPP participants regarding the confidentiality of the LPP, professionalism standards, and communication and resolution techniques.

3. Composition of the Committee. Upon invitation and consent, the Committee will be comprised of the following members:

A. The Chief Judge of the Thirteenth Judicial Circuit;

B. The President of the Hillsborough County Bar Association, or the President's designee;

C. At least 15 circuit or county judges or quasi-judicial officers from the Thirteenth Judicial Circuit;

D. One representative from each of the voluntary bar associations within the Thirteenth Judicial Circuit, including:

i. Asian Pacific American Bar Association of Tampa Bay
ii. Brandon Bar Association
iii. Carrollwood Community Bar Association
iv. Federal Bar Association
v. George Edgecomb Bar Association
vi. Hillsborough Association for Women Lawyers
vii. LGBT Bar Association of Tampa Bay
viii. Plant City Bar Association
ix. South Asian Bar Association
x. Tampa Bay Bankruptcy Bar Association
xi. Tampa Bay Catholic Lawyers Guild
xii. Tampa Bay Hispanic Bar Association
xiii. Tampa Bay Paralegal Association
xiv. Temple Terrace Bar Association;

E. One representative from each of the following Inns of Court, including:

i. Bruce Jacob–Chris Altenbernd Criminal Appellate Inn of Court
ii. Chester H. Ferguson–Morris E. White Inn of Court
iii. Herbert G. Goldberg–Ronald Cacciatore Criminal Law Inn of Court
iv. J. Clifford Cheatwood Inn of Court
v. Stann Givens Family Law Inn of Court
vi. Tampa Bay Workers Compensation Inn of Court
vii. William Reece Smith, Jr. Litigation Inn of Court

F. One representative from each of the following Sections, Committees, and Divisions of the Hillsborough County Bar Association, including:

i. Appellate Practice Section
ii. Bench Bar Committee
iii. Collaborative Law Section
iv. Community Services Committee
v. Construction Law Section
vi. Corporate Counsel Section
vii. Criminal Law Section
viii. Diversity Committee
ix. Elder Law Section
x. Eminent Domain Section
xi. Environmental & Land Use Section
xii. Health Care Law Section
xiii. Immigration & Nationality Section
xiv. Intellectual Property Law Section
xv. Labor & Employment Law Section
xvi. Law Day Committee
xvii. Leadership Institute
xviii. Marital & Family Law Section
xix. Mediation & Arbitration Law Section
xx. Military & Veterans Affairs Committee
xxi. Professionalism & Ethics Section
xxii. Real Property, Probate & Trust Law Section
xxiii. Securities Law Section
xxiv. Senior Counsel Section
xxv. Solo/Small Firm Practitioners Section
xxvi. Tax Law Section
xxvii. Trial & Litigation Section
xxviii. Workers' Compensation Section
xxix. Young Lawyers Division
xxx. 5K Pro Bono River Run;

G. One representative from each of the following local law schools:

i. Stetson University College of Law
ii. Western Michigan University Cooley Law School;

H. One representative from the American Board of Trial Advocates;

I. One representative from the Hillsborough County Association of Criminal Defense Lawyers;

J. One representative from each of the following local government law offices:

i. Attorney General's Office
ii. City Attorney's Office—City of Tampa
iii. Hillsborough County Attorney's Office
iv. Public Defender's Office
v. Regional Counsel's Office

vi. State Attorney's Office; and

K. Any other lawyer appointed by the Chief Judge or nominated by the Hillsborough County Bar Association President or Executive Chair of the Committee that practices within the Thirteenth Judicial Circuit and has demonstrated adherence to the professional standards of conduct set forth in the *Oath of Admission to the Florida Bar, The Florida Bar Creed of Professionalism, The Florida Bar Professionalism Expectations, The Rules Regulating The Florida Bar*, and the decisions of The Florida Supreme Court relating to professionalism.

4. Committee Responsibilities

A. *Meetings.* The Committee will meet periodically during the year to consider and review the professionalism efforts in Hillsborough County.

B. *Annual Report.* The Committee will submit an annual report on the status of professionalism and professionalism activities in the Thirteenth Judicial Circuit to the Chief Justice of the Florida Supreme Court and The Florida Bar's Standing Committee on Professionalism.

C. *Oversight.* The Committee will oversee and train members of the LPP.

5. Local Professionalism Panel (LPP)

A. *LPP Policies and Procedures.*

i. Initial Complaints. Any person may initiate a professionalism complaint against a member of The Florida Bar practicing within the Thirteenth Judicial Circuit through the LPP. A person making such complaint will be referred to as the "Complainant." Any complaint regarding a lawyer's compliance with the *Oath of Admission to the Florida Bar, The Florida Bar Creed of Professionalism, The Florida Bar Professionalism Expectations, The Rules Regulating the Florida Bar*, or the decisions of the Florida Supreme Court, should be directed to the LPP Subcommittee Co–Chairs. The lawyer that is the subject of the complaint will be referred to as the "Respondent." Matters or complaints may also be referred to the LPP by the Attorney Consumer Assistance and Intake Program (ACAP) created by the Florida Bar.

ii. Initial Screening Committee. An Initial Screening Committee consisting of five judges appointed by the Executive Chair will review initial complaints to provide consistency, guidance, and recommendations to the LLP Subcommittee Co–Chairs.

iii. Referral by LPP Co–Chair to LPP Panel. After receiving and reviewing a complaint, if, after consultation with the Initial Screening Committee, an LPP Co–Chair deems the referral appropriate for diversion to the LPP, the Co–Chair will select and refer the complaint to a three-member panel (Panel) from the LPP to hear, act upon, and resolve any unprofessional conduct. Each Panel must include at least one judge.

iv. LPP Panel Review. The Panel will initially meet without the Respondent to review the complaint and determine whether the complaint merits a full Panel meeting with the Respondent. If the Panel agrees and the alleged violation is not serious, one member of the Panel may wish to contact the Respondent informally to discuss the complaint and make recommendations to address such behavior, when appropriate. In more serious cases, the full Panel may decide to meet with the Respondent to review the complaint and determine whether the Respondent may benefit from various training programs offered within the Thirteenth Judicial Circuit locally or The Florida Bar, including Ethics School, Professionalism Workshops, Practice Resource Institute, Stress Management Workshop, Florida Lawyers Assistance, Inc., and the Trust Accounting Workshop. If the Panel deems the unprofessional conduct so egregious that it cannot appropriately dispose of the matter locally, the Panel will refer the matter back to the Co–Chair of the LPP, who will then refer the matter to ACAP.

v. LPP Resolution. After a Panel has reviewed and addressed a complaint and determined the Respondent has sufficiently complied with any recommended action, the Panel should report to the LPP Co–Chair that the matter has been successfully resolved. If a Respondent fails to meet with a Panel after sufficient notice, or if after a Panel review with the Respondent, the Respondent refuses to complete any recommended action, the Panel will refer the matter back to the LPP Co–Chair for referral to ACAP.

B. *Confidentiality.* All referrals, names of Respondents, communications within the Panels and with the Respondents will remain confidential. See Section 3.5 of the *Code for Resolving Professionalism Complaints.*

6. Peer Review Program. In 1997 the Thirteenth Judicial Circuit, in conjunction with the Hillsborough County Bar Association Professional Conduct Committee and Young Lawyers Section, established the Hillsborough County Bar Association Peer Review Program (Peer Review Program) to address behavior which, although not egregious enough to invoke formal disciplinary process or sanctions, falls below the high standards expected of attorneys including the Hillsborough County Bar Association's Standards of Professional Courtesy. The Peer Review Program has been in place and used in this circuit since its creation in 1997.

The definition of "unprofessional conduct" under the *Code for Resolving Professionalism Complaints* is "substantial or repeated violations of the *Oath of Admission to the Florida Bar, The Florida Bar Creed of Professionalism, The Florida Bar Professionalism Expectations, The Rules Regulating the Florida Bar*, or the decisions of the Florida Supreme Court." It is envisioned that the LPP, in addition to resolving complaints of alleged unprofessional conduct by attorneys, will also address less substantial or single violations of the above-referenced standards of behavior by attorneys. These less substantial or single violations attorney standards of behavior were previously addressed under the Peer Review Program. In this regard, matters previously referred to the Peer Review Program will be referred to the LPP in accordance with the provisions of this administrative order.

7. Previous Administrative Order Superseded. This administrative order supersedes Administrative Order S–2015–056 *(Professionalism Committee).*

8. Effective Date This administrative order is effective February 1, 2019.

ENTERED in Tampa, Hillsborough County, Florida, on January 29, 2019.

Ronald N. Ficarrotta
Chief Judge

S–2018–016. SEXUAL HARASSMENT POLICY AND PROCEDURES FOR COMPLAINTS AGAINST JUDGES

IN THE THIRTEENTH JUDICIAL CIRCUIT HILLSBOROUGH COUNTY, FLORIDA

ADMINISTRATIVE ORDER S–2018–016

(Supersedes Administrative Order S–2004–071)

SEXUAL HARASSMENT POLICY AND PROCEDURES FOR COMPLAINTS AGAINST JUDGES

The Florida Supreme Court amended the Sexual Harassment Policy and Procedures for Complaints against Justices and Judges earlier this year. *See* Administrative Order AOSC18–6 (February 16, 2018). As a result, it is necessary to update the Sexual Harassment Policy and Procedures for Complaints against Judges in this circuit. Accordingly, it is ORDERED:

1. Policy. It is the policy of the Thirteenth Judicial Circuit to foster a workplace free of sexual harassment or sexual misconduct. Sexual harassment occurs if there are unwelcome sexual advances; unwelcome requests for sexual favors; or unwelcome verbal or physical conduct of a sexual nature from or involving an employee's supervisors, peers, subordinates or other persons in contact with an employee during the course of the conduct of the employee's business when:

A. Submission to such conduct is either explicitly or implicitly a term or condition of employment; or

B. Submission to or rejection of such conduct by an individual is used as the basis for employment decisions affecting such individual or as the basis for any official action; or

C. Such conduct has the purpose or effect of interfering with an individual's work performance or creates a persistently intimidating and hostile environment, as that term is defined in state and federal law.

Sexual misconduct is any behavior of a sexual nature that is committed without consent or by force, intimidation, coercion, or manipulation. Sexual misconduct can occur between strangers or acquaintances, including people involved in an intimate or sexual relationship, and is not necessarily actionable sexual harassment.

It is the policy of the Thirteenth Judicial Circuit that all complaints of sexual harassment or sexual misconduct against any judge will be treated seriously and acted upon promptly. The following procedures apply to complaints against judges made by employees of the court system, applicants for employment with the court system, and when applicable, attorneys, litigants, or other members of the public. Compliance with these procedures by the chief judge constitutes a presumption of compliance with the disciplinary responsibilities under Canon 3D(1) of the Florida Code of Judicial Conduct.

2. Notification. The chief judge designates the court administrator to be responsible for receiving and documenting complaints of sexual harassment or sexual misconduct against judges of the Hillsborough County Court and the Thirteenth Judicial Circuit Court.

Any employee or applicant for employment with the court system who believes that he or she is the subject of sexual harassment or sexual misconduct by a county court judge or a circuit court judge should report his or her complaint in writing, or if the person prefers he or she may submit the complaint orally. The complaint may be submitted to any of the following: the chief judge, the court administrator, or the chief of human resources. If the person receiving the complaint is not the chief judge, the person receiving the complaint should forward it to the chief judge for investigation in accordance with section 4.

Student interns working for the state courts system who believe they are the subject of sexual harassment or sexual misconduct may use these complaint procedures, but in all instances, should submit a complaint to their college or university in accordance with the school sexual harassment complaint procedures.

If any person has difficulty writing out the complaint and the person requests assistance in reducing the complaint to writing, or if the person prefers to submit the complaint orally, the chief judge or designee must designate a person who will not be involved in the investigation or adjudication of the complaint to aid the complainant in reducing the complaint to writing.

If the chief judge is the subject of a complaint, the employee or applicant should report the complaint to the court administrator who will refer such complaint to the circuit judge having the longest continuous service as a judge in accordance with Florida Rule of Judicial Administration 2.215(c). The circuit judge to whom such a complaint is referred will assume all complaint investigation and resolution duties as provided for in these procedures. The circuit judge to whom such a complaint is referred will also be responsible for maintaining any records pertaining to the complaint.

If an employee or applicant chooses not to file a formal complaint, and any person designated in these procedures to receive complaints has actual knowledge or receives information that a substantial likelihood exists that a judge has engaged in sexual harassment or sexual misconduct, the person may inquire into the matter and take appropriate action.

3. Time for Filing Complaints. In order to ensure that the Thirteenth Judicial Circuit complaint procedures can be utilized without risk of precluding the filing of a charge of discrimination with state or federal entities, an employee or applicant should report an incident of sexual harassment within 90 days of the date of occurrence. Any complaint of sexual misconduct should also be reported within 90 days of the date of occurrence.

4. Investigation. A complaint of sexual harassment or sexual misconduct against a judge will be investigated promptly and thoroughly. If a complaint has been made to the chief judge, he or she may designate another person to make an initial inquiry into the complaint.

The chief judge or the chief judge's designee will interview the complainant within 5 days of the submission of the complaint to ascertain relevant facts and circumstances. If the complainant does not divulge names or details of the incident(s), the chief judge or the chief judge's designee will rely upon any information that is available. If another person has been designated to make an initial inquiry into the complaint, the designee will report details of the complaint, including any relevant facts, circumstances, and information, to the chief judge within 10 days of the submission of the complaint.

If the chief judge or the chief judge's designee determines the complaint is unfounded or insufficient to constitute sexual harassment, he or she may decline to pursue any action on the complaint.

If the chief judge or the chief judge's designee determines the complaint is facially sufficient to constitute sexual harassment, the chief judge may appoint an investigating officer or officers to investigate the complaint or may take any other action appropriate under the circumstances.

If the chief judge or the chief judge's designee determines the complaint is insufficient to constitute sexual harassment, but determines that it indicates potential sexual misconduct, the chief judge or the chief judge's designee may take any action appropriate to address the circumstances, including, but not limited to, appointing an investigating officer or officers to investigate the complaint.

The chief judge or investigating officer(s) will interview the complainant, the judge implicated, and witnesses, if any, and will review relevant materials. If any investigating officers have been appointed, they will submit a written report to the chief judge within 30 days of the submission of the complaint for formal investigation.

5. Resolution. The chief judge will determine the course of action for internal resolution of the complaint and may appoint another person to recommend the course of action for internal resolution. If the chief judge is the subject of a complaint, the circuit judge having the longest continuous service as a judge will determine the course of action for internal resolution of the complaint and may appoint another person to recommend the course of action for internal resolution.

If the chief judge or the chief judge's designee determines the complaint, including any relevant facts, circumstances, and information, is insufficient to constitute sexual harassment, the chief judge or designee may attempt to resolve the complaint informally through mutual conciliation by meeting with the complainant and the subject judge to discuss a method of resolution, including alternative dispute resolution. In attempting to resolve the complaint, the chief judge or designee may counsel or take other appropriate direct action with the judge involved.

If the complaint and investigation reasonably indicate that the subject judge engaged in activity that constitutes sexual harassment, constitutes sexual misconduct, or otherwise raises a substantial question as to the judge's fitness for office, the chief judge must refer the complaint and all written documentation pertaining to the complaint to the Judicial Qualifications Commission.

To the extent not otherwise prohibited by statute or rule, a written summary of the resolution will be provided to the complainant within a reasonable time after a determination is made and any resulting action is taken.

6. Documentation and Confidentiality. All information pertaining to a complaint of sexual harassment must be documented and maintained by the chief judge or the chief judge's designee.

All records made or received by any person in accordance with these complaint procedures are exempt from public disclosure under Florida Rule of Judicial Administration 2.420(c)(3)(A). Such records are exempt from public disclosure for the duration of an initial inquiry, formal investigation and resolution of the complaint, and at all times thereafter, unless the records are forwarded to the Judicial Qualifications Commission.

In accordance with Florida Rule of Judicial Administration 2.420(c)(3)(A) and rule 23(a) of the Rules of the Judicial Qualifications Commission, if records pertaining to a complaint are forwarded to the Judicial Qualifications Commission, such records will remain confidential until any formal charges against the judge are filed by the Investigative Panel of the Commission with the clerk of the Florida Supreme Court.

Records within the possession of the chief judge or the chief judge's designee pertaining to a complaint that has been forwarded to the Judicial Qualifications Commission will become public only upon formal charges being filed with the clerk of the Florida Supreme Court.

7. Referral to the Judicial Qualifications Commission. The Judicial Qualifications Commission is responsible for investigating all reported instances of judicial misconduct. These procedures do not preclude the referral of a complaint against a judge at any time by any person to the Judicial Qualifications Commission. If a complaint against a judge has been referred to the Judicial Qualifications Commission, no further action by a chief judge is required.

For anyone wishing to file a complaint, the Commission's mailing address is Post Office Box 141106, Tallahassee, Florida 32317. The Commission's executive director can be contacted by telephone at (850) 488–1581 or by e-mail at contact@floridajqc.com.

8. Referral to the Florida Commission on Human Relations or the United States Equal Employment Opportunity Commission. These procedures do not preclude the filing of a charge of employment discrimination with the Florida Commission on Human Relations (FCHR) or the United States Equal Employment Opportunity Commission (EEOC). For anyone wishing to file a complaint, the FCHR is located at 4075 Esplanade Way, Room 100, Tallahassee, Florida 32399. The telephone number for the FCHR is (850) 488–7082 or 1–800–342–8170. The EEOC office with jurisdiction over complaints arising in the Thirteenth Judicial Circuit is located at 501 East Polk Street, Suite 1000, Tampa, Florida 33602. The telephone number for the EEOC is 1–800–669–4000.

9. Previous Administrative Order Superseded. This administrative order supersedes Administrative Order S–2004–071 (*Sexual Harassment Policy and Complaint Procedures against Judges*).

10. Effective Date. This administrative order is effective immediately.

ENTERED in Tampa, Hillsborough County, Florida on May 16, 2018.

Ronald N. Ficarrotta
Chief Judge

S–2018–006. ATTORNEY'S FEES IN EXTRAORDINARY AND UNUSUAL CASES

IN THE THIRTEENTH JUDICIAL CIRCUIT HILLSBOROUGH COUNTY, FLORIDA

ADMINISTRATIVE ORDER S–2018–006

(Supersedes Administrative Order S–2014–043)

ATTORNEY'S FEES IN EXTRAORDINARY AND UNUSUAL CASES

The United States Constitution and Florida Constitution and laws require the provision of certain due process services to indigent persons in enforcing their rights under such authorities. The Florida Supreme Court in *Makemson v. Martin County*, 491 So. 2d 1109 (Fla. 1986), held that it is within the inherent power of Florida's trial courts to allow, in extraordinary and unusual cases, departure from the attorney's fees statute when necessary to ensure that an attorney who has served the public by representing a client is not compensated in an amount which is confiscatory of the attorney's time, energy and talents.

Section 27.5304(12), Florida Statutes, provides for an evidentiary hearing by the chief judge or a single chief judge designee when private court-appointed counsel seeks attorney's fees in an extraordinary and unusual case where the flat fee may be insufficient. It is necessary for the proper and efficient administration of the courts to appoint a chief judge designee to handle the evidentiary hearings when private court-appointed counsel seeks attorney's fees in an extraordinary and unusual case where the flat fee may be insufficient and to provide procedures for the processing of motions for attorney fees in extraordinary and unusual cases.

By the power vested in the chief judge under article V, section 2(d) of the Florida Constitution; section 43.26, Florida Statutes; and Florida Rule of Judicial Administration 2.215(b)(2), it is therefore **ORDERED:**

1. **Chief Judge Designee**. All motions for an order approving payment of court-appointed attorney's fees in excess of the limits prescribed in section 27.5304, Florida Statutes, and the General Appropriations Act must be scheduled for an evidentiary hearing with Administrative Judge of the Circuit Criminal Division Samantha L. Ward. All motions for an order approving payment of court-appointed attorney's fees in excess of the limits prescribed in section 27.5304, Florida Statutes, and the General Appropriations Act must be heard only by Judge Samantha Ward. If Judge Samantha Ward becomes unavailable to consider a motion, such matter will be reset on Judge Ward's docket. Judge Samantha Ward is the single chief judge designee for the Thirteenth Judicial Circuit and will hear all motions in all cases under section 27.5304(12), Florida Statutes, including criminal, dependency, delinquency, guardianship, and mental health cases.

2. **Contents of Motion**. All motions for an order approving payment of court-appointed attorney's fees in excess of the limits prescribed in section 27.5304, Florida Statutes, and the General Appropriations Act must include a copy of the intended billing, together with supporting affidavits and all other necessary documentation that was supplied to the Justice Administrative Commission along with the commission's letter stating its objection. The motion must also specify the number of witnesses interviewed or deposed or both, describe the complexity of the factual and legal issues, and specify the length of trial.

3. **Previous Administrative Order Superseded**. This administrative order supersedes Administrative Order S–2014–043 (*Attorney's Fees in Extraordinary & Unusual Cases*).

4. **Effective Date**. This administrative order is effective March 1, 2018.

ENTERED in Tampa, Hillsborough County, Florida, on February 22, 2018.

Ronald N. Ficarrotta
Chief Judge

S–2016–024. JURY MANAGEMENT

IN THE THIRTEENTH JUDICIAL CIRCUIT HILLSBOROUGH COUNTY, FLORIDA

ADMINISTRATIVE ORDER S–2016–024

(Supersedes Administrative Order S–2013–009)

JURY MANAGEMENT

Chapter 2016–52, Laws of Florida, amended section 40.013, Florida Statutes, providing that certain persons incapable of caring for themselves may be permanently excluded from jury service upon request. In light of this statutory amendment, it is necessary to update procedures for jury management in this circuit. By the power vested in the chief judge under article V, section 2(d), Florida Constitution; section 43.26, Florida Statutes; and Florida Rule of Judicial Administration 2.215(b)(2), it is therefore **ORDERED:**

1. **Jury Clerk & Jury Services.** The clerk of the court will assign deputy clerks to be designated as *jury clerks*. Jury clerks will comprise the department known as *Jury Services,* located in or near the jury auditorium. Jury clerks will be responsible for: summoning jurors; processing jurors' requests to be excused; checking in jurors on the automated jury system; assisting in the qualifications of jurors; preparing the jury list after excuses have been determined; making juror assignments to courtrooms; updating payroll; preparing letters of attendance for employers upon jurors' requests; and preparing paperwork for juror compensation.

2. **Jury Duty Judge.** Annually the chief judge enters an administrative order assigning circuit and county judges as duty judges to, among other duties, consider and act upon requests to be excused from jury service. The judge assigned for the respective week will be designated as the *jury duty judge*. Jury duty judges may affect changes in weekly assignment dates upon notification to Jury Services.

3. **Juror Summonses and Questionnaires.** Jury Services will be responsible for summoning jurors approximately five weeks in advance of the actual reporting date. Juror questionnaires will be mailed to prospective jurors with the summons. Supplemental juror questionnaires may be utilized in appropriate cases.

4. **Disqualified and Excused Jurors.** The jury clerk will send to each person summoned for jury service a form that

solicits information to determine whether the person is disqualified or excused from jury service under section 40.013, Florida Statutes. To be disqualified or excused from jury service, a prospective juror must complete the applicable form and return it to Jury Services along with any supporting documentation.

The jury clerk will excuse a prospective juror prior to the juror reporting for duty for any of the reasons set forth in the following sections of the Florida Statutes: 40.013(1), 40.013(2), 40.013(3), 40.013(4), 40.013(7), 40.013(8), 40.013(9) or 40.013(10). If any prospective juror requests to be excused from jury service for a reason set forth in section 40.013(5) or 40.013(6), Florida Statutes, prior to the juror reporting for duty, the jury clerk will direct such request to the jury duty judge.

Any request to be excused from jury service made to any judge will be directed to the jury duty judge. Any judge may excuse a prospective juror by communicating that request to the jury duty judge. The jury duty judge will honor another judge's decision to excuse and will notify the jury clerk in writing. The jury duty judge may excuse a prospective juror after that juror reports for duty.

5. Qualification of Venire. To assure prospective jurors are qualified under sections 40.01 and 40.013, Florida Statutes, the jury duty judge will qualify all prospective jurors unless the jury duty judge advises the jury clerk that another judge has agreed to perform the qualifying duty or advises that the jury clerk should perform the qualifying duty instead.

6. Scheduling. All administrative judges of subject matter divisions that conduct jury trials will send a yearly schedule of their divisions' designated jury trial weeks to Jury Services.

All jurors will be impaneled on Mondays of each week except for the week of Thanksgiving and any week in December the chief judge may designate. If a holiday falls on a Monday, jurors will be impaneled on the next working day after the Monday holiday.

Judges should make every effort to select all juries needed for the week on Monday. Juries are not to be selected on Tuesdays, Wednesdays, Thursdays, or Fridays except in extraordinary circumstances. Unless specifically reserved by a judge with the approval of the chief judge, no jurors will be available for service in the jury auditorium on Tuesdays, Wednesdays, Thursdays, or Fridays. If it is absolutely necessary for a judge to impanel a jury on a Tuesday, Wednesday, Thursday, or Friday, the judge or the judge's judicial assistant, after approval by the chief judge, must contact Jury Services by Monday with the exact size of the panel the judge wishes to reserve for Tuesday, Wednesday, Thursday or Friday.

7. Jury Panel Sizes. In accordance with Florida Supreme Court Administrative Order AOSC06–13, the panel sizes for any jury trial will be as follows:

Type of Case	Panel Size
Death penalty cases	No greater than 50
Other 12–person juries and life felonies	No greater than 40
Sexual battery cases with a child	No greater than 30
Sexual battery cases with no child	No greater than 25
Other circuit criminal cases	No greater than 22
Other circuit civil cases	No greater than 22
Domestic violence cases	No greater than 16
Driving under the influence cases	No greater than 16
Other county cases	No greater than 14

The presiding judge may deviate from these panel size guidelines as indicated in the attached table.

8. Reporting and Assignment Procedures. Unless disqualified, excused or otherwise advised by the jury clerk, all jurors should report to the Edgecomb Courthouse auditorium on the second floor on Mondays at 8:00 a.m. or 10:30 a.m., or as otherwise indicated on the jury summons. After jurors have taken the oath and are qualified by the jury duty judge or jury clerk, the jury clerk will assign the jurors to each court as requested.

No judge may request a panel be sent to the courtroom unless there is a case ready to go to trial and all parties are present in the courtroom. Bailiffs will report to the auditorium when instructed by their judges to escort jurors to the assigned courtrooms. Bailiffs must report to the jury auditorium and enter their judge's name on the sign-up sheet, which is located on the front counter in the Jury Services designated work area. Bailiffs may report as early as 7:30 a.m.

Bailiffs must be present in the jury auditorium immediately after the prospective jurors are qualified to enable the jury clerk to fill a panel. Jury Services will fill panels in the order listed on the sign-up sheet as long as the respective bailiff is present. For example, if Bailiff #1 on the sign-up sheet is not present in the auditorium at the time the clerk is filling a panel, but Bailiff #2 is present, then Jury Services will skip Bailiff #1, and then fill the panel for Bailiff #2.

Every judge should attempt to begin voir dire within 30 minutes of the jury panel arriving at the courtroom. If voir dire does not begin within 30 minutes, the judge should consider returning the panel to the jury auditorium for use by other judges.

After a jury is selected in the courtroom, the court clerk will determine from the judge when jurors will be needed again and call or send an e-mail message to the jury clerk in the auditorium to determine if jurors are needed to return to the auditorium. If additional jurors are needed in a courtroom, or if jurors are needed for the selection of another trial, the court clerk will call the jury clerk and request the required number be sent to the courtroom. The bailiff will go to Jury Services and escort jurors to the courtroom. Courtroom clerks will update juror attendance.

9. Electronic Devices. Use of electronic devices by jurors is governed by Florida Rule of Judicial Administration 2.451(b).

10. Previous Administrative Order Superseded. This administrative order supersedes Administrative Order S–2013–009 (*Jury Management*).

11. Effective Date. This administrative order is effective July 1, 2016.

It is ORDERED in Tampa, Hillsborough County, Florida, on this 10th day of June, 2016.
Ronald N. Ficarrotta, Chief Judge

Attachment: Panel Size Guidelines

Panel Size Guidelines

Panel Size Guidelines for Typical Cases			Guidelines for Exempted Cases**
Case Type	Guideline	Acceptable Deviations* (with approval of presiding judge)	
Death penalty cases	No greater than 50	Plus 3 for each additional defendant; or Plus 3 for lengthy trials; or Plus 3 for high profile trials; or Plus 3 for extraordinary circumstances.	Jury Panel Size to be Established by the Presiding Judge and Parties (Prompt notification to jury managers will be required.)
Other 12 person juries (criminal or civil) and life felonies	No greater than 40	Plus 3 for each additional defendant/party; or Plus 3 for lengthy trials; or Plus 3 for high profile trials; or Plus 3 for extraordinary circumstances.	
Sexual battery cases w/ child	No greater than 30	Plus 3 for each additional defendant; or Plus 3 for lengthy trials; or Plus 3 for high profile trials; or Plus 3 for extraordinary circumstances.	
Sexual battery cases no child	No greater than 25	Plus 3 for each additional defendant; or Plus 3 for lengthy trials; or Plus 3 for high profile trials; or Plus 3 for extraordinary circumstances.	
Other circuit criminal cases	No greater than 22	Plus 2 for each additional defendant; or Plus 2 for lengthy trials; or Plus 2 for high profile trials; or Plus 2 for extraordinary circumstances.	
Other circuit civil cases	No greater than 22	Plus 2 for each additional party; or Plus 2 for lengthy trials; or Plus 2 for high profile trials; or Plus 2 for extraordinary circumstances.	
Domestic violence cases	No greater than 16	Plus 2 for each additional party; or Plus 2 for lengthy trials; or Plus 2 for high profile trials; or Plus 2 for extraordinary circumstances.	
Driving under the influence cases	No greater than 16	Plus 2 for each additional defendant; or Plus 2 for lengthy trials; or Plus 2 for high profile trials; or Plus 2 for extraordinary circumstances.	
Other county cases	No greater than 14	Plus 2 for each additional defendant/party; or Plus 2 for lengthy trials; or Plus 2 for high profile trials; or Plus 2 for extraordinary circumstances.	

*These deviations from the guidelines must be approved by the presiding judge. Deviations may be cumulative given case specifics. However, such deviations should not exceed 20 jurors above the guideline. Lengthy trials are those predicted to last more than five days. High profile trials are those receiving a significant amount of publicity as determined by the presiding judge. Extraordinary circumstances are any other factors that may impact the voir dire process as determined by the presiding judge.

**Exemptions may be granted for complex, lengthy, or high profiles cases as determined by the presiding judge.

A–2013–006. STANDING RECUSAL ORDERS & STANDING RECUSAL ADMINISTRATIVE ORDERS

IN THE THIRTEENTH JUDICIAL CIRCUIT COURT HILLSBOROUGH COUNTY, FLORIDA

ADMINISTRATIVE ORDER A–2013–006

(Amends Administrative Orders A–1994–123, A–2000–039, A–2001–079, A–2004–011, A–2004–036, A–2004–039, A–2004–040, A–2005–193, A–2008–060, A–2008–103, A–2009–028, A–2010–036, A–2010–081, A–2011–037, A–2011–057, A–2012–002, A–2012–025, A–2012–057, A–2013–004 and A–2013–005)

STANDING RECUSAL ORDERS & STANDING RECUSAL ADMINISTRATIVE ORDERS

When a judge makes a professional decision to be administratively disqualified in cases in which a particular attorney is involved, the judge either issues his or her own standing recusal order or requests that the chief judge enter an administrative order to accomplish the same result. Until recent times, standing recusal orders and standing recusal administrative orders simply directed the Clerk of the Circuit Court (clerk) to automatically reassign a case upon a subject attorney appearing as counsel in the case.

The standing recusal orders and standing recusal administrative orders are intended to enable the clerk to reassign a case from a judge's division as soon as a subject attorney files and serves a party's first pleading or paper. Under the specific language used in most standing recusal orders and standing recusal administrative orders, the clerk automatically reassigns a case—even a case which may have been pending before a judge for years—anytime a subject attorney files a notice of appearance.

This procedure could result in unnecessary delay, allow for judge shopping, and create the appearance of impropriety. Accordingly this administrative order is entered to amend all standing recusal orders and all standing recusal administrative orders. A party bringing into a case an attorney who is the subject of a standing recusal order or standing recusal administrative order will initially be deemed to have waived the judge's disqualification. See *Sume v. State*, 773 So. 2d 600 (Fla. 1st DCA 2000) quoting *Town Centre of Islamorada, Inc. v. Overby*, 592 So. 2d 774, 776 (Fla. 3d DCA 1992) (explaining that "a party may not bring an attorney into a case after it has been assigned to a judge, and then move to disqualify the judge on grounds that the judge has a bias against the attorney.")

The entry of this administrative order is not intended to suggest that any attorney who is the subject of a standing recusal order or standing recusal administrative order has acted inappropriately. The entry of this administrative order is merely intended to avoid the appearance of impropriety and to standardize the process by which the clerk assigns and reassigns cases based on standing recusal orders and standing recusal administrative orders.

By the power vested in the chief judge under article V, section 2(d), Florida Constitution; section 43.26, Florida Statutes; and Florida Rule of Judicial Administration 2.215 (b)(2), it is therefore **ORDERED:**

1. **Definitions.** For purposes of this administrative order, the following terms have the following meanings:

A. **"Standing recusal administrative order"** means any administrative order entered by the chief judge directing the clerk to reassign a pending case from a division in which a subject judge is presiding to another division because the subject judge has made a professional decision to be disqualified in cases in which a subject attorney is an attorney of record.

B. **"Standing recusal order"** means any order entered by a subject judge directing the clerk to reassign a pending case from a division in which the subject judge is presiding to another division because the subject judge has made a professional decision to be disqualified in cases in which a subject attorney is an attorney of record.

C. **"Subject attorney"** means any attorney who is the subject of a standing recusal order or standing recusal administrative order.

D. **"Subject judge"** means any judge who has made a professional decision to be disqualified in cases in which a subject attorney is an attorney of record.

2. **Duty of Attorney to Advise Client of Judicial Conflict.** Rule 4–1.4(b) of the Rules Regulating The Florida Bar imposes upon a lawyer the duty to explain a matter to the extent reasonably necessary to permit a client to make informed decisions regarding the representation. If a proceeding is already pending before a subject judge, this professional duty obligates an attorney to disclose to a client the existence of a standing recusal order or a standing recusal administrative order between the subject attorney and the subject judge. See *Sume v. State*, 773 So. 2d 600, 602 (Fla. 1st DCA 2000).

3. **Conditions on Standing Recusal Orders and Standing Recusal Administrative Orders.** Whenever a subject judge is presiding in any subject matter division and there is a standing recusal order or standing recusal administrative order in effect, the clerk will reassign all cases of a subject attorney to another division only if the subject attorney files and serves a party's first pleading or paper in the proceeding.

Because a subject attorney is professionally obligated to notify a client of the existence of a standing recusal order or a standing recusal administrative order between the subject attorney and the subject judge and may not interject conflict into a case, if a subject attorney appears in a proceeding pending before a subject judge after the party's first pleading or paper is filed and served, the clerk is directed to not automatically reassign the proceeding to another division.

Nothing in this provision precludes any party from filing a motion for judicial disqualification under Florida Rule of Judicial Administration 2.330.

4. **Standing Recusal Orders Amended.** This administrative order amends all standing recusal orders entered prior to the effective date of this administrative order and all future standing recusal orders. The clerk is directed to provide the chief judge a copy of all standing recusal orders entered by any judge of this circuit and to provide to the chief judge a copy of any standing recusal order entered by a judge after the effective date of this administrative order.

5. **Previous Standing Recusal Administrative Orders Amended.** This administrative order amends all standing recusal administrative orders entered prior to the effective date of this administrative order. According to the records in the custody of the court's general counsel office, the following standing recusal administrative orders were entered prior to the effective date of this administrative order and are therefore amended:

NUMBER	TITLE
A–1994–123	*Automatic Reassignment of Certain Cases of the Judge Ronald Ficarrotta (Joseph Ficarrotta)*
A–2000–039	*Automatic Reassignment of Certain Cases of Judge Chet Tharpe (Norman Cannella, Sr.)*
A–2001–079	*Automatic Reassignment of Certain Cases of Judge Chet A. Tharpe (Taryn X. Temmer)*
A–2004–011	*Automatic Reassignment of Certain Cases of the Honorable D. Michelle Sisco (Lyann Goudie, William Hanlon, Bill Jung, and Paul Sisco)*
A–2004–036	*Automatic Reassignment of Certain Cases of the Honorable D. Michelle Sisco (Any attorney from the law firm of Trombley & Hanes)*
A–2004–039	*Automatic Reassignment of Certain Cases of the Honorable E. Lamar Battles (Any attorney from the law firm of de la Parte & Gilbert, P.A.)*

NUMBER	TITLE
A–2004–040	*Automatic Reassignment of Certain Cases of the Honorable Charles Ed Bergmann (Beth G. Reineke)*
A–2005–193	*Automatic Reassignment of Certain Cases of the Honorable Chet A. Tharpe (Eric J. Kuske)*
A–2008–060	*Automatic Reassignment of Certain Cases of the Honorable Kimberly Fernandez (Curry Law Group, P.A.)*
A–2008–103	*Automatic Reassignment of Certain Cases of the Honorable Denise A. Pomponio (Dominic Fariello and Darrigo and Diaz, P.A.)*
A–2009–028	*Automatic Reassignment of Certain Cases of the Honorable Catherine M. Catlin (Elizabeth "Betsy" Hapner and any attorneys associated with the law firm of Carey and Millison P.A.)*
A–2010–036	*Automatic Reassignment of Certain Cases of the Honorable Matthew C. Lucas (Richard M. Rocha, Michael R. Rocha, and any attorneys associated with the law firm of Bricklemyer, Smolker & Bolves, P.A.)*
A–2010–081	*Automatic Reassignment of Certain Cases of the Honorable Paul L. Huey (Catherine W. Real)*
A–2011–037	*Automatic Reassignment of Certain Cases of the Honorable Bernard C. Silver (Michael C. Addison, William J. Terry, Alan Von Spiegelfeld, Edward Waller, Joryn Jenkins, and any attorney associated with the law firm of Trenam, Kemker, Scharf, Barkin, Frye, O'Neill & Mullis P.A. or the law firm of Shutts & Bowen, LLP)*
A–2011–057	*Automatic Reassignment of Certain Cases of the Honorable Christopher C. Sabella (Any attorney associated with the law firm of Banker Lopez Gassler, P.A. and any attorney associated with The Yerrid Law Firm, P.A.)*
A–2012–002	*Automatic Reassignment of Certain Cases of the Honorable Lisa D. Campbell (Carl Roland Hayes)*
A–2012–025	*Automatic Reassignment of Certain Cases of the Honorable Richard A. Nielsen (Martha Irene Weed)*
A–2012–057	*Automatic Reassignment of Certain Cases of the Honorable Paul L. Huey (Patricia Palma)*
A–2013–004	*Automatic Reassignment of Certain Cases of the Honorable Margaret Courtney (Patrick B. Courtney)*
A–2013–005	*Automatic Reassignment of Certain Cases of the Honorable Elizabeth G. Rice (Barry Cohen, Lyann Goudie, Zilia C. Vasquez, and any attorney associated with the law firm of Sterns Weaver Miller Weissler Alhadeff & Sitterson, P.A. or the law firm of Glenn Rasmussen, P.A.)*

6. Effective Date. This administrative order is effective immediately.

It is ORDERED in Tampa, Hillsborough County, Florida, on this 23rd day of January, 2013.

Manuel Menendez, Jr., Chief Judge

S–2012–032. CERTIFIED PROCESS SERVERS

IN THE THIRTEENTH JUDICIAL CIRCUIT HILLSBOROUGH COUNTY, FLORIDA

ADMINISTRATIVE ORDER S–2012–032 (Supersedes Administrative Order S–1999–076)

CERTIFIED PROCESS SERVERS

In 1988, the Florida Legislature enacted the Florida Certified Process Server Act (sections 48.25 through 48.31, Florida Statutes), placing certified process servers under the jurisdiction of the chief judge. The Act establishes eligibility criteria for persons applying to become a certified process server and empowers the chief judge to prescribe additional rules and requirements regarding eligibility of certified process servers. It is necessary for the prompt and efficient administration of justice to update the procedures and eligibility requirements used to approve individuals who are designated as certified process servers in this circuit.

By the power vested in the chief judge under article V, section 2(d), Florida Constitution; section 43.26, Florida Statutes; the Florida Certified Process Server Act; and Florida Rule of Judicial Administration 2. 215(b)(2), it is therefore **ORDERED:**

1. List. The Administrative Office of the Courts for the Thirteenth Judicial Circuit (AOC) and the Clerk of the Circuit Court (clerk) will maintain a list of approved certified process servers who meet the requirements prescribed in this administrative order. The list may be amended to add or delete names of individuals in accordance with provisions of this administrative order. The clerk will make the list available to all individuals who file civil actions.

2. Eligibility. In addition to fulfilling the eligibility requirements in section 48.29, Florida Statutes, a certified process server applicant must also:

A. *Education.* Successfully complete the process server course offered by Hillsborough Community College.

B. *Examination.* Pass a written examination which will be administered by the AOC. The examination will be administered annually. A passing grade is fixed at a minimum of seventy-five percent (75%).

C. *Character and Fitness.* Conduct oneself in accordance with Florida law. Each certified process server is a representative of this circuit and will be issued an identification card bearing the seal of the Thirteenth Judicial Circuit. As a representative of this circuit, a person is not eligible to be placed on the list of certified process servers if the person (i) is registered or required to register as a sexual offender as defined in section 943.0435, Florida Statutes; (ii) has been designated as a sexual predator under section 775.21, Florida Statutes; or (iii) has a record of any conviction of any of the following criminal offenses:

- Murder or attempted murder (§ 782.04, Florida Statutes);
- Attempted felony murder (§ 782.051, Florida Statutes);
- Manslaughter (§ 782.07, Florida Statutes);
- Aggravated assault (§ 784.021, Florida Statutes);
- Aggravated battery or attempted aggravated battery (§ 784.045, Florida Statutes);
- Aggravated stalking (§ 784.048, Florida Statutes);
- Kidnapping or attempted kidnapping (§ 787.01, Florida Statutes);
- False imprisonment of a child under the age of 13 (§ 787.02(3), Florida Statutes);
- Luring or enticing a child (§ 787.025, Florida Statutes);
- Sexual battery or attempted sexual battery (§ 794.011, Florida Statutes);
- Lewd or lascivious battery, molestation, conduct or exhibition, or attempted lewd or lascivious battery, molestation, conduct or exhibition (§ 800.04, Florida Statutes);
- Arson or attempted arson (§ 806.01(1), Florida Statutes);
- Robbery or attempted robbery (§ 812.13, Florida Statutes);
- Carjacking or attempted carjacking (§ 812.133, Florida Statutes);
- Home invasion robbery or attempted home invasion robbery (§ 812.135, Florida Statutes);
- Lewd or lascivious offense upon or in the presence of an elderly or disabled person or attempted lewd or lascivious offense upon or in the presence of an elderly or disabled person (§ 825.1025, Florida Statutes);
- Sexual performance by a child or attempted sexual performance by a child (§ 827.071);
- Computer pornography (§ 847.0135(2), Florida Statutes);
- Lewd or lascivious exhibition on a computer (§ 847.0135(5)(b), Florida Statutes);
- Transmission of child pornography (§ 847.0137, Florida Statutes);
- Selling or buying minors (§ 847.0145, Florida Statutes); or
- Any offense committed in another jurisdiction which would be an offense listed above if that offense had been committed in Florida.

Any certified process server applicant whose application indicates a record of: (1) a withhold of adjudication for any felony listed above; (2) a felony conviction for an offense not listed above; (3) two or more revocations or suspensions of a driver license; or (4) a currently revoked or suspended driver license, will have the application reviewed by the Judicial Panel for a determination on whether the applicant should be added to the approved certified process server list.

3. **Application.** Individuals seeking certified process server designation must submit an application to the AOC on a prescribed form and pay the required fee. The application form may be found at www.fljud13.org.

4. **Proof of Liability Insurance.** Prior to an applicant's name being added to the approved certified process servers, the applicant must provide the AOC with proof of insurance, in the form of a certificate of insurance or policy in the amount of one hundred thousand dollars ($100,000.00) coverage per person and three hundred thousand dollars ($300,000.00) per incident for the benefit of any person wrongfully damaged by malfeasance, neglect of duty or incompetence of the applicant in connection with duties as a certified process server. The certified process servers, the chief judge, and "The Thirteenth Judicial Circuit" must be named as insureds or certificate holders under the insurance policy. The insurance policy must contain a provision that the AOC will be given 30 days' notification of any cancellation, expiration, termination or change in policy.

5. **AOC Review of Applications.** Completed applications will be reviewed by a representative of the AOC for verification of the applicant's compliance with the eligibility requirements of the Florida Statutes and this administrative order. If the AOC representative determines that an applicant meets all of the statutory eligibility requirements and the requirements in sections two and four of this administrative order, then the applicant's name will be added to the list of approved certified process servers. If the AOC representative determines that an applicant does not meet all of the statutory and administrative eligibility requirements, then the applicant will not be added to the approved certified process server list.

If the AOC representative is unable to determine whether an applicant meets all of the statutory and administrative eligibility requirements or if an applicant's application indicates a record of (1) a withhold of adjudication for any felony listed in section 2(C) of this administrative order; (2) a felony conviction for an offense not listed in section 2(C) of this administrative order; (3) two or more revocations or suspensions of a driver license; or (4) a currently revoked or suspended driver license, then the applicant's application and other documentation will be referred to the Judicial Panel for a determination.

All applicants will be notified of the AOC representative's determination, including applications that have been referred to the Judicial Panel for the final determination. If an applicant wishes to challenge an unfavorable determination made solely by the AOC representative, an applicant may request in writing, within 30 days of notice of the unfavorable determination, that the application be reviewed by the Judicial Panel.

6. **Judicial Panel Consideration of Applications.** The Judicial Panel, consisting of the administrative judges of the General Civil and County Civil Divisions and the associate administrative judge of the Family Law Division, will be the chief judge's designees under the Florida Certified Process Server Act. The Judicial Panel is clothed with broad discretion to make determinations considering whether an application will be added to the approved certified process server list.

The Judicial Panel will consider (1) all applications referred if the AOC representative is unable to determine whether an applicant meets all of the statutory and administrative eligibility requirements; (2) all timely requests to review an unfavorable initial determination by the AOC representative; and (3) all applications which indicate a record of (a) a withhold of adjudication for any felony listed in section 2(C) of this administrative order; (b) a felony conviction for an offense not listed in section 2(C) of this administrative order; (c) two or more revocations or suspensions of a driver license; or (d) a currently revoked or suspended driver license. All applicants will be notified of the Judicial Panel's decision by an AOC representative.

If the Judicial Panel's decision on an application is unanimous, then the decision is final. If a Judicial Panel's unfavorable decision on an application is not unanimous, then the applicant may request reconsideration by the Judicial Panel in writing, within 30 days of notice of the Judicial Panel's initial decision. Any majority or unanimous decision by the Judicial Panel on reconsideration is final. The applicant will be notified of the Judicial Panel's decision on reconsideration by an AOC representative.

7. Recertification. Designation as a certified process server is valid for one year. Designations may be renewed annually on the anniversary of the designation upon timely clearing a criminal record search and paying the renewal fee.

8. Identification Card. Certified process servers must, while serving process, carry the official certified process server identification card of the Thirteenth Judicial Circuit and display it to anyone who requests information on the process server's authority to serve process.

9. Return of Service of Process. The return of execution of process must be made by a certified process server on an Affidavit of Service form adopted by the AOC. The uniform Affidavit of Service form may be found at http://www.fljud13.org/formspage.asp.

10. Fees and Additional Procedures. The chief judge will determine application fees and approve additional internal procedures governing the certified process server program. The fees and additional procedures will be posted at www.fljud13.org.

11. Complaints. Any written complaint received by the chief judge or the AOC regarding the conduct of a certified process servers will be forwarded to the certified process server for a written response. The complainant will be provided a copy of the certified process server's response and may, within 30 days of notice of the response, submit a reply. The complaint, response, and reply, if any, will be reviewed by an AOC representative and if necessary, the matter will be investigated if resources are available. If necessary, the matter may be referred to the Judicial Panel for a determination. The complainant and certified process server will be notified of the resolution of the complaint.

12. Removal. A certified process server's name may be removed from the approved list of certified process servers for any malfeasance, misfeasance, neglect of duty, incompetence, conviction of a felony or a crime involving moral turpitude or dishonesty, or failure to comply with any of the provisions of this administrative order. The Judicial Panel will determine whether any certified process server's name should be removed from the approved list of certified process servers. The applicant will be notified of the Judicial Panel's decision by an AOC representative.

If the Judicial Panel's decision to remove a certified process server's name from the approved list is unanimous, then the decision is final. If the Judicial Panel's decision to remove a certified process server's name from the approved list is not unanimous, the certified process server may, within 30 days from notice of the Panel's decision, submit information to the chief judge as to why the Panel's non-unanimous decision should not be followed. The chief judge will review the Panel's determination and the applicant's information. The applicant will be notified of the chief judge's final action by an AOC representative.

Notice of removal of any certified process server's name from the list of approved certified process servers will be made to the clerk.

13. Previous Administrative Order Superseded. This administrative order supersedes Administrative Order S–1999–076 (*Certified Process Servers*).

14. Effective Date. This administrative order is effective July 1, 2012.

It is ORDERED in Tampa, Hillsborough County, Florida, on this 18th day of June, 2012.

Manuel Menendez, Jr., Chief Judge

S–2012–031. DELIVERY OF PROPOSED ORDERS

IN THE THIRTEENTH JUDICIAL CIRCUIT HILLSBOROUGH COUNTY, FLORIDA

ADMINISTRATIVE ORDER S–2012–031

DELIVERY OF PROPOSED ORDERS

The 2012 General Appropriations Act has significantly reduced the budgets of the Clerks of the Circuit Court throughout the state. For decades, in a spirit of goodwill, the Hillsborough County Clerk of Court (Clerk) has partnered with the Bar and the Court by performing duties that, while not specifically authorized by Florida law, assisted in the disposition of court cases. Because of the recent budget reductions, the Clerk can no longer perform certain duties that are not specifically mandated by statute.

Several administrative orders governing procedures in various subject matter divisions of the court require counsel to deliver proposed orders to the presiding judge for signature. Many times attorneys have delivered proposed orders to the Clerk instead of the presiding judge. In these circumstances, the Clerk has graciously delivered the proposed orders to the respective presiding judges. The Clerk's resources can no longer support this gratuitous function.

The several administrative orders governing delivery of proposed orders to the presiding judge will be amended in the near future to provide notice to attorneys that proposed orders delivered to the Clerk, instead of the presiding judge, may be destroyed by the Clerk instead of delivered by the Clerk to the presiding judge. Until the various amended administrative orders are entered in the coming weeks, this administrative order is entered on an emergency basis.

By the power vested in the chief judge under article V, section 2(d), Florida Constitution; section 43.26, Florida Statutes; and Florida Rule of Judicial Administration 2.215(b)(2), it is therefore **ORDERED**:

1. Applicability. This administrative order applies to all divisions of the Thirteenth Judicial Circuit Court and the Hillsborough County Court.

2. Delivery of Proposed Orders to the Presiding Judge. Any proposed order prepared by counsel at the direction of the presiding judge or in conformance with an administrative order must be delivered to the individual presiding judge. Proposed orders may be delivered to the presiding judge via hand delivery, United States Postal System, or other private package delivery service. Proposed orders are not to be delivered to the Clerk.

If delivery of a proposed order is accomplished via the United States Postal System or other private package delivery service, the outside of the envelope or package must contain the presiding judge's name, address and office number. The post office box address of the Clerk must not be used to submit any proposed order.

In order to assist in the delivery of proposed orders to the respective presiding judges, a current judicial directory is attached to this administrative order. Judges are located in one of three court facilities: (1) Edgecomb Courthouse, 800 East Twiggs Street, Tampa, Florida 33602; (2) Criminal Courthouse Annex, 401 North Jefferson Street, Tampa, Florida 33602; or (3) Plant City Courthouse, 301 North Michigan Avenue, Plant City, Florida 33563. The judicial directory is updated as necessary and the most current judicial directory may be accessed at the following link: http://www.fljud13.org/JudicialDirectory.aspx. [1]

3. Clerk Authorized to Destroy Any Proposed Order Received. If the Clerk receives any proposed order intended for signature by a judge, the clerk is not responsible for delivery of the proposed order to the presiding judge. If the Clerk receives a proposed order intended for signature by a judge, the Clerk is authorized to destroy the proposed order without notice.

4. Effective Date. This administrative order is effective on July 1, 2012.

It is ORDERED in Tampa, Hillsborough County, Florida, on this 18th day of June, 2012.

____

Manuel Menendez, Jr., Chief Judge

[1] Because of judicial reassignments taking effective on June 25, 2012, a revised judicial directory will be posted on the court's website on June 25, 2012.

S-2007-038. PHOTOGRAPHING, RECORDING OR BROADCASTING IN COURTHOUSE FACILITIES

IN THE THIRTEENTH JUDICIAL CIRCUIT HILLSBOROUGH COUNTY, FLORIDA

ADMINISTRATIVE ORDER S-2007-038

(Supersedes Administrative Order S-1996-109)

PHOTOGRAPHING, RECORDING OR BROADCASTING IN COURTHOUSE FACILITIES

WHEREAS Florida Rule of Judicial Administration 2.450 ("Rule 2.450") provides for technological coverage of judicial proceedings; and

WHEREAS Rule 2.450 does not authorize photographing, recording or broadcasting in the corridors, hallways, or lobbies of courthouse facilities; and

WHEREAS photographing, recording or broadcasting in the corridors, hallways, or lobbies of courthouse facilities has the potential of disrupting other court proceedings and functions and creating safety hazards; and

WHEREAS Florida Rule of Judicial Administration 2.215(b) authorizes the chief judge to regulate the use of the courthouse facilities; and

WHEREAS the undersigned chief judge wishes to delegate authority under Rule 2.450 to the presiding judges for determining location of media equipment in the courtrooms; and

WHEREAS the court must carefully balance the media's news gathering right with the dignity of the judicial process and safety concerns of the public; and

WHEREAS it is necessary for the efficient and proper administration of justice in the Thirteenth Judicial Circuit to update the procedures regarding photographing, recording or broadcasting in the courthouse facilities; it is therefore

ORDERED:

1. Definitions. For purposes of this administrative order, the following terms have the following meanings:

"Courthouse facility" means any building or other structure in which judicial proceedings may be conducted, including, but not limited to: the George Edgecomb Courthouse (800 East Twiggs Street, Tampa); the Courthouse Annex (800 East Kennedy Boulevard, Tampa); the Courthouse North Annex (801 East Twiggs Street, Tampa); the building located at 700 East Twiggs Street, Tampa; the Traffic Court Complex (known as Floriland Business Center—9309 North Florida Avenue, Tampa); and the Plant City Courthouse (302 North Michigan Street, Plant City).

"Photographing, recording or broadcasting" means using portable television cameras, still cameras, cellular telephone cameras, audio system equipment or any other electronic device to take a photograph, make a record or transmit as a broadcast.

2. Obstructionist Conduct Prohibited. No person, including but not limited to, photographers, videographers, news reporters, and other media personnel, shall obstruct or impede in any way the progress of persons on their way into or out from any courtroom or judicial chambers or office, nor shall any person obstruct the ingress or egress of courthouse facilities.

3. Limitations on Photographing, Recording or Broadcasting in a Courthouse Facility.

A. *Lobbies.* Except as provided in this subsection, neither photographing, recording, nor broadcasting is permitted in the lobbies of any courthouse facility from 8:00 a.m. to 5:30 p.m. Subject to the limitations in section 2 of this administrative order, photographing, recording, or broadcasting is only permitted in designated areas in the first floor lobby of the George Edgecomb Courthouse at any reasonable time. *See* attached diagram. Any individual or organization seeking the use of the lobby in any courthouse facility except the Edgecomb Courthouse for photographing, recording or broadcasting before 8:00 a.m. or after 5:30 p.m. shall provide advanced notice to the chief judge or the chief judge's designee.

B. *Corridors and Hallways.* Neither photographing, recording, nor broadcasting is permitted in any corridors or hallways of any courthouse facility between 8:00 a.m. and 5:30 p.m., unless otherwise authorized by the chief judge or the chief judge's designee. Any individual or organization seeking the use of a corridor or hallway of any courthouse facility for photographing, recording or broadcasting before 8:00 a.m. or after 5:30 p.m. shall provide advanced notice to the chief judge or the chief judge's designee.

C. *Staircases and Stairwells.* Neither photographing, recording nor broadcasting is permitted at any time in any staircases or stairwells in any courthouse facility.

D. *Courtrooms*

i. Court in Session. Subject to the limitations enumerated in Florida Rule of Judicial Administration 2.450(a), media coverage of judicial proceedings shall be allowed. The position of any cameras, audio system equipment or any other electronic devices to take a photograph, make a record or transmit as a broadcast shall be determined by the presiding judge. The court's public information officer may assist the presiding judge in determining an appropriate courtroom location for the media equipment.

ii. Court out of Session. Any individual or organization seeking the use of any courtroom for photographing, recording or broadcasting during a time when court is not in session shall make advanced application to the chief judge or the chief judge's designee. An individual or organization shall receive specific authorization from the chief judge or the chief judge's designee prior to photographing, recording or broadcasting in a courtroom during any time when court is not in session.

E. *Media Room.* On-camera interviews may be conducted at any time in the designated media room.

F. *Noise Reduction.* Any photographing, recording, or broadcasting permitted in a courthouse facility under this administrative order shall be conducted in such fashion as to cause minimum noise and distraction.

4. Court Orders. To the extent any judge enters an order regarding the control of persons in courthouse facility hallways, corridors, courtrooms or judicial chambers that is more restrictive than the provisions in this administrative order, all persons, including media personnel, shall recognize and comply with such order.

5. Media Coverage of Judicial Proceedings Not Effected. This administrative order in no way is intended to restrict the ability of the media to cover public judicial proceedings as provided in Rule 2.450.

6. Sanctions. Any person who willfully violates this administrative order shall be subject to the contempt powers of the court and to other appropriate disciplinary measures.

7. Posting of this Administrative Order. This administrative order shall be posted in a prominent place in each courthouse facility and on the Thirteenth Judicial Circuit's Internet web site.

8. Previous Administrative Order Superseded. This administrative order supersedes Administrative Order S–1996–109.

9. Effective Date. This administrative order is effective immediately.

DONE AND ORDERED in chambers in Tampa, Hillsborough County, Florida this 28th day of March, 2007.

Manuel Menendez, Jr., Chief Judge

Attachment—Media area of the first floor lobby of the George Edgecomb Courthouse

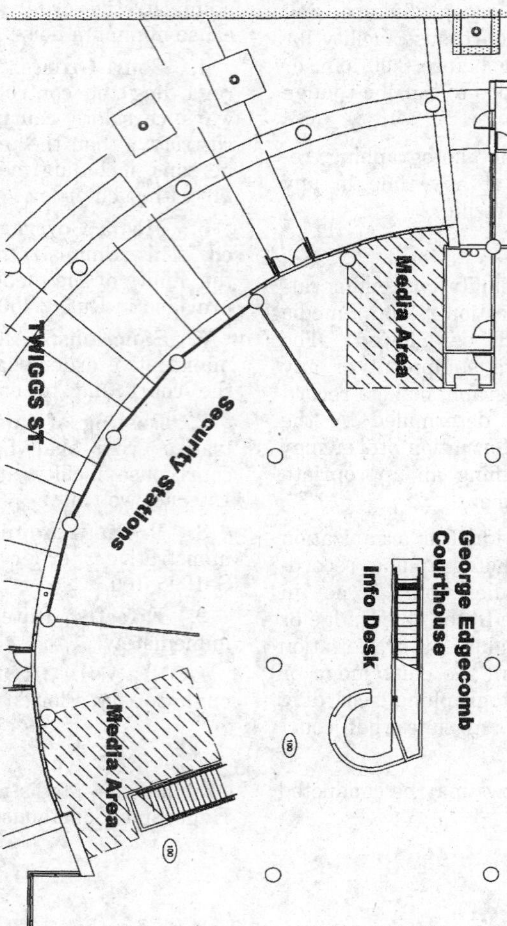

S–2007–036. NOTICE OF CHANGE OF CONTACT INFORMATION

IN THE THIRTEENTH JUDICIAL CIRCUIT FOR HILLSBOROUGH COUNTY, FLORIDA

ADMINISTRATIVE ORDER S–2007–036

NOTICE OF CHANGE OF CONTACT INFORMATION

WHEREAS Florida Rule of Judicial Administration 2.515 requires attorneys and *pro se* litigants to provide an address and telephone number on each paper or pleading filed with the court; and

WHEREAS attorneys and *pro se* litigants experience changes of address or telephone numbers or both during the pendency of litigation; and

WHEREAS the court, the Clerk of the Court ("clerk") and other parties need to be advised of such address and telephone number changes to provide proper notice or service of papers and pleadings; and

WHEREAS the courts and the clerk are not uniformly receiving timely notice of change of address or telephone number or both from all attorneys and *pro se* litigants; and

WHEREAS the courts and the clerk receive notices of change of address or telephone number or both where the notice does not identify the case number(s) associated with the attorney or *pro se* litigant; it is therefore

ORDERED:

1. **Change of Address & Telephone Number Form.** The clerk shall provide a change of address and telephone number form for use by attorneys *and pro se* litigants which complies with the requirements of this administrative order.

2. **Duty of Attorneys and *Pro Se* Litigants.** Every attorney and *pro se* litigant who is governed by Florida Rule of Judicial Administration 2.515 shall promptly provide the clerk and all parties with written change of address information or telephone number information or both, including the case number for each case associated with the attorney or *pro se* litigant on the form provided by the clerk.

3. **Reliance on Obsolete Contact Information.** Unless attorneys and *pro se* litigants who experience a change of address or telephone number or both comply with this administrative order, the courts, clerk and other parties have a right

to rely on the address and telephone number appearing in the most recent paper or pleading filed in a court file.

4. Effective Date. This administrative order is effective April 2, 2007.

DONE AND ORDERED in chambers in Tampa, Hillsborough county, Florida this 21st day of March, 2007.

Manuel Menendez, Jr., Chief Judge

REQUEST FOR CHANGE OF ADDRESS

Printed Name of Requestor ____________________ Telephone Number (required) ____________________

FAX Number: ____________________ E-Mail: ____________________

☐ Check if this is a change from current Telephone Number, FAX Number, or E-Mail Address on file with the Clerk.

Relationship to Requestor

_____ Self _____ Attorney _____ Legal Guardian _____ Personal Representative

Old Address:

Street No. ____ Street Name ____

City ____ State ____ Zip Code ____

New Address:

Street No. ____ Street Name ____

City ____ State ____ Zip Code ____

The Clerk will only change the contact information in cases specified below.

Case #	Case Style (Parties involved in the case)	Court Area (Family Law, Circuit Civil, Circuit Criminal, etc)	Effective Date

PLEASE USE ADDITIONAL FORMS AS NECESSARY TO INCLUDE ANY AND ALL CASES.

Signature of Requestor ____________________ Date of Request ____________________

For Office Use Only:
Request Completed: ____________ Clerk Completing Request: ____________

S–2005–128. COURT REPORTING PLAN

IN THE THIRTEENTH JUDICIAL CIRCUIT COURT FOR HILLSBOROUGH COUNTY, FLORIDA

ADMINISTRATIVE ORDER S–2005–128

(Supersedes Administrative Orders S–1995–069, S–1996–098 and S–2002–037)

COURT REPORTING PLAN

WHEREAS Florida Rule of Judicial Administration 2.070(g)(2) requires the chief judge to enter an administrative order developing and implementing a circuit-wide plan for court reporting of all judicial proceedings required to be reported at public expense; and

WHEREAS the following plan for court reporting services was developed after consideration of guidelines issued by the Office of the State Courts Administrator and a report on *Court Reporting in Florida's Trial Courts Post–Revision 7* issued by the Florida Supreme Court Commission on Trial Court Performance and Accountability; and

WHEREAS Florida Rule of Judicial Administration 2.070(g)(3) authorizes the use of electronic recording for judicial proceedings as a substitute for traditional stenographic court reporting; and

WHEREAS fiscal considerations require the increased use of digital court reporting of judicial proceedings; and

WHEREAS Florida Rule of Judicial Administration 2.070(h) requires the development and implementation of procedures to expedite the preparation of transcripts of trials in cases in which the death penalty is sought and in capital post-conviction proceedings; it is therefore

ORDERED:

1. Definitions and Designations. For the purpose of this administrative order, the following terms have the following meanings:

A. *"Circuit Court Reporter".* "Circuit Court Reporter" means Contractor, Contractor Personnel, or any person employed by the Administrative Office of the Courts for the Thirteenth Judicial Circuit ("AOC"), who meets the AOC's qualifications for delivery of court reporting services and whose duties include operating a stenographic machine in the courtrooms or hearing rooms of the Thirteenth Judicial Circuit.

B. *Classes of court reporters.* The State Court System has established three classes of court reporters: Court Reporter I, Court Reporter II and Digital Court Reporters. Court Reporter I and Court Reporter II are specific to the stenographic skill level of the position. For the purpose of this administrative order, persons performing court reporting in the Thirteenth Judicial Circuit shall be designated as Circuit Court Reporters or Digital Court Reporters.

C. *"Contractor".* "Contractor" means any person or entity with whom the Court Administrator of the Thirteenth Judicial Circuit contracts to provide court reporting services for judicial proceedings required to be reported at public expense.

D. *"Contractor Personnel".* "Contractor Personnel" includes and is collectively defined as employees, independent contractors, subcontractors, agents, assigns, students or interns of the Contractor.

E. *"Court reporting".* "Court reporting" means the act of making a verbatim record of the spoken word, whether by the use of written symbols, stenomask equipment or electronic devices, in any judicial proceedings pending in any of the courts of this circuit.

F. *"Digital Court Reporter".* "Digital Court Reporter" means Contractor, Contractor Personnel, or any person employed by the AOC, who meets the AOC's qualifications for delivery of court reporting services and whose duties include operating digital electronic recording equipment in the courtrooms or hearing rooms of the Thirteenth Judicial Circuit.

G. *"Digital court reporting".* "Digital court reporting" means the process of digitally capturing and recording, with the assistance of encoding hardware and software, the complete verbatim Multi–Media Court Record of any and all judicial proceedings.

H. *"Equipment".* "Equipment" means all hardware, software, storage, appliances, accessories and peripherals necessary to provide for the monitoring, recording, distribution, storage, archiving, assembling or production of the court verbatim record.

I. *"Judicial proceedings".* "Judicial proceedings" means all communications which take place in open court between the judge (including general magistrates and hearing officers) and the lawyers or other parties to the proceedings, and the testimony of any witnesses. Judicial proceedings include, but are not limited to, courtroom hearings, chamber or hearing room hearings, pre-trial conferences, jury trials, non-jury trials, motion or docket hearings, plea hearings, status review hearings, arraignments, dispositions, sentencing hearings, injunction hearings, detention and shelter hearings, bond hearings, post-conviction relief proceedings, first appearance proceedings, sworn statements and all other matters relating to the court's business. This term does not include any other matters that may have been monitored or recorded at the same time but which were not part of the court's business and which would likely not have been reported by a trained court reporter (such as private conversations between a lawyer and a client or between co-counsel).

J. *"Multi–Media Court Record".* "Multi–Media Court Record" means any combination of the digital audio file, metadata file, text file, annotated file and video file that is generated from the performance of court reporting.

K. *"Server".* "Server" means a computer that hosts an application or collects data from remote computer stations.

L. *"Services".* "Services" includes and is collectively defined as digital court reporting services and transcription services.

M. *"Transcription".* "Transcription" means the process of converting the complete verbatim Multi–Media Court Record generated by a Digital Court Reporter or the notes, disks or tapes generated by a Circuit Court Reporter, into a text file as a printed certified transcript.

2. Court Reporting Transition.

A. *State Responsibility.* Pursuant to Article V, Revision 7 of the Florida Constitution, court reporting services in Florida's court system, which had traditionally been a county's cost and responsibility, became the State of Florida's cost and responsibility effective July 1, 2004.

B. *Trial Court Performance and Accountability Commission.* It is the responsibility of the Florida Supreme Court Commission on Trial Court Performance and Accountability ("Commission") to review the operations and management of the state's court reporting systems.

C. *Statewide Plan.* In February 2005, the Commission released policy recommendations for court reporting services in a report titled *Court Reporting in Florida's Trial Courts Post–Revision 7.* The Commission developed a Statewide Plan for the Effective Use and Management of Court Reporting Services, and recommended that the goals, objectives and strategies in the plan be utilized at the circuit and state level in operating and managing court reporting services.

3. Hybrid Model of Court Reporting

A. *Overview.* In accordance with the goals, objectives and strategies outlined by the Commission, the Thirteenth Judicial Circuit, through its Court Reporting Committee, adopted a hybrid model of court reporting. The hybrid model utilizes a combination of stenographic, digital, centralized and video media for capturing the record in all judicial proceedings where court reporting is required at public expense. The staffing for this model includes employee and contractual resources. As of the effective date of this administrative order: (1) the Contractor is the University of South Florida Board of Trustees on behalf of WUSF–TV; (2) stenographic court reporting services are provided by Circuit Court Reporters; and (3) digital court reporting services are provided by Record Transcripts, Incorporated. It is anticipated that centralized court reporting services will be used by general magistrates and hearing officers. [1]

B. *Stenographic Court Reporting.* Stenographic Court Reporting utilizes real-time stenographic reporters employed or contracted by the AOC.

C. *Digital Court Reporting.* Digital Court Reporting is a total managed service by a contractual digital service provider.

This total managed service provides a 1:1 digital reporter coverage ratio per court division. This service also provides the equipment, management, maintenance and support of the equipment utilized in operating the digital court reporting system.

D. *Centralized Court Reporting.* Centralized Court Reporting is a digital court reporting model in which several courtrooms or hearing rooms are monitored and recorded simultaneously utilizing digital audio and video systems from a centralized location where the digital court record is captured, annotated and indexed.

E. *Video Court Reporting.* Video Court Reporting is the combination of a digital and video court reporting system and tools utilized to monitor and record remote court appearances in the courtroom or hearing room for events where the audio alone is insufficient to capture the record.

4. Management and Use of Court Reporting

A. *Court Administrator as Manager.* The Court Administrator, or his or her designee, is responsible for the management of delivering court reporting services for all judicial proceedings required to be reported at public expense.

B. *Circuit Court Reporters.* Circuit Court Reporters provide court reporting services to designated felony divisions. [2]

C. *Digital Court Reporters.* Digital Court Reporters provide Services to the following divisions of the court: (a) juvenile dependency and delinquency (includes detention and shelter hearings on weekends and holidays); (b) domestic violence (civil injunction cases and misdemeanor cases, Tampa and Plant City); (c) drug courts; (d) designated felony divisions; (e) misdemeanor (Tampa and Plant City); and (f) first appearance and emergency (daily, including weekends and holidays). [3]

D. *New Divisions, Judicial Reassignments and Emergencies.* In addition to the divisions designated in the previous subsection, it is anticipated that any newly created divisions, judicial reassignments or emergency circumstances requiring court reporting services at public expense will be covered by Digital Court Reporters when feasible.

E. *Substitution of Court Reporters.* Any felony divisions currently utilizing Circuit Court Reporters to provide court reporting services are subject to having Digital Court Reporters provide the Services under any of the following conditions: (a) state budgetary constraints; (b) directives of the Florida Supreme Court, the Office of the State Courts Administrator or the Trial Court Budget Commission; or (c) shortage of available Circuit Court Reporters for any given period of time, including but not limited to: vacation, illness, hiring restrictions or limitations, staff attrition or other shortfalls.

F. *Capital Cases.* Pursuant to Florida Rule of Judicial Administration 2.070(h), where available, a Circuit Court Reporter who has the capacity to provide real-time transcription of the judicial proceedings shall be used for court reporting services in capital cases. If real-time transcription services are not available, the use of a computer-aided transcription qualified court reporter will be utilized. Where available, scopists, text editors or alternating court reporters will be utilized to expedite the finalization of the certified transcript. Reasonable restrictions on work assignments by Circuit Court Reporters will be implemented to ensure transcript production in capital cases is given a priority.

5. Qualifications of Court Reporters

A. *Circuit Court Reporters.* Circuit Court Reporters shall hold a current certification as a Registered Professional Reporter or other higher-level certification from the National Court Reporter's Association. Circuit Court Reporters who do not hold a current certification may be approved by the Court Administrator or his or her designee based on past experience and demonstrated proficiency in stenographic court reporting.

B. *Digital Court Reporters.* The Contractor shall be responsible for providing qualified and trained Digital Court Reporters to perform the Services. The Contractor shall also be responsible for any training, certification or continuing education associated with the Digital Court Reporters performing the Services.

6. Reliability of the Record

A. *Contractor's Responsibility.* The Contractor, through Contractor Personnel, shall be responsible for capturing, managing, maintaining and storing the complete verbatim Multi–Media Court Record in all judicial proceedings reported at public expense utilizing digital court reporting.

B. *Equipment Usage.* All equipment utilized in the delivery of court reporting services by the Circuit Court Reporters and the Digital Court Reporters shall be operated and maintained in such a manner and under such conditions to ensure the reliability of capturing the record.

C. *Monitoring of the Recordings.* All judicial proceedings captured by the digital court reporting system shall be monitored to ensure the audio level and sound quality of the recording does not jeopardize the ability to play back recorded audio or the ability to transcribe judicial proceedings. If the audio level of the recording is not sufficient to produce a reliable record, the Digital Court Reporter shall immediately notify the presiding judge. It shall also be the Digital Court Reporter's responsibility to notify the presiding judge if the Digital Court Reporter becomes aware of matters other than the judicial proceedings being recorded (such as private conversations between a lawyer and a client or between co-counsel).

D. *Testing Prior to Court Sessions.* Prior to the beginning of each court session captured by the digital court reporting system, all equipment shall be tested by the Digital Court Reporter to establish all microphones, appliances and peripherals are operating at a level sufficient to ensure the recording of the record, playback of the audio and production of a transcript.

E. *Judge's Responsibility in Digital Court Reporting Proceedings.* In all proceedings in which digital court reporting is utilized, judges should remind participants to speak into the microphone and identify themselves for the record prior to speaking.

F. *Court Reporter's Notification to Judge of Inaudibility.* If a Circuit Court Reporter or a Digital Court Reporter is unable to hear a participant during the course of a judicial proceeding, the court reporter shall request the judge to direct and remind the participants to respond verbally and speak with sufficient volume to ensure a reliable record is captured.

G. *Counsel's Responsibility in Digital Court Reporting Proceedings.* It shall be counsel's responsibility to notify and request the presiding judge to direct court personnel to mute a microphone if counsel wishes to have confidential conversations with clients or other persons in an area where counsel believes such conversations may be recorded by the digital court reporting system.

H. *Tampering of Equipment.* Any observed incident of tampering with the equipment utilized in the delivery of court reporting services shall immediately be brought to the presiding judge's attention.

7. Transcription

A. *Requests.* An individual may request and obtain, without court order, a transcript of any reported or recorded judicial proceeding unless a record of such proceeding is deemed confidential (such as juvenile proceedings and Baker Act proceedings). Requests for transcripts of judicial proceedings reported or recorded at public expense shall be made to the Circuit Court Reporters or to the Digital Court Reporters who provided the reporting or recording service.

B. *Production.* When a transcript of a judicial proceeding or a portion of a judicial proceeding is requested from either the Circuit Court Reporters or from the Digital Court Reporters, an accurate and timely transcript shall be produced in accordance with Florida Rule of Judicial Administration 2.070(e) and Florida Rule of Appellate Procedure 9.200(b).

C. *Capital Cases.* Circuit Court Reporters who report in capital cases shall, pursuant to Florida Rule of Appellate Procedure 9.142(a)(2), file with the clerk of the lower tribunal on clearly labeled computer disks, sufficient copies of these transcripts for the clerk of the lower tribunal to include the disks in the record transmitted to the court and to the parties.

8. Safekeeping of the Record

A. *Circuit Court Reporters' Records.* Circuit Court Reporters shall manage, maintain, store and retain all stenographic notes, disks, tapes and transcripts from all judicial proceedings in a safe and secure place. Such records shall be retained in accordance with Florida Rule of Judicial Administration 2.075.

B. *Transfer of Circuit Court Reporters' Records to the AOC Server.* Circuit Court Reporters, with assistance from the Court Communications and Technology Services ("CCTS") staff, are responsible for the transfer and downloading of all data files onto the court server from all judicial proceedings reported in designated felony divisions. This server is owned, managed, maintained and supported by the AOC to ensure the integrity and safekeeping of the record.

C. *Multi–Media Court Record.* The Contractor, through Contractor Personnel, shall: (a) maintain the complete verbatim Multi–Media Court Record of all judicial proceedings reported at public expense in an archivable and retrievable format for the purpose of digital audio playback and transcription production; (b) be responsible for the daily management and maintenance of the metadata database, the database and data files which contain the verbatim Multi–Media Court Record; and (c) retain the complete verbatim Multi–Media Court Records and printed transcripts in accordance with Florida Rule of Judicial Administration 2.075.

D. *Court Communications and Technology Services' Responsibility.* The CCTS department shall be responsible for the daily management, maintenance and support of the AOC data distribution networks, audio/visual systems, video systems and sub systems in all courtrooms that utilize digital court reporting. CCTS shall manage, maintain, support and provide daily server administration to the AOC's primary digital audio server and back-up server to ensure the integrity and safekeeping of the Multi–Media Court Record.

E. *Contractor's Server.* The Contractor or Contractor Personnel shall own, manage, maintain and support its own server(s) and back-up server(s) for the purpose of storing, archiving and retrieving the verbatim Multi–Media Court Record in order to ensure the integrity and safekeeping of the record.

F. *Compliance with AOC Policies.* The Contractor and all Contractor Personnel shall comply with all policies and standard operating procedures established by the AOC, including, but not limited to, security and confidentiality policies and procedures.

9. Annotations and Indexing of the Multi–Media Record. To ensure the reliability, integrity, safekeeping and accurate transcription of the record, Digital Court Reporters shall capture, monitor, annotate, catalog and index the verbatim Multi–Media Court Record.

10. Ownership of the Records. To ensure the reliability, integrity, safekeeping and accurate transcription of the record, the AOC shall retain ownership of the complete verbatim Multi–Media Court Record generated in all judicial proceedings required to be reported at public expense. The Multi–Media Court Record shall remain the property of the AOC regardless of where the Multi–Media Court Record resides. The AOC shall also retain ownership of the complete verbatim court record generated by all Circuit Court Reporters.

11. On-Site Support. To ensure the reliability, integrity, safekeeping and accurate transcription of the record, the Contractor and CCTS shall maintain daily on-site support and management personnel.

12. Emergency Back–Up Plan. In all proceedings in which the type and means of court reporting equipment or services specified in this order are not available due to emergency circumstances, the chief judge or his or her designee may utilize and implement whatever other means of reporting is available to capture the court record.

13. Signage. Appropriate signs shall be placed outside all courtrooms and hearing rooms where digital court recording or monitoring is being utilized to capture the record. Such signs shall provide notice to all who enter the courtroom or hearing room of the use of digital court reporting and that any conversations may be recorded.

14. Constraints

A. *Prohibition Against Divulging or Transcribing Statements or Conversations Not Part of a Judicial Proceeding.* Anyone who has or gains access to any recordings produced from the Multi–Media Court Record shall not reveal, divulge or transcribe for anyone, any statements, matters or conversations monitored, intercepted or recorded by any digital recording system in the courts of Hillsborough County, Florid a, except those matters which occurred in open court and are directly related to the judicial proceeding at the time the monitoring was conducted or the recording made.

B. *Divulging or Transcribing Statements or Conversations Not Part of a Judicial Proceeding Only Upon Court Order.* Anyone who has or gains access to any recordings produced from the Multi–Media Court Record shall be prohibited from revealing, transcribing or utilizing in any fashion, any matters monitored or recorded except those occurring during judicial proceedings, unless otherwise provided by specific order of the court. Any such order shall only be entered after all the parties monitored or recorded have been properly noticed of the request for information or the request for a transcript. If the parties cannot stipulate to the distribution of the recording or transcript, such an order shall only be entered after the court has held a hearing on the matter.

15. Previous Administrative Orders Superseded. This administrative order supersedes Administrative Orders S–1995–069, S–1996–098 and S–2002–037.

16. Effective Date. This administrative order is effective immediately.

DONE AND ORDERED in chambers in Tampa, Hillsborough County, Florida, this 11th day of August, 2005.

\s\ Manuel Menendez, Jr.
Manuel Menendez, Jr., Chief Judge

1 Currently the court reporting needs of general magistrates and hearing officers are met through the use of electronic analog tape recording.

2 As of the effective date of this administrative order, Circuit Court Reporters provide court reporting services to nine (9) felony divisions.

3 As of the effective date of this administrative order, Digital Court Reporters provide Services to nineteen (19) divisions of the Thirteenth Judicial Circuit.

Civil

S–2018–060. COUNTY CIVIL DIVISION

IN THE THIRTEENTH JUDICIAL CIRCUIT HILLSBOROUGH COUNTY, FLORIDA

ADMINISTRATIVE ORDER S–2018–060

(Supersedes Administrative Order S–2017–040)

COUNTY CIVIL DIVISION

It is necessary for the proper and efficient administration of justice to update the assignment of cases in the County Civil Division in light of the newly-established County Civil Division "S" and to clarify that municipal and county ordinance violations are assigned to their respective county civil divisions regardless of whether the government initiates the action by citation or notice to appear.

By the power vested in the chief judge under article V, section 2(d), Florida Constitution; section 43.26, Florida Statutes; and Florida Rule of Judicial Administration 2.215(b)(2), it is ORDERED:

1. Divisions. Non-traffic civil matters of the county court will be administered by 11 judicial divisions. The judicial divisions are designated as Division "H," Division "I," Division "J," Division "K," Division "L," Division "M," East Division "Q," Division "S," Division "T" (non-criminal non-traffic infractions), Division "U" and East Division "Y." *See* Administrative Order S–2013–033 (*East Division*) or any successor administrative order for the geographic boundaries of the East Division. The Clerk of the County Court ("clerk") will designate on the progress docket the division to which each case is assigned.

2. Assignment of Cases.

A. *Non–Criminal Non–Traffic Infractions.*

i. Tampa. All non-criminal non-traffic infraction cases in which the infraction occurs outside of the East Division boundaries, including but not limited to, cases involving consumer protection (section 162.21, Florida Statutes, and Hillsborough County Ordinance 06–22), vessels (section 327.73, Florida Statutes), wildlife (section 372.83, Florida Statutes), juvenile smoking near school property (section 386.212, Florida Statutes), litter (section 403.413(6)(a), Florida Statutes), and juvenile possession and purchase of tobacco products (section 569.11, Florida Statutes) will be assigned to Division "T."

ii. Plant City. All non-criminal non-traffic infraction cases in which the infraction occurs within the East Division boundaries will be assigned to Division "Q" or Division "Y" according to the first letter of the alleged offender's last name. If the first letter of the alleged offender's last name is "A" through "L," the case will be assigned to East County Division "Q." If the first letter of the alleged offender's last name is "M" through "Z," the case will be assigned to East County Division "Y."

B. *Municipal Ordinance Violations and County Ordinance Violations.*

i. Definitions. The term "municipal ordinance violation" means a violation of a municipal ordinance initiated by citation or notice to appear in which the potential punishment does not include incarceration although the court may exercise its civil contempt powers when trying to coerce compliance with a court order. The term "county ordinance violation" means a violation of a Hillsborough County ordinance initiated by citation or notice to appear in which the potential punishment does not include incarceration although the court may exercise its civil contempt powers when trying to coerce compliance with a court order.

ii. Municipal Ordinance Violations.

a. Tampa & Temple Terrance. All City of Tampa and City of Temple Terrance municipal ordinance violation cases will be assigned to Division "T."

b. Plant City. All City of Plant City municipal ordinance violation cases will be assigned to Division "Q" or Division "Y" according to the first letter of the alleged offender's last name. If the first letter of the alleged offender's last name is "A" through "L," the case will be assigned to East County Division "Q." If the first letter of the alleged offender's last name is "M" through "Z," the case will be assigned to East County Division "Y."

iii. County Ordinance Violations.

a. Tampa. All county ordinance violations, including civil citations and notices to appear to enforce a county code or ordinance under part II of Chapter 162, Florida

Statutes, and Hillsborough County Ordinance 14–28, in which the offense occurred outside of the East Division boundaries, will be assigned to Division "T."

b. Plant City. All county ordinance violations, including civil citations and notices to appear to enforce a county code or ordinance under part II of Chapter 162, Florida Statutes, and Hillsborough County Ordinance 14–28, in which the offense occurred within the East Division boundaries, will be assigned to Division "Q" or Division "Y" according to the first letter of the alleged offender's last name. If the first letter of the alleged offender's last name is "A" through "L," the case will be assigned to East County Division "Q." If the first letter of the alleged offender's last name is "M" through "Z," the case will be assigned to East County Division "Y."

iv. Arraignments. All municipal ordinance violations and all county ordinance violations will be set for arraignment by the clerk upon receipt of the citation or notice to appear, except when the respective municipality or Hillsborough County notifies the clerk that the respondent is at risk for default under section 162.21(3)(c), Florida Statutes, in which event the clerk will set the citation for a default hearing. When a county ordinance violation or a municipal ordinance violation is set for an arraignment or hearing, the clerk will serve the notice of the event to the respondent in accordance with Florida Rule of Judicial Administration 2.516.

C. *Animal Cases.*

i. Tampa & Plant City. All animal custody cases (section 828.073, Florida Statutes) and animal control citations (section 828.27, Florida Statutes, and Hillsborough County Animal Ordinance 00–26, as amended by Ordinance 03–08) will be assigned to Division "T."

ii. Appeals. All appeals of dangerous dog classifications (section 767.12, Florida Statutes), in accordance with section 2 of Chapter 2016–16, Laws of Florida, will be assigned to the civil appellate division—Circuit Civil Division "X."

D. *Civil Actions.*

i. Tampa. All other county civil cases in which a defendant resides outside of the East Division boundaries, the cause of action accrued outside of the East Division boundaries, or the property in litigation is located outside of the East Division boundaries will be assigned to a Tampa division using a random assignment system to assign cases to Divisions "H," "I," "J," "K," "L," "M," "S," and "U" at a ratio of 8:10:6:5:8:10:10:4 through June 30, 2019. Effective July 1, 2019, cases will be assigned to a Tampa division using a random assignment system to assign cases to Divisions "H," "I," "J," "K," "L," "M," "S," and "U" at a ratio of 8:10:6:5:8:10:5:4.

ii. Plant City. All other county civil cases in which a defendant resides within the East Division boundaries, the cause of action accrued within the East Division boundaries, or the property in litigation is located within the East Division boundaries will be assigned to one of the two East county civil divisions—East County Civil Division "Q" or East County Civil Division "Y"—based on a random equitable distribution. It is the responsibility of the plaintiff's attorney or plaintiff, if self-represented, to advise the clerk if the case meets the criteria for assignment to the East Division.

E. *Re–Filed Cases.* Cases re-filed after being dismissed either voluntarily or involuntarily will be assigned to the same division to which the case was originally assigned. It will be the responsibility of the plaintiff or his or her attorney to advise the clerk so that the proper assignment can be made.

3. Reassignment of Case upon Judge's Disqualification.

A. *Non–Criminal Non–Traffic Infraction Cases and Municipal and County Ordinance Violation Cases.* If the judge presiding in Division "T" enters an order of disqualification, the clerk will reassign the case to one of the two Tampa civil traffic divisions—Civil Traffic Division "F" or Civil Traffic Division "N"—based on a random equitable distribution. If either of the judges presiding in East Divisions "Q" or "Y" enters an order of disqualification in a non-criminal non-traffic infraction case or a municipal or county ordinance violation case, the clerk will reassign the case to the other East Division. If both East Division judges have entered orders of disqualification, the clerk will reassign the case to Tampa Division "T."

B. *Other County Civil Cases.* If a judge presiding in any other Tampa division enters an order of disqualification, the clerk will randomly and equitably reassign the case to another Tampa division. If either of the judges presiding in East Divisions "Q" or "Y" enters an order of disqualification in any other county civil case, the clerk will reassign the case to the other East Division. If both East Division judges have entered orders of disqualification in any other county civil case, the clerk will reassign the case randomly and equitably to one of the Tampa divisions.

4. Jurisdictional Statement. Every complaint or statement of claim will state either the exact total amount claimed or the value of the property involved, exclusive of costs, interest and attorney's fees **OR** one of the five following statements: (1) this claim does not exceed $99.99, exclusive of costs, interest and attorney's fees; (2) this claim exceeds $99.99, but does not exceed $500, exclusive of costs, interest and attorney's fees; (3) this claim exceeds $500, but does not exceed $2,500, exclusive of costs, interest and attorney's fees; (4) this claim exceeds $2,500, but does not exceed $5,000, exclusive of costs, interest and attorney's fees; or (5) this claim exceeds $5,000, but does not exceed $15,000, exclusive of costs, interest and attorney's fees.

5. Court Registry Fee. In accordance with Florida law, the clerk is entitled to be paid a registry fee when the clerk accepts money for deposit into the registry of the court. When a person is required by law or court order to deposit a specified sum of money into the registry of the court, the person making the deposit must pay the amount of the registry fee to the clerk in addition to the amount of the deposit. If the registry fee is not paid at the time of the deposit, the clerk will deduct the amount of the registry fee from the deposit. The court has jurisdiction to determine the sufficiency of a deposit when a registry fee is not paid and which party is responsible for payment of the registry fee. The clerk will assist the public in calculating the amount of the registry fee.

6. Orders of Disbursement from the Court Registry.

A. *Request for Clerk's Statement of Available Registry Funds.* At any time a party seeks an order directing the clerk to disburse funds from the court registry, prior to filing a motion, the party must request the clerk to provide a statement showing available funds in the court registry. The statement will indicate the date and time the available funds were verified by the clerk. The clerk will develop and post on the clerk's website (www.hillsclerk.com) a form entitled *Request for Clerk's Statement of Available Registry Funds.*

B. *Motion for Disbursement of Registry Funds.* The party must attach a copy of the clerk's Statement of Available Registry Funds to the motion for disbursement of funds, file and serve the motion on all parties and legal counsel for the clerk. If the party seeking disbursement objects to the amount listed in the clerk's Statement of Available Registry Funds, the motion must identify the basis for the objection, and set the motion for hearing. If the party seeking disbursement does not object to the amount listed in the clerk's Statement of Available Registry Funds, the motion must confirm the stated amount is the proper amount of disbursement and request the entry of an order, without a hearing, if no other party files and serves a written objection within five days after service of the motion.

C. *Change in Registry Balance.* If any party becomes aware of any change to the court registry balance after the issuance of the initial clerk's Statement of Available Registry Funds, that party must obtain an updated clerk's Statement of Available Registry Funds and provide copies to the other party and to the court prior to the hearing on the motion seeking disbursement. If an updated clerk's Statement of Available Registry Funds is not presented at the hearing on the motion seeking disbursement, then the amount identified in the initial clerk's Statement of Available Registry Funds will be deemed the correct amount available for disbursement.

D. *Disbursement Orders to Account for Clerk Fees.* All proposed orders submitted to the court for disbursement from the court registry must contain the phrase "less clerk fees" immediately after the total requested disbursement amount (for example, Total: $12,000, less clerk fees). If the amount in the order exceeds the amount held in the court registry, the clerk will disburse the available amount in the registry, less clerk fees, at the time of the entry of the order (pro rata if disbursement is made to multiple parties).

7. Captions. After the assignment of a case to a division, all subsequent documents filed in the case will bear on the first page, as part of the caption of the case, the case number and letter of the assigned division.

8. Page Numbering. Every page of a filed document will be consecutively numbered and indicate the total number of pages of the document at the bottom of each page. For example, "Page 1 of 4," "Page 2 of 4," etc.

9. Multi–Count Complaints, Judgments, Executions and Satisfactions.

A. *Jurisdiction.* A multi-count complaint, in which each count demands money or involves property valued at a sum not exceeding the maximum jurisdictional amount of the court, exclusive of costs, interest and attorney's fees, will be filed in the county court, regardless of whether the total sum of money or property demanded in all counts exceeds the maximum jurisdictional amount of the court, exclusive of costs, interest and attorney's fees.

B. *Applicable Court Rules.* The Florida Small Claims Rules will apply in cases in which each count of a multi-count complaint demands money or property not exceeding $5,000, exclusive of costs, interest and attorney's fees. The Florida Rules of Civil Procedure will apply in cases in which one or more of the counts in a multi-count complaint demands money or property exceeding $5,000 in value, exclusive of costs, interest and attorney's fees.

C. *Judgment.* A final judgment rendered as a result of a multi-count action will be prepared on one final judgment form. Each count will be separately designated and totaled.

D. *Execution.* A writ of execution issued as a result of a multi-count final judgment will separately designate the total award rendered on each count.

E. *Satisfaction of Judgment.* A satisfaction of judgment resulting from the entry of a multi-count final judgment will separately designate which counts of the multi-count final judgment are being satisfied.

10. Personal Injury Protection (PIP) Cases. The following provisions apply to all personal injury protection insurance coverage cases:

A. *Applicability of Rules of Civil Procedure.* In accordance with Florida Small Claims Rule 7.020, all rules of the Florida Rules of Civil Procedures apply to PIP cases.

B. *Summons.* Accordingly, the clerk will not automatically set an initial pretrial conference date. Instead, the clerk will issue a summons in accordance with Form 1.902 of the Florida Rules of Civil Procedure.

C. *Response to Complaint.* A Defendant must serve a response within 20 days of the date of service of Plaintiff's complaint.

D. *Discovery Served with Complaint.* If Plaintiff serves a discovery request upon a Defendant contemporaneously with Plaintiff's complaint, the Defendant must serve its response to the discovery within 45 days of the date of service of Plaintiff's complaint.

E. *Setting Matters on the Court's Docket.* A party's counsel may set matters on the presiding judge's docket in accordance with sections 13–15 of this administrative order.

F. *Mediation.*

i. Required Mediation. All parties are required to mediate their case(s) prior to trial. The mediation conference will be conducted in accordance with chapter 44, Florida Statutes and Florida Rule of Civil Procedure 1.750. The mediation conference will be conducted by a mediator certified by the Florida Supreme Court and appointed by the circuit's County Civil Diversion Program.

ii. Sanctions for Failure to Mediate. Any party's failure to mediate in accordance with this provision may result in involuntary dismissal, default judgment, or other appropriate sanctions, including, without limitation, a monetary assessment as provided in the Rules of Civil Procedure.

iii. Settlement Notification. If a case settles prior to the mediation conference, a self-represented Plaintiff or Plaintiff's counsel must notify the circuit's County Civil Diversion Program of the settlement of the case and cancellation of the mediation conference. The circuit's County Civil Diversion Program may be contacted at: George Edgecomb

Courthouse, 800 East Twiggs Street, Room 208, Tampa, Florida 33602—Telephone: (813) 272-5642, press 2—Facsimile: (813) 301-3706.

11. Small Claims Pre-Trial Conferences. Except for PIP cases, the clerk will keep the court's pre-trial conference calendar and, in accordance with Florida Small Claims Rule 7.050(d), will notify the parties of the pre-trial conference date and time. The clerk will set the pre-trial conferences in small claims cases not more than 50 days from the date of the filing of the complaint or statement of claim, in accordance with Florida Small Claims Rule 7.090(b).

12. Consolidation.

A. *Judge with Lowest Case Number Makes Decision.* When two or more cases, regardless of their nature, involving common questions of law or fact are pending in the County Civil Division and might appropriately be considered or tried together, but which are assigned to different subdivisions of the County Civil Division, the judge assigned to the division in which the lower case number is pending may, upon a party's motion or upon the judge's own motion, transfer the case(s) with the higher case number(s) to the judge's division with the lower case number. Upon any reassignment, the clerk will make an appropriate notation on the progress docket(s), and thereafter the issues in all such cases will be heard, tried and determined by the judge assigned to the division making the reassignment. Once made, any reassignment will be permanent notwithstanding that such cases may not be ultimately tried together.

B. *Notice.* If cases are consolidated, the party filing the motion to consolidate is responsible for providing copies of the order of consolidation for filing in the reassigned cases. If the cases are consolidated upon the judge's own motion, the judge will designate the party responsible for providing copies of the order of consolidation for filing in the reassigned cases.

C. *Future Documents.* After consolidation, each pleading, document or order filed must show in the caption, the style and case number of all of the reassigned cases which have been consolidated. Each pleading, document or order will be filed only in the case into which the other cases have been consolidated.

13. Motions.

A. *Obtaining Hearing Time.* Attorneys may obtain available hearing times and schedule hearings on a judge's calendar by accessing the Judicial Automated Workflow System (JAWS) at https://jaws.fljud13.org/System/login.aspx or by telephoning the judge's judicial assistant. Self-represented parties may identify and obtain available hearing times on a judge's calendar by telephoning the judge's judicial assistant.

B. *Setting Motion for Hearing.* All motion hearings will be arranged and approved by the judge through the judge's judicial assistant and be coordinated with all other parties prior to a notice of hearing being served. Attorneys filing motions will arrange to have the motions set for hearing immediately. Self-represented parties will file the motion with the clerk who will arrange to have the motion timely set for hearing.

C. *Notice of Hearing.* Every notice of hearing will state the length of time reserved on the judge's calendar for the hearing and specify which matters are to be heard. Attorneys must not file a notice of hearing specifying the hearing on "all pending motions;" however, for purposes of case management and efficiency, a judge may set a hearing for "all pending motions." There will be no cross-noticing on hearing times unless the opposing counsel or self-represented party contacts the judge's office and determines if the docket will accommodate hearing additional matters at the same time. Additionally, a copy of the notice of hearing will be sent to the judge's judicial assistant within seven days from the date the hearing time is reserved with the judge's office. If the notice of hearing is not timely sent to the judge's judicial assistant, the time may be canceled and reassigned by the court upon notice to the defaulting party.

14. Motions to Compel Discovery—Order without Hearing.

A. *Motion.* Florida Rule of Civil Procedure 1.380(a)(2) requires that a motion to compel discovery "must include a certification that the movant, in good faith, has conferred or attempted to confer with the person or party failing to make the discovery in an effort to secure the information or material without court action." When a motion to compel discovery complying with Rule 1.380(a)(2) alleges the absence of a response or objection to discovery and there has been no request for an extension of time to respond, the court, without a hearing, may enter an order requiring compliance with the original discovery request within 10 days of the signing of the order, provided no written showing of good cause has been filed by the non-moving party.

B. *Proposed Order.* Unless the presiding judge directs otherwise, if all parties are represented by attorneys, none of whom have been excused from e-mail service under Florida Rule of Judicial Administration 2.516, the movant's attorney must submit to the court a proposed order through the JAWS. If any party is self-represented or represented by an attorney who has been excused from e-mail service by the court under Rule 2.516, the movant or movant's attorney must submit to the presiding judge sufficient hard copies of the proposed order along with stamped, addressed envelopes.

15. Motions to Set Case for Trial. All motions to set case for trial will contain a certificate by the party or attorney filing such motion that the party or attorney has discussed the subject matter of the motion with all other parties or attorneys and has been unable to reach agreement concerning the setting of the case for trial or that the opposing parties or attorneys have failed to respond.

16. Trials.

A. *Obtaining Time for Non-Jury Trial.* Attorneys may obtain available times and schedule non-jury trials on a judge's calendar by accessing the JAWS or by telephoning the judge's judicial assistant. Self-represented parties may identify and obtain available non-jury times on a judge's calendar by telephoning the judge's judicial assistant.

B. *Setting Case for Jury Trial.* Any party requesting a jury trial will send a copy of the demand for jury trial to the assigned judge within seven days from the date of filing the demand. The parties in every case will determine as nearly as possible the amount of time which will be necessary for the final hearing or trial before scheduling with the judge. All jury trials will be set by the judge of the division to which each case is assigned or reassigned. The case may be set for trial by an order based upon stipulation of the parties or as provided by the Florida Small Claims Rules or the Florida Rules of Civil Procedure.

C. *Notice of Trial.* A copy of the notice of trial will be sent to the judge's judicial assistant within seven days from the time the trial time is reserved with the judge's office. If the notice of trial is not timely sent to the judge's judicial assistant, the time may be canceled and reassigned by the court upon notice to the defaulting party.

17. Jury Instructions. Requested special instructions will be titled and distinctly indicate the party submitting the instructions. The instructions will be numbered consecutively and contain no more than one instruction per page. Each requested special instruction will be understandable, brief, non-argumentative, will embrace only one subject, and the principle stated in the request will not be repeated in subsequent requests. Except for standard jury instructions, all requested instructions will be accompanied by a citation of authorities supporting the proposition of law stated in such instructions. A copy of all requested instructions will be submitted to the court at least seven days prior to trial, or such other period as the court may require.

18. Cancellations. The court must be notified immediately if the parties have resolved the issues of a matter set for hearing or trial so that the court's time can be allotted to other cases or matters. The party setting the hearing, or the plaintiff in the case of a final hearing or trial, will be responsible for contacting the judge or the judge's judicial assistant and all other parties and witnesses to advise of the cancellation. Attorneys must cancel the hearing through the JAWS if the hearing was scheduled on the JAWS.

19. Continuances. Attorneys seeking a continuance of a scheduled trial or hearing will make a good faith application stating the justification for a continuance and will arrange to have the request heard immediately upon learning that a continuance is needed, unless all parties have agreed to the continuance and secured the approval of the court. Self-represented parties seeking a continuance of a scheduled trial or hearing will file a good faith application stating the justification for a continuance. The clerk will arrange to have the self-represented party's request forwarded to the judge for consideration to be heard timely upon learning that a continuance is needed, unless all parties have agreed to the continuance and secured the approval of the court.

20. Court Reporter. If a party wishes to have a court reporter present during any hearing or trial, it is that party's responsibility to secure the services of a court reporter, including the payment of all court reporter fees. See also Administrative Order S–2016–015 (*Civil Court Reporting*).

21. Emergencies.

A. *Assigned Case.* Application for emergency relief in an assigned case will be made to the judge of the division to which the case is assigned. If the judge of any division is for any reason absent from the courthouse, any emergency application in any case assigned to that judge's division will be presented to the judge present in the courthouse whose County Civil Division next follows in alphabetical sequence the division in which the case is pending. The term "present in the courthouse" includes being in a hearing, a jury trial or non-jury trial. If all of the County Civil Division judges are absent from the courthouse, any emergency application in an assigned case will be presented to the duty judge for that particular week. Duty judge assignments may be accessed at www.fljud13.org. The judge will review the request as soon as it is reasonably possible.

B. *Unassigned Case.* An unassigned case is a matter which has not been assigned to a division because the clerk's office is not and will not be open within a reasonable time. Application for emergency relief in an unassigned case may be made to the chief judge or the chief judge's designee. If the chief judge or designee is unavailable, then the application will be made to the duty judge assigned for that particular week. As soon thereafter as the clerk's office is open, any such application and any order entered will be filed with the clerk and the assignment of the case will be made by the clerk in accordance with the provisions established in this administrative order.

C. *Court's Determination.* Any judge to whom an emergency application is presented will determine whether an emergency actually exists, whether the requested relief is suitable for *ex parte* consideration if such a request is being made, and whether a hearing with notice to the adverse party is required pursuant to Florida Rule of Civil Procedure 1.610. If the judge determines that a hearing with notice is required, the hearing must be scheduled in the division in which the case is pending. If the judge determines that an emergency does not exist or denies the emergency request without a hearing, the requesting party is not authorized to present the emergency request to any other judge other than the judge assigned to the division in which the case is or will be pending.

22. Orders and Judgments.

A. *Consultation with Opposing Counsel or Party.* Unless the presiding judge directs otherwise, prior to submitting a proposed order for the court's consideration after a hearing, the counsel or party submitting the proposed order must consult with opposing counsel or the opposing party within five days after the court's decision and make a genuine effort to agree on the language of the proposed order.

B. *Timely Submission.* All proposed orders or judgments must be submitted to the court by the attorney or party directed to prepare the order within 10 days after the court's decision.

C. *Submission of Proposed Orders and Judgments.*

i. JAWS—All Parties Represented by Counsel. Unless the presiding judge directs otherwise, if all parties are represented by attorneys, none of whom have been excused from e-mail service under Florida Rule of Judicial Administration 2.516, an attorney who is requested to submit a proposed order or judgment will do so through the JAWS. Prior to submitting a proposed order or judgment, the attorney must review the presiding judge's webpage to determine that judge's format preference (Microsoft Word v. PDF) and comply with the preferred format.

Prior to the submission of a proposed order or judgment to the presiding judge through the JAWS, the submitting attorney will be required to certify that one of the following statements is true: (i) all parties have agreed to the content of the proposed order or judgment; (ii) opposing counsel objects to the content of the proposed order or judgment and intends to submit a different version of the proposed order or judgment; or (iii) opposing counsel has not responded within five business days of being provided the proposed order or judgment.

ii. Hard Copies and Envelopes—Self-Represented Party or Party's Attorney Excused from E-Service. If any party is self-represented or represented by an attorney who has been excused from e-mail service by the court under Rule 2.516, the party or attorney who is requested to submit a proposed order or judgment will do so by submitting to the presiding judge sufficient hard copies of the proposed order or judgment along with stamped, addressed envelopes.

D. *Title.*

i. Proposed Order. All proposed orders submitted will contain in the title of the order the exact nature of the court's ruling. Phrasing such as "order granting ..." or "order denying ..." is preferred over "order on ..."

ii. Judgments. All final judgments will state in the title whether it is entered against the plaintiff or defendant. Any final judgment which is not against all plaintiffs or all defendants named in the action will state the name of each party against whom judgment is rendered in the title. For example, a final judgment against all defendants in an action will be titled "Final Judgment against All Defendants." A final judgment against only one or two named defendants in an action will be titled "Final Judgment against Defendant, John Doe." A final judgment in favor of a landlord for possession will be titled "Final Judgment for Possession—Count I." A final judgment in favor of an owner or landlord for past due rents will be titled "Final Judgment for Past Due Rents—Count II."

E. *Required Statement.* An order must not be submitted to a judge unless the order contains one of the following: (1) a statement of the hearing date during which the subject matter of the order was argued before the court; (2) a statement that the matter was submitted *ex parte*; or (3) a statement that the matter was presented by stipulation. All proposed orders based on a stipulation must be submitted as a separate document apart from the stipulation.

F. *Objections.* Any attorney or party who objects to the entry of a proposed order which has been submitted to the presiding judge must immediately notify the judge's office via telephone or e-mail. If the objection notification is made by e-mail, the opposing attorney or party must be copied on the e-mail message. The objecting attorney or party must submit an alternative proposed order within five days of communicating the objection. If an alternative proposed order has not been received by the court within five days, the court will consider the objection withdrawn.

23. Post-Judgment Motions, Orders of Contempt and Orders of Arrest. All post-judgment motions for contempt and related notices of hearing may be served in accordance with Florida Rule of Judicial Administration 2.516. However, all post-judgment orders of contempt will be served on the subject person personally before any orders of arrest are signed. All orders of arrest will contain the following statement:

"That all singular sheriffs of the State of Florida do arrest and produce instanter before this Court ________ or if not subject to apprehension during the hours that this Court is in session, do arrest and take into custody ________ and produce him/her before this Court at the earliest opportunity, to show cause, if any, why the Order Adjudicating Contempt should not be enforced."

24. Dismissal Docket. The clerk will prepare a dismissal docket for the respective County Civil Divisions in accordance with the applicable Rules of Civil Procedure and Small Claims Rules. The date and time of each dismissal docket will be fixed by the presiding judge of the respective divisions.

25. Judicial Preferences. Attorneys and self-represented litigants should review and comply with the internal division preferences posted on the presiding judge's webpage.

26. Professional Conduct, Professionalism Expectations and Professional Courtesy. Counsel will adhere to The Florida Bar's Guidelines for Professional Conduct (https://www.floridabar.org/prof/presources/presources002/). The Florida Bar's Professionalism Expectations (https://www.floridabar.org/wp-content/uploads/2017/04/professionalism-expectations.pdf) and the Hillsborough County Bar Association's Standards of Professionalism (http://hillsbar.site-ym.com/?page=Professionalism). Each judge may announce and enforce additional requirements, or may excuse compliance with any provision(s) of the Guidelines, Expectations, or Standards as that judge deems appropriate.

27. Previous Administrative Order Superseded. This administrative order supersedes Administrative Order S-2017-040 (*County Civil Division*).

28. Effective Date. This administrative order is effective January 1, 2019.

ENTERED in Tampa, Hillsborough County, Florida, on December 17, 2018.

Ronald N. Ficarrotta
Chief Judge

S-2018-040. NON-BINDING ARBITRATION

IN THE THIRTEENTH JUDICIAL CIRCUIT HILLSBOROUGH COUNTY, FLORIDA

ADMINISTRATIVE ORDER S-2018-040

(Supersedes Administrative Order S-2014-027)

NON-BINDING ARBITRATION

Section 44.103, Florida Statutes, provides that a court may refer any contested civil action to non-binding arbitration in accordance with rules adopted by the Florida Supreme Court. Florida Rule of Civil Procedure 1.800 excludes certain matters from arbitration. Rule 1.810 provides for the selection and compensation of arbitrators. Rule 1.820 establishes certain hearing procedures for non-binding arbitration and authorizes the chief judge to establish other procedures for the expeditious and orderly operation of the arbitration hearing.

In accordance with section 44.103(5), Florida Statutes, and Florida Rule of Civil Procedure 1.820(g)(3), it is necessary to provide a method by which the arbitration decision may be filed under seal with the clerk so that the decision is not made known to the presiding judge unless no timely request for a trial de novo is made.

By the power vested in the chief judge under article V, section 2(d), Florida Constitution; section 43.26, Florida Statutes; and Florida Rule of Judicial Administration 2.215(b)(2), it is ORDERED:

1. **Selection of Arbitrators.** The court's Mediation & Diversion Services Program will maintain a list of qualified persons who have agreed to serve as arbitrators.

2. **Scheduling of Arbitration Hearing(s).** If the parties cannot stipulate to the date, time and location of the arbitration hearing, the presiding judge will decide these matters. Unless otherwise ordered by the presiding judge, within 20 days of the date of the order referring parties to non-binding arbitration, a hearing must be scheduled and must be held within 90 days of the order. Any additional hearings will be held in accordance with the time standards set forth in Florida Rule of Civil Procedure 1.820.

3. **Case Summary.** Unless the chief arbitrator directs otherwise, the parties must each submit a case summary to each arbitrator no later than 10 days before the scheduled hearing.

4. **Presentation.** The hearing will be conducted in an informal manner. While it is expected that presentation of the case will be made primarily by counsel for the parties and will be in the form of an opening and closing statement at trial, witnesses may be present and give live testimony as they would in a regular trial. If counsel for the parties opt for the abbreviated form of hearing, counsel will present only factual representations supportable by reference to discovery materials, signed statements of witnesses, stipulations and other documents.

5. **Compensation.** Arbitrators will be compensated in accordance with section 44.103, Florida Statutes, and Rule 11.100 of the Florida Rules for Court–Appointed Arbitrators. Payment must be made directly to the arbitrator by the conclusion of the arbitration hearing.

6. **Arbitration Decision.** Within 10 days of the final adjournment of the arbitration hearing, the arbitrators must notify the parties, or their counsel, of the arbitrators' decision by service in accordance with Florida Rule of Judicial Administration 2.516. At the time the parties are served with the decision, the arbitrators must file the decision with the Clerk of the Circuit Court (clerk). Arbitrators are required to file their decision under seal so that the decision is not made known to the presiding judge.

A. *Decision Filed Electronically.* If the chief arbitrator electronically files the arbitrators' decision with the clerk through the e-Portal, the chief arbitrator must, at the time of filing, file a separate "Notice of Sealed Nonbinding Arbitration Decision." Upon the filing of a Notice of Sealed Nonbinding Arbitration Decision, the clerk must maintain the arbitration decision as sealed unless no request for trial de novo is filed within 20 days of service on the parties of the decision. If a request for trial de novo is timely filed, the clerk will continue to maintain the arbitrators' decision under seal. The clerk will ensure that the arbitrators' decision is not made known to the presiding judge during the period it remains sealed.

B. *Decision Filed by Hard Copy.* If the chief arbitrator does not electronically file the arbitrators' decision, then the chief arbitrator must file a hard copy of the decision with the clerk by submitting it in a separate sealed manila envelope labeled "Nonbinding Arbitration Decision" followed by the style of the case and case number. The face of the envelope must indicate that the contents are exempt from public access in accordance with Florida Rule of Civil Procedure 1.820(g)(3). Upon receipt, the clerk will stamp the outside of the manila envelope with the date and time of filing and document the date and time of filing in the clerk's case maintenance system. The clerk will not make the arbitrator's decision known to the presiding judge unless no request for trial de novo is filed within 20 days of service on the parties of the decision. If a request for trial de novo is timely filed, the clerk will continue to maintain the arbitrators' decision under seal.

7. **Previous Administrative Order Superseded.** This administrative order supersedes Administrative Order S–2014–027 (*Non–Binding Arbitration*).

8. **Effective Date.** This administrative order is effective October 1, 2018.

ENTERED in Tampa, Hillsborough County, Florida, on September 14, 2018.

Ronald N. Ficarrotta
Chief Judge

S–2017–070. CIRCUIT CIVIL DIVISION

IN THE THIRTEENTH JUDICIAL CIRCUIT HILLSBOROUGH COUNTY, FLORIDA

ADMINISTRATIVE ORDER S–2017–070

(Supersedes Administrative Orders S–2016–061, S–2016–060, S–2012–009, S–2006–093 and S–1989–085)

CIRCUIT CIVIL DIVISION

It is necessary for the proper and efficient administration of justice to update the administrative provisions in the Circuit Civil Division and to consolidate the provisions of other administrative orders into this administrative order.

By the power vested in the chief judge under article V, section 2(d), Florida Constitution; section 43.26, Florida Statutes; and Florida Rule of Judicial Administration 2.215(b)(2), it is ORDERED:

1. **Divisions**

A. *Generally.* Civil matters of the circuit court will be administered by the following 19 divisions: Division "A," Division "B," Division "C," Division "D," Division "E," Division "F," Division "G," Division "H," Division "I," Division "J," Division "K," Division "L" (Business Court), Division "M" (Mortgage Foreclosure), East Division "R," East Division "T," Division "T" (Involuntary Civil Commitment of Sexually Violent Predators), Division "Y" (Tobacco), Division "Z" (Asbestos Litigation), and Trial Division 1. Divisions "A," "B," "C," "D," "E," "F," "G," "H," "I," "J," and "K" are standard Tampa civil divisions. Divisions "L," "M," "T," "Y," "Z," and Trial Division 1 are specialty civil divisions. East Divisions "R" and "T" are standard Plant City civil divisions, responsible for handling civil actions filed in the East Division in accordance with this administrative order and Administrative Order S–2013–033 or any successor administrative order.

B. *Specialty Divisions*

i. Business Court. Business Court Division "L" is responsible for handling business actions and certain complex business litigation in accordance with Local Rule 3 and Administrative Order S–2013–021 or any successor administrative order.

ii. Mortgage Foreclosure. Mortgage Foreclosure Division "M" is responsible for handling residential mortgage foreclosure cases filed on or before December 31, 2012 in accordance with this administrative order.

iii. Involuntary Civil Commitment of Sexually Violent Predators

a. Filing of New Cases. The Clerk of the Circuit Court (clerk) will assign all petitions filed by the state attorney in accordance with section 394.914, Florida Statutes—styled as "In Re: Commitment of ________" followed by the name of the person alleged to be a sexually violent predator to Circuit Civil Division "T."

b. Rules of Procedure. The Florida Rules of Civil Procedure for Involuntary Commitment of Sexually Violent Predators apply to all cases in Division "T."

iv. Tobacco

a. Filing of New Cases .T he clerk will assign all civil actions concerning allegations of personal injury or wrongful death arising out of the use of or exposure to tobacco products to Circuit Civil Division "Y." Counsel must mark all complaints with the Division "Y" designation prior to filing. All tobacco cases will be managed during the pretrial stage in Division "Y" until the case is activated for trial. The term "activated for trial" means that a case is ready for trial according to the case management order.

b. Transfer to Standard Division upon Activation for Trial. When a case is activated for trial, the presiding judge of Division "Y" will direct the clerk to reassign the case, using a random equitable distribution, to one of the standard circuit civil divisions.

v. Asbestos

a. Filing of New Cases. The clerk will assign all civil actions concerning allegations of personal injury or wrongful death arising out of exposure to asbestos to Circuit Civil Division "Z." Counsel must mark all complaints with the Division "Z" designation prior to filing.

b. Case Processing. Asbestos cases will be processed according to the omnibus order that is currently in effect.

vi. Trial Division. Trial Division 1 is responsible for handling jury and non-jury trials in accordance with this administrative order.

2. Allocation of Cases. Except as provided in section 1.B. of this administrative order, the clerk will assign all other civil actions and all civil-related extraordinary writ petitions to the standard civil divisions by a random equitable distribution.

3. Extraordinary Writ Petitions. If a petition is civil in nature, any petition filed with the clerk for writ of mandamus, quo warranto, certiorari, prohibition, or all writs necessary or proper to complete the exercise of the court's jurisdiction must be identified as an extraordinary writ petition in the caption of the petition. In addition to filing with the clerk through the e-portal, the movant must immediately hand deliver, mail or e-mail a copy of the extraordinary writ petition to the judge of the assigned division. A courtesy copy of all subsequent written submissions must be immediately hand delivered or mailed to the judge of the assigned division by the party filing the original subsequent written submission with the clerk.

4. Florida Contraband Forfeiture Act Cases. Sections 932.701 through 932.7062, Florida Statutes, establish procedural requirements in the application of the Florida Contraband Forfeiture Act. [1]

If a person entitled to notice timely submits to the seizing agency a request for an adversarial preliminary hearing, the seizing agency will file the notice of seizure with the clerk. The seizing agency must then (A) contact the court to set a hearing date and time for the adversarial preliminary hearing, (B) serve a copy of the notice of hearing on the claimant(s) and provide a copy of the notice to the court, and (C) file the original notice of hearing with the clerk.

Upon the filing of a complaint, if no adversarial preliminary hearing has been requested, the seizing agency will submit a proposed order to the court so that the court may determine whether probable cause exists. Unless the presiding judge directs otherwise, the proposed order should be submitted electronically through the Judicial Automated Workflow System (JAWS), which may be accessed at the following link: http://jaws.fljud13.org/system/login.aspx. Prior to submitting the proposed order, the seizing agency must review and comply with the divisional provisions posted on the presiding judge's webpage to determine that judge's format preference (Microsoft Word v. searchable PDF). If the presiding judge does not have divisional provisions posted, then the attorney should submit the proposed order in searchable PDF.

5. Foreclosure Cases

A. *Mediation.* The Hillsborough County Bar Foundation is designated as the mediation provider for the Thirteenth Judicial Circuit to provide and manage the mediation of residential mortgage foreclosure cases on a case-by-case basis. Mediation services provided by the Hillsborough County Bar Foundation will include maintaining a web-enabled information platform, the coordination of the collection and exchange of financial documents, coordinating and scheduling the mediation conference, providing mediation facilities, assignment of a mediator and other related administrative tasks associated with the mediation conference. If the presiding judge determines that a case is appropriate for mediation, the judge will enter a Uniform Order of Referral to Foreclosure Mediation. Parties wishing to utilize mediation services other than those provided through the Hillsborough County Bar Foundation must follow the provisions set out in the order of referral.

B. *Foreclosure Judgment Packet*

i. Contents. The foreclosure judgment packet must include the following documents:

- Proposed Uniform Final Judgment of Foreclosure (sale date will be inserted by the court at the time of the hearing) with sufficient copies. The most current Uniform Final Judgment form, which must be used, may be accessed at www.fljud13.org.
- Certificate of Sale;
- Certificate of Disbursements;
- Certificate of Title; and
- Three copies of stamped addressed envelopes.

ii. Timing of Delivery. If the moving party's counsel is attending the hearing in person, the counsel must bring the foreclosure judgment packet to the hearing; counsel should not send the packet to the judge's office prior to the hearing. If the moving party's counsel is attending the hearing telephonically, foreclosure judgment packets must be received by the presiding judge's office at least five business days prior to the scheduled hearing date for the motion for summary judgment.

C. *Judicial Sales*

i. Notice of Sale and Proof of Publication. The original Notice of Sale and Proof of Publication must be filed with the clerk at least 24 hours prior to the scheduled sale date.

ii. Electronic Sales. Judicial sales will be held on non-holiday weekdays, under sections 45.031(10) and 45.035(1) and (3), Florida Statutes, by electronic means only. All judgments or orders scheduling or rescheduling judicial sales will indicate that the sale will be conducted electronically online at http://www.hillsborough.realforeclose.com. All electronic sales will begin at 10:00 a.m. and continue until all scheduled sales have been completed.

iii. Bidding Increments. All tendered bids must be in increments of at least $100.00.

iv. Debarment for Failure to Pay. Any successful bidder who cannot pay the required deposit at the time of the judicial sale or who fails to pay the balance of the bid or other required costs of the judicial sale within the time required by the clerk will be reported to the judge who ordered the judicial sale. The court may enter an order debarring that bidder from participating in future judicial sales for a period of time, up to one month, or longer if such conduct is found to have been repetitive within the past 12 months.

v. Cancellation of Foreclosure Sale

a. Deadline. The deadline for cancellation of a judicial sale and for payment of the clerk's sale fee is no later than 8:00 a.m. on the day of the scheduled sale.

b. Upon Plaintiffs Notice of Cancellation. The clerk will cancel any scheduled foreclosure sale at least two hours before the scheduled foreclosure sale date and time upon receipt of a Notice of Cancellation of Foreclosure Sale filed electronically by plaintiff's counsel no later than 8:00 a.m. on the day of the scheduled sale. The uniform Notice of Cancellation of Foreclosure Sale form may be accessed at www.fljud13.org. The clerk will notify the online vendor of all cancellations of judicial sales.

c. Upon Suggestion of Bankruptcy. Unless otherwise directed by the presiding judge or a United States Bankruptcy Judge, the clerk will cancel any scheduled foreclosure sale upon receipt of a suggestion of bankruptcy on behalf of a named defendant in a pending foreclosure action no later than 8:00 a.m. on the day of the scheduled sale.

d. Upon Plaintiff's Failure to Pay Additional Filing Fee. If any difference between the estimated amount in controversy of the claim and the actual value of the claim causes there to be an additional filing fee owed by the plaintiff under section 28.241(1)(a), Florida Statutes, the plaintiff must pay the additional fee prior to the judicial sale. If any additional filing fee owed is not paid prior to the judicial sale, the clerk will cancel the judicial sale.

vi. Judicial Sale Fees. In accordance with section 45.035(3), Florida Statutes (2017), the clerk is entitled to receive an electronic sale service charge that "shall be assessed as costs and paid when filing for an electronic sale date." The clerk will assess this electronic sale service charge and the plaintiff will pay the service charge each time the plaintiff files for an electronic sale date.

D. *Verified Motion for Writ of Possession.* If a purchaser seeks an order directing the Clerk to issue a writ of possession, a verified motion must be filed swearing or affirming that the 30–day notice of termination was delivered to the tenant and the tenant failed to vacate the premises at the conclusion of the 30–day period or that the purchaser is not required to provide notice because one of the exceptions under 83.561(3), Florida Statutes, apply, in which case the purchaser must specify which exception or exceptions apply. A Uniform Verified Motion for Writ of Possession may be accessed at www.fljud13.org.

E. *Applicability.* All subsections of this section apply to residential mortgage foreclosure cases. Only subsections B (Foreclosure Judgment Packet) and C (Judicial Sale) of this section apply to non-residential mortgage foreclosure cases.

6. Consolidation of Cases. When two or more civil cases, regardless of the nature, involving common questions of law or fact, are pending in the Circuit Civil Division, which might be appropriately considered or tried together, but which are assigned to different divisions of the Circuit Civil Division, the judge assigned to the division which has the lowest case number may, upon appropriate motion or on the judge's own motion, transfer the case(s) with the higher number(s) to the division with the lowest case number. Upon any such transfer, the clerk will make appropriate notation upon the progress docket. Thereafter, the issues in all such cases will be heard, tried and determined by the judge assigned to the division consolidating such cases. Any such transfer will remain permanent regardless of whether such cases are ultimately tried together. After consolidation, each pleading, paper or order filed in a consolidated action must show in the caption, the style and case number of all of the transferred cases which have been consolidated.

7. Re–Filed Cases. Any case which was formerly assigned to a division of the Circuit Civil Division but which was dismissed and thereafter re-filed will be assigned to the division to which the case was originally assigned. The party re-filing the case must identify in writing to the clerk the division to which the case was originally assigned.

8. Reassignment of Case upon Judge's Disqualification

A. *Tampa Standard Divisions.* If the judge assigned to one of the Tampa standard civil divisions enters an order of disqualification, the clerk will reassign the case to another of the standard Tampa civil divisions based on a random equitable distribution.

B. *Plant City Divisions.* If either of the judges assigned to East Divisions "R" or "T" enters an order of disqualification, the clerk will reassign the case to the other East Circuit Division. If both of the judges in East Divisions "R" and "T" enter an order of disqualification, the clerk will reassign the case to a standard Tampa civil division based on a random equitable distribution.

C. *Business Court.* If the judge assigned to Division "L" enters an order of disqualification on a case originally transferred into Division "L" from another Circuit Civil Division, the clerk will transfer the case back to the division from which the case was transferred. If the judge assigned to Division "L" enters an order of disqualification on a case originally assigned to Division "L," the clerk will reassign the case to a standard Tampa civil division based on a random equitable distribution.

D. *Mortgage Foreclosure Cases Prior to 2013.* If a senior judge temporarily assigned to Division "M" enters an order of disqualification, the case will remain assigned to Division "M" but the case managers will ensure that all future proceedings are scheduled before a senior judge other than the senior judge who entered the order of disqualification. If all senior judges covering Division "M" enter orders of disqualification, the clerk will reassign the case to a standard Tampa civil division based on a random equitable distribution.

E. *Involuntary Civil Commitment of Sexually Violent Predator Cases.* If the judge assigned to Division "T" enters an order of disqualification, the clerk will reassign the case to a trial division in the Circuit Criminal Division based on a random equitable distribution.

F. *Tobacco Cases at the Pretrial Stage.* If the judge assigned to Division "Y" enters an order of disqualification, the clerk will reassign the case to a standard Tampa civil division based on a random equitable distribution.

G. *Asbestos Cases.* If the judge assigned to Division "Z" enters an order of disqualification, the clerk will reassign the case to a standard Tampa civil division based on a random equitable distribution.

9. Approval of Settlement of Minors' and Incompetents' Claims. A petition seeking court approval of the settlement of a claim on behalf of a minor or incompetent must comply with Florida Probate Rule 5.636 and Sections 744.301 and 744.387, Florida Statutes. The court will conduct a hearing to determine if the settlement is in the best interest of the minor or incompetent and if the attorney's fees and costs are fair and reasonable. Unless excused by the court, the minor or incompetent must be present at the hearing as well as the parent, next friend or guardian. The attorney must have the most recent medical report of the treating physician available for the court. If court approval is requested of a settlement for less than the actual value of the claim because of policy limits, evidence indicating the amount of insurance coverage must be produced at the hearing.

10. Motions

A. *Certification by Attorney.* Except for a motion (i) for injunctive relief; (ii) for judgment on the pleadings; (iii) for summary judgment; (iv) to dismiss or to permit maintenance of a class action; (v) to dismiss for failure to state a claim upon which relief can be granted; or (vi) to involuntarily dismiss an action, before the moving party or moving party's counsel files any other motion, the party or counsel must confer with the opposing party or opposing counsel in a good faith effort to resolve the issues raised by the motion. The moving party or moving party's counsel must file with the motion a statement certifying that the moving party or moving party's counsel has conferred with the opposing party or opposing party's counsel—either in person, by telephone, or by video conferencing device—and stating whether the party or counsel agree on the resolution of the motion.

A certification to the effect that opposing party or opposing party's counsel was unavailable for a conference before filing a motion is insufficient to satisfy the parties' obligation to confer. The moving party or moving party's counsel must describe, with particularity, all of the efforts undertaken to accomplish dialogue with the opposing party or opposing party's counsel prior to filing the subject motion.

The moving party or moving party's counsel retains the duty to contact the opposing party or opposing party's counsel expeditiously after filing and to supplement the motion promptly with a statement certifying whether, or to what extent, the parties have resolved the issue(s) presented in the motion.

B. *Motions to Compel—Order Without Hearing.* When a motion to compel that complies with the good faith certification in Florida Rule of Civil Procedure 1.380(a)(2)—motion "must include a certification that the movant, in good faith, has conferred or attempted to confer with the person or party failing to make the discovery in an effort to secure the information or material without court action"—alleges the absence of a response or objection to discovery and there has been no request for an extension of time to respond, the court, without a hearing, may enter an order requiring compliance with the original discovery request within 10 days of the signing of the order, provided no written showing of good cause has been filed by the non-moving party. The movant must submit to the court a proposed order in accordance with § 12 of this administrative order.

C. *Other Non–Evidentiary Pretrial Motions*

i. Non–Foreclosure Cases. A non-evidentiary pretrial motion may be ruled upon without a hearing. Any attorney wishing to invoke this provision may send an e-mail to the divisional e-mail address requesting that the court consider a particular motion, which is attached to the email message, without a hearing. The attorney must copy all parties or counsel for the parties on the request. If no objection is filed within 10 days of the request stating good cause why a hearing on the motion should be granted, the court will then rule on the motion without a hearing or direct that a hearing be scheduled. The movant must submit to the court a proposed order in accordance with § 12 of this administrative order.

ii. Foreclosure Cases. Unless the presiding judge directs otherwise, a copy of all non-evidentiary motions must be served on the presiding judge when the original motion is filed with the clerk. The presiding judge may decide to rule on a non-evidentiary motion without a hearing unless a hearing is required under section 702.10, Florida Statutes. Unless the presiding judge directs otherwise, a party may not set a non-evidentiary motion for hearing until at least 30 days have elapsed from the date of service of a copy of the motion on the presiding judge. The movant must submit to the court a proposed order in accordance with § 12 of this administrative order.

D. *Summary Judgment Motions in Foreclosure Cases*

i. Prerequisites to Scheduling Hearing. Prior to selecting a mortgage foreclosure summary judgment hearing date on the JAWS, attorneys of record for plaintiffs must file with the clerk the motion for summary judgment and a uniform affidavit titled "Affidavit of Compliance with Foreclosure Procedures." The uniform affidavit form may be accessed at www.fljud13.org. The affidavit swears or affirms that certain requisite actions have been completed and the dates on which they have occurred. Hearings scheduled on the JAWS prior to the filing of the summary judgment motion and the affidavit may be cancelled by the court without notice.

ii. Original Note or Lost Instrument Affidavit Required. If an affidavit of lost instrument is filed with the clerk, the affidavit must contain an agreement to indemnify the maker(s) or provide other adequate consideration. See § 673.3091(2), Fla. Stat. ("The court may not enter judgment in favor of the person seeking enforcement unless it finds that the person required to pay the instrument is adequately protected."); see also § 702.11, Fla. Stat, (establishing reasonable means of adequate protection). These requirements are in addition to the pleading procedures set forth in section 702.015, Florida Statutes.

11. Hearings

A. *Scheduling.* Attorneys may obtain available hearing times and schedule hearings on a judge's calendar by telephoning or e-mailing the judge's judicial assistant or accessing the JAWS. In foreclosure cases pending in Division "M," attorneys must set hearings in Section I or II on the JAWS. Self-represented parties may identify available hearing times and schedule hearings on a judge's calendar by telephoning or e-mailing the judge's judicial assistant. In foreclosure cases pending in Division "M," self-represented parties may schedule hearings by contacting the case manager in Section I at sectionIrmf@fljud13.org or Section II at sectionIIrmf@fljud13.org. The court may unilaterally cancel without notice any hearing set on the JAWS if the court has already entered an order on a non-evidentiary motion.

B. *Telephonic.* Telephonic hearings are governed by Florida Rule of Civil Procedure 1.451 and Florida Rule of Judicial Administration 2.530. For any multi-party telephonic hearings, all parties must be conferenced into the call prior to the call being placed to the presiding judge's office or courtroom. For any foreclosure case pending in Division "M," attorneys must use CourtCall (http://www.courtcall.com) or another comparable telephonic court appearance program for all telephonic appearances for summary judgment motions and other motion hearings.

C. *Notice of Hearing.* All notices of hearing must state the length of the time reserved on the judge's calendar for the hearing or must state that the hearing is on the Uniform Motion Calendar and must specify which matters are being heard. The court finds it helpful if the notice of hearing also specifies the date that the motion was filed. Counsel and self-represented parties are not authorized to indicate that the hearing will be on "all pending motions;" rather, the matter(s) being heard must be set out with particularity. There will be no cross-noticing on hearing time unless the opposing counsel or opposing party contacts the judge's office and determines if the docket will accommodate hearing additional matters at the same time.

D. *Cancellation.* If any hearing is canceled or rescheduled, the attorney or self-represented party setting the hearing must notify the judge's judicial assistant and the opposing counsel or opposing party as soon as possible of the cancellation. If the hearing was scheduled on JAWS, attorneys must also cancel the hearing through JAWS. In foreclosure cases, cancellations less than 20 days before the hearing date require a written notice of cancellation filed with an explanation of the reason for the cancellation.

E. *Uniform Motion Calendar*

i. Availability. Each standard civil division will, and any specialty civil division may, maintain a Uniform Motion Calendar on a regular basis. Each attorney setting any appropriate motion for hearing on the Uniform Motion Calendar must ascertain the presiding judge's availability prior to serving notice.

ii. Time Limitation. Hearings are limited to 10 minutes per case with time to be allocated to the parties by the judge. The 10 minutes includes the time necessary for the judge to review documents, memoranda, and cases.

iii. Types of Matters. Parties and counsel may only schedule matters on the Uniform Motion Calendar if they can be heard within 10 minutes. The court will not hear contempt matters and testimonial matters on the Uniform Motion Calendar. Procedural matters will not be heard unless counsel for the moving party files a certification with the motion in accordance with section 10.A. of this administrative order.

iv. Complexity. At the hearing, the judge may order that a further hearing be scheduled if the matter appears too complex to handle on the Uniform Motion Calendar.

12. Orders. Except when the court enters a Uniform Final Judgment of Foreclosure (as referenced in section 5.B. of this administrative order), the following provisions apply to orders after a hearing:

A. *Consultation with Opposing Counsel or Opposing Self–Represented Party.* Unless the presiding judge directs otherwise, prior to submitting a proposed order for the court's consideration after a hearing, the counsel or self-represented party directed to submit the proposed order must consult with opposing counsel or the opposing self-represented party within three business days after the court's decision and make a genuine effort to agree on the language of the proposed order.

B. *Cover Letter.* Prior to submitting a cover letter with a stipulated proposed order, the attorney must review and comply with the internal division procedures posted on the presiding judge's webpage to determine that judge's preference on the use of cover letters for stipulated proposed orders.

C. *Timely Submission.* Proposed orders on motions scheduled on the Uniform Motion Calendar must be submitted to the judge within three days of the judge's ruling. Unless the presiding judge directs otherwise, proposed orders on all other motions must be submitted to the judge by the attorney or self-represented party directed to prepare the order within 10 business days after the judge's ruling. If the attorney or self-represented party designated to prepare the order fails to timely submit a proposed order, the attorney for the opposing party or the opposing self-represented party may submit a proposed order within five business days after the initial time period.

D. *Submission of Proposed Orders and Judgments*

i. JAWS—All Parties Represented by Counsel. Unless the presiding judge directs otherwise, if all parties are represented by attorneys, none of whom have been excused from e-mail service under Florida Rule of Judicial Administration 2.516, an attorney who is requested to submit a proposed order must do so through the JAWS. Prior to submitting a proposed order, the attorney must review and comply with the internal division procedures posted on the presiding judge's webpage to determine that judge's format preference (Microsoft Word v. searchable PDF). If the presiding judge does not have divisional provisions posted, then the attorney should submit the proposed order in searchable PDF.

ii. Hard Copies and Envelopes Self–Represented Party, Party's Attorney Excused from E–Service or Presiding Judge's Direction. If any party is self-represented or represented by an attorney who has been excused from e-mail service by the court under Rule 2.516 or if the presiding judge directs, the self-represented party or attorney who is requested to submit a proposed order or judgment must do so by submitting to the presiding judge sufficient hard copies of the proposed order or judgment along with stamped, addressed envelopes.

E. *Title.* The title of every proposed order submitted must contain the subject matter of the pleading or motion upon which the ruling is made and must fairly apprise the reader of the action being ordered. Phrasing such as "order granting ..." or "order denying ..." is preferred over "order on ...".

F. *Form.* The first paragraph of all proposed orders must state the date or dates on which the hearing or trial took place. In all proposed orders, the page containing the court's signature must also contain substantive language of the proposed order so that a proposed order does not contain a signature page consisting only of the court's signature. Each page, except for the first page, must contain a page number.

13. Orders of Disbursement from the Court Registry

A. *Request for Clerk's Statement of Available Registry Funds.* At any time a party seeks an order directing the clerk to disburse funds from the court registry, prior to filing a motion, the party must request the clerk to provide a statement showing available funds in the court registry. The statement will indicate the date and time the available funds were verified by the clerk. The clerk will develop and post on the clerk's website (www.hillsclerk.com) a form entitled *Request for Clerk's Statement of Available Registry Funds.*

B. *Motion for Disbursement of Registry Funds.* The party must attach a copy of the clerk's Statement of Available Registry Funds to the motion for disbursement of funds, file and serve the motion on all parties and legal counsel for the clerk. If the party seeking disbursement objects to the amount listed in the clerk's Statement of Available Registry Funds, the motion must identify the basis for the objection, and set the motion for hearing. If the party seeking disbursement does not object to the amount listed in the clerk's Statement of Available Registry Funds, the motion must confirm the stated amount is the proper amount of disbursement and request the entry of an order, without a hearing, if no other party files and serves a written objection within five days after service of the motion.

C. *Change in Registry Balance.* If any party becomes aware of any change to the court registry balance after the issuance of the initial clerk's Statement of Available Registry Funds, that party must obtain an updated clerk's Statement of Available Registry Funds and provide copies to the other party and to the court prior to the hearing on the motion seeking disbursement. If an updated clerk's Statement of Available Registry Funds is not presented at the hearing on the motion seeking disbursement, then the amount identified in the initial clerk's Statement of Available Registry Funds will be deemed the correct amount available for disbursement.

D. *Disbursement Orders to Account for Clerk Fees.* All proposed orders submitted to the court for disbursement from the court registry must contain the phrase "less clerk fees" immediately after the total requested disbursement amount (for example, Total: $12,000, less clerk fees). If the amount in the order exceeds the amount held in the court registry, the clerk will disburse the available amount in the registry, less clerk fees, at the time of the entry of the order (pro rata if disbursement is made to multiple parties).

14. Final Judgments. All final judgments must state in the title whether they are entered against plaintiff(s) or defendant(s). Any final judgment which is not against all plaintiffs or all defendants named in the action will additionally state the name of each party against whom judgment is rendered. For example, a final judgment against all defendants in an action will be titled "Final Judgment against Defendants." A final judgment against only one of two named defendants in an action will be titled "Final Judgment against Defendant, John Doe."

15. Jury Trials

A. *Trial Division 1.* Multi-week cases may be scheduled in Trial Division 1 as set forth below. If the presiding judge of a standard division has conferred with the presiding judge of Trial Division 1 and determined that the schedule in Trial Division 1 may accommodate the trial, the presiding judge in Trial Division 1 will enter an order setting case for pretrial and trial. All pretrial motions will be heard in the standard divisions and even after a case is set for pretrial and trial in Trial Division 1, no pretrial motions will be heard in Trial Division 1.

B. *Standard Divisions.* The judge of each standard division will schedule the weeks in which jury trials will be held in that division and will determine the number of cases to be set for trial in any given week. The judge will determine the order to be assigned to each case scheduled for trial in that judge's division.

C. *Uniform Order.* Uniform orders setting pre-trial and trial for jury cases must be used. Uniform orders can be found at www.fljud13.org.

16. Exhibits

A. *Generally.* Each exhibit must be identified numerically, starting with number 1. Each exhibit must be preceded by a cover sheet indicating the exhibit number and the party submitting the exhibit. All exhibits must be listed, in numerical order, on a separate paper that sets forth the case caption, identifies the party submitting the exhibits and includes columns with the following headings: Exhibit Number, Document Description, Date Identified, Date Admitted, and With or Without Objection. No markings should be made in the "Identified" and "Admitted" columns. These columns are to be used by the courtroom clerk to record the exhibits that are offered into evidence and those that are received into evidence. Each party must provide a paper copy of the Exhibit List to the courtroom clerk before the start of the evidentiary hearing or trial. The courtroom clerk will file the completed Exhibit List after the conclusion of the evidentiary hearing or trial.

B. *Format (Electronic or Paper).* Unless the presiding judge directs otherwise, parties represented by counsel must file electronically-stored exhibits, except that paper exhibits may be used in all cases in which any party is self-represented.

C. *Electronically–Stored Exhibits*

i. Format. Each numbered and marked exhibit must include an Exhibit Cover Sheet and be electronically stored in an individual Portable Document Format (PDF) file. Each PDF file must have a unique identification name and number (e.g. Plaintiff's Exhibit 1).

a. Fifty Megabytes or Less. If the number of exhibits listed on a party's Exhibit List are 50 megabytes or less, the party submitting the exhibits must e-file them with the Exhibit List as a separate attachment to a filing titled "Notice of Filing [Party's Name]'s Exhibit List for [Trial or Evidentiary Hearing]. The e-filing of the Exhibit List and exhibits via the E–Portal will effectuate a party's delivery of exhibits to the opposing party or parties.

b. More than 50 Megabytes. If the number of exhibits listed on a party's Exhibit List are in excess of 50 megabytes, the exhibits must be stored on a Universal Serial Bus (USB) flash drive or compact disc (CD) in a file named with the case name, case number, and the party introducing the exhibits (e.g. Smith v. Jones, 14–CA–123456, Plaintiff's Exhibits for [Trial or Evidentiary Hearing]. Parties may exchange exhibits by delivering a CD or USB flash drive containing the exhibits to the opposing party or parties by the time set forth in the court's pretrial order for exchange of exhibits. A CD or USB flash drive containing the Exhibit List and the electronically stored exhibits must be delivered to the courtroom clerk before the start of the trial or evidentiary hearing.

ii. Use in Court. The electronically-stored exhibits will be considered the official exhibits for purposes of trial or the evidentiary hearing. However, a party using exhibits during the examination of a witness must, at the commencement of the party's questioning of the witness, provide paper copies of the exhibits to be used during the examination of the witness to the court, the witness, and other parties. Paper exhibits used during the examination of a witness will be removed from the courtroom following their use by the party using the paper exhibits.

iii. Additional Exhibits. If additional exhibits are offered or introduced during the course of the evidentiary hearing or trial that were not either e-filed or included on the USB flash drive or CD furnished to the courtroom clerk, a complete set of the additional exhibits introduced into evidence must be e-filed as separate attachments to a filing titled "Notice of Filing [Party's Name]'s Additional Exhibits" within seven days following the conclusion of the evidentiary hearing or trial.

D. *Paper Exhibits*

i. Submitting Exhibits to the Court. At the commencement of an evidentiary hearing or trial, each party must deliver to the courtroom clerk the original and one copy of the Exhibit List and all exhibits to be introduced into evidence in paper format. Original exhibits must not be stapled or permanently bound. Additional copies of the exhibits, either stapled or in binders or folders must be provided for use by witnesses, opposing counsel or party, and the presiding judge. Any exhibits introduced at hearing or trial that have not been premarked should be tendered to and marked by the courtroom clerk as they are presented in evidence.

ii. Large Items or Non–Paper Exhibits. Items other than paper documents to be introduced into evidence must be photographed, accompanied by an Exhibit Cover Sheet, and listed on the Exhibit List. Paper documents larger than 8½ × 11 inches must be listed on the Exhibit List and accompanied by a reduced 8½ × 11–inch copy and an Exhibit Cover Sheet. Counsel must attach Exhibit Cover Sheets to both the original physical exhibit and the photograph or reduced copy of the exhibit (substitutes), identifying the exhibits and corresponding substitutes with the same exhibit number. Unless the court orders otherwise, at the conclusion of the trial or evidentiary hearing at which the exhibits are offered, if the clerk has custody of the substitutes, the clerk will return the corresponding original exhibits to counsel. If an appeal is taken, substitutes will be included in the record on appeal.

iii. Disposal. The clerk may dispose of any unclaimed paper exhibits in accordance with Florida Rule of Judicial Administration 2.430(f). Parties will bear all costs associated with reclaiming exhibits.

17. Dismissal Docket. The clerk will prepare a dismissal docket for the respective Circuit Civil Divisions in accordance with the applicable Rules of Civil Procedure.

18. Emergencies

A. *Temporary Injunctions.* Applications for temporary injunctions without notice must comply with Florida Rule of Civil Procedure 1.610.

B. *Emergency Matters in an Assigned Case.* Application for emergency relief in an assigned case must be filed with the clerk with the term "Emergency" in its title. When filing through the E–Portal, the moving party must also indicate on the E–Portal interface's "Review and Submit" tab that the document being filed is deemed an "Emergency Filing." A judge will review the request as soon as reasonably possible.

i. Handling by a Judge Assigned to the Circuit Civil Division. The clerk will promptly notify and present the emergency matter to the presiding judge of the division to which the case is assigned. If the clerk makes the notification and presentation via e-mail, the clerk must verify that the judge is actually aware of the pending emergency matter. If the judge of any division is for any reason absent from the courthouse, any emergency application in any case assigned to that judge's division will be presented by the clerk to the judge present in the courthouse whose Circuit Civil Division next follows in alphabetical sequence the division in which the case is pending. The term "present in the courthouse" includes being in a hearing, a jury trial or non-jury trial.

Any judge assigned to the Circuit Civil Division who issues an *ex parte* order must personally conduct the return hearing unless the judge of the division in which the case is pending agrees to conduct the hearing. All emergency motion handling orders will be issued by the court, served on the parties, and delivered to the chambers of the judge of the division in which the case is pending for any necessary follow-up action. All emergency motion handling orders must be served to the parties by e-mail, facsimile, or regular United States mail.

If the reviewing judge determines that an emergency does not exist or denies the emergency request without a hearing, the requesting party is prohibited from presenting the emergency request to any other judge except the judge presiding in the division to which the case is assigned.

ii. Handling by Duty Judge. If there are no Circuit Civil Division judges present in the courthouse when an application for emergency relief is made in an assigned case, then the emergency matter will be presented to the duty judge. If the duty judge is a judge assigned to the Circuit Civil Division, the judge will handle the matter in accordance with section 18.B.i. of this administrative order above. If the duty judge is not assigned to the Circuit Civil Division, then the duty judge will handle the matter as set forth below.

If a duty judge issues an *ex parte* order and determines that the nature of the emergency requires that a return hearing be conducted imminently, the duty judge will personally conduct the return hearing. If a duty judge issues an *ex parte* order and determines that the nature of the emergency allows the return hearing to be scheduled with the judge presiding in the division in which the case is pending, the emergency motion and the *ex parte* order entered by the duty judge will be presented to the judge presiding in the division to which the case is assigned. The judge presiding in the division in which the case is pending may vacate any order issued by the duty judge before, after, or in lieu of the return hearing.

If a duty judge determines that an emergency does not exist or denies the emergency request without a hearing, the requesting party must not present the emergency request to any other judge except the judge presiding in the division to which the case is assigned.

C. *Emergency Matters in an Unassigned Case.* An unassigned case is a matter which has not been assigned to a Circuit Civil Division because the clerk's office is not and will not be open within a reasonable time. Application for emergency relief in an unassigned case will be made to the chief judge or the chief judge's designee, if the chief judge is unavailable. Otherwise, the application will be made to the duty judge. As soon as the clerk's office is open, any application and any order entered will be filed and the clerk will assign the case in accordance with section 2 of this administrative order.

19. Professional Conduct and Courtroom Decorum. Counsel will adhere to The Florida Bar's Guidelines for Professional Conduct (https://www.floridabar.org/prof/presources/presources002/), The Florida Bar's Professionalism Expectations (https://www.floridabar.org/wpcontent/uploads/2017/04/professionalism-expectations.pdf) and the Hillsborough County Bar Association's Standards of Professionalism (http://hillsbar.siteym.com/?page=Professionalism). Each judge may announce and enforce additional requirements, or may excuse compliance with any provision(s) of the Guidelines, Expectations, or Standards as that judge deems appropriate.

20. Previous Administrative Orders Superseded. This administrative order supersedes Administrative Orders S–2016–061 *(General Civil Division Procedures),* S–2016–060 *(Foreclosure Procedures),* S–2012–009 *(Tobacco Division),* S–2006–093 *(General Civil Division "J" ("Jimmy Ryce Act" Cases)),* and S–1989–085 *(Creation of Division "Z," Assignment and Transfer of Asbestos Litigation).*

21. Effective Date. This administrative order is effective January 1, 2018.

ENTERED in Tampa, Hillsborough County, Florida, on December 27, 2017.

Ronald N. Ficarrotta
Chief Judge

1 The initial application for probable cause determination is assigned to the judge presiding in County Criminal Division "C." See Administrative Order S–2017–067 *(County Criminal Division).*

S–2017–038. FRIVOLOUS LITIGATION SANCTION ORDERS

IN THE THIRTEENTH JUDICIAL CIRCUIT HILLSBOROUGH COUNTY, FLORIDA

ADMINISTRATIVE ORDER S–2017–038

FRIVOLOUS LITIGATION SANCTION ORDERS[1]

Access to Florida state courts is a right enjoyed by all persons under Article V, section 21 of the Florida Constitution, regardless of legal representation. When a person abuses his or her right to access to the courts however, the courts have an obligation to balance the litigant's right of access and the need of the courts to prevent repetitious and frivolous filings.

The frequent frivolous filing of meritless cases has the detrimental effect of consuming an inordinate amount of judicial time and resources—time and resources that therefore are not devoted to resolving potentially meritorious claims presented in other cases before the court.

Courts have the inherent authority to prohibit the deliberate and continual filing of frivolous actions that demonstrate an egregious abuse of the judicial process and ultimately interfere with the timely administration of justice. See generally *Bolton v. SE Property Holdings, LLC,* 127 So. 3d 746 (Fla. 1st DCA 2013); *Delgado v. Hearn,* 805 So. 2d 1017 (Fla. 2nd DCA 2001); and *State v. Spencer,* 751 So. 2d 47 (Fla. 1999).

The entry of this administrative order is necessary to protect the constitutional right of access to the courts for *all* litigants and permit the court to devote its finite resources to the consideration of legitimate claims filed in the Thirteenth Judicial Circuit.

By the power vested in the chief judge under article V, section 2(d), Florida Constitution; section 43.26, Florida Statutes; and Florida Rules of Judicial Administration 2.215(b)(2), it is ORDERED:

1. **Injunctive Sanction Order Defined.** For purposes of this administrative order, the term *injunctive sanction order* means an order-based on the court's detailed findings after notice and an opportunity to respond[2] that a litigant has egregiously abused the judicial process by filing frivolous documents—enjoining the litigant from filing further documents with the court or with the clerk unless the document is signed by a member in good standing of The Florida Bar.

2. **Necessary Provisions in Injunctive Sanction Orders.** All injunctive sanction orders should include provisions that allow the Clerk of the Court (clerk) to (A) place any submissions received by the litigant after entry of the injunctive sanction order into an inactive file; and (B) accept from the litigant, file, and submit to the appellate court a notice of appeal. *G. W. v. Rushing,* 22 So. 3d 819 (Fla. 2d DCA 2009).

3. **Injunctive Sanction Orders Issued in the Circuit Civil Division.** When a judge presiding in a Circuit Civil Division enters an injunctive sanction order, the clerk is directed to not only apply the injunctive sanction order to the specific lettered division of the presiding judge who entered the order, but to also apply the injunctive sanction order to any new action subsequently filed by that litigant, regardless of what division of the Circuit Civil Division the new case would be assigned, unless the judge's injunctive sanction order specifically limits the order's application to the individual case.

4. **Injunctive Sanction Orders Issued in the County Civil Division.** When a judge presiding in a County Civil Division enters an injunctive sanction order, the clerk is directed to not only apply the injunctive sanction order to the specific lettered division of the presiding judge who entered the order, but to also apply the injunctive sanction order to any new action subsequently filed by that litigant, regardless of what division of the County Civil Division the new case would be assigned, unless the judge's injunctive sanction order specifically limits the order's application to the individual case.

5. **Copies of Injunctive Sanction Orders Forwarded to Chief Judge.** Upon issuing an injunctive sanction order, the issuing judge must forward a copy of the injunctive sanction order to the chief judge electronically to enable the chief judge to distribute the injunctive sanction order to the judges of the affected division(s).

6. **Effective Date.** This administrative order is effective immediately and applies to all injunctive sanction orders issued prospectively.

ENTERED in Tampa, Hillsborough County, Florida on June 5, 2017.

Ronald N. Ficarrotta, Chief Judge

[1] This administrative order applies only to injunctive sanction orders issued under the court's inherent powers through case law; it does not apply to prefiling orders issued under the Florida Vexatious Litigation Law (§ 68.093, Florida Statutes).

[2] See *Bolton v. SE Property Holdings, LLC,* 127 So. 3d 746 (Fla. 1st DCA 2013).

S–2016–055. CIVIL APPELLATE DIVISION

IN THE THIRTEENTH JUDICIAL CIRCUIT HILLSBOROUGH COUNTY, FLORIDA

ADMINISTRATIVE ORDER S–2016–055

(Supersedes Administrative Order S–2016–010)

CIVIL APPELLATE DIVISION

Article V, Section 5(b) of the Florida Constitution and Florida Rule of Appellate Procedure 9.030(c) empower the circuit court with jurisdiction of appeals when provided by general law. Since 2000, Appellate Division "X"—a specialized subdivision of the Circuit Civil Division—has enhanced the deliberative process and provided greater uniformity in the disposition of appeals.

It is necessary for the proper and efficient administration of the courts to update the provisions in the appellate division to include the newly established Circuit Civil Division "E" and increase the number of appellate panels.

By the power vested in the chief judge under article V, section 2(d), Florida Constitution; section 43.26, Florida Statutes; and Florida Rule of Judicial Administration 2.215(b)(2), it is ORDERED:

1. **Purpose.** The purpose of Division "X" is to consider and dispose of: all appeals from the Hillsborough County Court Civil Division; all appeals in accordance with section 318.33, Florida Statutes, and Florida Traffic Court Rule 6.630(e); all appeals of dangerous dog classifications, penalties, or both in accordance with section 767.12, Florida Statutes; all appeals from final administrative orders of local government code enforcement boards; and all appeals of non-final orders when provided by general law.

2. **Three–Judge Panels.** All civil appeals invoking the appellate jurisdiction of the circuit court in accordance with Florida Rule of Appellate Procedure 9.030(c)(1) will be heard by three-judge panels.

3. **Composition of Panels.** An appeal will be assigned by the Clerk of the Circuit Court (clerk) to one of 28 appellate panels in a blind and equitable fashion. The 28 appellate panels are to be comprised of the judges assigned to the general civil divisions as follows:

PANEL NUMBER	DIVISIONS OF THE GENERAL CIVIL DIVISION		
1	A	G	I
2	B	H	J
3	C	F	H
4	D	A	K
5	E	F	R
6	F	B	I
7	G	C	J
8	H	I	K
9	I	C	E
10	J	I	L
11	K	B	C
12	L	R	T
13	R	A	B
14	T	F	C
15	A	T	G
16	B	R	D
17	C	T	J
18	D	E	J
19	E	K	G
20	F	H	R
21	G	A	L
22	H	K	D
23	I	A	D
24	J	T	L
25	K	L	B
26	L	E	H
27	R	F	G
28	T	E	D

4. Presiding Judge.

A. *Designation.* The judge assigned to the lettered division first named on each panel above will be the presiding judge of the panel.

B. *Authority.* The presiding judge will have full charge of the proceedings, provided that upon the absence or inability of the presiding judge to act, the judge of the panel longest in continuous service may be substituted. The presiding judge will: (a) discharge the administrative duties of the panel, including scheduling oral argument sessions or oral-argument-waived conferences; (b) rule on all non-dispositive motions; (c) preside at all sessions; and (d) author any written opinion when the presiding judge is in the majority (When the presiding judge is in the minority, this responsibility will be discharged by the panel judge in the majority longest in continuous service.).

C. *Non–Dispositive Motions.* In order to facilitate expeditious disposition of appeals, the presiding judge may enter orders concerning matters encompassed within the following Florida Rules of Appellate Procedure:

- 9.040(b) (transfer to appropriate court of proceeding in inappropriate court);
- 9.040(d) (motions to amend);
- 9.200(e) (motions to enforce preparation and transmittal of record);
- 9.200(f) (motions to correct or supplement record);
- 9.300 (motions for extension of time);
- 9.320 (motions relating to oral argument);
- 9.360 (motions relating to joinder and substitution of parties);
- 9.370 (motions relating to amicus curiae);
- 9.420 (motions relating to service); and
- 9.440 (motions relating to admission or withdrawal of attorneys).

5. Disqualification. In a case where a judge on a panel finds it necessary in the interest of justice to be disqualified, the judge will enter an order and refer the matter to the clerk for assignment of another judge in accordance with a blind and equitable rotation system. If the judge who is disqualified was the presiding judge of the panel, then the reassigned judge will become the presiding judge.

6. Judicial Automated Workflow System (JAWS). Attorneys appearing in appeals pending in the circuit court are required to associate themselves with the appeal on the Judicial Automated Workflow System (JAWS) so that as motions and briefs are filed and orders are entered all parties are served electronically.

7. Practice Pointers. Parties and counsel are encouraged to refer to the Appellate Practice Pointers located on the circuit's webpage.

8. Briefs. All briefs must be filed and served according to the provisions of Florida Rule of Appellate Procedure 9.210 and Florida Rule of Judicial Administration 2.516, except that parties are only required to file an original without a paper copy, All documents filed must be in searchable PDF. Parties and counsel are encouraged to provide the court with copies of ordinances, regulations, and policies when relying on such local authority. These authorities may be provided electronically as an appendix to the brief or by hard copy.

9. Motions. All motions must conform to the provisions of Florida Rule of Appellate Procedure 9.300 and be served in accordance with Florida Rule of Judicial Administration 2.516.

10. Decision. After oral argument, or after discussion of a case in an oral-argument-waived conference, the panel will take a preliminary vote. Cases will be decided by majority vote. The court's opinion will follow the format approved by the court. The opinion and any concurring or dissenting opinions will be filed with the clerk.

11. Rehearing or Clarification & Mandate. If no motion for rehearing or clarification has been timely filed, the clerk will prepare the mandate for issuance in accordance with Florida Rule of Appellate Procedure 9.340. If a motion for rehearing or clarification has been timely filed, the judicial panel will consider the motion. When a decision on the motion for rehearing or clarification is entered, the presiding judge will notify the clerk to issue the mandate.

10.[1] Clerk. In addition to the duties enumerated above, the clerk will also perform all ministerial functions and discharge all clerical duties traditionally fulfilled by clerks in Florida appellate courts.

11.[1] Previous Administrative Order Superseded. This administrative order supersedes Administrative Order S–2016–010 (*Civil Appellate Division*).

12.[1] Effective Date. This administrative order is effective January 3, 2017.

ENTERED in Tampa, Hillsborough County, Florida, on November 29, 2016.

Ronald N. Ficarrotta, Chief Judge

1 So as in original.

S–2016–015. CIVIL COURT REPORTING

IN THE THIRTEENTH JUDICIAL CIRCUIT HILLSBOROUGH COUNTY, FLORIDA

ADMINISTRATIVE ORDER S–2016–015

(Supersedes Administrative Order S–2003–020)

CIVIL COURT REPORTING

Florida Rule of Judicial Administration 2.535 defines the term *civil court reporter* as a court reporter who performs court reporting services in civil proceedings not required to be reported at public expense, and who meets the Florida Supreme Court's certification, training, and other qualifications for court reporting. Rule 2.535 also designates civil court reporters as officers of the court while acting as reporters in a judicial proceeding.

It is necessary for the proper and efficient administration of justice to update procedures for court reporting of all civil judicial proceedings.

By the power vested in the chief judge under article V, section 2(d), Florida Constitution; section 43.26, Florida Statutes; and Florida Rule of Judicial Administration 2.215(b)(2), it is therefore **ORDERED:**

1. Civil Judicial Proceeding

For purposes of this administrative order, the term *civil judicial proceeding* means a hearing or trial conducted before a judge, magistrate, or hearing officer concerning a matter pending in the Circuit Civil Division, the Family Law Division, or the County Civil Division.

2. Notices of Hearing

All notices of hearing for civil judicial proceedings will specify whether or not the party setting a matter for hearing will be securing the services of a court reporter.

3. Party's Responsibility to Secure Court Reporter

In a civil judicial proceeding in which a court reporter is requested, it is the responsibility of the party, or the party's attorney, to secure the services of a court reporter or court reporting firm prior to the proceeding. All costs associated with the court reporter's appearance will be the responsibility of the party or parties requesting the court reporter. This provision does not preclude the taxation of costs as authorized by law. *See* Fla. R. Jud. Admin. 2.535(b).

4. Official Record

There will only be one official record at a civil judicial proceeding taken by one court reporter. Attorneys must resolve any conflicts among themselves prior to the proceeding.

5. Previous Administrative Order Superseded

This administrative order supersedes Administrative Order S–2003–020 (*Court Reporting Procedures for Civil Proceedings*).

6. Effective Date

This administrative order is effective May 1, 2016.

It is ORDERED in Tampa, Hillsborough County, Florida on this 22nd day of April, 2016.

Ronald N. Ficarrotta
Chief Judge

S–2008–164. MEDIATION OF COUNTY CIVIL CASES

IN THE THIRTEENTH JUDICIAL CIRCUIT HILLSBOROUGH COUNTY, FLORIDA

ADMINISTRATIVE ORDER S–2008–164

(Supersedes Administrative Order S–1999–006)

MEDIATION OF COUNTY CIVIL CASES

Chapter 44, Florida Statutes, and Florida Rule of Civil Procedure 1.700 provide for court-ordered mediation of contested civil actions, except those matters expressly excluded by rule or law. The County Civil Diversion Program has been established as a court program under Mediation and Diversion Services to implement an equitable and expeditious alternative dispute resolution process for county civil cases. It is necessary for the proper and efficient administration of justice in the County Civil Division to update procedures for the mediation of county civil cases through the County Civil Diversion Program.

By the power vested in me under Florida Rule of Judicial Administration 2.215(b)(2), it is therefore **ORDERED:**

1. **Court Referral of County Civil Cases to Mediation**

All issues in county civil cases may be referred to mediation by the presiding judge unless excluded by statute or court rule. All court-ordered referrals will be made through the County Civil Diversion Program ("Program"). Matters referred to the Program will be handled by Florida Supreme Court certified county court mediators. See Florida Rule for Certified and Court–Appointed Mediators 10.100 for certifications requirements.

An Order Referring Parties to County Civil Mediation ("Order of Referral") will be prepared by the court. Upon execution of the Order of Referral, the court will notify the Program of the case and forward the case file and the original Order of Referral to the Program. The Program will provide the Clerk of the Circuit Court, County Civil Division ("clerk") with the original Order of Referral and mail copies of the Order of Referral to each party or party's counsel of record.

2. **Selection of Mediators and Scheduling**

Upon receipt of an Order of Referral to the Program, program staff will assign a certified mediator and will arrange the mediation conference date and time. If the parties wish to select a private mediator to handle their mediation conference they must contact the Program within 10 days from the date of the Order of Referral and provide the Program with the name of the mediator and the date and time of the mediation conference.

3. **Deferment**

Within 15 days of the Order of Referral, any party may file a motion to defer the mediation conference. The moving party will use best efforts to set the motion to defer for hearing prior to the scheduled date for the mediation conference. If a hearing on the motion to defer cannot be set prior to the mediation conference date the moving party will, more than 48 hours before the originally scheduled mediation conference, take necessary steps to reschedule the mediation conference. Failure to comply with this time standard may result in the imposition of monetary sanctions as determined by the court. Notice of the hearing on the motion to defer will be provided to all parties, the Program, and the appointed mediator. The court will forward to the Program a copy of any order granting a deferment of the mediation conference. If a deferment has been granted, the order will include the actual period of deferral and another mediation conference will be scheduled.

4. **Rescheduling or Cancellation Prior to Mediation**

The parties or their counsel must notify the Program of any rescheduling no later than 48 hours, excluding weekends and legal holidays, before the scheduled mediation conference. The petitioner, or if petitioner is represented by counsel, petitioner's counsel must notify the Program in writing if the mediation conference must be cancelled because a settlement has been reached or the case has been dismissed more than 48 hours prior to the scheduled mediation conference.

5. **Disqualification or Withdrawal of Mediator**

A party may move at any time to disqualify a mediator. The court will forward to the Program a copy of any order disqualifying a mediator. If a mediator has been disqualified or has withdrawn, a new mediator will be assigned by the Program. Rescheduling may be necessary to accommodate the substitute mediator.

6. **Mediation Conference**

The mediator will be in control of the mediation conference at all times. If a resolution is imminent or likely, the mediator may, at his or her discretion and with the agreement of the parties, schedule another mediation conference. The mediator will then arrange a date and time for the subsequent mediation conference with the parties and notify the Program. The Program will prepare a notice of additional mediation conference and provide a copy to each party. Upon completion of mediation, the mediator will return a completed Outcome of Service form to the Program office within 48 hours of the mediation conference.

7. **Report to the Court**

The Program will submit to the court a report stating whether or not the parties appeared for the mediation conference, and whether or not any agreement was reached.

8. **Agreements**

Agreements reached during the mediation conference will be memorialized, completed and submitted in accordance with Florida Civil Rule of Procedure 1.730(b).

9. **Fees**

Fees for court-ordered mediations will be assessed and collected in accordance with section 44.108, Florida Statutes. If payment of any fee owed is not made by the time of the scheduled mediation conference, the mediation conference will not take place. Payment may be by check (payable to the "Clerk of the Circuit Court"), money order, cash or credit card (Visa / MasterCard / Discover). Credit card payments cannot be made over the phone.

If a party fails to appear at a scheduled mediation conference, or fails to make payment by the time of the mediation conference, or fails to provide at least 24 hours prior written notice to the Program of the cancellation of a mediation conference, the party will be billed for the cancelled mediation conference.

10. Invoicing

The Program will be responsible for generating invoices for all parties participating in the mediation conference. An invoice for payment will outline each party's portion of the mediation cost. The clerk will accept payment, on behalf of the Program, of the amount due from the parties; however, the clerk will accept payment only in the amount specified on the invoice for payment. All payments made to the clerk will be accompanied by the invoice for payment.

11. Statistical Data

All parties ordered by the court to mediation will provide data as requested by the Program for statistical purposes. The data will remain confidential to the extent that any data published will contain no identify information.

12. Previous Administrative Order Superseded

This administrative order supersedes Administrative Order S–1999–006 (*In Re: General Procedures for County Civil Cases Court–Ordered to Mediation*).

13. Effective Date

This administrative order is effective January 1, 2009.

It is ORDERED in Tampa, Hillsborough County, Florida, on this 3rd day of December, 2008.

Manuel Menendez, Jr., Chief Judge

Criminal–Misdemeanor & Felony

S–2018–066. COUNTY CRIMINAL DIVISION

IN THE THIRTEENTH JUDICIAL CIRCUIT HILLSBOROUGH COUNTY, FLORIDA

ADMINISTRATIVE ORDER S–2018–066

(Supersedes Administrative Order S–2018–049)

COUNTY CRIMINAL DIVISION

Based on the elevation of the administrative judge of the County Criminal Division to the circuit court, it is necessary for the proper and efficient administration of justice to adjust the assignment of municipal and county ordinance violations. By the power vested in the chief judge under article V, section 2(d), Florida Constitution; section 43.26, Florida Statutes; and Florida Rule of Judicial Administration 2.215(b)(2); it is ORDERED:

1. Definitions. For the purposes of this administrative order, the following terms have the following meanings:

"Clerk" means the Clerk of the County Court or any deputy clerks.

"County ordinance violation" means a violation of a Hillsborough County ordinance which (a) is initiated by summons, notice to appear, or arrest; (b) includes incarceration as potential punishment; and (c) excludes county ordinance violations assigned to the County Civil Division.

"Domestic violence case" means any misdemeanor case arising from the conduct of one family or household member (as defined in section 741.28, Florida Statutes) against another, including assault, battery, harassment, stalking, and misdemeanor violations of section 741.31, Florida Statutes.

"Municipal ordinance violation" means a violation of an ordinance of a municipality which (a) is initiated by summons, notice to appear, or arrest; (b) includes incarceration as potential punishment; and (c) excludes municipal ordinance violations assigned to the County Civil Division.

"Open court" means in a courtroom or in a publicly accessible hearing room with the judge, the clerk, the state attorney or an assistant state attorney, the defendant, and if represented by an attorney, the defendant's attorney being present.

2. Divisions. There are 11 criminal divisions of the County Court, including Division "O." See Administrative Order S–2017–066 (*Criminal Division "O"—Preliminary Proceedings*) or any subsequent administrative order for the provisions governing this specialized subdivision of the county criminal division. Divisions "A," "B," "C," "D," "E," "F" (domestic violence), "G," "O," and "R" (trial division) are based in Tampa. East County Divisions "P" and "X" are based in Plant City. See Administrative Order S–2013–033 (*East Division*) or any subsequent administrative order for the geographical boundaries of the East Division.

3. Assignment of Cases.

A. *East County Misdemeanor and Criminal Traffic Offenses.* The clerk will assign all misdemeanor offenses (including domestic violence cases) and criminal traffic offenses in which the offense occurred within the East Division boundaries to East County Criminal Divisions "P" or "X" based on the first letter of the defendant's last name according to the following alphabetical distribution:

DIVISION	FIRST LETTER OF DEFENDANT'S LAST NAME
"P"	A, B, C, D, E, F, G, H, I, J, K, L
"X"	M, N, O, P, Q, R, S, T, U, V, W, X, Y, Z

B. *Tampa Misdemeanor and Criminal Traffic Offenses.* Except for domestic violence cases, the clerk will assign all other misdemeanor offenses and criminal traffic offenses in which the offense occurred outside of the East Division boundaries to a county criminal division based on the first letter of the defendant's last name according to the following alphabetical distribution:

DIVISION	FIRST LETTER OF DEFENDANT'S LAST NAME
"A"	G, O, S, U
"B"	B, F, P
"C"	D, M, N, X, Y
"D"	C, K, R
"E"	H, L, W

"G"	A, E, J, I, Q, T, V, Z

C. *Domestic Violence Criminal Offenses.* All domestic violence cases which involve defendants domiciled outside of the East Division boundaries will be assigned to Division "F." If a defendant who has a domestic violence case pending or who is on probation in Division "F," East County Criminal Division "P" or East County Criminal Division "X" is subsequently charged with a new misdemeanor charge that is not a domestic violence case, the new misdemeanor charge will be assigned to a county criminal division according to the assignment provisions in this administrative order. If a defendant is on probation in a division other than Division "F" or East County Criminal Divisions "P" or "X" and is subsequently charged with a domestic violence case, the clerk will file the domestic violence case in Division "F" or East County Criminal Divisions "P" or "X" and the probation case will remain the division in which it is pending.

D. *County Ordinance Violations.*

i. Plant City Courthouse. The clerk will assign all county ordinance violations in which the offense occurred within the East Division boundaries to East County Criminal Divisions "P" or "X" based on the first letter of the defendant's last name according to the following alphabetical distribution:

DIVISION	FIRST LETTER OF DEFENDANT'S LAST NAME
"P"	A, B, C, D, E, F, G, H, I, J, K, L
"X"	M, N, 0, P, Q, R, S, T, U, V, W, X, Y, Z

ii. Tampa Courthouse. The clerk will assign all county ordinance violations in which the offense occurred outside of the East Division boundaries to County Criminal Division "G" unless ancillary to a criminal offense.

E. *Municipal Ordinance Violations.*

i. Plant City Courthouse. The clerk will assign all City of Plant City municipal ordinance violations to East County Criminal Division "P" or "X" based on the first letter of the defendant's last name according to the following alphabetical distribution:

DIVISION	FIRST LETTER OF DEFENDANT'S LAST NAME
"P"	A, B, C, D, E, F, G, H, I, J, K, L
"X"	M, N, O, P, Q, R, S, T, U, V, W, X, Y, Z

ii. Tampa Courthouse. The clerk will assign all City of Tampa and City of Temple Terrance municipal ordinance violations to County Criminal Division "G."

F. *Scheduling of Ordinance Violations.* If a notice to appear contains a court date and it is signed by the defendant, the clerk will set the case for arraignment on that date. If the notice to appear contains a court date but is not signed by the defendant, the clerk will mail notice or issue a summons to the defendant for arraignment on that date. If a notice to appear or arrest affidavit consists of both a criminal offense and a municipal ordinance violation, the clerk must treat the municipal ordinance violation as ancillary and assign the case in accordance with the assignment provisions for the criminal offense.

G. *Consolidation.* When two or more misdemeanor offenses are pending, which may be appropriately considered or tried together, but which are assigned to different divisions due to the implementation of the alphabetical distribution system above, the case or cases will be reassigned to the division in which the case with the oldest offense date is pending.

H. *Transfer of Pending Cases to Probation Division.* Except as provided in section 3(C) of this administrative order dealing with domestic violence cases, if a defendant is on misdemeanor probation in one division and has a misdemeanor case or cases pending in other divisions, then all pending misdemeanor cases of the defendant will be transferred to the division in which the defendant is on probation.

I. *Violation of Probation.* The clerk will assign all violation of probation hearings to the county criminal division in which the defendant was sentenced to probation.

J. *Transfer between Tampa and Plant City.* When a new criminal traffic or misdemeanor case is filed in a Tampa division, the clerk's office in Tampa will determine if the defendant has any cases pending in the East Division (Plant City). Cases pending in both Tampa and Plant City on the same defendant will be assigned to the division with the oldest offense date and transferred appropriately.

4. Initial Probable Cause Determination under the Florida Contraband Forfeiture Act.

A. *Assignment of Probable Cause Application.* When a seizure of property is made under the Florida Contraband Forfeiture Act, the seizing law enforcement agency must timely apply *ex parte* to the presiding judge of County Criminal Division "C" for an initial order determining whether probable cause exists for the seizure of the property.

B. *Process.* Applications and orders will be filed in the Clerk's Administrative File via the following process. Law enforcement agency attorneys will submit their application via e-mail to the judicial assistant of County Criminal Division "C" who will forward the application to the clerk of court for assignment of a Clerk's Administrative File number. Upon the judge determining whether probable cause exists, the judicial assistant will notify the law enforcement agency attorney, request an appropriate order be submitted, and provide the Clerk's Administrative File number that has been assigned to the application. The law enforcement agency attorney will then submit a proposed order through the Judicial Automated Workload System (JAWS) using the Clerk's Administrative File number. The proposed order will then be automatically submitted to the judge's work queue on JAWS.

C. *Confidentiality.* If the law enforcement agency wishes the court to seal any portion of the application or sworn affidavit, it must e-mail to the judicial assistant of County Criminal Division "C" a separate Motion to Determine Confidentiality of Court Records simultaneously with the application. In accordance with the procedure outlined in Florida Rule of Judicial Administration 2.420(e), the application and sworn affidavit "must be treated as confidential by the clerk pending the court's ruling on the motion." Upon the judge making a decision on the Motion to Determine Confidentiality of Court Records, the judicial assistant will notify the law enforcement agency attorney, request an appropriate order be submitted, and provide the Clerk's Administrative File number that has been assigned to the application and motion. The law enforcement agency attorney will then submit a proposed order through the JAWS using the Clerk's Administrative File number.

D. *Complaint Filed in the Circuit Civil Division.* If the seizing law enforcement agency files a complaint to proceed against the contraband article, the complaint will be filed in the Circuit Civil Division. All adversarial preliminary hearings under the Florida Contraband Forfeiture Act will be scheduled in an assigned division of the Circuit Civil Division. See Administrative Order S–2017–070 (*Circuit Civil Division*) or any successor administrative order.

5. Emergency Matters. When the judge of any division is absent for any reason, any emergency application applying to a case assigned to such division may be presented and heard by the administrative judge or a designee of the administrative judge.

6. Arraignments.

A. *Notice to Appear or Released from Custody.* Arraignments for persons who are issued a notice to appear or who are released from custody pre-trial will be heard in the division assigned under section 3 of this administrative order.

B. *Persons Still Incarcerated.* Arraignments for persons arrested and still incarcerated on a misdemeanor charge will be heard via audiovisual technology in Courtroom 17. The presiding judge of County Criminal Division "F" is assigned to preside over the arraignment hearings. Arraignment hearings will be held semiweekly on non-holiday weeks and may be scheduled by the presiding judge of County Criminal Division "F" once per week on a holiday week. The administrative judge will maintain a schedule of county criminal division judges who will cover over the arraignment dockets on a rotating basis when the presiding judge of County Criminal Division "F" is on leave.

C. *Persons Scheduled for Arraignment in Assigned Division but then Incarcerated on Subsequent Charge.* Any person who is scheduled for arraignment in the standard division assigned under section 3 of this administrative order but who is then incarcerated in jail on a subsequent charge will not be transported by the sheriff to the assigned courtroom. Instead, the arraignment for the person on the misdemeanor charge(s) will be heard by the presiding judge of County Criminal Division "F" via audiovisual technology in Courtroom 17 according to the following procedure. The clerk in the assigned division will receive a jail sheet from the bailiff indicating the defendants who are scheduled for arraignment that day and are incarcerated in the county jail. When the defendant's case is called in the assigned standard division, the clerk will announce the next available arraignment date in County Criminal Division "F" and annotate the case abstract with this information. The arraignment will then be set for that next available date in Courtroom 17.

7. Motions.

A. *Setting Motion for Hearing.* To set a motion for hearing, the attorney must contact the judicial assistant in the appropriate division to obtain a motion calendar date. All motions, other than a Motion for Discharge or Motion for Speedy Trial, that are intended to be scheduled for hearing must be e-filed simultaneously with a Notice of Hearing after coordinating the hearing time with the opposing attorney or party.

B. *Deadline.* All motions and notices of hearing must be filed by at least 12:00 noon on the business day before the scheduled hearing. If a motion and notice of hearing are not timely filed, the motion will not appear on the calendar and it will be deemed abandoned until properly noticed in accordance with this section.

C. *Case Law.* Any party wishing to use case law for arguing in support of or in opposition to a filed motion must provide an electronic copy of the case law along with a copy of the notice of hearing and motion to the presiding judge's office and to opposing counsel or opposing party at least two business days prior to the motion hearing.

D. *Modification of Bail.* Except for bond and release on recognizance motions which are filed and heard in Division "O" prior to a defendant's scheduled arraignment, all other motions for modification of bail will be scheduled and heard in the division assigned under section 3 of this administrative order.

E. *Speedy Trial.* Motions for Discharge, Motions for Speedy Trial, and Notices of Expiration of Time for Speedy Trial are the only motions and notices accepted by the clerk without a Notice of Hearing. Upon receipt of a Motion for Discharge, Motion for Speedy Trial, or a Notice of Expiration of Time for Speedy Trial, the clerk will immediately contact the judicial assistant for a hearing time. After obtaining a hearing time, the clerk will notify all necessary parties.

F. *Motions filed by Self–Represented Parties.* The clerk will e-mail all motions filed by self-represented parties to the presiding judge and judicial assistant. If the motion needs to be set for hearing, the judicial assistant will send a memorandum with the date, time and necessary instructions for the clerk to send appropriate notice to the parties involved.

8. Setting Cases for Trial. If a defendant is entitled to a jury trial but elects to have a non-jury trial, the defendant must personally sign and file with the court a *Waiver of Jury Trial* form. A written document requesting a trial date without specifying a jury or non-jury trial will be deemed a request for a jury trial unless a *Waiver of Jury Trial* form has been previously filed. If a non-jury trial date is to be set at arraignment or pre-trial conference, and a *Waiver of Jury Trial* form has not been filed, the defendant must be present at the arraignment or pre-trial conference.

9. Jury Pre–Trial Conference.

A. *Presence of Defendant.* The defendant must be present at any jury pre-trial conference unless the defendant has signed and filed a written *Waiver of Appearance.*

B. *Presence of Attorneys.* The attorneys who are to conduct a jury trial are expected to appear at the pre-trial conference. If an attorney who is to conduct the trial does not attend the pre-trial conference, the attorney who appears must be fully advised about the case and be fully prepared to resolve any issues which may arise.

C. *Resolution of Pre–Trial Motions.* Except for good cause shown, all evidentiary and other motions must be filed, heard and resolved prior to the pre-trial conference.

D. *Completion of Discovery.* All discovery, including the taking of depositions, must be completed before the pre-trial conference.

E. *Plea Negotiations.* The parties are encouraged to discuss plea negotiations before the pre-trial conference. If the court approves the negotiations, a plea will be accepted at the pre-trial conference or at such time designated by the court.

F. *Continuance.* Any continuance granted after the pre-trial conference will be governed by Florida Rule of Criminal Procedure 3.190(f) and will be granted only upon written motion and order.

G. *Ready for Jury Trial.* By agreeing at the pre-trial conference that a case is ready for jury trial, the parties represent to the court that:

i. The attorneys are fully prepared for trial.

ii. The witnesses expected to testify at the trial have been interviewed, if desired, and will be present at trial.

iii. All discovery is complete and all pre-trial motions have been considered and resolved.

10. Trial Division. The presiding judge of County Criminal Trial Division "R" will be available on a weekly basis to assist the other criminal divisions in selecting juries and trying cases. If a case has been transferred to Division "R" for trial, the presiding judge of Division "R" will be responsible for sentencing hearings, retrials, re-sentencing hearings and any post-trial motions affecting the sentence filed in accordance with Rule of Criminal Procedure 3.800. The presiding judge of Division "R" will not consider postconviction motions under Florida Rules of Criminal Procedure 3.801 or 3.850. In accordance with section 3(I) of this administrative order, all violation of probation hearings on cases in which the sentence was pronounced by the presiding judge of Division "R" will be heard by the presiding judge of Division "R" unless the judge presiding in the county criminal division in which the case was originally pending is available and agrees to handle the VOP matter.

11. Criminal Traffic Offenses.

A. *Failure to Appear.* Upon the filing of a uniform traffic citation, the clerk will automatically set a court date and notify the defendant at the address provided on the citation or at the address listed on the most recent filing in the court file. If the defendant fails to appear at the hearing set by the clerk, the court may issue a capias for the arrest of the defendant, together with a Form D–6 (license suspension). The capias will be issued with an appropriate bond amount to ensure the defendant's appearance before the court. A capias may be issued when the defendant is a minor, but the minor will be released on the minor's own recognizance.

B. *Companion Civil Traffic Infractions.* When a defendant receives a criminal traffic citation together with a companion citation for a civil infraction, all citations will, when possible, remain together and will be scheduled on the court's calendar on the same date.

C. *Plea.* All persons charged with a criminal traffic offense must enter a plea in open court before the judge. Any person charged with a criminal traffic offense and who enters a plea of not guilty in open court will not be permitted to change such plea unless in open court.

12. Attorney of Record. In accordance with the spirit of Florida Rule of Judicial Administration 2.505(f), once an attorney appears on the record representing a defendant, that attorney is the attorney of record until relieved by a written order of the court. No attorney of record will be permitted to withdraw unless a motion to withdraw is filed, heard and granted at least 30 days prior to trial.

13. Reassignment of Case upon Judge's Disqualification.

A. *East County.* If either of the judges presiding in East County Criminal Divisions "P" or "X" enters an order of disqualification, the clerk will reassign the case to the other East county criminal division. If both east county criminal division judges have entered orders of disqualification in a non-domestic violence case, the clerk will reassign the case to a Tampa county criminal division based on the first letter of the defendant's last name according to the following alphabetical distribution:

DIVISION	FIRST LETTER OF DEFENDANT'S LAST NAME
"A"	G, O, S, U
"B"	B, F, P
"C"	D, M, N, X, Y
"D"	C, K, R
"E"	H, L, W
"G"	A, E, J, I, Q, T, V, Z

B. *Domestic Violence Cases.* If either of the judges presiding in East County Criminal Divisions "P" or "X" enters an order of disqualification in a domestic violence case, the clerk will reassign the case to the other east county criminal division. If both east county criminal division judges have entered orders of disqualification in a domestic violence case, the clerk will reassign the case to Tampa County Criminal Division "F." If the judge assigned to County Criminal Division "F" enters an order of disqualification, the clerk will reassign the case to a Tampa county criminal division based on the first letter of the defendant's last name according to the following alphabetical distribution:

DIVISION	FIRST LETTER OF DEFENDANT'S LAST NAME
"A"	G, O, S, U
"B"	B, F, P
"C"	D, M, N, X, Y
"D"	C, K, R
"E"	H, L, W
"G"	A, E, J, I, Q, T, V, Z

C. *Trial Division Cases.* If the judge assigned to County Criminal Trial Division "R" enters an order of disqualification, the clerk will reassign the case back to the division from which the case was transferred to Division "R."

D. *Other County Criminal Cases.* If a judge presiding in any other Tampa division enters an order of disqualification on any case, including municipal ordinance or county ordinance violation cases, the clerk will randomly and equitably reassign the case to another Tampa county criminal division.

14. Professional Conduct and Courtroom Decorum. Counsel will adhere to The Florida Bar's Guidelines for Professional Conduct (https://www.floridabar.org/prof/presources/presources002/). The Florida Bar's Professionalism Expectations (https://www.floridabar.org/wp–content/uploads/2017/04/professionalism–expectations.pdf), and the Hillsborough County Bar Association's Standards of Professionalism (http://hillsbar.site–vm.com/?page=Professionalism). Each judge may announce and enforce additional requirements, or may excuse compliance with any provision(s) of the Guidelines, Expectations or Standards as that judge deems appropriate.

15. Previous Administrative Order Superseded. This administrative order supersedes Administrative Order S–2018–049 (*County Criminal Division*).

16. Effective Date. This administrative order is effective January 1, 2019.

ENTERED in Tampa, Hillsborough County, Florida, on December 28, 2018.

Ronald N. Ficarrotta
Chief Judge

S–2018–047. BOND MATTERS

IN THE THIRTEENTH JUDICIAL CIRCUIT COURT HILLSBOROUGH COUNTY, FLORIDA

ADMINISTRATIVE ORDER S–2018–047

(Supersedes Administrative Order S–2018–009)

BOND MATTERS

Criminal defendants brought before the courts of this circuit are many times released on bail provided by them, bail bond agents or non-bail bond agent third parties. The purpose of bail is to relieve an accused of pretrial incarceration. A bail bond is a three-party contract between the state, the accused, and the surety whereby the accused is released to the custody of the surety, and the surety guarantees to the state the appearance of the accused at all criminal proceedings for which the surety bond is posted. Chapter 903, Florida Statutes (chapter 903), sets forth provisions for bail bond exoneration, forfeiture, judgment, remission and cancellation.

It is necessary to revise previously established procedures to provide for the proper and efficient administration of justice in this circuit for bail bond exoneration, forfeiture, judgment, remission, and cancellation.

By the power vested in the chief judge under article V, section 2(d), Florida Constitution; section 43.26, Florida Statutes; and Florida Rule of Judicial Administration 2.215(b)(2), it is therefore ORDERED:

1. Application. This administrative order applies to all circuit criminal, county criminal, and criminal traffic cases in which a defendant has been released on a bail bond in accordance with the provisions of chapter 903.

2. Types of Bonds. The county and circuit courts will not accept personal property of any kind other than a bail bond posted by a licensed surety to satisfy the bail requirements of chapter 903 or a cash bond. Real property bonds are discouraged. "Blanket bonds" are prohibited. A blanket bond is one bail bond that provides for the release of a defendant on more than one charge or case. Any judge setting or granting monetary bail will set a separate and specific bail amount for each charge or offense. When bail is posted, each charge or offense requires a separate bond.

3. Parties. For purposes of this administrative order, the following terms identifying the parties have the following meanings:

A. The term "petitioner" refers to a bail bond agent or surety and includes corporate sureties, corporate bond agencies, individual sureties, individual bail bond agents and cash bond depositors.

B. The term "defendant" refers to the accused and is the principal on the bail bond.

C. The term "clerk" refers to the Office of the Clerk of Court.

D. The term "state" refers to the Office of the State Attorney.

E. The term "clerk's legal counsel" refers to the legal department attorney(s) of the clerk.

4. Motions and Applications for Relief. Motions and applications for relief under chapter 903 must be filed with the clerk through the Florida Courts e-filing portal in the appropriate division (i.e. felony, misdemeanor or traffic). Except for motions and applications filed in First Appearance /Emergency Division "O," motions and applications must be court and case specific and may not address more than a single court division (e.g. a motion in a felony case may not address misdemeanor bonds in the same pleading). Motions and applications must list each bond power number for which relief is sought. Motions and applications must certify service of copies to the state and the clerk's legal counsel. Unless stated otherwise in this administrative order, all motions and applications will be filed without a notice of hearing. All motions and applications must be accompanied by the proof of the payment of the Hillsborough County Sheriff's transportation costs in the manner set forth in section 13 of this administrative order, when applicable. When practical, motions must be filed with the required fees and costs prepaid by the petitioner.

All supporting documentation attached to motions or applications, including but not limited to docket information and recommitment certificates, must be clearly legible and the applicable entries, cases, and charges must be highlighted or noted. Motions and applications to the court must be filed by the attorney for the corporate petitioner; a corporation cannot represent itself in court without a licensed attorney. However, if the surety is a natural person and individually and personally liable on the bond such that the forfeiture or judgment would be entered against a natural person, then that non-corporate surety may proceed without an attorney.

5. Forms. Sample motions, applications and proposed orders to be used with the provisions of this administrative order can be located at www.fljud13.org under the section entitled "Forms." Attorneys must use these sample motions, applications, and proposed orders when proceeding under the provisions of this administrative order.

6. Setting Hearings. Whenever a hearing is permitted, such hearing must be set by contacting the judicial assistant in the division to which the case is assigned and a notice of hearing must be filed with the clerk, with service provided to the clerk's legal counsel and the state, when appropriate. It will be the responsibility of the petitioner to set the matter for hearing before the assigned division judge when the state or the clerk's legal counsel files an objection to the relief requested.

Prior to scheduling a hearing with the assigned judge, counsel must consult with opposing counsel as to the date and the time required for such hearing. When appropriate, all motions must be filed simultaneously with a notice of hearing containing the scheduled hearing time.

7. Notices of Hearings. Except for an Application for Remission of Forfeiture [which requires 20 days' notice] and an Application for Exoneration [which requires three days' notice], the courts will refuse to hear any motion relating to chapter 903 unless at least five days' notice has been provided to both the state and the clerk's legal counsel. A petitioner may only set a hearing on a Motion to Discharge Forfeiture Before Judgment and a Motion to Set Aside Final Judgment of Forfeiture when an objection is filed by the state or the clerk's legal counsel, or when the petitioner objects to the payment of costs or the amount to be remitted. Any notice of hearing must clearly reference the title of the motion to be heard, the date and time for when the motion will be heard, and the location where the parties should appear.

8. Emergency Matters. Emergency matters may be set and heard provided that: (1) leave of court is first obtained, (2) the petitioner attempts to speak with the clerk's legal counsel, and the state when appropriate, to obtain their consent to the relief sought or the setting of the emergency hearing, and the emergency pleading recites that the clerk's legal counsel, and the state when appropriate, were contacted in accordance with this requirement, and (3) notice and copies of all motions with exhibits are provided to both the state and the clerk's legal counsel. The court may grant leave to file emergency motions in instances where the time periods contemplated by this administrative order and the provisions of chapter 903 would render the relief sought moot.

9. Orders. Proposed orders for all bail bond related pleadings must be filed along with the bail bond motion / application packet. The clerk's legal counsel will be responsible for uploading an agreed order to the division judge through the Judicial Automated Workflow System (JAWS). The clerk's legal counsel must not submit any order through JAWS until all parties have had a minimum of three business days to respond to the motion / application, excluding the day of service.

10. Time. The time periods statutorily established in chapter 903 must be strictly followed. Unless the tolling of a time period is specifically authorized under chapter 903 for the relief sought, the filing of a motion or application will not toll any time period. The computation of any time period relating to the filing of a document with the clerk will be determined by Florida Rules of Judicial Administration 2.525(f)(3) and chapter 903.

11. Application of Rules of Civil Procedure. Bail bonds are contracts and civil in nature and the Florida Rules of Civil Procedure apply to bail bond proceedings.

12. Surrender or Recommitment. Surrender or recommitment of a defendant will not be made to the court.

13. Transportation Costs. The Hillsborough County Sheriff's Office Transportation Section posts on its' website a Transportation Costs Rate Sheet (*See* www.hcso.tampa.fl.us). The Transportation Costs Rate Sheet in existence at the time of the chapter 903 proceeding, or the actual receipt given to the petitioner by the Hillsborough County Sheriff's Office, will be considered prima facie evidence of the transportation costs owed or paid by the petitioner. Transportation costs of a defendant with multiple cases need only be paid once and must be paid in conjunction with the lowest case number (i.e. transportation costs would be paid in the lowest numbered felony case and such payment would be referenced in a companion misdemeanor or traffic case pleading and proposed order).

14. Surrender Prior to Forfeiture Exoneration [§ 903.21, Florida Statutes]. A petitioner seeking to be relieved of liability on a bond under sections 903.21(1) and (2), Florida Statutes, must, prior to the scheduled appearance date insured by the bond, file an Application for Exoneration and proposed order with the clerk that includes the facts and legal arguments in support of exoneration. Any application under sections 903.21(1) and (2), Florida Statutes, must be filed with the clerk in the appropriate division and the following must be attached to the application: (1) a certificate acknowledging the defendant's surrender from the official who had custody of the defendant at the time bail was taken or the official into whose custody the defendant would have been placed if she or he had been committed, (2) a copy of the bond(s) from which exoneration is sought, and (3) an acknowledgment from petitioner or petitioner's counsel that the state and the clerk's legal counsel were provided three days' notice of application for an order of exoneration together with copies of the official's certificate and the bond.

A petitioner seeking to be relieved of liability on a bond under section 903.21(3), Florida Statutes, must, prior to the scheduled appearance date insured by the bond, file an Application for Exoneration and proposed order with the clerk that includes the facts and legal arguments in support of exoneration. Any application under section 903.21(3), Florida Statutes, must be filed with the clerk in the appropriate division and the following must be attached to the application: (1) documentation from the holding jail or prison that the defendant is in custody, (2) documentation substantiating that the person in custody is in fact the correct defendant, and (3) documentation indicating the petitioner agrees to pay the transportation costs of returning the defendant to the jurisdiction of the court. Costs will include any state and local assessments authorized by sections 938.01(1), and 943.25, Florida Statutes, and any costs to the state, sheriff, and clerk recoverable in accordance with chapter 903.

The clerk's legal counsel will file and serve his or her response to an Application of Exoneration filed under section 903.21(1) and (2) or (3), Florida Statutes, after the 3 days' notice has expired. If an objection is filed by the clerk or state, or the petitioner disagrees with the amount of costs to be paid, it will be the responsibility of the petitioner's counsel to set the matter for hearing to determine the appropriateness of the discharge or the amount of costs to be paid. Prior to scheduling a hearing with the assigned judge, counsel must consult with opposing counsel as to the date and the time required for such hearing. A notice of hearing must be filed with the clerk, with service provided to both the state and the clerk's legal counsel. Time is of the essence as the petitioner must obtain an order prior to the scheduled appearance date insured by the bond.

If the criteria for exoneration are met and the clerk's legal counsel or the state have no objection to the relief requested, the clerk's legal counsel will submit the proposed order to the assigned judge for disposition via JAWS.

15. Capias Recall and Vacating or Setting Aside Bond Forfeitures [§ 903.26, Florida Statutes]. A motion to recall a capias may be filed in conjunction with a motion to vacate or set aside a related bond forfeiture. All permitted motions or petitions to recall a capias and address a related bond forfeiture must comply with the requirements of chapter 903 and this administrative order. The petitioner, or a defendant, must file a motion to vacate or set aside bond forfeiture along with a proposed order in sufficient time to obtain an order no later than the 61st day from the date of the notice of forfeiture. A motion to vacate or set aside forfeiture does not toll the statutory time period before the entry of a judgment in accordance with section 903.27, Florida Statutes.

A. *Defendant's Motion to Recall Capias, Vacate Forfeiture and Reinstate Bond [Procedural or Due Process Grounds].* A defendant, self-represented, through counsel, or in concert with the surety petitioning to have a capias recalled and the forfeiture vacated on procedural or due process grounds, must, prior to the expiration of the statutory time period set forth in section 903.26(2)(a), Florida Statutes, file with the clerk a Motion to Recall Capias, Vacate Forfeiture and Reinstate Bond along with a proposed order in sufficient time to obtain an order no later than the 61st day from the date of the notice of forfeiture. The vacating of a bail bond forfeiture is an equitable proceeding and is based on some procedural or due process error in the entry of the forfeiture (i.e. deficient notice). A surety has no legal basis to object to a procedural or due process reinstatement of the bond. If a capias is withdrawn or recalled for a due process violation and the forfeiture is vacated, the parties return to their pre-forfeiture status, and the bond will remain in full force and effect. The surety will not be liable for any clerk or statutory fees associated with the original vacated forfeiture.

The Motion to Recall Capias, Vacate Forfeiture and Reinstate Bond must provide the bond power number and surety information and must be served on the state, the clerk's legal counsel and the surety, if the surety agent has not joined in or approved the motion. Nothing in this administrative order affects the court's inherent ability to vacate the forfeiture on the court's own motion and reinstate the bond. If the court recalls or withdraws the capias, then the court will vacate the forfeiture and reinstate the bond.

While it is the intention of this administrative order to simultaneously resolve the bond forfeiture in conjunction with the capias proceeding, should the bond forfeiture not be addressed for any reason, nothing in this administrative order affects the surety's ability to later address the bond forfeiture in accordance with the provisions of chapter 903 and this administrative order.

B. *Defendant's Motion to Recall Capias, Set Aside Forfeiture and Reinstate Bond [Non–Procedural or Non–Due Process Grounds].* A defendant, self-represented, through counsel, or in concert with the surety petitioning to have a capias recalled and the forfeiture set aside on non-procedural or non-due process grounds, must, prior to the statutory time period set forth in section 903.26(2)(a), Florida Statutes, file with the clerk a Motion to Recall Capias, Set Aside Forfeiture and Reinstate Bond along with a proposed order in sufficient time to obtain an order no later than the 61st day from the date of the notice of forfeiture. The setting aside of a bail bond forfeiture that does not involve a procedural or due process error is an equitable proceeding and requires the agreement of the surety to reinstate the bond.

The Motion to Recall Capias, Set Aside Forfeiture and Reinstate Bond must provide the bond power number and surety information and must be served on the state and the clerk's legal counsel, together with the surety, if the surety has not previously joined in or approved of the motion. Nothing in this administrative order affects the court's inherent ability to set aside the forfeiture on the court's own motion and reinstate the bond subject to the approval from the surety on the original bond.

i. Surety's Objection to Bond Reinstatement. A surety's filed objection to the bond reinstatement will automatically prevent the forfeiture from being addressed and the bond reinstated by the court in accordance with section 903.31(2), Florida Statutes. The surety's objection to the bond reinstatement does not affect the court's inherent discretion to recall its capias. The only valid grounds for discharging a forfeiture are set forth in section 903.26, Florida Statutes. As such, the recalling of a capias is not a legal ground to discharge the bond forfeiture.

ii. Surety's Failure to Address Bond Reinstatement. If the court recalls or withdraws the capias, the court may not reinstate the bond in accordance with section 903.31(2), Florida Statutes. The setting aside or withdrawal of a capias has no effect on the reinstatement of a bond. If the bond forfeiture is not addressed for any reason, nothing in this administrative order affects the surety's ability to address the bond forfeiture in accordance with the provisions of chapter 903 and this administrative order. However, should the forfeiture not be discharged or set aside in sufficient time to obtain an order no later than the 61st day from the date of the notice of forfeiture under section 903.26(2)(a), Florida Statutes, the clerk will enter a final judgment in accordance with section 903.27, Florida Statutes.

16. Bond Forfeiture Discharge—Court Discharge [§ 903.26(5)(a) or (b), Florida Statutes]. A petitioner seeking to have a bond forfeiture discharged under section 903.26(5)(a) or (b), Florida Statutes, must file their motion along with a proposed order in sufficient time to obtain an order no later than the 61st day from the date of the notice of forfeiture. The court will refuse to hear, and the clerk will not discharge, any forfeiture when a Motion to Discharge Forfeiture Before Judgment is not filed in accordance with the time periods set forth in this administrative order.

The petitioner must attach to the motion a copy of the Notice of Forfeiture as well as documentation supporting the claim that: (1) it was impossible for the defendant to appear as required or within 60 days after the date of the required appearance due to circumstances beyond the defendant's control (in accordance with section 903.26(5)(a), Florida Statutes, the potential adverse economic consequences of appearing as required may not be considered as constituting a ground for such a determination), or (2) at the time of the required appearance or within 60 days after the date of the required appearance, the defendant was confined in an institution or hospital, was confined in any county, state, federal, or immigration detention facility, was deported, or is deceased. Proper documentation of confinement must be from the institution, hospital, or detention facility in which the defendant was confined at the time of the required appearance or within 60 days after the date of the required appearance and must specify the dates of confinement. Proper documentation of death or deportation must specify the date of death or deportation. Proof of the confinement, death or deportation and that the confined, deceased or deported person is the defendant must be shown by admissible evidence. The Motion to Discharge Forfeiture Before Judgment must also have attached documentation from the Hillsborough County Sheriff's Office, or one of its approved contractors, stating the cost of returning the defendant to Hillsborough County. The petitioner must serve copies of the Motion to Discharge Forfeiture Before Judgment on the state and the clerk's legal counsel.

The clerk's legal counsel will file and serve his or her response to a Motion filed under section 903.26(a) or (b), Florida Statutes. If an objection is filed, or the petitioner disagrees with the amount of costs to be paid, it will be the responsibility of the petitioner to set the matter for hearing to determine the appropriateness of the discharge or the amount of costs to be paid. Prior to scheduling a hearing with the assigned judge, counsel must consult with opposing counsel as to the date and the time required for such hearing. A notice of hearing must be filed with the clerk, with service provided to both the state and the clerk's legal counsel. Time is of the essence as the petitioner must obtain an order no later than the 61st day from the date of the notice of forfeiture, or the clerk will enter a final judgment in accordance with section 903.27, Florida Statutes.

If the clerk's legal counsel has no objection to the relief sought, the clerk's legal counsel will submit the proposed order to the assigned judge for disposition via JAWS. An Order Discharging Bond Forfeiture Before Judgment entered under sections 903.26(5)(a) or (b), Florida Statutes, will only discharge the forfeiture, and provide for payment of any costs authorized by chapter 903 and sections 938.01(1) and 943.25, Florida Statutes. If an Order Discharging Bond Forfeiture Before Judgment has not been entered on or before the 61st day from the date of the notice of forfeiture and the bond is secured other than by money and bonds authorized in section 903.16, Florida Statutes, the clerk will, without delay, enter a Final Judgment of Forfeiture in accordance with section 903.27, Florida Statutes.

17. Bond Forfeiture Discharge—Court Discharge [§ 903.26(5)(c), Florida Statutes]. A petitioner seeking to have a bond forfeiture discharged under section 903.26(5)(c), Florida Statutes, must file their motion along with a proposed order in sufficient time to obtain an order no later than the 61st day from the date of the notice of forfeiture. The court will refuse to hear, and the clerk will not discharge, any forfeiture when a Motion to Discharge Order of Forfeiture Before Judgment is not filed in accordance with the time periods set forth herein.

The petitioner must attach to the motion a copy of the Notice of Forfeiture as well as documentation supporting the claim that: (1) there was a surrender or arrest of the defendant at the time of the required appearance or within 60 days after the date of the required appearance in any county, state, or federal jail or prison, and (2) a hold has been placed to return the defendant to the jurisdiction of the court. In addition, the petitioner must attach documentation from the Hillsborough County Jail indicating whether the defendant was arrested or surrendered within Hillsborough County or outside of Hillsborough County and highlight in such documentation any applicable charge(s) and case number(s) for which the defendant has been recommitted. If the arrest or surrender was outside of Hillsborough County, the documentation must include the cost of transporting the defendant back to Hillsborough County or a notation that the defendant was allowed to post a new bond at the surrender or arrest location. The petitioner must serve copies of the Motion to Discharge Forfeiture Before Judgment on the state and the clerk's legal counsel.

The clerk's legal counsel will file and serve his or her response to a motion filed under section 903.26(5)(c), Florida Statutes. If an objection is filed, or the petitioner disagrees with the amount of costs to be paid, it will be the responsibility of the petitioner to set the matter for hearing to determine the appropriateness of the discharge or the amount of costs to be paid. Prior to scheduling a hearing with the assigned judge, counsel must consult with opposing counsel as to the date and the time required for such hearing. A notice of hearing must be filed with the clerk, with service provided to both the state and the clerk's legal counsel. Time is of the essence as the petitioner must obtain an order no later than the 61st day from the date of the notice of forfeiture, or the clerk will enter a final judgment in accordance with section 903.27, Florida Statutes.

If no objection is received from the clerk's legal counsel or the state, the clerk's legal counsel will submit the proposed order to the assigned judge via JAWS. The court will condition a discharge or remission on the payment of costs and the expenses incurred by an official in returning the defendant to the jurisdiction of the court. Costs will include any state and local assessments authorized by sections 938.01(1), and 943.25, Florida Statutes, and any costs to the state, sheriff, and clerk recoverable in accordance with chapter 903.

18. Bond Forfeiture Discharge—Court Discharge [§ 903.26(5)(d), Florida Statutes]. A petitioner seeking to have a bond forfeiture discharged under section 903.26(5)(d), Florida Statutes, must file their motion along with a proposed order in sufficient time to obtain an order no later than the 61st day from the date of the notice of forfeiture. The court will refuse to hear, and the clerk will not discharge, any forfeiture when a Motion to Discharge Forfeiture Before Judgment is not filed in accordance with the time periods set forth in this administrative order.

The petitioner must attach to the motion a copy of the Notice of Forfeiture as well as documentation supporting the claim that: (1) the state is unwilling to seek extradition of the fugitive defendant within 30 days after a request by the surety agent to do so, and (2) contingent upon the surety agent's consent to pay all costs and the expenses incurred by an official in returning the defendant to the jurisdiction of the court, up to the penal amount of the bond. Proof of the state's unwillingness to extradite the defendant must be shown by admissible evidence. The petitioner must serve copies of the

Motion to Discharge Forfeiture Before Judgment on the state and clerk's legal counsel.

The clerk's legal counsel will file and serve his or her response to a motion filed under section 903.26(5)(d), Florida Statutes. If an objection is filed, or the petitioner disagrees with the amount of costs to be paid, it will be the responsibility of the petitioner to set the matter for hearing to determine the appropriateness of the discharge or the amount of costs to be paid. Prior to scheduling a hearing with the assigned judge, counsel must consult with opposing counsel as to the date and the time required for such hearing. A notice of hearing must be filed with the clerk, with service provided to both the state and the clerk's legal counsel. Time is of the essence as the petitioner must obtain an order no later than the 61st day from the date of the Notice of Forfeiture, or the clerk will enter a final judgment in accordance with section 903.27, Florida Statutes.

If no objection is received from the clerk's legal counsel or the state, the clerk's legal counsel will submit the proposed order to the assigned judge via JAWS. The court will condition a discharge on the surety agent's consent to pay all costs and the expenses incurred by an official in returning the defendant to the jurisdiction of the court, up to the penal amount of the bond. Costs will include any state and local assessments authorized by sections 938.01(1), and 943.25, Florida Statutes, and any costs to the state, sheriff, and clerk recoverable in accordance with chapter 903.

19. Bond Forfeiture Discharge—Clerk's Discharge [§ 903.26(8), Florida Statutes]. A petitioner seeking to have a bond forfeiture discharged under section 903.26(8), Florida Statutes, must, prior to the entry of a judgment in accordance with section 903.27, Florida Statutes, file with the clerk an Application for Clerk's Discharge of Forfeiture Before Judgment ("Application"). The petitioner must attach to the Application a copy of the Notice of Forfeiture, as well as documentation supporting the claim that: (1) the defendant is arrested and returned to the county of the jurisdiction of the court, or (2) has posted a new bond for the case at issue before judgment. Proper documentation will be in the form of an affirmation by the sheriff or the chief correctional officer indicating that the defendant has been arrested or surrendered and returned to Hillsborough County. In accordance with section 903.26(8), Florida Statutes, a clerk's discharge of the forfeiture of a bond is conditioned on the payment of any costs and expenses incurred in returning the defendant to Hillsborough County. Costs will include any state and local assessments authorized by sections 938.01(1), and 943.25, Florida Statutes, and any costs to the state, sheriff, and clerk recoverable in accordance with chapter 903.

If the petitioner fails to pay the costs and expenses incurred in returning the defendant to the county of jurisdiction, the clerk will not discharge the forfeiture of the bond. If the petitioner and the sheriff fail to agree on the amount of said costs, then the court, after notice to the sheriff and the state, will determine the amount of the costs. It will be the responsibility of the petitioner to set the matter for hearing to determine the amount of costs to be paid. Prior to scheduling a hearing with the assigned judge, counsel must consult with opposing counsel as to the date and time required for such hearing. A notice of hearing must be filed with the clerk, with service provided to both the state and the clerk's legal counsel.

20. Bond Forfeiture to Judgment [§ 903.27, Florida Statutes]. A bond forfeiture must be paid, or discharged by court order, on or before the 61st day from the date of the Notice of Forfeiture, or the clerk will enter a judgment against the surety in accordance with section 903.27, Florida Statutes, and let execution issue.

A. *New Case File.* When a forfeiture in a county criminal case (i.e. misdemeanor or traffic) goes to Final Judgment, the clerk will create a new circuit case file with a new case number for the purpose of addressing the forfeiture only and randomly assign the new case to one of the standard divisions in the Circuit Criminal Division. A defendant's underlying county criminal case(s) will remain assigned to the appropriate County Criminal Division.

When a forfeiture in a circuit criminal case goes to Final Judgment, the clerk will create a new circuit case file. The petitioner must file any Motion to Set Aside Final Judgment of Forfeiture or Motion to Stay Execution of Final Judgment with the clerk in the Circuit Criminal Division to which the new case has been assigned and must include both the new court case number and the original court case number on the motions, when applicable.

B. *Satisfying the Final Judgment of Forfeiture.* To satisfy the Final Judgment of Forfeiture, the surety must pay it within 35 days of the judgment's entry.

C. *Contesting the Final Judgment of Forfeiture.* If the petitioner wants to contest the entry of final judgment, it must file a Motion to Set Aside Final Judgment of Forfeiture or Motion to Stay Execution of Final Judgment of Forfeiture. The motion must be accompanied by payment of the Final Judgment of Forfeiture to the clerk, which amount will be held in escrow until such time as the court has disposed of the Motion to Set Aside Final Judgment of Forfeiture or the Motion to Stay Execution of Final Judgment of Forfeiture.

A Motion to Set Aside Final Judgment of Forfeiture or Motion to Stay Execution of Final Judgment of Forfeiture must have attached a copy of the Final Judgment of Forfeiture and documentation indicating that the defendant has been arrested or surrendered to the Hillsborough County Jail. In addition, the petitioner must attach documentation from the Hillsborough County Jail indicating whether the defendant was arrested or surrendered within Hillsborough County or outside of Hillsborough County and highlight in such documentation any applicable charge(s) and case number(s) for which the defendant has been recommitted. If arrest or surrender was outside of Hillsborough County, the documentation must include the cost of transporting the defendant back to the county or a notation that the defendant was allowed to post a new bond at the arrest or surrender location. The petitioner must serve copies of any Motion to Set Aside Final Judgment of Forfeiture or Motion to Stay Execution of Final Judgment of Forfeiture on the clerk's legal counsel.

The setting aside of any Final Judgment of Forfeiture will be subject to the payment of costs which may include any state and local assessments authorized by sections 938.01(1), and 943.25, Florida Statutes, and any costs to the state, sheriff, and clerk in accordance with chapter 903.

D. *Clerk's Response.* The clerk's legal counsel will file and serve his or her response indicating approval or objection to the Motion to Set Aside Final Judgment of Forfeiture or

Motion to Stay Execution of Final Judgment. If an objection to a Motion to Set Aside Final Judgment of Forfeiture or Motion to Stay Execution of Final Judgment is filed by the clerk's legal counsel, it will be the responsibility of the petitioner to set the matter for hearing before the assigned division judge. Prior to scheduling a hearing with the assigned judge, counsel must consult with opposing counsel as to the date and the time required for such hearing. A notice of hearing must be filed with the clerk, with service provided to the clerk's legal counsel.

21. Remission of Forfeiture [§ 903.28, Florida Statutes]. An application for remission of forfeited bonds must be filed within two years from the date of the forfeiture. The prerequisites for remission of forfeited funds are that: (1) there was no breach of the bond, and (2) the defendant has been surrendered or apprehended. In addition, if a Final Judgment of Forfeiture has been entered in accordance with section 903.27, Florida Statutes, a petitioner will not be eligible for remission unless a timely Motion to Set Aside Final Judgment of Forfeiture has been granted and a copy of the corresponding order is attached to the Application for Remission of Forfeiture.

A petitioner seeking remission of forfeiture of bail bonds must file an Application for Remission of Forfeiture and an Affidavit in Support of Application for Remission of Forfeiture with the clerk and serve the same on the state and the clerk's legal counsel. The Application for Remission of Forfeiture must also include: (1) a receipt for payment of the forfeiture, (2) an affidavit from the surety documenting any claimed attempt at procuring or causing the apprehension or surrender of the defendant, (3) documentation indicating that the defendant has been arrested or surrendered, and (4) a proposed Order Granting Remission of Forfeiture. If the arrest or surrender of the defendant was outside of Hillsborough County, the documentation must include the cost of transporting the defendant back to Hillsborough County.

The clerk's legal counsel will file and serve his or her response to the Application for Remission of Forfeiture. The state will review its file to determine whether prosecution of the case has been thwarted by the delay. The state must file any objection to the Application for Remission of Forfeiture setting forth its objections and serve a copy of its objection to the clerk's legal counsel and to the petitioner's attorney indicating either: (1) the prosecution of the case has been thwarted, or (2) the state cannot determine whether prosecution of the case has been thwarted. Recoverable costs incurred by the state (i.e. subpoenas, service of process, witness fees, etc.), if any, must be affirmatively listed by the state in their timely filed objection to the Application for Remission of Forfeiture, and if not listed in the objection, it will be presumed that the state has no such recoverable costs.

If an objection is filed, or the petitioner disagrees with the amount of costs to be paid, it will be the responsibility of the petitioner to set the matter for hearing before the assigned division judge. Prior to scheduling a hearing with the assigned judge, counsel must consult with opposing counsel as to the date and the time required for such hearing. The petitioner must file and serve a notice of hearing and provide at least 20 days' notice to the clerk's legal counsel and the state before a hearing on the Application for Remission of Forfeiture. The petitioner must also provide the clerk's legal counsel and the state with copies of all papers, applications, and affidavits related to the Application for Remission of Forfeiture.

Costs will be deducted from the amount of the remission. The costs may include state and local assessments authorized by sections 938.01(1) and 943.25, Florida Statutes, unpaid sheriff's costs, when a Final Judgment has been entered and set aside, and any costs the clerk or state of Florida is entitled to recover under chapter 903.

22. Return of Cash Bonds [§ 903.286, Florida Statutes]. The clerk will withhold from the return of a cash bond, posted on behalf of a defendant by a person other than a licensed bail bond agent or surety, sufficient funds to pay any unpaid costs of prosecution, costs of representation as provided by sections 27.52 and 938.29, Florida Statutes, court fees, court costs, and criminal penalties, in all of a defendant's Thirteenth Judicial Circuit cases.

23. Cancellation of Surety Bonds [§ 903.31, Florida Statutes]. Within 10 business days after the conditions of a bond have been satisfied or the forfeiture discharged or remitted, the court will order the bond cancelled and, if the surety has attached a certificate of cancellation to the original bond, the clerk will furnish an executed certificate of cancellation to the surety without cost.

The following will satisfy the conditions of a bond that has not been declared forfeited before the 36 month expiration: (1) an adjudication of guilt or innocence, or an acquittal, or (2) if a period of 36 months has passed since the original bond was posted, or (3) a withholding of an adjudication of guilt. If no formal charges are brought against the defendant within 365 days after arrest, the court will order the bond canceled unless good cause is shown by the state.

The original appearance bond does not guarantee the following: (1) a deferred sentence, or (2) an appearance during or after a presentence investigation, or (3) an appearance during or after appeals, or (4) conduct during or appearance after admission to a pretrial intervention program, or (5) placement in a court-ordered program, including a residential mental health facility, or (6) payment of fines, or (7) attendance at educational or rehabilitation facilities the court otherwise provides in the judgment.

If the original appearance bond has been forfeited or revoked, the bond will not be reinstated without approval from the surety on the original bond.

24. Previous Administrative Order Superseded. This administrative order supersedes Administrative Order S–2018–009 *(Bond Matters)*.

25. Effective Date. This administrative order is effective December 1, 2018.

Entered in Tampa, Hillsborough County, Florida, on November 15, 2018.

Ronald N. Ficarrotta
Chief Judge

S–2018–022. UNIFORM BAIL BOND SCHEDULE

**IN THE THIRTEENTH JUDICIAL CIRCUIT
HILLSBOROUGH COUNTY, FLORIDA**

ADMINISTRATIVE ORDER S–2018–022

(Supersedes Administrative Order S–2014–023)

UNIFORM BAIL BOND SCHEDULE

The uniform bail bond schedule has traditionally listed certain criminal offenses for which a person arrested is ineligible for release pending the first appearance hearing. Section 825.1035(11)(b), Florida Statutes (2018), provides that any person who is arrested for a violation of an injunction for protection against the exploitation of a vulnerable adult must be held in custody until brought before the court. Section 903.046, Florida Statutes, provides that any person arrested, who is a sexual offender or a sexual predator is not eligible for release on bail or a surety bond until the person's first appearance hearing, unless the arrest is for a misdemeanor offense under chapter 316, Florida Statutes. Section 947.141, Florida Statutes, requires that certain state supervised offenders who are arrested on a felony charge must be held for up to 72 hours pending a decision by the Florida Commission on Offender Review to issue a warrant charging the offender with violation of the conditions of release. It is necessary for the proper administration of justice to update the uniform bail bond schedule to reference these statutory provisions.

By the power vested in the chief judge under article V, section 2(d), Florida Constitution; section 43.26, Florida Statutes; and Florida Rule of Judicial Administration 2.215(b)(2), it is therefore **ORDERED:**

1. General. The following bail bond schedule is established so that persons arrested for certain criminal offenses may be released on a bail bond prior to the person's first appearance hearing. This schedule is not intended to bind any judge conducting first appearance hearings or bail bond hearings. When determining bail, judges should consider the criteria set out in section 903.046, Florida Statutes, and Florida Rule of Criminal Procedure 3.131.

2. First Appearance Hearing Required. The following persons who are arrested will not be released on a bail bond pending the arrested person's first appearance hearing. The judge presiding at the first appearance hearing will determine the appropriate amount of bail bond, if any.

- Anyone who at the time of arrest is known to be on pretrial release;
- Anyone who is determined to be on felony probation or felony community control;
- Anyone who is determined to be a sexual offender or a sexual predator unless the arrest is for a misdemeanor offense under chapter 316, Florida Statutes (§ 903.046(2)(m), Fla. Stat.);
- Anyone who is arrested for any of the criminal offenses listed below
    - Capital Felony
    - Life Felony
    - First Degree Felony Punishable by Life
    - Attempt/Solicitation/Conspiracy to Commit First Degree Murder
    - Carjacking
    - Sexual Battery
    - Escape
    - Attempt/Solicitation/Conspiracy to Commit Second Degree Murder
    - DUI Manslaughter
    - Retaliating Against a Witness (§ 914.23, Fla. Stat.)
    - Failure of Defendant on Bail to Appear (§ 843.15, Fla. Stat.)
    - Domestic Violence (§ 741.2901(3), Fla. Stat.)
    - Violation of Domestic Violence Injunction (§ 741.30(9)(b), Fla. Stat.)
    - Violation of Repeat Violence Injunction when the alleged violation involves repeat violence (§ 784.046(9)(b), Fla. Stat.)
    - Violation of Pretrial Release when original arrest was for domestic violence (§ 741.29(6), Fla. Stat.)
    - Violation of Injunction for Protection against Exploitation of a Vulnerable Adult (§ 825.1035(11), Fla. Stat. (2018))
    - Trafficking Offenses
    - Arson
    - Aggravated Child Abuse
    - Gang–Related Offenses (Ch. 874, Fla. Stat.)
- Any offender who is on release supervision under sections 947.1405, 947.146, 947.149, or 944.4731, Florida Statutes and who is arrested on a felony charge (§ 947.141(2), Fla. Stat.). If the first appearance judge determines there is probable cause for the arrest, the offender must continue to be detained without bond for up to 72 hours, pending a decision by the Florida Commission on Offender Review to issue a warrant charging the offender with violation of the conditions of release.

3. Warrants. Bail for persons arrested on a violation of probation warrant or a failure to appear warrant will be set in the amount provided for in the warrant itself. If the violation of probation warrant or failure to appear warrant is silent as to a bail bond amount, then there will be no bond, pending the arrested person's next appearance before the judge assigned to handle the violation of probation or failure to appear matter. Bail for arrest warrants will be set in the amount provided for in the warrant itself. If the arrest warrant is silent as to a bail bond amount, then the bail will be set in accordance with the provisions of this administrative order.

4. Schedule. Except as provided in sections 2 and 3 of this administrative order, any person arrested for a criminal offense may be released on a bail bond in an amount based on the designated classification and degree of the offense. Persons arrested for the following classifications and degrees of criminal offenses may be released on a bail bond in the corresponding amount:

First Degree Felony	$15,000
Second Degree Felony	$ 7,500
Third Degree Felony	$ 2,000
First Degree Misdemeanor & non-felony DUI	$ 500
Second Degree Misdemeanor	$ 250
City or County Ordinance Violation	$ 250

5. Previous Administrative Order Superseded. This administrative order supersedes Administrative Order S–2014–023 (*Uniform Bail Bond Schedule*).

6. Effective Date. This administrative order is effective July 1, 2018.

ENTERED in Tampa, Hillsborough County, Florida, on June 27, 2018.

Ronald N. Ficarrotta
Chief Judge

S–2017–037. DRUG COURT

IN THE THIRTEENTH JUDICIAL CIRCUIT HILLSBOROUGH COUNTY, FLORIDA

ADMINISTRATIVE ORDER S–2017–037

(Supersedes Administrative Order S–2010–013)

DRUG COURT

Section 397.334, Florida Statutes, codifies the Florida Legislature's intent to implement treatment-based drug court programs in each judicial circuit. In 1992, the Thirteenth Judicial Circuit first established the Drug Court division to serve as a specialized division of the Circuit Criminal Division.

It is necessary for the proper and efficient operation of the Thirteenth Judicial Circuit to update the administrative provisions in Drug Court.

By the power vested in the chief judge under article V, section 2(d), Florida Constitution; section 43.26, Florida Statutes; and Florida Rules of Judicial Administration 2.215(b)(2) and 2.215(e)(3), it is ORDERED:

1. Purpose. The purpose of the drug court division is to provide a non-adversarial forum, in addition to the pre-trial intervention program, whereby an individual who meets the eligibility criteria and voluntarily chooses to avail himself or herself of the benefits of drug court treatment may do so by pleading guilty and entering into a drug court treatment program as determined by the judge presiding in the drug court division.

2. Definitions. For purposes of this administrative order, the following terms have the following meanings:

A. *Co-defendant case* means two or more defendants charged, in the same case, with at least one drug offense (*e.g.* constructive possession of a controlled substance).

B. *Community sanctions* means probation, drug offender probation, community control, or community control II.

C. *Drug court model* means a case management system for drug offenses in which court-supervised drug treatment is used rather than litigation (*i.e.*, no trials or pre-trial motions). The treatment may include, but is not limited to, community sanctions, varying levels of drug treatment, and incarceration in accordance with the Criminal Punishment Code. The drug court model applies a protocol which includes the use of in-court substance abuse evaluators to aid the presiding judge in fashioning appropriate substance abuse treatment, conditions of community sanctions, and case reviews every four to six weeks as needed.

D. *Drug offense* means a felony violation of chapter 893, Florida Statutes.

E. *Drug treatment* means outpatient, intensive day-night, residential, or in-jail treatment programs.

F. *Felony* has the same meaning as provided in section 775.08(1), Florida Statutes.

G. *Forcible felony* means any felony listed in section 776.08, Florida Statutes.

H. *Guilty plea* means a plea of guilty to a criminal charge pursuant to Florida Rules of Criminal Procedure 3.170(a) and 3.172(d) in which the defendant either acknowledges his or her guilt or acknowledges that he or she feels the plea to be in his or her best interest.

I. *Non-violent felony* means a third degree felony violation of chapter 810 or any other felony offense that is not a forcible felony as defined in section 776.08, Florida Statutes.

J. *Standard division* means any of the following divisions of the Circuit Criminal Division: "A," "B," "C," "D," "E," "F," "G," and "I."

K. *Violent felony* means any forcible felony except a third degree felony violation of chapter 810.

L. *VOP* means violation of probation, violation of drug offender probation, violation of community control, or violation of community control II.

3. Drug Court Division "W"—Pre-Trial Intervention Program. Drug Court Division "W" serves as the pre-trial intervention program division. To be eligible for voluntary admission into Drug Court Division "W," a defendant must meet the following criteria: (a) be charged with a nonviolent felony; (b) identified as having a substance abuse problem; and (c) not previously been convicted of a felony.

Defendants will be required to enter into an agreement for treatment, but will not be required to enter a plea of guilty or *nolo contendere* to the charges that caused them to be assigned to drug court. Successful completion of the drug treatment program will result in dismissal of the charge(s) against the defendant. *See* § 948.08, Fla. Stat.

4. Drug Court Division "Y"—Post-adjudicatory Drug Court. Drug Court Division "Y" serves as the post-adjudicatory treatment-based drug court division handling eligible drug offenses. These drug offenses will be strictly managed by the presiding judge according to the traditional drug court model. Drug Court Division "Y" will handle all eligible cases through final disposition, including VOPs.

A. *Initial Case Filings.* All third degree felony drug offenses and all second degree felony purchase or possession of a controlled substance cases, except co-defendant cases, along with any accompanying non-violent felony offenses and misdemeanor offenses, will initially be filed in Drug Court Division "Y." All other drug offenses, including all co-defendant cases, will be filed in a standard division according to the assignment provisions in Administrative Order S–2017–009 (*Circuit Criminal Division*) or successor administrative orders.

B. *Drug Court Division "Y" Eligibility.* In order for a case to remain pending in Drug Court Division "Y" after the initial filing, the following criteria must be met: (a) the defendant has a substance abuse problem; (b) the defendant's Criminal Punishment Code scoresheet total sentence points are 60 points or fewer; (c) the current offense is a nonviolent felony; (d) the defendant wishes to participate in the drug court model; and (e) the defendant does not wish in any way to contest the criminal charges.

C. *Transfer to Drug Court Division "W".* Upon motion of either party or the court's own motion, if a defendant is eligible for the drug court pre-trial intervention program, the defendant's case(s) will be transferred from Drug Court Division "Y" to Drug Court Division "W."

5. Arraignments in Drug Court Division "Y".

A. *Information Provided to Defendant.* At arraignment, all police reports and Criminal Punishment Code scoresheets, including relevant prior criminal history, will be provided by the Office of the State Attorney to the defendant to afford the defendant a meaningful opportunity to discuss options with counsel, to be verified for eligibility, and to be evaluated by a court substance abuse evaluator if desired.

B. *Verification of Eligibility.* At arraignment, the presiding judge in Drug Court Division "Y" will verify that all cases meet the eligibility criteria for Drug Court Division "Y." If any case does not meet the eligibility criteria for Drug Court Division "Y," the judge will direct the clerk to transfer the case to a standard division for disposition.

C. *Defendant's Decision.* For those cases meeting the eligibility criteria for Drug Court Division "Y," at arraignment the defendant will either: (a) decide to contest the charges; (b) decide to participate in the drug court model; or (c) request more time to decide whether to contest the charges or to participate in the drug court model.

i. Decision to Contest Charges. If, at arraignment, the defendant decides to contest the charges, then the presiding judge in Drug Court Division "Y" will direct the clerk to transfer the case to a standard division for disposition.

ii. Decision to Participate in the Drug Court Model. If, at arraignment, the defendant decides to participate in the drug court model, the defendant must enter a guilty plea and then be set for sentencing.

iii. Request More Time for Decision. If, at arraignment, the defendant requests more time to decide whether to contest the charges or to participate in the drug court model, then the presiding judge in Drug Court Division "Y" may set a subsequent date to accept a plea. The subsequent date should be no more than 21 days from the date of arraignment, absent good cause shown. During this period, no pre-trial motions will be heard other than motions for pre-trial release or bond reductions.

a. Not Guilty Plea & Transfer of Case. If, on the subsequent plea date, the defendant decides to contest any charge and plead not guilty, then the judge will direct the clerk to transfer the case to a standard division for disposition.

b. Guilty Plea & Participation in the Drug Court Model. If, on the subsequent plea date, the defendant decides to participate in the drug court model, the defendant must enter a plea of guilty and then be set for sentencing.

6. Sentencing in Drug Court Division "Y". The defendant's sentence will be imposed by the presiding judge in Drug Court Division "Y" after the defendant is assessed at sentencing by a court substance abuse evaluator to determine appropriate treatment options. Except as provided in section 7 of this administrative order, any defendant sentenced in Drug Court Division "Y" will remain in Drug Court Division "Y" until final disposition of the case.

7. VOP in Drug Court Division "Y".

A. *Technical VOP.* If a VOP arises as a result of any violation that does not involve a new criminal charge, the presiding judge in Drug Court Division "Y" will handle the VOP in accordance with the drug court model to final disposition.

B. *Violent Felony Charges.* If a VOP arises as a result of a new violent felony charge, the new charge and corresponding VOP will be transferred from Drug Court Division "Y" to a standard division for disposition.

C. *Non–Violent Felony Charges.* If a VOP arises as a result of a new non-violent felony charge, the presiding judge in Drug Court Division "Y" will handle the VOP in accordance with the drug court model unless the defendant wishes to contest the new substantive charge. If the defendant decides to contest only the new substantive charge, then the presiding judge in Drug Court Division "Y" will direct the clerk to transfer the new substantive charge and corresponding VOP to a standard division for disposition. Otherwise, all VOPs will remain in Drug Court Division "Y."

8. Hearing for Entry or Denial Into Drug Court Division "Y". If there is an issue or question as to the defendant's eligibility for drug court in accordance with the law (i.e. substance abuse problem), or if the state does not recommend a defendant for admission to drug court under section 397.34, Florida Statutes, the court may hold a hearing to determine if the defendant will be allowed to enter or remain in Drug Court Division "Y,"

9. Co–Defendant Cases. All co-defendant cases will be initially filed in a standard division according to the assignment provisions in Administrative Order S–2017–009 (*Circuit Criminal Division*) or successor administrative orders.

A. *Discretionary Transfer to Drug Court Division "Y".* Any defendant in a co-defendant case may be transferred to Drug Court Division "Y" by the presiding judge in a standard division if such defendant meets the following criteria: (a) the defendant's Criminal Punishment Code scoresheet total sentence points are 60 points or fewer; (b) the current offense is a nonviolent felony; (c) the defendant wishes to participate in the drug court model; and (d) the defendant does not wish in any way to contest the criminal charges. If the presiding judge in a standard division decides to allow an eligible defendant in a codefendant case to be transferred to Drug Court Division "Y," the case will be transferred to Drug Court Division "Y" for acceptance of a guilty plea and sentencing.

B. *Disposition of Remaining Cases in Standard Division.* Any defendant in a co-defendant case who (a) does not have a Criminal Punishment Code scoresheet with total sentence points of 60 points or fewer; (b) has a violent felony offense pending; (c) does not wish to participate in the drug court model; or (d) desires in any way to contest the criminal charges will not be eligible for transfer to Drug Court Division "Y" and will remain in the standard division for disposition.

10. Transfer of Case From Another Division to Drug Court Division "Y".

A. *Transfers Generally.* If at any time the presiding judge in another division determines that (a) the defendant's

Criminal Punishment Code scoresheet total sentence points are 60 points or fewer; (b) the current offense is a nonviolent felony; (c) the defendant wishes to participate in the drug court model; and (d) the defendant does not wish in any way to contest the criminal charges, the judge may transfer the case to Drug Court Division "Y," subject to the limitation in section 11 of this administrative order. If a judge decides to transfer such a case in which a defendant has not entered a plea or has not been adjudicated for the pending criminal charge, the presiding judge will direct the clerk to transfer the case to Drug Court Division "Y" for acceptance of a guilty plea and sentencing. The clerk will place the case on the Drug Court Division docket within seven days.

B. *Transfer of Eligible Departure Sentences.* For offenses committed on or after July 1, 2009, if a defendant's offense is a non-violent felony, the defendant scores 60 points or fewer on the Criminal Punishment Code scoresheet, and the presiding judge determines that the defendant is amenable to the services of a post-adjudicatory treatment-based drug court, the judge may transfer the case to Drug Court Division "Y," subject to the limitation in section 11 of this administrative order. If a judge decides to transfer such a case to Drug Court Division "Y," the case will be transferred to Drug Court Division "Y" for acceptance of a guilty plea and sentencing.

C. *Transfer of Eligible VOP Cases From Division "K".* For any VOP ease pending in Circuit Criminal Division "K" in which the underlying offense was committed on or after July 1, 2009, the judge may transfer the VOP to Drug Court Division "Y," subject to the limitation in section 11 of this administrative order, if (a) a defendant's underlying offense is a non-violent felony; (b) the defendant scores 60 points or fewer on the Criminal Punishment Code scoresheet including violation points; and (c) the presiding judge in Division "K" determines that the defendant is amenable to the services of a post-adjudicatory treatment-based drug court. If the Division "K" judge decides to transfer such a case to Drug Court Division "Y," the case will be transferred to Drug Court Division "Y" for acceptance of an admission and sentencing or modification.

D. *Transfer of Certain Probation–Sentenced Cases.* If the presiding judge in another division determines that a defendant who has been sentenced to probation for a non-violent felony is particularly amenable to the services of a post-adjudicatory treatment-based drug court, the defendant scores 60 points or fewer on the Criminal Punishment Code scoresheet, and the presiding judge in Drug Court Division "Y" consents to the transfer of the case, the presiding judge in the other division may transfer the supervision of probation to Drug Court Division "Y."

11. Transfer of Case From Drug Court Division "Y" to a Standard Division. If a case is transferred from Drug Court Division "Y" to a standard division for any reason, such case will not be transferred back to Drug Court Division "Y" except with the consent of the presiding judge in Drug Court Division "Y."

All cases transferred from Drug Court Division "Y" to a standard division will be reassigned as provided in Administrative Order S–2017–009 (*Circuit Criminal Division*) or successor administrative orders, unless the case originated from a standard division. If a case is transferred into Drug Court Division "Y" from a standard division (*see* sections 9 and 10 of this administrative order) and is subsequently transferred out of Drug Court Division "Y," such case will be reassigned back to the standard division from which the case originated.

For any case transferred from Drug Court Division "Y," the clerk will provide notification in open court of the standard division to which the case is reassigned.

12. Acting County Court Judge. The judge assigned to Drug Court Division "Y" is appointed as an acting county court judge for the purpose of presiding over misdemeanor charges as specified in this administrative order.

13. Drug Court Oversight Committee. The Drug Court Oversight Committee will continue to oversee drug court operations in order to ensure proper training of court personnel and correct implementation of the drug court model. The committee is charged with recommending strategies to maintain the quality and effectiveness of drug court and to ensure that the many treatment options now available for drug court remain viable. The Drug Court Oversight Committee is comprised of representatives from the Public Defender' Office, State Attorney's Office, Administrative Office of the Courts, Community Corrections' Office of the Department of Corrections, Hillsborough County Sheriff's Office, treatment providers, and judicial representatives as determined by the chief judge.

14. Previous Administrative Order Superseded. This administrative order supersedes Administrative Order S–2010–013 (*Drug Court*).

15. Effective Date. This administrative order is effective June 1, 2017.

ENTERED in Tampa, Hillsborough County, Florida on May 30, 2017.

Ronald N. Ficarrotta, Chief Judge

S–2017–009. CIRCUIT CRIMINAL DIVISION

IN THE THIRTEENTH JUDICIAL CIRCUIT HILLSBOROUGH COUNTY, FLORIDA

ADMINISTRATIVE ORDER S–2017–009

(Supersedes Administrative Order S–2016–062)

CIRCUIT CRIMINAL DIVISION

It is necessary to update the provisions in the Circuit Criminal Division in order to clarity the eligibility criteria of the newly-established Mental Health Criminal Division.

By the power vested in the chief judge under article V, section 2(d), Florida Constitution; section 43.26, Florida Statutes; and Florida Rule of Judicial Administration 2.215(b)(2), it is ORDERED:

1. Definitions. For purposes of this administrative order, the following terms have the following meanings:

A. *Capital sexual battery* means a violation of section 794.011(2)(a), Florida Statutes.

B. *Co-defendant case* means two or more defendants charged, in the same case, with at least one felony offense.

C. *Drug court division* means Circuit Criminal Division "W" (Pre–Trial Drug Court Intervention) or Division "Y" (Drug Court Model).

D. *Drug court model* means a case management system for drug offenses in which court supervised drug treatment is used rather than litigation (*i.e.*, no trials or pre-trial motions). The treatment may include community sanctions, varying levels of drug treatment and incarceration in accordance with the Criminal Punishment Code. The drug court model applies a protocol which includes the use of in-court substance abuse evaluators to aid the presiding judge in fashioning appropriate substance abuse treatment, conditions of community sanctions, and case reviews every four to six weeks as needed.

E. *Drug offense* means a felony violation of chapter 893, Florida Statutes.

F. *Even distribution* means, in the context of case assignments, a system where each standard division receives the appropriate number of cases within each of the five categories of cases (capital, RICO, capital sexual battery, appeals, and all other types) so that the difference between newly-assigned cases in any two standard divisions is not more than one.

G. *Felony* has the same meaning as provided in section 775.08(1), Florida Statutes.

H. *Pending case* means a case in which any matter is pending before the court after an indictment or information is filed or any case in which a probation or community control sentence is still in effect. A probation or community control sentence is not considered "still in effect" if such sentence has been terminated early.

I. *Proposed Division.*

i. Proposed Division for Capital. RICO and Capital Sexual Battery Cases. *Proposed division* for capital, RICO, and capital sexual battery cases means an assignment of a standard division based on an even distribution made by the Clerk of the Circuit Court (clerk) upon the filing of a criminal report affidavit after arrest. This term also means an assignment of a standard division for capital, RICO, and capital sexual battery cases based on an even distribution by the clerk at the request of the State Attorney's Office (state attorney's office) upon the referral of a criminal investigation to the state attorney's office prior to an arrest, i.e. direct file cases.

ii. Proposed Division for All Other Cases. *Proposed division* for all non-capital, non–RICO, and non-capital sexual battery cases means an assignment of a standard division based on an even distribution made by the clerk upon the filing of a criminal report affidavit after arrest. This term also means an assignment of a standard division made by the clerk at the request of the state attorney's office upon the referral of a criminal investigation to the state attorney's office prior to an arrest, i.e. direct file cases.

J. *Specialized division* means any of the following Circuit Criminal Divisions: Division "J" (Post–Conviction Relief Matters), Division "K" (Violation of Probation and Community Control), Division "M" (Mental Health Court), Division "O" (First Appearance / Emergency) or Division "V" (Veterans Treatment Court).

K. *Standard division* means any of the following Circuit Criminal Divisions: Division "A," Division "B," Division "C," Division "D," Division "E," Division "F," Division "G," or Division "I."

L. *Trial division* means any of the following Circuit Criminal Divisions: Trial Division 1, Trial Division 2, or Trial Division 3.

M. *VOP* means violation of probation, violation of drug offender probation, violation of community control, violation of community control II, and violation of juvenile commitment or violation of juvenile community control imposed as a consequence of a juvenile having been sentenced as an adult.

2. Division "J"—Postconviction Relief Matters.

A. *Motions Scheduled and Disposed of in Division "J".* The following motions filed on and after the effective date of this administrative order will be scheduled and disposed of in Circuit Criminal Division "J":

- All initial motions seeking postconviction relief in accordance with Florida Rule of Criminal Procedure 3.850 and all related motions (*e.g.* motions to appoint counsel and motions for rehearing); and
- All motions seeking postconviction relief by defendants who have been sentenced to death in accordance with Florida Rules of Criminal Procedure 3.851 and 3.852 and all related motions (e.g. motions for competency evaluations).

B. *Motions Assigned to and Disposed of in the Division in which the Case was Last Pending.* The following motions filed on and after the effective date of this administrative order will be assigned to and disposed of in the division in which the case was last pending:

- All motions seeking to correct, modify or reduce a sentence in accordance with Florida Rules of Criminal Procedure 3.800(a), 3.800(b), 3.800(c), and all related motions (*e.g.* motions to set hearings and motions to appoint counsel);
- All motions seeking a correction of jail credit in accordance with Florida Rule of Criminal Procedure 3.801;
- All motions seeking postconviction DNA testing in accordance with Florida Rule of Criminal Procedure 3.853;
- All motions related to initial Rule 3.850 motions filed on or before February 29, 2016 (*e.g.* motions to set hearings and motions to appoint counsel); and
- Any other matter that reopens or addresses a closed case.

3. Division "K"—Violation of Probation.

A. *Technical Violation.* All VOP matters arising in any standard division as a result of any alleged violation not involving a new felony charge will be scheduled and disposed of in Circuit Criminal Division "K."

B. *New Misdemeanor Charge Violation.* All other VOP matters arising in any standard division as a result of any alleged violation involving a new misdemeanor charge, including the new misdemeanor charge, will be scheduled and disposed of in Division "K." If a defendant is on felony probation and misdemeanor probation when a new misdemeanor charge is allegedly committed by the defendant, any VOP arising in a county criminal division will be scheduled and disposed of in Division "K." The judge assigned to Division "K." is hereby appointed as an acting county court judge for the purpose of presiding over such misdemeanor charges.

C. *Proposed Warrant.* For standard division cases, all proposed warrants for any technical VOP and for any alleged violation involving a new misdemeanor charge, should be presented to the judge assigned to Division "K" for review and action.

D. *New Felony Charge Violation.* Any VOP matter arising in a standard division as a result of any alleged violation involving a new felony charge will be filed and disposed of in the standard division in which the case was last pending. Any VOP matter arising in a standard division as a result of any alleged violation involving a new felony charge and an alleged technical violation will be filed and disposed of in the standard division in which the case was last pending.

E. *Violation in Drug Court Case.* All VOP matters arising in Circuit Criminal Division "Y" as a result of any alleged violation will be filed and disposed of in Division "Y" and handled according to the administrative provisions for Drug Court.

4. Division "M"—Mental Health Court. Mental Health Criminal Division "M," colloquially known as Mental Health Court, provides court-supervised diversion for eligible defendants who are identified as having a mental illness into available mental health treatment programs in accordance with an agreement between the defendant and the State Attorney's Office. In light of limited resources, the presiding judge of Mental Health Court is empowered to suspend the transfer or filing of eligible cases into the Mental Health Court if the pending criminal caseload in Mental Health Court reaches 40 cases.

5. Division "V"—Veterans Treatment Court. Veterans Treatment Court—consisting of both a pretrial intervention program component and a post-adjudicatory component—diverts eligible veterans with service-related issues into available treatment programs for veterans without compromising the safety of the public. For more information on Division "V," see Administrative Order S–2015–012 or successor administrative orders.

6. Division "W"—Pre-Trial Drug Intervention. Drug Court Division "W" is the pre-trial intervention program division available to defendants who have been charged with a third degree felony drug offense and who have not been previously adjudicated guilty of a felony. Defendants will be required to enter into an agreement for drug treatment, but will not be required to enter a plea of guilty or *nolo contendere* to the charges that caused them to be assigned to drug court. Successful completion of the drug treatment program will result in dismissal of the charge(s) against the defendant. *See* § 948.08, Fla. Stat. For more information on Division "W," see Administrative Order S–2010–013 or successor administrative orders.

7. Division "Y"—Drug Court Model. Drug Court Division "Y" is the drug court division to handle eligible drug offenses. These drug offenses will be strictly managed by the presiding judge according to the traditional drug court model. Division "Y" will handle all eligible cases (as provided in the administrative order on drug court, Administrative Order S–2010–013 or successor administrative orders) through final disposition, including VOPs.

8. Administrative and Associate Administrative Judges. An administrative judge is designated to assist with the administrative supervision of the Circuit Criminal Division. Associate administrative judges are designated to assist with the administrative supervision of the standard divisions, the drug court divisions and the specialized divisions. The administrative judge and associate administrative judges are designated by a separate administrative order.

9. Assignment of Cases.

A. *Division "O".*

i. Criminal Report Affidavit and Arrest. Upon the filing of a criminal report affidavit and booking of a defendant through the Hillsborough County Sheriff's Office, the clerk will designate a sequential case number, designate a proposed division, and assign the case to Division "O." The clerk will notate these designations and assignment in the progress docket of the case. All matters will remain assigned to Division "O" until a charging decision has been made by the state attorney's office or grand jury. If an information is filed, the clerk will then transfer the case to a circuit criminal division as provided in this administrative order.

ii. Direct File Cases. If the state attorney's office files an information prior to the arrest of a defendant (direct file cases), the clerk will designate a sequential case number, reveal the proposed division, and assign the case to Division "O." The clerk will notate the proposed division in the progress docket of the case. The clerk will transfer the case to a circuit criminal division after the defendant has been arrested and booked on that case.

iii. Indictments. If the state attorney's office files an indictment prior to the arrest of a defendant, in accordance with section 905.26, Florida Statutes, the clerk will not disclose that an indictment has been filed until the defendant has been arrested. Once an indicted defendant is arrested, the clerk will publicly designate a sequential case number, designate a proposed division, notate the designated proposed division in the progress docket of the case, and assign the case to Division "O" for the first appearance hearing. Thereafter, the clerk will transfer the case to the assigned circuit criminal division.

B. *Circuit Criminal Division Assignment.* Simultaneous with the filing of any indictment or information, the state attorney's office will notify the clerk in writing if any named defendant has any pending case, and if so, the division to which the pending case is assigned. Using the information provided to the clerk by the state attorney's office, the clerk will transfer a case from Division "O" to a circuit criminal division using the following process:

i. First Degree Murder. All newly filed cases charging first degree murder will be assigned to the division that was identified as the proposed division. All pending cases involving any defendant charged in the indictment will be transferred to the division to which the first degree murder case is assigned.

ii. RICO. All newly filed cases charging RICO will be assigned to the division that was identified as the proposed division. All pending cases involving any defendant charged in the indictment or information will be transferred to the division to which the RICO case is assigned.

iii. Capital Sexual Battery. All newly filed cases charging capital sexual battery will be assigned to the division that was identified as the proposed division. All pending cases involving any defendant charged in the indictment or information will be transferred to the division to which the capital sexual battery case is assigned.

iv. Third Degree Felony Drug Offense. All newly filed eligible third degree felony drug offenses will be assigned to Division "Y" in accordance with Administrative Order S–2010–013 (*Drug Court*) or any successor administrative order.

v. All Other Cases.

a. Single Defendant, No Pending Case(s). If the defendant has no co-defendants and no pending cases, the newly filed case will be assigned to the division that was identified as the proposed division. In the event of multiple proposed divisions, the newly filed case will be assigned to the division that was the earliest assigned proposed division.

b. Single Defendant, Pending Case(s). If the defendant has no co-defendants, but does have a pending case or cases, the newly filed case will be assigned to the division that has the lowest pending case number. All of the defendant's pending cases will be transferred to the assigned division if necessary.

c. Co–Defendants, No Pending Case(s). If a newly filed case involves co-defendants, none of whom has a pending case, the newly filed case will be assigned to the division that was identified as the proposed division. In the event of multiple proposed divisions, the newly filed case will be assigned to the division that was the earliest assigned proposed division.

d. Co–Defendants, Pending Case(s). If a newly filed case involves co-defendants, any one of whom has a pending case, the newly filed case will be assigned to the division that has the lowest pending case number. All co-defendants' pending cases will be transferred to the assigned division if necessary. If co-defendants have pending cases in different divisions, all pending cases will be transferred to the division that has the lowest pending case number.

C. *Re–Filed Cases.* Whenever any case assigned to a division of the Circuit Criminal Division is dismissed by the state attorney's office (*nolle prossed*) and is thereafter re-filed, the re-filed case will be assigned to the division to which the case was originally assigned. The state attorney's office must identify in writing to the clerk the division to which the case was originally assigned.

D. *Appeals.* Upon the filing of a notice of appeal from a county court criminal division, the clerk will designate a sequential case number and assign the appeal to a standard division in the Circuit Criminal Division based on an even distribution.

E. *Habeas Corpus Petitions.* All habeas corpus petitions will be assigned to the Circuit Criminal Division in which the underlying case was last pending except petitions involving custody of minors who have not been charged as adults and petitions filed under the provisions of "The Baker Act." Petitions involving custody of minors who have not been charged as adults will be assigned to the Juvenile Delinquency Division. Petitions filed under the provisions of "The Baker Act" will be assigned to the Probate, Guardianship, Mental Health and Trust Division.

F. *Second District Court of Appeal Commissioner Petitions.* All belated appeal petitions, and any other matter referred to the chief judge by the Second District Court of Appeal for appointment of a commissioner, will be assigned to the judge presiding in Division "J" unless the presiding judge of Division "J" is ineligible. If the judge presiding in Division "J" is not eligible to be a commissioner in a particular case because of the appellate court's criteria, the administrative judge of the Circuit Criminal Division will be assigned as the commissioner of the Second District Court of Appeal.

10. Reassignment Upon Disqualification.

A. *Standard Division.* If any judge presiding in a standard division enters an order of disqualification, the clerk will reassign the case to one of the other standard divisions based on an even distribution.

B. *Drug Court or Specialized Division.* If any judge presiding in a drug court division or a specialized division enters an order of disqualification, the clerk will reassign the case to the standard division in which the case would have been pending if not for the establishment of the drug court division or specialized division. If the case was transferred from a standard division to a drug court division or specialized division, the clerk will reassign the case back to the standard division from which the case was previously transferred.

C. *Trial Division.* If any judge presiding in a trial division enters an order of disqualification, the clerk will reassign the case back to the standard division from which the case was previously transferred to the trial division.

11. Identification of Court Reporters. The clerk must ensure that the names of court reporters and the names of court reporting entities, if applicable, are captured in the progress docket for all court proceedings.

12. Bond Reduction and Release on Recognizance.

A. *Criminal Case.* If defense counsel seeks either the reduction of bond or release on recognizance, defense counsel will contact the assistant state attorney assigned to the case or that attorney's immediate supervisor. If counsel are able to stipulate to the conditions of a defendant's release, such stipulation will be reduced to writing and delivered to the office of the presiding judge for consideration and approval. If the presiding judge is not available, the stipulation will be presented to the administrative judge of the Circuit Criminal Division or the administrative judge's designee for consideration and approval. When counsel are unable to stipulate to the conditions of a defendant's release, defense counsel may schedule a hearing with the presiding judge and file an application for modification of bail with notice of hearing in accordance with Florida Rule of Criminal Procedure 3.131(d)(2).

B. *VOP Matter.* In cases involving an alleged VOP, applications for modification of bail will be submitted to the judge assigned to the division in which the alleged violation is pending or scheduled. Applications for modification of bail in such cases will not be heard at first appearance or in Division "O" without the specific concurrence of the judge assigned the violation, or in that judge's absence, the administrative judge of the Circuit Criminal Division, an associate administrative judge or the chief judge. If defense counsel schedules a hearing for the reduction of bond or release on recognizance, defense counsel will notify the defendant's probation officer of the scheduled hearing so that probation information can be made available for the hearing.

13. Arraignments.

A. *Written Notice.* The clerk will provide written notice of arraignment to defendants who are not incarcerated as well as all surety and counsel of record. The clerk will provide written notice of the trial date or disposition date as well as any scheduled pre-trial conference date to all defendants, defense counsel and surety.

B. *Timely Hearings.* Each circuit criminal division will handle arraignments involving incarcerated defendants on a timely basis. The arraignment hearings must be scheduled by the clerk and set to be heard on the respective judge's docket within seven days (excluding weekends and holidays) after the filing of the information or indictment. If an indictment or information has been filed prior to the arrest of a defendant, arraignment hearings must be scheduled by the clerk and set to be heard on the respective judge's docket within seven days (excluding weekends and holidays) after the arrest of the defendant.

C. *Monthly Report.* The clerk will provide a monthly report to the chief judge indicating, by circuit criminal division, any case involving an incarcerated defendant where the clerk is unable to schedule the arraignment hearing within the prescribed time. The report will include the name of the defendant, the case number, and the reason for non-compliance. If all incarcerated defendants in a circuit criminal division are arraigned within the 7–day time period, the report should include a statement to this effect.

14. Score Sheet, Plea Offer, and Police Report. Whenever possible, the state attorney's office will prepare a criminal punishment code score sheet and furnish a copy of it together with a plea offer to defense counsel at or prior to arraignment. Likewise, the state attorney's office should provide a copy of any available police reports to defense counsel at arraignment.

15. Revocation of Probation or Community Control Involving Incarcerated Defendants.

A. *Timely Hearings.* Each circuit criminal division will handle first time hearings on revocations of probation or community control involving incarcerated defendants on a timely basis. The revocation hearings must be scheduled by the clerk and set to be heard on the respective judge's docket no later than seven working days (excluding weekends and holidays) after the arrest of the defendant.

B. *Monthly Report.* The clerk will provide a monthly report to the chief judge indicating, by circuit criminal division, any case involving an incarcerated defendant where the clerk is unable to schedule such a revocation hearing within the prescribed time. The report will include the name of the defendant, the case number, and the reason for non-compliance. If all incarcerated defendants in a circuit criminal division are able to have their revocation hearings scheduled within the 7–day time period, the report should include a statement to this effect.

16. Plea Agreements. If the assistant state attorney and the defense counsel or unrepresented defendant reach a plea agreement, the case will be placed on the assigned judge's calendar as quickly as possible for a change of plea.

17. Motions.

A. *Time of Hearing.* All motions will be heard prior to pre-trial conference unless such opportunity did not exist or the defendant was not aware of the grounds for the motion prior to the pre-trial conference. If there is no pre-trial conference, then motions will be heard prior to the date of the trial. The court in its discretion, however, may entertain any motion at any time.

B. *Scheduling of Hearing.* Prior to filing any motion and scheduling a hearing with the assigned judge, counsel should consult with opposing counsel as to the date and the time required for such hearing. Counsel will contact the judicial assistant of the assigned judge and obtain a hearing time.

C. *Timely Notice of Hearing.* Except for demands for speedy trial and motions for discharge, all motions must be filed simultaneously with a notice of hearing containing the scheduled hearing time. Counsel must file all motions and attached notices of hearing no later than 12:00 noon the day preceding the scheduled hearing. All matters not in compliance with this requirement will not appear on the calendar and will be deemed abandoned until properly noticed.

D. *Submission of Legal Authority.* All legal authority relied upon in support of the motion should be provided to the court and opposing party at least three days prior to the motion hearing.

E. *Response From State Attorney.* A copy of any motion which is subject to a traverse, demurrer, or other responsive pleading by the state attorney should be delivered to and received by the assistant state attorney assigned to the case or that attorney's immediate supervisor at least five working days prior to any scheduled hearing. A copy of the traverse, demurrer, or other responsive pleading should be delivered to and received by the defense counsel at least two working days prior to the hearing. It is suggested that hand delivery or electronic mail be utilized by all counsel.

18. Orders.

A. *Submission of Proposed Orders and Judgments.*

i. Judicial Automated Workflow System (JAWS)—All Parties Represented by Counsel. Unless the presiding judge directs otherwise, if all parties are represented by attorneys, none of whom have been excused from e-mail service under Florida Rule of Judicial Administration 2.516, an attorney who is requested to submit a proposed order or judgment must do so through the JAWS. Prior to submitting a proposed order or judgment, the attorney must review the presiding judge's webpage to determine that judge's format preference. Attorneys must comply with the presiding judge's formatting preference (Microsoft Word v. PDF) when submitting a proposed order or judgment through the JAWS.

ii. Hard Copies and Envelopes—Self–Represented Party or Party's Attorney Excused from E–Service. If any party is self-represented or represented by an attorney who has been excused from e-mail service by the court under Rule 2.516, the party or attorney who is requested to submit a proposed order or judgment will do so by submitting to the presiding judge sufficient hard copies of the proposed order or judgment along with stamped, addressed envelopes.

B. *Title.* All proposed orders will contain, in the title of the order, the exact nature of the court's ruling and must fairly apprise the reader of the action being ordered. Phrasing such as "order granting . . ." or "order denying . . ." is preferred over "order on . . ."

C. *Form.* No proposed order will be submitted to a judge unless such order contains in the body of the order a reference to the date(s) of the hearing during which the subject matter of the order was argued before the court and the names of the parties and counsel present.

D. *Objections.* Any attorney or party who objects to the entry of a proposed order which has been submitted to the presiding judge must immediately notify the judge's office via telephone or e-mail. If the objection notification is made by e-mail, the opposing attorney or party must be copied on the e-mail message. The objecting attorney or party must submit an alternative proposed order within two days of communicating the objection. If an alternative proposed order has not been received by the court within two days, the court will consider the objection withdrawn.

19. Speedy Trial. Demands for speedy trial, notices of expiration of speedy trial time, and motions for discharge will automatically be calendared by the clerk within five days of filing. Within 24 hours of the filing of a demand for speedy trial, a notice of expiration of speedy trial time, or a motion for discharge, the clerk will notify the presiding judge of the filing.

20. Depositions. No deposition or any part of a deposition will be accepted by the clerk for filing unless accompanied by a written certificate stating the contents are necessary for the decision of a matter pending before the court.

21. Competency and Involuntary Hospitalization Hearings.

A. *Appointment of Mental Health Experts.* Upon the granting of either a motion to determine competency or motion to determine the need for involuntary hospitalization, the assigned judge will appoint at least two mental health experts from an approved list compiled by the Administrative Office of the Courts to examine the defendant and set the matter for further hearing.

B. *Timely Submission of Evaluation Report.* Unless otherwise required by the court, the examining mental health experts need not be present at the scheduled hearing if the expert has electronically submitted to both the court and counsel the evaluation report at least 24 hours in advance of the scheduled hearing.

C. *Need for Evidentiary Hearing.* If counsel are unable to stipulate to the admission of the evaluation reports as evidence, the matter will be set for a further evidentiary hearing and the examining mental health experts will be notified that their presence is required for such hearing.

22. Appearance and Withdrawal. The appearance of an attorney and termination of the appearance of an attorney must comply with Florida Rule of Judicial Administration 2.505. If a defendant discharges counsel, it will be the responsibility of that defendant to either proceed as a self-represented party or obtain substitute counsel in sufficient time to meet established trial dates or other scheduled proceedings.

23. Continuance Policy.

A. *Uniform Motions and Orders.* Florida Rule of Judicial Administration 2.545(e) requires all judges to apply a firm continuance policy. To implement this policy and provide accountability for continuances, uniform motions for continuance and uniform orders on motions for continuance will be used. Uniform motions for continuance and orders on motions for continuance can be found at www.fljud13.org. Counsel seeking a continuance must file a uniform motion for continuance and notice of hearing and must be present for hearing on the motion.

B. *No Continuances Based Solely on Stipulations.* No trial, hearing, or other proceeding will be continued upon stipulation of counsel alone.

C. *Timing of Filing and Hearing.* All motions for continuance of a trial or VOP hearing will be filed and heard prior to the scheduled trial or VOP hearing date.

D. *Failure to Complete Discovery.* Failure to complete discovery will not constitute cause for a continuance unless such failure is brought to the attention of the court at least five working days in advance of any scheduled trial or hearing date and is not the result of lack of diligence in pursuing such discovery. Except for good cause shown, no continuance will be granted because a witness has not been served with a subpoena, unless the moving party has attempted service at least five working days before the return date.

24. Witness and Exhibit Lists. Prior to the commencement of trial or at such other time as the court may direct, counsel will file written witness and exhibit lists with the courtroom clerk and provide copies to the presiding judge, court reporter, and opposing counsel.

25. Jury Instructions. Prior to the commencement of jury selection or at such other time as the court may direct, counsel will provide to the court and opposing counsel all requested jury instructions.

26. Trial Weeks.

A. *Trial Docket.* Each standard division will schedule weekly trial dockets in accordance with the trial calendar published by the administrative judge of the Circuit Criminal Division. The trial calendar may be modified by the assigned judge if deemed necessary. If a division's trial docket is not taken up with its own cases, the judge of that division will be available to try cases which cannot be reached in other divisions.

B. *Availability of Trial Divisions.* Each trial division will be available on a weekly basis to handle the trials of cases transferred from the standard divisions. On those occasions when a trial division's docket is not taken up with the trial of cases, the trial division judge will notify the administrative judge and be available, as determined by the administrative judge, to preside and handle any matters on a circuit criminal division's calendar. If there are no circuit criminal division matters to be handled by the trial division, the trial division judge will then notify all judges of the circuit and county courts and be available, as determined by the administrative judge, to handle any and all matters as needed.

27. Calendar Assistance. If a division's calendar is not taken up with its own cases, that judge will notify all judges in the Circuit Criminal Division of his or her availability to assist with the handling of any matters on a calendar. If none of the Circuit Criminal Divisions require assistance, then that judge will notify all judges of the circuit and county courts and be available, as determined by the administrative judge, to handle any and all matters as needed.

28. Cases Transferred for Trial.

A. *Pre–Trial Motions.* Once a case is transferred by a standard division to a trial division or other division for trial, no pre-trial motions will be entertained by the judge to whom the case has been transferred for trial unless the judge consents to doing so.

B. *Sentencing Matters.* Once a case has been transferred for trial to another division, the division to which the case has been transferred will be responsible for sentencing hearings, retrials, re-sentencing hearings and any post-trial motions affecting the sentence filed in accordance with Rule of Criminal Procedure 3.800.

C. *Post–Conviction Motions.* Trial divisions will not consider motions under Florida Rules of Criminal Procedure 3.801, 3.850, 3.851, or 3.853. See section 2 of this administrative order.

D. *Re–Trials.* If a mistrial is declared or the Second District Court of Appeal remands a case for re-trial, any retrial will be held in the division in which the trial was held unless another division judge is available and agrees to conduct the re-trial.

E. *VOP Matters.* Except as provided in section 3 of this administrative order, all VOP hearings will be heard in the division in which the case was originally assigned unless the sentencing judge is available and agrees to handle the VOP matter.

29. Time–Served Sentences. Whenever a defendant who is in custody is sentenced to "time served," the defendant will be released from custody immediately upon completion of out-processing from the Hillsborough County Jail. Out-processing will be completed as soon as possible upon the return of the defendant from court to the jail facility and will include the determination of outstanding warrants, capiases, or other lawful orders detaining the defendant on other charges; verification of identification; and return of property.

30. Court Information to be Provided to Sheriff. The clerk must ensure the Sheriffs Office Detention Department receives on a daily basis all information captured by the clerk during all court proceedings for each Circuit Criminal Division.

31. Court–Appointed Private Attorneys. Court-appointed private attorneys must follow the procedures for payment of fees and costs promulgated by the Justice Administrative Commission ("JAC"), which may be accessed at http://www.justiceadmin.org.

32. Emergency Matters.

A. *Assigned Judge.* All circuit criminal division judges will be available to handle emergency matters arising in their respective divisions during normal business hours unless arrangements have been made with another judge to substitute during any absence. Any matter arising under Florida Rule of Criminal Procedure 3.191 (*Speedy Trial*) is considered an emergency matter. The administrative judge of the Circuit Criminal Division will handle emergency matters if the assigned or substitute judge is not available. If the administrative judge is absent from the courthouse, emergency matters will be presented to an associate administrative judge. If the associate administrative judges are absent from the courthouse, emergency matters will be presented to the duty judge assigned for that particular week. (*See* www.fljud13.org for duty judge assignments).

B. *Assigned Assistant Public Defender and Assistant State Attorney.* The Public Defender and State Attorney will ensure that at least one assistant public defender and one assistant state attorney are assigned by their respective offices to handle emergency matters arising during non-business hours. The Sheriff's Office will maintain the respective emergency duty mobile telephone numbers of the Public Defender's Office and the State Attorney's Office for use by the duty judge.

33. Sealing or Expunging Criminal Records.

A. *Assignment of Petition.* All petitions to expunge or seal criminal records in accordance with sections 943.0583, 943.0585, or 943.059 will be filed in the division in which the underlying criminal case was last pending. Petitions must include all applicable case numbers. If the state has not filed a traverse or demurrer in accordance with Florida Rule of Criminal Procedure 3.692 within 14 days from the date of service of the petition, the clerk will present the petition to the administrative judge for entry of an appropriate order. If the state has timely filed a traverse or demurrer, the clerk will present the petition and the state's response to the judge presiding in the division in which the petition is pending.

B. *Report of Unpaid Fees. Charges, and Costs.* Prior to the court signing an order granting expunction or sealing of a criminal history record or any part of a criminal history record, the clerk will report to the assigned judge the amount of all court-related fees, charges and costs unpaid in the case.

C. *Felony Reduced to a Misdemeanor.* If a felony criminal report affidavit is reduced to a misdemeanor and filed in the county court, that affidavit will also be sealed or expunged by the clerk and law enforcement agencies upon the entry of an order sealing or expunging the misdemeanor case which states both case numbers.

D. *Public Defender to Receive Copy of Order.* The clerk will provide to the public defender a certified copy of all orders to expunge or seal criminal history records.

34. Professional Conduct and Courtroom Decorum. Counsel will adhere to The Florida Bar's Guidelines for Professional Conduct (http://www.floridabar.org). The Florida Bar's Professionalism Expectations (http://www.floridabar.org) and the Hillsborough County Bar Association's Standards of Professional Courtesy (http://www.hillsbar.com). Each judge may announce and enforce additional requirements, or may excuse compliance with any provision(s) of the Guidelines, Expectations, or Standards as that judge deems appropriate.

35. Previous Administrative Order Superseded. This administrative order supersedes Administrative Order S–2016–062 (*Circuit Criminal Division Procedures*).

36. Effective Date. This administrative order is effective April 1, 2017.

ENTERED in Tampa, Hillsborough County, Florida on March 15, 2017.

Ronald N. Ficarrotta, Chief Judge

S–2016–032. VETERANS TREATMENT COURT

IN THE THIRTEENTH JUDICIAL CIRCUIT HILLSBOROUGH COUNTY, FLORIDA

ADMINISTRATIVE ORDER S–2016–032

(Supersedes Administrative Order S–2015–012)

VETERANS TREATMENT COURT

In furtherance of implementing provisions of the "T. Patt Maney Veterans' Treatment Intervention Act" (sections 16–20 of Chapter 2012–159, Laws of Florida), it is necessary and appropriate to make changes to the current Hillsborough County Veterans Court to focus on a greater number of veterans suffering from military-service related mental illness, traumatic brain injury, substance abuse disorder, or psychological problems who enter the criminal justice system.

Consolidation of the separate misdemeanor and felony veterans treatment courts will facilitate continued effective and efficient operation of a Veterans Treatment Court. This consolidated specialized Veterans Treatment Court will enable consideration of the unique nature of the issues related to veterans, the need for appropriate treatment in an environment conducive to wellness, as well as the continuing necessity to ensure the protection of the public.

The Veterans Treatment Court will expeditiously and efficiently divert veterans with service-related issues into available veteran treatment programs without compromising the safety of the public. This specialized court division will increase the efficiency of the criminal court system and permit access to state, local and federal services and resources by utilizing Veterans Administration and Veteran Mentor Volunteer resources and support systems.

The Veterans Treatment Court consists of both a Pretrial Intervention Program component and a Post–Adjudicatory component.

By the authority vested in the chief judge under article V, section 2(d), Florida Constitution; section 43.26, Florida Statutes; and Florida Rule of Judicial Administration 2.215(b)(2), it is therefore **ORDERED:**

1. Establishment. Circuit Criminal Division "V" is hereby established as the Veterans Treatment Court division handling all eligible cases.

2. Limited Caseload. Subject to the availability of resources, the presiding Veterans Treatment Court judge is empowered with discretion to temporarily suspend the transfer or direct filing of any eligible cases into the Veterans Treatment Court. If the presiding judge decides to temporarily suspend the transfer or direct filing of any future eligible cases into Veterans Treatment Court, the judge must provide written notice of the suspension to the Public Defender's Office, the State Attorney's Office, the Clerk of Court (clerk), the Veterans Administration, the administrative judge of Circuit Criminal Division, and the chief judge.

3. Eligibility Criteria for Pretrial Intervention Program. In order to participate in the Pretrial Intervention Program component of the Veterans Treatment Court, a defendant must meet the following criteria:

A. *Misdemeanor Cases—section 948.16, Florida Statutes*

i. Veteran or Servicemember. The defendant is a veteran, as defined in section 1.01, Florida Statutes, including a veteran who is discharged or released under a general discharge, or a servicemember, as defined in section 250.01, Florida Statutes.

ii. Service–Related Condition. The defendant suffers from a military service-related mental illness, traumatic brain injury, substance abuse disorder, or psychological problem.

iii. Voluntary Participation. The defendant voluntarily agrees to participate in the Veterans Treatment Court for a period of time based on the program's requirements and the treatment plan for the offender.

iv. Eligible Criminal Offenses. The defendant is charged with a city ordinance violation, a county ordinance violation, or a misdemeanor offense.

v. Second Chance Denial. The court may deny the defendant admission into the misdemeanor pretrial veterans treatment intervention program if the defendant has previously entered a court-ordered veterans treatment program.

B. *Felony Cases—section 948.08, Florida Statutes*

i. Veteran or Servicemember. The defendant is a veteran, as defined in section 1.01, Florida Statutes, including a veteran who is discharged or released under a general discharge, or a servicemember, as defined in section 250.01, Florida Statutes.

ii. Service–Related Condition. The defendant suffers from a military service-related mental illness, traumatic brain injury, substance abuse disorder, or psychological problem.

iii. Voluntary Participation. The defendant is eligible for voluntary admission into the pretrial Veterans Treatment Court upon motion of either party or the court's own motion.

iv. Eligible Criminal Offenses. The defendant is charged with a felony, other than a felony listed in section 948.06(8)(c), Florida Statutes.

v. Second Chance Denial. The court may deny the defendant admission into the pretrial veterans treatment intervention program if (1) the defendant was previously offered admission to a pretrial veterans treatment intervention program at any time before trial and the defendant rejected that offer on the record; or (2) the defendant has previously entered a court-ordered veterans treatment program.

C. *Veterans Administration Services or Other Resources.* The defendant must be eligible to receive services for evaluation and treatment planning through the Veterans Administration and Veteran Mentor Volunteer resources and support systems, or other available court-approved state, local, or federal resources.

4. Process for Identifying, Transferring and Assessing Eligible Pretrial Intervention Program Cases

A. *Transfer by Clerk.* Efforts should be made to identify potentially eligible defendants as early in their entrance to the criminal justice system as possible. The task of initial identification should be the responsibility of all entities involved, including the court, defense counsel, the Office of the State Attorney, the Hillsborough County Sheriff's Office at booking, and the defendant. The issue of eligibility for Veterans Treatment Court may be raised at any court proceeding by the defendant, defense counsel, the Office of the State Attorney, or the court, during which the waiver of speedy trial requirement must be addressed. Unless the presiding judge has provided notice of a temporary suspension of any future eligible cases into Veterans Treatment Court under section two of this administrative order, if any entity involved in the proceedings indicates on the record the belief that the defendant is eligible for the Pretrial Intervention Program component of Veterans Treatment Court and the presiding judge finds that the defendant appears to be eligible, the court will transfer the case to the Veterans Treatment Court. The clerk will set the case on the next Veterans Treatment Court docket. This transfer will occur without the necessity of a written court order.

B. *Cases Filed Directly into Veterans Treatment Court.* If cases that appear to be eligible for the Pretrial Intervention Program component of the Veterans Treatment Court are identified prior to the State Attorney's Office filing criminal charges, the case may be directly filed into Veterans Treatment Court unless the presiding judge has provided notice of a temporary suspension of any future eligible cases under section two of this administrative order.

C. *Assessment by Veterans Administration.* Prior to the first hearing in Veterans Treatment Court, the defendant should be assessed by the Veterans Justice Outreach Liaison for verification that the defendant meets eligibility criteria in subsections 3 A and B of this administrative order.

D. *Confirmation of Eligibility.* At the defendant's first hearing in Veterans Treatment Court, the presiding judge will confirm the defendant's eligibility for the program, provide appropriate instructions and information about the program, and confirm the defendant's willingness to enter into a participation agreement and take part in treatment.

E. *Waiver of Speedy Trial.* Upon acceptance into the Veterans Treatment Court, the defendant voluntarily agrees to waive speedy trial.

F. *Discharge from Veterans Court.* If at any point it is determined that the defendant is not eligible for or unwilling to participate in Veterans Treatment Court, or the defendant is otherwise unsuccessfully discharged from Veterans Treatment Court, the case will be transferred back to the criminal division from which it originated. If the case was not assigned to a criminal division prior to transfer to Veterans Treatment Court, the case will be assigned to a criminal division by the clerk in accordance with the applicable administrative order on assignment of cases and transferred to that division. The case will be set for a disposition in the new division and copies of the transfer order will be provided to all parties.

G. *Assistance by the Administrative Office of the Courts.* To the extent resources are available, the Administrative Office of the Courts will facilitate the process by which a defendant is assessed in conjunction with the Veterans Treatment Court Oversight Committee; coordinate the procedure by which the written assessment is furnished to the State Attorney's Office, defense counsel, and judge; assist the court in managing its caseload; compile statistics; and maintain the necessary documents to demonstrate compliance with any funding requirements.

5. Participation in the Pretrial Intervention Program Component of Veterans Treatment Court

A. *Coordinated Strategy.* The Veterans Treatment Court participant will be subject to a coordinated strategy developed by the veterans treatment intervention team. The coordinated strategy is modeled after the therapeutic jurisprudence principles and key components in section 397.334(4), Florida Statutes, with treatment specific to the needs of veterans and servicemembers. The coordinated strategy may include a protocol of sanctions that may be imposed upon the participant for noncompliance with program rules. The protocol of sanctions may include, but need not be limited to, placement in a treatment program offered by a licensed service provider, placement in a jail-based treatment program, or serving a period of incarceration within the time limits established for contempt of court. The coordinated strategy must be provided in writing to the participant before the participant agrees to enter into a pretrial veterans treatment invention program or other pretrial intervention program.

B. *Court Hearings.* The defendant is required to attend court hearings as set by the Veterans Treatment Court judge. The defendant must participate in continued assessment and treatment and engage in discharge planning. This participation must include the voluntary and truthful provision of information to the court and all collaborating entities in the assessment and treatment process.

6. Disposition of Case

A. *Successful.* At the end of the pretrial intervention program period, the court must consider the recommendation of the treatment program and the state attorney. The court may also consider other arguments or recommendations of the parties. If the court determines that the defendant has successfully completed Veterans Treatment Court, the court must dismiss the charges.

B. *Unsuccessful.* If the court at any time determines that the participant should be unsuccessfully discharged from Veterans Treatment Court, including failure of the participant to provide truthful necessary information, the court will order the case transferred back to the criminal division from which it originated. If the case was not assigned to a criminal division prior to being assigned or transferred to the Veterans Treatment Court, the case will be assigned to a criminal division by the clerk in accordance with the applicable administrative order on assignment of cases and transferred to that division. The case will be set for a disposition in the new division and copies of the transfer order will be provided to all parties.

7. New Arrests

A. *Eligible Charge(s) or Violation(s).* If, while participating in the Pretrial Intervention Program component of Veterans Treatment Court, a defendant is arrested for a new charge eligible for admission to Veterans Treatment Court, the Veterans Treatment Court judge will determine whether or not the defendant remains amenable for treatment and should be allowed to continue to participate in the program. The judge will hear from the parties and consider the recommendation of the treatment program in determining whether the defendant will remain in the Pretrial Intervention Program. If so, and the defendant agrees, the new charge will be transferred to Veterans Treatment Court. If the Veterans Treatment Court judge determines that the defendant should not remain in Veterans Treatment Court, the defendant will be unsuccessfully discharged by the court entering an order transferring the case(s). The case will then be set for a disposition in the new division and copies of the transfer order will be provided to all parties.

B. *Ineligible Charge(s)* If, while participating in Veterans Treatment Court, a defendant is arrested for a new charge not eligible for Veterans Treatment Court, the presiding judge may unsuccessfully discharge the defendant from the Veterans Treatment Court by entering an order transferring the case(s) in accordance with the transfer procedure in section 4F of this administrative order. The case will be set for a disposition in the new division and copies of the transfer order will be provided to all parties.

8. Expunction of Records. Any person whose charges are dismissed after successful completion of the Pretrial Intervention Program component of Veterans Treatment Court, if otherwise eligible, may have his or her arrest record of the dismissed charges expunged in accordance with section 943.0585, Florida Statutes. Petitions to Expunge for such defendants must be filed in Veterans Treatment Court and handled in accordance with section 32 of Administrative Order S–2016–025 (*Circuit Criminal Division Procedures*) or any successor administrative orders.

9. Post–Adjudicatory Program Component of Veterans Treatment Court—Section 394.47891, Florida Statutes

A. *Eligibility Criteria.* In order to participate in the Post–Adjudicatory Program component of Veterans Treatment Court, a defendant must meet the following criteria:

i. Veteran or Servicemember. The defendant must be a veteran, as defined in section 1.01, Florida Statutes, including a veteran who was discharged or released under a general discharge, or a servicemember, as defined in section 250.01, Florida Statutes.

ii. Service–Related Condition. The defendant suffers from a military service-related mental illness, traumatic brain injury, substance abuse disorder, or psychological problem.

iii. Criminal Offense. The defendant is charged with or convicted of a criminal offense.

B. *Acceptance Procedure.* Admission into the Post–Adjudicatory Program component of Veterans Treatment Court must be in accordance with chapter 921, Florida Statutes, in a manner that appropriately addresses the severity of the mental illness, traumatic brain injury, substance abuse disorder, or psychological problem through services tailored to the individual needs of the participant, and based on the sentencing court's assessment of the defendant's criminal history, military service, substance abuse treatment needs, mental health treatment needs, amenability to the services of the program, the recommendation of the state attorney and the victim, if any, and the defendant's agreement to enter the program.

C. *Transfer of Case*

i. Sentenced by Standard Criminal Division Judge. An eligible post-adjudicatory case may be transferred from a standard criminal division to Veterans Treatment Court via written order (1) after acceptance of an open plea of guilty or nolo contendre and imposition of sentence by another judge which includes successful completion of the Veterans Treatment Court Program; or (2) after a sentencing hearing following a guilty verdict, and imposition of sentence by another judge that includes successful completion of the Veterans Treatment Court Program. If a case is transferred to Veterans Treatment Court after imposition of sentence by a judge in another criminal division, the case will proceed in the same manner as cases in the Pretrial Intervention Program component.

ii. Sentenced by Veterans Treatment Court Judge. A veteran or servicemember who suffers from a military service-related condition and whose criminal case is pending in a standard criminal division may request that the case be transferred to Veterans Treatment Court prior to entering a plea. If the standard criminal division judge determines the case appropriate for transfer, the judge will enter a written order transferring the case to Veterans Treatment Court so that the Veterans Treatment Court judge may accept the plea and impose sentence at the first hearing. Part of the sentence will include successful completion of the Veterans Treatment Court program. After imposition of sentence, the case will proceed in the same manner as cases in the Pretrial Intervention Program component.

D. *Violation of Probation, Drug Offender Probation or Community Control*

i. Technical Violations. If a defendant in the post-adjudicatory component of Veterans Treatment Court is accused of violating probation, drug offender probation or community control not involving a new criminal charge, the alleged violation will be handled by the Veterans Treatment Court judge.

ii. New Eligible Criminal Charge Violations. If a defendant in the post-adjudicatory component of Veterans Treatment Court is accused of violating probation, drug offender probation or community control involving a new criminal charge that is eligible for the Pretrial Intervention Program component of the Veterans Treatment Court, the new charge and alleged violation will be handled in the Veterans Treatment Court if the presiding judge in the Veterans Treatment Court determines the new charge appropriate for transfer.

iii. New Ineligible Criminal Charge Violations. If a defendant in the post-adjudicatory component of Veterans Treatment Court is accused of violating probation, drug offender probation or community control involving a new criminal charge that is not eligible for the Pretrial Intervention Program component of Veterans Treatment Court, the new charge and alleged violation will be transferred back to the criminal division from which it originated. If the original case was not assigned to a criminal division prior to transfer to Veterans Treatment Court, the new charge and alleged violation will be assigned to a criminal division by the clerk in accordance with the applicable administrative order on assignment of cases and transferred to that division. The case will be set for a disposition in the new division and copies of the transfer order will be provided to all parties.

E. *Modifications of Probation, Drug Offender Probation or Community Control.* Motions to modify or terminate probation, drug offender probation or community control on Post–Adjudicatory participants will be heard in Veterans Treatment Court. If the case has been transferred from a Veterans Treatment Court division to another division, motions will be heard in the division assigned at the time the motion is filed.

10. Confidential Records. Prior to submitting to the mental health and substance abuse assessment, and any other assessments as deemed necessary by the court or any collaborating treatment entity, the defendant must consent to a waiver of confidentiality of the defendant's confidential treatment records, allowing communications between the various providers, the Veterans Administration, and the court for verification of the defendant's eligibility for Veterans Treatment Court and the continued monitoring of the defendant's compliance in the program. If the defendant refuses to agree to waive confidentiality for the purposes of verification and monitoring in Veterans Treatment Court, the defendant will not be eligible for, or allowed to continue in, Veterans Treatment Court. No other use or disclosure of confidential records is authorized.

Patient treatment records are deemed confidential as provided by Florida law and generally must not be filed in the court file. If it is necessary that a treatment record or report or any portion of a treatment record or report be filed with the clerk for placement in the court file of a defendant in Veterans Treatment Court, the filer must also file a "Motion to Determine Confidentiality of Court Records" in accordance with Florida Rule of Judicial Administration 2.420. The court will enter any appropriate order in accordance with Rule 2.420.

11. Veterans Treatment Court Oversight Committee. The Veterans Treatment Court Oversight Committee is hereby established to oversee Veterans Treatment Court operations in order to ensure proper training of court personnel and correct implementation of the Veterans Treatment Court model. The committee is charged with recommending strategies to maintain the quality and effectiveness of Veterans Treatment Court and to ensure that the many treatment options now available for Veterans Treatment Court remain viable.

The Veterans Treatment Court Oversight Committee is comprised of the Public Defender or designee, the State Attorney or designee, the Trial Court Administrator or designee, a representative of the Veterans Administration, the Hillsborough County Sheriff or designee, the chair of the Hillsborough County Bar Association's Military and Veterans Affairs Committee or designee, a representative of any other service provider identified by the State Attorney's Office or the Public Defender's Office, the presiding judge in Veterans Treatment Court, the administrative judge of the Veterans Treatment Court, the administrative judge of the Criminal Justice Division, and the chief judge or designee.

The Veterans Treatment Court Oversight Committee will meet at least twice per year.

12. Previous Administrative Order Superseded. This administrative order supersedes Administrative Order S–2015–012 (*Veterans Treatment Court*).

13. Effective Date. This administrative order is effective October 1, 2016.

It is ORDERED in Tampa, Hillsborough County, Florida on this 4th day of August, 2016.

Ronald N. Ficarrotta, Chief Judge

S–2010–012. BLANKET DISCOVERY

IN THE THIRTEENTH JUDICIAL CIRCUIT HILLSBOROUGH COUNTY, FLORIDA

ADMINISTRATIVE ORDER S–2010–012

BLANKET DISCOVERY

The State Attorney and the Public Defender both recognize that in certain cases the institution of a Blanket Notice of Defendant's Intent to Participate in Discovery and Defendant's Demand for Favorable and Impeachment Information ("Blanket Notice and Demand"), pursuant to Florida Rule of Criminal Procedure 3.220 and Florida Rule of Juvenile Procedure 8.060, will promote efficiency without prejudicing the defendant or the state.

The Public Defender has submitted a Blanket Notice and Demand to the State Attorney, a copy of which is attached to this administrative order. The State Attorney has agreed to accept the attached Blanket Notice and Demand thereby obligating him and his office to comply with the applicable provisions of Florida Rule of Criminal Procedure 3.220 within 15 days after the later of: (1) the filing of the charging document or (2) the appointment of the Office of the Public Defender in any Circuit Court non-indictment criminal case. The State Attorney has also agreed to comply with Florida Rule of Juvenile Procedure 8.080 within 5 days after the later of: (1) the filing of the charging document or (2) the appointment of the Office of the Public Defender in the Juvenile Division of the Circuit Court.

Pursuant to Florida Rule of Criminal Procedure 3.220(b)(1) and (b)(4), Florida Rule of Juvenile Procedure 8.060(a)(1) and (b), *Brady v. Maryland*, 373 U.S. 83 (1963); *United States v. Agurs*, 427 U.S. 97 (1976); *United States v. Bagley*, 473 U.S. 667 (1985); and *Kyles v. Whitley*, 514 U.S. 419 (1995), the Public Defender has submitted the attached Blanket Notice and Demand as full and complete notices of intent to participate in discovery, in the absence of filing a timely Notice of Opting Out of the Blanket Notice and Demand.

The Public Defender has agreed to provide the State Attorney with a written Notice of Opting Out of the provisions of her Blanket Notice and Demand if discovery is not desired in any particular case. Any Notice of Opting Out will be filed at or before arraignment and before acceptance of any discovery materials.

By the power vested in the chief judge under Florida Rule of Judicial Administration 2.215(b)(2), it is therefore **ORDERED:**

1. Non-indictment Circuit Criminal Cases. For purposes of discovery pursuant to Florida Rule of Criminal Procedure 3.220, the attached Blanket Notice and Demand is determined to be filed in each Circuit Court non-indictment criminal case at the time of the appointment of the Office of the Public Defender, except in those limited cases in which the Office of the Public Defender has timely filed and submitted to the State Attorney a Notice of Opting Out of the Blanket Notice and Demand.

2. Juvenile Delinquency Cases. For purposes of discovery pursuant to Florida Rule of Juvenile Procedure 8.060, the attached Blanket Notice and Demand is determined to be filed in each juvenile delinquency case at the time of the appointment of the Office of the Public Defender, except in those limited cases in which the Office of the Public Defender has timely filed and submitted to the State Attorney a Notice of Opting Out of the Blanket Notice and Demand.

3. Full and Complete Notices. The Blanket Notice and Demand is to be treated as full and complete Notices of Intent to Participate in Discovery pursuant to Florida Rule of Criminal Procedure 3.220(b)(1) and (b)(4) and Florida Rule of Juvenile Procedure 8.060(a)(1) and (b) and pursuant to *Brady v. Maryland,* 373 U.S. 83 (1963); *United States v. Agurs,* 427 U.S. 97 (1976); *United States v. Bagley,* 473 U.S. 667 (1985); and *Kyles v. Whitley,* 514 U.S. 419 (1995).

4. Timely Notice of Opting Out. The Public Defender agrees to provide the State Attorney with a written Notice of Opting Out of the Blanket Notice and Demand if discovery is not desired in any particular case. Any Notice of Opting Out will be filed and submitted to the State Attorney at or before arraignment and before acceptance of any discovery materials.

5. Effective Date. This administrative order is effective February 1, 2010.

It is ORDERED in Tampa, Hillsborough County, Florida, on this 25th day of January, 2010.

Manuel Menendez, Jr.
Chief Judge

Guardianship, Probate, Mental Health & Trust

S–2018–021. GUARDIANSHIP PROCEEDINGS

IN THE THIRTEENTH JUDICIAL CIRCUIT HILLSBOROUGH COUNTY, FLORIDA

ADMINISTRATIVE ORDER S–2018–021

(Supersedes Administrative Order S–2017–012)

GUARDIANSHIP PROCEEDINGS

In light of a new cause of action for an injunction for protection against exploitation of a vulnerable adult becoming law on July 1, 2018 (Chapter 2018–100, Laws of Florida), it is necessary for the proper and efficient administration of justice in this circuit to update the administrative provisions governing guardianship proceedings in this circuit. By the power vested in the chief judge under article V, section 2(d), Florida Constitution; section 43.26, Florida Statutes; and Florida Rule of Judicial Administration 2.215(b)(2), it is ORDERED:

1. Assignment of Cases

A. *Generally.* All proceedings under section 393.12 (guardian advocate); chapter 744 (Florida Guardianship Law); chapter 747 (conservatorship); and section 825.1035 (injunction for protection against exploitation of a vulnerable adult), Florida Statutes (2018), will be assigned to Probate, Guardianship, Mental Health and Trust Division "A" unless the person with a developmental disability, alleged incapacitated person, or alleged vulnerable adult resides in the East Circuit Division boundaries, or the absentee was domiciled in the East Circuit Division boundaries, or the absentee's property's is located in the East Circuit Division boundaries in which event the guardian advocate, guardianship, conservatorship, or injunction for protection proceedings will be assigned to East Circuit Division "U" or East Circuit Division "W" on a random equitable basis. See Administrative Order S–2013–033 or any successor administrative order for the East Division boundaries.

B. *Mental Health Companion Cases.* All mental health companion cases in which the subject of the case is also the subject of a pending guardianship case in the East Division will be assigned to the same East Division in which the guardianship case is pending. For purposes of this administrative order, the term "mental health companion case" means a proceeding in which a petition to determine incapacity (section 744.3201, Florida Statutes), a suggestion of capacity (section 744.464, Florida Statutes), or a petition under the Adult Protective Services Act (chapter 415, Florida Statutes) has been filed and the subject of the petition or suggestion is also the subject of a pending guardianship case.

C. *Injunctions for Protection against Exploitation of a Vulnerable Adult and Pending Guardianship Proceeding.* In accordance with section 825.1035(2)(f), Florida Statutes (2018), if a proceeding concerning a vulnerable adult under chapter 744 is pending at the time of a filing of a petition for an injunction for protection against exploitation of a vulnerable adult, the petition must be filed in the guardianship proceeding.

2. Applicability

A. *Guardian Advocacy.* Unless otherwise provided in chapter 393, Florida Statutes, or in the applicable Florida Probate Rules, any proceeding on a petition for the appointment of a guardian advocate will be governed by the provisions in this administrative order. The term "guardian" as used in this administrative order also applies to a guardian advocate. The notice required to a person with a developmental disability who is the subject of a petition filed under section 393.12, Florida Statutes, may be satisfied by filing proof of service on counsel for the person with a developmental disability and that such counsel has waived notice on behalf of his or her client.

B. *Guardianship.* Unless otherwise provided in chapter 744, Florida Statutes, or in the applicable Florida Probate Rules, all guardianship proceedings will be governed by the provisions in this administrative order. Minor guardianships are also addressed in Administrative Order S–2011–014 *(Child Custody Proceedings).*

C. *Conservatorship.* Unless otherwise provided in chapter 747, Florida Statutes, or in the applicable Florida Probate Rules, any proceeding on a conservatorship will be governed by the provisions in this administrative order. The term "guardian" as used in this administrative order also applies to a conservator.

D. *Injunctions for Protection against Exploitation of a Vulnerable Adult.* Unless otherwise provided in section 825.1035, Florida Statutes (2018), all petitions for injunctions for protection against exploitation of a vulnerable adult will be governed by the provisions in this administrative order.

3. Dismissal of Petition for Incapacity. A petition to determine incapacity, once filed, may not be voluntarily dismissed. A motion to dismiss filed by any person must be scheduled for hearing for the court's consideration. The motion must state with specificity the reasons for the dismissal and whether the petitioner stipulates to pay the costs of the examining committee and court appointed attorney for the alleged incapacitated person. Corresponding proposed orders dismissing the petition will be provided to the court at the time the motion to dismiss is heard.

4. Application for Appointment as Guardian. Every proposed guardian seeking appointment by the court must file an application for appointment as guardian that is signed by the proposed guardian under penalties of perjury. Professional guardians must update their application annually by filing either a list of current wards served by the guardian or a complete application for appointment as guardian. Professional guardians must denote any *pro bono* cases in the initial application and annual updates to their application. Nonprofit corporate guardians must file quarterly disclosure statements, in lieu of an application for appointment as guardian, denoting any *pro bono* cases.

5. Appointment of Guardian

A. *Professional Guardians.* Professional guardians seeking appointment must establish a professional guardian file with the Clerk of the Circuit Court (clerk) and submit documentation that the requirements of sections 744.2002, 744.2003, and 744.3135, Florida Statutes, have been satisfied.

In addition to the credit and criminal history investigation documentation contained within a professional guardian's file maintained by the clerk under section 744.3135, Florida Statutes, professional guardians must submit the following items, which the clerk will maintain in the professional guardian's file:

(i) Application for appointment as guardian and annual updates, or quarterly disclosure statements for nonprofit corporate guardians, in accordance with section 744.3125, Florida Statutes;

(ii) Proof of blanket fiduciary bond required by section 744.2003, Florida Statutes;

(iii) Evidence of completion of instruction and training, including continuing education required by section 744.2003, Florida Statutes.

(iv) Proof of registration with the Statewide Public Guardianship Office under section 744.2002, Florida Statutes; and

(v) Evidence of passage of the approved competency examination required by section 744.2003, Florida Statutes.

Additionally, each professional guardian is responsible for maintaining individual records of attendance at continuing education programs. The records must include the date, hours, title, location, and sponsor of the course and the certificate of attendance if provided. At least 8 of the 16 hours of continuing education required by section 744.2003, Florida Statutes, every two years must be directly related to ethics, guardianship duties, or care of the ward. Verification of continuing education course attendance must be filed in the professional guardian file.

B. *Nonprofessional Guardians.* Prior to the hearing on the appointment of the guardian, the court will conduct a state and national criminal background investigation of all proposed nonprofessional guardians. In order to complete the criminal background investigation, the proposed nonprofessional guardian must supply his or her date of birth and social security number. Additionally, any proposed nonprofessional guardian of the property must file a full credit report taken within the last year. A copy of the entire free annual credit report from Equifax, Experian, or TransUnion is acceptable. The court may require a nonprofessional guardian to submit to a level 1 or level 2 background screening and credit check under section 744.3135, Florida Statutes. In accordance with section 744.3135, the clerk will maintain a separate file on each guardian appointed by the court and retain in the guardian file documentation of the results of any investigation conduct under the section.

6. Constructive Service—Affidavit of Diligent Search and Inquiry. To obtain constructive service in a guardianship case, all counsel and interested persons (if unrepresented) must complete and file an affidavit of diligent search and inquiry substantially similar to the affidavit designated as Florida Rule of Civil Procedure Form 1.924. A uniform Affidavit of Diligent Search and Inquiry can be found at www.fljud13.org.

7. Service of Injunctions for Protection against Exploitation of Vulnerable Adults. In accordance with section 825.1035, Florida Statutes (2018), any sworn law enforcement officer in Hillsborough County may effect service within their jurisdiction of the petition, financial affidavit, notice of hearing, and any temporary ex parte injunction, as applicable. A law enforcement officer performing service under this statutory provision must use service and verification procedures consistent with those of the sheriff.

8. Referral to General Magistrate. Administrative provisions regarding referrals to a general magistrate are memorialized in a separate administrative order that may be found online at www.fljud13.org under the section titled "Administrative Orders." Judges should not refer petitions for injunctions for protection against exploitation of a vulnerable adult to a general magistrate.

9. Reassignment of Case upon Judge's Disqualification. If the judge presiding in Probate, Guardianship, Mental Health and Trust Division "A" enters an order of disqualification in a guardianship case, the case will be reassigned by the clerk on a random equitable basis to one of the Tampa Family Law Divisions. If either of the judges presiding in East Circuit Division "U" or "W" enters an order of disqualification in a guardianship case, the clerk will reassign the case to the other division. If both judges assigned the East Circuit Divisions "U" and "W" enter orders of disqualification in a guardianship case, the clerk will reassign the case to Tampa Probate, Guardianship, Mental Health and Trust Division "A."

10. Setting of Hearings

A. *Obtaining Hearing Time.* Attorneys may obtain available hearing times and schedule hearings on a judge's calendar by accessing the Judicial Automated Workflow System (JAWS) at https://jaws.fljud13.org/System/login.aspx or by e-mailing the judge's judicial assistant at the appropriate divisional e-mail address:

- Probate, Guardianship, Mental Health and Trust Division "A"—probatedivisiona@fljud13.org.
- East Circuit Division "U"—eastcirdivu@fljud13.org.
- East Circuit Division "W"—eastcirdivw@fljud13.org.

Unrepresented interested persons are encouraged to obtain hearing times and schedule hearings on a judge's calendar by e-mailing the judge's judicial assistant at the appropriate divisional e-mail address above.

B. *Notice of Hearing.* All notices of hearing must state the length of the time reserved on the judge's calendar for the hearing and specify the matters to be heard. The party filing a notice of hearing must provide a copy of the notice to the presiding judge's judicial assistant. A notice indicating that the hearing will be on "all pending motions" is not authorized. The matter to be heard must be set out with particularity. There will be no cross-noticing on hearing times unless the opposing counsel or opposing interested person contacts the judge's office and determines whether the docket will accommodate hearing additional matters at the same time and all parties agree to including the additional matters to be heard.

C. *Cancellation or Rescheduling.* If any hearing is cancelled or rescheduled, the attorney or unrepresented interested person setting the hearing is responsible for notifying the judge's judicial assistant and the opposing counsel or opposing interested person as soon as possible of the cancellation. Attorneys must also cancel the hearing through JAWS if the hearing was scheduled on JAWS.

11. Hearings. Any petition, pleading, motion, or other document that is the subject of a hearing or a conference set before the court must be filed with the clerk no later than five days before the matter is to be considered. A hearing on any such petition, pleading, motion, or other document not so filed may be postponed until another hearing is scheduled. Courtesy copies of any case law, statutes, or other authority relied upon for the hearing must be provided to the judge at the hearing.

12. Court Reporters. The court will not provide court reporters for hearings, except for recordings for proceedings on petitions for injunctions for protection against exploitation of a vulnerable adult. If an attorney or unrepresented interested person wishes to have a court reporter present during any hearing, it is that attorney's or unrepresented interested person's responsibility to contact the court reporter to arrange for the presence of such reporter. *See also* Administrative Order S–2016–015 *(Civil Court Reporting)*.

13. Emergencies. Application for emergency relief in a case must be made to the presiding judge. All petitions for injunctions for protection against exploitation of a vulnerable adult are considered applications for emergency relief.

If the presiding judge is the judge assigned to Probate, Guardianship, Mental Health and Trust Division "A" and is for any reason absent from the courthouse, then emergency application in any case assigned to that judge's division will be presented to the judge assigned Drug Court Division "Z" if that judge is present in the courthouse. If the judge assigned Drug Court Division "Z" is absent from the courthouse, then the case will be presented to the duty judge assigned for that particular week. Duty judge assignments may be accessed at www.fljud13.org. The judge will review the request as soon as it is reasonably possible.

If the presiding judge is either of the judges presiding in East Circuit Division "U" or "W," and is for any reason absent from the courthouse, then emergency application in any case assigned to that judge's division will be presented to the judge of the other East Circuit guardianship division if that judge is present in the courthouse. If both judges assigned the East Circuit Divisions "U" and "W" are unavailable, then any emergency matter will be assigned to any other judge assigned to the East Division who is present in the courthouse. If all judges assigned to the East Division are unavailable, then the emergency matter will be presented to the judge assigned to Tampa Probate, Guardianship, Mental Health and Trust Division "A."

"Present in the courthouse" includes being in a hearing, a jury trial, or nonjury trial.

Matters scheduled for hearing as an emergency may not be heard with less than 48 hours' actual prior notice to an opposing interested person unless all interested persons agree.

14. Adversary Proceedings. In an adversary proceeding as defined by Florida Probate Rule 5.025, the following provisions apply:

A. *Case Management Conference.* All petitioners must schedule a case management conference within 60 days of commencing an adversary proceeding. All trials or final hearings of adversary proceedings must be set by the court entering a Uniform Order Setting Adversary Proceeding for Trial and Pretrial Conference (Nonjury). Uniform orders may be found at www.fljud13.org. Once scheduled, a hearing may not be cancelled unilaterally by counsel.

B. *Military Service—Memorandum for Certificate of Military Service.* If a petitioner does not know whether the respondent is on active duty in a branch of the military service of the United States, the petitioner must complete a memorandum for certificate of military service substantially similar to the memorandum designated as Florida Family Law Rule of Procedure Form 12.912(a). A uniform Memorandum for Certificate of Military Service can be found at www.fljud13.org.

C. *Default Judgment—Affidavit of Military Service.* If a petitioner seeks a default judgment and the respondent has been properly served and has not responded to the petition, the petitioner must complete and file an affidavit of military service substantially similar to the affidavit designated as Florida Family Law Rule of Procedure Form 12.912(b). A uniform Affidavit of Military Service can be found at www.fljud13.org.

D. *Motions to Compel—Order Without Hearing.* When a motion to compel that complies with the good faith certification in Florida Rule of Civil Procedure 1.380(a)(2)—motion "must include a certification that the movant, in good faith, has conferred or attempted to confer with the person or party failing to make the discovery in an effort to secure the information or material without court action"—alleges the absence of a response or objection to discovery and there has been no request for an extension of time to respond, the court, without a hearing, may enter an order requiring compliance with the original discovery request within 10 days of the signing of the order, provided no written showing of good cause has been filed by the non-movant.

Unless the presiding judge directs otherwise, if all parties are represented by attorneys, none of whom have been excused from e-mail service under Florida Rule of Judicial Administration 2.516, the movant's attorneys must submit to the court a proposed order through the JAWS in searchable PDF format. If any party is unrepresented or represented by an attorney who has been excused from e-mail service under Rule 2.516, the movant or movant's attorney must submit to the presiding judge sufficient hard copies of the proposed order along with stamped, addressed envelopes.

E. *Motions to Set Case for Trial—Certificate by Attorney.* All motions to set a case for trial must contain a certificate by the attorney or party filing such motion that the attorney or party has discussed the subject matter of the motion with all other attorneys or parties and has been unable to reach agreement concerning the setting of the case for trial, or that the opposing attorneys or parties have failed to respond.

15. Orders

A. *Consultation with Opposing Counsel or Party.* Unless the presiding judge directs otherwise, prior to submitting a proposed order for the court's consideration after a hearing, the counsel submitting the proposed order must consult with opposing counsel or unrepresented party within five days after the court's decision and make a genuine effort to agree on the language of the proposed order.

B. *Timely Submission.* All proposed orders must be submitted to the court by the attorney directed to prepare the order within 10 days after the court's decision.

C. *Submission of Proposed Orders*

i. JAWS—All Parties Represented by Counsel None of Whom are Excused from E–Service. Unless the presiding judge directs otherwise, if all parties are represented by attorneys, none of whom have been excused from e-mail service under Florida Rule of Judicial Administration 2.516, an attorney who is requested to submit a proposed order will do so through the JAWS in searchable PDF.

All proposed orders submitted to the presiding judge must include a cover letter certifying that one of the following statements is true: (i) all parties have agreed to the content of the proposed order or (ii) opposing counsel has not responded within five business days of being provided the proposed order.

If, after consultation with opposing counsel or the appropriate interested person, the parties cannot agree on the language in the proposed order to be submitted to the court, then the attorney or interested person submitting the proposed order must document in the cover letter that the opposing counsel or opposing interested person has registered an objection and specifically state what the objection is. At the time the cover letter and proposed order is submitted to the court, a copy must simultaneously be sent to all parties and interested persons or their counsel. If an objection is registered, the court will determine if a hearing is necessary to resolve the dispute.

ii. Hard Copies and Envelopes—Unrepresented Party or Party's Attorney Excused from E–Service. If any party is unrepresented or represented by an attorney who has been excused from e-mail service under Rule 2.516, the party or attorney who is requested to submit a proposed order will do so by submitting to the presiding judge sufficient hard copies of the proposed order along with stamped, addressed envelopes.

iii. Title. The title of every proposed order submitted must contain the subject matter of the pleading or motion upon which the ruling is made and must fairly apprise the reader of the action being ordered. Phrasing such as "order granting ..." or "order denying ..." is preferred over "order on ...."

iv. Form. In all proposed orders, the page containing the court's signature must also contain substantive language of the proposed order so that a proposed order does not contain a signature page consisting only of the court's signature. Each page, except for the first page, must contain a page number.

16. Substitution of Counsel and Resident Agent. Any stipulation for the substitution of counsel for a guardian must be signed by the attorneys involved and by the guardian. If the former attorney is the designated resident agent for the guardian, then the former attorney should resign, and a new resident agent should be designated. This rule will not affect the right of a guardian to change attorneys, so long as notice is given to the former attorney.

17. Mediation. The court may, on its own motion or on the motion of the guardian or other interested person, refer adversary matters to mediation. If the mediation order is entered on the motion of the guardian, conservator, or other interested person, an order with sufficient copies and stamped, addressed envelopes will be provided for the service of the copies of the mediation order.

18. Approval of Settlement of Minor and Incompetent Claims. A petition seeking court approval of the settlement of a claim on behalf of a minor or incompetent person must comply with Florida Probate Rule 5.636 and sections 744.301 and 744.387, Florida Statutes.

The court will conduct a hearing to determine if the settlement is in the best interest of the minor or incompetent person and if the attorney's fees and costs are fair and reasonable. Unless excused by the court, the minor or incompetent person must be present at the hearing as well as the parent, next friend or guardian. The attorney must have available for the court the most recent medical report of the treating physician.

In situations where approval of a settlement for less than the actual value of the claim is requested because of policy limits, evidence indicating the amount of insurance coverage must be produced at the hearing. If a guardian ad litem report is required based on the amount of the settlement, a courtesy copy must be provided to the court at least 48 hours prior to the hearing.

19. Mandatory Depository

A. *Minor Guardianships.* Unless waived or otherwise ordered by the court, in every guardianship of the property of a minor ward, a depository must be designated (in accordance with section 69.031, Florida Statutes) for deposit of all cash owned by or owed to the ward, wherever located. For good cause shown, the court may waive the necessity of a depository, in which case a bond will be required.

B. *All Other Guardianships of the Property.* Unless waived or otherwise ordered by the court, in every guardianship of the property, except a minor guardianship (see above), the guardian must place in a restricted depository all cash assets or cash-equivalent assets of the ward. A one-time sum of $3,000, or any other amount specified by the court, may be maintained outside of the depository for payment of the ward's initial expenses, including costs incurred with the establishment of the guardianship proceeding and payment of the examining committee. The ward's income need not be placed in the restricted depository, unless otherwise ordered by the court.

20. Reports and Plans

A. *Initial Guardianship Report and Plan.* Every guardian must file an initial guardianship report and plan, as required by sections 744.362, 744.363, and 744.365 Florida Statutes, within the statutory timeframe, unless waived by the court. The reporting period for the initial report and plan will begin with the date that letters of guardianship were signed by the court and end the following year on the last day of the anniversary month in which the letters of guardianship were signed.

B. *Annual Guardianship Plan.* Beginning the year after the initial plan is filed, a guardian of the person must file the annual guardianship plan as required by sections 744.367 and 744.3675, Florida Statutes. The reporting period for the annual plan is prospective and will begin on the first day of the first month following the end of the reporting period for the initial plan and end the following year on the last day of the anniversary month in which the letters of guardianship were signed. If a ward is in a persistent vegetative condition and the guardian wishes to use substantially the same plan as in previous years, then the guardian must provide a reasonable basis for doing so.

C. *Annual Guardianship Accounting.* A guardian of the property must file the annual guardianship accounting as required by sections 744.367 and 744.3678, Florida Statutes, on a fiscal-year basis. The fiscal year will be deemed to end on the last day of the anniversary month in which the letters of guardianship were signed. Therefore, the reporting period for the first annual accounting will begin with the date that letters of guardianship were entered and end on the last day of the anniversary month in which the letters of guardianship were signed. Thereafter, the reporting period for all future accountings will begin on the first day of the first month following the month in which letters of guardianship were signed by the court and end the following year, on the last day of the anniversary month in which the letters of guardianship were signed. Accountings must include all property interests of the ward regardless of how the property is titled unless specifically exempted under section 744.3678, Florida Statutes.

D. *Format.* All reports must include the guardian's signature, current address, current telephone number with area code, and e-mail address. Additionally, all reports must include the signature of the attorney of record, the attorney's current address, current telephone number with area code, e-mail address, and Florida Bar number.

E. *Timeliness.* All reports must be signed under penalties of perjury and filed within 90 days after the last day of the anniversary month in which the letters of guardianship were signed by the court. If the reports cannot be filed in the time required by law, a motion for extension of time must be filed within the respective time period. Reports must not be filed prior to the end of the applicable reporting period.

F. *Audit Fees.* Audit fees must be paid to the clerk in accordance with sections 744.365 and 744.3678, Florida Statutes.

G. *Simplified Accounting Procedures.* Under the appropriate circumstances, the guardian may use the simplified accounting procedures under section 744.3679, Florida Statutes, or file a verified petition clearly indicating the justification for the court to allow simplified plans or waive the requirement of annual accountings. If the court grants a petition to allow simplified plans, the guardian must use the court's approved form.

21. Guardian's Fees. All petitions to the court for approval of compensation to a guardian must be accompanied by an itemized description of the services provided for which fees are sought. This itemization of services must be provided in chronological date order and in line-item format, with each line-item entry containing a specific description of the services rendered, the date listed with the amount of time expended on each service in one-tenth (0.10) of an hour increments. This information must also state the rate charged and amount sought to be approved. Notices to, or the signed consent of, the guardian of the property or the Veterans Administration or both must be submitted with the petition for guardian's fees, if applicable. No payment of guardian fees and expenses may be made without the entry of a court order approving the fees and expenses. Fees will be awarded by the court after applying the analysis specified in section 744.108, Florida Statutes. When fees are awarded, the approved amount must be transferred in full from the ward's account.

All petitions for guardian's fees must reference all prior fees paid and the billing time period included. A petition must not exceed a billing time period of one year. The first petition for guardian's fees may be filed as early as three months after letters of guardianship are signed; however, the first fee petition will not be approved until the inventory is filed by the guardian and approved by the court. Thereafter, a petition for guardian's fees should be filed every six months and will not be approved if statutorily required reports are delinquent, without a court-ordered extension. Instances of non-compliance with statutory, administrative, or court-ordered requirements may result in a reduction of a guardian's fees. Any reductions imposed by the court for such non-compliance will not become final until the guardian has had an opportunity to be heard on the matter.

The fee structure for professional guardians will vary and be based primarily upon a guardian's years of experience as a professional guardian. For any individual serving as a non-professional guardian, the chief judge will approve a rate of pay for reasonable and necessary services provided to the ward or on behalf of the ward within the scope of the guardian's duties as guardian.

Guardians must not charge in a petition for guardian's fees for time spent to prepare the billing itemization or any other documentation associated with petitioning the court for guardian's fees. Additionally, time spent to discuss with court staff or to review orders or directions from the court as a result of a guardian's non-compliance with court-ordered, statutory, or administrative obligations, and time spent to produce amended documents as a result of such non-compliance, must not be charged in the petition for guardian's fees.

All petitions for guardian's fees must include the following certification immediately before the guardian's signature:

> *I certify that all current reports, including, but not limited to: initial plan, annual plan, inventory, annual accounting, or final accounting, and the educational requirements, if applicable, have been filed. (Professional guardians must add the following sentence: I further certify that my professional guardian file is current and complies with all statutory and administrative requirements.)*

22. Attorney's Fees. The attorney for a guardian may petition the court for approval of attorney's fees *ex parte* at any time if the guardian has executed a written consent or has joined in the petition. Any petition for attorney's fees must contain an itemized billing statement for the attorney's service with the amount of time expended on each service in one-tenth (0.10) of an hour increments. If the attorney and the guardian cannot agree upon a fee or if an objection to the attorney's fees is made by an interested person, a hearing must be set before the court. If attorney's fees are paid to the attorney by the guardian without prior court approval, the guardian must attach an itemized billing statement for the fees, in accordance with the provisions of section 744.108, Florida Statutes, to the annual accounting in which the disbursement for the attorney's fees is documented. Any written consent of the guardian to the requested fees must be filed contemporaneously with the fee petition or motion.

23. Court Reviews. The Elder Justice Center, as a court program under the auspices of the Thirteenth Judicial Circuit Court, is utilized by the court to initially review filings and documentation related to guardianship cases and report to the court based upon its reviews. The Elder Justice Center guardianship court staff will review: (a) professional guardian files for annual statutory compliance; (b) guardians' petitions for fees and compensation as requested by the court; (c) initial reports; (d) annual plans; and (e) accountings. The results of the review will be reduced to writing for the court and filed in each corresponding case file. Elder Justice Center staff will be authorized to participate in guardianship hearings, as requested by the court, to address issues related to their reviews. Staff members will also serve as court monitors when appointed by the court to report on the welfare of the ward and conditions of the guardianship.

Additionally, the court may select a number of guardianship files for a comprehensive audit of all transactions. The audit may be conducted by a court monitor, the clerk, the Elder Justice Center, a general magistrate, or anyone else designated by the court.

24. Change of Guardian's Contact Information. All guardians must promptly advise the court, via written notice filed with the clerk, of any change of his or her name, address, telephone number, or e-mail address. The notice requirements in the Florida Probate Rules must be complied with at all times. In accordance with Florida Probate Rule 5.060, any interested person who desires notice may file a written request for notice of further proceedings. Such persons must indicate a current residence, post office address, and e-mail address. A new address designation must be filed by the requesting person when any address changes occur. Any person filing a request for notice must also provide a copy of the request to the clerk for forwarding to the guardian's attorney or the guardian, if not represented by counsel. Thereafter, the interested person must receive notice of further proceedings and must receive copies of subsequent pleadings and papers by the movant as long as such person remains an interested person.

25. Change of Ward's Residence. If the ward's residence changes to a new location within Hillsborough County or to an adjacent county, the guardian must inform the court, in writing, in accordance with section 744.1098(2), Florida Statutes. In accordance with section 744.1098(1), Florida Statutes, a guardian may not, without prior court approval, change the residence of the ward to another state or to a non-adjacent county. If a ward's permanent residence is changed to a county other than Hillsborough County, the guardian and the guardian's attorney must file all appropriate pleadings and proposed orders to have venue of the guardianship case transferred to the court in the appropriate county.

26. Death of the Ward. Within 30 days after the death of the ward, the guardian must file a notice of death. A certified copy of the ward's death certificate must be applied for within 15 days of the ward's death and filed immediately upon receipt.

The guardian of the property must file a final report in compliance with section 744.527, Florida Statutes, and Florida Probate Rule 5.680, unless waived in writing by all necessary interested persons, and petition for discharge, unless extended by court order. Any objections to the final accounting or discharge are required to be filed in accordance with Florida Probate Rule 5.680.

27. Motions to Withdraw. Any motion to withdraw as attorney for a guardian that is based upon lack of client contact must include all diligent efforts made by the attorney to locate the guardian. Any motion to withdraw as attorney for a guardian must include the name, address, and telephone number of the financial institution where the guardianship funds are located; the account number(s); and the current balance on all accounts, together with verifying account documentation. If this information is not obtainable by counsel, the motion to withdraw as attorney for guardian must detail all diligent efforts made to secure this information and documentation for the court. Termination of representation must comply with Rule 4–1.16 of the Rules Regulating The Florida Bar.

28. Dismissal Docket. The clerk will prepare an order to show cause docket in accordance with the applicable Florida Rules of Civil Procedure and the applicable Florida Probate Rules.

29. Professional Conduct and Courtroom Decorum. Counsel must adhere to The Florida Bar's Guidelines for Professional Conduct (https://www.floridabar.org/prof/presources/presources002/). The Florida Bar's Professionalism Expectations (https://www.floridabar.org/wp-content/uploads/2017/04/professionalism-expectations.pdf) and the Hillsborough County Bar Association's Standards of Professionalism (http://hillsbar.site-ym.com/?page=Professionalism). Each judge may announce and enforce additional requirements, or may excuse compliance with any provision(s) of the Guidelines, Expectations or Standards as that judge deems appropriate.

30. Previous Administrative Order Superseded. This administrative order supersedes Administrative Order S–2017–012 (*Guardianship Procedures*).

31. Effective Date. This administrative order is effective July 1, 2018.

ENTERED in Tampa, Hillsborough County, Florida on June 18, 2018.

Ronald N. Ficarrotta
Chief Judge

S–2017–010. PROBATE PROCEDURES

IN THE THIRTEENTH JUDICIAL CIRCUIT HILLSBOROUGH COUNTY, FLORIDA

ADMINISTRATIVE ORDER S–2017–010

(Supersedes Administrative Orders S–2014–037)

PROBATE PROCEDURES

It is necessary for the prompt and efficient administration of justice to update the procedures in the probate division. By the power vested in the chief judge under article V, section 2(d), Florida Constitution; section 43.26, Florida Statutes; and Florida Rule of Judicial Administration 2.215(b)(2), it is ORDERED:

1. Assignment of Cases. All proceedings under the Florida Probate Code (chapters 731, 732, 733, 734 and 735, Florida Statutes) are assigned to Probate, Guardianship, Mental Health and Trust Division "A" unless the decedent was domiciled in the East Division boundaries. If the decedent was domiciled in the East Division boundaries, the probate proceedings are assigned to East Circuit Division "U" or East Circuit Division "W" based on a random equitable distribution system. See Administrative Order S–2013–033 or any successor administrative order for the East Division boundaries.

Independent torts filed by or against a personal representative, a beneficiary, or an interested person are assigned to the Circuit Civil Division.

2. Transfer of Case. If it becomes apparent to either the administrative judge of the Probate, Guardianship, Mental Health and Trust Division or the administrative judge of the Circuit Civil Division, or both, that a proceeding has been erroneously filed in either of the two divisions, the administrative judges will consult with each other and determine the appropriate division for the proceeding. Either administrative judge may enter an order transferring a proceeding from one subject matter division to another with the consent of the other administrative judge. If the administrative judges do not agree on the appropriate subject matter division for a proceeding, the chief judge will make the decision.

3. Consolidation of Case. Consolidation of a case pending in the Probate, Guardianship, Mental Health and Trust Division with an independent, but related, action that is appropriately filed in the Circuit Civil Division is disfavored unless the right to jury trial, if any, has been waived by all parties in the action pending in the Circuit Civil Division.

4. Description of Real and Personal Property. Each item of real or personal property identified in a petition, order or other document must be listed with a complete and correct description. To the extent possible, the description should include:

A. *Real property:* a complete legal description and mailing address.

B. *Corporate stocks:* the current name of the corporation, the number of shares, the class, and such other information as may be necessary to sufficiently identify the stock.

C. *Bonds, debentures, and other debt obligations:* the name of the issuer, the original principal amount, the interest rate, the series (if applicable), and the maturity date.

D. *Amounts receivable that are secured under mortgages or security agreements:* the date of the obligation, the identity of the obligor, the original principal balance, and the record book and page number or other filing or recording reference.

E. *Rights of action:* a brief description of the nature of the action, the style of the action, the name of the court in which the action is pending, and the court's case number.

F. *Accounts at banks:* the name and location of the savings and loan association, brokerage firm, or other financial institution; the type of account; the account number; the principal balance or value; and, in the case of a brokerage account, a description of the assets held.

G. *Vehicles and boats:* year, make, type, and serial number.

Each item of tangible personal property must be separately described if it is valued at more than S500 or specifically devised.

Counsel must determine if it is appropriate to file a Notice of Confidential Information within Court Filing or a Motion to Determine Confidentiality of Court Records in accordance with Florida Rule of Judicial Administration 2.420.

5. Substitution of Counsel and Resident Agent. Any stipulation for the substitution of counsel for a personal representative or other represented person must be signed by the attorneys involved and by the personal representative or other represented person. If the former attorney is the designated resident agent for the personal representative, then the former attorney should resign, and a new resident agent should be designated. This rule will not affect the right of a personal representative to change attorneys, so long as notice is given to the former attorney.

6. Reassignment of Case upon Judge's Disqualification. If the judge assigned to Probate, Guardianship, Mental Health and Trust Division "A" enters an order of disqualification, the case will be reassigned by the clerk in a random and equitable fashion to one of the standard Circuit Civil Divisions, If either of the judges presiding in East Circuit Division "U" or "W" enters an order of disqualification, the clerk will reassign the case to the other division. If both judges assigned to East Circuit Divisions "U" and "W" enter orders of disqualification, the clerk will reassign the case to Tampa Probate, Guardianship, Mental Health and Trust Division "A."

7. Setting of Hearings.

A. *Obtaining Hearing Time.* Attorneys may obtain available hearing times and schedule hearings on a judge's calendar by accessing the Judicial Automated Workflow System (JAWS) at https://jaws.fljud13.org/System/login.aspx or by e-mailing the judge's judicial assistant at the appropriate divisional e-mail address:

- Probate, Guardianship, Mental Health and Trust Division "A"—probatedivisiona@fljud13.org.
- East Circuit Division "U"—eastcirdivu@fljud13.org.
- East Circuit Division "W"—eastcirdivw@fljud13.org.

Unrepresented interested persons are encouraged to obtain hearing times and schedule hearings on a judge's calendar by e-mailing the judge's judicial assistant at the appropriate divisional e-mail address above.

B. *Notice of Hearing.* All notices of hearing must state the length of the time reserved on the judge's calendar for the hearing and specify the matters to be heard. The party filing a notice of hearing must provide a copy of the notice to the presiding judge's judicial assistant. A notice indicating that the hearing will be on "all pending motions" is not authorized. The matter to be heard must be set out with particularity. There will be no cross-noticing on hearing times unless the opposing counsel or opposing interested person contacts the judge's office and determines whether the docket will accommodate hearing additional matters at the same time and all parties agree to including the additional matters to be heard.

C. *Cancellation or Rescheduling.* If any hearing is cancelled or rescheduled, the attorney or unrepresented interested person setting the hearing is responsible for notifying the judge's judicial assistant and the opposing counsel or opposing interested person as soon as possible of the cancellation. Attorneys must also cancel the hearing through JAWS if the hearing was scheduled on JAWS.

8. Court Reporters. The court does not provide court reporters for hearings. If an attorney or unrepresented interested person wishes to have a court reporter present during any hearing, it is that attorney's or unrepresented interested person's responsibility to contact the court reporter and arrange for the court reporter's attendance. *See also* Administrative Order S–2016–015 *(Civil Court Reporting)*.

9. Hearings. Any petition, pleading, motion, or other document that is the subject of a hearing or a conference set before the court must be filed with the clerk no later than five days before the hearing or conference. Consideration of any petition, pleading, motion, or other document not so filed may be postponed until another hearing is scheduled. Courtesy copies of any case law, statutes, or other authority relied upon for the hearing must be provided to the judge at the hearing.

10. Emergency Hearing. Application for emergency relief in a probate case must be made to the presiding judge of the division in which the case is pending.

If the presiding judge is the judge assigned to Probate, Guardianship, Mental Health and Trust Division "A" and is for any reason absent from the courthouse, then emergency application in any case assigned to that judge's division will be presented to the administrative judge of the Circuit Civil Division. If the administrative judge of the Circuit Civil Division is absent from the courthouse, any emergency application will be presented to the duty judge. (*See* www.fljud13.org for duty judge assignment).

If the presiding judge is either of the judges presiding in East Circuit Division "U" or "W," and is for any reason absent from the courthouse, then emergency application in any probate case assigned to that judge's division will be presented to the judge of the other East Circuit probate division if that judge is present in the courthouse. If both judges assigned to the East Circuit Divisions "U" and "W" are absent from the courthouse, then any emergency matter will be assigned to any other judge assigned to the East Division who is present in the courthouse. If all judges assigned to the East Division are absent from the courthouse, then the emergency matter will be presented to the judge assigned to Probate, Guardianship. Mental Health and Trust Division "A" in Tampa.

"Absent from the courthouse" means being physically located outside of the respective court facility. The term does not include being in a hearing, jury trial, or non-jury trial.

Matters scheduled for hearing as an emergency may not be heard with less than 48 hours' actual prior notice to an opposing interested person unless all interested persons agree.

11. Orders.

A. *Consultation with Opposing Counsel or Interested Person.* Unless the presiding judge directs otherwise, prior to counsel submitting a proposed order for the court's consideration, counsel must consult with opposing counsel or the appropriate interested person within five days after the court's decision and make a genuine effort to agree on the language of the proposed order.

B. *Timely Submission.* All proposed orders must be submitted to the court by the attorney directed to prepare the order within 10 days after the court's decision.

C. *Submission of Proposed Orders.*

i. JAWS—All Parties Represented by Counsel None of Whom are Excused from E-Service. Unless the presiding judge directs otherwise, if all parties are represented by attorneys, none of whom have been excused from e-mail service under Florida Rule of Judicial Administration 2.516, an attorney who is requested to submit a proposed order will do so through the JAWS in searchable PDF.

All proposed orders submitted to the presiding judge must include a cover letter certifying that one of the following statements is true: (i) all parties have agreed to the content of the proposed order or (ii) opposing counsel has not responded within five business days of being provided the proposed order.

If, after consultation with opposing counsel or the appropriate interested person, the parties cannot agree on the language in the proposed order to be submitted to the court, then the attorney or interested person submitting the proposed order must document in a cover letter that the opposing counsel or opposing interested person has registered an objection and specifically state what the objection is. At the time the cover letter and proposed order is submitted to the court, a copy must simultaneously be sent to all parties and interested persons or their counsel. If an objection is registered, the court will determine if a hearing is necessary to resolve the dispute.

ii. Hard Copies and Envelopes—Unrepresented Interested Person or Party's Attorney Excused from E–Service. If any interested person is unrepresented or if any party is represented by an attorney who has been excused from e-mail service under Rule 2.516, the interested person or attorney who is requested to submit a proposed order must do so by submitting to the presiding judge sufficient hard copies of the proposed order along with stamped, addressed envelopes.

iii. Title. The title of every proposed order submitted must contain the subject matter of the pleading or motion upon which the ruling is made and must fairly apprise the reader of the action being ordered. Phrasing such as "order granting ..." or "order denying ..." is preferred over "order on ...."

iv. Form. In all proposed orders, the page containing the court's signature must also contain substantive language of the proposed order so that a proposed order does not contain a signature page consisting only of the court's signature. Each page, except for the first page, must contain a page number.

12. **Adversary Proceedings.** In an adversary proceeding as defined by Florida Probate Rule 5.025, the following provisions apply:

A. *Case Management Conference.* A case management conference will be scheduled by the petitioner within 60 days of the commencement of an adversary proceeding as defined by Rule 5.025. All trials of adversary proceedings must be set by a uniform order setting pre-trial and nonjury trial. Uniform orders can be found at www.fljud13.org.

B. *Military Service—Memorandum for Certificate of Military Service.* If a petitioner does not know whether the respondent is on active duty in a branch of the military service of the United States, the petitioner must complete a memorandum for certificate of military service substantially similar to the memorandum designated as Florida Family Law Rule of Procedure Form 12.912(a). A uniform Memorandum for Certificate of Military Service can be found at www.fljud13.org.

C. *Default Judgment—Affidavit of Military Service.* If a petitioner seeks a default judgment and the respondent has been properly served and has not responded to the petition, the petitioner must complete and file an affidavit of military service substantially similar to the affidavit designated as Florida Family Law Rule of Procedure Form 12.912(b). A uniform Affidavit of Military Service can be found at www.fljud13.org.

D. *Motions to Compel—Order Without Hearing.* When a motion to compel that complies with the good faith certification in Florida Rule of Civil Procedure 1.380(a)(2)—motion "must include a certification that the movant, in good faith, has conferred or attempted to confer with the person or party failing to make the discovery in an effort to secure the information or material without court action"—alleges the absence of a response or objection to discovery and there has been no request for an extension of time to respond, the court, without a hearing, may enter an order requiring compliance with the original discovery request within 10 days of the signing of the order, provided no written showing of good cause has been filed by the non-moving party.

Unless the presiding judge directs otherwise, if all parties are represented by attorneys, none of whom have been excused from e-mail service under Florida Rule of Judicial Administration 2.516, the movant's attorneys must submit to the court a proposed order through the JAWS in searchable PDF format. If any interested person is unrepresented or if any party is represented by an attorney who has been excused from e-mail service under Rule 2.516, the movant or movant's attorney must submit to the presiding judge sufficient hard copies of the proposed order along with stamped, addressed envelopes.

E. *Motions to Set Case for Trial—Certificate by Attorney.* All motions to set a case for trial must contain a certificate by the attorney filing such motion that the attorney has discussed the subject matter of the motion with the opposing counsel or unrepresented interested person and has been unable to reach agreement concerning the setting of the case for trial, or that opposing counsel or unrepresented person has failed to respond.

13. **Order to Show Cause Docket.** The clerk will prepare an order to show cause docket in accordance with the applicable Florida Probate Rules and the applicable Florida Rules of Civil Procedure.

14. **Professional Conduct and Courtroom Decorum.** Counsel must adhere to The Florida Bar's Guidelines for Professional Conduct (www.floridabar.org). The Florida Bar's Professionalism Expectations (www.floridabar.org) and the Hillsborough County Bar Association's Standards of Professional Courtesy (www.hillsbar.com). Each judge may announce and enforce additional requirements, or may excuse compliance with any provision(s) of the Guidelines, Expectations, or Standards as that judge deems appropriate.

15. **Previous Administrative Order Superseded.** This administrative order supersedes Administrative Order S–2014–037 *(Probate Procedures)*.

16. **Effective Date.** This administrative order is effective February 1,2017.

ENTERED in Tampa, Hillsborough County, Florida, on January 31, 2017.

Ronald N. Ficarrotta, Chief Judge

S–2015–025. BAKER ACT HEARINGS

IN THE THIRTEENTH JUDICIAL CIRCUIT HILLSBOROUGH COUNTY, FLORIDA

ADMINISTRATIVE ORDER S–2015–025

(Supersedes Administrative Order S–2011–047)

BAKER ACT HEARINGS

Because of limited resources in the state courts system, the Offices of the Public Defender and State Attorney of the Thirteenth Judicial Circuit, it is necessary to reduce the number of mental health receiving facilities at which Baker Act hearings are scheduled.

The number of receiving facilities for Baker Act patients has grown over the years and additional future growth is anticipated. As a result, it is necessary to consolidate the locations where Baker Act hearings occur. The current Baker Act receiving facilities have been consulted and have provided input with regard to locations to be used as sites for Baker Act hearings.

A memorandum of understanding has been executed between the local Baker Act receiving facilities, the Sun Coast Region of the Department of Children and Family Services, the Administrative Office of the Courts for the Thirteenth Judicial Circuit, the Office of the Public Defender of the Thirteenth Judicial Circuit, and the Office of the State Attorney of the Thirteenth Judicial Circuit regarding the limitation of Baker Act hearings to three facilities. The memorandum of understanding recognizes the responsibilities of all affected entities to ensure the efficient administration of justice while protecting the rights of the patients as well as the safety of all parties.

Notwithstanding the memorandum of understanding, if circumstances necessitate relocating Baker Act hearings from a host facility to the courthouse, the administrative judge of the Probate, Guardianship and Trust Division is delegated the discretion to schedule hearings at the courthouse in addition to host facilities.

By the power vested in the chief judge under Article V, section 2(d), Florida Constitution; section 43.26, Florida Statutes; and Florida Rule of Judicial Administration 2.215(b)(2), it is therefore ORDERED:

1. **Definitions.** For purposes of this administrative order, the following terms have the following meanings:

A. **"Receiving facility"** means any public or private facility designated by the Department of Children and Families to receive and hold involuntary patients under emergency conditions or for psychiatric evaluation and to provide short-term treatment. The term does not include a county jail.

B. **"Host facility"** means a receiving facility which has been classified to serve as a facility at which Baker Act hearings will be conducted.

C. **"Transporting facility"** means a receiving facility which has not been classified to serve as a facility at which Baker Act hearings will be conducted; therefore, the facility is required to provide transportation to a host facility.

2. **Host Facility.**

A. *Criteria.* The classification of a receiving facility as a host facility or as a transporting facility is subject to change based on the following criteria: (a) number of petitions for involuntary placement filed with the Clerk of the Circuit Court by receiving facilities; (b) number of hearings conducted; (c) number of physicians at the receiving facilities; and (d) number of petitions filed which include minor children at receiving facilities.

B. *Change in Classification.* The Administrative Office of the Courts will provide a minimum of 90 days notice of any change of status of a receiving facility with respect to a facility's classification as a host facility or a transporting facility.

C. *Locations.* The three receiving facility locations initially classified as host facilities for the convening of Baker Act hearings are: (i) Mental Health Care, Inc.; (ii) BayCare Health System at St. Joseph's Hospital; and (iii) IASIS Health Care at Memorial Hospital. All transporting facilities will transport their patients to one of the classified host facilities for hearings.

D. *Adequacy of Hearing Room.* Each host facility is required to hold hearings in a room which is of adequate size and decorum, with sufficient dignity to elicit the customary respect afforded to court proceedings. During court proceedings, the United States flag and the State of Florida flag will be displayed, as well as the seal of the Thirteenth Judicial Circuit and a nameplate of the presiding General Magistrate.

3. **Newly Designated Receiving Facility to be Classified as Transporting Facility.** If a hospital is newly designated as a Baker Act receiving facility within the circuit, the newly designated receiving facility will be classified as a transporting facility.

4. **Hearing Schedule.** The schedule for Baker Act hearings at host facilities will be established by the administrative judge of the Probate, Guardianship and Trust Division for all of the Baker Act receiving facilities. The administrative judge of the Probate, Guardianship and Trust Division may schedule Baker Act hearings at the courthouse if circumstances necessitate such action and adequate notice is provided to the parties.

5. **Effective Date.** This administrative order is effective May 1, 2015.

It is ORDERED in Tampa, Hillsborough County, Florida, on this 15 day of April, 2015.

Ronald N. Ficarrotta, Chief Judge

Unified Family Court - Juvenile

S-2018-064. JUVENILE DELINQUENCY DIVISION

IN THE THIRTEENTH JUDICIAL CIRCUIT HILLSBOROUGH COUNTY, FLORIDA

ADMINISTRATIVE ORDER S-2018-064

(Supersedes Administrative Order S-2018-008)

JUVENILE DELINQUENCY DIVISION

Administrative Order S-2018-054 established Juvenile Mental Health Delinquency Division "B." In light of the creation of this specialized subdivision of the Juvenile Delinquency Division, it is necessary provide a mechanism for transferring eligible cases to this new subdivision.

By the power vested in the chief judge under article V, section 2(d), Florida Constitution; section 43.26, Florida Statutes; and Florida Rule of Judicial Administration 2.215(b)(2), it is ORDERED:

1. **Divisions & Application of Administrative Order.** There are two standard subdivisions in the Juvenile Delinquency Division: Divisions "A" and "F." There are also the following specialized subdivisions in the Juvenile Delinquency

Division: Juvenile Mental Health Delinquency Division "B," Juvenile Drug Court Division "E," and Unified Family Court Juvenile Crossover Division "M," which is also a partial standard subdivision. This administrative order governs matters in Division "A," Juvenile Mental Health Delinquency Division "B," Division "F," and Unified Family Court Juvenile Crossover Division "M" only to the extent delinquency matters are handled in Division "M." This administrative order does not govern matters in Juvenile Drug Court Division "E" and it does not govern dependency matters in Unified Family Court Juvenile Crossover Division "M."

2. Assignment of Cases.

A. *Children and Families in Need of Services Petitions and Truancy Petitions.* All petitions under chapter 984, Florida Statutes, will be assigned to Unified Family Court Juvenile Crossover Division "M."

B. *Sex–Related Offenses.* All sex-related offenses will be assigned to Unified Family Court Juvenile Crossover Division "M." For purposes of this administrative order, the term "sex-related offense" means a violation of section 787.06(3)(b), (d), (f), and (g) (human trafficking involving commercial sexual activity); 794.011 (sexual battery); 794.08 (female genital mutilation); 796.04 (forcing, compelling, or coercing another to become a prostitute); 796.05 (deriving support from the proceeds of prostitution); 796.07 (prostitution); 800.02 (unnatural and lascivious acts); 800.03 (exposure of sexual organs); 800.04 (lewd or lascivious offenses committed upon or in the presence of persons less than 16 years of age); 810.14 (voyeurism); 810.145 (video voyeurism); 825.1025 (lewd or lascivious offenses committed upon or in the presence of an elderly person or disabled adult); 826.04 (incest); 827.071 (sexual performance by a child); 828.126 (sexual activities involving animals); 847.011 (obscenity); 847.012 (sale or distribution of materials harmful to minors); 847.0133 (sale or distribution of obscene materials to minors); 847.0135 (computer pornography); 847.0137 (transmission of pornography by electronic device); 847.0138 (transmission of material harmful to a minor by electronic device); or 847.0141 (sexting—noncriminal first violations and second and subsequent criminal violations), Florida Statutes.

C. *New Delinquency Cases.*

i. Criminal Report Affidavit—Juvenile Assessment Center. For all juveniles taken into custody and not detained in accordance with Florida Rule of Juvenile Procedure 8.045(c), the notice to appear issued to the child must indicate the division in which the child will appear. If a juvenile (1) has a pending case or cases; (2) is on probation or commitment status; (3) has ever had a pending case or cases; or (4) was ever on probation or commitment status, the division on the notice to appear will be the division in which the pending case is pending or had been pending or the division in which the juvenile is on probation or commitment status or had been on probation or commitment status. If the juvenile has no pending case(s), has never had a pending case, is not on probation or commitment status, and has never been on probation or commitment status, the division on the notice to appear will be designated based on the juvenile's last name according to the following schedule:

DIVISION	FIRST LETTER OF JUVENILE'S LAST NAME
"A"	P, Q, R, S, T, U, V, W, X, Y, Z
"F"	F, G, H, I, J, K, L, M, N, O
"M"	A, B, C, D, E

ii. Delinquency Petition—Single defendant, no pending or previous case(s). If a juvenile has no co-defendants and has never had a pending case or been on probation or commitment status, the newly filed delinquency petition will be assigned to one of the juvenile delinquency divisions based on the juvenile's last name according to the following schedule:

DIVISION	FIRST LETTER OF JUVENILE'S LAST NAME
"A"	P, Q, R, S, T, U, V, W, X, Y, Z
"F"	F, G, H, I, J, K, L, M, N, O
"M"	A, B, C, D, E

iii. Delinquency Petition—Single defendant pending or previous case(s). If a juvenile has no co-defendants but has a pending case or cases or is on probation or commitment status or has had a pending case or cases or has been on probation or commitment status, the newly filed petition will be assigned to the division in which the other case is pending or had been pending, unless the juvenile's pending case is in Juvenile Mental Health Delinquency Division "B." If a juvenile's pending case is in Juvenile Mental Health Delinquency Division "B," the newly filed petition will be assigned to Division "B" only by order of the presiding judge of Division "B." The decision to transfer the new charge to Division "B" will be made on a case-by-case basis after consultation with the parties.

iv. Delinquency Petition—Co-defendants, no pending or previous case(s). If a newly filed petition involves co-defendants, none of whom has a pending case or have ever had a pending case or are not on probation or commitment status or have never been on probation or commitment status, the newly filed petition will be assigned to one of the juvenile delinquency divisions based on the lowest case number of the co-defendants.

v. Delinquency Petition—Co-defendants, pending or previous case(s). If a newly filed petition involves co-defendants, any one of whom has a pending case or have ever had a pending case or is on probation or commitment status or has ever been on probation or commitment status, the newly filed petition will be assigned to the division that has or had the lowest case number. If there is more than one pending case or had been more than one pending case, the newly filed petition will be assigned to the division handling the lowest pending case number or the division that had previously handled the lowest pending case number. All co-defendants' pending cases will be transferred to the assigned division if necessary. If co-defendants have or have had pending cases in different divisions, all pending cases will be transferred to the division which has or had the lowest case number, unless any defendant has a case pending in Division "M" solely because of the case's status as a sex-related offense (see § 2B of this administrative order) or because of the case's dual crossover status or any defendant has a case pending in Juvenile Mental Health Delinquency Division "B" (see § 3 of this administrative order). If any defendant has a case pending in Division "M" solely because of the case's status as a sex-related offense or because of the case's dual crossover status, that defendant's case(s) will be transferred into Division "M," apart from any other co-defendant(s). If any defendant has a case pending in Juvenile Mental Health Delinquency Division "B," that defendant's case(s) will be transferred into Division "B," apart from any other co-defendant(s), for the presiding judge of Division "B" to determine whether the new charge will remain pending in Division "B."

D. *Competency to Proceed.*

i. Determination. When a juvenile's competency is believed to be at issue, the attorney of record will file a motion to determine competency in the respective division in which the child's case is pending. The juvenile's case will remain pending in the respective division while the child's competency is being evaluated. In accordance with section 985.19(1)(b), Florida Statutes, the court will determine competency at a hearing with findings of fact based on a written evaluation of the child's mental condition made by the appointed mental health professionals.

ii. Competent to Proceed. If the court finds the juvenile competent to proceed, the juvenile will remain in the respective division unless the court and both parties agree that the juvenile's behavioral or mental health issues may be more appropriately addressed in Juvenile Mental Health Delinquency Division "B" in accordance with section 3D of this administrative order.

iii. Incompetent to Proceed. If the court finds the juvenile incompetent to proceed, the court will enter an appropriate order in accordance with section 985.19(1)(c), Florida Statutes. Upon the issuance of an order determining incompetency, the clerk will transfer the juvenile's case(s) to Juvenile Mental Health Delinquency Division "B" and all case related matters will be addressed in Division "B" while the juvenile is incompetent.

iv. Restoration of Competency. Upon restoration of competency, a goal of the Juvenile Mental Health Delinquency Court is for the juvenile to be offered appropriate diversionary programs upon agreement between the parties. Juveniles may be offered a diversionary program and remain in Division "B" for further monitoring. If the parties do not agree to a diversion pathway, the court will transfer the competent juvenile to the original division for disposition of the case through plea, motion, adjudicatory hearing, or other agreed upon resolution.

3. Juvenile Mental Health Delinquency Division "B".

A. *Purpose.* Juvenile Mental Health Delinquency Division "B" has been established as the specialized subdivision to monitor juveniles found incompetent to proceed and juveniles with behavioral or mental health issues.

B. *Transfer of Pending Incompetent to Proceed Cases.* On or before the effective date of this administrative order, the clerk will transfer all juveniles who have been previously found incompetent to proceed to Juvenile Mental Health Delinquency Division "B."

C. *Transfer of Future Incompetent to Proceed Cases.* On and after the effective date of this administrative order, the clerk will transfer all juveniles who are found incompetent to proceed to Juvenile Mental Health Delinquency Division "B" in accordance with section 2D of this administrative order.

D. *Behavioral or Mental Health Issues.* By agreement of the parties and the court, certain juveniles with behavioral or mental health issues may be eligible for transfer to Juvenile Mental Health Delinquency Division "B" prior to being found incompetent to proceed. Upon court approval, defense counsel will prepare and submit a transfer order for all eligible juveniles together with the diversionary agreement. The clerk will transfer the eligible juveniles to Division "B" upon receipt of the transfer order. All case related matters will be addressed in Division "B."

E. *New Criminal Charge.* If a juvenile is charged with a new criminal offense while the juvenile has a case or cases pending in Juvenile Mental Health Delinquency Division "B," the new charge may be transferred to Division "B" by order of the presiding judge of Division "B." The decision to transfer the new charge to Division "B" will be made on a case-by-case basis after consultation with the parties.

4. Reassignment of Case upon Judge's Disqualification. If either of the judges presiding in Juvenile Delinquency Division "A" or "F" enters an order of judicial disqualification, the clerk will reassign the case to the other division. If both standard juvenile delinquency subdivision judges have entered orders of disqualification, the clerk will reassign the case to the judge presiding in Unified Family Court Juvenile Crossover Division "M." If the judge presiding in Division "M" enters an order of disqualification, the clerk will reassign the case randomly to one of the standard subdivisions in the Juvenile Delinquency Division unless the case was previously pending in both of the divisions in which situation the case is to be reassigned to Juvenile Dependency Specialty Division "V." If the judge presiding in Juvenile Mental Health Delinquency Division "B" enters an order of disqualification, the clerk will reassign the case to the original division.

5. Petitions and Motions. All detention petitions, delinquency petitions, petitions under chapter 984, Florida Statutes, motions and any other documents seeking relief in a juvenile delinquency action must be filed with the clerk in accordance with Florida Rule of Judicial Administration 2.525 and served in accordance with Rule 2.516. Hearings on these matters will be scheduled through the clerk.

Prior to filing any motion and scheduling a hearing, counsel should consult with opposing counsel as to the date and the time required for such hearing. If a motion is not simultaneously filed with a notice of hearing, the motion will be deemed abandoned, and the clerk will not calendar it.

Counsel must file all motions and notices of hearing no later than 12:00 noon the day preceding the scheduled hearing. All matters not in compliance with this requirement will not appear on the calendar and will be deemed abandoned until properly noticed.

All petitions, motions, or other documents will have the name of the court, uniform case number, and division letter for that child or children, and will be styled in accordance with Florida Rule of Juvenile Procedure 8.025 or 8.620.

All petitions, motions, or other documents will also contain the name, address, telephone number, e-mail address, and Florida Bar number of the attorney of record and an indication of which party the attorney represents, all of which information will appear directly below the signature line.

Unless the presiding judge directs otherwise, any case law that counsel or a party wishes the court to consider in support of or in opposition to any motion set for hearing should be cited in the motion or submitted to the court at least 24 hours prior to the hearing on the motion.

6. Orders and Judgments.

A. *Timely Submission.* All proposed orders or judgments, except detention and disposition orders, will be submitted to the court by the attorney designated by the court within two days of the court's decision. Detention and disposition orders will be submitted to the court immediately after the hearing.

B. *Entity to Prepare Proposed Orders.* Unless the presiding judge directs otherwise, the following general guidelines will also apply:

i. Detention Orders will be prepared by the Department of Juvenile Justice.

ii. Depending upon the party that prevails, all Pre-Disposition Orders will be prepared by either counsel for the prevailing party (the state attorney's office, the public defender's office, or defense counsel representing the child) or as otherwise directed by the presiding judge.

iii. Disposition Orders will be prepared by the clerk.

C. *Submission of Proposed Orders and Judgments.* Unless the presiding judge directs otherwise, an attorney who is requested to submit a proposed order or judgment will do so through the Judicial Automated Workflow System (JAWS). Prior to submitting a proposed order or judgment, the attorney must review and comply with the presiding judge's webpage to determine that judge's format preference (Microsoft Word v. PDF). If the presiding judge does not have divisional provisions posted, then the attorney should submit the proposed order in searchable PDF.

D. *Title.* All proposed orders and judgments submitted to the judges will contain, in the title of the order, the exact nature of the court's ruling and must fairly apprise the reader of the action being ordered. Phrasing such as "order granting ..." or "order denying ..." is preferred over "order on ..."

E. *Form.* No proposed order or judgment will be submitted to a judge unless such order contains in the body of the order a reference to the date(s) of the hearing during which the subject matter of the order or judgment was argued before the court and the names of the parties and counsel present. Every proposed order and judgment will also contain the name of the court, uniform case number, and division letter, and will be styled in accordance with Florida Rule of Juvenile Procedure 8.025 or 8.620. Any submission of a proposed order or judgment by an attorney will be considered a representation that the attorney has read it and that it is submitted in good faith in accordance with the findings and decision of the court.

F. *Objections.* Any attorney or party who objects to the entry of a proposed order which has been submitted to the presiding judge must immediately notify the judge's office via telephone or e-mail. If the objection notification is made by e-mail, the opposing attorney or party must be copied on the e-mail message. The objecting attorney or party must submit an alternative proposed order within two days of communicating the objection. If an alternative proposed order has not been received by the court within two days, the court will consider the objection withdrawn.

7. Cancellation of Hearings. No hearing may be canceled without the consent of all parties, approval of the court and notice to the clerk.

8. Continuances. A continuance may be granted by order of the court either before or during a hearing for good cause shown. Counsel seeking a continuance will file an appropriate motion and notice of hearing prior to the scheduled hearing date and be present for the hearing on the motion. No hearing or other proceeding will be continued upon stipulation of counsel alone. Failure to complete discovery will not constitute cause for a continuance unless such failure is brought to the attention of the court at least five working days in advance of any scheduled hearing date and the failure is not the result of lack of diligence in pursuing discovery. Except for good cause shown, no continuance will be granted because a witness has not been served with a subpoena.

9. Scheduling Conflicts. Attorneys who have scheduled hearings or trials in more than one court at the same time will notify the affected judges and opposing counsel prior to the hearing date if the conflict might substantially affect the attorney's ability to meet his or her obligation. *See* Fla. R. Jud. Admin. 2.550.

10. Emergency Matters. Judges will be available to handle emergency matters arising in their respective divisions unless prior arrangements have been made with another judge for substitution during an absence. The associate administrative judge of the Juvenile Delinquency Division will handle emergency matters if an assigned or substitute judge is not available.

11. Court-Appointed Private Attorneys. Court-appointed private attorneys from the chief judge registry must follow the procedures for payment of fees and costs promulgated by the Justice Administrative Commission. Such Justice Administrative Commission procedures can be accessed at http://www.justiceadmin.org.

12. Professional Conduct and Courtroom Decorum. Counsel will adhere to The Florida Bar's Guidelines for Professional Conduct (https://www.floridabar.org/prof/presources/presources002/). The Florida Bar's Professionalism Expectations (https://www.floridabar.org/wpcontent/uploads/2017/04/professionalism-expectations.pdf) and the Hillsborough County Bar Association's Standards of Professionalism (http://hillsbar.sitevm.com/?page=Professionalism). Each judge may announce and enforce additional requirements, or may excuse compliance with any provision(s) of the Guidelines, Expectations, or Standards as that judge deems appropriate.

13. Previous Administrative Order Superseded. This administrative order supersedes Administrative Order S-2018-008 (*Juvenile Delinquency Division*).

14. Effective Date. This administrative order is effective January 1, 2019.

ENTERED in Tampa, Hillsborough County, Florida on December 28, 2018.

Ronald N. Ficarrotta
Chief Judge

S–2018–033. JUVENILE DEPENDENCY DIVISION

IN THE THIRTEENTH JUDICIAL CIRCUIT HILLSBOROUGH COUNTY, FLORIDA

ADMINISTRATIVE ORDER S–2018–033

(Supersedes Administrative Order S–2017–045)

JUVENILE DEPENDENCY DIVISION

General magistrates assist judges in the Juvenile Dependency Division with judicial reviews and other post-adjudicatory motions. Based on a redeployment of magistrate resources effective January 1, 2019, it is necessary for the proper and efficient administration of justice to update the provisions governing assignment of juvenile dependency cases to the general magistrates.

By the power vested in the chief judge under article V, section 2(d), Florida Constitution; section 43.26, Florida Statutes; and Florida Rule of Judicial Administration 2.215(b)(2), it is ORDERED:

1. **Divisions.** Juvenile dependency matters will be administered by seven judicial divisions. The judicial divisions are designated as Division "C," Division "D," Division "I" (Independent Living Transition Services), Division "J" (Dependency Drug Court), Division "M" (Dependency Crossover), Division "S" and Division "V" (Dependency Specialty).

2. **Assignment of Cases.** Upon the filing of a shelter petition, the Clerk of the Circuit Court (clerk) will designate a case number and assign the petition using a random equitable assignment system to Division "C," "D" or "S." The clerk will assign all subsequently-filed petitions, except petitions involving a minor seeking special immigrant status, to the division to which the shelter petition was assigned. If an initial shelter petition was not filed, the clerk will assign all other new petitions (dependency, child abuse injunctions, and termination of parental rights), except petitions involving a minor seeking special immigrant status, using a random equitable assignment system to Division "C," "D" or "S."

3. **Shelter Hearings.** For purposes of this provision, the term "dependency judge" means any judge assigned to the Juvenile Dependency Division or a judge or senior judge who has previously presided over dependency proceedings.

Regardless of the division assignment, all shelter petitions will be considered at a shelter hearing conducted by a dependency judge each non-holiday weekday at 1:30 p.m. The dependency judges presiding in Divisions "C," "D," "J," "M," "S," and "V" will preside over shelter hearings on a weekly rotating basis. Judges presiding in other subject matter divisions who have previously presided over dependency proceedings may offer assistance in the shelter hearing rotation schedule. The associate administrative judge of the Juvenile Dependency Division will maintain the schedule of judges presiding over weekly shelter dockets.

The clerk will assign an arraignment date at the shelter hearing. All parties present at the shelter hearing will be informed of the arraignment date assigned to their case. The court will advise any parent of the right to have counsel present and appoint registry counsel to indigent parents unless intelligently waived. Court-appointed attorneys will be assigned to cover shelter hearings on a weekly basis. The associate administrative judge of the Juvenile Dependency Division will maintain a list of court-appointed attorneys eligible for appointment and the weekly schedule of assignments.

4. **Dependency Petitions Involving a Minor Seeking Special Immigrant Status.** Petitions for dependency involving a minor seeking special immigrant status will be assigned to Dependency Specialty Division "V." To assist the clerk in identifying such petitions the party filing the petition must title the petition "Petition for Dependency Involving Minor Seeking Special Immigrant Status."

5. **Petitions for Child Abuse Injunctions.** If the dependency judge issues a temporary injunction, the return hearing will be scheduled by the clerk in Family Law Division "G" or "H" based on a random equitable basis. If a motion to modify or dissolve a final injunction is filed, the motion will be heard in the division in which the return hearing was conducted.

6. **Termination of Parental Rights Petitions.** The judges presiding in Divisions "C," "D" and "S" will coordinate with the judges presiding in Juvenile Crossover Division "M" and Juvenile Dependency Specialty Division "V" regarding adjudicatory and post-disposition hearings in termination of parental rights cases.

7. **Reactivation of Protective Services.** If a motion is filed to reactivate protective services supervision on a closed case or if a new shelter, dependency, or termination of parental rights petition is filed concerning a new child born into a family with an already existing case, the motion or petition will be assigned to the division in which the corresponding case was last pending or is currently pending. If the Office of the Attorney General, Division of Children's Legal Services (CLS) or Guardian Ad Litem Program (GAL) files such a motion or petition, the CLS or GAL will include the appropriate division designation on the first page of the motion or petition. If the clerk discovers any inaccuracy in the division designation on the motion or petition, the clerk will rectify such inaccuracy so that the motion or petition is filed in the appropriate division. If any other person files such a motion or petition, the clerk will file the motion or petition and immediately consult with the associate administrative judge for determination of the appropriate division assignment.

8. **Juvenile Divisions "M" and "V".** The presiding judges in Divisions "M" and "V" are responsible for providing equitable backup relief to the Juvenile Dependency Division. Backup responsibilities include, but are not limited to: handling all dependency related petitions under chapters 984 (CINS/FINS), Florida Statutes; presiding over adjudicatory, disposition and post-disposition hearings in dependency cases; presiding over adjudicatory and post-disposition hearings in termination of parental rights cases; covering any juvenile dependency division's docket matters when the regularly assigned judge is unavailable and handling any other matters that might appear on a juvenile dependency division's calendar. Prior to transferring any matter from Division "C," "D," or "S" to Division "M" or "V" in accordance with this provision, the affected presiding judges must consult with each other. A case may be transferred to Division "M" or "V" only

by an Order of Transfer issued by the presiding judge of Division "M" or "V."

9. Dependency Drug Court Division "J". For purposes of this provision, the term "drug court model" means a case management system for parents, guardians and any other person seeking custody of a child in which court supervised drug treatment is used in promoting substantial compliance with a case plan. The treatment may include, but is not limited to, varying levels of drug treatment enforced by the court through its contempt powers or implementation of sanctions or both. The drug court model applies a protocol which utilizes case managers, substance abuse evaluators and treatment modalities to aid the court in fashioning appropriate substance abuse treatment and utilizing frequent case reviews as needed.

At shelter hearings, in accordance with established eligibility criteria, substance abuse evaluators will identify and notify the presiding judge of any case in which the drug court model may be appropriate. If the substance abuse evaluator has identified a case in which the drug court model may be appropriate, at any time after the disposition hearing, the presiding judge in Division "C," "D," "M," "S" or "V" may transfer that case to Dependency Drug Court Division "J" for court supervision under the drug court model.

10. General Magistrates

A. *Appointments.* Tracy L. Ellis, Nancy Neaves and Joan Montagno are appointed as general magistrates of the Juvenile Dependency Division. The general magistrates serve under the direction of the associate administrative judge of the Juvenile Dependency Division.

B. *General Magistrate Divisions.* Divisions "GM–1," "GM–2," and "GM–3" are established as general magistrate divisions within the Dependency Division. The general magistrates are assigned to the general magistrate divisions as follows:

General Magistrate Division	General Magistrate
"GM—1"	Tracy L. Ellis
"GM—2"	Nancy Neaves
"GM—3"	Joan Montagno

C. *Case Assignments*

i. Case Number Assignment. Any dependency matter referred by the court to a general magistrate will be assigned via the Judicial Automated Workflow System (JAWS) to either General Magistrate Division "GM–1," "GM–2," or "GM–3."

Except as provided in section 10.C.ii. of this administrative order dealing with the assignment of related cases, the assignment of a referred matter to a general magistrate will be determined by the last two digits of the case number according to the following table:

GM–1 TRACY ELLIS	GM–2 NANCY NEAVES		GM–3 JOAN MONTAGNO
01	00	50	51
03	02	52	53
05	04	54	55
07	06	56	57
09	08	58	59
11	10	60	61
13	12	62	63
15	14	64	65
17	16	66	67
19	18	68	69
21	20	70	71
23	22	72	73
25	24	74	75
27	26	76	77
29	28	78	79
31	30	80	81
33	32	82	83
35	34	84	85
37	36	86	87
39	38	88	89
41	40	90	91
43	42	92	93
45	44	94	95
47	46	96	97
49	48	98	99

ii. Related Case Exception to Case Number Assignment. Notwithstanding the case number, if the court refers a matter to a general magistrate in a case concerning a new child born into a family with an already existing dependency case, the order of referral for the new child will assign the matter to the same general magistrate who is already handling or who previously handed the related dependency case. This exception does not apply if the court has terminated jurisdiction of the related case based on the adoption of the child or if the court no longer has jurisdiction of the related case.

D. *Referral.* The general magistrates may hear any juvenile dependency case referred for the purpose of judicial review or any other related matter authorized by the Florida Rules of Juvenile Procedure. Upon the filing of any juvenile dependency matter that may be referred to a general magistrate, any party may submit to the judge assigned to the case a proposed Order of Referral to the General Magistrate. Any objection to a referral must be in writing and filed within 10 days of the date of service of the signed order of referral. If an objection is filed, the case will remain with the judge.

E. *Hearing.* When a matter is referred to the general magistrate, the matter referred will be set for hearing on a specific date and at a specific time before the general magistrate. The general magistrate will proceed with the hearing and the preparation and filing of reports in the manner set out in Florida Rule of Juvenile Procedure 8.257.

11. Reassignment of Case upon Judge's Disqualification. If a judge in Juvenile Dependency Division "C," "D," or "S" enters an order of disqualification, the clerk will reassign the case randomly and equitably to one of the other two standard divisions in the Juvenile Dependency Division. If all three judges in Juvenile Dependency Division "C," "D," and "S" enter orders of disqualification, the clerk will randomly and equitably reassign the case to Juvenile Crossover Division "M" or Juvenile Dependency Specialty Division "V."

If the presiding judge in Juvenile Crossover Division "M" enters an order of disqualification, the clerk will reassign the case to Juvenile Dependency Specialty Division "V." If the presiding judge in Juvenile Dependency Specialty Division "V" enters an order of disqualification, the clerk will reassign the case to Juvenile Crossover Division "M." If both presiding judges in Divisions "M" and "V" enter orders of disqualification, the clerk will reassign the case to a standard division in accordance with the above paragraph.

If all of the judges in Juvenile Dependency Division "C," "D," "S," "M" and "V" enter orders of disqualification, the clerk will transfer the case to a deputy clerk assigned to the Family Law Division for random reassignment to one of the divisions in the Family Law Division.

If the presiding judge in Dependency Drug Court Division "J" enters an order of disqualification, the clerk will reassign the case to the Dependency Division from which the case was originally transferred to Division "J."

If the presiding judge in Independent Living Transition Services Division "I" enters an order of disqualification, the clerk will reassign the case to the Dependency Division from which the case was originally transferred to Division "I."

12. Motions, Petitions and Other Documents

A. *Scheduling*

i. Attorneys. Attorneys may obtain available hearing times and schedule hearings on a judge's calendar by accessing JAWS at: https://jaws.fljud13.org/System/login.aspx or by telephoning the judge's judicial assistant.

ii. Self–Represent Litigants. After any self-represented litigant files a motion with the clerk, a representative of the Dependency Case Management Unit will contact the self-represented litigant for scheduling of the matter on the assigned judge's calendar or other necessary action. Self-represented litigants may obtain a form motion at: http://www.fljud13.org/Portals/0/Forms/pdfs/fiu/dependency_pkt.pdf.

B. *Form.* Every motion, petition or other document must have the name of the court, uniform case number, and division letter for the child or children, and must be styled in accordance with Florida Rule of Juvenile Procedure 8.220.

C. *Notices of Hearing.* Every notice of hearing must state the length of time reserved on the judge's calendar for the hearing and specify which matters are to be heard. Notices of hearing specifying that the hearing is on "all pending motions" will not be accepted for filing. There will be no cross-noticing on hearing time unless the opposing counsel or party contacts the judge's judicial assistant and determines if the docket will accommodate hearing additional matters at the same time.

13. Orders and Judgments

A. *Consultation with Opposing Counsel or Party.* Unless the presiding judge directs otherwise, prior to submitting a proposed order for the court's consideration after a hearing, the attorney or self-represented litigant submitting the proposed order must consult with opposing counsel or the opposing self-represented litigant within five days after the court's decision and make a genuine effort to agree on the language of the proposed order.

B. *Objections.* If, after consultation with opposing counsel or the opposing self-represented litigant, the parties cannot agree on the language in the proposed order or judgment to be submitted to the court, then the attorney or self-represented litigant submitting the proposed order or judgment must document in a cover letter that the opposing party or counsel has registered an objection and specifically state what the objection is. At the time the cover letter and proposed order or judgment is submitted to the court, a copy must simultaneously be sent to all parties or their attorneys. If an objection is registered, the court will determine if a hearing is necessary to resolve the dispute.

C. *Timely Submission.* All proposed orders or judgments will be submitted to the court by the attorney or self-represented litigant directed to prepare the order within 10 days of the court's decision. If the designated attorney or self-represented litigant fails to timely submit a proposed order or judgment, the attorney for the opposing party or the opposing self-represented litigant may submit a proposed order or judgment within 5 days after the initial ten-day period.

D. *Submission of Proposed Orders and Judgments*

i. JAWS—All Parties Represented by Counsel. Unless the presiding judge directs otherwise, if all parties are represented by attorneys, none of whom have been excused from e-mail service under Florida Rule of Judicial Administration 2.516, an attorney who is requested to submit a proposed order or judgment will do so through the JAWS. Attorneys must comply with the presiding judge's formatting preference (Microsoft Word v. PDF) posted on the presiding judge's webpage when submitting a proposed order or judgment through the JAWS. If the presiding judge has not posted a preference, a proposed order or judgment should be submitted through JAWS in PDF.

Prior to the submission of a proposed order or judgment to the presiding judge through the JAWS, the submitting attorney will be required to certify that one of the following statements is true: (i) all parties have agreed to the content of the proposed order or judgment; (ii) an included cover letter documents the specific objection(s) to the proposed order or judgment; or (iii) opposing counsel has not responded within five business days of being provided the proposed order or judgment.

ii. Hard Copies and Envelopes—Self–Represented Party or Party's Attorney Excused from E–Service. If any party is self-represented or represented by an attorney who has been excused from e-mail service by the court under Rule 2.516, the party or attorney who is requested to submit a proposed order or judgment will do so by submitting to the presiding judge sufficient hard copies of the proposed order or judgment along with stamped, addressed envelopes.

E. *Title.* All proposed orders and judgments submitted to the judges must contain, in the title of the order, the exact nature of the court's ruling and must fairly apprise the reader of the action being ordered. Phrasing such as "order granting ..." or "order denying ..." is preferred over "order on ..."

F. *Form.* No proposed order or judgment will be submitted to a judge unless the order contains in the body of the order a reference to the date(s) of the hearing during which the subject matter of the order or judgment was argued before the court and the names of the parties and counsel present. Every proposed order and judgment must also contain the name of the court, uniform case number, and division letter for the child or children, and be styled in accordance with Florida Rule of Juvenile Procedure 8.220. Any submission of a proposed order or judgment by an attorney will be considered a representation that the attorney has read it and that it is submitted in good faith in accordance with the findings and decision of the court.

14. Cancellation of Hearings. No hearing may be canceled without the consent of all parties, approval of the court, and notice to the clerk.

15. Continuances. In accordance with Florida Rule of Juvenile Procedure 8.255(f), the court may grant a continuance for good cause shown, as permitted by law. *See* § 39.0136, Fla. Stat. Counsel seeking a continuance will file an appropriate motion and notice of hearing and will be present for hearing on the motion. All motions for continuance will explain what effect the motion will have on the progress of the case. *See* Fla. R. Jud. Admin. 2.545(e). No hearing or other proceeding will be continued upon stipulation of counsel alone. All motions for continuance of a hearing will be filed and heard prior to the scheduled hearing date.

Failure to complete discovery will not constitute cause for a continuance unless such failure is brought to the attention of the court at least five working days in advance of any scheduled hearing date and the failure is not the result of lack of diligence in pursuing such discovery. Except for good cause shown, no continuance will be granted because a witness has not been served with a subpoena, unless the moving party has attempted service at least five working days before the return date.

16. Emergency Matters. All judges will be available to handle emergency matters arising in their respective divisions unless arrangements have been made with another judge to substitute during any absence. The associate administrative judge of the Juvenile Dependency Division will handle emergency matters if the assigned or substitute judge is not available.

17. Professional Conduct and Courtroom Decorum. Counsel must adhere to The Florida Bar's Guidelines for Professional Conduct (https://www.floridabar.org/prof/presources/presourcesQ02/), The Florida Bar's Professionalism Expectations (https://www.floridabar.org/wp-content/uploads/2017/04/professionalism-expectations.pdf), and the Hillsborough County Bar Association's Standards of Professional Courtesy (http://hillsbar.site-ym.com/?page=Professionalism). Each judge may announce and enforce additional requirements, or may excuse compliance with any provision(s) of the Guidelines, Expectations, or Standards as that judge deems appropriate.

18. Attorneys' Obligation to Notify Court of Other Proceedings. Counsel are obligated to notify the court, as soon as it becomes known to counsel, of the existence of any other court proceeding in the Thirteenth Judicial Circuit or any other jurisdiction that may be relevant to the subject matter before the court affecting the custody, visitation, or support of a child.

19. Previous Administrative Order Superseded. This administrative order supersedes Administrative Order S–2017–045 (*Juvenile Dependency Division*).

20. Effective Date. In order to timely populate General Magistrate Division "GM–3" with referrals, section 10 of this administrative order is effective immediately. All other provisions of this administrative order are effective January 1, 2019. General Magistrate Division "GM–3" will begin hearing cases on January 9, 2019.

ENTERED in Tampa, Hillsborough County, Florida on August 13, 2018

Ronald N. Ficarrotta
Chief Judge

S–2011–046. PARENTAL NOTICE OF ABORTION ACT CASES

IN THE THIRTEENTH JUDICIAL CIRCUIT HILLSBOROUGH COUNTY, FLORIDA

ADMINISTRATIVE ORDER S–2011–046

(Supersedes Administrative Order S–2006–200)

PARENTAL NOTICE OF ABORTION ACT CASES

The Parental Notice of Abortion Act (hereinafter "Act"), section 390.01114, Florida Statutes, provides that a termination of pregnancy may not be performed or induced upon a minor unless the physician performing or inducing the termination of pregnancy has given at least 48 hours actual notice to one parent or to the legal guardian of the pregnant minor of his or her intention to perform or induce the termination of pregnancy. The Act further provides for judicial waiver of notice to the parents or legal guardian. The court is required to give these proceedings precedence over other pending matters to the extent necessary to ensure that the court reaches a decision within three (3) business days after a petition is filed.

It is necessary for the prompt and efficient administration of justice to update the procedures for handling parental notice of abortion act cases to ensure that proceedings under this Act are handled in an expeditious manner. By the power vested in the chief judge under article V, section 2(d), Florida Constitution; section 43.26, Florida Statutes; and Florida Rule of Judicial Administration 2.215(b)(2), it is therefore **ORDERED:**

1. Filing of Petition. All petitions seeking a judicial waiver of the notice requirements of section 390.01114, Florida Statutes, will be filed in the Juvenile Dependency Division.

2. Assignment of Case. Immediately upon filing, the Clerk of the Circuit Court (hereinafter "clerk") will assign the petition to one of the Unified Family Court divisions by using a random equitable distribution system. For purposes of this administrative order only, a Unified Family Court division is a division within any of the following subject matter divisions: Domestic Relations / Family Law, Domestic Violence, Juvenile Dependency, Juvenile Dependency Crossover and Juvenile Dependency Specialty.

The clerk will immediately contact the judge presiding in the division to which the petition is assigned by telephoning or otherwise communicating with the assigned judge's judicial assistant. If the judicial assistant or assigned judge cannot be immediately contacted, the clerk will notify any other Unified Family Court division judge using a random equitable distribution system. If none of the Unified Family Court division judges are available, the clerk will contact the duty judge who will handle the matter.

3. Appointment of Counsel. If the petitioner is not represented by counsel and has requested counsel in the petition, the clerk or the assigned judge's judicial assistant will contact the next attorney on the registry of attorneys approved in the Chief Judge Registry which can be found on the Thirteenth Judicial Circuit's webpage at www.fljud13.org. If the attorney is not available to assist the petitioner, the next attorney on the registry should be contacted until an attorney is located to represent the petitioner.

If the petitioner is not represented by counsel and has not requested counsel in the petition, the judge should immediately conduct a hearing to advise the petitioner she has a right to court-appointed counsel at no cost to her, and after inquiry, appoint counsel if requested by the petitioner or as the circumstances require.

4. Three (3) Business Day Rule. Proceedings arising out of these petitions will be given precedence over other pending matters and will be heard in closed court immediately, on the same day the petition is filed, if possible. If a hearing cannot be held immediately, the clerk will coordinate a hearing time with the assigned judge and then provide notice of the hearing to the petitioner pursuant to Rule 8.805(d). The court must rule and issue written findings of fact and conclusions of law (see Florida Rule of Juvenile Procedure Forms 8.990 and 8.991) within three business days from the time the petition is filed, except that the three business day limitation may be extended at the request of the petitioner. If the court fails to rule within the three business day period and an extension has not been requested, the petitioner may immediately petition for a hearing upon the expiration of the three business day period to the chief judge who will ensure a hearing is held within 48 hours after receipt of the minor's petition and an order is entered within 24 hours after the hearing.

5. Transcript. If the assigned judge is a judge presiding in the Domestic Relations / Family Law Division (division without court reporters provided by the court), the judicial assistant will immediately contact the court operations department so that a court reporter can be assigned for the hearing. If the assigned judge is the duty judge, the judge may consider conducting the hearing on a weekend day or holiday after conducting juvenile shelter and detention hearings so that a court reporter is available for the hearing. An expedited transcript must be produced by the court reporter as soon after the hearing as possible and immediately delivered to the court for inclusion with the court's written findings.

6. Confidentiality. As provided by section 390.01116, Florida Statutes, and Florida Rule of Juvenile Procedure 8.835(a), any information including the petition, documents, transcripts, recordings of cases, and any other information that could be used to identify a minor who has petitioned the court for a judicial waiver of parental notice of termination of pregnancy is confidential and exempt from public disclosure. As provided by Rule 8.835(b), the court file shall be sealed unless otherwise ordered by the court. Judges are encouraged to (1) hold such hearings at a place and time that will provide the maximum privacy to the minor; (2) ensure that unauthorized persons are not in the courtroom or hearing room; (3) ensure that unauthorized persons cannot see or hear the proceedings; and (4) recognize the sensitive nature of these proceedings.

7. Previous Administrative Order Superseded. This administrative order supersedes Administrative Order S–2006–200 *(Parental Notice of Abortion Act Cases)*.

8. Effective Date. This administrative order is effective October 1, 2011.

It is ORDERED in Tampa, Hillsborough County, Florida, on this 30th day of September, 2011.

Manuel Menendez, Jr.
Chief Judge

S–2011–014. CHILD CUSTODY PROCEEDINGS

IN THE THIRTEENTH JUDICIAL CIRCUIT HILLSBOROUGH COUNTY, FLORIDA

ADMINISTRATIVE ORDER S–2011–014

CHILD CUSTODY PROCEEDINGS

It is necessary for the prompt and efficient administration of justice in this circuit to clarify the assignment procedures for petitions for custody of a minor child and petitions for guardianships of the person for a minor child. By the power vested in the chief judge under Article V, section 2(d), Florida Constitution; section 43.26, Florida Statutes; and Florida Rule of Judicial Administration 2.215(b)(2), it is therefore ORDERED:

1. Chapter 751 Proceedings—Temporary Custody of Minor Children by Extended Family

A. *Uncontested Proceedings.* If a petition for temporary or concurrent custody of a minor child by extended family, filed in accordance with section 751.03, Florida Statutes, alleges it is an uncontested proceeding supported by the written consent of each living parent or documented abandonment by any living parent who has not consented, the petition will be filed with the Clerk of the Circuit Court ("clerk") to be heard in the Domestic Relations / Family Law Division. A parent's consent must be in writing and notarized unless given in court under oath. The case will be assigned to a specific division based on the assignment procedures for the Domestic Relations / Family Law Division. A petition to establish, modify, or terminate temporary or concurrent custody filed under chapter 751, Florida Statutes, must be accompanied by a Uniform Child Custody Jurisdiction and Enforcement Act Affidavit ("UCCJEA Affidavit"), Family Law Form 12.902(d) and served on the parents.

B. *Contested Proceedings.* If a petition for temporary custody of a minor child by extended family, filed in accordance with section 751.03, Florida Statutes, alleges unfitness of a living parent, the petition will be initially filed with the clerk to be heard in the Domestic Relations / Family Law Division. The case will be assigned to a specific division based on the assignment procedures for the Domestic Relations / Family Law Division. A petition to establish, modify, or terminate temporary custody which has been filed under chapter 751, Florida Statutes, must be accompanied by a UCCJEA Affidavit, Family Law Form 12.902(d), and served on the parents.

C. *Pending Dependency Proceedings.* If a shelter or dependency petition regarding the minor child has been filed with the clerk prior to the chapter 751 petition being filed in accordance with sections 1A or 1B of this administrative order or if a shelter or dependency petition is filed during the pendency of a chapter 751 proceeding, the presiding domestic relations / family law division judge may consider transferring the chapter 751 petition to the appropriate division of the Juvenile Dependency Division.

2. Section 744.3021, Florida Statutes—Guardians of Minors. A petition for a custody arrangement in a guardianship of the person for a minor child under section 744.3021, Florida Statutes, based on the voluntary consent of all living parents, will be filed with the clerk and assigned to the Probate, Guardianship, & Trust Division. The petition must be accompanied by a UCCJEA Affidavit, Family Law Form 12.902(d). Upon review of the petition, the court will determine if a guardianship of the person for a minor child should be established.

If a guardianship of the person for a minor child is established and a parent later withdraws the consent, the parent must file a notarized notice of withdrawal of consent with the clerk and serve the notice on all interested parties and the court. The parent, guardian, or any interested person may afterwards file a petition for discharge of the guardian and termination of the guardianship. A hearing must be scheduled with the court prior to the termination of guardianship.

3. Chapter 61 and Chapter 742 Proceedings—Dissolution of Marriage and Paternity. When a parent files an action against another parent seeking timesharing or custody of a minor child, the action will be filed with the clerk pursuant to either Chapter 61 Dissolution of Marriage or Chapter 742 Paternity Action, as applicable, to be heard in the Domestic Relations / Family Law Division in accordance with Administrative Order S–2011–009 (*Family Law Procedures*) or its successor. The procedures for Chapter 61 and Chapter 742 proceedings may be found in the Family Law Procedures Administrative Order and any other applicable administrative orders.

4. Notice of Related Cases. Attorneys and parties must notify the court, by filing Family Law Form 12.900(h), upon awareness of the existence of any other court proceeding in any jurisdiction that may be relevant to the subject matter before the court. A copy of any relevant orders must be provided to the court. This obligation is a continuing one throughout the proceeding.

5. Change of Minor Child's Residence. A custodian or guardian must not, without prior court approval, change the permanent residence of the minor child. If a minor child whose custody arrangement has been granted by court order is moved to a new residence with court approval, the custodian or guardian must inform the court of the minor child's new address in writing within 30 days after the move. A custodian or guardian does not need prior court approval for a temporary change of residence for the purpose of schooling or holiday.

6. Notice of Change of Custodian's or Guardian's Contact Information. A custodian or guardian of minor children must promptly advise the court, via written notice filed with the clerk in the case in which the custodian or guardian was granted custody, of any change of his or her name, telephone number, or e-mail address. Notice must be filed with the clerk within 30 days of such change and must list the case number.

7. Death of the Minor Child. Within 15 days of a minor child's death, the custodian or guardian must apply for a certified copy of the minor child's death certificate. A certified copy of the minor child's death certificate must be filed with the clerk immediately upon receipt. If a certified copy of the minor child's death certificate is not filed within 30 days of the minor child's death, the custodian or guardian must file a notice of death with the clerk.

8. Adoption of the Minor Child. Whenever a child whose custody arrangement has been granted by court order under Chapter 751 or Chapter 744 is subject to a petition for adoption, counsel for the adoption petitioner must present to the adoption court an order terminating the custody arrangement established under Chapter 744 or Chapter 751 at the same time the final judgment of adoption is presented. The original of this order must be promptly filed with the clerk. If the adoption is finalized in another circuit, a notice of adoption must be filed with the court which granted the Chapter 744 or Chapter 751 custody arrangement order within 30 days following the adoption of a minor child along with a petition to terminate the custody arrangement order.

9. Other Administrative Orders. This administrative order is meant to supplement and not replace administrative orders establishing court procedures for guardianship, family law, and dependency proceedings.

10. Effective Date. This administrative order will be effective April 1, 2011.

It is ORDERED in Tampa, Hillsborough County, Florida on this 30th day of March, 2011.

Manuel Menendez, Jr.
Chief Judge

S–2010–094. ADOPTIONS NEEDED NOW PROJECT

IN THE THIRTEENTH JUDICIAL CIRCUIT HILLSBOROUGH COUNTY, FLORIDA

ADMINISTRATIVE ORDER S–2010–094

ADOPTIONS NEEDED NOW PROJECT

In most termination of parental rights cases, the time period between the final order terminating parental rights and the final order of adoption is significant. With support from the Thirteenth Judicial Circuit Pro Bono Committee, the L. David Shear Children's Law Center of Bay Area Legal Services and Hillsborough Kids, Incorporated have been collaborating to expedite final adoptions of foster children. The collaborative project—Adoptions Needed Now—focuses on foster children five years old and younger and includes older siblings. The Adoptions Needed Now project, through funding from The Florida Bar Foundation, has secured services of pro bono attorneys to act as attorneys ad litem.

Florida Rule of Juvenile Procedure 8.217 authorizes the court to appoint an attorney ad litem for a child in a dependency case. By the power vested in the chief judge under Florida Rule of Judicial Administration 2.215(b)(2), it is therefore ORDERED:

1. Adoptions Needed Now Attorneys Ad Litem. An Attorney Ad Litem volunteering through the Adoptions Needed

Now project may be appointed by the court to represent any child for whom the attorney seeks appointment. Appointment may be sought by a motion filed by the prospective Attorney Ad Litem, by a verbal request of a Children's Law Center Attorney Ad Litem, or by both written motion and verbal request.

2. **Effective Date.** This administrative order is effective immediately.

It is ORDERED in Tampa, Hillsborough County, Florida, on this 11th day of October, 2010.

Manuel Menendez, Jr., Chief Judge

S–2010–012. BLANKET RECOVERY

Publisher's Note: Order S–2010–012 is replicated under the heading, 'Criminal.'

S–2005–153. INTERVIEWS OF ABUSE VICTIMS UNDER AGE 16 OR PERSONS WITH A DEVELOPMENTAL DISABILITY

IN THE THIRTEENTH JUDICIAL CIRCUIT COURT FOR HILLSBOROUGH COUNTY, FLORIDA

ADMINISTRATIVE ORDER S–2005–153

(Supersedes Administrative Order S–2005–050)

INTERVIEWS OF ABUSE VICTIMS UNDER AGE 16 OR PERSONS WITH A DEVELOPMENTAL DISABILITY

WHEREAS section 914.16, Florida Statutes, requires the chief judge to establish reasonable limits on the number of interviews of a victim under the age of 16 in child and sexual abuse cases arising out of sections 794.011, 800.04, or 827.03, Florida Statutes, or of a victim who is a person with a developmental disability in abuse cases arising out of sections 794.011, 800.02, 800.03, or 825.102, Florida Statutes; and

WHEREAS such limitations are necessary to protect victims from potential psychological damage of repeated interrogation; and

WHEREAS Chapter 39, Florida Statutes, assures that all children before the court because of abuse or neglect shall receive certain protection; and

WHEREAS Florida Rule of Criminal Procedure 3.220(h)(4) requires that the deposition of children under the age of 16 be videotaped unless otherwise ordered by the court; and

WHEREAS it is in the best interest of a victim who is under the age of 16 or who is a person with a developmental disability to limit the number of interviews of the victim in abuse cases; and

WHEREAS Florida law establishes that the Court has control of its own records; and

WHEREAS these considerations are balanced with the rights of the public and the person charged with a violation of the law; and

WHEREAS it is more efficient and effective to record interviews on digital video disks ("DVDs") instead of on videocassette tapes; it is therefore

ORDERED:

The following procedures shall apply to interviews of victims who are under the age of 16 or who are persons with a developmental disability in child abuse, disable adult abuse, child sexual abuse and disabled adult sexual abuse cases:

1. **Definitions**

For purposes of this administrative order, the following terms have the following meanings:

"DCF" means the Department of Children and Family Services and, if contracted to perform child protective investigations under section 39.3065, Florida Statutes, the Hillsborough County Sheriff.

"Interview" means any procedure in which the victim is required to provide a detailed account or demonstration of the nature and circumstances of the abuse, but this definition does not include a history obtained for the purposes of medical or psychological diagnosis or treatment or an initial contact with the victim by law enforcement or DCF to assess the validity of the complaint or the need to take protective measures on behalf of the victim. If the assessment can be made without the necessity of obtaining a statement from the victim, such shall be the preferred procedure. "Interview" does not include the taking of a deposition.

2. **Officer Training**

All law enforcement agencies within the Thirteenth Judicial Circuit are hereby requested and urged to implement appropriate training of officers in the area of child abuse investigations and to put in place, where not already in existence, standard operating procedures for conducting the investigation of all child abuse, disabled adult abuse, child sexual abuse and disabled adult sexual abuse cases.

3. **Medical History**

A medical history of a victim for the purposes of a forensic medical examination or for psychological diagnosis or treatment should be limited to that which is necessary to facilitate the forensic medical examination of the victim or the diagnosis and indication of treatment for any psychological concern, and not for law enforcement purposes.

4. **Coordination of Investigations**

All parties and agencies involved in the investigation and prosecution of all cases of abuse involving a victim who is under the age of 16 or who is a person with a developmental disability should coordinate their investigations so that the number of interviews of the victim is limited. To the extent possible, the Child Protection Team, the Guardian ad Litem Program, and whatever agency is designated to conduct medical examinations of a victim of child sexual abuse shall rely on the interview of the victim conducted jointly by the representatives of law enforcement, DCF, and the Children's Justice Center. A criminal investigation shall be coordinated, whenever possible, with the child protection investigation of DCF. *See* section 39.306, Florida Statutes.

5. **Limitation on Number of Interviews**

The number of interviews to be conducted of a victim who is under the age of 16 or who is a person with a developmental disability should be limited as follows:

A. Two interviews by the investigating law enforcement agency including an initial interview by a specially designated and trained child abuse investigator, and a follow up interview by a specially trained detective or a trained Children's Justice Center interviewer only if necessary, and such additional interview being limited in scope as much as possible to assure minimal impact on the victim;

B. One interview by a member of the State Attorney's Office Sexual Offender Division, plus a subsequent contact to prepare the victim for defense depositions, if scheduled, a subsequent contact to prepare the victim for trial testimony if the victim is to testify and any additional contacts necessary to address litigation issues; and

C. One interview by DCF, unless such interview is conducted jointly with law enforcement.

6. **Additional Interviews**

Additional interviews may be allowed by order of the trial judge upon a showing of good cause. Additional interviews shall be limited in scope as much as possible to assure minimal impact on the victim.

7. **Setting, Manner, Timing and Location of Interviews**

All interviews shall be conducted in a setting and manner intended to minimize the traumatic effects of the interview on the victim who is under the age of 16 or who is a person with a developmental disability. The interviews by law enforcement, the State Attorney's Office, and DCF shall be held as soon as practical after notification of the alleged abuse. Recorded interviews should be conducted at the Children's Justice Center or another appropriate facility as designated by the chief judge.

8. **Interviewer**

Any individual who conducts any interview shall be specifically trained in techniques for interviewing victims who are under age 16 or who are persons with a developmental disability. The interviewer may be from one of the following: the Children's Justice Center, law enforcement, DCF, the State Attorney's Office, or as specified in the Child Protective Investigations of Sexual Abuse Protocol and approved by the chief judge.

All interviews should be conducted by one individual regardless of whether more than one agency or individual is requesting the interview. This procedure does not preclude any proper agency or individual requesting the interview from having questions necessary for their investigation asked of the victim.

9. **Recording of Interview**

All interviews conducted at the Children's Justice Center shall be recorded on two original digital video disks ("DVDs"), or on one original DVD while simultaneously producing a digital electronic recording for electronic storage. One original DVD shall be designated the "Court DVD" and sealed to verify authenticity and for use in court. The other original DVD or the digital electronic recording shall be maintained by the Children's Justice Center or the Court Business Center for purposes of review by the State Attorney's Office, DCF, or law enforcement.

10. **Maintenance of Recordings**

Both original DVD recordings shall be kept in accordance with procedures established by Florida Statutes, the Children's Justice Center, and the Administrative Office of the Courts. All original videotapes of any interviews recorded pursuant to previous administrative orders shall also be kept in accordance with these procedures. These procedures shall be precise and uniform to establish a proper chain of custody.

11. **Investigative or Prosecutorial Copy of Recordings**

Upon request of the appropriate law enforcement agency, the State Attorney's Office, or DCF, a copy of the DVD, videotape or digital recording will be produced for the respective entities to assist in their investigations and prosecutions and to enable compliance with discovery obligations. Any such request should be made to the Children's Justice Center. The Children's Justice Center shall instruct the Court Business Center to duplicate the original recording, and requesting representatives of the respective entities shall execute an acknowledgment that the recording was received. Any recording released to any of these entities shall remain confidential to the extent provided by the Florida Statutes and shall be returned to the Children's Justice Center for storage or destruction when no longer needed by the respective entities. The Court Business Center is not authorized to release copies of any DVD, videotape or digital recording unless specifically instructed to do so by representatives of the Children's Justice Center.

12. **Duplication of Recordings**

Any person who is in possession of any original recording or any copy released pursuant to this administrative order or through discovery shall not duplicate it for disclosure to anyone, without prior written order of the court. However, duplicates of copies of recordings may be made by the State Attorney's Office for compliance with its discovery obligations under Florida Rule of Criminal Procedure 3.220 without an order of the court. Duplicates may also be made for discovery purposes under Florida Rule of Juvenile Procedure 8.245 without such order of the court. Any other requests for duplicates should be made to the Children's Justice Center, and the requesting party shall pay the costs associated with the production of the duplicate. All Florida Statutes relating to confidentiality of child abuse records, including section 39.202, shall apply to the original recordings and any and all duplicates.

13. **Depositions**

All discovery depositions of victims or witnesses under the age of 16 taken pursuant to Florida Rule of Criminal Procedure 3.220(h)(4) or Florida Rule of Juvenile Procedure 8.245(e) should be conducted at the Children's Justice Center.

14. **Sanctions**

Failure to abide by the procedures set forth in this administrative order may result in sanctions as allowed by Florida law. Upon notification of violation of this order, the court shall hold a hearing to determine whether violations occurred and impose appropriate sanctions.

15. Previous Administrative Order Superseded

This administrative order supersedes Administrative Order S-2005-050.

16. Effective Date

This administrative order is effective October 1, 2005.

DONE AND ORDERED in Chambers at Tampa, Hillsborough County, Florida on this 15th day of September, 2005.

\s\ J. Rogers Padgett
J. Rogers Padgett, Acting Chief Judge

Unified Family Court - Domestic Relations

S-2018-052. FAMILY LAW DIVISION

IN THE THIRTEENTH JUDICIAL CIRCUIT HILLSBOROUGH COUNTY, FLORIDA

ADMINISTRATIVE ORDER S-2018-052

(Supersedes Administrative Order S-2017-068)

FAMILY LAW DIVISION

In light of the establishment of new violence injunction subdivision "K," it is necessary for the efficient and proper administration of justice to adjust the allocation of cases in the Family Law Division. By the power vested in the chief judge under article V, section 2(d), Florida Constitution; section 43.26, Florida Statutes; and Florida Rule of Judicial Administration 2.215(b)(2), it is ORDERED:

1. Scope. This administrative order applies to each of the following types of actions: (A) Dissolution of Marriage; (B) Support Unconnected With Dissolution; (C) Temporary Custody by Extended Family Member; (D) Paternity, including child support, time-sharing and disestablishment of paternity; (E) Violence Injunctions (domestic violence, repeat violence, dating violence, sexual violence, and stalking); (F) Termination of Parental Rights Pending Adoption; (G) Adoption; and (H) Change of Name.

2. Allocation of Cases.

A. *Cases Other than Violence Injunctions.* Upon filing of a petition commencing one or more of the above-enumerated case types, other than violence injunctions, the Clerk of the Circuit Court ("clerk") will determine whether the same parties were involved in a previously filed petition of the same or substantially related type. If so, the subsequently filed petition will be assigned to the same division in which the previously filed petition was assigned. For purposes of this paragraph, any cases of the type referenced in section 1A though 1D of this administrative order involving the same marriage or same child or children are "substantially related." A termination of parental rights case pending adoption is always substantially related to the subsequent adoption. If the case is not substantially related to a previously filed case involving the same parties, the clerk will assign the newly filed petition to the Tampa Family Law Divisions using a random and equitable assignment system. The clerk will assign newly filed petitions in the East Division using a random and equitable system to East Circuit Division "R" or East Circuit Division "T." *See* Administrative Order S-2013-033 (*East Division*) or any successor administrative order for the geographic boundaries of the East Division.

B. *Self-Representation Case Identification.* For tracking purposes, new cases filed under section 2A of this administrative order in which all parties are self-represented will be assigned to a subdivision within each Family Law Division and the East Division. The subdivision will be a two-letter designation. The designation will be "AP," "BP," "CP," "DP," "EP," "FP," "IP," "JP," "RP" or "TP." The first letter designates the respective Family Law Division or the East Division to which the case is assigned and the second letter—"P"—designates that the case involves only self-represented litigants. The subdivision designation will assist the court and the Case Management Unit in tracking and managing self-represented litigation cases.

C. *Violence Injunctions.*

i. Assignment of Petitions. Upon receipt of a petition for an injunction for protection against domestic violence, repeat violence, dating violence, sexual violence, or stalking (collectively referred to as a "petition for protection against violence"), the clerk will determine whether the same parties were involved in a previously filed petition for protection against violence.

(a) Petitions Involving Same Parties to a Previously Filed Petition. If the clerk determines the same parties were involved in a previously-filed petition for protection against violence, the subsequently-filed petition will be assigned to the same division in which the previously-filed petition was assigned, except that if the previously-filed petition was assigned to East Division "S" or "V," the subsequently-filed petition will only be assigned to East Division "S" or "V" if one of the parties currently resides within the East Division boundaries.

(b) Petitions Not Involving Same Parties to Previously Filed Petition. If the clerk determines the same parties were not involved in a previously filed petition for protection against violence and the petitioner does not reside within the East Division boundaries, the clerk will assign the newly filed petition randomly to one of the three family law violence injunction divisions, Family Law Division "G," "H" or "K," using a ratio of 2:1:1. If the clerk determines the same parties were not involved in a previously filed petition for protection against violence and the petitioner resides within the East Division boundaries, the clerk will assign the newly filed petition to East Division "S" or "V" on a random equitable basis.

(c) Related Family Law Case / Motions to Consolidate or Transfer. Assignment of petitions for protection against violence will proceed according to this section even when another family law case may be pending between the same parties. Motions to consolidate or transfer a petition for protection against violence action into another family law case will be heard by the judge assigned to the division in which the other family law action is pending. A decision to consolidate or transfer may only consolidate or transfer the petition for protection against violence into the family law case, not vice versa.

ii. Review of Petitions.

(a) Presiding Judge Review. Petitions filed between 8:00 a.m. and 3:29 p.m. on non-holiday weekdays will be reviewed on a rotational basis by one of the presiding judges of Family Law Division "G," "H" or "K" if the petition for protection against violence is filed in Tampa or reviewed by one of the presiding judges of East Division "S" or "V" if the petition for protection against violence is filed in Plant City. The associate administrative judge of the violence injunction divisions will maintain the judicial rotation schedule for reviewing petitions and strive to ensure that one of the presiding judges of the violence injunction divisions is available to review petitions on as many non-holiday weekdays as possible.

(b) Coverage Judge Review. For petitions filed between 8:00 a.m. and 3:29 p.m. on non-holiday weekdays, when the presiding judges of East Divisions "S" and "V" are both on leave at the same time, the clerk will first determine if any other judge in the East Division is available to review the petition. If the presiding judges of East Divisions "S" and "V" are both on leave at the same time and there are no other East Division judges available, the clerk will submit the petition to a presiding judge of Family Law Division "G," "H" or "K" for review. If all three judges of the Tampa violence injunction divisions are on leave at the same time, petitions will be reviewed on a rotational basis by a judge assigned to the Unified Family Court (UFC) divisions. Any violence injunction division judge who needs coverage by a UFC division judge to review petitions must provide as much advance notice to the administrative judge of the UFC as possible, but no later than 90 days before coverage is needed. The administrative judge of the UFC will maintain a schedule of judges assigned to the UFC divisions who will review petitions for protection against violence when all of the presiding judges of the violence injunction divisions are on leave at the same time.

(c) Duty Judge Review. The duty judge will review petitions filed between 3:30 p.m. and 7:59 a.m. on non-holiday weekdays and petitions filed on weekends in accordance with the applicable duty judge administrative order.

iii. Return Hearings. When a temporary injunction for protection against violence is entered ex parte, the return hearing on the petition will be heard by the judge presiding in the division to which the petition is assigned. The return hearing must not be delayed pending any request to consolidate or transfer the violence injunction action to the domestic relations / family law division. For Plant City cases, if the judge presiding in the division to which the petition is assigned is not available to conduct the return hearing, the judge will coordinate with one of the other presiding judges of the East Division to cover the return hearings. For Tampa cases, if the judge presiding in the division to which the petition is assigned is not available to conduct the return hearing, the judge will attempt to coordinate with one of the other two presiding judges of the violence injunction divisions to cover the return hearings. If all three judges assigned to the violence injunction divisions are on leave at the same time, the return hearings will be conducted on a rotational basis by a judge assigned to the UFC divisions based on the schedule maintained by the administrative judge of the UFC divisions. Any violence injunction division judge who needs return hearing coverage by a UFC division judge must provide as much advance notice to the administrative judge of the UFC as possible but no later than 90 days before coverage is needed.

D. *Cases Involving Special Immigrant Juvenile Status.* Any petition requesting that the court make the necessary findings to permit a juvenile to apply for Special Immigrant Juvenile Status will be scheduled and disposed of in the dependency division to which the administrative judge of the Unified Family Court is assigned. If a judge assigned to any of the family law divisions determines that a pending petition is requesting such relief, the judge will confer with the administrative judge of the Unified Family Court so that the petition can be scheduled and disposed of in the Unified Family Court administrative judge's division.

E. *Cases Seeking Expedited Affirmation of Parental Status of Gestational Surrogacy.* The clerk will assign any petition filed in accordance with section 742.16, Florida Statutes, seeking an expedited affirmation of parental status of gestational surrogacy, to the Family Law Division to which the associate administrative judge is assigned. If the judge assigned to any of the other family law divisions determines that a petition is requesting an expedited affirmation of parental status of gestational surrogacy, the judge will enter an Order of Transfer transferring the case to the associate administrative judge's division.

F. *Single Division for All Actions Involving Same Parties.* If more than one family law action involving the same parties or the same child or children is pending in more than one family law division, except for a petition for protection against violence action pending in Family Law Division "G," "H" or "K" or East Divisions "S" or "V," such cases will be consolidated in the division with the lowest case number. The parties or their attorneys will be responsible for initiating the transfer if not accomplished by the court.

3. Service of Temporary Injunctions for Protection. In accordance with sections 741.30(8)(a)1 and 784.046(8)(a)1, Florida Statutes, any sworn law enforcement officer in Hillsborough County may serve petitions and temporary injunctions for protection against domestic violence, repeat violence, sexual violence, dating violence, and stalking.

4. Reassignment of Case upon Judge's Disqualification.

A. *Family Law Cases.* If a judge presiding in Family Law Division "A," "B," "C," "D," "E," "F," "I" or "J" enters an order of disqualification, the clerk will reassign the case to another of these Tampa family law divisions on a random equitable basis. If either of the judges presiding in East Divisions "R" or "T" enters an order of disqualification in a family law case, the clerk will reassign the case to the other East Division. If both East Division judges have entered orders of disqualification in a family law case, the clerk will reassign the case to a Tampa Family Law Division on a random equitable basis.

B. *Violence Injunction Cases.* If any of the judges presiding in Family Law Divisions "G," "H" or "K" enters an order of disqualification, the clerk will randomly reassign the violence injunction case to one of the other two Tampa violence injunction division. If all three judges assigned to Family Law Divisions "G," "H" and "K" enter orders of disqualification, the clerk will reassign the violence injunction case to one of the remaining Tampa family law divisions on a random equitable basis, unless there is a family law action pending between the same parties, in which event the violence injunction case will be assigned to the same division in which such other case is pending.

If either of the judges presiding in East Divisions "S" or "V" enters an order of disqualification in a violence injunction case, the clerk will reassign the case to the other East Division. If both judges assigned to East Divisions "S" and "V" enter orders of disqualification, the clerk will reassign the case to a Tampa violence injunction division on a random equitable basis, unless there is a family law action pending between the same parties, in which event the violence injunction case will be assigned to the same division in which such other case is pending.

5. Standing Temporary Order for Family Law Cases. Upon the filing of any petition commencing an action governed by this administrative order, except for violence injunctions, change of name, and adoption cases, the clerk will provide the petitioner with two copies of the Standing Temporary Order for Family Law Cases ("Standing Temporary Order"). The Standing Temporary Order is a tool used to educate the parties in a family law case at the outset of litigation of their duties and responsibilities concerning the treatment of their children, if any, and the preservation of their assets. The Standing Temporary Order will be signed by the associate administrative judge of the Family Law Division. The petitioner must serve a copy of the Standing Temporary Order along with a copy of the initial process and original petition. The Standing Temporary Order will remain in effect until further order of the court.

6. Case Management Order.

A. *Generally.* Upon the filing of any petition commencing or reopening an action governed by this order, except for violence injunctions, change of name and adoption cases, an Order Setting First Case Management Conference ("Case Management Order") will be entered. The Case Management Order is a mechanism by which the court will take charge of all cases at an early stage in the litigation and control the progress of the case thereafter until the case is concluded. The Case Management Order will be signed by the presiding judge of the respective family law division and apply to all domestic relations cases.

B. *Service.* If the petitioner is represented by counsel, the clerk will provide petitioner's counsel with two copies of the Case Management Order and petitioner's counsel must serve a copy of the Case Management Order along with a copy of the initial process and original petition and copy of the Standing Temporary Order. If the petitioner is self-represented, the Administrative Office of the Courts Case Management Unit will be responsible for serving a copy of the Case Management Order on both parties.

C. *Rescheduled Conference.* A case management conference may only be rescheduled by order of the court. Either party may move the court for entry of an order continuing the initial case management conference to a later date by sending to the judge's chambers a jointly signed stipulation and proposed order ratifying the stipulation. The stipulation must state: (1) respondent has been properly served and an answer has been filed; (2) both parties have exchanged financial affidavits and complied with mandatory disclosure requirements; (3) if there are any minor children, that both parties have completed the parenting course and filed their respective certificates of completion; (4) that mediation has been completed or is scheduled and will not be cancelled except by order of court; and (5) the date and time of the new case management conference that has been provided by the judicial assistant and cleared by both parties, which is within 60 days of the originally-scheduled date.

D. *Cancellation.* A case management conference may only be canceled if (1) the case settles prior to the date of the case management conference; (2) the written settlement agreement is provided to the presiding judge; and (3) the presiding judge authorizes the cancellation. A final disposition form and final judgment must be submitted to the court within 10 days of the cancellation, if no hearing is required to prove the elements of the case. If a hearing is required to prove the elements of the case, the case management conference will be used for the final hearing unless an earlier date is cleared and properly calendared.

E. *Production of Evidence.* Counsel and self-represented parties should be prepared, at the case management conference, to provide evidence of the statutory residence requirement and that the marriage is irretrievably broken. The court may take evidence at the case management conference of the statutory residence requirement and the irretrievably broken marriage in order to avoid scheduling a future uncontested dissolution hearing if the case settles after the case management conference.

7. Notice of Related Cases Form. Petitioners must file a Notice of Related Cases form (Florida Family Law Rules of Procedure Form 12.900(h)) with the clerk along with the initial pleading in a family law case, even if there are no related cases.

8. Attorney & Party Information. In all filed pleadings and other documents, an attorney must state the following information directly below the signature line: the attorney's name; address; telephone number, including area code; Florida Bar number; primary e-mail address; secondary e-mail address, if any; and the party whom the attorney represents. In all filed pleadings and other documents, all self-represented litigants must state the following information directly below the signature line: the party's name; address; and telephone number, including area code. A self-represented litigant may also provide an e-mail address with this information.

9. Pleadings, Financial Affidavits and Other Documents.

A. *Pleadings.* All pleadings and other documents must be filed with the clerk in accordance with Florida Rule of Judicial Administration 2.525 and served in accordance with Rule 2.516. A courtesy copy of all pleadings and other documents should be brought to the court for use by the court and the opposing party.

B. *Financial Affidavits.* The title page of a financial affidavit must designate the date the affidavit was signed and the name of the affiant. The financial affidavit requirements of the Family Law Rules of Procedure will be applicable to all temporary hearings and trials including modification proceedings in which child support or alimony may be involved. Sufficient copies of all financial affidavits and other exhibits must be brought to the hearing or trial for use by the court and parties.

C. *Specific Requirements.* It is incumbent upon the attorney or self-represented party to review each individual judge's webpage for any specific requirements of the judge including, but not limited to, whether memorandum of law, documentary evidence or other papers must be delivered in advance of a scheduled court hearing.

10. Modification Proceedings—Attachments. In all modification proceedings involving financial matters, in addition to the current financial affidavit filed, there must also be attached to the initial modification pleading a copy of the last financial affidavits submitted to the court by the parties together with a copy of the final judgment and the most recent modification order, if any, entered in the cause. A copy of any stipulation or property settlement agreement incorporated into such judgment or modification order must also be attached. Failure to do so may result in the imposition of sanctions, including an award of attorney's fees to the other party.

11. Uniform Motion Calendar / Open Docket / Motion Docket.

A. *Calendar.* A Uniform Motion Calendar / Open Docket is provided in each Family Law Division, at least one day per week per judge, unless holidays, illness, vacations, judges' meetings or education programs present a conflict. Each judge will select a day and time to hold the judge's uniform motion calendar / open docket.

B. *Time Limitation.* Uniform Motion Calendar / Open Docket hearings are non-evidentiary except for uncontested final hearings and will be limited to seven minutes per case. The time limitation will include the time necessary for the judge to review documents, memoranda and cases.

C. *Types of Matters Heard.* Uniform Motion Calendar / Open Docket hearings may include, but are not limited to: motions to compel discovery, motions for protective orders, motions to withdraw, uncontested final hearings, and motions to continue. Complex matters will not be heard during the uniform motion calendar / open docket time.

D. *Scheduling.*

i. JAWS. Attorneys and parties do not need to reserve calendar time with the judicial assistant for a hearing on the Uniform Motion Calendar / Open Docket if the hearing has been reserved through the Judicial Automated Workflow System ("JAWS") which may be accessed at the following link on the court's website: https://jaws.fljud13.org/System/login.aspx. However, counsel or a self-represented moving party must file a notice of hearing with the clerk and serve notice upon opposing counsel or a self-represented party in accordance with the applicable rules of procedure.

ii. Motion Docket. In any division that uses a Motion Docket, the docket will be available online through JAWS for scheduling hearings up to 30 minutes in length. The hearing time contemplates presentation by both sides; if the scheduling party knows its presentation is 15 minutes in length, a 30–minute hearing should be scheduled to provide adequate time for both sides. The Motion Docket is for 15–minute or 30–minute hearings (up to two 15–minutes blocks of time may be reserved). The scheduling party may contact the judicial assistant to obtain alternative hearing times if unable to clear time on the Motion Docket with opposing counsel or self-represented party.

iii. E–Mail. For hearings not scheduled through JAWS, the preferred method for scheduling is via e-mail rather than telephone. Divisional e-mail addresses may be accessed via the judicial directory posted on the court's webpage. For any scheduling request, the requesting party should e-mail the judicial assistant for hearing time(s) and copy the opposing party. The judicial assistant will provide a minimum of two available dates/times to the requesting party, with a copy to the opposing party by "replying to all." If the requesting party sends the dates to the opposing party or attorney (whichever is applicable) by e-mail, the responding party or a representative in the attorney's office must respond via e-mail within two business days of receipt of the request. If the responding party or attorney fails to respond via e-mail within two business days, the requesting party may select the hearing date and time of his or her choice.

12. Motions.

A. *Generally.* Motions are filed with the clerk, and they are not brought to the attention of the court until called up for hearing by the parties or their respective counsel. Counsel or a self-represented moving party must review each individual judge's webpage to determine whether the division judge requires a courtesy copy of the motion to be delivered to the judge in advance of a scheduled hearing.

B. *Notice.* All pleadings or motions seeking relief in a family law action must be served on the party or counsel not less than five days prior to the hearing. If motions or pleadings are not timely served, the court may continue the hearing to a later date. Pleadings or motions requesting emergency relief may be exempt from this five-day service requirement upon a finding of emergency status by the judge before whom such motion or pleading is to be heard.

C. *Piggybacking Motions.* There will be no cross noticing on hearing time or "piggybacking" one motion upon a previously scheduled motion without timely notice to the parties and the court. No "piggybacked" motion will be heard unless it is determined by the court that the docket will accommodate the hearing of the additional matters at the scheduled time. The motions will be heard in the order in which they are scheduled.

D. *Discovery Motions & Motions to Set Case for Trial.*

i. General. All motions to compel discovery, for compulsory physical examination, and to set case for trial must contain a certificate by the attorney filing such motion that the attorney has discussed the subject matter of the motion with the opposing counsel and has been unable to reach agreement concerning the disputed discovery or the setting of the case for trial, or that opposing counsel has failed to respond.

ii. Order Issued without Hearing for Failure to Respond. If a party has failed to file or serve any response, objection, or request for an extension to a discovery request or mandatory disclosure, and the deadline to provide such response(s) has expired, then the opposing party may serve a motion to compel discovery and include an order compelling responses to the discovery or mandatory disclosure, which may be delivered to the assigned judge for consideration without a hearing. In addition to the certification required in section 12D(i) above, such motion must also include a certification that the non-moving party has: (1) failed to respond or object in any way to the discovery request or mandatory disclosure, whether by filing with the clerk or by communicating with the moving party, and (2) that the non-moving party has made no request, whether by filing with the clerk or by communicating with the moving party, for any extension of time. The moving party utilizing this procedure must submit the proposed order to the Court via JAWS or with delivery of hard copies of the proposed order with sufficient copies, envelopes, and postage to facilitate service to all parties. The proposed order must allow the non-responding party no less than 10 days to provide responses to the discovery request or mandatory disclosure. The motion, proposed order, and any correspondence to the Court accompanying the same must reference this section of this administrative order and that the relief sought by the moving party is for judicial consideration without a hearing.

The procedure described in this section is intended to provide an alternative, expedited method for obtaining an order compelling discovery or mandatory disclosure in those instances where there has been a complete failure by the non-moving party to provide any response, objection, or request for extension. Because an award of expenses may only be granted after an opportunity for hearing under Florida Rule of Family Law Procedure 12.380, a party electing to utilize this procedure to obtain discovery must not include any request within the motion to recover attorney's fees or costs associated with such motion.

E. *Motions for Continuance.* In accordance with Florida Rule of Judicial Administration 2.545(e) and Florida Family Law Rule of Procedure 12.460, all motions for continuance must be signed by the litigant requesting the continuance as well as the litigant's attorney, unless made at trial, or good cause is shown.

13. Notices of Hearing. All notices of hearing must be on a document separate from the pleading or motion for which the hearing is scheduled. All notices of hearing will clearly state if a court reporter will be provided.

14. Cancellation of Hearings. All hearings scheduled for two hours or more must be approved by the presiding judge and should be scheduled by order of the court. Whether scheduled by order of the court or by notice of hearing, a hearing of two hours or more may not be canceled without approval of the court. Other hearings may be canceled on 24 hours' notice by the attorney or party scheduling them. Any attorney or party cancelling a hearing of less than two hours must notify the opposing party or their counsel *and the court.*

15. Temporary Relief Matters.

A. *Hearing Prerequisites of Moving Party.* The party seeking temporary relief must:

i. File with the clerk the appropriate Uniform Motion for Temporary Relief which may be accessed at http://www.fljud13.org/Forms.aspx;

ii. Attach to the motion a proposed temporary time-sharing plan if the case involves a minor child or minor children;

iii. Attach, if not previously filed, a financial affidavit in compliance with Rule 12.285(d)(1);

iv. File a notice of hearing reflecting the date and time obtained from the court;

v. Serve a copy of the above documents on the opposing party; and

vi. Serve on the opposing party/counsel, but do not file with the clerk, the documents required under Rule 12.285(d)(2)–(4).

B. *Hearing Prerequisites of Responding Party.* Within 10 days after being served with the Motion for Temporary Relief (15 days if service was made by mail), the party against whom the temporary relief is being sought will file and serve a response to the motion stating what, if any, temporary relief the responding party contends is appropriate. When applicable, the responding party will propose an alternate time-sharing plan. The responding party will attach a financial affidavit in compliance with Florida Family Law Rule of Procedure 12.285(d)(1) and will serve the response and financial affidavit upon the opposing party. Contemporaneously, the responding party must serve upon the opposing party, but not file with the clerk or with the judge, the documents required in Rule 12.285(d)(2)–(4). Any temporary relief sought by the responding party may be asserted by cross-motion at that time.

C. *Temporary Relief Mediation.* Temporary relief matters must be mediated prior to being heard by the court. The presiding judges are authorized to enter an order naming the mediator and setting the time of mediation on an *ex parte* basis upon motion by either party if the parties cannot schedule mediation by agreement. The presiding judge has discretion to move forward with the request for temporary relief if the responding party cancels or refuses to attend mediation.

D. *Temporary Relief Mediation Cover Sheet.* To initiate the mediation process with the court's Mediation and Diversion Services Program (Program), the attorney or the self-represented party will submit a Temporary Relief Cover Sheet to the Program, with a copy of the motion requesting temporary relief. Temporary Relief Cover Sheets are available from the court, the Program, the Case Management Unit, and may be accessed at http://www.fljud13.org/Forms.aspx.

E. *Temporary Attorney's Fees.* If the relief sought includes temporary attorney's fees, the seeking party must file an attorney's fee affidavit at least seven business days before the hearing. The attorney's fee affidavit must set forth fees and costs to date and anticipated hours, fees and costs reasonably expected to be incurred through the final hearing.

F. *Exhibits and Temporary Relief Memorandum.* At least 72 hours prior to the scheduled temporary relief hearing, the parties will exchange exhibits and each will file and serve a copy of a Temporary Relief Hearing Memorandum using the uniform Temporary Relief Hearing Memorandum that may be accessed at http://www.fljud13.org/Forms.aspx.

G. *Court Action for Unresolved Issues.* If the issues are not resolved through mediation, a temporary relief hearing should be scheduled for the earliest available date following the scheduled mediation conference. The hearing should be scheduled within 14 business days of the request for hearing, if possible. Hearings that will involve complex temporary support matters or other temporary relief matters, such as custody or visitation issues, or hearings to exceed one hour, may be scheduled for a date beyond 14 business days.

16. Attorney's Fees Hearings for Requests exceeding $50,000. When a party seeks an award of attorney's fees and costs exceeding $50,000 after a final hearing or seeks an interim award of attorney's fees and costs exceeding $50,000 for which fees and costs have already been incurred, the hearing on the matter will be set using a uniform order that may be accessed at http://www.fljud13.org/Forms.aspx. The requesting party will be responsible for scheduling the hearing time and submitting a completed uniform order to the presiding judge.

17. Extraordinary Relief.

A. *Temporary Injunctions.* Applications for temporary injunctions without notice must comply with Florida Family Law Rule of Procedure 12.610 or Florida Rule of Civil Procedure 1.610. All applications for injunctive relief for protection against domestic violence, repeat violence, dating violence, sexual violence, or stalking must be filed with the clerk's office through the Family Law violence injunction division of the Thirteenth Judicial Circuit in accordance with sections 741.30, 784.046, or 784.0485, Florida Statutes.

B. *Emergency Matters in an Assigned Case.* Application for emergency relief in an assigned case must be filed with the clerk with a request for emergency handling. A judge will review the request as soon as it is reasonably possible.

i. Handling by a Judge Assigned to the Family Law Division. The clerk will promptly present the matter, along with the paper court file if electronic images are not available in the case maintenance system, and the emergency motion handling order form, to the judge of the division to which the case is assigned. When the judge is absent from the courthouse, any emergency application in a case assigned to that judge's division will be presented to the family law judge present in the courthouse whose division next follows in alphabetical sequence (Divisions "A" through "F," "I" and "J" only). "Present in the courthouse" includes being in a hearing or trial. If uncertain about a judge's presence in the courthouse, the clerk will inquire at the bailiff station, and if the bailiff reports that the assigned judge is not present, the clerk will present the matter to the next judge in alphabetical letter division sequence.

Any judge assigned to the Family Law Division who issues an *ex parte* order must hold the return hearing personally, unless the judge of the division in which the case is pending agrees to hold the hearing. All emergency motion handling orders must be docketed by the clerk and delivered, along with the paper court file if electronic images are not available in the case maintenance system, to the chambers of the judge of the division in which the case is pending for any necessary follow-up action. All emergency motion handling orders must be served to the parties by facsimile, e-mail, or regular United States mail.

If the reviewing judge determines that an emergency does not exist or denies the emergency request without a hearing, the requesting party is prohibited from presenting the emergency request to any other judge except the judge presiding in the division to which the case is assigned.

ii. *Handling by a Duty Judge.* If there are no family law judges present in the courthouse when an application for emergency relief in an assigned case is made, then the emergency matter will be presented to the duty judge. If the duty judge is a judge assigned to the Family Law Division, the judge will handle the matter in accordance with section 17B.i. of this administrative order above. If the duty judge is not assigned to the Family Law Division, then the duty judge will handle the matter as set forth below.

If a duty judge issues an *ex parte* order and determines that the nature of the emergency requires that a return hearing be conducted imminently, the duty judge will conduct the return hearing personally. If a duty judge issues an *ex parte* order and determines that the nature of the emergency allows the return hearing to be scheduled with the judge presiding in the division in which the case is pending, then the clerk will, by the next business day, deliver the emergency motion, the *ex parte* order entered by the duty judge, and the paper court file if electronic images are not available in the case maintenance system, to the judge presiding in the division to which the case is assigned. If a duty judge issues an *ex parte* order and determines that the nature of the emergency allows the return hearing to be scheduled with the judge presiding in the division in which the case is pending, such determination is conditioned upon the understanding that the judge presiding in the division in which the case is pending may vacate any order issued by the duty judge before, after, or in lieu of the return hearing.

All emergency motion handling orders must be docketed by the clerk and delivered, along with the paper court file if electronic images are not available in the case maintenance system, to the chambers of the judge of the division in which the case is pending for any necessary follow-up action. All emergency motion handling orders must be served to the parties by facsimile, e-mail, or regular United States mail.

If a duty judge determines that an emergency does not exist or denies the emergency request without a hearing, the requesting party must not present the emergency request to any other judge except the judge presiding in the division to which the case is assigned.

C. *Emergency Matters in an Unassigned Case.* An unassigned case is a matter that has not been assigned to a Family Law Division because the clerk's office is not and will not be open within a reasonable time. Application for emergency relief in an unassigned case may be made to the chief judge or the chief judge's designee. Otherwise, the application will be made to the duty judge. As soon as the clerk's office is open, any such application and any such order will be properly filed with the clerk and the assignment of the case will be made by the clerk in accordance with section 2 of this administrative order.

18. Professional Courtesy in Clearing Hearing Dates and Deposition Dates. A good faith effort to clear all hearing dates and deposition dates with opposing counsel or a self-represented party is required prior to notices being filed. This fact should be shown on the face of the notice itself by inserting the following at the very bottom of the notice after the certificate of service: *"The above hearing/deposition has* *been cleared with opposing counsel's (party's) calendar on (date)."* In the alternative, if it has not been possible to reach opposing counsel's office (party) to clear the date or if opposing counsel (party) has failed to respond, the following language should be used: *"The above hearing/deposition date has not been cleared with opposing counsel's/party's calendar because (state reason) ..."*

19. Interpreters. At the time of any hearing or trial in which a witness who does not speak English is to be presented, it is the responsibility of the party offering the non-English speaking witness to provide a disinterested, qualified interpreter at the initial expense of the offering party.

20. Trials and Pretrial Conferences—Scheduling. In all cases in which a trial is scheduled for more than four hours, a pretrial conference will be scheduled. A pretrial memorandum must be served at least three days prior to the pretrial conference. A uniform order setting trial and pretrial conference will be entered. All trials must be scheduled in accordance with Florida Rule of Civil Procedure 1.440 and Florida Family Law Rule of Procedure 12.440, or by stipulation waiving such procedure.

21. Uncontested Trials—Limit. Judges will provide block time for uncontested trials. Some divisions permit use of Uniform Motion Calendar / Open Docket time for uncontested trials. Attorneys must ascertain from the individual judge's office the day and time provided for such trials. Each attorney or firm may be limited to the number of uncontested sessions.

22. Orders and Judgments.

A. *Consultation with Opposing Counsel or Self–Represented Party.* Unless the presiding judge directs otherwise, prior to submitting a proposed order or judgment for the court's consideration after a hearing, the counsel or self-represented party directed to submit the proposed order must consult with opposing counsel or the opposing self-represented party within five business days after the court's decision and make a genuine effort to agree on the language of the proposed order.

B. *Objection.* If, after consultation with opposing counsel or the opposing self-represented party, the parties cannot agree on the language in the proposed order or judgment to be submitted to the court, then the attorney or self-represented party submitting the proposed order or judgment must document in a cover letter that the opposing party or counsel has registered an objection and specifically state what the objection is. At the time the cover letter and proposed order or judgment is submitted to the court, a copy must simultaneously be sent to all parties or their attorneys. If an objection is registered, the court will determine if a hearing is necessary to resolve the dispute.

C. *Timely Submission.* The attorney or self-represented party directed to prepare the order or judgment must submit the proposed order or judgment to the court by within 10 business days after the court's decision. If the attorney or self-represented party designated to prepare the order or judgment fails to timely submit a proposed order or judgment, the attorney for the opposing party or the opposing self-represented party may submit a proposed order or judgment within five business days after the initial ten-day period.

D. *Submission of Proposed Orders and Judgments.*

i. JAWS—All Parties Represented by Counsel. Unless the presiding judge directs otherwise, if all parties are represented by attorneys, none of whom have been excused from e-mail service under Florida Rule of Judicial Administration 2.516, an attorney who is requested to submit a proposed order or judgment will do so through the JAWS. Prior to submitting a proposed order or judgment, the attorney must review the presiding judge's webpage and comply with the presiding judge's formatting preference (Microsoft Word v. PDF) when submitting a proposed order or judgment through the JAWS.

Prior to the submission of a proposed order or judgment to the presiding judge through the JAWS, the submitting attorney will be required to certify that one of the following statements is true: (i) all parties have agreed to the content of the proposed order or judgment; (ii) opposing party or counsel has not responded within five business days of being provided the proposed order or judgment; or (iii) opposing party or counsel has registered an objection and the cover letter states what the objection is.

Competing proposed orders or judgments must not be submitted through the JAWS.

ii. Hard Copies and Envelopes—Self–Represented Party or Party's Attorney Excused from E–Service. If any party is self-represented or represented by an attorney who has been excused from e-mail service by the court under Rule 2.516, the self-represented party or attorney who is requested to submit a proposed order or judgment must do so by submitting to the presiding judge sufficient hard copies of the proposed order or judgment along with stamped, addressed envelopes.

E. *Title.* The title of every proposed order and judgment submitted must contain the subject matter of the pleading or motion upon which the ruling is made and must fairly apprise the reader of the action being ordered. Phrasing such as "order granting ..." or "order denying ..." is preferred over "order on ...".

F. *Form.* The first paragraph of all proposed orders and judgments must state the date or dates on which the hearing or trial took place. In all proposed orders or judgments, the page containing the court's signature must also contain substantive language of the proposed order or judgment so that a proposed order or judgment does not contain a signature page consisting only of the court's signature. Each page, except for the first page, must contain a page number.

G. *Income Withholding Order.* If an order or final judgment provides for payment of alimony or child support by income withholding order, the income withholding order must be submitted contemporaneously with the order or final judgment.

H. *Settlement Agreements.* Unless the presiding judge directs otherwise, either the entire settlement agreement must be recited word for word in the final judgment or it must be attached and incorporated into the final judgment. Notwithstanding the above, the judgment must recite provisions of the settlement agreement pertaining to shared or sole parental responsibility, time-sharing, child support and alimony.

I. *Orders Granting Motions to Withdraw.* Any order granting an attorney's motion to withdraw under Florida Rule of Judicial Administration 2.505(f)(1) must include a statement that the party whose attorney is withdrawing is obligated to provide the court and the opposing attorney or opposing self-represented party a written notice of any change to the party's mailing address, telephone number, and e-mail address (if available) if the party intends to remain self-represented.

J. *Final Disposition Form.* A Final Disposition Form must be submitted at the time of submission of a final order or judgment to the court.

23. Court Registry Fee. In accordance with Florida law, the clerk is entitled to be paid a registry fee when the clerk accepts money for deposit into the registry of the court. When a person is required by law or court order to deposit a specified sum of money into the registry of the court, the person making the deposit must pay the amount of the registry fee to the clerk in addition to the amount of the deposit. If the registry fee is not paid at the time of the deposit, the clerk will deduct the amount of the registry fee from the deposit. The court has jurisdiction to determine the sufficiency of a deposit when a registry fee is not paid and which party is responsible for payment of the registry fee. The clerk will assist the public in calculating the amount of the registry fee.

24. Orders of Disbursement from the Court Registry.

A. *Request for Clerk's Statement of Available Registry Funds.* At any time a party seeks an order directing the clerk to disburse funds from the court registry, prior to filing a motion, the party must request the clerk to provide a statement showing available funds in the court registry. The statement will indicate the date and time the available funds were verified by the clerk. The clerk will develop and post on the clerk's website (www.hillsclerk.com) a form entitled *Request for Clerk's Statement of Available Registry Funds.*

B. *Motion for Disbursement of Registry Funds.* The party must attach a copy of the clerk's Statement of Available Registry Funds to the motion for disbursement of funds, file and serve the motion on all parties and legal counsel for the clerk. If the party seeking disbursement objects to the amount listed in the clerk's Statement of Available Registry Funds, the motion must identify the basis for the objection, and set the motion for hearing. If the party seeking disbursement does not object to the amount listed in the clerk's Statement of Available Registry Funds, the motion must confirm the stated amount is the proper amount of disbursement and request the entry of an order, without a hearing, if no other party files and serves a written objection within five days after service of the motion.

C. *Change in Registry Balance.* If any party becomes aware of any change to the court registry balance after the issuance of the initial clerk's Statement of Available Registry Funds, that party must obtain an updated clerk's Statement of Available Registry Funds and provide copies to the other party and to the court prior to the hearing on the motion seeking disbursement. If an updated clerk's Statement of Available Registry Funds is not presented at the hearing on the motion seeking disbursement, then the amount identified in the initial clerk's Statement of Available Registry Funds will be deemed the correct amount available for disbursement.

D. *Disbursement Orders to Account for Clerk Fees.* All proposed orders submitted to the court for disbursement from the court registry must contain the phrase "less clerk fees" immediately after the total requested disbursement amount (for example. Total: $12,000, less clerk fees). If the amount in the order exceeds the amount held in the court registry, the clerk will disburse the available amount in the registry, less clerk fees, at the time of the entry of the order (pro rata if disbursement is made to multiple parties).

25. Children and Court. In accordance with Florida Family Law Rule of Procedure 12.407, children must not be brought to the courthouse for any reason without prior approval of the court authorizing a child's appearance on any day when any hearing, mediation, or other related court proceeding is scheduled to occur, except in uncontested adoption cases and in an emergency situation.

26. The Rules of Courtroom Civility. The judges, general magistrates and hearing officers assigned to the Family Law Division expect that all litigants, whether or not they are represented by attorneys, will conduct themselves in an appropriate fashion so that all parties will be afforded a fair opportunity to present their case. Specific rules have been established to assist litigants in meeting appropriate standards of conduct when appearing in court. These Rules of Courtroom Civility may be accessed at http://www.fljud13.org/Forms.aspx.

27. Professional Conduct and Courtroom Decorum. Counsel must also adhere to The Florida Bar's Guidelines for Professional Conduct (https://www.floridabar.org/prof/presources/presources002/), The Florida Bar's Professionalism Expectations (https://www.floridabar.org/wp–content/uploads/2017/04/professionalism–expectations.pdf), and the Hillsborough County Bar Association's Standards of Professionalism (http://hillsbar.site–ym.com/?page=Professionalism). Each judge may announce and enforce additional requirements, or may excuse compliance with any provision(s) of the Guidelines, Expectations, or Standards as that judge deems appropriate.

28. Forms and Procedure. Suggested forms to be used with the provisions of this administrative order may be accessed at www.fljud13.org under the section titled "Forms." Each division judge's webpage should be reviewed for additional procedural requirements specific to that judge.

29. Other Family Law Subjects. Provisions for other family law subjects, such as the central governmental depository, the child support enforcement program under Title IV–D, mediation, general magistrates and hearing officers, adoption records, adoption procedures and collaborative family law practice can be found in separate administrative orders. These administrative orders, like all procedural administrative orders, may be accessed at www.fljud13.org under the section titled "Administrative Orders."

30. Previous Administrative Order Superseded. This administrative order supersedes Administrative Order S–2017–068 (*Family Law Division*).

31. Effective Date. This administrative order is effective January 7, 2019.

ENTERED in Tampa, Hillsborough County, Florida, on December 3, 2018.

Ronald N. Ficarrotta
Chief Judge

S–2018–034. GENERAL MAGISTRATES AND CHILD SUPPORT ENFORCEMENT HEARING OFFICERS IN THE FAMILY LAW DIVISION

IN THE THIRTEENTH JUDICIAL CIRCUIT HILLSBOROUGH COUNTY, FLORIDA

ADMINISTRATIVE ORDER S–2018–034

(Supersedes Administrative Order S–2018–024)

GENERAL MAGISTRATES AND CHILD SUPPORT ENFORCEMENT HEARING OFFICERS IN THE FAMILY LAW DIVISION

Many post-judgment matters are brought before the judges in the Family Law Division. The interests of the public and of the litigants require a flexible and speedy resolution of these matters. Florida Family Law Rule of Procedure 12.490 provides for the appointment of general magistrates. Florida Family Law Rule of Procedure 12.491 provides for the usage of child support enforcement hearing officers in non–Title IV–D cases upon administrative order of the chief justice. By administrative order dated February 27, 1998, the chief justice of the Florida Supreme Court ordered that hearing officers may be utilized in this circuit to consider proceedings for the establishment, enforcement and modification of support in non–Title IV–D cases.

Based on a redeployment of magistrate resources effective January 1, 2019, it is necessary for the proper and efficient administration of justice to update the provisions governing assignment of cases to the general magistrates and hearing officers in the Family Law Division.

By the power vested in the chief judge under article V, section 2(d), Florida Constitution; section 43.26, Florida Statutes; and Florida Rule of Judicial Administration 2.215(b)(2), it is ORDERED:

1. Appointments. Mary Lou Cuellar–Stilo, Jon Johnson, Joan Montagno, Jennifer Sarmiento, and Vicki Reeves are appointed as general magistrates and as child support enforcement hearing officers in the Family Law Division and East Circuit Divisions "R" and "T" (Plant City).

2. General Magistrate / Hearing Officer Divisions. Divisions "GM–1," "GM–2," "GM–3," "GM–4," and "GM–5" are established as General Magistrate / Hearing Officer Divisions in the Family Law Division and East Circuit Divisions "R" and "T" (Plant City). The general magistrates / hearing officers are assigned to the general magistrate / hearing officer divisions as follows:

General Magistrate / Hearing Officer Division	General Magistrate / Hearing Officer
"GM—1"	Mary Lou Cuellar–Stilo
"GM—2"	Jon Johnson
"GM—3"	Joan Montagno
"GM—4"	Jennifer Sarmiento
"GM—5"	Vicki Reeves

3. Case Assignments. Any post-judgment family law matter referred by the court to the general magistrates or hearing officers will be assigned via the Judicial Automated Workflow System (JAWS) to either General Magistrate / Hearing Officer Division "GM–1," "GM–2," "GM–3," "GM–4," or "GM–5." The assignment of a referred matter will be determined by the last two digits of the case number according to the following table:

GM–1 MARY LOU CUELLAR–STILO	GM–2 JON JOHNSON	GM–3 JOAN MONTAGNO	GM–4 JENNIFER SARMIENTO	GM–5 VICKI REEVES
00	01	02	03	50
04	05	06	07	54
08	09	10	11	58
12	13	14	15	62
16	17	18	19	66
20	21	22	23	70
24	25	26	27	74
28	29	30	31	78
32	33	34	35	82
36	37	38	39	86
40	41	42	43	90
44	45	46	47	94
48	49		51	98
52	53		55	
56	57		59	
60	61		63	
64	65		67	
68	69		71	
72	73		75	
76	77		79	
80	81		83	
84	85		87	
88	89		91	
92	93		95	
96	97		99	

4. General Magistrate Powers. General magistrates may hear and make recommendations on post-judgment family law matters, excluding Title IV–D cases.

5. Referral to General Magistrate

A. *General Procedures.* All post-judgment family law matters, excluding Title IV–D child support issues, will be referred by the court to a general magistrate. Contemporaneous with the filing of any post-judgment family law matter, the party filing the matter must file and serve on all parties either (1) a Motion for Referral to General Magistrate, or (2) an Objection to Referral to General Magistrate.

No pre-judgment matters will be referred to the general magistrates.

When motions concerning discovery, continuances, or withdrawal of counsel relate to a matter referred to and pending before the general magistrate, such motions must be set before and heard by the general magistrate without further order of referral by the court. A separate order of referral is required for all contempt matters. See *Young v. Young*, 816 So. 2d 1267 (Fla. 3d DCA 2002).

B. *Referral Orders*

i. JAWS—All Parties Represented by Counsel. In the absence of an Objection to Referral to General Magistrate, if all parties are represented by attorneys, none of whom has been excused from e-mail service under Florida Rule of Judicial Administration 2.516, the judge will enter an appropriate order of referral generated by using the JAWS.

ii. Hard Copies and Envelopes—Self–Represented Party or Party's Attorney Excused from E–Service. In the absence of an Objection to Referral to General Magistrate, if any party is self-represented or represented by an attorney who has been excused from e-mail service by the court under Rule 2.516, the self-represented party or attorney who filed the post-judgment family law matter must submit to the presiding judge stamped, addressed envelopes for conformed copies of an order of referral to be mailed.

C. *Objection to Referral.* Any objection to a referral, in accordance with Florida Family Law Rule of Procedure 12.490(b), must be in writing and filed within 10 days of the date of service of the order of referral. In accordance with section 5A of this administrative order, a party filing a post-judgment matter may file an objection to referral contemporaneous with the filing of the post-judgment matter which obviates the need for an order of referral being entered. If an objection is filed, the matter will remain to be heard by the presiding judge in the respective division, except that, when the magistrate is acting as a child support enforcement hearing officer under section 8 of this administrative order, the court will not entertain any objection to the referral of post-judgment child support matters. When a case is referred to a general magistrate, and there is no objection to the referral, the action must be set for hearing before the assigned magistrate in the manner prescribed in the referral order. The general magistrate will proceed with the hearings and the preparation and filing of reports in the manner set forth in Florida Family Law Rule of Procedure 12.490.

D. *Exceptions.* If exceptions are filed pursuant to Rule 12.490(f), the general magistrate will retain authority to correct any errors or omissions or both in the original report by filing a corrected or amended report at any time prior to the court's ruling on the exceptions. If the general magistrate intends to correct or amend the report, the general magistrate will notify the parties or their attorneys within 15 days of receipt of a copy of any exceptions filed. Such reservation of authority by the general magistrate does not restrict the jurisdiction of the circuit court to proceed on the exceptions previously filed, nor does the reservation of authority by the general magistrate prevent a party from filing exceptions to the corrected or amended report. If no exceptions are filed, the general magistrate has authority to correct any errors or omissions in the original report at any time before the court enters judgment on the report. If a corrected or amended report is filed, a new 10–day exceptions period will begin.

6. Mandatory Mediation Required. In accordance with Administrative Order S–2009–107 (*Mediation of Family Law Cases*), a prerequisite to schedule a post-judgment hearing before a judge or general magistrate is the submission of the issues to mediation. The general magistrate may decline to schedule a hearing unless a mediation appointment is scheduled, but may not defer setting the hearing until after the mediation actually occurs. The magistrate is authorized to determine if one party is obstructing the scheduling of mediation, and upon such finding may set a hearing in the absence of a scheduled mediation. If the parties appear for a hearing and had scheduled but failed to complete the mediation, the magistrate may continue the hearing until the mediation is completed, or may proceed with the hearing if the party who is not responsible for the failure to complete the mediation so requests.

7. Child Support Enforcement Hearing Officer Powers. The persons appointed as general magistrates by this administrative order are also appointed as child support enforcement hearing officers, under Florida Family Law Rule of Procedure 12.491, solely for conducting proceedings involving the enforcement and modification of non–Title IV–D child support issues. When acting as child support enforcement hearing officers under this administrative order, the hearing officers will have all the powers and duties as provided in Rule 12.491. Unlike referral of matters to a general magistrate which requires the consent of all parties, referral of matters to the child support enforcement hearing officers under Rule 12.491 does not require the consent of any party and therefore a party may not lodge any objection to the referral.

8. Automatic Referral to Child Support Enforcement Hearing Officer. Upon the filing of any post-judgment action where the sole issue is the enforcement or modification of non–Title IV–D child support, the action is automatically referred to a child support enforcement hearing officer without order of court being required. The child support enforcement hearing officer will proceed with the hearing and the preparation and filing of a recommended order as provided in Florida Family Law Rule of Procedure 12.491. No objections to a referral to a child support enforcement hearing officer under this section will be entertained by the court. Either party may set the action for hearing before the assigned child support enforcement hearing officer.

9. Contempt Hearings. In all contempt hearings in which the general magistrate or hearing officer recommends immediate incarceration, a recommendation and order will be promptly prepared and then reviewed by the judge assigned to the division in which the matter is pending. If the assigned judge is absent from the courthouse, the contempt matter will be reviewed by the family law judge present in the courthouse whose division next follows in alphabetical sequence the division in which the case is pending. Recognizing the need for expediency, if the court is attending to other judicial matters the court must recess as soon as is practicable and immediately review the magistrate's or hearing officer's recommendation. If the court ratifies the magistrate's or hearing officer's recommendation, the general magistrate or hearing officer will recall the case and the bailiff will take the contemnor into. If the court determines that a hearing before the court is necessary, the matter will be scheduled on an emergency basis and must be heard immediately.

10. Time Standards. General magistrates will file and serve copies of the report and recommendations on all parties within 60 days from the date of the hearing. Child support enforcement hearing officers will submit a recommended order to the assigned judge within 60 days from the date of the hearing. Each general magistrate and child support hearing officer will maintain a log of cases under advisement and must submit a bi-monthly memorandum to the associate administrative judge of the Family Law Division detailing any and all cases that have been held under advisement for more than 60 days. General magistrates and child support enforcement hearing officers must not maintain a case under advisement for more than 90 days from the date of the hearing.

11. Previous Administrative Order Superseded. This administrative order supersedes Administrative Order S–2018–024 (*General Magistrates and Child Support Enforcement Hearing Officers in the Family Law Division*).

12. Effective Date. In order to timely populate General Magistrate Division "GM–5" with referrals, section 3 of this administrative order is effective September 1, 2018. All other provisions of this administrative order are effective January 1, 2019. General Magistrate Division "GM–5" will begin hearing cases on January 2, 2019.

ENTERED in Tampa, Hillsborough County, Florida, on August 29, 2018.

Ronald N. Ficarrotta
Chief Judge

S–2016–015. CIVIL COURT REPORTING

IN THE THIRTEENTH JUDICIAL CIRCUIT HILLSBOROUGH COUNTY, FLORIDA

ADMINISTRATIVE ORDER S–2016–015

(Supersedes Administrative Order S–2003–020)

CIVIL COURT REPORTING

Florida Rule of Judicial Administration 2.535 defines the term *civil court reporter* as a court reporter who performs court reporting services in civil proceedings not required to be reported at public expense, and who meets the Florida Supreme Court's certification, training, and other qualifications for court reporting. Rule 2.535 also designates civil court reporters as officers of the court while acting as reporters in a judicial proceeding.

It is necessary for the proper and efficient administration of justice to update procedures for court reporting of all civil judicial proceedings.

By the power vested in the chief judge under article V, section 2(d), Florida Constitution; section 43.26, Florida Statutes; and Florida Rule of Judicial Administration 2.215(b)(2), it is therefore **ORDERED:**

1. Civil Judicial Proceeding. For purposes of this administrative order, the term *civil judicial proceeding* means a hearing or trial conducted before a judge, magistrate, or hearing officer concerning a matter pending in the Circuit Civil Division, the Family Law Division, or the County Civil Division.

2. Notices of Hearing. All notices of hearing for civil judicial proceedings will specify whether or not the party setting a matter for hearing will be securing the services of a court reporter.

3. Party's Responsibility to Secure Court Reporter. In a civil judicial proceeding in which a court reporter is requested, it is the responsibility of the party, or the party's attorney, to secure the services of a court reporter or court reporting firm prior to the proceeding. All costs associated with the court reporter's appearance will be the responsibility of the party or parties requesting the court reporter. This provision does not preclude the taxation of costs as authorized by law. *See* Fla. R. Jud. Admin. 2.535(b).

4. Official Record. There will only be one official record at a civil judicial proceeding taken by one court reporter. Attorneys must resolve any conflicts among themselves prior to the proceeding.

5. Previous Administrative Order Superseded. This administrative order supersedes Administrative Order S–2003–020 (*Court Reporting Procedures for Civil Proceedings*).

6. Effective Date. This administrative order is effective May 1, 2016.

It is ORDERED in Tampa, Hillsborough County, Florida on this 22nd day of April, 2016.

Ronald N. Ficarrotta
Chief Judge

S–2015–048. ADOPTION PROCEDURES

IN THE THIRTEENTH JUDICIAL CIRCUIT HILLSBOROUGH COUNTY, FLORIDA

ADMINISTRATIVE ORDER S–2015–048

(Supersedes Administrative Order S–2014–041)

ADOPTION PROCEDURES

The Florida Adoption Act (chapter 63, Florida Statutes) provides a multitude of procedural and technical requirements designed to ensure that basic safeguards in adoption-related proceedings are met.

In an effort to ensure that all parties adhere to the statutory and other requirements for adoption filings, it is necessary to adopt uniform procedures for filing documents and providing sufficient time for the court to review all pleadings and required filings prior to the final hearing.

It is also necessary for the proper and efficient administration of justice to update the assignment procedures so that chapter 63 adoption cases are assigned to the divisions of the Family Law Divisions on a random equitable basis.

By the power vested in the chief judge under article V, section 2(d), Florida Constitution; section 43.26, Florida Statutes; and Florida Rule of Judicial Administration 2.215(b)(2), it is therefore **ORDERED:**

1. Allocation of Cases. All actions under chapter 63, Florida Statutes, are assigned to one of the divisions of the Family Law Division on a random equitable basis. All adoption cases pending in any of the divisions of the Family Law Division on the effective date of this administrative order will remain pending in the respective divisions.

2. **Applicability.** The procedures outlined below apply to any actions under chapter 63, Florida Statutes, including termination of parental rights pending adoption proceedings and adoption proceedings.

3. **Required Documents Filed Prior to Final Hearing.** The court must conduct a final hearing in all termination of parental rights pending adoption and adoption proceedings arising under chapter 63.

Petitioner(s) must file all documents required to be filed under chapter 63 at least 21 days in advance of the scheduled final hearing. A petitioner's failure to file any required document at least 21 days in advance of a final hearing may result in the cancellation of the hearing by the court, unless the court recognizes good cause for a shortened time frame.

A. *Termination of Parental Rights Pending Adoption Proceedings.* In addition to the documents required by section 63.087, Florida Statutes, other documents which must be timely filed prior to the hearing include, but are not limited to:

- Certificate of search of the Florida Putative Father Registry (section 63.054, Florida Statutes);
- All affidavits of inquiry, diligent search, and service (section 63.088, Florida Statutes);
- A certified copy of the minor's birth certificate as provided in section 4 of this administrative order;
- Interview summaries or statements, if applicable (section 63.082(3)(b), Florida Statutes); and
- Any acknowledgment or affidavit (section 63.085, Florida Statutes).

B. *Adoptions Proceedings.* In addition to the documents required by section 63.112, Florida Statutes, other documents which must be timely filed prior to the hearing include, but are not limited to:

- Report of the final home investigation, if applicable (section 63.125, Florida Statutes);
- Affidavit of expenses and receipts, if applicable (section 63.132, Florida Statutes); and
- Any acknowledgment or affidavit, if applicable (section 63.085, Florida Statutes).

4. **Birth Certificate.** Unless other grounds are shown, at the time of the filing of a petition for termination of parental rights, section 63.062(1)(b)4., Florida Statutes, requires the father's consent to the termination of his parental rights pending adoption if he is listed on the child's birth certificate. It is therefore critical for the Court to be aware of whether the child's birth certificate names a father to determine if consent is necessary. Accordingly, in termination of parental rights proceedings under chapter 63 (including proceedings involving joint petitions), a certified copy of the child's birth certificate must be filed, except that if the child's adoptive name is listed on the birth certificate, the certified copy must be filed in the related adoption file and a copy with the child's adoptive name redacted must be filed in the termination of parental rights proceeding.

5. **Required Inquiry.** In any termination of parental rights pending adoption proceeding in which the Petitioner does not submit a sworn affidavit as prescribed by section 63.088(4), Florida Statutes, the Petitioner must ensure that the persons identified in that statutory subsection are present at the hearing and prepared to address each inquiry enumerated under the statute. In addition, by way of notice filed with the Clerk of the Circuit Court, Petitioner must alert the court of its intent to have the required inquiry conducted orally at the hearing. The notice must be filed at least 30 days in advance of the final hearing. This provision also applies to cases in which one hearing is held on the joint petition for termination of parental rights and adoption.

6. **Separate Proceedings.** Except in cases where joint petitions are expressly permitted under chapter 63, a petition for termination of parental rights pending adoption and the petition for adoption must be filed under separate case numbers. Failure to comply with this provision may result in dismissal of the petition without prejudice or denial of the requested relief, or both. Reports to the court of intended placement under section 63.092, Florida Statutes, and petitions for declaratory statement under section 63.102, Florida Statutes, if applicable, must be filed in the adoption proceeding.

7. **Statement Regarding Jurisdiction in TPR Proceedings.** If a Notice of Related Cases form (required in all actions filed in the Family Law Division under Administrative Order S–2014–022 (*Unified Family Court*)) or Uniform Child Custody Jurisdiction and Enforcement Act information (required in a petitioner's first pleading or an attached affidavit under section 61.522, Florida Statutes) lists a separate action that may affect the court's jurisdiction to proceed in the termination of parental rights proceeding, the Petitioner must file a Statement Regarding Jurisdiction either within the body of the petition, or as a stand-alone document at the time the original petition is filed.

The Statement Regarding Jurisdiction must contain a brief statement of the relationship of the actions and any other information relevant to the Court's jurisdiction to proceed. The Petitioner must attach, or file no later than 21 days prior to the final hearing, certified copies of the most recent order(s) from another court that (1) involves a child custody determination concerning the minor child; or (2) addresses the jurisdiction of that court over the child subject to the proceeding in this Court.

To the extent the Petitioner is unable to obtain the court order(s), Petitioner must state this and explain the circumstances arising within the Statement Regarding Jurisdiction.

8. **Previous Administrative Order Superseded.** This administrative order supersedes Administrative Order S–2014–041 (*Adoption Procedures*).

9. **Effective Date.** This administrative order is effective September 1, 2015.

It is ORDERED in Tampa, Hillsborough County, Florida, on this 26 day of August, 2015.

Ronald N. Ficarrotta, Chief Judge

S–2014–062. ADOPTION RECORDS

IN THE THIRTEENTH JUDICIAL CIRCUIT COURT HILLSBOROUGH COUNTY, FLORIDA

ADMINISTRATIVE ORDER S–2014–062 (Supersedes Administrative Order S–2006–161)

ADOPTION RECORDS

Section 63.162(2), Florida Statutes, provides that all papers and records pertaining to an adoption are confidential and subject to inspection only upon order of the court.

Attorneys for adoptive parents need access to adoption court files and without the entry of this administrative order, counsel for adoptive parents would be required to file a motion to unseal an adoption court file in virtually every case.

Section 28.29, Florida Statutes, requires the Clerk of the Circuit Court ("clerk") to record all final judgments of civil actions in the official records, but the recording of a final judgment of adoption in the official records would frustrate the confidentiality provisions of section 63.162(2), Florida Statutes.

By the power vested in the chief judge under article V, section 2(d), Florida Constitution; section 43.26, Florida Statutes; and Florida Rule of Judicial Administration 2.215(b), it is therefore **ORDERED**:

1. Access to Court File by Adoptive Parents' Attorney. An attorney of record for the adoptive parents may have access to the respective adoption court file while the adoption is pending. The adoption is pending from the initial filing until the time expires to file an appeal and, if filed, determined by the appellate court.

2. Final Judgments.

i. *Certified Copies for Adoptive Parents' Attorney.* If requested by an attorney of record for the adoptive parents, and subject to payment of the appropriate fees, the clerk will provide to an attorney of record for the adoptive parents certified copies of the final judgment of adoption.

ii. *No Recording.* Unless otherwise ordered by the presiding judge in the respective Unified Family Court division, the clerk must not release final judgments of adoption from the court file for recording in the official records.

3. Previous Administrative Order Superseded. This administrative order supersedes Administrative Order S–2006–161 (*Adoption Records*).

4. Effective Date. This administrative order is effective January 1, 2015.

It is ORDERED in Tampa, Hillsborough County, Florida on this 5th day of December, 2014.

Manuel Menendez, Jr., Chief Judge

S–2014–022. UNIFIED FAMILY COURT

IN THE THIRTEENTH JUDICIAL CIRCUIT HILLSBOROUGH COUNTY, FLORIDA

ADMINISTRATIVE ORDER S–2014–022 (Supersedes Administrative Order S–2014–016)

UNIFIED FAMILY COURT

In *In Re: Report of the Family Court Steering Committee,* 794 So. 2d 518 (Fla. 2001), the Florida Supreme Court endorsed the creation of a unified family court system in the circuit courts of Florida. The Court's concept of "one family, one judge" or "one family, one team" to coordinate multiple cases involving one family was expected to improve the resolution of disputes within the judicial system for children and families. Since 2001, this circuit has implemented various strategies to improve the resolution of disputes involving children and families.

In *In re Amendments to the Florida Rules of Judicial Administration and In re Amendments to the Florida Family Law Rules of Procedure*, 39 Fla. L. Weekly S25 (January 16, 2014), the Florida Supreme Court adopted Rule 12.003 which requires that all related family cases must be handled before one judge "unless impractical." Although the implementation of a "one family, one judge" approach may present challenges, we now implement the "one family, one judge" concept in accordance with the most recent decision of the Florida Supreme Court.

By the power vested in the chief judge under article V, section 2(d), Florida Constitution; section 43.26, Florida Statutes; and Florida Rule of Judicial Administration 2.215(b)(2), it is therefore **ORDERED:**

1. Unified Family Court Division. For purposes of this administrative order, "Unified Family Court Division" means any of the following divisions of the Thirteenth Judicial Circuit:

Subject Matter Division	Letter
Domestic Relations / Family Law	A
Domestic Relations / Family Law	B
Domestic Relations / Family Law	C
Domestic Relations / Family Law	D
Domestic Relations / Family Law	E
Domestic Relations / Family Law	F
Domestic Relations / Family Law	I
Domestic Relations / Family Law (East)	R
Domestic Relations / Family Law (East)	T
Title IV–D Child Support	Y
Domestic Violence	G
Domestic Violence	H
Domestic Violence (East)	S
Domestic Violence (East)	V
Juvenile Delinquency	A
Juvenile Delinquency	B
Juvenile Delinquency	F
Juvenile Drug Court	E
Juvenile Dependency	C
Juvenile Dependency	D
Juvenile Dependency	S
Independent Living Transition Services	I
Dependency Drug Court	J
Delinquency–Dependency Crossover	M
Dependency Specialty	V

2. Unified Family Court Cases. All judges assigned to Unified Family Court Divisions will preside over "family cases" involving a single family in accordance with this administrative order, including but not limited to: dissolution of marriage; annulment; support unconnected with dissolution of marriage; paternity; child support; UIFSA; custodial care of and access to children; proceedings for temporary or concurrent custody of minor children by extended family; adoption; name change; declaratory judgment actions related to premarital, marital, or postmarital agreements; civil domestic violence, repeat violence, dating violence, stalking, and sexual violence injunctions; juvenile dependency; termination of parental rights; juvenile delinquency; emancipation of a minor; CINS/FINS; truancy; and modification and enforcement of orders entered in these cases.

3. Notice of Related Cases Form. In accordance with Florida Rule of Judicial Administration 2.545(d), petitioners in all Unified Family Court Divisions, except the Domestic Relations / Family Law Divisions, must complete and file a Notice of Related Cases form in conformity with Florida Family Law Rules of Procedure Form 12.900(h) if any related cases are pending and known or reasonably ascertainable.

Petitioners in the Domestic Relations / Family Law Divisions must complete and file a Notice of Related Cases form in conformity with Florida Family Law Rules of Procedure Form 12.900(h) even if there are no related cases.

In accordance with Rule 2.545(d)(4), the petitioner must file the Notice in each of the related cases that are currently open and pending with the court. **The petitioner must serve the Notice on: (a) all other parties in each of the related cases; (b) the respective presiding division judges; and (c) the administrative judge of the Unified Family Court.**

The Clerk of the Circuit Court ("clerk") will provide Notice of Related Cases forms and instructions for completion to all petitioners or their attorneys in all Unified Family Court Divisions.

4. Administrative Judge Duties. Upon service of a Notice of Related Cases form on the Administrative Judge of the Unified Family Court, the administrative judge will determine if it is practical to transfer or consolidate the related family cases. If the administrative judge determines that it is practical to transfer or consolidate two or more related family cases, the administrative judge will enter an order transferring or consolidating the related family cases and specifying which Unified Family Court Division will hear the cases. If the administrative judge determines that it is impractical to transfer or consolidate related family cases, the administrative judge will enter an order giving a reason for such determination.

The administrative judge of the Unified Family Court is the final arbiter on whether related family cases involving the same parties or children should be transferred or consolidated to one division.

The administrative judge of the Unified Family Court will be assisted in the judge's duties under this administrative order by the clerk and by the court's Case Management Unit.

5. Inconsistent Provisions of Other Administrative Orders. If any provisions of this administrative order are inconsistent with the provisions of any other administrative order, the provisions of this administrative order control.

6. Previous Administrative Order Superseded. This administrative order supersedes Administrative Order S–2014–016 (*Unified Family Court).*

7. Effective Date. This administrative order is effective April 1, 2014.

It is ORDERED in Tampa, Hillsborough County, Florida, on this 27th day of March, 2014.

Manuel Menendez, Jr., Chief Judge

S–2012–041. COLLABORATIVE FAMILY LAW PRACTICE

IN THE THIRTEENTH JUDICIAL CIRCUIT HILLSBOROUGH COUNTY, FLORIDA

ADMINISTRATIVE ORDER S–2012–041

COLLABORATIVE FAMILY LAW PRACTICE

In the 1990s the collaborative family law practice model was adopted in jurisdictions both in the United States and abroad by common law and by statute. In Florida, the creation of family law divisions and necessary support services in the 1990s and the adoption of the Model Family Court in 2001 reflected the recognition of the Florida Supreme Court and Florida Legislature that families in conflict needed a non-litigation forum to restructure family relationships. The Florida Supreme Court recognized that family cases needed "a system that provided nonadversarial alternatives and flexibility of alternatives; a system that preserved rather than destroyed family relationships; . . . and a system that facilitated the process chosen by the parties." *In re Report of the Family Law Steering Committee*, 794 So. 2d 518, 523 (Fla. 2001).

The Florida Supreme Court's acceptance of recommendations for a model family court is consistent with the principles of the collaborative practice model because the collaborative process empowers parties to make their own decisions guided and assisted by counsel in a setting outside of court. The Thirteenth Judicial Circuit supports the philosophy that the interdisciplinary collaborative practice model may be a suitable alternative to full scale adversarial litigation in family law cases if the parties agree to such a model.

By the power vested in the chief judge under article V, section 2(d), Florida Constitution; section 43.26, Florida Statutes; and Florida Rule of Judicial Administration 2.215(b)(2), it is therefore ORDERED:

1. Collaborative Practice Model. The collaborative practice model is confidential and utilizes interest-based negotiation to resolve disputes through the structured assistance of collaboratively trained professionals, including but not limited to lawyers, financial professionals, mental health professionals, mediators, and other neutral professionals. The collaborative practice model is authorized in the Thirteenth Judicial Circuit of Florida to resolve dissolution of marriage cases and other family law matters according to the following procedures.

2. Role of Collaborative Professionals.

A. *Collaborative Lawyers.* The collaborative lawyers advise and counsel their respective clients, facilitate negotiation, and create written agreements.

B. *Neutral Mental Health Professionals/Neutral Facilitators.* The neutral mental health professional, mediator, or other neutral facilitator is available to both parties and may work to:

i. Prioritize parties' concerns;

ii. Help develop conflict resolution skills;

iii. Develop co-parenting skills;

iv. Help the parties focus on the needs of the children;

v. Enhance communication skills;

vi. Reduce misunderstandings;

vii. Assist in focus on working toward resolution; and

viii. Perform any other activity agreed upon by the team.

C. *Neutral Financial Professional.* The neutral financial professional is available to both parties and may assist in the following activities:

i. Provide the parties with necessary financial scenarios and analyses regarding the division of assets, liabilities, and support, both child and spousal;

ii. Provide analysis of the nature and composition of specific marital assets (e.g. retirement, capital gain consideration, tax implication, etc.);

iii. Take responsibility for gathering all relevant financial information;

iv. Assist development of and understanding of any valuation processes;

v. Assist with estate planning issues; and

vi. Perform any other activity agreed upon by the team.

3. Participation Agreement. If the parties and professionals desire to use the collaborative practice model, they must enter into a contractual commitment (Participation Agreement) to negotiate a settlement without using the court system to decide any issues of the parties. The lawyers and other retained professionals or consultants, who are entitled to be paid for their services in the collaborative process, will be paid by the parties in accordance with the terms of their Participation Agreement. The Participation Agreement must provide that if a full settlement of all issues is not reached then the collaborative attorneys must withdraw. The Participation Agreement should also contain a provision on the extent of maintaining confidentiality of oral or written communication exchanged during the collaborative process. This confidentiality provision must comply with Florida law and rules of court. As a resource for Participation Agreements and other documents, practitioners and parties may review the website of the International Academy of Collaborative Professionals, which is accessible at the following link: http://www.collaborativepractice.com.

4. Timing of Process. The parties may participate in the collaborative practice model either before or after a petition for dissolution of marriage or any other family law matter is filed.

A. *Pre–Filing Collaborative Cases.* If the collaborative process is utilized prior to filing a petition for dissolution or other family law matter, the parties must file the Participation Agreement with the Clerk of the Circuit Court (Clerk) as a separate document at the same time as the petition. If the parties have come to a full settlement of all issues prior to filing, then the parties may jointly petition for an uncontested family law action and set this matter for an uncontested final hearing. In such a case, the 20–day waiting period will be deemed waived by the parties.

B. *Post–Filing Collaborative Cases.* If the collaborative process is to be utilized after an initial pleading has already been filed with the Clerk, then the parties must file the Participation Agreement with the Clerk and notify the presiding judge. Upon notice to the presiding judge, the court will abate the court proceedings. A collaborative status conference will be held within six months of the abatement. The proceeding will remain abated until either an uncontested dissolution of marriage or a motion to withdraw by counsel is heard by the court. Periodic status conferences may be scheduled at the presiding judge's discretion.

5. Collaborative Status Conference. Upon the filing of a Participation Agreement, an Order Setting First Collaborative Status Conference will be entered. The Collaborative Status Conference Order will be signed by the presiding judge. The Clerk will provide the filing attorney with two copies of the Collaborative Status Conference Order, and the filing attorney must distribute a copy of the Collaborative Status Conference Order to the other engaged collaborative professionals, including the other attorney.

A. *Continuance.* A collaborative status conference may only be rescheduled by order of the court. Either party may move the court for entry of an order continuing the initial collaborative status conference to a later date by sending to the judge's chambers a jointly-signed stipulation and proposed order ratifying the stipulation. The stipulation must state that the new date and time of the collaborative status conference has been provided by the judicial assistant and cleared by both parties, which new date is within 60 days of the originally-scheduled date.

B. *Cancellation.* A collaborative status conference may only be cancelled if (i) the parties have reached a full settlement prior to the date of the conference and the parties have scheduled an uncontested final hearing prior to the date of the status conference; (ii) the presiding judge authorizes the cancellation; or (iii) the parties file and serve upon the presiding judge a joint stipulated notice to dismiss the matter.

6. Exchange of Information. During the collaborative process, no formal discovery procedures will be used, unless agreed upon by the parties. The parties will make a full and candid exchange of information so that a proper resolution of the case can occur, which will include a full disclosure of the nature and extent of all assets and liabilities, income of the parties, and all relevant information concerning the parties' children. Any material change in the information provided must be promptly updated and exchanged.

7. Case Management. During the collaborative process, the court will not set a hearing or trial in the case, except for periodic status conferences, or impose discovery deadlines. The court will not adjudicate any dispute between the parties. If a party seeks affirmative relief by petition or motion, the collaborative process will cease. If a full settlement has been reached, the collaborative lawyers will ask the court to approve the settlement agreement. If an agreement has not been reached, the collaborative attorneys must withdraw from representation.

During the collaborative process, the parties may, from time to time, resolve temporary issues in an executed writing. If agreed upon by the parties, the court may ratify and approve any such temporary agreements by reference or otherwise. If the collaborative process breaks down, the parties agree to abide by the terms of all court-ratified temporary agreements once litigation ensues.

8. **Termination of the Collaborative Process.** If the collaborative process breaks down or a full settlement is not reached, then

A. Counsel for the parties must withdraw;

B. All engaged professionals are disqualified from testifying as witnesses, experts, or otherwise, regarding the case, unless the parties mutually agree in writing; and

C. The professionals' work product created or exchanged during the collaborative process cannot be used in any judicial proceedings unless the parties otherwise mutually agree in writing.

9. **Effective Date.** This administrative order is effective August 1, 2012.

It is ORDERED in Tampa, Hillsborough County, Florida, on this 31st day of July, 2012.

Manuel Menendez, Jr.

S–2011–046. PARENTAL NOTICE OF ABORTION ACT CASES

Publisher's Note: Administrative Order S-2011-046 available under the topical heading of "Unified Family Court - Juvenile."

S–2011–014. CHILD CUSTODY PROCEEDINGS

Publisher's Note: Administrative Order S-2011-014 available under the topical heading of "Unified Family Court – Juvenile."

S–2009–107. MEDIATION OF FAMILY LAW CASES

IN THE THIRTEENTH JUDICIAL CIRCUIT HILLSBOROUGH COUNTY, FLORIDA

ADMINISTRATIVE ORDER S–2009–107 (Supersedes Administrative Orders S–2008–163)

MEDIATION OF FAMILY LAW CASES

Chapter 44, Florida Statutes, and Florida Family Law Rule of Procedure 12. 740 provide for mediation of family law actions. The Family Diversion Program has been established as a court program under Mediation and Diversion Services to implement an equitable and expeditious alternative dispute resolution process for family law cases. It is necessary for the proper and efficient administration of justice in the Unified Family Court Domestic Relations / Family Law Division to update procedures for the mediation of family law cases through the Family Diversion Program.

By the power vested in the chief judge under Florida Rule of Judicial Administration 2.215(b)(2), it is therefore **ORDERED:**

1. **Court Referral of Family Matters to Mediation**

All issues in marriage dissolution and post dissolution proceedings and in domestic proceedings between unmarried parents may be referred to mediation by the presiding judge unless excluded by statute or court rule. All court-ordered referrals will be made through the Family Diversion Program ("Program"). Matters referred will be handled by Florida Supreme Court certified family mediators. See Florida Rule for Certified and Court–Appointed Mediators 10.100 for certification requirements.

An Order Referring Parties to Family Mediation will be prepared by the court. The court will forward the original order to the Clerk of the Circuit Court, Family Law Division ("clerk"). A copy of the order will be mailed by the court to each party or party's counsel of record and a copy will be provided to the Program.

2. **Selection of Mediators and Scheduling**

The parties or their counsel will have 10 days from the date of the Order Referring Parties to Family Mediation in which to select a mediator and notify the Program of the selection. The petitioner or petitioner's counsel will be solely responsible for notifying the Program. If a certified private mediator is selected instead of a Program mediator, the parties should also propose a date and time for a conference. If a certified private mediator is selected, the petitioner or petitioner's counsel should notify the Program of the mediator, proposed date and proposed time. If the parties select a Program mediator, upon notification by the petitioner or petitioner's counsel of the mediator selected, the Program will arrange the conference date and time. If selections of a particular mediator, date and time for a conference are not made within 10 days from the date of the Order Referring Parties to Family Mediation, such decisions will be made by the Program. In any case, the Program will provide written notice to the parties of the mediator, date, time and location of the mediation conference.

3. **Deferment**

Within 15 days of the Order Referring Parties to Family Mediation, any party may file a motion to defer the mediation conference. The moving party will use best efforts to set the motion to defer for hearing prior to the scheduled date for the mediation conference. If a hearing on the motion to defer cannot be set prior to the mediation conference date the moving party will, more than 48 hours before the originally scheduled conference, take necessary steps to reschedule the conference. Failure to comply with this time standard may result in the imposition of monetary sanctions as determined by the court. Notice of the hearing on the motion to defer will be provided to all parties, the Program, and the appointed mediator. The court will forward to the Program a copy of any order granting a deferment of the mediation conference. If a deferment has been granted, the order will include the actual period of deferral and another mediation conference will be scheduled.

4. **Mandatory Post–Judgment Mediation**

Whenever a post-judgment family law case is initiated, as a prerequisite to scheduling a hearing before the presiding judge or general magistrate, the parties will submit such issues to mediation. Such post-judgment matters are hereby automatically referred to the Program without further order of the court. The party initiating the post-judgment action will have the responsibility of initially contacting the Program to arrange for its service.

A. Scheduling

The Program will set a reasonable time for a mediation conference on the matter(s) in controversy. The conference will be held within the time frames outlined in Rule 12.740(e), unless the parties agree to an extension of time or the court, for good cause, extends the time. The Program will notify the parties and their respective attorneys of the time and place of the mediation conference.

B. Discovery Not Limited

Nothing in this administrative order will be construed as limiting the parties or their attorneys from scheduling discovery prior to the mediation conference.

C. Non–Applicability

This mandatory post-judgment mediation requirement will not apply when the Department of Revenue brings an action as plaintiff or pursuant to chapter 409, Florida Statutes.

5. Waiver of Mandatory Mediation

Notwithstanding the provisions of section 4 of this administrative order, any party may request the presiding judge to waive the requirement of mandatory mediation of post-judgment parenting plan or time-sharing disputes. The judge will waive such requirement in cases where the judge finds there has been a history of domestic violence that would compromise the mediation process. The judge may also waive the requirement if it appears mediation of the issues would not be appropriate under the circumstances of the case or because of exigent circumstances a hearing before the judge should be expedited.

6. Mediation Conference

The mediator will be in control of the mediation conference at all times. If a resolution is imminent or likely, the mediator may, at his or her discretion and with the agreement of the parties, schedule another mediation conference. The mediator will then arrange a date and time for the subsequent conference with the parties and notify the Program. The Program will prepare a notice of additional mediation conference and provide a copy to each party. Upon completion of mediation, the mediator will return a completed Outcome of Service form to the Program office within 48 hours of the mediation conference.

7. Report to the Court

The Program will submit to the court a report stating whether or not the parties appeared for the mediation conference, and whether or not any agreement was reached.

8. Agreements

Agreements reached during mediation must be memorialized, completed and submitted in accordance with Florida Family Rule of Procedure 12.740(f).

9. Rescheduling or Cancellation Prior to Mediation

The parties or their counsel must notify the Program of any rescheduling no later than 48 hours, excluding weekends and legal holidays, before the scheduled mediation conference. Petitioner, or if petitioner is represented by counsel, petitioner's counsel, must notify the Program in writing if the mediation must be cancelled because a settlement has been reached or the case has been dismissed more than 48 hours prior to the scheduled conference.

10. Disqualification or Withdrawal of Mediator

A party may move at any time to disqualify a mediator. The court will forward to the Program a copy of any order disqualifying a mediator. If a mediator has been disqualified or has withdrawn, a new mediator will be assigned by the Program. Rescheduling may be necessary to accommodate the substitute mediator.

11. Fees

Fees for court-ordered mediation sessions will be assessed and collected in accordance with section 44.108, Florida Statutes. If proof of income is not provided, the fee will be as provided for in section 44.108(2)(a). If payment of any owed fees is not made by the time of the scheduled mediation session, the mediation session will not take place. Payment may be by check (payable to the "Clerk of the Circuit Court"), money order, cash or credit card (Visa / MasterCard / Discover). Credit card payments cannot be made over the telephone.

If a party fails to appear at a scheduled mediation session, or fails to make payment by the time of the mediation session, or fails to provide at least 24 hours prior written notice to the Program of the cancellation of a mediation session, the party will be billed for the cancelled mediation session.

12. Invoicing

The Program will be responsible for generating invoices for all parties participating in the mediation conference. An invoice for payment will outline each party's portion of the mediation cost. The clerk will accept payment, on behalf of the Program, of the amount due from the parties; however, the clerk will accept payment only in the amount specified on the invoice for payment. All payments made to the clerk will be accompanied by the invoice for payment.

13. Statistical Data

All parties ordered by the court to mediation will provide data as requested by the Program for statistical purposes. The data will remain confidential to the extent that any data published will contain no identifying information.

14. Previous Administrative Orders Superseded

This administrative order supersedes Administrative Order S–2008–163 (*Mediation of Family Law Cases*).

15. Effective Date

This administrative order is effective January 1, 2010.

It is ORDERED in Tampa, Hillsborough County, Florida, on this 28th day of October, 2009.

Manuel Menendez, Jr., Chief Judge

Fifteenth Judicial Circuit (Palm Beach County)

ADMINISTRATIVE ORDERS

LOCAL RULES

1.001. DIVISIONS OF COURT.
1.002. [RESCINDED BY ORDER NO. 12.015–3/10, EFFECTIVE MARCH 5, 2010.].
1.003. ORDERS/JUDGMENTS SUBMITTED FOR SIGNATURE.
1.004. UNIFORM MOTION CALENDAR AND SPECIALLY SET HEARINGS.
1.005. REPORTING DATE FOR ANNUAL ACCOUNTINGS BY GUARDIANS OF THE PROPERTY.
1.006. PETITIONS FOR REHEARING.
1.007. NOT APPROVED BY THE SUPREME COURT.
1.008. [VACATED BY ORDER OF THE COURT, EFFECTIVE MAY 15, 2001.].

GENERAL RULES

GENERAL ADMINISTRATIVE MATTERS

2.101. PREPARATION & DISTRIBUTION OF ADMINISTRATIVE ORDERS.
2.102. ADMINISTRATIVE ORDER NUMBERING SYSTEM.
2.103. ADDITIONAL COURT HOLIDAYS.
2.104. DESIGNATION OF RECORD NEWSPAPER.
2.105. FIFTEENTH CIRCUIT PROFESSIONALISM PANEL.
2.106. PRO BONO SERVICE.
2.107. USE OF COURTHOUSE ROOMS FOR DEPOSITIONS AND NURSING MOTHERS.

SECURITY, EMERGENCY, AND OTHER PROCEDURES

2.201. COURTHOUSE SECURITY AND SCREENING.
2.202. SECURITY OF JUDICIAL CORRIDORS.
2.203. COURT EMERGENCY MANAGEMENT GROUP.
2.204. CONTAINMENT AND REMOVAL OF BIO–HAZARDOUS/INFECTIOUS WASTE.
2.205. COURT DISASTER AND EMERGENCY PROCEDURES.
2.206. DISASTER AND EMERGENCY PROCEDURES IN CRIMINAL AND DEPENDENCY MATTERS.
2.207. REQUESTS FOR ACCOMMODATIONS UNDER THE AMERICANS WITH DISABILITIES ACT.
2.208. PROCEDURES FOR SPECIAL INTEREST/HIGH PROFILE PROCEEDINGS.

COURT FILES, RECORDS AND CASES

2.301. PAPER COURT FILES.
2.302. COMPANION, REFILED, AND TRANSFERRED CASES.
2.303. CONFIDENTIALITY/SEALING OF COURT HEARINGS AND RECORDS.
2.304. REQUEST FOR PUBLIC JUDICIAL RECORDS.
2.305. MICROFILMING SEALED COURT RECORDS.
2.306. MOTIONS, ORDERS, AND JUDGMENTS.
2.307. CASE ADVANCEMENT IN NON–CRIMINAL MATTERS.
2.308. UNIFORM INTRACIRCUIT CONFLICT RESOLUTION PROCEDURE.
2.309. EXEMPLIFICATION CERTIFICATES.
2.310. SERVICE BY EMAIL.
2.311. NOTICES OF CHANGE OF ADDRESS, SUBSTITUTION/WITHDRAWAL OF COUNSEL, AND DESIGNATION OF ATTORNEY OF RECORD.
2.312. ELECTRONIC FILING OF DOCUMENTS.
2.313. ASSIGNMENT OF CRIMINAL AND CIVIL CONTEMPT CASES.
2.314. ELECTION PROCEDURES.

JURY MANAGEMENT AND JURORS

2.401. JURY MANAGEMENT.
2.402. JURY PANELS.
2.403. JURY SERVICE COMPENSATION DONATION PROGRAM.

WITNESS MANAGEMENT, COURT REPORTING, AND INTERPRETERS

2.501. WITNESS MANAGEMENT OFFICE.
2.502. PROCEDURES FOR SCHEDULING AND RECORDING DEPOSITIONS AT WITNESS MANAGEMENT OFFICE.
2.503. COURT REPORTING SERVICES.
2.504. COURT REPORTER'S APPOINTMENT, APPEARANCE FORMS AND TRANSCRIPTS IN CIVIL CASES.
2.505. COURT REPORTING PLAN FOR DEATH PENALTY TRIALS AND CAPITAL POST–CONVICTION PROCEEDINGS.
2.506. COURT INTERPRETER POLICIES.
2.507. [VACATED AND SET ASIDE BY ORDER 2.507-11/16, EFFECTIVE NOVEMBER 1, 2016.].
2.508. CONTRACTUAL COURT INTERPRETERS ADDITIONAL COMPENSATION FOR SPANISH & CREOLE AND ADDITIONAL COMPENSATION FOR EXOTIC LANGUAGES.

EXPERT, DUE PROCESS, AND COURT APPOINTED COUNSEL

2.601. SELECTION AND PAYMENT OF COURT APPOINTED EXPERTS.
2.602. ESTABLISHMENT OF REVIEW PANEL FOR SELECTION OF COURT APPOINTED EXPERTS.
2.603. DUE PROCESS COSTS.
2.604. COURT APPOINTED COUNSEL.
2.606. APPOINTMENT OF CHIEF JUDGE DESIGNEE TO HEAR REQUESTS BY GENERAL REGISTRY ATTORNEYS FOR ADDITIONAL COMPENSATION.

PROCESS SERVERS

2.701. CERTIFIED PROCESS SERVERS.
2.702. RETURN OF SERVICE FORM.
2.703. RECOVERY OF CERTIFIED PROCESS SERVER COSTS.
2.704. EXTENSION OF RECIPROCITY TO CERTIFIED PROCESS SERVERS OF THE ELEVENTH JUDICIAL CIRCUIT.
2.705. CERTIFIED PROCESS SERVERS, REMOVAL FOR FAILURE TO RENEW CERTIFICATION OR BOND.
2.706. GRIEVANCE REVIEW COMMITTEE.

Administrative Orders

Local Rules

1.001. DIVISIONS OF COURT

IN THE CIRCUIT COURT OF THE FIFTEENTH JUDICIAL CIRCUIT IN AND FOR PALM BEACH COUNTY, FLORIDA

Local Rule No. 1

Revision 1

IN RE: DIVISIONS OF COURT

Pursuant to the authority conferred by rule 2.050(b), Fla.R.Jud.Admin., it is

ORDERED that: Six divisions of the Circuit Court are created for the administration and management of court proceedings.

(1) Appellate Division

(2) Civil Division

(3) Criminal Division

(4) Family Law Division

(5) Foreclosure Division

(6) Probate & Guardianship Division

Three divisions of the County Court for Palm Beach County are created for the administration and management of court proceedings.

(1) Civil Division

(2) Criminal Division

(3) Domestic Violence Division

DONE and **SIGNED** in Chambers at West Palm Beach, Florida, this 21st day of October, 1998.

Walter N. Colbath, Jr.
Chief Judge

Adopted January 15, 1999, effective June 1, 1999.

1.002. [RESCINDED BY ORDER NO. 12.015–3/10, EFFECTIVE MARCH 5, 2010.]

1.003. ORDERS/JUDGMENTS SUBMITTED FOR SIGNATURE

IN THE CIRCUIT COURT OF THE FIFTEENTH JUDICIAL CIRCUIT IN AND FOR PALM BEACH COUNTY, FLORIDA

Local Rule No. 3

IN RE: ORDERS/JUDGMENTS SUBMITTED FOR SIGNATURE

..........:

Pursuant to the authority conferred by rule 2.050(b), Fla.R.Jud.Admin., it is

ORDERED as follows:

(1) At the commencement of any motion hearing (including the uniform motion calendar), the moving party shall furnish the Court with a proposed order or judgment together with sufficient copies and stamped, addressed envelopes for all parties.

(2) When a party is directed to prepare and furnish a proposed order to the Court, that party shall furnish a copy of the proposed order or judgment to opposing counsel prior to submission to the Court. Furthermore, the submitting party shall provide the Court with sufficient copies and stamped, addressed envelopes to permit mailing to all parties.

(3) Unless the Court directs otherwise, proposed orders on non-motion calendar hearings shall be prepared by the prevailing or designated counsel and shall be submitted to the Court for consideration within seventy-two hours after the hearing.

(4) Unless the Court directs otherwise, a proposed final judgment in accord with a jury verdict shall be submitted to the Court for its consideration within seventy-two hours of the return of the verdict.

DONE and SIGNED in Chambers at West Palm Beach, Florida, this 31st day of January, 1991.

Daniel T. K. Hurley
Chief Judge

Adopted January 31, 1991, effective April 23, 1991.

1.004. UNIFORM MOTION CALENDAR AND SPECIALLY SET HEARINGS

IN THE CIRCUIT COURT OF THE FIFTEENTH JUDICIAL CIRCUIT IN AND FOR PALM BEACH COUNTY, FLORIDA

Local Rule No. 4

IN RE: UNIFORM MOTION CALENDAR **AND SPECIALLY SET HEARINGS**

Pursuant to the authority conferred by Rule 2.215(e), Fla. R. Jud. Admin., it is **ORDERED** as follows:

1. Circuit and County Court judges in each division shall conduct a Uniform Motion Calendar on days and at a time specified by the judges of the division.

2. Prior to filing and serving a Notice of Hearing for a Uniform Motion Calendar hearing or a specially set hearing, the attorney noticing the motion for hearing shall attempt to resolve the matter and shall certify the good faith attempt to resolve. [1]

3. The term "attempt to resolve the matter" in paragraph 2 shall require counsel to make reasonable efforts to speak to one another (in person or via telephone) and engage in reasonable compromises in a genuine effort to resolve or narrow the disputes before seeking Court intervention. [2] All parties are to act courteously and professionally in the attempted resolution of the disputes prior to filing and serving a Notice of Hearing including responding timely to counsel who initiated the attempt to resolve the matter.

4. All notices of hearings for matters scheduled on the Uniform Motion Calendar or on a special setting shall set forth directly above the signature block, the below certifications without modification and shall designate with a check mark or other marking the specific certification(s) that apply:

_________ *Movant's attorney has spoken in person or by telephone with the attorney(s) for all parties who may be affected by the relief sought in the motion in a good faith effort to resolve or narrow the issues raised.*

_________ *Movant's attorney has attempted to speak in person or by telephone with the attorney(s) for all parties who may be affected by the relief sought in the motion.*

_________ *One or more of the parties who may be affected by the motion are self represented.*

5. Failure to make a good faith attempt at resolving the issues may, in the Court's discretion, result in the motion being stricken from the Uniform Motion Calendar or specially set hearing and/or the imposition of sanctions. The Court may waive the good faith attempt at resolving the issues in appropriate circumstances.

6. The attorney attending the hearing on behalf of the movant, as well as any attorney who is covering the hearing for another attorney, shall be prepared to specify to the Court the efforts made to confer when the parties' attorneys have not spoken.

7. To the extent reasonable, the movant's attorney shall advise the Court in advance of the hearing of cancellation, or resolution of some or all of the issues raised by the motion.

8. On Uniform Motion Calendar, hearings shall be limited to ten minutes per case. If two parties, each side shall be allotted five minutes. If more than two parties, the time shall be allocated by the Court. The ten-minute time limitation shall include the time necessary for the Court to review documents, memoranda, case authority, etc.

9. The moving party must furnish the Court with a copy of the motion to be heard together with a copy of the notice of hearing. Also, all parties shall furnish the Court with copies of all relevant documents, pleadings and case authority which they wish the Court to consider.

10. Except in the criminal division, counsel shall not make appointments with the Court's judicial assistant but shall file and serve opposing counsel with a Notice of Hearing pursuant to the applicable rules of procedure, and the Standards of Professional Courtesy and Civility (the "Standards"), which have been endorsed by the judges of the Fifteenth Judicial Circuit. The Standards are available on the Fifteenth Judicial Circuit and the Palm Beach County Bar Association websites.

11. Cases on the uniform motion calendar will be called for hearing in the order in which they appear on the sign-in sheet for that day. Failure of any party to appear at the time set for the commencement of the calendar shall not prevent a party from proceeding with the hearing. If a party called for hearing chooses to wait for an absent party, the matter will be passed over but shall retain its position on that day's calendar.

DONE and **SIGNED** in Chambers at West Palm Beach, Palm Beach County, Florida, this 18th day of July, 2017.

Krista Marx
Chief Judge

Adopted January 31, 1991, effective April 23, 1991. Amended effective June 17, 2015; June 6, 2017; July 18, 2017.

1 The requirements of this rule do not apply when the moving party or non-moving party is pro se.

2 The requirements of this rule do not preclude the use of e-mail or other written communication in an effort to resolve a pending motion. Compliance with this rule, including "making reasonable efforts to speak to one another" in person or by telephone before filing and serving a Notice of Hearing is required when e-mail or other written communication efforts are unsuccessful.

1.005. REPORTING DATE FOR ANNUAL ACCOUNTINGS BY GUARDIANS OF THE PROPERTY

IN THE CIRCUIT COURT OF THE FIFTEENTH JUDICIAL CIRCUIT IN AND FOR PALM BEACH COUNTY, FLORIDA

Local Rule NO. 5

IN RE: REPORTING DATE FOR ANNUAL ACCOUNTINGS BY GUARDIANS OF THE PROPERTY

..........:

WHEREAS, the Legislature amended section 744.367(2), Florida Statutes (Supp. 1990), to permit the Court to designate one of two time frames (calendar year or fiscal year) for submission of annual accountings by guardians of the property; and

WHEREAS, the Supreme Court promulgated rule 5.695(a)(2), Fla.R.P.&G.P., to implement the foregoing legislation; and

WHEREAS, the Court in the Fifteenth Judicial Circuit, can best fulfill its responsibility to review these accountings if they are received on a fiscal- year basis;

NOW, THEREFORE, it is ORDERED as follows:

(1) This local rule shall establish the reporting date for all guardians of the property unless the Court, by written order entered subsequent to the effective date of this rule, shall establish a different reporting date for an individual case.

(2) In the Fifteenth Judicial Circuit, guardians of the property shall file their annual accountings on a fiscal-year basis.

(3) The term "fiscal year" shall be individualized for each guardianship of the property, i.e., the "fiscal year" for each guardianship of the property shall terminate on the last day of the month during which the guardian of the property received his or her letters of guardianship.

(4) Annual accountings by guardians of the property shall be filed on or before the first day of the fourth month after the end of the fiscal year established by this local rule.

DONE and SIGNED in Chambers at West Palm Beach, Florida, this 8th day of November, 1991.

Daniel T. K. Hurley
Chief Judge

Adopted November 8, 1991, effective April 28, 1992.

1.006. PETITIONS FOR REHEARING

IN THE CIRCUIT COURT OF THE FIFTEENTH JUDICIAL CIRCUIT IN AND FOR PALM BEACH COUNTY, FLORIDA

Local Rule No. 6

IN RE: PETITIONS FOR REHEARING

..........:

With the exception of motions for new trial or rehearing pursuant to rule 1.530, Fla.R.Civ.P., or similar procedural rule, no petition for rehearing, motion for reconsideration, or like pleading, shall be set for oral argument except upon court order. The petition or motion shall be filed with the clerk and a copy shall be furnished to the assigned judge along with a copy of the original order. Upon consideration of the matter, the judge shall either deny the petition or motion or shall set it for oral argument.

DONE and SIGNED in Chambers at West Palm Beach, Florida, on this 19th day of February, 1993.

Daniel T. K. Hurley
Chief Judge

Adopted February 19, 1993, effective April 28, 1993.

1.007. NOT APPROVED BY THE SUPREME COURT

1.008. [VACATED BY ORDER OF THE COURT, EFFECTIVE MAY 15, 2001.]

General Rules

General Administrative Matters

2.101. PREPARATION & DISTRIBUTION OF ADMINISTRATIVE ORDERS

IN THE CIRCUIT COURT OF THE FIFTEENTH JUDICIAL CIRCUIT IN AND FOR PALM BEACH COUNTY, FLORIDA

ADMINISTRATIVE ORDER NO. 2.101–9/08 *

IN RE: PREPARATION & DISTRIBUTION OF ADMINISTRATIVE ORDERS

Pursuant to the authority conferred by Florida Rule of Judicial Administration 2.215, it is **ORDERED** as follows:

1. The Chief Judge shall sign one original of all administrative orders in blue ink. The chief judge's judicial assistant shall then **electronically distribute copies** to comply with the following procedures.

2. The following procedure shall govern the distribution of all administrative orders except special administrative orders, i.e., those found in chapter 12.

a. The chief judge's judicial assistant shall file the **blue ink** original signature with the clerk, shall retain one copy and shall transmit one copy to the administrative office of the courts for processing.

b. The Administrative Office of the Court shall be responsible for maintaining an up-to-date listing of all administrative orders in the Court's website.

3. The Administrative Office of the Court shall be responsible for maintaining a read-only library of all administrative orders. The read-only library entitled "adminord" can be accessed **on the shared directory.** The chief judge's judicial assistant will, for information purposes only, electronically transmit a copy of the administrative order to an Administrative Order Distribution List which list will be approved by the Chief Judge and maintained by the Office of Court Technology.

4. Special administrative orders shall be handled as follows:

a. The chief judge's judicial assistant shall file the blue ink signature original with the clerk, shall retain one copy, shall transmit one copy to the administrative office of the courts and shall send one copy to the individual(s) named in the order.

b. The administrative office of the courts shall maintain the order on file only, the special administrative orders shall not be distributed.

5. Administrative orders shall contain series number and topic numbers and shall be followed by numbers indicating the month and year of issuance e. g. 2.101 9/08.

6. When an administrative order is updated or issued in place of an existing order, the new order shall contain an asterisk after the order number and a footnote below the body of the order shall indicate that the new order "supersedes admin. order no. (old order no.)."

DONE and **SIGNED** in Chambers at West Palm Beach, Palm Beach County, Florida, this 29 day of September, 2008.

Kathleen J. Kroll
Chief Judge

Adopted effective September 29, 2008.

* supersedes admin. order 11.016–8/99

2.102. ADMINISTRATIVE ORDER NUMBERING SYSTEM

IN THE CIRCUIT COURT OF THE FIFTEENTH JUDICIAL CIRCUIT IN AND FOR PALM BEACH COUNTY, FLORIDA

ADMINISTRATIVE ORDER NO. 2.102–9/08 *

IN RE: ADMINISTRATIVE ORDER NUMBERING SYSTEM

The orderly administration of justice within the Fifteenth Judicial Circuit of Florida requires that administrative orders be reviewed and that out-of-date administrative orders be vacated and set aside. Administrative Orders should also be set forth in an efficient and user friendly manner. A complete review of the administrative orders occurred in September, 2008. Some administrative orders were changed in number only while other administrative orders had substantive changes.

NOW, THEREFORE, pursuant to the authority conferred by Florida Rule of Judicial Administration 2.215, it is **ORDERED** as follows:

A. With the exception of Local Rules (Series 1),Series 12, and Administrative Order Numbers 11.033 (Order Establishing JIS), 11.040 (JIS System Security), 3.018 (Banner Computer System), and 2.052 (In Re: Anthony Martin) all current administrative orders are hereby vacated effective October 15, 2008. There shall be a new Administrative Order numbering system that will clearly identify the matter the administrative order is to address. The Administrative Orders which were signed between September 29, 2008 and October 14, 2008 will be effective as of October 15, 2008. New administrative orders shall be numbered in accordance with the applicable series as set forth below.

B. The new numbering system shall be as follows:

1. Series 1—Local Rules
2. Series 2—General Orders
   a. Series 2.100—General Administrative Matters
   b. Series 2.200—Security, Emergency and Other Procedures
   c. Series 2.300—Court Files, Court Records and Cases
   d. Series 2.400—Jury Management and Jurors
   e. Series 2.500—Witness Management, Court Reporting and Interpreters
   f. Series 2.600—Experts, Due Process and Court Appointed Counsel
   g. Series 2.700—Process Servers
   h. Series 2.800—Alternative Dispute Resolution
   i. Series 2.900—OPEN
3. Series 3—Civil Orders
   a. Series 3.100—Administrative Matters
   b. Series 3.200—Circuit Civil—Pretrial and Trial
   c. Series 3.300—Foreclosures and Judicial Sales
   d. Series 3.400—Eminent Domain
   e. Series 3.500—Forfeiture
   f. Series 3.600—County Civil—Pretrial and Trial
   g. Series 3.700—OPEN
   h. Series 3.800—OPEN
   i. Series 3.900—Special Civil Administrative Orders
4. Series 4—Criminal Orders
   a. Series 4.100—Administrative Matters
   b. Series 4.200—First Appearance & Bond
   c. Series 4.300—Pretrial and Trial Management
   d. Series 4.400—Sentencing and Related Post Sentencing Matters
   e. Series 4.500—Circuit Criminal
   f. Series 4.600—County Criminal
   g. Series 4.700—Restraining Orders/Domestic Violence
   h. Series 4.800—Inmates
   i. Series 4.900—Special Criminal Administrative Orders
5. Series 5—Unified Family Court Orders
   a. Series 5.100—UFC Administrative Matters
   b. Series 5.200—Family Division Pretrial/Trial
   c. Series 5.300—Alimony, Child Support, Custody and Visitation
   d. Series 5.400—Domestic Relations—Post Judgment
   e. Series 5.500—Special Family Administrative Orders
   f. Series 5.600—Delinquency
   g. Series 5.700—Dependency
   h. Series 5.800—Special Juvenile Administrative Orders
   i. Series 5.900—OPEN
6. Series 6—Probate/Guardianship/Mental Health/Substance Abuse Orders
   a. Series 6.100—Administrative Matters
   b. Series 6.200—Probate
   c. Series 6.300—Guardianship/Mental Health/Substance Abuse
   d. Series 6.400—OPEN
   e. Series 6.500—OPEN
   f. Series 6.600—OPEN
   g. Series 6.700—OPEN
   h. Series 6.800—OPEN
   i. Series 6.900—OPEN
7. Series 7—Prisoner Litigation/Writs/Post Conviction
   a. Series 7.100—Prisoner Litigation
   b. Series 7.200—Writs
   c. Series 7.300—Post Conviction
   d. Series 7.400—OPEN
   e. Series 7.500—OPEN
   f. Series 7.600—OPEN
   g. Series 7.700—OPEN
   h. Series 7.800—OPEN
   i. Series 7.900—OPEN
8. Series 8—Appeals
   a. Series 8.100—General Appellate Information
   b. Series 8.200—OPEN
   c. Series 8.300—OPEN
   d. Series 8.400—OPEN
   e. Series 8.500—OPEN
   f. Series 8.600—OPEN
   g. Series 8.700—OPEN
   h. Series 8.800—OPEN
   i. Series 8.900—OPEN
9. Series 9—OPEN
10. Series 10—Traffic Orders
   a. Series 10.100—Criminal Traffic Matters
   b. Series 10.200—Civil Traffic Matters
   c. Series 10.300—Civil Traffic Hearing Officers
   d. Series 10.400—Civil Traffic Infraction Procedures
   e. Series 10.500—Driver Programs/Court Costs
   f. Series 10.600—OPEN
   g. Series 10.700—OPEN
   h. Series 10.800—OPEN

i. Series 10.900—OPEN

11. Series 11—Internal Policies and Procedures

a. Series 11.100—County and Circuit Judges

b. Series 11.200—Senior Judges, Trial Division Judges and Magistrates

c. Series 11.300—Branch Courthouses

d. Series 11.400—Judicial Chambers

e. Series 11.500—Miscellaneous Judiciary

f. Series 11.600—Judicial Staff

g. Series 11.700—Human Resources

h. Series 11.800—Technology

i. Series 11.900—OPEN

12. Series 12—Special Appointments

a. Series 12.100—Acting Chief Judge

b. Series 12.200—Acting County Court Judges/Acting Circuit Court Judges

c. Series 12.300—Emergency Procedures/Filings

d. Series 12.400—Appointments of Judges as Commissioners

e. Series 12.500—Miscellaneous

A conversion chart listing the former Administrative Order numbers will be available on the Court's website.

DONE and **ORDERED** in Chambers at West Palm Beach, Palm Beach County, Florida this 29 day of September, 2008.

Kathleen J. Kroll
Chief Judge

Adopted effective September 29, 2008.

* supersedes admin. order 2.001–9/92

2.103. ADDITIONAL COURT HOLIDAYS

IN THE CIRCUIT COURT OF THE FIFTEENTH JUDICIAL CIRCUIT IN AND FOR PALM BEACH COUNTY, FLORIDA

ADMINISTRATIVE ORDER NO. 2.103–09/08 *

IN RE: ADDITIONAL COURT HOLIDAYS

The State Courts System Personnel Rules and Regulations 4.07 (3) permits the chief judge to designate Good Friday, Rosh Hashanah and Yom Kippur as additional legal holidays. It would be an appropriate sign of respect and religious tolerance to cancel court activities in Palm Beach County on Good Friday, Rosh Hashanah and Yom Kippur so that litigants, court personnel and attorneys may observe these important holy days.

NOW, THEREFORE, pursuant to the authority conferred by Florida Rule of Judicial Administration 2.215, it is **ORDERED** as follows:

1. All court activities, including judicial and public sales, in Palm Beach County are suspended on Good Friday, Rosh Hashanah and Yom Kippur. These days shall be recognized holidays for all judicial offices.

2. Nothing in this Order shall conflict with First Appearance scheduling.

DONE and **SIGNED** in Chambers at West Palm Beach, Palm Beach County, Florida, this 29 day of September, 2008.

Kathleen J. Kroll
Chief Judge

Adopted effective September 29, 2008.

* supersedes admin. order no. 2.026–06/01

2.104. DESIGNATION OF RECORD NEWSPAPER

IN THE CIRCUIT COURT OF THE FIFTEENTH JUDICIAL CIRCUIT IN AND FOR PALM BEACH COUNTY, FLORIDA

ADMINISTRATIVE ORDER NO. 2.104—8/15*

IN RE: DESIGNATION OF RECORD NEWSPAPER

In August 2015, a majority of the judges in the Fifteenth Judicial Circuit voted by written ballots to designate *The Palm Beach Post* as the record newspaper for the Fifteenth Judicial Circuit of Florida.

NOW, THEREFORE, pursuant to the authority conferred by Florida Rule of Judicial Administration 2.215, it is **ORDERED** as follows:

Effective October 1, 2015, *The Palm Beach Post* is designated as the record newspaper for the Fifteenth Judicial Circuit of Florida with all of the responsibilities, obligations and entitlements conferred by section 50.0711, Florida Statutes (2015).

DONE and **SIGNED** in Chambers at West Palm Beach, Palm Beach County, Florida, this 12 day of August, 2015.

Jeffrey Colbath
Chief Judge

Adopted effective September 29, 2008. Amended effective August 12, 2015.

* Supersedes admin. order no. 2.104–9/08.

2.105. FIFTEENTH CIRCUIT PROFESSIONALISM PANEL

IN THE CIRCUIT COURT OF THE FIFTEENTH JUDICIAL CIRCUIT IN AND FOR PALM BEACH COUNTY, FLORIDA

ADMINISTRATIVE ORDER NO. 2.105–11/16 *

IN RE: FIFTEENTH CIRCUIT PROFESSIONALISM PANEL

In May of 1990, the Board of Governors of the Florida Bar approved Ideals and Goals of Professionalism, hereinafter referred to as the "*Ideals.*" In June of 1990, the Board of Directors of the Palm Beach County Bar Association approved Standards of Professional Courtesy ("*1990 Standards*") to educate attorneys unfamiliar with the customary practices in Palm Beach County. The *1990 Standards* were endorsed by the Judges of the Fifteenth Judicial Circuit. In 1997, the Chief Judge of the Fifteenth Judicial Circuit, through an administrative order, created a Professionalism Council to meet with and counsel attorneys whose conduct appeared to violate the *Ideals* and/or the *1990 Standards*.

On June 11, 1998, the Chief Justice of the Florida Supreme Court issued an administrative order directing the Chief Judge of each circuit to create and maintain in continuous operation a Circuit Committee on Professionalism. The Chief Judge of the Fifteenth Judicial Circuit designated the Professionalism Committee of the Palm Beach County Bar Association as the Circuit Professionalism Committee. The Professionalism Committee of the Palm Beach County Bar Association and the President of the Palm Beach County Bar Association have worked with this Court to maintain an active professionalism committee and to assist in counseling members of the Bar who engage in conduct inconsistent with the Ideals or Standards.

In September 2007, the Board of Directors of the Palm Beach County Bar Association approved revised Standards of Professional Courtesy ("*2007 Standards*"). In October 2007, the judges of the Fifteenth Judicial Circuit and Palm Beach County voted and approved the *2007 Standards*.

In September 2011, the Florida Supreme Court added the civility provision in the Oath of Admission to the Florida Bar. On June 6, 2013, the Supreme Court of Florida, in opinion SC13–688, adopted the Code for Resolving Professionalism Complaints and directed the Chief Judge of each circuit to create a Local Professionalism Panel to receive and resolve professionalism complaints. In June of 2013, the Fifteenth Judicial Circuit amended its Administrative Order to reconstitute the Professionalism Council as the Professionalism Panel.

On May 28, 2014, the Board of Directors of the Palm Beach County Bar Association approved revised Standards of Professional Courtesy and Civility ("*2074 Standards*"). These *2014 Standards* were endorsed by the judges of the Fifteenth Judicial Circuit and Palm Beach County in June 2014. In January 2015, The Florida Bar Board of Governors replaced the Ideals and Goals of Professionalism with the Professionalism Expectations ("Expectations").

NOW, THEREFORE, pursuant to the authority conferred by Florida Rule of Judicial Administration 2.215, it is **ORDERED** as follows:

1. The Fifteenth Judicial Circuit Professionalism Council is hereby designated the local professionalism panel in accordance with SC13–688. The Panel is composed of the President of the Palm Beach County Bar Association, or his/her designee, a current or former representative of The Florida Bar Board of Governors for the Fifteenth Judicial Circuit, the Chairperson of the Palm Beach County Bar Association's Professionalism Committee and three members of the Florida Bar and/or retired Judges selected by the Chief Judge. The Chief Judge shall not be a member of the Panel but may preside over the Panel.

2. The purpose of the Panel is to meet with attorneys who have conducted themselves in a manner inconsistent with the *Expectations* or *2014 Standards* in order to discuss such conduct and counsel attorneys to avoid future conduct inconsistent with the *Expectations* or *2014 Standards*. The Panel shall have no authority to discipline any attorney or to compel any attorney to appear before the Panel. The Panel may also counsel attorneys if it determines such counseling will further the goals of the *Expectations* or *2014 Standards*. The following procedures shall generally govern the proceedings of the Panel:

a. *Initiation by Judicial Officer or Quasi Judicial Officer:*

1) When any Judge, Magistrate or Traffic Hearing Officer within the Fifteenth Judicial Circuit determines that an attorney has engaged in conduct inconsistent with the *Expectations* or *2014 Standards*, the Judge, Magistrate or Traffic Hearing Officer may refer the matter to the Professionalism Panel via the Chairperson of the Palm Beach County Bar Association's Professionalism Committee.

2) The Chairperson of the Palm Beach County Bar Association's Professionalism Committee, on behalf of the Panel, shall address a letter to the attorney involved inviting that attorney to meet with the Panel on a date and time specified.

b. *Initiation by Attorney/Non–Attorney:*

1) If an attorney observes conduct on the part of another attorney that he or she believes is inconsistent with the *Expectations* or *2014 Standards*, that attorney may request that the Panel consider the matter by directing a letter or e-mail to the Chairperson of Palm Beach County Bar Association's Professionalism Committee.

2) If a non-attorney person is directly and adversely affected by conduct on the part of an attorney that is inconsistent with the *Expectations* or *2014 Standards*, that person may request that the Panel consider the matter by directing a letter or e-mail to the Chairperson of the Palm Beach County Bar Association's Professionalism Committee.

3) The request shall be limited to ten (10) pages inclusive of exhibits.

4) The Chairperson of the Palm Beach County Bar Association's Professionalism Committee shall review the request, shall notify the respondent attorney of the request, may request a response and shall determine whether the matter justifies a referral to the Panel. If a matter is referred to the Panel, the Chairperson of the Palm Beach County Bar Association's Professionalism Committee shall address a letter to the attorney involved inviting the attorney to meet with the Panel on a date and time specified.

c. *Initiation by the Florida Bar's Attorney Consumer Assistance and Intake Program (ACAP)*

1) The Professionalism Panel may accept referrals sent by ACAP.

2) The Chairperson of the Palm Beach County Bar Association's Professionalism Committee shall review the request, shall notify the respondent attorney of the request, may request a response and shall determine whether the matter justifies a referral to the Panel. If a matter is referred to the Panel, the Chairperson of the Palm Beach County Bar Association's Professionalism Committee shall address a letter to the attorney involved inviting the attorney to meet with the Panel on a date and time specified.

d. Any letter sent to an attorney by the Panel (paragraph a above) or the Professionalism Committee (paragraph b and c above) requesting that an attorney appear before the Panel shall identify the conduct alleged to be inconsistent with the *Expectations* or *2014 Standards* and the *Expectations* or 2014 *Standards* potentially implicated and shall advise the attorney that the Panel meeting is not a disciplinary proceeding. A copy of the *Expectations* and 2014 *Standards* shall be included in the correspondence.

e. The Panel will meet at the date and time specified in the letter. The purpose of the meeting shall be to discuss with the attorney his or her conduct and ways the attorney should act in the future to be consistent with the *Expectations* or *2014 Standards.* The Chairperson of the Palm Beach County Bar Association's Professionalism Committee may send a letter summarizing the Panel's discussions to the respondent attorney and to the Palm Beach County Bar Association for publication in the *Bulletin* with the name(s) deleted.

f. If the respondent attorney fails to appear, the Panel shall discuss the conduct inconsistent with the *Expectations* or *2014 Standards* and shall summarize the Panel's discussions by letter to the respondent attorney. The Chairperson of the Palm Beach County Bar Association's Professionalism Committee may send a letter summarizing the Panel's discussions to the Palm Beach County Bar Association for publication in the *Bulletin* with the name(s) deleted. Consistent with the provisions of paragraph 4 of this Order, the Panel may consider the Respondent's failure to appear in determining whether referral to ACAP is appropriate.

3. The *Expectations* and *2014 Standards* apply to all counsel practicing law in this circuit and their staff, *pro se* litigants appearing before the courts of this circuit, and all persons entering an appearance before the courts of this circuit.

4. Pursuant to Section 2.1 of Supreme Court Opinion SC13–688, the Palm Beach County Professionalism Panel has discretion to refer any appropriate complaints to the Florida Bar Attorney Consumer Assistance and Intake Program (ACAP).

DONE AND SIGNED, in Chambers, at West Palm Beach, Palm Beach County, Florida, this 7 day of November, 2016.

Jeffrey Colbath
Chief Judge

Adopted September 29, 2008. Amended effective September 23, 2010; June 20, 2013; November 19, 2014; November 7, 2016.

*supersedes admin. order 2.105–6/14 [**PUBLISHER'S NOTE:** This order incorrectly refers to the 6/14 version of the rule. The correct rule being superseded is 2.105–11/14.]

2.106. PRO BONO SERVICE

IN THE CIRCUIT COURT OF THE FIFTEENTH JUDICIAL CIRCUIT IN AND FOR PALM BEACH COUNTY, FLORIDA

ADMINISTRATIVE ORDER NO. 2.106–9/08 *

IN RE: PRO BONO SERVICE

The Florida Supreme Court has held that "every lawyer . . . who is a member of The Florida Bar has an obligation to represent the poor when called upon by the courts and that each lawyer has agreed to that commitment when admitted to practice law in this state," In re Amendments to Rules Regulating the Florida Bar, 573 So.2d 800, 806 (Fla. 1990). The Supreme Court approved a modification of recommendation No. 24 of The Florida Bar/Florida Bar Foundation Joint Commission on the Delivery of Legal Services to the Indigent in Florida which requires each circuit to develop a plan to provide pro bono legal services to the circuit's indigent population, see In re Amendments to Rules Regulating the Florida Bar, 598 So.2d 41 (Fla. 1992). The Legal Aid Society of Palm Beach County, Inc. has served the poor for over thirty years and presently has the expertise and resources to administer this circuit's pro bono plan. The chief judge of each judicial circuit is mandated to appoint and convene a circuit pro bono committee.

NOW, THEREFORE, pursuant to the authority conferred by Florida Rule of Judicial Administration 2.215, it is **ORDERED** as follows:

GOAL

1. Each member of the Florida Bar who practices in the Fifteenth Judicial Circuit should perform pro bono service by providing free legal service to the poor (125% of federal poverty income level standard) through the circuit's pro bono program which shall be administered by the Legal Aid Society of Palm Beach County, Inc.

2. A lawyer's obligation to provide pro bono legal services to the poor may be fulfilled by any of the methods set forth in the pro bono rules.

ADMINISTRATIVE AGENCY

3. The Legal Aid Society of Palm Beach County, Inc. is designated as the administrative agency to implement this circuit's pro bono plan.

4. The administrative agency shall

a. provide intake and referral of clients;

b. provide malpractice insurance and litigation costs;

c. establish quality control procedures;

d. provide training and staff support for pro bono attorneys; and

e. undertake other responsibilities as directed by the circuit's pro bono committee to implement the circuit's pro bono plan.

5. The administrative agency shall submit to the circuit pro bono committee, by December 31st of each year, an annual report with recommendations to update the plan.

6. The administrative agency shall prepare a report by December 31st of each year listing each attorney who rendered pro bono service that year, the attorney's bar number, and the nature and extent of the attorney's service. This report shall be provided to the chief judge and to the circuit pro bono committee.

CIRCUIT PRO BONO COMMITTEE

7. A circuit pro bono committee shall be established to plan, develop, prepare in written form, coordinate and establish the circuit's voluntary pro bono plan. The committee shall discharge all additional responsibilities imposed by the pro bono rules.

8. The circuit pro bono committee shall consist of the following:

a. Three (3) representatives recruited from and selected by the Palm Beach County Bar Association one being a member of the North County Section, one being a member of the Young Lawyers Section and one being a member-at-large.

b. One (1) representative recruited from and selected by the South County Bar Association.

c. One (1) representative from and selected by the F. Malcolm Cunningham, Sr., Bar Association.

d. One (1) representative from and selected by the Florida Association of Women Lawyers (Palm Beach County Chapter)

e. One (1) representative from and selected by the Hispanic Bar Association of Palm Beach County.

f. One (1) representative from and selected by the Palm Beach County Association of Criminal Defense Lawyers.

g. One (1) representative from and selected by the Palm Beach County Justice Association.

h. One (1) public member selected by the other members of the circuit pro bono committee.

i. One (1) client eligible member selected by the other members of the circuit pro bono committee, and

j. The executive director of the Legal Aid Society of Palm Beach County, Inc.

k. The Legal Aid Society's pro bono coordinator.

l. One (1) representative from Florida Rural Legal Services, Inc.

m. The chief judge or a judge designated by the chief judge.

9. Any other organized local bar association can petition the circuit pro bono committee for inclusion as a representative to the committee.

10. The circuit pro bono committee shall meet at least once a year to review and, if necessary, revise the circuit's plan. Further, the committee shall monitor the manner in which the administrative agency is implementing the plan consistent with the policies and procedures established by the committee.

11. The chief judge shall provide The Florida Supreme Court with a copy of the circuit's plan together with any revisions and a copy of the administrative agency's annual report.

DONE and **SIGNED** in Chambers at West Palm Beach, Palm Beach County, Florida, this 29 day of September, 2008.

Kathleen J. Kroll
Chief Judge

Adopted effective September 29, 2008.

* supersedes admin. order no. 2.030–12/96

2.107. USE OF COURTHOUSE ROOMS FOR DEPOSITIONS AND NURSING MOTHERS

IN THE CIRCUIT COURT OF THE FIFTEENTH JUDICIAL CIRCUIT IN AND FOR PALM BEACH COUNTY, FLORIDA

ADMINISTRATIVE ORDER NO. 2.107–12/18 *

IN RE: USE OF COURTHOUSE ROOMS FOR DEPOSITIONS AND NURSING MOTHERS

Security concerns might arise when taking depositions in private offices. Court Administration has designated specific rooms at the Main Judicial Center, South County Branch Courthouse and the North County Branch Courthouse to be used for criminal or civil depositions. Additionally, privacy is needed for nursing mothers. Court Administration has designated a specific room at the Main Judicial Center to be used by nursing mothers.

NOW, THEREFORE, pursuant to the authority conferred by Florida Rule of Judicial Administration 2.215, it is **ORDERED** as follows:

1. Main Judicial Center:

a. Rooms 4.2004, 4.2005, 4.2006, 4.2007, 4, 2008, 4.2010 and 4, 2011 may be used for depositions in criminal and civil matters on Wednesday and Thursday afternoons (1:00 p.m.–5:00 p.m.), and all day on Mondays and Fridays (8:00 a.m.–5:00 p.m.)

b. Rooms 4.2004, 4.2005, 4.2006, 4.2007, 4.2008, 4.2010 and 4.2011 are not available on Tuesdays (8:00 a.m.–5:00 p.m.), and on Wednesday and Thursday mornings (8:00 a.m.–12:00 p.m.) as they are permanently reserved for the Alternative Dispute Resolution Office.

c. Room 4.2003 is designated as a Nursing Mothers Room. Access to the Nursing Mothers Room is made by contacting Court Administration at 561–355–2431.

2. South County Branch Courthouse:

a. Rooms 2E–207, 2E–208 and 2E–209 may be used for depositions in criminal and civil matters during working hours on Mondays, Tuesdays, Thursdays and Fridays (8:00 a.m.–5:00 p.m.)

b. Rooms 2E–207, 2E–208 and 2E–209 are not available on Wednesdays (8:00 a.m.–5:00 p.m.) as they are permanently reserved for the Alternative Dispute Resolution Office.

c. Rooms 2W–151 and 2W–152 are permanently reserved for the Alternative Dispute Resolution Office.

d. Hearing Room A

1) Hearing Room A will be available for depositions in Dependency matters only and are set through the Witness Management Office located at the Main Judicial Center.

2) Witness Management will notify the South County Law Library and Central Recording of scheduled dependency depositions. Attorneys shall contact the South County Law Librarian upon arrival at the South County Courthouse to obtain access to Hearing Room A.

3) Hearing Room A is equipped with digital recording.

4) Digital Recording of criminal matters falls under Administrative Order 2.501 and 2.502 (Witness Management).

3. North County Branch Courthouse:

a. Room 2.715 may be used for depositions in criminal and civil matters during working hours on Mondays, Tuesdays, Wednesdays, Thursdays and Fridays (8:00 a.m.–5:00 p.m.)

b. Room 2.716 may be used for depositions in criminal and civil matters during working hours on Mondays, Wednesdays, Thursdays and Fridays (8:00 a.m.–5:00 p.m.). It is not available on Tuesdays (8:00 a.m.—5:00 p.m.) as it is permanently reserved for the Alternative Dispute Resolution Office.

4. The deposition rooms are available on a first come/first serve basis. The Administrative Office of the Court does not schedule usage of the rooms for private depositions. In instances where all rooms are occupied or a conflict exists, the Administrative Office of the Court may be contacted for assistance in securing another appropriate location within the facility.

5. This Administrative Order does not apply to those depositions taken through the Witness Management Office in accordance with Administrative Order 2.501.

DONE and **SIGNED** in Chambers at West Palm Beach, Palm Beach County, Florida, this 11th day of December, 2018.

Krista Marx
Chief Judge

Adopted effective September 29, 2008. Amended effective January 5, 2009; December 22, 2009; December 11, 2018.

* supersedes admin, order 2.107–12/09

Security, Emergency, and Other Procedures

2.201. COURTHOUSE SECURITY AND SCREENING

IN THE CIRCUIT COURT OF THE FIFTEENTH JUDICIAL CIRCUIT IN AND FOR PALM BEACH COUNTY, FLORIDA

ADMINISTRATIVE ORDER NO. 2.201–1/19 *

IN RE: COURTHOUSE SECURITY AND SCREENING

Threats and acts of violence directed toward witnesses, jurors, litigants, lawyers, court personnel, judges and others demonstrate the need for appropriate security at the county courthouse and at all courthouse annexes as part of the necessary regulation of those facilities. Florida Rule of Judicial Administration 2.215(b)(7), as amended in 2012, now specifies that, "The chief judge shall regulate the use of all court facilities, ..." It is therefore appropriate, after consultation with and consideration of the recommendations of the Palm Beach County Sheriff's Office as well as the Palm Beach County Department of Facilities and Development Operations, that certain security measures be specified by Administrative Order.

NOW, THEREFORE, pursuant to the authority conferred by Florida Rule of Judicial Administration 2.215, it is **ORDERED** as follows:

A. General Provisions

1. All persons, with the exception of those specifically enumerated in section B1 below, are prohibited from carrying or possessing firearms, weapons or destructive devices, as defined in section 790.001, Florida Statutes (2018), in the county courthouse or any courthouse annex (hereinafter collectively referred to as the "courthouse") in Palm Beach County.

2. All persons are prohibited from carrying or being in possession of any other device(s) or instrument(s) that could be used or perceived to be used as a physical threat to persons, or property, in the Courthouse/annexes in Palm Beach County. Prohibitions may include but are not limited to pocket knives, ammunition, fireworks, caustic or flammable liquids. To enforce this prohibition the court, with the financial support of the Board of County Commissioners of Palm Beach County, hereby authorizes the establishment of a court security detail.

3. A security detail is empowered to stop all persons entering the courthouse, with the exception of those persons specifically enumerated in the section D1 and D2 below, and condition the right of entry upon the entrant's willingness to submit to a search of their person and/or personal effects to include purses, pocketbooks, briefcases, containers, packages, pagers, cellular phones, electronic devices and any other item deemed necessary for inspection by the security detail. All persons refusing to submit to a search shall be denied access to the courthouse. Searches shall be conducted through the least intrusive means practicable. The purpose of the search is to insure the safety of the occupants of the courthouse. Nonetheless, discovery of illegal weapons, contraband as defined in section 932.701, Florida Statutes (2011), or other violations of criminal statutes will result in the immediate notification of law enforcement so that a seizure and an arrest may be effectuated. Sworn members of the Court Security Detail/Palm Beach County Sheriff shall be responsible for performing all law enforcement functions for the 15th Judicial Circuit at each of its court facilities.

B. Firearm Prohibition Exemptions

1. The following shall be exempt from the prohibition against carrying firearms into the courthouse:

a. sworn members of the court security detail, including court deputies, and Palm Beach County Sheriff's Office deputies assigned as back-up to the security detail;

b. Palm Beach County Sheriff's Office deputies assigned to guard prisoners in the courthouse;

c. judges;

d. law enforcement officers responding to a call for emergency assistance in the courthouse;

e. effective January 1, 2019, law enforcement officers from law enforcement departments whose jurisdiction is within Palm Beach County and who are wearing Class 1 or Class 2 uniforms (standard uniform) including officers of the Palm Beach County Sheriff's Office (PBSO) not previously identified in this section, who are appearing at a Palm Beach County Courthouse while carrying out their official duties and subject to the following conditions:

(1) Each law enforcement officer will provide to a PBSO deputy stationed at the entrance/ screening area of the courthouse, his/her agency identification along with his/her subpoena which shall identify the deputy, the proceeding, and the date of appearance.

(2) Photographs of Class 1 and Class 2 uniforms from all law enforcement agencies will be maintained by PBSO. Only those uniforms deemed acceptable in the photographs will be permitted.

(3) Only firearms carried in a Level 3 holster may be retained.

(4) A daily log will be maintained as a courthouse security record by PBSO listing the name and ID number of each deputy and his/her purpose for entering the courthouse.

(5) All Judges and Magistrates maintain the authority to either permit or prohibit firearm possession in their respective courtrooms. Secure gun lockers, provided for and maintained by PBSO, will be strategically placed in secure locations for use by deputies appearing as part of their official duties in courtrooms where firearm retention is prohibited.

(6) The PBSO Policies and Procedures Manual will be updated to inform all deputies of the change in courthouse security procedures as well as the courthouse security protocols that would apply to the deputies at a Palm Beach County Courthouse while carrying out their official duties.

C. Nonexempt Persons

1. No one shall be permitted to carry a weapon into the courthouse unless the person is specifically exempted under section B1 above.

2. For law enforcement officers, other than those specified in paragraph B1, the long-standing policy in this county requiring law enforcement officers to check their weapons shall remain in force and effect. A gun locker shall be provided in close proximity to the front entry of the courthouse.

3. Prior to gaining entry into the courthouse, any law enforcement officer, other than those identified in paragraph B1, carrying a legally-authorized firearm or other weapon shall surrender the weapon to the security detail. The weapon shall be held under lock and shall be returned to the owner when leaving the courthouse.

D. Admission Searches

1. When entering the courthouse/annexes through designated judicial access points in the secured garage or secured parking areas, the following shall be exempt from the search requirement:

a. all circuit court judges of the Fifteenth Judicial Circuit;

b. all county court judges of Palm Beach County;

c. the Clerk of the Court;

d. the Court Administrator;

e. Domestic and Juvenile Magistrates;

f. General Counsel.

2. When entering through the general public entrances to the courthouse/annexes during normal hours of operation all persons, with the exception of 15th Judicial Circuit Judges, Palm Beach County Court Judges, Domestic and Juvenile Magistrates showing valid courthouse identification, and firefighters and EMS technical and transport personnel responding to a call for emergency assistance in the courthouse, shall be subject to screening including those other individuals listed in paragraph D1.

3. Other than those persons identified in paragraphs B1 and D1, any person entering the courthouse/annexes during normal hours of operation shall enter through authorized entrances and shall pass through a magnetometer (metal detector).

4. Any person who activates the metal detector must empty his or her pockets and pass through the device a second time. If, after the second pass through, the metal detector is again activated, the person shall be subject to a security search to identify all objects which activated the metal detector.

5. Prior to passing through the metal detector, any person carrying a package, briefcase, container, purse, pocketbook, pager, cellular phone or any other electronic device shall place such items on the X-ray conveyor belt and/or shall submit it to the security detail for visual inspection up to and including activation if applicable.

6. Should the X-ray machine disclose what may be a weapon, the container shall be subject to a manual search.

7. The examiner shall not read any written material disclosed during a search.

8. If illegal firearms, weapons, destructive devices or contraband, as defined above, are discovered during a search, the appropriate law enforcement authority shall be notified immediately so that an arrest and seizure might be effectuated.

E. Packages and Letters

1. All packages and letters entering the Palm Beach County Courthouse shall either pass through a metal detector or be inspected. In the case of boxes of materials and supplies delivered through the courthouse loading dock, the inspection shall be to ensure that the integrity of the carton has not been compromised. If a carton appears to have been opened and resealed, the carton shall be inspected to ensure that no firearms, weapons or destructive devices have been placed in the carton.

2. If illegal firearms, weapons, destructive devices or contraband, as defined above, are discovered during a search, the appropriate law enforcement authority shall be notified immediately so that an arrest and seizure may be effectuated.

F. NOTICE. The following notice shall be posted in a conspicuous place at all courthouse entrances:

"FOR THE PROTECTION OF THE PUBLIC, ALL PERSONS ENTERING THESE PREMISES MUST PASS THROUGH THE MAGNETOMETER (METAL DETECTOR). IF THE DETECTOR REGISTERS, THAT PERSON WILL BE SUBJECT TO A LIMITED SEARCH. ALL PACKAGES, BRIEFCASES, POCKETBOOKS OR OTHER ITEMS CARRIED BY A PERSON MUST BE OFFERED FOR INSPECTION IF SUCH PERSON WISHES TO ENTER THE BUILDING. ALL WEAPONS, INCLUDING LEGALLY–AUTHORIZED FIREARMS, MUST BE SURRENDERED PRIOR TO GAINING ENTRY INTO THE COURTHOUSE AND MAY BE RECLAIMED UPON LEAVING THE COURTHOUSE. ILLEGAL WEAPONS OR OTHER CONTRABAND DISCOVERED IN THE COURSE OF THESE SEARCH PROCEDURES WILL BE SEIZED."

DONE and **SIGNED** in Chambers at West Palm Beach, Palm Beach County, Florida, this 2nd day of January, 2019.

Krista Marx
Chief Judge

Adopted effective September 29, 2008. Amended effective October 20, 2010; March 27, 2012; January 2, 2019.

* supersedes admin, order 2.201–3/12

2.202. SECURITY OF JUDICIAL CORRIDORS

IN THE CIRCUIT COURT OF THE FIFTEENTH JUDICIAL CIRCUIT IN AND FOR PALM BEACH COUNTY, FLORIDA

ADMINISTRATIVE ORDER NO. 2.202–9/08 *

IN RE: SECURITY OF JUDICIAL CORRIDORS

For security reasons, the judicial corridors in the Palm Beach County Courthouse were designed and constructed to be restricted access areas, limited primarily to judges and their staff, court personnel, clerks, and bailiffs. Jurors and prisoners have on occasion been permitted to enter and exit courtrooms by means of the judicial corridors. Judges and court personnel have expressed safety and other concerns regarding such a practice. The Executive Committee has unanimously approved adoption of procedures designed to limit and regulate juror and prisoner access to the judicial corridors.

NOW, THEREFORE, pursuant to the authority conferred by Florida Rule of Judicial Administration 2.215, it is **ORDERED** as follows:

1. Jurors. Ingress and egress by jurors to the judicial corridors shall be prohibited unless the presiding judge determines that exceptional circumstances exist which require their presence. In those unusual or exception instances such as high-profile cases where the judge determines that the jurors require access from the courtroom by way of the judicial corridor, the court security officer shall loudly announce "Jurors coming through" or some other appropriate call to indicate to the working personnel the jurors' momentary presence as they are escorted as a group out of the judicial corridor to the jury assembly room or other appropriate location for release.

2. Prisoners. Only in exigent circumstances, such as when the elevator is inoperable, shall prisoners be permitted to ingress or egress the courtroom by way of the judicial corridor. On any such occasion, the court security officer or deputy shall loudly announce to the working personnel within the corridor "Prisoner(s) coming through" to indicate the presence of a temporary security concern.

DONE and **SIGNED** in Chambers, in West Palm Beach, Palm Beach County, Florida, this 29 day of September, 2008.

Kathleen J. Kroll
Chief Judge

Adopted effective September 29, 2008.

* supersedes admin. order 11.029–4/97

2.203. COURT EMERGENCY MANAGEMENT GROUP

IN THE CIRCUIT COURT OF THE FIFTEENTH JUDICIAL CIRCUIT IN AND FOR PALM BEACH COUNTY, FLORIDA

ADMINISTRATIVE ORDER NO. 2.203–1/13 *

IN RE: COURT EMERGENCY MANAGEMENT GROUP

The Supreme Court desired the development of emergency preparedness/disaster recovery guidelines for the State Court System. A Fifteenth Judicial Circuit Court Emergency Management Group (CEMG), comprised of representative of Circuit Court, County Court, State Attorney, Public Defender, Clerk of Court, Sheriff and Palm Beach County Board of County Commissioners developed emergency preparedness/disaster recovery guidelines and procedures for the Fifteenth Circuit for use in the event of (1) a significant threat to the well-being of employees and the general public; i.e. terrorist acts, bomb threats, biological, environment; (2) a significant threat due to natural disasters, i.e. hurricane floods; (3) or other possible emergency situations which may occur and have an adverse impact on life and safety.

NOW, THEREFORE, pursuant to the authority conferred by Florida Rule of Judicial Administration 2.215, it is **ORDERED** as follows:

1. The Fifteenth Judicial Circuit adopts the Court's Comprehensive Emergency Management Plan ("CEMP") developed by the Court Emergency Management Group. In the event of an emergency, the Fifteenth Judicial Circuit will follow the procedures outlined in the CEMP.

2. As identified in the CEMP, training programs for judges and court personnel will be conducted on a regular basis. Such training shall include specialized training for responding to bomb threats, medical emergencies, fire alarms and biological/environmental threats.

3. The Court Emergency Management Group shall be required to meet regularly to ensure the draft emergency plan is available for presentation to the chief judge on or before May 1st of each year.

4. As directed by the Supreme Court and pursuant to Section 252.365, Florida Statutes, Debra Oats shall serve as Emergency Coordinating Officer (ECO) and Barbara Dawicke as the alternate Emergency Coordinating Officer, each serving as the Fifteenth Circuit's liaison with State Emergency Operations Center.

DONE and **SIGNED** in Chambers at West Palm Beach, Palm Beach County, Florida, this 8 day of January, 2013.

Peter D. Blanc
Chief Judge

Adopted effective September 29, 2008. Amended effective April 1, 2009; June 30, 2009; January 8, 2013.

* supersedes administrative order 2.203–6/09

2.204. CONTAINMENT AND REMOVAL OF BIO–HAZARDOUS/INFECTIOUS WASTE

IN THE CIRCUIT COURT OF THE FIFTEENTH JUDICIAL CIRCUIT IN AND FOR PALM BEACH COUNTY, FLORIDA

ADMINISTRATIVE ORDER NO. 2.204–9/08 *

IN RE: CONTAINMENT AND REMOVAL OF BIO–HAZARDOUS/INFECTIOUS WASTE

To ensure the safe collection and disposal of bio-hazardous /infectious waste material(s) which may be introduced during courtroom proceedings, Palm Beach County has set forth policies and procedures for waste containment and removal which are also consistent with Administrative Order No. 2.203–9/08 (as amended).

NOW, THEREFORE, pursuant to the authority conferred by Florida Rule of Judicial Administration 2.215, it is **ORDERED** as follows:

1. In those instances when a court proceeding may require the containment and removal of bio-hazardous/infectious waste material or any material perceived to be a health risk, the bailiff assigned to that proceeding shall immediately contact Palm Beach County Facilities Management at 355–2255. Custodial services shall deliver immediately a special waste receptacle for disposal of such materials when appropriate or necessary, the bailiff shall notify PBC Facilities to remove the waste receptacle or when a replacement is needed.

2. Palm Beach County Facilities will be responsible for disposing the waste by a certified waste disposal provider on contract with Palm Beach County.

DONE and **SIGNED,** in Chambers, at West Palm Beach, Palm Beach County, Florida, on this 29 day of September, 2008.

Kathleen J. Kroll
Chief Judge

Adopted effective September 29, 2008.

* supersedes admin. order 11.041–3/01

2.205. COURT DISASTER AND EMERGENCY PROCEDURES

IN THE CIRCUIT COURT OF THE FIFTEENTH JUDICIAL CIRCUIT IN AND FOR PALM BEACH COUNTY, FLORIDA

ADMINISTRATIVE ORDER NO. 2.205–7/12*

IN RE: COURT DISASTER AND EMERGENCY PROCEDURES

During a disaster or emergency the courts will likely be unable to operate under normal rules and procedures.

NOW, THEREFORE, pursuant to the authority conferred by Florida Rule of Judicial Administration 2.215, it is **ORDERED** as follows:

1. When a disaster or emergency is declared by either the Governor, pursuant to Florida Statutes s. 252.36(2), or the Board of County Commissioners, pursuant to Florida Statutes § 52.38 and County Ordinance 92–37, this administrative order shall take precedence over all other administrative orders of the court if in conflict except Administrative Order 2.203 which adopts the Court Emergency Management Plan. This administrative order shall also take effect if, in the opinion of the Chief Judge, a disaster or emergency is imminent and it is in the interest of the efficient administration of justice to invoke these emergency procedures.

2. The court will coordinate its efforts under the guidance of the Chief Judge or his or her designee, and will work in conjunction with the county's emergency management team. The court will provide the necessary Judges and personnel to handle first appearances, detention hearings, domestic violence petitions, and other matters determined to be an emergency by the Duty Judge or a Judge assigned to hear those matters.

GENERAL MATTERS

3. Initial notification.

a. When the Chief Judge is notified that a state of emergency has been declared by either the Governor or the Board of County Commissioners, or the Chief Judge determines that this order shall take effect, the Chief Judge shall notify the Court Administrator. Contemporaneous with the implementation of this order, the Court shall activate its Continuity of Operations Plan ("COOP").

b. The Court Administrator shall establish a telephone number (561) 355–6744 which will be equipped with a message advising all court personnel of the disaster or emergency, the status of court proceedings and whether or not they should report to their places of employment.

c. All court personnel are to remain in contact with the courts through this phone line. In the event there is a loss of telephone service, communication will be achieved through local radio, television and newspaper reports.

4. Communications.

a. The Chief Judge or his or her designee shall notify, through Dialogic, the Clerk of the Court, State Attorney, Public Defender, Sheriff, Department of Juvenile Justice and the Department of Children and Families of the status of court functions during an emergency.

b. It shall be the responsibility of these agencies to provide the Chief Judge with the name and telephone number of the person to receive such notification.

c. The Court Administrator or her designee shall be responsible for all news releases regarding court activities and will coordinate with the county administrative offices with reference to the operational status of court facilities.

d. The Palm Beach County Sheriff's Office shall assign radios, if available, to the Chief Judge and Court Administrator. The radios shall be accompanied by instructions on basic operating procedures.

5. Court Operations.

a. The following buildings are designated as operational centers of the courts during an emergency:

1) Gun Club Road Criminal Justice Complex
2) Main Courthouse
3) South County Courthouse
4) North County Courthouse
5) Belle Glade Courthouse

b. The County, in consultation with the Chief Judge, shall designate the location(s) to be used or may designate any other facility as a temporary court facility.

COURT PROCEEDINGS

6. Bond Schedules. During the period of any emergency declared by the Governor or the Board of County Commissioners, or when ordered by the Chief Judge, the bond schedule established by Administrative Order 4.202–8/11 (as amended), shall remain in effect.

7. **Court Hearings and Judicial Staffing.**

a. With the exception of first appearance hearings, detention hearings (dependency and delinquency) and emergencies, all court dockets and foreclosure sales are suspended during a declared emergency until the Chief Judge has determined that normal court activities can be resumed.

b. In the case of a hurricane, the Chief Judge shall designate a Judge who will respond to the Gun Club Road Criminal Justice Complex. The Chief Judge shall also designate an alternate Judge who will be dispatched to the Gun Club Road Criminal Justice Complex only in the event the Chief Judge determines that the services of an additional Judge will be required.

c. The Sheriffs Office shall provide accommodations for the Judges, Court Administrator, Deputy Clerks of Court, State Attorney Office employees and Public Defender Office employees during the hurricane and its aftermath until the Judges are relieved by order of the Chief Judge.

d. These Judges shall be responsible for conducting first appearance, juvenile detention and emergency hearings during a declared emergency.

e. Other Judges may be assigned to assist in these duties by the Chief Judge.

f. If it is not physically possible to transport juveniles to the court for detention hearings, those hearings may be conducted in the absence of the juvenile defendants. In all such cases, the Public Defender shall be appointed to represent the absent juvenile.

g. The Chief Judge or the Chief Judge's designee shall petition the Florida Supreme Court for a tolling of all statutory and rule authorized time limits during the time of the emergency, until normal court activities can be resumed.

h. The Court Administrator or her (his) designee shall respond to the county's emergency operations center no later than four hours before the landfall of a hurricane and shall act as the court's representative at the emergency operations center.

i. The Chief Judge, emergency Duty Judge(s), State Attorney, Public Defender, Clerk of Court, and Court Administrator shall confer during an emergency to determine the workload and staffing requirements of court facilities.

8. **Transportation.**

a. If the roads are **not** passable, and upon request, the Palm Beach County Sheriff's Office shall provide transportation for the emergency Duty Judge(s) and other Judges as well as the Court Administrator, Deputy Clerks of Court, State Attorney Office employees and Public Defender Office employees assigned to conduct first appearance, juvenile shelter, juvenile detention or Domestic Violence Injunction hearings.

b. The declaration of a state of emergency by the Governor or the Board of County Commissioners shall constitute an emergency authorizing the transportation of juveniles in a police vehicle pursuant to Florida Statutes § 39.044(3).

9. **Resumption of Normal Court Procedures.**

a. The Chief Judge shall determine when normal court procedures may be resumed.

b. The general public, court personnel and state agencies shall be notified of the resumption of normal court procedures in the same manner as they were notified of the emergency suspension of court procedures.

c. Prior to the resumption of normal court procedures, the county shall survey all court buildings to determine the following:

1) the condition of the building;

2) the existence of electrical and water service to the building;

3) telephone service to and within the building;

4) the availability of security within the building; and

5) the availability of access routes to the building.

d. The County, in consultation with the Chief Judge, shall coordinate with county personnel to determine when court facilities will be available for use by the court personnel and the general public.

DONE and **SIGNED** in Chambers at West Palm Beach, Palm Beach County, Florida, this 13th day of July, 2012.

Peter D. Blanc
Chief Judge

Adopted effective June 22, 2009. Amended effective July 13, 2012.
*supersedes admin. order no. 2.205–6/09

2.206. DISASTER AND EMERGENCY PROCEDURES IN CRIMINAL AND DEPENDENCY MATTERS

IN THE CIRCUIT COURT OF THE FIFTEENTH JUDICIAL CIRCUIT IN AND FOR PALM BEACH COUNTY, FLORIDA

ADMINISTRATIVE ORDER NO. 2.206–9/08 *

IN RE: DISASTER AND EMERGENCY PROCEDURES IN CRIMINAL AND DEPENDENCY MATTERS

The Fifteenth Judicial Circuit has adopted disaster and emergency procedures in Admin. Order 2.205–9/08. Those procedures do not address the handling of children in foster care or offenders on community control or housed in the Probation and Restitution Center or in a non-secure treatment bed.

NOW, THEREFORE, pursuant to the authority conferred by Florida Rule of Judicial Administration 2.215, it is **ORDERED** as follows:

CRIMINAL MATTERS

1. Whenever a disaster or emergency is declared as provided for in Admin. Order 2.205–9/08, the Correctional Probation Administrator for the Department of Corrections, Probation and Parole Services, in and for the Fifteenth Judicial Circuit, in consultation with the Department of Corrections Central and Regional Offices, as outlined in the Florida Department of Corrections Region IV Hurricane Disaster Control Plan, is hereby authorized to allow offenders that are placed on community control and/or ordered by the courts as a

special condition of supervision to be placed in the Probation and Restitution Center or a non-secure treatment bed, to leave their approved residence or court-ordered treatment program and go to a safe and temporary shelter approved by the Correctional Probation Administrator.

2. Offenders are to remain at their approved safe and temporary shelter until they receive other instructions from Probation and Parole Services. Offenders are to return to their approved residence or court-ordered treatment facility within forty-eight hours after being advised by Probation and Parole Services that it is safe to return.

3. If an offender's approved residence or court-ordered treatment facility is determined to be unsafe, the offender shall immediately contact Probation and Parole Services for further instructions.

4. In the event that an approved residence or treatment facility is determined to be unsafe by Probation and Parole Services, the Correctional Probation Administrator shall assign the offender to a safe residence or treatment facility and shall notify the presiding judge accordingly.

DEPENDENCY MATTERS

5. Whenever a disaster or emergency is declared as provided for in Admin. Order 2.205–9/08, the Department of Children and Families ("Department") and/or the community-based care provider agency that contracts or subcontracts with the Department to provide case management or other services to children and their families ("Provider"), is authorized to allow children in the custody of the Department and/or under their supervision to go to a safe and temporary location, including out of county and/or state, without court order or permission of the presiding Judge.

6. At all times the Department shall maintain responsibility of all children who are relocated pursuant to this Administrative Order and shall establish procedures to ensure that the Department is advised of the planned relocation of all children in its care.

7. The Department/Provider shall make reasonable efforts to ensure that daily contact is made with their staff to report on the location of the children and their families, and report to the Court accordingly. Within twenty-four hours of relocation or notification from the caregiver, the Department must notify the Court of the location of the children and that the children have been placed under appropriate supervision and are safe.

8. The children shall be returned to their original placement as soon as it is determined that it is safe and suitable. Notice of the children's return shall be given to the Court. A hearing may be set by the administrative juvenile judge as soon as the emergency situation abates at which the Department shall certify the location of any children who have not been returned to their original placements.

DONE and **SIGNED** in Chambers at West Palm Beach, Palm Beach County, Florida, this 29 day of September, 2008.

Kathleen J. Kroll
Chief Judge

Adopted effective September 29, 2008.

* supercedes admin. order 2.036 9/94

2.207. REQUESTS FOR ACCOMMODATIONS UNDER THE AMERICANS WITH DISABILITIES ACT

IN THE CIRCUIT COURT OF THE FIFTEENTH JUDICIAL CIRCUIT IN AND FOR PALM BEACH COUNTY, FLORIDA

ADMINISTRATIVE ORDER NO. 2.207–1/15 *

IN RE: REQUESTS FOR ACCOMMODATIONS UNDER THE AMERICANS WITH DISABILITIES ACT

The Americans with Disabilities Act of 1990 (ADA), 42 U.S.C § 12101 et seq., requires reasonable accommodations be provided to qualified persons with disabilities so they might participate fully in court programs, services, activities, and benefits. Florida Rule of Judicial Administration 2.540 requires specific ADA language be included in all notices of court proceedings.

NOW THEREFORE, in accordance with the authority vested in the chief judge by Rule 2.215 (b) (2), Florida Rules of Judicial Administration it is **ORDERED** as follows:

1. All summonses and communications noticing court proceedings, proceedings before general masters, and mediation proceedings shall include the following language which shall, be in bold face, 14–point Times New Roman or Courier font:

"If you are a person with a disability who needs any accommodation in order to participate in this proceeding, you are entitled, at no cost to you, to the provision of certain assistance. Please contact Tammy Anton, Americans with Disabilities Act Coordinator, Palm Beach County Courthouse, 205 North Dixie Highway West Palm Beach, Florida 33401; telephone number (561) 355–4380 at least 7 days before your scheduled court appearance, or immediately upon receiving this notification if the time before the scheduled appearance is less than 7 days; if you are hearing or voice impaired, call 711."

2. The required language must also be provided in Spanish and Creole.

3. Spanish and Creole translations of the above notice are attached.

DONE and **SIGNED** in Chambers, at West Palm Beach, Palm Beach County, Florida, this 13 day of January, 2015.

Jeffrey J. Colbath
Chief Judge

This notice is provided pursuant to Administrative Order No. 2.207–1/15

"If you are a person with a disability who needs any accommodation in order to participate in this proceeding, you are entitled, at no cost to you, to the provision of certain assistance. Please contact Tammy Anton, Americans with Disabilities Act Coordinator, Palm Beach County Courthouse, 205 North Dixie Highway West Palm Beach, Florida 33401; telephone number (561) 355–4380 at least 7 days before your scheduled court appearance, or immediately upon receiving this notification if the time before the scheduled appearance is less than 7 days; if you are hearing or voice impaired, call 711."

"Si usted es una persona minusválida que necesita algún acomodamiento para poder participar en este procedimiento, usted tiene derecho, sin tener gastos propios, a que se le provea cierta ayuda. Tenga la amabilidad de ponerse en contacto con Tammy Anton, 205 N. Dixie Highway, West Palm Beach, Florida 33401; teléfono número (561) 355–4380, por lo menos 7 días antes de la cita fijada para su comparecencia en los tribunales, o inmediatamente después de recibir esta notificación si el tiempo antes de la comparecencia que se ha programado es menos de 7 días; si usted tiene discapacitación del oído o de la voz, llame al 711."

"Si ou se yon moun ki enfim ki bezwen akomodasyon pou w ka patisipe nan pwosedi sa, ou kalifye san ou pa gen okenn lajan pou w peye, gen pwovizyon pou jwen kèk èd. Tanpri kontakte Tammy Anton, kòòdonatè pwogram Lwa pou ameriken ki Enfim yo nan Tribinal Konte Palm Beach la ki nan 205 North Dixie Highway, West Palm Beach, Florida 33401; telefòn li se (561) 355–4380 nan 7 jou anvan dat ou gen randevou pou parèt nan tribinal la, oubyen imedyatman apre ou fin resevwa konvokasyon an si le ou gen pou w parèt nan tribinal la mwens ke 7 jou; si ou gen pwoblèm pou w tande oubyen pale, rele 711."

Adopted effective September 29, 2008. Amended effective June 28, 2010; February 1, 2012; September 13, 2012; January 13, 2015.
*supersedes admin. order 2.207–9/12

2.208. PROCEDURES FOR SPECIAL INTEREST/HIGH PROFILE PROCEEDINGS

IN THE CIRCUIT COURT OF THE FIFTEENTH JUDICIAL CIRCUIT IN AND FOR PALM BEACH COUNTY, FLORIDA

ADMINISTRATIVE ORDER NO. 2.208–2/09 *

IN RE: PROCEDURES FOR SPECIAL INTEREST/HIGH PROFILE PROCEEDINGS

"The unhindered and untrammeled functioning of our courts is part of the very foundation of our constitutional democracy," Cox v. Louisiana, 379 U.S. 559, 562, 85 S.Ct. 476, 13 L.Ed.2d 487 (1965). The Florida Supreme Court has said that "a trial court has the inherent power to control the conduct of the proceedings before it, and it is the trial court's responsibility to protect a defendant in a criminal prosecution from inherently prejudicial influences which threaten fairness of [the] trial and the abrogation of . . . constitutional rights," State ex rel. Miami Herald Publishing Co. v. McIntosh, 340 So.2d 904, 909 (Fla. 1976); and

Florida Rule of Judicial Administration 2.450 (2007), Technological Coverage of Judicial Proceedings, sets forth procedures to govern special interest/high visibility proceedings. Rule 2.450 delineates procedures and special accommodations to ensure full access without compromising the right of any litigant to a fair and orderly trial and to preserve the peace and ensure the safety and security of persons and property.

NOW, THEREFORE, pursuant to the authority conferred by Florida Rule of Judicial Administration 2.215, it is **ORDERED** as follows:

1. When the chief judge and the judge assigned to preside over a proceeding of great public interest, have consulted and determined that the Plan for Special Interest/High Profile Proceedings ("the Plan") should be in effect, the chief judge, or the judge assigned to preside over such proceeding, shall enter a written order implementing the Plan ("Written Order"). As soon as practicable, the court administrator, or designee, shall meet with the trial judge to discuss any specific requests that the trial judge may have regarding the implementation of the Plan. The trial judge shall be notified of any meeting of the Media Committee by the court administrator or designee. A copy of the Written Order shall be distributed by the court administrator to Palm Beach County Sheriffs Office Court Security ("PBSO") and County's Facilities Department ("FDO"). Any changes by the trial judge to the Written Order must be made in writing with copies provided to PBSO and FDO.

IMPLEMENTATION PLAN

2. The court administrator is authorized to effectuate the Plan to achieve the goals of the court's Written Order. The court administrator a) shall provide a copy of the Written Order implementing the Plan, and any changes to the Written Order, to the Media Committee and the High Profile Committee and 2) shall post a simple notice near the entrance to the courtroom which states that the Plan is in effect. Notification of the implementation of the Plan will also occur through the Court's website and/or email notification system.

3. The court administrator is authorized, on behalf of the court, to seek the advice, assistance and expertise of any private or governmental entity in the effectuation and implementation of the Plan.

COURT PRESS OFFICER

4. The court administrator shall designate a member of the court's administrative staff to serve as the court's press officer. This person shall serve as the director of the High Profile Media Center, the liaison between the court and the media, and the liaison between the court, PBSO, and FDO. Additionally, this person shall issue press credentials to members of the media covering the high profile case. The court administrator shall also appoint an acting press officer, who shall act if the court press officer is unavailable at any time. The court administrator will provide the name of the court press officer and court acting press officer to PBSO and FDO at the time the Written Order is provided to PBSO and FDO.

ESTABLISHMENT OF MEDIA COMMITTEE

5. The court's press officer, upon proper notice, shall convene a meeting of interested media representatives for the purpose of establishing a Media Committee and a High Profile Committee.

6. The Media Committee shall consist of one representative from television, radio, and print media ("Media Committee"). The High Profile Committee shall consist of the trial judge or designee, the trial court administrator or designee, and a representative of PBSO and FDO. The High Profile Committee will work with the Media Committee to meet and effectively execute the Media Committee's decisions.

The Media Committee shall:

a. Designate (1) the pool television camera person for coverage inside the courtroom, (2) the pool still photographer for coverage inside the courtroom, (3), the pool audio person for coverage inside the courtroom, (4) the pool television camera person for coverage outside the courtroom, (5) the pool still photographer for coverage outside the courtroom, (6) the pool audio person for coverage outside the courtroom, (7) the pool print reporter for coverage outside the courtroom, and (8) the pool web videographer for coverage outside the courtroom.

b. Determine and report to the High Profile Committee the needs of the media center including, but not limited to, the capacity, hours of access, and the furniture and technology amenities desired. The needs of the media center are to be provided to the High Profile Committee in writing unless otherwise agreed to by the Media Committee and the High Profile Committee.

c. Allocate, from among those holding court-issued press credentials, courtroom seating assignments in the area reserved for media representatives. This allocation shall be made on a daily basis and shall be reported to the court's press officer. Proper press credentials will entitle the bearer to enter the courtroom and utilize the reserved area.

d. Oversee the distribution and dissemination of all pool reports to the media.

The High Profile Committee shall:

e. Oversee the distribution and dissemination of all court information related to the high profile case that is to be made available to the media.

f. Work with the media on requests for unique parking needs not otherwise covered by the Administrative Order, and propose solutions.

g. Work closely with the Media Committee to accommodate other special needs of the media, and to ensure proper security.

h. Create a written record of its decisions which will be forwarded to the Court Press Officer who will forward it to the trial judge. The trial judge can incorporate the High Profile Committee's decisions into the Written Order (or amendments thereto) implementing the Plan.

MEDIA CENTER

7. A High Profile Media Center created for the high profile proceeding will be located in the main courthouse unless the Chief Judge determines otherwise after a hearing at which the High Profile Media Committee and Media Committee were noticed. The hearing may be requested by the Media Committee or the High Profile Media Committee. If the Media Committee determines that the existing media center located on the fourth floor of the courthouse does not meet the needs of the media for coverage of the High Profile case, FDO will report to the Media Committee, within twenty-four (24) hours of receiving the Media Committee's notice and requirements pursuant to 6b above, areas available in the Courthouse which can be made available to serve as a temporary media center ("High Profile Media Center"). If requested by the Media Committee, FDO can at that time, also identify other available areas that are located in adjacent properties. FDO's report will identify how each area meets or does not meet the needs of the media identified by the Media Committee including the amount of space for tables and chairs and whether remote real time viewing of the court proceedings is possible. The Media Committee shall then select a location for the High Profile Media Center from among the choices identified by FDO. If the spaces identified by FDO are insufficient to meet the reasonable needs of the media, the High Profile Committee will meet with the Media Committee to review the options. This facility, under the supervision of the court's press officer, will be open during normal working hours and for reasonable extended hours to media representatives with court-issued press credentials. Duplicate copies of exhibits and other court documents will be released in this facility by the press officer, and may, in addition, be posted on the court's website. Space for media initiated interviews will also be provided in the High Profile Media Center. Pursuant to Palm Beach County Policy CW-O-024, press conferences are not permitted at the Main Courthouse or at branch courthouses.

COURTROOM ADMITTANCE

8. The trial judge, as designee of the Chief Judge, shall set forth in the Written Order a specified location in the courtroom for the pool television camera person, the pool still photographer, and the pool audio person. The trial judge shall choose a location that preserves a clear egress path from the courtroom for safety reasons. Other than the pool cameras designated in the Written Order, no other cameras shall be operated in the courtroom. These persons shall strictly comply with Rule 2.450, Florida Rules of Judicial Administration (2007), Technological Coverage of Judicial Proceedings, and the orders of the trial judge.

9. Taking into consideration the recommendations by the Media Committee, the High Profile Committee shall decide the location outside the courtroom for the pool television camera person, the pool still photographer, the pool audio person, the pool print reporter and the pool web videographer. No other television cameras, still cameras, or other broadcasting or recording equipment shall be operated directly outside the courtroom. PBSO shall announce the presence of jurors, potential jurors, or witnesses outside the courtroom, and enforce the prohibition of any media commentary or interviews in the presence of jurors, potential jurors, or those witnesses which have not yet testified in the case. The Written Order shall require attorneys to advise witnesses who are to provide testimony that upon their arrival near or outside the courtroom they are to identify themselves to PBSO as witnesses so that they do not remain in the area being used by the pool media persons outside the courtroom.

10. The trial judge shall designate a specified number of seats in the public area of the courtroom for the following categories of individuals: (a) parties' family, friends and court designees, (b) media representatives, and (c) general public. Categories "a" and "c" will be regulated by the trial court's bailiff or court security deputy. Category "b" will be allocated by the media committee.

11. Admission to the public section of the courtroom shall be gained by presenting a pass which shall be issued on the first floor of the courthouse on a first-come-first-admitted basis. The pass shall be valid for one session only i.e., morning, afternoon or evening. With the exception of court-ordered recesses during a regular session, an observer must surrender the pass on leaving the courtroom.

OTHER RELATED ACTIVITIES /REQUIREMENTS

12. By arrangement with the court's press officer, the courtroom will be made available to the media before the court proceeding, for installation of necessary equipment and cables; however, the court's bailiff, or court security deputy, must be present in the courtroom to supervise all such activities.

13. The Court's security policy requires all persons and equipment entering the courthouse to pass through electronic security devices. Additional case-specific requirements and checks shall be enforced by PBSO to maintain safety and security.

14. The use of laptop computers and personal digital assistants (PDA's), for example: Blackberries and Treos, will be permitted, unless otherwise determined by the trial judge, inside the courtroom but shall not be used as photographic equipment. No recording is permitted in the courtroom other than by designated pool persons, unless specifically permitted by the trial judge or detailed in the trial judge's Written Order.

15. The pool media persons shall be permitted to accompany persons entering and leaving the courtroom for the purposes of media coverage, so long as the individual does not object and the safety and security of persons and property in the courthouse are not adversely affected. No media commentary or interviews shall be conducted in the presence of jurors, potential jurors, or witnesses in the case.

16. All media representatives who are NOT designated pool persons, do NOT hold courtroom access passes and are covering the proceeding which is the subject of the Plan are prohibited from the areas inside or directly outside the courtroom in which the high profile case is pending. All such persons may cover the high profile proceeding elsewhere in the courthouse, other than the side of the floor on which the high profile case is pending, so long as the safety and security of persons and property in the courthouse are not adversely affected.

17. All facility related inquiries are to be directed to the Business and Community Agreements Manager at FDO at (561) 233–0232. All inquiries relating to court proceedings are to be directed to the Court Press Officer at (561) 355–2431.

18. No temporary structures of any kind may be erected in the areas immediately adjacent to the courthouse without the express permission of FDO.

19. The Court and FDO may rely on PBSO to assist with ensuring compliance with guidelines.

20. Private vehicles may be parked in public parking lots and garages or in metered spots available in the downtown West Palm Beach area. Public parking is available in the Judicial Center Parking Garage. Space in this garage is limited and available on a first-come, first-served basis. No overnight parking is allowed in this garage.

NOTE: Parking in any reserved spaces will result in vehicles being towed.

21. Two parking spaces in the loading dock have been reserved for media/television transmission vehicles during high profile trials. One of the parking spaces will be allotted to the "pool" television station. The allocation of the second parking space will be determined by the Media Committee and the recipient of the parking space must provide any required audio/video feeds to off site media. Offsite satellite trucks must be parked in approved locations. FDO will coordinate parking with the West Palm Beach municipal government as needed.

22. Cables which are placed across sidewalks or streets are to be covered in such a way that they do not impede the flow of vehicular or pedestrian traffic. All cabling must conform to the policies and ordinances of the County and the City of West Palm Beach. All cables must be located so as not constitute a safety hazard or an obstruction to pedestrian traffic.

DONE and **ORDERED** in Chambers at West Palm Beach, Palm Beach County, Florida, this 17th day of February, 2009.

Kathleen J. Kroll
Chief Judge

Adopted effective September 29, 2008. Amended effective February 17, 2009.

* supersedes administrative order 2.208–9/08

Court Files, Records and Cases

2.301. PAPER COURT FILES

IN THE CIRCUIT COURT OF THE FIFTEENTH JUDICIAL CIRCUIT IN AND FOR PALM BEACH COUNTY, FLORIDA

ADMINISTRATIVE ORDER NO. 2.301–11/14*

IN RE: PAPER COURT FILES

While the Fifteenth Judicial Circuit is moving towards electronic court files, paper files continue to exist. Administrative Order 2.312 governs e-filing and the electronic court file. Written procedures are still necessary to govern the paper file.

NOW, THEREFORE, pursuant to the authority conferred by Florida Rule of Judicial Administration 2.215, it is **ORDERED** as follows:

A. Procedures Applicable To Judge's Offices.

1. Cancellations and additions to prior file requests should be made by calendar notation, request form or telephone call.

2. Files are not to be removed from judges' offices.

3. Nothing herein precludes a judge from requesting a file to be delivered at any time.

B. Procedures Of The Clerk's Office Fileroom.

1. Only the last volume of a requested file will be delivered, unless otherwise specified.

2. File runs will be made as needed.

DONE and **SIGNED** in Chambers at West Palm Beach, Palm Beach County, Florida, this 19 day of November, 2014.

Jeffrey Colbath
Chief Judge

Adopted effective September 29, 2008. Amended effective November 19, 2014.

*supersedes admin. order no. 2.301–9/08

2.302. COMPANION, REFILED, AND TRANSFERRED CASES

IN THE CIRCUIT COURT OF THE FIFTEENTH JUDICIAL CIRCUIT IN AND FOR PALM BEACH COUNTY, FLORIDA

ADMINISTRATIVE ORDER 2.302–9/08 *

IN RE: COMPANION, REFILED, AND TRANSFERRED CASES

Sound principles of judicial economy require the establishment of procedures to govern the assignment of companion, refiled and transfer of cases for pretrial management purposes.

NOW, THEREFORE, pursuant to the authority conferred by Florida Rule of Judicial Administration 2.215, it is **ORDERED** as follows:

A. Companion Cases.

1. When two or more cases concerning the same subject matter ("companion cases") are filed with the court at the same time, the attorney filing the cases shall notify the Clerk of Court, in writing, that companion cases are being filed.

a. The clerk, utilizing the blind-assignment system, shall select one judge and assign all designated companion cases to that judge.

b. The clerk shall file a written notice that the cases have been assigned in compliance with this order and a copy of this notice shall be served with the summons and complaint.

2. If companion cases are filed at different times and are assigned to different judges, or if cases filed pursuant to paragraph 1 above were not assigned to the same judge, it shall be the continuing duty of counsel of record to notify, in writing, all judges involved and to file a motion to transfer the cases to the judge with the lowest numbered case.

3. In the interest of judicial economy, companion cases may be consolidated for discovery and/or trial, and the order of consolidation shall specify either or both. When such a consolidation is ordered, the case files shall remain separate and pleadings shall continue to be filed in their appropriate file. Companion cases shall not be consolidated into one pleading file.

4. Motions and Orders must be filed separately in each case. The caption of any pleading or order shall only bear the underlying case number with no reference to the companion case number.

5. A transfer may be initiated by the Court on its own motion.

B. Refiled Cases.

6. When a case is voluntarily dismissed and, is subsequently refiled, the newly-filed action shall be assigned to the division of court in which the original action was assigned. It is the duty of the attorney or the party refilling the action to advise the clerk of the prior voluntary dismissal.

C. Case Management In Multiple Court Divisions.

7. Multiple Court Divisions shall consist of those court divisions as set forth in Local Rule 1 (Appellate Division, Civil Division, Criminal Division, Family Law Division, Foreclosure Division, and Probate/Guardianship Division).

8. When a significant number of actions are pending in more than one Court Division that involve the same or similar parties, or are substantially similar in subject matter, or arise from the same transaction or occurrence, the Chief Judge in consultation with the affected Division Judges, may appoint a managing judge to oversee case management.

9. Each separate action that is transferred for pretrial purposes requires a separate order, to be rendered by the Chief Judge, the division judge or the managing judge to whom the case is assigned. Each suit shall maintain its independent status with respect to the rights of the parties involved. Any objections to the transfer shall be made to the managing judge.

10. The extent of the managing judge's duties shall be determined by the Case Management Order.

11. Motions shall be filed under the assigned case number and in the division to which the case is assigned irrespective of the managing judge's division.

DONE and **SIGNED**, in Chambers, at West Palm Beach, Palm Beach County, Florida, this 29 day of September, 2008.

Kathleen J. Kroll
Chief Judge

Adopted effective September 29, 2008.

* supersedes admin. order 2.009–6/07

2.303. CONFIDENTIALITY/SEALING OF COURT HEARINGS AND RECORDS

IN THE CIRCUIT COURT OF THE FIFTEENTH JUDICIAL CIRCUIT IN AND FOR PALM BEACH COUNTY, FLORIDA

ADMINISTRATIVE ORDER NO. 2.303–3/18 *

IN RE: CONFIDENTIALITY/SEALING OF COURT HEARINGS AND RECORDS **

The Florida constitution mandates that the public shall have access to court records, subject only to certain enumerated limitations that are restricted by operation of state law, federal law, or court rule. The Florida Supreme Court has stated that the news media has been the public surrogate on the issue of courtroom closure and must be given an opportunity to be heard prior to a court's ruling on closure. *The Miami Herald Publishing Co. v. Lewis*, 426 So. 2d 1 (Fla. 1982). Florida Rule of Judicial Administration 2.420 is the rule of procedure governing the confidentiality of court records and must be followed prior to making a record confidential and thus inaccessible by the public (i.e. sealed).

Rule 2.420 addresses categories of court documents that 1) the clerk must maintain as confidential, 2) procedures a party must follow when filing a confidential document, 3) procedures a party must follow when seeking to make other court documents confidential, and 4) sanctions for violation of the rule. The rule also requires publication by the Clerk of Court of certain notices and orders.

- Rule 2.420(c) sets forth the types of documents that are confidential and exempt from public view.

• Rule 2.420(d)(1) sets forth the 22 categories of documents that the Clerk of Court must maintain as confidential.

• Rule 2.420 (d)(2) sets forth the obligations of the filer to file a "Notice of Confidential Information Within Court Filing" when the filer submits one of the 22 categories of documents for filing in a case that is not already maintained as confidential. This requires the filer to identify the precise location of the confidential information within the document being filed.

• Rule 2.420(d)(2) further sets forth the clerk's obligation to review such a notice to ensure that it pertains to one of the 22 categories of documents and the procedures the Clerk of Court is to undertake when the notice is improperly filed.

• Rule 2.420(d)(3) sets forth the ability of a filer of a document to file a "Motion to Determine Confidentiality of Court Records" when the filer seeks to have information not contained within the 22 categories of documents treated as confidential and exempt from public view.

• Rule 2.420(e) sets forth the procedure the filer must follow when filing a Motion to Determine Confidentiality of trial court records in non criminal cases, the discretion of the judge to require public notice of the hearing, the time frame within which to hold a hearing, the time frame within which an order must issue, the time frame within which a copy of the order must be published by the clerk both on its website and in a prominent public location in the courthouse, and the time frame within which the order must remain published.

• Rule 2.420(f) sets forth the procedure the filer must follow when filing a Motion to Determine Confidentiality of trial court records in criminal cases, the time frame within which to hold a hearing, the time frame within which an order must issue, and the requirement that the Clerk of Court must be directed by the Court to publish a copy of the order.

• Rule 2.420 (h) sets forth the procedures when a movant seeks to make an oral motion to determine the confidentiality of trial court records.

• Rule 2.420) (i) sets forth the sanctions provision of the rule.

NOW, THEREFORE, pursuant to the authority conferred by Florida Rule of Judicial Administration 2.215, it is **ORDERED** as follows:

1. Confidentiality of Court Records Under Rule of Judicial Administration 2.420

a. *Notice of Hearing on Motion to Determine Confidentiality.* When the Notice of Hearing on the Motion to Determine Confidentiality of Court Records is to be published, the Notice of Hearing will be sent to the Communications Department at the Clerk and Comptroller's Office in accordance with paragraph 3 below and within the time frame provided by the Court.

b. *Order on Motion to Determine Confidentiality in Non Criminal Cases.* Following the issuance of an order on the Motion to Determine Confidentiality of Court Records in non criminal cases, the requesting party must ensure that the Clerk of Court has received a copy of the order for filing and publication in accordance with Rule 2.420(e)(4). The order on the Motion to Determine Confidentiality is to also be sent to the Communications Department at the Clerk and Comptroller's Office in accordance with paragraph 3 below.

c. *Order on Motion to Determine Confidentiality in Criminal Cases.* Following the issuance of an order on the Motion to Determine Confidentiality of Court Records in criminal cases, and at the direction of the Court, the requesting party must ensure that the Clerk of Court is provided with a copy of the order so that it can be filed and published in accordance with the Court's directions. Any order is also to be sent to the Communications Department at the Clerk and Comptroller's Office in accordance with paragraph 3 below.

2. Court Proceedings

a. *The Miami Herald Publishing Co. v. Lewis*, 426 So. 2d 1 (Fla. 1982) applies to the closure of court proceedings and notice to the media.

b. The moving party will also provide the "notice to the media" to the Communications Department at the Clerk and Comptroller's Office for publication in accordance with paragraph 3 below.

3. Publication by Clerk's Office. When Rule of Judicial Administration 2.420 requires, or upon order of court, the moving party will also provide the applicable documents to the Clerk's Office Communication Department for publication.

a. The email address to which such documents are to be sent is: Communications@mypalmbeachclerk.com

b. The Clerk and Comptroller's office will publish such documents on its website at www.mypalmbeachclerk.com/sealedcases.aspx and on the bulletin boards located in the respective lobbies of the division in which they are filed (Circuit Civil—Room 3.23; Unified Family Court—Room 3.22; and County Civil—Room 2.22).

4. Opening of Sealed/Confidential File. The Clerk of Court, or a deputy clerk, is hereby authorized to open any paper court file sealed by operation of law or court order, or access any sealed electronic file, for the purpose of filing documents pertinent to the particular file, as well as for microfilming or imaging files, and for preparing a record on appeal. The Clerk, or deputy clerk, shall reseal the file immediately upon completion of the task, with the date and time of the unsealing clearly noted on the docket along with the initials of the deputy clerk.

5. Adult Parties and Attorneys of Record. In all matters except adoption and surrogacy cases, the Clerk of Court will make the contents of a sealed file available to adult parties and their attorneys of record. The contents of adoption and surrogacy files shall not be made available to any person absent a court order.

6. Sanctions. If a motion to seal/make court records confidential is not made in good faith and is not supported by a sound legal and factual basis, the court may impose sanctions upon the movant.

DONE AND SIGNED in Chambers in West Palm Beach, Palm Beach County, Florida this 7 day of March, 2018.

Krista Marx
Chief Judge

Adopted effective September 29, 2008. Amended effective September 22, 2009; March 7, 2018.

* supersedes admin, order 2.303–9/09

** Due to the rewrite of the prefatory language as well as the rewrite of paragraphs 1–3, new language is not bolded in those sections. New language is bolded in paragraphs 4–6.

2.304. REQUEST FOR PUBLIC JUDICIAL RECORDS

IN THE CIRCUIT COURT OF THE FIFTEENTH JUDICIAL CIRCUIT IN AND FOR PALM BEACH COUNTY

ADMINISTRATIVE ORDER NO. 2.304–4/10 *

IN RE: REQUEST FOR PUBLIC JUDICIAL RECORDS

Florida Rule of Judicial Administration 2.420 sets forth those records of the judicial branch of government to which the public shall have access.

Certain records of the judiciary are confidential and exempt and are therefore not deemed public records.

In order to ensure that those judicial records which are public are provided timely to the requestor it is

NOW, THEREFORE, pursuant to the authority conferred by Florida Rule of Judicial Administration 2.215, it is **ORDERED** as follows:

1. All public records request made to the Fifteenth Judicial Circuit must be made in writing.

2. The recipient of a request for public records of the Fifteenth Judicial Circuit is to forward the original request to the Office of General Counsel within 2 days of receipt. The recipient is to also retain a copy of the request.

3. The Office of General Counsel will immediately forward a response to the requestor acknowledging receipt of the public record's request with a copy to the original recipient of the request and to any court employee (including county employees under the supervision of the court), judicial assistant or judicial officer (if applicable) about whom the request was related.

4. Any court employee (including county employees under the supervision of the court), judicial assistant or judicial officer from whom the public records request is sought, will provide the requested public documents to the Office of General Counsel within a reasonable period of time. The Office of General Counsel will review the documents to ensure that confidential and/or exempt information is not included. The Office of General Counsel will forward to the court employee, judicial assistant or judicial officer for review the documents that have been compiled (or will make available the documents available for inspection should the response be too large to forward) and will notify the court employee, judicial assistant or judicial officer of the time period available for review. After the time period for review has expired, the Office of General Counsel will forward the public records to the requestor with a copy of the letter to the court employee (including county employees under the supervision of the court), judicial assistant or judicial officer about whom the records were sought (if applicable).

5. Assistance is available to those court employees (including county employees under the supervision of the court), judicial assistants or judicial officers who need to retrieve technical information.

6. The cost of copies of public records is as follows:

a. $.15 per one sided copy

b. $.20 per one two sided copy

c. Mail, facsimile and scanning fees (if applicable)

Documents will not be released until the payment for the records has been received. The requestor will be informed whether the payment is to be made by check or money order and whether it is to be payable to the State of Florida or the Board of County Commissioners.

7. The cost of retrieval and copying of public records, which by their nature or volume require extensive use of information technology resources or extensive clerical or supervisory assistance by personnel of the judiciary, or both, will incur a special service charge. The special service charge is a reasonable fee that will be imposed, in addition to the actual cost of duplication, which is based on the cost incurred for such extensive use of information technology recourses or the labor cost of the personnel providing the service that is actually incurred for the clerical and supervisory assistance required.

8. At the direction of the Chief Judge, fees can be waived in fairness to the public.

DONE AND SIGNED in Chambers in West Palm Beach, Palm Beach County, Florida, this 19 day of April 2010.

Peter D. Blanc
Chief Judge

Adopted effective September 29, 2008. Amended effective March 31, 2009; April 19, 2010.

* supersedes admin. order 2.304–3/09

2.305. MICROFILMING SEALED COURT RECORDS

IN THE CIRCUIT COURT OF THE FIFTEENTH JUDICIAL CIRCUIT IN AND FOR PALM BEACH COUNTY, FLORIDA

ADMINISTRATIVE ORDER NO. 2.305–9/08 *

IN RE: MICROFILMING SEALED COURT RECORDS

It may be necessary for the Clerk of Court to microfilm court files to conserve space.

NOW, THEREFORE, pursuant to the authority conferred by Florida Rule of Judicial Administration 2.215, it is **ORDERED** as follows:

1. The Clerk of Court, as he or she deems necessary, is authorized to microfilm sealed and unsealed court files.

2. The clerk shall utilize the following procedure for microfilming sealed court files:

a. Sealed court files, or any sealed document in a court file, shall be microfilmed on a separate microfilm and shall be kept separate and apart from the microfilm of unsealed court files.

b. The clerk shall keep a separate list of sealed files and sealed portions of files which shall be cross-referenced with the cases.

c. The list of cases containing sealed material shall be indexed numerically by case number. The reels containing the sealed microfilmed materials shall be kept in a locked cabinet by the clerk.

d. The clerk shall permit viewing of the microfilm of sealed court files only upon order of the Court. Furthermore, the clerk shall ensure that the viewer who obtained the order to see a specific file or document is allowed access only to that file or document. To ensure this, viewing will be allowed only under a deputy clerk's supervision.

e. Any items sealed by order of the Court must be stamped and docketed by the clerk.

f. After microfilming a sealed file or portion of file, the "hard copy" may be destroyed by the clerk by shredding. The microfilmed copy, however, shall be retained and shall not be destroyed unless there has been full compliance with Rule 2.430(j), Fla.R.Jud.Admin.

DONE and **SIGNED** in Chambers at West Palm Beach, Palm Beach County, Florida, this 29 day of September, 2008.

Kathleen J. Kroll
Chief Judge

Adopted effective September 29, 2008.

* supersedes admin. order 2.025 9/92

2.306. MOTIONS, ORDERS, AND JUDGMENTS

IN THE CIRCUIT COURT OF THE FIFTEENTH JUDICIAL CIRCUIT IN AND FOR PALM BEACH COUNTY, FLORIDA

ADMINISTRATIVE ORDER NO. 2.306–9/08 *

IN RE: MOTIONS, ORDERS, AND JUDGMENTS

Each order entered should clearly identify the parties who are to receive a copy of the court order.

Florida Rule of Civil Procedure 1.080(h)(1) permits the court to require orders and judgments to be prepared by a party, for the party to furnish the court with stamped, addressed envelopes for service of the order or judgment, and may require the proposed order and judgments be furnished to all parties before entry by the court of the order or judgment.

NOW, THEREFORE, pursuant to the authority conferred by Florida Rule of Judicial Administration 2.215, it is **ORDERED** as follows:

1. All judgments and orders filed in this Circuit shall specify the name and address of all persons who are to receive copies.

2. In matters governed by the rules of civil procedure, including family matters, the attorney for the either the moving party or the party required to prepare an order or judgment, shall provide the court with a stamped, addressed envelope for each party who is to receive a copy of the order or judgment.

DONE and SIGNED in Chambers at West Palm Beach, Palm Beach County, Florida this 29 day of September, 2008.

Kathleen J. Kroll
Chief Judge

Adopted effective September 29, 2008.

* supersedes admin. order 2.033 8/93

2.307. CASE ADVANCEMENT IN NON–CRIMINAL MATTERS

IN THE CIRCUIT COURT OF THE FIFTEENTH JUDICIAL CIRCUIT IN AND FOR PALM BEACH COUNTY, FLORIDA

ADMINISTRATIVE ORDER NO.: 2.307–9/08 *

IN RE: CASE ADVANCEMENT IN NON–CRIMINAL MATTERS

Pursuant to Rule of Judicial Administration 2.545(c), in any non-criminal action, assigned a priority status by statute, rule of procedure, case law or otherwise, if a party is of the good faith opinion that the case has not been properly advanced on the docket or has not received priority in scheduling consistent with its priority case status, after having filed the notices required by Rule 2.545(c)(1), then the party may seek review of such action by motion.

NOW, THEREFORE, pursuant to the authority conferred by Florida Rule of Judicial Administration 2.215, it is **ORDERED** as follows:

A party who files a motion regarding advancement of a non criminal matter shall direct the motion to the administrative judge of that division of the court unless it is that particular administrative judge before whom the case is currently pending. In that event the motion shall be directed to the chief judge.

DONE and **SIGNED** in Chambers, in West Palm Beach, Palm Beach County, Florida this 29 day of September, 2008.

Kathleen J. Kroll
Chief Judge

Adopted effective September 29, 2008.

* supersedes admin. order 2.067-10/02

2.308. UNIFORM INTRACIRCUIT CONFLICT RESOLUTION PROCEDURE

IN THE CIRCUIT COURT OF THE FIFTEENTH JUDICIAL CIRCUIT IN AND FOR PALM BEACH COUNTY, FLORIDA

ADMINISTRATIVE ORDER NO. 2.308–09/08 *

IN RE: UNIFORM INTRACIRCUIT CONFLICT RESOLUTION PROCEDURE

Intracircuit scheduling conflicts may arise for parties having more than one pending case.

NOW, THEREFORE, pursuant to the authority conferred by Florida Rule of Judicial Administration 2.215, it is **ORDERED** as follows:

1. This order shall be utilized to resolve intracircuit conflicts.

2. The judges affected by an intracircuit scheduling conflict shall initially confer and determine priorities considering such factors as the age of the case, the number of parties and attorneys involved, the estimated time needed for trial, and the availability of witnesses.

3. The following priorities shall apply in the event that the judges affected cannot resolve an intra-circuit scheduling conflict:

a. Appellate proceedings in a District Court of Appeal or the Supreme Court of Florida.

b. Felony trials set pursuant to motion for discharge [Rule 3.191(i), Fla. R.Crim.P.].

c. Misdemeanor trials set pursuant to motion for discharge [Rule 3.191(i), Fla.R.Crim.P.].

d. Capital trials where the death penalty is an issue and hearings on Rule 3.850 motions when the death penalty has been imposed.

e. Termination of parental rights and dependency cases.

f. Noncapital felony jury trials.

g. Misdemeanor jury trials.

h. Civil jury trials.

i. Civil non-jury trials estimated to last four days or more.

j. Court ordered mediation and arbitration.

k. Circuit court non-jury trials estimated to last less than four days including violations of probation or community control and Rule 3.850 motions.

l. County court non-jury trials including violations of probation.

m. Motions requiring evidentiary hearing.

n. Traffic infraction hearings.

o. Other motions or proceedings.

p. Depositions.

4. In cases of equal dignity, the oldest case shall have priority. The date of filing shall determine the age of the cases. Criminal defendants in custody shall have priority over other criminal defendants.

DONE and **SIGNED** in Chambers at West Palm Beach, Palm Beach County, Florida, this 29 day of September, 2008.

Kathleen J. Kroll
Chief Judge

Adopted effective September 29, 2008.

* supercedes administrative order 2.013–6/01

2.309. EXEMPLIFICATION CERTIFICATES

IN THE CIRCUIT COURT OF THE FIFTEENTH JUDICIAL CIRCUIT IN AND FOR PALM BEACH COUNTY, FLORIDA

ADMINISTRATIVE ORDER NO. 2.309–9/08 *

IN RE: EXEMPLIFICATION CERTIFICATES

From time-to-time the Clerk of Court is required to provide exemplified certifications which are required to authenticate or exemplify a Court document. The Clerk of Court must maintain an adequate supply of exemplification certificates to ensure a timely response for exemplified requests.

NOW, THEREFORE, pursuant to the authority conferred by Florida Rule of Judicial Administration 2.215, it is **ORDERED** as follows:

When required by the Clerk of Court, it shall be the responsibility of the Chief Judge to sign blank exemplification certificates. In the absence of the Chief Judge, the Duty Judge shall sign such certificates. The certificates shall be used for the sole purpose of providing parties with exemplified copies of Court orders.

DONE and **SIGNED**, in Chambers, at West Palm Beach, Palm Beach County, Florida, this 29 day of September, 2008.

Kathleen J. Kroll
Chief Judge

ATTACHMENT

EXEMPLIFICATION CERTIFICATION

STATE OF FLORIDA
COUNTY OF PALM BEACH

I, ________________, Judge of the Circuit Court of the Fifteenth Judicial Circuit, in and for Palm Beach County, Florida, DO HEREBY CERTIFY that SHARON BOCK, whose name is subscribed to the foregoing certificate and attestation, is the duly appointed and qualified Clerk of the Circuit Court of the Fifteenth Judicial Circuit, in and for Palm Beach County, Florida, and that the seal thereto affixed is the genuine seal of the said Court, and that the said certificate and attestation are in due form and made by the proper officer, and full faith and credit are due and ought to be given to all of the official acts of said Clerk, as well in courts of judicature as elsewhere.

IN TESTIMONY WHEREOF, I have hereunto set my hand at West Palm Beach, Palm Beach County, Florida this ___ day of _________, ___.

____
Judge of the Circuit Court
of Palm Beach County, Florida

STATE OF FLORIDA
COUNTY OF PALM BEACH

I, SHARON BOCK, Clerk of the Circuit Court of the Fifteenth Judicial Circuit, in and for Palm Beach County, Florida, DO HEREBY CERTIFY that the Honorable ________________ is a Judge of the Circuit Court of Palm Beach County, Florida, duly commissioned, qualified and acting, and that the signature of the foregoing certificate and attestation is genuine and in his/her own proper handwriting, and that full faith and credit are due and ought to be given to all of his/her official acts as well in courts of judicature as elsewhere.

IN TESTIMONY WHEREOF, I have hereunto set my hand at West Palm Beach, Palm Beach County, Florida this ___ day of _________, ___.

SHARON BOCK
CLERK OF THE CIRCUIT COURT
PALM BEACH COUNTY, FLORIDA
BY: ________________
Deputy Clerk

*Note: This document is used for providing exemplified copies of court orders.

Adopted effective September 29, 2008.

* supersedes admin. order 2.063–2/01

2.310. SERVICE BY EMAIL

IN THE CIRCUIT COURT OF THE FIFTEENTH JUDICIAL CIRCUIT IN AND FOR PALM BEACH COUNTY, FLORIDA

ADMINISTRATIVE ORDER NO. 2.310–1/18 *

IN RE: SERVICE BY EMAIL

Pursuant to Florida Rule of Judicial Administration 2.516, all attorneys who have not been exempted by a rule of procedure or by an order of the court, must serve and accept court filings by email. Florida Rule of Judicial Administration 2.516 makes it optional for judges to serve court orders and receive other documents by email.

NOW, THEREFORE, pursuant to the authority conferred by Florida Rule of Judicial Administration 2.215, it is **ORDERED** as follows:

1. When an attorney is no longer counsel of record, the attorney must provide notice to the Clerk and Comptroller's Office in accordance with Administrative Order 2.311–2/13 (as amended). Until such time as the Clerk and Comptroller's records the notice and the e-portal service lists are updated by the parties, the attorney may continue to receive electronic service by the court.

2. Unless otherwise instructed or permitted by the assigned divisional judge or magistrate, attorneys and self-represented litigants are not to email courtesy copies of e-filed documents to the judge or court staff. This applies to the divisional and individual email addresses.

3. All self help packets distributed by the Clerk and Comptroller's Office are to include an Email Designation **Form** along with instructions on e-serving. The form is attached as Exhibit "A".

4. Email addresses of self represented litigants are to be added to the Clerk's Showcase Case Maintenance System only:

a. When a self represented litigant files through the e-portal and includes an email address.

b. Upon the filing of a designation of email address.

DONE and **SIGNED**, in Chambers, at West Palm Beach, Palm Beach County, Florida, this 8 day of January, 2018.

Krista Marx
Chief Judge

Exhibit "A"

E–SERVICE INSTRUCTIONS FOR SELF REPRESENTED PARTIES

Pursuant to the Florida Rule of Judicial Administration 2.516, self-represented parties involved in any type of case in any Florida court, may, but are not required to, serve on the opposing party's attorney court documents by e-mail.

E-mail Service to/from an Opposing Party: Self-represented parties opting to serve court documents by e-mail may do so by designating a primary e-mail address (and up to 2 secondary e-mail addresses) for receiving service in that proceeding. This designation only informs the other side of your email address. Once a party has filed an e-mail address designation in a proceeding, all court documents **and orders** required or permitted to be served on a party must be served by e-mail unless the parties otherwise agree or a court orders otherwise.

Form of Email: E-mail service is made by attaching a copy of the document to be served in PDF format to an e-mail. The e-mail's subject line must state "SERVICE OF COURT DOCUMENT" in all capital letters, followed by the case number of the relevant proceeding. The body of the e-mail must identify the: (1) court in which the proceeding is pending; (2) case number; (3) name of the initial party on each side; (3) title of each document served with that e-mail; (4) sender's name; (5) sender's telephone number. The e-mail and attachments together may not exceed 5 megabytes in size; emails that exceed the size requirement must be divided into separate e-mails (no one of which may exceed 5 megabytes) and labeled sequentially in the subject line. Documents served by e-mail may be signed by "/s/", "/s" or "s/" as long as the document filed with the Clerk's Office is signed in accordance with the applicable rule of procedure.

Service Dates: Service by e-mail is deemed complete on the date it is sent. E-mail service is treated as service by mail for the computation of time. When, in addition to service by e-mail, the sender also utilizes another means of service provided for in the Rules of Judicial Administration, the computation of time will be based on the method of service that has the shortest response time.

Filing of Documents: The Rules of Judicial Administration require that all documents be filed with the court either before service on the opposing party or immediately thereafter. Documents are deemed filed when they are filed with the clerk of court. If the sender learns that the e-mail did not reach the address of the person to be served, the sender must immediately send another copy by e-mail, or serve by a means authorized by subdivision (b)(2) of the Rules of Judicial Administration.

IN THE CIRCUIT/COUNTY COURT OF THE FIFTEENTH JUDICIAL CIRCUIT IN AND FOR PALM BEACH COUNTY, FLORIDA

CASE NO.: ________

________________________,
Plaintiff/Petitioner

v.

________________________,
Defendant/Respondent.

NOTICE OF DESIGNATION OF EMAIL ADDRESS FOR E–SERVICE

I, (full legal name) ________, designate my e-mail address(es) below (up to 3 different email address) to opt in E-service in this case.

Primarily Email Address: ____________________

Secondary Email Address: ____________________

Other Email Address: ____________________

1. By completing this form I am authorizing the Court, the Clerk of the Fifteenth Judicial Circuit of Florida and the opposing party to send copies of orders/judgment, notices or other written communications or pleadings to me through my designated e-mail and NOT through regular U.S. Mail.

2. I understand that I must keep the clerk's office and the opposing party or parties notified of my current mailing and e-mail address(es) and that all future orders/judgment, notices or other written communications or pleadings in this lawsuit will be served at the email address(es) provided above.

3. I will ensure the software filters have been removed from my computer, so it does not interfere with my ability to receive any of the above documents.

I certify that a copy of this document was {check all used}: ( ) e-mailed ( ) mailed ( ) faxed ( ) hand-delivered to the person(s) listed below on {date} ________.

Other party or his/her attorney

Name: ______________________

Address: ______________________

City, State, Zip: ______________________

Fax Number: ______________________

E–Mail Address(es): ______________________

Dated: ______________ ______________________

Signature of Party

IF A NONLAWYER HELPED YOU FILL OUT THIS FORM, HE/SHE MUST FILL IN THE BLANKS BELOW:

[fill in all blanks] This form was prepared for the: {choose only one} ( ) Petitioner ( ) Respondent

This form was completed with the assistance of:

{name of individual} ______________________

{name of business} ______________________

{street} ______________________

{city} ________, {state} ________ {telephone number} ___

Adopted effective October 1, 2012. Amended effective April 10, 2013; May 14, 2014; January 8, 2018.

* supersedes admin. order 2.310–5/14

2.311. NOTICES OF CHANGE OF ADDRESS, SUBSTITUTION/WITHDRAWAL OF COUNSEL, AND DESIGNATION OF ATTORNEY OF RECORD

IN THE CIRCUIT COURT OF THE FIFTEENTH JUDICIAL CIRCUIT IN AND FOR PALM BEACH COUNTY, FLORIDA

ADMINISTRATIVE ORDER NO. 2.311–2/13

IN RE: NOTICES OF CHANGE OF ADDRESS, SUBSTITUTION/WITHDRAWAL OF COUNSEL, AND DESIGNATION OF ATTORNEY OF RECORD

Pursuant to Florida Rule of Judicial Administration 2.515, every pleading and other document of a party represented by an attorney shall be signed by at least one attorney of record whose current record Florida Bar address, telephone number, including area code, primary e-mail address and secondary e-mail addresses, if any, and Florida Bar number shall be included. Pursuant to Florida Rule of Judicial Administration 2.505(f), an order of substitution or withdrawal of counsel must be entered prior to a change of counsel. The Rules of Judicial Administration do not address the notification process when there is a change of attorney within the law firm representing a party. A random review of files showed that many attorneys and law firms are not clearly notifying the Clerk & Comptroller's office of a change of address, change of attorney within the law firm of record or directing the Clerk and Comptroller to update the record following a substitution or withdrawal of counsel and therefore the Clerk & Comptroller's records may not reflect correct information. Incorrect addresses and inaccurate attorney/firm information compromises the judiciary's ability to accurately serve orders by mail and email.

NOW, THEREFORE, pursuant to the authority conferred by Florida Rule of Judicial Administration 2.215, it is **ORDERED** as follows:

1. When a law firm with attorneys practicing in the Fifteenth Judicial Circuit changes its mailing or email address, it shall file a copy of the Notice of Change of Counsel's Address, attached hereto as Exhibit "A", in each and every case number in which it is the law firm of record.

2. When an attorney practicing in the Fifteenth Judicial Circuit changes his or her mailing or email address, he or she shall file a copy of the Notice of Change of Counsel's Address, attached hereto as Exhibit "A", in each and every case number in which he or she is the attorney of record.

3. The title of a proposed order on a Motion for Substitution of Counsel or Motion to Withdraw shall clearly direct the Clerk to update counsel of record or update the applicable mailing addresses.[1]

a. If the title of an order granting the substitution of counsel does not specifically direct the Clerk of Court to change counsel of record or the body of the order does not provide the new counsel's contact information, new counsel of record shall file a Notice of Substitution of Counsel, attached hereto as Exhibit "B", in each case file in which the court has ordered that the attorney be substituted in as counsel of record.

b. If the title of an order granting the withdrawal of counsel does not specifically direct the Clerk of Court to update the file with new contact information for the party, or the body of the order does not contain the new contact information, the withdrawing counsel shall file a Notice of Withdrawal of Counsel, attached hereto as Exhibit "C", in each case file in which the attorney's motion to withdraw as counsel has been granted.

4. If the initial attorney of record is no longer associated with the law firm which is prosecuting or defending an action, a Stipulation for Substitution of Counselor a Notice of Change of Attorney of Record and Directions to the Clerk to Update Attorney Information must be filed in order to ensure that the case is no longer linked to the initial attorney of record, attached hereto as Exhibit "D".[2]

5. If an attorney of record remains with the law firm which is prosecuting or defending an action, but is no longer working on the case or is replaced internally within the law firm, the new attorney from the law firm shall file in each applicable court file either a Stipulation for Substitution of Counsel or a Notice of Change of Attorney of Record and Directions to

Clerk to Update Attorney Information, attached hereto as Exhibit "D".

6. The filing of a Stipulation of Substitution of Counsel or a Notice of Change of Attorney for situations outlined in paragraphs 4 and 5 above will be deemed to be an order granting the substitution of counsel under Rule of Judicial Administration 2.505(f)(2).[3]

7. The Clerk & Comptroller's Office will, upon receipt of a Notice of Change of Counsel's Address, an Order Substituting Counsel, an Order Granting the Withdrawal of Counsel, a Notice of Substitution of Counsel, a Notice of Withdrawal of Counsel, a Stipulation of Substitution of Counsel as provided in paragraph 4 and 5 above or a Notice of Change of Attorney of Record as provided for in paragraph 4 and 5 above, update the clerk's records to reflect the current counsel and current addresses and docket the item within a reasonable time of the receipt of the filing.

DONE and **SIGNED**, in Chambers, at West Palm Beach, Palm Beach County, Florida, this 25th day of February, 2013.

Peter D. Blanc
Chief Judge

EXHIBIT "A"

IN THE CIRCUIT COURT OF THE FIFTEENTH JUDICIAL CIRCUIT IN AND FOR PALM BEACH COUNTY, FLORIDA
CASE NO.:

Plaintiff/Petitioner,

v.

Defendant/Respondent.
____________________/

NOTICE OF CHANGE OF ADDRESS & DIRECTIONS TO CLERK TO CHANGE ADDRESS

___ Please be advised that the undersigned LAW FIRM has changed its mailing address to:

___ Please be advised that the undersigned LAW FIRM has changed its email address to:

___ Please be advised that the undersigned ATTORNEY has changed his/her mailing address to:

___ Please be advised that the undersigned ATTORNEY has changed his/her email address to:

____

CERTIFICATE OF SERVICE

EXHIBIT "B"

IN THE CIRCUIT/COUNTY COURT OF THE FIFTEENTH JUDICIAL CIRCUIT IN AND FOR PALM BEACH COUNTY, FLORIDA
CASE NO.:

Plaintiff/Petitioner,

v.

Defendant/Respondent.
____________________/

NOTICE OF SUBSTITUTION OF COUNSEL & DIRECTIONS TO CLERK TO CHANGE COUNSEL OF RECORD

Please be advised that by an order of the court dated ________ the undersigned attorney/law firm has been substituted as counsel for NAME OF PARTY. The ________ (name of law firm/attorney) should be removed as counsel of record. Copies of documents and pleadings should be sent to the undersigned at the address below.

INSERT ADDRESS HERE

____
Signature of Attorney

CERTIFICATE OF SERVICE

EXHIBIT "C"

IN THE CIRCUIT/COUNTY COURT OF THE FIFTEENTH JUDICIAL CIRCUIT IN AND FOR PALM BEACH COUNTY, FLORIDA
CASE NO.:

Plaintiff/Petitioner,

v.

Defendant/Respondent..
____________________/

NOTICE OF WITHDRAWAL OF COUNSEL & DIRECTIONS TO CLERK TO UPDATE FILE WITH NEW CONTACT INFORMATION

Please be advised that by an order of the court dated ________ the undersigned attorney/law firm has withdrawn as counsel for NAME OF PARTY. The ________ (name of law firm/attorney) should be removed as counsel of record. Copies of documents and pleadings should be sent to the NAME OF PARTY at the following address:

INSERT ADDRESS HERE

____
Signature of Attorney

CERTIFICATE OF SERVICE

EXHIBIT "D"

IN THE CIRCUIT/COUNTY COURT OF THE FIFTEENTH JUDICIAL CIRCUIT IN AND FOR PALM BEACH COUNTY, FLORIDA
CASE NO.:

Plaintiff/Petitioner,

v.

Defendant/Respondent.

______________________/

NOTICE OF CHANGE OF ATTORNEY OF RECORD & DIRECTIONS TO CLERK TO UPDATE ATTORNEY INFORMATION

Please be advised that while the law firm of _________ is still the law firm representing the plaintiff/defendant NAME, Attorney _________ is now counsel of record. Attorney _________ should be removed as counsel of record.

____

Signature of Attorney

CERTIFICATE OF SERVICE

Adopted effective February 25, 2013.

1 For example "Order Granting Plaintiffs Motion for Substitution of Counsel and Directing Clerk of Court to Change Counsel of Record".

2 The Clerk's Office links a case to an attorney's Florida Bar ID number and not to a firm.

3 New counsel from a separate law firm will still need an order from the trial judge.

2.312. ELECTRONIC FILING OF DOCUMENTS

IN THE CIRCUIT COURT OF THE FIFTEENTH JUDICIAL CIRCUIT IN AND FOR PALM BEACH COUNTY, FLORIDA

ADMINISTRATIVE ORDER NO. 2.312–11/14 *

IN RE: ELECTRONIC FILING OF DOCUMENTS

Florida Rule of Judicial Administration 2.520 requires all documents filed in any court to be filed by electronic transmission in accordance with Florida Rule of Judicial Administration 2.525. In order to assist with the implementation of electronic filing in the Fifteenth Judicial Circuit, administrative procedures must also be implemented.

NOW, THEREFORE, pursuant to the authority conferred by Florida Rule of Judicial Administration 2.215, it is **ORDERED** as follows:

A. Original Documents.

1. Except for those documents specified in paragraphs B, C, D and E below, when an original document, or a document containing an original signature, is required to be filed by rule, statute, or other law, the original document must be filed with the Clerk of Court.

2. When presented with an original document, the Clerk of Court will maintain the original document in a file with the assigned case number unless otherwise directed by a court order.

3. Original documents also include any document for which an electronic signature has not been authorized by law or a document which requires a seal, raised embossment, or has a tactile requirement.

4. Other than those documents specified in paragraphs B, C, D and E below, a copy of an original document shall not be e-filed with the E–Filing Portal if the original is to be filed with the Clerk of Court. If the Clerk of Court is able to determine that a copy of the original document is erroneously e-filed, the Clerk of Court is to note in the docket which document is the paper filing and which document is the electronic filing.

B. Affidavits.

1. Copies of affidavits shall be e-filed.

2. The e-filed copy is to show the full scripted signatures as reflected on the original affidavit.

3. The original affidavit need only be filed in original paper format with the Clerk of Court if required by law, court order, or divisional instructions.

4. If the original affidavit is filed with the Clerk of Court, the Clerk shall retain the affidavit in accordance with paragraph A.

5. As a matter of best practices, the original affidavit should be maintained in the filer's possession for a minimum of one (1) year after final disposition and time for appeal of the case. E–filing a copy of an affidavit does not eliminate the potential need to present the original affidavit for evidentiary or record purposes.

C. Returns of Service.

1. Copies of returns of service shall be e-filed.

2. The e-filed copy is to show the full scripted signatures as reflected on the original return of service.

3. The original return of service need only be filed in original paper format with the Clerk of Court if required by law, court order, or divisional instructions.

4. If the original return of service is filed with the Clerk of Court, the Clerk shall retain the return of service in accordance with paragraph A.

5. As a matter of best practices, the return of service should be maintained in the filer's possession for a minimum of one (1) year after final disposition and time for appeal of the case. E–filing a copy of a return of service does not eliminate the potential need to present the original return of service for evidentiary or record purposes.

D. Verified Documents.

1. Complaints and other pleadings, papers, or documents which are verified by an attorney, party, or person, are to be electronically filed and a paper copy shall not be filed with the Clerk except upon order of court or as required by the trial judge's divisional instructions.

2. Verified documents are to contain a full scripted signature and not an electronic signature such as /s, s/, or /s/.

3. The verified document need only be filed in original paper format with the Clerk of Court if required by law, court order, or divisional instructions.

4. If the verified document is filed with the Clerk of Court, the Clerk shall retain the verified document in accordance with paragraph A.

5. As a matter of best practices, the verified document should be maintained in the filer's possession for a minimum of one (1) year after final disposition and time for appeal of the case. E–filing a verified document does not eliminate the potential need to present the original document for evidentiary or record purposes.

E. Court Ordered Original Paper Filings. Judges may require additional original documents to be paper filed. The judge should set forth a listing of those documents in divisional instructions or in an applicable order.

F. Memoranda of Law.

Memoranda of Law may be electronically filed. Courtesy Copies must be separately sent to the judge in accordance with the judge's divisional instructions. Memoranda of law shall not exceed the technical size limitations as set forth by the Florida Supreme Court and shall not exceed any page limitation as set forth by the divisional judge.

G. Paper and Electronic Copies.

1. The filer shall not provide the Clerk of Court with a paper copy unless otherwise required by rule, statute, or court order.

2. Other than an original paper document that is required by rule, statute, or order to be maintained in the court file, the Clerk of Court may follow Rule 2.525(c)(6), Florida Rules of Judicial Administration, with regard to the disposal of the paper document.

3. Electronic courtesy copies shall not be sent to the judicial offices except as provided for in the judicial officer's divisional instructions.

H. Non Conforming Documents.

1. *Integrity of Court Record:* The integrity of the court record is dependent on the quality of the documents received through the e-Filing Portal. Filers must ensure that documents e-filed are accurate, properly formatted, legible, and meet applicable e-filing portal standards. Documents must also be rotated in the proper orientation to allow images to be viewed as intended. Images that are not rotated to the proper orientation will result in documents displaying on the docket as sideways or upside-down.

2. *Correspondence:* Letters will not be made part of the court file unless ordered by the judge. The Clerk of Court may reject any correspondence that does not have a court order or instructions to permit the filing. This includes a Notice of Filing Correspondence. The Clerk of Court shall place the filing into the E–Filing Portal Pending Queue and notify the filer that the document is not being accepted for filing. After proper notice to the filer, the Clerk of Court shall follow the Florida Supreme Court Standards for Electronic Access to the Courts guidelines and place the filing in the Judicial Review Queue.[1]

3. *Proposed Orders/Proposed Judgments:* Proposed orders and proposed judgments are not to be electronically or paper filed with the Clerk of Court. This includes a Notice of Filing Proposed Order or Notice of Filing Proposed Judgment. If proposed orders, proposed judgments and other documents intended for entry by the court are submitted through the E–Filing Portal, the Clerk is directed to place the filing that contains those documents in the E–Filing Portal Pending Queue and notify the filer that the document is not being accepted for filing. After proper notice to the filer, the Clerk of Court shall follow the Florida Supreme Court Standards for Electronic Access to the Courts guidelines and place the filing in the Judicial Review Queue. In the event the proposed order or proposed judgment is attached to a motion, the Clerk will docket the filing as a motion and shall notate in the docket text that a proposed unsigned order or proposed unsigned judgment was attached.

4. *Wrong Jurisdiction/Invalid Case Number:* The Clerk of Court may reject documents that are e-filed in the wrong county or with an invalid case number. The Clerk of Court shall place the filing into the E–Filing Portal Pending Queue and notify the filer that the document is not being accepted for filing. After proper notice to the filer, the Clerk of Court shall follow the Florida Supreme Court Standards for Electronic Access to the Courts guidelines and place the filing in the Judicial Review Queue.

5. *Corrupted Documents:* Filings which are not accepted by the E–Filing Portal and/or the Clerk's Office for non-compatible settings (i.e. nonconforming DPI or failure to comply with submission standards) or which are unreadable will be placed in the E–Filing Portal Pending Queue. The Clerk of Court will notify the filer that the document is not being accepted for filing. If, after proper notice, the filer has not corrected the error, the Clerk of Court shall docket the nonconforming filing with the notation that the filing is "Nonconforming—Corrupted".

6. *Final Disposition Forms:* Form 1.998 requires the prevailing party, or the plaintiff if there is no prevailing party, to file a Final Disposition Form at the conclusion of the court proceeding. Final Disposition Forms filed prior to the conclusion of the matter will be placed into the E–Filing Portal Pending Queue and the Clerk will notify the filer that the document is not being accepted for filing. After proper notice to the filer, the Clerk of Court shall follow the Florida Supreme Court Standards for Electronic Access to the Courts guidelines and place the filing in the Judicial Review Queue.

7. *Non–Compliant Documents:* Electronically filed documents which do not comply with the Florida Rules of Judicial Administration, the Florida Supreme Court's Administrative Orders or this Administrative Order, and which have not already been addressed above, shall be placed in the E–Filing Portal Pending Queue and the Clerk will notify the filer that the document is not being accepted for filing. After proper notice to the filer, the Clerk of Court shall follow the Florida Supreme Court Standards for Electronic Access to the Courts guidelines and place the filing in the Judicial Review Queue.

8. *Non–Court Related Documents:* The Clerk's Office is authorized to reject documents which from the face of the document are clearly misfiled (i.e. wrong case name and number) or not meant to be included as part of the court file (i.e. personal documents of the filer). The Clerk of Court shall place the document into the E–Filing Portal Pending Queue and notify the filer that the document is not being accepted for filing. After proper notice to the filer, the Clerk of Court shall follow the Florida Supreme Court Standards for Electronic Access to the Courts guidelines and place the filing in the Judicial Review Queue. If the filer intended to file the document, the filer can move the court to direct the Clerk of Court to accept the filing.

9. *Batched Documents:* A pleading or paper uploaded to the E–Filing Portal shall not be combined with another pleading or paper to form one document.[2] Each e-filed document must be submitted as a distinct item. Filings which are not accepted by the Clerk's Office as a result of multiple filings being "batched" together as one document, will be placed into the E–Filing Portal Pending Queue. The Clerk of Court will notify the filer that the filing was improperly batched. If,

after proper notice, the filer has not corrected the error, the Clerk of Court shall docket the nonconforming filing with the notation that the filing is "Nonconforming—Batched Document". Only the title of the first document in the batch filing will be listed in the docket.

10. *Duplicate Filings:*

a. Electronic and Paper Filings: If the Clerk of Court is able to determine at the time of docketing that an electronic filing is a duplicate of a pleading or document that was erroneously paper filed, the Clerk of Court will docket with the notation "Duplicate Filing".

b. Electronic Replacement Filings: If after the Clerk of Court notifies a filer that a filing was placed in the pending queue and the filer, rather than correcting the filing, files a replacement document, the Clerk of Court can move the filing from the pending queue to the Judicial Queue in accordance with the Florida Supreme Court Standards for Electronic Access to the Courts guidelines. If the filer intended to file the initial document in addition to the replacement document, the filer can move the court to direct the Clerk of Court to accept the filing.

I. Signatures.

1. Except as specified above, the placement by an attorney or party or interested person of a "/s" "s/" or "/s/" or the placement of an image of a signature on the signature line of an electronically filed paper shall be accepted as the signature and shall represent to the court that the filer is in possession of the originally executed document.

2. Signatures on verified pleadings and affidavits shall be in accordance with paragraphs B, C and D above.

J. Envelopes. Envelopes for service of orders and other documents shall be provided as follows:

1. *Envelopes for Service by the Court.* When mail service is required, envelopes for service of orders, with postage prepaid, shall be provided directly to the court with paper copies of the order to be conformed.

2. *Envelopes for Service by the Clerk.* When an attorney or party requests service of documents by the Clerk of Court, whether those documents are e-filed or filed in paper form, the attorney or party shall provide to the Clerk's Office postage pre-paid envelopes. If postage paid envelopes are not provided to the Clerk of Court for service, the Clerk of Court does not have to mail out the subject document. In such cases, the Clerk of Court will notate on the docket that service of the document did not occur due to failure of party to provide postage paid envelopes.

K. Multiple Cases. If a single document is to be filed in two or more cases, the document must be submitted in a separate e-filing transaction for each case. If a document is e-filed with multiple case numbers, the Clerk of Court will only docket the pleading under the case number referenced in the e-Filing Portal.

L. Confidential Information. The Notice of Confidential Information, as required by Rule of Judicial Administration 2.420, must be a document separate from the pleading or paper containing the confidential information and must be uploaded and e-filed in the same transaction.

M. Emergency Motions and Documents Treated as Emergencies.

1. *E-Filed Emergency Motions:* When an Emergency Motion or emergency document is e-filed, the filer shall flag the motion **or document** as an emergency by clicking on the emergency box in the E-Filing Portal.

a. With the exception of Family Law cases, the Clerk shall forward the emergency filing as follows:

1) If the Judicial Office utilizes a divisional email address, the Clerk's Office shall immediately scan and email the motion **or document** to the divisional judge through the Court Administration's divisional email address.

a) If the Clerk does not receive an electronic confirmation that the emergency filing was received by the judicial assistant or judge within three (3) hours or by the end of business, whichever occurs first, then the clerk shall personally contact the Judge's office to verify the Emergency Motion was received.

b) If the Clerk is not able to verify with the Judge or Judicial Assistant that the Emergency Motion was received, the Clerk shall hand deliver the motion to the Judge.

2) If a divisional email address is not utilized, the Clerk's Office shall hand deliver the Emergency Motion to the judicial office.

b. In family law cases, the Clerk is directed to forward specific motions to the email boxes designated by Court Administration. The administrative judge of the family courts or his/her designee, after consultation with the family division judges, shall identify and provide to the Clerk a list of the motions and the email addresses.

2. *Paper Filed Emergency Motions:* When an Emergency Motion is filed in paper with the Clerk's Office, the Clerk shall, if the Judicial Office utilizes a divisional email address, immediately scan and email the motion to the divisional judge through the Court Administration's divisional email address and shall contact the Judge's office to verify the Emergency Motion was received. If the Clerk is not able to reach the Judicial Assistant to verify the motion was received, the Clerk shall hand deliver the motion to the Judge. If a divisional email address is not utilized, the Clerk's Office shall hand deliver the Emergency Motion to the judicial office. If filed after hours, the Clerk will bring the paper document to the duty judge.

3. The following will be deemed and treated as an emergency and will follow the procedures as set forth in Paragraph M:

a. The filer electronically files the motion and flags the motion as an emergency in the E-Filing Portal system. The title of the pleading or paper shall also include the word "Emergency".

b. The filer paper files the motion with the Clerk's Office and titles the motion as an "Emergency Motion".

c. The filer paper files or electronically files a Demand for Speedy Trial, Notice of Speedy Trial, or Notice of Expiration of Speedy Trial.

d. The filer electronically or paper files a Motion for Disqualification/Recusal.

e. The filer electronically or paper files a Writ of Habeas Corpus.

f. The filer paper files or electronically files a Mandate returned to the Clerk by the District Court of Appeals or Florida Supreme Court, or the Circuit Court files a Mandate to the County Court.

g. The filer electronically or paper files a document deemed an emergency in accordance with Administrative Orders 3.206 (Emergency Motions in Circuit Civil), 3.607 (Emergency Motions in County Civil), 4.101 (Administrative Matters in Criminal Cases), 5.203 (Emergency Hearings in Domestic Relations Cases), 5.806 (Emergency Matters in Juvenile Cases), 6.104 (Emergency Hearings in Probate and Guardianship Matters, Domestic/Dating/Stalking/Repeat Violence Petitions[3] and affidavits alleging violations of Domestic/Dating/Stalking/Repeat Violence Injunctions, and Motions to Stay Issuance of Writs of Possession.

h. The filer electronically or paper files a Petition for Rehearing, Motion for Reconsideration or like document pursuant to Local Rule 6.

N. Court Calendars and Child Support Enforcement Ledger. For those judicial officers who request paper calendars, the Clerk's Office shall continue to print the calendars for the County Civil Pretrial Dockets, Civil Domestic Violence Dockets, Traffic Dockets and Criminal Dockets. In addition, the Clerk's Office shall continue to print the Child Support Enforcement Ledgers for First Appearances and Enforcement Hearings upon request by the Court.

O. Docket Codes. The Clerk's Office shall collaborate with the Administrative Office of the Court to create docket codes for electronic viewing and for statistical reporting purposes.

P. Access by Court and Court Staff to Unredacted Filings. In accordance with In Re: Florida Rules of Judicial Administration, 124 So.3d 819 (Fla. 2013), judges and court staff will have access to unredacted images of electronically filed or paper filed documents.

Q. Hard Copy of Court Files. The Court and Clerk agree to move forward cooperatively and expeditiously in accordance with Standard 4.1 of the Florida Supreme Court Standards for Electronic Access to the Courts (Jan. 2013 update, version 8.0).

R. Electronic Access. The Clerk should have images of filed pleadings and documents available for electronic viewing by the Court in its Banner System and its Showcase System (when e-filing is required in criminal, juvenile and traffic divisions and when civil filings are converted to the Showcase system) in the time period as set forth in the FCC guidelines. Matters that are time sensitive must be treated as a priority. The Clerk shall continue to provide a direct link to Court Administration's Judicial Viewer: Integrated Case Management System ("ICMS").

S. Pro Hac Vice. Attorneys who have received a Pro Hac Vice ("PHV") e-filing number are not permitted to appear or e-file in a case until an order of the court granting appearance in that case has been entered.

T. Pro Se Litigants. Pro se litigants who e-file, must opt in to e-service in accordance with paragraph 1 of Administrative Order 2.310 and register their email address(es) at www.15thcircuit.com/html/onlineservices.

U. Electronic Issuances by Clerk of Court. In accordance with court rule or statute, the Clerk of Court may electronically issue and release any document, including but not limited to summons, subpoenas, notices of default, and writs.

V. Motions Regarding Terms and Conditions of Confinement. The filer is required to provide a copy of any motion pertaining to terms and conditions of confinement for inmates currently incarcerated either in a secure correctional facility, hospital, or In-house Arrest program to either the Palm Beach County Sheriffs Office or the Department of Corrections based upon the inmate's location. Motions pertaining to Furlough, Transport, and Modification of Bond (or other similar type motions) shall be forwarded to the Palm Beach County Sheriff's Office at InmateRecordsNoFile@pbso.org. Motions relating to Early Termination of Probation and Modification of Probation (or other similar type motions) shall be forwarded to the Department of Corrections at: Circuit15AdminMailbox@mail.dc.state.fl.us.

DONE and **SIGNED**, in Chambers, at West Palm Beach, Palm Beach County, Florida, this 19 day of November 2014.

Jeffrey Colbath
Chief Judge

Adopted effective June 1, 2013. Amended effective September 20, 2013; November 19, 2014.

* supersedes admin. order 2.312–9/13.

1The Judicial Review Queue is the repository for electronic filings that conflict with applicable rules and/or filing standards. Filings moved to this queue will not be placed on the court docket absent a court order.

2For example, a Motion for Summary Judgment shall not be in the same document as the Notice of Hearing. However, documents and related exhibits, when those exhibits are referenced sequentially in the initial document may be combined for filing purposes to form one document. (For example, a Motion for Summary Judgment with Exhibits A—D.)

3Domestic/Dating/Stalking/Repeat Violence Petitions shall be forwarded to the judge in accordance with Administrative Order 5.501.

2.313. ASSIGNMENT OF CRIMINAL AND CIVIL CONTEMPT CASES

IN THE CIRCUIT COURT OF THE FIFTEENTH JUDICIAL CIRCUIT IN AND FOR PALM BEACH COUNTY, FLORIDA

ADMINISTRATIVE ORDER 2.313–6/15

IN RE: ASSIGNMENT OF CRIMINAL AND CIVIL CONTEMPT CASES

In order to maintain accurate court records, it is necessary to initiate a misdemeanor case whenever a defendant is adjudicated guilty of direct criminal contempt or charged with indirect criminal contempt. The initiation of a misdemeanor case number is for record-keeping purposes only, and does not affect the status of the contempt for appellate purposes. *See Schaab v. State*, 33 So. 3d 763 (Fla. 4th DCA 2010) (holding that misdemeanor case number did not affect the status of the contempt as a Circuit Court matter because contempt arose from felony proceeding).

NOW, THEREFORE, pursuant to the authority conferred by Florida Rule of Judicial Administration 2.215, it is **ORDERED** as follows:

1. Cases involving criminal contempt shall be treated as follows:

a. In direct criminal contempt proceedings, the clerk of court shall initiate a misdemeanor case upon the filing of the judgment of guilt of contempt. *See* Fla. R. Crim. P. 3.830. The case shall be assigned to the same division as the case from which the direct criminal contempt proceeding arose.

b. In indirect criminal contempt proceedings, the clerk of court shall initiate a misdemeanor case upon the filing of the Order to Show Cause. *See* Fla. R. Crim. P. 3.840(a). The case shall be assigned to the same division as the case from which the indirect criminal contempt proceeding arose.

2. The clerk shall not open a new case number for civil contempt proceedings.

DONE and **SIGNED**, in Chambers, at West Palm Beach, Palm Beach County, Florida, this 22 day of June, 2015.

Jeffrey Colbath
Chief Judge

Adopted effective June 22, 2015.

2.314. ELECTION PROCEDURES

IN THE CIRCUIT COURT OF THE FIFTEENTH JUDICIAL CIRCUIT IN AND FOR PALM BEACH COUNTY, FLORIDA

ADMINISTRATIVE ORDER 2.314—11/18

IN RE: ELECTION PROCEDURES

During local, state and federal elections, issues may arise during the voting period that require immediate judicial involvement. Lawsuits may be filed after hours when the clerk's office is closed. A managing judge is necessary to address election related issues to ensure a timely response, consistency, and transparency. Procedures need to be in place to ensure the orderly administration of justice.

NOW, THEREFORE, pursuant to the authority conferred by Florida Rule of Judicial Administration 2.215, it is **ORDERED** as follows:

1. The Chief Judge, or his/her designee, will be the judicial officer who will oversee lawsuits involving the election process in Palm Beach County which is filed from one week prior to election day (including primary election day) until the official election results are certified and returned to the secretary of state. This includes lawsuits filed by a candidate, the candidate's party organization, the supervisor of elections, the media, or an interested party.

2. New filings will be marked in the e-portal as "emergency" in order for the Clerk's Office to docket the filing and bring it to the attention of the Chief Judge or designee.

a. The Clerk will assign the case to a circuit civil division using the case type "CA" and assign the case to Division "CHJD".

b. To ensure that the filing is identified as an election filing, the word "election" is to appear in the title of the filing. If the word "election" is not included in the title of the filing, then the filing may not be treated as an election related filing by the Clerk's Office and may not be addressed on an expedited basis by the Chief Judge or designee.

3. If a filing is made after business hours, the filing party will provide a courtesy copy to the Chief Judge, or designee, at the following email address: CAD–ChiefJudge@pbcgov.org. The Clerk's Office will docket any filings immediately upon the office's opening.

4. The Chief Judge's judicial assistant, or designee's judicial assistant, shall conduct after-hours communication with the noticed parties only via email unless otherwise instructed by the Chief Judge or designee.

DONE and **SIGNED**, in Chambers, at West Palm Beach, Palm Beach County, Florida, this 14 day of November, 2018.

Krista Marx
Chief Judge

Adopted effective November 14, 2018.

Jury Management and Jurors

2.401. JURY MANAGEMENT

IN THE CIRCUIT COURT OF THE FIFTEENTH JUDICIAL CIRCUIT IN AND FOR PALM BEACH COUNTY, FLORIDA

ADMINISTRATIVE ORDER NO. 2.401–9/08 *

IN RE: JURY MANAGEMENT

Florida Statute section 40.001 designates the chief judge of each judicial circuit as having "overall authority and responsibility for the management, operation and oversight of the jury system within his or her circuit". Florida Statute section 40.001 assigns certain and specific responsibilities regarding the processing of jurors to the clerk of the circuit court. In accordance with Florida Statute 40.001, the Chief Judge may also designate to the clerk of the circuit court additional duties consistent with jury management, operations and oversight. The Court is desirous of maintaining a jury system which best meets the varied needs of this circuit.

NOW, THEREFORE, pursuant to the authority conferred by Florida Rule of Judicial Administration 2.215, it is **ORDERED** as follows:

The clerk of the circuit court shall

1. Maintain ongoing communications with judicial offices to ensure adequate jury pools;

2. Prepare an annual budget that is adequate for performing the jury tasks required. A copy of the annual budget shall be provided to the Chief Judge and Trial Court Administrator thirty (30) days after the close of the state's fiscal year.

3. Maintain an automated jury system. Modifications require advance approval from the chief judge

4. Prepare jury management reports as may be required by the office of the chief judge.

DONE and **SIGNED** in Chambers at West Palm Beach, Palm Beach County, Florida, this 29 day of September, 2008.

Kathleen J. Kroll
Chief Judge

Adopted effective September 29, 2008.

* supersedes admin. order 2.015–06/04

2.402. JURY PANELS

IN THE CIRCUIT COURT OF THE FIFTEENTH JUDICIAL CIRCUIT IN AND FOR PALM BEACH COUNTY, FLORIDA

ADMINISTRATIVE ORDER NO. 2.402–7/13*

IN RE: JURY PANELS

Effective jury management is a responsibility of the courts of Florida. The Chief Justice of Florida, by order dated October 8, 1990, has mandated standard panel sizes for certain types of cases.

NOW, THEREFORE, pursuant to the authority conferred by Florida Rule of Judicial Administration 2.215, it is **ORDERED** as follows:

IMPLEMENTATION OF ORDER

1. The chief judge or designee shall be responsible for implementing the provisions of this order.

STANDARD PANEL SIZES

2. Pursuant to the Chief Justice's order, panel sizes for cases involving single defendants shall be as follows:

a.	CAPITAL CASES (in which the death penalty is sought):	50
b.	OTHER 12–PERSON JURIES & LIFE FELONIES:	30
c.	CIRCUIT CRIMINAL JURIES:	22
d.	COUNTY COURT CRIMINAL JURIES:	16
e.	CIRCUIT CIVIL JURIES:	16
f.	COUNTY COURT CIVIL JURIES:	14

3. If a judge determines special circumstances require an enlarged panel (equal or greater than two (2) times the allowable panel size), the requesting judge must obtain the written concurrence of the chief judge before the Jury Office can honor the request.

REQUESTS FOR JURY PANELS

4. To ensure that a sufficient number of jurors will be on hand and available for jury duty, each division shall notify the jury office no later than 3:00 p.m. the day before a trial is scheduled to start. Likewise, the Jury Office must be placed on notice immediately when a jury trial is canceled. When requesting jurors, the following information must be provided to the Jury Office: (a) the style of the case, (b) case number, (c) the case type, and (d) schedule time for panel to report to the courtroom.

5. The Jury Office shall not hold a requested panel for longer than one hour beyond the original requested time. If the panel is not taken within this period, the jurors shall be returned to the general pool.

6. Judicial assistants, courtroom clerks, and bailiffs shall not order jury panels without the express authorization of the trial judge. When requesting, staff shall provide the correct case number and judge's name when ordering jurors.

POSTPONEMENTS

7. Only the chief judge or the jury judge may excuse a person from jury service.

8. The jury manager shall have the discretion to grant no more than two postponements which, together, shall not exceed a term of six months. All requested postponements which exceed 6 months shall be submitted to the chief judge or designee for consideration.

SPECIAL PROVISIONS

9. The jury office must be placed on notice if jurors will have a break in their scheduled jury service.

10. Hours of operation for the Jury Office are 8:00 a.m. through 5:00 p.m.

11. Lunch hours for jurors are scheduled 12:00 to 1:00 p.m.

12. Early release of jurors is permitted, however, the Jury Office shall maintain a pool of not less than 50 prospective jurors at all times. All jurors in the jury pool may be released after 2:30 p.m. daily unless a judge or judicial office has made a request to keep the jury pool until 4:45 p.m.

DONE and **SIGNED** in Chambers at West Palm Beach, Palm Beach County, Florida, this 26 day of July, 2013.

Jeffrey J. Colbath
Chief Judge

Adopted effective September 29, 2008. Amended effective December 14, 2009; August 29, 2011; July 26, 2013.

*supersedes admin. order 2.402—8/11

2.403. JURY SERVICE COMPENSATION DONATION PROGRAM

IN THE CIRCUIT COURT OF THE FIFTEENTH JUDICIAL CIRCUIT IN AND FOR PALM BEACH COUNTY, FLORIDA

ADMINISTRATIVE ORDER 2.403—9/08 *

IN RE: JURY SERVICE COMPENSATION DONATION PROGRAM

Florida Statute § 40.24(8) authorizes the Chief Judge to establish a jury service compensation donation program. Florida Statute § 40.24(8) directs the Clerk of Court to provide written notice at the conclusion of their service that jurors have the option to donate their compensation.

NOW, THEREFORE, pursuant to the authority conferred by Florida Rule of Judicial Administration 2.215, it is **ORDERED** as follows:

1. At the start of each fiscal year, the Guardian Ad Litem's Office and the Clerk and Comptroller shall designate and provide notice to the Chief Judge and Trial Court Administrator the recipient of that fiscal year's donated juror compensation.

2. At the close of each fiscal year, the Guardian Ad Litem's Office and the Clerk and Comptroller shall provide an accounting of the donated juror compensation funds to the Chief Judge and Trial Court Administrator. The Guardian Ad Litem's Office shall provide documentation that the funds were used for services for children for whom the Guardians Ad Litem were appointed.

DONE and **SIGNED**, in Chambers, at West Palm Beach, Palm Beach County, Florida this 29 day of September, 2008.

Kathleen J. Kroll
Chief Judge

Adopted effective September 29, 2008.

* supersedes admin. order 2.057–10/03

Witness Management, Court Reporting, and Interpreters

2.501. WITNESS MANAGEMENT OFFICE

IN THE CIRCUIT COURT OF THE FIFTEENTH JUDICIAL CIRCUIT IN AND FOR PALM BEACH COUNTY, FLORIDA

ADMINISTRATIVE ORDER NO. 2.501–1/18 *

IN RE: WITNESS MANAGEMENT OFFICE

Florida Rule of Judicial Administration 2.535(h)(4) permits the Chief Judge to authorize the use of electronic reporting for discovery depositions in criminal cases. Electronic reporting of criminal discovery depositions will reduce the cost of case preparation without diminishing access to discoverable information.

NOW, THEREFORE, pursuant to the authority conferred by Florida Rule of Judicial Administration 2.215, it is **ORDERED** as follows:

1. The Fifteenth Judicial Circuit's Witness Management Office ("WMO") will provide electronic reporting of depositions to attorneys from the Office of the Public Defender, Office of Regional Criminal Conflict, Office of the State Attorney and Court Appointed Attorneys when a civilian or law enforcement witness is being deposed in a criminal, dependency, or delinquency case.

2. The coordination and scheduling of depositions at the Main Judicial Complex is to be completed through the Witness Management Online Scheduling application. The coordination and scheduling of depositions at the South County Courthouse, Hearing Room A, is to be completed by emailing CAD-witnessmanagementoffice@pbcgov.org in accordance with Administrative Order 2.502.

3. The WMO at the Main Judicial Complex is located on the 5th Floor of the courthouse in room 5.1500 and is available for criminal, juvenile, and dependency cases pending at any courthouse in the Fifteenth Judicial Circuit.

4. The WMO at the South County Courthouse is located in Hearing Room A on the Second Floor and is available for depositions scheduled only in cases pending in Division D and Division JS. To gain access to Hearing Room A, parties must check-in with the Law Librarian.

DONE and **SIGNED** in Chambers at West Palm Beach, Palm Beach County, Florida, this 8 day of January 2018.

Krista Marx
Chief Judge

Adopted effective September 29, 2008. Amended effective June 22, 2009; August 3, 2010; January 8, 2013; June 1, 2016; January 8, 2018.

* supersedes admin. order 2.501–6/16

2.502. PROCEDURES FOR SCHEDULING AND RECORDING DEPOSITIONS AT WITNESS MANAGEMENT OFFICE

IN THE CIRCUIT COURT OF THE FIFTEENTH JUDICIAL CIRCUIT IN AND FOR PALM BEACH COUNTY, FLORIDA

ADMINISTRATIVE ORDER NO. 2.502–3/18 *

IN RE: PROCEDURES FOR SCHEDULING AND RECORDING DEPOSITIONS AT WITNESS MANAGEMENT OFFICE

To assist with the scheduling and recording of depositions at the Witness Management Office ("WMO") uniform procedures must be implemented.

NOW, THEREFORE, pursuant to the authority conferred by Florida Rule of Judicial Administration 2.215, it is **ORDERED** as follows:

A. SCHEDULING DEPOSITIONS

1. The coordination and scheduling of depositions at the Main Judicial Complex is to be completed via the Witness Management Online Scheduling application. The coordination and scheduling of depositions at the South County Courthouse, Hearing Room A, is to be completed by emailing CAD-witnessmanagementoffice@pbcgov.org

2. In accordance with the Standards of Professional Courtesy and Civility, adopted by the Fifteenth Judicial Circuit, depositions are to be scheduled with sufficient notice (at least five business days) except upon agreement of the parties and on a date and time that is mutually convenient to all interested persons.

a. Witnesses who are not law enforcement are to be directed to appear at Witness Management, 205 North Dixie Highway, West Palm Beach, Florida Room 5.1500.

b. Counsel is responsible for forwarding copies of the Notice of Deposition to the parties and witnesses. WMO does not distribute copies.

3. Counsel must complete the Witness Management Online Scheduling form in its entirety.

4. If counsel is notified that a subpoena has not or cannot be served, counsel must timely cancel or reschedule the deposition through the Witness Management Online Scheduling application or be subject to a fee as set forth in paragraph B2 below.

5. Failure to follow the scheduling procedures may result in WMO services being delayed or denied.

B. FEE SCHEDULE

1. WMO will invoice the appropriate agency a $10.00 fee per witness at the conclusion of each month. Invoices are sent out via email to the State Attorney Office, Public Defender Office and Office of Conflict Counsel. Invoices are sent via US mail to the Justice Administrative Commission. Checks should be made payable to Palm Beach Board of County Commissioners and mailed to the WMO: Palm Beach County Courthouse 205 North Dixie Hwy Room 5.1500 West Palm Beach, FL 33401.

2. Failure of an attorney to appear at a properly scheduled deposition without providing at least one hour's notice will result in a fee being assessed against the non appearing attorney in the amount of $25.00 and shall cause WMO to file a certificate of nonappearance with the clerk. Failure to appear by a subpoenaed witness at a properly scheduled deposition may result in the imposition of sanctions and shall cause the WMO to file a certificate of nonappearance with the clerk. WMO will copy defense counsel, the state, and the law enforcement agency.

C. OPERATING PROCEDURES

1. Electronically recorded depositions shall be conducted in accord with Florida Rule of Criminal Procedure 3.220(h), and in compliance with the procedures outlined in this Administrative Order.

2. A staff member of the WMO, who is a Notary Public, shall operate and monitor all digital recordings and equipment. The depositions may be recorded remotely. The staff member shall ensure the production of a high-quality audio record on the network.

3. The WMO shall design an indexing and web-based system to permit ready access by authorized persons to the master recording. This system shall be designed to protect the integrity and ensure the security of the master recording.

4. The master recording shall not be removed from the custody of the WMO without an order from the Chief Judge or the appropriate trial judge.

5. For The Record ("FTR") Log Notes are provided by WMO with all pertinent information including:

a. The swearing in is the first time logged (when the deposition starts).

b. Anytime a deposition is stopped, and/or resumes.

c. Exhibits.

d. Conclusion of the deposition.

6. Counsel should indicate on the record if the deponent wishes to read a copy of the transcript.

7. The following information is to be stated on the record at the beginning of the deposition.

a. The name (correct spelling) of every person who speaks during the deposition.

b. The correct spelling of all the names of persons mentioned during the deposition, if they are difficult to understand.

c. The correct spellings for schools, streets, cities, bars/taverns, stores, medical terms, medicines, legal terms, et cetera.

d. The name and spelling of the attorney, whom they represent, and if they are from the State Attorney's Office or from the Public Defender's Office.

e. Business cards should be obtained to insure the correct mailing address —and telephone number.

8. **Exhibits.** Unless instructed otherwise by the attorneys or deponent, exhibits are to be marked as follows:

a. On the front of the exhibit where they will not interfere with the sketch or printed material on the exhibit.

b. As Defendant's Exhibit 1 or State's Exhibit A for Identification, in large, legible handwriting, depending upon which side is entering the exhibits.

c. With the Defendant's name, Deponent's name, and the date of the deposition.

d. With the technician's initials.

EXAMPLE: Defendant's Exhibit 1 for Identification
7/5/90
Deponent Myers
DLS

e. All exhibits are marked and collected at the conclusion of the deposition.

9. **Audible Answers.**

a. The attorneys should inform the deponents, prior to administering the oath, that they must answer any and all questions posed to them in a loud and audible manner and not mumble their answers or nod their heads.

b. Electronic Recording Technicians will inform the deponent that everything is being tape-recorded, and that nods of the head, be they in the affirmative or the negative, are not picked up by the machine, so they must speak as clearly as possible

10. **Certified Questions.** The attorney shall be responsible for certifying any question they asked and which the deponent has refused to answer, and the words "certified question" after the time.

11. At the end of a deposition, the attorney should ask the deponent if he/she wishes to read or waive (reading and signing the deposition if it is transcribed). If the question to read or waive is not asked at the conclusion of the deposition the transcript will be marked as a read for the witness.

D. DUPLICATE RECORDINGS

1. The WMO shall have the capability of providing duplicate copies of all recorded depositions.

2. Upon request of defense counsel or the state, the WMO shall produce, within a reasonable time, a duplicate of the master recording which shall be provided to the requesting party. If requested, the duplicate recording shall be accompanied by a certificate indicating the duplicate recording is a true and correct reproduction of the master recording.

3. **CD Prices.**

Regular service $10 (5–7 days)

Overnight service $20 (24 hours)

4. **Digital Share (State Agencies Only).**

Regular service $5 (2–3 days)

Overnight service $10 (24 hours)

5. A certified duplicate CD may be played in open court for the purpose of impeaching a deponent/witness.

E. TRANSCRIPTIONS

1. Electronically recorded deposition transcripts may be requested by using the Online Transcript Request Form at: https://e-services.co.palm-beach.fl.us/wmtrans/

2. An Order to Transcribe, listing all witnesses and dates of depositions signed by the judge, must be provided to the WMO in all Court Appointed and Indigent cases paid for by the Justice Administrative Commission.

3. Transcripts shall be certified to be a true and accurate copy of the recorded deposition.

4. The WMO shall maintain a list of qualified personnel who shall be certified with AAERT as official transcribers. Upon receipt of an order or approved request to transcribe, the WMO, using a rotation plan, shall assign the project to a certified transcriber. In the event that a certified transcriptionist is not available, the WMO may assign the task to the court's computer-aided transcription (C.A.T.) program.

5. Under normal circumstances, transcripts shall be prepared and delivered within five (5) days of receipt of the order by WMO. If expressly ordered by the court, transcripts shall be prepared on an overnight (24 hour) basis.

6. The certified transcriber shall prepare and provide a digital version of each requested deposition to the WMO. The WMO will distribute the transcript to appropriate parties. The transcriptionist is responsible for invoicing and payment arrangements. The invoice shall be included with the transcript.

7. Transcribed depositions shall conform to the requirements set forth in Rule of Judicial Administration 2.535. Charges for transcribed depositions shall be in accordance with this fee schedule:

Digital Transcript Regular Service (5 days)	**$2.00** per page
Digital Transcript Overnight Service (24 hours)	**$3.00** per page
Printed Transcript	**Additional $1.00 per page**
Reprint	**$1.00 per page**

8. Certified transcribers are responsible for invoicing and securing financial arrangements for the transcripts they produce.

DONE and **SIGNED** in Chambers at West Palm Beach, Palm Beach County, Florida, this 29 day of March, 2018.

Krista Marx
Chief Judge

Adopted effective September 29, 2008. Amended effective June 1, 2016; March 29, 2018.

* supersedes admin. order no. 2.502–6/16

2.503. COURT REPORTING SERVICES

IN THE CIRCUIT COURT OF THE FIFTEENTH JUDICIAL CIRCUIT IN AND FOR PALM BEACH COUNTY, FLORIDA

ADMINISTRATIVE ORDER NO. 2.503–6/18 *

IN RE: COURT REPORTING SERVICES

The State of Florida has established and funded court reporter positions for all judicial proceedings required by law to be reported at public expense. The Court's administrative office is charged with the responsibility of supervising court reporting functions.

NOW, THEREFORE, pursuant to the authority conferred by Florida Rule of Judicial Administration 2.215, it is **ORDERED** as follows:

1. The Court Reporting Services Department ("Department") shall continue as established within the administrative office of the court. A manager of the Department shall be appointed by the Trial Court Administrator.

2. Subdivisions of the Department shall include Computer Assisted Transcription ("CAT"), Digital Court Reporting ("DCR"), and Central Recording ("CR").

3. CAT and DCR technology may be utilized for any judicial proceeding including depositions in County and Circuit Courts of the Fifteenth Judicial Circuit.

4. The Manager shall:

a. Direct and manage the affairs of all court reporting services provided within this circuit, inclusive of maintaining the schedules for the circuit and county courts.

b. Implement policies and procedures for the effective administration of the programs.

c. In conjunction with the Trial Court Administrator, develop and administer a budget for the effective and efficient administration of the programs.

d. Provide and coordinate the appropriate training of stenographers/digital court reporters/electronic transcribers/scopist assigned to circuit and county courts.

e. Recommend the establishment of new programs to ensure keeping pace with the latest court reporting technology.

f. Develop retention and retrieval policies and procedures to ensure timely and adequate production of transcripts.

5. Stenographers, digital court reporters, electronic transcribers and scopist who are contractual may be assigned to the CAT and DCR court reporting programs. Agreements for contractual stenographers/digital court reporters/electronic transcribers/scopist must be approved by the Manager and Trial Court Administrator. All contractual stenographers, digital court reporters, electronic transcribers, and scopist will be required to enter into an agreement for services and certain contractors may be required to pay an annual processing fee. A current list of all contractual stenographers, digital court reporters, electronic transcribers and scopist shall be maintained by court reporting services.

6. All contractual stenographers, digital court reporters, electronic transcribers, and scopist utilized by the Fifteenth Circuit must meet certification requirements established by the Court. Proof of certification may be required from time to time by the Trial Court Administrator.

7. Requests to the Department for transcript and/or digital recording production at public expense shall be accompanied by a court order.

8. If **appellate** transcripts are requested for a specific date on which both trial and other proceedings (voir dire, motions in limine, etc.) take place, then the Department will not produce transcripts of any proceeding except for trial, unless such other proceeding is more specifically requested in the Notice of Designation.

9. The Department will produce transcripts of voir dire/ jury selection only in the following circumstances:

a) when voir dire or jury selection is specifically included in the Statement of Judicial Acts to be Reviewed; or

b) when the Notice of Designation states that a transcript of voir dire/jury selection is necessary for considering one of the judicial acts listed in the Statement of Judicial Acts to be Reviewed.

10. Transcripts of all judicial proceedings, including depositions, shall comply with Rule of Judicial Administration 2.535(e).

11. A schedule of fees shall be established by the Department. A copy of the fee schedule is attached hereto as Exhibit "A".[1] All transcript production shall be in accordance with the fee schedule, except that the Office of the Public Defender, the Office of the State Attorney, and the Office of Regional Conflict Counsel shall be billed as set forth in the Fifteenth Judicial Circuit Court Reporting Statement of Services. Court appointed counsel and private counsel representing indigent defendants for costs shall comply with court orders and the requirements of the Justice Administration Committee for payment.

12. The Court Reporting Services Department shall maintain a list of Frequently Asked Questions on the circuit's website at: http://15thcircuit.co.palm–beach.ft.us/court–reporters **A copy of the Frequently Asked Questions is attached hereto as Exhibit "B".**[2]

DONE and **SIGNED** in Chambers at West Palm Beach, Palm Beach County, Florida, this 29 day of June, 2018.

Adopted effective September 29, 2008. Amended effective June 1, 2012; January 18, 2013; June 8, 2015; January 25, 2017; June 29, 2018.

* supersedes admin. order 2.503–1/17

1 Exhibit A not attached. Please go to http://15thcircuit.com for an up to date list of fees for court reporting

2 Exhibit B not attached. Please visit the court's website for the Frequently Asked Questions

2.504. COURT REPORTER'S APPOINTMENT, APPEARANCE FORMS AND TRANSCRIPTS IN CIVIL CASES

IN THE CIRCUIT COURT OF THE FIFTEENTH JUDICIAL CIRCUIT IN AND FOR PALM BEACH COUNTY, FLORIDA

ADMINISTRATIVE ORDER NO. 2.504–9/08 *

IN RE: COURT REPORTER'S APPOINTMENT, APPEARANCE FORMS AND TRANSCRIPTS IN CIVIL CASES

Court reporting services are not provided by the court for civil proceedings. The expeditious preparation of transcripts is essential to the orderly and efficient administration of justice. Justice requires that all parties have notice when a transcript is requested by any party.

NOW, THEREFORE, pursuant to the authority conferred by Florida Rule of Judicial Administration 2.215, it is ORDERED as follows:

1. It shall be the duty of a party desiring the presence of a court reporter at any civil trial or hearing to secure the presence of a court reporter. The court reporter shall complete the attached "Court Reporter Appearance" form and file it with the clerk prior to the commencement of the proceeding.

2. The court reporter shall transcribe the proceeding at the request of any party to the litigation. When a party requests a transcript or a portion thereof, the court reporter shall notify all other parties of the request.

DONE and **SIGNED** in Chambers at West Palm Beach, Palm Beach County, Florida, this 29 day of September, 2008.

Kathleen J. Kroll
Chief Judge

* supercedes admin. order no. 2.012–3/94

ATTACHMENT

IN THE CIRCUIT COURT OF THE FIFTEENTH JUDICIAL CIRCUIT IN AND FOR PALM BEACH COUNTY, FLORIDA

CASE NO.

v. (Short style)

COURT REPORTER APPEARANCE

Date of Proceeding:

Agency:

Address:

Phone:

Name of Reporter:

Retained by:

Contact agency for rates.

Signature of Reporter

(To be completed by Reporter and filed with Court)

Adopted effective September 29, 2008.

2.505. COURT REPORTING PLAN FOR DEATH PENALTY TRIALS AND CAPITAL POST–CONVICTION PROCEEDINGS

IN THE CIRCUIT COURT OF THE 15TH JUDICIAL CIRCUIT IN AND FOR PALM BEACH COUNTY, FLORIDA

ADMINISTRATIVE ORDER NO. 2.505–9/08 *

IN RE: COURT REPORTING PLAN FOR DEATH PENALTY TRIALS AND CAPITAL POST–CONVICTION PROCEEDINGS

The Supreme Court of Florida adopted rule of judicial administrative, Rule 2.535(h), requiring the chief judge of each circuit to enter an administrative order developing and implementing a circuit-wide plan to expedite the preparation of transcripts in all cases in which the death penalty is sought and in capital post-conviction proceedings.

NOW, THEREFORE, pursuant to the authority conferred by Florida Rule of Judicial Administration 2.215, it is **ORDERED** as follows:

1. Whenever and where available, the court reporting manager of the 15th Judicial Circuit shall assign a court reporter who has the capacity to provide real-time transcription to report trials in which the State seeks the death penalty and in capital post-conviction proceedings.

2. If real-time transcription services are not available, the use of a computer-aided transcription qualified court reporter shall be assigned to report these trials and proceedings.

3. The circuit's court reporting manager is directed to use scopists, text editors, alternating court reporters or other means to expedite the finalization of the certified transcript for these trials and proceedings.

4. The circuit's court reporting manager will impose reasonable restrictions on work assignments by employee or contract court reporters to ensure that transcript production in capital cases is given a priority.

5. The court reporting manager for the 15th Judicial Circuit is further directed and authorized to put into effect any other measures as allowed by law or rule to expedite the preparation and finalization of transcripts in these cases.

DONE and **SIGNED** at West Palm Beach, Palm Beach County, Florida this 29 day of September, 2008.

Kathleen J. Kroll
Chief Judge

Adopted effective September 29, 2008.
* supersedes admin. order 4.052 6/02

2.506. COURT INTERPRETER POLICIES

IN THE CIRCUIT COURT OF THE FIFTEENTH JUDICIAL CIRCUIT IN AND FOR PALM BEACH COUNTY, FLORIDA

ADMINISTRATIVE ORDER NO. 2.506–1/14 *

IN RE: COURT INTERPRETER POLICIES

Cases sometimes involve persons who require the assistance of a foreign language interpreter or sign language interpreter when attending court proceedings. The role of the interpreter is to facilitate communication between the court and non–English speaker(s) ("NES") during criminal court proceedings. Interpreter Services are provided to the Criminal Divisions of the Circuit, County, and Juvenile Court, as well as Domestic Violence Injunction proceedings. Qualified language and sign interpreters for NES and hearing impaired individuals are ordered by the court, as mandated by sections 90.606 and 90.6063, Florida Statutes, and under the provisions of the Americans with Disabilities Act for hearing impaired individuals, for all courts.

The Court Interpreter Department of Court Administration ("Court Interpreter Office") consists of a director, a supervising interpreter and full-time Spanish and Creole staff interpreters. The court also contracts with free-lance interpreters for Sign Language, Spanish, Creole, and other exotic languages. In an effort to ensure the effective administration of justice, it is necessary that a policy be established to provide certain basic principles concerning the use of interpreters assigned to Court Interpreter Department in the Fifteenth Judicial Circuit ("Staff Interpreters").

NOW, THEREFORE, pursuant to the authority conferred by Florida Rule of Judicial Administration 2.215, it is **ORDERED** as follows:

1. Staff interpreters are assigned to the Main, South, North, West and Gun Club court facilities. Interpreter services are provided to the Criminal Divisions of the Circuit, County and Juvenile Court, as well as Domestic Violence Injunction proceedings and dependency proceedings. Interpreter services shall only be utilized for individuals appearing before the court. Spoken language interpreter services shall not be provided for persons summoned for jury service.

2. Interpreter services may only be requested by a judge, judicial assistant, trial clerk, attorney of record or Court Administration. If the services of an interpreter are needed at a hearing, the attorney must so inform the judicial assistant when scheduling the hearing or they must contact the court interpreter's office directly. Opposing counsel must inform the judicial assistant of the need for interpreter services as soon as counsel is made aware of the need or they must coordinate the scheduling directly with the interpreter's office. If interpreter services are needed for a trial or plea or for a witness who will testify in court, the attorney shall so inform the court at the pre-trial conference. Requests shall be made no less than two (2) business days in advance of the scheduled date for Spanish, Creole and American Sign Language interpreters, and no less than ten (10) business days in advance of the scheduled date for unique languages, which shall include all languages other than Spanish, Creole and American Sign Language. Once the need for an interpreter has been determined, the requesting party must contact the Court Interpreter Office via email: CAD–CourtInterpreters@pbcgov.org. Same day requests should be made by telephone at 561–355–2434 and shall be covered whenever possible, depending upon the availability of resources.

3. When staff interpreter services are needed to assist in more trials than the Court Interpreter Office has personnel to cover, cases will be given priority in the following order: (1) capital cases; (2) cases in which speedy trial has not been waived and the end of the speedy trial time period is most quickly approaching; and (3) by the severity of the offense. In the event of a conflict concerning the severity of the offense, the chief judge or his/her designee shall decide which case will be given precedence. Cases for which staff interpreter services were not available on the preceding day will be given priority the following day, if possible.

4. The presiding judge shall call cases involving the use of staff interpreters before other matters, but shall not be required to interrupt a proceeding that has already begun.

Staff interpreters shall move to their next assignment if the presiding judge does not utilize the interpreter's services within 15 minutes of their arrival or the conclusion of the immediate case before the court, whichever occurs first. The Court Interpreter Office will be notified when the staff interpreter is to return to the courtroom if the case for which their services are required is ready to be heard. When staff interpreters are requested for a general trial call, only one staff interpreter shall be present to assist with possible pleas or negotiations. Every effort shall be made to minimize the length of time the staff interpreter must remain in the courtroom.

5. Trials requiring foreign language interpretation shall be coordinated with the Court Interpreter Office no less than two (2) business days in advance from the scheduled date for Spanish and Creole interpreters and for languages other than Spanish and Creole, no less than ten (10) business days in advance of the scheduled date. Jury trials involving interpreters are scheduled as "time certain" trials within a trial period. Only when a request is made for a time certain trial, which includes estimated days of service required, will the Court Interpreter Office guarantee the presence of interpreters for the duration of said trial.

6. Staff interpreters shall not be required to provide interpretation to defendants without the presence of defendant's counsel, unless directed by the court.

7. Staff interpreters shall not be required to sit in the jury box with a defendant and shall not accompany an attorney into a holding cell to conduct "in-custody" client interviews except where a unique circumstance occurs which requires the court to proceed to a holding cell to advise a defendant of certain consequences of his actions where a defendant refuses to leave a holding cell.

8. The staff interpreter may assist an attorney with conducting a brief "in-custody" client exchange, such as updating or conveying an offer, within the courtroom. This shall only occur under unique circumstances as the presiding judge may deem necessary. When necessary, the judge shall instruct the staff interpreter to assist an attorney with communicating with an "in-custody" client once the defendant is brought into the courtroom.

9. Staff interpreters shall not accompany defendants or any other NES individual to the Clerk's Office, Probation Office, or to any other destination.

10. Staff interpreters may sight translate brief court documents during a court proceeding, but shall not explain court documents, procedures, or otherwise communicate with litigants outside of the court proceeding. Staff interpreters shall not be required to translate disposition reports or case plans during court proceedings due to the excessive length of the document.

11. Staff interpreters shall not translate audio or video recordings during court proceedings.

12. Court Administration will seek the services of a freelance interpreter if the target language is Spanish or Creole and a staff interpreter is unavailable to cover the assignment, or the target language is not offered by the Court Interpreter Office. The Court Administrator must approve all individual or agency contracts. Free–lance, Federal or State certified interpreters will have right of first refusal on any assignment over court-qualified and otherwise qualified interpreters.

13. Staff interpreter services will be available for initial appearance and other proceedings during weekends and holidays. Spanish and Creole interpreters are always present during weekend and holiday sessions. If the need for an interpreter for a language other than Spanish or Creole, including American Sign Language, were to arise during the weekend, the clerk's office may request that the staff interpreter present during the proceeding attempt to call a freelance interpreter to cover the assignment or call Language Line services to request the assistance of an interpreter telephonically.

14. Staff interpreter services are provided for NES parents or guardians of a minor who are directly involved in a juvenile court proceeding. Staff interpreter services are provided to any NES individual who is served a summons to appear before the court due to his or her direct involvement in a minor's juvenile court proceeding.

15. The use of headsets and wireless microphones shall be used in all venues wherever possible.

16. Every effort must be made to obtain the most qualified staff interpreter for each court proceeding.

DONE AND SIGNED in Chambers at West Palm Beach, Palm Beach County Florida, this 7th day of January, 2014.

Jeffrey J. Colbath
Chief Judge

Adopted effective September 29, 2008. Amended effective January 8, 2013; January 7, 2014.

*supersedes admin. order 2.506–1/13

2.507. [VACATED AND SET ASIDE BY ORDER 2.507-11/16, EFFECTIVE NOVEMBER 1, 2016.]

2.508. CONTRACTUAL COURT INTERPRETERS ADDITIONAL COMPENSATION FOR SPANISH & CREOLE AND ADDITIONAL COMPENSATION FOR EXOTIC LANGUAGES

IN THE CIRCUIT COURT OF THE FIFTEENTH JUDICIAL CIRCUIT IN AND FOR PALM BEACH COUNTY, FLORIDA

ADMINISTRATIVE ORDER NO. 2.508–9/08 *

IN RE: CONTRACTUAL COURT INTERPRETERS ADDITIONAL COMPENSATION FOR SPANISH & CREOLE AND ADDITIONAL COMPENSATION FOR EXOTIC LANGUAGES

The Court requires the services of contractual multi-language interpreters at various court locations. Contractual interpreters are compensated for court appearances as set forth in their Contractual Services Agreement for On Call Foreign Language Interpreters with the State of Florida. From time to time it is necessary to provide additional interpreters due to demand and due to the need to interpret languages not interpretable by the court's staff.

NOW, THEREFORE, pursuant to the authority conferred by Florida Rule of Judicial Administration 2.215, it is **ORDERED** as follows:

The Court Administrator for the Fifteenth Judicial Circuit is hereby authorized to approve requests for additional compensation for Spanish and Creole interpreters and for additional compensation for exotic languages interpreters with a maximum rate of $35.00 per hour not to exceed 8 hours per day for Spanish and Creole interpreters and a maximum rate of $100.00 per hour for exotic language interpreters.

DONE and **SIGNED** in Chambers at West Palm Beach, Palm Beach County, Florida, this 29 day of September, 2008.

Kathleen J. Kroll
Chief Judge

Adopted effective September 29, 2008.
* supersedes admin. order no. 2.069–3/04

Expert, Due Process, and Court Appointed Counsel

2.601. SELECTION AND PAYMENT OF COURT APPOINTED EXPERTS

IN THE CIRCUIT COURT OF THE FIFTEENTH JUDICIAL CIRCUIT IN AND FOR PALM BEACH COUNTY, FLORIDA

ADMINISTRATIVE ORDER NO. 2.601–06/17 *

IN RE: SELECTION AND PAYMENT OF COURT APPOINTED EXPERTS

Chapter 2005–236, Laws of Florida, amends various Florida Statutes concerning the appointment and funding of competency experts and mental health professionals. The statutory amendments are based on the general premise that the court system should be responsible for the payment of most experts it appoints to determine competence to proceed and certain other experts for other purposes.

Florida Statute § 916.115 provides for the appointment of experts to examine a defendant who may be incompetent to proceed to trial. Rules of Criminal Procedure 3.210 et seq. establish the procedure for the examination of a defendant who is alleged to be incompetent to stand trial.

Florida Statute § 916.301 provides for the appointment of experts to examine a defendant who may be incompetent to proceed to trial due to intellectual disability or autism.

Florida Statute § 921.137 and Florida Rule of Criminal Procedure 3.203 provide for the appointment of experts to examine a death-sentenced prisoner, or a defendant charged with a capital felony and facing a death sentence, who may be mentally retarded and therefore barred from receiving a death sentence.

Florida Statute § 985.19 provides for the appointment of experts to examine a juvenile who may be incompetent to proceed to trial. Rule of Juvenile Procedure 8.095 establishes the procedure for examination of a juvenile who is alleged to be incompetent to proceed.

Florida Statute § 394.4655 and § 394.467(6) provide for an independent examination of persons who are subject to involuntary placement under the Baker Act.

Florida Rule of Family Procedure 12.363 and Florida Statute § 61.20 provides for the appointment of an expert to conduct an examination, evaluation, testing or interview of a minor child.

Florida Rule of Family Procedure 12.364 and Florida Statute § 61.20 provides for the appointment of an investigator to conduct a social investigation and study when the issue of time-sharing, parental responsibility, ultimate decision-making, or a parenting plan for a minor child is in controversy.

The source of compensation for various types of expert witnesses must be clarified in order to provide for the orderly appointment of expert witnesses.

NOW, THEREFORE, pursuant to the authority conferred by Florida Rule of Judicial Administration 2.215, it is **ORDERED** as follows:

1. This administrative order shall govern the compensation of all experts and professionals seeking payments from public funds in all court matters except Probate and Guardianship as provided for in A.O 6.301 (as amended).

2. The Criminal Courts of the Fifteenth Judicial Circuit shall use a uniform order when appointing experts to examine the competency of a defendant (Exhibits "A" and "B")**.

3. The Juvenile Courts of the Fifteenth Judicial Circuit shall use a uniform order when appointing experts to examine the competency of a child (Exhibit "C" and "D")**.

4. The Family Courts of the Fifteenth Judicial Circuit shall use uniform orders when appointing experts to examine the mental health of a child in a family court matter (Exhibits "E")**.

5. The Family Courts of the Fifteenth Judicial Circuit shall use uniform orders when appointing investigators to conduct a social investigation when the issue of time-sharing, parental responsibility, ultimate decision-making, or a parenting plan for a minor child is in controversy in a family court matter (Exhibits "F")**.

6. The Juvenile Courts of the Fifteenth Judicial Circuit shall use a uniform order when appointing experts to examine the mental condition of a juvenile (Exhibit "G")**.

7. Payment for medical and psychological evaluations are subject to the following conditions:

a. Compensation for the expert's time to testify will be paid at a rate determined by the expert and the party who is requesting the expert's appearance. If no rate is agreed upon, then the rate shall be in accordance with those set forth below.

b. Except for allowable travel time, the rate shall be constant, i.e., there shall be no distinction between trial testimony and other professional services such as testimony at deposition, preparation time, correspondence time, telephone time, etc.

c. Experts who are retained by the State Attorney, Public Defender, Office of Criminal Conflict and Civil Regional Counsel or private counsel ("Contracting Party") and who are subsequently appointed by the Court, will be paid by Court Administration the lesser of the rate agreed to in the contract between the Expert and the Contracting Party or the fee as provided for in this Administrative Order. Should the agreement between the Expert and the Contracting Party be a flat rate that includes an examination and testimony, then Court Administration will have no additional obligation to the Expert.

d. The Expert's bill or invoice submitted for reimbursement shall detail the actual amount of time spent for the examination as well as for the preparation of the report. The bills submitted for reimbursement must be itemized to indicate in-court time, travel time, preparation time, etc., and be accompanied by a copy of the court order appointing said expert. Invoices are to show actual time expended by the Expert regardless of whether the Expert is being paid a flat fee. All invoices must be submitted within thirty days following the end of the month in which services are provided or compensation may be denied.

HOURLY RATES

8. Unless good cause is shown, all experts providing professional services within Dade, Broward, Palm Beach, Martin, St. Lucie and Okeechobee counties who apply for compensation pursuant to the terms of this order shall be compensated as follows:

a. All medical doctors, including psychiatrists, shall be compensated at a flat rate of $500 per adult competency evaluation. Payment by Court Administration will not exceed a total of $500.00 for the examination and preparation of report (including travel time). Examinations for defendants housed in the Belle Glade jail facility, Treasure Coast Forensic Treatment Center and South Florida Evaluation and Treatment Center will be paid a flat rate of $550.00 for the examination and preparation of the report including travel time. Examinations to determine intellectual disability performed as part of the competency examination will be paid at a flat rate of $650.00 for the competency/intellectual disability examinations. Neuropsychological evaluations will be paid at a rate of $800.00 per evaluation including examination and preparation. All medical doctors, including psychiatrists, shall be compensated at a flat rate of $350 per juvenile competency evaluation. Payment by Court Administration will not exceed a total of $350.00 for the examination and preparation of a report (including travel time). Testifying at court will be paid at a rate of $150.00 per hour, not to exceed a total of $300.00. If a doctor is not able to complete a scheduled examination due to the defendant either not showing up or refusing to participate in the examination, all medical doctors, including psychiatrists, shall be compensated at a flat rate of $200 per evaluation.

b. All psychologists shall be compensated at a flat rate of $500.00 per adult competency evaluation. Payment by Court Administration will not exceed a total of $500.00 for the examination and preparation of a report (including travel time). Examinations for defendants housed in the Belle Glade jail facility, Treasure Coast Forensic Treatment Center and South Florida Evaluation and Treatment Center will be paid a flat rate of $550.00 for the examination and preparation of the report including travel time. Examinations to determine intellectual disability performed as part of the competency examination will be paid at a flat rate of $650.00 for the competency/intellectual disability examinations. Neuropsychological evaluations will be paid at a rate of $800.00 per evaluation including examination and preparation. All psychologists, shall be compensated at a flat rate of $350 per juvenile competency evaluation. Payment by Court Administration will not exceed a total of $350.00 for the examination and preparation of a report (including travel time). Testifying at court will be paid at a rate of $150.00 per hour, not to exceed a total of $300.00. If a doctor is not able to complete a scheduled examination due to the defendant either not showing up or refusing to participate in the examination, all psychologists, shall be compensated at a flat rate of $200 per evaluation.

c. Other Experts retained by the Court not listed above will be paid an hourly rate as agreed to between the expert and the contracting party but no more than a total of $500.00 for examination, preparation of report and testimony (including travel time). Travel time is compensated at $50.00/hour (actual time) which amount is not to exceed 1 hour in each direction.

d. Other experts (e.g., fingerprints, blood, ballistics, jury selection, etc.) shall be compensated by the appropriate party on a case-by-case basis after entry of an agreed order having the concurrence of the State Attorney, Justice Administrative Commission and the defendant or after a hearing in open court attended by the above listed parties.

e. Compensable travel time will be paid at a rate of $50.00 per hour (or fraction thereof) but no more than one hour for time expended from the point of departure to the arrival destination.

f. The Court may, in consultation with Court Administration, exercise its discretion to adjust the hourly rates set forth above or utilize agreements for per diem payment to compensate experts from outside the six-county area.

RESPONSIBILITY FOR PAYMENT

9. The responsibility for payment is as follows:

Orders pursuant to Florida Statute § 916.115 (adult competency)

a. When, on written motion by either counsel for the defendant, a *pro se* defendant, or the State Attorney, or upon the Court's own motion, the Court orders an adult competency evaluation pursuant to Florida Statute § 916.115(2), the Court shall select and pay for one expert. If the expert opines that the defendant is competent to stand trial and either party requests a second expert, the requesting party shall select and pay for the expert. If the expert opines the defendant is incompetent to stand trial and either party requests a second expert, the Court shall select and pay for the second expert.

b. When an expert is appointed by the Court pursuant to Florida Statute § 916.115(2) to evaluate the competence of the defendant to proceed and the defense also requests that the defendant be examined for sanity at the time of the offense, the Court will pay only for that portion of the expert's fees relating to the evaluation of competency to proceed at the rates established in this Administrative Order or in the Contract between Court Administration and the Expert. The expert's fee for the sanity evaluation shall be paid by the defense.

Orders pursuant to Florida Statute § 916.301 (adult competency: intellectual disability or autism)

c. When, pursuant to Florida Statute § 916.301, the Court orders the adult competency evaluation for a defendant whose suspected mental condition is intellectual disability or autism, the Court shall select and pay for one expert. The Court may order the Agency for Persons with Disabilities to also examine the defendant.

Orders pursuant to Florida Statute § 921.137 (intellectual disability)

d. When experts are appointed by the Court to evaluate a defendant or prisoner to determine whether the defendant or prisoner is mentally retarded and barred from execution, pursuant to Florida Statute § 921.137 and Florida Rule of Criminal Procedure 3.203(c)(3), the Court shall select, appoint and pay for the experts.

e. When the State Attorney requests an appointment of an expert under Florida Rule of Criminal Procedure 3.203(c)(2) and an expert is appointed pursuant to Florida Statute § 921.137, the State Attorney shall select and pay for the expert.

f. When an expert is otherwise appointed to determine a defendant's or prisoner's intellectual disability as a bar to execution, the Court shall select and pay for the expert(s).

Orders pursuant to Florida Statute § 985.19 (juvenile competency)

g. When an evaluation of a juvenile defendant is ordered pursuant to Florida Statute § 985.19 to determine if the juvenile defendant is incompetent to proceed due to mental illness, the Court will select, appoint and pay for the expert(s).

h. When an evaluation of a juvenile defendant is ordered pursuant to Florida Statute § 985.19(*l*)(e) to determine if the juvenile defendant is incompetent to proceed due to intellectual disability, the Agency for Persons with Disabilities shall examine the juvenile in accordance with Florida Rule of Juvenile Procedure 8.095.

Orders pursuant to Family Rule of Procedure 12.363 and 12.364 and Florida Statute § 61.20 (social investigation)

i. When the issue of visitation, parental responsibility, or residential placement of a child is ordered pursuant to Florida Statute 61.20, the court, on motion of any party or the court's own motion, may appoint an expert for an examination, evaluation, testing, or interview of any minor child.

j. When the issue of time-sharing, parental responsibility, ultimate decision-making, or a parenting plan for a minor child is in controversy, the court, on motion of any party or the court's own motion, may appoint an investigator under section 61.20, Florida Statutes.

k. The parties may agree to appointment of the expert, upon approval of the court. The parties are responsible for payment.

APPOINTMENT OF EXPERTS

10. When an expert is appointed or reappointed by the Court pursuant to Rule of Criminal Procedure 3.212 to perform a periodic evaluation of a defendant who has been found incompetent to proceed, or appointed or reappointed by the Court pursuant to Rule of Criminal Procedure 3.213 after an adjudication of not guilty by reason of insanity, the Court shall select and pay for one expert. Provided the same expert is under contract with the Court, the Court will generally reappoint for subsequent evaluations the same expert who performed the last examination of the defendant. On the Court's own motion, or a motion of the State or defense showing good cause, the Court may appoint a new expert by rotation from the list of experts under contract with the Fifteenth Judicial Circuit.

11. Except for those cases where the Court selects and appoints the expert or those cases pending in the Mental Health Specialty Division, whenever counsel for either the defendant or the State Attorney requests the appointment of an expert to determine competence to proceed or insanity, that attorney shall prepare a form Order Directing Examination of Defendant's Mental Condition for the Court's signature. The Order should be prepared and submitted to the Court within five days. The form Orders for use in the Fifteenth Judicial Circuit are attached to and incorporated into this Administrative Order as Exhibits A and B. The form Orders may be amended without further amendment to this Administrative Order.

12. Except where an expert is reappointed to do an examination or evaluation, the appointment of an expert by the Court will be by rotation from the list of experts under contract with the Fifteenth Judicial Circuit.

13. Experts appointed by the Court will be entitled to the appropriate compensation determined in this Administrative Order (as amended) or in the expert's contract with the Fifteenth Judicial Circuit if different. For an expert to be paid for services rendered, the expert's report and testimony must explicitly address each of the factors and follow the procedures set out in the applicable chapter of the Florida Statutes and in the applicable Florida Rules of Court.

14. Experts retained by the Public Defender or Office of Criminal Conflict and Civil Regional Counsel ("Regional Counsel) pursuant to Florida Statute § 29.006 or by the State Attorney pursuant to Florida Statute § 29.005, shall be paid from the respective budgets of the Public Defender, Regional Counsel or the State Attorney. An expert retained by court-appointed counsel, by counsel for a defendant who is indigent for costs, or by a defendant who is indigent for costs shall, pursuant to Florida Statute § 29.007, be paid by the Justice Administrative Commission. Prior court approval is required for such experts retained pursuant to Florida Statute § 29.007. If the State Attorney needs a court order of appointment to ensure that a State-retained expert has access to the defendant, the State Attorney shall pay for the expert notwithstanding the Court's order of appointment.

15. This Administrative Order does not restrict the ability of the Court to otherwise appoint an expert pursuant to other Florida Rules of Court.

16. This Administrative Order does not affect the appointment or payment of experts under Administrative Order 6.301 (as amended) Probate and Guardianship Division Compensation for Attorneys, Examining Committee Members, and Other Experts Relating to Guardianship Matter nor social/home study investigations under Florida Statute § 61.20 or Florida Rule of Family Law 12.363 and Florida Rule of Family Law 12.364.

DONE AND SIGNED in Chambers in West Palm Beach, Palm Beach County, Florida, this 20 day of June, 2017.

Jeffrey Colbath
Chief Judge

Adopted effective December 2, 2010. Amended effective August 1, 2011; November 16, 2011; July 17, 2015; June 20, 2017.

* supersedes admin. order no. 2.601–07/15

** Exhibits not reproduced with this order.

2.602. ESTABLISHMENT OF REVIEW PANEL FOR SELECTION OF COURT APPOINTED EXPERTS

IN THE CIRCUIT COURT OF THE FIFTEENTH JUDICIAL CIRCUIT IN AND FOR PALM BEACH COUNTY, FLORIDA

ADMINISTRATIVE ORDER NO. 2.602–9/08 *

RE: ESTABLISHMENT OF REVIEW PANEL FOR SELECTION OF COURT APPOINTED EXPERTS

In an effort to provide for the orderly appointment and review of experts, the Fifteenth Judicial Circuit is desirous of establishing a review panel consisting of professionals who shall screen applicants to determine whether or not the expert is qualified to participate on the Expert List. If the panel selects an expert to participate on the List, the expert will be provided with a contract and will be added to the Expert List upon execution of the contract.

Pursuant to Rule of Judicial Administration 2.215, the Chief Judge has the authority to adopt administrative orders necessary to ensure the operation of the court system.

NOW, THEREFORE, pursuant to the authority conferred by Florida Rule of Judicial Administration 2.215, it is **ORDERED** as follows:

1. All experts who wish to be considered to be part of the Fifteenth Judicial Circuit's "Expert List" must complete the Fifteenth Judicial Circuit's Expert Application and return the application to the Administrative Office of Court.

2. A review panel is hereby created and shall consist of the Administrative Judges of the Circuit Criminal, Probate/Guardianship and Unified Family Court Divisions.

3. The review panel shall screen all applicants who meet the minimum criteria as set forth in the Fifteenth Judicial Circuit's Expert Application to determine whether or not an applicant should be added to the Expert List. Additionally, the review panel may review the expert's performance during the contractual period and make recommendations to the Chief Judge based upon its findings.

DONE and **SIGNED** in Chambers at West Palm Beach, Florida, this 29 day of September, 2008.

Kathleen J. Kroll
Chief Judge

Adopted effective September 29, 2008.

* supersedes admin. order 2.073–6/08

2.603. DUE PROCESS COSTS

IN THE CIRCUIT COURT OF THE FIFTEENTH JUDICIAL CIRCUIT IN AND FOR PALM BEACH COUNTY, FLORIDA

ADMINISTRATIVE ORDER NO. 2.603–1/15 *

IN RE: DUE PROCESS COSTS

In the event that a person makes application for a determination of indigency for the sole purpose that public funds be used to pay due process costs, the following procedure in accordance with Florida Statute 27.52 (2013) shall be sufficient unless determined otherwise by the presiding judge. Florida Statute 27.5304 sets forth the procedure for private counsel to seek payment for indigent cases from the Justice Administrative Commission.

NOW, THEREFORE, pursuant to the authority conferred by Florida Rule of Judicial Administration 2.215, it is **ORDERED** as follows:

A. Application & Motion for Determination of Indigency. The individual applying for a determination of indigency must file with the Clerk of Court, both a completed Florida Supreme Court approved Application for Indigency and a Motion to Determine Indigency.

B. Requirements of Motions Filed by Privately Retained Counsel. Privately retained counsel must submit a written motion that includes the following information:

1. Clarification as to whether the legal services are being provided *pro bono* or being paid for by the client or a third party (without disclosing the name of the third party).

2. If the legal services are being paid for by the client or a third party, the amount of the attorney's fee.

3. Specific due process services to be obtained; i.e.: court reporting, psychological evaluations, depositions.

4. The known costs or estimated costs for such services.

5. The justification for the cost for these services.

6. An indigency affidavit utilizing the form approved by the Florida Supreme Court.

7. Certification that copies of the motion were provided to all attorneys of record, including the State Attorney, Justice Administrative Commission, and the Administrative Office of the Court.

C. Requirements of Court Orders Stemming From Motions Filed by Privately Retained Counsel:

1. Upon hearing argument of counsel, the court shall make its findings, utilizing the attached form order, or special order disclosing:

a. Whether the defendant is indigent for due process costs only;

b. Whether privately retained counsel is providing legal services *pro bono* or whether the legal fees are being paid for by the defendant or a third party (without disclosing the name of the third party);

c. Specific amount of due process costs approved;

d. Notice that Counsel is required to use the services offered by the 15th Judicial Circuit; i.e.: court reporting, psychological evaluations, depositions.

2. Copies of the signed order shall be furnished to all attorneys of record, including the State Attorney, the Justice Administrative Commission, and the court file.

DONE AND SIGNED in Chambers at West Palm Beach, Palm Beach County, Florida this 9 day of January, 2015.

Jeffrey Colbath
Chief Judge

☐ IN THE CIRCUIT COURT OF THE FIFTEENTH JUDICIAL CIRCUIT

☐ IN THE COUNTY COURT IN AND FOR PALM BEACH COUNTY, FLORIDA

STATE OF FLORIDA, DIVISION ☐ Criminal ☐ Juvenile Delinquency

vs.

CASE NO.: ____________________

____

Defendant

ORDER DECLARING DEFENDANT INDIGENT FOR DUE PROCESS COSTS

This matter came before the Court pursuant to Administrative Order 2.603–11/14 (as amended) on the written motion of the Defendant to be declared indigent for due process costs, and the Court having heard argument of counsel and being otherwise advised in the premises, **FINDS** that:

a. Counsel for the Defendant is ______________, and is privately retained.

b. ☐ Counsel is providing the legal services *pro bono*, **or** ☐ A third party is paying for legal services **or** _____ Defendant is paying for the legal services.

c. The Defendant ☐ filed ☐ did not file the approved Affidavit of Indigent Status.

d. Counsel ☐ provided ☐ did not provide a copy of the motion to the State Attorney, Justice Administrative Commission, Administrative Office of the Court, and the co-defendant(s), if any.

e. The Defendant ☐ justified ☐ did not justify the fee for said legal services.

f. The Defendant requested due process costs for: court reporting * ☐ deposition(s) * ☐ subpoena(s) ☐ investigator(s) ☐ expert(s) * ☐ appeal ☐ other ____________

g. The Defendant requested due process costs in the amount of $ __________.

h. The Defendant justified due process costs in the amount of $ __________.

i. The Defendant ☐ is ☐ is not indigent for due process costs.

Therefore, it is **ORDERED** that:

1. Defendant's motion is ☐ **GRANTED** ☐ **DENIED.**

2. The due process costs and amounts approved are: ☐ court reporting $ __________ *

☐ deposition(s) $ __________ * ☐ subpoena(s) $ __________ ☐ investigator $ ___.

☐ expert(s) $ __________ appeal $ __________ ☐ other $ __________.

3. The due process costs shall not exceed $ __________.

4. Other: ______________________________

* Counsel is required to use the services offered by the 15th Judicial Circuit

DONE AND ORDERED in Palm Beach County, Florida on this _____ day of __________, 20 _____.

____

☐Circuit Court ☐ County Court Judge

Adopted effective September 29, 2008. Amended effective January 9, 2015.

* supersedes admin. order 2.603–9/08

2.604. COURT APPOINTED COUNSEL

IN THE CIRCUIT COURT OF THE FIFTEENTH JUDICIAL CIRCUIT IN AND FOR PALM BEACH COUNTY, FLORIDA

ADMINISTRATIVE ORDER NO. 2.604–5/15 *

IN RE: COURT APPOINTED COUNSEL

Florida Statute § 27.40 sets forth the duties and responsibilities of the Chief Judge in establishing a registry of attorneys for appointment to represent defendants in criminal and juvenile delinquency cases in which both the Office of the Public Defender and the Office of Criminal Conflict and Civil Regional Counsel are unable to provide representation due to a conflict of interest. Florida Statute § 27.40 further sets forth the duties and responsibilities of the Chief Judge in establishing a registry of attorneys for appointment to represent parents in dependency actions and alleged incapacitated wards in guardianship cases when the Office of Criminal Conflict and Civil Regional Counsel is unable to provide representation due to a conflict of interest.

NOW, THEREFORE, pursuant to the authority conferred by Florida Rule of Judicial Administration 2.215, it is **ORDERED** as follows:

1. In order to be eligible to receive **court** appointments, attorneys must apply with the Administrative Office of the Court ("AOC") and be approved in accordance with the AOC's procedures. The AOC's procedures may include convening a committee to review the applications and interview the attorneys applying to be on the **Court Appointed** Registry ("Committee"). A copy of the AOC's application procedures can be found on the Circuit's website at www.15thcircuit.com.

3. [1] All **court appointed** attorneys must execute a yearly contract with the Justice Administrative Commission ("JAC") to receive compensation. The annual JAC contract must be signed no later than July 15 of each fiscal year. Failure to annually execute the JAC contract by July 15 of each fiscal year may result in the automatic removal from the limited and general registries. Newly approved attorneys will have **until July 15,** or thirty (30) days from the date of approval to sign a contract, **whichever is later.**

4. Rates of compensation are set forth by the JAC except for those guardianship/mental health cases which do not involve indigent persons.

5. Once approved by the AOC and after the execution of a contract with the JAC, the attorney's name will be placed on an electronic wheel (for qualifying categories) which wheel is maintained by the Clerk of Court.

6. Registry Applications:

a. Attorneys must complete an AOC application. Applications will be accepted from **May 1–May 15.**

b. All attorneys must complete an Attorney Certification Form, which is included in the application packet, to certify that they meet certain requirements and to specify whether they are willing to accept as full payment the flat fees as required by Florida Statute § 27.5304 for certain categories of cases.

7. Capital Cases:

a. Except upon special motion or order, no lawyer shall be appointed to more than two pending capital trial cases (where the state has not waived the death penalty), either as lead counsel or co-counsel or a combination thereof. A lawyer shall notify the court when an order of appointment would be in violation of this Administrative Order.

b. Attorneys qualified for capital appeal counsel under the Rule shall be placed on a separate list. Except upon special motion or order, no attorney shall be appointed to more than two pending capital appeals.

c. Members of the bar have no right to appointment as conflict attorneys in capital cases and those appointed are expected to provide representation commensurate with the seriousness of the charge.

d. When in the opinion of the trial judge a capital case list attorney has failed to provide representation to a defendant commensurate with the seriousness of the offense, the trial judge may inform Court Administration that the attorney does not meet the qualifications to receive capital appointments.

8. Removal from the Conflict Attorney Limited and General Registries:

a. Where there are compelling circumstances, the trial judge (or magistrate hearing the matter) may recommend to the Chief Judge that the attorney be removed from the **Court Appointed** Attorney Registry (collectively the "Conflict Attorney Registry").

b. Upon receipt of the information indicating that compelling circumstances exist to remove an attorney from the Conflict Attorney Registry, the Chief Judge may request a meeting with the attorney to discuss the circumstances or refer the matter to the Committee for review and a recommendation as to whether the attorney should remain on the registry. After meeting with the attorney or after review of the Committee's recommendation, the Chief Judge will determine whether or not the attorney should remain on the Conflict Attorney Registry.

DONE and **SIGNED** in Chambers at West Palm Beach, Palm Beach County, Florida, this 8 day of May, 2015.

Jeffrey Colbath
Chief Judge

Adopted effective September 29, 2008. Amended effective May 4, 2015; May 8, 2015.

* supersedes admin. order no. 2.604–5/4/15

1 So in original.

2.606. APPOINTMENT OF CHIEF JUDGE DESIGNEE TO HEAR REQUESTS BY GENERAL REGISTRY ATTORNEYS FOR ADDITIONAL COMPENSATION

IN THE CIRCUIT COURT OF THE FIFTEENTH JUDICIAL CIRCUIT IN AND FOR PALM BEACH COUNTY, FLORIDA

ADMINISTRATIVE ORDER NO. 2.606–6/17 *

IN RE: APPOINTMENT OF CHIEF JUDGE DESIGNEE TO HEAR REQUESTS BY GENERAL REGISTRY ATTORNEYS FOR ADDITIONAL COMPENSATION

Chapter 2012–123, Laws of Florida, effective July 1, 2012, amends Section 27.5304(12)(b), Florida Statutes, and requires the Chief Judge, or a single designee, to hear and determine motions filed by court appointed counsel which seek to exceed fee limits.

NOW, THEREFORE, pursuant to the authority conferred by Florida Rule of Judicial Administration 2.215, effective July 1, 2017 it is **ORDERED** as follows:

Judge Dina Keever–Agrama, who is currently assigned as the Circuit Court Judge at the Criminal Justice Complex, will act as the Chief Judge's designee to hear all requests for additional compensation by attorneys on the general registry in accordance with Florida Statute § 27.5304. Should a motion be filed for additional attorney's fee in excess of the limits prescribed by Florida Statute 27.5304 and the General Appropriations Act, the motion will be sent to Judge Keever–Agrama's office and hearings will be scheduled by the Judicial Assistant.

DONE and **SIGNED** in Chambers at West Palm Beach, Palm Beach County, Florida, this 20 day of June, 2017.

Jeffrey J. Colbath
Chief Judge

Adopted effective July 9, 2012. Amended effective June 25, 2014; June 20, 2017.

* supersedes Admin. Order No. 2.606–6/14

Process Servers

2.701. CERTIFIED PROCESS SERVERS

IN THE CIRCUIT COURT OF THE FIFTEENTH JUDICIAL CIRCUIT IN AND FOR PALM BEACH COUNTY, FLORIDA

ADMINISTRATIVE ORDER NO. 2.701—12/11 *

IN RE: CERTIFIED PROCESS SERVERS

The Florida Certified Process Server Act, Florida Statutes 48.25 through 48.31, expressly vests in the Chief Judge the authority to establish an approved list of process servers who have met the requirements for certification under the Florida Certified Process Server Act and the requirements set forth by the Fifteenth Judicial Circuit of Florida.

NOW, THEREFORE, pursuant to the authority conferred by Florida Rule of Judicial Administration 2.215, it is **ORDERED** as follows:

Standards and requirements are established for Certified Process Servers to be eligible to be included on the approved list for the Fifteenth Judicial Circuit. The Administrative Office of the Courts of the Fifteenth Judicial Circuit of Florida (hereinafter "AOC") shall maintain the said List of Approved Certified Process Servers. Individuals seeking certification as process servers within the Fifteenth Judicial Circuit must comply with the following conditions:

CERTIFICATION OF PROCESS SERVERS

1. Individuals seeking certification must submit an application with a reasonable processing fee, as set forth by the Administrative Office of the Courts, and must fulfill the following requirements:

a. The applicant shall be a permanent resident of the State of Florida; shall be at least eighteen (18) years of age; and must have no mental or legal disability.

b. The applicant shall submit to a background investigation which shall include a review of the applicant's criminal record, if any exists.

c. The applicant shall obtain and file with the application a certificate of good conduct which specifies all of the following:

(1) There is no pending criminal case against the applicant.

(2) There is no record of any felony conviction.

(3) There is no record of a conviction of a misdemeanor involving moral turpitude or dishonesty within the past five (5) years.

d. Persons who have completed an application and satisfied the requirements set forth in paragraphs 1(a)–(c) shall submit to a written examination, testing the applicant's knowledge of the laws and rules regarding the service of process. A passing examination score is hereby fixed at eighty percent (80%). The content, frequency and location of the examination shall be approved by the Chief Judge.

e. The applicant shall execute a performance bond with a surety company authorized within this County in the amount of Five Thousand Dollars ($5,000. 00) as provided in § 48.29(2)(g), Florida Statute. Such bond must remain in force and effect during the certification period. The bond shall either be recorded by the Clerk of the Court with a certified copy provided to the AOC or the original bond is to be surrendered to the AOC. The bond shall be renewed on an annual basis unless the bond is for a period greater than 1 year. A certified process server shall at all times have a valid bond in the amount of $5,000.00 or an amount as required by Florida law.

f. Applicants who successfully complete the written examination shall take an oath that he or she will honestly, diligently, and faithfully exercise the duties of a certified process server.

g. The Certified Process Server Examination is strictly confidential and according to Florida Statute 119.07 (3)(a) is exempt from public records. However, anyone taking the examination has the right to review his or her own completed examination. Those interested in reviewing their examination must make a request to the AOC and shall be allowed a total of fifteen (15) minutes to review the examination.

h. An applicant who completes the requirements set forth in Chapter 48 and set forth in this Administrative Order shall be eligible to be placed on the approved list of process servers to serve initial non-enforceable civil process as may be authorized in 48.27, Florida Statute.

2. An approved list of certified process servers for the Fifteenth Judicial Circuit shall be established by the Chief Judge each year. The identification card issued to each certified process server shall be renewed annually, upon proof of good standing and current bond. At the time of renewal, a reasonable renewal fee set by the Chief Judge shall be due from each process server.

3. Certified process servers approved by the Fifteenth Judicial Circuit shall comply with all rules, case law and statutes pertaining to service of process and will be expected to keep up to date with any new provisions within said rules, case law and statutes.

4. In the event any certified process server is the subject of any sanction or penalty with respect to his or her certification to serve process in another circuit, the process server must comply with the following:

a. Promptly report the sanction or penalty to the AOC in writing.

b. Respond to any inquires by the AOC concerning the report.

c. Report in writing that the penalty or sanction has been complied with.

5. In the event of any suspension or revocation of a certified process server's authority to serve process in another circuit, the AOC shall notify the Chief Judge, who may refer the matter to the Certified Civil Process Servers Grievance Committee for review and a report.

6. A certified process server from the approved List of Certified Process Servers eligible to serve process within the Fifteenth Judicial Circuit may be removed from the List for good cause upon a recommendation of the Grievance Committee and approval by the Chief Judge. Good cause shall include, but shall not be limited to malfeasance, misfeasance, neglect of duty or incompetence in connection with the duties of a certified process server.

7. Nothing herein shall limit the power of the Chief Judge to take whatever action the Chief Judge deems appropriate with respect to a sanctioned, suspended or revoked process server without the necessity of referral to the grievance committee.

8. Results of any suspensions or revocation of certificates will be made available by the Administrative Office of the Court.

DONE and **ORDERED** in Chambers at West Palm Beach, Palm Beach County, Florida this 7 day of December, 2011.

Peter D. Blanc
Chief Judge

Adopted effective September 29, 2008. Amended effective December 7, 2011.

* supersedes admin. order 2.701–9/08

2.702. RETURN OF SERVICE FORM

IN THE CIRCUIT COURT OF THE FIFTEENTH JUDICIAL CIRCUIT IN AND FOR PALM BEACH COUNTY, FLORIDA

ADMINISTRATIVE ORDER NO. 2.702—9/08 *

IN RE: RETURN OF SERVICE FORM

Florida Statute section 48.27 allows the Chief Judge to establish an approved list of individuals designated as certified process servers, and these persons are authorized to serve initial nonenforceable civil process within the circuit. Florida Statute section 48.29(6)(b), provides that "return of service shall be made by a certified process server on a form which has been reviewed and approved by the court".

NOW, THEREFORE, pursuant to the authority conferred by Florida Rule of Judicial Administration 2.215, it is **ORDERED** as follows:

1. Certified process servers shall utilize and complete a form captioned "RETURN OF SERVICE", containing the following information:

a. The court, the case number and the caption of the case;

b. The date and time when process was received by the certified process server;

c. The date and time when process was executed;

d. A description narrative of the specific manner of execution;

e. The name and physical description of the person on whom process was executed;

f. If a person was served in a representative capacity, the position occupied by the person;

g. The signature of the certified process server;

h. The printed name and identification number of the certified process server; and

i. A statement that the person serving process is a certified process server, in good standing, in the judicial circuit in which the process was served.

2. A return of service form which contains additional information than required by part "A" above, shall not be invalidated on that basis.

3. The signature of the certified process server need not be notarized, nor does it need to be in affidavit form. Only persons appointed to serve papers in a particular case (i.e., elisors) shall make proof of service by affidavit as required by Rule 1.070 of the Florida Rules of Civil Procedure.

DONE and **SIGNED** in Chambers at West Palm Beach, Palm Beach County, Florida, this 29 day of September, 2008.

Kathleen J. Kroll
Chief Judge

Adopted effective September 29, 2008.

* supersedes admin. order 2.018—8/96

2.703. RECOVERY OF CERTIFIED PROCESS SERVER COSTS

IN THE CIRCUIT COURT OF THE FIFTEENTH JUDICIAL CIRCUIT IN AND FOR PALM BEACH COUNTY, FLORIDA

ADMINISTRATIVE ORDER NO. 2.703–9/08 *

IN RE: RECOVERY OF CERTIFIED PROCESS SERVER COSTS:

The Legislature has enacted sections 48.25–48.31, Florida Statutes (2007) to provide for certified process servers. A party recovering judgment is entitled to recover all legal costs and charges under section 57.041, Florida Statutes (2007).

NOW, THEREFORE, pursuant to the authority conferred by Florida Rule of Judicial Administration 2.215, it is **ORDERED** as follows:

1. A party shall supply proof of the necessity for using a certified process server when applying for an award of the costs of such services in all actions except those proceeding under Florida Statutes Chapter 51, Summary Procedure.

2. Absent submission of appropriate proof in cases proceeding other than under Florida Statutes Chapter 51, a party shall be limited to recovering the cost of process service by the sheriff or other authorized enforcement personnel.

DONE and **SIGNED** in Chambers at West Palm Beach, Palm Beach County, Florida, this 29 day of September, 2008.

Kathleen J. Kroll
Chief Judge

Adopted effective September 29, 2008.

* supersedes admin. order 2.028 9/92

2.704. EXTENSION OF RECIPROCITY TO CERTIFIED PROCESS SERVERS OF THE ELEVENTH JUDICIAL CIRCUIT

IN THE CIRCUIT COURT OF THE FIFTEENTH JUDICIAL CIRCUIT IN AND FOR PALM BEACH COUNTY, FLORIDA

ADMINISTRATIVE ORDER NO. 2.704–12/11 *

IN RE: EXTENSION OF RECIPROCITY TO CERTIFIED PROCESS SERVERS OF THE ELEVENTH JUDICIAL CIRCUIT

The Legislature has enacted the Florida Certified Process Server Act, section 48.25–31, Florida Statutes (2007). The Circuit Courts of the Eleventh and Fifteenth Judicial Circuits (Miami–Dade and Palm Beach Counties) have implemented the Act by creating standards and requirements concerning certification and promulgating lists of certified process servers. Florida Statute section 48.29(4) empowers the chief judge of each circuit to prescribe additional rules and requirements regarding the eligibility of a person to become a certified process server. The Circuit Courts of Dade and Palm Beach Counties have agreed to extend reciprocity to certified process servers in order to promote the efficient administration of justice by allowing for service of process throughout a large section of southeast Florida's urban corridor.

NOW, THEREFORE, pursuant to the authority conferred by Florida Rule of Judicial Administration 2.215, it is **ORDERED** as follows:

1. Reciprocity is extended to certified process servers of the Eleventh Judicial Circuit upon the conditions set forth below.

2. Process servers who are certified in the Eleventh Judicial Circuit (Miami–Dade County) will be certified in the Fifteenth Judicial Circuit (Palm Beach County), without sitting for an examination, upon satisfying the following conditions:

a. Complete the circuit's application form and tender the normal processing fee.

b. Execute a performance bond with a surety company authorized within this County in the amount of Five Thousand Dollars ($5,000.00) as provided in § 48.29(2)(g), Florida Statute. Such bond must remain in force and effect during the certification period. The bond shall either be recorded by the Clerk of the Court with a certified copy provided to the Administrative Office of the Court or the original bond is to be surrendered to the Administrative Office of the Court.

c. Tender a letter or certificate of good standing from the Clerk of the Circuit Court of the Eleventh Judicial Circuit or the Administrative Office of the Court of the Eleventh Judicial Circuit.

d. Complete any required training course.

DONE and **SIGNED** in Chambers at West Palm Beach, Palm Beach County, Florida, this 7 day of December, 2011.

Peter D. Blanc
Chief Judge

Adopted effective September 29, 2008. Amended effective December 7, 2011.

* supersedes admin. order 2.704–9/08

2.705. CERTIFIED PROCESS SERVERS, REMOVAL FOR FAILURE TO RENEW CERTIFICATION OR BOND

IN THE CIRCUIT COURT OF THE FIFTEENTH JUDICIAL CIRCUIT IN AND FOR PALM BEACH COUNTY, FLORIDA

ADMINISTRATIVE ORDER 2.705–9/08 *

IN RE: CERTIFIED PROCESS SERVERS, REMOVAL FOR FAILURE TO RENEW CERTIFICATION OR BOND

Florida Statute § 48.25, The Florida Certified Process Server Act (the "Act"), authorizes the creation of an approved list of certified process servers. The Act requires each certified process server to renew his or her certification and bond on an annual basis.

NOW, THEREFORE, pursuant to the authority conferred by Florida Rule of Judicial Administration 2.215, it is **ORDERED** as follows:

Any person who fails to renew his or her certification and fails to keep his/her bond current, will be removed from the approved list of certified process servers as of the expiration of the bond.

DONE and **SIGNED** in Chambers at West Palm Beach, Palm Beach County, Florida this 29 day of September, 2008.

Kathleen J. Kroll
Chief Judge

Adopted effective September 29, 2008.

* supersedes admin. order 2.021 9/92

2.706. GRIEVANCE REVIEW COMMITTEE

IN THE CIRCUIT COURT OF THE FIFTEENTH JUDICIAL CIRCUIT IN AND FOR PALM BEACH COUNTY, FLORIDA

ADMINISTRATIVE ORDER NO. 2.706–9/08 *

IN RE: GRIEVANCE REVIEW COMMITTEE

Florida Statute section 48.31(1), The Florida Certified Process Server Act, provides that the "[a] certified process server may be removed from the list of certified process servers for any malfeasance, misfeasance, neglect of duty, or incompetence, as provided by court rule". Florida Statute section 48.29 provides that "[t]he chief judge of the circuit may, from time to time by administrative order, prescribe additional rules and requirements regarding the eligibility of a person to become a certified process server or to have his name maintained on the list of certified process servers". The chief judge may receive written complaints alleging malfeasance, misfeasance, neglect of duty or incompetence by certified process servers. The Chief Judge is unable to investigate each of these complaints personally, and a collegial body of volunteer attorneys appointed to sit as a review committee, pursuant to the inherent powers of this Court, could provide a neutral forum for investigating and making recommendations about alleged malfeasance, misfeasance, neglect of duty or incompetence by certified process servers.

NOW, THEREFORE, pursuant to the authority conferred by Florida Rule of Judicial Administration 2.215, it is **ORDERED** as follows:

1. The Chief Judge shall appoint, from time to time, at least three attorneys to serve as voting committee members and two process servers to serve as advisory committee members for addressing process server complaints.

2. These volunteer attorneys shall constitute a grievance review committee to review written complaints about alleged acts of malfeasance, misfeasance, neglect of duty or incompetence by a certified process server for this judicial circuit. The grievance review committee members can seek advisory opinions from the process server(s) appointed by the Chief Judge or the Fifteenth Circuit's General Counsel.

3. The volunteer attorneys, acting as a collegial body, are authorized to conduct fact gathering proceedings, make findings of fact and, as deemed appropriate, make recommendations to the Chief Judge. The volunteer attorneys shall adhere to procedural guidelines set forth in Administrative Order No. 2.707–9/08 (as amended). Any party appearing before them shall have the right to a *de novo* review before the Chief Judge.

4. To the extent granted by law, the volunteer attorneys shall be immune from the subpoena power or otherwise from any requirement to testify concerning power or otherwise from any requirement to testify concerning matters related to or within the course and scope their responsibilities as committee members. No matter which occurs during any hearing or fact finding by the volunteer attorneys shall be admissible in evidence in any subsequent hearing or proceeding.

DONE and **SIGNED** in Chambers at West Palm Beach, Palm Beach County, Florida, this 29 day of September, 2008.

Kathleen J. Kroll
Chief Judge

Adopted effective September 29, 2008.

* supersedes admin. order no. 2.020—7/02

2.707. PROCEDURAL GUIDELINES FOR CERTIFIED PROCESS SERVER GRIEVANCE REVIEW COMMITTEE

IN THE CIRCUIT COURT OF THE FIFTEENTH JUDICIAL CIRCUIT IN AND FOR PALM BEACH COUNTY, FLORIDA

ADMINISTRATIVE ORDER NO. 2.707–12/11 *

IN RE: PROCEDURAL GUIDELINES FOR CERTIFIED CIVIL PROCESS SERVER GRIEVANCE REVIEW COMMITTEE

The Court has promulgated administrative order number 2.706–9/08, authorizing the creation of a grievance review committee to investigate complaints about certified process servers.

NOW, THEREFORE, pursuant to the authority conferred by Florida Rule of Judicial Administration 2.215, it is **ORDERED** as follows:

1. The purpose of these rules is to provide an orderly method for the Certified Civil Process Grievance Review Committee, created pursuant to Administrative Order 2.706, to hear and evaluate disputes concerning the service of civil process and to make the determination required under Section 48.31, Florida Statutes (2011).

2. The Certified Civil Process Grievance Review Committee shall hereinafter be referred to as "Committee."

3. Each convened committee shall consist of two (2) attorneys previously appointed by the Chief Judge to serve as voting committee members and no less than one (1) certified process server previously appointed by the Chief Judge to serve as an advisory committee member to handle the business before the Committee. Administrative matters may be addressed by one attorney committee member.

4. If at any time a Committee member feels that there is a conflict of interest concerning the evaluation of a claim, then the Committee member may excuse himself/herself from further proceedings with regard to the claim by advising the other Committee members of the conflict and taking no further part in the proceedings. The proceeding may be reset in order for another member to be assigned to hear the grievance. Any conflict of interest urged by a party to the proceeding shall be noticed in the final report. In the event that any Committee member previously appointed by the Chief Judge is not available for a meeting to evaluate a complaint, then the Committee, upon the concurrence of two or more members, may request a member of the Florida Bar regularly practicing in the Fifteenth Judicial Circuit to serve as a temporary member of the Committee for the purpose of reviewing the complaint.

5. All complaints by a complainant shall be written. If the complainant verbally contacts any Committee member or the Chief Judge's Office, the complainant shall be advised that the complaint must be put in writing and sent to the **Chief Judge's** office. The complaint shall include the complainant's mailing address.

6. Upon receipt of a written complaint, the Chief Judge will forward the complaint to the Certified Civil Process Program Manager ("Program Manager"). The Program Manager will review the complaint to ensure that it is a matter within the purview of the Committee. If the complaint is not related to a certified process server's alleged misfeasance, malfeasance or neglect of duty, the Program Manager will inform the complainant of such fact. If the complaint does allege misfeasance, malfeasance or neglect of duty, the Program Manager will convene a Committee to review the complaint and take any other action consistent with the committee's duties and obligations.

7. The Program Manager shall mail a Notice of Meeting not less than fifteen days prior to the meeting to the complainant and the affected process server advising them of the time and date of the meeting. The notice shall be signed by the Chief Judge. Service of the notice of the meeting shall be effected by mailing the notice, first class U.S. mail, to the address provided by the process server in his/her application and to the complainant at the address indicated in the written complaint. Any inquiries on scheduling of the meeting shall be directed to the Program Manager.

8. The notice of the meeting shall be on a form to be prescribed by the Committee, and shall be in the nature of an order of referral from the Chief Judge to the Committee for a review under these rules.

9. Other matters which may be referred to the Committee consist of suspensions or revocations of authority to serve process in other circuits/jurisdictions. In addition, the Chief Judge or Program Manager may refer to the Committee any information about an incident involving a process server which is indicative of malfeasance, misfeasance or neglect of duty. In such cases, the Program Manager shall be the complainant and provide the Grievance Committee with information concerning the incident.

11. [1] At its discretion, the Committee may meet periodically and as necessary to handle the grievance complaints and other business before it.

12. The meeting shall commence promptly at the appointed time and place. The place of the meeting shall be at the discretion of the Committee, and may be held anywhere in Palm Beach County.

13. The Committee reserves the right to set meetings before or after regular business hours for the benefit of the Committee members, the certified civil process servers and the public.

14. The Committee's proceedings shall be informal and shall not rely strictly on rules of evidence.

15. In the event either the complainant or the process server does not appear at the appointed time and place for the meeting, then that person's non-appearance shall be noted in the Committee's report, and the Committee will continue the meeting and take evidence from the individuals present and make a recommendation accordingly.

16. The Committee shall advise the participants at the commencement of the meeting that it is not the Committee's position to make any adjudication or to issue or enforce any sanction against either the complainant or the process server. The parties shall further be advised it is not within the scope of the Committee's authority to make any finding or recommendation as to whether any service effected binds the participant to the jurisdiction of the court, requires a response to the paper served, or has any other substantive legal effect. The participants shall be advised that the function of the Committee is simply to make a recommendation as requested by the Chief Judge as to whether the conduct of the process server constitutes malfeasance, misfeasance, neglect of duty or incompetence, as set forth in section 48.31, Florida Statutes (2011).

17. The complainant and the process server are each limited to fifteen minutes for their presentation unless the Committee increases the time limit based upon exceptional circumstances. If there are more than two complainants or two process servers involved, the Committee shall have discretion to otherwise apportion time, and shall advise the participants at the start of the meeting. The fifteen minute time period shall include such time as is reasonably necessary for the Committee to review any documentary, photographic, or other evidence presented by a participant.

18. The Committee will encourage the participants at the meeting to try to reach some mutually acceptable resolution. If such resolution is reached, then it will be recorded in the Committee's report of proceedings. The recommendation of the Committee may consist of a recommendation of no action, a recommendation of a letter of reprimand to the process server, a recommendation of suspension of the circuit court's authority to serve process, a recommendation of a fine, recommendation of a warning to the civil process server, a recommendation of suspension of the civil process server's license, or a recommendation of termination as a civil process server.

19. The function of the Committee is simply to provide a recommendation. The Committee will provide the recommendation to the Chief Judge through a written report.

20. The Committee will advise the complainant and the certified process server at the conclusion of the hearing that they have a right to apply to the Chief Judge for further review of the matter and an independent evaluation of the Committee's recommendation consistent with paragraph 25 below.

21. The Committee's report shall contain a brief summary of the information and documents provided and the conclusions drawn by the Committee. The report shall also contain a statement of recommended disposition, and a brief statement of reasons supporting the recommendation. It is to be emphasized that these are simply recommendations, subject to denovo review by the Chief Judge who shall have final say over disposition of any complaint brought hereunder.

22. The Committee's report shall be final when it has been circulated to the Committee members and each Committee member's approval has been noted on the report.

23. Once the Committee's report is approved by the Committee members, there shall be no opportunity for re-hearing, amendment or modification by the Committee or further proceedings with respect to the claim that was before the Committee. All further business concerning the claim shall be taken before the Chief Judge.

24. The Chief Judge shall review the report of the Committee and enter an Administrative order adopting, modifying or rejecting the Committee's recommendation. The Administrative Order will set forth what, if any, sanctions are to be imposed.

25. If the complainant or the certified process server disagree with the Administrative Order entered by the Chief Judge, the complainant or certified process server may file a written request to the Chief Judge requesting that the Chief Judge modify the Administrative Order, convene a subsequent proceeding, or take such other action as may be deemed appropriate. The written request must be sent by United States Mail within twenty (20) days of the date the Administrative Order was entered. Relief under this provision is discretionary with the Chief Judge.

26. The Committee further adopts and incorporates herein such procedures and standards as are set forth in the Administrative Order (No. 2. 706–9/08) creating the Committee.

25. [2] These rules and procedures may be amended from time to time by either the Chief Judge or by a majority vote of the Committee, subject to approval by the Chief Judge.

DONE and **SIGNED** in Chambers at West Palm Beach, Palm Beach County, Florida, this 7 day of December, 2011.

Peter D. Blanc
Chief Judge

Adopted effective September 29, 2008. Amended effective December 7, 2011.

* supersedes admin, order 2.707–9/08

1 Numbering as provided in original.

2 Numbering as provided in original.

2.708. PROCEDURES FOR REPORTING ARRESTS, CONVICTIONS, SANCTIONS OR PENALTIES IMPOSED ON CERTIFIED PROCESS SERVERS

IN THE CIRCUIT COURT OF THE FIFTEENTH JUDICIAL CIRCUIT IN AND FOR PALM BEACH COUNTY, FLORIDA

ADMINISTRATIVE ORDER NO. 2.708–1/12 *

IN RE: PROCEDURES FOR REPORTING ARRESTS, CONVICTIONS, SANCTIONS OR PENALTIES IMPOSED ON CERTIFIED PROCESS SERVERS

The Florida Legislature has enacted sections 48.25—48.31, Florida Statutes, to provide for certified process servers. The Administrative Office of the Courts of the Fifteenth Judicial Circuit of Florida (hereinafter "AOC") maintains an approved list of individuals who have satisfied the requirements of the statute and other administrative requirements to merit certification as certified process server. Florida Statute § 48.29(4), provides that the Chief Judge of the Circuit may, from time to time by administrative order, prescribe additional rules and requirements regarding the eligibility of a person to become a certified process server or to have his name maintained on the list of certified process servers. Florida Statute § 48.29 (7)(A), provides that a person may qualify as a certified process server and have his or her name entered on the list of more than one Circuit. The Chief Judge/AOC from time to time receives information from other jurisdictions regarding sanctions or penalties imposed on process servers certified in their jurisdiction.

NOW, THEREFORE, pursuant to the authority conferred by Florida Rule of Judicial Administration 2.215, it is **ORDERED** as follows:

1. In the event any certified process server of the Fifteenth Judicial Circuit is arrested or charged with a misdemeanor or felony in any jurisdiction, the process server must promptly report the arrest/charge to the AOC in writing.

2. In the event any certified process server of the Fifteenth Judicial Circuit is the subject of any sanction or penalty with respect to his or her certification to serve process in another circuit, the process server must comply with the following:

a. Promptly report the sanction or penalty to the AOC in writing.

b. Respond to any inquires by the AOC concerning the report.

c. Report in writing that the penalty or sanction has been complied with.

3. In the event of any suspension or revocation of a certified process server's authority to serve process in another circuit, the AOC shall make a report to the Chief Judge, who may refer the matter to the Certified Civil Process Servers Grievance Committee for review and a report. In such case, the AOC shall be the complainant and provide the Grievance Committee with information concerning the suspension or revocation.

4. In the event the Chief Judge or the AOC receives information about an incident which is significantly indicative of malfeasance, misfeasance or neglect of duty by a certified civil process server, the AOC may report the matter to the Chief Judge, who may refer the matter to the Certified Civil Process Server Grievance Committee for review and report. In such a case, the AOC shall be the complainant and provide the Grievance Committee with information concerning the incident.

5. Nothing herein shall limit the power of the Chief Judge to take whatever action he/she deems appropriate without the necessity of referral to Grievance Committee.

DONE and **ORDERED** in Chambers at West Palm Beach, Palm Beach County, Florida, this 11 day of January, 2012.

Peter D. Blanc
Chief Judge

Adopted effective September 29, 2008. Amended effective January 11, 2012.

* supersedes admin. order 2.708–9/08

2.709. PROCESS SERVERS SECTION 48.29(e) GUIDELINES

IN THE CIRCUIT COURT OF THE FIFTEENTH JUDICIAL CIRCUIT IN AND FOR PALM BEACH COUNTY, FLORIDA

ADMINISTRATIVE ORDER NO. 2.709–9/08 *

IN RE: PROCESS SERVERS SECTION 48.29 (e) GUIDELINES

The Fifteenth Judicial Circuit has established a certification program for process servers. A misdemeanor involving "moral turpitude or dishonesty" may invalidate a person's certification or make them ineligible for certification as a process server. Section 48.29 (e), Florida Statutes (2007) does not specifically cite offenses which relate to moral turpitude.

NOW, THEREFORE, pursuant to the authority conferred by Florida Rule of Judicial Administration 2.215, it is **ORDERED** as follows:

Reference shall be made to Addendum I to this Administrative Order for citing specific offenses, which relate to acts of "moral turpitude and dishonesty". Further, Addendum I shall serve as a guideline for purposes of clarifying the interpretation of Section 48.29 (e), Florida Statutes (2007).

DONE and **SIGNED,** in Chambers, at West Palm Beach, Palm Beach County, Florida this 29 day of September, 2008.

Kathleen J. Kroll
Chief Judge

Adopted effective September 29, 2008.

* supersedes admin. order 3.011–8/97

ATTACHMENT

ADDENDUM I

§316.193	Driving under the influence.
§316.1935	Fleeing or attempting to elude police.
§414.39	Fraud; social and economic assistance.
§784.011	Assault.
§784.03	Battery.
§784.048	Stalking; definitions; penalties.
§784.05(2)	Culpable negligence inflicts personal injury.
§790.01(1)	Carrying concealed weapons.
§790.10	Improper exhibition of dangerous weapons or firearms.
§790.27	Alteration or removal of firearm serial number.
§794.027	Duty to report sexual battery; penalties.
§796.07	Prohibiting prostitution, etc.; evidence; penalties; definitions.
§800.02	Unnatural and lascivious act.
§800.03	Exposure of sexual organs.
§806.101	False alarms of fires.
§806.13	Criminal mischief; penalties; penalty for minor.
§810.08	Trespass in structure or conveyance.
§812.014(2)(d)	Theft.
§812.015	Retail & farm theft.
§812.14	Trespass & larceny with relation to utility fixtures.
§817.235	Personal property; removing or altering identification marks.
§817.49	False reports of commission of crimes; penalty.
§817.563	Sale of controlled substance.
§817.565	Urine testing, fraudulent practices; penalties.
827.03(1)(3)	Child abuse.
§831.30	Fraud in obtaining medicinal drugs.

§831.31(1)(b)	Counterfeit controlled substance.
§832.05(2)(4)	Worthless checks, drafts and debit card orders.
§837.012	Perjury.
§837.05	False reports to law enforcement authorities.
§837.06	False official statement.
§839.20	Refusal to execute criminal process.
§843.02	Resisting officer without violence to his person.
§843.06	Neglect or refusal to aid peace officer.
§843.085	Unlawful use of police badges or other indicia of authority.
§847.011(1)(2)	Prohibition of certain acts in connection with obscene, lewd, etc., materials; penalty.
§856.021	Loitering or prowling; penalty.
§870.01	Affrays and riots.
§876.17	Placing burning or flaming cross in public place.
§876.18	Placing burning or flaming cross on property of another.
§893.13(1)(a)(3)	Prohibited acts; penalties.
§914.22(2)	Tampering with a witness, victim, or informant.
§944.35(3)	Malicious battery on inmates.
§944.35(4)(b)	Untruthful report.
§944.36	Permitting inmates to escape.
§944.37	Acceptance of unauthorized compensation; penalty.
§944.38	Acceptance of remuneration from contractor; dealing or barter with prisoners; interest in contract; penalty.
§944.39	Interference with prisoners; penalty.
§944.47	Introduction, removal, or possession of certain articles unlawful, penalty.

Alternative Dispute Resolution

2.801. ALTERNATIVE DISPUTE RESOLUTION OFFICE

IN THE CIRCUIT COURT OF THE FIFTEENTH JUDICIAL CIRCUIT IN AND FOR PALM BEACH COUNTY, FLORIDA

ADMINISTRATIVE ORDER NO. 2.801–9/08 *

IN RE: ALTERNATIVE DISPUTE RESOLUTION OFFICE

Rule 2.215(b)(3), Fla.R.Jud.Admin., mandates the chief judge to "develop an administrative plan for the efficient and proper administration of all courts within [the] circuit". The public policy of this state favors amicable settlement of disputes through mediation and arbitration, thus avoiding litigation, see, e.g., Schnurmacher Holding, Inc. v. Noriega, 542 So.2d 1327 (Fla. 1989). The Fifteenth Judicial Circuit has established a number of alternative dispute resolution programs in furtherance of this public policy and to reduce delay. The establishment of an Alternative Dispute Resolution Office will increase the court's effectiveness and provide for coordination of existing and new programs to foster the amicable settlement of disputes;

NOW, THEREFORE, pursuant to the authority conferred by Florida Rule of Judicial Administration 2.215, it is **ORDERED** as follows:

1. An Alternative Dispute Resolution Office is hereby established for the Fifteenth Judicial Circuit of Florida.

2. The Alternative Dispute Resolution Office shall:

a. Direct and manage the affairs of the circuit's alternative dispute resolution programs.

b. Implement all policies and procedures for the effective administration of the programs.

c. Recommend new and revised policies and procedures.

d. Recommend and draft proposed administrative orders for the chief judge's signature to implement new and revised policies.

e. Develop and administer, in consultation with the court administrator, a budget for the effective administration of the programs.

f. Provide for and coordinate and/or conduct appropriate training of circuit personnel, program contractors, and program volunteers in conformity with state law and applicable court rules.

g. Recommend the establishment of new programs and changes in existing programs to insure coordination and efficiency.

h. Perform other duties as assigned by the chief judge and court administrator.

DONE and **SIGNED** in Chambers at West Palm Beach, Palm Beach County, Florida, this 29 day of September, 2008.

Kathleen J. Kroll
Chief Judge

Adopted effective September 29, 2008.

* supersedes admin. order no. 2.010–10/03

2.802. ARBITRATORS

IN THE CIRCUIT COURT OF THE FIFTEENTH JUDICIAL CIRCUIT IN AND FOR PALM BEACH COUNTY, FLORIDA

ADMINISTRATIVE ORDER NO. 2.802–9/08 *

IN RE: ARBITRATORS

The Florida Legislature has enacted section 44.106, Florida Statutes, to provide for standards and procedures of those persons who are eligible and qualified to serve as arbitrators. Rules 11.010 through 11.130, Fla. R. Arb. establish qualifications and standards of professional conduct for those individuals who are interested in serving as arbitrators. Rule 1.810(a), Fla.R.Civ.P. requires the chief judge to maintain a list of individuals who are determined eligible and qualified to act as arbitrators;

NOW, THEREFORE, pursuant to the authority conferred by Florida Rule of Judicial Administration 2.215, it is **ORDERED** as follows:

1. The Alternative Dispute Resolution Office shall maintain a list of those individuals who have provided evidence that they have met the qualifications set forth in the applicable rules, and have agreed to serve as arbitrators,

2. Those individuals listed with the Alternative Dispute Resolution Office and those added hereafter by addendum, are determined to be eligible and qualified to serve as arbitrators in the Fifteenth Judicial Circuit of Florida with all the power and duties conferred by Chapter 44, Florida Statutes and Rules 1.700, 1.810–1.830, Florida Rules of Civil Procedure.

3. This order shall take effect as of the date hereon and continue until revoked by subsequent order of this Court.

DONE and **SIGNED** in Chambers at West Palm Beach, Palm Beach County, Florida, this 29 day of September 2008.

Kathleen J. Kroll
Chief Judge

Adopted effective September 29, 2008.

* supersedes admin. order no. 3.004–6/04

2.803. COUNTY COURT CIVIL MEDIATION PROGRAM

IN THE CIRCUIT COURT OF THE FIFTEENTH JUDICIAL CIRCUIT IN AND FOR PALM BEACH COUNTY, FLORIDA

ADMINISTRATIVE ORDER NO. 2.803–9/8 *

IN RE: COUNTY COURT CIVIL MEDIATION PROGRAM

The Legislature has enacted sections 44.1011–108, Florida Statutes (2007), permitting court-ordered mediation. The Supreme Court has promulgated the Florida Rules for Certified and Court–Appointed Mediators, setting forth the qualifications for county court mediators. The Fifteenth Judicial Circuit has established an Alternative Dispute Resolution Office to facilitate mediation alternatives to judicial action, see Admin. Order No. 2.801–9/8 (as amended). The Florida Legislature has enacted section 44.108, Florida Statutes (2007), to provide for the collection of fees when court ordered mediation services are provided by the Alternative Dispute Resolution Office;

NOW, THEREFORE, pursuant to the authority conferred by Florida Rule of Judicial Administration 2.215, it is **ORDERED** as follows:

1. A county court civil mediation program is hereby established.

2. The judges of the civil division of the county court are authorized to refer all appropriate cases, with the exception of small claims cases, to the Alternative Dispute Resolution Office.

3. Cases shall be referred to mediation through a uniform court order which, among other things, shall permit the parties to select a mediator. In instances where the parties in a County Court case cannot agree upon the selection of a mediator within ten (10) days of the Order of Referral, the Court shall utilize a certified County Court mediator who is on staff or contracted with the Alternative Dispute Resolution Office.

4. All orders referring county court civil cases to mediation at the Alternative Dispute Resolution Office shall contain a directive requiring the parties to pay to the clerk of court, no later than 10 days prior to the date of the mediation session, the appropriate fees as determined by the clerk of court and defined in section 44.108 Florida Statutes (2007).

5. No mediation sessions will be held for any party who fails to make the required payment herein above set forth.

DONE and **SIGNED** in Chambers at West Palm Beach, Palm Beach County, Florida, this 29 day of September, 2008.

Kathleen J. Kroll
Chief Judge

Adopted effective September 29, 2008.

* supersedes admin. order no. 9.003–6/4

2.804. CIRCUIT COURT CIVIL MEDIATION PROGRAM

IN THE CIRCUIT COURT OF THE FIFTEENTH JUDICIAL CIRCUIT IN AND FOR PALM BEACH COUNTY, FLORIDA

ADMINISTRATIVE ORDER NO. 2.804—9/08 *

IN RE: CIRCUIT COURT CIVIL MEDIATION PROGRAM

Circuit Court mediation has grown into an established industry in the community and it is no longer necessary for the Court to underwrite an office for the support of Circuit Court civil mediation.

NOW, THEREFORE, pursuant to the authority conferred by Florida Rule of Judicial Administration 2.215, it is **ORDERED** as follows:

1. Parties requiring mediation of Circuit Court civil cases are expected to make outside arrangements.

2. Mediation rooms inside the Courthouse will remain available for Circuit Court Civil mediation to accommodate special circumstances, such as security concerns. These rooms can be reserved through the Alternative Dispute Resolution Office by obtaining a court order.

3. Procedures regarding Domestic Relations Mediation can be found in Administrative Order No. 5.208 9/08 (as amended).

DONE and SIGNED in Chambers at West Palm Beach, Palm Beach County, Florida, this 29 day of September, 2008.

Kathleen J. Kroll
Chief Judge

Adopted effective September 29, 2008.

* supersedes admin. order 3.003–10/03

2.805. JUVENILE DEPENDENCY MEDIATION PROGRAM

IN THE CIRCUIT COURT OF THE FIFTEENTH JUDICIAL CIRCUIT IN AND FOR PALM BEACH COUNTY, FLORIDA

ADMINISTRATIVE ORDER NO. 2.805–9/08 *

IN RE: JUVENILE DEPENDENCY MEDIATION PROGRAM

The Fifteenth Judicial Circuit has established a number of Alternative Dispute Resolution Office programs, and has created an Alternative Dispute Resolution Office to provide coordination of existing and new programs to foster amicable settlement of disputes. The legislature has enacted Section 39.4075 of the Florida Statutes dealing with referral of dependency cases to mediation. It is in the best interest of the citizens of the Fifteenth Judicial Circuit to continue the Juvenile Dependency Mediation Pilot Program created in January 2004.

NOW, THEREFORE, pursuant to the authority conferred by Florida Rule of Judicial Administration 2.215, it is **ORDERED** as follows:

1. A Juvenile Dependency Mediation Program is herewith established under the auspices of the Alternative Dispute Resolution Office of the court.

2. A Dependency Mediation Committee is hereby created with members being appointed by the Chief Judge.

3. Procedures for the juvenile mediation program shall be established by the Dependency Mediation Committee and approved by the Chief Judge.

4. All shelter cases shall go to dependency mediation including direct filed cases. Cases may also be referred by juvenile division judges.

5. No fees for the conducting of Juvenile Dependency Mediation shall be collected by the Alternative Dispute Resolution Office.

6. Any agreement executed by all the parties and approved by the court shall become part of the court record.

DONE and **SIGNED** in Chambers at West Palm Beach, Palm Beach County, Florida, this 29 day of September, 2008.

Kathleen J. Kroll
Chief Judge

Adopted effective September 29, 2008.

* supersedes admin. order no. 7.007–6/04

2.806. [VACATED AND SET ASIDE BY ORDER 2.806-3/18, EFFECTIVE MARCH 29, 2018.]

2.807. FUNDING OF MEDIATION AND ARBITRATION

IN THE CIRCUIT COURT OF THE FIFTEENTH JUDICIAL CIRCUIT IN AND FOR PALM BEACH COUNTY, FLORIDA

ADMINISTRATIVE ORDER NO. 2.807–9/08 *

IN RE: FUNDING OF MEDIATION AND ARBITRATION

Pursuant to Administrative Order No. 2.801–9/08 (as amended) the Alternative Dispute Resolution Office has been established for the Fifteenth Judicial Circuit. Pursuant to Florida Statute § 44.102(c), a Family Mediation Program has been established for the Fifteenth Judicial Circuit. The Alternative Dispute Resolution administers the Family Mediation Program. Pursuant to 44.108, when court ordered meditation services are provided by the Circuit's mediation program;

NOW, THEREFORE, pursuant to the authority conferred by Florida Rule of Judicial Administration 2.215, it is **ORDERED** as follows:

1. Upon a finding of indigency by the Clerk or Family Division Judge, mediation fees shall be waived.

2. When utilizing the Court's mediation, the fee is defined in Section 44.108 Florida Statutes.

3. Parties required to pay the mediation fee shall make payment to the Clerk of Court no less than 10 days prior to the mediation date.

4. When appearing for the scheduled mediation, proof of payment or indigency status must be provided prior to proceeding with the mediation.

DONE and SIGNED in Chambers at West Palm Beach, Palm Beach County, Florida, this 29 day of September, 2008.

Kathleen J. Kroll
Chief Judge

Adopted effective September 29, 2008.

* supersedes admin. order no. 5.025–06/04

Civil Orders

Administrative Matters

3.101. CIVIL JURY TRIALS AT BRANCH COURTHOUSES

IN THE CIRCUIT COURT OF THE FIFTEENTH JUDICIAL CIRCUIT IN AND FOR PALM BEACH COUNTY, FLORIDA

ADMINISTRATIVE ORDER NO. 3.101—9/08 *

IN RE: CIVIL JURY TRIALS AT BRANCH COURTHOUSES

The assignment of jury trials at the Fifteenth Judicial Circuit's Main Courthouse continues to be the most efficient use of the Circuit's court facilities, as well as the most convenient assembly point for the jury pool. Intermittently a courtroom becomes temporarily available at a branch courthouse. The regulation of the use of courtrooms is a duty of the chief judge.

NOW, THEREFORE,pursuant to the authority conferred by Florida Rule of Judicial Administration 2.215, it is **ORDERED** as follows:

1. In civil actions, if the presiding judge deems it appropriate and efficient to conduct a jury trial at a branch courthouse (as designated in Administrative Order No. 11.301–9/08), then the judge shall contact the Court Administrator who shall advise the judge of the dates when a courtroom at that facility will be available.

2. On the judge's specific request, the courtroom will be reserved for that judge. If the trial runs beyond the dates reserved, it will be concluded at the Main Courthouse.

3. Jury selection will be conducted at the Main Courthouse.

DONEand **SIGNED** in Chambers in West Palm Beach, Palm Beach County, Florida this day 29 of September, 2008.

Kathleen J. Kroll
Chief Judge

Adopted effective September 29, 2008.

* supersedes admin. order 3.017–1/03

3.102. CASE DISTRIBUTION COUNTY CIVIL

IN THE CIRCUIT COURT OF THE FIFTEENTH JUDICIAL CIRCUIT IN AND FOR PALM BEACH COUNTY, FLORIDA

ADMINISTRATIVE ORDER 3.102–1/19 *

IN RE: CASE DISTRIBUTION COUNTY CIVIL

County Court Civil cases are assigned to the Central, North, South, and West County Courthouses and a fair and equitable distribution of the caseload is required.

NOW, THEREFORE, pursuant to the authority conferred by Florida Rule of Judicial Administration 2.215, it is **ORDERED** as follows:

All County Court–Civil Division cases, excluding civil infractions that are assigned to a Traffic Hearing Officer, shall be filed and assigned pursuant to the zip code designations provided below:

A. Courthouse Location.

1. *West County Courthouse.* 2950 State Road 15, Belle Glade, Florida 33430, shall be assigned all civil cases within zip code(s):

Belle Glade	33430
Canal Point	33438
Bryant	33439
Clewiston	33440
Wellington	33414
Wellington	33449
Lake Harbor	33459
Pahokee	33476
Pelican Lake	33491
South Bay	33493
Loxahatchee	33470

2. *North County Courthouse.* 3188 PGA Blvd., Palm Beach Gardens, Florida 33418, shall be assigned all civil cases within zip code(s):

Jupiter	33458
Jupiter	33468
Jupiter	33477
Jupiter	33478
Lake Park	33403
North Palm Beach	33408
Palm Beach Gardens	33418
Tequesta Inlet	33469
West Palm Beach	33410
West Palm Beach	33412
West Palm Beach	33419
West Palm Beach	33420

3. *South County Courthouse.* 200 W. Atlantic Ave. Delray Beach, Florida 33444, shall be assigned all civil cases within zip code(s):

Boca Raton	33427
Boca Raton	33428
Boca Raton	33429
Boca Raton	33431
Boca Raton	33432
Boca Raton	33433
Boca Raton	33434
Boca Raton	33486
Boca Raton	33487
Boca Raton	33496
Boca Raton	33498
Boca Raton	33499
Boca Raton	33481
Boca Raton	33488
Boca Raton	33497
Delray Beach	33446
Delray Beach	33447
Delray Beach	33483
Delray Beach	33484
Delray Beach	33444
Delray Beach	33445
Delray Beach	33448
Delray Beach	33482
Boynton Beach	33424
Boynton Beach	33425
Boynton Beach	33426
Boynton Beach	33435
Boynton Beach	33436
Boynton Beach	33437
Boynton Beach	33472
Boynton Beach	33473
Boynton Beach	33474
Lake Worth	33463
Lake Worth	33467
Manalapan	33462
Palm Springs	33461
Tampa	33687

4. *Central Courthouse (Main).* 205 North Dixie Hwy. West Palm Beach, Florida 33401, shall be assigned all civil cases within zip code(s):

West Palm Beach	33401
West Palm Beach	33402
West Palm Beach	33404
West Palm Beach	33405
West Palm Beach	33406
West Palm Beach	33407
West Palm Beach	33409
West Palm Beach	33411
West Palm Beach	33413
West Palm Beach	33415
West Palm Beach	33416

West Palm Beach	33417
West Palm Beach	33421
West Palm Beach	33422
West Palm Beach	33423
Lake Worth	33454
Lake Worth	33460
Lake Worth	33464
Lake Worth	33465
Lake Worth	33466
Palm Beach	33480
South Palm Beach	33480

B. Special Instructions.

CASE TYPE ASSIGNMENTS

1. All evictions cases shall be filed based upon the zip code of the premises subject to eviction.

2. All other county court civil types shall be filed based upon zip code of the plaintiff unless represented by counsel, in which case, the business address of counsel will be substituted.

3. All other county court civil cases filed with zip codes other than those specified in Section I of this order shall be assigned to the Central Courthouse.

4. All county court civil cases filed absent a zip code shall be assigned to the Central Courthouse.

5. The Clerk of Court shall program its computer system to ensure all Central County Court Civil Divisions (RE, RE, RP, RJ, and RL) are assigned all categories of case type (small claims –00, evictions–01, standard civil–02, replevin–28, non-monetary actions–29 and replevin–30).

6. Animal abuse cases filed pursuant to Florida Statutes Section 828.073 shall be initially assigned by computer system and then reassigned by the Clerk's office to ensure equitable distribution of this case type across all appropriate divisions.

DONE and **SIGNED** in Chambers, at West Palm Beach, Palm Beach County, Florida this 11 day of January, 2019.

Krista Marx
Chief Judge

Adopted effective September 29, 2008. Amended effective November 1, 2010; January 8, 2013; March 1, 2016; September 21, 2016; January 11, 2019.

* supersedes admin, order no. 3.102–09/16

3.103. [VACATED AND SET ASIDE BY ORDER 3.103-1/13, EFFECTIVE JANUARY 8, 2013.]

3.104. TRANSFER OF CIVIL CASES FROM COUNTY COURT TO CIRCUIT COURT

IN THE CIRCUIT COURT OF THE FIFTEENTH JUDICIAL CIRCUIT IN AND FOR PALM BEACH COUNTY, FLORIDA.

ADMINISTRATIVE ORDER NO. 3.104–6/09 *

IN RE: TRANSFER OF CIVIL CASES FROM COUNTY COURT TO CIRCUIT COURT

Amended claims, counter claims, cross claims and third party claims filed in county court matters may necessitate the transfer of the original county court claim to circuit court.

NOW, THEREFORE, pursuant to the authority conferred by Florida Rule of Judicial Administration 2.215, it is **ORDERED** as follows:

1. When an amended claim, counter claim, cross claim or third party claim filed in a county court case is within the jurisdiction of the circuit court, the county court judge may determine that, for judicial economy, the matter remain before the county court judge.

2. If the matter remains before the county court judge, the judge shall have all the jurisdiction and powers of a circuit judge of the Fifteenth Judicial Circuit of Florida to resolve the case.

3. A uniform order of transfer, a copy of which is attached hereto as Exhibit "A", shall be used by the affected county court judge.

DONE and **SIGNED** in Chambers at West Palm Beach, Palm Beach County, Florida, this 29 day of June, 2009.

Kathleen J. Kroll
Chief Judge

* supersedes admin. order no. 3.104–9/08

"EXHIBIT A"

IN THE COUNTY COURT IN AND FOR PALM BEACH COUNTY, FLORIDA

CASE NO.

v.

________________:

ORDER ON MOTION TO TRANSFER CAUSE TO CIRCUIT COURT

THIS CAUSE was considered upon Motion to Transfer Cause to Circuit Court, and it appearing that an amended claim, counterclaim, crossclaim or third party claim was filed, which claim exceeds the jurisdiction of the county court, and it further appearing that there exists an administrative order controlling this situation authorizing the assigned county judge circuit court jurisdiction, it is,

ORDERED and **ADJUDGED** as follows:

1. This cause is hereby transferred to circuit court upon payment of the required fee. A circuit court case number will thereupon be assigned.

2. If the moving party has not paid the transfer fee within thirty days of the filing of this order, then this order shall be vacated automatically and the moving party's pleadings shall be deemed to seek relief not exceeding jurisdiction of county court.

3. (check one)

___The **undersigned** County Court Judge, **or this division's successor judge,** shall serve as the presiding circuit judge until the case is resolved. The Clerk shall designate the **circuit** case number in the following format: Case No. 01–1234 A( ), PENDING IN COUNTY COURT DIVISION R( ), and all counsel shall so designate all pleadings hereafter. **If, thereafter, the case needs to be randomly reassigned,**

the reassignment shall be to the circuit civil division assigned when the circuit case number was obtained.

___The undersigned County Court Judge declines to hear the matter as an Acting Circuit Judge and the Clerk is directed to randomly assign the matter to a Circuit Judge.

DONE and **SIGNED** in Chambers at West Palm Beach, Florida, this ___ day of __________, 20 ___.

____
County Court/Acting Circuit Judge

Adopted effective September 29, 2008. Amended effective June 29, 2009.

3.105. [VACATED AND SET ASIDE BY ORDER 3.105-1/13, EFFECTIVE JANUARY 8, 2013.]

3.106. CORRECTING SCRIVENER'S ERRORS IN CIRCUIT AND COUNTY CIVIL CASES

IN THE CIRCUIT COURT OF THE FIFTEENTH JUDICIAL CIRCUIT IN AND FOR PALM BEACH COUNTY

ADMINISTRATIVE ORDER 3.106—11/14

IN RE: CORRECTING SCRIVENER'S ERRORS IN CIRCUIT AND COUNTY CIVIL CASES

Tanner v. State, 744 So.2d 101722 (Fla. 4th DCA 1997) finds that the Clerk of Court may not refuse to accept documents which contain scrivener's errors in the caption. To ensure accurate court records and the timely administration of justice, corrections to scrivener errors must be addressed.

NOW, THEREFORE, pursuant to the authority conferred by Florida Rule of Judicial Administration 2.215, it is **ORDERED** as follows:

The Clerk and Comptroller's Office shall correct scrivener errors in the caption or case number of a civil court filing so that the filing can be docketed in the correct court file.

DONE and **ORDERED,** in Chambers, at West Palm Beach, Palm Beach County, Florida this 19 day of November, 2014.

Jeffrey Colbath
Chief Judge

Adopted effective November 19, 2014.

Circuit Civil – Pretrial and Trial

3.201. UNIFORM MOTION CALENDAR PRACTICE

IN THE CIRCUIT COURT OF THE FIFTEENTH JUDICIAL CIRCUIT IN AND FOR PALM BEACH COUNTY, FLORIDA

ADMINISTRATIVE ORDER NO. 3.201–2/18 *

IN RE: UNIFORM MOTION CALENDAR PRACTICE

________________________________:

The Circuit Civil Judges, in accordance with Local Rule No. 4, have determined that two options be available for Uniform Motion Practice

NOW, THEREFORE, pursuant to the authority conferred by Florida Rule of Judicial Administration 2.215, it is **ORDERED** as follows:

1. The Circuit Civil Division Uniform Motion Calendar will be held either from:

a. 8:45 a.m.—9:30 a.m. Monday through Thursday; or

b. 8:30 a.m.—9:30 a.m. Tuesday through Thursday.

2. The divisional web page will list the judge's UMC schedule.

DONE and **ORDERED** in Chambers at West Palm Beach, Palm Beach County, Florida this 23 day of February, 2018.

Krista Marx
Chief Judge

Adopted effective September 29, 2008. Amended effective February 23, 2018.

* supersedes administrative order 3.201–9/08

3.202. MOTIONS TO COMPEL DISCOVERY

IN THE CIRCUIT COURT OF THE FIFTEENTH JUDICIAL CIRCUIT IN AND FOR PALM BEACH COUNTY, FLORIDA

ADMINISTRATIVE ORDER NO. 3.202–9/08 *

IN RE: MOTIONS TO COMPEL DISCOVERY

1. No motions to compel discovery will be heard unless the motion or notice of hearing bears a certificate of moving counsel to the effect that he or she contacted opposing counsel and attempted to resolve the discovery dispute without a hearing, but that the matter could not be resolved.

2. When a motion to compel discovery alleges a complete failure to respond or object to discovery, and that there has been no request for extension, an ex parte order may be entered by the court requiring compliance with the original discovery demand within 10 days of the signing of the order. The movant shall submit the proposed order and addressed, stamped envelopes for the court's consideration.

DONE and ORDERED in Chambers at West Palm Beach, Florida, this 29 day of September, 2008.

Kathleen J. Kroll
Chief Judge

Adopted effective September 29, 2008.

* supersedes admin. order 3.010–2/97

3.203. UNIFORM PRETRIAL PROCEDURES IN CIVIL ACTIONS

IN THE CIRCUIT COURT OF THE FIFTEENTH JUDICIAL CIRCUIT IN AND FOR PALM BEACH COUNTY, FLORIDA

ADMINISTRATIVE ORDER NO. 3.203–9/08 *

IN RE: UNIFORM PRETRIAL PROCEDURES IN CIVIL ACTIONS

Pursuant to the authority conferred by Florida Rule of Judicial Administration 2.215, it is **ORDERED** as follows:

Pursuant to Rule 1.200, Florida Rules of Civil Procedure and Rule 2.545, Rules of Judicial Administration, the attached orders (except for the time deadlines) shall constitute the uniform pretrial orders for circuit court civil actions. Time deadlines may vary in the orders.

DONE and **ORDERED** in Chambers at West Palm Beach, Palm Beach County, Florida, this 29 day of September, 2008.

Kathleen J. Kroll
Chief Judge

Adopted effective September 29, 2008.

* supersedes admin. order no. 3.001–6/05

ATTACHMENT 1

IN THE FIFTEENTH JUDICIAL CIRCUIT IN AND FOR PALM BEACH COUNTY, FLORIDA

CASE NO.

Plaintiff,

vs.

Defendant.

________________________/

ORDER SETTING JURY TRIAL AND DIRECTING PRETRIAL AND MEDIATION PROCEDURES

I. SCHEDULING

This action is set for jury trial on the calendar beginning ________ at 9:45 o'clock a.m. **YOU MUST APPEAR AT 9:00 O'CLOCK A.M. ON FRIDAY, , IN COURTROOM ___, PALM BEACH COUNTY COURTHOUSE, 205 NORTH DIXIE HIGHWAY, WEST PALM BEACH, FLORIDA FOR THE JURY CALENDAR CALL.** (___ days reserved).

The trial will be scheduled sometime during the calendar beginning ________, at a date and time to be provided at the calendar call, subject to the court's ordering a later case setting.

II. UNIFORM PRETRIAL PROCEDURE

A. On the last business day no later than **120 DAYS PRIOR TO CALENDAR CALL**, the parties shall exchange lists of all trial exhibits, names and addresses of all trial witnesses, and names and addresses of all expert witnesses.

B. On the last business day no later than **60 DAYS PRIOR TO CALENDAR CALL**, the parties shall exchange lists of names and addresses of all rebuttal witnesses.

C. In addition to names and addresses of each expert retained to formulate an expert opinion with regard to this cause, both on the initial listing and on rebuttal, the parties shall provide:

1. the subject matter about which the expert is expected to testify;

2. the substance of the facts and opinions to which the expert is expected to testify;

3. a summary of the grounds for each opinion;

4. a copy of any written reports issued by the expert regarding this case; and

5. a copy of the expert's curriculum vitae.

D. On the last business day no later than **30 DAYS PRIOR TO CALENDAR CALL**, the parties shall confer and:

1. discuss settlement;

2. simplify the issues and stipulate, in writing, as to as many facts and issues as possible;

3. prepare a Pre–Trial Stipulation in accordance with paragraph E; and

4. list all objections to trial exhibits.

E. PRETRIAL STIPULATIONS MUST BE FILED. It shall be the duty of counsel for the Plaintiff to see that the Pre–Trial Stipulation is drawn, executed by counsel for all parties, and filed with the Clerk no later than **20 DAYS PRIOR TO CALENDAR CALL**. UNILATERAL PRE-TRIAL STATEMENTS ARE DISALLOWED, UNLESS APPROVED BY THE COURT, AFTER NOTICE AND HEARING SHOWING GOOD CAUSE. Counsel for all parties are charged with good faith cooperation in this regard. The Pre–Trial Stipulation shall contain in separately numbered paragraphs:

1. a list of all pending motions including MOTIONS IN LIMINE and FRYE MOTIONS requiring action by the Court and the dates those motions are set for hearing (MOTIONS IN LIMINE and FRYE HEARINGS shall not be heard the day of trial or thereafter.)

2. stipulated facts which require no proof at trial which may be read to the trier of fact;

3. a statement of all issues of fact for determination at trial;

4. each party's numbered list of trial exhibits with specific objections, if any, to schedules attached to the Stipulation;

5. each party's numbered list of trial witnesses with addresses (including all known rebuttal witnesses); the list of witnesses shall be on separate schedules attached to the Stipulation;

6. a statement of estimated trial time;

7. names of attorneys to try case; and

8. number of peremptory challenges per party.

F. FILING OF PRE–TRIAL STIPULATION. Failure to file the Pre–Trial Stipulation or a Court Approved Unilateral Stipulation as above provided may result in the case being stricken from the Court's calendar at its sounding or other sanctions.

G. ADDITIONAL EXHIBITS, WITNESSES OR OBJECTIONS. At trial, the parties shall be strictly limited to exhibits and witnesses disclosed and objections reserved on the schedules attached to the Pre–Trial Stipulation prepared in accordance with paragraphs D and E, absent agreement specifically stated in the Pre–Trial Stipulation or order of the Court upon good cause shown. Failure to reserve objections constitutes a waiver. A party desiring to use an exhibit or witness discovered after counsel have conferred pursuant to paragraph D shall immediately furnish the Court and other counsel with a description of the exhibit or with the witness' name and address and the expected subject matter of the witness' testimony, together with the reason for the late discovery of the exhibit or witness. Use of the exhibit or witness may be allowed by the Court for good cause shown or to prevent manifest injustice.

H. DISCOVERY. Unless otherwise agreed in the Pre–Trial Stipulation, all discovery must be completed no later than **10 DAYS BEFORE THE DATE SET FOR CALENDAR CALL**, absent agreement for later discovery specifically stated in the Pre–Trial Stipulation or for other good cause shown.

I. PRE–TRIAL CONFERENCE. No pre-trial conference pursuant to Fla. R. Civ. P. 1.200 is set by the Court on its own motion. If a pre-trial conference is set upon motion of a party, counsel shall meet and prepare a stipulation pursuant to paragraphs D and E and file the stipulation no later than **5 DAYS BEFORE THE CONFERENCE**. Failure to request a pre-trial conference in a timely fashion constitutes a waiver of the notice of requirement of Rule 1.200. Motions for Summary Judgment will not be heard at any pre-trial conference.

J. UNIQUE QUESTIONS OF LAW. Prior to calendar call, counsel for the parties are directed to exchange and simultaneously submit to the Court appropriate memoranda with citations to legal authority in support of any unique legal questions which may reasonably be anticipated to arise during the trial.

K. MODIFICATION TO UNIFORM PRE–TRIAL PROCEDURE. Upon written stipulation of the parties filed with the court, the Pre–Trial Procedure, except for items II D–F, inclusive, may be modified in accordance with the parties' stipulation, except to the extent that the stipulation may interfere with the Court's scheduling of the matter for trial or hinder the orderly progress of the trial.

L. PREMARKING EXHIBITS. Prior to trial, each party shall meet with and assist the clerk in marking for identification all exhibits, as directed by the clerk.

M. DEPOSITION DESIGNATIONS. No later than **20 DAYS PRIOR TO CALENDAR CALL**, each party shall serve his, her, or its designation of depositions, or portions of depositions, each intends to offer as testimony in his, her or its case in chief. No later than **10 DAYS PRIOR TO CALENDAR CALL**, each opposing party shall serve his, her, or its counter (or "fairness") designations to portions of depositions designated, together with objections to the depositions, or portions thereof, originally designated. No later than calendar call, each party shall serve his, her or its objections to counter designations served by an opposing party.

III. MEDIATION

A. All parties are required to participate in mediation.

1. The appearance of counsel who will try the case and representatives of each party with full authority to enter into a complete compromise and settlement is mandatory. If insurance is involved, an adjuster with authority up to the policy limits or the most recent demand, whichever is lower, shall attend.

2. At least **ONE WEEK BEFORE THE CONFERENCE**, all parties shall file with the mediator a brief, written summary of the case containing a list of issues as to each party. If an attorney or party filing the summary wishes its content to remain confidential, he/she must advise the mediator in writing when the report is filed.

3. All discussions, representations, and statements made at the mediation conference shall be privileged consistent with Florida Statutes sections 44.102 and 90.408.

4. The mediator has no power to compel or enforce a settlement agreement. If a settlement is reached, it shall be the responsibility of the attorneys or parties to reduce the agreement to writing and to comply with Florida Rule of Civil Procedure 1.730(b), unless waived.

B. The Plaintiff's attorney shall be responsible for scheduling mediation. The parties should agree on a mediator. If they are unable to agree, any party may apply to the Court for appointment of a mediator in conformity with Rule 1.720 (f), Fla. R. Civ. P. The lead attorney or party shall file and serve on all parties and the mediator a Notice of Mediation giving the time, place, and date of the mediation and the mediator's name. The mediator shall be paid $175.00 per hour, unless otherwise agreed by the parties.

C. Completion of mediation is a prerequisite to trial. If mediation is not conducted, or if a party fails to participate in mediation, the case may be stricken from the trial calendar, pleadings may be stricken, and other sanctions may be imposed.

D. Any party opposing mediation may proceed under Florida Rule of Civil Procedure 1,700(b).

IV. NONCOMPLIANCE

NONCOMPLIANCE WITH ANY PORTION OF THIS ORDER MAY RESULT IN THE STRIKING OF THE CASE, WITNESSES, OR EXHIBITS, OR IMPOSITION OF SUCH OTHER SANCTIONS AS ARE JUST.

DONE AND ORDERED in West Palm Beach, Palm Beach County, Florida this ___ day of __________, 2005.

____

Circuit Court Judge

ATTACHMENT 2

IN THE FIFTEENTH JUDICIAL CIRCUIT IN AND FOR PALM BEACH COUNTY, FLORIDA

CASE NO.

Plaintiff,

vs.

Defendant.

______________________/

ORDER SETTING NON–JURY TRIAL AND DIRECTING PRETRIAL AND MEDIATION PROCEDURES

I. SCHEDULING

This action is set for non-jury trial on the calendar beginning __________ at 9:45 o'clock a.m. **YOU MUST APPEAR AT 10:00 O'CLOCK A.M. ON FRIDAY, , IN COURTROOM ___, PALM BEACH COUNTY COURTHOUSE, 205 NORTH DIXIE HIGHWAY, WEST PALM BEACH, FLORIDA FOR THE NON–JURY CALENDAR CALL.** (__________ days reserved).

The trial will be scheduled sometime during the calendar beginning ________, at a date and time to be provided at the calendar call, subject to the court's ordering a later case setting.

II. UNIFORM PRETRIAL PROCEDURE

A. On the last business day no later than **60 DAYS PRIOR TO CALENDAR CALL**, the parties shall exchange lists of all trial exhibits, names and addresses of all trial witnesses, and names and addresses of all expert witnesses.

B. On the last business day no later than **30 DAYS PRIOR TO CALENDAR CALL**, the parties shall exchange lists of names and addresses of all rebuttal witnesses.

C. In addition to names and addresses of each expert retained to formulate an expert opinion with regard to this cause, both on the initial listing and on rebuttal, the parties shall provide:

1. the subject matter about which the expert is expected to testify;

2. the substance of the facts and opinions to which the expert is expected to testify;

3. a summary of the grounds for each opinion;

4. a copy of any written reports issued by the expert regarding this case; and

5. a copy of the expert's curriculum vitae.

D. On the last business day no later than **20 DAYS PRIOR TO CALENDAR CALL**, the parties shall confer and:

1. discuss settlement;

2. simplify the issues and stipulate, in writing, as to as many facts and issues as possible;

3. prepare a Pre–Trial Stipulation in accordance with paragraph E; and

4. list all objections to trial exhibits.

E. PRETRIAL STIPULATIONS MUST BE FILED. It shall be the duty of counsel for the Plaintiff to see that the Pre–Trial Stipulation is drawn, executed by counsel for all parties, and filed with the Clerk no later than **20 DAYS PRIOR TO CALENDAR CALL**. UNILATERAL PRE-TRIAL STATEMENTS ARE DISALLOWED, UNLESS APPROVED BY THE COURT, AFTER NOTICE AND HEARING SHOWING GOOD CAUSE. Counsel for all parties are charged with good faith cooperation in this regard. The Pre–Trial Stipulation shall contain in separately numbered paragraphs:

1. a list of all pending motions requiring action by the Court and the dates those motions are set for hearing;

2. stipulated facts which require no proof at trial which may be read to the trier of fact;

3. a statement of all issues of fact for determination at trial;

4. each party's numbered list of trial exhibits with specific objections, if any, to schedules attached to the Stipulation;

5. each party's numbered list of trial witnesses with addresses (including all known rebuttal witnesses); the list of witnesses shall be on separate schedules attached to the Stipulation;

6. a statement of estimated trial time;

7. names of attorneys to try case.

F. FILING OF PRE–TRIAL STIPULATION. Failure to file the Pre–Trial Stipulation or a Court Approved Unilateral Stipulation as above provided may result in the case being stricken from the Court's calendar at its sounding or other sanctions.

G. ADDITIONAL EXHIBITS, WITNESSES OR OBJECTIONS. At trial, the parties shall be strictly limited to exhibits and witnesses disclosed and objections reserved on the schedules attached to the Pre–Trial Stipulation prepared in accordance with paragraphs D and E, absent agreement specifically stated in the Pre–Trial Stipulation or order of the Court upon good cause shown. Failure to reserve objections constitutes a waiver. A party desiring to use an exhibit or witness discovered after counsel have conferred pursuant to paragraph D shall immediately furnish the Court and other counsel with a description of the exhibit or with the witness' name and address and the expected subject matter of the witness' testimony, together with the reason for the late discovery of the exhibit or witness. Use of the exhibit or witness may be allowed by the Court for good cause shown or to prevent manifest injustice.

H. DISCOVERY. Unless otherwise agreed in the Pre–Trial Stipulation, all discovery must be completed no later than **10 DAYS BEFORE THE DATE SET FOR CALENDAR CALL**, absent agreement for later discovery specifically stated in the Pre–Trial Stipulation or for other good cause shown.

I. PRE–TRIAL CONFERENCE. No pre-trial conference pursuant to Fla. R. Civ. P. 1.200 is set by the Court on its own motion. If a pre-trial conference is set upon motion of a party, counsel shall meet and prepare a stipulation pursuant to paragraphs D and E and file the stipulation no later than **5 DAYS BEFORE THE CONFERENCE**. Failure to request a pre-trial conference in a timely fashion constitutes a waiver of the notice of requirement of Rule 1.200. Motions for Summary Judgment will not be heard at any pre-trial conference.

J. UNIQUE QUESTIONS OF LAW. On the date of trial, counsel for the parties are directed to submit to the Court appropriate memoranda with citations to legal authority in support of any unique legal questions which may reasonably be anticipated to arise during the trial.

K. MODIFICATION TO UNIFORM PRE–TRIAL PROCEDURE. Upon written stipulation of the parties filed with the Court, the Pre–Trial Procedure, except for items II D–F, inclusive, may be modified in accordance with the parties' stipulation, except to the extent that the stipulation may interfere with the Court's scheduling of the matter for trial or hinder the orderly progress of the trial.

L. PREMARKING EXHIBITS. Parties shall pre-mark all exhibits in the manner customarily used by the Clerk of Court.

M. DEPOSITION DESIGNATIONS. No later than **20 DAYS PRIOR TO CALENDAR CALL**, each party shall serve his, her, or its designation of depositions, or portions of depositions, each intends to offer as testimony in his, her or its case in chief. No later than **10 DAYS PRIOR TO CALENDAR CALL**, each opposing party shall serve his, her, or its counter (or "fairness") designations to portions of depositions designated, together with objections to the depositions, or portions thereof, originally designated. No later than calendar call, each party shall serve his, her or its objections to counter designations served by an opposing party.

III. MEDIATION

A. All parties are required to participate in mediation.

1. The appearance of counsel who will try the case and representatives of each party with full authority to enter into a complete compromise and settlement is mandatory. If insurance is involved, an adjuster with authority up to the policy limits or the most recent demand, whichever is lower, shall attend.

2. At least **ONE WEEK BEFORE THE CONFERENCE**, all parties shall file with the mediator a brief, written summary of the case containing a list of issues as to each party. If an attorney or party filing the summary wishes its content to remain confidential, he/she must advise the mediator in writing when the report is filed.

3. All discussions, representations, and statements made at the mediation conference shall be privileged consistent with Florida Statutes sections 44.102 and 90.408.

4. The mediator has no power to compel or enforce a settlement agreement. If a settlement is reached, it shall be the responsibility of the attorneys or parties to reduce the agreement to writing and to comply with Florida Rule of Civil Procedure 1.730(b), unless waived.

B. The Plaintiff's attorney shall be responsible for scheduling mediation. The parties should agree on a mediator. If they are unable to agree, any party may apply to the Court for appointment of a mediator in conformity with Rule 1.720 (f), Fla. R. Civ. P. The lead attorney or party shall file and serve on all parties and the mediator a Notice of Mediation giving the time, place, and date of the mediation and the mediator's name. The mediator shall be paid $175.00 per hour, unless otherwise agreed by the parties.

C. Completion of mediation is a prerequisite to trial. If mediation is not conducted, or if a party fails to participate in mediation, the case may be stricken from the trial calendar, pleadings may be stricken, and other sanctions may be imposed.

D. Any party opposing mediation may proceed under Florida Rule of Civil Procedure 1,700(b).

IV. NONCOMPLIANCE

NONCOMPLIANCE WITH ANY PORTION OF THIS ORDER MAY RESULT IN THE STRIKING OF THE CASE, WITNESSES, OR EXHIBITS, OR IMPOSITION OF SUCH OTHER SANCTIONS AS ARE JUST.

DONE AND ORDERED in West Palm Beach, Palm Beach County, Florida this ___ day of ________, 2005.

____
Circuit Court Judge

3.204. PREPARATION OF JUDGMENTS AND ORDERS

IN THE CIRCUIT COURT OF THE FIFTEENTH JUDICIAL CIRCUIT IN AND FOR PALM BEACH COUNTY, FLORIDA

ADMINISTRATIVE ORDER NO. 3.204–9/08 *

IN RE: PREPARATION OF JUDGMENTS AND ORDERS

1. When instructed by the court to prepare an order or judgment, counsel shall submit the proposed order or judgment within 10 working days. A copy of the proposed order or judgment shall be mailed, delivered, "faxed", or read telephonically to opposing counsel at least one day prior to submission to the court. If designated counsel fails to submit a proposed order within 10 days, opposing counsel shall notify the judge's judicial assistant in writing.

2. Objections to proposed orders or judgments: Should opposing counsel object to a proposed order or judgment prepared by designated counsel, opposing counsel shall notify the judge's judicial assistant immediately by telephone, and submit an alternate within 5 days.

3. Copies and envelopes: Counsel preparing the proposed order or judgment shall furnish the court with sufficient copies and stamped, addressed envelopes for service on the opposing parties.

4. The title of every order or judgment submitted shall contain the subject matter pursuant to rule 1.100, Fla.R.Civ.P. The submission of an order or judgment to a judge shall constitute a representation that the attorney has read it, and that it accurately sets forth the findings and decision of the court.

5. Signature page: No order or judgment shall contain a signature page that does not include a portion of the text of the order or judgment.

DONE and **SIGNED** in Chambers at West Palm Beach, Palm Beach County, Florida, this 29 day of September, 2008.

Kathleen J. Kroll
Chief Judge

Adopted effective September 29, 2008.

* supersedes admin. order 3.009–6/96

3.205. CLOSURE OF FILES

IN THE CIRCUIT COURT OF THE FIFTEENTH JUDICIAL CIRCUIT IN AND FOR PALM BEACH COUNTY, FLORIDA

ADMINISTRATIVE ORDER NO. 3.205–9/08 *

IN RE: CLOSURE OF FILES

It is imperative for the court to have an accurate and meaningful count of the numbers and types of actions pending. The clerk of court has experienced difficulty in interpreting court orders and judgments to determine when a case should be closed for statistical purposes. This problem is particularly acute in the civil division due to multiple parties, counterclaims, cross claims and third-party claims.

NOW, THEREFORE, pursuant to the authority conferred by Florida Rule of Judicial Administration 2.215, it is **ORDERED** as follows:

1. When the presiding judge of a pending civil action desires that a particular order or judgment close the case, for statistical purposes only, then the judge shall place a BLUE–COLORED "CLOSED" designation under the case number in the caption of the judgment or order. Any such "CLOSED"

designation shall be made only in accordance with the Florida Supreme Court Summary Reporting System ("SRS") Guidelines.

2. Upon receipt of an order or judgment bearing the blue "CLOSED" designation, the clerk shall close out the case for statistical purposes and shall denote in accordance with established SRS procedure the basis upon which the case has been closed. If the clerk cannot immediately determine from the judgment or order the basis upon which the judge has relied upon in designating the case as "CLOSED," the clerk shall return it to the judge with a request that the judge specify one of the following reasons for disposition:

Cases Disposed

Before Hearing	___
After Hearing	___
By Default	___
By Judge	___
Non–Jury Trial	___
Jury Trial	___
Other	___

2.[1] This administrative order shall have no effect on the rights, duties, or obligations of the parties in the litigation.

DONE and **SIGNED** in Chambers at West Palm Beach, Palm Beach County, Florida, this 29 day of September 2008.

Kathleen J. Kroll
Chief Judge

Adopted effective September 29, 2008.

* supersedes admin. order no. 3.002–6/99

[1] So in original, two para. 2.

3.206. EMERGENCY HEARINGS IN CIRCUIT CIVIL MATTERS

IN THE CIRCUIT COURT OF THE FIFTEENTH JUDICIAL CIRCUIT IN AND FOR PALM BEACH COUNTY, FLORIDA

ADMINISTRATIVE ORDER NO. 3.206–1/09

IN RE: EMERGENCY HEARINGS IN CIRCUIT CIVIL MATTERS

Pursuant to the authority conferred by Florida Rule of Judicial Administration 2.215, it is **ORDERED** as follows:

1. Requests for Emergency Hearings shall be decided by each judge on the Emergency Motion alone.

2. Upon receiving a request for an emergency hearing, the judge shall decide whether an emergency exists, and if so, shall schedule a hearing, enter any ex parte order deemed necessary, or take any other appropriate action.

DONE and **SIGNED** in Chambers at West Palm Beach, Palm Beach County, Florida, this 22 day of January, 2009.

Kathleen J. Kroll
Chief Judge

Adopted effective January 22, 2009.

Foreclosures and Judicial Sales

3.301. FORECLOSURE SALES AND CANCELATION OF FORECLOSURE SALES

IN THE CIRCUIT COURT OF THE FIFTEENTH JUDICIAL CIRCUIT IN AND FOR PALM BEACH COUNTY FLORIDA

ADMINISTRATIVE ORDER 3.301–11/12 *

IN RE: FORECLOSURE SALES AND CANCELATION OF FORECLOSURE SALES

It appears that routinely 20% to 50% of foreclosure sales scheduled online end up canceling just prior to the foreclosure sale being held and that many of these canceled sales are subsequently reset. The compelling interest of efficient and effective case management requires a proper process and procedure be established to properly address the requested cancelation of a foreclosure sale. The Florida Supreme Court has amended the Florida Rules of Civil Procedure to require that an order canceling a foreclosure sale be entered before a foreclosure sale can be canceled and created a form motion to cancel sale. *See In re: Amendments to the Florida Rules of Civil Procedure; In re: Amendments to the Florida Rules of Civil Procedure—Form 1.996 (Final Judgment of Foreclosure)*, 35 Fla. L. Weekly S97 (Fla. Feb. 11, 2010).

NOW, THEREFORE, pursuant to the authority conferred by Florida Rule of Judicial Administration 2.215 it is ORDERED as follows:

A. Online Foreclosure Sales.

1. In accordance with section 45.031(10), Florida Statutes (2012), the Fifteenth Judicial Circuit conducts online electronic judicial foreclosure sales.

2. All proposed foreclosure Final Judgments and all Notices of Sale shall contain the following location for the online judicial foreclosure sale:

www.mypalmbeachclerk.clerkauction.com

3. Foreclosure Plaintiffs shall submit the $70.00 Clerk Sale Fee prior to the sale date. The Clerk shall not issue the Certificate of Title until the $70.00 clerk sale fee, and all other fees, are paid.

4. Foreclosure Plaintiffs shall submit the Proof of Publication at least three (3) business days before the online sale date.

5. All parties to the foreclosure action, as well as all foreclosure sale bidders/participants, shall abide by and follow the administrative policy of the Clerk & Comptroller's Judicial Sales Procedure found at www.mypalmbeachclerk.com.

B. Cancelation of Foreclosure Sales.

1. Effective May 15, 2010, regardless of any contrary language contained in a previously issued Final Judgment, a court order is required to cancel any scheduled foreclosure sale.

2. The Clerk is hereby prohibited from canceling a scheduled foreclosure sale without a court order except in cases where a bankruptcy petition has been filed.

3. Failure to provide proof of publication or pay the clerk sale fee prior to the sale is not grounds for canceling a sale. The certificate of sale will not, however, issue unless proof of publication has been received by the Clerk's Office.

4. Motion to Cancel Sale and Reschedule Sale:

a. Any party seeking to cancel and reschedule a foreclosure sale shall file a written motion in the same format Exhibit "A" which is attached hereto. The Motion and Order shall include the number of times the sale has been canceled.

b. This motion shall be filed at least seven (7) business days before the sale date and must be set on the Uniform Motion Calendar.

c. All motions to cancel foreclosure sales that result in the case being reopened shall include payment of the $50 reopen fee and be accompanied by a proposed order that is in the same format as the Order on the Motion to Cancel and Reschedule Foreclosure Sale form that is attached hereto as Exhibit "B."

DONE and **ORDERED**, in Chambers, at West Palm Beach, Palm Beach County, Florida this 16th day of November, 2012.

Peter D. Blanc
Chief Judge

IN THE CIRCUIT COURT OF THE FIFTEENTH JUDICIAL CIRCUIT
IN AND FOR PALM BEACH COUNTY, FLORIDA

______________, Case No.:
Plaintiff, Division:

vs.

______________,
Defendant(s)

______________________/

MOTION TO CANCEL AND RESCHEDULE FORECLOSURE SALE

Plaintiff, by and through undersigned counsel, moves to cancel and reschedule the mortgage foreclosure sale scheduled in the instant matter and in support thereof states:

1. On __________, this Court entered a Final Judgment of Foreclosure pursuant to which a foreclosure sale was scheduled for __________, 20 ___. **There have been __________ (number) prior court orders canceling sales entered on (mm/dd/yy) & docket entry number of all prior cancelations.**

2. The sale needs to be canceled for the following reason(s):

a. ___ Plaintiff and Defendant are continuing to be involved in loss mitigation;

b. ___ Defendant is negotiating for the sale of the property that is the subject of this matter and Plaintiff wants to allow the Defendant an opportunity to sell the property and pay off the debt that is due and owing to Plaintiff.

c. ___ Defendant has entered into a contract to sell the property that is the subject of this matter and Plaintiff wants to give the Defendant an opportunity to consummate the sale and pay off the debt that is due and owing to Plaintiff.

d. ___ Defendant has filed a Chapter ___ Petition under the Federal Bankruptcy Code;

e. ___ Plaintiff has ordered but has not received a statement of value/appraisal for the property;

f. ___ Plaintiff and Defendant have entered into a Forbearance Agreement;

g. ___ Other

____

____

____

WHEREFORE, Plaintiff respectfully requests this Court enter an order canceling the foreclosure sale and order that it be rescheduled and requests such other and further relief as this Court deems just and proper.

____
, Esquire

I HEREBY CERTIFY that a true and correct copy of the foregoing Motion has been furnished by Email, United States Mail, facsimile or hand delivery to __________ this ___ day of ___, 20 ___.

____
, Esquire

IN THE CIRCUIT COURT OF THE FIFTEENTH JUDICIAL CIRCUIT
IN AND FOR PALM BEACH COUNTY, FLORIDA

______________, CASE NUMBER:
Plaintiff,

vs.

______________,
Defendant(s)

______________________/

ORDER ON MOTION TO CANCEL AND RESCHEDULE FORECLOSURE SALE

THIS CAUSE came before this Court on Plaintiff's Motion to Cancel and Reschedule Foreclosure Sale. **There having been ___ (number) prior cancelations of sales in this cause and** this Court being fully advised rules as follows:

It is hereby **ORDERED AND ADJUDGED:**

___ Plaintiff's motion is denied.

___ Plaintiff's motion is granted. The foreclosure sale is hereby canceled. The new sale date shall be __________ at 10:00 a.m. The sale will be conducted at: www.mypalmbeachclerk.clerkauction.com. Plaintiff shall prepare a Notice of Sale and send a copy to all parties. The original must be filed with the Clerk's office. Plaintiff shall submit a copy of the Notice of Sale to a newspaper of general circulation for publication pursuant to F.S. 45.031(2).

DONE AND ORDERED in West Palm Beach, Palm Beach County, Florida this ___ day of __________, 20 ___.

CIRCUIT JUDGE

Adopted effective September 29, 2008. Amended effective May 5, 2010; March 1, 2012; November 16, 2012.

* supersedes admin. order no. 3.301–3/12

3.302. FORECLOSURE DIVISION—"AW"

IN THE CIRCUIT COURT OF THE FIFTEENTH JUDICIAL CIRCUIT IN AND FOR PALM BEACH COUNTY, FLORIDA

ADMINISTRATIVE ORDER NO. 3.301–8/17 *

IN RE: FORECLOSURE DIVISION—"AW"

In the interest of judicial economy, Division "AW" is being closed and its cases reassigned to the circuit civil divisions. To aid in a smooth transition of the reassignment of cases, procedures need to be implemented.

NOW, THEREFORE, pursuant to the authority conferred by Florida Rule of Judicial Administration 2.215, it is **ORDERED AND ADJUDGED** as follows:

A. New Case Filings.

1. Effective at the close of business on August 18, 2017, the Clerk and Comptroller shall cease assigning newly filed residential foreclosure cases to Division "AW".

2. The Clerk and Comptroller shall randomly assign any newly filed residential foreclosure cases to the existing circuit civil divisions.

B. Reassignment of Newly Reopened Cases.

1. Effective at the close of business on August 18, 2017, the Clerk and Comptroller shall not reopen any cases in Division "AW".

2. The Clerk and Comptroller shall randomly reassign any newly reopened cases to the existing circuit civil divisions. The Clerk and Comptroller shall prepare a Notice of Reassignment and serve it on the Plaintiff either electronically or by United States Mail.

a. The Notice of Reassignment shall be docketed and available for public viewing within one business day of the reassignment,

b. The Notice of Reassignment shall contain a directive to the Plaintiff to serve the Notice of Reassignment on all parties, in accordance with Rule of Judicial Administration 2.516.

c. The Clerk and Comptroller, shall, within one business day, file and serve the Notice of Reassignment on the Plaintiff.

3. Within three (3) business days of receipt of the Notice of Reassignment of the newly reopened case, the Plaintiff shall serve, in accordance with Rule of Judicial Administration 2.516, a copy of the Notice of Reassignment on all parties who have not been dismissed or dropped from the action. The Plaintiff shall also file a Notice of Service of the Notice of Reassignment ("Notice of Service") with the Clerk and Comptroller. The Notice of Service is to include a complete service list.

4. Any motion, including an emergency, which arises out of the newly reopened case, shall be set for hearing in the circuit civil division in which it has been reassigned according to that division's procedures.

C. Active Cases. Residential foreclosure cases, in open and reopened status, will be processed as follows:

1. *First 1.215 Cases:* No later than August 30, 2017, Court Administration is directed to provide to the Clerk and Comptroller a list of 1,215 foreclosure cases in open and reopened status pending in Division "AW".

a. The Clerk and Comptroller is directed to begin randomly reassigning the identified 1,215 cases to the circuit civil divisions on August 31, 2017.

b. No later than September 8, 2017, the Clerk and Comptroller is to provide to Court Administration a list of the circuit civil divisions to which the cases were reassigned.

c. The Clerk and Comptroller will prepare a Notice of Reassignment and serve it on the Plaintiff either electronically or by United States Mail.

1) The Notice of Reassignment shall be docketed and available for public viewing within twenty-four (24) hours of the reassignment.

2) The Notice of Reassignment shall contain a directive to the Plaintiff to serve the Notice of Reassignment on all parties, in accordance with Rule of Judicial Administration 2.516. The Clerk and Comptroller shall file and serve the Notice of Reassignment on the Plaintiff no later than September 8, 2017.

3) Within seven (7) business days of the service of the Notice of Reassignment, the Plaintiff shall serve in accordance with Rule of Judicial Administration 2.516 a copy of the Notice of Reassignment on all parties who have not been dismissed or dropped from the action. The Plaintiff shall also file a Notice of Service of the Notice of Reassignment ("Notice of Service") with the Clerk and Comptroller. The Notice of Service is to include a complete service list.

2. *Second 1.215 Cases:* No later than September 8, 2017, Court Administration is directed to provide to the Clerk and Comptroller a second list of 1,215 foreclosure cases in open and reopened status pending in Division "AW".

a. The Clerk and Comptroller is directed to begin randomly reassigning the identified second set of 1,215 cases to the circuit civil divisions on September 11, 2017.

b. No later than September 18, 2107, the Clerk and Comptroller is to provide to Court Administration a list of the divisions to which the cases were reassigned.

c. The Clerk and Comptroller will prepare a Notice of Reassignment and serve it on the Plaintiff either electronically or by United States Mail.

1) The Notice of Reassignment shall be docketed and available for public viewing within twenty-four (24) hours of the reassignment.

2) The Notice of Reassignment shall contain a directive to the Plaintiff to serve the Notice of Reassignment on all parties, in accordance with Rule of Judicial Administration 2.516. The Clerk and Comptroller shall file and serve the Notice of Reassignment on the Plaintiff no later than September 18, 2017.

3) Within seven (7) business days of the service of the Notice of Reassignment, the Plaintiff shall serve, in accordance with Rule of Judicial Administration 2.516, a copy of the Notice of Reassignment on all parties who have not been dismissed or dropped from the action. The Plaintiff shall also file a Notice of Service of the Notice of Reassignment ("Notice of Service") with the Clerk and Comptroller. The Notice of Service is to include a complete service list.

3. *Any Remaining Cases:* No later than September 18, 2017, Court Administration is directed to provide to the Clerk and Comptroller a list of any remaining foreclosure cases assigned to Division "AW".

a. Effective September 19, 2017, the Clerk and Comptroller is directed to randomly reassign any remaining cases from Division "AW" to the circuit civil divisions.

b. No later than September 26, 2017, The Clerk and Comptroller is to provide to Court Administration the divisions to which the cases were reassigned.

c. The Clerk and Comptroller will prepare a Notice of Reassignment and serve it on the Plaintiff either electronically or by United States Mail.

1) The Notice shall be docketed and available for public viewing within twenty-four (24) hours of the reassignment.

2) The Notice shall contain a directive to the Plaintiff to serve the Notice of Reassignment on all parties, in accordance with Rule of Judicial Administration 2.516. The Clerk and Comptroller shall file and serve the Notice of Reassignment on the Plaintiff no later than September 26, 2017.

3) Within seven (7) business days of the service of the Notice of Reassignment, the Plaintiff shall serve a copy of the Notice of Reassignment, in accordance with Rule of Judicial Administration 2.516, on all parties who have not been dismissed or dropped from the action. The Plaintiff shall also file a Notice of Service of the Notice of Reassignment ("Notice of Service") with the Clerk and Comptroller which Notice of Service is to include a complete service list.

D. Cases Set for Uniform Motion Calendar.

1. Cases that are set for Uniform Motion Calendar (UMC) in Division "AW" prior to the redistribution of cases, will remain as currently scheduled on the Division "AW" UMC calendar.

2. Because the on-line scheduling program for Division "AW" only permits scheduling for cases assigned to Division "AW", parties are to check the Clerk's docket, located at www.mypalmbeachclerk.com, prior to scheduling a UMC hearing to ensure that a reassignment has not occurred. Reassigned cases should be set for UMC in front of the newly assigned division unless previously set for trial, calendar call or summary judgment in Division "AW" as set forth in paragraph E below.

E. Cases Set for Trial, Calendar Call or Summary Judgment Hearing.

1. Cases scheduled for a trial, calendar call or summary judgment hearing, in Division "AW" from the date of this order through December 31, 2017, will have the trial, calendar call, or summary judgment motion, heard by a judge covering Division "AW" despite the reassignment.

2. Motions for continuance of trials, calendar calls, or summary judgments scheduled in Division "AW" from the date of this order through December 31, 2017, will be set before the newly assigned judge.

3. No case will be heard in Division "AW" after December 31, 2017.

F. Emergency Motions. Emergency Motions should be referred to the Newly Assigned Division upon reassignment. For cases reassigned to a newly created circuit civil division "AK", the Clerk and Comptroller will, through September 30, 2017, hand deliver the Emergency Motion to the Division "AW" case manager.

G. List of Reassigned Cases. Court Administration shall post a complete listing of reassignments on the Fifteenth Judicial Circuit Website at www.15thcircuit.com.

DONE AND SIGNED in Chambers in West Palm Beach, Palm Beach County, Florida this 18 day of August, 2017.

KRISTA MARX
Chief Judge

Adopted effective September 29, 2008. Amended effective June 22, 2009; November 20, 2009; May 5, 2010; May 1, 2011; July 12, 2011; March 1, 2012; November 16, 2012; June 18, 2013; August 18, 2017.
* supersedes Admin. Order 3.302–6/13

3.303. FILING OF BANKRUPTCY DURING FORECLOSURE PROCEEDING

IN THE CIRCUIT COURT OF THE FIFTEENTH JUDICIAL CIRCUIT IN AND FOR PALM BEACH COUNTY

ADMINISTRATIVE ORDER 3.303—9/08 *

IN RE: FILING OF BANKRUPTCY DURING FORECLOSURE PROCEEDING

There has been an increase number of foreclosure actions pending in Division AW, which are being affected by the filing a bankruptcy petitions under Title 11, United States Code. It has become necessary to implement a procedure whereby the Clerk of Court for the Fifteenth Judicial Circuit is promptly notified of such bankruptcy filings and the concomitant invocation of the automatic stay pursuant to 11 U.S.C. section 362. The failure of filing proper notification of the bankruptcy action with the Clerk of Court has resulted in a significant increase in the cancellation or invalidation of pending foreclosure sales, and the unnecessary expenditure of valuable court resources. This Court has determined that the implementation of the following described procedure is necessary to avoid further misuse of Court resources.

NOW, THEREFORE, pursuant to the authority conferred by Florida Rule of Judicial Administration 2.215, it is **ORDERED** as follows:

1. Every attorney who represents a debtor or bankrupt who is a defendant to a foreclosure action pending in Division AW or, in the case of an individual(s) named as a defendant in a pending foreclosure action, every such defendant shall, upon the filing of a bankruptcy petition, immediately deliver to the Clerk of Court either:

a. A copy of the Bankruptcy Petition commencing such bankruptcy case; or

b. A Notice or Suggestion of Bankruptcy, styled in the pending foreclosure action, reflecting the case name and number of the bankruptcy case, and the date upon which the bankruptcy petition was filed.

2. If at the time of the filing of the bankruptcy petition a foreclosure sale has been scheduled, counsel for the defendant(s), or if unrepresented the defendant pro se, shall deliver a copy of the Petition or Suggestion of Bankruptcy to the Clerk of Court, 205 North Dixie Highway, Room 3.23, Attention–Foreclosure Department, West Palm Beach, Florida 33401, prior to the date and time of the scheduled foreclosure sale.

DONE and **ORDERED** in Chambers, at West Palm Beach, Palm Beach County, Florida this 29 day of September, 2008.

Kathleen J. Kroll
Chief Judge

Adopted effective September 29, 2008.

* supersedes admin. order 3.013—4/00

3.304. FORECLOSURE JUDGMENTS

IN THE CIRCUIT COURT OF THE FIFTEENTH JUDICIAL CIRCUIT IN AND FOR PALM BEACH COUNTY, FLORIDA

ADMINISTRATIVE ORDER 3.304–12/17 *

IN RE: FORECLOSURE JUDGMENTS

Uniform and clear procedures will assist the Clerk and Comptroller with post judgment foreclosure processes.

NOW, THEREFORE, pursuant to the authority conferred by Florida Rule of Judicial Administration 2.215 it is **ORDERED** as follows:

1. All proposed final judgments of foreclosure are to conform to Florida Rule of Civil Procedure Form 1.996.

2. The Clerk and Comptroller will issue a Writ of Possession after issuance of the Certificate of Title and upon an order of the Court which is separate from the Final Judgment. If a Final Judgment contains language directing the Clerk of Court to issue a Writ of Possession "without further order of the court", the Clerk will disregard such language unless the judge has affixed his or her initials next to that specific instruction.

3. A foreclosure sale will only be canceled by the Clerk and Comptroller in accordance with Administrative Order 3.301. If a final judgment contains language regarding the cancellation of the sale that does not comport with Administrative Order 3.301, the Clerk will disregard such language unless the judge has affixed his or her initials next to that specific instruction.

4. In addition to any specifically described and approved costs contained in the final judgment, the Clerk & Comptroller is hereby authorized to credit the Plaintiff with and pay the post judgment interest, the sale fee, and the costs of publication of the foreclosure sale incurred subsequent to the date of the final judgment upon the filing of an affidavit of the plaintiff or the plaintiff's attorney, together with the invoice of costs. All other costs must be approved by court order.

5. Upon the entry of the foreclosure judgment, the Plaintiff shall:

a. Submit to the Clerk & Comptroller the following: four (4) sets of envelopes addressed to all parties in the case with sufficient postage attached for the Clerk to mail the following documents: the Final Judgment, Certificate of Sale, Certificate of Title and Certificate of Disbursements.

b. Prepare a Notice of Sale, file it with the Clerk & Comptroller, send a copy to all parties and submit a copy of the Notice of Sale to a newspaper of general circulation for publication pursuant to F.S. Section 45.031(2).

6. All parties to the foreclosure action, as well as all foreclosure sale bidders/participants, shall abide by and follow the administrative policy of the Clerk & Comptroller's Judicial Sales Procedure found at www.mypalmbeachclerk.com.

DONE and **ORDERED,** in Chambers, at West Palm Beach, Palm Beach County, Florida this 18 day of December, 2017.

Krista Marx
Chief Judge

Adopted effective September 29, 2008. Amended effective May 5, 2010; March 21, 2012; December 18, 2017.

* supersedes admin. order no. 3.304–3/12.

3.305. [VACATED AND SET ASIDE BY ORDER 3.305-7/10, EFFECTIVE JULY 16, 2010.]

3.306. [VACATED AND SET ASIDE BY ORDER 3.306-7/10, EFFECTIVE JULY 16, 2010.]

3.307. PROTECTING TENANTS AT FORECLOSURE ACT OF 2009

IN THE CIRCUIT COURT OF THE FIFTEENTH JUDICIAL CIRCUIT IN AND FOR PALM BEACH COUNTY, FLORIDA

ADMINISTRATIVE ORDER 3.307–7/09

IN RE: PROTECTING TENANTS AT FORECLOSURE ACT OF 2009

The Federal Protecting Tenants at Foreclosure Act, Pub. L. No. 111–22 [S 896] §§ 701–04, 123 Stat. 1632 ("Protecting Tenants at Foreclosure Act of 2009") law became effective on May 20, 2009. The Writs of Possession against tenants in possession issued by the court must comply with the new federal law.

NOW, THEREFORE, pursuant to the authority conferred by Florida Rule of Judicial Administration 2.215, it is **ORDERED** as follows:

Effective August 3, 2009, A Motion for Writ of Possession must contain a certification from the attorney filing the motion as follows:

I HEREBY CERTIFY that there are no tenants in possession of the subject property or, if there are tenants in possession, such tenants have been provided with notice as required by the Federal Protecting Tenants at Foreclosure Act, Pub. L. No. 111–22 [S 896] §§ 701–04, 123 Stat. 1632 ("Protecting Tenants at Foreclosure Act of 2009"), and this motion does not seek an order that violates the tenants' right to continued occupancy under the Federal Protecting Tenants at Foreclosure Act.

DONE and **ORDERED**, in Chambers, at West Palm Beach, Palm Beach County, Florida this 27 day of July, 2009.

Peter D. Blanc
Chief Judge

Adopted effective July 27, 2009.

3.308. CASE MANAGEMENT OF RESIDENTIAL FORECLOSURE CASES AND MANDATORY MEDIATION REFERRAL

IN THE CIRCUIT COURT OF THE FIFTEENTH JUDICIAL CIRCUIT IN AND FOR PALM BEACH COUNTY, FLORIDA

ADMINISTRATIVE ORDER NO.: 3.308–11/14 *

IN RE: CASE MANAGEMENT OF RESIDENTIAL FORECLOSURE CASES AND MANDATORY MEDIATION REFERRAL

Administrative Order 3.308–1/12 is obsolete due to the Supreme Court's entering Administrative Order AOSC11–44 which dissolved the Statewide Managed Mediation Program.

NOW THEREFORE, it is hereby **ORDERED** that Administrative Order 3.308–1/12 is vacated and set aside.

DONE AND SIGNED in Chambers at West Palm Beach, Palm Beach County, Florida this 19 day of November, 2014.

Jeffrey J. Colbath
Chief Judge

Adopted effective July 12, 2010. Amended effective January 12, 2012; November 19, 2014.

* supersedes admin. order 3.308–1/12

3.310. [VACATED AND SET ASIDE BY ORDER 3.310-1/13, EFFECTIVE JANUARY 8, 2013.]

3.311. DISPOSAL OF FORECLOSURE TRIAL EXHIBITS

IN THE CIRCUIT COURT OF THE FIFTEENTH JUDICIAL CIRCUIT IN AND FOR PALM BEACH COUNTY, FLORIDA

ADMINISTRATIVE ORDER NO. 3.311–4/12

IN RE: DISPOSAL OF FORECLOSURE TRIAL EXHIBITS

Florida Rule of Judicial Administration 2.430(g) provides that all exhibits, except exhibits from criminal proceedings, shall be retained by the clerk until 90 days after a judgment has become final and if an exhibit is not withdrawn, the clerk may destroy or dispose of the exhibits after 30 days notice. Original Promissory Notes and Mortgages are routinely filed as exhibits in foreclosure trials. These original documents may need to be preserved should the parties renegotiate the loan following completion of the trial.

NOW, THEREFORE, pursuant to the authority conferred by Florida Rule of Judicial Administration 2.215, it is **ORDERED AND ADJUDGED** as follows:

1. Original notes and mortgages taken into evidence in foreclosure cases will be retained by the clerk in accordance with the Rules of Judicial Administration.

2. If, after the Clerk provides the parties the requisite 30 days notice of destruction, original notes and mortgages have not been retrieved by the parties, the Clerk will place the note and mortgage in the Court file and maintain it in accordance to Records' Retention laws.

3. Parties can seek a Court Order for the return of those original notes and mortgages which were placed in the court file in accordance with this Administrative Order. The Clerk will replace returned original documents from court files with a photocopy.

DONE and **SIGNED** in Chambers at West Palm Beach, Palm Beach County, Florida, this 10 day of April 2012.

Peter D. Blanc
Chief Judge

Adopted effective April 10, 2012.

3.312. REQUIRED SUBMISSION OF SERVICE LISTS IN RESIDENTIAL FORECLOSURE CASES AND PROCEDURES FOR SCHEDULING TRIALS

IN THE CIRCUIT COURT OF THE FIFTEENTH JUDICIAL CIRCUIT IN AND FOR PALM BEACH COUNTY, FLORIDA

ADMINISTRATIVE ORDER NO. 3.312–3/13 *

IN RE: REQUIRED SUBMISSION OF SERVICE LISTS IN RESIDENTIAL FORECLOSURE CASES AND PROCEDURES FOR SCHEDULING TRIALS

In an effort to improve the administration of justice in the area of residential foreclosure litigation, it has become necessary for the Court to seek the assistance of plaintiff's counsel in clarifying case status and properly identifying service lists for the purpose of providing proper notice to all parties to pending residential foreclosure cases.

NOW, THEREFORE, pursuant to the authority conferred by Florida Rule of Judicial Administration 2.215, it is **ORDERED AND ADJUDGED** as follows:

A. Service Lists.

1. Plaintiffs, through counsel, with the exception of plaintiffs that are Associations governed by Florida Statute Chapters 718, 719, 720, or 723, shall identify all open residential foreclosure cases pending in Division AW (pending cases are cases that have not had a Final Judgment entered or, if previously entered, has been vacated) in the Fifteenth Judicial Circuit (Palm Beach County) in which the firm acts as plaintiff's counsel and shall provide the following for each individual case:

a. A cover letter identifying the case number and the case style;

b. A current, accurate service list for ALL parties, including plaintiff's counsel, defense counsel, and pro se defendants as appropriate (mailing and e-mail addresses, as applicable);

c. Pre-addressed, postage paid **standard business** size mailing envelopes for the entire service list, including plaintiff's counsel, with the case number referenced on the face of the envelopes;

d. An accurate and fully executed Foreclosure Case Status Form (attached hereto as Exhibit A). All parties listed on the Complaint must be addressed on the Status Form and it must indicate whether case is at issue.

2. Plaintiff shall provide the information required in Section 1 above as follows:

a. The deadline for receipt for cases filed in 2007 or earlier is March 8, 2013;

b. The deadline for receipt of cases filed in 2008 is March 15, 2013;

c. The deadline for receipt of cases filed in 2009 is March 29, 2013;

d. The deadline for receipt of cases filed before July 1, 2010 is April 12, 2013;

e. Currently, cases filed after July 1, 2010, are exempt from this Administrative Order.

3. Plaintiff shall deliver the required items in Section 1 addressed to Senior Judges, Foreclosure Division, Palm Beach County Courthouse, 205 North Dixie Highway, West Palm Beach, FL 33401.

a. Items must be received within the applicable timeframes;

b. Early submissions are encouraged and will be accepted. Please do not hold these items until the deadline. Partial deliveries are encouraged and you may deliver these items as soon as they are ready.

4. In addition to the foregoing, for each individual case plaintiff shall file with the Clerk of the Courts its Notice of Compliance with this order and attach thereto a copy of the updated Service List and a copy of the Foreclosure Case Status Form [1].

5. Failure to comply with the foregoing requirements may result in the imposition of sanctions, including contempt of court and/or dismissal.

6. It is the Court's intention to allow plaintiffs to electronically provide all information required herein, with the exception of stamped, addressed envelopes for service lists which must still be delivered. Until the availability of such a system is announced, all parties must comply with the procedures specified herein in paper format. Postponing or delaying efforts to comply with this order while waiting for the availability of an electronic process will not be considered good cause to avoid the imposition of sanctions.

7. Plaintiff's counsel must register with the Fifteenth Judicial Circuit's eService system no later than March 29, 2013, by going to www.15thcircuit.com/onlineservices.

B. Scheduling Trials.

1. For residential foreclosure cases pending 36 months or more, it is the intention of the Court to begin setting blocks of residential foreclosure cases for trial beginning with the oldest pending cases and working forward. Firms that wish to take advantage of group scheduling of trials are not exempted from compliance with this order. However, if a firm wishes to notice a group of cases for trial, it must check to make sure that each case is at issue and must provide the Court with courtesy copies of the Notices for Trial in a manner that allows the Court to identify those cases which should be set for trial as a group. The Court will determine the proper number of cases that should be grouped together for trial at any given time.

2. Foreclosure trials will be scheduled in blocks by the Court and may be distributed among the various civil division judges as well as among the Senior Judges assigned to the Foreclosure Division. The Court reserves the right to schedule trials among the various other judges of this county and circuit as their schedules permit.

3. a. In an effort to promote consistency and improve the administration of justice, all motions to continue trial, to strike trial date, to reschedule trial, or any other motions which affect the scheduling of trials already set, including but not limited to motions to amend, motions for extension of time, and motions to withdraw, shall be heard only by the Chief Judge or his or her designee on Wednesdays between 10:30 and 11:45 a.m. or Thursdays between 10:30 and 11:45 a.m. in locations to be announced.

b. Motions specified in 3.a. above shall not be heard by the Senior Judges in the Foreclosure Division or by the Judges assigned to the standard civil divisions, even those divisions in which the case is set for trial.

c. Failure to comply with the provisions of this section may result in the imposition of sanctions.

4. Continuances shall be granted only for good cause and all parties requesting a finding of good cause shall bring with them to the hearing on the motion a proposed order specifying the good cause, and providing a space for the Court to specify by date a deadline for the parties to bring the case to issue or to otherwise eliminate the good cause supporting the continuance. The same order shall provide a space for the Court to set a status hearing for the parties before the same judge within seven (7) days after the previously specified deadline date. The same order shall also include an option for denial of the motion. (A copy of the form Order Granting / Denying Motion to Continue Trial is attached hereto as Exhibit B.)

5. The proposed order shall specify that, absent exceptional circumstances, the failure to appear for the status hearing or to comply with the deadline to bring the case to issue may result in sanctions, including dismissal. The party bringing the motion and proposed order shall also bring stamped, addressed envelopes for all parties, including the moving party.

DONE and **SIGNED** in Chambers at West Palm Beach, Palm Beach County, Florida, this 22 day of March, 2013.

Peter D. Blanc
Chief Judge

EXHIBIT B

IN THE CIRCUIT COURT OF THE FIFTEENTH JUDICIAL CIRCUIT IN AND FOR PALM BEACH COUNTY, FLORIDA

CIVIL DIVISION AW

CASE NO.

____________________,

Plaintiff(s),

vs

____________________,

Defendant(s).

____________________/

ORDER GRANTING/DENYING MOTION TO CONTINUE TRIAL

THIS MATTER came before the Court upon the Motion to Continue Trial filed by the Plaintiff(s) / Defendant(s). The Plaintiff(s) / Defendant(s) allege(s) that good cause for continuation of trial is based upon the following facts:

(to be completed by moving party)

Based upon the circumstances of the instant case, the Court finds these facts sufficient /insufficient to establish good cause. It is therefore

ORDERED AND ADJUDGED as follows:

___ The Motion to Continue Trial is DENIED and this case remains set for trial.

OR

___ The Motion to Continue Trial is GRANTED and this matter is stricken from the current trial docket. The parties shall have until __________ to eliminate the good cause for continuance specified above or to resolve any other issues that would prevent the Court from setting this matter for trial.

A status hearing is set for __________, 2013, at ___ a.m./p.m. to determine compliance with this order.

Failure to timely comply with the terms of this order may result in the imposition of sanctions, including dismissal, without prejudice.

DONE AND ORDERED at West Palm Beach, Palm Beach County, Florida, this ___ day of _________, 2013.

____

PETER D. BLANC, Chief Judge

Adopted effective February 1, 2013. Amended March 22, 2013.

* supersedes admin. order no. 3.312–2/13

1 Form not attached.

3.313. FORECLOSURE DIVISION CASE STATUS REPORTING REQUIREMENTS

IN THE CIRCUIT COURT OF THE FIFTEENTH JUDICIAL CIRCUIT IN AND FOR PALM BEACH COUNTY, FLORIDA

ADMINISTRATIVE ORDER 3.313–11/13

IN RE: FORECLOSURE DIVISION CASE STATUS REPORTNG * REQUIREMENTS

Pursuant to Florida Supreme Court Administrative Order 13–51, each chief judge is required to issue an administrative order to provide direction to the clerk regarding a change in the status of a foreclosure case.

NOW, THEREFORE, pursuant to the authority conferred by Florida Rule of Judicial Administration 2.215, it is **ORDERED** as follows:

1. The Clerk of Court shall create a code for inactive pending and reopened foreclosure cases. As defined by the Foreclosure Initiative Data Collection Plan, "A case is considered in an inactive status when court activity on that case is suspended pending resolution of an issue external to the court or that does not directly involve the court in resolving that issue; for example, awaiting the results of an appeal or the disposition of a related case. A case placed in an inactive status is not closed and does not need to be reopened when the case returns to active status, regardless of the length of time involved." Accordingly, "A case is considered to be in a reopened inactive status if the activity on all outstanding post-judgment actions is held in abeyance pending resolution of some issue external to the court or that does not directly involve the court in resolving that issue. In this circumstance, the court is not actively working to resolve the matter(s)."

2. The Clerk of Court shall utilize the inactive code when the following instances occur: a stay of bankruptcy is filed, a case is on hold pending appeal, or when directed by the presiding judge.

3. Court Administration shall create a report of inactive cases, and review the report on a monthly basis to identify cases that should be returned to an active status.

4. The Clerk of Court shall return a case to an active status when directed by the presiding judge or the chief judge.

DONE and **ORDERED,** in Chambers, at West Palm Beach, Palm Beach County, Florida this 22 day of November, 2013.

Jeffrey Colbath
Chief Judge

Adopted effective November 22, 2013.

* So in original.

3.314. [VACATED AND SET ASIDE BY ORDER 3.314-4/15, EFFECTIVE APRIL 16, 2015.]

3.315. REASSIGNMENT OF RESIDENTIAL FORECLOSURE CASES

IN THE CIRCUIT COURT OF THE FIFTEENTH JUDICIAL CIRCUIT IN AND FOR PALM BEACH COUNTY, FLORIDA

ADMINISTRATIVE ORDER NO.: 3.315—5/15

IN RE: REASSIGNMENT OF RESIDENTIAL FORECLOSURE CASES

There are currently approximately 6,400 residential foreclosure cases pending in foreclosure division "AW". There are on average between 1,200–1,300 cases pending in the eleven Circuit Civil Divisions. The temporary supplemental funding provided by the Florida Legislature for the fifteen case managers and six rotating senior judges to assist with the backlog of pending foreclosure cases will end on June 30, 2015. In order to ensure that the foreclosure cases have adequate judicial resources, the approximately 2,800 pending foreclosure cases filed from 2007 through 2013 will be randomly reassigned to the Circuit Civil Divisions. The reassignment will occur in phases over a four week period.

NOW, THEREFORE, pursuant to the authority conferred by Florida Rule of Judicial Administration 2.215, it is **ORDERED AND ADJUDGED** as follows:

A. 2007–2011 Cases Without a Final Judgment.

1. No later than May 22, 2015, Court Administration is directed to provide to the Clerk of Court a list of foreclosure cases pending in Division "AW" and which were initiated between January 2007 and December 2011 and which do not currently have a final judgment of foreclosure entered, including those cases where a Final Judgment has been vacated.

2. Effective May 26, 2015, the Clerk of Court is directed to randomly reassign from Division "AW" to the Circuit Civil Divisions the 2007–2011 cases identified by Court Administration.

3. No later than June 1, 2015, the Clerk of Court shall provide to Court Administration a list of the divisions to which the cases were reassigned.

4. The Clerk of Court shall prepare a Notice of Reassignment and serve either electronically or by United States Mail the Notice of Reassignment on the Plaintiff.

a. The Notice shall be docketed and the case docket, which will list the new judicial division, will be updated on the Clerk and Comptroller's website within twenty-four (24) hours of the reassignment.

b. The Notice shall contain a directive to the Plaintiff to serve the Notice of Reassignment on all parties, in accordance with Rule of Judicial Administration 2.516. The Clerk of Court shall file and serve the Notice of Reassignment on the Plaintiff no later than June 1, 2015.

5. Within seven (7) business days of the service of the Notice of Reassignment, the Plaintiff shall serve in accordance with Rule of Judicial Administration 2.516 a copy of the Notice of Reassignment on all parties who have not been dismissed or dropped from the action. The Plaintiff shall also file a Notice of Service of the Notice of Reassignment ("Notice of Service") with the Clerk of Court. The Notice of Service is to include a complete service list.

B. 2013 Cases Filed Between June 2013 and December 2013 without a Final Judgment.

1. No later than May 29, 2015, Court Administration is directed to provide to the Clerk of Court a list of foreclosure cases pending in Division AW and which were initiated between June 2013 and December 2013 and which do not currently have a final judgment of foreclosure entered, including those cases where a Final Judgment has been vacated. This shall include foreclosure case numbers between 2013–CA–010000 through 2013–CA–020000.

2. Effective June 1, 2015, the Clerk of Court is directed to randomly reassign from Division "AW" to the circuit civil divisions the 2013 cases identified by Court Administration.

3. No later than June 8, 2015, the Clerk of Court shall provide to Court Administration a list of the divisions to which the cases were reassigned.

4. The Clerk of Court shall prepare a Notice of Reassignment and serve either electronically or by United States Mail the Notice of Reassignment on the Plaintiff.

a. The Notice shall be docketed and the case docket, which will list the new judicial division, will be updated on the Clerk and Comptroller's website within twenty-four (24) hours of the reassignment.

b. The Notice shall contain a directive to the Plaintiff to serve the Notice of Reassignment on all parties, in accordance with Rule of Judicial Administration 2.516. The Clerk of Court shall file and serve the Notice of Reassignment on the Plaintiff no later than June 8, 2015.

5. Within seven (7) business days of the service of the Notice of Reassignment, the Plaintiff shall serve, in accordance with Rule of Judicial Administration 2.516, a copy of the Notice of Reassignment on all parties who have not been dismissed or dropped from the action. The Plaintiff shall also file a Notice of Service of the Notice of Reassignment ("Notice of Service") with the Clerk of Court. The Notice of Service is to include a complete, current and accurate service list.

C. 2013 Cases Filed Between January 2013 and June 2013 without a Final Judgment.

1. No later than June 5, 2015, Court Administration is directed to provide to the Clerk of Court a list of foreclosure cases pending in Division "AW" and which were initiated between January 2013 and June 2013 and which do not currently have a final judgment of foreclosure entered, including those cases where a Final Judgment has been vacated. This shall include foreclosure case numbers between 2013–CA–000001 through 2013–CA–009999.

2. Effective June 8, 2015, the Clerk of Court is directed to randomly reassign from Division AW to the circuit civil divisions the 2013 cases identified by Court Administration.

3. No later than June 15, 2015, the Clerk of Court shall provide to Court Administration a list of the divisions to which the cases were reassigned.

4. The Clerk of Court shall prepare a Notice of Reassignment and serve, either electronically or by United States Mail, the Notice of Reassignment on the Plaintiff.

a. The Notice shall be docketed and the case docket, which will list the new judicial division, will be updated on the Clerk and Comptroller's website within twenty-four (24) hours of the reassignment.

b. The Notice shall contain a directive to the Plaintiff to serve the Notice of Reassignment on all parties, in accordance with Rule of Judicial Administration 2.516. The Clerk of Court shall file and serve the Notice of Reassignment on the Plaintiff no later than June 15, 2015.

5. Within seven (7) business days of the service of the Notice of Reassignment, the Plaintiff shall serve a copy of the Notice of Reassignment, in accordance with Rule of Judicial Administration 2.516, on all parties who have not been dismissed or dropped from the action. The Plaintiff shall also file a Notice of Service of the Notice of Reassignment ("Notice of

Service") with the Clerk of Court. The Notice of Service is to include a complete service list.

D. 2012 Cases without a Final Judgment.

1. No later than June 12, 2015, Court Administration is directed to provide to the Clerk of Court a list of foreclosure cases pending in Division "AW" and which were initiated between January 2012 and December 2012 and which do not currently have a final judgment of foreclosure entered, including those cases where a Final Judgment has been vacated.

2. Effective June 15, 2015, the clerk is directed to randomly reassign from Division "AW" to the circuit civil divisions the 2012 cases identified by Court Administration.

3. No later than June 22, 2015, clerk shall provide to Court Administration the divisions to which the cases were reassigned.

4. The Clerk of Court shall prepare a Notice of Reassignment and serve, either electronically or by United States Mail, the Notice of Reassignment on the Plaintiff.

a. The Notice shall be docketed and the case docket, which will list the new judicial division, will be updated on the Clerk and Comptroller's website within twenty-four (24) hours of the reassignment.

b. The Notice shall contain a directive to the Plaintiff to serve the Notice of Reassignment on all parties, in accordance with Rule of Judicial Administration 2.516. The Clerk of Court shall file and serve the Notice of Reassignment on the Plaintiff no later than June 22, 2015.

5. Within seven (7) business days of the service of the Notice of Reassignment, the Plaintiff shall serve a copy of the Notice of Reassignment, in accordance with Rule of Judicial Administration 2.516, on all parties who have not been dismissed or dropped from the action. The Plaintiff shall also file a Notice of Service of the Notice of Reassignment ("Notice of Service") with the Clerk of Court which Notice of Service is to include a complete service list.

E. post Judgment Cases.

1. All Division AW cases that are currently closed or in a "reopen" status as of June 22, 2015 and which have had a final judgment entered and which have not been vacated, will remain in Division "AW" for all post judgment motions.

2. Cases transferred from Division "AW" to a circuit civil division and which are subsequently closed and reopened will remain in the newly assigned circuit civil division.

F. pending 2014 and 2015 Cases and Newly Filed Cases.

1. 2014 and 2015 cases will remain in Division "AW".

2. Newly filed residential foreclosure cases will be assigned to Division "AW".

G. Cases Set for Uniform Motion Calendar.

1. Cases that are set for Uniform Motion Calendar (UMC) in Division "AW" prior to the redistribution of cases, will remain as currently scheduled on the Division "AW" UMC calendar regardless of year.

2. Once the case is reassigned, the on-line scheduling program for Division "AW" will only permit scheduling for cases which remain in Division "AW". The Clerk's docket, www.mypalmbeachclerk.com, should be checked prior to scheduling a UMC hearing to ensure that a reassignment has not been made.

H. 2007–2013 Cases Set for Summary Judgment Hearing, Special Set Hearing or Case Management Conference in Division "AW".

1. 2007–2013 cases currently scheduled for a summary judgment hearing, special set hearing or case management conference in Division "AW" from the date of this order through June 30, 2015, will have the summary judgment hearing, special set hearing, or case management conference heard by the judge assigned to Division "AW" despite the reassignment.

2. If the parties file a motion to continue the summary judgment hearing, special set hearing or case management conference and are precluded from scheduling Motions for Continuance on the Division "AW" online UMC calendar due to the reassignment, the motions for continuances will be heard by the Division "AW" judge at the time of the scheduled motion for summary judgment, special set hearing or case management conference.

3. No reassigned cases shall have motions set for hearing in Division "AW" after June 30, 2015.

I. cases Set on a Circuit Civil Divisions Trial Docket Through June 30, 2015.

1. 2007–2013 cases that have been set on a circuit civil division's trial docket, will remain set for trial regardless of the new divisional assignment.

a. If the parties file a motion to continue the trial and are precluded from scheduling Motions for Continuance on the Division "AW" online UMC calendar due to the reassignment, the motions for continuances will be heard by the trial judge at the time of the scheduled trial.

b. Any motions for new trial, rehearing or reconsideration will be heard by the Judge that conducted the trial. Any other post judgment motions will be heard in the newly assigned division.

2. 2014–2015 cases that have been set on a circuit civil division's trial docket shall remain set for trial.

a. Any pretrial motions, including Motions for Continuances are to set in accordance with the procedures outlined in the trial order.

b. Any motions for new trial, rehearing, or reconsideration will be heard by the judge who conducted the trial. Any other post judgment motions will be heard in Division AW.

c. The cases shall remain assigned to division AW, and will return to AW following the trial date, regardless of continuance or a post judgment proceeding.

J. 2007–2013 Cases where the Final Judgments are Subsequently Vacated, Dismissals are Subsequently Set Aside or are Remanded by the Fourth District Court of Appeals. Any 2007–2013 cases where the final judgments are vacated, dismissals set aside or are reversed by the Fourth District Court of Appeals shall be randomly reassigned to one of the eleven circuit civil divisions.

K. List of Reassigned Cases. Court Administration shall post a complete listing of reassignments on the Fifteenth Judicial Circuit Website at www.15thcircuit.com.

L. Case Management. As defined in the Foreclosure Initiative Data Collection Plan, adopted by the Florida Supreme Court, Court Administration shall continue to monitor the:

1. Time to Disposition—this statistic measures the length of time between filings and disposition and is frequently presented as an average percentage of cases that have been resolved within established time frames

2. Age of pending foreclosure case—this statistic measures the age of the active cases that are pending before the court.

3. Clearance Rate—this statistic measures the ratio of dispositions to new case filings and assesses whether the court is keeping pace with its incoming caseload.

DONE AND ORDERED this 5 day of May, 2015 in chambers in West Palm Beach, Palm Beach County, Florida.

Jeffrey J. Colbath
Chief Judge

Adopted effective May 5, 2015.

3.316. DISBURSEMENT OF FORECLOSURE SALE PROCEEDS

IN THE CIRCUIT COURT OF THE FIFTEENTH JUDICIAL CIRCUIT IN AND FOR PALM BEACH COUNTY, FLORIDA

ADMINISTRATIVE ORDER 3.316–12/17

IN RE: DISBURSEMENT OF FORECLOSURE SALE PROCEEDS

When surplus funds remain after the sale of foreclosed properties, an order is required for the Clerk and Comptroller to distribute surplus funds. Florida Statute § 45.032(3)(a) requires the court to order the clerk to deduct any applicable service charges from surplus funds following a foreclosure sale. Proposed orders submitted by parties may fail to include language stating "less clerk's fees".

NOW THEREFORE, pursuant to the authority conferred by Florida Rule of Judicial Administration 2.215 it is **ORDERED** as follows:

1. After an Owner's Claim for Mortgage Foreclosure Surplus is filed with the Clerk and Comptroller, the Clerk and Comptroller will forward the Owner's Claim to the assigned judge with a cover memo provided by Court Administration.

2. Except as provided in paragraph 3 below, the Clerk and Comptroller is authorized to deduct its fees and costs when an Order on Disbursement of Foreclosures Sale Proceeds is filed. The Clerk and Comptroller may deduct its fees and costs regardless of whether the order contains the language "less clerk's fees".

3. If the sale is vacated due to an error of the court or clerk, the Clerk and Comptroller's office will not deduct its fees and will refund the full amount to the buyer after an order is entered by the court reflecting that the Clerk will not recover its fees.

4. If a party disputes the Clerk and Comptroller's entitlement to fees or costs, the party may seek relief with an appropriate motion to the court.

DONE and **ORDERED,** in Chambers, at West Palm Beach, Palm Beach County, Florida this 18 day of December, 2017.

Krista Marx
Chief Judge

Adopted effective December 18, 2017.

Eminent Domain

3.401. "QUICK–TAKE" EMINENT DOMAIN PROCEEDINGS

IN THE CIRCUIT COURT OF THE FIFTEENTH JUDICIAL CIRCUIT IN AND FOR PALM BEACH COUNTY, FLORIDA

ADMINISTRATIVE ORDER NO. 3.401–9/08 *

IN RE: "QUICK–TAKE" EMINENT DOMAIN PROCEEDINGS

It is the public policy of the state to expedite eminent domain proceedings. The instruction of special procedures regarding the scheduling of "quick-take" hearings would contribute to the realization of the state's policy,

NOW, THEREFORE, pursuant to the authority conferred by Florida Rule of Judicial Administration 2.215, it is **ORDERED** as follows:

1. The Clerk of Court shall maintain a separate rotation list of civil division judges which shall be utilized to assure random and even apportionment of eminent domain cases.

2. A public body intending to file an eminent domain action in which a "quick-take" procedure will be utilized, may—prior to the time the case is filed—file a pleading styled, "Notice of Intent to File Eminent Domain Proceeding." The notice shall designate the proposed style of the case, the street address of the land sought to be condemned and the names and addresses of the owners/proposed defendants. A copy of the authorizing public document/resolution shall be attached as an exhibit to the notice.

3. The Clerk of Court, upon receiving the notice of intent, shall randomly select a judge from the eminent domain rotation list and shall disclose the judge's name by marking it on the notice of intent.

4. Counsel for the condemning authority may then take a copy of the notice of intent to the designated judge's judicial assistant and obtain the date of the court's next non-jury calendar scheduled not less than ninety (90) days from the date of the filing of the notice of intent. The judicial assistant shall add the proposed eminent domain case to the non-jury calendar and the "quick-take" hearing shall receive priority over all other non-emergency matters.

DONE and **SIGNED** in Chambers at West Palm Beach, Palm Beach County, Florida, this 28 day of September, 2008.

Kathleen J. Kroll
Chief Judge

Adopted effective September 29, 2008.

* supersedes admin. order 3.006–9/92

Forfeiture

3.501. PROCEDURE FOR FORFEITURE PROCEEDINGS

IN CIRCUIT COURT OF THE FIFTEENTH JUDICIAL CIRCUIT IN AND FOR PALM BEACH COUNTY, FLORIDA

ADMINISTRATIVE ORDER NO. 3.501–7/16 *

IN RE: PROCEDURE FOR FORFEITURE PROCEEDINGS

The Florida Contraband Forfeiture Act was revised effective July 1, 2016. The Act gives persons who own, possess, or otherwise have a claim to the property to be seized or which has been seized certain rights, including the opportunity to be heard at an adversarial preliminary hearing. The Act refers to proceedings involving the Court, the Office of the Clerk of Courts, the seizing agency, and others in the forfeiture process for whom it is necessary to have a uniform procedure throughout the Fifteenth Judicial Circuit in order to implement the provisions of the Act.

NOW, THEREFORE, pursuant to the authority conferred by Florida Rule of Judicial Administration 2.215, it is **ORDERED** as follows:

The procedures set forth in this administrative order shall be followed whenever property has been seized or is the subject of an application for seizure under the Act.

A. Application for Ex Parte Probable Cause Order.

1. Florida Statute 932.703(2)(a) requires a seizing agency to apply, within 10 business days after the date it has seized property under the Florida Contraband Forfeiture Act, to a court of competent jurisdiction for an order determining whether probable cause exits for the seizure of the property.

2. A seizing agency or its counsel within the jurisdiction of the Fifteenth Judicial Circuit will bring the application for a probable cause determination and a sworn affidavit to the assigned duty judge during normal business hours. The duty judge shall review the application in accordance with Florida Statute 932.703(1)(2).

3. If probable cause is found, the duty judge will return the signed probable cause order to the officer or attorney requesting the order. A form Order on Application for Probable Cause Pursuant to the Florida Contraband Forfeiture Act is attached as Exhibit A (finding probable cause) and Exhibit B (finding that statutory requirements have not been met or there is no probable cause).

4. If probable cause is not found, any amended application filed within the statutory time period will state "Amended Application" and list the dates of all previous submissions and the name of the judge to whom the submission was made.

B. Case Filing. Upon the filing of the Notice of Forfeiture, Complaint, Seizure Warrant or Lis Pendens by the seizing agency, the Clerk shall collect from the seizing agency any required filing fee and bond and will assign the forfeiture matter a case number from the Civil Division of the Circuit Court in and for the Fifteenth Judicial Circuit. The Clerk shall randomly assign the forfeiture case to one of the Judges of the Civil Division.

C. Adversarial Preliminary Hearing.

1. Any request for an adversarial preliminary hearing will be made in accordance with Florida Statute s. 932.703(3).

2. If a request for an adversarial preliminary hearing is made prior to the seizing agency filing a pleading or document that creates a civil case, the Clerk of Court will open a civil case filing, assign a case number, and randomly assign the case to a circuit civil division.

3. Within ten (10) days or as soon as practicable from the date of notification of a request for an adversarial preliminary hearing, the assigned judge's office will set the matter for hearing in accordance with Florida Statute s. 932.703(3).

a. If the assigned judge's calendar is suspended, the seizing agency or its attorney is to contact the assigned judge's alternate, as set forth in Administrative Order 11.106, to set the matter for hearing before the alternate judge.

b. If the alternate judge's calendar is suspended, or if the alternate judge is not able to provide a hearing date within the statutorily required time period, the seizing agency or its attorney is to contact the office of the administrative judge of the circuit civil division to determine if another judge is available to hear the matter within the statutorily required time period.

DONE AND ORDERED in Chambers at West Palm Beach, Palm Beach County, Florida, on this 19 day of July 2016.

Jeffrey Colbath
Chief Judge

Exhibit "A"

IN THE CIRCUIT COURT OF THE FIFTEENTH JUDICIAL CIRCUIT IN AND FOR PALM BEACH COUNTY, FLORIDA

IN RE THE FORFEITURE OF: (describe property)

______________________________/

EX–PARTE ORDER GRANTING APPLICATION FOR PROBABLE CAUSE PURSUANT TO THE FLORIDA CONTRABAND FORFEITURE ACT

THIS CAUSE came before the Court on (seizing agency's) Application for Probable Cause pursuant to Florida Statute 932.703(2)(a) to forfeit (describe property). The Court has reviewed the seizing agency's Application for Probable Cause and the accompanying sworn affidavit. The Court finds as follows:

1. The seizing agency filed the Application for Probable Cause within ten (10) business days from the date of seizure.

2. After a review of the Application for Probable Cause the Court has determined, pursuant to 932.703(2)(b), that at least one of the following has taken place (check all that apply):

___ The owner of the property was arrested for a criminal offense that forms the basis for determining that the property is a contraband article under s. 932.701 (Fla. Stat. s. 932.703(1)(a));

___ The owner of the property cannot be identified after a diligent search, or the person in possession of the property denies ownership and the owner of the property cannot be identified by means that are available to the employee or agent of the seizing agency at the time of the seizure (Fla. Stat. s. 932.703(1)(a)1);

___ The owner is a fugitive from justice or is deceased (Fla. Stat. s. 932.703(1)(a)2);

___ An individual who does not own the property is arrested for a criminal offense that forms the basis for determining that the property is a contraband article under 932.701 and the owner of the property had actual knowledge of the criminal activity. (Fla. Stat. s. 932.703(1)(a)3);

___ The owner of the property agrees to be a confidential informant as defined in s. 914.28. (Fla. Stat. s. 932.703(1)(a)4);

___ The property is a monetary instrument (Fla. Stat. s. 932.703(1)(a)5).

3. The Court finds that probable cause exists for the forfeiture of the above described property. The property will be held by the seizing agency until the issue of a determination of title is resolved pursuant to the procedures set forth in the Florida Contraband Forfeiture Act.

DONE AND ORDERED in Chambers in West Palm Beach, Palm Beach County, Florida this ________ day of ________, 2016.

____

Circuit/County Judge

Exhibit "B"
IN THE CIRCUIT COURT OF THE FIFTEENTH JUDICIAL CIRCUIT IN AND FOR PALM BEACH COUNTY, FLORIDA
IN RE THE FORFEITURE OF: (describe property)

______________________________/

EX–PARTE ORDER DENYING APPLICATION FOR PROBABLE CAUSE PURSUANT TO THE FLORIDA CONTRABAND FORFEITURE ACT

THIS CAUSE came before the Court on (seizing agency's) Application for Probable Cause pursuant to Florida Statute 932.703(2)(a) to forfeit (describe property). The Court has reviewed the seizing agency's Application for Probable Cause and the accompanying sworn affidavit. The Court finds as follows: (check all that apply):

___ The seizing agency did not apply for the probable cause determination within ten (10) business days after the date of seizure.

___ After a review of the Application for Probable Cause the Court has determined, pursuant to 932.703(2)(b), none of the statutory requirements set forth in s. 932.703(1)(a) have been met. The owner of the property has not been arrested nor have any of the exceptions set forth in s. 932.703(1)(a) apply.

___ Probable cause does not exist for the property seizure under the Florida Contraband Forfeiture Act.

Pursuant to Florida Statute s. 932.703(2)(d), since there has been a finding that the requirements in s. 932.703(1)(a) have not been satisfied or that no probable cause has been found to exist for the seizure, the seizing agency will release any hold, lien, lis pendens, or other civil encumbrance on the above described property within five (5) days from the date of this order.

DONE AND ORDERED in Chambers in West Palm Beach, Palm Beach County, Florida this ________ day of ________, 2016.

____

Circuit/County Judge

Adopted effective September 29, 2008. Amended effective July 19, 2016.

* supersedes admin. order no. 3.501–9/08

County Court – Pretrial and Trial

3.601. SMALL CLAIMS SUMMONS

IN THE CIRCUIT COURT FOR THE FIFTEENTH JUDICIAL CIRCUIT IN AND FOR PALM BEACH COUNTY, FLORIDA

ADMINISTRATIVE ORDER NO. 3.601 9/08 *

IN RE: SMALL CLAIMS SUMMONS

The Supreme Court has promulgated for use in small claims actions "FORM 7.322 SUMMONS/NOTICE TO APPEAR FOR PRETRIAL CONFERENCE". A form summons for small claims actions has been used in this circuit. Through the use in practice of such form of summons, the county courts in this circuit had encountered problems specific to small claims cases which may be corrected by way of addition to the form summons currently in use The county court judges have been consulted with respect to such additions to the small claims summons which have been incorporated into the form of summons attached hereto.

NOW, THEREFORE, pursuant to the authority conferred by Florida Rule of Judicial Administration 2.215, it is **ORDERED** as follows:

The following form of summons is hereby adopted (which shall include translation into both Spanish and Creole as attached hereto), and shall be used in all small claims actions in the Fifteenth Judicial Circuit.

DONE and **SIGNED** in Chambers at West Palm Beach, Palm Beach County, Florida, this 29 day of September, 2008.

Kathleen J. Kroll
Chief Judge

Adopted effective September 29, 2008.

* supersedes Adm. Order No. 9.008–4/03

ATTACHMENT

IN THE COUNTY COURT IN AND FOR PALM BEACH COUNTY, FLORIDA

CASE NO:
UNIFORM CASE NO:
DOCUMENT TRACKING NO:

PLAINTIFF(S)

–VS-

DEFENDANT(S)

SUMMONS/NOTICE TO APPEAR FOR
PRE–TRIAL CONFERENCE

STATE OF FLORIDA—NOTICE TO PLAINTIFF(S) AND DEFENDANT(S)

NAME OF DEFENDANT

DEFENDANT'S ADDRESS

PHONE NUMBER (IF AVAILABLE)

YOU MUST APPEAR IN PERSON OR BY ATTORNEY AT: ___, ON ___ AT ___, ROOM # ___ FOR A PRE–TRIAL CONFERENCE BEFORE A JUDGE OF THIS COURT.

IMPORTANT READ CAREFULLY

BOTH SIDES SHALL BRING ALL PAPERS, PHOTOS AND/OR DOCUMENTS THAT YOU NEED FOR COURT. DO NOT BRING WITNESSES.

THE DEFENDANT(S) MUST TIMELY APPEAR IN COURT ON THE ABOVE DATE TO AVOID A DEFAULT JUDGMENT. THE PLAINTIFF(S) MUST TIMELY APPEAR TO AVOID A JUDGMENT OF DISMISSAL. NEITHER PARTY IS EXCUSED FROM ATTENDING THE PRE–TRIAL CONFERENCE EVEN IF A WRITTEN MOTION OR ANSWER IS FILED. THE DATE AND TIME OF THE PRETRIAL CONFERENCE CANNOT BE RESCHEDULED WITHOUT GOOD CAUSE AND PRIOR COURT APPROVAL.

WHEN YOU COME TO THE PRE–TRIAL CONFERENCE, YOU WILL MEET WITH A TRAINED MEDIATOR TO TRY TO SETTLE THE CASE. YOU MUST PERSONALLY ATTEND UNLESS YOU HAVE A LAWYER WHOM YOU HAVE GIVEN FULL AUTHORITY TO SETTLE YOUR CASE WITHOUT FURTHER DISCUSSION WITH YOU.

IF PLAINTIFF OR DEFENDANT IS A CORPORATION, A CORPORATE OFFICER (PRESIDENT, VICE PRESIDENT, SECRETARY OR TREASURER) OR CORPORATE DIRECTOR SHALL APPEAL. AN EMPLOYEE OF THE CORPORATION MAY APPEAR WITH FULL WRITTEN SETTLEMENT AUTHORITY FROM A CORPORATE OFFICER OR DIRECTOR.

IF THE CASE DOES NOT SETTLE THE PARTIES WILL MEET WITH THE JUDGE. THE JUDGE WILL DECIDE IF THERE IS ANY POSSIBLE ISSUE FOR TRIAL. IF THERE IS NOT, THE JUDGE WILL DECIDE THE CASE AT THAT TIME. OTHERWISE, YOU WILL BE GIVEN A TRIAL DATE. BE PREPARED TO TELL THE NUMBER OF WITNESSES TO BE CALLED AT TRIAL AND HOW LONG IT WILL TAKE TO TRY THE CASE.

IF YOU HAVE TROUBLE SPEAKING OR UNDERSTANDING ENGLISH, YOU MUST BRING WITH YOU TO THE PRE–TRIAL CONFERENCE AND TRIAL SOMEONE WHO IS FLUENT IN ENGLISH AND YOUR OWN LANGUAGE.

RIGHT TO VENUE. THE LAW GIVES THE PERSON OR COMPANY WHO HAS SUED YOU THE RIGHT TO FILE IN ANY ONE OF SEVERAL PLACES AS LISTED BELOW. HOWEVER, IF YOU HAVE BEEN SUED IN ANY PLACE OTHER THAN ONE OF THESE PLACES, YOU, AS THE DEFENDANT(S) HAVE THE RIGHT TO REQUEST THAT THE CASE BE MOVED TO A PROPER LOCATION OR VENUE. A PROPER LOCATION OR VENUE MAY BE ONE OF THE FOLLOWING: 1) WHERE THE CONTRACT WAS ENTERED INTO; 2) IF SUIT IS ON UNSECURED PROMISSORY NOTE, WHERE NOTE IS SIGNED OR WHERE MAKER RESIDES; 3) IF SUIT IS TO RECOVER PROPERTY OR TO FORECLOSE A LIEN, WHERE THE PROPERTY IS LOCATED; 4) WHERE THE EVENT GIVING RISE TO THE SUIT OCCURRED; 5) WHERE ANY ONE OR MORE OF THE DEFENDANT(S) SUED RESIDES; 6) ANY LOCATION AGREED TO IN A CONTRACT; 7) IN AN ACTION FOR MONEY DUE IF THERE IS NO AGREEMENT WHERE SUIT MAY BE FILED, WHERE PAYMENT IS TO BE MADE.

IF YOU, AS THE DEFENDANTS(S), BELIEVE THE PLAINTIFF(S) HAS/HAVE NOT SUED IN ONE OF THESE CORRECT PLACES, YOU MUST APPEAR ON YOUR COURT DATE AND ORALLY REQUEST A TRANSFER, OR YOU MUST FILE A WRITTEN REQUEST FOR TRANSFER IN AFFIDAVIT FORM (SWORN TO UNDER OATH) WITH THE COURT SEVEN (7) DAYS PRIOR TO YOUR FIRST COURT DATE AND SEND A COPY TO THE PLAINTIFF(S) OR PLAINTIFF(S) ATTORNEY, IF ANY.

A COPY OF THE STATEMENT OF CLAIM SHALL BE SERVED WITH THIS SUMMONS.

"IF YOU ARE A PERSON WITH A DISABILITY WHO NEEDS ANY ACCOMMODATION IN ORDER TO PARTICIPATE IN THIS PROCEEDING, YOU ARE ENTITLED AT NO COST TO YOU, TO THE PROVISION OF CERTAIN ASSISTANCE. PLEASE CONTACT NICOLE SAUNDERS, ADA COORDINATOR IN THE ADMINISTRATIVE OFFICE OF THE COURT, PALM BEACH COUNTY COURTHOUSE, 205 NORTH DIXIE HIGHWAY, ROOM 5.2500, WEST PALM BEACH, FLORIDA 33401; TELEPHONE NUMBER (561) 355–4380 WITHIN TWO (2) WORKING DAYS OF YOUR RECEIPT OF THIS SUMMONS; IF YOU ARE HEARING OR VOICE IMPAIRED, CALL 1–800–955–8771".

DATED AT PALM BEACH COUNTY, FLORIDA ON

SHARON R. BOCK, CLERK OF COURT

BY:

DEPUTY CLERK

EN EL TRIBUNAL DEL CONDADO, EN Y DEL CONDADO DE PALM BEACH, FLORIDA

CAUSA NO:

DEMANDANTE(S),

vs.

DEMANDADO(S)

CITACIÓN/NOTIFICACIÓN PARA COMPARECER A UNA CONFERENCIA PREVIA AL JUICIO

NOMBRE DEL DEMANDADO

DIRECCIÓN DEL DEMANDADO

NÚMERO DE TELÉFONO (SI ESTÁ DISPONIBLE)

ESTADO DE LA FLORIDA—NOTIFICACIÓN A LOS DEMANDANTES Y A LOS DEMANDADOSUSTED DEBE COMPARECER PERSONALMENTE, Ó POR MEDIO DE SU ABOGADO, AL, EL DÍA ___, A LAS ___ AM/PM, SALA ___ PARA UNA CONFERENCIA PREVIA AL JUICIO ANTE EL JUEZ DE ESTE TRIBUNAL.

IMPORTANTE, LEA CUIDADOSAMENTE

LAS DOS PARTES DEBEN TRAER TODOS LOS PAPELES, FOTOGRAFÍAS Y/Ó DOCUMENTOS QUE NECESITEN EN EL TRIBUNAL. NO TRAIGA A LOS TESTIGOS.

EL DEMANDADO(S) DEBE COMPARECER PUNTUALMENTE AL TRIBUNAL EN LA FECHA INDICADA ARRIBA PARA EVITAR UNA SENTENCIA EN REBELDÍA. EL DEMANDANTE(S) DEBE COMPARECER PUNTUALMENTE PARA EVITAR UNA SENTENCIA EN DESESTIMACIÓN. NINGUNA DE LAS DOS PARTES ESTÁ EXEMPTA DE COMPARECER A LA CONFERENCIA PREVIA AL JUICIO AUNQUE SE HAYA REGISTRADO UNA RESPUESTA O UNA PETICIÓN POR ESCRITO. LA FECHA Y LA HORA DE LA CONFERENCIA PREVIA AL JUICIO NO SE PUEDEN REPROGRAMAR SIN UNA JUSTIFICACIÓN VÁLIDA Y SIN APROBACIÓN PREVIA DEL TRIBUNAL.

CUANDO USTED VIENE A UNA CONFERENCIA PREVIA AL JUICIO, USTED DEBE REUNIRSE CON UN MEDIADOR CAPACITADO PARA TRATAR DE RESOLVER LA CAUSA. USTED DEBE ASISTIR PERSONALMENTE, A MENOS QUE TENGA UN ABOGADO A QUIEN LE HAYA DADO UN PODER COMPLETO PARA RESOLVER SU CAUSA SIN NECESIDAD DE CONSULTAR CON USTED.

SI EL DEMANDANTE Ó EL DEMANDADO ES UNA SOCIEDAD ANÓNIMA, COMPARECERÁ UN FUNCIONARIO DE LA EMPRESA (PRESIDENTE, VICEPRESIDENTE, SECRETARIO Ó TESORERO) Ó UN DIRECTOR DE LA EMPRESA. UN EMPLEADO DE LA EMPRESA PUEDE COMPARECER CON AUTORIDAD PLENA Y SUFICIENTE PARA TRANSACCIÓN DE UNA CONTROVERSIA JUDICIAL, POR ESCRITO, DE UN FUNCIONARIO Ó DIRECTOR DE LA EMPRESA.

SI LA CAUSA NO SE RESUELVE, LAS PARTES SE REUNIRÁN CON EL JUEZ. EL JUEZ DECIDIRÁ SI HAY RAZÓN PARA UN JUICIO. SI NO LA HAY, EL JUEZ DECIDIRÁ LA CAUSA EN ESE MOMENTO; DE LO CONTRARIO, LE DARÁN UNA FECHA PARA EL JUICIO. ESTÉ PREPARADO PARA DECIR CUANTOS TESTIGOS SE VAN A LLAMAR PARA EL JUICIO Y CUANTO TIEMPO VA A DURAR EL JUICIO.

SI USTED TIENE PROBLEMAS PARA HABLAR Ó ENTENDER INGLÉS, USTED DEBE TRAER A LA CONFERENCIA PREVIA AL JUICIO, Y AL JUICIO, A ALGUIEN QUE HABLE CON FLUIDEZ INGLÉS Y EL IDIOMA QUE USTED HABLA.

DERECHO A COMPETENCIA TERRITORIAL: LA LEY LE CONFIERE A LA PERSONA O A LA ENTIDAD QUE LO HA DEMANDADO A USTED EL DERECHO A REGISTRAR LA DEMANDA EN UNO DE VARIOS LUGARES QUE SE ENUMERAN A CONTINUACIÓN. SIN EMBARGO, ST A USTED LO HAN DEMANDADO EN ALGÚN OTRO LUGAR DIFERENTE A UNO DE LOS ENUMERADOS, USTED, SIENDO EL DEMANDADO(S), TIENE DERECHO A PEDIR QUE LA CAUSA SEA TRASLADADA A OTRO LUGAR APROPIADO. UN LUGAR APROPIADO PUEDE SER UNO DE LOS SIGUIENTES: 1) DONDE SE HIZO EL CONTRATO; 2) SI LA DEMANDA ES SOBRE UN PAGARÉ NO GARANTIZADO, DONDE SE FIRMÓ EL PAGARÉ O DONDE VIVE QUIEN LO EJECUTÓ; 3) SI LA DEMANDA ES PARA RECUPERAR UNA PROPIEDAD O PARA EMPRENDER UNA EJECUCIÓN HIPOTECARIA, DONDE ESTÁ UBICADA LA PROPIEDAD; 4) DONDE OCURRIÓ EL ACONTECIMIENTO QUE OCASIONÓ LA DEMANDA; DONDE RESIDE UNO Ó MÁS DE LOS DEMANDADO(S); 6) CUALQUIER LUGAR ACORDADO POR CONTRATO; 7) EN UNA ACCIÓN PARA COBRAR DINERO, SI NO HAY UN ACUERDO EN CUANTO AL LUGAR DONDE DEBE REGISTRASE LA DEMANDA, SE LLEVARÁ A CABO DONDE TIENEN QUE HACERSE LOS PAGOS.

SI USTED, COMO DEMANDADO, CREE QUE EL DEMANDANTE HA/NO HA REGISTRADO LA DEMANDA EN UNO DE ESTOS LUGARES APROPIADOS, USTED DEBE COMPARECER A SU CITA EN EL TRIBUNAL Y PEDIR LA TRANSFERENCIA VERBALMENTE, Ó USTED DEBE REGISTRAR UNA PETICIÓN FOR ESCRITO EN FORMA DE ACTA JURAMENTADA (HECHA BAJO JURAMENTO) EN EL TRIBUNAL SIETE (7) DÍAS ANTES DE SU PRIMERA CITA EN EL TRIBUNAL Y DEBE ENVIAR UNA COPIA AL DEMANDANTE(S) Ó AL ABOGADO DEL DEMANDANTE(S).

UNA COPIA DE LA DECLARACIÓN DE DEMANDA DEBE SER ENTREGADA CON LA CITACIÓN.

"SI USTED ES UNA PERSONA INCAPACITADA, QUE NECESITA AYUDA PARA PODER PARTICIPAR EN ESTE PROCEDIMIENTO, USTED TIENE DERECHO, SIN COSTO ALGUNO, A RECIBIR CIERTA AYUDA. POR FAVOR PÓNGASE EN CONTACTO CON NICOLE SAUNDERS, COORDINADOR DE ADA (AYUDA PARA INCAPACITADOS) EN LA OFICINA DE ADMINISTRACIÓN DEL TRIBUNAL DEL CONDADO DE PALM BEACH, 205 NORTH DIXIE HIGHWAY, SALA 5.2500, WEST PALM BEACH, FLORIDA 33401; NÚMERO DE TELÉFONO (561) 355–4380 DURANTE LOS DOS DÍAS DESPUÉS DE QUE USTED HA RECIBIDO ESTA CITACIÓN. SI USTED TIENE UNA INCAPACIDAD DE AUDICIÓN O DE HABLA, LLAME AL 1–800–955–8771" FECHADO EN EL CONDADO DE PALM BEACH, FLORIDA,

SHARON R. BOCK, SECRETARIA DEL TRIBUNAL

NAN TRIBINAL KI REGLE TI ZAFE NAN E
POU KOMIN PALM BEACH, FLORIDA

NIMERO KA:

PLEYAN(YO),

KONT

AKIZE(YO).

DEMANN/AVETISMAN POU PARET POU KONFERANS AVAN PWOSE

ETA FLORID—AVETISMAN POU PLEYAN(YO) AK AKIZE(YO)

NON AKIZE AN

ADRES AKIZE AN

NIMERO TELEFON (SI GENYEN)

OU DWE PARET AN PESONN OU VOYE AVOKA OU NAN:, NAN DAT A ___ MATEN/APREMIDI, NAN SAL ___ POU KONFERANS AVAN PWOSE A DEVAN YON JUJ NAN TRIBUNAL SA.

ENPOTAN LI AVEK ATANSYON

TOU DE PATI YO DWE POTE TOUT PAPYE, TOUT FOTO AVEK/OUBYEN TOUT DOKIMAN KE OU BEZWEN NAN TRIBUNAL LA. PA VINI AK TEMWEN OU YO.

AKIZE AN (YO) DWE PARET A LE NAN TRIBUNAL LA NAN DAT KE YO DI A POU EVITE KE YO PRAN JIJMAN DEYE DO LI (YO). PLEYAN AN (YO) DWE PARET A LE TOU POU EVITE YON JIJMAN KI KA RANVWAYE KA A. OKENN NAN DE PATI YO PA KA PALA POU PATISIPE NAN KONFERANS AVAN PWOSE A MENM SI YON DEMANN TA FET PA EKRI OU YON LET AK REPONS TA NAN DOSYE A. DAT AK LE KONFERANS AVAN PWOSE A PA KA CHANJE SAN BON JAN REZON VALAB EPI TOU PA AVAN KE TRIBINAL LA TONBE DAKO.

JOU OU VINI POU KONFERANS AVAN PWOSE A, OU VA RANKONTRE AK YON MEDYATE KI ANTRENE KI VA ESEYE RANJE ZAFE A. OU DWE VINI AMWENSKE OU GEN YON AVOKA KE OU BAY OTORIZASYON NET ALE POU REGLE KA A SAN PA GEN OKENN LOT DISKISYON KI FET AK OU.

SI PLEYAN AN OUBYEN DEFANDAN AN SE YON KONPAYI, YON OFISYEL KONPAYI A (PREZIDAN, VISPREZIDAN, SEKRETE OUBYEN TREZORYE) OU DIREKTE KONPAYI A DWE KONPARET. YON ANPLOYE KONPAYI A KAPAB PARET AK YON PAPYE OTORIZASYON EKRI SOU ANTANT KI SIYEN PA YON OFISYEL KONPAYI A OU DIREKTE A.

SI KA A PA RIVE NAN YON ANTANT, TOU DE PATI YO PRAL RANKONTRE JUJ LA. JUJ LA VA DESIDE SI GEN KEK REZON POU ALE NAN PWOSE. SI PA GENYEN, JIJ LA VA DESIDE SOU KA LE SA A. OTREMAN, YO VA BA OU YON DAT POU AL NAN PWOSE. PREPARE OU POU DI KI VALE TEMWEN POU YO RELE JOU PWOSE A EPI TOU KONBYEN TAN SA AP PRAN POU FE PWOSE A.

SI OU GEN PWOBLEM PALE AK KONPRANN ANGLE, OU DWE VINI NAN KONFERANS AVAN PWOSE A AK NAN PWOSE A AVEK YON MOUN KI KONN PALE LANG PA OU A AK ANGLE BYEN.

DWA POU CHANJE LOKASYON OUBYEN(VENUE): LA LWA BAY MOUN NAN OU KONPAYI AN KI ASIYEN OU LAN DWA POU POTE PLENT NAN YON NAN PLAS SA YO KI NAN LIS SA. MEN, SI YO POTE PLENT POU OU NAN YON PLAS KI PA YON NAN PLAS SA YO, OU MENM KOM AKIZE (YO) GEN DWA POU MANDE DEPLASE KA A EPI VOYE–L NAN LOKASYON OUBYEN(VENUE) KOTE–L DWE YE A. YON BON JAN LOKASYON OUBYEN (VENUE) KAPAB YON NAN SA YO:

1) KOTE KONTRA A TE ANTRE A (PRAN PLAS); 2) SI PWOSE A BAZE SOU YON MOSO PAPYE EKRI KI PA ASIRE, OU BEZWEN KOTE PAPYE A TE SIYEN AN OU BYEN KOTE MOUN KI FE PAPYE A ABITE; 3) SI PWOSE A SE POU KAPAB JWEN DWA PWOPRIYETE OU ANKO, OUBYEN POU RETIRE DWA PWOPRIYETE OU EPI VANN LI POU PEYE YON DET, OU BEZWEN PLAS KOTE PWOPRIYETE A YE; 4) KI KOTE EVENMAN KI MENNEN OU DEVAN LETA TE PASE; 5) KI KOTE DEFANDAN AN (YO) KE YO MENNEN DEVAN LA JISTIS LA ABITE. 6) NINPOT LOKASYON KE OU TE DAKO NAN KONTRA A; 7) NAN YON ZAFE KI REGADE LAJAN OU DWE SI PA GEN ANTANT KI FET KOTE POU OU POTE PLENT, KOTE LAJAN AN DWE PEYE.

SI OU KOM AKIZE AN (YO), KWE KE PLEYAN AN (YO) POTE OU PA POTE PLENT NAN YON NAN PLAS KOREK SA YO, OU DWE PARET NAN DAT RANDEVOU TRIBUNAL OU A, EPI MANDE YON TRANSFE AK PWOP BOUCH OU, OUBYEN OU DWE RANPLI YON DEMANN PA EKRI POU TRANSFE A NAN YON FOM (AFFIDAVIT) SOU SEMAN A TRIBUNAL LA (7) JOU AVAN PREMYE DAT OU DWE PARET NAN TRIBUNAL LA EPI VOYE YON KOPI BAY PLEYAN AN (YO) OUBYEN AVOKA PLEYAN AN (YO), SI GENYEN.

OU DWE BAY YON KOPI DEKLARASYON PLENT LAN ANSANM AK LOD POU KONPARET LA.

≪SI OU SE YON MOUN KI GEN YON ENFIMITE KI BEZWEN YON ARANJMAN ESPESYAL POU OU KA PATISIPE NAN PWOSE A, OU GEN DWA MANDE SA SAN PEYE LAJAN, PASKE GEN PWOVIZYON POU KEK ED KONSA. TANPRI KONTAKTE NICOLE SAUNDERS, KOODINATE ADA NAN OFIS ADMINISTRASYON TRIBINAL LA, REJYON TRIBUNAL PALM BEACH, 205 NORTH DIXIE HIGHWAY, CHANM 5.2500, WEST PALM BEACH, FLORIDA 33401; NIMERO TELEFON (561) 355–4380 NAN ESPAS (2) JOU BIWO OUVE APRE OU FIN RESEVWA LOD POU KONPARET LA; SI OU BèBè (PA KA PALE) OU BYEN SOUD (PA KA TANDE), RELE 1–800–955–8771.≫

DATE NAN REJYON PALM BEACH, FLORIDA

SHARON R. BOCK, SEKRETE TRIBUNAL LA

3.602. RESIDENTIAL EVICTION SUMMONS

IN THE CIRCUIT COURT OF THE FIFTEENTH JUDICIAL CIRCUIT IN AND FOR PALM BEACH COUNTY, FLORIDA

ADMINISTRATIVE ORDER NO.: 3.602–11/14 *

IN RE: RESIDENTIAL EVICTION SUMMONS

The contents of the attached form of residential eviction summons is in substantial compliance with Form 1.923 and is consistent with the aforementioned need for modification and has been translated into both Spanish and Creole languages.

NOW, THEREFORE, pursuant to the authority conferred by Florida Rule of Judicial Administration 2.215, it is **ORDERED** as follows:

1. The attached form of summons is hereby adopted and shall be used in all residential eviction cases in the Fifteenth Judicial Circuit.

2. A copy of the forms shall be posted on the circuit's website in both Word and PDF formats.

DONE and **SIGNED** in Chambers at West Palm Beach, Palm Beach County, Florida, this 19 day of November, 2014.

Jeffrey Colbath
Chief Judge

IN THE COUNTY/CIRCUIT COURT, IN AND FOR PALM BEACH COUNTY, FLORIDA

CASE NO.

Plaintiff(s),

v.

Defendant(s).
____________________________/

EVICTION SUMMONS/RESIDENTIAL

TO DEFENDANT(S):

PLEASE READ CAREFULLY

YOU ARE BEING SUED BY: ____________________ to require you to move out of the place where you are living for the reasons given in the attached complaint.

You are entitled to a trial to determine whether you can be required to move, but you MUST do ALL of the things listed below. You must do them **within 5 days** (not including Saturday, Sunday, or any legal holiday) after the date these papers were given to you or to a person who lives with you or were posted at your home.

THE THINGS YOU MUST DO ARE AS FOLLOWS:

1. **You must** write down the reason(s) **in English** why you think you should not be forced to move. The written reason(s) must be given to the clerk of the court at **any one of** the following Palm Beach County Courthouses:

- **205 North Dixie Highway, Suite 2.2200, West Palm Beach, FL 33401**
- **200 W. Atlantic Ave., Delray Beach, FL 33444**
- **3188 PGA Blvd., Palm Beach Gardens, FL 33410**
- **2950 State Road 15, Room S–100, Belle Glade, FL 33430**

2. **You must** mail or give a copy of your written reason(s) to: ____________________________ Plaintiff/Plaintiffs Attorney, whose address is: ____.

3. **You must** pay to the clerk of the court the amount of rent that the attached complaint claims to be due and any rent that becomes due until the lawsuit is over. If you believe that the amount claimed in the complaint is incorrect, you should file with the clerk of the court a motion to have the court determine the amount to be paid. If you file a motion, you must attach to the motion any documents supporting your position and mail or give a copy of the motion to the plaintiff/plaintiff's attorney.

4. IF YOU DO NOT DO ALL OF THE THINGS SPECIFIED ABOVE WITHIN 5 WORKING DAYS AFTER THE DATE THAT THESE PAPERS WERE GIVEN TO YOU OR TO A PERSON WHO LIVES WITH YOU OR WERE POSTED AT YOUR HOME, YOU MAY BE EVICTED WITHOUT A HEARING OR FURTHER NOTICE.

5. If the attached complaint also contains a claim for money damages (such as unpaid rent), you must respond to that claim separately. You must write down the reasons why you believe that you do not owe the money claimed. The written reasons must be given to the clerk of the court at the address specified in paragraph (1) above, and you must mail or give a copy of your written reasons to the plaintiff/plaintiff's attorney at the address specified in paragraph (2) above. This must be done within 20 days after the date these papers were given to you or to a person who lives with you. This obligation is separate from the requirement of answering the claim for eviction within 5 working days after these papers were given to you or to a person who lives with you or were posted at your home.

If you are a person with a disability who needs any accommodation in order to participate in this proceeding, you are entitled, at no cost to you, to the provision of certain assistance. Please contact the Americans with Disabilities Act Coordinator, Palm Beach County Courthouse, 205 North Dixie Highway West Palm Beach, Florida 33401; telephone number (561) 355–4380 at least 7 days before your scheduled court appearance, or immediately upon receiving this notification if the time before the scheduled appearance is less than 7 days; if you are hearing or voice impaired, call 711.

IF YOU HAVE TROUBLE SPEAKING OR UNDERSTANDING ENGLISH, YOU MUST BRING WITH YOU SOMEONE WHO IS FLUENT WITH BOTH ENGLISH AND YOUR OWN LANGUAGE AND WHO HAS THE ABILITY TO TRANSLATE AND INTERPRET BOTH LANGUAGES.

THE STATE OF FLORIDA: To Each Sheriff of the State: You are commanded to serve this summons and a copy of the complaint in this lawsuit on the above-named defendant.

DATED on __________

SHARON R. BOCK, CLERK
BY: ____________________
As Deputy Clerk

EN LOS TRIBUNALES DE CONDADO/CIRCUITO EN Y DEL CONDADO DE PALM BEACH, FLORIDA

CAUSA NO.

Demandante(s),

v.

Demandado(s).
____________________________/

NOTIFICACION DE DESALOJO/RESIDENCIAL

AL DEMANDADO O LOS DEMANDADOS:

SIRVASE LEER CON CUIDADO

USTED ESTA SIENDO DEMANDADO POR: __________ para exigirle que desaloje el lugar donde reside por los motivos que se expresan en la demanda adjunta. Usted tiene derecho a llevar la causa a juicio para determinar si se le puede exigir que se mude, pero ES NECESARIO que haga TODO lo que se le pide a continuación en un plazo de **5 días** (no incluidos los sábados, domingos, ni días feriados) a partir de la fecha en que estos documentos se le entregaron a usted o a una persona que vive con usted, o se colocaron en su casa.

USTED DEBERA HACER LO SIGUIENTE:

1. **Deberá** escribir **en inglés** el (los) motivo(s) por el (los) cual(es) cree que no se le debe obligar a mudarse. El (Los) motivo(s) debera(n) entregarse por escrito al secretario del tribunal **en cualquiera de los siguientes** tribunales del Condado de Palm Beach:

- **205 North Dixie Highway, Suite 2.2200, West Palm Beach, FL 33401**
- **200 W. Atlantic Ave., Delray Beach, FL 33444**
- **3188 PGA Blvd., Palm Beach Gardens, FL 33410**
- **2950 State Road 15, Room S–100, Belle Glade, FL 33430**

2. **Deberá** enviar por correo o darle su(s) motivo(s) por escrito a: __________ Demandante/Abogado del Demandante __________ Dirección.

3. **Deberá** pagarle al secretario del tribunal el monto del alquiler que la demanda adjunta reclama como adeudado, así como cualquier alquiler pagadero hasta que concluya el litigio. Si usted considera que el monto reclamado en la demanda es incorrecto, deberá presentarle al secretario del tribunal una moción para que el tribunal determine el monto que deba pagarse. Si usted presenta una moción, deberá adjuntarle a ésta cualesquiera documentos que respalden su posición, y enviar por correo o entregar una copia de la misma al demandante/abogado del demandante.

4. SI USTED NO LLEVA A CABO LAS ACCIONES QUE SE ESPECIFICAN ANTERIORMENTE EN UN PLAZO DE 5 DIAS LABORABLES A PARTIR DE LA FECHA EN QUE ESTOS DOCUMENTOS SE LE ENTREGARON A USTED O A UNA PERSONA QUE VIVE CON USTED, O SE COLOCARON EN SU CASA, SE LE PODRA DESALOJAR SIN NECESIDAD DE CELEBRAR UNA AUDIENCIA NI CURSARSELE OTRO AVISO

5. Si la demanda adjunta también incluye una reclamaciôn por daños y perjuicios pecuniarios (tales como el incumplimiento de pago del alquiler), usted deberá responder a dicha reclamación por separado. Deberá exponer por escrito los motivos por los cuales considera que usted no debe la suma reclamada, y entregarlos al secretario del tribunal en la dirección que se especifica en el párrafo (1) anterior, así como enviar por correo o entregar una copia de los mismos al demandante/abogado del demandante en la dirección que se especifica en el párrafo (2) anterior. Esto deberá llevarse a cabo en un plazo de 20 días a partir de la fecha en que estos documentos se le entregaron a usted o a una persona que vive con usted. Esta obligación es aparte del requisito de responder a la demanda de desalojo en un plazo de 5 días a partir de la fecha en que estos documentos se le entregaron a usted o a una persona que vive con usted, o se colocaron en su casa.

Si usted es una persona minusválida que necesita algún servicio especial para poder participar en este procedimiento, usted tiene derecho, sin cargo para usted, a que se le provea cierta ayuda. Tenga la amabilidad de ponerse en contacto con: Americans with Disabilities Act Coordinator, Palm Beach County Courthouse, 205 N. Dixie Highway, West Palm Beach, Florida 33401; teléfono número (561) 355–4380, por lo menos 7 días antes de la cita fijada para su comparecencia en los tribunales, o inmediatamente después de recibir esta notificatión si el tiempo antes de la comparecencia que se ha programado es menos de 7 días; si usted tiene una discapacidad del oído o de la voz, llame al 711.

Si usted tiene dificultad en hablar o entender el idioma inglés, debe traer con usted una persona que hable bien inglés y el idioma que usted habla, y que sea capaz de traducir e interpretar ambos idiomas.

NAN TRIBINAL KONTE /SIKWI, NAN E POU KONTE PALM BEACH, FLORIDA

NIMEWO KA A.

Moun ki pote plent lan(yo),

kont

Akize a (yo).

______________________/

SITASYON POU METE MOUN DEYÓ NAN KAY POU AKIZE A (YO):

TANPRI LI AVÈK ATANSYON

GEN YON PWOSÈ KONT OU PA: __________

Ki mande w pou w sòti kote ou abite kounye a la pou rezon sa yo ke yo bay nan konplent ki atache a.

Ou gen dwa a yon jijman pou detèmine si yo ka mande w pou w sòti, men ou DWE fè TOUT bagay ki nan lis anba a. Ou dwe fè yo **nan espas 5 jou** (Samdi, Dimanch, ou jou fèt legal pa ladan 1) aprè dat ke yo ba w papye sa yo, oubyen yon moun ki abite avèk ou, oubyen yo te plake yo sou pòt kay ou.

MEN BAGAY KE OU DWE FÈ YO:

1. **Ou dwe** ekri rezon an (yo) pouki ou panse ke yo pa dwe fòse w sòti **ann anglè.** Ou dwe bay rezon sa yo pa ekri a Sekretè Tribinal **ki nan nenpòt nan adrès nou bay pi ba** la a, ki nan Tribinal Konte Palm Beach:

- **205 North Dixie Highway, Suite 2.2200, West Palm Beach, FL 33401**
- **200 W. Atlantic Ave., Delray Beach, FL 33444**
- **3188 PGA Blvd., Palm Beach Gardens, FL 33410**
- **2950 State Road 15, Room S–100, Belle Glade, FL 33430**

2. **Ou dwe** poste ou bay yon kopi rezon pa ekri a (yo) a:

____

Avoka Moun ki pote plent lan (yo), ki nan adrès: __________

____

3. **Ou dwe** peye Sekretè Tribinal la valè kòb lwaye ke konplent yo atache a di ou dwe ak nenpòt lòt lajan lwaye ke ou vin dwe jis le pwosè a fini. Si ou kwè ke valè lajan yo mande nan konplent lan pa korèk, ou dwe ranpli yon mosyon nan sekretarya Tribinal la pou Tribinal la ka detèmine ki valè ou dwe peye. Si w ranpli yon mosyon, ou dwe atache nan mosyon an nenpòt dokiman ki sipòte pozisyon w lan, epi voye pa lapòs oubyen bay yon kopi mosyon an a Akoka Moun ki pote plent lan (yo).

4. SI OU PA FÈ TOUT BAGAY YO ESPESIFYE ANLÈ A NAN ESPAS 5 JOU KOTE BIWO OUVÈ APRÈ DAT KE TE YO FIN BA W PAPYE SA YO, OUBYEN A YON MOUN KI ABITE NAN MENM KAY AVÈK OU, OUBYEN YO TE PLAKE YO SOU PÓT KAY OU, YO KA METE OU DEYÒ SAN YON JIJMAN, OUBYEN SAN YON LÒT NOTIS.

5. Si konplent ki atache a gen ladan I tou reklamasyon pou peye lajan pou (tankou lajan lwaye ou pa peye), ou dwe reponn reklamasyon sa separe. Ou dwe ekri rezon an (yo) pouki ou kwè ke ou pa dwe lajan yo mande a. Ou dwe bay rezon sa yo pa ekri a Sekretè Tribinal la nan adrès ki espesifye nan paragraf (1) anlè a, epi ou dwe voye pa lapòs oubyen bay yon kopi rezon pa ekri ou a (yo) a Avoka Moun ki pote plent lan (yo) nan adrès ki espesifye nan paragraf (2) anlè a. Sa dwe fèt nan espas 20 jou aprè dat yo te ba w papye sa yo, oubyen yon moun ki abite avèk ou. Obligasyon sa li separe de demand pou reponn a reklamasyon pou sòti nan kay la nan espas 5 jou kote biwo ouvè aprè yo te ba w paye yo, oubyen yon moun ki abite avèk ou, oubyen yo te plake yo sou pòt kay ou.

"Si ou se yon moun ki enfim ki bezwen akomodasyon pou w ka patisipe nan pwosedi sa, ou kalifye san ou pa gen okenn lajan pou w peye, gen pwovizyon pou jwen kèk éd. Tanpri kontakte, kòòdonatè pwogram Lwa pou Ameriken ki Enfim yo nan Tribinal Konte Palm Beach la ki nan 205 North Dixie Highway, West Palm Beach, Florida 33401; telefòn li se (561) 355–4380 nan 7 jou anvan dat ou gen randevou pou parèt nan Tribinal la, oubyen imedyatman apre ou fin resevwa konvokasyon an si lè ou gen pou w parèt nan tribinal la mwens ke 7 jou; si ou gen pwoblèm pou w tande oubyen pale, rele 711."

SI OU GEN PWOBLÈM PALE OU KONPRANN ANGLÈ, OU DWE VINI AK YON MOUN KI PALE NI ANGLÈ BYEN AK LANG OU PALE A, E KI KA TRADWIE ENTÈPRETE TOU DE LANG YO.

Adopted effective September 29, 2008. Amended effective January 17, 2012; November 19, 2014.

* supersedes admin. order 3.602–1/12

3.603. COUNTY COURT MOTION PRACTICE

IN THE CIRCUIT COURT OF THE FIFTEENTH JUDICIAL CIRCUIT IN AND FOR PALM BEACH COUNTY, FLORIDA

ADMINISTRATIVE ORDER NO. 3.603–9/08 *

IN RE: COUNTY COURT MOTION PRACTICE

Local Rule No. 4 does not apply to the County Court. Motion practice in the County Court would benefit from the procedure set forth in paragraph (2) of Local Rule No. 4. The County Court judges have been consulted and have overwhelmingly approved such provisions for application to County Court;

NOW, THEREFORE, pursuant to the authority conferred by Florida Rule of Judicial Administration 2.215, it is **ORDERED** as follows:

1. Prior to scheduling a hearing for any motion before the County Court, other than continuances and extensions of time, the party or attorney noticing the motion shall attempt to resolve the matter and shall certify the good faith attempt to resolve.

2. Motions for continuances and extensions of time (other than to obtain service of process) shall include a certification by the moving party or attorney that the movant has made a good faith effort to contact the opponent and shall further state whether there is any objection to the motion.

DONE and **SIGNED** in Chambers at West Palm Beach, Palm Beach County, Florida, this 29 day of September, 2008.

Kathleen J. Kroll
Chief Judge

Adopted effective September 29, 2008.

* supersedes admin. order 9.007–2/96

3.604. MOTIONS TO COMPEL DISCOVERY IN COUNTY CIVIL MATTERS

IN THE CIRCUIT COURT OF THE FIFTEENTH JUDICIAL CIRCUIT IN AND FOR PALM BEACH COUNTY, FLORIDA

ADMINISTRATIVE ORDER NO. 3.604–9/08 *

IN RE: MOTIONS TO COMPEL DISCOVERY IN COUNTY CIVIL MATTERS

1. No motions to compel discovery will be heard unless the motion or notice of hearing bears a certificate of moving counsel to the effect that he or she contacted opposing counsel and attempted to resolve the discovery dispute without a hearing, but that the matter could not be resolved.

2. When a motion to compel discovery alleges a complete failure to respond or object to discovery, and that there has been no request for extension, an ex parte order may be entered by the court requiring compliance with the original discovery demand within 10 days of the signing of the order. The movant shall submit the proposed order and addressed, stamped envelopes for the court's consideration.

DONE and **SIGNED** in Chambers at West Palm Beach, Palm Beach County, Florida, this 29 day of September, 2008.

Kathleen J. Kroll
Chief Judge

Adopted effective September 29, 2008.

* supersedes admin. order 9.009 3/97

3.605. COUNTY COURT CIVIL JURY TRIALS—BRANCH COURTHOUSE REQUESTS

IN THE CIRCUIT COURT OF THE FIFTEENTH JUDICIAL CIRCUIT IN AND FOR PALM BEACH COUNTY, FLORIDA

ADMINISTRATIVE ORDER 3.605–5/17 *

IN RE: COUNTY COURT CIVIL JURY TRIALS—BRANCH COURTHOUSE REQUESTS

County Court civil cases are assigned to court divisions in the various branch courthouses. The courthouse located in West Palm Beach is the central courthouse for the county and is the courthouse in which jury trials are held. When a party in a county court civil action assigned to the branch courthouse requests a trial by jury, the case will need to be transferred to the central courthouse for jury trial.

NOW, THEREFORE, pursuant to the authority conferred by Florida Rule of Judicial Administration 2.215, it is ordered that;

Upon written order of the judge assigned to a county civil division in a branch courthouse, a county court civil action pending in a branch courthouse in which a jury trial is requested shall, upon the case becoming at issue and a notice of trial filed by either party, be transferred to the central courthouse for jury trial. The Office of Clerk and Comptroller shall randomly assign such cases among the civil divisions of the county court.

DONE AND ORDERED in Chambers at West Palm Beach, Palm Beach County, Florida, on this 11 day of May, 2017.

Jeffrey Colbath
Chief Judge

Adopted effective September 29, 2008. Amended effective May 11, 2017.

* supersedes admin. order 3.605–9/08

3.606. COUNTY CIVIL COVER SHEET

IN THE CIRCUIT COURT OF THE FIFTEENTH JUDICIAL CIRCUIT IN AND FOR PALM BEACH COUNTY, FLORIDA

ADMINISTRATIVE ORDER NO.: 3.606–12/12 *

IN RE: COUNTY CIVIL COVER SHEET

In an effort to promote more informed judicial decision making, the Fifteenth Judicial Circuit has identified the need to revise the Civil Cover Sheet to identify PIP and Wage Dispute matters in the county and small claims court.

NOW, THEREFORE, pursuant to the authority conferred by Florida Rule of Judicial Administration 2.215, it is **ORDERED** as follows:

1. All parties filing a County Civil Case Type and/or a Small Claims matter are hereby required to utilize the attached Civil Cover Sheet.

2. At the time of filing, the Clerk and Comptroller shall direct any party who does not provide this form to the Self Service Center for assistance and/or provide the form at the appropriate cost.

DONE AND SIGNED in Chambers, at West Palm Beach, Palm Beach County, Florida this 21 day of December, 2012.

Peter D. Blanc
Chief Judge

IN THE COUNTY COURT OF THE FIFTEENTH JUDICIAL CIRCUIT IN AND FOR PALM BEACH COUNTY, FLORIDA

CASE NUMBER: ________
DIVISION: ________

IN RE: THE MATTER OF:

____________________,
PLAINTIFF[1]

v.

____________________,
DEFENDANT
____________________ /

COUNTY & SMALL CLAIMS CIVIL COVER SHEET

I. TYPE OF CASE (Place an x in one box only. If the case fits more than one type of case, select the most definitive.)

TORTS

☑ *Auto negligence*
☑ *Professional malpractice*
☑ *Products liability*
☑ *Other negligence*

OTHER CIVIL

☑ *Challenge to proposed constitutional amendment*
☑ *Condominium*
☑ *Contracts*
☑ *Civil Replevin*
☑ *Eviction*
☑ *Foreclosure*
☑ *Arbitration/Foreign Judgment*
☑ ***Personal Injury Protection (PIP) (claims up to $5,000)***
☑ ***Personal Injury Protection (PIP) (claims from $5,000.01–$15,000.00)***
☑ *Real property/Mortgage foreclosure*
☑ ***Wage Dispute (claims up to $5,000)***
☑ ***Wage Dispute (claims from $5,000.01–$15,000.00)***
☑ ***Other County Civil*** ________
☑ ***Small Claims other than Wage Dispute and PIP***

II. IS JURY TRIAL DEMANDED IN COMPLAINT?

☑ Yes

☑ No

III. CLAIMS/PARTIES

Has there been a previous case filed in Palm Beach County/15th Judicial Circuit which involved the same claim against the same adverse party and which was voluntarily or involuntarily dismissed?

☑ Yes. Please provide the appropriate case number(s) ________.

☑ No

I CERTIFY that the information I have provided in this cover sheet is accurate to the best of my knowledge and belief.

Signature ________________ Fla. Bar # ____________
Attorney or party (Bar # if attorney)

________________ Date ____________
(type or print name)

Adopted effective September 29, 2008. Amended effective December 19, 2012; December 21, 2012.

* supersedes admin. order 3.606–12/12 (dated 12/19/12)

3.607. EMERGENCY HEARINGS IN COUNTY CIVIL MATTERS

IN THE CIRCUIT COURT OF THE FIFTEENTH JUDICIAL CIRCUIT IN AND FOR PALM BEACH COUNTY, FLORIDA

ADMINISTRATIVE ORDER NO. 3.607–11/14

IN RE: EMERGENCY HEARINGS IN COUNTY CIVIL MATTERS

Pursuant to the authority conferred by Florida Rule of Judicial Administration 2.215, it is **ORDERED** as follows:

1. Requests for Emergency Hearings shall be decided by each judge on the Emergency Motion alone,

2. Upon receiving a request for an emergency hearing, the judge shall decide whether an emergency exists, and if so, shall schedule a hearing, enter any ex parte order deemed necessary, or take any other appropriate action.

3. The following are considered emergencies in county civil matters:

a. Motions to Stay Writ of Possession

b. Motions to Restore Utility Service

c. Requests for Relief for Prohibited Practices under Florida Statute 83.67

d. Motions to Cancel Foreclosure Sale when sale is within two (2) business days from date of filing motion.

4. The emergency filing will be forwarded to the divisional judge in accordance with Administrative Order 2.312.

DONE and **SIGNED** in Chambers at West Palm Beach, Palm Beach County, Florida, this 19 day of November, 2014

Jeffrey Colbath
Chief Judge

Adopted effective November 19, 2014.

Special Civil Administrative Orders

3.901. CODE ENFORCEMENT CITATION SYSTEM AND FINAL JUDGMENT FORMS

IN THE CIRCUIT COURT OF THE FIFTEENTH JUDICIAL CIRCUIT IN AND FOR PALM BEACH COUNTY, FLORIDA

ADMINISTRATIVE ORDER NO. 3.901–9/08 *

IN RE: CODE ENFORCEMENT CITATION SYSTEM AND FINAL JUDGMENT FORMS

The Florida Legislature, pursuant to section 162.21, Florida Statutes (2007), has enabled counties and municipalities to issue citations to persons reasonably believed to have committed civil infractions in violation of duly enacted codes or ordinances. The contents of the citation and enforcement procedures are specifically prescribed in the enabling legislation.

NOW, THEREFORE, pursuant to the authority conferred by Florida Rule of Judicial Administration 2.215, it is **ORDERED** as follows:

The following forms and procedures are adopted for all code enforcement cases that shall come before the Palm Beach County Courts.

A. Forms

1. Approved Citation Form attached hereto as Exhibit "A" front and back sides.

2. Approved Final Judgment Forms attached hereto as Exhibit "B1" and "B2".

B. Procedures

The following basic procedures shall apply:

1. The municipality or county must enact a valid Code Enforcement Citation System Ordinance.

2. After notice and a reasonable time to comply, (not to exceed 30 days), The county or the municipal code enforcement officer may issue the citation appearing in Exhibit A (attached hereto).

3. Upon receipt of the citation, the party may either pay the amount set forth in the citation or request a hearing in the County Court.

4. If the party fails to timely pay the applicable fine and fails to appear or request a hearing, the clerk of court shall so advise the appropriate county court judge by the submission of a proposed Default and Final Judgment. (see Exhibit B1).

5. If the case proceeds to hearing and a violation is found, the Court shall order the amount of the fine, (not to exceed $500 per violation), and shall enter a Final Judgment against the party as set forth in Exhibit B2.

6. It shall be the responsibility of the appropriate municipality or county to file any appropriate lien and record any judgments entered into the public records.

C. Fee schedule

Approved Fee Schedule For Uncontested Violations Which May Be Paid By Mail:

CODE ORDINANCE VIOLATIONS COUNTY COURT UNIFORM SCHEDULE LOCAL ORDINANCE VIOLATIONS

	FINE	COSTS	TOTAL
Class I	$50	$8.00	$ 58.00
Class II	$75	$8.00	$ 83.00
Class III	$125	$8.00	$133.00
Class IV	$250	$8.00	$258.00

DONE and SIGNED in Chambers at West Palm Beach, Palm Beach County, Florida this 29 day of September, 2008.

Kathleen J. Kroll
Chief Judge

* supersedes admin. order 9.002–10/96

FLORIDA UNIFORM CODE CITATION	NO. 00 x ☐ City Ordinance ☐ County Code
County of/ City of **COUNTY OF PALM BEACH** 3400 Belvedere Road West Palm Beach, Florida 33406 (407) 233-5500	

The undersigned certified that he had just and reasonable grounds to believe, and does believe that on:

Day of Week	Month	Day	Year	Time		AM / PM

Name (*print*)	First	MI	Last
Street			

City		State		Zip
Telephone Number	Date of Birth	Race	Sex	Height

Violation Description

Code Section No.

Location of Violation: ☐Uninc. ☐Inc.

Classification of Violation	Fine up to $500 if contested and costs
	Fine, if paid within 10 days + $8 costs **Amount: $**

NOTICE: *This citation is issued pursuant to section 462.21, Fla. Stat. The violation for which you are charged is a civil infraction. Your signature below does not constitute an admission of guilty however, willful refusal to sign and accept this citation is a misdemeanor of the 2nd degree as provided S.775.082 or 775.083 Fla. Stat. Failure to pay the applicable civil penalty or request a hearing from the Clerk of the Court within 10 days shall constitute a waiver of your right to contest this citation, and judgment may be entered against you for an amount of up to $500. per infraction*

Signature of Individual

Signature of Officer ID #

Print Name

Title of Officer

DATE/TIME OF ISSUANCE		
TIME		AM / PM
Month	Day	Year

WHITE Clerk's Office YELLOW Individual PINK Code Enforcement BLUE Clerk's Office

YOU MAY MAIL THE AMOUNT INDICATED ON THE REVERSE SIDE OF THIS CITATION ALONG WITH THE COPY OF YOUR CITATION TO:

CLERK OF THE COURT
P. O. BOX 3544
WEST PALM BEACH, FLORIDA 33402

Payment may be made at the location listed below between 8:30 a.m. and 4:30 p.m. Monday through Friday.

Cashier's Check, Money Orders, or Checks shall be made payable to Palm Beach County.

ALL FEES MUST BE REMITTED IN U.S. FUNDS

All fine amounts include the basic fine with State Administrative fees added per Section 943.25, Florida Statutes ($3.00).

You may request a hearing or pay the fine within 10 days in person or by mail at one of the locations listed below:

Central Courthouse
205 North Dixie Highway
W. Palm Beach, FL 33401
(561) 355-2994

North County Courthouse
3188 PGA Boulevard
Palm Beach Gardens, FL 33410
(561) 355-2994

South County Courthouse
200 W. Atlantic Avenue
Delray Beach, FL 33445
(561 355-2994

Glades Courthouse
38844 State Road 80
Belle Glade, FL 33430
(561) 355-2994

CODE ORDINANCE VIOLATIONS
COUNTY COURT UNIFORM TIME SCHEDULE
LOCAL ORDINANCE VIOLATIONS

	Fine	Costs	Total
Class I	$ 50	$ 8	$ 58
Class II	$ 75	$ 8	$ 83
Class III	$125	$ 8	$133
Class IV	$250	$ 8	$258

If you elect a hearing and are found to have committed the infraction the judge may impose a penalty not to exceed $500.00 plus court costs, per infraction.

You may request a hearing by indicating below:

I hereby request a hearing.

Signature Date

Exhibit "A"

EXHIBIT "B1"

IN THE COUNTY COURT OF THE FIFTEENTH JUDICIAL CIRCUIT IN AND FOR PALM BEACH COUNTY, FLORIDA

CASE NO.:

Plaintiff,

v.

Defendant.

_____________________/

DEFAULT AND FINAL JUDGMENT

THIS CAUSE came before the Court upon notice from the Clerk of Court that the Defendant has failed to timely respond to the above-captioned citation and is therefore in default. Accordingly, a default is hereby entered against the Defendant herein. Upon said default, it is hereby

ORDERED AND ADJUDGED that the Plaintiff recover from the Defendant the sum of $ ________, including costs, which sum shall bear interest at the prevailing statutory rate, and for which let execution issue.

DONE and SIGNED in chambers at West Palm Beach, Palm Beach County, Florida, this ___ day of ________, 20 ___.

____

County Court Judge

EXHIBIT "B2"

IN THE COUNTY COURT OF THE FIFTEENTH JUDICIAL CIRCUIT IN AND FOR PALM BEACH COUNTY, FLORIDA

CASE NO.:

Plaintiff,

v.

Defendant.

_____________________/

FINAL JUDGMENT

THIS CAUSE came before the Court upon citation issued against the Defendant.

IT IS ADJUDGED that the Plaintiff shall recover from the Defendant the principal sum of $ ________, plus costs in the amount of $ ________, for a total of $ ________, which sum shall bear interest at the prevailing statutory rate, and for which let execution issue.

DONE AND SIGNED in chambers at West Palm Beach, Palm Beach County, Florida, this ___ day of ________, 20 ___.

____

County Court Judge

Adopted effective September 29, 2008.

3.902. PREMARITAL PREPARATION COURSE AND MOTIONS TO WAIVE DELAY OF MARRIAGE LICENSE'S EFFECTIVE DATE

IN THE CIRCUIT COURT OF THE FIFTEENTH JUDICIAL CIRCUIT IN AND FOR PALM BEACH COUNTY, FLORIDA

ADMINISTRATIVE ORDER NO. 3.902–5/10 *

IN RE: PREMARITAL PREPARATION COURSE AND MOTIONS TO WAIVE DELAY OF MARRIAGE LICENSE'S EFFECTIVE DATE

Florida Statutes Section 741.0305 permits reduction of a marriage license application fee upon completion of a premarital preparation course and authorizes a judicial circuit to designate certain providers to offer such courses. The effective date of a marriage license is delayed three days for Florida residents if the couple has not submitted valid certificates of completion of a premarital preparation course. A county court judge is authorized to waive the delayed effective date for good cause, under Florida Statutes Section 741.04(3). Most couples applying to waive the effective date do so without benefit of counsel, and may be unaware of the proper form in which such requests should be made. It will promote efficiency and fairness if a standard form is made available to request that the delay be waived.

NOW, THEREFORE, pursuant to the authority conferred by Florida Rule of Judicial Administration 2.215, it is **ORDERED** as follows:

1. **Premarital Preparation Course:**

a. A Premarital Preparation Course shall be established within the Fifteenth Judicial Circuit and maintained by the Administrative Office of the Court. The Clerk of Court shall make the roster available to all parties requesting a marriage license.

b. Instructors shall be eligible to provide the premarital preparation course under Chapter 741 of the Florida Statutes if they fall within one of the categories set forth in the Chapter, to wit:

1) A psychologist licensed under chapter 490;

2) A clinical social worker licensed under chapter 491;

3) A marriage and family therapist licensed under chapter 491;

4) A mental health counselor licensed under chapter 491;

5) An official representative of a religious institution which is recognized under s. 496.404(20), F.S., if the representative has relevant training;

6) A school counselor certified to offer premarital preparation courses.

c. All area course providers wishing to be added to the roster for this circuit shall complete and submit the registration form, which shall be available from the Administrative Office of the Court. The Administrative Office of the Court shall be responsible for generating and maintaining the roster of area course providers, and for providing the roster to the Clerk.

2. **Motions to Waive Delay of Effective Date:**

The Clerk of Court shall make the form, attached as Exhibit A, available to all parties requesting that the delayed effective date of their marriage license be waived.

DONE and **SIGNED**, in Chambers, at West Palm Beach, Palm Beach County, Florida this 4 day of May, 2010.

Peter D. Blanc
Chief Judge

* supersedes admin. order 3.902–9/08

EXHIBIT A

IN THE COUNTY COURT OF THE FIFTEENTH JUDICIAL CIRCUIT IN AND FOR PALM BEACH COUNTY, FLORIDA

In Re: The Marriage License of

and

__________ /

MOTION FOR WAIVER OF DELAY OF EFFECTIVE DATE OF MARRIAGE LICENSE

The undersigned bride and groom request this Honorable Court to grant an exception to the delay of the effective date of the marriage license, and allege the following:

1. The undersigned bride and groom are both residents of the State of Florida.

2. The undersigned have not attended or completed a premarital preparation course for the following reason(s): __________. The undersigned cannot wait for the marriage ceremony to be delayed three (3) days from the date of application of the marriage license for the following reason(s):

____

____

3. The undersigned submit the reason(s) set forth above constitutes hardship and good cause for waiver of the delayed effective date of the marriage license.

Sworn and submitted this ___ day of __________, 20 ___.

______________________ ______________________
Bride's Signature Groom's Signature

STATE OF FLORIDA

COUNTY OF __________

Sworn to or affirmed and subscribed before me this ___ day of __________, 20 ___, by __________ (name of groom) and __________ (name of bride), who are either personally known to me OR who produced identification (Type of Identification Produced __________).

____

Signature of Notary Public or Deputy Clerk

(Print, type, or stamp name of deputy clerk or commissioned name of notary public)

IN THE COUNTY COURT OF THE FIFTEENTH JUDICIAL CIRCUIT IN AND FOR PALM BEACH COUNTY, FLORIDA

In Re: The Marriage License of

and

__________ /

ORDER

This matter came before the Court on the Motion of the applicants to the marriage license as set forth above. The Court having reviewed the Motion and being fully advised in the premises, the Motion is hereby:

( ) Granted. The reasons set forth in the motion constitute good cause for the waiver of the delayed effective date of the marriage license. Any marriage license issued to these applicants shall become effective immediately.

( ) Denied. The reasons set forth in the motion do not constitute good cause for the waiver of the delayed effective date of the marriage license. Any marriage license issued to these applicants shall be delayed three (3) days from the date of application.

DONE and ORDERED in Chambers at West Palm Beach, Florida, this ___ day of __________, 20 ___.

____
(Signature of Presiding Judge)

Adopted effective September 29, 2008. Amended effective May 4, 2010.

3.903. [VACATED AND SET ASIDE BY ORDER 3.903-1/13, EFFECTIVE JANUARY 8, 2013.]

3.904. [VACATED AND SET ASIDE BY ORDER 3.904-8/13, EFFECTIVE AUGUST 22, 2013.]

3.905. PREPAYMENT OF FEE FOR FILING COMPLAINT OF REPLEVIN AGAINST LAW ENFORCEMENT AGENCY

IN THE CIRCUIT COURT OF THE FIFTEENTH JUDICIAL CIRCUIT IN AND FOR PALM BEACH COUNTY, FLORIDA

ADMINISTRATIVE ORDER NO.: 3.905–1/15 *

IN RE: PREPAYMENT OF FEE FOR FILING COMPLAINT OF REPLEVIN AGAINST LAW ENFORCEMENT AGENCY

During the performance of a law enforcement officer's duties, firearms may be removed from an individual and taken into custody of the law enforcement agency. When no court case is filed, it may be necessary for the individual to file an action in Replevin against the law enforcement agency in order to seek to obtain the return of the firearm. To file an action for Replevin requires the payment of a filing fee which may exceed the value of the weapon.

Pursuant to the authority conferred by Florida Rule of Judicial Administration 2.215, it is hereby **ORDERED** as follows:

The Clerk of Court shall not require prepayment of a filing fee when an individual files a Writ of Replevin against a law enforcement agency for the return of a firearm, pistol or other property that has been seized and is being held by a Law Enforcement Agency when no charges or related case have been filed.

DONE and **SIGNED** in Chambers at West Palm Beach, Palm Beach County, Florida, this 9 day of January, 2015.

Jeffrey Colbath
Chief Judge

Adopted effective October 19, 2010. Amended effective January 9, 2015.

* supersedes admin. order 3.905–10/10

3.906. ADMINISTRATIVE CLOSURE OF REOPENED COUNTY COURT CIVIL ACTIONS

IN THE CIRCUIT COURT OF THE FIFTEENTH JUDICIAL CIRCUIT, IN AND FOR PALM BEACH COUNTY, FLORIDA

ADMINISTRATIVE ORDER NO.: 3.906–3/12

IN RE: ADMINISTRATIVE CLOSURE OF REOPENED COUNTY COURT CIVIL ACTIONS

County Court civil cases may be reopened after entry of final judgment in order for final process to be issued pursuant to Florida Statute Chapter 56. Cases reopened after final judgment for money damages can be administratively closed and notice under Florida Rule of Civil Procedure 1.420 is not required. Park Finance of Broward, Inc. v. Jones, ___ So.3d ___; 36 Fla. L. Weekly D1505 (Fla. 4th DCA July 13, 2011). There currently exists over 1,800 county civil cases and over 2,800 small claims cases that have had no record activity since December 31, 2008. According to the Clerk and Comptroller's docketing system, the docket sheets for each of these "reopened" cases include a docket code indicating that some type of final judgment has been entered in the matter. The Court is responsible for managing its caseload pursuant to the Florida Rule of Judicial Administration 2.545, and the administration of justice would be furthered by administratively closing those "reopened" cases which have been dormant for at least three years as the personnel time involved in manually retrieving and reviewing the files is cost prohibitive.

Pursuant to the authority conferred by Florida Rule of Judicial Administration 2.215, it is hereby **ORDERED** as follows:

1. County civil reopened cases that have had no record activity since December 31, 2008 and have a docket code indicating a final judgment was entered are hereby administratively closed. A list of those cases are attached hereto and incorporated herein as Exhibit A [1].

2. Small claims reopened cases that have had no activity since December 31, 2008 and have a docket code indicating a final judgment was entered are hereby administratively closed. A list of those cases are attached hereto and incorporated herein as Exhibit B [2].

3. Due to practical and resource limitations, the Clerk & Comptroller is hereby directed to effectuate the closing process by entering a docket code in the case management system to administratively close the case and by associating the scanned image of this order to that docket entry. The Clerk & Comptroller is not required to manually file a hard copy of this order in each physical case file. If a party files written notice asserting that their case was administratively closed in error, the clerk shall reopen the file without charge to the party.

4. Court Technology is hereby directed to post Exhibits "A" and "B" on the circuit's website for a period of at least 90 days.

DONE and **SIGNED** in Chambers at West Palm Beach, Palm Beach County, Florida, this 28 day of March, 2012.

Peter D. Blanc
Chief Judge

Adopted effective March 28, 2012.

1 Attachment not included.

2 Attachment not included.

3.907. PALM BEACH COUNTY WAGE DISPUTE DOCKET AND CREATION OF "WD" DIVISION

IN THE CIRCUIT COURT OF THE FIFTEENTH JUDICIAL CIRCUIT IN AND FOR PALM BEACH COUNTY, FLORIDA

ADMINISTRATIVE ORDER NO. 3.907–3/15 *

IN RE: PALM BEACH COUNTY WAGE DISPUTE DOCKET AND CREATION OF "WD" DIVISION

Palm Beach County and Legal Aid Society of Palm Beach County have entered into an agreement in an effort to assist those individuals in disputes regarding unpaid wages. In order to increase the fair, effective, and efficient resolution of these disputes, a specialized docket is hereby created and one Judge shall preside over this docket.

NOW, THEREFORE, pursuant to the authority conferred by Florida Rule of Judicial Administration 2.215, it is **ORDERED** as follows:

1. The Administrative Office of the Court's Technology Department created Division "WD" and all Wage Dispute cases within the small claims jurisdiction of the court shall be assigned to this Division.

2. Pursuant to Administrative Order 3.606, the Plaintiff is required to file a Civil Cover Sheet for all newly filed County Civil Cases. The Clerk and Comptroller shall review the Civil Cover Sheet to determine if a case is a small claims wage dispute, and if so, the Clerk and Comptroller shall assign the case to Division "WD". In the event a case is identified as a small claims wage dispute and the case was not assigned to Division "WD", the divisional judge may prepare an Order of Reassignment to the Wage Dispute Division.

3. At the time of filing, if the case is filed by a pro-se litigant, the Clerk and Comptroller shall provide the litigant with a copy of the attached handout (in English, Spanish or Creole) referring the litigant to the Legal Aid Society of Palm Beach County.

4. A County Judge will preside over this docket and hearings shall take place at the Palm Beach County Courthouse on the last Thursday of each month, subject to change by the presiding Judge, beginning at 10:00 a.m. Additional docket sessions will be scheduled depending on the volume of cases.

5. The Alternative Dispute Resolution Office shall work with the volunteer mediators to identify a team of mediators to coordinate and attend pre-suit mediation and to appear during pretrial hearings to assist in the resolution of these cases.

6. The Administrative Office of the Court, in collaboration with the [1], will facilitate collection and maintenance of the statistical data for the program. In addition to tracking the number of cases assigned to the Division, number of cases scheduled for hearing, and court disposition, a record of the funds recovered shall be maintained on a monthly basis.

7. In the event that the presiding judge in Division WD determines that the circumstances of any particular case assigned to Division WD indicate that the case would be appropriate for transfer to a regular civil division, the judge will direct the Clerk and Comptroller to randomly reassign that case.

DONE and **SIGNED,** in Chambers, at West Palm Beach, Palm Beach County, Florida, this 9 day of March, 2015.

Jeffrey Colbath
Chief Judge

Adopted effective December 19, 2012. Amended effective March 9, 2015.

* supersedes admin. order 3.907—12/12.

1 http://www.legalaidpbc.org/

3.908. ESTABLISHMENT OF ENGLE PROGENY TOBACCO LITIGATION TRIAL DIVISION AND REALLOCATION OF DIVISION 'AI' CASES

IN THE CIRCUIT COURT OF THE FIFTEENTH JUDICIAL CIRCUIT IN AND FOR PALM BEACH COUNTY, FLORIDA

ADMINISTRATIVE ORDER NO. 3.908–2/16

RE: ESTABLISHMENT OF ENGLE PROGENY TOBACCO LITIGATION TRIAL DIVISION AND REALLOCATION OF DIVISION "AI" CASES

To better serve the citizens of Palm Beach County, the Fifteenth Judicial Circuit has found that a more effective and efficient use of judicial resources is best achieved by transferring Engle Progeny Tobacco Litigation cases to one division to be presided over by one judge.

NOW, THEREFORE, pursuant to the authority conferred by Florida Rule of Judicial Administration 2.215, it is **ORDERED** as follows:

1. Effective February 1, 2016, all Engle Progeny Tobacco cases shall be transferred to Circuit Civil Division "AI".

2. The Clerk of Court shall reassign all of the Engle Progeny Tobacco cases listed in the attached Exhibit "A" [1] into Circuit Civil Division "AI".

3. In order to equalize the judicial caseload of the reassignment of the tobacco cases into Circuit Civil Division "AI", the Clerk of Court shall randomly reassign all the cases listed in the attached Exhibit "B" [2] from Circuit Civil Division "AI" amongst the other Circuit Civil Divisions.

4. No later than February 18, 2016, the Clerk of Court shall provide to Court Administration a list of the divisions to which the cases were reassigned.

5. The Clerk of Court shall prepare a Notice of Reassignment and serve either electronically or by United States Mail the Notice of Reassignment on the Plaintiff.

a. The Notice shall be docketed and available for public viewing within twenty-four (24) hours of the reassignment.

b. The Notice shall contain a directive to the Plaintiff to serve the Notice of Reassignment on all parties, in accordance with Rule of Judicial Administration 2.516. The Clerk of Court shall file and serve the Notice of Reassignment on the Plaintiff no later than February 18, 2016.

6. Within seven (7) business days of the service of the Notice of Reassignment, the Plaintiff shall serve in accordance with Rule of Judicial Administration 2.516, a copy of the Notice of Reassignment on all parties who have not been dismissed or dropped from the action. The Plaintiff shall also file a Notice of Service of the Notice of Reassignment ("Notice of Service") with the Clerk of Court. The Notice of Service is to include a complete and accurate service list.

DONE and **SIGNED** in Chambers at West Palm Beach, Palm Beach County, Florida, this 1 day of February, 2016.

Jeffery J. Colbath
Chief Judge

Adopted effective February 1, 2016.

1 Exhibit A not attached.

2 Exhibit B not attached.

3.909. CREATION OF CIRCUIT DIVISION 'AK'

IN THE CIRCUIT COURT OF THE FIFTEENTH JUDICIAL CIRCUIT IN AND FOR PALM BEACH COUNTY, FLORIDA

ADMINISTRATIVE ORDER NO. 3.909–8/17

IN RE: CREATION OF CIRCUIT CIVIL DIVISION "AK"

In the interest of judicial economy and to increase efficiency, a twelfth Circuit Civil Division is created and will be titled Division "AK".

NOW, THEREFORE, pursuant to the authority conferred by Florida Rule of Judicial Administration 2.215, it is **ORDERED AND ADJUDGED** as follows:

A. Creation of Division.

1. Effective August 23, 2017, the Clerk and Comptroller will create Circuit Civil Division "AK" in its case maintenance system ("Showcase") for the sole purpose of transferring cases.

2. The Clerk and Comptroller shall not assign any newly filed cases to this division until September 1, 2017.

B. Transfer of Pending Circuit Civil Cases.

1. Court Administration will identify an equal number of cases from each of the eleven circuit civil divisions to be transferred to Division "AK" and provide the list to the Clerk and Comptroller.

2. Upon receipt of the list of cases, the Clerk and Comptroller will reassign the identified cases to Division "AK".

3. The Clerk of Court will prepare a Notice of Reassignment and serve it on the Plaintiff either electronically or by United States Mail.

a. The Notice of Reassignment shall be docketed and available for public viewing within twenty-four (24) hours of the reassignment.

b. The Notice of Reassignment shall contain a directive to the Plaintiff to serve the Notice of Reassignment on all parties, in accordance with Rule of Judicial Administration 2.516. The Clerk of Court shall file and serve the Notice of Reassignment on the Plaintiff no later than August 29, 2017.

4. Within seven (7) business days of the service of the Notice of Reassignment, the Plaintiff shall serve in accordance with Rule of Judicial Administration 2.516 a copy of the Notice of Reassignment on all parties who have not been dismissed or dropped from the action. The Plaintiff shall also file a Notice of Service of the Notice of Reassignment ("Notice of Service") with the Clerk of Court. The Notice of Service is to include a complete service list.

5. When, at the time of the transfer, a case has a hearing scheduled in the original division during August, 2017, the hearing date will remain as scheduled and will be heard by the judge before whom the hearing was originally scheduled. Any hearing scheduled beyond September 1, 2017, shall be reset in Division "AK" by the parties.

6. When, at the time of the transfer, a case is set for trial during August, 2017, the trial date will remain as scheduled and will be heard by the judge before whom the trial was set. Any trial scheduled after September 1, 2017, is to be reset in Division AK by the parties.

7. A list of the transferred cases will be maintained by the Administrative Office of the Court, and will be posted on the Fifteenth Judicial Circuit's website.

C. Assignment of Newly Filed Cases. Division "AK" will be activated in the Clerk's case maintenance system ("Showcase") on September 1, 2017. The Clerk and Comptroller will then randomly assign all newly filed cases amongst the twelve circuit civil divisions.

D. Emergency Matters. Any emergency matter that arises prior to September 1, 2017, is to be referred to the previously assigned division for disposition.

DONE and SIGNED in Chambers at West Palm Beach, Palm Beach County, Florida, this 23rd day of August, 2017

Krista Marx
Chief Judge

Adopted effective September 1, 2017.

3.910. WEB–BASED VIDEO CONFERENCING

IN THE CIRCUIT COURT OF THE FIFTEENTH JUDICIAL CIRCUIT IN AND FOR PALM BEACH COUNTY, FLORIDA

ADMINISTRATIVE ORDER NO. 3.910 1/19

IN RE: WEB–BASED VIDEO CONFERENCING IN CIRCUIT CIVIL DIVISIONS

Florida Rule of Judicial Administration 2.530 provides that a judge may direct that communication equipment be used for a motion hearing, pretrial conference or a status conference with notice to the parties and consideration of any objections to the use of the equipment. The use of video conferencing in non-evidentiary court events improves the efficiency of the judiciary and provides a savings to the public.

NOW, THEREFORE, pursuant to the authority conferred by Florida Rule of Judicial Administration 2.215, it is **ORDERED** as follows:

1. A web-based video conferencing technology project will commence February 1, 2019 in circuit civil divisions for non-evidentiary hearings.

2. Participation by each Circuit Civil division is optional. A current list of participating divisions can be found at https://15thcircuit.com/services/court–technology/approved–video. Each division will have its own rules and instructions that participants are to follow.

3. Only vendors registered with the Fifteenth Judicial Circuit's Court Technology Office can be used to provide web-based video conferencing services as part of this project.

a. Companies can register to be an approved vendor by emailing a completed, signed Video Appearance Acceptable Use Policy form, found at https://15thcircuit.com/services/court–technology/approved–video, to CAD–Video_Appearances@pbcgov.org.

b. Parties can locate approved vendors at: https://15thcircuit.com/services/court–technology/approved–video.

4. Web-based video conferencing technology will be available when all parties have signed and filed the Acceptable Use Policy found at https://15thcircuit.com/services/court–technology/approved–video.

5. Costs for the web-based video conferencing are to be borne by the parties in accordance with the approved vendor's policies.

6. All forms, notices and links for the Video Appearance Project are available on the Circuit's website at the following link: https://15thcircuit.com/services/court–technology/approved–video

DONE AND SIGNED in chambers in West Palm Beach, Palm Beach County, Florida this 31 day of January, 2019

Krista Marx
Chief Judge

Adopted effective January 31, 2019.

Criminal Orders

Administrative Matters

4.101. ADMINISTRATIVE PROCEDURES IN THE CRIMINAL DIVISION

IN THE CIRCUIT COURT OF THE FIFTEENTH JUDICIAL CIRCUIT IN AND FOR PALM BEACH COUNTY

ADMINISTRATIVE ORDER NO. 4.101 6/17 *

IN RE: ADMINISTRATIVE PROCEDURES IN THE CRIMINAL DIVISION

Pursuant to the authority conferred by Florida Rule of Judicial Administration 2.215, it is hereby **ORDERED** that the following administrative procedures are established for the Criminal Division of the Circuit and County Court:

A. Filing of Capital Cases.

1. All capital cases will be assigned by the Clerk of Court on a rotating basis amongst the judges in the Circuit Criminal Division.

a. This assignment will occur upon arrest of the defendant(s), the filing of a direct file arrest warrant, or filing of an indictment.

b. This rotational assignment shall be separate from, and independent of, the non-capital wheel.

c. Any divisional assignments made under the previous Administrative Order for cases not yet filed will be canceled by the Clerk and, upon the arrest of the defendant, the filing of a Direct File Arrest Warrant, or the filing of an Indictment, will be assigned to the division next on the rotational assignment.

2. The assignment of capital cases shall be made without reference to any other felony charge involving the same defendant. If a capital case is assigned to a division that is different than a lower numbered felony case involving the same defendant, the State shall file a motion to transfer the lower numbered felony case to the division to which the capital case is assigned.

B. Filing of Non–Capital Cases. With the exception of those cases assigned to Division Y pursuant to Administrative Order 4.502, the Clerk of Court shall assign all non-capital cases on a rotating basis among the judges in the Criminal Division using a blind-assignment process.

C. Captions to Include Division Assignments. The caption of all pleadings and notices filed in the criminal division shall include the letter designation of the division to which the case is assigned.

D. Arraignment.

1. When a defendant appears at first appearance and an information has not been filed, arraignment shall be scheduled thirty (30) days from the date of arrest at the Criminal Justice Complex.

2. When an information is filed prior to the expiration of thirty (30) days, the arraignment of a defendant in custody will be rescheduled on Tuesday afternoons at 1:30 p.m. in Division "KK2" at the Criminal Justice Complex, unless waived in writing.

3. If formal charges are not filed by:

a. the thirtieth (30th) day following the arrest or service of a capias for a defendant in custody, the defendant shall be brought to a first appearance hearing for further proceedings consistent with F.R.Cr.P. 3.134.

b. the arraignment date for Defendants on pre-trial release, the Court shall take action consistent with F.R.Cr.P. 3.134. In the event the State Attorney subsequently files formal charges relating to such an arrest or service of a capias, the Clerk shall proceed with the provisions set forth in F.R.Cr.P. 3.131(j).

4. Arraignment for defendants released from custody shall be set on the day of the week designated by the Judge of the assigned felony division following the **thirtieth (30th)** day after the date of arrest **or as soon as practicable.**

a. Prior to release, the defendant must sign a "Notice of Arraignment" which shall be completed by the Booking Office, indicating that the defendant is to report to the assigned Felony Division Courtroom in the Palm Beach County Courthouse, West Palm Beach, Florida at 8:45 a.m. on the day of arraignment.

b. Notwithstanding the above provision, a defendant charged with Felony–Driving with a Suspended License who has been released on bond prior to arraignment, shall be set for an arraignment at the Criminal Justice Courtroom, Div. "KK2", at 1:30 p.m. on the Tuesday following the 45th day after the date of arrest.

5. No Defendant shall be released from custody without signing for a court date.

6. Unmarried minors shall not be arraigned on any criminal charge prior to notification of parents or guardian, unless otherwise ordered by the court. The state attorney shall, upon the filing of the accusatory writ, notify the Clerk of the defendant's minority status and address of parents. The Clerk shall immediately notify the defendant's parents or guardian of the charge(s) and if unable to do so, notify the judge at arraignment. The Clerk's notification shall be pursuant to F.S. 925.07 (1991).

7. All persons released from custody shall comply with the conditions of the undertaking as set forth in the Florida Rules of Criminal Procedure and any other conditions set by the Court.

a. The defendant shall keep his/her attorney and the Clerk notified at all times of his/her correct mailing address.

b. The mailing of a notice to the last address furnished to the Clerk by the defendant shall constitute service of the notice when it is mailed at least five (5) days (excluding Saturday, Sunday, and holidays), prior to the date of the required appearance.

8. If a defendant is on pre-trial release, the filing of an information or indictment shall not cause a capias to be issued except by order of the judge assigned the case.

E. Upfiled Charges. When a misdemeanor charge has been upfiled to a felony charge, the county court judge assigned to the misdemeanor charge is hereby designated to act as a first appearance judge on the felony charge for purposes of imposing conditions of bail and/or setting the amount of bond. Should the county court judge choose to accept the designation as a first appearance judge and set the conditions of bail or the amount of bond, then the defendant will not be brought before a judge at the Criminal Justice Complex.

F. Assignment of Companion Cases (Involving One Defendant Only or Multiple Defendants) within the Criminal Division of the Circuit Court.

1. When a defendant has more than one case pending against him/her, all cases will be reassigned to the division having the case with the lowest case number, provided however, this shall not apply to defendants charged under Section A above. The assignment shall occur at the time of the arrest.

2. Co-defendants arrested at the same time will be assigned a separate case number by the Clerk. Upon filing of the Information by the State, the defendant with the lowest booking number determines the division assignment for all of the defendants. If a co-defendant has a case already pending in another division, then all defendants are transferred into that division, regardless of the booking number.

3. When a defendant has more than one case pending against him/her and the case has more than one defendant, reassignment of any case shall occur only upon motion, hearing, and order of court in the transferring division. However, transfer shall be done only with the consent of the Judge of the division into which the case is being transferred.

G. Setting and Resetting Cases for Trial.

1. In capital cases, when an indictment has been filed, the Clerk will contact the division Judicial Assistant to secure an arraignment date. After the defendant is arraigned, the file will be sent to the division Judge for setting of trial date or other action.

2. All other cases shall be set for trial at the direction of the Judge presiding in each division.

3. Upon the receipt of a demand for speedy trial, the Clerk shall immediately notify the Judicial Assistant of the assigned division for further action by the Judge consistent with the Florida Rules of Criminal Procedure.

H. Calendar Review and Call.

1. If the criminal division uses a calendar call system, the notice for trial shall designate the date and time of the calendar call and the trial period following same.

2. At the calendar call the Court shall set the order of cases for trial. All cases ready for trial will be given a specific trial date or placed on call. Any potential conflict shall be brought to the attention of the Court at the calendar call, or as soon as possible, or shall be considered waived.

3. All defendants who are not in custody shall be present at calendar call unless their attendance has been waived by the Court prior to the date of the calendar call.

4. Defendants who are in custody will not automatically be brought to Court. Unless the defendant's presence is requested by defense counsel by giving notice to the Judicial Assistant prior to Noon of the day preceding calendar call, the defendant's presence shall be deemed waived. This section may be modified at the option of the division Judge.

I. Scheduling Hearings.

1. As to the County Criminal Division, the clerk shall continue to set Case Disposition hearings when a plea of not guilty and a waiver of Arraignment is filed by the attorney of record.

2. Counsel shall schedule hearings through the Judicial Assistant and shall notice opposing counsel in accordance with the Rules of Criminal Procedure. Upon obtaining a hearing time, counsel shall file a notice of hearing with the Clerk of Court immediately. No hearing shall be scheduled with less than five (5) days notice unless agreed to by all parties.

3. All Notices of Hearing shall contain a statement setting forth that counsel has made a good faith effort to resolve the issues raised without a hearing, but has been unable to do so.

4. *Emergency Hearings:* Contact Judicial Assistant.

5. Whenever the Court determines that a case should be heard, but appropriate notices have not been filed with the Clerk, the Judicial Assistant shall notify the Clerk in writing when the case is to be heard.

J. Sentencing.

1. Where a pre-sentence investigation (PSI) is not ordered, the Court shall schedule sentencing in approximately fifteen (15) days from a plea of guilty or no contest, or upon a finding of guilt, unless otherwise ordered by the Court.

2. When a PSI is ordered, the Court shall schedule sentencing approximately forty (40) days from the time of ordering the PSI, and the PSI shall be due within thirty (30) days from the finding of guilt. It shall be the responsibility of the Department of Corrections to specifically request additional time, if needed, to complete the PSI.

3. The Court shall be responsible for insuring the defendant is sentenced without undue delay and shall notify all parties of the sentencing hearing.

K. Release of Defendant Upon Verdict of Not Guilty. Upon a verdict of not guilty in a criminal case the defendant shall immediately be released from custody upon that cause and shall not be further restrained in that cause.

L. Mandates From Appellate Courts. Upon the receipt of a Mandate from an Appellate Court, the Clerk shall send a memorandum to all parties acknowledging receipt of the Mandate with a copy attached. The Clerk shall forward the original Mandate to the appropriate Judge, to be set for a status conference within seven (7) days.

M. Emergency Matters. In the event it is necessary to contact a Judge or court employee for an emergency matter, the Court Administrator will maintain a confidential list of telephone numbers of both Judges and Judicial Assistants. The list will have limited distribution.

DONE and SIGNED, in Chambers, at West Palm Beach, Palm Beach County, Florida this 6 day of June, 2017.

Jeffrey J. Colbath
Chief Judge

Adopted effective September 29, 2008. Amended effective March 5, 2009; March 11, 2013; July 1, 2016; January 27, 2017; June 6, 2017.

* supersedes admin. order 4.101–1/17

4.102. JUDGES ASSIGNED TEMPORARILY TO CRIMINAL DIVISION: SENTENCING AND POST CONVICTION MATTERS

IN THE CIRCUIT COURT OF THE FIFTEENTH JUDICIAL CIRCUIT IN AND FOR PALM BEACH COUNTY, FLORIDA

ADMINISTRATIVE ORDER NO. 4.102–9/08 *

IN RE: JUDGES ASSIGNED TEMPORARILY CRIMINAL DIVISION: SENTENCING AND POST CONVICTION MATTERS

Pursuant to the authority conferred by Florida Rule of Judicial Administration 2.215, it is hereby **ORDERED** that to insure the proper completion of cases tried by judges assigned temporarily to the criminal division, the following procedures are established:

1. Judges temporarily assigned will handle the motion for new trial, sentencing, and motion for mitigation in any trial conducted by them which results in conviction.

a. When a presentence investigation (P.S.I.) is ordered, the clerk shall furnish the judge's judicial assistant with a copy of the commitment form ordering the P.S.I. (If the judge is retired or from another circuit, the form will be delivered to the division assigned the case.) If a P.S.I. report is not received within thirty (30) days, the judge's judicial assistant shall contact the Probation and Parole Department.

b. The judge's judicial assistant shall schedule the date and time of any motion for new trial, sentencing and motion for mitigation. He/she shall notify the clerk's office, parties, and counsel, and obtain the services of a court reporter.

c. After the disposition of the motion for new trial, sentencing, and motion for mitigation, the case shall be reassigned to the judge to whom the case was originally assigned, for disposition of any other post-conviction matter.

2. Judges temporarily assigned may conduct plea conferences. In this event, when sentence is withheld pending the receipt of a presentence investigation, the case shall be reassigned to the judge to whom it was originally assigned. The judge shall impose sentence and determine all post conviction matters.

3. The court reporter reporting plea bargaining conferences before any judge temporarily assigned to the criminal division shall, within seven (7) days from the plea conference, furnish a transcript of it to the judicial assistant of the judge to whom the case was originally assigned. The judge shall file the transcript with the clerk of court at sentencing.

4. The clerk shall furnish the regular division judicial assistant a copy of the commitment form ordering the P.S.I., and he/she shall be responsible for the proper scheduling of sentencing, hearings, and post-conviction matters as set forth in paragraphs b and c, in Section 1 above.

DONE and **SIGNED** in Chambers at West Palm Beach, Palm Beach County, Florida, this 29 day of September, 2008.

Kathleen J. Kroll
Chief Judge

Adopted effective September 29, 2008.

* supersedes admin. order 4.004–9/92

4.103. [VACATED AND SET ASIDE BY ORDER 4.103-1/17, EFFECTIVE JANUARY 27, 2017.]

4.104. DIVISION ASSIGNMENT FOR MOTIONS FOR INVESTIGATIVE SUBPOENA FOR PATIENT RECORDS

IN THE CIRCUIT COURT OF THE FIFTEENTH JUDICIAL CIRCUIT IN AND FOR PALM BEACH COUNTY, FLORIDA

ADMINISTRATIVE ORDER 4.104–9/08 *

IN RE: DIVISION ASSIGNMENT FOR MOTIONS FOR INVESTIGATIVE SUBPOENA FOR PATIENT RECORDS

Sound principles of judicial economy require the establishment of procedures to govern the assignment of State Attorney motions for authorization to issue investigative subpoenas. Florida Statute § 395.3025(4), requires, upon an objection by the patient, the State Attorney to obtain court authorization prior to the issuance of State Attorney investigative subpoenas for patient records.

NOW, THEREFORE, pursuant to the authority conferred by Florida Rule of Judicial Administration 2.215, it is **ORDERED** as follows:

Upon the State's filing of a motion for authorization to execute an investigative subpoena for patient records, the Clerk of Court will assign the motion a case number and division assignment and the motion will be heard before the assigned division at the setting of the State.

DONE and **SIGNED**, in Chambers, at West Palm Beach, Palm Beach County, Florida, this 29 day of September, 2008.

Kathleen J. Kroll
Chief Judge

Adopted effective September 29, 2008.

* supersedes admin. order 4.040—3/98

4.105. REQUIRED DNA TESTING

IN THE CIRCUIT COURT OF THE FIFTEENTH JUDICIAL CIRCUIT IN AND FOR PALM BEACH COUNTY, FLORIDA

ADMINISTRATIVE ORDER 4.105–9/08 *

IN RE: REQUIRED DNA TESTING

The success and effectiveness of the DNA database is contingent upon compliance with Florida Statutes § 943.325 (governing certain convictions), § 948.03(5)(h) (governing certain probationers and community controllees) and § 947.1405 (governing certain inmates under a control release program).

NOW, THEREFORE, pursuant to the authority conferred by Florida Rule of Judicial Administration 2.215, it is **ORDERED** as follows:

In the event a trial judge inadvertently fails to order any required DNA sample under any statutory requirement, the responsibility for causing the samples to be timely drawn and collected shall remain with the appropriate agency designated by law.

DONE and **SIGNED**, in Chambers, at West Palm Beach, Palm Beach County, Florida this 29 day of September, 2008.

Kathleen J. Kroll
Chief Judge

Adopted effective September 29, 2008.

* supersedes admin orders 4.044–8/99 and 4.045–8/99

4.106. [VACATED AND SET ASIDE BY ORDER 4.106-3/18, EFFECTIVE MARCH 29, 2018.]

4.107. [VACATED AND SET ASIDE BY ORDER 4.107–4/12, RETROACTIVE EFFECTIVE APRIL 2, 2012]

4.108. CORRECTING SCRIVENER'S ERRORS IN CRIMINAL CASES

IN THE CIRCUIT COURT OF THE FIFTEENTH JUDICIAL CIRCUIT IN AND FOR PALM BEACH COUNTY

ADMINISTRATIVE ORDER 4.108–9/08 *

IN RE: CORRECTING SCRIVENER'S ERRORS IN CRIMINAL CASES

Tanner v. State, 744 So.2d 101722 (Fla. 4th DCA 1997) finds that the Clerk of Court may not refuse to accept documents which contain scrivener's errors in the caption. The administration of criminal justice and judicial economy are best served by the prompt correction of more substantive errors as well.

NOW, THEREFORE, pursuant to the authority conferred by Florida Rule of Judicial Administration 2.215, it is **ORDERED** as follows:

1. The Office of the Clerk of Court shall correct scrivener's errors in the caption of both pleadings and orders in criminal cases.

2. The Office of the Clerk of Court may correct substantive errors or omissions contained in orders, provided that the information is available from another document in the court file, not including the court event form. Correction shall be made to the original document so that it conforms to the source document in the court file.

3. If the information is not available, the originating party shall be responsible for the correction or revision

DONE and **ORDERED**, in Chambers, at West Palm Beach, Palm Beach County, Florida this 29 day of September, 2008.

Kathleen J. Kroll
Chief Judge

Adopted effective September 29, 2008.

* supersedes administrative order 4.046–10/99

First Appearance and Bond

4.201. FIRST APPEARANCE HEARINGS

IN THE CIRCUIT COURT OF THE FIFTEENTH JUDICIAL CIRCUIT IN AND FOR PALM BEACH COUNTY, FLORIDA

ADMINISTRATIVE ORDER NO. 4.201–4/18 *

IN RE: FIRST APPEARANCE HEARINGS

First Appearance hearings involve the participation of various court personnel and officers of the court. Procedures are to be implemented to ensure uniformity at first appearance hearings. Rule of Judicial Administration Rule 2.215(b) gives the chief judge of the circuit the authority to require that all judges of the court, other court officers, and court personnel comply with all court and judicial branch policies, administrative orders, procedures and administrative plans.

NOW, THEREFORE, pursuant to the authority conferred by Florida Rule of Judicial Administration 2.215, it is **ORDERED** as follows:

A. Time and Place of First Appearance Hearings.

1. All persons in custody at the Palm Beach County Detention Center annexes shall be brought to a first appearance hearing within twenty-four (24) hours of their arrest except those exempted by Rule 3.130(a), F.R.Cr.P. See Paragraph 3 below.

2. *Generally.* First appearance hearings for all defendants, except those specified in Paragraph 3, shall be held in the Criminal Justice Courtroom, 3228 Gun Club Road, West Palm Beach, Florida, at 9:30 a.m. Monday–Friday and 9:00 a.m. Saturday, Sunday and holidays and the Belle Glade Courthouse, 2950 State Road 15, Belle Glade, Florida at 8:30 a.m. Monday through Friday. These times may be modified with the approval of the chief judge.

3. *Exceptions to 24–Hour Rule for First Appearance Hearings*

a. Violation of Probation on a Felony Charge. If the defendant is also charged with an additional substantive offense, he/she shall be taken to a first appearance hearing on the new charge(s) only. For the violation of felony probation, follow the procedures in Administrative Order No. 4.401–3/13 (as amended).

b. Failure to Appear at Felony Arraignment. All Defendants arrested for failure to appear for felony arraignment shall be set for Tuesday mornings at 9:00 a.m. at the Criminal Justice Complex, or on Monday mornings at 9:00 a.m. at the Belle Glade Courthouse.

c. Failure to Appear at any other Felony Court Proceeding. The Judicial Assistant of the assigned Felony Division shall be notified of the defendant's re-arrest and shall set a court hearing as soon as is practicable.

d. Failure to Appear for any Misdemeanor charge. Cases assigned to the Central, North, South, and Belle Glade Courthouses, with the exception of Failure to Appear for Misdemeanor Domestic Violence and Misdemeanor DUI, the person shall be brought before Division KK Monday though Sunday on the next work day after the Clerk receives the booking slip. Persons arrested for Failure to Appear for Misdemeanor Domestic Violence or Misdemeanor DUI shall be brought before the presiding judge of the assigned division for a hearing within 48 hours of the arrest excluding weekends and holidays.

e. Contempt of Court (not Occurring on a Weekend or Holiday*). The Judicial Assistant of the Judge issuing the contempt order shall be notified and shall schedule a hearing before the Judge as soon as is practicable. *If the contempt order is executed such that the next day is a weekend or holiday, the individual shall be brought to first appearance at the Criminal Justice Complex or Belle Glade Courthouse.

f. Material Witness. The witness shall be brought before the first appearance judge. The witness shall be held separate from the regular first appearance population.

g. Bond Surrenders and Extraditions. On weekends and holidays, bond surrenders and extraditions shall not be brought to first appearance hearings, but shall be brought to first appearances at the next regular work day. (SPECIAL NOTE: Persons in custody on a Bond Surrender who have not previously had a first appearance on the charge shall be brought to first appearance as though it were the original arrest.)

h. Up–files. Those cases that are up-filed from misdemeanors to felonies and which the county court judge set the conditions of bail and/or the amount of the bond may be heard by the county court judge presiding over the misdemeanor. See Admin. Order 4.101.

Note: Limited first appearance hearings may be held in the branch courthouses on days and at times designated by the judge assigned to the branch courthouse.

4. *Personnel in Attendance.* The following personnel shall be present:

a. A Judge

b. A Deputy Clerk of the Court

c. A State Attorney or Assistant State Attorney and a Public Defender or Assistant Public Defender

d. A Courtroom Deputy designated by the Palm Beach County Sheriff's Office

e. Deputy Sheriffs as may be needed for security

f. Court Interpreters (see Paragraph I below)

g. A Digital Court Reporter and

h. A minimum of two (2) representatives from Pretrial Services Program.

1) A court representative presents/clarifies information contained in interviews.

2) An O.R. agreement sign-up representative to explain O.R. bond guidelines and secure the defendant's signature on the agreement. The O.R. sign-up representative shall also screen for supervised O.R. acceptance, explain to the supervised O.R. client the conditions of supervised O.R. and schedule an orientation appointment for supervised O.R.

B. Responsibility for Flow of Documents.

1. The Sheriff's Office will provide the Clerk with:

a. The Rough Arrest

b. The Probable Cause Affidavit, Warrant, Capias or Citation

c. Sheriff's Office Booking Face Sheet

2. The Sheriff's Office will provide a copy of the criminal history, when available, to the State's representative for use by the Court.

3. The Clerk shall present to the Judge:

a. A First Appearance List

b. The Rough Arrest

c. The Probable Cause Affidavit

d. The Probable Cause Order

e. The completed Application for Criminal Indigency Status filed by the Defendant;

f. Sheriff's Office Booking Face Sheet.

4. The Palm Beach County Sheriff's Office will provide to the State Attorney, thirty (30) minutes prior to the hearing:

a. Sheriff's Office First Appearance List

b. Clerk's PALMS/First Appearance Criminal History

c. Rough Arrest and Probable Cause Affidavit as provided by the Sheriff's Office

d. Warrant or Capias as provided by the Sheriff's Office

e. Access to original Citation for review, if available.

f. Sheriff's Office Booking Face Sheet.

5. The Clerk shall indicate on the first appearance record and court file when foreign language interpreters are needed.

6. The Pretrial Services Court Representatives shall present to the Judge:

a. The PTS interview

b. In applicable cases, the reason an interview does not exist

C. Appointment of Counsel and Affidavit of Indigency.

1. In appropriate cases if the defendant is determined to be indigent and therefore unable to obtain an attorney at the time of first appearance, a public defender, an attorney from the Office of Criminal Conflict and Civil Regional Counsel, or a conflict attorney, should be appointed for all purposes. Whenever possible the indigency determination should be made at first appearance.

2. Unless the defendant has retained private counsel, prior to the first appearance hearing the Public Defender is authorized to consult with all defendants. The Clerk shall determine whether the defendant is indigent with the right of the defendant to appeal the indigency determination to the judge. If indigent, the Public Defender's Office will be appointed to represent the defendant.

3. Should there be a conflict of interest with the Public Defender's Office, the Office of Criminal Conflict and Civil Regional Counsel will be appointed.

4. If there is a conflict of interest with the Office of Criminal Conflict and Civil Regional Counsel, then the Clerk of Court shall appoint an attorney from the list of court appointed attorneys maintained by the Clerk of Court.

5. The Clerk of Court shall promptly notify the judge or the judge's judicial assistant of the name of the conflict attorney.

6. Upon receipt of the notification by the Clerk of Court, the judicial assistant shall notify the conflict attorney of the appointment.

D. Mental Competency.

1. If a defendant appears to be imminently dangerous to himself or others, or if a mental evaluation is appropriate to determine the proper release for a defendant, the Court may order a mental examination and/or treatment.

2. When so ordered, the Clerk shall note the order on the disposition form and provide a copy to the mental health staff.

E. Arraignments. Misdemeanors. The presiding Judge may arraign and sentence at first appearance hearings. The Judge shall make the Public Defender available for defendants who are sentenced and/or arraigned at first appearance.

F. Juvenile Cases.

1. Juvenile cases shall be heard before adult cases.

2. The Department of Children and Families and Department of Juvenile Justice shall notify the Clerk's Office by 8:00 a.m. on weekends and holidays if hearings are necessary and will be responsible for the notification of parents, and for the presence of the children and a counselor.

3. The counselor shall present at the hearing all documents and evidence relating to the need for detention to the Court and State Attorney.

G. Security. The Sheriff's Office will be responsible for security during first appearance hearings and will inform the presiding Judge if special circumstances require a different procedure either in the number of defendants brought into the courtroom, or the order in which defendants should be called.

H. Court Record at First Appearance.

1. The clerk shall prepare a first appearance record reflecting the action taken during the hearing and shall supply a copy to the Sheriff.

2. The proceeding shall be electronically recorded under the supervision of the Court's Administrative Office.

I. Non–English Speaking Defendants

1. A Spanish and Creole interpreter will be available on a regular basis.

2. Detention Center Intake shall notify Court Administration, as soon as possible, whenever an individual is booked into the Detention Center who communicates only in a language other than Spanish, Creole or English.

3. When a defendant speaks a language or dialect for which an interpreter cannot be obtained within twenty-four (24) hours, the defendant should nonetheless be brought to first appearance for probable cause and preliminary bond determinations in accordance with this Order.

J. Emergency Petitions for Injunctions for Protection. Emergency Petitions for Injunctions for Protection may be heard immediately following first appearances on weekends and holidays.

K. Modifications to the First Appearance Procedures. Personnel listed in section A.4. above and their respective offices shall not make any changes to the procedures listed in this Administrative Order nor shall they implement any internal procedures which substantially affects the First Appearance hearings without first consulting the Chief Judge. This paragraph does not apply to the Sheriff when acting within the executive branch of government.

DONE AND SIGNED in Chambers, at West Palm Beach, Palm Beach County, Florida this 4th day of April, 2018.

Krista Marx
Chief Judge

Adopted effective September 29, 2008. Amended effective October 23, 2009; May 10, 2010; March 11, 2013; August 29, 2013; April 3, 2018; April 4, 2018.

* supersedes admin. order 4.201–4/18 (dated April 3, 2018)

4.202. SCHEDULE OF BONDS AND PROCEDURES RELATING TO PRE–FIRST APPEARANCE RELEASE

IN THE CIRCUIT COURT OF THE FIFTEENTH JUDICIAL CIRCUIT IN AND FOR PALM BEACH COUNTY, FLORIDA

ADMINISTRATIVE ORDER NO. 4.202–5/14 *

IN RE: SCHEDULE OF BONDS AND PROCEDURES RELATING TO PRE–FIRST APPEARANCE RELEASE

The Fifteenth Judicial Circuit has established a system for the release of persons accused of crimes on bond prior to the first appearance hearing. It is necessary to establish a uniform schedule to designate those offenses eligible for bond release prior to first appearance and the amount of such bond,

NOW, THEREFORE, pursuant to the authority conferred by Florida Rule of Judicial Administration 2.215, it is **ORDERED** as follows:

I. Crimes Not Eligible for Bond Prior to First Appearance. The following offenses are crimes of violence and persons charged with these offenses shall not be eligible for release on bond prior to a first appearance hearing, unless otherwise specified on an active warrant.

STATUTE	DESCRIPTION	DEGREE
806.01(1)	Arson, 1st Degree	F1
806.031(2)	Arson/Great Bodily Harm	F2
784.021	Assault/Aggravated	F3
784.021	Assault/Aggravated Law Enforcement Officer	F2
784.08(2)(c)	Assault/Aggravated/on Person 65 or Older	F2
784.021(1)(a)	Assault/Aggravated/With Deadly Weapon	F3
784.041	Battery/Felony Battery	F3
784.045	Battery/Aggravated	F2
784.045(1)(a)	Battery/Aggravated/Great Bodily Harm	F2
784.045(1)(a)	Battery/Aggravated/Great Bodily Harm/F/Arm	F1
784.045	Battery/Aggravated/Law Enforcement Officer	F1

784.045(1)(b)	Battery/Aggravated/of a Pregnant Victim	F2
784.045(1)(a)	Battery/Aggravated/With a Firearm	F2
784.08(2)(c)	Battery on a Person 65 or Older	F3
790.161(3)	Bomb, Destructive Device/Cause Bodily Harm	F1
790.161(4)	Bomb, Destructive Device/Causing Death	FC
810.02(2)(b)	Burglary/Armed	**F1–PBL**
810.02(3)	Burglary/Occupied	F2
810.02(3)(b)	Burglary/Occupied Structure, Conveyance With Mask	F1
810.02(3)	Burglary/Unoccupied Dwelling	F2
810.02(2)(a)	Burglary/With Assault or Battery	**F1–PBL**
810.02(2)(a)	Burglary/With Assault or Battery/Armed	**F1–PBL**
827.03(2)(a)	Child Abuse/Aggravated	**F1**
847.0135	**Computer Pornography/Prohibited Comp Use/Travel to Meet Minor**	**F3–F2**
790.19	Deadly Missile/Shoot, Throw	F2
741.28(1)	Domestic Violence** 1	Varies
741.31	Domestic Violence, Violation of Injunction	M1
893.135	Drug Trafficking, in general	F1
316.193(3)(c)(3)	DUI Manslaughter	F2
316.193(3)(c)(2)	DUI Serious Bodily Injury	F3
825.102(1)	Elderly, Disabled Adult/Abuse/Great Bodily Harm	F3
825.102(2)	**Elderly, Disabled Adult/Aggravated Abuse/Great Bodily Harm**	**F1**
944.40	Escape	F2
787.02(3)	False Imprisonment of Child Under Age 13	**F1–PBL**

790.15(2)	Firearm/Discharge From a Vehicle	F2
790.23	Firearm/Possession by Felon	F2
790.115(2)(c)	Firearm/School Property/Possession	F3
790.115(2)(d)	Firearm/School Property/Discharge	F2
790.07(2)	Firearm/Use, Display While Committing a Felony	F2
787.01(2)	Kidnapping	**F1–PBL**
782.09	Killing of Unborn Child by Injury to Mother	**F3–FC**
782.11	Killing/Unnecessary, to Prevent Unlawful Act	F2
316.027(2)(b)	Leave Scene of Accident/Death	F2
800.04	Lewd and Lascivious Assault on Child	F2
322.34(6)	License Cancel/Sus/Revoked/No Driver's License Causing Death or Serious Bodily Injury	F3
870.03	Looting	F3
782.07	Manslaughter	F2
782.07	Manslaughter/With a Deadly Weapon	F1
782.04(1)	Murder, 1st Degree	FC
782.04(1)	Murder, 1st Degree/Attempt	F1
782.04(1)	Murder, 1st Degree/Conspire	F1
782.04(1)	Murder, 1st Degree/Law Enforcement Officer	FC
782.04(2)	Murder, 2nd Degree	**F1–PBL**
782.04(2)	Murder, 2nd Degree/Attempt	F2
782.04(3)	Murder, 2nd Degree/Felony	**F1–PBL**
782.04(2)	Murder, 2nd Degree/Law Enforcement Officer	**LIFE**
782.04(2)	Murder, 2nd Degree/With a Deadly Weapon/Att	F1
782.04(4)	Murder, 3rd Degree	F2

782.04(4)	Murder, 3rd Degree/Attempt	F3
782.04(4)	Murder, 3rd Degree/Law Enforcement Officer	**LIFE**
782.04(4)	Murder, 3rd Degree/With a Firearm	F1
847.011	**Prohibition of Acts in Connection w/ Obscene/Lewd etc. materials when depicting minor or repeat offender**	**F3**
914.23	Retaliate Against Witness/Bodily Injury	F2
812.13(2)(b)	Robbery/Armed	F1
812.13(2)(b)	Robbery/Armed/Attempt	F2
812.13(2)(b)	Robbery/Armed/Conspiracy	F2
812.13(2)(b)	Robbery/Armed/Principal	F1
812.133(2)**(b)**	Robbery/Carjacking	F1
812.133(2)(a)	Robbery/Carjacking/Armed	**F1–PBL**
812.133(2)(b)	Robbery/Carjacking/Attempt	**F2**
812.13(2)(a)	Robbery/Deadly Weapon, Firearm/Attempt	F2
812.135	Robbery/Home Invasion	F1
812.13(2)(a)	Robbery/Deadly Weapon, Firearm	**F1–PBL**
812.13(2)(c)	Robbery/Strong–arm/Masked	F1
812.13(2)(c)	Robbery/Strong–arm	F2
812.13(2)(c)	Robbery/Strong–arm/Attempt	F3
794.011(5)	Sexual Battery/By Physical Force	F2
794.011(5)	Sexual Battery/By Physical Force/Attempt	F3
794.011(5)	Sexual Battery/By Physical Force/Gang	F1
794.011(4)	Sexual Battery/By Threats	F1
794.023	Sexual Battery/Multiple Perpetrators Fel 2 Deg/ Fel 1 Deg	F1–LIFE
794.011(2)	Sexual Battery/On a Minor/Attempt	F1
794.011(3)	Sexual Battery/With a Deadly Weapon/Attempt	F2
794.011(3)	Sexual Battery/With a Deadly Weapon/Force	**LIFE**
943.0435	**Sexual Offender/Failure to Register/Notify**	**F3–F2**
827.071	**Sexual Performance by a Child**	**F3–F2**
775.21(6)(j)	**Sexual Predators Act/ Fail to Notify/Residence**	**F2**
790.221	Short–Barrel Shotgun, Rifle, Machine Gun/Possession	F2
784.048(3)	Stalking/Aggravated	F3
784.048(4)	Stalking/Aggravated/Court Order	F3
914.22	Tampering with a Witness, Victim, or Informant	F3–LIFE
836.05	Threats/Extortion	F2
847.0138	**Transmission of Material Harmful to Minors /Electronic Device/Equipment**	F3
322.34(6)(b)	Vehicular Homicide/Driving While License Canceled, Suspended or Revoked Causing Death or Serious Bodily Injury	F3
782.07 1(1)**(b)**	Vehicular Homicide/Failure to Stop	**F1**
782.071(1)**(a)**	Vehicular Homicide/Operate in Reckless Manner	**F2**
782.072(2)	Vessel Homicide/Failure to Stop	F1
782.072(1)	Vessel Homicide/Operate in Reckless Manner	F2
741.29(6)	Violation of a condition of Pre-trial Release	M1
790.07(1)	Weapon/Use, Display While Committing a Felony	F3
790.115(2)(d)	Weapon, Firearm/School Property/Discharge	F2

790.115(1)	Weapon, Firearm/School Property/Exhibit	F3

1 **741.28 Domestic violence; definitions [in part].
(1) "Domestic Violence" means any assault, aggravated assault, battery, aggravated battery, sexual assault, sexual battery, stalking, aggravated stalking, or any criminal offense resulting in physical injury or death of one family or household member by another who is or was residing in the same single dwelling unit.
(2) "Family or household member" means spouses, former spouses, persons related by blood or marriage, persons who are presently residing together as if a family or who have resided together in the past as if a family, and persons who have a child in common regardless of whether they have been married or have resided together at any time.

II. Bond Schedule for Crimes Not Listed Above. Persons arrested for crimes other than those listed above shall be eligible for bond release prior to first appearance according to the following schedule and provisions:

A. *Felonies:*

1. OFFENSES AND BOND AMOUNT:

OFFENSE	BOND
FIRST–DEGREE FELONIES	
Palm Beach County Resident	$15,000.00
Florida Resident, Not Palm Beach County	$20,000.00
Out–of–State Resident	$25,000.00
SECOND–DEGREE FELONIES	
Palm Beach County Resident	$ 5,000.00
Florida Resident, Not Palm Beach County	$ 7,500.00
Out–of–State Resident	$10,000.00
THIRD–DEGREE FELONIES	
Palm Beach County Resident	$ 3,000.00
Florida Resident, Not Palm Beach County	$ 4,500.00
Out–of–State Resident	$ 5,000.00

2. *Provisions Relating to Felony Bonds*

a. The amount of bond is increased by $10,000.00 in each category when the individual is arrested outside the State of Florida.

b. If a person is currently on bond or on personal recognizance release for a felony, a first-degree misdemeanor or the crime of driving while impaired, the arrestee shall not be eligible for a bond under this schedule. Rather, the arrestee shall be held and brought before a judge at the next first appearance hearing. If a person is currently on bond for a second-degree misdemeanor, the bond specified in this order or in administrative order 10.001–1/95 shall be doubled. In the event the person is on a personal recognizance release, the bond shall be set at $250.00 per charge.

c. Effective October 1, 2006 a separate and specific bond shall be set for each charge or offense

d. A separate and specific bond shall be set for each charge or offense.

B. *Misdemeanors/Traffic Crimes/Violations of Municipal and County Ordinances:*

1. OFFENSES AND BOND AMOUNT

FIRST–DEGREE STALKING MISDEMEANORS	
Palm Beach County Permanent Resident	$ 500.00
Florida Resident, Not Palm Beach County	$ 750.00
Out–of–State Resident	$ 1,000.00
LOITERING IN RELATION TO PROSTITUTION, PROSTITUTION, ATTEMPTING TO HIRE OR HIRING A PROSTITUTE OR ANY OTHER VIOLATION OF § 796.07 FLA. STAT.	
Palm Beach County Permanent Resident	$ 250.00
Adjoining County Permanent Resident (Broward, Okeechobee, Hendry or Martin Counties)	$ 250.00
Florida Resident, Not Palm Beach County or Adjoining County	$ 500.00
Out–of–State Resident	$ 500.00
REFUSAL TO SIGN NOTICE TO APPEAR, TRAFFIC CITATION	
Palm Beach County Permanent Resident	O.R.
Adjoining County Permanent Resident (Broward, Okeechobee, Hendry or Martin Counties)	O.R.
Florida Resident, Not Palm Beach County or Adjoining County	O.R.
Out–of–State Resident	O.R.
HAS AN OUTSTANDING FTA ON A CRIMINAL CHARGE	
Palm Beach County Permanent Resident	$250.00
Adjoining County Permanent Resident	$250.00

(Broward, Okeechobee, Hendry or Martin Counties)	
Florida Resident, Not Palm Beach County or Adjoining County	$500.00
Out–of–State Resident	$500.00

FIRST DEGREE MISDEMEANORS OTHER THAN THOSE LISTED ABOVE (OR EQUIVALENT ORDINANCE VIOLATION); DUI UBA, OR OFFENSE CARRYING A MINIMUM MANDATORY JAIL SENTENCE

Palm Beach County Permanent Resident	O.R.
Adjoining County Permanent Resident	O.R.
(Broward, Okeechobee, Hendry or Martin Counties)	
Florida Resident, Not Palm Beach County or Adjoining County	O.R.
Out–of–State Resident	O.R.

SECOND DEGREE MISDEMEANORS OTHER THAN THOSE LISTED ABOVE (OR EQUIVALENT ORDINANCE VIOLATION); RECKLESS DRIVING

Palm Beach County Permanent Resident	O.R.
Adjoining County Permanent Resident	O.R.
(Broward, Okeechobee, Hendry or Martin Counties)	O.R.
Florida Resident, Not Palm Beach County or Adjoining County	O.R.
Out–of–State Resident	O.R.

TRAFFIC CRIME OF NO REGISTRATION

Palm Beach County Permanent Resident	O.R.
Adjoining County Permanent Resident	O.R.
(Broward, Okeechobee, Hendry or Martin Counties)	
Florida Resident, Not Palm Beach County or Adjoining County	O.R.
Out–of–State Resident	O.R.

2. PROVISIONS RELATING TO BONDS FOR MISDEMEANORS, TRAFFIC CRIMES AND VIOLATIONS OF MUNICIPAL AND COUNTY ORDINANCES:

a. The above bond schedule shall be utilized by the booking desk of the Palm Beach County Jail.

b. A permanent resident of Palm Beach, Broward, Okeechobee, Hendry or Martin County is defined as a person who can provide proof of a current permanent address in one of these counties. A post office box alone will not suffice.

c. In all cases where a defendant is arrested for misdemeanor assault or battery upon a spouse, ex-spouse, boyfriend, girlfriend, ex-boyfriend or ex-girlfriend, no bond shall be available prior to the first appearance hearing.

d. Defendants with Existing Bonds: If a person is currently on bond or is on personal recognizance release for a felony, a first-degree misdemeanor, second-degree misdemeanor or the crime of driving while impaired, the arrestee shall not be eligible for a bond under this schedule. Rather, the arrestee shall be held and brought before a judge at the next first-appearance hearing as set forth above.

e. Pursuant to Section 903.046 (d), Florida Statutes (2007), any defendant who failed to appear on the day of any required court proceeding in the case at issue and who was later arrested shall not be eligible for a recognizance bond or for any form of bond which does not require a monetary undertaking or commitment equal to or greater than $2,000.00 or twice the value of the monetary commitment or undertaking of the original bond, whichever is greater. Notwithstanding anything in this paragraph, the court has discretion in determining conditions of release if the defendant proves circumstances beyond his or her control for the failure to appear.

f. Effective October 1, 2006 a separate and specific bond shall be set for each charge or offense.

C. *Release to Electronic Monitoring*

1. Should no prohibition be stated by the first appearance judge, the Palm Beach County Sheriff's Office shall have the discretion, subject to its own standards and guidelines, to release a defendant who remains in the Sheriff's custody after ten (10) consecutive days and whose total bond amount for all pending charges is $3,000.00 or less, to the Sheriff's Electronic Monitoring Program.

2. The Sheriff's Office shall also have discretion to waive all or part of the cost of the program in those circumstances the Sheriff's Office deems appropriate.

3. Should the presiding first appearance judge object to the defendant's release to the Sheriff's Office electronic monitoring program, the objection shall be noted by the Clerk of Court and the defendant may not be released into the Sheriff's Office electronic monitoring program without further court order.

4. Nothing contained herein eliminates or modifies the Court's authority to address these issues in a separate proceeding at the request of either party.

III. First Appearance When an accused is brought to a first appearance hearing, all proceedings are governed by Crim. Rule 3.131 and the bonds for pre-first appearance release under this administrative order shall cease to be effective.

DONE and **SIGNED** in Chambers at West Palm Beach, Palm Beach County, Florida, this 16 day of May, 2014.

Jeffrey Colbath, Chief Judge

Adopted effective September 29, 2008. Amended effective October 1, 2010; November 16, 2010; August 30, 2011; May 16, 2014.

* Supersedes admin. order no. 4.202–8/11.

4.203. PROPERTY BONDS

IN THE CIRCUIT COURT OF THE FIFTEENTH JUDICIAL CIRCUIT IN AND FOR PALM BEACH COUNTY, FLORIDA

ADMINISTRATIVE ORDER NO. 4.203–9/08 *

IN RE: PROPERTY BONDS

NOW, THEREFORE, pursuant to the authority conferred by Florida Rule of Judicial Administration 2.215, it is **ORDERED** as follows:

In order to establish a uniform system for the release of defendants on property bonds the following procedures are established and shall be followed unless otherwise ordered by the judge presiding over the cause:

1. A surety for the release of a defendant on a property bond must file an affidavit in accordance with section 903.09, Florida Statutes (1991), and shall otherwise qualify under section 903.05, Florida Statutes (1991).

2. Property pledged as surety for the bond shall be located in the State of Florida.

3. The surety shall execute an appearance bond, an approved form for which is attached to this order as exhibit A.

4. The surety shall execute a mortgage deed to secure the appearance bond, an approved form for which is attached to this order as exhibit B.

5. The surety shall provide an appraisal of any property pledged to secure the bond in order to insure the sufficiency of said property as collateral. Any such appraisal shall have been performed no more than twelve months prior to the date of the bond.

6. The surety shall provide a title insurance policy insuring the title to such property in the name of Palm Beach County in an amount equal to the amount of the bond, plus any outstanding mortgages or liens on the property.

7. Once the above requirements are satisfied, the defendant and/or his counsel are responsible for recording said mortgage in favor of Palm Beach County, for obtaining a file stamped copy of the recorded mortgage from the clerk's office and filing the file stamped copy of the recorded mortgage in the criminal case file.

8. Upon compliance with all of the above conditions, the defendant may be released upon the property bond.

9. At the conclusion of the case and the termination of the requirements of the bond, the defendant's attorney and the assistant state attorney assigned to the case will prepare a stipulated motion for exoneration of bond and satisfaction of lien, setting forth all of the conditions showing the defendant's compliance and the reasons for exoneration of the bond. Along with this motion, counsel will submit a proposed order exonerating the bond and releasing the lien to be signed by the appropriate judge. The court then will forward the signed order to the defense counsel who is responsible for filing the order with the clerk of court for Palm Beach County. The defendant's attorney shall also prepare a satisfaction of mortgage lien which may be executed by the clerk of court for Palm Beach County and returned to the defendant's attorney who is then responsible for filing the satisfaction of mortgage.

DONE and **SIGNED** in Chambers at West Palm Beach, Palm Beach County, Florida, this 29 day of September, 2008.

Kathleen J. Kroll
Chief Judge

* supersedes admin. order 4.014–9/92

IN THE CIRCUIT COURT OF THE FIFTEENTH JUDICIAL CIRCUIT IN AND FOR PALM BEACH COUNTY, FLORIDA

CASE NO.

STATE OF FLORIDA,

vs.

, APPEARANCE BOND FOR _____

Defendant.

______________________:

I(We), the undersigned, (jointly and severally) acknowledge that I(we) and my(our) personal representatives are bound to pay to Palm Beach County the sum of ___ dollars ($ ___).

The conditions of this bond are that the defendant, _________ is to appear before _________, Circuit Court Judge for the Fifteenth Judicial Circuit, in and for Palm Beach County, Florida, at West Palm Beach, Florida, and at such other places as the defendant may be required to appear in the above-styled matter as may be ordered by the judge or by the Circuit Court of the Fifteenth Judicial Circuit, in and for Palm Beach County, Florida, or any other court to which the defendant may be removed or the cause transferred; that the defendant is not to depart the State of Florida, or the jurisdiction of any other court to which the defendant may be removed or the cause transferred after he has appeared in such other court pursuant to the terms of this bond, except in accordance with such orders or warrants as may be issued by the judge or the Circuit Court of the Fifteenth Judicial Circuit in and for Palm Beach County, Florida, or such other court to which the defendant may be removed or the cause transferred; that the defendant is to abide by any judgment entered in such matter by surrendering himself to serve any sentence imposed and obeying any order or direction in connection with such judgment as the court imposing it may prescribe, and to obey and perform the further conditions of bond attached hereto and made a part hereof;

If the defendant appears as ordered and otherwise obeys and performs the foregoing conditions of this bond, then this bond is to be void, but if the defendant fails to obey or perform any of these conditions, payment of the amount of this bond shall be due forthwith. The forfeiture of this bond for any breach of its conditions may be declared by any circuit court within the State of Florida having cognizance of the above entitled matter at the time of such breach and if the bond is forfeited and if the forfeiture is not set aside or remitted, judgment may be entered upon motion in such circuit court against each debtor jointly and severally for the amount above stated together with interest and costs, and execution may be issued and payment secured as provided by the laws of the State of Florida.

EXHIBIT A

It is agreed and understood that this is a continuing bond (including any proceeding on appeal or review) which shall continue in full force and effect until such time as the undersigned are duly exonerated.

This bond is signed this ___ day of __________, 20 ___ at West Palm Beach, Florida.

____
SURETY

BY ______________________________
(as agent)

____
Street Address

____
City State Zip Code
Phone: ______________

____
DEFENDANT

____
Street Address

____
City State Zip Code

Phone: ______________

Signed and acknowledged before me this ____ day of __________, 20 ___.

Approved: ______________
Judge/Sheriff

MORTGAGE DEED

THIS INDENTURE executed this ___ day of __________, 20 ___ by, ______________ hereinafter called the Obligor/Mortgagor in favor of Palm Beach County hereinafter called the Obligee/Mortgagee.

WITNESSETH that in consideration of a ___ personal surety bond collateralized by this indenture, hereby grants, bargains, sells, aliens, remises, conveys and confirms unto the Obligee/Mortgagee that certain land of which the Obligor/Mortgagor is now seized and in possession situate in __________ County, Florida, more particularly described as follows:

SUBJECT to restrictions, reservations, easements and covenants of record, if any, to the extent that same are valid and enforceable. (Subject to all the terms, covenants and conditions of the Declaration of Condominium.)

THIS Indenture is being made to the Obligee/Mortgagee as a personal surety to assure the presence of __________ to appear in court to answer to charges pending against him in the Circuit Court of the Fifteenth Judicial Circuit in and for Palm Beach County, Florida, in case number __________. Should __________ not appear in the aforementioned court whenever ordered by the judge thereof, then this Indenture will be due and payable in full.

TO HAVE AND TO HOLD the same, together with the tenements, hereditaments and appurtenances thereto belonging, and the rents, issues and profits thereof, unto the mortgagee, in fee simple.

AND the Obligor/Mortgagor covenants with the Obligee/Mortgagee that the Obligor/Mortgagor is indefeasibly seized of said land in fee simple; that the Obligor/Mortgagor has good right and lawful authority to convey said land as aforesaid; that the Obligor/Mortgagor will make such further assurances to perfect the fee simple title to said land in the Obligee/Mortgagee as may reasonably be required; that the Obligor/Mortgagor hereby fully warrants the title to said land and will defend the same against the lawful claims of all persons whomsoever, and that said land is free and clear of all encumbrances except a prior mortgage of __________ with __________.

EXHIBIT B

IN WITNESS WHEREOF, the said Obligor/Mortgagor has hereunto signed and sealed these presents the day and year first written above.

____
Obligor/Mortgagor

____
Obligor/Mortgagor

____
Witness

____
Witness

STATE OF FLORIDA)
:
COUNTY OF ______________)

I HEREBY CERTIFY that on this day, before me, an officer duly authorized in the State and County aforesaid to take acknowledgments, personally appeared to me known to be the person or persons described in and who executed foregoing instrument and who acknowledged before me that the instrument was executed for the purposes therein expressed.

WITNESS my hand and official seal, this ___ day of __________, 20 ___.

____
NOTARY PUBLIC, State of Florida

My commission expires:

Adopted effective September 29, 2008.

4.204. SURETY BONDS AND CASH BONDS

IN THE CIRCUIT COURT OF THE FIFTEENTH JUDICIAL CIRCUIT IN AND FOR PALM BEACH COUNTY, FLORIDA

ADMINISTRATIVE ORDER NO. 4.204–9/08 *

IN RE: SURETY BONDS AND CASH BONDS

NOW, THEREFORE, pursuant to the authority conferred by Florida Rule of Judicial Administration 2.215, it is **ORDERED** as follows:

1. All surety bond contracts submitted to the Sheriff or Clerk for the release of a prisoner shall specifically indicate that the prisoner is returnable to either the county court or the circuit court, provided, however, that the filed information arises from the original booking for which the bond was posted.

2. The Clerk and the Sheriff shall not accept a surety bond contract for the release of a prisoner unless the contract contains the above provisions.

3. In any instance where a cash bond is set, the Sheriff shall accept a surety bond in the same amount for the release of a prisoner.

DONE and **SIGNED** in Chambers at West Palm Beach, Palm Beach County, Florida, this 29 day of September, 2008.

Kathleen J. Kroll
Chief Judge

Adopted effective September 29, 2008.

* supersedes admin. order no. 4.015–10/93

4.205. FORFEITURE AND DISCHARGE OF SURETY AND CASH BONDS

IN THE CIRCUIT COURT OF THE FIFTEENTH JUDICIAL CIRCUIT IN AND FOR PALM BEACH COUNTY, FLORIDA

ADMINISTRATIVE ORDER 4.205–11/16 *

IN RE: FORFEITURE AND DISCHARGE OF SURETY AND CASH BONDS

It is statutorily mandated that surety bonds be forfeited and that agents and cash bond depositors should automatically have their bonds discharged upon the happening of certain events. Florida Statute § 903.26 requires a bond to be forfeited if the defendant fails to appear in court as required and if the proper prerequisites are followed. Florida Statute § 903.26(2)(b) requires that upon issuance of a warrant or capias for a defendant who has failed to appear as required, the Clerk of Court shall promptly notify the trial judge of the existence of a surety or cash bond available for forfeiture and, once forfeited, the Clerk shall automatically enter such forfeiture. Florida Statute § 903.26(2)(a) requires the Clerk of Court, within five (5) days of such forfeiture, to mail the statutorily required notice of forfeiture to the surety. Failure of the surety bond agent to pay the forfeiture within sixty (60) days of the mailing of the statutorily required notice shall preclude any surety application for remission pursuant to Florida Statute § 903.28. If the forfeiture is timely paid, the surety shall be entitled to the remission provisions of Florida Statute § 903.28.

It will benefit the Court, Clerk of Court, surety bond agents and cash depositors to reiterate those events both covered and not addressed by statute and be set forth herein by administrative order. Nothing in this Administrative Order shall be deemed as superseding, modifying, or changing existing and controlling statutory and case law.

NOW, THEREFORE, pursuant to the authority conferred by Florida Rule of Judicial Administration 2.215, it is **ORDERED** as follows:

1. The Clerk shall automatically discharge a forfeiture if the trial court recalls or quashes the warrant or capias for the defendant within sixty (60) days of the forfeiture of a bond.

2. The Clerk shall, within ten (10) business days of notice of the following, unless good cause is shown, discharge the bond, as to a specific charge or charges whether secured by cash or surety, in any case that one of the following events has occurred:

a. A qualifying event listed in Florida Statutes §§ 903.20, 903.21, 903.22, 903.31(1)

b. A *nolle prosequi* or "no file" announced or filed by the State Attorney's Office or a dismissal of charges entered by the court. A change in charge does not constitute a nolle prosequi or "no-file."

c. A defendant's admission to a pretrial intervention program. *See* F.S. § 903.31(2).

d. When all felony charges have been reduced to a misdemeanor. The discharge does not apply to non-monetary conditions of release, without prejudice to the state or defense to seek a modification of the non-monetary conditions.

3. When a felony charge is increased in severity or an additional charge is added and the defendant is not rearrested, the Clerk, prior to the matter being addressed by the court, shall maintain the current bond without prejudice to the state or defense to seek a modification of the bond.

4. When a felony charge is decreased in severity to a lesser felony, the Clerk shall maintain the current bond, without prejudice to the state or defense to seek a modification of the bond, The state agrees to provide a copy of the indictment or information, as soon as practicable, to the defense upon filing, or amending to, a lesser felony charge.

5. When there are multiple charges and the counts change (either increased or decreased), the bond amounts will stay the same as previously set for the original counts that remain, notwithstanding the charge. If the charges remain the same but the counts they are assigned to differ, the bonds remain as previously set per charge, not count.

6. The Clerk shall discharge any bond on a felony charge when that felony charge has been no filed. Any bond on accompanying misdemeanor charge(s) shall remain in effect without prejudice for the state or defense to seek a modification of bond.

7. When a defendant is in custody, the state shall inform the first appearance judge at the 30 day return hearing, whether charges have been filed, including the nature of the charges, and any request for extension pursuant to Florida Rule of Criminal Procedure 3.134(2). If the state has filed lesser felony charges, the matter of bond modification, including non monetary conditions, may be addressed by the first appearance judge, or set for arraignment/bond hearing before the assigned trial division judge.

8. The Clerk of Court shall immediately issue a final judgment of forfeiture pursuant to Florida Statute § 903.27(1) if the surety fails to pay the forfeiture within the required sixty (60) day time period. If however, the fugitive defendant is surrendered to Palm Beach County authorities prior to the Clerk's entry of the final judgment of forfeiture the Clerk of Court shall discharge the forfeiture, and release the surety or if paid, remit to the surety 100% of the monies paid so long as the surety pays all costs and expenses associated with the return of the defendant to Palm Beach County. *See* F.S. § 903.26(8).

9. In order to challenge the validity of the final judgment of forfeiture, the surety must pay the amount of the judgment within thirty five (35) days of issuance by the Clerk. *See* Florida Statute §§ 903.27(4), (5).

10. Pursuant to Florida Statute § 903.286, the Clerk of Court shall withhold from the return of a cash bond posted on behalf of a defendant by a person other than a bail bond agent licensed pursuant to Chapter 684, Florida Statutes, sufficient funds to pay any unpaid cost of prosecution, costs of representation court fees, court costs and criminal penalties.

11. Prior to the expiration of a bond in the thirty-sixth (36) month as provided for in Florida Statute s. 903.31(1), the Clerk shall schedule before the appropriate division judge a "Status Hearing on Surety Bond". This hearing shall be scheduled during the thirty-fourth (34) month after the issuance of the original appearance surety bond.

12. If so agreed to between the Clerk of Court and the surety, statutorily required notice to the surety may be made by electronic mail.

DONE and **SIGNED,** in Chambers, at West Palm Beach, Palm Beach County, Florida, this 21 day of November, 2016.

Jeffrey Colbath
Chief Judge

Adopted effective September 29, 2008. Amended effective February 21, 2012; January 21, 2014; April 25, 2014; November 21, 2016.

* supersedes admin, order 4.205–4/14

4.206. PRETRIAL RELEASE PROGRAM

IN THE CIRCUIT COURT OF THE FIFTEENTH JUDICIAL CIRCUIT IN AND FOR PALM BEACH COUNTY, FLORIDA

ADMINISTRATIVE ORDER NO. 4.206–1/15

IN RE: PRETRIAL RELEASE PROGRAM

The establishment of procedures for pretrial release promotes the efficient and uniform administration of justice. Pretrial release programs provide the court with verified background information on defendants held in jail prior to their First Appearance Court hearing.

NOW, THEREFORE, pursuant to the authority conferred by Florida Rule of Judicial Administration 2.215, it is **ORDERED** as follows:

1. This Order is to govern the administrative procedures needed to implement the laws of Florida and the Florida Rules of Criminal Procedure relating to pretrial release.

2. The Justice Services Department of Palm Beach County will administer and supervise the Pretrial Release Program in the Fifteenth Judicial Circuit ("Palm Beach County Pretrial Release Program").

3. The Palm Beach County Pretrial Release Program qualifies as the designated organization referred to in Florida Rule of Criminal Procedure 3.131(b)(1)(D).

4. Any person who a judge deems eligible for pretrial release may be released into the Palm Beach County Pretrial Release Program after first appearance provided that the Palm Beach County Pretrial Release Program certifies to the judge that it has investigated or otherwise verified:

a. The circumstances of the accused person's family, employment, financial resources, character, mental condition, and length of residence in the community;

b. The accused person's record of convictions, of appearances at court proceedings, or flight to avoid prosecution, or failure to appear at court proceedings; and

c. Other facts necessary to assist the court in its determination of the indigence of the accused person and whether she or he should be released under the supervision of the Pretrial Release Program.

5. Palm Beach County Pretrial Release Program will follow the judge's instruction as to whether the defendant is to report by telephone or "in person".

6. Unless the fee is waived by the Court, defendants placed in the Palm Beach County Pretrial Release Program shall pay an administrative fee to Palm Beach County in order to participate in the program.

7. Palm Beach County Pretrial Release Program will submit a sworn affidavit informing the Court when a defendant fails to comply with any or all conditions of the pretrial release. The Defendant's failure to comply with any of the pretrial conditions may result in the immediate disqualification of the accused from participating in the pretrial release program or other lawful sanction deemed appropriate by the Court.

8. If a person released under this program violates any condition of release or is arrested for a crime for which probable cause has been found by a judge, Palm Beach County Pretrial Release Program shall apply to the First Appearance judge (if charges have not been filed) or the judge assigned to try the defendant's criminal case (if charges have been filed) to have his/her release revoked and have a warrant issued for his/her arrest.

9. If any pretrial conditions of release have changed, such as change of address or change of employment, Pretrial Services shall file a Notice of Change of Pretrial Condition ("Notice") with the First Appearance judge (if charges have not been filed) or the judge assigned to try the defendant's criminal case (if charges have been filed) and provide a form Order on the Notice of Change of Pretrial Conditions ("Order") as set forth in the Notice and Order attached as Exhibit "A".

10. Pretrial Services shall provide a quarterly report to the Administrative Judges of Circuit and County Criminal as to the number of referrals, number of defendants accepted into the program, the number of warrants filed for breach of pretrial release conditions, and bond amounts for defendants placed on SOR with an accompanying bond.

DONE and **SIGNED** in Chambers, at West Palm Beach, Palm Beach County, Florida this 9 day of January, 2015.

Jeffrey Colbath
Chief Judge

EXHIBIT "A"

IN THE CIRCUIT COURT OF THE FIFTEENTH JUDICIAL CIRCUIT IN AND FOR PALM BEACH COUNTY FLORIDA

CASE NO.: ____________
Division: ____________

STATE OF FLORIDA

vs.

____
Defendant
____________/

PRETRIAL SERVICES PROGRAM'S NOTICE OF CHANGE OF PRETRIAL CONDITIONS

The Pretrial Services Program of Palm Beach County ("PTS") files this Notice of Change of Pretrial Conditions.

PTS hereby notifies the court of the following changes in the Defendant's circumstances:

☐ Defendant's residence address has changed

☐ Defendant's work status has changed

☐ Defendant is in a treatment facility

☐ Defendant is a full time student

☐ Other ____________

Under penalties of perjury, I declare that I have read the foregoing Notice of Change of Pretrial Conditions and the facts contained therein are true and correct.

By:

Signature: ____________

Printed name: ____________

Title: ________ Telephone Number: ____________

Date: ____________

Copy provided to:

State Attorney's Office

Defense Counsel ________ (insert name and address)

IN THE CIRCUIT/COUNTY COURT OF THE FIFTEENTH JUDICIAL CIRCUIT IN AND FOR PALM BEACH COUNTY FLORIDA

CASE NO.: ____________
Division: ____________

STATE OF FLORIDA

vs.

DEFENDANT
____________/

ORDER MODIFYING SUPERVISED CONDITIONS OF RELEASE

THIS CAUSE having come before the Court on Pretrial Services' Notice of Change of Pretrial Conditions, and the Court having reviewed the Notice and being otherwise duly advised in the premises hereby ORDERS as follows:

☐ 1. The Defendant will have no contact with the victim either directly or indirectly.

☐ 2. Victim contact permitted with ________. **This condition in no way alters or preempts any contact provision in any other order in any other case.**

☐ 3. The Defendant will stay away from the following persons and/or location(s): ________.

☐ 4. The Defendant will abide by a curfew of ________.

☐ 5. The Defendant will not consume or possess any alcohol, drugs or narcotics unless prescribed by a licensed physician.

☐ 6. The Defendant will not knowingly be on the premises of any commercial or private establishment whose primary purpose is the sale or consumption of alcoholic beverages.

☐ 7. The Defendant will enter outpatient drug treatment.

☐ 8. The Defendant will enter and successfully complete, at his/her own expense, the following treatment(s)/program(s): ____________

☐ 9. The Defendant will undergo random standard alcohol and drug testing, at his/her own expense.

☐ 10. The Defendant will not possess, carry, nor own any weapons or firearms.

☐ 11. The Defendant will report to SOR by telephone ________ per week.

☐ 12. Other: ____________

DONE AND ORDERED in Chambers/Open Court in Palm Beach County, Florida this ________ day of ________, 20 ________

____
Circuit/County Court Judge

Copies provided to:
State Attorney's Office—Division __________
Defense Counsel __________________ (insert name)
Palm Beach County SOR

Adopted effective January 9, 2015.

Pretrial and Trial Management

4.301. DISCOVERY STIPULATION BETWEEN STATE ATTORNEY & PUBLIC DEFENDER IN ADULT CRIMINAL CASES

IN THE CIRCUIT COURT OF THE FIFTEENTH JUDICIAL CIRCUIT IN AND FOR PALM BEACH COUNTY, FLORIDA

ADMINISTRATIVE ORDER NO. 4.301–3/16 *

IN RE: DISCOVERY STIPULATION BETWEEN STATE ATTORNEY & PUBLIC DEFENDER IN ADULT CRIMINAL CASES

The attached stipulation between the State Attorney and Public Defender for the Fifteenth Judicial Circuit will promote the efficient administration of justice and, thus, is in the public interest;

NOW, THEREFORE, pursuant to the authority conferred by Florida Rule of Judicial Administration 2.215, it is **ORDERED** as follows;

The attached stipulation between the Offices of the State Attorney and Public Defender for the Fifteenth Judicial Circuit of Florida was ratified and accepted on August 24, 2015. This stipulation shall govern the process of demanding and responding to discovery in all adult criminal matters, except capital murder cases or as otherwise agreed to in the attached signed stipulation, in the Circuit Court for the Fifteenth Judicial Circuit of Florida and in the County Court for Palm Beach County, Florida.

DONE and **SIGNED** in Chambers at West Palm Beach, Palm Beach County, Florida, this 8th day of March, 2016.

Jeffrey Colbath
Chief Judge

DISCOVERY STIPULATION

The Office of the State Attorney, Fifteenth Judicial Circuit, by and through the undersigned State Attorney, and the Office of the Public Defender, Fifteenth Judicial Circuit, by and through the undersigned Public Defender, stipulates as follows:

1. In every criminal and delinquency case, except capital murder cases or otherwise agreed in this Stipulation, where the Office of the Public Defender is appointed subsequent to the filing of an information, indictment or delinquency petition, the State Attorney shall provide discovery in accordance with Fla.R.Crim.P.3.220 and Fla.R.Juv.P. 8.060 without the necessity of filing a "Notice of Discovery". Unless there is a Notice filed pursuant to paragraph 3 herein, the Public Defender will be participating in discovery in all criminal and delinquency cases, except capital murder cases, and will have the obligations of reciprocal discovery pursuant to Fla.R.Crim.P. 3.220 and Fla.R.Juv P. 8.060.

2. This Stipulation shall remain in full force and effect unless either party withdraws specifically in writing from the Stipulation.

3. The Office of the Public Defender shall have the obligation to notify the Office of the State Attorney that, in a particular case, it does not desire to participate in discovery so as to not be obligated to provide reciprocal discovery. Notification shall be in writing and filed at the time of the appointment of the Office of the Public Defender.

4. This Stipulation shall not apply to specially appointed public defenders or conflict attorneys.

5. Upon withdrawal from a case after receiving discovery, it is the responsibility of the Office of the Public Defender to forward the discovery to the newly retained attorney or appointed conflict attorney.

This stipulation is hereby entered into this 24th day of August, 2015.

Dave Aronberg
State Attorney, 15th Judicial Circuit

Carey Haughwout
Public Defender, 15th Judicial Circuit

Adopted effective September 29, 2008. Amended effective March 8, 2016.

* supersedes admin. order 4.301–9/08

4.302. PAPERWORK FOR NEGOTIATED PLEAS

IN THE CIRCUIT COURT OF THE FIFTEENTH JUDICIAL CIRCUIT IN AND FOR PALM BEACH COUNTY, FLORIDA

ADMINISTRATIVE ORDER 4.302–9/08 *

IN RE: PAPERWORK FOR NEGOTIATED PLEAS

The State Attorney's Office has been responsible for filling out all necessary paperwork attendant to negotiated pleas since the early 1980's. Since said time, the required paperwork has increased from approximately four documents to ten or more at the present time. To continue to require the State Attorney to be responsible for filling out all the paperwork impresses an inordinate burden upon that office.

NOW, THEREFORE, pursuant to the authority conferred by Florida Rule of Judicial Administration 2.215, it is **ORDERED** as follows:

1. The State Attorney's Office shall be responsible for filling out the following documents.

a. Plea Sheet

b. Victim Notification Sheet

c. Guideline Score Sheet

d. Judgment

e. Restitution Order

2. The Clerk shall be responsible for filling out the following documents:

a. Fingerprint Form

b. Department of Corrections Check List

c. Sentence Order

3. Defense counsel shall be responsible for filling out the following forms:

a. Rights Sheet

b. Juvenile Waiver (where appropriate)

c. Cost Order

DONE and **SIGNED,** in Chambers, at West Palm Beach, Palm Beach County, Florida this 29 day of September, 2008.

Kathleen J. Kroll
Chief Judge

Adopted effective September 29, 2008.

* supersedes admin. order 4.043–6/99

4.303. STIPULATIONS FOR CONTINUANCES OF TRIAL DATES IN CRIMINAL ACTIONS

IN THE CIRCUIT COURT OF THE FIFTEENTH JUDICIAL CIRCUIT IN AND FOR PALM BEACH COUNTY, FLORIDA

ADMINISTRATIVE ORDER NO. 4.303–9/08 *

IN RE: STIPULATIONS FOR CONTINUANCES OF TRIAL DATES IN CRIMINAL ACTIONS

All stipulations for continuance must be in writing, signed by counsel, filed, and presented to the judge for signature, at least twenty-four (24) hours before the trial day, excluding Saturdays, Sundays, and holidays. No case shall be considered continued unless ordered by the court.

1. The stipulation shall contain the following information:

a. Date of defendant's arrest;

b. Whether a waiver of speedy trial has been filed;

c. The reason for the request;

d. Whether the cause of continuance arose after the case was set for trial;

e. Whether trial had been continued previously and, if so, the number of times;

f. The amount of time requested, and the reason for the length of time requested;

g. Whether the defendant is in jail.

2. No case shall be continued on the day of trial except for extraordinary circumstances which could not have been anticipated before the day of trial.

DONE and **SIGNED** in Chambers at West Palm Beach, Palm Beach County, Florida, this 29 day of September, 2008.

Kathleen J. Kroll
Chief Judge

Adopted effective September 29, 2008.

* supersedes admin. order 4.003–9/92

4.304. WITNESS COMPENSATION/REIMBURSEMENT

IN THE CIRCUIT COURT OF THE FIFTEENTH JUDICIAL CIRCUIT IN AND FOR PALM BEACH COUNTY, FLORIDA

ADMINISTRATIVE ORDER NO. 4.304–9/08 *

IN RE: WITNESS COMPENSATION/REIMBURSEMENT

Guidelines have been established for the payment of witnesses under Florida Statute sections 92.142 and 112.061.

NOW, THEREFORE, pursuant to the authority conferred by Florida Rule of Judicial Administration 2.215, it is **ORDERED** as follows:

1. The subpoenaing party (Public Defender, State Attorney, etc.), when making arrangements for witnesses to appear, is responsible for informing the witnesses of the travel costs for which they will be reimbursed and advising them that receipts must be obtained for travel fare, tolls, parking, hotel, communication expense, and cab or bus fares.

2. The Clerk of Court shall make payments that comply with sections 92.142 and 112.061, Florida Statutes (2007).

DONE and **SIGNED** in Chambers at West Palm Beach, Palm Beach County, Florida, this 29 day of September, 2008.

Kathleen J. Kroll
Chief Judge

Adopted effective September 29, 2008.

* supersedes admin. order 4.016–12/92

4.305. SUBPOENAS ISSUED TO LAW ENFORCEMENT OFFICERS

IN THE CIRCUIT COURT OF THE FIFTEENTH JUDICIAL CIRCUIT IN AND FOR PALM BEACH COUNTY, FLORIDA

ADMINISTRATIVE ORDER NO. 4.305–9/08 *

IN RE: SUBPOENAS ISSUED TO LAW ENFORCEMENT OFFICERS

All subpoenas to law enforcement officers shall be served in accordance with the Florida Rules of Criminal Procedure and the Florida Statutes, except that subpoenas or notices to appear may be served upon the department or agency employing the witness, under the following conditions:

1. A statement shall be filed with the clerk of the circuit court (criminal division) by the individual officer appointing his or her department or agency as agent for the officer for the purpose of receiving subpoenas, and service upon the department or agency shall constitute personal service upon the officer.

2. A statement shall be filed with the clerk of the circuit court stating the department or agency agrees to pay the court reporter's per diem rate whenever the officer, without justifiable excuse and proper notification, fails to respond to a subpoena properly left with the agency.

3. This procedure is applicable only when the subpoena is left with the agency at least seventy-two (72) hours in advance of the required testimony.

DONE and **SIGNED** in Chambers at West Palm Beach, Palm beach County, Florida, this 29 day of September, 2008.

Kathleen J. Kroll
Chief Judge

Adopted effective September 29, 2008.
* supersedes admin. order 4.012–9/92

4.306. MOTIONS TO DEPOSE

IN THE CIRCUIT COURT OF THE FIFTEENTH JUDICIAL CIRCUIT IN AND FOR PALM BEACH COUNTY, FLORIDA

ADMINISTRATIVE ORDER NO. 4.306–9/08 *

IN RE: MOTIONS TO DEPOSE

Pursuant to the authority conferred by Florida Rule of Judicial Administration 2.215, it is **ORDERED** as follows:

1. All motions to depose shall be in writing and shall specify the basis for good cause.

2. No motion to depose will be heard unless the motion bears a certificate of moving counsel stating that he or she contacted opposing counsel and attempted to resolve the issue without a hearing, but that the matter could not be resolved.

DONE and **SIGNED** in Chambers at West Palm Beach, Palm Beach County, Florida, this 29 day of September, 2008.

Kathleen J. Kroll
Chief Judge

Adopted effective September 29, 2008.
* supersedes admin. order 10.022–5/97

4.307. RESCISSION OF NO CONTACT ORDERS

IN THE CIRCUIT COURT OF THE FIFTEENTH JUDICIAL CIRCUIT IN AND FOR PALM BEACH COUNTY, FLORIDA

ADMINISTRATIVE ORDER NO. 4.307–8/12 *

IN RE: RESCISSION OF NO CONTACT ORDERS

The Sheriff of Palm Beach County enters all No Contact Orders into the Palm Beach Sheriff's Office PALMS system. There is a need to have a uniform procedure by which the Palm Beach County Sheriff's Office is notified that a No Contact Order is no longer in effect by operation of law or by rescission of court order. The status and disposition of No Contact Orders must be accurately reflected within the PALMS system to ensure victim and defendant constitutional rights.

NOW, THEREFORE, pursuant to the authority conferred by Florida Rule of Judicial Administration 2.215, it is **ORDERED** as follows:

1. Except as provided by section 921.244, Florida Statutes, the rescission of a No Contact Order shall occur when:

a. The State enters a nolle pros as to the charges, or

b. The State enters a "no file" as to the charges and no down-filed or related charges arising from the same incident remain open; or

c. The No Contact Order is not a part of a plea agreement; or

d. The No Contact Order is to be rescinded; or

e. Probation is terminated.

2. All nolle proses/"no files" shall be filed in writing. In the event the State enters a nolle pros or "no file" and it contains "clerk and sheriff to rescind No Contact Order" the Clerk shall rescind the No Contact Order, retroactive to the date the case was closed and/or a nolle pros was filed.

3. In the event there is not a written nolle pros or "no file" and the case is otherwise closed, the clerk is hereby directed to rescind the no contact order, retroactive to the date the case was closed.

4. When the No Contact Order is rescinded, an Order Rescinding the No Contact Order (attached hereto as "Exhibit A") shall be executed by the presiding judge. For the convenience of the parties, the Administrative Office of the Court will maintain form orders in the courtroom.

5. Upon the rescission of a No Contact Order, the Clerk of the Court is directed to provide immediate electronic notification of the rescission to the Palm Beach County Sheriff's Central Records Office and to send a hard copy of the Order within 48 hours.

6. The Palm Beach County Sheriff's Office shall immediately record the rescission order in the PALMS system.

DONE and **SIGNED**, in Chambers, at West Palm Beach, Palm Beach County, Florida this 22nd day of August, 2012.

Peter D. Blanc
Chief Judge

* supersedes admin. order 4.307–6/11

IN THE CIRCUIT COURT OF THE FIFTEENTH JUDICIAL CIRCUIT IN AND FOR PALM BEACH COUNTY, FLORIDA

BOOKING NO: ______________________

CASE NO: ______________________

DIVISION: ______________________

STATE OF FLORIDA,

vs.

(Last Name), (First Name), Defendant/

ORDER RESCINDING NO CONTACT ORDER

This matter having come before the Court, the Court finds that:

☐ the State Attorney has entered a nolle pros as to the charges.

☐ the State Attorney has entered a "No File" as to the charges and no down-filed or related charges arising from the same incident remain open.

☐ the case has been concluded by plea.

☐ the Defendant has been found not guilty at trial.

☐ a motion to rescind the No Contact Order has been granted.

☐ probation has been revoked or terminated.

Wherefore, it is hereby **ORDERED** and **ADJUDGED** that the No Contact Order previously entered in this case is hereby rescinded.

DONE and **ORDERED**, in Chambers, at Palm Beach County, Florida this ________ day of ________, 20 ___.

____
Judge

Adopted effective September 29, 2008. Amended effective July 1, 2009; December 22, 2009; June 29, 2011; August 22, 2012.

4.308. RECALL OF CAPIASES IN NOLLE PROSSED CASES

IN THE CIRCUIT COURT OF THE FIFTEENTH JUDICIAL CIRCUIT IN AND FOR PALM BEACH COUNTY, FLORIDA

ADMINISTRATIVE ORDER 4.308–9/08 *

IN RE: RECALL OF CAPIASES IN NOLLE PROSSED CASES

The court may direct the clerk to issue a capias for a defendant's arrest if the defendant fails to appear in court (Florida Rule of Criminal Procedure 3.730 and Florida Rule of Traffic Court 6.190). Capiases may remain active in closed cases, which have been nolle prossed by the State without a court hearing or dismissed because of an inactive status pursuant to Administrative Order 4.605–9/08 (as amended).

NOW, THEREFORE, pursuant to the authority conferred by Florida Rule of Judicial Administration 2.215, it is **ORDERED** as follows:

1. Capiases are hereby recalled on felony, misdemeanor and traffic crimes that have been nolle prossed by the State without a court hearing or that have been dismissed because of inactive status pursuant to an Administrative Order 4.605–9/08 (as amended).

2. The clerk is authorized to take appropriate steps to implement this order.

DONE and **SIGNED** in Chambers at West Palm Beach, Palm Beach County, Florida, this 29 day of September, 2008.

Kathleen J. Kroll
Chief Judge

Adopted effective September 29, 2008.

* supersedes admin. order 10.023 8/97

Sentencing and Related Post Sentencing Matters

4.401. PROCEDURES FOR ARRESTS WITH WARRANTS FOR VIOLATIONS OF PROBATION

IN THE CIRCUIT COURT OF THE FIFTEENTH JUDICIAL CIRCUIT IN AND FOR PALM BEACH COUNTY, FLORIDA

ADMINISTRATIVE ORDER NO. 4.401–8/13 *

IN RE: PROCEDURES FOR ARRESTS WITH WARRANTS FOR VIOLATIONS OF PROBATION

The establishment of procedures for arrests with warrants for violation of probation would promote the efficient and uniform administration of justice.

NOW, THEREFORE, pursuant to the authority conferred by Florida Rule of Judicial Administration 2.215, it is **ORDERED** as follows:

1. At the time a warrant is issued, the judge may set a bond, indicating the amount on the warrant, and shall indicate the scope of the warrant (i.e., Florida only, national, intent to extradite).

2. The sheriff shall notify the Clerk and the Probation Office immediately upon a probationer from this County being booked into the Palm Beach County Detention Center.

3. In all felony cases where the probationer has posted bond or been released on his own recognizance prior to the preliminary hearing, the preliminary hearing shall be heard on the third Friday following the release on bond or recognizance.

4. In all misdemeanor and traffic crime cases where the probationer has posted bond or been released on his own recognizance prior to the preliminary hearing, the preliminary hearing shall be heard on the trial court's next scheduled monthly VOP date (the Deputy Administrative Judge for the County Court Criminal Division shall be responsible for providing the Clerk's Office with the master schedule).

5. All persons arrested on a Misdemeanor Violation of Probation warrant, who are not released on bond or O.R. pursuant to said warrant, shall be brought before the presiding judge of the assigned division for preliminary hearing forthwith, except on weekends and holidays, when such person shall be brought before the first appearance judge. All persons arrested on a Misdemeanor Violation of Probation warrant arising from North or South satellite shall be brought before the first appearance judge Monday through Sunday.

6. All persons arrested on a Felony Violation of Probation warrant, who are not released on bond or O.R. pursuant to said warrant, shall be brought before the assigned divisional judge or a judge covering the assigned division on the next business day following the defendant's arrest.

7. Individuals with Belle Glade cases (both misdemeanor and felony) shall be brought before the judge sitting in Belle Glade on the next business day following the defendant's arrest.

DONE and **SIGNED** in Chambers at West Palm Beach, Palm Beach County, Florida, this 29 day of August, 2013.

Jeffrey J. Colbath
Chief Judge

Adopted effective September 29, 2008. Amended effective May 10, 2010; August 29, 2013.

* supersedes admin. order 4.401–5/10

4.402. PROCEDURES FOR WARRANTLESS ARRESTS FOR VIOLATION OF PROBATION AND COMMUNITY CONTROL

IN THE CIRCUIT COURT OF THE FIFTEENTH JUDICIAL CIRCUIT IN AND FOR PALM BEACH COUNTY, FLORIDA

ADMINISTRATIVE ORDER NO. 4.402–9/08 *

IN RE: PROCEDURES FOR WARRANTLESS ARRESTS FOR VIOLATION OF PROBATION AND COMMUNITY CONTROL

The establishment of procedures for arrests without warrants for violation of probation and violation of community control would promote the efficient and uniform administration of justice. Florida Statute section 948.06(1) (2007), authorizes any law enforcement officer to arrest, without warrant, a probationer or offender in community control who has violated his or her probation or community control in a material respect, and forthwith return him or her to the court granting such probation or community control. Florida Rule of Criminal Procedure 3.130(a) requires a first appearance within 24 hours of arrest;

NOW, THEREFORE, pursuant to the authority conferred by Florida Rule of Judicial Administration 2.215, it is **ORDERED** as follows:

A. Booking Procedures.

1. The sheriff shall notify the Clerk of Court and the Probation Office immediately upon a probationer from this County being booked into the Palm Beach County Detention Center.

2. The Sheriff is directed to prepare a separate booking for every violation of probation or community control. To facilitate this, law enforcement is directed to prepare a separate probable cause affidavit for each violation of probation or community control.

3. Immediately following the arrest without a warrant of a probationer or offender in community control, or no later than the first working day following the arrest, the Sheriff shall notify the supervising authority (i.e. Department of Corrections or Pride, Inc.) of the arrest.

4. A probationer or offender in community control arrested without a warrant shall not be eligible for release prior to his or her appearance before the first appearance judge, or the judge placing him/her on probation or community control.

B. First Appearance.

1. *Probable Cause/Bond.*

a. The probationer or offender in community control shall be brought within 24 hours of his or her arrest to a first appearance hearing, before the court granting such probation or community control within the Fifteenth Judicial Circuit, or if arrested on a weekend/holiday before the first appearance judge, to determine if there is probable cause to believe the probationer or offender in community control has violated his or her probation or community control in a material respect.

b. If probable cause is not found, the judge may grant an additional 72 hours for probable cause to be presented to the court or may order the individual's release on his or her own recognizance (O.R.).

c. If probable cause is found, the probationer or offender in community control shall, subject to the judge's discretion be released on bond, or be ordered held in custody.

2. *Extra–Territorial Probation and Community Control.*

a. If the court granting such probation or community control is outside the Fifteenth Judicial Circuit, the probationer or offender in community control shall be brought before a judge within 24 hours of his or her arrest for a first appearance hearing, to determine if there is probable cause to believe the probationer or offender in community control has violated his or her probation or community control in a material respect.

b. If probable cause is not found, the judge may grant an additional 72 hours for probable cause to be presented to the court or may order the individual's release on his or her own recognizance (O.R.).

c. If probable cause is found, the probationer or offender in community control shall, subject to the first appearance judge's discretion be released on bond, or be ordered held in custody.

d. For those offenders held in custody, the clerk shall schedule the probationer or offender in community control for another appearance before the first appearance judge within 10 days, to determine if the Sheriff, State and/or the Department of Corrections have made sufficient arrangements for the individual's return to the court granting such probation or community control.

e. If still in custody after 10 days, and a warrant and/or hold has not been issued, then absent good cause to the contrary the individual shall be released on his or her own recognizance (O.R.).

C. Affidavits of Violation.

1. Within 10 working days following notification by the Sheriff of the arrest of a probationer or offender in community control, the supervising authority (i.e. D.O.C. or Pride, Inc.) shall file an affidavit of probation or community control violation.

2. If such affidavit is not filed within 10 days, an offender in custody shall be brought back before the court and, absent good cause to the contrary, shall be released on his or her own recognizance (O.R.).

D. Hearings on Violation of Probation/Community Control.

1. In all felony cases where the probationer has posted bond or been released on his own recognizance prior to the preliminary hearing, the preliminary hearing shall be heard on the third Friday following the release on bond or recognizance.

2. In all misdemeanor and traffic crime cases where the probationer has posted bond or been released on his own recognizance, prior to the preliminary hearing shall be heard on the trial court's next scheduled monthly VOP date (the Deputy Administrative Judge for the County Court Criminal Division shall be responsible for providing the Clerk's Office with the master schedule.)

3. All hearings subsequent to the first appearance hearings contained herein shall be scheduled by the court placing the individual on probation and/or community control.

E. Danger to Public Hearings.

1. If the offender is under supervision for any offense listed below, the court will hold a "danger to the public hearing" and make a finding that the probationer or offender is not a danger to the public prior to release:

Florida Statute Chapter 794;	**Florida Statute § 800.04(4),(5), or (6);**
Florida Statute § 827.071;	**Florida Statute § 847.0154**

2. A "danger to the public hearing" will be held if the offender is a registered sexual predator, a registered sexual offender, or is under supervision for a criminal offense for which he or she would meet the registration criteria as set forth in Florida Statute §§ 775.21, 943.0435 or 944.607.

DONE AND SIGNED in Chambers at West Palm Beach, Palm Beach County, Florida, this 29 day of September, 2008.

Kathleen J. Kroll
Chief Judge

Adopted effective September 29, 2008.

* supersedes admin. orders 2.068–1/03; 4.005 11/99

4.403. PROBATION/COMMUNITY CONTROL COST OF SUPERVISION

IN THE CIRCUIT COURT OF THE FIFTEENTH JUDICIAL CIRCUIT IN AND FOR PALM BEACH COUNTY, FLORIDA

ADMINISTRATIVE ORDER NO. 4.403–9/08 *

IN RE: PROBATION/COMMUNITY CONTROL COST OF SUPERVISION

Section 948.09, Florida Statutes, provides that any person ordered by the Court to be placed on probation, drug offender probation, or community control, "must, as a condition of any placement, pay the department a total sum of money equal to the total month or portion of a month of supervision times the Court–Ordered amount, but not to exceed the actual per diem costs of the supervision.". The Court believes that all offenders should bear to the extent possible the costs of supervision to minimize the economic impact on the taxpayers of the State of Florida. Each defendants, prior to entering a plea of guilty or nolo contendere, should be aware of the costs of supervision if probation is to be imposed.

NOW, THEREFORE, pursuant to the authority conferred by Florida Rule of Judicial Administration 2.215, it is **ORDERED** as follows:

1. Unless otherwise exempted or ordered by the Court, every defendant placed on probation or community control by the Circuit Court in and for Palm Beach County, Florida shall pay the sum of $50.00 per month as and for the costs of supervision for probation and/or community control. In addition thereto, probationers and/or community controllees shall also pay a four percent (4%) surcharge provided by statute for a total of $52.00 per month.

2. The Correctional Probation Circuit Administrator of the Fifteenth Judicial Circuit may exempt all or part of the court ordered cost of supervision if the offender's financial status changes during the supervision period.

DONE and **SIGNED** in Chambers at West Palm Beach, Palm Beach County, Florida, this 29 day of September, 2008.

Kathleen J. Kroll
Chief Judge

Adopted effective September 29, 2008.

* supersedes admin. order 4.035–7/97

4.404. POLICIES AND PROCEDURES REGARDING IN–HOUSE ARREST AND ELECTRONIC MONITORING PROGRAMS

IN THE CIRCUIT COURT OF THE FIFTEENTH JUDICIAL CIRCUIT IN AND FOR PALM BEACH COUNTY, FLORIDA

ADMINISTRATIVE ORDER NO. 4.404–9/08 *

IN RE: POLICIES AND PROCEDURES REGARDING IN–HOUSE ARREST AND ELECTRONIC MONITORING PROGRAMS

The Palm Beach County Sheriff's Office conducts a program known as the In–House Arrest Program (Monitoring Pre–Trial Detainee's, Direct filed Juvenile and Adult, and County Sentenced Adults) and the Department of Corrections, Parole and Probation Office, conducts a program known as the Electronic Monitoring Program (Monitoring State Sentenced Adults), both programs will be hereinafter referred to as the responsible agencies. Both programs rely upon electronic monitoring (Global Positioning Satellite and Radio Frequency) with a transmitter affixed to the ankle of the person to be monitored. In the interest of public safety, persons being monitored must strictly comply with the constraints placed upon them by the Court, and strictly comply with the rules and regulations placed upon them by the Responsible Agency;

NOW, THEREFORE, pursuant to the authority conferred by Florida Rule of Judicial Administration 2.215, it is **ORDERED** as follows:

1. Whenever a person on Electronic Monitoring through the Department of Corrections, Office of Community Corrections or In–House Arrest under the Palm Beach County Sheriff's Office is required to be within the confines of his/her residence, he/she shall be physically within the residence at all times, i.e., he/she is prohibited from being outside the residential walls.

2. If an alarm is reported by the monitoring company the responsible agency shall immediately investigate and take appropriate action to determine if there has been a bonafide equipment failure not caused, in any respect, by the person being monitored.

3. In the event the representative of the responsible agency determines that there was no bonafide equipment failure, then the person being monitored shall be taken into custody immediately. If the responsible agent deems the violation to not be willful a warrant may be requested from the sentencing judge for a Notice to Appear within the next business day.

4. Persons on In–House Arrest under the Palm Beach county Sheriff's Office or Electronic Monitoring under the Department of Corrections, Office of Community Corrections shall strictly comply with all constraints placed on them from the Courts, and shall strictly comply with all of the rules and regulations of the responsible agencies.

5. In the event a representative of the responsible agency determines that the person being monitored has not strictly complied with all constraints placed on them by the Court, or strictly complied with all of the rules and regulations of the responsible agency, the person being monitored shall be taken into custody immediately unless the responsible agent deems the violation to not be willful a warrant may be requested from the sentencing judge for a Notice to Appear within the next business day.

6. Any person whose case originated from circuit or county criminal court and who is taken into custody, shall be held without bond and shall, on the next working day, be brought before the judge presiding over his or her case for further disposition at the discretion of the presiding judge.

7. A copy of this Administrative Order shall be furnished to every person presently being monitored and every person placed on the monitor in the future.

DONE and **SIGNED** in Chambers at West Palm Beach, Palm Beach County, Florida, this 29 day of September, 2008.

Kathleen J. Kroll
Chief Judge

Adopted effective September 29, 2008.

* supersedes admin. order 2.051–5/06 except as it pertains to juveniles

4.405. APPLICATION OF FUNDS RECEIVED FROM PROBATIONER

IN THE CIRCUIT COURT OF THE FIFTEENTH JUDICIAL CIRCUIT IN AND FOR PALM BEACH COUNTY, FLORIDA

ADMINISTRATIVE ORDER NO. 4.405–9/08 *

IN RE: APPLICATION OF FUNDS RECEIVED FROM PROBATIONER

Persons placed on probation or community control may be required to make monetary payments through the Department of Corrections for multiple purposes. There is a need for consistency within the Fifteenth Judicial Circuit as to how monies shall be applied. The interests of victims are paramount in the view of the court.

NOW, THEREFORE, pursuant to the authority conferred by Florida Rule of Judicial Administration 2.215, it is **ORDERED** as follows:

The order in which monetary payments are to be distributed are as follows:

1. First, to any Restitution Order by the Court as a condition of probation until fully paid. Provided, this shall not apply to probationers while residing in a restitution center who shall pay in accordance with the rules of the center, then

2. Second, according to statutory priority, to any Court costs imposed as a condition of probation, until fully paid, and thereafter

3. Third, to costs of supervision as determined by Administrative Order 4.403–9/08 (as amended)

4. Court Costs Which Are a Condition of Probation. If at the end of the probationary period the probationer has made a good faith effort to make payment of the court courts or exceptional circumstances exist where the probationer is unable to pay the court costs, then the probation officer shall, upon termination of the probationary period, present to the judge a cost judgment for entry.

DONE and **SIGNED,** in Chambers, at West Palm Beach, Palm Beach County, Florida this 29 day of September, 2008.

Kathleen J. Kroll
Chief Judge

Adopted effective September 29, 2008.

* supersedes admin. order 4.038–11/02

4.406. RESTITUTION TO CRIME VICTIMS

IN THE CIRCUIT COURT OF THE FIFTEENTH JUDICIAL CIRCUIT IN AND FOR PALM BEACH COUNTY, FLORIDA

ADMINISTRATIVE ORDER NO. 4.406–9/08 *

IN RE: RESTITUTION TO CRIME VICTIMS

Section 775.089, Florida Statutes (2007), mandates that defendants make restitution to crime victims. Section 775.089(11), Florida Statutes (2007), authorizes the court to order the clerk to collect and dispense restitution payments section 775.089(12)(a), Florida Statutes (2007), permits the issuance of income deduction orders to facilitate prompt and full restitution.

NOW, THEREFORE, pursuant to the authority conferred by Florida Rule of Judicial Administration 2.215, it is **ORDERED** as follows:

STANDARD FORMS

1. To fulfill the statutory requirement that separate orders be entered for restitution and income deduction, see section 775.089(12)(a)(1), Florida Statutes (2007), orders substantially like those attached, see appendix "A", Order for Restitution, and appendix "B", Order for Income Deduction, are recommended for the court's use.

2. The assistant state attorney responsible for the case shall complete a clerk's data sheet to accompany each income deduction order. The completed data sheet see appendix "C" shall be forwarded to the clerk's support department.

3. The clerk's support department shall mail a notice to each payor as provided in appendix "D".

4. The clerk's support office shall provide forms, see appendix "E", which shall be used to give notice and request a hearing in the event of a contest regarding an income deduction order.

IMPLEMENTATION BY THE CLERK

5. Upon the entry of an income deduction order pursuant to section 775.089(12)(a)(1), Florida Statutes (2007), payments shall be processed through the clerk's support department.

6. The clerk of court ("clerk") is authorized to impose and collect an initial processing fee of twenty dollars ($20.00). This fee shall be charged for each payor on which the income deduction order is served. The $20.00 fee shall be deducted from the first payment received under the income deduction order.

7. The clerk is authorized to charge and collect a service charge of two dollars ($2.00) on all restitution payments processed through the support department.

8. The clerk's support department's responsibilities shall be limited to the collection and disbursement of funds received through income deduction orders. The support department shall not be responsible for investigative functions to locate the defendant or his employer.

9. Each month the support department shall prepare a thirty-day delinquency report. This report shall be delivered to the criminal felony division clerk for subsequent pickup by the various probation agencies. The monthly report shall contain the following information:

a. Defendant's name

b. Case number(s)

c. Probation agency code

d. Date of the last payment received and the amount paid

e. Balance due based on income deduction order

f. Total amount due the victim

g. Victim's name

10. Upon receipt of a payer's personal check, the clerk is authorized to withhold disbursement for a reasonable time to ensure that the check clears. If a personal check is returned by the bank, then the clerk is authorized to notify that payer that all future payments must be made by certified check or cashier's check in lieu of personal check.

DONE and **SIGNED** in Chambers at West Palm Beach, Palm Beach County, Florida, this 29 day of September, 2008.

Kathleen J. Kroll
Chief Judge

Adopted effective September 29, 2008.

* supersedes admin. order 4.020–9/92

4.407. DISTRIBUTION OF UNCLAIMED RESTITUTION

IN THE CIRCUIT COURT OF THE FIFTEENTH JUDICIAL CIRCUIT IN AND FOR PALM BEACH COUNTY, FLORIDA

ADMINISTRATIVE ORDER 4.407–9/08 *

IN RE: DISTRIBUTION OF UNCLAIMED RESTITUTION

Pursuant to the authority conferred by Florida Rule of Judicial Administration 2.215, it is **ORDERED** as follows:

1. When restitution is ordered by the Court and is subsequently collected by the Clerk's Office or PRIDE, and the victim who is to receive this court ordered restitution is unable to be located, these funds shall be disbursed to the Crimes Compensation Trust Fund of the Office of the Attorney General, Division of Victim Services, Department of Legal Affairs, The Capitol, Tallahassee, Florida 32399–1050.

2. Such disbursement should clearly designate these funds as Unclaimed Restitution because of the unknown whereabouts of the victims.

3. Should this victim later be located or come forward, they may claim any funds paid on their behalf by sending a notarized written request to the Crimes Compensation Trust Fund.

DONE and **ORDERED**, in Chambers, at West Palm Beach, Palm Beach County, Florida this 29 day of September, 2008.

Kathleen J. Kroll
Chief Judge

Adopted effective September 29, 2008.

* supersedes admin. order 4.039–7/03; 10.025 12/97

4.408. [VACATED AND SET ASIDE BY ORDER 4.408-5/15, EFFECTIVE MAY 26, 2015.]

4.409. WEEKEND SENTENCES

IN THE CIRCUIT COURT OF THE FIFTEENTH JUDICIAL CIRCUIT IN AND FOR PALM BEACH COUNTY, FLORIDA

ADMINISTRATIVE ORDER NO. 4.409–9/08 *

IN RE: WEEKEND SENTENCES

Defendants are sometimes permitted to serve their sentence on weekends and such is a privilege and not a right;

NOW, THEREFORE, pursuant to the authority conferred by Florida Rule of Judicial Administration 2.215, it is **ORDERED** as follows:

1. Persons who exhibit any of the conduct specified below shall be deemed to have violated an implied condition of their sentence and, therefore shall be held at the Stockade and brought before the sentencing judge or his/her alternate on the next regular business day.

a. Persons who fail to show up as scheduled.

b. Persons who report intoxicated for booking physical, or weekend time.

c. Persons who report late.

d. Persons who fail to do work as assigned by jail staff.

e. Persons who appear for weekends who have previously failed to appear without having been excused by the sentencing judge.

f. Any violation of the weekend rules imposed by the Sheriff's Office.

2. In the event a prisoner is held pursuant to a reason cited above, the jail personnel shall file a brief affidavit stating the reason(s) for such detention, including breathalyzer results if applicable. This affidavit shall accompany the court file at the hearing before the sentencing judge.

3. Persons failing to appear and persons failing to obtain their physical examination or complete the booking process shall be reported, in writing, by jail personnel to the sentencing judge by the following Tuesday after the missed weekend. The sentencing judge shall advise jail personnel as to what action he/she wants taken in the case prior to the next weekend.

DONE and **SIGNED** in Chambers at West Palm Beach, Palm Beach County, Florida, this 29 day of September, 2008.

Kathleen J. Kroll
Chief Judge

Adopted effective September 29, 2008.

* supersedes admin. order 10.010–3/93

4.410. DEPARTMENT OF CORRECTIONS REENTRY PROGRAM "THINKING FOR A CHANGE"

IN THE CIRCUIT COURT OF THE FIFTEENTH JUDICIAL CIRCUIT IN AND FOR PALM BEACH COUNTY, FLORIDA

ADMINISTRATIVE ORDER NO. 4.410–9/12

IN RE: DEPARTMENT OF CORRECTIONS REENTRY PROGRAM "*THINKING FOR A CHANGE*"

The Department of Corrections is utilizing a Reentry Program entitled *Thinking for a Change* which program was developed by the National Institute of Corrections. This free program is designed to assist offenders by combining cognitive restructuring theory with cognitive skills theory to create an innovative and integrated curriculum designed to help individuals in the Criminal Justice System take control of their lives by taking control of their thinking. In the corrections field the targeted behavior is a reduction in reoffending, and cognitive behavioral interventions have been found to be an evidence-based practice for achieving this goal. The Department of Corrections is desirous of expanding this program to those individuals who are ordered to perform community service hours as part of a felony sentence.

NOW, THEREFORE, pursuant to the authority conferred by Florida Rule of Judicial Administration 2.215, it is **ORDERED** as follows:

1. An offender ordered to perform community service hours may choose to participate in the *Thinking for a Change* program in lieu of performing community service hours. The offender shall be credited with an hour of community service for each hour the offender attended the *Thinking for a Change* program.

2. Individuals who have been sentenced to community service as part of a felony case are eligible.

3. The Department of Corrections Court Officer shall notify the Court upon the offender completing the program.

DONE and **SIGNED** in Chambers at West Palm Beach, Palm Beach County, Florida, this 12 day of September, 2012.

Peter D. Blanc
Chief Judge

Adopted effective September 12, 2012.

4.411. ALTERNATIVE SANCTIONS PROGRAM FOR FELONY OFFENDERS

IN THE CIRCUIT COURT OF THE FIFTEENTH JUDICIAL CIRCUIT IN AND FOR PALM BEACH COUNTY, FLORIDA

ADMINISTRATIVE ORDER NO. 4.411—11/18 *

IN RE: ALTERNATIVE SANCTIONS PROGRAM FOR FELONY OFFENDERS

There are a substantial number of technical violations that do not involve a new arrest or other serious violation. Recidivism may be reduced by utilizing collaborative efforts among the courts, probation and law enforcement to hold the offender accountable and apply swift and certain sanctions for technical violations of probation. Alternatives to incarcerating felony offenders with technical probation violations can reduce the court docket of probation hearings; reduce the workload of prosecutors and defense attorneys involved with many technical violation hearings; reduce law enforcement resources required to serve violation warrants for certain technical violations; reduce jail population for offenders pending violation hearings; and offer the offender an alternative to a violation hearing in court, allowing the offender to remain engaged in employment, school, treatment, etc. while taking immediate responsibility for his/her actions and consequences of those actions.

A key component of the Alternative Sanctions Program is the Home Builders Institute, Inc (HBI) administered by the Florida Department of Corrections (FDC). The HBI's program prepares individuals with the skills and experience needed for successful careers through pre-apprenticeship training, job placement services, certification programs, textbooks and curricula. Participants have an opportunity to learn about careers in the construction trades, earn an industry recognized pre-apprenticeship credential, and receive assistance with job placement. HBI Offenders who wish to participate in the HBI program, must adhere to FDC's attendance, dress code, and supervision policy. Further, any unemployed offenders can voluntarily be referred to this program by their probation officer in lieu of completing court costs. Upon successful completion of the program, full credit for court costs will be given. This benefit is retroactive for offenders who have already successfully completed the HBI program.

NOW, THEREFORE, pursuant to the authority conferred by Florida Rule of Judicial Administration 2.215, it is **ORDERED** as follows:

1. The Alternative Sanctions Program is hereby created in the Fifteenth Judicial Circuit, Palm Beach County, for felony case types.

2. Eligibility. To be eligible for the program, offenders must have been placed on probation under the supervision of the Department of Corrections by a judge in the Fifteenth Judicial Circuit, have stable community ties, and have a stable residence in Florida.

a. Offenders who are eligible for the program include probation offenders and drug offenders.

b. The program only applies to offenders charged with a non-violent third degree felony or less, and who have committed certain technical violations addressed in the Alternative Sanctions Program Violation/Sanction Matrix included in section three (3) of this order

c. The threat an offender poses to public safety is the most important factor in determining eligibility. Offenders with a lengthy (three or more prior felony convictions) or violent criminal history, including sex offenders, are not eligible to be in the program.

d. Offenders who have new law violations, are absconders, or have violated a "no contact" condition of supervision are not eligible for the program.

e. No offender who has three or more previous violations is eligible for the program.

3. Qualifying Technical Violations and Approved Sanctions. The following matrix lists the specific technical violations that may be addressed through the Alternative Sanctions Program process for offenders who were sentenced in Palm Beach County, Florida. Each technical violation includes a list of sanctions determined and approved by the court for the probation officer to select from when reporting these technical violations, based on the individual offender's circumstances at the time of the violation.

ALTERNATIVE SANCTIONS PROGRAM VIOLATION/SANCTION MATRIX

VIOLATION	APPROVED LIST OF SANCTIONS
Condition (1): failed to report as instructed (more than 40 days)	1. Weekly call in for 6 weeks 2. Daily call in for 30 days 3. Report 2x a month for 60 days
Condition (3): Failed to report changes in residence or employment without first procuring the officer's consent (or notifying immediately if evicted from residence or laid off from job)	1. Weekly call in for 6 weeks 2. Twice a month reporting for 3 months 3. Weekly reporting for 6 weeks
Condition (6): Found to be associating with person(s) engaged in criminal activity	1. Curfew from 8 pm to 6 am for 90 days (can be modified by probation officer for treatment/work purposes) 2. Weekly call in for 6 weeks 3. 25 hours public service work
Condition (7): Positive drug test for non-prescribed drugs (first occurrence)	1. Drug evaluation and successfully complete treatment if determined necessary 2. Increase level of treatment program up to and including residential 3. Curfew from 8 pm to 6 am for 90 days (can be modified by probation officer for treatment/work purposes) 4. Weekly reporting for 6 weeks
Condition (7): Positive drug test for non-prescribed drugs (second occurrence)	1. Drug evaluation and successfully complete treatment if determined necessary 2. Increase level of treatment program up to and including residential 3. Weekly reporting for 6 weeks
Condition (8): Failure to maintain employment	1. Weekly reporting with job search logs until employed 2. Daily reporting with job search logs until employed 3. Curfew from 8 pm to 6 am for 90 days (can be modified by probation officer for treatment/work purposes) 4. Participate and successfully complete the HBI program
Condition (10): Failure to pay monetary obligations (excludes restitution)	1. If unemployed—daily job search or participate and successfully complete the HBI program 2. If employed—weekly payments payable by money order 3. Curfew from 8 pm to 6 am for 90 days (can be modified by probation officer for treatment/work purposes) 4. Weekly call in until monetary obligations current 5. Extend probation to auto term upon completion of all conditions.*
Condition (11): Failure to submit to random testing as directed	1. Weekly reporting as instructed by Probation Officer 2. Reporting 3 times a week as instructed by Probation Officer 3. Curfew from 8 pm to 6 am for 90 days (can be modified by probation officer for treatment/work purposes)
Special Condition (1): Failure to attend treatment evaluation or treatment session as scheduled	1. Curfew from 8 pm to 6 am until evaluation completed 2. Weekly reporting until evaluation completed 3. Daily call in until evaluation completed
Special Condition (8): Failure to complete community service hours as instructed	1. Daily reporting until community hours completed if unemployed 2. Weekly reporting until community hours completed if employed 3. Participate and successfully complete the HBI program if in lieu of court costs
Special Condition (9): Failure to remain at residence during curfew period	1. Weekly reporting for 3 months

*Affidavit will be filed with this sanction to toll the supervision. Once the offender completes the supervision, the Affidavit will be dismissed.

4. Alternative Sanctions Program Process.

a. The probation officer shall inform offenders who have committed violations enumerated in section 3 that they may participate in the Alternative Sanctions Program for administrative disposition of the violation. No offender is required to participate in the Alternative Sanctions Program and may opt for a formal violation of probation proceeding in Circuit Court.

b. If the offender admits the violation, agrees to accept the administrative sanction(s) recommended by the probation officer, and agrees to waive his/her formal violation hearing to modify his/her sentence, the probation officer will prepare an "Alternative Sanctions Program Technical Violation Notification", which will provide details of the circumstances of the technical violation that occurred and the probation officer's recommended sanction, based on the sanctions listed in the approved matrix. If the offender agrees to participate in the Alternative Sanctions Program, he/she will sign the second section of this form titled "Alternative Sanctions Program Waiver of Formal VOP/VOCC Hearing, Admission of Violation, and Acceptance of Sanctions", which will be submitted to the Court once the probation officer signs and dates the form.

c. The judge shall review the "Alternative Sanctions Program Technical Violation Notification" and waiver form submitted and, if the judge agrees that the technical violation should be addressed via the Alternative Sanctions Program and agrees with the recommended sanction, the judge will sign the "Order—Alternative Sanctions Program". If the judge does not agree with the particular sanction recommended by the officer or does not agree that the technical violation should be addressed via the Alternative Sanctions Program, the judge shall reflect further instructions on the order.

d. The Clerk of Court shall collaborate with the Administrative Office of the Court to create a unique docket code to track each Alternative Sanctions Order entered for statistical reporting purposes.

e. Upon court approval, the probation officer will instruct the offender on the sanction imposed by the court and instruct the offender to take actions necessary to ensure the sanction is executed immediately. Failure to complete the imposed sanction as instructed will result in a violation report, affidavit and warrant being submitted to the court citing the original condition that was violated.

5. The Alternative Sanctions Program shall be administered by the Administrative Office of the Court and the Florida Department of Corrections.

DONE AND ORDERED, in Chambers at West Palm Beach, Palm Beach County, Florida, this 20 day of November, 2018.

Krista Marx
Chief Judge

Adopted effective May 2, 2013. Amended effective November 27, 2017; November 20, 2018.

* supersedes admin. order 4.411- 11/17*

4.412. ALTERNATIVE SANCTIONS FOR MISDEMEANOR OFFENDERS

IN THE CIRCUIT COURT OF THE FIFTEENTH JUDICIAL CIRCUIT IN AND FOR PALM BEACH COUNTY, FLORIDA

ADMINISTRATIVE ORDER NO.: 4.412–3/16

IN RE: ALTERNATIVE SANCTIONS FOR MISDEMEANOR OFFENDERS

A substantial number of technical violations of probation by misdemeanants do not involve a new arrest or other serious violation. Court dockets can be reduced; the workload of prosecutors and attorneys involved in misdemeanor violations can be reduced; law enforcement resources can be directed to more significant public safety concerns; the jail population can be reduced; and, alternatives to incarceration can be provided by allowing an offender to remain productive in the community while taking responsibility for the offender's actions.

The alternative sanctions described herein are advisory only and are offered merely as guidelines to offenders and probation officers to resolve violations as alternatives to incarcerating offenders.

NOW, THEREFORE, pursuant to the authority conferred by Florida Rule of Judicial Administration 2.215, it is **ORDERED** as follows:

1. The Misdemeanor Alternative Sanctions Program is created in the Fifteenth Judicial Circuit, Palm Beach County, Florida for alleged violations as set forth in paragraph 5.

2. **Eligibility.** Participating in the alternative sanctions program for misdemeanor probation violations is within the discretion of the trial judge based upon the nature of the underlying offense, an offender's criminal history, the nature of the alleged violation, and any other factor a judge may lawfully consider.

3. Alternative sanctions are not available to offenders who have new law violations, who abscond, or who have violated a "no contact" condition of probation.

4. An offender who has participated in alternative sanctions twice during probation is ineligible to again be considered for alternative sanctions.

5. The following matrix describes the alleged violation and corresponding alternative sanction(s). All time periods (weekly, monthly) required herein run consecutively.

VIOLATION	APPROVED LIST OF SANCTIONS
A. Failing to report for the initial or any subsequent probation meeting	1. Daily call-in for 10 days 2. Weekly call-in for 4 weeks
B. Changing residence or employment without prior notice to probation officer or traveling outside Palm Beach County without permission of court or probation officer	1. Daily call-in for 10 days
C. Positive drug test for non-prescribed substances; alcohol use	1. Frequency of random substance use tests increased 2. Substance abuse evaluation and successfully complete recommended treatment (for non-DUI underlying charge offenders 3. 10 hours of community service
D. Failing to submit to required random substance use testing	1. Will be considered as a positive test result with the sanctions described in subparagraph, C. above, applied
E. Failing to submit timely to substance use evaluation or attend treatment session(s) as recommended in an evaluation	1. Weekly reporting until substance use evaluation and recommended treatment are completed 2. 10 hours of community service
F. Failing to initiate contact with, failing to submit timely to a recommended evaluation, or failing to begin or remain current with recommended treatment, or any other programmatic condition of probation not otherwise specified herein	1. Weekly reporting until the programmatic condition of probation is satisfied 2. 10 hours of community service

6. The misdemeanor probation provider has agreed to inform offenders who have committed violation(s) described herein that he/she may accept and perform alternative sanctions to resolve alleged violation(s) administratively. No offender is required to participate in alternative sanctions and may contest an alleged violation(s). Accepting alternative sanctions waives preliminary hearing on a violation of probation.

7. The misdemeanor probation provider has agreed to file an affidavit of violation of probation when first becoming aware of the violation(s). The affidavit shall indicate whether the probation officer will attempt to resolve the violation(s) through alternative sanctions. If so, the court shall issue a notice to appear to the offender. The probationary term resumes upon the earliest to occur of the probation officer either filing a document withdrawing the affidavit or withdrawing the affidavit on the record.

8. If the offender admits the violation to the probation officer, this admission shall be without prejudice to the offender and cannot be used against the offender as any proof of the alleged violation(s) in any future proceeding.

9. If the offender admits the violation and accepts alternative sanctions, the probation officer and offender shall both sign and date a form indicating what sanctions have been accepted. This form shall be submitted to the court, to which will be attached a copy of the affidavit of violation of probation. If the court accepts the offender's offer to perform alternative sanctions, the court shall sign an order so indicating, and describe therein the alternative sanctions accepted. If the court does not accept the offender's offer to perform alternative sanctions, the order shall so indicate and set a date, time, and place for a preliminary hearing on the alleged violation(s). A form copy of the order is attached hereto as Exhibit "A".

10. Upon court approval, the probation officer shall inform the offender that he/she is to begin complying immediately with the alternative sanctions. The probation officer shall file a report indicating whether the offender has successfully completed alternative sanctions. Failing to comply with the alternative sanctions shall result in the offender being prosecuted under the affidavit of violation.

11. No offender shall be eligible to participate in alternative sanctions for alleged violation(s) occurring while subject to previously accepted alternative sanctions.

12. Offenders are eligible to resolve alleged violations through alternative sanctions no more than twice during probation.

13. The Clerk of Court shall create a unique docket code to track each Alternative Sanctions Order entered for statistical reporting purposes.

DONE AND ORDERED in chambers at West Palm Beach, Palm Beach County, Florida, this 8 day of March, 2016.

Jeffrey Colbath
Chief Judge

EXHIBIT A

IN THE COUNTY COURT OF THE FIFTEENTH JUDICIAL CIRCUIT
IN AND FOR PALM BEACH COUNTY, FLORIDA
COUNTY CRIMINAL DIVISION: __
CASE NO: ____________

STATE OF FLORIDA,

vs.

____________,
Defendant.
____________/

ORDER IMPLEMENTING ALTERNATIVE SANCTIONS FOR VIOLATING PROBATION

Defendant's alleged violation of probation pursuant to the Affidavit of Violation of Probation signed by the probation officer on the __ day of ________, 20 __, has been resolved by implementing the following alternative sanction set forth in Administrative Order 4.412:

Alternative Sanctions: ____________

Defendant waives preliminary and final hearings on the violation of probation. Defendant acknowledges that a violation of probation alleged to have occurred while complying with the above-specified alternative sanction(s) shall not be eligible to be resolved through additional alternative sanctions.

DONE AND ORDERED at West Palm Beach, Palm Beach County, Florida, this __ day of ________, 20 __.

____
County Court Judge

Adopted effective March 8, 2016.

Circuit Criminal

4.501. INTERVIEWS OF YOUNG VICTIMS IN CHILD AND SEXUAL ABUSE CASES

IN THE CIRCUIT COURT OF THE FIFTEENTH JUDICIAL CIRCUIT IN AND FOR PALM BEACH COUNTY, FLORIDA

ADMINISTRATIVE ORDER NO. 4.501–7/12 *

IN RE: INTERVIEWS OF YOUNG VICTIMS IN CHILD AND SEXUAL ABUSE CASES

Section 914.16, Florida Statutes (2012), authorizes the chief judge to establish limits on the number of interviews that a minor victim must submit to for law enforcement or discovery purposes.

NOW, THEREFORE, pursuant to the authority conferred by Florida Rule of Judicial Administration 2.215, it is **ORDERED** as follows:

1. This order shall apply to the investigation and prosecution of all cases of abuse under Sections 794.011, 800.04, or 827.03 when the victim is under thirteen years of age or a victim of a violation of Sections 794.011, 800.02, 800.03, or 825.102 who is a person with mental retardation as defined in Section 393.063(42), at the time the interviews are sought.

2. For purposes of this order the term "interview" is defined as any procedure in which the child victim is required to provide a factual recitation of the circumstances surrounding the allegation of abuse. The term "interview" does not include the following:

a. Information obtained for the purpose of medical or psychological diagnosis for treatment.

b. An initial contact with the victim by law enforcement and/or Florida Department of Children and Families to assess validity of complaint or need to take protective measures on behalf of the victim.

c. Contacts with DCF legal, victim services (sexual assault/domestic violence) counselors, guardians ad litem, or assistant state attorneys seeking to carry out responsibilities as designated by statute.

d. Actual court testimony of victim.

e. Re-contact with the victim for the purpose of expanding/clarifying a previous statement prior to the filing of formal charges.

3. In accord with the foregoing and the need to act in the best interest of child victims of abuse, it is ordered that no child victim of abuse shall be subject to more than four interviews in the course of the investigation and prosecution of an incident of abuse except upon order of the court. These interviews shall be as follows:

a. The first interview shall be conducted within a reasonable time for the validation of the complaint. The interview when feasible shall be held at a Child Protection Team Facility in Palm Beach County. When applicable, this interview will be attended by law enforcement, a representative from DCF, Victim Services (sexual assault/domestic violence), the State Attorney's Office, and the Child Protection Team. When applicable, DCF shall, prior to scheduling a forensic interview, contact the law enforcement agency of jurisdiction and coordinate a mutually agreeable date and time for both law enforcement and DCF to attend the forensic interview. All attending agencies shall meet prior to the interview and make reasonable efforts to coordinate and produce all necessary information in the course of that interview. To minimize the traumatic effects to the child, all interviews shall be conducted by no more than two persons. This interview shall be recorded whenever possible to ensure that other parties have the opportunity to hear the child's statement.

b. The second interview by law enforcement, with the State Attorneys approval, may occur prior to the filing of formal charges and may include DCF, Victim Services (sexual assault/ domestic violence) or the Child Protection Team.

c. The third interview will be conducted under the rules governing depositions. The deposition shall be conducted in a setting and manner intended to minimize the traumatic effects of the interview on the victim. Defense counsel shall notice all parties including the guardian ad litem consistent with Crim. Proc. Rule 3.220(h).

d. If necessary, law enforcement may meet with the victim for the purpose of expanding/ clarifying any facts necessary. Additional interviews shall be allowed only by order of the court upon motion for good cause shown. Additional interviews shall be limited in scope to assure minimal impact on the victim.

DONE and **SIGNED** in Chambers at West Palm Beach, Palm Beach County, Florida, this 2nd day of July, 2012.

Peter D. Blanc
Chief Judge

Adopted effective September 29, 2008. Amended effective July 2, 2012.

* supersedes admin. order 4.501–09/08

4.502. CIRCUIT CRIMINAL CASE ASSIGNMENT

IN THE CIRCUIT COURT OF THE FIFTEENTH JUDICIAL CIRCUIT IN AND FOR PALM BEACH COUNTY, FLORIDA

ADMINISTRATIVE ORDER NO. 4.502–6/17 *

IN RE: CIRCUIT CRIMINAL CASE ASSIGNMENT

The Fifteenth Circuit's pending felony caseload will be allocated to streamline the processing of cases in a fair, timely and cost effective manner. Procedures must be established to insure the proper completion of cases tried by Judges assigned to the felony criminal division.

NOW, THEREFORE, pursuant to the authority conferred by Florida Rule of Judicial Administration 2.215, effective July 1, 2017, it is **ORDERED** as follows:

1. **Newly Filed Cases.**

a. The Clerk of the Court shall randomly assign felony cases arising east of the twenty mile bend (those cases that fall outside the area handled by the Palm Beach County Sheriff's Office District V Substation) to divisions R, S, U, V, W, X and Z.

b. With the exception of capital cases which are covered by Administrative Order 4.101, the Clerk of the Court shall assign felony cases arising west of the twenty mile bend (those cases that fall within the area handled by the Palm Beach County Sheriffs Office District V Substation) to Division Y. All cases assigned to Division Y will remain at the West County Courthouse until one party requests, in writing, a trial by jury. If the Division Y Judge transfers the case to the main courthouse, the clerk of court shall randomly assign the case to a Circuit Criminal Division located at the Main Courthouse.

2. **Master Calendar.**

a. *Divisions R, S, U, V, W, X and Z.*

1) Out-of-custody arraignments shall be conducted on Thursdays.

2) In-custody arraignments will be handled at the Gun Club complex pursuant to Administrative Order 4.101.

3) Calendar calls may be conducted as determined by the presiding Judge. Any case that is not resolved may be sent to a Trial Division Judge regardless of the length of the trial.

b. *Division Y.*

1) In custody and out of custody arraignments shall be conducted on Monday mornings at the West County Courthouse.

2) All post-arraignment demands for jury trial made by the State or the Defense shall be in writing.

c. *Division T.* Division T cases will be set in accordance with Administrative Order 4.906.

DONE AND SIGNED in Chambers, at West Palm Beach, Palm Beach County, Florida this 20 day of June, 2017.

Jeffery Colbath
Chief Judge

Adopted effective December 16, 2008. Amended effective March 1, 2009; October 2, 2009; May 29, 2013; March 4, 2014; July 25, 2016; June 20, 2017.

* supersedes admin. order 4.502–7/16

4.503. CIRCUIT CRIMINAL CASE DISPOSITION

IN THE CIRCUIT COURT OF THE FIFTEENTH JUDICIAL CIRCUIT IN AND FOR PALM BEACH COUNTY

ADMINISTRATIVE ORDER NO. 4.503–10/09 *

IN RE: CIRCUIT CRIMINAL CASE DISPOSITION

The Fifteenth Judicial Circuit is assessing the effectiveness of the case-flow management system to ensure that a timely and just disposition of all Circuit Criminal cases exists. The pending caseload report provided for each of the Felony divisions reflects cases that are neither open nor require judicial action. In an effort to evaluate this system and obtain accurate pending caseload data, the following administrative procedures are hereby established:

A. CLOSURE OF COURT FILES.

1. The Clerk and Comptroller is hereby directed to close a Court File in the event the following is filed:

a. a Sentencing Order (even if this includes a concurrent sentence with another case number);

b. a case has been down-filed to misdemeanor charges;

c. proof of death consisting of an official death certificate or any official notification of death by the Department of Highway Safety and Motor Vehicles;

d. a no file/information reflecting all open counts;

e. a nolle prosse reflecting all open counts;

f. cases assigned to pretrial intervention (these cases shall be designated on the absentee docket);

g. ruled upon extradition cases; and

h. cases in which defendants are found not guilty by reason of insanity (court retains jurisdiction for a period of time as required by Statute and therefore the Clerk shall maintain the Court file until further order of the Court).

2. When the presiding judge of a pending criminal case desires that a particular order or judgment close the case, for statistical purposes only, then the judge shall place a red-colored "clerk please close file" designation under the case number in the caption of the judgment or order. Any such closed designation shall be made in accordance with the Florida Supreme Court Summary Reporting System ("SRS") Guidelines.

3. Upon receipt of an order or judgment bearing the red-colored "clerk please close file" designation, the clerk shall close out the case for statistical purposes and shall denote in accordance with established SRS procedure the basis upon which the case has been closed. If the clerk cannot immediately determine from the judgment or order the basis upon which the judge has relied upon in designating the case as "closed" the clerk shall forward the Court file to the Administrative Office of the Court, Criminal Case Manager.

B. ABSENTEE DOCKET. The Clerk and Comptroller is hereby directed to assign the following cases to the absentee docket: Pretrial Intervention, Jimmy Ryce and defendants found incompetent to proceed.

DONE AND SIGNED in Chambers, at West Palm Beach, Palm Beach County, Florida this 2 day of October, 2009.

Peter D. Blanc
Chief Judge

Amended effective June 22, 2009; October 2, 2009.

* supersedes admin. order 4.503–6/09

4.504. [VACATED AND SET ASIDE BY ORDER 4.504-4/13, EFFECTIVE APRIL 10, 2013.]

County Criminal

4.601. COUNTY COURT CRIMINAL PROCEDURES

IN THE CIRCUIT COURT OF THE FIFTEENTH JUDICIAL CIRCUIT IN AND FOR PALM BEACH COUNTY, FLORIDA

ADMINISTRATIVE ORDER NO. 4.601–9/08 *

IN RE: COUNTY COURT CRIMINAL PROCEDURES

Pursuant to the authority conferred by Florida Rule of Judicial Administration 2.215, it is **ORDERED** as follows:

1. CAPTIONS TO INCLUDE DIVISION ASSIGNMENTS. The caption of all pleadings and notices filed in the county criminal division shall include the letter designation of the division to which the case is assigned.

2. NOTICE TO APPEAR. Consistent with Rule 3.125, Fla. R. Crim. P., persons authorized by this order to be released on their own recognizance shall be given a Notice to Appear.

3. BOND SCHEDULE. A uniform bond release schedule for misdemeanors and county or municipal ordinance violations is set forth in Administrative Order 4.202 9/08 as amended. Persons arrested for the violation of a county or municipal ordinance or a misdemeanor who are not released on their own recognizance with a notice to appear, shall be transported to the appropriate facility for booking.

4. MISDEMEANOR MENTAL HEALTH DIVERSION. Notwithstanding the foregoing, if a person is arrested for any of the following:

Trespass (FEC railroad tracks only), F.S. 810.09(1)(a), (2)(a), and (2)(b);

Possession of Paraphernalia, F.S. 893.147 (1)(b)

Disorderly Conduct, F.S. 877.03

Disorderly Intoxication, F.S. 856.011(1)

Open Container, C.O. 93–14

Giving a False Name Upon Being Arrested or Detained, F.S. 901.36 (1);

Panhandling, C.O. 54–146;

Lodging in Public, C.O. 15–29

and it appears to the Arresting Officer or the Booking Officer that there may be mental health issues, the defendant may be referred to the Mental Health Diversion Specialist (MHDS) for assessment. If the MHDS determines that the person is suitable for mental health assistance, he/she shall make the appropriate referral. If the defendant agrees to follow up with the referral, the defendant shall be released from jail and be given a Notice to Appear in Court for the Tuesday following the arranged referral.

5. MUNICIPAL PROSECUTORS. Each municipality which retains a prosecutor for municipal ordinance violations shall give prompt written notice to the clerk of the county court, with copies to the state attorney and court administrator. The notice shall include the name, business address and telephone number of each prosecutor.

6. MUNICIPAL ORDINANCE HEARINGS. Upon the filing of citation or Notice to Appear to which the defendant pleads "not guilty", the clerk of the county court shall provide notice of the hearing to the defendant and the municipality.

7. MUNICIPAL PARKING VIOLATIONS. Other than traffic citations prepared and supplied by the Department of Highway Safety & Motor Vehicles pursuant to Section 316.650, Florida Statutes (2007), municipal citations for parking violations shall be administratively processed by the respective municipalities and shall not be made returnable or payable to or through the county court. Each municipality shall be entirely responsible for collection of fines and penalties and the money so collected shall not be under the supervision or control of the county court system. If provided by appropriate municipal ordinance, nonpayment of a parking citation to the issuing agency within the time designated, and continued failure to pay within the time as specified in the agency's follow-up notice, shall permit the municipality to institute proceedings in the county court against the nonpaying violator. The follow-up notice referred to shall be a prerequisite to initiation of proceedings in the county court.

8. ARREST WARRANTS BEFORE CASE ASSIGNED TO A DIVISION. When an arrest warrant is needed by a law enforcement officer before a case has been assigned to a trial division, the arresting officer shall contact the assistant state attorney on duty who, in turn, shall contact the county court judge assigned to hold first appearance hearings or, if after normal court hours, the duty judge. The judge shall determine whether probable cause exists to issue a warrant. If probable cause exists, the judge shall issue the arrest warrant.

DONE and **SIGNED** in Chambers at West Palm Beach, Palm Beach County, Florida, this 29 day of September, 2008.

Kathleen J. Kroll
Chief Judge

Adopted effective September 29, 2008.

* supersedes admin. order 10.001–3/08

4.602. ASSIGNMENT OF CASES—CRIMINAL DIVISION, COUNTY COURT

IN THE CIRCUIT COURT OF THE FIFTEENTH JUDICIAL CIRCUIT IN AND FOR PALM BEACH COUNTY, FLORIDA

ADMINISTRATIVE ORDER NO. 4.602–2/12 *

IN RE: ASSIGNMENT OF CASES—CRIMINAL DIVISION, COUNTY COURT

Administrative Order No. 11.101–9/08, sets forth this circuit's policy concerning the assignment of judges, appointment of administrative judges and assignment of cases and requires that the Clerk of Court equitably and randomly assign cases "within the division in which the cases are filed". The County Court, Criminal Division cases are assigned to the divisions by various means, in order to provide an efficient process of handling the large number of criminal cases, in addition to allowing for an equitable and random assignment of cases.

NOW, THEREFORE, pursuant to the authority conferred by Florida Rule of Judicial Administration 2.215, it is **ORDERED** as follows:

Cases filed in the County Court, Criminal Division, shall be assigned to divisions in the main courthouse as follows:

1. Traffic crimes and misdemeanors, other than domestic violence, shall be assigned to a trial division by the Clerk of Court. The clerk of court shall assign all misdemeanor and criminal traffic cases on a rotating basis among the judges in the County Court Division using a blind filing process;

2. Misdemeanors down-filed from felony arrests shall be randomly assigned to a trial division and set by the Clerk of Court for arraignment to be held within ten days of filing;

3. Except for domestic violence cases arising within the geographical jurisdiction of the West County Courthouse, all domestic violence cases shall be assigned to the designated domestic violence divisions.

4. When a defendant has more than one case pending against him/her, and that information is known to the clerk, the clerk shall assign all cases, except cases involving domestic violence, to the division having the case with the lowest number. Pending shall include cases on appeal.

5. When a defendant is on probation and is charged in a new case, and that information is known to the clerk, the clerk shall assign the case to the division which placed the defendant on probation unless the new charge involves domestic violence.

6. If the state enters a nolle prosequi and subsequently refiles the case, the newly-filed case shall be assigned to the division in which the original case was assigned, unless the refiled charge involves domestic violence, in which case, the newly filed case shall be assigned to the designated domestic violence divisions, unless it arose within the geographical jurisdiction of the West County Courthouse. It is the duty of the state to advise the clerk of the earlier nolle prossed case.

DONE and **SIGNED** in Chambers at West Palm Beach, Palm Beach County, Florida, this 21 day of February, 2012.

Peter D. Blanc
Chief Judge

Adopted effective September 29, 2008. Amended effective February 21, 2012.

* supersedes admin order no. 4.602–9/08

4.603. COUNTY CRIMINAL REGIONS/BRANCH COURTHOUSES

IN THE CIRCUIT COURT OF THE FIFTEENTH JUDICIAL CIRCUIT IN AND FOR PALM BEACH COUNTY, FLORIDA

ADMINISTRATIVE ORDER NO. 4.603–9/08 *

IN RE: COUNTY CRIMINAL REGIONS/BRANCH COURTHOUSES

The court is committed to providing judicial services at convenient locations consistent with the efficient and sound administration of justice and the court has concluded that the foregoing principle dictates that county civil services be provided at the branch courthouses in addition to the main county courthouse;

NOW, THEREFORE, pursuant to the authority conferred by Florida Rule of Judicial Administration 2.215, it is **ORDERED** as follows:

A. County Criminal Division Regions.

1. The Criminal Division of the County Court, Palm Beach County, Florida, shall be divided into four separate regions—The Northern Region Southern Region, Western Region and Central Region.

2. All cases assigned to the Northern Region will be heard in the North County Courthouse, 3188 PGA Boulevard, Palm Beach Gardens, Florida, 33410.

3. All cases assigned to the Southern Region will be heard in the South County Courthouse, 200 West Atlantic Avenue, Delray Beach, Florida, 33444.

4. All cases assigned to the Western Region will be heard in the West County Courthouse, 3884 State Road 80, Belle Glade, Florida

5. All cases assigned to the Central Region will be heard in the Main Courthouse, 205 North Dixie Highway, West Palm Beach, Florida, 33401.

B. Jurisdictional Areas.

1. The geographical jurisdictional area of the NORTHERN REGION shall be as follows: Bounded on the South by the northern city limits of West Palm Beach, and on the west by State Road 710 (Beeline Highway).

2. The geographical jurisdictional area of the SOUTHERN REGION shall be as follows: the boundary shall be the

northern city limits of Lantana and continuing south to Lantana Road and West to the North–South boundary of 20 mile Bend.

3. The geographical jurisdictional area of the WESTERN REGION shall be as follows: That portion of Palm Beach County, Florida, lying west of a north-south line at 20–Mile Bend.

4. The geographical jurisdictional area of the MAIN/CENTRAL COURTHOUSE shall be as follows: All areas within Palm Beach County not included in paragraphs 1–3 above.

DONE and **SIGNED** in Chambers at West Palm Beach, Palm Beach County, Florida, this 29 of September, 2008.

Kathleen J. Kroll
Chief Judge

Adopted effective September 29, 2008.

* supersedes admin. order 2.006–12/05 (as it pertains to county criminal)

4.604. REQUESTS FOR CONTINUANCE OF MISDEMEANOR ARRAIGNMENTS AT BRANCH COURTHOUSES

IN THE CIRCUIT COURT OF THE FIFTEENTH JUDICIAL CIRCUIT IN AND FOR PALM BEACH COUNTY, FLORIDA

ADMINISTRATIVE ORDER NO. 4.604–9/08 *

IN RE: REQUESTS FOR CONTINUANCE OF MISDEMEANOR ARRAIGNMENTS AT BRANCH COURTHOUSES

There is an increasing volume of misdemeanor arraignments scheduled at the Branch Courthouses and there is a concomitant increase in the requests for continuance of arraignment filed by the defendant. A written request for continuance signed by the defendant operates as a waiver of speedy trial. The Office of the State Attorney has agreed to the continuance of arraignment one time for a period of no more than thirty (30) days upon the filing of a written request for continuance signed by the defendant.

NOW, THEREFORE, pursuant to the authority conferred by Florida Rule of Judicial Administration 2.215, it is **ORDERED** as follows:

1. Cases set for misdemeanor arraignment at the branch courthouses shall be continued by the clerk once for a period of no more than thirty (30) days if a written request for continuance is filed by the defendant prior to the originally scheduled arraignment date and time.

2. The defendant's written request for continuance shall be made part of the court file.

DONE AND SIGNED in Chambers at West Palm Beach, Palm Beach County, Florida this 29 day of September, 2008.

Kathleen J. Kroll
Chief Judge

Adopted effective September 29, 2008.

* supersedes admin. order 10.013–8/99 (as it pertains to misdemeanor arraignments)

4.605. INACTIVE MISDEMEANOR CASES

IN THE CIRCUIT COURT OF THE FIFTEENTH JUDICIAL CIRCUIT IN AND FOR PALM BEACH COUNTY, FLORIDA

ADMINISTRATIVE ORDER NO. 4.605–8/14*

IN RE: INACTIVE MISDEMEANOR CASES

The State Attorney for the Fifteenth Judicial Circuit has indicated that he does not object to the dismissal of cases where the defendant is deceased.

NOW, THEREFORE, pursuant to the authority conferred by Florida Rule of Judicial Administration 2.215, it is **ORDERED** as follows:

1. When the Clerk obtains documentation evidencing that the defendant in a misdemeanor case is deceased, the case is deemed dismissed without further order of the court and the Clerk is hereby directed to close the case.

2. The Clerk shall provide notice of such dismissal to the Office of the State Attorney and defense counsel of record, if any.

3. Administrative Order 10.102–8/14 (as amended) governs the inactive criminal traffic cases not covered in this Administrative Order.

DONE and **SIGNED** in Chambers at West Palm Beach, Palm Beach County, Florida, this 25 day of August, 2014.

Jeffrey Colbath
Chief Judge

Adopted effective September 29, 2008. Amended effective August 25, 2014.

* supersedes admin. order 4.605–9/08

4.606. TRANSPORTING OF IN–CUSTODY COUNTY COURT CRIMINAL OFFENDERS

IN THE CIRCUIT COURT OF THE FIFTEENTH JUDICIAL CIRCUIT IN AND FOR PALM BEACH COUNTY

ADMINISTRATIVE ORDER NO. 4.606–6/09

IN RE: TRANSPORTING OF IN–CUSTODY COUNTY COURT CRIMINAL OFFENDERS

The transportation of incarcerated individuals charged with misdemeanor and criminal traffic offenses from the Palm Beach County Jail to the North County and South County branch courthouses requires the expenditure of additional funds and personnel than is required if an incarcerated individual was transported to the Main Judicial Complex.

In an effort to assist the taxpayers of Palm Beach County with the rising cost associated with transporting incarcerated offenders to and from the Palm Beach County Jail and the Branch Courthouses, the County Court Criminal Judges have agreed to a procedure to minimize the cost of transportation while protecting the due process rights of the individuals.

NOW, THEREFORE, pursuant to the authority conferred by Florida Rule of Judicial Administration 2.215, it is **ORDERED** as follows:

1. In-custody offenders charged with misdemeanor or criminal traffic offenses shall not be transported to the South County Branch Courthouse or the North County Branch Courthouse unless otherwise specifically ordered by the Branch Courthouse Judge assigned to the matter.

2. All in-custody offenders charged with misdemeanor or criminal traffic offenses who do not resolve their case(s) at the Criminal Justice Complex located at 3228 Gun Club Road, West Palm Beach, Florida pursuant to Administrative Order 4.201, shall make their court appearances before a County Court Criminal Judge located at the Main Courthouse.

3. In-custody defendants previously assigned to a South or North County division shall not be transported.

4. The Clerk and Comptroller shall randomly assign the above cases to a County Court Criminal Judge located at the Main Judicial Complex.

DONE AND SIGNED in Chambers, at West Palm Beach, Palm Beach County, Florida this 22 day of June, 2009.

Kathleen J. Kroll
Chief Judge

Adopted effective June 22, 2009.

4.607. MISDEMEANOR IN–CUSTODY CASES

IN THE CIRCUIT COURT OF THE FIFTEENTH JUDICIAL CIRCUIT IN AND FOR PALM BEACH COUNTY

ADMINISTRATIVE ORDER NO. 4.607–7/12*

IN RE: MISDEMEANOR IN–CUSTODY CASES

Due to the rising cost associated with housing inmates, the criminal justice stakeholders met to develop a procedure to save taxpayer dollars, maximize resources and increase efficiency. Additionally, it is anticipated that this procedure will assist with reducing the jail population.

NOW, THEREFORE, pursuant to the authority conferred by Florida Rule of Judicial Administration 2.215, it is **ORDERED** as follows:

1. **Next Day Returns and/or Failures to Appear.** Effective **July 16, 2012**, all next day returns and/or failure to appear misdemeanants, except those set forth in paragraph 2 below, shall be brought before the assigned divisional judge the next business day following their arrest. In the event, the divisional judge is out of the office, the defendant shall be brought before the alternate judge. In the event, both the divisional judge and alternate judge are out of the office, the Palm Beach County Sheriff's Office shall contact the Administrative Judge of the County Criminal Division to determine which judge the defendant shall be brought before.

The above procedure shall apply unless the warrant specifically indicates that the defendant shall be brought before the divisional judge only. If the warrant specifically states that the defendant shall appear before the divisional judge and he/she is out of the office, the defendant shall appear before first appearance judge at Criminal Justice Complex. Based upon the unavailability of the judge who issued the warrant, the presiding first appearance judge shall have discretion to consider bond modification. As defined in Administrative Order 4.606, defendants shall not be transported to the North and South Annexes. Therefore, these defendants shall appear before a judge for first appearance located at the Criminal Justice Complex.

2. **Misdemeanor Violation of Probation Hearings.** With the exception of cases assigned to the North, South, and Belle Glade courthouses, all VOP misdemeanor in-custody hearings shall be heard by the divisional judge on the next business day following the defendant's arrest. In the event the divisional judge is not available, the defendant shall be brought to the Criminal Justice Complex, Gun Club Road. As defined in Administrative Order 4.606, those defendants who have cases assigned to the North and South courthouses shall be brought to the Criminal Justice Complex, Gun Club Road. Cases assigned to Belle Glade shall be brought to the West County Courthouse, State Road 80.

DONE AND SIGNED in Chambers, at West Palm Beach, Palm Beach County, Florida this 12th day of July, 2012.

Peter D. Blanc
Chief Judge

Adopted effective July 14, 2009. Amended effective July 12, 2012.

*supersedes admin order no. 4.607–7/09

4.608. INTOXILYZER 8000 LITIGATION

IN THE CIRCUIT COURT OF THE FIFTEENTH JUDICIAL CIRCUIT IN AND FOR PALM BEACH COUNTY, FLORIDA

ADMINISTRATIVE ORDER NO.: 4.608–4/15

IN RE: INTOXILYZER 8000 LITIGATION

There are cases pending in the County Criminal Divisions in which defendants have filed motions to suppress breath tests for alleged violations of Rule 11D–8.004(2) of the Administrative Code ("Motion to Suppress"). These cases involve similar, related, or identical issues. To promote judicial economy and to assist in the coordination of case management, these cases should be assigned to a single judge for hearing and ruling upon the Motion to Suppress.

NOW, THEREFORE, pursuant to the authority conferred by Florida Rule of Judicial Administration 2.215, it is **ORDERED** as follows:

1. All Driving Under the Influence cases pending or filed in the county court criminal divisions in which a defendant files a Motion to Suppress as defined above and files a Consent to Participate shall be temporarily assigned to County Court Criminal Division "B" for purposes of having the Motion to Suppress, and all matters preliminary thereto, heard and ruled upon. The party filing the Consent to Participate must comply with the requirements in the "Order Granting Motion for Temporary Assignment to Division "B" for Hearing and Ruling on Motion to Suppress" in *State v. Cook*, 2013CT02104 attached hereto as Exhibit A.

2. All cases affected by this Administrative Order shall remain in the County Court Criminal Division to which the case was originally assigned for trial and shall not be designated as a case pending in Division "B." No case shall be set for trial except upon order by the judge presiding in the division to which the case was originally assigned.

3. All pleadings in any case assigned pursuant to this Administrative Order shall bear the following notation: "Intoxilyzer 8000."

DONE and ORDERED in Chambers, at West Palm Beach, Palm Beach County, Florida this 15 day of April, 2015.

JEFFREY COLBATH
Chief Judge

EXHIBIT "A"

IN THE COUNTY COURT OF THE FIFTEENTH JUDICIAL CIRCUIT IN AND FOR PALM BEACH COUNTY, FLORIDA

CASE NO.: 2013CT021047—DIVISION "B"

STATE OF FLORIDA

vs.

BRIAN MICHAEL COOK
Defendant.
/

ORDER GRANTING MOTION FOR TEMPORARY ASSIGNMENT TO DIVISION "B" FOR HEARING AND RULING ON MOTION TO SUPPRESS

THIS CAUSE came before the Court on the Defendant's Motion for Temporary Assignment to Division "B" for Hearing and Ruling on a Motion to Suppress Breath Test Due to Violation of Rule 11D–8.004(2) of Administrative Code ("Motion to Suppress"). Motions to Suppress have been filed in cases pending in all of the county court criminal divisions which contain the substantive claims as set forth in the Motion to Suppress filed in the instant action and dated November 21, 2014 (docket entry 134). The State filed on January 21, 2015, two responses to the Motion to Suppress as reflected in docket entry 149 and 152 and has filed an Amended Response to Defendant's Motion for *En Masse* Proceedings, Filings, and Hearing (now referred to as the Motion to Temporary Assignment) and provided the Court with additional case law. After carefully examining and considering the motion, having reviewed the court file and record, as well as the arguments presented by the Parties, and being otherwise fully advised in the premises, it is

ORDERED AND ADJUDGED that the Court **grants** the Defendant's Motion for Temporary Assignment to Division "B" for Hearing and Ruling on the Motion to Suppress. It is further

ORDER AND ADJUDGED that the following procedures shall be followed:

1. The motion to be heard by the Division "B" judge is the Defendant's Motion to Suppress Breath Test Due to Violations of Rule 11D–8.004(2) of the Administrative Code (hereinafter "Substantive Motion") filed on November 21, 2014 in docket entry 134.

2. The hearing will begin on June 3, 2015 at 9:00 a.m. in Courtroom 2E and will continue through June 4, 2015 at 5:00 p.m. subject to change by agreement by the parties or court order.

3. The case of *State of Florida v. Brian Michael Cook*, 2013CT021047 will act as the lead case for those defendants represented by the private defense bar and by the public defender's office.

4. Any party wishing to participate in the proceedings must contact Brian Gabriel, Esq., counsel for the named defendant and lead counsel for the Motion to Suppress. Mr. Gabriel is directed to file a Notice of Consent to Temporary Assignment and a Notice of Adoption of the Substantive Motion on behalf of any party wishing to participate in the proceedings. The documents should be filed under the individual party's respective case number. These documents must be filed no later than April 16, 2015 at 5:00 p.m. Lead counsel for State v. Cook will provide copies of the forms to the parties seeking temporary assignment. Failure to file said documents will result in the party being barred from being included under this Order.

5. Cases assigned to Divisions B, C, E, L, M, and P in which a Notice of Consent for Temporary Assignment has been timely filed will be considered part of the proceedings.

6. By April 20, 2015 at 5:00 p.m., Mr. Gabriel will file with the Clerk of Court, under the lead case number, a Master List of all defendants who have opted for the temporary assignment to Division B. The list shall include each defendant's name, case number, and divisional assignment. A courtesy copy of the Master List must also be sent to the chambers of each divisional judge and the Administrative Judge.

7. Any party wishing to participate in the proceedings who is represented by The Office of the Public Defender shall file a Notice of Consent to Temporary Assignment and an Adoption of the Substantive Motion under his or her respective individual case number by April 13, 2015 at 5:00 p.m.

8. By April 20, 2015 at 5:00 p.m., the Officer of the Public Defender will file with the Clerk of Court, under the lead case number, a Master List of all defendants who have opted for the temporary assignment to Division B. The list shall include each defendant's name, case number, and divisional assignment. A courtesy copy of the Master List must also be sent to the chambers of each divisional judge and the Administrative Judge.

9. By agreement of all undersigned Judges, Judge Leonard Hanser will preside over the hearing on the Motion to Suppress and all matters preliminary therefore, and issue an Order on the "substantive motion" that will bind all cases in the class.

10. Any issues relating to the hearing and which need to be addressed prior to the hearing will be filed under the lead case numbers and heard by Judge Leonard Hanser. The parties are directed to contact Judge Hanser's Judicial Assistant for divisional instructions prior to setting any matters for the group.

11. On or before May 18, 2015 at 5:00 p.m., the parties shall submit a joint stipulation of exhibits that will be introduced into evidence.

12. Approximately twenty-one (21) days prior to the scheduled hearing, there will be a Case Management Status Check before Judge Hanser where the parties will update the Court on the state of the case and pending hearing.

13. All cases made part of the class, and temporarily assigned to Division "B," shall remain in the Criminal Division to which the case was originally assigned for trial and shall not be designated as a case pending in Division "B." No case shall be set for trial except upon order by the judge presiding in the Division to which the case was originally assigned.

DONE AND ORDERED in Chambers at West Palm Beach, Palm Beach County, Florida this ___ day of ________, 2015.

Adopted effective April 15, 2015.

Restraining Orders/Domestic Violence

4.701. RESTRAINING ORDERS—VICTIM/WITNESS PROTECTION ACT

IN THE CIRCUIT COURT OF THE FIFTEENTH JUDICIAL CIRCUIT IN AND FOR PALM BEACH COUNTY, FLORIDA

ADMINISTRATIVE ORDER NO.4.701–9/08 *

IN RE: RESTRAINING ORDERS—VICTIM/WITNESS PROTECTION ACT

Section 914.24, Florida Statutes (2007), provides a remedy to prevent the harassment of a victim or witness in a criminal case.

NOW, THEREFORE, pursuant to the authority conferred by Florida Rule of Judicial Administration 2.215, it is **ORDERED** as follows:

1. All application for restraining order pursuant to section 914.24, Florida Statutes (2007), shall be filed before the duty judge on forms provided by the state attorney.

2. Petitions for restraining orders against harassment or intimidation shall be filed with the clerk of circuit court, criminal division, without fee.

3. The duty judge hearing the petition for restraining order shall retain jurisdiction of the matter until the issuance of or until the time is past for the issuance of the protection order [section 914.24(2)(a), Florida Statutes (2007)].

4. Upon issuance of a restraining order, the clerk shall provide the Sheriff with a certified copy of the order. This order shall be served upon the respondent within 24 hours of its issuance. If an affidavit of insolvency is filed, service shall be without costs.

DONE and **SIGNED** in Chambers at West Palm Beach, Palm Beach County, Florida, this 29 day of September, 2008.

Kathleen J. Kroll
Chief Judge

Adopted effective September 29, 2008.

* supersedes admin. order 4.008–9/92

Inmates

4.801. [VACATED AND SET ASIDE BY ORDER 4.801-9/12, EFFECTIVE SEPTEMBER 4, 2012.]

4.802. PERSONS IN CUSTODY FOR OUT–OF–COUNTY HOLDS

IN THE CIRCUIT COURT OF THE FIFTEENTH JUDICIAL CIRCUIT IN AND FOR PALM BEACH COUNTY, FLORIDA

ADMINISTRATIVE ORDER NO. 4.802 9/08 *

IN RE: PERSONS IN CUSTODY FOR OUT–OF–COUNTY HOLDS

Pursuant to the authority conferred by Florida Rule of Judicial Administration 2.215, it is **ORDERED** as follows:

1. In order to relieve overcrowded conditions at the Palm Beach County Jail, all persons being held in custody pursuant to a hold for an out-of-county misdemeanor, traffic or related contempt warrant shall be released within seventy-two (72) hours if not picked up by the authorities requesting the hold. If the hold is for a neighboring county, which is defined as Dade, Broward, Hendry, Okeechobee, Martin or St. Lucie counties, the prisoner shall be released within forty-eight (48) hours.

2. The Palm Beach County Sheriff's Office will, immediately upon booking an individual in this category, notify the requesting authorities of the contents of this Administrative Order and that the requested person is in custody.

DONE and **SIGNED** in Chambers at West Palm Beach, Palm Beach County, Florida, this 29 day of September, 2008.

Kathleen J. Kroll
Chief Judge

Adopted effective September 29, 2008.

* supersedes admin. order 4.010–9/92

Special Criminal Administrative Orders

4.901. JIMMY RYCE INVOLUNTARY CIVIL COMMITMENT FOR SEXUAL VIOLENT PREDATORS TREATMENT AND CARE ACT

IN THE CIRCUIT COURT OF THE FIFTEENTH JUDICIAL CIRCUIT IN AND FOR PALM BEACH COUNTY, FLORIDA

ADMINISTRATIVE ORDER NO. 4.901–9/08 *

IN RE: JIMMY RYCE INVOLUNTARY CIVIL COMMITMENT FOR SEXUAL VIOLENT PREDATORS TREATMENT AND CARE ACT

The Florida Legislature in Chapter 98–64, Laws of Florida, enacted the Jimmy Ryce Involuntary Civil Commitment for Sexually Violent Predators' Treatment and Care Act (hereinafter referred to as the Jimmy Ryce Act). The Jimmy Ryce Act establishes procedures for reviewing and litigating an involuntary civil commitment of an individual determined to be a sexually-violent predator. It is incumbent upon this Court to establish guidelines for the implementation of the Jimmy Ryce Act.

NOW, THEREFORE, pursuant to the authority conferred by Florida Rule of Judicial Administration 2.215, it is **ORDERED** as follows:

1. In all cases litigated under the Jimmy Ryce Act, the Clerk of Court shall assign such cases to the Criminal Division which presided over the underlying case.

2. Pursuant to Fla. Stat. 394.916, all cases litigated under the Jimmy Ryce Act must be given priority on the trial docket and set for trial within thirty (30) days of filing.

DONE and **SIGNED**, in chambers, at West Palm Beach, Palm Beach County, Florida this 29 day of September, 2008.

Kathleen J. Kroll
Chief Judge

Adopted effective September 29, 2008.

* supersedes admin. order 2.054–4/02

4.902. VEHICLE IMMOBILIZATION

IN THE CIRCUIT COURT OF THE FIFTEENTH JUDICIAL CIRCUIT IN AND FOR PALM BEACH COUNTY, FLORIDA

ADMINISTRATIVE ORDER NO. 4.902–1/18 *

IN RE: VEHICLE IMMOBILIZATION

Florida Statute 316.193(6)(d) requires the Court to order the immobilization/impoundment of the vehicle which was driven by, or in the actual physical control of the person convicted of violating the provisions of Florida Statutes 316.193. In order to ensure that immobilization entities operating in Palm Beach County are in compliance with all statutory requirements, the Administrative Office of the Fifteenth Judicial Circuit hereby establishes a vehicle immobilization/impoundment program.

NOW, THEREFORE, pursuant to the authority conferred by Florida Rule of Judicial Administration 2.215, it is **ORDERED** as follows:

1. A vehicle immobilization/impoundment program is permanently established within the Fifteenth Judicial Circuit.

2. Court Administration will maintain a list of the names and numbers of all immobilization agencies that meet the requirements of Florida Statute 316.193(13) and which operate and provide all the essential services associated with the immobilization/impoundment of vehicles pursuant to F.S. 316.193(6)(d) and in accordance with the directives of the Court.

3. Companies seeking to have their names placed on Court Administration's list, must submit an application showing proof that all of the requirements of Florida Statute 316.193(13) have been fulfilled along with an initial processing fee of $500.00. Applications to be an approved Vehicle Immobilizer will be accepted from May 1–May 31 of each year.

5. [1] Once the application has been reviewed by Court Administration and approved by the Chief Judge, and it is confirmed that the requirements of Florida Statute 316.193(13) have been met, the immobilization agency will be added to Court's List of Approved Vehicle Immobilizers. Companies who fail to comply with the statutory requirements or who, in the Chief Judge's discretion, are engaging in practices which compromise the integrity of the court, may be removed from the circuit's approved list of immobilization agencies.

6. Immobilization agencies must provide notice to the Chief Judge of their intent to renew their active status on the circuit's immobilization list in accordance with the directions from Court Administration. At the time of the annual renewal, a renewal fee of $500.00 is due from the immobilization agency to offset the administrative costs associated with the Vehicle Immobilization Program. A list of the vehicles immobilized during the preceding year must be submitted with the Notice of Intent to Renew.

7. Immobilization agencies have an ongoing responsibility to inform Court Administration of any new employees, agents or independent contractors working on the company's behalf who will be immobilizing vehicles in the Fifteenth Judicial Circuit as well as any other changes affecting their status as a qualified immobilization agency.

a. After a qualifying immobilization agency hires a new employee or retains a new independent contractor, it shall immediately submit proof that the person has no disqualifying criminal history.

b. No new employee, agent or independent contractors will be permitted to immobilize vehicles in the Fifteenth Judicial Circuit unless and until the company has received written notice from Court Administration that the employee has been approved.

c. A $50.00 processing fee will be required for each new employee/independent contractor that Court Administration must confirm complies with the statutory requirements

7. [2] Immobilization agencies on the list maintained by the Fifteenth Judicial Circuit shall comply with all rules and statutes pertaining to vehicle immobilization and will be expected to keep up to date with any new provisions within said rules and statutes.

8. Approved immobilization agencies will provide to the Director of Criminal Court Operations at the Clerk & Comptroller's Office an affidavit as required by Florida Statute 316.193(13)(a)l (2017). The Clerk & Comptroller's Office will forward the affidavit to Court Administration for placement in the agency's file.

9. The immobilization agency will also provide monthly a list of the cases in which a vehicle was impounded or immobilized along with the number of days the vehicle was impounded.

10. The approved immobilizing agencies shall submit to the Administrative Office of the Court a proposed fee schedule for their immobilizations. The fee schedule shall be reviewed by Court Administration on an annual basis and must be approved by the Administrative Office of the Court prior to it being imposed.

11. Attached to this administrative order are forms of Certificate of Completion and Notice of Non Completion to be used by the approved vehicle immobilization companies.

DONE and **SIGNED** in Chambers at West Palm Beach, Palm Beach County, Florida this 8 day of January, 2018.

Krista Marx
Chief Judge

IN THE COUNTY COURT IN AND FOR PALM BEACH COUNTY, FLORIDA

Case Number: ______

STATE OF FLORIDA

v.

______
Defendant.

______/

VEHICLE IMMOBILIZATION CERTIFICATE OF COMPLETION

The undersigned authorized immobilizer of ______ hereby certifies that Defendant ______ in case number ______ has paid the required immobilization fee and the vehicle has been immobilized in accordance with the Court's Order of Immobilization and Administrative Order 4.902.

Received the sum of $ ______ Dollars on ______ Method of Payment: ☐ Cash ☐ Money Order ☐ Cashier's Check

REMARKS: ______

Odometer Reading at time immobilization device installed: ______
Date: ______ Time: ______ Def./Owner Initials: ______
Immobilizer's Initials: ______
Odometer Reading at time immobilization device removed: ______
Date: ______ Time: ______ Def./Owner Initials: ______
Immobilizer's Initials: ______

______ Signature of Immobilizer ______ Company Name

______ Printed Name of Immobilizer ______ Company Address

Date: ______ ______ Company Address

cc: Court File
Defendant
Probation

______ Company Telephone Number

IN THE COUNTY COURT IN AND FOR PALM BEACH COUNTY, FLORIDA

Case Number: ______

STATE OF FLORIDA

v.

______
Defendant.

______/

VEHICLE IMMOBILIZATION NOTICE OF NON COMPLETION

The undersigned authorized immobilizer of ______ hereby certifies that Defendant ______ in case number ______ has **NOT** had the vehicle immobilized in accordance with the Court's Order and Administrative Order 4.902.

REMARKS: ______

______ Signature of Immobilizer ______ Company Name

______ Printed Name of Immobilizer ______ Company Address

______ Company Address

Date: ______ ______ Company Telephone Number

cc: Court File Defendant Probation

Adopted effective September 29, 2008. Amended effective July 22, 2009; April 26, 2011; January 8, 2018.

* supersedes admin. order 4.902–4/11

1 Numbered as in original.

2 Numbered as in original.

4.903. [VACATED AND SET ASIDE BY ORDER 4.903-1/13, EFFECTIVE JANUARY 8, 2013.]

4.904. PALM BEACH COUNTY DRUG COUNT/ASSIGNMENT OF DIVISION "KD"

IN THE CIRCUIT COURT OF THE FIFTEENTH JUDICIAL CIRCUIT IN AND FOR PALM BEACH COUNTY, FLORIDA

ADMINISTRATIVE ORDER NO. 4.904–9/08 *

IN RE: PALM BEACH COUNTY DRUG COURT/ASSIGNMENT OF DIVISION "KD"

In April 1999 after and pursuant to unanimous vote of the criminal court judges of the Fifteenth Judicial Circuit, the Palm Beach County Criminal Justice Commission (CJC) successfully submitted an application to the Drug Courts Program Office of the U.S. Department of Justice for a Drug Court planning grant of $30,000. The Palm Beach County Board of County Commissioners approved the required matching grant of $10,000 from the County Drug Abuse Trust Fund. Upon receipt of that planning grant a Drug Court Planning Committee was created with County Court Judge Nelson E. Bailey as Chairperson. In August 2000 after and pursuant to unanimous vote of the Drug Abuse Trust Fund Committee, $275,000 was allotted to be used for Drug Court treatment. The Drug Court Planning Committee proposed the Drug Court be operational at the existing "first appearance" and "arraignment" court at the Criminal Justice Complex at Gun Club Road in West Palm Beach.

NOW, THEREFORE, pursuant to the authority conferred by Florida Rule of Judicial Administration 2.215, it is **ORDERED** as follows:

1. Palm Beach County Drug Court will hear such qualified drug related charges pursuant to criteria set forth in Division KD procedural manual.

2. A County Court Judge assigned to the Criminal Justice Complex/Gun Club Facility, shall preside as a Circuit Judge over the Palm Beach County Drug Court.

3. Drug Court shall be designated as Division KD for case assignment purposes, and that upon receipt of appropriate orders of the Court transferring individual cases to the Drug Court, the Clerk of the Circuit Court, Palm Beach County, shall assign those designated cases to "Division KD, Drug Court."

4. Drug Court hours of operation shall be Monday through Friday at 1:00 p.m. for Drug Court First Appearances in Courtroom #1 of the Gun Club Courthouse, and Monday and Fridays at 1:00 p.m. for Drug Court Status Check Hearings in Courtroom #2 of the Gun Club Courthouse.

5. To allow for the scheduling of Drug Court at the Gun Club Courthouse, the "Civilian & Jail MM/TC V.O.P. Hearings" will be assigned to West Palm Beach Courthouse Divisions on a random, equitable, rotational basis.

6. In all cases in which defendants have been referred to Drug Court but they subsequently elect not to participate in the program, or they are rejected from the program for any reason, or they are removed from the program prior to entry of a plea of guilty or nolo contendere, then the Drug Court and/or Clerk of Court shall transfer those defendants' cases back to the cases' previously assigned divisions for further consideration.

7. Felony offenders participating in the Palm Beach County Drug Court Program shall be supervised mutually by Drug Court staff and the Florida Department of Corrections staff, in accordance with the procedures and orders of the Drug Court.

8. The Drug Court program office shall maintain statistics in a format compatible with CJIS development.

DONE and **SIGNED,** in Chambers, at West Palm Beach, Palm Beach County, Florida, this 29 day of September, 2008.

Kathleen J. Kroll
Chief Judge

Adopted effective September 29, 2008.

* supersedes admin. order 10.033–8/00

4.905. PALM BEACH COUNTY VETERANS' DOCKET/AND CREATION OF "VA" DIVISION

IN THE CIRCUIT COURT OF THE FIFTEENTH JUDICIAL CIRCUIT IN AND FOR PALM BEACH COUNTY, FLORIDA

ADMINISTRATIVE ORDER NO. 4.905–11/10

IN RE: PALM BEACH COUNTY VETERANS' DOCKET/ AND CREATION OF "VA" DIVISION

A report by the Substance Abuse and Mental Health Services Administration's Center for Mental Health Services National GAINS Center determined that on any given day, veterans account for nine (9) out of every one hundred (100) individuals in U.S. jails and prisons. Statistics show that in the Fifteenth Judicial Circuit, approximately sixty (60) veterans enter the criminal justice system on a monthly basis.

In 2010, the Chief Judge of the Fifteenth Judicial Circuit formed a Veterans' Committee comprised of stakeholders from the Judiciary, Office of the State Attorney, Office of the Public Defender, the Clerk and Comptroller's Office, Pride Probation, Department of Corrections, Veteran's Association, Stand Down House, Vietnam Veterans of America, Law Enforcement and Court Administration. The Committee's goal was to improve public safety by providing meaningful treatment to address the needs of veterans while reducing recidivism.

The Veterans' Committee determined that a need existed for a Veterans' Docket staffed by a full time case coordinator who will work on individualized treatment plans to address existing substance abuse, mental health, homelessness and employment issues of veterans charged with misdemeanor, municipal ordinance violations, county ordinance violations, and felony crimes. The case coordinator will link the veterans to services available at the Veteran's Hospital and local Community Service Providers with the goal of having the veterans become crime free citizens. The Veteran's Association agreed to fund the case coordinator to establish an individualized treatment plan for veterans. The Veterans' Committee also determined that a Volunteer Mentor Program, made up entirely of specially trained veteran volunteers, is a critical component of the Veterans' Docket, As such, the Stand Down House and Vietnam Veterans of America have agreed to oversee the Mentor Program and to coordinate training and background checks of the mentors.

NOW, THEREFORE, pursuant to the authority conferred by Florida Rule of Judicial Administration 2.215, it is **ORDERED** as follows:

1. Effective November 11, 2010, Veterans' Day, the Palm Beach County Veterans' Docket ("Veterans' Docket") is hereby established. The Veterans' Docket will hear qualified charges pursuant to criteria which will be set forth in the Veterans' Treatment Docket procedural manual which will be found at www.15thcircuit.com.

2. County Judge Ted Booras will preside over this docket and hearings shall take place at the Criminal Justice Complex/Gun Club Facility.

3. The Clerk and Comptroller shall designate all Veteran cases as Division "VA" for case assignment purposes. Upon receipt of court orders transferring individual cases to the Veterans' Docket, the Clerk of the Circuit Court shall assign those designated cases to Division "VA", Veterans' Docket.

4. The Veterans' Docket shall occur on the first (1st) and third (3rd) Thursday of each month, subject to change by the presiding Judge, beginning at 1:30 p.m. in Courtroom 1 of the Criminal Justice Complex ("Gun Club") Courthouse.

5. In all cases in which defendants have been referred to the Veterans' Docket, but subsequently either elect not to participate in the program, are rejected from the program for any reason, or are removed from the program prior to entry of a plea of guilty or nolo contendere, then the Clerk and Comptroller, or Criminal Case Manager, shall transfer those

cases back to the previously assigned divisions for further proceedings.

6. In those cases where felony and misdemeanor offenders participating in the Palm Beach County Veterans' Docket are placed on probation, they shall be supervised in the normal course by the Florida Department of Corrections staff or Pride Probation.

7. A Mentor Program is hereby created and will be overseen by The Stand Down House and Vietnam Veterans of America who will conduct trainings and background checks on the assigned mentors.

8. The Administrative Office of the Court, in collaboration with the Veteran's Association and Palm Beach County Pretrial Services, will facilitate collection and maintenance of the statistical data for the program.

9. The case coordinator, funded by the Veteran's Association, shall attend all case staffings and court sessions.

DONE and **SIGNED,** in Chambers, at West Palm Beach, Palm Beach County, Florida, this 10 day of November, 2010.

Peter D. Blanc
Chief Judge

Adopted effective November 10, 2010.

4.906. MENTAL HEALTH SPECIALTY DIVISION "T"

IN THE CIRCUIT COURT OF THE FIFTEENTH JUDICIAL CIRCUIT IN AND FOR PALM BEACH COUNTY, FLORIDA

ADMINISTRATIVE ORDER NO. 4.906–9/17 *

IN RE: MENTAL HEALTH SPECIALTY DIVISION "T"

Research has shown that specialized dockets can enhance the expediency, effectiveness, and quality of judicial administration. Persons charged with serious crimes who may have a mental illness, intellectual disability, autism or traumatic brain injury that impacts their ability to understand the court process require specialized management through the criminal justice system. These defendants require mental health evaluations to determine if they are competent to face their charges.

In order to more efficiently and effectively address this special population, the Mental Health Specialty Division (also referred to as Division "T") was created so that defendants could be addressed by one dedicated judge and judicial assistant, attorneys, and enhanced case management services. A Mental Health Specialty Division Team is comprised of the Division "T" Judge, Assistant State Attorney(s) assigned to Division "T", Assistant Public Defender(s) Assigned to Division "T" and the court administration mental health case manager.

NOW, THEREFORE, pursuant to the authority conferred by Florida Rule of Judicial Administration 2.215, it is **ORDERED** as follows:

A. Eligibility.

1. There must be a written motion alleging the defendant to be Incompetent to Proceed due to Mental Illness, Intellectual Disability, Autism, Traumatic Brain Injury or a finding of Not Guilty by Reason of Insanity.

2. The defendant must be charged with a felony and it must be either the first time the issue of competency is being raised or it is upon subsequent motion with agreement of the parties or by order of court.

3. Defendants who have already been found Not Guilty by Reason of Insanity may be transferred on agreement of the presiding Mental Health Specialty Division Judge.

B. Procedures Prior to and After Transfer of Cases.

1. Motions to Appoint Expert to Determine Competency made by Mental Health Specialty Division Team:

a. Motions to Appoint Expert to Determine Competency made by the Judge, Assistant Public Defender or Assistant State Attorney assigned to the Mental Health Specialty Division, will be forwarded directly to the Mental Health Case Manager and the Division T Judicial Assistant. If the case is specially set for trial or on a trial docket within 45 days from the date the motion to transfer is filed, the Mental Health Case Manager shall alert the divisional judge and the divisional judge may, at his or her discretion, keep the case in his or her division.

b. The Division T Judicial Assistant will prepare the Order Temporarily Reassigning the Case to Division T, Order Granting Examination of Defendant's Competency and Order Setting Hearing in Division T for a Competency Status Check.

c. The Division T Judicial Assistant will contact the Mental Health Case Manager who will provide the name of **one** expert whose name is obtained from the list of eligible competency experts to evaluate the defendant.

2. Motions to Appoint Expert to Determine Competency made by parties other than the Mental Health Specialty Division Team:

a. When a motion to appoint expert to determine competency is made by anyone other than the Judge, Assistant Public Defender or Assistant State Attorney assigned to the Mental Health Specialty Division, then the attorney or party submitting the Motion to Appoint Expert to Determine Competency must have the Divisional Judge hear the motion and if granted sign the Order Temporarily Reassigning Case to Division T.

b. The attorney or party shall email a copy of the signed order transferring the case to Division T to the Mental Health Case Manager and the Division T Judicial Assistant. The Order Granting Examination of Defendant's Competency and Order Setting Hearing in Division "T" for a Competency Status Check will be prepared by the Division T Judicial Assistant.

c. The Division T Judicial Assistant will contact the Mental Health Case Manager who will provide the name of one expert whose name is obtained from the list of eligible competency experts to evaluate the defendant.

3. Special Circumstances—The Motion to Appoint Expert to Determine Competency must set forth any special circumstances that require the need for a neuropsychological exam, an exam for a person with Intellectual Disability or Autism, or

when the defendant does not speak English and the exam must be performed in another language.

4. The Clerk and Comptroller shall:

a. maintain the original divisional assignment for statistical reporting purposes while the case is temporarily assigned to Division "T".

b. identify cases temporarily transferred to Division "T" with a "M.H." designation

c. transfer the case back to the original trial division, remove the M.H. designation, and set the matter on the next available docket if the defendant is found competent to proceed.

5. If the Court finds the Defendant Incompetent to Proceed or Not Guilty by Reason of Insanity, the case will stay in the Mental Health Specialty Division until such time as the defendant is found competent or the Court's Jurisdiction is terminated.

C. Disqualification. If the Mental Health Specialty Division Team determines that a defendant is not eligible for the Mental Health Specialty Division, the case will be immediately sent back to the original assigned division.

DONE and **SIGNED**, in Chambers,at West Palm Beach, Palm Beach County, Florida, this 5th day of September, 2017.

KRISTA MARX
Chief Judge

Adopted effective March 9, 2015. Amended effective September 5, 2017.

* supersedes admin. order 4.906–3/15

4.907. DESTRUCTION OF EVIDENCE BY LAW ENFORCEMENT

IN THE CIRCUIT COURT OF THE FIFTEENTH JUDICIAL CIRCUIT IN AND FOR PALM BEACH COUNTY, FLORIDA

ADMINISTRATIVE ORDER NO.: 4.907–6/15

IN RE: DESTRUCTION OF EVIDENCE BY LAW ENFORCEMENT:

Florida Statute 893.12(a) requires the Court to order the destruction of all substances controlled by Chapter 893 and all listed chemicals, which substances or chemicals are handled, delivered, possessed, or distributed contrary to any provisions stated in the Chapter, and all such controlled substances or listed chemicals the lawful possession of which is not established or the title to which cannot be ascertained, are declared to be contraband, are subject to seizure and confiscation by any person whose duty it is to enforce the provisions of the Chapter. Additionally, Florida Statute 893.12(a) authorizes the court to order such controlled substances or listed chemicals forfeited and destroyed. Florida Statute 379.338 permits the forfeiture and disposal of illegally taken wildlife, freshwater fish and saltwater fish upon court order.

Pursuant to the authority conferred by Florida Rule of Judicial Administration 2.215, it is hereby **ORDERED** that the following procedures are established for the destruction and/or forfeiture pursuant to Florida Statute 893.12 and 379.338:

1. A request for an order permitting the destruction of suspected controlled substance or a request for forfeiture of wildlife, freshwater fish or saltwater fish ("Request") shall be forwarded to Court Administration/Criminal Case Manager by electronic mail at CAD–criminalcasemanager@pbcgov.org as follows:

a. For pending cases, the request must be signed by both counsel for the law enforcement agency and the State Attorney's Office.

b. For closed cases, the request must be signed by either counsel for the law enforcement agency or the State Attorney's Office.

2. The request shall comply with the applicable statutory requirements for judicial review.

3. The Criminal Case Manager will forward the request to the Administrative Judge assigned to the Circuit Criminal Division for his/her review no earlier than the sixteenth (16th) day after the Request is received.

4. The Administrative Judge assigned to the Circuit Criminal Division will review the request and enter any applicable order.

5. The Criminal Case Manager will forward the original order to the Clerk's Office to be recorded in the official records for Palm Beach County, Florida.

6. The criminal case manager will email a copy of the order to the attorneys who made the Request. A copy will be maintained by Court Administration.

DONE and SIGNED in Chambers at West Palm Beach, Palm Beach County, Florida, this 22 day of June, 2015.

Jeffrey Colbath
Chief Judge

Adopted effective June 22, 2015.

4.908. [VACATED AND SET ASIDE BY ORDER 4.908-11/15, EFFECTIVE NOVEMBER 23, 2015.]

4.909. DRIVING WHILE LICENSE SUSPENDED COURT (DUS)

IN THE CIRCUIT COURT OF THE FIFTEENTH JUDICIAL CIRCUIT

ADMINISTRATIVE ORDER NO.: 4.909–10/17 *

IN RE: DRIVING WHILE LICENSE SUSPENDED COURT (DUS)

In order to assist individuals trying to regain their driver's license while they pay their fines and court costs, all citations issued for "driving while license suspended" will be assigned to a specialized diversion court (DUS Court). Law Enforcement has agreed to provide individuals qualifying for DUS court with a Uniform Traffic Citation requiring the defendant to appear to DUS Court.

NOW, THEREFORE, pursuant to the authority conferred by Florida Rule of Judicial Administration 2.215, it is **ORDERED** as follows:

1. All "driving while license suspended" cases, except those which resulted from Driving Under the Influence or certain other serious offenses which carry a statutory license suspension as part of the sentence, shall be assigned to division "DUS".

2. Cases assigned to the Central Courthouse shall be scheduled on Thursdays beginning at 1:30 p.m. in Courtroom 2D. The Clerk of Court shall provide each law enforcement agency with a time frame to stagger the docket flow.

3. Cases assigned to the North County region shall be scheduled on Wednesdays at 1:30 p.m. Cases assigned to the South County region shall be scheduled on Tuesdays at 8:30 a.m. Cases assigned to the West County region shall be scheduled on Thursdays at 9:00 a.m.

4. The Offices of the State Attorney and Public Defender for the Fifteenth Judicial Circuit of Florida have agreed to this diversion court as evidenced by a Stipulation, a copy of which is attached as Exhibit "A". Private defense counsel and counsel with the Office of Criminal Conflict and Civil Regional Counsel may file a motion to transfer qualifying cases to the DUS Division.

5. The County Court judges located at the Main Courthouse have agreed to hear the DUS docket on a rotating basis. The Judicial Assistant for the Administrative Judge of the County Criminal Division will prepare a schedule each year designating which judge will preside over the docket. This schedule will be provided to the Clerk of Court for scheduling purposes.

6. County Court Cases. A County Court Judge who presides over the DUS docket may address concurrent traffic infractions and county criminal cases (any court financial obligations) for purposes of case disposal regarding costs.

7. Circuit Cases. Unless a standing order retaining jurisdiction over felony court costs is entered by a Circuit Judge, the County Court Judge presiding over the DUS docket is vested with the authority of a Circuit Judge to modify a felony court cost order that affects the DUS defendant's ability to reinstate his or her driver's license.

8. The Clerk of Court shall forward to the Administrative County Criminal Judge, or any other person designated by the Chief Judge, any DUS motions and/or correspondence filed by a defendant that has not been assigned to the DUS division. The Administrative Judge will either rule on the motion/correspondence in chambers or schedule a hearing on same.

9. The inclusion of felony cases on this specialized docket will take effect on November 15, 2017 and the specialized docket shall continue until further order of this Court.

DONE and **SIGNED** in Chambers at West Palm Beach, Palm Beach County, Florida, this 30th day of October, 2017.

Krista Marx
Chief Judge

DUS DIVERSION COURT STIPULATION

The Office of the State Attorney, Fifteenth Judicial Circuit, by and through the undersigned State Attorney and the Office of the Public Defender, Fifteenth Judicial Circuit, by and through the undersigned Public Defender, stipulate as follows:

1) At arraignment, Driving under Suspension cases will be reviewed for eligibility into the DUS diversion court. The Public Defender or private defense attorney will look up the status of the drivers license in court and speak with the State Attorney as to whether the defendant is eligible for diversion.

2) The followingis a list of eligible DUS cases:

1. Unpaid Infractions
2. Child support
3. Financial responsibility/Insurance/Judgments
4. Points suspensions
5. Noncurrent 893 suspensions
6. Noncurrent DUI suspensions
7. Noncurrent HTO suspensions

3) The following is a list of non-eligible cases:

1. Felony DUS cases
2. Cases involving crashes
3. Current 893 suspensions
4. Felony DUI, DUI involving accidents, and current DUI suspensions
5. Current HTO suspensions
6. Permanent suspensions

4) The procedure for non-eligible cases will remain unchanged.

5) If eligible and participating in the program, the defendant will waive speedy trial and sign a deferred prosecution agreement. The defendant may be allowed up to 3 months to obtain a valid license. The SAO will not be required to turn over discovery on these cases while the defendant is in the diversion program. The defendant will be assessed $50.00 cost of prosecution.

6) At the conclusion of the time allotted for the deferred prosecution, if the defendant has been in compliance, has committed no new criminal law violations, and obtained a valid drivers license, the state will Nolle Prosse the case.

7) As a part of this pilot project, a new A.O. will issue to give the DUS diversion judge concurrent jurisdiction over PBC infractions. Additionally, the A.O. will provide the DUS diversion judge with concurrent jurisdiction over PBC criminal cases for purposes of case disposal regarding costs.

8) After 3 months, if the defendant is unable to obtain a lawful permit or a valid driver's license, the defendant has the option to enter into a Plea and Pass Agreement. The case will be passed for sentencing for 6 months. At sentencing, if the defendant has obtained a valid driver's license, the State will vacate the defendant's plea and enter a Nolle Prosse.

9) Both the State Attorney and Public Defender may withdraw from this stipulation at any time,

This stipulation is hereby entered into this 29 day of March, 2016.

Dave Aronberg
State Attorney
15th Judicial Circuit
Carey Haughwout

Public Defender
15th Judicial Circuit

Adopted effective April 4, 2016. Amended effective November 15, 2017.

* Supersedes admin., order 4.909–4/16

4.910. CREATION OF CIRCUIT CRIMINAL DIVISION "Z" AND TRANSFER OF 450 PENDING FELONY CASES

IN THE CIRCUIT COURT OF THE FIFTEENTH JUDICIAL CIRCUIT IN AND FOR PALM BEACH COUNTY, FLORIDA

ADMINISTRATIVE ORDER NO. 4.910–5/17

IN RE: CREATION OF CIRCUIT CRIMINAL DIVISION "Z" AND TRANSFER OF 450 PENDING FELONY CASES

In the interest of judicial economy and to increase efficiency, a seventh Felony Division is created and will be titled Division "Z".

NOW, THEREFORE, pursuant to the authority conferred by Florida Rule of Judicial Administration 2.215, it is **ORDERED AND ADJUDGED** as follows:

A. Creation of Division

1. Effective May 11, 2017, the Clerk and Comptroller shall create Circuit Criminal Division "Z" in its case maintenance system ("Showcase") for the sole purpose of scheduling cases.

2. The Clerk and Comptroller shall not assign any newly filed cases to this division until 450 cases have been transferred to Division "Z" in accordance with Paragraph B below.

B. Transfer of Pending Felony Cases

1. Court Administration's criminal case manager will identify approximately 75 cases from each of the six circuit criminal divisions to be transferred to Division "Z" for a total of approximately 450 transferred cases.

2. The criminal case manager and/or judicial assistant will prepare for the divisional judge an Order to Transfer for each of the identified cases.

3. Upon receipt of the electronically filed Order to Transfer, the Clerk and Comptroller will reassign the identified case to Division "Z".

4. Where a transferred case has a hearing scheduled in the original division at the time of the transfer, the hearing date will remain as scheduled until July 10, 2017; any hearing scheduled beyond July 10, 2017 shall take place in Division "Z".

5. Where a transferred case is set for trial in the original division at the time of transfer, the trial date will remain as scheduled unless the trial is scheduled after July 10, 2017; if the trial is scheduled after July 10, 2017, the trial will be heard in Division "Z".

6. A list of the transferred cases will be maintained by the Administrative Office of the Court.

C. Assignment of Newly Filed Cases

Division Z will be activated in the Clerk's case maintenance system ("Showcase") on July 10, 2017.

Upon transfer of the 450 pending felony cases in accordance with paragraph B above, the Clerk and Comptroller shall assign newly filed cases in the following manner:

- Division "R" twelve and half percent (12.5%)
- Division "S" twelve and half percent (12.5%)
- Division "U" twelve and half percent (12.5%)
- Division "V" twelve and half percent (12.5%)
- Division "W" twelve and half percent (12.5%)
- Division "X" twelve and half percent (12.5%)
- Division "Z" twenty-five percent (25%)

D. Monitoring of Caseloads

1. The Administrative Office of the Court will monitor the pending caseloads for each of the Circuit Criminal Divisions to ensure equity amongst the divisions.

2. When Division "Z" has received 657 cases (which includes the approximately 450 transferred cases and 207 newly filed cases) the Administrative Office of the Court will notify the Clerk and Comptroller that the case assignment percentages are equal and newly filed cases are to be allocated randomly amongst the seven felony divisions in accordance with AO 4.101.

E. Post Conviction Motions and Violation of Probation Matters

All Post Conviction Motions and Violation of Probation matters filed in Felony Division "T" shall be reassigned to Division "Z".

DONE and SIGNED in Chambers at West Palm Beach, Palm Beach County, Florida, this 11 day of May, 2017

Jeffrey Colbath
Chief Judge

Adopted effective May 11, 2017.

Unified Family Court

UFC Administrative Matters

5.101. UNIFIED FAMILY COURT JURISDICTION

IN THE CIRCUIT COURT OF THE FIFTEENTH JUDICIAL CIRCUIT IN AND FOR PALM BEACH COUNTY, FLORIDA

ADMINISTRATIVE ORDER NO. 5.101–1/19 *

IN RE: UNIFIED FAMILY COURT JURISDICTION

The Florida Supreme Court, in In Re: Report of the Family Court Steering Committee, 94 So.2d 518 (Fla. 2001), ("Family Courts IV"), directed each Circuit to submit revised local rules, or an Administrative Order, implementing a Unified Family Court consistent with its approved recommendations. The Florida Supreme Court further directed each Circuit to make every effort to resolve family disputes in a fair, timely, efficient and cost effective manner.

The Fifteenth Judicial Circuit shall assist litigants with cases involving family issues to avoid conflicting decisions and minimize inconvenience to the family and of maximizing all resources readily available to assist with resolving familial related case litigation. The Fifteenth Judicial Circuit seeks to facilitate open and effective communication between judges, court staff, attorneys and social service providers to better serve the litigants. The Fifteenth Judicial Circuit, in compliance of the Supreme Court's directives, has created a Unified Family Court Mission:

Unified Family Court is a fully integrated, comprehensive approach to handling all cases involving children and families, while at the same time resolving family disputes in a fair, timely, efficient and cost-effective manner.

NOW, THEREFORE, pursuant to the authority conferred by Florida Rule of Judicial Administration 2.215, it is **ORDERED** as follows:

A. Unified Family Court Jurisdiction.

1. The Unified Family Court shall include Judicial Divisions FA, FC, FD, FW, JA, JL, JK, JM, JO, JS, FI, FH, FJ, FX, FY, FZ, IB, IC, ID, IH, II, IJ, IY, IX, IZ, County Court Division DV–TD, and CHJD. The clerk shall only assign risk protection orders to the CHJD Division.

2. All Unified Family Court judges shall be assigned as Juvenile Court judges, as Mental Health and Guardianship Court judges and as Family Court judges,

3. At a minimum, the Unified Family Court of the Fifteenth Judicial Circuit shall include the following case types: dissolution of marriage; division and distribution of property arising out of a dissolution of marriage; annulment; support unconnected with dissolution of marriage; paternity; disestablishment of paternity; child support; URESA/UIFSA; custodial care of and access to children; proceedings for temporary or concurrent custody of minor children by extended family; adoption; name change; declaratory judgment actions related to premarital, marital, or post marital agreements; civil domestic, repeat, sexual and dating violence injunctions; juvenile dependency; termination of parental rights; emancipation of a minor; CINS/FINS; truancy; modification and enforcement of orders entered in these cases; juvenile delinquency; criminal domestic violence; stalking; cyber stalking; all mental health and guardianship cases, including but not limited to petition for determination of incapacity and petition for appointment of guardian; Marchman Act; Baker Act; and risk protection orders.

4. Two or more cases listed in paragraph A3 above constitute a "related case" when any of the parties are either presently or were ever previously involved in litigation.

B. Unified Family Court Case Assignment.

1. Unified Family Court shall be divided into four separate regions: the Central Courthouse. Judicial Divisions FA, FC, FD, IB, IC, ID, JK, JL, JM, JO and DV–TD; the South County Courthouse, Judicial Divisions FX, FY, FZ, IX, IY, IZ and JS; the North County Courthouse, Judicial Divisions FH, FJ, FI, IH, II, IJ and the West County Courthouse, Judicial Divisions FW and JA, and the Criminal Justice Complex, Judicial Division CHJD.

2. In all cases except delinquency, dependency, mental health, probate, guardianship, risk protection orders, Department of Revenue (DOR), and private adoptions, the Clerk is hereby responsible to determine case assignment based upon the zip code designations of the petitioner's residential address. Cases will not be assigned by the address of the attorney. Cases will remain in the same division they were originally filed in, regardless if the parties move their residence. This includes cases that are reopened for enforcement and/or modification—these cases will remain in the original division in which they were filed. Assignment of delinquency and dependency matters are set forth in Administrative Order 5.102. Assignment of mental health, probate, and guardianship cases are set forth in Administrative Order 6.102. Assignment and procedures related to risk protection orders are set forth in Administrative Order 6.312.

3. The Clerk of Court shall assign juvenile Marchman Act petitions to a juvenile judge when there is an open dependency and/or delinquency case. The clerk of court is directed to forward the initial assessment petition to the appropriate magistrate per A.O. 6.101 for hearing. After the initial determination is made, the magistrate and juvenile judge will confer whether to transfer the services petition to the juvenile judge under UFC or if the magistrate should continue to hear the case. The assigned juvenile judge will sign the orders for both assessment and services hearings. For Statistical Reporting System (SRS) purposes, the juvenile Marchman Act case will remain designated as a "MH" case type.

4. The Clerk shall randomly assign family law cases properly filed, among the family law divisions sitting at that location.

5. Upon receipt of any Petition or Complaint filed with a Notice of Related Case Form, for relief over which UFC has jurisdiction, the Clerk shall determine whether any of the parties were previously involved in litigation seeking any of the relief set forth herein. Any subsequently filed petition and/or motion shall be assigned to the division of UFC which heard the first case in the following manner:

a. When two or more domestic relations or two or more juvenile cases exist, the newly filed case shall be assigned to the same division as the previous case, if active within four years of the newly filed petition.

b. Civil domestic violence cases shall be assigned in accordance with Administrative Order 5.501.

c. Civil domestic violence cases with a pending criminal domestic violence case shall be assigned to division DV–TD. If a juvenile or domestic relations case also is pending with the case(s) in division DV–TD, the DV–TD judge shall refer all matters related to the minor children to the juvenile or family judge. The juvenile or family judge shall be noticed by the case manager who identified the related case to ensure there are no conflicting orders.

d. Juvenile dependency and delinquency cases shall be assigned in accordance with Administrative Order 5.102.

e. When a juvenile, mental health, or guardianship case is pending, along with a domestic relations case, the case manager who identified the related case shall prepare a UFC Identification Form and submit to the appropriate judges to confer and determine the best method of handling these cases.

6. Department of Revenue ("DOR") cases are exempt from the above and shall be assigned to a division at either the Main Courthouse or West County Courthouse. When DOR is no longer involved in the case, then the case may be re-assigned in accordance with the procedure described herein upon order of the Court. All DOR cases shall be set for hearing in the designated branches, according to their divisional assignments. If there are two or more related DOR cases in different divisions, the DOR Magistrates shall confer and determine the best method of handling these cases.

7. In the event a case must be transferred because of disqualification or recusal by the judge to which the case was previously assigned or elimination of a division, the Clerk shall, by random selection, reassign the case to another division within the same circuit, excluding West Branch division.

8. When there is no pending dependency case, the Clerk's Office shall randomly assign a Termination of Parental Rights action filed by an individual pursuant to Florida Statute Chapter 39 to the Juvenile Division.

C. Unified Family Court Regions/Domestic Relations Case Types.

1. *South County Courthouse.* With the exception of Department of Revenue family law cases, all cases filed and assigned in the Unified Family Court wherein the petitioner's residential zip code address lies within the South County service area shall be assigned to the South County Courthouse. The residential zip codes designating the South County service area are as follows:

Boynton Beach 33424
Boynton Beach 33425
Boynton Beach 33426
Boynton Beach 33435
Boynton Beach 33437
Boynton Beach 33473
Boynton Beach 33474
Boynton Beach 33435
Boynton Beach 33427
Boynton Beach 33428
Boynton Beach 33429
Boynton Beach 33431
Boynton Beach 33432
Boynton Beach 33433
Boynton Beach 33434
Boynton Beach 33481
Boynton Beach 33486
Boca Raton 33487
Boca Raton 33488
Boca Raton 33496
Boca Raton 33497
Boca Raton 33498
Boca Raton 33499
Delray Beach 33444
Delray Beach 33445
Delray Beach 33446
Delray Beach 33447
Delray Beach 33448
Delray Beach 33482
Delray Beach 33483
Delray Beach 33484
Gulfstream 33483
Highland Beach 33487
Ocean Ridge 33435

2. *North County Courthouse.* With the exception of Department of Revenue family law cases, all cases filed and assigned in the Unified Family Court wherein the petitioner's residential zip code address lies within the North County service area shall be assigned to the North County Courthouse. The residential zip codes designating the North County service area are as follows:

Greenacres 33413
Greenacres 33415
Haverhill 33409
Haverhill 33417
Juno Beach 33408
Juno Beach 33410
Jupiter 33458
Jupiter 33468
Jupiter 33469
Jupiter 33477
Jupiter 33478
Lake Park 33403
Loxahatchee 33470
Mangonia Park 33407
North Palm Beach 33408
Palm Beach Gardens 33403
Palm Beach Gardens 33408
Palm Beach Gardens 33410
Palm Beach Gardens 33419
Palm Beach Gardens 33420
Palm Beach Shores 33404
Riviera Beach 33404
Riviera Beach 33407
Riviera Beach 33412
Riviera Beach 33419
Riviera Beach 33420
Royal Palm Beach 33411
Royal Palm Beach 33412
Tequesta 33469
Wellington 33414
West Palm Beach 33403
West Palm Beach 33404
West Palm Beach 33407
West Palm Beach 33408
West Palm Beach 33409
West Palm Beach 33410
West Palm Beach 33411
West Palm Beach 33412
West Palm Beach 33417

West Palm Beach 33418
West Palm Beach 33419
West Palm Beach 33420

3. *West County Courthouse.* Civil domestic violence, repeat violence, dating violence and sexual violence cases are assigned to Division FW at West County Courthouse. Domestic relations cases shall be assigned to Division FW. All family cases filed, including Department of Revenue family law active cases, wherein the petitioner's residential zip code address lies within the West County service area, shall be assigned to the West County Courthouse.

Belle Glade 33430
Canal Point 33438
Clewiston 33440
Lake Harbor 33459
Pahokee 33476
South Bay 33493
Pelican Lake 33491

4. *Central (Main) Courthouse.* All cases filed and assigned in the Unified Family Court, including Department of Revenue family law active cases, wherein the petitioner's residential zip code address lies within the Central service area, shall be assigned to the central Courthouse.

Atlantis 33462
Boynton Beach 33436
Boynton Beach 33472
Bryant 33439
Cloud Lake 33416
Glen Ridge 33406
Golfview 33416
Greenacres 33463
Greenacres 33467
Haverhill 33422
Hypoluxo 33462
Lantana 33462
Lake Clarke Shores 33406
Lake Worth 33454
Lake Worth 33460
Lake Worth 33461
Lake Worth 33462
Lake Worth 33463
Lake Worth 33464
Lake Worth 33465
Lake Worth 33466
Lake Worth 33449
Manalapan 33462
Palm Beach 33480
Palm Springs 33461
Lake Worth 33467
Royal Palm Beach 33421
South Palm Beach 33480
Village of Golf 33406
Village of Wellington 33421
Wellington 33467
West Palm Beach 33401
West Palm Beach 33402
West Palm Beach 33405
West Palm Beach 33406
West Palm Beach 33416
West Palm Beach 33421
West Palm Beach 33422
West Palm Beach 33423

5. *Petitioner Lives Outside of Palm Beach County.* If the case is properly filed in Palm Beach County, and if the Petitioner lives outside of Palm Beach County and the Respondent resides in Palm Beach County, then the case shall be assigned per the Respondent's residential address. If the Respondent's address is not known immediately, then the case shall be temporarily assigned to Central Courthouse, and then re-assigned by the Respondent's residential address when received. Should the Respondent not live in Palm Beach County, but the Petitioner lives in either Broward or Miami–Dade county, then the case shall be assigned to the South County Courthouse. Should the Respondent not live in Palm Beach County, but the Petitioner lives in either Martin, St. Lucie, Indian River or Okeechobee county, then the case shall be assigned to the North County courthouse. All other cases filed by petitioners residing outside of Palm Beach County shall be assigned to the Central Courthouse.

D. Unified Family Court Elements.

1. *The Unified Family Court Bench.* judges assigned to UFC shall have received training or have extensive experience in family, juvenile, and county criminal court.

2. *General Magistrates.* General Magistrates shall be utilized to supplement the work of judges within Unified Family Court when a presiding judge determines that a referral of a case is appropriate, consistent with Administrative Order 5.104.

3. *Case Management.* UFC Case managers and case managers assigned pursuant to A.O. 6.312, will serve to coordinate related cases and assist litigants, case parties and the judiciary with various court processes and to monitor movement of cases through the judicial process.

4. *Identification and Coordination of Related Cases.* The Clerk and Comptroller will be responsible for initially identifying related open or closed cases upon filing of a new case or reopened on a petition for modification. Upon initial identification, the Clerk shall enter the related cases into the related case field in the Clerk's case management system (Showcase) in the newly filed case and any open case or reopened petition for modification.

5. Upon in-depth screening, UFC Case Managers will coordinate and link any open or closed related cases as well. As described in paragraph A.7., the judge or judges will decide whether all or some of the cases should be assigned to the same judge or coordinated in a manner to conserve judicial resources, avoid inconsistent court orders and eliminate multiple appearances on the same issue.

6. *Alternative Dispute Resolution.* UFC shall maximize use of alternative dispute resolution of family matters and issues as authorized by sections 44.102 and 39.4075, Florida

Statutes, and Florida Family Law Rules of Procedure 12.740 and 12.741 and Florida Juvenile Rule of Procedure 8.290.

7. *Technology.* The 15th Judicial Circuit shall use available technology to access information essential to case management and coordination, to print forms and notices, to generate statistical reports to provide public and inter-agency access to records.

8. *Domestic Violence.* The 15th Judicial Circuit shall work to ensure that cases involving domestic/repeat/dating/sexual violence/cyber stalking or stalking are identified and managed in a manner that is organized, timely and sensitive to the special dynamics involved in these cases.

E. Unified Family Court Screening, Case Identification and Coordination.

1. At the time of filing any case type delineated in paragraph A3 above, except risk protection orders, a fully completed Notice of Related Case shall be filed with the Court by the Petitioner in accordance with Rule 2.545(d), Florida Rules of Judicial Administration. If there appears to be a related case that has not been identified, the attorney or litigant may file a Notice with the Clerk and Comptroller's office requesting a review of the cases by providing the related cases, identified by Case Number and an explanation of why the cases are related.

2. Pursuant to Administrative Order 5.109, the moving party or the attorney for the moving party shall provide the name, current address and date of birth of the petitioner(s), the respondent(s) and each minor child listed in any newly or reopened Unified Family Court cases as defined in paragraph A3 above by filing a fully completed "Date of Birth Form" with the Clerk of Court. When the petitioner is a governmental agency, the petitioner does not need to provide its name, current address or date of birth.

3. Once related cases are identified, case managers will notify each of the judges involved in the cases. The judges will then confer to determine whether assignment of both cases to one judge will serve in the best interest of the family or whether another method of coordination should be utilized.

4. UFC case managers shall review the filings along with the Notice of Related Case form and draft the Order Transferring Unified Family Court Case if directed by the Judge.

5. Upon Order of the Court or notification from court staff, the Clerk shall enter related case information into the case management system for all related cases identified.

6. Pursuant to Family Law Rule of Procedure 12.006, the Clerk is directed to docket copies of orders transferring related cases, Final Judgments and any order related to a change in the custody of minor child(ren) in each related case involving the same parties, in which the judge/court staff has listed all relevant case numbers in the Order or Final Judgment.

7. Unified Family Court procedures shall be evaluated routinely by the Chief Judge or his/her designee to determine its effectiveness in implementing this Circuit's goal of addressing family law matters in a comprehensive, coordinated manner.

8. The Fifteenth Judicial Circuit's FLAG (Family Law Advisory Group) and the involved stakeholders shall continue to provide input regarding the Fifteenth Judicial Circuit's Unified Family Court.

DONE and SIGNED in Chambers at West Palm Beach, Palm Beach County, Florida, this 3rd day of January 2019.

Krista Marx
Chief Judge

Adopted effective September 29, 2008. Amended effective July 22, 2009; October 2, 2009; April 13, 2010; October 31, 2011; May 31, 2013; June 5, 2015; August 4, 2016; January 3, 2019.

* supersedes admin, order 5.101–8/16

5.102. ASSIGNMENT OF DELINQUENCY AND DEPENDENCY CASES

IN THE CIRCUIT COURT OF THE FIFTEENTH JUDICIAL CIRCUIT IN AND FOR PALM BEACH COUNTY, FLORIDA

ADMINISTRATIVE ORDER NO. 5.102–11/09 *

IN RE: ASSIGNMENT OF DELINQUENCY AND DEPENDENCY CASES

Administrative Order No. 11.101 sets forth this Circuit's policy concerning the assignment of judges, appointment of administrative judges and assignment of cases requiring that the Clerk of the Court equitably and randomly assigns cases within the division in which the cases are filed. The cases assigned to the Juvenile Subdivision of the Unified Family Court Division are assigned on a geographical basis, in order to provide an efficient and consistent process in handling those cases.

NOW, THEREFORE, pursuant to the authority conferred by Florida Rule of Judicial Administration 2.215, it is **ORDERED** as follows:

A. General Rules.

1. Delinquency cases filed on or after April 20, 2009, are deemed to arise where the crime occurs. If no zip code exists for the location of the crime, then the case shall be deemed to arise where the child resides. If no zip code is known for the residency of the child, then the case shall be assigned to the Main Judicial Complex according to the blind-assignment system.

2. Dependency cases are deemed to arise where the mother resides. If no zip code is known for the residency of the mother, then the case shall be deemed to arise where the child resides. If no zip code is known for the residency of the child, then the case shall be deemed to arise where the father resides. If no zip code is known for the residency of the mother, child or father, then the case shall be assigned according to the blind-assignment system.

3. Upon motion of either party, the court will consider reassigning a juvenile case.

B. Assignment of Cases to The West County Courthouse.

1. The Clerk of the Court shall assign delinquency and dependency cases arising west of the twenty mile bend (those cases that fall within the area handled by the Palm Beach County Sheriff District V Substation) to Division "JA" located at the West County Courthouse.

C. Assignment of Cases to The South County Courthouse.

1. The Clerk of Court shall assign delinquency and dependency cases arising in the following zip codes to Division "JS" to be located at the South County Courthouse.

Boynton Beach 33424	Boca Raton 33487
Boynton Beach 33425	Boca Raton 33488
Boynton Beach 33426	Boca Raton 33496
Boynton Beach 33435	Boca Raton 33497
Boynton Beach 33436	Boca Raton 33498
Boynton Beach 33437	Boca Raton 33499
Boynton Beach 33472	Delray Beach 33444
Boynton Beach 33474	Delray Beach 33445
Briny Breezes 33435	Delray Beach 33446
Boca Raton 33427	Delray Beach 33447
Boca Raton 33428	Delray Beach 33448
Boca Raton 33429	Delray Beach 33482
Boca Raton 33431	Delray Beach 33483
Boca Raton 33432	Delray Beach 33484
Boca Raton 33433	Gulfstream 33483
Boca Raton 33434	Highland Beach 33487
Boca Raton 33481	Ocean Ridge 33435
Boca Raton 33486	

D. Assignment of Cases to The Main Judicial Complex.

1. The Clerk of the Court shall assign delinquency and dependency cases arising east of the twenty mile bend as defined above, and not arising from a zip code listed in paragraph B1 above, to the appropriate juvenile court division at the Main Judicial Complex.

2. *Assignment of Delinquency Cases*

a. The Clerk shall randomly assign the delinquency cases amongst the juvenile division judges at the Main Judicial Complex in accordance with Administrative Order 11.101–8/09 (as amended).

b. Any known siblings in delinquency cases shall be assigned to the division having the lowest case number regardless of case status (pending or closed).

c. If, rather than file separate counts in the same petition, the state elects to file separate cases concerning the same factual situation, the assistant state attorney filing the cases shall notify the clerk, in writing, that companion cases are being filed. A companion case is a case wherein the delinquent has multiple cases in the system. The clerk, in turn, utilizing the blind-assignment system, shall select one judge and assign all designated companion cases to that judge.

d. If companion cases are assigned to different judges, it shall be the continuing duty of the state to notify, in writing, all judges involved and to file a motion to reassign the cases to the judge with the lowest numbered case.

e. If the state enters a nolle prosequi and subsequently refiles the case, the newly-filed case shall be assigned to the division of court in which the original case was assigned. It is the duty of the state to advise the clerk of the earlier nolle prossed case.

f. Violations of Probation: Upon the filing of a violation of probation, the case shall be assigned to the division which handled the underlying charge, regardless of timeframe. Cases will remain in the same division they were originally filed in, regardless of whether the parent or child changes their residence. This includes reopened or modification cases.

g. In the event a juvenile is currently in a diversionary program and is arrested again and is thus the subject of an entirely new case, the juvenile's new case should be assigned to the judge who had been randomly selected at the time the child was put into the diversionary program, if a judge was so assigned.

3. *Assignment of Dependency Cases*

a. The Clerk shall randomly assign the delinquency cases amongst the juvenile division judges at the Main Judicial Complex in accordance with Administrative Order 11.101–08/09 (as amended).

b. If a delinquency or dependency case is active for the minor parent of the child for whom a petition of dependency was filed, the clerk shall assign the dependency action to the division in which the child's minor parent has a pending dependency or delinquency matter. If both parents have pending matters before a juvenile court, the dependency action will be assigned to the judge presiding over the mother's active juvenile matter.

4. *Assignment of "Cross Over" Cases*

a. In the event, the parties and/or child have an existing dependency case and the child enters the delinquency system, the same judge/division shall be assigned the delinquency case, regardless of case status (pending or closed). The same shall apply to a dependency case where there is an existing delinquency case.

b. Any known siblings in delinquency cases shall be assigned to the division having the lowest case number.

5. In the event a case must be transferred because of disqualification or recusal by the judge to which the case was previously assigned or elimination of a division, the clerk shall, by random selection, unless otherwise specified in the case of division closure, reassign the case to another division within the Main Courthouse, excluding South and West Branch divisions.

DONE AND SIGNED in Chambers at West Palm Beach, Palm Beach County, Florida, this 6 day of November, 2009, *nunc pro tunc* November 2, 2009.

Peter D. Blanc
Chief Judge

Adopted effective September 29, 2008. Amended effective July 1, 2009; October 2, 2009; November 6, 2009.

* supersedes admin. order no. 5.102–11/09

5.103. [VACATED AND SET ASIDE BY ORDER 5.103-6/17, EFFECTIVE JUNE 16, 2017.]

5.104. APPOINTMENT OF MAGISTRATES UNIFIED FAMILY COURT CASES

IN THE CIRCUIT COURT OF THE FIFTEENTH JUDICIAL CIRCUIT IN AND FOR PALM BEACH COUNTY, FLORIDA

ADMINISTRATIVE ORDER 5.104–11/16 *

IN RE: APPOINTMENT OF MAGISTRATES UNIFIED FAMILY COURT CASES

Unified Family Court proceedings include but are not limited to cases involving support, alimony, custody, time-sharing, juvenile dependency, attorney's fees, and substance abuse. These types of cases comprise a substantial portion of this Circuit Court's workload both as to the number of cases and the amount of judicial time connected with disposition of same. The interests of the public and of the litigants require a flexible, speedy and final resolution of these cases. These interests can be better served by the utilization of a General Magistrate system.

The Florida Family Law Rules of Procedure, specifically Rule 12.490 and Rule 12.491 authorize the Chief Circuit Judge to appoint General Magistrates to preside over a myriad of post-judgment non-child support matters and child support establishment, enforcement and modification; Florida Rules of Juvenile Procedure, Rules 8.257 (juvenile dependency) and 8.625 (families and children in need of services); Florida Probate Rules, Rule 5.697 (guardianship proceedings); as well as Florida Statutes Chapters 394 (Baker Act) and 397 (Marchman Act) proceedings. In 1989 the Chief Justice of the Florida Supreme Court authorized this Circuit to effectuate the appointment of General Magistrates in accordance with these Rules and Florida Statutes.

NOW, THEREFORE, pursuant to the authority conferred by Florida Rule of Judicial Administration 2.215, it is **ORDERED** as follows:

A. Office of General Magistrate.

1. The Office of General Magistrate of the Fifteenth Judicial Circuit is hereby established for the express purpose of assisting the Circuit Judges in their above-described Unified Family Court workload.

2. Each General Magistrate in this Circuit is appointed and authorized to function within all of the types of proceedings enumerated above.

3. Each General Magistrate in this Circuit is also appointed and authorized to function as a Child Support Hearing Officer consistent with the Florida Family Law Rules of Procedure, Rule 12.491 as well as a General Magistrate pursuant to a valid Order of Referral in accordance with Rule 12.490.

4. General Magistrates shall be appointed by the Chief Judge of the Circuit and shall serve at the pleasure of the Chief Judge of the Circuit and a majority of the Circuit Judges of this Circuit.

5. Separate orders of appointment shall be entered for each General Magistrate upon his or her appointment by the Circuit.

6. General Magistrates shall be invested with all powers and authority under Florida law and the appropriate Florida Family Law Rules of Procedure, Florida Juvenile Rules of Procedure, and Florida Probate and Guardianship Rules of Procedure.

7. General Magistrates shall discharge their duties and obligations at the direction of the Chief Judge of the Circuit, the Administrative Judge of the Unified Family Court, and the Unified Family Court Judges for whom they serve.

B. Emergency Matters.

1. Because of the time limitations procedurally inherent in the General Magistrate system, post-judgment emergency matters, as set forth in Administrative Order 5.203, shall be forwarded to the Circuit Judges directly by the Clerk of the Circuit Court and not to the General Magistrates.

2. If the Circuit Judge determines by order that the matter is not an emergency, then it may be referred and/or assigned to the General Magistrate for disposition.

C. Record of Proceedings.

1. Consistent with the Florida Family Law Rules of Procedure, the Florida Juvenile Rules of Procedure, the Florida Probate and Guardianship Rules of Procedure and Florida Statutes Chapters 394 and 397, all proceedings before General Magistrates shall be electronically reported with equipment provided by this Circuit's Office of Court Administration.

2. Copies of the recordings or a transcript of the proceedings may be obtained in accordance with Administrative Order 2.503–1/13 (as amended).

D. Assignment to General Magistrate for Child Support and Matters in the Nature of Support Pursuant to Florida Rule of Family Procedure 12.491. Pursuant to Florida Family Law Rule of Procedure 12.491, all child support matters, regardless of whether titled "child support", are hereby assigned to the General Magistrates and Child Support Hearing Officers. When pleadings and motions relating to child support are filed, except those including a request for attorney's fees, no additional referral to the General Magistrate or Child Support Hearing Officer is required.

E. Order of Referral to General Magistrate Pursuant to Florida Rule of Family Procedure 12.490.

1. A General Magistrate will solely preside over all matters related to a motion or petition which is referred to the General Magistrate, without objection, pursuant to Florida Rule of Family Procedure *12.490* Such matters may include but not are limited to discovery matters, dismissal motions, continuances, motions for temporary relief, motion for child testimony, motion to appoint guardian ad litem, parenting coordinator, social investigations, motions to appear telephonically, and motions to withdraw.

2. Each order of referral to a General Magistrate will state with specificity the matter being referred and the name of the specific general magistrate to whom referral is being made. As set forth in paragraph 3 below, for internal caseflow management purposes, each order of referral will identify only <u>one</u> motion or pleadings.

a. Upon a self-represented party filing for post-judgment relief in a motion or pleadings, the Clerk of the Court will forward the motion or pleadings to the appropriate family case management email inboxes for review and processing. Upon receipt and review, the case manager shall immediately prepare the appropriate Order of Referral to General Magistrate and forward to the General Magistrate for review and approval. If the Magistrate determines the Order of Referral to General Magistrate is appropriate, the family case manager will forward the Order of Referral to the presiding Judge for execution and distribution to the parties.

b. The type of motions or pleadings that will be sent to the family case management email inboxes for review and processing has been previously established with the Clerk of the Court and will be modified from time to time, if deemed necessary.

c. If the filing party is represented by counsel, and the matter involves issues other than solely child support, the filing party shall submit an order of referral contemporaneous with the initial filing to the presiding Judge for execution and distribution to the parties unless notice of a preemptory objection has been filed.

3. In order to effectively administer the affairs of the court, there is to be only one motion or pleading per Proposed Order of Referral to General Magistrate. Any Proposed Order of Referral to the General Magistrate which contains reference to multiple motions or pleadings will not be considered. The Proposed Order of Referral to the General Magistrate must include the following:

a. The specific title of the pleading or motion;

b. The name of the party filing the motion or pleadings;

c. The date the motion or pleadings was filed;

d. The assigned Magistrate's hearing room number listed immediately above the style of the case.

4. If an amended motion or pleading is filed raising new substantive non child support matters, an Amended Order of Referral is required.

5. Any objection to an Order of Referral to a General Magistrate will identify the date of the Order of Referral which is the subject of the objection. The party filing the objection will provide a copy of the objection to the General Magistrate to whom the referral was made, or, in the event of a preemptory objection, to the General Magistrate to whom the referral would have been made. No order of referral will be forwarded to the presiding judge if a preemptory objection has been filed. The General Magistrate will prepare a proposed order on the objection for the Circuit Judge who will rule upon the objection in writing.

6. The following matters are not appropriate for and will not be referred or assigned to this circuit's General Magistrates:

a. Motion to Vacate Recommended Order (Child Support) per Rule 12.491;

b. Exceptions to Report per Rule 12,490;

c. Domestic Violence Proceedings (except child support enforcement) per Rule 12.490;

d. All prejudgment proceedings including discovery and motions connected therewith;

e. Bifurcation of attorney's fees hearing after Judge has ruled on underlying action or motion;

f. Bifurcation of initial action for dissolution of marriage after Judge grants dissolution of marriage and refers everything else;

g. Motion for Rehearing of Order on an action or motion heard and issued by the Judge;

h. Motion for Clarification of Order on an action or motion heard and issued by the Judge;

i. Emergencies of any type;

j. Criminal Contempt/Criminal Rule to Show Cause per Rule 3.840;

k. Commitment Proceedings arising from a contempt order which was heard and issued by a Judge;

l. First Appearance Hearings on Commitment Order arrests;

m. Paternity Establishment (contested);

n. Paternity Disestablishment (contested);

o. Ex Parte Injunction;

p. Reversal and remand from appellate court of trial court proceedings heard and ruled upon by Judge.

q. Uncontested relocation pursuant to section 61.13001

r. Writs re: Habeas Corpus & Ne Exeat and all other original Writs

DONE and **SIGNED** in Chambers at West Palm Beach, Palm Beach County, Florida, this 7 day of November, 2016.

Jeffrey Colbath
Chief Judge

Adopted effective May 21, 2009. Amended effective July 30, 2015; November 7, 2016.

* supersedes admin. order 5.104–07/15.

5.105. PROCEDURES FOR PRIVATE PLACEMENT ADOPTION PROCEEDINGS PURSUANT TO FLORIDA STATUTE CHAPTER 63

IN THE CIRCUIT COURT OF THE FIFTEENTH JUDICIAL CIRCUIT IN AND FOR PALM BEACH COUNTY, FLORIDA

ADMINISTRATIVE ORDER NO. 5.105–1/12 *

IN RE: PROCEDURES FOR PRIVATE PLACEMENT ADOPTION PROCEEDINGS PURSUANT TO FLORIDA STATUTE CHAPTER 63

Chapter 63 of the Florida Statutes provides for the private adoption of children through adoption agencies or attorney intermediaries ("adoption entities"). Adoption proceedings are filed at the Main Judicial Center and the branch courthouses. Uniform procedures will ensure the timely disposition of the adoption proceedings.

NOW, THEREFORE, pursuant to the authority conferred by Florida Rule of Judicial Administration 2.215, it is **ORDERED** as follows:

A. Petition for Termination of Parental Rights.

1. If a Petition for Termination of Parental Rights ("TPR") is required in an adoption proceeding, the TPR must be filed separate from and prior to the filing of the Petition for Adoption in accordance with Florida Statute 63.102. In accordance with Florida law, a Petition for Declaratory Statement seeking prior approval of fees and costs can be filed at any time after an agreement is reached between the birth mother and the adoptive parents but will be assigned a case number separate and apart from the TPR. Pursuant to Chapter 63, the Clerk will only assess one filing fee.

2. In order to ensure that a responsive pleading by a putative or legal father is accepted for filing and properly docketed, the Clerk & Comptroller's office is directed to

initiate a TPR proceeding, and to generate a ease number, upon either the filing of a Petition for Termination of Parental Rights or upon the filing of a Notice of Intended Adoption Plan.

3. The Clerk's Office will assign the TPR a case number separate from the Petition for Adoption or the Petition for Declaratory Statement/Petition for Prior Approval of Fees and Costs ("Petition for Declaratory Statement"). If the Petition for Declaratory Statement is filed prior to the TPR, a Notice of Related Case will be filed with the TPR indicating the division to which the Petition for Declaratory Statement has been assigned.

4. All pleadings, motions or other papers filed in the TPR shall be presented to the Clerk for filing as separate documents and multiple pleadings, motions or other papers shall not be filed under one Notice of Filing. Should various pleadings, motions or other papers be filed under one Notice of Filing, the Clerk shall separately index and docket each pleading, motion or other paper.

5. Each court filing will contain the TPR case number and have a title that provides a clear description in order for the Clerk to identify the pleading for indexing and docketing.

6. An internal case management review of the file will be undertaken by the Court prior to the setting of the Final Hearing on the Petition for Termination of Parental Rights.

7. All proposed orders shall contain a signature line with the judge's name typewritten below.

B. Petition for Adoption.

1. The Petition for Adoption shall be assigned to the same family division that the Petition for Termination of Parental Rights or Petition for Declaratory Statement was assigned.

a. The Clerk shall not charge a filing fee for the Petition for Adoption if a filing fee for the Petition for Termination of Parental Rights had previously been paid.

b. A Notice of Related Case Form shall also be filed with each Petition for Adoption. The Notice of Related Case Form shall include the requested information for both the Petition for Termination of Parental Rights case as well as any other case that had been filed and which addressed the placement, adoption or care of the unborn or born child.

c. If a Petition for Declaratory Statement was previously filed, the Petition for Adoption shall be assigned the same case number and made part of that case file.

2. All pleadings, motions or other papers filed in the Petition for Adoption shall be presented to the Clerk for filing as separate documents and multiple pleadings, motions or other papers shall not be filed under one Notice of Filing. Should various pleadings, motions or other papers be filed under one Notice of Filing, the Clerk shall separately index and docket each pleading, motion or other paper.

3. Each court filing will contain the Petition for Adoption case number and have a title that provides a clear description in order for the Clerk to identify the pleading for indexing and docketing.

4. An internal case management review of the file will be undertaken by the Court prior to the setting of the Final Hearing on the Petition for Adoption.

5. All proposed orders shall contain a signature line with the judge's name typewritten below.

6. Pleadings wherein attorney's fees or costs/expenses are sought in excess of $5,000.00 will contain sufficient detail such that the Court can review the invoice for reasonableness and determine whether the requested fees are in accordance with Rule 4–1,5 of the Rules Regulating the Florida Bar. At the judge's discretion, a hearing may be set so that testimony concerning the fees or costs/expenses may be presented to the Court.

7. In accordance with Florida Statute § 63.102(3), the Petition for Adoption may be dismissed if it is not filed within 60 days after the entry of the final judgment terminating parental rights.

C. Petition for Declaratory Statement.

1. When a Petition for Declaratory Statement as to an Adoption Contract is filed by the adoption entity, the Clerk of Court shall accept for filing the Petition for Declaratory Statement with the same confidentiality procedures as is required for a Petition for Adoption.

2. The Clerk shall charge the same filing fee as is charged for the filing of a Petition for Adoption. No additional filing fee shall be assessed for the filing of the Petition for Declaratory Statement if a filing fee has been paid for the TPR. The case number assigned to the Petition for Declaratory Statement shall be assigned to a subsequently filed Petition for Adoption.

DONE and **SIGNED** in Chambers at West Palm Beach, Palm Beach County, Florida, this 30 day of January, 2012.

Peter D. Blanc
Chief Judge

Amended effective May 1, 2011; January 30, 2012.

* supersedes admin. order 5.105–5/11.

5.106. NOTICE OF RELATED CASES FORM IN UNIFIED FAMILY COURT CASES

IN THE CIRCUIT COURT OF THE FIFTEENTH JUDICIAL CIRCUIT IN AND FOR PALM BEACH COUNTY, FLORIDA

ADMINISTRATIVE ORDER 5.106–3/15 *

IN RE: NOTICE OF RELATED CASES FORM IN UNIFIED FAMILY COURT CASES

Florida Rule of Judicial Administration 2.545(d) requires that Family Law Form 12.900(h), Notice of Related Cases Form, be filed with the initial pleading/petition in family cases which cases include, but are not limited to, dissolution of marriage, child support, adoption, juvenile delinquency, juvenile dependency, termination of parental rights matters, civil domestic, repeat, sexual and dating violence injunctions, criminal domestic violence injunctions, stalking injunctions and cyber stalking injunctions. Florida Rule of Judicial Administration 2.545(d)(7) requires "The notice of related cases shall be served on all parties in the related cases, the presiding judges, and the chief judge or family law administrative judge."

NOW, THEREFORE, pursuant to the authority conferred by Florida Rule of Judicial Administration 2.215, it is **ORDERED** as follows:

1. The case manager assigned to the division in which the case is pending shall serve as the designee of the chief judge, division judge, and the administrative judges of the family and juvenile divisions for purposes of receiving the notice of related case as required by Florida Rule of Judicial Administration 2.545(d)(4).

2. All information required by the Family Law Form 12.900(h) shall be included within the form itself and no additional documents or papers shall be attached to the Notice of Related Case without the prior approval of the Chief Judge.

3. A copy of the Notice of Related Case shall be sent to the case manager either electronically or mailed to the case manager at the postal address of Administrative Office of the Court, Unified Family Court Case Management, 205 North Dixie Highway, West Palm Beach, Florida 33401. In an effort to conserve resources, the Notice of Related Case should be sent electronically whenever possible.

4. A listing of the case managers can be found at http://15thcircuit.co.palm-beach.fl.us/web/guest/ufc-case-management.

DONE and SIGNED, in Chambers at West Palm Beach, Palm Beach County, Florida this 9 day of March, 2015.

Jeffrey Colbath
Chief Judge

Amended effective June 1, 2011; October 31, 2011; March 9, 2015.

* supersedes Admin. Order 5.106–10/11

5.107. ASSIGNMENT OF NEWLY FILED CASES IN UNIFIED FAMILY COURT SOUTH COUNTY FAMILY DIVISIONS "FX" "FY" AND "FZ"

IN THE CIRCUIT COURT OF THE FIFTEENTH JUDICIAL CIRCUIT IN AND FOR PALM BEACH COUNTY, FLORIDA

ADMINISTRATIVE ORDER NO. 5.107–12/13*

ASSIGNMENT OF NEWLY FILED CASES IN UNIFIED FAMILY COURT SOUTH COUNTY FAMILY DIVISIONS "FX" "FY" AND "FZ"

In the interest of judicial economy and to increase the efficiency of service to litigants, the Fifteenth Judicial Circuit created Unified Family Division "FX" on August 12, 2011. Based upon review of then pending South County Family and Probate/Guardianship caseloads and rotations, effective January 22, 2013, the judge assigned to Division "FZ" was no longer assigned a Probate/Guardianship division and the ratio assignment for newly filed family cases was modified.

Based upon current review of the pending South County Family and Probate/Guardianship caseloads and new rotations in January 2014, Court Administration intends to re-open Probate/Guardianship Division "IZ". Therefore, the ratio assignment for newly filed family cases requires adjustment.

NOW, THEREFORE, pursuant to the authority conferred by Florida Rule of Judicial Administration 2.215, it is **ORDERED AND ADJUDGED** as follows:

A. Assignment of Cases. Effective December 1, 2013, newly filed South County Family Division cases shall be randomly assigned in the following manner: Division "FX" thirty-four percent (34%), Division "FY" thirty-three percent (33%), and Division "FZ" thirty-three percent (33%).

B. Monitoring of Caseloads. The Administrative Office of the Court shall monitor the pending caseloads for each of the South County Family Divisions to ensure equity amongst the divisions in light of other assignments.

DONE and **SIGNED** in Chambers at West Palm Beach, Palm Beach County, Florida, this 16 day of December, 2013 *nunc pro tunc* December 1, 2013.

Jeffrey Colbath, Chief Judge

Adopted effective August 8, 2011. Amended effective January 22, 2013; December 11, 2013.

* supersedes admin. order 5.107–1/13

5.108. [VACATED AND SET ASIDE BY ORDER 5.108-12/16, EFFECTIVE RETROACTIVELY AS OF OCTOBER 1, 2014.]

5.109. DATE OF BIRTH FORM FOR UNIFIED FAMILY COURT CASE IDENTIFICATION

IN THE CIRCUIT COURT OF THE FIFTEENTH JUDICIAL CIRCUIT IN AND FOR PALM BEACH COUNTY, FLORIDA

ADMINISTRATIVE ORDER NO. 5.109–1/17 *

IN RE: DATE OF BIRTH FORM FOR UNIFIED FAMILY COURT CASE IDENTIFICATION

In compliance with the Supreme Court's directives, the Fifteenth Judicial Circuit's Unified Family Court is desirous of assisting litigants with cases involving family issues to avoid conflicting decisions, minimize inconvenience to the family, and maximize all resources readily available to assist with resolving familial related case litigation. To capture related cases for the family accurately and pursuant to Administrative Order 5.101, additional information is needed for efficient case management of these cases. Rule of Judicial Administration 2.425 permits otherwise sensitive information to be included in court documents when the court so orders.

NOW, THEREFORE, pursuant to the authority conferred by Florida Rule of Judicial Administration 2.215, it is **ORDERED** as follows:

1. The Unified Family Court division shall utilize the local "Date of Birth Form" to capture additional information for the family for better identification of related cases for each family. A copy of "Date of Birth Form" is attached hereto as exhibit "A".

2. The moving party or the attorney for the moving party shall provide the name, current address and date of birth of the petitioner(s), the respondent(s) and each minor child listed in any newly or reopened case types in the Unified Family Court, as listed in paragraph 3 below, by filing a fully completed "Date of Birth Form" with the Clerk of Court. When the petitioner is a governmental agency, the petitioner does not need to provide its name, current address or date of birth.

3. The form is to be provided in the following case UFC types: dissolution of marriage; division and distribution of property arising out of a dissolution of marriage; annulment; support unconnected with dissolution of marriage; paternity; disestablishment of paternity; child support; URESA/UIFSA; custodial care of and access to children; proceedings for temporary or concurrent custody of minor children by extended family; adoption; name change; declaratory judgment actions related to premarital, marital, or post marital agreements; civil domestic, repeat, sexual and dating violence injunctions; juvenile dependency; termination of parental rights; emancipation of a minor; CINS/FINS; truancy; modification and enforcement of orders entered in these cases; juvenile delinquency; criminal domestic violence; stalking; cyber stalking; all mental health and guardianship cases.

4. The Clerk of Court shall enter into its case maintenance system the information on the Date of Birth Form for Unified Family Court.

5. The Clerk of Court will enter into its case maintenance system the name and date of birth of a minor child as a confidential party on each family case.

6. The Clerk of Court will redact the date of birth and the name of a minor child in the "Date of Birth Form" prior to docketing.

7. Such procedures shall be evaluated routinely by the Chief Judge or his/her designee to determine its effectiveness in implementing this Circuit's goal of addressing family law matters in a comprehensive, coordinated manner.

DONE and **SIGNED** in Chambers at West Palm Beach, Palm Beach County, Florida, this 27 day of January 2017.

Jeffrey Colbath
Chief Judge

[Attachment]

IN THE CIRCUIT COURT OF THE FIFTEENTH JUDICIAL CIRCUIT IN AND FOR PALM BEACH COUNTY, FLORIDA

Case No: ____________
Division: ____________

____________________,
Petitioner,

and

____________________,
Respondent.

Date of Birth Form for Unified Family Court

Instructions

Pursuant to Administrative Order 5.109, this form is to be completed and filed with the Clerk's Office in all new and reopened Unified Family Court ("UFC") cases. UFC case types include but are not limited to all family, juvenile, mental health, domestic violence and guardianship cases. A detailed list of UFC case types can be found in Administrative Order 5.101.
Sensitive Information in this document (month and day of birth/names of minors) will be redacted by the Clerk and will not be accessible by the general public.

Information

Petitioner's Name ____________ Petitioner's D.O.B

Petitioner's Address ____________

//

Respondent's Name ____________ Respondent's D.O.B

Respondent's Address ____________

//

Child's Name ____________ Child's D.O.B

Child's Name ____________ Child's D.O.B

Child's Name ____________ Child's D.O.B

Child's Name ____________ Child's D.O.B

Child's Name ____________ Child's D.O.B

*Please attach an additional page for additional Party or Child

Filed by: ____________
Type/Print your name

15th Judicial Circuit—Date of Birth Form for Unified Family Court

Adopted effective September 1, 2016. Amended effective January 27, 2017.

* supersedes admin. order 5.109–9/16

5.110. PROCEDURES FOR NAME CHANGE PETITIONS

IN THE CIRCUIT COURT OF THE FIFTEENTH JUDICIAL CIRCUIT IN AND FOR PALM BEACH COUNTY, FLORIDA

ADMINISTRATIVE ORDER NO. 5.110–5/17

IN RE: PROCEDURES FOR NAME CHANGE PETITIONS

Section 68.07 of the Florida Statutes provides for the change of the name of any person residing in the State of Florida in the county in which he or she is domiciled. Name Change proceedings are filed at the Main Judicial Center and the branch courthouses. Uniform procedures will ensure the appropriate review and timely disposition of Name Change proceedings.

NOW, THEREFORE, pursuant to the authority conferred by Florida Rule of Judicial Administration 2.215, it is **ORDERED** as follows:

A. Case Filings

1. Name Change Petitions, except for those filed under Florida Statute section 68.07(9), will be assigned in accordance with Administrative Order 5.101. If a related Domestic Relations case is identified at initial screening or on the Notice of Related Case Form, the Clerk of Court shall assign the newly filed case to the same division as the previous case.

2. Except if a former name is being restored, the petitioner must submit electronic fingerprints for a state and national criminal history records check. A final judgment cannot be entered without the results of the state and national records check.

3. Pursuant to Fifteenth Judicial Circuit Administrative Order 5.307, a copy of a Live Birth Certificate for any minor

child(ren) involved in a Petition for Change of Name must be filed in the case.

4. Pursuant to Fifteenth Judicial Circuit Administrative Order 5.109, a Date of Birth Form for all parties, including minor child(ren) involved in a Petition for Change of Name must be filed in the case.

B. Review of the Cases

1. An internal case management review of the file will be undertaken by the Court prior to the setting of the Final Hearing on any Petition for Change of Name.

2. Upon filing of a criminal history records check, the Clerk of Court is directed to notify the appropriate court administration email inbox for review and processing.

3. If the Petition for Change of Name is incomplete or requires additional information or documentation, the Court will enter a status order outlining the deficiencies or missing information.

4. Failure to comply with the Court's requirements on the status order could result in the dismissal of the case.

C. Hearing and Disposition of the Cases

1. A hearing will only be set on a Petition for Change of Name after the Court's case management review of the file.

2. *Filings by Self Represented Litigants:* Upon completion of the case management review and determination by the Court that the case is ready for the entry of a Final Judgment, the case manager will prepare an Order Setting Hearing on the Case and/or Prepare Final Judgment of Name Change, depending on the divisional procedures.

3. *Filings by Attorneys:* Upon completion of the case management review and determination by the Court that the case is ready for the entry of a Final Judgment, the judicial assistant will, in accordance with divisional procedures, contact the attorneys to set the case for a final hearing.

DONE AND SIGNED in Chambers at West Palm Beach, Palm Beach County, Florida, this 5/16/ day of May, 2017.

Jeffrey J. Colbath
Chief Judge

Adopted effective May 16, 2017.

5.111. PROCEDURES FOR TEMPORARY AND CONCURRENT CUSTODY PROCEEDINGS

IN THE CIRCUIT COURT OF THE FIFTEENTH JUDICIAL CIRCUIT IN AND FOR PALM BEACH COUNTY, FLORIDA

ADMINISTRATIVE ORDER NO. 5.111–6/17

IN RE: PROCEDURES FOR TEMPORARY AND CONCURRENT CUSTODY PROCEEDINGS

Chapter 751 of the Florida Statutes provides for the temporary or concurrent custody of a minor child to an extended family member having physical custody of the minor child, to enable the custodian to provide for the welfare of and give complete care to the child. Temporary and concurrent custody proceedings are filed at the Main Judicial Center and the branch courthouses. Uniform procedures will ensure the timely disposition of the temporary and concurrent custody proceedings.

NOW, THEREFORE, pursuant to the authority conferred by Florida Rule of Judicial Administration 2.215, it is **ORDERED** as follows:

A. Case Filings.

1. Temporary and Concurrent Custody Petitions will be assigned in accordance with Administrative Order 5.101. If a related Domestic Relations case is identified at initial screening or on the Notice of Related Case Form, the Clerk of Court shall assign the newly filed case to the same division as the previous case.

2. The Clerk of Court shall forward Temporary and Concurrent Custody Petitions filed by self represented litigants to the case manager divisional email inboxes.

3. An internal case management review of the file will be undertaken by the Court prior to the setting of the Final Hearing on the Petition for Temporary or Concurrent Custody.

4. Pursuant to Fifteenth Judicial Circuit Administrative Order 5.307, a copy of a Live Birth Certificate for any minor child(ren) involved in a Petition for Temporary or Concurrent Custody must be filed in the case.

5. Pursuant to Fifteenth Judicial Circuit Administrative Order 5.109, a Date of Birth Form for all parties, including minor child(ren) involved in a Petition for Temporary or Concurrent Custody, must be filed in the case.

6. If the Petition for Temporary or Concurrent Custody is incomplete or requires additional information or documentation, the Court will enter a status order outlining the deficiencies or missing information.

7. Failure to comply with the Court's requirements on the status order could result in the dismissal of the case.

B. Hearing and Disposition of the Cases.

1. *Filings by Self Represented Litigants:* Upon completion of the case management review, the case manager will prepare an Order Setting Hearing on the Case.

2. *Filings by Attorneys:* A hearing is not to be requested unless there is compliance with the checklist attached as Exhibit A, a completed copy of which is to be filed, and the attorney believes that there is full compliance with Chapter 751. Requests for hearings are to be made in accordance with the Divisional Instructions.

DONE and **SIGNED** in Chambers at West Palm Beach, Palm Beach County, Florida, this 16 day of June, 2017.

Jeffrey Colbath
Chief Judge

[Exhibit "A"]

Case Name and Number:

CHECKLIST FOR PETITION FOR TEMPORARY OR CONCURRENT CUSTODY

I. PETITIONER QUALIFICATIONS:

___ A. Petitioner must be:

___ 1. An extended family member who has the signed, notarized consent of the child's legal parents. *See* § 751.02(1)(a).

- OR –

___ 2. An extended family member caring full time for the child and with whom the child is presently living. *See* § 751.02(1)(b).

___ B. If filing for concurrent custody, Petitioner must also:

___ 1. Currently have physical custody of the child and have had physical custody of the child for at least 10 days in any 30–day period within the last 12 months; *See* § 751.02(2)(a).

- AND –

___ 2. Not have signed, written document from a parent sufficient to enable the custodian to do all of the things necessary to care for the child which are available to custodians who have an order issued under section 751.05, Florida Statutes. *See* § 751.02(2)(b).

___ C. Extended family members include:

___ 1. A family member within the 3rd degree from the child, (brother, sister, grandparent, aunt, uncle, cousin, great grandparent, great aunt, great uncle). *See* § 751.011.

- OR –

___ 2. A stepparent currently married to the parent of the child and not a party to any lawsuit currently pending in any court involving one or both of the child's parents as an adverse party. *See* § 751.011,

II. THE PETITION:

___ A. Petitions for custody are styled "In the Interest of . . ., a minor child(ren)."

NOTE: It is acceptable if the child is referred to by his or her initials throughout the Petition. *See* Fla. R. Jud. Admin. 2.425.

___ B. The petition must be <u>signed</u> and <u>verified</u> and state the following:

___ 1. The name, date of birth, and current address of the child.

___ 2. The names and current addresses of the child's parents.

___ 3. The names and current addresses of the persons with whom the child has lived during the past 5 years.

___ 4. The places where the child has lived during the past 5 years.

___ 5. Information concerning any custody proceeding in this or any other state with respect to the child.

___ 6. The residence and post office address of the petitioner.

___ 7. The petitioner's relationship to the child.

___ 8. Any temporary or permanent orders for child support, the court entering the order, and the case number, if any.

___ 9. Any temporary or permanent orders for protection entered on behalf of or against either the petitioner, or the child, the court entering the order, and the case number.

___ 10. A statement that it is in the best interest of the child for the petitioner to have custody.

___ 11. A statement of the period of time the petitioner is requesting temporary custody, and a statement of the reasons supporting that request.

See § 751.03(1–13) and Florida Family Law Form 12.970(a).

___ C. If <u>concurrent</u> custody is being requested, the petition must also state:

___ 1. The time periods during the last 12 months that the child lived with the petitioner;

___ 2. The type of document, if any, provided by the parent(s) to enable the petitioner to act on behalf of the child;

___ 3. The services or actions that the petitioner is unable to obtain or undertake without an order of custody; AND

___ 4. Whether each parent has consented in writing to the entry of an order of concurrent custody.

See § 751.03(8).

___ D. If <u>temporary</u> custody is being requested, the petition must also state:

___ 1. Include the consent of the child's parents; or

___ 2. State the specific acts or omissions of the parents which demonstrate that the parents have abused, abandoned, or neglected the child as defined in Chapter 39.

See § 751.03(9).

III. ATTACHMENTS TO THE PETITION:

___ A. The birth parents' consent to the temporary or concurrent custody, and any documents that enable the petitioner to act on behalf of the child.

The consent should substantially follow the form of Florida Family Law Forms 12.970(c) or (d).

___ B. **If consent has NOT been provided,** notice (personal or constructive) must be given to the parents. *See* § 751.04.

___ 1. Proof of Service;

- OR –

___ 2. Affidavit of Diligent Search and Inquiry and proof of publication. *See* Florida Family Law Form 12.913(c) and Family Law Rule 12.070. All search inquiries must be conducted on the Affidavit of Diligent Search.

___ C. **If one of the parents of the child is deceased,** a certified copy of the death certificate.

___ D. **If either parent files an answer and objects to a temporary custody petition,** a hearing must be set for the court to determine whether the child's parents are unfit to provide for the care and control of the child. The court must find that the parent has abused, abandoned, or neglected the child as defined in Chapter 39. § 751.05(3)(b).

If a parent objects to a concurrent custody petition, the petitioner has the option of converting the petition to a petition for temporary custody. § 751.05(3)(a).

___ E. A copy of the child's birth certificate.

___ F. A Uniform Child Custody Jurisdiction and Enforcement Act Affidavit. *See* § 61.503(3) and § 61.522. *See also* Florida Family Law Form 12.902(d).

___ G. **If an order was granted by another court** in this, or any other state, concerning the custody of the child, that order must be attached to the petition.

___ H. A Notice of Related Cases Form. *See* Florida Family Law Form 12.900(h).

___ I. A Family Court Cover Sheet. *See* Florida Family Law Form 12.928.

___ J. If obtaining a **default** on petitions that have been served, a **Non–Military Affidavit.** *See* Florida Family Law Form 12.912(b). If petitioner knows or does not know whether the parent is on active duty, petitioner must file a **Memorandum for Certificate of Military Service**. *See* Florida Family Law Form 12.912(a).

___ K. **If a non-lawyer helps the petitioner complete the forms,** that person must provide a copy of a Disclosure from Nonlawyer. *See* Florida Family Law Form 12.900(a).

Adopted effective June 16, 2017.

Domestic Relations Pretrial/Trial

5.201. UNIFORM MOTION CALENDAR PRACTICE IN UNIFIED FAMILY COURT

IN THE CIRCUIT COURT OF THE FIFTEENTH JUDICIAL CIRCUIT IN AND FOR PALM BEACH COUNTY, FLORIDA

ADMINISTRATIVE ORDER 5.201–6/15 *

IN RE: UNIFORM MOTION CALENDAR PRACTICE IN UNIFIED FAMILY COURT

The Family Court Judges, in accordance with Local Rule No. 4, have specified that Uniform Motion Calendar (UMC) shall be held by all family divisions.

NOW, THEREFORE, pursuant to the authority conferred by Florida Rule of Judicial Administration 2.215, it is **ORDERED** as follows:

1. Uniform Motion Calendar (hereinafter referenced as "UMC") shall occur weekly in the Family Divisions of the Circuit Court of the Fifteenth Judicial Circuit pursuant to the following general schedule which is subject to adjustment based upon each particular Judge's calendar and conflicts. Please refer to paragraph 7 for detailed divisional schedules.

2. The purpose of the UMC is to provide a forum in which to resolve non-evidentiary procedural motions and uncontested Family Division proceedings, such as dissolution of marriage actions, within the framework of hearings that do not exceed 10 minutes.

a. Contested proceedings including dissolution of marriage, paternity, support, custody, time-sharing and non-routine non-evidentiary motions are not appropriate to be scheduled on UMC and will not be heard during the UMC.

b. Matters that will exceed 10 minutes, which time includes reviewing documents and motions as well as time for argument, must be scheduled for a special set hearing.

3. All non-evidentiary/procedural motions scheduled for the UMC must contain a "good-faith" certification in either the motion or notice of hearing verifying that a good faith effort has been made to contact the opposing attorney or the opposing *pro se* party to discuss and make an effort to resolve by agreement the issues framed for hearing prior to filing the notice of hearing on said motion. Failure to adhere to this requirement may result in the motion being stricken from the UMC and/or the imposition of sanctions, in the court's discretion. The court may waive this "good-faith" certification requirement.

4. No attorneys or *pro se* parties are permitted to cross-notice or "piggyback" one motion upon a previously scheduled motion set by the opposing side, unless (a) both sides agree and (b) the maximum time limit of 10 minutes per case set forth hereinabove will not be exceeded.

a. The Court will only allow a maximum of 3 (three) motions in one given case to be set.

b. If time permits, the court in its discretion may, however, defer the hearings on any cross-noticed motions which both sides have agreed may be heard but which cannot be dealt with in the 10 minute time limit until all other motions scheduled on UMC related to other cases have been addressed.

c. If time permits the court may elect to address the cross-noticed motion.

d. The court reserves the option of taking certain UMC motions out of order based upon emergent or exigent scheduling or other circumstances.

5. Each moving party is obligated to bring an order that can be completed by the Circuit Judge or General Magistrate during the hearing reflecting his or her ruling together with the appropriate pre-addressed, stamped return envelopes. If the court requires that a more detailed order be prepared, the attorney who is directed to prepare the order shall do so and submit same within 5 working days of said hearing together with the appropriate pre-addressed, stamped return envelopes unless the Judge or General Magistrate has indicated in their divisional instructions that proposed orders may be sent by email.

6. No Motions for Reconsideration, Motions for Rehearing or Motions for Clarification are permitted on the UMC Docket. Please refer to Local Rule 6 for more information.

7. The UMC Schedule for the Family Divisions of this Circuit is as follows:

a. Central County Courthouse:

1) Division "FA"
Wednesday: 8:30 a.m.–10:00 a.m.

2) Divisions "FC" & "FD"
Tuesday, Wednesday, and Thursday
8:45 a.m.–9:30 a.m.

b. North County Courthouse:

1) Division "FH"
Tuesday and Wednesday
8:30 a.m.–9:15 a.m.

2) Division "FI"
Tuesday and Wednesday
8:45 a.m.–9:30 a.m.

3) Divisions "FJ"
Tuesday and Wednesday
8:45 a.m.–9:30 a.m.

c. South County Courthouse **(all divisions):**
Tuesday, Wednesday and Thursday
8:45 a.m.–9:30 a.m.

d. West County Courthouse **(Division FW)**
Wednesday: 1:45 p.m.–2:30 p.m.

8. To obtain the UMC schedule for the UFC Magistrates, please refer to each Magistrate's webpage for divisional instructions.

9. The above-described UMC schedule is subject to change. Prior to scheduling any UMC Calendar hearing, attorneys and their staff should consult the Fifteenth Judicial Circuit's website (www.15thcircuit.com) to review the judge's calendar suspension dates.

DONE AND ORDERED in Chambers at West Palm Beach, Palm Beach County, Florida this 5 day of June, 2015.

Jeffrey Colbath
Chief Judge

Adopted effective May 21, 2009. Amended effective November 6, 2009; June 5, 2015.

* supersedes admin. order 5.201–11/09

5.202. MOTIONS TO COMPEL DISCOVERY IN FAMILY LAW CASES

IN THE CIRCUIT COURT OF THE FIFTEENTH JUDICIAL CIRCUIT IN AND FOR PALM BEACH COUNTY, FLORIDA

ADMINISTRATIVE ORDER NO. 5.202–5/09 *

IN RE: MOTIONS TO COMPEL DISCOVERY IN FAMILY LAW CASES

Pursuant to the authority conferred by Florida Rule of Judicial Administration 2.215, it is **ORDERED** as follows:

1. Hearings on Motions to Compel Discovery: No motions to compel discovery will be heard unless the motion or notice of hearing contains a "good-faith" certification by the moving counsel or moving *pro se* party to the effect that he or she has already contacted opposing counsel or the opposing party, if that party is unrepresented, and attempted to resolve the discovery dispute without a hearing, but that the matter could not be resolved.

2. Ex Parte Motion to Compel: When a motion to compel discovery alleges a complete failure to respond or object to discovery and affirmatively states that no timely request for extension of time has been served, an ex parte order on the motion may be entered by the court which requires compliance with the original discovery demand within 10 days of the signing of the order. No hearing is required. The moving part shall submit a proposed order along with a copy of the motion to compel directly to the court along addressed, stamped envelopes for the court's consideration. A copy of all materials provided to the court in accordance with this rule shall be timely provided by the moving party to opposing counsel or the opposing party, if that party is unrepresented.

DONE and **SIGNED** in Chambers at West Palm Beach, Palm Beach County, Florida, this 21 day of May, 2009.

Kathleen J. Kroll
Chief Judge

Adopted effective May 21, 2009.

* supersedes admin. order 5.011

5.203. EMERGENCY MATTERS IN FAMILY LAW CASES

IN THE CIRCUIT COURT OF THE FIFTEENTH JUDICIAL CIRCUIT IN AND FOR PALM BEACH COUNTY, FLORIDA

ADMINISTRATIVE ORDER NO. 5.203–1/17 *

IN RE: EMERGENCY MATTERS IN FAMILY LAW CASES

Pursuant to the authority conferred by Florida Rule of Judicial Administration 2.215, it is **ORDERED** as follows:

1. Requests for emergency hearings or emergency relief shall be decided by each judge on the Emergency Motion alone. Upon receiving a request for an emergency hearing or emergency relief, the judge shall decide whether an emergency exists, and if so, shall schedule a hearing, enter any ex parte order deemed necessary, or take any other appropriate action.

2. Motions for Emergency Hearings will be denied unless there are sufficient allegations to establish that there is:

a. An imminent risk of substantial physical harm to a minor child; or

b. A child is about to be illegally removed from this Court's jurisdiction.

3. Motions for Child Pick Up, regardless of whether titled "emergency", will be treated as an emergency matter.

4. Motions for immediate payment of child support and/or alimony or for timesharing usually do not meet the standard for emergency relief.

DONE and **SIGNED** in Chambers at West Palm Beach, Palm Beach County, Florida, this 24 day of January, 2017.

Jeffrey Colbath
Chief Judge

Adopted effective May 21, 2009. Amended effective January 24, 2017.

* supersedes admin, order 5.203–5/09

5.204. PREPARATION OF JUDGMENTS AND ORDERS

IN THE CIRCUIT COURT OF THE FIFTEENTH JUDICIAL CIRCUIT IN AND FOR PALM BEACH COUNTY, FLORIDA

ADMINISTRATIVE ORDER 5.204–5/09 *

IN RE: PREPARATION OF JUDGMENTS AND ORDERS

Pursuant to the authority conferred by Florida Rule of Judicial Administration 2.215, it is **ORDERED** as follows:

A. Preparation of Orders and Judgments.

1. When instructed by the court to prepare an order or judgment, the designated attorney or *pro se* party shall submit the proposed order or judgment within 5 business days unless ordered otherwise.

2. A copy of the proposed order or judgment shall be mailed, hand-delivered, emailed or faxed to the opposing attorney or *pro se* party for review.

3. The proposed order or judgment submitted to the court shall be accompanied by a transmittal letter or memo confirming that opposing counsel or *pro se* party approved the contents thereof or alternatively, confirming that 5 business days have expired since the proposed order or judgment has been submitted to the opposing attorney or *pro se* party and that no response was received objecting to same.

B. Objections to Proposed Orders or Judgments.

1. Should the opposing attorney or *pro se* party object to a proposed order or judgment prepared by the designated attorney or *pro se* party, the objection letter or memo from the designated attorney or *pro se* party shall issue immediately and indicate that:

a. there is an objection;

b. identify the objection; and

c. submit an alternate proposed order or judgment within 5 business days.

2. If the objecting attorney or *pro se* party fails to submit the alternated proposed order within that time fame, then, the court may in its discretion construe the objection as abandoned and proceed to enter the proposed order.

3. Alternatively, the court may, in its discretion, enter the order or judgment it deems accurately reflects the *ore tenus* ruling; require the parties to share the initial cost of furnishing a transcript or record of the hearing {but reserving jurisdiction to reassess as appropriate between the parties} to the court to help reconcile the conflict within 10 business days and/or schedule a hearing on the objection to resolve the dispute. This is the exclusive remedy to address the objection.

4. In no event may an attorney or *pro se* party schedule a hearing during the U.M.C. Calendar to determine the correct form of the disputed proposed order or judgment.

C. Title—Representation as to Accuracy.

1. The title of every order or judgment submitted shall identify the subject matter thereof pursuant to Florida Rules of Civil Procedure, Rule 1.100.

2. The submission of a proposed order or judgment to a Circuit Judge or General Magistrate shall constitute a representation that the submitting attorney or *pro se* party has read it, and that it accurately sets forth the findings and ruling of the court.

D. Pages.

1. Each page of the proposed order judgment shall contain a header reflecting the style of the case, the case number as well as the page number.

2. No order or judgment shall contain a signature page that does not include a portion of the text of the order or judgment.

E. Copies and Envelopes.

1. The designated attorney or *pro se* party preparing the proposed order or judgment shall include the names **and** addresses of the opposing attorney or if none, the *pro se* party.

2. The designated attorney or *pro se* party preparing the proposed order or judgment shall also furnish the court with a sufficient number of copies and stamped, pre-addressed envelopes for service of the order or judgment.

DONE and **SIGNED** in Chambers at West Palm Beach, Palm Beach County, Florida, this 21 day of May, 2009.

Kathleen J. Kroll
Chief Judge

Adopted effective May 21, 2009.

* supersedes admin. order 5.013–9/92

5.205. UNCONTESTED MATTERS

IN THE CIRCUIT COURT OF THE FIFTEENTH JUDICIAL CIRCUIT IN AND FOR PALM BEACH COUNTY, FLORIDA

ADMINISTRATIVE ORDER NO. 5.205–5/09 *

IN RE: UNCONTESTED MATTERS

Pursuant to the authority conferred by Florida Rule of Judicial Administration 2.215, it is **ORDERED** as follows:

1. Uncontested Dissolutions. Uncontested dissolutions include only those cases where the parties have entered into a written property settlement agreement or a default has been entered or an answer and waiver has been filed, and minimal testimony taking five minutes or less to present is required relative to parental responsibility, time-sharing, child support or alimony.

2. Final Hearings on Uncontested Dissolutions.

a. Final hearings on uncontested dissolutions of marriage are heard during the uniform motion calendar (See Administrative Order 5.201).

b. It is the responsibility of the party noticing the matter for final hearing to send a copy of the Notice of Final Hearing to the uniform motion calendar clerk no less than four (4) business days before the uncontested final hearing, so that the file will be available at the final hearing.

c. Any default, answer or waiver being relied upon must be contained in the court file when presented to the judge at final hearing.

d. The following shall be submitted to the Court at the conclusion of the Final Hearing:

1) Final Judgment (original and sufficient number of copies for the parties)

2) Income Deduction Order (original and sufficient number of copies for the parties)

3) Notice to Payor (original and sufficient number of copies for the parties)

4) Support Information Sheet (S.I.S. form)

5) Final Disposition forms

6) Pre-addressed, stamped envelopes for the parties

7) Pre-addressed, stamped envelope to the Payor with sufficient postage to transmit the Notice to Payor via CERTIFIED United States Mail—RETURN RECEIPT REQUESTED.

3. **Simplified Dissolutions.**

a. Each judge hearing such matters shall set aside time each week to hear simplified and uncontested *pro se* dissolutions of marriage.

b. Such hearings shall be scheduled by the Unified Family Court Case Manager.

c. Before final hearing, the parties to every uncontested *pro se* dissolution of marriage involving minor children shall mediate all issues pertaining to child custody, support, and time-sharing with the family mediator in the Alternative Dispute Resolution Office, Room 6.2100, Central County Courthouse unless the parties have already signed a written settlement agreement resolving all of the issues involved in the case.

d. A signed mediation or settlement agreement shall be presented to the Court at final hearing and shall contain within it, or have attached to it, a parenting plan consistent with the minimum requirements of Florida law.

4. **Uncontested Adoptions.** Uncontested adoptions must be scheduled with judicial assistant.

5. **Name Changes.**

a. Petitions for change of name shall be submitted to the assigned judge for consideration on an *ex-parte* basis. A Final Disposition Form and pre-addressed stamped envelopes shall also be included.

b. The judge will schedule a hearing after reviewing the court file, should one be necessary.

DONE and **SIGNED** in Chambers at West Palm Beach, Palm Beach County, Florida, this 21 day of May, 2009.

Kathleen J. Kroll
Chief Judge

Adopted effective May 21, 2009.

* supersedes admin. order 5.004–10/03

5.206. MOTION AND EVIDENTIARY HEARINGS

IN THE CIRCUIT COURT OF THE FIFTEENTH JUDICIAL CIRCUIT IN AND FOR PALM BEACH COUNTY, FLORIDA

ADMINISTRATIVE ORDER NO. 5.206–5/09 *

IN RE: MOTION AND EVIDENTIARY HEARINGS

Pursuant to the authority conferred by Florida Rule of Judicial Administration 2.215, it is **ORDERED** as follows:

1. Each judge shall set aside time each week for hearing motions requiring presentation of evidence which is too complex for consideration on the Uniform Motion Calendar.

2. The moving party shall reserve hearing time with the judicial assistant. No moving party may reserve more than one hour for a motion hearing without court approval. The judicial assistant will obtain the files in advance for these hearings.

3. A party may request a hearing requiring more than one hour by

a. filing a "Request for Hearing in Excess of One Hour" with the clerk, and providing a copy of the request to the court's judicial assistant; or

b. filing a motion requesting more than one hour of hearing time and then setting that motion for hearing on the Court's Uniform Motion Calendar. Any request or motion requesting a hearing in excess of one hour shall include a good-faith estimate of the time required to complete the hearing on the substantive motion and an explanation as to why the additional time is necessary.

4. Scheduled hearings may be cancelled only upon

a. filing of a Notice of Withdrawal of the motion; or

b. settlement of the underlying motion along with the submission of a proposed agreed order on the motion to the Judge prior to the scheduled hearing; or

c. entry of a order cancelling the hearing by the judge.

5. Should the matter settle prior to hearing, it is the responsibility of the moving party to immediately submit the proposed agreed order and to inform the judicial assistant so that the hearing time may be used for another purpose.

6. A party shall not cross-notice or "piggyback" a motion upon a previously scheduled motion set by opposing counsel, unless both parties agree, the time originally reserved for the hearing will be adequate to hear both motion, and the Court, in its discretion, elects to hear the cross-noticed or "piggy backed" matter.

DONE and **SIGNED** in Chambers at West Palm Beach, Palm Beach County, Florida, this 21 day of May, 2009.

Kathleen J. Kroll
Chief Judge

Adopted effective May 21, 2009.

* supersedes admin. order 5.005–9/92

5.207. TEMPORARY RELIEF IN FAMILY DIVISION

IN THE CIRCUIT COURT OF THE FIFTEENTH JUDICIAL CIRCUIT IN AND FOR PALM BEACH COUNTY, FLORIDA

ADMINISTRATIVE ORDER NO. 5.207–10/10 *

IN RE: TEMPORARY RELIEF IN FAMILY DIVISION

1. All temporary relief issues, including but not limited to support, time-sharing, equitable distribution, residence, fees, and costs shall be scheduled on the court's evidentiary motion calendar.

2. Temporary relief hearings will be scheduled for not more than thirty (30) minutes per case unless otherwise ordered by the court.

3. No temporary relief hearing shall be set unless the parties have first submitted to mediation and an impasse has been reported.

4. Failure to appear for mediation when scheduled shall result in the imposition of costs upon one or both of the parties. Once set, the mediation date cannot be changed without agreement of both parties or order of the court. Temporary relief settlements shall immediately be reduced to writing and signed by both parties. The settlement agreement shall then be submitted to the Court along with a proposed order approving the settlement.

5. Temporary relief hearings may be canceled only upon order of the judge (including following settlement).

6. The order scheduling mediation and a temporary relief hearing shall be prepared by counsel.

7. Should both parties file temporary relief applications, the matters shall be heard at the same time unless the Court deems it impracticable. Hearings on subsequent applications for temporary relief shall be set with authorization of the assigned judge.

DONE and **SIGNED** in Chambers at West Palm Beach, Palm Beach County, Florida, this 21 day of October, 2010.

Peter D. Blanc
Chief Judge

Adopted effective May 21, 2009. Amended effective October 21, 2010.

* supersedes admin. order no. 5.207–5/09

5.208. FAMILY MEDIATION

IN THE CIRCUIT COURT OF THE FIFTEENTH JUDICIAL CIRCUIT IN AND FOR PALM BEACH COUNTY, FLORIDA

ADMINISTRATIVE ORDER NO. 5.208–12/17 *

IN RE: FAMILY MEDIATION

Pursuant to the authority conferred by Florida Rules of Judicial Administration 2.215, it is **ORDERED** as follows:

1. All parties, whether **self-represented** or represented by counsel, are encouraged to seek such mediation and resolution prior to initiating any legal action through the Court.

2. Court personnel will set matters for mediation at the instruction of the presiding judge.

3. In cases where minor children are involved, mediators will prepare an appropriate parenting plan, a child support guidelines work sheet, and calculate child support (with allocation if more than one minor child is involved) and attach the child support guidelines worksheet to the signed settlement agreement.

4. The parties are to share the costs of such mediation as provided for by Florida law.

5. Parties may elect to use a private mediator, certified in family mediation for mediation of any matter. If the parties' income statutorily permits, they shall be eligible to receive the services of the family mediation department of the Alternative Dispute Resolution Office (Administrative Order 2.801–9/08 as amended) to reach an amicable settlement of the issues or controversy.

DONE and **SIGNED** in Chambers at West Palm Beach, Palm Beach County, Florida, this 18 day of December, 2017.

Krista Marx
Chief Judge

Adopted effective May 21, 2009. Amended effective December 18, 2017.

* supersedes admin. order no. 5.208–5/09

5.209. TRIAL SCHEDULING IN UNIFIED FAMILY COURT—FAMILY DIVISION

IN THE CIRCUIT COURT OF THE FIFTEENTH JUDICIAL CIRCUIT IN AND FOR PALM BEACH COUNTY, FLORIDA

ADMINISTRATIVE ORDER 5.209–5/09 *

IN RE: TRIAL SCHEDULING IN UNIFIED FAMILY COURT—FAMILY DIVISION

Pursuant to the authority conferred by Florida Rule of Judicial Administration 2.215, it is **ORDERED** as follows:

1. A pending action shall be scheduled for non-jury trial by filing an original notice or motion to set cause for non-jury trial with the Clerk, with copies served on the opposing side, the presiding Circuit Judge or General Magistrate, and if appropriate, the attorney ad litem, guardian ad litem and any attorney who has noticed a charging lien in the action to be scheduled for non-jury trial.

2. The notice or motion to set cause for non-jury trial shall be in writing and shall:

a. Identify the relevant pleadings to be disposed of by title and date, any ancillary motions that the party desires be heard in conjunction therewith;

b. A certification that the pleadings are "closed" and that the action is ripe and ready to be set for non-jury trial;

c. A realistic time estimate for the non-jury trial.

3. Pre-addressed, stamped envelopes for the persons identified in paragraph 1 above shall be attached to the Court's copy of the notice or motion to set cause for non-jury trial.

4. The Circuit Judge or General Magistrate may, sua sponte or in consultation with one another or the case manager, issue an order scheduling non-jury trial. A pre-hearing or case management conference or calendar call may be used by the Circuit Judge or General Magistrate when scheduling the non-jury trial.

5. Attorneys, attorneys ad litem, and guardians ad litem may file a Notice of Unavailability advising the court of any trial, vacation and other relevant conflicts, if known and/or as same arise.

6. An attorney or pro se party may seek the entry of a pretrial order by the Circuit Judge or General Magistrate by including that request in the notice or motion to set cause for non-jury trial, or by filing a separate motion seeking same.

7. Non-jury trials shall be scheduled for a specific day and time whenever possible.

8. Once a non-jury trial is scheduled it will not be cancelled unless:

a. the action is voluntarily dismissed; or

b. a written settlement agreement accompanied by an order disposing of the matter which shall be submitted to the Circuit Judge for signature {or in the case of the General Magistrate for review and for submission to the Circuit Judge}. The Order must be accompanied by a Final Disposition form to ensure the Clerk's closure of the pending action on its docket; or

c. upon motion properly noticed for disposition on the Uniform Motion Calendar and in conformity with the Florida Rules of Civil Procedure; or

d. upon emergency or such other circumstance that within the discretion of the presiding Circuit Judge or General Magistrate is an appropriate basis for cancellation.

DONE AND ORDERED at West Palm Beach, Palm Beach County, Florida this 21 day of May, 2009.

Kathleen J. Kroll
Chief Judge

Adopted effective May 21, 2009.

* supersedes admin. order 5.008–9/92

5.210. INTERPRETERS AND DOCUMENT TRANSLATION IN FAMILY DIVISION CASES

IN THE CIRCUIT COURT OF THE FIFTEENTH JUDICIAL CIRCUIT IN AND FOR PALM BEACH COUNTY, FLORIDA

ADMINISTRATIVE ORDER NO. 5.210–5/09 *

IN RE: INTERPRETERS AND DOCUMENT TRANSLATION IN FAMILY DIVISION CASES

NOW, THEREFORE, pursuant to the authority conferred by Florida Rule of Judicial Administration 2.215, it is **ORDERED** as follows:

1. Interpreters for hearings and/or trials:

a. The Fifteenth Circuit does not provide interpreters for non-English speaking parties or witnesses in Family Division, Unified Family Court hearings. An attorney or *pro se* party is responsible for providing a disinterested, qualified interpreter at a hearing or trial to interpret for the non-English speaking party and/or witness(es). See Administrative Order 2.506–9/08 (as amended).

b. For each appearance before the Court, the interpreter shall file a notice of appearance which shall include his or her name, business address, telephone number and credentials as well as the name of the person who initially retained the interpreter.

c. The attorney or *pro se* party seeking to utilize the interpreter has the burden of

1) demonstrating the interpreter's disinterest;

2) demonstrating the interpreter's qualifications; and

3) bearing the responsibility for initial payment of the fees and costs associated with the interpreter's services, subject to those fees and costs being assessed by the Court between the parties as appropriate.

2. Interpreters for Documents:

a. Any documents written in a language other than English which a party seeks to introduce into evidence at a hearing or trial, must be accompanied by a verbatim translation of the document.

b. If made by a United States Embassy or Consulate employee, agent or representative or by some other qualified, certified interpreter, the appropriate documentation corroborating the authenticity of the translation, including a certificate stating his or her name, business address and telephone number, credentials and the name of the person initially retaining the interpreter to perform the translation.

DONE and **SIGNED** in Chambers at West Palm Beach, Palm Beach County, Florida, this 21 day of May, 2009.

Kathleen J. Kroll
Chief Judge

Adopted effective May 21, 2009.

* supersedes admin. order 5.019–9/92

5.211. PETITIONS FOR MODIFICATION

IN THE CIRCUIT COURT OF THE FIFTEENTH JUDICIAL CIRCUIT IN AND FOR PALM BEACH COUNTY, FLORIDA

ADMINISTRATIVE ORDER 5.211–5/09 *

IN RE: PETITIONS FOR MODIFICATION

Pursuant to the authority conferred by Florida Rule of Judicial Administration 2.215, it is **ORDERED** as follows:

1. Petitions for Modification must be filed with the clerk along with the appropriate filing fee, if applicable, and served on the opposing party.

2. Such petitions shall carry the same case number as the final judgment or order for which modification is sought, and shall remain assigned to the same division where that final judgment or order was obtained unless a divisional reassignment has occurred pursuant to Administrative Order 5.101–1/09 (as amended) or 5.102–9/08 (as amended).

DONE AND ORDERED at West Palm Beach, Palm Beach County, Florida this 21 day of May, 2009.

Kathleen J. Kroll
Chief Judge

Adopted effective May 21, 2009.

* supersedes admin. order 5.007–9/92

5.212. ORDER TO ATTEND PARENT EDUCATION AND FAMILY STABILIZATION COURSE

IN THE CIRCUIT COURT OF THE FIFTEENTH JUDICIAL CIRCUIT IN AND FOR PALM BEACH COUNTY, FLORIDA

ADMINISTRATIVE ORDER NO. 5.212–2/17 *

IN RE: ORDER TO ATTEND PARENT EDUCATION AND FAMILY STABILIZATION COURSE, AND TO FILE FINANCIAL DISCLOSURE AND CHILD SUPPORT GUIDELINE WORKSHEET IN PATERNITY & DISSOLUTION OF MARRIAGE CASES WITH MINOR CHILDREN

Florida Statute §§ 61.21(4), (5) and (9), Florida Statute § 61.30(1)(a), and Florida Family Law Rule of Procedure 12.285(b)(2), (e), and (k), require that parties to a dissolution of marriage proceeding with minor children or a paternity action that involves issues of parental responsibility are required to complete the Parent Education and Family Stabilization Course prior to the entry of a final judgment by the court. Each party is also required to file and serve a completed notarized Financial Affidavit and Child Support Guidelines Worksheet in order for the Court to determine and award child support for a minor child.

NOW, THEREFORE, pursuant to the authority conferred by Florida Rule of Judicial Administration 2.215, it is **ORDERED** as follows:

1. All parties to dissolution of marriage proceeding with minor children or a paternity action that involves issues of parental responsibility shall attend and complete the Parent Education and Family Stabilization Course approved by the Florida Department of Children and Families.

2. A list of approved providers of such courses may be found at either the Palm Beach County Law Library or the Clerk and Comptroller's website at http://www.mypalmbeachclerk.com/divorce.aspx. This list may also be found on the Florida Department of Children and Families website at: http://www.dcf.state.fl.us/programs/childwelfare/stabilization/.

3. For dissolution of marriage actions, the petitioner must complete the course within 45 days after the filing of the petition, and all other parties must complete the course within 45 days after service of the petition unless excused by the court. For paternity actions, the petitioner must complete the course within 45 days after filing the petition, and any other party must complete the course within 45 days after an acknowledgment of paternity by that party, an adjudication of paternity of that party, or an order granting time-sharing to or support from that party unless excused by the court. The parties shall be responsible for the course fees.

4. Both the Petitioner and the Respondent, or their legal counsel, must each file a "Certificate of Attendance" with the Clerk of the Court immediately after completing the class and prior to entry of a final judgment in the case. Unless the trial judge excuses a party from attending for good cause, a final judgment will not be issued until the Certificate of Attendance for both parties has been filed with the Clerk's Office.

5. The requirement to attend the course may be waived in appropriate circumstances, including instances where the parties are attending or have already completed a parenting program approved by the Florida Department of Children and Families, and the trial judge concludes that a repeat attendance is unnecessary. Any party seeking to be excused from attendance, for good cause, must file a written motion alleging the grounds constituting good cause. Unless excused by court order, the Court may hold any parent failing to attend the required course in contempt, or may order that the parent be denied shared parental responsibility or visitation, or may otherwise sanction that parent as the Court deems appropriate.

6. Nothing in this Order shall be construed to require the parties to attend an approved parenting course together.

7. Nothing in this Order shall prohibit judges from ordering parties to attend a parenting course in cases not subject to this Order.

8. Each party shall file and serve a completed, notarized Financial Affidavit in substantial conformity with Florida Family Law Rules of Procedure Form 12.902(b), if the party's gross income is less than $50,000.00 or Florida Family Rules of Procedure Form 12.902(c), if the party's gross annual income is $50,000.00 or greater.

9. The parties shall file and serve a complete Child Support Guidelines Worksheet in substantial conformity with Florida Family Law Rules of Procedure Form 12.902(e).

10. The parties cannot waive the requirement that Financial Affidavits and a Child Support Guidelines Worksheet be filed and served. No Final Judgment determining child custody and visitation may be entered absent determination of child support and child support may not be determined without the information required to be disclosed in the Financial Affidavits and Child Support Guidelines Worksheet.

11. The Financial Affidavits and Child Support Guidelines Worksheet must be served within forty-five (45) days of service of the petition on Respondent but, in any event, at least five (5) days before Court ordered mediation, absent agreement of the parties in writing or Court order.

12. In cases affected by this Order, the Clerk & Comptroller shall advise the parties of the requirements of this Order and instructions and information on how to access a list of providers by:

a. Posting the "Notice of Requirement" provided by Court Administration in all Self Help and Family Clerk of Court locations.

b. Providing a link on the Clerk & Comptroller's website to the Florida Department of Children and Families website for a list of approved providers.

13. In cases in which the petitioning party is self-represented (pro se), or the pro se parties (Petitioner and Respondent) have waived service of process, the Clerk & Comptroller shall distribute this Administrative Order as follows:

a. If the filing party appears at the Clerk's Office at the time of filling, the Clerk shall provide a copy of this Administrative Order to the filing party and shall mail a copy to the responding party with a preaddressed stamped envelope provided to the Clerk by the filing party.

b. If both parties appear at time of filing, the Clerk shall provide a copy of this AO to both parties at such time.

c. If the filing party mails the petition to the Clerk's office for filing, the filing party shall include self addressed stamped envelopes so that the Clerk can forward copies of this AO to the Petitioner and Respondent. If the Petitioner fails to provide envelopes, the clerk shall nevertheless forward copies of this AO to the Petitioner and Respondent.

d. In cases in which the self-represented (pro se) parties, have designated a proper email address and have opted into email service, the Clerk & Comptroller may furnish this Administrative Order via Electronic Mail to the self-represented (pro se) party.

e. The Clerk & Comptroller shall docket a single copy of this Administrative Order in the court file.

14. In cases where the petitioning party is self-represented (pro se), and the Clerk & Comptroller has forwarded the petition directly to the Palm Beach County Sheriff for service, the Clerk & Comptroller shall also provide a copy of this Administrative Order, along with the summons, to the Sheriff for service upon the Respondent. The Clerk & Comptroller shall docket a single copy of this Administrative Order in the court file.

15. In cases where the petitioning party is represented by counsel at the time of case initiation, a copy of this Administrative Order shall be electronically filed at the time the Petition is filed. A copy of this Administrative Order shall also accompany the summons to be served on the Respondent. Failure to include this Administrative Order with the summons will not affect the validity of service of the Petition.

16. A copy of this Administrative Order, which is to be included with the service packet for the respondent, can be found on the Fifteenth Judicial Circuit website at www.15thcircuit.com/adminorders. Petitioner's attorney shall be responsible for establishing that Respondent was provided with a copy of this Administrative order.

DONE AND SIGNED in Chambers at West Palm Beach, Palm Beach County, Florida, this 21 day of February, 2017.

Jeffrey J. Colbath
Chief Judge

Adopted effective January 2, 2014. Amended effective September 9, 2014; November 8, 2016; February 21, 2017.

* supersedes admin. order 5.212–11/16

Alimony, Child Support, and Time Sharing

5.301. ARREARAGE CALCULATION REQUIREMENT

IN THE CIRCUIT COURT OF THE FIFTEENTH JUDICIAL CIRCUIT IN AND FOR PALM BEACH COUNTY, FLORIDA

ADMINISTRATIVE ORDER NO. 5.301–5/09 *

IN RE: ARREARAGE CALCULATION REQUIREMENT

Pursuant to the authority conferred by Florida Rule of Judicial Administration 2.215, it is **ORDERED** as follows:

1. Payments made through the Florida State Disbursement Unit.

a. In any action to enforce the payment of an alleged arrearage in child support, alimony or any other monetary court ordered payment term, if the term(s) are payable through Florida State Disbursement Unit (i.e. .S.D.U.) then, in that event, a certified copy of the Family Law Case History (a/k/a C.S.E. Ledger) is presumptively valid for purposes of establishing the arrearage balance(s). It is the burden of the moving party to present a current, certified copy of the C.S.E. Ledger to the court at hearing.

b. If, however, direct payments were made toward these term(s), rather than through S.D.U., then, in that event, it is the obligation of the moving party to provide a written calculation identifying the date(s), amount(s) paid and to provide copies of documents corroborating the direct payments to the opposing attorney or *pro se* party no less than five (5) days prior to the evidentiary hearing.

2. Direct payments.

a. In any action to enforce the payment of an alleged arrearage in child support, alimony or any other monetary court ordered payment term, if the term(s) are payable directly rather than through S.D.U., it is the burden of the moving party to provide a written calculation sheet reflecting the manner in which the arrearage was calculated, plus interest due if sought.

b. The arrearage calculation sheet shall identify the date(s) and amount(s) of non-payment. A copy of such arrearage and interest calculation sheet shall be presented to the opposing attorney or *pro se* party no less than 5 days prior to evidentiary hearing thereon, and the court at hearing.

3. Failure to adhere to the requirements of this Administrative Order may, in the discretion of the Court, result in a denial or a deferral of a hearing on the request for the relief sought by the moving party.

DONE and **SIGNED** in Chambers at West Palm Beach, Palm Beach County, Florida, this 21 day of May, 2009.

Kathleen J. Kroll
Chief Judge

Adopted effective May 21, 2009.

* supersedes admin. order 5.010–10/03

5.302. REDIRECTION OF CHILD SUPPORT PAYMENTS

IN THE CIRCUIT COURT OF THE FIFTEENTH JUDICIAL CIRCUIT IN AND FOR PALM BEACH COUNTY, FLORIDA

ADMINISTRATIVE ORDER NO. 5.302–5/09 *

IN RE: REDIRECTION OF CHILD SUPPORT PAYMENTS

Pursuant to the authority conferred by Florida Rule of Judicial Administration 2.215, it is **ORDERED** as follows:

1. State Disbursement Unit, upon receipt of payment of child support for a child for whom payments are being made as Temporary Assistance to Needy Families (TANF) or for whom the services of the Child Support Enforcement Unit have been retained, shall transmit the support payment, less the service fee, to the Department of Revenue. Department of Revenue shall have the right to serve as complainant in any enforcement proceeding so long as the department provides such support.

2. The Department of Revenue shall file with the clerk an affidavit stating when aid or services covered in Paragraph 1 are being provided and attach thereto an Acknowledgment of Assignment of Rights to Support or a Contract and Power of Attorney, signed by the recipient of the services.

3. Upon termination of the payments or services, the Department of Revenue shall file a notice of cancellation, and the State Disbursement Unit shall thereafter forward the support received to the person designated to receive said support pursuant to the Order of support in said action.

4. Payments received by the State Disbursement Unit are to be allocated pursuant to Florida Statutes.

DONE and **SIGNED** in Chambers at West Palm Beach, Palm Beach County, Florida, this 21 day of May, 2009.

Kathleen J. Kroll
Chief Judge

Adopted effective May 21, 2009.

* supersedes admin. order 5.016–10/03

5.303. TIME STANDARDS FOR POST JUDGMENT ENFORCEMENT ORDERS IN TITLE IV/DEPARTMENT OF REVENUE CASES

IN THE CIRCUIT COURT OF THE FIFTEENTH JUDICIAL CIRCUIT IN AND FOR PALM BEACH COUNTY, FLORIDA

ADMINISTRATIVE ORDER NO. 5.303–5/09 *

IN RE: TIME STANDARDS FOR POST JUDGMENT ENFORCEMENT ORDERS IN TITLE IV/DEPARTMENT OF REVENUE CASES

Administrative Order Number 5.108–2/09 (as amended) establishes the office of Unified Family Court Magistrate. Magistrates schedule and conduct post final judgment enforcement proceedings and make findings of facts, conclusions of law and recommendations pursuant to Rules 1.490, Fla.R.Civ.P. and 12.491, Fla.Fam.L.R.P. Post judgment enforcement motions in Title IV cases must be promptly ruled upon.

NOW, THEREFORE, pursuant to the authority conferred by Florida Rule of Judicial Administration 2.215, it is **ORDERED** as follows:

1. General Magistrates shall ensure that proposed recommended orders are promptly submitted to the appropriate circuit judge.

2. General Magistrates shall ensure that agreed or proposed recommended orders received from the parties, if approved, are submitted to the appropriate circuit judge within 3 working days of receipt by the general magistrate.

3. General Magistrates shall conduct commitment hearings on motions for commitment filed in Title IV cases within six (6) weeks of the motion being filed with the clerk of court.

4. General Magistrates shall submit their reports and proposed orders on Title IV motions for commitment to the circuit court judge within one (1) week of the commitment hearing.

DONE and **SIGNED** in Chambers at West Palm Beach, Palm Beach County, Florida, this 21 day of May, 2009.

Kathleen J. Kroll
Chief Judge

Adopted effective May 21, 2009.

* supersedes admin. order 5.027–10/04

5.305. [VACATED AND SET ASIDE BY ORDER 5.305–1/18, EFFECTIVE JANUARY 8, 2018.]

5.306. [VACATED AND SET ASIDE BY ORDER 5.306–9/14, RETROACTIVELY EFFECTIVE SEPTEMBER 9, 2014.]

5.307. FILING OF CERTIFICATES OF LIVE BIRTH IN FAMILY LAW CASES

IN THE CIRCUIT COURT OF THE FIFTEENTH JUDICIAL CIRCUIT IN AND FOR PALM BEACH COUNTY, FLORIDA

ADMINISTRATIVE ORDER NO. 5.307–7/15

IN RE: FILING OF CERTIFICATES OF LIVE BIRTH IN FAMILY LAW CASES

Chapter 68.07, Florida Statutes, allows the parents of a minor child to file a Petition for Change of Name. Chapter 751, Florida Statutes, allows for the filing of a Petition for Temporary Custody by Extended Family Members and a Petition for Concurrent Custody. Chapter 742, Florida Statutes, allows the mother of a child or the putative father of a child to file a Petition to Determine Paternity. The Court often deems necessary to review the Certificate of Live Birth of the minor child(ren) to make a determination and appropriate decision in these cases.

NOW, THEREFORE, pursuant to the authority conferred by Florida Rule of Judicial Administration 2.215, it is **ORDERED** as follows:

1. In the interest of the judicial economy and to increase the efficiency in processing time of these cases, the Court is mandating the filing of a Live Birth Certificate for any minor child(ren) involved in any Petition for Change of Name for a Minor, Petition for Temporary Custody by Extended Family Members, Petition for Concurrent Custody and Petition to Determine Paternity.

2. The Petitioner or Petitioner's attorney shall file a copy of the Live Birth Certificate for any minor child(ren) involved in these cases at the time of initiating the case.

3. In a Petition to Determine Paternity, wherein the Mother is the Respondent, the Mother or Mother's attorney shall file a copy of the Live Birth Certificate for the minor child(ren) involved in the case upon filing of an Answer.

4. The original Live Birth Certificate document will not be required unless specifically requested by the Court.

5. Pursuant to Florida Rules of Judicial Administration, Rule 2.425 any filed Live Birth Certificate for the minor child(ren) shall be deemed confidential.

6. The Clerk of the Court is directed to include appropriate instructions for filing of a Live Birth Certificate for the minor child(ren) in all self help packages affected by this administrative order.

DONE AND SIGNED in Chambers at West Palm Beach, Palm Beach County, Florida, this 7 day of July, 2015.

Jeffrey J. Colbath
Chief Judge

Adopted effective July 7, 2015.

5.308. ADMINISTRATIVE CHILD SUPPORT CASES

IN THE CIRCUIT COURT OF THE FIFTEENTH JUDICIAL CIRCUIT IN AND FOR PALM BEACH COUNTY, FLORIDA

ADMINISTRATIVE ORDER NO. 5.308–1/17 *

IN RE: ADMINISTRATIVE CHILD SUPPORT CASES

Florida Statute § 409.2563(8) requires the Department of Revenue ("DOR") to file with the clerk of the circuit court a certified copy of an administrative support order rendered by the Division of Administrative Hearings pursuant to

§ 409.2563. The statute further gives the clerk the authority to initiate a judgment upon delinquency by the obligor. Florida Statute § 409.2563(10) sets forth the authority of the circuit court to review, enforce or enter an order superseding an administrative support order entered by an administrative law judge of the Division of Administrative Hearings. Florida Statute § 409.2563(10)(a) provides that an obligor or DOR has the right to seek judicial review of an administrative support order or a final order denying an administrative support order.

Uniform practices are necessary for the administration of the alternate procedures set forth under § 409.2563 which are filed in the Fifteenth Judicial Circuit. There is currently not an established form or procedure for the circuit court to supersede an administrative support order entered by an administrative law judge of the Division of Administrative Hearings.

NOW, THEREFORE, pursuant to the authority conferred by Florida Rule of Judicial Administration 2.215, it is **ORDERED** as follows:

1. **Administrative Support Cases "AS".**

a. Administrative support orders filed with the Clerk of Court by DOR pursuant to Florida Statute § 409.2563(8) shall by coded by the Clerk's Office as an "AS" case.

b. If the Clerk of Court or DOR issues to the obligor any notice of delinquency, notice of intent to suspend a driver's license or motor vehicle registration in accordance with § 61.13016, or notice of intent to suspend a professional license or certification in accordance with § 61.13015, such notice will be filed and docketed in the "AS" case.

2. **Domestic Relations Cases "PR".**

a. When a party seeks affirmative relief from the circuit court to supersede or modify an administrative child support order, or if the obligor files a petition or notice contesting the delinquency set forth in paragraph lb above, the Clerk will:

1) docket the new pleadings under the existing case number when an open or closed domestic relations case exists with *both* parties, and it is a case involving dissolution, paternity, or in any manner dealing with support, and has not been dismissed;

2) create a *new* Domestic Relations Case with the "DR" Court type, when none of the above domestic relations cases exists for these same parties.

b. A filing fee will not be assessed when an obligor files a petition or notice contesting the delinquency or suspension of driver's license set forth in paragraph 1b above in the Administrative Support cases.

c. A filing fee will not be assessed when no superseding order has been entered and the parties in an Administrative Support case file a pleading to seek relief from the circuit court. Examples of such pleadings are motions to pay direct, motion to stop child support, motion to lift bank levy or motion to reinstate driver's license.

d. A filing fee will be assessed when affirmative relief is sought to supersede or modify an administrative child support order.

3. Following the docketing of the Notice of Contest or any document which disputes the notice of delinquency, notice of intent to suspend a driver's license or motor vehicle registration in accordance with § 61.13016, or notice of intent to suspend a professional license or certification in accordance with § 61.13015 in the Administrative Support cases, the Clerk shall promptly forward the documents to the appropriate child support hearing officer to be addressed.

a. DOR will e-file the notice of delinquency, notice of intent to suspend a driver's license or motor vehicle registration in accordance with § 61.13016 or notice of intent to suspend a professional license or certification in accordance with § 61.13015 within three business days after receipt of the notice of hearing.

b. The Clerk will docket the notice of delinquency, notice of intent to suspend a driver's license or motor vehicle registration in accordance with § 61.13016 in the newly created domestic relations case along with a copy of the final administrative support order and Income Deduction/Withholding order, if any.

4. To provide assistance and fair access to the courts for the self represented litigant, the Unified Family Court of the Fifteenth Judicial Circuit shall create a self help package for the pro se litigants that will include relevant documents and forms required for filing along with procedural directions in these cases. The package shall be made available at any of the Self Help Centers in each Courthouse location or at the Fifteenth Judicial Circuit's website at http://15thcircuit.co.palm–beach.fl.us/web/guest/courtdivision/family.

DONE AND SIGNED this 24 day of January, 2017, in Chambers at West Palm Beach, Palm Beach County, Florida.

Jeffrey J. Colbath
Chief Judge

Adopted effective February 8, 2016. Amended effective July 25, 2016; January 24, 2017.

* supersedes admin. order 5.308–7/16

5.309. RECALL OF CERTAIN DOR CHILD SUPPORT WRITS OF BODILY ATTACHMENT

IN THE CIRCUIT COURT OF THE FIFTEENTH JUDICIAL CIRCUIT IN AND FOR PALM BEACH COUNTY, FLORIDA

ADMINISTRATIVE ORDER NO. 5.309–10/17

IN RE: RECALL OF CERTAIN DOR CHILD SUPPORT WRITS OF BODILY ATTACHMENT

The Palm Beach County Sheriff's Office and the Department of Revenue (DOR) have identified over 200 outstanding active DOR Child Support Writs of Bodily Attachment (Writs) in Palm Beach County. These cases are set forth in Exhibit "A" which is attached to this Administrative Order. DOR has reviewed and agrees that the list of cases attached in Exhibit "A" are all either closed, cold cases, or cases where the non-custodial parent is now paying via income deduction or Income withholding order. DOR has moved for the recall of these outstanding writs as the manpower required for service and execution and record-keeping, along with the physical housing and storage of these writs, places a tremendous burden on the Palm Beach County Sheriff's Office, Clerk of Court, and DOR. DOR agrees that these writs should be quashed.

NOW, THEREFORE, pursuant to the authority conferred by Florida Rule of Judicial Administration 2.215, it is **ORDERED** as follows:

1. All outstanding Department of Revenue Child Support writs issued in the cases set forth in Exhibit "A" [1] are hereby **RECALLED AND QUASHED.** Any related outstanding motions for contempt filed by the Department of Revenue on these cases are **DENIED.**

2. The Palm Beach County Clerk of Court shall deliver to PBSO one certified copy of this Administrative Order which shall serve as the Order to Recall and Quash for each case set forth in Exhibit "A" as if separately ordered.

3. The recalling of the active writ does not terminate a party's obligation to pay child support as required by a Final Order of Final Judgment entered by the Court.

4. The party owed child support, either on its own, with a private attorney, or with renewed services from the DOR Child Support Enforcement Program, may seek remedies for enforcement with the court.

5. The Clerk of Court is to file a copy of this Administrative Order in the identified cases.

DONE and **SIGNED** in Chambers at West Palm Beach, Palm Beach County, Florida, this 4th day of October, 2017.

Krista Marx
Chief Judge

Adopted effective October 4, 2017.

1 Exhibit A not included.

Special Domestic Relations Administrative Orders

5.501. DOMESTIC, REPEAT, DATING AND SEXUAL VIOLENCE INJUNCTIONS

IN THE CIRCUIT COURT OF THE FIFTEENTH JUDICIAL CIRCUIT IN AND FOR PALM BEACH COUNTY, FLORIDA

ADMINISTRATIVE ORDER NO. 5.501–5/09 *

IN RE: DOMESTIC, REPEAT, DATING AND SEXUAL VIOLENCE INJUNCTIONS

NOW, THEREFORE, pursuant to the authority conferred by Florida Rule of Judicial Administration 2.215, it is **ORDERED** as follows:

A. Case Assignment of Petition for Temporary Injunctions.

1. Upon receiving a petition for domestic violence or repeat violence temporary injunction under section 741.30 or 784.046, Florida Statutes (2007), where no "transfer order" exists transferring all matters to a single division for handling by one or the same judge, the Clerk of Court and Comptroller shall assign the case to one of the following Unified Family Court divisions: FA, FB, FC, FD, FH, FI, FY, FZ, FW or county court division TD.

2. Upon receiving a petition for domestic violence or repeat violence temporary injunction under section 741.30 or 784.046, Florida Statutes (2007), where a "transfer order" exists transferring all matters to a single division for handling by one or the same judge, the Clerk of Court and Comptroller shall assign the case to the division as directed by the existing transfer order. In the unlikely event that more than one transfer order exists, the Clerk of Court and Comptroller shall assign the case based upon the most recent transfer order.

3. The Clerk of Court and Comptroller shall promptly deliver the Verified Petition for Temporary Injunction, Order Identifying Unified Family Court Case (if the parties or child have a juvenile case), the complete file and all necessary documents and information to the Unified Family Court Division/Judge assigned to the case for a prompt ruling or decision by the judge. If the judge executes the Order Identifying Unified Family Court Case at that time, then the Clerk of Court and Comptroller shall deliver the file, Order and necessary documents to the newly assigned judge/division.

4. In the event the assigned Unified Family Court Division/Judge is unavailable, then the Clerk of Court and Comptroller shall promptly deliver the Verified Petition for Temporary Injunction along with the complete file and all necessary documents in the following order:

a. Assigned Judge's Alternate; if unavailable then to the

b. Administrative Judge for the division to which the case has been assigned; if unavailable then to the

c. Duty Judge

B. Scheduling of The Final/Extension Hearing.

1. Upon the entry of a temporary injunction under section 741.30 or 784.046, Florida Statutes (2007), in those cases where no "transfer order exists" transferring all matters to a single division for handling by one or the same judge, the Clerk of Court and Comptroller shall forthwith schedule the final/extension hearing on the assigned judge's next regularly scheduled domestic violence "designated" block hearing time.

2. Upon the entry of a temporary injunction under section 741.30 or 784.046, Florida Statutes (2007), in those cases where a "transfer order exists" transferring all matters to a single division for handling by one or the same judge, the Clerk of Court and Comptroller shall forthwith schedule the final/extension hearing on the assigned judge's next regularly scheduled domestic violence "designated" block hearing time. In the unlikely event the assigned judge has not established a regularly scheduled domestic violence "designated" block hearing time, then the Clerk of Court and Comptroller shall promptly and forthwith:

a. First contact the assigned judge's judicial assistant and obtain a hearing date and time.

b. Second, if unsuccessful, then immediately contact the administrative judge to obtain a hearing date and time.

C. Processing Procedures.

1. Procedures for processing an alleged violation of an injunction for protection against domestic violence shall in accordance with Section 741.31, Florida Statutes (2007).

2. To ensure the prompt and expeditious handling of any alleged violation, the Office of the State Attorney is designated as the appropriate law enforcement agency for investigation of any affidavit alleging the commission of a crime. The State

Attorney may refer the affidavit to the Sheriff of Palm Beach County or any other appropriate law enforcement agency for further investigation if necessary.

DONE and SIGNED in Chambers at West Palm Beach, Palm Beach County, Florida, this 21 day of May, 2009.

Kathleen J. Kroll
Chief Judge

Adopted effective May 21, 2009.

* supersedes admin. order 5.018–2/08

5.502. SERVICE OF DOMESTIC, REPEAT, SEXUAL AND DATING VIOLENCE INJUNCTIONS

IN THE CIRCUIT COURT OF THE FIFTEENTH JUDICIAL CIRCUIT IN AND FOR PALM BEACH COUNTY, FLORIDA

ADMINISTRATIVE ORDER NO. 5.502–5/09 *

IN RE: SERVICE OF DOMESTIC, REPEAT, SEXUAL AND DATING VIOLENCE INJUNCTIONS

Florida Statute § 741.30(8)(a)(1) and Florida Statute § 784.046(8)(a)(1) provide that the Chief Judge of each circuit, in consultation with the appropriate Sheriff, may authorize a law enforcement agency within the Chief Judge's jurisdiction to effect service of domestic violence, repeat violence, sexual violence and dating violence injunctions. The undersigned Chief Judge has consulted with the Sheriff of Palm Beach County with regard to which law enforcement agencies within Palm Beach County have received the training necessary to effectively serve domestic violence, repeat violence, sexual violence and dating violence injunctions, pursuant to Florida Statute § 741.30(8)(a)(1) and Florida Statute § 784.046(8)(a)(1) and who may be therefore be authorized to effect service of such injunctions.

NOW, THEREFORE, pursuant to the authority conferred by Florida Rule of Judicial Administration 2.215, it is **ORDERED** as follows:

1. When presented with a serviceable copy of an injunction for protection against domestic violence, repeat violence, sexual violence or dating violence, the following law enforcement agencies are authorized to effect service of process:

1. The City of Atlantis Police Dept.
2. The City of Boca Raton Police Dept.
3. The City of Boynton Beach Police Dept.
4. The City of Delray Beach Police Dept.
5. The Florida Atlantic University Police Dept.
6. The City of Greenacres Police Dept.
7. The Town of Gulf Stream Police Dept.
8. The Town of Highland Beach Police Dept.
9. The Town of Juno Beach Police Dept.
10. The Town of Jupiter Police Dept.
11. The Jupiter Inlet Colony Police Dept.
12. The Town of Lake Clarke Shores Police Dept.
13. The Town of Lantana Police Dept.
14. The Town of Manalapan Police Depart.
15. The Village of North Palm Beach Police Dept.
16. The Town of Ocean Ridge Police Dept.
17. The Town of Palm Beach Police Dept.
18. The City of Palm Beach Gardens Police Dept.
19. The Town of Palm Beach Shores Police Dept.
20. The Village of Palm Springs Police Dept.
21. The City of Riviera Beach Police Dept.
22. The School Board of Palm Beach County Police Dept.
23. The Town of South Palm Beach Police Dept.
24. The Village of Tequesta Police Dept.
25. The City of West Palm Beach Police Dept.

2. Any law enforcement officer effectuating service of process pursuant to this administrative order shall complete the attached "Exhibit 1"[1] as proof of service and shall promptly fax a copy of "Exhibit 1" to the Palm Beach County Sheriffs Office Validations at area code (561) 688–3457. Additionally, the law enforcement officer shall call in the return of service to Palm Beach County Sheriff's Office Validations at (561) 688–3452.

3. The Court Services Bureau of the Palm Beach County Sheriffs Office shall provide a copy of the faxed proof of service to the Clerk of Court DVRV Division on the next business day following receipt of the faxed proof of service.

DONE and **SIGNED** in Chambers at West Palm Beach, Palm Beach County, Florida, this 21 day of May, 2009.

Kathleen J. Kroll
Chief Judge

Adopted effective May 21, 2009.

* supersedes admin. order 5.028–5/95

1 Exhibit 1 not included.

5.504. ESTABLISHMENT OF NORTH COUNTY DOMESTIC RELATIONS DIVISION "FJ" AND SHIFT OF ZIP CODES 33413, 33414 AND 33415 TO THE NORTH COUNTY COURTHOUSE

IN THE CIRCUIT COURT OF THE FIFTEENTH JUDICIAL CIRCUIT IN AND FOR PALM BEACH COUNTY, FLORIDA

ADMINISTRATIVE ORDER NO. 5.504–7/09

ESTABLISHMENT OF NORTH COUNTY DOMESTIC RELATIONS DIVISION "FJ" AND SHIFT OF ZIP CODES 33413, 33414 AND 33415 TO THE NORTH COUNTY COURTHOUSE

The Fifteenth Judicial Circuit has identified a need to better serve the citizens of Palm Beach County by creating an additional Domestic Relations Division thereby ensuring that cases move through the Family Division in a smooth and expeditious manner.

NOW, THEREFORE, pursuant to the authority conferred by Florida Rule of Judicial Administration 2.215, it is **ORDERED AND ADJUDGED** as follows:

A. Establishment of North County, Family Division.

1. Effective July 28, 2009, the Administrative Office of the Court, Court Technology is hereby directed to establish Division "FJ".

B. Assignment of Cases to Division "FJ".

1. Effective August 31, 2009, the Clerk and Comptroller shall assign domestic relations cases to the North County

Courthouse according to the zip codes outlined in Administrative Order 5.101–7/09. Newly filed and re-opened cases shall be assigned as follows:

- •50% to division "FJ"
- •25% to division "FH"
- •25% to division "FI"

Cases shall be assigned as defined by Administrative Order 5.101–7/09.

2. The Family Court Case Manager assigned to this project shall prepare an Order of Reassignment to the North County Courthouse for each case identified in a pending status for zip codes 33413, 33414 and 33415. These cases shall be reassigned to division "FJ".

C. Reassignment of Pending Cases in Division "FI" and "FH".

1. By August 31, 2009, the Clerk and Comptroller is directed to have reassigned the randomly selected cases listed on the attached report to division "FJ".

DONE and **SIGNED** in Chambers at West Palm Beach Palm Beach County, Florida, this 30 day of July, 2009.

Peter D. Blanc
Chief Judge

Adopted effective July 30, 2009.

5.505. [VACATED AND SET ASIDE BY ORDER 5.505–9/14, RETROACTIVELY EFFECTIVE SEPTEMBER 9, 2014.]

5.506. [VACATED AND SET ASIDE BY ORDER 5.506-2/14, EFFECTIVE FEBRUARY 6, 2014.]

5.507. SOUTH COUNTY ASSIGNMENT OF REPEAT VIOLENCE, DATING VIOLENCE, AND STALKING VIOLENCE INJUNCTIONS

IN THE CIRCUIT COURT OF THE FIFTEENTH JUDICIAL CIRCUIT IN AND FOR PALM BEACH COUNTY, FLORIDA

ADMINISTRATIVE ORDER NO. 5.507—2/19*

IN RE: SOUTH COUNTY ASSIGNMENT OF REPEAT VIOLENCE, DATING VIOLENCE, AND STALKING VIOLENCE INJUNCTIONS

In the interest of judicial economy and to increase the efficiency of service to litigants, the Fifteenth Judicial Circuit has identified the need to assign Petitions for Repeat Violence Injunctions, Dating Violence Injunctions, and Stalking Violence Injunctions, except when there is a related case, to a county criminal division of the court.

NOW, THEREFORE, pursuant to the authority conferred by Florida Rule of Judicial Administration 2.215, it is **ORDERED AND ADJUDGED** as follows:

1. The Palm Beach County Clerk and Comptroller's Office shall assign Petitions for Repeat Violence Injunctions, Dating Violence Injunctions, and Stalking Violence Injunctions as set forth below:

a. When there is a related case pursuant to Administrative Order 5.101, the Clerk and Comptroller will assign the newly filed petition to the division of the court where the related matter had been assigned.

b. When there is no related case, cases filed in the South County Region shall be assigned to Division "D".

2. The county criminal judge assigned to Division "D" has been appointed to serve as circuit judge in accordance with Administrative Order 11.110.

DONE and **SIGNED** in Chambers at West Palm Beach, Palm Beach County, Florida, this 1 day of February, 2019.

Krista Marx
Chief Judge

Adopted effective January 14, 2019. Amended effective February 1, 2019.

* supersedes admin. order 5.507- 1/19

Delinquency

5.601. JUVENILES PROSECUTED IN THE COUNTY COURT

IN THE CIRCUIT COURT OF THE FIFTEENTH JUDICIAL CIRCUIT IN AND FOR PALM BEACH COUNTY, FLORIDA

ADMINISTRATIVE ORDER 5.601–9/08 *

IN RE: JUVENILES PROSECUTED IN THE COUNTY COURT

Florida Statute 985.265(5)(a) prohibits the detention of any juvenile in an adult facility who is transferred to adult court on a misdemeanor offense. Florida Statute 318.143(3) prohibits the detention of any juvenile in an adult facility who is charged with traffic misdemeanor offenses or infractions.

NOW, THEREFORE, pursuant to the authority conferred by Florida Rule of Judicial Administration 2.215, it is **ORDERED** as follows:

When a juvenile is taken into custody on a capias for any misdemeanor or traffic offense, failure to appear, or violation of probation or community control for such offense, the following shall occur:

1. The juvenile shall be delivered to the Booking area of the jail for processing the capias, setting bond and fingerprinting.

2. The juvenile and parent shall be give a Notice to Appear before the Judge who issued the capias.

3. If the juvenile cannot make bond, this Order hereby allows the Sheriff to release the juvenile directly to his/her parent.

4. If the parent cannot be located, the arresting officer shall deliver the youth to the Juvenile Assessment Center.

5. The Department of Juvenile Justice staff shall then make every effort to either locate the parent or an approved shelter on all traffic cases.

6. On criminal misdemeanor cases, the Department of Juvenile Justice shall detain the juvenile pursuant to Florida Statutes 985.265(5)(a). The juvenile shall be brought before the Judge who issued the capias, within twenty-four (24) hours, excluding weekends and holidays.

7. The County Court Judge shall set aside a daily time period for delivery of said juvenile before the court. Further use of the juvenile detention center after this initial hearing is prohibited unless there is a finding of contempt of court as set forth in Florida Statutes 316.635(4).

DONE and SIGNED, in Chambers at West Palm Beach, Palm Beach County, Florida this 29 day of September, 2008.

Kathleen J. Kroll
Chief Judge

Adopted effective September 29, 2008.

* supersedes admin. order 7.011–2/99

5.602. JUVENILE RESTITUTION

IN THE CIRCUIT COURT OF THE FIFTEENTH JUDICIAL CIRCUIT IN AND FOR PALM BEACH COUNTY, FLORIDA

ADMINISTRATIVE ORDER NO. 5.602–9/08 *

IN RE: JUVENILE RESTITUTION

Victims of crime should be compensated in full as quickly and equitably as possible.

NOW, THEREFORE, pursuant to the authority conferred by Florida Rule of Judicial Administration 2.215, it is **ORDERED** as follows:

1. Restitution in juvenile offender cases is joint and several, unless otherwise ordered by the Court.

2. Restitution disbursement shall be directed by the Clerk of Court first to the victim and then, after the victim has been fully compensated, to any insurance company claimant.

3. When victims are multiple, restitution shall be disbursed pro rata by the Clerk of Court, unless a priority has been assigned by the Court.

4. If the Court gives no indication as to how to apply a restitution payment, the payment shall be applied pro rate to a juvenile's cases with outstanding restitution.

5. If restitution payment of less than $15.00 is received, the Clerk of Court may hold such payment for thirty (30) days.

6. Upon entry of a Civil Restitution Order, any and all juvenile offender court cases associated by order(s) of joint and several restitution are no longer considered active court cases; therefore, restitution shall be pursued by civil remedy.

DONE and SIGNED in Chambers at West Palm Beach, Palm Beach County, Florida this 29 day of September, 2008.

Kathleen J. Kroll
Chief Judge

Adopted effective September 29, 2008.

* supersedes admin. order 7.016–6/01

5.603. DELINQUENCY DRUG COURT

IN THE CIRCUIT COURT OF THE FIFTEENTH JUDICIAL CIRCUIT IN AND FOR PALM BEACH COUNTY, FLORIDA

ADMINISTRATIVE ORDER NO. 5.603–5/15 *

IN RE: DELINQUENCY DRUG COURT

According to a national research study, four out of every five children and teens (ages 10–17) in the juvenile justice system (1.9 out of 2.4 million arrests are either under the influence of alcohol or drugs while committing a crime, test positive for drugs, are arrested for committing an alcohol or drug offense, admit to having substance abuse and addiction problems, or share some combination of these characteristics). A reduction in juvenile substance abuse can make a significant impact on the community by reducing law enforcement and detention/jail costs while promoting public safety.

NOW, THEREFORE, pursuant to the authority conferred by Florida Rule of Judicial Administration 2.215, it is **ORDERED** as follows:

1. Delinquency Drug Court is hereby established in the Fifteenth Judicial Circuit of Florida.

2. The treatment portion of the program will consist of a three-phase treatment model, including individual and group counseling, random urinalysis and other support services.

3. Participants for the program will be selected by the Drug Court Team. A youth is eligible to enter the program if the following conditions are satisfied:

a. Participant must be:

1) Between the ages of 14 and 17

2) Reside in Palm Beach County

3) Youth and advocate agree to participate; <u>and</u>

b. Participant must meet ONE of the following criteria (b1, b2, b3 or b4):

1) 985.345 Cases. Meets criteria as outlined in F.S. 985.345

a) Has not previously been adjudicated for a felony; <u>and</u>

b) Is charged with a felony of the second or third degree for:

i) Purchase or possession of a controlled substance under Chapter 893;

ii) Tampering with evidence;

iii) Solicitation for purchase of a controlled substance; <u>or</u>

iv) Obtaining a prescription by fraud

2) Deferred Prosecution Cases. Any filed misdemeanor <u>or</u> non-violent, second or third degree felony offense(s) where youth is <u>not</u> on Probation and WITH WRITTEN AGREEMENT FROM THE OFFICE OF THE STATE ATTORNEY where:

a) There is evidence of a substance abuse problem; <u>and</u>

b) Victim is in agreement (only on victim cases)

c) Youth has not been enrolled in a diversion program for a felony non-drug offense

d) Youth has not previously been found to have committed a non–Chapter 893 felony

e) Youth has not previously been found to have committed more than 2 felony drug offenses

f) Youth is not charged with a firearm, sale of controlled substance or a sex offense

g) Youth has not previously participated (signed contract) in any juvenile drug court

3) Probation Cases. Youth may be placed in Delinquency Drug Court as a condition of Probation or is currently on Probation and requests to modify Probation; **and**

a) Youth has not previously participated (signed contract) in any juvenile drug court (youth either completed or was unsuccessfully terminated prior to current charge(s) being filed); and

b) Youth is not charged with any offense involving a firearm, sale of controlled substance or a sex offense

4. The Delinquency Drug Court Team will consist of the following: Delinquency Drug Court Judge, Delinquency Drug Court Coordinator, State Attorney (Juvenile), Public Defender (Juvenile), treatment provider(s), Department of Juvenile Justice representative, Youth Court representative, Clerk of Court representative, Juvenile Case Manager and a school representative.

5. The Delinquency Drug Court Team shall meet prior to each Drug Court session to review current cases and make determinations on new referrals.

6. Staffing will be conducted by the Delinquency Drug Court Team to determine if potential candidates will be admitted into Delinquency Drug Court. If a youth is accepted into Delinquency Drug Court, the youth and his/her advocate agree to participate in Delinquency Drug Court and will be required to successfully complete the program.

DONE AND SIGNED in Chambers, at West Palm Beach, Palm Beach County, Florida, this 14 day of May, 2015.

Jeffrey Colbath
Chief Judge

Adopted effective September 29, 2008. Amended effective February 11, 2009; November 13, 2010; September 12, 2013; May 14, 2015.

* supersedes admin. order 5.603–9/13

5.604. JUVENILE IN–HOUSE ARREST AND ELECTRONIC MONITORING PROGRAMS

IN THE CIRCUIT COURT OF THE FIFTEENTH JUDICIAL CIRCUIT IN AND FOR PALM BEACH COUNTY, FLORIDA

ADMINISTRATIVE ORDER NO. 5.604–9/08 *

IN RE: JUVENILE IN–HOUSE ARREST AND ELECTRONIC MONITORING PROGRAMS

The Palm Beach County Sheriff's Office conducts a program known as the In–House Arrest Program. The Palm Beach County Sheriff's Office has agreed to include a limited number of Juvenile Court Detainees in their program subject to budget constraints. The program relies upon electronic monitoring (Global Positioning Satellite and Radio Frequency) with a transmitter affixed to the ankle of the person to be monitored. In the interest of public safety, persons being monitored must strictly comply with the constraints placed upon them by the Court, and strictly comply with the rules and regulations placed upon them by the Palm Beach County Sheriff's Office.

NOW, THEREFORE, pursuant to the authority conferred by Florida Rule of Judicial Administration 2.215, it is **ORDERED** as follows:

1. The Juvenile Judge shall sign a detention order placing the juvenile into secure detention with a special temporary release to the Palm Beach County Sheriff's Office In–House Arrest Program and specifying the date of release from secure detention.

2. The juvenile will receive the same court dates that he/she would otherwise be assigned as a secure detainee.

3. Any juvenile from the Juvenile Court who is taken into custody for any violation of the court order or the program's rules and regulations, shall be delivered to the Juvenile Assessment Center and detained at the Palm Beach Regional Juvenile Detention Center on the original secure detention order, and will be released from the In–House Arrest Program on the same date of release specified in the original detention order.

4. The transporting deputy shall provide a written or verbal description of how the juvenile violated house arrest to the Department of Juvenile Justice Probation Officer at the Juvenile Assessment Center, who will convey that information to the Juvenile Detention Center, Court, state attorney and public defender.

5. A juvenile on In–House Arrest under the Palm Beach County Sheriff's Office is required to be within the confines of his/her residence, he/she shall be physically within the residence at all times, i.e., he/she is prohibited from being outside the residential walls.

6. A copy of this Administrative Order shall be furnished to every person presently being monitored and every person placed on the monitor in the future.

DONE and **SIGNED** in Chambers at West Palm Beach, Palm Beach County, Florida, this 29 day of September, 2008.

Kathleen J. Kroll
Chief Judge

Adopted effective September 29, 2008.

* supersedes Administrative Order 2.051–5/06 (as it pertains to juveniles)

5.605. COMPANION AND REFILED JUVENILE CASES

IN THE CIRCUIT COURT OF THE FIFTEENTH JUDICIAL CIRCUIT IN AND FOR PALM BEACH COUNTY, FLORIDA

ADMINISTRATIVE ORDER NO. 5.605–9/08 *

IN RE: COMPANION AND REFILED JUVENILE CASES

Sound principles of judicial economy require the establishment of procedures to govern the assignment of companion and refiled cases.

NOW, THEREFORE, pursuant to the authority conferred by Florida Rule of Judicial Administration 2.215, it is **ORDERED** as follows:

1. If, rather than file separate counts in the same information or indictment, the state elects to file separate cases concerning the same factual situation, the assistant state attorney filing the cases shall notify the clerk, in writing, that companion cases are being filed. The clerk, in turn, utilizing the blind-assignment system, shall select one judge and assign all designated companion cases to that judge. When this procedure is employed, the clerk shall file a written notice that the cases have been assigned in compliance with this order.

2. If companion cases are assigned to different judges, it shall be the continuing duty of the state to notify, in writing, all judges involved and to file a motion to reassign the cases to the judge with the lowest numbered case.

3. If the state enters a nolle prosequi and subsequently refiles the case, the newly-filed case shall be assigned to the division of court in which the original case was assigned. It is the duty of the state to advise the clerk of the earlier nolle prossed case.

4. If a conflict exists between this administrative order and the procedures outlined in Administrative Order 5.102 9/08 (as amended) pertaining to dependency and delinquency assignments, Administrative Order 5. 102 shall govern.

DONE and **SIGNED** in Chambers at West Palm Beach, Palm Beach County, Florida, this 29 day of September, 2008.

Kathleen J. Kroll
Chief Judge

Adopted effective September 29, 2008.

* supersedes admin. order 4.006–9/92 (as it pertains to juveniles)

5.606. CORRECTING SCRIVENER'S ERRORS IN JUVENILE CASES

IN THE CIRCUIT COURT OF THE FIFTEENTH JUDICIAL CIRCUIT IN AND FOR PALM BEACH COUNTY

ADMINISTRATIVE ORDER 5.606—9/08 *

IN RE: CORRECTING SCRIVENER'S ERRORS IN JUVENILE CASES

Tanner v. State, 744 So.2d 101722 (Fla. 4th DCA 1997) finds that the Clerk of Court may not refuse to accept documents which contain scrivener's errors in the caption. The administration of criminal justice and judicial economy are best served by the prompt correction of more substantive errors as well.

NOW, THEREFORE, pursuant to the authority conferred by Florida Rule of Judicial Administration 2.215, it is **ORDERED** as follows:

1. The Office of the Clerk of Court shall correct scrivener's errors in the caption of both pleadings and orders in delinquency cases.

2. The Office of the Clerk of Court may correct substantive errors or omissions contained in orders, provided that the information is available from another document in the court file, not including the court event form. Correction shall be made to the original document so that it conforms to the source document in the court file.

3. If the information is not available, the originating party shall be responsible for the correction or revision

DONE and **ORDERED,** in Chambers, at West Palm Beach, Palm Beach County, Florida this 29 day of September, 2008.

Kathleen J. Kroll
Chief Judge

Adopted effective September 29, 2008.

* supersedes administrative order 4.046–10/99 (as it pertains to delinquency cases)

5.607. FIRST APPEARANCE HEARINGS JUVENILE MATTERS

IN THE CIRCUIT COURT OF THE FIFTEENTH JUDICIAL CIRCUIT IN AND FOR PALM BEACH COUNTY, FLORIDA

ADMINISTRATIVE ORDER NO. 5.607–9/08

IN RE: FIRST APPEARANCE HEARINGS JUVENILE MATTERS

Pursuant to the authority conferred by Florida Rule of Judicial Administration 2.215, it is hereby **ORDERED** as follows:

Administrative Order 4.201 9/08 (as amended) will provide the procedures for those juveniles who are taken to First Appearances.

DONE and SIGNED in Chambers, at West Palm Beach, Palm Beach County, Florida this 29 day of September, 2008.

Kathleen J. Kroll
Chief Judge

Adopted effective September 29, 2008.

5.608. APPLICATION OF FUNDS RECEIVED FROM PROBATIONER IN JUVENILE PROCEEDINGS

IN THE CIRCUIT COURT OF THE FIFTEENTH JUDICIAL CIRCUIT IN AND FOR PALM BEACH COUNTY, FLORIDA

ADMINISTRATIVE ORDER NO. 5.608–6/12

IN RE: APPLICATION OF FUNDS RECEIVED FROM PROBATIONER IN JUVENILE PROCEEDINGS

Juveniles placed on probation may be required to make monetary payments through the Office of the Clerk and Comptroller for multiple purposes. There is a need for consistency within the Fifteenth Judicial Circuit as to how monies shall be applied. The interests of victims are paramount in the view of the court.

NOW, THEREFORE, pursuant to the authority conferred by Florida Rule of Judicial Administration 2.215, it is **ORDERED** as follows:

The order in which monetary payments are to be distributed are as follows:

1. First, to any restitution ordered by the Court as a condition of probation until fully paid, then

2. Second, to the Public Defender application fee according to statutory priority, until fully paid, then

3. Third, to Crimes Compensation Trust Fund imposed as a condition of probation pursuant to F.S. 938.03, until fully paid, and then

4. Fourth, to any court costs ordered by the Court as a condition of probation pursuant to F.S. 775.083(2).

DONE and **SIGNED,** in Chambers, at West Palm Beach, Palm Beach County, Florida this 19 day of June, 2012.

Peter D. Blanc
Chief Judge

Adopted effective June 19, 2012.

5.609. DISCOVERY STIPULATION BETWEEN STATE ATTORNEY & PUBLIC DEFENDER IN JUVENILE DELINQUENCY CASES

IN THE CIRCUIT COURT OF THE FIFTEENTH JUDICIAL CIRCUIT IN AND FOR PALM BEACH COUNTY, FLORIDA

ADMINISTRATIVE ORDER NO. 5.609–3/16

IN RE: DISCOVERY STIPULATION BETWEEN STATE ATTORNEY & PUBLIC DEFENDER IN JUVENILE DELINQUENCY CASES

The attached stipulation between the State Attorney and Public Defender for the Fifteenth Judicial Circuit will promote the efficient administration of justice and, thus, is in the public interest;

NOW, THEREFORE, pursuant to the authority conferred by Florida Rule of Judicial Administration 2.215, it is **ORDERED** as follows:

The attached stipulation between the Offices of the State Attorney and Public Defender for the Fifteenth Judicial Circuit of Florida was ratified and accepted on August 24, 2015. This stipulation shall govern the process of demanding and responding to discovery in all juvenile delinquency cases in the Circuit Court for the Fifteenth Judicial Circuit of Florida.

DONE and **SIGNED** in Chambers at West Palm Beach, Palm Beach County, Florida, this 8 day of March, 2016.

Jeffrey Colbath
Chief Judge

DISCOVERY STIPULATION

The Office of the State Attorney, Fifteenth Judicial Circuit, by and through the undersigned State Attorney, and the Office of the Public Defender, Fifteenth Judicial Circuit, by and through the undersigned Public Defender, stipulates as follows:

1. In every criminal and delinquency case, except capital murder cases or otherwise agreed in this Stipulation, where the Office of the Public Defender is appointed subsequent to the filing of an information, indictment or delinquency petition, the State Attorney shall provide discovery in accordance with Fla.R.Crim.P.3.220 and Fla.R.Juv.P. 8.060 without the necessity of filing a "Notice of Discovery". Unless there is a Notice filed pursuant to paragraph 3 herein, the Public Defender will be participating in discovery in all criminal and delinquency cases, except capital murder cases, and will have the obligations of reciprocal discovery pursuant to Fla.R.Crim.P. 3.220 and Fla.R.Juv P. 8.060.

2. This Stipulation shall remain in full force and effect unless either party withdraws specifically in writing from the Stipulation.

3. The Office of the Public Defender shall have the obligation to notify the Office of the State Attorney that, in a particular case, it does not desire to participate in discovery so as to not be obligated to provide reciprocal discovery. Notification shall be in writing and filed at the time of the appointment of the Office of the Public Defender.

4. This Stipulation shall not apply to specially appointed public defenders or conflict attorneys.

5. Upon withdrawal from a case after receiving discovery, it is the responsibility of the Office of the Public Defender to forward the discovery to the newly retained attorney or appointed conflict attorney.

This stipulation is hereby entered into this 24th day of August 2015.

Dave Aronberg
State Attorney, 15th Judicial Circuit

Carey Haughwout
Public Defender, 15th Judicial Circuit

Adopted effective March 8, 2016.

Dependency

5.701. ATTORNEY AD LITEM PROGRAM

IN THE CIRCUIT COURT OF THE FIFTEENTH JUDICIAL CIRCUIT IN AND FOR PALM BEACH COUNTY, FLORIDA

ADMINISTRATIVE ORDER NO. 5.701–9/08 *

IN RE: ATTORNEY AD LITEM PROGRAM

It is within the Court's discretion to appoint Attorneys Ad Litem to represent children in dependency cases. The Children's Services Council of Palm Beach County has funded the Legal Aid Society of Palm Beach County, Inc. to establish and administer an Attorney Ad Litem program to represent foster children, ages birth to twelve years and their siblings, and assist them in obtaining their goal of permanence in dependency cases. The Children's Services Council of Palm Beach County has authorized the Legal Aid Society of Palm Beach County, Inc. to expand their current program in order to administer an Attorney Ad Litem program to represent dependent children placed in the care of relatives. The program intends to begin by representing children ages birth to five years and their siblings in the juvenile division, and assist them in obtaining their goal of permanence in dependency cases.

NOW, THEREFORE, pursuant to the authority conferred by Florida Rule of Judicial Administration 2.215, it is **ORDERED** as follows:

1. The Attorney Ad Litem program, known as the Foster Children's Project, is established and administered by the Legal Aid Society of Palm Beach County, Inc., to provide legal representation to foster children in dependency cases and to advocate for their right to permanence as provided by statute.

2. An Attorney Ad Litem shall be appointed to represent each child, age birth to twelve years, who is placed into the custody of the Department of Children and Families at the shelter hearing or each child, age birth through five years, who is placed into the custody of relatives at the shelter hearing who meet the program's internal qualifications for appointment. The Attorney Ad Litem shall also represent all siblings of any qualifying child. Representation shall commence immediately after the Court makes a finding of probable cause and signs an order of appointment.

3. The Attorney Ad Litem program shall represent a maximum of 420 children. If a child is removed from foster care the program shall be discharged from further representation of that child.

4. The Attorney Ad Litem from the Foster Children's Project may decline appointment if the caseload of the Attorney Ad Litem has reached capacity. If a child achieves permanence as defined by Chapter 39, the Attorney Ad Litem shall be discharged from further representation of that child. The Attorney Ad Litem may seek discharge for other reasons as provided by law.

5. The Clerk of the Juvenile Division shall provide the daily shelter calendar to the Attorney Ad Litem office by facsimile each weekday. The Clerk shall indicate which children qualify for appointment of an Attorney Ad Litem by placing the child's date of birth next to his or her name on the shelter docket.

DONE AND SIGNED in Chambers in West Palm Beach, Palm Beach County, Florida, this 29 day of September, 2008.

Kathleen J. Kroll
Chief Judge

Adopted effective September 29, 2008.

* supersedes admin. order 7.015–11/03

5.702. FAMILY DRUG COURT

IN THE CIRCUIT COURT OF THE FIFTEENTH JUDICIAL CIRCUIT IN AND FOR PALM BEACH COUNTY, FLORIDA

ADMINISTRATIVE ORDER 5.702–7/16 *

IN RE: FAMILY DRUG COURT

Florida Statute Chapter 39 requires the Court to rehabilitate parents with substance abuse problems to promote the parents' ability to regain custody of their child(ren). In 2009, Palm Beach County's Division of Justice Services, in conjunction with the Administrative Office of the Court, Department of Children and Families' (DCF's) Substance Abuse and Mental Health Office, applied for and was awarded a three year grant from the Office of Justice Programs to develop a Family Drug Court program in the Fifteenth Judicial Circuit. The Family Drug Court addresses substance abuse and other issues affecting the parents and their child(ren) in new dependency petitions. It offers a comprehensive and systematic approach to the treatment of substance abuse problems of parents while limiting the risk of physical and emotional harm to children with the ultimate goal of reunification. Essential components of the Family Drug Court program are cross agency and interdisciplinary training and ongoing data sharing and analysis.

NOW THEREFORE, pursuant to the authority conferred by the Florida Rule of Judicial Administration 2.215, it is **ORDERED** as follows:

1. A Family Drug Court is hereby established in the Fifteenth Judicial Circuit of Florida in the juvenile division "JL".

2. The treatment portion of the program will consist of a five phase model and participants will be required to participate in evidence based treatment, submit to frequent random drug testing, appear at regular court status hearings, and comply with other court conditions geared to accountability, rehabilitation, long-term sobriety and cessation of criminal activity.

3. The Family Drug Court will operate with a "team approach" with a minimum of the following team members: Judge, Family Drug Court Coordinator, Dependency Case Managers (ChildNet/Children's Home Society), Family Intervention Specialists (Drug Abuse Foundation), Children's Legal Services, Attorneys for the Parent's, Attorneys for the Children, the Guardian Ad Litem's Office, Substance Abuse Treatment providers and an Education Liaison.

4. Family Drug Court Hearings and Team Staffings are held on Wednesday afternoons.

5. The Family Drug Court Team will have discretion regarding the acceptance of new cases. At a minimum, potential Family Drug Court cases will be identified when: at least one parent has substance abuse issues; the primary goal for the family is reunification; the parent(s) admit to the abuse/neglect allegation; case jurisdiction is in Palm Beach County;

6. Clients with a history of the following exclusionary criteria are automatically excluded from participation in the Family Drug Court: alleged sexual perpetrators; persons who are incompetent; individuals who suffer from an un-stabilized mental disorder (paranoia, hallucinations, delusions, mania) lack of medical stabilization, failure to follow medical regime, or other functional impairment that would inhibit effective program participation; individuals with advanced terminal illness; individuals with an extensive history of violent or criminal offenses; individuals on methadone maintenance or pain management regime.

7. Upon identifying a case meeting the aforementioned eligibility criteria, the Court may present the Family Drug Court program option to the parent and explain that Family Drug Court is a voluntary program which offers wraparound, supportive services to parents with allegations of alcohol and drug use who are seeking reunification with their child(ren).

8. If the parent agrees to voluntarily submit to the Family Drug Court program option, the following procedures shall occur:

a. The identified participant(s) in the Family Drug Court will be scheduled for a Family Group Conference.

b. The Family Drug Court Coordinator shall meet with the parent deemed eligible for Drug Court to perform the intake, clinical screening and brief assessment for participant(s).

c. The parent will be referred to the Drug Abuse Foundation for an assessment within 72 hours.

d. The Drug Abuse Foundation will provide a treatment recommendation to the Family Drug Court Coordinator and the Dependency Case Manager.

e. The participant will attend an Arraignment Hearing within twenty eight days of the Shelter Hearing, wherein their Consent to the allegations in the Petition will be entered and the Initial Drug Court Hearing will be set within one week. If Arraignment has already occurred, an Initial Drug Court Hearing will be set within one week of an eligible client's agreement to participate in the program.

9. All Family Drug Court participants shall be responsible for compliance with the terms and conditions as set forth in the Family Drug Court acknowledgment and agreement forms, as otherwise ordered by the Court, and as set forth in Chapter 39, Florida Statutes.

DONE and ORDERED in Chambers at West Palm Beach, Palm Beach County this 25 day of July, 2016

JEFFREY J. COLBATH
Chief Judge

Adopted effective June 28, 2010. Amended effective July 25, 2016.

* supersedes admin. order 5.702–6/10

5.703. JUVENILE JUDICIAL REVIEW ORDERS

IN THE CIRCUIT COURT OF THE FIFTEENTH JUDICIAL CIRCUIT IN AND FOR PALM BEACH COUNTY, FLORIDA

ADMINISTRATIVE ORDER NO.: 5.703–3/11 *

IN RE: JUVENILE JUDICIAL REVIEW ORDERS

To reduce the costs incurred by the Court for the photocopying and mailing of juvenile judicial review orders and to increase the efficiency of the judicial review process, a six month pilot project was undertaken from August, 2010 through February, 2011, whereby juvenile judicial review orders were served via electronic mail. The Department of Children and Families, the Guardian Ad Litem's office, the Office of Criminal Conflict and Civil Regional Counsel, the Legal Aid Society of Palm Beach County, as well as the court appointed conflict attorneys (collectively the "entities") have all agreed, as shown by the Memorandum of Understanding attached to this Administrative Order as Exhibit "A", to continue to receive service of the Judicial Review orders by electronic mail.

NOW, THEREFORE, pursuant to the authority conferred by Florida Rule of Judicial Administration 2.215, it is **ORDERED** as follows:

1. Copies of Judicial Review orders issued as a result of a Judicial Review hearing conducted by a General Magistrate at the Main Judicial Center or the South County Courthouse or by a Judge or General Magistrate at the West County Courthouse will be forwarded to The Department of Children and Families, the Guardian Ad Litem's office, the Office of Criminal Conflict and Civil Regional Counsel, Legal Aid Society Juvenile Advocacy Project, Legal Aid Society Foster Children's Project and the court appointed conflict attorneys.

2. Each of the above named entities, including the individual court appointed dependency conflict counsel, will provide to the assistant to the Juvenile General Magistrate and West County Judge, an "intake" email address(es) to which scanned copies of judicial review orders will be sent.

3. Independent Living Reviews are specifically excluded.

DONE and **SIGNED** in Chambers, at West Palm Beach, Palm Beach County, Florida, this 14 day of March, 2011.

Peter D. Blanc
Chief Judge

Adopted effective August 11, 2010. Amended effective March 14, 2011.

* supersedes admin. order 5.703–8/10

5.704. INDEPENDENT LIVING REVIEW (ILR) COURT

IN THE CIRCUIT COURT OF THE FIFTEENTH JUDICIAL CIRCUIT IN AND FOR PALM BEACH COUNTY, FLORIDA

ADMINISTRATIVE ORDER NO.: 5.704–2/15 *

IN RE: INDEPENDENT LIVING REVIEW (ILR) COURT

Florida Statute Section 409.1451 provides that the Department of Children and Families, its agents, or community-based providers, shall administer a system of independent living transition services to enable older children in foster care and young adults who exit foster care to make the transition to self-sufficiency as adults. The goals of independent living transition services are to assist older children in foster care and young adults who were formerly in foster care to obtain life skills and education for independent living and employment, to have a quality of life appropriate for their age, and to assume personal responsibility for becoming self-sufficient adults.

Since 2007, the Fifteenth Judicial Circuit, in partnership with the Department of Children and Families, Child and Family Connections (now ChildNet), Vita Nova Inc., Guardian Ad Litem Office, Palm Beach County Legal Aid Society, Palm Beach County Clerk and Comptroller, Department of Juvenile Justice, Agency for Persons with Disabilities, Palm Beach County School District, Office of Regional Conflict Counsel, Conflict Team, and Independent Living partners have been monitoring youth in licensed care in an Independent Living Review (ILR) Court. The purpose of the Independent Living Review Court is to evaluate a youth's progress in developing independent living skills and take the necessary steps to help the youth obtain his/her goals.

NOW, THEREFORE, pursuant to the authority conferred by Florida Rule of Judicial Administration 2.215, it is **ORDERED** as follows:

1. An Independent Living Review (ILR) Court is hereby established. All dependent youth, ages 17 and older, who are in licensed care will be placed on an ILR Court Docket to be heard by the Divisional Judge. The youth will have the first hearing within 90 days of his/her 17th birthday. The Divisional Judge will have discretion to bring younger dependent youth into the ILR Court.

2. The youth will have the discretion to request the ILR/Judicial Review/Permanency Hearing continue to be heard by the General Magistrate. At the last Judicial Review prior to the first scheduled ILR, the youth shall be given the option to have the ILR/Judicial Review/Permanency Hearing continue to be heard before the Magistrate. If the youth chooses this option, the Order on Judicial Review/Permanency Hearing shall reflect that all further ILR/Judicial Review/Permanency Hearings for the youth shall continue to be heard by the General Magistrate. If applicable, the youth's hearing shall be set at the same time as his/her sibling(s) before the General Magistrate.

3. Eligible youth will be identified by the Juvenile Court Case Manager through a monthly listing of youth ages 17 and over in foster care. The listing is sent to the Juvenile Court Operations Manager by ChildNet.

4. The Juvenile Court Case Manager will prepare the initial Order transferring the youth into ILR Court and cancelling any previously scheduled JR Hearings. All subsequent ILR Court hearings will be scheduled on the Divisional Judge's ILR docket by the Clerk and Comptroller.

5. The ILR case shall be opened with the Order to Transfer a dependent youth's case to ILR Court. The Clerk and Comptroller shall create a new case file and establish a new case number in the Divisional ILR Court. The Clerk and Comptroller shall designate all ILR Court cases as Division "ILR" for case assignment purposes. The transfer of a dependent youth's case to the ILR Court will not affect any remaining family members to a dependency case filed in the original dependency division and the family's case file number will remain unchanged. When the youth is given a new case number an Order linking UFC cases will also be completed by the Juvenile Court Case Manager. Youth without siblings or youth who choose to have their case stay with the General Magistrate will not receive a new case number.

6. When a new ILR case number has been assigned, after the transfer of a dependent youth's case to the ILR Court, new documents filed regarding the dependent youth will be filed in the dependent youth's ILR court file. The Clerk and Comptroller shall copy the following documents from the old dependency file and place them in the new ILR court file: petition for shelter, order for shelter, petition for adjudication of dependency, order for adjudication of dependency, case plan, and previous JR Orders. After transfer of a dependent youth's case to the ILR Court, a Judicial Review conducted for the youth's siblings will <u>not</u> address the dependant youth who is assigned to ILR Court. While the dependent youth assigned to ILR Court is welcome to attend the Judicial Review for his/her siblings, no portion of the Judicial Review for the dependent youth's siblings will address the tasks, needs, or services of the dependent youth assigned to ILR Court.

7. Any party who wishes to cancel or reset an ILR hearing must do so by motion to the Divisional ILR Court and provide notice to all parties.

8. The ILR Court will occur as listed on the Divisional Judge's scheduled ILR docket time:

- Division JA: as needed
- Division JK: bi-weekly
- Division JL: bi-weekly
- Division JM: as needed
- Division JO: weekly
- Division JS: weekly

9. All parents who have a reunification case plan and the parents' legal counsel shall be noticed about every hearing.

10. All youth shall be noticed of every hearing and their attendance is mandatory, unless good cause is shown in writing at least ten (10) days prior to the hearing as to why the youth cannot attend.

11. All JRSSRs and Independent Living Transition Plans shall be filed with the Court at least 72 hours prior to the hearing. The JRSSRs and Independent Living Transition plan shall contain the most updated information regarding the information listed on the ILR Court Checklist attached as Exhibit A.

12. All JRSSRs with all requisite supporting documentation and Independent Living Transition Plans shall be emailed to the Divisional Juvenile Court Case Manager and all counsel of record at least 72 hours prior to the hearing.

13. The ILR hearing will be considered a Judicial Review and/or Permanency Review hearing and heard by the Divisional Judge.

14. The dependent youth will stay in ILR Court even if the youth is on runaway status.

15. The ILR hearing is to be heard by the Divisional Judge and approximately twenty (20) minutes is to be allotted to hear the case. At the hearing, the Court will review the needs of the youth, discuss future plans (vocational and educational goals), review compliance with case plan tasks, review services for the youth, and most importantly, allow the youth to voice his/her concerns and become engaged in the decision-making process. The next hearing will be scheduled within four to six months, unless an earlier date is needed.

16. Following the hearing, copies of the signed Order shall be distributed by Department's attorney to the following case parties: youth, parent(s)/guardian(s), attorney for youth, attorney(s) for parent(s), Dependency Case Manager and Life Coaches (as applicable) assigned to the youth.

17. If a dependent youth's placement changes from licensed care to relative care, the Department's attorney and youth's attorney shall IMMEDIATELY provide a copy of the Order of Modification of Placement to the Divisional Juvenile Court Case Manager. The youth's case shall be removed from the ILR Court docket and placed on the Divisional Dependency docket. The Divisional Juvenile Court Case Manager shall prepare an Order cancelling the ILR, directing the Clerk to close out the ILR case and setting a new JR hearing.

18. If a youth who is currently under extended jurisdiction to age 19 wishes to opt into extended foster care and extend jurisdiction to age 21 (or age 22 if young adult is disabled) and he/she has completed an extended foster care application which has been approved by ChildNet, Children's Legal Services (CLS) shall file a signed Agreed Order to Extended Jurisdiction within 14 days. A Juvenile Court Case Manager shall then set the case for a Hearing on Approval of Case Plan and Setting Independent Living Review (ILR) within 14 days of receiving the Order. The Clerk shall assign the previously designated ILR case number.

19. If a youth who is currently in care and turned 18 after January 1, 2014, his/her jurisdiction shall be automatically extended to age 21 (or age 22 if young adult is disabled). If not already set, a Juvenile Court Case Manager shall set the case for a Hearing on Approval of Case Plan and Setting Independent Living Review (ILR) within 14 days of receiving the Order. The Clerk shall assign the previously designated ILR case number.

20. If a youth has no open jurisdiction and wishes to opt back into care and he/she has completed an extended foster care application which has been approved by ChildNet, Children's Legal Services (CLS) shall file a signed Agreed Order to Reopen Jurisdiction within 14 days. A Juvenile Court Case Manager shall then set the case for a Hearing on Approval of Case Plan and Setting Independent Living Review (ILR). The Clerk shall assign the previously designated ILR case number.

DONE AND SIGNED in Chambers, at West Palm Beach, Palm Beach County, Florida, this 27 day of February, 2015.

Jeffrey Colbath
Chief Judge

Exhibit "A"—Revised 7/1/2014

ILR Court Checklist

1. School: Specific School Name, location, GPA, extracurricular activities- (especially important if youth is out of county), progress in school.

2. Current Case Plan Goal and Goal Date

3. Placement: Specific Placement Name (not generic, for example "group home") and location (which county) and any issues with placement. What is the living arrangement for post–18 and backup plan? Is there an Order removing the disability of non–age?

4. Mental Health/Substance Abuse: Details on mental health and substance abuse treatment-assessments completed, is youth participating in treatment or therapy- how often, where, progress, *current medications*, etc.

5. Work: Is youth working? Where and for how long?

6. DJJ/Criminal: Any pending DJJ or criminal cases in or out of county and status.

7. Special Needs: Any other needs youth might have (i.e.: assistance with getting documents, benefits, etc.) Does the youth wish to extend jurisdiction? Does the youth have a master trust account; is he/she receiving SSI, if necessary has an APD application been made? Current IL services and/or RTI? Does the child have a bank account, birth certificate, SS card and Medicaid card?

Adopted effective June 20, 2012. Amended effective February 27, 2015.

* supersedes admin. order 5.704–6/12

Special Juvenile Administrative Orders

5.801. DISCOVERY REQUESTS OF DEPARTMENT OF CHILDREN AND FAMILIES

IN THE CIRCUIT COURT OF THE FIFTEENTH JUDICIAL CIRCUIT IN AND FOR PALM BEACH COUNTY, FLORIDA

ADMINISTRATIVE ORDER NO. 5.801–9/08 *

IN RE: DISCOVERY REQUESTS OF DEPARTMENT OF CHILDREN AND FAMILIES

Section 39.202, Florida Statutes, require court orders prior to releasing information which is otherwise discoverable pursuant to Rule 3.220, Florida Rules of Criminal Procedure.

NOW, THEREFORE, pursuant to the authority conferred by Florida Rule of Judicial Administration 2.215, it is **ORDERED** as follows:

1. This order shall apply to the prosecution of all cases in which there was an investigation of the same facts and occurrences by both a law enforcement agency and the State of Florida Department of Childrens and Families.

2. The agents of the Department of Children and Families, and other persons having access to confidential information under section 39.202, Florida Statutes, are hereby required to comply with discovery requests made pursuant to the Florida Rules of Criminal Procedure regarding disclosure of confidential information obtained through or from abuse investigations under Chapter 39, Florida Statutes, and may testify at trial without further order of the Court.

3. Further, said information obtained remains confidential and shall not be publicly disclosed by any prosecuting or defending attorney unless said attorney has obtained prior authorization from the Court that public disclosure is necessary to resolve an issue pending before the Court in accordance with section 39.202 Florida Statutes.

DONE and **SIGNED** in Chambers at West Palm Beach, Palm Beach County, Florida, this 29 day of September, 2008.

Kathleen J. Kroll
Chief Judge

Adopted effective September 29, 2008.

* supersedes admin order 4.025–6/93

5.802. JUDICIAL WAIVER OF PARENTAL NOTICE OF ABORTION

IN THE CIRCUIT COURT OF THE FIFTEENTH JUDICIAL CIRCUIT IN AND FOR PALM BEACH COUNTY, FLORIDA

ADMINISTRATIVE ORDER NO.: 5.802–9/08 *

IN RE: JUDICIAL WAIVER OF PARENTAL NOTICE OF ABORTION

Florida Statute 390.01114 states minors may petition the Court for a waiver of parental notice requirements concerning their request to terminate pregnancy. Cases filed pursuant to Florida Statute 390.01114 require the Court's prompt attention.

NOW, THEREFORE, pursuant to the authority conferred by Florida Rule of Judicial Administration 2.215, it is **ORDERED** as follows:

1. Petitions filed by minors requesting the Court for a waiver of parental requirements shall be assigned to the Juvenile Division.

2. The clerk shall promptly deliver the petition and complete file to the appropriate juvenile judge based on the alphabetical range into which the juvenile's last name falls.

3. All petitions filed pursuant to Florida Statute 390.01114 shall be heard in Juvenile Court in the Central Courthouse within forty-eight (48) hours. Petitions filed after 4:00 P.M. on Friday will be heard by the Duty Judge. If Petitioner waives the forty-eight (48) hour requirement, the case will be heard in Juvenile Division on the first day of the regularly scheduled court calendar.

4. Proceedings arising out of these petitions shall be given precedence over other pending matters in Juvenile Court.

5. The Clerk of Court shall be present for all 390.01114 proceedings and shall maintain a confidential record of the evidence and findings of each case.

DONE and **SIGNED** in Chambers at West Palm Beach, Palm Beach County, Florida this 29 of September, 2008.

Kathleen J. Kroll
Chief Judge

Adopted effective September 29, 2008.

* supersedes admin. order 5.044–6/05

5.803. ESTABLISHMENT OF THE SOUTH COUNTY UNIFIED FAMILY COURT JUVENILE DIVISION "JS" AND THE REASSIGNMENT OF EXISTING CASES IN THE "JM" DIVISION

IN THE CIRCUIT COURT OF THE FIFTEENTH JUDICIAL CIRCUIT IN AND FOR PALM BEACH COUNTY, FLORIDA

ADMINISTRATIVE ORDER NO. 5.803–4/09

ESTABLISHMENT OF THE SOUTH COUNTY UNIFIED FAMILY COURT JUVENILE DIVISION "JS" AND THE REASSIGNMENT OF EXISTING CASES IN THE "JM" DIVISION

The Fifteenth Judicial Circuit has identified a need to better serve children and families by expanding Unified Family Court to the South County Annex thereby ensuring children and families are linked to local services in the community.

NOW, THEREFORE, pursuant to the authority conferred by Florida Rule of Judicial Administration 2.215, it is **ORDERED AND ADJUDGED** as follows:

A. Creation of Division "JS" and Assignment of Cases.

1. Effective April 20, 2009, Court Administration is hereby directed to establish a South County Juvenile Division, Division "JS".

2. The Clerk of Court shall assign delinquency and dependency cases according to the zip codes outlined in Administrative Order 5.102–4/09 (as amended).

3. Division "JS" will also include the transfer of all existing delinquency and dependency cases currently assigned to Divisions "JK", "JL", "JM" and "JO" according to the requirements set forth in Administrative Order 5.102–4/09 (as amended).

4. No later than June 1, 2009, Division "JS" will be completely established.

5. Division "JS" cases will initially be located at the Main Judicial Complex until it is relocated to the South County Courthouse on July 6, 2009.

B. Reassignment of Newly Filed and Existing Division "JM" Cases.

1. Effective April 20, 2009, newly filed delinquency and dependency cases at the Main Judicial Complex shall not be assigned to division "JM". Alphabetical assignments comprising Division JM shall be distributed as follows:

Alphabetical Assignment from Division JM	To Division
S, X, and Z	JL
T, U, W and Y	JK
R and V	JO

2. No later than June 1, 2009, those cases in Division "JM," that were not transferred to Division "JS" in accordance with Administrative Order 5. 102—4/09 shall be transferred/reassigned to the three remaining Main County Courthouse divisions according to the following alphabetical assignment:

Alphabetical Assignment from Division JM	To Division
S, X, and Z	JL
T, U, W and Y	JK
R and V	JO

3. In transferring existing cases with the applicable South County zip code to Division "JS" and reassigning existing Division "JM" cases to the other three divisions, it is contemplated that subsequent Administrative Orders may be entered to facilitate the bulk transfer/reassignment of such cases.

4. To the extent that this Administrative Order differs from Administrative Order 5.102, this Administrative Order controls. Upon the completion of the establishment of the South County UFC Division and the entire transfer of all applicable cases, Administrative Order 5.102 will be reviewed and amended, if necessary.

C. Order Transferring/Reassigning Cases.

1. An order transferring a case to Division JS, or reassigning a case, will be filed in each case with a copy mailed to the parties.

2. The order of transfer may be signed by the Chief Judge, the Administrative Judge, or the Division Judge.

3. For judicial economy, a transfer/reassignment order may list one or more cases to be transferred/reassigned. A certified copy of the order will be deemed to be an original and have the same force and effect as an original.

4. If a transfer/reassignment order has more than one case listed, only one copy of the order will be sent to the following: State Attorney's Office, Public Defender's Office, Office of Criminal Conflict and Civil Regional Counsel, Department of Children and Families, court appointed attorneys having contracts with the Justice Administrative Commission, Guardian Ad Litem Office and the Department of Juvenile Justice.

DONE and **SIGNED** in Chambers at West Palm Beach, Palm Beach County, Florida, this 14 day of April, 2009.

Kathleen J. Kroll
Chief Judge

Adopted effective April 14, 2009.

5.804. CROSSOVER CASE NOTIFICATION

IN THE CIRCUIT COURT OF THE FIFTEENTH JUDICIAL CIRCUIT IN AND FOR PALM BEACH COUNTY, FLORIDA

ADMINISTRATIVE ORDER NO.: 5.804–11/10

IN RE: CROSSOVER CASE NOTIFICATION

For purposes of this Administrative Order, a crossover case is defined as a case involving a child in both the delinquency and dependency systems. These children experience a unique set of issues that are best served by the cooperation of all parties involved in both their delinquency case(s) and dependency case(s). In order to ensure that the child's needs and rights are adequately represented in both arenas, the parties agree that notification needs to 1 be provided to the Department of Children and Families, the Department of Juvenile Justice, Court Administration, the Statewide Office of the Guardian Ad Litem Program, Office of Criminal Conflict and Civil Regional Counsel, the Legal Aid Society of Palm Beach County, the Office of the State Attorney, the Office of the Public Defender, and court appointed conflict attorneys when a crossover case is identified.

NOW, THEREFORE, pursuant to the authority conferred by Florida Rule of Judicial Administration 2.215, it is **ORDERED** as follows:

1. Cases where a child is involved in both the dependency and delinquency systems ("crossover case") may be identified by the Court, the Department of Children and Families, the Department of Juvenile Justice, the Statewide Office of the Guardian Ad Litem Program, Office of Criminal Conflict and Civil Regional Counsel, the Legal Aid Society of Palm Beach County, the Office of the State Attorney, the Office of the Public Defender, or court appointed conflict attorneys.

2. Once a crossover case is identified, notification will be provided to the Court, the Department of Children and Families, the Department of Juvenile Justice, the Statewide Office of the Guardian Ad Litem Program, Office of Criminal Conflict and Civil Regional Counsel, the Legal Aid Society of Palm Beach County, the Office of the State Attorney, the Office of the Public Defender, and court appointed conflict attorneys that a crossover case exists. Notice will include the information set forth in the attached Exhibit "A" and be made by the appropriate party.

3. This administrative order, in accordance with Florida Statutes sections 985.04(1) and 39.0132(3), will permit the parties identified in this Administrative Order to share with each other the information contained in Exhibit "A". The information contained within each notification shall be used appropriately and ethically in order to advocate effectively for their respective clients and to disregard information pertaining to an individual child to whom their agency/program is not appointed.

DONE and **SIGNED** in Chambers, at West Palm Beach, Palm Beach County, Florida, this 22 day of November, 2010

Peter D. Blanc
Chief Judge

EXHIBIT "A"

CROSSOVER NOTIFICATION
Name of youth: ______
Youth's date of birth: ______
Judge/Division: ______
DEPENDENCY CASE # ______
Next court hearing: ______ at ___:___ AM/PM
Hearing Type: ______
Hearing location: ______
Case Worker: ______
Case Worker E-mail: ______
Case Worker Phone: ______
DELINQUENCY CASE # ______
Next court hearing: ______ at ___:___ AM/PM
Hearing Type: ______
Hearing location: ______
Probation Officer: ______
Probation Officer E-mail: ______
Probation Officer Phone: ______

Adopted effective November 22, 2010.

5.805. TRUANCY COURT

IN THE CIRCUIT COURT OF THE FIFTEENTH JUDICIAL CIRCUIT IN AND FOR PALM BEACH COUNTY, FLORIDA

ADMINISTRATIVE ORDER NO.: 5.805–9/13 *

IN RE: TRUANCY COURT:

Florida Statute Section 1003.21 states that all children who are either six years of age, who will be six years old by February 1 of any school year, or who are older than six years of age but who have not attained the age of 16 years, must attend school regularly during the entire school term. Florida Statute Section 1003.27 sets forth the court procedure and penalties for the enforcement of the statutory provisions relating to compulsory school attendance. The Fifteenth Judicial Circuit, in partnership with the School District of Palm Beach County, and the Children's Services Council of Palm Beach County has implemented the Student Attendance with Family Engagement (S.A.F.E.) Truancy Court program. The S.A.F.E. program will offer a comprehensive and systematic holistic approach designed to reengage students in the educational environment and increase attendance by addressing issues within the family system.

NOW, THEREFORE, pursuant to the authority conferred by Florida Rule of Judicial Administration 2.215, it is **ORDERED** as follows:

1. A Truancy Court pilot program is hereby established in Division "JL".

2. The Office of the Clerk and Comptroller and Court Administration shall schedule the initial hearing and distribute the Notice to Appear.

3. Actions filed under Florida Statute 1003.27 shall be assigned a Juvenile Dependency ("DP") case number.

4. Proceedings may be initiated by the Executive Officer of the Court (Chief Judge) or his designee. The Designee shall be the circuit's Juvenile Court Operations Manager.

5. The treatment portion of the program will consist of participants working with social service agencies, attending regular court appearances and complying with other court-ordered conditions.

6. Truancy Court hearings will be held at a date and time to be determined by the Court.

DONE AND SIGNED in Chambers, at West Palm Beach, Palm Beach County, Florida, this 10 day of September, 2013.

Jeffrey J. Colbath
Chief Judge

Adopted effective November 7, 2011. Amended effective September 10, 2013.

* supersedes admin. order 5.805–11/11.

5.806. EMERGENCY MOTIONS AND REQUESTS FOR EMERGENCY HEARINGS IN JUVENILE MATTERS

IN THE CIRCUIT COURT OF THE FIFTEENTH JUDICIAL CIRCUIT IN AND FOR PALM BEACH COUNTY, FLORIDA

ADMINISTRATIVE ORDER NO. 5.806–11/14

IN RE: EMERGENCY MOTIONS AND REQUESTS FOR EMERGENCY HEARINGS IN JUVENILE MATTERS

Pursuant to the authority conferred by Florida Rule of Judicial Administration 2.215, it is **ORDERED** as follows:

1. Emergency Motions and Requests for Emergency Hearings filed in dependency or delinquency matters shall be immediately brought to the judge to which the juvenile case is assigned. If the judge assigned to the case is not available, the emergency matter shall be brought to the judge's alternate. If the judge's alternative is not available, then the emergency matter shall be brought to any available juvenile judge. If no juvenile judge is available, the emergency matter shall then be brought to the duty judge.

2. The request for an emergency hearing will be decided on the Emergency Motion alone. Upon receiving a request for an emergency hearing, the judge shall decide whether an emergency exists, and if so, shall schedule a hearing, enter any ex parte order deemed necessary, or take any other appropriate action.

3. Motions for Emergency Hearings will be denied unless there are sufficient allegations to establish that there is:

a. An imminent risk of substantial physical harm to a minor child; or

b. A child is about to be illegally removed from this Court's jurisdiction.

DONE and **SIGNED** in Chambers at West Palm Beach, Palm Beach County, Florida, this 19 day of November, 2014.

Jeffrey Colbath
Chief Judge

Adopted effective November 19, 2014.

5.807. CHAPTER 39 ADOPTIONS

IN THE CIRCUIT COURT OF THE FIFTEENTH JUDICIAL CIRCUIT IN AND FOR PALM BEACH COUNTY, FLORIDA

ADMINISTRATIVE ORDER NO.: 5.807–7/17

IN RE: CHAPTER 39 ADOPTIONS

A case in which a minor becomes available for adoption after the parental rights of each parent have been terminated by a judgment entered pursuant to chapter 39 is governed by section 39.812 and Chapter 63, Florida Statutes. All documents necessary for the adoption must be filed prior to the final hearing. A checklist of the required documents would assist the court in ensuring a timely disposition of the matter.

NOW, THEREFORE, pursuant to the authority conferred by Florida Rule of Judicial Administration 2.215, it is **ORDERED AND ADJUDGED** as follows:

1. A final hearing will not be scheduled on Petition for Adoption unless a Notice of Compliance with Statutory Requirements for Adoption Initiated Under Chapter 39, Florida Statutes ("Notice of Compliance") along with a fully completed Checklist has been filed.

2. A copy of the Notice of Compliance with the Checklist is attached as Exhibit "A".

DONE AND SIGNED in Chambers, at West Palm Beach, Palm Beach County, Florida, this 18th day of July, 2017.

Krista Marx
Chief Judge

EXHIBIT "A"

IN THE CIRCUIT COURT OF THE FIFTEENTH JUDICIAL CIRCUIT IN AND FOR PALM BEACH COUNTY, FLORIDA

JUVENILE DIVISION "__"
CASE NO.:

In the Matter of the Adoption of

[ADOPTIVE NAME]
A minor child.
_________________/

NOTICE OF COMPLIANCE WITH STATUTORY REQUIREMENTS FOR ADOPTION INITIATED UNDER CHAPTER 39, FLORIDA STATUTES

The undersigned hereby notifies the Court that 1) the attached checklist has been reviewed and substantially complied with as evidenced by the reviewer's initials; 2) all required information and documentation pertaining to this adoption has been provided to the Court; and 3) that this matter is now ready to be set for final hearing.

Date: _____________

[Attorney Name], Esq.
[Firm Name]
[Firm Address]
[Email/Phone Number]
[Florida Bar Number]

CHAPTER 39 ADOPTION CHECKLIST

Pursuant to section 63.037, Florida Statutes (2016), a case in which a minor becomes available for adoption after the parental rights of each parent have been terminated by a judgment entered pursuant to chapter 39, is governed by section 39.812 and Chapter 63, Florida Statutes.

THE FOLLOWING CHECKLIST INCLUDES THE INFORMATION AND DOCUMENTATION REQUIRED FOR ADOPTION PROCEEDINGS INITIATED UNDER CHAPTER 39.

Please initial next to each entry indicating review and completion or mark the paragraph number of the petition where the information is located. If you are unable to obtain the information, please provide an explanation at the end of the checklist. If the entry is not applicable to the adoption please mark "NA" for Not Applicable.

I. PETITION FOR ADOPTION

_____ A. The primary residence of prospective adoptive parents must be in Florida, except when adopting a special needs child as defined in § 409.166 Fla. Stat.

_____ B. Adoption Entities may place a child out of state only in certain instances covered by § 63.207 Fla. Stat. If the Adoption Entity is placing the Minor Child out of state, it must file the proper Interstate Compact on the Protection of Children (ICPC) documentation pursuant to § 409.401 Fla. Stat.

_____ C. The Petition for Adoption must be filed in the division of the circuit court which entered the judgment terminating parental rights, unless a motion for change of venue is granted pursuant to § 47.122. §§ 39.812(5); 63.102(2) Fla. Stat.

_____ D. The Adoption Petition may not be filed until the judgment terminating parental rights becomes final. § 39.812(5), Fla. Stat.

Date Final Judgment of TPR final: _________/___/___

Date Adoption Petition filed: _________/___/___

___ E. The Adoption Petition must be signed and verified by the petitioner(s), filed with the clerk of the court, and shall state pursuant to § 63.112 Fla. Stat.:

___ 1. The date and place of birth of the person to be adopted, if known;

___ 2. The name to be given to the person to be adopted;

___ 3. The date petitioner acquired custody of the minor;

___ 4. The name of the Adoption Entity placing the minor, if any;

___ 5. The full name, age, and place and duration of residence of the petitioner;

___ 6. The marital status of the petitioner, including the date and place of marriage, if married, and divorces, if applicable to the adoption by a stepparent;

___ 7. A statement that the petitioner is able to provide for the material needs of the child;

___ 8. A description and estimate of the value of any property of the person to be adopted;

___ 9. The case style and date of entry of the TPR Judgment or, if the adoptee is an adult or a minor relative or a stepchild of the petitioner, the address, if known, of any person whose consent to the adoption is required and, if such person has not consented, the facts or circumstances that excuse the lack of consent to justify a termination of parental rights; and

___ 10. The reasons why the petitioner desires to adopt the person.

II. ATTACHMENTS/EXHIBITS TO PETITION FOR ADOPTION

The following documents **must** be attached to, or filed along with, the petition for adoption pursuant to section 39.812, Florida Statutes:

___ A. A copy of the consent executed by the department must be *attached to* the petition, unless waived pursuant to § 63.062(7). *See* § 39.812(5), Fla. Stat.

___ B. statement, signed by the prospective adoptive parents, acknowledging receipt of all information required to be disclosed under § 63.085(2); and

___ C. A form provided by the department which details the social and medical history of the child **and** each parent **and** includes the social security number and date of birth for each parent, if such information is available or readily obtainable.

The following documents **must** be filed with along with the petition for adoption pursuant to Chapter 63, Florida Statutes:

___ A. A certified copy of the court judgment terminating parental rights under chapter 39.

___ B. Favorable Preliminary Homestudy. A preliminary homestudy must be conducted before placing the minor in the intended adoptive home. § 63.092(3), Fla. Stat. The homestudy must be conducted within 1 year of child custody pursuant to 63.092(3), Fla. Stat.

Section 63.092(3)(a)–(h) requires the following:

___ 1. Documentation of interview with the adoptive parents;

___ 2. Records check with the department's central abuse registry and criminal records checks through FDLE (See § 39.0138, Fla. Stat.);

___ 3. An assessment of the physical environment of the home;

___ 4. A determination of the financial security of the adoptive parents;

___ 5. Documentation of counseling and education of the adoptive parents on adoptive parenting;

___ 6. Documentation that information on adoption and the adoption process has been provided to the adoptive parents;

___ 7. Documentation that information on support services available in the Community has been provided to the adoptive parents; and

___ 8. A copy of each signed acknowledgement of receipt of the disclosure required by § 63.085(2), Fla. Stat.

___ C. A copy of any declaratory statement previously entered by the court pursuant to section 63.102.

___ D. Certificate of the results of the search of Florida Putative Father Registry provided in section 63.054(7). *See* § 63.037, Fla. Stat.

This document is required ONLY if a search was previously completed and documentation of the search is not contained in the case file.

___ E. Documentation that an interview was held with the minor, if older than 12 years of age, unless the court, in the best interest of the minor, dispenses with the minor's consent under section 63.062(1)(c).

___ F. Final Home Investigation. The final home investigation must be conducted before the adoption becomes final. The investigation may be conducted by a licensed child-placing agency or a professional in the same manner as provided in section 63.092 to ascertain whether the adoptive home is a suitable home for the minor and whether the proposed adoption is in the best interest of the minor.

• Unless ordered by the court, no final home investigation, report or recommendation is required when the placement is a stepparent adoption or an adult adoption or when the minor is a relative of one of the adoptive parents. § 63.125(1), Fla. Stat.

• Section 63.125(3)–(5) requires the following in the Final Home Investigation:

___ 1. Evaluation of placement with a recommendation on granting the Petition for Adoption;

___ 2. The information from the Preliminary Home Study;

___ 3. Reports of the two post placement visits (one must be in the home);

___ 4. The family social and medical history as provided in § 63.082.

___ 5. Any other information relevant to the suitability of the intended adoptive home.

___ 6. Any other relevant information, as provided in rules that the department may adopt.

___ G. Uniform Child Custody Jurisdiction Enforcement Act (UCCJEA) Affidavit.

___ H. Indian Child Welfare Act (ICWA) Affidavit.

The following is **NOT** required for adoption proceedings initiated under chapter 39. *See* Fla. Stat. § 63.037:

• Requirement for search of the Florida Putative Father Registry provided in section 63.054(7), if a search was previously completed and documentation of the search is contained in the case file;

• Disclosure requirements for the adoption entity provided in section 63.085(1);

• However, adoptions initiated under Chapter 39 are not exempt from the disclosure requirements of section 63.085(2), Florida Statutes. *See* § 39.812, Fla. Stat.

• General provisions governing termination of parental rights pending adoption provided in section 63.087;

• Notice and service provisions governing termination of parental rights pending adoption provided in section 63.088; and

• Procedures for terminating parental rights pending adoption provided in section 63.089.

Comments: ______________________________

____

____

____

Adopted effective July 18, 2017.

Probate/Guardianship/Mental Health/Substance Abuse

Administrative Matters

6.101. PROBATE AND GUARDIANSHIP DIVISION REGIONS, HEARING SITES AND ASSIGNMENT CRITERIA

IN THE CIRCUIT COURT OF THE FIFTEENTH JUDICIAL CIRCUIT IN AND FOR PALM BEACH COUNTY, FLORIDA

ADMINISTRATIVE ORDER NO. 6.101–1/13 *

IN RE: PROBATE AND GUARDIANSHIP DIVISION REGIONS, HEARING SITES AND ASSIGNMENT CRITERIA

The court is committed to providing judicial services at convenient locations consistent with the efficient and sound administration of justice and the court has concluded that the foregoing principle dictates that probate and guardianship services be provided at the branch courthouses in addition to the main county courthouse;

NOW, THEREFORE, pursuant to the authority conferred by Florida Rule of Judicial Administration 2.215, it is **ORDERED** as follows:

A. Probate & Guardianship Division Regions.

1. The Probate & Guardianship Division of the Circuit Court, Palm Beach County, Florida, shall be divided into three separate regions—The Northern Region, Southern Region, and Central Region.

2. All cases assigned to the Northern Region will be heard in the North County Courthouse, 3188 PGA Boulevard, Palm Beach Gardens, Florida 33410

3. All cases assigned to the Southern Region will be heard in the South County Courthouse, 200 West Atlantic Avenue, Delray Beach, Florida 33444.

4. All cases assigned to the Central Region will be heard in the Main Courthouse, 205 North Dixie Highway, West Palm Beach, Florida 33401.

B. Northern Region. The cities to be served within the NORTHERN REGION, together with their presently existing zip code numbers are as follows:

JUNO BEACH	33408
JUNO BEACH	33410 *
JUPITER	33458
JUPITER	33468
JUPITER	33477
JUPITER	33478
LAKE PARK	33403
MANGONIA PARK	33407
NORTH PALM BEACH	33408
PALM BEACH GARDENS	33410 *
PALM BEACH GARDENS	33418
PALM BEACH SHORES	33404
RIVIERA BEACH	33404
TEQUESTA INLET	33469
WEST PALM BEACH	33403

WEST PALM BEACH	33404
WEST PALM BEACH	33407
WEST PALM BEACH	33410 *
WEST PALM BEACH	33412
WEST PALM BEACH	33418
WEST PALM BEACH	33419
WEST PALM BEACH	33420

*Note: Juno Beach, Palm Beach Gardens and West Palm Beach overlap zip code 33410

C. Southern Region. The cities to be served within the SOUTHERN REGION, together with their presently existing zip code number are as follows:

ATLANTIS	33462
BOYNTON BEACH	33424
BOYNTON BEACH	33425
BOYNTON BEACH	33426
BOYNTON BEACH	33435
BOYNTON BEACH	33436
BOYNTON BEACH	33437
BRINY BREEZES	33435
BOCA RATON	33428
BOCA RATON	33429
BOCA RATON	33431
BOCA RATON	33432
BOCA RATON	33433
BOCA RATON	33434
BOCA RATON	33481
BOCA RATON	33486
BOCA RATON	33487
BOCA RATON	33496
BOCA RATON	33498
BOCA RATON	33499
DELRAY BEACH	33444
DELRAY BEACH	33445
DELRAY BEACH	33446
DELRAY BEACH	33447
DELRAY BEACH	33483
DELRAY BEACH	33484
GREENACRES CITY	33463 *
GREENACRES CITY	33461 *
GULFSTREAM	33483
HIGHLAND BEACH	33487
HYPOLUXO	33462
LAKE WORTH	33454
LAKE WORTH	33460
LAKE WORTH	33462
LAKE WORTH	33463 *
LAKE WORTH	33464
LAKE WORTH	33465
LAKE WORTH	33466
LAKE WORTH	33467
LANTANA	33462
MANALAPAN	33462
OCEAN RIDGE	33435
PALM SPRINGS	33461 *

*Note: Greenacres City and Palm Springs overlap zip code 33461
Greenacres City and Lake Worth overlap zip code 33463

D. Central Region. The geographical jurisdictional area of the CENTRAL REGION shall be as follows: All areas within Palm Beach County not contained within the Northern and Southern Regions.

E. General Provisions.

1. This order shall not alter or amend subject matter jurisdiction of the Probate & Guardianship Division as previously established by administrative orders.

2. *Assignment Criteria.* All cases presently filed within the Division of this Court and all future cases so filed, will be assigned to either the Central, Northern or Southern Region based upon the following criteria:

a. New Probate and Incapacity/Guardianship cases filed by privately retained counsel shall be assigned to the region reflecting the office address of the first attorney to petition the court for the administration of the estate or the petition to determine incapacity. Assignment of all incapacity and guardianship cases initiated by the Department of Children and Families or by an attorney hired to represent that agency, shall be determined by the residence address of the alleged incapacitated person.

b. Out-of-state or out-of-county attorneys submitting original petitions to the court: If the attorney's address is in Broward, Dade or Monroe counties, all such matters shall be assigned to the Southern Region. If the attorney's address is in Martin, St. Lucie, Okeechobee or Indian River Counties, all such matters shall be assigned to the Northern Region. All other out of county and out of state matters shall be assigned to the Central Region.

c. Beginning September 1, 2010, assignment of Summary Administration and Disposition of Property Without Administration cases initiated by pro se litigants shall be determined by the last residential address of the decedent and those initiated by privately retained counsel shall be assigned to the region reflecting the office address of the initiating attorney.

d. As to the presently filed cases, the assignment criteria shall be established by the office address of the first attorney presently representing the personal representative(s) of the probate estate or the attorney representing the guardian of the property and if there be none, then the attorney representing the guardian of the person.

e. All cases involving the Developmental Disabilities Prevention and Community General Provisions (F.S. 393); Protective Services, (F.S. 415), the residence address of the patient will be determinative of proper assignment but for those Persons incarcerated and those without known residence addresses whose cases shall be heard in the Main Courthouse.

f. All Baker Act (F.S. 394) and Marchman Act (F.S. 397) cases shall be assigned to and heard in the appropriate region based upon the Respondent's residential zip code, unless the Petitioner is a licensed services provider (hospital or treatment center) or the Respondent's residential address is unknown. Except as stated below in subparagraph g., the Clerk is directed to override cases assigned to the Central Region by zip code and assign those cases to the Northern Region. Until further notice, all even numbered Marchman Act (F.S. 397) cases designated for the Central Region shall be assigned and heard in Division IH in the Northern Region, and all odd numbered Marchman Act (F.S. 397) cases designated for the Central Region shall be assigned and heard in Division II in the Northern Region.

g. Any emergency hearings (including, but not limited to, Petitions for Involuntary Examination) pursuant to the

Baker Act (F.S. 394) or the Marchman Act (F.S. 397) shall be heard in the Courthouse in which the Petitioner files the Petition, regardless of whether or not the case otherwise falls within that region based upon the Respondent's zip code.

h. All communicable disease cases will be assigned to the Main Courthouse.

i. Belle Glade matters will be assigned and processed without change.

j. Two or more cases filed in the below list constitute a "related case" and the Clerk of Court is directed to assign the subsequently filed case to the same division. Cases shall be linked in the Clerk's computer system.

1) The Estate or Trust proceedings for the deceased ward shall remain in the division for the Guardianship proceedings.

2) If assets of two (2) or more individuals adjudicated incapacitated are significantly interrelated so that one division should hear the guardianship proceedings for all individuals. These cases shall be assigned to the same division. Example: Incapacitated husband and wife.

3) If minor guardianships proceedings are opened for siblings with the same guardian of the property the cases shall be assigned to the same division.

4) All Estate and Non-relief Trust matters filed relating to a decedent shall be assigned to the Judge assigned to the first case opened.

5) All Petitions to Determine Incapacity, Petition to Appoint an Emergency Temporary Guardian and Petition to Appoint a Plenary or Limited Guardian for the same alleged incapacitated person, shall be assigned to the same Division.

6) In all of the above situations if these cases are not filed simultaneously, all cases shall be assigned to the division where the first case was assigned. It is the responsibility of the attorney of record to notify the Clerk of the Circuit Court in writing that related cases exist. If the related cases are filed by different attorneys it is the responsibility of the attorney filing the latter case to notify the Clerk of the Circuit Court in writing at the time of filing that related cases are pending before the Court.

3. The court reserves jurisdiction to change assignment between the regions utilizing the general principles of law governing a request for change.

DONE and **SIGNED** in Chambers at West Palm Beach, Palm Beach County, Florida, this 8th day of January, 2013.

Peter D. Blanc
Chief Judge

Adopted effective September 29, 2008. Amended effective December 17, 2008; August 23, 2010; January 11, 2012; January 8, 2013.

* supersedes admin. order no. 6.101–1/12

6.102. MATTERS TO BE FILED IN PROBATE AND GUARDIANSHIP DIVISION

IN THE CIRCUIT COURT OF THE FIFTEENTH JUDICIAL CIRCUIT IN AND FOR PALM BEACH COUNTY, FLORIDA

ADMINISTRATIVE ORDER NO. 6.102–9/08 *

IN RE: MATTERS TO BE FILED IN PROBATE AND GUARDIANSHIP DIVISION

Pursuant to the authority conferred by Florida Rule of Judicial Administration 2.215, it is **ORDERED** as follows:

1. The following matters, except those specified below, shall be filed with and conducted by the Probate and Guardianship Division of the Court. All proceedings pertaining to:

a. Florida Probate Code (Ch. 731–35 F.S.);

b. Florida Guardianship Law (Ch. 744 F.S.);

c. Conservators and Curators (Ch. 747 F.S.);

d. Trusts (complaints filed under Ch. 736 F.S. or Ch. 86 F.S. relating to the administration of, or rights of beneficiaries in trusts);

e. Baker Act (Ch. 394 F.S.);

f. Hal S. Marchman Alcohol and Other Drug Services Act (Ch. 397 F.S.);

g. Adult Protective Services Act (Sec. 415.105 F.S.);

h. Compulsory Treatment and Commitment of Persons Afflicted with Tuberculosis (Sec. 392.55, 392.56, 392.57 F.S.); and

i. All proceedings for determination of incapacity pursuant to Ch. 744 F.S.

2. All actions properly filed with the Probate and Guardianship Division which contain a cognizable right to trial by jury may be transferred to the appropriate Civil Division at the option of the Probate and Guardianship Division presiding judge.

3. Action seeking relief in the nature of constructive and resulting trusts shall be filed in the Civil Division. All independent civil actions filed against an estate or trust as a result of an objection to a claim filed against a decedent's estate pursuant to F.S. Section 733.702, et al., or against a trust pursuant to F.S. Section 736.1008 shall be filed in the Civil Division

DONE AND SIGNED in Chambers at West Palm Beach, Palm Beach County, Florida, this 29 day of September, 2008.

KATHLEEN J. KROLL
Chief Judge

Adopted effective September 29, 2008.

* supersedes admin. order 6.012–7/07

6.103. ASSIGNMENT OF CASES SOUTH COUNTY PROBATE/GUARDIANSHIP MENTAL HEALTH AND SUBSTANCE ABUSE DIVISIONS "IX" "IY" AND "IZ"

IN THE CIRCUIT COURT OF THE FIFTEENTH JUDICIAL CIRCUIT IN AND FOR PALM BEACH COUNTY, FLORIDA

ADMINISTRATIVE ORDER NO. 6.103–12/13 *

ASSIGNMENT OF CASES SOUTH COUNTY PROBATE/GUARDIANSHIP MENTAL HEALTH AND SUBSTANCE ABUSE DIVISIONS "IX" "IY" AND "IZ"

In the interest of judicial economy and to increase the efficiency of service to litigants, the Fifteenth Judicial Circuit created two additional Probate and Guardianship Divisions "IX" and "IZ" on August 12, 2011. Based upon review of the pending South County Family and Probate/Guardianship caseloads and judicial rotations, effective January 22, 2013, Probate Division "IZ" was temporarily closed and the pending cases were evenly divided between probate divisions "IX" and "IY" and newly filed Probate/Guardianship/Marchman and Mental Health/Substance Abuse cases were assigned only to divisions "IX" and "IY".

Court Administration will re-open Probate/Guardianship Division "IZ" effective December 1, 2013. Therefore, the ratio assignment for newly filed Probate/Guardianship/Marchman and Mental Health/Substance Abuse cases requires adjustment.

NOW, THEREFORE, pursuant to the authority conferred by Florida Rule of Judicial Administration 2.215, it is **ORDERED AND ADJUDGED** as follows:

1. Effective December 1, 2013, newly filed South County Probate/Guardianship/Marchman and Mental Health/Substance Abuse cases shall be randomly assigned in the following manner: Division "IX" thirty-three percent (33%), Division "IY" thirty-three percent (33%), and Division "IZ" thirty-four percent (34%).

2. All Ex-parte and emergency hearings scheduled in Division "IZ" prior to the rotations on January 22, 2014 (should any arise) will be heard by the divisional Judges in Divisions "IX" and "IY" in the following manner: Division "IX" will handle odd numbered cases, and Division "IY" will handle even numbered cases. Following rotations on January 22, 2014, the Judge assigned to the Division "IZ" will handle all cases assigned to that Division.

3. The Administrative Office of the Court shall monitor the pending caseloads for each of the South County Family Divisions to ensure equity amongst the divisions in light of other assignments.

4. To the extent that this Administrative Order differs from Administrative Order 6.101–1/13 (as amended), this Administrative Order controls.

DONE and **SIGNED** in Chambers at West Palm Beach, Palm Beach County, Florida, this 30 day of December, 2013 *nunc pro tunc* December 1, 2013.

Jeffrey Colbath
Chief Judge

Adopted effective August 29, 2011. Amended effective January 22, 2013; December 30, 2013.

* supersedes admin. order 6.103–1/13

6.104. EMERGENCY HEARINGS IN PROBATE AND GUARDIANSHIP MATTERS

IN THE CIRCUIT COURT OF THE FIFTEENTH JUDICIAL CIRCUIT IN AND FOR PALM BEACH COUNTY, FLORIDA

ADMINISTRATIVE ORDER NO. 6.104–11/14

IN RE: EMERGENCY HEARINGS IN PROBATE AND GUARDIANSHIP MATTERS

Pursuant to the authority conferred by Florida Rule of Judicial Administration 2.215, it is **ORDERED** as follow:

1. Requests for Emergency Hearings shall be decided by each judge on the Emergency Motion alone. Upon receiving a request for an emergency hearing, the judge shall decide whether an emergency exists, and if so, shall schedule a hearing, enter any ex parte order deemed necessary, or take any other appropriate action.

2. Motions for Emergency Hearings in Guardianship matters will be denied unless there are sufficient allegations to establish that there is:

a. An imminent risk of substantial physical harm to the alleged incapacitated person or ward;

b. An imminent risk of substantial waste to the alleged incapacitated person or ward's property or finances;

c. An alleged incapacitated person or ward is about to be illegally removed from this Court's jurisdiction;

d. An Appointment of an Emergency Court Monitor or Emergency Temporary Guardian in accordance with Florida Statute s. 744.1075 and s. 744.3031.

3. Motions for immediate payment of funds usually do not meet the standard for emergency relief.

4. The emergency filing will be forwarded in accordance with Administrative Order 2.312.

DONE and **SIGNED** in Chambers at West Palm Beach, Palm Beach County, Florida, this 19 day of November, 2014.

Jeffrey Colbath
Chief Judge

Adopted effective November 19, 2014.

6.105. ESTABLISHMENT OF NORTH COUNTY PROBATE/GUARDIANSHIP MENTAL HEALTH AND SUBSTANCE ABUSE DIVISION "IJ"

IN THE CIRCUIT COURT OF THE FIFTEENTH JUDICIAL CIRCUIT IN AND FOR PALM BEACH COUNTY, FLORIDA

ADMINISTRATIVE ORDER NO. 6.105–12/14

ESTABLISHMENT OF NORTH COUNTY PROBATE/GUARDIANSHIP MENTAL HEALTH AND SUBSTANCE ABUSE DIVISION "IJ"

For efficiency purposes, in North County, the Domestic Relations, Probate, Guardianship, Mental Health, and Substance abuse cases shall be equally divided among three divisions.

NOW, THEREFORE, pursuant to the authority conferred by Florida Rule of Judicial Administration 2.215, it is **ORDERED AND ADJUDGED** as follows:

A. Establishment of North County, Probate/Guardianship Hybrid Division. Effective **January 1, 2015**, the Administrative Office of the Court, Court Technology is hereby directed to establish Division **"IJ"**.

B. Assignment of Cases to Family Division.

1. Effective **January 1, 2015**, the Clerk and Comptroller shall assign **probate/guardianship, mental health, substance abuse and** domestic relations cases to the North County

Courthouse according to the zip codes outlined in Administrative Order 5.101. Newly filed and re-opened cases shall be assigned as follows:

- 34% to division "FJ" **and "IJ"**
- 33% to division "FH" **and "IH"**
- 33% to division "FI" **and "II"**

2. Family cases shall be assigned as defined by Administrative Order 5.101.

DONE and **SIGNED** in Chambers at West Palm Beach, Palm Beach County, Florida, this 19 day of December, 2014.

Jeffrey Colbath
Chief Judge

Adopted effective January 1, 2015.

6.106. ESTABLISHMENT OF MAIN COURTHOUSE PROBATE/GUARDIANSHIP DIVISIONS "IC" AND "ID" AND ASSOCIATING DOMESTIC RELATIONS DIVISION

IN THE CIRCUIT COURT OF THE FIFTEENTH JUDICIAL CIRCUIT IN AND FOR PALM BEACH COUNTY, FLORIDA

ADMINISTRATIVE ORDER NO 6.106–10/17

IN RE: ESTABLISHMENT OF MAIN COURTHOUSE PROBATE/GUARDIANSHIP DIVISIONS "IC" AND "ID" AND ASSOCIATING DOMESTIC RELATIONS DIVISIONS

In the interest of judicial economy and to increase the efficiency of service to litigants, two new Probate/Guardianship Divisions will be created at the Main Branch. Cases shall be equally divided among the three Probate/Guardianship Divisions located at the Main Branch. Similar to the North County and South County Domestic Relations/Probate hybrid divisions, one judge will preside over a Probate/Guardianship Division and a Domestic Relations Division.

NOW, THEREFORE, pursuant to the authority conferred by Florida Rule of Judicial Administration 2.215, it is **ORDERED AND ADJUDGED** as follows:

A. Creation of Divisions.

1. Effective October 25, 2017, the Clerk and Comptroller shall create Probate/Guardianship Division "IC" and this Division shall be associated with Domestic Relations Division "FC". One Judge shall preside over both divisions.

2. Effective October 25, 2017, the Clerk and Comptroller shall create Probate/Guardianship Division "ID" and this Division shall be associated with Domestic Relations Division "FD". One Judge shall preside over both divisions.

3. Effective October 25, 2017, the Clerk and Comptroller shall associate the existing Probate/Guardianship Division "IB" with Domestic Relations Division "FA". One Judge shall preside over both divisions.

B. Transfer of Pending Probate/Guardianship Cases.

1. The Clerk and Comptroller shall reassign the attached list of pending Probate/Guardianship Division "IB" cases among the two new Probate/Guardianship Divisions "IC" and "ID" in order to equally balance the caseload among the Probate/Guardianship Divisions. The reassignment of all cases shall be completed by December 1, 2017.

2. Cases currently scheduled for a hearing in Division "IB" shall be heard before the new divisional judge starting December 1, 2017.

3. Emergency or time sensitive matters on transferred cases shall be heard by the Division "IB" Judge until December 1, 2017.

4. The Clerk and Comptroller will electronically serve a copy of the Notice of Reassignment on all attorneys who are listed with the E–Portal as counsel on cases in Division "IB". Within seven (7) business days of the service of the Notice of Reassignment, counsel representing the petitioner will serve, in accordance with Rules of Judicial Administration 2.515, a copy of the Notice of Reassignment on all parties not listed in the E–Portal and who have not been dropped or dismissed from the action. If the petitioner is self- represented, then counsel representing the Respondent will serve a copy of the Notice of Reassignment as set forth above. Counsel serving the Notice of Reassignment will also file a Notice of Service of the Notice of Reassignment ("Notice of Service") with the Clerk of Court. The Notice of Service is to include a complete, current and accurate service list.

C. Assignment of Newly Filed Probate/Guardianship Cases and Domestic Relations Cases.

1. Starting December 1, 2017, the Clerk and Comptroller shall assign all Domestic Violence cases equally among Family Divisions "FA", "FC", and "FD". All other Domestic Relations case types shall be assigned 100% to Division "FA" until such time as the Division reaches the average number of pending cases, not to exceed a two-month time frame. Therefore, Divisions "FC" and "FD" shall not receive any newly filed Domestic Relations case types, with the exception of Domestic Violence case types. However, in the event that a related case is filed, the Clerk and Comptroller shall override Showcase and assign the newly filed case to the same division as the related case.

2. Starting December 1, 2017, the Clerk and Comptroller shall assign all Probate/Guardianship cases equally among the three Probate/Guardianship "IB", "IC", and "ID" Divisions.

D. Monitoring of Caseloads.

1. The Administrative Office of the Court will monitor the pending caseloads for each Domestic Relation Division to ensure equity amongst the divisions.

2. The Administrative Office of the Court will notify the Clerk and Comptroller by email as to when the case counter for the Domestic Relations Divisions shall be set to equally assign newly filed cases.

DONE and **SIGNED** in Chambers at West Palm Beach, Palm Beach County, Florida, this 24th day of October, 2017.

Krista Marx
Chief Judge

Adopted effective December 1, 2017.

Probate

6.201. PRE–HEARING REVIEW OF PROBATE DOCUMENTS

IN THE CIRCUIT COURT OF THE FIFTEENTH JUDICIAL CIRCUIT IN AND FOR PALM BEACH COUNTY, FLORIDA

ADMINISTRATIVE ORDER NO. 6.201–9/08 *

IN RE: PRE–HEARING REVIEW OF PROBATE DOCUMENTS

A pre-hearing review of pleadings and documents by a case manager or other qualified court personnel in the probate division will promote full compliance with statutory and procedural requirements.

NOW, THEREFORE, pursuant to the authority conferred by Florida Rule of Judicial Administration 2.215, it is **ORDERED** as follows:

All matters, which are to be presented to a probate judge during motion calendar (ex parte hour) shall be submitted first to a probate case manager or other qualified court personnel.

DONE and **SIGNED** in Chambers at West Palm Beach, Palm Beach County, Florida, this 29 day of September, 2008.

Kathleen J. Kroll
Chief Judge

Adopted effective September 29, 2008.

* supersedes admin. order 6.009–2/93

6.202. FORMAL ADMINISTRATION CHECKLIST FOR CLOSING ESTATES

IN THE CIRCUIT COURT OF THE FIFTEENTH JUDICIAL CIRCUIT IN AND FOR PALM BEACH COUNTY, FLORIDA

ADMINISTRATIVE ORDER NO. 6.202–9/08 *

IN RE: FORMAL ADMINISTRATION CHECKLIST FOR CLOSING ESTATES

The Court is committed to providing efficient judicial services and streamlining the estate administration process. The completion, by the attorney of record, of a pre-closing checklist before submission of an order of discharge of the personal representative will promote compliance with statutory and procedural requirements.

NOW, THEREFORE, pursuant to the authority conferred by Florida Rule of Judicial Administration 2.215, it is **ORDERED** as follows:

1. The Clerk of the Court (Probate Division) shall, upon request, issue a Checklist for Closing Estates involving Formal Administration. The checklist shall include all docketed information as it appears in the Clerk's records at the time the checklist is requested.

2. Thereafter, each proposed order of discharge filed in an estate must be accompanied by such checklist, on which the attorney of record for the estate shall attest to the filing of all required documents as disclosed on the checklist. Any proposed order of discharge which is not accompanied by a properly completed checklist shall not be reviewed by the Court.

DONE and **SIGNED** in Chambers at West Palm Beach, Palm Beach County, Florida, this 29 day of September, 2008.

Kathleen J. Kroll
Chief Judge

Adopted effective September 29, 2008.

* supersedes admin. order 6.013–12/96

Guardianship/Mental Health/Substance Abuse

6.301. PROBATE & GUARDIANSHIP DIVISION COMPENSATION FOR ATTORNEYS AND EXAMINING COMMITTEE MEMBERS

IN THE CIRCUIT COURT OF THE FIFTEENTH JUDICIAL CIRCUIT IN AND FOR PALM BEACH COUNTY, FLORIDA

ADMINISTRATIVE ORDER NO.: 6.301–6/17 *

IN RE: PROBATE & GUARDIANSHIP DIVISION COMPENSATION FOR ATTORNEYS AND EXAMINING COMMITTEE MEMBERS

This order shall govern the compensation of members of the examining committee and attorneys appointed for a person alleged to be incapacitated or appointed pursuant to Chapters 392, 393, 394, 397, and 415, Florida Statutes.

NOW, THEREFORE, pursuant to the authority conferred by Florida Rule of Judicial Administration 2.215, it is **ORDERED** as follows:

A. Court Appointed Attorneys.

1. *Alleged Incapacitated Persons Who Are Not Deemed Indigent.* Attorneys appointed to represent alleged incapacitated persons in contested or uncontested matters and who are not found indigent shall receive a reasonable fee as set forth in Florida Statute § 744.331(7) (2014) (as amended). The petition for attorney fees must be accompanied by an affidavit addressing the pertinent considerations set forth in Rule 4–1.5(b), Rules Regulating the Florida Bar, supported by an itemized schedule of time and effort which shall be served upon counsel for the guardian. Should the alleged incapacitated person substitute his or her own counsel for counsel appointed by the court, a reasonable fee will be awarded by the court to the court-appointed counsel.

2. *Alleged Incapacitated Persons Who Are Deemed Indigent.*

a. Uncontested matters:

1) If the alleged incapacitated person is indigent and the Office of Criminal Conflict and Civil Regional Counsel is not appointed to an uncontested matter, or withdraws from an uncontested matter, an appointed attorney will

receive for services rendered the total sum of $400 from the inception of the appointment through discharge.

2) Should the alleged incapacitated person substitute his or her own counsel for counsel appointed by the court, the fee to the court appointed counsel is not to exceed $400.00.

b. Contested matters and matters pursuant to Florida Statute §§ 392, 393, 394, 397, 415:

1) Except for those cases in which the Office of Criminal Conflict and Civil Regional Counsel is appointed in contested matters or those matters pursuant to Florida Statute §§ 392, 393, 394, 397, 415, court appointed counsel in indigent cases will be paid a rate as set forth by the Justice Administrative Commission.

2) If the alleged ward is indigent, and the Office of Criminal Conflict and Civil Regional Counsel is not appointed or has withdrawn, the petition, affidavit and itemized schedule of time and effort shall be served on the Justice Administration Commission, 227 North Bronough, Suite 2100, Tallahassee, Florida 32302 for payment.

B. Examining Committee Members.

1. Examining committee members shall receive a flat fee for services rendered in all cases regardless of indigency and regardless of whether the matter is contested.

a.	Medical Doctors (including Psychiatrists)	$350
b.	Psychologists or Ph.D. in relevant area	$300
c.	Registered Nurse, Nurse Practitioner, Master's Level Practitioner in relevant field with license approved by the Clinical Social Work, Marriage and Family Therapy, and Mental Health Counseling Board of the Florida Medical Quality Assurance Services	$100
d.	Lay Person	$ 75

2. Examining committee members shall be paid an hourly fee for in court testimony regardless of indigency and regardless of whether the matter is contested. Fractional hours of testimony shall be prorated. No fee will be paid by the court for travel time, preparation time or depositions. **Payment for testimony is capped at two (2) hours total.**

a.	Medical Doctors (including Psychiatrists)	$200/hour
b.	Psychologists or Ph.D. in relevant area	$150/hour
c.	Registered Nurse, Nurse Practitioner, Master's Level Practitioner in relevant field with license approved by the Clinical Social Work, Marriage and Family Therapy, and Mental Health Counseling Board of the Florida Medical Quality Assurance Services	$100/hour
d.	Lay Person	$ 75/hour

3. Court Administration shall pay the fees of the examining committee members in the event that the proceedings are dismissed because:

a. the alleged ward is found to not be incapacitated and the court makes a finding that the petition was not filed in bad faith; or

b. the alleged ward dies prior to a determination of incapacity; or

c. the proceedings are dismissed prior to a determination of incapacity but after the examining committee has completed their evaluations.

4. If a medical doctor or psychologist is not able to complete a scheduled examination due to the alleged ward either not showing up or refusing to participate in the examination, all medical doctors and psychologists shall be compensated at a flat rate of $150 per scheduled evaluation. If a registered nurse, nurse practitioner, master's level practitioner in relevant field with license approved by the Clinical Social Work, Marriage and Family Therapy, and Mental Health Counseling Board of the Florida Medical Quality Assurance Services, or a lay person is not able to complete a scheduled examination due to the alleged ward either not showing up or refusing to participate in the examination, all registered nurses, nurse practitioners, master's level practitioners in relevant field with license approved by the Clinical Social Work, Marriage and Family Therapy, and Mental Health Counseling Board of the Florida Medical Quality Assurance Services, and lay people shall be compensated at a flat rate of S50 per scheduled evaluation.

DONE and SIGNED in Chambers at West Palm Beach, Palm Beach County, Florida, this 14 day of June, 2017.

Jeffrey Colbath
Chief Judge

Adopted effective September 29, 2008. Amended effective January 8, 2013; July 20, 2015; June 14, 2017.

* supersedes admin. order 6.301–7/15

6.302. DISCOVERY REQUESTS OF DEPARTMENT OF CHILDREN AND FAMILIES

IN THE CIRCUIT COURT OF THE FIFTEENTH JUDICIAL CIRCUIT IN AND FOR PALM BEACH COUNTY, FLORIDA

ADMINISTRATIVE ORDER NO. 6.302–9/08 *

IN RE: DISCOVERY REQUESTS OF DEPARTMENT OF CHILDREN AND FAMILIES

Section 415.107(2), Florida Statutes, require court orders prior to releasing information which is otherwise discoverable pursuant to Rule 3.220, Florida Rules of Criminal Procedure.

NOW, THEREFORE, pursuant to the authority conferred by Florida Rule of Judicial Administration 2.215, it is **ORDERED** as follows:

1. This order shall apply to the prosecution of all cases in which there was an investigation of the same facts and occurrences by both a law enforcement agency and the State of Florida Department of Children and Families.

2. The agents of the Florida Department of Children and Families and other persons having access to confidential information under section 415.107, Florida Statutes, are hereby required to comply with discovery requests made pursuant to the Florida Rules of Criminal Procedure regarding disclosure of confidential information obtained through or from abuse investigations under Chapter 415, Florida Statutes, and may testify at trial without further order of the Court.

3. Information obtained remains confidential and shall not be publicly disclosed by any prosecuting or defending attorney unless said attorney has obtained prior authorization from the Court that public disclosure is necessary to resolve an issue pending before the Court in accordance with section 415.107(2), Florida Statutes.

DONE and **SIGNED** in Chambers at West Palm Beach, Palm Beach County, Florida, this 29 day of September, 2008.

Kathleen J. Kroll
Chief Judge

Adopted effective September 29, 2008.

* supersedes admin order 4.025–6/93

6.304. APPOINTMENT OF MAGISTRATE—MENTAL HEALTH AND GUARDIANSHIP

IN THE CIRCUIT COURT OF THE FIFTEENTH JUDICIAL CIRCUIT IN AND FOR PALM BEACH COUNTY, FLORIDA

ADMINISTRATIVE ORDER NO. 6.304–9/08 *

IN RE: APPOINTMENT OF MAGISTRATE—MENTAL HEALTH AND GUARDIANSHIP

This circuit has a substantial mental health and guardianship caseload. Florida Statutes require the court to conduct timely hearings to determine if a person needs to be involuntarily examined at and/or committed to a mental health treatment program. Florida Statutes also require that guardianships file annual plans and/or accountings. The interests of the public and litigants involved in mental health proceedings require flexible and speedy resolutions because of the exigency of the subject matter. The current resources of the court and the time available to conduct such hearings in mental health proceedings are limited. The interests of the public and the wards who are the subject of guardianship proceedings mandate that the welfare and needs of wards are met, that wards assets are being appropriately managed and expenses paid. Such guardianship proceedings require flexible and speed resolutions. The current resources of the court and time available to conduct guardianship review and enforcement functions are limited.

NOW, THEREFORE, pursuant to the authority conferred by Florida Rule of Judicial Administration 2.215, it is **ORDERED** as follows:

1. Magistrates shall be appointed to hear all matters arising from Marchman, Baker and Tuberculosis Control Acts within the Fifteenth Circuit.

2. Magistrates shall be responsible for recommending examination, treatment and designation of the treatment facilities to the Court; shall conduct contempt hearings relative to violations of court order; document such findings of fact and conclusions of law and render a report making recommendations to the appropriate judicial office together with a recommended order based upon the report.

3. The duties and responsibilities of a Magistrate shall not be limited to the above stated functions but rather shall serve under the direction and at the appointment of the Circuit Court as the Court's judicial representative on all mental health matters.

4. Magistrates shall be appointed to assist the court to hear certain matters arising from Florida's Guardianship Law within the Fifteenth Circuit.

5. Magistrates shall be responsible for reviewing guardianship plans and accountings when problems are discovered by the Clerk of Circuit Court's auditors, shall schedule and conduct status conference and order to show cause hearings for non-compliance with annual guardianship plans and accountings or other enforcement functions pertaining to orders of the court, document such findings of fact, conclusions of law and render a report making recommendations to the appropriate judicial office together with a recommended order based upon the report.

6. The duties and responsibilities of a Magistrate shall not be limited to the above stated functions but rather shall serve under the direction and at the appointment of the Circuit Court.

7. By separate order, the chief judge shall appoint magistrates, members of the Florida Bar, to serve as judicial officers of the Circuit Court of the Fifteenth Judicial Circuit in accordance with rules 1.490(a), Fla.R.Civ.P.; 12.490 and 12.491, Fla.Fam.L.R.P., *5.267, Fla.R.Guardianship P.* and rule 2.215, Fla.R.Jud.Admin. and in conformity with Florida Statutes Chapters 397, 394, 392 and 744.

DONE and **SIGNED** in Chambers at West Palm Beach, Palm Beach County, Florida, this 29 day of September, 2008.

Kathleen J. Kroll
Chief Judge

Adopted effective September 29, 2008.

* supersedes admin. order no. 6.005–10/04

6.305. CIVIL DRUG COURT

IN THE CIRCUIT COURT OF THE FIFTEENTH JUDICIAL CIRCUIT IN AND FOR PALM BEACH COUNTY, FLORIDA

ADMINISTRATIVE ORDER NO. 6.305–7/11 *

IN RE: CIVIL DRUG COURT

Article V, Section 7, of the Florida Constitution states that "[a] circuit or county court may hold civil and criminal trials and hearings in any place within the territorial jurisdiction of the court as designated by the chief judge of the circuit". The City of Riviera Beach has offered to provide facilities within the City of Riviera Beach located at 2051 Martin Luther King Boulevard, Riviera Beach, Florida 33404, so that the court may conduct civil commitment hearings for drug and alcohol abuse pursuant to Chapter 397, Florida Statutes (2010). There exists an urgent need to provide treatment modalities for drug and alcohol abuse outside of the criminal justice system, i.e., without the taint of arrest and conviction. Various agencies and entities have offered their resources and cooperation to support a community-based drug court.

NOW, THEREFORE, pursuant to the authority conferred by Florida Rule of Judicial Administration 2.215, it is **ORDERED** as follows:

1. A community drug court is hereby established to conduct civil commitment hearings and to commit alcohol and drug abusers to treatment programs ("Civil Drug Court").

2. The chief judge, by separate order, shall assign a judge or special magistrate to preside over the community-based drug court.

3. The facility, located at 2051 Martin Luther King Boulevard, in the City of Riviera Beach, is hereby designated as an approved location at which the Circuit Court for the Fifteenth Judicial Circuit may conduct civil commitment hearings pursuant to Chapter 397, Florida Statutes (2010).

4. Adult and juvenile civil commitment hearings will be scheduled on Saturdays with juvenile hearings in the morning and adult hearings in the afternoon.

5. A clerk from the Fifteenth Judicial Circuit Court shall be designated by the Chief Operation Officer/Clerk & Comptroller to assist the judge in civil commitment hearings.

6. The appointed clerk is authorized and ordered to transport the necessary court files to the civil commitment hearings.

7. In the event a clerk is unable to attend the hearings, an employee of the City of Riviera Beach, who is assigned to work at this Community Drug Court, is authorized to take custody of the court files of cases scheduled to be heard at 2051 Martin Luther King Boulevard, Riviera Beach, Florida 33404.

8. The clerk is hereby authorized and ordered to make necessary court files available to the municipal employee assigned to work at Community Drug Court as needed.

DONE and **SIGNED** in Chambers at West Palm Beach, Palm Beach County, Florida, this 6 day of July, 2011.

Peter D. Blanc
Chief Judge

Adopted effective September 29, 2008. Amended effective July 5, 2011; July 6, 2011.

* supersedes admin. order 6.305–7/11 (dated 7/5/11)

6.306. GUARDIANSHIP MATTERS TO BE AUDITED BY CLERK & COMPTROLLER

IN THE CIRCUIT COURT OF THE FIFTEENTH JUDICIAL CIRCUIT IN AND FOR PALM BEACH COUNTY, FLORIDA

ADMINISTRATIVE ORDER NO.: 6.306–12/10

IN RE: GUARDIANSHIP MATTERS TO BE AUDITED BY CLERK & COMPTROLLER

Persons who are placed in guardianship need an effective and efficient review of guardianship accountings, plans, and inventories. Florida Statute 744.368 sets forth statutory time frames within which guardianship accountings, plans and inventories must be reviewed. Different levels of review may be necessary to provide a thorough audit of the files.

NOW THEREFORE, pursuant to the authority conferred by Florida Rule of Judicial Administration 2.215, it is **ORDERED** as follows:

A. Level 1 Audit.

1. The Clerk shall:

a. Conduct the statutorily required audit/review of all initial, annual, simplified, interim, trust or final accountings, plans and inventories pursuant to Chapter 744, Florida Statutes. This review shall consist of a desk review (worksheet) of the guardianship reports in conjunction with the supporting documentation filed with the report.

b. Prepare and forward to the Court the file and the Clerk's review along with a proposed order approving the initial, annual, interim or final accounting, plan or inventory.

c. Prepare and forward to the General Magistrate or Judge a Notice of Delinquency and an Order Setting Contempt Hearing if an initial an annual report is not timely filed.

d. Send correspondence to the guardian/attorney stating the discrepancies and allowing reasonable time for a response if there is a discrepancy. If there is no response, the Clerk will prepare a Notice of Delinquency and an Order Setting Contempt Hearing which will be submitted to the General Magistrate or Judge.

2. Upon review of the file, the Clerk will determine if a Level 2 or Level 3 audit is needed.

B. Level 2 & Level 3 Audits.

1. If the Clerk determines that a Level 2 Audit is necessary the Clerk will:

a. Examine the guardianship report and attempt to verify selected questionable items.

b. Conduct limited inquiries and/or requests for supporting documentation to resolve the issues.

c. Submit to the General Magistrate or Judge the file and audit report identifying any discrepancies within 90 days after the filing of the verified inventory and accountings pursuant to Florida Statute sec. 744.368. If the 90 day time period is insufficient to complete the audit, the Clerk shall file an Ex–Parte Motion for Extension of Time to Complete Review, along with a proposed order.

d. If the filed documents are insufficient to properly audit the account at any stage in the review or documents are not produced timely upon written request by the Clerk, the Clerk will prepare an order for the Court to order the guardian to file the report within 15 days after the service of the order upon her or him or show cause why she or he should not be compelled to do so as provided by Florida Statute 744.3685.

e. If the documents are still not forthcoming after service of the above order, the Clerk shall notify the Court that the documents were not timely received and will request that a hearing be set.

f. Determine if a Level 3 Audit is necessary.

2. If the Clerk determines that a Level 3 Audit is necessary the Clerk will:

a. Examine and attempt verification of all significant items pertinent to the guardianship report.

b. Conduct a detailed review of the accounts and attendant transactions which may include third party confirmation.

c. Submit to the General Magistrate or Judge the file and audit report identifying any discrepancies within 90 days after the filing of the verified inventory and accountings pursuant to Florida Statute sec. 744.368. If the 90 day time period is insufficient to complete the audit, the Clerk shall file an Ex–Parte Motion for Extension of Time to Complete Review, along with a proposed order.

d. If the filed documents are insufficient to properly audit the account at any stage in the review or documents are not produced timely upon written request by the Clerk, the Clerk will prepare an order for the Court to order the guardian to file the report within 15 days after the service of the order upon her or him or show cause why she or he should not be compelled to do so as provided by Florida Statute 744.3685.

e. If the documents are still not forthcoming after service of the above order, the Clerk shall notify the Court that the documents were not timely received and will request that a hearing be set.

C. Quality Control Sample. Each year the Clerk shall randomly select a sample of guardianships and perform a comprehensive audit of related transactions and records. From the selected sample, the Clerk will conduct a Level 2 or Level 3 audit as described above.

D. Confidentiality. In accordance with Florida Statute 744.3701(1) & (2), any data included in the reports and supporting documentation prepared by the Clerk auditor which came directly from the guardianship reports shall remain confidential and not available for review by the general public without a court order.

DONE AND ORDERED in Chambers at West Palm Beach, Palm Beach County, Florida this 20 day of December, 2010.

PETER D. BLANC
Chief Judge

Adopted effective December 20, 2010.

6.307. [VACATED AND SET ASIDE BY ORDER 6.307–1/18, EFFECTIVE JANUARY 8, 2018.]

6.308. ADMINISTRATIVE CLOSURE OF BAKER ACT CASES

IN THE CIRCUIT COURT OF THE FIFTEENTH JUDICIAL CIRCUIT IN AND FOR PALM BEACH COUNTY, FLORIDA

ADMINISTRATIVE ORDER 6.308–8/15

IN RE: ADMINISTRATIVE CLOSURE OF BAKER ACT CASES

A circuit court may take action in cases filed pursuant to Florida Statute § 394.451 ("The Baker Act") up to two years from the date of filing. Petitioners may seek a six (6) month extension following the filing of the action. There are currently over 325 Baker Act Cases which have been pending longer than two years from the date of the case filing and which have had no activity for at least seven (7) months. The Court is responsible for managing its caseload pursuant to Florida Rule of Judicial Administration 2.545. The administration of justice would be furthered by administratively closing cases that are pending beyond the statutorily required time period as the personnel time involved in manually reviewing the files is costly.

Pursuant to the authority conferred by Florida Rule of Judicial Administration 2.215, it is hereby **ORDERED** as follows:

1. Pending Baker Act cases that were filed prior to June 30, 2013 and which have had no activity for at least seven (7) months are hereby administratively closed. A list of those cases are attached hereto and incorporated herein as Exhibit "A"[1].

2. Due to practical and resource limitations, the Clerk & Comptroller is hereby directed to effectuate the closing process by entering a docket code in the case management system to administratively close the case and by entering text stating the case is closed pursuant to Administrative Order 6.308. The Clerk & Comptroller is not required to manually file a hard copy of this order should a physical case file exist.

3. If a party files a written notice asserting that a case was administratively closed in error, the clerk shall reopen the file without charge to the party.

4. Court Technology is hereby directed to post Exhibit "A" on the circuit's website for a period of at least 90 days.

DONE AND SIGNED in Chambers at West Palm Beach, Palm Beach County, Florida this 24 day of August, 2015.

Jeffrey J. Colbath
Chief Judge

Adopted effective August 24, 2015.

[1] Exhibit A not included.

6.309. ADMINISTRATIVE CLOSURE OF MARCHMAN ACT CASES

IN THE CIRCUIT COURT OF THE FIFTEENTH JUDICIAL CIRCUIT IN AND FOR PALM BEACH COUNTY, FLORIDA

ADMINISTRATIVE ORDER 6.309–8/15

IN RE: ADMINISTRATIVE CLOSURE OF MARCHMAN ACT CASES

A circuit court may take action in cases filed pursuant to Florida Statute § 397.301 ("Hal S. Marchman Alcohol and Other Drug Services Act") up to 150 days from the date of filing of a treatment order. If applicable, at the conclusion of the 60–day period of court-ordered involuntary treatment, a service provider may seek a 90 day extension following the filing of the action. There are currently over 130 Marchman Cases which have had no activity for at least 150 days. The Court is responsible for managing its caseload pursuant to Florida Rule of Judicial Administration 2.545. The administration of justice would be furthered by administratively closing cases that are pending beyond the statutorily required time period as the personnel time involved in manually reviewing the files is costly.

Pursuant to the authority conferred by Florida Rule of Judicial Administration 2.215, it is hereby **ORDERED** as follows:

1. Pending Marchman Act cases which have had no activity for 150 days are hereby administratively closed. A list of those cases are attached hereto and incorporated herein as Exhibit "A"[1].

2. Due to practical and resource limitations, the Clerk & Comptroller is hereby directed to effectuate the closing process by entering a docket code in the case management system to administratively close the case and by entering text stating the case is closed pursuant to Administrative Order 6.309. The Clerk & Comptroller is not required to manually file a hard copy of this order should a physical case file exist.

3. If a party files a written notice asserting that a case was administratively closed in error, the clerk shall reopen the file without charge to the party.

4. Court Technology is hereby directed to post Exhibit "A" on the circuit's website for a period of at least 90 days.

DONE AND SIGNED in Chambers at West Palm Beach, Palm Beach County, Florida this 24 day of August, 2015.

Jeffrey J. Colbath
Chief Judge

Adopted effective August 24, 2015.

1 Exhibit A not included.

6.310. PROFESSIONAL GUARDIAN REGISTRY & APPOINTMENT OF PROFESSIONAL GUARDIAN

IN THE CIRCUIT COURT OF THE FIFTEENTH JUDICIAL CIRCUIT IN AND FOR PALM BEACH COUNTY, FLORIDA

ADMINISTRATIVE ORDER NO. 6.310–10/16

IN RE: PROFESSIONAL GUARDIAN REGISTRY & APPOINTMENT OF PROFESSIONAL GUARDIAN

Chapter 744, Florida Statutes, authorizes court appointment of professional guardians, subject to the considerations set forth in Section 744.312, Florida Statutes. The Office of the Public and Professional Guardians in the Department of Elder Affairs provides a current list of registered professional guardians, who are also listed on the Department of Elder Affairs website. There is both a need for a fair and impartial manner of selecting professional guardians and the appointment of guardians to serve indigent wards on a pro bono basis.

NOW THEREFORE, pursuant to the authority conferred by Florida Rule of Judicial Administration 2.215, it is **ORDERED** as follows:

1. In order to be eligible to be appointed as a professional guardian in the Fifteenth Judicial Circuit, a professional guardian must annually apply for and be appointed to the Fifteenth Judicial Circuit's Professional Guardian Registry ("Registry").

a. Applications for the appointment period of January 1, 2017–June 30, 2017 are to be submitted to the Administrative Office of the Court from November 1– December 15, 2016. Applications are to be sent only by email to:

CAD-professionalguardians@pbcgov.org

Failure to timely submit an application will result in the professional guardian not being appointed to the Registry.

b. To be appointed during subsequent fiscal years (July 1 – June 30), applications are to be submitted to the Administrative Office of the Court from May 1–15 of each year. Applications are to be sent only by email to:

CAD-professionalguardians@pbcgov.org

Failure to timely submit an annual application will result in the professional guardian not being appointed to the Registry.

c. To be reappointed during subsequent fiscal years (July 1–June 30), renewal applications are to be submitted to the Administrative Office of the Court from May 1–May 15 for professional guardians who were appointed to the Registry the preceding fiscal year. Applications are to be sent only by email to:

CAD-professionalguardians@pbcgov.org

Failure to timely submit a renewal application will result in the professional guardian not being reappointed to the Registry and will require a new application (not renewal) should the professional guardian seek to be reappointed during another fiscal year.

2. A professional guardian will be appointed to the registry upon completion of all of the following:

a. satisfaction of the requirements for registration by the Office of Public and Professional Guardian.

b. completion of an application to be placed on the Registry ("Application") during the time period specified by the Administrative Office of the Court ("AOC").

c. sign an agreement to be bound by the application's terms and conditions including any billing procedures.

d. sign an agreement to accept a pro bono appointment as professional guardian in accordance with the terms of the application each application year.

3. Once approved by the AOC, the name of professional guardian will be included on the Registry which will be maintained by the Clerk's Office. The Clerk will maintain separate wheels on the Registry based upon the professional guardian's specialized skills and education.

4. Should the interested parties and/or family members not agree on a professional guardian from the Registry, the Court will contact the Clerk of Court who will select a professional guardian whose name next appears on the applicable wheel. If the Court declines to appoint the professional guardian whose name was provided by the Clerk, the Court will make the necessary findings as required by Section 744.312(4)(a), Florida Statute. The Court will inform the Clerk and obtain the name of the next professional guardian on the applicable wheel.

5. A Professional Guardian may be removed from the Professional Guardian Registry as follows:

a. *Suspension or Revocation of Registration:* When the AOC is notified by the Office of Public and Professional Guardian that a professional guardian's registration is suspended or revoked, the AOC will notify the Clerk to immediately remove the professional guardian from the Registry. The professional guardian may provide information to the AOC that the suspension or revocation is no longer in effect. The AOC, in consultation with the Chief Judge and probate judges, will determine whether the professional guardian is to be reinstated on the Registry.

b. *Recommendation by Judicial Officer:* When a judicial officer recommends to the Chief Judge or AOC to remove a professional guardian from the Registry, the Chief Judge may request a meeting with the professional guardian to discuss the circumstances or refer the matter to a committee appointed by the Chief Judge for review and a recommendation as to whether the professional guardian should remain on the registry. After meeting with the professional guardian, or after review of the Committee's recommendation, the Chief Judge will determine whether or not the professional guardian should remain on the Registry.

c. *Non acceptance of Pro Bono Appointment:* When the professional guardian fails to accept a pro bono appointment, the Chief Judge or AOC, in consultation with the probate judges, will determine if there was good cause for the professional guardian to not accept the pro bono appointment. The professional guardian will not be required to have more than one (1) pro bono appointment by the Court at a time.

d. *Violation of Law or Standards of Practice:* When the Clerk's Inspector General provides information to the Chief Judge or AOC of a professional guardian's violation of Florida Guardianship Law, Florida Criminal Code, or a significant violation of the standards of practice by a professional guardian, the Chief Judge or AOC will consult with the probate judges to determine whether such violations require removal from the Registry. If it is found that such violations require removal, the Chief Judge or AOC will notify the Clerk to remove the professional guardian from the Registry.

DONE and SIGNED in Chambers at West Palm Beach, Palm Beach County, Florida, this 26 day of October 2016.

Jeffrey Colbath
Chief Judge

Adopted effective October 26, 2016.

6.311. INVOLUNTARY COMMITMENT (BAKER ACT) AND VOLUNTARY COMMITMENT PROCEEDINGS

IN THE CIRCUIT COURT OF THE FIFTEENTH JUDICIAL CIRCUIT IN AND FOR PALM BEACH COUNTY, FLORIDA

ADMINISTRATIVE ORDER NO. 6.311–8/18 *

IN RE: INVOLUNTARY COMMITMENT (BAKER ACT) AND VOLUNTARY COMMITMENT PROCEEDINGS

Florida Statute §§ 394.451–394.47892 governs involuntary commitment (Baker Act) and voluntary commitment proceedings. Florida Statute section 394.4625 is specific to voluntary admission of minors.

Florida Statute § 394.4625 does not provide any process for the filing of the application nor for the manner in which the hearing is to be held. Representatives of Court Administration, the Clerk and Comptroller's Office, and the receiving facilities have met to discuss a process that will meet the needs of the parties while complying with the statute.

Florida Statute § 394.4625 does not address the confidentiality of the minor's name in applications for voluntary commitment or petitions for involuntary commitment. In order to ensure that the hearings are held in a timely manner, and protection of a minor's identity is maintained as required by Rule of Judicial Administration 2.525, internal processes are to be implemented.

Neither the statutes governing Baker Act proceedings, nor the rules of procedure, address the closure of cases when a facility withdraws its Petition or Application for admission.

NOW, THEREFORE, pursuant to the authority conferred by Florida Rule of Judicial Administration 2.215, it is **ORDERED** as follows:

A. Minors

1. *Procedures for the Filing of Applications for Voluntary Admission of a Minor.* Applications for voluntary admission for a person age 17 or under to a mental health facility ("Voluntary Application") will be accepted for filing at the main courthouse and branch courthouse locations.

a. Upon receipt of the filing, the Clerk and Comptroller will provide the filer with copies of the Demographic Information Sheet, a copy of which is attached as Exhibit A.

b. Voluntariness hearings will be added to the Magistrate's schedule for Baker Act Hearings.

2. *Additional Procedures for both Voluntary Applications and Involuntary Petitions of Minors.*

a. Upon receipt of a Voluntary Application or an Involuntary Petition ("Involuntary Petition") of a minor, the Clerk and Comptroller will open a case using the minor's initials.

b. The Clerk will treat the filing of an Voluntary Application or an Involuntary Petition to include a Motion to Determine Confidentiality of Court Records pursuant to Florida Rule of Judicial Administration 2.420(d)(3) and will maintain the file as confidential pending court order.

B. Withdrawal of Petition/Application by Facility for Minors and Adults. If prior to a hearing a patient is discharged, or the Voluntary or Involuntary Petition is withdrawn, and the receiving facility has not filed a Notification to Court of Withdrawal of Petition for Hearing, the Magistrate's staff will request a copy of the Notification of Withdrawal or Discharge from the facility. After the notice reporting the discharge or withdrawal is filed, the Clerk and Comptroller will report the matter as "closed".

DONE and **SIGNED** in Chambers at West Palm Beach, Palm Beach County, Florida, this 28 day of August, 2018.

Krista Marx
Chief Judge

EXHIBIT A

DEMOGRAPHIC INFORMATION SHEET—VOLUNTARY ADMISSION OF MINOR

Instructions: Each item must be fully completed and furnished to the Clerk of the Circuit Court at the time the Application for Voluntary Admission is filed with the Clerk.

Name of Minor: ________ **Minor's D.O.B.** ________
Name of Minor's Parent(s) ________
Legal Guardian Present: ______ **Yes** ______ **No**

If Parents No Longer Married Has Final Judgment/ Marital Settlement Agreement/Parenting Plan Been Provided to Facility/Court: _____ Yes _____ No
If So, Who Is Authorized to Make Healthcare Decisions Regarding Minor? ____________________

If Not Parents, Has Document(s) Been Provided to Facility/Court Identifying Legal Guardian? _____ Yes _____ No
If So, Who Is Authorized to Make Healthcare Decisions Regarding Minor? ____________________
I have attached copy of Final Judgment of Dissolution of Marriage (with Marital Settlement Agreement and/or Parenting Plan—OR—Order Appointing Guardian and Letters of Guardianship): _____ Yes _____ No

-OR-

I will furnish the document at hearing before General Magistrate or Circuit Judge: _____ Yes _____ No

Minor's Parent(s)/Guardian(s) Name(s) and Address(es)?

Name: ____________	**Name:** ____________
Address: ____________	**Address:** ____________
____________	____________
Phone Number: ____________	**Phone Number:** ____________
Email address: ____________	**Email address:** ____________

Adopted effective May 21, 2018. Amended effective August 28, 2018.

* supersedes admin. order 6.311–5/18

6.312. RISK PROTECTION ORDERS

IN THE CIRCUIT COURT OF THE FIFTEENTH JUDICIAL CIRCUIT IN AND FOR PALM BEACH COUNTY, FLORIDA

ADMINISTRATIVE ORDER NO 6.312–12/18 *

IN RE: RISK PROTECTION ORDERS

Florida Statute section 790.401 sets forth the procedures from filing to disposition of Petitions for Risk Protection Order. Internal processes are to be implemented to effectuate the court's obligations under the statute.

NOW, THEREFORE, pursuant to the authority conferred by Florida Rule of Judicial Administration 2.215, it is **ORDERED** as follows:

1. A Petition for Risk Protection Order ("RPO") or a Petition for an Ex Parte Temporary Risk Protection Order ("TRPO") filed by a law enforcement agency under section 790.401 may be electronically filed at any time or paper filed at any branch of the Clerk and Comptroller's office during normal business hours. Normal business hours means from 8:00 a.m.–4:00 p.m. Monday through Friday except court holidays. The Petitioner should include all relevant information including arrest history or related case information that involves the Respondent.

2. RPO's and TRPO's which are electronically filed after 4:00 p.m. Monday through Friday, on weekends, and on court holidays, will not be addressed until the next business day. A Petitioner who electronically files a TRPO after 4:00 p.m. Monday through Friday, on weekends, and on court holidays may bring the filing to the attention of the Clerk's Office at the Gun Club Courthouse in accordance with paragraph 8.

3. Upon receipt of a RPO or TRPO, the Clerk and Comptroller shall assign the case to a probate/guardianship division using the case type "RP" and assign the case to Division "CHJD".

4. The RPO and TRPO, while assigned to Division "CHJD" will be heard by the judge assigned to the Mental Health Division "T".

5. Upon the filing of the RPO or TRPO during regular business hours, the Clerk and Comptroller will immediately notify the judge assigned to the Mental Health Division "T" and forward the petition and all necessary documents and information to the judge assigned to the case, via the designated electronic email account for a prompt ruling or decision by the judge. For RPO's and TRPO's electronically filed outside of normal business hours, the Clerk and Comptroller will, on the next business day, retrieve the filings from the queue and immediately forward to the judge assigned to the Mental Health Division "T" for prompt ruling or decision.

6. In the event the judge assigned to the Mental Health Division "T" is unavailable, the Division "T" alternate will hear the TRPO or RPO. In the event the alternate is unavailable, the Duty Judge will hear the TRPO or RPO.

7. The following applies to Petitions for RPO and TRPO:

a. Hearings on Petitions for TRPO and RPO will be held at the Gun Club Courthouse.

b. Hearings on Petitions for TRPO that are filed on regular business days will have a hearing set at a time designated by the Division "T" judge.

c. Hearings on Petitions for TRPO that are filed on weekends and court holidays will be heard on the first appearance docket.

d. Hearings on Petitions for RPO will be scheduled before the Division "T" judge.

e. Three day compliance hearings will be scheduled on regular business days before the Division "T" judge.

f. A law enforcement officer may appear by phone for the TRPO hearing.

8. On weekends and court holidays, the Clerk's Office is to accept paper filed TRPO's between 6:00 a.m.—10:00 a.m. (or until the end of First Appearances) at the Clerk's Office located at 3228 Gun Club Road West Palm Beach, Florida ("Gun Club Courthouse").

9. The duty judge assigned to cover First Appearances on weekends and court holidays will hear TRPO's which were filed at the Gun Club Courthouse in accordance with paragraph 8 above and schedule any follow up hearings on the Division "T" calendar in accordance with paragraph 7b above.

10. Florida Statute § 790.401(5)(a) provides that the Chief Judge of each circuit, in consultation with the appropriate sheriff, may authorize a law enforcement agency within the Chief Judge's jurisdiction to effect service of the RPO and TRPO. The undersigned Chief Judge has consulted with the Sheriff of Palm Beach County with regard to which law enforcement agencies within Palm Beach County have received the training necessary to effectively serve RPOs and TRPOs. The following agencies are hereby authorized to serve RPO's and TRPO's.

1. The City of Atlantis Police Dept.
2. The City of Boca Raton Police Dept.
3. The City of Boynton Beach Police Dept.
4. The City of Delray Beach Police Dept.

5. The Florida Atlantic University Police Dept.
6. The City of Greenacres Police Dept.
7. The Town of Gulf Stream Police Dept.
8. The Town of Highland Beach Police Dept.
9. The Town of Juno Beach Police Dept.
10. The Town of Jupiter Police Dept.
11. The Jupiter Inlet Colony Police Dept.
12. The Town of Lake Clarke Shores Police Dept.
13. The Town of Lantana Police Dept.
14. The Town of Manalapan Police Dept.
15. The Village of North Palm Beach Police Dept.
16. The Town of Ocean Ridge Police Dept.
17. The Town of Palm Beach Police Dept.
18. The City of Palm Beach Gardens Police Dept.
19. The Town of Palm Beach Shores Police Dept.
20. The Village of Palm Springs Police Dept.
21. The City of Riviera Beach Police Dept.
22. The School Board of Palm Beach County Police Dept.
23. The Town of South Palm Beach Police Dept.
24. The Village of Tequesta Police Dept.
25. The City of West Palm Beach Police Dept.

11. The Clerk and Comptroller's office will forward a certified copy of the order and a copy of the law enforcement agency's petition to the petitioning agency for service. If the petitioning agency is not one of the agencies listed in paragraph 10, then the Clerk and Comptroller's office will forward a certified copy of the order and a copy of the petition to the Palm Beach County Sheriff's Office for service.

12. The Clerk and Comptroller's office shall be responsible for notifying the Department of Agriculture and Consumer Services at RPO@FreshFromFlorida.com of the issuance of the RPO or TRPO within three business days after the entry of the order.

13. Upon the filing by law enforcement of the background information checklist created by the Palm Beach County Sheriffs Office, which includes information from the Clerk's Comprehensive Case Information System ("COS"), the Clerk and Comptroller's Office will forward the checklist to the presiding judge.

14. Court Administration, through its criminal case manager, will screen for cases pending in the Fifteenth Judicial Circuit wherein the Respondent is a party. In the event there is an active case wherein the Respondent is a party, the criminal case manager will notify the judge presiding over the active case, as well as any divisional case manager, of the newly filed TRPO/RPO.

DONE and **SIGNED** in Chambers at West Palm Beach, Palm Beach County, Florida, this 11th day of December 2018.

Krista Marx
Chief Judge

Adopted effective May 21, 2018. Amended effective December 11, 2018.

* supersedes admin. order 6.312–5/18

6.313. EXPLOITATION OF VULNERABLE ADULT INJUNCTIONS

IN THE CIRCUIT COURT OF THE FIFTEENTH JUDICIAL CIRCUIT IN AND FOR PALM BEACH COUNTY, FLORIDA

ADMINISTRATIVE ORDER NO. 6.313–12/18

IN RE: EXPLOITATION OF VULNERABLE ADULT INJUNCTIONS

Florida Statute sections 825.1035 and 825.1036 sets forth the procedures from filing to disposition of Injunctions for Protection Against Exploitation of a Vulnerable Adult. Internal processes are to be implemented to effectuate the court's obligations under the statute.

NOW, THEREFORE, pursuant to the authority conferred by Florida Rule of Judicial Administration 2.215, it is **ORDERED** as follows:

A. Case Assignment of Petition for Injunctions or Temporary Injunctions.

1. Upon receiving a petition for injunction—or temporary injunction—for protection against exploitation of a vulnerable adult, shall assign the case to one of the following Probate/Guardianship Division: IB, IC, ID, IH, II, IJ, IX, IY, IZ.

2. The Clerk and Comptroller will check its case maintenance system and CCIS to determine if there is a pending action under Chapter 744 or another related case.

a. If a Chapter 744 case is pending in the Fifteenth Judicial Circuit, the Petition will be filed in the open guardianship case.

b. If a Chapter 744 case is pending in another circuit, the Clerk and Comptroller will open a case in the guardianship division and inform the assigned judge so that a transfer order can be issued.

c. If a related UFC case is pending in the Fifteenth Judicial Circuit, the Clerk and Comptroller will follow in the procedures outlined in Administrative Order 5.101.

3. The Clerk and Comptroller shall promptly deliver the Verified Petition for Injunction or Temporary Injunction and all necessary documents and information to the judge assigned to the case, via the designated electronic email accounts as per the divisional instructions for a prompt ruling or decision by the judge.

a. If the Clerk does not receive an Order addressing the Temporary Petition for Injunction, within three (3) hours or by the end of business, whichever occurs first, the Clerk shall personally contact the judge's office to verify the temporary petition was received.

b. If the Clerk does not receive either an order setting hearing or confirmation of receipt of the Petition for Injunction by end of business, the Clerk shall personally contact the judge's office to verify the petition was received.

c. In the event the assigned judge is unavailable and a Temporary Petition for Injunction is received, then the Clerk and Comptroller shall promptly deliver the Temporary Injunction and all necessary documents and information in the following order:

1) Assigned judge's alternate; if unavailable then to the

2) Administrative Judge for the division to which the case has been assigned; if unavailable then to the

3) Duty Judge

B. Scheduling of Hearing. Upon the entry of a temporary injunction, or upon the filing of the petition for injunction if temporary relief is not requested, the judge reviewing the matter will schedule the hearing on the assigned judge's next regularly scheduled domestic violence "designated" block hearing time. The clerk will docket the notice of hearing and place the date and time of the hearing on the Judge's calendar in the clerk's docketing system.

C. Assistance With Violations of Injunctions. The Clerk and Comptroller is the office designated as the central intake point for injunction violations and where the petitioner can receive assistance in the preparation of the affidavit in support of violation.

D. Service of Injunctions for Protection Against Exploitation of a Vulnerable Adult.

1. Florida Statute § 825.1035(10)(a)1.c provides that the Chief Judge of each circuit, in consultation with the appropriate sheriff, may authorize a law enforcement agency within the Chief Judge's jurisdiction to effect service of the injunction and temporary injunction. The undersigned Chief Judge has consulted with the Sheriff of Palm Beach County with regard to which law enforcement agencies within Palm Beach County have received the training necessary to effectively serve the injunctions and temporary injunctions. The following agencies are hereby authorized to serve the injunctions and temporary injunctions.

1. The City of Atlantis Police Dept.
2. The City of Boca Raton Police Dept.
3. The City of Boynton Beach Police Dept.
4. The City of Delray Beach Police Dept.
5. The Florida Atlantic University Police Dept.
6. The Town of Gulf Stream Police Dept.
7. The Town of Highland Beach Police Dept.
8. The Town of Juno Beach Police Dept.
9. The Town of Jupiter Police Dept.
10. The Jupiter Inlet Colony Police Dept.
11. The Town of Lake Clarke Shores
12. The Town of Lantana Police Dept. Police Dept.
13. The Town of Manalapan Police Depart.
14. The Village of North Palm Beach Police Dept.
15. The Town of Ocean Ridge Police Dept.
16. The Town of Palm Beach Police Dept.
17. The City of Palm Beach Gardens Police Dept.
18. The Town of Palm Beach Shores Police Dept.
19. The Village of Palm Springs Police Dept.
20. The City of Riviera Beach Police Dept.
21. The School Board of Palm Beach County Police Dept.
22. The Town of South Palm Beach Police Dept.
23. The Village of Tequesta Police Dept.
24. The City of West Palm Beach Police Dept.

2. The Clerk and Comptroller's office will forward a certified copy of the order and a copy of the petition to the law enforcement agency for service

DONE and **SIGNED** in Chambers at West Palm Beach, Palm Beach County, Florida, this 31st day of December, 2018.

Krista Marx
Chief Judge

Adopted effective December 31, 2018.

Prisoner Litigation/Writs/Post Convictions

Prisoner Litigation

7.101. TELEPHONIC APPEARANCE BY PRISONERS/INMATES IN NON–CRIMINAL DIVISIONS OF THE COURT

IN THE CIRCUIT COURT OF THE FIFTEENTH JUDICIAL CIRCUIT IN AND FOR PALM BEACH COUNTY, FLORIDA

ADMINISTRATIVE ORDER NO. 7.101–9/08 *

IN RE: TELEPHONIC APPEARANCE BY PRISONERS/INMATES IN NON–CRIMINAL DIVISIONS OF THE COURT

Numerous prisoners in custody throughout the State of Florida and the United States have filed and continue to file civil actions in this circuit. Their transportation to and from this circuit for non-criminal non-evidentiary hearings has become extremely expensive and an unwarranted security risk.

NOW, THEREFORE, pursuant to the authority conferred by Florida Rule of Judicial Administration 2.215, it is **ORDERED** as follows:

1. In non-evidentiary hearings before the civil, probate/guardianship and Unified Family Court divisions of the court involving prisoners in custody, said prisoners shall make their appearance telephonically.

2. It shall be the responsibility of the Office of the State Attorney General or the institution having custody of the prisoner to arrange for the prisoner's telephonic appearance with the Court's judicial assistant and all other interested parties and/or counsel.

3. The costs of the telephonic appearance shall be borne by the institution having custody of the prisoner in lieu of the prisoner's transportation expenses and live appearance before the court.

4. The judge presiding over any prisoner's case may require the live appearance of the prisoner for a non-evidentiary hearing upon a showing of good cause and in the exercise of the court's sound discretion.

5. This order shall not apply to evidentiary hearings although evidentiary hearings may be conducted telephonically with the stipulation and agreement of all parties and/or counsel including the prisoner.

DONE and **SIGNED** in Chambers at West Palm Beach, Palm Beach County, Florida, this 29 day of September, 2008.

Kathleen J. Kroll
Chief Judge

Adopted effective September 29, 2008.

* supersedes admin. order 3.007–1/95

7.102. PRISONER LITIGATION

IN THE CIRCUIT COURT OF THE FIFTEENTH JUDICIAL CIRCUIT IN AND FOR PALM BEACH COUNTY

ADMINISTRATIVE ORDER NO. 7.102–3/18 *

IN RE: PRISONER LITIGATION

Filings by prisoners are frequently mistitled resulting in the document being filed in the wrong division of court. Prisoners may be required to pay portions of their court costs and fees in accordance with Florida Statute § 57.081, § 57.082, and § 57.085 and an indigency review must be undertaken by the Clerk and Comptroller's office. Procedures need to be implemented to ensure timely review of the filings, assignment to the correct division of the court, and payment of required fees and costs.

NOW, THEREFORE, pursuant to the authority conferred by Florida Rule of Judicial Administration 2.215, it is **ORDERED** as follows:

A. Nature of Filing Not Clear on the Face of the Document.

1. When the Clerk and Comptroller receives a new civil lawsuit or correspondence from a prisoner as defined by Florida Statute § 57.085(1) (excluding clearly delineated writs and post conviction motions as addressed in Administrative Orders 7.201 and 7.301) where it is not clear on the face of the pleading or correspondence as to whether the prisoner is seeking a writ of habeas corpus, post conviction relief, collateral criminal relief, or filing a civil lawsuit unrelated to a the prisoner's substantive criminal matter, the Clerk and Comptroller's Office shall forward the matter to the Office of General Counsel, Administrative Office of the Court, to determine whether the matter seeks post conviction relief, collateral criminal relief, or other relief.

2. The Office of General Counsel will review the file and submit recommendations to the Chief Judge as to whether the prisoner seeks post conviction relief, collateral criminal relief, or other relief

3. An Order will be entered by the Chief Judge, or another judge, instructing the Clerk and Comptroller's Office as to whether the matter seeks post conviction relief, seeks collateral criminal relief and is therefore exempt from Florida Statute § 57.085, or seeks other relief and therefore must comply with Florida Statute § 57.085.

B. Filing Which Seeks Post Conviction Relief.

1. If it is ordered that the matter seeks post conviction relief, the Clerk and Comptroller will close the newly created civil case and file the prisoner's post conviction motion in the underlying criminal case file.

2. The post conviction motion will be handled in accordance with Administrative Order 7.301.

C. Filing Which Seeks Collateral Criminal Relief (Clerk's Determination of Indigency under § 57.081).

1. If it is ordered that the matter seeks collateral criminal relief and the Plaintiff/Petitioner has requested indigency status the Clerk and Comptroller will determine whether the prisoner has provided documentation as required by Florida Statute § 57.081.

a. If the prisoner has not furnished the appropriate documentation for the Clerk and Comptroller's Office to make a determination of indigency, the Clerk and Comptroller will forward to the prisoner the applicable indigency forms attached to this Administrative Order as Exhibit 1.

b. The Clerk and Comptroller will determine whether the Plaintiff/Petitioner is indigent and must submit to a payment plan pursuant to Florida Statutes §§ 57.081 and 57.082. Any document that may have been provided by the Plaintiff/Petitioner pursuant to § 57.085 will be considered in the Clerk and Comptroller's determination under § 57.081 and § 57.082.

2. If the prisoner initiates a case that will be assigned to a civil division, the following applies:

a. The Clerk and Comptroller's Office will also conduct a preliminary screening to the best of its ability to determine whether the Plaintiff/Petitioner has any other matters seeking collateral criminal relief pending in the Fifteenth Judicial Circuit.

b. If another proceeding seeking collateral criminal relief is pending, the Clerk and Comptroller's office shall assign the new litigation a civil case number and assign it to the civil judge assigned to the file with the lowest pending case number.

c. If no other proceeding seeking collateral criminal relief is pending, the Clerk and Comptroller's office shall assign the new litigation a case number and randomly assign the case to a civil judge.

d. A representative of the Clerk and Comptroller's Office will immediately notify the assigned judge of the new litigation.

D. Filing Which Seeks Other Relief (Clerk's Determination of Indigency under § 57.085).

1. When a prisoner intervenes in or initiates a judicial proceeding other than a collateral criminal proceeding, and seeks to defer the prepayment of court costs and fees because of indigence, a determination of indigency is to be completed by the Clerk.

a. The Clerk and Comptroller will determine whether the prisoner is indigent and has provided documentation as required by Florida Statute § 57.085.

1) If the prisoner has not furnished the appropriate documentation for the Clerk and Comptroller's Office to make a determination of indigency, the Clerk and Comptroller will forward to the prisoner the applicable indigency forms attached to this Administrative Order as Exhibit 2.

2) If under Florida Statute § 57.085, the affidavit states that the prisoner has twice in the preceding three years has been adjudicated indigent, the Clerk and Comptroller will forward the matter to the assigned judge to determine whether the prisoner should be granted leave to seek a determination of indigency pursuant to § 57.085.

b. If the prisoner initiates a case that will be assigned to a civil division, the following applies:

1) The Clerk and Comptroller's Office will also conduct a preliminary screening to the best of its ability to determine whether the Plaintiff/Petitioner has any other civil matters (non family) pending in the circuit or county court.

2) If another civil proceeding is pending in the same court (circuit or county), the Clerk and Comptroller's office shall assign the new litigation a civil case number and assign it to the civil judge assigned to the file with the lowest pending case number.

3) If no other proceeding seeking civil relief is pending, the Clerk and Comptroller's office shall assign the new litigation a case number and randomly assign the case to a civil judge.

2. *Orders to Pay Costs.*

a. This administrative order shall serve as the order required by Florida Statute § 57.085(4) to require the prisoner to make an initial partial payment of costs and fees prior to service of process. After reviewing the preceding 6 months of the prisoner's trust account records, or less if imprisoned for a shorter period of time, the clerk is hereby directed to assess an initial partial payment, of at least 20% of the average monthly balance as follows:

1) If the average balance is $10.00 or less, no initial partial payment is required.

2) If the average balance is greater than SI0.00 but not more than $25.00, the initial partial payment due is $5.00.

3) If the average balance is greater than $25.00 but not more than $50.00, the initial partial payment due is $15.00.

4) If the average balance is greater than $50.00 but not more than $75.00, the initial partial payment due is $30.00.

5) If the average balance is greater than $75.00, the initial partial payment due is $50.00.

b. This administrative order shall serve as the order required by Florida Statute § 57.085(5) to require the prisoner to make monthly payments of no less than 20% of the balance of the prisoner's trust account as payment of court costs and fees. When the Clerk has found the prisoner to be indigent under § 57.085, the Clerk is hereby directed to forward to the Department of Corrections or the local detention facility a memorandum setting forth the prisoner's name and case number and the amount of the outstanding court costs and fees, along with a copy of this Administrative Order, for the imposition of the lien as required by Florida Statute § 57.085(5). As fees and costs continue to accrue, the Clerk will update the Department of Corrections or the detention facility with the current amount due and owing.

3. *Review of Legal Sufficiency.*

a. The Clerk and Comptroller's Office will immediately notify the assigned judge of the new litigation following receipt of the partial payment as set forth in paragraph D 2 a above, or, if no partial payment is due, following the determination of indigency as set forth in D 1 above.

b. The assigned judge, in accordance with Florida Statute § 57.085(6), will review the claim(s) to determine whether it is legally sufficient to state a cause of action for which the court has jurisdiction and may grant relief.

DONE AND SIGNED, in Chambers, at West Palm Beach, Palm Beach County, Florida this 29 day of March, 2018.

Krista Marx
Chief Judge

* supersedes admin. order 7,102–5/12

EXHIBIT "1"

IN THE CIRCUIT/COUNTY COURT OF THE FIFTEENTH JUDICIAL CIRCUIT IN AND FOR PALM BEACH COUNTY, FLORIDA
CASE NO: ________

____
Plaintiff/ Petitioner or In the Interest Of

vs.

____
Defendant / Respondent

APPLICATION FOR DETERMINATION OF CIVIL INDIGENT STATUS PURSUANT TO § 57.081

Notice to Applicant: If you qualify for civil indigence you must enroll in the Clerk's Office payment plan and pay a one-time administrative fee of $25.00. This fee shall not be charged for Dependency or Chapter 39 Termination of Parental Rights actions.

1. **I have ___ dependents.** *(Include only those persons you list on your U.S. income tax return)*
Are you married? ___ Yes ___ No
Does your spouse work? ___ Yes ___ No   Annual Spouse Income? $ ________.

2. **I have a net income of $______** paid ( ) weekly ( ) every two weeks ( ) semi-monthly ( ) monthly ( ) yearly ( ) other ____.
(Net income is your total income including salary, wages, bonuses, commissions, allowances, overtime, tips and similar payments, ***minus*** *deductions required by law and other court-ordered payments such as child support.)*

3. **I have other income** paid ( ) weekly ( ) every two weeks ( ) semi-monthly ( ) monthly ( ) yearly ( ) other ________
(check "Yes" and fill in the amount if you have this kind of income, otherwise check "No")

Second Job . . . . No ___ Yes ___ $ ________
Veterans' benefits . . . . No ___ Yes ___ $ ________
Workers Compensation . . . . No ___ Yes ___ $ ________
Social Security benefits
For you . . . . No ___ Yes ___ $ ________
For your child(ren) . . . . No ___ Yes ___ $ ________

Income from absent family members . . . No ___ Yes ___ $ ________
Stocks/bonds . . . . No ___ Yes ___ $ ________
Unemployment compensation . . . . No ___ Yes ___ $ ________
Rental Income . . . . No ___ Yes ___ $ ________
Union Payments . . . . No ___ Yes ___ $ ________
Dividends or interest . . . . No ___ Yes ___ $ ________
Retirement/pensions . . . . No ___ Yes ___ $ ________
Other kinds of income not on the list . . . No ___ Yes ___ $ ________
Gifts . . . . No ___ Yes ___ $ ________

I understand that I will be required to make payments for fees and costs to the clerk in accordance with Florida Statute 57,082(5), as provided by law, <u>although I may agree to pay more if I choose to do so.</u>

4. **I have other assets:** *(check "yes" and fill in the value of the property, otherwise check "No")*

Cash . . . . No ___ Yes ___ $ ________
Savings Account . . . . No ___ Yes ___ $ ________
Bank account(s) . . . . No ___ Yes ___ $ ________
Stocks/bonds . . . . No ___ Yes ___ $ ________
Certificates of deposit
or Money market accounts . . . . No ___ Yes ___ $ ________
Homestead Real Property * . . . . No ___ Yes ___ $ ________
Motor Vehicle * . . . . No ___ Yes ___ $ ________
Boats * . . . . No ___ Yes ___ $ ________
Non-homestead real property * . . . . No ___ Yes ___ $ ____
* Show loans on these assets in paragraph 5.
Check one: I ( ) DO ( ) DO NOT expect to receive more assets in the near future.
The asset is ________________

5. **I have total liabilities and debts of $ ___ as follows:**
Motor Vehicle $ ______, Home $ ______, Other Real Estate Property $ ______, Child Support paid direct $ ______, Credit Cards $ ______, Medical Bills $ ______, Cost of medicines (monthly) $ ______, Other $ ______.

6. I have a private lawyer in this case . . . . No ____ Yes ____

A person who knowingly provides false information to the clerk or the court in seeking a determination of indigent status under s. 57.082, F.S. commits a misdemeanor of the first degree, punishable as provided in s.775.082, F.S. or s. 775.083, F.S. **I attest that the information I have provided on this application is true and accurate to the best of my knowledge.**

Signed this ____ day of ______, 20 ___.

______________________ Signature of Applicant for Indigent Status

______________________ Print Full Legal Name

______________________ Date of Birth

______________________ Driver's License or ID Number

______________________ Phone number

______________________ Address, City, State, Zip Code

CASE NO. ______________

CLERK'S DETERMINATION

Based on the information in this Application, I have determined the applicant to be

______ Indigent

______ Not Indigent,

according to s. 57.082, F.S.

Dated this ___ day of ______, 20 ___

Clerk of the Circuit Court

____

By:

This form was completed with the assistance of:

____

Clerk/Deputy Clerk/Other authorized person.

APPLICANTS FOUND NOT TO BE INDIGENT MAY SEEK REVIEW BY THE CHIEF JUDGE.

THERE IS NO FEE FOR THIS REVIEW.

Sign here if you want the Chief Judge to review the clerk's decision.

____

Signature

____

Printed Name

____

Date

EXHIBIT "2"

IN THE CIRCUIT COURT OF THE FIFTEENTH JUDICIAL CIRCUIT IN AND FOR PALM BEACH COUNTY, FLORIDA

CASE NUMBER: ______________

____

v.

____

AFFIDAVIT OF INDIGENCY PURSUANT TO § 57.085

STATE OF FLORIDA COUNTY OF ______________

Before me personally appeared {Name} ______________

Who after being sworn states:

1. My full name is: ______________
and I am also known by the following alias(es) and nicknames:

____

____

2. I am currently incarcerated at {Name of facility}:

____

Located in {city and state}:

____

My prisoner identification number is:

____

My full mailing address is:

____

3. I was found guilty or plead guilty/no contest to the following crime(s) (list Courts, case numbers, offenses, date of convictions and sentences imposed):

____

____

____

4. The nature and amount of my current income are as follows: (list the source, entitlement and amount of any income you now receive):

____

____

5. I own the following real property (land) (describe the nature and location of real property};

____

____

6. I own the following tangible and intangible property worth more than $100 (describe any property or possessions you own worth more than $100 and list an approximate value for each):

____

____

____

7. I am in possession of cash in the amount of: ______

8. The balances of all checking, savings and money-market accounts held by me are as follows (list the financial institution and the current balance for each account):

____

____

____

9. The names and ages of my dependents are as follows:

____

____

____

10. I owe the following debts (include the names of all creditors and the amount owed to each}:

____

____

____

____

____

11. My monthly expenses are as follows (list all monthly expenses and the amount of each}:

____

____

____

____

I have been adjudicated indigent twice in the preceding 3 years, under F.S. 57.085 (Fla. Stat.) certified indigent under F.S. 57.081 (Fla. Stat.) or authorized to proceed as an indigent under 28 U.S.C. 1915 by a federal court on the following occasions list each Court, case name and number, and date of adjudication, certification or authorization to proceed as an indigent. **Do NOT include any criminal prosecutions in which you were adjudicated indigent:**

☐ Yes ☐ No

List each Court, case name and number, and date of adjudication, certification or authorization to proceed as an indigent. **Do NOT list any criminal prosecutions in which you were adjudicated indigent:**

____

____

____

____

____

____

THE PRISONER MUST ATTACH TO THIS AFFIDAVIT A PHOTOCOPY OF THE PRISONER'S TRUST ACCOUNT RECORDS FOR THE PRECEDING SIX (6) MONTHS OR FOR THE LENGTH OF THE PRISONER'S INCARCERATION, WHICHEVER PERIOD IS SHORTER.

I am presently unable to pay court costs and fees. Under penalty of perjury, I swear or affirm that all statements in this affidavit are true and complete.

DATED: ______________________________

Signature of Prisoner: ______________________________

Printed Name of Prisoner: ______________________________

Address: ______________________________

____

City, State, Zip ______________________________

STATE OF FLORIDA
COUNTY OF {name} ______________________________

Sworn to (or affirmed) and subscribed before me on
{date} __________, 20 ___, by
{name} ______________________________
NOTARY PUBLIC—STATE OF FLORIDA {Print, type or stamp commissioned name of notary}
______ Personally known ______ Produced identification

Type of identification produced ______________________________
CASE NO.: ______________________________

CLERK'S DETERMINATION OF INDIGENT STATUS

Based on the information in the affidavit for indigent status, the above named applicant
______________________________ is determined to be:
name of applicant

____ indigent
____ not indigent
according to 200% of the Federal Poverty Guidelines.
Date: ______________ Signature: ______________________________
Deputy Clerk

Adopted effective September 29, 2008. Amended effective June 25, 2009; May 25, 2012; March 29, 2018.

Writs

7.201. FILING OF WRITS

IN THE CIRCUIT COURT OF THE FIFTEENTH JUDICIAL CIRCUIT IN AND FOR PALM BEACH COUNTY

ADMINISTRATIVE ORDER NO. 7.201–6/09 *

IN RE: FILING OF WRITS

Pursuant to the authority conferred by Florida Rule of Judicial Administration 2.215, it is **ORDERED** that the following procedures will govern the handling of Writs.

A. Generally.

1. All Writs are to be filed in Circuit Civil.

2. All Extraordinary Writs shall be coded by the Clerk & Comptroller's Office as case type "EW".

B. Petitions for Writ of Habeas Corpus.

1. Upon the filing of a Petition for Writ of Habeas Corpus, the Clerk and Comptroller's Office shall conduct a preliminary screening to the best of its ability to determine whether the Petitioner has any other writs pending in any other court in the Fifteenth Judicial Circuit.

2. If another writ is pending, the Clerk and Comptroller's office shall assign the Petition for Writ of Habeas Corpus a civil case number and assign it to the judge assigned to the pending writ with the lowest case number. If no other writ is pending, the Clerk and Comptroller's office shall assign the writ a civil case number and randomly assign the Petition for Writ of Habeas Corpus to a circuit judge as follows:

a. All "Family" Writs of Habeas Corpus regarding parents incarcerated as a result of an order entered by a UFC Division Judge are to be assigned to the UFC Division Judge who entered the particular order.

b. All "Mental Health/Substance Abuse" Writs of Habeas Corpus regarding individuals incarcerated or placed in patient as a result of a Baker Act, Marchman Act, or other order entered by a Probate/Guardianship Division judge are to be assigned to the Probate/Guardianship Judge who entered the particular order.

c. All other Writs of Habeas Corpus are to be given a civil case number and randomly assigned to a Circuit Civil Division Judge.

3. No filing fee for the Petition for Writ of Habeas Corpus will be required of the Petitioner.

4. A representative of the Clerk and Comptroller's Office will immediately bring the Petition for Writ of Habeas Corpus to the assigned Judge along with any other writ filed by the same Petitioner that is pending before the assigned Judge.

5. If the assigned judge determines that the Petition for Writ of Habeas Corpus is seeking post conviction relief, an Order will be entered transferring the file to the Circuit Criminal Division.

6. The Clerk and Comptroller's Office will transfer the file to Circuit Criminal and address the matter in accordance with Administrative Order 7.301–9/08 (as amended).

C. Petitions for All Writs (Other Than Habeas Corpus) by Persons in Custody.

1. Upon the filing by an individual in custody of a Petition for a Writ NOT entitled "Habeas Corpus", the Clerk and Comptroller's Office shall assign the Petition a case number.

2. If by the face of the pleading the Clerk and Comptroller's office can determine that the Petition is seeking post conviction relief (i.e. the initial pleading states it is a Writ Corum Nobis but cites to Criminal Rule of Procedure 3.850 or 3.800), then the Clerk shall transfer the matter to the criminal division which handled the trial proceedings.

3. If by the face of the pleading the Clerk and Comptroller's office can determine that the Petition is not seeking collateral criminal relief (i. e. writ of quo warranto), then:

a. The Clerk and Comptroller will determine whether the plaintiff is indigent and has provided documentation as required by Florida Statute § 57.085.

1) If the prisoner has not furnished the appropriate documentation for the Clerk and Comptroller's Office to make a determination of indigency, the Clerk and Comptroller will forward to the prisoner the applicable indigency forms attached to this Administrative Order as Exhibits 1 and 2.

2) If under Florida Statute § 57.085, the affidavit states that the prisoner has twice in the preceding three years has been adjudicated indigent, the Clerk and Comptroller will forward the matter to the assigned judge for determination of indigency pursuant to 57.085.

b. Upon resolution of the Clerk's Determination of Indigency, a representative of the Clerk and Comptroller's Office will immediately bring the file to the assigned Judge.

c. The assigned Judge, in accordance with Florida Statute § 57.085(6), will review the claims(s) to determine whether the pleading is legally sufficient to state a cause of action for which the court has jurisdiction and may grant relief. If the pleading, or a portion thereof, is legally sufficient, then the Court shall enter an appropriate order regarding the merits of the petition. Under Florida Statute § 57.085(6)(a–d), the Judge shall dismiss all or part of an indigent prisoner's claim which:

1) Fails to state a claim for which relief may be granted; or

2) Seeks monetary relief from a defendant who is immune from such relief; or

3) Seeks relief for mental or emotional injury where there has been not related allegation of a physical injury; or is frivolous, malicious, or reasonable appears to be intended to harass one or more named defendants.

4. If the pleading states "Writ of Mandamus" or if, by the face of the pleading, the Clerk and Comptroller cannot determine whether the pleading seeks post conviction relief or whether it does not seek collateral criminal relief, the Clerk and Comptroller will forward the file to the Office of General Counsel, Administrative Office of the Court, to determine whether the Writ seeks collateral criminal relief ("collateral criminal proceedings"), seeks other civil relief or seeks post conviction relief.

a. The Office of General Counsel will review the file and submit recommendations to the Chief Judge or Civil Trial Division Judge as to whether the Petitioner seeks collateral criminal relief, seeks other civil relief or seeks post conviction relief.

b. An Order will be entered by the Chief Judge, the Civil Trial Division Judge, or another judge, instructing the Clerk and Comptroller's Office as to whether the matter seeks collateral criminal relief and is therefore exempt from Florida Statute § 57.085, seeks other civil relief and therefore must comply with Florida Statute § 57.085, or whether it seeks post conviction relief and is to be transferred to the criminal division.

5. If it is ordered that the Writ seeks collateral criminal relief and the plaintiff has requested indigency status:

a. The Clerk and Comptroller will determine whether the plaintiff is indigent and must submit to a payment plan pursuant to Florida Statutes §§ 57.081 and 57.082. Any document that may have provided by the plaintiff pursuant to § 57.085 will be considered in the Clerk and Comptroller's determination under § 57.081 and § 57.082.

b. The Clerk and Comptroller's Office will also conduct a preliminary screening to the best of its ability to determine whether the Petitioner has any other Writs seeking collateral criminal relief pending in the Fifteenth Judicial Circuit.

c. If another Writ seeking collateral criminal relief by the Petitioner is pending, the Clerk and Comptroller's office shall assign the new litigation a civil case number and assign it to the civil judge assigned to the Writ with the lowest pending case number. If no other Writ seeking collateral criminal relief is pending, the Clerk and Comptroller's office shall assign the new litigation a case number and randomly assign the case to a civil judge.

d. Upon resolution of the Clerk's Determination of Indigency, a representative of the Clerk and Comptroller's Office will immediately bring the file to the assigned Judge.

6. If it is ordered that the Writ seeks other civil relief and the plaintiff has requested indigency status:

a. The Clerk and Comptroller will determine whether the plaintiff is indigent and has provided documentation as required by Florida Statute § 57.085.

1) If the prisoner has not furnished the appropriate documentation for the Clerk and Comptroller's Office to make a determination of indigency, the Clerk and Comptroller will forward to the prisoner the applicable indigency forms attached to this Administrative Order as Exhibits 1 and 2.

2) If under Florida Statute § 57.085, the affidavit states that the prisoner has twice in the preceding three years has been adjudicated indigent, the Clerk and Comptroller

will forward the matter to the assigned judge for determination of indigency pursuant to 57.085.

b. Upon resolution of the Clerk's Determination of Indigency, a representative of the Clerk and Comptroller's Office will immediately bring the file to the assigned Judge.

c. The assigned Judge, in accordance with Florida Statute § 57.085(6), will review the claims(s) to determine whether the pleading is legally sufficient to state a cause of action for which the court has jurisdiction and may grant relief. If the pleading, or a portion thereof, is legally sufficient, then the Court shall enter an appropriate order regarding the merits of the petition. Under Florida Statute § 57.085(6)(a–d), the Judge shall dismiss all or part of an indigent prisoner's claim which

1) Fails to state a claim for which relief may be granted; or

2) Seeks monetary relief from a defendant who is immune from such relief; or

3) Seeks relief for mental or emotional injury where there has been not related allegation of a physical injury; or

4) Is frivolous, malicious, or reasonable appears to be intended to harass one or more named defendants.

7. If it is ordered that the matter seeks post conviction relief, the matter will be transferred to the criminal division and assigned to the division which handled the trial. The Post Conviction Motion will be handled in accordance with Administrative Order 8.401 9/08 as amended.

D. Petitions for All Writs (Other Than Habeas Corpus) Filed by Pro Se Litigants Not in Custody. Upon the filing by a pro se litigant not in custody of a Petition for a Writ NOT entitled "Habeas Corpus", the Clerk and Comptroller's Office shall treat the filing as a civil matter and proceed accordingly.

DONE and SIGNED in Chambers at West Palm Beach, Palm Beach County, Florida this 25 day of June, 2009.

Kathleen J. Kroll
Chief Judge

Adopted effective September 29, 2008. Amended effective June 25, 2009.

* supersedes admin. order 7.201 9/08

Post Convictions

7.301. FILING OF POSTCONVICTION MOTIONS

IN THE CIRCUIT COURT OF THE FIFTEENTH JUDICIAL CIRCUIT IN AND FOR PALM BEACH COUNTY

ADMINISTRATIVE ORDER NO. 7.301–3/18 *

IN RE: FILING OF POSTCONVICTION MOTIONS

A uniform procedure should govern the assignment of postconviction motions.

NOW, THEREFORE, pursuant to the authority conferred by Florida Rule of Judicial Administration 2.215, it is **ORDERED** as follows:

1. Upon the filing of any postconviction motion, the Clerk and Comptroller's Office shall reopen the criminal case file and assign the postconviction motion to the division that handled the substantive criminal case.

2. All postconviction motions filed with the Clerk and Comptroller's office shall be docketed with a "POST" designator.

3. When a postconviction motion referencing Florida Rule of Criminal Procedure 3.850 or titled "Motion for Postconviction Relief or a variation thereof is filed, the Clerk and Comptroller shall notify the office of General Counsel, Administrative Office of the Court of the filing by sending a copy to CAD–CriminalDep@pbcgov.org. The Office of General Counsel will review the filing for timeliness and oath and, upon completion of the review, will forward the motion to the divisional judge.

4. When a postconviction motion other than a 3.850 is filed, [1] the Clerk and Comptroller shall notify the divisional judge of the postconviction motion.

5. A filing that is deemed to be a petition for an extraordinary writ shall be transferred to the circuit civil division and given a civil case number. A circuit civil judge will handle the **filing** in accordance with Administrative Order 7.201.

6. When a State's response is required, the State Attorney's Office shall also email an electronic copy of the response to pcmotions@pbcgov.org in Microsoft Word format or in an editable PDF.

7. When the Office of the State Attorney files a motion seeking an extension of time to a trial court's order directing the State to respond to a motion for postconviction relief, the State shall include the following information which information shall be bolded:

a. Date postconviction motion was filed;

b. Date(s) of prior requests for extension(s) of time to file response;

c. Amount of additional time granted for each request for extension of time;

d. Detailed reason why the additional time is needed.

DONE AND SIGNED in Chambers at West Palm Beach, Palm Beach County, Florida this 29 day of March 2018.

Krista Marx
Chief Judge

Adopted effective September 29, 2008. Amended effective July 21, 2009; December 20, 2010; March 29, 2018.

* supersedes admin. order 7.301–12/10.

1 This includes but is not limited to: motions to withdraw a plea, motions to correct illegal sentence, motions to correct jail credit, motions based upon newly discovered evidence, motions for DNA testing, and any motions referencing Florida Rules of Criminal Procedure 3.170, 3.800, 3.801, 3.851, and 3.853.

Appeals

8.101. APPEALS FROM COUNTY COURT AND LOCAL ADMINISTRATIVE AGENCIES; PETITIONS FOR EXTRAORDINARY WRIT

IN THE CIRCUIT COURT OF THE FIFTEENTH JUDICIAL CIRCUIT IN AND FOR PALM BEACH COUNTY, FLORIDA

ADMINISTRATIVE ORDER NO.: 8.101–5/18 *

IN RE: APPEALS FROM COUNTY COURT AND LOCAL ADMINISTRATIVE AGENCIES; PETITIONS FOR EXTRAORDINARY WRIT

The Circuit Court is charged with the responsibility of hearing and ruling on appeals and petitions for extraordinary writs from County Court and local administrative bodies. Administrative orders 8.101 and 8.102 have been combined into the current 8.101. Due to a combination of the two administrative orders, no holding indicating change is reflected below.

NOW, THEREFORE, pursuant to the authority conferred by Florida Rule of Judicial Administration 2.215, it is ORDERED as follows:

I. THE APPELLATE COURT

A. Panels, Divisions of the Court, and Assignment of Cases.

1. *Panels:* The Circuit Appellate Court fulfills its appellate responsibilities through monthly panels comprised of three judges which shall hear the following matters:

a. All appeals invoking the appellate jurisdiction of the circuit court, pursuant to Fla. R. App. P. 9.030(c).

b. All petitions for extraordinary writs which are filed pursuant to Fla. R. App. P. 9.030(c) and which seek review of a lower tribunal ruling, except for those qualifying Writs of Habeas Corpus and other Emergency Writs that are ruled up on by the Presiding Judge.

2. *Divisions of the Court:* Appeals and petitions for extraordinary writs filed in the circuit appellate court shall be assigned to either Division "AC" or Division "AY".

a. Appeals and petitions for extraordinary writs arising from county court criminal proceedings shall be assigned to Division "AC".

b. Appeals and petitions for extraordinary writs arising from county court civil proceedings shall be assigned to Division "AY".

c. Appeals and petitions for extraordinary writs arising from administrative proceedings shall be assigned to Division "AY".

3. *Assignment of Judges:*

a. Cases assigned to Division "AY" and "AC"

1) A panel may be composed of three judges assigned to the North County Courthouse or the South County Courthouse. A branch courthouse panel will not hear appeals arising from one of its county court divisions.

2) The chief judge, or designee, shall assign judges to the panels and designate a presiding judge in an equitable and fair manner so that no undue burden falls upon any single judge or group of judges.

3) The chief judge may assign any circuit judge to an "AC" or "AY" panel as needed.

b. Cases assigned to Division "AC". Cases assigned to Division "AC" will be heard by a panel composed of three judges from the circuit criminal and UFC/juvenile judges located at the Main Judicial Complex, or from circuit judges assigned to a branch courthouse as specified above. UFC/family judges may sit on an "AC" panel as needed.

c. Cases assigned to Division "AY"

1) Appeals and petitions from county civil proceedings will be heard by a panel composed of three judges from the circuit civil and UFC/family judges located at the Main Judicial Complex, or from circuit judges assigned to a branch courthouse as specified above. UFC/juvenile judges may sit on an "AY" panel as needed.

2) Appeals and petitions from administrative proceedings may be heard by a panel composed of circuit criminal judges, circuit civil judges, UFC judges, and circuit judges assigned to branch courthouses. A county judge may be specially appointed to sit as a circuit judge, however, there can be no more than one county court judge assigned to a panel.

4. *Presiding Judge:*

a. The presiding judge must be a circuit judge.

b. For panels held at the Main Judicial Complex, the presiding judge is to be a judge assigned to the circuit civil or circuit criminal divisions.

c. The presiding judge shall have the following responsibilities:

1) To rule on non dispositive motions. Dispositive motions shall be decided by the full panel for that month;

2) To discharge the administrative duties of the panel, including scheduling oral argument sessions and/or oral-argument-waived conferences;

3) To preside at all sessions;

4) To assign the writing of opinions among the panel members when the presiding judge is in the majority; however, when the presiding judge is in the minority, this responsibility shall be discharged by the most senior judge in the majority;

5) To rule upon Emergency Petitions for Writs of Habeas Corpus or other Emergency Petitions filed pursuant to Fla. R. App. P. 9.030(c) which seek review of a lower tribunal ruling.

d. If the presiding judge is unavailable, then his/her responsibilities may be discharged by one of the two other panel members. If the other two panel members are unavailable, then the presiding judge's responsibilities may be discharged by the circuit civil or circuit criminal administrative judge or, if unavailable, a circuit judge.

B. Oral Arguments.

1. When oral argument is requested by a party, it will be granted by the court only in those cases where a majority of

the panel genuinely believes it is necessary for disposition of the cause.

2. Oral arguments shall be scheduled on any case when requested by two members of the panel of assigned judges, though not requested by the parties.

C. Opinions.

1. The final opinion shall be circulated together with a face sheet on which each panel member shall indicate their concurrence or dissent. (See attached FORM "A").

2. The face sheet together with the majority opinion and any concurring or dissenting opinions shall be filed with the clerk.

D. Determination of Causes En Banc.

1. *En Banc Proceedings, Generally*

a. En banc hearings and rehearings shall not be ordered unless the case is of exceptional importance or unless necessary to maintain uniformity in the circuit court's appellate decisions.

b. An en banc panel shall be comprised as follows:

1) En banc criminal panels bearing the designation 'AC shall be comprised of the judges from the circuit criminal divisions located at the Main Judicial Complex.

2) En banc civil panels bearing the designation 'AY' shall be comprised of the judges from the circuit civil divisions located at the Main Judicial Complex.

3) Any judge who sat on the three judge panel that initially reviewed the matter now before the en banc panel may also sit on the en banc panel. Such judge may sit on the en banc panel even if such judge is no longer assigned to the applicable circuit criminal or circuit civil division.

c. An en banc decision shall be by a majority of the judges on the en banc panel who participate and vote on the case. If there is no majority decision of the en banc panel, then the decision of the original three panel members shall stand as the decision of the court.

2. *Hearings En Banc*

a. A hearing en banc may only be ordered by the court on its own motion. A party may not request an en banc hearing.

b. At any time after the three judge panel confers, any judge on that panel may poll the judges comprising the en banc panel to determine whether a majority of the en banc panel desires a hearing en banc. A majority of the judges compromising the en banc panel may order that a proceeding pending before the court be determined en banc.

3. *Rehearings En Banc*

a. A rehearing en banc may be ordered by the court on its own motion or on motion of a party. Within the time prescribed by Florida Rule of Appellate Procedure 9.330, a party may move for an en banc rehearing solely on the grounds that the case is of exceptional importance or that such consideration is necessary to maintain uniformity in the court's decisions. A motion based on any other ground shall be stricken. A response may be served within ten (10) days of service of the motion.

b. Any judge on the original three judge panel may poll the judges comprising the en banc panel to determine whether a majority of the en banc panel desires a rehearing en banc. A vote by the en banc panel will not be taken on a party's motion requesting en banc rehearing unless requested by a judge on the original three judge panel. Judges who did not sit on the original panel are under no obligation to consider a party's motion unless a vote is requested.

c. A motion for rehearing en banc must contain a statement as required by Florida Rule of Appellate Procedure 9.331(d)(2).

d. A motion for rehearing en banc shall be disposed of by order. If rehearing en banc is granted, the court may limit the issues to be reheard, require the filing of additional briefs, and may require additional argument.

II. RESPONSIBILITIES OF THE PARTIES

The parties will be provided a copy of Form B—Notice to Attorneys and Parties—by the Clerk in accordance with Part III below. Form B sets forth the parties' responsibilities and is incorporated herein.

III. THE CLERK OF COURT

A. Duties of the Clerk of Court.

1. The clerk shall perform all functions and discharge all duties traditionally fulfilled by clerks in Florida's Fourth District Court of Appeal. See Manual of Internal Operating Procedures, Fourth District Court of Appeal.

2. Upon receipt of the Notice of Appeal or Petition for Extraordinary Writ arising from the county court, the clerk will input the party and attorney information from the lower court for the petitioner/appellant and respondent/appellee.

3. The Clerk will link together the applicable lower court case with the appellate case in its case maintenance system.

4. The Clerk's duties include but are not limited to the following:

a. Original Notice of Appeal: filing and docketing the original notice of appeal in the lower court case and a copy in the appellate case and providing a copy of the notice of appeal to the Trial Court Law Clerk/Staff Attorney's Office.

b. Acknowledgment of New Case and Designation to Court Reporter: filing and docketing in Division AC cases (criminal appeals), the designation to Court Reporter, the Court Reporter's Acknowledgement in the appellate case.

c. Overdue Fees:

1) notifying the Appellant/Petitioner as to whether the required appellate filing fee or record on appeal fee has not been paid in full. Such notice shall be filed in the appellate court file with a courtesy copy forwarded to the Trial Court Law Clerk/Staff Attorney's Office.

2) notifying the Trial Court Law Clerk/Staff Attorney's Office when the Appellant/Petitioner has paid an overdue fee. Such notice shall be filed in the appellate court file with a courtesy copy forwarded to the Trial Court Law Clerk/Staff Attorney's Office.

d. Form B: forwarding copies of the "notice to attorneys and parties" (See attached FORM "B") to all parties after receipt of the notice of appeal or petition for extraordinary writ.

e. Motions: filing and docketing all requests for extension of time and motions relating to the appeal in the appellate case and forwarding copies of all motions to the Trial Court Law Clerk/Staff Attorney's Office.

f. Briefs: filing and docketing all briefs (initial/petition, answer/response and reply) in the appellate case and forwarding the 3 courtesy copies of briefs filed by the parties to the Trial Court Law Clerk/Staff Attorney's Office.

g. Transmitting the record on appeal to the Trial Court Law Clerk/Staff Attorney's Office.

h. Mandates: issuing the mandates in accordance with Fla. R. App. P. 9.340.

B. Monthly Reports.

1. The clerk shall, pursuant to Fla. R. Jud. Admin. 2.215(b)(6), prepare and provide monthly civil reports to the Chief Judge and Staff Attorney Office, and prepare and provide monthly criminal reports to the Chief Judge, Staff Attorney Office, the Office of the State Attorney, and the Office of the Public Defender.

2. The monthly reports shall be due on the first of each month.

3. The Reports shall list all of the appeals and petitions for extraordinary writ pending in the division. The listing shall be in sequential order utilizing the filing date of the notice of appeal or petition and shall contain as follows:

a. the appellate case number;

b. the style of the case (e.g., Jones v. State):

c. the date on which the notice of appeal or petition was filed;

d. the date a request for oral argument is filed, if applicable;

e. the date on which oral argument or an oral-argument-waived conference was held, if applicable;

f. the date on which the court's decision was issued; and

g. the date on which the mandate was issued.

IV. TRIAL COURT LAW CLERK/STAFF ATTORNEY

The Trial Court Law Clerks/Staff Attorney's Office shall:

1. maintain a log of all pending appeals;

2. perform case management responsibilities under the supervision and direction of the presiding judge;

3. review all motions and prepare orders under the supervision and direction of the presiding judge;

4. prepare bench memoranda for all cases;

5. assist in drafting of opinions under the direction and supervision of a member of the appellate panel;

6. prepare the calendars for oral argument sessions and oral-argument-waived conferences ("panel");

7. distribute copies of all Court orders to parties of record;

8. distribute copies of the court's opinions as follows:

a. FLW Supplement;

b. Main Courthouse Law Library;

c. County Civil Judges (if a civil decision), or County Criminal Judges (if criminal decision);

d. Office of General Counsel;

e. Parties of Record.

DONE and **SIGNED** in Chambers at West Palm Beach, Palm Beach County, Florida, this 21 day of May 2018.

Krista Marx
Chief Judge

FORM "A"

IN THE CIRCUIT COURT OF THE FIFTEENTH JUDICIAL CIRCUIT IN AND FOR PALM BEACH COUNTY, FLORIDA

CASE NO.:
L.T. NO.:

Opinion/Decision filed:

,

Appeal/Petition from the [Lower Tribunal] [in and for Palm Beach County], , [Judge].

Appellant/Petitioner(s),

v.

,

Appellee/Respondent(s).

Date of Appeal/Petition:

/
____

DATE OF PANEL: ______________________________
PANEL JUDGES: __________, __________, __________
AFFIRMED/REVERSED/OTHER: ______________________
DECISION BY: ______________________________

CONCURRING:	) DISSENTING:	) CONCURRING SPECIALLY:	)
	) With/Without Opinion	) With/Without Opinion	)
	)	)	)
	)	)	)
Date:	) Date:	) Date:	)
	)	)	)
	)	)	)
Date:	) Date:	) Date:	)
	)	)	)
	)	)	)
Date:	) Date:	) Date:	)

FORM "B"

IN THE CIRCUIT COURT OF THE FIFTEENTH JUDICIAL CIRCUIT IN AND FOR PALM BEACH COUNTY, FLORIDA

APPELLATE DIVISION OF THE CIRCUIT COURT

IMPORTANT NOTICE TO ATTORNEYS AND PARTIES **Revised 5/18**

Unless there are exigent circumstances, the court will strictly enforce the following procedures to assist in the prompt and orderly disposition of matters under review:

1. NOTICE OF APPEAL: The notice of appeal shall be substantially in the form prescribed by rule 9.900(a). The Caption shall contain the name of the lower tribunal, the name of the trial court judge, the name and designation of at least 1 party on each side, and the case number in the lower tribunal. The notice shall contain the name of the court to which the appeal is taken, the date of rendition, and the nature of the order to be reviewed. Except in criminal cases, a conformed copy of the order or orders designated in the notice of appeal shall be attached to the notice together with any order entered on a timely motion postponing rendition of the order or orders appealed. See Fla. R. App. P. 9.110(d) and 9.130(c).

2. BRIEFS: Each brief must be served and filed as follows:

a. To Parties: One (1) copy of each brief and appendix must be served on counsel for each party separately represented;

b. To Clerk's Office: Filing with Clerk:

1) E-filing. Briefs shall be e-filed in accordance with Florida Rule of Judicial Administration 2.525.

2) Physical filing. Any briefs that are physically filed (rather than e–filed) with the Clerk's office must be secured with a binder clip and without brief covers on opaque, white, unglossed 8 ½ by 11 inch paper. See Fla. R. App. P. 9.210.

c. Courtesy Copies for the Court:

1) Paper courtesy copies. In addition to filing a copy of the brief and appendix with the clerk, parties must provide three (3) paper courtesy copies of each brief and appendix. The paper courtesy copies shall be submitted to the Clerk and the Clerk shall forward the courtesy copies to the court appellate liaison. Each of the three paper courtesy copies of the briefs and appendices must be securely bound by a staple in the upper left-hand corner or, if they are too voluminous to be securely stapled, by any other secure means (such as a notebook or by spiral binding). The Court will reject paper courtesy copies held together by rubber band, binder clip, or any other insecure means.

2) Electronic courtesy copy. In addition to providing paper courtesy copies, the parties must send an electronic courtesy copy of each brief. The electronic copy must be sent in PDF format with bookmarks to any appendices. The forwarding email must contain the title and docket number of the case, and the name of the attached document. The electronic courtesy copy must be sent via email as follows:

a) for civil appeals and petitions: **civilappeals@pbcgov.org**

b) for criminal appeals and petitions: **criminalappeals@pbcgov.org**

c) for administrative agency appeals and petitions: **adminappeals@pbcgov.org**

3. APPENDIX: An appendix shall be filed as a single PDF with bookmarks unless the size exceeds that permitted by rule or the Standards of the Florida Court Technology Commission. If the filing of one PDF exceeds the permitted megabytes, then the exhibits shall be grouped together so that there are as few separate PDFs as possible.

4. MOTIONS:

a. Excessive and unnecessary motion practice is discouraged and may result in the imposition of sanctions under Fla. R. App. P. 9.410.

b. Any record material necessary for resolution of a motion should be attached as an appendix.

c. Motions are to also contain an express representation, except on motions where clearly inappropriate, that opposing counsel has been contacted and will or will not stipulate to the relief requested.

d. Any request for action or relief should be clearly set forth in the form of a motion styled in the case which reflects "Fifteenth Judicial Circuit" at the top, the case name, this court's case number, and the lower tribunal case number. See Fla. R. App. P. 9.300.

e. The moving party shall file the original and one copy of all motions.

5. RESPONSES TO MOTIONS: Responses to motions shall be served within 10 days after service of the motion. No reply will be considered unless specifically authorized by the court. Any unauthorized reply will be stricken without consideration. Fla. R. App. P. 9.300.

6. EXTENSIONS OF TIME:

a. Attorneys are responsible for seeing that the time schedule set out in the Appellate Rules is followed and that the record and briefs are filed on time. Requests for extension of time should be filed in compliance with Fla. R. App. P. 9.300(a).

b. In lieu of an agreed motion for extension of time to file an initial, answer, or reply brief, pursuant to Fla. R. App. P. 9.300(a), or an agreed motion for extension of time to file a response to a petition for extraordinary writ or a reply to a response, the court will accept a notice from a party that the parties have agreed to a specific extension of time. This notice shall state as follows:

> Counsel for [movant] has consulted opposing counsel or self represented litigant who has agreed that the time for serving [movant's] [initial/answer/response/reply] brief may be extended for ________ days to ________ [date].

An agreed notice of extension of time will be accepted for up to a total of 120 days for an initial or answer brief, and 60 days for a response for a petition for extraordinary writ or reply brief. The notice need not be signed by both parties. No order will issue from the court. This procedure shall apply to criminal, civil, and administrative appeals and petitions for extraordinary writs. It shall not apply to any expedited or emergency appeals or any cases in which the court has ordered that additional extensions are not permitted.

c. No extensions of time will be granted in expedited cases.

d. No motion for extension of time will be granted that does not contain a certificate that opposing counsel has been contacted and stating whether the motion is opposed.

e. A motion for extension of time served after the time for serving the brief has expired may not be granted absent a showing of good cause.

f. Motions for extensions of time for reply briefs are discouraged.

g. Failure to comply with these standards may result in dismissal or in striking an untimely brief or in other sanctions.

7. ORAL ARGUMENT: Oral Argument will be granted by the court only in those cases where it is genuinely believed necessary for disposition of the cause. Oral argument will be limited to twenty (20) minutes per side with exceptions only by motion and order of the court. Requests should be filed in conformity with Fla. R. App. P. 9.320.

8. RELATED CASES: All parties have the obligation to advise the Court in writing, as soon as possible, of any other cases pending before this Court involving related issues.

9. CERTIFICATES OF SERVICE: All motions, notices, briefs and appendices are required to have a certificate of service. See Fla. R. App. P. 9.420(d).

10. EXHIBITS: If a party desires to include one or more articles of physical evidence, excluding documents, in the record on appeal, the party shall first seek permission from the court.

11. SUPPLEMENTAL AUTHORITY: A party's brief should contain all relevant authority published prior to submission of the brief. A Notice of Supplemental Authority should cite to newly discovered cases (copy of opinion to be attached to Notice) with a clear designation of the point on appeal to which the authority is pertinent.

12. REHEARING: Although motions for rehearing are permitted by Fla. R. App. P. 9.330, they should be rare. The court strongly discourages the practice of routinely filing such motions or those which merely re-argue the merits or question the court's decision. Where there has been an award of attorney's fees on appeal in connection with our decision on the merits, additional attorney's fees will be awarded upon a denial of a motion for rehearing.

13. PARTIES:

Pro Se	An individual is entitled to represent herself or himself in a civil proceeding but he or she must comply with the Florida Appellate Rules of Procedure. Failure to properly comply with rules of procedure can reach a point where such failure amounts in an abuse of judicial process properly subjecting the appeal to a dismissal with prejudice. For information on Pro Se Appeals go to: http://prose.flabarappellate.org/default.asp
Businesses	A corporation or limited liability company may not represent itself through non-lawyer employees, officers, or shareholders even where the non-lawyer purporting to represent the corporation is the sole shareholder of the corporation.

14. CHANGE OF ADDRESS: All attorneys representing parties in this court and parties representing themselves must promptly notify this court of any change of address by filing a Notice of Change of Address and updating in the court's online system at: https://e-services.co.palm-beach.fl.us/scheduling/login.php?ref=/scheduling/

15. FILING FEE: In all appeals and cases originating in the circuit appellate court, at the time the certified copy of the notice of appeal, petition, or other initial pleading is filed, the Clerk shall require the payment of a fee as required by law. Parties may file an affidavit of indigency with the Clerk's Office if unable to pay the required filing fee. Failure to pay such fee, after notice from the court, may result in the dismissal of the case. The payment shall not be exacted in advance in criminal appeals in which the defendant has been adjudicated insolvent for the purpose of an appeal, or in appeals in which the state is the petitioner/appellant.

Adopted effective September 29, 2008. Amended effective January 5, 2009; June 22, 2009; July 5, 2011; April 2, 2012; December 19, 2012; May 16, 2017; May 21, 2018.

* supersedes admin. order no. 8.101–5/17 (amended as to Form B only)

8.102. ASSIGNMENT OF APPELLATE PANELS

IN THE CIRCUIT COURT OF THE FIFTEENTH JUDICIAL CIRCUIT IN AND FOR PALM BEACH COUNTY, FLORIDA

ADMINISTRATIVE ORDER NO. 8.102–5/17 *

IN RE: ASSIGNMENT OF APPELLATE PANELS

Administrative Order 8.102 has been merged with Administrative Order 8.101–5/17.

NOW THEREFORE, it is hereby **ORDERED** that Administrative Order 8.102–4/09 is vacated and set aside.

DONE AND SIGNED in Chambers at West Palm Beach, Palm Beach County, Florida this 16 day of May, 2017.

Jeffrey Colbath, Chief Judge

Adopted effective September 29, 2008. Amended effective April 28, 2009; May 16, 2017.

* supersedes admin. order 8.102–4/09*

Traffic

Criminal Traffic Matters

10.101. REQUESTS FOR CONTINUANCE OF TRAFFIC CRIME ARRAIGNMENTS AT BRANCH COURTHOUSES

IN THE CIRCUIT COURT OF THE FIFTEENTH JUDICIAL CIRCUIT IN AND FOR PALM BEACH COUNTY, FLORIDA

ADMINISTRATIVE ORDER NO. 10.101–9/08 *

IN RE: REQUESTS FOR CONTINUANCE OF TRAFFIC CRIME ARRAIGNMENTS AT BRANCH COURTHOUSES

There is an increasing volume of traffic crime arraignments scheduled at the Branch Courthouses and there is a concomitant increase in the requests for continuance of arraignment filed by the defendant. A written request for continuance signed by the defendant operates as a waiver of speedy trial. The Office of the State Attorney has agreed to the continuance of arraignment one time for a period of no more than thirty (30) days upon the filing of a written request for continuance signed by the defendant.

NOW, THEREFORE, pursuant to the authority conferred by Florida Rule of Judicial Administration 2.215, it is **ORDERED** as follows:

1. Cases set for traffic crime arraignment at the branch courthouses shall be continued by the clerk once for a period of no more than thirty (30) days if a written request for continuance is filed by the defendant prior to the originally scheduled arraignment date and time.

2. The defendant's written request for continuance shall be made part of the court file.

DONE AND SIGNED in Chambers at West Palm Beach, Palm Beach County, Florida this 29 day of September, 2008.

Kathleen J. Kroll
Chief Judge

Adopted effective September 29, 2008.

* supersedes admin. order 10.013–8/99 (as it pertains to traffic crimes)

10.102. INACTIVE TRAFFIC CRIMINAL CASES

IN THE CIRCUIT COURT OF THE FIFTEENTH JUDICIAL CIRCUIT IN AND FOR PALM BEACH COUNTY, FLORIDA

ADMINISTRATIVE ORDER NO. 10.102–8/14 *

IN RE: INACTIVE TRAFFIC CRIMINAL CASES

The State Attorney for the Fifteenth Judicial Circuit has indicated that he does not object to the dismissal of cases where the defendant is deceased.

NOW, THEREFORE, pursuant to the authority conferred by Florida Rule of Judicial Administration 2.215, it is **ORDERED** as follows:

1. When the Clerk obtains documentation evidencing that the defendant in a criminal traffic case is deceased, the case is deemed dismissed without further order of the court and the Clerk is hereby directed to close the case.

2. The Clerk shall provide notice of such dismissal to the Office of the State Attorney and defense counsel of record, if any.

3. Administrative Order 4.605–8/14 (as amended) governs the inactive misdemeanor cases.

DONE and **SIGNED** in Chambers at West Palm Beach, Palm Beach County, Florida, this 25 day of August, 2014.

Jeffrey Colbath
Chief Judge

Adopted effective September 29, 2008. Amended effective August 25, 2014.

*supersedes admin. order 10.102–9/08

10.103. TRAFFIC CRIMES & INFRACTIONS ASSOCIATED WITH A FELONY CHARGE

IN THE CIRCUIT COURT OF THE FIFTEENTH JUDICIAL CIRCUIT IN AND FOR PALM BEACH COUNTY, FLORIDA

ADMINISTRATIVE ORDER NO. 10.103–5/15

IN RE: TRAFFIC CRIMES & INFRACTIONS ASSOCIATED WITH A FELONY CHARGE

In the interest of judicial economy and to promote more informed judicial decision making, procedures must be established to ensure that traffic crimes and traffic infractions which are scheduled before a county court judge (collectively "traffic offenses") and which are associated with a felony charge are heard by the court simultaneously. This practice will avoid multiple appearances by witnesses and law enforcement.

NOW, THEREFORE, pursuant to the authority conferred by Florida Rule of Judicial Administration 2.215, it is **ORDERED** as follows:

1. Newly Filed Cases.

a. When the State Attorney's Office determines that an information shall be filed on a felony charge which is related to a traffic offense, the state attorney may reference the traffic citation case number in the top right hand corner of the information if such case number is known.

b. Based upon the case number listed in the information document, the Clerk of Court shall schedule the traffic offense and the felony case before the assigned Felony Judge, and the Felony calendar shall reflect both case numbers.

2. Cases Identified After Filing.

a. In the event that a traffic offense associated with a felony charge is identified prior to the felony case being resolved, the assigned county court judge shall direct the clerk to schedule the traffic offense at the next scheduled felony court date to be heard by the felony division judge.

b. The Clerk of Court shall list both the felony and traffic offense case numbers on the felony calendar.

3. Cases Pending After Disposition of Felony Case. If the traffic offense is not resolved with the felony case, the clerk shall schedule the traffic offense before the county court judge presiding in the division in which the traffic offense was originally assigned.

DONE AND SIGNED in Chambers, at West Palm Beach, Palm Beach County, Florida this 22 day of May, 2015.

Jeffrey Colbath
Chief Judge

Adopted effective May 22, 2015.

Civil Traffic Matters

10.201. TRAFFIC INFRACTION HEARINGS INVOLVING FATALITIES

IN THE CIRCUIT COURT OF THE FIFTEENTH JUDICIAL CIRCUIT IN AND FOR PALM BEACH COUNTY, FLORIDA

ADMINISTRATIVE ORDER NO. 10.201–9/08 *

IN RE: TRAFFIC INFRACTION HEARINGS INVOLVING FATALITIES

The proper administration of justice suggests that the sensitive nature of fatality-involved traffic infractions merits specially set hearings.

NOW, THEREFORE, pursuant to the authority conferred by Florida Rule of Judicial Administration 2.215, it is **ORDERED** as follows:

1. Traffic infraction hearings involving fatalities which are, in accordance with current practice, scheduled in the Main Courthouse shall be segregated from other traffic infractions and then assigned to the Civil Division Judges of the County Court who sit in the Main Courthouse on a rotation basis after the entry of any plea. (Fatality-involved traffic infraction hearings which are scheduled in satellite courthouse facilities shall be segregated from other traffic infractions and then forwarded to the appropriately assigned satellite courthouse judge as outlined below).

2. Upon assignment of such fatality-involved traffic infraction, the Clerk shall then forward to such assigned judge, forthwith, the court file which shall include the citation, witness lists, and a request for designation of hearing.

3. The assigned judge shall, upon receipt of the court file and its contents, promptly designate a courtroom, a hearing date and time, and immediately return the file with the designations to the Clerk. The Clerk shall, within 5 business days thereafter, issue all subpoenas and notices of hearing to all proper parties, counsel, and witnesses. The hearing date designated by the assigned judge shall afford at least 45 days in advance of the designated hearing to accommodate preparation of such notices and subpoenas and for service of same. However, the 45–day minimum is subject to speedy trial considerations pursuant to Rule 6.325, Fla. R. Traffic Court.

4. The Clerk of Court shall assign a courtroom clerk to be present on the date and time scheduled for such fatality-involved traffic infraction.

DONE and **SIGNED** in Chambers at West Palm Beach, Palm Beach County, Florida, this 29 day of September, 2008.

Kathleen J. Kroll
Chief Judge

Adopted effective September 29, 2008.

* supersedes admin. order 9.010 9/99

Civil Traffic Hearing Officers

10.301. CIVIL TRAFFIC INFRACTION HEARING OFFICER PROGRAM

IN THE CIRCUIT COURT OF THE FIFTEENTH JUDICIAL CIRCUIT IN AND FOR PALM BEACH COUNTY, FLORIDA

ADMINISTRATIVE ORDER NO. 10.301–8/17 *

IN RE: CIVIL TRAFFIC INFRACTION HEARING OFFICER PROGRAM

On March 5, 1991, the Civil Traffic Infraction Hearing Officer Program approved by the Supreme Court was established in Palm Beach County. The program was confirmed in Administrative Order No. 10.005–9/92. Since the 2002 Order, statutory and other changes warrant revision to the Order. Therefore, in order to continue the efficient operation of the Civil Traffic Infraction Hearing Officer Program in Palm Beach County and in accordance with Florida Statutes and the Florida Rules of Traffic Procedure; and in order to provide for the orderly appointment and compensation of civil traffic infraction hearing officers, it is

NOW, THEREFORE, pursuant to the authority conferred by Florida Rule of Judicial Administration 2.215, it is **ORDERED** as follows:

1. The existence of the Civil Traffic Infraction Hearing Officer Program in Palm Beach County is affirmed and continued from the date of establishment detailed above.

2. The Civil Traffic Infraction Hearing Officer (THO) shall be selected by the Chief Judge. As many individuals may be selected to serve as THO's as may be necessary to ensure that traffic infraction cases are disposed of timely and efficiently.

3. THO's shall:

a. Execute an oath of office;

b. Serve part-time and at the pleasure of the Chief Judge;

c. Hear and consider all traffic infraction proceedings, including parking ticket hearings;

d. Preside over calendars scheduled during the week and on weekends at traffic court locations throughout Palm Beach County;

e. Have the power to accept pleas from Defendants, hear and rule upon motions, decide the guilt or innocence of any person, adult or juvenile charged with any civil traffic infraction, and adjudicate or withhold adjudication in the same manner as a county court judge under the statutes, rules and procedures presently existing or as subsequently amended.

4. However, THO's shall not:

a. Have the power to hold any person in contempt of court, but shall be permitted to file a verified motion for order of contempt with an appropriate state trial court judge pursuant to Florida Rule of Criminal Procedure 3.840;

b. Hear a case involving an accident resulting in injury or death;

c. Hear a criminal traffic offense case or a case involving a civil traffic infraction issued in conjunction with a criminal traffic offense; or

d. Have the power to suspend a Defendant's driver's license pursuant to Florida Statute 316.655(2).

5. Any THO regularly scheduled to preside over a calendar will be an independent contractor and must enter into a contract with the Fifteenth Judicial Circuit before serving as a THO. The compensation for contract THO's will be as provided in his or her contract with the Fifteenth Judicial Circuit. A court employee qualified under Florida Rule of Traffic Court 6.630 may preside over a calendar as part of his or her regular duties when determined necessary by the County Administrative Judge or the Chief Judge.

6. The following attorneys have completed, or are in the process of completing, the required training. Once training has been completed, they are approved to act as Hearing Officers and are hereby appointed (or reappointed as the case may be) and are authorized to hear proceedings in Palm Beach County, Florida until further order of this Court.

Parnel Auguste
Sara Blumberg
Elliot Brooks
Cathy Chimera
Jack Goldberger
Daniel Haverman

James Kehoe
John Kurtz
Michele Lenoff
James McGlynn
Steven Miller
Marshall Osofsky
Donia Roberts
Lloyd Routman
Steven Rubin

7. THO's shall perform their duties in accordance with Florida Statutes, Rules of Court, the Code of Judicial Conduct, applicable Administrative Orders, relevant case law and the terms and conditions of the contract between the THO and the Fifteenth Judicial Circuit.

8. Matters of contempt arising from the THO's calendars shall be heard by the County Court Judge assigned to the applicable traffic division.

9. Upon the timely request of a Defendant in a Notice of Appearance or in a written plea pursuant to F.R.T.C. 6.630(n), a case shall be assigned to the county court judge assigned to the applicable traffic division instead of scheduling the case to be heard by a THO.

10. Appeals from dispositions of the THO's shall be filed in the Circuit Court.

11. All actions taken before this date by previously appointed THO's are hereby confirmed.

12. Other THO's may be appointed as deemed necessary by the Chief Judge.

13. The THO program will be supervised by judges designated by the Chief Judge and administered by a THO ("Administrative THO") designated by the Chief Judge.

14. The Clerk and Comptroller shall provide deputy clerks to perform normal courtroom duties during traffic infraction hearings.

15. The Chief Courtroom Deputy shall assign a courtroom deputy to attend and assist the THO's during traffic infraction hearings.

DONE and **SIGNED** in Chambers at West Palm Beach, Palm Beach County, Florida I this 29th day of August, 2017 *nunc pro tunc to* April 28, 2017.

Krista Marx
Chief Judge

Adopted effective September 29, 2008. Amended effective July 22, 2009; November 23, 2009; September 1, 2010; October 5, 2010; March 13, 2012; June 11, 2013; June 30, 2014; June 30, 2016; November 1, 2016; April 28, 2017.

* supersedes administrative order no. 10.301–11/16

Civil Traffic Infraction Procedures

10.401. ASSIGNMENT OF CIVIL TRAFFIC INFRACTIONS

IN THE CIRCUIT COURT OF THE FIFTEENTH JUDICIAL CIRCUIT IN AND FOR PALM BEACH COUNTY

ADMINISTRATIVE ORDER NO. 10.401–9/12 *

IN RE: ASSIGNMENT OF CIVIL TRAFFIC INFRACTIONS

The efficient administration of the Traffic Division requires a uniform policy concerning assignment of traffic infractions to the various courthouses within the county.

NOW, THEREFORE, pursuant to the authority conferred by Florida Rule of Judicial Administration 2.215, it is **ORDERED** as follows:

1. All traffic infractions will be assigned to the courthouse facility assigned to the specific law enforcement agency as set forth below, with the exception of red light camera citations issued pursuant to F.S. 316.0083 and parking tickets, which may be scheduled in any county courthouse facility regardless of which agency issued the citation.

2. Citations issued by the following departments will be assigned to the Main Judicial Center:

a. West Palm Beach
b. Lake Clarke Shores
c. Town of Palm Beach
d. Palm Springs
e. Greenacres
f. Palm Beach Sheriff's Office
 1) Traffic 06MB
 2) District 1 (West Palm Beach)
 3) District 8 (Wellington)
 4) District 9 (Royal Palm Beach)
 5) Airport District.

3. Citations issued by the following departments will be assigned to the North County Courthouse:

a. Palm Beach Gardens
b. Florida Highway Patrol
 1) Troop J NB
 2) Troop K NB
 3) Troop L NB
c. Riviera Beach
d. Tequesta
e. Juno Beach
f. Jupiter
g. Palm Beach Shores
h. North Palm Beach
i. Palm Beach County Sheriff's Office
 1) District 2 (Mangonia Park)
 2) District 3 (North Palm Beach)
 3) District 10 (Lake Park)
 4) District 15 (Acreage/Loxahatchee)
 5) Traffic 06NB

4. Citations issued by the following departments will be assigned to the South County Courthouse:

a. Boca Raton

b. Boynton Beach

c. Delray Beach

d. Gulfstream

e. Highland Beach

f. Hypoluxo

g. Lantana

h. Manalapan

i. Ocean Ridge

j. South Palm Beach

k. Florida Atlantic University

l. Atlantis

m. Florida Highway Patrol

1) Troop J SB

2) Troop K SB

3) Troop L SB

n. Department of Transportation

o. SunPass (toll) violations issued pursuant to Florida Statute 316.1001.

p. Palm Beach County Sheriff's Office

1) District 4 (Delray Beach)

2) District 6 (Western Boynton Beach/Delray)

3) District 7 (Boca Raton)

4) District 14 (Lake Worth)

5) Traffic 06SB

5. Citations issued by the following departments will be assigned to the West County Courthouse:

a. Florida Highway Patrol west of the 20 mile bend

b. Department of Transportation west of 20 mile bend

c. Palm Beach County Sheriff's Office

1) District 5 (Western Palm Beach County)

2) District 11 (South Bay)

3) District 12 (Pahokee)

4) District 13 (Belle Glade)

5) Traffic 06WB

6. The traffic hearing schedule for each of these facilities shall remain as currently in place but may be adjusted from time to time as needed.

7. Cases that are scheduled to appear before a county court civil judge will be assigned in accordance with Administrative Order 3.102–11/10 (as amended).

8. Cases that are scheduled to appear before a county court criminal judge will be assigned in accordance with Administrative Order 4.603–9/08 (as amended).

DONE and ORDERED in Chambers at West Palm Beach, Palm Beach County, Florida, this 24 day of September, 2012.

PETER D. BLANC
Chief Judge

Adopted effective September 29, 2008. Amended effective August 17, 2010; September 24, 2012.

* supersedes admin. order no. 10.401–8/10

10.402. CIVIL TRAFFIC INFRACTION HEARING CONTINUANCES

IN THE CIRCUIT COURT OF THE FIFTEENTH JUDICIAL CIRCUIT IN AND FOR PALM BEACH COUNTY, FLORIDA

ADMINISTRATIVE ORDER NO: 10.402–3/16 *

IN RE: CIVIL TRAFFIC INFRACTION HEARING CONTINUANCES

The efficient administration of the Traffic Division requires a uniform policy concerning requests for continuances of infraction hearings. Procedures for the scheduling of traffic infraction hearings must be consistent with the policy to prevent forum shopping before judges and traffic hearing officers. The Judges of the County Court have determined that the defendant and law enforcement agency (or its designee) in a civil traffic infraction case should be allowed a Clerk of Court's administrative continuance of a pretrial hearing and/or trial, so long as the request for continuance is in writing and filed with the Clerk not less than one (1) business day prior to a scheduled pretrial date or not less than fourteen (14) calendar days prior to a scheduled trial date.

NOW, THEREFORE, pursuant to the authority conferred by Florida Rule of Judicial Administration 2.215, it is **ORDERED** as follows:

1. **Continuance Request by a Defendant.**

a. A defendant in a civil traffic infraction case is hereby allowed one ex parte administrative continuance of a scheduled pretrial hearing upon written request, provided such request is filed with the Clerk of Court not later than one (1) business day prior to the scheduled pretrial hearing. A continuance allowed pursuant to this subsection shall constitute a waiver of speedy trial. Upon the receipt of the defendant's timely written request for continuance of the pretrial, the Clerk shall provide notice of the new pretrial date, place, and time to the defendant.

b. A defendant in a civil traffic infraction case is hereby allowed one ex parte administrative continuance of a scheduled trial date upon written request, provided such request is filed with the Clerk of Court not later than fourteen (14) calendar days prior to the scheduled trial date. The date of the trial shall not be included in calculating the fourteen (14) day time period. The continuance of the trial date shall constitute a waiver of speedy trial. Upon the allowance of the administrative continuance of a trial date, the Clerk of Court shall provide notice of the new trial date, place and time to the defendant, the law enforcement agency which issued the citation, and to all witnesses that have been subpoenaed for trial.

c. Any untimely filed written request for a Clerk's administrative continuance, and any other request for continuance, which by this Administrative Order may not be allowed by the Clerk of Court, shall be assigned to and ruled upon ex parte by the Administrative Traffic Hearing Officer, or such other person designated by the Chief Judge. If such request is not ruled upon before the scheduled pretrial hearing or trial date, then the request shall remain on the docket of the scheduled pretrial hearing or trial, at which time the Official will rule on the request in open court.

d. Notwithstanding anything to the contrary in the preceding subsections, if a defendant has sought and obtained one continuance of a pretrial hearing date (whether a Clerk's administrative continuance or a continuance granted by an Official), no Clerk's administrative pretrial hearing continuance shall be allowed. If a defendant has sought and obtained one continuance of a trial date (whether a Clerk's administrative continuance or a continuance granted by an Official), no Clerk's administrative trial date continuance shall be allowed at the request of the defendant.

2. Continuance Request by a Law Enforcement Agency.

a. A law enforcement agency (or its designee) in a civil traffic infraction case is hereby allowed one ex parte administrative continuance of a scheduled trial date upon written request for same, provided such request is filed with the Clerk of Court not later than fourteen (14) calendar days prior to the scheduled trial date. The date of the trial shall not be included in calculating the fourteen (14) day time period. Upon the allowance of the administrative continuance of a trial date, the Clerk of Court shall provide notice of the new trial date, place, and time to the defendant, the law enforcement agency which issued the citation, and to all witnesses that have been subpoenaed for trial.

b. Any request for a continuance of a civil traffic infraction trial date may be filed by a representative of the law enforcement agency which issued the citation. The law enforcement agency shall use the "Law Enforcement Agency Request For Continuance" form ("Form"), attached as Exhibit "A", in seeking a continuance of a trial date. If a request for continuance by the law enforcement agency is filed but the law enforcement agency does not utilize the approved Form, the Clerk shall accept the paper for filing but not continue the trial date, and instead, the request shall be ruled upon as provided in paragraph 2(c) of this Order. The Form is available through the Administrative Office of the Court.

c. Any untimely filed written request for a Clerk's administrative continuance, and any other request for continuance, which by this Administrative Order may not be allowed by the Clerk (including a timely request for continuance which is not filed utilizing the approved Form), shall be assigned to and ruled upon ex parte by the Administrative Traffic Hearing Officer, or such other person designated by the Chief Judge. If such request is not ruled upon before the scheduled trial date, then the request shall remain on the docket of the scheduled trial, at which time the Official will rule on the request in open court.

d. Notwithstanding anything to the contrary in the preceding subsections, if the law enforcement agency has sought and obtained one continuance of a trial date (whether a Clerk's administrative continuance or a continuance granted by an Official), no Clerk's administrative trial date continuance shall be allowed at the request of the law enforcement agency.

DONE and **ORDERED** in Chambers at West Palm Beach, Palm Beach County, Florida, this 11 day of March, 2016

Jeffrey Colbath
Chief Judge

EXHIBIT "A"

IN THE COUNTY COURT OF THE FIFTEENTH JUDICIAL CIRCUIT
IN AND FOR PALM BEACH COUNTY, FLORIDA

State of Florida Case No.:

v.

____
______________/
Defendant.

LAW ENFORCEMENT AGENCY REQUEST FOR CONTINUANCE

1. My name is ______________
2. I work for ______________
3. I was served with a subpoena for trial in this case on ______________.
4. The date of trial is: ______________
5. I am requesting a continuance because:
   - ☐ Vacation/Leave: My vacation/leave plans were made on ______________
   - ☐ Training: I was told I was attending this training on ______________
   - ☐ Other: ______________
6. My return date from training/leave/vacation/other is: ______________
7. If this request for continuance is not filed with the Clerk at least 14 days before the trial date, please state why (add more space if necessary): ______________

Respectfully submitted,

____
(Signed name)

____
(Printed name)

____
(Name, address, and phone number of agency)

Adopted effective September 29, 2008. Amended effective April 30, 2009; March 11, 2016.

* supersedes Admin. Order 10.402–4/09

10.403. TRAFFIC INFRACTION MOTIONS AND CORRESPONDENCE

IN THE CIRCUIT COURT OF THE FIFTEENTH JUDICIAL CIRCUIT IN AND FOR PALM BEACH COUNTY

ADMINISTRATIVE ORDER NO. 10.403–7/14 [1]

IN RE: TRAFFIC INFRACTION MOTIONS AND CORRESPONDENCE

The efficient administration of the Traffic Division requires a uniform policy concerning motions and correspondence that are filed in traffic infraction cases.

NOW, THEREFORE, pursuant to the authority conferred by Florida Rule of Judicial Administration 2.215, it is **ORDERED** as follows:

1. Procedures Before Entry of A Timely Filed Not Guilty Plea in Traffic Infraction Cases.

a. The Clerk of Court shall forward, to the division judge designated by the Chief Judge for ruling, any motion and/or correspondence filed by a defendant who has not yet entered a timely filed plea of not guilty in a traffic infraction case. The Judge will either rule on the motion/correspondence in chambers or schedule a hearing on same.

b. The Clerk of Court shall also forward the related case file.

2. Procedures For All Other Traffic Infraction Cases.

a. The Clerk of Court shall forward to the Administrative Traffic Hearing Officer, or any other person designated by the Chief Judge, any motion and/or correspondence filed by a defendant that has not been assigned to a judicial division and which may be heard by a Traffic Hearing Officer for ruling. With the exception of timely filed Motions and Correspondence to Mitigate or for New Trial filed pursuant to Florida Rules of Traffic Procedure 6.490(b) or 6.550, the Administrative Traffic Hearing Officer will either rule on the motion/correspondence in chambers or schedule a hearing on same.

b. Motions and Correspondence to Mitigate or for New Trial that are timely filed pursuant to Florida Rules of Traffic Procedure 6.490(b) or 6.550, shall be ruled upon by the Traffic Hearing Officer who presided over the disposition of the case unless the orderly administration of justice will be impeded in which case paragraph 2(a) shall apply.

c. The Clerk of Court shall forward the related case file to the Administrative Traffic Hearing Officer or any other person designated by the Chief Judge.

3. **Procedures for Motions and Correspondence in Cases That Have Been Assigned to a Judicial Division.**

a. When a motion or correspondence is filed with the Clerk in any traffic infraction case that has been assigned to a judicial division, the Clerk shall forward the motion and/or correspondence with the related case file to the assigned judge for ruling.

b. The procedure for resolving any motion or request for continuance shall be governed by Administrative Order 10.402–9/08 (as amended) or any subsequently entered Administrative Order pertaining to same.

4. **Procedures in Toll & Sun Pass Violations.** Notwithstanding the above, in any such case which has not been assigned to a judicial division in which the defendant is charged with a violation of Florida Statute 316.1001 (toll and Sun Pass violations), the Clerk shall forward the motion and/or correspondence with the related case file to the Administrative Traffic Hearing Officer or any other person designated by the Chief Judge for ruling.

5. **Oral Argument/Hearing.**

a. Motions pertaining to traffic infraction cases that do not require a mandatory court hearing shall not be set for oral argument/hearing.

b. Upon receipt of a motion and/or a notice of hearing, the Clerk shall follow the procedures set forth in paragraphs 1–4 above. After consideration of the motion, a Judge or Traffic Hearing Officer shall either grant or deny the motion or set it for oral argument/hearing.

DONE and ORDERED in Chambers at West Palm Beach, Palm Beach County, Florida, this 29 day of July, 2014.

Jeffrey Colbath
Chief Judge

Adopted effective September 29, 2008. Amended effective June 22, 2009; November 23, 2009; July 29, 2014.

1 supersedes admin. order 10.403–11/09.

10.404. PRE–TRIAL CONFERENCES IN CIVIL TRAFFIC INFRACTION CASES HEARD BY CIVIL TRAFFIC INFRACTION HEARING OFFICERS

IN THE CIRCUIT COURT OF THE FIFTEENTH JUDICIAL CIRCUIT IN AND FOR PALM BEACH COUNTY, FLORIDA

ADMINISTRATIVE ORDER NO. 10.404- 1/15/19 *

IN RE: PRE–TRIAL CONFERENCES IN CIVIL TRAFFIC INFRACTION CASES HEARD BY CIVIL TRAFFIC INFRACTION HEARING OFFICERS

The utilization of Pre–Trial Conferences is a successful method of fairly and effectively reducing the number of trials in civil traffic infraction cases assigned to Civil Traffic Infraction Hearing Officers when a defendant has entered a plea of not guilty.

NOW, THEREFORE, pursuant to the authority conferred by Florida Rule of Judicial Administration 2.215, it is **ORDERED** as follows:

1. Except as otherwise provided herein, a Pre–Trial Conference shall be conducted before a trial may be scheduled in all civil traffic infraction cases over which a Civil Traffic Infraction Hearing Officer has jurisdiction and in which there is no unsatisfied D–6 and a defendant has entered a plea of not guilty. A Pre–Trial Conference shall not be scheduled by the Clerk and it shall not be conducted with respect to:

a. Any SunPass violation charged under F.S. Section 316.1001; or

b. Any civil traffic infraction case, other than a red light camera violation, in which an affidavit of identity is filed wherein a defendant raises identity as an issue stating that he or she is not the person who received the citation.

2. Continuance and/or reset requests of a Pre–Trial Conference made prior to the Pre–Trial Conference shall be governed by Administrative Order 10.402–9/08 (as amended).

3. **At the Pre–Trial Conference:**

a. All motions relating to defects in the charging document shall be made in writing and heard at the Pre–Trial Conference, or they are waived. Once waived, no such matter shall be revisited. However, all motions relating to defects in the charging document, or any other motion made at the Pre–Trial Conference, may be denied without prejudice to renew at trial.

b. The defendant shall state whether he or she desires to change his or her plea to either no contest or guilty, or to maintain the plea of not guilty. If the defendant maintains the plea of not guilty, the case shall be set for trial. If the defendant changes his or her plea to no contest or guilty, the defendant's right to a trial shall be deemed to be waived, and the Hearing Officer shall impose the appropriate disposition after the defendant is offered an opportunity to offer any mitigating circumstances.

c. If a defendant has filed an affidavit of defense, identity, or admission before the Pre–Trial Conference, the Hearing Officer shall excuse the defendant's absence and review the affidavit to determine the intent of same. If the Hearing Officer determines that the defendant is actually seeking to plead no contest or guilty, the Hearing Officer shall impose an appropriate disposition. If the affidavit raises a defense to the citation, the Hearing Officer shall set the case for trial.

4. Failure to Appear at the Pre–Trial Conference:

a. The failure of a defendant to appear at the Pre–Trial Conference scheduled pursuant to this Administrative Order may subject the defendant to the sanctions provided in § 318.15(1), Florida Statutes, and Fla. R. Traf. Ct. 6.600.

b. Notwithstanding the foregoing, the Hearing officer may, in his or her discretion, alternatively set the case for trial or reset the Pre–Trial Conference.

c. A defendant who has failed to appear at a pre-trial hearing scheduled on a Saturday or via video shall not be rescheduled for another Saturday or video hearing. Those cases shall be rescheduled during the normal business week at the courthouse.

5. As used in this Administrative Order, the "Pre–Trial Conference shall be deemed a "pre-trial hearing" for the purpose of Administrative Order 10.401–9/08 (as amended) and a "hearing" for the purpose of applying or construing any applicable Florida Statute (e.g. F.S. Section 318.15(1)) or the Florida Traffic Court Rules (e.g. Fla. R. Traf. Ct. 6.430(c)).

DONE and ORDERED in Chambers at West Palm Beach, Palm Beach County, Florida this 15th day of January, 2019.

Krista Marx
Chief Judge

Adopted effective September 29, 2008. Amended effective August 3, 2010; April 6, 2011; January 11, 2019; January 15, 2019.

* supersedes admin order 10.404–1/19 (signed on January 11, 2019)

10.405. WITNESS SUBPOENAS IN CIVIL TRAFFIC INFRACTION HEARINGS

IN THE CIRCUIT COURT OF THE FIFTEENTH JUDICIAL CIRCUIT IN AND FOR PALM BEACH COUNTY, FLORIDA

ADMINISTRATIVE ORDER NO. 10.405–9/08 *

IN RE: WITNESS SUBPOENAS IN CIVIL TRAFFIC INFRACTION HEARINGS

Witnesses are subpoenaed to appear at civil traffic infraction hearings and due to the large number of hearings set, a number of the final hearings are continued prior to the hearing date due to conflicts. It is expensive and time consuming to cause amended subpoenas to be served on witnesses.

NOW, THEREFORE, pursuant to the authority conferred by Florida Rule of Judicial Administration 2.215, it is **ORDERED** as follows:

1. The Clerk is directed to add the following language to the body of witness subpoenas issued for civil traffic infractions:

> You are ordered to appear at the time and date indicated above or, if the hearing is re-set, at the re-set time and date. If the hearing is re-set, you will be notified of the re-set time and date by mail only.

2. If a hearing is re-set, the Clerk shall so notify all witnesses for which she has a return of service indicating the witness was served, by U.S. mail, postage pre-paid, at the address where the witness was served, using the form attached as Exhibit A.

3. The Clerk shall issue subpoenas to all witnesses for the re-set hearing date for whom the subpoena was returned unexecuted or for whom no return was received.

DONE and **SIGNED,** in Chambers, at West Palm Beach, Palm Beach County, Florida this 29 day of September, 2008.

Kathleen J. Kroll
Chief Judge

* supersedes admin. order 10.035–11/00

EXHIBIT A

TO: (witness name) Citation: (citation number)
(address)
(city, state, zip) Defendant: (name)

Issuing Officer: (name)

RESET FROM: (date)

Pursuant to subpoena previously served and Administration Order ________, you are hereby notified that you must appear at the (courthouse, name, address, courtroom#) on (date) at (time) to testify regarding the action referenced above. This case has been reset from its original hearing date.

IF YOU FAIL TO APPEAR, YOU MAY BE IN CONTEMPT OF COURT. Please contact the Clerk's office (phone number) one day prior to the above date to verify the time or the hearing.

TO COLLECT WITNESS FEE: (Clerk to insert current procedure)

I hereby certify that a copy hereof has been furnished to the addressee above by US mail, postage prepaid, this ___ day of ______, 200 ___.

____
Clerk of the Court

Adopted effective September 29, 2008.

10.406. SATURDAY AND VIDEO CONFERENCE TRAFFIC COURT LIMITED TO SELF REPRESENTED INDIVIDUALS

IN THE CIRCUIT COURT OF THE FIFTEENTH JUDICIAL CIRCUIT IN AND FOR PALM BEACH COUNTY, FLORIDA

ADMINISTRATIVE ORDER NO.: 10.406 9/08 *

IN RE: SATURDAY AND VIDEO CONFERENCE TRAFFIC COURT LIMITED TO SELF REPRESENTED INDIVIDUALS

Saturday and video conference traffic court hearings were implemented in order to accommodate the schedules of people who would not normally be at the courthouse and there are a limited number of cases that can be heard on Saturday or at community service centers where the video conference hearings originate.

NOW, THEREFORE, pursuant to the authority conferred by Florida Rule of Judicial Administration 2.215, it is **ORDERED** as follows:

1. Saturday and video conference traffic court hearings shall not be available to attorneys since attorneys are expected to be able to appear without undue inconvenience during the normal working week at the courthouse.

2. Attorneys are directed to request cases be rescheduled if they acquire cases of persons who have already been scheduled for Saturday traffic court.

3. The Clerk is also directed that Saturday and video conference traffic court be limited to individuals representing themselves.

4. Due to the popularity of the Saturday and video conference traffic court hearings, and the limited number of cases that can be scheduled on those dockets, any person desiring to appear at a Saturday or video conference traffic court hearing must waive their right to a speedy trial.

DONE and **SIGNED** in Chambers in West Palm Beach, Palm Beach County, Florida, this 29 day of September, 2008.

Kathleen J. Kroll
Chief Judge

Adopted effective September 29, 2008.

* supersedes admin. order 10.039–1/05

10.407. [VACATED AND SET ASIDE BY ORDER 10.407–1/19, EFFECTIVE JANUARY 11, 2019.]

10.409. INACTIVE TRAFFIC CITATIONS OF DECEASED DEFENDANTS

IN THE CIRCUIT COURT OF THE FIFTEENTH JUDICIAL CIRCUIT IN AND FOR PALM BEACH COUNTY, FLORIDA

ADMINISTRATIVE ORDER NO. 10.409–10/11 *

IN RE: INACTIVE TRAFFIC CITATIONS OF DECEASED DEFENDANTS

The Judges of the County Court of Palm Beach County, Florida, have determined that the following is necessary and proper for the disposition of traffic cases.

NOW, THEREFORE, pursuant to the authority conferred by Florida Rules of Judicial Administration 2.215, it is **ORDERED** as follows:

The Clerk and Comptroller's Office is ordered to dismiss any citation and satisfy any D–6 issued to anyone who is deceased. Proof of death shall consist of an official death certificate or any official notification of death by the Department of Highway Safety and Motor Vehicles or the Department of Health (Vital Statistics). If any of these cases have an outstanding or unsatisfied D–6 and/or any unpaid fines/costs, the Clerk, pursuant to Florida Rule of Traffic Court 6.575, shall vacate same.

DONE and **SIGNED** in Chambers at West Palm Beach, Palm Beach County Florida, this 5 day of October, 2011.

Peter D. Blanc
Chief Judge

Adopted effective February 24, 2009. Amended effective October 5, 2011.

* supersedes admin. order 10.409–2/09

Driver Programs/Court Costs

10.501. REQUESTS FOR EXTENSIONS OF TIME TO COMPLETE DRIVING SCHOOL

IN THE CIRCUIT COURT OF THE FIFTEENTH JUDICIAL CIRCUIT IN AND FOR PALM BEACH COUNTY, FLORIDA

ADMINISTRATIVE ORDER NO. 10.501–9/08 *

IN RE: REQUESTS FOR EXTENSIONS OF TIME TO COMPLETE DRIVING SCHOOL

In Palm Beach County there are a significant number of written requests for extensions of time within which to enroll in defensive driving school. The Court has discretion to grant extensions of time to enroll in and complete driving school. The County Court Judges of Palm Beach County have unanimously endorsed the granting of an extension of time to complete driving school upon the written request of a defendant.

NOW, THEREFORE, pursuant to the authority conferred by Florida Rule of Judicial Administration 2.215, it is **ORDERED** as follows:

1. The Clerk of the Court may permit up to ninety (90) days from election to complete a defensive driving school.

2. Any extension encompassing the periods set forth above shall advise the defendant that no further extensions of time will be granted absent extraordinary circumstances.

3. If a D–6 license suspension was issued in a traffic infraction case based upon the defendant's failure to enroll in or complete the defensive driving school, an extension of time is not automatically granted. In that event, the file and request shall be forwarded to the judge or traffic hearing officer for ruling.

DONE and **SIGNED** in Chambers in West Palm Beach, Palm Beach County, Florida, this 29 day of September, 2008.

Kathleen J. Kroll
Chief Judge

Adopted effective September 29, 2008.

* supersedes admin. order no. 10.019–11/02

10.502. DUI AND DRIVER IMPROVEMENT PROGRAM REQUISITES

IN THE CIRCUIT COURT OF THE FIFTEENTH JUDICIAL CIRCUIT IN AND FOR PALM BEACH COUNTY, FLORIDA

ADMINISTRATIVE ORDER NO: 10.502–11/09 *

IN RE: DUI, DRIVER IMPROVEMENT AND CHILD RESTRAINT SAFETY PROGRAMS

The Department of Highway Safety and Motor Vehicles is responsible for the certification of DUI and Driver Improvement Programs. The Chief Judge has the authority to authorize DUI, driver improvement programs, and child restraint safety programs to operate within his/her jurisdiction. All DUI and Driver Improvement programs must provide like-program elements to ensure the citizens of Palm Beach County participate in programs which are equitable with one another.

NOW, THEREFORE, pursuant to the authority conferred by Florida Rule of Judicial Administration 2.215, it is **ORDERED** as follows:

A. DUI and Driver Improvement Programs

1. DUI and Driver Improvement Programs being established in Palm Beach County must provide the following services and that Certification within the Fifteenth Circuit shall be given only to programs meeting these prerequisites.

2. All DUI and Driver Improvement programs must provide services in or near the Belle Glade area on an as needed basis for client enrollment, evaluation and/or consultation. All schedules are subject to review by Chief Judge.

3. All DUI and Driver Improvement programs **MUST** provide bilingual services to ensure clients have full access to programs service(s).

4. All DUI and Driver Improvement programs must comply with Americans with Disabilities Act, 1990 for those clients requiring a reasonable accommodation.

5. Driver Improvement programs must electronically report students' course completions to the Clerk of Court within ten (10) days of said completion.

B. Child Restraint Safety Program. The "Child Saver Program" operated by the Safety Council of Palm Beach County Inc. is approved as a child restraint safety program as required by Florida Statute 316.613(5) (2009).

DONE and **SIGNED** in Chambers, West Palm Beach, Florida, Palm Beach County, this 23 day of November, 2009.

Peter D. Blanc
Chief Judge

Adopted effective September 29, 2008. Amended effective November 23, 2009.

* supersedes administrative order 10.502–9/08

10.503. FAILURE TO COMPLY WITH DRIVERS IMPROVEMENT SCHOOL ELECTIONS

IN THE CIRCUIT COURT OF THE FIFTEENTH JUDICIAL CIRCUIT IN AND FOR PALM BEACH COUNTY, FLORIDA

ADMINISTRATIVE ORDER NO.: 10.503–01/19 *

IN RE: FAILURE TO COMPLY WITH DRIVERS IMPROVEMENT SCHOOL ELECTIONS.

NOW, THEREFORE, pursuant to the authority conferred by Florida Rule of Judicial Administration 2.215, it is **ORDERED** as follows:

1. That in those cases where the individual cited has previously elected to attend, either a 4 hour or 8 hour driver improvement course, and has subsequently failed to successfully complete the necessary course within 90 days, the Clerk shall do the following:

a. refer the case to the Administrative Traffic Hearing Officer or any other person designated by the Chief Judge for entry of an order adjudicating the defendant guilty of the infraction charged; and

b. notify the Department of the failure to comply; and

c. collect all outstanding statutory civil penalties, late fees, reinstatement fees, deferral fees and reset fees, if applicable.

2. The provisions in this order shall supersede any previous orders or memoranda directed toward any of the matters contained herein, and any such previous orders or memoranda in conflict herewith are rescinded.

DONE and **SIGNED** in Chambers at West Palm Beach, Palm Beach County, Florida this 11 day of January, 2019.

Krista Marx
Chief Judge

Adopted effective September 29, 2008. Amended effective January 11, 2019.

* supersedes admin, order 10.503–9/08

Internal Policies and Procedures

County and Circuit Judges

11.101. ASSIGNMENT OF JUDGES

IN THE CIRCUIT COURT OF THE FIFTEENTH JUDICIAL CIRCUIT IN AND FOR PALM BEACH COUNTY, FLORIDA

ADMINISTRATIVE ORDER NO. 11.101–01/19 *

IN RE: ASSIGNMENT OF JUDGES

Rule 2.215, Fla.R.Jud.Admin., states that "[t]he chief judge shall assign judges to the courts and divisions, and shall determine the length of each assignment;"

NOW, THEREFORE, pursuant to the authority conferred by Florida Rule of Judicial Administration 2.215, it is **ORDERED, effective January 22, 2019,** as follows:

CIRCUIT COURT CIVIL DIVISION

AA G. Joseph Curley
AB Janis Keyser
AD Jaimie Goodman
AE Jeffrey D. Gillen
AF Edward Artau
AG Donald Hafele
AH Lisa Small*
AI Cymonie Rowe
AJ Scott Kerner
AN Howard Coates, Jr.
AO James Nutt
AK Meenu Sasser

CIRCUIT COURT CIVIL DIVISION

FORECLOSURE DIVISION

AW CLOSED [1]

CIRCUIT COURT UNIFIED FAMILY COURT

FAMILY DIVISION /DOMESTIC DIVISION

FA Maxine Cheesman
FB Temporarily Closed
FC Kathleen Kroll
FD Sarah Willis
FH Rosemarie Scher*
FI Karen Miller
FJ Scott Suskauer
FX Charles Burton
FY Samantha Schosberg Feuer
FZ Jessica Ticktin**
FW Sherri Collins**

JUVENILE DIVISION

JK Carolyn Bell
JL [2] Gregory Keyser
JM [3] Kirk Volker
JO [4] James Martz*
JS Luis Delgado
JA [5] Kirk Volker

CIRCUIT COURT CRIMINAL DIVISION

R Jeffrey Colbath
S Daliah Weiss
T/KK2 [6] Dina Keever–Agrama**
U Laura Johnson
V John Kastrenakes
W Glenn D. Kelley*
X Joseph Marx
Y Sherri Collins**
Z Cheryl Caracuzzo

CIRCUIT COURT PROBATE & GUARDIANSHIP DIVISION

IB Maxine Cheesman
IC Kathleen Kroll
ID Sarah Willis
IX Samantha Schosberg Feuer
IY Charles Burton*
IZ Jessica Ticktin**
IH Rosemarie Scher
II Karen Miller
IJ Scott Suskauer

COUNTY COURT CIVIL DIVISION

RA Sherri Collins
RB August Bonavita
RD Reginald Corlew
RE Ashley Zuckerman
RF/WD Sandra Bosso–Pardo
RJ Paige Gillman
RL Edward Garrison
RH Frank Castor*
RS Marni Bryson

COUNTY COURT CRIMINAL DIVISION

B Leonard Hanser
C Sheree Cunningham*
D/DR Paul Damico
E Robert Panse
H/NC Frank Castor
L Bradley Harper
M Mark Eissey
P Sara Alijewicz
BG Sherri Collins
DV/TD Debra Moses Stephens
KK1/KD [6] Ted Booras

TRIAL DIVISION

Caroline Shepherd

BRANCH COURTHOUSES

Gun Club Facility: Dina Keever–Agrama [7] [8]*** Ted Booras [6]

North County Courthouse: Rosemarie Scher *&** Karen Miller Frank Castor Scott Suskauer

West County Courthouse Sherri Collins** Kirk Volker [3]

South County Courthouse: Samantha Schosberg Feuer Charles Burton Marni Bryson Jessica Ticktin** Reginald Corlew Paul Damico Luis Delgado

To insure equitable distribution of caseloads, unless otherwise provided in these administrative orders, the Clerk of Court shall assign cases by random selection to judges within the divisions in which the cases are filed. Should a reassignment be required due to disqualification or recusal, the Clerk of Court shall, when possible, randomly reassign the case to a judge within the Division at the same courthouse. For those Divisions where there is only one judge, or where all judges are unable to preside over the case, reassignment shall be as follows:

1. Foreclosure Division to Circuit Civil Divisions.
2. Probate/Guardianship/Mental Health Division:

a. Branch Courthouse Divisions to Main Courthouse Division

b. Main Courthouse Division to North County Division

3. Juvenile Divisions

a. South County Division to Main Courthouse Divisions

b. West County Division to Main Courthouse Divisions

4. Family Divisions:

a. Branch Courthouse Divisions to Main Courthouse Divisions

b. Main Courthouse Divisions to North County Divisions

5. County Court Criminal Divisions

a. North County Division to Main Courthouse Divisions

b. South County Division to Main Courthouse Divisions

c. West County Division to Main Courthouse Divisions

6. County Court Civil Divisions

a. North County Division to Main Courthouse Divisions

b. South County Divisions to Main Courthouse Divisions

c. West County Division to Main Courthouse Divisions

DONE and **SIGNED** in Chambers at West Palm Beach, Palm Beach County, Florida, this 11 day of January, 2019.

Krista Marx
Chief Judge

*Administrative Judge

**Administrative Judge of Satellite Courthouse

Amended effective January 17, 2012; June 15, 2012; July 2, 2012; January 22, 2013; July 1, 2013; December 2, 2013; December 1, 2014; January 9, 2015; April 6, 2015; June 1, 2015; July 15, 2015; November 10, 2015; February 9, 2016; July 5, 2016; August 5, 2016; October 31, 2016; January 17, 2017; March 22, 2017; June 20, 2017; August 29, 2017; January 16, 2018; February 16, 2018; July 16, 2018; October 1, 2018; January 22, 2019.

* supersedes Admin. Order No. 11.101–12/18*

1 Please refer to Administrative Order 3.302–8/17 for further instructions.

2 Assignment includes Family Drug Court.

3 Assignment includes Belle Glade Division 'JA' (Delinquency and Dependency) on Monday's {effective March 2, 2015}.

4 Assignment includes Delinquency Drug Court.

5 Assignment includes Makemson Hearings.

6 Assignment includes Veterans' Court.

7 Assignment includes Criminal Mental Health Court.

8 Assignment includes Adult Drug Court.

11.102. ADMINISTRATIVE JUDGES AND EXECUTIVE COMMITTEE

IN THE CIRCUIT COURT OF THE FIFTEENTH JUDICIAL CIRCUIT IN AND FOR PALM BEACH COUNTY, FLORIDA

ADMINISTRATIVE ORDER NO. 11.102–01/19 *

IN RE: ADMINISTRATIVE JUDGES AND EXECUTIVE COMMITTEE

Rule 2.215, Fla.R.Jud.Adm., states that "[t]he chief judge may designate a judge in any court or court division of circuit or county courts as "Administrative Judge" of any court or division to assist with the administrative supervision of the court or division." It is deemed necessary and appropriate for the efficient administration of the circuit court to appoint administrative judges of the several divisions.

NOW, THEREFORE, pursuant to the authority conferred by Florida Rule of Judicial Administration 2.215, it is **ORDERED, effective January 22, 2019,** as follows:

CIRCUIT COURT

Civil Division

Lisa Small

All Family Courts

Rosemarie Scher

Juvenile

James Martz

Criminal Division

Glenn Kelley

Probate & Guardianship Division

Charles Burton

COUNTY COURT

Civil Division

Frank Castor

Criminal Division

Sheree Cunningham

BRANCH COURTHOUSES

Gun Club

Dina Keever–Agrama

North County

Rosemarie Seller

West County

Sherri Collins

South County

Jessica Ticktin

MAGISTRATES

Maxine Williams

Administrative judges shall be a member of and attend the Fifteenth Circuit's Judicial Executive Committee meetings, schedule and preside over divisional meetings as needed, and be responsible for the efficient operation of their division.

DONE and **SIGNED** in Chambers at West Palm Beach, Palm Beach County, Florida, this 11 day of January, 2019.

Krista Marx
Chief Judge

Amended effective January 31, 2011; July 15, 2011; October 13, 2011; January 17, 2012; January 22, 2013; July 1, 2013; January 17, 2014; January 9, 2015; July 30, 2015; March 7, 2016; May 10, 2016; November 2, 2016; January 17, 2017; January 16, 2018; July 2, 2018; October 1, 2018; January 22, 2019.

* supersedes admin. order 11.102—9/18.

11.103. JUDICIAL SENIORITY

IN THE CIRCUIT COURT OF THE FIFTEENTH JUDICIAL CIRCUIT IN AND FOR PALM BEACH COUNTY, FLORIDA

ADMINISTRATIVE ORDER NO. 11.103–12/12 *

IN RE: JUDICIAL SENIORITY

Pursuant to the authority conferred by Florida Rule of Judicial Administration 2.215, it is **ORDERED** as follows:

1. Seniority among judges in the Fifteenth Judicial Circuit shall be determined by the length of time that a person has served as a judge, whether or not continuous, on any court of the State of Florida.

2. If a judge has served on one court throughout his or her tenure, the length of time in service will determine the judge's seniority. If, however, the judge has served on more than one state court, the judge's seniority will be determined by adding the years of service on all state courts.

3. If two or more judges have served the same length of time, the judge who has served more years as a circuit judge in the Fifteenth Judicial Circuit shall have seniority.

DONE and **SIGNED** in Chambers at West Palm Beach, Palm Beach County, Florida, this 6th day of December, 2012.

Peter D. Blanc
Chief Judge

Adopted effective September 29, 2008. Amended effective December 6, 2012.

* supersedes admin order 11.103–9/08

11.104. SENIORITY LISTING OF JUDGES

IN THE CIRCUIT COURT OF THE FIFTEENTH JUDICIAL CIRCUIT IN AND FOR PALM BEACH COUNTY, FLORIDA

ADMINISTRATIVE ORDER NO. 11.104–01/19*

IN RE: SENIORITY LISTING OF JUDGES

Seniority among the circuit and county court courts is as follows:

SENIORITY OF JUDGES
CIRCUIT AND COUNTY COURT

JUDGE	JUDICIAL COMMISSION	CIRCUIT COURT COMMISSION	COUNTY COURT COMMISSION
Edward A. Garrison	01/06/81 (1st) 01/08/13 (2nd)	01/03/89 (Retired 6/30/10)	01/06/81 01/08/13
Kathleen J. Kroll	01/07/85	02/14/94	01/07/85
Jeffrey J. Colbath	10/05/92	01/07/03	10/05/92
Sheree Cunningham	01/04/94	----------	01/04/94
Krista Marx	01/05/99	01/04/05	01/05/99
Donald Hafele	04/01/99	10/31/08	04/01/99
Charles E. Burton	05/08/00	11/02/05	05/08/00
Debra Moses Stephens	06/19/00	----------	06/19/00
Paul Damico	11/15/01	----------	11/15/01
Laura S. Johnson	01/07/03	01/03/17	01/07/03
Karen M. Miller	01/07/03	01/07/03	----------
Joseph Marx	08/01/03	08/26/09	08/01/03
Mark Eissey	01/04/05	----------	01/04/05
Sandra Bosso-Pardo	01/31/05	----------	01/31/05
James Martz	01/06/06	09/20/10	01/06/06
Reginald Corlew	04/03/06	----------	04/03/06
Janis Keyser	04/03/06	06/10/11	04/03/06
Ted Booras	01/02/07	----------	01/02/07
Frank Castor	01/02/07	----------	01/02/07
Glenn Kelley	01/22/07	01/22/07	----------
August Bonavita	05/18/09	----------	05/18/09
John S. Kastrenakes	06/01/09	06/01/09	----------
Caroline Shepherd	06/01/09	----------	06/01/09

Meenu Sasser	06/05/09	06/05/09	------------
Leonard Hanser	12/07/09	----------	12/07/09
Lisa Small	01/04/11	01/04/11	----------
Marni Bryson	01/04/11	----------	01/04/11
Gregory Keyser	01/31/11	02/02/12	01/31/11
Rosemarie Scher	10/05/11	10/05/11	----------
Robert Panse	12/05/11	----------	12/05/11
Daliah H. Weiss	06/01/12	11/01/16	06/01/12
Jeffrey D. Gillen	01/04/13	01/04/13	----------
Edward Artau	12/31/14	12/31/14	----------
Kirk Volker	12/31/14	12/31/14	----------
Samantha Schosberg Feuer	01/06/15	01/06/15	--------
Jaimie Goodman	01/06/15	01/06/15	--------
Jessica Ticktin	01/06/15	01/06/15	--------
Howard Coates, Jr.	02/19/15	02/19/15	--------
Cheryl Caracuzzo	04/03/15	04/03/15	--------
Scott Ira Suskauer	07/17/15	07/17/15	--------
Dina A. Keever-Agrama	07/27/15	07/27/15	--------
Cymonie Rowe	07/26/16	07/26/16	--------
Sherri Collins	12/30/16	----------	12/30/16
Luis Delgado	01/03/17	01/03/17	----------
Bradley Harper	01/03/17	----------	01/03/17
James Nutt	01/03/18	01/03/18	----------
G. Joseph Curley	02/16/18	02/16/18	----------
Carolyn Bell	05/07/18	05/07/18	----------
Paige Gillman	12/03/18	----------	12/03/18
Sara Alijewicz	01/08/19	----------	01/08/19
Maxine Cheesman	01/08/19	01/08/19	----------
Scott Kerner	01/08/19	01/08/19	----------
Sarah Willis	01/08/19	01/08/19	----------
Ashley Zuckerman	01/08/19	----------	01/08/19

DONE and **SIGNED** in Chambers at West Palm Beach, Palm Beach County, Florida, this 29 day of January, 2019.

Krista Marx
Chief Judge

Amended effective January 31, 2011; July 15, 2011; October 13, 2011; January 17, 2012; June 15, 2012; January 14, 2013; April 6, 2015; July 27, 2015; July 5, 2016; August 5, 2016; November 6, 2016; February 10, 2017; March 6, 2017; August 29, 2017; January 18, 2018; February 20, 2018; July 9, 2018; December 4, 2018; January 24, 2019.

* supersedes Admin. Order No. 11.104–12/18*

11.105. JUDICIAL ROTATION POLICY

IN THE CIRCUIT COURT OF THE FIFTEENTH JUDICIAL CIRCUIT IN AND FOR PALM BEACH COUNTY, FLORIDA

ADMINISTRATIVE ORDER NO. 11.105–1/18 *

RE: JUDICIAL ROTATION POLICY

Rule 2.215 of the Rules of Judicial Administration mandates that the Chief Judge shall develop an administrative plan for the efficient and proper administration of the courts within the circuit. The Judges of this circuit should have an opportunity to serve in divisions of their choice and should also share in the responsibility of serving in those divisions which are less sought after assignments. This administrative order has been agreed to by the majority of the Circuit and County Court Judges of this circuit.

NOW, THEREFORE, pursuant to the authority conferred by Florida Rule of Judicial Administration 2.215, it is **ORDERED** as follows:

The following shall be the policy in the Fifteenth Judicial Circuit governing rotation between divisions of the circuit and county court, including assignments to and from the north, south, Belle Glade and Gun Club satellite facilities:

1. Except for good cause and in the best interests of the court, assignments shall be for a minimum of two years and a maximum of five years, unless circumstances dictate otherwise, commencing the day after the July 4th holiday in July of each year. Should a mid-term assignment be made, the term shall be deemed to commence on the day after the next July 4th holiday. The Chief Judge, upon leaving office, shall be allowed to choose his or her first divisional assignment.

2. In making assignments to and from divisions, the Chief Judge in keeping with the tenor of this order, shall consider the following factors, assigning each the weight the Chief Judge deems appropriate on a case by case basis:

a. Public interest

b. Judge's preference and previous assignments

c. Length of time in present assignment vis-a-vis other judges in the same division

d. Length of time to anticipated retirement

e. Length of time to judge's next election date

f. Geographical proximity of judge's residence and assignment location

g. Judge's expertise relative to present and contemplated assignment

h. Seniority

i. Any additional pertinent considerations

3. If a division utilizes e-service, on-line scheduling, or has implemented a fileless or paperless system ("technological practices"), any judge rotating into the division must continue to use the technological practices unless excused by the Chief Judge. The incoming judge and judicial assistant shall meet with the current assigned judge and judicial assistant to discuss the divisional operation in effect. Court Technology shall ensure that the email accounts are installed onto the incoming judge's computer and iPad and that the incoming judge has access to these email accounts.

4. When a judge rotates out of a division ("outgoing judge"), the judge will review his or her caseload to determine whether the judge should retain any case based upon court rule, statute, or for purposes of judicial economy.

a. If the outgoing judge determines that a case should be retained, the outgoing judge will consult with the judge rotating in to the division ("incoming judge"). The incoming judge will have the final determination as to whether the case should be retained by the outgoing judge.

b. If outgoing judge retains the case, the outgoing judge will enter an order notifying the parties and the clerk's office.

1) When the outgoing judge is rotating within the same division of the court (i.e. one civil division to another civil division), the case will be transferred to the outgoing judge's new division.

2) When the outgoing judge is rotating to a different division of the court (i.e. a civil division to a family division), the case will remain assigned to the original division but will be handled by the outgoing judge.

c. If the outgoing judge is transferring to a division that requires court proceedings to be recorded by the Court Reporting Office, the judicial assistant will ensure that any hearings on the retained case will occur in a courtroom equipped for digital court recording.

5. Following a rotation(s), issues may arise as to whether the original trial judge or the current divisional judge should hear a matter. To avoid confusion the following applies:

a. Any case returned to a division following an appeal will be heard by the judge currently assigned to that division unless court rule, statute or judicial economy provides otherwise. Examples of judicial economy would include but not be limited to requiring the division judge to expend an unreasonable amount of time to familiarize himself/herself with the case compared to the original trial judge who is still a member of the judiciary; determination of prevailing party in complex litigation; direction by appellate court requiring written findings or rulings. If it is the opinion of the division judge that the case should be handled by the original trial judge, then the division judge shall confer with the original trial judge. If the judges cannot agree, the divisional judge will hear the matter.

b. Cases returned for resentencing will be heard by the sentencing judge if the sentencing judge is still a member of the judiciary.

c. *Statement of the Evidence.* The original trial judge who has since rotated out of the division, if available, shall be responsible for settling and approving a Statement of the Evidence as required by Florida Rule of Appellate Procedure 9.200(b)(4).

DONE AND SIGNED in Chambers at West Palm Beach, Palm Beach County, Florida, this 18 day of January, 2018.

Krista Marx
Chief Judge

Adopted effective September 29, 2008. Amended effective June 6, 2013; August 23, 2013; January 10, 2014; January 18, 2018.

* supersedes administrative order 11.105–10/17

11.106. ALTERNATE ASSIGNMENTS

IN THE CIRCUIT COURT OF THE FIFTEENTH JUDICIAL CIRCUIT IN AND FOR PALM BEACH COUNTY, FLORIDA

ADMINISTRATIVE ORDER NO. 11.106–01/19 *

IN RE: ALTERNATE ASSIGNMENTS

To promote the efficient administration of justice, judges are designated as "alternates" to preside over emergency matters when the paired judge is away from the courthouse.

NOW, THEREFORE, pursuant to the authority conferred by Florida Rule of Judicial Administration 2.215, **effective January 22, 2019** it is **ORDERED** as follows:

1. Alternates shall coordinate with one another to ensure that one of them will be in the courthouse during normal court hours.

2. If alternates are both scheduled to be absent from the courthouse for periods of vacation, etc. then it shall be the responsibility of-each judge to procure emergency coverage for his or her division by another judge.

3. If for any reason alternate judges do not carry out this responsibility, then the duty judge shall preside over emergency matters in such divisions.

4. The following is a listing of the alternate judges:

CIRCUIT COURT CIVIL

Judge J. Keyser / Judge Small / Judge Nutt
Judge Coates, Jr. / Judge Curley/ Judge Sasser
Judge Gillen / Judge Artau
Judge Rowe / Judge Hafele
Judge Kerner / Judge Goodman

CIRCUIT COURT FAMILY DIVISION

DOMESTIC DIVISION

Judge Cheesman / Judge Willis / Judge Kroll

JUVENILE DIVISION

Judge G. Keyser / Judge Volker
Judge Martz / Judge Bell

CIRCUIT COURT CRIMINAL DIVISION

Judge J. Marx / Judge Caracuzzo

Judge Weiss / Judge Colbath

Judge Kastrenakes / Judge Johnson / Judge Kelley

CIRCUIT COURT PROBATE/GUARDIANSHIP DIVISION

Judge Cheesman / Judge Willis / Judge Kroll

COUNTY COURT DIVISIONS

Judge Zuckerman / Judge Bosso Pardo

Judge Garrison/ Judge Gillman

Judge Hanser / Judge Stephens

Judge Panse / Judge Eissey

Judge Harper / Judge Cunningham

Judge Bonavita / Judge Alijewicz

NORTH COUNTY COURTHOUSE

Judge Suskauer / Judge Castor [1] Judge Miller / Judge Scher

Magistrate Jean–Adel Williams / Magistrate Kirigin

WEST COUNTY COURTHOUSE

Judge Collins [2]

SOUTH COUNTY COURTHOUSE

Judge Delgado / Judge Burton / Judge Schosberg Feuer / Judge Ticktin

Judge Corlew / Judge Bryson / Judge Damico

Magistrate Baker / Magistrate Bassaline

CRIMINAL JUSTICE COMPLEX / GUN CLUB

Judge Keever–Agrama / Judge Booras

MAGISTRATES / MAIN COURTHOUSE

Magistrate Fanelli (DOR) / Magistrate James Williams (DOR)

Magistrate Printz / Magistrate Maxine Williams / Magistrate Zeitenberg

DONE and **SIGNED**, in Chambers, at West Palm Beach, Florida, this 11 day of January, 2019.

Krista Marx
Chief Judge

Amended effective November 12, 2010; January 31, 2011; January 17, 2012; March 21, 2012; July 2, 2012; January 23, 2013; July 1, 2013; January 17, 2014; April 6, 2015; June 2, 2015; February 25, 2016; May 10, 2016; July 6, 2016; August 5, 2016; November 1, 2016; January 25, 2017; March 20, 2017; June 20, 2017; August 18, 2017; January 16, 2018; February 16, 2018; July 16, 2018; October 1, 2018; January 22, 2019.

* supersedes Admin. Order No. 11.106–8/18

1 Judge Castor is the only County Judge located at the North County Courthouse. As such, the Circuit Judges located there must assist as his alternate.

2 Judge Collins is the only County Judge located at the Belle Glade Complex. As such, the Gun Club Judges will serve as his alternate with all Circuit matters being handled by Judge Keever–Agrama and all County matters handled by Judge Booras. Exception being for all Juvenile matters, Division JM (currently Judge Volker) will serve as the alternate.

11.107. JUDICIAL LEAVE POLICY

IN THE CIRCUIT COURT FOR THE FIFTEENTH JUDICIAL CIRCUIT IN AND FOR PALM BEACH COUNTY, FLORIDA

ADMINISTRATIVE ORDER NO. 11.107–1/18 *

RE: JUDICIAL LEAVE POLICY

The Judicial Administration Section of the Conference of Circuit Judges has reviewed the leave practices in existence in other judicial branches throughout the United States. The American Bar Association's National Conference of Special Court Judges has recommended criteria for sound leave policies to include no less than 21 nor more than 30 working days of vacation leave per year. Judicial officers, unlike state employees, cannot accumulate annual and medical leave for which they are compensated at the termination of services. Judicial officers are considered to be available for duty twenty-four hours a day and are often required to serve on weekends and after hours without compensatory time. Judicial annual leave assures that judges have sufficient time away from the bench to maintain good health and effectiveness and to permit time for rejuvenation and renewal. The establishment of the following judicial leave policy ensures that judges are accountable for the time they are away from the bench while simultaneously emphasizing that some leave time is in the best interests of a properly functioning judiciary.

Judicial leave does not encompass sick leave, educational leave, military leave, leave to serve on court committees or other leave in the furtherance of justice. All judges are expected to participate, as both faculty and students, in approved continuing judicial education programs. Judges are also encouraged as part of their regular judicial responsibilities to participate in professional meetings and conferences that advance the administration of justice or the public's understanding of the judicial system, to serve on commissions and committees of state and national organizations that contribute to the improvement of the law or the administration of justice, and to serve on Supreme Court appointed or intra-circuit assignments or committees. A judicial office is a public office rather an employment status, and therefore the establishment of a judicial annual leave policy cannot be required by law and is entirely voluntary on the part of the State Court System. Most, if not all, of the circuits in Florida have adopted judicial leave policies that provide judges with no less than 21 nor more than 30 working days of vacation leave per year.

Florida Rule of Judicial Administration 2.205(2)(C) requires justices of the Florida Supreme Court to notify the Chief Justice of contemplated absences from the court and the reasons therefore. Florida Rule of Judicial Administration 2.210(2)(F) requires judges of the district courts to notify the

Chief Judge of the District of any contemplated absence from the court and the reasons therefore.

NOW, THEREFORE, pursuant to the authority conferred by Florida Rule of Judicial Administration 2.215, it is **ORDERED** as follows:

1. Circuit court and county court judges are expected to take no more than 30 working days of annual leave. For the purposes of this administrative order, "annual leave" means "time away from judicial duties to provide opportunities for rest, relaxation and personal pursuits." Annual leave does not encompass sick leave, educational leave, military leave, leave to serve on court committees or other leave in the furtherance of justice. The taking of annual leave shall not interfere with the efficient administration of a judicial officer's docket.

2. Judicial officers are to notify the Chief Judge of any contemplated extended absence from the court. An extended absence means an absence of more than 5 business days. Before any contemplated extended absence is taken, a judicial officer must notify the chief judge of his or her intention to be out for an extended absence and indicate the specific date(s) and the reasons therefore. Judicial officers are to notify their alternates of the dates of contemplated absences—extended or otherwise—in accordance with Administrative Order 11.106.

3. Because all judges are constitutional officers and professional public servants, each judge shall self report judicial leave by maintaining within their office an accurate record of the annual leave time taken. Such records shall be available for inspection by the chief judge or his/her designee.

4. Unused judicial annual leave does not accrue from year to year. No judge shall be entitled to be paid for those hours of judicial annual leave not taken within a calendar year.

5. Nothing herein prevents a chief judge, upon good cause shown on a case by case basis, from allowing judicial annual leave in excess of 30 working days.

DONE AND ORDERED in Chambers in West Palm Beach, Palm Beach County, Florida this 18 day of January, 2018.

Krista Marx
Chief Judge

Adopted effective September 29, 2008. Amended effective January 18, 2018.

* supersedes admin. order 11.107–9/08

11.108. DUTY JUDGE/EMERGENCIES

IN THE CIRCUIT COURT OF THE FIFTEENTH JUDICIAL CIRCUIT IN AND FOR PALM BEACH COUNTY, FLORIDA

ADMINISTRATIVE ORDER NO. 11.108–9/08 *

IN RE: DUTY JUDGE/EMERGENCIES

The prompt and efficient administration of justice requires a judge to be available in chambers during work, hours and on call after work hours to handle emergency matters.

NOW, THEREFORE, pursuant to the authority conferred by Florida Rule of Judicial Administration 2.215, it is **ORDERED** as follows:

DEFINITION OF "EMERGENCY"

1. By separate administrative order, the chief judge shall promulgate an annual duty roster so that a judge, commonly referred to as the "duty judge," shall be available at all times to handle applications for search warrants, pen registers, petitions for ex parte injunctive relief to prevent domestic violence, and other emergency matters. In this context, the term "emergency" encompasses the foregoing ex parte applications and other matters of extreme urgency, i.e., matters of life and death or instances of irreparable harm. Not included in this definition are matters of extreme urgency in cases which have been assigned to a trial division if the assigned trial judge or his or her alternate is present in the courthouse.

HOURS

2. The "duty judge," shall be available from 8:30 a.m. to 5:00 p.m. each work day at the county courthouse in West Palm Beach. Before leaving the courthouse each work day, the "duty judge" shall call the domestic violence clerk at extension 4506 to determine whether they are processing any last minute petitions and, if so, the duty judge must remain at the courthouse until the petition is completed, reviewed and acted upon by the "duty judge". On holidays and weekends, the duty judge shall be available from 9:00 a.m. until approximately noon at the Criminal Justice Complex on Gun Club Road in West Palm Beach. After-hours coverage shall be provided through an on-call system in which the duty judge can be reached by telephone through the communications division of the Palm Beach County Sheriff's Office or by fax through personnel of the Palm Beach County Victim Services for those cases wherein there is filed a petition for ex parte injunctive relief to prevent domestic violence.

RESPONSIBILITIES

3. Whether a judge should clear his or her calendar to be available to handle the duty judge's responsibilities is a matter left to the discretion of each judge. If a judge maintains a normal or reduced workload during the duty judge assignment period, that judge is obligated to stop what he or she is doing to accommodate duty judge responsibilities.

4. First Appearances—Holidays & Weekends. The duty judge shall preside at holiday and weekend first appearance hearings which shall commence at 9:00 a.m. at the Criminal Justice Complex on Gun Club Road in West Palm Beach.

5. After–Hours Injunctive Relief. Emergency intake and processing of ex parte applications for injunctive relief to prevent domestic violence, see section 741.30, Florida Statutes (2007), between the hours of 5:00 p.m. and 8:00 a.m. on weekdays as well as on all holidays and weekends, shall be the responsibility of personnel of the Palm Beach County Victim Services who have been specially appointed as Deputy Clerks to perform these functions. The duty judge shall be available at the Criminal Justice Complex on holidays and weekends between the hours of 9:00 a.m. and approximately noon to rule upon domestic violence petitions. Similarly, the duty judge shall be available after normal business hours at a location with access to a computer or facsimile machine to rule upon domestic violence petitions. See Section 26.20, Florida Statutes (2007). The Sheriff of Palm Beach County is herewith authorized and empowered to accept a domestic violence injunction with a faxed signature or electronic signature sent by the duty judge's court email address for service of process.

6. **Extension Hearings.** Extension hearings shall be scheduled before the Family Division Judge to which the case is assigned.

TRANSFER OF RESPONSIBILITY AND EQUIPMENT

7. The transfer of responsibility from one duty judge to the next shall occur at 8:30 a.m. on Monday of each week, including those weeks in which Monday is a holiday. A cellular phone, to allow for telephonic contact, and a fax machine, to permit receipt of after-hours petitions for injunctive relief in domestic violence cases, shall be provided to the duty judge. A loose-leaf binder containing relevant statutes, rules and case law shall be provided to the duty judge. This material will also be available to the duty judge on the court's computer system. The equipment and information shall be transferred from one duty judge to the next at the beginning of the duty assignment.

OPERATING PRINCIPLES

8. Every judge in the circuit shall be assigned to preside at weekend and holiday first appearance hearings. All County Court Judges are hereby temporarily assigned to serve as Circuit Judges while functioning as a Duty Judge and they are vested with all and singular the powers and prerogatives conferred by the Constitution and Laws of the State of Florida upon a Circuit Court Judge.

9. Judges stationed at courthouse annexes and at the Criminal Justice Complex shall serve on holiday and weekend duty with such duty limited to first appearances only. However, the duty assignment shall be limited to first appearance hearings only. The duty judge assigned to the previous week day assignment shall be responsible for the transfer of equipment as delineated in Section 7 of this Administrative Order.

10. Duty judge assignments shall rotate in alphabetical order except that no judge should be required to serve more than one holiday weekend in a calendar year, in which case the Chief Judge may alter the schedule as necessary to ensure fairness and equity. The Chief Judge may also make adjustments to ensure that judges assigned to the courthouse annexes and Criminal Justice Complex are not assigned the same holiday weekend duty in successive years.

11. Alterations or substitutions in the published annual duty judge roster must be done in writing with a copy sent to Court Administration.

12. When possible, all annex duty judge assignments will be rotated from year-to-year to ensure no annex judge is assigned the same weekend/holiday.

DONE and **SIGNED** in Chambers at West Palm Beach, Palm Beach County, Florida, this 29 day of September, 2008.

Kathleen J. Kroll
Chief Judge

Adopted effective September 29, 2008.

* supersedes admin. order 2.004 12/00

11.109. DUTY JUDGE ROSTER

IN THE CIRCUIT COURT OF THE FIFTEENTH JUDICIAL CIRCUIT
IN AND FOR PALM BEACH COUNTY, FLORIDA

ADMINISTRATIVE ORDER NO. 11.109–11/18 *

IN RE: DUTY JUDGE ROSTER

WHEREAS, a duty judge is responsible for weekend first appearance hearings, the issuance of search warrants and other emergency matter, see Administrative Order 11.108;

NOW, THEREFORE, the following judges are assigned for the period specified below.

DUTY PERIOD **12/31/18 – 1/5/20**	**FIRST APPEARANCES**	**JUDGE**
	▲ January 1	*Bryson
December 31 – January 6		Caracuzzo
	January 5 & January 6	*Ticktin
January 7 – January 13		Garrison
	January 12 & January 13	*Suskauer
January 14 – January 20		Coates
	January 19 & 20	*Bryson
	▲ January 21	*Castor
January 21 – January 27		Colbath
	January 26 & January 27	*Scher
January 28 – February 3		Cunningham
	February 2 & February 3	*Miller
February 4– February 10		Curley
	February 9 & February 10	*Keever-Agrama
February 11 – February 17		Eissey
	February 16 & February 17	*Schosberg Feuer
February 18 – February 24		Cheesman
	February 23 & February 24	*Delgado
February 25 – March 3		Gillman
	March 2 & March 3	*Damico
March 4 – March 10		Gillen
	March 9 & March 10	*Corlew
March 11 – March 17		Goodman
	March 16 & March 17	*Collins

March 18 – March 24		Hafele
	March 23 & March 24	*Castor
March 25 – March 31		Hanser
	March 30 & March 31	*Burton
April 1 – April 7		Harper
	April 6 & April 7	*Booras
April 8 – April 14	April 13 & April 14	Johnson
	▲ April 19	*Burton
April 15 – April 21	April 20 & April 21	Kastrenakes
April 22 – April 28	April 27 & April 28	Kelley
April 29 – May 5	April 4 & May 5	Kerner
May 6 – May 12	May 11 & May 12	G. Keyser
May 13– May 19	May 18 & May 19	J. Keyser
May 20 – May 26	May 25 & May 26	Kroll
	▲ May 27	*Scher
May 27 – June 2	June 1 & June 2	Martz
June 3 – June 9	June 8 & June 9	Gillman
June 10– June 16	June 15 & June 16	Nutt
June 17 – June 23	June 22 & June 23	Panse
June 24 – June 30	June 29 & June 30	Rowe
	▲ July 4	*Corlew
	▲ July 5	*Damico
July1 – July 7	July 6 & July 7	Sasser
July 8 – July 14	July 13 & July 14	Small
July 15 – July 21	July 20 & July 21	Shepherd
July 22 – July 28	July 27 & July 28	Moses Stephens
July 29 – August 4	August 3 & August 4	Volker
August 5 – August 11	August 10 & August 11	Zuckerman
August 12 – August 18	August 17 & August 18	Willis
August 19 – August 25	August 24 & August 25	Weiss
August 26 – September 1	August 31 & September 1	Alijewicz
	▲ September 2	*Schosberg Feuer
September 2 – September 8	September 7 & September 8	Bell
September 9– September 15	September 14 & September 15	Bonavita
September 16 – September 22	September 21 & September 22	Bosso Pardo
September 23 – September 29	September 28 & September 29	Caracuzzo
	▲ September 30	*Delgado
September 30 – October 6	October 5 & October 6	Cheesman
	▲ October 9	*Keever-Agrama
October 7 – October 13	October 12 & October 13	Coates
October 14 – October 20	October 19 & October 20	Colbath
October 21 – October 27	October 26 & October 27	Cunningham
October 28 – November 3	November 2 & November 3	Curley

November 4 – November 10	November 9 & November 10	Eissey
	▲ November 11	*Miller
November 11 – November 17	November 16 & November 17	Garrison
November 18 – November 24	November 23 & November 24	Gillen
	▲November 28	*Suskauer
	▲ November 29	*Ticktin
November 25 – December 1	November 30 & December 1	J. Marx
December 2 – December 8	December 7 & December 8	Goodman
December 9 – December 15	December 14 & December 15	Hafele
December 16 – December 22	December 21 & December 22	Hanser
	▲ December 25	*Collins
December 23 – December 29	December 28 & December 29	Harper
December 30 – January 5		Johnson
	▲ January 1, 2020	*Booras
	January 4 & 5	TBA on 2020 Roster

DONE and SIGNED in Chambers at West Palm Beach, Florida, this 28th day of November, 2018.

Krista Marx
Chief Judge

▲ Denotes Court Holidays Observed

*Denotes Weekend Duty and/or Holiday Duty for Satellite Judges. Please note that Satellite Judges **are not** required to be on call with a pager/cell phone. This assignment is solely to cover first appearances.

(NOTE FROM CHIEF JUDGE: All duty judges should be in contact with Judge Dina Keever and/or Judge Booras prior to presiding at any first appearances.

Additionally, weekend duty judge(s) should call Gun Club lobby, 688–4658, five minutes prior to arrival to arrange escort into facility through judicial access)

Amended effective November 30, 2010; November 21, 2011; November 25, 2013; December 1, 2014; January 9, 2015; June 1, 2015; November 23, 2015; December 15, 2016; March 22, 2017; January 1, 2018; May 8, 2018; December 31, 2018.

* Supersedes Administrative Order 11.109–5/18*

11.110. APPOINTMENT OF CIRCUIT JUDGES AS ACTING COUNTY JUDGES COUNTY JUDGES AS ACTING CIRCUIT JUDGES

IN THE CIRCUIT COURT OF THE FIFTEENTH JUDICIAL CIRCUIT IN AND FOR PALM BEACH COUNTY, FLORIDA

ADMINISTRATIVE ORDER NO. 11.110 –9/18 *

IN RE: APPOINTMENT OF CIRCUIT JUDGES AS ACTING COUNTY JUDGES COUNTY JUDGES AS ACTING CIRCUIT JUDGES

It is necessary for the prompt dispatch of the business of the circuit and county courts, that circuit judges be temporarily assigned to duty in the county court and that county judges be temporarily assigned to duty in the circuit court.

NOW, THEREFORE, pursuant to the authority conferred by Florida Rule of Judicial Administration 2.215, it is **ORDERED** as follows:

1. Each circuit judge of the Fifteenth Judicial Circuit of Florida is hereby assigned and designated to hear, conduct, try and determine county court cases that are brought before the judge as a temporary judge of the Palm Beach County Court, and thereafter to dispose of all matters considered by the judge, including emergency and duty judge matters for the next six months.

2. Further, each county court judge of Palm Beach County is hereby assigned and designated to hear, conduct, try and determine circuit court cases that are brought before the judge as a temporary judge of the Fifteenth Judicial Circuit Court, and thereafter to dispose of all matters considered by the judge, including emergency and duty judge matters for the next six months.

DONE and **SIGNED** in Chambers at West Palm Beach, Palm Beach County, Florida, this 28 day of September, 2018.

Krista Marx
Chief Judge

Amended effective March 31, 2011; October 13, 2011; April 12, 2012; September 28, 2012; April 1, 2013; June 24, 2014; October 1, 2014; April 6, 2015; November 2, 2016; March 31, 2017; March 29, 2018; September 28, 2018.

* supersedes Admin. Order No. 11.110–4/18

11.111. TRANSFER OF CASES FROM COUNTY COURT TO CIRCUIT COURT

IN THE CIRCUIT COURT OF THE FIFTEENTH JUDICIAL CIRCUIT IN AND FOR PALM BEACH COUNTY, FLORIDA

ADMINISTRATIVE ORDER NO. 11.111–9/08

IN RE: TRANSFER OF CASES FROM COUNTY COURT TO CIRCUIT COURT

Amended claims, counter claims, cross claims and third party claims filed in county civil court matters may necessitate the transfer of the original county court claim to circuit civil court. The upfiling of misdemeanor charges to felony charges may occur while a defendant is before a county criminal court judge.

NOW, THEREFORE, pursuant to the authority conferred by Florida Rule of Judicial Administration 2.215, it is **ORDERED** as follows:

1. Procedures for the transfer of county civil cases to circuit civil is set forth in Administrative Order 3.104 9/08 (as amended).

2. Procedures for the setting of bond when a misdemeanor charge is upfiled to a felony is set forth in Administrative Order 4.101 9/08 as amended.

DONE and **SIGNED** in Chambers at West Palm Beach, Palm Beach County, Florida, this 29 day of September, 2008.

Kathleen J. Kroll
Chief Judge

Adopted effective September 29, 2008.

11.112. HANDLING CAPITAL CASES

IN THE CIRCUIT COURT OF THE FIFTEENTH JUDICIAL CIRCUIT IN AND FOR PALM BEACH COUNTY, FLORIDA

ADMINISTRATIVE ORDER NO. 11.112–7/09

IN RE: HANDLING CAPITAL CASES

Pursuant to Rule of Judicial Administration 2.215(b)(10) judges must attend certain judicial education courses to become qualified to hear death penalty cases.

NOW, THEREFORE, pursuant to the authority conferred by Florida Rule of Judicial Administration 2.215, it is **ORDERED** as follows:

Once a circuit judge has taken the "Handling Capital Cases" course ("HCC") offered through the Florida College of Advanced Judicial Studies and has become HCC qualified, the circuit judge must remain HCC compliant by attending the HCC refresher course during each of the judge's subsequent continuing judicial education reporting periods regardless of whether the judge is assigned to the criminal division.

DONE and **SIGNED** in Chambers at West Palm Beach, Palm Beach County, Florida, this 14 day of July, 2009.

Peter D. Blanc
Chief Judge

Adopted effective July 14, 2009.

11.113. REASSIGNMENT OF CASES AFTER DISQUALIFICATION OR RECUSAL

IN THE CIRCUIT COURT OF THE FIFTEENTH JUDICIAL CIRCUIT IN AND FOR PALM BEACH COUNTY, FLORIDA

ADMINISTRATIVE ORDER 11.113–9/17

IN RE: REASSIGNMENT OF CASES AFTER DISQUALIFICATION OR RECUSAL

The Clerk and Comptroller is required to randomly assign cases amongst the divisions of the Court in accordance with Administrative Order 11.101. In order to ensure equitable distribution of case assignments, it is necessary to create procedures for the assignment of cases following judicial disqualification or recusal.

NOW, THEREFORE, pursuant to the authority conferred by Florida Rule of Judicial Administration 2.215, it is **ORDERED** as follows:

1. Upon entry of an order granting a motion for disqualification pursuant to Rule of Judicial Administration 2.330 or upon entry of an Order of Recusal, the Clerk and Comptroller will forward a copy of the Notice of Reassignment to the judge to whom the case was reassigned.

2. The Clerk and Comptroller will randomly assign a new case to the transferring judge's division pursuant to existing ShowCase case maintenance system programming processes.

3. Upon taking the bench, a judicial officer will provide to the Clerk and Comptroller the names and The Florida Bar numbers of attorneys, as well as the names of parties, who are to be listed on the judicial officer's standing order of recusal. A copy will be sent to the Chief Judge and Court Technology.

4. Standing orders of recusal as to parties or attorneys will be reviewed at least two times per year.

a. Court Administration will provide the current list of standing recusals to judicial officers no later than November 15 and May 15 of each year.

b. Judicial officers are to review their list of standing recusals and, no later than December 15 and June 15 of each year, either affirm that there are no changes to the list or provide any changes to the Clerk and Comptroller with a copy to the Chief Judge and Court Technology.

5. If a case is assigned to a judge with a party or attorney who is on the judge's standing order of recusal, the clerk shall randomly reassign the case in accordance with Administrative Order 11.101 without further order of the court.

DONE and **SIGNED**, in Chambers, at West Palm Beach, Palm Beach County, Florida, this 20th day of September, 2017.

KRISTA MARX
Chief Judge
Adopted effective September 20, 2017.

Senior Judges, Trial Division Judges and Magistrates

11.201. SENIOR JUDGES

IN THE CIRCUIT COURT OF THE FIFTEENTH JUDICIAL CIRCUIT IN AND FOR PALM BEACH COUNTY, FLORIDA

ADMINISTRATIVE ORDER NO. 11.201–12/17 *

IN RE: SENIOR JUDGES

The use of Senior Judges aid in the administration of justice.

NOW, THEREFORE, pursuant to the authority conferred by Florida Rule of Judicial Administration 2.215, it is **ORDERED** as follows:

1. All requests for senior judge assistance shall be coordinated with the Court's Administrative Office and require the approval of the Chief Judge.

a. Prior to seeking the approval of the Chief Judge, the trial judge must first seek coverage from other judges in his or her division. The administrative judge for the division in which coverage is sought, shall assist the trial judge in obtaining coverage.

b. The trial judge may request a specific senior judge so long as the senior judge meets the qualifications.

c. Court Administration will attempt to secure the requested senior judge and will contact the trial judge if unable to secure the requested senior judge.

d. No additional expense may be incurred by choosing a specific senior judge unless there is prior approval by the Chief Judge.

2. To ensure equitable and fair distribution of the work, Court Administration will utilize a selection wheel when a specific senior judge is not requested. Using the wheel, senior judges will be notified by phone and/or e-mail of the date of service and the division/type of work.

3. Coverage shall comply with all rules, guidelines and recommendations regarding Senior Judges as set forth by the Supreme Court including the requirement that the covering senior judge be certified for the type of work to be performed.

4. Requests for Senior Judge time shall be governed by the following guidelines:

a. Coverage for Judges on vacation, attending educational meetings or conferences and voluntarily assisting with the work of other courts are of the lowest priority.

b. Senior Judges should not be assigned first degree murder cases or trials/**hearings** scheduled for more than five days. These matters should be handled by the Judge in the division to which the case is assigned. Exceptions for coverage in extended trials may be made for good cause shown to the Chief Judge.

c. When short-term emergencies arise, Judges should attempt to procure assistance from their alternate or via an inter-office request for assistance directed to all other judicial offices.

5. Volunteer Senior Judges. Senior judges may volunteer their time pursuant to the following guidelines:

a. A need for Senior Judge assistance must exist and the Chief Judge must approve the volunteer days at least one week in advance of the work.

b. A courtroom for the additional work must be available. Courtrooms cannot be reserved more than two weeks in advance because of the shortage of empty courtrooms and the frequent need to accommodate other court proceedings.

c. When applicable, the following must also be available, arranged by the *requesting* Judge's Judicial Assistant:

1) a clerk

2) a recorded courtroom (if juvenile, criminal, or domestic violence)

3) court reporting staff to monitor the courtroom

4) a Palm Beach County Sheriff's deputy

d. Volunteer Senior Judges cannot also provide senior judge assistance for which they are compensated in the same month of the volunteer work.

e. Senior Judges who choose to serve as a volunteer Senior Judge must first sign a waiver, for each period of volunteer senior judge work, agreeing not to seek compensation within the same calendar month that they will serve as a volunteer Senior Judge. The waiver must be signed prior to commencing work. A copy of the waiver is attached as Exhibit "A".

f. If the senior judge has already provided fee based services in a calendar month, volunteer days cannot start until the following month.

g. Volunteer Senior Judges will not be paid, retroactively, for work conducted as a volunteer even if Senior Judge days remain in the Circuit's allocation.

h. Volunteer Senior Judge will not receive preferential treatment for paid Senior Judge work.

DONE and **SIGNED** in Chambers at West Palm Beach, Palm Beach County, Florida, on this 18 day of December, 2017.

Krista Marx
Chief Judge

Exhibit "A"

FIFTEENTH JUDICIAL CIRCUIT VOLUNTEER SENIOR JUDGE WAIVER OF PAYMENT

I, ________, a senior judge qualified in the State of Florida, hereby consents to be temporarily assigned to judicial service in the courts of the Fifteenth Judicial Circuit without compensation.

The judicial services to be provided without compensation will occur during the month of __________. These are for assignments that I have volunteered to accept. No assignment has been scheduled to last longer than five days.

I understand and agree that I cannot both perform volunteer work and paid work in the same calendar month.

I understand and agree that should I be assigned paid senior judge work in the same calendar month that I have provided volunteer senior judge services, that I will forgo any payment due to me.

I understand and agree that regardless of whether there are senior judge funds remaining at the end of the fiscal year, I will not be entitled to seek reimbursement for volunteer services.

I understand and agree that Administrative Order 11.201 governs the use of Senior Judges (both paid and volunteer).

A completed Service Log (available in the Circuit's Human Resources Department) will be provided to the Chief Judge at the end of each calendar month in which volunteer services are provided.

____
Name

____
Signature

____
Date

Adopted effective September 29, 2008. Amended effective December 18, 2017.

* supersedes admin. order no. 11.201–9/08

11.202. TRIAL DIVISION JUDGES

IN THE CIRCUIT COURT OF THE FIFTEENTH JUDICIAL CIRCUIT IN AND FOR PALM BEACH COUNTY, FLORIDA

ADMINISTRATIVE ORDER NO. 11.202–7/13 *

IN RE: TRIAL DIVISION JUDGES

The use of trial divisions has been shown to be an effective case management tool.

NOW, THEREFORE, pursuant to the authority conferred by Florida Rule of Judicial Administration 2.215, it is **ORDERED** as follows:

1. There shall be established a Trial Division in the Circuit Criminal and County Criminal Divisions and at the South County Courthouse.

2. The Trial Division's main purpose is to preside over trials.

3. Each Trial Division judge shall provide monthly to his or her Administrative Judge and the Chief Judge a report containing the following information:

a. *List of Trials:*

1) the number of trials completed each month;

2) the types of case or offense(s) charged;

3) the number of days spent on each trial;

4) the verdict of each trial;

5) whether the trial was jury or non jury;

6) the division and name of the judge before whom the case was pending;

7) the case number corresponding to each case.

b. *List of Pleas, Settlements and Continuances:*

1) a list of all cases sent to TD resulting in a negotiated settlement or open plea;

2) a list of all cases wherein a continuance was granted and whether the case was sent back to the assigned division;

3) the division and name of the judge before whom the case was pending;

4) the case number corresponding to each case;

5) any motion, other than a Motion in Limine, prior to trial.

DONE AND SIGNED in Chambers at West Palm Beach, Palm Beach County, Florida, this 19th day of July 2013.

Jeffrey J. Colbath
Chief Judge

Adopted effective September 29, 2008. Amended effective July 19, 2013.

* supersedes admin. order 11.202–9/08

11.203. APPOINTMENT OF MAGISTRATES

IN THE CIRCUIT COURT OF THE FIFTEENTH JUDICIAL CIRCUIT IN AND FOR PALM BEACH COUNTY, FLORIDA

ADMINISTRATIVE ORDER NO. 11.203—5/18 *

IN RE: APPOINTMENT OF MAGISTRATES

The Court has entered administrative orders establishing the office of magistrate in family law matters (Administrative Order 5.104), juvenile matters (administrative order 5.104) and mental health matters (Administrative Order 6.304).

NOW, THEREFORE, pursuant to the authority conferred by Florida Rule of Judicial Administration 2.215, it is **ORDERED** as follows:

The following are hereby appointed to serve as magistrates with all of the authority, responsibility and power conferred by the Florida Rules of Civil Procedure, Florida Family Law Rules of Procedure, Florida Rules of Juvenile Procedure, Florida Rules of Probate Procedure and Florida Statutes.

Thomas Baker, Esq.

Peter Bassaline, Esq.

Judette Fanelli, Esq.

Diane M. Kirigin, Esq.

Jennifer Printz, Esq.

James Williams, Esq.

Jean–Adel Williams, Esq.

Maxine Williams, Esq.

Temi Zeitenberg, Esq.

DONE and SIGNED in Chambers at West Palm Beach, Palm Beach County, this 8 day of May, 2018.

Krista Marx
Chief Judge

Adopted effective September 29, 2008. Amended effective June 30, 2010; February 11, 2013; August 14, 2013; September 5, 2014; January 9, 2015; May 10, 2016; April 9, 2018; May 8, 2018.

* supersedes admin. order 11.203–4/18

11.204. RESTRICTIONS ON MAGISTRATES QUALIFYING FOR PUBLIC OFFICE

IN THE CIRCUIT COURT OF THE FIFTEENTH JUDICIAL CIRCUIT IN AND FOR PALM BEACH COUNTY, FLORIDA

ADMINISTRATIVE ORDER NO. 11.204–9/08 *

IN RE: RESTRICTIONS ON MAGISTRATES QUALIFYING FOR PUBLIC OFFICE

The Fifteenth Judicial Circuit employs Magistrates to assist the court in adjudicating matters in both the Family and Probate Divisions of the courts. The duties of the Magistrates must be performed in a timely and efficient manner. It is impractical to expect that a campaign for elective office can be conducted during the evening and weekend hours as the time and energy demands of a campaign for elective office would necessarily effect the ability of a Magistrate to devote his or her full attention to the duties of office.

NOW, THEREFORE, pursuant to the authority conferred by Florida Rule of Judicial Administration 2.215, it is **ORDERED** as follows:

1. A Magistrate must submit, at least twenty (20) days prior to the first day of the qualification period, a written resignation which is to be effective no later than the first day that the magistrate qualifies for an elected office.

2. If a written resignation is not submitted, the Magistrate's employment with the Fifteenth Judicial Circuit shall cease on the date the Magistrate files qualifying papers for an elective office.

DONE AND SIGNED, in Chambers, at West Palm Beach, Palm Beach County, Florida, this 29 day of September, 2008.

Kathleen J. Kroll
Chief Judge

Adopted effective September 29, 2008.

* supersedes admin. order 2.037–3/05

Branch Courthouses

11.301. BRANCH COURTHOUSES

IN THE CIRCUIT COURT OF THE FIFTEENTH JUDICIAL CIRCUIT IN AND FOR PALM BEACH COUNTY, FLORIDA

ADMINISTRATIVE ORDER NO. 11.301–1/13 *

IN RE: BRANCH COURTHOUSES

The orderly administration of justice will benefit by providing some judicial services at branch court facilities outside the county seat.

NOW, THEREFORE, pursuant to the authority conferred by Florida Rule of Judicial Administration 2.215, it is **ORDERED** as follows:

The following geographic locations and facilities are officially designated as branch courthouses:

A. Designation of Branch Courthouses.

1. *West County Courthouse.* **2950 SR #15,** Belle Glade, Florida 33430

2. *South County Courthouse.* 200 W. Atlantic Avenue, Delray Beach, FL 33444

3. *North County Courthouse.* 3188 PGA Boulevard, Palm Beach Gardens, FL 33418

4. *Criminal Justice Gun Club Road.* 3228 Gun Club Road, West Palm Beach, FL 33406

B. Branch Courthouse Procedures.

1. Parties bringing matters on for hearing may, at their option, notice them at one of the branch courthouses, provided the offices of all opposing counsel are located within such described branch courthouse area. By agreement of counsel and the presiding judge, any matter covered by this order may be heard at a branch courthouse.

2. Notice requirements are the same in all cases, and appointments shall be made with the judicial assistant of the assigned judge for all matters, including ex parte, to insure that files needed are present at the hearing.

3. In all matters except traffic, cases must have been filed and a number assigned, before such matters can be heard at a branch courthouse.

C. Branch Courthouse Jurisdictional Boundaries.

1. To determine the assignment of County Court Civil cases see Administrative Order 3.102–11/10 (as amended).

2. To determine the assignment of Domestic Relations cases, see Administrative Order 5.101–9/08 (as amended).

3. To determine the assignment of Delinquency and Dependency cases, see Administrative Order 5.102–10/11(as amended).

4. To determine the assignment of Probate/Guardianship cases, see Administrative Order 6.101–1/12 (as amended).

5. To determine the assignment of Domestic Violence Repeat Violence cases, see Administrative Order 5.501–5/09 (as amended).

6. To determine the assignment of Civil Traffic Infraction Traffic cases, see Administrative Order 10.401–9/12 (as amended).

D. Jury Trials.

1. Administrative Order 3.101–9/08 (as amended) governs the procedures for circuit and county civil jury trials pending at the Main/Central Judicial Complex to be heard at a branch courthouse.

2. Administrative Order 3.605–9/08 (as amended) governs the procedures for transferring county civil cases pending at a branch courthouse when a jury trial has been requested.

DONE AND SIGNED in Chambers at West Palm Beach, Palm Beach County, Florida, this 8th day of January, 2013.

Peter D. Blanc
Chief Judge

Adopted effective September 29, 2008. Amended effective January 8, 2013.

* supersedes admin. order no. 11.301–9/08

11.302. HEARINGS HELD OUTSIDE MAIN OR BRANCH COURTHOUSES

IN THE CIRCUIT COURT OF THE FIFTEENTH JUDICIAL CIRCUIT IN AND FOR PALM BEACH COUNTY, FLORIDA

ADMINISTRATIVE ORDER NO. 11.302–9/08 *

IN RE: HEARINGS HELD OUTSIDE MAIN OR BRANCH COURTHOUSES

Circumstances may require that an evidentiary hearing be conducted outside of a designated courthouse. Article V, Section 7, Florida Constitution, authorizes the chief judge to designate any place within the territorial jurisdiction of the court where a Circuit or County Court may hold civil or criminal hearings.

NOW, THEREFORE, pursuant to the authority conferred by Florida Rule of Judicial Administration 2.215, it is **ORDERED** as follows:

Hearings may be conducted at the following facilities and locations:

1. **Main Detention Center**
3228 Gun Club Road
West Palm Beach, FL 33406

2. **County Stockade**
State Road 80
Loxahatchee, FL

3. **Any County Jail Facility**
Located within Palm Beach County

4. **Palm Beach County Governmental Center**
301 N. Olive Avenue
West Palm Beach, FL 33401

5. Any medical or mental health facility in Palm Beach County.

6. Any governmental facility as designated by the Chief Judge.

DONE and **SIGNED** in Chambers at West Palm Beach, Palm Beach County, Florida, this 29 of September, 2008.

Kathleen J. Kroll
Chief Judge

Adopted effective September 29, 2008.

* supersedes admin. order 2.007–9/92

Judicial Chambers

11.401. NEW JUDGES—FURNITURE AND SUPPLIES

IN THE CIRCUIT COURT OF THE FIFTEENTH JUDICIAL CIRCUIT IN AND FOR PALM BEACH COUNTY, FLORIDA

ADMINISTRATIVE ORDER NO. 11.401–9/08 *

IN RE: NEW JUDGES—FURNITURE AND SUPPLIES

Pursuant to the authority conferred by Florida Rule of Judicial Administration 2.215, it is **ORDERED** as follows:

The Office of the Court Administrator shall bear the responsibility to consult with the newly-elected or appointed judge to explain the purchasing guidelines for furniture and supplies and order the appropriate material so that they are available for use upon the arrival of the new judge.

DONE and **SIGNED** in Chambers at West Palm Beach, Palm Beach County, Florida, this 29 day of September, 2008.

Kathleen J. Kroll
Chief Judge

Adopted effective September 29, 2008.

* supersedes admin. order 11.019–9/92

11.402. JUDICIAL RESEARCH MATERIALS AND LIBRARIES

IN THE CIRCUIT COURT OF THE FIFTEENTH JUDICIAL CIRCUIT IN AND FOR PALM BEACH COUNTY, FLORIDA

ADMINISTRATIVE ORDER NO. 11.402–7/18 *

IN RE: JUDICIAL RESEARCH MATERIALS AND LIBRARIES

Access to case law and legal treatises is essential to the discharge of the court's constitutional responsibilities.

NOW, THEREFORE, pursuant to the authority conferred by Florida Rule of Judicial Administration 2.215, it is **ORDERED** as follows:

1. A bench library containing the following volumes shall be established in every courtroom **and shall remain in the courtroom upon rotation of the divisional judge:**

Florida Statutes

Florida Rules of Court–State

Florida Standard Jury Instructions in Criminal Cases (Criminal Judges)

Florida Standard Jury Instructions in Civil Cases (Civil Judges)

2. There shall be a court law library in the Main Courthouse, South County Courthouse, and North County Courthouse.

3. Each court law library will have available paper subscriptions to the Florida Law Weekly, Florida Law Weekly Supplement, and the Florida Law Weekly Federal for use by the public and the judiciary.

4. An electronic edition of Florida Law Weekly, Florida Law Weekly Supplement, and the Florida Law Weekly Federal is available for use by the judiciary and court staff.

5. Any request by a judge for additional research resources must be in writing and approved by the Chief Judge and limited to $400 per judge each fiscal year.

6. All judicial libraries shall be maintained by the law library staff.

DONE and SIGNED in Chambers at West Palm Beach, Palm Beach County, Florida, this 6 day of July, 2018.

Krista Marx
Chief Judge

Adopted effective September 29, 2008. Amended effective January 8, 2013; July 6, 2018.

* Supersedes admin. order 11.402-1/13

Miscellaneous Judiciary

11.501. LEGAL REPRESENTATION FOR JUDICIAL OFFICERS AND EMPLOYEES

IN THE CIRCUIT COURT OF THE FIFTEENTH JUDICIAL CIRCUIT IN AND FOR PALM BEACH COUNTY, FLORIDA

ADMINISTRATIVE ORDER NO.: 11.501–9/08 *

IN RE: LEGAL REPRESENTATION FOR JUDICIAL OFFICERS AND EMPLOYEES

Judges, Magistrates, Hearing Officers, and other court employees, could be sued as a result of their employment with the Fifteenth Judicial Circuit.

NOW, THEREFORE, pursuant to the authority conferred by Florida Rule of Judicial Administration 2.215, it is **ORDERED** as follows:

1. In such instances where a judicial officer is sued in his or her official capacity or as a result of his or her employment with the Fifteenth Judicial Circuit, the judicial officer or employee shall forward suit papers to the Fifteenth Judicial Circuit's General Counsel. General Counsel will forward the suit papers, along with a request for legal representation from the Office of the Attorney General, to:

Office of the State Courts Administrator
Legal Affairs and Education Division
Florida Supreme Court Building
500 South Duval Street
Tallahassee, Florida 32399–1900
Telephone (850) 922–5109; Fax (850) 410–5301

2. If monetary damages are sought, General Counsel will also send a written request for legal representation from the Office of the Attorney General, to:

Division of Risk Management
Bureau of State Liability Claims
200 East Gaines Street, Room 439
Tallahassee, Florida 32399–0300
Telephone (850) 413–3122; Fax (850) 488–6992

3. At the request of a judge, magistrate or hearing officer, General Counsel will monitor the case.

DONE and **SIGNED** in Chambers at West Palm Beach, Palm Beach County, Florida, this 29 day of September, 2008.

Kathleen J. Kroll
Chief Judge

Adopted effective September 29, 2008.

* supersedes admin. order 11.010–5/04

11.502. FLOWER FUND

IN THE CIRCUIT COURT OF THE FIFTEENTH JUDICIAL CIRCUIT IN AND FOR PALM BEACH COUNTY, FLORIDA

ADMINISTRATIVE ORDER NO. 11.502–12/14 *

IN RE: FLOWER FUND

Pursuant to the authority conferred by Florida Rule of Judicial Administration 2.215, it is **ORDERED** as follows:

1. By agreement of the judges, a "flower fund" has been established. As the fund becomes depleted, each judge will be requested to make a donation to replenish the fund.

2. Expenditures from the fund shall be by check which shall require the signature of the chief judge and either the court administrator or the finance director. Expenditures from the flower fund shall be limited to "in-house" situations, e.g., expressions of sympathy, get-well or congratulations to judges, judicial assistants or other court staff as approved by the chief judge.

3. A list of the approved uses of the Flower Fund is attached as Exhibit "A".

4. Each judge shall be provided with an annual report listing all expenditures from the fund.

DONE and **SIGNED** in Chambers at West Palm Beach, Palm Beach County, Florida, this 29 day of December, 2014.

Jeffrey J. Colbath
Chief Judge

"Exhibit A"

The following recommendations are made with regard to the type of things the Flower Fund should be used for:

- Flowers for Judges who are ill
- Flowers for Judge's spouse who is ill
- Flowers for Court Administrator who is ill
- Flowers for Judge's family members who died
- Donations to Memorial Funds: Hospice, Church, Temple, Charity
- Get well cards
- Sympathy cards
- Law Clerk lunches (no more than 2 times a year)
- Retirement party for Judge (no more than 5 family members gratis)

• Retirement gifts for Judge and his or her Judicial Assistant (if also retiring)

• Retirement gift for Judicial Assistant (if served the courts more than 10 years)

• Breakfast, Lunch or Dinner for Legislative delegation

• Breakfast, Lunch or Dinner for County Commissioners or Administration (with purpose of obtaining funding or services for courts or Judicial needs)

• Breakfast, Lunch or Dinner for Media (with stated purpose to improve the relationship with the court or the Judiciary)

• Breakfast or Lunch for volunteers with the courts (no more than 1 time per year)

The following are the recommended amounts to be spent on the above:

• $50.00 for flowers plus whatever delivery charge there is

• $50.00 for donations to memorial funds

• Cost of the card

• $15.00 (which includes tip) for Law Clerks lunch

• Discretion of Chief Judge for Breakfast, Lunch or Dinner for Legislative delegation, County Commissioner/Administration and Media Board

• $15.00 (which includes tip) for volunteer lunch or at the discretion of Chief Judge

• At the discretion of the Chief Judge for Retirement parties

• $150.00 for Retirement party gift for Judge

• $50.00 for Retirement party gift for Judicial Assistant

Adopted effective September 29, 2008. Amended effective December 29, 2014.

* supersedes admin, order 11.502—9/08

11.503. CIRCUIT CONTRACTS

IN THE CIRCUIT COURT OF THE FIFTEENTH JUDICIAL CIRCUIT IN AND FOR PALM BEACH COUNTY, FLORIDA

ADMINISTRATIVE ORDER NO. 11.503–9/12

IN RE: CIRCUIT CONTRACTS

Florida Statute § 43.26 (2011) permits the Chief Judge of a judicial circuit to delegate to the Trial Court Administrator the authority to bind the circuit in contract.

NOW, THEREFORE, pursuant to the authority conferred by Florida Rule of Judicial Administration 2.215, it is **ORDERED** as follows:

Barbara L. Dawicke, Trial Court Administrator for the Fifteenth Judicial Circuit, is delegated the authority to bind the Fifteenth Judicial Circuit in contract until such order has been revoked or rescinded, or upon termination of her employment with the Fifteenth Judicial Circuit.

DONE and **SIGNED** in Chambers at West Palm Beach, Palm Beach County, Florida, this 4 day of September, 2012.

Peter D. Blanc
Chief Judge

Adopted effective September 4, 2012.

11.504. CIRCUIT ADMINISTRATIVE PLAN

IN THE CIRCUIT COURT OF THE FIFTEENTH JUDICIAL CIRCUIT IN AND FOR PALM BEACH COUNTY, FLORIDA

ADMINISTRATIVE ORDER NO. 11.504–12/18

IN RE: CIRCUIT ADMINISTRATIVE PLAN

Florida Rule of Judicial Administration 2.215(b)(3) requires the chief judge of each judicial circuit to establish an administrative plan for the efficient and proper administration of all courts within the respective circuit. The Fifteenth Judicial Circuit's administrative orders as set forth in the attached appendix, provide additional details of the Circuit's plan.

NOW, THEREFORE, pursuant to the authority conferred by Florida Rule of Judicial Administration 2.215, it is **ORDERED** as follows:

1. **Prompt Disposition of Cases.**

a. In order to provide for the prompt disposition of cases, the Clerk of Court randomly assigns cases to court division with regard to percentages or methods of assigning cases as set forth in administrative orders entered by the chief judge.

b. Judges are expected to adhere to Supreme Court Administrative Order No. AOSC 14–66—*In Re: Diligent Performance of Judicial Duties* — and Judicial Canon 3, wherein our courts are required to "[d]ispose of all judicial matters promptly, efficiently, and fairly."

2. **Assignment of Judges.**

a. In order to provide for the assignment of judges and in order to ensure each judge is qualified to serve in any division, the chief judge in conjunction with the administrative judges, will periodically review judicial assignments. Judges are rotated to different divisions approximately every two years and to the extent the needs of the circuit allow. By doing so, the capabilities of the judges are developed so that each judge will eventually be qualified to serve in any division. Caseload data from the Circuit's Judicial Viewer regarding trends in case filings and other factors are considered in determining whether to create a new section within a division.

b. To assist with the administrative supervision of the court and division, the chief judge assigns administrative judges to the various court divisions pursuant to administrative order.

c. Judicial assignments for circuit judges include the Civil Division, Criminal Division, Probate & Guardianship Division, Family Law Division (comprised of family and juvenile) and Appellate Divisions. Judicial Assignments for county court judges include the Civil Division, Criminal Division and Domestic Violence Division. The chief judge may assign a judge to temporary work in another division when the need-requires.

d. Each judge is also assigned to serve as duty judge on a rotating basis. The duty judge is responsible for reviewing and signing arrest and search warrants and reviewing applications for ex-parte probable cause orders in civil forfeiture matters, and handling other emergency matters. During weekends and court holidays, the duty judge is also responsible for presiding over first appearances, detention hearings, and shelter hearings, as well as reviewing requests for domestic violence injunctions, risk protection orders, and other emergency matters.

e. All circuit judges are appointed to temporary county court duties and all county court judges are appointed to temporary circuit court duties twice per year pursuant to administrative order. The judges are assigned to temporary duty for the purposes of fulfilling duty judge obligations as well as hearing and disposing of all matters for an assignment that may be outside of their respective circuit/county court.

f. Administrative orders and schedules are entered by the Chief Judge and routinely updated where necessary.

3. **Assignment of Other Court Officers.** General Magistrates are assigned to the Family, Dependency, and Mental Health divisions pursuant to administrative order. Hearing Officers are assigned to preside over Title IV–D child support cases.

4. **Assignment of Other Court Personnel.**

a. The Circuit is organized into an Administrative Office of the Court (AOC) with the Trial Court Administrator selected in accordance with Florida Rule of Judicial Administration 2.215(b), and each judge having control over the selection and retention of his/her judicial assistant.

b. The AOC supports the Fifteenth Judicial Circuit by managing the administrative functions of the court, including human resources, court technology, case management, court reporting, purchasing, facilities management, budget and finance, research and statistical analysis, and public information and emergency management.

c. The Office of the General Counsel provides legal advice to the Chief Judge, Trial Court Administrator, the judicial officers, and senior members of Court Administration.

d. The AOC also oversees and supervises the operation of all court programs. Such programs include: Unified Family Court case management; Mental Health Court, Drug Court; Foreclosures Unit; Trial Court Law Clerks; Court Reporters; Interpreters; Mediation staff; and Information Technology and Video Operations staff.

5. **Case Management of Dockets.** The Administrative Office of the Court provides monthly reports to the Judges and Magistrates on the status of pending cases by division. Performance measurement reports may be accessed on demand through the Circuit's Judicial Viewer System (JVS).

6. **Regulation and Use of Courtrooms.** The Fifteenth Judicial Circuit has courtrooms located at the Main Judicial Complex, South Complex, North Complex, West Complex, and the Criminal Justice Complex. A list of courtroom assignments is maintained by the Administrative Office of the Court.

7. **Periodic Review of Inmates in the County Jail.** The Palm Beach County Sheriff's Office provides a monthly report of inmates to the Public Safety Coordinating Council/Corrections Task Force, which meets to discuss inmate population and other corrections issues.

DONE AND ORDERED in Chambers in West Palm Beach, Palm Beach County, Florida, this 14th day of December, 2018.

Krista Marx
Chief Judge

Adopted effective December 14, 2018.

Judicial Staff

11.601. JUDICIAL ASSISTANTS' ENTRY RATE OF COMPENSATION

IN THE CIRCUIT COURT OF THE FIFTEENTH JUDICIAL CIRCUIT IN AND FOR PALM BEACH COUNTY, FLORIDA

ADMINISTRATIVE ORDER NO.: 11.601–6/11 *

IN RE: JUDICIAL ASSISTANTS' ENTRY RATE OF COMPENSATION

Administrative Order 11.601–9/08 is obsolete in that the rate of compensation is not governed by Administrative Order.

NOW THEREFORE, it is **ORDERED** that Administrative Order 11.601–9/08 is vacated and set aside.

DONE and **SIGNED** in Chambers at West Palm Beach, Palm Beach County, Florida, this 30 day of June, 2011.

Peter D. Blanc
Chief Judge

Adopted effective September 29, 2008. Amended effective June 30, 2011.

* supersedes admin. order no. 11.601–9/08

11.602. JUDICIAL ASSISTANT COVERAGE

IN THE CIRCUIT COURT OF THE FIFTEENTH JUDICIAL CIRCUIT IN AND FOR PALM BEACH COUNTY, FLORIDA

ADMINISTRATIVE ORDER NO. 11.602–1/13 *

IN RE: JUDICIAL ASSISTANT COVERAGE

Administrative/secretarial coverage for the judiciary should be operated in the most efficient means possible.

NOW, THEREFORE, pursuant to the authority conferred by Florida Rule of Judicial Administration 2.215, it is **ORDERED** as follows:

1. All Judicial Assistants shall make the appropriate arrangements for coverage to the extent possible, at least 2 weeks prior to taking time off, beginning with their alternate. The Judicial Assistant shall set up an "out of office reply" for all emails received that indicates that the Judicial Assistant is out of the office and the duration of the absence. The email shall also identify the covering Judicial Assistant, as well as all appropriate contact information. Additionally, the Judicial Assistant shall create a voice mail message that also indicates that he/she is out of the office and the duration of the absence. The voice mail message shall also identify the covering Judicial Assistant and contain all appropriate contact information.

2. If an emergency should arise that requires a Judicial Assistant to be out of the office, regardless of duration, he/she is required to contact and coordinate coverage with his/her alternate. The absent Judicial Assistant shall also be required to remotely change his/her voice mail message to state that he/she is out of the office and shall identify the alternate/covering Judicial Assistant, as well as include all contact information for same.

3. In the event the absent Judicial Assistant is unable to arrange coverage after due diligence, he/she shall contact the Judicial Assistant to the Administrative Judge who will assist in securing coverage for the affected division. The Administrative Judge can seek assistance from Court Administration.

4. The Court Administrator is authorized to temporarily reassign a Judicial Assistant whose Judge may be absent due to an extended leave to work within other areas of the circuit until the Judge's return to work.

5. For the purposes of this Administrative Order, the Judicial Assistant's alternate shall be defined in Administrative Order 11.106.

DONE and **SIGNED** in Chambers at West Palm Beach, Palm Beach County, Florida, this 8 day of January, 2013.

Peter D. Blanc
Chief Judge

Adopted effective September 29, 2008. Amended effective January 8, 2013.

* supersedes admin. order 11.602–9/08

11.603. TRIAL COURT LAW CLERKS INTERNAL OPERATING PROCEDURES

IN THE CIRCUIT COURT OF THE FIFTEENTH JUDICIAL CIRCUIT IN AND FOR PALM BEACH COUNTY, FLORIDA

ADMINISTRATIVE ORDER NO. 11.603–9/08 *

IN RE: TRIAL COURT LAW CLERKS INTERNAL OPERATING PROCEDURES

The Legislature has funded law clerk/staff attorney positions to assist the judiciary in the Fifteenth Judicial Circuit in the discharge of its responsibilities.

NOW, THEREFORE, pursuant to the authority conferred by Florida Rule of Judicial Administration 2.215, it is **ORDERED** as follows:

1. General Counsel, in consult with the Chief Judge, is responsible for the hiring, assignment and deployment of the Trial Court Law Clerks, and any other such issue as the Chief Judge shall assign to General Counsel. General Counsel shall develop a Trial Court Law Clerk Program and shall annually consult with a Trial Court Law Clerk Committee to ensure that the Trial Court Law Clerk program is meeting the demands of the judiciary. The Trial Court Law Clerk Committee shall be composed of no less than four members of the judiciary to be appointed by the Chief Judge and shall include at least one judge from both the county and circuit court.

2. Assignments for the Trial Court Law Clerks shall be prioritized as follows:

a. *Priority 1.* Emergency Assignments—those assignments which require a legal response within twenty-four (24) hours. These assignments are to be given top priority over any other assignment a trial court law clerk may have pending. This applies to both Circuit and County assignments.

b. *Priority 2.* Criminal and Civil Appeals—including county court, criminal, administrative, extraordinary writs and post conviction motions.

c. *Priority 3.* General Research Assignments—assignments which are based upon a specific case and can be reasonably scheduled with other pending assignments.

d. *Priority 4.* Teaching Materials—legal and related research for judges' teaching materials for Conference and OSCA programs.

e. *Priority 5.* Supreme Court Committees—legal and related research for Supreme Court Committees

f. *Priority 6.* Scholarly writings—Trial Court Law Clerks will be available for assignments related to articles for bar journals or judicial magazines on an "as available basis". These assignments have the lowest priority rating in terms of Trial Court Law Clerk assignments.

3. When a judge seeks the assistance of a Trial Court Law Clerk, the Judge shall clearly state the assignment's required completion date. The Judge shall use, unless impracticable, the "Assignment Request Form" which is sent out semi-annually to all judges and judicial assistants. When making assignments, the judge shall first contact the Division Coordinator assigned to that judge's division. In an emergency situation, a judge may contact directly a Trial Court Law Clerk assigned to the Judge's division provided that other priority assignments do not conflict.

4. Upon completion of an assignment which required extensive research and writing by the Trial Court Law Clerk, the Trial Court Law Clerk shall promptly submit to the judge an Assignment/Evaluation Form which shall be completed by both the Trial Court Law Clerk and the judge. The original of the form shall be sent by the judge to the General Counsel and a copy delivered to the Trial Court Law Clerk. These forms may be used by General Counsel in evaluation and assessing the performance of Trial Court Law Clerks.

5. Should the number of assignments given to the Trial Court Law Clerks from any one judge greatly exceed the number of assignments from other judges in the same division at the same time, the judge who has made the greater number of assignments will be asked to either curtail the assignments or have some of his/her assignments be reprioritized.

6. Trial Court Law Clerks assigned to the North County and South County courthouses will accept assignments from the judges assigned to such courthouse as well as from General Counsel. Trial Court Law Clerks assigned to either the North County or South County courthouses may be required to work from the Main Courthouse as the demands of the judiciary require.

7. Trial Court Law Clerks will have an annual performance appraisal by General Counsel.

8. In accordance with the Office of State Court Administrators, Trial Court Law Clerks are entitled to forty (40) hours of paid administrative leave to attend a bar review course in preparation for the Florida Bar exam. This forty (40) hours of paid administrative leave is only available once during the Trial Court Law Clerk's employment with the Fifteenth Judicial Circuit. Trial Court Law Clerks are entitled to two (2) days of paid leave when sitting for the Florida Bar exam. This two (2) day paid leave is available whenever a Trial Court Law Clerk sits for the Florida Bar exam during his or her employment. Whether to grant additional leave to prepare for the Florida Bar Exam is within the discretion of the General Counsel and Chief Judge. At no time, however, will more than twenty-eight (28) days of leave (paid or unpaid) be permitted. Failure to pass the Florida Bar exam within one (1) year of employment will result in the termination of employment. Failure to pass the Florida Bar exam after two attempts (regardless of whether the exam was taken while employed as a trial court law clerk) will result in termination of employment.

9. A trial court clerkship at the Main Courthouse will be for a period of no more than two (2) years. Trial court clerkships at the North County and South County courthouses, as well as permanent division coordinators, may last for a period of time greater than two (2) years when agreed upon by General Counsel, the Chief Judge and the Trial Court Law Clerk in consultation with administrative judge assigned to the respective satellite courthouse.

10. Trial Court Law Clerks will maintain time sheets as required by the Office of State Court Administrators. Time sheets will be electronically submitted no later than the seventh day of the following month.

11. Vacation or other leave must be approved by General Counsel at least two (2) weeks in advance of the requested date unless circumstances do not otherwise permit. Vacation or other leave requests may be denied if another Trial Court Law Clerk in the same assigned division has already requested leave.

12. General Counsel or the Chief Judge shall review the assignments of the Trial Court Law Clerks periodically and may reassign Trial Court Law Clerks to different divisions. Reassignment decisions will be made upon consideration of factors including, but not limited to, length of assignment, seniority, preference, experience and performance.

DONE and **SIGNED**, in Chambers, at West Palm Beach, Palm Beach County, Florida, this 29, day of September, 2008.

Kathleen J. Kroll
Chief Judge

Adopted effective September 29, 2008.

* supersedes admin. order no. 11.021–11/01

11.604. CODE OF CONDUCT FOR TRIAL COURT LAW CLERKS

IN THE CIRCUIT COURT OF THE FIFTEENTH JUDICIAL CIRCUIT IN AND FOR PALM BEACH COUNTY, FLORIDA

ADMINISTRATIVE ORDER NO. 11.604–9/08 *

IN RE: CODE OF CONDUCT FOR TRIAL COURT LAW CLERKS

Trial Court Law Clerks have special ethical obligations as a result of their employment with the court.

NOW, THEREFORE, pursuant to the authority conferred by Florida Rule of Judicial Administration 2.215, it is **ORDERED** as follows:

The attached Code of Conduct for Law Clerks is adopted to govern the activities of the trial court law clerks on the court's staff in the Fifteenth Judicial Circuit.

DONE and **SIGNED** in Chambers at West Palm Beach, Palm Beach County, Florida, this 29 day of September, 2008.

Kathleen J. Kroll
Chief Judge

* supersedes admin. order 11.023–9/92

ATTACHMENT

CODE OF CONDUCT FOR LAW CLERKS

CANON 1

A LAW CLERK SHOULD UPHOLD THE INTEGRITY AND INDEPENDENCE OF THE JUDICIARY AND THE OFFICE

An independent and honorable judiciary is indispensable to justice in our society. A law clerk should observe high standards of conduct so that the integrity and independence of the judiciary may be preserved. The provisions of this Code should be construed and applied to further that objective. The standards of this Code shall not affect or preclude other more stringent standards required by law, by court order, or by direction of the appointing judge.

CANON 2

A LAW CLERK SHOULD AVOID IMPROPRIETY AND THE APPEARANCE OF IMPROPRIETY IN ALL ACTIVITIES

A law clerk should not engage in any activities that would put into question the propriety of the law clerk's conduct in carrying out the duties of the office. A law clerk should not allow family, social, or other relationships to influence official conduct or judgment. A law clerk should not lend the prestige of the office to advance the private interests of others; nor should the law clerk convey or permit others to convey the impression that they are in a special position to influence the law clerk.

CANON 3

A LAW CLERK SHOULD PERFORM THE DUTIES OF THE OFFICE IMPARTIALLY AND DILIGENTLY

The official duties of a law clerk take precedence over all other activities. Official duties include all the duties of the office prescribed by law, resolution of the Judicial Conference of the United States, the court in which the law clerk serves, and the appointing judge. In the performance of these duties, the following standards apply:

A. A law clerk should respect and comply with the law and should conduct himself or herself at all times in a manner that promotes public confidence in the integrity and impartiality of the judiciary and of the office.

B. A law clerk should maintain professional competence in the profession. A law clerk should be dignified, courteous, and fair to all persons with whom the law clerk deals in the law clerk's official capacity. A law clerk should diligently discharge the responsibilities of the office. A law clerk should bear in mind the obligation to treat fairly and courteously the general public as well as the legal profession.

C. The relationship between judge and law clerk is essentially a confidential one. A law clerk should abstain from public comment about a pending or impending proceeding in the court in which the law clerk serves. A law clerk should never disclose to any person any confidential information received in the course of the law clerk's duties, nor should the law clerk employ such information for personal gain. This subsection does not prohibit a law clerk from making public statements in the course of official duties to the extent authorized by the appointing judge. A law clerk should inform the appointing judge of any circumstance or activity of the law clerk that might serve as a basis for disqualification of the judge, e.g., a prospective employment relation with a law firm, association of the law clerk's spouse with a law firm or litigant, etc.

CANON 4

A LAW CLERK MAY ENGAGE IN ACTIVITIES TO IMPROVE THE LAW, THE LEGAL SYSTEM, AND THE ADMINISTRATION OF JUSTICE

A law clerk, subject to the proper performance of official duties, may engage in the following law related activities:

A. A law clerk may speak, write, lecture, teach, and participate in other activities concerning the law, the legal system, and the administration of justice.

B. A law clerk may serve as a member, officer, or director of an organization or governmental agency devoted to the improvement of the law, the legal system, or the administration of justice.

C. A law clerk may promote the development of professional organizations and foster the interchange of technical information and experience with others in the profession. A law clerk may make himself or herself available to the public at large for speaking engagements and public appearances designed to enhance the public's knowledge of the operation of the court system.

CANON 5[2]

A LAW CLERK SHOULD REGULATE EXTRA–OFFICIAL ACTIVITIES TO MINIMIZE THE RISK OF CONFLICT WITH OFFICIAL DUTIES

A. Vocational Activities. A law clerk may write, lecture, teach and speak on none legal subjects and engage in the arts, sports, and other social and recreational activities, if such vocational activities do not detract from the dignity of the office or interfere with the performance of official duties.

B. Civic and Charitable Activities. A law clerk may participate in civic and charitable activities that do not detract from the dignity of the office or interfere with the performance of official duties. A law clerk may official action with respect to the case;

(f) a loan from a lending institution in its regular course of business on the same terms generally available to persons who are not law clerks;

(g) a scholarship or fellowship awarded on the same terms and based on the same criteria applied to other applicants; or

(h) any other gift, bequest, favor or loan, only if:

(i) the donor has not sought and is not seeking to do business with the court or other entity served by the law clerk; or

(ii) the donor is not a party or other person who has had or is likely to have any interest in the performance of the law clerk's official duties.

(3) A law clerk should report the value of any gift, bequest, favor, or loan as required by statute or by the Judicial Conference of the United States.

D. Practice of Law. A law clerk shall not practice law in any federal, state, or local court, or undertake to perform legal services for any private client in return for remuneration. This prohibition, however, shall not be construed to preclude the performance of routine legal work necessary to the management of the personal affairs of the law clerk or a member of the law clerk's family, so long as:

(1) Such work is done without compensation or for nominal compensation;

(2) It does not require any act, including the entry of an appearance in a court of the United States, that would suggest that the position of Law Clerk is being misused, that preferential treatment is being sought by virtue of the holding of that position, or that would otherwise be inconsistent with the law clerk's primary responsibility to the court; and

(3) so long as such activity does not have actual conflict or appear in conflict with court duties or will not reflect adversely on the court or create the appearance of impropriety.

A law clerk should ascertain and observe any limitations imposed by the appointing judge or the court on which the appointing judge serves concerning the practice of law by a former law clerk before the judge or the court.

CANON 6

A LAW CLERK SHOULD REGULARLY FILE ANY REQUIRED REPORTS OF COMPENSATION RECEIVED FOR ALL EXTRA–OFFICIAL ACTIVITIES

A law clerk may receive compensation and reimbursement of expenses for all extra-official activities permitted by this Code, if the source of such payments does not influence or give the appearance of influencing the law clerk in the performance of official duties or otherwise give the appearance of impropriety, subject to the following restrictions:

A. Compensation. Compensation should not exceed a reasonable amount nor should it exceed that normally received by others for the same activity.

B. Expense Reimbursement. Expense reimbursement should be limited to the actual cost of travel, food, and lodging reasonably incurred by a law clerk and, where appropriate to the occasion, by the law clerk's spouse. Any payment in excess of such an amount is compensation.

C. Public Reports. A law clerk should make and file such reports as may be prescribed by law or by the Judicial Conference of the United States.

Notwithstanding the above, a law clerk shall not receive any salary, or any supplementation of salary, as compensation for official services from any source other than the Government of the United States.

CANON 7

A LAW CLERK SHOULD REFRAIN FROM POLITICAL ACTIVITY

A. Political Activity. A law clerk should refrain from political activity; a law clerk should not act as a leader or hold office in a political organization; a law clerk should not make speeches for or publicly endorse a political organization or candidate; a law clerk should not solicit funds for or contribute to a political organization, candidate for political or public office; a law clerk should not otherwise engage in political activities.

EFFECTIVE DATE OF COMPLIANCE

Persons to whom this Code becomes applicable should arrange their affairs as soon as reasonably possible to comply with it and should do so in any event within thirty days of the appointment.

Adopted effective September 29, 2008.

[2] So in original. Canon 5 appears to be missing text.

Human Resources

11.701. CIVIL RIGHTS COMPLAINT PROCEDURE

IN THE CIRCUIT COURT OF THE FIFTEENTH JUDICIAL CIRCUIT IN AND FOR PALM BEACH COUNTY, FLORIDA

ADMINISTRATIVE ORDER NO. 11.701–7/18 *

IN RE: CIVIL RIGHTS COMPLAINT PROCEDURE

This procedure is adopted pursuant to Administrative Order In Re: Personnel Rules and Regulations issued by the Chief Justice of the Supreme Court on September 23, 1993 and sets forth the steps to be taken to investigate and provide for a prompt and equitable resolution to complaints of discrimination in employment decisions.

Only complaints of discrimination, by and against officers and employees of the Fifteenth Judicial Circuit, because of race, religion, sex (including pregnancy discrimination and sexual harassment), national origin, age, disability, sexual orientation, marital status or familial status, veteran status, and gender identity or expression should be filed using the procedures described herein.

NOW, THEREFORE, pursuant to the authority conferred by Florida Rule of Judicial Administration 2.215, it is **ORDERED** as follows:

A. Intake Officer.

1. The Honorable Sandra Bosso–Pardo, Main Courthouse, 205 N Dixie Highway, West Palm Beach, Florida 33401, is hereby appointed as the intake officer who shall be responsible for receiving and documenting complaints of discrimination by and against Fifteenth Judicial Circuit officers and employees.

2. If for any reason the intake officer cannot or should not perform her duties, the Chief Judge shall appoint an alternate.

B. Procedure.

1. All complaints of discrimination shall be treated seriously and acted upon promptly. Any officer, employee, or applicant for employment, who believes that he or she is a victim of discrimination, should report the matter either orally or in writing, to the intake officer or the employee's supervisor, within ninety (90) days of the date of the alleged violation. If reported to the supervisor, the supervisor will report the complaint to the intake officer.

2. The intake officer shall interview the officer or employee the complaint is against and report the details of the complaint to the Chief Judge within five (5) working days. Complaints of discrimination under the Americans with Disabilities Act shall also be referred to the Court's ADA Coordinator. The Chief Judge may attempt to resolve the complaint, informally, through mutual conciliation, or appoint an investigative officer(s) who will make an investigation and report to the Chief Judge on this matter.

3. If mutual conciliation is agreed upon by the complainant and the officer or employee the complaint is against, the Chief Judge, or an appointed representative, will meet with the individuals involved to discuss the nature of the complaint and methods for resolution. The Chief Judge, his or her appointed representative, or the individuals involved, may recommend alternative dispute resolution as a method for resolving the complaint. Alternative dispute resolution may be initiated at any stage of this procedure.

4. If an investigative officer(s) is appointed:

a. The investigative officer(s) shall:

1) Interview the complainant concerning the nature and facts of the complaint.

2) Interview the officer or employee the complaint is against to obtain his or her understanding of the complaint, and his or her perception of the facts of the complaint. The officer or employee the complaint is against may prepare a written response to the complaint.

3) Interview any witnesses as the investigative officer(s) deem necessary.

4) Prepare and submit a written report to the Chief Judge describing the nature and facts of the complaint.

b. All interviews shall be under oath and recorded either steno graphically or electronically.

c. The Chief Judge shall make a determination of the validity of the complaint. The Chief Judge may meet with all individuals concerned with a goal toward mutual resolution, dismiss the complaint, authorize appropriate discipline up to and including dismissal, or refer the complaint to the appropriate outside agency. The Chief Judge may meet with the complainant and the officer or employee the complaint is against, either separately or together, and inform them of his or her decision.

C. Confidentiality. As provided in the Supreme Court Administrative Order In Re: Personnel Rules and Regulations issued on September 23, 1993, all recorded statements and written materials developed through the use of this procedure are confidential pursuant to Rule 2.420, Public Access to Judicial Records, Florida Rules of Judicial Administration.

D. Complainant's Other Rights.

1. Irrespective of these internal procedures, the complainant retains the right before, during, or after the proceedings, to seek remedy outside the court's internal procedure as provided by law. The complainant may file a charge with the EEOC, or with the Florida Commission on Human Relations (FCHR). The EEOC may be reached toll free at (800) USA EEOC. The FCHR is located at 325 John Knox Road, Building F, Suite 240, Tallahassee, Florida, 32303–4113.

2. Additionally, the Judicial Qualifications Commission, under Article V, Section 12, of the Florida Constitution, has the jurisdiction to investigate all reported instances of judicial misconduct. The Judicial Qualifications Commission is located at Room 102, The Historic Capitol, Tallahassee, Florida, 32399–6000. **Michael L. Schneider,** Executive Director, can be contacted at (850) 488–1581.

3. The Board of Governors of The Florida Bar, by authority of the Supreme Court and under its Rules and Regulations, has the jurisdiction to investigate all reported instances of misconduct by members of The Florida Bar. The Florida Bar is located at 650 Appalachee Parkway, Tallahassee, Florida, 32399–2300.

E. Records. All records of complaints of discrimination and their resolution shall be documented and maintained by the intake officer. If an investigation takes place and the investigative officer has submitted a written report to the Chief Judge, any record of any resulting disciplinary action will be maintained in the disciplined employee's personnel file.

F. Complaints Against Judges. The Supreme Court's Sexual Harassment Policy and Procedures for Sexual Harassment Complaints Against Justices and Judges is hereby adopted for the Fifteenth Judicial Circuit. The policies and procedures set forth in AOSC18–6 located at http://www.floridasupremecourt.org/clerk/adminorders/2018/AOSC18-6.pdf are made a part of this Administrative Order.

DONE and **SIGNED** in Chambers at West Palm Beach, Palm Beach County, Florida, this 5 day of July, 2018.

Krista Marx
Chief Judge

Adopted effective September 29, 2008. Amended effective September 26, 2016; July 5, 2018.

* supersedes admin. order no. 11.701–9/16

11.702. CODE OF CONDUCT FOR NONJUDICIAL COURT EMPLOYEES

IN THE CIRCUIT COURT OF THE FIFTEENTH JUDICIAL CIRCUIT IN AND FOR PALM BEACH COUNTY, FLORIDA

ADMINISTRATIVE ORDER NO. 11.702–9/16 *

IN RE: CODE OF CONDUCT FOR NONJUDICIAL COURT EMPLOYEES

NOW, THEREFORE, pursuant to the authority conferred by Florida Rule of Judicial Administration 2.215, it is **ORDERED** as follows:

The American Judicature Society's Model Code of Conduct, which is attached [1] along with an addendum to Section Five (E) is herewith adopted as a recommended guideline for all nonjudicial employees in the Fifteenth Judicial Circuit and reads as follows:

No Court Employee shall discriminate on the basis of nor manifest, by words or conduct, bias or prejudice based on race, religion, sex (including pregnancy discrimination and sexual harassment), national origin, age, disability, sexual orientation, marital status or familial status, veteran status, gender identity or expression, or political affiliation in the conduct of service to the court.

DONE and **SIGNED** in Chambers at West Palm Beach, Palm Beach County, Florida, this 22 day of September, 2016.

Jeffrey Colbath
Chief Judge

* supersedes admin. order 11.702–9/08

1 Attachment not included.

11.703. GIFT POLICY

IN THE CIRCUIT COURT OF THE FIFTEENTH JUDICIAL CIRCUIT IN AND FOR PALM BEACH COUNTY, FLORIDA

ADMINISTRATIVE ORDER NO. 11.703–9/08 *

IN RE: GIFT POLICY

It is the policy of the Fifteenth Judicial Circuit that all court employees and all courtroom deputies serving in the courts are prohibited from accepting gifts from any person or entity who has had, now has, or foresee ably will have business before the courts.

This policy shall be printed in appropriate publications prior to holiday periods with a request to attorneys and others for assistance in complying with the policy.

DONE and **SIGNED** in Chambers at West Palm Beach, Palm Beach County, Florida, this 29 day of September, 2008.

Kathleen J. Kroll
Chief Judge

Adopted effective September 29, 2008.

* supersedes admin. order 11.009 9/92

11.704. POLICIES FOR USE OF PERSONAL COMPUTERS BY JUDGES AND COURT PERSONNEL

IN THE CIRCUIT COURT OF THE FIFTEENTH JUDICIAL CIRCUIT IN AND FOR PALM BEACH COUNTY, FLORIDA

ADMINISTRATIVE ORDER NO. 11.704 9/08 *

IN RE: POLICIES FOR USE OF PERSONAL COMPUTERS BY JUDGES AND COURT PERSONNEL

All judges and court personnel in the Fifteenth Judicial Circuit have been furnished or have access to personal computers ("PC's") to assist them in their work-related functions and assignments. There is a recognized need to promulgate uniform policies to ensure the safety of the network and compliance with state and federal licensing and intellectual property laws.

NOW, THEREFORE, pursuant to the authority conferred by Florida Rule of Judicial Administration 2.215, it is **ORDERED** as follows:

1. The Court's computer systems (including the Court's computer equipment, software, e-mail system and Internet access) may be used only for a purpose that is court- or law-related, or that involves other legitimate matters.

2. Using the Court's computer system for the purposes of any employment outside the State Court's System or for private commercial or business purposes is prohibited.

3. To ensure safe and effective computing with the Court's networked systems:

a. Application settings, operating system software settings, or network configuration settings of your machine are not to be changed as each workstation has been configured to ensure safe and effective computing with the Court's networked systems.

b. Material from unknown web sites, additional software, or upgrades to existing standard court software should not be downloaded or transferred to a court computer as it can result in software incompatibilities, destruction of data, or licensing violations. Changes to the workstation should only be made by the systems administrators.

c. Peer-to-peer software (e.g., Kazaa, Napster, WinMX) should not be downloaded on any court computer system. The use of peer-to-peer applications consumes large amounts of network resources and exposes the computer and the Court network to viruses, worms, spyware, and other security threats.

4. All state and county employees who work in the court system shall comply with the Computer Use Policy that is to be signed by all employees and which is retained in the employee's personnel file. A copy of the Computer Use Policy is attached as Exhibit "A".

5. Definitions.

a. "Court-related" means that the purpose furthers legitimate interests of the courts.

b. "Law-related" means that the purpose promotes a better understanding of the law and legal trends.

c. "Other legitimate matters" are activities relevant to users' personal life or family that do not detract from the Court's dignity or routine functions, and that do not interfere with the timely performance of the normal work duties.

DONE and **SIGNED** in Chambers, in West Palm Beach, Palm Beach County, Florida, this 29 day of September, 2008.

Kathleen J. Kroll
Chief Judge

* supersedes admin. order 2.045–4/97

EXHIBIT "A"

THE FIFTEENTH JUDICIAL CIRCUIT
COMPUTER USE POLICY

I. ACCEPTABLE USE

The security of the Fifteenth Judicial Circuit's ("Court") data and systems is a top priority. The Court's systems administrators and Palm Beach County's ISS department go to great lengths to ensure that our software and systems are as secure as possible in order to reduce the risks of virus attacks, compromise of the network systems and services, and legal issues. To make our computing environment as safe as possible, your systems administrators are directed to ensure that the following policies are followed.

1. Employees and judges using the Court's computer systems (including the Court's computer equipment, software, e-mail system and Internet access) may do so only for a purpose that is court- or law-related, or that involves other legitimate matters. "Court-related" means that the purpose furthers legitimate interests of the courts. "Law-related" means that the purpose promotes a better understanding of the law and legal trends. "Other legitimate matters" are activities relevant to users' personal life or family that do not detract from the Court's dignity or routine functions, and that do not interfere with the timely performance of the normal work duties. Using the Court's computer system for the purposes of any employment outside the State Courts System or for private commercial or business purposes is prohibited.

2. The Court is the owner of the computer systems and has the right to access, monitor, inspect, and disclose, for legitimate Court business reasons, all information and materials entered, created, transmitted, accessed, received or stored on the systems. The Court's right to access, monitor, inspect and disclose extends to all aspects of the computer systems, including Internet use and e-mail. Users of the Court's computer systems have no reasonable expectation of privacy in information and materials entered, created, transmitted, accessed, received or stored on the Court's computer systems.

3. Unique, unnecessary software, configuration settings (desktop wallpaper) and personal files are not supported and may be lost with little or no advanced notice. The Court's computing needs are fulfilled through the use of a standardized and periodically updated workstation configuration. In the event of a workstation failure or when extensive software upgrades are necessary, your workstation may need to be "rebuilt" using the standard configuration. In such cases, it is the user's responsibility to restore settings and data that are not court or law-related.

4. To ensure safe and effective computing with the Court's networked systems:

a. Do not change the application settings, operating system software settings, or network configuration settings of your machine. Your workstation has been configured to ensure safe and effective computing with the Court's networked systems.

b. Never download material from unknown web sites, install additional software, or upgrade existing standard court software. This includes software obtained via the Internet, e-mail, CD–ROM or diskette. Doing so can result in software incompatibilities, destruction of data, licensing violations or worse. Changes to the workstation should only be made by the systems administrators.

c. Do not download or install peer-to-peer software (e.g., Kazaa, Napster, WinMX) on any court computer system. The use of peer-to-peer applications consumes large amounts of network resources and exposes your computer and the Court network to viruses, worms, spyware, and other security threats. Use of this type of application could expose you and the Court to legal liability for the distribution of pirated computer software, copyrighted music and movies, etc.

5. Always "lock" your workstation before leaving it unattended and do not attempt to modify screen-saver settings. All workstations should be set to a default screen-saver that will automatically "lock" the workstation after being left idle for 30 minutes. If you leave your workstation before the screen-saver has engaged, you should lock your workstation manually by pressing the windows and the "L" key.

6. Do not share your password or account with anyone. Authorized users are responsible for the security of their passwords and accounts.

7. Save all work-related files in the proper location as outlined below. Data that is lost due to a system failure or other unplanned event cannot be recovered unless it is stored in the appropriate location; nor can the confidentiality and integrity of files be guaranteed if they are not stored in the appropriate location. It is a good practice to save your work frequently.

8. With any system, storage capacity is neither limitless nor free. Therefore, we all must cooperate to avoid intentional or unintentional "abuse" of network resources. In this regard, it is important to recognize that inappropriate utilization of network storage capacity by just a few end-users can, and may, result in insufficient storage capacity for all. Activities that are not work-related are particularly noteworthy from the standpoint of file storage. Typical examples of files that are not work-related are nonstandard screen-savers, graphics (including photos), files, music, e-mail, CD–ROM or diskette. The problem with such items is that they are generally large and consume an inordinate amount of system storage capacity. In this regard, you may have a Personal folder on your workstation identified as "Personal" to store files that are: a) not work-related and b) qualify as "other legitimate matters" as per this policy regarding acceptable use. Items stored here will be your responsibility to maintain and may be subject to loss in the event of a system failure.

9. All hosts used by judges and employees (e.g., laptops, tablet pc, home computers) that are connected to the court network via ethernet cable, wireless, dial-up, or VPN, shall be continually executing approved virus-scanning software with a current virus database, and the operating system shall be patched with the most current service packs, patches, and/or hotfixes as recommended by your systems administrator. There will be mandatory routine maintenance for all court-owned portable computing devices.

10. Upon leaving work at the end of the day, save your work, exit from any open applications, and restart your computer (this will leave your computer in a locked state). Several maintenance tasks are performed on the Court's systems after working hours but may fail to occur if your computer is turned off at night. Some of the tasks may cause loss of data if you have not saved your work in progress and closed open applications.

11. Court users should adhere to these policies at all times. Compliance with the terms of the Court's Computer Use Policies is a condition of employment. Violation of the policies may subject users to disciplinary action, up to and including dismissal. If you have any questions or concerns regarding these policies, please feel free to contact your systems administrator.

II. PASSWORDS

12. Passwords are an important aspect of computer security. They are the front line of protection for user accounts. A poorly chosen password may result in the compromise of the network. All judges and employees are responsible for taking the appropriate steps, as outlined below, to select and secure their passwords.

13. Court-related (i.e., Windows workstation/e-mail, VPN account, CMS, etc.) passwords should never be written down or stored on-line. Try to create strong passwords that you can easily remember, but would be hard for someone else to guess.

14. There is no need to share passwords in order to share work documents. If you are out of the office and another court employee or judge needs access to a work document that you have stored in your network folder, upon approval by the supervisor, the systems administrator can assist with this request.

15. If an account or password is suspected to have been compromised, contact your systems administrator immediately.

III. E-MAIL [2]

16. Appropriate Use of E-mail—The Court's e-mail system provides a valuable communication link and should be used for court-related, law-related or other legitimate purposes as outlined in Section I. E-mail messages go out under the Court's address, which is essentially the Court's "electronic letterhead." Thus, e-mail should not include any information that would reflect poorly on the Court (e.g., "off-color" comments, insensitive jokes, racial slurs) or that may be construed as representing the opinion/policy of the Court proper. Do not forward e-mail reports about computer viruses, profit-making schemes, or "chain letters." Users' e-mail can be retrieved and may be disclosed in response to a subpoena or court order, or an investigation concerning misconduct. Global e-mails (for example, e-mails addressed to SC–Everyone, OSCA–Everyone) or mass e-mails (e-mails sent to multiple users) should only be sent for official court business. Global and mass e-mails may not be used for non-court sponsored solicitations, such as advertising the sale of personal property, fundraising activities, and communications promoting political positions or actions.

17. Accessing the Court's E-mail System via the Web—When accessing webmail, do not configure the login to remember your password. Do not leave the computer device without logging out of webmail and closing the Internet Explorer page.

18. Accessing Outside E-mail—Accessing web-based e-mail accounts (such as HotMail, YahooMail, NetscapeMail, etc.) while at work is strongly discouraged but will be permitted during break periods. If you must do so for court-related, law-related or other legitimate purposes, consult your systems administrator regarding the service you must use and the appropriate use of that service. More importantly, do not open or download e-mail attachments from a web-based e-mail account.

19. Suspicious or Questionable E-mail—It is not uncommon for false virus warnings, known as "hoaxes" to be inappropriately sent in mass via e-mail by mal-intentioned individuals on the Internet. Forwarding hoaxes to others puts undue strain on the Court's systems and can create unnecessary confusion or even panic. If you receive an e-mail that is suspicious, unsolicited, appears to be a spoof or a hoax, or contains a warning, immediately contact your systems administrator. Do not open the e-mail and do not forward the e-mail to anyone.

20. Attachment Blocking—Certain e-mail file attachments that are commonly used to spread viruses may be blocked from entering our e-mail system. If you are not able to receive a court or law related e-mail attachment because it is being blocked, please contact your systems administrator for assistance.

21. Attachment Size Limitations—There is a size limit on e-mail attachments coming into and leaving our e-mail system. This limit protects our e-mail system from unnecessary strain. If you are not able to send or receive a court or law related e-mail attachment, please contact your system administrator who can assist you with other options for transferring files. We have no control over the attachment size limits that other entities enforce.

22. E-mail and Public Records Requirements—All records made or received in connection with the transaction of official business by the Court are public records. These records must be retained for specified amounts of time, and are subject to public disclosure, upon request. Public record e-mails are transitory if they are created merely for communication of information, rather than to perpetuate knowledge. Transitory e-mails do not set policy, establish guidelines or procedures, certify a transaction, or become a receipt. Transitory e-mails include those that involve only short-lived administrative matters, such as scheduling meetings, suggesting revisions to a document that has yet to be finalized, or requesting supplies. A transitory e-mail can be deleted once it is obsolete, or superseded by other records. E-mails concerning only personal matters are not public record unless the volume of personal emails can be viewed as interfering with or affecting job performance.

23. E-mail Retention—All e-mail transmitted on the Court's e-mail system will be archived for the purpose of complying with the retention requirements as provided for in the Florida Rules of Judicial Administration. Employees should be aware that all e-mail will be archived and maintained indefinitely.

IV. HARASSMENT

24. The Fifteenth Judicial Circuit's policy is to provide a safe and comfortable workplace for all employees. This includes freedom from harassment based on race, religion, sex, national origin, age or disability. Sending any offensive messages by means of the Court's computer or E-mail system will not be tolerated. Failure to comply with this policy may result in discipline up to and including dismissal.

25. Should you receive any improper messages via E-mail or over the Internet at your work email address or work computer, you should immediately report the situation to your supervisor. Should you receive any improper messages via E-mail or over the Internet at your personal email account or personal computer from a co-worker or supervisor, you should immediately report the situation to your supervisor. If for any reason you are unable to advise your supervisor, bring the matter to the attention of the Trial Court Administrator or the Human Resource Manager. The Trial Court Administrator and/or Human Resource personnel will investigate any reported instances of misuse of the Court's computer system or unwanted and improper electronic communications from co-workers or supervisors. Failure to report the dissemination of offensive material may result in disciplinary action.

V. APPLICABILITY

26. This policy applies to all State employees and to all County-funded Court employees.

EMPLOYEE ACKNOWLEDGEMENT AND CONSENT

I acknowledge that I have read and understand the Court's Computer Use Policies. I understand that the Court and/or Palm Beach County is the owner of the Court's computer systems, and has the right to access, monitor, inspect and disclose, for legitimate Court business reasons, information and materials contained or stored on the computer systems. I understand that the Court's right to access, monitor, inspect and disclose extends to information and materials concerning users' Internet use and e-mail. I understand that adherence to the computer use policies is required as a condition of employment, and I consent to the terms of the policies.

____
Employee Signature

____
Employee Printed Name

____
Date

Adopted effective September 29, 2008.

2 includes Instant Messenger where applicable

11.705. INTERNS AND VOLUNTEERS

IN THE CIRCUIT COURT OF THE FIFTEENTH JUDICIAL CIRCUIT IN AND FOR PALM BEACH COUNTY, FLORIDA

ADMINISTRATIVE ORDER NO. 11.705–3/11

IN RE: INTERNS AND VOLUNTEERS

Volunteers and interns play an important role in helping the circuit function efficiently while at the same time learning about the judicial branch of government. Volunteers and interns are brought to the circuit either through Court Administration or directly by individual judges. Because of the confidentiality of the work involved and the different levels of supervision provided, a clear explanation of the role of court administration, judges, volunteers, needs to be clearly set forth. Moreover, guidelines and screening processes must be in place with regard to volunteers and interns in order to ensure the security of the court, including the safety of its employees and its computer system, and to ensure that there is sufficient office space, technological resources, and proper supervision.

NOW, THEREFORE, pursuant to the authority conferred by Florida Rule of Judicial Administration 2.215, it is **ORDERED** as follows:

A. Volunteers Through Court Administration. These are local residents, including students, retirees or anyone with an interest in learning about and assisting with the administration of court programs. These volunteers have a set schedule but may work for a specific or an indefinite time period. Potential assignments may include administrative or in-court duties. Students may receive course credit if approved by both Court Administration and the educational institution in advance. A court administration employee is assigned to arrange the volunteer's work schedule and to supervise the duties of the volunteer; but it is the responsibility of the volunteer to record work hours, if needed.

1. *Applications*:

a. Applications for volunteer positions are accepted year-round, for either ongoing or specific time frames. Areas in which volunteers are needed to assist are posted on the Fifteenth Circuit's website and with www.volunteermatch.org.

b. Volunteers may specify the hours during which they are available and must be more than 18 years of age.

ç. The volunteer applicant must complete the application form located on the circuit's website. The volunteer program does not have the extensive educational element of an internship.

2. *Interview*: An interview is arranged with Court Administration to discuss the match between the applicant's skills or preferences and the work available.

3. *Computer Access/Badge/Parking*:

a. The volunteer will be required to undergo a background and reference check.

b. The volunteer will be provided with photo ID badge that does not allow access to secure areas of the courthouse.

c. If needed for assigned work, the volunteer may be given a computer user account.

d. Volunteers will not be given a parking pass to the employee parking garage. Volunteers will be eligible to receive a daily stamp from Court Administration to validate a parking ticket for the employee parking garage.

e. Training will be conducted by the court employee who is responsible for supervising the volunteer.

f. Court Administration will be responsible for collecting the volunteer's badge and cancelling any computer accounts upon the volunteer's separation from the circuit.

B. Interns Through Court Administration. These are college, graduate school and law school students or graduates who are working with the court for a specific period of time with structured hours and work assignments along with an educational component. Interns sometimes receive course credit, pro bono or community service hours. There is a structured program run in conjunction with law schools or universities. A court administration employee supervises the interns, accounts for the interns' time and, when applicable, reports the time to the school in order for credit to be received.

1. *Applications*: Applications for internship positions are accepted and reviewed by the Trial Court Administrator, General Counsel or their designee.

2. *Interview*: Applicants are screened and those qualified will undergo an interview.

3. *Computer Access/Badge/Parking*:

a. The intern applicants will undergo and satisfactorily pass a background and reference check.

b. The interns are given a computer user account (if needed for their work), LEXIS and WESTLAW password (where applicable).

c. The interns will receive a photo ID badge that allows access to secure areas of the courthouse.

d. A parking pass to the employee parking garage may be obtained.

e. The interns will be trained by the Court Administration employee who will be supervising them.

f. Court Administration will be responsible for collecting the interns' badges and cancelling any computer accounts upon the interns' separation from the circuit.

C. Personal Interns/Volunteers to Judge. These are individuals who assist a judge without utilizing Court Administration's application and interview process.

1. *Application*: At judge's discretion.

2. *Interview*: At judge's discretion.

3. *Computer Access/Badge/Parking*:

a. Personal interns/volunteers will not be issued computer user accounts.

b. Personal interns/volunteers will not be issued badges.

c. Personal interns/volunteers will not be given parking passes to the employee parking garage. Personal interns/volunteers will be eligible for a daily stamp from Court Administration to validate a parking ticket for the employee parking garage.

d. Personal interns/volunteers will need to be supervised by the judge or the judge's judicial assistant.

DONE and **SIGNED** in Chambers at West Palm Beach, Palm Beach County, Florida this 31 day of March, 2011.

Peter D. Blanc
Chief Judge

Adopted effective March 31, 2011.

Technology

11.801. COURT WEBSITE

IN THE CIRCUIT COURT OF THE FIFTEENTH JUDICIAL CIRCUIT IN AND FOR PALM BEACH COUNTY, FLORIDA

ADMINISTRATIVE ORDER NO.: 11.801–9/08 *

IN RE: COURT WEBSITE

A court website can provide information that can assist both the public and members of the bar.

NOW, THEREFORE, pursuant to the authority conferred by Florida Rule of Judicial Administration 2.215, it is **ORDERED** as follows:

1. All materials posted must be related to court business.

2. All materials to be posted on the website must be reviewed and approved by the Chief Judge, the Court Administrator, or their authorized designee.

3. To post information on the website, the information must be submitted to Court Technology. Requests outside the established scope of content on the website must be submitted to the Court Administrator or a designee for approval prior to publication. The exception to this rule is calendar—related information, or other approved divisional information posted directly by a judge or judicial assistant on their divisional website.

4. For case related information, such as signed orders to be posted on the website, the link will list the case name, case number and the title of the document being posted (i.e. Smith v. Jones –2008–000123 "AN"—Order on Motion for Summary Judgment).

DONE AND SIGNED in chambers at West Palm Beach, Palm Beach County, Florida, this 29 day of September, 2008.

Kathleen J. Kroll
Chief Judge

Adopted effective September 29, 2008.

* supersedes admin. order 11.047–6/05

11.802. ORGANIZATION OF A JUSTICE SYSTEMS POLICY BOARD

IN THE CIRCUIT COURT OF THE FIFTEENTH JUDICIAL CIRCUIT IN AND FOR PALM BEACH COUNTY, FLORIDA

ADMINISTRATIVE ORDER 11.802–6/09

IN RE: ORGANIZATION OF A JUSTICE SYSTEMS POLICY BOARD

A Criminal Justice Information System ("CJIS") Task Force Policy Component Agreement was entered into in January, 1992 by the State Attorney, Chief Judge, Sheriff, Clerk of Court and Public Defender, and thereafter a Justice Information Systems Policy Board was created on March 6, 1995 by agreement between and among the Chief Judge, Public Defender, Sheriff, Clerk of Court, State Attorney and the Board of County Commissioners to ensure the effective sharing of justice information technology in an accurate and timely manner which furthers the constitutional purpose of the participating agencies and increases the efficiency and effectiveness of the justice system. There is a need for compatibility on the part of all contemplated justice information technology projects and a further need to provide a forum for information technology project reporting and discussion as agreed by the Justice Information Systems Policy Board members in the Memorandum of Understanding dated May 7, 2008 which is attached hereto as Exhibit "A".

NOW, THEREFORE, pursuant to the authority conferred by Florida Rule of Judicial Administration 2.215, it is **ORDERED** as follows:

1. **Justice Information Systems Policy Board ("Policy Board").** This Policy Board will provide the forum for court information technology project reporting, information sharing and discussion to ensure coordinated use, data sharing (to the extent consistent with legal restrictions or requirements), integration and efficient utilization of justice information technology in the Fifteenth Judicial Circuit. The Policy Board shall consist of the Chief Judge, the State Attorney, the Public Defender, the Clerk, the Sheriff, a representative from the Board of County Commissioners, the President of the Palm Beach County Bar Association or designee, the President of the South Palm Beach County Bar Association or designee and a member of the Criminal Justice Commission. The Chief Judge shall be chair of the committee unless a majority of the Policy Board vote otherwise.

2. **Information Sharing and Reporting.** The Policy Board meetings will provide a forum for discussing individual member agencies technology projects, directions and priorities which have a potential impact on other member agencies. Additionally the Policy Board will create a forum for obtaining member input on.

Exhibit A

MEMORANDUM OF UNDERSTANDING

The Chief Judge, Public Defender, State Attorney and Clerk & Comptroller of the Fifteenth Judicial Circuit, along with the Sheriff of Palm Beach County and representatives of the Palm Beach County Board of County Commissioners, Palm Beach County Bar Association, South Palm Beach County Bar Association and Palm Beach County Criminal Justice Commission collectively sitting as the Justice Information Systems Policy Board, agree to work to ensure the effective sharing of criminal justice information in an accurate and timely manner which furthers the constitutional purpose of the participating agencies and increases the efficiency and effectiveness of the justice system.

To accomplish this goal, the participating agencies agree to:

1. Create and establish formal plans for information sharing;

2. Identify the objectives and benefits of information sharing for the participants;

3. Provide a forum for discussing those individual technology projects, directions and priorities of the member agencies which have a potential impact on other member agencies as

well as provide a forum for discussing the integration of said projects.

4. Support information sharing by involving agency representatives when appropriate in the formulation of plans and projects, consistent with Florida law;

5. Support government transparency by providing public access to information when consistent with Florida law.

Dated this 7 day of May, 2008.

Kathleen J. Kroll Chief Judge	Carey Haughwout Public Defender	Barry Krischer State Attorney
Sharon Bock Clerk & Comptroller	Ric Bradshaw Sheriff	Robert Weisman County Administrator
Bard Rockenbach Palm Beach County Bar Assn.	Mark Osherow South Palm Beach County Bar Assn.	Gerald Richman Palm Beach County Criminal Justice Commission

Adopted effective June 30, 2009.

11.803. JIS SYSTEM SECURITY

IN THE CIRCUIT COURT OF THE FIFTEENTH JUDICIAL CIRCUIT IN AND FOR PALM BEACH COUNTY, FLORIDA

ADMINISTRATIVE ORDER NO. 11.803–9/08 *

IN RE: JIS SYSTEM SECURITY

Security policies, procedures and standards were developed by the JIS Project and adopted by the JIS Policy Board. The JIS Policy Board voted on May 10, 2000 specifically to direct ISS to carry out its responsibility as database and server administrator in accordance with the rules outlined in the security policies. ISS presently carries out the responsibility as database and server administrator.

NOW, THEREFORE, pursuant to the authority conferred by Florida Rule of Judicial Administration 2.215, it is **ORDERED** as follows:

All individuals and offices who have the ability to enter information into the Banner System shall comply with the Information Resource Security Policies adopted by the JIS Policy Board directing ISS to carry out its responsibility as database and server administrator in accordance with the rules outlined therein.

DONE and **SIGNED** in Chambers, at West Palm Beach, Palm Beach County, Florida this 29 day of September, 2008.

Kathleen J. Kroll
Chief Judge

Adopted effective September 29, 2008.

* supersedes admin. order 11.040–9/00

11.804. FILING OF CASES WITH MORE THAN 999 PARTIES IN THE BANNER COMPUTER SYSTEM

IN THE CIRCUIT COURT OF THE FIFTEENTH JUDICIAL CIRCUIT IN AND FOR PALM BEACH COUNTY, FLORIDA

ADMINISTRATIVE ORDER NO.: 3.018–3/03

ADMINISTRATIVE ORDER NO.: 3.018–3/03

IN RE: FILING OF CASES WITH MORE THAN 999 PARTIES IN THE BANNER COMPUTER SYSTEM

WHEREAS, the new Banner Court Computer System becomes operational on February 18, 2003 in the Circuit Civil Division; and

WHEREAS, the new Banner Court Computer System has a limitation allowing no more than 999 parties per case; and

WHEREAS, occasionally a case is filed which contains more than 999 parties;

NOW, THEREFORE, it is **ORDERED,** that upon receipt of any case filing which contains more than 999 parties, the Clerk of Court shall distribute the number of parties to additional, consecutive case numbers by a blocking method as appropriate and that all pleadings shall be referenced by the lowest assigned case number in the Banner Court Computer System. All other case numbers so assigned shall only be used for indexing or recording pleadings upon the lowest case number having reached its limit on available data space. Furthermore, the Clerk of Court shall charge one filing fee for this type of case.

DONE AND SIGNED in Chambers at West Palm Beach, Florida, this 12th day of March, 2003.

Edward Fine
Chief Judge

Special Appointments

12.015. RESCISSION OF LOCAL RULE 2

IN THE CIRCUIT COURT OF THE FIFTEENTH JUDICIAL CIRCUIT IN AND FOR PALM BEACH COUNTY, FLORIDA

ADMINISTRATIVE ORDER NO. 10–12.015–3/10

IN RE: RESCISSION OF LOCAL RULE 2

Local Rule 2, dated September 8, 1994, and created in accordance with Florida Statute § 40.225, provides for an alternative method for drawing a jury venire. A majority of the judges in Palm Beach County agree that since Palm Beach County jurors are drawn from a list of names delivered by the Department of Highway Safety and Motor Vehicles, in accordance with Florida Statute § 40.011, there is no longer a need for an alternative method of drawing a jury venire. In a vote taken on February 17, 2010, a majority of the county court and circuit judges agreed that Local Rule 2 should be rescinded.

NOW, THEREFORE, pursuant to the authority conferred by Florida Rule of Judicial Administration 2.215, it is **ORDERED** as follows:

Local Rule 2 is hereby rescinded.

DONEand SIGNED in Chambers at West Palm Beach, Florida, this 5 day of March, 2010.

Peter D. Blanc
Chief Judge

Adopted effective March 5, 2010.

12.063. MOTION, NOTICE AND JUDGMENTS OF DISMISSAL; NOTICES OF LACK OF PROSECUTION AND NOTICES OF HEARINGS ON MOTIONS TO DISMISS FOR LACK OF PROSECUTION

IN THE CIRCUIT COURT OF THE FIFTEENTH JUDICIAL CIRCUIT IN AND FOR PALM BEACH COUNTY, FLORIDA

ADMINISTRATIVE ORDER NO. 08–12.063–6/08 *

IN RE: MOTION, NOTICE AND JUDGMENTS OF DISMISSAL; NOTICES OF LACK OF PROSECUTION AND NOTICES OF HEARINGS ON MOTIONS TO DISMISS FOR LACK OF PROSECUTION

An extraordinary number of county court small claims and civil division cases exist wherein there has been no record activity for a minimum of six months and ten months respectively. An inordinate amount of judicial time and resources will be expended in the execution of the Small Claims "Motion, Notice and Judgment of Dismissals", and "Notices of Lack of Prosecution and Notices of Hearings on Motions to Dismiss for Lack of Prosecution" entered in civil division cases. Ink stamped signatures of the county court civil judges, administered by assistants working under the authority and direction of the county court civil judges, will expedite the routine handling of these orders.

THEREFORE, it is **ORDERED** that ink stamped signatures of the county court civil judges may be used on Small Claims "Motion, Notice and Judgment of Dismissals", and "Notices of Lack of Prosecution and Notices of Hearings on Motions to Dismiss for Lack of Prosecution" entered in civil division cases, when affixed by authorized individuals, from the date of this Administrative Order through **December 31, 2008.** Each county court civil judge will provide a list, signed by the judge, of those individuals who are authorized to utilize the judge's signature stamp on the "Motion, Notice and Judgment of Dismissals" and "Notices of Lack of Prosecution and Notices of Hearings on Motions to Dismiss for Lack of Prosecution".

DONE and ORDERED in Chambers at West Palm Beach, Florida, this 27th day of June, 2008.

Kathleen J. Kroll
Chief Judge

Adopted effective June 27, 2008.

* supersedes Admin. Order 07–12.103–12/07.

12.076. EXTENSION OF TIME FOR PAYMENT OF FEES, FINES AND COURT COSTS UNTIL AUGUST 20th, 2008 DUE TO EFFECTS FROM TROPICAL STORM FAY

IN THE CIRCUIT COURT OF THE FIFTEENTH JUDICIAL CIRCUIT IN AND FOR PALM BEACH COUNTY, FLORIDA

ADMINISTRATIVE ORDER NO. 08–12.076–8/08

IN RE: EXTENSION OF TIME FOR PAYMENT OF FEES, FINES AND COURT COSTS UNTIL AUGUST 20th, 2008 DUE TO EFFECTS FROM TROPICAL STORM FAY

WHEREAS, due to the closure of all Palm Beach County Judicial Complexes from August 19th, 2008 at 8:00 a.m. through 8:00 a.m., August 20th, 2008 this Court finds it appropriate to issue this Administrative Order for an extension of time for the payment of all Fees, Fines and/or Court Costs until Wednesday, August 20th, 2008.

NOW, THEREFORE, it is ORDERED as follows:

1. The Clerk of the Court shall hereby issue an extension of time for the payment of all Fees, Fines and / or Court Costs until Wednesday, August 20th, 2008.

DONE AND SIGNED in Chambers at the Palm Beach County Courthouse, West Palm Beach, Florida, on this 20th day of August, 2008.

KATHLEEN J. KROLL
Chief Judge

Adopted effective August 20, 2008.

12.081. EXTENSION OF TIME FOR PAYMENT OF FEES, FINES AND COURT COSTS UNTIL NOVEMBER 7TH, 2005 DUE EFFECTS FROM HURRICANE WILMA

IN THE CIRCUIT COURT OF THE FIFTEENTH JUDICIAL CIRCUIT IN AND FOR PALM BEACH COUNTY, FLORIDA

ADMINISTRATIVE ORDER NO. 12.081–11/05

IN RE: EXTENSION OF TIME FOR PAYMENT OF FEES, FINES AND COURT COSTS UNTIL NOVEMBER 7TH, 2005 DUE EFFECTS FROM HURRICANE WILMA

WHEREAS, due to the closure of the Palm Beach County, Main Judicial Center from October 24th, 2005 through and 8:00 a.m., October 31st, 2005, the North County Complex from October 24th, 2005 through 8:00 a.m, November 1st, 2005; the South County Judicial Complex and Belle Glade Judicial Complex from October 24th, 2005 through 8:00 a.m., November 7th, 2005 this Court finds it appropriate to issue this Administrative Order for an extension of time for the payment of all Fees, Fines and /or Court Costs until Monday, November 7th, 2005.

NOW, THEREFORE, it is ORDERED as follows:

1. The Clerk of the Court shall hereby issue an extension of time for the payment of all Fees, Fines and / or Court Costs until Monday, November 7th, 2005.

DONE AND SIGNED in Chambers at the Palm Beach County Courthouse, West Palm Beach, Florida, on this 3rd day of November, 2005.

KATHLEEN J. KROLL
Chief Judge

Adopted effective November 3, 2005.

12.084. EXTENSION OF TIME FOR PAYMENT OF FEES, FINES AND COURT COSTS UNTIL AUGUST 31ST, 2006 DUE TO EFFECTS FROM TROPICAL STORM ERNESTO

IN THE CIRCUIT COURT OF THE FIFTEENTH JUDICIAL CIRCUIT IN AND FOR PALM BEACH COUNTY, FLORIDA

ADMINISTRATIVE ORDER NO. 06–12.084–8/06

IN RE: EXTENSION OF TIME FOR PAYMENT OF FEES, FINES AND COURT COSTS UNTIL AUGUST 31ST, 2006 DUE TO EFFECTS FROM TROPICAL STORM ERNESTO

WHEREAS, due to the closure of all Palm Beach County Judicial Complexes from August 29th, 2006 at 4:00 p.m. through 8:00 a.m., August 31st, 2006 this Court finds it appropriate to issue this Administrative Order for an extension of time for the payment of all Fees, Fines and/or Court Costs until Thursday, August 31st, 2006.

NOW, THEREFORE, it is ORDERED as follows:

1. The Clerk of the Court shall hereby issue an extension of time for the payment of all Fees, Fines and / or Court Costs until Thursday, August 31st, 2006.

DONE AND SIGNED in Chambers at the Palm Beach County Courthouse, West Palm Beach, Florida, on this 31st day of August, 2005.

KATHLEEN J. KROLL
Chief Judge

Adopted effective August 31, 2005.

12.301. ORDER TEMPORARILY ASSIGNING THE HONORABLE CAROLINE SHEPHERD AS AN ACTING CIRCUIT JUDGE

IN THE CIRCUIT COURT OF THE FIFTEENTH JUDICIAL CIRCUIT IN AND FOR PALM BEACH COUNTY, FLORIDA

ADMINISTRATIVE ORDER NO.: (2018)12.301–12/18

IN RE: ORDER TEMPORARILY ASSIGNING THE HONORABLE CAROLINE SHEPHERD AS AN ACTING CIRCUIT JUDGE

It is necessary for the orderly and prompt dispatch of cases within the jurisdiction of the Circuit Court that a County Court Judge be assigned to temporary duty as a Circuit Judge. Administrative Order 11.110–3/17 currently authorizes a County Court Judge to serve as a Circuit Judge.

NOW THEREFORE, pursuant to the authority conferred by Florida Rule of Judicial Administration 2.215, it is **ORDERED** as follows:

1. The Honorable Caroline Shepherd, Judge of the County Court in and for Palm Beach County, Florida, is hereby assigned effective January 1, 2019, to temporarily serve as a Circuit Judge for the Fifteenth Judicial Circuit of Florida for purposes of reviewing, hearing, and determining matters pending in the Trial Division.

2. Judge Caroline Shepherd is vested with all and singular powers and prerogatives conferred by the Constitution and laws of the State of Florida upon a Circuit Judge.

3. This order shall remain in full force and effect for six months from January 1, 2019.

DONE and **ORDERED** in Chambers at West Palm Beach, Palm Beach County, Florida, this 31st day of December, 2018.

Krista Marx
Chief Judge

Adopted effective January 1, 2019.

12.501. RESET OF FORECLOSURE SALES CANCELED DUE TO TROPICAL STORM ERIKA AUGUST 31, 2015

IN THE CIRCUIT COURT OF THE FIFTEENTH JUDICIAL CIRCUIT IN AND FOR PALM BEACH COUNTY, FLORIDA

ADMINISTRATIVE ORDER 15–12.501–9/15

IN RE: RESET OF FORECLOSURE SALES CANCELED DUE TO TROPICAL STORM ERIKA AUGUST 31, 2015

On Monday, August 31, 2015, Tropical Storm Erika caused the closure of the courts in the Fifteenth Judicial Circuit and resulted in the cancelation of the foreclosure sales scheduled on August 31, 2015.

NOW THEREFORE, pursuant to the authority conferred by Florida Rule of Judicial Administration 2.215 it is **ORDERED** as follows:

1. A list of cases wherein a sale date was scheduled for Monday, August 31, 2015, is attached hereto and incorporated herein as Exhibit A[1].

2. Foreclosure sales which were scheduled for August 31, 2015 shall be rescheduled by Plaintiff's counsel or a *pro* se plaintiff.

3. Plaintiff's counsel or a *pro se* plaintiff shall file a Motion to Reset Sale Date and schedule same on the Uniform Motion Calendar within 30 days from the date of this Administrative Order.

DONE and **ORDERED,** in Chambers, at West Palm Beach, Palm Beach County, Florida this 1 day of September, 2015.

Jeffrey J. Colbath
Chief Judge

Adopted effective September 1, 2015.

[1] Attachment not included.

12.502. PUBLICATION OF NON-CONFIDENTIAL RECORDS IN A CASE OF SIGNIFICANT PUBLIC INTEREST

IN THE CIRCUIT COURT OF THE FIFTEENTH JUDICIAL CIRCUIT IN AND FOR PALM BEACH COUNTY, FLORIDA

ADMINISTRATIVE ORDER NO. 12–12.502–3/12

IN RE: PUBLICATION OF NON-CONFIDENTIAL RECORDS IN A CASE OF SIGNIFICANT PUBLIC INTEREST

Supreme Court Administrative Order 07–49 permits the Chief Judge to direct that all non-confidential records in a case be made available electronically when the case is of significant public interest. Although it is not the prerogative of this Court to determine which pending case or cases could be considered of great public interest, the case of State v. Goodman, 2010CF005829AXXMB has been deemed to be a Special Interest/High Profile case pursuant to Fifteenth Judicial Circuit Administrative Order 2.208–2/09. Consequently and pursuant to the aforesaid Fifteenth Circuit Administrative Order, both a Media Committee and a High Profile Committee have been created to assist with the public dissemination of information in relation to the State v. Goodman case. To assist these committees in responding to the increased demand for public information in connection with this case, it does appear that it would ease the burden of providing public records to interested persons by having such public records available in an electronic fashion.

NOW, THEREFORE, pursuant to the authority conferred by Florida Rule of Judicial Administration 2.215, it is **ORDERED AND ADJUDGED** as follows:

When so requested by the trial judge in the case of State v. Goodman, the Clerk of Court shall make available on its website public records/court pleadings in case number 2010CF005829AXXMB.

DONE and **SIGNED** in Chambers at West Palm Beach, Palm Beach County, Florida, this 6 day of March, 2012.

Peter D. Blanc
Chief Judge

Adopted effective March 6, 2012.

12.503. INTERIM POLICY ON ELECTRONIC RELEASE OF COURT RECORDS

IN THE CIRCUIT COURT OF THE FIFTEENTH JUDICIAL CIRCUIT IN AND FOR PALM PEACH COUNTY

ADMINISTRATIVE ORDER 12–12.503–6/12 *

IN RE: INTERIM POLICY ON ELECTRONIC RELEASE OF COURT RECORDS

Due to the implementation of the Clerk and Comptroller's "Showcase" computer system, and the ability of the public to access imaged documents through Showcase at computer terminals within the courthouse, the need for the "EZ View System" is obsolete.

NOW, THEREFORE, pursuant to the authority conferred by Florida Rule of Judicial Administration 2.215, it is **ORDERED** as follows:

Administrative Order 07–12.015–2/07 which required the Clerk and Comptroller to maintain the EZ View Subscription System is hereby VACATED.

DONE and **ORDERED**, in Chambers, at West Palm Beach, Palm Beach County, Florida this 20 day of June, 2012.

Peter D. Blanc
Chief Judge

Adopted effective June 21, 2012.

* supersedes administrative order 07–12.015–2/07

12.509. RESET OF FORECLOSURE SALES CANCELED DUE TO TROPICAL STORM ISAAC ON AUGUST 27, 2012 AND AUGUST 28, 2012

IN THE CIRCUIT COURT OF THE FIFTEENTH JUDICIAL CIRCUIT IN AND FOR PALM BEACH COUNTY, FLORIDA

ADMINISTRATIVE ORDER 12–12.509–10/12

IN RE: RESET OF FORECLOSURE SALES CANCELED DUE TO TROPICAL STORM ISAAC ON AUGUST 27, 2012 AND AUGUST 28, 2012

On Monday, August 27, 2012, and Tuesday, August 28, 2012, Tropical Storm Isaac caused the closure of the courts in the Fifteenth Judicial Circuit; and resulted in the cancelation of the foreclosure sales scheduled during August 27, 2012 and August 28, 2012.

NOW THEREFORE, pursuant to the authority conferred by Florida Rule of Judicial Administration 2.215 it is **ORDERED** as follows:

1. A list of cases wherein a sale date was scheduled for August 27, 2012 and August 28, 2012 is attached hereto and incorporated herein as Exhibit A [1] and Exhibit B [2] respectively.

2. Foreclosure sales which were scheduled for August 27, 2012 and August 28, 2012 shall be rescheduled by Plaintiff's counsel or a *pro* se plaintiff

3. Plaintiff's counsel or a *pro se* plaintiff shall file a Motion to Reset Sale Date and schedule same on the Uniform Motion Calendar within 30 days from the date of this Administrative Order.

DONE and **ORDERED,** in Chambers, at West Palm Beach, Palm Beach County, Florida this 2 day of October, 2012.

Peter D. Blanc
Chief Judge

Adopted effective October 2, 2012.

1 Attachment not included.

2 Attachment not included.

12.703. ORDER PERMITTING CLERK TO ACCEPT PAPER FILINGS BY ATTORNEYS

IN THE CIRCUIT COURT OF THE FIFTEENTH JUDICIAL CIRCUIT IN AND FOR PALM BEACH COUNTY, FLORIDA

ADMINISTRATIVE ORDER NO.: 2017–12.703–9/17

IN RE: ORDER PERMITTING CLERK TO ACCEPT PAPER FILINGS BY ATTORNEYS

THIS MATTER came before the Court upon the request of the Clerk and Comptroller to accept paper filings by attorneys who are unable to file through the E–Portal due to power outages caused by Hurricane Irma.

NOW, THEREFORE, pursuant to the authority conferred by Florida Rule of Judicial Administration 2.215, it is **ORDERED** as follows:

The Clerk and Comptroller is hereby authorized to accept paper filings from attorneys/law offices that, at the time of filing, are without power due to Hurricane Irma.

DONE and **ORDERED** in Chambers at West Palm Beach, Palm Beach County, Florida, this 13 day of September, 2017.

Peter D. Blanc
Acting Chief Judge

Adopted effective September 13, 2017.

Seventeenth Judicial Circuit (Broward County)

LOCAL RULES

ADMINISTRATIVE ORDERS

CIVIL ORDERS

CRIMINAL ORDERS

COUNTY ORDERS

GENERAL ORDERS

2018–63–GEN. PROCEDURE FOR APPOINTMENT OF COUNSEL IN CRIMINAL AND CIVIL PROCEEDINGS.

2018–16–GEN. SEXUAL HARASSMENT POLICY AND COMPLAINT PROCEDURES FOR COURT EMPLOYEES AND OTHERS.

2018–15–GEN. SEXUAL HARASSMENT POLICY AND PROCEDURES FOR SEXUAL HARASSMENT COMPLAINTS AGAINST JUDGES.

2018–10–GEN. PROVISION OF ADA ACCOMMODATIONS.

2018–4–GEN. USE OF CELLULAR TELEPHONES AND OTHER PORTABLE ELECTRONIC DEVICES.

2017–33–GEN. AMENDED ADMINISTRATIVE ORDER REGARDING MOTIONS FOR REHEARING.

2016–8–GEN. PROFESSIONALISM PANEL.

2013–50–GEN. PROCEDURES FOR MEDICAL EXAMINER AS TO AUTOPSY RECORDS.

2013–26–GEN. PROCEDURES FOR E–FILING AND COURT RECORDS.

2011–22–GEN. REPORTING OF PROCEEDINGS REQUIRED BY LAW.

2011–15–GEN. COURT INTERPRETERS PROGRAM.

2010–81–GEN. PRO BONO COMMITTEE.

PROBATE ORDERS

2018–79–PRC. FINGERPRINTING OF GUARDIANS FOR CRIMINAL INVESTIGATIONS.

2018–58–PRC. PETITIONS FOR INJUNCTION FOR PROTECTION AGAINST EXPLOITATION OF A VULNERABLE ADULT.

2018–33–PRC. PILOT MEDIATION PROGRAM FOR INCAPACITY AND GUARDIANSHIP PROCEEDINGS.

2017–043–PRC. ADMINISTRATIVE ORDER REGARDING DELINQUENT AND NON–COMPLIANT GUARDIANSHIP REPORTS/DELINQUENT EDUCATIONAL CERTIFICATES/UNPAID AUDIT FEES.

2016–33–PRC. ADMINISTRATIVE ORDER AS TO BAKER ACT PROCEDURES.

2016–24–PRC. ADMINISTRATIVE ORDER ESTABLISHING EMERGENCY TEMPORARY GUARDIANSHIP PROCEDURES.

2011–26–PRC. ADMINISTRATIVE ORDER ESTABLISHING FILING PROCEDURES FOR THE PROBATE DIVISION.

2009–89–PRC. ADMINISTRATIVE ORDER REQUIRING CREDIT AND CRIMINAL BACKGROUND INVESTIGATION.

IV–07–B–1. REFERRAL OF GUARDIANSHIP FILES WHERE REQUIRED DOCUMENTS HAVE NOT BEEN FILED.

IV–06–A–16. ADULT ABUSE AND NEGLECT RECORDS AND GUARDIANSHIP APPLICATIONS.

IV–05–A–26. GUARDIANSHIP APPLICATIONS FOR APPOINTMENT AND DISCLOSURE STATEMENTS.

UNIFIED FAMILY ORDERS

2018–107–UFC. COLLABORATIVE DISPUTE RESOLUTION PILOT PROCESS.

2018–94–UFC. PROCEDURE FOR HEARINGS ON CHILD SUPPORT WRITS OF ARREST.

2018–87–UFC. 2018 UNIFIED FAMILY COURT PLAN.

2018–74–UFC. DOMESTIC VIOLENCE CASES.

2017–77–UFC. ADMINISTRATIVE ORDER ADOPTING AND AUTHORIZING THE USE OF A STATUS QUO TEMPORARY ORDER IN DISSOLUTION OF MARRIAGE AND PATERNITY ACTIONS IN THE SEVENTEENTH JUDICIAL CIRCUIT OF FLORIDA.

2017–19–UFC. ADMINISTRATIVE ORDER MANDATING PARENT EDUCATION AND FAMILY STABILIZATION COURSE.

2016–35–UFC. ADMINISTRATIVE ORDER AS TO JUVENILE DRUG COURT PROGRAM.

2016–6–UFC. ADMINISTRATIVE ORDER AS TO VOLUNTARY DEPENDENCY DRUG COURT PROGRAM.

2016–4–UFC. ADMINISTRATIVE ORDER ESTABLISHING EARLY CHILDHOOD COURT.

2015–11–UFC. ADMINISTRATIVE ORDER PROHIBITING DESTRUCTION OF UNIFIED FAMILY COURT DOMESTIC VIOLENCE COURT RECORDS.

2015–10–UFC. ADMINISTRATIVE ORDER ESTABLISHING PROCEDURES FOR FAMILY DIVISION EMERGENCY MATTERS.

2014–22–UFC. ADMINISTRATIVE ORDER AS TO DEPARTMENT OF REVENUE TITLE IV–D CASES.

2014-14-UFC. ADMINISTRATIVE ORDER DIRECTING CLERK OF COURTS WITH REGARD TO DISMISSED CIVIL OR FAMILY CASES.

2010–11–UFC [1]. SECOND AMENDED ADMINISTRATIVE ORDER ESTABLISHING PROCEDURE FOR APPOINTMENT OF CRIMINAL MENTAL HEALTH EVALUATORS.

2009–76–UFC. ADMINISTRATIVE ORDER REQUIRING ESTABLISHMENT SUPPORT DEPOSITORY ACCOUNT.

2008–141–UFC. ADMINISTRATIVE ORDER DESIGNATING DEPOSITORY FOR CHILD SUPPORT AND ALIMONY PAYMENTS.

V–06–N–1. JUDICIAL WAIVER OF PARENTAL NOTICE OF TERMINATION OF PREGNANCY.

Local Rules

RULE NO. 1A. COURT DIVISIONS

IN THE CIRCUIT COURT OF THE SEVENTEENTH JUDICIAL CIRCUIT, IN AND FOR BROWARD COUNTY, FLORIDA

LOCAL RULE NO. 1A

(Redrafted but unchanged)

IN RE:

COURT DIVISIONS

In accordance with the authority vested in the Chief Judge by Rule 2.050 of the Florida Rules of Judicial Administration, it is

ORDERED that:

Five divisions of the Circuit Court are created for the administration and management of court proceedings.

(1) General Civil Division

(2) Criminal Division

(3) Probate Division

(4) Juvenile Division

(5) Family Division

The Family Court Division hears all suits, proceedings, or matters that affect one family. These shall include dissolution of marriage, simplified dissolution of marriage, child custody and support, URESA, domestic violence, name changes, adoptions, paternity suits, modification proceedings, support without dissolution, and juvenile dependency.

DONE AND ORDERED in chambers in Fort Lauderdale, Broward County, Florida this 6th day of October, 1999.

/s/DALE ROSS
DALE ROSS, Chief Judge

RULE NO. 2B. ALTERNATIVE METHOD OF DRAWING JURY VENIRE PURSUANT TO 40.225, FLORIDA STATUTES

IN THE CIRCUIT COURT OF THE SEVENTEENTH JUDICIAL CIRCUIT, IN AND FOR BROWARD COUNTY, FLORIDA

LOCAL RULE 2B

IN RE: ALTERNATIVE METHOD OF DRAWING JURY VENIRE PURSUANT TO 40.225, FLORIDA STATUTES

/

WHEREAS, the source of jury selection in the Seventeenth Judicial Circuit, in and for Broward County, Florida is defined by Chapter 40, Florida Statutes.

WHEREAS, the source list for jury selection shall be certified by the Clerk of the Circuit Court of the Seventeenth Judicial Circuit in and for Broward County (the "Clerk").

WHEREAS, the Clerk's Technology Department is designated the official custodian of the computer files to be used in the selection of petit and grand juries and shall at all times be charged with seeing that the files and equipment to be used in such selection are not accessible to anyone other than those directly involved in the selection of venire as herein provided.

It is hereby RESOLVED:

A. The Clerk, in accordance with Florida Statutes, Chapter 40.02(3), shall direct the Clerk's Technology Department to rebuild the Jury Master file in the following manner:

1. The source file that is used to create the Jury Master file in the IBM 3090 mainframe is maintained by the Office of Information Technology of Broward County. Upon completion of the creation of the Jury Master file, the source tape is copied to tape storage for the purpose of certification and is kept secure by the Clerk.

2. Upon the direction of the Chief Judge or his designee, pursuant to the provisions of Chapter 40.221 and Chapter 40.02(3), Florida Statutes, the Director of Jury Administration enters the jury requirements for a selection into his/her computer terminal. The Clerk approves all requirements prior to the selection process. The Clerk's Technology Department requests the Office of Information Technology to run the Jury Selection process based on a predefined schedule. All jurors previously deferred to the current selection date are added to the file. Once the deferrals are added to the file, the remainder of jurors needed from the Master file are randomly selected in accordance with random number generator (See Attachment A for random selection method). These jurors are added to the Jury Pool file which contains the jurors summoned for the year. Following the selection process, summonses are produced, passed through a glue-folder and mailed.

B. Security is essential to the selection process. In order to control unauthorized personnel from entering the computer facility, electronic security measures are enforced using a key card. Individual key cards are monitored through a centralized database. All software applications are protected by a computerized password security system.

DONE AND ORDERED, in chambers in Fort Lauderdale, Broward County, Florida this 1st day of July, 2004.

/s/DALE ROSS
DALE ROSS, Chief Judge

SEVENTEENTH JUDICIAL CIRCUIT

Attachment A

Juror Selection Random Number Generation Procedure

The computer program which generates random numbers, used for the selection of jurors, was provided by the Florida State Court Administrator's Office. The formula was developed by Dr. G. Marsaglia and B. Narasimhan of Florida State University.

Seed Generation

At the beginning of each year a file is built containing a record for each julian day (1–365) and 4 seed values associated with each day. The seed values are derived from a list provided by the State Court Administrator's Office.

When the selection process is initiated the current julian day (stored in the computer) is matched with the associated record in the julian date file and the four seed values are utilized to begin the random number generation.

Algorithm

The attached paper 'Toward A Universal Random Number Generator' authored by Dr. George Marsaglia, explains the algorithm used to generate random numbers.

RULE NO. 3. TRAFFIC VIOLATIONS BUREAU COURT COSTS, TRAFFIC AND MISDEMEANOR CASES

IN THE CIRCUIT COURT OF THE SEVENTEENTH JUDICIAL CIRCUIT, IN AND FOR BROWARD COUNTY, FLORIDA

LOCAL RULE NO. 3

IN RE:

TRAFFIC VIOLATIONS BUREAU :
COURT COSTS, TRAFFIC AND :
MISDEMEANOR CASES :

In accordance with the authority vested in the Chief Judge by Rule 2.050 of the Florida Rules of Judicial Administration, it is

ORDERED that:

1. Pursuant to Rule 6.100(a) Florida Rules of Practice and Procedure for Traffic Courts, there is hereby established a Traffic Violations Bureau within the office of the Clerk of the County Court, which bureau shall perform such duties as are prescribed by said rule.

2. In accordance with the provisions of Rule 6.470(b), Florida Rules of Practice and Procedure for Traffic Courts, in cases where no hearing is required or held and the offender admits the commission of the offense by forfeiting a bond or paying the penalty, the following costs shall be deducted from the penalty by the Traffic Violations Bureau:

(a) Three dollars for all infractions of bicycle regulations, Section 316.11, Florida Statutes, and infractions of pedestrian regulations, Section 316.057, Florida Statutes.

(b) Six dollars for all non-moving traffic infractions, and

(c) Ten dollars for all moving infractions.

DONE AND ORDERED in chambers in Fort Lauderdale, Broward County, Florida this First day of November, 1988.

/s/MIETTE K. BURNSTEIN
MIETTE K. BURNSTEIN, Chief Judge

RULE NO. 4. APPROVAL OF NATIONAL HIGHWAY SAFETY COUNCIL DEFENSIVE DRIVING COURSE

IN THE CIRCUIT COURT OF THE SEVENTEENTH JUDICIAL CIRCUIT, IN AND FOR BROWARD COUNTY, FLORIDA

LOCAL RULE NO. 4

IN RE:

APPROVAL OF NATIONAL HIGHWAY :
SAFETY COUNCIL DEFENSIVE :
DRIVING COURSE :

In accordance with the authority vested in the Chief Judge by Rule 2.050 of the Florida Rules of Judicial Administration, it is

ORDERED that:

Pursuant to the provisions of Rule 6.110(a), Florida Rules of Practice and Procedure for Traffic Courts, the Defensive Driving course sponsored by the National Highway Safety Council is approved as a school to which attendance may be required by a court handling traffic cases and infractions, or to which attendance may be elected by persons cited for non-mandatory appearance traffic infractions.

Any other school or course may apply to the Chief Judge for designation as an approved school by submitting its credentials and course program in writing to the Court Administrator, who shall evaluate same and recommend approval or disapproval thereof to the Chief Judge. Any school disapproved by the Chief Judge may appeal such decision by petition to the Traffic Court Review Committee, as authorized by Rule 6.110(b).

DONE AND ORDERED in chambers in Fort Lauderdale, Broward County, Florida this First day of November, 1988.

/s/MIETTE K. BURNSTEIN
MIETTE K. BURNSTEIN, Chief Judge

RULE NO. 5. APPROVAL OF D.W.I. COUNTERATTACK SCHOOL

IN THE CIRCUIT COURT OF THE SEVENTEENTH JUDICIAL CIRCUIT, IN AND FOR BROWARD COUNTY, FLORIDA

LOCAL RULE NO. 5

IN RE:

APPROVAL OF D.W.I. :
COUNTERATTACK SCHOOL :

In accordance with the authority vested in the Chief Judge by Rule 2.050 of the Florida Rules of Judicial Administration, it is

ORDERED that:

Pursuant to the provisions of Rule 6.110(a), Florida Rules of Practice and Procedure for Traffic Courts, the D.W.I. Counterattack School operated by the Broward County Commission on Alcoholism, Inc., is designated as an approved school to which attendance may be required by the Courts of this circuit.

A copy of the annual audit furnished by said school to the Florida D.W.I. Counterattack School shall be simultaneously furnished to the Court Administrator of the Seventeenth Judicial Circuit.

DONE AND ORDERED in chambers in Fort Lauderdale, Broward County, Florida this First day of November, 1988.

/s/MIETTE K. BURNSTEIN
MIETTE K. BURNSTEIN, Chief Judge

RULE NO. 7. VACATED AND SUPERSEDED BY ADMINISTRATIVE ORDER NO. 2010–47–GEN

RULE NO. 8. ORDERS FOR SIGNATURE–CIVIL DIVISION

IN THE CIRCUIT COURT OF THE SEVENTEENTH JUDICIAL CIRCUIT, IN AND FOR BROWARD COUNTY, FLORIDA

LOCAL RULE NO. 8

IN RE:

ORDERS FOR SIGNATURE :
Civil Division :
:

In accordance with the authority vested in the Chief Judge by Rule 2.050 of the Florida Rules of Judicial Administration, it is

ORDERED that:

In addition to the requirements of Rule 1.080 (h) (1), Florida Rules of Civil Procedure, a party submitting an Order or Judgment shall furnish the Court with sufficient copies together with stamped envelopes addressed to all parties entitled to receive a copy.

Proposed Orders or Judgments must be furnished opposing counsel prior to submission to the court. Proposed orders or judgments must be titled to conform with the motion to which it refers. Language in the order or judgment not agreed as conforming to the court's pronouncement shall be brought to the attention of the court.

The proposed order shall indicate date of the hearing on which the order is predicated.

Attorneys for the movant shall have at Motion Calendar Hearings all proposed orders and judgments together with the appropriate stamped envelopes where applicable.

Unless the Court directs otherwise, proposed orders on non–Motion Calendar Hearings must be prepared by the prevailing or designated counsel and submitted to the Court for consideration within 48 hours after said hearing. Copies of all such orders, after entry, shall be conformed and mailed by the Clerk of Court, or the judge's secretary, within 48 hours.

Final judgments pursuant to a jury verdict shall be submitted to the Court for its consideration within 48 hours following rendition of said verdict.

DONE AND ORDERED in chambers in Fort Lauderdale, Broward County, Florida this 1st day of June, 1989.

/s/MIETTE K. BURNSTEIN
MIETTE K. BURNSTEIN, Chief Judge

RULE NO. 10A. UNIFORM MOTION CALENDAR, EX PARTE MOTIONS TO COMPEL DISCOVERY, AND SCHEDULING OF SPECIAL SET HEARINGS FOR CIRCUIT CIVIL AND FAMILY HEARINGS

IN THE CIRCUIT COURT OF THE SEVENTEENTH JUDICIAL CIRCUIT, IN AND FOR BROWARD COUNTY, FLORIDA

LOCAL RULE NO. 10A

IN RE: UNIFORM MOTION CALENDAR, EX PARTE MOTIONS TO COMPEL DISCOVERY, AND SCHEDULING OF SPECIAL SET HEARINGS FOR CIRCUIT CIVIL AND FAMILY HEARINGS

In accordance with the authority vested in the Chief Judge by Rule 2.215(e) of the Florida Rules of Judicial Administration, it is **ORDERED** that:

UNIFORM MOTION CALENDAR

1. The Circuit Court Judges of the general civil/family divisions (excluding juvenile/dependency) shall maintain a uniform motion calendar from 8:45 A.M. to 9:30 A.M., Monday through Thursday. Business and Complex Litigation divisions shall set any motion calendars per their procedures. All parties shall be prepared to proceed at 8:45 A.M., and if one party fails to timely appear, the matter may proceed on the merits in that party's absence. A party is defined as: (1) any entity or individual that is represented by counsel; or (2) any self-represented person.

2. All motions set on motion calendar shall be scheduled electronically using the 17th Judicial Circuit Online Scheduling System, which can be found at http://www.17th.flcourts.org/index.php/self-help/online-scheduling. Any person scheduling a motion calendar shall set same a minimum of five (5) days in advance of the hearing: Self-represented parties may obtain permission to utilize the Online Scheduling System. Prior to setting any matter on uniform motion calendar, the party or parties noticing the motion shall attempt to resolve the matter by direct communication with all parties, and shall also certify a good faith attempt to resolve or narrow the issues contained in the motion. Direct communication means by oral or written communication, including by telephone, in person, email, or text messaging. All time requirements regarding the scheduling of hearings shall be governed by the Florida Rules of Civil Procedure, Florida Family Law Rules of Procedure, or Florida Rules of Judicial Administration, as applicable.

3. All persons scheduling cases on motion calendar or special set hearings shall review the practices and procedures of the assigned judge at http://www.17th.flcourts.org. As a matter of courtesy to the court, the moving party shall bring to the uniform motion calendar hearing a hard copy of the motion(s), pleading(s), or underlying document(s) that is/are the subject of the hearing. Failure to comply with this requirement of Rule 10A may result in sanctions, including an award of attorney's fees, or the suspension of online scheduling privileges.

4. To comply with the above good faith certification, every party scheduling a motion for a uniform motion calendar hearing **shall** execute the following certification in the body of the notice of hearing: *I hereby certify that A) the movant has conferred or attempted to confer with all parties or self-represented parties who may be affected by the relief sought in the motion in a good faith effort to resolve the issues raised in the motion; and B) the issues in the motion may be heard and resolved by the court within five (5) minutes.*

5. Cancelling Motion Calendar Hearings. The scheduling party **shall** utilize the Online Scheduling System to cancel any hearing. The filing of a notice of cancellation, without also cancelling using the Online Scheduling System, is insufficient to cancel a uniform motion calendar hearing. Only the scheduling party or the court may cancel a uniform motion calendar hearing. The cancelling party shall also generate an email advising all parties of the cancellation of the hearing. It is the responsibility of all parties to check their email regarding the cancellation of hearings. Cancelling pending uniform motion calendar hearings in this manner is a courtesy to other parties who may schedule their matter in the cancelled time slot.

6. Hearings requiring the presentation of evidence are **NOT** permitted on uniform motion calendar, unless permitted by the division judge. Additionally, multiple discovery matters, including lengthy or complex disputes regarding interrogatories or requests for production, that exceed the five (5) minute limitation on uniform motion calendar hearings, **shall** not be scheduled on uniform motion calendar, unless otherwise permitted by the assigned judge. However, motions to approve minor settlements in civil cases may be scheduled on uniform motion calendar. Any motion to withdraw from a case must evidence service on the client.

7. Ex parte matters, non-evidentiary motions, and uncontested proceedings for adoptions, paternity, or dissolution of marriage may be heard on uniform motion calendar, provided such matters can be heard and resolved by the court in five (5) minutes, as required by the certification in paragraph 4 above.

8. No more than a total of two (2) matters per case may be scheduled on any one uniform motion calendar day, unless otherwise approved by the division judge. Parties shall review each Judge's practices and procedures for guidance. This information can be found at http://www.17th.flcourts.org.

9. Any party requesting relief shall bring to the uniform motion calendar hearing a prepared proposed order with sufficient copies for all parties. The party submitting the order(s) for entry by the court shall be responsible to serve such order(s) on all interested parties, as required by applicable rules of the Florida Rules of Judicial Administration.

10. Judges have limits on the number of cases that can be scheduled using the Online Scheduling System. If you are unable to schedule your matter on a specific date, it is likely because the docket is full and there are no additional time slots available. Please schedule on an alternate date.

11. Agreed Orders. All agreed orders shall be uploaded and transmitted to the court via the 17th Circuit Court agreed order portal. Information relating to uploading an agreed order can be found at http://www.17th.flcourts.org/index.php/self-help/eorders. Agreed orders that are permitted to be uploaded, include: (1) orders which are agreed as to the form and content; (2) Local Rule 10A ex parte orders; (3) orders which are the result of a ruling by the court in which the language is agreed to by all parties; (4) final judgments approved by the court at a hearing; (5) any order which a judge orders a party to submit via the online agreed order portal; and (6) orders re-validating subpoenas for trial. No correspondence should be uploaded with any agreed order. Any final order or final judgment approving a stipulation for dismissal or settlement agreement shall not be uploaded for approval until the stipulation or settlement agreement is electronically filed and accepted by the Clerk of Court.

12. When a motion to compel alleges a complete failure to respond or object to discovery, and no request for extension has been filed, an ex parte order may be entered requiring compliance with the original discovery demand within ten (10) days of the execution of the order. The moving party must submit a proposed order via the 17th Judicial Circuit online agreed order portal indicating a complete failure to respond to the discovery citing non-compliance with Local Rule 10A. Any ex parte discovery order under this rule shall not contain language regarding attorney's fees. Sanctions may be imposed if discovery is not completed within ten (10) days from the date the judge executes the ex parte order.

SPECIAL SET HEARINGS

1. All matters, other than uniform motion calendar hearings, shall be scheduled in accordance with the practices and procedures of each individual judge. This information can be found at http://www.17th.flcourts.org. All pleadings, affidavits, or other materials shall be provided to the court as required by each judge's published practices and procedures. The parties are directed to comply with all time requirements as set forth in the Florida Rules of Civil Procedure, Florida Family Law Rules of Procedure, or the Florida Rules of Judicial Administration, as applicable.

2. Cancelling Special Set Hearings. It shall be the responsibility of the scheduling party to utilize the Online Scheduling System to cancel any hearing set using the Online Scheduling System. The filing of a notice of cancellation, without also cancelling using the Online Scheduling System, is insufficient to cancel a special set hearing. The cancelling party shall also generate an email advising all parties and the court's judicial assistant of the cancellation of the hearing. It is the responsibility of all parties to check their email regarding the cancellation of hearings. Any special set hearing that is scheduled by the court may only be cancelled when: (1) the parties have reached an agreement on the matter(s) subject of the specially set hearing; (2) there exists an emergency; or (3) the court has approved the cancellation. Cancelling in this manner is a courtesy to other litigants who may schedule their matter in the cancelled time slot. Email addresses for each division can be located on each individual judge's practices and procedures webpage on the Seventeenth Judicial Circuit's website.

3. All special set hearings shall contain the following language in the body of the notice of hearing: *I hereby certify that I have made a good faith attempt to resolve this matter by having direct communication about the matter with all parties, prior to my noticing this motion for hearing.* Direct communication means by oral or written communication, including by telephone, in person, email, or text messaging.

4. Prior to appearing before the court, the parties shall have direct communication regarding the issues raised in the pending motion, and all parties shall be prepared to certify at the hearing that they have made a good faith effort to resolve the issues, as required to be included in the notice of hearing by paragraph (3) above.

5. Failure to comply with the procedures designated in Local Rule 10A may result in a hearing being stricken from the docket, suspension of online scheduling privileges, an award of attorney's fees, or such other sanction as may be permitted by Florida law or other rules of court.

MOTIONS FOR EMERGENCY RELIEF

1. Any motion seeking emergency relief as to any circuit civil or family matter shall comply with existing Administrative Orders governing emergencies, which can be found at http://www.17th.flcourts.org/index.php/rules-and-policies/administrative-orders.

DONE AND ORDERED in Fort Lauderdale, Broward County, Florida, on ________.

Jack Tuter, Chief Judge

Amended effective January 23, 2018.

RULE NO. 11. COUNTY COURT CIVIL EX PARTE MOTIONS TO COMPEL DISCOVERY AND SPECIAL SET HEARINGS

IN THE CIRCUIT COURT OF THE SEVENTEENTH JUDICIAL CIRCUIT, IN AND FOR BROWARD COUNTY, FLORIDA

LOCAL RULE NO. 11

IN RE:

COUNTY COURT CIVIL :
EX PARTE MOTIONS TO COMPEL :
DISCOVERY AND SPECIAL SET HEARINGS :

In accordance with the authority vested in the Chief Judge by Florida Rule of Judicial Administration 2.050, it is

ORDERED that:

EX PARTE MOTIONS TO COMPEL DISCOVERY

1. When a motion to compel discovery alleges a complete failure to respond or object to discovery, and there has been no request for extension, a county judge may enter an ex parte order requiring compliance with the original discovery demand within ten (10) days of entry of the order. Movant shall submit the proposed order and the envelopes. Sanctions may be imposed if discovery is not completed within ten (10) days from the date of entry of the ex parte order, necessitating a hearing on a motion to compel, or if a party fails to appear for a properly noticed hearing on a motion to compel.

SPECIAL SET HEARINGS

2. Special set hearings in county court may only be canceled by parties if an agreement on the merits has been reached and the parties have entered into a written stipulation or with court approval.

3. Prior to setting a special set hearing, the party or attorney noticing the motion for hearing shall attempt to resolve the matter and shall certify the good faith attempt to resolve.

4. To comply with the above, every attorney setting a hearing shall execute the following certification: I hereby certify that I have made a good faith attempt to resolve this matter prior to my noticing this motion for hearing.

5. Prior to appearing before the court, the parties shall discuss the issues raised in the pending motion, and both parties shall be prepared to certify at the hearing they have made a good faith effort to resolve the issues.

6. Failure to comply with the procedures designated in the above paragraphs may result in the hearing being stricken from the docket or such other sanctions as the court deems appropriate.

DONE AND ORDERED in Fort Lauderdale, Broward County, Florida this 29th day of June, 2001.

/s/DALE ROSS
DALE ROSS, Chief Judge

Administrative Orders

Civil Orders

2018–76–CIV. VOLUNTEER PROFESSIONALISM AND CIVILITY MAGISTRATE PILOT PROGRAM

IN THE CIRCUIT COURT OF THE SEVENTEENTH JUDICIAL CIRCUIT IN AND FOR BROWARD COUNTY, FLORIDA

Administrative Order 2018–76–Civ / 2018–76–UFC

ADMINISTRATIVE ORDER AUTHORIZING VOLUNTEER PROFESSIONALISM AND CIVILITY MAGISTRATE PILOT PROGRAM

(a) Pursuant to Article V, section 2(d) of the Florida Constitution, and section 43.26, Florida Statutes, the chief judge of each judicial circuit is charged with the authority and the power to do everything necessary to promote the prompt and efficient administration of justice.

(b) In order to promote professionalism and civility among lawyers appearing in the Seventeenth Judicial Circuit, and in accordance with the authority vested in the chief judge by Article V, section 2(d) of the Florida Constitution, section 43.26, Florida Statutes, and Florida Rule of Judicial Administration 2.215, it is hereby **ORDERED**:

(1) A Professionalism and Civility Magistrate Pilot Program (the "Program") is hereby created for Circuit Civil and Unified Family Court matters, as set forth in this Administrative Order.

(2) *Purpose*. The purpose of the Program is to promote and better enforce the appropriate level of professionalism and civility among the lawyers practicing in the Circuit Civil divisions of the Seventeenth Judicial Circuit.

(3) The Large Law Firm Committee of the Broward County Bar Association (the "Committee") will create and maintain a list of attorneys willing to volunteer their time to serve as Magistrates (the "List"). The List shall include the name of the attorney, and his or her address, telephone number, and email address. Attorneys will be invited to participate as a Magistrate by the Committee through: (i) direct invitation by the Committee; or (ii) advertisement in the Broward County Bar Association Barrister. Magistrates will serve on a volunteer basis and will receive no compensation for their service. The Committee shall provide a copy of the List to the Chief Judge and the Circuit Judges participating in the Program on the first business day of each month.

(4) The Committee shall ensure that each attorney that is approved to serve as a Magistrate satisfies the requirements set forth herein and is otherwise qualified to serve as a Magistrate. Each Magistrate must have a minimum of twenty (20) years of civil litigation experience and have his or her primary office location in Broward County, Florida.

(5) A Magistrate may be appointed by a Circuit Court Judge presiding in a civil division participating in the Program in appropriate cases where the parties' dispute arises from a lack of civility in the courtroom, discovery or other interaction with counsel that undermines the integrity or professionalism of the legal profession, including:

a. Non-routine discovery disputes involving conduct that has occurred on more than one occasion;

b. Non-routine discovery disputes where one party and/or counsel's conduct is the subject of multiple motions by the opposing party;

c. Conduct that is the subject of a motion for sanctions that the court determines may have prima facie merit based on the parties' written submissions; and

d. Repetitive disregard for scheduling protocols consistent with the presiding judge's practices and procedures, and applicable local rules and Florida Rules of Civil Procedure.

(6) The required order of appointment is attached hereto as Attachment "A".[1] Upon notification of his or her appointment, the Magistrate shall, within ten (10) days of the date of the order of appointment, conduct a conflict check and notify the presiding judge whether he or she accepts the appointment by filing a "Notice of Acceptance of Appointment" with the Clerk of the Court. Each party shall have three (3) business days from the entry of the order of appointment to file an objection. Any objection to the appointment shall be resolved by the assigned division judge. If neither party files an objection to the order of appointment, the parties are deemed to have consented to the appointment.

(7) Within five (5) business days of acceptance by the Magistrate of the appointment, the Magistrate shall provide the parties, via email, with a schedule for written submissions and a hearing date. Within five (5) business days of the Magistrate's initial email, each party shall electronically file with the Clerk of the Court and serve their initial position paper, with a courtesy copy provided to the Magistrate via email. Within five (5) business days of submission of the initial position papers, each party shall electronically file with the Clerk of the Court and serve a response brief, with courtesy copies provided to the Magistrate via email. The time for filing initial and response briefs may be modified by the Magistrate as appropriate.

(8) A hearing shall be held before the Magistrate within ten (10) business days of the filing of the parties' response briefs. The hearing will be held at the Magistrate's office and shall be limited to one (1) hour in duration, unless otherwise ordered by the Magistrate. The parties may present oral argument and submit affidavits or live testimony, as needed and permitted by the Magistrate. The Magistrate shall retain any documents or evidence submitted that is not otherwise electronically filed and part of the court record. The attendance at the hearing by an attorney's client is permitted, but is not mandatory. The plaintiff shall be responsible for securing the services of a court reporter, with the eventual cost of such services to be taxed as determined by the Magistrate.

(9) The Magistrate shall issue and file with the Clerk of the Court a Report and Recommendation ("R&R") within ten (10)

business days of the hearing, with courtesy copies to the parties and the referring judge. The R&R may include a suggested award of attorney's fees and costs or other relief, including:

a. The appointment of a special master for ruling on discovery issues or presiding over depositions;

b. The implementation of special procedures for communication between counsel;

c. Other relief as appropriate under the circumstances.

(10) Any objection(s) to the R&R shall be filed within ten (10) days of the date of the R&R. Upon timely filed objections to the R&R, the referring judge may set the matter for a hearing in his or her discretion. If objections to the R&R are not timely filed, the referring judge may take appropriate action and issue any orders pertaining to the R&R.

(11) The Chief Judge will determine which Circuit Civil and Unified Family Court Divisions shall participate in the Program.

(12) This Administrative Order supersedes and vacates Administrative Orders 2018–72–Civ and 2018–72–UFC.

DONE AND ORDERED in Chambers, Fort Lauderdale, Florida, Broward County, Florida, this 4th day of September, 2018.

Jack Tuter
Chief Judge

1 Attachment A not included.

2018–46–CIV. PETITIONS FOR RISK PROTECTION ORDERS

IN THE CIRCUIT COURT OF THE SEVENTEENTH JUDICIAL CIRCUIT IN AND FOR BROWARD COUNTY, FLORIDA

Administrative Order 2018–46–Civ

ADMINISTRATIVE ORDER GOVERNING PETITIONS FOR RISK PROTECTION ORDERS PURSUANT TO SECTION 790.401, FLA. STAT.

(a) Pursuant to Article V, section 2(d) of the Florida Constitution, and section 43.26, Florida Statutes, the chief judge of each judicial circuit is charged with the authority and the power to do everything necessary to promote the prompt and efficient administration of justice.

(b) Florida Rule of Judicial Administration 2.215(b)(3) states the chief judge "shall, considering available resources, ensure the efficient and proper administration of all courts within [this] circuit."

(c) On March 9, 2018, Governor Rick Scott signed into law Senate Bill 7026, also known as the Marjory Stoneman Douglas High School Public Safety Act, which, among other things, enacted section 790.401, Florida Statutes, and amended certain provisions of Florida's Baker Act.

(d) Section 790.401, Florida Statutes, as enacted by the Florida Legislature, permits law enforcement agencies and officers to file a petition with the Circuit Court for the issuance of a Risk Protection Order. The statute requires the Clerk of the Court and the petitioning party to provide certain information to the Court.

(e) In accordance with the authority vested in the chief judge by Article V, section 2(d) of the Florida Constitution, section 43.26, Florida Statutes, and Florida Rule of Judicial Administration 2.215, it is hereby **ORDERED**:

I. Duties of the Clerk of the Court, Section 790.401, Florida Statutes

(1) Upon receipt of a newly-filed petition for risk protection order, the Clerk of the Court shall conduct a search of its records to determine if the respondent:

a. has had prior, or is currently involved in, any mental health or Baker Act cases;

b. was or currently is a Respondent in an action for a Risk Protection Order;

c. was or currently is the subject of a no contact order issued in an action for stalking, domestic, sexual, or dating violence under sections 741.30, 784.046, or 784.0485, Florida Statutes; or

d. was or currently is a defendant in a criminal action, including misdemeanor, felony, or traffic infraction cases.

(2) After conducting the searches set out above, the Clerk of the Court shall immediately file with the Court a certificate of compliance listing the case number(s) of the related case(s) found or certifying no prior or pending cases could be found after a diligent search. The Clerk of the Court shall utilize the "Certificate of Compliance" form attached hereto as Attachment "A."

(3) Upon receipt of a newly-filed petition for a risk protection order, the Clerk of the Court shall inform the Court of the filing by sending a notification to RPO@17th.flcourts.org, which shall include the case number.

(4) All petitions for risk protection orders shall be designated RPO by the Clerk of the Court and assigned to judicial divisions as directed by the Chief Judge or designee.

(5) Upon issuance of an order required to be served pursuant to section 790.401(5)(a), Florida Statutes, the Clerk of the Court shall forward a certified copy of the order and a copy of the law enforcement agency's petition to the petitioning law enforcement agency or the Broward Sheriff's Office, as applicable, for service by such agency.

(6) The Clerk of the Court shall, within three (3) business days after the issuance of a temporary *ex parte* or final risk protection order, forward a copy of the order and all available identifying information concerning the respondent to the Florida Department of Agriculture and Consumer Affairs.

II. Duties of the Petitioner, Section 790.401, Florida Statutes

(1) In determining whether grounds exist for the issuance of a risk protection order, including a temporary *ex parte* risk protection order, the court may consider any relevant evidence, including evidence relating to factors set forth in section 790.401(3)(c), Florida Statutes. Prior to filing a petition for a risk protection order, including a request for an *ex parte* risk protection order, the petitioning agency shall conduct a

search of law enforcement databases to determine whether the respondent:

a. has, within the past twelve (12) months, committed an act or threat of violence against himself/herself or others;

b. has or has had in the past, serious or recurring mental health issues;

c. was or currently is, a respondent in an action for a risk protection order and whether he/she violated a prior risk protection order;

d. was or currently is, the subject of a no contact order issued under sections 741.30, 784.046, or 784.0485, Florida Statutes;

e. has used or has threatened to use, a weapon against himself/herself or others;

f. has unlawfully or recklessly displayed or brandished a firearm;

g. has threatened physical force against or stalked another person;

h. in this State, or any other State, was arrested, convicted, had adjudication withheld or pled nolo contendere to a crime involving violence or a threat of violence;

i. has a history of abusing alcohol or controlled substances; and

j. recently acquired a firearm or ammunition.

(2) If the petitioning law enforcement agency discovers any of the above information or other relevant evidence during its search of law enforcement databases, the petitioning agency shall file such information with the Clerk of the Court, unless already included in its' petition.

(3) All petitions for a risk protection order shall:

a. allege the respondent poses a significant danger of causing personal injury to himself/herself or others by having a firearm or ammunition in his/her custody or control or by purchasing, possessing, or receiving a firearm or any ammunition;

b. be accompanied by an affidavit, based on *personal knowledge*, setting forth the specific statements, actions, or facts that give rise to a reasonable fear of significant dangerous acts by the respondent;

c. identify the quantities, types, and location of all firearms and ammunition the petitioner believes to be in the respondent's current ownership, possession, custody, or control, or the attempts by the petitioning agency to identify and investigate whether the respondent owns, controls, or possesses firearms or ammunition; and

d. identify whether there is a known existing protection order governing the respondent under sections 741.30, 784.046, or 784.0485, Florida Statutes, or under any other applicable statute.

(4) The petitioning agency shall attach to its petition a physical description and location of the respondent. The law enforcement agency shall use a form that is substantially similar to Attachment "B."

(5) Upon service of any paper required to be served under section 790.401(5)(a), Florida Statutes, the law enforcement agency effecting service shall file a return of service with the Clerk of the Court as prescribed by the Florida Rules of Civil Procedure.

(6) Within seventy-two (72) hours of service of a temporary *ex parte* or final risk protection order, the law enforcement officer or agency taking possession of any firearm or ammunition owned by the respondent, or a license to carry a concealed weapon or firearm issued under section 790.06, Florida Statutes, shall issue a receipt identifying all firearms and the quantity and type of ammunition that has been surrendered, and any concealed weapons license surrendered, and shall file said receipt with the Clerk of the Court.

III. General Provisions

(1) The Clerk of the Court, any law enforcement agency or officer located within Broward County, and the judicial officers and staff of the Seventeenth Judicial Circuit, may communicate via electronic means as prescribed by the Florida Rules of Judicial Administration on any matter relating to notification of petitions for risk protection orders or service of risk protections orders.

(2) All law enforcement agencies filing petitions for risk protection orders pursuant to section 790.401, Florida Statutes, shall provide the Clerk of the Court and Court Administration Office of the General Counsel an email address for communications pertaining to service and notification of petitions for risk protection orders. The email address shall be provided to the Court's designated risk protection order email address at RPO@17th.flcourts.org, and to the Clerk of the Court designated risk protection order email address at RPO@browardclerk.org.

(3) When requested by a law enforcement agency authorized to effect service under section 790.401, Florida Statutes, the Clerk of the Court may transmit to the petitioning agency via email, facsimile or other electronic transmission permitted under the Florida Rules of Judicial Administration, a copy of any pleading or order required to be served under section 790.401, Florida Statutes.

(4) Pending approval of final forms from the Office of the State Courts Administrator as required by section 790.401(14), petitioning law enforcement agencies or officers shall utilize the interim template petition attached hereto as Attachment "C."

(5) Upon the filing of a petition for a temporary *ex parte* risk protection order, the court must conduct an *ex parte* hearing on the day the petition is filed or on the next business day. Unless ordered otherwise, all *ex parte* hearings contemplated under section 790.401, Florida Statutes shall be conducted by telephonic conference. All *ex parte* hearings will be scheduled by the Court and it shall be the responsibility of the petitioning party to make the affiant or affiants of the petition available for a telephonic conference call as prescribed by the Court. Upon notification of the date and time for the *ex parte* hearing, the petitioning law enforcement agency shall provide the Court with a direct telephone number or conference call-in information to RPO@17th.flcourts.org.

(6) Three (3) day return hearings relating to the surrender of firearms or ammunition may be conducted by telephone, in person or as otherwise ordered by the presiding judge. The Court may cancel the three (3) day return hearing based on

the filing of an affidavit demonstrating that the respondent is in compliance with the *ex parte* or final order.

(7) The petitioning agency and the Clerk of the Court shall comply with the requirements of Florida Rules of Judicial Administration pertaining to the confidentiality of court records, including the filing by the petitioning agency of appropriate notices of filing confidential information. In cases involving a juvenile respondent, the Court will strive to balance a juvenile's right to privacy against public safety. In order to effect service of process under section 790.401, Florida Statutes, a juvenile respondent shall be identified by full name.

This Administrative Order supersedes and vacates Administrative Order 2018–27–Civ.

DONE AND ORDERED in Chambers, Fort Lauderdale, Broward County, Florida, this 1st day of June, 2018.

Jack Tuter
Chief Judge

Attachment "A"
IN THE CIRCUIT COURT OF THE SEVENTEENTH JUDICIAL CIRCUIT IN AND FOR BROWARD COUNTY, FLORIDA

Petitioner,

v. Case Number: RPO
Judge:

Respondent.

______________________/

CLERK'S CERTIFICATE OF COMPLIANCE PURSUANT TO ADMINISTRATIVE ORDER 2018–27–CIV

I HEREBY certify that pursuant to Administrative Order 2018–27–Civ, "Administrative Order Governing Petitions for Risk Protection Orders Pursuant to Section 790.401, Fla. Stat.," the Clerk has conducted a search for all previous and currently pending cases involving the Respondent.

☐ Listed below are all of the aforementioned cases involving the Respondent:

☐ After a diligent search and inquiry of the Clerk's records, there are no previous or currently pending cases involving the Respondent.

Brenda D. Forman

By______________________

ATTACHMENT"B"

RESPONDENT DESCRIPTION INFORMATION

ATTENTION LAW ENFORCEMENT OFFICERS, PLEASE REMOVE THIS SHEET PRIOR TO SERVICE. PLEASE DO NOT GIVE THIS SHEET TO THE RESPONDENT.

SECTION I: RESPONDENT'S NAME

Respondent's Full Name: ______________

Nickname/Alias: ______________

SECTION II: PHYSICAL DESCRIPTION:

Race: ________ Sex: ________ Date of Birth: ________ Age: ________

Height: ________ Weight: ________ Hair Color: ________ Eye Color: ________

Other Marks/Scars/Tattoos: ________

SECTION III: RESPONDENTS CURRENT ADDRESS

Address: ________ City: ________ State: ________ Zip: ________

Phone No: ________

Work Address: ________ City: ________ State: ________ Zip: ________

Hangouts: ________

SECTION IV: RESPONDENT'S CLOSE RELATIVES

Name: ________ Relationship: ________

Address: ________ City: ________ State: ________ Zip: ________

Phone No: ________

SECTION V: LICENSE/VEHICLE INFORMATION DRIVER LICENSE

State: ________ Number: ________

SECTION VI: LETHALITY ASSESSMENT (Indicate yes, no, or unknown. If yes, add details.)

Does Respondent have any weapons? ________
Does Respondent have a drug problem? ________
Does Respondent have an alcohol problem? ________
Does Respondent have children in his/her care? ________
Is the Respondent wanted by police? ________
Does Respondent have a criminal record? ________
Is the Respondent expecting this Order? ________

PLEASE ATTACH A PHOTOGRAPH OF RESPONDENT IF YOU HAVE ONE

Attachment "C"
IN THE CIRCUIT COURT OF THE SEVENTEENTH JUDICIAL CIRCUIT, IN AND FOR BROWARD COUNTY, FLORIDA

Petitioner (Law Enforcement Officer/Agency),

v. Case No.: ________ RPO
Division: ________

Respondent.

______________________/

PETITION FOR RISK PROTECTION ORDER AND REQUEST FOR TEMPORARY EX PARTE RISK PROTECTION ORDER

SECTION I. PETITIONER

1. Petitioner's full legal name or name of petitioning agency: ________

2. Petitioner's law enforcement office/agency is located at {*street address, city, state and zip code*}: ________

SECTION II. RESPONDENT

1. Respondent's full legal name: ________

2. Respondent's current address: {*street address, city, state, and zip code*}

____

3. Physical description of Respondent:

Race: __________ Sex: __________ Male __________ Female __________ Date of Birth: ____________________

Height: __________ Weight: __________ Eye Color: __________ Hair Color: ____________________

4. Distinguishing marks or scars: __________

5. Vehicle: {*make/model*}__________ Color: __________ Tag Number: ____________________

6. Other names Respondent goes by: {*aliases or nicknames*}____________________

7. Respondent's email address: {*if known*}__________

8. Respondent's Driver's License number: {*if known*}____

9. Respondent's attorney's name, address, and telephone number: {*if known*}____________________

____

SECTION III. BASIS FOR PETITION

In support of this Petition the undersigned Law Enforcement Officer/Agency alleges:

1. Respondent poses a significant danger of causing personal injury to himself/herself or others by having a firearm or any ammunition in his/her custody or control or by purchasing, possessing, or receiving a firearm or any ammunition.

2. A sworn affidavit alleging specific statements, actions, or facts based on personal knowledge that give rise to a reasonable fear of significant dangerous acts by the Respondent is attached to this petition and incorporated by reference.

3. The attached sworn affidavit includes a list of the quantities, types, and locations of all firearms and ammunition believed to be in the Respondent's ownership, possession, custody, or control.

4. Respondent poses a significant danger of injury to himself/herself or others by having in his/her control, or by purchasing, possessing, or receiving, a firearm or ammunition.

5. Relevant evidence for the Court's consideration is detailed in the attached affidavit and demonstrates that the Respondent:

☐ was involved in a recent act or threat of violence against himself/herself or others;

☐ engaged in an act or threat of violence, including but not limited to acts or threats of violence against himself/herself, within the past 12 months;

☐ may have recurring mental health issues or is seriously mentally ill;

☐ has violated a risk protection order or no contact order issued under sections 741.30, 784.046, or 784.0485, Florida Statutes;

☐ is the subject of a previous or existing risk protection order;

☐ has violated a previous or existing risk protection order;

☐ has been convicted of, had adjudication withheld on, or pled *nolo contendere* in Florida or in any other state to a crime that constitutes domestic violence as defined in section 741.28, Florida Statutes;

☐ has used, or threatened to use, against himself/herself or others, any weapons;

☐ has unlawfully or recklessly used, displayed or brandished a firearm;

☐ has used or threatened to use on a recurring basis physical force against another person or has stalked another person;

☐ has been arrested for, convicted of, had adjudication withheld, or pled *nolo contendere* to a crime involving violence or a threat of violence in Florida or in any other state;

☐ has abused or is abusing controlled substances or alcohol;

☐ has recently acquired firearms or ammunition;

☐ other (Detail additional relevant information below).

SECTION IV. FIREARMS AND/OR AMMUNITION

Respondent owns, has, and/or is known to have guns or other weapons, including: {*list firearms and/or ammunition*}

SECTION V. EXISTING PROTECTION ORDERS

☐ There is a known existing protection order governing the Respondent under s. 741.30, s. 784.046, or s. 784.0485 or under any other applicable statute.

☐ There are no existing protection orders governing the Respondent under s. 741.30, s. 784.046, or s. 784.0485 or under any other applicable statute.

☐ Petitioner is without knowledge as to whether there are any known existing protection orders governing Respondent under s. 741.30, s. 784.046, or s. 784.0485 or under any other applicable statute.

SECTION VI. NOTICE

☐ Petitioner has made a good faith effort to provide notice to a family or household member of the Respondent and to any known third party who may be at risk of violence in compliance with section 790.401(2)(f), Florida Statutes;

OR

☐ Petitioner will take the following steps to provide notice as required by section 790.401(2)(f), Florida Statutes:

____

____

____

SECTION VII. TEMPORARY RISK PROTECTION ORDER AND FINAL RISK PROTECTION ORDER

For the foregoing reasons, Petitioner requests the Court to enter a TEMPORARY RISK PROTECTION ORDER until a hearing a hearing can be held and which requires Respondent to:

1. Immediately surrender all firearms and ammunition in his or her custody, control, or possession and any license to carry a concealed weapon or firearm to the {*name of law enforcement agency*}; ____________________

2. Not have in his/her custody, control, or possession any firearm or ammunition while this Order is in effect;

3. Not purchase, possess, receive, or attempt to purchase or receive, a firearm or ammunition while this order is in effect; and

4. Abide by any other lawful relief the Court deems appropriate.

Additionally, for the foregoing reasons, petitioner requests the Court to enter a RISK PROTECTION ORDER to remain in effect for a period the Court deems appropriate, up to an including, but not exceeding, twelve (12) months.

WHEREFORE, Petitioner requests that this Honorable Court enter (1) a Temporary Ex Parte Risk Protection Order; and (2) a final Risk Protection Order to remain in effect for a period the Court deems appropriate, up to and including but not exceeding twelve (12) months.

Respectfully submitted this ________ day of ________, 20 ___.

____

Signature of Petitioner

____

Law Enforcement Agency

____

____

Service Address

2018–23–CIV. LOCAL LAW ENFORCEMENT AGENCIES TO EFFECT SERVICE

IN THE CIRCUIT COURT OF THE SEVENTEENTH JUDICIAL CIRCUIT IN AND FOR BROWARD COUNTY, FLORIDA

Administrative Order 2018–23–CIV

ADMINISTRATIVE ORDER AUTHORIZING LOCAL LAW ENFORCEMENT AGENCIES TO EFFECT SERVICE PURSUANT TO SECTION 790.401, FLORIDA STATUTES

(a) Pursuant to Article V, section 2(d) of the Florida Constitution, and section 43.26, Florida Statutes, the chief judge of each judicial circuit is charged with the authority and the power to do everything necessary to promote the prompt and efficient administration of justice.

(b) Florida Rule of Judicial Administration 2.215(b)(3) states the chief judge "shall, considering available resources, ensure the efficient and proper administration of all courts within this circuit."

(c) On March 9, 2018, Governor Rick Scott signed into law Senate Bill 7026, also known as the Marjory Stoneman Douglas High School Public Safety Act, which, among other things, created section 790.401, Florida Statutes, and amended certain provisions of Florida's Baker Act.

(d) Section 790.401(5)(a), Florida Statutes, mandates service of risk protection orders and related documents take precedence over the service of other documents, unless the other documents are of a similar emergency nature, and permits the Chief Judge, in consultation with the Sheriff, to authorize local law enforcement agencies within Broward County to effect service as required under section 790.401, Florida Statutes.

(e) In accordance with the authority vested in the chief judge by Article V, section 2(d) of the Florida Constitution, section 43.26, Florida Statutes, and Florida Rule of Judicial Administration 2.215, it is hereby **ORDERED**:

(1) The Broward Sheriff's Office shall remain the primary agency responsible for serving temporary ex-parte and final risk protection orders for individuals who reside in or can be found in Broward County. Any law enforcement agency enumerated below may continue to have the Broward Sheriff's Office effect service under section 790.401, Florida Statutes, until their officers are sufficiently trained and prepared to effect service.

(2) After consultation with the Sheriff, the undersigned, as Chief Judge, authorizes the following local law enforcement agencies to effect service as required under section 790.401, Florida Statutes:

Coral Springs PD
Coconut Creek PD
Davie Police PD
Fort Lauderdale PD
Hallandale Beach PD
Hillsboro Beach PD
Hollywood PD
Lauderhill PD
Lighthouse Point PD
Margate PD
Miramar PD
Pembroke Pines PD
Plantation PD
Sunrise PD
Wilton Manors PD

(3) Any local law enforcement agency enumerated above which **chooses not** to effect service under section 790.401, Florida Statutes, shall notify the Sheriff in writing. The law enforcement agencies listed above are only permitted to effect service on pleadings, orders, or notices as prescribed in section 790.401, Florida Statutes.

(4) When the Respondent resides, or can be found, within the jurisdictional boundary of the law enforcement agency that filed the Petition, and that agency has agreed to effect service—absent an agreement with another law enforcement agency to effect service—that agency is responsible to effect service. If the Respondent resides outside the jurisdictional boundary of the petitioning agency, the petitioning agency shall be responsible for arranging service with a law enforcement agency where the Respondent resides or can be found. Nothing in this Administrative Order prevents local law enforcement agencies in Broward County from working harmoniously with the Broward Sheriff's Office to effect service, or from adopting an inter-local agreement as to service under section 790.401, Florida Statutes.

(5) A local law enforcement agency effecting service pursuant to section 790.401, Florida Statutes, shall use the service and verification procedures consistent with those of the Sheriff. The Sheriff may provide educational training to local law enforcement agencies on its service and verification procedures and on statutory requirements for service of process under Florida law. Any law enforcement agency effecting service under section 790.401, Florida Statutes, must do so in accord with Florida law and the mandate of section

790.401(5)(a), Florida Statutes that ***"[s]ervice under this section takes precedence over the service of other documents unless the other documents are of a similar emergency nature."***

(6) Any local law enforcement agency electing to effect service pursuant to section 790.401, Florida Statutes, shall maintain an e-mail address for communication with the Court, Clerk of the Courts, and the Sheriff, and provide such e-mail address to the Court at RPO@17th.flcourts.org.

(7) The Clerk of the Circuit Court in Broward County shall furnish the Broward Sheriff's Office or local law enforcement agencies, as applicable, with appropriate copies of all such orders and related documents issued for petitions filed pursuant to section 790.401, Florida Statutes, in order for the Broward Sheriff's Office or the local law enforcement agency to effectuate service.

DONE AND ORDERED in Chambers, Fort Lauderdale, Florida, Broward County, this 2nd day of April, 2018.

Jack Tuter
Chief Judge

2017–71–CIV. PROCEDURES FOR NON–BINDING ARBITRATION

IN THE CIRCUIT COURT OF THE SEVENTEENTH JUDICIAL CIRCUIT IN AND FOR BROWARD COUNTY, FLORIDA

Administrative Order No. 2017–71–Civ

CORRECTED ADMINISTRATIVE ORDER UPDATING PROCEDURES FOR NON–BINDING ARBITRATION

(a) Florida Rule of Judicial Administration 2.215 (b) (3) states the Chief Judge "shall, considering available resources, ensure the efficient and proper administration of all courts within [this] circuit."

(b) Section 44.103, Florida Statutes and Florida Rules of Civil Procedure require the Chief Judge to establish procedures with regard to non-binding arbitration for contested Circuit Court and County Court civil actions.

(c) In accordance with the authority vested in the Chief Judge by Florida Rule of Judicial Administration 2.215, it is hereby **ORDERED**:

(1) The Chief Judge shall approve applicants for addition to the list of individuals qualified to serve as arbitrators for Circuit and County Court civil matters. Pursuant to Florida Rule for Court–Appointed Arbitrators 11.130, arbitrators serve at the pleasure of the Chief Judge.

(2) Individuals seeking to and qualified to serve as an arbitrator for Circuit and/or County Court civil matters are required to complete the "Arbitrator Application for the Seventeenth Judicial Circuit." A copy of this application is attached as Exhibit A. Applications are also available from the Court Mediation and Arbitration Program, Room 19150, Broward County Courthouse, 201 S.E. 6th Street, Fort Lauderdale, Florida 33301. Completed applications should be returned to the Court Mediation and Arbitration Program, Room 19150, Broward County Courthouse, 201 S.E. 6th Street, Fort Lauderdale, Florida 33301.

(3) The required order of referral to non-binding arbitration and notice of arbitration hearing for civil actions other than personal injury protection (PIP) cases are attached as Exhibit B and the procedures and requirements of non-binding arbitration are incorporated by reference.

(4) The required order of referral to non-binding arbitration and notice of arbitration hearing for PIP cases are attached as Exhibit C and the procedures and requirements of non-binding arbitration are incorporated by reference.

(5) Only arbitrators who meet the qualifications set forth in Florida Rules for Court–Appointed Arbitrators 11.010 and 11.020 shall be approved by the Chief Judge and appointed by the presiding judge in civil actions. The individuals meeting the qualifications of Florida Rules for Court–Appointed Arbitrators 11.010 and 11.020 shall be separately designated on the list of qualified arbitrators as either a member of The Florida Bar or not a member of The Florida Bar.

(6) If a party to the action has been declared indigent by the Clerk of the Courts the case shall not be referred to arbitration.

(7) If an arbitrator fails to submit the statistical summary to the Court Mediation and Arbitration Program, then in the discretion of the Chief Judge, the arbitrator may be removed from the list of qualified arbitrators for this Circuit. The statistical summary is attached as Exhibit D.

(8) This Administrative Order vacates and supersedes Administrative Order 2009–45–Civ.

DONE AND ORDERED in Chambers, Fort Lauderdale, Broward County, Florida, this 4th day of December, 2017, *nunc pro tunc* to December 1, 2017.

Jack Tuter
Chief Judge

EXHIBIT "A"

ARBITRATOR APPLICATION FOR THE SEVENTEENTH JUDICIAL CIRCUIT

Instructions: This application must be filled out in its entirety if you wish to be considered for inclusion on the list of qualified arbitrators for the Broward County Court and Seventeenth Judicial Circuit. Please print legibly or type. A copy of your Training Certificate and, if applicable, a copy of your Florida Bar Card must be included with your application. Please attach a copy of your current resume or curriculum vitae and a statement as to any experience as an arbitrator. You must return the application with supporting documentation to:

Court Mediation and Arbitration Program
Broward County Courthouse, Room 19150
201 S.E. Sixth Street
Fort Lauderdale, Florida 33301

Full Legal Name ______

Principle Business Address ______

Business Address in Broward County, Florida to conduct arbitration hearings ______

Business Phone: ______

Business Fax: ______

Email Address: ______

Member of The Florida Bar ☐ Yes ☐ No

Have you completed Florida Supreme Court approved Arbitration Training? ☐ Yes ☐ No

Please check all types of cases for which you are seeking appointment:

☐ Consumer	☐ Personal Injury
☐ Contract	☐ Products Liability
☐ Eminent Domain	☐ Property Damage
☐ Employment	☐ Real Property/Mortgage Foreclosure

☐ Malpractice ☐ Other (please indicate) ________
☐ PIP

____
Signature

____
Date Signed

EXHIBIT "B"

☐IN THE COUNTY COURT IN AND FOR BROWARD COUNTY, FLORIDA
☐ IN THE CIRCUIT COURT OF THE SEVENTEENTH JUDICIAL CIRCUIT IN AND FOR BROWARD COUNTY, FLORIDA

Case Number
Division

Plaintiff,

v.

Defendant.

______________________/

ORDER REFERRING CASE TO ARBITRATION
(Single Arbitrator)

THE COURT ☐sua sponte/☐upon the motion of a party, hereby refers the above captioned matter to non-binding arbitration as authorized by statute and rules of procedure. It is ORDERED as follows:

1. The parties shall within fifteen (15) days of the date of this Order select an arbitrator from those individuals authorized to conduct arbitrations for this County/Circuit. The parties shall file the original joint notice of the name, address, and telephone number of the selected arbitrator with the Court Mediation and Arbitration Program, Room 19150, Broward County Courthouse, 201 S.E. Sixth Street, Fort Lauderdale, Florida 33301.

2. If the parties cannot agree, the Court appoints the following arbitrator:

   Name ________________________

   Address ________________________
   ____
   ____

   Telephone Number ________________________

3. The parties shall provide the arbitrator with a copy of this Order.

4. The first arbitration hearing shall be held within sixty (60) days of the date of this Order in Broward County, Florida.

5. The arbitrator within thirty (30) days of this Order shall notify the parties of the date, time and place of the arbitration hearing. The form Notice of Arbitration Hearing is attached and all terms are incorporated by reference into this Order.

6. If there is lack of cooperation and/or a failure to meet the time limits imposed by this Order, the arbitrator shall file a Notice of Non–Compliance and shall serve same upon counsel for each party and all self-represented parties with a courtesy copy to the undersigned Judge and the Court Mediation and Arbitration Program.

7. The arbitrator shall complete the Arbitrator Statistical Summary Form and return it to the Court Mediation and Arbitration Program within twenty (20) days after the time for filing any motions directed to the written decision has expired.

DONE AND ORDERED in Chambers, Fort Lauderdale, Broward County, Florida on this ________ day of ________________, 20____.

____
County Judge/Circuit Judge

Copies furnished:
Counsel of Record
Parties of Record
Court Mediation and Arbitration Program, Room 19150, Broward County Courthouse, 201 S.E. Sixth Street, Fort Lauderdale, Florida 33301

If you are a person with a disability who needs any accommodation in order to participate in this proceeding, you are entitled, at no cost to you, to the provision of certain assistance. Please contact ________________________

________________________ at least 7 days before your scheduled court appearance, or immediately upon receiving this notification if the time before the scheduled appearance is less than 7 days; if you are hearing or voice impaired, call 711.

☐IN THE COUNTY COURT IN AND FOR BROWARD COUNTY, FLORIDA
☐ IN THE CIRCUIT COURT OF THE SEVENTEENTH JUDICIAL CIRCUIT IN AND FOR BROWARD COUNTY, FLORIDA

Case Number
Division

Plaintiff,

v.

Defendant.

______________________/

ARBITRATOR ACCEPTANCE FORM
(Single Arbitrator)

In accordance with the Order Referring Case to Arbitration:

( ) The undersigned parties hereby agree to the arbitrator(s) assigned by the Judge.

( ) The undersigned parties **did not agree on the selection** of an arbitrator(s) selected by the Judge. Within fifteen (15) days of the signed Order Referring Case to Arbitration, they have selected the following arbitrator:

Name ________________________

Address ________________________
____

Telephone Number ________________________

____
Attorney for Plaintiff/Plaintiff's Signature Date

____
Attorney for Defendant/Defendant's Signature Date

PLEASE RETURN ORIGINAL TO:

Court Mediation and Arbitration Program, Broward County Courthouse, Room 19150, 201 S.E.
6th Street, Fort Lauderdale, Florida 33301
Tel. (954) 831–6313
Fax (954) 831–6079

☐IN THE COUNTY COURT IN AND FOR BROWARD COUNTY, FLORIDA
☐ IN THE CIRCUIT COURT OF THE SEVENTEENTH JUDICIAL CIRCUIT IN AND FOR BROWARD COUNTY, FLORIDA

Case Number
Division

Plaintiff,

v.

Defendant.

______________________/

NOTICE OF ARBITRATION HEARING
(Single Arbitrator)

You are hereby notified that the court-ordered arbitration in this matter shall take place as follows:

Name of Arbitrator ________________________

Address of Arbitration ________________________
____

Date of Arbitration ________________________

Time of Arbitration ________________________

ARBITRATION PROCEDURES

1. The parties and arbitrator shall comply with Florida Rules of Civil Procedure 1.700, 1.800, 1.810, and 1.820.
2. The parties and arbitrator shall comply with section 44.103, Florida Statutes.
3. The arbitrator shall be compensated in an amount not to exceed $1,500.00 per day, unless otherwise agreed to by the parties and arbitrator. The parties shall equally be responsible for the arbitrator's compensation.
4. A minimum fee of $175.00 shall be paid to the arbitrator ten (10) days prior to the commencement of arbitration. The parties shall equally be responsible for the arbitrator's minimum compensation.
5. Any compensation due the arbitrator upon conclusion of the hearing shall be equally paid by the parties.
6. The arbitrator shall have the power to administer oaths or affirmations and conduct the arbitration proceedings.
7. Individual parties or authorized representatives of corporate parties shall attend the arbitration hearing, unless excused in advance for good cause by the arbitrator. If a party, an authorized representative of a corporate party, or an attorney for any party fails to attend an arbitration hearing, the arbitrator may proceed with the arbitration hearing and enter his or her written decision.
8. When the parties, attorneys, and witnesses are at the arbitration hearing, the arbitrator shall make all decisions with regard to the proceedings.
9. The arbitration hearing shall be conducted as follows:
   a. each party will present an opening statement;

b. each party will present evidence or testimony;
c. each party will present a final summation.

10. The arbitrator in his or her decision shall indicate which party prevailed on each claim, counter-claim, or cross-claim. The arbitrator's decision shall also indicate if a party is required to pay costs or attorney's fees, as applicable, and the amount of the fees and costs to be awarded.
11. The arbitrator shall file his or her decision and the original of any transcripts with the Clerk of the Courts in a sealed envelope and on the face of the envelope indicate the contents are exempt from public access pursuant to Florida Rule of Civil Procedure 1.820 (g) (3).
12. Florida Rules of Civil Procedure 1.080 and 1.090 shall govern the manner in which the arbitrator shall serve his or her decision upon the parties and the time by which the parties must file any motions directed to the decision. A copy of any motion directed to the decision shall also be served upon the arbitrator.

CERTIFICATE OF SERVICE

I HEREBY CERTIFY that a true and correct copy of the foregoing was served by ☐ hand delivery/☐ mail/☐ telecopier and mail upon

____

____

______________________________on

______________________, 20____.

Signature of Arbitrator ______________________

Printed Name of Arbitrator ______________________

If you are a person with a disability who needs any accommodation in order to participate in this proceeding, you are entitled, at no cost to you, to the provision of certain assistance. Please contact ______________________

____

at least 7 days before your scheduled court appearance, or immediately upon receiving this notification if the time before the scheduled appearance is less than 7 days; if you are hearing or voice impaired, call 711.

☐IN THE COUNTY COURT IN AND FOR BROWARD COUNTY, FLORIDA
☐ IN THE CIRCUIT COURT OF THE SEVENTEENTH JUDICIAL CIRCUIT IN AND FOR BROWARD COUNTY, FLORIDA

Case Number
Division

Plaintiff,

v.

Defendant.

______________________/

ORDER REFERRING CASE TO ARBITRATION
(Panel Arbitration)

THE COURT ☐sua sponte/☐upon the motion of a party, hereby refers the above-captioned matter to a non-binding arbitration panel as authorized by statute and rules of procedure. It is ORDERED as follows:

1. The parties shall within fifteen (15) days of the date of this Order each select an arbitrator from those individuals authorized to conduct arbitrations for this County/Circuit. The arbitrators selected by the parties shall select a third arbitrator from those individuals authorized to conduct arbitrations for this County/Circuit who shall serve as the chief arbitrator.
2. The parties shall file the original joint notice of the names, addresses, and telephone numbers of the selected arbitrators on the panel with the Court Mediation and Arbitration Program, Room 19150, Broward County Courthouse, 201 S.E. Sixth Street, Fort Lauderdale, Florida 33301.
3. If the parties cannot agree, the Court appoints the following arbitrators:

Name ______________________
Chief Arbitrator
Address ______________________

____

Telephone Number ______________________

Name ______________________
Address ______________________

Telephone Number ______________________

Name ______________________

Address ______________________

____

Telephone Number ______________________

4. The parties shall provide the arbitrators with a copy of this Order.
5. The first arbitration hearing shall be held within sixty (60) days of this Order in Broward County, Florida.
6. The chief arbitrator within thirty (30) days of this Order shall notify the parties of the date, time and place of the arbitration hearing. The form Notice of Arbitration Hearing is attached and all terms are incorporated by reference into this Order.
7. If there is lack of cooperation and/or a failure to meet the time limits imposed by this Order, the chief arbitrator shall file a Notice of Non–Compliance and shall serve same upon counsel for each party and all self-represented parties with a courtesy copy to the undersigned Judge and the Court Mediation and Arbitration Program.
8. The chief arbitrator shall complete the Arbitrator Statistical Summary Form and return it to Court Mediation and Arbitration Program within twenty (20) days after the time for filing any motions directed to the written decision has expired.

DONE AND ORDERED in Chambers, Fort Lauderdale, Broward County, Florida on this ________ day of ______________, 20____

____
County Judge/Circuit Judge

Copies furnished:
Counsel of Record/Parties of Record
Court Mediation and Arbitration Program, Room 19150, Broward County Courthouse, 201 S.E. Sixth Street, Fort Lauderdale, Florida 33301

If you are a person with a disability who needs any accommodation in order to participate in this proceeding, you are entitled, at no cost to you, to the provision of certain assistance. Please contact ______________________

____

at least 7 days before your scheduled court appearance, or immediately upon receiving this notification if the time before the scheduled appearance is less than 7 days; if you are hearing or voice impaired, call 711.

☐IN THE COUNTY COURT IN AND FOR BROWARD COUNTY, FLORIDA
☐ IN THE CIRCUIT COURT OF THE SEVENTEENTH JUDICIAL CIRCUIT IN AND FOR BROWARD COUNTY, FLORIDA

Case Number
Division

Plaintiff,

v.

Defendant.

______________________/

ARBITRATOR ACCEPTANCE FORM
(Panel Arbitration)

In accordance with the Order Referring Case to Arbitration:

( ) The undersigned parties hereby agree to the arbitrators assigned by the Judge.

( ) The undersigned parties **did not agree on the selection** of an arbitrators selected by the Judge. Within fifteen (15) days of the signed Order, they have selected the following arbitrators:

Name, Chief Arbitrator ______________________

Address ______________________

____

Telephone Number ______________________

Name ______________________

Address ______________________

____

Telephone Number ______________________
Name ______________________

Address ______________________

____

Telephone Number ______________________

Attorney for Plaintiff/Plaintiff's Signature Date

______________________ ______________

Attorney for Defendant/Defendant's Signature Date

PLEASE RETURN ORIGINAL TO:

Court Mediation and Arbitration Program, Broward County Courthouse, Room 19150, 201 S. E.
6th Street, Fort Lauderdale, Florida 33301
Tel. (954) 831–6313

Fax: (954) 831–6079
☐IN THE COUNTY COURT IN AND FOR BROWARD COUNTY, FLORIDA
☐ IN THE CIRCUIT COURT OF THE SEVENTEENTH JUDICIAL CIRCUIT IN AND FOR BROWARD COUNTY, FLORIDA

Case Number
Division

Plaintiff,

v.

Defendant.

______________________/

NOTICE OF ARBITRATION HEARING
(Panel Arbitration)

You are hereby notified that the court-ordered arbitration in this matter shall take place as follows:

Name of Chief Arbitrator ______________________

Name of Arbitrator ______________________

Name of Arbitrator ______________________

Address of Arbitration ______________________

____

____

Date of Arbitration ______________________

Time of Arbitration ______________________

ARBITRATION PROCEDURES

1. The parties and arbitrators shall comply with Florida Rules of Civil Procedure 1.700, 1.800, 1.810, and 1.820.
2. The parties and arbitrators shall comply with section 44.103, Florida Statutes.
3. Each arbitrator shall be compensated in an amount not to exceed $1,500.00 per day, unless otherwise agreed to by the parties and arbitrators. The parties shall equally be responsible for the arbitrators's compensation.
4. A minimum fee of $175.00 shall be paid to each arbitrator ten (10) days prior to the commencement of arbitration. The parties shall equally be responsible for the arbitrators' minimum compensation.
5. Any compensation due the arbitrators upon conclusion of the hearing shall be equally paid by the parties.
6. The arbitrators shall have the power to administer oaths or affirmations and conduct the arbitration proceedings.
7. Individual parties or authorized representatives of corporate parties shall attend the arbitration hearing, unless excused in advance for good cause by the chief arbitrator. If a party, an authorized representative of a corporate party, or an attorney for any party fails to attend an arbitration hearing, the arbitrators may proceed with the arbitration hearing and enter their written decision.
8. When the parties, attorneys, and witnesses are at the arbitration hearing, the arbitrators shall make all decisions with regard to the proceedings.
9. The arbitration hearing shall be conducted as follows:
   a. each party will present an opening statement;
   b. each party will present evidence or testimony;
   c. each party will present a final summation.
10. The arbitrators in their decision shall indicate which party prevailed on each claim, counterclaim, or cross-claim. The decision of the arbitrators shall also indicate if a party is required to pay costs or attorney's fees, as applicable, and the amount of the fees and costs to be awarded.
11. The chief arbitrator shall file the decision and the original of any transcripts with the Clerk of the Courts in a sealed envelope and on the face of the envelope indicate the contents are exempt from public access pursuant to Florida Rule of Civil Procedure 1.820 (g) (3).
12. Florida Rules of Civil Procedure 1.080 and 1.090 shall govern the manner in which the chief arbitrator shall serve the decision upon the parties and the time by which the parties must file any motions directed to the decision. A copy of any motion directed to the decision shall also be served upon the arbitrators.

CERTIFICATE OF SERVICE

I HEREBY CERTIFY that a true and correct copy of the foregoing was served by ☐ hand delivery/☐ mail/☐ telecopier and mail upon

____

____

______________________ on

______________________, 20____.

Signature of Arbitrator ______________________

Printed Name of Arbitrator ______________________

If you are a person with a disability who needs any accommodation in order to participate in this proceeding, you are entitled, at no cost to you, to the provision of certain assistance. Please contact ______________________

____

at least 7 days before your scheduled court appearance, or immediately upon receiving this notification if the time before the scheduled appearance is less than 7 days; if you are hearing or voice impaired, call 711.

EXHIBIT "C"

IN THE COUNTY COURT IN AND FOR BROWARD COUNTY, FLORIDA

Case Number:
Division:

Plaintiff,

v.

Defendant.

______________________/

ORDER REFERRING PERSONAL INJURY PROTECTION CASE TO ARBITRATION
(Single Arbitrator)

THE COURT sua sponte [ ] OR [ ] upon the motion of a party, hereby refers the above-caption matter to non-binding arbitration as authorized by statute and rules of procedure. It is ORDERED as follows:

1. The parties shall within fifteen (15) days of the date of this Order select an arbitrator from those individuals authorized to conduct arbitrations for this County/Circuit. The parties shall file the original joint notice of the name, address, and telephone number of the selected arbitrator with the Court Mediation and Arbitration Program, Room 19150, Broward County Courthouse, 201 S.E. Sixth Street, Fort Lauderdale, Florida 33301.

2. If the parties cannot agree, the Court appointed the following arbitrator:

   Name ______________________

   Address ______________________

   ____

   Telephone Number ______________________

3. The parties shall provide the arbitrator with a copy of this Order.

4. The arbitrator shall be entitled to a fee of $750.00 and the time limit for the arbitration hearing is three (3) hours, subject to any written agreement entered into between the parties and arbitrator. The fee shall be paid as follows: $ ____ Plaintiff and $ ____ Defendant, unless otherwise agreed to by the parties.

5. The first arbitration hearing shall be held within sixty (60) days of the date of this Order in Broward County, Florida.

6. The arbitrator within thirty (30) days of the date of this Order shall notify the parties of the date, time and place of the arbitration hearing. The form Notice of Arbitration Hearing is attached and all terms are incorporated by reference into this Order.

7. If there is a lack of cooperation and/or a failure to meet the time limits imposed by this Order, the arbitrator shall file a Notice of Non–Compliance and shall serve same upon counsel for each party and all self-represented litigants with a courtesy copy to the undersigned Judge and the Court Mediation and Arbitration Program.

8. The arbitrator shall complete the Arbitrator Statistical Summary Form and return it to the Court Mediation and Arbitration Program within twenty (20) days after the time for filing any motions directed to the written decision has expired.

DONE AND ORDERED in Chambers, Fort Lauderdale, Broward County, Florida, this ________ day of ________, 20____.

____
County Judge

Copies furnished:
Counsel of Record
Parties of Record
Court Mediation and Arbitration Program, Room 19150, Broward County Courthouse, 201
S.E. Sixth Street, Fort Lauderdale, Florida 33301

If you are a person with a disability who needs any accommodation in order to participate in this proceeding, you are entitled, at no cost to you, to the provision of certain assistance. Please contact ______________ [name of coordinator for arbitrator], ADA coordinator, ______________________ [address of coordinator for arbitrator] at ______________________ [telephone number of coordinator for arbitrator], at least seven (7) days before your scheduled court appearance, or immediately upon receiving this notification if the time before the scheduled appearance is less than seven (7) days; if you are hearing or voice impaired, call 711.

IN THE COUNTY COURT IN AND FOR BROWARD COUNTY, FLORIDA

Case Number:
Division:

Plaintiff,

v.

Defendant.

______________________/

ARBITRATOR ACCEPTANCE FORM
(Single Arbitrator—Personal Injury Protection Case)

In accordance with Order Referring Personal Injury Protection Case to Arbitration:

[ ] The undersigned parties hereby agree to the arbitrator(s) assigned by the Judge.

[ ] The undersigned parties **did not agree on the selection** of the arbitrator(s) selected by the Judge. Within fifteen (15) days of the Order Referring Personal Injury Protection Case to Arbitration, they have selected the following arbitrator:

Name ______________________

Address ______________________

____

Telephone Number ______________________

______________________ ______________________
Attorney for Plaintiff/Plaintiff's Signature Date

______________________ ______________________
Attorney for Defendant/Defendant's Signature Date

PLEASE RETURN ORIGINAL TO:
Court Mediation and Arbitration Program, Broward County Courthouse, Room 19150, 201 S.E. Sixth Street, Fort Lauderdale, Florida 33301
Tel. (954) 831–6313
Fax (954) 831–6079

IN THE COUNTY COURT IN AND FOR BROWARD COUNTY, FLORIDA

Case Number:
Division:

Plaintiff,

v.

Defendant.

______________________/

NOTICE OF ARBITRATION HEARING
(Single Arbitrator—Personal Injury Protection Case)

You are hereby notified that the court-ordered arbitration in this matter shall take place as follows:

Name of Arbitrator ______________________

Address of Arbitration ______________________

____

Date of Arbitration ______________________

Time of Arbitration ______________________

ARBITRATION PROCEDURES

1. The parties and arbitrator shall comply with Florida Rule of Civil Procedure 1.700, 1.800, 1.810, and 1.820.
2. The parties and arbitrator shall comply with section 44.103, Florida Statutes.
3. The arbitrator shall be compensated in an amount not to exceed $750.00 for a three (3) hour hearing, unless otherwise agreed to by the parties and arbitrator. The parties shall be responsible for the arbitrator's compensation as set forth in the Order Referring Personal Injury Protection Case to Arbitration unless otherwise agreed to by the parties.
4. A minimum fee of $100.00 shall be paid to the arbitrator ten (10) days prior to the commencement of arbitration. The parties shall be responsible for the arbitrator's minimum compensation as set forth in the Order Referring Personal Injury Protection Case to Arbitration unless otherwise agreed to by the parties.
5. Any compensation due the arbitrator upon conclusion of the hearing shall be paid by the parties as set forth in the Order Referring Personal Injury Protection Case to Arbitration unless otherwise agreed to by the parties.
6. The arbitrator shall have the power to administer oaths or affirmations and conduct the arbitration proceedings.
7. Individual parties or authorized representatives of corporate parties shall attend the arbitration hearing, unless excused in advanced for good cause by the arbitrator. If a party, an authorized representative of corporate parties, or an attorney for any party fails to attend an arbitration hearing, the arbitrator may proceed with the hearing and enter his or her written decision.
8. When the parties, attorneys, and witnesses are at the hearing, the arbitrator shall make all decisions with regard to the proceedings.
9. The arbitration hearing shall be conducted as follows:
   a. each party will present an opening statement;
   b. each party will present evidence or testimony;
   c. each party will present a final summation.
10. The arbitrator in his or her decision shall indicate which party prevailed on each claim, counterclaim, or crossclaim. The arbitrator's decision shall also indicate if a party is required to pay costs or attorney's fees, as applicable, and the amount of the fees and costs to be awarded.
11. The arbitrator shall file his or her decision and the original of any transcripts with the Clerk of the Courts in a sealed envelope and on the face of the envelope indicate the contents are exempt from public access pursuant to Florida Rule of Civil Procedure 1.820 (g) (3).
12. Florida Rules of Civil Procedure 1.080 and 1.090 shall govern the manner in which the arbitrator shall serve his or her decision upon the parties and the time by which the parties must file any motions directed to the decision. A copy of any motion directed to the decision shall also be served upon the arbitrator.

CERTIFICATE OF SERVICE

I HEREBY CERTIFY that a true and correct copy of the foregoing was served by [ ] hand delivery / [ ] mail / [ ] telecopier and mail upon ______________________

____

______________________on

______________________, 20____.

Signature of Arbitrator ______________________

Printed Name of Arbitrator ______________________

If you are a person with a disability who needs any accommodation in order to participate in this proceeding, you are entitled, at no cost to you, to the provision of certain assistance. Please contact ______________ [name of coordinator for arbitrator], ADA coordinator, ______________ [address of coordinator for arbitrator] at ______________ [telephone number of coordinator for arbitrator], at least seven (7) days before your scheduled court appearance, or immediately upon receiving this notification if the time before the scheduled appearance is less than seven (7) days; if you are hearing or voice impaired, call 711.

IN THE COUNTY COURT IN AND FOR BROWARD COUNTY, FLORIDA

Case Number:
Division:

Plaintiff,

v.

Defendant.

______________________/

ORDER REFERRING PERSONAL INJURY PROTECTION CASE TO ARBITRATION
(Panel Arbitration)

THE COURT [ ] sua sponte OR [ ] upon the motion of a party, hereby refers the above-captioned matter to a non-binding arbitration panel as authorized by statute and rules of procedure. It is ORDERED as follows:

1. The plaintiff and defendant shall within fifteen (15) days of that date of this Order each select an arbitrator from those individuals authorized to conduct arbitrations for this County/Circuit. The arbitrators selected by the parties shall select a third arbitrator from those individuals authorized to conduct arbitrations for this County/Circuit who shall serve as the chief arbitrator.
2. The parties shall file the original joint notice of the names, addresses, and telephone numbers of the selected arbitrators on the panel with the Court Mediation and Arbitration Program, Room 19150, Broward County Courthouse, 201 S.E. Sixth Street, Fort Lauderdale, Florida 33301.
3. If the parties cannot agree, the Court appoints the following arbitrators:

Name ______________________

Chief Arbitrator ______________________

Address ______________________

Telephone Number ______________________

Name ______________________

Address ______________________

____

Telephone Number ______

Name ______

Address ______

______

Telephone Number ______

4. Each arbitrator shall be entitled to a fee of $750.00 and the time limit for the arbitration hearing is three (3) hours subject to any written agreement entered into between the parties and arbitrators. The fee shall be paid as follows: $ ____ Plaintiff and $ ____ Defendant, unless otherwise agree to by the parties.
5. The parties shall provide the arbitrators with a copy of this Order.
6. The first arbitration hearing shall be held within sixty (60) days of the date of this Order in Broward County, Florida.
7. The chief arbitrator within thirty (30) days of the date of this Order shall notify the parties of the date, time and place of the arbitration hearing. The form Notice of Arbitration hearing is attached and all terms are incorporated by reference into this Order.
8. If there is a lack of cooperation and/or a failure to meet the time limits imposed by this Order, the chief arbitrator shall file a Notice of Non–Compliance and shall serve same upon counsel for each party and all self-represented litigants with a courtesy copy to the undersigned Judge and the Court Mediation and Arbitration Program.
9. The chief arbitrator shall complete the Arbitrator Statistical Summary Form and return it to Court Mediation and Arbitration Program within twenty (20) days after the time for filing any motions directed to the written decision has expired.

DONE AND ORDERED in Chambers, Fort Lauderdale, Broward County, Florida, this ______ day of ______, 20 ____.

______
County Judge

Copies furnished:
Counsel of Record
Parties of Record
Court Mediation and Arbitration Program, Room 19150, Broward County Courthouse, 201 S.E. Sixth Street,
Fort Lauderdale, Florida 33301

If you are a person with a disability who needs any accommodation in order to participate in this proceeding, you are entitled, at no cost to you, to the provision of certain assistance. Please contact ______ [name of coordinator for arbitrator], ADA coordinator, ______ [address of coordinator for arbitrator] at ______ [telephone number of coordinator for arbitrator], at least seven (7) days before your scheduled court appearance, or immediately upon receiving this notification if the time before the scheduled appearance is less than seven (7) days; if you are hearing or voice impaired, call 711.

IN THE COUNTY COURT IN AND FOR BROWARD COUNTY, FLORIDA

Case Number:
Division:

Plaintiff,

v.

Defendant.

______/

ARBITRATOR ACCEPTANCE FORM
(Panel Arbitration—Personal Injury Protection Case)

In accordance with Order Referring Personal Injury Protection Case to Arbitration:

[ ] The undersigned parties hereby agree to the arbitrator(s) assigned by the Judge.

[ ] The undersigned parties **did not agree on the selection** of the arbitrator(s) selected by the Judge. Within fifteen (15) days of the Order Referring Personal Injury Protection Case to Arbitration, they have selected the following arbitrators:

Name ______

Chief Arbitrator ______

Address ______

Telephone Number ______

Name ______

Address ______

______

Telephone Number ______

Name ______

Address ______

______

Telephone Number ______

______
Attorney for Plaintiff/Plaintiff's Signature Date

______
Attorney for Defendant/Defendant's Signature Date

PLEASE RETURN ORIGINAL TO:
Court Mediation and Arbitration Program, Broward County Courthouse, Room 19150, 201 S.E. Sixth Street, Fort Lauderdale, Florida 33301
Tel. (954) 831–6313
Fax (954) 831–6079

IN THE COUNTY COURT IN AND FOR BROWARD COUNTY, FLORIDA

Case Number:
Division:

Plaintiff,

v.

Defendant.

______/

NOTICE OF ARBITRATION HEARING
(Panel Arbitration—Personal Injury Protection Case)

You are hereby notified that the court-ordered arbitration in this matter shall take place as follows:

Name of Chief Arbitrator ______

Name of Arbitrator ______

Name of Arbitrator ______

Address of Arbitration ______

______

______

Date of Arbitration ______

Time of Arbitration ______

ARBITRATION PROCEDURES

1. The parties and arbitrators shall comply with Florida Rules of Civil Procedure 1.700, 1.800, 1.810, and 1.820.
2. The parties and arbitrators shall comply with section 44.103, Florida Statutes.
3. Each arbitrator shall be compensated in an amount not to exceed $1,500.00 per day, unless otherwise agreed to by the parties and arbitrators. The parties shall equally be responsible for the arbitrators's compensation.
4. A minimum fee of $175.00 shall be paid to each arbitrator ten (10) days prior to the commencement of arbitration. The parties shall equally be responsible for the arbitrators minimum compensation.
5. Any compensation due the arbitrators upon conclusion of the hearing shall be equally paid by the parties.
6. The arbitrators shall have the power to administer oaths or affirmations and conduct the arbitration proceedings.
7. Individual parties or authorized representatives of corporate parties shall attend the arbitration hearing, unless excused in advance for good cause by the chief arbitrator. If a party, an authorized representative of a corporate party, or an attorney for any party fails to attend an arbitration hearing, the arbitrators may proceed with the arbitration hearing and enter their written decision.
8. When the parties, attorneys, and witnesses are at the arbitration hearing, the arbitrators shall make all decisions with regard to the proceedings.
9. The arbitration hearing shall be conducted as follows:
   a. each party will present an opening statement;
   b. each party will present evidence or testimony;
   c. each party will present a final summation.
10. The arbitrators in their decision shall indicate which party prevailed on each claim, counter-claim, or cross-claim. The decision of the arbitrators shall also indicate if a party is required to pay costs or attorney's fees, as applicable, and the amount of the fees and costs to be awarded.
11. The chief arbitrator shall file the decision and the original of any transcripts with the Clerk of the Courts in a sealed envelope and on the face of the

envelope indicate the contents are exempt from public access pursuant to Florida Rule of Civil Procedure 1.820 (g) (3).

12. Florida Rules of Civil Procedure 1.080 and 1.090 shall govern the manner in which the chief arbitrator shall serve the decision upon the parties and the time by which the parties must file any motions directed to the decision. A copy of any motion directed to the decision shall also be served upon the arbitrators.

CERTIFICATE OF SERVICE

I HEREBY CERTIFY that a true and correct copy of the foregoing was served by ☐ hand delivery/☐ mail/☐ telecopier and mail upon

____

____

______________________________________on

______________________________, 20____.

Signature of Arbitrator ______________________

Printed Name of Arbitrator ______________________

If you are a person with a disability who needs any accommodation in order to participate in this proceeding, you are entitled, at no cost to you, to the provision of certain assistance. Please contact ______________

______________ at least 7 days before your scheduled court appearance, or immediately upon receiving this notification if the time before the scheduled appearance is less than 7 days; if you are hearing or voice impaired, call 711.

EXHIBIT "D"

ARBITRATION STATISTICAL SUMMARY

Style of Case ______________________

Case Number ______________________

Judge ______________________ ☐Circuit ☐County

Date of Arbitration ______________________

Number of Hearing(s) ______________________

Hours ______________________

Total Charges

Type of Case (Primary basis for lawsuit)

☐ Consumer
☐ Contract
☐ Eminent Domain
☐ Employment
☐ Malpractice
☐ PIP
☐ Personal Injury
☐ Products Liability
☐ Property Damage
☐ Real Property/Mortgage Foreclosure
☐ Other (please indicate) ______________

A party to the arbitration filed a motion seeking a trial de novo after no later than twenty (20) days after the final decision was served? ☐ Yes ☐ No

Signature of Arbitrator ______________________

Printed Name of Arbitrator ______________________

Date ______________________

RETURN TO:
Court Mediation and Arbitration Program
Broward County Courthouse
Room 19150
201 S. E. 6th Street
Fort Lauderdale, Florida 33301
Tel: (954) 831–6313
Fax: (954) 831–6079

2017–60–CIV. TRANSPORT OF INDIVIDUALS SUBJECT TO INVOLUNTARY CIVIL COMMITMENT PROCEEDINGS

IN THE CIRCUIT COURT OF THE SEVENTEENTH JUDICIAL CIRCUIT IN AND FOR BROWARD COUNTY, FLORIDA

Administrative Order No. 2017–60–Civ

ADMINISTRATIVE ORDER REGARDING THE TRANSPORT OF INDIVIDUALS SUBJECT TO INVOLUNTARY CIVIL COMMITMENT PROCEEDINGS PURSUANT TO PART V, CHAPTER 394, FLORIDA STATUTES, IN THE WEST TOWER OF THE BROWARD COUNTY COURTHOUSE

(a) The Seventeenth Judicial Circuit is compelled to handle cases involving the involuntary civil commitment of sexually violent predators pursuant to Part V, Chapter 394, Florida Statutes.

(b) Pursuant to Administrative Order 2015–8–Civ, all open and active cases filed pursuant to Part V, Chapter 394, Florida Statutes, are assigned to Circuit Civil Division 07.

(c) These proceedings require extensive case management to comply with applicable laws and rules of procedure, and often require the attendance of those individuals who have been involuntarily committed and are placed at the Civil Commitment Center.

(d) It is incumbent upon the Broward Sheriff's Office to assist in the movement and transport of these individuals within the West Tower of the Broward County Courthouse when their attendance is required for court proceedings.

(e) In accordance with the authority vested in the Chief Judge pursuant to Article V, section 2(d) of the Florida Constitution, section 43.26, Florida Statutes, and Florida Rule of Judicial Administration 2.215, it is hereby **ORDERED**:

(1) The Broward Sheriff's Office shall cooperate with representatives of the Civil Commitment Center to permit entry into the West Tower of the Broward County Courthouse and assure that any individual subject to proceedings pursuant to Part V, Chapter 394, Florida Statutes, is transported to any courtroom as ordered by the presiding judge.

(2) The Broward Sheriff's Office shall also assist representatives of the Civil Commitment Center to ensure that these individuals are able to safely exit the West Tower of the Broward County Courthouse for transport back to the Civil Commitment Center.

DONE AND ORDERED in Chambers, Fort Lauderdale, Florida, this, 27th day of September, 2017.

Jack Tuter
Chief Judge

2017–35–CIV. PROCEDURES FOR DIRECT FILING OR REASSIGNMENT OF CIRCUIT CIVIL CASES TO A COMPLEX BUSINESS OR COMPLEX TORT DIVISIONS

IN THE CIRCUIT COURT OF THE SEVENTEENTH JUDICIAL CIRCUIT IN AND FOR BROWARD COUNTY, FLORIDA

Administrative Order No. 2017–35–Civ

AMENDED ADMINISTRATIVE ORDER ESTABLISHING PROCEDURES FOR DIRECT FILING OR REASSIGNMENT OF CIRCUIT CIVIL CASES TO A COMPLEX BUSINESS OR COMPLEX TORT DIVISION

(a) Florida Rule of Judicial Administration 2.215 (b) (3) states the chief judge "shall, considering available resources, ensure the efficient and proper administration of all courts within [this] circuit."

(b) In accordance with the authority vested in the chief judge by Florida Rule of Judicial Administration 2.215, it is hereby **ORDERED**:

(1) Florida Rule of Civil Procedure 1.201 shall govern the designation of a case as complex and thereafter the management of the case to final disposition.

(2) A case may be directly filed or reassigned/transferred to a complex litigation division (business or tort) only as set forth in this Administrative Order.

(3) *Direct Filing of New Cases into a Complex Business or Complex Tort Division.* Any party seeking to direct file an original complaint meeting the criteria as set forth in this Administrative Order, into a complex business or tort division, shall complete form "B" and e-file same with the Clerk of the Courts at the time of filing. The Clerk of the Courts shall thereafter randomly assign the case to a complex business or tort division as set forth in this Administrative Order. (See Form "B" attached). Any case directly filed into a complex litigation division not meeting the criteria set forth in this Administrative Order may be reassigned by the Administrative Judge of the Circuit Civil Division or the Chief Judge presently assigned to Division (07).

(4) *Reassignment of Pending Cases to a Complex Business or Tort Division.* A party seeking to reassign a **tort case** to a complex litigation division shall file a motion and set a hearing before the assigned division judge. The division judge, on his or her own motion, may also request the case be reassigned to a complex litigation division. The division judge, at the time of the hearing, will determine if the case meets the requirements of this Administrative Order for reassignment to a complex litigation division. In cases involving complex **tort** matters, if the division judge has sufficient time and resources to handle the matter, he or she may keep the case and not recommend transfer to a complex **tort** division. Upon a recommendation by the division judge to transfer a case to a complex litigation division, the Chief Judge presently assigned to Division (07) may reassign the case consistent with criteria set forth in this Administrative Order.

As it pertains to **business cases**, a party seeking to transfer a case to the complex business division shall set a hearing before the Chief Judge presently assigned to Division (07) on the Court's transfer calendar which will be on Wednesday mornings at 8:45 a.m. Requests for scheduling a business case for transfer shall be made through the Court's judicial assistant. A form (Form "A") as attached to this Administrative Order shall accompany any motion to transfer/reassign a case to a complex litigation division. All requests to transfer **business** cases to a complex business division shall be set on the Court's transfer calendar. A motion to transfer/reassign a **tort** case shall be transferred as set forth above.

Upon the denial of a request for transfer of a **tort** case to a complex division, any party may request a hearing before the Chief Judge presently assigned to Division (07) for final consideration as to whether the matter meets criteria for transfer to a complex litigation division. Any such request for a hearing shall be accompanied by use of (Form "A") and scheduled on the Court's transfer calendar on Wednesday mornings at 8:45 a.m.

Factors to be considered regarding a dispute over the transfer to a complex litigation division include: (1) the length of time needed for trial; (2) number of times the case has been set or reset for trial; (3) age of the case; (4) number of parties in the case; (5) complexity of the subject matter of the case; (6) availability of the division judge to hear the case; and (7) any prejudice that might inure to a party if the case is transferred.

(5) The Chief Judge presently assigned to Division (07) or the Administrative Judge of the Circuit Civil Division may decline reassignment of a case to a complex litigation division. If such a situation arises, the case will remain assigned to the division randomly determined at the time of filing.

(6) A case may be directly filed or reassigned/transferred to a complex **business** division based on a number of factors including: (1) the nature of the case; (2) complexity of the issues; (3) complexity of the discovery; (4) number of parties in the case; **and** (5) if the subject matter of the case meets one or more of the following:

(a) the amount in controversy exceeds $150,000.00 and is a Uniform Commercial Code non-consumer related transaction;

(b) the amount in controversy exceeds $500,000.00 and arises from the purchase and sale of a business or the assets of a business (including non-consumer contract disputes, commercial foreclosures which are accompanied by requests/motions for appointment of receiver or assignment of rents);

(c) the amount in controversy exceeds $150,000.00 and involves the sale of goods or services by or to business entities;

(d) the amount in controversy exceeds $150,000.00 and involves non-consumer bank or brokerage accounts (including loan, deposit, cash management, and investment accounts);

(e) the amount in controversy exceeds $150,000.00 and arises from the purchase, sale, or lease of commercial real or personal property or security interests;

(f) the amount in controversy exceeds $500,000.00 and relates to construction litigation (non–personal injury);

(g) the amount in controversy exceeds $150,000.00 and is a franchisee/franchisor dispute;

(h) the amount in controversy exceeds $150,000.00 and concerns professional malpractice of non-medical professionals in connection with rendering services to a business entity;

(i) the amount in controversy exceeds $150,000.00 and relates to the internal affairs, governance, dissolution, liquidation rights, or obligations between or among owners of a business entity (shareholders, partners, members);

(j) the amount in controversy exceeds $150,000.00 and concerns the liability or indemnity of officers, directors, managers, trustees, members or partners functioning as managers of a business entity;

(k) the amount in controversy exceeds $150,000.00 and relates to trade secrets;

(*l*) the amount in controversy exceeds $150,000.00 and relates to non-compete agreements;

(m) the amount in controversy exceeds $150,000.00 and is an intellectual property claim; or

(n) the amount in controversy exceeds $150,000.00 and arises under state securities laws or antitrust statutes.

Further, the following **business** cases described in A–H below, meeting the criteria as set forth in this Administrative Order, **shall** be directly filed or reassigned/transferred to the complex business division:

A) All UCC non-consumer claims which exceed $150,000.00;

B) All commercial foreclosure cases exceeding $500,000.00 which are accompanied by a request/motion for appointment of a receiver or assignment of rents;

C) All cases in which the subject matter is an Assignment for the Benefit of Creditors;

D) All business dissolutions and related shareholder/partnership/limited liability company disputes;

E) Any business case where the subject matter relates to trade secrets where the amount in controversy exceeds $150,000.00;

F) All business cases involving Non–Competition Agreements or disputes where the amount in controversy exceeds $150,000.00;

G) Disputes involving the confirmation of non-consumer arbitration awards;

H) All shareholder derivative actions where the amount in controversy exceeds $150,000.00.

(7) Post-judgment matters and proceedings supplementary are generally not subject to transfer to a complex litigation division absent approval from the Chief Judge presently assigned to Division (07).

(8) Personal injury cases, construction claims with personal injuries, eminent domain, professional negligence, and class action cases that meet either the time duration or complexity criteria as set forth in this Administrative Order may qualify for transfer to a complex litigation division. Personal injury or other tort related cases seeking transfer to a complex litigation division, meeting the criteria above, must require a minimum of (10) days for trial.

(9) *Class Actions*. Class Actions may be subject to assignment/reassignment to a complex business division subject to the following limitations:

a) the amount in controversy regarding the class action exceeds $250,000.00 exclusive of claims for attorney fees;

b) a class action has been previously certified by the division judge and the matter will take substantial judicial management of the class or issues relating to the class;

c) any other class action in which the division judge, Chief Judge presently assigned to Division (07), and the Administrative Judge of the Circuit Civil Division agree meet the criteria for transfer to a complex litigation division.

(10) The division judge and counsel of record should strive to make an early determination as to whether a case may qualify for transfer to a complex litigation division and make a timely motion to transfer. Factors to be considered regarding a dispute over transfer to a complex division include: (1) the length of time needed for trial; (2) number of times the case has been set or reset for trial; (3) age of the case; (4) number of parties in the case; (5) complexity of the subject matter of the case; (6) availability of the division judge to hear the case; and (7) any prejudice that might inure to a party if the case is transferred.

(11) Cases subject to transfer to a complex litigation division pursuant to this Administrative Order shall be reassigned to a particular complex litigation division based on the nature, type, duration, complexity of the case, workload of the judges serving in the complex litigation divisions, and any other factor(s) within the discretion of the Chief Judge presently assigned to Division (07) and Administrative Judge of the Circuit Civil Division.

(12) Should a judge presiding over a case in a complex litigation division be disqualified or enter an order of recusal, the matter shall be reassigned by the Chief Judge presently assigned to Division (07) or the Administrative Judge of the Circuit Civil Division utilizing the criteria set forth in this Administrative Order.

(13) Requests for direct filing or reassignment to a complex litigation division shall be accompanied by a notice/motion utilizing the forms attached to this Administrative Order.

(14) The Clerk of the Courts is directed to furnish each judge assigned to a complex litigation division a list of newly filed or assigned cases each month.

(15) This Administrative Order vacates and supersedes Administrative Order 2014–16–Civ.

DONE AND ORDERED in Chambers, Fort Lauderdale, Broward County, Florida, this 28th day of July, 2017.

Jack Tuter
Chief Judge

FORM "A"

(To be utilized only when seeking to reassign or transfer a pending case into a complex business or tort division)

IN THE CIRCUIT COURT OF THE SEVENTEENTH JUDICIAL CIRCUIT IN AND FOR BROWARD COUNTY, FLORIDA

Case Number xx-xxxxxx CACE (xx)

Plaintiff(s)

v.

Defendant(s).

MOTION REQUESTING TRANSFER OF BUSINESS CASE OR TORT CASE FROM GENERAL CIVIL DIVISION TO A COMPLEX LITIGATON DIVISION

The undersigned seeks transfer of the above entitled case to a complex litigation division (business or tort) and certifies this action is appropriate for assignment/reassignment to a complex litigation division (business or tort), and complies with Administrative Order 2017–35–Civ in that:

The case meets the criteria for one or more of the following categories:

☐ the amount in controversy exceeds $150,000.00 and is a Uniform Commercial Code non-consumer related transaction

☐ the amount in controversy exceeds $500,000.00 and arises from the purchase and sale of businesses or the assets of a business (including non-consumer contract disputes, commercial foreclosures which are accompanied by requests/motions for appointment of receiver or assignment of rents)

☐ the amount in controversy exceeds $150,000.00 and the sale of goods or services by or to business entities

☐ the amount in controversy exceeds $150,000.00 and involves non-consumer bank or brokerage accounts (including loan, deposit, cash management, and investment accounts)

☐ the amount in controversy exceeds $150,000.00 and arises from the purchase, sale, financing, or lease of commercial real or personal property or security interests

☐ the amount in controversy exceeds $150,000.00 and relates to construction litigation (non-personal injury) and/or surety bonds

☐ the amount in controversy exceeds $150,000.00 and is a franchisee/franchisor dispute

☐ the amount in controversy exceeds $150,000.00 and concerns professional malpractice of non-medical professionals in connection with rendering services to a business entity
☐ the amount in controversy exceeds $150,000.00 and involves non-competition agreements
☐ the action involves confirmation of a non-consumer arbitration award that exceeds $150,000.00
☐ this action is a shareholder derivative action and the amount in controversy exceeds $150,000.00
☐ this is an action predicated on an assignment for the benefit of creditors
☐ the amount in controversy exceeds $150,000.00 and is an insurance coverage dispute, bad faith litigation, or a third party indemnity action against insurers arising under policies issued to a business entity
☐ personal injury claims, construction claims with personal injury, eminent domain, professional negligence and class action cases that meet either the time duration or complexity requirements (Personal Injury cases must exceed 10 days for trial)
Is this a class action case where the amount in controversy exceeds $250,000.00?
☐ Yes ☐ NO

[Attorney Signature Block]

CERTIFICATE OF SERVICE
FORM "B"
(To be utilized when filing an original complaint)
IN THE CIRCUIT COURT OF THE SEVENTEENTH JUDICIAL CIRCUIT IN AND FOR BROWARD COUNTY, FLORIDA
NOTICE OF INTENT TO FILE NEW CASE IN THE COMPLEX BUSINESS OR TORT DIVISION
THIS ACTION IS APPROPRIATE FOR ASSIGNMENT TO A COMPLEX BUSINESS OR TORT DIVISION AND COMPLIES WITH REQUIREMENTS FOR FILING IN SUCH COMPLEX LITIGATION DIVISION AS SET FORTH IN ADMINISTRATIVE ORDER 2017–35–Civ.
Is this a **tort** case which meets the criteria of Administrative Order 2017–35–Civ?
YES ______ NO ______

Is this a **business** case which meets the criteria of Administrative Order 2017–35–Civ?
YES ______ NO ______

Is this a class action case?
YES ______ NO ______

I CERTIFY the information herein is accurate and this case meets the criteria pursuant to Administrative Order 2017–35–Civ for filing in the complex business or tort division of the Seventeenth Judicial Circuit.
Signature of attorney ______________________
Florida Bar #
Name, Address and Phone Number

2016–16–CIV. TRANSFER OF WATER DAMAGE CASES

IN THE CIRCUIT COURT OF THE SEVENTEENTH JUDICIAL CIRCUIT IN AND FOR BROWARD COUNTY, FLORIDA

Order Number 2016–16–Civ

AMENDED ADMINISTRATIVE ORDER REGARDING TRANSFER OF WATER DAMAGE CASES

(a) Florida Rule of Judicial Administration 2.215(b) (3) states the chief judge shall "considering available resources, ensure the efficient and proper administration of all courts within [this] circuit."

(b) The Circuit and County courts are experiencing the filing of cases by a homeowner or third party vendor or assignee for the same incident seeking insurance coverage. In order to efficiently utilize judicial resources these cases, if possible, should be heard by one judge.

(c) In accordance with the authority vested in the chief judge by Florida Rule of Judicial Administration 2.215, it is ordered:

1. If there is a pending county court case regarding water damage with a companion circuit court case based upon the same incident a party may seek the transfer of the case to circuit court.

2. The party seeking transfer shall file a motion in the county court case for hearing before the assigned judge. The county court judge may grant or deny the transfer.

3. If the county case is transferred to circuit court, the circuit judge shall determine how the cases will proceed taking into consideration Florida Rule of Civil Procedure 1.270.

4. Once the case is transferred from county to circuit court it shall remain a companion case of the circuit case until final resolution and may not be transferred back to county court.

5. A copy of the order granting the transfer shall be provided to the circuit judge by the moving party within 5 days of the order being signed.

DONE AND ORDERED in chambers at Fort Lauderdale, Broward County, Florida on March 11, 2016 nunc pro tunc to March 4, 2016.

Peter M. Weinstein
Chief Judge

2014–32–CIV. CIRCUIT CIVIL AND COUNTY CIVIL EMERGENCY MATTERS

IN THE CIRCUIT COURT OF THE SEVENTEENTH JUDICIAL CIRCUIT IN AND FOR BROWARD COUNTY, FLORIDA

Order Number 2014–32–Civ 2014–32–CO

AMENDED ADMINISTRATIVE ORDER AS TO CIRCUIT CIVIL AND COUNTY CIVIL EMERGENCY MATTERS

(a) Florida Rule of Judicial Administration 2.215(b)(3) states the chief judge shall "considering available resources, ensure the efficient and proper administration of all courts within [this] circuit."

(b) Pleadings and Motions filed as emergencies disrupt court procedures and interrupt work on cases that are currently pending. Consequently, an attorney or party who seeks "emergency" review loses credibility when the court determines there is no true emergency. See, *USAA Cas. Ins. Co. V. Pembroke Pines MRI, Inc., 24 So. 3d 588* (Fla. 4th DCA 2009).

(c) In accordance with the authority vested in the chief judge by Florida Rule of Judicial Administration 2.215, it is ordered:

(1) If a party in a civil case has an emergency matter it shall be presented to the assigned division judge. If the division judge is absent or otherwise unavailable, the matter shall be taken to the Office of the Trial Court Administrator who shall attempt to locate an alternate judge for assignment prior to the matter being presented to the civil duty judge or county relief judge. The circuit judges shall have all the power and jurisdiction of a county judge if he or she is assigned an emergency county court matter. The county judges shall have all the power and jurisdiction of a circuit judge if he or she is assigned an emergency circuit court matter.

Any party requesting emergency relief for any motion, appeal or petition shall file a separate notice of "Request for Emergency Relief." The "Request for Emergency Relief" shall be filed simultaneously with the motion, appeal or petition for which emergency relief is sought. The required form is attached as Exhibit A to this order.

(2) Attorneys shall file the Request for Emergency Relief with the Efiling Authority Portal and bring the receipt of the filing to the Clerk of Court. Attorneys shall also ensure that they select the emergency option to indicate the filing is in compliance with this Administrative Order. The Clerk of Court shall locate the Request for Emergency Relief in the pending queue and if appropriate, immediately accept the document or advise the filing attorney of deficiencies to be corrected for acceptance. The filing attorney shall only proceed to the division judge or the Office of the Trial Court Administrator upon the Clerk of Court's acceptance and docketing of the Request for Emergency Relief.

(3) Self represented parties may register with the Efiling Authority Portal and file the Request for Emergency Relief with the Efiling Authority Portal and bring the receipt of the filing to the Clerk of Court. The necessary form is located on the website for the 17th Judicial Circuit at www.17th.flcourts.org. The Clerk of Court shall locate the Request for Emergency Relief in the pending queue and if appropriate, immediately accept the document or advise the filing party of deficiencies to be corrected for acceptance. The filing party shall only proceed to the division judge or the Office of the Trial Court Administrator upon the Clerk of Court's acceptance and docketing of the Motion for Emergency Relief.

(4) If a self represented party does not file the Request for Emergency Relief with the Efiling Authority Portal then the party shall bring the original motion and request to the Clerk of Court for filing.

(5) No emergency motion shall be afforded emergency relief until the court determines whether an emergency exists. An emergency is defined as a matter that will result in irreparable harm, death or result in a manifest injury if immediate relief is not afforded. Matters which do not meet this definition shall not be submitted to the court as an "emergency".

(6) Any party or attorney who violates this Administrative Order by requesting emergency relief without an objectively reasonable basis is subject to sanctions pursuant to Section 57.105, Fla. Stat., or any other sanction as authorized by law, rule of procedure, or case.

(7) This Administrative Order vacates and supersedes Administrative Order II–90–A–3.

DONE AND ORDERED in chambers at Fort Lauderdale, Broward County, Florida on September 30, 2014.

Peter M. Weinstein
Chief Judge

Form "A"

IN THE CIRCUIT/COUNTY COURT OF THE 17TH JUDICIAL CIRCUIT IN AND FOR BROWARD COUNTY

Case No.:
Judge/Division:

______________________/

REQUEST FOR EMERGENCY RELIEF

The attached motion, appeal or petition meets criteria for consideration for emergency relief pursuant to Amended Administrative Order 2014–32–CIV/2014–32–CO:

1. The nature of the emergency:

____
____
____
____
____

2. If an order is at issue, the name of the Judge and date of the order:

____

3. This request for emergency relief has not been previously denied by any Judge.

I hereby certify there exists a reasonably objective basis to request emergency relief as set forth in the attached motion.

Name ______________________________
Address ______________________________
______________ Phone ______________________
Dated: ______________________________

____
Signature of Counsel or Self–Represented Party

CERTIFICATE OF SERVICE TO ALL COUNSEL/PARTIES

2014–17–CIV. RESIDENTIAL MORTGAGE FORECLOSURES

IN THE CIRCUIT COURT OF THE SEVENTEENTH JUDICIAL CIRCUIT IN AND FOR BROWARD COUNTY, FLORIDA

Order Number 2014–17–Civ

ADMINISTRATIVE ORDER AS TO RESIDENTIAL MORTGAGE FORECLOSURES

(a) Florida Rule of Judicial Administration 2.215(b)(3) states the chief judge shall "considering available resources, ensure the efficient and proper administration of all courts within [this] circuit."

(b) Supreme Court Administrative Order AOSC13–28, Final Report and Recommendations of the Foreclosure Initiative Workgroup, emphasized the necessity to review the current Circuit procedures for residential mortgage foreclosure procedures.

(c) The Florida Legislature authorized and designated funds to utilize senior judges and general magistrates to assist with the backlog of residential mortgage foreclosure cases.

(d) In accordance with the authority vested in the chief judge by Florida Rule of Judicial Administration 2.215, it is ordered:

(1) The Clerk of Court shall assign all residential foreclosure cases to Division 11.

(2) All open and pending cases in Division 11 are divided into two (2) tiers. Tier 1 cases are cases that appear ready for

final hearing or dismissal. Tier 2 cases are all other open and pending mortgage residential foreclosure cases. Tier 1 cases shall be set for hearing or trial. Tier 2 cases shall be scheduled for case management conferences.

(3) Parties shall refer to the Foreclosure Procedures posted on the 17th Circuit website for additional instructions.

(4) Cases set for summary judgment shall have the foreclosure affidavit, attached as Exhibit A, completed by the attorney for the plaintiff and presented to the presiding judge at the summary judgment hearing. The Clerk of the Court shall post on his webpage the foreclosure affidavit in both a word format and pdf format at no cost to attorneys and the public.

(5) All pending motions shall be scheduled for hearing on or before the date set for Summary Judgment.

(6) Any party seeking to cancel a residential foreclosure sale shall file and serve on all parties a motion as contained in Form 1.996(b) of the Florida Rules of Civil Procedure. The motion shall be noticed for hearing, with service on all parties at least ten (10) court business days after filing. The Clerk of Courts shall not cancel any residential foreclosure sale without the entry of an order canceling and resetting the sale except if a Petition for Bankruptcy was filed in federal court. Plaintiff shall ensure that a Notice of Sale is published as required by law and the proof of publication is filed with the Clerk of Courts in all residential mortgage foreclosure cases.

(7) The attorneys who submit an order or judgment for entry in residential foreclosure case shall be responsible for providing to all parties a conformed copy of the order or judgment upon entry.

(8) The Clerk of Court shall reflect the disposition of residential mortgage foreclosure cases as indicated on the final disposition form filed by the plaintiff or as directed by a judge or the judge's designee.

(9) This Order vacates and supersedes Administrative Orders 2013–59–Civ.

DONE AND SIGNED, in Chambers, at Broward County, Fort Lauderdale, Florida, on April 15, 2014.

Peter M. Weinstein
Chief Judge

EXHIBIT A
IN THE CIRCUIT COURT OF THE SEVENTEENTH JUDICIAL CIRCUIT IN AND FOR BROWARD COUNTY, FLORIDA

Case Number CACE ____ (11)

Plaintiff,
v.

Defendant(s).

________________ /

AFFIDAVIT OF COMPLIANCE WITH ADMINISTRATIVE ORDER AS TO SUMMARY JUDGMENT HEARINGS

On this date personally appeared before me, this undersigned authority, duly authorized to administer oaths and take acknowledgments, ________ Esq., who after being first duly sworn, upon his or her oath, deposes and states:

1. Original filing fee has been properly adjusted up or down to reflect the actual value of the claim in the Final Judgment:

[ ] No additional fee required; or

[ ] Additional filing fee enclosed; or

[ ] Plaintiff to get a refund from the Clerk of Court.

2. [ ] Elements and Certification were filed with the Complaint for cases filed on or after July 1, 2013, pursuant to Section 702.015, Fla. Stat.; or

[ ] Elements and Certification not applicable as case filed before July 1, 2013.

3. Service of Process is completed on all parties and any and all proof has been filed in this action.

Defendant (s)	Date Served	Date of Default	Date of Answer	Affirmative Def.
________	________	________	________	Yes/No
________	________	________	________	Yes/No
________	________	________	________	Yes/No
________	________	________	________	Yes/No
________	________	________	________	Yes/No

Documents:

1. Current Notice of Hearing sent to all parties. Yes/No
2. Affidavit of Non–Military Service [ ] was or [ ] was not filed for defendants who have not answered.
3. Defendant filed bankruptcy Yes/No
   Date stay was lifted ________
4. Original promissory was filed Yes/No or an Affidavit of Lost Promissory Note was filed on ________ and adequate protection is provided by:
   [ ] Written indemnification
   [ ] Surety bond
   [ ] Letter of credit
   [ ] Deposit of cash collateral
   [ ] Other Security approved by the court
5. Motion for Final Judgment was completed and filed:
   [ ] Summary Final Judgment Date Filed ___
   [ ] Order to Show Cause Date Filed ___
   [ ] Other Order ________________ Date Filed ___
6. Motion to Dismiss Yes/No Date Filed ___
7. Affidavit of Guardian Ad Litem filed Yes/No Date Filed ___ $ ________
8. Affidavit of Indebtedness. Date Filed ___ $ ________
9. Affidavit of Costs. Date Filed ___ $ ________
10. Affidavit of Attorney's Fees Date Filed ___ $ ________
11. There are no pending motions Yes/No

The information requested above is located in the court file. The dates reflect the information in the court file.

FURTHER AFFIANT SAYETH NAUGHT.

Attorney's Signature:
____

Attorney's Name:
____

Attorney's Bar #:
____

Sworn to and subscribed before me this ___ day of ________, 20__. The undersigned notary public specifies that Affiant's signature is the signature being notarized and that Affiant personally appeared before the notary public at the time of notarization. Affiant is [ ] personally known or [ ] produced identification. Type of identification produced ________.

____

Notary Public—State of Florida

My Commission Expires: ________________

2014–14–CIV. DISMISSED CIVIL OR FAMILY CASES

IN THE CIRCUIT COURT OF THE SEVENTEENTH JUDICIAL CIRCUIT IN AND FOR BROWARD COUNTY, FLORIDA

Order Number 2014–14–CIV 2014–14–UFC 2014–14–CO

ADMINISTRATIVE ORDER DIRECTING CLERK OF COURTS WITH REGARD TO DISMISSED CIVIL OR FAMILY CASES

(a) Florida Rule of Judicial Administration 2.215(b)(3) states the chief judge shall "considering available resources, ensure the efficient and proper administration of all courts within [this] circuit."

(b) In accordance with the authority vested in the chief judge by Florida Rule of Judicial Administration 2.215, it is ordered:

(1) If a civil or family case is disposed by voluntary dismissal or court ordered dismissal without prejudice the Clerk of Courts shall determine if a prior case was filed with the same parties and cause of action. If the Clerk of Courts determines there was a prior case with the same parties and cause of action the Clerk shall assign the newly filed case to the division assigned to the first case.

(2) If the Clerk of Courts does not assign the newly filed case as required by this Administrative Order the parties shall notify the division judge assigned to the dismissed action of the newly filed action. The division judge for the dismissed action, or the Administrative Judge of the Division, shall order the newly filed action transferred from division to which the newly filed action was assigned.

DONE AND ORDERED in chambers at Fort Lauderdale, Broward County, Florida on May 2, 2014.

Peter M. Weinstein
Chief Judge

2013–54–CIV. CASE STATUS REPORTING REQUIREMENTS FOR REAL PROPERTY MORTGAGE FORECLOSURE CASES

IN THE CIRCUIT COURT OF THE SEVENTEENTH JUDICIAL CIRCUIT IN AND FOR BROWARD COUNTY, FLORIDA

Order Number 2013–54–Civ

AMENDED ADMINISTRATIVE ORDER ESTABLISHING CASE STATUS REPORTING REQUIREMENTS FOR REAL PROPERTY MORTGAGE FORECLOSURE CASES (to correct a scrivener's error in the first order)

(a) Florida Rule of Judicial Administration 2.215(b)(3) states the chief judge shall "considering available resources, ensure the efficient and proper administration of all courts within [this] circuit."

(b) The Florida Supreme Court adopted requirements for FY 2013–2014 Foreclosure Initiative Data Collection Plan in AOSC 13–51 which directed the adoption of a circuit administrative order.

(c) In accordance with the authority vested in the chief judge by Florida Rule of Judicial Administration 2.215, it is ordered:

(1) The Clerk of Courts (Clerk) is directed to comply with the requirements of the FY 2013–2014 Foreclosure Initiative Data Collection Plan adopted by the Florida Supreme Court in AOSC 13–51.

(2) If the Clerk is aware of any event which may change the status of a real property mortgage foreclosure case, he shall immediately notify the judge assigned to Division 11.

(3) The Court shall enter orders as necessary upon the change of status of a real property mortgage foreclosure case. The form of the orders is attached to this Administrative Order.

DONE AND ORDERED in chambers at Fort Lauderdale, Broward County, Florida on December 16, 2013.

Peter M. Weinstein
Chief Judge

IN THE CIRCUIT COURT OF THE SEVENTEENTH JUDICIAL CIRCUIT IN AND FOR BROWARD COUNTY, FLORIDA

Case Number CACE

________________________,
Plaintiff,
v.

________________________,
Defendant.

ORDER PLACING CASE ON INACTIVE STATUS DUE TO:

This case came before the Court, and the Court has been advised that the Plaintiff/Defendant have/has moved to place the case on INACTIVE status due to:

☐ Bankruptcy stay, Case No. ___ [BKST]

☐ Case pending resolution of another case, Case No. ___ [CPRC]

☐ Written agreement of the parties [BWAP]

☐ Appeal pending [AP]

☐ Motion to stay or abate due to Department of Justice/Attorney General settlement [DOJ/AG]

☐ Other (a reason must be provided in writing by the presiding judge or designee) [OTH] ________________

The Clerk of Court is therefore directed to remove this case from the ACTIVE status, and designate it as an INACTIVE case category based on the reason checked above. The parties must return the case to active status by motion, with notice to all parties, within 30 days of the termination of grounds for inactive status, and seek an order of court returning it to active status.

DONE and ORDERED in ________ County, Florida, this ___ day of ________ 20 ___.

____
Circuit Judge

IN THE CIRCUIT COURT OF THE SEVENTEENTH JUDICIAL CIRCUIT IN AND FOR BROWARD COUNTY, FLORIDA

Case Number CACE

_______________________,
Plaintiff,
v.
_______________________,
Defendant.

ORDER RETURNING CASE TO ACTIVE STATUS DUE TO:

This case came before the Court, and the Court has been advised that the Plaintiff/Defendant have/has moved to place the case on ACTIVE status due to:

☐ Plaintiff/defendant stipulates that the bankruptcy stay has been lifted, Case No. ___ [BKST LFT]

☐ Plaintiff/defendant stipulates that related case has been disposed, Case No. ___ [CPCS DISP]

☐ By written agreement of the parties [BWAP]

☐ Plaintiff/defendant stipulates that pending appeal has been disposed [AP DISP]

☐ Plaintiff/defendant stipulates that Department of Justice/Attorney General review is complete [DOJ/AG DISP]

☐ Other (a reason must be provided in writing by the presiding judge or designee) [OTH DISP] ________

The Clerk of Court is therefore directed to remove this case from the INACTIVE status, and designate it as an ACTIVE case based on the reasons checked above.

DONE and ORDERED in ________ County, Florida, this ___ day of ________ 20 ___.

____
Circuit Judge

2012–16–CIV. ELECTRONIC FILING PROCEDURES FOR THE CIVIL DIVISION

IN THE CIRCUIT COURT OF THE SEVENTEENTH JUDICIAL CIRCUIT IN AND FOR BROWARD COUNTY, FLORIDA

Order Number 2012–16–Civ

ADMINISTRATIVE ORDER ESTABLISHING ELECTRONIC FILING PROCEDURES FOR THE CIVIL DIVISION

(a) Florida Rule of Judicial Administration 2.215(b)(3) states the chief judge shall "considering available resources, ensure the efficient and proper administration of all courts within [this] circuit."

(b) The Florida Supreme Court no longer requires the filing of original pleadings or papers filed electronically in the Seventeenth Circuit.

(c) In accordance with the authority vested in the chief judge by Florida Rule of Judicial Administration 2.215, it is ordered:

(1) This Administrative Order incorporates by reference all provisions of Florida Supreme Court Administrative Order No. AOSC09–30, In Re: Statewide Standards for Electronic Access to the Courts and AOSC10–31, In Re: Electronic Filing of Documents in the Probate Division for the electronic filing of documents with the Clerk of the Circuit Court (herein Clerk) as now in effect or as may be amended from time to time.

(2) Attorneys may electronically file pleadings and papers on existing cases in circuit civil divisions 1, 7, 9, 19, 26 and 27.

(3) The following documents may be scanned and efiled; however, the original must be filed with the Clerk:

a. Documents ordered by the Court; and

b. Original documents required by law or rule of procedure to be filed with the Clerk.

(4) Self represented individuals shall file pleadings and papers with the Clerk.

(5) The filing date of an efiled document is when the last page is received by the Clerk. If the Clerk has a vendor providing electronic court record services, the vendor must comply with this Administrative Order and the Clerk shall endorse upon each electronically transmitted document the date and time of receipt.

(6) The Clerk within twenty four (24) hours of receipt of an electronic document shall either accept or reject the electronic document for filing and send electronic notice to the filer.

(7) The placement of a "/s/" or the image of a signature by an attorney or party or affected non-party signature line on an electronically filed document shall be accepted as the signature and shall verify to the Court the filer is in possession of the originally executed document. Notwithstanding the manner in which an electronic document is signed the originally executed pleading or paper shall be maintained in the filer's possession for a minimum of one (1) year after final disposition and time for appeal of the case. The originally executed document shall be produced for filing or inspection as directed by the Court.

(8) The electronic filing of a document does not modify any filing deadlines as required by law, rule of procedure, or court order.

(9) If a document filed electronically is not received due to:

a. an error in the transmission of the document to the Clerk or any vendor of the Clerk to provide electronic court record filing services which is unknown to an attorney or party or affected non party, or

b. a failure to process the electronic document when received by the Clerk or rejection by the Clerk, or

c. any other technical problems experienced by the attorney or party or affected non party,

the Court may, after an evidentiary hearing and upon satisfactory proof, enter an order permitting the document to be filed nunc pro tunc to the date it was first attempted to be sent electronically.

(10) The Clerk or any vendor of the Clerk providing electronic court record filing services shall provide to the judiciary

the entire electronic filing data export upon acceptance by the Clerk as part of the transfer of electronic transmission.

(11) The Clerk or any vendor of the Clerk providing electronic court record filing services shall not charge any state court entity or statutorily exempt entity or individual for electronically filing documents. Any non-exempt attorney or party electronically filing documents shall pay any and all statutory fees to the Clerk.

(12) This Administrative Order shall govern the initial use of the Florida Courts Efiling Portal for the Circuit Civil Division but does not alleviate the Clerk from complying with the Chief Judge's conditions of approval of the Clerk's efiling plan, which were included in the Florida Courts Technology Commission's approval of the plan.

DONE AND ORDERED in chambers at Fort Lauderdale, Broward County, Florida on March 2, 2012.

Peter M. Weinstein
Chief Judge

2011–27–CIV. RESIDENTIAL EVICTION SUMMONS

IN THE CIRCUIT COURT OF THE SEVENTEENTH JUDICIAL CIRCUIT IN AND FOR BROWARD COUNTY, FLORIDA

Order Number 2011–27–Civ

ADMINISTRATIVE ORDER AS TO RESIDENTIAL EVICTION SUMMONS

(a) Florida Rule of Judicial Administration 2.215(b)(3) states the chief judge shall "develop an administrative plan for the efficient and proper administration of all courts within that circuit."

(b) The form for residential eviction summons located in the Florida Rules of Civil Procedures requires modifications as to the order of the contents but the attached form is otherwise in substantial compliance with Form 1.923.

(c) In accordance with the authority vested in the chief judge by Florida Rule of Judicial Administration 2.215, it is ordered:

The attached form for residential evictions is adopted for the Seventeenth Judicial Circuit and Broward County Courts. The attached form shall be used by all Plaintiffs seeking a residential eviction in a Seventeenth Judicial Circuit or Broward County Court.

DONE AND ORDERED at Fort Lauderdale, Broward County, Florida on May 23, 2011.

Victor Tobin
Chief Judge

Form 1.923. Eviction Summons/Residential

TO:

Defendant(s)

PLEASE READ CAREFULLY

You are being sued by __________ to require you to move out of the place where you are living for the reasons given in the attached complaint.

You are entitled to a trial to determine whether you can be required to move, but a Judge may order you to move without a trial **unless you have done ALL of the things listed below. You must do them within 5 days** (not including Saturday, Sunday, or any legal holiday) after the date these papers were given to you or to a person who lives with you or were posted at your home.

THE THINGS YOU MUST DO ARE AS FOLLOWS:

(1) **Pay to the clerk of the court the amount of rent that the attached complaint claims to be due and any rent that becomes due until the lawsuit is over**. In addition, you must pay the Clerk's registry fee of 3% of the first $500.00 deposit and 1.5% of each subsequent $100.00. The Clerk will only accept cash, certified check or a money order or an attorney's trust account check, made payable to the Clerk of Courts.

(2) If you believe that the amount claimed in the complaint is incorrect, you should **file with the clerk** of the court a motion to have the court determine the amount to be paid. If you file a motion, **you must attach to the motion any documents supporting your position and mail or give a copy of the motion to the plaintiff/plaintiff's attorney.**

(3) Write down the reason(s) why you think you should not be forced to move. (You still must deposit the rent in the court registry.) The written reason(s) must be given to the Clerk of the Court at 201 S.E. 6th Street, Ft. Lauderdale, FL 33301, within the time limit, and you must also mail or give a copy of your written reason(s) to the Plaintiff's attorney, or if the Plaintiff has no attorney, to the Plaintiff(s) at:

____

IF YOU DO NOT DO ALL OF THE THINGS SPECIFIED ABOVE WITHIN 5 WORKING DAYS AFTER THE DATE THAT THESE PAPERS WERE GIVEN TO YOU OR TO A PERSON WHO LIVES WITH YOU OR WERE POSTED AT YOUR HOME, YOU MAY BE EVICTED WITHOUT A HEARING OR FURTHER NOTICE.

(4) If the attached complaint also contains a claim for money damages (such as unpaid rent), you must respond to that claim separately. You must write down the reasons why you believe that you do not owe the money claimed. The written reasons must be given to the clerk of the court at the address specified in paragraph (1) above, and you must mail or give a copy of your written reasons to the plaintiff/plaintiff's attorney at the address specified in paragraph (2) above. This must be done within 20 days after the date these papers were given to you or to a person who lives with you. This obligation is separate from the requirement of answering the claim for eviction within 5 working days after these papers were given to you or to a person who lives with you or were posted at your home.

If you are a person with a disability who needs any accommodation in order to participate in this proceeding, you are entitled, at no cost to you, to the provision of certain assistance. Please contact the ADA Coordinator, Room 470, 201 S.E. 6th Street, Ft. Lauderdale, FL 33301, (954) 831–7721 at least 7 days before your scheduled court appearance, or immediately upon receiving this notifica-

tion if the time before the scheduled appearance is less than 7 days; if you are hearing or voice impaired, call 711.

The court does not provide interpreters for civil hearings. You must provide your own interpreter or bring someone to translate for you.

THE STATE OF FLORIDA:

To Each Sheriff of the State: You are commanded to serve this summons and a copy of the complaint in this lawsuit on the above-named defendant.

DATED on ______________________

Clerk of the Courts
By ______________________
As Deputy Clerk

2009–12–CIV. SUMMARY JUDGMENT FORECLOSURE PROCEDURES

IN THE CIRCUIT COURT OF THE SEVENTEENTH JUDICIAL CIRCUIT IN AND FOR BROWARD COUNTY, FLORIDA

Order Number 2009–12–Civ

ADMINISTRATIVE ORDER ESTABLISHING SUMMARY JUDGMENT FORECLOSURE PROCEDURES

(a) Florida Rule of Judicial Administration 2.215(b) (3) states the chief judge shall "develop an administrative plan for the efficient and proper administration of all courts within that circuit."

(b) The volume of cases set for summary judgment in foreclosure proceedings requires a uniform procedure to assist the judges in expeditiously hearing the motions.

(c) In accordance with the authority vested in the chief judge by Florida Rule of Judicial Administration 2.215, it is ordered:

(1) Effective February 9, 2009 the foreclosure worksheet attached as Exhibit A shall be completed by the attorney for the plaintiff and presented to the presiding judge at the summary judgment hearing.

(2) The attorney for the plaintiff, in addition to completing the foreclosure worksheet shall also locate and mark with a tab all documents referenced on the foreclosure worksheet.

(3) The attorney for the plaintiff shall file the original foreclosure worksheet with the Clerk of Circuit Court.

(4) The Clerk of Circuit Court shall post on his webpage the foreclosure worksheet in both a word format and pdf format at no cost to attorneys and the public.

(5) All motions to dismiss shall be scheduled for hearing on or before the date set for Summary Judgment.

DONE AND ORDERED in chambers at Fort Lauderdale, Broward County, Florida on February 9, 2009.

Victor Tobin
Chief Judge

EXHIBIT A

SEVENTEENTH JUDICIAL CIRCUIT UNIFORM FORECLOSURE WORKSHEET

Date ____________ Case # ____________

Plaintiff ____________ Defendants ____________

The information requested below must be located in the court file and must be marked for the presiding judge. The dates should reflect the information in the court file. Please print legibly when completing this worksheet.

Defendant(s)	Date Served	Date of Default	Date of Answer	Affirmative Defenses
______	______	______	______	☐Yes ☐ No
______	______	______	______	☐Yes ☐ No
______	______	______	______	☐Yes ☐ No
______	______	______	______	☐Yes ☐ No
______	______	______	______	☐Yes ☐ No
______	______	______	______	☐Yes ☐ No

Documents	Date Filed	
Non military affidavit (with Dept. of Defense Manpower Form)	______	☐Yes ☐ Not Applicable
Motion to Dismiss	______	
Original promissory note	______	☐ Attached
Affidavit of lost promissory note	______	☐ Attached
Original/copy of recorded mortgage	______	
Original/copy of assignment of mortgage	______	
Affidavit of Indebtedness	______	$______
Affidavit of Costs	______	$______
Affidavit of Attorney's Fees	______	$______
Affidavit of GAL Fees	______	$______

Verification

Legal description	☐Yes ☐ No
Names of all parties	☐Yes ☐ No

Spelling of all parties names ☐Yes ☐ No
Plaintiff is proper mortgagee ☐Yes ☐ No
Bankruptcy ☐Yes ☐ No ☐ Stay lifted
I HEREBY CERTIFY that I have personally reviewed the court file and verified all of the information and entries on this foreclosure worksheet.

____
Attorney Signature

____
Printed Name of Attorney

____
Florida Bar Number

Criminal Orders

2018–115–CRIM. FIRST APPEARANCE DIVISION

IN THE CIRCUIT COURT OF THE SEVENTEENTH JUDICIAL CIRCUIT IN AND FOR BROWARD COUNTY, FLORIDA

Administrative Order No. 2018–115–Crim

FIRST APPEARANCE DIVISION

(a) Florida Rule of Judicial Administration 2.215(b)(3) states the Chief Judge "shall, considering available resources, ensure the efficient and proper administration of all courts within [this] circuit."

(b) A First Appearance Division is established to ensure every arrested person may be taken before a judicial officer as required by law or rule of procedure.[1]

(c) It shall be the responsibility of all judges presiding over first appearance to determine probable cause and examine the custody status of all persons appearing before the first appearance judge. Public safety shall be the overwhelming consideration of all judges who establish a monetary bond, place persons on pretrial release or release the person on their own recognizance. For those persons who do not pose a threat to public safety, all judges shall first consider non-monetary release conditions.

(d) In accordance with the authority vested in the Chief Judge by Article V. section 2(d) of the Florida Constitution, section 43.26, Florida Statutes, and Florida Rule of Judicial Administration 2.215, it is hereby **ORDERED:**

(1) All first appearance proceedings shall be open to the public, except proceedings otherwise designated as confidential by court rule or Florida Statutes.

(2) *Date and Time.*

(a) General. A First Appearance docket shall be conducted at 8:30 a.m. and 1:00 p.m., Monday through Friday of each week. Any individual who was arrested, and completed processing at the Broward County Jail or other detention facility no later than 4:00 a.m., shall be placed on the 8:30 a.m. docket, except as otherwise provided in this Administrative Order. Any individual arrested and completed processing at the Broward County Jail or other detention facility no later than 9:00 a.m. shall be placed on the afternoon docket, except as otherwise provided in this Administrative Order. Nothing in this Administrative Order precludes the judge presiding in first appearance to alter the schedule for judicial efficiency.

(b) On court holidays, Saturdays, and Sundays, the First Appearance docket shall be conducted at 8:30 a.m. only. First Appearance matters held on court holidays, Saturdays, and Sundays include shelter hearings, juvenile detention hearings, and misdemeanor and felony domestic violence matters.

(c) During any natural disaster or emergency closure of the courts, the Chief Judge shall determine the time and/or location for conducting first appearance hearings.

(d) Individuals arrested for violations of probation or community control shall not be taken before the first appearance judge, unless otherwise required under this Administrative Order, but shall be taken before the appropriate judge as set forth in paragraphs (9) and (10) of this Administrative Order.

(3) *Location.* The First Appearance hearings will be held in Room 4155 of the Broward County Courthouse–West Tower, 201 S.E. Sixth Street, Fort Lauderdale, Florida, 33301, with video links to any and all facilities where the arrested individual is detained by the Broward County Sheriff.

(4) *Required Attendance.* The following individuals shall be present at the First Appearance hearings: First Appearance Judge[2] (First Appearance Judge), Clerk of the Courts or her designee (herein Clerk), State Attorney or his designee (herein State Attorney), Public Defender or his designee (herein Public Defender), Court Video Operator/Digital Court Reporter, Sheriff or his designee(s) (herein Sheriff) as necessary to provide security, Court Bailiff assigned by the Sheriff, Pre–Trial Services[3] or designee(s) (herein Director), and the individual being detained by the Sheriff.

A Spanish Interpreter and Creole Interpreter shall be on call/available for the scheduled First Appearance dockets on Monday through Friday. A Spanish Interpreter shall be on call/available for the scheduled First Appearance dockets on Saturdays, Sundays, and court holidays. If an interpreter is required and none is available, the First Appearance Judge shall determine if there is probable cause to continue to detain the individual and reset the matter for the next court business day on the afternoon docket so that an interpreter may be present at the hearing. The First Appearance Judge shall advise the Trial Court Administrator's Interpreter Services of the case number, date and time of the hearing, and language required.

If the First Appearance Judge determines the detained individual voluntarily refuses to attend the First Appearance hearing, the First Appearance Judge shall determine probable cause for the absent individual as required by law or rule of procedure.

(5) *Representation at First Appearance.* All persons arrested for and/or charged with violating a state statute, or

county or municipal ordinance are entitled to representation by legal counsel at first appearance.

If the accused has not retained private counsel to represent them, and if the accused is indigent and arrested for and/or charged with violating a state statute, the Office of the Public Defender shall be appointed to represent the accused at first appearance. The representation shall continue until the Clerk makes a determination on the accused's application for indigent status. Should the Clerk determine the accused is not indigent, or if the accused does not submit an application for criminal indigent status within seven (7) days after being brought before the Court for his or her first appearance hearing, the Office of the Public Defender shall be discharged from representation without further order of the Court.

If the accused has not retained private counsel to represent them, and if the accused is indigent and arrested for and/or charged with violating a county or municipal ordinance, and the county or municipality has not entered into an agreement with the Public Defender pursuant to section 27.51, Florida Statutes to represent individuals arrested for only county or municipal ordinance violations, the arresting entity shall have an attorney or attorneys present at First Appearance for appointment by the presiding judge for indigent individuals Monday to Friday at 9:30 a.m. and 1:30 p.m. On weekends and court holidays, the municipality shall have an attorney present at First Appearance between the hours of 9:00 a.m. and 10:00 a.m.

If the county or municipality has not entered into an agreement with the State Attorney pursuant to section 27.02, Florida Statutes to prosecute county or city municipal ordinance violations, the arresting entity shall have an attorney present at First Appearance Monday to Friday at 9:30 a.m. and 1:30 p.m. On weekends and court holidays, the arresting entity shall have an attorney present at First Appearance between the hours of 9:00 a.m. and 10:00 a.m.

The county and each municipality shall provide the Chief Judge, Clerk, Sheriff, and First Appearance Judge the name of the attorney who is prosecuting violations on its behalf and the name of the attorney to be appointed for indigent individuals charged with only a county or municipal ordinance no later than the first of each month.

(6) *Required Pleadings/Papers.*

(a) The following documents shall be provided to the First Appearance Judge at the first appearance hearing for each individual: (i) booking slip; (ii) probable cause affidavit or other document setting forth the reasons for the individual's arrest; (iii) Pretrial Services Report; and (iv) the individual's criminal history information,[4] if completed. Broward Pretrial Services shall also provide to the Court, Public Defender and State Attorney a risk assessment report objectively assessing risk factors for the accused.

(b) The Clerk or Broward Pretrial Services shall provide a copy of the booking slip, probable cause affidavit, risk assessment evaluation or other document setting forth the reasons for the individual's arrest and any other paper as required by law or rule of procedure to the State Attorney, Public Defender, and Director.

(c) The Clerk or Sheriff shall prepare and provide to the First Appearance Judge, Administrative Judge of the County Court, State Attorney, Public Defender, Director, and Sheriff or Clerk a printed list of all cases heard at each First Appearance docket. The Clerk and Sheriff shall confer to determine which entity will be responsible for providing the printed list as required by this provision.

(7) All individuals in the custody of the Sheriff being detained because of an arrest, warrant, capias, or order shall be brought before the First Appearance Judge for a hearing within twenty-four (24) hours of his or her arrest as required by law or rule of procedure, unless otherwise indicated in this Administrative Order.

(8) *Second Hearing before the First Appearance Judge.* If any individual is still being detained on a misdemeanor charge or county or municipal ordinance violation and has not been released from the Sheriff's detention facility within two (2) days after being granted bond or pretrial release at his or her first appearance hearing, or if any individual is detained on a non-violent second or third degree felony charge, which is not an offense listed in section 907.041(4), Florida Statutes, and has not been released from the Sheriff's detention facility within two (2) days after being granted bond or approved for release under the supervision of Pre–Trial Release program at his or her first appearance hearing, there shall be a second hearing before the First Appearance Judge on the first court business day that is not a weekend or court holiday at the afternoon docket for first appearance hearings. The Director shall prepare the list of individuals eligible for a second hearing and forward the list to the Clerk. The Clerk shall thereafter prepare and distribute a copy of the second hearing docket to the First Appearance Judge, Administrative Judge of the County Court, State Attorney, Public Defender, Office of Criminal Conflict and Civil Regional Counsel, Sheriff, and attorney retained by the county or each municipality to represent individuals charged with only a county or municipal ordinance violation.

(9) *In Custody Felony Violation of Probation.*

(a) All persons arrested on a felony warrant for violation of probation or community control shall be transported, upon arrest, to the Broward County Main Jail.

(b) The Broward Sheriff's Office shall ensure that all persons arrested Monday–Thursday and on Sunday on a felony warrant for violation of probation or community control and who are held with no bond or who are unable to post a monetary bond are taken directly to the division judge presiding over their case the next court business day following their arrest.

(c) Individuals arrested on a Friday, Saturday, or court holiday on a felony warrant for violation of probation or community control and who are held with no bond or who are unable to post a monetary bond shall be taken before the division judge presiding over their case the next court business day following their arrest.

(d) It shall be the responsibility of the Department of Corrections and the Clerk to ensure that all necessary paperwork, including pleadings, warrants, etc., relating to the allegations of violation of probation or community control is provided to the Court, Public Defender, and State Attorney contemporaneously with the Defendant's court appearance.

(e) The Clerk, Sheriff, or Department of Corrections shall prepare and provide to each division judge, the State Attorney and Public Defender, a daily (Monday–Friday) printed list of all cases to be heard by each division judge in accordance with this section.

(f) All persons arrested on a felony warrant for violation of probation or community control, the basis of which is a new law violation, shall be taken before the First Appearance Judge in accordance with this Administrative Order. A subsequent hearing for persons arrested for and/or charged with a new law violation and a violation of probation or community control pursuant to section 948.06, Florida Statutes, shall be held by the division judge presiding over their case two (2) days following their arrest, or the next court business day if the second day is a weekend or court holiday.

(g) In any case where the assigned division judge is unavailable, the Clerk or Sheriff shall notify the Administrative Judge of the Circuit Criminal Division in order for a hearing to be scheduled before an available judge. If the Administrative Judge of the Circuit Criminal Division is unavailable, the Clerk or Sheriff shall notify the Chief Judge.

(10) *In Custody Misdemeanor Violation of Probation.*

(a) All persons arrested on a misdemeanor warrant for violation of probation shall be transported, upon arrest, to the Broward County Main Jail.

(b) All persons arrested Monday–Thursday and on Sunday on a misdemeanor warrant for violation of probation for a case with a designation 10, and who are held with no bond or who are unable to post a monetary bond, shall be taken directly to the division judge presiding over their case the next court business day following their arrest.

(c) Individuals arrested on a Friday, Saturday, or court holiday on a misdemeanor warrant for violation of probation for a case with a designation of 10 and who are held with no bond or who are unable to post a monetary bond shall be taken directly to the division judge presiding over their case the next court business day following their arrest.

(d) All persons arrested Monday–Thursday and on Sunday on a misdemeanor warrant for violation of probation for a case with a designation of 20, 30, or 40, and who are held with no bond or who are unable to post a monetary bond, shall be taken before the Chairperson of the County Criminal Division the next court business day following their arrest for appropriate action, including reassignment to another judicial officer if necessary.

(e) Individuals arrested on a Friday, Saturday, or court holiday on a misdemeanor warrant for violation of probation for a case with a designation of 20, 30, or 40, and who are held with no bond or who are unable to post a monetary bond shall be taken before the Chairperson of the County Criminal Division the next court business day following their arrest for appropriate action, including reassignment to another judicial officer if necessary.

(f) All persons arrested on a misdemeanor warrant for violation of probation, the basis of which is a new law violation, shall be taken before the First Appearance Judge in accordance with this Administrative Order.

(g) In any case where the assigned division judge is unavailable, the Clerk or Sheriff shall notify the Chairperson for the County Criminal Division in order for a hearing to be scheduled before an available judge. If the Chairperson for the County Criminal Division is unavailable, the Clerk or Sheriff shall notify the Chief Judge.

(11) *Misdemeanor Domestic Violence.* All persons arrested for and/or charged with misdemeanor domestic violence shall have first appearance proceedings before the judge assigned to Division MV/57, except as provided in Section (2)(b) of this Administrative Order.

(12) *Felony Domestic Violence.* All persons arrested for and/or charged with felony domestic violence shall have first appearance proceedings before the judge assigned to Division FV/GC/57, except as provided in Section (2)(b) of this Administrative Order.

(13) *Extradition Warrants and Extradition Hearings.* **Effective January 7, 2019**, if an individual is detained on a warrant requesting or requiring extradition, the Sheriff shall provide a docket of cases to be heard to the judge presiding in Division MT with a copy to the State Attorney, Public Defender, and Clerk. All hearings required by law or rule of procedure shall be heard by the judge presiding in Division MT in courtroom WW5155 on Tuesdays and Thursdays at 1:00 p.m. or as otherwise indicated by the court, excluding court holidays. In the event the judge presiding in Division MT is unavailable or otherwise absent, these matters shall be heard by such other judge as may be designated by the Chief Judge from time to time. The Broward Sheriff's Office shall be responsible for transporting any individuals for extradition hearings.

(14) *Felony Capias Arrests.* If an individual is detained on a felony capias, the Clerk shall set the case on the presiding judge's next court business day docket.

(15) *Misdemeanor Capias Arrests.* Unless an individual is held with no bond, any individual arrested on a misdemeanor capias shall appear before the First Appearance Judge who shall have authority to modify the bond or set pretrial release conditions. If an individual is held with no bond on a misdemeanor capias for a case with a designation of 20, 30, or 40, the judge shall direct the Clerk to set the case before the Chairperson of the County Criminal Division the next court business day following his or her arrest for appropriate action. If an individual is held with no bond on a misdemeanor capias for a case with a designation of 10, the judge shall direct the Clerk to set the case on the county criminal division judge's next court business day docket.

(16) *Civil Detentions.* If an individual is detained on any civil writ or other noncriminal order requiring detention, excluding a writ of arrest for failure to pay child support, the Sheriff shall advise the presiding division judge, Administrative Judge for the division, and the Chief Judge of the individual's detention. If the civil writ or other non-criminal order requiring detention, excluding a writ of arrest for failure to pay child support, is not a case pending in Broward County or the Seventeenth Judicial Circuit, the Sheriff shall advise the Administrative Judge for the division and the Chief Judge of the individual's detention. In the absence of the Chief Judge and Administrative Judge for the division, the Sheriff shall advise the Circuit Civil Duty Judge of the individual's detention.

(17) *All Other Authorized Detentions.* If an individual is otherwise detained by the Sheriff for any reason in which there is no pending case in Broward County or the Seventeenth Judicial Circuit, the Sheriff shall advise the Chief Judge of the individual's detention. In the absence of the Chief Judge, the Sheriff shall advise the Circuit Criminal and Circuit Civil Duty Judges. This includes any such person arrested on a civil warrant or contempt order.

(18) *Additional Charges or Amended Charges.* If an individual in custody is charged with additional crimes or the initial charges are otherwise amended, the individual shall be heard on the next First Appearance docket as to the additional crimes or amended charges as required by law or rule of procedure.

(19) *Filing of Formal Charges.* If an individual remains in the custody of the Sheriff for thirty (30) days from the date of arrest without formal charges being filed, a hearing shall be held before the First Appearance on the 33rd day following the individual's arrest. It shall be the responsibility of the Broward Sheriff's Office, State Attorney and/or Public Defender to bring such cases to the attention of the Court. It shall be the responsibility of the Broward Sheriff's Office and/or State Attorney to advise the Court in such cases where the individual is unrepresented by legal counsel.

(20) *Authority of First Appearance Judge.* Any judge presiding at any hearing authorized by this Administrative Order shall have the full power and authority of a county judge or circuit judge, as necessary, based upon the matter presented for a determination.

(21) *Notification.* It shall be the responsibility of the Broward Sheriff's Office, Department of Detention to advise the Chief Judge of any person who is not facing a criminal charge or charges and who is confined in the Broward County Jail for more than thirty (30) days.

(22) This Administrative Order vacates and supersedes Administrative Order 2018–89–Crim. Any and all other Administrative Orders, not inconsistent with this Administrative Order and not vacated remain in full force and effect.

DONE AND ORDERED in Chambers at Fort Lauderdale, Broward County, Florida on this 27th day of December, 2018.

Carol-Lisa Phillips
Acting Chief Judge

[1] If the arrested person is a minor and not being held on charges filed as an adult by the State Attorney, he or she will not be brought before the First Appearance Judge except on court holidays or weekends. If the arrested person is a minor, he or she will be brought before the judge presiding over detention hearings Monday through Friday. The procedures for juvenile detention hearings are established by separate Administrative Order. If the minor is charged with a misdemeanor criminal traffic offense, he or she shall be treated as an adult as required by law.

[2] Monday through Friday dockets for all first appearance matters except misdemeanor and felony domestic violence cases will be heard by a county court judge assigned pursuant to a separate Administrative Order. A circuit or county court judge will be assigned to all First Appearance duties by memorandum from the Chief Judge to preside at dockets held on Saturdays, Sundays, and court holidays. If a judge assigned to a First Appearance docket is not able to preside, for any reason, he or she shall secure a replacement and advise the Chief Judge, Trial Court Administrator, Administrative Judge for the County Court, Chairperson for the County Criminal Division, and Clerk, in writing, of his or her replacement. If the judge is not able to provide written notice, he or she shall verbally advise the Chief Judge, Administrative Judge for the County Court, Chairperson for County Criminal Division, and Clerk, and thereafter provide written notice. In the event a judge resigns or retires, the judge appointed or elected to fill the vacancy shall be responsible to preside at the dockets assigned to the judge who resigned or retired.

[3] Pre–Trial Services shall prepare an objective risk assessment on each defendant with a crime except if the criminal charge is a capital felony or a first degree felony punishable by life. Pre–Trial Services shall assess the risk of the defendant's failure to appear at future court hearings and risk of performance on community supervision. The risk assessment tool shall consider, *inter alia*, the defendant's criminal history, prior failures to appear, and community ties.

[4] Administrative Order III–97–A–13A remains in effect. If the criminal history is not provided at the time of booking as set forth in Administrative Order III–97–A–13A, the criminal history shall be provided by the Sheriff.

2018–9–CRIM. ALTERNATIVE SANCTIONS PROGRAM FOR MISDEMEANOR OFFENDERS

IN THE CIRCUIT COURT OF THE SEVENTEENTH JUDICIAL CIRCUIT IN AND FOR BROWARD COUNTY, FLORIDA

Administrative Order No. 2018–9–CRIM

ADMINISTRATIVE ORDER ESTABLISHING AN ALTERNATIVE SANCTIONS PROGRAM FOR MISDEMEANOR OFFENDERS

(a) There is a substantial number of technical violations of probation by misdemeanants that do not involve a new arrest or other serious violations.

(b) Arresting and incarcerating certain non-violent offenders for minor and technical violations of probation is both expensive and nonproductive.

(c) There is research to support that recidivism may be reduced by utilizing collaborative efforts among the courts, probation and law enforcement to hold the offender accountable and apply swift and certain sanctions for technical violations of probation.

(d) Providing an administrative option for processing technical violations of probation will have the potential to offer benefits including:

i. Reducing the court docket of probation and violation hearings;

ii. Reducing the workload of prosecutors and defense attorneys involved with many technical violation hearings;

iii. Reducing law enforcement resources required to serve violation warrants for certain technical violations;

iv. Reducing jail population for offenders pending violation hearings; and

v. Offering the offender an alternative to a violation hearing in court, which will allow the offender to remain engaged in employment, school, treatment, etc., and allow the offender to take immediate responsibility for their actions and consequences of those actions.

(e) In accordance with the authority vested in the Chief Judge by Florida Rule of Judicial Administration 2.215 and section 948.06, Florida Statutes, it is hereby **ORDERED**:

1. *Misdemeanor Alternative Sanctions Program.* There is created in the Seventeenth Judicial Circuit, Broward County, Florida, a program that shall be known as the Misdemeanor Alternative Sanctions Program (herein referred to as "Misdemeanor ASP") for alleged violations as set forth in Section 3 of this Administrative Order.

2. *Eligibility.* To be eligible for the program, offenders must have been placed on probation under the supervision of the Broward Sheriff's Office by a judge in Broward County, Florida, and have stable community ties. Offenders who are eligible for the program include misdemeanor probation offenders. The program only applies to offenders who have committed certain technical violations addressed in the Misdemeanor Alternative Sanctions Program Violation/Sanction Matrix set forth in Section 3 of this Administrative Order. The threat an offender poses to public safety is the most important factor in determining eligibility. Participation in the Misdemeanor ASP is within the discretion of the trial judge based upon the nature of the underlying offense, an offender's criminal history, the nature of the alleged violation, and any other factor a judge may lawfully consider. The following individuals/offenders are not eligible for participation in the Misdemeanor ASP: (1) offenders charged with misdemeanor domestic violence, regardless of adjudication; and (2) offenders who have new violations, are absconders, or have violated a "no contact" condition of supervision. An eligible offender may participate in the Misdemeanor ASP no more than three (3) times.

3. *Qualifying Technical Violations and Approved Sanctions.* The following matrix lists the specific technical violations that may be addressed through the Misdemeanor ASP process for offenders who were sentenced in Broward County, Florida. Each technical violation includes a list of sanctions determined and approved by the court for the probation officer to select from when reporting these technical violations, based on the individual offender's circumstances at the time of the violation. An offender's participation in the Misdemeanor ASP and completion of any alternative sanctions does not excuse the offender's compliance with any other conditions of probation or completion of any statutorily mandated program(s) or requirement(s).

MISDEMEANOR ALTERNATIVE SANCTIONS PROGRAM VIOLATION/SANCTION MATRIX

VIOLATION	APPROVED LIST OF SANCTIONS
Condition (1): Failed to report changes in residence or employment without first procuring the officer's consent (or notifying immediately if evicted from residence or laid off from job)	1. Weekly call in for 30 days 2. Report 2 times per month for 1 month
Condition (1): Failed to request permission prior to leaving the county/country	1. Report 2 times per month for 2 months 2. Report weekly for 1 month
Condition (2): Reported late; failed to report as instructed, but reported within 20 calendar days	1. Weekly call in for 30 days 2. Report 2 times per month for 1 month
Condition (5): Positive drug test for non-prescribed drugs (first occurrence)	1. Weekly drug testing for 2 months 2. Drug evaluation and treatment, if recommended
Condition (5): Failure to submit to random testing as directed	1. Weekly drug testing for 30 days 2. Attend 10 AA/NA meetings within 10 days
Condition (6): Failure to maintain employment	1. Attend and complete BSO Employability Skills workshop 2. Submit job search logs to officer weekly
Condition (7): Failure to answer inquiries truthfully (depending on nature of question, response, and reason for being untruthful, consequence will vary)	1. Weekly call in for 30 days 2. Report weekly for 30 days
Condition (8): Failure to comply with officer's instructions (depending on nature of instruction and reason for not complying, consequence will vary)	1. Weekly call in for 30 days 2. 16 hours of community service with BSO
Condition (9): Failed to pay Cost of Supervision (COS)	1. Submit job search logs to Officer weekly 2. No recreational travel until payments are current 3. Community service hours with BSO at $10.00 per hour until payments become current

4. *Misdemeanor Alternative Sanctions Program Process.*

A. The probation officer shall inform offenders who have committed violations enumerated in Section 3 of this Administrative Order that they may participate in the Misdemeanor ASP for administrative disposition of the violation. No offender is required to participate in the Misdemeanor ASP and may opt for a formal violation of probation proceeding in County Court.

B. If the offender admits the violation, agrees to accept the administrative sanction recommended by the probation officer, and agrees to waive a formal violation hearing, the probation officer will prepare a Misdemeanor Alternative Sanctions Program Technical Violation Notification, which will provide details of the circumstances of the technical violation that occurred and the probation officer's recommended sanction, based on the sanctions listed in the approved matrix. If the offender agrees to participate in the Misdemeanor ASP, the offender will sign the second section of this form titled Offender's Waiver of Formal VOP Hearing, Admission of Violation, and Acceptance of Sanctions. These forms as well as the Misdemeanor Alternative Sanctions Program Technical Violation Notification will be submitted to the Court, State Attorney, and Defense Attorney via an electronic drop box once the probation officer signs and dates the form. If the offender elects to discontinue participation in the Misdemeanor ASP, the offender's prior admission to the technical violation may not be used as evidence in subsequent proceedings pursuant to section 948.06(1)(h)7., Florida Statutes.

C. The judge shall review the submitted forms and, if the judge agrees that the technical violation should be addressed via the Misdemeanor ASP and agrees with the recommended sanction, the judge will sign the Order—Misdemeanor Alternative Sanctions Program. If the judge does not agree with the particular sanction recommended by the officer or does not agree that the technical violation should be addressed via the Misdemeanor ASP, the judge shall reflect further instructions on the order. If the judge does not approve the use of the Misdemeanor ASP, any admission(s) of violation by the Defendant given as a condition of agreeing to enter into the Misdemeanor ASP may not be used as evidence in subsequent proceedings pursuant to section 948.06(1)(h)7., Florida Statutes.

D. Upon court approval, the probation officer will instruct the offender on the sanction imposed by the court and instruct the offender to take actions necessary to ensure the sanction is executed immediately. Failure to complete the imposed sanction as instructed will result in a violation report, affidavit and warrant being submitted to the court for the original underlying violation. Failure to complete the imposed sanction shall not constitute additional grounds for violation.

E. No sentencing points will be assessed by virtue of entering into or failing to complete the Misdemeanor ASP.

5. ADMINISTRATION. The Misdemeanor ASP shall be administered by the Broward County Court of the Seventeenth Judicial Circuit and the Broward Sheriff's Office.

6. EFFECTIVE DATE. This Administrative Order shall take effect on March 5, 2018, and shall remain in effect until further order of this Court.

DONE AND ORDERED in Fort Lauderdale, Broward County, Florida, this 6th day of February, 2018.

Jack Tuter
Chief Judge

Attachment "A"

IN THE COUNTY COURT OF THE SEVENTEENTH JUDICIAL CIRCUIT, IN AND FOR BROWARD COUNTY, FLORIDA

STATE OF FLORIDA Judge/Division
Case No. ____

vs.

____
Defendant

MISDEMEANOR ALTERNATIVE SANCTIONS PROGRAM TECHNICAL VIOLATION NOTIFICATION

Original Charge: ________

Term of Supervision: ________ to ______________

Offender Eligible: ☐

Date of Violation(s): ________ ☐ First or ☐ Second Violation

Technical violation that occurred: ________

Sanctions/consequence to be imposed in the discretion of the Court: ______________

OFFENDER'S WAIVER OF FORMAL VOP HEARING, ADMISSION OF VIOLATION, AND ACCEPTANCE OF SANCTIONS

By signing below I understand that I have the right to a formal violation of probation hearing before the Court; however, I am agreeing to waive this right along with waiving the following rights to:

- be represented by legal counsel;
- subpoena and present witnesses and evidence in my defense and to present any defense I might have to the judge;
- require a written statement from a factfinder as to the evidence relied on and the reasons for the sanction imposed;
- see and hear witnesses testify or confront witnesses against me; and
- require the State of Florida to prove my guilt before a neutral and detached hearing body.

I also acknowledge that I am aware of the right to contest and appeal any order entered by the Court and hereby waive this right to appeal all matters except the legality of my sentence. No one has coerced me, pressured me, made any threats against me, or promised me anything to convince me to give up these rights.

I am agreeing to voluntarily participate in the Misdemeanor Alternative Sanctions Program and understand I can discontinue participation in the Misdemeanor Alternative Sanctions Program at any time before the issuance of the court order imposing the recommended sanction. I am admitting to the technical violation(s) of probation listed above with the understanding that I will be required to complete the additional sanction(s) listed above.

I further understand that if I fail to complete the additional sanction(s) within the time specified, a formal violation of probation report, affidavit and warrant will be forwarded to the Court. I understand that if the Court determines I have violated my probation, I may be sentenced as authorized by law.

I understand the Court reserves the right to accept or reject my request to participate in the Misdemeanor Alternative Sanctions Program.

______________________ ______________________
Offender Signature / Date Officer Signature / Date

Typed/Printed Name Typed/Printed Name & Telephone Number

____
Supervisor Signature / Date

Attachment "B"

IN THE COUNTY COURT OF THE SEVENTEENTH JUDICIAL CIRCUIT,
IN AND FOR BROWARD COUNTY, FLORIDA

STATE OF FLORIDA Judge/Division ____

Case No. _______

VS

____

Defendant

ORDER

MISDEMEANOR ALTERNATIVE SANCTIONS PROGRAM

It appears that the Defendant has materially violated one or more conditions of probation but has not committed a new law violation and is otherwise eligible to participate in the Misdemeanor Alternative Sanctions Program.

☐ The Court has reviewed the Misdemeanor Alternative Sanctions Program Technical Violation Notification and Offender's Waiver of Formal VOP Hearing, Admission of Violation, and Acceptance of Sanctions form, a copy of which is attached, and approves the following sanction selected: __________.

Accordingly, it is hereby ORDERED:

1. The Defendant shall complete the sanction selected.

2. The Broward Sheriff's Office is directed to forward a violation of probation report, affidavit and warrant to the Court in the event the Defendant fails to satisfactorily complete the sanction selected.

OR

☐ The Court does not approve the use of the Misdemeanor Alternative Sanctions Program and directs the Broward Sheriff's Office to submit a violation of probation report, affidavit and warrant to address the alleged violation.

OR

☐ The Court hereby sets this matter for a reprimand hearing on __________, 20 __________. The Defendant and probation officer shall attend this hearing. The Broward Sheriff's Office shall provide notice of hearing to the Defendant.

DONE AND ORDERED in Chambers, Fort Lauderdale, Broward County, Florida, this __________ day of __________, 20 __________.

____

COUNTY COURT JUDGE

2018–8–CRIM. ALTERNATIVE SANCTIONS PROGRAM FOR FELONY OFFENDERS

IN THE CIRCUIT COURT OF THE SEVENTEENTH JUDICIAL CIRCUIT IN AND FOR BROWARD COUNTY, FLORIDA

Administrative Order No. 2018–8–CRIM

ADMINISTRATIVE ORDER ESTABLISHING AN ALTERNATIVE SANCTIONS PROGRAM FOR FELONY OFFENDERS

(a) There is a substantial number of technical violations of probation by felons that do not involve a new arrest or other serious violations.

(b) Arresting and incarcerating certain non-violent offenders for minor and technical violations of probation is both expensive and nonproductive.

(c) There is research to support that recidivism may be reduced by utilizing collaborative efforts among the courts, probation and law enforcement to hold the offender accountable and apply swift and certain sanctions for technical violations of probation.

(d) Providing an administrative option for processing technical violations of probation will have the potential to offer benefits including:

i. Reducing the court docket of probation and violation hearings;

ii. Reducing the workload of prosecutors and defense attorneys involved with many technical violation hearings;

iii. Reducing law enforcement resources required to serve violation warrants for certain technical violations;

iv. Reducing jail population for offenders pending violation hearings; and

v. Offering the offender an alternative to a violation hearing in court, which will allow the offender to remain engaged in employment, school, treatment, etc., and allow the offender to take immediate responsibility for their actions and consequences of those actions.

(e) In accordance with the authority vested in the Chief Judge by Florida Rule of Judicial Administration 2.215 and section 948.06, Florida Statutes, it is hereby **ORDERED**:

1. *Felony Alternative Sanctions Program.* There is created in the Seventeenth Judicial Circuit, Broward County, Florida, a program that shall be known as the Felony Alternative Sanctions Program (herein referred to as "Felony ASP") for alleged violations as set forth in Section 3 of this Administrative Order.

2. *Eligibility.* To be eligible for the program, offenders must have been placed on probation or community control under the supervision of the Department of Corrections in Broward County, Florida, and have stable community ties. Except as provided herein, offenders who are eligible for the Felony ASP include probation offenders, drug offenders, and community control supervision offenders. The program only applies to offenders who have committed certain technical violations addressed in the Alternative Sanctions Program Violation/Sanction Matrix included in Section 3 of this Administrative Order. The threat an offender poses to public safety is the most important factor in determining eligibility. The following individuals/offenders are not eligible for participation in the Felony ASP: (1) offenders whose supervision offense is a "dangerous crime" as described in section 907.041(4)(a), Florida Statutes, regardless of adjudication; (2) offenders with a lengthy prior criminal history; (3) persons with cases in repeat offender court, felony drug court, or domestic violence; and (4) offenders who have new law violations, are absconders,

or have violated a “no contact” condition of supervision. An eligible offender may participate in the Felony ASP no more than three (3) times.

3. *Qualifying Technical Violations and Approved Sanctions.* The following matrix lists the specific technical violations that may be addressed through the Felony ASP process for offenders who were sentenced in Broward County, Florida. Each technical violation includes a list of sanctions determined and approved by the court for the probation officer to select from when reporting these technical violations, based on the individual offender’s circumstances at the time of the violation. An offender’s participation in the Felony ASP and completion of any alternative sanction(s) does not alter or reduce an offender’s obligation to complete all other conditions of probation or community control imposed by the court.

FELONY ALTERNATIVE SANCTIONS PROGRAM VIOLATION/SANCTION MATRIX

VIOLATION	APPROVED LIST OF SANCTIONS
Condition (1): Reported late; failed to report as instructed, but reported within 40 calendar days	1. Weekly call in for 2 months 2. Report 2 times per month for 2 months 3. Weekly reporting for 2 months
Condition (2): Failed to pay Cost of Supervision (COS)	1. Submit job search logs to PO weekly 2. No recreational travel for 3 months 3. Submit a monthly budget until payments are current
Condition (3): Failed to report changes in residence or employment without first procuring the officer's consent (or notifying immediately if evicted from residence or laid off from job), but reported that change within 40 calendar days after the change	1. Weekly call in for 2 months 2. Report 2 times per month for 2 months 3. 8 p.m. to 6 a.m. curfew for 2 months
Condition (3): Failed to request permission prior to leaving the county/country, but did report and/or return within 10 working days after leaving	1. Report 2 times per month for 3 months 2. Report weekly for 2 months 3. 8 p.m. to 6 a.m. curfew for 2 months
Condition (6): Found to be associating with person(s) engaged in criminal activity	1. 8 p.m. to 6 a.m. curfew for 2 months 2. 25 CSH within 30 days 3. Thinking for a Change (T4C) program
Condition (7): Positive drug test for non-prescribed drugs (first occurrence)	1. Drug evaluation and successfully complete treatment recommended 2. Weekly drug testing for 2 months 3. 8 p.m. to 6 a.m. curfew for 2 months
Condition (7): Positive drug test for non-prescribed drugs (second occurrence)	1. Increase level of treatment up to residential 2. Weekly drug testing for 3 months 3. 8 p.m. to 6 a.m. curfew for 3 months
Condition (8): Failure to maintain employment	1. Attend 3 sessions with DOC Employment Specialist 2. Submit job search logs to PO weekly

	3. Complete HBI program
Condition (9): Failure to answer inquiries truthfully (depending on nature of question, response, and reason for being untruthful, consequence will vary)	1. Weekly call in for 2 months 2. 25 CSH within 30 days 3. Thinking for a Change (T4C) program
Condition (9): Failure to comply with officer's instructions (depending on nature of instruction and reason for not complying, consequence will vary)	1. Weekly call in for 2 months 2. 25 CSH within 30 days 3. Thinking for a Change (T4C) program
Condition (10): Failure to pay restitution or court costs when there is 90 days or more remaining on probation	1. Submit job search logs daily (if unemployed) 2. Create a payment plan and budget 3. No recreational travel until current with payments
Condition (11): Failure to submit to random testing as directed	1. Weekly drug testing for 2 months 2. Attend 10 AA/NA meetings within 30 days 3. 8 p.m. to 6 a.m. curfew for 2 months
Special Condition (1): Failure to attend treatment evaluation or treatment session as scheduled	1. Weekly reporting until evaluation completed or missed session is made up 2. Curfew from 7 p.m. to 6 a.m. until evaluation completed or missed session is made up 3. 25 CSH within 30 days
Special Condition (8): Failure to complete community service hours as instructed	1. Daily call in until current 2. Weekly reporting until current 3. No recreational travel until in compliance
Special Condition (9): Failure to remain at residence during curfew period	1. Weekly reporting for 2 months 2. GPS for 2 months 3. 25 CSH within 30 days
Community Control Condition (16): Failure to maintain approved schedule – unapproved absence from required location (negligence in getting home late, stopping at store on way home without permission)	1. GPS for 2 months 2. 25 CSH within 30 days 3. Thinking for a Change (T4C) program

4. *Felony Alternative Sanctions Program Process.*

A. The probation or community control officer shall inform offenders who have committed violations enumerated in Section 3 of this Administrative Order that they may participate in the Felony ASP for administrative disposition of the violation. No offender is required to participate in the Felony ASP and may opt for a formal violation of probation proceeding in Circuit Court.

B. If the offender admits the violation, agrees to accept the administrative sanction recommended by the probation or community control officer, and agrees to waive a formal violation hearing, the probation or community control officer will prepare a Felony Alternative Sanctions Program Technical Violation Notification, which will provide details of the circumstances of the technical violation that occurred and the probation or community control officer's recommended sanction, based on the sanctions listed in the approved matrix. If the offender agrees to participate in the Felony ASP, the offender will sign the second section of this form titled Offender's Waiver of Formal VOP Hearing, Admission of Violation, and Acceptance of Sanctions. These forms as well as the Felony Alternative Sanctions Program Technical Violation Notification will be submitted to the Court, State Attorney, and Defense Attorney via an electronic drop box once the probation or community control officer signs and dates the form. If the offender elects to discontinue participation in the Felony ASP, the offender's prior admission to the technical violation may not be used as evidence in subsequent proceedings pursuant to section 948.06(1)(h)7., Florida Statutes.

C. The judge shall review the submitted forms and, if the judge agrees that the technical violation should be addressed via the Felony ASP and agrees with the recommended sanction, the judge will sign the Order—Felony Alternative Sanctions Program. If the judge does not agree with the particular sanction recommended by the officer or does not agree that the technical violation should be addressed via the Felony ASP, the judge shall reflect further instructions on the order. If the judge rejects the Department's recommendation to place a Defendant into the Felony ASP, any admission(s) of violation by the Defendant given as a condition of agreeing to enter into the Felony ASP may not be used as evidence in subsequent proceedings pursuant to section 948.06(1)(h)7., Florida Statutes.

D. Upon court approval, the probation or community control officer will instruct the offender on the sanction imposed by the court and instruct the offender to take actions necessary to ensure the sanction is executed immediately. Failure to complete the imposed sanction as instructed will result in a violation report, affidavit and warrant being submitted to the court for the original underlying violation. Failure to complete the imposed sanction shall not constitute additional grounds for violation.

E. No sentencing points will be assessed by virtue of entering into or failing to complete the Felony ASP.

F. This Administrative Order and the Felony ASP shall not affect the Department's use of Technical letters.

5. *Administration.* The Felony ASP shall be administered by the Broward County Circuit Court of the Seventeenth Judicial Circuit and the Florida Department of Corrections.

6. *Effective Date.* This Administrative Order shall take effect on March 5, 2018, and shall remain in effect until further order of this Court.

DONE AND ORDERED in Fort Lauderdale, Broward County, Florida, this 6th day of February, 2018.

Jack Tuter
Chief Judge

Attachment "A"

IN THE CIRCUIT COURT OF THE SEVENTEENTH JUDICIAL CIRCUIT, IN AND FOR BROWARD COUNTY, FLORIDA

STATE OF FLORIDA

VS

Judge/Division

DC No. ____

____
Defendant

Docket/UC No. _____

FELONY ALTERNATIVE SANCTIONS PROGRAM TECHNICAL VIOLATION NOTIFICATION

Original Charge: __________

Term of Supervision: ________ to ______________

Offender Eligible: ☐

Date of Violation(s): ________ ☐ First or ☐ Second Violation

Technical violation that occurred: ________

Sanctions/consequence to be imposed in the discretion of the Court: ______________________

OFFENDER'S WAIVER OF FORMAL VOP/VOCC HEARING, ADMISSION OF VIOLATION, AND ACCEPTANCE OF SANCTIONS

By signing below I understand that I have the right to a formal violation of probation or community control hearing before the Court; however, I am agreeing to waive this right along with waiving the following rights to:

- be represented by legal counsel,
- subpoena and present witnesses and evidence in my defense and to present any defense I might have to the judge,
- require a written statement from a factfinder as to the evidence relied on and the reasons for the sanction imposed,
- see and hear witnesses testify or confront witnesses against me, and
- require the State of Florida to prove my guilt before a neutral and detached hearing body.

I also acknowledge that I am aware of the right to contest and appeal any order entered by the Court and hereby waive this right to appeal all matters except the legality of my sentence. No one has coerced me, pressured me, made any threats against me, or promised me anything to convince me to give up these rights.

I am agreeing to voluntarily participate in the Felony Alternative Sanctions Program and understand I can discontinue participation in the Felony Alternative Sanctions Program at any time before the issuance of the court order imposing the recommended sanction. I am admitting to the technical violation(s) of probation or community control listed above with the understanding that I will be required to complete the additional sanction(s) listed above.

I further understand that if I fail to complete the additional sanction(s) within the time specified, a formal violation of probation or community control report, affidavit and warrant will be forwarded to the Court. I understand that if the Court determines I have violated my probation, I may be sentenced as authorized by law.

I understand the Court reserves the right to accept or reject my request to participate in the Felony Alternative Sanctions Program.

_____________________	_____________________
Offender Signature/ Date	Officer Signature /Date
Typed/Printed Name	Typed/Printed Name & Telephone Number

____
Supervisor Signature/ Date

Attachment "B"

STATE OF FLORIDA

IN THE CIRCUIT COURT OF THE SEVENTEENTH JUDICIAL CIRCUIT, IN AND FOR BROWARD COUNTY, FLORIDA

VS

Judge/Division ________

DC No. ____

____
Defendant

Docket/UC No. _____

ORDER
ALTERNATIVE SANCTIONS PROGRAM

It appears that the Defendant has materially violated one or more conditions of probation or community control but has not committed a new law violation and is otherwise eligible to participate in the Felony Alternative Sanctions Program.

☐ The Court has reviewed the Alternative Sanctions Technical Violation Notification and Offender's Waiver of Formal VOP/VOCC Hearing, Admission of Violation, and Acceptance of Sanctions form, a copy of which is attached, and approves the following sanction selected: _________.

Accordingly,

IT IS ORDERED:

1. The Defendant shall complete the sanction selected.

2. The Department of Corrections is directed to forward a violation of probation or community control report, affidavit and warrant to the Court in the event the Defendant fails to satisfactorily complete the sanction selected.

OR

☐ The Court does not approve the use of the Alternative Sanctions Program and directs the Department of Corrections to submit a violation of probation or community control report, affidavit and warrant to address the alleged violation.

OR

☐ The Court hereby sets this matter for a reprimand hearing on _________, 20 ________. The Defendant and probation officer shall attend this hearing. The Department of Corrections shall provide notice of hearing to the Defendant.

DONE AND ORDERED in Chambers, Broward County, Florida, this _________ day of _________, 20 _____.

____
CIRCUIT JUDGE

2017–63–CRIM. INTRODUCTION OF EVIDENCE CONTAINING HIGH–POTENCY NARCOTICS

IN THE CIRCUIT COURT OF THE SEVENTEENTH JUDICIAL CIRCUIT IN AND FOR BROWARD COUNTY, FLORIDA

Administrative Order No. 2017–63–Crim

ADMINISTRATIVE ORDER GOVERNING THE INTRODUCTION OF EVIDENCE CONTAINING HIGH–POTENCY NARCOTICS

(a) Pursuant to Article V, section 2(d) of the Florida Constitution and section 43.26, Florida Statutes, the Chief Judge is charged with the authority and the power to do everything necessary to promote the prompt and efficient administration of justice.

(b) Florida Rule of Judicial Administration 2.215 (b) (3) states the Chief Judge shall "develop an administrative plan" and "shall, considering available resources, ensure the efficient and proper administration of all courts within [this] circuit."

(c) The court has seen a steady increase in the number of opioid-related arrests.

(d) There has also been a dramatic increase in the prevalence of high-potency narcotics that are so strong accidental contact with or inhalation of such substances can be deadly.

(e) The health, safety, and welfare of those who conduct business within the courthouses of the Seventeenth Judicial Circuit, including employees and citizens, are of primary concern to this Court.

(f) In an effort to ensure the health and safety of all persons within each courthouse of the Seventeenth Judicial Circuit and to prevent any accidental exposure, this Court recognizes a need to establish a procedure for introducing evidence that contains or may contain high-potency narcotics ("HPN Exhibits").

(g) In accordance with the authority vested in the Chief Judge pursuant to Article V, section 2(d) of the Florida Constitution, section 43.26, Florida Statutes, and Florida Rule of Judicial Administration 2.215, it is hereby **ORDERED:**

(1) HPN Exhibits are those that contain or may contain high-potency narcotics which are highly toxic and may be fatal, including, but not limited to the following: Fentanyl (Actiq, Fentora, Duragesic, Subsys, Abstral, Lazanda, Ionsys, Onsolis, Duragesic–100, Duragensic–50, Duragensic, Duragensic–75, Sublimace, Duragensic–25, and Duragensic–12); Carfentanil; Remifentanil; Alfentanil; Sufentanil; and other related high-potency narcotics.

(2) In the event any party intends to introduce HPN Exhibits in any court proceeding, the party intending to introduce the evidence must file a notice of its possession of an HPN Exhibit no later than fifteen (15) days prior to hearing, unless a shorter time is permitted by the presiding Judge.

(3) The court shall conduct a hearing to determine if the HPN Exhibit(s) can be introduced by admission, statement of fact, photographs, stipulations and/or certificate of analysis.

(4) If the parties are unable to reach an agreement or stipulation at the hearing, the trial clerk(s) shall promptly notify a supervisor in the trial clerk division or evidence clerk division of the Clerk of the Courts.

(5) In the event that HPN Exhibits are brought into any courtroom or other public space of the Seventeenth Judicial Circuit courthouses for any purpose, including trial, the HPN Exhibits shall be double-bagged in clear heat-sealed packaging, sealed inside a manila envelope, and clearly labeled. Further, the HPN Exhibits must be handled, labeled, and packaged in accordance with all relevant and applicable policies that may be established by federal or local law enforcement, which may be amended from time to time to ensure the safety of all court participants.

(6) At any hearing, if the parties are unable to stipulate to alternative presentations of the evidence and an HPN Exhibit is to be introduced into evidence, the court shall discuss with the parties and decide upon the protective gear that may be worn by trial participants, including but not limited to, attorneys, court deputies, court reporters, trial clerk(s), evidence clerk(s), and the court. The court shall also decide whether the jury may handle the HPN Exhibit(s) and what, if any, protections shall be in place for the benefit of the jurors.

(7) The trial clerk(s) shall promptly notify an evidence clerk supervisor in the event that HPN Exhibits are marked as exhibits.

(8) This Administrative Order shall be effective immediately and shall continue until further order of this Court.

(9) This Administrative Order supersedes any provisions in prior Administrative Orders which may be inconsistent.

DONE AND ORDERED in Chambers, Fort Lauderdale, Florida, this 5th day of October, 2017.

Jack Tuter
Chief Judge

2017–59–CRIM. PROCEDURES FOR THE RELEASE OF CERTAIN INMATES UPON THE ISSUANCE OF A HURRICANE WATCH/WARNING OR OTHER NATURAL DISASTER

IN THE CIRCUIT COURT OF THE SEVENTEENTH JUDICIAL CIRCUIT IN AND FOR BROWARD COUNTY, FLORIDA

Administrative Order No. 2017–59–Crim

ADMINISTRATIVE ORDER ESTABLISHING PROCEDURES FOR THE RELEASE OF CERTAIN INMATES UPON THE ISSUANCE OF A HURRICANE WATCH/WARNING OR OTHER NATURAL DISASTER

(a) Pursuant to Article V, section 2(d) of the Florida Constitution and section 43.26, Florida Statutes, the Chief Judge is charged with the authority and the power to do everything necessary to promote the prompt and efficient administration of justice.

(b) Florida Rule of Judicial Administration 2.215 (b) (3) states the Chief Judge shall "develop an administrative plan" and "shall, considering available resources, ensure the efficient and proper administration of all courts within [this] circuit."

(c) The Broward County Board of County Commissioners have designated the Sheriff of Broward County, Florida as the Chief Correctional Officer for Broward County, pursuant to section 951.061, Florida Statutes, and Section 18–01 of the Broward County Code of Ordinances.

(d) As a result of the Seventeenth Judicial Circuit's location and susceptibility to sustaining hurricanes and other natural disasters, it is necessary to establish emergency procedures to permit the release of certain inmates from the custody of the Broward Sheriff's Office Department of Detention before or after a natural disaster strikes.

(e) In accordance with the authority vested in the Chief Judge pursuant to Article V, section 2(d) of the Florida Constitution, section 43.26, Florida Statutes, and Florida Rule of Judicial Administration 2.215, it is hereby **ORDERED:**

(1) When a hurricane watch or warning is issued by the National Weather Service, or any other natural disaster has happened or is imminent to occur in Broward County, Florida, such as a hurricane, flood, tornado, or other catastrophic event, the Broward Sheriff, or his designee, acting as Chief Correctional Officer, is hereby authorized to release, at his discretion and after consultation with the Chief Judge, any inmate sentenced to the custody of the Sheriff who has no more than thirty (30) days remaining on his/her sentence, excepting those inmates under mandatory sentence.

(2) Further in his discretion during such an emergency, the Sheriff, or his designee, acting as the Chief Correctional Officer may, after consultation with the Chief Judge, release any other person in the custody of the Sheriff who does not pose a threat to the safety of the citizens of Broward County, Florida.

(3) This Administrative Order shall be immediately effective and shall continue from year to year unless voided, modified, vacated, or otherwise suspended by subsequent order of the court.

DONE AND ORDERED in Chambers, Fort Lauderdale, Florida, this 27th day of September, 2017.

Jack Tuter
Chief Judge

2016–13–CRIM. IMMOBILIZATION AGENCIES

IN THE CIRCUIT COURT OF THE SEVENTEENTH JUDICIAL CIRCUIT IN AND FOR BROWARD COUNTY, FLORIDA

Order Number 2016–13–Crim

ADMINISTRATIVE ORDER AS TO IMMOBILIZATION AGENCIES

(a) Florida Rule of Judicial Administration 2.215(b)(3) states the chief judge shall "develop an administrative plan for the efficient and proper administration of all courts within that circuit."

(b) Section 316.193(13), Fla. Stat., establishes the conditions for a business entity to immobilize vehicles. The Seventeenth Judicial Circuit and Broward County judges want to standardize the addition of a business entity to a list of eligible immobilization agencies.

(c) In accordance with the authority vested in the chief judge by Florida Rule of Judicial Administration 2.215, it is ordered:

(1) This Administrative Order shall govern the addition of a business entity to a list of eligible immobilization agencies.

(2) A business entity seeking to immobilize vehicles pursuant to Section 316.193, Fla. Stat., shall submit the required affidavit to the Clerk of Court and complete the attached application. The original application and copy of the affidavit shall be provided to the Chairperson for the County Criminal Division.

(3) The Chairperson for the County Criminal Division shall review the application and affidavit and provide notice to the Clerk of Court if a business entity shall be included on the list of eligible immobilization agencies. Upon approval the Clerk of Court shall include the business entity on a list of eligible immobilization agencies and provide an updated list to all judges.

(4) All approved immobilization agencies shall provide a monthly report to the Chairperson for the County Criminal Division which provides the case numbers and status of the immobilization for the vehicles.

(5) Any business entity seeking to immobilize vehicles pursuant to Section 316.193, Fla. Stat. must comply with this Administrative Order on or before July 1, 2016. If a business entity has not complied on or before July 1, 2016 and been approved by the Chairperson for the County Criminal Division it must cease all operations to immobilize vehicles for Broward County or Seventeenth Judicial Circuit cases.

DONE AND ORDERED in chambers at Fort Lauderdale, Broward County, Florida on Mar. 1, 2016.

Peter M. Weinstein
Chief Judge

BROWARD COUNTY SEVENTEENTH JUDICIAL CIRCUIT VEHICLE IMMOBILIZATION APPLICATION

Name of Business ______________

Business Address ______________

Telephone Number ______________

Email Address ______________

Type of Business Entity ______________

Name of Principals/Officers/Directors/Shareholders of Business Entity

____

License(s) for Business Entity

Type ______________

Municipal or County ______________

Expiration Date ______________

License(s) for each Principals/Officers/Directors/Shareholders of Business Entity

Name of Individual ______________

Type ______________

Municipal or County ______________

Expiration Date ______________

Attach a copy of the affidavit provided to the Clerk of Court

AFFIDAVIT OF COMPLIANCE

________ (Name of Company) by and through its authorized agent ________ (Name of Affiant) being duly sworn deposes and says:

1. ________ (Name of Affiant) is the ________ (Title of Affiant) for ________ (Name of Company).

2. ________ (Affiant) has the authority to execute this Affidavit of Compliance on behalf of ________ (Name of Company).

3. ________ (Name of Company) has verifiable experience in immobilizing vehicles as reflected on the attached list of cases for Miami–Dade, Broward, or Palm Beach County from January 1, 2015 to date.

4. ________ (Name of Company) maintains accurate and complete records of all payments for the immobilization, copies of all documents pertaining to the court's order of impoundment or immobilization, and any other documents relevant to each immobilization for a least 3 years from the date of the court order.

5. ________ (Name of Company) employs and assigns persons to immobilize vehicles that meet the requirements of § 316.193, Fla. Stat.

6. ________ (Name of Company) employs and assigns a person to immobilize a vehicle who is not adjudicated incapacitated under § 744.331, or a similar statute in another state; involuntarily placed in a treatment facility for the mentally ill under chapter 394, or a similar law in any other state; or diagnosed as having an incapacitating mental illness unless a psychologist or psychiatrist licensed in this state certifies that he or she does not currently suffer from the mental illness.

7. ________ (Name of Company) employs and assigns a person to immobilize a vehicle who is not a chronic and habitual user of alcoholic beverages to the extent that his or her normal faculties are impaired; has not been committed under chapter 397, former chapter 396, or a similar law in any other state; has not been found to be a habitual offender under § 856.011(3), or a similar law in any other state; or not have had any convictions under this section, or a similar law in any other state, within 2 years before the affidavit is submitted.

8. ________ (Name of Company) employs and assigns a person to immobilize a vehicle who has not have been committed for controlled substance abuse or have been found guilty of a crime under chapter 893, or a similar law in any other state, relating to controlled substances in any other state.

9. ________ (Name of Company) employs and assigns a person to immobilize a vehicle who has not been found guilty of or entered a plea of guilty or nolo contendere to, regardless of adjudication, or been convicted of a felony, unless his or her civil rights have been restored.

10. ________ (Name of Company) employs and assigns a person to immobilize a vehicle who is a citizen or legal resident alien of the United States or was granted authorization to seek employment in this country by the United States Bureau of Citizenship and Immigration Services.

11. ________ (Name of Company) conducted a state criminal history check through the Florida Department of Law Enforcement for each person it employs and assigns person to immobilize a vehicle.

12. This Affidavit is being executed as a condition precedent to ________ (Name of Company) being included on the list of companies for Broward County and the Seventeenth Judicial Circuit that may immobilize a vehicle.

I understand that I am swearing or affirming under oath to the truthfulness of the claims made in this Affidavit of Compliance and that the punishment for knowingly making a false statement includes fines and/or imprisonment.

Date executed: ________

____
Signature of Affiant

____
Printed Name of Affiant

____
Title of Affiant

STATE OF FLORIDA
COUNTY OF ______

SWORN TO OR AFFIRMED before me on ______ by ______ who is ___ personally known or ______ produced the following identification ______.

____

Signature of Notary Public
Stamp of Notary Public

2015–14–CRIM. BOND SCHEDULE

IN THE CIRCUIT COURT OF THE SEVENTEENTH JUDICIAL CIRCUIT IN AND FOR BROWARD COUNTY, FLORIDA

Order Number 2015–14–Crim

ADMINISTRATIVE ORDER ESTABLISHING A BOND SCHEDULE

(a) Florida Rule of Judicial Administration 2.215(b)(3) states the chief judge shall "develop an administrative plan for the efficient and proper administration of all courts within that circuit."

(b) The County is under a Federal decree with regard to the jail population. To balance the space limitations of the jail and the need to protect the public, it is necessary to establish a bond schedule to allow for the release of individuals arrested for certain crimes prior to a First Appearance Hearing.

(c) However, the Court finds that the bond determination for certain serious offenses requires individual determination by a First Appearance Judge. As a result, individuals arrested for certain serious crimes shall not be released until a judicial determination of the conditions of release at a First Appearance Hearing.

(d) The First Appearance Judge may set bond and the conditions of release in accord with Florida Rule of Criminal Procedure 3.131, after consideration of the factors listed in Rule 3.131 and Section 903.046, Florida Statutes, including the nature and circumstances of the charged offense, the defendant's ties to the community, and the defendant's criminal history. In accordance with the authority vested in the chief judge by Florida Rule of Judicial Administration 2.215, it is ordered effective May 18, 2015:

(1) Any individual arrested and taken into custody in Broward County shall be provided an initial bond or no bond in accordance with the attached schedule. The term no bond shall also include hold for magistrate. The bond schedule may be amended from time to time without notice. The official copy of the most current schedule shall be maintained in Court Administration and posted on the Seventeenth Judicial Circuit's web page.

(2) If the charge does not have an initial bond, or if the individual is not able to post bond, the individual shall be brought before a judge for a First Appearance Hearing.

(3) If an individual is arrested for more than one misdemeanor arising out of the same incident, but no felonies, the initial bond shall be determined by the severest misdemeanor charge with all remaining misdemeanor charges being issued a notice to appear at booking. A notice to appear may not be issued at arrest or booking for a misdemeanor driving under the influence, boating under the influence, driving while intoxicated, prostitution, or domestic violence.

(4) If an individual is arrested for one or more misdemeanors and felonies arising out of the same incident then the initial bond shall be determined by the severest felony charge with the misdemeanor charge or misdemeanor charges being issued a notice to appear at booking. A notice to appear may not be issued at arrest or booking for a misdemeanor driving under the influence, boating under the influence, driving while intoxicated, prostitution, or domestic violence.

(5) If an individual is arrested for a charge not on the attached schedule, the initial bond is established as follows:

Charge	Coding	Bond Amount
Capital Offense	6FY	No Bond
First Degree Life Felony		No Bond
First Degree Felony	7FY	$7,500.00
Second Degree Felony	2FY	$3,500.00
Third Degree Felony	3FY	$1,000.00
Fist[1] Degree Misdemeanor	1MY	$100.00
Second Degree Misdemeanor	2MY	$25.00

[1] So in original.

(6) This Administrative Order rescinds and supersedes Administrative Order III–04C–6B and 2013–27–Crim on May 18, 2015.

DONE AND ORDERED in chambers at Fort Lauderdale, Broward County, Florida on April 23, 2015.

Peter M. Weinstein
Chief Judge

2012–35–CRIM. VETERANS TREATMENT INTERVENTION COURT PROGRAM

IN THE CIRCUIT COURT OF THE SEVENTEENTH JUDICIAL CIRCUIT IN AND FOR BROWARD COUNTY, FLORIDA

Order Number 2012–35–Crim

ADMINISTRATIVE ORDER ESTABLISHING VETERANS TREATMENT INTERVENTION COURT PROGRAM

(a) Florida Rule of Judicial Administration 2.215(b)(3) states the chief judge shall "considering available resources, ensure the efficient and proper administration of all courts within [this] circuit."

(b) The United States Department of Veterans Affairs (Department) is able to assist the court with the provision of services for veterans eligible to receive benefits from the Department who are arrested for municipal ordinance violations, misdemeanors, and felonies. The services provided by the Department will provide meaningful treatment for veterans that is anticipated will reduce recidivism and improve public safety.

(c) The Department has agreed to provide the Circuit with a Veterans Justice Outreach (VJO) Coordinator one (1) day per week to develop individualized treatment plans for each veteran in an effort to alleviate the problems that resulted in the veteran's arrest.

(d) Individuals have also agreed to provide a volunteer mentor program comprised of specially trained volunteers to assist veterans with the treatment plan and other needs available from the Department.

(e) In accordance with the authority vested in the chief judge by Florida Rule of Judicial Administration 2.215, it is ordered:

(1) *General Provisions.*

a. A Veterans Treatment Intervention Court Program (court program) is established for county and circuit criminal cases effective May 7, 2012.

b. The judge assigned to preside over this court program shall establish the day and time of the hearings.

c. The VJO Coordinator shall be at all court hearings and case staffing.

d. An individual (defendant) must be a veteran or servicemember to be transferred to this court program.

e. At the time of booking at a jail or at first appearance, an attempt shall be made to determine if the defendant is a veteran or servicemember. If the defendant is identified as a veteran, his or her name shall be provided to the VJO Coordinator to determine eligibility for services from the Department.

f. The Clerk of Courts shall assign all cases to a county or circuit criminal division subject to entry of a transfer order to this court program.

g. The division judge and court program judge must sign a written court order of transfer for cases sent to this program.

h. The Clerk of Courts shall designate, after transfer, county cases with the division alpha MVC and circuit cases with the division alpha VF.

i. If a defendant is terminated from this court program for any reason, the case shall be transferred to the originally assigned division for further proceedings.

j. The defendant must suffer from a military-related mental illness, traumatic brain injury, substance abuse disorder, or psychological problem.

k. The number of participants may be limited subject to funding for community programs and Department programs.

l. Impact Broward is responsible for implementing a mentor program in conjunction with the services provided by the Department.

m. After hearing, and with the agreement of the State, cases not otherwise qualified for this court program, may be transferred.

(2) *Felony Pretrial Intervention Programs.*

a. A defendant is eligible for a pretrial intervention program if he or she meets the requirements of § 948.08, Fla. Stat.

b. A transfer to this court program may not be ordered until arraignment to allow the defendant sufficient time to consult with counsel, voluntarily agree to enter the court program, waive the right to a speedy trial, and review the proposed coordinated strategy while in a pretrial intervention program.

c. The State, defendant, or court may make the motion for transfer to this court program.

(3) *Misdemeanor Pretrial Intervention Programs.*

a. A defendant is eligible for a pretrial intervention program if he or she meets the requirements of § 948.16, Fla. Stat.

b. A defendant may be eligible for a pretrial intervention program for other charges agreed to by the State Attorney.

c. The State may object to a case being transferred to this court program as authorized by § 948.16, Fla. Stat.

d. A transfer to the court program may not be ordered until arraignment to allow the defendant sufficient time to consult with counsel, voluntarily agree to enter the court program, waive the right to a speedy trial, and review the proposed coordinated strategy while in a pretrial intervention program.

e. The State, defendant, or court may make the motion for transfer to this court program. A hearing shall be held with the State, defense counsel (if any), and defendant present to provide evidence or argument that supports transfer to this court program.

(4) *Felony Post Adjudicatory Program.*

a. The defendant is eligible for probation or community control pursuant to Chapter 921, Fla. Stat.

b. The defendant is convicted of a criminal offense and sentenced pursuant to Chapter 921, Fla. Stat., by a division judge.

c. A defendant seeking a downward departure may be transferred to this program if:

i. a plea of guilty or no contest is entered before the division judge;

ii. a waiver of the right to be sentenced by the division judge is entered on the record;

iii. files a written motion for downward departure as required by law and the criminal rules of procedure; and

iv. agrees that if the motion is denied the judge assigned to this court program may sentence the defendant.

d. If a defendant is placed on probation or community control, he or she shall be supervised as all other defendants.

DONE AND ORDERED in chambers at Fort Lauderdale, Broward County, Florida on May 7, 2012.

Peter M. Weinstein
Chief Judge

2010–14–CRIM. FELONY DRUG COURT DIVISIONS

IN THE CIRCUIT COURT OF THE SEVENTEENTH JUDICIAL CIRCUIT IN AND FOR BROWARD COUNTY, FLORIDA

Order Number 2010–14–Crim

ADMINISTRATIVE ORDER AS TO FELONY DRUG COURT DIVISIONS

(a) Florida Rule of Judicial Administration 2.215(b)(3) states the chief judge shall "develop an administrative plan for the efficient and proper administration of all courts within that circuit."

(b) § 948.08(6), Fla. Stat., authorizes the chief judge to establish a drug court program to include programs as authorized by § 948.08, Fla. Stat., and § 397.334, Fla. Stat.

(c) In accordance with the authority vested in the chief judge by Florida Rule of Judicial Administration 2.215, it is ordered:

(1) General Conditions

(a) Cases eligible for transfer to the felony drug court divisions, subject to any other conditions established by law, rule, or this Administrative Order, are:

(i) defendants eligible for a pretrial substance abuse education and treatment intervention program as authorized by § 948.08(6), Fla. Stat., [1] or

(ii) defendants who enter pleas, receive eighteen (18) months probation and agree to a substance abuse treatment program, [2] or

(iii) defendants referred by another circuit criminal judge for drug court monitoring. [3]

(b) Entry into the felony drug court is voluntary and subject to funding for pretrial and post adjudicatory programs.

(c) A defendant who elects not to enter into felony drug court or pleads to probation without treatment will be transferred to the originally assigned circuit criminal division by the drug court division judge.

(d) The Clerk of Court shall randomly assign transferred cases to the drug court divisions as required by any and all directives either by Administrative Order or other directive from the Chief Judge. This provision is directed only to those matters wherein the Clerk of Court is requiring the entry of an administrative order for internal operating procedure that does not require an administrative order.

(2) Pretrial Intervention

(a) The Broward Sheriff's Office of Pretrial Services will expeditiously interview on a daily basis the in custody arrestees to preliminarily determine eligibility to participate in a pretrial substance abuse education and treatment intervention program and inform the First Appearance Judge if the individual should participate in a pretrial drug court program. The First Appearance Judge may order the arrestee into the drug court pretrial release program offered by the Broward Sheriff's Office if the conditions set forth at § 948.08(2), Fla. Stat., are met.

(b) In addition to any other conditions of participation imposed by the Broward Sheriff's Office of Pretrial Services drug court program, the following conditions are also imposed:

(i) The defendant must immediately report to and attend the Drug Court Treatment Program as directed by the Broward Sheriff's Office of Pretrial Services; and

(ii) The individual must personally appear at all court hearings as instructed by the Broward Sheriff's Office of Pretrial Services officer and/or counselor.

(c) The Broward Sheriff's Office of Pretrial Services will furnish on a weekly basis to the Department of Corrections, a list of the individuals preliminarily determined to be eligible for pretrial substance abuse education and treatment intervention program and on pretrial release together with the applicable booking sheet, probable cause affidavit, criminal records investigation report, and pretrial drug court release order.

(d) If an arrested individual posts a cash or surety bond, the Broward Sheriff's Office of Pretrial Services shall review the criminal history if the arrest was for a qualifying charge and may be eligible for a pretrial substance abuse education and treatment intervention program. [4]

(e) The Broward Sheriff's Office of Pretrial Services will advise the Clerk of Circuit Court the cases where the defendant is out on bond or in his pretrial release program that shall be set in a drug court division for arraignment and/or judicial determination of eligibility to participate in the drug court program.

(f) At arraignment or pretrial determination, the defendant may:

(i) Opt into a pretrial substance abuse education and treatment intervention program; [5] or

(ii) Opt out of a pretrial substance abuse education and treatment intervention program with his or her case transferred to a non drug court circuit criminal division for an additional arraignment and further proceedings.

(g) The participation requirements for a pretrial substance abuse education and treatment intervention program are:

(i) A minimum of one (1) year and no more than eighteen (18) months attendance at the Broward Sheriff's Office Drug Court Treatment Program or approved alternative treatment program.

(ii) Substantial compliance with all terms of the pretrial substance abuse education and treatment intervention program; all orders of the court including attendance at all status hearings; the rules and regulations of the Broward Sheriff's Office Drug Court Treatment Program or approved alternative treatment program; and the rules and regulations of the Department of Corrections.

(h) At the one (1) year anniversary of entry into a pretrial substance abuse education and treatment intervention program the court shall conduct a status conference and determine if:

(i) The defendant successfully completed all terms and conditions of the pretrial substance abuse education and treatment intervention program.

(ii) The defendant is successfully finishing all terms and conditions of the pretrial substance abuse education and treatment intervention program and will complete same within the next six (6) months.

(iii) The defendant did not successfully complete all terms and conditions of the pretrial substance abuse education and treatment intervention program and will not complete same within the next six (6) months.

(iv) The court may determine if there are extraordinary circumstances and order continued treatment.

(i) At the eighteen (18) month anniversary of entry into a pretrial substance abuse education and treatment intervention program the court shall conduct a status conference and determine if the defendant did or did not successfully complete the pretrial substance abuse education and treatment intervention program. If the defendant did not successfully complete the pretrial substance abuse education and treatment intervention program, absent extraordinary circumstances, the case shall be transferred to the originally assigned circuit criminal division for all future hearings.

(3) Pretrial Intervention Pilot Project.

(a) This program is limited to forty (40) defendants who are identified as having a substance abuse problem or substance addiction, meet the requirements for pretrial intervention, and

(i) are charged with non-violent third degree felony offenses as provided in Chapter 810, Fla. Stat., or

(ii) are charged with an offense that is not a forcible felony as defined in § 776.08, Fla. Stat.

(b) The initial forty (40) defendants participating in the pretrial intervention pilot project will be selected as follows:

(i) cases currently transferred to a drug court division for which an assessment is being conducted to determine if the individual has a substance abuse problem or substance addiction; or

(ii) upon request of the defendant for cases pending in a criminal division upon completion of screening to determine if the individual has a substance abuse problem or substance addiction and agreement of the criminal division judge.

(c) The judge assigned to a drug court division shall order a professional substance abuse/addiction assessment at the defendant's first hearing in the division and reset the defendant for a hearing to determine attendance at the Broward Sheriff's Office Drug Court Treatment Program or approved alternative treatment program as determined by the drug court division judge.

(d) If a victim of the crime for which the defendant is charged is entitled to restitution, the defendant must agree to pay restitution and complete payment by the time he or she completes the pretrial intervention pilot project. The agreement to enter the pretrial intervention pilot project will contain a provision for restitution and a payment plan. [6] The judge may extend participation in the pretrial intervention pilot project for the defendant to complete payment of restitution to the victim.

(e) The Drug Court Manager shall separately track the individuals in the pretrial intervention pilot project and advise the Administrative Judge of the Circuit Criminal Division when capacity is reached or if space is available for additional participants.

(f) In an effort to provide as many individuals as possible with an opportunity to participate in the pretrial intervention pilot project and due to resource limitations, an individual is limited to one second qualifying case if it is a drug offense within the provisions of § 948.08(6), Fla. Stat.

(g) All other provisions of the Administrative Order as to pretrial intervention and termination apply to this pretrial intervention pilot project.

(4) Post Adjudicatory Pilot Expansion Project.

(a) This program is limited to three hundred fifty (350) defendants who are identified as having a substance abuse problem or substance addiction, meet the requirements for a post adjudicatory drug court program, and qualify pursuant to §§ 397.334 or 948.01, Fla. Stat.

(b) The criminal division judge to whom the case is assigned shall direct the defendant seeking entry into the post adjudicatory pilot expansion project to complete a screening assessment to determine if the defendant has a substance abuse problem or substance addiction. The criminal division judge upon receipt of the screening assessment, review of the defendant's criminal history, and sentencing score sheet may transfer the case to a drug court division in lieu of sentencing the defendant to prison after imposing all conditions of probation which shall include the post adjudicatory probation requirements as set forth herein.

(c) The judge assigned to a drug court division shall order a professional substance abuse/addiction assessment at the defendant's first hearing in the division and reset the defendant for a hearing to determine attendance at the Broward Sheriff's Office Drug Court Treatment Program or approved alternative treatment program as determined by the drug court division judge.

(d) All other provisions of the Administrative Order that pertain to post adjudicatory drug court and termination apply to this post adjudicatory pilot expansion project.

(5) Post Adjudicatory Drug Court.

(a) The participation requirements for the drug court program are:

(i) A maximum of twenty four (24) months attendance at the Broward Sheriff's Office Drug Court Treatment Program or approved alternative treatment program.

(ii) Substantial compliance with all terms of probation; all orders of the court including attendance at status hearings; the rules and regulations of the Broward Sheriff's Office Drug Court Treatment Program or approved alternative treatment program; and the rules and regulations of the Department of Corrections.

(b) At the one (1) year anniversary of the order of probation the court shall conduct a status conference and determine if:

(i) The defendant successfully completed all terms and conditions of probation.

(ii) The defendant is successfully finishing all terms and conditions of probation and will complete same within the next twelve (12) months.

(iii) The defendant did not successfully complete all terms and conditions of probation and will not complete same within the next twelve (12) months. The court may determine if there are extraordinary circumstances and order continued treatment.

(c) At the second (2d) anniversary of probation the court shall conduct a status conference and determine if the defendant did or did not successfully complete the drug court program. If the defendant did not successfully complete the drug court program, absent extraordinary circumstances and an order extending treatment, the case shall be transferred to the originally assigned circuit criminal division by the Clerk of Court for all future hearings based upon the defendant's failure to successfully complete a post adjudicatory drug court program.

(d) A defendant may seek early termination of probation upon successful completion of a post adjudicatory drug court program.

(6) Discharge from Drug Court.

(a) there is an outstanding capias for a period of six (6) months for an individual in a pretrial substance abuse education and treatment intervention program;

(b) there is an outstanding capias for a period of three (3) months for an individual in a post adjudicatory drug court program; or

(c) new felony criminal charges are filed other than drug crimes encompassed within the provisions of § 948.08(6), Fla. Stat.; or

(d) violation of probation not encompassed within the provisions of § 948.08(6), Fla. Stat.

(7) This Administrative Order vacates and supersedes Administrative Order Number 2009–54–Crim.

DONE AND ORDERED in chambers at Fort Lauderdale, Broward County, Florida on January 22, 2010.

Victor Tobin
Chief Judge

1 In an effort to provide as many individuals as possible with an opportunity to participate in drug court programs and due to resource limitations, an individual is limited to two (2) cases for entry into a pretrial substance abuse education and treatment program.

2 If the defendant has not completed probation and a substance abuse education and treatment intervention program within two (2) years after commencement of probation, the case shall be transferred, as long as there is no order extending treatment, from a drug court division to the originally assigned circuit criminal division by the drug court division judge.

3 If a case is transferred to drug court from another circuit criminal division for drug court monitoring and if the defendant is then charged with a violation of probation or arrested and prosecution commenced for a felony not set forth in § 948.08(6), Fla. Stat., the case shall be transferred back to the originally assigned circuit criminal division for proceedings with regard to the violation of probation or additionally filed charges.

4 To expedite and encourage immediate participation by an individual released from jail on bond, the Broward Sheriff's Office of Pretrial Services will notify the arrested individual of the possibility of participating in the drug court pretrial substance abuse education and treatment intervention program. The notice shall contain information as to where the arrested individual is to report or whom to contact if interested in receiving additional information.

5 If a defendant opts in, he or she shall execute an agreement to comply with the pretrial substance abuse education and treatment intervention program and all pretrial intervention requirements of the Florida Department of Corrections. The pretrial substance abuse education and treatment intervention program may require residential treatment.

6 If the State, victim, and defendant are unable to agree as to the amount of restitution, the judge assigned to a drug court division shall conduct an evidentiary hearing to determine the amount of restitution.

III–07–I–1. CAREER CRIMINAL/HABITUAL OFFENDER SECTION

IN THE CIRCUIT COURT OF THE SEVENTEENTH JUDICIAL CIRCUIT IN AND FOR BROWARD COUNTY, FLORIDA

ADMINISTRATIVE ORDER NO:III–07–I–1

IN RE: CAREER CRIMINAL/HABITUAL OFFENDER SECTION

WHEREAS, The Legislature has determined that a substantial and disappropriate number of serious crimes are committed in Florida by a relatively small group of multiple and repeat felony offenders, Section 775.0841, Florida Statutes (2006); and

WHEREAS, The Legislature has concluded that priority should be given to the prosecution of career criminals, and the Legislature supports increased efforts by the State to investigate and prosecute career criminals, Section 775.0841, Florida Statutes (2006); and

WHEREAS, The Legislature has continued to recognize that priority be given to career criminal cases by its passage of the "Officer Evelyn Gort and All Fallen Officers Career Criminal Act of 1995"; and

WHEREAS, The Legislature has empowered agencies within the criminal justice system to employ enhanced management efforts and resources for the prosecution of career criminals, Section 775.0843, Florida Statutes (2006); and

WHEREAS, Local Rules, under the umbrella of Article V, Section 20(c)(10) of the Florida Constitution, create divisions or subdivisions within the circuit courts, this Administrative Order, pursuant to Florida Rules of Judicial Administration 2.215 and consistent with prior rulings of the Florida Supreme Court, has the express and exclusive objective of facilitating and advancing the efficient administration of justice in the Broward Circuit Criminal Courts; and

WHEREAS, Consistent with Florida Supreme Court holdings, this Order merely creates a section of the circuit court's criminal division, a matter within the broad administrative authority of this circuit's Chief Judge. Case No.: 81,017, In Re: Administrative Order of the Fourth Judicial Circuit—No. 88–21, (Career Criminal Project), unreported, (Fla. 1993); and

WHEREAS, The designation of a specialized section, within the criminal division, to hear cases limited to career criminals and/or repeat violent offenders promotes the efficiency of judicial administration.

ORDER

NOW, THEREFORE, pursuant to the authority conferred by Florida Rules of Judicial Administration 2.215(b)(2), it is ORDERED, effective immediately:

1. All cases pending on or filed after December 2, 1996, in which the State Attorney files a Designation indicating that at least one of the defendants meets the following criteria, shall be randomly assigned to division "FW" and "FX" in the criminal division of the circuit court.

CRITERIA

VIOLENT CAREER CRIMINAL

(a) The charged offense is any felony included within enumerated felonies of Florida Statute 775.084(1)(c) 1:

1. Any forcible felony, as described in s. 776.08;
2. Aggravated stalking, as described in s. 784.048(3) and 4;
3. Aggravated child abuse, as described in s. 827.03;
4. Lewd, lascivious, or indecent conduct, as described in s. 800.04;
5. Escape, as described in s. 944.40; or
6. A felony violation of chapter 790 involving the use or possession of a firearm.

AND

(b) The defendant has previously been convicted as an adult three (3) or more times for an offense in this state or other qualified offense that is enumerated in Florida Statute 775.084(1)(c)1.

(c) The defendant has been incarcerated in a state prison or a federal prison.

(d) The primary felony offense for which the defendant is charged is alleged to have been committed on or after October 1, 1995, and within 5 years after the conviction of the last prior enumerated felony or within 5 years after the defendant's release, on parole or otherwise, from a prison sentence or other commitment imposed as a result of a prior conviction for an enumerated felony, whichever is later.

(e) The defendant has not received a pardon for any felony or other qualified offense that is necessary for the operation of this paragraph.

(f) A conviction of a felony or other qualified offense necessary to the operation of this paragraph has not been set aside in any post-conviction proceeding.

(g) In order to be counted as a prior felony for purposes of the operation of this paragraph, the felony must have resulted in a conviction sentenced separately from any other felony conviction that is to be counted as a prior felony.

HABITUAL VIOLENT FELONY OFFENDER

(a) The charged offense is a violent felony of the second degree or higher included within the enumerated violent felonies of Florida Statute 775.084(1)(b)1, or its attempt or conspiracy which is a second degree or higher felony, AND

(b) The defendant must have at least one (1) prior conviction for an enumerated violent felony, or its attempt or conspiracy. Florida Statute 775.084(1)(b)1 enumerates the violent felonies as:

1. Arson
2. Sexual Battery
3. Robbery
4. Kidnapping
5. Aggravated Child Abuse
6. Aggravated Assault
7. Murder
8. Manslaughter
9. Unlawful throwing, placing, or discharging of a destructive device or bomb
10. Armed Burglary
11. Aggravated Battery; or
12. Aggravated Stalking

(c) The felony for which the Defendant is charged is alleged to have been committed within Five (5) years of the date of the conviction of the last prior enumerated felony or within Five (5) years of the Defendant's release, on parole or otherwise, from a prison sentence or other commitment imposed as a result of a prior conviction for an enumerated felony, whichever is later; AND

(d) The Defendant has not received a pardon on the ground of innocence for any crime that is necessary for the operation of this paragraph; AND

(e) A conviction of a crime necessary to the operation of this paragraph has not been set aside in any post-conviction proceeding.

HABITUAL FELONY OFFENDER

(a) 1. The charged offense is a violent felony of the second degree or higher included within the enumerated felonies of Florida Statute 775.084(1)(b)1, or its attempt or conspiracy which is a second degree or higher felony; AND

2. The Defendant has been convicted of at least two (2) prior felonies.

(b) 1. The charged offense is a non-violent Second Degree or higher felony, excluding sale, delivery, purchase or trafficking in controlled substances, and burglaries; AND

2. The Defendant has at least Three (3) prior felony convictions, or Two (2) prior enumerated violent felony convictions as set forth in Florida Statute 775.084(1)(b)1.

(c) 1. The charged offense is a non-violent Burglary of the second degree or higher; AND

2. The Defendant has at least Two (2) prior felony convictions.

(d) The felony for which the Defendant is charged is alleged to have been committed within Five (5) years of the date of the conviction of the defendant's last prior felony: or other qualified offense, or within Five (5) years of the defendant's release, on parole or otherwise, from a prison sentence or other commitment imposed as a result of a prior conviction for a felony or other qualified offense, whichever is later;

(e) The felony for which the defendant is charged, and at least one of the prior felony convictions is not a violation of Florida Statute 893.13 relating to the purchase or the possession of a controlled substance;

(f) The defendant has not received a pardon for any felony or other qualified offense that is necessary for the operation of this paragraph; AND

(g) A conviction of a felony or other qualified offense necessary to the operation of this paragraph has not been set aside in any post-conviction proceeding.

(h) In order to be counted as a prior felony for purposes of the operation of this paragraph, the felony must have resulted in a conviction sentenced separately prior to the current offense and, if two or more prior felony convictions are required, at least one of the prior felonies must have resulted in a conviction sentenced separately from any other felony conviction that is to be counted as a prior felony.

CAPITAL MURDER

2. Effective immediately no capital (death) murder cases shall be filed in either divisions "FW" or "FX", but shall randomly assigned in the normal non-special assignment divisions (FA through FK, FP and FY).

On a case by case basis, Judge Gardiner "FW" may transfer her pending capitol murder cases to Division FX (Backman).

CASES FILED AFTER DECEMBER 2, 1996

3. In cases filed on or after December 2, 1996, in which the State Attorney prior to the defendant's arraignment, files a Designation indicating the state's intent to seek habitualization and its good faith belief that at least one defendant in a specified case meets the criteria set forth in paragraph one above, then upon timely receipt of the state's Designation, the Clerk shall transfer and randomly assign the case to Division "FW" or "FX". The State may establish its good faith belief that a defendant meets the criteria by attaching to the Designation a printout of the defendant's qualifying criminal convictions.

4. Cases shall be transferred to Division "FW" or "FX" after a defendant's arraignment, upon motion by the state setting forth facts to demonstrate (1) that at least one defendant in the case meets the criteria set forth in paragraph one above, and (2) that good cause exists why the state failed to file its Designation prior to defendant's arraignment.

5. Cases shall be transferred out of Division "FW" and "FX" and randomly assigned upon timely motion by the defendant or the state when it is shown by the movant that the defendant does not meet the criteria set forth in paragraph above.

REASSIGNMENT OF NON-QUALIFYING CASES

6. All cases not qualifying for divisions "FW" and "FX" which are pending or assigned to the judges who will preside over divisions "FW" and "FX", shall be reassigned and distributed equally among divisions prior to the effective date of this Order.

MULTIPLE CASES

7. If a defendant in a case assigned to Division "FW" or "FX" has one or more felony cases pending in another division, the pending case(s) shall be transferred to Division FW or FX, without the necessity of any Motion or Order.

WARRANT & CAPIAS CASES

8. All cases in which a warrant or capias was issued but not served prior to December 2, 1996, and where the state has filed a Designation indicating that the defendant meets the criteria set forth in paragraph one above, shall be randomly assigned to Division "FW" or "FX".

POST-JUDGMENT MATTERS

9. All post-judgment matters, e.g., reversals of sentence or judgment, motions for post-conviction relief, Writs of Habeas Corpus, etc., resulting from cases assigned to a division "FW" or "FX" judge prior to the effective date of this order shall continue to be handled by that division "FW" or "FX" judge.

VIOLATION OF PROBATION

10. If a defendant in a case assigned to Division "FW" or "FX" has one or more violations of probation or community control cases pending in another division, the pending case(s) shall be transferred to Division "FW" or "FX" without the necessity of any Motion or Order.

However, each division shall be assigned capital cases (excluding sexual capital cases) in the normal felony rotation.

DONE AND ORDERED in Chambers at Fort Lauderdale, Broward County, Florida on this the 23rd day of May 2007.

Dale Ross
Chief Judge

III–06–W–1A. CRIMINAL CASES: PUBLIC ACCESS TO COURT RECORDS

IN THE CIRCUIT COURT OF THE SEVENTEENTH JUDICIAL CIRCUIT, IN AND FOR BROWARD COUNTY, FLORIDA

ADMINISTRATIVE ORDER NO.: III–06–W–1A

IN RE: CRIMINAL CASES: PUBLIC ACCESS TO COURT RECORDS

To ensure the public has access to court records as set forth in Fla. R. Jud. Admin. 2.051 based upon the entry of orders by judges of this Circuit and the interpretation of said orders by the Clerk of Court, in accordance with the authority vested in the Chief Judge by Fla. R. Jud. Admin. 2.050, it is

It is Ordered and Adjudged that the Clerk of the Court shall forthwith examine any case files which have been removed from the public records of the Court and from public access, to determine if an Order of Expungement has been entered. In the event, no Order of Expungement has been entered and the case has been removed from Public Access subject to the provisions of this Administrative Order, the Clerk of the Court shall forthwith reinstate the case number and the defendant's name in the public records of the Court and on public access sites.

Furthermore, all docket entries and case notations shall be reinstated to public record, excluding any plea agreement and deferral of sentence, in the event sentence has not been imposed, or judgment and Sentence in the event sentence has been imposed. The Court file shall remain sealed pending further court order.

Any interested party may petition the Judge of the assigned trial division for access to the Court file.

DONE AND ORDERED in chambers in Fort Lauderdale, Broward County, Florida this 21st day of August 2006.

Dale Ross
Chief Judge

III–06–S–1A. MENTAL HEALTH COURT SUBDIVISION

IN THE CIRCUIT COURT OF THE SEVENTEENTH JUDICIAL CIRCUIT, IN AND FOR BROWARD COUNTY, FLORIDA

ADMINISTRATIVE ORDER NO.: III–06–S–1A

IN RE: MENTAL HEALTH COURT SUBDIVISION WITHIN THE CIRCUIT CRIMINAL DIVISION

In accordance with the authority vested in the Chief Judge by Rule 2.050, Florida Rules of Judicial Administration:

IT IS ORDERED that effective January 17, 2006, Administrative Order No. III–03–S–1, which created the Mental Health Court Subdivision within the Circuit Criminal Division, is hereby amended as follows:

I. ELIGIBILITY

A. Mentally Ill, Mentally Retarded or Autistic and Probation Eligible

1. Defendants formally charged with non-violent third degree felonies (wherein "violent" offenses include those enumerated in Florida Statutes, Section 775.084) and who score Any Non–State Prison under the Florida Sentencing Guidelines/Criminal Punishment Code, who are mentally ill, mentally retarded, or autistic, and who desire to be considered for admission into said division, shall be transferred by the Clerk of Court to the Felony Mental Health Division unless excluded pursuant to paragraph I.A.2. below, after:

a. The Defendant has pled guilty or no contest before the trial judge,

b. The Defendant has waived his or her right to be sentenced by the assigned trial judge and expressed a desire to be transferred and sentenced by the Felony Mental Health Division Judge,

c. A certificate of eligibility has been filed by a mental health court placement coordinator, and

d. A written transfer order has been filed.

2. Defendants charged with criminal traffic related offenses, defendants whose sentence includes a minimum mandatory, unless eligible for a youthful offender sentence, pursuant to Florida Statute, and defendants whose cases are qualified for and assigned to the Career Criminal/Habitual Offender Section pursuant to Administrative Order No. III–99–I–1 or the Domestic Violence Court pursuant to Administrative Order No. II–01–H–4A, or subsequent related orders governing said section and court, are not eligible for the Felony Mental Health Division pursuant to paragraph I.A.1. above.

B. Mentally Ill, Mentally Retarded or Autistic and Seeking a Downward Departure

1. Defendants whose sentence, if convicted, mandates prison under the Florida Sentencing Guidelines/Criminal Punishment Code, who are mentally ill, mentally retarded, or autistic, and who desire to be considered for admission into said division, who move for a downward departure, pursuant to Florida Statutes, Section 921.0016(4)(d) or Section 921.0026(2)(d), shall be transferred by the Clerk of Court to the Felony Mental Health Division for said hearing, unless excluded pursuant to paragraph I.B.2. below, after:

a. The Defendant has pled guilty or no contest before the trial judge,

b. The Defendant has waived his or her right to be sentenced by the assigned trial judge and expressed a desire to be transferred and sentenced by the Felony Mental Health Division Judge,

c. A certificate of eligibility has been filed by a mental health court placement coordinator [1],

d. A written motion for downward departure has been filed, and

e. A written transfer order has been filed.

2. If said motion for downward departure is denied by the Felony Mental Health Division Judge, the defendant shall still be sentenced by the Felony Mental Health Division Judge, acting in his capacity as a Circuit Court Judge, in accordance with the laws of the State of Florida.

3. Defendants charged with criminal traffic related offenses, defendants whose sentence includes a minimum mandatory, unless eligible for a youthful offender sentence, pursuant to Florida Statute, and defendants whose cases are qualified for and assigned to the Career Criminal/Habitual Offender Section pursuant to Administrative Order No. III–99–I–1 or the Domestic Violence Court pursuant to Administrative Order No. II–01–H–4A, or subsequent related orders governing said section and court, are not eligible for the Felony Mental Health Division pursuant to paragraph I.B.1. above.

C. Competency and Insanity

1. Any defendant adjudged incompetent to proceed by the referring court, contesting competency or commitment, found not guilty by reason of insanity, returned from forensic commitment for either competency restoration or treatment for insanity, on conditional release after commitment for competency restoration, or on conditional release after being found not guilty by reason of insanity, shall have his or her case transferred, upon filing of a transfer order, by the Clerk of Court to the Felony Mental Health Division for the determination of placement and/or commitment.

2. The above provisions shall not divest other Circuit Criminal Courts of their authority to enter orders of incompetency and forensic commitment in uncontested cases. After a finding that a Defendant has been declared incompetent to proceed and requires forensic commitment, the case shall be transferred by the Clerk of the Court, upon filing of a transfer order, to the Felony Mental Health Division, until such time as the Defendant is restored to competency.

3. However, any defendant who contests their competency, or who does not meet the criteria for forensic commitment, or who contests commitment as stated in paragraph I.C.1., shall be transferred:

a. With at least two competency evaluations that are not older than ninety (90) days, and

b. Upon filing of a transfer order, to Felony Mental Health Court for a competency hearing, placement hearing and order of commitment or the formulation and imposition of a conditional release order.

4. The only time a case may be transferred to the Felony Mental Health Division by the Clerk of the Court, upon filing of a transfer order, without at least two competency evaluations, in compliance with paragraph I.C.3., is when a defense attorney has ordered confidential competency evaluations and the Defendant declines to release those reports to the Court.

5. Any defendant committed to a forensic facility for competency restoration or treatment for insanity, or on conditional release on the date this order is effective is eligible for the Felony Mental Health Division. The Clerk of Court shall transfer, upon filing of a transfer order, those cases to Felony Mental Health Division upon the filing of any violation of conditional release, requests for status, modification or reprimands, or upon return of the defendant from a forensic hospital.

6. Upon a determination of competency, the Felony Mental Health Division Judge shall utilize the above criteria to determine whether the case should remain in the Felony Mental Health Division. If it is determined that the case does not qualify for the Felony Mental Health Division, it shall be transferred, upon filing of a transfer order, back to the original division.

7. Defendants whose cases are qualified for and assigned to the Career Criminal/Habitual Offender Section pursuant to Administrative Order No.: III–99–I–1 or the Domestic Violence Court pursuant to Administrative Order No.: II–01–H–4A, or subsequent related orders governing said section and court, are not eligible for the Felony Mental Health Division pursuant to paragraph I.C.1., I.C.2., I.C.3., I.C.4. and I.C.5. above.

8. Defendants whose cases are qualified for and assigned to the Drug Court, pursuant to Administrative Order No.: III–05–E–3A, or subsequent related orders governing said court, who are declared to be incompetent to proceed, are deemed eligible for the Felony Mental Health Court. After a finding that a Defendant has been declared incompetent to proceed, the case shall be transferred by the Clerk of the Court, upon filing of a transfer order, to the Felony Mental Health Division, until such time as the Defendant is restored to competency. Once the Defendant is restored to competency, the case shall be transferred, upon filing of a transfer order, back to the Drug Court Division, unless the Defendant elects to remain in the Felony Mental Health Division to resolve his or her case.

II. FELONY MENTAL HEALTH PROBATION

1. Any defendant on Felony Mental Health Probation, as set forth in Administrative Order III–02–N–1A or subsequent related orders governing Felony Mental Health Probation, at the time of the effective date of this order, shall immediately be transferred by the Clerk of Court to the Felony Mental Health Division.

2. If the defendant qualifies for Felony Mental Health Probation, the criteria set forth in Administrative Order III–02–N–1A or subsequent related orders governing Felony Mental Health Probation shall be complied with.

3. Due to the limited mental health resources in the community, Felony Mental Health Probation, as set forth in Administrative Order No. III–02–N–1A, will only be used for the monitoring and supervision of defendants eligible for the Felony Mental Health Division, except as provided in section II.5. below. The Felony Mental Health Division Judge will preside over status, reprimand and violation hearings for defendants who are on Felony Mental Health Probation, except as provided in section II.5. below.

4. Due to the limited mental health resources in the community, defendants ineligible for the Felony Mental Health Division, as set forth above, shall not be transferred to the Felony Mental Health Division for monitoring or supervision by any other criminal court.

5. Defendants whose cases are qualified for and assigned to the Career Criminal/Habitual Offender Section pursuant to Administrative Order No. III–99–I–1 or the Domestic Violence Court pursuant to Administrative Order No. II–01–H–4A, or subsequent related orders governing said section and court may, if the presiding judge in that section/court deems it appropriate and such is a legally permissible sentence, be sentenced to Felony Mental Health Probation, so long as the criteria set forth in Administrative Order III–02–N–IA or subsequent related orders governing Felony Mental Health Probation is complied with. The monitoring and supervision of such probation shall then be handled by the Career Criminal/Habitual Offender Section or Domestic Violence Court judge who placed the defendant on Felony Mental Health Probation.

III. DISQUALIFICATION

1. A defendant is no longer eligible for the Felony Mental Health Division if:

a. The defendant is not mentally ill, mentally retarded, or autistic,

b. The defendant indicates that he or she no longer desires to participate in the Felony Mental Health Division.

c. The defendant demands a trial or hearing on a motion to determine legal issues unrelated to mental health.

This section, (paragraph III.1.), shall not apply to paragraph I.B.2.

2. If the Court determines that the defendant is no longer sufficiently participating in or benefiting from the Felony Mental Health Division; or that the defendant poses a great threat to public safety, he or she is no longer eligible for the Felony Mental Health Division.

3. If the defendant is arrested for or charged with any new offense, the defendant is no longer eligible for the Felony Mental Health Division without the consent of the Felony Mental Health Division Judge and the State as to any or all of the defendant's cases.

4. If the defendant was admitted pursuant to section IV. of this order, and the State determines that the defendant is no longer sufficiently participating in or benefiting from the program, he or she is no longer eligible for the Felony Mental Health Division and will be transferred, upon the filing of a transfer order, back to the original division upon notice of revocation filed by the State.

5. If a defendant is determined to be ineligible for the Felony Mental Health Division, the case shall be transferred, by the filing of a transfer order, back to the original division. Thereupon, the defendant's right to a speedy trial and formal discovery may be reinstated upon a written demand.

IV. EXCEPTIONS AND VICTIM CONSENT

1. Defendants who do not meet any of the above criteria may be admitted only with the consent of the Felony Mental Health Division Judge, the State, the victim and the defendant.

2. The defendant or the defendant's immediate family may not personally contact the victim or the victim's immediate family to acquire the victim's consent.

V. TRANSFER OF CASES

1. Motions for transfer into the Felony Mental Health Division may be made sua sponte by any court or ore tenus, with the defendant present if feasible, by the Defense or the State accompanied by documentation, testimony, or any other specific evidence that would convince the court in support thereof. After transfer by the referring court, the case will be heard by the Felony Mental Health Division Judge, who shall make the final determination of a defendant's eligibility.

2. Any motion or notice to transfer a defendant into the Felony Mental Health Division, unless specifically objected to by defense counsel, shall be deemed a waiver of the defendant's right to a speedy trial and formal discovery, other than providing documentation relating to defendant's mental health status and all available statements and police reports.

3. If the Felony Mental Health Judge determines that a defendant is mentally ill, mentally retarded or autistic and meets the criteria as set forth in sections I.A., I.B., I.C. or IV, the defendant is eligible for the Felony Mental Health Division. If a defendant is eligible for the Felony Mental Health Division, all of the defendant's eligible felony cases as well as all of the defendant's misdemeanor cases eligible for the Mental Health Subdivision within the County Criminal Division pursuant to Administrative Order VI–00–I–1 or subsequent related orders governing said division, including violations of probation or community control, shall be consolidated and transferred, by the filing of a transfer order, by the Clerk of Court to the assigned Felony Mental Health Division Judge.

4. Prior to a defendant being accepted into the Felony Mental Health Division, appropriate waivers of confidentiality shall be obtained.

5. If a Defendant is currently on Mental Health Probation and is charged with a new felony offense, the new case(s) shall not automatically be transferred to the Felony Mental Health Division, without first meeting the criteria for eligibility pursuant to paragraphs I.A., I.B. or I.C.

6. If a Defendant is currently on conditional release due to incompetency, and is charged with a new felony offense, the new case(s) shall not automatically be transferred to the Felony Mental Health Division, without first meeting the criteria for eligibility pursuant to paragraph I.C. and obtaining competency evaluations that are dated within ninety (90) days of the date of the transfer order.

7. If a Defendant is currently on conditional release due to a finding of not guilty by reason of insanity, and is charged with a new felony offense, the new case(s) shall not automatically be transferred to the Felony Mental Health Division, without first meeting the criteria for eligibility pursuant to paragraphs I.A., I.B. or I.C.

VI. ADMINISTRATION

IT IS FURTHERMORE ORDERED that Judge Martin Bidwill is hereby designated as the Judge assigned to this specialized court. In that capacity, Judge Bidwill will be responsible for administering the Felony Mental Health Division and coordinating the role of the judiciary with the functions of the Department of Children and Family Services, Henderson Mental Health Center, Nova Southeastern Outpatient Care Clinic, private mental health care providers, Department of Corrections, County Court Probation, Broward County Court Alternatives, Pretrial Services Program and Broward Regional Health Planning Council. In that Judge Bidwill has proven himself to be learned in the field of mental health and possesses a unique understanding with respect to the needs of the mentally ill, and handles said cases accordingly, without compromising the safety of the public, the Office of the State Attorney concurs in the assignment of Judge Bidwill, and if for some reason Judge Bidwill ceases to preside over said division, any judicial replacement is subject to consultation with the Office of the State Attorney, the Office of the Public Defender and the criminal defense bar.

IT IS FURTHERMORE ORDERED that the Honorable Mark A. Speiser shall serve as Judge Bidwill's alternate. For the purpose of presiding over the above-mentioned misdemeanor cases, Judge Bidwill is hereby appointed as an acting County Court Judge in order to enter orders which are necessary, fit and proper, and/or as required by law.

IT IS FURTHERMORE ORDERED that this order supercedes any conflicting language in any previous administrative orders concerning mental health in these criminal courts.

DONE AND ORDERED in Chambers at Fort Lauderdale, Broward County, Florida on this the 17th day of January, 2006.

Dale Ross
Chief Judge

[1] Provision I.B.1.c. has been vacated by administrative order 2016–39–CRIM.

III–06–A–8. DISCOVERY STIPULATION BETWEEN STATE ATTORNEY AND PUBLIC DEFENDER

IN THE CIRCUIT COURT OF THE SEVENTEENTH JUDICIAL CIRCUIT IN AND FOR BROWARD COUNTY, FLORIDA

ADMINISTRATIVE ORDER NO. III–06–A–8

IN RE: DISCOVERY STIPULATION BETWEEN STATE ATTORNEY AND PUBLIC DEFENDER

In accordance with the authority vested in the Chief Judge by Rule 2.050, Florida Rules of Judicial Administration, and in order to promote efficient administration of justice and the prompt and orderly disposition of cases within the Seventeenth Judicial Circuit, and whereas State Attorney and Public Defender have entered into the attached Discovery Stipulation.

Now therefore it is ORDERED that the attached Stipulation entered into between the Office of the State Attorney, Seventeenth Judicial Circuit, and the Office of the Public Defender, Seventeenth Judicial Circuit, is hereby ratified and accepted for all circuit and county courts having jurisdiction over criminal cases in the Seventeenth Judicial Circuit.

This order vacates Administrative Order III–90–A–8.

DONE AND ORDERED in chambers in Fort Lauderdale, Broward County, Florida this 12th day of January, 2006.

Dale Ross
Chief Judge

III–03–S–1. MENTAL HEALTH COURT SUBDIVISION

IN THE CIRCUIT COURT OF THE SEVENTEENTH JUDICIAL CIRCUIT, IN AND FOR BROWARD COUNTY, FLORIDA

ADMINISTRATIVE ORDER NO. III–03–S–1

IN RE: CREATION OF A MENTAL HEALTH COURT SUBDIVISION WITHIN THE CIRCUIT CRIMINAL DIVISION

In accordance with the authority vested in the Chief Judge by Rule 2.050, Florida Rules of Judicial Administration:

WHEREAS, this Circuit has recognized that the creation of "specialized courts" within other divisions of the Court has enhanced the expediency, effectiveness and quality of Judicial Administration;

WHEREAS, the rapidly increasing number of felony cases involving mentally ill, mentally retarded, or autistic defendants has contributed to congesting and overburdening the court dockets in the Circuit Court Criminal Division, and,

WHEREAS, a centralized Mental Health program would increase the efficiency of the criminal court system in this Circuit, and

IT IS NOW THEREFORE;

ORDERED that:

Effective November 3, 2003, for a period of one year, a part time Felony Mental Health Subdivision shall be operational within the Circuit Court Criminal Division to preside over cases deemed eligible in this Order.

I. ELIGIBILITY

A. Mentally Ill, Mentally Retarded or Autistic and Probation Eligible

1. Defendants formally charged with non-violent third degree felonies (wherein "violent" offenses include those enumerated in Florida Statutes, Section 775.084) and who score Any Non–State Prison under the Florida Sentencing Guidelines/Criminal Punishment Code, who are mentally ill, mentally retarded, or autistic, and who desire to be considered for admission into said division, shall be transferred by the Clerk of Court to the Felony Mental Health Division upon the filing of a written transfer order, unless excluded pursuant to paragraph I.A.2. below.

2. Defendants charged with criminal traffic related offenses, defendants whose sentence includes a minimum mandatory sentence pursuant to Florida Statute, and defendants whose cases are qualified for and assigned to the Career Criminal/Habitual Offender Section pursuant to Administrative Order No. III–99–I–1 or the Domestic Violence Court pursuant to Administrative Order No. II–01–H–4A, or subsequent related orders governing said section and court, are not eligible for the Felony Mental Health Division pursuant to paragraph I.A.1. Above.

B. Mentally Ill, Mentally Retarded or Autistic and Seeking a Downward Departure

1. Defendants whose sentence, if convicted, mandates prison under the Florida Sentencing Guidelines/Criminal Punishment Code, who are mentally ill, mentally retarded, or autistic, and who desire to be considered for admission into said division, who move for a downward departure, pursuant to Florida Statutes, Section 921.0016(4)(d) or Section 921.0026(2)(d), shall be transferred by the Clerk of Court to the Felony Mental Health Division for said hearing, upon the filing of a written motion for downward departure and transfer order, unless excluded pursuant to paragraph I.B.2. below. If said motion for downward departure is denied by the Felony Mental Health Division Judge, the defendant shall be deemed ineligible for said division.

2. Defendants charged with criminal traffic related offenses, defendants whose sentence includes a minimum mandatory sentence pursuant to Florida Statute, and defendants whose cases are qualified for and assigned to the Career Criminal/Habitual Offender Section pursuant to Administrative Order No. III–99–I–1 or the Domestic Violence Court pursuant to Administrative Order No. II–01–H–4A, or subsequent related orders governing said section and court, are not eligible for the Felony Mental Health Division pursuant to paragraph I.B.1. above.

C. Competency and Insanity

1. Any defendant adjudged incompetent to proceed by the referring court, contesting competency or commitment, found not guilty by reason of insanity, returned from forensic commitment for either competency restoration or treatment for insanity, on conditional release after commitment for competency restoration, or on conditional release after being found not guilty by reason of insanity, shall have his or her case transferred, upon filing of a transfer order, by the Clerk of Court to the Felony Mental Health Division for the determination of placement and/or commitment.

2. The above provisions shall not divest other Circuit Criminal Courts of their authority to enter orders of competency and forensic commitment in non-contested cases. However, any defendant who does not meet the criteria for forensic commitment, or who contests commitment as stated in paragraph I. C.1., shall be transferred, upon filing of a transfer order, to Felony Mental Health Court for commitment hearing and order of commitment or the formulation and imposition of a conditional release order.

3. Any defendant committed to a forensic facility for competency restoration or treatment for insanity, or on conditional release on the date this order is effective is eligible for the Felony Mental Health Division. The Clerk of Court shall transfer, upon filing of a transfer order, those cases to Felony Mental Health Division upon the filing of any violation of conditional release, requests for status, modification or reprimands, or upon return of the defendant from a forensic hospital.

4. Upon a determination of competency, the Felony Mental Health Division Judge shall utilize the above criteria to deter-

mine whether the case should remain in the Felony Mental Health Division. If it is determined that the case does not qualify for the Felony Mental Health Division, it shall be transferred, upon filing of a transfer order, back to the original division.

5. Defendants whose cases are qualified for and assigned to the Career Criminal/Habitual Offender Section pursuant to Administrative Order No. III–99–I–1 or the Domestic Violence Court pursuant to Administrative Order No. II–01–H–4A, or subsequent related orders governing said section and court, are not eligible for the Felony Mental Health Division pursuant to paragraph I.C.1., I.C.2. and I.C.3. above.

II. FELONY MENTAL HEALTH PROBATION

1. Any defendant on Felony Mental Health Probation, as set forth in Administrative Order III–02–N–1A or subsequent related orders governing Felony Mental Health Probation, at the time of the effective date of this order, shall immediately be transferred by the Clerk of Court to the Felony Mental Health Division.

2. If the defendant qualifies for Felony Mental Health Probation, the criteria set forth in Administrative Order III–02–N–1A or subsequent related orders governing Felony Mental Health Probation shall be complied with.

3. Due to the limited mental health resources in the community, Felony Mental Health Probation, as set forth in Administrative Order No. III–02–N–1A, will only be used for the monitoring and supervision of defendants eligible for the Felony Mental Health Division, except as provided in section II.5. below. The Felony Mental Health Division Judge will preside over all status, reprimand and violation hearings for defendants who are on Felony Mental Health Probation, except as provided in section II.5. below.

4. Due to the limited mental health resources in the community, defendants ineligible for the Felony Mental Health Division, as set forth above, shall not be transferred to the Felony Mental Health Division for monitoring or supervision by any other criminal court.

5. Defendants whose cases are qualified for and assigned to the Career Criminal/Habitual Offender Section pursuant to Administrative Order No. III–99–I–1 or the Domestic Violence Court pursuant to Administrative Order No. II–01–H–4A, or subsequent related orders governing said section and court may, if the presiding judge in that section/court deems it appropriate and such is a legally permissible sentence, be sentenced to Felony Mental Health Probation, so long as the criteria set forth in Administrative Order III–02–N–1A or subsequent related orders governing Felony Mental Health Probation is complied with. The monitoring and supervision of such probation shall then be handled by the Career Criminal/Habitual Offender Section or Domestic Violence Court judge who placed the defendant on Felony Mental Health Probation.

III. DISQUALIFICATION

1. If a defendant is not mentally ill, mentally retarded, or autistic; indicates that he or she no longer desires to participate in the Felony Mental Health Division; or at any time demands a trial or hearing on a motion to determine legal issues unrelated to mental health, he or she is no longer eligible for the Felony Mental Health Division.

2. If the Court determines that the defendant is no longer sufficiently participating in or benefiting from the Felony Mental Health Division; or that the defendant poses a great threat to public safety, he or she is no longer eligible for the Felony Mental Health Division.

3. If the defendant is arrested for or charged with any new offense, the defendant is no longer eligible for the Felony Mental Health Division without the consent of the Felony Mental Health Division Judge and the State as to any or all of the defendant's cases.

4. If the defendant was admitted pursuant to section IV. of this order, and the State determines that the defendant is no longer sufficiently participating in or benefiting from the program, he or she is no longer eligible for the Felony Mental Health Division and will be transferred, upon the filing of a transfer order, back to the original division upon notice of revocation filed by the State.

5. If a defendant is determined to be ineligible for the Felony Mental Health Division, the case shall be transferred, by the filing of a transfer order, back to the original division. Thereupon, the defendant's right to a speedy trial and formal discovery may be reinstated upon a written demand.

IV. EXCEPTIONS AND VICTIM CONSENT

1. Defendants who do not meet any of the above criteria may be admitted only with the consent of the Felony Mental Health Division Judge, the State, the victim and the defendant.

2. The defendant or the defendant's immediate family may not personally contact the victim or the victim's immediate family to acquire the victim's consent.

V. TRANSFER OF CASES

1. Motions for transfer into the Felony Mental Health Division may be made sua sponte by any court or ore tenus, with the defendant present if feasible, by the Defense or the State accompanied by documentation, testimony, or any other specific evidence that would convince the court in support thereof. After transfer by the referring court, the case will be heard by the Felony Mental Health Division Judge, who shall make the final determination of a defendant's eligibility.

2. Any motion or notice to transfer a defendant into the Felony Mental Health Division, unless specifically objected to by defense counsel, shall be deemed a waiver of the defendant's right to a speedy trial and formal discovery, other than providing documentation relating to defendant's mental health status and all available statements and police reports.

3. If the Felony Mental Health Judge determines that a defendant is mentally ill, mentally retarded or autistic and meets the criteria as set forth in sections I.A., I.B., I.C. or IV., the defendant is eligible for the Felony Mental Health Division. If a defendant is eligible for the Felony Mental Health Division, all of the defendant's eligible felony cases as well as all of the defendant's misdemeanor cases eligible for the Mental Health Subdivision within the County Criminal Division pursuant to Administrative Order VI–00–I–1 or subsequent related orders governing said division, including violations of probation or community control, shall be consolidated and transferred, by the filing of a transfer order, by the Clerk of Court to the assigned Felony Mental Health Division Judge.

4. Prior to a defendant being accepted into the Felony Mental Health Division, appropriate waivers of confidentiality shall be obtained.

VI. ADMINISTRATION

IT IS FURTHERMORE ORDERED that Judge Mark A. Speiser is hereby designated as the Judge assigned to this specialized court. In that capacity, Judge Speiser will be responsible for administering the Felony Mental Health Division and coordinating the role of the judiciary with the functions of the Department of Children and Family Services, Henderson Mental Health Center, Nova Southeastern Outpatient Care Clinic, private mental health care providers, Department of Corrections, County Court Probation, Broward County Court Alternatives, Pretrial Services Program and Broward Regional Health Planning Council. In that Judge Speiser has proven himself to be learned in the field of mental health and possesses a unique understanding with respect to the needs of the mentally ill, and handles said cases accordingly, without compromising the safety of the public, the Office of the State Attorney concurs in the assignment of Judge Speiser, and if for some reason Judge Speiser ceases to preside over said division, any judicial replacement is subject to consultation with the Office of the State Attorney, the Office of the Public Defender and the criminal defense bar.

IT IS FURTHERMORE ORDERED that the Honorable Ginger Lerner–Wren shall serve as Judge Speiser's alternate, and for such purpose is hereby appointed as an acting Circuit Court Judge in order to enter orders which are necessary, fit and proper, and/or as required by law. For the purpose of presiding over the above-mentioned misdemeanor cases, Judge Speiser is hereby appointed as an acting County Court Judge in order to enter orders which are necessary, fit and proper, and/or as required by law.

IT IS FURTHERMORE ORDERED that this order supercedes any conflicting language in any previous administrative orders concerning mental health in these criminal courts.

DONE AND ORDERED in Chambers at Fort Lauderdale, Broward County, Florida on this the 17th day of October, 2003.

Dale Ross
Chief Judge

III–03–R–1. NOTICE OF EXPIRATION OF SPEEDY TRIAL; MOTION FOR DISCHARGE; DEMAND FOR SPEEDY TRIAL

IN THE CIRCUIT COURT OF THE SEVENTEENTH JUDICIAL CIRCUIT, IN AND FOR BROWARD COUNTY, FLORIDA

ADMINISTRATIVE ORDER NO. III–03–R–1

IN RE: NOTICE OF EXPIRATION OF SPEEDY TRIAL; MOTION FOR DISCHARGE; DEMAND FOR SPEEDY TRIAL

WHEREAS, Notices of Expiration of Speedy Trial, Motions for Discharge and Demands for Speedy Trial in criminal, juvenile and traffic infraction cases often require expedited hearings and, pursuant to Florida Rule of Criminal Procedure 3.191, Rule of Juvenile Procedure 8.090 and Traffic Court Rule 6.325, the setting of such is the responsibility of the Court; and,

WHEREAS, attorneys representing Defendants have on occasion included Notices of Expiration of Speedy Trial, Motions for Discharge, and Demands for Speedy Trial together with other motions, resulting in routine scheduling of hearings on said motions; and,

WHEREAS, there have been delays in the scheduling of Notices of Expiration of Speedy Trial, Motions for Discharge, and Demands for Speedy Trial it is hereby:

ORDERED that;

1. All Notices of Expiration of Speedy Trial, Motions for Discharge, and Demands for Speedy Trial shall be filed as separate pleadings with correct descriptive titles.

2. The attorneys filing Notices of Expiration of Speedy Trial, Motions for Discharge, and Demands for Speedy Trial, are to simultaneously provide the Judge or Traffic Hearing Officer to whom the case is assigned a copy of the motion(s).

3. The Clerk of Court shall provide the Judge or Hearing Officer to whom a case is assigned, by hand delivery, copies of Notices of Expiration of Speedy Trial, Motions for Discharge, and Demand for Speedy Trial on the day of filing.

DONE AND ORDERED in Chambers at Fort Lauderdale, Broward County, Florida on this the 12th day of March, 2003.

Dale Ross
Chief Judge

County Orders

2017–65–CO. PROCEDURES FOR APPOINTMENT OF MEDIATORS

IN THE CIRCUIT COURT OF THE SEVENTEENTH JUDICIAL CIRCUIT IN AND FOR BROWARD COUNTY, FLORIDA

Administrative Order No. 2017–65–CO

AMENDED ADMINISTRATIVE ORDER ESTABLISHING PROCEDURES FOR APPOINTMENT OF MEDIATORS IN COUNTY COURT CASES AND UNIFORM ORDERS OF REFERRAL

(a) Florida Rule of Judicial Administration 2.215 (b) (3) states the Chief Judge shall "develop an administrative plan" and "shall, considering available resources, ensure the efficient and proper administration of all courts within [this] circuit."

(b) A uniform procedure for the appointment of mediators in County Court cases will assist with the resolution of cases.

(c) In accordance with the authority vested in the Chief Judge by Florida Rule of Judicial Administration 2.215, it is hereby **ORDERED**:

(1) *Small Claims Cases.* The Trial Court Administrator's Office of Court Mediation and Arbitration, in accordance with Florida Rule of Civil Procedure 1.750(c) and Florida Small Claims Rule of Procedure 7.090(f), shall schedule mediators for mediation conferences to be held at or immediately after the pretrial conferences. If the parties invoke the Florida Rules of Civil Procedure for a small claims case then mediation shall occur as set forth herein for County Court cases.

(2) *Residential Eviction Cases.* The parties shall within five (5) days of entry of the Order of Referral to Mediation in a residential eviction case submit a stipulation as to the designation of the mediator to the division judge. The parties shall provide a copy of the stipulation to the Court Mediation and Arbitration Program in Room 19150, Broward County Courthouse, 201 S.E. Sixth Street, Fort Lauderdale, Florida 33301. If the parties fail to submit a stipulation as to the designation of the mediator, the Court shall refer the case to the Court Mediation and Arbitration Program to select a mediator by rotation and provide the date and time of the mediation to the parties. The parties shall pay the costs of mediation as set forth in the Order of Referral.

(3) *County Court Cases (including Non–Residential Evictions).* The parties shall within fifteen (15) days of entry of the Order of Referral to Mediation submit a stipulation as to the designation of the mediator to the division judge. The parties shall provide a copy of the stipulation to the Court Mediation and Arbitration Program in Room 19150, Broward County Courthouse, 201 S.E. Sixth Street, Fort Lauderdale, Florida 33301. If the parties fail to submit a stipulation as to the designation of the mediator, then the Court may appoint a private mediator or the Court Mediation and Arbitration Program.

(4) *Orders of Referral.* The attached orders of referral shall be used by the Judges and parties.

(5) This Administrative Order vacates and supersedes Administrative Order 2012–1–CO.

DONE AND ORDERED in Chambers, Fort Lauderdale, Broward County, Florida, this 10th day of October, 2017 *nunc pro tunc* to October 6, 2017.

Jack Tuter
Chief Judge

IN THE COUNTY COURT IN AND FOR BROWARD COUNTY, FLORIDA

__________ CASE NO.: ____COCE _

Plaintiff, JUDGE: __________

v.

____

Defendant.

__________/

ORDER REFERRING CASE TO MEDIATION (COUNTY COURT)

THE COURT [ ] sua sponte/[ ] upon the motion of a party, hereby refers the above captioned matter to mediation as authorized by statute and rules of procedure. It is ORDERED as follows:

1. **Appointment of Mediator**

The parties shall within fifteen (15) days of the date of this Order submit to the undersigned Judge and file with the Clerk of the Courts a stipulation as to the designation of a mediator. The parties shall within the same time period provide a copy of the stipulation to the Court Administration Court Mediation and Arbitration Program (CMAP) in Room 19150, Broward County Courthouse, 201 S.E. Sixth Street, Fort Lauderdale, Florida 33301.

If the parties fail to timely submit and file a stipulation as to the designation of a mediator, the Court orders the following:

[ ] The Court appoints as mediator:

Name: __________

Address: __________

Telephone: __________

[ ] Court Mediation and Arbitration Program shall coordinate the date, time, and location for the mediation.

2. If the mediator stipulated to by the parties or appointed by the Court cannot serve, the parties shall either submit a stipulation with order thereon designating a substitute mediator or advise the court so that a substitute mediator can be appointed by the Court.

3. The mediation shall be held within sixty (60) days from the date of this Order in Broward County, Florida unless both parties and the mediator agree to another location. If the parties cannot agree on a mediation date falling within this deadline, the mediator shall unilaterally set the mediation conference. Any party having a conflict with the date chosen by the mediator must file a motion for continuance with the Court explaining what specific efforts were made by the parties to agree on a date and why no agreement could be reached.

4. The appearance of all parties, and their counsel, in person is **MANDATORY**. If a business entity (i.e. an insurance company, corporation, association, partnership) is a party, a bona fide representative employed by that company shall also appear having full authority to settle. If the Court has approved the absence of a party, the attorney must have full and complete authority to settle from the client and authority to execute any mediation agreement on behalf of the client, without further consultation. **Full authority means the individual representing the plaintiff has the authority to dismiss the claim and to pay up to the full amount of the counterclaim and the individual representing the defendant has the authority to pay up to the full amount of the claim.**

5. CONTINUANCES MAY BE GRANTED ONLY BY THE COURT UPON TIMELY WRITTEN MOTION FOR GOOD CAUSE SHOWN. Even if the parties mutually agree to continue mediation, they must receive the permission of the Court and file the appropriate motions in a timely manner. PARTIES SHALL NOT UNILATERALLY CANCEL MEDIATION FOR ANY REASON EXCEPT SETTLEMENT OF THE CASE AND NOTIFICATION OF SUCH SETTLEMENT IS PROVIDED IN WRITING TO THE COURT.

6. Parties utilizing the CMAP shall pay the Clerk of the Courts for mediation in advance of the mediation session being scheduled. Parties using the designated mediator shall pay the mediator directly in advance of the mediation session being scheduled. For those parties using the designated mediator, payment shall be made within fifteen (15) days of the date of this Order and not less than five (5) days prior to the scheduled mediation date. A session shall not exceed one and one-half hours (1.5 hours), unless both parties agree. For those cases using the CMAP, each party in the case, including cases with multiple parties, shall pay the Clerk of the Courts sixty dollars ($60.00) per session prior to the commencement of the mediation. If a party was declared indigent the fee is not required from that party. If additional sessions are needed, the parties must pay the Clerk of the Courts in advance and a follow-up mediation appointment will be scheduled.

FAILURE TO PAY BY ANY PARTY WILL PREVENT THE SCHEDULING OF A MEDIATION SESSION. THE JUDGE WILL BE NOTIFIED THAT THE PARTY OR PARTIES FAILED TO PAY. THE CASE WILL BE REFERRED BACK TO THE JUDGE FOR SANCTIONS WHICH MAY INCLUDE AN AWARD OF MEDIATOR FEES, ATTORNEY'S FEES, OTHER COSTS, OR OTHER APPROPRIATE REMEDIES.

7. Regarding this Order of referral to mediation, the Court determines that:

[ ] The Plaintiff(s) and the Defendant(s) shall share equally in the cost of mediation

[ ] The Plaintiff(s) shall pay the full amount for all parties in the mediation

[ ] The Defendant(s) shall pay the full amount for all parties in the mediation

[ ] The Clerk of the Courts has certified that the [ ] Plaintiff and/or [ ] the Defendant is/are indigent

[ ] Other (Please Specify) ____________________.

If a cost for mediation is imposed above, you may object to mediation on grounds of financial hardship or on any ground set forth in Fla. R. Civ. P. 1.700 within fifteen (15) days of the date of this Order.

8. **All parties are responsible for full compliance with each provision of this Order.** The Court shall have the power to impose sanctions as authorized by the Florida Rules of Civil Procedure, for the following:

a. Failure to attend and/or participate in good faith at the mediation conference without good cause;

b. Failure to pay the mediation fee within the time period set forth in this Order;

c. Failure to obey this Order;

d. Failure of the parties to appear;

e. Failure of a representative to appear with full authority to settle, without further consultation;

f. Failure of an attorney to appear with full authority to act on behalf of the client, if the Court has granted the absence of a party;

g. Failure to obtain permission of the Court for a continuance.

9. Plaintiffs and Defendants shall present a brief written summary of the case to the mediator, at least one week before the mediation conference. This summary shall include a list of outstanding issues in the case.

10. The conferences are governed by the Mediation Confidentiality and Privilege Act as well as applicable rules of procedure.

11. Parties utilizing their own private mediators shall pay the mediator directly based upon arrangements the parties make with the mediator. In addition, the private mediator is responsible for all administrative functions pertaining to the mediation including securing a space outside courthouse locations. Any private mediator chosen is subject to all relevant provisions of this Order, including deadlines.

12. Parties shall notify the CMAP if settlement is reached prior to a scheduled mediation date. Mediation shall not be canceled until a copy of the settlement is provided to CMAP and the Court. There shall be no refunds for payments made to CMAP. Because of related work done upon referral of a case to mediation to a designated mediator, a minimum of one hour of designated mediator time is deemed earned as of the fifteen (15) day payment deadline specified in paragraph 6 above, even if the parties settle prior to the mediation date.

13. If a settlement or partial settlement is reached, it shall be reduced to writing in the presence of the mediator, signed by all parties or their counsel, and promptly submitted to the Court.

14. Within ten (10) days following the completion of mediation, the designated mediator or the private mediator shall complete and file the mediation report via the eportal. For cases using the CMAP, within thirty (30) days following completion of mediation, the mediator shall complete and return the Statistical Information Sheet, Mediator Timesheets, and State Invoice to the CMAP, Director, Broward County Courthouse, Room 19150, 201 SE 6th St., Fort Lauderdale, FL 33301.

15. The parties are responsible for providing their own interpreter, if one is needed. Neither the Court nor the CMAP Office provides interpreters for County Court Civil cases.

DONE AND ORDERED in Chambers, Broward County, Florida, this ________ day of ____________________, 20____.

____

COUNTY JUDGE

Copies furnished:
Plaintiff
Defendant
Mediator

If you are a person with a disability who needs any accommodation in order to participate in this proceeding, you are entitled, at no cost to you, to the provision of certain assistance. Please contact Diana Sobel, Room 20140, 201 S.E. Sixth Street, Fort Lauderdale, Florida 33301, 954–831–7721 at least 7 days before your scheduled court appearance, or immediately upon receiving this notification if the time before the scheduled appearance is less than 7 days; if you are hearing or voice impaired, call 711.

IN THE COUNTY COURT IN AND FOR BROWARD COUNTY, FLORIDA

CASE NO.: COCE

Plaintiff(s), DIVISION: ___

JUDGE: ________

v.

Defendant(s).

_________________/

ORDER REFERRING CASE TO COURT MEDIATOR IN COUNTY COURT (SMALL CLAIMS)

The Court hereby refers this case to mediation as authorized by Florida Rules of Civil Procedure, Florida Small Claims Rules, and Chapter 44, Florida Statutes.

All parties are ordered to attend the mediation conference to be held on ______, 20 __ at ______ at the Broward County Courthouse located at 201 SE Sixth Street, West Tower, Room 19150, Fort Lauderdale, Broward County, Florida. The telephone number for the Court Administration Mediation and Arbitration Program (CMAP) offices is 954–831–6076.

The general rules governing the settlement conference are:

1. The appearance of all parties in person is **MANDATORY.** If the Court has granted the absence of any party, an attorney appearing on behalf of a party must have full and complete authority to settle and execute a mediation agreement without further consultation. If a business entity (i.e. an insurance company, corporation, association, partnership) is a party, a representative of that company must appear having full authority to settle. A non-lawyer representative may appear on behalf of a party to small claims mediation if the representative has the party's signed written authority to appear and has full authority to settle without further consultation. **Full authority includes having complete authority to dismiss the claim, to pay up to the full amount of any counterclaim, or the individual representing the defendant has the authority to pay up to the full amount of the claim.**

2. The Court shall have the power to impose sanctions for failure to attend the mediation conference or failure to comply with the terms of paragraph 1, including the imposition of costs and attorney's fees.

3. All discussions, representations and statements made in the mediation conference or in the furtherance of mediation shall be confidential and privileged commencing with the date of this Order.

4. There shall be no charge to the parties for the mediation services in Small Claims Court for services provided by the CMAP at pre-trial unless the mediation has to be reset due to any party's failure to comply with the terms of this Order.

5. If a settlement or partial settlement is reached, it shall be reduced to writing in the presence of the mediator, signed by all parties or their counsel, and promptly submitted to the Court for review and approval.

6. All provisions contained in this Order may be enforced by contempt proceedings or other appropriate sanctions.

7. The parties are responsible for providing their own interpreter, if one is needed. Neither the Court nor the CMAP Office provides interpreters for civil cases.

DONE AND ORDERED in Chambers, Broward County, Florida this ______ day of ________, 20 ___.

____

COUNTY JUDGE

Copies furnished:
Counsel of Record/Parties of Record
Court Mediation and Arbitration Program, Room 19150, Broward County Courthouse
201 S.E. Sixth Street, Fort Lauderdale, Florida 33301

If you are a person with a disability who needs any accommodation in order to participate in this proceeding, you are entitled, at no cost to you, to the provision of certain assistance. Please contact Diana Sobel, Room 20140, 201 S.E. Sixth Street, Fort Lauderdale, Florida 33301, 954–831–7721 at least 7 days before your scheduled court appearance, or immediately upon receiving this notification if the time before the scheduled appearance is less than 7 days; if you are hearing or voice impaired, call 711.

IN THE COUNTY COURT IN AND FOR BROWARD COUNTY, FLORIDA

Case No.: ______COCE

Judge: ______

Plaintiff(s),

vs.

Defendant(s),

_________________/

ORDER REFERRING CASE TO MEDIATION (COUNTY COURT—RESIDENTIAL EVICTION CASE)

THE COURT hereby refers the above captioned matter to mediation as authorized by statute and rules of procedure. It is hereby **ORDERED** as follows:

1. Unless the parties select their own mediator as provided in paragraph (2) below, the parties shall attend mediation through Court Administration's Court Mediation and Arbitration Program (CMAP) located in the West Tower, Room 19150, Broward County Courthouse, 201 S.E. Sixth Street, Fort Lauderdale, Florida 33301. The phone number is (954) 831–6309. CMAP shall coordinate the date, time, and location for the mediation session.

2. If the parties desire to select their own mediator, they shall within five (5) days of the date of entry of this Order file a stipulation with the Clerk of the Courts as to the designation of the mediator. The parties shall provide a copy of the stipulation to the CMAP office located in the West Tower, Room 19150, Broward County Courthouse, 201 S.E. Sixth Street, Fort Lauderdale, Florida 33301. If the parties cannot agree on their own mediator, they must use the CMAP mediator as specified in paragraph (1) above.

3. The mediation shall be held within fifteen (15) days of the date of this Order, unless both parties agree to extend the mediation deadline.

4. CONTINUANCES MAY BE GRANTED ONLY BY THE COURT UPON TIMELY WRITTEN MOTION FOR GOOD CAUSE SHOWN. Even if the parties mutually agree to

continue mediation, they must receive the permission of the Court and file the appropriate motions in a **timely** manner. PARTIES SHALL NOT UNILATERALLY CANCEL MEDIATION FOR ANY REASON EXCEPT SETTLEMENT OF THE CASE AND NOTIFICATION OF SUCH SETTLEMENT IS PROVIDED IN WRITING TO THE COURT.

5. The appearance of all parties, and their counsel, in person is **MANDATORY**. If the Court has granted the absence of a party, the attorney must have full and complete authority to settle from the client and authority to execute any mediation agreement on behalf of the client, without further consultation. If a business entity (i.e. an insurance company, corporation, association, partnership) is a party, a representative employed by that entity shall also appear having full authority to settle. **Full authority means the individual representing the plaintiff has the authority to dismiss the claim and to pay up to the full amount of the counterclaim and the individual representing the defendant has the authority to pay up to the full amount of the claim.**

6. Regarding this Order of referral to mediation, the court determines that:

— This is a residential eviction case and there is no charge to either party if CMAP is used.

— Other (Please specify): ______________

7. The Court shall have the power to impose sanctions as authorized by the Florida Rules of Civil Procedure, for the following:

a. Failure to attend and/or participate in good faith at the mediation conference without good cause;

b. Failure to obey this Order;

c. Failure of the parties to appear;

d. Failure of a representative to appear without full authority to settle, without further consultation;

e. Failure of an attorney to appear without full authority to act on behalf of his/her client, if the Court has granted the absence of a party;

f. Failure to obtain permission of the Court for a continuance;

g. Failure to pay the mediator's fee within the time period set forth in this order.

8. The conferences are governed by the Mediation Confidentiality and Privilege Act as well as applicable rules of procedure.

9. Parties shall notify CMAP if settlement is reached prior to a scheduled mediation date. Mediation shall not be canceled until a copy of the settlement is provided to CMAP and the Court.

10. If a settlement or partial settlement is reached, it shall be reduced to writing in the presence of the mediator, signed by all parties or their counsel, and promptly submitted to the Court.

11. Within ten (10) days following the completion of mediation, the mediator shall complete and return the Statistical Information Sheet to the CMAP, County Court Coordinator, Broward County Courthouse, Room 19150, 201 SE 6th St., Fort Lauderdale, FL 33301.

12. The parties are responsible for providing their own interpreter, if one is needed. Neither the Court nor the CMAP Office provides interpreters for County Court Civil cases.

DONE AND ORDERED in Chambers, Fort Lauderdale, Broward County, Florida, this __________ day of ______________________________, 20 _____.

____

COUNTY JUDGE

Copies furnished to the parties and CMAP

If you are a person with a disability who needs any accommodation in order to participate in this proceeding, you are entitled, at no cost to you, to the provision of certain assistance. Please contact Diana Sobel, Room 20140, 201 S.E. Sixth Street, Fort Lauderdale, Florida 33301, 954–831–7721 at least 7 days before your scheduled court appearance, or immediately upon receiving this notification if the time before the scheduled appearance is less than 7 days; if you are hearing or voice impaired, call 711.

2014–32 CO. CIRCUIT CIVIL AND COUNTY CIVIL EMERGENCY MATTERS

Publisher's Note: For text of order, see Order 2014–032–CIV under the Civil Orders heading, supra.

2014–26–CO. VACATING COUNTY ADMINISTRATIVE ORDER 2009–26–CO

IN THE CIRCUIT COURT OF THE SEVENTEENTH JUDICIAL CIRCUIT IN AND FOR BROWARD COUNTY, FLORIDA

Order Number 2014–26–CO

ADMINISTRATIVE ORDER VACATING COUNTY ADMINISTRATIVE ORDER 2009–26–CO

(a) Florida Rule of Judicial Administration 2.215(b)(3) states the chief judge shall "considering available resources, ensure the efficient and proper administration of all courts within [this] circuit."

(b) A review of the Civil Administrative Order 2009–26–CO indicates a need to vacate it as the judges assigned to the West Satellite Courthouse can hear additional small claims cases.

(c) In accordance with the authority vested in the chief judge by Florida Rule of Judicial Administration 2.215, it is ordered

Civil Administrative Order 2009–26–CO is vacated.

DONE AND ORDERED in chambers at Fort Lauderdale, Broward County, Florida on June 12, 2014.

Jack Tuter
Acting Chief Judge

2014–14–CO. DISMISSED CIVIL OR FAMILY CASES

Publisher's Note: For text of order, see Order 2014–14–CIV under the Civil Orders heading, supra.

2014–3–CO. CIVIL TRAFFIC INFRACTIONS

IN THE CIRCUIT COURT OF THE SEVENTEENTH JUDICIAL CIRCUIT IN AND FOR BROWARD COUNTY, FLORIDA

Order Number 2014–3–CO

ADMINISTRATIVE ORDER AS TO CIVIL TRAFFIC INFRACTIONS

(a) Florida Rule of Judicial Administration 2.215(b)(3) states the chief judge shall "considering available resources, ensure the efficient and proper administration of all courts within [this] circuit."

(b) In accordance with the authority vested in the chief judge by Florida Rule of Judicial Administration 2.215, it is ordered:

A. RESOLUTION OF CIVIL TRAFFIC INFRACTIONS

(1) All law enforcement officers shall include with any civil traffic citation issued in Broward County, Florida, not requiring a mandatory hearing, a Court approved "mailer", which shall provide the necessary instructions to resolve the citation administratively with the Clerk of Court or before the Court including the civil penalty and shall also be available on the Clerk of the Court's website.

(2) Traffic infraction citations shall indicate in the court information section the following:

a. "See Mailer" in lieu of indicating the civil penalty on the citation.

b. "Must comply within thirty (30) days of issuance of the citation."

c. The Defendant's signature is not required if the citing officer certifies by checking the appropriate box that the defendant received the citation unless it is a civil traffic infraction that requires a mandatory appearance.

(3) Any failure to include 2(a), 2(b), 2(c) information in the citation or mailer shall not result in the dismissal of any citation, unless the defendant shows that he or she did not receive the information and suffered prejudice as a result of not receiving the citation, not having the civil penalty or other available choices for resolving the citation provided at the time of the traffic stop.

B. CLERK OF THE COURT "GUILTY" OR "NO CONTEST" ADMINISTRATIVE PLEAS

(1) The Clerk of Court is authorized to:

a. Upon the entry of a plea of **no contest** or **guilty** impose an eight (8) hour state approved driver improvement course. This election is in lieu of payment of the civil penalty and is extended by authority of this order as an alternative for an individual who is unable to qualify for the option of a four (4) hour state approved driver improvement course in accordance with the provision of Section 318.14(9), Florida Statutes. This election is not available to an individual who has made the same election within the preceding twelve (12) months or five (5) times ever or to drivers who hold a Commercial Driver's License. Expenses will include the course tuition plus statutory court costs in the same amount as provided in Section 318.14 (9), Florida Statutes. Upon successful completion of this option, adjudication would be withheld.

b. In cases where the individual cited has previously elected to attend, either a four (4) hour or eight (8) hour driver improvement course, and subsequently failed to successfully complete the necessary course and/or pay the required expenses within ninety (90) days, the Clerk of Court shall do the following:

i. enter an adjudication for the person cited to be guilty of the infraction charged;

ii. issue a D6 Driver license suspension notice; and

iii. collect the statutory civil penalties, late fees, reinstatement fees, deferral fees and reset fees, if applicable. A credit shall be given toward the civil penalty for any court costs already paid.

c. If a no contest plea is filed with the Clerk of Court and the individual has improperly elected to attend a state approved driver improvement course because he or she made the same election within the preceding twelve (12) months, or more than five (5) times in a lifetime, the Clerk of Court shall enter an adjudication and assess points, but no additional fine or costs shall be imposed.

(2) Enter a D6 driver's license suspension notice as to any cited person who fails to resolve the citation or file a plea as required by law. The D6 license suspension may be lifted by the clerk as follows:

i. filing a plea of no contest or guilty and assessment of the civil penalty, costs, and/or points as required by law; or

ii. dismissal of the citation(s) as authorized by law upon the presentation of proper proof of compliance and the payment of the statutory costs and payment of any statutory late fees; or

iii. imposition of a four (4) hour state approved driver improvement course. This election is in lieu of payment of the civil penalty and in accordance with the provisions of Section 318.14(9), Florida Statutes, along with the payment of any statutory late fees; or

iv. filing a plea of not guilty and having the matter reset 1 time for a court appearance upon the payment of any statutory late fees. Subsequent requests for resets must go before the court to grant or deny at its discretion.

(3) Assign any case to a judge, if there is a timely written request within thirty (30) days of the issuance citation, and if there is no timely written request the case will be referred to a civil traffic hearing officer for pre-trial conference after filing of a plea of not guilty. Until a judicial assignment is made, no county court judge shall dispose of any such case by accepting a plea of guilty or no contest.

C. COURT APPEARANCES AND NOT GUILTY PLEAS

(1) A **not guilty** plea may **only** be entered as follows:

a. a written plea of not guilty filed with the Clerk of Court; or

b. a written affidavit of defense filed with the Clerk of Court along with the posting of the required bond in the amount of court costs currently $90.00 for any citation not involving an accident; or

c. a written affidavit of defense filed with the Clerk of Court along with the posting of the required bond in the amount of court costs currently $100.00 for any citation that does involve an accident.

(2) Once a **not guilty** plea is entered the Clerk of Court is authorized to:

a. set the case for a pre-trial conference or trial if it is a photo enforcement infraction;

b. accept and defer payments up to sixty (60) days, for the civil penalty, from the date the Clerk of Court processes the option for a civil penalty or other statutory costs or fees imposed by law;

c. utilize postmark, an electronic receipt or reference number date or any other date required by law as the compliance date.

(3) A defendant shall appear at a properly noticed traffic court proceedings as follows:

a. in person at the scheduled location, date and time;

b. through counsel of record at the scheduled location, date and time;

c. by affidavit of defense in accordance with section C(1) of this Administrative Order and applicable law;

d. by any other means at the discretion of the Judge of Civil Traffic Hearing Officer including via telephone and/or other electronic modalities that are permitted by law and accepted by the Circuit.

(4) Enter a D6 driver's license suspension notice as to any cited person who fails to appear after being properly noticed for a scheduled traffic infraction proceeding as required by law. The D6 license suspension may be lifted by the clerk as follows:

a. filing a plea of not guilty and having the matter reset 1 time for a court appearance upon the payment of any statutory late fees;

b. upon Order of the Court upon payment of any statutory late fees;

c. upon the entry of a guilty plea after payment of the civil penalty, costs, and/or points as required by law;

d. imposition of a four (4) hour state approved driver improvement course. This election is in lieu of payment of the civil penalty and in accordance with the provisions of Section 318.14 (9), Florida Statutes, along with the payment of any statutory late fees;

e. upon the entry of any other resolution permitted under section B(2)of this Administrative Order that applies.

D. This Order vacates and supersedes Administrative Order VI–99–A–3.

DONE AND ORDERED in chambers at Fort Lauderdale, Broward County, Florida on February 6, 2014.

Peter M. Weinstein
Chief Judge

2010–38–CO. MISDEMEANOR DRUG COURT DIVISION

IN THE CIRCUIT COURT OF THE SEVENTEENTH JUDICIAL CIRCUIT IN AND FOR BROWARD COUNTY, FLORIDA

ORDER NUMBER 2010-38-CO

ADMINISTRATIVE ORDER AS TO MISDEMEANOR DRUG COURT DIVISION

(a) Florida Rule of Judicial Administration 2.215(b)(3) states the chief judge shall "develop an administrative plan for the efficient and proper administration of all courts within that circuit."

(b) § 948.16(1), Fla. Stat., authorizes the chief judge to establish a drug court program to include programs as authorized by § 397.334, Fla. Stat.

(c) In accordance with the authority vested in the chief judge by Florida Rule of Judicial Administration 2.215, it is ordered:

(1) Cases eligible for transfer to the misdemeanor drug court division are:

(a) defendants eligible for a pretrial substance abuse education and treatment intervention program as authorized by § 948.16(1), Fla. Stat., [1] or

(b) defendants referred by another county criminal judge for drug court probation after sentencing. [2]

(2) Entry into misdemeanor drug court is voluntary. The defendant upon entry into a pretrial substance abuse education and treatment intervention program shall sign an agreement setting forth the terms of the pretrial substance abuse education and treatment intervention program. If the defendant voluntarily enters misdemeanor drug court probation he or she shall sign a document listing the terms of probation.

(3) A defendant is preliminarily qualified to participate in a pretrial substance abuse education and treatment intervention program or probation if the charged offense is set forth at § 948.16(1), Fla. Stat., [3] or other charges agreed to by the State Attorney.

(4) An eligible defendant may seek to transfer his or her case to misdemeanor drug court by filing a written motion or by ore tenus motion and having the matter heard either by the originally assigned county criminal division judge or misdemeanor drug court division judge. Additionally a judge may sua sponte order the transfer of a case to the misdemeanor drug court division. The State, defendant, and defense counsel, if any, shall be present at the hearing and may present evidence that supports transfer of the case to the misdemeanor drug court division. [4]

(5) The judge assigned to the misdemeanor drug court division at the defendant's drug court arraignment or upon transfer of a case to the misdemeanor drug court division shall make the final determination of the defendant's eligibility for voluntary entry in the misdemeanor pretrial substance abuse education and treatment intervention program or probation. The State Attorney shall advise the Court if the defendant is eligible to participate in the available misdemeanor drug court programs.

(6) Any defendant electing to voluntarily enter into misdemeanor drug court must:

(a) sign an agreement setting forth all terms and conditions of participation;

(b) attend a pretrial substance abuse education and treatment intervention program or probation substance abuse education and treatment intervention program for a minimum of six (6) months;

(c) substantially comply with all terms of probation or the terms of the pretrial substance abuse education and treatment intervention program (which shall include all approved alternative programs);

(d) substantially comply with all court orders.

(7) At the six (6) month anniversary of entry into a pretrial substance abuse education and treatment intervention program or probation the court shall conduct a status conference and determine if:

(a) The defendant successfully completed all terms and conditions of the pretrial substance abuse education and treatment intervention program and/or probation.

(b) The defendant is successfully finishing all terms and conditions of the pretrial substance abuse education and treatment intervention program and/or probation and will complete same within the next six (6) months.

(c) The defendant did not successfully complete all terms and conditions of the pretrial substance abuse education and treatment intervention program and/or probation and will not complete same within the next six (6) months. The court may determine if there are extraordinary circumstances and order continued treatment.

(8) A defendant transferred to misdemeanor drug court may be terminated if:

(a) there is an outstanding capias for a period of thirty (30) days; or

(b) new criminal charge(s) or violation of probation is/are filed;

(c) he or she is no longer participating in the pretrial substance abuse education and treatment intervention program or other approved program; or

(d) he or she poses a danger to public safety; or

(e) he or she requests a trial.

(9) A defendant shall be terminated if he or she is charged with a violent felony crime or felony sex crime.

(10) Administrative Order vacates and supersedes Administrative Order 2009–92–CO.

DONE AND ORDERED in chambers at Fort Lauderdale, Broward County, Florida on ________.

Victor Tobin
Chief Judge

[1] The defendant's participation in a State Attorney pretrial drug diversion program will not exclude the transfer of the case from the State Attorney's program to a court supervised pretrial substance abuse education and treatment intervention program. A defendant who was arrested and is prosecuted for a violent felony crime or sex felony crime is not eligible to enter misdemeanor drug court.

[2] If a case is transferred to drug court from another county criminal division for drug court probation and if the defendant is then charged with a violation of probation or arrested and prosecution commenced for a crime not set forth in § 948.16(1), Fla. Stat., the case may be transferred back to the originally assigned county criminal division for proceedings with regard to the violation of probation or additionally filed misdemeanor charges after hearing before the judge assigned to the misdemeanor drug court division.

[3] If the State Attorney objects to a case being transferred to drug court based upon allegations the defendant was dealing or selling the controlled substance which is the basis for the arrest, he or she shall advise the court. If the objection is sustained the defendant's case shall be transferred to the originally assigned county criminal division from drug court or with consent of the defendant the misdemeanor drug court judge may proceed with final disposition of the case.

[4] If the defendant requests a hearing before the judge assigned to the misdemeanor drug court division, the Clerk of County Court shall provide a notice to the State Attorney, defense counsel, and defendant of the date and time for a hearing. The judge assigned to the misdemeanor drug court division shall be responsible for the entry of a transfer order if the case is accepted into the misdemeanor drug court division.

VI–07–N–1. MISDEMEANOR DIVERSION PROGRAM FOR THE OFFENSE OF DRIVING WHILE LICENSE SUSPENDED

IN THE CIRCUIT COURT OF THE SEVENTEENTH JUDICIAL CIRCUIT, IN AND FOR BROWARD COUNTY, FLORIDA

ADMINISTRATIVE ORDER NO.: VI–07–N–1

IN RE: ORDER CONCERNING CREATION OF THE MISDEMEANOR DIVERSION PROGRAM FOR THE OFFENSE OF DRIVING WHILE LICENSE SUSPENDED

WHEREAS, this Circuit has recognized that the creation of specialized diversion programs have enhanced the expediency, effectiveness, and quality of Judicial Administration;

WHEREAS, it is essential that a new strategy be implemented to focus upon individuals charged with the Misdemeanor Criminal Traffic offense of Driving While License Suspended (DWLS) who seek an opportunity to regain and retain their driving privileges;

WHEREAS, this Circuit recognizes that it is in the interest of Public Safety that its drivers should be encouraged to drive safely with a valid driver's license, with proper equipment, with proper insurance coverage and with sufficient driver education;

WHEREAS, this Circuit recognizes that it in the pursuit of Justice and the Public Interest that individuals be encouraged to pay or make recompense for child support, fines, court costs and other financial responsibilities;

WHEREAS, this Circuit has recognized that the administration of such a program should be open to persons who wish to enter the program provided they follow all rules and regulations as determined by the Broward County Sheriff's Office Probation Department (herein after referred to as "Probation") as well as the State Attorney's Office for Broward County (herein after referred to as "the State");

In accordance with the authority vested in the Chief Judge by Rule 2.050 of the Florida Rules of Judicial Administration it is

NOW AND THEREFORE ORDERED that:

Effective February 1, 2007 persons arrested for or charged with the Misdemeanor Offense of DWLS, who are otherwise eligible, may participate in the Broward County Misdemeanor Diversion Program for DWLS as created by the Broward County State Attorney's Office (herein after referred to as "the Program"). The Program is strictly on a voluntary basis. The Program will be operated and enforced by Probation and the State. An eligible person, or his or her attorney may request admission into the Program within 30 days of the arraignment, or if no arraignment is held due to the filing of a written plea, within 30 days after a written plea of not guilty is filed, or within 30 days of the inception of the Program. The applicant shall apply through the Probation department before the first status conference or calendar call.

I. ELIGIBILITY

A. The applicant must be charged in the instant offense with Misdemeanor DWLS where the license was **only** suspended for failure to pay penalty, failure to appear, failure to complete traffic school (except D.U.I. school), failure to pay child support or failure to satisfy financial responsibility/insurance/judgments.

B. The applicant cannot have been previously or currently classified as a Habitual Traffic Offender.

C. The applicant cannot have had their license previously or currently permanently suspended or revoked.

D. The applicant may not have any convictions or suspensions on his/her license for the offense of DUI or a Chapter 893 violation.

E. The applicant cannot have a prior withhold of adjudication or adjudication for a felony driving/traffic offense in this state or any other jurisdiction.

F. The instant offense cannot have involved a traffic crash where the applicant was deemed by law enforcement to be at fault.

G. The instant offense cannot have been part of a Felony charge or arrest.

H. The applicant cannot have had the instant offense previously disposed of by way of plea or trial, and then subsequently vacated or set aside said plea, conviction or sentence.

I. The instant charge may be for any eligible DWLS charge, but the applicant is **only** allowed to complete the Program once. At the inception of the Program, all eligible charges that the applicant has pending may be included

J. It is permissible for the applicant to have previously entered another diversion program.

K. It is permissible for the applicant to have a limited prior criminal history, except as noted above, but whether such will cause the applicant to be ineligible will be determined by the State on a case-by-case basis.

II. PROGRAM REQUIREMENTS

A. Diversion Phase

1. The applicant, upon acceptance into the Program, must abide by the rules and regulations of the Program, including, but not limited to, a written admission of guilt and an educational component.

2. The participant must take all necessary steps to obtain a valid Florida's Driver's License, including paying or satisfying all outstanding citations, fines and court costs, fees, child support payments and judgments.

3. All vehicles owned and operated by the participant must have valid motor vehicle insurance.

4. All previously cited equipment violations must be corrected.

5. The participant, if necessary, may have to complete driving school, as determined by Probation, and the Department of Highway Safety and Motor Vehicles.

6. The participant must be gainfully employed or actively seek employment. The Broward County Sheriff's Office D.O.C.C. Employment Program can be used to assist with such.

7. While in the Program, any arrest or charge for any criminal offense, or traffic infraction that is a moving violation, will result in automatic termination of the participant's participation in the Program.

8. The participant will have up to 90 days to complete the diversion phase of the Program, but may successfully complete the diversion phase as soon as all conditions are satisfied. The diversion phase of the Program may be extended by Probation only if the participant is unable to complete for financial reasons, but is continuing to make his or her best efforts to do so.

B. Disposition and Probation Phase

1. Upon successful completion of the above diversion phase, the participant will resolve the DWLS charge by way of a **guilty** plea to the changed charge of No Valid Driver's License, as well as pleading guilty or no contest to any other accompanying charges.

2. The negotiated sentence for the changed charge will consist of an Adjudication to the charge of No Valid Driver's License, six (6) months of non-reporting administrative probation (with no early termination). Special conditions of said probation will be that the participant must maintain a valid driver's license here in the State of Florida, may not commit any criminal offenses, or civil traffic infractions that are moving violations, and that the participant maintain motor vehicle insurance for all vehicles owned or operated by the participant.

III. PROCEDURAL CONSIDERATIONS

A. If an applicant indicates a desire to participate in the Program, an initial Preliminary Recommendation Memorandum will be completed by an Assistant State Attorney from the County Court division.

B. The applicant shall sign the form and waive his or her Right to Discovery and a Speedy Trial. If the applicant is represented by an attorney, the attorney shall also sign the form. If an interpreter is utilized the interpreter shall also sign the form.

C. The original form (white) shall be filed with the Clerk. The blue copy shall be sent to the Program. The yellow copy shall be kept by the applicant. The pink copy shall be retained by the State.

D. The applicant must obtain a copy of his or her driving record either from the Court Clerk while in the courtroom or at the Clerk of Court counter for a cost, and with such and the yellow copy of the form, the applicant shall go to probation and sign up for the Program no later than the end of the following business day.

E. In order to participate in the Program the applicant must be a legal resident of the United States, with a verifiable address. If the applicant is a citizen of another country, the applicant must provide proof that he or she was in the country legally when the offense was committed.

F. Once accepted, the participant must remain in the country while the case is pending, unless the participant is deployed to active military duty, is a student studying abroad, or is a foreign national who no longer has permission to remain in the United States

G. If the participant has more than one open eligible criminal traffic matter pending, the Clerk shall transfer all eligible criminal traffic matters to the division with the open eligible criminal traffic matter with the earliest incident date, regardless of where located. If the participant has any open traffic infractions (pending or open due to outstanding obligations) that the participant cannot readily dispose of or satisfy, unless the matter has already been submitted to a collection agency, said matters shall be transferred to the division with the open eligible criminal traffic matter with the earliest incident date, regardless of where located. The Program will assist the Clerk in identifying such cases by providing a list of prospective matters for transfer.

H. Once all eligible matters are consolidated before one Judge as noted above, the Judge may dispose of pending outstanding monetary obligations by ordering public works or community service as provided by law. Such may be done in open court or upon review of financial affidavits provided by the Program to the Judge in chambers. If such is ordered, the Program will provide public works projects or community service opportunities and monitor compliance with the Court's orders.

I. It is solely within the discretion of the State to make any exceptions to or waivers of the above eligibility requirements, Program requirements, or procedural considerations.

DONE AND ORDERED in Chambers at Fort Lauderdale, Broward County, Florida on this the 26th day of January, 2007.

Dale Ross
Chief Judge

VI–02–D–3. COURT COSTS AND ASSESSMENTS IN COUNTY COURT

IN THE CIRCUIT COURT OF THE SEVENTEENTH JUDICIAL CIRCUIT, IN AND FOR BROWARD COUNTY, FLORIDA

ADMINISTRATIVE ORDER NO. VI–02–D–3

IN RE: COURT COSTS AND ASSESSMENTS IN COUNTY COURT; CLERK'S COSTS IN CERTAIN TRAFFIC INFRACTIONS; AND DISTRIBUTION OF COSTS, ASSESSMENTS, TRAFFIC FINES, AND OTHER PENALTIES.

In accordance with the authority vested in the Chief Judge by Rule 2.050 of the Florida Rules of Judicial administration, and pursuant to applicable statutes, rules and Motion adopted by the Broward County Board of County Commissioners on December 7, 1982, it is ORDERED that:

The Clerk of Court will record on all disposition documents, as an assessed court cost, all mandatory and discretionary court costs as required or mandated by law including state statute, rule of court, county, municipal or local ordinance. Should the presiding judge order a reduction or waver in a discretionary court cost the Clerk of Court will record as an assessed cost that amount as ordered or directed.

Mandatory Costs

Court Costs
Criminal Justice Standards and Training Trust Fund
Crimes Compensation Trust Fund
Local Government Criminal Justice Trust Fund
Safe Neighborhood Assessment

Mandatory Costs in Specific Cases

Crime Stoppers Trust Fund
Emergency Medical Trust Fund
County Alcohol and other Drug Abuse Trust Fund
Domestic Violence Trust Fund

Local Option Mandatory Costs

Criminal Justice Education and Training
Delinquency Prevention
Teen Courts

Discretionary Costs

Operating Trust Fund of the Department of Law Enforcement Court Facilities Service Charge

Subsequent to the effective date of this order, should additional court costs be mandated by state statute, local ordinance, Rule of Court, or other authority, the Clerk of Court is ordered to record the same as required by this administrative order.

Wherever a conflict arises between the court costs set forth in this Administrative Order and state statute or local ordinance, the state statute or local ordinance shall prevail.

SECTION I. COURT COSTS AND ASSESSMENTS WHERE HEARING IS HELD CIVIL TRAFFIC INFRACTIONS

A. Court costs and assessments for law enforcement training shall be assessed in the County Court in the sum of at least $25.00 in the following cases:

1. In each civil traffic infraction case where a hearing is held to determine whether a civil infraction was committed, except where the alleged offender is found "not guilty" or the court determines that the traffic infraction was not committed. Such costs and assessments shall be assessed when any person admits that a civil traffic violation was committed and when the offender is found to have committed the infraction, notwithstanding that the Court may withhold setting a civil penalty or entering judgment thereon or, after setting a civil penalty, the Court may suspend its payment. Such court costs and assessments for law enforcement training shall be in addition to any civil penalty set or imposed by the Court.

2. Court costs, including the assessments for law enforcement training, shall not be waived by the Court except upon compliance with the provisions of Section 939.05, Florida Statutes.

B. The court costs and assessments for law enforcement training provided for in A above shall be paid by the Clerk of County Court and remitted on a monthly basis, as follows:

1. The first $20.00 shall be paid to and retained by Broward County as court costs.

2. The next $3.00 shall be paid and remitted to the Department of Revenue for deposit in the State treasury for law enforcement training; provided, however that no such assessment shall be made against any person convicted for violation

of any state statute, municipal ordinance, or county ordinance relating to the parking of vehicles.

3. If Broward County or any municipality has adopted an ordinance assessing an additional $2.00 for local law enforcement training and has filed a certified copy of such ordinance with the Clerk of County Court, then the next $2.00 shall be paid to Broward County or to any such municipality for local law enforcement training, depending upon (a) whether the infraction or violation occurred or was committed within the unincorporated area of Broward County or within a municipality whose law enforcement services are provided by the Broward County Sheriff's Office, or (b) whether the infraction or violation occurred or was committed within the territorial jurisdiction of any such municipality; provided, however, that no such assessment shall be made against any person convicted for violation of any state statute, municipal ordinance, or county ordinance relating to the parking of vehicles. Such assessments shall be remitted by the Clerk to qualifying municipalities and Broward County on a monthly basis for local law enforcement training; provided, however, that if the municipal law enforcement services are or have been provided to any such municipality by the Broward County Sheriff's Office, then the next $2.00 assessment shall be remitted to Broward County rather than to such municipality for local law enforcement training, In any case, where all of the provisions of this subsection 3 are not complied with, the said $2.00 shall be paid to and retained by Broward County.

4. If the Court withholds adjudication after holding a hearing in a case involving a civil traffic infraction and only assesses court costs against the offender all court costs in excess of $25.00 shall be paid to the municipality in which the civil traffic infraction was committed or to Broward County if committed in the unincorporated area of the county, and all such court costs in excess of $25.00 shall be remitted by the Clerk on a monthly basis to such municipality or to Broward County.

5. If the Court directs the payment of "court costs" without specifying any dollar amount, the total sum of $25.00 for court costs and assessment for law enforcement training is thereby assessed in addition to any penalty and/or fine imposed by the Court. Such $25.00 shall be collected by the Clerk and paid and remitted as provided in B above.

SECTION II. COURT COSTS AND ASSESSMENTS WHERE HEARING IS HELD CRIMINAL TRAFFIC AND MISDEMEANORS VIOLATIONS

A. Court costs and assessments for law enforcement training shall be assessed in the County Court in the sum of at least $26.00 in the following cases:

1. In each criminal traffic case where a hearing is held to determine whether a criminal traffic or misdemeanor violation was committed, except where the alleged offender is found "not guilty" or the Court determines that the criminal traffic or misdemeanor violation was not committed. Such costs and assessments shall be assessed when any person admits that a criminal traffic or misdemeanor violation was committed and when the offender is found to have committed the infraction, notwithstanding that the Court may withhold setting a criminal penalty or entering judgment thereon or, after setting a criminal penalty, the Court may suspend its payment. Such court costs and assessments for law enforcement training shall be in addition to any criminal penalty imposed by the court.

2. Court costs, including the assessments for law enforcement training, shall not be waived by the Court except upon compliance with the provision of Section 939.05, Florida Statutes.

B. The court costs and assessments for law enforcement training provided for in A above shall be paid by the Clerk of County Court and remitted on a monthly basis, as follows:

1. The first $21.00 shall be paid to and retained by Broward County as court costs.

2. The next $3.00 shall be paid and remitted to the Department of Revenue for deposit in the State Treasury for law enforcement training; provided, however, that no such assessment shall be made against any person convicted for violation of any state statute relating to the parking of vehicles.

3. If Broward County or any municipality has adopted an ordinance assessing an additional $2.00 for local law enforcement training and has filed a certified copy of such ordinance with the Clerk of the County Court, then the next $2.00 shall be paid to Broward County or to any such municipality for local law enforcement training, depending upon (a) whether the violation occurred or was committed within the unincorporated area of Broward County or within a municipality whose law enforcement services are provided by the Broward County Sheriff's Office, or (b) whether the violation occurred or was committed within the territorial jurisdiction of any such municipality; provided, however, that no such assessment shall be made against any person convicted for violation of any state statute regarding the parking of vehicles. Such assessments shall be remitted by the Clerk to qualifying municipalities and Broward County on a monthly basis for local law enforcement training; provided, however, that if the municipal law enforcement services are or have been provided to any such municipality by the Broward County Sheriff's Office, then the next $2.00 assessment shall be remitted to Broward County rather than to such municipality for local law enforcement training. In any case, where all of the provisions of this subsection 3 are not complied with, the said $2.00 shall be paid to and retained by Broward County.

4. If the Court withholds adjudication after holding a hearing in a case involving a criminal traffic violation and only assesses court costs against the offender, all court costs in excess of $26.00 shall be paid to the municipality in which the criminal traffic violation was committed or to Broward County if committed in the unincorporated area of the county, and all such court costs in excess of $26.00 shall be remitted by the Clerk on a monthly basis to such municipality or to Broward County.

5. If the Court directs the payment of "court costs" without specifying any dollar amount, the total sum of $26.00 for court costs and assessments for law enforcement training is thereby assessed in addition to any penalty and/or fine imposed by the Court. Such $26.00 shall be collected by the Clerk and paid and remitted as provided in B above.

6. The Clerk shall collect all surcharges which are statutorily imposed in addition to the above court costs and assessments.

SECTION III. COURT COSTS AND ASSESSMENTS WHERE HEARING IS HELD MUNICIPAL ORDINANCE VIOLATIONS

A. Court costs and assessments for law enforcement training shall be assessed in County Court in the sum of at least $26.00 in the following cases:

1. In each municipal ordinance violation where a hearing is held to determine whether a municipal ordinance violation was committed, except where the alleged offender is found "not guilty" or the Court determines that the municipal ordinance violation was not committed. Such costs and assessments shall be assessed when any person admits that a municipal ordinance violation was committed and when the offender is found to have committed the violation, notwithstanding that the Court may withhold setting a municipal ordinance penalty or entering judgment thereon or, after setting a penalty, the Court may suspend its payment. Such court costs and assessments for law enforcement training shall be in addition to any municipal ordinance penalty imposed by the Court.

2. Court costs, including the assessments for law enforcement training, shall not be waived by the Court except upon compliance with the provisions of Section 939.05, Florida Statutes.

B. The court costs and assessments for law enforcement training provided for in A above shall be paid by the Clerk of County Court and remitted on a monthly basis, as follows:

1. The first $21.00 shall be paid to and retained by Broward County as court costs, provided, however, that the violation occurred in the jurisdiction of a municipality which is not represented by their own City Prosecutor.

2. If a municipal ordinance violation occurred in a municipality which is represented by their own City Prosecutor, then the first $10.50 in B (1) above shall be paid to and retained by Broward County and the next $10.50 shall be paid to and retained by the municipality in whose jurisdiction the violation occurred.

3. The next $3.00 shall be paid and remitted to the Department of Revenue for deposit in the State Treasury for law enforcement training; provided however, that no such assessments shall be made against any person convicted for violation of any state statute or municipal ordinance relating to the parking of vehicles.

4. If Broward County or any such municipality has adopted an ordinance assessing an additional $2.00 for local law enforcement training and has filed a certified copy of such ordinance with the Clerk of the County Court, then the next 2.00 shall be paid to any such municipality or to Broward County for local law enforcement training, depending upon (a) whether the violation occurred or was committed within a municipality whose law enforcement services are provided by the Broward County Sheriff's Office, or (b) whether the municipal ordinance violation occurred or was committed within the territorial jurisdiction of any such municipality; provided, however, that no such assessment shall be made against any person convicted for violation of a municipal ordinance violation relating to the parking of vehicles. Such assessments shall be remitted by the Clerk to qualifying municipalities and Broward County on a monthly basis for local law enforcement training; provided, however, that if the municipal law enforcement services have been provided to any municipality by the Broward County Sheriff's Office, then the next $2.00 assessment shall be remitted to Broward County rather than to such municipality for local law enforcement training. In any case, where all of the provisions of this Section 4 are not complied with, the said $2.00 shall be paid to and retained by Broward County.

5. If the Court withholds adjudication after holding a hearing in a case involving a municipal ordinance violation, and only court costs are assessed against the offender, all court costs in excess of $26.00 shall be paid to the municipality in which the violation was committed.

6. If the Court directs the payment of "court costs" without specifying any dollar amount, the total sum of $26.00 for court costs and assessments for law enforcement training is thereby assessed in addition to any penalty and/or fine imposed by the Court. Such $26.00 shall be collected by the Clerk and paid and remitted as provided in B above.

7. The Clerk shall collect all surcharges which are statutorily imposed in addition to the above court costs and assessments.

SECTION IV. COURT COSTS AND ASSESSMENTS NO HEARING HELD

A. The Clerk of the County Court is hereby authorized to add to the penalty, Pursuant to F.S. 318.18(11), in each traffic infraction case where no hearing is required or held and the offender admits the commission of the offense by forfeiting a bond or paying the penalty by mail or in person the following:

1. Three dollars ($3.00) for each infraction of bicycle regulations, Section 316.2065, Florida Statutes, and for each infraction of pedestrian regulations, Section 316.130, Florida Statutes.

2. Six dollars ($6.00) for each nonmoving traffic infraction.

3. Ten dollars ($10.00) for each moving infraction.

B. The costs collected by the Clerk pursuant to A above shall be paid to Broward County and shall be remitted by the Clerk on a monthly basis.

C. In addition to the costs provided in A above, the Clerk of the County Court shall, subject to the limitation stated in subsection 6 hereof, collect and remit on a monthly basis to the Department of Revenue for deposit in the State Treasury as assessment of $3.00 for law enforcement training in the following cases:

1. From each bond estreature and forfeited bail bond related to charges for violation of a state penal or criminal statute, including misdemeanors and criminal traffic offenses.

2. From each bond estreature and forfeited bail bond related to charges for violation of a county or municipal ordinance.

3. In no event shall such an assessment for law enforcement training be made against any person who is convicted for or who admits or pleads guilty to violation of any state statute, municipal ordinance, or county ordinance related to the parking of vehicles.

SECTION V. DISTRIBUTION OF TRAFFIC FINES AND CERTAIN COSTS

Effective as of October 1, 1996, the Clerk of the County Court is hereby directed to pay to each municipality the penalty or fine paid for each traffic infraction and for each criminal traffic violation which occurred or was committed within the territorial jurisdiction of a municipality, together with all court costs in connection therewith payable to such municipality pursuant to the provisions of Section I (B)(4) above, regardless of whether such traffic infraction is consolidated with and reported under the case number of another criminal traffic violation or non-traffic offense, and regardless of whether such criminal traffic violation is consolidated with and reported under the case number of another non-traffic offense. Such penalties or fines and court costs under Section I(B) (4) shall be remitted to each municipality hereafter on a monthly basis.

SECTION VI. UNIFORM COMPLIANCE SCHEDULE

A. The Clerk of County Court is hereby directed to apply a Uniform Compliance Schedule of thirty (30) days to all civil infractions including those infractions associated with Personal Injury Protection Insurance.

SECTION VII. EFFECTIVE DATE

This Administrative order replaces Administrative Order VI–97–D–3 issued on April 14, 1997.

DONE AND ORDERED at Fort Lauderdale, Broward County, Florida this 7th day of June, 2002.

Dale Ross
Chief Judge

General Orders

2019–6–GEN. PROCEDURES FOR CIRCUIT COURT APPEALS AND PETITIONS FOR EXTRAORDINARY WRITS

IN THE CIRCUIT COURT OF THE SEVENTEENTH JUDICIAL CIRCUIT IN AND FOR BROWARD COUNTY, FLORIDA

Administrative Order 2019–6–Gen

ADMINISTRATIVE ORDER UPDATING PROCEDURES FOR CIRCUIT COURT APPEALS AND PETITIONS FOR EXTRAORDINARY WRITS

(a) Pursuant to Article V, section 2(d) of the Florida Constitution and section 43.26, Florida Statutes, the chief judge of each judicial circuit is charged with the authority and power to do everything necessary to promote the prompt and efficient administration of justice.

(b) Florida Rule of Judicial Administration 2.215(b)(3) states the chief judge "shall, considering available resources, ensure the efficient and proper administration of all courts within [this] circuit."

(c) The Circuit Court is charged with the responsibility of hearing and ruling on appeals and petitions for extraordinary writs from the County Court and local administrative bodies. To ensure the proper use of judicial resources and efficient disposition of such cases, it is necessary to update the Circuit's appellate procedures.

(d) In accordance with the authority vested in the chief judge by Article V, section 2(d) of the Florida Constitution, section 43.26, Florida Statutes, and Florida Rule of Judicial Administration 2.215, it is hereby **ORDERED**:

(1) *Assignment of Civil Appeals and Petitions for Extraordinary Writs.*

(a) All county civil appeals and appeals from local administrative bodies to the Circuit Court shall be assigned by the Clerk of the Court ("Clerk") to Division AP.

(b) Petitions for writs seeking certiorari, habeas corpus, mandamus, quo warranto, or prohibition filed with the Clerk, including any petition arising out of a county criminal case, shall be assigned to Division AW.

(c) Petitions for extraordinary writs relating to a circuit criminal case are not to be assigned to Division AW.

i. The Clerk shall immediately forward all petitions for extraordinary writs relating to a circuit criminal case to the assigned division consistent with the Clerk's protocol for notifying the Court as to the filing of postconviction motions in circuit criminal cases.

ii. The Clerk shall file the petition as a docket entry in the circuit criminal case.

(2) *Assignment of Criminal Appeals.* All county criminal appeals and civil traffic infraction appeals to the Circuit Court shall be assigned by the Clerk to Division AC.

(3) *General Procedures for Circuit Appeals.*

(a) There shall be a three-judge panel of circuit court judges to consider all circuit civil appeals and a separate three-judge panel to consider all circuit criminal appeals. Petitions for extraordinary writs will be assigned to Division AW, but the Administrative Judge of the Circuit Civil Division may transfer the petition to the circuit criminal panel or general circuit civil division, when appropriate based on the nature of the petition.

(b) The Administrative Judge of the Circuit Civil Division shall assign three judges to serve on the circuit civil appellate panel and shall appoint one of the three judges as the presiding judge of the panel. The Administrative Judge of the Circuit Criminal Division shall assign three judges to serve on the circuit criminal appellate panel and shall appoint one of the three judges as the presiding judge of the panel. The term of the appointment shall be for six (6) months, unless extended by the Administrative Judge of the Circuit Civil Division or Administrative Judge of the Circuit Criminal Division, as appropriate, or the Chief Judge. Assignments shall be made by memorandum.

(c) If a judge assigned to a panel recuses himself or herself, the Administrative Judge of the Circuit Civil Division or Administrative Judge of the Circuit Criminal Division, as appropriate, or the Chief Judge, shall assign a judge to be the third member of the panel. Assignments shall be made by a memorandum.

(d) The presiding judge shall:

i. Discharge the administrative duties of the panel, including scheduling conferences at least once a month, and oral argument sessions, when necessary;

ii. Preside at all sessions;

iii. Set a schedule for duty assignments among the panel members to determine all non-dispositive motions and other issues raised by the parties or the Court *sua sponte*;

iv. Assign the writing of opinions among the panel members when the presiding judge is in the majority; however, when the presiding judge is in the minority, the most senior judge on the panel shall discharge this responsibility for the majority.

(e) If the presiding judge is unavailable, then one of the two other panel members may discharge his or her responsibilities. If all members of a panel are unavailable, then the Administrative Judge of the Circuit Civil or Circuit Criminal Division, as appropriate, may discharge the presiding judge's responsibilities. If the administrative judges are unavailable, then the circuit civil or circuit criminal duty judge, as appropriate, may discharge the presiding judge's responsibilities.

(f) Oral Arguments.

i. Requests for oral argument made by a party will be granted only in those cases where a majority of the appellate panel genuinely believes it is necessary for disposition of the cause.

ii. Oral arguments shall be scheduled on any case when requested by two members of the appellate panel, even if not requested by the parties.

(g) After oral argument, or after the discussion of a case in conference, the panel shall take a preliminary vote. Cases shall be decided by majority vote.

(h) En banc matters shall comply with Florida Rule of Appellate Procedure 9.331. The references to the judges of the district court of appeal shall be read as judges of the circuit civil or circuit criminal division for the purposes of this Administrative Order. The judges sitting en banc are limited to those judges eligible for assignment to an appellate panel.

(i) All motions for rehearing must comply with Florida Rule of Appellate Procedure 9.300.

(4) *Clerk of the Court Duties.*

(a) The Clerk shall perform all functions, and discharge all duties, traditionally fulfilled by the clerk of the Fourth District Court of Appeal.

(b) The Clerk shall accept electronically filed notices of appeal and petitions for extraordinary writs as prescribed by law.

(c) If the Clerk assigns a case to a division not in compliance with this Administrative Order, the Administrative Judge of the Circuit Civil or Circuit Criminal Division, as appropriate, may enter an order directing the Clerk to transfer the case to the appropriate division or court. The Clerk shall forthwith change the division coding to reflect the proper division on its case maintenance software.

(d) The Clerk shall prepare the index to the record on appeal and transmit the record on appeal for county to circuit court appeals as required by the Florida Rules of Appellate Procedure. If the Clerk is not able to comply with the times set forth in Florida Rule of Appellate Procedure 9.200 for the preparation of the index and transmission of the record on appeal, the Clerk shall file a notice indicating the additional time required to prepare the index and transmit the record on appeal. Such additional time shall not exceed fifty (50) days. If the Clerk requires in excess of fifty (50) days, a motion shall be filed with the Court.

(e) It is the obligation of the appellant or petitioner to ensure the Clerk complies with the duties as established by Florida Rule of Appellate Procedure 9.200.

(f) The Clerk shall issue a mandate as required by Florida Rule of Appellate Procedure 9.340. Upon issuance of a mandate, the Clerk shall provide a copy of the mandate and opinion or order disposing of said case to Florida Law Weekly Supplement and the Broward County Law Library.

(g) The Clerk shall return the record on appeal to the county court no later than ten (10) court business days after the issuance of the mandate or dismissal of the appeal.

(5) *Extensions of Time.*

(a) In lieu of a motion pursuant to Florida Rule of Appellate Procedure 9.300(a), parties or counsel may agree to no more than two (2) extensions of time to file an initial brief that, in the aggregate, shall not exceed a combined total of 120 days. Parties or counsel may agree to no more than two (2) extensions of time for the filing of the answer brief that, in the aggregate, shall not exceed a combined total of sixty (60) days. Any notice or motion for extension of time must be filed before the expiration date of the time period. Any motion for additional time must be for a period of sixty (60) days or less. The nonmoving party shall have ten (10) days to file an opposition, if any.

(b) Cases in Division AP shall have an automatic thirty (30) day extension of time from the date of service of the index to the record on appeal if the Clerk files a notice seeking additional time.

(c) No order shall issue from the Court on any agreed extension or automatic Clerk extension.

(d) The notice as set forth in Exhibit A shall be filed with the Clerk by the parties to the appeal. Any notice of agreement of extension of time to file a brief that is in excess of the times authorized by this Administrative Order may be stricken by the Court.

(e) This provision for extension of time for briefs does not apply to expedited appeals, emergency appeals, or petitions for extraordinary writs. If the parties do not agree to an extension, or a party seeks an extension of time in excess of the times authorized herein, the party seeking the extension shall file a motion, pursuant to Florida Rule of Appellate Procedure 9.300(a), that sets forth the total time granted by agreement or by order of this Court. If a party has filed a motion seeking an extension and the Court's ruling on the pending motion is still outstanding, the party should not file a subsequent motion seeking an extension.

(6) *Mandatory Electronic Courtesy Copies.*

(a) The appellant or petitioner shall add the Court to the service list at the time of creating the appellate case in the Florida Courts E–Filing Portal using the following email address: appeals@17th.flcourts.org. Service via this email address is to provide a courtesy copy to the Court.

(b) Any self-represented party may register with the Florida Courts E–Filing Portal to send and receive filings. If a self-represented party does not provide electronic copies, then the party shall provide a paper courtesy copy to the Court. The paper courtesy copies for the Court must be timely delivered to Appellate Division c/o Office of the General Counsel at the Office of the Trial Court Administrator, 201 S.E. 6th Street, Suite 20170, Fort Lauderdale, Florida 33301. This address should only be used for providing courtesy copies of documents already filed with the Clerk.

(c) It is the responsibility of the attorney or self-represented litigant submitting an electronic copy to remove any metadata prior to transmission. All electronic copies shall comply with applicable Florida Rules of Judicial Administration, including rules 2.420, 2.425, and 2.526.

(7) *Proposed Orders.*

(a) Proposed orders shall not be submitted to the chambers of a panel member.

(b) Any proposed order(s) shall be submitted to the Court at appeals@17th.flcourts.org in either a Word or Rich Text Format. All other electronic copies of documents submitted to the court shall be submitted in PDF format.

(8) *Requests for Emergency Treatment.*

(a) Pleadings and motions filed as emergencies disrupt court procedures and interrupt work on cases that are currently pending. Consequently, an attorney or party who seeks "emergency" review or treatment of a motion or appellate matter loses credibility when the court determines there is no true emergency. *See USAA Cas. Ins. Co. v. Pembroke Pines MRI, Inc.*, 24 So. 3d 588 (Fla. 4th DCA 2009).

(b) For purposes of this Administrative Order, an "emergency" is a matter that will cause irreparable harm, death or result in a manifest injury if immediate relief is not afforded. Matters that do not meet this definition shall not be submitted to the Court as an "emergency." An exigency that is caused by the lack of diligence of the moving party shall not constitute an "emergency."

(c) A party requesting emergency treatment for any motion, appeal, or petition shall file a separate document entitled "Request for Emergency Treatment." The separate "Request for Emergency Treatment" (herein "Request") shall be filed simultaneously with the motion, appeal, or petition for which emergency treatment is sought. The Request shall not exceed two (2) pages in length and shall state succinctly:

i. The nature of the emergency;

ii. The date the order at issue was entered; and

iii. The date of the event that constitutes the basis for request emergency treatment, *i.e.*, the deadline.

Both the Request and matter sought to be treated as an emergency shall be filed with the Florida Courts E–filing Portal, with a copy served on the Court at appeals@17th.flcourts.org.

(d) Self-represented parties may register with the Florida Courts E–filing Portal and file the Request with the Florida Courts E–filing Portal. The party shall bring the receipt of the filing to the Clerk of Court. The Clerk of Court shall locate the Request in the pending queue and if appropriate, immediately accept the document or advise the filing party of deficiencies to be corrected for acceptance. If a self-represented party does not file the Request and corresponding motion with the Florida Courts E–filing Portal then the party shall bring the original motion and Request to the Clerk of Court for filing. Upon acceptance of the filing, the Clerk of Court shall hand deliver a hard copy to the Office of the General Counsel in the Office of the Trial Court Administrator to be forwarded to the appellate division for appropriate action.

(e) If the party seeks a stay, the Request and corresponding motion shall indicate whether it has applied for relief in the trial court and the date and outcome of any ruling on such motion(s). The attorney or self-represented party requesting emergency treatment shall certify that the request for emergency treatment is made in good faith.

(f) No matter shall be afforded emergency treatment unless the Court determines that an emergency exists.

(e) Any party or attorney who requests emergency treatment without an objectively reasonable basis for doing so is subject to sanctions pursuant to section 57.105, Florida Statutes, or any other sanction as authorized by law, rule of procedure, or case law.

(9) *Opinions.* The court will provide electronic copies of orders and opinions to the attorneys of record and registered self-represented litigants via the E–Filing Portal. A self-represented litigant will receive a copy of an order or opinion by regular U.S. mail if the individual has not provided an email address to the Court.

(10) *Communications with the Appellate Division.* All parties must review and comply with the Guidelines for Communications with the Appellate Division.

(11) *Self–Represented Parties.*

(a)All self-represented parties are referred to The Self–Represented (Pro Se) Appellate Handbook.[1]

(b)A hard copy of The Self–Represented (Pro Se) Appellate Handbook may be viewed in the Appeals Division of the Clerk of Court, Room 4140 of the Broward County Courthouse–West Wing, 201 S.E. 6th Street, Fort Lauderdale, Florida 33301.

(12) This Administrative Order vacates and supersedes Administrative Order 2018–93–Gen.

DONE AND ORDERED in Chambers, Fort Lauderdale, Florida this 7th day of January, 2019.

Jack Tuter
Chief Judge

[1] http://prose.flabarappellate.org/default.asp

2018–82–GEN. MEDIA

IN THE CIRCUIT COURT OF THE SEVENTEENTH JUDICIAL CIRCUIT IN AND FOR BROWARD COUNTY, FLORIDA

Administrative Order No. 2018–82–Gen

ADMINISTRATIVE ORDER GOVERNING MEDIA

(a) Pursuant to Article V, section 2(d) of the Florida Constitution and section 43.26, Florida Statutes, the Chief Judge of each judicial circuit is charged with the authority and the power to do everything necessary to promote the prompt and efficient administration of justice.

(b) The safe and orderly use of court facilities, and the minimization of activities which disrupt or interfere with the fair, orderly and peaceable conduct of court business requires the imposition of provisions governing the media and media coverage of judicial proceedings.

(c) Pursuant to Florida Rule of Judicial Administration 2.450 (a), media coverage of public judicial proceedings is "[s]ubject at all times to the authority of the presiding judge to: (i) control the conduct of proceedings before the court; (ii) ensure decorum and prevent distractions; and (iii) ensure the fair administration of justice in the pending cause."

(d) The court must balance the constitutional right to a free press with the constitutional right to a fair trial.

(e) Special interest and/or high visibility proceedings require procedures and special accommodations to ensure full access to public judicial proceedings without compromising the right of any litigant to a fair and orderly trial.

(f) Standards governing media coverage of judicial proceedings must contain safeguards to ensure media coverage will not detract from or degrade court proceedings, impair or interrupt the orderly procedures of the court, or otherwise interfere with a fair trial.

(g) The lack of a uniform, statewide definition of media that has kept pace with the dramatic and rapidly evolving use of new technologies, forums and mediums for gathering and disseminating information and news to the public has posed significant challenges and requires the imposition of certain guidelines.

(h) In all judicial proceedings in the Seventeenth Judicial Circuit, the presiding judge has the authority to determine whether the case he or she is presiding over is a special interest/high profile case and to determine whether to invoke the special interest/high profile case procedures established by this Administrative Order.

(I) In accordance with the authority vested in the Chief Judge by Florida Rule of Judicial Administration 2.215, it is hereby **ORDERED**:

I. GENERAL PROVISIONS APPLICABLE TO ALL MEDIA FOR ALL PROCEEDINGS

A. Definitions

(1) *Courthouse Facility.* For purposes of this Order, "Courthouse facility" means any building or structure in which judicial proceedings may be conducted, including, but not limited to: (1) Broward County Central Judicial Complex located at 201 S.E. Sixth Street, Fort Lauderdale, Florida 33301; (2) North Regional Courthouse located at 1600 West Hillsboro Boulevard, Deerfield Beach, Florida 33442; (3) South Regional Courthouse located at 3550 Hollywood Boulevard, Hollywood, Florida 33021; and (4) West Regional Courthouse located at 100 North Pine Island Road, Plantation, Florida 33324.

(2) *Courtroom.* For purposes of this Order, "courtroom(s)" means courtrooms, hearing rooms and any other place(s) used to conduct court proceedings, unless specifically stated otherwise.

(3) *Media.* For purposes of this Order, "media" is defined as: 1) traditional print and broadcast communication channels, such as radio, television, newspapers, and magazines, through which news and information is disseminated that reach or influence people widely for newsworthy, entertainment, or other purposes; 2) motion picture entities, including documentary and independent filmmakers; and 3) the next generation of digital, computerized or networked information and communication technologies, not directly associated with traditional print and/or broadcast media entities and defined as:

> An online entity which was a previously established, independent site that contains regularly updated original news content above and beyond links, forums, troubleshooting tips and reader contributions; said content is thoroughly reviewed by an independent editor before publication; has readership or viewership of more than 1000 per month; and has previously covered the judicial branch for the six (6) months immediately prior to requesting to cover proceedings in this Circuit. Fan sites, web logs or blogs and portable websites do not qualify as media.

The individual and/or entity requesting to cover any judicial proceeding in this Circuit must demonstrate proof it meets the definition of media.

B. Conduct

(1) All media representatives must read this Administrative Order and Florida Rule of Judicial Administration 2.450 governing technological coverage of judicial proceedings, as well as all administrative orders governing the use of cellular telephones and other portable electronic devices in courtrooms in the Seventeenth Judicial Circuit.

(2) All media representatives should always: (i) display proper media credentials and/or identification supplied to them by their employer; (ii) exhibit proper courtroom decorum; and (iii) dress professionally. Eating, drinking or chewing gum during court proceedings is strictly prohibited.

(3) No media representative shall enter the well of the courtroom at any time, unless otherwise permitted by the presiding judge, Chief Judge, or Trial Court Administrator.

(4) As outlined in Florida Rule of Judicial Administration 2.450, only one video camera and operator, one still camera and operator, and one audio recording device and operator are permitted to cover a court proceeding unless additional equipment is authorized by the presiding judge or Chief Judge. The placement of additional cameras inside a courtroom is at the discretion of the presiding judge. Additional cameras and recording devices not otherwise authorized for use by the presiding judge or Chief Judge shall remain in the off position and stowed so as not to disrupt the proceedings. Use of laptop computers and cellular telephones or other electronic devices is permitted as provided by separate administrative order. Cabling of extension cords and power supplies is prohibited in the courtroom. All media representatives may view open court proceedings provided there is available seat-

ing. Unless otherwise specified by the presiding judge, Chief Judge or Trial Court Administrator, seating for media representatives is on a first-come basis.

(5) Media access to a courtroom is granted at the time the deputy opens the courtroom to the public. All media equipment is subject to search at any time. All set-up and breakdown of cameras and recording devices must be done when court is not in session (prior to the commencement of the proceedings) or during breaks. Media may not set-up once a proceeding has begun. Video cameras must be operated from a tripod and from a location as designated by the presiding judge, Chief Judge, or Trial Court Administrator. Cameras and recording devices must operate silently and not produce distracting light. Photographers must position themselves in a location as designated by the presiding judge, Chief Judge, or Trial Court Administrator. Still photographers shall not shoot video, unless no other video camera is present. Media representatives shall not engage in any movement or discussions that attract undue attention.

(6) Assignment of a video and/or still pool camera is the sole responsibility of the media. The media shall designate: (1) a pool video camera person for coverage inside the courtroom; (2) a pool still photographer for inside the courtroom; (3) a pool video camera person for coverage outside the courtroom; and (4) a pool still photographer for outside the courtroom. Those designated as the "pool" positions must be able to provide a feed or copy of the proceedings to all other media outlets present at the time with equipment capable of recording the proceedings. The court will not resolve any disagreements or conflicts among any media outlets desiring to cover a legal proceeding.

(7) Media representatives may not record audio of "sidebar" or "bench" conferences. There shall be no in court recording or broadcast while court is in recess, except as may be necessary for members of the media to setup or troubleshoot equipment or to capture the appearance of a litigant entering or leaving the courtroom. To protect the attorney-client privilege, the effective right to counsel, and the due process of all litigants, including victims and the families of victims, there shall be no recording or broadcast of conferences that occur in court between attorneys and their clients, between co-counsel, or between counsel and the presiding judge held at the bench. Upon the conclusion or recess of proceedings being covered by the media (including after recording a litigant leaving the courtroom), any video or audio recording (including live streaming), if applicable, shall cease so as to avoid the inadvertent capture of any of the aforementioned types of communications. Interviews of jurors after their release from service is at the individual juror's discretion and must be conducted in a location not otherwise prohibited by this Administrative Order. The purpose and intent of this paragraph is not to prevent the media from covering legal proceedings, but to protect the vital due process rights of all litigants, including victims and their families.

(8) So as not to interfere with court proceedings or with a litigant's rights, no interviews are permitted: (i) within or immediately outside the courtroom at any time; (ii) in the presence of a juror or prospective juror; or (iii) within any Courthouse facility which unreasonably interferes with the safety, security, or movement of persons in any courtroom, doorway, hallway, and other areas of any Courthouse facility, or which disrupts any court proceeding. Additionally, media representatives shall not station themselves or their equipment in public areas of any Courthouse facility in any manner that unreasonably interferes with the safety, security, or movement of persons of which is disruptive to any court proceeding to be determined on a case-by-case basis at the discretion of Court Administration or the Broward Sheriff's Office. Further, when court is not in session, media may not film or take photographs in courtrooms without prior permission from the Chief Judge or Trial Court Administrator. So as not to present a risk to public safety, no media shall chase, or record while walking, any parties within the Courthouse facility.

(9) Satellite trucks and/or remote/live trucks must be parked or stationed in an area designated by the City of Fort Lauderdale and/or the Broward Sheriff's Office.

(10) At all times, the procedures set forth in this Administrative Order are subject to the authority of the presiding judge, Chief Judge, or Trial Court Administrator who may modify these procedures to control the conduct of pending proceedings, ensure the fair administration of justice, or ensure public safety consistent with Florida Rule of Judicial Administration 2.450.

II. ADDITIONAL PROCEDURES FOR SPECIAL INTEREST/HIGH PROFILE PROCEEDINGS

(1) The Chief Judge or the presiding judge of any judicial proceeding may instruct Court Administration to implement the Special Interest/High Profile Procedures set forth in this Administration Order.

(2) Upon implementation of these procedures, Court Administration will, as soon as practicable, convene a meeting of all interested media representatives for the purpose of creating a media committee to establish protocols for the specific case.

(3) When possible, the media committee shall consist of at least one print media representative, one television broadcast media representative, and one audio broadcast representative, as well as a member or members of Court Administration designated by the Trial Court Administrator to act as a liaison between the court and media. Additionally, representatives from Broward County Facilities Management Division/Security, the Clerk of the Courts, and the Broward Sheriff's Office may be asked to attend a meeting of the media committee, if deemed necessary.

(4) The duties of the media committee shall include:

a. Selection of a media representative to act as a liaison between the media and the court for the duration of the case;

b. Designation of the pool camera operators and pool camera positions in accordance with Florida Rule of Judicial Administration 2.450;

c. Evaluation of parking needs and availability, and, if necessary, the facilitation of a lottery system for media parking;

d. Evaluation of courtroom seating and, if necessary, the facilitation of a lottery system for media seating in the courtroom;

e. Determination of a process for dissemination of information to include timely access to examine and photograph submitted evidence; and

f. Identification of other special needs of the media, including access through courthouse security, staging of equipment, additional power requirements, and any other issue.

(5) At all times, the Special Interest/High Profile Procedures set forth in this Administrative Order are subject to the authority of the presiding judge, Chief Judge, or Trial Court Administrator who may modify these procedures to control the conduct of pending proceedings, ensure the fair administration of justice, or ensure public safety consistent with Florida Rule of Judicial Administration 2.450.

This Administrative Order supersedes and vacates Administrative Order 2018–70–Gen.

DONE AND ORDERED in Chambers, Fort Lauderdale, Broward County, Florida, this 17th day of September, 2018.

Jack Tuter
Chief Judge

2018–63–GEN. PROCEDURE FOR APPOINTMENT OF COUNSEL IN CRIMINAL AND CIVIL PROCEEDINGS

IN THE CIRCUIT COURT OF THE SEVENTEENTH JUDICIAL CIRCUIT IN AND FOR BROWARD COUNTY, FLORIDA

Administrative Order No. 2018–63–Gen

ADMINISTRATIVE ORDER ESTABLISHING PROCEDURE FOR APPOINTMENT OF COUNSEL IN CRIMINAL AND CIVIL PROCEEDINGS AND ESTABLISHMENT OF DUE PROCESS SERVICE PROVIDER RATES

(a) Section 27.40, Florida Statutes, sets forth the duties and responsibilities of the Chief Judge in establishing a registry of attorneys, to be provided to the Clerk of the Court, for appointment of counsel as authorized by law. Such duties and responsibilities include the authority to restrict the number of attorneys on the registry.

(b) In accordance with the authority vested in the Chief Judge by Article V, section 2(d) of the Florida Constitution, sections 43.26 and 27.40, Florida Statutes, and Florida Rule of Judicial Administration 2.215, it is hereby **ORDERED**:

(1) *Appointment to Registry.* The selection, approval, and continuation of attorneys on the Registry is a privilege, not a right and is dependent upon qualifications, training, and other factors as determined solely by the Chief Judge. The number of appointments an attorney receives is subject to the number of cases filed, the number of cases for which the Office of Public Defender (Public Defender) or Office of Criminal Conflict and Civil Regional Counsel (Regional Counsel) cannot provide representation, and the number of attorneys on the Registry. Attorneys will be added to the Registry on a quarterly basis based on the State of Florida's fiscal year, which is July 1 to June 30. Applications to be added to the Registry must be submitted no later than the first of the month preceding the start of each quarter (i.e., June 1, September 1, December 1, and March 1). Applications received after this date will not be considered until the following quarter. Applications can be located on the following webpage of the Seventeenth Judicial Circuit: www.17th.flcourts.org/court-appointed-attorneys/. Each attorney approved to be added to the Registry is responsible for entering into any and all Agreements required by the Justice Administrative Commission (JAC). The Chief Judge will advise the JAC and Clerk of the Court (Clerk) of the names of the attorneys approved to be on the Registry. Attorneys' names will not be sent to the Clerk for addition to the Registry until the Chief Judge is notified by the JAC that the attorney has executed any and all required agreements with the JAC.

(2) *Notices.*

(A) Unless otherwise noted herein, any notice required to be provided under this Administrative Order shall be sent in writing to the designated email addresses below:

(i) Notice to the Chief Judge shall be sent to isc@17th.flcourts.org.

(ii) Notice to the Clerk shall be sent to CACS@browardclerk.org.

(iii) Notice to the JAC shall be in the manner required by the JAC.

(iv) Notice to the Administrative Judge of the Probate Division shall be sent to isc@17th.flcourts.org.

(B) Notices between the Chief Judge and Clerk shall be in an electronic format.

(C) The e-mail addresses of judges, general magistrates, and court administration employees are exempt from public access and shall not be disclosed by the Clerk to any individual who is not employed by the Clerk.

(3) *General Requirements.*

(A) The attorney must be a member of The Florida Bar in good standing.

(B) The attorney must have either a principle office in Broward County, Florida or a permanent physical office location in Broward County, Florida to meet with clients.

(C) The attorney must have either a telephone number with an area code for Broward County, Florida, or a toll-free number for the receipt of telephone calls from clients.

(D) The attorney must provide notice to the Chief Judge, Clerk, and JAC of any change in address, telephone number or e-mail address, and must also provide notice to the Clerk if the attorney is unavailable to accept appointments for any period of time. If the attorney is appointed to a case which is confidential or exempt from public access pursuant to rule of court or statute, the attorney shall advise the JAC in writing that the name of the client, pleadings/papers, or progress docket is confidential or exempt from public access and must be redacted prior to any public dissemination.

(E) The attorney must notify the Chief Judge if he or she is under investigation by The Florida Bar, under a criminal investigation, or has pending criminal charges. Upon delivery of the notice, the attorney will be immediately suspended from the Registry for all future appointments pending the outcome of The Florida Bar investigation, criminal investigation or criminal charges, and subsequent review by the Chief Judge of the outcome. The Chief Judge is the sole decision-maker if the attorney is to be reinstated to or removed from the Registry. The Chief Judge has the authority to suspend or remove an attorney from the Registry even if the attorney fails to provide notice.

(F) The attorney must notify the Chief Judge if he or she is held in contempt by a court of competent jurisdiction. Upon delivery of the notice, the attorney will be immediately suspended from the Registry for all future appointments pending review by the Chief Judge of the circumstances surrounding the contempt. The Chief Judge is the sole decision-maker if the attorney is to be reinstated to or removed from the Registry. The Chief Judge has the authority to suspend and/or remove an attorney from the Registry even if the attorney fails to provide notice.

(G) An attorney approved to be added to the Registry may not reassign or subcontract a case on which the attorney has been appointed to another attorney or allow another attorney to appear at a critical stage of the case to which the attorney has been appointed.

(4) *Additional Probate Division Requirements.* In addition to the general requirements set forth in Paragraph (2) above, attorneys approved for Probate Division categories must comply with the following requirements.

(A) All private attorneys on any Probate Division Registry category are required to maintain in full force and effect malpractice insurance with a liability limit of at least $300,000.00 during any period of time the attorney is on the Registry. The attorney must submit proof of legal malpractice insurance being in full force and effect within ten (10) days of the expiration of any policy during the fiscal year to the Chief Judge. Failure to provide proof within ten (10) days of the expiration of any policy will result in an immediate suspension from the Registry until proof of insurance is provided. If the attorney fails to provide proof within thirty (30) days of the policy expiration, the attorney will be removed from the Registry and required to reapply if he or she seeks reinstatement to the Registry.

(B) The initial Continuing Legal Education (CLE) for private attorneys seeking appointments for Adult Protective Services, Developmentally Disabled Adults, Emergency Temporary Guardianships, and Incapacity is ten (10) hours of guardianship, mental health, or elder law topics in the twelve (12) months preceding application and appointment to the Registry. Acceptable CLE courses shall include advance directives, legislative updates, mental health, capacity, any and all aspects of elder law, and courses of other similar nature but shall not include estate planning, mediation training, family law matters, or arbitration training.

(C) Private attorneys receiving appointments on a fiscal year basis, which is defined as July 1 to June 30, for Adult Protective Services, Developmentally Disabled Adults, Emergency Temporary Guardianships, and Incapacity are required to complete six (6) hours of CLE in the areas of elder law, guardianship, or mental health. Acceptable CLE courses shall include advance directives, legislative updates, mental health, capacity and courses of other similar nature but shall not include estate planning, mediation training, family law matters, or arbitration training. The private attorney must provide proof no later than June 15 of each year that the attorney remains on the Registry that he or she has met the annual CLE requirement to the Administrative Judge of the Probate Division. Failure to provide proof will result in an immediate suspension from the Registry until proof of CLE is provided. If the attorney fails to provide proof by September 1, the attorney will be removed from the Registry and required to reapply if he or she seeks reinstatement to the Registry.

(D) Private attorneys receiving appointments for Baker Act, Marchman Act, or Admission of Inmate to Mental Health Facility cases are required to attend any course presented by the Department of Children and Families or Department of Corrections, as applicable and available, with regard to these areas. The attorney must provide proof within ninety (90) days of the course that he or she did attend. Failure to provide proof will result in an immediate suspension from the Registry until proof of attendance is provided. If the attorney fails to provide proof within six (6) months after notice of the deficiency the attorney will be removed from the Registry and required to reapply if he or she seeks reinstatement to the Registry.

(5) *Removal from the Registry.*

(A) An attorney may be removed from the Registry if he or she:

(i) Resigns. The attorney shall immediately send notice to the JAC as required by the JAC. The notice shall specifically state those categories from which the attorney is resigning. A copy of the notice shall be provided by the attorney to the Chief Judge and Clerk and shall be relied upon, at the time of receipt, for the removal of the attorney from the Registry as set forth in the notice. A copy of the notice shall be delivered to the Chief Judge by e-mail to isc@17th.flcourts.org. The copy to the Clerk should be delivered to CACS, Room 18130, Broward County Courthouse, 201 S.E. Sixth Street, Fort Lauderdale, Florida 33301 and via email to CACS@browardclerk.org. If an attorney later decides he or she wants to be reinstated to the Registry, the attorney must submit a new application to be considered by the Chief Judge.

(ii) Fails to comply with terms of contract with the JAC. The Chief Judge may provide notice to an attorney of any failure to comply with the terms of the contract with the JAC and provide the attorney with an opportunity to respond prior to removal from the Registry.

(iii) Fails to notify the Chief Judge, Clerk, and JAC of any change in status. The removal may be temporary until such time as the attorney notifies the Chief Judge, Clerk, and JAC or may be permanent, in the discretion of the Chief Judge, based upon the nature of the change of status. The Chief Judge shall advise the Clerk if any attorney is removed from the Registry.

(iv) Fails to attend hearings, except for good cause as determined by the presiding judge or general magistrate. The Chief Judge shall advise the Clerk if any attorney is removed from the Registry.

(v) Fails to maintain a valid e-mail address for communication with the Chief Judge, Clerk and JAC. The Chief Judge shall advise the Clerk if any attorney is removed from the Registry.

(vi) Fails to enter into any and all agreement(s) and addendums to agreement(s) as required by the JAC on or before the last weekday of August for each fiscal year the attorney is eligible for inclusion on the Registry. Entering into any and all agreements and addendums to agreements as required by the JAC is solely the responsibility of the attorney. The Chief Judge shall advise the Clerk if any attorney is removed from the Registry.

(vii) Fails to enter into any and all other agreement(s) and addendums to agreement(s) as required by JAC within thirty (30) days of a request by the JAC. The Chief Judge shall advise the Clerk if any attorney is removed from the Registry.

(viii) Has his or her contract terminated by the JAC.

(ix) Terminates his or her contract with the JAC.

(x) Reassigns or subcontracts a case to another attorney, or allows another attorney to appear at a critical stage of the case to which the attorney has been appointed.

(xi) Fails to comply with any provision of this Administrative Order.

(B) If an attorney is disbarred or suspended, has surrendered his or her license to practice law in this State, or is not a member in good standing with The Florida Bar, the attorney must promptly notify the Chief Judge in writing. The Chief Judge has the authority to remove an attorney from the Registry who (1) is disbarred or suspended, (2) has surrendered his or her license to practice law in this State, or (3) is not in good standing with The Florida Bar, even if the attorney fails to provide notice. An attorney removed for any reason set forth in this paragraph, upon reinstatement to The Florida Bar, will be required to submit a new application to be considered by the Chief Judge for reinstatement to the Registry.

(C) At any time an attorney is removed from and later reinstated to the Registry, the attorney will be placed at the bottom of the list for rotation for the category for which the attorney is eligible to receive appointments.

(6) *Selection of Attorney from Registry.*

(A) The judge or general magistrate shall advise the Clerk that a name of an attorney from the Registry is required on a case when Regional Counsel is not authorized by law to provide representation or an order is entered granting his withdrawal. The judge or general magistrate shall provide the Clerk with the name of the individual for whom counsel is being appointed, the case number, and type of case. Upon such notification, the Clerk shall provide the judge with the name of a Registry attorney.

(B) An attorney from the Registry shall be selected for the respondent in all Chapter 744 proceedings unless the judge advises the Clerk the respondent is indigent.

(C) The attorney appointed to a case has an obligation to ensure:

(i) the Public Defender cannot accept the case pursuant to law; or

(ii) the Public Defender has filed a motion to withdraw and an order of withdrawal has been entered by the presiding judge; **and**

(iii) Regional Counsel cannot accept the case pursuant to law; or

(iv) Regional Counsel has filed a motion to withdraw and an order of withdrawal has been entered by the presiding judge.

If the attorney cannot ascertain the above information, the attorney shall set the matter for a status conference before the presiding judge with notice to the Public Defender and/or Regional Counsel, as applicable.

(D) It shall be the responsibility of the judge to determine if an attorney is eligible for appointments in a Registry category prior to notifying the Clerk of an order of appointment not in rotating order. By way of example, it shall be the responsibility of the judge to determine if the attorney representing the parent in the dependency proceedings is eligible to represent the parent in termination of parental rights proceedings.

(E) The Clerk shall, within one (1) business day of entry of the order of appointment mail a copy of the order to the Public Defender, Regional Counsel, or private attorney. If time is of the essence it shall be the responsibility of the judge to notify the attorney of his or her appointment to represent a defendant, parent, or respondent.

(F) Attorneys shall be selected in strict rotation of the Registry, unless the presiding judge makes a finding of good cause on the record for appointing an attorney not in strict rotation.

(G) The following shall be considered good cause for selecting an attorney not in strict rotation of the Registry, including but not limited to:

(i) The attorney was previously appointed to represent the client in another case. This shall include cases which are simultaneously pending or filed after the initial representation and the Public Defender and Regional Counsel cannot provide representation.

(ii) Florida Statutes or Florida rules of court require an immediate hearing and the attorney next in rotation fails to respond to telephone calls. The judicial assistant for the judge making the appointment shall allow a minimum of one (1) hour to contact the attorney as provided by the Clerk. If the attorney does not return the telephone call within one (1) hour or declines the case, the judicial assistant shall contact the Clerk and request the name of the attorney next on the Registry for that category of cases. This procedure shall continue until such time as an attorney accepts the appointment. **This provision only applies to Emergency Temporary Guardianship proceedings and Parental Notification Waiver proceedings.**

(iii) Florida Statutes or Florida rules of court require the appointment of the previously appointed attorney.

(H) If the Clerk is advised an attorney is appointed out of order, the Clerk shall update the Registry to ensure that the attorney is placed at the bottom of the Registry category in which the case was assigned.

(7) *List of Attorneys on Registry.* The Clerk shall provide to the Chief Judge a copy of the Registry on the first business day of each month in an electronic format(s) as determined by the Chief Judge.

(8) *Scheduling of Attorneys for Dependency Shelter Hearings.*

(A) The Clerk shall schedule attorneys on a quarterly basis to attend the scheduled hearings for dependency shelter hearings. The quarters are based on the State of Florida's fiscal year, which is July 1 to June 30, and the quarters are as follows: July to September (first quarter); October to December (second quarter); January to March (third quarter); and April to June (fourth quarter).

(B) The Administrative Judge for Unified Family Court or his or her designee will notify the Clerk as to the dates, times, and locations of the shelter hearings at least thirty (30) days prior to the start of each quarter.

(C) The Clerk shall select two (2) names of private attorneys from the Dependency Registry, assign a dummy case number for the purpose of selecting names from the Dependency Registry and otherwise schedule private attorneys to appear on weekdays which are not court holidays or days on which the court is otherwise closed. The Clerk shall provide an electronic copy of the schedule to the judges presiding at the shelter hearings, the judicial assistants for the judges presiding at the shelter hearings, the private attorneys on the Dependency Registry, and Regional Counsel no later than the third (3rd) business day of the month preceding the start of each quarter.

(D) Appointments of private attorneys from the Dependency Registry shall not be on a first come, first serve basis. The Clerk's Shelter list shall designate one attorney as the first attorney, and the other attorney as the second attorney. The first attorney on this list shall be given the first appointment for which a Dependency Registry attorney is needed, the second attorney shall be given the second appointment, the first attorney the third appointment, and so on. The attorneys shall be rotated between the first position and second position for each successive scheduled date to assure an equitable distribution of appointments of private attorneys from the Dependency Registry.

(E) If an attorney scheduled to appear at the Shelter hearings cannot appear at the time of the Shelter hearing, the scheduled attorney may trade their designated date with another attorney from the Dependency Registry, who the scheduled attorney shall designate to appear in their place. There shall be no substitutions for a non-appearing attorney as Dependency Registry attorneys are only permitted to trade scheduled dates. The attorneys must provide advance notice to the Clerk of the trade. Notice shall include the names of the attorneys and the dates which have been traded.

(F) When an attorney from the Dependency Registry is appointed for a parent at a Shelter hearing, the Clerk shall update the Dependency Registry to reflect the attorney's appointment for a dependency case and place the attorney at the bottom of the Dependency Registry for dependency appointments.

(G) The procedures as outlined for Shelter hearings is to provide parents and children with an expedited process to determine if a child should remain out of his or her home.

(9) *Scheduling of Attorneys for Emergency Temporary Guardianship Hearings.*

(A) The Clerk shall schedule private attorneys on a quarterly basis to attend the scheduled hearings for emergency temporary guardianship hearings. The quarters are based on the State of Florida's fiscal year, which is July 1 to June 30, and the quarters are as follows: July to September (first quarter); October to December (second quarter); January to March (third quarter); and April to June (fourth quarter).

(B) The general magistrates for the probate division shall advise the Clerk at least thirty (30) days prior to the commencement of each quarter the dates, times, and locations of the emergency temporary hearings.

(C) Upon securing the information as to the dates, times, and locations of the emergency temporary guardianship hearings, the Clerk shall schedule private attorneys to appear at the date, time, and location of the emergency temporary guardianship hearings. The Clerk shall select one (1) name of a private attorney from the Registry who is approved for emergency temporary guardianship hearings, assign a dummy case number for the purpose of selecting names from the Registry and otherwise schedule private attorneys to appear at the emergency temporary guardianship hearings.

(D) The Clerk shall provide an electronic copy of the proposed schedule to the private attorneys who shall have five (5) business days to accept the date and time to appear for emergency temporary guardianship hearings. If the private attorney fails to accept the date and time, he or she shall not be scheduled for that date and the Clerk shall select another private attorney from the Registry.

(E) If an attorney, after accepting, is unable to appear at the scheduled date and time, the attorney shall notify the Clerk who shall select another attorney from the Registry.

(F) At the time of finalizing the emergency temporary guardianship hearing schedule, or upon changes to the schedule, the Clerk shall provide an electronic copy to the probate division judges, the judicial assistants for the probate division judges, the general magistrates for the probate division, the administrative assistants for the general magistrates for the probate division, and the private attorneys. The Clerk shall also post a copy of the schedule in his or her office for the probate division.

(G) Upon the filing of the emergency petition and incapacity petition, the Clerk shall update the Registry to reflect the attorney's appointment and drop the attorney to the bottom of the Registry categories for emergency temporary guardianship proceedings and incapacity proceedings.

(10) *Fees.*

(A) Fees for private attorneys shall be those as established by statute or the General Appropriations Act, whichever shall apply at the time of appointment.

(B) It is the responsibility of the attorney to maintain any and all records required by the JAC to receive compensation at the conclusion of the case to which the attorney is appointed.

(C) The private attorneys scheduled for or appearing at dependency shelter hearings are not entitled to receive fees unless an order of appointment is entered by the judge appointing the attorney to the dependency case at the time of the shelter hearings.

(D) The private attorneys scheduled for emergency temporary guardianship hearings are not entitled to receive fees unless a case is filed with the Clerk wherein a determination of incapacity and appointment of an emergency temporary guardian is sought.

(E) If an attorney seeks fees in excess of those established by statute or the General Appropriations Act, whichever shall apply at the time of appointment, the attorney shall comply with all statutory requirements.

(F) If an attorney withdraws from the case and intends to seek a portion of the flat fee for representation of the defendant, parent, or respondent, the attorney shall file a motion in the case with service upon the JAC and the subsequently appointed attorney. The attorney subsequently appointed shall, at the conclusion of the case, provide notice to the prior attorney that the case is concluded so that:

(i) both attorneys can file any and all appropriate requests for fees with the JAC; and

(ii) both attorneys can file a motion before the presiding judge for an allocation of the flat fee.

(G) It shall be the responsibility of the withdrawn attorney to set the motion for hearing before the presiding judge with notice to the JAC and the subsequently appointed attorney.

(H) If the respondent in a Chapter 744 proceeding is not determined indigent by the Clerk, then the attorney appointed from the Registry shall be entitled to fees and costs pursuant to Chapter 744 and is not required to file a motion for extraordinary fees.

(11) Appointment of a Non–Registry Attorney.

(A) A non-Registry attorney may be appointed if:

(i) There are no attorneys on the Registry for a category of cases requiring appointment of counsel; or

(ii) All attorneys on the Registry for a category of cases have withdrawn or declined the appointment of the case; or

(iii) All attorneys on the Registry for a category are precluded by statute or rule of court from accepting any additional appointments.

(B) The presiding judge shall set forth in the order of appointment that the Public Defender and Regional Counsel are unable to represent the individual and one of the reasons from paragraph (11)(A) of this Administrative Order.

(C) The attorney appointed shall be ordered to execute any and all Agreements required by the JAC to be compensated and for payment of due process expenses.

(D) The Clerk shall, within one (1) business day of entry of the order of appointment, send a copy to the private attorney. If expedited notice of the appointment is required, the judicial assistant or general magistrate shall provide verbal notice to the private attorney.

(12) *Complaints.*

(A) Any interested person may advise the presiding judge, in writing, of any matter set forth in section 27.40(9), Florida Statutes. Upon receipt of the written document with regard to any matter set forth in section 27.40(9), Florida Statutes, the presiding judge shall set the matter for hearing with notice to the attorney, individual for whom the attorney was appointed to represent, the individual who notified the court, and any other attorney who has made an appearance in the case. At the conclusion of the hearing, the presiding judge shall enter an order which includes a recitation of facts as well as whether the attorney should be suspended or removed from the Registry for a specific period of time. A copy of the written complaint and order shall be provided to the Chief Judge at the conclusion of the hearing. The Chief Judge shall make the final decision as to whether a private attorney is temporarily or permanently removed from the Registry.

(B) Any judge presiding over a matter in which an attorney has been appointed to represent a party may advise the Chief Judge, in writing, of any matter concerning the adequacy of the attorney's representation, including any violation of this Administrative Order, and the Chief Judge or his or her designee shall promptly inquire into the circumstances. Upon receipt of the information and subsequent inquiry, the Chief Judge shall be the sole decision-maker as to whether the attorney is suspended from the Registry for a period of time or removed from the Registry.

(13) *Appellate Case Registry Requirements.*

(A) Criminal Division. The Clerk and judge shall confer to determine if the private attorney selected has the qualifications as set forth herein to represent the defendant on appeal. The judge can require the private attorney selected by the Clerk to provide proof of meeting the requirements as set forth herein prior to entering the order of appointment. If the determination is made the private attorney does not meet the requirements as set forth herein to represent the defendant on appeal, the private attorney should not be appointed with the reason noted by the judge, so that the attorney remains at the top of the Registry category for the next appointment. The necessity of the judge and Clerk conferring as to the appointment of a private attorney is required as the Appropriation categories, Registry categories, and qualifications may differ, and it is the responsibility of the judge to ensure that a qualified private attorney is appointed.

(i) Misdemeanor
Registry Category: Appellate
Appropriations Category: Misdemeanor Appeals
Length of Bar Membership: 2 years
CLE Requirement: 10 hours of CLE in appellate law **OR** 5 hours of CLE in appellate law and 5 hours of CLE in criminal law for the last reporting cycle or current reporting cycle
Experience: 3 criminal appeals **OR** 5 criminal trials

(ii) Second and Third Degree Felony
Registry Category: Appellate
Appropriations Category: Felony Appeals
Length of Bar Membership: 2 years
CLE Requirement: 10 hours of CLE in appellate law **OR** 5 hours of CLE in appellate law and 5 hours of CLE in criminal law for the last reporting cycle or current reporting cycle
Experience: 3 criminal appeals **OR** 5 criminal trials

(iii) Non–Capital Appeals
Registry Category: Appellate
Appropriations Category: Felony Appeals

Length of Bar Membership: 3 years

CLE Requirement: 10 hours of CLE in appellate law for the last reporting cycle or current reporting cycle

Experience: 5 criminal appeals **OR** 10 criminal trials (The 10 criminal trials shall be defined as at least 5 felony trials and 3 criminal appeals.)

(iv) Death Penalty Appeals

Registry Category: Appellate—Capital

Appropriations Category: Capital Appeals

Length of Bar Membership: 5 years

CLE Requirement: 12 hours of CLE in defense of capital cases at least every 24 months

Appellate or Criminal Practice Percentage: 33%

Experience:

A. 5 years of experience in criminal law **AND** prepared a brief for an appeal for at least 1 case which had a sentence of death imposed **AND** experience as lead counsel in the appeal of at least 3 felony convictions, in federal or state court, of which at least 1 was an appeal of a murder conviction; **OR**

B. Lead counsel in the appeal of at least 6 felony convictions in federal or state court, of which at least 2 were appeals of a murder conviction

(v) Involuntary Commitment of Sexually Violent Predators and Complex Appeals

Registry Category: Appellate

Appropriations Category: Civil Appeal

Length of Bar Membership: 4 years

CLE Requirement: 10 hours of CLE in appellate criminal law for the last reporting cycle or current reporting cycle

Appellate Experience: 5 criminal appeals, at least 3 of which are non-capital appeals

Appellate or Criminal Practice Percentage: 33%

(B) Dependency Division. The Clerk and judge shall confer to determine if the private attorney selected has the qualifications as set forth herein to represent the party appealing. The judge can require the private attorney selected by the Clerk to provide proof of meeting the requirements as set forth herein prior to entering the order of appointment. If the determination is made the private attorney does not meet the requirements as set forth herein to represent the party appealing, the private attorney should not be appointed with the reason noted by the judge and an indication why, so that the private attorney remains at the top of the Registry category for the next appointment. The necessity of the judge and Clerk conferring as to the appointment of a private attorney is required as the Appropriation categories, Registry categories, and qualifications may differ, and it is the responsibility of the judge to ensure that a qualified private attorney is appointed.

(i) Dependency and Termination of Parental Rights

Registry Category: Appellate–Dependency

Appropriations Category: Dependency Appeals; TPR Appeals

The Appropriations category used will depend on the type of appeal.

Length of Bar Membership: 2 years

CLE Requirement: 3 hours of dependency CLE for the last reporting cycle or current reporting cycle

Appellate, Dependency or Family Practice Percentage: 25%

Appellate Experience:

A. 3 years of experience in dependency or appellate law **AND** lead counsel in at least 3 contested dependency trials **AND** 3 contested termination of parental rights trials; **OR**

B. Demonstrate knowledge through the practice of family law

(ii) Parental Notification Waiver

Registry Category: Appellate–Dependency

Appropriations Category: Civil Appeal

Length of Bar Membership: 5 years

CLE Requirement: review of the ACLU materials with a statement of same on the application

Experience: A minimum of 5 constitutional law appeals. In addition, attorneys shall be familiar with the youth, privacy and constitutional issues relating to reproductive rights.

(iii) Children/Families in Need of Services

Registry Category: Appellate–Dependency

Appropriations Category: Civil Appeal

Length of Bar Membership: 2 years

CLE Requirement: 3 hours of dependency CLE for the last reporting cycle or current reporting cycle

Appellate, Dependency or Family Practice Percentage: 25%

Appellate Experience:

A. 3 years of experience in dependency or appellate law **AND** lead counsel in at least 3 contested dependency trials **AND** 3 contested termination of parental rights trials; **OR**

B. Demonstrate knowledge through the practice of family law

(C) Juvenile Delinquency Appeals. The Clerk and judge shall confer to determine if the private attorney selected has the qualifications as set forth herein to represent the minor child on appeal. The judge can require the private attorney selected by the Clerk to provide proof of meeting the requirements as set forth herein prior to entering the order of appointment. If the determination is made the private attorney does not meet the requirements as set forth herein to represent the minor on appeal, the attorney should not be appointed with the reason noted by the judge and an indication why, so that the private attorney remains at the top of the registry category for the next appointment. The necessity of the judge and Clerk conferring as to the appointment of a private attorney is required as the Appropriation categories, Registry categories, and qualifications may differ, and it is the responsibility of the judge to ensure that a qualified private attorney is appointed.

(i) Misdemeanor

Registry Category: Appellate

Appropriations Category: Juvenile Delinquency Appeals

Length of Bar Membership: 2 years

CLE Requirement: 10 hours of CLE in appellate law **OR** 5 hours of CLE in appellate law and 5 hours of CLE in criminal law for the last reporting cycle or current reporting cycle

Experience: 3 criminal appeals **OR** 5 criminal trials

(ii) Second and Third Degree Felony

Registry Category: Appellate

Appropriations Category: Juvenile Delinquency Appeals

Length of Bar Membership: 2 years

CLE Requirement: 10 hours of CLE in appellate law **OR** 5 hours of CLE in appellate law and 5 hours of CLE in criminal law for the last reporting cycle or current reporting cycle

Experience: 3 criminal appeals **OR** 5 criminal trials

(iii) First Degree and Life Felony Appeals

Registry Category: Appellate

Appropriations Category: Juvenile Delinquency Appeals

Length of Bar Membership: 3 years

CLE Requirement: 10 hours of CLE in appellate law for the last reporting cycle or current reporting cycle

Experience: 5 criminal appeals **OR** 10 criminal trials (The 10 criminal trials shall be defined as at least 5 felony trials and 3 criminal appeals)

(14) *Criminal Division Registry Requirements.* Each of the following Criminal Division Registry categories shall also be used for the appointment of counsel, based upon the charge for which the appointment is required: Violation of probation and/or violation of community control (Appropriations Category: Violation of Probation–Misdemeanor (includes VOCC); contempt proceedings (Appropriations Category: Contempt Proceedings); extradition (Appropriations Category: Extradition); 3.850 and 3.800. (Appropriations Category: Post conviction—3.850 and 3.800).

(A) Misdemeanor and Criminal Traffic

Registry Category: Misdemeanor

Appropriations Category: Misdemeanor; Criminal Traffic

Length of Bar Membership: 1 year

CLE Requirement: 10 hours of criminal law CLE for the last each reporting cycle or current reporting cycle

Trial Experience: 3 state or federal jury or nonjury trials

(B) Third Degree Felony

Registry Category: Third Degree Felony

Appropriations Category: Felony—3rd Degree

Length of Bar Membership: 2 years

CLE Requirement: 10 hours of criminal law CLE for the last reporting cycle or current reporting cycle and demonstrated compliance with Fla. R. Crim. P. 3.113.

Trial Experience: Minimum of 5 criminal jury trials

(C) Second Degree Felony

Registry Category: Second Degree Felony

Appropriations Category: Felony—2nd Degree

Length of Bar Membership: 2 years

CLE Requirement: 10 hours of criminal law CLE for the last reporting cycle or current reporting cycle and demonstrated compliance with Fla. R. Crim. P. 3.113.

Trial Experience: Minimum of 7 criminal jury trials, 2 of which must be felony trials

(D) First Degree Felony

Registry Category: First Degree/Life Felony

Appropriations Category: Felony—1st Degree

Length of Bar Membership: 5 years

CLE Requirement: 10 hours of criminal law CLE for the last each reporting cycle or current reporting cycle and demonstrated compliance with Fla. R. Crim. P. 3.113.

Trial Experience: 15 Criminal trials, 10 of which shall be jury trials and at least 5 of the jury trials in felony cases

Criminal Practice Percentage: 50%

(E) Life Felony

Registry Category: First Degree/Life Felony

Appropriations Category: Felony—Life; Felony—PBL

Length of Bar Membership: 5 years

CLE Requirement: 10 hours of criminal law CLE for the last reporting cycle or current reporting cycle and demonstrated compliance with Fla. R. Crim. P. 3.113.

Trial Experience: 15 Criminal trials, 10 of which shall be jury trials and at least 5 of the jury trials in felony cases

Criminal Practice Percentage: 50%

(F) Capital Sexual Battery

Registry Category: Capital Sexual Battery

Appropriations Category: Capital Sexual Battery

Length of Bar Membership: 5 years

CLE Requirement: 10 hours of criminal law CLE for the last reporting cycle or current reporting cycle and demonstrated compliance with Fla. R. Crim. P. 3.113.

Trial Experience: 15 Criminal trials, 10 of which shall be jury trials and at least 5 of the jury trials in felony cases

Criminal Practice Percentage: 50%

(G) First Degree Murder (Death Penalty waived at time of appointment)

Registry Category: First Degree/Life Felony

Appropriations Category: Felony—Life

Length of Bar Membership: 5 years

CLE Requirement: 10 hours of criminal law CLE for the last reporting cycle or current reporting cycle and demonstrated compliance with Fla. R. Crim. P. 3.113.

Trial Experience: 15 Criminal trials, 10 of which shall be jury trials and at least 5 of the jury trials in felony cases

Criminal Practice Percentage: 50%

(H) Capital (Death Penalty not waived at the time of appointment)

(i) Lead Counsel

Registry Category: Capital

Appropriations Category: Capital—1st Degree Murder (Lead Counsel)

Length of Bar Membership: 5 years

Additional Requirements: Fla. R. Crim. P. 3.112; Fla. R. Crim. P. 3.113.

Trial Experience: Lead trial counsel in no fewer than 9 state or federal jury trials of serious and complex cases which were tried to completion, as well as prior experience as lead defense counsel or co-counsel in at least 2 state or federal cases tried to completion in which the death penalty was sought. In addition, of the 9 jury trials which were tried to completion, the attorney should have been lead counsel in at least 3 cases in which the charge was murder; or alternatively, of the 9 jury trials, at least 1 was a murder trial and an additional 5 were felony jury trials.

Criminal Practice Percentage: 50%

(ii) Co–Counsel

Registry Category: Capital Co–Counsel

Appropriations Category: Capital—1st Degree Murder (Co–Counsel)

Length of Bar Membership: 3 years

Additional Requirements: Fla. R. Crim. P. 3.112; Fla. R. Crim. P. 3.113.

Trial Experience: Lead counsel or co-counsel in no fewer than 3 state or federal jury trials of serious and complex cases which were tried to completion, at least 2 of which were trials in which the charge was murder; or alternatively, of the 3 jury trials, at least 1 was a murder trial and 1 was a felony jury trial

Criminal Practice Percentage: 50%

(I) Involuntary Civil Commitment of Sexually Violent Predator Cases (Chapter 394, Part V)

Registry Category: Jimmy Ryce

Appropriations Category: Baker Act/Mental Health–Ch. 394, F.S.

Length of Bar Membership: 5 years

CLE Requirement: 10 hours of criminal law CLE for the last reporting cycle or current reporting cycle

Trial Experience: 15 Criminal trials, 10 of which shall be jury trials and at least 5 of the jury trials in felony cases

Criminal Practice Percentage: 50%

(15) *Dependency Division Registry Requirements*

(A) Dependency

Registry Category: Dependency;

Appropriations Category: Dependency

The Dependency Registry category shall be used by the Clerk when scheduling attorneys to appear at Shelter Hearings.

Length of Bar Membership: 1 year

CLE Requirement: 3 hours of dependency CLE for the last reporting cycle or current reporting cycle

Family or Dependency Practice Percentage: 25%

Trial Experience: 30 hours of hearing time representing a parent or child. The hearing hours shall consist of at least 6 shelter hearings, 3 dependency hearings, and 1 termination of parental rights hearing

(B) Termination of Parental Rights Cases (Chapter 39 and 63 Proceedings)

Registry Category: Termination of Parental Rights

Appropriations Category: Termination of Parental Rights—Ch. 39, F.S.; Termination of Parental Rights—Ch. 63, F.S. The selection of an appropriations category is dependent on the chapter under which the action is filed.

Length of Bar Membership: 2 years

CLE Requirement: 3 hours of dependency CLE for the last reporting cycle or current reporting cycle

Family or Dependency Practice Percentage: 25%

Trial Experience: 10 dependency trials **OR** 1 year of dependency experience

(C) Parental Notification Waiver Cases

Registry Category: Judicial Waiver

Appropriations Category: Parental Notification of Abortion Act

Length of Bar Membership: 2 years

CLE Requirement: review of the ACLU materials with a statement of same on the application

Trial Experience: Minimum of 5 criminal or civil trials **OR** 5 adjudicatory/evidentiary hearings. In addition, attorneys shall be familiar with the youth, privacy and constitutional issues relating to reproductive rights. The attorney should also have an interest in working with teens.

(D) Children/Families in Need of Services Cases

Registry Category: Dependency

Appropriations Category: CINS/FINS—Ch. 984, F.S.

Length of Bar Membership: 1 year

CLE Requirement: 3 hours of dependency CLE for the last reporting cycle or current reporting cycle

Family or Dependency Practice Percentage: 25%

Trial Experience: 30 hours of hearing time representing a parent or child. The hearing hours shall consist of at least 6 shelter hearings, 3 dependency hearings, and 1 termination of parental rights hearing

(E) Emancipation

Registry Category: Dependency

Appropriations Category: Emancipation

Length of Bar Membership: 1 year

CLE Requirement: 3 hours of dependency for the last reporting cycle or current reporting cycle

Family or Dependency Practice Percentage: 25%

Trial Experience: 30 hours of hearing time representing a parent or child. The hearing hours shall consist of at least 6 shelter hearings, 3 dependency hearings, and 1 termination of parental rights hearing

(F) Children with Special Needs

Registry Category: Children with Special Needs

Appropriations Category: Guardian Ad Litem

Length of Bar Membership: 2 years

CLE Requirement: 3 hours of dependency CLE for the last reporting cycle or current reporting cycle

Family or Dependency Practice Percentage: 25%

Trial Experience: 10 dependency trials **OR** 1 year of dependency experience

(16) *Juvenile Delinquency Registry Requirements.* Each of the following Juvenile Delinquency Division Registry categories shall also be used for the appointment of counsel, based upon the charge for which the appointment is required: violation of probation and/or violation of community control (Appropriations Category: Violation of Probation [VOCC] Juvenile Delinquency).

(A) Misdemeanor

Registry Category: Juvenile–Misdemeanors

Appropriations Category: Juvenile Delinquency—Misdemeanor

Length of Bar Membership: 1 year

CLE Requirement: 10 hours of criminal law CLE for the last reporting cycle or current reporting cycle

Trial Experience: 5 adjudicatory hearings **OR** 3 criminal jury trials one of which is a second degree felony or higher

(B) Third Degree Felony

Registry Category: Juvenile–Third Degree Felony

Appropriations Category: Juvenile Delinquency—3d Degree

Length of Bar Membership: 3 years

CLE Requirement: 10 hours of criminal law CLE for the last reporting cycle or current reporting cycle

Trial Experience: 5 adjudicatory hearings **OR** 3 criminal jury trials with at least 1 a second degree felony or higher

(C) Second Degree Felony

Registry Category: Juvenile–Second Degree Felony

Appropriations Category: Juvenile Delinquency—2nd Degree

Length of Bar Membership: 3 years

CLE Requirement: 10 hours of criminal law CLE for the last reporting cycle or current reporting cycle

Trial Experience: 5 adjudicatory hearings **OR** 3 criminal jury trials with at least 1 a second degree felony or higher

(D) First Degree or Life Felony

Registry Category: Juvenile–First Degree and Life Felony

Appropriations Category: Juvenile Delinquency—1st Degree

Felony; Juvenile Delinquency—Felony Life

The selection of an appropriations category is determined by the charge for which the minor is tried or pleads.

Length of Bar Membership: 3 years

CLE Requirement: 10 hours of criminal law CLE for the last reporting cycle or current reporting cycle

Criminal Practice Percentage: 50%

Trial Experience: 5 adjudicatory hearings **OR** 3 criminal jury trials with at least 1 a second degree felony or higher

(17) *Probate Division Registry Requirements.*

(A) Adult Protective Services

Registry Category: Probate–Adult Protective Services

Appropriations Category: Adult Protective Services- Ch. 415, F.S.

CLE Requirement: 10 hours of CLE for topics including guardianship, mental health, or elder law for the last reporting cycle or current reporting cycle

Trial Experience: Minimum of 10 cases representing a respondent in APS proceedings and/or developmentally disabled adult proceedings and/or incapacity proceedings

(B) Developmentally Disabled Adults

Registry Category: Probate–Developmentally Disabled Adults

Appropriations Category: Developmentally Disabled Adult

CLE Requirement: 10 hours of CLE for topics including guardianship, mental health, or elder law for the last reporting cycle or current reporting cycle

Trial Experience: 10 cases representing a respondent in APS proceedings and/or developmentally disabled adult proceedings and/or incapacity proceedings

(C) Emergency Temporary Guardianships

Registry Category: Probate—Emergency Temporary Guardianship

Appropriations Category: Guardianship–Emergency–Ch. 744, F.S.

Probate—Emergency Temporary Guardianship Registry category shall be used by the Clerk when scheduling attorneys to appear at emergency hearings before the general magistrates or if there is a Petition for Emergency Temporary Guardianship to be heard at a time other than established for emergency temporary guardianship hearings.

CLE Requirement: 10 hours of guardianship CLE for the last reporting cycle or current reporting cycle

Trial Experience: Minimum of 10 cases representing a respondent in APS proceedings and/or developmentally disabled adult proceedings and/or incapacity and/or emergency temporary guardianship proceedings (may also include 10 cases representing a guardian or proposed guardian in developmentally disabled adult proceedings or Chapter 744 proceedings)

(D) Guardianship Incapacity, Extraordinary Proceedings, and Restoration

Registry Category: Incapacity

Appropriations Category: Guardianship—Ch. 744, F.S.

CLE Requirement: 10 hours of guardianship CLE for the last reporting cycle or current reporting cycle

Trial Experience: 10 cases representing a respondent in APS proceedings and/or developmentally disabled adult proceedings and/or incapacity and/or emergency temporary guardianship proceedings (may also include 10 cases representing a guardian or proposed guardian in developmentally disabled adult proceedings or Chapter 744 proceedings)

(E) Medical Procedures

Registry Category: Probate–Baker Act

Appropriations Category: Medical Procedures–Section 394.459(3), F.S.

Experience: Education or training with regard to mental health issues

(F) Mental Health

Registry Category: Probate–Baker Act

Appropriations Category: Baker Act/Mental Health–Ch. 394, F.S.

CLE Requirement: online course at http://mhlp.fmhi.usf.edu/training/tdetail.cfm?id="47" with a copy of the certificate of completion

Experience: Education or training with regard to mental health issues

(G) Substance Abuse

Registry Category: Probate—Marchman Act

Appropriations Category: Marchman Act/Substance Abuse—Ch. 397, F.S.

Experience: Education or training with regard to substance abuse issues

(H) Tuberculosis

Registry Category: Probate–Tuberculosis

Appropriations Category: Tuberculosis—Ch. 392, F.S.

Experience: Education or training with regard to tuberculosis

(I) Admission of Inmate to Mental Health Facility

Registry Category: Department of Corrections Mental Health

Appropriations Category: Admission of Inmate to Mental Health Facility

Experience: Education or training with regard to mental health issues

(18) *Due Process Provider Rates.*

(A) The due process provider rates for costs incurred on or after July 1, 2010 shall comply with the due process provider rates, as established by the Legislature. The private attorney shall also comply with all requirements of the JAC for approval of costs and payment of costs.

(B) The due process provider rates for the period of time October 1, 2007 to June 30, 2010 were:

(i) ***Expert Witness Fees***

Category	Fee Rate
Downward Departure Examination	$400.00 per examination and report
Expert Witness	$150.00 per hour
Expert Witness—Out of Court	$110.00 per hour

Category	Fee Rate
Expert Witness—Waiting to Testify at Court Proceeding or Deposition	$70.00 per hour
Expert Witness—Travel	$60.00 per hour
Expert Witness	$1,580.00 per case
Insanity Evaluations	$150.00 per hour
Investigators	$38.00 per hour
Investigators	$840.00 per case
Medical Doctors—Deposition and In Court	$150.00 per hour
Medical Doctors—Out of Court	$130.00 per hour
Other Pre–Trial Expert—In Court	$100.00 per hour
Other Pre–Trial Expert—Out of Court	$77.00 per hour
Psychological (Competency) Examination	$250.00 per examination
Psychologist—In Court	$140.00 per hour
Psychologist—Out of Court	$130.00 per hour
Psychologist—Waiting to Testify at Court Proceeding or Deposition	$85.00 per hour

(ii) ***Interpreters***

Creole	$35.00 per hour, one (1) hour minimum and $8.75 for each quarter hour thereafter
French	$50.00 per hour, one (1) hour minimum and $12.50 for each quarter hour thereafter.
Portuguese	$50.00 per hour, one (1) hour minimum and $12.50 for each quarter hour thereafter.
Sign	$50.00 to 75.00 per hour, two (2) hour minimum and travel expenses, and $18.75 for each quarter hour thereafter
Spanish	$35.00 per hour, one (1) hour minimum and $8.75 for each quarter hour thereafter
Other	$50.00 per hour, two (2) hour minimum and $12.50 for each quarter hour thereafter

(iii) ***Court Reporters***

(a) Appearance Fees

Time Period	Fee
Transcription of recorded investigative statements, discovery, or reports	1 to 5 recorded items $25.00 Each additional recorded item $5.00
8:30 a.m. until noon	$100.00
1:30 p.m until 5:00 p.m.	$100.00
Not scheduled for 8:30 a.m. to noon or 1:30 p.m. until 5:00 p.m.	$30.00 per hour with a 2 hour minimum
Real time from 8:30 a.m. until noon	$150.00
Real time from 1:30 p.m. until 5:00 p.m.	$150.00
Real time not scheduled for 8:30 a.m. to noon or 1:30 p.m. until 5:00 p.m.	$45.00 per hour with a 2 hour minimum

(b) Transcripts and ASCII Disk of Transcript

Delivery Time	Number	Cost per page
24 hours (overnight)	Original and 2	$ 7.50
	Each additional copy	$ 1.10
3 business days	Original and 2	$ 6.50
	Each additional copy	$ 1.10
6 business days	Original and 2	$ 5.50
	Each additional copy	$ 1.10
10 business days	Original and 2	$ 5.00
	Each additional copy	$ 1.10
Appeals	Original and 2 and disks	$5.00
Non certified (a transcript prepared by an individual other than the court reporter taking the proceeding)	Original and 2	$4.00
Recorded investigative statements, discovery, or reports—same day	Original and 1	$7.85
Recorded investigative statements, discovery, or reports—24 hours (overnight)	Original and 1	$5.10

Delivery Time	Number	Cost per page
Recorded investigative statements, discovery, or reports—10 business days	Original and 1	$2.75
Recorded investigative statements, discovery, or reports—3 business days	Original and 1	$4.15
	Each additional copy	$1.00

(C) The due process provider rates for the period of time July 1, 2004 to September 30, 2007 were those as established by the Indigent Services Committee.

(19) *References.* Any and all references to the Chief Judge, Clerk, Administrative Judge, judge, general magistrate, Public Defender, or Regional Counsel shall include his or her designee.

(20) This Administrative Order vacates and supersedes Administrative Order 2018–40–Gen.

DONE AND ORDERED in chambers in Fort Lauderdale, Broward County, Florida on this 18th day of July, 2018.

Jack Tuter
Chief Judge

2018–16–GEN. SEXUAL HARASSMENT POLICY AND COMPLAINT PROCEDURES FOR COURT EMPLOYEES AND OTHERS

IN THE CIRCUIT COURT OF THE SEVENTEENTH JUDICIAL CIRCUIT IN AND FOR BROWARD COUNTY, FLORIDA

Administrative Order No. 2018–16–GEN

ADMINISTRATIVE ORDER ADOPTING SEXUAL HARASSMENT POLICY AND COMPLAINT PROCEDURES FOR COURT EMPLOYEES AND OTHERS

(a) Pursuant to Florida Rule of Judicial Administration 2.215 (b) (1), the Chief Judge is "the administrative officer of the courts within [this] circuit and shall, consistent with branch-wide policies, direct the formation and implementation of policies and priorities for the operation of all courts and officers within [this] circuit."

(b) The creation and implementation of uniform procedures for court personnel and others to report any alleged occurrence(s) of sexual harassment is necessary to fulfill the Seventeenth Judicial Circuit's longstanding policy to make the workplace free of sexual harassment.

(c) Pursuant to the authority vested in the Chief Judge by Florida Rule of Judicial Administration 2.215, it is hereby **ORDERED**:

(1) The Seventeenth Judicial Circuit Sexual Harassment Policy and Complaint Procedures, attached hereto as Attachment "A" and incorporated herein, is hereby adopted and shall be implemented immediately in the Seventeenth Judicial Circuit.

(2) This policy shall apply to all court personnel of the Seventeenth Judicial Circuit without regard to position funding, i.e., county, state, or other payroll classification, and contractors or vendors of the Circuit depending on the Circuit's control over and business relationship with such contractor or vendor.

(3) The Sexual Harassment Policy and Procedures for Sexual Harassment Complaint against Justice and Judges, adopted and implemented in the Seventeenth Judicial Circuit pursuant to Administrative Order 2018–15–Gen shall govern the reporting of and procedures for handling complaints of sexual harassment against judges.

(4) The Office of the Trial Court Administrator shall, as soon as practicable, distribute the attached policy to all court personnel of the Seventeenth Judicial Circuit and obtain signed confirmations of receipt of said policy from all employees, excluding constitutional officers.

(5) This Administrative Order supersedes and vacates Administrative Order 2018–6–Gen.

DONE AND ORDERED in Chambers, Fort Lauderdale, Broward County, Florida, this 23rd day of February, 2018.

Jack Tuter
Chief Judge

ATTACHMENT"A"

SEVENTEENTH JUDICIAL CIRCUIT SEXUAL HARASSMENT POLICY AND COMPLAINT PROCEDURES

I. POLICY

It is the policy of the Seventeenth Judicial Circuit to make the workplace free of sexual harassment or sexual misconduct. Sexual harassment occurs if there are unwelcome sexual advances; unwelcome requests for sexual favors; or unwelcome verbal or physical conduct of a sexual nature from or involving an employee's supervisor(s), peer(s), subordinates or other persons in contact with an employee during the course of the conduct of the employee's business when:

1. Submission to such conduct is either explicitly or implicitly a term or condition of employment; or

2. Submission to or rejection of such conduct by an individual is used as the basis for employment decisions affecting such individual; or

3. Such conduct has the purpose or effect of interfering with an individual's work performance or creates an intimidating, hostile, or offensive work environment.

Sexual misconduct is any behavior of a sexual nature that is committed without consent or by force, intimidation, coercion, or manipulation. Sexual misconduct can occur between strangers or acquaintances, including people involved in an intimate or sexual relationship, and is not necessarily actionable sexual harassment.

The Seventeenth Judicial Circuit condemns any sexual harassment or sexual misconduct and advances the position that anyone in contact with the Seventeenth Judicial Circuit should feel empowered to bring any such inappropriate activity to the attention of all proper authorities. Anyone authorized to investigate or pursue a complaint of sexual harassment or sexual misconduct hereunder must always maintain an open-door policy that fosters the free expression of any complaint. The Chief Judge or Chief Judge's designee has the authority to take any administrative action necessary to protect the complainant from further sexual harassment or sexual misconduct and from retaliation related to a complaint hereunder.

It is the policy of the Seventeenth Judicial Circuit that complaints of sexual harassment or sexual misconduct will be treated seriously and acted upon promptly. Such conduct, whether committed (1) by or against court employees or applicants for employment, or (2) by contractors or vendors of the Court against court employees or other contractors or vendors of the Court, is strictly prohibited and will not be tolerated. Any court employee engaging in such prohibited conduct will be subjected to disciplinary action up to and including termination of employment. Complaints against non-employees of the Seventeenth Judicial Circuit, including contractors or vendors of the Court, will be investigated and addressed based on the Circuit's control over and business relationship with the alleged harasser.

II. NOTIFICATION

a. Complaints Against Judges

Complaints against a judge should be reported and addressed as provided in the Sexual Harassment Policy and Procedures for Sexual Harassment Complaints against Justices and Judges, adopted and implemented in the Seventeenth Judicial Circuit pursuant to Administrative Order 2018–15–Gen.

b. Complaints Against Co–Employees and Supervisors

Complaints against co-employees should be reported to the complainant's immediate supervisor. If the complainant believes that reporting the conduct of co-employees to his or her supervisor would be futile, or if the employee has a complaint against his or her supervisor, the employee should report the conduct to the Human Resources Chief of Personnel. The individual to whom the complaint is made shall immediately report the complaint to the Trial Court Administrator, who will in turn notify the Chief Judge. The Chief Judge will appoint persons to investigate all complaints against employees. Such persons may include the General Counsel, Chief Deputy Court Administrator, and/or the Human Resources Chief of Personnel.

The appointed person(s) shall investigate all complaints under this section promptly and thoroughly. The investigation may include interviews of the complainant and alleged harasser to ascertain relevant facts and circumstances. Such interviews, if deemed necessary, shall occur within five (5) days of the submission of the complaint, where feasible. If the complainant does not divulge names or details of the incident(s), the appointed person(s) will rely upon information that is available, to the extent possible. After due consideration of all available information, the appointed person(s) shall expeditiously report the nature and facts of the complaint to the Chief Judge and Trial Court Administrator. The Chief Judge and/or Trial Court Administrator shall make a determination based upon the complaint and the report, and shall take appropriate corrective action, which may include disciplinary action up to and including termination of employment.

If any person has difficulty writing out the complaint and the person requests assistance in reducing the complaint to writing or if the person prefers to submit the complaint orally, the Chief Judge, Trial Court Administrator, or Human Resources Chief of Personnel, as appropriate, shall designate a person, who will not be involved in the investigation or adjudication of the complaint, to aid the person in reducing the complaint to writing.

c. Complaints against the Trial Court Administrator

Complaints against the Trial Court Administrator shall be brought directly to the attention of the Chief Judge. The Chief Judge shall determine the procedure for addressing the complaint, as specified in Section II.b. above.

Upon completion of any investigation, the Chief Judge shall make a determination based thereon and shall take appropriate corrective action.

d. Complaints against Contractors or Vendors of the Court

This section applies to complaints made by: (1) court employees against contractors or vendors of the court; (2) contractors or vendors of the court against court employees; and (3) contractors or vendors of the court against other contractors or vendors of the court.

Complaints by court employees against contractors or vendors of the court should be reported to the complainant's immediate supervisor, who will in turn notify the Trial Court Administrator and Chief Judge. If the court employee believes that reporting the conduct to his or her supervisor would be futile, the employee should report the conduct to the Trial Court Administrator, who in turn will notify the Chief Judge. The Chief Judge shall determine the procedure for addressing the complaint, as specified in Section II.b. above. Complaints by court employees against contractors or vendors of the court will be investigated and addressed based on the Circuit's control over and business relationship with the alleged harasser.

Complaints by contractors or vendors of the court against court employees should be reported to the Trial Court Administrator, who will in turn notify the Chief Judge and the Human Resources Chief of Personnel. The Chief Judge shall determine the procedure for addressing the complaint, as specified in Section II.b. above.

Complaints by contractors or vendors of the court against other contractors or vendors of the court should be reported to the Trial Court Administrator, who will in turn notify the Chief Judge. The Chief Judge shall determine the procedure for addressing the complaint, as specified in Section II.b. above. Complaints by contractors or vendors of the court against other contractors or vendors of the court will be investigated and addressed based on the Circuit's control over and business relationship with the alleged harasser.

e. Student Interns/Volunteers

Student interns or volunteers working for the Seventeenth Judicial Circuit who believe they are the subject of sexual harassment or sexual misconduct may use these complaint procedures, but in all instances, should submit a complaint to their college or university in accordance with school sexual harassment complaint procedures.

III. Time for Filing Complaints

In order to ensure that Seventeenth Judicial Circuit complaint procedures can be utilized without risk of precluding the filing of a charge of discrimination with state or federal entities, any individual who believes that he or she has been the subject or target of sexual harassment should report such incident within 90 days of the date of occurrence.

IV. Documentation and Confidentiality

All information pertaining to a complaint and investigation of sexual harassment or sexual misconduct must be conducted in a professional, confidential, and expeditious manner. Nothing in this Policy guarantees protection from public access other than as provided in Florida or federal law, or court rule.

All records made or received by the Chief Judge or the Chief Judge's designee through use of this Policy and complaint procedures are exempt from public disclosure under Florida Rule of Judicial Administration 2.420. Such records of complaints against employees are exempt until a determination of probable cause is found. Any record of resulting disciplinary action will be maintained in the disciplined employee's personnel file.

Such records of complaints against judges are exempt from public disclosure for the duration of an initial inquiry, formal investigation and resolution of the complaint, and at all times thereafter, unless the records are forwarded to the Judicial Qualifications Commission. If records pertaining to a complaint against a judge are forwarded to the Judicial Qualifications Commission, such records will be confidential under Florida Rule of Judicial Administration 2.420 and rule 23, Rules of the Judicial Qualifications Commission, until any formal charges against the judge are filed by the Investigative Panel of the commission with the Clerk of the Florida Supreme Court.

Records within the possession of any judge or court staff pertaining to a complaint that has been forwarded to the

Judicial Qualifications Commission will become public upon formal charges being filed with the clerk of the Florida Supreme Court.

V. Protection from Retaliation

In no case will an employee be disciplined or otherwise retaliated against for opposing sexual harassment or sexual misconduct in the workplace by reporting in good faith any violation of this Policy. However, any employee who is in receipt of a complaint of sexual harassment or sexual misconduct or has knowledge of a violation of this Policy and fails to take action by reporting the matter may be subject to disciplinary action up to an including termination of employment. Any employee who knowingly files a false complaint of sexual harassment or other discrimination against another person shall be subject to disciplinary action up to and including termination of employment.

VI. Referral to the Florida Commission on Human Relations or the United States Equal Employment Opportunity Commission

This Policy does not preclude the filing of a charge of employment discrimination with the Florida Commission on Human Relations or the Equal Employment Opportunity Commission.

For anyone wishing to file such a complaint, the Florida Commission on Human Relations (FCHR) is located at: 4075 Esplanade Way, Room 110, Tallahassee, Florida 32399. The telephone number for the FCHR is: (850) 488–7082 or 1–800–342–8170.

The United States Equal Employment Opportunity Commission (EEOC) office with jurisdiction over complaints arising in Florida is the Miami District Office located at 100 SE 2nd Street, Suite 1500, Miami, Florida 33131. The telephone number for the EEOC Miami District Office is: 1–800–669–4000.

2018–15–GEN. SEXUAL HARASSMENT POLICY AND PROCEDURES FOR SEXUAL HARASSMENT COMPLAINTS AGAINST JUDGES

IN THE CIRCUIT COURT OF THE SEVENTEENTH JUDICIAL CIRCUIT IN AND FOR BROWARD COUNTY, FLORIDA

Administrative Order No. 2018–15–GEN

ADMINISTRATIVE ORDER REGARDING SEXUAL HARASSMENT POLICY AND PROCEDURES FOR SEXUAL HARASSMENT COMPLAINTS AGAINST JUDGES

(a) On February 16, 2018, the Supreme Court of Florida issued AOSC18–6, *In re: Sexual Harassment Policy and Procedures for Complaints against Justices and Judges*, adopting the Sexual Harassment Policy and Procedures for Sexual Harassment Complaints against Justices and Judges and directing chief judges of the circuit courts to adopt and implement this policy and procedures for complaints in their respective courts.

(b) Pursuant to the authority vested in the Chief Judge by Florida Rule of Judicial Administration 2.215 and under mandate from the Supreme Court of Florida in *In Re: Sexual Harassment Policy and Procedures for Complaints against Justices and Judges*, it is hereby **ORDERED** as follows:

(1) The Sexual Harassment Policy and Procedures for Sexual Harassment Complaints against Justices and Judges attached hereto and incorporated herein is adopted and shall be immediately implemented in the Seventeenth Judicial Circuit Court of Florida.

(2) The Office of the Trial Court Administrator shall, as soon as practicable, distribute the attached policy to all court personnel of the Seventeenth Judicial Circuit and obtain signed confirmations of receipt of said policy from all employees, excluding constitutional officers.

(3) This Administrative Order supersedes and vacates Administrative Order I–04–D–4A.

DONE AND ORDERED in Chambers, Fort Lauderdale, Florida, this 23rd day of February, 2018.

Jack Tuter
Chief Judge

SEXUAL HARASSMENT POLICY AND PROCEDURES FOR SEXUAL HARASSMENT COMPLAINTS AGAINST JUSTICES AND JUDGES

1. Policy. The chief justice's implementation of this policy is under his or her authority as the administrative officer of the judicial branch and of the supreme court pursuant to rule 2.205(a)(2)(B), Florida Rules of Judicial Administration.

It is the policy of the Florida Supreme Court to foster a workplace free of sexual harassment, or sexual misconduct. Sexual harassment occurs if there are unwelcome sexual advances; unwelcome requests for sexual favors; or unwelcome verbal or physical conduct of a sexual nature from or involving an employee's supervisors, peers, subordinates or other persons in contact with an employee during the course of the conduct of the employee's business when:

1. Submission to such conduct is either explicitly or implicitly a term or condition of employment; or

2. Submission to or rejection of such conduct by an individual is used as the basis for employment decisions affecting such individual or as the basis for any official action; or

3. Such conduct has the purpose or effect of interfering with an individual's work performance or creates a persistently intimidating and hostile environment, as that term is defined in state and federal law.

Sexual misconduct is any behavior of a sexual nature that is committed without consent or by force, intimidation, coercion, or manipulation. Sexual misconduct can occur between strangers or acquaintances, including people involved in an intimate or sexual relationship, and is not necessarily actionable sexual harassment.

The Florida Supreme Court and the entire state court system condemn any sexual harassment or sexual misconduct and advance the position that anyone in contact with the state courts system should feel empowered to bring any such inappropriate activity to the attention of all proper authorities, including and especially the Florida Supreme Court. Anyone authorized to investigate or pursue a complaint of sexual harassment or sexual misconduct hereunder must always maintain an open-door policy that fosters the free expression of any complaint. The chief justice or chief justice's designee has the authority to take any administrative action necessary to protect the complainant from further sexual harassment or sexual misconduct and from retaliation related to a complaint hereunder.

It is the policy of the Florida Supreme Court that all complaints of sexual harassment or sexual misconduct against any justice or judge within the state courts system will be treated seriously and acted upon promptly. The following procedures apply to complaints against justices or judges made by employees of the court system, applicants for employment with the court system, and when applicable attorneys, litigants, or other members of the public. Compliance with these procedures by the chief justice, the chief justice's designee, or a chief judge constitutes a presumption of compliance with the disciplinary responsibilities under Canon 3(D)1 of the Code of Judicial Conduct.

2. Notification. The chief justice may designate any court system officer or employee to be responsible for receiving and documenting complaints of sexual harassment or sexual misconduct against justices of the Supreme Court, judges of the district courts of appeal, or judges of any of the trial courts.

Any employee or applicant for employment with the court system who believes that he or she is the subject of sexual harassment by a justice of the Supreme Court, a judge of any of the district courts of appeal, or a judge of any of the trial courts should submit his or her complaint in writing, or if the person prefers he or she may submit the complaint orally. The complaint may be submitted to any of the following: the chief justice or his or her designee; a local administrator, such as a Trial Court Administrator, human resource manager or Marshal; or the Chief of Human Resources at the Office of the State Courts Administrator (OSCA). If the person receiving the complaint is not the chief justice, the chief justice's designee hereunder, or a chief judge, the person receiving the complaint should forward it to the chief justice, the chief justice's designee hereunder, or the chief judge of the court in which the subject judge serves for an investigation pursuant to section 4, below. Student interns working for the state courts system who believe they are the subject of sexual harassment may use these complaint procedures, but in all instances, should submit a complaint to their college or university in accordance with school sexual harassment complaint procedures.

If any person has difficulty writing out the complaint and the person requests assistance in reducing the complaint to writing or if the person prefers to submit the complaint orally, the chief justice, local administrator, or OSCA Chief of Human Resources, as appropriate, shall designate a person, who will not be involved in the investigation or adjudication of the complaint, to aid the person in reducing the complaint to writing.

If the chief justice is the subject of a complaint, the employee or applicant should submit the complaint to the inspector general of the Supreme Court, who will refer the complaint to the most senior justice, excluding the chief justice. The justice to whom such a complaint is referred will assume all complaint investigation and resolution duties for which the chief justice otherwise would be responsible. The justice to whom such a complaint is referred also will be responsible for maintaining records pertaining to the complaint.

If an employee or applicant chooses not to file a formal complaint, and any person designated hereunder to receive complaints has actual knowledge or receives information that a substantial likelihood exists that a justice or judge has engaged in sexual harassment or sexual misconduct, the person may inquire into the matter and take appropriate action.

3. Time for Filing Complaints. In order to ensure that Florida Supreme Court complaint procedures can be utilized without risk of precluding the filing of a charge of discrimination with state or federal entities, an employee or applicant should report an incident of sexual harassment within 90 days of the date of occurrence.

4. Investigations. A complaint of sexual harassment or sexual misconduct against a justice or judge will be investigated promptly and thoroughly. If a complaint has been made, the chief justice, the chief justice's designee hereunder, or the chief judge of the court in which the subject judge serves may designate another person to make an initial inquiry into the complaint.

The chief justice, chief justice's designee, or a chief judge of the court in which the subject judge serves will interview the complainant within five days of the submission of the complaint to ascertain relevant facts and circumstances. If the complainant does not divulge names or details of the incident(s), the chief justice or chief justice's designee, or the chief judge of the court in which the subject judge serves will rely upon any information that is available. If another person has been designated to make an initial inquiry into the complaint, the designee will report details of the complaint, including any relevant facts, circumstances, and information, to the chief justice within ten days of the submission of the complaint.

If the chief justice, chief justice's designee, or the chief judge of the court in which the subject judge serves determines the complaint is unfounded or is insufficient to constitute sexual harassment, he or she may decline to pursue any action on the complaint.

If the chief justices, chief justice's designee, or the chief judge of the court in which the subject judge serves determines the complaint is facially sufficient to constitute sexual harassment, the chief justice, chief justice's designee, or the chief judge of the court in which the subject judge serves may appoint an investigating officer or officers to formally investigate the complaint, or may take any other action appropriate under the circumstances.

If the chief justice or chief justice's designee determines the complaint is insufficient to constitute sexual harassment, but nevertheless indicates potential sexual misconduct, the chief justice or chief justice's designee may take any action appropriate to address the circumstances, including but not limited to appointing an investigating officer or officers to formally investigate the complaint.

The chief justice, chief justice's designee, the chief judge of the court in which the subject judge serves, or investigating officer will interview the complainant, the justice or judge implicated, and witnesses, if any, and will review relevant documents. If any investigating officers have been appointed, they will submit a written report to the chief justice, chief justice's designee, or the chief judge of the court in which the subject judge serves within thirty days of the submission of the complaint for formal investigation.

5. **Resolution.** The chief justice, or pursuant to rule 2.205(a)(2)(D), Florida Rules of Judicial Administration, the other most senior justice if the chief justice is the subject of a complaint, shall determine the course of action for internal resolution of the complaint, and may appoint another person, other than the subject of the complaint, to recommend the course of action for internal resolution.

If the chief justice or chief justice's designee determines the complaint, including any relevant facts, circumstances, and information, is insufficient to constitute sexual harassment, the chief justice, chief justice's designee, or the chief judge of the court in which the subject judge serves may attempt to resolve the complaint informally through mutual conciliation by meeting with the complainant and the subject justice or judge to discuss a method of resolution, including alternative dispute resolution. In attempting to resolve the complaint, the chief justice, chief justice's designee, or the chief judge of the court in which the subject judge serves may counsel or take other appropriate direct action with the justice or judge involved.

If the complaint and investigation reasonably indicate that the subject justice or judge engaged in activity that constitutes sexual harassment, constitutes sexual misconduct, or otherwise raises a substantial question as to a justice's or judge's fitness for office, the chief justice, chief justice's designee, or the chief judge of the court in which the subject judge serves shall refer the complaint and all written documentation pertaining to the complaint to the Judicial Qualifications Commission.

To the extent not otherwise prohibited by statute or rule, a written summary of the resolution will be provided to the complainant within a reasonable time after a determination is made and any action pursuant thereto is taken.

6. **Documentation and Confidentiality.** All information pertaining to a complaint of sexual harassment must be documented and maintained by the chief justice, chief justice's designee, or the chief judge of the court in which the subject judge serves whichever officer took final action on the resolution of the complaint.

All records made or received by any person pursuant to these complaint procedures are exempt from public disclosure as provided in rule 2.420(c)(3)(A), Florida Rules of Judicial Administration. Such records are exempt from public disclosure for the duration of an initial inquiry, formal investigation and resolution of the complaint, and at all times thereafter, unless the records are forwarded to the Judicial Qualifications Commission.

If records pertaining to a complaint are forwarded to the Judicial Qualifications Commission, such records will be confidential under rule 2.420(c)(3)(A), and rule 23(a), Rules of the Judicial Qualifications Commission, until any formal charges against the justice or judge are filed by the Investigative Panel of the Commission with the clerk of the Florida Supreme Court.

Records within the possession of any justice, judge, or court staff and pertaining to a complaint that has been forwarded to the Judicial Qualifications Commission will become public upon formal charges being filed with the clerk of the Florida Supreme Court.

7. **Referral to the Judicial Qualifications Commission.** The Judicial Qualifications Commission is responsible for investigating all reported instances of judicial misconduct. These procedures do not preclude the referral of a complaint against a justice or judge at any time by any person to the Judicial Qualifications Commission. If a complaint has been referred to the Judicial Qualifications Commission, no further action by the chief justice or chief justice's designee is required.

For anyone wishing to file such a complaint, the Commission's mailing address is P.O. Box 141106, Tallahassee, Florida 32317. The Commission's Executive Director, can be contacted by telephone at 850–488–1581 or by email at contact@floridajqc.com.

8. **Referral to the Florida Commission on Human Relations or the United State Equal Employment Opportunity Commission.** These procedures do not preclude the filing of a charge of employment discrimination with the Florida Commission on Human Relations or the United States Equal Employment Opportunity Commission.

For anyone wishing to file such a complaint, the Florida Commission on Human Relations (FCHR) is located at: 4075 Esplanade Way Room 110 Tallahassee, FL32399. The telephone number for the FCHR is: 850–488–7082 or 1–800–342–8170.

The United States Equal Employment Opportunity Commission (EEOC) office with jurisdiction over complaints arising in Florida is the Miami District Office located at 100 SE 2nd Street, Suite 1500, Miami, FL 33131. The telephone number for the EEOC Miami District office is: 1–800–669–4000.

9. **Referral to the Chief of Human Resources, Office of the State Courts Administrator.** For anyone wishing to file a complaint under this policy, the Chief of Human Resources, OSCA is located at: 500 South Duval Street Tallahassee, Florida 32399–1925. The telephone number is 850–617–4028.

2018–10–GEN. PROVISION OF ADA ACCOMMODATIONS

IN THE CIRCUIT COURT OF THE SEVENTEENTH JUDICIAL CIRCUIT IN AND FOR BROWARD COUNTY, FLORIDA

Administrative Order 2018–10–Gen

ADMINISTRATIVE ORDER REGARDING PROVISION OF ADA ACCOMMODATIONS

(a) Florida Rule of Judicial Administration 2.215 (b) (3) states the Chief Judge "shall, considering available resources, ensure the efficient and proper administration of all courts within [this] circuit."

(b) Florida Rule of Judicial Administration 2.540 governs Requests for Accommodations by Persons with Disabilities.

(c) In accordance with the authority vested in the Chief Judge by Florida Rule of Judicial Administration 2.215, it is hereby **ORDERED**:

(1) The Trial Court Administrator shall post the following information on the Seventeenth Judicial Circuit's web page and at each courthouse location: (a) the procedures for re-

questing accommodations from the court or court administration program; and (b) the grievance procedures that allow for the resolution of complaints.

(2) The Clerk of the Courts and any individual or entity contracting with the Seventeenth Judicial Circuit shall comply with the requirements of Florida Rule of Judicial Administration 2.540.

(3) All matters noticed or ordered for a hearing or conference before a judge or quasi-judicial officer or court administration program shall contain, in bold face, 14–point Times New Roman or Courier font, the following:

If you are a person with a disability who needs any accommodation in order to participate in this proceeding, you are entitled, at no cost to you, to the provision of certain assistance. Please contact Diana Sobel, Room 20140, 201 S.E. Sixth Street, Fort Lauderdale, Florida 33301, 954–831–7721 at least 7 days before your scheduled court appearance, or immediately upon receiving this notification if the time before the scheduled appearance is less than 7 days; if you are hearing or voice impaired, call 711.

(4) The Administrative Order vacates and supersedes Administrative Order 2014–5–Gen.

DONE AND ORDERED in Chambers, Fort Lauderdale, Broward County, Florida on this 12th day of February, 2018.

Jack Tuter
Chief Judge

2018–4–GEN. USE OF CELLULAR TELEPHONES AND OTHER PORTABLE ELECTRONIC DEVICES

IN THE CIRCUIT COURT OF THE SEVENTEENTH JUDICIAL CIRCUIT IN AND FOR BROWARD COUNTY, FLORIDA

Administrative Order No. 2018–4–Gen

ADMINISTRATIVE ORDER REGARDING THE USE OF CELLULAR TELEPHONES AND OTHER PORTABLE ELECTRONIC DEVICES IN COURTROOMS[1] AND COURT PROCEEDINGS

(a) Pursuant to Article V, section 2(d) of the Florida Constitution and section 43.26, Florida Statutes, the Chief Judge of each judicial circuit is charged with the authority and the power to do everything necessary to promote the prompt and efficient administration of justice.

(b) The safe and orderly use of court facilities, and the minimization of activities which disrupt or interfere with the fair, orderly and peaceable conduct of court business requires the imposition of provisions regarding the utilization of electronic devices in courtrooms by members of the public, attorneys, litigants, and members of the media.

(c) The regulation of cellular telephones and other electronic devices is within the Court's inherent authority to take supervisory and administrative actions necessary to implement its judicial functions.

(d) The Court's longstanding commitment to making courts open to the public and accessible to the media is of paramount importance in fashioning the regulations set forth herein.

(e) The court recognizes the increasing use of mobile devices for business purposes and the trend towards "paperless" offices, but proper decorum is required in all courtrooms and court proceedings.

(f) The overall purposes of this Administrative Order is to secure litigants' rights to a fair and impartial proceeding while providing the public, attorneys, and members of the media access to the proceedings.

SPECIFIC FINDINGS

(1) The Court has seen a consistent increase in the public's and media's use of devices such as cellular telephones to take video and still photographs during court proceedings. These activities can disrupt courtroom proceedings, cause safety concerns and reduce the dignity necessary for such proceedings.

(2) Standards must be established to balance the use of portable electronic devices with the competing needs and desires of the Court, Judges, media, litigants, defendants, attorneys, and members of the public during court proceedings.

(3) Media coverage of judicial proceedings is "[s]ubject at all times to the authority of the presiding judge to: (i) control the conduct of proceedings before the court; (ii) ensure decorum and prevent distractions; and (iii) ensure the fair administration of justice in the pending cause." Fla. R. Jud. Adm. 2.450(a).

(4) The Court must balance the constitutional right to a fair trial with the constitutional right to a free press.

(5) The standards must contain safeguards to ensure that media coverage and public attendance at court proceedings does not detract from or degrade those proceedings, impair or interrupt the Court's orderly procedures, or otherwise interfere with a fair trial.

(6) The increasing use of portable electronic devices or equipment has proven to be a tremendous burden and distraction for courtroom deputies continually removed from their primary duty of providing security to instead managing the usage of portable electronic devices or equipment by attendees of court proceedings. Court deputies cannot quickly ascertain what type of device is being utilized, for what purpose it is being used, and who may be allowed to use such technology. The more involved courtroom security becomes in managing technology as opposed to managing security, the more perilous the safety and security of those who enter the courthouse becomes. This issue is directly alleviated by banning types of usage of certain electronic devices from court proceedings and requiring any media representatives to display proper media credentials or identification supplied to them by their employer.

(7) It is within the Court's discretion whether to permit the use of laptop computers, cellular telephones, or similar portable electronic devices during a court proceeding. Traditionally, all portable electronic devices have been prohibited from the courtroom and there is no court rule that specifically permits the use of cellular telephones, laptop computers or similar portable electronic devices in a courtroom. The display of proper media credentials or identification by members of the media is the most effective and least burdensome method available to allow court security to instantly identify some of those individuals (who are usually not known to court security) who may utilize specified equipment without unduly interfering with their primary duty of providing security.

ACCORDINGLY, to facilitate the efficient administration of justice, in accordance with the authority vested in the chief judge pursuant to Florida Rule of Judicial Administration 2.215, it is hereby **ORDERED**:

I. CELLULAR TELEPHONES.

(1) *Public.* Members of the public may not use or display cellular telephones in any courtroom or during any court proceeding. All cellular telephones must be turned off or placed in silent or vibrate mode and shall not be used, viewed or otherwise displayed while in any courtroom.

(2) *Attorneys.* **With the permission of the presiding Judge**, attorneys, including those who are not the attorney of record, may utilize cellular telephones for texting, organizational functions, research and writing functions, and other data transmission functions. Cellular telephones and other similar electronic devices cannot be used to record or send photographs, video, or audio. All cellular telephones must be placed in either silent or vibrate mode. All Bluetooth and similar wireless devices must be turned off, removed from the wearer and secured out of sight.

(3) *Media.* Members of the media should always display proper media credentials or identification supplied to them by their employer. Members of the media exhibiting appropriate media credentials or identification supplied to them by their employer may utilize cellular telephones for texting, organizational functions, research and writing functions, and other data transmission functions. Cellular telephones and other similar electronic devices cannot be used to record or send photographs, video, or audio. All cellular telephones must be placed in either silent or vibrate mode. All Bluetooth and similar wireless devices must be turned off, removed from the wearer and secured out of sight.

(4) *Court Employees & Certain Contractual Vendors.* Court employees and certain contractual vendors including, but not limited to interpreters, court reporters, court technology personnel, and in-court clerks may use cellular telephones for texting, organizational functions, research and writing functions, and other data transmission functions in the course of their official duties. All cellular telephones must be placed in either silent or vibrate mode. In rare instances, with the permission of the presiding Judge, a court employee may use a cellular telephone to make or receive telephone calls while in the courtroom.

II. LAPTOP COMPUTERS, SIMILAR DEVICES AND OTHER PORTABLE ELECTRONIC DEVICES.[2]

(1) *Public.* Use of laptop computers and other portable electronic devices by members of the general public is **prohibited unless permission is granted from the presiding judge.**

(2) *Attorneys and Litigants Representing Themselves.* Attorneys and litigants representing themselves may use a laptop computer or other portable electronic device when their case is in session and they are actively participating in the proceeding. Attorneys may use electronic devices to conduct research, check calendars, check or send emails and perform other related tasks when seated in the well of the courtroom or during lengthy calendar calls while awaiting their cases to be called when they are in an area designated by the presiding Judge for attorneys. No computer or other electronic device can be used to record or send photographs, video, or audio. The transmission of materials on a computer to other peripheral devices also in use during the proceeding, and specifically in advancement of the proceeding, is permissible. For example, the transmission and display of a power point presentation is allowable.

(3) *Court Employees & Certain Contractual Vendors.* Court employees and certain contractual vendors including, but not limited to, interpreters, court reporters, court technology personnel, and in-court clerks may use laptop computers and other portable electronic devices as necessary in the course of their official duties.

(4) *Media.*

a. Media representatives may use laptop computers or similar electronic devices provided the devices operate silently on the user's lap and do not require additional seating space. Media representatives should always display proper media credentials or identification supplied to them by their employer. No laptop computer shall be used to record or send photographs, video, or audio. Use of a laptop computer shall be used solely to record and transmit text data. Only laptop computers or similar devices with virtual or silent keyboards are permitted and they must operate on battery power. Cabling of extension cords and power supplies is prohibited. Other devices equipped with virtual keyboards such as tablets (e.g., iPads and similar electronic devices) may be utilized for text recording and transmission. A presiding Judge may exclude laptop computers or similar devices or other portable electronic devices from the courtroom.

b. The operation of any permitted devices in a courtroom must be in a manner that does not disturb or disrupt the proceedings or distract the participants.

c. Media representatives attending any court proceeding and using a laptop computer or similar device shall generally sit in the row of seating as designated by the presiding Judge, Chief Judge or Trial Court Administrator so as to lessen the distraction to others.

III. GENERAL PROVISIONS.

(1) Nothing in this Administrative Order is intended to apply to persons who require electronic devices (or services requiring the use of electronic devices) under the Americans with Disabilities Act except that electronic devices cannot be used to record or send photographs, video or audio during a proceeding unless specifically approved by the presiding Judge.

(2) Court Deputies should instruct anyone violating this Administrative Order to cease. Violating this Administrative Order may result in temporary or permanent removal of a cellular telephone or other electronic device. If Court Deputies remove any device from a person, it shall be at the presiding Judge's direction and pursuant to this Administrative Order. If the conduct continues, the presiding Judge can

direct the person be removed from the courtroom. Anyone violating this Administrative Order may face contempt proceedings and/or other sanctions as permitted by law. Media representatives failing to abide by this Administrative Order may be precluded, in the future, from using portable electronic devices during court proceedings.

This Administrative Order supersedes and vacates Administrative Order 2017–39–Gen.

DONE AND ORDERED at Fort Lauderdale, Florida, this 17th day of January, 2018.

Jack Tuter
Chief Judge

[1] As used herein, the term "courtroom(s)" includes courtrooms, hearing rooms and any other places used to conduct court proceedings, unless specifically stated otherwise.

[2] As used herein, the phrase "laptop computers or similar devices" includes traditional laptop computers, as well as tablets, iPads and all other similar devices, unless specifically stated otherwise.

2017–33–GEN. AMENDED ADMINISTRATIVE ORDER REGARDING MOTIONS FOR REHEARING

IN THE CIRCUIT COURT OF THE SEVENTEENTH JUDICIAL CIRCUIT IN AND FOR BROWARD COUNTY, FLORIDA

Administrative Order No. 2017–33–Gen

AMENDED ADMINISTRATIVE ORDER REGARDING MOTIONS FOR REHEARING

(a) Florida Rule of Judicial Administration 2.215 (b) (3) states the chief judge "shall, considering available resources, ensure the efficient and proper administration of all courts within [this] circuit."

(b) Motions [1] for Rehearing and/or Reconsideration are submitted to the judges routinely with request for a hearing. Due to increased caseloads and time constraints, the judge, after review of any Motion for Rehearing/Reconsideration may rule on the merits of the motion without further hearing or set the matter for oral argument at the judge's discretion.

(c) In accordance with the authority vested in the chief judge by Florida Rule of Judicial Administration 2.215, it is hereby **ORDERED**:

(1) Effective immediately, upon the filing of a Motion for Rehearing and/or Reconsideration with the Clerk of the Courts, the filing party shall provide a courtesy copy to the division judge or judge who entered the order subject to the Motion for Rehearing and/or Reconsideration along with stamped envelopes addressed to all parties.

(2) A Memorandum of Law shall be incorporated into the Motion for Rehearing and/or Reconsideration with the legal basis for the Court to grant the relief requested.

(3) Upon review of the Motion for Rehearing and/or Reconsideration, the division judge or judge who entered the order subject to the Motion for Rehearing and/or Reconsideration may grant the motion, set the motion for a hearing, or deny the motion. The parties shall not schedule the Motion for Rehearing and/or Reconsideration for a hearing unless otherwise directed to do so by the division judge or judge who entered the order subject to the Motion for Rehearing and/or Reconsideration.

(4) This Administrative Order does not apply to Motions for New Trial, which shall be governed by the applicable rule of procedure.

(5) This Administrative Order vacates and supersedes Administrative Order 2010–47–Gen.

(6) Local Rule 7 remains vacated.

DONE AND ORDERED in Chambers, Fort Lauderdale, Broward County, Florida, this 28th day of July, 2017.

Jack Tuter
Chief Judge

[1] This Administrative Order shall also apply to Petitions for Rehearing and/or Reconsideration.

2016–8–GEN. PROFESSIONALISM PANEL

IN THE CIRCUIT COURT OF THE SEVENTEENTH JUDICIAL CIRCUIT IN AND FOR BROWARD COUNTY, FLORIDA

Order Number 2016–8–Gen

SEVENTEENTH CIRCUIT PROFESSIONALISM PANEL

WHEREAS, the Florida Supreme Court has adopted standards of professional behavior codified in: (1) the Oath of Admission to The Florida Bar; (2) The Florida Bar Creed of Professionalism; (3) The Florida Bar Professionalism Expectations; (4) The Rules Regulating The Florida Bar; (5) the decisions of the Florida Supreme Court ("Standards of Professional Behavior"); and

WHEREAS, the Board of Directors of the Broward County Bar Association has approved the Standards of Professional Courtesy and Civility for South Florida (attached hereto as Exhibit A); and

WHEREAS, the Florida Supreme Court's Standards of Professional Behavior and the Standards of Professional Courtesy and Civility for South Florida are hereinafter collectively referred to as the "*Standards of Professionalism*"; and

WHEREAS, the *Standards of Professionalism* apply to all attorneys practicing law in the Seventeenth Judicial Circuit; and

WHEREAS, on June 6, 2013 and January 29, 2015, the Supreme Court of Florida, in opinions SC13–688 and SC15–75, adopted and amended the Code for Resolving Professionalism Complaints and directed the Chief Judge of each circuit to create a Local Professionalism Panel to receive and resolve professionalism complaints.

NOW, THEREFORE, pursuant to the authority conferred by the Florida Supreme Court and Florida Rule of Judicial Administration 2.215, it is ORDERED as follows:

1. **Establishment of Local Professionalism Panel.**

a. The Seventeenth Judicial Circuit Professionalism Panel ("Panel") is hereby constituted and is designated the Local Professionalism Panel in accordance with SC13–688 and SC15–75.

b. The Panel shall consist of not less than fifteen (15) or more than twenty-one (21) members selected and appointed from time to time by the Chief Judge of the Seventeenth Judicial Circuit. The Chief Judge shall strive to select members that represent a cross-section of the Circuit with due consideration to such matters as, but not limited to, geographic location, diversity, discipline, reputation or bar activities.

c. The Chief Judge of the Seventeenth Judicial Circuit shall appoint the Chairperson of the Panel. The Vice–Chairperson of the Panel shall be elected by the members of the Panel.

d. The Chief Judge shall not be a member of the Panel but may preside over the Panel.

e. Meetings may be called by the Chairperson, the Chief Judge, or a majority of the membership. Notice of any meeting shall be given to each Panel member in such manner as deemed appropriate by the Chairperson of the Panel, and e-mail or telephonic notice is specifically approved.

f. Members of the Panel shall serve at the discretion of the Chief Judge. The membership of the Panel, as it changes from time to time, shall be posted on the Seventeenth Judicial Circuit website.

2. Purpose of Local Professionalism Panel. The purpose of the Panel is to promote adherence to the *Standards of Professionalism,* receive, screen, evaluate and act upon complaints of unprofessional conduct and resolve those complaints informally, if possible, or refer to The Florida Bar if appropriate or necessary. The Panel may discuss the complaint, if appropriate, with the complainant, witnesses and the attorney alleged to have engaged in unprofessional conduct (the "Respondent Attorney"). The Panel shall address conduct inconsistent with the *Standards of Professionalism* in an informal, nonpunitive, and educational manner. The Panel shall have no authority to discipline any attorney or to compel any attorney to appear before the Panel. The Panel may counsel attorneys if it determines such counseling will further the goals of the *Standards of Professionalism.*

3. Panel Procedures. The following procedures shall generally govern the proceedings of the Panel:

a. *Initiation by Judicial Officer or Quasi–Judicial Officer.* When any Judge or Quasi–Judicial Officer within the Seventeenth Judicial Circuit determines that an attorney has engaged in conduct inconsistent with the *Standards of Professionalism,* he or she may refer the matter to the Panel via the Chairperson of the Panel.

b. *Initiation by Attorney/Non–Attorney.*

i. If an attorney observes conduct on the part of another attorney that he or she believes in good faith, is inconsistent with the *Standards of Professionalism,* that attorney may request that the Panel consider the matter by completing a referral form and submitting it to the Chairperson of the Panel.

ii. If a non-attorney is directly and adversely affected by conduct on the part of an attorney that is allegedly inconsistent with the *Standards of Professionalism,* that person may request the Panel consider the matter by completing a referral form and submitting it to the Chairperson of the Panel.

The request shall be limited to two (2) pages exclusive of exhibits.

c. *Initiation by the Florida Bar's Attorney Consumer Assistance and Intake Program (ACAP).*

d. *Review.*

i. The Chairperson of the Panel shall review the request, shall notify the Respondent Attorney of the request, may request a response, and shall determine whether the matter justifies a referral to the Panel. If a matter is referred to the Panel, the Chairperson of the Panel shall address a letter to the Respondent Attorney inviting the attorney to meet with the Chairperson or members of the Panel on a date and time specified.

ii. Any letter sent to a Respondent Attorney by the Panel requesting that the Respondent Attorney appear before the Panel shall identify the conduct alleged to be inconsistent with the *Standards of Professionalism* and the *Standards of Professionalism* potentially implicated and shall advise the attorney that the Panel meeting is not a disciplinary proceeding.

iii. The Chairperson, alone or the Chairperson with any number of Panel members to be designated by the Chairperson, may meet at the date and time specified in the letter. The purpose of the meeting shall be to discuss with the Respondent Attorney his or her conduct *and* attempt to resolve the conduct or behavior alleged to be inconsistent with the *Standards of Professionalism.* The Chairperson of the Panel may send a letter summarizing the Panel's discussions to the Respondent Attorney.

iv. If the Respondent Attorney fails to appear, the designated members of the Panel shall discuss the alleged conduct inconsistent with the *Standards of Professionalism* and may summarize the Panel's discussions by letter to the Respondent Attorney. Consistent with the provisions of this Order, the Panel may consider the Respondent Attorney's failure to appear in determining whether referral to ACAP is appropriate.

(4) General Matters.

a. The Panel members should endeavor to resolve all referrals in a timely manner.

b. Upon conferring with each other and conducting an investigation, the Panel members involved may proceed and resolve the issues in the following non-punitive, educational and constructive manner to provide the Respondent Attorney with an incentive for self–improvement:

i. The Chairperson may issue an oral or written decision to the Respondent Attorney;

ii. The Panel, in its discretion, may also refer the Respondent Attorney to the Broward County Bar Association's Mentorship program or may communicate with an assisting mentor of the Respondent;

iii. The Panel may recommend the Respondent Attorney attend "The Florida Bar's Ethics School," which is an eight (8) hour ethics course, or any other course(s) deemed appropriate;

iv. The Panel may advise the Respondent Attorney with recommendations that will assist the attorney in the future;

v. The Panel, in appropriate circumstances, may refer the Respondent Attorney to "Florida Lawyers Assistance" or other similar, appropriate program(s), for assistance with drug, alcohol, and/or emotional problems;

vi. Pursuant to Section 2.1 of the Supreme Court Opinion SC13–688, the Panel has the discretion to direct any referrals to ACAP depending upon the nature and severity of the referral; or

vii. The Panel may form any other such solutions that the Panel may deem as appropriate or necessary.

c. All records regarding referrals to the Panel will be handled in the same manner as set forth in the Supreme Court Opinion SC13–688 and as outlined in Rule 3–7.1 of *The Rules Regulating the Florida Bar* regarding the confidentiality of disciplinary investigations and proceedings.

This Administrative Order vacates and supersedes Administrative Order 2013–53–Gen.

DONE AND ORDERED in chambers at Fort Lauderdale, Broward County, Florida on February 16, 2016.

Peter M. Weinstein
Chief Judge

Standards of Professional Courtesy and Civility for South Florida

Preamble

Attorneys are often retained to represent their clients in disputes or transactions. The practice of law is often an adversarial process. Attorneys are ethically bound to zealously represent and advocate in their clients' best interests. Nonetheless, certain standards of professional courtesy exist that must be observed in the courtroom, the board room, or any other setting in which an attorney is present.

The following standards of professional courtesy describe the conduct expected of attorneys practicing before courts and other tribunals in South Florida, including Broward, Indian River, Martin, Miami–Dade, Monroe, Okeechobee, Palm Beach, and St. Lucie counties. These standards are not meant to be exhaustive, but instead to set a tone or guide for conduct not specifically covered by these standards. The overriding principles promoted by these standards are good-faith, civil and respectful communication between counsel and similar cooperation with judges, arbitrators, mediators, clerks, court staff, witnesses and non-parties.

These standards have been codified with the intent that their dissemination will educate and remind attorneys and their clients that attorneys practicing in South Florida are expected to behave professionally and civilly at all times. In 1990, the Board of Governors of The Florida Bar adopted the Ideals and Goals of Professionalism. In 2011, the Florida Supreme Court amended its oath of attorney admission ("Oath of Attorney Admission") to require that attorneys taking the oath pledge to opposing parties and counsel "fairness, integrity, and civility, not only in court, but also in all written and oral communications." In 2013, the Florida Supreme Court issued an opinion entitled *In re: Code for Resolving Professionalism Complaints* (SC13–688) that requires each judicial circuit in Florida to create a local professionalism panel to hear grievances for professionalism and civility violations. These standards below should be read together with the Ideals and Goals of Professionalism, the Oath of Attorney Admission, and the Florida Supreme Court's opinion aimed at improving attorneys' professionalism and civility.

I. Scheduling

1. Attorneys should endeavor to provide opposing counsel and pro se litigants (collectively, "opposing counsel"), parties, witnesses, and other affected persons, sufficient notice of depositions, hearings and other proceedings, except upon agreement of counsel, in an emergency, or in other circumstances compelling more expedited scheduling. As a general rule, actual notice should be given that is no less than five (5) business days for in-state depositions, ten (10) business days for out-of-state depositions and five (5) business days for hearings.

2. Attorneys should communicate with opposing counsel prior to scheduling depositions, hearings and other proceedings, so as to schedule them at times that are mutually convenient for all interested persons. Further, sufficient time should be reserved to permit a complete presentation by counsel for all parties. Upon receiving an inquiry concerning a proposed time for a hearing, deposition, meeting or other proceeding, a lawyer should promptly agree to the proposal or offer a counter suggestion that is as close in time as is reasonably available, and attorneys should cooperate with each other when conflicts and calendar changes are reasonably necessary. Only after making a reasonable effort to confer with opposing counsel should attorneys unilaterally schedule depositions, hearings or other matters.

3. Attorneys should notify opposing counsel, the court or other tribunal, and others affected, of scheduling conflicts as soon as they become apparent. Further, attorneys should cooperate with one another regarding all reasonable rescheduling requests that do not prejudice their clients or unduly delay a proceeding and promptly offer reasonable alternative dates to reschedule a matter.

4. Attorneys should promptly notify the court or other tribunal of any resolution between parties that renders a scheduled court appearance unnecessary or otherwise moot.

5. Attorneys should grant reasonable requests by opposing counsel for extensions of time within which to respond to pleadings, discovery and other matters when such an extension will not prejudice their client or unduly delay a proceeding.

6. Attorneys should cooperate with opposing counsel during trials and evidentiary hearings by disclosing with reasonable advance notice the identities of all witnesses reasonably expected to be called and the length of time needed to present the attorney's client's case, except when a client's material rights would be adversely affected. The attorneys also should cooperate with the calling of witnesses out of turn when the circumstances justify it.

II. Discovery

1. Attorneys should pursue discovery requests that are reasonably related to the matter at issue. Attorneys should not use discovery for the purpose of harassing, embarrassing or causing the adversary to incur unnecessary expenses.

2. Attorneys should not use discovery for the purpose of causing undue delay or obtaining unfair advantage.

3. Attorneys should ensure that responses to reasonable discovery requests are timely, organized, complete and consistent with the obvious intent of the request. Attorneys should not produce documents in a way calculated to hide or obscure the existence of documents. A response to a request to produce should refer to each of the items in the request and the responsive documents should be produced as they correspond to each request or as they are kept in the usual course of business.

III. Conduct Directed to Opposing Counsel, the Court/Tribunal, and Other Participants in the Proceedings

1. As it brings dishonor to the legal profession, attorneys should refrain from criticizing or denigrating opposing counsel, the court/tribunal and their staff, the parties, and witnesses before clients, the public, and the media.

2. Attorneys should be, and should impress upon their clients and witnesses the need to be, courteous and respectful and not rude or disruptive with the court/tribunal, opposing counsel, parties and witnesses.

3. Attorneys should make an effort to explain to witnesses the purpose of their required attendance at depositions, hearings or trials. Absent compelling circumstances, attorneys should give adequate notice to non-party witnesses before the scheduling of their depositions, advance notice of a subpoena for a deposition, hearing or trial. Attorneys further should attempt to accommodate the schedules of witnesses when resetting their appearance and promptly notify them of any cancellations.

4. Attorneys should respect and abide by the spirit and letter of all rulings of the court and advise their clients to do the same.

5. Attorneys and their staff should a) act and speak civilly and respectfully to courtroom deputies and bailiffs, clerks, court reporters, judicial assistants and law clerks; b) be selective in inquiries posed to judicial assistants as their time and resources are limited; and c) familiarize themselves with the court's administrative orders, local rules and each judge's published standing orders, practices and procedures.

IV. Candor to the Court/Tribunal and Opposing Counsel

1. Attorneys should not knowingly misstate, misrepresent, or distort any fact or legal authority to the court, tribunal or opposing counsel and shall not mislead by inaction or silence. Further, if this occurs unintentionally and is later discovered, the attorney immediately should disclose and correct the error. Attorneys, likewise, should affirmatively notify the court or tribunal of controlling legal authority that is contrary to their client's legal position.

2. Attorneys immediately should notify opposing counsel of all oral or written communications with the court or other tribunal, except those involving only scheduling or administrative matters.

3. Copies of any submissions to the court or other tribunal (such as e-mails, correspondence, motions, pleadings, memoranda or law, legal authorities, exhibits, transcripts, etc.), should be simultaneously provided to opposing counsel by e-mail or delivery of an electronic or hard copy. For example, if a memorandum of law is hand-delivered to the court, a copy should be simultaneously e-mailed or hand-delivered to opposing counsel.

4. Attorneys should submit factual or legal argument to a court in a motion or memorandum of law and not in the form of an e-mail or letter. Tribunals other than courts, however, may permit more informal means than a motion or memorandum of law for the submission of factual or legal argument.

5. Attorneys should draft proposed orders promptly after a hearing or decision and the orders should fairly and adequately represent the ruling of the court or tribunal. Attorneys should promptly provide, either orally or in writing, proposed orders to opposing counsel for approval. In response, opposing counsel should communicate promptly any objections to the drafting attorney. The drafting attorney then should promptly submit a copy of the proposed order to the court or other tribunal and state whether opposing counsel agrees or objects to the form of the order.

6. Attorneys should draft agreements and other documents promptly after the discussions or agreement so as to fairly reflect the true intent of the parties. Where revisions are made to an agreement or other document, attorneys should point out, redline or otherwise highlight any such additions, deletions or modifications for opposing counsel.

V. Efficient Administration

1. Attorneys should refrain from actions intended primarily to harass or embarrass and should refrain from actions which cause unnecessary expense or delay.

2. Attorneys should, whenever possible, prior to filing or upon receiving a motion, contact opposing counsel to determine if the matter can be resolved in whole or in part. This may alleviate the need for filing the motion or allow submission of an agreed order in lieu of a hearing.

3. Attorneys should, whenever appropriate, discuss discovery planning. Attorneys should also endeavor to stipulate to all facts and legal authority not reasonably in dispute.

4. Attorneys should encourage principled negotiations and efficient resolution of disputes on their merits.

2013–50–GEN. PROCEDURES FOR MEDICAL EXAMINER AS TO AUTOPSY RECORDS

IN THE CIRCUIT COURT OF THE SEVENTEENTH JUDICIAL CIRCUIT IN AND FOR BROWARD COUNTY, FLORIDA

Order Number 2013–50–Gen

ADMINISTRATIVE ORDER ESTABLISHING PROCEDURES FOR MEDICAL EXAMINER AS TO AUTOPSY RECORDS

(a) Florida Rule of Judicial Administration 2.215(b)(3) states the chief judge shall "considering available resources, ensure the efficient and proper administration of all courts within [this] circuit."

(b) Chapter 406, Fla. Stat., governs the duties of medical examiners, including but not limited to, utilizing autopsy photos, video, or audio recordings.

(c) The Medical Examiner for Broward County presents to groups and organizations as to the results of reckless behavior or lectures on pathology as well as authoring articles and holding medical quality assurance/peer review conferences and seeks to use autopsy records.

(d) The Medical Examiner for Broward County requires an expedited procedure to secure authorization to use autopsy records which are otherwise confidential and exempt from public access pursuant to § 406.135, Fla. Stat.

(e) In accordance with the authority vested in the chief judge by Florida Rule of Judicial Administration 2.215, it is ordered:

(1) If the Medical Examiner for Broward County files an action to authorize his or her use of autopsy records for public dissemination it shall be assigned to the division for the Administrative Judge of the Circuit Criminal Division.

(2) Upon the filing of the action, the Medical Examiner for Broward shall provide a courtesy copy to the Administrative Judge of the Circuit Criminal Division so that an expedited hearing may be held unless the interested parties agree to waive the necessity of a hearing.

DONE AND ORDERED in chambers at Fort Lauderdale, Broward County, Florida on September 26, 2013.

Peter M. Weinstein
Chief Judge

2013–26–GEN. PROCEDURES FOR E–FILING AND COURT RECORDS

IN THE CIRCUIT COURT OF THE SEVENTEENTH JUDICIAL CIRCUIT IN AND FOR BROWARD COUNTY, FLORIDA

Order Number 2013–26–Gen

ADMINISTRATIVE ORDER ESTABLISHING PROCEDURES FOR E–FILING AND COURT RECORDS

(a) Florida Rule of Judicial Administration 2.215(b)(3) states the chief judge shall, considering available resources, ensure the efficient and proper administration of all courts within [this] circuit."

(b) Florida Rule of Judicial Administration 2.236 established the Florida Courts Technology Commission (FCTC) to oversee the use of technology for case management and case maintenance.

(c) The Clerk of the Courts received approval from the FCTC on December 31, 2010 for e-filing that included the following conditions:

(1) The Broward County Clerk of Court must continue to provide paper to the judiciary until the chief judge authorizes the elimination of paper files. At such time, the Broward County Clerk of Court must convert all documents, beginning on the date the Supreme Court or Florida Courts Technology Commission's (FCTC) approval to a searchable document.

(2) The Broward County Clerk of Court shall continue to accept paper filings at no charge, other than statutorily authorized fees.

(3) The Clerk of Court's implementation of e-filing must comply with the chief judge's approval letter of November 9, 2010.

(4) The ability of the chief judge to enter administrative orders to impose related requirements with regard to e-filing.

(d) The chief judge's November 9, 2010 approval of the Clerk of the Courts e-filing plan included the following requirements:

(1) The judges must have access to electronically filed and served documents in cases either via the e-Filing Authority Portal or his office.

(2) There shall be a continuation of paper cases, files and documents until the chief judge approves the electronic processes that replace the paper file.

(3) The electronic file provided to the court must meet or exceed the capabilities and ease of use currently provided by paper case files, for both in court and out of court use.

(4) The application shall not have a negative operational impact on the court.

(e) Florida Rule of Judicial Administration 2.525 requires approval of local "procedures, programs and standards" for electronic filing. The revised opinion in SC11–399, implementing mandatory e-filing for attorneys, did not significantly amend the requirements for e-filing plan approval in effect in 2010.

(f) The 17th Circuit Court is committed to the use of e-filing as a step in managing electronic court records and electronic court processes. The Court is in the process of implementing a case management workflow system. The Court must proceed carefully to ensure that the transition to electronic court records and electronic court processes does not have a negative impact on the operations of the Court. Moreover, at this time the electronic file provided to the court by the Clerk of Court does not meet or exceed the capabilities and ease of use provided by a paper case file as the electronic file is not in a searchable PDF format.

(g) Administrative Orders 2011–26–PRC, 2011–53–UFC, and 2012–16–Civ implementing e-filing all state "[the] Administrative Order shall govern the initial use of the Florida Courts Efiling Portal for the ... division ... but does not alleviate the Clerk from complying with the Chief Judge's conditions of approval of the Clerk's efiling plan which were included in the Florida Courts Technology Commission's approval of the plan." The Administrative Orders were not vacated or superseded by Florida Rule of Judicial Administration 2.525. In accordance with the authority vested in the chief judge by Florida Rule of Judicial Administration 2.215, it is ordered effective immediately:

(1) The Clerk of Courts shall provide for probate cases either an all paper court file or an all electronic court file in a searchable PDF format. There shall be no hybrid court files for the probate division.

(2) The Clerk of Courts shall provide either an all paper court file or an all electronic court file in searchable PDF format for criminal (circuit and county), delinquency, or dependency cases commencing October 1, 2013. There shall be no hybrid court files for the criminal, delinquency, or dependency divisions.

(3) The Clerk of Courts may determine if a file shall be provided in an all paper format or an all electronic court file in searchable PDF format but cannot provide a hybrid file for the probate, criminal (circuit and county), delinquency, or dependency divisions unless authorized in writing by the chief judge.

(4) The Clerk of Courts shall accept paper pleadings and documents from an attorney when the attorney:

a. has a deadline for the filing of a document and the e–Filing Authority Portal is not operational to accept filings or does not validate the case type subject to the deadline; or

b. has an emergency matter that requires immediate judicial review that cannot wait for acceptance[1] by the Clerk of Courts after filing with the e-Filing Authority Portal.

DONE AND ORDERED in chambers at Fort Lauderdale, Broward County, Florida on May 31, 2013.

Peter M. Weinstein
Chief Judge

[1] The Clerk of Courts on May 28, 2013 indicated that is approximately a ten (10) business day delay from the filing of a document with the e–Filing Authority and acceptance by his office. Litigants represented by attorneys should not be denied immediate judicial review in emergencies with electronic filing when immediate judicial review was available with paper filings.

2011–22–GEN. REPORTING OF PROCEEDINGS REQUIRED BY LAW

IN THE CIRCUIT COURT OF THE SEVENTEENTH JUDICIAL CIRCUIT IN AND FOR BROWARD COUNTY, FLORIDA

Order Number 2011–22–Gen

ADMINISTRATIVE ORDER AS TO REPORTING OF PROCEEDINGS REQUIRED BY LAW OR RULE OF COURT OR AT PUBLIC EXPENSE

(a) The 17th Judicial Circuit utilizes electronic and digital recording of proceedings as required by law or rule of court.

(b) The cost of providing services to users of the court system has increased since 2003 with public funds being spent for the utilization of electronic, or digital, or video recording or the transcription of same.

(c) In accordance with the authority granted to the chief judge pursuant to Florida Rules of Judicial Procedure 2.215 and 2.535, it is ordered:

(1) *Definitions.* The terms as used throughout this Administrative Order shall have the following meaning.

(A) "Electronic and digital recording" is the capture of proceedings either electronically, digitally, or by video.

(B) "Court Reporter" is an individual qualified to operate a stenographic machine to take notes of proceedings and thereafter produce a transcript. It shall also include an individual who listens to and produces a transcript of an electronic and digital recording of a proceeding.

(C) "Court reporting agency" is a business entity which provides court reporters through a contract with the circuit to make a verbatim record of proceedings and prepare transcripts of proceedings.

(D) "Digital Court Reporter" is an individual who operates electronic and digital recording equipment for proceedings.

(E) "Official court record" shall be either the electronic and digital recording or the stenographic notes of the proceeding prior to a transcript being typed of the proceedings. If a transcript of the electronic and digital recording or the stenographic notes is prepared upon filing with the Clerk of Court it shall be the official court record.

(F) "Proceeding" is all criminal proceedings, juvenile proceedings, and any other matter before a judge or general magistrate or hearing officer when a verbatim record is required by law or rule of court, but does not include any communications which are protected by the attorney client privilege, or work product privilege, or are otherwise not part of the public proceeding before the judge or general magistrate or hearing officer and are private in nature. If there are in camera or side bar matters heard by the presiding judge, those proceedings are part of the proceeding, but are exempt from public access, and shall only be available to the court, party to the action, and the attorney for the party as otherwise set forth herein. All proceedings shall be captured by electronic and digital recording unless otherwise exempted herein.

(G) "Transcript" is the typed verbatim record by a court reporter of the electronic and digital recording of a proceeding or the stenographic notes of a proceeding.

(H) "Verbatim record" includes all forms in which information of proceedings is received and stored.

(2) *Establishment of Court Reporting Services.*

(A) An office titled Court Reporting Services is established and will be under the auspices of the Trial Court Administrator. The purpose of Court Reporting Services is to provide electronic and digital recording of proceedings required by law or rule of court and to provide transcripts of said proceedings. There shall be a Director of Court Reporting Services.

(B) The Director shall direct and manage the affairs of all electronic and digital reporting and shall implement policies and procedures for the effective administration of the program.

(C) The Director shall report to the Trial Court Administrator or designee for day-to-day operations. The Chief Judge or designee shall establish qualifications for Court Reporting Services staff to insure qualified court reporters or digital court reporters with the ability to record proceedings, transcribe proceedings, and certify the correctness of the transcript.

(3) *Electronic and Digital Recording of Proceedings.*

(A) When proceedings are being recorded as the official court record, the digital court reporter monitoring the recording shall immediately notify a designated in-court official when the quality of the recording is doubtful. The proceedings shall be suspended until the equipment is operating properly.

(B) The digital court reporter shall maintain a detailed, accurate, legible record of all proceedings recorded on any media for electronic and digital recordings. All recording media shall be properly identified, together with the recording log, and will be stored for a period of time as prescribed by the Rules of Judicial Administration by Court Reporting Services.

(4) *Capital Cases.*

(A) When the State of Florida prosecutes a case seeking the death penalty, where available, the court reporter shall use "real-time" technology.

(B) Upon an appeal of the trial court capital case proceedings, and service of a designation to the court reporter, transcripts shall:

(i) be prepared as required by the Florida Rules of Appellate Procedure; and

(ii) be prepared as required by an Administrative Order or policy/procedure required by the appellate jurisdiction; and

(iii) be in consecutively numbered volumes not to exceed two hundred (200) pages per volume; and

(iv) have each page consecutively numbered; and

(v) have the first page of each volume with an index which contains the names of the witnesses, list of items offered into evidence, list of items entered into evidence, with the page numbers where each is located.

(C) Transcripts of capital cases where the death penalty is imposed are a priority and the court reporter shall use all available methods of production to expedite same for filing in the appellate proceedings.

(D) When transcripts of capital cases where the death penalty is imposed are ordered and due, the court reporter shall not appear at any proceeding until the transcript is prepared and delivered as required by law, court order, or rule of court.

(5) *Unified Family Court.*

(A) All proceedings before general magistrates and/or hearing officers shall be by electronic and digital recording even if a court reporter is retained by a party to the case. An attorney or a party may retain the services of a court reporter if he or she does not want the proceeding to be by electronic and digital recording.

(B) Proceedings before judges shall be by electronic and digital recording only as required by law or rule of court.

(6) *Transcription of Electronic and Digital Proceedings.*

(A) Court Reporting Services and court reporters shall prepare transcripts of proceedings to meet deadlines as established by law, court order, or rule of court.

(B) Any party having an interest in a court action may order a transcription of any electronic and digital recording on file, or request a copy of the original electronic and digital recording. Only Court Reporting Services may prepare the transcript as the official court record from an electronic and digital recording.

(C) If the proceeding is confidential and exempt from public access pursuant to law or rule of court and the party requesting the transcription is not an attorney, party of record, or court staff in the performance of his or her duties, the requesting party must secure an order granting the request for the transcription or copy of the proceeding from the presiding judge.

(D) Written requests for transcription or copy of any electronic and digital recording shall be sent to Court Reporting Services and shall designate with particularity that portion of the proceeding which is to be transcribed. The request must include:

(i) style of case; and

(ii) date of proceedings; and

(iii) name of presiding judge or general magistrate or hearing officer; and

(iv) location where recording occurred; and

(v) information with regard to the portion requested if not the entire proceeding.

(7) *Appellate Transcription of Electronic and Digital Proceedings.*

(A) Court Reporting Services is represented by Court Administration's Office of General Counsel when any pleadings or papers are filed with a court having appellate jurisdiction.

(B) As required by R. Regulating Fla. Bar 4–4.2, a copy of the designation served upon Court Reporting Services pursuant to Fla. R. App. P. 9.200(b) or any other paper filed with the appellate court, shall be served upon Court Administration's Office of General Counsel at Broward County Courthouse, Room 880A, 201 S.E. Sixth Street, Fort Lauderdale, Florida 33301.

(C) In the event a party serving a designation to Court Reporting Services does not receive an acknowledgement as contemplated by Fla. R. App. P. 9.200(b), the party shall contact Court Administration's Office of General Counsel to determine the status of the acknowledgment.

(8) *Transcription Costs for Electronic, Digital, or Video Proceedings by Court Reporting Services.*

(A) All privately ordered transcripts require an initial 50% deposit and the balance is due upon receipt. No transcript shall be released by Court Reporting Services until payment has been made in full.

(B) Payment for privately ordered transcripts shall be made payable to the State of Florida by attorney trust account check, money order, or official bank check.

(C) Rates for Court Reporting Services.

Delivery Time	Number	Cost per page
24 hours (overnight)	Original and two (2)	$ 7.50
	Each additional copy	$ 1.10
Three (3) business days	Original and two (2)	$ 6.50
	Each additional copy	$ 1.10
Six (6) business days	Original and two (2)	$ 5.50
	Each additional copy	$ 1.10
Ten (10) business days	Original and two (2)	$ 5.00
	Each additional copy	$ 1.10
Appeals	Original and two (2) and disks	$ 5.00
	Each additional copy	$ 1.10

The cost for a copy of compact disk, which is not transcribed, is $25.00.

(D) At the time of delivery of a transcript Court Reporting Services shall certify that it is a "true and correct stenographic record from the electronic and digital recording of the proceeding."

(E) If any dispute arises as to whether the transcript accurately reflects the electronic and digital recording, the attorneys and/or parties shall first attempt to resolve the matter with the Director of Court Reporting Services or designee. If the attorneys and/or parties are not able to resolve the matter with the Director of Court Reporting Services, then the matter shall be resolved by the presiding judge.

(9) *Court Reporter Qualifications.*

(A) A court reporter appearing for a proceeding in a circuit court must have the ability to provide a current stenographic dictionary in a digital format which sets forth his or her manner of writing verbatim records to every court reporting agency on whose behalf he or she appears.

(B) A court reporter appearing for a proceeding in a circuit court must have the ability to provide an ASCII disk of all transcribed proceedings.

(C) A court reporter must have the ability to produce a transcript as required by law and rule or court which is accurate.

(10) *Retention of Records.*

(A) All verbatim records shall be maintained for the period of time required by the Florida Rules of Judicial Administration in effect at the time the record was made. The court reporter, court reporting agency, and Court Reporting Services have the obligation to maintain the verbatim records.

(B) The Clerk of Court shall maintain all verbatim records in his custody and possession as required by the Florida Rules of Judicial Administration.

(C) A court reporting agency shall secure from every court reporter that appears on behalf of the court reporting agency at a proceeding all verbatim records and thereafter maintain custody and control of same.

(D) The court reporter at least yearly or upon other request of the court reporting agency who secured his or her services for a proceeding shall provide a current stenographic dictionary in a digital format which sets forth his or her manner of writing verbatim records.

(E) The court reporter shall provide to the court reporting agency on whose behalf he or she appeared, on a monthly basis, a translated disk of all circuit criminal and juvenile proceedings, along with an ASCII disk of all transcribed criminal and juvenile proceedings.

(11) *Contact Information for Court Reporters.*

(A) All court reporters, as an officer of the court, appearing in a Broward County or 17th Judicial Circuit court shall provide the following at the time of each appearance:

(i) his or her full name; and

(ii) the name of the court reporting agency contracting with the court reporter; and

(iii) his or her address at which pleadings or papers can be served; and

(iv) his or her telephone number at which he or she may be reached.

(B) The Clerk of Court shall place the contact information with regard to the court reporter in the court file.

(C) A court reporter shall have a continuing duty to provide a current address and telephone number to the court reporting agency on whose behalf he or she appeared to record the proceeding as long as he or she is required to maintain the verbatim record.

(12) In the event a court reporter or court reporting agency fails to provide a transcript, upon motion filed by any party, the presiding judge may issue an order for rule to show cause why the court reporter or court reporting agency shall not be held in contempt. Unless otherwise set forth in the order for rule to show cause the proceeding shall be a civil contempt hearing.

(13) Notices shall be posted in every courtroom, chambers, or hearing room where proceedings are recorded by electronic, or digital, or video equipment that any and all conversations may be recorded. If an attorney, litigant, or any other individual present at the hearing does not want his or her conversation recorded, he or she should exit the location of the hearing, or mute the microphone, or ask the presiding judge to make other arrangements to preclude the contents of the conversation being captured by electronic, digital, or video equipment.

(14) This Administrative Order shall not preclude the judge, attorneys of record, and parties from all consenting to the proceedings being "off the record."

(15) This Administrative Order vacates and supersedes Administrative Order 2008–16–Gen.

DONE AND ORDERED in chambers at Fort Lauderdale, Broward County, Florida on April 20, 2011.

Victor Tobin
Chief Judge

2011–15–GEN. COURT INTERPRETERS PROGRAM

IN THE CIRCUIT COURT OF THE SEVENTEENTH JUDICIAL CIRCUIT IN AND FOR BROWARD COUNTY, FLORIDA

Order Number 2011–15–Gen

ADMINISTRATIVE ORDER AS TO COURT INTERPRETERS PROGRAM

(a) Florida Rule of Judicial Administration 2.215(b)(3) states the chief judge shall "develop an administrative plan for the efficient and proper administration of all courts within that circuit."

(b) Florida statutes and rules of procedure establish the Courts duties and requirements for providing interpreters for court hearings and trials.

(c) In accordance with the authority vested in the chief judge by Florida Rule of Judicial Administration 2.215, it is ordered:

(1) The Trial Court Administrator shall operate a Court Interpreters Program and implement any and all procedures necessary to meet the requirements and duties established by law or rules of procedure for the provision of interpreters at court hearings and trials pursuant to Florida Statutes §§ 90.606. 90.6063 and Florida Rule of Judicial Administration 2.560.

(2) All foreign language interpreters shall provide services at the central courthouse unless otherwise authorized by the Chief Judge or Trial Court Administrator. If a foreign language interpreter is required for a court proceeding, which is not a trial or complex hearing, at a satellite courthouse the

translation shall be provided via the remote interpreter system. If the foreign language interpreter is required for a trial or complex hearing the case may be transferred to the central courthouse for further judicial action.

(3) Any interpreter who is a State Courts System employee or contractor with the Circuit shall not interpret any audio recording, video recording, digital document, or written evidence which a party is introducing into evidence or referring to at a trial or hearing. If an audio recording, video recording, digital document, or written evidence is sought to be introduced or referenced at a trial or hearing it is the responsibility of the offering party to have the audio recording, video recording, digital document, or written evidence translated into English at the offering party's expense and provide the transcript of the English translation to the opposing party a reasonable amount of time prior to the trial or hearing. The party offering the audio recording, video recording, digital document, or written evidence shall provide to the Court at the trial or hearing the transcript of the English translation. DONE AND ORDERED in chambers at Fort Lauderdale, Broward County, Florida on March 24, 2011.

Victor Tobin
Chief Judge

2010–81–GEN. PRO BONO COMMITTEE

IN THE CIRCUIT COURT OF THE SEVENTEENTH JUDICIAL CIRCUIT IN AND FOR BROWARD COUNTY, FLORIDA

Administrative Order 2010–81–Gen

ADMINISTRATIVE ORDER AS TO THE PRO BONO COMMITTEE FOR THE SEVENTEENTH JUDICIAL CIRCUIT

(a) Florida Rule of Judicial Administration 2.215(b)(3) states the chief judge shall "develop an administrative plan for the efficient and proper administration of all courts within that circuit."

(b) Rule Regulating The Florida Bar 4–6.5(c) requires a Pro Bono Committee for the Circuit.

(c) In accordance with the authority vested in the chief judge by Florida Rule of Judicial Administration 2.215 and Rule Regulating The Florida Bar 4–6.5(c), it is ordered:

(1) The Pro Bono Committee for the Seventeenth Judicial Circuit shall be comprised of the following members:

(A) The Chief Judge or designee;

(B) The President or designee of the Asian Pacific American Bar Association of South Florida;

(C) The President or designee of the South Florida Chapter of the Association of Corporate Counsel;

(D) The President or designee of the Bankruptcy Bar Association of Southern District of Florida;

(E) The President or designee of the Association of South Florida Mediators and Arbitrators;

(F) The President or designee of the B'nai B'rith Justice Unit No. 5207;

(G) The President or designee of the Broward Association of CDL;

(H) The President or designee of the Broward Christian Legal Society;

(I) The President or designee of the Broward County Bar Association;

(J) The President or designee of the Broward County Hispanic Bar Association;

(K) The President or designee of the Broward County Christian Lawyers Association;

(L) The President or designee of the Broward County Justice Association;

(M) The President or designee of the Broward Chapter of the Florida Association for Women Lawyers;

(N) The President or designee of the Caribbean Bar Association;

(O) A representative of Coast to Coast Legal Aid of South Florida, Inc.;

(P) A representative of FIU College of Law Educational Advocacy Clinic;

(Q) The President or designee of the Cuban American Bar Association;

(R) A representative of The Florida Bar Board of Governors from the Seventeenth Judicial Circuit;

(S) A representative of Florida Immigrant Advocacy Center;

(T) A representative of Florida Institutional Legal Services, Inc.;

(U) A representative of Florida Justice Institute;

(V) The President or designee of the Florida Muslim Bar Association;

(W) The President or designee of the Gay and Lesbian Lawyers Association of South Florida;

(X) The President or designee of the Haitian Lawyers Association, Inc.;

(Y) The President or designee of the Intellectual Property Law Association of South Florida;

(Z) A representative of Legal Aid Service of Broward County, Inc.;

(AA) The President or designee of the Nova University Chapter of the Florida Association for Women Lawyers;

(BB) The President or designee of the Broward County Chapter of the Federal Bar Association;

(CC) The President or designee of the Puerto Rican Bar Association;

(DD) The President or designee of the Fort Lauderdale Chapter of FLABOTA;

(EE) The President or designee of the North Broward Bar Association;

(FF) The President or designee of the South Broward Bar Association;

(GG) The President or designee of the Stephen R. Booher American Inn of Court;

(HH) The President or designee of the T.J. Reddick Bar Association;

(II) The Director or designee of the Nova Southeastern University Public Interest Law Center;

(JJ) A representative of Broward Lawyers Care;

(KK) A client of pro bono services and resident of Broward County as nominated and elected by the Seventeenth Judicial Circuit's Pro Bono Committee; and

(LL) A public member who is a resident of Broward County as nominated and elected by the Seventeenth Judicial Circuit's Pro Bono Committee.

(2) The members of the Seventeenth Judicial Circuit's Pro Bono Committee were determined from the list of voluntary bar associations, pro bono providers, and legal assistance providers with a presence or membership in Broward County as available from The Florida Bar web page. If a member of the Pro Bono Committee becomes aware of another voluntary bar association, pro bono provider, or legal assistance provider with a presence or membership in Broward County that should have a representative on the Seventeenth Judicial Circuit's Pro Bono Committee he or she shall provide the information to the Chief Judge.

(3) The Chief Judge of the Seventeenth Judicial Circuit or designee shall convene the first meeting of 2010 for the Pro Bono Committee. The Committee shall thereafter appoint its Chair.

(4) Broward Lawyers Care is designated to provide coordination and administrative support for the Seventeenth Judicial Circuit's Pro Bono Committee.

(5) Broward Lawyers Care shall assist the Seventeenth Judicial Circuit's Pro Bono Committee with meeting the requirements of Rule Regulating The Florida Bar 4–6.5(c)(2).

(6) Governance and terms of service shall be determined by the Seventeenth Judicial Circuit's Pro Bono Committee.

(7) The Seventeenth Judicial Circuit's Pro Bono Committee shall meet at least semi-annually or as determined by the Chair at the Broward County Courthouse, 201 S.E. Sixth Street, Fort Lauderdale, Florida 33301 or elsewhere as agreed by the Committee. Those members in attendance at a meeting shall constitute a quorum to conduct the business of the Seventeenth Judicial Circuit's Pro Bono Committee.

(8) This Administrative Order vacates and supersedes Administrative Orders I–98–K–2 and 2010–34–Gen.

DONE AND ORDERED at Fort Lauderdale, Broward County, Florida on November 17, 2010.

Victor Tobin
Chief Judge

Probate Orders

2018–79–PRC. FINGERPRINTING OF GUARDIANS FOR CRIMINAL INVESTIGATIONS

IN THE CIRCUIT COURT OF THE SEVENTEENTH JUDICIAL CIRCUIT IN AND FOR BROWARD COUNTY, FLORIDA

Administrative Order 2018–79–PRC

ADMINISTRATIVE ORDER REQUIRING FINGERPRINTING OF GUARDIANS FOR CRIMINAL INVESTIGATIONS

(a) Pursuant to Article V, section 2(d) of the Florida Constitution, and section 43.26, Florida Statutes, the chief judge of each judicial circuit is charged with the authority and the power to do everything necessary to promote the prompt and efficient administration of justice.

(b) Florida Rule of Judicial Administration 2.215(b)(3) states the Chief Judge "shall, considering available resources, ensure the efficient and proper administration of all courts within [this] circuit."

(c) Section 744.3135, Florida Statutes, authorizes credit and criminal investigations for nonprofessional and professional guardians, which includes the use of fingerprints.

(d) The Federal Bureau of Investigation no longer processes hard copy applicant fingerprint cards and, as a result, the Florida Department of Law Enforcement no longer accepts such cards.

(e) In accordance with the authority vested in the chief judge pursuant to Article V, section 2(d) of the Florida Constitution, section 43.26, Florida Statutes, and Florida Rule of Judicial Administration 2.215, it is hereby **ORDERED**:

(1) All non-professional proposed guardians shall submit fingerprints electronically at the time of his or her initial application to be appointed guardian. All other documents required by the court to complete a credit and criminal background investigation shall be submitted directly to the Clerk of the Court.

(2) Professional guardians, including all employees of professional guardians, are required to undergo criminal history record checks as set forth in section 744.3135, Florida Statutes. Professional guardians, including all employees of professional guardians, shall submit fingerprints electronically and are only required to resubmit fingerprints for a criminal history record check to be performed pursuant to section 744.3135, Florida Statutes, if the fingerprints are not retained by the Florida Department of Law Enforcement. It is the responsibility of the professional guardian and their respective employees to determine whether fingerprints need to be resubmitted in order to comply with the requirements of section 744.3135, Florida Statutes. All other documents required by the Court to complete the credit and criminal investigations pursuant to section 744.3135, Florida Statutes, must be submitted no later than January 15th every year.

(3) This Administrative Order supersedes and vacates Administrative Order 2012–50–PRC.

DONE AND ORDERED in Chambers, Fort Lauderdale, Broward County, Florida, this 6th day of September, 2018.

Jack Tuter
Chief Judge

2018–58–PRC. PETITIONS FOR INJUNCTION FOR PROTECTION AGAINST EXPLOITATION OF A VULNERABLE ADULT

IN THE CIRCUIT COURT OF THE SEVENTEENTH JUDICIAL CIRCUIT IN AND FOR BROWARD COUNTY, FLORIDA

Administrative Order 2018–58–PRC

ADMINISTRATIVE ORDER GOVERNING PETITIONS FOR INJUNCTION FOR PROTECTION AGAINST EXPLOITATION OF A VULNERABLE ADULT

(a) Pursuant to Article V, section 2(d) of the Florida Constitution, and section 43.26, Florida Statutes, the chief judge of each judicial circuit is charged with the authority and the power to do everything necessary to promote the prompt and efficient administration of justice.

(b) Florida Rule of Judicial Administration 2.215(b)(3) states the chief judge "shall, considering available resources, ensure the efficient and proper administration of all courts within [this] circuit."

(c) The Florida Legislature enacted section 825.1036, Florida Statutes, which is effective July 1, 2018 and which creates a cause of action for an injunction for protection against the exploitation of a vulnerable adult.

(d) In accordance with the authority vested in the chief judge by Article V, section 2(d) of the Florida Constitution, section 43.26, Florida Statutes, and Florida Rule of Judicial Administration 2.215, it is hereby **ORDERED**:

(1) A petition for injunction against exploitation of a vulnerable adult may be filed by:

a. A vulnerable adult in imminent danger of being exploited;

b. The guardian of a vulnerable adult in imminent danger of being exploited;

c. A person or organization acting on behalf of the vulnerable adult with the consent of the vulnerable adult or his or her guardian; or

d. A person who simultaneously files a petition for determination of incapacity and appointment of an emergency temporary guardian with respect to the vulnerable adult.

A petition for injunction against exploitation of a vulnerable adult must be sworn, and allege the existence of exploitation, or the imminent exploitation, of the vulnerable adult, and must include the specific facts and circumstances for which relief is sought. The form petition attached hereto as Attachment "A" is approved for use in the Seventeenth Judicial Circuit. The petitioning party shall also submit as an exhibit to the petition information on the respondent's physical description and location, and the petitioner may utilize the form attached hereto as Attachment "B."

(2) All petitions for injunction against exploitation of a vulnerable adult shall be assigned by the Clerk of the Court to a probate division. If there is a proceeding pertaining to the vulnerable adult under Chapter 744, Florida Statutes pending at the time of filing, the petition <u>**must**</u> be filed in that proceeding.

(3) When a petition for an injunction against exploitation of a vulnerable adult is filed, the Clerk of the Court shall notify the assigned division judge or the judge's designee of the filing no later than one (1) business day after the date of filing. If filed through the e-portal, the filing should be designated by the filing party as an "emergency," so that the Clerk and judge may be aware of the need for review and entry of a written order.

(4) Upon notification of the filing, the assigned division judge shall immediately review the petition and shall enter either: (1) a temporary ex parte injunction for protection against exploitation of a vulnerable adult pending a full hearing; or (2) a written order denying the petition on an ex parte basis, with the specific legal grounds stated therein, and setting a full hearing. When reviewing an ex parte petition, the court may consider all relevant factors, including those expressly set forth in section 825.1035(6), Florida Statutes. In all instances in which a full hearing is required under section 825.1035, Florida Statutes, the presiding judge shall strive to schedule such hearing on the earliest possible date, but in no event more than fifteen (15) days from the date the petition is filed. An ex parte temporary injunction entered pursuant to section 825.1035, Florida Statutes, is valid for a fixed period not to exceed fifteen (15) days.

(5) The Clerk of the Court shall comply with the obligations set forth section 825.1035(4), Florida Statutes, including providing simplified petition forms and instructions for completion thereof, assisting petitioners in filing petitions pursuant to section 825.1035, Florida Statutes, and providing a copies of all petitions filed and orders entered pursuant to section 825.1035, Florida Statutes to the adult protective services program.

(6) The Clerk of the Court shall furnish a copy of the petition, financial affidavit, notice of hearing, and any temporary injunction to the Sheriff of the county in which the respondent resides or can be found, who shall serve it upon the respondent as soon thereafter as possible on any day of the week and at any time of the day or night. The Clerk of the Court shall also furnish to the Sheriff such information on the respondent's physical description and location as is required by the Florida Department of Law Enforcement.

(7) If the vulnerable adult is not the petitioner, the Clerk of the Court shall furnish a copy of the petition, financial affidavit, notice of hearing, and any temporary injunction to the Sheriff of the county in which the vulnerable adult resides or can be found, who shall serve it upon the vulnerable adult as soon thereafter as possible on any day of the week and at any time of the day or night. The Clerk of the Court shall also furnish to the Sheriff such information on the respondent's physical description and location as is required by the Florida Department of Law Enforcement and as provided by the petitioner.

(8) At the request of the Sheriff, the Clerk of the Court may transmit an injunction that has been certified by the Clerk of the Court via facsimile or other electronic means as contemplated and permitted by the Florida Rules of Judicial Administration, which electronic copy may be served in the same manner as a certified copy.

(9) Within twenty-four (24) hours after the court issues an injunction pursuant to section 825.1035, Florida Statutes, the Clerk of the Court must forward a certified copy of the order

to the Sheriff with jurisdiction over the residence of the petitioner for service in accordance with section 825.1035, Florida Statutes.

(10) Within twenty-four (24) hours after service of an injunction issued under section 825.1035, Florida Statutes, the law enforcement officer who served the injunction must forward the written proof of service to the sheriff with jurisdiction over the residence of the petitioner.

(11) Within twenty-four (24) hours of receiving a certified copy of an injunction issued under section 825.1035, Florida Statutes, the Sheriff must make information related to the injunction available statewide by electronically transmitting such information to the Florida Department of Law Enforcement.

(12) Within twenty-four (24) hours after the Sheriff or other law enforcement officer has made service upon the respondent and the Sheriff has been so notified, the Sheriff must make information relating to the service available to other law enforcement agencies by electronically transmitting such information to the Florida Department of Law Enforcement.

(13) Within twenty-four (24) hours of the termination, expiration, or court order rendering an injunction issued under section 825.1035, Florida Statutes no longer effective, the Clerk of the Court must notify the Sheriff receiving original notification of the injunction, and the Sheriff, within twenty-four (24) hours of receiving such notification from the Clerk of the Court, shall notify the Florida Department of Law Enforcement of such court action.

(14) A permanent injunction issued pursuant to section 825.1035, Florida Statutes may be modified or dissolved by the court upon proper application by the petitioner, respondent, or vulnerable adult. The court shall promptly hear a motion to modify or dissolve an injunction issued under section 825.1035, Florida Statutes.

DONE AND ORDERED in Chambers, Fort Lauderdale, Broward County, Florida, this 3rd day of July, 2018.

Jack Tuter
Chief Judge

Attachment "A"

IN THE CIRCUIT COURT OF THE SEVENTEENTH JUDICIAL CIRCUIT,
IN AND FOR BROWARD COUNTY, FLORIDA

______________________,

Petitioner,

v. Case No.: __________

______________________,

Respondent,

______________________/

PETITION FOR INJUNCTION FOR PROTECTION AGAINST EXPLOITATION OF A VULNERABLE ADULT

Before me, the undersigned authority, personally appeared Petitioner __________ who has been sworn and says that the following statements are true:

1. The vulnerable adult resides at: ______________________
____
2. The respondent resides at: ______________________
____
3. The respondent's last known place of employment is: ___
____
4. The physical description of the respondent is:
Race: ______________________
Sex: ______________________
Date of Birth: ______________________
Height: ______________________
Weight: ______________________
Eye Color: ______________________
Hair Color: ______________________
Distinguishing marks or scars: ______________________
5. Aliases of the respondent are: ______________________
6. The respondent is associated with the vulnerable adult as follows: ______________________
____
7. The following describes (1) any other cause of action currently pending between the petitioner and the respondent, any proceeding under chapter 744 concerning the vulnerable adult, and any previous or pending attempts by the petitioner to obtain an injunction for protection against exploitation of the vulnerable adult in this or any other circuit, (2) related case numbers, if available, and (3) the results of any such attempts: ______________________
____
____
____
8. The following describe the petitioner's knowledge of any reports made to (1) a government agency, including, but not limited to, the Department of Elderly Affairs, the Department of Children and Families, and the adult protective services program relating to the abuse, neglect, or exploitation of the vulnerable adult, (2) any investigations performed by a government agency relating to abuse, neglect, or exploitation of the vulnerable adult, and (3) the results of any such reports or investigations: ______________________
____
____
____
9. The petitioner knows the vulnerable adult is either a victim of exploitation or the petitioner has reasonable cause to believe the vulnerable adult is, or is in imminent danger of becoming, a victim of exploitation because the respondent has caused the following incidents or caused the following threats of exploitation: ______________________
____
____
____
____
____
10. The following describes (1) the petitioner's knowledge of the vulnerable adult's dependence on the respondent for care,

(2) alternative provisions for the vulnerable adult's care in the absence of the respondent, if necessary, (3) available resources the vulnerable adult has in order to access such alternative provisions, and (4) the vulnerable adult's willingness to use such alternative provisions: ____________

____

____

____

11. The petitioner knows the vulnerable adult maintains assets, accounts, or lines of credit at the following financial institutions (provide name, address, and account number of each):

Name	Address	Account Number

12. The petitioner believes that the vulnerable adult's assets to be frozen are (check one):

a. Worth less than $1500 ____________

b. Worth between $1500 and $5000 ____________

c. Worth more than $5000 ____________

13. The petitioner genuinely fears imminent exploitation of the vulnerable adult by the respondent.

14. The petitioner seeks an injunction for the protection of the vulnerable adult, including (mark appropriate section or sections):

a. ☐ Prohibiting the respondent from having any direct or indirect contact with the vulnerable adult

b. ☐ Immediately restraining the respondent from committing any acts of exploitation against the vulnerable adult

c. ☐ Freezing the assets of the vulnerable adult held at (name and address of depository or financial institution) even if titled jointly with the respondent, or in the respondent's name only, in the court's discretion ____________

____

____

____

____

d. ☐ Freezing the credit lines of the vulnerable adult at (name and address of financial institution) even if jointly with the respondent, in the court's discretion ____________

____

____

____

e. ☐ Providing any terms the court deems necessary for the protection of the vulnerable adult or his or her assets, including any injunctions or directives to law enforcement agencies.

15. If the court enters an injunction freezing assets and credit lines, the petitioner believes that the critical expenses of the vulnerable adult will be paid for or provided by the following persons or entities: ____________

____

____

____

____

____

16. The petitioner requests that the following expenses be paid notwithstanding the freeze (for each expense, list the name of the payee, address, account number if known, amount to be paid, and a brief explanation of why payment is critical):

____

____

____

____

____

____

I ACKNOWLEDGE THAT PURSUANT TO SECTION 415.1034, FLORIDA STATUTES, ANY PERSON WHO KNOWS, OR HAS REASONABLE CAUSE TO SUSPECT, THAT A VULNERABLE ADULT HAS BEEN OR IS BEING ABUSED, NEGLECTED, OR EXPLOITED HAS A DUTY TO IMMEDIATELY REPORT SUCH KNOWLEDGE OR SUSPICION TO THE CENTRAL ABUSE HOTLINE. I HAVE REPORTED THE ALLEGATIONS IN THIS PETITION TO THE CENTRAL ABUSE HOTLINE.

I HAVE READ EACH STATEMENT MADE IN THIS PETITION AND EACH SUCH STATEMENT IS TRUE AND CORRECT. I UNDERSTAND THAT THE STATEMENTS MADE IN THIS PETITION ARE BEING MADE UNDER PENALTY OF PERJURY PUNISHABLE AS PROVIDED IN SECTION 837.02, FLORIDA STATUTES.

Dated: ____________ ____________

Signature of Party

Printed Name: ____________

Address: ____________

City, State, Zip: ____________

Telephone Number: ____________

Fax Number: ____________

Designated E-mail Address(es): ____________

STATE OF FLORIDA
COUNTY OF ____________

Sworn to or affirmed and signed before me on ____________, 20 ___, by ____________

____

NOTARY PUBLIC or DEPUTY CLERK

Printed Name: ____________

☐ Personally known
☐ Produced identification: ____________

ATTACHMENT "B"

RESPONDENT DESCRIPTION INFORMATION

ATTENTION LAW ENFORCEMENT OFFICERS, PLEASE REMOVE THIS SHEET PRIOR TO SERVICE. PLEASE DO NOT GIVE THIS SHEET TO THE RESPONDENT.

SECTION I: RESPONDENT'S NAME

Respondent's Full Name: ______________________

Nickname/Alias: ______________________

SECTION II: PHYSICAL DESCRIPTION:

Race: ________ Sex: ________ Date of Birth: ________ Age: ______________________

Height: ________ Weight: ________ Hair Color: ________ Eye Color: ______________________

Other Marks/Scars/Tattoos: ______________________

SECTION III: RESPONDENTS CURRENT ADDRESS

Address: ________ City: ________ State: ________ Zip: ______________________

Phone No: ______________________

Work Address: ________ City: ________ State: ________ Zip: ______________________

Hangouts: ______________________

SECTION IV: RESPONDENT'S CLOSE RELATIVES

Name: ________ Relationship: ______________________

Address: ________ City: ________ State: ________ Zip: ______________________

Phone No: ______________________

SECTION V: LICENSE/VEHICLE INFORMATION DRIVER LICENSE

State: ________ Number: ________

SECTION VI: LETHALITY ASSESSMENT (Indicate yes, no, or unknown. If yes, add details.)

Does Respondent have any weapons? ________

Does Respondent have a drug problem? ________

Does Respondent have an alcohol problem? ________

Does Respondent have children in his/her care? ________

Is the Respondent wanted by police? ________

Does Respondent have a criminal record? ________

Is the Respondent expecting this Order? ________

PLEASE ATTACH A PHOTOGRAPH OF RESPONDENT IF YOU HAVE ONE

2018–33–PRC. PILOT MEDIATION PROGRAM FOR INCAPACITY AND GUARDIANSHIP PROCEEDINGS

IN THE CIRCUIT COURT OF THE SEVENTEENTH JUDICIAL CIRCUIT IN AND FOR BROWARD COUNTY, FLORIDA

Administrative Order No. 2018–33–PRC

ADMINISTRATIVE ORDER EXTENDING PILOT MEDIATION PROGRAM FOR INCAPACITY AND GUARDIANSHIP PROCEEDINGS

(a) Pursuant to Article V, section 2(d) of the Florida Constitution, and section 43.26, Florida Statutes, the Chief Judge of each judicial circuit is charged with the authority and the power to do everything necessary to promote the prompt and efficient administration of justice.

(b) Florida Rule of Judicial Administration 2.215(b)(3) states the chief judge "shall, considering available resources, ensure the efficient and proper administration of all courts within [this] circuit."

(c) Pursuant to Administrative Order 2016–54–PRC, a pilot mediation program for incapacity and guardianship proceedings was established for the period of time December 1, 2017 to December 31, 2017 to determine if the legal fees and costs for such proceedings could be reduced by use of this alternate dispute resolution as well as determine if judicial efficiency is improved.

(d) In accordance with the authority vested in the chief judge by Florida Rule of Judicial Administration 2.215, it is hereby **ORDERED**:

(1) The pilot mediation program established pursuant to Administrative Order 2016–54–PRC for incapacity and guardianship proceedings governed by Chapter 744, Florida Statutes, is extended for the period of time January 1, 2018 to December 31, 2019. This does not include minor guardianships, VA guardianships, or guardianships initiated from Chapter 415 proceedings. Chapter 44, Florida Statutes, and Florida Rule of Civil Procedure 1.720 shall govern the program, except as modified by the order of referral to address the specific time restraints associated with incapacity and guardianship proceedings.

(2) The petitioner or interested persons may request the incapacity or guardianship proceedings be referred to mediation. In appropriate cases the General Magistrate will also be authorized to suggest to the petitioner and interested persons that they consider mediation. The mediator must be Supreme Court certified as a family or civil mediator with a primary office located in Broward County, Florida. An Order of Referral to Mediation shall be entered only if the petitioner and respondent agree.

(3) If the petitioner or respondent determine that mediation is appropriate for a case a motion shall be filed with the court. A motion for mediation shall be set before the General Magistrate assigned to the case for hearing. This Administrative Order shall be an order of referral to the General Magistrate as required by Florida Probate Rule 5.095, if the petitioner and respondent consent. If there is no consent by petitioner or respondent or if an interested person objects, the motion for mediation shall be set for hearing before the assigned judge.

(4) The Court will select a mediator from a list it maintains. The Administrative Judge for the Probate Division shall determine the mediators on the list, and the mediators shall be selected by strict rotation.

(5) The petitioner shall provide a copy of the examining committee reports to the appointed mediator.

(6) The examining committee reports shall not be deemed stale during the period from the entry of the order of referral to mediation to an incapacity hearing if the hearing is not held as required by Chapter 744, Florida Statutes. If the petitioner, respondent, or interested person thinks there is a change in circumstances from the initial evaluations and the date of any incapacity hearing then a motion shall be filed with the court requesting re-evaluations of the respondent.

(7) The election to mediate will toll all time requirements imposed by Chapter 744, Florida Statutes, pertaining to incapacity and/or guardianship proceedings for adults.

(8) The order of referral attached hereto as Attachment "A" shall be used during the pilot mediation program.

(9) This Administrative Order vacates Administrative Order 2016–54–PRC.

DONE AND ORDERED in Chambers, Fort Lauderdale, Broward County, Florida on this 26th day of April, 2018, *nunc pro tunc* to January 1, 2018.

Jack Tuter
Chief Judge

Attachment "A"
IN THE CIRCUIT COURT OF THE SEVENTEENTH JUDICIAL CIRCUIT IN AND FOR BROWARD COUNTY, FLORIDA

Case Number:
Division:

IN RE:

ORDER REFERRING CASE TO MEDIATION

THE COURT hereby refers the above-captioned matter to mediation as authorized by Chapter 44, Florida Statutes, the Florida Rules of Civil Procedure, and as modified herein. It is hereby ORDERED as follows:

1. The court appoints as mediator:

Name ____________________
Address ____________________
Telephone Number ____________________

2. If the mediator appointed by the court cannot serve, the court shall be notified so that a substitute mediator can be appointed.

3. The petitioner shall provide the examining committee reports to the mediator at least five (5) business days prior to the mediation session.

4. The mediator shall be entitled to compensation at the rate of $350.00 per hour. The respondent shall have no obligation to pay mediation fees unless ordered by the court after the mediation session. If the petitioner or an interested person objects to the mediator's fee, an objection shall be filed and set for hearing prior to the mediation session. If the petitioner or interested persons do not object to the mediator's fees, the petitioner or interested persons who have filed competing petitions and attend the mediation session shall pay the total fee at the close of the mediation, unless otherwise agreed to by the petitioner and interested persons at the mediation session, or ordered by the court. The mediator shall be entitled to an initial fee of $350.00 to be paid by petitioner at least five (5) business days prior to the mediation session. The payment of the initial fee shall be credited against the total mediator fees for the session. If the petitioner or interested persons at the mediation session do not pay the balance of the mediator's fees and the mediator is required to institute collection proceedings, the mediator shall be entitled to fees of $350.00 per hour for enforcement.

5. The first mediation conference shall be held in Broward County, Florida within twenty (20) days from the entry of this Order.

6. Petitioner's counsel is responsible for coordinating the date, time, and place of the mediation conference within five (5) days of this Order. Petitioner's counsel shall provide written notice to the respondent and interested persons of the date, time, and place of the mediation conference. Petitioner's counsel is responsible for providing a copy of this Order to the mediator.

7. The petitioner, respondent, guardian, and counsel for petitioner, respondent, and guardian must attend mediation in person. Interested persons shall attend if he or she will contest any mediated agreement. The provisions of Florida Rule of Civil Procedure 1.720(c) do not apply to incapacity or guardianship proceeding mediation.

8. The court may impose sanctions for failure to appear at a duly noticed mediation conference as authorized by the Florida Rules of Civil Procedure.

9. The Mediation Confidentiality and Privilege Act govern the conference pursuant to this Order.

10. Mediations as ordered for referral herein are governed by the Florida Rules of Civil Procedure and Chapter 44, Florida Statutes, as now in effect or as may be amended from time to time.

DONE AND ORDERED in Chambers, Fort Lauderdale, Broward County, Florida on __________, 20 ______.

____
Circuit Judge

Copies furnished:
Counsel of Record
Petitioner
Respondent
Interested Persons

If you are a person with a disability who needs any accommodation in order to participate in this proceeding, you are entitled, at no cost to you, to the provision of certain assistance. Please contact ________ at least 7 days before the mediation conference or immediately upon receiving notification of the date for mediation if the time before the scheduled conference is less than 7 days; if you are hearing or voice impaired, call 711.

2017–043–PRC. ADMINISTRATIVE ORDER REGARDING DELINQUENT AND NON–COMPLIANT GUARDIANSHIP REPORTS/DELINQUENT EDUCATIONAL CERTIFICATES/UNPAID AUDIT FEES

IN THE CIRCUIT COURT OF THE SEVENTEENTH JUDICIAL CIRCUIT IN AND FOR BROWARD COUNTY, FLORIDA

Administrative Order No. 2017–43–PRC

ADMINISTRATIVE ORDER REGARDING DELINQUENT AND NON–COMPLIANT GUARDIANSHIP REPORTS/DELINQUENT EDUCATIONAL CERTIFICATES/UNPAID AUDIT FEES

(a) Florida Rule of Judicial Administration 2.215(b)(3) states the chief judge shall "develop an administrative plan" and "shall, considering available resources, ensure the efficient and proper administration of all courts within [this] circuit."

(b) The preparation of report and recommendations by the General Magistrates when an Order to Show Cause is issued for failure to file timely as provided by applicable Florida Statutes (Chapter 744) and Florida rules of court, is an inefficient use of judicial resources as many of the guardianship reports and educational certificates are filed before the hearing date and time. The time used by the General Magistrates to prepare the report and recommendations are better utilized for other matters referred for hearing.

(c) In accordance with the authority vested in the chief judge by Florida Rule of Judicial Administration 2.215, it is hereby **ORDERED**:

(1) If the delinquent report, delinquent educational certificate or amended report is filed with the Efiling Authority Portal prior to the commencement of the hearing on the Order to Show Cause, and "Odyssey" reflects that the filing of said document has been accepted and not rejected by the Clerk of the Courts:

a) The guardian attorney and guardian/guardian advocate do not need to appear at the date and time stated in the Order to Show Cause;

b) The Order to Show Cause shall be automatically dismissed without the necessity for a Report and Recommendation by the General Magistrate or an Order Approving the Report and Recommendation.

(2) If the delinquent report, or amended report, as filed, is audited and is found to be "non-compliant" by the Clerk of the Courts, a subsequent Order to Show Cause may be issued requiring the mandatory appearance of the guardian attorney and guardian/guardian advocate.

(3) If the Court determines that the above referenced self-executing provision in paragraph (1) of this Order appears to be intentionally misused by the guardian/guardian advocate and/or the guardian attorney, the Court may enter an Order to Show Cause requiring a mandatory appearance of the guardian attorney and guardian/guardian advocate that shall not be automatically dismissed by way of the same self-executing provision in paragraph (1) of this Order.

(4) The failure to pay the required audit fee(s) will also result in the Court entering an Order to Show Cause requiring a mandatory appearance of the guardian attorney and guardian/guardian advocate.

DONE AND ORDERED in Chambers at Fort Lauderdale, Broward County, Florida on this 14th day of August, 2017.

Jack Tuter, Chief Judge

2016–33–PRC. ADMINISTRATIVE ORDER AS TO BAKER ACT PROCEDURES

IN THE CIRCUIT COURT OF THE SEVENTEENTH JUDICIAL CIRCUIT IN AND FOR BROWARD COUNTY, FLORIDA

Order Number 2016–33–PRC

ADMINISTRATIVE ORDER AS TO BAKER ACT PROCEDURES

(a) Florida Rule of Judicial Administration 2.215(b)(3) states the chief judge shall "develop an administrative plan for the efficient and proper administration of all courts within that circuit."

(b) Chapter 394, Part I, Florida Statutes, commonly referred to as The Baker Act authorizes judges to enter ex parte orders for involuntary examination. The judges seek the least restrictive manner to link individuals with community mental health services to determine if an individual requires transfer for an involuntary examination or if community mental health services are available.

(c) In accordance with the authority vested in the chief judge by Florida Rule of Judicial Administration 2.215, it is ordered:

(1) Upon the filing of a Petition and Affidavit Seeking Ex Parte Order Requiring Involuntary Examination, the Clerk of Court shall forward the court records to the assigned judge.

(2) The judge shall determine if the allegations are or are not sufficient for further assessment of the respondent.

(3) If the allegations are insufficient for an involuntary examination it shall be denied.

(4) If the judge determines the allegations may be sufficient for an involuntary examination it shall be granted and require Henderson Behavioral Health to perform an outpatient evaluation to determine if the respondent meets The Barker Act criteria for an involuntary examination or if community mental health services are a least restrictive means to meet the respondent's needs.

(5) The Petition and order granting shall be forwarded by the Clerk of Court to Henderson Behavioral Health by secure email. The Clerk of Court shall call Henderson Behavioral Health to inform it that an order was sent by email.

(6) Upon receipt of the order, the Mobile Crisis Response Team at Henderson Behavioral Health shall review the court records and thereafter assess the respondent. If the clinician is unable to conduct an evaluation to determine if the respondent meets the criteria for an involuntary examination he or she shall be transported to the nearest receiving facility for continuation of said involuntary examination. The respondent shall be transported by the Broward Sheriff or any Deputy Broward Sheriff or any other authorized law enforcement officer to the nearest receiving facility.

(7) Upon receipt of the order, the Mobile Crisis Response Team at Henderson Behavioral Health shall review the court records and thereafter assess the respondent. If the clinician conducts the evaluation and determines the respondent meets the criteria for an involuntary examination and there are no community mental health services which can meet his or her needs, the respondent shall be transported to the nearest receiving facility. The respondent shall be transported by the Broward Sheriff or any Deputy Broward Sheriff or any other authorized law enforcement officer to the nearest receiving facility.

(8) Upon receipt of the order, the Mobile Crisis Response Team at Henderson Behavioral Health shall review the court records and thereafter assess the respondent. If the clinician conducts the evaluation and determines the respondent does not meet the criteria for an involuntary examination and there are community mental health services which can meet his or her needs, the respondent shall be referred to the community resources.

(9) Henderson Behavioral Health shall provide monthly statistics to the Probate Division Administrative Judge with the number of respondents who met criteria for transport to the nearest receiving facility and the number of respondents who did not meet criteria.

(10) This Administrative Order vacates and supersedes Administrative Order I–98–A18.

DONE AND ORDERED in chambers at Fort Lauderdale, Broward County, Florida on June 24, 2016.

/s/ Peter M. Weinstein

Peter M. Weinstein, Chief Judge

2016–24–PRC. ADMINISTRATIVE ORDER ESTABLISHING EMERGENCY TEMPORARY GUARDIANSHIP PROCEDURES

IN THE CIRCUIT COURT OF THE SEVENTEENTH JUDICIAL CIRCUIT IN AND FOR BROWARD COUNTY, FLORIDA

Order Number 2016–24–PRC

ADMINISTRATIVE ORDER ESTABISHING[1] EMERGENCY TEMPORARY GUARDIANSHIP PROCEDURES

(a) Florida Rule of Judicial Administration 2.215(b)(3) states the chief judge shall "develop an administrative plan for the efficient and proper administration of all courts within [the Seventeenth] circuit."

(b) In accordance with the authority vested in the chief judge by Florida Rule of Judicial Administration 2.215, it is ordered:

(1) Petitions for Appointment of an Emergency Temporary Guardian filed pursuant to section 744.3031, Florida Statutes, are hereby referred to the general magistrates for the Probate Division pursuant to Florida Probate Rule 5.095. All Petitions for Appointment of an Emergency Temporary Guardian and all other required documents shall be filed with the Clerk of Court at least 24 hours before the hearing on the petition is scheduled to commence. Notice of the Petition for Appointment of an Emergency Temporary Guardian and Notice of Hearing on the Petition must be served on the alleged incapacitated person and on his/her attorney at least 24 hours before the hearing, unless the petitioner demonstrates that substantial harm to the alleged incapacitated person would occur if the 24–hour notice were given.

(2) Any interested person may object to the referral of the Petition for Appointment of an Emergency Temporary Guardian at the time of the hearing before the general magistrate. If an objection is raised, the general magistrate shall notify the assigned judge's office of the objection and secure a time from the assigned judge to hear the matter the same day. If the assigned judge is absent from the courthouse, the general magistrate shall contact the Administrative Judge to secure a hearing time for the same day. If the Administrative Judge is also absent from the courthouse, the general magistrate shall contact the Civil Duty Judge to hear the matter the same day.

(3) Each general magistrate for the Probate Division shall set aside one (1) hour per week to hear Petitions for Appointment of an Emergency Temporary Guardian. Each general magistrate shall post the day and time of his/her hearings for the appointment of an emergency temporary guardian and shall provide a copy to the Clerk of Court.

(4) If the need arises for the appointment of an emergency temporary guardian, other than at the times previously designated by the general magistrates, the petitioner's attorney should contact the general magistrates to secure a date and time for the hearing. If neither general magistrate is able to hold a hearing within forty eight (48) hours of the request then the petitioner's attorney should contact the assigned judge to secure a date and time for the hearing.

(5) The general magistrates **will not** entertain any Petitions for Appointment of an Emergency Temporary Guardian without the court file, a Petition to Determine Incapacity as to the Respondent filed at least 24 hours in advance of the hearing, and the statutory 24–hour notice of hearing. Attorneys for petitioners shall pick up the file from the Probate Mental Health Division of the Clerk of Court and take it to the hearing.

(6) If during the hearing the general magistrate determines that an emergency exists wherein any delay would place the alleged incapacitated person's health or assets in imminent danger, the general magistrate will provide the petitioner's attorney with an "URGENT SLIP." The slip, when accompanied by the court file, will allow the attorney to take the file to the assigned judge to enter an order as to the general magistrate's recommendations.

(7) This Administrative Order vacates and supersedes Administrative Order 2009–91–PRC.

DONE AND ORDERED in chambers at Fort Lauderdale, Broward County, Florida on April 21, 2016.

/s/ Peter M. Weinstein

Peter M. Weinstein

Chief Judge

[1] So in original.

2011–26–PRC. ADMINISTRATIVE ORDER ESTABLISHING FILING PROCEDURES FOR THE PROBATE DIVISION

IN THE CIRCUIT COURT OF THE SEVENTEENTH JUDICIAL CIRCUIT IN AND FOR BROWARD COUNTY, FLORIDA

Order Number 2011–26–PRC

ADMINISTRATIVE ORDER ESTABLISHING ELECTRONIC FILING PROCEDURES FOR THE PROBATE DIVISION

(a) Florida Rule of Judicial Administration 2.215(b)(3) states the chief judge shall "develop an administrative plan for the efficient and proper administration of all courts within that circuit."

(b) The Florida Supreme Court no longer requires the filing of original pleadings or papers filed electronically in the Seventeenth Circuit's probate division.

(c) In accordance with the authority vested in the chief judge by Florida Rule of Judicial Administration 2.215, it is ordered:

(1) This Administrative Order incorporates by reference all provisions of Florida Supreme Court Administrative Order No. AOSC09–30, In Re: Statewide Standards for Electronic Access to the Courts and AOSC10–31, In Re: Electronic Filing of Documents in the Probate Division for the electronic filing of documents with the Clerk of the Circuit Court (herein Clerk) as now in effect or as may be amended from time to time.

(2) Effective immediately attorneys may electronically file pleadings and papers for cases in the probate division.

(3) The following documents may be scanned and efiled; however, the original must be filed with the Clerk:

a. Last Will and Testament for estate cases;

b. Last Will and Testament deposited with the Clerk;

c. Pre-need Guardian Declarations;

d. Bonds;

e. Death certificates;

f. Returns of service;

g. Documents ordered by the Court; and

h. Original documents required by law or rule of procedure to be filed with the Clerk.

(4) Self represented individuals shall file pleadings and papers with the Clerk until registration procedures are developed for filing via the Florida Courts Efiling Portal.

(5) The filing date of a document is when the last page is received by the Clerk. If the Clerk has a vendor providing electronic court record services, the vendor must comply with this Administrative Order and the Clerk shall endorse upon each electronically transmitted document the date and time of receipt.

(6) The Clerk within twenty four (24) hours of receipt of an electronic document shall either accept or reject the electronic document for filing and send electronic notice to the filer.

(7) The placement of a "/s/" or the image of a signature by an attorney or party or interested person's signature line on an electronically filed document shall be accepted as the signature and shall verify to the Court the filer is in possession of the originally executed document. Notwithstanding the manner in which an electronic document is signed the originally executed pleading or paper shall be maintained in the filer's possession for a minimum of one (1) year after final disposition and time for appeal of the case. The originally executed document shall be produced for filing or inspection as directed by the Court.

(8) The electronic filing of a document does not modify any filing deadlines as required by law, rule of procedure, or court order.

(9) If a document filed electronically is not received due to:

a. an error in the transmission of the document to the Clerk or any vendor of the Clerk to provide electronic court record filing services which is unknown to an attorney or party, or

b. a failure to process the electronic document when received by the Clerk or rejection by the Clerk, or

c. any other technical problems experienced by the attorney or party,

the Court may, after an evidentiary hearing and upon satisfactory proof, enter an order permitting the document to be filed *nunc pro tunc* to the date it was first attempted to be sent electronically.

(10) The Clerk or any vendor of the Clerk providing electronic court record filing services shall provide to the judiciary the entire electronic filing data export upon acceptance by the Clerk as part of the transfer of electronic transmission.

(11) The Clerk or any vendor of the Clerk providing electronic court record filing services shall not charge any state court entity or statutorily exempt entity or individual for electronically filing documents. Any non-exempt attorney or party electronically filing documents shall pay any and all statutory fees to the Clerk.

(12) This Administrative Order shall govern the initial use of the Florida Courts Efiling Portal for the probate division but does not alleviate the Clerk from complying with the Chief Judge's conditions of approval of the Clerk's efiling plan which were included in the Florida Courts Technology Commission's approval of the plan.

(13) This Administrative Order vacates and supersedes Administrative Order 2009–79–PRC.

DONE AND ORDERED at Broward County, Florida on April 29, 2011.

s/Victor Tobin
Victor Tobin, Chief Judge

2009–89–PRC. ADMINISTRATIVE ORDER REQUIRING CREDIT AND CRIMINAL BACKGROUND INVESTIGATION

IN THE CIRCUIT COURT OF THE SEVENTEENTH JUDICIAL CIRCUIT IN AND FOR BROWARD COUNTY, FLORIDA

Order Number 2009–89–PRC

ADMINISTRATIVE ORDER REQUIRING CREDIT AND CRIMINAL BACKGROUND INVESTIGATION

(a) Florida Rule of Judicial Administration 2.215(b)(3) states the chief judge shall "develop an administrative plan for the efficient and proper administration of all courts within that circuit."

(b) In accordance with the authority vested in the chief judge by Florida Rule of Judicial Administration 2.215, it is ordered:

(1) In an effort to assure the appointment of qualified guardians and guardian advocates all prospective guardians and guardian advocates must submit to an investigation of his/her credit history and criminal background check.

(2) Guardianship personnel will be authorized to obtain the required investigatory information.

(3) All nonprofessional guardians and guardian advocates shall undergo periodic and recurring credit and criminal investigation at least once every calendar year, at the time of the

filing of the annual accounting and/or plan. If no accounting or plan is required, on the anniversary date of the letters of guardianship or letters of guardian advocate.

(4) All professional guardians shall be required to submit to an annual background investigation on or before every January 15th. All professional guardians shall register with the Statewide Public Guardianship Office pursuant to the Administrative Rules of the Department of Elder Affairs.

(5) All guardians shall have a continuing affirmative duty to disclose adverse information relating to their credit and criminal backgrounds.

(6) The cost for the criminal and credit investigation, for nonprofessional guardians, professional guardians, professional guardians' staff with a fiduciary responsibility to a ward, and prospective guardians, shall be $50.00. The check for the criminal and credit investigation cost shall be made payable to the Clerk of Court. The Clerk of Court shall forward all such payments he receives to the Board of County Commissioners.

(7) The cost for the criminal and credit investigation for proposed guardian advocates and appointed guardian advocates is waived both initially and annually thereafter.

(8) The statutorily authorized fee for the fingerprint card processing shall be paid by the nonprofessional guardians, professional guardians, professional guardians' staff with a fiduciary responsibility to a ward, and prospective guardians. The check for the fingerprint card processing shall be made payable to the Florida Department of Law Enforcement. The proposed guardian and proposed guardian advocate who are nonprofessionals shall be required to submit to an initial fingerprint card processing only unless otherwise ordered by the Court. All professional guardians and employees of a professional guardian with a fiduciary obligation to a ward shall annually submit to a fingerprint card processing unless waived by the Court.

(9) Professional guardians may elect to have their fingerprints submitted to the Court electronically. Electronic fingerprints must be taken by a vendor approved by the Statewide Public Guardianship Office.

(10) Any individual who is fingerprinted and whose prints are not discernible, as informed by the Clerk of Court, may have his or her fingerprints waived, upon the following conditions:

(a) If the fingerprints are taken at the Broward County Courthouse by the designated Court Deputy after two (2) attempts.

(b) If the fingerprints are not taken at the Broward County Courthouse by the designated Court Deputy for the first two (2) attempts then the third (3) attempt at fingerprinting must be done at the Broward County Courthouse by the designated Court Deputy.

(11) If the proposed guardian, guardian, or employee of a professional guardian with a fiduciary obligation to a ward, is advised that his or her fingerprints are not discernible after two (2) cards were printed by a designated Court Deputy at the Broward County Courthouse or after three (3) attempts with the final attempt by a designated Court Deputy at the Broward County Courthouse, then the attorney for the proposed guardian or professional guardian shall file a motion with the Court seeking waiver of the fingerprint requirement. The Court will review the request and enter an order either granting or denying the waiver of fingerprinting of the proposed guardian, guardian, or employee of a professional guardian with a fiduciary obligation to a ward. The order granting the waiver will be for all future fingerprinting requirements for the individual.

(12) If the Guardianship Investigation Office when performing the credit and criminal investigation determines that the proposed guardian or guardian fails to meet the requirements to be appointed or remain as guardian, or has failed to complete the guardianship education requirements, or has failed to pay the criminal/credit investigation cost the matter is hereby referred to a general magistrates pursuant to the provisions of Florida Probate Rule 5.095. The general magistrate upon receipt of the information from the Guardianship Investigation Office that the proposed guardian or guardian fails to meet the requirements to be appointed or remain as guardian or has failed to complete the guardianship education requirements or has failed to pay the criminal/credit investigation cost shall set same for hearing and provide notice to the proposed guardian or guardian and proposed guardian's attorney or guardian's attorney. Any interested person may object to the general magistrate hearing the matter by serving and filing an objection to the general magistrate hearing the matter. The notice of hearing as served by the general magistrate shall contain notice that an interested person can object to the general magistrate hearing the matter.

DONE AND ORDERED in chambers at Fort Lauderdale, Broward County, Florida on July 27, 2009.

s/Victor Tobin
Victor Tobin, Chief Judge

IV–07–B–1. REFERRAL OF GUARDIANSHIP FILES WHERE REQUIRED DOCUMENTS HAVE NOT BEEN FILED

IN THE CIRCUIT COURT OF THE SEVENTEENTH JUDICIAL CIRCUIT IN AND FOR BROWARD COUNTY, FLORIDA

ADMINISTRATIVE ORDER NO.: IV–07–B–1

IN RE: REFERRAL OF GUARDIANSHIP FILES WHERE REQUIRED DOCUMENTS HAVE NOT BEEN FILED

In accordance with the authority vested in the Chief Judge by Florida Rule of Judicial Administration 2.215 and § 744.3125 and § 744.3135, Florida Statutes, which provide that each prospective guardian must complete an application for appointment and the court may require background investigations of non-professional guardians and shall require same for professional guardians, it is hereby

ORDERED as follows:

The following procedure is effective immediately:

1. Initial Background Investigations in Minor and Voluntary Guardianships

a. If a proposed guardian(s) fails to file the paperwork needed to complete the background investigation within sixty (60) days of the date of filing of a Petition for Guardian of a Minor or a Petition for Voluntary Guardian, the Clerk shall notify the proposed guardian(s) in writing of the deficiency within ten (10) days.

b. If the proposed guardian(s) fails to file the required paperwork to complete the background investigation within ten (10) days of the written notification sent by the Clerk, the file is hereby referred to the assigned General Magistrate for hearing.

2. Annual Investigations

a. If the guardian(s) fails to file all documents required to complete the annual application for investigation within fifteen (15) days of the date due, the Clerk shall notify the guardian(s) in writing of the deficiency no later than twenty five (25) days after the original due date of the required documents.

b. If the guardian(s) fails to file the documents necessary to complete the annual background investigation within ten (10) days of the written notification sent by the Clerk, the file is hereby referred to the assigned General Magistrate for hearing.

3. Any interested person may object to the referral of this matter. The interested person shall file a notice of objection in the guardianship file, secure time on the assigned judge's docket for the hearing, and provide notice to counsel and all interested persons.

This Order supersedes Administrative Order IV–04–B–1.

DONE and ORDERED in Chambers at Broward County this 8th day of February, 2007.

/s/DALE ROSS
DALE ROSS
Chief Judge

IV–06–A–16. ADULT ABUSE AND NEGLECT RECORDS AND GUARDIANSHIP APPLICATIONS

IN THE CIRCUIT COURT OF THE 17TH JUDICIAL CIRCUIT IN AND FOR BROWARD COUNTY, FLORIDA

ADMINISTRATIVE ORDER NO.: IV–06–A–16

IN RE: ADULT ABUSE AND NEGLECT RECORDS AND GUARDIANSHIP APPLICATIONS

In accordance with the authority vested in the Chief Judge by Fla. R. Jud. Administration 2.050 and § 744.3135, Fla. Stat., which provides, in part, that the Court may require a nonprofessional guardian and shall require a professional guardian or public guardian and all employees of a professional guardian who have a fiduciary obligation to a ward submit to a credit history and background screening, it is hereby:

ORDERED that:

1. Effective April 1, 2006, all nonprofessional guardians and guardian advocates shall submit initially to a level 2 background screening as required under § 435.04, Fla. Stat.

2. Effective April 1, 2006, all professional guardians, public guardians, and employees of a professional guardian who have a fiduciary obligation to a ward, who have not previously submitted to a level 2 background screening as required under § 435.04, Fla. Stat. shall submit the required documents for a level 2 background screening no later than May 31, 2006.

3. Annually, thereafter, if a professional guardian hires employees with a fiduciary obligation to the ward, who have not previously submitted to a level 2 background screening shall be required to do so at the next annual investigation requirements for the professional guardian.

4. The Department of Children and Family Services, shall provide information to the Court via the Guardianship Investigation Office, for all level 2 background investigations, whether the individuals has a confirmed report of abuse, neglect, or exploitation pursuant the Chapter 415, Fla. Stat., which has been uncontested or upheld.

This Order shall supersede Administrative Order IV–97–A–16.

DONE AND ORDERED in Chambers in Fort Lauderdale, Broward County, Florida on this 10th day of January, 2006.

/s/DALE ROSS
DALE ROSS, Chief Judge

IV–05–A–26. GUARDIANSHIP APPLICATIONS FOR APPOINTMENT AND DISCLOSURE STATEMENTS

IN THE CIRCUIT COURT OF THE SEVENTEENTH JUDICIAL CIRCUIT IN AND FOR BROWARD COUNTY, FLORIDA

ADMINISTRATIVE ORDER NO.: IV–05–A–26

IN RE: GUARDIANSHIP APPLICATIONS FOR APPOINTMENT AND DISCLOSURE STATEMENTS

In accordance with the authority vested in the Chief Judge pursuant to Fla. R. Jud. Admin. 2.050 and in accordance with § 744.3125, Fla. Stat. which requires the filing of Applications for Appointment and Disclosure Statements, in order to comply with the statutory requirements and protect wards, it is hereby:

ORDERED that:

1. All guardians, except for corporate guardians, shall use and file the attached Application for Appointment as Guardian effective October 1, 2005.

2. All nonprofit corporate guardians shall use and file the attached Disclosure Statement effective October 1, 2005.

3. All employees of a professional guardian shall use and file the attached Employee Statement with a Fiduciary Obligation to a Ward effective October 1, 2005.

4. This order supersedes Administrative Order IV–01–A–26.

DONE AND ORDERED in Chambers in Fort Lauderdale, Broward County, Florida on this 15th day of September, 2005.

/s/DALE ROSS
DALE ROSS, Chief Judge

IN THE CIRCUIT COURT FOR THE 17TH JUDICIAL CIRCUIT IN AND FOR BROWARD COUNTY, FLORIDA

IN RE: GUARDIANSHIP OF Case Number
Judge:

______________________/

APPLICATION FOR APPOINTMENT AS GUARDIAN

Pursuant to § 744.3125, Fla. Stat., the undersigned submits this Application for Appointment as Guardian of ______ (the Ward) and submits the following information (whenever the space is insufficient, attach additional pages):

1. Name: ______
2. Social Security Number: ______
3. Date and Place of Birth: ______
4. Residence address: ______

______

5. Mailing address: ______

______

6. U.S. Citizen? Yes ______ No ______

7. Employer's name and address: ______

______

Applicant's position: ______

8. Marital status and name of spouse, if any: ______

9. Home telephone number: ______

10. Length of residence in county wherein application is filed ______

11. If currently serving as guardian for any other ward, list names of each ward, court file number(s), circuit court(s) in which the case(s) is/are pending and whether applicant is acting as the limited or plenary guardian of the person or property or both: (attach additional pages if necessary): ______

12. Does applicant have any physical disabilities?: ______

If yes, please describe and state whether such disability may affect applicant's ability, in any degree, to serve as guardian ______

13. Has applicant ever been treated for the following:

a. Mental condition? Yes ______ No ______

b. Alcohol? Yes ______ No ______

c. Drugs? Yes ______ No ______

d. Other? Yes ______ No ______

Nature of Condition: ______

If yes was answered to any of the above, please state date, time, location of treatment and name of physician or professional involved ______

14. Has applicant ever been judicially determined to have committed abuse or neglect against a child as defined by Florida Statutes? Yes ______ No ______

15. Has applicant ever been the subject of a confirmed report of abuse, neglect, or exploitation which has been contested or upheld pursuant to the provisions of Sections 415.104 and 415.1075, Florida Statutes? Yes ______ No ______

16. Has applicant ever been charged with fraud, misrepresentation or perjury in a judicial or administrative proceeding? Yes ______ No ______

17. Has applicant ever been:

a. Charged with a felony? Yes ______ No ______

b. Arrested for a felony? Yes ______ No ______

c. Convicted of a felony? Yes ______ No ______

d. Entered a plea of guilty or no contest to a felony? Yes ______ No ______

If yes, to any of the above, please furnish details, including type of offense, location and final disposition: ______

18. Has applicant ever been:

a. Charged with any crime other than a felony? Yes ______ No ______

b. Arrested for any crime other than a felony? Yes ______ No ______

c. Convicted of any crime other than a felony? Yes ______ No ______

d. Entered a plea of guilty or no contest to a crime other than a felony? Yes ______ No ______

If yes, to any of the above, please furnish details, including type of offense, location and final disposition: ______

19. Has applicant ever held a position which required bonding? Yes ______ No ______

20. Has applicant, in the past, ever served as guardian of a person or of a person's property? Yes ______ No ______

If yes, please describe below, including reason for termination of fiduciary position: ______

21. Has applicant ever been held in contempt of court or removed as a guardian? Yes ______ No ______

If yes, please describe below: ______

22. Has applicant ever filed for bankruptcy? Yes ______ No ______

If yes, please state date and location of court: ______

23. What is applicant's relationship to the alleged incapacitated person (or ward, if renewal application)? ______

24. Is applicant, or applicant's business or corporation or other business entity a creditor of or providing professional, personal or business services to the incapacitated person? Yes ______ No ______

If yes, please furnish details: ______

25. Is applicant employed by a business, corporation or other business entity which is providing professional, personal or business services to the incapacitated person? Yes ______ No ______

If yes, please furnish details: __________

26. Is applicant a health care provider for the alleged incapacitated person? Yes __________ No __________

27. Educational history of applicant

	Name and Address	Degree	Date
High School			
College			
Other			

28. List applicant's employment experience for the past 10 years beginning with the most recent date

Name and Address	Date	Reason for Leaving

29. Has applicant ever been discharged from employment? Yes __________ No __________

If yes, please explain: __________

30. Has applicant ever been a member of the armed forces of the U.S.? Yes __________ No __________

If yes, what branch, dates and military serial number: ___

31. PERSONAL REFERENCES. Please give the names, addresses and telephone numbers of three (3) responsible persons who have been closely associated with applicant and who have known applicant for five (5) years or more, not including relatives or spouse

Name and address	Telephone Number

32. Does applicant possess any special educational qualifications (financial, business, or otherwise) that uniquely qualifies applicant to be appointed as guardian? Yes __________ No __________

If yes, please describe: __________

33. Has applicant received instruction and training which covered the legal duties and responsibilities of a guardian, the rights of an incapacitated person, the availability of local resources to aid a ward, and the preparation of habilitation plans and annual guardianship reports, including financial accounting for the ward's property? Yes __________ No __________

If yes, indicate when and where training was received. If the instruction and training was the professional guardianship class required by 744.1085 then please also state whether you have taken the professional guardian competency examination. If you have taken the professional guardian competency examination, please attach proof that you passed the examination. Proof of passing the professional guardian competency examination is required only for initial applications. __________

____

Under penalties of perjury, I declare that I have read the foregoing, and the facts alleged are true, to the best of my knowledge and belief.

Signed on __________, 20 ___

____
Applicant

Effective October 1, 2005

IN THE CIRCUIT COURT OF THE SEVENTEENTH JUDICIAL CIRCUIT IN AND FOR BROWARD COUNTY, FLORIDA

IN RE: NONPROFIT CORPORATION (Insert Name)

__________/

DISCLOSURE STATEMENT

Pursuant to § 744.3125, Fla. Stat., the undersigned submits this Disclosure Statement for the quarter beginning __________ and ending __________ and submits the following information (whenever the space provided is insufficient, attach additional pages):

1. Name of Nonprofit Corporate Guardian __________
2. Nonprofit Corporate Guardian's Address __________

____

3. This Nonprofit Corporation is organized under Florida law for (please circle one)

Religious or Charitable Purposes.

4. Nonprofit Corporate Guardian's phone number __________
5. Professional Guardian's name and social security number __________

____

6. Has the Nonprofit Corporation's Professional Guardian ever been treated for the following? If yes, please indicate which professional guardian.

a. Mental condition? Yes _____ No _____

b. Alcohol? Yes _____ No _____

c. Drugs? Yes _____ No _____

d. Other? Yes _____ No _____

Nature of Condition __________

If yes was answered to any of the above, please state date, time, location of treatment and name of physician or professional involved __________

____

7. Has the Nonprofit Corporation's Professional Guardian listed ever been judicially determined to have committed abuse or neglect against a child as defined by Florida Statutes? Yes __________ No __________

If yes, please indicate which professional guardian __________

8. Has the Nonprofit Corporation's Professional Guardian ever been the subject of a confirmed report of abuse, neglect, or exploitation which has been contested or upheld pursuant to the provisions of Sections 415.104 and 415.1075, Florida Statutes? Yes ________ No ________

9. Has the Nonprofit Corporation's Professional Guardian ever been charged with fraud, misrepresentation or perjury in a judicial or administrative proceeding? Yes ________ No ________

10. Has the Nonprofit Corporation's Professional Guardian ever been

a. Charged with a felony? Yes _____ No _____

b. Arrested for a felony? Yes _____ No _____

c. Convicted of felony? Yes _____ No _____

d. Entered a plea of guilty or no contest to a felony? Yes _____ No _____

If yes, to any of the above, please furnish details, including type of offense, location and final disposition ________

11. Has the Nonprofit Corporation's Professional Guardian ever been:

a. Charged with any crime other than a felony? Yes _____ No _____

b. Arrested for any crime other than a felony? Yes _____ No _____

c. Convicted of any crime other than a felony? Yes _____ No _____

d. Entered a plea of guilty or no contest to a crime other than a felony? Yes _____ No _____

12. Has the nonprofit corporation's professional guardian ever been denied bond or had a bond forfeited? Yes _____ No _____

If yes, please provide details, including the name of surety and the date(s) ________

13. Has the nonprofit corporation's professional guardian ever been held in contempt of court or removed as guardian? Yes ________ No ________

If yes, please describe ________

14. Has the nonprofit corporation's professional guardian ever filed bankruptcy? Yes ________ No ________

If yes, please state date and location of court ________

15. Has the nonprofit corporation's professional guardian, or applicant's business, corporation or other business entity ever been a creditor of, or providing professional or business services to any incapacitated person prior to appointment as guardian? Yes ________ No ________

If yes, please furnish details ________

16. Has the nonprofit corporation's professional guardian ever been a health care provider for any alleged incapacitated person prior to appointment as guardian? Yes ________ No ________

17. Educational history of the nonprofit corporation's professional guardian

	Name and Address	Degree	Date
High School			
College			
Other			

18. Has the nonprofit corporation's professional guardian received the minimum of 40 hours of instruction and training as required by Florida Statutes? Yes ________ No ________

19. Please list the nonprofit corporation's professional guardian's continuing education as required by Florida Statutes

Class	Credit Hours	Date

20. List the names of all wards for whom the corporation is acting as guardian, the court file number and circuit court in which each case is pending and a statement as to whether the corporation is acting as limited or plenary guardian of the person or property or both, of each ward.

____

____

____

I hereby certify that the nonprofit corporation filing this disclosure statement is a nonprofit corporation organized for religious or charitable purposes under Florida law. Under penalties of perjury I declare that I have read the foregoing, and the facts alleged are true, to the best of my knowledge and belief.

________ ________
Applicant's signature Date

Effective 10/1/2005

IN THE CIRCUIT COURT FOR THE 17TH JUDICIAL CIRCUIT IN AND FOR BROWARD COUNTY, FLORIDA

IN RE: GUARDIANSHIP OF ________/ Case Number
Judge:

EMPLOYEE STATEMENT WITH A FIDUCIARY OBLIGATION TO A WARD

__________, as an employee of __________, a professional guardian, hereby provides the following information:

1. Has employee ever been judicially determined to have committed abuse or neglect against a child as defined by Florida Statutes? Yes __________ No __________

2. Has employee ever been the subject of a confirmed report of abuse, neglect, or exploitation which has been contested or upheld pursuant to the provisions of Sections 415.104 and 415.1075, Florida Statutes? Yes __________ No __________

3. Has employee ever been charged with fraud, misrepresentation or perjury in a judicial or administrative proceeding? Yes __________ No __________

4. Has employee ever been:

a. Charged with a felony? Yes ___ No ___

b. Arrested for a felony? Yes ___ No ___

c. Convicted of a felony? Yes ___ No ___

d. Entered a plea of guilty or no contest to a felony? Yes ___ No ___

If yes, to any of the above, please furnish details, including type of offense, location and final disposition __________

____

5. Has employee ever been:

a. Charged with any crime other than a felony? Yes ___ No ___

b. Arrested for any crime other than a felony? Yes ___ No ___

c. Convicted of any crime other than a felony? Yes ___ No ___

d. Entered a plea of guilty or no contest to a crime other than a felony? Yes ___ No ___

If yes, to any of the above, please furnish details, including type of offense, location and final disposition: __________

____

6. Has employee ever held a position which required bonding? Yes __________ No __________

7. Has employee ever filed for bankruptcy? Yes __________ No __________

If yes, please state date and location of court: __________

____

____

Under penalties of perjury, I declare that I have read the foregoing, and the facts alleged are true, to the best of my knowledge and belief.

Signed on __________, 20 ___

____

Employee

Effective October 1, 2005

Unified Family Orders

2018–107–UFC. COLLABORATIVE DISPUTE RESOLUTION PILOT PROCESS

IN THE CIRCUIT COURT OF THE SEVENTEENTH JUDICIAL CIRCUIT IN AND FOR BROWARD COUNTY, FLORIDA

Administrative Order 2018–107–UFC

ADMINISTRATIVE ORDER ESTABLISHING COLLABORATIVE DISPUTE RESOLUTION PILOT PROCESS FOR DISSOLUTION OF MARRIAGE AND PATERNITY CASES

(a) Pursuant to Article V, section 2(d) of the Florida Constitution and section 43.26, Florida Statutes, the chief judge of each judicial circuit is charged with the authority and power to do everything necessary to promote the prompt and efficient administration of justice.

(b) Florida Rule of Judicial Administration 2.215(b)(3) states the chief judge "shall, considering available resources, ensure the efficient and proper administration of all courts within [this] circuit."

(c) The collaborative dispute resolution process is a non-adversarial alternative to litigation that helps the parties maintain a working relationship and avoid the emotional and financial toll of litigation and encourages the peaceful resolution of disputes through a voluntary settlement process. *See* § 61.55, Fla. Stat.

(d) In accordance with the authority vested in the Chief Judge by Article V, section 2(d) of the Florida Constitution, section 43.26, Florida Statute, and Florida Rule of Judicial Administration 2.215, it is hereby **ORDERED, effective December 7, 2018**:

(1) The Collaborative Dispute Resolution Pilot Process ("Collaborative Process") is authorized for a period of six (6) months in the Seventeenth Judicial Circuit of Florida to resolve dissolution of marriage and paternity actions and all attendant issues therein according to the requirements of this Administrative Order and applicable Florida Statutes and Florida Family Law Rules Procedure. Prior to the expiration of the six (6) months, all pertinent parties will meet to review case statistics and the success of the Collaborative Process.

(2) The Collaborative Process is limited to dissolution of marriage and paternity cases where:

i. Both parties are self-represented with children in common of the relationship;

ii. There are no pending or prior related civil domestic cases where a final judgment has been entered involving the parties and/or the minor children in common of the relationship;

iii. There are no pending or prior related criminal domestic violence cases involving the parties and/or the minor children in common of the relationship; and

iv. The parties voluntarily agree to engage in the Collaborative Process by executing a collaborative law participation agreement.

(3) Cases shall be screened for eligibility by Court Administration Family Case Management upon the filing of an answer. If the action is eligible for the Collaborative Process, a case management conference shall be set on the presiding judge's next available case management docket. At the case management conference, the presiding judge, along with the collaborative process team comprised of collaborative law attorneys, and a mental health professional and a financial professional, shall explain the Collaborative Process to the parties.

(4) If, after the case management conference the parties voluntarily agree to participate in the Collaborative Process, they shall execute and file with the court a collaborative law participation agreement. Upon notice of filing of such agreement, the presiding judge shall enter an order staying the action for a period not to exceed ninety (90) days. The presiding judge may require the parties to file periodic status reports as to whether the collaborative process is ongoing or concluded.

(5) The Collaborative Process concludes or terminates upon the occurrence of an event or events as set forth in section 61.57, Florida Statutes or Florida Rule of Family Procedure 12.745, but shall not exceed ninety (90) days from the order staying the proceedings.

DONE AND ORDERED in Chambers, Fort Lauderdale, Florida, this 6th day of December, 2018.

Jack Tuter
Chief Judge

2018–94–UFC. PROCEDURE FOR HEARINGS ON CHILD SUPPORT WRITS OF ARREST

IN THE CIRCUIT COURT OF THE SEVENTEENTH JUDICIAL CIRCUIT IN AND FOR BROWARD COUNTY, FLORIDA

Administrative Order 2018–94–UFC

ADMINISTRATIVE ORDER ESTABLISHING PROCEDURE FOR HEARINGS ON CHILD SUPPORT WRITS OF ARREST ON DEPARTMENT OF REVENUE CASES ONLY

(a) Pursuant to Article V, section 2(d) of the Florida Constitution and section 43.26, Florida Statutes, the chief judge of each judicial circuit is charged with the authority and power to do everything necessary to promote the prompt and efficient administration of justice.

(b) Florida Rule of Judicial Administration 2.215(b)(3) states the chief judge "shall, considering available resources, ensure the efficient and proper administration of all courts within [this] circuit."

(c) In accordance with the authority vested in the Chief Judge by Article V, section 2(d) of the Florida Constitution, section 43.26, Florida Statute, and Florida Rule of Judicial Administration 2.215, it is hereby **ORDERED**:

(1) Any person who is detained on a civil writ for failure to comply with an order to pay child support where the Florida Department of Revenue (DOR) is a party shall be brought to a room of the West Wing of the Broward County Courthouse designated by the Broward Sheriff's Office at 1:30 p.m. the next court business day following his or her arrest. The Broward Sheriff's Office shall be responsible for reserving and designating the appropriate room each day.

(2) An attorney for the DOR shall be physically present in the room designated by the Broward Sheriff's Office at 1:30 p.m. each court business day.

(3) If an agreement is reached between DOR and the individual detained on the writ, the attorney for DOR shall prepare and deliver an order to the Judge assigned to Backup Domestic Violence coverage. The judge assigned to Backup Domestic Violence coverage shall be available between the hours of 1:30 p.m. and 2:30 p.m. each court business day for which he or she is assigned to such duty in order to execute any such order.

(4) If an agreement cannot be reached between DOR and the individual detained on the writ, the attorney for DOR shall contact the assigned judge so that a hearing can occur. If the assigned judge is unavailable, the attorney for DOR shall contact the judge assigned to Backup Domestic Violence duty who shall immediately hold a hearing.

(5) Upon arresting an individual on a writ of arrest for failure to comply with an order to pay child support, the Broward Sheriff's Office shall notify appropriate individuals with DOR and Court Administration and advise as to the date and time the individual will be transported to the room location designated by the Broward Sheriff's Office.

(6) For all cases not involving DOR, the Broward Sheriff's Office shall contact the assigned judge to coordinate the scheduling of the hearing and transportation of the individual.

(7) This Administrative Order supersedes and vacates Administrative Order 2018–88–UFC.

DONE AND ORDERED in Chambers, Fort Lauderdale, Broward County, Florida, this 24th day of October, 2018.

Jack Tuter
Chief Judge

2018–87–UFC. 2018 UNIFIED FAMILY COURT PLAN

IN THE CIRCUIT COURT OF THE SEVENTEENTH JUDICIAL CIRCUIT IN AND FOR BROWARD COUNTY, FLORIDA

Administrative Order 2018–87–UFC

ADMINISTRATIVE ORDER FOR THE 2018 UNIFIED FAMILY COURT PLAN

(a) Pursuant to Article V, section 2(d) of the Florida Constitution and section 43.26, Florida Statutes, the chief judge of each judicial circuit is charged with the authority and power to do everything necessary to promote the prompt and efficient administration of justice.

(b) Florida Rule of Judicial Administration 2.215(b)(3) states the chief judge "shall, considering available resources, ensure the efficient and proper administration of all courts within [this] circuit."

(c) The Florida Supreme Court in *In re Report of Family Court Steering Comm.*, 794 So. 2d 518 (Fla. 2001), directed the Circuit Courts to establish Unified Family Plans. This Circuit has established a plan that is being updated to reflect the best practices that will assist with judicial resources and the needs of families.

(d) In accordance with the authority vested in the chief judge by Article V, section 2(d) of the Florida Constitution, section 43.26, Florida Statutes, and Florida Rule of Judicial Administration 2.215, it is hereby **ORDERED**:

(1) The 2018 Unified Family Court Plan for the Seventeenth Judicial Circuit is attached to this Administrative Order.

(2) This Administrative Order vacates and supersedes Administrative Order 2017–22–UFC.

DONE AND ORDERED in Chambers at Fort Lauderdale, Broward County, Florida, this 17th day of October, 2018.

Jack Tuter
Chief Judge

2018 UNIFIED FAMILY COURT PLAN FOR THE SEVENTEENTH JUDICIAL CIRCUIT

I. Unified Family Court. The Unified Family Court (herein UFC) for the Seventeenth Judicial Circuit (herein Circuit) was established in 1994. Since 1994, the Circuit has continued with developing policy and procedures to implement a UFC for families. This Plan shall apply to UFC concurrently with the Circuit's Administrative Orders. If this Plan is in conflict with any statute, rule of procedure, or case law, the Plan is automatically amended to comply with the statute, rule of procedure, or case law.

II. Goal Of UFC. The goal is to create a fully integrated, comprehensive approach to handling cases involving children and families to maximize judicial resources and efficiency, avoid inconsistent court orders, and reduce court hearings for a family. To accomplish this goal the Circuit, whenever possible, will assign one judge to one family.

III. UFC Divisions. UFC contains the following four (4) divisions: (1) Delinquency; (2) Dependency; (3) Domestic Violence (civil and criminal); and (4) Family.

The Chief Judge will determine the judges assigned to UFC by Administrative Order as authorized by statute and rules of procedure. The Chief Judge will appoint general magistrates and hearing officers to UFC by Administrative Order, if funding is available, as authorized by statute and rules of procedure. The Chief Judge, by separate Administrative Order, will appoint an Administrative Judge and Chairpersons for UFC.

The judges, general magistrates, and hearing officers assigned to UFC may be required to attend educational courses as to domestic relations, domestic violence, dependency, delinquency, mediation, diversity, sensitivity and problem-solving as required by the Chief Justice of the Supreme Court of Florida or the Chief Judge.

IV. Assignment of UFC Cases. The Clerk of the Circuit Court (herein Clerk) shall assign UFC cases to the divisions as follows:

a. *Delinquency*

i. Cases filed pursuant to Chapter 985, Florida Statutes

b. *Dependency*

i. Cases filed pursuant to Chapter 39, Florida Statutes

1. Drug Court
2. Early Childhood Court

ii. CINS/FINS

iii. Petition for Judicial Waiver of Parental Notice of Termination of Pregnancy

iv. Motions to Intervene for Private Adoptions pursuant to Chapter 63, Florida Statutes, if there is a pending dependency case

c. *Domestic Violence*

i. Criminal Domestic Violence (any and all arrests and/or prosecutions for domestic violence as defined by Chapter 741, Florida Statutes, or stalking, sexual violence and dating violence as defined by Chapter 784, Florida Statutes)

ii. Civil Domestic Violence

1. Injunction for Protection against Dating Violence
2. Injunction for Protection against Domestic Violence
3. Injunction for Protection against Repeat Violence
4. Injunction for Protection against Sexual Violence
5. Injunction for Protection against Stalking (includes cyberstalking)

d. *Family*

i. Adoption

ii. Amend Birth Certificate

iii. Amend Marriage Certificate

iv. Annulment

v. Change of Name

vi. Declaratory actions related to premarital, marital, or post martial agreements

vii. Dissolution of Marriage (including modification and enforcement)

viii. Extraordinary Writs (if the underlying case is a UFC case)

ix. Florida Judgment Modification (including modification and enforcement)

x. Partition/Domestic (including modification and enforcement)

xi. Paternity (including modification and enforcement)

xii. Petition To Enforce Foreign Custody Order (including modification and enforcement)

xiii. Petition for Temporary Custody by Extended Family (including modification and enforcement)

xiv. Separate Maintenance (including modification and enforcement)

xv. Simplified Dissolution of Marriage (including modification and enforcement)

xvi. Timesharing for Minor Children (including modification and enforcement)

xvii. Title IV–D (including but not limited to Child Support, Child Custody, Paternity, and Uniform Interstate Family Support Act) (including modification and enforcement)

xviii. Uniform Interstate Family Support Act (including modification and enforcement)

V. Assignment of Cases to Achieve one Family, One Judge. The Circuit, whenever possible, will assign one family to one judge. To accomplish the assignment of one family to one judge, the parties to UFC cases shall comply with Florida Rule of Judicial Administration 2.545(d) by filing the notice of related case using the Florida Supreme Court approved form. Each judge presiding over a UFC case shall make an inquiry at the earliest possible date to determine if the parties currently have any UFC cases pending in the Seventeenth Judicial Circuit or any other judicial circuit located in the State of Florida. The Clerk will review his or her case maintenance system at the time a UFC case is filed to determine along with the notice of related case and conduct a name search of the parents, children, or other party for all UFC cases. If the Clerk determines there are open UFC cases for a parent, child, or other party, the Clerk shall assign the case as follows:

a. *Delinquency*

i. If a sua sponte shelter hearing is required for a minor to be released from a Department of Juvenile Justice facility or for any other reason and heard by a delinquency judge, the case shall be subsequently assigned to a dependency division.

ii. If there is an open and pending family case or civil domestic violence case at the time of filing the delinquency case, the case shall be assigned to a delinquency division JF. This is the only case the Clerk may direct file in division JF.

iii. If a delinquency case is filed after the dependency case, and the dependency case is closed for less than twelve (12) months, the delinquency case shall be assigned to a dependency division.

iv. If a delinquency case is filed after the dependency case, and protective supervision and jurisdiction have been terminated in the dependency case, the delinquency case shall be assigned to a delinquency division.

v. If a delinquency case is filed after a family or civil domestic violence case is closed for more than twelve (12) months, the delinquency case shall be assigned to a delinquency division.

vi. If there is an open and pending delinquency case at the time of filing the dependency case, the delinquency case shall be transferred to a dependency division unless there is a pending disposition before the delinquency division or a final hearing was commenced.

vii. If there is an open and pending delinquency case at the time of filing a criminal domestic violence case the case shall be assigned to a criminal domestic violence division with coordinated case management for both cases.

b. *Dependency*

i. If there is an open and pending family case at the time of filing the dependency case, the family case shall be transferred to the same dependency division.

ii. If there is an open and pending dependency case at the time of filing a Petition for Judicial Waiver of Parental Notice of Termination of Pregnancy the case shall be assigned to the same dependency division.

iii. If a family case is filed after the dependency case, and protective supervision has been terminated but jurisdiction has been retained in the dependency case, the new family case shall be assigned to the family division, unless the predominant issues in the family case concern custody of a minor child or minor children, including but not limited to timesharing or paternity, then the family case shall be assigned to the dependency division in which the dependency case was pending.

iv. If a family case is filed after the dependency case, and protective supervision and jurisdiction have been terminated in the dependency case, the family case shall be assigned to a family division, unless the predominant issues in the family case concern custody of the minor children, including but not limited to timesharing or paternity, then the matter shall be assigned to the dependency division in which the dependency case was pending.

v. If there is an open and pending civil domestic violence case at the time of filing the dependency case, the civil domestic violence case shall be assigned to a dependency division.

vi. If a civil domestic violence case involving a child in a dependency case is filed after the dependency case, and protective supervision has been terminated but jurisdiction has been retained in the dependency case, the civil domestic violence case shall be assigned to the dependency division in which the dependency case was pending.

vii. If a civil domestic violence case is filed after the dependency case, and protective supervision and jurisdiction have been terminated in the dependency case, the civil domestic violence case shall be assigned to a civil domestic violence division.

viii. If there is an open and pending delinquency case at the time of filing the dependency case, the dependency case shall be assigned to a dependency division. The related delinquency case will thereafter be transferred to a dependency division unless there is a pending disposition before the delinquency division or a final hearing was commenced.

ix. If a delinquency case is filed after the dependency case, and protective supervision and jurisdiction have been terminated in the dependency case, the delinquency case shall be assigned to a delinquency division.

c. *Domestic Violence*

i. If there is an open and pending family case at the time of filing the civil domestic violence case, the civil domestic violence case shall be assigned to the family division in which the family case is pending.

ii. If a civil domestic violence case is filed after the family case, and the family case is closed for less than twelve (12) months, the civil domestic violence case shall be assigned to the family division in which the family case was assigned.

iii. If a civil domestic violence case is filed after the family case, and the family case is closed for more than twelve (12) months, the civil domestic violence case shall be assigned to a civil domestic violence division.

iv. If there is an open and pending dependency case at the time of filing the civil domestic violence case, the case shall be assigned to a dependency division.

v. If a civil domestic violence case involving a child in a dependency case is filed after the dependency case, and protective supervision has been terminated but jurisdiction has been retained in the dependency case, the civil domestic violence case shall be assigned to a dependency division in which the dependency case was pending.

vi. If a civil domestic violence case is filed after the dependency case, and protective supervision and jurisdiction have been terminated in the dependency case, the civil domestic violence case shall be assigned to a civil domestic violence division.

vii. If there is an open and pending delinquency case at the time of filing the civil domestic violence case, the case shall be assigned to the civil domestic violence cross over division.

viii. Criminal domestic violence cases shall be assigned to a criminal domestic division.

d. *Family*

i. If there is no open and pending UFC case at the time of filing the family case it shall be assigned to a family division.

ii. If there is an open and pending dependency case at the time of filing the family case, the case shall be assigned to a dependency division.

iii. If a family case is filed after the dependency case, and protective supervision has been terminated but jurisdiction has been retained in the dependency case, the family case shall be assigned to the family division, unless the predominant issues in the family case concern custody of a minor child or minor children, including but not limited to timesharing or paternity, then the family case shall be assigned to the dependency division in which the dependency case was pending.

iv. If a family case is filed after the dependency case, and protective supervision and jurisdiction has terminated in the dependency case, the family case shall be assigned to a family division, unless the predominant issues in the family case concern a minor child or minor children, including but not limited to timesharing or paternity, then the matter shall be assigned to the dependency division in which the dependency case was pending.

v. If a civil domestic violence case is filed after the family case, as long as the family case is closed for less than twelve (12) months, the civil domestic violence case shall be assigned to the family division in which the family case was pending.

vi. If a civil domestic violence case is filed after the family case, as long as the family case is closed for more than twelve (12) months, the civil domestic violence case shall be assigned to a civil domestic violence division.

vii. If there is an open and pending delinquency case at the time of filing the family case, excluding DOR cases, the case shall be assigned to the family cross over division.

e. *General Magistrates.* The General Magistrate assignment at the time of filing a family case shall be the General Magistrate for all family and civil domestic violence related cases. If there is a dependency related case, the dependency General Magistrate assignment shall be for all related cases.

VI. Transfer of Cases Between UFC Divisions to Achieve One Family, One Judge

a. If at any time a judge assigned to a UFC division is advised that a family has more than one (1) pending UFC case a transfer order shall be entered by the judge. Transfer of cases may occur as follows:

i. If there is an open dependency case then all other civil domestic violence, delinquency and family cases shall be transferred to the dependency division to which the case is pending.

ii. If there is an open family case then all other civil domestic violence and dependency cases filed thereafter shall be transferred to the dependency division to which the dependency case is pending.

iii. If there is an open family case then all other civil domestic violence and delinquency cases shall be transferred to Division JF/29.

iv. If a minor is a co-defendant for a delinquency case with an open dependency case then only his or her delinquency case shall be transferred to the dependency division with the pending case.

v. If a minor is a co-defendant for a delinquency case with an open family case then only his or her delinquency case shall be transferred to the cross over family division.

b. All parties to a UFC case have an obligation to advise any judge assigned to a UFC case if there is more than one (1) pending case for a family. The parties to UFC cases shall comply with Florida Rule of Judicial Administration 2.545(d) by filing the notice of related case using the Florida Supreme Court approved form.

c. This plan does not preclude the assigned judges from conferring between themselves and deviating from the assignments of cases set forth herein to meet the best interests of the family. The Administrative Judge of Unified Family Court or the Chairpersons of the Delinquency, Dependency, and Family Divisions may enter transfer orders as needed for these cases. In all instances, the Administrative Judge for the Unified Family Court shall be the final arbiter as to whether the transfer of a case is appropriate.

VII. Assignment of Cases/Transfer of Cases Between Delinquency Divisions. It is in the best interest of a minor for one judge to dispose of all delinquency proceedings. This will alleviate the possibility of conflicting orders if a minor's cases are not heard by one judge and confusion by the child and parents as to hearing dates.

a. If a minor has an open and pending case at the time a new case is filed, the new filed case shall be assigned to the same division as the open and pending case. This shall include minors whose case or cases have reached a disposition but probation or commitment supervision remains outstanding.

b. If a minor has more than one case in which probation or conditional release was ordered but not completed then all cases shall be transferred to the division with the oldest case number.

c. If more than one minor has a case filed arising from the same incident, all companion cases shall be assigned to the division with the oldest case. The determination of oldest case numbers for all minors shall be determined first by an open and pending probation case for any of the companion minors. If there is not an open and pending probation case, then by an open conditional release case for any of the companion minors. If there is not an open or pending conditional release case for any companion minor then by an open and pending commitment case for any of the companion minors. If there is not an open and pending probation, conditional release, or commitment case for any companion minors, then by the oldest case number. All companion cases for which the minors receive probation, commitment or is on conditional release shall be assigned to the division with the oldest case number.

If any delinquency division receives assignment/transfer of cases in excess of the percentages established by Administrative Order there shall be no adjustment of caseloads due to the procedures to secure one judge for one minor's delinquency proceedings.

If there are pending delinquency cases with other UFC cases the judges shall confer to determine if an order of transfer of cases shall be entered or if the cases shall receive coordinated case management.

VIII. Delinquency Detentions, Arraignments, and Hearings. All minors who are charged with a crime arising from the same incident shall be set for a hearing on the same day, before the same judge, determined by the division assignment.

IX. Court Records. The Clerk shall maintain court records as required by law or rule. All court records related to a family shall be delivered by the Clerk to the presiding judge at the time of a hearing.

X. Child Support Enforcement. The Plan invokes Florida Family Law Rule of Procedure 12.491 as to Title IV–D and non–Title IV–D child support enforcement proceedings.

XI. The Family Law Advisory Group (FLAG). FLAG is an ad hoc committee of stakeholders established pursuant to the recommendations of the Florida State Family Court Steering Committee. FLAG is chaired by the UFC Administrative Judge or designee and members include judges, general magistrates, court administration employees, Clerk of Court staff attorneys, social service providers, and other community stakeholders. FLAG seeks to ensure effective communication between stakeholders while supporting the judicial branch. FLAG shall meet at least quarterly.

XII. Trial Court Administrator Programs. The Circuit's Trial Court Administrator shall provide, if funding is available, the following programs for UFC.

a. Case Management

b. Juvenile Alternative Sanctions

c. Teen Court

d. Early Childhood Court Community Coordinator

e. Mediation

f. Court Projects

g. Court Reporting for court proceedings as required by statute, rule of procedure, or case law

h. Interpreters as required by law

XIII. Clerk of Court Programs.

a. Self–Represented Self Help Unit

b. Domestic Violence Intake Unit

c. Depository (non–Title IV–D cases and alimony cases)

XIV. State of Florida Resources.

a. Florida Guardian Ad Litem Program

b. Department of Revenue (interstate and intrastate child support matters)

XV. Other Resources.

a. Supervised Visitation Programs

b. Parenting Education and Family Stabilization Courses. All parents who are parties to a dissolution of marriage or paternity case are ordered to attend a course pursuant to section 61.21, Florida Statutes. Information as to courses is available from the Clerk or the Department of Children and Families Website[1]

c. Seventeenth Judicial Circuit webpage (www.17th.flcourts.org)

d. Florida State Courts web page (www.flcourts.org)

e. Clerk web page (www.browardclerk.org)

f. Broward County Bar Association (http://www.browardbar.org)

g. Legal Aid (http://www.legalaid.org/coasttocoast)

h. The Florida Bar—Lawyer Referral Service (http://www.floridabar.org/tfb/TFBConsum.nsf/48E76203493B82AD852567090070C9B9/EC2322E512B83D1E85256B2F006CC812?OpenDocument#InformationörČonsumers)

[1] http://www.dcf.state.fl.us/programs/childwelfare/docs/ParentEducationAndFamilyStabilization.pdf

2018–74–UFC. DOMESTIC VIOLENCE CASES

IN THE CIRCUIT COURT OF THE SEVENTEENTH JUDICIAL CIRCUIT IN AND FOR BROWARD COUNTY, FLORIDA

Administrative Order 2018–74–UFC

ADMINISTRATIVE ORDER AS TO DOMESTIC VIOLENCE CASES

(a) Pursuant to Article V, section 2(d) of the Florida Constitution, and section 43.26, Florida Statutes, the chief judge of each judicial circuit is charged with the authority and the power to do everything necessary to promote the prompt and efficient administration of justice.

(b) Florida Rule of Judicial Administration 2.215(b)(3) states the chief judge "shall, considering available resources, ensure the efficient and proper administration of all courts within [this] circuit."

(c) The Florida Supreme Court mandated the creation of Unified Family Courts in each circuit to meet the unique needs of families. The Seventeenth Judicial Circuit in recognition of The Florida Supreme Court established a Unified

Family Court which includes civil and criminal domestic violence cases.

(d) In accordance with the authority vested in the chief judge by Article V, section 2(d) of the Florida Constitution, section 43.26, Florida Statutes, Florida Rule of Judicial Administration 2.215, it is hereby **ORDERED**:

(1) *General Provisions.*

a. The term domestic violence as set forth in this Administrative Order shall be as defined in Chapter 741, Florida Statutes and Chapter 784, Florida Statutes, as now in effect or as may be amended from time to time.

b. Civil domestic violence are the court proceedings seeking an injunction.

c. Criminal domestic violence are those cases wherein an individual is arrested and/or prosecuted for a crime.

(2) *Civil Domestic Violence.*

a. Civil domestic violence cases shall be assigned to Division 59 or Division 63 by the Clerk of the Court (Clerk) unless otherwise designated in the Circuit's Unified Family Court Plan. Division 59 and Division 63 shall hold the evidentiary hearings for civil domestic cases for the fifteen (15) day returns.

b. The Clerk during court business hours shall assist individuals with seeking injunctions for dating violence, domestic violence, repeat violence, stalking, and sexual violence at the Broward County Courthouse at 201 S.E. Sixth Street, Fort Lauderdale, Florida 33301 or at any Satellite Courthouse as determined by the Clerk.

c. The Clerk shall deliver a copy of all court records, during court business hours, to a judge at the Central Courthouse for review and entry of appropriate orders within one (1) hour of the filing. If the petition is filed at a Satellite Courthouse, the Clerk shall deliver a copy of all court records, during court business hours, to a judge at the Central Courthouse for review and entry of appropriate orders within two (2) hours of the filing.

d. A judge shall review and enter appropriate orders within one (1) hour of receipt of the court file.

e. If the judge assigned to Division 59 or Division 63 is absent from the courthouse or needs assistance with hearings or review of petitions, another Unified Family Court judge shall assist the assigned judge.

f. If a division judge is unavailable to hear a domestic violence case within a statutorily mandated period, the backup domestic violence judge shall hear the case when originally scheduled, or during the backup judge's assigned time to hear domestic violence cases, or if no time is available then on the next Friday at 1:30 p.m.

g. The Administrative Judge for Unified Family Court shall prepare and distribute the schedule for Unified Family Court judges to provide assistance to Division 59 and Division 63.

h. If the judge assigned to Division 59 is disqualified from a case the case shall be reassigned to Division 63.

i. If the judge assigned to Division 63 is disqualified from a case the case shall be reassigned to Division 59.

(3) *After Hours Civil Domestic Violence Procedures.*

a. Starting January 1, 2019, an individual seeking a civil domestic violence injunction between the hours of 5:00 p.m. to 8:30 a.m. on Monday to Thursday, or 5:00 p.m. Friday to 8:30 a.m. Monday, or any court holiday, or any other day that the court is closed is advised to contact Women In Distress of Broward County, Inc. Crisis Line at 954–761–1133.[1]

b. Women In Distress of Broward County, Inc. ("Women In Distress") has agreed to assist the Circuit to conduct an initial screening of risk and make referrals to available community resources to alleviate the risk of harm to the individual. If community resources are available the individual will be directed to the resource(s) and provided instructions on how to seek a civil domestic violence injunction during normal court business hours.

c. If Women In Distress determines that available community resources will not alleviate the risk of harm or an individual requests to file a petition and seek an order, then the Clerk or designee shall be contacted to assist the individual.

d. The Clerk or designee shall travel to the Broward County Courthouse at 201 S.E. Sixth Street, Fort Lauderdale, Florida 33301 upon receipt of a telephone call from Women In Distress to assist with the preparation of the petition and related documents. The Clerk or designee shall respond to the courthouse within one (1) hour, or as soon as possible, of receiving a call from Women In Distress. Upon the filing of the petition and related documents, the Clerk or designee shall contact the Civil Duty Judge who shall review the petition and related documents for entry of appropriate orders.

e. The Civil Duty Judge shall review the petition and related documents received from the Clerk as soon as possible. The Clerk may email or fax the petition and related documents to the Civil Duty Judge.

f. The Civil Duty Judge, after review of the petition and related documents, shall enter any order(s) as appropriate and return the order to the Clerk by email, fax, or in person.

g. The Clerk shall certify any and all orders received by email or fax for distribution as required law. The orders received by email or fax shall be deemed originals and included in the court records by the Clerk.

(4) *Extension of Injunctions Upon Court Closure.*

a. If the Chief Judge directs the closure of the Seventeenth Judicial Circuit court on a day or days not a Saturday, Sunday, or court holiday, then all injunctions and injunctions ready to expire where motions to extend have been filed are extended until further order of the court.

b. If the Chief Judge directs the closure of the Seventeenth Judicial Circuit court on a day or days not a Saturday, Sunday, or court holiday, then all cases set for hearing on that date are extended until further order of the court.

c. Any hearings set on a day the Chief Judge directed closure of the courts shall be re-noticed for hearing with service of the re-notice upon the parties within twenty (20) days of the reopening of the courts. The Clerk shall prepare and serve all re-notices or other papers required to reset the hearings.

(5) *Criminal Domestic Violence.*

a. Felony domestic violence cases shall be assigned to Division FV/GC/57 by the Clerk unless otherwise designated in the Circuit's Unified Family Court Plan.

b. Misdemeanor domestic violence cases shall be assigned to Division 57/MV by the Clerk unless otherwise designated in the Circuit's Unified Family Court Plan.

c. The Clerk shall not assign to Divisions FV/GC/57 or 57/MV any criminal domestic violence case charged by indictment or information by the State of Florida that involves: i) murder in the first degree; ii) child abuse; iii) juvenile matters; or iv) sex offenses unless between "family or household members."[2]

d. The Clerk shall not assign to Divisions FV/GC/57 or 57/MV any criminal domestic violence case charged by indictment or information by the State of Florida if the defendant has another criminal case, violation of probation case, or violation of community control case pending in another circuit criminal division. The new domestic violence case shall be assigned to the same circuit criminal division assigned the defendant's pending case(s).

e. If a criminal domestic violence case is inadvertently assigned to a criminal division other than FV, GC, 57, or MV, the case shall be transferred to the appropriate Unified Family Court criminal domestic violence division by the assigned division judge.

f. The judges assigned to the Unified Family Court criminal domestic violence divisions are alternates for each other for emergency matters.

g. If the judge assigned to the circuit criminal domestic violence division enters an order of disqualification or recusal, the Clerk shall assign the case to the county criminal domestic violence division.[3] If the judge assigned to the county criminal domestic violence division enters an order of disqualification or recusal, the Clerk shall assign the case to the circuit criminal domestic violence division.[4]

h. The Broward County Sheriff at the time of booking shall review and identify each arrest for criminal domestic violence charges. Any and all documents provided by the Broward County Sheriff's Office to the Court or Clerk as to a criminal domestic violence arrest shall be clearly and prominently marked or stamped "Domestic Violence."

i. The Clerk shall, as to criminal domestic violence cases, clearly and prominently mark or stamp the case file and court records to reflect the nature of the case as "Domestic Violence."

j. Any individual arrested for criminal domestic violence shall be processed, booked, and held at the main jail until after his or her first appearance.

k. If an individual is detained on a criminal domestic violence misdemeanor violation of probation warrant with no bond or is unable to post bond, he or she shall have an initial hearing on the violation of probation as required by law or rule of procedure at the date and time as set by the county criminal court domestic violence judge.

This Administrative Order vacates and supersedes Administrative Order 2016–5–UFC on January 1, 2019.

DONE AND ORDERED in Chambers at Fort Lauderdale, Broward County, Florida on 17th day of August, 2018.

Jack Tuter
Chief Judge

1 Administrative Order 2016–5–UFC remains in effect until January 1, 2019, and the after-hours domestic violence procedures shall continue to be followed until January 1, 2019. As such, up until January 1, 2019, individuals seeking a civil domestic violence junction between the hours of 5:00 p.m. to 8:30 a.m. on Monday to Thursday, or 5:00 p.m. Friday to 8:30 a.m. Monday, or any court holiday, or any other day that the court is closed shall contact Henderson Behavioral Health Crisis Line at 954–463–0911.

2 "Family or household members" are those individuals as defined by applicable Florida Statutes as now in effect or as may be amended from time to time.

3 By separate Administrative Order the judge assigned to the county criminal domestic violence division is designated an acting circuit court judge.

4 By separate Administrative Order the judge assigned to the circuit criminal domestic violence division is designated an acting county court judge.

2017–77–UFC. ADMINISTRATIVE ORDER ADOPTING AND AUTHORIZING THE USE OF A STATUS QUO TEMPORARY ORDER IN DISSOLUTION OF MARRIAGE AND PATERNITY ACTIONS IN THE SEVENTEENTH JUDICIAL CIRCUIT OF FLORIDA

IN THE CIRCUIT COURT OF THE SEVENTEENTH JUDICIAL CIRCUIT IN AND FOR BROWARD COUNTY, FLORIDA

Administrative Order No. 2017–77–UFC

ADMINISTRATIVE ORDER ADOPTING AND AUTHORIZING THE USE OF A STATUS QUO TEMPORARY ORDER IN DISSOLUTION OF MARRIAGE AND PATERNITY ACTIONS IN THE SEVENTEENTH JUDICIAL CIRCUIT OF FLORIDA

(a) Florida Rule of Judicial Administration 2.215(b)(3) states the Chief Judge "shall, considering available resources, ensure the efficient and proper administration of all courts within [this] circuit."

(b) The Seventeenth Judicial Circuit ("Circuit") is compelled to handle family law cases involving dissolution of marriage and paternity.

(c) In dissolution of marriage and paternity actions, the Circuit seeks to: (1) promote the stability of families engaged in such actions; (2) provide guidance to parties in an effort to help parties pattern their behavior and conduct in ways that reduce the negative impact that such proceedings have on the children and all parties involved; and (3) reduce the number of "emergency" hearings during the beginning stages of dissolution of marriage and paternity actions, thereby promoting the stability and preserving the resources of the parties and the court.

(d) It is in the best interest of the parties and any child or children involved, as the case may be, that parents in a dissolution of marriage or paternity action learn about the various problems, duties, and responsibilities of litigation and parenting following separation and divorce, and that the parties preserve their assets and comply with court rules and court orders.

(d) * The judges assigned to the Unified Family Division of the Seventeenth Judicial Circuit, after receiving input from the local Family Law Bar, support the use of a status quo temporary order to be utilized in dissolution of marriage and paternity actions, in an effort to achieve the aforementioned goals.

(e) The undersigned finds that it is in the best interest of the parties and any minor child or children of the parents in dissolution of marriage and paternity actions to adopt and authorize the use of the status quo temporary order in this Circuit, as may be modified as deemed appropriate by the presiding judges in such actions.

(d) * In accordance with the authority vested in the Chief Judge by section 43.26, Florida Statutes, and Florida Rule of Judicial Administration 2.215, it is hereby **ORDERED, effective January 2, 2018**:

(1) The Status Quo Temporary Domestic Relations Order, With or Without Minor Children (hereinafter referred to as "Order"), attached hereto as Exhibit "A" is hereby adopted and authorized for use in dissolution of marriage and paternity actions in the Seventeenth Judicial Circuit of Florida, as may be generally amended from time to time. The use of the Order is discretionary with each judge, and the terms and conditions of the Order may be modified, terminated, or amended as deemed appropriate by the presiding judge in such actions. If a judge permits the use of the Order, the judge shall indicate such and provide a link to a copy of the Order on his or her Division Procedures.

(2) It shall be the responsibility of the Petitioner and/or counsel for Petitioner to provide the Respondent(s) with a copy of the Order by including it with the petition at time of service.

(3) The Clerk of the Courts shall post a copy of the Order on its website to ensure that it is readily available to the Petitioner and/or Petitioner's counsel when the case is filed.

(4) Any failure to comply with the Order may result in appropriate sanctions against the offending party, as permitted by Florida law.

(5) This Administrative Order shall take effect on January 2, 2018, and shall remain in effect until further order of this Court.

DONE AND ORDERED in Chambers, Fort Lauderdale, Florida, this 12th day of December, 2017.

Jack Tuter, Chief Judge

EXHIBIT "A"

IN THE CIRCUIT COURT OF THE SEVENTEENTH JUDICIAL CIRCUIT IN AND FOR BROWARD COUNTY, FLORIDA

STATUS QUO TEMPORARY DOMESTIC RELATIONS ORDER, WITH OR WITHOUT MINOR CHILDREN, ISSUED PURSUANT TO ADMINISTRATIVE ORDER 2017–77–UFC

The following Status Quo Temporary Domestic Relations Order, With or Without Minor Children (hereinafter "Order") shall apply to both Petitioner and Respondent in an original dissolution of marriage or paternity action. This Order shall be in effect as to the Petitioner upon filing of the petition; and with regard to the Respondent, upon service of the summons and petition or upon waiver and acceptance of service. The Order shall remain in effect during the pendency of the action unless modified, terminated or vacated, or amended by further order of the presiding judge in the action.

It is in the best interests of the parties in a dissolution of marriage or paternity action to learn about the problems, duties and responsibilities that may arise during their dissolution of marriage or paternity proceeding. It is also important for the parties to preserve their assets, act in the best interests of their children and comply with Court orders and applicable Court rules. Therefore, the parties are hereby advised:

1. **NO RELOCATION OF CHILDREN.** Unless there is a prior court order, domestic violence injunction (permanent or temporary) or agreement signed by both parties, to the contrary, neither party will permanently remove, cause to be removed, nor permit the removal of any minor child of the parties to a location greater than fifty (50) miles from the principal residence of a parent. The intent of this restriction is not to prohibit temporary travel within the State of Florida. Neither party shall apply for any passport nor passport services on behalf of any child or children, without an order of the court from the presiding judge.

2. **CHILD SUPPORT.** Unless there is a prior court order, domestic violence injunction (permanent or temporary) or agreement signed by both parties, if the parties have minor children and choose to live apart while the action is pending, the parent with whom the children are not residing for a majority of the time should make voluntary payments of child support to the other parent, prior to the entry of an order requiring payment of child support. Child support should in an amount as determined by the Uniform Child Support Guidelines, section 61.30, Florida Statutes. Since child support can be ordered retroactive to the date of filing the petition, it is advisable that the party making payment keep proof of the payments and bring them to court. Signed receipts should be obtained for any cash payments. Parent/child access and child support are separate and distinct under the law. Accordingly, a child's right to access to his or her parent is not contingent upon the payment of child support.

3. **SHARED PARENTING GUIDELINES.** These guidelines apply unless there is a prior court order, domestic violence injunction (permanent or temporary) or agreement of the parties to the contrary. The safety, financial security, and mental well-being of the children involved in these cases are of paramount concern. It is mandatory that parents complete a parenting class and know, understand, and follow the Court's guidelines for parents in dissolution cases with children. The parties are ordered to abide by the principles of shared parental responsibility, which means:

3.1. Both parents shall confer with each other so that major decisions affecting the welfare of the children shall be determined jointly. Such decisions include, but are not limited to, education, discipline, religion, medical, and general upbringing.

3.2. Each parent shall exercise, in the utmost good faith, his and her best efforts at all times to encourage and foster the maximum relations, love, and affection between the minor children of the parties and the other parent. Neither parent shall impede, obstruct, or interfere with the exercise by the other parent of his or her right to companionship with the minor children.

3.3. Each parent shall have access to records and information pertaining to the minor children, including, but not limited to, medical, dental, and school records.

3.4. Neither parent shall make any disparaging remarks about the other parent or quiz the children as to the other parent's private life. It is the children's right to be spared from experiencing and witnessing any animosity or ill-feeling, if any should occur, between the parents, and the minor children should be encouraged to maintain love, respect, and affection for both parents.

3.5. The relationship between the parents shall be courteous and respectful as possible, relatively formal, low-key, and public.

3.6. Each parent has a duty to communicate directly with the children concerning his/her relationship with them to the extent warranted by their age and maturity. Neither parent can expect the other parent to continually act as a "buffer" or "go-between." For example, should either parent be unable to exercise time-sharing, that parent should explain this directly to the child.

3.7. Both parents shall be entitled to participate in and attend special activities in which the minor children are engaged, such as religious activities, school programs, sports events and other extracurricular activities, and important social events in which the children participate. Each parent should keep the other notified of these events.

3.8. The children shall not be referred to by any other last name than the one listed on their birth certificate.

3.9. Each parent has a duty to discuss with the other parent the advantage and disadvantages of all major decisions regarding the children and to work together in an effort to reach a joint decision. For example, this duty would include an obligation to discuss a decision to remove a child from public school in order to enroll the child in private school.

3.10. Neither parent shall conceal the whereabouts of the children, and each parent will keep the other advised at all times of the residential address and phone numbers where the children will be staying while with the other parent. Each parent shall notify the other immediately of any emergency pertaining to any child of the parties.

3.11. Each party shall provide to the other party his or her residence address, residence, work, and cellular telephone numbers, and e-mail address. Each party shall notify the other party, in writing, of any and all changes in his or her residence address and residence, work, and cellular telephone numbers, and e-mail address. Such notification shall be done within five (5) days of any such change and shall include the complete new address or complete new telephone number(s) and/or e-mail address.

4. REQUIRED ATTENDANCE IN A 4–HOUR PARENTING COURSE. Section 61.21, Florida Statutes. All parties to dissolution of marriage proceedings with minor children or to paternity proceedings shall be required to complete the Parent Education and Family Stabilization Course prior to the entry by the Court of a final judgment, as follows:

4.1. *Required Attendance.* For **dissolution of marriage actions**, the Petitioner must complete the course within forty-five (45) days after the filing of the petition, and all other parties must complete the course within forty-five (45) days after service of the petition. For **paternity actions**, the Petitioner must complete the course within forty-five (45) days after filing the petition, and any other party must complete the course within forty-five (45) days after an acknowledgement of paternity by that party, an adjudication of paternity of that party, or an order granting time-sharing to or support from that party. The presiding judge may excuse a party from attending the parenting course for good cause. The programs are educational and designed to assist parents and children in making transitions during and after the divorce. A certificate of completion for each party must be filed with the Clerk of the Courts prior to the entry of a final judgment.

4.2. *Cost.* Each party shall pay their respective cost of the Parent Education and Family Stabilization Course. The cost is determined by the agencies providing the different programs. No person shall be refused permission to attend because of inability to pay.

4.3. *Non–Compliance.* If either party does not attend and complete the Parent Education and Family Stabilization Course, upon filing of an affidavit of non-compliance, the presiding judge will enter an Order to Show Cause and will schedule a hearing date. At the hearing, the non-complying party will demonstrate why he or she has not attended the Parent Education and Family Stabilization Course. The presiding judge may impose sanctions, including a stay of proceedings, or any other sanction the presiding judge finds just and permissible under Florida law.

5. MEDIATION. Unless there is a prior court order, domestic violence injunction (permanent or temporary) or agreement signed by both parties, the parties are required to attend mediation prior to any final hearing or as otherwise ordered by the Court. The parties may utilize the mediation services provided by this Circuit's in-house mediators or the services of a private mediator.

6. CONDUCT OF THE PARTIES DURING THE CASE. Both parties are ordered to refrain from physical, verbal, or any other form of harassment of the other, including, but not limited to, acts done in person or by telephone, email, or text messaging at their residence or at work.

7. DISPOSITION OF ASSETS AND CASE. Neither party in a dissolution of marriage action will conceal, damage, nor dispose of any asset, whether jointly or separately owned, nor will either party dissipate the value of any asset (for example, by adding a mortgage to real estate), except by written consent of the parties or an order of court. Neither party will cancel nor cause to be canceled any utilities, including telephone, electric, or water and sewer. Notwithstanding, the parties may spend their income in the ordinary course of their business, personal, and family affairs. Neither party will conceal, hoard, nor waste jointly-owned funds, whether in the form of cash, bank accounts, or other highly liquid assets, except that said funds can be spent for the necessities of life. The use of funds or income after separation must be accounted for and justified as reasonable and necessary for the necessities of the party or to preserve marital assets or pay marital debts. Attorney's fees and costs are necessities and must be accounted for by each party. Both parties are accountable for all money or property in their possession after separation and during the dissolution of marriage proceedings. Any party who violates this provision will be required to render an accounting and may be later sanctioned for wasting a marital asset. To the extent there are pending contracts or transactions affected by this paragraph, the affected party may seek relief from the presiding judge, on an expedited basis, if the parties are unable to resolve the issue.

8. PERSONAL AND BUSINESS RECORDS. Neither party will, directly nor indirectly, conceal from the other or destroy any family records, business records, or any records in income, debt, or other obligations.

9. INSURANCE POLICIES. Any insurance policies in effect at the time the petition was filed, shall not be terminated, allowed to lapse, modified, borrowed against, pledged, or otherwise encumbered by either of the parties or at the direction of either party. This includes medical, hospital and/or dental insurance for the other party or the minor children. Neither party shall change the beneficiaries of any existing life insurance policies. Additionally, each party shall maintain all existing insurance policies in full force and effect, without change of their terms, unless agreed to in writing by both parties. All policy premiums will continue to be paid in full on a timely basis, unless there is an order of the court by the presiding judge or written agreement of the parties to the contrary. In order to modify this provision, or any other provision, the party must follow the procedure set forth in Paragraph 13.

10. ADDITIONAL DEBT. Neither party in a dissolution of marriage action may incur any unreasonable debts or additional personal debt which would bind the other spouse, including, but not limited to, further borrowing against any credit line secured by the family residence, further encumbering any assets, or unreasonably using credit/bank cards or cash advances against said cards, except with the written consent of the parties or order of the court by the presiding judge. The parties are strongly urged to temporarily refrain from using joint credit cards, except for absolute necessities and only as a last resort. Abuse of credit, especially the other spouse's credit, offends the Court's sense of equity and will be dealt with accordingly.

11. SANCTIONS. The presiding judge will sanction any party who fails, without good cause, to satisfactorily comply with the rules pertaining to the production of financial records and other documents, or fails, without good cause, to answer interrogatories or attend a deposition. When setting hearings, conferences, and depositions, an attorney must make a good faith effort to coordinate the date and time with opposing counsel.

12. JUDICIAL ENFORCEMENT. Failure to comply with the terms of this Order may result in appropriate sanctions against the offending party, as permitted by Florida law.

13. SERVICE AND APPLICATIONS OF THIS ORDER. The Petitioner or Petitioner's attorney shall serve a copy of this Order with a copy of the petition. This Order shall bind the Petitioner upon the filing of this action and shall become binding on the Respondent upon service of the initial pleading. This Order shall remain in full force and effect until further order of the court. Any part of this Order not changed by some later order or subsequent written agreement of the parties remains in effect. Nothing in this Order shall preclude either party from applying to the presiding judge for further temporary orders or any temporary injunction. Should either party wish to modify this Order, an appropriate motion must be filed with the Family Division of the Broward County Clerk of Courts, and set on uniform motion calendar for the Court to determine the scheduling of a hearing. An evidentiary hearing on a motion seeking enforcement or modification of this Order shall be accorded priority on the Court's calendar. This entire Order will terminate once a final judgment is entered.

DONE AND ORDERED in Chambers, Fort Lauderdale, Broward County, Florida, this 12th day of December, 2017.

Jack Tuter, Chief Judge

* Lettering as provided by the court.

2017-19-UFC. ADMINISTRATIVE ORDER MANDATING PARENT EDUCATION AND FAMILY STABILIZATION COURSE

IN THE CIRCUIT COURT OF THE SEVENTEENTH JUDICIAL IN AND FOR BROWARD COUNTY, FLORIDA

Order Number 2017-19-UFC

ADMINISTRATIVE ORDER MANDATING PARENT EDUCATION AND FAMILY STABILIZATION COURSE

(a) Florida Rule of Judicial Administration 2.215(b)(3) states the chief judge shall "considering available resources, ensure the efficient and proper administration of all courts within [this] circuit."

(b) Section 61.21, Florida Statutes, requires parents to attend a Parent Education and Family Stabilization Course if there are issues of parental responsibility.

(c) In accordance with the authority vested in the chief judge by Florida Rule of Judicial Administration 2.215, it is ordered:

(1) When a dissolution of marriage action with children or paternity action is filed with Clerk of Court the parents are required to attend a Parent Education and Family Stabilization Course.

(2) The Clerk of Courts shall provide the petitioning party or attorney notice of this Administrative Order and a link to the approved providers of a Parent Education and Family Stabilization Course.

(3) The parents shall attend the course as required by Section 61.21, Florida Statutes and file a copy with the Clerk of Court proof of completion.

(4) The failure to complete or file a certificate of completion will not preclude a parent from seeking emergency relief at any time.

(5) The petitioner must file a certificate of completion prior to the final hearing. If the responding party has defaulted in the action or failed to complete the course, a final hearing may be scheduled by the petitioner; however, the petitioner must

bring to the Court's attention the respondent's failure to comply with this Administrative Order.

(6) This Order vacates and supersedes Administrative Order No. II–00–F–6.

DONE AND ORDERED in chambers at Fort Lauderdale, Broward County, Florida on April 19, 2017.

Peter M. Weinstein, Chief Judge

2016–35–UFC. ADMINISTRATIVE ORDER AS TO JUVENILE DRUG COURT PROGRAM

IN THE CIRCUIT COURT OF THE SEVENTEENTH JUDICIAL CIRCUIT IN AND FOR BROWARD COUNTY, FLORIDA

Order Number 2016–35–UFC

ADMINISTRATIVE ORDER AS TO JUVENILE DRUG COURT PROGRAM

(a) Florida Rule of Judicial Administration 2.215(b)(3) states the chief judge shall "develop an administrative plan for the efficient and proper administration of all courts within that circuit."

(b) Section 985.345(1), Florida Statutes, authorizes the establishment of a juvenile drug court program to include programs as authorized by section 985.345, Florida Statutes, and section 397.334, Florida Statutes.

(c) In accordance with the authority vested in the chief judge by Florida Rule of Judicial Administration 2.215, it is ordered:

(1) A juvenile drug court program is established as authorized by sections 985.345 and 397.334, Florida Statutes.

(2) Cases eligible for transfer to the juvenile drug court are juveniles charged or for which a petition was filed by the State Attorney:

(a) for the offenses set forth at section 985.345, Florida Statutes.

(b) for any misdemeanor or non-violent second or third degree felony offense or offenses when the juvenile is not on probation and there is evidence of substance abuse.

(c) the juvenile is placed in Drug Court as a condition of probation. The juvenile will be under the supervision of the Drug Court judge while on probation who shall issue any warrant for violation of probation and dispose of any violations of probation.

(3) The criteria for participation in the juvenile drug court program are:

(a) The juvenile and at least one parent or legal guardian of the juvenile must reside in Broward County.

(b) The juvenile must be at least 14 years old at the time of acceptance into the juvenile drug court program. Some exceptions may apply for extenuating circumstances.

(c) The juvenile must be able to successfully complete the juvenile drug court program prior to turning 19 years old.

(d) The juvenile must be physically and mentally able to understand the juvenile drug court requirements and comply with the requirements of participation.

(4) Entry into a delinquency pretrial substance abuse and education treatment intervention program or other treatment program in juvenile drug court is voluntary after being provided and signing a written coordinated strategy as required by section 985.345(2), Florida Statutes. The written coordinated strategy is the agreement setting forth the terms and conditions of participation in juvenile drug court. The written coordinated strategy must at a minimum be signed by the juvenile and at least one parent or legal guardian of the juvenile.

(5) Upon entry into juvenile drug court the case will be transferred from the assigned juvenile division to the juvenile drug court division and set on the next available docket.

(6) The State Attorney may object to a case being transferred to juvenile drug court and request a preadmission hearing upon a belief the minor was dealing or selling controlled substances. The court, after a hearing, shall determine if the preponderance of the evidence excludes transfer of the case to juvenile drug court.

(7) A juvenile is excluded from juvenile drug court if:

(a) he or she has a prior record of violent felony or sexual felony offenses; or

(b) the pending charges may result in direct filed charges as an adult; or

(c) he or she has a prior felony adjudication not charged under Chapter 893 of the Florida Statutes.

(8) A juvenile may be terminated, after hearing, from juvenile drug court if:

(a) he or she is arrested for an additional offense; or

(b) he or she is not able to complete the juvenile delinquency pretrial substance abuse education and treatment intervention program or treatment program; or

(c) he or she is unable to obtain ninety (90) days of continuous abstinence prior to completion of the juvenile delinquency pretrial substance abuse education and treatment intervention program or other treatment program; or

(d) his or her current offense is likely to merit commitment; or

(e) he or she poses a threat to public safety; or

(f) he or she has an outstanding pick up order in excess of thirty (30) days.

(9) The minimum time of participation for a misdemeanor offense is six (6) months. The minimum time of participation for a felony offense is nine (9) months. If a juvenile successfully completes the drug court program his or her case may be dismissed as authorized by section 985.345, Florida Statutes.

(10) The time limitations may be extended if there are extenuating circumstances as decided by the Court.

(11) If the juvenile does not successfully comply with the written coordinated strategy, the court may order continuation in an education, treatment, or urine monitoring program.

(12) "Any child whose charges are dismissed after successful completion of the treatment-based drug court program, if otherwise eligible, may have his or her arrest record and plea of nolo contendere to the dismissed charges expunged under [section] 943.0585[, Florida Statutes]."

(13) Upon a juvenile's termination from juvenile drug court his or her case will be transferred to the originally assigned juvenile division.

(14) This Administrative Order vacates and supersedes Administrative Order 2009–116–UFC.

DONE AND ORDERED in chambers at Fort Lauderdale, Broward County, Florida on June 27, 2016.

/s/ Peter M. Weinstein

Peter M. Weinstein, Chief Judge

2016–6–UFC. ADMINISTRATIVE ORDER AS TO VOLUNTARY DEPENDENCY DRUG COURT PROGRAM

IN THE CIRCUIT COURT OF THE SEVENTEENTH JUDICIAL CIRCUIT IN AND FOR BROWARD COUNTY, FLORIDA

Administrative Order 2016–6–UFC

ADMINISTRATIVE ORDER AS TO VOLUNTARY DEPENDENCY DRUG COURT PROGRAM

(a) Florida Rule of Judicial Administration 2.215(b) states the chief judge shall "develop an administrative plan for the efficient and proper administration of all courts within that circuit."

(b) Chapter 39, Florida Statutes, authorizes the establishment of voluntary substance abuse programs for dependency cases for the rehabilitation of parents to promote reunification and stable home environments for children.

(c) In accordance with the authority vested in the chief judge by Florida Rule of Judicial Administration 2.215, it is ordered:

(1) A voluntary dependency drug court is established as authorized by Chapter 39, Florida Statutes.

(2) The dependency divisions shall identify cases which may be appropriate for dependency drug court using the following criteria:

a. substance use/abuse involvement or co-occurring disorder (substance abuse and mental health) is noted on the petition for shelter or dependency or identified by the court and reunification is the goal; and

b. the parent resides in Broward County; and

c. no more than forty five (45) days have elapsed since removal of the child (ren) or an arraignment on a straight petition. This time requirement can only be waived by the judge assigned to dependency drug court or upon approval of a general magistrate's recommendation on a case by case basis.

(3) A parent may not elect to participate in dependency drug court if:

a. judicially determined a sexual predator;

b. judicially determined a pedophile;

c. judicially determined to have caused severe physical or sexual abuse on a minor;

d. diagnosed with a terminal illness with less than six (6) months to live; or

e. diagnosed with a mental health illness which will substantially impair participation in a substance abuse treatment program.

(4) Upon identifying a case meeting the eligibility criteria, the court shall:

a. refer the parent(s) to a dependency drug court orientation;

b. refer the parent(s) to a comprehensive assessment by the Family Intervention Specialist (herein FIS) on a specific date and at a specific time if the parent indicates a willingness to participate in the dependency drug court program;

c. hold a drug court acceptance hearing after orientation and assessment to:

i. hear from a representative of the dependency drug court program as to the parent(s) probability of complying with the dependency drug court program requirements;

ii. allow the parent and his or her attorney to sign the "Agreement to Participate in Dependency Drug Court" if the parent is allowed to participate in dependency drug court; the parent(s) consent to the petition and a finding of dependency as to the child(ren).

iii. set a dependency drug court status hearing.

(5) Upon transfer to the dependency drug court the parent(s) will attend status hearings and all other statutorily mandated hearings until completion of the requirements of the dependency drug court tasks or termination from dependency drug court. Cases may be referred to a general magistrate as authorized by law and rules of procedure.

(6) This Administrative Order vacates and supersedes Administrative Order 2011–42–UFC.

DONE AND ORDERED in chambers at Fort Lauderdale, Broward County, Florida on January 13, 2016.

/s/ Peter M. Weinstein

Peter M. Weinstein, Chief Judge

2016–4–UFC. ADMINISTRATIVE ORDER ESTABLISHING EARLY CHILDHOOD COURT

IN THE CIRCUIT COURT OF THE SEVENTEENTH JUDICIAL CIRCUIT IN AND FOR BROWARD COUNTY, FLORIDA

Administrative Order 2016–4–UFC

ADMINISTRATIVE ORDER ESTABLISHING EARLY CHILDHOOD COURT

(a) Florida Rule of Judicial Administration 2.215(b) states the chief judge shall "develop an administrative plan for the efficient and proper administration of all courts within that circuit."

(b) Chapter 39, Florida Statutes, authorizes the establishment of an early childhood court to promote reunification and stable home environments for children from birth to age 5.

(c) In accordance with the authority vested in the chief judge by Florida Rule of Judicial Administration 2.215, it is ordered:

(1) An early childhood court is established as authorized by Chapter 39, Florida Statutes.

(2) The dependency division judges at the time of the shelter hearing but no later than arraignment shall identify cases which may be appropriate for early childhood court using all of the following criteria:

a. The child is under the age of 5.

b. The child was allegedly exposed to abuse, abandonment, or neglect and sheltered from the parent.

c. The child and parent reside in Broward County.

(3) If the parent has substance use, substance abuse or co-occurring mental health disorder, they may be admitted to the early childhood court after a court hearing. The parent at the time of the court hearing shall provide information as to current treatment for the substance abuse or mental health condition(s) or be willing to participate in treatment for the substance abuse or mental health condition.

(4) A parent may not participate in early childhood court if:

a. judicially determined a sexual predator;

b. judicially determined a pedophile;

c. judicially determined to have caused severe physical or sexual abuse on a minor;

d. diagnosed with a terminal illness with less than six (6) months to live;

e. the child is diagnosed with a terminal illness with less than six (6) months to live;

f. the alleged perpetrator of an "egregious" act on the child;

g. has a no contact order as to the child;

h. willfully failed to protect the child from the alleged abuse;

i. the alleged perpetrator of sexual abuse of a child; or

j. incarcerated for 6 months or longer.

(5) Upon identifying a case meeting the eligibility criteria, the court shall:

a. offer the early childhood court option to one or both parents;

b. explain that early childhood court is a voluntary program which offers wraparound, supportive services to a parent who seeks reunification with his or her child;

c. order a comprehensive assessment by the Early Childhood Court Child Parent Psychotherapist if the parent indicates a willingness to participate in the early childhood court program;

d. request that the parent and his or her attorney to sign the "Consent to Participate in Early Childhood Court" if the parent agrees to participate in early childhood court which shall include all terms of participation; and

e. set an early childhood court status hearing.

(6) A case will be transferred into early childhood court upon acceptance by the Early Childhood Court Judge. Upon transfer to early childhood court the parent will attend status hearings and all other statutorily mandated hearings until completion of early childhood court tasks or termination from early childhood court.

(7) Cases may be referred to a general magistrate as authorized by law and rules of procedure.

DONE AND ORDERED in chambers at Fort Lauderdale, Broward County, Florida on January 13, 2016.

/s/ Peter M. Weinstein

Peter M. Weinstein, Chief Judge

2015–11–UFC. ADMINISTRATIVE ORDER PROHIBITING DESTRUCTION OF UNIFIED FAMILY COURT DOMESTIC VIOLENCE COURT RECORDS

IN THE CIRCUIT COURT OF THE SEVENTEENTH JUDICIAL CIRCUIT IN AND FOR BROWARD COUNTY, FLORIDA

Order Number 2015–11–UFC

ADMINISTRATIVE ORDER PROHIBITING DESTRUCTION OF UNIFIED FAMILY COURT DOMESTIC VIOLENCE COURT RECORDS

(a) Florida Rule of Judicial Administration 2.215(b)(3) states the chief judge shall "considering available resources, ensure the efficient and proper administration of all courts within [this] circuit."

(b) Florida Rule of Judicial Administration 2.430 authorizes the disposition and destruction of domestic violence injunction files. The judges hearing these cases need the files preserved for a period of time longer than required by Florida Rule of Judicial Administration 2.430 to comply with litigants' due process rights.

(c) In accordance with the authority vested in the chief judge by Florida Rule of Judicial Administration 2.215, it is ordered:

(1) The Clerk of Court is directed to immediately cease the physical destruction and disposition of Unified Family Court Domestic Violence Court Records as may be authorized by Florida Rule of Judicial Administration 2.430.

(2) The Clerk of Court shall note on the physical court file, progress docket, and on the electronic court records the court records are not to be physically destroyed or disposed of without further court order.

(3) The Clerk of Court may permanently record all paper documents in the court file, including the parties contact information, and thereafter request authorization for the physical destruction and disposition of the paper documents.

(4) The Clerk of Court shall not destroy or dispose of any electronic court records.

(5) The court records subject to this order are any and all arrests and/or prosecutions for domestic violence as defined by Chapter 741, Fla. Stat., or stalking, sexual violence and dating violence as defined by Chapter 784, Fla. Stat., Injunction for Protection against Dating Violence, Injunction for Protection against Domestic Violence, Injunction for Protection against Repeat Violence, Injunction for Protection against Sexual Violence, and Injunction for Protection against Stalking (which includes cyber stalking).

DONE AND ORDERED in chambers at Fort Lauderdale, Broward County, Florida on March 25, 2015.

s/ Peter M. Weinstein
Peter M. Weinstein, Chief Judge

2015–10–UFC. ADMINISTRATIVE ORDER ESTABLISHING PROCEDURES FOR FAMILY DIVISION EMERGENCY MATTERS

IN THE CIRCUIT COURT OF THE SEVENTEENTH JUDICIAL CIRCUIT IN AND FOR BROWARD COUNTY, FLORIDA

Order Number 2015–10–UFC

ADMINISTRATIVE ORDER ESTABLISHING PROCEDURES FOR FAMILY DIVISION EMERGENCY MATTERS

(a) Florida Rule of Judicial Administration 2.215(b)(3) states the chief judge shall "develop an administrative plan for the efficient and proper administration of all courts within that circuit."

(b) In accordance with the authority vested in the chief judge by Florida Rule of Judicial Administration 2.215, it is ordered:

(1) *Child Emergencies.* A child emergency is a matter of imminent or impending abuse, neglect or abandonment affecting the health, safety, or welfare of a child. Florida Statute section 39.201 mandates certain alleged abuses be reported. If the allegations fall within the statute, the matter shall be reported to the Abuse Hotline, 1–800–96–ABUSE. A written verified motion shall be filed and signed by the filing party. A copy of the written verified motion shall be provided to the opposing party and the divisional judge. Visitation is not an emergency. See, Florida Statute section 61.13(4). A UCCJEA affidavit shall be filed and a copy of the affidavit shall be provided to the divisional judge.

(2) *Child Pick Up Orders and Injunctions Related to Children.* The Florida Supreme Court Approved Family Law Forms in 12.941 shall be the exclusive forms to be used. Only those with standing by virtue of Florida law are entitled to relief. A UCCJEA affidavit shall be filed and a copy of the written verified motion and affidavit shall be provided to the divisional judge. Four copies of proposed orders which comply with the rule shall accompany the copy of the motion to the judge.

(3) *Ex Parte Emergencies and Injunctions Not Related to Children.* An emergency that is not a child emergency is defined by Florida Rule of Civil Procedure 1.610(a) (1) (A), as a matter in which "immediate and irreparable injury, loss or damage will result" and for which there is no adequate remedy at law." A written verified motion, providing for ex-parte or relief with notice, shall be filed in which Florida Rule of Civil Procedure 1.610 is strictly followed, with a copy to the divisional judge. Four copies of a proposed order which complies with the rule shall accompany the copy of the motion to the judge.

(4) *Priority.* The judge is required to determine if the facts demonstrate an emergency and whether a hearing should be set on an expedited basis. An emergency shall be given priority on the Court's calendar with short notice.

(5) *Certification and Sanctions.* All emergency motions shall be verified and shall include a certification by the lawyer or self represented litigant that the motion is an emergency and the lawyer or self represented litigant is acting in good faith in seeking such relief. Sanctions shall be considered by the divisional judge for the filing of emergency motions that do not comply with this administrative order.

(6) *Alternate Assignment.* When the divisional judge is absent from the courthouse and an emergency matter has been filed in an assigned case, application may be made to the Court Administrator in Room 880 who will assign the matter to one of the judges of that division in accordance with a schedule of assignments made pursuant to instructions of the Chief Judge. The judge so assigned shall consider the matter after determining if it is an emergency.

(7) This Administrative Order rescinds and supersedes Administrative Order 2008–60–UFC

(8) The Clerk of Courts shall provide a copy of this order along with the initial pleadings to the petitioning party or attorney for service on the respondent.

DONE AND ORDERED in chambers at Fort Lauderdale, Broward County, Florida on March 16, 2015.

s/ Peter M. Weinstein
Peter M. Weinstein, Chief Judge

2014–22–UFC. ADMINISTRATIVE ORDER AS TO DEPARTMENT OF REVENUE TITLE IV–D CASES

IN THE CIRCUIT COURT OF THE SEVENTEENTH JUDICIAL CIRCUIT IN AND FOR BROWARD COUNTY, FLORIDA

Order Number 2014–22–UFC

ADMINISTRATIVE ORDER AS TO DEPARTMENT OF REVENUE TITLE IV–D CASES

(a) Florida Rule of Judicial Administration 2.215(b)(3) states the chief judge shall "considering available resources, ensure the efficient and proper administration of all courts within [this] circuit."

(b) The statutory scheme as set forth in Chapter 409, Florida Statutes, envisions that only those matters authorized by statute, paternity and child support but not parenting or timesharing matters may be litigated in Title IV–D cases and all other litigation shall occur in a separate action.

(c) The filing of counter claims and/or third party claims in Title IV–D actions which are not paternity or child support, but include parenting or timesharing matters is not consistent with Chapter 409, Fla. Stat., which results in inefficient case management and disposition of cases.

(d) In accordance with the authority vested in the chief judge by Florida Rule of Judicial Administration 2.215, it is ordered:

(1) The Respondent in a Title IV–D case shall not file a counter claim or third party claim for parenting or time sharing matters but shall file a separate action for those claims.

(2) The Clerk of Court upon the filing of a Title IV–D action or separate action shall review his records to determine if there is any pending case with the obligor and obligee to ensure the cases are assigned to one judicial division and one general magistrate division.

DONE AND ORDERED in chambers at Fort Lauderdale, Broward County, Florida on May 6, 2014.

s/Peter M. Weinstein
Peter M. Weinstein, Chief Judge

2014-14-UFC. ADMINISTRATIVE ORDER DIRECTING CLERK OF COURTS WITH REGARD TO DISMISSED CIVIL OR FAMILY CASES

Publisher's Note: For text of order, see Order 2014–14–CIV under the Civil Orders heading, supra.

2010–11–UFC[1]. SECOND AMENDED ADMINISTRATIVE ORDER ESTABLISHING PROCEDURE FOR APPOINTMENT OF CRIMINAL MENTAL HEALTH EVALUATORS

IN THE CIRCUIT COURT OF THE SEVENTEENTH JUDICIAL CIRCUIT IN AND FOR BROWARD COUNTY, FLORIDA

Order Number 2010–10–Crim; 2010–11–UFC

SECOND AMENDED ADMINISTRATIVE ORDER ESTABLISHING PROCEDURE FOR APPOINTMENT OF CRIMINAL MENTAL HEALTH EVALUATORS

(a) Chapters 916 and 985, Fla. Stat., sets forth the duties of the judicial branch with regard to evaluations of defendants.

(b) § 29.004, Fla. Stat., determines the state court system obligations to pay for an expert witness.

(c) The Seventeenth Judicial Circuit (herein Circuit) enters into contracts with psychologists and psychiatrics to provide evaluations and reports as required by law.

(d) In accordance with the authority vested in the Chief Judge by Florida Rule of Judicial Administration 2.215, it is ordered effective January 25, 2010, as follows:

(1) All psychiatrists and psychologists (herein expert) upon execution of a contract to provide services to the Circuit shall be assigned to one or more categories for appointments.[2] An expert's failure to comply with the contract requirements, including but not limited to time requirements and report formats, may result in termination of the contract and the experts removal from the registry.

(2) If a judge or general magistrate requires an expert for an evaluation and report which the state court system is obligated to pay he or she shall contact the Trial Court Administrator's Court Projects (herein Court Projects). The judge or general magistrate shall provide to Court Projects the name of the defendant, type of ordered evaluation, the case number, location of the individual, and next court date.

(3) Upon receipt of the required information Court Projects shall access an electronic rotational registry to select the names of three (3) experts for the ordered evaluation and the requesting judge or general magistrate shall appoint one of the experts from the names provided. Court Projects shall thereafter process the order of appointment and coordinate the receipt of all required reports.

(4) If a judge or general magistrate requires a re-evaluation to determine if the defendant is now competent to proceed to trial, Court Projects shall access the electronic rotational registry to select the names of three (3) experts for presentation to the judge or general magistrate. A judge or general magistrate may choose one of the experts from the names provided, or instead may choose another expert listed on the registry, not in rotation, if that expert previously provided an opinion regarding the defendant's competency within the last twelve (12) months.

DONE AND ORDERED in chambers at Fort Lauderdale, Broward County, Florida on October 4, 2010.

s/Victor Tobin
Victor Tobin, Chief Judge

[1] Alternative citation 2010-10-CRIM.

[2] The categories are as follows: autism, adult competency, criteria for hospitalization (incompetent), criteria for hospitalization(insane), domestic violence risk assessment, juvenile competency, neuropsychological evaluation, mental retardation, psychological assessments (residential placement, sentencing, penalty phase, competency to waive Miranda), and violence risk assessment. The categories may change from time to time based upon statutory changes or appropriations.

2009–76–UFC. ADMINISTRATIVE ORDER REQUIRING ESTABLISHMENT SUPPORT DEPOSITORY ACCOUNT

IN THE CIRCUIT COURT OF THE SEVENTEENTH JUDICIAL CIRCUIT IN AND FOR BROWARD COUNTY, FLORIDA

Order Number 2009–76–UFC

ADMINISTRATIVE ORDER REQUIRING ESTABLISHMENT SUPPORT DEPOSITORY ACCOUNT

(a) Florida Rule of Judicial Administration 2.215(b)(3) states the chief judge shall "develop an administrative plan for the efficient and proper administration of all courts within that circuit."

(b) The volume of unified family cases that include a final judgment or order for support requires a uniform procedure to establish a depositoiry[1] account for the receipt, disbursement, and enforcement of support obligations.

(c) In accordance with the authority vested in the chief judge by Florida Rule of Judicial Administration 2.215, it is ordered:

(1) The attorney of record for a party receiving support shall establish a depository account with the Clerk of the Circuit Court within ten (10) days of the final judgment or order establishing a support obligation. If the party entitled to receive support does not have an attorney then the party shall establish a depository account with the Clerk of the Circuit Court within ten (10) days of the final judgment or order establishing a support obligation.

(2) At the time of establishing the depository account with the Clerk of Circuit Court the attorney and/or party shall complete any and all forms required by the Clerk of Circuit Court and provide a copy of the final judgment or order establishing the support obligation.

(3) If a final judgment or order establishing a support obligation is modified, a copy of the modified order shall be

provided to the Clerk of Circuit Court's depository staff within (10) days of the final judgment or order modifying the support obligation.

DONE AND ORDERED in chambers at Fort Lauderdale, Broward County, Florida on July 1, 2009.

s/Victor Tobin
Victor Tobin, Chief Judge

1 So in original.

2008–141–UFC. ADMINISTRATIVE ORDER DESIGNATING DEPOSITORY FOR CHILD SUPPORT AND ALIMONY PAYMENTS

IN THE CIRCUIT COURT OF THE SEVENTEENTH JUDICIAL CIRCUIT IN AND FOR BROWARD COUNTY, FLORIDA

Order Number 2008–141–UFC

ADMINISTRATIVE ORDER DESIGNATING DEPOSITORY FOR CHILD SUPPORT AND ALIMONY PAYMENTS

(a) Florida Rule of Family Law 12.611 authorizes the chief judge to establish by administrative order a depository for support payments.

(b) Chapter 61, Fla. Stat., has a scheme for the payment of support either through a county depository or the State Depository Unit.

(c) In accordance with the authority vested in the chief judge by Florida Rule of Judicial Administration 2.215, effective October 1, 2008, it is ordered:

(1) The depository for non Title IV–D, alimony, and non Income Deduction Order cases for Broward County shall be the Clerk of the Circuit Court. Any individual ordered to make payments for which the Clerk of Circuit Court is the named depository shall mail his or her payment by money order or other form of certified funds to Clerk of the Circuit Court, P.O. Box 14248, Fort Lauderdale, Florida 33302.

(2) The depository for Title IV–D and Income Deduction Order cases, except alimony only, for Broward County shall be the State Disbursement Unit. Any individual ordered to make payments for which the State Disbursement Unit is the named depository shall mail his or her payment by money order or other form of certified funds to State Disbursement Unit, P.O. Box 8500, Tallahassee, Florida 32314.

(3) The payor and payee of a support obligation shall cooperate with the depository receiving support payments by providing any and all information required for the processing of payments.

(4) The payor shall be responsible to pay any and all service fees and charges imposed by Clerk of the Circuit Court or the State Disbursement Unit as authorized by Chapter 61, Fla. Stat., unless otherwise ordered by the court.

(5) The Clerk of the Circuit Court and the State Disbursement Unit shall comply with any and all federal and state laws or regulations with regard to the collection and disbursement of support.

(6) This Administrative Order supersedes and vacates Administrative Order 2007–61–UFC.

DONE AND ORDERED in chambers at Fort Lauderdale, Broward County, Florida on October 1, 2008.

s/Victor Tobin
Victor Tobin, Chief Judge

V–06–N–1. JUDICIAL WAIVER OF PARENTAL NOTICE OF TERMINATION OF PREGNANCY

IN THE CIRCUIT COURT OF THE SEVENTEENTH JUDICIAL CIRCUIT IN AND FOR BROWARD COUNTY, FLORIDA

ADMINISTRATIVE ORDER NO.: V–06–N–1

IN RE: JUDICIAL WAIVER OF PARENTAL NOTICE OF TERMINATION OF PREGNANCY

_______________/

WHEREAS, petitions to waive the parental notification of termination of pregnancy are sensitive matters involving minors, for which s. 390.01114 and 390.01116, Florida Statutes require that a confidential record be maintained, that the hearings are held confidential and closed to the public, that the court file be sealed and the minor's identity remain anonymous; and

WHEREAS, proceedings for a judicial waiver of parental notice of termination of pregnancy are subject to the Rules of Juvenile Procedure, rules 8.800, 8.805, 8.810, 8.815, 8.820, and 8.835; and

WHEREAS, section 390.01114, Florida Statutes requires that the court make a ruling on the petition within 48 hours of filing; and

THEREFORE, in accordance with the authority vested in the Chief Judge by rule 2.050 of the Florida Rules of Judicial Administration and pursuant to section 390.01114 and 390.01116 Florida Statutes, and rules 8.800 through 8.835, Florida Rules of Juvenile Procedure,

IT IS ORDERED THAT:

1. Case Assignment: The Clerk of Court shall assign the petition to waive parental notification of termination of pregnancy pursuant to s. 390.01114, Florida Statutes to a Juvenile Dependency Division of the Unified Family Court to be heard by the judge presiding over that division. The Clerk shall immediately forward the petition and court file to the assigned judge.

2. Confidentiality: The court file and hearings on the petition to waive parental notification of termination of pregnancy are confidential and closed to the public pursuant to s. 390.01114(4)(e), Florida Statutes. The court file shall be sealed and the identity of the minor shall remain anonymous.

3. Right to Counsel: The minor child shall be advised in writing of her right to court-appointed counsel, and counsel shall be appointed for the child at her request without cost to the minor. The Clerk of Court shall provide the minor with a written notice of her right to counsel. The presiding judge shall appoint counsel from the Judicial Waiver wheel upon request from the petitioner/child. Compensation of court-

appointed counsel shall be as established by the circuit Indigent Services Committee.

4. Notice: The Clerk shall notice the petitioner and counsel for the petitioner of the date, time and location of the hearing. The notice shall be provided by the Clerk of Court to the petitioner on the same day the petition is filed before the minor leaves the courthouse.

5. Hearings During Normal Business Hours: Court proceedings for the waiver of parental notification of termination of pregnancy must be given precedence over other pending matters to the extent necessary to ensure that the court reaches a decision promptly. Hearings on petitions to waive parental notification of termination of pregnancy shall be held within 48 hours of filing by the assigned judge during normal business hours. The court shall rule, and must issue written findings of fact and conclusions of law within 48 hours after the petition is filed. The 48 hour limitation may be extended at the request of the minor. If the assigned judge is not available, then the petition shall be heard by an alternate for the assigned judge during normal business hours.

6. Review of Petitions and Hearings on Weekends or Court Holidays:

a. Petitions filed after 12:00 p.m. on a Friday or any other day of the week immediately after which the courthouse will be closed for one day or more, which can not be heard in accordance with paragraph 5. above, shall be heard by the judge presiding over first appearances, detention and shelter hearings.

b. These proceedings shall be held in courtroom 241 or another courtroom equipped to record proceedings. The Clerk shall provide petitioner and counsel for the petitioner notice in accordance with paragraph 4. above, to be present for hearing on the petition at 9:00 a.m. in room 241 the day after the petition is filed. The hearing on the petition shall be held immediately after the judge presiding over first appearances has heard juvenile detention, dependency shelter, and adult first appearance hearings. The courtroom must be cleared as the proceeding is closed to the public and confidential. The hearing shall be recorded by the equipment configured for that courtroom.

c. In the event that the judge presiding over first appearances is unavailable to hold a hearing, then the Civil Duty Judge shall hold a hearing in a courtroom equipped to record proceedings, at 9:00 AM the day after the petition is filed, or as soon thereafter as is practicable.

d. The court shall rule, and must issue written findings of fact and conclusions of law within 48 hours after the petition is filed. The 48 hour limitation may be extended at the request of the minor.

7. If the court fails to rule or enter an order within 48 hours of filing and the minor has not requested an extension of time, then the petition is deemed granted, and the parental notice requirement is waived. An order so indicating shall be entered by the assigned judge, his or her alternate or the judge presiding over first appearances in accordance with paragraphs 1, 5, and 6 above.

8. This order rescinds and replaces Administrative Order: V–05–N–1, and is effective upon execution.

DONE AND ORDERED in chambers at Fort Lauderdale, Broward County, Florida on this 9th day of February, 2006.

/s/DALE ROSS
DALE ROSS, Chief Judge

Eighteenth Judicial Circuit (Brevard and Seminole Counties)

ADMINISTRATIVE ORDERS

19–11. DOMESTIC RELATIONS—REQUIREMENT TO COMPLETE THE PARENT EDUCATION AND FAMILY STABILIZATION COURSE.

19–08–S. JUVENILES—SEXTING BY MINORS–SECTION 847.0141, FLORIDA STATUTES.

18–55–B. CLERK OF COURT—UNIFORM BREVARD COUNTY COURT CRIMINAL AND TRAFFIC PROCEDURES.

18–42–B. MISDEMEANOR AND FELONY CHARGES ARISING OUT OF THE SAME CIRCUMSTANCES.

18–40. USE OF THERAPY ANIMALS OR FACILITY DOGS IN PROCEEDINGS INVOLVING A SEXUAL OFFENSE OR CHILD ABUSE, ABANDONMENT, OR NEGLECT.

18–26–S. CRIMINAL—MODIFICATION OF MONETARY BOND AMOUNTS AND BOND CONDITIONS.

18–23 (A1). MENTAL HEALTH—RISK PROTECTION ORDERS.

18–22–S (A1). CRIMINAL BAIL SCHEDULE FOR SEMINOLE COUNTY.

18–21–B. BAIL SCHEDULE.

18–18–B. PROBATE & GUARDIANSHIP—PETITIONS TO SELL REAL PROPERTY.

18–13–S. ADMINISTRATIVE RULES—ORDER ESTABLISHING COURT INTERPRETER POLICY.

18–12–S. CRIMINAL—STANDARDIZED SEMINOLE COUNTY ARREST AFFIDAVIT.

18–06–S. DRUG COURT—FELONY SUBSTANCE ABUSE PRE–TRIAL INTERVENTION.

17–46–B. PROBATE AND GUARDIANSHIP—FINGERPRINTING OF GUARDIANS.

17–40–B. JAIL—FARM TIME—ALTERNATIVE TO INCARCERATION PROGRAM (ATIP).

17–38. PROBATE AND GUARDIANSHIP—ESTABLISHING SURETY BONDS FOR PUBLIC GUARDIANS.

17–37. MENTAL HEALTH—CONFIDENTIALITY OF EXAMINING COMMITTEE REPORTS.

17–30–S. CRIMINAL—ALTERNATIVE SANCTIONS PROGRAM.

17–29–B. CRIMINAL—ALTERNATIVE SANCTIONS PROGRAM.

17–28. JUVENILE—ALL CHILDREN IN THE JUVENILE DIVISION REPRESENTED BY THE OFFICE OF THE PUBLIC DEFENDER.

17–24 (A1). [SUPERSEDED BY ORDER 18–40, EFFECTIVE AUGUST 23, 2018.].

17–20–B. MENTAL HEALTH—MARCHMAN ACT HEARINGS—TELEPHONIC APPEARANCE OF QUALIFIED PROFESSIONALS.

17–19 (A1). FEES—ESTABLISHMENT OF DUE PROCESS SERVICE PROVIDER RATES AND POLICIES GOVERNING THE APPOINTMENT OF EXPERT WITNESSES.

17–18. ATTORNEYS—COURT APPOINTED ATTORNEY PROCEDURE FOR APPOINTMENT OF COUNSEL IN CRIMINAL AND CIVIL PROCEEDINGS.

17–17–S. DOMESTIC RELATIONS—FAMILY DIVISION—STANDING TEMPORARY ORDER IN DOMESTIC RELATIONS CASES SUCH AS DISSOLUTION OF MARRIAGE, PATERNITY AND DOMESTIC VIOLENCE.

17–16–B. CRIMINAL—PROCEDURES FOR E-WARRANTS FOR SEARCH AND ARREST WARRANTS.

17–15. CLERK OF COURT—ELECTRONIC FILING.

17–14–S. ADMINISTRATIVE RULES—ORDER ESTABLISHING GUIDELINES FOR PUBLIC ASSEMBLY AND ESTABLISHMENT OF RESTRICTED AREAS FOR PUBLIC PROTESTS.

17–11–B. MENTAL HEALTH—BAKER ACT PROCEEDINGS.

17–08–S. MEDIATION—FAMILY LAW MEDIATION PROGRAM.

16–42–B. ADOPTIONS—CRIMINAL CHECKS.

16–38–B. DOMESTIC VIOLENCE—GEOGRAPHIC ASSIGNMENT FOR INJUNCTIONS FOR PROTECTION (OTHER THAN DOMESTIC VIOLENCE).

16–35–B. DOMESTIC RELATIONS—FAMILY DIVISION PARTIES.

16–34–B. [SUPERSEDED BY ORDER 17-23-B, EFFECTIVE JUNE 1, 2017.].

16–32–B. ADMINISTRATIVE ORDERS—RESCINDS ADMINISTRATIVE ORDER 14–22–B.

16–31–S. CIVIL—CONTRABAND FORFEITURE ACT PROCEDURES.

16–30–B. MEDIATION—FAMILY MEDIATION MANDATORY REFERRAL OF ALL CONTESTED FAMILY LAW CASES TO MEDIATION.

16–25–S. CRIMINAL–MISDEMEANOR PROBATION SERVICES IN SEMINOLE COUNTY.

16–18–S. [SUPERSEDED BY ORDER 17–30–S, EFFECTIVE JUNE 28, 2017.].

16–17–B. [SUPERSEDED BY ORDER 17–29–B, EFFECTIVE JUNE 28, 2017.].

16–15–S (A1). [SUPERSEDED BY ORDER 18-02-S, EFFECTIVE JANUARY 22, 2018.].

16–15–S. [SUPERSEDED BY ORDER 16-15-S (A1), EFFECTIVE SEPTEMBER 1, 2016.].

16–11. COURT REPORTING.
16–05–S (A). [SUPERSEDED BY ORDER 17-26-S, EFFECTIVE JUNE 20, 2017.].
16–05–S. [SUPERSEDED BY ORDER 16–05–S (AMD), EFFECTIVE JUNE 30, 2016.].
16–04–S. MENTAL HEALTH—MARCHMAN ACT HEARINGS—TELEPHONIC APPEARANCE OF QUALIFIED PROFESSIONALS.
16–03–S. ADMINISTRATIVE ORDERS—RESCINDS ADMINISTRATIVE ORDERS.
16–02–B (A1). [SUPERSEDED BY ORDER 18–21–B, EFFECTIVE MAY 22, 2018.].
16–02–B. [SUPERSEDED BY ORDER 16–02–B (A1), EFFECTIVE JULY 5, 2016.].
16–01–B. CRIMINAL—ASSIGNMENT OF CASES ASSOCIATED WITH THE JIMMY RYCE INVOLUNTARY CIVIL COMMITMENT ACT.
15–47. [SUPERSEDED BY ORDER 18–44, EFFECTIVE NOVEMBER 7, 2018.].
15–44–S. [SUPERSEDED BY ORDER 18–45–S, EFFECTIVE NOVEMBER 7, 2018.].
15–43–B. [SUPERSEDED BY ORDER 17-33-B, EFFECTIVE SEPTEMBER 1, 2017.].
15–42–S. CRIMINAL BAIL SCHEDULE FOR SEMINOLE COUNTY.
15–40. PROBATE AND GUARDIANSHIP—FILING ANNUAL GUARDIANSHIP REPORTS.
15–39. [SUPERSEDED BY ORDER 17–18, EFFECTIVE APRIL 17, 2017.].
15–36–B. [SUPERSEDED BY ORDER 18–52–B, EFFECTIVE NOVEMBER 14, 2018.].
15–35. ATTORNEYS—APPOINTMENT OF PUBLIC DEFENDER IN BAKER ACT PROCEEDING.
15–29–S. SUPERSEDED BY ADMINISTRATIVE ORDER NO. 16–05–S.
15–26. ABORTION—ASSIGNMENT OF CASES ADDRESSING A MINOR'S REQUEST FOR JUDICIAL WAIVER OF PARENTAL NOTICE OF ABORTION.
15–24. CLERK OF COURT–CONFIDENTIALITY OF COURT RECORDS.
15–22 (A1). DOMESTIC RELATIONS—EIGHTEENTH JUDICIAL CIRCUIT BATTERERS' INTERVENTION PROGRAM.
15–19–B (A1). ADMINISTRATIVE ORDERS—RESCINDS ADMINISTRATIVE ORDER.
15–18 (A1). SUPERSEDED BY ADMINISTRATIVE ORDER NO. 16–11.
15–17. DOMESTIC RELATIONS—PARENTING COORDINATION IN HIGH CONFLICT FAMILY LAW CASES.
15–15–B. CRIMINAL—NOTICE OF EXPIRATION OF SPEEDY TRIAL/MOTION FOR DISCHARGE/DEMAND FOR SPEEDY TRIAL.
15–13–S. CRIMINAL—EMPACT–ELECTRONIC MONITORING OF DEFENDANTS AS A CONDITION OF PRE–TRIAL RELEASE—GENERAL GUIDELINES AND SPECIFICALLY IN DOMESTIC VIOLENCE MATTERS.
15–10–B. DOMESTIC RELATIONS—ORDERS AND JUDGMENTS IN TANDEM WITH THE POLICIES AND PROCEDURES OF THE SCHOOL BOARD OF BREVARD COUNTY.
15–07. ADMINISTRATIVE ORDERS—RESCINDS ADMINISTRATIVE ORDERS.
14–39–B. CLERK OF COURT—PROCEDURES FOR PROCESSING CHILD SUPPORT PAYMENTS.
14–37–B. SUPERSEDED BY ADMINISTRATIVE ORDER NO. 16-34-B.
14–32–S. SUPERSEDED BY ADMINISTRATIVE ORDER NO. 15–42–S.
14–31–S. CRIMINAL—PROCEDURES FOR SEARCH AND ARREST WARRANTS IN SEMINOLE COUNTY.
14–30. ADMINISTRATIVE PROCEDURES—ESTABLISHMENT OF LOCAL PROFESSIONALISM PANEL.
14–22–B. SUPERSEDED BY ADMINISTRATIVE ORDER NO. 16-32-B.
14–18–B. PROCESS SERVERS—PROCEDURES FOR APPOINTMENT OF CERTIFIED PROCESS SERVERS AND GRIEVANCES.
14–05. [SUPERSEDED BY ORDER 19–11, EFFECTIVE JANUARY 24, 2019].
14–04 (A1). DOMESTIC RELATIONS—COLLABORATIVE CONFLICT RESOLUTION IN DISSOLUTION OF MARRIAGE CASES.
13–42–S. SUPERSEDED BY ADMINISTRATIVE ORDER NO. 17-08-S.
13–41. FORECLOSURE—CASES STATUS REPORTING REQUIREMENTS.
13–40–S. [SUPERSEDED BY ORDER 18–12–S, EFFECTIVE MARCH 8, 2018.].
13–38–B. DOMESTIC RELATIONS—FAMILY DIVISION—STANDING TEMPORARY DOMESTIC RELATIONS ORDER.
13–37–B. TRAFFIC—PLEA OF NO CONTEST AND REQUEST FOR WITHHOLD OF ADJUDICATION PROGRAM.
13–32–S. FORECLOSURE-MORTGAGE FORECLOSURE SALES—CANCELLATION BY CLERK.
13–28. CRIMINAL—"THINKING FOR A CHANGE" PROGRAM IN LIEU OF PERFORMING COMMUNITY SERVICE HOURS FOR A FELONY SENTENCE.
13–27–B. SUPERSEDED BY ADMINISTRATIVE ORDER NO. 16-17-B.
13–24–B (A1). [SUPERSEDED BY ORDER 18–55–B, EFFECTIVE DECEMBER 20, 2018.].
13–19–B (A1). CRIMINAL—ALERTS/REPORTS FROM ELECTRONIC MONITORING COMPANIES CONCERNING POSSIBLE VIOLATIONS OF ELECTRONIC MONITORING RULES.
13–18–S. SUPERSEDED BY ADMINISTRATIVE ORDER NO. 16-18-S.
13–17–S. FORECLOSURE—RESIDENTIAL MORTGAGE FORECLOSURE NOTICE OF LIMITED APPEARANCE FOR MEDIATION ONLY.
13–16–S. FORECLOSURE—RESIDENTIAL MORTGAGE FORECLOSURE MEDIATION NOTICE.
13–15. [SUPERSEDED BY ORDER 17-15, EFFECTIVE MARCH 24, 2017.].

13–11–B. SUPERSEDED BY ADMINISTRATIVE ORDER NO. 16-30-B.

12–33–B. DOMESTIC RELATIONS—TEMPORARY ORDER GOVERNING BATTERERS' INTERVENTION PROGRAMS.

12–28–B. COURT COSTS—INSURANCE COVERAGE IN COUNTY COURT—COMMUNITY SERVICE.

12–27–S. JUVENILE DEPENDENCY—DISCOVERY IN ALL CHILD DEPENDENCY CASES IN THE JUVENILE DIVISION.

12–25–S. MEDIATION—MANDATORY MEDIATION CIRCUIT COURT SEMINOLE COUNTY OWNER-OCCUPIED RESIDENTIAL MORTGAGE FORECLOSURES.

12–18–B. JAIL—BREVARD COUNTY JAIL TESTING OF DETAINEES, INMATES, AND OTHER PERSONS AND DISCLOSURE OF TEST RESULTS.

12–17–B. ADOPTIONS—OBJECTION TO NOTICE OF ADOPTION.

12–14–S. COUNTY COURT—MISDEMEANOR VETERANS' TREATMENT COURT.

12–09–S. MENTAL HEALTH COURT.

12–08. FORECLOSURE PROCEDURE—ORDER DIRECTING COUNSEL TO SERVE COPIES OF NOTICES OF HEARING, ORDERS AND JUDGMENTS IN RESIDENTIAL MORTGAGE CASES.

11–38–B. COUNTY COURT—MISDEMEANOR VETERANS' TREATMENT COURT.

11–29–B. CRIMINAL—STANDARDIZED BREVARD COUNTY ARREST AFFIDAVIT.

11–24. DOMESTIC RELATIONS—FAMILY DIVISION—MODEL FAMILY COURT.

11–22–B (A1). CRIMINAL—STANDARDIZED BREVARD COUNTY ARREST AFFIDAVIT.

11–15–S. JUVENILE COURT AND PROSECUTION ALTERNATIVES FOR YOUTH PROGRAM PROCEDURE.

11–14–B (A4). SUPERSEDED BY ADMINISTRATIVE ORDER NO. 16-35-B.

11–12–B. SUPERSEDED BY ADMINISTRATIVE ORDER NO. 16–01–B.

11–10–S. [SUPERSEDED BY ORDER 17–17–S, EFFECTIVE MARCH 27, 2017.].

10–33–B. JAIL—DISTRIBUTION OF SUMMARIES OF CRIMINAL HISTORY NCIC/FCIC OF DEFENDANTS APPEARING AT FIRST APPEARANCE AT BREVARD COUNTY JAIL.

10–30–S. JUVENILE—DEPENDENCY MEDIATION—FLORIDA STATUTES CHAPTER 39 MANDATORY REFERRAL OF ALL CONTESTED DEPENDENCY CASES TO MEDIATION.

10–26–B. DOMESTIC RELATIONS—FAMILY DIVISION PARTIES REQUIRED TO READ CERTAIN ADMINISTRATIVE ORDERS.

10–24–B. [SUPERSEDED BY ORDER 17-40-B, EFFECTIVE OCTOBER 2, 2017.].

10–10–B. SUPPORT—CHILD SUPPORT—REDIRECTION OF PAYMENTS AND ACCOUNT MAINTENANCE IN FORMER TITLE IV–D CHILD SUPPORT ENFORCEMENT CASES.

10–07–B. SUPERSEDED BY ADMINISTRATIVE ORDER NO. 16–02–B.

09–26–B. SUPERSEDED BY ADMINISTRATIVE ORDER NO. 16–42–B.

09–19–S. DOMESTIC RELATIONS—FAMILY DIVISION—SUPPLEMENTAL PETITIONS FOR MODIFICATION.

09–17–S (A2). CRIMINAL—GPS ELECTRONIC MONITORING—POST–SENTENCING ALTERNATIVES FOR NON–VIOLENT OFFENDERS.

09–15–B. CRIMINAL—ON SITE VIOLATIONS OF PROBATION AND COMMUNITY CONTROL; FAILURE TO APPEAR, AND VIOLATION OF PROBATION WARRANTS.

09–14–B (A2). MEDIATION—MANDATORY MEDIATION CIRCUIT COURT BREVARD COUNTY OWNER OCCUPIED RESIDENTIAL MORTGAGE FORECLOSURE.

09–07–B (A1). CRIMINAL—PRETRIAL RELEASE PROGRAM—EXPANSION OF THE RELEASE AUTHORITY OF THE PRETRIAL RELEASE PROGRAM.

09–06. COURTROOM DECORUM AND PROCEDURE.

08–26–S. [SUPERSEDED BY ORDER 18–13–S, EFFECTIVE MARCH 19, 2018.].

08–24. FEES—COSTS OF DEFENSE; PUBLIC DEFENDER APPLICATION FEE.

07–36–B. [SUPERSEDED BY ORDER 17-46-B, EFFECTIVE DECEMBER 4, 2017.].

07–26–S. CRIMINAL—BAIL SCHEDULE FOR SEMINOLE COUNTY.

07–12–S. CRIMINAL—WORK RELEASE PROGRAM SEMINOLE COUNTY.

07–06–S. CRIMINAL—ADULT CONSEQUENCE PROGRAM.

06–12–B. ARBITRATION—QUALIFICATIONS FOR APPOINTMENT OF ARBITRATORS IN CIVIL CASES.

06–06–S (A2). SUPERSEDED BY ADMINISTRATIVE ORDER NO. 16-15-S.

05–50. APPEALS TO CIRCUIT COURT.

05–46–B. CRIMINAL—RELEASE ON RECOGNIZANCE/SIGNATURE BOND IN VIOLATION OF MISDEMEANOR PROBATION CASES.

05–45–B. DOMESTIC VIOLENCE—CHILDREN ATTENDING DOMESTIC VIOLENCE INJUNCTION HEARINGS.

05–27. [SUPERSEDED BY ORDER 17-38, EFFECTIVE SEPTEMBER 25, 2017.].

05–23–B. ARBITRATION—CREATION AND MAINTENANCE OF CIRCUIT LIST OF QUALIFIED ARBITRATORS; COURT ORDERED ARBITRATION IN CIRCUIT CIVIL CASES & COUNTY COURT; COMPENSATION AND PROCEDURES.

05–02–S. JUDGES—ACTING AS MAGISTRATES/FIRST APPEARANCE DUTIES.

02–19–S. [SUPERSEDED BY ORDER 18–02–S (A1), EFFECTIVE DECEMBER 18, 2018.].

01–19–S. [SUPERSEDED BY ORDER 18–06–S, EFFECTIVE FEBRUARY 8, 2018.].

97–5. [RESCINDED BY ORDER 17-39, EFFECTIVE SEPTEMBER 25, 2017.].

91–140–CR. [SUPERSEDED BY ORDER 18–42–B, EFFECTIVE SEPTEMBER 13, 2018.].

Administrative Orders

19–11. DOMESTIC RELATIONS—REQUIREMENT TO COMPLETE THE PARENT EDUCATION AND FAMILY STABILIZATION COURSE

IN THE CIRCUIT COURT OF THE EIGHTEENTH JUDICIAL CIRCUIT

ADMINISTRATIVE ORDER NO.: 19–11 SUPERSEDES 14–05

IN RE: DOMESTIC RELATIONS—REQUIREMENT TO COMPLETE THE PARENT EDUCATION AND FAMILY STABILIZATION COURSE IN DISSOLUTION OF MARRIAGE PROCEEDING WITH MINOR CHILDREN OR A PATERNITY ACTION THAT INVOLVES ISSUES OF PARENTAL RESPONSIBILITY

The Family Division Judges of the Eighteen Judicial Circuit have determined that a substantial portion of family law cases filed involve custody and visitation with minor children, and that a divorce or separation of their parents may detrimentally affect the children and the family relationships of the separating parents; that the children often become innocent unintended victims of the problems and "wars" of their parents; and the Court being concerned with the potential harmful impact on the children in such situations, including possible loss of self-esteem and pride, feelings of guilt in causing their parent's break-up, weakened trust and feelings of loyalty, anger, and the economic and social impact of the break-up of the home, all of which may lead to decrease in school performance, social difficulties, grief, problems with anger, guilt syndromes, depression, unacceptable behavior, anxiety about intimate relationships, concerns about betrayal and abandonment, feelings of being unloved, and viewing the world as unsafe and unreliable; and the Court being desirous of providing a means to assist both the parents and the children in coping with the break-up of their home; and to insure that the parents understand and are aware of the perspective of the children and the potential psychological and emotional trauma of the children; and to provide education resulting in recognition by the parents of the signs of trauma or distress in the children related to the separation or divorce and methods of assisting the children to cope with the trauma or distress beneficially, which will hopefully better society, and refocus the energies of the parents in a constructive rather than destructive manner to protect their children, and in consideration thereof

IT IS HEREBY ORDERED that successful completion of the Parent Education and Family Stabilization Course is a required policy for all parties to dissolution of marriage proceeding with minor children or a paternity action that involves issues of parental responsibility as a condition precedent to obtaining a Final Judgment. A party may be excused from attending the parenting course or from completing the parenting course within a certain time period, provided the court determines that the party has shown good cause. For dissolution of marriage actions, the petitioner must complete the course within 45 days after the filing of the petition, unless excused by the court. All other parties must complete the course within 45 days after service of the petition. For paternity actions, the petitioner must complete the course within 45 days after filing the petition, unless excused by the court. Any other party must complete the course within 45 days after an acknowledgement of paternity by that party, an adjudication of paternity of that party, or an order granting visitation to or support from that party. Each party to a dissolution or paternity action shall file proof of compliance with the court prior to the entry of the final judgment.

All parties are required to complete the parenting course as quickly as possible.

A copy of the "Standing Order of Referral Requiring Parties to Attend the Parent and Education Stabilization Course" (ATTACHMENT 1) shall be provided at the time of filing to the Petitioner by the Clerk of the Court and a copy of said Order shall be served on the opposing party(s) by Petitioner. Said Order of Referral shall be attached to the original pleadings by the Clerk of the Court.

IT IS FURTHER ORDERED that each provider offering a parenting course must be approved by the Department of Children and Family Services. The Department of Children and Family Services shall provide the Clerk of Court with a list of approved course providers and sites at which the Parent Education and Family Stabilization Course may be completed. The list shall be made available to the parties so that they may attend the parenting class of their choice.

The Department of Children and Family Services may remove a provider who violates these requirements, or its implementing rules, from the list of approved course providers.

IT IS FURTHER ORDERED that all parties to a modification of a final judgment involving shared parental responsibilities, custody, or visitation may be required to complete a court-approved parenting course prior to the entry of an order modifying the final judgment.

IT IS FURTHER ORDERED a reasonable fee may be charged to each parent attending the course.

IT IS FURTHER ORDERED that if any parent fails to attend the required Parent Education and Family Stabilization course, the court may hold the defaulting parent in contempt.

IT IS FURTHER ORDERED that the court may, with or without motion of either party, prohibit the parenting course from being taken together, if there is a history of domestic violence between the parties.

Done and Ordered this 24th day of January, 2019.

TONYA RAINWATER
CHIEF JUDGE

ATTACHMENT 1

IN THE CIRCUIT COURT OF THE EIGHTEENTH JUDICIAL CIRCUIT

STANDING ORDER OF REFERRAL REQUIRING PARTIES TO ATTEND PARENT EDUCATION AND FAMILY STABILIZATION COURSE

WHEREAS, pursuant to Administrative Order, the Petition filed herein includes a request for relief involving minor children of the parties. It is thereupon

ORDERED AND ADJUDGED that each of the parties shall attend a Parent Education and Family Stabilization Course. For dissolution of marriage actions, the petitioner must complete the course within 45 days after the filing of the petition, unless excused by the court. All other parties must complete the course within 45 days after service of the petition. For paternity actions, the petitioner must complete the course within 45 days after filing the petition, unless excused by the court. Any other party must complete the course within 45 days after an acknowledgement of paternity by that party, an adjudication of paternity of that party, or an order granting visitation to or support from that party. A list of providers may be obtained from the Clerk of the Court or from their website, Brevard County www.brevardclerk.us, Seminole County www.seminoleclerk.org. Each party is responsible for contacting the providers, scheduling attendance, completion of the seminar and payment of the seminar fee.

Upon completion of the seminar, you must submit your Certificate of Completion to the Clerk of the Court, Brevard County Clerk of Court, P.O. Box 219, Titusville, Florida, 32781–0219, along with the above case number, Seminole County Clerk of Court, P.O. Box 8099, Sanford, FL 32772–8099, along with the above case number.

This parenting course, ordered by the court, shall apply regardless of whether the parties were legally married and in family cases involving family member visitation, etc.

Copies provided to:

Petitioner by ___ hand delivery ___ mail

Respondent by ___ mail ___ attached to Summons

Dated: ________ Clerk of the Court

By: ______________________
Deputy Clerk

19–08–S. JUVENILES—SEXTING BY MINORS–SECTION 847.0141, FLORIDA STATUTES

IN THE CIRCUIT COURT OF THE EIGHTEENTH JUDICIAL CIRCUIT IN AND FOR SEMINOLE COUNTY FLORIDA

ADMINISTRATIVE ORDER NO.: 19–08–S
SUPERSEDES 17–22–S

IN RE: JUVENILES—SEXTING BY MINORS–SECTION 847.0141, FLORIDA STATUTES

WHEREAS, Florida Statute provides elements defining when a minor commits the offense of sexting in violation of section 847.0141(1);

WHEREAS, a minor for purposes of section 847.0141, Florida Statutes, is defined in section 847.001(8), Florida Statutes, as a person under the age of eighteen years;

WHEREAS, the Sheriff of Seminole County has established a Sexting and Cyber–Safety Awareness Program to address civil and criminal sexting violations pursuant to section 847.0141, Florida Statutes;

WHEREAS, the Seminole County Sheriff's Office Sexting and Cyber–Safety Awareness Program is administered by the Seminole County Sheriff's Office Prosecution Alternatives for Youth (PAY) Program;

WHEREAS, the Seminole County Sheriff's Office has also agreed to oversee Community Work Service performed pursuant to Sexting case violations including non-criminal civil citation cases;

WHEREAS, pursuant to Article V, section 2(d) of the Florida Constitution and section 43.26, Florida Statutes, the chief judge of each judicial circuit is charged with the authority and the power to do everything necessary to promote the prompt and efficient administration of justice; and

WHEREAS, pursuant to the chief judge's constitutional and statutory responsibility for administrative supervision of the courts within the circuit and to create and maintain an organization capable of effecting the efficient, prompt, and proper administration of justice for the citizens of this State, the chief judge is required to exercise direction, see Fla. R. Jud. Admin. 2.215(b)(2), (b)(3);

NOW, THEREFORE, I, Tonya Rainwater, in order to facilitate the efficient operation of the administration of justice, and pursuant to the authority vested in me as Chief Judge of the Eighteenth Judicial Circuit of Florida, Seminole County, under Florida Rule of Judicial Administration 2.215, hereby order the following, effective immediately, and to continue until further order:

1. First-time violations of section 847.0141, Florida Statutes, are designated as non-criminal violations that are to be heard by the Circuit Judges assigned to hear juvenile delinquency matters. *See* § 985.0301(1)(b), Fla. Stat. (2015).

2. First-time violators must sign and accept a citation indicating a promise to appear before the Juvenile Court. *(ATTACHMENT 1)*

3. Pursuant to section 847.0141(3)(a)1., Florida Statutes, the citation must contain all of the following:

a. The date and time of issuance.

b. The name and address of the minor to whom the citation is issued.

c. A thumbprint of the minor to whom the citation is issued.

d. Identification of the noncriminal violation and the time it was committed.

e. The facts constituting reasonable cause.

f. The specific section of law violated.

g. The name and authority of the citing officer.

h. The procedures that the minor must follow to contest the citation, perform the required community service, pay the civil penalty, or participate in a cyber- safety program.

4. The Civil Sexting Citation must also contain a statement that the first-time violator is required to appear in court for a hearing, set a court date for not less than 45 days from the date of the offense nor more than 60 days from the date of offense and any instructions for handling of the citation in lieu of appearance at said court hearing.

5. The Civil Sexting Citation shall also advise the first-time violator that in lieu of appearing in Court, pursuant to section 847.0141(3)(a), Florida Statutes, first-time violators may complete the Sexting and Cyber–Safety Awareness Program administered through the PAY Program. The first-time violator must satisfy attendance completion and provide proof of such to the Clerk of Court—Juvenile Division within 30 days after receipt of the citation. Upon proof of completion presented to the clerk, the clerk will cancel the hearing date and will mail notice of the cancellation of the hearing to the first-time violator. Furthermore, the Clerk may terminate the case upon receipt of proof of completion of the Sexting and Cyber–Safety Awareness Program.

6. The Civil Sexting Citation shall further advise that failure to provide proof of completion of the Sexting and Cyber–Safety Awareness Program within 30 days after receipt of the citation will require the first-time violator's appearance in Court on the scheduled arraignment date.

7. A minor who completes the Sexting and Cyber–Safety Awareness Education Program shall be issued a certificate of completion containing the minor's name, citation or case number and the date of completion.

8. All Civil Sexting Citations shall be filed with the Clerk of the Court Juvenile Division and copies provided to the minor and the Seminole County PAY Program Administrator.

9. Second and subsequent violations of section 847.0141, Florida Statutes, are criminal violations and will be processed as any other delinquent act or violation of law.

10. The Civil Sexting Citation attached to this Administrative Order is recognized as the Civil Sexting Citation for use in Seminole County and is incorporated herein as part of this Order.

DONE AND ORDERED this 9th day of January, 2019.

TONYA RAINWATER
CHIEF JUDGE

18–55–B. CLERK OF COURT—UNIFORM BREVARD COUNTY COURT CRIMINAL AND TRAFFIC PROCEDURES

IN THE CIRCUIT COURT OF THE EIGHTEENTH JUDICIAL CIRCUIT IN AND FOR BREVARD COUNTY, FLORIDA

ADMINISTRATIVE ORDER NO: 18–55–B
SUPERSEDES 13–24–B AMENDED

IN RE: CLERK OF COURT—UNIFORM BREVARD COUNTY COURT CRIMINAL AND TRAFFIC PROCEDURES

WHEREAS, the Brevard County Judges have previously delegated authority and discretion to the Clerk of the Court to: continue, reschedule, re-enter, or cancel criminal (including county and municipal ordinance violations) and traffic court appearances: extend the deadline for payment of fines and court costs; issue D–6 clearances in advance of an emergency identification hearing; recall specific types of bench warrants without express court order; accept pleas of guilty or no contest in civil infraction cases, withholding or imposing an adjudication of guilt as appropriate; and assess fines and court costs, all without individual court orders; and

WHEREAS, the Clerk's exercise of the aforesaid authority and discretion has greatly assisted in reducing County Court dockets and demands upon county judges and their judicial assistants for decisions on routine matter; and

WHEREAS, uniformity among the County Court Divisions as to the nature and amount of authority and discretion so delegated would be beneficial; and

WHEREAS, the amounts of various fines of court costs required by law have not been specifically or clearly fixed by statute, court rule or administrative order with regard to certain offenses; and

WHEREAS, the goal of fair, consistent and efficient administration of justice will be better served if the aforesaid matters are treated uniformly throughout the county according to the traffic laws of the State of Florida and the oral or written orders of the Judges of this circuit and their judicial assistants; it is hereby;

ORDERED AS FOLLOWS:

1. Continuing, Rescheduling, Re–Entry, Cancelling and Scheduling Court Dates:

A. *Continuances*:

1. The Clerk shall have the authority to continue criminal (traffic and misdemeanor) first appearances cases one time, without court order, at the personal, written or telephonic request of a defendant who has not already failed to appear in the cause. The continuance shall be to the division's next available docket leaving sufficient time to provide notice. Defendants requesting a continuance in person, by telephone or in writing waive their right to a speedy trial. Defendants requesting a continuance in writing or by telephone shall be required to immediately submit to the clerk a written acknowledgement of the waiver of speedy trial bearing the case number(s), new court time and date, and signature. The deputy clerk authorizing a continuance shall note when and by what means the request for continuance was received, and the new court date granted. Defendants represented by counsel shall be instructed to contact their attorney with their request for a continuance.

2. The Clerk shall have the authority to continue civil traffic, parking and animal control hearings one time, at the request of either the defendant or law enforcement, to the division's next available docket if the request for continuance is received at least five business days before the hearing date, so as to allow the Clerk sufficient time to notify all parties and witnesses of the rescheduled hearing date. A request for continuance within five business days of the hearing shall be made to the assigned judge and if the judge grants the continuance, the Clerk shall use best efforts to notify the participants.

3. No second appearance, violation of probation first appearance or hearing, non-jury trial, docket sounding or jury trial shall be continued by the Clerk without the

approval of the judge to whom the case is assigned. Defendants represented by counsel shall be instructed to contact their attorney with the request for continuance.

B. *Rescheduling*:

1. The Clerk shall have authority to reschedule, without court approval, criminal and civil first appearances dates erroneously assigned to an incorrect time, date or docket by law enforcement, surety or pre-trial release officer, when the error is detected sufficiently in advance so as to allow notification of the defendant by mail. The Clerk shall also notify defense counsel, the State Attorney, where appropriate, and the party making the erroneous assignment.

2. The Clerk shall have authority to reschedule, without court approval, criminal and civil first appearance dates where the defendant appears in court as instructed, on an erroneous date assigned by law enforcement, surety or pre-trial release officer, when the case does not appear on the docket and the court file is not readily available. The Clerk shall notify defense counsel, the State Attorney, where appropriate, and the party making the erroneous assignment. The defendant shall be required to acknowledge the rescheduled court date in writing.

3. Cases rescheduled under sub-paragraphs one and two above shall be assigned to the next available correct docket in the appropriate division, allowing sufficient time for notification of the other parties by mail.

C. *Re–Entry of Criminal Cases After Failure to Appear*:

1. Unless instructed otherwise by the assigned judge, the Clerk shall have authority to re-enter a defendant who has failed to appear:

a. at a first appearance;

b. as ordered at the jail or work farm; or,

c. in response to an order to show cause as to unpaid fines, costs or community service.

2. Upon re-entering such a defendant, the Clerk shall schedule such defendant for appropriate proceedings before the assigned judge. All other defendants requesting re-entry following a failure to appear shall be instructed to turn themselves into the Brevard County Sheriff's Department.

3. The Clerk shall promptly activate and facilitate the issuance of bench warrants as ordered upon any failure to appear, unless instructed otherwise by the assigned judge. Warrants shall not be held or recalled by the Clerk without the judge's approval and defendants seeking to have warrants recalled shall be instructed to direct their request to the judge issuing the warrant.

D. *Setting Civil Traffic Hearings*:

1. If requested by the Defendant, the Clerk shall have authority to set a civil hearing within thirty-one days of the issuance of the citation.

2. A defendant timely demanding a civil traffic infraction hearing <u>and</u> requesting to submit an affidavit of defense in lieu of a personal appearance shall be required to post bond, a cashier's check or money order in the amount of the original civil penalty, plus applicable costs, as a condition precedent to the scheduling of the hearing.

E. *Setting Emergency I.D. Hearings*: The Clerk shall have the authority to schedule a civil emergency I.D. hearing for a defendant whose driver's history reflects a Brevard County <u>civil</u> traffic infraction conviction when the defendant's license or driving privilege is then under suspension for that infraction and the defendant swears that he or she was not the driver to whom the citation was issued. The Clerk shall have the authority in civil <u>and criminal</u> traffic charges to issue a D–6 clearance ("suspended in error"), in advance of the civil I.D. hearing, or re-entered criminal court date [under, I(C)(1)], without charge, when, in the discretion of the Clerk, the defendant has a credible basis for requesting the civil I.D. hearing or criminal re-entry. When possible, a civil emergency I.D. hearing should be scheduled before the division to which the citation would have been originally assigned, at a date no less than three weeks subsequent, so as to allow sufficient time to subpoena the officer issuing the citation.

F. *Cancellation of Court Dates*:

1. The Clerk shall have the authority to cancel a court date and dismiss the pending contempt charge for uncompleted community service and other court-ordered programs and schools if the defendant provides written proof of compliance to the Clerk at least five business days prior to the scheduled court hearing.

2. The Clerk shall have the authority to cancel a civil traffic infraction hearing at the request of a defendant wishing to enter a plea of guilty under F.S. s. 318(14)(4), to make and election to attend traffic school under s. 318.14(9) or to plead no contest and provide proof of compliance for offenses listed in the chart at IV.B below. The request may be made at any time before the hearing. The Clerk shall send written notice of the cancellation to the witnesses within 24 hours of receiving the request for cancellation from the defendant. The defendant must pay applicable fines and costs at the time of the cancellation.

2. Extensions of Time for Payment of Fines and Court Costs, Driver Improvement School and Proof of Compliance for Certain Traffic Offenses:

A. *Criminal Fines and Court Costs*: If requested by the Defendant prior to the due date, the Clerk shall have the authority to grant a one-time 60–day extension for the payment of traffic and misdemeanor criminal fines and court costs, at the request of the defendant who is not on probation for the offense. The Clerk also has the authority pursuant to F.S. s. 28.246(2) to enter into scheduled payment plans with defendants. A defendant on probation shall be referred to the probation officer, who may elect to submit an appropriate extension request and order to the judge who placed the defendant on probation.

B. *Civil Traffic, Parking, Animal Control and Marine Violation Penalties*: The Clerk shall have the authority to grant a one-time extension for the payment of civil penalties and court costs. The length of such extension shall not be later than a date which is 90 days from the date of the offense set forth in the citation. The Clerk also has the authority pursuant to F.S. s. 28.246(2) to enter in to scheduled payment plans with defendants for payment within a reasonable amount of time.

3. Conversion of Fines and DUI Court Costs to Community Service Hours and Vice Versa: The Clerk shall not have the authority to convert civil or criminal fines, court costs or delinquency fees to community service or to convert community service to fines. Persons seeking such conversions must obtain permission from the Court.

4. Authorized Dispositions of Criminal and Civil Citations Without Court Order:

A. *Pleas for Traffic Infractions*:

1. Guilty Pleas: Pursuant to F.S. s. 318.14(4) and this Order, the Clerk shall have the authority to accept pleas of guilty for civil traffic infractions in person or in absentia. The Clerk shall enter an adjudication of guilt and assess the application fines and costs.

2. Driver Improvement School Election:

A. Pursuant to F.S. s. 318.14(9) and this Order, the Clerk shall have the authority to accept driver improvement school elections in person or in absentia for violations for which a court appearance is not mandatory. The Clerk shall accept the election, withhold adjudication and assess all applicable fines and costs. After making the election, the driver shall provide proof of school attendance within 90 days of the date of the infraction unless an extension of time is granted in accordance with Sec. II.B, above.

B. The Clerk shall have the authority to accept a Driver Improvement School Certificate as timely, without judicial approval, when a certificate of completion is submitted within one year of the date of infraction, but which clearly shows a completion date within 90 days of the date of the infraction.

C. The driver shall be responsible for payment of all fees previously imposed by the Clerk related to the untimely submission of the Driver Improvement School Certificate.

D. If a driver elects to attend Driver Improvement School, but subsequently fails to timely complete the course, the Clerk shall adjudicate the driver guilty pursuant to F.S. S 318.15(1)(b).

3. Bicycle helmet violations: Pursuant to F.S. 316.2065(3)(e) and this Order, the clerk shall have the authority to accept a receipt showing purchase of a bicycle helmet on or after the citation date and dismiss the citation. Upon submission of appropriate proof, the clerk shall dismiss the citation and make note on the docket that proof was verified. This option shall not be available to a defendant who has made a prior election under this provision. If proof of purchase is presented outside of the defendant's 30 day compliance period, a late fee is due. The defendant's right to exercise this option expires once the citation is referred to a collection agency for collection.

4. Proof of compliance: Pursuant to this Order, the Clerk shall have the authority to accept pleas of no contest in person or in absentia for the traffic infractions set forth below, to withhold adjudication of guilt and to assess authorized fines and costs. The person shall provide proof of compliance to the Clerk as prescribed below. This option shall not be available to a defendant who has made an election under this provision within the preceding 12 months. For infractions marked with an asterisk*, below, the Clerk shall dismiss the citation and assess the maximum fee allowed by rule or statute ($10.00 in 2010) if the person provides proof that he was in compliance at the time of violation.

B. *Traffic Offenses which may be remedied by providing proof of compliance to the Clerk:*

1. Criminal offenses:

Florida Statute	Offense	Proof of Compliance
320.02(1)	Operating unregistered vehicle	Vehicle currently registered
320.02(4)	Failure to notify DHSMV of change of address	Proof of notification of change of address
320.131	Unlawful use of temporary tag if tag was expired less than 6 months	Vehicle currently registered
320.38	Non-resident exemption not allowed (FL resident without out-of-state tag)	Current Florida registration
322.03(1)	No valid license	Florida license valid at time of violation
322.03(5)*	License expired more than 6 months	Current Florida license
322.031	Non-resident exemption not allowed (FL resident with out-of-state license)	Current Florida license
322.16	Violation of restriction requiring glasses or hearing aid	Functioning glasses or hearing aid
322.32(1)	Possession of cancelled, suspended or revoked license	Reinstated license
322.57(2)	Driving motorcycle without motorcycle endorsement	License with motorcycle endorsement

2. Civil offenses:

Florida Statute	Offense	Proof of Compliance
316.646(1)*	Failure to display proof of insurance	Proof of insurance
320.0605*	Failure to exhibit registration upon demand	Proof of registration
320.07(3)*	Registration expired less than 6 months	Proof that vehicle is currently registered
322.065*	License expired less than 6 months	Current license
322.15(1)*	Failure to exhibit license upon demand	Proof of valid license

3. Time limits for proof of compliance and payment of fines and costs: The defendant must enter a plea of no contest to the above listed infractions by the first court appearance date (if criminal and companion civil), or within thirty days of the issuance of the civil citation (if no companion criminal). Pursuant to Traffic Court Rule 6.291(c) and this Order, the Clerk shall have the authority to continue the first appearance date for up to sixty days for a criminal defendant making this election but unable to provide proof of compliance at the time of said election. A defendant so continued may show proof of compliance and pay the required fine and court costs at any time prior to or at the continued first appearance date. Defendants requesting a continuance in person, by telephone or in writing waive their right to speedy trial. Defendants requesting a continuance in writing or by telephone shall be required to immediately

submit to the clerk a written acknowledgment of waiver of speedy trial bearing the case number(s), new court time and date, and signature.

C. *Offenses with Unspecified Minimum Civil Penalties:* Leaving child unattended in vehicle, F.S. s.316.6135: If not charged as a criminal violation under s. 316.6135(1)(a) or (4), the fine for a nonmoving violation of this provision is $60.

D. *Tender of Less Than Correct Civil Penalty and Court Costs*: If a defendant timely tenders, by mail or in person, a civil penalty and court costs sum totaling less than that required by law, the Clerk shall have the authority to dispose of the citation by accepting the lesser amount, if the defendant submits his or her copy of the citation and it confirms that the officer incorrectly indicated the sum required. In such cases, the civil penalty so accepted shall be allocated on a prorated basis, as provided by law, after deduction of court costs. If a defendant timely tenders, by mail or in person, a civil penalty and court costs sum less than that required by law, and does not submit his or her copy of the citation, or if it appears from a review of the citation that the officer provided a correct sum, the Clerk shall have authority to allow the defendant a thirty day extension for payment of the correct balance due, plus an additional $5.00 civil penalty.

DONE AND ORDERED this 20th day of December, 2018.

TONYA RAINWATER
CHIEF JUDGE

18–42–B. MISDEMEANOR AND FELONY CHARGES ARISING OUT OF THE SAME CIRCUMSTANCES

IN THE CIRCUIT COURT OF THE EIGHTEENTH JUDICIAL CIRCUIT IN AND FOR BREVARD COUNTY, FLORIDA

ADMINISTRATIVE ORDER NO: 18–42–B

SUPERSEDES 91–140 CR

IN RE: MISDEMEANOR AND FELONY CHARGES ARISING OUT OF THE SAME CIRCUMSTANCES

WHEREAS, defendants are frequently charged with felony and misdemeanor (criminal traffic and non–traffic) offenses which arise out of the same circumstances; and

WHEREAS, under F.S. 26.012(2)(d), the circuit court has exclusive original jurisdiction of all misdemeanors (criminal traffic or otherwise) arising out the same circumstances as a felony which is also charged; and

WHEREAS, such misdemeanors arising out the same circumstances as a felony are frequently separated, given separate case numbers, and assigned separate court dates before separate judges; and

WHEREAS, such separation of a misdemeanor arising out of the same circumstances as a felony is contrary to law and the conservation of judicial economy;

THEREFORE IT IS ORDERED that:

1. Any misdemeanors (criminal traffic or otherwise) or ordinance violations which arise out of the same circumstances as a felony shall not be separated from the felony.

2. When a felony arrest is made, the law enforcement agency should include, on the felony arrest report, any misdemeanors (criminal traffic or otherwise), or ordinance violations which arose out of the same circumstances as the felony. The uniform traffic citation number of any citation actually issued a defendant should be notated with the respective criminal traffic charge on the arrest form.

3. Booking officers, bondsman and pre-trial release officers should give a defendant being released before seeing a judge an appropriate felony court date to cover all related felonies, misdemeanors (criminal traffic or otherwise), and ordinance violations listed on the arrest report.

4. Upon receipt of an arrest report including felonies, misdemeanors (criminal traffic or otherwise), or ordinance violations, the court clerk shall assign a felony ("CF") case number to include all such related charges, including any criminal traffic charges for which the arresting officer may have issued a uniform traffic citation.

5. Court clerks and judges assigned to first appearances at the jail shall provide a defendant an appropriate felony court date to cover all felonies, misdemeanors (criminal traffic or otherwise), and ordinance violations arising out of the same circumstances and included on a single arrest report.

6. All felonies, misdemeanors (criminal traffic or otherwise), and ordinance violations arising out of the same circumstances shall be included in a single indictment or information. For the Clerk's tracking purposes, the indictment or information shall include, along with the "CF" case number, the uniform traffic citation numbers for any criminal traffic charges issued by the arresting officer or State Attorney's office.

7. In the event of an improper separation of felonies, misdemeanors (criminal traffic or otherwise), or ordinance violations arising out of the same circumstances, a court, may on its own motion or that of the State or Defense, consolidate such offenses.

8. In the event the State reduces all pending felony charge to a misdemeanor, then any remaining related misdemeanors (criminal traffic or otherwise), or ordinance violations shall forthwith be reassigned a "MM" case number and be transferred to the appropriate division of the county court.

9. Any civil traffic infractions which arise out of the same circumstances as a felony shall receive their own "TR"case number.

DONE AND ORDERED this 13th day of September, 2018.

TONYA RAINWATER
CHIEF JUDGE

18–40. USE OF THERAPY ANIMALS OR FACILITY DOGS IN PROCEEDINGS INVOLVING A SEXUAL OFFENSE OR CHILD ABUSE, ABANDONMENT, OR NEGLECT

IN THE CIRCUIT COURT OF THE EIGHTEENTH JUDICIAL CIRCUIT

ADMINISTRATIVE ORDER NO.: 18–40
SUPERSEDES 17–24 AMENDED

IN RE: ADMINISTRATIVE RULES—PROTOCOL IN EIGHTEENTH JUDICIAL CIRCUIT FOR USE OF

THERAPY ANIMALS OR FACILITY DOGS IN PROCEEDINGS INVOLVING A SEXUAL OFFENSE OR CHILD ABUSE, ABANDONMENT, OR NEGLECT

WHEREAS, section 92.55(5), Florida Statutes, authorizes the Court to establish conditions it finds just and appropriate when taking the testimony of a victim or witness under the age of 18, a person who has an intellectual disability, or a sexual offense victim or witness;

WHEREAS, pursuant to Article V, section (2)(d) of the Florida Constitution, and section 43.26(1)(e), Florida Statutes, the Chief Judge of each judicial circuit is charged with the authority and the power to do everything necessary to promote the prompt and efficient administration of justice; and

WHEREAS, it is necessary to provide specific guidelines for the presence and conduct of therapy animals or facility dogs inside the courthouses in the Eighteenth Judicial Circuit in any proceeding involving a sexual offense or child abuse, abandonment, or neglect;

NOW, THEREFORE, in accordance with the authority vested in the Chief Judge pursuant to Rule 2.215, Florida Rules of Judicial Administration, it is **ORDERED:**

1. The use of therapy animals or facility dogs to assist a victim or witness under the age of 18, a person who has an intellectual disability, or a sexual offense victim or witness, to testify with the assistance of a therapy animal or facility dog in any proceeding involving a sexual offense or child abuse, abandonment, or neglect is a decision to be made by the presiding judge or magistrate in accordance with section 92.55, Florida Statutes. This Administrative Order does not preclude the presiding judge from entering orders with additional procedures to those outlined herein for the use of therapy animals or facility dogs in that judge's courtroom.

2. **Written Motion and Court Order Required for Use of a Therapy Animal or Facility Dog in Courthouse.** If the Office of the State Attorney, the Office of the Public Defender, the Florida Department of Children and Families, the Guardian ad Litem, or privately retained counsel determine pursuant to section 92.55, Florida Statutes, that the presence and use of a therapy animal or facility dog may aid in the testimony of a child, victim, or witness at a hearing, trial or deposition, that agency or individual shall file a written motion in the official court file in the case requesting court approval for the use of a therapy animal or facility dog with a copy of the motion and notice of the hearing on the motion to all interested parties, including the Americans with Disabilities Act (ADA) Coordinator in Court Administration and the Sheriff's Office. [1] The moving party shall be solely responsible for informing all interested parties in any changes in date and/or time of the scheduled hearing on the motion, including notice to the Sheriff's Office. Prior to the hearing on the motion, the moving party shall contact an approved therapy animal or facility dog provider to determine the availability of a therapy team and use of one of their therapy animals or facility dogs. [2]

3. **Costs and Fees Paid by Moving Party.** The moving party is responsible for the costs and fees charged by the therapy animal and facility dog providers for this service.

4. **Written Court Order, Scheduling & Coordinating Appearances.** Once the therapy animal or facility dog's presence is approved by the presiding judge in a written order filed in the official court file and copied to the Americans with Disabilities Act (ADA) Coordinator in Court Administration in addition to the Sheriff's Office, the therapy animal/facility dog team is permitted into the courthouse for all scheduled court events as well as case related events scheduled by another agency. All appearances must be scheduled and coordinated with the ADA Coordinator in Court Administration so that the team will be granted access into the courthouse by court security. The handler and the therapy animal/facility dog will be subject to the same security screening measures as the public when entering the courthouse.

5. **Third Party/Representative's Presence Required.** It is the responsibility of the moving party to ensure that an appropriate third party/representative is present at all times with the therapy animal/facility dog team while aiding in the testimony of a child/victim/witness in a courthouse facility. [3] An appropriate third party/representative of the moving party is one who has no personal interest in the case; for example, a Guardian ad Litem volunteer or a State Attorney victim advocate. The third party and therapy animal/facility dog handler shall use best efforts to minimize contact between the animal therapy/facility dog team and the public and other courthouse employees. At no time shall the dog/animal be permitted to be alone with any child/victim/witness without the presence of the third party/representative of the moving party.

6. **Therapy Animal and Facility Dog Provider Requirements.** The approved therapy animal and facility dog providers shall:

a. Ensure that the therapy animal/facility dog has been trained, evaluated, and certified as a therapy animal/facility dog pursuant to industry standards and provides unobtrusive emotional support to children and adults in facility settings.

b. Ensure that handlers and therapy animals/facility dogs have completed any and all therapy training and have passed a nationally recognized skills and aptitude test and evaluation by an organization that certifies the team as appropriate to provide animal assisted therapy.

c. Ensure that therapy animals/facility dogs have been examined by a Florida veterinarian to ensure good health within the past year and all immunizations, including rabies vaccination, are current.

d. Ensure that every therapy animal/facility dog is properly registered/licensed in the State of Florida.

e. Carry a minimum of one million dollars ($1,000,000) in liability insurance with a rider that includes therapy animals/facility dogs on the premises of the courthouse facility and naming the appropriate county (Brevard or Seminole County) as a named insured. The Chief Judge may waive this requirement on a case by case basis.

f. Provide a copy of the insurance liability insurance rider page to the appropriate county attorney's office and Court Administration.

g. Ensure that all therapy animals and facility dogs will be leashed at all times with the handler in control of the animal/dog and the leash.

h. Advise handlers to refrain from all overt displays of emotion during all court proceedings.

i. Advise handlers to take measure to ensure that the therapy animal or facility dog is out of the view of the jury and not making noises to indicate the presence of the dog/animal.

j. Ensure that handlers will adhere to their certifying organizations' policies regarding grooming and zoonotic disease/parasite control in attempts to reduce allergens and/or parasites.

k. Ensure that handles will inquire if there are any known allergies or concerns prior to entering an elevator.

l. Ensure that handlers are aware that their therapy animals/facility dogs are strictly prohibited from entering any deli, cafeteria, eatery, or restaurant within any courthouse facility.

m. Ensure that handlers are responsible for arriving early enough to exercise the therapy animal/facility animal to avoid any elimination issues. All therapy animals/facility dogs must be trained not to eliminate indoors. Outdoor elimination shall be cleaned up by the handler using proper disposal methods to control odors, etc.

n. Ensure that any incidents are immediately reported to the presiding judge, the Office of the Chief Judge, and Court Administration. Reportable incidents include any injury to a person or an animal; situations with a high potential that an injury could have occurred either to a person or an animal, even though no one was hurt at the time; situations with a perception of an accident or injury, and damages to property, including animal elimination in the courthouse facility. The Incident Report Form C, is available on the circuit's website at http://flcourts18.org/.

o. Ensure that all handlers have completed a fingerprinted national criminal background check and provided a current copy of the same to Court Administration, Harry T. and Harriette V. Moore Justice Center, 2825 Judge Fran Jamieson Way, Viera, Florida 32940. The information contained therein and specific findings are confidential and the approved provider will be advised in writing as to whether the specific individual handler is approved or not approved to provide services to the Eighteenth Judicial Circuit. The cost associated for the fingerprinting will be paid by the approved therapy animal and facility dog provider.

p. Ensure that all handlers will immediately report to Court Administration any incident that may change the status of their background check, including but not limited to any arrest, conviction, or other incident involving law enforcement.

q. Ensure that handlers will maintain the confidentiality of all information whether written or verbal, received through the scope of interaction with the individual testifying including, but not limited to, names and information pertaining to the individuals testifying and their families. Handlers will sign an oath of confidentiality. The Oath of Confidentiality Form A is located on the Circuit's website at http://flcourts18.org/.

r. Ensure that all handlers have received, acknowledged, and endorsed an Acknowledgement of Terms and Conditions Sheet. The Acknowledgment of Terms and Conditions Form B is located on the Circuit's website at http://flcourts18.org/.

s. Ensure that every therapy animal/facility dog handler shall carry with and produce their certifying organization identification card and an identification card bearing their association or employment with the approved provider and shall produce same upon request by any court official. Additionally, all therapy animals or facility dogs shall be clearly identified by a dog therapy vest, neckerchief, or other identifying garment.

t. Inform handlers that the handler and the therapy animal or facility dog are subject to the same security screening measures as the public when entering a courthouse facility.

7. **Approved Animal Therapy and Facility Dog Providers.** All approved therapy animal/facility dog providers and their contact information shall be listed on the Eighteenth Judicial Circuit website at http://flcourts18.org. Any organization seeking approval to be added as an approved provider must submit the following information to Court Administration for the Eighteenth Judicial Circuit:

a. A written request for approval; and

b. Company information including years established, present services provided, number of therapy animals and facility dogs available, and presently certified as set forth in this Order, availability of handlers to provide proper services, and any other information which demonstrates the ability to comply with the terms and conditions of this Order; and

c. Proof of proper insurance as set forth in paragraph 6(e) of this Order.

The Chief Judge of the Eighteenth Judicial Circuit shall determine, in his/her sole discretion, whether an organization is an approved provider for the Eighteenth Judicial Circuit.

DONE AND ORDERED this 23rd day of August, 2018.

JOHN M. HARRIS
CHIEF JUDGE

1 "Sheriff's Office" in this Administrative Order refers to the Sheriff's Office in the respective county (Brevard or Seminole) where the movant requests for therapy animal or facility dog to assist.

2 A list of approved therapy animal and facility dog providers and their contact information is listed on the Eighteenth Judicial Circuit's website located at http://flcourts18.org/.

3 The "third party" is not a judicial officer or court administration staff. It is inappropriate for the court or court staff to actively participate or interact with the therapy animal or facility dog in any capacity because the animal's presence is a support mechanism for victims/witnesses. See Fla. Code Jud. Conduct, Canons 3C(2) and 3B(5), (7), (9).

18–26–S. CRIMINAL—MODIFICATION OF MONETARY BOND AMOUNTS AND BOND CONDITIONS

IN THE CIRCUIT COURT OF THE EIGHTEENTH JUDICIAL CIRCUIT IN AND FOR SEMINOLE COUNTY, FLORIDA

ADMINISTRATIVE ORDER NO.: 18–26–S

IN RE: CRIMINAL—MODIFICATION OF MONETARY BOND AMOUNTS AND BOND CONDITIONS UPON THE FILING OF AN INFORMATION CHARGING DIFFERENT CRIMES THAN THOSE CONTAINED IN THE ARREST REPORT

WHEREAS, pursuant to section 903.02(4), Florida Statutes, bond is set according to the Bond Schedule Administrative Order to correspond with the specific charges brought against a defendant in the arrest affidavit; and

WHEREAS the Office of the State Attorney has the exclusive discretion to charge any crimes supported by the sworn facts and is not bound by the charges for which a defendant is arrested; and

WHEREAS the bond set at first appearance may not be appropriate for the charges formally brought by the State Attorney; and

WHEREAS the Clerk of the Court releases the posted bond when the charges brought by the State reference a different chapter of the Florida Statutes from those upon which a defendant is arrested, eliminating the monetary incentive for a defendant to appear at all scheduled court hearings to answer for the charges.

NOW, THEREFORE, it is ORDERED:

1. When the State files an Information charging only misdemeanor(s) in a case where the defendant was originally arrested for a felony offense but has not yet posted the felony bond:

a. The Clerk of the Court shall immediately assign the case a misdemeanor case number; and

b. The case shall be removed from the felony docket to which it was originally assigned, and the felony arraignment shall be cancelled; and

c. The misdemeanor case shall be set on the next First Appearance docket. The First Appearance Judge is authorized to modify the previous bond amount and conditions pursuant to the controlling Bond Schedule and other relevant factors and shall set the case for an arraignment before the duly assigned County Court Judge; and

d. All parties shall be provided the opportunity to be heard regarding the modified bond amount and conditions.

2. When the State files an Information charging a defendant, who is not in custody, with crime(s) arising from a different chapter of the Florida Statutes than the original offense(s) for which the defendant was arrested:

a. The State shall indicate on the filed Information that "This Information, as a charging document, encompasses all charges contained in this case. The Seminole County Sheriff's Office shall substitute the charge(s) indicated on this Information for those on the corresponding arrest report, criminal traffic citation, arrest warrant, or summons/capias report. The bond(s) shall not be released and shall remain as last set under this case number. The bond(s) shall apply to each charge indicated on this Information in order of highest bond to lowest bond."

b. When the Information contains the above notation, the Clerk shall not release the bond. The Clerk of the Court shall transfer the bond(s) so as to apply to the new charge(s) filed in the State's Information. If there is any question as to what bond is to be transferred to the charge(s) filed in the State's Information, the Clerk of the Court is to assign each bond, beginning with the greatest bond from the arrested offense(s), in descending order, to each of the charge(s) filed in the State's Information.

c. The parties may move the assigned court to modify the bond as permitted by law.

DONE AND ORDERED this 5th day of June, 2018.

John M. Harris
Chief Judge

18–23 (A1). MENTAL HEALTH—RISK PROTECTION ORDERS

IN THE CIRCUIT COURT OF THE EIGHTEENTH JUDICIAL CIRCUIT

ADMINISTRATIVE ORDER NO: 18–23
AMENDED SUPERSEDES 18–23

IN RE: MENTAL HEALTH—RISK PROTECTION ORDERS

WHEREAS, it is the intent of the legislature as expressed in Section 790.401 Florida Statutes ("The Risk Protection Order Act") to temporarily prevent individuals who are at high risk of harming themselves or others from accessing firearms or ammunition, and

WHEREAS, a judicial procedure has been created under The Risk Protection Order Act that allows law enforcement officers or agencies to obtain a court order temporarily restricting a person's access to firearms and ammunition in situations where that person poses a significant danger of harming himself or herself or others by possessing a firearm or ammunition, and

WHEREAS, it is critical to adopt local procedures that will respect and protect the constitutional rights of respondents and due process of law; and

WHEREAS, it is necessary in the 18th Circuit for the efficient administration of justice to adopt policies and procedures for the handling of petitions filed under The Risk Protection Order Act, including filing requirements, service on court personnel, and the manner and procedure for scheduling the various hearings provided under The Risk Protection Order Act; and

WHEREAS, pursuant to Rule 2.215, Florida Rules of Judicial Administration, the Chief Judge is charged with ensuring the efficient and proper administration of all courts with the circuit;

NOW THEREFORE, it is ORDERED as follows:

1. A Petition for Risk Protection Order may be filed by a law enforcement officer or law enforcement agency in the county where the Petitioner's law enforcement office is located or the county where the respondent resides. The petition shall be in compliance with Section 790.401(e)–(g).

2. A Petitioner may include in the Petition for Risk Protection Order a request for a Temporary Risk Protection Order pursuant to section 790.401(4) Florida Statutes. Any such request shall be in compliance with section 790.401(4)(a).

3. Petitions for Risk Protection Order shall be assigned to the Guardianship/Mental Health Division in both Brevard County and Seminole County, and shall be assigned a MH case number.

4. The Brevard County Sheriff's Office and the Seminole County Sheriff's Office are authorized to file petitions for Risk Protection Order on behalf of any law enforcement agencies within their respective jurisdictions and with whom a Risk Protection Order filing agreement has been entered. The entry of such an agreement does not preclude any law enforcement officer or agency from filing a Petition for Risk Protection Order on its own behalf.

5. In Brevard County Only: All petitions for Risk Protection Order shall be filed electronically via the statewide efiling portal. Approved forms for use in Brevard County can be found at http://flcourts18.org/rpo. A petition for Risk Protection Order filed in Brevard County shall include BrevardRPO@flcourts18.org and digitalcourtreporters@flcourts18.org in the service list. Upon filing, the following shall occur:

a. A petition for Risk Protection Order that includes a request for a Temporary Risk Protection Order shall be presented to the initial appearance judge either on the day the petition is filed or the following day. The initial appearance judge shall review the petition and pursuant to Section 790.401(4)(d), hold a temporary ex parte Risk Protection Order hearing.

b. If impossible or impractical to have the temporary ex parte hearing before the initial appearance judge, the petitioner may seek review and an ex parte hearing before the Duty Judge, the Chief Judge or any other judge. The temporary ex parte Risk Protection Order hearing may be in person or by telephone, at the discretion of the judge holding the hearing, and need not be recorded.

6. In Seminole County Only: All petitions for Risk Protection Order shall be filed electronically via the statewide efiling portal. Approved forms for use in Seminole County can be found at http://flcourts18.org/rpo. Petitions for Risk Protection Order filed in Seminole County shall include SeminoleRPO@flcourts18.org and Seminoledigitalcourtreporters@flcourts18.org in the service list. Upon filing, the following shall occur:

a. Should a petition for Risk Protection Order filed in Seminole County on a weekday, include a request for a Temporary Risk Protection Order, it shall be presented to the business duty judge either on the day the petition is filed or the following day. The business duty judge shall review the petition and pursuant to Section 790.401(4)(d), and hold a temporary ex parte Risk Protection Order hearing. If impossible or impractical to have the temporary ex parte hearing before the business duty judge, the petitioner may seek review and an ex parte hearing before the after-hours duty Judge, Chief Judge or any other judge.

b. Should a petition for Risk Protection Order filed in Seminole County after close of business day on Friday and before opening of business day on Monday, include a request for a Temporary Risk Protection Order, it shall be presented to the after-hours duty judge. The after-hours duty judge shall review the petition and pursuant to Section 790.401(4)(d), and hold a temporary ex parte Risk Protection Order hearing. If impossible or impractical for the temporary ex parte hearing before the after-hours duty judge, the petitioner may seek review and an ex parte hearing before the Chief Judge or any other judge. The temporary ex parte Risk Protection Order hearing may be in person or by telephone, at the discretion of the judge holding the hearing, and need not be recorded.

7. All other hearings under Section 790.401, including compliance hearings, final hearings, hearings on a request to vacate or to extend a Risk Protection Order, shall be heard in the Guardianship/Mental Health division and shall be recorded.

8. Nothing in this Administrative Order shall be deemed to conflict with or otherwise modify the rights, responsibilities and obligations of Petitioners, Respondents, the Clerk of Court, Sheriff or the Courts as provided in the Risk Protection Order Act.

DONE AND ORDERED this 2nd day of August, 2018.

JOHN M. HARRIS
CHIEF JUDGE

18–22–S (A1). CRIMINAL BAIL SCHEDULE FOR SEMINOLE COUNTY

IN THE CIRCUIT COURT OF THE EIGHTEENTH JUDICIAL CIRCUIT IN AND FOR SEMINOLE COUNTY, FLORIDA

ADMINISTRATIVE ORDER NO.: 18–22–S AMENDED

SUPERSEDES 18–22–S

IN RE: CRIMINAL BAIL SCHEDULE FOR SEMINOLE COUNTY

Bail is an essential part of the criminal justice system, and a bail schedule is hereby promulgated so that law enforcement officers and booking officers can set bonds on arrests prior to first appearance. This schedule is not binding upon first appearance judges, who have the responsibility to review arrests at first appearance and set conditions of release pursuant to Rule 3.131 of the Florida Rules of Criminal Procedure and section 903.046 Florida Statutes.

Within this bail schedule, special provisions setting bail for specific offenses control over general provisions that may also be applicable to the specific offense.

Under the provisions of Florida Statute 903.02(4), a separate and specific bail amount must be set for each offense charged.

Bail will have a condition in every case that the defendant will have no direct or indirect contact with the alleged victim, if there is one in the case; and that the defendant shall remain from criminal activity of any kind.

IT IS ADJUDGED:

I. OFFENSES FOR WHICH NO BAIL SHALL BE SET UNTIL THE INITIAL APPEARANCE PROCEEDING BEFORE A JUDGE

1. Capital Felony

2. Life Felony

3. First Degree Felony Punishable by Life

4. First Degree Felony (Violent)

5. Second Degree Felony (Violent–with at least one prior violent felony conviction)

6. Attempt/Solicitation/Conspiracy to Commit First Degree Murder

7. Persons who are arrested for a felony while released on bail for a separate felony

8. Armed Robbery (Firearm or Dangerous Weapon)

9. Armed Burglary (Firearm or Dangerous Weapon)

10. Carjacking

11. Armed Home Invasion (Firearm or Dangerous Weapon)

12. Kidnapping

13. Drug Trafficking and Conspiracy to traffic in drugs

14. Sale or Delivery of a Controlled Substance (3rd Offense or more)

15. Manufacture of Methamphetamine

16. RICO Act Violations (F.S. 895.03)

17. Escape from DOC or Rehabilitation Reentry Program or other correctional facility

18. Attempt/Solicitation/Conspiracy to Commit Second Degree Murder

19. Aggravated Stalking

20. Domestic Violence (Any felony or misdemeanor offense defined in F.S. 741.28(1))

21. Violations of Domestic Violence Injunctions, Repeat Violence Injunctions, Dating Violence Injunctions or Sexual Violence Injunctions, regardless of the nature of the alleged violation.

22. Violation of any Condition of Release where the underlying offense is one of Domestic Violence

23. Burglary with an Assault or Battery

24. Violations of Felony Probation or Community Control unless

a. There is a violation of probation warrant, which, on its face, provides that the probationer does not meet the qualifications for a "danger to public" hearing as defined in Florida Statute 948.06(4) (as amended by the "Jessica Lunsford Act"), and

b. Such violation of probation warrant sets a bond amount.

25. Any criminal offense if the defendant is currently on felony probation or community control

26. Persons who are arrested for a felony who, because of their prior criminal record, qualify for sentencing on the arrested felony as a "Habitual Violent Felony Offender"; "Three–time Violent Felony Offender"; "Violent Career Criminal" or "Prison Release Reoffender".

27. Persons who are arrested for Possession of a Firearm by a Convicted Felon;

28. Any felony involving the use or threatened use of a firearm.

29. DUI Manslaughter

30. DUI 4th Offense or More.

NOTE TO INITIAL APPEARANCE JUDGES: "Unless charged with a capital offense or an offense punishable by life imprisonment and the proof of guilt is evident or the presumption is great, every person charged with a crime shall be entitled to pretrial release on reasonable conditions ... If no conditions of release can reasonably protect the community from risk of physical harm to persons, assure the presence of the accused at trial, or assure the integrity of the judicial process, the accused may be detained." Fla. R. Crim. P. 3.131(a).

II. ARRESTEES SUBJECT TO THE JESSICA LUNSFORD ACT

1. The Jessica Lunsford Act requires a judge to make a finding that a probationer or an offender on community control who is arrested for violating his/her probation or community control is not a "danger to public" prior to his/her release with or without bail where the probationer or offender in community control is:

a. A registered sexual predator, or

b. A registered sexual offender, or

c. Under supervision for any criminal offense prescribed in Chapter 794 (Sexual Battery); Section 800.04(4) (Lewd or Lascivious Battery); Section 800.04(5) (Lewd or Lascivious Molestation); Section 800.04(6) (Lewd or Lascivious Conduct); Section 827.01 (Sexual Performance by a Child), or Section 847.0145 (Selling or Buying of Minors), or

d. Under supervision for a criminal offense for which he/she would meet the registration criteria in Section 775.21, Section 943.0435, or Section 944.607 but for the effective date of those sections.

2. A probationer who is subject to the provisions of the "Jessica Lunsford Act" shall not be released on bail unless there is a judicial finding that he or she is not a danger to the public. If there is no such finding on the face of the warrant, the offender shall be held without bail, even if the warrant provides a specific bail amount.

3. If the judge who issued the warrant expressly states that the offender is not a danger to the public, bail shall be set in the amount provided for in the warrant.

4. If the warrant issuing judge does not include a finding that the offender is not a danger to the public and the offender is thereby held without bail, the First Appearance Judge may, in their discretion, hold the hearing and make findings as provided in Fla. Stat. § 948.06(4). If the First Appearance Judge does not hold this hearing, the court shall set the case for a status hearing in the assigned criminal division within 72 hours of the First Appearance hearing.

III. SPECIFIC OFFENSES

OFFENSE	RESIDENCY			
	LOCAL	FLORIDA	OUT–OF–STATE	OUT–OF–COUNTRY
1. Third Degree Murder	$15,000	$20,000	$25,000	$35,000
2. Manslaughter	$15,000	$20,000	$25,000	$35,000
3. Vehicular Homicide	$15,000	$20,000	$25,000	$35,000
4. Leaving Scene of Accident Involving Death/Personal Injury	$15,000	$20,000	$25,000	$35,000
5. Burglary of an Occupied Dwelling	$15,000	$20,000	$25,000	$35,000
6. All other non-armed Burglaries	$5,000	$8,000	$10,000	$15,000
7. Sexual Offenses—First Degree Felony	$35,000	$40,000	$50,000	$60,000

8.	Sexual Offenses—Second Degree Felony	$15,000	$20,000	$25,000	$35,000
9.	Sexual Offenses—Third Degree Felony	$5,000	$8,000	$10,000	$15,000
10.	DUI Involving Personal Injury	$15,000	$20,000	$25,000	$35,000
11.	DUI—Third Offense	$5,000	$8,000	$10,000	$15,000
12.	Aggravated Fleeing or Attempting to Elude	$15,000	$20,000	$25,000	$35,000
13.	Fleeing or Attempting to Elude	$5,000	$8,000	$10,000	$15,000
14.	Sale or Delivery of a Controlled Substance (Second Offense)	$35,000	$40,000	$50,000	$60,000
15.	Sale or Delivery of a Controlled Substance (First Offense)	$15,000	$20,000	$25,000	$35,000
16.	Possession of a Listed Chemical	$25,000	$30,000	$35,000	$40,000
17.	Computer Crimes Involving Child Pornography or Soliciting Sexual Conduct by a Child	$35,000	$40,000	$50,000	$60,000
18.	Failure to Register as a Sex Offender	$15,000	$20,000	$25,000	$35,000

IV. NON-ENUMERATED FELONIES

	OFFENSE	RESIDENCY			
		LOCAL	FLORIDA	OUT-OF-STATE	OUT-OF-COUNTRY
1.	First Degree Felony (Non–Violent)	$15,000	$20,000	$25,000	$35,000
2.	Second Degree Felony (Violent)	$15,000	$20,000	$25,000	$35,000
3.	Second Degree Felony (Non–Violent)	$5,000	$8,000	$10,000	$15,000
4.	Third Degree Felony (Violent—with at least one prior violent felony conviction)	$15,000	$20,000	$25,000	$35,000
5.	Third Degree Felony (Violent)	$5,000	$8,000	$10,000	$15,000
6.	Third Degree Felony (Non–Violent)	$2,000	$3,000	$5,000	$8,000

V. WARRANTS

Bond for persons arrested on a violation of felony probation shall be set as provided for in the warrant itself, if and only if, the warrant provides that the probationer does not meet the qualifications of a "danger to public" hearing as defined in Florida Statute 948.06(4) (as amended by the "Jessica Lunsford Act"); otherwise, such person shall be held without bond pending the initial appearance before a judge.

Bond for persons arrested on a violation of misdemeanor probation warrant, a failure to appear warrant, or an arrest warrant shall be set as provided for in the warrant itself. If the warrant is silent as to a bond amount, the bond shall be set as otherwise provided in this Administrative Order.

VI. MISDEMEANORS

Rule 3.125(b) provides:

1. "If a person is arrested for an offense declared to be a misdemeanor of the first or second degree or for violation of a municipal or county ordinance triable in the county, and demand to be taken before a magistrate is not made, notice to appear may be issued by the arresting officer unless:

a. The accused fails or refuses to sufficiently identify himself or herself or supply the required information;

b. The accused refuses to sign the notice to appear;

c. The officer has reason to believe that the continued liberty of the accused constitutes an unreasonable risk of bodily injury to the accused or others;

d. The accused has no ties with the jurisdiction reasonably sufficient to assure the accused's appearance or there is substantial risk that the accused will refuse to respond to the notice;

e. The officer has any suspicion that the accused may be wanted in any jurisdiction; or

f. It appears that the accused has previously failed to respond to a notice or a summons or has violated the conditions of any pretrial release program.

2. Pursuant to Fla. Stat. 907.041(3), pretrial release is presumed to be appropriate for initial misdemeanor arrests when a Notice to Appear is not issued, unless the Seminole County Sheriff's Office Pretrial Release Division determines that nonmonetary release is not appropriate for the reasons set forth in 907.041(3) or (4). The Seminole County Sheriff's Office Pretrial Release Division shall recommend the appropriate level of PTR supervision, as defined below:

a. PTR: Weekly telephonic reporting or reporting through a Web-based software application.

b. Supervised PTR: Report as directed to the probation division based on the conditions set forth in the Pretrial Release Conditions.

c. EMPACT: Report as directed to the probation division based on the conditions set forth in the Pretrial Release Conditions.

The first appearance court retains the discretion to adopt the recommendation and release the defendant on PTR, release the defendant on a more or less restrictive level of PTR, or reject the PTR recommendation and set an appropriate monetary bond. The first appearance judge may impose any reasonable conditions of PTR.

3. The Seminole County Sheriff's Office shall notify the Office of the State Attorney of any violations of PTR release conditions which did not result in the defendant's arrest. The Office of the State Attorney may seek to revoke PTR as provided by law.

4. If PTR is deemed to be insufficient or unavailable pursuant to Fla. Stat. 907.041, bond shall be set as follows,

unless the particular circumstances in the case necessitate a higher bond be set to ensure the defendant's presence at all court hearings or for the protection of the public:

OFFENSE	BAIL
DUI (First Offense)	$500
DUI (Second Offense)	$1,000
Criminal Traffic Offenses	$500
First Degree Misdemeanors	$500
Second Degree Misdemeanor	$263
Violations of conditions of release where the underlying offense is not one of Domestic	$1,000

5. As to all individuals arrested for the offense of DUI, any release must also comply with the criteria set forth in Fla. Stat. § 316.193(9).

6. The Sheriff's Office may recommend a defendant for release on PTR at any time, including when a monetary bond has previously been set. If the Seminole County Sheriff's Office Pretrial Release Division finds that a detainee should properly be released on PTR, it shall follow the above procedures in making a recommendation as to the appropriate level of supervision and shall have the case set on the next first appearance docket.

Definitions. The following definitions apply to this bail schedule:

1. Local Resident—A person qualifies as a local resident if his/her principal place of domicile is located in Seminole County, Florida and has been so for a period of three (3) months.

2. Florida Resident—A person qualifies as a Florida resident if his/her principal place of domicile is located in the State of Florida and has been so for a period of three (3) months.

3. Out of State Resident—A person qualifies as an out of state resident if his/her principal place of domicile is located outside the State of Florida but in another state within the United States and he/she is a United States citizen or he/she is a foreign national and his/her principal place of domicile is in another state within the United States and has been so for a period of six (6) months and he/she is in possession of such documents as permit a current domicile within the United States or such permit is otherwise corroborated.

4. Out of County Resident—A person qualifies as an out of country resident if he/she is not domiciled in the United States or is not a United States citizen and his/her principal place of domicile is in the United States but has been so for less than six (6) months whether permitted or not.

5. Violent Offense—An offense qualifies a violent offense if it involves physical harm or bodily injury or threat of same.

6. Non–Violent Offense—An offense qualifies as a non—violent offense if it involves no physical harm or bodily injury or threat of same.

VIII. SPECIAL CONDITIONS OF RELEASE—DUTY OF RELEASE OFFICER

1. General Conditions for Pretrial Release Applicable to All Cases

a. The defendant shall refrain from criminal activity of any kind.

b. The defendant shall refrain from any contact of any type with the victim(s), except through pretrial discovery pursuant to Florida Rules of Criminal Procedure. F.S. 903.47

c. The defendant shall comply with all other conditions of pretrial release.

2. Persons Arrested for Domestic Violence, Repeat, Sexual, and Dating Violence; Order of No Contact. Any person who is arrested in Seminole County for an offense of domestic violence, repeat violence, sexual violence or dating violence shall be furnished an Order of No Contact (Attachment 1) [1] stating the conditions of pretrial release. Persons arrested for any of the above noted offenses shall not be released until they have been instructed on the special conditions set forth in the Order of No Contact and have signed a court approved written notice acknowledging instruction on the special conditions of pretrial release.

3. Persons Arrested for Sexual Offenses or Child Abuse. Any person who is arrested for a sexual offense or for child abuse shall, as an additional condition of release, be prohibited from having direct or indirect contact with victim(s), victim(s)' family, or residence(s) of the victim(s). Persons arrested who have committed a sexual offense or child abuse shall not be released until they have been instructed of these special conditions by the pretrial release officer and have signed a written notice approved by the court.

4. Persons on Probation–Department of Corrections: Any person who is arrested in Seminole County and who is on probation with supervision by the Department of Corrections, Probation and Parole Services, shall, as an additional condition of release, report to their Probation Officer with the Department of Corrections, Probation and Parole services before 4:00 p.m. on the first business day following release. An offender is considered to be on probation if he is on parole or under any other type of supervision status by the Department of Corrections.

5. Persons on Probation—Seminole County Probation Department. Any person who is arrested in Seminole County and who is on probation with supervision by the Seminole County Probation Department, shall, as an additional condition of release, report to Seminole County Probation Department, Sanford, Florida, before 4:00 p.m. on the first business day following release.

IX. EFFECT OF FILING NOTICE OF NO INFORMATION OR NOLLE PROSEQUI

If a person arrested for any offense(s) occurring within Seminole County is admitted to bail and the State Attorney files a notice of No Information or Nolle Prosequi with respect to all charges arising out of a single arrest, the Sheriff shall without further order of the Court, release the person from custody as to the charges named. As to the named charges and person, all bail undertaking, not defaulted, shall be canceled, all sureties shall be exonerated, and all release on recognizance obligations shall be discharged without further order of the Court. A bench warrant or capias which may be outstanding and is yet unserved upon a named individual for a specified charge shall also be canceled upon the filing of a No

Information or Nolle Prosequi without further order of the Court.

X. COMPLIANCE WITH THIS ADMINISTRATIVE ORDER

Upon receipt of the person arrested the booking officer shall review the arrest form to ensure that the arresting officer has properly set the initial bond according to this administrative order. The booking officer is authorized to make changes to the bond amount reflected on the arrest form to properly comply with this order but in considering changes the booking officer shall consider any information in the arrest form that the arresting officer believed called for a higher bond and shall defer to that judgment. However, any bond set shall not exceed the amount of bail set forth in the bond schedule

DONE AND ORDERED this 13th day of June, 2018.

JOHN M. HARRIS
CHIEF JUDGE

1 Attachment 1 not included

18–21–B. BAIL SCHEDULE

IN THE CIRCUIT COURT OF THE EIGHTEENTH JUDICIAL CIRCUIT IN AND FOR BREVARD COUNTY

ADMINISTRATIVE ORDER NO: 18–21–B

SUPERSEDES 16–02–B AMENDED

IN RE: BAIL SCHEDULE

Bail is an essential part of the criminal justice system, and a bail schedule is hereby promulgated so that law enforcement officers making warrantless arrests can set bail for those arrests. This schedule is for law enforcement officers setting bail prior to first appearance. It does not bind in any way judges conducting first appearance hearings or judges conducting bond hearings. The judges may set bail at any reasonable amount utilizing the factors set forth in Rule 3.131(b)(3) of the Florida Rules of Criminal Procedure and Section 903.046 Florida Statutes. **However, judges must be mindful that bail cannot be set at "None" for a new substantive offense unless it is punishable by death or life imprisonment and the proof of guilt is evident or the presumption great.**

In this bail schedule, special provisions setting a bail amount for specific offenses control over general provisions that might also be applicable to the specific offense. A separate and specific bail amount must be set for each offense charged.

Bail will have a condition on it in every case that the defendant will have no direct or indirect contact with the alleged victim; and that the defendant shall refrain from criminal activity of any kind.

I. OFFENSES FOR WHICH NO BAIL IS TO BE GRANTED THE DEFENDANT PENDING THE INITIAL APPEARANCE PROCEEDING BEFORE A JUDGE

1. Capital Felony

2. Life Felony

3. First Degree Felony Punishable by Life

4. First Degree Felony (Violent)

5. Second Degree Felony (Violent–with at least one prior violent felony conviction)

6 Attempt/Solicitation/Conspiracy to Commit First Degree Murder

7. Persons who are arrested for a felony while released on bail for a separate felony

8. Armed Robbery (Firearm or Dangerous Weapon)

9. Armed Burglary (Firearm or Dangerous Weapon)

10. Carjacking

11. Armed Home Invasion (Firearm or Dangerous Weapon)

12. Kidnapping

13. Drug Trafficking and Conspiracy to traffic in drugs

14. Sale or Delivery of a Controlled Substance (3rd Offense or more)

15. Manufacture of Methamphetamine

16. RICO Act Violations (F.S. 895.03)

17. Escape from DOC or Rehabilitation Reentry Program or other correctional facility

18. Attempt/Solicitation/Conspiracy to Commit Second Degree Murder

19. Aggravated Stalking

20. Domestic Violence (Any Felony or misdemeanor offense defined in F.S. 741.28(1))

21. Violations of Domestic Violence Injunctions, Repeat Violence Injunctions, Dating Violence Injunctions or Sexual Violence Injunctions, regardless of the nature of the alleged violation.

22. Violation of any Condition of Release where the underlying offense is one of Domestic Violence

23. Burglary with an Assault or Battery

24. Violations of Felony Probation or Community Control, unless

a. There is a violation of probation warrant, which, on its face, provides that the probationer does not meet the qualifications for a "danger to public" hearing as defined in Florida Statute 948.06(4) (as amended by the "Jessica Lunsford Act"), and

b. Such violation of probation warrant sets a bond amount.

25. Any criminal offense if the defendant is currently on felony probation or community control.

26. Persons who are arrested for a felony who, because of their prior criminal record, qualify for sentencing on the arrested felony as a "Habitual Violent Felony Offender"; "Threetime Violent Felony Offender"; "Violent Career Criminal" or "Prison Releasee Reoffender".

27. Persons who are arrested for Possession of a Firearm by a Convicted Felon or any felony involving the use or threatened use of a firearm.

28. DUI Manslaughter

29. DUI 4th Offense or More

30. Violation of a Risk Protection Order or Temporary Risk Protection Order.

NOTE TO INITIAL APPEARANCE JUDGES: "Unless charged with a capital offense or an offense punishable by life imprisonment and the proof of guilt is evident or the presumption is great, every person charged with a crime shall be entitled to pretrial release on reasonable conditions. If no conditions of release can reasonably protect the community from risk of physical harm to persons, assure the presence of the accused at trial, or assure the integrity of the judicial process, the accused may be detained." Rule 3.131(a), Fla. R. Crim. Pro.

ADDITIONAL NOTE TO INITIAL APPEARANCE JUDGES: The Jessica Lunsford Act requires a judge to make a finding that a probationer or an offender in community control who is arrested for violating his/her probation or community control is not a "danger to public" prior to his/her release with or without bail where the probationer or offender in community control is:

1. A registered sexual predator, or

2. A registered sexual offender, or

3. Under supervision for any criminal offense prescribed in Chapter 794 (Sexual Battery); Section 800.04(4) (Lewd or Lascivious Battery); Section 800.04(5) (Lewd or Lascivious Molestation); Section 800.04(6) (Lewd or Lascivious Conduct); Section 827.071 (Sexual Performance by a Child), or Section 847.0145 (Selling or Buying of Minors), or

4. Under supervision for a criminal offense for which he/she would meet the registration criteria in Section 775.21, Section 943.0435, or Section 944.607 but for the effective date of those sections;

II. SPECIFIC OFFENSES

	OFFENSE	LOCAL	RESIDENCY FLORIDA	OUT–OF STATE	OUT–OF COUNTRY
1.	Third Degree Murder	15,000	20,000	25,000	35,000
2.	Manslaughter	15,000	20,000	25,000	35,000
3.	Vehicular Homicide	15,000	20,000	25,000	35,000
4.	Leaving Scene of Accident Involving Death/Personal Injury	15,000	20,000	25,000	35,000
5.	Burglary of an Occupied Dwelling	15,000	20,000	25,000	35,000
6.	All Other Non–Armed Burglaries	5,000	8,000	10,000	15,000
7.	Sexual Offenses First Degree Felony	35,000	40,000	50,000	60,000
8.	Sexual Offenses Second Degree Felony	15,000	20,000	25,000	35,000
9.	Sexual Offenses Third Degree Felony	5,000	8,000	10,000	15,000
10.	DUI Involving Personal Injury	15,000	20,000	25,000	35,000
11.	DUI Third Offense	5,000	8,000	10,000	15,000
12.	Aggravated Fleeing or Attempting to Elude	15,000	20,000	25,000	35,000
13.	Fleeing or Attempting to Elude	5,000	8,000	10,000	15,000
14.	Sale or Delivery of a Controlled Substance (Second Offense)	35,000	40,000	50,000	60,000
15.	Sale or Delivery of a Controlled Dangerous Substance (First Offense)	15,000	20,000	25,000	35,000
16.	Possession of a Listed Chemical	25,000	30,000	35,000	40,000
17.	Computer Crimes Involving Child Pornography or Soliciting Sexual Conduct by a Child	35,000	40,000	50,000	60,000
18.	Failure to Register as a Sex Offender	15,000	20,000	25,000	35,000
III.	**NON–SPECIFICALLY ENUMERATED FELONIES**				
1.	First Degree Felony (Non–Violent)	15,000	20,000	25,000	35,000
2.	Second Degree Felony (Violent)	15,000	20,000	25,000	35,000
3.	Second Degree Felony (Non–Violent)	5,000	8,000	10,000	15,000
4.	Third Degree Felony (Violent With at Least One Prior Violent Felony Conviction)	15,000	20,000	25,000	35,000
5.	Third Degree Felony (Violent)	5,000	8,000	10,000	15,000
6.	Third Degree Felony (Non–Violent)	2,000	3,000	5,000	8,000

IV. WARRANTS: Bond for persons arrested on a violation of felony probation shall be set as provided for in the warrant itself, if and only if, the warrant provides that the probationer does not meet the qualifications for a "danger to public" hearing as defined in Florida Statute 948.06(4) (as amended by the "Jessica Lunsford Act"); otherwise, such person shall be held without bond pending the initial appearance proceedings

Bond for persons arrested on a violation of misdemeanor probation warrant, a failure to appear warrant, or an arrest warrant shall be set as provided for in the warrant itself. If the warrant is silent as to a bond amount, the bail shall be set as otherwise provided in this Administrative Order.

V. MISDEMEANORS: Rule 3.125(b) provides:

"If a person is arrested for an offense declared to be a misdemeanor of the first or second degree or for violation of a municipal or county ordinance triable in the county, and demand to be taken before a magistrate is not made, notice to appear may be issued by the arresting officer unless:

1. The accused fails or refuses to sufficiently identify himself or herself or supply the required information;

2. The accused refuses to sign the notice to appear;

3. The officer has reason to believe that the continued liberty of the accused constitutes an unreasonable risk of bodily injury to the accused or others;

4. The accused has no ties with the jurisdiction reasonably sufficient to assure the accused's appearance or there is substantial risk that the accused will refuse to respond to the notice;

5. The officer has any suspicion that the accused may be wanted in any jurisdiction; or

6. It appears that the accused has previously failed to respond to a notice or a summons or has violated the conditions of any pretrial release program."

Rule 3.125(c) provides:

"If the arresting officer does not issue a notice to appear because of one of the exceptions listed in (b)(1) through (b)(6) and takes the accused to police headquarters, the booking officer may issue a notice to appear if the officer determines that there is a likelihood that the accused will appear as directed, based on a reasonable investigation of:

1. Residence and length of residence in the community;

2. Family ties in the community;

3. Employment record;

4. Character and mental condition;

5. Past record of convictions; or

6. Past history of appearance at court proceedings."

If a defendant is not released on a "Notice to Appear", pursuant to Rule 3.125, bond shall be set, pending first appearance, as follows:

DUI (Second Offense)	1,000
First Degree Misdemeanors/Criminal Traffic Offenses/DUI (First Offense)	500
Second Degree Misdemeanor	250
Violations of Conditions of Release Where the Underlying Offense is Not One of Domestic Violence	1,000

"As to all individuals arrested for the offense of DUI, any release must also comply with the criteria set forth in F.S. 316.193(9)."

VI. DEFINITIONS: The following definitions apply to this bond schedule:

1. Local Resident —A person qualifies as a local resident if his/her principal place of domicile is located in Brevard County, Florida and has been so for a period of three (3) months.

2. Florida Resident—A person qualifies as a Florida resident if his/her principal place of domicile is located in the State of Florida and has been so for a period of three (3) months.

3. Out of State Resident—A person qualifies as an out of state resident if his/her principal place of domicile is located outside the State of Florida but in another state within the United States and he/she is a United States citizen or he/she is a foreign national and his/her principal place of domicile is in another state within the United State and has been so for a period of six (6) months and he/she is in possession of such documents as permit a current domicile within the United States or such permit is otherwise corroborated.

4. Out of Country Resident—A person qualifies as an out of country resident if he/she is not domiciled in the United States or is not a United States citizen and his/her principal place of domicile is in the United States but has been so for less than six (6) months whether permitted or not.

5. Violent Offense—An offense qualifies as a violent offense if it involves physical harm or bodily injury or threat of same.

6. Non- Violent Offense—An offense qualifies as a non-violent offense if it involves no physical harm or bodily injury or threat of same.

VII. MISDEMEANOR WARRANT NOTIFICATION MAILER.

Defendants, who have an active misdemeanor warrant or capias, may be released on their own recognizance by compliance with the "Misdemeanor Warrant Notification Mailer" process. Specifically, a Brevard County Sheriff's Deputy anywhere within the geographical boundaries of Brevard County is authorized to release the defendant when the defendant timely presents the Misdemeanor Warrant Mailer, and the defendant other qualifies for release under this provision. The process consists of mailing the defendant a "Brevard County Sheriff's Office Misdemeanor Warrant Notification Mailer". These Misdemeanor Warrant Notification Mailers will be sent by first class mail to the defendant's last known address. The defendant, who receives the Misdemeanor Warrant Notification Mailer, would be instructed to bring proper identification along with the Misdemeanor Warrant Notification Mailer to any deputy sheriff within Brevard County. The deputy upon receiving the Misdemeanor Warrant Notification Mailer would complete an arrest affidavit (923.01) to include the court date. The defendant would be released without having to post the bond amount that is listed on the warrant/capias. All defendant releases of the Misdemeanor Warrant Notification Mailers shall be for non-violent misdemeanor crimes only. No defendant shall be released under this process for warrants/capias that include any felony, crime of violence, failure to appear, pay or appears, violation of probation in which a cash or surety bond has been set, violation of probation where the defendant is a registered sexual offender or registered sexual predator, or violations of probation where the defendant is also on felony probation or community control. In addition, under this program, no defendant will be released for any crime that involves domestic violence violations. The defendant will be required to respond to the Misdemeanor Warrant Notification Mailer within 20 days of United States Postal Service postmarking. Once the time period has expired, the bond amount originally listed on the warrant/capias will remain in effect. The Misdemeanor Warrant Notification Mailer is person specific and not warrant/capias specific

VIII. SPECIAL CONDITIONS OF RELEASE—
DUTY OF RELEASE OFFICER

1. **Persons Arrested for Sexual Offenses or Child Abuse.** Any person who is arrested for a sexual offense or for child abuse shall, as an additional condition of release, be prohibited from having direct or indirect contact with victim(s), victims(s)' family, or residence(s) of the victim(s).

2. **Duty of Pretrial Release Officer.** Persons arrested who have committed a sexual offense or child abuse shall not be released until they have been instructed of these special conditions by the pretrial release officer and have signed a written notice approved by the court.

3. **Persons Arrested for Domestic Violence, Repeat, Sexual, and Dating Violence; Order of No Contact.** Any person who is arrested in Brevard County for an offense of domestic violence, repeat violence, sexual violence or dating violence shall be furnished an Order of No Contact (Attachment 1[1]) stating the conditions of pretrial release. Persons arrested for any of the above noted offenses shall not be released until they have been instructed on the special conditions set forth in the Order of No Contact and have signed a court approved written notice acknowledging instruction on the special conditions of pretrial release.

IX. COMPLIANCE WITH THIS
ADMINISTRATIVE ORDER

Upon receipt of the person arrested by the Brevard County Sheriff, the booking officer shall review the 923.01 arrest form to ensure that the arresting officer has properly set the initial bond according to this administrative order. The booking officer is authorized to make changes to the bond amount reflected on the 923.01 arrest form to properly comply with this order but in considering changes the booking officer shall consider any information in the 923.01 arrest form that the arresting officer believed called for a higher bond and shall defer to that judgment. However, any bond set shall not exceed the amount of bail set forth in the bail schedule.

DONE AND ORDERED this 22nd day of May, 2018.

JOHN M. HARRIS
CHIEF JUDGE

[1] Attachment 1 not included

18–18–B. PROBATE & GUARDIANSHIP—PETITIONS TO SELL REAL PROPERTY

IN THE CIRCUIT COURT OF THE EIGHTEENTH JUDICIAL CIRCUIT OF FLORIDA IN AND FOR BREVARD COUNTY, FLORIDA

ADMINISTRATIVE ORDER NO.: 18–18–B

IN RE: PROBATE & GUARDIANSHIP—PETITIONS TO SELL REAL PROPERTY

Whereas, section 744.361, Florida Statutes, requires that a guardian shall act in good faith, shall act in the Ward's best interests, and protect and preserve the property of a Ward.

Whereas, section 744.441(12), Florida Statutes, authorizes a guardian to sell, mortgage, or lease any real or personal property, including homestead property, upon approval of the Court.

Whereas, section 744.441(21), Florida Statutes, authorizes a guardian to enter into contracts that are appropriate for, and in the best interest of, the Ward, upon approval of the Court.

Whereas, section 744.447, Florida Statutes, requires the filing of a petition requesting authorization to act under section 744.441, which shall include:

1. The facts showing expediency or necessity for the action;

2. A description of any property involved;

3. The price and terms of a sale, mortgage, or other contract;

4. Whether the application conforms to the general terms of the guardianship report; and

5. Whether the Ward has been adjudicated incapacitated to act with respect to the rights to be exercised.

Whereas, section 744.381, Florida Statutes, authorizes the Court to appoint appraisers to appraise the property of the Ward that is subject to the guardianship when it deems necessary.

In order to further protect the real property of the Ward against exploitation, to avoid conflicts of interest and to avoid the appearance of impropriety in the sale of real property subject to a guardianship.

It is hereby ORDERED and ADJUDGED that all petitions to sell real property shall include the following:

1. Acknowledgment that an appraisal of the real property was performed within 60 days of the filing of the petition to sell real property. The appraisal shall be attached to the petition.

2. When a listing agreement is entered into, the real property shall be publicly listed for sale on the Multiple Listing Service ("MLS"); and

3. The petitioner shall disclose any known relationship or conflicts of interests, both familial and business related, between any of the following individuals or entities involved in the transaction to sell the Ward's real property: seller, seller's agent, buyer, buyer's agent or Guardian. The Guardian shall similarly attest to no known conflicts.

4. The Guardian may seek leave of Court to depart from the requirements of paragraph 1 and/or 2 for good cause shown prior to or at the time of filing any petition to sell real property.

DONE and ORDERED this 1st day of May, 2018.

JOHN M. HARRIS
CHIEF JUDGE

18–13–S. ADMINISTRATIVE RULES—ORDER ESTABLISHING COURT INTERPRETER POLICY

IN THE CIRCUIT COURT OF THE EIGHTEENTH JUDICIAL CIRCUIT IN AND FOR SEMINOLE COUNTY, FLORIDA

ADMINISTRATIVE ORDER NO.: 18–13–S

SUPERSEDES 08–26–S

IN RE: ADMINISTRATIVE RULES—ORDER ESTABLISHING COURT INTERPRETER POLICY

WHEREAS, pursuant to s. 2(d), Art. V of the Florida Constitution and section 43.26, Florida Statutes, the Chief Judge of each judicial circuit is charged with the authority and the power to do everything necessary to promote the prompt and efficient administration of justice; and

WHEREAS, cases sometimes involve persons who require the assistance of a foreign language interpreter or sign language interpreter when attending court proceedings; and

WHEREAS, the role of the Court's interpreter is to facilitate communication between the court and non–English speaker(s) (NES) and hearing impaired individuals during court proceedings. Interpreter services are provided to the County and Circuit Criminal Divisions, Juvenile Court, as well as Domestic Violence Injunction proceedings; and

WHEREAS, certified or duly qualified foreign language and sign interpreters as defined in Florida Rules 14.100 are ordered by the Court as mandated by sections 90.606 and 90.6063, Florida Statutes and under the provisions of the Americans with Disability Act, and

WHEREAS, in an effort to ensure the effective administration of justice, it is necessary that a policy be established to provide certain basic principles concerning court interpreters in Seminole County.

NOW, THEREFORE, pursuant to the authority vested in me as Chief Judge of the Eighteenth Judicial Circuit of Florida under Florida Rule of Judicial Administration 2.215, the Chief Judge orders that all judges, judicial assistants, trial clerks, and attorneys appearing in this Court, as well as Court Administration, shall abide by the following:

1. The Court's interpreter services shall only be utilized for individuals appearing before the court. The Court's interpreter shall not be used to cover mediations, except for Dependency cases, psychiatric evaluations or any other aspect of the judicial process. spoken language interpreter services shall not be provided for persons summoned for jury service.

2. The Court's interpreter services may only be requested by a judge, judicial assistant, trial clerk, or Court Administration. If the services of an interpreter are needed at a hearing or trial, the attorney must inform the judicial assistant when scheduling the hearing. Opposing counsel must inform the judicial assistant of the need for interpreter services as soon as counsel is made aware of the need. Once the need for an interpreter has been determined, the requesting party must contact Court Administration. If interpreter services are needed, the attorney shall inform court administration no less than five (5) business days in advance of the scheduled date for Spanish interpreters, and all other foreign languages. In proceedings expecting to last more than one hour, team interpreting should be utilized. Emergency requests and same day requests shall be covered whenever possible, depending upon the availability of resources.

3. When interpreter services are needed to assist in more than one trial, cases will be given priority in the following order: (1) capital cases; (2) cases in which speedy trial has not been waived and the end of the speedy trial time period is most quickly approaching; and (3) by the severity of the offense. In the event of a conflict concerning the severity of the offense, the chief judge or his designee shall decide which case will be given precedence. Cases for which interpreter services were not available on the preceding day will be given priority the following day.

4. The Court's interpreters shall not sit in the jury box with a defendant and shall not accompany an attorney into a holding cell to conduct "in-custody" client interviews, except when a unique circumstance occurs which requires the court to proceed to a holding cell to advise a defendant of certain consequences of his actions where a defendant refuses to leave a holding cell.

5. The Court's interpreters shall not hold discussions or offer interpretation to defendants unless directed by the court and in the presence of defendant's counsel. The interpreter may assist an attorney with conducting a brief "in-custody" client exchange, such as updating or conveying an offer, within the courtroom. This shall only occur under the direction of the presiding judge.

6. The Court's interpreters shall not assist defendants after court, except to receive court minutes, judgments and sentencing paperwork. The Court's Interpreters may assist NES individuals in preparing an affidavit to determine indigent status, if requested by the Court.

7. If foreign language audio or video recordings are to be used as evidence in a trial or hearing, the party offering the recordings shall have them transcribed and translated into English at his or her own expense, or as provided for indigent criminal defendants, and shall provide in advance a copy of the recordings, foreign language transcripts, and transcripts of the English translation to opposing counsel and the court. The court interpreter shall not interpret audio or video recordings during court proceedings.

8. If the need for an interpreter arises during the weekend or holiday, the trial clerk shall utilize the language line service.

9. The Court's interpreter services shall be provided for NES parents or guardians of a minor who are directly involved in a juvenile court proceeding. Interpreter services shall be provided to any NES individual who is served a summons to appear before the court due to his or her direct involvement in a minor's juvenile court proceeding.

10. The Court's interpreter services shall be provided for domestic, dating, repeat and sexual violence injunction hearings to indigent NES parties. At the time the case has been set for hearing, the clerk shall provide the parties an affidavit for indigency. Based upon the affidavit, the clerk shall notify Court Administration if there is an indication that interpreter services may be needed.

11. The use of headsets and wireless microphones is encouraged in the courtroom when available.

DONE AND ORDERED this 19th day of March, 2018.

JOHN M. HARRIS
CHIEF JUDGE

18–12–S. Criminal—Standardized Seminole County Arrest Affidavit

THE CIRCUIT COURT OF THE EIGHTEENTH JUDICIAL CIRCUIT IN AND FOR SEMINOLE COUNTY, FLORIDA

ADMINISTRATIVE ORDER NO.: 18–12–S

SUPERSEDES 13–40–S

IN RE: Criminal—Standardized Seminole County Arrest Affidavit

WHEREAS, in November 1998, Florida voters approved an amendment to Article V of the Florida Constitution, which relates to funding for the Judicial Branch of government. The amendment, referred to as Revision 7, changes how our courts will be funded. Revision 7 transfers financial responsibility from 67 counties to the State. The State of Florida largely now requires uniformity of statistical information for court related expenses and other matters.

WHEREAS, Florida Rules of Court (Rule 2.050) states that the chief judge *"shall exercise administrative supervision over all courts within the judicial circuit in the exercise of judicial power and over the judges and officers of the court"* and *"shall develop an administrative plan for the efficient and proper administration of all courts within that circuit"*, which includes a *"mandatory periodic review of the status of the inmates of the county jail;"* and

WHEREAS, standardization of Seminole County's Arrest Affidavit will increase efficiency, effectiveness, statistical information and sharing of information among various state, county and municipal agencies; and

WHEREAS, standardization of Seminole County's Arrest Affidavit will decrease inefficiency, court-related costs, labor hours, redundancy, data entry and clerical mistakes; and

WHEREAS, presently over ninety-five percent (95%) of all arrests booked into the Seminole County John E. Polk Facility utilize the same standardized arrest affidavit form; and

WHEREAS, Seminole County Police Chief Association will make recommendations to the standard Arrest Affidavit format in order to improve local law enforcement operations.

WHEREAS, the Standard Arrest Affidavit currently in use contains minor typographical errors which have now been corrected, Therefore, after due consideration,

IT IS ORDERED AND ADJUDGED that the Standard Affidavit of Arrest attached hereto as Exhibit "A [1]" is hereby adopted for use by all law enforcement agencies within Seminole County effective immediately.

DONE AND ORDERED this 8th day of March, 2018.

JOHN M. HARRIS
CHIEF JUDGE

1 Exhibit A not included.

18–06–S. DRUG COURT—FELONY SUBSTANCE ABUSE PRE–TRIAL INTERVENTION

IN THE CIRCUIT COURT OF THE EIGHTEENTH JUDICIAL CIRCUIT IN AND FOR SEMINOLE COUNTY, FLORIDA

ADMINISTRATIVE ORDER NO. 18–06–S

SUPERSEDES 01–19–S

IN RE: DRUG COURT—FELONY SUBSTANCE ABUSE PRE–TRIAL INTERVENTION

WHEREAS, the Florida Legislature has enacted Section 948.08(6)(a), Florida Statutes (1993), enabling the Chief Judge of the Eighteenth Judicial Circuit of Florida to approve a Pre–Trial Substance Abuse Education and Intervention Program; and

WHEREAS the proper implementation of a Pre-trial Substance Abuse Education and Intervention Program as authorized by Section 948.08(6)(a), Florida Statutes, would provide a valuable alternative to prosecution in appropriate drug cases; and

WHEREAS, a defendant's successful completion of a treatment program will result in the case being dismissed.

WHEREAS, when criminal charges are dismissed upon a defendant's successful completion of the Drug Court Program, court costs should not be imposed against the defendant.

WHEREAS, court costs should therefore be suspended while defendants are participating in the Drug Court Program during any period of probation and, upon successful completion of the program, such costs should be waived completely.

WHEREAS the Circuit Court of the Eighteenth Judicial Circuit In and For Seminole County wishes to establish a Drug Court Docket within the criminal division and designate a separate docket for cases assigned to "Drug Court":

NOW, THEREFORE, It is hereby ordered and adjudged:

1. That there is hereby established a Pre–Trial Substance Abuse Education and Intervention Program pursuant to Section 948.08(6)(a), Florida Statutes, supervised by the Seminole County Drug Court Team which will be known as "Drug Court";

2. That there shall be created a separate circuit criminal docket which shall be known as "Drug Court".

3. That the State Attorney shall notify the court in writing if it is requesting a preadmission hearing;

4. That the Department of Corrections shall notify the court, the State Attorney and defense counsel of any violation of the court order placing the defendant in the Program. This notification shall contain a recommendation whether the court should remove the defendant from the Program.

5. That any defendant that enters the Drug court Program pursuant to 948.08(6)(a), Florida Statutes, shall be transferred from the division s/he was originally assigned and placed on the "Drug Court" Docket.

6. That any defendant referred to the Track One "Tier One" of Seminole County Drug Court who elects not to participate or who is rejected by the Program or who is otherwise removed from the Program prior to entry of a plea of guilty or nolo contendre shall be transferred to the originally assigned criminal division for further proceedings.

7. That a Defendant referred to Track Two of Seminole County Drug Court, who elects not to participate or who is rejected by the Program or who is otherwise removed from the Program subsequent to his/her previously entered plea, shall be sentenced by the Adult Drug Court Judge upon termination from the program. However, should the Defendant be entitled to withdraw his plea, the Defendant shall be transferred to the originally assigned criminal division for further proceedings.

8. That should the Defendant be sentenced to a term of probation by the Adult Drug Court Judge and subsequently violate said probation, his/her violation shall be transferred to the originally assigned criminal division of the originating charge for further proceedings.

9. That any Seminole County Drug Court Team Member or the Department of Corrections shall immediately advise the court if, for any reason, either entity becomes unable to provide the services contemplated by this administrative order.

10. That any person admitted into the Pre–Trial Substance Abuse Education and Intervention Program may be admitted, as an outpatient or an inpatient client to approved Drug Court Program treatment providers:

DONE AND ORDERED this 8th day of February, 2018.

JOHN M. HARRIS
CHIEF JUDGE

17–46–B. PROBATE AND GUARDIANSHIP—FINGERPRINTING OF GUARDIANS

IN THE CIRCUIT COURT OF THE EIGHTEENTH JUDICIAL CIRCUIT OF FLORIDA IN AND FOR BREVARD COUNTY, FLORIDA

ADMINISTRATIVE ORDER NO.: 17–46–B

SUPERSEDES 07–36–B

IN RE: PROBATE AND GUARDIANSHIP—FINGERPRINTING OF GUARDIANS

In accordance with the authority vested in the Chief Judge by Rule 2.215, Florida Rules of Judicial Administration, and section 744.3135, Florida Statutes, which provides, in part, that the Court shall require all guardians to submit, at their own expense, to an investigation of his or her criminal background, it is hereby:

ORDERED that:

1. All non-professional proposed guardians shall submit fingerprints electronically at the time of initial application to be appointed guardian. All other documents required by the court to complete a credit and criminal background investigation shall be submitted directly to the Clerk of Court.

2. Professional guardians, including employees of professional guardians, shall submit fingerprints electronically and must be electronically reprinted every five (5) years. All other documents required by the Court to complete the annual credit and criminal investigation must be submitted no later than January 15th every year.

3. Any individual who is fingerprinted and whose prints are not discernible or rejected due to image quality, as informed by the Clerk of Court, may have his or her fingerprints waived after two (2) attempts.

4. If the proposed guardian, guardian, or employee of a professional guardian with a fiduciary obligation to a ward, is advised that his or her fingerprints are not discernible or rejected due to image quality, then the attorney for the proposed guardian, guardian, or professional guardian shall file a motion with the Court seeking waiver of the fingerprint requirement. The Court will review the request and enter an order either granting or denying the waiver of fingerprinting of the proposed guardian, guardian, or employee of a professional guardian with a fiduciary obligation to a ward. The order granting the waiver will be for all future fingerprinting requirements for the individual.

5. If a proposed guardian, guardian, or employee of a professional guardian with a fiduciary obligation to a ward has an order entered waiving fingerprints because his or her fingerprints are not discernible or rejected due to image quality, an alternative background investigation, both state and federal is required.

DONE and ORDERED this 4th day of December, 2017.

JOHN M. HARRIS
CHIEF JUDGE

17–40–B. JAIL—FARM TIME—ALTERNATIVE TO INCARCERATION PROGRAM (ATIP)

IN THE CIRCUIT COURT OF THE EIGHTEENTH JUDICIAL CIRCUIT IN AND FOR BREVARD COUNTY, FLORIDA

ADMINISTRATIVE ORDER NO.: 17–40–B

SUPERSEDES 10–24–B AMENDED

In Re: JAIL—FARM TIME—ALTERNATIVE TO INCARCERATION PROGRAM (ATIP)

This Administrative Order sets forth the procedure for acceptance into the Alternative To Incarceration Program (ATIP), which shall include individuals sentenced to work duty at the Sheriff's Farm located at 2955 Pluckebaum Road, Cocoa, Florida 32926, or other locations as determined by the Sheriff or the Sheriff's designee, as a part of being sentenced to the Brevard County Jail.

This Administrative Order applies to orders imposing incarceration in the Brevard County Jail in excess of 14 days either as a sentence or as a condition of probation. ATIP eligibility is extended only where such incarceration is imposed on a nonviolent charge that does not involve lewdness, sexual impropriety or a firearm and that is either a misdemeanor or a third degree felony. This Administrative Order also applies to orders directing that an individual to report to the Sheriff's Farm for work duty.

Judicial Determination of Eligibility

The sentencing order imposing such incarceration or an amendment thereto shall reflect a determination as to the defendant's eligibility for inclusion in the ATIP (e.g. "ATIP Eligible," "Not ATIP Eligible," or "ATIP Eligible After X Days") or impose work duty at the Sheriff's Farm. The defendant's eligibility for inclusion in the ATIP shall be governed by that determination.

In determining whether a defendant shall be deemed eligible for inclusion in the ATIP or to spend certain days at the Sheriff's Farm, the Court, in its discretion, may consider whether the defendant's early release from custody poses a danger of injury or damage to the person or property of another and may consider all other factors relative to benefits and detriments of the defendant's incarceration or service on the Sheriff's farm or elsewhere.

If the sentencing order does not address the defendant's ATIP eligibility, the State Attorney, the attorney for the defendant and/or the Sheriff's Jail Commander or his/her designee may request that the sentencing judge amend the sentencing order to reflect a determination as to ATIP eligibility.

Sheriff's Assessment

Upon receipt of an order imposing such incarceration and determining that the defendant is eligible for inclusion in the ATIP, the Sheriff's Jail Commander or his/her designee shall promptly assess whether:

1. The incarceration was imposed on a nonviolent misdemeanor or non-violent third-degree felony that did not involve lewdness, sexual impropriety or a firearm;

2. The incarceration did not constitute a mandatory jail sentence;

3. The defendant is not either serving any other sentence, the subject of any hold or the subject of any pending criminal charge;

4. The defendant is not on felony probation or community control;

5. The defendant has not previously been convicted of any violent crime, a crime involving lewd conduct or sexual impropriety, or any crime involving a firearm; and,

6. There exists a substantial likelihood that the defendant shall appear and perform assigned tasks at the Sheriff's Farm or such other location at which work is to be performed in connection with the ATIP.

If the Sheriff's Jail Commander or his/her designee determines that the defendant does not meet any of the foregoing criteria, such defendant shall be excluded from the ATIP.

Medical Evaluation

Upon assessing that the defendant qualifies for inclusion in the ATIP in accordance with the foregoing criteria, the Sheriff shall expedite the defendant's medical evaluation. The Sheriff shall be entitled to rely on the information provided by the defendant to the Sheriff or his/her employees or agents relative to the defendant's medical history and treatment, as well as with respect to the defendant's training, work experience and familiarization with various tools and equipment.

The Sheriff's Jail Commander or his/her designee may exclude from ATIP any defendant whose medical evaluation does not conclusively demonstrate that such defendant is capable of performing the types of work that may be assigned to the defendant without significant health risk to the defendant or others, Notwithstanding the foregoing, the Sheriff and the Sheriff's employees and agents shall not be liable to the defendant for the evaluation performed pursuant to this provision and the defendant shall sign a release in the form attached to this order if such defendant wishes to be sentenced to the ATIP.

Medical Coverage

Although the Sheriff has obtained a group-type accident insurance policy to provide some insurance benefits to defendants who are sentenced to the ATIP, neither the Sheriff nor the Brevard County Board of County Commissioners shall have any obligation to provide accident or medical insurance coverage or medical care and services to such defendants. Each defendant shall be responsible for the costs of medical care resulting from injuries incurred in performing work in connection with the ATIP to the extent not covered by medical insurance policies.

Acceptance into the ATIP

The Sheriff may accept a qualified defendant into the ATIP and release said person from the Brevard County Jail upon the defendant's voluntary, written agreement to comply with:

1. A schedule of work days equal to the number of days remaining on his or her incarceration, exclusive of any gain time or other discretionary sentence reduction; and,

2. The rules of the ATIP and the rules applicable to performing the work whether at the Sheriff's Farm or elsewhere.

3. Unless determined by the sentencing judge to be indigent, payment to the Sheriff's in the amount of $10.00 to cover daily subsistence cost obtained by the Sheriff relative to defendants who are injured while performing work in the ATIP.

No person shall be compelled to enter into the ATIP against his or her will.

Performance of Work

The Sheriff's Jail Commander or his/her designee may have a defendant who is sentenced to the ATIP perform work at the Sheriff's Farm or at other locations, under the supervision of employees or agents of the Sheriff. In addition, a defendant who is sentenced to the ATIP may be required to perform work at locations other than the Sheriff's Farm under the supervision of employees or agents of the Brevard County Board of County Commissioners.

Effect on Probation

If the defendant is sentenced to incarceration as a condition of probation and released into the ATIP, appearance at the Sheriff's Farm and completion of the assigned tasks at the Sheriff's Farm or elsewhere shall constitute a condition of the defendant's probation.

Acceptance into the ATIP shall not constitute a modification of the defendant's sentence or probation.

The defendant shall report to his or her probation officer within 24 hours of release (excluding weekends and holidays) that he or she has been released into the ATIP.

Failure to Appear and Perform

In the event that a person accepted into the ATIP or otherwise ordered to report to the Sheriff's Farm for work duty fails to appear and perform the assigned tasks at the Sheriff's Farm or elsewhere, the Sheriff's Jail Commander or his/her designee shall promptly notify the sentencing judge who may issue a bench warrant for the defendant's arrest and detention in the Brevard County Jail for the balance of his or her sentence.

In the event that the defendant is on probation, the Sheriff's Jail Commander or his/her designee shall promptly notify the defendant's probation officer, if any, who may submit an affidavit of violation of probation for issuance of a warrant for violation of probation.

Protection from Liability

The Sheriff of Brevard County and any and all sheriff's deputies, corrections officers, employees and agents, including, without limitation, the Sheriff's Jail Commander or his/her designee, shall be afforded protection from liability for damages arising from the fulfillment their duty pursuant to this Administrative Order, including, but not limited to supervising defendants who are performing work under the ATIP, to the extent provided by law. In addition, the Brevard County Board of County Commissioners and its employees and agents shall be afforded protection from liability for damages arising from the fulfillment of their duty pursuant to this Administrative Order, including, but not limited to supervising defendants who are performing work under the ATIP, to the extent provided by law. Moreover, as a condition of participating in the ATIP, the defendant shall sign a release in the form attached to this order if such defendant wishes to be sentenced to the ATIP.

DONE AND ORDERED this 2nd day of October, 2017.

JOHN M. HARRIS
CHIEF JUDGE

ATTACHMENT

RELEASE, HOLD HARMLESS AND INDEMNIFICATION AGREEMENT

I, the undersigned, for and in consideration of the opportunity to participate in the Alternative to Incarceration Program pursuant to Administrative Order ________ (hereinafter, the "**ATIP**") and the benefit flowing from the services being provided by the Sheriff of Brevard County, Florida, and his employees and agents, and the Brevard County Board of County Commissioners and its employees and agents, (hereinafter, collectively the **"RELEASED PARTY"**), hereby release and agree to defend, indemnify and save harmless, and shall defend, indemnify and hold harmless, the **RELEASED PARTY** from and against any and all liability, claims, demands, suits, actions, losses, damages, expenses, fees or fines, of any kind and nature, arising or growing out of or in any way connected with the undersigned's participation in the **ATIP**, INCLUDING DUE TO THE NEGLIGENCE OF THE **RELEASED PARTY**.

I FULLY UNDERSTAND THAT: (i) I WILL BE PERFORMING WORK IN THE **ATIP** WHICH MAY FROM TIME TO TIME BE VERY DANGEROUS AND SUCH WORK MAY INVOLVE RISKS AND DANGERS OF SERIOUS BODILY INJURY, INCLUDING PERMANENT DISABILITY, PARALYSIS AND DEATH ("**RISKS**"); (ii) THESE **RISKS** AND DANGERS MAY BE CAUSED BY MY ACTIONS OR INACTIONS OR THE ACTIONS OR INACTIONS OF OTHERS PARTICIPATING IN THE **ATIP**, THE RULES OF THE **ATIP**, OR THE NEGLIGENCE OF THE **RELEASED PARTY**; (iii) THERE MAY BE OTHER **RISKS** NOT KNOWN TO ME OR THAT MAY NOT BE READILY FORESEEABLE AT THIS TIME; AND (iv) THE SOCIAL AND ECONOMIC LOSSES AND DAMAGES THAT COULD RESULT FROM THOSE **RISKS** COULD BE SEVERE AND COULD PERMANENTLY CHANGE MY FUTURE.

I HEREBY ACCEPT AND ASSUME ALL SUCH **RISKS**, KNOWN AND UNKNOWN, AND ASSUME ALL RESPONSIBILITY FOR THE LOSSES, COSTS AND DAMAGES FOLLOWING SUCH INJURY, DISABILITY, PARALYSIS OR DEATH, EVEN IF CAUSED, IN WHOLE OR IN PART, BY THE NEGLIGENCE OF THE **RELEASED PARTY**.

This Release shall be binding upon my assigns, successors, personal representatives, executors, administrators and heirs.

This Release shall be governed by the laws of the State of Florida and any action brought to interpret or enforce this Release shall be brought exclusively in the appropriate state court situated in Brevard County, Florida.

I HAVE READ THIS RELEASE, HOLD HARMLESS AND INDEMNIFICATION AGREEMENT, UNDERSTAND THAT BY SIGNING IT I GIVE UP SUBSTANTIAL RIGHTS I WOULD OTHERWISE HAVE TO RECOVER DAMAGES FOR LOSSES OCCASIONED BY THE RELEASEES FAULT, AND SIGN IT VOLUNTARILY AND WITHOUT INDUCEMENT.

____
DATE SIGNATURE OF RELEASOR

____
Printed Name: ________________________________
OF RELEASOR

____
SIGNATURE OF WITNESS

Printed Name: ________________________________
OF WITNESS

17–38. PROBATE AND GUARDIANSHIP—ESTABLISHING SURETY BONDS FOR PUBLIC GUARDIANS

IN THE CIRCUIT COURT OF THE EIGHTEENTH JUDICIAL CIRCUIT OF FLORIDA

ADMINISTRATIVE ORDER NO.: 17–38

SUPERSEDES 05–27

IN RE: PROBATE AND GUARDIANSHIP—ESTABLISHING SURETY BONDS FOR PUBLIC GUARDIANS

WHEREAS, Section 744.2102, Florida Statutes (2004) requires that a public guardian file a surety bond in the amount fixed by a majority of judges within each judicial circuit; and

WHEREAS, a majority of the judges within the Eighteenth Judicial Circuit have approved a proposal that the amount of such surety bond shall be $15,000.00.

It is hereby Ordered and Adjudged that public guardians holding that office under Section 701, et.seq., Florida Statutes in the Eighteenth Judicial Circuit shall file a surety bond with the Clerk of the Circuit Court in the amount of $15,000.00

Done and Ordered this 25th day of September 2017.

JOHN M. HARRIS
CHIEF JUDGE

17–37. MENTAL HEALTH—CONFIDENTIALITY OF EXAMINING COMMITTEE REPORTS

IN THE CIRCUIT COURT OF THE EIGHTEENTH JUDICIAL CIRCUIT OF FLORIDA

ADMINISTRATIVE ORDER NO.: 17–37

IN RE: MENTAL HEALTH—CONFIDENTIALITY OF EXAMINING COMMITTEE REPORTS

F.S. 744.331(3)(a) requires that, within 5 days after a petition for determination of incapacity has been filed, the court shall appoint an examining committee of three members consisting of a psychiatrist or other physician, and two other members who must be either a psychologist, gerontologists, another psychiatrist, or other physician, a registered nurse, nurse practitioner, licensed social worker, a person with an advanced degree in gerontology from an accredited institution of higher education or other person who by knowledge, skill, experience, training or education may, in the court's discretion, advise the court in the form of an expert opinion.

F.S. 744.331(3) (g) requires that each committee member's report must include *inter alia*:

1. To the extent possible, a diagnosis, prognosis and recommended course of treatment.

2. An evaluation of the alleged incapacitated person's ability to retain her or his rights, including, without limitation, the rights to marry; vote; contract; manage or dispose of property; have a driver license; determine her or his residence; consent to medical treatment; and make decisions affecting her or his social environment.

3. The results of the comprehensive examination and the committee member's assessment of information provided by the attending or family physician, if any.

4. A description of any matters with respect to the which the person lacks the capacity to exercise rights, the extent of that incapacity, and the factual basis for the determination that the person lacks that capacity.

In sum, an examining committee's report contains intimately sensitive information regarding an alleged incapacitated person.

Effective July 1, 2017, the Florida Legislature amended section 744.331(3)(e), Florida Statutes, regarding the filing of examining committee reports in relation to a Petition to Determination of Incapacity. Section 744.331(3)(e), Florida Statutes provides in part "Each member of the examining committee must file his or her report with the clerk of court within 15 days after appointment."

As a consequence of this amendment, an examining committee report filed with the Clerk becomes a public record in accordance with Florida Rule of Judicial Administration 2.420(a) and (b)(1)(A) since the examining committee report is not specifically exempted from the right of public access by statute or Rule.

In accordance with the authority vested in the Chief Judge by the Florida Rule Judicial Administration 2.215, to exercise administrative supervision over the courts within the circuit and to control dockets; and in order to protect the confidentiality of the mental and physical health assessment of alleged incapacitated persons, it is ORDERED:

Examining committee reports filed in mental health cases in conjunction with a Petition to Determine Incapacity are deemed confidential and are subject to inspection only by the court, the clerk or the clerk's representative, the petitioner, the petitioner's attorney, the alleged incapacitated person and the alleged incapacitated person's attorney. Access to the examining committee's reports may be granted to other individuals upon the filing of a Motion to Unseal Examining Committee's Reports based upon good cause, in the mental health case.

DONE AND ORDERED this 25th day of September, 2017.

JOHN M. HARRIS
CHIEF JUDGE

17–30–S. CRIMINAL—ALTERNATIVE SANCTIONS PROGRAM

IN THE CIRCUIT COURT OF THE EIGHTEENTH JUDICIAL CIRCUIT, IN AND FOR SEMINOLE COUNTY, FLORIDA.

ADMINISTRATIVE ORDER NO: 17–30–S

SUPERSEDES 16–18–S

IN RE: CRIMINAL—ALTERNATIVE SANCTIONS PROGRAM

Whereas, there is a substantial number of technical violations that do not involve a new arrest or other serious violations; and,

Whereas, arresting and incarcerating certain non-violent offenders for minor violations of probation or community control is both expensive and nonproductive; and,

Whereas, there is research to support that recidivism may be reduced by utilizing collaborative efforts among the courts, probation and law enforcement to hold the offender accountable and apply swift and certain sanctions for technical violations of probation or community control; and

Whereas, an administrative option for processing technical violations will have the potential to offer benefits including:

- Reducing the court docket of probation and community control violation hearings;
- Reducing the workload of prosecutors and defense attorneys involved with many technical violation hearings;
- Reducing law enforcement resources required to serve violation warrants for certain technical violations;
- Reducing jail population for offenders pending violation hearings; and
- Offering the offender an alternative to a violation hearing in court, which will allow the offender to remain engaged in employment, school, treatment, etc. and allow the offender to take immediate responsibility for his/her actions and consequences of those actions

NOW, THEREFORE, IT IS ORDERED:

1. Alternative Sanctions Program: There is created in Seminole County a program that shall be known as the Alternative Sanctions Program.

2. Eligibility: To be eligible for the program, offenders must have been placed on probation or community control under the supervision of the Department of Corrections by a judge in Seminole County, have stable community ties, and have a stable residence in Seminole County, Florida. Offenders who are eligible for the program include probation offenders, drug offenders, and community control supervision offenders. The program only applies to offenders who have committed certain technical violations addressed in the Alternative Sanctions Program Violation/Sanction Matrix included in this order. The threat an offender poses to public safety is the most important factor in determining eligibility. Offenders with a lengthy or violent criminal history, including sex offenders, are not eligible to be in the program. Additionally, offenders who have new law violations, are absconders, or have violated a "no contact" condition of supervision are not eligible for the program. No offender who has three or more previous violations is eligible for the program.

3. Qualifying Technical Violations and Approved Sanctions: The following matrix lists the specific technical violations that may be addressed through the Alternative Sanctions Program process for offenders who were sentenced in Seminole County, Florida. Each technical violation includes a list of sanctions determined and approved by the court for the probation officer to select from when reporting these technical violations, based on the individual offender's circumstances at the time of the violation.

ALTERNATIVE SANCTIONS PROGRAM VIOLATION/SANCTION MATRIX

VIOLATION	APPROVED LIST OF SANCTIONS
Condition (1): Reported late; failed to report as instructed	1. Weekly call in for 6 weeks 2. Report 2x a month for 60 days 3. Thinking for Change program through DOC 4. Attend Step Forward/ Job skills class 5. Attend a Lifeskills/Career Readiness class as directed by DOC. 6. Participate in 3 sessions with the DOC employment specialist. 7. Attend and complete Moral Reconation Therapy classes through DOC. 8. Attend and participate in the DOC onsite GED/Adult Education program
Condition (3): Failed to report changes in residence or employment without first procuring the officer's consent (or notifying immediately if evicted from residence or laid off from job)	1. Weekly call in for 6 weeks 2. Twice a month reporting for 3 months 3. Weekly reporting for 6 weeks 4. Attend Step Forward/Job Skills class 5. Attend a Lifeskills/Career Readiness class as directed by DOC 6. Thinking For Change program through DOC 7. Participate in 3 sessions with DOC employment specialist. 8. Attend and participate in the DOC on site GED/Adult Education program 9. Attend and complete Moral Reconation Therapy classes through DOC.
Condition (3): Failed to request permission prior to leaving the county	1. Weekly call in for 6 weeks 2. Twice a month reporting for 60 days 3. Weekly reporting for 6 weeks at discretion of PO.
Condition (6): Found to be associating with person(s) engaged in criminal activity	1. Curfew from 8 p.m. to 6 a.m. for 90 days (can be modified by PO for treatment or work purposes) 2. Weekly call in for 6 weeks 3. 25 hours public service work 4. Thinking for Change class through DOC 5. Attend a Lifeskills/Career Readiness class as directed by DOC 6. Attend and participate in the DOC onsite GED/Adult Education program 7. Participate in 3 sessions with DOC Employment Specialist 8. Attend Step Forward/Job Skills class 9. Attend and complete Moral Reconation Therapy classes through DOC
Condition (7): Positive drug test for non-prescribed drugs (first occurrence)	1. Drug evaluation and successfully complete treatment determined necessary 2. Increase level of treatment program up to and including residential 3. Curfew from 8 p.m. to 6 a.m. for 90 days (can be modified by PO for treatment or work purposes) 4. Thinking for Change class through DOC 5. Attend a Lifeskills/Career Readiness class as directed by DOC 6. Attend 90 days NA/AA meetings 7. Attend and complete Moral Reconation Therapy classes through DOC 8. Attend and participate in the DOC onsite GED/Adult Education program
Condition (7): Positive drug test for non-prescribed drugs (second occurrence)	1. Drug evaluation and successfully complete treatment determined necessary 2. Increase level of treatment program up to and including residential 3. Curfew from 8 p.m. to 6 a.m. for 90 days (can be modified by PO for treatment or work purposes) 4. Thinking for Change class through DOC 5. Attend a Lifeskills/Career Readiness class as directed by DOC 6. Attend 90 days NA/AA meetings 7. Attend and complete Moral Reconation Therapy classes through DOC 8. Attend and participate in the onsite GED/Adult Education program through DOC
Condition (8): Failure to maintain employment	1. Weekly reporting with Job Search logs until employed 2. Daily reporting with job search logs until employed

VIOLATION	APPROVED LIST OF SANCTIONS
	3. Curfew from 8 p.m. to 6 a.m. for 90 days (can be modified by PO for treatment or work purposes) 4. Attend 3 sessions with the DOC Employment Specialist 5. Attend the Step Forward/Employment Skills program. 6. Thinking for Change class through DOC 7. Attend and participate in the DOC onsite GED/Adult Education program 8. Attend a Lifeskills/Career Readiness class as directed by DOC 9. Attend and complete Moral Reconation Therapy classes through DOC
Condition (9): Failure to comply with officer's instructions (depending on nature of instruction and reason for not complying, consequence will vary)	1. Weekly call in for 4 weeks 2. 8 hours Community service work 3. Thinking for Change class through DOC 4. Attend a Lifeskills/Career Readiness class as directed by DOC 5. If employment related, participate in three sessions with DOC Employment Specialist 6. Attend Step Forward/Job Skills class 7. Attend and complete Moral Reconation Therapy classes through DOC
Condition (10): Failure to pay monthly monetary obligations as stipulated by the Court	1. If unemployed-daily job search 2. If employed-monthly budgeting 3. Curfew from 8 p.m. to 6 a.m. (can be modified by PO for treatment or work purposes) 4. Weekly call in until monetary obligations are current 5. Extend probation to auto term upon completion of all conditions 6. Attend Lifeskills/Career Readiness class as directed by DOC. 7. Participate in three sessions with DOC Employment Specialist 8. Attend and participate in the DOC onsite GED/Adult Education program as directed by PO 9. Attend Step Forward/Job Skills class
Condition (11): Failure to submit to random testing as directed	1. Weekly reporting by 11 am 2. Reporting 3 times per week by 11 am 3. Curfew from 8 p.m. until 6 a.m. for 90 days (can be modified by PO for treatment or work purposes) 4. Attend Lifeskills/Career Readiness class as directed by DOC 5. Substance abuse evaluation and treatment determined necessary 6. Thinking for Change class through DOC 7. Attend 90 days NA/AA meetings 8. Attend and complete Moral Reconation Therapy classes through DOC
Special Condition (1): Failure to attend treatment evaluation or treatment session as scheduled	1. Curfew from 8 p.m. to 6 a.m. until evaluation is completed 2. Weekly reporting until evaluation is completed 3. Daily call in until evaluation is completed
	4. Thinking for Change class through DOC 5. Attend and complete Moral Reconation Therapy classes through DOC 6. Attend and participate in the DOC onsite GED/Adult Education program. 7. Attend 90 Days NA/AA meetings
Special Condition (8): Failure to complete community service hours as instructed	1. Daily reporting until community service hours completed/current, if unemployed 2. Weekly reporting until community service hours completed/current, if employed 3. Thinking for Change class through DOC 4. Attend and participate in the DOC onsite GED/Adult Education program
Special Condition (9): Failure to remain at residence during curfew period	1. Weekly reporting for three months 2. Electronic Monitoring for 30 days 3. Attend and participate in the DOC onsite GED/Adult Education program.
Community Control Condition (16): Failure to maintain approved schedule—unapproved absence from required location (negligence in getting home late, stopping at store on way home without permission)	1. Electronic Monitoring for 30 days 2. 10 Hours Community Service work 3. 20 Hours Community Service work 4. Thinking for Change class through DOC 5. Attend Lifeskills/Career Readiness class as directed by DOC. 6. Attend and complete Moral Reconation Therapy classes through DOC 7. Attend and participate in the DOC onsite GED/Adult Education program.

4. Alternative Sanctions Program Process:

A. The probation or community control officer shall inform offenders who have committed violations enumerated in section 3 that they may participate in the Alternative Sanctions Program for administrative disposition of the violation. No offender is required to participate in the Alternative Sanctions Program and may opt for a formal violation of probation or community control proceeding in Circuit Court.

B. If the offender admits the violation, agrees to accept the administrative sanction(s) recommended by the probation officer, and agrees to waive his/her formal violation hearing to modify his/her sentence, the probation officer will prepare an "Alternative Sanctions Program Technical Violation Notification", which will provide details of the circumstances of the technical violation that occurred and the probation officer's recommended sanction, based on the sanctions listed in the approved matrix. If the offender agrees to participate in the Alternative Sanctions Program, he/she will sign the second section of this form titled "Alternative Sanctions Program Waiver of Formal VOP/VOCC Hearing, Admission of Violation, and Acceptance of Sanctions", which will be submitted to the Court once the probation officer signs and dates the form.

C. The judge shall review the "Alternative Sanctions Program Technical Violation Notification" and waiver form submitted and, if the judge agrees that the technical violation should be addressed via the Alternative Sanctions Program and agrees with the recommended sanction, the judge will sign the "Order—Alternative Sanctions Program". If the judge does not agree with the particular sanction recommended by the officer or does not agree that the technical violation should be addressed via the Alternative Sanctions Program, the judge shall reflect further instructions on the order.

D. Upon court approval the probation officer will instruct the offender on the sanction imposed by the court and instruct the offender to take actions necessary to ensure the sanction is executed immediately. Failure to complete the imposed sanction as instructed will result in a violation report, affidavit and warrant being submitted to the court.

5. **Administration:** The Alternative Sanctions Program shall be administered by the Seminole County Circuit Court and the Florida Department of Corrections.

DONE and ORDERED this 28th day of June, 2017.

JOHN D. GALLUZZO
CHIEF JUDGE

17–29–B. CRIMINAL—ALTERNATIVE SANCTIONS PROGRAM

IN THE CIRCUIT COURT OF THE EIGHTEENTH JUDICIAL CIRCUIT, IN AND FOR BREVARD COUNTY, FLORIDA.

ADMINISTRATIVE ORDER NO: 17–29–B

SUPERSEDES 16–17–B

IN RE: CRIMINAL—ALTERNATIVE SANCTIONS PROGRAM

Whereas, there is a substantial number of technical violations that do not involve a new arrest or other serious violations; and,

Whereas, arresting and incarcerating certain non-violent offenders for minor violations of probation or community control is both expensive and nonproductive; and,

Whereas, there is research to support that recidivism may be reduced by utilizing collaborative efforts among the courts, probation and law enforcement to hold the offender accountable and apply swift and certain sanctions for technical violations of probation or community control; and

Whereas, an administrative option for processing technical violations will have the potential to offer benefits including:

• Reducing the court docket of probation and community control violation hearings;

• Reducing the workload of prosecutors and defense attorneys involved with many technical violation hearings;

• Reducing law enforcement resources required to serve violation warrants for certain technical violations;

• Reducing jail population for offenders pending violation hearings; and

• Offering the offender an alternative to a violation hearing in court, which will allow the offender to remain engaged in employment, school, treatment, etc. and allow the offender to take immediate responsibility for his/her actions and consequences of those actions

NOW, THEREFORE, IT IS ORDERED:

1. **Alternative Sanctions Program:** There is created in Brevard County a program that shall be known as the Alternative Sanctions Program.

2. **Eligibility:** To be eligible for the program, offenders must have been placed on probation or community control under the supervision of the Department of Corrections by a judge in Brevard County, have stable community ties, and have a stable residence in Brevard County, Florida. Offenders who are eligible for the program include probation offenders, drug offenders, and community control supervision offenders. The program only applies to offenders who have committed certain technical violations addressed in the Alternative Sanctions Program Violation/Sanction Matrix included in this order. The threat an offender poses to public safety is the most important factor in determining eligibility. Offenders with a lengthy or violent criminal history, including sex offenders, are not eligible to be in the program. Additionally, offenders who have new law violations, are absconders, or have violated a "no contact" condition of supervision are not eligible for the program. No offender who has three or more previous violations is eligible for the program.

3. **Qualifying Technical Violations and Approved Sanctions:** The following matrix lists the specific technical violations that may be addressed through the Alternative Sanctions Program process for offenders who were sentenced in Brevard County, Florida. Each technical violation includes a list of sanctions determined and approved by the court for the probation officer to select from when reporting these technical violations, based on the individual offender's circumstances at the time of the violation.

ALTERNATIVE SANCTIONS PROGRAM VIOLATION/SANCTION MATRIX

VIOLATION	APPROVED LIST OF SANCTIONS
Condition (1): Reported late; failed to report as instructed	1. Weekly call in for 6 weeks 2. Twice a month reporting for 3 months 3. Weekly reporting for 6 weeks 4. Attend Good will Job club class 5. Attend a Lifeskills/Career Readiness class as directed by DOC 6. Thinking for Change program through DOC 7. Participate in 3 sessions with DOC Employment Specialist. 8. Attend and complete Moral Reconation Therapy classes through DOC
Condition (3): Failed to report changes in residence or employment without first procuring the officer's consent (or notifying immediately if evicted from residence or laid off from job)	1. Weekly call in for 6 weeks 2. Twice a month reporting for 3 months 3. Weekly reporting for 6 weeks 4. Attend Good will Job club class 5. Attend a Lifeskills class as directed by DOC 6. Thinking for Change program through DOC 7. Participate in 3 sessions with DOC Employment Specialist. 8. Attend and complete Moral Reconation Therapy classes through DOC 9. Attend and participate in the DOC on site GED/Adult Education classes.
Condition (3): Failed to request	1. Weekly call in for 6 weeks

VIOLATION	APPROVED LIST OF SANCTIONS
permission prior to leaving the county	2. Twice a month reporting for 60 days 3. Weekly reporting for 6 weeks at discretion of PO. 4. Participate in one weekend at the Brevard County Sheriff's Office work farm.*
Condition (6): Found to be associating with person(s) engaged in criminal activity	1. Curfew from 8 p.m. to 6 a.m. for 90 days (can be modified by PO for treatment or work purposes) 2. Weekly call in for 6 weeks 3. 25 hours public service work 4. Thinking for Change class through DOC 5. Attend a Lifeskills/Career Readiness class as directed by DOC 6. Attend the GED program if deemed appropriate through PO 7. Participate in 3 sessions with DOC Employment Specialist 8. Attend Good will job club class 9. Participate in 2 weekends at the Brevard County Sheriff's Office work farm.* 10. Attend and complete Moral Reconation Therapy classes through DOC. 11. Attend and participate in the DOC on site GED/Adult Education classes.
Condition (7): Positive drug test for nonprescribed drugs (first occurrence)	1. Drug evaluation and successfully complete treatment determined necessary 2. Increase level of treatment program up to and including residential 3. Curfew from 8 p.m. to 6 a.m. for 90 days (can be modified by PO for treatment or work purposes) 4. Thinking for Change class through DOC 5. Attend a Lifeskills/Career Readiness class as directed by DOC 6. Participate in 2 weekends at the Brevard County Sheriff's work farm* 7. Attend 90 days NA/AA meetings 8. Attend and complete Moral Reconation Therapy classes through DOC. 9. Attend and participate in the DOC on site GED/Adult Education classes.
Condition (7): Positive drug test for nonprescribed drugs (second occurrence)	1. Drug evaluation and successfully complete treatment determined necessary 2. Increase level of treatment program up to and including residential 3. Curfew from 8 p.m. to 6 a.m. for 90 days (can be modified by PO for treatment or work purposes) 4. Thinking for Change class through DOC 5. Attend a Lifeskills/Career Readiness class as directed by DOC 6. Participate in 2 weekends at the Brevard County Sheriff's work farm* 7. Attend and participate in the DOC on site GED/Adult Education classes. 8. Attend 90 days NA/AA meetings.

VIOLATION	APPROVED LIST OF SANCTIONS
	9. Attend and complete Moral Reconation Therapy classes through DOC.
Condition (8): Failure to maintain employment	1. Weekly reporting with Job Search logs until employed 2. Daily reporting with job search logs until employed 3. Curfew from 8 p.m. to 6 a.m. for 90 days (can be modified by PO for treatment or work purposes) 4. Attend 3 sessions with the DOC Employment Specialist 5. Attend the Good will job club class 6. Thinking for Change class through DOC 7. Participation in the GED program through DOC 8. Attend a Lifeskills/Career Readiness class as directed by DOC 9. Participate in 3 weekends at the Brevard County Sheriff's office work farm.* 10. Attend and complete Moral Reconation Therapy classes through DOC
Condition (9): Failure to comply with officer's instructions (depending on nature of instruction and reason for not complying, consequence will vary)	1. Weekly call in for 4 weeks 2. 8 hours Community service work 3. Thinking for Change class through DOC 4. Attend a Lifeskills/Career Readiness class as directed by DOC 5. If employment related, participate in three sessions with DOC Employment Specialist 6. Attend Goodwill Job Club class 7. Participate in 1 weekend at the Brevard County Sheriff's work farm* 8. Attend and complete Moral Reconation Therapy classes through DOC
Condition (10): Failure to pay monthly monetary obligations as stipulated by the Court	1. If unemployed-daily job search 2. If employed-monthly budgeting 3. Curfew from 8 p.m. to 6 a.m. (can be modified by PO for treatment or work purposes) 4. Weekly call in until monetary obligations are current 5. Extend probation to auto term upon completion of all conditions* 6. Attend Lifeskills/Career Readiness class as directed by DOC. 7. Attend and participate in three sessions with DOC Employment Specialist 8. Attend and participate on site GED/Adult Education program as directed by PO 9. Attend Good will job club class
Condition (11): Failure to submit to random testing as directed	1. Weekly reporting by 11 am 2. Reporting 3 times per week by 11 am 3. Curfew from 8 p.m. until 6 a.m. for 90 days (can be modified by PO for treatment or work purposes) 4. Attend Lifeskills/Career Readiness class as directed by DOC 5. Substance abuse evaluation and treatment determined necessary 6. Thinking for Change class through DOC 7. Attend and complete Moral Reconation Therapy classes through DOC

VIOLATION	APPROVED LIST OF SANCTIONS
	8. Attend 90 NA/AA meetings.
Special Condition (1): Failure to attend treatment evaluation or treatment session as scheduled	1. Curfew from 8 p.m. to 6 a.m. until evaluation is completed 2. Weekly reporting until evaluation is completed 3. Daily call in until evaluation is completed 4. Thinking for Change class through DOC 5. Attend and complete Moral Reconation Therapy classes through DOC 6. Attend and participate in on site GED/Adult Education program as directed by PO.
Special Condition (8): Failure to complete community service hours as instructed	1. Weekly reporting until community service hours completed/current, if employed 2. Enrollment in Thinking for Change class through DOC 3. Requirement to serve one weekend on the Brevard County Sheriff's Office Work Farm. 4. Attend and participate in on site GED/Adult Education program as directed by PO.
Special Condition (9): Failure to remain at residence during curfew period	1. Weekly reporting for three months 2. Electronic Monitoring for 30 days 3. Participate in 2 weekends at the Brevard County Sheriff's work farm* 4. Attend and participate in on site GED/Adult Education program as directed by PO.
Community Control Condition (16): Failure to maintain approved schedule—unapproved absence from required location (negligence in getting home late, stopping at store on way home without permission)	1. Electronic Monitoring for 30 days 2. 10 Hours Community Service work 3. 20 Hours Community Service work 4. Thinking for Change class through DOC 5. Attend Lifeskills/Career Readiness class as directed by DOC. 6. Participate in 2 weekends at the Brevard County Sheriff's work farm* 7. Attend and complete Moral Reconation Therapy classes 8. Attend and participate in on site GED/Adult Education program as directed by PO

* Weekends at the work farm are to be considered a Saturday and Sunday at a minimum of 8 hours each day.

4. Alternative Sanctions Program Process

A. The probation or community control officer shall inform offenders who have committed violations enumerated in section 3 that they may participate in the Alternative Sanctions Program for administrative disposition of the violation. No offender is required to participate in the Alternative Sanctions Program and may opt for a formal violation of probation or community control proceeding in Circuit Court.

B. If the offender admits the violation, agrees to accept the administrative sanction(s) recommended by the probation officer, and agrees to waive his/her formal violation hearing to modify his/her sentence, the probation officer will prepare an "Alternative Sanctions Program Technical Violation Notification", which will provide details of the circumstances of the technical violation that occurred and the probation officer's recommended sanction, based on the sanctions listed in the approved matrix. If the offender agrees to participate in the Alternative Sanctions Program, he/she will sign the second section of this form titled "Alternative Sanctions Program Waiver of Formal VOP/VOCC Hearing, Admission of Violation, and Acceptance of Sanctions", which will be submitted to the Court once the probation officer signs and dates the form.

C. The judge shall review the "Alternative Sanctions Program Technical Violation Notification" and waiver form submitted and, if the judge agrees that the technical violation should be addressed via the Alternative Sanctions Program and agrees with the recommended sanction, the judge will sign the "Order Alternative Sanctions Program". If the judge does not agree with the particular sanction recommended by the officer or does not agree that the technical violation should be addressed via the Alternative Sanctions Program, the judge shall reflect further instructions on the order.

D. Upon court approval the probation officer will instruct the offender on the sanction imposed by the court and instruct the offender to take actions necessary to ensure the sanction is executed immediately. Failure to complete the imposed sanction as instructed will result in a violation report, affidavit and warrant being submitted to the court.

5. Administration. The Alternative Sanctions Program shall be administered by the

Brevard County Circuit Court and the Florida Department of Corrections.

DONE and ORDERED this 28th day of June, 2017.

JOHN D. GALLUZZO
CHIEF JUDGE

17–28. JUVENILE—ALL CHILDREN IN THE JUVENILE DIVISION REPRESENTED BY THE OFFICE OF THE PUBLIC DEFENDER

IN THE CIRCUIT COURT OF THE EIGHTEENTH JUDICIAL CIRCUIT OF FLORIDA

ADMINISTRATIVE ORDER NO: 17–28

SUPERSEDES 91–139

IN RE: JUVENILE—ALL CHILDREN IN THE JUVENILE DIVISION REPRESENTED BY THE OFFICE OF THE PUBLIC DEFENDER

Pursuant to Rule 8.060, Florida Rules of Juvenile Procedure, a child may make a written demand to participate in discovery in juvenile cases.

This Court has been informed of an agreement submitted by the Public Defender and the State Attorney to eliminate the necessity of filing a written demand for discovery in each juvenile case.

Upon filing a Notice of Discovery with the Chief Judge of the Eighteenth Judicial Circuit, requesting compliance in all juvenile cases in the Eighteenth Judicial Circuit, this agreement allows the Public Defender, when appointed, to participate in all discovery authorized by Rule 8.060, Florida Rules of Juvenile Procedure, except when electing not to participate. When choosing not to participate the Public Defender shall file a "Notice of Intent Not To Participate In Discovery" with the Court and the State.

The State Attorney has informed this Court of its concurrence in this working agreement.

It is therefore **ORDERED:**

In all juvenile cases where the Public Defender is appointed, except where the Public Defender has filed a "Notice of Intent Not to Participate in Discovery", the State Attorney and Public Defender shall fully participate in discovery as provided by the Juvenile Rules of Procedure. The State Attorney shall disclose and permit inspection, copying, testing, and photographing of all material provided for in Rules 8.060 and 8.245, Florida Rules of Juvenile Procedure, within the State's possession or control within five (5) days after a Petition is filed or after an Answer to Demand for Discovery is filed, whichever occurs first. The Public Defender will notify the State of its intent to copy all available discovery, and the State shall make the same available the next working day. Discovery materials actually obtained by a secretary for the Public Defender's office will be deemed to have been demanded and received irrespective of any written notice to the contrary.

The prosecuting attorney, pursuant to Rule 8.060 and Brady v. Maryland, 373 U.S. 83 (1963), shall disclose to the Public Defender any material information within the State's possession or control which tends to negate the guilt of the child as to the offense charged.

If subsequent to compliance with this Order, the prosecuting attorney discovers additional witnesses or material which the prosecuting attorney would have been under a duty to disclose or produce at the time of such previous compliance, the prosecuting attorney shall promptly disclose or produce such witnesses or material in the same manner as required under this order for initial discovery.

If a child elects to participate in discovery, either through filing the appropriate notice or by participating in the discovery process outlined in this agreement, the child through his/her Public Defender shall comply with all requirements of Rule 8.060(b), Florida Rules of Juvenile Procedure.

If problems arise which cannot be satisfactorily resolved, suspension of this procedure will become effective upon the filing of written notice with this Court.

DONE and ORDERED this 27th day of June, 2017.

JOHN D. GALLUZZO
CHIEF JUDGE

17–24 (A1). [SUPERSEDED BY ORDER 18–40, EFFECTIVE AUGUST 23, 2018.]

17–20–B. MENTAL HEALTH—MARCHMAN ACT HEARINGS—TELEPHONIC APPEARANCE OF QUALIFIED PROFESSIONALS

IN THE CIRCUIT COURT OF THE EIGHTEENTH JUDICIAL CIRCUIT IN AND FOR BREVARD COUNTY, FLORIDA

ADMINISTRATIVE ORDER NO: 17–20–B

IN RE: MENTAL HEALTH—MARCHMAN ACT HEARINGS—TELEPHONIC APPEARANCE OF QUALIFIED PROFESSIONALS

WHEREAS, Florida's Marchman Act, Chapter 397, Florida Statutes, provides for hearings on petitions for involuntary treatment; and

WHEREAS, Florida Rules of Civil Procedure provide for the telephonic appearance of witnesses at hearing only "(1) by agreement of the parties or (2) for good cause shown upon written request of a party upon reasonable notice to all other parties." Fla. R. Civ. P. 1.451; Fla. R. Jud. Admin. 2.530; and

WHEREAS, electronic testimony may be taken "only if a notary public or other person authorized to administer oaths in the witness's jurisdiction is present with the witness and administers the oath consistent with the laws of the jurisdiction." Fla. R. Civ. P. 1.451; Fla. R. Jud. Admin. 2.530; and

WHEREAS, Florida Rule of Judicial Administration 2.530 further requires that the "[t]he cost for the use of the communication equipment is the responsibility of the requesting party unless otherwise directed by the court." Fla. R. Jud. Admin. 2.530; and

WHEREAS it would impose a hardship and undue expense for the treating professionals in Marchman Act proceedings to appear in person; and

NOW THEREFORE WHEREAS it is in the best interests of the parties to have a qualified professional available to testify, whether in person or through electronic communication, and pursuant to the authority vested in me as Chief Judge of the Eighteenth Judicial Circuit of Florida, under Rule 2.215, of the Florida Rules of Judicial Administration; It is hereby **ORDERED**:

1. In Marchman Act hearings for involuntary treatment, treating professionals may appear by telephone without the prior written request or notice to the parties required under Fla. R. Civ. P. 1.451 and Fla. R. Jud. Admin. 2.530.

2. Such testimony will be authorized only if a notary public or other person authorized to administer oaths in the witness's jurisdiction is present with the witness and administers the oath consistent with the law of the jurisdiction.

DONE AND ORDERED this 24th day of April, 2017.

JOHN D. GALLUZZO
CHIEF JUDGE

17–19 (A1). FEES—ESTABLISHMENT OF DUE PROCESS SERVICE PROVIDER RATES AND POLICIES GOVERNING THE APPOINTMENT OF EXPERT WITNESSES

IN THE CIRCUIT COURT OF THE EIGHTEENTH JUDICIAL CIRCUIT OF FLORIDA

ADMINISTRATIVE ORDER NO.: 17–19 AMENDED

SUPERSEDES 17–19

IN RE: FEES—ESTABLISHMENT OF DUE PROCESS SERVICE PROVIDER RATES AND POLICIES GOVERNING THE APPOINTMENT OF EXPERT WITNESSES

WHEREAS, pursuant to section 27.425, Florida Statutes, due process costs are allocated in the General Appropriations Act; and

WHEREAS the total amount expended for providers of due process services in eligible cases may not exceed the amount budgeted in the General Appropriations Act; and

WHEREAS the Florida Supreme Court issued AOSC17–12 in which it standardized the appropriate costs for the provision of certain due process costs to improve the processes for appointing experts and containing costs. The Court directed each judicial circuit to implement the standardized rate structure no later than July 1, 2017.

NOW, THEREFORE, it is ORDERED:

1. In accordance with AOSC17–12, the Eighteenth Judicial Circuit will pay the following rates for the identified due process costs.

A. *Expert Witness Fees:*

1. Psychological/Adult and Juvenile Competency Evaluation Fees:

a.	Evaluation and record	$350
b.	Follow–up with same expert	$350
c.	No show rate	$140
d.	Testifying, including wait time	$150/hr (2 hour max)
e.	Out–of–County Travel	$75/hr

2. Guardianship Examining Committee

The following fee schedule for the Guardianship Examining Committee shall apply:

a. $350 for the M.D. or D.O. committee member;
b. $300 for the Ph.D committee member;
c. $250 for the ARNP, RN, MSW, LPN, LCSW or Lay Person committee member

3. Developmental Disability Examining Committee

The following fee schedule for the Developmental Disability Examining Committee shall apply:

a. $350 for the physician committee member;
b. $250 for other committee members

B. *Court Reporter Fees*

1. Brevard County:

a. Appearance Fees:

Standard Reporting	$30.00/hr
Weekend/Holiday	$45.00/hr
Real–Time	$50.00/hr

(1–1/2 hour minimum per initial appearance)

b. Transcripts—Standard:

Original for pleas only (per page)	$3.50/per pg
Original (includes 1 copy/per page)	$4.50/per pg
Additional Original Reprints (per page)	$1.00/per pg
ASCII DISK (per disk)	$5.00/disk
E–TRANSCRIPT (per transmission)	$10.00/transmit

c. Transcripts—Expedited:

1. Delivery on or before the next work day after the order:

Original for pleas only (per page)	$6.00
Original (includes 1 copy/per page)	$7.00
Additional Original Reprints (per page)	$1.00

2. Delivery after one but within three work days of the order:

Original for pleas only (per page)	$4.50
Original (includes 1 copy/per page)	$5.50
Additional Original Reprints (per page)	$1.00

d. Shipping Expenses:

Actual amount expended.

2. Seminole County:

a. Appearance Fees:

Standard Reporting	$40.00/hr
Weekend/Holiday	$60.00/hr
Real–Time	$50.00/hr
No Show/No Notice	$40.00/hr

b. Transcripts:

Original (per page)	$3.50
Each Copy (per page)	$1.75
ASCII DISK (per disk)	$25.00

c. Daily Copy:

Original (per page)	$6.00
Each Copy (per page)	$3.25

d. Expedited Copy:

Original (per page)	$4.50
Each copy (per page)	$1.90

e. Other Transcripts/Real–Time:

Certified daily copy (per page)	$6.00
Uncertified daily copy (per page)	$3.00

f. Shipping:

Actual amount expended.

C. *Interpreter Fees:*

1. Brevard County:

Arabic	$90.00/hr (2 hr min.)
Brazilian Portuguese	$75.00/hr (2 hr min.)
Cantonese	$150.00/hr (2 hr min.)
Czechoslovakian	$100.00/hr (2 hr min.)
Dutch	$100.00/hr (2 hr min.)
French	$75.00/hr (2 hr min.)
German	$90.00/hr (2 hr min.)
Greek	$100.00/hr (2 hr min.)
Haitian Creole	$75.00/hr (2 hr min.)
Hungarian	$100.00/hr (2 hr min.)
Indonesian	$100.00/hr (2 hr min.)
Italian	$80.00/hr (2 hr min.)
Japanese	$150.00/hr (2 hr min.)
Korean	$90.00/hr (2 hr min.)
Mandarin Chinese	$150.00/hr (2 hr min.)
Polish	$100.00/hr (2 hr min.)
Russian–Ukrainian	$90.00/hr (2 hr min.)
Serbo–Croatian	$100.00/hr (2 hr min.)
Spanish	$40.00/hr (1 hr min.)

Spanish–Certified	**$60.00/hr (2 hr min.)**
Tagalog	$100.00/hr (2 hr min.)
Thai	$90.00/hr (2 hr min.)
Turkish	$100.00/hr (2 hr min.)
Vietnamese	$150.00/hr (2 hr min.)
Sign Language	**$70.00/assignment (2 hr min.)**
	$35.00 half hr thereafter
Language Line	$2.50—$4.50/minute

Spanish is a 2–hour minimum when going to Titusville or the Sharpes Detention Center.

2. Seminole County:

Spanish	$45/hour (2 hr min.)
All other foreign languages	**$75—$90/hr (2 hour min.)**
Sign Language	$70/hour (2 hr min.)
Language Line	$2.50—$4.50/minute

2. The following policies and procedures governing the appointment and payment of expert witness fees are hereby established:

A. *Orders pursuant to Florida Statute § 916.115 (adult competency)*

1. When, on written motion by either counsel for the defendant, a *pro se* defendant, or the State Attorney, or upon the Court's own motion, the Court orders an adult competency evaluation pursuant to Florida Statute § 916.115(2), the Court shall select and pay for **one expert. If any party objects to the report of the appointed expert, the Court will appoint a second expert at the expense of the objecting party. If the Court requests any additional expert evaluation, the Court shall be responsible for the payment.**

2. When an expert is appointed by the Court pursuant to Florida Statute § 916.115(2) to evaluate the competence of the defendant to proceed and the defense also requests that the defendant be examined for sanity at the time of the offense, the Court will pay only for that portion of the expert's fees relating to the evaluation of competency to proceed at the rate established in this Administrative Order and the defense will be responsible for the sanity portion of said evaluation.

B. *Orders pursuant to Florida Statute § 916.301 (adult competency: intellectual disability or autism)*

1. When, pursuant to Florida Statute § 916.301, the Court orders an adult competency evaluation for a defendant whose suspected mental condition is intellectual disability or autism, the Court shall select and pay for one expert. The Court may order the Agency for Persons with Disabilities to also examine the defendant.

C. *Orders pursuant to Florida Statute § 921.137 (intellectual disability)*

1. When experts are appointed by the Court to evaluate a defendant or prisoner to determine whether the defendant or prisoner is intellectually disabled and barred from execution, pursuant to Florida Statute § 921.137 and Florida Rule of Criminal Procedure 3.203(c)(3), the Court shall select, appoint and pay for the expert.

2. When the State Attorney requests an appointment of an expert under Florida Rule of Criminal Procedure 3.203(c)(2) and an expert is appointed pursuant to Florida Statute § 921.137, the State Attorney shall select and pay for the expert.

3. When an expert is otherwise appointed to determine a defendant's or prisoner's intellectual disability as a bar to execution, the Court shall select and pay for the expert(s).

D. *Orders pursuant to Florida Statute § 985.19 (juvenile competency)*

1. When an evaluation of a juvenile defendant is ordered pursuant to Florida Statute § 985.19 to determine if the juvenile defendant is incompetent to proceed due to mental illness, the Court will select, appoint and pay for the expert.

2. When an evaluation of a juvenile defendant is ordered pursuant to Florida Statute § 985.19(1)(e) to determine if the juvenile defendant is incompetent to proceed due to intellectual disability, the Agency for Persons with Disabilities shall examine the juvenile in accordance with Florida Rule of Juvenile Procedure 8.095.

E. *Orders pursuant to Family Rule of Procedure 12. 363 and 12.364 and Florida Statute § 61.20 (social investigation)*

1. When the issue of visitation, parental responsibility, or residential placement of a child is ordered pursuant to Florida Statute 61.20, the court, on motion of any party or the court's own motion, may appoint an expert for an examination, evaluation, testing, or interview of any minor child.

2. When the issue of time-sharing, parental responsibility, ultimate decision-making, or a parenting plan for a minor child is in controversy, the court, on motion of any party or the court's own motion, may appoint an investigator under section 61.20, Florida Statutes.

3. The parties may agree to appointment of the expert, upon approval of the court. The parties are responsible for payment.

F. *Appointment of Experts*

1. When an expert is appointed or reappointed by the Court pursuant to Rule of Criminal Procedure 3.212 to perform a periodic evaluation of a defendant who has been found incompetent to proceed or appointed or reappointed by the Court pursuant to Rule of Criminal Procedure 3.213 after an adjudication of not guilty by reason of insanity, the Court shall select and pay for one expert. Provided the same expert is under contract with the Court, the Court will generally reappoint for subsequent evaluations the same expert who performed the last examination of the defendant. On the Court's own motion, or a motion of the State or defense showing good cause, the Court may appoint a new expert by rotation from the list of experts under contract with the Eighteenth Judicial Circuit.

2. Except where an expert is reappointed to do an examination or evaluation, the appointment of an expert by the Court will be by rotation from the list of experts under contract with the Eighteenth Judicial Circuit.

3. Experts retained by the Public Defender or Office of Criminal Conflict and Civil Regional Counsel ("Regional Counsel) pursuant to Florida Statute § 29.006 or by the State Attorney pursuant to Florida Statute § 29.005, shall be paid from the respective budgets of the Public Defender,

Regional Counsel or the State Attorney. An expert retained by court-appointed counsel, by counsel for a defendant who is indigent for costs, or by a defendant who is indigent for costs shall, pursuant to Florida Statute § 29.007, be paid by the Justice Administrative Commission. Prior court approval is required for such experts retained pursuant to Florida Statute § 29.007. If the State Attorney needs a court order of appointment to ensure that a State-retained expert has access to the defendant, the State Attorney shall pay for the expert notwithstanding the Court's order of appointment.

3. This Administrative Order does not restrict the ability of the Court to otherwise appoint an expert pursuant to other Florida Rules of Court.

4. Any expert seeking to provide those services in the above-listed areas shall enter into a contract with Court Administration agreeing to the above rates. Court Administration shall maintain a registry of all contracted experts from which such experts will be selected. If no expert from the registry is available for service, Court Administration shall seek experts contracted with other local Judicial Circuits before seeking the services of an uncontracted provider.

5. The Court shall select experts from the Court Administration registry unless the interests of justice require that a non-registry expert be appointed. Non–registry experts shall be compensated at the rates set forth herein. Expert witness fees in excess of the established rates may only be approved by the Court when there is a manifest necessity. The Chief Judge or his/her designee must approve in advance the payment of any fees or compensation above the standard rates.

6. Any complaint or grievance regarding a court approved expert witness shall be in writing and submitted to Court Administration for review by the Chief Judge or his/her designee.

7. Expert witnesses in disciplines not specifically identified in this Administrative Order shall be paid circuit-determined contractual rates.

8. These rates shall be incorporated into any contract executed or renewed effective July 1, 2017.

DONE AND ORDERED this 15th day of June, 2017.

JOHN D. GALLUZZO
CHIEF JUDGE

17–18. ATTORNEYS—COURT APPOINTED ATTORNEY PROCEDURE FOR APPOINTMENT OF COUNSEL IN CRIMINAL AND CIVIL PROCEEDINGS

IN THE CIRCUIT COURT OF THE EIGHTEENTH JUDICIAL CIRCUIT OF FLORIDA

ADMINISTRATIVE ORDER NO.: 17–18

SUPERSEDES 15–39

IN RE: ATTORNEYS—COURT APPOINTED ATTORNEY PROCEDURE FOR APPOINTMENT OF COUNSEL IN CRIMINAL AND CIVIL PROCEEDINGS

WHEREAS, pursuant to Section 27.40, Florida Statutes, and in accordance with Florida Rule of Judicial Administration 2.215 setting forth the duties and responsibilities of the Chief Judge in establishing a registry of attorneys, to be provided to the Clerk of Courts for appointment of counsel as authorized by law in cases in which the Office of the Public Defender and the Office of Regional Conflict Counsel are unable to provide representation due to conflict of interest or otherwise, the terms outline herein are in effect in the Eighteenth Judicial Circuit for services performed on or after July 1, 2014.

NOW, THEREFORE, it is ORDERED:

REGISTRY:

1. The Registry will be used only when representation cannot be legally or ethically provided by the Office of the Public Defender and the Office of Regional Conflict Counsel. § 27.40(2), Fla. Stat. Where a conflict precludes representation by the Office of the Public Defender and the Office of Regional Conflict Counsel, of a Defendant having multiple pending cases, a single registry attorney will be cross appointed to represent the Defendant in all cases the Defendant has pending at the time of the appointment.

2. The Chief Judge of the Eighteenth Judicial Circuit shall compile a list of attorneys in private practice, designated by county and category of cases and provide the list to the Clerk of Court in each county. § 27.40(3)(a), Fla. Stat. The court shall appoint attorneys in rotating order as their names appear on the registry, unless the court makes a finding of good cause on the record for appointing an attorney out of order. § 27.40(3)(b), Fla. Stat. The Clerk of Court is responsible for maintaining the registry and providing the court with the name of the attorney for appointment.

3. There will be an annual open enrollment period for attorneys seeking initial admission to the court's Registry. Applications for the Registry will only be accepted by Court Administration during the open enrollment period which will begin May 1 and run through May 31 of each year. Should the Chief Judge determine there is a need for additional attorneys on one or more specific Registry lists, the Chief Judge may appoint qualified attorneys outside the open enrollment period.

APPOINTMENT TO THE REGISTRY:

To be considered for placement on the Court's Registry, an attorney must be a member in good standing of the Florida Bar and submit a completed application to Court Administration in the county in which the attorney is seeking inclusion. At any time, the Chief Judge may limit the number of attorneys to a specific registry. Applicants may be denied admission to the registry with or without cause. Applicants must disclose any active Florida Bar complaints or investigations in writing to the Chief Judge. The Chief Judge has the authority to deny applicants with active Bar complaints pending the outcome of the investigation.

REGISTRY STANDARDS: All registry attorneys must:

1. Meet any minimum requirements established in general law for court appointment.

2. Be available to vigorously represent indigent defendants in cases requiring court appointment of conflict private counsel. Certify that they will be available to appear in Court whenever required by the presiding judge in any case in which they are appointed.

3. Accept appointments within their category list(s) without regard to the type of crime or proceeding involved.

4. Abide by the terms of the contract for services with the Justice Administrative Commission, herein after referred to as "JAC", and this Administrative Order.

5. Maintain an office to meet with clients in the county in which the attorney is seeking inclusion. For purposes of meeting this requirement, the address listed with the Florida Bar shall be the sole criteria. Attorneys on the capital case registry must maintain an office within fifty (50) miles of the county correctional facility in which the Defendant is incarcerated.

6. In addition to the Clerk of Court and JAC, immediately notify Court Administration of any change in his or her status or contact information.

CATEGORY–SPECIFIC STANDARDS: In addition to the qualifications stated above, any attorney requesting to be placed on the Court's Registry must certify they meet the following category-specific standards:

1. **Capital Cases:**

a. Must meet the requirements for lead counsel set forth in rule 3.112(f), Florida Rules of Criminal Procedure; or

b. Must meet the requirements for co-counsel set forth in rule 3.112(g), Florida Rules of Criminal Procedure.

2. **Felony Cases (excluding capital cases):**

a. Must be a member in good standing with The Florida Bar for no less than three years.

b. Must meet the requirements set forth in rule 3.113, Florida Rules of Criminal Procedure.

c. Must be familiar with the practice and procedures of the criminal courts in the Eighteenth Circuit.

d. Must be an experienced and active trial practitioner with no fewer than 5 criminal jury trials.

3. **Misdemeanor Cases**

a. Must be a member in good standing with The Florida Bar for the previous 12 months.

b. Must be familiar with the practice and procedures of the criminal courts in the Eighteenth Circuit.

4. **Criminal Appeals Cases:**

a. Must be a member in good standing with The Florida Bar for no less than two years.

b. Must have completed a minimum of 10 hours of CLE devoted to appellate law.

c. Must meet the requirements for appellate counsel set forth in rule 3.112(h), Florida Rules of Criminal Procedure for appointment on a capital appeal.

5. **Juvenile Delinquency Cases:**

a. Must be a member in good standing with The Florida Bar for the previous 12 months.

b. Must be familiar with the practice and procedure of delinquency proceedings.

c. Must be experienced trial practitioner with no fewer than three delinquency dispositions or three state or federal non-jury trials.

d. Must have completed a minimum of 10 hours of CLE devoted to delinquency law or legal advocacy for children within the last 3 years.

6. **Guardianship Cases:**

a. Must be familiar with the practice and procedure of guardianship proceedings.

b. Must have represented a party in a guardianship case in the past three years.

c. Must have completed no less than eight hours of a guardianship education class or six hours of credit in one or more Florida Bar CLE guardianship cases.

7. **Marchman Act/Baker Act Cases:**

a. Must be a member in good standing with The Florida Bar for no less than two years.

b. Must be familiar with the practice and procedures of Marchman Act and Baker Act proceedings.

8. **Jimmy Ryce Cases:**

a. Must be a member in good standing with The Florida Bar for no less than two years.

b. Must have acted as lead or co-counsel in at least one Jimmy Ryce/Sexually Violent Predator Act commitment trial.

9. **Termination of Parental Right/Dependency Cases:**

a. Must be familiar with the practice and procedure of juvenile dependency and termination of parental rights proceedings.

b. Must have represented a party in a dependency case in the past three years.

c. Must appear at any shelter hearings that he or she is scheduled to attend by the Clerk of Court for the Circuit Court. An attorney that does not appear at shelter or other hearings as scheduled may be removed from the list.

10. **Juvenile Dependency and TPR Appeals:**

a. Must have represented a party as lead counsel or secondary counsel in two different appellate cases over the last five years, including the preparation and filing of a brief with the District Court of Appeal or with the Supreme Court of Florida.

ATTORNEY'S FEES:

1. Attorneys shall be compensated in accordance with the schedule of fees prescribed by the Florida Statutes and the General Appropriations Act in effect at the time of Attorney's date of appointment.

2. Attorneys seeking compensation for extraordinary and unusual effort pursuant to section 27.5304(12), Florida Statutes, must motion the Court for an evidentiary hearing. The hearing must be conducted by the Chief Judge or his or her single designee for Brevard and Seminole cases.

RESIGNATION FROM REGISTRY:

1. An attorney may resign from the registry upon request if he or she submits the resignation in writing to the Chief Judge and the Justice Administrative Commission. The notice shall state if the attorney is resigning from all categories to which the attorney is entitled to receive appointments or only some categories to which the attorney is entitled to receive appointments. The attorney shall complete work on all cases assigned prior to the resignation date.

2. If an attorney later seeks to be reinstated to the registry, the attorney must file a new application during the open enrollment period to be considered by the Chief Judge.

REGISTRY COMPLAINTS: If a written complaint is received by the Chief Judge or Court Administration regarding a Registry Attorney, a copy of the written complaint shall be immediately forwarded to the attorney to whom the written complaint concerns. The attorney will then have up to thirty (30) days to respond to the written complaint, if he/she so chooses. The Chief Judge will make a determination as to whether or not the complaint contains merit and should be considered.

REMOVAL FROM REGISTRY: An attorney may be removed from the Registry for any of the following:

1. Failure to remain in good standing with The Florida Bar.

2. Failure to comply with all terms of the JAC contract and this Administrative Order.

3. Failure to renew or maintain his or her JAC contract.

4. Failure to attend hearings, except for good cause as determined by the presiding judge or general magistrate.

5. Reassigning or subcontracting an assigned case to another attorney.

6. Failure to report an active Bar complaint, investigation, or disciplinary action.

DONE AND ORDERED this 17th day of April, 2017.

JOHN D. GALLUZZO
CHIEF JUDGE

17–17–S. DOMESTIC RELATIONS—FAMILY DIVISION—STANDING TEMPORARY ORDER IN DOMESTIC RELATIONS CASES SUCH AS DISSOLUTION OF MARRIAGE, PATERNITY AND DOMESTIC VIOLENCE

IN THE CIRCUIT COURT OF THE EIGHTEENTH JUDICIAL CIRCUIT IN AND FOR SEMINOLE COUNTY, FLORIDA

ADMINISTRATIVE ORDER NO.: 17–17–S

SUPERSEDES 11–10–S

IN RE: DOMESTIC RELATIONS—FAMILY DIVISION—STANDING TEMPORARY ORDER IN DOMESTIC RELATIONS CASES SUCH AS DISSOLUTION OF MARRIAGE, PATERNITY AND DOMESTIC VIOLENCE

Whereas certain issues recur in family court actions including but not limited to Paternity and Dissolution of Marriage actions involving minor children and it is in the best interest of the parties and the children of the action to order certain temporary relief, it is hereby Ordered and Adjudged as follows:

1. **Relocation of Children.** Neither party shall change their residence beyond a fifty (50) mile radius from their current residence, nor shall either party change a child's customary school district or day care arrangement without the written agreement of both parties or an order of this court.

2. **Child Support.** In most cases, child support will ultimately be ordered retroactive to the date when the parties discontinued residing together in the same household with the child. To avoid the accumulation of retroactive arrearages, the parent who has the obligation (based on income and contact) should immediately begin making voluntary payments of child support even prior to the entry of an order requiring payment of child support. The parties should review Section 61.30, Florida Statutes to assist in determining an appropriate child support amount. Any payments made by one parent to the other parent during this retroactive period shall be considered by the court in determining any retroactive arrearage. Receipts should be retained.

3. **Parenting Class Requirement.** Pursuant to Section 61.21, Florida Statutes, both parties in a Dissolution of Marriage proceeding involving children, must complete the Parent Education and Family Stabilization Course, and provide proof of the course's completion, within forty-five (45) days after receipt of this order. Completion of this course is required in both uncontested and contested cases and is a condition precedent to entry of final judgment. Additionally, the attached "shared parenting guidelines" are provided to assist both parties with better understanding their parental responsibilities throughout the duration of a dissolution case. While these guidelines are not specifically ordered by the court at this time, compliance or noncompliance with them shall be considered by the court in future child related matters.

4. **Non–Disparagement.** Neither party shall disparage the other party to, or in the presence of, the minor child(ren), nor permit any third person to do so.

5. **No Harassment.** Both parties are enjoined from harassing the other party, whether by telephone or in person, or otherwise, at home or the other parties' place of employment or any other place the other party may be found.

6. **Mutual Restraining Order.** Unwanted physical contact between married couples and domestic partners may be a crime and will be vigorously prosecuted. Failure to obey this order may result in the issuance of a restraining order or contempt proceedings. Contempt of court is punishable by a jail sentence.

7. **Property.** Property generally includes all assets acquired during the marriage, individually or jointly, such as gifts to each other during marriage; all vested and non-vested benefits, rights and funds accrued during marriage in retirement, pension, profit sharing, annuities, deferred compensation, insurance plans and programs; land, houses, buildings, furniture, TVs, VCRs, appliances, household furnishings, motor vehicles, funds, money market accounts, IRAs, 401–Ks and other accumulations. Neither party shall sell, donate, pledge, conceal, damage, encumber, or otherwise dispose of any marital or non-marital property without the prior written consent of the other party or court order. These restrictions exclude cash, checking accounts or other sources of funds customarily used to pay ongoing living expenses of the parties or marital debt or other recurring marital obligations of the parties, limited to the amounts actually required to pay those recurring obligations. Both parties shall be held accountable for all money or property possessed during the marriage and after separation.

8. **Insurance Policies.** Any insurance policies, including but not limited to health, auto, life, homeowners, disability, etc., in effect at the time of the filing of the Petition for Dissolution of Marriage shall not be cancelled, allowed to lapse, concealed, modified, borrowed against, pledged or otherwise encumbered by either of the parties, or at the direction of either party, unless there is written consent by both parties or a court order. Both parties shall continue to pay premiums in a timely manner unless there is a written consent by both parties or a court order.

9. **Personal and Business Records.** Neither party may, directly or indirectly, conceal from the other, or destroy, any family records, business records, income records, debt records, or records of any other obligations.

10. **Additional Debt.** Both parties are prohibited from incurring any additional debt which would operate to bind the other party or mutual property. This prohibition specifically includes, but is not limited to, the use of joint credit cards, which shall be used exclusively for the necessities of life and only as a means of last resort. Any party using a joint credit card must be prepared to justify any charges as reasonable for necessities.

11. **Application and Term of this Order.** The Clerk of Court shall provide a copy of this order to the Petitioner or Petitioner's counsel when the Petition for Dissolution of Marriage or Paternity Complaint is filed. The Petitioner shall attach and serve a copy of this order to the process to be served on the Respondent along with the Petition for Dissolution of Marriage. This order shall become binding on the Petitioner upon the filing of this action and binding on the Respondent upon service of this order. This order shall remain in full force and effect until the entry of a final judgment, a dismissal of this cause, or until the entry of a subsequent temporary order, whichever shall occur first.

DONE AND ORDERED this 27th day of March, 2017.

JOHN D. GALLUZZO
CHIEF JUDGE

SHARED PARENTING GUIDELINES

The safety, financial security, and well-being of the children involved in this case are the court's primary concern. Parents should follow these guidelines until the entry of a subsequent order by the court.

It is the law, except in certain rare circumstances, that both parents will share parental responsibility for all minor children involved in this case. The law requires parents to share the children's time and to participate together in making all important decisions concerning the children. The law expects parents to put aside their feelings and cooperate on all decisions involving the children. Therefore, parents must recognize the following:

Children have a right to a loving, open and continuing relationship with *both parents*. They have the right to express love, affection, and respect for one parent in the presence of the other parent.

Neither parent may alienate a child's affection for the other parent.

Parents must separate any bad feelings for one another from their duties as parents. Their duty is to share the children's time and share in making parenting decisions. Children must be free to draw their own conclusions about each parent, without the prejudicial influences of the other parent.

Children have the right to *never* hear a parent, or a relative or friend of a parent, run down or degrade the other parent.

Children have the right to be free from guilt because the parents have decided to *separate*. They are entitled to honest answers to questions about changes taking place in family makeup.

Parents should *never* be so preoccupied with their own problems that they fail to meet the children's needs. Separation of the parents usually has a worse impact on the children than on the parents, a fact both parents should never forget.

Each parent should openly, honestly, respectfully, and regularly communicate with the other parent to avoid misunderstandings. They should never argue about the children in front of them.

Parents should discuss *all* differences regarding their separation and financial issues between them and parenting decisions out of the presence of the child. Both parents should always try to present a united front in handling any problems with the children.

Generally, children have the right to regular and continuing contact with both parents. Parents should arrange all visitations and exchanges together and not through the child. The child should never be the messenger between the parents.

Plans for contact with children should be kept and *never cancelled* unless absolutely necessary. If plans change, children should be given an explanation, preferably in advance, and by the parent causing the cancellation.

Common courtesies (politeness, promptness, readiness, calling to notify if one is going to be late) should always be observed when picking up and dropping off children. These times can be very stressful on children, so it is imperative that parents always behave as responsible adults.

Between visits, children should be encouraged to contact the absent parent by letter and phone, frequently and continuously.

Parent/child access and child support, while they may be emotionally connected, are **separate and distinct** under the law. Accordingly, a child's right of access to his or her parent is not contingent upon the payment of child support.

A child should **never** be the delivery person for support payments.

Both parents are entitled to participate in and attend all special activities in which their children are engaged, such as religious activities, school programs, sports events, and other extracurricular activities and programs.

17-16-B. CRIMINAL—PROCEDURES FOR E-WARRANTS FOR SEARCH AND ARREST WARRANTS

IN THE CIRCUIT COURT OF THE EIGHTEENTH JUDICIAL CIRCUIT IN AND FOR BREVARD COUNTY, FLORIDA

ADMINISTRATIVE ORDER NO: 17–16–B

IN RE: CRIMINAL—PROCEDURES FOR E–WARRANTS FOR SEARCH AND ARREST WARRANTS

WHEREAS it is necessary and proper for the prompt and efficient administration of justice in Brevard County to establish procedures for applying for search and arrest warrants; and

WHEREAS the Florida Legislature had authorized the use of an electronic warrant system; and

WHEREAS in the interest of speedy, efficient and proper administration of justice, Brevard County has adopted an electronic warrant system.

IT IS ORDERED as follows:

1. General Provisions

a. Brevard County has adopted an electronic warrant system (hereinafter E–warrant System) as the preferred method for submitting applications for search and arrest warrants. It is anticipated all the Brevard County law enforcement agencies and judges will eventually be approved and trained on the E–warrant System. The goal is for the majority of search and arrest warrants to be processed via the E–warrant System instead of paper submissions.

b. Law enforcement officers, who have received training and approval on the E–warrant System, should use the E–warrant System.

c. Unless required by law, felony warrants are not required to be approved by the State Attorney's Office prior to submission, but it is recommended that law enforcement officers have the State review warrants prior to submission if possible.

d. A copy of the Spouse Abuse/Weekend Jail & Holiday Schedule will be provided, on a monthly basis to all Law Enforcement Agencies via email. Law enforcement officers should consult said schedule to ascertain the name of the appropriate judge to whom the warrant application should be directed.

Due to possible changes in the schedule after distribution, all agencies should check the courts extranet page prior to contacting a judge's office for warrants at http://extranet.flcourts18.org/extranet/.

e. If a judge declines to execute a warrant based upon a finding of no probable cause, the warrant shall be presented to the <u>same</u> judge if resubmitted after changes are made to the affidavit.

2. Warrants During Business Hours—E–Warrant System

a. The law enforcement officer shall direct the affidavit and E–warrant to the Business Hours Duty Judge, unless the matter is ongoing, in which case they shall be directed to the judge who granted the first warrant in the case.

b. After uploading the electronically signed sworn affidavit and e-warrant, the officer shall phone the assigned judge's office. In an ongoing case, the officer shall phone the appropriate judge's office. The judicial assistant will bring the matter to the judge's attention at the earliest appropriate time.

3. Warrants During Business Hours—Paper Warrants

a. The E-warrant System should not be used if:

1. The law enforcement officer has a good faith belief that the search or arrest warrant is exceptionally sensitive;

2. The law enforcement agency has not been trained and approved to use the E–warrant system; or

3. When the E-warrant system is not operating.

In all other circumstances, law enforcement officers are strongly encouraged to use the E–warrant System. However, law enforcement officers may, at their own discretion, elect to submit a warrant application in paper form.

b. The law enforcement officer shall direct the affidavit and warrant to the Business Hours Duty Judge, unless the matter is ongoing, in which case they shall be directed to the Judge who granted the first warrant in the case.

c. After preparing the affidavit and warrant, the officer shall phone the assigned judge's office. In an ongoing case, the officer shall phone the appropriate judge's office. The judicial assistant will arrange with the officer a time for the officer to see the judge.

4. Emergency Warrants During Business Hours

a. If an emergency exists, the law enforcement officer must advise the assigned judges office, who will immediately locate an available judge.

b. An emergency is when the law enforcement officer has a good faith belief that unless a warrant is signed and executed immediately, it will frustrate an arrest, endanger lives, or permit the destruction of evidence.

c. The judge will determine if the law and the totality of the circumstances require immediate attention.

5. Emergency Warrants After Hours

a. For emergency search and arrest warrants after hours, on weekends, holidays or any time the courthouse is closed, the law enforcement officer shall contact the After–Hours Duty Judge by calling the duty judge. If after several attempts the officer is unable to contact the duty judge, the officer should call the Brevard County Sheriff's Department. The BCSO will then attempt to contact the duty judge on their home or cell phone and notify the judge that the officer is trying to make contact.

b. The law enforcement officer should not contact the duty judge until the affidavit and warrant have been prepared and/or uploaded to the E–warrant System and are ready for review and signature.

c. If the officer is using a paper warrant instead of an e-warrant, they should make arrangements with the duty judge for presenting the judge with the affidavit and warrant.

Done and Ordered this 15th day of March, 2017.

JOHN D. GALLUZZO
CHIEF JUDGE

17–15. CLERK OF COURT—ELECTRONIC FILING

IN THE CIRCUIT COURT OF THE EIGHTEENTH JUDICIAL CIRCUIT OF FLORIDA

ADMINISTRATIVE ORDER NO: 17–15

SUPERSEDES 13–15

IN RE: CLERK OF COURT—ELECTRONIC FILING

WHEREAS, Florida's courts have made great advances in the use of technology to improve and enhance efficiency in the court system;

WHEREAS, technologies are rapidly emerging, and the judicial branch is committed to improving the administration of justice, and enhancing public access and service;

WHEREAS, electronic filing is being utilized and the Clerk of Court will receive certain documents that are not appropriate for electronic filing;

WHEREAS, to enable the Clerk to take prompt action to reject incorrect or incomplete documents;

WHEREAS, to facilitate the efficient operation of the administration of justice, and pursuant to the authority vested in me as Chief Judge of the Eighteenth Judicial Circuit of Florida pursuant to Rule 2.215, Florida Rules of Judicial Administration,

IT IS HEREBY ORDERED:

1. The Clerk of the Court in Brevard County, Florida, and the Clerk of the Court in Seminole County, Florida, are hereby authorized to reject for electronic filing documents in accordance with Florida Courts Technology Commission's Electronic Standards.

2. Any party whose pleading has been rejected for electronic filing by the Clerk of Court and the party believes the pleading was erroneously rejected, the party may move the Chief Judge or the Administrative Judge to review the Clerk's action and provide appropriate relief, if necessary.

DONE AND ORDERED this 24th day of March, 2017.

JOHN D. GALLUZZO
CHIEF JUDGE

17–14–S. ADMINISTRATIVE RULES—ORDER ESTABLISHING GUIDELINES FOR PUBLIC ASSEMBLY AND ESTABLISHMENT OF RESTRICTED AREAS FOR PUBLIC PROTESTS

IN THE CIRCUIT COURT OF THE EIGHTEENTH JUDICIAL CIRCUIT, IN AND FOR, SEMINOLE COUNTY, FLORIDA.

ADMINISTRATIVE ORDER NO: 17–14–S

SUPERSEDES 13–14–S AMENDED AND 14–17–S

IN RE: ADMINISTRATIVE RULES—ORDER ESTABLISHING GUIDELINES FOR PUBLIC ASSEMBLY AND ESTABLISHMENT OF RESTRICTED AREAS FOR PUBLIC PROTESTS

WHEREAS, pursuant to Article V, section 2(d) of the Florida constitution and section 43.26, Florida Statutes, the chief judge of each judicial circuit is charged with the authority and the power to do everything necessary to promote the prompt and efficient administration of justice; and

WHEREAS, pursuant to the chief judge's constitutional and statutory responsibility for administrative supervision of the courts within the circuit and to create and maintain an organization capable of effecting the efficient, prompt, and proper administration of justice for the citizens of the State, the chief judge is required to exercise direction, *see* Fla.R.Jud.Admin. 2.215(b)(2), (b)(3); and

WHEREAS, to ensure the safe and orderly use of court facilities, and to minimize activities which unreasonably disrupt, interrupt, and interfere with the fair and orderly conduct of court business, and the orderly and peaceable conduct of court business in a neutral forum free of actual or perceived partiality; and

WHEREAS, recent events in Seminole County, Florida, have sparked demonstrations and other expressive conduct on some of the grounds of the three (3) courthouses serving the courts in Seminole County, Florida, which if unrestricted can lead to interference with the ingress and egress of persons appearing in court at said courthouses for exercising their lawful rights; and

WHEREAS, further evaluation has demonstrated the need to specify items prohibited on the grounds of all three (3) courthouses serving the courts in Seminole County; and

WHEREAS, restriction upon expressive conduct and lawful assembly to express grievances outside of these courthouses is necessary to serve the State's compelling interest to allow unrestricted access to said courthouses; and

WHEREAS, any such restriction must be narrowly drawn to achieve that end; and

WHEREAS, such regulation is a proper exercise of the Court's inherent authority to take supervisory and administrative actions necessary to implement its judicial functions; and

WHEREAS, the power of courts to punish for contempt is of immemorial antiquity, and is inherent in all courts as a necessary power belonging to them in order to enable them to accomplish the purposes for which they were designed; that is, the orderly trial and decision of causes, the enforcement of public order, the prevention of interferences with their proceedings, and the enforcement of the due respect belonging to them as institutions of the country;

NOW THEREFORE, I, John D. Galluzzo, in order to facilitate the efficient administration of justice, pursuant to the authority vested in me as Chief Judge of the Eighteenth Judicial Circuit of Florida under Florida Rule of Judicial Administration 2.215, hereby order the following, effective **immediately,** and to continue until further order:

1. Any person seeking to engage in oral protest, display a sign to express his or her opinion as to any subject, or otherwise wishing to express an opinion on any subject, on the grounds of any of the courthouses in Seminole County, Florida shall be restricted to conducting such activity in the areas described in this order.

2. No person may wear any garment with patches, insignias, writing or colors that would demonstrate an affiliation with any group or organization supportive of any person or cause that would be disruptive to open court proceedings in any courthouse or restricted areas.

3. Under no circumstances shall anyone interfere with the rights of any other person to lawfully enter and leave any of the three (3) courthouses in Seminole County, Florida.

4. The areas within which all expressive conduct is restricted are as follows, see attachments:

a. At the **Seminole County Criminal Justice Center**, 101 Eslinger Way, Sanford, Florida, 32773, the designated protest area is approximately 100' from the front door, beginning east of the fountain, continuing east toward the retention pond to (but not including) the paved circle drive, not to encroach on the thoroughfares in the parking lot or any parking spaces or any of the main entrance and exit doors to the building. Each designated area will allow citizens to gather up to the sidewalks, measuring one hundred and thirty feet east to west and twenty-five feet north to south.

A designated media area will be located east of (but not including) the paved circle drive continuing east towards Hwy. 17–92, not to encroach on the thoroughfares in the parking lot or any parking spaces, measuring one hundred five feet east to west, and ninety feet north to south.

b. At the **Seminole County Juvenile Justice Center**, 190 Eslinger Way, Sanford, Florida, 32773, the designated protest area is the sidewalks along Eslinger Way and the grassy area southeast of the Juvenile Justice Center between Eslinger Way and fifteen (15) feet east of the main entrance of the Juvenile Justice Center not to include the parking lot.

c. At the **Seminole County Civil Courthouse**, 301 North Park Ave., Sanford, Florida, 32771, the designated protest area is the sidewalks along North Park Ave., East Seminole Blvd., and North Hood Ave. Protesters may not encroach on the walkways on the east and west main entry doors from the sidewalks to the building, or the reserved employee parking lot located on the south side of the building.

5. To ensure public safety, the following items are strictly prohibited on court-house grounds: Weapons of any type, including fire arms, fireworks and other explosive devices, bladed instruments, ammunition, batons/clubs, taser/stun guns, chemical sprays, contraband, and any other hazardous materials. This restriction also prohibits weapons and firearms on courthouse grounds carried by concealed weapon permit (CWP) holders. Other prohibited items (unless authorized by advance permit from Seminole County) include: musical speakers, loud speakers or sound amplifiers of any kind, chairs, coolers, backpacks, signage affixed to wood, piping or metal, tents or temporary structures, any type of vendor sales or service, alcoholic beverages, portable generators, cooking grills, open fires, or any other item deemed dangerous by the Sheriff's Office. Only preauthorized vehicles with special permits issued by Seminole County are permitted to remain overnight. Prohibited items found on courthouse grounds may be confiscated by the Sheriff's Office. Non-permitted vehicles may be towed.

6. Persons assembling on courthouse grounds may be subject to a physical search of their person and handheld possessions. Handheld possessions include, but are not limited to, bags, purses, wallets, wheelchairs, carriages, strollers, electronic devices, briefcases, packages, etc. Persons refusing to be searched may be denied access to courthouse grounds, including the Public Assembly Zone.

7. Law enforcement is authorized to separate any demonstrators with conflicting points of view to different parts of the designated area. Law enforcement is also authorized to alter the buffer zones between persons assembled to reduce crowding and create a safer environment. Law enforcement is further authorized to temporarily disband persons assembled on courthouse grounds should public safety be threatened.

8. The Seminole County Sheriff's Office, the Sanford Police Department, or any other law enforcement agency designated by the Seminole County Sheriff is authorized to advise anyone who is in possession of prohibited items or engaging in activity described herein in an area on courthouse grounds other than designated herein to cease and desist immediately and remove themselves to the restricted area if they wish to peacefully protest, after having provided to those persons a copy of this order. Anyone who is observed continuing to engage in such conduct as contemplated by this order may face indirect civil contempt of court proceedings. If found in contempt of court, penalties include confinement, fine or both.

DONE and ORDERED this 27th day of February, 2017.

JOHN D. GALLUZZO
CHIEF JUDGE

17–11–B. MENTAL HEALTH—BAKER ACT PROCEEDINGS

IN THE CIRCUIT COURT OF THE EIGHTEENTH JUDICIAL CIRCUIT IN AND FOR BREVARD COUNTY, FLORIDA

ADMINISTRATIVE ORDER NO.: 17–11–B

IN RE: MENTAL HEALTH—BAKER ACT PROCEEDINGS

The 18th Judicial Circuit Court adopts the following procedures when Baker Act proceedings are heard by a General Magistrate pursuant to sec. 394.467(6)(a)3., Florida Statutes (2016) and Fla. R. Civ. P. 1.490:

1. Upon filing, all cases seeking involuntary inpatient placement under sec. 394.467(3), Florida Statutes (2016), continued involuntary inpatient placement under sec. 394.467(7), Florida Statutes (2916); involuntary outpatient placement under sec. 394.4655(4), Florida Statutes (2016); or a petition seeking consent for procedures listed under sec. 394.4598(7), shall be referred to a duly-appointed Magistrate of the 18th Judicial Circuit. This Administrative Order shall act as a blanket Order of Referral for those cases. This order does not prohibit those proceedings from being heard by a county or circuit judge.

2. Upon conclusion of the hearing, the Magistrate will inquire whether the parties agree to waive the exceptions period provided under rule 1.490(h), Fla.R.Civ.Pro. If the parties waive the exceptions period, a Circuit Judge will immediately review the Recommended Order and, if appropriate, adopt it as the Court's order.

3. Exceptions to the Magistrate's Recommended Order shall be filed promptly but in no event later than 10 days after service of the report and recommendation. A copy of the exceptions shall be delivered to the Circuit Judge assigned to the probate/mental health division.

4. Upon filing exceptions, the Court will arrange a hearing on the exceptions within 4 business days after the date of filing. The record for purposes of the hearing on the exceptions, will consist of the court's file, the recommended order, and the audio recording of the testimony presented at the hearing on the petition. No transcript will be required. The party filing the exceptions shall have the burden of so notifying the Digital Court Reporter and ensuring that copies of the audio recording are provided to the parties and the court. The attorney for the patient may waive the patient's appearance at the exceptions hearing. If the patient's appearance is not waived, the exceptions hearing will be held at the facility where the patient is being treated.

5. An order disposing of the exceptions will be filed within 3 days of the date of the hearing on the exceptions, unless the parties and court agree to a longer period.

Done and Ordered this 21st day of February, 2017

JOHN D. GALLUZZO
CHIEF JUDGE

17–08–S. MEDIATION—FAMILY LAW MEDIATION PROGRAM

IN THE CIRCUIT COURT OF THE EIGHTEENTH JUDICIAL CIRCUIT IN AND FOR SEMINOLE COUNTY, FLORIDA.

ADMINISTRATIVE ORDER NO.: 17–08–S

SUPERSEDES 13–42–S

IN RE: MEDIATION—FAMILY LAW MEDIATION PROGRAM

WHEREAS, this Administrative Order is adopted under the provisions of Chapter 44 and Chapter 61 of the Florida Statutes.

WHEREAS, pursuant to Florida Statute 44.102(2)(c) quoted in pertinent part "A court, under rules adopted by the Supreme Court; in circuits in which a family mediation program has been established and upon a court finding a dispute, shall refer to mediation all or part of custody, visitation, or other parental responsibility issues as defined is s. 61.13. Upon motion or request of a party, a court shall not refer any case to mediation if it finds there has been a history of domestic violence that would compromise the mediation process."

WHEREAS, pursuant to Florida Statute 61.183(1) "In any proceeding in which the issues of parental responsibility, primary residence, access to, visitation with, or support of a child are contested, the court may refer the parties to mediation in accordance with the rules promulgated by the Supreme Court."

WHEREAS, pursuant to Florida Statute 44.102(2)(b) quoted in pertinent part "A court, under rules adopted by the Supreme Court, may refer to mediation all or any part of a filed civil action for which mediation is not required under this section". The court relies on this provision to mandatorily refer to mediation all paternity actions under Florida Statutes 742 and all issues of property and indebtedness filed in any family law case regardless of the pendency of any issues involving children.

WHEREAS, a Family Mediation Program is required under F.S. 44.102(2)(c) in order for the courts in the Eighteenth Judicial Circuit, Seminole County, to mandatorily refer all family law matters with disputed or contested issues regarding children to mediation. In accordance with the statute, the Family Law Mediation Department for Seminole County, Florida is hereby created under this order. This Order adopts and establishes procedures to set the standards for operation of this court based program.

WHEREAS, all mediators serving in the Seminole County Family Law Mediation Department must be Florida Supreme Court Certified Family Law Mediators.

WHEREAS, the Family Law Mediation Program for Seminole County, Florida is developed to serve families with a combined gross income of $100,000.00 or less.

IT IS HEREBY ORDERED AND ADJUDGED:

1. All contested family law cases not specified as exceptions herein are referred to mediation. Mediation must be completed before any hearing on temporary or final matters by the presiding judge. If a temporary matter has been referred to the General Magistrate and a party files a timely objection, the objection must include the date, time, mediator (if private) and place of the mediation in order for it to be deemed valid. A family law case is deemed contested or disputed upon the filing with the Clerk of Court of an initial or supplemental petition seeking relief and when any form of responsive paper or pleading is filed unless the responsive filing can only be construed as an admission to all allegations of the initial or supplemental petition. The effective date of this order of referral is the date in which a respondent files the first responsive paper or pleading to any initial or supplemental petition and the response has been docketed by the Clerk of Court.

2. As paternity actions under Florida Statutes Chapter 742 raise virtually identical issues to issues relating to children in dissolution of marriage actions under Florida Statutes Chapter 61 and as the bests interests of children are a paramount concern to the courts of the Eighteenth Judicial Circuit, Seminole County, all paternity actions under Florida Statutes Chapter 724 are referred to mandatory mediation under the same conditions and standards as dissolution of marriage actions under Florida Statutes Chapter 61. Reference herein to family law cases or family law matters includes paternity actions.

3. Mediation for all pending family law cases is required before any court hearing on any temporary matters or trial is scheduled before the presiding judge.

4. The following matters are deemed to be not contested or are considered not suitable for a mandatory referral to mediation. These matters are not to be set with the Seminole County Family Law Mediation Program;

a. Actions in which a default has been entered by the clerk or the trial court and the default has not been set aside;

b. Actions for enforcement and contempt in which no other issues are pled;

c. Actions in which the parties are in agreement and have filed with the clerk of court a fully executed Marital Settlement Agreement and, in cases involving children, a fully executed Parenting Plan;

d. Actions in which the trial court has entered an order dispensing with mediation due to a history of domestic violence;

e. Actions in which the trial court has entered an order dispensing with mediation for any cause accepted by the court, and

f. Pre-suit mediations.

5. Other than the general referral to mediation herein, including the requirement that mediation be completed before temporary or final hearings are heard before the presiding judge, this order will not serve as any limitation on mediation or any form of dispute resolution between the parties not set with Seminole County Family Law Mediation Department.

6. Scheduling Mediation Sessions:

a. The program administrator, or a person specifically designated by Court Administration, are the only person(s) authorized to coordinate and set mediation sessions for the Seminole County Family Law Mediation Program.

b. Mediation scheduling is initiated by receipt of the court approved form titled "*Information for Scheduling Mediation*" or a form substantially in compliance. Failure to fully complete all information may result in substantial delays.

c. The program administrator will initiate telephone contact to coordinate the scheduling with both parties. If any party cannot be reached by two attempts on two calls made on two separate business days and two different times of day, the program administrator will set the mediation session not less than 21 days from the date of the last attempt.

d. The program administrator will honor a request by both parties to schedule mediation with a specific mediator. Unilateral selection of a mediator over the other party's objection will not be honored. If the parties disagree on selection of a mediator, designation of the mediator must be determined by the court. If the parties have no mediator preference the program administrator will select a mediator from the court approved mediators within the program.

e. The program administrator reserves the right to reassign mediators to specific cases in an effort to effectively manage the program.

7. Required Documentation:

a. The Program Administrator will not schedule a case for a mediation session until the parties have filed and the clerk of court has docketed a current financial affidavit substantially in compliance with Form 12.902(b) Florida Family Law Forms promulgated by the Florida Supreme Court. A financial affidavit is deemed current if it has been filed within two years of the first mediation scheduling attempt so long as the parties' income has not changed. The parties shall also bring to mediation their pay stubs or other pay records covering the month preceding the date of the mediation session.

8. Attendance and Sanctions:

a. Pursuant to Florida Family Law Rule of Procedure 12.740 and in accordance with the uniform Order of Referral and Requirement to Attend Mediation with the Seminole County Family Mediation Program appearance of a party is by personal appearance not less than 15 minutes before the scheduled session start time through the scheduled start time. No party making a proper appearance is required to wait more than 15 minutes after the scheduled start time when the opposing party has made no appearance. Each party must pay all applicable mediation fees regardless of the other party's failure to appear.

b. Sanctions for failure of a party to appear are governed by Florida Family Law Rule of Procedure 12.741 which provides as follows: "If a party fails to appear at a duly noticed mediation conference without good cause, or knowingly and willfully violates any confidentiality provision under section 44.405, Florida Statutes, the court upon motion shall impose sanctions, including an award of mediator and attorneys' fees and other costs, against the party".

c. Specific costs required by the Seminole County Family Law Mediation Program are also assessed pursuant to the uniform Order of Referral and Requirement to Attend Family Mediation. All program costs and cost setting procedures are detailed herein.

d. All parties have a right to counsel of an attorney licensed to practice law in the State of Florida. In the discretion of the mediator and with the agreement of the parties the mediation session may proceed in the absence of counsel unless otherwise court ordered (Florida Statute 44.1011(2)(d). No party or the mediator is required to wait for counsel delayed and unable to appear at mediation within 15 minutes after the scheduled session start time. By definition (F.S, 44.1011(2)(d) the conduct of a family law mediation is to be conducted by the parties. When counsel for a party does not show and when the opposing party agrees to proceed, the party whose counsel is absent will be required to make a decision to proceed or not to proceed without counsel. A decision not to proceed will not be treated as a failure to appear but the refusal to proceed is a unilateral cancellation with assessment of costs as addressed herein.

e. Appearance of a party by telephone or electronic device is allowed by stipulation of the parties prior to the mediation or by court order. Both parties are obligated to timely notify the program administrator of any agreement or court order allowing appearance of a party by telephone or electronic device and the specific manner of appearance. The program administrator must be able to confirm in advance the party appearing electronically must have continuous access to a fax machine requiring not more than 5 minutes time per transmission.

9. Cancellation and Mediation Resets:

a. All Seminole County Family Law Mediation Department mediation sessions are scheduled by uniform court orders. Scheduled mediations sessions can be reset or cancelled anytime and under any conditions by court order. Absent court order, the courts allow that a scheduled mediation with the Seminole County Family Law Mediation Department may be cancelled or reset without cost or court sanction upon receipt to the program administrator, a signed stipulation from both parties not later than three (3) working days prior to the scheduled mediation date.

b. No party may unilaterally cancel or reset a mediation session.

c. All mediation fees must be paid to the Clerk of Court before the scheduled mediation session or the session may be cancelled.

10. Mediation Fees:

a. Mediation fees for the Seminole County Family Law Mediation Program are set by Florida Statute and by the adoption of this Administrative Order along with the uniform Order of Referral and Requirement to Attend Family Mediation.

b. The Seminole County Family Law Mediation Program can only accept cases in which the combined gross annual income of the parties is $100,000.00 or less.

c. The following mediation session fees shall be collected by the Clerk of Court:

1. One hundred twenty dollars ($120.00) per person per scheduled session when the parties combined gross annual income is greater than $50,000.00, but less than $100,000.00 per year;

2. Sixty dollars ($60.00) per person per scheduled session when the parties combined gross annual income is less than $50,000.00 per year.

3. Any person who is determined to be indigent by the Clerk of Court will not be charged a session fee. Only an authorized Deputy Clerk of Court may make an indigent determination. If the Clerk of Court denies a request for indigent status the matter may be reviewed by the judge assigned to the specific case.

d. Mediation session fees are paid directly to the Clerk of Court, Family Division located at 301 North Park Avenue, Sanford, FL 32771. Payments are accepted in the form of cash, check, cashier's check, certified check or money order only. No third party checks will be accepted.

e. Mediation session costs are set by Florida Statute cannot be waived. Nonpayment of these fees may cause the mediation session to be cancelled by the program administrator.

f. Each mediation session is set for up to three (3) hours from the scheduled start time. Any extension of a mediation session over three hours requires agreement of the parties and the mediator. If subsequent sessions are scheduled or if the scheduled session exceeds three (3) hours the parties are required to pay an additional session cost at the applicable rates described above.

g. If a mediation session is not cancelled or reset by joint stipulation within three (3) working days from the scheduled session date, the party initiating or making the reset or cancellation request must pay the cost for the scheduled session and the session costs for any reset mediation session. The opposing party not initiating the reset or cancellation request will have the present session fee carried over to any future reset mediation session. The family mediation program administrator must receive the joint stipulation signed by both parties no later than 5:00 p.m. within the three (3) full business days prior, and not including, the original scheduled mediation date for fees to be waived.

h. All mediation fees must be paid in advance of the scheduled session pursuant to the uniform Order of Referral to mediation.

i. If a party fails to pay mediation fees in advance, the mediation session may be cancelled. No subsequent mediations (resets, continuances or supplemental sessions) will be scheduled if fees are outstanding. Any party who fails to pay the mediation fees is subject to judicial sanctions.

11. Conduct of Mediation:

a. Mediators in the Seminole County Family Mediation Program shall conduct mediation in accordance with the Florida Rules for Certified and Court–Appointed Mediators and the Standards of Professional Conduct promulgated by the Florida Supreme Court.

b. For each mediation session the mediator shall report the mediation results, attendance of parties or failure to appear, full settlement, partial settlement or continuance on the court approved report form.

DONE AND ORDERED this 9th day of January, 2017.

JOHN D. GALLUZZO
CHIEF JUDGE

16–42–B. ADOPTIONS—CRIMINAL CHECKS

IN THE CIRCUIT COURT OF THE EIGHTEENTH JUDICIAL CIRCUIT IN AND FOR BREVARD COUNTY, FLORIDA

ADMINISTRATIVE ORDER NO.: 16–42–B

SUPERSEDES 09–26–B

IN RE: ADOPTIONS—CRIMINAL CHECKS

In all adoptions before the Circuit Court for Brevard County, Florida, involving a minor or an adult as adoptee and a preliminary home study under section 63.092, Florida Statutes, is neither required by Chapter 63, Florida Statutes, nor ordered by the Court in a particular case, the Petitioner shall send a copy of the adoption Petition to the Program Administrator at the Florida Department of Children and Families ("Department"), 375 Commerce Parkway, Suite 101, Rockledge, Florida 32955. The Petitioner shall also provide the name of the judge assigned to the Petitioner's adoption case. (The Petitioner may verify the Department's receipt of this information by calling (321) 637–7383).

The Department will immediately, upon receiving a copy of the adoption Petition from the Petitioner, conduct a FCIC criminal records check on the Petitioner through the Records and Warrants Division of the Brevard County Sheriff's Office and a child abuse check on the Petitioner from the Department's own records. Within twenty (20) days from receipt of the adoption Petition, the Department shall inform the judge assigned to the Petitioner's adoption case of the results of Petitioner's FCIC/abuse registry background checks. The Court in any particular case may expressly waive in writing such criminal and child abuse check by the Department.

The social security number and date of birth of the Petitioner will be set forth in all adoption Petitions in order for the criminal and abuse registry checks to be performed pursuant to this Administrative Order.

Done and Ordered this 6th day of December, 2016.

JOHN D. GALLUZZO
CHIEF JUDGE

16–38–B. DOMESTIC VIOLENCE—GEOGRAPHIC ASSIGNMENT FOR INJUNCTIONS FOR PROTECTION (OTHER THAN DOMESTIC VIOLENCE)

IN THE CIRCUIT COURT OF THE EIGHTEENTH JUDICIAL CIRCUIT IN AND FOR BREVARD COUNTY, FLORIDA

ADMINISTRATIVE ORDER NO.: 16–38–B

IN RE: Domestic Violence–Geographic Assignment for Injunctions for Protection (other than Domestic Violence)

Upon the filing of an Injunction for Protection Against Repeat Violence, Sexual Violence or Dating Violence pursuant to F.S. 784.046, or a Petition for Injunction Against Stalking pursuant to F.S. 784.048, if the clerk has determined that no related cases exist, the clerk shall geographically assign the cases to the county judges assigned to hear civil cases in Titusville, Viera and Melbourne according to the following criteria:

1. The Petitioner's address shall be utilized to determine assignment by zip code. If Petitioner does not reside in Brevard County, or Petitioner's address is unavailable, the Respondent's address shall be utilized to determine assignment.

2. The following zip codes will be assigned to the Civil Division County Judge presiding in Titusville, Florida: 32754, 32780, 32781, 32796, 32926 and 32952.

3. The following zip codes will be assigned to the Civil Division County Judge presiding in Viera, Florida: 32920, 32922, 32925, 32927, 32937, 32940, 32953, and 32955.

4. The following zip codes will be assigned to the Civil Division County Judge presiding in Melbourne, Florida: 32901, 32903, 32904, 32905, 32907, 32908, 32909, 32931, 32934, 32935, 32950, 32951, and 32976.

If the clerk has determined that a related case exists pursuant to existing rules, then the clerk shall forward the Petition to the Family Circuit Division Judge to whom the related case is assigned, for review and determination for coordination with the related case before the assigned Family Division Judge. In that case, the related injunction matter shall be assigned to the Family Division Judge.

If a closed case is reopened, the clerk shall reassign the case to the County Judge currently presiding in the civil division pursuant to the geographic assignment procedures set forth herein, using the most current address available for each party in making this determination. If both parties no longer reside in Brevard County, the clerk may use any prior address of the Petitioner to determine the proper assignment.

This procedure shall be effective for relevant cases filed or reopened on or after September 26, 2016.

DONE and ORDERED this 21st day of September, 2016

JOHN D. GALLUZZO

CHIEF JUDGE

16–35–B. DOMESTIC RELATIONS—FAMILY DIVISION PARTIES

IN THE CIRCUIT COURT OF THE EIGHTEENTH JUDICIAL CIRCUIT IN AND FOR BREVARD COUNTY, FLORIDA

ADMINISTRATIVE ORDER NO.: 16–35–B
SUPERSEDES 11–14–B 4TH AMENDED

IN RE: DOMESTIC RELATIONS—FAMILY DIVISION PARTIES REQUIRED TO READ CERTAIN ADMINISTRATIVE ORDERS

WHEREAS the court sitting and adjudging Domestic Relations cases in the 18th Judicial Circuit in and for Brevard County believes it is appropriate and wise that parties to a dissolution of marriage case read and become familiar with certain relevant Administrative Orders.

NOW THEREFORE pursuant to the authority vested in the Chief Judge by Rule 2.215 of the Florida Rules of Judicial Administration and Section 43.26 of Florida Statutes, it is Ordered that the 18th Judicial Circuit's website shall contain the following Administrative Orders for inspection and reading:

1. In all cases:

a. IN RE: Mediation—Family Mediation Mandatory Referral Of All Contested Family Law Cases To Mediation

b. IN RE: Domestic Relations—Collaborative Conflict Resolution In Dissolution Of Marriage Cases

c. IN RE: Domestic Relations—Family Division–Standing Temporary Relations Order

d. IN RE: Domestic Relations—Family Division- Model Family Court

2. The following additional administrative orders must be read if there are minor children of the marriage:

a. IN RE: Domestic Relations—Requirement To Complete The Parent Education And Family Stabilization Course In Dissolution Of Marriage Proceeding With Minor Children Or A Paternity Action That Involves Issues Of Parental Responsibility

b. IN RE: Domestic Relations—Parenting Coordinators In High Conflict Family Law Cases

The petitioner/respondent upon reading the Administrative Orders required shall execute the statement attached hereto (Attachment A) and file said statement with the clerk of court.

DONE AND ORDERED this 9th day of September, 2016.

JOHN D. GALLUZZO
CHIEF JUDGE

ATTACHMENT A

IN THE CIRCUIT COURT FOR THE EIGHTEENTH JUDICIAL CIRCUIT IN AND FOR BREVARD COUNTY, FLORIDA

CASE NO.: ____________

In re: The Matter/Marriage of:

______________, Petitioner,

and

______________, Respondent.

ATTESTATION

I, ________ (___ petitioner ___ respondent) have read the administrative orders required to be read in Administrative Order 16–35–B.
Signature: ____________ Date: ____________

Printed Name: ____________

16–34–B. [SUPERSEDED BY ORDER 17-23-B, EFFECTIVE JUNE 1, 2017.]

16–32–B. ADMINISTRATIVE ORDERS—RESCINDS ADMINISTRATIVE ORDER 14–22–B

IN THE CIRCUIT COURT OF THE EIGHTEENTH JUDICIAL CIRCUIT IN AND FOR BREVARD COUNTY, FLORIDA

ADMINISTRATIVE ORDER NO.: 16–32–B

SUPERSEDES 14–22–B

IN RE: ADMINISTRATIVE ORDERS—RESCINDS ADMINISTRATIVE ORDER 14–22–B

Pursuant to Dougan v. Bradshaw, No. 4D15–2123, 2016 WL 3745378 (Fla. 4th DCA, July 13, 2016);

It is hereby ordered that Administrative Order 14–22–B In Re: Mental Health—Procedures for Return of Firearms Involving Baker Act Actions is hereby rescinded.

DONE AND ORDERED this 17th day of August, 2016

JOHN D. GALLUZZO

CHIEF JUDGE

16–31–S. CIVIL—CONTRABAND FORFEITURE ACT PROCEDURES

IN THE CIRCUIT COURT OF THE EIGHTEENTH JUDICIAL CIRCUIT IN AND FOR SEMINOLE COUNTY, FLORIDA

ADMINISTRATIVE ORDER NO.: 16–31–S

IN RE: CIVIL—CONTRABAND FORFEITURE ACT PROCEDURES

WHEREAS, The Florida Contraband Forfeiture Act sets forth the procedural requirements governing the forfeiture of contraband articles. See §§ 932.701–932.7062, Florida Statutes, and

WHEREAS, Florida Statute 932.703(2016), now provides that when a seizure of property is made under the Florida Contraband Forfeiture Act, the seizing agency shall apply, within 10 business days after the date of seizure, to a court of competent jurisdiction, for an order determining whether probable cause exists for the seizure of the property, and

WHEREAS, in most instances involving property forfeiture a criminal arrest involving the claimant or potential claimant has been made and a related Circuit Criminal Case number exists, and

WHEREAS, Civil Forfeiture involves court proceedings which occur prior to the filing of a Forfeiture Complaint and therefore prior to the assignment of a Civil Court Case number associated with the Forfeiture, and

WHEREAS, an Administrative Order will assist in the provision of uniform procedures, address the filing and maintenance of documentation and provide for the uniform disposition of forfeiture proceedings and ensure consistency amongst all seizing agencies within the courts of the Eighteenth Judicial Circuit—Seminole County.

NOW, THEREFORE, I, John D. Galluzzo, in order to facilitate the efficient operation of the administration of justice, and pursuant to the authority vested in me as Chief Judge of the Eighteenth Judicial Circuit of Florida, Seminole County in accordance with Article V, section 2, Florida Constitution, pursuant to Rule of Judicial Administration 2.215, and section 43.26, Florida Statutes, hereby order the following, effective for forfeiture seizures of property which occur on or after July 1, 2016 within Seminole County, and to continue until further order:

It is hereby ORDERED:

A. Circuit Civil Forfeiture Proceedings Generally

1. In accordance with section 932.704(2), Florida Statutes, of the Florida Contraband Forfeiture Act, all civil forfeiture cases shall be heard before a Circuit Judge. In Seminole County, Complaints filed seeking forfeiture shall be assigned to any civil section judge in the same manner other circuit civil cases are assigned.

B. Notice of Seizure & Right to Adversary Preliminary Hearing

1. Section 932.703(3), Florida Statutes, includes a right to an Adversarial Preliminary Hearing upon request. Pursuant to this statute a specific notice of this right must be provided by the seizing agency. All law enforcement agencies within the Eighteenth Judicial Circuit—Seminole County shall use "Attachment A"—Notice of Forfeiture Seizure/Right to Adversarial Preliminary Hearing in substantially the same format.

2. When any person receiving the Notice of Forfeiture Seizure/ Right to Adversarial Preliminary Hearing, requests an Adversarial Preliminary Hearing in conformity with the statute, the seizing agency is then required to set the hearing within 10 days of receipt of said request, or as soon as practicable thereafter. Adversarial Preliminary Hearings held prior to the filing of a Forfeiture Complaint shall be scheduled with a Circuit Judge assigned to the Civil/Family Court Division and heard pursuant to the Judicial rotation schedule set by the Civil/Family Court Judges. For the purpose of documenting proper notice of the hearing, in the absence of an existing Civil case number, the Notice of Hearing shall be filed under the Criminal Clerk Case number and filed in the Criminal Case file. The attorney setting the hearing shall make sure the hearing is coordinated with the Civil Court Judge and that the notice is also provided to the Civil Judge who will be hearing the matter.

3. Upon the filing of a Complaint for Forfeiture, all documents pertaining to an Adversarial Preliminary Hearing regarding the same Property shall be transferred by the clerk to the Court file maintained for the Complaint. The Seizing agency shall be responsible for filing a Notice with the Court under the criminal case number indicating the need for the transfer of paperwork to the civil case file listed by civil case number and no further Order is needed by the Court to authorize the transfer. If an Adversarial Preliminary Hearing is conducted and no Complaint for Forfeiture is subsequently filed, the documents pertaining to the Adversarial Preliminary

Hearing shall remain filed under the Circuit Criminal Case number.

C. Application for an Ex–Parte Order Finding Probable Cause for Seizure

1. Effective July 1, 2016, to obtain a ruling pursuant to section 932.703(2)(a), Florida Statutes, the seizing agency shall, within 10 business days of the seizure, submit an Ex–Parte Application for a 10–day Probable Cause Forfeiture Seizure Determination "Attachment B" with an accompanying affidavit to the court for ex-parte review and ruling. The submission packet must include both a proposed Ex–Parte Order Finding Probable Cause for Seizure "Attachment C–1" and a proposed Ex–Parte Order Denying Probable Cause for Seizure "Attachment C–2". The Ex–Parte Application for the 10–day Probable Cause Determination and the proposed orders shall be in substantially the same format.

2. Submission of such Applications and Proposed Orders may be by use of the e-warrant system in the same manner that search warrants and arrest warrants are submitted. The submission by the e-warrant system shall indicate "Search Warrant" and also identify the submission as a Civil Forfeiture. Ex parte probable cause affidavits shall not be submitted after business hours to the Court for review but shall be submitted during regular business hours to a Circuit Judge assigned to the Civil/Family Court Division pursuant to Judicial rotation set by the Civil/Family Court Judges. All 10–day Probable Cause Applications, supporting affidavits and Orders determining Probable Cause shall include the agency case number if there is a corresponding agency case number and under the case number the terms "Civil Forfeiture."

3. After the assigned Judge has made his/her findings, the Application for Probable Cause, the affidavit in support of such application, and the court order determining probable cause shall be retained by counsel for the submitting seizing agency or the submitting agency affiant in the absence of counsel and shall be filed as further provided in this Administrative Order.

If a formal Complaint for forfeiture is filed with the Clerk of the Court—Circuit Civil Division, the Application for Probable Cause, the affidavit in support of such application and the Court Order Finding Probable Cause shall be filed as attachments to the Civil Forfeiture Complaint. The affidavit used in support of the Probable Cause Order shall be sufficient to support the Complaint for Forfeiture, however a supplemental affidavit containing additional facts may also be submitted.

4. If a Civil Forfeiture Complaint is not filed with the Clerk of the Court—Circuit Civil Division, then the Application for Probable Cause, the affidavit in support of such application and the Court Order determining Probable Cause shall be filed with the Clerk of the Court—Criminal Division within 60 days of the seizure where a corresponding criminal arrest was made. The filing shall be in the clerk case which corresponds to the agency case number and such case number shall be clearly noted.

5. If a Civil Forfeiture Complaint is not filed with the Clerk of the Court—Circuit Civil Division, and there is also no corresponding criminal case filed with the Circuit Criminal Division, then the Probable Cause Application, supporting affidavit and Court Order determining Probable Cause shall be retained by the submitting agency pending direction from the Court issuing the Probable Cause Order.

6. In all cases where a Forfeiture Complaint is not filed, a Civil Forfeiture Return "Attachment B–1" shall be prepared indicating that a Formal Forfeiture Complaint was not filed. If an agreement with the owner/claimant was reached in lieu of the filing of a Forfeiture Complaint, then such disposition shall also be reflected on the Civil Forfeiture Return. The Civil Forfeiture Return shall be filed or maintained in the same manner as the Application for Probable Cause and other related documents when a Formal Complaint for Forfeiture is not filed.

7. Pursuant to State Statute, no additional Probable Cause determination will be required if a 10–day Ex Parte Order Finding Probable Cause for Forfeiture Seizure has been entered. The entry of an Order finding Probable Cause for seizure does not negate a claimant's right to request an Adversarial Preliminary Hearing.

8. No filing fee is required for submission of a 10 Day Application for Probable Cause Finding as these are handled as ex parte requests similar to arrest and search warrants. No filing fee is required for the scheduling and handling of the Adversarial Preliminary Hearing unless a Circuit Civil Case number is requested.

D. Complaint for Forfeiture and § 932.704(5)(c), Florida Statutes, Administrative Order

1. Section 932.704(5)(c), Florida Statutes, states that the court shall require any claimant who desires to contest the forfeiture to file and serve upon the attorney for the seizing agency any responsive pleading and affirmative defenses within 20 days after the receipt of the complaint. To comply with this provision, the court shall include this notifying language advising the claimant of the responsive pleading requirements in any Order finding Probable Cause for Seizure. The seizing agency shall include a copy of the Order Finding Probable Cause with the Complaint and summons to be served upon the claimant.

2. Upon filing of the Complaint and accompanying documents as set forth in Section C.3 of this order and payment of the appropriate filing fee, clerk fees and posting of bond pursuant to section 932.704(4), Florida Statutes, the Clerk of the Court shall open a circuit civil case which shall be treated in all regards as a civil proceeding.

3. Bond may be by surety or by cash. Upon resolution of the Forfeiture Complaint, the court shall direct disposition of the bond. If the Court orders payment of bond to the claimant, the seizing agency shall deposit payment with the clerk along with any authorized clerk fees so that payment may be provided to the claimant by the clerk. Upon payment to the clerk by the seizing agency, the clerk shall release the surety from further obligation.

DONE AND ORDERED this 4th day of August, 2016.

JOHN D. GALLUZZO

CHIEF JUDGE

"ATTACHMENT A"

NOTICE OF FORFEITURE SEIZURE AND RIGHT TO ADVERSARIAL PRELIMINARY HEARING

SEMINOLE COUNTY SHERIFF'S OFFICE
Sheriff Donald F. Eslinger

NOTICE OF SEIZURE OF PROPERTY FOR FORFEITURE AND RIGHT TO ADVERSARIAL PRELIMINARY HEARING

DATE: ______________________ AGENCY NO.: ______________________

TO: ______________________
(Name)
______________________ ______________________
(Address) *(City/State/Zip)*

RE: ______________________
(List of all property seized for forfeiture, i.e. currency, guns, tools, etc.)

OR, if vehicle seized, insert information below:

(Year) ________ (Make) ________ (Model) ________ (Color) ________

(Vehicle Identification Number) ______________________

On ____________, 201____ the above-described property was seized from ______________________ ______________________, Seminole County, Florida, by the Seminole County Sheriff's Office pursuant to the provisions of the Florida Contraband Forfeiture Act, Florida Statutes 932.701-932.7062. This is separate from any seizure for evidentiary purposes. Although an ex parte probable cause determination by a judge will be sought within 10 days of seizure by the seizing agency, you are advised that you have a right to request an adversarial preliminary hearing to determine whether probable cause exists to believe that said property has been or is being used in violation of the Florida Contraband Forfeiture Act. If you do not request an adversarial preliminary hearing you still have the right to contest the forfeiture action at a later date. If you would like to request a post seizure adversarial hearing, you must request the hearing in writing, by certified mail, return receipt requested, within fifteen (15) days of your receipt of this notice. You must send your request to the Seminole County Sheriff's Office, Attention: General Counsel, 100 Bush Boulevard, Sanford, Florida 32773. A court hearing will be set within ten (10) days after your request is received or as soon as practicable thereafter.

SHERIFF DONALD F. ESLINGER

By: ______________________
Deputy Sheriff / ID #

____
Supervisor Authorizing/Reviewing Probable Cause for Seizure
Supervisor / ID #

The undersigned acknowledges receipt of a copy of this notice.

______________________ ______________________
Signature of Recipient Witness to Claimant Receiving a Copy of this Notice

____
Date Received

If claimant refuses to sign, please indicate the refusal in the signature line.

(If the Notice is mailed it must be sent by certified mail, return receipt requested within 5 working days after the seizure.)

Certified Mail Receipt #: ______________ Date Mailed: ______________

"ATTACHMENT B"

IN THE CIRCUIT COURT OF THE EIGHTEENTH JUDICIAL CIRCUIT IN AND FOR SEMINOLE COUNTY, FLORIDA

Agency Case No: ______________________

CIVIL FORFEITURE

EX–PARTE APPLICATION FOR 10 DAY PROBABLE CAUSE FORFEITURE SEIZURE DETERMINATION

COMES NOW the Petitioner, __________ (insert agency), by and through undersigned counsel, pursuant to section 932.703(2), Florida Statutes, and says:

1. On __________ (date), (insert agency), seized for forfeiture the following described property:(Property Description)

2. This application is being presented within 10 business days of seizing that property;

3. The requirements specified in 932.703(1)(a) Florida Statutes, have been satisfied based on the fact that one or more of the following facts as indicated below exist:

__________ The owner of the property was arrested for a criminal offense that forms the basis for determining that the property is a contraband article under section 932.701, Florida Statutes;

_________ The owner of the property cannot be identified after a diligent search or the person in possession of the property denies ownership and the owner of the property cannot be identified by means that were available to the employee or agent of the seizing agency at the time of the seizure;

_________ The owner of the property is a fugitive from justice or is deceased;

_________ An individual who does not own the property was arrested for a criminal offense that forms the basis for determining that the property is a contraband article under section 932.701, Florida Statutes, and the owner of the property, had actual knowledge of the criminal activity;

_________ The owner of the property has agreed to be a confidential informant as defined in section 914.28, Florida Statutes;

_________ The property is a monetary instrument.

4. The description of the property and the facts and circumstances surrounding the seizure are contained in the attached affidavit of _________ (Name of Officer), which is incorporated as if fully set forth herein.

WHEREFORE, Petitioner requests an Order Finding Probable Cause for Seizure pursuant to section 932.703(2), Florida Statutes.

ATTESTATION

I HEREBY ATTEST that a copy of this Application and attached affidavit has been submitted to a Judge of the Circuit Court, Seminole County, Florida this ___ day of _________, 20___.

____

Attorney signature block

"ATTACHMENT B–1"

IN THE CIRCUIT COURT OF THE EIGHTEENTH JUDICIAL CIRCUIT IN AND FOR SEMINOLE COUNTY, FLORIDA

CIVIL FORFEITURE RETURN

AGENCY: ____________________

AGENCY CASE NUMBER: ____________________

IF ARREST—NAME OF ARRESTEE IN CRIMINAL CASE: ____________________

FORFEITURE FILING DETERMINATION:

_________ Forfeiture proceeding authorized by Agency Head and Complaint Filed Civil Court Case Number: _________

_________ Forfeiture Complaint will not be filed.

_________ Settlement Agreement Reached

DATED this _________ day of _________, 20___.

____

Attorney Name

Florida Bar No.

Contact Information

"ATTACHMENT C–1"

IN THE CIRCUIT COURT OF THE EIGHTEENTH JUDICIAL CIRCUIT IN AND FOR SEMINOLE COUNTY, FLORIDA

IN RE: FORFEITURE OF: _____ AGENCY CASE NO. _________

(Description of Property) _______ CIVIL FORFEITURE

EX–PARTE ORDER FINDING PROBABLE CAUSE FOR SEIZURE

THIS MATTER having come before this Court pursuant to section 932.703(2), Florida Statutes, within ten (10) business days of seizure of the above-described property by the (insert name of seizing Law Enforcement Agency) and the Court having reviewed the sworn affidavit of (Insert LEO Name), FINDS:

1. The seizing agency applied for the probable cause determination within 10 business days of the date of the seizure.

2. The requirements specified in paragraph (1)(a) of section 932.703, Florida Statutes, have been satisfied based on the fact that one or more of the following facts exist as indicated below:

A. _________ The owner of the property was arrested for a criminal offense that forms the basis for determining that the property is a contraband article under section 932.701, Florida Statutes; and/or

B. Exception to Owner of Property Arrest requirement exists as indicated:

_________ Regardless of whether an arrest of the owner of the property was or was not made, the owner of the property cannot be identified after a diligent search or the person in possession of the property denies ownership and the owner of the property cannot be identified by means that were available to the employee or agent of the seizing agency at the time of the seizure;

_________ Regardless of whether an arrest of the owner of the property was or was not made the owner is a fugitive from justice or is deceased;

_________ Regardless of whether an arrest of the owner of the property was or was not made, an individual who does not own the property was arrested for a criminal offense that forms the basis for determining that the property is a contraband article under section 932.701, Florida Statutes, and the owner of the property had actual knowledge of the criminal activity;

_________ Regardless of whether an arrest of the owner of the property was or was not made, the owner of the property agrees to be a confidential informant as defined in section 914.28, Florida Statutes; or

_________ Regardless of whether an arrest of the owner of the property was or was not made the property is a monetary instrument.

3. Probable cause exists to seize the above-described property under the Florida Contraband Forfeiture Act.

Therefore, the Court having found that the requirements of Florida Statute section 932.703(1)(a) were satisfied and that probable cause exists for the seizure, it is ORDERED and ADJUDGED as follows:

1. The Court authorizes continued seizure of the subject contraband property by the seizing law enforcement agency or an agency or agent on their behalf, pending a determination of title to the property upon the Filing of a Complaint for Forfeiture and pursuant to the procedures defined in the Florida Contraband Forfeiture Act.

2. Pursuant to section 943.704(5)(c), Florida Statutes, any claimant who desires to contest the forfeiture action upon the Filing of a Complaint for Forfeiture by or on behalf of the seizing agency shall file and serve upon the attorney representing the seizing agency any responsive pleadings and affirmative defenses. Therefore, upon the filing of a Civil Complaint for Forfeiture, the seizing Agency shall serve a Certified Copy of the Complaint along with a copy of this Order Finding Probable Cause upon all claimants.

3. Claimants are Notified upon service of this Order and a Complaint for Final Order of Forfeiture of the following: THAT AS A CLAIMANT OR POTENTIAL CLAIMANT WHO CLAIMS AN INTEREST IN THE SEIZED PROPERTY, YOU HAVE TWENTY (20) DAYS FROM SERVICE OF A COPY OF THE COMPLAINT FOR FORFEITURE AND A COPY OF THIS ORDER FINDING PROBABLE CAUSE, TO FILE IN THIS COURT, ANY RESPONSIVE PLEADING, ANSWER, AND/OR AFFIRMATIVE DEFENSES TO THE COMPLAINT FOR FORFEITURE. SAID PLEADINGS SHALL INCLUDE A SHORT AND PLAIN STATEMENT DEMONSTRATING A VALID PROPERTY INTEREST IN THAT WHICH IS CLAIMED, SUFFICIENT TO CONFER STANDING TO APPEAR IN THIS CAUSE.

4. YOU ARE FURTHER COMMANDED TO SERVE A COPY OF SUCH ANSWER OR RESPONSIVE PLEADING WITHIN SAID TIME PERIOD UPON THE ATTORNEY WHO FILED THE COMPLAINT FOR FORFEITURE. FAILURE TO FILE AND SERVE SUCH ANSWER OR PLEADING WITHIN SAID TIME PERIOD SHALL RESULT IN THE ENTRY OF A DEFAULT PURSUANT TO FLORIDA RULE OF CIVIL PROCEDURE 1.500(a), AND A FINAL ORDER OF FORFEITURE.

5. The seizing Agency as described herein is ordered to restrain the seized property by the least restrictive means to protect against disposal, waste, or continued illegal use of such property, pending disposition of the property pursuant to the Florida Contraband Forfeiture Act.

DONE AND ORDERED in Chambers, in Sanford, Seminole County, Florida, this _________ day of _________, 20.

____

CIRCUIT JUDGE

"ATTACHMENT C–2"

IN THE CIRCUIT COURT OF THE EIGHTEENTH JUDICIAL CIRCUIT IN AND FOR SEMINOLE COUNTY, FLORIDA

IN RE: FORFEITURE OF: ______ **AGENCY CASE NO.:** ______

(Description of Property): ______ **CIVIL FORFEITURE**

EX–PARTE ORDER DENYING PROBABLE CAUSE FOR SEIZURE

THIS MATTER having come before this Court pursuant to section 932.703(2), Florida Statutes, of the above-described property by the Application of the (Seizing Law Enforcement Agency) and the Court having reviewed the Application and the sworn supporting affidavit described therein, the COURT FINDS as indicated below:

__________ The seizing agency did not apply for the probable cause determination within 10 business days of the date of the seizure, AND/OR;

__________ The requirements specified in paragraph (1)(a) of section 932.703, Florida Statutes, have not been satisfied, AND/OR

__________ The Agency has not established probable cause for the seizure based upon the Court's review of the supporting affidavit made part of the Application for the 10–day Probable Cause for Seizure Determination.

Therefore, the Court having found that the requirements of Florida Statute section 932.703(1) were not satisfied for the reasons indicated herein, it is HEREBY ORDERED:

Any forfeiture hold, lien, lis pendens, or other civil encumbrance shall be released in conformity with the Florida Contraband Forfeiture Act within 5 days of receipt of this Order. This Order is separate from any criminal evidentiary hold on said property.

DONE AND ORDERED in Chambers, in Sanford, Seminole County, Florida, this ___ day of _________, 20 ___.

____

CIRCUIT JUDGE

16–30–B. MEDIATION—FAMILY MEDIATION MANDATORY REFERRAL OF ALL CONTESTED FAMILY LAW CASES TO MEDIATION

IN THE CIRCUIT COURT OF THE EIGHTEENTH JUDICIAL CIRCUIT IN AND FOR BREVARD COUNTY, FLORIDA

ADMINISTRATIVE ORDER NO.: 16–30–B

SUPERSEDES 13–11–B

IN RE: MEDIATION—FAMILY MEDIATION MANDATORY REFERRAL OF ALL CONTESTED FAMILY LAW CASES TO MEDIATION

Whereas, mediation is a process whereby a neutral third party acts to encourage the resolution of disputes through a non-adversarial process and assists the parties in reaching a mutually acceptable agreement; and

Whereas, certain disputes that include family matters in marriage dissolution and post-dissolution proceedings, in domestic proceedings between unmarried parents, and modifications thereof; and matters of juvenile dependency can be amicably and expeditiously resolved through mediation prior to hearing by the Court; and

Whereas, the mediation process can result in cost and schedule efficiencies to the parties; and

Whereas, mediation of certain matters promotes prompt and efficient administration of justice by the Court; reduces litigation; and reduces Court dockets; and

Whereas, applicable provisions of Florida Statute Chapter 44—Mediation Alternatives to Judicial Action; Chapter 61—Dissolution of Marriage, Support, Time-sharing; and Chapter 39—Proceedings Relating to Children; and the applicable provisions of the Florida Rules of Civil Procedure, Family Procedure, and Juvenile Procedure, as they relate to Family Mediation and Dependency Mediation, and the Order to Family Mediation are incorporated into this Order.

IT IS HEREBY ORDERED THAT:

1. **Family Mediation Program:** The Family Mediation Program ("Program") shall be governed by applicable Florida Statutes and Rules of Procedure. The Program office staff shall be responsible for scheduling mediations as ordered by the Court for matters including, but not limited to, shared parental responsibility, time-sharing, child support, alimony, and division of property and debt, juvenile dependency, and any other domestic disputes appearing on the court docket. This Program will be administered under the direction of the Office of the Trial Court Administrator and the Chief Judge of the Eighteenth Judicial Circuit and shall include both staff mediator(s) and contract mediators.

2. **Family Mediators:** The Family Mediation Program shall appoint only mediators who are Florida Supreme Court Certified Family Mediators. The Program staff shall be responsible for referring applicable cases to private mediation.

3. **Mandatory Referral of All Contested Pre–Judgment and Post–Judgment Family Law Matters:**

a. Any party who seeks to schedule a final hearing for either a pre-judgment family law matter or a modification of a post-judgment matter, including domestic proceedings between unmarried parents, shall first participate in a mediation conference through the Family Mediation Program herein established, or through a private mediator, unless otherwise ordered by the Court.

b. An Order to Family Mediation will be prepared by the presiding Judge.

c. Petitioner, or counsel of record, must notify the Mediation Office of any settlement or dismissal of the action prior to the mediation.

4. **Required Documentation:**

a. Current Financial Affidavits for BOTH parties MUST be filed prior to obtaining an Order to Family Mediation. This requirement applies to mediations before temporary hearings or final trials. This requirement is necessary to adequately determine if the parties' income meets statutory program eligibility requirements in accordance with Florida Statute 44. If the parties are not financially eligible, the mediation may be cancelled immediately, even if all parties appear at the mediation session.

b. If Financial Affidavits are not filed, the mediation will not be scheduled, and an Order to Family Mediation will not be issued.

5. **Domestic Violence:**

a. Pursuant to Florida Statute 44, upon motion or request of a party, the Court shall not refer any case to mediation if it finds there has been a history of domestic violence that would compromise the mediation process. The issuance of a temporary or final injunction alone is insufficient to establish that the mediation process is compromised.

6. **Fees, Session Length, and Failure to Appear:**

a. The fees for mediation are defined by Florida Statute 44, are based upon the parties' combined income, and are established per scheduled session. Fees defined by that Statute shall be paid in full by the parties prior to the scheduled mediation session(s). Failure to pay all mediation fees prior to the scheduled mediation session(s) may result in the Court's imposition of sanctions.

b. The Order to Family Mediation shall be accompanied by an invoice which identifies the mediation fee owed and the due date. Fees must be paid prior to the scheduled mediation, whether or not the other party has paid the fees. If applicable, an approved Application of Civil Indigent Status must be submitted to the Mediation Program on or before the payment due date.

c. If a party fails to pay an assessed mediation fee, the initial mediation shall be conducted. At the discretion of the ADR Director, no subsequent mediation session will be scheduled or conducted until all prior assessed mediation fees are paid in full.

d. Failure to pay a mediation fee shall result in the mediation office filing a report to the Court, identifying the party who failed to pay the fee pursuant to the applicable governing documents.

e. Mediation sessions shall be scheduled for up to three hours. Parties and counsel must appear at the mediation conference on time and must pay the required mediation fee prior to the time the mediation conference is scheduled to begin. Session length shall not be extended due to the failure of parties and/or counsel to arrive punctually or the failure to pay required fees.

f. If either party or counsel fails to appear or causes the mediation to be cancelled due to tardiness, that party, or counsel, shall be charged the combined total of both parties' fees for the missed mediation session, regardless of indigency. The mediation will be rescheduled after fees have been paid.

7. **Appearance by Telephone:**

a. Approval to appear by telephone is required by the Mediation Office, at least ten (10) business days prior to the mediation session. The following circumstances will be considered in granting approval:

1. The party must live outside of Brevard, Orange, Seminole, Osceola, Indian River, and Volusia Counties;

2. The party is on active military duty outside of Brevard County;

3. The party is incarcerated.

b. Any party requesting to appear by telephone shall submit a current Financial Affidavit and proof of income to the Mediation Office at least ten (10) business days prior to the mediation or their request will not be granted, and they will be expected to appear in person. Failure to do so will result in a report to the Court of "Failure to Appear."

8. **Record Keeping:** The Family Mediation Program shall keep a record of the case name, number, assigning judge,

mediator, the attorneys, and the outcome of the mediation in all cases referred to the Family Mediation Program.

DONE AND ORDERED this 2 day of August, 2016.

JOHN D. GALLUZZO

CHIEF JUDGE

16–25–S. CRIMINAL–MISDEMEANOR PROBATION SERVICES IN SEMINOLE COUNTY

IN THE CIRCUIT COURT OF THE EIGHTEENTH JUDICIAL CIRCUIT OF FLORIDA IN AND FOR SEMINOLE COUNTY, FLORIDA

ADMINISTRATIVE ORDER NO.: 16–25–S

IN RE: CRIMINAL–MISDEMEANOR PROBATION SERVICES IN SEMINOLE COUNTY

WHEREAS, pursuant to Article V, section 2(d) of the Florida Constitution and section 43.26, Florida Statutes, the chief judge of each judicial circuit is charged with the authority and the power to do everything necessary to promote the prompt and efficient administration of justice; and

WHEREAS, pursuant to the chief judge's constitutional and statutory responsibility for administrative supervision of the courts within the circuit and to create and maintain an organization capable of effecting the efficient, prompt, and proper administration of justice for the citizens of this State, the chief judge is required to exercise direction, see Fla. R. Jud. Admin. 2.215(b)(2), (b)(3); and

WHEREAS, Seminole County's Probation Division is a division of Seminole County's Department of Public Safety and the Probation Division is comprised of several independent yet interrelated work programs, which provide services and supervision to offenders in community-based settings; and

WHEREAS, Seminole County and the Sheriff have agreed to the transfer of the administration and oversight of the Probation Division from the County's Department of Public Safety to the Sheriff and have memorialized this agreement in an executed Interlocal Agreement effective July 1, 2016; and

WHEREAS, pursuant to the Interlocal Agreement entered into between the Seminole County and the Sheriff, the Eighteenth Judicial Circuit also approves the Seminole County Sheriff's Office as the public entity to provide supervision to individuals placed on supervision whether by probation or a pre-trial diversion program or any form of supervision ordered by the Courts in Seminole County to be supervised by probation or supervision services at the County level.

WHEREAS, pursuant to Florida Statute 948.09 person's placed on misdemeanor probation by a county court judge must contribute not less than $40.00 per month, as decided by the sentencing court, to the Court approved public or private entity providing misdemeanor supervision.

WHEREAS, the costs of supervision assessed for County Court supervision, have been set at no less than $60.00 as evidenced in a memorandum dated July 8, 2008.

IT IS THEREFORE, ORDERED AND ADJUDGED;

1. The Seminole County Sheriff's Office is recognized as the authorized provider of Seminole County Probation supervision services previously provided by Seminole County's Department of Public Safety Probation Division.

2. Persons currently being supervised by Seminole County Department of Public Safety Probation Division shall be under the supervision of the Sheriff beginning July 1, 2016.

3. Persons ordered to supervision to be supervised at the county level beginning on or after July 1, 2016 shall be ordered to supervision by the Sheriff.

4. County Court monthly supervision costs shall be assessed at no less than $60.00.

5. Any fees, costs, restitution payments or special assessments currently in effect or collected as a function or part of Probation when under the supervision of the County shall continue to be in effect, collected and assessed by the SHERIFF.

6. This administrative order is effective July 1, 2016.

DONE AND ORDERED this 27th day of June, 2016.

JOHN D. GALLUZZO

CHIEF JUDGE

16–18–S. [SUPERSEDED BY ORDER 17–30–S, EFFECTIVE JUNE 28, 2017.]

16–17–B. [SUPERSEDED BY ORDER 17–29–B, EFFECTIVE JUNE 28, 2017.]

16–15–S (A1). [SUPERSEDED BY ORDER 18-02-S, EFFECTIVE JANUARY 22, 2018.]

16–15–S. [SUPERSEDED BY ORDER 16-15-S (A1), EFFECTIVE SEPTEMBER 1, 2016.]

16–11. COURT REPORTING

IN THE CIRCUIT COURT OF THE EIGHTEENTH JUDICIAL CIRCUIT OF FLORIDA

ADMINISTRATIVE ORDER NO.: 16–11

SUPERSEDES 15–18 AMENDED

IN RE: COURT REPORTING

Whereas, rule 2.535(h)(3), Florida Rules of Judicial Administration, requires that the chief judge, after consultation with the circuit and county court judges in the Eighteenth Judicial Circuit, shall enter an administrative order developing and implementing a circuit-wide plan for the court reporting of all proceedings required to be reported at public expense using either full or part-time court employees or independent contractors;

Whereas, rule 2.535(h)(4), Florida Rules of Judicial Administration, permits the Chief Judge after consultation with the circuit and county judges of the Eighteenth Judicial Circuit, to enter a circuit-wide plan that authorizes electronic recording of court proceedings and subsequent transcription by approved court reporters or approved transcriptionists of any judicial proceedings; and

Whereas, rule 2.535(i), Florida Rules of Judicial Administration requires the chief judge of each circuit to enter an administrative order developing and implementing a circuit-wide plan for court reporting in all trials in which the State seeks the death penalty and in capital post-conviction proceedings;

I. Definitions and Designations. For the purpose of this Administrative Order, the following terms have the following definitions and designations:

A. *Circuit Court Reporter.* "Circuit court reporter" means a contractor, contractor personnel, or any person employed by the Administrative Office of the Courts for the Eighteenth Judicial Circuit ("AOC"), who meets the AOC's qualifications for delivery of court reporting services and whose duties include operating a stenographic machine in the courtrooms or hearing rooms of the Eighteenth Judicial Circuit.

B. *Classes of Court Reporters.* The State Court System has established three classes of court reporters: Court Reporter I, Court Reporter II, and Digital Court Reporters. Court Reporter I and Court Reporter II are specific to the stenographic skill level of the position. For the purpose of this Administrative Order, persons performing court reporting in the Eighteenth Judicial Circuit shall be designated as Circuit Court Reporters or Digital Court Reporters.

C. *Contractor.* "Contractor" means any person or entity with whom the Court Administrator of the Eighteenth Judicial Circuit contracts to provide court reporting services for judicial proceedings required to be reported at public expense.

D. *Contractor Personnel.* "Contractor personnel" includes and is collectively defined as employees, independent contractors, subcontractors, agents, assigns, students, or interns of the contractor.

E. *Court Reporting.* "Court Reporting" means the act of making a verbatim record of the spoken word, whether by use of written symbols, stenomask equipment, stenographic equipment, or electronic devices, in any judicial proceedings pending in any of the courts of this circuit.

F. *Digital Court Reporter.* "Digital court reporter" means a Contractor, Contractor Personnel, or any person employed by the Administrative Office of the Courts for the Eighteenth Judicial Circuit, who meets the AOC's qualifications for delivery of court reporting services and whose duties include digitally recording proceedings held in the courtrooms or hearing rooms of the Eighteenth Judicial Circuit.

G. *Digital Court Reporting.* "Digital court reporting" means the process of digitally capturing and recording, with the assistance of encoding hardware and software, the complete verbatim Multi–Media Court Record of any and all judicial proceedings.

H. *Equipment.* "Equipment" means all hardware, software, storage, appliances, accessories, and peripherals necessary to provide for the monitoring, recording, distribution, storage, archiving, assembling, or production of the court verbatim record.

I. *Judicial Proceedings.* "Judicial proceedings" means all communications which take place in open court between the judge (including general magistrates and hearing officers) and the lawyers or other parties to the proceeding, and the testimony of any witnesses. Judicial proceedings, include, but are not limited to courtroom hearings, chamber or hearing room hearings, pre-trial conferences, jury trials, non-jury trials, motion or docket hearings, plea hearings, status review hearings, arraignments, dispositions, sentencing hearings, injunction hearings, detention and shelter hearings, bond hearings, post-conviction relief proceedings, first appearance proceedings, sworn statements, and all other matters relating to the court's business. This term does not include any other matters that may have been monitored or recorded at the same time but which were not part of the court's business and which would likely not have been reported by a trained circuit court reporter (such as, private conversations between a lawyer and client or between co-counsel

J. *Multi–Media Court Record.* "Multi–Media Court Record" means any combination of the digital audio file, metadata file, text file, annotated file, and video file that is generated from the performance of court reporting.

K. *Server.* "Server" means a computer that hosts an application or collects date from remote computer stations.

L. *Services.* "Services" includes and is collectively defined as digital court reporting services and transcription services.

M. *Transcription.* "Transcription" means the process of converting the complete verbatim Multi–Media Court Record generated by a Digital Court Reporter or the notes, disks, or tapes generated by a Circuit Court Reporter, into a text file as a printed certified transcript.

N. *Centralized Court Reporting.* "Centralized Court Reporting" is a digital court reporting model in which several courtrooms or hearing rooms are monitored and recorded simultaneously utilizing digital audio and video systems from a centralized location where the digital court record is captured, annotated, and indexed.

O. *Video Court Reporting.* "Video Court Reporting" is the combination of a digital and video court reporting system and tools utilized to monitor and record remote court appearances in the courtroom or hearing room for events where the audio alone is insufficient to capture the record.

II. Hybrid Model of Court Reporting. The Eighteenth Judicial Circuit currently uses a hybrid model of court reporting. The hybrid model utilizes a combination of stenographic, digital, centralized and video media for capturing the record in all judicial proceedings where court reporting is required at public expense. This model incorporates multiple service delivery strategies for the reporting or recording of all proceedings required to be reported or recorded at public expense. The plan utilizes both independent contract court reporters and employee digital court recorders.

III. Applicable Proceedings. This Administrative Order and the contracts entered into in accordance with this Administrative Order, former Administrative Order Number 04–33, and the other authorities cited herein shall apply to all criminal and juvenile proceedings, including depositions, and any other judicial proceedings required by law or the court to be reported or recorded at public expense, as required by rule 2.535, Florida Rules of Judicial Administration.

IV. Methods of Reporting

A. *Stenographic Recording.* In any required proceeding set forth in paragraph II above, stenographic reporting by a court reporter as defined by rule 2.535, Florida Rules of Judicial Administration, may be utilized.

B. *Electronic Recording.* The term "electronic recording" shall include audio tape recording, videocassette tape recording, or recording by any other electronic means, including but not limited to, digital or other technology.

V. Independent Contract Court Reporters. Court reporting services as defined by rule 2.535(h)(3), Florida Rules of Judicial Administration, may be provided by independent contractors subject to contracts entered into between the Administrative Office of the Court and the court reporters.

A. A request for proposal shall be issued in Brevard County and in Seminole County for contracted court reporting services.

B. The proposal shall clearly state the relationship between the contractor(s) (court reporter(s)) and the Courts as being independent:

1. The contractor(s) shall pay any and all applicable taxes, comply with all pertinent state and federal statutes, and is solely responsible for any tax withholding from its employees or subcontractors;

2. The contractor(s) shall hire, compensate, supervise, terminate, set the hours of work for members of their work force, and control and direct the manner in which the work is performed;

3. The contractor(s) shall not be provided office space at the courthouse(s), and shall not perform office work and/or transcription services on court property;

4. The contractor(s) shall furnish their own equipment, supplies and pay their own travel, training and continuing education expenses.

C. The Court Administrator and the contractor(s) shall enter into a contract that:

1. States the fee schedule for services provided;

2. Sets the term of the contract;

3. Describes the scope of services and specific requirements;

4. Sets the qualifications of proposers;

5. Describes possible sanctions for non-compliance;

6. Outlines the methods for invoicing and payment;

7. States minimum insurance coverage requirements; and

8. Establishes a policy for record storage and ownership.

D. The trial court administrator or designee shall be the contract manager.

VI. Electronic Recording and Transcription. In accordance with rule 2.535(h)(4), Florida Rules of Judicial Administration, the Chief Judge hereby authorizes that the electronic recording and subsequent transcription by persons other than circuit court reporters of any judicial proceedings, including depositions, that are otherwise required to be reported by a circuit court reporter.

A. *Digital Court Recording Office*

1. Authorized Proceedings. The Administrative Office of the Courts, Digital Court Recording Office, is authorized to capture the record for criminal and civil judicial proceedings required by law or by rules of court to be reported or recorded at public expense. Parties to civil actions shall arrange for an independent court reporter to record those proceedings that the Court is not required to record or report at public expense.

2. Digital Court Reporters

A. Court Administrator as Manager. The Court Administrator, or his or her designee, is responsible for the management of delivering court reporting services for all judicial proceedings required to be reported at public expense.

B. Qualifications and Training. The Court Administrator, or his or her designee, is responsible for providing qualified and trained Digital Court Reporters to perform the services, in addition to being responsible for any training, certification, or continuing education associated with the Digital Court Reporters performing the services.

C. Officers of the Court. Employees of the Digital Court Recording Office are considered officers of the court and shall not disclose or discuss any confidential information to which they may be privy. As officers of the court, employees must comply with all applicable Florida statutes, court rules, and other requirements as established by the State Courts System. Each employee must sign an Oath of Confidentiality, which will be maintained in his or her personnel file. Failure to comply with the Oath of Confidentiality is grounds for termination of employment.

B. *Reliability of the Record.* The digital recording equipment shall comply with all statewide standards for digital recording as established by the Florida Courts Technology Commission. To ensure a reliable record of proceedings, the following procedures and directives are prescribed to be applied in all cases wherein any judge directs electronic recording.

1. Digital Court Recording Office's Responsibility. The Digital Court Recording Office shall be responsible for capturing, managing, maintaining, and storing the complete verbatim Multi–Media Court Record in all judicial proceedings reported at public expense utilizing digital court recording.

2. Operation of Electronic Equipment. The Court's electronic recording equipment shall be operated by employees of the Administrative Office of the Courts and/or by such other persons designated by the Court Administration and the Chief Judge. All equipment utilized by the digital court reporters shall be operated and maintained in such a manner and under such conditions to ensure the reliability of capturing the record. These employees shall operate the electronic recording equipment in such manner and under such conditions as to ensure the production and safekeeping of an understandable recording capable of being transcribed into a reliable record.

3. Monitoring the Recordings. The Digital Court Reporters shall monitor the recording input and shall immediately signal or notify the trial judge or presiding official, or such other person designated by the trial judge, when the quality of the recording is in question or doubtful.

4. Testing prior to Court Sessions. Prior to beginning of each court session captured by the digital court reporting system, all equipment shall be tested by the Digital Court Reporter to establish all microphones, appliances, and peripherals are operating at a level sufficient to ensure the

recording of the record, playback of the audio, and production of a transcript.

5. Responsibilities of Other Court Personnel. When digital court recording is utilized in a courtroom or hearing room, all court personnel are expected to comply with this Administrative Order.

A. Trial Judges, General Magistrates and Hearing Officers. In all proceedings in which digital court reporting is utilized, judges should remind participants:

1. The proceeding is being recorded and/or monitored;

2. All questions need verbal responses;

3. Each participant shall identify self, spell their names for the record, speak clearly, loudly, and distinctly into or near a microphone;

4. Counsel shall not speak at the same time that witnesses or other counsel are speaking or otherwise improperly interrupt or obstruct the recording of another's speech;

5. All physical and visible happenings and events are reported in sound;

6. Notify the court if equipment has been tampered with or is not functioning;

7. The proceedings will be stopped when needed to remedy any matter preventing an adequate recording

8. Protect the recording equipment; and

9. Signify when it is appropriate to use Mute button;

10. Seminole County Only: The Chief Judge hereby orders and designates as of January 15, 2014 that all Baker Act Proceedings in Seminole County shall be preserved by digital recording means using equipment provided by Court Administration which shall be operated by the Magistrate without the need for an electronic reporter to be present. The Magistrate shall maintain custody of the equipment and record until surrendering it to Court Administration for preservation on or before the end of the work day of the scheduled hearing. Court Administration shall pick up and deliver the recording device to the Magistrate.

B. Court Deputy. The court deputy should assist the trial judge as needed or desired in maintaining courtroom discipline and should be constantly alert for signals from the trial judge and clerks to communicate with others and to remedy any circumstances interfering with the making of an adequate recording. The court deputy shall ensure that all participants refrain from tampering with equipment including the inappropriate use of microphone mute buttons or the unauthorized removal of microphones from their original location.

C. Counsel. All participating counsel must be constantly aware of the special requirements for making a clear, reliable, and transcribable recording. Counsel must speak loudly, distinctly, and only from a position at or near a microphone. Counsel must make all directions and explanations verbally and should aid and direct all witnesses as needed. Counsel should use the push to mute feature on the counsel table when engaging in privileged communications. Counsel should instruct all parties at the table to do the same. Counsel should also identify themselves and spell their names before speaking for the first time in court each day. Attorneys shall inform their clients of the method of recording being utilized and take necessary precautions to protect disclosure of confidential communication during the proceeding.

C. *Alteration or Circumvention of Recording System Prohibited.* Alteration or circumvention of the court's recording system is prohibited. This includes, but is not limited to, unplugging a microphone, repositioning a microphone, covering a microphone, or permanently engaging a microphone's mute switch with books, rubber bands, or other objects. All parties shall work on the assumption that their conversations are being recorded while in the courtroom. The mute switches provided are designed for brief moments of private consultation. Parties desiring to have extended private conversations should take appropriate measures such as, but not limited to, requesting that the recording system be put in "Off Record" mode or leaving the courtroom. Persons who tamper with the digital recording equipment, including the microphones, may be held in contempt of court.

D. *Retention of Electronic Recordings*

1. Cassette Taped Recordings. The Clerk of Court shall provide storage space and safekeeping for all taped recordings of court proceedings for the appropriate record retention period.

2. Digital Recordings. The Digital Court Recording Office is responsible for providing storage space and safekeeping for all digital recordings of court proceedings for the appropriate record retention period. The Digital Court Recording Office is the custodian of digital court recordings that it has recorded. The Digital Court Recording Office shall follow court orders regarding sealed and expunged files, and to what extent recordings of proceedings in those cases should be released. Digital recordings currently in the possession of the Clerk of the Court will be properly stored and safeguarded by the Clerk of the Court until transferred to the Digital Court Recording Office.

E. *Transcription*

1. Transcriber. Proceedings electronically recorded and where said recordings are the official record will be transcribed only by the Digital Court Recording Office, or by a contracted firm or individual who is capable of producing an accurate and quality transcript. All persons performing court reporting transcription services shall comply with all applicable court rules and standards established by the State Courts System and the Chief Judge of this circuit.

2. Request for Transcript and Fees. Any individual may request and obtain, without a court order, a transcript of any reported or recorded judicial proceeding unless a record of such proceeding is deemed confidential (such as, juvenile and Baker Act proceedings). In order to obtain a transcript, a person must make a written request and pay the requisite fees to the transcriber. An original and at least one copy of proceedings shall be transcribed and the transcriber shall file the original with the clerk.

3. Requests for Copies of Tapes and Digital Recordings. All requests for a written transcript or a copy of an original recording must be submitted in writing to the Digital Court Recording Office. The form to be utilized for any written request is available from the Digital Court Recording Office

or on-line on the website of the Eighteenth Judicial Circuit. If the request is for transcripts or copies of original recordings which may include confidential information, including but not limited to juvenile dependency, the request must be accompanied by an appropriate court order. If you are a party or attorney of record in a juvenile delinquency cases, a court order is not needed for the recording.

4. Production. When a transcript of a judicial proceeding or a portion of a judicial proceeding is requested from the Circuit Court Reporters or from the Digital Court Reporters, an accurate and timely transcript shall be produced in accordance with rule 2.535(f), Florida Rules of Judicial Administration, and rule 9.200(b), Florida Rules of Appellate Procedure.

5. Original Transcript of Proceedings to be Filed. Unless otherwise ordered by the Court, the original transcript of the proceeding shall be filed with the Clerk of Court.

6. On–Record Events When Court Reporter Present. The digital recording is the official record for all proceedings except when a court reporter is present and paid for with state funds.

In circumstances where both a circuit court reporter is present and the digital recording equipment is used, a request for the digital recording may be made pursuant to the appropriate request procedures. If the court reporter is present and paid for with state funds, the Digital Court Recording Office will notify the requestor that the digital recording is not the "official court record."

If a circuit court reporter records a proceeding (trial, hearing, or other court event), the request for a transcript of the proceeding shall be submitted to the court reporter.

No juvenile recordings will be released without a court order, except in juvenile delinquency cases where the requestor is a party or an attorney of record. Exceptions to this policy may be considered and granted by the Chief Judge upon a showing of extraordinary circumstances.

7. Off–Record Events. Electronic recording by the Digital Court Recording Office of off-record discussions or conversations were not made pursuant to any court rule, law or ordinance, and were not recorded in connection with the transaction of official business of the judiciary. As such, any incidental electronic recordings of off-record discussions or conversations do not constitute a record of the judicial branch to which the public is entitled access, as defined by rule 2.420, Florida Rules of Judicial Administration. In addition, all off-record conversations between attorneys and their clients are protected by the attorney-client privilege and shall remain confidential. The Digital Recording Office shall review recordings to be given to the public at large to ensure that matters protected from disclosure by court rule or Florida law are not disseminated. Anyone who has or gains access to any recordings produced from the electronic court record shall not reveal, divulge, utilize in any fashion, or transcribe any attorney-client statements, conversations, or similar confidential communications that are monitored, intercepted, and/or recorded in the courts of the Eighteenth Judicial Circuit, unless otherwise provided by specific order of the Court.

8. Certification of Transcripts or Electronic Recordings. All persons transcribing digital recordings, whether court personnel or independent contract transcriptionist, shall certify the transcript as a true and accurate text of the digital recording of the proceeding or deposition. All court personnel providing a copy of the original recording on electronic medium, such as compact disk, shall certify the copy to be true and accurate. If any portion of the recording is redacted from a copy of the audio recording, the Digital Court Reporter shall provide in the certification an accurate record of the date and time of the redaction and indicate that the redaction is for an off-record conversation as the term is utilized in paragraph 8. If any dispute arises as to whether any transcript truly discloses what occurred, the disputing party shall motion the presiding court for settlement of the dispute, and, upon order of the court, the transcript shall be made to conform accordingly.

Copies of audio/video recordings may be made available to attorneys of record, parties to a case, and self-represented litigants upon request so long as an acknowledgement is provided with the copy that states confidential information may be contained on the recording, further dissemination of confidential information contained on the recording is prohibited, and violation of the prohibition against the dissemination may subject the requestor to an action for contempt of court.

9. Capital Cases

A. In all trials in which the State seeks the death penalty, and in capital post-conviction proceedings, in-court stenographic court reporting services must be used. The use of digital court reporting as the court reporting system is prohibited. If available, Real-time or CAT stenography may be used. All persons approved by the Court to perform court reporting transcription services shall give priority to capital cases in the production of transcripts, and shall use all measures necessary to expedite the preparation of the transcript, including but not limited to:

1. Where available, the use of an approved court reporter who has the capacity to provide real-time transcription of the proceedings;

2. If real-time transcription services are not available, the use of a computer-aided transcription qualified court reporter;

3. The use of scopists, text editors, alternating court reporters, or other means to expedite the finalization of the certified transcript; and

4. The imposition of reasonable restrictions on work assignments by employee or contract approved court reporters to ensure that transcript production in capital cases is given a priority.

B. The Court Reporter in these cases shall provide, upon request, transcripts of individual testimony within 48 hours of the request.

C. The Court Reporter shall be paid from state funds to prepare and provide the finalized and certified transcript in these cases within 30 days of the end of the trial or proceeding.

D. "Loaning out" of stenographic notes is prohibited in capital cases to ensure that the court reporter has immediate access to the notes for production of the transcript.

E. Use of only the digital recording to transcribe a proceeding without the in-court stenographic reporter's notes is prohibited unless those notes are destroyed or lost.

F. Judges shall give immediate instruction to the court reporter to begin transcription upon the return of the verdict in capital cases and immediately initiate an order approving the production of the transcript.

G. The contracted court reporting agency shall assure that any court reporter assigned to death penalty or capital post-conviction proceedings is aware and capable of complying with these requirements.

H. In the event of an appeal, the appealing party is responsible for the payment of transcripts.

F. *Depositions.* Depositions may be electronically recorded. The party scheduling an electronically recorded deposition shall be responsible for safekeeping the recording of any testimony. Any party requesting transcription shall be responsible for notifying all parties that transcription is being requested and obtaining a competent transcriber. Depositions in criminal cases may be scheduled at the Office of the State Attorney, the Office of the Public Defender, or at any other location, if the parties agree.

VII. Fees and Rates

A. *Electronic Court Recording.* Fee schedules for transcripts or copies of electronically recorded proceedings or depositions required to be reported at public expense shall be on file in the Digital Court Recording Office.

B. *Court Recording by Independent Contractors.* Fees and rates for the recording and transcription by independent contract court reporters of court proceedings or deposition required to be reported at public expense shall be as set forth in the court reporting contracts.

VIII. Signage. Appropriate signs shall be placed outside all courtrooms and hearing rooms where digital court recording or monitoring is being utilized to capture the records. Signs noticing the use of microphones shall also be posted on the counsel table and podiums. The signs shall provide notice to all who enter the courtroom or hearing room of the use of digital court recording and that any conversations may be recorded.

IX. On–Site Support. To ensure the reliability, integrity, safekeeping, and accurate transcription of the record, the Digital Court Recording Office shall maintain daily on-site support and management personnel.

X. Emergency Back–Up Plan. In all proceedings in which the type and means of court reporting equipment or services specified in this Order are not available due to emergency circumstances, the Chief Judge or his or her designee may utilize and implement whatever other means of reporting is available to capture the court record.

XI. Ownership of the Official Record. The Court shall retain ownership and control over the official record whether it is in paper or electronic format. The Court reserves the right to full and complete access to any unedited notes, paper tapes, electronic files, and audio and video recordings used to create the official record.

XI. Effective Date. This Administrative Order is effective immediately.

DONE AND ORDERED this 4th of April, 2016.

JOHN D. GALLUZZO

CHIEF JUDGE

16–05–S (A). [SUPERSEDED BY ORDER 17-26-S, EFFECTIVE JUNE 20, 2017.]

16–05–S. [SUPERSEDED BY ORDER 16–05–S (AMD), EFFECTIVE JUNE 30, 2016.]

16–04–S. MENTAL HEALTH—MARCHMAN ACT HEARINGS—TELEPHONIC APPEARANCE OF QUALIFIED PROFESSIONALS

IN THE CIRCUIT COURT OF THE EIGHTEENTH JUDICIAL CIRCUIT IN AND FOR SEMINOLE COUNTY, FLORIDA

ADMINISTRATIVE ORDER NO: 16–04–S

IN RE: MENTAL HEALTH—MARCHMAN ACT HEARINGS—TELEPHONIC APPEARANCE OF QUALIFIED PROFESSIONALS

WHEREAS, Florida's Marchman Act, Chapter 397, Florida Statutes, provides for hearings on petitions for involuntary treatment; and

WHEREAS, Florida Rules of Civil Procedure provide for the telephonic appearance of witnesses at hearing only "(1) by agreement of the parties or (2) for good cause shown upon written request of a party upon reasonable notice to all other parties." Fla. R. Civ. P. 1.451; Fla. R. Jud. Admin. 2.530; and

WHEREAS, electronic testimony may be taken "only if a notary public or other person authorized to administer oaths in the witness's jurisdiction is present with the witness and administers the oath consistent with the laws of the jurisdiction." Fla. R. Civ. P. 1.451; Fla. R. Jud. Admin. 2.530; and

WHEREAS, Florida Rule of Judicial Administration 2.530 further requires that the "[t]he cost for the use of the communication equipment is the responsibility of the requesting party unless otherwise directed by the court." Fla. R. Jud. Admin. 2.530; and

WHEREAS the treating professionals in Marchman proceedings are located outside of Seminole County, and it would impose a hardship and extraordinary cost for them to appear in person; and

NOW THEREFORE WHEREAS it is in the best interests of the parties to have a qualified professional available to testify, whether in person or through electronic communication, and pursuant to the authority vested in me as Chief Judge of the Eighteenth Judicial Circuit of Florida, under Rule 2.215, of the Florida Rules of Judicial Administration;

It is hereby **ORDERED**:

1. In Marchman Act hearings for involuntary treatment, treating professionals may appear by telephone without the prior written request or notice to the parties required under Fla. R. Civ. P. 1.451 and Fla. R. Jud. Admin. 2.530.

2. Such testimony will be authorized only if a notary public or other person authorized to administer oaths in the witness's jurisdiction is present with the witness and administers the oath consistent with the law of the jurisdiction.

DONE AND ORDERED this 5th day of February, 2016.

JOHN D. GALLUZZO
CHIEF JUDGE

16–03–S. ADMINISTRATIVE ORDERS—RESCINDS ADMINISTRATIVE ORDERS

IN THE CIRCUIT COURT OF THE EIGHTEENTH JUDICIAL CIRCUIT IN AND FOR SEMINOLE COUNTY, FLORIDA

ADMINISTRATIVE ORDER NO.: 16–03–S
SUPERSEDES ORDERS LISTED IN THIS A.O.

IN RE: ADMINISTRATIVE ORDERS—RESCINDS ADMINISTRATIVE ORDERS

WHEREAS, administrative orders from time to time become obsolete;

IT IS ORDERED, that the following administrative orders are hereby rescinded:

15–46–S SUPERSEDES 00–26–S: In Re: Judges—Caseload Assignment—Reassignment of Cases Assigned to Judge Debra Steinberg Nelson

15–27–S: In Re: Criminal—First Appearance Administrative Order for Operation "Cyber Summer" June 22 through 29, 2015 in Seminole County

15–28–S: In Re: Criminal—First Appearance Administrative Order for Operation "Cyber Summer" June 22 through 29, 2015 in Seminole County

DONE AND ORDERED this 2nd day of February, 2016.

JOHN D. GALLUZZO
CHIEF JUDGE

16–02–B (A1). [SUPERSEDED BY ORDER 18–21–B, EFFECTIVE MAY 22, 2018.]

16–02–B. [SUPERSEDED BY ORDER 16–02–B (A1), EFFECTIVE JULY 5, 2016.]

16–01–B. CRIMINAL—ASSIGNMENT OF CASES ASSOCIATED WITH THE JIMMY RYCE INVOLUNTARY CIVIL COMMITMENT ACT

IN THE CIRCUIT COURT OF THE EIGHTEENTH JUDICIAL CIRCUIT IN AND FOR BREVARD COUNTY FLORIDA

ADMINISTRATIVE ORDER NO.: 16–01–B
SUPERSEDES 11–12–B

IN RE: CRIMINAL—ASSIGNMENT OF CASES ASSOCIATED WITH THE JIMMY RYCE INVOLUNTARY CIVIL COMMITMENT ACT

Whereas, proceedings conducted pursuant to the Jimmy Ryce Involuntary Civil Commitment of Sexually Violent Predators Act, § 394.10—394.931, Fla. Stat. (1999) (hereinafter referred to as "the Act"), are recognized to be civil in nature, governed by the Florida Rules of Civil Procedure and Florida Rules of Evidence applicable to civil cases.

Whereas, the civil nature of said proceedings is evidenced by the Florida Legislature's express intent to create a civil commitment procedure for the long term care and treatment of sexually violent predators, referenced in § 394.10, Fla. Stat.; and

Whereas, establishment of a fair and orderly process for the assignment of all cases related to the Act is necessary in order to promote the proper distribution of cases among court divisions, clear directives for the Clerk of Court, and the efficient use of judicial resources;

It is Ordered:

1. Each petition initially filed by the Office of the State Attorney seeking commitment of a person pursuant to the Act shall be assigned a civil case number bearing case category abbreviation "MH" for "Mental Health".

2. No filing fee shall be required.

3. Cases opened by initial petitions shall be assigned to the circuit criminal division alphabetically by the first letter of the defendant's last name in accordance with the Criminal Caseload Assignment of Cases in Felony Criminal Department of the Circuit Court of Brevard County, Florida.

4. A petition which is re-filed pursuant to § 394.917, Fla. Stat., and any petition for release after commitment, shall bear the same case number as the initial petition, and the re-opened case shall remain in the previously assigned division.

5. Pursuant to § 394.921, Fla. Stat., all psychological or psychiatric reports, drug and alcohol reports, treatment records, medical records, or victim impact statements which are submitted to the Court or admitted into evidence during any proceedings related to the Act shall be part of the record but shall be sealed, and may be opened only pursuant to a court order.

Done and Ordered this 11th day of January, 2016.

JOHN D. GALLUZZO
CHIEF JUDGE

15–47. [SUPERSEDED BY ORDER 18–44, EFFECTIVE NOVEMBER 7, 2018.]

15–44–S. [SUPERSEDED BY ORDER 18–45–S, EFFECTIVE NOVEMBER 7, 2018.]

15–43–B. [SUPERSEDED BY ORDER 17–33-B, EFFECTIVE SEPTEMBER 1, 2017.]

15–42–S. CRIMINAL BAIL SCHEDULE FOR SEMINOLE COUNTY

IN THE CIRCUIT COURT OF THE EIGHTEENTH JUDICIAL CIRCUIT IN AND FOR SEMINOLE COUNTY, FLORIDA

ADMINISTRATIVE ORDER NO.: 15–42–S
SUPERSEDES 14–32–S

IN RE: CRIMINAL BAIL SCHEDULE FOR SEMINOLE COUNTY

Bail is an essential part of the criminal justice system, and a bail schedule is hereby promulgated so that law enforcement officers and booking officers can set bonds on arrests prior to first appearance. This schedule is not binding upon first appearance judges, who have the responsibility to review arrests at first appearance and set conditions of release pursuant to Rule 3.131 of the Florida Rules of Criminal Procedure and section 903.046 Florida Statutes.

Within this bail schedule, special provisions setting bail for specific offenses control over general provisions that may also be applicable to the specific offense.

Under the provisions of Florida Statute 903.02(4), a separate and specific bail amount must be set for each offense charged.

Bail will have a condition in every case that the defendant will have no direct or indirect contact with the alleged victim, if there is one in the case; and that the defendant shall remain from criminal activity of any kind.

IT IS ADJUDGED:

I. Offenses for Which No Bail Shall Be Set Until the Initial Appearance Proceeding Before a Judge.

1. Capital Felony
2. Life Felony
3. First Degree Felony Punishable by Life
4. First Degree Felony (Violent)
5. Second Degree Felony (Violent-with at least one prior violent felony conviction)
6. Attempt/Solicitation/Conspiracy to Commit First Degree Murder
7. Persons who are arrested for a felony while released on bail for a separate felony
8. Armed Robbery (Firearm or Dangerous Weapon)
9. Armed Burglary (Firearm or Dangerous Weapon)
10. Carjacking
11. Armed Home Invasion (Firearm or Dangerous Weapon)
12. Kidnapping
13. Drug Trafficking and Conspiracy to traffic in drugs
14. Sale or Delivery of a Controlled Substance (3rd Offense or more)
15. Manufacture of Methamphetamine
16. RICO Act Violations (F.S. 895.03)
17. Escape from DOC or Rehabilitation Reentry Program or other correctional facility
18. Attempt/Solicitation/Conspiracy to Commit Second Degree Murder
19. Aggravated Stalking
20. Domestic Violence (Any Felony or misdemeanor offense defined in F.S. 741.28(1))
21. Violations of Domestic Violence Injunctions, Repeat Violence Injunctions, Dating Violence Injunctions or Sexual Violence Injunctions, regardless of the nature of the alleged violation.
22. Violation of any Condition of Release where the underlying offense is one of Domestic Violence
23. Burglary with an Assault or Battery
24. Violations of Felony Probation or Community Control unless

    a. There is a violation of probation warrant, which, on its face, provides that the probationer does not meet the qualifications for a "danger to public" hearing as defined in Florida Statute 948.06(4) (as amended by the "Jessica Lundsford Act"), and

    b. Such violation of probation warrant sets a bond amount.

25. Any criminal offense if the defendant is currently on felony probation or community control
26. Persons who are arrested for a felony who, because of their prior criminal record, qualify for sentencing on the arrested felony as a "Habitual Violent Felony Offender"; "Three-time Violent Felony Offender"; "Violent Career Criminal" or "Prison Release Reoffender".
27. Persons who are arrested for Possession of a Firearm by a Convicted Felon;
28. Any felony involving the use of threatened use of a firearm.
29. DUI Manslaughter
30. DUI 4th Offense or More.

NOTE TO INITIAL APPEARANCE JUDGES: "Unless charged with a capital offense or an offense punishable by life imprisonment and the proof of guilt is evident or the presumption is great, every person charged with a crime shall be entitled to pretrial release on reasonable conditions. If no conditions of release can reasonably protect the community from risk of physical harm to persons, assure the presence of the accused at trial, or assure the integrity of the judicial process, the accused may be detained." Fla. R. Crim. P.

II. Arrestees Subject to the Jessica Lunsford Act.

1. The Jessica Lundsford Act requires a judge to make a finding that a probationer or an offender on community control who is arrested for violating his/her probation or community control is not a "danger to public" prior to his/her release with or without bail where the probationer or offender in community control is:

a. A registered sexual predator, or

b. A registered sexual offender, or

c. Under supervision for any criminal offense prescribed in Chapter 794 (Sexual Battery); Section 800.04(4) (Lewd or Lascivious Battery); Section 800.04(5) (Lewd or Lascivious Molestation); Section 800.04(6) (Lewd or Lascivious Conduct); Section 827.01 (Sexual Performance by a Child), or Section 847.0145 (Selling or Buying of Minors), or

d. Under supervision for a criminal offense for which he/she would meet the registration criteria in Section 775.21, Section 943.0435, or Section 944.607 but for the effective date of those sections.

2. A probationer who is subject to the provisions of the "Jessica Lunsford Act" shall not be released on bail unless there is a judicial finding that he or she is not a danger to the public. If there is no such finding on the face of the warrant, the offender shall be held without bail, even if the warrant provides a specific bail amount.

3. If the judge who issued the warrant expressly states that the offender is not a danger to the public, bail shall be set in the amount provided for in the warrant.

4. If the warrant issuing judge does not include a finding that the offender is not a danger to the public and the offender is thereby held without bail, the First Appearance Judge may, in their discretion, hold the hearing and make findings as provided in Fla. Stat. § 948.06(4). If the First Appearance Judge does not hold this hearing, the court shall set the case for a status hearing in the assigned criminal division within 72 hours of the First Appearance hearing.

III. SPECIFIC OFFENSES

OFFENSE	RESIDENCY			
	LOCAL	FLORIDA	OUT-OF-STATE	OUT-OF-COUNTRY
1. Third Degree Murder	$15,000	$20,000	$25,000	$35,000
2. Manslaughter	$15,000	$20,000	$25,000	$35,000
3. Vehicular Homicide	$15,000	$20,000	$25,000	$35,000
4. Leaving Scene of Accident Involving Death/Personal Injury	$15,000	$20,000	$25,000	$35,000
5. Burglary of an Occupied Dwelling	$15,000	$20,000	$25,000	$35,000
6. All other non-armed Burglaries	$5,000	$8,000	$10,000	$15,000
7. Sexual Offenses – First Degree Felony	$35,000	$40,000	$50,000	$60,000
8. Sexual Offenses – Second Degree Felony	$15,000	$20,000	$25,000	$35,000
9. Sexual Offenses – Third Degree Felony	$5,000	$8.000	$10,000	$15,000
10. DUI Involving Personal Injury	$15,000	$20,000	$25,000	$35,000
11. DUI – Third Offense	$5,000	$8,000	$10,000	$15,000
12. Aggravated Fleeing or Attempting to Elude	$15,000	$20,000	$25,000	$35,000
13. Fleeing or Attempting to Elude	$5,000	$8,000	$10,000	$15,000
14. Sale or Delivery of a Controlled Substance (Second Offense)	$35,000	$40,000	$50,000	$60,000
15. Sale or Delivery of a Controlled Substance (First Offense)	$15,000	$20,000	$25,000	$35,000
16. Possession of a Listed Chemical	$25,000	$30,000	$35,000	$40,000
17. Computer Crimes Involving Child Pornography or Soliciting Sexual Conduct by a Child	$35,000	$40,000	$50,000	$60,000
18. Failure to Register as a Sex Offender	$15,000	$20,000	$25,000	$35,000

IV. NON-SPECIFICALLY ENUMERATED FELONIES

OFFENSE	RESIDENCY			
	LOCAL	FLORIDA	OUT-OF-STATE	OUT-OF-COUNTRY
1. First Degree Felony (Non-Violent)	$15,000	$20,000	$25,000	$35,000
2. Second Degree Felony (Violent)	$15,000	$20,000	$25,000	$35,000
3. Second Degree Felony (Non-Violent)	$5,000	$8,000	$10,000	$15,000
4. Third Degree Felony (Violent—with at least one prior violent felony conviction)	$15,000	$20,000	$25,000	$35,000
5. Third Degree Felony (Violent)	$5,000	$8,000	$10,000	$15,000
6. Third Degree Felony (Non-Violent)	$2,000	$3,000	$5,000	$8,000

V. Warrants. Bond for persons arrested on a violation of felony probation shall be set as provided for in the warrant itself, if and only if, the warrant provides that the probationer does not meet the qualifications of a "danger to public" hearing as defined in Florida Statute 948.06(4) (as amended by the "Jessica Lundsford Act"); otherwise, such person shall be held without bond pending the initial appearance before a judge.

Bond for persons arrested on a violation of misdemeanor probation warrant, a failure to appear warrant, or an arrest warrant shall be set as provided for in the warrant itself. If the warrant is silent as to a bond amount, the bail shall be set as otherwise provided in this Administrative Order.

VI. Misdemeanors. Rule 3.125(b) provides:

1. If a person is arrested for an offense declared to be a misdemeanor of the first or second degree or for violation of a municipal or county ordinance triable in the county, and demand to be taken before a magistrate is not made, notice to appear may be issued by the arresting officer unless:

a. The accused fails or refuses to sufficiently identify himself or herself or supply the required information;

b. The accused refuses to sign the notice to appear;

c. The officer has reason to believe that the continued liberty of the accused constitutes an unreasonable risk of bodily injury to the accused or others;

d. The accused has no ties with the jurisdiction reasonably sufficient to assure the accused's appearance or there is substantial risk that the accused will refuse to respond to the notice;

e. The officer has any suspicion that the accused may be wanted in any jurisdiction; or

f. It appears that the accused has previously failed to respond to a notice or a summons or has violated the conditions of any pretrial release program.

2. If a defendant is not released on a "Notice to Appear", pursuant to Rule 3.125, bond shall be set, pending first appearance, as follows:

OFFENSE	BAIL
DUI (First Offense)	$500
DUI (Second Offense)	$1,000
Criminal Traffic Offenses	$500
First Degree Misdemeanors	$500
Second Degree Misdemeanor	$250
Violations of conditions of release where the underlying offense is not one of Domestic Violence	$1,000

3. As to all individuals arrested for the offense of DUI, any release must also comply with the criteria set forth in Fla. Stat. § 316.193(9).

VII. Definitions. The following definitions apply to this bail schedule:

1. *Local Resident.* A person qualifies as a local resident if his/her principal place of domicile is located in Seminole County, Florida and has been so for a period of three (3) months.

2. *Florida Resident.* A person qualifies as a Florida resident if his/her principal place of domicile is located in the State of Florida and has been so for a period of three (3) months.

3. *Out of State Resident.* A person qualifies as an out of state resident if his/her principal place of domicile is located outside the State of Florida but in another state within the United States and he/she is a United States citizen or he/she is a foreign national and his/her principal place of domicile is in another state within the United States and has been so for a period of six (6) months and he/she is in possession of such documents as permit a current domicile within the United States or such permit is otherwise corroborated.

4. *Out of County Resident.* A person qualifies as an out of country resident if he/she is not domiciled in the United States or is not a United States citizen and his/her principal place of domicile is in the United States but has been so for less than six (6) months whether permitted or not.

5. *Violent Offense.* An offense qualifies a violent offense if it involves physical harm or bodily injury or threat of same.

6. *Non–Violent Offense.* An offense qualifies as a non—violent offense if it involves no physical harm or bodily injury or threat of same.

VIII. Special Conditions of Release—Duty of Release Officer.

1. *General Conditions for Pretrial Release Applicable to All Cases.*

a. The defendant shall refrain from criminal activity of any kind.

b. The defendant shall refrain from any contact of any type with the victim(s), except through pretrial discovery pursuant to Florida Rules of Criminal Procedure. F.S. 903.47

c. The defendant shall comply with all other conditions of pretrial release.

2. *Persons Arrested for Domestic Violence, Repeat, Sexual, and Dating Violence; Order of No Contact.* Any person who is arrested in Seminole County for an offense of domestic violence, repeat violence, sexual violence or dating violence shall be furnished an Order of No Contact (Attachment 1) stating the conditions of pretrial release. Persons arrested for any of the above noted offenses shall not be released until they have been instructed on the special conditions set forth in the Order of No Contact and have signed a court approved written notice acknowledging instruction on the special conditions of pretrial release.

3. *Persons Arrested for Sexual Offenses or Child Abuse.* Any person who is arrested for a sexual offense or for child abuse shall, as an additional condition of release, be prohibited from having direct or indirect contact with victim(s), victim(s)' family, or residence(s) of the victim(s). Persons arrested who have committed a sexual offense or child abuse shall not be released until they have been instructed of these special conditions by the pretrial release officer and have signed a written notice approved by the court.

4. *Persons on Probation—Department of Corrections.* Any person who is arrested in Seminole County and who is on probation with supervision by the Department of Corrections, Probation and Parole Services, shall, as an additional condition of release, report to their Probation Officer with the Department of Corrections, Probation and Parole services before 4:00 p.m. on the first business day following release. An offender is considered to be on probation if he is on parole or under any other type of supervision status by the Department of Corrections.

5. *Persons on Probation—Seminole County Probation Department.* Any person who is arrested in Seminole County and who is on probation with supervision by the Seminole County Probation Department, shall, as an additional condition of release, report to Seminole County Probation Department, Sanford, Florida, before 4:00 p.m. on the first business day following release.

IX. Effect of Filing Notice of No Information or Nolle Prosequi. If a person arrested for any offense(s) occurring within Seminole County is admitted to bail and the State Attorney files a notice of No Information or Nolle Prosequi with respect to all charges arising out of a single arrest, the Sheriff shall without further order of the Court, release the person from custody as to the charges named. As to the named charges and person, all bail undertaking, not defaulted, shall be canceled, all sureties shall be exonerated, and all release on recognizance obligations shall be discharged without further order of the Court. A bench warrant or capias which may be outstanding and is yet unserved upon a named individual for a specified charge shall also be canceled upon the filing of a No Information or Nolle Prosequi without further order of the Court.

X. Compliance With This Administrative Order. Upon receipt of the person arrested the booking officer shall review the arrest form to ensure that the arresting officer has properly set the initial bond according to this administrative order. The booking officer is authorized to make changes to the bond amount reflected on the arrest form to properly comply with this order but in considering changes the booking officer shall consider any information in the arrest form that the arresting officer believed called for a higher bond and shall defer to that judgment. However, any bond set shall not exceed the amount of bail set forth in the bond schedule.

DONE AND ORDERED this 12th day of October, 2015.

JOHN D. GALLUZZO

CHIEF JUDGE

ATTACHMENT 1

ORDER OF NO CONTACT IN CASES OF DOMESTIC VIOLENCE, REPEAT VIOLENCE, SEXUAL VIOLENCE, AND DATING VIOLENCE

Pursuant to Florida Statute 903.047, all persons arrested for domestic violence, repeat violence, sexual violence, or dating violence shall as conditions of pretrial release abide by the following conditions:

(a) Refrain from criminal activity of any kind.

(b) Refrain from any contact of any type with the victim except through pretrial discovery pursuant to the Florida Rules of Criminal Procedure.

The term "no contact" prohibits all oral or written communication either in person, telephonically, electronically, or by any other means either directly or indirectly through a third party with the victim or any other person named in the order.

(c) Refrain from having any physical or violent contact with the victim or other named person or his or her property.

(d) Refrain from being within 500 feet of the victim's or other named person's residence even if the victim or other named person shared the residence with the arrestee at the time of arrest.

(e) Refrain from being within 500 feet of the victim's or other named person's vehicle, place of employment, or other specified location frequented regularly by such person.

THIS ORDER OF NO CONTACT IS EFFECTIVE IMMEDIATELY AND IS ENFORCEABLE FOR THE DURATION OF PRETRIAL RELEASE OR UNTIL MODIFIED BY THE COURT.

The undersigned release officer acknowledges instructing the arrestee on the above conditions and furnishing the arrestee with a copy of the Order of No Contact.

The undersigned arrestee acknowledges being instructed on the conditions of pretrial release contained in the Order of No Contact and being furnished with a copy of the Order of No Contact.

This Order of No Contact applies to the following named persons and addresses:

____

____

____

____

Release Officer	Defendant/Arrestee
Date	Date

15–40. PROBATE AND GUARDIANSHIP—FILING ANNUAL GUARDIANSHIP REPORTS

IN THE CIRCUIT COURT OF THE EIGHTEENTH JUDICIAL CIRCUIT OF FLORIDA

ADMINISTRATIVE ORDER NO.: 15–40

SUPERSEDES 92–28 & 98–8

IN RE: PROBATE AND GUARDIANSHIP—FILING ANNUAL GUARDIANSHIP REPORTS

WHEREIN, pursuant to Florida Statute 744.367(2), the Court may require the filing of annual accountings on a fiscal year basis, and

WHEREIN, the filing of annual accountings on a fiscal year basis will allow the Clerk to maintain a more balanced workload and will spread the judicial labor required to review and take action on these reports more evenly.

IT IS THEREFORE ADJUDGED:

1. Annual accountings shall be filed by guardians of property on a fiscal year basis.

2. A fiscal year is deemed to end on the last day of the anniversary month in which the letters of guardianship were signed.

3. The annual accounting shall cover the fiscal year including the anniversary month in which the letters of guardianship were signed.

4. Each annual accounting shall be filed on or before the first day of the fourth month after the anniversary date of the letters of guardianship. (For example, if the anniversary date is January 17, the annual accounting shall be filed no later than May 1.)

5. Annual plans shall be filed by guardians of the person pursuant to Florida Statute 744.367(1).

6. This Order shall take effect immediately. The Clerk is directed to provide notice of the contents of this order to guardians in all future cases and in all pending cases.

DONE and ORDERED this 15th day of September, 2015.

JOHN D. GALLUZZO
CHIEF JUDGE

15–39. [SUPERSEDED BY ORDER 17–18, EFFECTIVE APRIL 17, 2017.]

15–36–B. [SUPERSEDED BY ORDER 18–52–B, EFFECTIVE NOVEMBER 14, 2018.]

15–35. ATTORNEYS—APPOINTMENT OF PUBLIC DEFENDER IN BAKER ACT PROCEEDING

IN THE CIRCUIT COURT OF THE, EIGHTEENTH JUDICIAL CIRCUIT

ADMINISTRATIVE ORDER NO.: 15–35

IN RE: ATTORNEYS—APPOINTMENT OF PUBLIC DEFENDER IN BAKER ACT PROCEEDING

Whereas, 394–467(4), Florida Statutes requires the appointment of the public defender to represent a person who is the subject of a petition for involuntary placement within one (1) working day after the filing of the petition, unless the person is otherwise represented by counsel, and

Whereas, it has been determined that the issuance of an administrative order covering all such cases would be more efficient than issuing individual orders of appointment in each applicable case,

Now therefore, I, John D. Galluzzo, Chief Judge of the Eighteenth Judicial Circuit hereby order the appointment of the Public Defender of the Eighteenth Judicial Circuit of Florida to represent persons who are the subjects of petitions for involuntary placement filed in the Eighteenth Judicial Circuit pursuant to 394.467(4) Florida Statutes. The Public Defender shall not be appointed in those cases where the subjects are represented by private counsel. The Clerk of Court shall notify the Public Defender of all cases in which the office is appointed pursuant to the terms of this order.

DONE AND ORDERED this 31st day of July, 2015.

JOHN D. GALLUZZO
CHIEF JUDGE

15–29–S. SUPERSEDED BY ADMINISTRATIVE ORDER NO. 16–05–S

15–26. ABORTION—ASSIGNMENT OF CASES ADDRESSING A MINOR'S REQUEST FOR JUDICIAL WAIVER OF PARENTAL NOTICE OF ABORTION

IN THE CIRCUIT COURT OF THE EIGHTEENTH JUDICIAL CIRCUIT

ADMINISTRATIVE ORDER NO.: 15–26 SUPERSEDES 11–23

IN RE: ABORTION—ASSIGNMENT OF CASES ADDRESSING A MINOR'S REQUEST FOR JUDICIAL WAIVER OF PARENTAL NOTICE OF ABORTION

Whereas, due to the enactment of the Parental Notice of Abortion Act, Section 390.01114, Florida Statutes, effective October 1, 2011, pregnant minors may petition the court for a judicial waiver of the parental notice requirements; and

Whereas, in order to promote judicial economy and efficiency in the assignment and management of cases filed pursuant to this legislation, and to ensure that court proceedings filed under this Act are given precedence over other pending matters to the extent necessary to reach a decision promptly, it is necessary that these cases be assigned in the most efficient manner.

Accordingly, it is hereby ordered;

1. **Case Assignment.** The Clerk of Court shall assign the Petition Seeking Judicial Waiver of Parental Notice to a circuit judge. Immediately thereafter, the clerk of court shall forward the petition and court file to the assigned judge.

Brevard County Only: Petitions shall be assigned to the existing family law and juvenile divisions on a rotating basis.

Seminole County Only: Petitions shall be assigned to the juvenile divisions on a rotating basis.

2. **3 Business–Day Rule.** Proceedings arising out of these petitions shall be given precedence over other pending matters and shall be heard in closed court in a prompt fashion. The court shall rule and issue written findings of fact and conclusions of law within 3 business days after the petition is filed, except that the 3 business-day limitation may be extended at the request of the minor. If the court fails to rule within the 3 business-day period and an extension has not been requested, the minor may immediately petition for a hearing upon the expiration of the 3 business-day period to the chief judge of the circuit, who must ensure a hearing is held within 48 hours after receipt of the minor's petition and an order is entered within 24 hours after the hearing.

3. **Review of Petitions and Proceedings on Weekends or Court Holidays.** If a petition is filed between the hours of 12:00 p.m. noon and 5:00 p.m. and the next day falls on a court holiday or a weekend, the clerk of court shall provide the court files to the emergency duty judge immediately. The emergency duty judge is authorized to hear proceedings arising from this petition at either the jail or the courthouse.

4. **Right to Court Appointed Counsel.** The clerk shall advise the minor that she has a right to counsel, without cost, at the time the petition is filed. If the petitioner requests counsel, the court shall appoint counsel for her.

5. **Confidentiality.** Any information in documents relating to the petition, and which could be used to identify the minor, is confidential. The court file shall be sealed and the minor's identity shall remain anonymous. All hearings under this section, including appeals, shall remain confidential and closed to the public, as provided by court rule.

6. **Expedited Appeal.** If the circuit court does not grant the judicial waiver of notice, the minor has the right to appeal. An appellate court must rule within 7 days after receipt of appeal, but a ruling may be remanded with further instruction for a ruling within 3 business days after the remand. The reason for overturning a ruling on appeal must be based on abuse of discretion by the court and may not be based on the weight of the evidence presented to the circuit court since the proceeding is a nonadversarial proceeding.

Done and Ordered this 27th day of May, 2015.

JOHN M. HARRIS
CHIEF JUDGE

15–24. CLERK OF COURT–CONFIDENTIALITY OF COURT RECORDS

IN THE CIRCUIT COURT OF THE EIGHTEENTH JUDICIAL CIRCUIT OF FLORIDA

ADMINISTRATIVE ORDER NO: 15–24

SUPERSEDES 13–23

IN RE: CLERK OF COURT—CONFIDENTIALITY OF COURT RECORDS

This Administrative Order implements the Florida Supreme Court's amendments to Rule 2.420, Florida Rules of Judicial Administration {*In re: Amendments to Florida Rule of Judicial Administration 2.420*, 124 So.3d 819 (Fla. 2013); *In re: Amendments to Florida Rule of Judicial Administration 2.420*, 156 So.3d 499 (Fla. 2015)}.

Pursuant to the Chief Judge's authority under Rule 2.215, Florida Rules of Judicial Administration, to exercise administrative supervision over the courts within the circuit and to control dockets; and in order to provide a uniform method for ensuring the confidentiality of court records when such confidentiality is required by law or found warranted by court order, to ensure that materials are not unintentionally designated as confidential, and to provide a procedure whereby the public can request review of orders determining confidentiality of records, it is hereby

ORDERED that:

1. All requests and orders regarding the confidentiality of trial court records shall comply with Rule 2.420, Florida Rules of Judicial Administration.

2. The filer of any document containing confidential information shall, at the time of filing, file with the clerk a "Notice of Confidential Information within Court Filing" indicating that either the entire document is confidential or identifying the precise location of the confidential information within the document. If an entire court file is maintained as confidential, the filer of a document is not required to file the notice form.

3. The "Notice of Confidential Information within Court Filing" may be used, after-the-fact, by the filer, a party, or any affected non-party when confidential information or documents were not initially identified by the filer and are not being maintained as confidential by the clerk of court. The notice must state the title and type of document, date of filing (if known), date of document, docket entry number, and must indicate that the entire document is confidential or identify the precise location of the confidential information within the document.

4. A form "Notice of Confidential Information within Court Filing" accompanies this Administrative Order. See Attachment A.

5. Pursuant to Rule 2.420(d)(1)(A), the clerk of court shall designate and maintain the confidentiality of any information contained within a court record described by any of subdivisions (c)(1) through (c)(6) of Rule 2.420.

6. Pursuant to Rule 2.420(d)(1)(B), matters which should automatically be made confidential by the clerk of court without necessity of a court order, include:

i. Chapter 39 records relating to dependency matters, termination of parental rights, guardians ad litem, child abuse, neglect, and abandonment. §§ 39.0132(3), 39.0132(4)(a), Fla. Stat.

ii. Adoption records. § 63.162, Fla. Stat.

iii. Social Security, bank account, charge, debit, and credit card numbers. § 119.0714(1)(i)–(j), (2)(a)–(e), Fla. Stat. (Unless redaction is requested pursuant to § 119.0714(2), Fla. Stat., this information is exempt only as of January 1, 2012.)

iv. HIV test results and the identity of any person upon whom an HIV test has been performed. § 381.004(2)(e), Fla. Stat.

v. Records, including test results, held by the Department of Health or its authorized representatives relating to sexually transmissible diseases. § 384.29, Fla. Stat.

vi. Birth records and portions of death and fetal death records. §§ 382.008(6), 382.025(1), Fla. Stat.

vii. Information that can be used to identify a minor petitioning for a waiver of parental notice when seeking to terminate pregnancy. § 390.01116, Fla. Stat.

viii. Clinical records under the Baker Act. § 394.4615(7), Fla. Stat.

ix. Records of substance abuse service providers which pertain to the identity, diagnosis, and prognosis of and service provision to individuals. § 397.501(7), Fla. Stat.

x. Clinical records of criminal defendants found incompetent to proceed or acquitted by reason of insanity. § 916.107(8), Fla. Stat.

xi. Estate inventories and accountings. § 733.604(1), Fla. Stat.

xii. The victim's address in a domestic violence action on petitioner's request. § 741.30(3)(b), Fla. Stat.

xiii. Protected information regarding victims of child abuse or sexual offenses. §§ 119.071(2)(h), 119.0714(1)(h), Fla. Stat.

xiv. Gestational surrogacy records. § 742.16(9), Fla. Stat.

xv. Guardianship reports and orders appointing court monitors, and orders relating to findings of no probable cause in guardianship cases. §§ 744.1076, 744.3701, Fla. Stat.

xvi. Grand jury records. §§ 905.17, 905.28(1), Fla. Stat.

xvii. Records acquired by courts and law enforcement regarding family services for children. § 984.06(3)–(4), Fla. Stat.

xviii. Juvenile delinquency records. §§ 985.04(1), 985.045(2), Fla. Stat.

xix. Records disclosing the identity of persons subject to tuberculosis proceedings and records held by the Department of Health or its authorized representatives relating to known or suspected cases of tuberculosis or exposure to tuberculosis. §§ 392.545, 392.65, Fla. Stat.

xx. Complete presentence investigation reports. Fla. R. Crim. P. 3.712.

xxi. Forensic behavioral health evaluations under Chapter 916. § 916.1065, Fla. Stat.

xxii. Eligibility screening, substance abuse screening, behavioral health evaluations, and treatment status reports for defendants referred to or considered for referral to a drug court program. § 397.334(10)(a), Fla. Stat.

7. A form "Motion to Determine Confidentiality of Court Records" accompanies this Administrative Order. See Attachment B.

8. A form "Order Granting/Denying Motion to Determine Confidentiality of Court Records Pursuant to Fla. R. Jud. Admin. 2.420(c)(9)" accompanies this Administrative Order. See Attachment C.

9. Pursuant to Rule 2.420(e)(4), within 10 days following the entry of an order granting a request to determine the confidentiality of court records in noncriminal cases, the clerk must post a copy of the order on the clerk's website and in a prominent public location in the courthouse; the order must remain posted in both locations for no less than 30 days.

DONE AND ORDERED this 22nd day of April, 2015.

JOHN M. HARRIS
CHIEF JUDGE

ATTACHMENT A

IN THE CIRCUIT COURT OF THE EIGHTEENTH JUDICIAL CIRCUIT

IN AND FOR ______________ COUNTY, FLORIDA

CASE NO: ________

____

Plaintiff/Petitioner,

v.

____

Defendant/Respondent.

______________________/

NOTICE OF CONFIDENTIAL INFORMATION WITHIN COURT FILING

Pursuant to Florida Rule of Judicial Administration 2.420(d)(2), I hereby certify:

( ) (1) I am filing herewith a document containing confidential information as described in Rule 2.420(d)(1)(B) and that:

(a) The title/type of document is __________, and:

(b) ( ) the entire document is confidential, or

( ) the confidential information within the document is precisely located at: __________

OR

( ) (2) A document was previously filed in this case that contains confidential information as described in Rule 2.420(d)(1)(B), but a Notice of Confidential Information within Court Filing was not filed with the document and the confidential information was not maintained as confidential by the clerk of court. I hereby notify the clerk that this confidential information is locate [1] as follows:

(a) Title/type of document: __________;

(b) Date of filing (if known): __________;

(c) Date of document: __________;

(d) Docket entry number: __________;

(e) ( ) Entire document is confidential, or

( ) Precise location of confidential information in document: __________.

____
Filer's Signature

CERTIFICATE OF SERVICE

I HEREBY CERTIFY that a copy of the foregoing was furnished by (e–mail)(delivery)(mail)(fax) on: (All parties and Affected Non–Parties. Note: If the name or address of a Party or Affected Non–Party is confidential DO NOT include such information in this Certificate of Service. Instead, serve the State Attorney or request Court Service. See Rule 2.420(k)). __________, on __________, 20 ____.

Name ______________________
Address ______________________
Phone ______________________
Florida Bar No. (if applicable) ________
E–mail Address ______________________

ATTACHMENT B

IN THE CIRCUIT COURT OF THE EIGHTEENTH JUDICIAL CIRCUIT

IN AND FOR ________ COUNTY, FLORIDA

CASE NO: ________

____

Plaintiff/Petitioner,

v.

____

Defendant/Respondent.

______________________/

MOTION TO DETERMINE CONFIDENTIALITY OF COURT RECORDS

The undersigned, by and through his/her attorney, moves the Court pursuant to Florida Rule of Judicial Administration 2.420 for an order determining the confidentiality of court records.

a. The undersigned's attorney has given written notice of the subject motion to all affected non-parties [*specify names of non–parties]*, and filed copies of the notice provided. The notice identified this case by docket number; described the confidential information without revealing it; specified the location of the information in the court record; and advised that if the motion is denied by the court then the subject material will not be treated as confidential by the clerk.

b. The particular court records or portion of a record that the movant seeks to have determined as confidential is/are:

____

[Describe with as much specificity as possible without revealing the information subject to the confidentiality determination.]

c. The movant seeks an order determining confidentiality of the following information relative to this ________ [specify type of case, such as civil action, dissolution of marriage, paternity, etc.] case: [*select all that apply*]

___ the party's name on the progress docket.

___ particular documents within the court file, specifically ___.

___ the entire court file, but not the progress docket.

___ the entire court file and the progress docket.

d. The legal bases for determining the court records to be confidential are as follows: ___.

[Cite to specific rule, statute, case(s) that apply.]

e. *[For rule 2.420(c)(7) or (c)(8) motions]* The specific legal authority and applicable legal standards for determining such court records to be confidential are: ___.

f. *[For rule 2.420(c)(9) motions]* Confidentiality is required to protect the following interest(s): [*select any/all that apply*]

___ 1. Preventing a serious and imminent threat to the fair, impartial, and orderly administration of justice, specifically: ___.

___ 2. A trade secret.

___ 3. A compelling government interest, specifically ___.

___ 4. Obtaining evidence to determine the legal issues in a case;

___ 5. Avoiding substantial injury to innocent third parties, specifically ___.

___ 6. Avoiding substantial injury to a party by the disclosure of matters protected by a common law or privacy right not generally inherent in this type of proceeding, specifically: ___.

___ 7. Complying with established public policy set forth in the Florida or United States Constitution or statutes or Florida rules or case law, specifically: ___ *[cite]*.

g. There is no less restrictive measure available to protect this/these interest(s), and the degree, duration and manner of confidentiality ordered herein are no broader than necessary to protect the interest(s).

Wherefore, the undersigned **REQUESTS** that:

The Court finds that ___ documents are confidential and the following materials related to this matter shall be reserved from public access: [*select all that apply*]

___ 1. The party's name on the progress docket. On the public progress docket, the Clerk of the Circuit Court shall substitute the following for the party's name: ___. Further, the Clerk shall ensure that the party's name is redacted from all public materials in the file and that the final judgment is recorded in a manner that does not reveal the identity of the party. However, the progress docket and the file shall otherwise remain available to the public.

___ 2. The following documents within the court file: ___. However, the file and progress docket shall otherwise remain available to the public subject to any substitution of a party's name set forth above.

___ 3. The entire court file. However, the progress docket shall remain open to the public subject to any substitution of a party's name set forth above.

___ 4. The entire court file and the progress docket. The progress docket shall not be available on any public information system. However, the case number shall remain public.

Submitted and filed this ___ day of ___, 20 ___.

___
Attorney's Signature

I certify that this motion is made in good faith and is supported by a sound factual and legal basis. ___ Party's Signature/Attorney's Signature

CERTIFICATE OF SERVICE

I HEREBY CERTIFY that a copy of the foregoing was furnished by (e–mail)(delivery)(mail)(fax) on: ___ (See Rule 2.420(k)), ___, on ___, 20 ___.

Name ___
Address ___
Phone ___
Florida Bar No. ___
E–mail Address ___

ATTACHMENT C

IN THE CIRCUIT COURT OF THE EIGHTEENTH JUDICIAL CIRCUIT
IN AND FOR ___ COUNTY, FLORIDA

CASE NO: ___

___
Plaintiff/Petitioner,
v.

___
Defendant/Respondent.
___/

ORDER GRANTING/DENYING MOTION TO DETERMINE CONFIDENTIALITY OF COURT RECORDS PURSUANT TO FLA. R. JUD. ADMIN. 2.420(c)(9)

THIS MATTER is before the Court on the Motion to Determine Confidentiality of Court Records filed by ___ *[insert name of party]* pursuant to rule 2.420(c)(9), Florida Rule of Judicial Administration. ___ *[insert name of party]* seeks an order determining the confidentiality of the following information relative to this ___ [specify type of case, such as civil action, dissolution of marriage, paternity, etc.] case: [*select all that apply*]

___ the party's name on the progress docket.

___ particular documents within the court file, specifically ___.

___ the entire court file, but not the progress docket.

___ the entire court file and the progress docket.

This motion *[was/was not]* contested and a hearing *[was/was not]* conducted *[if conducted, include date.]*

Having considered the arguments of the parties, legal authority, and otherwise being fully advised, the Court **DENIES** the motion because the moving party has failed to establish that confidentiality of the information is necessary to protect any interest under Rule 2.420(c)(9).

—**OR**—

The Court **GRANTS** the motion as follows:

1. Confidentiality of the information is required to protect the following interest(s): [*select all that apply*]

___ a. Preventing a serious and imminent threat to the fair, impartial, and orderly administration of justice, specifically: ________.

___ b. A trade secret.

___ c. A compelling government interest, specifically ________.

___ d. Obtaining evidence to determine the legal issues in a case;

___ e. Avoiding substantial injury to innocent third parties, specifically ________.

___ f. Avoiding substantial injury to a party by the disclosure of matters protected by a common law or privacy right not generally inherent in this type of proceeding, specifically: ________.

___ g. Complying with established public policy set forth in the Florida or United States Constitution or statutes or Florida rules or case law, specifically: ________.

2. The Court further finds that no less restrictive measure is available to protect this/these interest(s), and that the degree, duration and manner of confidentiality ordered herein are no broader than necessary to protect the interest(s).

IT IS HEREBY ORDERED:

The Clerk of the Circuit Court is hereby directed to treat as confidential immediately the following materials related to this matter and to keep such materials from public access: [*select all that apply*]

___ 1. The party's name on the progress docket. On the public progress docket, the Clerk of the Circuit Court shall substitute the following for the party's name: ________. Further, the Clerk shall ensure that the party's name is redacted from all public materials in the file and that the final judgment is recorded in a manner that does not reveal the identity of the party. However, the progress docket and the file shall otherwise remain available to the public.

___ 2. The following documents within the court file: ________. However, the file and progress docket shall otherwise remain available to the public subject to any substitution of a party's name set forth above.

___ 3. The entire court file. However, the progress docket shall remain open to the public subject to any substitution of a party's name set forth above.

___ 4. The entire court file and the progress docket. The progress docket shall not be available on any public information system. However, the case number shall remain public.

It is further **ORDERED** that any materials treated as confidential pursuant to this Order may be disclosed only as follows:

1. to any judge of this Circuit for case-related reasons;
2. to the Chief Judge or his or her designee;
3. to authorized government agencies;
4. to the following specific individuals: ________; or
5. by further order of the Court.

It is further **ORDERED** that, within 10 days of the date of this Order, the Clerk shall post a copy of this Order in a prominent public location *[specify courthouse at which order is being signed]* and the Clerk's website for a period of 30 days to provide public notice.

It is further **ORDERED** that the Clerk is hereby authorized to open any materials determined to be confidential pursuant to this Order for the purpose of filing, microfilming or imaging files, or transmitting a record to an appellate tribunal. The materials shall be treated as confidential immediately upon completion of the filing.

DONE AND ORDERED in Chambers, at [*Courthouse Location*], this ___ day of ________, 20 ___.

____
(Judge Signature)

[1] So in original.

15–22 (A1). DOMESTIC RELATIONS—EIGHTEENTH JUDICIAL CIRCUIT BATTERERS' INTERVENTION PROGRAM

IN THE CIRCUIT COURT OF THE EIGHTEENTH JUDICIAL CIRCUIT OF FLORIDA

ADMINISTRATIVE ORDER NO.: 15–22 AMENDED

SUPERSEDES 15–22

IN RE: DOMESTIC RELATIONS—EIGHTEENTH JUDICIAL CIRCUIT BATTERERS' INTERVENTION PROGRAM

WHEREAS, section 741.325, Florida Statutes, establishes the requirements batterer's intervention programs must meet in order to be included on the circuit court's list of batterers' intervention programs, pursuant to section 741.30(6)(a)5, Florida Statutes;

NOW, THEREFORE, in order to facilitate the efficient operation of the administration of justice, and pursuant to the authority vested in me as Chief Judge of the Eighteenth Judicial Circuit of Florida under Florida Rule of Judicial Administration 2.215,

IT IS HEREBY ORDERED as follows:

In order to be included on the 18th Judicial Circuit's list of batterers' intervention programs, such program must provide to Court Administration in Brevard County, 2825 Judge Fran Jamieson Way, Viera, FL 32950 or Seminole County, 301 N. Park Avenue, Suite 301, Sanford, FL 32771 the following:

1. The program schedule;

2. Program content;

3. Fee schedule, including sliding scale or reduced fee options;

4. Locations where programs are offered;

5. Contact information;

6. The program model, and if it is other than the Duluth Model, proof that the model is accepted by the domestic violence prevention community as an effective model; and

7. A completed "Affidavit to be placed on the Batterers' Intervention Program Provider List in the 18th Circuit" (Attachment A).

All batterers' intervention programs currently on the 18th Judicial Circuit list of batterers' intervention programs shall have 30 days from the date of this order to submit the required information identified above to remain on the list.

Any changes to the information provided by a batterers' intervention program in 1 through 7 above, must be provided to the Court Administration in Brevard County or Seminole County immediately.

DONE AND ORDERED this 24th day of November, 2015.

JOHN D. GALLUZZO

CHIEF JUDGE

Eighteenth Judicial Circuit—Court Administration—Brevard & Seminole Counties Batterers' Intervention Program Provider Affidavit

I, ______________________________ (Authorized Representative's Name), being duly sworn, hereby certify, sear [1] and/or affirm that the following information is true and correct:

1. I am over 18 years of age, am sui juris, and am otherwise competent to make this affidavit.

2. I make this affidavit based upon my personal knowledge.

3. I am the ______________________________ (Title or Position through which affiant is authorized) of ______________________________ (Legal Name of Batterers' Intervention Program Provider—BIP Provider)

4. I have the authority to act on behalf of and to bind the BIP Provider.

5. The BIP Provider provides a batterer's intervention program course for individuals who have been ordered to attend a batterer's intervention program by the court.

6. I am aware that pursuant to 741.30(6)(a)5, Florida Statutes, when the court orders the respondent to participate in a batterer's intervention program, the court, or any entity designated by the court, must provide the respondent with a list of batterers' intervention programs from which the respondent must choose a program in which to participate. I am submitting this affidavit in order to have the BIP Provider placed on the list of eligible programs in the 18th Judicial Circuit Court.

7. The BIP Provider program meets each of the following requirements:

A. The primary purpose of the program is victim safety and the safety of children, if present.

B. The batterer is held accountable for acts of domestic violence.

C. The program is at least 29 weeks in length and includes 24 weekly sessions, plus appropriate intake, assessment, and orientation programming.

D. The program content is based on the below listed psychoeducational model that addresses tactics of power and control by one person over another. Model Name or Description: ____________________

E. The program is funded by a user fee in the amount of ____________________ paid by the batterers who attend the program, which allows them to take responsibility for their acts of violence. An exception is made for local, state, or federal programs that fund batterers' intervention programs in whole or in part.

8. Except in cases of actual conflict of interest, the BIP Providers cannot reject a referral on the basis of race, color, religion (creed), gender, gender expression, age, national origin (ancestry), disability, marital status, sexual orientation, or military status.

9. The BIP Provider currently and will continue to satisfy all criteria to be included on the list of batterer's interventions programs, and that the BIP Provider should be included on the Court's list of providers.

10. I understand that the BIP Provider is responsible for continuously meeting the statutory requirements for batterer intervention programs.

11. The Court may audit the BIP Provider's program as necessary to ensure compliance with the Florida statutes. I understand that such audit may include a survey of participants of the BIP Provider's program. The BIP Provider will fully cooperate with any efforts to conduct such audit.

12. I understand that it is my responsibility to IMMEDIATELY notify the Court if the BIP Provider no longer meets any of the statutory requirements. This notification must be sent to the Court Administration office in Brevard or Seminole County, at which time the BIP Provider's name will be immediately removed from the court's list of providers.

13. I further understand that failure to notify the court when the BIP Provider is no longer in compliance with the statute may constitute fraud for which I and/or the BIP Provider may be subject to liability.

14. I understand that if I no longer am employed by or represent the BIP Provider, I or the BIP provider must contact the courts immediately and the BIP Provider must issue an affidavit by the new legal representative or the BIP Provider in order to remain on the list of eligible providers.

I DECLARE UNDER PENALTY OR PERJURY, under the laws of the State of Florida that the statements and facts indicated in this Affidavit or [2] true and correct.

______________________________ ____________________

(Name) (Date)

Printed Name: ______________________________

Address: ______________________________

City, State, Zip: ______________________________

Phone Number: ______________________________

Email address: ______________________________

STATE OF FLORIDA

COUNTY OF ____________________

Sworn to (or affirmed) and subscribed before me this ____ day of ____________, ______, by ______________________________ (name of person making statement).

____

(Signature of Notary Public—State of Florida)

____

(Print, Type, or Stamp Commissioned Name of Notary Public)

(NOTARY SEAL)

☐ Personally Known OR ☐ Produced Identification

Type of Identification Produced: ☐ Driver's License: ______ ☐ Other: ______

[1] So in original.

[2] So in original.

15–19–B (A1). ADMINISTRATIVE ORDERS—RESCINDS ADMINISTRATIVE ORDER

IN THE CIRCUIT COURT OF THE EIGHTEENTH JUDICIAL CIRCUIT IN AND FOR BREVARD COUNTY, FLORIDA

ADMINISTRATIVE ORDER NO.: 15–19–B AMENDED

SUPERSEDES 15–19–B

IN RE: ADMINISTRATIVE ORDERS—RESCINDS ADMINISTRATIVE ORDER

WHEREAS, administrative orders from time to time become obsolete;

IT IS ORDERED, that the following administrative orders are hereby rescinded:

15–19–B: In Re: Foreclosure—Residential Mortgage Foreclosure Department, Brevard County

DONE AND ORDERED this 22nd day of July, 2015

JOHN D. GALLUZZO
CHIEF JUDGE

15–18 (A1). SUPERSEDED BY ADMINISTRATIVE ORDER NO. 16–11

15–17. DOMESTIC RELATIONS—PARENTING COORDINATION IN HIGH CONFLICT FAMILY LAW CASES

IN THE CIRCUIT COURT OF THE EIGHTEENTH JUDICIAL CIRCUIT OF FLORIDA

ADMINISTRATIVE ORDER NO: 15–17

Supersedes 11–34–B AMENDED

IN RE: DOMESTIC RELATIONS—PARENTING COORDINATION IN HIGH CONFLICT FAMILY LAW CASES

WHEREAS, children caught in the middle of high parental conflict are more likely to be harmed; and

WHEREAS, it is the public policy of the State of Florida to assure that each minor child has frequent and continuing contact with both parents after the parents separate or the marriage of the parties is dissolved and to encourage parents to share the rights, responsibilities, and joys of childrearing; and

WHEREAS, the Florida Supreme Court adopted a guiding principle encouraging a family court process to "empower families through skills development, assist them to resolve their own disputes, provide access to appropriate services, and offer a variety of dispute resolution forums where the family can resolve problems without additional emotional trauma," as set forth in *In re Report of the Family Court Steering Committee (Family Courts IV)*, 794 So. 2d 518, 522 (Fla. 2001); and

WHEREAS, parenting coordination is a process whereby an impartial third person, called a parenting coordinator, helps the parties implement their parenting plan by facilitating the resolution of disputes between parents and/or legal guardians, providing education, making recommendations to the parties and, with the prior approval of the parties and the court, making decisions within the scope of the court order of appointment; and

WHEREAS, the use of parenting coordinators promotes the best interests of minor children and their parents in high conflict cases by reducing the duration and severity of parental conflict, thereby protecting children from the harmful effects of such conflict; and

WHEREAS, in that parenting coordination provides a form of alternative dispute resolution that enhances the purposes of Chapter 61, Florida Statutes, the legislature enacted Section 61.125, Florida Statutes, to establish the procedures for the proper administration of parenting coordination within the State of Florida, thereby obviating the need for the adoption of separate provisions for this Circuit; and

WHEREAS, Section 61.125, Florida Statutes, became effective on October 1, 2009; and

WHEREAS, this Circuit has developed certain forms that are relevant to the Circuit that will assist with the effectuation of the provisions set forth in Section 61.125, Florida Statutes; and

WHEREAS the Supreme Court of Florida promulgated Rule 12.742 of the Florida Family Law Rules of Procedure encaptioned Parenting Coordination on January 28, 2010; and

NOW, THEREFORE WHEREAS the Supreme Court of Florida issued AOSC14–64 on November 14, 2014, calling for uniformity throughout the state in the implementation of section 61.125 Florida Statutes and adopting a uniform statewide parenting coordination application form, pursuant to the authority vested in me as Chief Judge of the Eighteenth Judicial Circuit of Florida, under Rule 2.215, of the Florida Rules of Judicial Administration;

It is hereby **ORDERED**:

1. The provisions set forth in Section 61.125, Florida Statutes, shall be followed in this Circuit regarding parenting coordination.

2. A parenting coordinator must meet all the required qualifications set forth in Section 61.125 (4) Florida Statutes. A parenting coordinator so qualified must submit an application in substantial compliance with AOSC14–64 to be listed on the roster of parenting coordinators for this circuit to the Chief Judge or designee(s). The court shall only appoint a parenting coordinator that is currently listed on the roster of parenting coordinators for this or another circuit in Florida. The Chief Judge or designee(s) shall determine whether to approve the application. The roster of approved parenting coordinators will be kept by Court Administration.

3. The following forms, attached hereto, are hereby adopted and shall be used in carrying out the provisions of Section 61.125, Florida Statutes:

a. Order of Referral to Parenting Coordinator.

b. Report of General Magistrate on Motion for Referral to Parenting Coordinator.

c. Response by Parenting Coordinator.

4. The parties shall provide to the Parenting Coordinator a copy of a notice of hearing for any hearing scheduled with the court for any matter that is within the scope of the Order of Referral to Parental Coordination. During hearings when addressed by the court, the Parenting Coordinator may testify on the subjects of the parties' compliance with the Order of Referral to Parenting Coordination and the appropriateness of maintaining the case in parenting coordination. However, the Parenting Coordinator may not set a hearing with the court.

5. The Parenting Coordinator may report to the court in writing on the subjects of the parties' compliance with the Order of Referral to Parenting Coordination and the appropriateness of maintaining the case in parenting coordination. The court itself may set a status hearing after reviewing the written report of the Parenting Coordinator.

6. Prior to the expiration of the Order of Referral to Parent Coordinator, the court will determine whether the order should be extended. Within thirty days of the expiration date of the Order of Referral to Parenting Coordinator, the parenting coordinator will notify in writing the judicial assistant of the court which entered the Order of Referral to Parenting Coordinator or the successor of the expiration date, and such written notice shall contain a recommendation as to whether the order should be extended. The Court may thereafter schedule a hearing to determine whether the order of Referral to Parenting Coordinator should be extended.

7. Process For Periodic Review Of Whether Parenting Coordinator Continues To Be Qualified, And Removal If No Longer Qualified. ("The chief judge or designee(s) in each judicial circuit shall establish a process to periodically review whether a parenting coordinator continues to be qualified and shall remove a parenting coordinator immediately from the roster if the coordinator is no longer qualified." Fla. Sup. Ct. AO14–64, p. 4) At least once per year, the Chief Judge or designee(s) will review the current roster of Parenting coordinators and determine if the individuals continue to meet the requirements for inclusion on the roster. Each parenting coordinator listed on the roster shall immediately notify the Chief Judge of any circumstance that would affect that person's continued qualification to serve as a Parenting Coordinator pursuant to F.S. 61.125.

8. Any appeal pertaining to a Parenting Coordinator's inclusion on or removal from the list of approved Parenting Coordinators shall be heard and decided by the Chief Judge or designee(s) whose decision shall be final.

DONE AND ORDERED this 10th day of February, 2015.

JOHN M. HARRIS
CHIEF JUDGE

ATTACHMENT

IN THE CIRCUIT COURT OF THE EIGHTEENTH JUDICIAL CIRCUIT, IN AND FOR ________ COUNTY, FLORIDA.

CASE NO: ____________________

________,

Petitioner,

and

________,

Respondent.

ORDER OF REFERRAL TO PARENTING COORDINATOR

The Court considered the ☐ motion of the court, ☐ joint motion of the parties, ☐ motion of a party, reviewed the court file, considered the testimony presented. Based on this information, the court FINDS that:

A. Appropriateness of Process: This matter is appropriate for parenting coordination and it is in the best interest of the child(ren).

B. Parenting Coordination Process: Parenting coordination is a child-focused alternative dispute resolution process whereby a parenting coordinator assists the parties in creating or implementing their parenting plan by facilitating the resolution of disputes, providing education and making recommendations to the parties; and, with the prior consent of the parties and approval of the court, making limited decisions within the scope of this order of referral.

C. Parenting Coordinator: A parenting coordinator is an impartial third person whose role is to assist the parties in successfully creating or implementing a parenting plan.

D. Selection of Parenting Coordinator: ________ shall serve as the parenting coordinator.

The parenting coordinator was selected by:

___ the parties' agreement.

___ the court.

E. History of Domestic Violence: Based upon testimony and evidence presented and a review of related court records, the court has determined:

___ There is no history of domestic violence.

___ There has been a history of domestic violence, and:

___ Each party has had an opportunity to consult with an attorney or domestic violence advocate before this court has accepted the parties consent; and

Each party has consented to this referral and the consent has been given freely and voluntarily.

It is therefore, **ORDERED:**

1. *Parenting Coordinator:* The parties are referred to parenting coordination for an initial period of ________ months (not to exceed two years):

a. The parenting coordinator shall file a response to this Order within 30 days accepting or declining the appointment. The response to the appointment must be in substantial compliance with Form 12.984(b).

b. The parties or their attorneys must provide to the parenting coordinator copies of all pleadings and orders related to domestic violence and any other pleadings and orders requested by the parenting coordinator related to parenting coordination.

2. *Meetings:* Unless prohibited herein as a domestic violence safeguard or by another court order, the parenting coordinator may meet with the parties and/or child (ren) together or separately, in person or by any electronic means.

3. *Domestic Violence Safeguards:* The parties shall adhere to all provisions of any injunction or conditions of bail, probation, or a sentence arising from criminal proceedings. In addition to any safety measures the parenting coordinator

deems necessary, the following domestic violence safeguards must be implemented:

(Choose all that apply)

___ None are necessary.

___ No joint meetings.

___ No direct negotiations.

___ No direct communications.

___ Other: ______________________________

4. *Role, Responsibility, and Authority of Parenting Coordinator.* The parenting coordinator shall have the following role, responsibility, and authority:

a. Assisting the parties in creating and implementing a parenting plan:

b. Facilitating the resolution of disputes regarding the creation or implementation of the Parenting Plan;

c. Recommending to the parties strategies for creating or implementing the Parenting Plan. Such recommendations may include that one or both parents avail themselves of accessible and appropriate community resources, including, but not limited to, random drug screens, parenting classes, and individual psychotherapy and/or family counseling, if there is a history or evidence that such referrals are appropriate;

d. Recommending to the parties changes to the Parenting Plan:

e. Educating the parties to effectively:

1. Parent in a manner that minimizes conflicts;

2. Communicate and negotiate with each other and their child(ren);

3. Develop and apply appropriate parenting skills;

4. Understand principles of child development and issues facing child(ren) when their parents no longer live together;

5. Disengage from the other parent when engagement leads to conflicts and non-cooperation;

6. Identify the sources of their conflict with each other and work individually and/or jointly to minimize conflict and lessen its deleterious effects on the child(ren); and

7. Allow the child (ren) to grow up free from the threat of being caught in the middle of their parents' disputes.

f. Facilitating the ability of both parents to maintain ongoing relationships with their children.

g. Reporting or communicating with the court concerning non-confidential matters as provided in paragraph 6 of this order;

h. Communicating with the parties and their child(ren), separately or together in person or by telephone, unless otherwise prohibited by court order or applicable law. The parenting coordinator shall determine the schedule for subsequent appointments:

i. Providing information to health care providers for the parents and the children, and to any third parties, when the parenting coordinator deems it is reasonably necessary.

5. *Scope of Authority:* The parenting coordinator shall make limited decisions within the scope of this order of referral. Limited decision making authority shall include, but may not be limited to:

____

6. *Fees and Costs for Parenting Coordination.*

a. (Choose all that apply)

___ The parties have consented to this referral to parenting coordination and have agreed that they have the present ability to pay parenting coordination fees.

___ The parties have consented to this referral to parenting coordination and the Court finds that: ___ petitioner ___ respondent ___ both parties has/have the present financial ability to pay the parenting coordination fees.

___ This order is without the consent or [1] the parties and the court has determined that: ___ petitioner ___ respondent ___ both parties has/have the financial ability to pay the parenting coordination fees & costs.

b. The court allocates payment of fees and costs for parenting coordination as follows:

_______ % shall be paid by the Father.

_______ % shall be paid by the Mother.

_______ % No fees as Family court Services to provide parenting coordination

Other:

c. If a party causes the parenting coordinator to expend an unreasonable and unnecessary amount of time, the Court may later determine that party will be solely responsible for payment of the parenting coordinator's fees and costs for such time expended or that the party shall reimburse the other party for the parenting coordinator's fees and cost paid by the other party for such time expended. Failure to pay the parenting coordinator's fees and costs in a timely manner may subject the party to sanctions for contempt of court.

d. The parenting coordinator shall not proceed until he/she is satisfied with the terms and conditions of payment for his/her services. Further, the parenting coordinator shall not perform nor continue to perform the parenting coordination services in this case unless all of his/her fees and costs are paid by the parties as ordered, and, in the event of nonpayment, the parenting coordinator shall file a Request for Status Conference, and the court may address the issue of non-payment of fees and costs.

7. *Confidentiality:* All communications made by, between, or among the parties and the parenting coordinator during parenting coordination sessions are confidential. The parenting coordinator and each party may not testify or offer evidence about communications made by a party or the parenting coordinator during the parenting coordination sessions, except if:

a. It is necessary to identify, authenticate, confirm, or deny a written agreement entered into by the parties during parenting coordination;

b. The testimony or evidence is necessary to identify an issue for resolution by the court without otherwise disclosing communications made by any party or the parenting coordinator;

c. The testimony or evidence is limited to the subject of a party's compliance with the order of referral to parenting coordination, orders for psychological evaluation, counseling ordered by the court or recommended by a health care provider, or for substance abuse testing or treatment.

d. The parenting coordinator is reporting that the case is no longer appropriate for parenting coordination;

e. The parenting coordinator is reporting that he or she is unable or unwilling to continue to serve and that a successor parenting coordinator should be appointed.

f. The testimony or evidence is necessary pursuant to s. 61.125(5)(b) or s. 61.125(8), Florida Statutes;

g. The parenting coordinator is not qualified to address or resolve certain issues in the case and a more qualified coordinator should be appointed;

h. The parties agree that the testimony or evidence be permitted; or

i. The testimony or evidence is necessary to protect any person from future acts that would constitute domestic violence under Chapter 741, Florida Statutes; child abuse, neglect, or abandonment under Chapter 39, Florida Statutes; or abuse, neglect, or exploitation of an elderly or disabled adult under Chapter 825, Florida Statutes.

8. *Agreement on Non–confidentiality:* The parties can agree to waive confidentiality of a specific communication or all communications. The waiver must be in writing, signed by the parties and their respective counsel. The waiver shall be filed with the court and a copy served on the parenting coordinator. Either party may revoke his or her waiver of confidentiality by providing written notice signed by that party. The revocation shall be filed with the court and a copy served on the other party and the parenting coordinator.

9. *Withdrawal Procedure:* With Court approval, the parenting coordinator may withdraw from the role of parenting coordinator. The parenting coordinator shall apply directly to the Court with a request to be discharged, and shall provide notice to the parties and their counsel of their request to withdraw. Either party may seek to terminate the parenting coordinator's services by filing a motion with the Court. The parenting coordinator's services may not be terminated by either of the parties (or at the request of both parties) without order of this court.

10. *Scheduling:* Each party shall contact the parenting coordinator within 10 days of the date of this order to schedule the first appointment. The parenting coordinator shall determine the schedule for subsequent appointments.

11. *Reservation of Jurisdiction:* This Court specifically reserves jurisdiction to enforce and/or modify the terms and conditions of this Order.

DONE AND ORDERED in ________ County, Florida, on this ___ day of ________, 2015.

____

Circuit Judge

Copies furnished to:
Name of Parties:
Counsel for Parties
Address of Counsel
Guardian Ad Litem
Address of GAL

ATTACHMENT

IN THE CIRCUIT COURT OF THE EIGHTEENTH JUDICIAL CIRCUIT, IN AND FOR ________ COUNTY, FLORIDA.

CASE NO.: ________________________

________,

Petitioner,

and

________,

Respondent.

REPORT OF GENERAL MAGISTRATE ON MOTION FOR REFERRAL TO PARENTING COORDINATOR

The above cause came before the undersigned General Magistrate on this ________ day of ________, 2015, upon the ☐ joint motion of the parties ☐ motion of a party, pursuant to Section 61.125, Florida Statutes, Florida Family Law Rules of Procedure, and the General Magistrate, having considered the evidence presented and after being otherwise advised in the premises, **FINDS, CONCLUDES AND RECOMMENDS** that:

A. Appropriateness of Process: This matter is appropriate for parenting coordination and it is in the best interest of the child(ren).

B. Parenting Coordination Process: Parenting coordination is a child-focused alternative dispute resolution process whereby a parenting coordinator assists the parties in creating or implementing their parenting plan by facilitating the resolution of disputes, providing education and making recommendations to the parties; and, with the prior consent of the parties and approval of the court, making limited decisions within the scope of this order of referral.

C. Parenting Coordinator: A parenting coordinator is an impartial third person whose role is to assist the parties in successfully creating or implementing a parenting plan.

D. Selection of Parenting Coordinator: ________ shall serve as the parenting coordinator.

The parenting coordinator was selected by:

___ the parties' agreement.

___ the court.

E. History of Domestic Violence: Based upon testimony and evidence presented and a review of related court records, the court has determined:

___ There is no history of domestic violence.

___ There has been a history of domestic violence, and:

___ Each party has had an opportunity to consult with an attorney or domestic violence advocate before this court has accepted the parties consent; and

___ Each party has consented to this referral and the consent has been given freely and voluntarily.

It is therefore, **ORDERED**:

1. *Parenting Coordinator:* The parties are referred to parenting coordination for an initial period of ________ months (not to exceed two years):

a. The parenting coordinator shall file a response to this Order within 30 days accepting or declining the appointment. The response to the appointment must be in substantial compliance with Form 12.984(b).

b. The parties or their attorneys must provide to the parenting coordinator copies of all pleadings and orders related to domestic violence and any other pleadings and orders requested by the parenting coordinator related to parenting coordination.

2. *Meetings:* Unless prohibited herein as a domestic violence safeguard or by another court order, the parenting coordinator may meet with the parties and/or child (ren) together or separately, in person or by any electronic means.

3. *Domestic Violence Safeguards:* The parties shall adhere to all provisions of any injunction or conditions of bail, probation, or a sentence arising from criminal proceedings. In addition to any safety measures the parenting coordinator deems necessary, the following domestic violence safeguards must be implemented:

(Choose all that apply)

___ None are necessary.

___ No joint meetings.

___ No direct negotiations.

___ No direct communications.

___ Other: ________________________________

4. *Role, Responsibility, and Authority of Parenting Coordinator.* The parenting coordinator shall have the following role, responsibility, and authority:

a. Assisting the parties in creating and implementing a parenting plan:

b. Facilitating the resolution of disputes regarding the creation or implementation of the Parenting Plan;

c. Recommending to the parties strategies for creating or implementing the Parenting Plan. Such recommendations may include that one or both parents avail themselves of accessible and appropriate community resources, including, but not limited to, random drug screens, parenting classes, and individual psychotherapy and/or family counseling, if there is a history or evidence that such referrals are appropriate;

d. Recommending to the parties changes to the Parenting Plan:

e. Educating the parties to effectively:

1. Parent in a manner that minimizes conflicts;

2. Communicate and negotiate with each other and their child(ren);

3. Develop and apply appropriate parenting skills;

4. Understand principles of child development and issues facing child(ren) when their parents no longer live together;

5. Disengage from the other parent when engagement leads to conflicts and non-cooperation;

6. Identify the sources of their conflict with each other and work individually and/or jointly to minimize conflict and lessen its deleterious effects on the child(ren); and

7. Allow the child (ren) to grow up free from the threat of being caught in the middle of their parents' disputes.

f. Facilitating the ability of both parents to maintain ongoing relationships with their children.

g. Reporting or communicating with the court concerning non-confidential matters as provided in paragraph 6 of this order;

h. Communicating with the parties and their child(ren), separately or together in person or by telephone, unless otherwise prohibited by court order or applicable law. The parenting coordinator shall determine the schedule for subsequent appointments:

i. Providing information to health care providers for the parents and the children, and to any third parties, when the parenting coordinator deems it is reasonably necessary.

5. *Scope of Authority:* The parenting coordinator shall make limited decisions within the scope of this order of referral. Limited decision making authority shall include, but may not be limited to:

____

6. *Fees and Costs for Parenting Coordination.*

a. (Choose all that apply)

___ The parties have consented to this referral to parenting coordination and have agreed that they have the present ability to pay parenting coordination fees.

___ The parties have consented to this referral to parenting coordination and the Court finds that: ___ petitioner ___ respondent ___ both parties has/have the present financial ability to pay the parenting coordination fees.

___ This order is without the consent o ²r the parties and the court has determined that: ___ petitioner ___ respondent ___ both parties has/have the financial ability to pay the parenting coordination fees & costs.

b. The court allocates payment of fees and costs for parenting coordination as follows:

________ % shall be paid by the Father.

________ % shall be paid by the Mother.

________ % No fees as Family court Services to provide parenting coordination

Other: ________________________________

c. If a party causes the parenting coordinator to expend an unreasonable and unnecessary amount of time, the Court may later determine that party will be solely responsible for payment of the parenting coordinator's fees and costs for such time expended or that the party shall reimburse the other party for the parenting coordinator's fees and cost paid by the other party for such time expended. Failure to pay the parenting coordinator's fees and costs in a timely manner may subject the party to sanctions for contempt of court.

d. The parenting coordinator shall not proceed until he/she is satisfied with the terms and conditions of payment for his/her services. Further, the parenting coordinator shall not perform nor continue to perform the parenting coordination services in this case unless all of his/her fees and costs are paid by the parties as ordered, and, in the event of nonpayment, the parenting coordinator shall file a Request for Status Conference, and the court may address the issue of non-payment of fees and costs.

7. *Confidentiality:* All communications made by, between, or among the parties and the parenting coordinator during parenting coordination sessions are confidential. The parenting coordinator and each party may not testify or offer evidence about communications made by a party or the parenting coordinator during the parenting coordination sessions, except if:

a. It is necessary to identify, authenticate, confirm, or deny a written agreement entered into by the parties during parenting coordination;

b. The testimony or evidence is necessary to identify an issue for resolution by the court without otherwise disclosing communications made by any party or the parenting coordinator;

c. The testimony or evidence is limited to the subject of a party's compliance with the order of referral to parenting coordination, orders for psychological evaluation, counseling ordered by the court or recommended by a health care provider, or for substance abuse testing or treatment.

d. The parenting coordinator is reporting that the case is no longer appropriate for parenting coordination;

e. The parenting coordinator is reporting that he or she is unable or unwilling to continue to serve and that a successor parenting coordinator should be appointed.

f. The testimony or evidence is necessary pursuant to s. 61.125(5)(b) or s. 61.125(8), Florida Statutes;

g. The parenting coordinator is not qualified to address or resolve certain issues in the case and a more qualified coordinator should be appointed;

h. The parties agree that the testimony or evidence be permitted; or

i. The testimony or evidence is necessary to protect any person from future acts that would constitute domestic violence under Chapter 741, Florida Statutes; child abuse, neglect, or abandonment under Chapter 39, Florida Statutes; or abuse, neglect, or exploitation of an elderly or disabled adult under Chapter 825, Florida Statutes.

8. *Agreement on Non–confidentiality:* The parties can agree to waive confidentiality of a specific communication or all communications. The waiver must be in writing, signed by the parties and their respective counsel. The waiver shall be filed with the court and a copy served on the parenting coordinator. Either party may revoke his or her waiver of confidentiality by providing written notice signed by that party. The revocation shall be filed with the court and a copy served on the other party and the parenting coordinator.

9. *Withdrawal Procedure:* With Court approval, the parenting coordinator may withdraw from the role of parenting coordinator. The parenting coordinator shall apply directly to the Court with a request to be discharged, and shall provide notice to the parties and their counsel of their request to withdraw. Either party may seek to terminate the parenting coordinator's services by filing a motion with the Court. The parenting coordinator's services may not be terminated by either of the parties (or at the request of both parties) without order of this court.

10. *Scheduling:* Each party shall contact the parenting coordinator within 10 days of the date of this order to schedule the first appointment. The parenting coordinator shall determine the schedule for subsequent appointments.

11. *Reservation of Jurisdiction:* This Court specifically reserves jurisdiction to enforce and/or modify the terms and conditions of this Order.

DONE AND ORDERED in ________ County, Florida, on this ___ day of ________, 2015.

____
General Magistrate

Copies furnished to:
Name of Parties:
Counsel for Parties
Address of Counsel
Guardian Ad Litem
Address of GAL

ATTACHMENT

IN THE CIRCUIT COURT OF THE EIGHTEENTH JUDICIAL CIRCUIT, IN AND FOR ________ COUNTY, FLORIDA.

CASE NO.: ________________

________,
Petitioner,
and
________,
Respondent.

RESPONSE BY PARENTING COORDINATOR

I, {*name*} ________ notify the Court and affirm the following:

1. **Acceptance.**

[Choose only *one*]

a. ___ I accept the appointment as parenting coordinator.

b. ___ I decline the appointment as parenting coordinator.

2. **Qualifications.**

[Choose only *one*]

a. ___ I meet the qualifications in section 61.125(4), Florida Statutes.

b. ___ I do not meet the qualifications in section 61.125(4), Florida Statutes. However, the parties have chosen me by mutual consent and I believe I can perform the services of a parenting coordinator because:

____

____

3. I am not aware of any conflict, circumstance, or reason that renders me unable to serve as the parenting coordinator

in this matter and I will immediately inform the court and the parties if such arises.

4. I understand my role, responsibility, and authority under the Order of Referral to Parenting Coordinator; Florida Family Law Rules of Procedure Form 12.984(a); section 61.125, Florida Statutes; Florida Family Law Rule of Procedure 12.742; and Rules for Qualified and Court Appointed Parenting Coordinators.

I hereby affirm the truth of the statements in this acceptance and understand that if I make any false representations in this acceptance, I am subject to sanctions by the Court.

______________ ______________
Date Signature

Printed Name: ______________

Address: ______________

City, State, Zip: ______________

Telephone Number: ______________

Email: ______________

Professional License # (if applicable) ______________

Professional Certification # (if applicable) ______________

IF A NONLAWYER HELPED YOU FILL OUT THIS FORM, HE/SHE MUST FILL IN THE BLANKS BELOW: [fill in *all* blanks]

Copies to:

Attorney for Parent #1 OR Parent #1 if not represented by Counsel

Attorney for Parent #2 OR Parent #2 if not represented by Counsel

I, {*full legal name and trade name of nonlawyer*} ________, a nonlawyer, whose address is {*street*} ________, {*city*} ________, {*state*} ________,{*phone*} ________, helped {*name*} ________, who is the parenting coordinator, fill out this form.

1 So in original.
2 So in original.

15–15–B. CRIMINAL—NOTICE OF EXPIRATION OF SPEEDY TRIAL/MOTION FOR DISCHARGE/DEMAND FOR SPEEDY TRIAL

IN THE CIRCUIT COURT OF THE EIGHTEENTH JUDICIAL CIRCUIT IN AND OF BREVARD COUNTY FLORIDA

ADMINISTRATIVE ORDER NO.: 15–15–B
SUPERSEDES 93–93–Cr–B

IN RE: CRIMINAL—NOTICE OF EXPIRATION OF SPEEDY TRIAL/MOTION FOR DISCHARGE/DEMAND FOR SPEEDY TRIAL

WHEREAS, notices of expiration of speedy trial, motions for discharge and demands for speedy trial in criminal cases often require expedited hearings; and,

WHEREAS, attorneys representing criminal defendants have on occasion included notices of expiration of speedy trial, motions for discharge, and demands for speedy trial together with other motions, resulting in routine scheduling of hearings on said motions; and,

WHEREAS, there have been delays in the scheduling of notices of expiration of speedy trial, motions for discharge, and demands for speedy trial it is hereby:

ORDERED that;

1. All notices of expiration of speedy trial, motions for discharge, and demands for speedy trial shall be filed as separate pleadings with correct descriptive titles.

2. The attorneys filing notices of expiration of speedy trial, motions for discharge, and demands for speedy trial, are to immediately provide the judge to whom the case is assigned a copy of said motion within 24 hours of filing, by hand delivery or email.

3. The Clerk of Court shall provide the judge to whom a criminal case is assigned by electronic means, copies of notices of expiration of speedy trial, motions for discharge, and demands for speedy trial within 24 hours of filing.

Done and Ordered this 27th day of January, 2015.

____
JOHN M. HARRIS
CHIEF JUDGE

15–13–S. CRIMINAL—EMPACT–ELECTRONIC MONITORING OF DEFENDANTS AS A CONDITION OF PRE–TRIAL RELEASE—GENERAL GUIDELINES AND SPECIFICALLY IN DOMESTIC VIOLENCE MATTERS

IN THE CIRCUIT COURT OF THE EIGHTEENTH JUDICIAL CIRCUIT IN AND FOR SEMINOLE COUNTY, FLORIDA

ADMINISTRATIVE ORDER NO.: 15–13–S
SUPERSEDES 14–07 S

IN RE: CRIMINAL—EMPACT–ELECTRONIC MONITORING OF DEFENDANTS AS A CONDITION OF PRETRIAL RELEASE—GENERAL GUIDELINES AND SPECIFICALLY IN DOMESTIC VIOLENCE MATTERS

Whereas, most criminal defendants are entitled to be released from custody pending disposition of the charges for which they were arrested; and

Whereas, the Seminole County Sheriff, and the Seminole County Probation Division, under the Florida Rule of Criminal Procedure 3.131(b)(1)(d), have the capability to electronically monitor defendants who are released from custody by nonintrusive means through a program known as Electronic Monitoring Protection and Crime Tracking (EMPACT); and Whereas, electronic monitoring can provide timely information to law enforcement regarding the activities of a defendant as they relate to compliance with conditions of release, including abstinence from criminal activity; and

Whereas, the Seminole County Sheriff and the State Attorney have requested authority to require defendants who meet specified criteria to be electronically monitored as a condition of pretrial release, in addition to reasonable or reduced bond, but not in lieu of bond, without compliance with the investigation and recommendation required by F.S. 907.041(3)(b); and

Whereas, F.S. 903.046 and Florida Rule of Criminal Procedure 3.131(b) permit the imposition of reasonable conditions of pretrial release that will protect the community from risk of physical harm to persons, assure the presence of the accused at trial or assure the integrity of the judicial process; and

Whereas, it is estimated that more than 1.3 million women are victims of physical assault by an intimate partner each year; and in 2006, in the State of Florida, there were 115,170 reported cases of domestic violence, 164 of which were domestic-related homicides; and from January, 2007, to July 2008, there were over 3,000 domestic violence incidents in Seminole County, of which 2,768 resulted in an arrest or criminal charges filed against the defendant; and since 2006, 13 Seminole County residents have fallen victim to domestic-related homicides and 7 domestic-related attempted homicides; and

Whereas, domestic violence is pervasive throughout our society and the use of electronic monitoring devices provides a non-intrusive method of monitoring an individual and has been proven to modify the behavior of certain defendants; and

Whereas, the Seminole County Sheriff's Office implemented such a program in 2003 known as EMPACT (Electronic Monitoring Protection and Crime Tracking), as a pretrial release condition for certain qualified defendants; and since that time the program has expanded to include a domestic violence and dating violence program, or DV EMPACT, which introduces an additional level of security by offering the ability to immediately notify the victim, law enforcement, and others of certain specified violations perpetrated by a defendant; and although this initiative should not be considered a failsafe assurance on behalf of the victim, it does provide a near to real time accounting of the defendant's whereabouts and activities, thereby enhancing both the security of the victim and the responsibility of the defendant to answer for violations of conditions of pretrial release;

Now, therefore, after due consideration,

IT IS ADJUDGED;

The following procedures and criteria shall be followed when defendants are released from custody by the Court upon the condition that they submit to electronic monitoring under the EMPACT program or other monitoring program and more specifically, shall be followed when defendants are released from custody by the Court upon the condition that they submit to electronic monitoring under the DV EMPACT program or similar electronic monitoring program approved by the Seminole County Sheriff:

1. The defendant must have a residence. The residence must have an operational telephone line if the electronic monitor requires a telephone line.

2. The defendant must be a resident of Seminole County, Florida, or have made arrangements to live in the contiguous counties of Lake, Orange, Brevard, Osceola, Polk or Volusia upon Court approval with verification that the electronic monitor program covers the defendant's new residence.

3. Defendants who have a serious medical condition that requires frequent care, or who are identified as psychotic, severely mentally retarded, currently suicidal, mentally incapable or unable to cope with the structure of electronic monitoring shall not be placed on an electronic monitor. Any Defendant that the Sheriff, any Police Agency in Seminole County, or the Seminole County Probation Division, determines is not mentally capable to cope with the structure of electronic monitoring shall notify the court immediately. The Defendant shall not be released until a further determination is made by the Court as to the Defendant's release conditions.

4. Defendants who have a condition of release to participate in the EMPACT or another electronic monitoring program shall be responsible for any damage or loss to equipment issued and shall pay a per diem cost to Seminole County.

5. The Seminole County Sheriff's Office and Seminole County Probation Division shall be responsible for collection of any fees related to the EMPACT program. In the event of non-payment for electronic monitoring services the Seminole County Sheriff's Office or Seminole County Probation Division may notify the Court of the Defendant's non-indigent status and recommend review by the Court.

6. The following categories of defendants may be placed upon electronic monitoring as a condition of pretrial release only after considering the availability of electronic monitoring equipment and the risk the defendant presents to the victim or the community:

A. Defendants with a pending violation of probation on a case involving domestic violence when the violation involves violence, unauthorized contact with the victim, or coming onto property forbidden by the probation order.

B. Defendants who have been taken into custody for violation of an injunction for protection against domestic violence, repeat violence, or dating violence.

C. Defendants who have been taken into custody for any domestic violence related offense.

D. Defendants who have been charged with stalking/aggravated stalking, with notice to the victim.

E. Any Defendant where the Court finds that the facts and circumstances warrant such monitoring.

7. Any defendant who breaches a condition of release while on electronic monitoring in a domestic violence case shall be taken into custody by any law enforcement officer upon probable cause and held until first appearance as provided by F.S. 901.15(13), F.S. 903.0471, and Seminole County Administrative Order Bail Schedule. In the event of a suspected breach of a condition of electronic monitoring, the Seminole County Sheriff's Office or Seminole County Probation Division shall notify the Court in writing so that the violation may be brought before the Court for review. Defendants shall have been informed in their Court minutes/order placing them on EMPACT that violations include, but not be limited to:

A. Equipment tampers or removals.

B. Willful exclusion zone violations.

C. Failure to comply with any conditions of release set by the Court.

D. Failure to comply with any of the program requirements set forth by the GPS Electronic Monitoring Program.

E. The defendant must refrain from criminal conduct of any kind.

F. The defendant must not have unauthorized contact with the victim.

G. All information provided to the Court, the Sheriff and any supervising agency, must be truthful.

H. Payment of per diem costs to Seminole County Sheriff's Office.

8. This Order supersedes and repeals all prior Administrative Orders on this subject of pre-trial release monitoring.

Done and Ordered this 14th day of January, 2015.

JOHN M. HARRIS
CHIEF JUDGE

15–10–B. DOMESTIC RELATIONS—ORDERS AND JUDGMENTS IN TANDEM WITH THE POLICIES AND PROCEDURES OF THE SCHOOL BOARD OF BREVARD COUNTY

IN THE CIRCUIT COURT OF THE EIGHTEENTH JUDICIAL CIRCUIT IN AND FOR BREVARD COUNTY, FLORIDA

ADMINISTRATIVE ORDER NO.: 15–10–B

IN RE: DOMESTIC RELATIONS—ORDERS AND JUDGMENTS IN TANDEM WITH THE POLICIES AND PROCEDURES OF THE SCHOOL BOARD OF BREVARD COUNTY

WHEREAS, it is necessary that orders and judgments in the family division not impact the schools of Brevard County as well as the School Board of Brevard County, and

WHEREAS, many of the Domestic Relations cases filed or pending in Brevard County involve parents of school-age children, and

WHEREAS, disputes between parents regarding school matters often disrupt the ability of schools and their staff to conduct their primary business of educating children,

Now, it is therefore ORDERED:

1. A parent who is a party to a pending Domestic Relations action shall include the other parent's name on the school contact list when registering or enrolling a child in school in Brevard County, unless that parent has a specific court order relieving the parent of this obligation. The parent shall include the other parent's name and contact information, along with any other necessary information required by the school. Should a parent fail to comply with this requirement, the other parent may supplement the contact list with the child's school to indicate the names of both legal parents as contact persons.

2. When registering or enrolling the child in school, the parent or parents shall designate the true residence of the child.

3. Parents shall not attempt to register or enroll a child in two different schools. If the true residence of a child is disputed for school purposes, the parties may submit that issue to the court for determination as part of the pending domestic relations case.

4. No domestic relations order will be entered which requires the School Board to provide transportation to the school for the child. The rules and policies of the School Board determine whether transportation is provided.

5. Nothing in this administrative order precludes parents from jointly placing a child in the school of their mutual choice, in compliance with established school board procedures.

This administrative order supersedes all previous court orders and judgments inconsistent with it. It shall also be a standing order governing the parties in a pending domestic relations case unless or until the Court has specifically addressed an issue within the scope of this administrative order and has entered an order that is specific to the parties in that pending case which conflicts with the provisions of this order.

Done and Ordered this 12th day of January, 2015.

JOHN M. HARRIS
CHIEF JUDGE

15–07. ADMINISTRATIVE ORDERS—RESCINDS ADMINISTRATIVE ORDERS

IN THE CIRCUIT COURT OF THE EIGHTEENTH JUDICIAL CIRCUIT

ADMINISTRATIVE ORDER NO.: 15–07 SUPERSEDES ORDERS LISTED IN THIS A.O.

IN RE: ADMINISTRATIVE ORDERS—RESCINDS ADMINISTRATIVE ORDERS

WHEREAS, administrative orders from time to time become obsolete; IT IS ORDERED, that the following administrative orders are hereby rescinded:

99–1 AMENDED SUPERSEDES 99–1: In Re: Clerk of Court—Use and Removal of Official Court Files from the Clerk's Office

03–26–B: In Re: Master—Appointment of General Master Valerie Brown in Brevard County Over Chapter 984 (Children and Families in Need of Services) Proceedings

09–16–B: In Re: Judges—Caseload Assignment—Reassignment of Cases Assigned to Judge Robert A. Wohn, Jr.

10–01–S: In Re: Judges—Caseload Assignment—Reassignment of Cases Assigned to Judge Alan A. Dickey

11–25–S: In Re: Judges—Caseload Assignment—Reassignment of Cases Assigned to Judge Alan A. Dickey

11–35–S: In Re: Judges—Caseload Assignment—Reassignment of Cases Assigned to Judge John D. Galluzzo

13–43–S Amended Supersedes 13–43–S: In Re: Judges—Caseload Assignment—Reassignment of Cases Assigned to Judge Alan A. Dickey

DONE AND ORDERED this 6th day of January, 2015

JOHN M. HARRIS
CHIEF JUDGE

14–39–B. CLERK OF COURT—PROCEDURES FOR PROCESSING CHILD SUPPORT PAYMENTS

IN THE CIRCUIT COURT OF THE EIGHTEENTH JUDICIAL CIRCUIT IN AND FOR BREVARD COUNTY, FLORIDA

ADMINISTRATIVE ORDER NO: 14–39–B

IN RE: CLERK OF COURT—PROCEDURES FOR PROCESSING CHILD SUPPORT PAYMENTS

The judges of Brevard County have decided that it is in the best interest of the litigants and constituents of the Family/Domestic Relations Division that the court implements a uniform method for applying payments and requiring their orderly processing by the Clerk and uniform accounting of the same.

NOW THEREFORE I, John M. Harris, pursuant to the authority vested in me as Chief Judge of the Eighteenth Judicial Circuit under Rule 2.050, Fla.R.Jud.Admin, cause the same to take effect and

IT IS ORDERED:

1. For the purpose of ensuring that the Clerk's administrative fees under Section 61.181, Florida Statutes are correctly deducted from the child support payments made directly to the Clerk, the Clerk shall determine the weekly rate of child support and/or arrearage amounts and shall implement this rate on a weekly basis, regardless support was calculated by the court on a biweekly, semi-monthly, monthly or other term in the support order.

2. The system shall not affect how the employer/respondent pays child support under the terms of the support order.

3. The Clerk shall be responsible for accounting for a 53–week year, when necessary.

4. This Administrative Order shall not alter or otherwise amend any portion of an order for support except otherwise provided herein.

DONE AND ORDERED this 19th day of November, 2014.

JOHN M. HARRIS
CHIEF JUDGE

14–37–B. SUPERSEDED BY ADMINISTRATIVE ORDER NO. 16-34-B

14–32–S. SUPERSEDED BY ADMINISTRATIVE ORDER NO. 15–42–S

14–31–S. CRIMINAL—PROCEDURES FOR SEARCH AND ARREST WARRANTS IN SEMINOLE COUNTY

IN THE CIRCUIT COURT OF THE EIGHTEENTH JUDICIAL CIRCUIT IN AND FOR SEMINOLE COUNTY, FLORIDA

ADMINISTRATIVE ORDER NO: 14–31–S

IN RE: CRIMINAL—PROCEDURES FOR SEARCH AND ARREST WARRANTS IN SEMINOLE COUNTY

WHEREAS it is necessary and proper for the prompt and efficient administration of justice in Seminole County to establish procedures for applying for search and arrest warrants; and

WHEREAS the Florida Legislature had authorized the use of an electronic warrant system; and

WHEREAS in the interest of speedy, efficient and proper administration of justice, Seminole County has adopted an electronic warrant system.

IT IS ORDERED as follows:

1. GENERAL PROVISIONS

a. Seminole County has adopted an electronic warrant system (hereinafter E–warrant System) as the preferred method for submitting applications for search and arrest warrants. It is anticipated all the Seminole County law enforcement agencies and Judges will eventually be approved and trained on the E–warrant System. The goal is for the majority of search and arrest warrants to be processed via the E–warrant System instead of paper submissions.

b. Law enforcement officers, who have received training and approval on the E warrant System, should use the E–warrant System.

c. Unless required by law, felony warrants are not required to be approved by the State Attorney's Office prior to submission, but it is recommended that law enforcement officers have the State review warrants prior to submission if possible.

d. A copy of the Seminole County Duty Judge roster will be provided, on a monthly basis, to the Seminole County Sheriff's Department COMM Center. Law enforcement officers should consult said roster to ascertain the name of the appropriate Judge to whom the warrant application should be directed.

e. If a Judge declines to execute a warrant based upon a finding of no probable cause, the warrant shall be presented to the same Judge if resubmitted after changes are made to the affidavit.

2. WARRANTS DURING BUSINESS HOURS—E–WARRANT SYSTEM

a. The law enforcement officer shall direct the affidavit and e-warrant to the Business Hours Duty Judge, unless the matter is ongoing, in which case they shall be directed to the Judge who granted the first warrant in the case.

b. After uploading the electronically signed sworn affidavit and e-warrant, the officer shall phone the judicial assistant (J A) for the Business Hours Duty Judge. In an ongoing case, the officer shall phone the appropriate Judge's JA. The JA will bring the matter to the Judge's attention at the earliest appropriate time. If the officer cannot reach the appropriate JA, he or she should phone Court Administration.

3. WARRANTS DURING BUSINESS HOURS—PAPER WARRANTS

a. The E–warrant System should not be used if:

1. The law enforcement officer has a good faith belief that the search or arrest warrant is exceptionally sensitive;
2. The law enforcement agency has not been trained and approved to use the E–warrant system; or
3. When the E–warrant system is not operating.

In all other circumstances, law enforcement officers are strongly encouraged to use the E–warrant System. However, law enforcement officers may, at their own discretion, elect to submit a warrant application in paper form.

b. The law enforcement officer shall direct the affidavit and warrant to the Business Hours Duty Judge, unless the matter is ongoing, in which case they shall be directed to the Judge who granted the first warrant in the case.

c. After preparing the affidavit and warrant, the officer shall phone the JA for the Business Hours Duty Judge. In an ongoing case, the officer shall phone the appropriate Judge's JA. The JA will arrange with the officer a time for the officer to see the Judge. If the officer cannot reach the appropriate JA, he or she should phone Court Administration.

4. EMERGENCY WARRANTS DURING BUSINESS HOURS

a. If an emergency exists, the law enforcement officer must advise the JA, who will immediately locate an available Judge.

b. An emergency is when the law enforcement officer has a good faith belief that unless a warrant is signed and executed immediately, it will frustrate an arrest, endanger lives, or permit the destruction of evidence.

c. The Judge will determine if the law and the totality of the circumstances require immediate attention.

5. EMERGENCY WARRANTS AFTER HOURS

a. For emergency search and arrest warrants after hours, on weekends, holidays or any time the courthouse is closed, the law enforcement officer shall contact the After–Hours Duty Judge by calling the duty judge phone. If after several attempts the officer is unable to contact the Duty Judge, the officer should call the Seminole County Sheriff's Department's COMM Center. The COMM Center will then attempt to contact the Duty Judge on their home or cell phone and notify the Judge that the officer is trying to make contact.

b. The law enforcement officer should not contact the Duty Judge until the affidavit and warrant have been prepared and/or uploaded to the E–warrant System and are ready for review and signature.

c. If the officer is using a paper warrant instead of an e-warrant, he or she should make arrangements with the Duty Judge for presenting the Judge with the affidavit and warrant.

Done and Ordered this 4th day of August, 2014.

JOHN M. HARRIS
CHIEF JUDGE

14–30. ADMINISTRATIVE PROCEDURES—ESTABLISHMENT OF LOCAL PROFESSIONALISM PANEL

PROFESSIONALISM IN THE CIRCUIT COURT OF FLORIDA, EIGHTEENTH JUDICIAL CIRCUIT

ADMINISTRATIVE ORDER NO.: 14–30

IN RE: ADMINISTRATIVE PROCEDURES—ESTABLISHMENT OF LOCAL PROFESSIONALISM PANEL

WHEREAS, in order to provide effective coordination of professionalism programs and activities throughout the Eighteenth Judicial Circuit and in accordance with the Florida Supreme Court's Administrative Order entitled In Re: Commission on Professionalism, dated June 11, 1998, mandating the establishment of a local Professionalism Committee in each judicial circuit; and

WHEREAS, the Chief Judge, in and for the Eighteenth Judicial Circuit shall serve as the Chair of the Eighteenth Circuit Professional Committee; and

WHEREAS, in the interest of promoting professionalism, a Professionalism Committee allows the bench and the Bar to coordinate professional activities for lawyers and judges in furtherance of and in an effort to maintain the highest standards of professionalism in the Eighteenth Circuit; and

WHEREAS, on June 6, 2013, the Florida Supreme Court entered Administrative Order No.: SC13–688 In Re: Code for Resolving Professionalism Complaints, mandating that a local subdivision of the Eighteenth Circuit Professionalism Committee be developed in each county of the Eighteenth Judicial Circuit to receive, screen and act upon complaints of unprofessional conduct and resolve those complaints informally, if possible, or refer them to The Florida Bar if necessary.

NOW THEREFORE, I, JOHN M. HARRIS, as Chief Judge of the Eighteenth Judicial Circuit of Florida and in accordance with Florida Rules of Judicial Administration 2.215(b)(2), hereby order the establishment of a separate Local Professionalism Panel (hereinafter referred to as "Panel") for Brevard and Seminole counties in the Eighteenth Judicial Circuit. The Panel shall be an entity independent of the Florida Bar, established at the local level for the purpose of resolving complaints of alleged unprofessional conduct amongst members of the Bar practicing in that circuit.

IT IS FURTHER ORDERED as follows:

1. A Panel consisting of respected attorneys in the community will be used to address alleged instances of improper conduct and will conduct proceedings in a constructive, non-punitive fashion.

2. Brevard and Seminole county shall each establish a Panel which shall operate under the guidance and supervision of the Eighteenth Circuit Chief Judge and the Eighteenth Circuit Professionalism Committee.

3. Each Panel shall consist of no less than seven (7) members of the Florida Bar in good standing in each of their respective counties, with one Panel member designated as the Panel Chair, as selected by the Chief Judge of the Circuit.

4. One member of each Panel shall serve as the Panel liaison and be responsible for communicating between the Chief Judge and the Circuit Professionalism Committee Chair, the Panel Chair and the Panel members. The liaison shall be responsible for coordinating meetings and distributing information. The liaison shall be the Panel Chair or his designee.

5. All Panel members shall be selected by the Chief Judge and/or Circuit Professionalism Chair.

6. Initially, all members of the Panel, other than the Panel Chair, shall be appointed to serve a one-year renewable term. The Panel Chair shall be appointed to serve a two-year renewable term. There are no term limits, the Chief Judge will appoint the Panel Chair at his discretion and appoint all Panel members.

7. Participation by attorneys on the Panel is strictly voluntary.

8. Appearances by attorneys before the Panel are also strictly voluntary but essential for the process to succeed and therefore are encouraged.

9. The judges of the Eighteenth Judicial Circuit may refer cases of perceived improper attorney conduct to the Panel for resolution, but are not obligated to make such referrals.

10. Each of the Eighteenth Judicial Circuit Local Professionalism Panels, for Brevard and Seminole counties, will otherwise be governed by the internal operating procedures attached hereto.

DONE AND ORDERED in this 24th day of July, 2014.

JOHN M. HARRIS
CHIEF JUDGE

EIGHTEENTH JUDICIAL CIRCUIT

PROFESSIONALISM COMMITTEE LOCAL PROFESSIONALISM PANEL

1. Standards and Purpose: The purpose of the Local Professionalism Panel (hereinafter referred to as "Panel") in the Eighteenth Judicial Circuit is to enhance professionalism among members of the Florida Bar practicing in this circuit. The Panel recognizes that the Rules Regulating the Florida Bar identify a minimal level of conduct and ethical standards for members of the Bar, failing which members may be subject to discipline. The Panel is not intended to address conduct that may violate these Rules. It is designed to encourage compliance with aspirational goals identified in:

a. "Ideals and Standards of Professional" promulgated by The Florida Bar;

b. "Guidelines for Professional Conduct" promulgated by The Trial Lawyers Section of The Florida Bar; and

c. Professionalism guidelines developed by the voluntary bar associations within the Eighteenth Judicial Circuit.

2. Initiation of a Complaint:

a. Attorneys may initiate a written complaint, signed by the attorney who observes the alleged conduct in question. Attorneys are encouraged, prior to referring conduct to the Panel, to discuss the situation with the other attorney involved in an effort to reach an amicable resolution consistent with the above-referenced professionalism standards and guidelines.

b. Judges, at their discretion, may also refer conduct for consideration by the Panel by initiating a signed, written complaint. Alternatively Judges may directly respond and/or provide advice with regard to conduct observed by the Judge that the Judge believes may be inconsistent with the above-referenced professionalism standards and guidelines.

c. The form required for initiation of a complaint is attached as Exhibit "A."

3. Procedure to Form Panel:

Complaints will be considered by the Panel consisting of no less than seven (7) members selected by the Chief Judge. A quorum for purposes of attorney review shall be comprised of at least three (3) members of the Panel who are in good standing with the Florida Bar plus the Panel Chair. The Chief Judge will appoint a Panel Chair for each county. The Panel must include at least one member who practices within the same field of specialty as the individual who is the subject of the complaint. Therefore, Panel additions are allowed if necessary during a term.

4. Review:

a. All complaints must be made in writing and submitted to the Panel via the Chief Judge of the Circuit or the Professionalism Committee Chair.

b. The Chief Judge will refer the complaint to the Panel Chair who will review the complaint and consult with the other members of the Panel to determine if any action should be taken. If, by majority, the Panel determines that the complaint may be resolved by a telephone consultation with the lawyer who is the subject of the complaint, or by an informal meeting, the matter may be resolved informally by such means.

c. In the event the complaint is not resolved by an informal telephone call, and a meeting (formal or informal) is required, the lawyer who is subject of the complaint will be furnished with a copy of the complaint and provided an opportunity to submit a written response.

d. If, by majority, the Panel determines that the complaint presents a serious violation, then the Panel will contact the referring lawyer and the lawyer who is the subject of the complaint and schedule a formal hearing. At said hearing, each party will have an opportunity to attend and present their positions. The hearing may be conducted with both the referring lawyer and the lawyer subject to the complaint present, in a mediation format, or in such other format as the Panel deems appropriate.

e. Upon conclusion of a formal hearing, the Panel will issue a written decision and submit it to the Chief Judge. Copies will be provided to both the referring lawyer and the lawyer who is the subject of the complaint. Among other things, the Panel may refer the subject lawyer to a mentor, and/or to Florida Lawyers Assistance, Inc., or The Florida Bar's Attorney Consumer Assistance Program.

5. Records:

A written record including the complaint, responses (if any), formal decision (if any), and memo outlining the resolution of the complaint, will be maintained by the Chief Judge for a period of sixty (60) days, after which said record will be destroyed. The Chief Judge will maintain Panel records, in docket form, identifying the complaint file number, the date the complaint was made, the manner in which the complaint was made, the manner in which the complaint was resolved, and the date of the resolution. These Panel records will **not** include the names of the referring or subject lawyers, but will be maintained in accordance with Rule 2.440, Florida Rules of Judicial Administration.

6. Confidentiality:

All Panel members, referring lawyers, and subject lawyers will be required to sign statements acknowledging:

a. Information disclosed during the Panel process is confidential and may not be disclosed to anyone except other Panel members, the referring lawyer, or the subject lawyers, and

b. The Panel conducts a voluntary, informal process intended to be non-punitive, educational and constructive. It will not result in the imposition of sanctions or discipline.

EXHIBIT "A"

LOCAL PROFESSIONALISM PANEL COMPLAINT FORM

Submit form to: (Check One)

___ Chief Judge, 18th Circuit

___ Brevard County Professionalism Committee Chair

___ Seminole County Professionalism Committee Chair

1. **Referring Attorney**:

Your Name: ______________________

Bar No.: ______________________

Address: ______________________

____

Telephone: ______________________

Fax: ______________________

☐ Check this box if you wish to discuss this issue with the Panel Chair of the Local Professionalism Panel prior to making a written complaint. Such discussions will be off the record and you may thereafter elect not to proceed with a written complaint. However, the Local Professionalism Panel cannot take formal action on an issue unless a written complaint is filed, including items 2 & 3 below.

2. **Attorney Being Referred**:

Name (if more than one, attach information to this form)

Name: ______________________

Bar No.: (if known) ______________________

Address: ______________________

____

Telephone: ______________________

Fax: ______________________

NOTE: THIS IS NOT A DISCIPLINARY PROCEEDING

3. **Alleged Violation** (please refer to specific Bar association guidelines, if possible): Use the reverse side of this form or attach additional pages if necessary. Please try to be brief, factual and non-judgmental. Please list and attach any papers requiring consideration or needed for clarification of the allegations discussed.

____

____

____

____

Signed ______________ Date: ______________

14–22–B. SUPERSEDED BY ADMINISTRATIVE ORDER NO. 16-32-B

14–18–B. PROCESS SERVERS—PROCEDURES FOR APPOINTMENT OF CERTIFIED PROCESS SERVERS AND GRIEVANCES

IN THE CIRCUIT COURT OF THE EIGHTEENTH JUDICIAL CIRCUIT IN AND FOR BREVARD COUNTY, FLORIDA

ADMINISTRATIVE ORDER NO: 14–18–B
SUPERSEDES 08–19–B Amended

IN RE: PROCESS SERVERS—PROCEDURES FOR APPOINTMENT OF CERTIFIED PROCESS SERVERS AND GRIEVANCES

WHEREAS, Secs. 48.25–48.31, Florida Statutes, authorizes the Chief Judge of each Circuit to qualify, appoint and remove certified process servers in the respective Circuits, it is therefore

ORDERED AND ADJUDGED that pursuant to the authority vested in me as Chief Judge of the Eighteenth Judicial Circuit of Florida, there shall be established an approved list of certified process servers, for Brevard County, who may be chosen by counsel without the necessity of a motion and order in each individual case, pursuant to the following requirements:

I. QUALIFICATION OF CERTIFIED PROCESS SERVERS TO BE INCLUDED ON THE APPROVED LIST. The prospective certified process server must meet and comply with the following requirements:

a. Be at least 18 years of age;

b. Have no mental or legal disability;

c. Be a permanent resident of the State of Florida;

d. Within the 5 years preceding application has not been convicted of any felony.

e. Within the 5 years preceding application, has not been convicted of a misdemeanor involving moral turpitude or dishonesty or a violation of the laws relating to controlled substances;

f. Applicant must complete with a passing grade an orientation program in service of process conducted by a designated representative of the Sheriff's Office and file with the Clerk of Court a certificate of successful completion of that program. The Orientation certificate will expire one year after date of testing. If applicant does not activate the new process server certification within that period of time, they must retake the orientation program.

g. File with the Clerk of Court proof that the applicant has obtained a bond in the amount of $5,000 with said bond to remain in effect as long as the certified process server is authorized to act. A certified process server, and if applicable, the employing agency, must notify the Clerk of Court if the bond lapses for any reason during the period of appointment.

h. Take and file with the Clerk of Court an oath of office that he/she will honestly, diligently, and faithfully fulfill the duties of a certified process server.

II. APPLICATION FOR APPOINTMENT. Any individual seeking appointment as a certified process server under this Order shall make his/her request for such appointment to the Clerk of Court. Such application shall be in affidavit form, filed with the Clerk of Court and shall include the following information:

a. The applicant's name, date of birth, and social security number.

b. The applicant's residence and business addresses and telephone numbers.

c. The names, addresses, and telephone numbers of the applicant's immediate supervisor and employer, if applicable.

d. The documents required by Paragraphs I (a) through (h) above.

e. The applicant must certify that the original has been delivered to the Clerk of Court.

f. Each application shall include non-refundable processing fees made payable to the Clerk of Court and Sheriff's Department (required to do the applicant's background check), Said fees shall be forwarded to the appropriate Clerk and Sheriff if the application facially meets the requirements set forth herein. If the application does not facially meet said requirements, the fees shall be returned to the applicant with the deficiencies pointed out.

III. BACKGROUND CHECK OF CERTIFIED PROCESS SERVER. Upon receiving application, the Sheriff's Office shall conduct a background investigation of the applicant. The investigation will include, but is not limited to, a check of criminal records and fingerprints. The Sheriff will advise the Clerk of Court of the results of the background investigation. The investigating role by the Sheriff's Office does not imply or create any right of control by the Sheriff over the certified process server. Neither the Sheriff, Clerk of Court, nor the Chief Judge or his/her designee, by virtue of this Order, shall bear any civil liability for a certified process server's action.

IV. APPOINTMENT

a. Upon the filing of the application and all supporting documents in proper form the Clerk of Court will submit an order to the Chief Judge or his/her designee who will either deny the application or grant same by Order. The Clerk of Court will add the successful applicant's name to the list of certified process servers. The Clerk of Court shall maintain a current list of the certified process servers.

b. The Clerk of Court shall issue an identification card to each certified process server bearing his/her identification number, printed name, signature, photograph, seal of the Circuit Court and an expiration date.

c. Proof of a $5,000 bond shall be filed with the Clerk of Court.

V. DUTIES. Each certified process server shall comply with all of the duties and responsibilities of certified process servers set forth in Sec.48.25 through 48.31 Florida Statutes and this Order, as the same now exists, and as it may hereafter be amended or modified.

VI. PERIOD OF APPOINTMENT. Any appointment granted under this Order, shall be valid until the expiration of the Order of Appointment, not to exceed a period of one year.

VII. RENEWAL

a. Persons appointed under this order may apply for renewal of appointment prior to, or upon, expiration of the Order of Appointment. Effective May 1, 2014, the applicant must attend and successfully complete an annual renewal program prior to the expiration of the date of the Order of Appointment. Said request for renewal shall contain all information required by Paragraph II a-f, above, shall be sent to the Clerk of Court and shall contain non-refundable processing fees payable to the Clerk, and the Sheriff. The Sheriff shall conduct such background information of the applicant as Sheriff deems necessary to determine the applicant's continued fitness and promptly report to the Clerk of Court a written evaluation by the Sheriff. Upon compliance, as determined by the Chief Judge, through the Clerk of Court, the certified process server shall continue in good standing until the expiration of the Order renewing appointment, have his/her identification card with new expiration date renewed by the Clerk of Court, and the name of the certified process server shall be continued on the list maintained by the Clerk of Court and the Court Administration office. Failure to renew properly shall cause the name of the certified process server automatically to be removed from the list and such person shall lose all standing as a certified **process server to and until such time as standing is re-established. If a certified process server does not attend and successfully complete an annual renewal program prior to the expiration date of the Order of Appointment, the applicant must submit to an orientation program and begin the process as if a new applicant.**

VIII. MAINTENANCE OF APPROVED LIST AND RELATED RECORDS

a. The Clerk of Court and the Court Administration office shall maintain for public inspection a current list of all persons authorized to act as a certified process server in Brevard County pursuant to the Order of Appointment or renewal signed by the Chief Judge or his/her designee.

b. The Clerk of Court shall maintain for public inspection a file containing copies of all approved applications, a file containing all Orders appointing individuals to the approved list of certified process servers, a file containing all Orders denying appointment, and a file containing all Orders removing individuals from the approved list of certified process servers.

c. The Clerk of Court for Brevard County shall provide a copy of the list of certified process servers to the Sheriff of Seminole County, the Seminole County Clerk of Court, and Court Administration in Brevard and Seminole Counties.

IX. REMOVAL FROM LIST OF CERTIFIED PROCESS SERVERS

Section 48.31(1), Florida Statutes, provides that "a certified process server may be removed from the list of certified process servers for any malfeasance, misfeasance, neglect of duty, or incompetence, as provided by court rule," and;

Section 48.29(4), Florida Statutes, provides that the chief judge of the circuit may, from time to time by administrative order, prescribe additional rules and requirements regarding the eligibility of a person to become a certified process server, and;

A certified process server may be removed from the list of process servers, and the process server's certification revoked, for any malfeasance, misfeasance, and neglect of duty or incompetence. Upon any complaint made, or on the chief judge's own motion, an order to show cause setting forth the grounds for the suggested removal may be directed to any certified process server by ordinary U.S. Mail to the process server's address set forth in the application, requiring that the process server appear before the chief judge at a time set and place to show cause why the process server should not be removed from said list. The chief judge shall conduct a hearing at which the process server may appear and offer evidence. The hearing shall be summary in nature, and the formal rules of evidence shall not apply. If, from the evidence, the chief judge finds the process server guilty of malfeasance, misfeasance, neglect of duty of duty or incompetence, the chief judge or circuit court judge designated by the chief judge may order the process server to be removed from the list and revoke the prior certification.

DONE AND ORDERED this 19th day of March, 2014.

JOHN M. HARRIS
CHIEF JUDGE

14–05. [SUPERSEDED BY ORDER 19–11, EFFECTIVE JANUARY 24, 2019]

14–04 (A1). DOMESTIC RELATIONS—COLLABORATIVE CONFLICT RESOLUTION IN DISSOLUTION OF MARRIAGE CASES

IN THE CIRCUIT COURT OF THE EIGHTEENTH JUDICIAL CIRCUIT

ADMINISTRATIVE ORDER NO. 14–04 AMENDED

SUPERSEDES 14–04

IN RE: DOMESTIC RELATIONS—COLLABORATIVE CONFLICT RESOLUTION IN DISSOLUTION OF MARRIAGE CASES

WHEREAS the courts of the Eighteenth Judicial Circuit believe that the collaborative conflict alternative dispute resolution model may be a suitable alternative to full scale adversarial litigation in cases involving dissolution of marriage should the parties so agree and

WHEREAS beginning in the 1990's the collaborative conflict alternative dispute resolution model has been adopted in several states both by common law and by statute, in the United States of America and

WHEREAS by means of example the Chief Judge of the State of New York Judith S. Kaye in her 2007 State of the Judiciary address stated the following concerning collaborative conflict alternative dispute resolution at page 11 of her 27–page address on February 26, 2007:

Collaborative Family Law Center

"Finally in the area of matrimonials, the Miller Commission concluded that, when used appropriately, ADR can reduce the delay expense and trauma of divorce. Following upon that conclusion, this year we will open the first court-based Collaborative Family Law Center in the nation. Parties and their attorneys who participate in this process agree, either before commencing an action or on court referral, to use their best efforts to resolve all issues relating to dissolution of marriage with minimum conflict and without litigation. The end result is a settlement agreement, which can then be used to obtain a divorce.

Our new Center, situated in downtown Manhattan, will serve New York City's five counties. There we will train attorneys, provide space for participants, and connect families with professional service such as child development specialists, financial services, mental health service and substance abuse treatment. We anticipate the spouses who choose this approach will find that the financial and emotional cost of divorce is reduced for everyone involved, surely a step in the right direction."

It is noteworthy that this Collaborative Law Center was enacted by the courts in New York without legislative approval and is a pilot project for the state.

NOW THEREFORE pursuant to the statutory authority vested in the Chief Judge by Rule 2.215 of the Florida Rules of Judicial Administration and section 43.26 Florida Statutes it is **ORDERED** that:

1. The collaborative conflict alternative resolution model is authorized to resolve dissolution of marriage, and all attendant issues therein according to the following definitions and specifications herein.

2. The collaborative conflict alternative resolution model is defined as a method of resolving dispute through structured assistance of collaborative professionals including lawyers, mental health professionals and financial planners.

3. If the parties and professionals desire to engage in collaborative conflict resolution they shall enter into a contractual commitment to negotiate a settlement without using the court system to decide any issues of the parties. A representative contractual commitment is attached hereto and made a part hereof as Exhibit 1.

4. The parties may participate in collaborative conflict alternative dispute resolution either before or after a petition for dissolution of marriage is filed. After a petition for dissolution of marriage is filed, if the parties are going to participate in collaborative conflict alternative dispute resolution, they must file the agreement to do so. That will abate court proceedings until either a hearing for an uncontested dissolution of marriage or a motion to withdraw by counsel is heard by the court. If the collaborative conflict alternative dispute resolution process is utilized prior to filing a petition of dissolution, the agreement must be filed when the petition for dissolution of marriage is filed. Thereafter the court proceedings will be abated until a hearing for an uncontested dissolution of marriage or a motion to withdraw is heard by the court.

5. Part of that contractual agreement is that counsel will withdraw from any further representation of the parties if an agreement is not reached.

6. The mental health professionals and financial planners engaged are disqualified from testifying as witnesses, expert or otherwise, regarding the case, and their writings are inadmissible in any judicial proceedings.

7. In order for a proper resolution of the case to occur, the parties agree to make a full and candid exchange of information. This includes full disclosure of the nature and extent of all assets, liabilities, and income of the parties and all relevant information concerning the parties' children. Any material change in the information provided must be promptly updated. No formal discovery procedures will be used requiring court order.

8. The parties agree to maintain the confidentiality of any oral or written communication relating to the subject matter of the dispute made by the parties or their lawyers or other participants in the collaborative conflict alternative resolution proceedings.

9. The lawyers and consultants are entitled to be paid for their services. The parties agree to pay them as part of their contract. If necessary, one party may be asked to pay all or a disproportionate share of the fees when the assets, liabilities, and income of the parties are compared. The determination of fees is subject to the collaborative agreement process also.

10. The rules of collaborative professionals are as follows:

The mental health professional may afford the child an opportunity to voice his or her concerns. As to the parties, the mental health professional is neutral and available to both parents in coaching them on the described activities:

a. Prioritize concerns.

b. Help develop conflict resolution skills.

c. Develop co-parenting skills.

d. Enhance communication skills.

e. Reduce misunderstandings.

f. Assist in working toward resolution.

The financial professional is available to both parties and likewise neutral and will assist in the following activities:

a. Provide each party with necessary financial planning regarding the division of assets, liabilities and support, both child and spousal.

b. Provide analysis of the nature and composition of specific marital assets (e.g. retirement, capital gain consideration, tax implication, etc.).

c. Take responsibility for neutrally gathering all relevant financial information.

d. Assist development for and understanding of any valuation processes.

e. Assist with estate planning issues.

The lawyers advise and counsel their respective clients. As they guide their client through the process, they analyze choices and consequences, evaluate costs and benefits of the choices, facilitate negotiation, and create written agreements.

11. During the collaborative conflict alternative dispute resolution process, the court will not adjudicate any dispute between the parties. If an agreement is reached, counsel will ask the court to approve the settlement agreement. If a settlement agreement is not reached, all collaborative law counsel will move to withdraw from further representation. During the time the parties are engaging in collaborative conflict alternative dispute resolution procedure, the court will not set a hearing or trial in the case, or impose discovery deadlines, or require compliance with scheduling orders, or dismiss the case. If the collaborative conflict resolution procedures result in a settlement, the case will be scheduled for a hearing on an uncontested dissolution of marriage. The parties will provide status reports to the court every 90 days, beginning from the date the signed collaborative law participation agreement is filed with the clerk.

DONE AND ORDERED this 3rd day of February, 2014.

JOHN M. HARRIS
CHIEF JUDGE

"EXHIBIT 1"

COLLABORATIVE LAW PARTICIPATION AGREEMENT

PURPOSE

(PARTY 1) and (PARTY 2) (the "parties") have chosen to use Collaborative Law to resolve their family differences. (PARTY 1) has engaged (LAWYER) and (PARTY 2) has engaged (LAWYER 2) as collaborative lawyers. The parties and their lawyers acknowledge that the essence of collaborative law is the shared belief that it is in the best interests of parties and their families to commit themselves to avoiding litigation.

We adopt this conflict resolution process, which relies on honesty, cooperation, integrity, and professionalism geared toward the future well-being of the restructured family. Our goal is to eliminate the negative economic, social, and emotional consequences of litigation. We commit to the collaborative law process to resolve our differences justly and equitably.

COMMITMENTS

We commit to a collaborative problem-solving process which is based on:

1. Identification of the values, goals and interests of each party;

2. Our empowerment to make decisions;

3. The collaborative lawyers' assistance to their respective clients in identifying issues, analyzing relevant information, developing options, and understanding their consequences.

COMMUNICATIONS

We agree to effectively and honestly communicate with each other. All written and verbal communications between us will be respectful and constructive. Settlement meetings will be focused on those issues necessary to the constructive resolution of the matter. We agree not to engage in unnecessary discussions of past events.

To maintain an objective and constructive process, we agree to discuss settlement of issues with each other only in the settlement conference setting, unless we agree otherwise. Settlement issues will not be discussed at unannounced times by telephone calls or appearances at the other party's residence or place of employment. The lawyers will meet together to plan agendas for settlement meetings and to draft or review documents, but no agreements will be made by the lawyers on behalf of the parties.

We shall maintain a high standard of integrity and shall not take advantage of each other or of known mistakes, errors of fact or law, miscalculations or other inconsistencies, but shall identify and correct them. However, a party may choose not to make known an error which disadvantages only that party.

Include the next two paragraphs if a minor child is involved:

We acknowledge that inappropriate communications regarding our dispute can be harmful to our child(ren). Communication with the minor child(ren) regarding disputed issues will occur only as agreed by us and our lawyers.

Our goal is to reach an agreement that promotes the best interests of the child(ren). Neither of us will seek a custody evaluation while the matter is in the collaborative law process. No collaborative lawyer will interview the minor child(ren) unless both of us agree, and the child(ren)'s therapist or neutral child specialist, if any, approves.

ALLIED PROFESSIONALS, EXPERTS AND ADVISORS

If allied professionals, experts or advisors (hereinafter referred to as "consultants") are needed, we will engage them jointly. We may engage consultants for purposes of valuation, cash flow analysis, tax issues, parenting issues, and any other issue that requires expert advice and/or recommendations, such as coaching by mental health professionals. We will agree in advance how consultants' fees will be paid. The consultants engaged are disqualified from testifying as witnesses, expert or otherwise, regarding this matter and their writings are inadmissible in any judicial proceeding in this matter. This disqualification does not apply to individuals engaged by the parties to assist them in other matters independent of the collaborative law process, such as preparation of tax returns and estate planning.

Consultants may communicate with each other, the parties, their lawyers, and any lawyers consulted for a second opinion during the collaborative law process.

INFORMATION

We agree to make such full and candid exchange of information as is necessary to make a proper evaluation of the case, including, but not limited to, full disclosure of the nature, extent, value of—and all developments affecting—our income, assets and liabilities, and all relevant matters concerning our child(ren). Any material change in information previously provided must be promptly updated. We authorize our respective lawyers to fully disclose all information which, in the lawyer's judgment, must be provided to other participants in order to fulfill this commitment.

No formal discovery procedures will be used unless specifically agreed to in advance. However, we may be required to sign a sworn statement making full and fair disclosure of our income, assets, and debts (a sworn inventory and appraisal).

We agree to maintain the confidentiality of any oral or written communications relating to the subject matter of the dispute made by us or our lawyers or other participants in the collaborative law process, whether before or after the institution of formal judicial proceedings. The collaborative law process is a form of settlement conference involving compromise negotiations. All communications, whether oral or written, and conduct of any party, lawyer, or consultant in the collaborative process constitute compromise negotiations under section 90.408 Florida Statutes and are, therefore, inadmissible. We agree that any oral communication or written material used in or made a part of the collaborative law process will only be admissible or discoverable if it is admissible or discoverable independent of the process. This paragraph does not apply to reports of abuse or neglect required by law, or to any sworn documents prepared in this matter, or to a fully executed collaborative law settlement agreement.

A party and/or his or her collaborative lawyer is free to disclose all information to either party's successor lawyer or to a lawyer hired to render a second opinion for that party.

AGREEMENTS

We may agree to the entry of temporary orders as in other family law matters. We agree to abide by the terms of the code of conduct set out as Exhibit "A" until it is modified by court order or written agreement. We understand that this agreement shall remain enforceable as a contract between the parties and may be the basis for a claim against the party violating its terms in the event of termination of this process. In such event, the collaborative lawyers shall withdraw as lawyers of record and, if required, shall consent to the substitution of litigation lawyers.

Any written agreement, whether partial or final, which is signed by us and our respective collaborative lawyers, may be filed with the court as a collaborative law settlement agreement. Such an agreement is retroactive to the date of the written agreement and may be made as the basis of a court order. The collaborative lawyers shall cooperate in preparing the documents necessary to effectuate the parties' agreement. Either or both collaborative lawyers shall be permitted to appear in court to have agreed judgment(s) entered.

LEGAL PROCESS

Suspension of Court Intervention. The parties and the lawyers agree that court intervention shall be suspended while the parties are using collaborative law procedures. Seeking court intervention for a judicially-imposed decision regarding a disputed issue automatically terminates the process.

Court Proceedings. The lawyers' representation is limited to the collaborative law process. Once the process is terminated, neither lawyer can participate in the pending matter in any manner, nor can the lawyer subsequently represent either party in a proceeding against the other.

No motion or document will be prepared or filed which would initiate court intervention, other than a Petition for Dissolution of Marriage, an Answer and Counter Petition, and Answer thereto. No hearing shall be set thereafter, other than to enter agreed orders and judgments or to withdraw as counsel.

Termination by Party. A party who has decided to terminate the collaborative law process shall notify his or her lawyer in writing. That party's lawyer shall then give prompt written notice to the other party through his or her lawyer and the court. Upon notice of termination of the process to the other lawyer, there will be a 30–day waiting period (unless there is an emergency) before any court hearing to permit each party to engage another lawyer and make an orderly transition. All written agreements shall remain effective until modified by agreement or court order. Either party may bring this provision to the attention of the court in requesting a postponement of a hearing.

If the process is terminated, whether by a party or a lawyer, both lawyers shall withdraw from the representation. If a party chooses to terminate the collaborative process by seeking court involvement, both lawyers shall withdraw from the representation. Neither collaborative lawyer (including any lawyer associated in the practice of law with the collaborative process) may serve as a litigation lawyer in this case or in any other matters between the parties thereafter. Each lawyer will cooperate in transferring the file to a new lawyer.

Termination by Lawyer. If a party refuses to disclose the existence of information which, in the lawyer's judgment, must be provided to other participants, or proposes to take an action that would compromise the integrity of the process, the collaborative law process must be terminated. If a party refuses to do so, their respective lawyer is authorized to terminate the process.

Withdrawal of Lawyer. Either collaborative lawyer may withdraw unilaterally from the collaborative law process by giving three days' written notice to his or her client and the other collaborative lawyer. Notice of withdrawal of a collaborative lawyer does not necessarily terminate the collaborative law process; however, in order for the process to continue, the party whose lawyer has withdrawn must engage a new collaborative lawyer who will agree in writing to be bound by this Participation Agreement. If the party whose lawyer has withdrawn chooses to represent himself or herself, the collaborative law process terminates and the other lawyer must withdraw.

LAWYER'S FEES AND EXPENSES

We understand that the lawyers and consultants are entitled to be paid for their services. We agree to make funds available to pay these fees. We understand that, if necessary, one party may be asked to pay all fees (including fees of the other party's lawyer) from his or her salary or from separate funds. We agree that, to the extent possible, all lawyers' fees and expenses (including consultant's fees) incurred by both parties shall be paid in full prior to entry of a final judgment.

UNDERSTANDINGS

We understand that each collaborative lawyer is independent from the other and each represents his or her client only in the collaborative law process. We further understand that each collaborative lawyer is an advocate for his or her client only. No legal duty, by contract or otherwise, is owed to a party by the other party's collaborative lawyer. No lawyer-client relationship exists between one party's collaborative lawyer and the other party by virtue of this Participation Agreement or the collaborative process.

We acknowledge that there is no guarantee that the collaborative process will be successful in resolving the matter. The process cannot eliminate concerns about the differences that have led to the current conflict. We are expected to assert their own interests and their respective collaborative lawyers will help each of them to do so. The process, even with full and honest disclosure, can involve intense good-faith negotiation, but best efforts will be used to create proposals that meet the interests of both parties. Compromise may be needed to reach a settlement of all issues. Although the likely outcome of a litigated result may be discussed, the threat of litigation will not be used.

We understand that by agreeing to this process, we are giving up certain rights, including the right to conduct formal discovery, the right to participate in adversarial court hearings and other procedures provided by the adversarial legal system, unless the process is terminated. The terms of this agreement may be modified only by written agreement signed by all participants. However, the prohibition against either lawyer representing their client in contested matters against the other party may not be modified. Both parties and their respective collaborative lawyers hereby pledge to comply with and to promote the spirit and letter of this agreement. Both parties and their collaborative lawyers acknowledge that they have read this agreement, understand its terms and conditions, and agree to abide by them.

Signed on _________.

____________________	____________________
(PARTY 1)	(PARTY 2)
Street Address	Street Address
City, State, Zip code	City, State, Zip code

____________________	____________________
(LAWYER 1)	(LAWYER 2)
Lawyer for (PARTY 1)	Lawyer for (PARTY 2)
SBN #	SBN #
Street Address	Street Address
City, State, Zip code	City, State, Zip code
Office Phone	Office Phone
Fax Number	Fax Number

Exhibit "A"

CODE OF CONDUCT

The parties agree NOT to:

1. Communicate with the other party in an offensive manner.

2. Place telephone calls without a legitimate purpose of communication.

3. Destroy, remove, conceal, encumber, transfer, or otherwise harm or reduce the value of the property of one or both of the parties.

4. Falsify in writing or falsely record information relating to the property of either party.

5. Damage or destroy the tangible property of one or both of the parties, including any document that represents or embodies anything of value.

6. Tamper with the tangible property of one or both of the parties, including any document that represents or embodies anything of value, thereby causing monetary loss to the other party.

7. Sell, transfer, assign, mortgage, encumber, or in any other manner alienate any of the property of either party, whether personally [1] or realty, and whether separate or community, except as specifically agreed to in writing.

8. Incur any indebtedness, including but not limited to borrowing against any credit line or unreasonably using credit cards or cash advances against credit or bank cards, except as specifically agreed to in writing, or as specified in this agreement.

9. Make withdrawals from any checking or savings account in any financial institution for any purpose, except as specifically agreed to in writing, or as specified in this agreement.

10. Spend any sum of cash in the possession of or subject to the control of either party for any purpose, except as specifically agreed to in writing, or as specified in this agreement.

11. Withdraw or borrow in any manner for any purpose from any retirement, profit-sharing, pension, death, or other employee benefit plan or employee savings plan or from any individual retirement account or Keogh account, except as specifically agreed to in writing.

12. Enter any safe-deposit box in the name of or subject to the control of either party, whether individually or jointly with others, unless the parties accompany each other and jointly enter the box for the sole purpose of inventorying or dividing its contents by mutual agreement.

13. Withdraw or borrow in any manner all or any part of the case surrender value of life insurance policies on the life of either party, except as specifically agreed to in writing.

14. Change or in any manner alter the beneficiary designation on any pension, retirement plan or insurance policy, except as specifically agreed to in writing.

15. Cancel, alter, fail to renew or pay premium, permit to lapse or in any manner affect or reduce the value of the present level of coverage of any life, disability, casualty, automobile, or health insurance policies insuring the parties' property or persons, except as specifically agreed to in writing.

16. Change any provisions of any existing trust or will or execute a new trust or will without the prior written consent of the other party.

17. Terminate or in any manner affect the service of water, electricity, gas, telephone, cable, television, or other contractual services, such as security, pest control, landscaping, or yard maintenance, at the residence of the other party or in any manner attempt to withdraw any deposits for service in connection with those services, except as specifically agreed to in writing.

18. Exclude the other party from the use and enjoyment of his or her respective residence.

19. Enter or remain on the premises of the residence of the other party without the other's consent.

20. Open or divert mail addressed to the other party, except as specifically agreed to in writing.

21. Sign or endorse the other party's name on any negotiable instrument, check, or draft, such as tax refunds, insurance payments, and dividends, or attempt to negotiate any negotiable instrument payable to the parties or the other party without the personal signature of the other party.

22. Take any action to terminate or limit credit or charge cards in the name of the parties or the other party, except as specifically agreed to in writing.

23. Transfer balances between credit cards or open new credit card amounts, except as specifically agreed to in advance in writing by the parties.

24. Pay more than the outstanding balance owed on a credit card or charge account, except as specifically agreed to in writing.

25. Take any actions to freeze or put a hold on any account with any financial institution from which the other party has the right to withdraw funds for purposes consistent with the authorizations contained in this agreement.

26. Operate or exercise control over the motor vehicles in the possession of the other party, except as specifically agreed to by the parties.

27. Discontinue or reduce the withholding for federal income taxes on either party's wages or salary, except as specifically agreed to in writing.

28. Destroy, dispose of, or alter any financial records of the parties, including but not limited to records from financial institutions (including canceled checks and deposit slips), all records of credit purchases or cash advances, tax returns, and financial statements.

29. Destroy, dispose of, or alter any relevant e-mail or other electronic data, whether stored on a hard drive or on a diskette or other electronic storage device.

30. Conduct surveillance of the other party's activities, including the use of an investigator, detective or other individual paid for or engaged by a party or third party, or use of electronic listening or tracking devices until this collaborative law process is terminated.

31. Engage in services of a stand-by litigation lawyer so long as the collaborative law process continues.

32. Exercise any stock options and warrants except as specifically authorized in advance by written agreement of the parties.

33. Exercise any general or limited power of attorney, whether or not recorded, granted by one party to the other.

34. Pay any indebtedness owed by the parties by either of them prior to the date the indebtedness is due, unless agreed to specifically in writing by the parties.

35. Create or contribute to, or reduce the value of or withdraw from or terminate, any trust of any kind or nature except as specifically authorized in advance by written agreement of the parties.

36. Make any gift of any kind or nature, other than usual and customary gifts to family members of either party or mutual friends or their child(ren).

37. Create or contribute to any Uniform Gifts/Transfers to Minor Act accounts or any trust of any kind or nature, except as specifically agreed to in advance in writing by the parties.

38. File any extension or form with the Internal Revenue Service with regard to federal tax liability for any years of the marriage that limits the other party's choice of filing status, unless agreed to in advance in writing by the parties.

39. File any federal income tax return or amendment to any federal income tax return for any year of the marriage during the pendency of the matter without first providing a true and correct copy of such proposed return to the lawyer of record for the other party at least 14 days in advance of the proposed tender to the Internal Revenue Service. This shall apply whether or not such filing is proposed to be by electronic methods or hard copy filing.

Either party may:

1. Make expenditures and incur indebtedness for reasonable and necessary living expenses for food, clothing, shelter, transportation, entertainment, education and medical care.

2. Make expenditures and incur indebtedness for reasonable lawyer's fees and consultants' fees and expenses in connection with this matter.

3. Make withdrawals from accounts in financial institutions only for the purposes authorized by this agreement.

4. Engage in acts, make expenditures, incur indebtedness, make investments, and acquire, sell and transfer assets, as is reasonable and necessary to the conduct of either party's usual investment activities, business and occupation, subject to all such activities being fully disclosed and accounted for to the other party.

1 So in original. Probably should be "personalty".

13–42–S. SUPERSEDED BY ADMINISTRATIVE ORDER NO. 17-08-S

13–41. FORECLOSURE—CASES STATUS REPORTING REQUIREMENTS

IN THE CIRCUIT COURT OF THE EIGHTEENTH JUDICIAL CIRCUIT OF FLORIDA

ADMINISTRATIVE ORDER NO: 13–41

RE: FORECLOSURE—CASES STATUS REPORTING REQUIREMENTS

Whereas AOSC13–51 requires each chief judge to issue an administrative order establishing a mechanism that enables judges and magistrates to provide explicit direction to each clerk of court's office with regard to designating a change in the status of a foreclosure case for statistical reporting purposes,

It is ordered:

The clerk of court shall designate a foreclosure case as inactive when court activity is suspended pending resolution of an issue external to the court or an issue that does not directly involve the court in resolving that issue. Examples of events that would move a case from active to inactive are:

1. When directed by the presiding judge because resolution of the case requires resolution of a related case; ongoing settlement negotiations or agreement by the parties; or the case is on hold pending appeal

2. A stay of bankruptcy

3. Any other reason found appropriate by the presiding judge.

The clerk of court shall designate a foreclosure case as active when the criteria in the above paragraph cease to exist.

Parties to the case, judges, magistrates, and court case managers shall notify the clerk of court in writing (fax, email, letter) when they are aware that the clerk of court should change a case status from active to inactive or vice versa.

DONE AND ORDERED this 30th day of October, 2013.

JOHN M. HARRIS
CHIEF JUDGE

13–40–S. [SUPERSEDED BY ORDER 18–12–S, EFFECTIVE MARCH 8, 2018.]

13–38–B. DOMESTIC RELATIONS—FAMILY DIVISION—STANDING TEMPORARY DOMESTIC RELATIONS ORDER

IN THE CIRCUIT COURT OF THE EIGHTEENTH JUDICIAL CIRCUIT IN AND FOR BREVARD COUNTY, FLORIDA

ADMINISTRATIVE ORDER NO: 13–38–B
SUPERSEDES 08–33–B

IN RE: DOMESTIC RELATIONS—FAMILY DIVISION—STANDING TEMPORARY DOMESTIC RELATIONS ORDER

Whereas certain issues recur in actions for dissolution of marriage and other actions in which child custody is an issue raised in the pleadings of either party, and it is in the best interest of the parties and the children to order certain temporary relief, it is hereby Ordered and Adjudged as follows in all such cases:

1. Relocation of Children: Neither party shall remove, cause to be removed, or permit the removal of any minor child(ren) of the parties from the State of Florida without the written agreement of both parties or an order from the court.

2. Child Support: In many circumstances, child support will ultimately be ordered retroactive to the date the initial petition for relief was filed. To avoid the accumulation of retroactive arrearages, the court encourages the non-residential parent to immediately begin making voluntary payments of child support even prior to the entry of an order requiring payment of support. The parties should review Section 61.30 Florida Statutes to assist in determining an appropriate child support amount.

3. Non–Disparagement: Neither party shall disparage the other party to or in the presence of the minor child(ren), nor permit any third person to do so.

4. Mutual Restraining Order: Both parties are enjoined from committing any physical acts of violence against the other. Both parties are further enjoined from threatening any acts of physical violence against the other.

5. No Harassment: Both parties are enjoined from harassing the other party, whether by telephone or in person, or otherwise, at home or the other parties' place of employment or any other place the other party may be found.

6. Insurance Policies and Survivor Benefit Plans (applicable to Dissolution of Marriage cases only): Any insurance policies, including but not limited to health, auto, life, homeowners, disability, etc., in effect at the time of the filing of the Petition for Dissolution of Marriage shall not be cancelled, modified, borrowed against, pledged or otherwise encumbered by either of the parties, or at the direction of either party, unless there is written consent by both parties or an order of the court.

7. Property (applicable to Dissolution of Marriage cases only): Property generally includes all assets acquired during marriage, individually or jointly, such as gifts to each other during marriage; all vested and non-vested benefits, rights and funds accrued during marriage in retirement, pension, profit sharing, annuities, deferred compensation, insurance plans and programs; land, houses, buildings, furniture, TVs, VCRs, appliances, household furnishings, motor vehicles, boats, motorcycles, aircraft, stocks, bonds, mutual funds, money market accounts, IRAs, 401–Ks and other liquid or non-liquid assets, including cash accumulations. Neither party shall sell, donate, pledge, encumber, or otherwise dispose of any marital or non-marital property without the prior written consent of the other party or court order other than cash, checking accounts or other sources of funds customarily used to pay ongoing living expenses of the parties or marital debt or other recurring marital obligations of the parties, limited to the amounts actually required to pay those recurring obligations. Additionally, the beneficiary will not be changed in any survivor benefit plans.

8. Reading Family Law Administrative Orders: The parties to a dissolution of marriage action are required to read certain administrative orders located at the 18th Judicial Circuit website: www.flcourts18.org. The parties thereafter will file a statement with the clerk of the court that they have read the orders identified on the website. Counsel representing the parties will distribute the Standing Temporary Domestic Relations order to their clients. A pro-se petitioner who files a petition for dissolution of marriage will be furnished this order by the clerk of the court when they file a petition for dissolution of marriage.

9. Term of This Order: This order shall remain in full force and effect until the entry of a final judgment, a dismissal of the cause, or as it relates to paragraphs 1,2,3,4,5,7 and 8 until the entry of a subsequent temporary order. However, as to paragraph 6, the entry of a subsequent temporary order will not abrogate paragraph 6 remaining in full force and effect unless the judge in the temporary order specifically addressed the requirements of insurance or survivor benefit plans.

Done and Ordered this 19th day of September, 2013.

JOHN M. HARRIS
CHIEF JUDGE

13–37–B. TRAFFIC—PLEA OF NO CONTEST AND REQUEST FOR WITHHOLD OF ADJUDICATION PROGRAM

IN THE CIRCUIT COURT OF THE EIGHTEENTH JUDICIAL CIRCUIT IN AND FOR BREVARD COUNTY, FLORIDA

ADMINISTRATIVE ORDER NO.: 13–37–B

IN RE: TRAFFIC—PLEA OF NO CONTEST AND REQUEST FOR WITHHOLD OF ADJUDICATION PROGRAM

WHEREAS, it has been determined that much time and expense can be saved by instituting a program with respect to certain traffic infractions that are assigned to Civil Traffic Infraction Hearing Officers by allowing, in certain circumstances, for the defendant to plead no contest and request the Civil Traffic Infraction Hearing Officer to withhold adjudication of guilt with respect to the civil traffic infraction for which the defendant is being charged; and,

WHEREAS, the Clerk of Court of Brevard County, Florida, has agreed to implement this program in terms of the administrative aspects thereof; and,

WHEREAS, Sheriff Wayne Ivey in his capacity as Sheriff of Brevard County, Florida, as the various chiefs of police of the local law enforcement agencies in Brevard County, Florida, have indicated their support for this program, because it will save significant taxpayer dollars and free up law enforcement officers and staff to address other needs of our community; and,

WHEREAS, the Florida Rules of Traffic Court as adopted by the Supreme Court of Florida authorizes and empowers the withholding of adjudication of guilt with respect to civil infractions not otherwise prohibited by statute or rules of procedure.

WHEREAS, the fact that the defendant does not participate in the program does not mean that the defendant cannot obtain a withhold of adjudication in a hearing before the traffic hearing officer or the court.

IT IS ORDERED that Civil Traffic Infraction Hearing Officers may, in the exercise of their discretion, accept a plea of no contest and withhold adjudication of guilt with respect to civil traffic infraction violations other than those determined to have resulted in a traffic crash, a charge of driving while one's driver's license is revoked or suspended, a charge of driving with no valid driver's license, and any civil infraction that would require a mandatory hearing pursuant to the provisions of Section 318.19, Florida Statutes; and it is

FURTHER ORDERED that when a request is made by a defendant to enter a plea of no contest and withhold adjudication of guilt, the Civil Traffic Infraction Hearing Officer assigned to the case shall render a decision within sixty (60) days of the filing of the conditional plea, and it is

FURTHER ORDERED that if the law enforcement officer that issued the uniform traffic citation has opposition to the providing the defendant with the remedy of having the adjudication of guilt withheld, such officer shall note on the uniform traffic citation that the officer opposes the adjudication of guilt, and it is

FURTHER ORDERED that the Clerk of Court shall develop a form to enable a defendant to enter a plea of no contest conditioned on the Civil Traffic Infraction Hearing Officer withholding an adjudication of guilt relative to the civil traffic infraction being charged pursuant to the uniform traffic citation issued by the law enforcement officer, and it is

FURTHER ORDERED that a defendant may request that a traffic infraction hearing be held before a County Court Judge, rather than before a Civil Traffic Infraction Hearing Officer, whereupon the authority provided by this administrative order shall be equally applicable to the County Court Judge hearing the matter.

DONE AND ORDERED this 11th day of September, 2013.

JOHN M. HARRIS
CHIEF JUDGE

13–32–S. FORECLOSURE–MORTGAGE FORECLOSURE SALES—CANCELLATION BY CLERK

IN THE CIRCUIT COURT OF THE EIGHTEENTH JUDICIAL CIRCUIT IN AND FOR SEMINOLE COUNTY, FLORIDA.

ADMINISTRATIVE ORDER NO.: 13–32–S

IN RE: FORECLOSURE –MORTGAGE FORECLOSURE SALES—CANCELLATION BY CLERK

The court finds that the Clerk of the Court should not proceed with a foreclosure sale when the clerk determines the sale has not been properly published according to law or when the defendant has obtained a stay in bankruptcy, even if no order has been entered cancelling the sale, it is therefore,

ORDERED that the Clerk of this Court is not to proceed with a mortgage foreclosure sale when the clerk determines that the sale has not been properly published according to law or that a stay in bankruptcy exists.

DONE and ORDERED this 28th day of June, 2013.

ALAN A. DICKEY
CHIEF JUDGE

13–28. CRIMINAL—"THINKING FOR A CHANGE" PROGRAM IN LIEU OF PERFORMING COMMUNITY SERVICE HOURS FOR A FELONY SENTENCE

IN THE CIRCUIT COURT OF THE EIGHTEENTH JUDICIAL CIRCUIT

ADMINISTRATIVE ORDER NO.: 13–28

IN RE: CRIMINAL—"THINKING FOR A CHANGE" PROGRAM IN LIEU OF PERFORMING COMMUNITY SERVICE HOURS FOR A FELONY SENTENCE

The Department of Corrections is utilizing a Reentry Program entitled Thinking for a Change which program was developed by the National Institute of Corrections. This free program is designed to assist offenders by combining cognitive restructuring theory with cognitive skills theory to create an innovative and integrated curriculum designed to help individuals in the Criminal Justice System take control of their lives by taking control of their thinking. In the corrections field the targeted behavior is a reduction in reoffending, and cognitive behavioral interventions have been found to be an evidence-based practice for achieving this goal. The Department of Corrections is desirous of expanding this program to those individuals who are ordered to perform community service hours as part of a felony sentence.

Now, Therefore, pursuant to the authority conferred by Florida Rule of Judicial Administration 2.215, it is Ordered as follows;

1. An offender ordered to perform community service hours may choose to participate in the "Thinking for a Change" program in lieu of performing community service hours. The offender shall be credited with an hour of community service for each hour the offender attended the "Thinking for a Change" program.

2. Individuals who have been sentenced to community service as part of a felony case are eligible.

3. The Department of Corrections Court Officer shall notify the Court upon the offender completing the program.

Done and Ordered this 24TH day of JUNE, 2013.

ALAN A. DICKEY
CHIEF JUDGE

13–27–B. SUPERSEDED BY ADMINISTRATIVE ORDER NO. 16-17-B

13–24–B (A1). [SUPERSEDED BY ORDER 18–55–B, EFFECTIVE DECEMBER 20, 2018.]

13–19–B (A1). CRIMINAL—ALERTS/REPORTS FROM ELECTRONIC MONITORING COMPANIES CONCERNING POSSIBLE VIOLATIONS OF ELECTRONIC MONITORING RULES

IN THE CIRCUIT COURT OF THE EIGHTEENTH JUDICIAL CIRCUIT IN AND FOR BREVARD COUNTY, FLORIDA

ADMINISTRATIVE ORDER NO.: 13–19–B
AMENDED SUPERSEDES 13–19–B

IN RE: CRIMINAL—ALERTS/REPORTS FROM ELECTRONIC MONITORING COMPANIES CONCERNING POSSIBLE VIOLATIONS OF ELECTRONIC MONITORING RULES

WHEREAS, Article I, section 14, of the Florida Constitution, and Florida Rule of Criminal Procedure 3.131(a) provide that every person charged with a crime or violation of a municipal or county ordinance shall be entitled to pretrial release on reasonable conditions, unless the person is charged with a capital offense or an offense punishable by life imprisonment and the proof of guilt is evident or the presumption is great;

WHEREAS, section 903.046, Florida Statutes, and Rule 3.131(b), Florida Rules of Criminal Procedure permit the imposition of reasonable conditions of pretrial release;

WHEREAS, electronic monitoring is a reasonable condition that allows for pretrial release pursuant to Article I, section 14 of the Florida Constitution, while also assuring the integrity of the judicial process and assisting in protecting the community from possible risk of physical harm to persons;

WHEREAS, electronic monitoring of probationers and community controlees help defendants to conform conduct to society's requirements by discouraging behaviors that are likely to lead to new law violations or other violations of supervision, Correa v. State, 43 So. 3d 738, 745 (Fla. 2d DCA 2010);

WHEREAS, e-mail or letter notifications from electronic monitoring companies sent directly to a judge or judges that serve as notification of possible violations by defendants of electronic monitoring rules, such as, location or activity restrictions, may constitute improper ex parte and hearsay communication, see e.g. Edwards v. State, 60 So. 3d 529 (Fla. 2d DCA 2011);

WHEREAS, pursuant to Article V, section 2(d) of the Florida Constitution and section 43.26(2)(e), Florida Statutes, the Chief Judge of each judicial circuit is charged with the authority and the power to do everything necessary to promote the prompt and efficient administration of justice;

It is **ORDERED:**

1. All notifications from electronic monitoring companies of possible violations by person(s) under electronic/GPS monitoring ("alleged violators") shall be immediately and directly sent only by the electronic monitoring companies to the law enforcement entity having jurisdiction over the alleged violator.

Law Enforcement shall coordinate with the State Attorney's Office to determine what further action will be taken.

2. E-mail or letter notifications that are sent in error to the judge's office by electronic monitoring companies will not be read by the judge or the judicial assistant.

DONE AND ORDERED this 20th day of May, 2013.

ALAN A. DICKEY
CHIEF JUDGE

13–18–S. SUPERSEDED BY ADMINISTRATIVE ORDER NO. 16-18-S

13–17–S. FORECLOSURE—RESIDENTIAL MORTGAGE FORECLOSURE NOTICE OF LIMITED APPEARANCE FOR MEDIATION ONLY

IN THE CIRCUIT COURT OF THE EIGHTEENTH JUDICIAL CIRCUIT, IN AND FOR SEMINOLE COUNTY, FLORIDA.

ADMINISTRATIVE ORDER NO: 13–17–S

IN RE: FORECLOSURE—RESIDENTIAL MORTGAGE FORECLOSURE NOTICE OF LIMITED APPEARANCE FOR MEDIATION ONLY

WHEREAS, mediation is required in certain residential foreclosures pursuant to the terms of Administrative Order No. 12–25–S; and

WHEREAS, many defendants in those cases are not represented by counsel and are unfamiliar with the mediation process; and

WHEREAS, Seminole County Legal Aid has received a grant to assist unrepresented defendants in the foreclosure process; and

WHEREAS, a number of lawyers have offered to assist unrepresented defendants on a limited basis pro bono;

NOW THEREFORE, in order to facilitate the efficient operation of the administration of justice, and pursuant to the authority vested in me as Chief Judge of the Eighteenth Judicial Circuit of Florida under Florida Rule of Judicial Administration 2.215,

IT IS HEREBY ORDERED that any attorney wishing to represent a defendant pro bono during the mediation process in a residential mortgage foreclosure case regardless of whether the attorney is referred by a program run by lawyer referral, legal aid, or legal services program or on the lawyer's own volition shall file a limited notice of appearance in the form attached as Exhibit A and serve copies on the parties and the assigned mediator. When the notice of limited appearance is filed the attorney must attend the mediation session unless allowed to withdraw by the court. When the mediation process is complete the attorney may file a notice of termination of representation and have no further duties in the case.

DONE and ORDERED this 3rd day of April, 2013.

ALAN A. DICKEY
CHIEF JUDGE

EXHIBIT A

IN THE CIRCUIT COURT OF THE EIGHTEENTH JUDICIAL CIRCUIT IN AND FOR SEMINOLE COUNTY, FLORIDA

_______________, CASE NO: _____
Plaintiff,

vs.

_______________,
Defendants.

_______________/

NOTICE OF LIMITED APPEARANCE FOR MEDIATION ONLY

TAKE NOTICE that the undersigned _________, submits this Notice of Limited Appearance on behalf of Defendant, _________, in the above-styled case for the following limited purpose of requesting, preparing and attending mediation session(s) as permitted under Administrative Order 12–25–S. This limited appearance is permissible in the Eighteenth Judicial Circuit pursuant to Administrative Order 13–17–S and is for the **limited purpose related to mediation** of owner-occupied properties.

Copies of all pleadings, filings and other correspondence must be served upon the defendant, _________ at the following address: _________, and not the undersigned.

Attached hereto is certification from the named defendant(s), certifying the nature of this counsel's appearance and authorizing a withdrawal of counsel after the filing of the mediator's report, the undersigned may file a Notice of Termination of Representation.

CERTIFICATE OF SERVICE

I certify that a copy hereto has been furnished to the parties listed on the attached service list by email; hand–delivery; mail; and/or fax on this ___ day of _________, 20 ___.

____
Name: _________
Florida Bar No _________
Address: _________
____

13–16–S. FORECLOSURE—RESIDENTIAL MORTGAGE FORECLOSURE MEDIATION NOTICE

IN THE CIRCUIT COURT OF THE EIGHTEENTH JUDICIAL CIRCUIT, IN AND FOR SEMINOLE COUNTY, FLORIDA.

ADMINISTRATIVE ORDER NO: **13–16–S**

IN RE: FORECOSLURE[1]—RESIDENTIAL MORTGAGE FORECLOSURE MEDIATION NOTICE

It has come to the attention of the court that the Clerk of this Court has been asked to include in the summons packet for residential mortgage foreclosures information about mediation that is outdated and incorrect in view of the adoption of Administrative Order No. 12–25–S. The court finds that for the benefit of the clerk and the parties that a standard notice in lieu of all others for those cases should be required by the court.

It is; therefore,

ORDERED and ADJUDGED that the Clerk of this Court include the Notice to Homeowner Defendants attached hereto as Exhibit A in the summons packet in every residential mortgage foreclosure case in Seminole County, Florida, to the exclusion of any other notice regarding mediation in those cases. Any other notice furnished by any other entity is to be discarded.

DONE and ORDERED this 1st day of April, 2013.

ALAN A. DICKEY
CHIEF JUDGE

EXHIBIT A

NOTICE TO HOMEOWNER DEFENDANTS

If you are a homeowner who occupies the property subject of this suit as your primary residence you are entitled to participate in MEDIATION to attempt to settle this legal action. You may be able to negotiate:

*Modification of the note and mortgage to retain the property

*Sale the property

*Surrender of the property

To preserve your rights you should either contact an attorney to file an Answer to the complaint or you must file an Answer with the court on your own, even if you chose mediation. An Answer must be filed as instructed in the Summons served on you.

A Seminole County Administrative Order requires mediation in any foreclosure of an owner occupied homestead if the homeowner requests it in writing in the case.

Successful mediation requires your active participation in full completion of financial applications and cooperation in scheduling financial counseling and mediation.

*You have a right to participate in scheduling the date and time of the mediation session.

*The plaintiff's attorney does not have the right to send you to a mediator selected by the Lender without your agreement.

SPECIAL NOTE: UNLESS YOU HAVE BEEN ADVISED BY YOUR ATTORNEY WHO IS REPRESENTING YOU IN THIS CASE (NOT THE LENDERS ATTORNEY) OR UNLESS YOU ARE EXCUSED BY THE TRIAL JUDGE YOU MUST ATTEND ALL SCHEDULED COURT PROCEEDINGS AND MEDIATION. (Bank representatives, mediation counselors and real estate professionals do not have the authority to excuse you).

BEWARE OF FORECLOSURE ASSISTANCE SCAMS; Foreclosure counseling is provided for **free** by the Foreclosure Mediation Program and through other Housing and Urban Development (HUD) agencies.

1 So in original.

13–15. [SUPERSEDED BY ORDER 17-15, EFFECTIVE MARCH 24, 2017.]

13–11–B. SUPERSEDED BY ADMINISTRATIVE ORDER NO. 16-30-B

12–33–B. DOMESTIC RELATIONS—TEMPORARY ORDER GOVERNING BATTERERS' INTERVENTION PROGRAMS

IN THE CIRCUIT COURT OF THE EIGHTEENTH JUDICIAL CIRCUIT IN AND FOR BREVARD COUNTY, FLORIDA

ADMINISTRATIVE ORDER NO.: 12–33–B

IN RE: DOMESTIC RELATIONS—TEMPORARY ORDER GOVERNING BATTERERS' INTERVENTION PROGRAMS

WHEREAS, per section 741.32, Florida Statutes, the Legislature has found that the incidence of domestic violence in this state is disturbingly high and that, despite the efforts of many to curb this violence, one person dies at the hands of a spouse, ex-spouse, or cohabitant approximately every three days. Further, a child who witnesses the perpetration of this violence becomes a victim as he or she hears or sees it occurring. This child is at high risk of also being the victim of physical abuse by the parent who is perpetrating the violence and, to a lesser extent, by the parent who is the victim. These children are also at a high risk of perpetrating violent crimes as juveniles and, later, becoming perpetrators of the same violence that they witnessed as children. Further, the Legislature has found that there should be standardized programming available to the justice system to protect victims and their children and to hold the perpetrators of domestic violence accountable for their acts. Finally, the Legislature recognizes that in order for batterers' intervention programs to be successful in protecting victims and their children, all participants in the justice system, as well as social service agencies and local and state governments, must coordinate their efforts at the community level; and

WHEREAS, the Department of Children and Families has historically been responsible for the statewide domestic violence program, which provides supervision, direction, coordination, and administration of activities related to domestic violence prevention and intervention services; and

WHEREAS, imperative to ending domestic violence is to ensure that batterers' intervention program providers have the necessary credentials, experience, and hands-on knowledge to ensure program effectiveness and offender compliance with a focus on victim safety; and

WHEREAS, batterers' intervention programs are an integral component to a comprehensive approach to domestic violence. Strong communication between providers of such programs and the criminal justice system is paramount to making sure perpetrators of domestic violence are held accountable and a change in behavior is attainable; and

WHEREAS, effective July 1, 2012, HB 7093 amends section 741.32, Florida Statutes, and other related statutes, terminating the Department of Children and Family Services Office for Certification and Monitoring of batterers' intervention programs with no further specification as to certification and oversight of said programs;

NOW, THEREFORE, in order to facilitate the efficient operation of the administration of justice, and pursuant to the authority vested in me as Chief Judge of the Eighteenth Judicial Circuit of Florida under Florida Rule of Judicial Administration 2.215,

IT IS HEREBY ORDERED that, **effective immediately** and to continue through and until June 30, 2013 unless further extended, as of the effective date of this Order, all current state certified batterers' intervention programs shall remain the sole referral source for the Eighteenth Judicial Circuit Court, Brevard County, until such time as the Court implements permanent measures to address the need created by House Bill 7093, effective July 1, 2012.

DONE AND ORDERED this 1st day of October, 2012.

ALAN A. DICKEY
CHIEF JUDGE

12–28–B. COURT COSTS—INSURANCE COVERAGE IN COUNTY COURT—COMMUNITY SERVICE

IN THE CIRCUIT COURT OF THE EIGHTEENTH JUDICIAL CIRCUIT IN AND FOR BREVARD COUNTY, FLORIDA

ADMINISTRATIVE ORDER NO.: 12–28–B

SUPERSEDES 96–27–B

In Re: COURT COSTS—Insurance Coverage in County Court—Community Service

Persons who have been assigned community service by the County Court of Brevard County as a condition of probation or otherwise, need medical insurance while performing such community service.

It is therefore ORDERED;

1. Anyone required to perform community service as a condition of probation or otherwise, shall have costs of $15.00 for each fifty (50) hours of community service or portion thereof.

2. The Judicial Correction Services, Inc., shall collect these funds in the same manner as supervision costs and shall distribute these costs accordingly.

These costs are imposed automatically, and do not require a specific Order of Court at the time of sentencing.

DONE AND ORDERED this 22nd day of August, 2012.

ALAN A. DICKEY
CHIEF JUDGE

12–27–S. JUVENILE DEPENDENCY—DISCOVERY IN ALL CHILD DEPENDENCY CASES IN THE JUVENILE DIVISION

IN THE CIRCUIT COURT OF THE EIGHTEENTH JUDICIAL CIRCUIT IN AND FOR SEMINOLE COUNTY, FLORIDA

ADMINISTRATIVE ORDER NO.: 12–27–S

IN RE: JUVENILE DEPENDENCY—DISCOVERY IN ALL CHILD DEPENDENCY CASES IN THE JUVENILE DIVISION

Pursuant to Rule 8.245, F.R.Juv.P., a party may make a written demand to participate in discovery in Child Dependency cases.

This court has been informed of an Agreement submitted by the Department of Children and Families Child Legal Services, Jaime Rivera, Esq., the Office of Regional Conflict Counsel, and the Guardian ad Litem Program, to eliminate the necessity of filing a written demand for discovery in each Child Dependency case.

Upon filing a Notice of Discovery with the Clerk of Court of Seminole County Florida, requesting compliance in all Child Dependency cases, this agreement allows The Department of Children and Families Child Legal Services, the Office of Regional Conflict Counsel, the Guardian ad Litem Program, and/or other privately retained counsel to participate in all discovery authorized by Rule 8.245, F.R.Juv.P., except when electing not to participate.

When choosing **not** to participate, a party shall file a "Notice of Intent Not To Participate in Discovery" with the court, the Department of Children and Families Child Legal Services office, the Office of Regional Conflict Counsel and any privately retained counsel making an appearance.

It is therefore **ORDERED:**

1. In all Dependency cases where the Department of Children and Families Child Legal Services, Guardian ad Litem Program, Office of Regional Conflict Counsel and/or privately retained attorneys are involved, except where a party has filed a "Notice of Intent Not to Participate in Discovery", the Department of Children and Families Child Legal Services, Guardian ad Litem Program, Office of Regional Conflict Counsel and/or privately retained attorneys shall, on a reciprocal basis, fully participate in discovery as provided by the Juvenile Rules of Procedure without further request or order on an ongoing basis.

2. The Department of Children and Families Child Legal Services, Guardian ad Litem Program, Office of Regional Conflict Counsel and/or privately retained attorneys shall reciprocally disclose and permit inspection, copying, testing, and photographing of all material provided for in Rule 8.245, F.R. Juv.P., within the possession or control of the Department of Children and Families Child Legal Services, Guardian ad Litem Program, Office of Regional Conflict Counsel and/or privately retained attorneys within five (5) days after a Petition is filed or after an Answer to Demand for Discovery is filed, whichever occurs first.

3. The Guardian ad Litem Program, Office of Regional Counsel and Office of Regional Conflict Counsel and privately retained attorneys will notify the Department of Children and Families Child Legal Services of its intent to copy all available discovery, and the Department of Children and Families Child Legal Services shall make the same available the next working day by either document, facsimile or other secure electronic means. Discovery materials actually obtained by a secretary for the Guardian ad Litem Program, Office of Regional Conflict Counsel and privately retained attorneys will be deemed to have been demanded and received irrespective of any written notice to the contrary.

4. The Department of Children and Families Child Legal Services, pursuant to F.R. Juv. P. 8.245 and *Brady v. Maryland*, 373 U.S. 83 (1963), shall disclose to the Guardian ad Litem Program, Office of Regional Conflict Counsel and/or privately retained attorneys any material information within the their possession or control which tends to negate the evidence or responsibility of the parent or caretaker as to the offense(s) alleged.

5. If, subsequent to compliance with this order, the Department of Children and Families Child Legal Services discovers additional witnesses or material which they would have been under a duty to disclose or produce at the time of such previous compliance, they shall promptly disclose or produce such witnesses or material in the same manner as required under this order for initial discovery.

6. All parties who elect to participate in discovery, either through filing the appropriate notice or by participating in the discovery process outlined in this agreement, shall comply with all requirements of Rule 8.245 (b), F. R. Juv. P.

7. If problems arise which cannot be satisfactorily resolved, suspension of this procedure will become effective upon Court Order pursuant to the filing of written Motion to Suspend the proceedings and notice for hearing with this Court.

This order applies to Seminole County Dependency Cases ONLY.

DONE and ORDERED this 22nd day of August, 2012

ALAN A. DICKEY
CHIEF JUDGE

12–25–S. MEDIATION—MANDATORY MEDIATION CIRCUIT COURT SEMINOLE COUNTY OWNER–OCCUPIED RESIDENTIAL MORTGAGE FORECLOSURES

IN THE CIRCUIT COURT OF THE EIGHTEENTH JUDICIAL CIRCUIT IN AND FOR SEMINOLE COUNTY, FLORIDA

ADMINISTRATIVE ORDER NO: 12–25–S SUPERSEDES 09–09–S AMENDED, 11–17–S and 12–12–S

IN RE: MEDIATION—MANDATORY MEDIATION CIRCUIT COURT SEMINOLE COUNTY OWNER–OCCUPIED RESIDENTIAL MORTGAGE FORECLOSURES

WHEREAS, high residential foreclosure rates are having a damaging impact on the economy of Seminole County, the State of Florida, and the financial community; and,

WHEREAS, owner-occupied residential foreclosures place increased strain on family relationships, leading to higher divorce rates, increased incidents of domestic violence, and adverse impacts on children; and,

WHEREAS, the Judges in the Seminole County Circuit Civil Divisions are routinely advised by owner-occupant litigants that it is difficult, if not outright impossible, to negotiate settlements due to the inability to communicate with appropriate representatives of the lender or the lender's attorneys after the complaint for foreclosure has been filed. In many of these cases, the first opportunity the owner/occupant litigants have to discuss the issues and attempt to resolve their differences is at a hearing on the lender's motion for summary judgment, at trial or later at the foreclosure sale. By that time in most cases, all judicial labor has been expended and the costs and attorney's fees have increased significantly. The failure of the parties to communicate in a timely fashion results in unnecessary waste of resources by the court, the court staff, and the clerk's office and could be obviated by pre-judgment mediation; and,

WHEREAS, Florida Rule of Civil Procedure 1.700(a) provides that a presiding judge may enter an order referring all or any part of a contested civil matter to mediation or arbitration; and

WHEREAS, foreclosure actions are equitable in nature, the law abhors a forfeiture, and the nature of a owner-occupied residential foreclosure mandates that the court give full, fair, and equitable consideration to all issues in these cases rather than deal with them in a summary fashion; and,

WHEREAS, the presiding Seminole Circuit Civil Division judges have determined that greater economy of limited judicial and clerk resources would occur if contested homeowner-occupied residential foreclosure cases in Seminole County were required to be scheduled for mediation before being set for final hearing;

NOW, THEREFORE, IT IS ORDERED:

1. For all homeowner-occupied residential mortgage foreclosure actions filed in Seminole County, Florida, and in which responsive pleadings or other filings asserting viable defenses or seeking any form of affirmative relief are filed by a homeowner Defendant, this order shall constitute an order of referral to mediation at Plaintiff's expense. Counsel for plaintiff shall coordinate and schedule the case for mediation prior to the date the matter is set for final or summary judgment hearing. The plaintiff may schedule mediation with any Supreme Court Certified Civil Mediator.

2. The plaintiff shall make a reasonable effort to coordinate the mediation with all parties and shall give the defendant homeowner(s) and any un-defaulted inferior lien holders reasonable advance notice of the date, time, and place of the mediation. When plaintiff gives notice of the mediation, plaintiff shall also give written notice identifying the lender's representative and attesting to the representative's authority to participate in mediation and settle on behalf of the lender.

3. Nothing in this Order is intended to prevent the plaintiff from filing all pleadings necessary to proceed to final or summary judgment and scheduling a hearing on a motion for summary judgment or a trial, so long as the hearing or trial is set to occur after the conclusion of the scheduled mediation session or mediation has been waived as permitted under paragraph 2 above.

4. Plaintiff shall provide lender's loan modification package to defendant(s) within ten (10) days after scheduling mediation, and the defendant(s) shall provide the completed package at least fifteen (15) days prior to the date of the mediation. Upon completion of the mediation, the mediator shall file a written report with fifteen (15) days from the date of the mediation. Plaintiff's representative may appear telephonically if all paperwork has been exchanged as set forth herein.

5. If defendant(s) fail to appear at a properly noticed mediation or if the matter impasses after mediation, the matter may be promptly noticed for final or summary judgment, provided all requirements of F.R.C.P. 1.510 have been met. If plaintiff fails to appear for mediation or no representative with full settlement authority appears, the action shall be dismissed without prejudice.

6. Lenders are encouraged to enter into pre-suit mediation to expedite the process and hopefully result in fewer foreclosures being filed.

DONE AND ORDERED this 26th day of July, 2012.

ALAN A. DICKEY
CHIEF JUDGE

12–18–B. JAIL—BREVARD COUNTY JAIL TESTING OF DETAINEES, INMATES, AND OTHER PERSONS AND DISCLOSURE OF TEST RESULTS

IN THE CIRCUIT COURT OF THE EIGHTEENTH JUDICIAL CIRCUIT IN AND FOR BREVARD COUNTY, FLORIDA

ADMINISTRATIVE ORDER NO.: 12–18–B

IN RE: JAIL—BREVARD COUNTY JAIL TESTING OF DETAINEES, INMATES, AND OTHER PERSONS AND DISCLOSURE OF TEST RESULTS

This Administrative Order sets forth the procedure for the testing of blood for detainees and inmates in the Brevard County Jail, as well as blood testing for other persons who come into contact with a person in such a way that significant exposure to bodily fluids has occurred.

This Administrative Order also sets forth the procedure for disclosure of blood test results.

WHEREAS, the legislature has previously and expressly authorized HIV and Hepatitis testing, and disclosure of the test results pursuant to court order, and under the direction of the Department of Children and Families, to the victim of criminal offenses which involve the transmission of bodily fluids, and disclosure also to public health agencies, pursuant to § 960.003(1), Fla. Stat.

WHEREAS, the legislature also authorizes an officer, firefighter or ambulance driver, paramedic, or emergency technician, acting within the scope of employment, who comes into contact with a person in such a way that significant exposure to bodily fluids has occurred, to request that the person be screened for sexually transmissible disease. If the person who provides exposure of bodily fluids to another, is unwilling to voluntarily submit to screening, the person so exposed is authorized to seek a court order, directing the person to submit to screening, where there is significant exposure and the screening is medically necessary to determine the course of treatment to be provided to the exposed person. § 384.287, Fla. Stat.

WHEREAS, disclosure must be immediate and consistent with legislative intent stated in § 384.287 and 960.003(1), Fla. Stat., to prevent unnecessary mental anguish.

WHEREAS, due to the fact that it is often difficult for the Circuit Court to enter an order immediately authorizing prompt testing and disclosure as intended by the legislature, this standing Administrative Order is intended to prevent such delays.

WHEREAS, this Administrative Order is further designed to harmonize competing interests of due process rights and expectations or privacy of detainees and inmates with society's special need to protect persons responsible for the care and custody of detainees and inmates carrying infectious diseases, thus allowing immediate testing and disclosure of the detainee's or inmate's blood test results in the least intrusive way by means of this standing Administrative Order, within the parameters of the case law, legislative intent, and statutory authority. Fosman v. State, 664 So.2d 1163 (Fla. 4th DCA 1995).

NOW THEREFORE, by the authority vested in me as Chief Judge of the Eighteenth Judicial Circuit and pursuant to the Florida Rules of Judicial Administration, it is:

ORDERED and **ADJUDGED**:

This Administrative Order shall be deemed to take effect as an Order authorizing blood testing and prompt disclosure of blood tests results under the circumstances set forth below.

1. Whenever any medical personnel, through or during the course of a detainee's or inmate's medical treatment, or any employee, agent, representative, contractor, or officer of the Brevard County Sheriff's Office, who is or has been responsible for the care and custody of a detainee or inmate, is exposed to the transmission of bodily fluids by a detainee or inmate who has been convicted or charged with an offense enumerated under § 775.0877(1)(a)–(n), Fla. Stat., this Administrative Order will take effect so that there will already be deemed to have been a court order entered in this Eighteenth Judicial Circuit, directing the offender to immediately undergo HIV testing, and the test results to be disclosed promptly to such persons affected or impacted by exposure. § 775.0877(2) and 960.003(3)(a), Fla. Stat. Testing and disclosure shall be immediate, consistent with legislative intent stated in § 960.003(1), Fla. Stat., to prevent unnecessary mental anguish.

2. Whenever an officer (i.e., full-time, part-time or auxiliary law enforcement officer, correctional officer or correctional probation officer), a firefighter or public health agency personnel, acting within the scope of employment, comes into contact with an arrestee, detainee or inmate in such a way that significant exposure to bodily fluids has occurred, sufficient to warrant a reasonably cautious person to be concerned for the health and safety of their own and their family's health regarding infection, it shall be deemed that a *voluntary submission* to immediate testing for a sexually transmissible disease and prompt disclosure of the results has been made § 384.287, Fla. Stat.

3. In the alternative, if the infected person, including a detainee or inmate is unwilling to voluntarily submit to testing, then the exposed person, may utilize this Administrative Order as the standing Order in effect, directing the person, including a detainee or inmate, to submit to immediate testing and prompt disclosure where there was significant exposure and the screening is medically necessary to determine the course of treatment. § 384.287, Fla. Stat., and § 960.003(1), (3), Fla. Stat. This immediate testing and disclosure is consistent with the policy and intent expressed by the legislature in § 960.003(1), (3), Fla. Stat., to prevent extreme mental anguish.

4. Further, all detainees or inmates who have already been tested for infectious disease, including Hepatitis and those detainees or inmates tested for HIV pursuant to § 775.0877 Fla. Stat., shall have their test results disclosed immediately to all medical personnel who have treated or examined them, and to all employees, agents, representatives, contractors, and officers of the Brevard County Sheriff's Office, who are or have been responsible for their care and custody. § 951.27 and 960.003, Fla. Stat. Even though no court order is necessary pursuant to § 951.27, Fla. Stat., this Administrative Order shall be deemed as an Order in effect, directing such immediate testing and disclosure.

5. Nothing herein prohibits an exposed person referred to above from seeking a court order that specifically addresses the individual circumstances, which may include, but not be limited too, blood testing for both the infected person, a detainee or inmate, for HIV, Hepatitis A, Hepatitis B and Hepatitis C.

6. This Administrative Order shall take effect immediately and remain in effect until further Order of the Court, and all terms and conditions set forth in this Administrative Order shall apply unless otherwise ordered by the Court.

DONE AND ORDERED this 20th day of June, 2012.

ALAN A. DICKEY
CHIEF JUDGE

12–17–B. ADOPTIONS—OBJECTION TO NOTICE OF ADOPTION

IN THE CIRCUIT COURT OF THE EIGHTEENTH JUDICIAL CIRCUIT IN AND FOR BREVARD COUNTY, FLORIDA

ADMINISTRATIVE ORDER NO.: 12–17–B

IN RE: ADOPTIONS—OBJECTION TO NOTICE OF ADOPTION

WHEREAS, in proceedings seeking an adoption under Chapter 63 of the Florida Statutes, if an unmarried biological father desires to contest the adoption plan, he must provide to the adoption entity (defined by Section 63.032(3) Florida Statutes) a copy of the verified response filed with the court as well as the claim of paternity filed with the Office of Vital Statistics.

NOW THEREFORE, in any petition for adoption, there must be a certification by the petitioner whether or not the unmarried biological father has provided a copy of a verified response filed with the court as well as the claim of paternity filed with the Office of Vital Statistics to the adoption entity.

DONE AND ORDERED this 20th day of June, 2012.

ALAN A. DICKEY
CHIEF JUDGE

12–14–S. COUNTY COURT—MISDEMEANOR VETERANS' TREATMENT COURT

IN THE CIRCUIT COURT OF THE EIGHTEENTH JUDICIAL CIRCUIT, IN AND FOR SEMINOLE COUNTY, FLORIDA

ADMINISTRATIVE ORDER NO.: 12–14–S

IN RE: COUNTY COURT—MISDEMEANOR VETERANS' TREATMENT COURT

WHEREAS, specialized courts can enhance the expediency, effectiveness and quality of judicial administration;

WHEREAS, it is essential that a new strategy be implemented to isolate and focus upon individuals arrested for misdemeanor offenses who are veterans who have been diagnosed with a service connected behavioral health issue, in view of the unique nature of behavioral health issues related to veterans, and the need for appropriate treatment in an environment conducive to wellness and not punishment, as well as the continuing necessity to insure the protection of the public;

WHEREAS, there is a recognized need to bring defendants qualified to participate in the Veterans' Treatment Court before a judge assigned to expeditiously and efficiently move veterans with service connected behavioral health issues from an overcrowded jail system into veteran treatment programs without compromising the safety of the public; and

WHEREAS, a centralized Veterans' Treatment Court that utilizes available Veteran Administration and Veteran Mentor Volunteer resources and support systems will increase the efficiency of the criminal court system in this circuit and permit better access to a continuing shrinkage of state and local resources and services;

NOW THEREFORE, by authority vested in me as Chief Judge and pursuant to the Florida Rules of Judicial Administration, it is

ORDERED:

1. A Veterans' Treatment Court shall be operational within the Seminole County Court Criminal Division to hear cases involving defendants who are veterans who are eligible for treatment, evaluation, or placement related to a behavioral health issue and who have been arrested for misdemeanors or criminal traffic offenses, with the exception of those charged with driving under the influence. Court approval will be considered upon the consent of the victim and the State Attorney and an agreement to participate by the defendant and the defendant's attorney. Veterans' Treatment Court may also hear cases in which a defendant is charged with a violation of county court probation for a nondriving under the influence offense with the consent of the county court judge of the criminal division to which the case is assigned.

2. Referrals into the program may be made *sua sponte* by any court, by Court Services, by the Forensic Program at the Seminole County Jail, the state attorney, the defense attorney, law enforcement, mental health providers, Veteran Organizations, or any other interested person. The criterion for admittance into the program requires verification by the Veterans Administration that the defendant is entitled to receive veteran services for treatment, evaluation, or placement related to a behavioral health issue.

3. Upon confirmation from the Veterans Administration that the defendant is entitled to receive veteran services for treatment, evaluation, or placement related to a behavioral health issue, and after approval of the parties set forth above, the Veterans' Treatment Court Judge shall enter an order transferring the case to Veterans' Treatment Court and directing the Clerk to place the case or cases, including any traffic criminal cases involving the accepted defendant, on the Misdemeanor Veterans' Treatment Court docket.

4. Prior to the Veterans' Treatment Court Judge transferring the case to the Veterans' Treatment Court docket, the defendant must enter a written waiver of speedy trial.

5. The case shall be transferred back to the original criminal division if a defendant fails, for any reason, to successfully participate and complete the Veterans' Treatment Court program and the defendant's right to a speedy trial may be reinstated upon a written demand.

6. Defendants who are accepted for participation in the Veterans' Treatment Court, and who voluntarily agree to participate in the Veterans' Treatment Court, shall, at the discretion of the State Attorney, enter into a Deferred Prosecution Agreement, unless charged with a violation of county probation. Additionally the court will enter an Order transferring the defendant's case(s) into the Veterans' Treatment Court as a court event.

7. Defendants accepted into the Veterans' Treatment Court will attend court hearings as ordered by the court, based on each defendant's needs. After the defendant's acceptance into the Veterans' Treatment Court, the defendant will participate in continued assessment and treatment and engage in discharge planning. The defendant's participation will end upon the successful completion of the discharge plan. The charges will be then dismissed by the State Attorney or the violation of probation will be dismissed by the Veterans' Treatment Court judge.

8. The public is entitled to access to judicial records, however, patient treatment records are an exception to this rule and are deemed confidential by Florida law. In the event a treatment record or report is placed in the court file of a Veterans' Treatment Court participant, the court will determine whether such report is a confidential patient record, exempt under Florida law from public access, and if the court finds the record is exempt the court will seal the document and mark the envelope with the date, description, and author of the document, whereupon access to the document will be limited to those authorized under Section 395.3025 and 393.13, Florida Statutes, or by court order.

DONE AND ORDERED, this 18th day of May, 2012.

ALAN A. DICKEY
CHIEF JUDGE

12–09–S. MENTAL HEALTH COURT

IN THE CIRCUIT COURT OF THE EIGHTEENTH JUDICIAL CIRCUIT OF FLORIDA IN AND FOR SEMINOLE COUNTY, FLORIDA

ADMINISTRATIVE ORDER NO.: 12–09–S

IN RE: MENTAL HEALTH COURT

WHEREAS, the Supreme Court of Florida, Steering Committee on Families and Children in the Court and its' subcommittee on mental health was charged with addressing the issues of persons with mental illnesses involved in the criminal justice system; and

WHEREAS, specialized courts can enhance the expediency, effectiveness and quality of judicial administration; and

WHEREAS, in view of the nature of mental illness and developmental disability, it is in the public interest and in the interest of justice that a new strategy be implemented to address persons who are mentally ill or developmentally disabled and who are arrested for nonviolent criminal offenses; and

WHEREAS, the Court in the interest of justice strives to balance the need for mentally ill and developmentally disabled defendants to receive appropriate treatment with the need for public safety; and

WHEREAS, there is a recognized need for the Court to expeditiously and efficiently move mentally ill or developmentally disabled defendants, who are qualified to participate in the Mental health Court from jail into the mental health system without compromising the safety of the public;

It is, therefore ORDERED:

1. Mental Health Court ("MHC") shall be operational within Seminole County Court Criminal Division as a program for cases involving defendants who are suffering from mental illness or a developmental disability and arrested for misdemeanors or criminal traffic offenses, and certain approved third-degree felonies. A county Court Judge ("MHC Judge"), appointed by the Chief Judge, shall preside over MHC. Referrals to MHC shall be made sua sponte by any court, by Court Services, by the Seminole county Jail Mental Health Specialist (masters level practitioners) at the Seminole County Jail, the state, the defense attorney, law enforcement, mental health providers, or any other interested person. Prior to the MHC Judge transferring the case to the MHC docket, the defendant must enter a written waiver of speedy trial, unless specifically objected to by defense counsel.

2. Referrals into the program may be made sua sponte by any court, by Court Services, by the Forensic Program at the Seminole County Jail, the State, the defense attorney, law enforcement, mental health providers, or any other interested person. The criterion for admittance into the program requires diagnosis by a mental health expert of (a) a current Axis I mental illness including Schizophrenia, Bi-polar Disorder, Recurrent Major Depressive Disorder, Post–Traumatic Stress Disorder, or other psychotic disorders of an unspecified nature or (b) a developmental disability as defined in Section 393.063(12), Florida Statutes.

3. Upon defendant's diagnosis of a current Axis I mental illness or developmental disability by a mental health expert, and the assigned judge's determination that the defendant is mentally ill or developmentally disabled and after approval of the parties set forth above, the Mental Health Court Judge shall enter an order transferring the case to Mental Health Court and directing the Clerk to place the case or cases, including any traffic criminal cases involving the accepted defendant, on the Misdemeanor Mental Health Court docket.

4. Prior to the Mental Health Court Judge transferring the case to the Mental Health Court docket, the defendant must enter a written waiver of speedy trial.

5. The case shall be transferred back to the original criminal division if a defendant fails, for any reason, to successfully participate and complete the Mental Health Court program and the defendant's right to a speedy trial may be reinstated upon a written demand.

6. Defendants who are accepted for participation in the Mental Health Court, and who voluntarily agree to participate in the Mental Health Court, shall, at the discretion of the State Attorney, enter into a Deferred Prosecution Agreement, unless charged with a violation of county probation. Additionally the court will enter an Order transferring the defendant's case(s) into the Mental Health Court as a court event.

7. Defendants accepted into the Mental Health Court will attend weekly court hearings as ordered by the court, based on each defendant's needs. After the defendant's acceptance into the Mental Health Court, the defendant will participate in

continued assessment and treatment and engage in discharge planning. The defendant's participation will end upon the successful completion of the discharge plan. The charges will be then dismissed by the State Attorney or the violation of probation will be dismissed by the Mental Health Court judge.

8. The public is entitled to access to judicial records, however, patient treatment records are an exception to this rule and are deemed confidential by Florida law. See sections 395.3025 (7), and 393.13, Florida Statutes (central records of clients who are determined to be eligible by the Department of Children and Family Services for development services). In the event a treatment record or report is placed in the court file of a Mental Health Court participant, the court will determine whether such report is a confidential patient record, exempt under Florida law from public access, and if the court finds the record is exempt the court will seal the document and mark the envelope with the date, description, and author of the document, whereupon access to the document will be limited to those authorized under Section 395.3025 and 393.13, Florida Statutes, or by court order.

DONE AND ORDERED, this 3rd day of April, 2012.

ALAN A. DICKEY
CHIEF JUDGE

12–08. FORECLOSURE PROCEDURE—ORDER DIRECTING COUNSEL TO SERVE COPIES OF NOTICES OF HEARING, ORDERS AND JUDGMENTS IN RESIDENTIAL MORTGAGE CASES

IN THE CIRCUIT COURT OF THE EIGHTEENTH JUDICIAL CIRCUIT OF FLORIDA

ADMINISTRATIVE ORDER NO.: 12–08

IN RE: FORECLOSURE PROCEDURE—ORDER DIRECTING COUNSEL TO SERVE COPIES OF NOTICES OF HEARING, ORDERS AND JUDGMENTS IN RESIDENTIAL MORTGAGE CASES

WHEREAS Florida Rule of Civil Procedure 1.080(h)(1) authorizes the court to direct the service of orders and judgments under its direction when necessary. The high volume of residential foreclosure cases precludes judicial assistants and case managers from performing other essential functions.

Florida Rule of Judicial Administration 2.215(b)(3) states the chief judge shall "develop an administrative plan for the efficient and proper administration of all courts within the circuit."

NOW THEREFORE in accordance with the authority vested in the chief judge by Florida Rule of Judicial Administration 2.215, it is **ORDERED:**

1. The attorney submitting an order or judgment for entry in a residential foreclosure case shall be responsible for mailing to all parties a conformed copy of the order or judgment upon entry.

2. A judge, case manager or judicial assistant may serve a conformed copy of an order entered *sua sponte* upon plaintiffs' counsel by mail, fax or e-mail to be copied and distributed to all other parties in the case.

Done and Ordered this 15th day of March, 2012.

ALAN A. DICKEY
CHIEF JUDGE

11–38–B. COUNTY COURT—MISDEMEANOR VETERANS' TREATMENT COURT

IN THE CIRCUIT COURT OF THE EIGHTEENTH JUDICIAL CIRCUIT, IN AND FOR BREVARD COUNTY

ADMINISTRATIVE ORDER NO.: 11–38–B

IN RE: COUNTY COURT—MISDEMEANOR VETERANS' TREATMENT COURT

WHEREAS, specialized courts can enhance the expediency, effectiveness and quality of judicial administration;

WHEREAS, it is essential that a new strategy be implemented to isolate and focus upon individuals arrested for misdemeanor offenses who are veterans who have been diagnosed with a service connected behavioral health issue, in view of the unique nature of behavioral health issues related to veterans, and the need for appropriate treatment in an environment conducive to wellness and not punishment, as well as the continuing necessity to insure the protection of the public;

WHEREAS, there is a recognized need to bring defendants qualified to participate in the Veterans' Treatment Court before a judge assigned to expeditiously and efficiently move veterans with service connected behavioral health issues from an overcrowded jail system into veteran treatment programs without compromising the safety of the public; and

WHEREAS, a centralized Veterans' Treatment Court that utilizes available Veteran Administration and Veteran Mentor Volunteer resources and support systems will increase the efficiency of the criminal court system in this circuit and permit better access to a continuing shrinkage of state and local resources and services;

NOW THEREFORE, by authority vested in me as Chief Judge and pursuant to the Florida Rules of Judicial Administration, it is

ORDERED:

1. A Veterans' Treatment Court shall be operational within the Brevard County Court Criminal Division to hear cases involving defendants who are veterans who are eligible for treatment, evaluation, or placement related to a behavioral health issue and who have been arrested for misdemeanors or criminal traffic offenses, with the exception of those charged with driving under the influence. Court approval will be considered upon the consent of the victim and the State Attorney and an agreement to participate by the defendant and the defendant's attorney. Veterans' Treatment Court may also hear cases in which a defendant is charged with a violation of county court probation for a nondriving under the influence offense with the consent of the county court judge of the criminal division to which the case is assigned.

2. Referrals into the program may be made *sua sponte* by any court, by Court Services, by the Forensic Program at the Brevard County Jail, the state attorney, the defense attorney, law enforcement, mental health providers, Veteran Organizations, or any other interested person. The criterion for admittance into the program requires verification by the Veterans Administration that the defendant is entitled to receive veteran services for treatment, evaluation, or placement related to a behavioral health issue.

3. Upon confirmation from the Veterans Administration that the defendant is entitled to receive veteran services for treatment, evaluation, or placement related to a behavioral health issue, and after approval of the parties set forth above, the Veterans' Treatment Court Judge shall enter an order transferring the case to Veterans' Treatment Court and directing the Clerk to place the case or cases, including any traffic criminal cases involving the accepted defendant, on the Misdemeanor Veterans' Treatment Court docket.

4. Prior to the Veterans' Treatment Court Judge transferring the case to the Veterans' Treatment Court docket, the defendant must enter a written waiver of speedy trial.

5. The case shall be transferred back to the original criminal division if a defendant fails, for any reason, to successfully participate and complete the Veterans' Treatment Court program and the defendant's right to a speedy trial may be reinstated upon a written demand.

6. Defendants who are accepted for participation in the Veterans' Treatment Court, and who voluntarily agree to participate in the Veterans' Treatment Court, shall, at the discretion of the State Attorney, enter into a Deferred Prosecution Agreement, unless charged with a violation of county probation. Additionally the court will enter an Order transferring the defendant's case(s) into the Veterans' Treatment Court as a court event.

7. Defendants accepted into the Veterans' Treatment Court will attend court hearings as ordered by the court, based on each defendant's needs. After the defendant's acceptance into the Veterans' Treatment Court, the defendant will participate in continued assessment and treatment and engage in discharge planning. The defendant's participation will end upon the successful completion of the discharge plan. The charges will be then dismissed by the State Attorney or the violation of probation will be dismissed by the Veterans' Treatment Court judge.

8. The public is entitled to access to judicial records, however, patient treatment records are an exception to this rule and are deemed confidential by Florida law. In the event a treatment record or report is placed in the court file of a Veterans' Treatment Court participant, the court will determine whether such report is a confidential patient record, exempt under Florida law from public access, and if the court finds the record is exempt the court will seal the document and mark the envelope with the date, description, and author of the document, whereupon access to the document will be limited to those authorized under Section 395.3025 and 393.13, Florida Statutes, or by court order.

DONE AND ORDERED, this 16th day of November, 2011.

ALAN A. DICKEY
CHIEF JUDGE

11–29–B. CRIMINAL—STANDARDIZED BREVARD COUNTY ARREST AFFIDAVIT

IN THE CIRCUIT COURT OF THE EIGHTEENTH JUDICIAL CIRCUIT IN AND FOR BREVARD COUNTY, FLORIDA

ADMINISTRATIVE ORDER NO.: 11–29–B

IN RE: Criminal—Standardized Brevard County Arrest Affidavit

WHEREAS, Florida Rules of Judicial Administration (Rule 2.050) states that the chief judge "shall exercise administrative supervision over all courts within the judicial circuit in the exercise of judicial power over the judges and officers of the court" and "shall develop an administrative plan for the efficient and proper administration of all courts within that circuit", which included a "mandatory periodic review of the status of the inmates of the county jail"; and

WHEREAS, the sheriff and municipal law enforcement agencies in Brevard County have historically used a standard arrest form which was at one time provided by the Clerk of the Court, but has now become the financial responsibility of each law enforcement agency; and

WHEREAS, many law enforcement agencies are generating forms or are considering programs that generate forms through their computer systems; and

WHEREAS, continued standardization of Brevard County's Arrest Affidavit will maintain efficiency, effectiveness, statistical information and sharing of information among various state, county and municipal agencies; and

WHEREAS, continued standardization of Brevard County's Arrest Affidavit will avoid inefficiency, court-related costs, labor hours, redundancy, data entry and clerical mistakes.

IT IS ORDERED AND ADJUDGED that the Standard Affidavit of Arrest attached hereto as Attachment "A", which shall include a Notice Of Confidential Information when required under Florida Rule of Judicial Administration 2.420(d)(2), is hereby adopted for use by all law enforcement agencies within Brevard County. Said Arrest Affidavit, whether pre-printed or computer generated, is required to maintain the same basic format in the inclusion and presentation of information to the court.

DONE AND ORDERED, this 21st day of September, 2011.

ALAN A. DICKEY
CHIEF JUDGE

FCIC CHECK ☐YES ☐NO

OBTS Number

ATTACHMENT "A"
ARREST/NOTICE TO APPEAR
PROBABLE CAUSE AFFIDAVIT/
JUVENILE REFERRAL

1. Arrest
2. Notice to Appear
3. Arrest Affidavit
4. Complaint Affidavit
5. Request for Capias
6. Juvenile Referral

Juvenile ☐

Agency ORI Number **FL 005035 A** | Agency Name | Agency Report Number

Check Type. Check as many as apply: ☐1. Felony ☐2. Traffic Felony ☐3. Misdemeanor ☐4. Traffic Misdemeanor ☐5. Ordinance ☐6. Other | Weapon Seized/Type ☐ Yes ☐ No | Agency Arrest Number

Location of Arrest (Include Name of Business) | City | Location of Offense Business Name, Address | City

Date of Arrest | Time of Arrest | BCSO Date | BCSO Time | Jail Date | Jail Time | Fingerprinted ☐ Identification Only ☐AFIS ☐Criminal By:

Date of Offense | FDLE Number | DOC Number | FBI Number

Name (Last, First, Middle) | Alias

Race: W-White I-American Indian B-Black O-Oriental/Asian | Sex | Date of Birth | Height | Weight | Eye Color | Hair Color | Complexion | Build

Scars, Marks, Tattoos, Unique Physical Features (Location, Type, Description) | Indication of: Y N Unk. Alcohol Influence ☐☐☐ Drug Influence ☐☐☐

Local Address (Street, Apt, Number) | (City) | (State) | (Zip) | Phone | Residence Type ☐ City. ☐County ☐ Florida ☐ Out of State

Permanent Address (Street, Apt, Number) or Parent's Name if Juv. | (City) | (State) | (Zip) | Phone | Parent Contacted Y ☐ N ☐

Business Address (Name, Street,) or Parent's Address if Juvenile | (City) | (State) | (Zip) | Phone | Occupation

Driver's License State/Number | Social Security Number | I.C.E. Number | Place of Birth | Citizenship

Co-Defendant Name (Last, First, Middle) | Race | Sex | Date of Birth or Age | ☐Arrested ☐ Felony ☐ Juvenile ☐ At Large ☐ Misdemeanor

Co-Defendant Name (Last, First, Middle) | Race | Sex | Date of Birth or Age | ☐Arrested ☐ Felony ☐ Juvenile ☐ At Large ☐ Misdemeanor

Activity: N. N/A, P. Possess, S. Sell, B. Buy, T. Traffic, R. Smuggle, D. Deliver, E. Use, K. Dispense / Distribute, M. Manufacture / Produce / Cultivate, Z. Other | Type: N. N/A, P. Possess, B. Barbiturate, C. Cocaine, E. Hemin, H. Hallucinogen, M. Marijuana, O. Opium / Derivative, P. Paraphernalia / Equipment, S. Synthetic, U. Unknown, Z. Other

Charge Description | Counts | ☐F.S. ☐Ord | Statute Violation Number | Violation of Section (ORD)

Activity | Drug Type | Amount/Unit | Bond Amount | Court Number

☐PC ☐ Capias ☐AC ☐BW ☐FW ☐PW ☐ Juv. PU ☐Citation | Date Issued | ☐ Writ. Att. ☐ Order of Arrest ☐Domestic Viol. Inj.

Charge Description | Counts | ☐F.S. ☐Ord | Statute Violation Number | Violation of Section (ORD)

Activity | Drug Type | Amount/Unit | Bond Amount | Court Number

☐PC ☐ Capias ☐AC ☐BW ☐FW ☐PW ☐ Juv. PU ☐Citation | Date Issued | ☐ Writ. Att. ☐ Order of Arrest ☐Domestic Viol. Inj.

The undersigned certifies and swears that he/she has just and reasonable grounds to believe, and does believe the above named Defendant committed the following violation of law:
On the day of , 2011 at ☐ A.M. ☐ P.M. (Specifically include facts constituting cause for arrest.)

Pursuant to Florida Statute 938.27 the investigative cost incurred by this agency is .

Continued for ☐ Narrative ☐ Charges

Mandatory Appearance In Court | **Location : Brevard County Courthouse, 2825 Judge Fran Jamieson Way, Viera, FL 32940**
Month | Day | Year | Time | ☐ A.M. ☐ P.M.

I AGREE TO APPEAR AT THE TIME AND PLACE DESIGNATED TO ANSWER THE OFFENSE CHARGED. I UNDERSTAND THAT SHOULD I WILLFULLY FAIL TO APPEAR BEFORE THE COURT AS REQUIRED BY THIS NOTICE TO APPEAR, THAT I MAY BE HELD IN CONTEMPT OF COURT AND A WARRANT FOR MY ARREST OR A TAKE INTO CUSTODY ORDER SHALL BE ISSUED.

Signature of Defendant/Juvenile | Signature of Juv. Parent/Custodian | Released to: (Name) | Date | Time

Miranda ☐ Warning | Hold for Other Agency Name: | Verified By | Date | Bonding Agency

Adults Only: ☐ Hold for First Appearance. ☐ Do Not Bond Out
Reason: | Bond # | Amount

I swear/affirm the above and attached is true and correct. ☐ Yes Investigator's/Complainant's
Signature
ID. No/Dist.
Name (Printed)

Sworn and subscribed before me, the undersigned authority this day of , 2011.
Signature
Type name
Notary/Law Enforcement Officer in Performance of Official Duties. Personally Known ☐ ID Produced ☐

Bond # | Amount
Returnable Court Date | Returnable Court Date
Court Location:
Page 1 of

Brevard County, FL

Narrative Continuation Page of

DEFENDANT/JUVENILE (Last, First, Middle)				Agency Report No.
				OBTS No.
Charge Description		Counts	☐ F.S. ☐ Ord.	Statute Violation Number / Violation of Section (ORD)
Activity	Drug Type	Amount/Unit	Bond Amount	Court Number
☐ PC ☐ Capias ☐ AC ☐ BW ☐ FW ☐ PW ☐ Juv. PU ☐ Citation			Date Issued	☐ Writ. Att. ☐ Order of Arrest ☐ Domestic Viol. Inj.
Charge Description		Counts	☐ F.S. ☐ Ord.	Statute Violation Number / Violation of Section (ORD)
Activity	Drug Type	Amount/Unit	Bond Amount	Court Number
☐ PC ☐ Capias ☐ AC ☐ BW ☐ FW ☐ PW ☐ Juv. PU ☐ Citation			Date Issued	☐ Writ. Att. ☐ Order of Arrest ☐ Domestic Viol. Inj.

Officer's Signature ______________________ Officer's Name Printed ______________________

NOTICE OF CONFIDENTIAL INFORMATION WITHIN COURT FILING

Pursuant to Florida Rule of Judicial Administration 2.420(d)(2), the filer of a court record at the time of filing shall indicate whether any confidential information is included within the document being filed; identify the confidentiality provision that applies to the identified information; and identify the precise location of the confidential information within the document being filed.

Title/Type of Document(s): ______________________________

Indicate the applicable confidentiality provision(s) below from Rule 2.420(d)(1)(B), by specifying the location within the document on the space provided:

____ Chapter 39 records relating to dependency matters, termination of parental rights, guardians ad litem, child abuse neglect, and abandonment. §39.1032(3), Fla. Stat. (If the document is filed within a Chapter 39 case, this form is not required.)

____ Adoption records. §63.162, Fla. Stat. (If the document is filed within a Chapter 63 adoption case, this form is not required)

____ Social Security, bank account, charge, debit, and credit card numbers in court records. §119.0714(1)(i)-(j), (2)(a)-(e), Fla. Stat. (Unless redaction is requested pursuant to §119.0714(2), this information is exempt only as of January 1, 2011)

____ HIV test results and patient identity within the HIV test results, §381.004(3)(e), Fla. Stat.

____ Sexually transmitted diseases - test results and identity within the test results when provided by the Department of Health or the department's authorized representative. § 384.29, Fla. Stat.

____ Birth and death certificates, including court-issued delayed birth certificates and fetal death certificates. §§382.008(6), 382.025(1)(a), Fla. Stat.

____ Identifying information in petition by minor for waiver of parental notice when seeking to terminate pregnancy. §390.01116, Fla. Stat. (If the document is filed within a Ch. 390 waiver of parental notice case, this form is not required)

____ Identifying information in clinical mental health records under the Baker Act. §394.4615(7), Fla. Stat.

____ Records of substance abuse service providers which pertain to the identity, diagnosis, and prognosis of and service provision to individuals who have received services from substance abuse service providers. § 397.501(7), Fla Stat.

____ Identifying information in clinical records of detained criminal defendants found incompetent to proceed or acquitted by reason of insanity. § 916.107(8), Fla. Stat.

____ Estate inventories and accountings. §733.604(1), Fla. Stat.

____ Victim's address in domestic violence action on petitioner's request. §741.30(3)(b), Fla. Stat.

____ Information identifying victims of sexual offenses, including child sexual abuse. §§119.071(2)(h), 119.0714(1)(h), Fla. Stat.

____ Gestational surrogacy records. §742.16(9), Fla. Stat.

____ Guardianship reports, and orders appointing court monitors in guardianship cases. §§744.1076, 744.3701, Fla. Stat.

____ Grand jury records. Ch. 905, Fla. Stat. (If the document is filed in Ch. 905 grand jury proceedings, this form is not required)

____ Information acquired by courts and law enforcement, regarding family services for children. §984.06(3)-(4), Fla. Stat. (If the document is filed in Ch. 984 family services for children case, this form is not required)

____ Juvenile delinquency records. §§985.04(1), 985.045(2), Fla. Stat. (If the document is filed in a Ch. 985 juvenile delinquency case, this form is not required)

____ Information disclosing the identity of persons subject to tuberculosis proceedings and records of the Department of Health in suspected tuberculosis cases. §§392.545, 392,65, Fla. Stat.

11–24. DOMESTIC RELATIONS—FAMILY DIVISION—MODEL FAMILY COURT

IN THE CIRCUIT COURT OF THE EIGHTEENTH JUDICIAL CIRCUIT

ADMINISTRATIVE ORDER NO: 11–24 SUPERSEDES 06–14

IN RE: DOMESTIC RELATIONS—FAMILY DIVISION—MODEL FAMILY COURT

WHEREAS, the Eighteenth Judicial Circuit is committed to developing a fully integrated, comprehensive approach to handling all cases involving children and families; [1]

WHEREAS, the Florida Supreme Court has adopted the following guiding principles as a foundation for defining and implementing a model family court; [2]

Children should live in safe and permanent homes;

The needs and best interests of children should be the primary consideration of any family court;

All persons, whether children or adults, should be treated with objectivity, sensitivity, dignity and respect;

Cases involving inter-related family law issues should be consolidated or coordinated to maximize use of court resources to avoid conflicting decisions and to minimize inconvenience to the families;

Family court processes should attempt to address the family's interrelated legal and non-legal problems, empower families through skills development, assist them to resolve their own disputes, provide access to appropriate services, and offer a variety of dispute resolution forums where the family can resolve problems without additional emotional trauma;

Whenever possible, parties and their attorneys should be empowered to select processes for addressing issues in their cases that are compatible with the family's needs, financial circumstances, and legal requirements;

The court is responsible for managing its cases with due consideration of the needs of the family, the litigants, and the issues presented by the case;

There should be a means of differentiating among cases so that judicial resources are conserved and cases are diverted to non-judicial and quasi-judicial personnel for resolution, when appropriate and consistent with the ends of justice;

Trial courts must coordinate and maximize court resources and establish linkages with community resources;

The court's role in family restructuring is to identify services and craft solutions that are appropriate for long-term stability and that minimize the need for subsequent court action;

Court services should be available to litigants at a reasonable cost and accessible without economic discrimination; and

Courts should have well-trained and highly-motivated judicial and non-judicial personnel.

NOW, THEREFORE, pursuant to the authority vested in me as the Chief Judge of the Eighteenth Judicial Circuit, in order to establish a Family Division that will meet the requirements of the Florida Supreme Court articulated In re Report of the Family Court Steering Committee, 794 So.2d 518 (Fla. 2001), and to better serve the needs of the citizens of the state of Florida, it is hereby ORDERED as follows:

I. JURISDICTION

The Family Court Division of the Eighteenth Judicial Circuit shall include, at a minimum, the following types of cases: [3]

A. dissolution of marriage

B. division and distribution of property arising out of dissolution of marriage

C. annulment

D. support unconnected with dissolution of marriage

E. paternity

F. child support

G. URESA/UIFSA

H. custodial care of and access to children

I. adoption

J. name change

K. declaratory judgment actions related to premarital, marital, or post marital agreements

L. civil domestic and repeat violence injunctions

M. juvenile dependency

N. termination of parental rights

O. juvenile delinquency

P. emancipation of a minor

Q. CINS/FINS

R. truancy

S. Marchman acts

T. modification and enforcement of orders entered in these cases.

II. ADMINISTRATIVE FAMILY LAW JUDGE

Pursuant to Rule 2.050(b)(5), Rules of Judicial Administration, an administrative judge for the Family Division shall be designated to oversee and coordinate the Eighteenth Judicial Circuit's comprehensive response to children and families in litigation. The Administrative Family Judge will manage the Family Division and be responsible for:

A. Coordinating the circuit's development of the overall plan for implementation of the family court concept;

B. Developing proposed policy, operating procedures, and administrative orders for implementation of the circuit's plan;

C. Monitoring and reporting progress toward implementation;

D. Coordinating the development of resources that may be required by various courts dealing with family matters (e.g., guardian ad litem, mediation services, drug referral and treatment, home studies, parenting classes, parenting coordinators, etc.) and assessing the possible integration of cases regarding involuntary commitments for drug and alcohol dependency or mental health, and as appropriate, guardianships;

E. Developing and facilitating communications with court-related entities on policy with respect to family cases, including but not limited to state attorneys, public defenders, the Department of Children and Families, the Department of Revenue, the Department of Juvenile Justice, hearing officers, magistrates, mediators, community social services entities, clerk of courts, and law enforcement agencies; and

F. Developing a means of orienting judges newly assigned to matters affecting children and families to the family court concept for integrating the court's response to cases involving the same family, including directing them to appropriate initial and continuing judicial education offerings and reference materials.

IIA. FAMILY ADMINISTRATIVE JUDGES

Because of the size of the Eighteenth Judicial Circuit, it is necessary to designate a separate administrative judge for both Brevard County and Seminole County. However, one of the two family administrative judges will be designated as the Circuit's Family Division Administrative Judge with primary supervisory responsibilities. The administrative judges shall work together to ensure genuine coordination of cases and a coordinated approach to the overall handling of cases and utilization of resources.

III. ROTATION OF JUDGES

Judges are assigned for one year rotation periods. Judges who are assigned to the Family Division for the first time or who have not served in the Family Division for two years, should receive mandatory training in the fundamentals of family law, domestic violence, juvenile dependency, and juvenile delinquency before assuming the assignment or within 60 days (when reasonably possible) after assuming the assignment.

It is the policy of the Eighteenth Judicial Circuit to ensure that all judges receive proper orientation and are well prepared to undertake their judicial assignments. Therefore, the chief judge will designate an experienced Family Division judge to function as a mentor to judges entering the division.

IV. ESSENTIAL ELEMENTS

A. Case Management. To the extent that existing staff and resources can be allocated, the Family Division shall receive case management services and support, including, but not limited to, the timely referral of cases to mediation, the timely referral of litigants with minor children to classes which help educate parents on ways to assist their minor children cope with their parents' separation, the referral of cases to the general magistrate, when appropriate, the scheduling of cases for pre-trial or status conferences, and the scheduling of cases for trial. Additionally, to the extent existing staff or resources can be allocated, the family division shall receive case management services and support to enable the family court judge to be aware of and to be able to identify all collateral cases affecting the parties involved.

B. Self Help. The Eighteenth Judicial Circuit shall ensure that Self Help programs exist so that litigants are provided with Florida Supreme Court approved forms, instructions, definitions, and procedural information consistent with Rule 12.750, Florida Family Law Rules of Procedure. As part of its intake function, the clerk of the circuit court shall provide ministerial assistance to pro se litigants. Ministerial assistance shall not include the providing of legal advice.

C. Domestic Violence. The Family Division Administrative Judge shall work with other judges within the division to develop a policy to ensure that the cases involving domestic violence are identified and managed in a manner that is organized, timely, and sensitive to the special dynamics involved in these cases.

D. Alternative Dispute Resolution. It is the policy of the Eighteenth Judicial Circuit to make maximum use of alternative dispute resolution (ADR) of family matters and issues as authorized by sections 44.102 and 39.4075, Florida Statutes, and Florida Family Law Rules of Procedure 12.740 and 12.741 and Florida Juvenile Rule of Procedure 8.290.

The court shall take necessary steps to ensure that a party who has been the victim of domestic violence and who does not wish to participate in mediation is not ordered to attend mediation.

E. Guardian Ad Litem ("GAL"). The Eighteenth Judicial Circuit will coordinate with the GAL Program to ensure representation of the best interests of children involved in cases with allegations of abuse, abandonment, and neglect.

F. General Magistrates. General Magistrates may be utilized to supplement the work of judges within the Family Division when a presiding judge determines that referral of a case is appropriate and consent of the parties is obtained. Referrals shall be made in accordance with relevant Rules of Juvenile and Family Procedure and any applicable administrative orders.

G. Custody Evaluation. To the extent existing staff and resources can be allocated, the family division shall receive home study reports from court evaluators in those cases involving a high degree of conflict and/or those cases involving allegations of abandonment, abuse, or neglect. To the extent the financial resources of the parties permit, judges may also order custody evaluations to be performed by mental health professionals.

H. Supervised Visitation. A list of approved supervision centers in each county shall be made available to each family division judge as well as to the Clerk's office.

I. Parenting Education. Pursuant to section 61.21, Florida Statutes, all parties to dissolution of marriage proceeding with minor children or a paternity action which involves issues of parental responsibility shall be required to complete the parent education and family stabilization course prior to the entry of the court's final judgment.

J. Counseling Services/Treatment Programs. Under the leadership of the Family Division Administrative Judge and in consultation with the Family Law Advisory Group, and others, the Eighteenth Judicial Circuit will develop strategies to enable the courts to be able to advise litigants of counseling services and treatment programs available in the appropriate county. Additionally, the strategies shall ensure that compliance is monitored when such services are court-ordered.

K. Security. Judges in the Family Division are aware of the special security issues attendant to family law matters. The Chief Judge shall consult and cooperate with the local sheriffs' departments to develop a plan to ensure that adequate and sufficient security personnel and equipment are available to ensure that Family Divisions are safe environments for judges, non-judicial staff, and the public.

L. Technology. The Eighteenth Judicial Circuit shall use available technology to access information essential to case management and coordination, to print forms and notices immediately, to generate statistical reports, to provide public and inter-agency access to records, and to allow teleconferencing and appearance of witnesses by electronic means.

V. IDENTIFICATION AND COORDINATION OF RELATED CASES

A. Provisions applicable to both Brevard and Seminole Counties.

1. The Eighteenth Circuit's plan for coordination of cases is based on the coordinated management model adopted by the Florida Supreme Court and is designed to take into account the individual needs and resources within each county in the circuit. Each county will utilize the one family—one team model, with a goal of having the vast majority of time-sharing decisions regarding a minor child be made by a single judge.

2. In identifying related cases, the Eighteenth Circuit recognizes that many family cases involve individuals and issues that are interrelated, but do not involve a family relationship or children. The case manager or the clerk will determine if any of the parties or children have pending or closed family cases. If they have pending or closed family cases, the Court will decide whether all or some of the cases should be assigned to the same judge or coordinated to conserve judicial resources, avoid inconsistent court orders, and eliminate multiple appearances on the same issue. Upon the filing of a case in the Family Division, the clerk shall conduct a search of existing family law cases to determine the existence of other litigation involving the same family. Additionally, at the time of the filing, the parties and/or their attorneys shall be required to complete an information sheet indicating, as appropriate, the existence of prior or pending cases involving the same parties. If possible, the party/attorney shall set forth the style, case number, and date of disposition of the case.

3. Cases involving the same child(ren) in family law cases and juvenile dependency cases are defined as cross-over cases. These cross-over cases shall be consolidated and assigned to the dependency division judge unless otherwise ordered by such judge.

4. When there exists a Department of Revenue action for child support and a dissolution of marriage action is subsequently filed, the Department of Revenue action for child support shall automatically be consolidated with the dissolution of marriage action and arrearages or credits from the prior Department of Revenue action will be transferred to the dissolution of marriage action. An exception to this order is a Department of Revenue action brought only for the purpose of recovering prior private public assistance payments. Such actions will not be consolidated with a subsequently filed dissolution of marriage action.

B. Provisions applicable to Brevard County only:

1. There shall be a unified family court division which will be presided over by the dependency division judge. Where there is a delinquency case filed against a minor child and such child is also the subject of an on-going dependency case, the delinquency division judge may refer such matter to the dependency division judge. The unified family court/dependency division judge will have the sole discretion to determine if such case will be accepted in the unified family court division after determining whether the acceptance of such case in the unified family court division will be in the child's best interest.

2. Cases involving the same parties in domestic violence cases and family law cases are defined as cross-over cases. If the family law case is filed first, the clerk will be directed to assign the cross-over domestic violence case to the judicial division which is handling the existing family law case. If a domestic violence case is filed first, the clerk will be similarly directed to assign the subsequently filed cross-over family law case to the judicial division which is assigned or within the past 6 months was assigned the domestic violence case.

C. Provisions applicable to Seminole County Only:

1. There shall be two unified family court divisions which will be presided over by the judges assigned to the dependency/delinquency divisions. Where there is a delinquency case filed against a minor child and such child is also the subject of an on-going dependency case, the delinquency/dependency judge may order the two cases be heard in a consolidated proceeding after determining such consolidation would be in the best interest of the minor child.

2. Cases involving the same parties in Unified Family Court injunctions and family law cases are defined as cross-over cases. If the family law case is filed first, the clerk will be directed to assign the cross-over Unified Family Court injunction to the judicial division which is handling the existing family law case. If the Unified Family Court injunction case is filed first, the clerk will be similarly directed to assign the subsequently filed cross-over family law case to the judicial division which is assigned or was previously assigned the Unified Family Court injunction even if the prior petition was dismissed. A Unified Family Court injunction is defined as a Petition for Injunction for Protection Against Domestic Violence where the domestic violence relationship arises as a result of the parties being currently or previously married, or if not currently or previously married, where the parties have a minor child in common.

VI. FAMILY LAW ADVISORY GROUP

The success of any family court is dependent upon effective communication among all stakeholders both in the judicial system and in the community. In each county, there is established a family law advisory group. The chair of the family law advisory group shall either be the administrative family judge or a family division judge appointed by the administrative family judge. Membership of the group shall be open to interested parties, to include but not be limited to, a representative from each of the following:

Judge(s), Domestic Relations
Judges(s), Dependency
Judge(s), Domestic Violence
Judges(s), Delinquency
Hearing Officer
General Magistrate
Trial Court Administrator
Case Manager
Self Help Center Director
Clerk of Court
Clerk's Office Staff
Mediators
Guardian ad Litem
Custody Evaluators
Parenting Course Providers
Supervised Visitation Providers
Parenting Coordinators
Process Servers
Private Attorneys
Public Defenders
State Attorneys
Legal Services/Legal Aid
Department of Revenue
Department of Children and Families
Department of Juvenile Justice
School Board/Dept. of Education
Law Enforcement
Local Government Officials
Community Organizers
Parents and Children (Consumers)
Certified Public Accountants
Faith-based Community Programs
Domestic Violence Advocates/Shelter Staff
Substance Abuse and Mental Health Providers
Batterers' Intervention Providers
Local Colleges, University Professionals

The Family Law Advisory Group shall meet quarterly, or more often, upon the call of the chairperson. The report on the progress of the group in meeting the goals of the model family court shall be submitted to the Chief Judge by December 1st of each year.

This Administrative Order shall become effective upon signing.

DONE AND ORDERED this 9th day of September, 2011.

ALAN A. DICKEY
CHIEF JUDGE

1 In re Report of the Commission on Family Courts, 633 So.2d 14, 17 (Fla. 1994).

2 See In re Report of the Family Court Steering Committee, 794 So.2d 518, 522 (Fla. 2001).

3 REQUIREMENT: See In re Report of the Family Court Steering Committee, 794 So.2d 518, 525 (Fla. 2001)

11–22–B (A1). CRIMINAL—STANDARDIZED BREVARD COUNTY ARREST AFFIDAVIT

IN THE CIRCUIT COURT OF THE EIGHTEENTH JUDICIAL CIRCUIT IN AND FOR BREVARD COUNTY, FLORIDA

ADMINISTRATIVE ORDER NO.: 11–22–B

IN RE: Criminal—Standardized Brevard County Arrest Affidavit

WHEREAS, Florida Rules of Judicial Administration (Rule 2.050) states that the chief judge "shall exercise administrative supervision over all courts within the judicial circuit in the exercise of judicial power over the judges and officers of the court" and "shall develop an administrative plan for the efficient and proper administration of all courts within that circuit", which included a "mandatory periodic review of the status of the inmates of the county jail"; and

WHEREAS, the sheriff and municipal law enforcement agencies in Brevard County have historically used a standard arrest form which was at one time provided by the Clerk of the Court, but has now become the financial responsibility of each law enforcement agency; and

WHEREAS, many law enforcement agencies are generating forms or are considering programs that generate forms through their computer systems; and

WHEREAS, continued standardization of Brevard County's Arrest Affidavit will maintain efficiency, effectiveness, statistical information and sharing of information among various state, county and municipal agencies; and

WHEREAS, continued standardization of Brevard County's Arrest Affidavit will avoid inefficiency, court-related costs, labor hours, redundancy, data entry and clerical mistakes.

IT IS ORDERED AND ADJUDGED that the Standard Affidavit of Arrest attached hereto as Attachment "A", which shall include a Notice Of Confidential Information when required under Florida Rule of Judicial Administration 2.420(d)(2), is hereby adopted for use by all law enforcement agencies within Brevard County. Said Arrest Affidavit, whether pre-printed or computer generated, is required to maintain the same basic format in the inclusion and presentation of information to the court.

DONE AND ORDERED, this ___ day of June, 2011.

J. PRESTON SILVERNAIL
CHIEF JUDGE

FCIC CHECK ☐YES ☐NO

OBTS Number

ATTACHMENT "A"
ARREST/NOTICE TO APPEAR
PROBABLE CAUSE AFFIDAVIT/
JUVENILE REFERRAL

1. Arrest
2. Notice to Appear
3. Arrest Affidavit
4. Complaint Affidavit
5. Request for Capias
6. Juvenile Referral

Juvenile ☐

Agency ORI Number FL 005035 A	Agency Name	Agency Report Number
Check Type. Check as many as apply: ☐1. Felony ☐ 2. Traffic Felony ☐ 3. Misdemeanor ☐ 4. Traffic Misdemeanor ☐ 5. Ordinance ☐ 6. Other	Weapon Seized/Type ☐ Yes ☐ No	Agency Arrest Number

Location of Arrest (Include Name of Business)	City	Location of Offense Business Name, Address	City

Date of Arrest	Time of Arrest	BCSO Date	BCSO Time	Jail Date	Jail Time	Fingerprinted ☐ Identification Only ☐AFIS ☐Criminal By:

Date of Offense	FDLE Number	DOC Number	FBI Number

Name (Last, First, Middle)	Alias

Race: W-White I-American Indian B-Black O-Oriental/Asian	Sex	Date of Birth	Height	Weight	Eye Color	Hair Color	Complexion	Build

Scars, Marks, Tattoos, Unique Physical Features (Location, Type, Description)	Indication of: Y N Unk. Alcohol Influence ☐ ☐ ☐ Drug Influence ☐ ☐ ☐

Local Address (Street, Apt, Number)	(City)	(State)	(Zip)	Phone	Residence Type ☐ City. ☐County ☐ Florida ☐ Out of State
Permanent Address (Street, Apt, Number) or Parent's Name if Juv.	(City)	(State)	(Zip)	Phone	Parent Contacted Y ☐ N ☐
Business Address (Name, Street,) or Parent's Address if Juvenile	(City)	(State)	(Zip)	Phone	Occupation

Driver's License State/Number	Social Security Number	I.C.E. Number	Place of Birth	Citizenship

Co-Defendant Name (Last, First, Middle)	Race	Sex	Date of Birth or Age	☐Arrested ☐ Felony ☐ Juvenile ☐ At Large ☐ Misdemeanor
Co-Defendant Name (Last, First, Middle)	Race	Sex	Date of Birth or Age	☐Arrested ☐ Felony ☐ Juvenile ☐ At Large ☐ Misdemeanor

Activity N. N/A P. Possess S. Sell B. Buy T. Traffic R. Smuggle D. Deliver E. Use K. Dispense / Distribute M. Manufacture / Produce / Cultivate Z. Other

Type N. N/A P. Possess B. Barbiturate C. Cocaine E. Heroin H. Hallucinogen M. Marijuana O. Opium / Derivative P. Paraphernalia / Equipment S. Synthetic U. Unknown Z. Other

Charge Description	Counts	☐F.S. ☐Ord	Statute Violation Number	Violation of Section (ORD)
Activity / Drug Type / Amount/Unit	Bond Amount		Court Number	
☐PC ☐ Capias ☐AC ☐BW ☐FW ☐PW ☐ Juv. PU ☐Citation	Date Issued		☐ Writ. Att. ☐ Order of Arrest	☐Domestic Viol. Inj.
Charge Description	Counts	☐F.S. ☐Ord	Statute Violation Number	Violation of Section (ORD)
Activity / Drug Type / Amount/Unit	Bond Amount		Court Number	
☐PC ☐ Capias ☐AC ☐BW ☐FW ☐PW ☐ Juv. PU ☐Citation	Date Issued		☐ Writ. Att. ☐ Order of Arrest	☐Domestic Viol. Inj.

The undersigned certifies and swears that he/she has just and reasonable grounds to believe, and does believe the above named Defendant committed the following violation of law:
On the 1st day of May 2008 at ☐ A.M. ☐ P.M. (Specifically include facts constituting cause for arrest.)

Pursuant to Florida Statute 938.27 the investigative cost incurred by this agency is

Continued for ☐ Narrative ☐ Charges

Mandatory Appearance In Court — **Location : Brevard County Courthouse, 2825 Judge Fran Jamieson Way, Viera, FL 32940**
Month Day Year Time ☐ A.M. ☐ P.M.

I AGREE TO APPEAR AT THE TIME AND PLACE DESIGNATED TO ANSWER THE OFFENSE CHARGED. I UNDERSTAND THAT SHOULD I WILLFULLY FAIL TO APPEAR BEFORE THE COURT AS REQUIRED BY THIS NOTICE TO APPEAR, THAT I MAY BE HELD IN CONTEMPT OF COURT AND A WARRANT FOR MY ARREST OR A TAKE INTO CUSTODY ORDER SHALL BE ISSUED.

Signature of Defendant/Juvenile	Signature of Juv. Parent/Custodian	Released to: (Name)	Date	Time
Miranda ☐ Warning	Hold for Other Agency Name:	Verified By	Date	Bonding Agency

Adults Only: ☐ Hold for First Appearance. ☐ Do Not Bond Out Reason:		Bond #	Amount
I swear/affirm the above and attached is true and correct. ☐ Yes Investigator's/Complainant's Signature ______ ID. No/Dist.	Sworn and subscribed before me, the undersigned authority this day of , 2011. Signature______	Bond #	Amount
	Type name Notary/Law Enforcement Officer in Performance of Official	Returnable Court Date	Returnable Court Date
Name (Printed)	Duties. Personally Known ☐ ID Produced ☐	Court Location:	Page 1 of

Brevard County, FL

Narrative Continuation Page of

DEFENDANT/JUVENILE (Last, First, Middle)				Agency Report No.	
				OBTS No.	
Charge Description		Counts	☐ F.S. ☐ Ord.	Statute Violation Number	Violation of Section (ORD)
Activity	Drug Type	Amount/Unit	Bond Amount	Court Number	
☐ PC ☐ Capias ☐ AC ☐ BW ☐ FW ☐ PW ☐ Juv. PU ☐ Citation			Date Issued	☐ Writ. Att. ☐ Order of Arrest	☐ Domestic Viol. Inj.
Charge Description		Counts	☐ F.S. ☐ Ord.	Statute Violation Number	Violation of Section (ORD)
Activity	Drug Type	Amount/Unit	Bond Amount	Court Number	
☐ PC ☐ Capias ☐ AC ☐ BW ☐ FW ☐ PW ☐ Juv. PU ☐ Citation			Date Issued	☐ Writ. Att. ☐ Order of Arrest	☐ Domestic Viol. Inj.

Officer's Signature ______________________ Officer's Name Printed ______________________

NOTICE OF CONFIDENTIAL INFORMATION WITHIN COURT FILING

Pursuant to Florida Rule of Judicial Administration 2.420(d)(2), the filer of a court record at the time of filing shall indicate whether any confidential information is included within the document being filed; identify the confidentiality provision that applies to the identified information; and identify the precise location of the confidential information within the document being filed.

Title/Type of Document(s): ____________________

Indicate the applicable confidentiality provision(s) below from Rule 2.420(d)(1)(B), by specifying the location within the document on the space provided:

___ Chapter 39 records relating to dependency matters, termination of parental rights, guardians ad litem, child abuse neglect, and abandonment. § 39.1032(3), Fla. Stat. (If the document is filed within a Chapter 39 case, this form is not required.)

___ Adoption records. § 63.162, Fla. Stat. (If the document is filed within a Chapter 63 adoption case, this form is not required)

___ Social Security, bank account, charge, debit, and credit card numbers in court records. § 119.0714(1)(i)–(j), (2)(a)–(e), Fla. Stat. (Unless redaction is requested pursuant to § 119.0714(2), this information is exempt only as of January 1, 2011)

___ HIV test results and patient identity within the HIV test results, § 381.004(3)(e), Fla. Stat.

___ Sexually transmitted diseases—test results and identity within the test results when provided by the Department of Health or the department's authorized representative. § 384.29, Fla. Stat.

___ Birth and death certificates, including court-issued delayed birth certificates and fetal death certificates. §§ 382.008(6), 382.025(1)(a), Fla. Stat.

___ Identifying information in petition by minor for waiver of parental notice when seeking to terminate pregnancy. § 390.01116, Fla. Stat. (If the document is filed within a Ch. 390 waiver of parental notice case, this form is not required)

___ Identifying information in clinical mental health records under the Baker Act. § 394.4615(7), Fla. Stat.

___ Records of substance abuse service providers which pertain to the identity, diagnosis, and prognosis of and service provision to individuals who have received services from substance abuse service providers. § 397.501(7), Fla Stat.

___ Identifying information in clinical records of detained criminal defendants found incompetent to proceed or acquitted by reason of insanity. § 916.107(8), Fla. Stat.

___ Estate inventories and accountings. § 733.604(1), Fla. Stat.

___ Victim's address in domestic violence action on petitioner's request. § 741.30(3)(b), Fla. Stat.

___ Information identifying victims of sexual offenses, including child sexual abuse. §§ 119.071(2)(h), 119.0714(1)(h), Fla. Stat.

___ Gestational surrogacy records. § 742.16(9), Fla. Stat.

___ Guardianship reports, and orders appointing court monitors in guardianship cases. §§ 744.1076, 744.3701, Fla. Stat.

___ Grand jury records. Ch. 905, Fla. Stat. (If the document is filed in Ch. 905 grand jury proceedings, this form is not required)

___ Information acquired by courts and law enforcement, regarding family services for children. § 984.06(3)–(4), Fla. Stat. (If the document is filed in Ch. 984 family services for children case, this form is not required)

___ Juvenile delinquency records. §§ 985.04(1), 985.045(2), Fla. Stat. (If the document is filed in a Ch. 985 juvenile delinquency case, this form is not required)

___ Information disclosing the identity of persons subject to tuberculosis proceedings and records of the Department of Health in suspected tuberculosis cases. §§ 392.545, 392,65, Fla. Stat.

11–15–S. JUVENILE COURT AND PROSECUTION ALTERNATIVES FOR YOUTH PROGRAM PROCEDURE

IN THE CIRCUIT COURT OF THE EIGHTEENTH JUDICIAL CIRCUIT IN AND FOR SEMINOLE COUNTY, FLORIDA

ADMINISTRATIVE ORDER NO.: 11–15–S

SUPERSEDES 09–21–S AMENDED

IN RE: JUVENILE COURT AND PROSECUTION ALTERNATIVES FOR YOUTH PROGRAM PROCEDURE

WHEREAS, the policy of the juvenile justice and delinquency system is to develop and implement effective programs to provide procedural and substantive due process, prompt, fair and just resolution of delinquency matters, prevent delinquency, to divert children from the traditional juvenile justice system, and to intervene at an early stage of delinquency. F.S. 985.02(1)(b).

WHEREAS, Seminole County, as part of a Delinquency Prevention Program is fortunate to have the Prosecution Alternatives for Youth Program (PAY), a delinquency prevention program that provides arbitration services, a Teen Court program, and other alternative services to divert children from the Court system.

WHEREAS, a diversion program is more effective if a child can enter the program as soon as possible after the child is taken into custody.

WHEREAS, an arraignment hearing is usually up to twenty one (21) days after a child is taken into custody.

WHEREAS, Delinquency Prevention programs would be more effective if children begin a program before their arraignment, and the judicial system would be more effective if the less serious cases were diverted from prosecution.

WHEREAS, as a condition to release from detention, probation, or other Court supervised activity, each juvenile subject to the jurisdiction of the Juvenile Division, Circuit Court, Seminole County, Florida shall be deemed to consent to the release of student records, including but not limited to: attendance, academic History, grades and school discipline records held by the School Board of Seminole County, Florida and the juvenile's current school of enrollment.

WHEREAS, in order to accomplish these goals, the child must sign a waiver of speedy trial and a release of his records to the Juvenile Court, Department of Juvenile Justice and his attorney, and shall meet with PAY officials prior to arraignment.

IT IS THEREFORE, ORDERED AND ADJUDGED;

1. When a juvenile is taken into custody by a law enforcement officer, charged with a delinquent act and given a notice to appear, the Department of Juvenile Justice (DJJ) shall submit, within 24 hours after a child is placed into detention or within 20 days after the date a child is taken into custody, a written recommendation to the State Attorney's Office that includes a copy of the original probable cause affidavit and a copy of the child's prior record as required by F.S. 985.145(1)(j).

2. If DJJ recommends non-judicial handling to the State Attorney, then the juvenile probation officer (JPO) must also include with the recommendation form a waiver of speedy trial form signed by the child and parent or guardian as required by the Department of Juvenile Justice Probation & Community Corrections Handbook, Chapter 4, page 4–15.

3. As a condition to release from detention, probation, or other Court supervised activity, each juvenile subject to the jurisdiction of the Juvenile Division, Circuit Court, Seminole County, Florida shall be deemed to consent to the release of student records, including but not limited to: attendance, academic history, grades and school discipline records held by the School Board of Seminole County, Florida and the juvenile's current school of enrollment.

4. If the State Attorney's Office is able to refer children to PAY prior to arraignment, the State Attorney's Office shall provide to PAY a copy of the referral as soon as it is filed with the Clerk, and PAY shall make every attempt to meet with the child and parent or guardian prior to the scheduled arraignment hearing.

5. The State Attorney's Office shall provide to PAY as soon as practicable after receipt from the Clerk a copy of the arraignment docket printed by the Clerk on the Thursday before arraignment. This copy will indicate the children who have been referred to PAY before arraignment.

6. Upon receipt of the docket from the State Attorney's Office, PAY will indicate on the docket which of the children referred to PAY have already met with PAY and signed up for the program and provide a copy of the docket to the State Attorney's Office and the Clerk of Court by the close of business on the Thursday before arraignment.

7. At the arraignment hearing, the State Attorney's Office will first announce the names of the children who have previously been referred to PAY, who have met with PAY prior to arraignment, and who are, therefore, excused from attending their arraignment and will then announce the names of the children who have not signed up to participate in PAY prior to arraignment. Those children will then be sent to the PAY office from the courtroom.

8. If a child is not present when their name is called, the arraignment hearing will be continued one week. If the child is also not present at the second arraignment hearing, and PAY has not advised the State Attorney's Office that the child has signed up for PAY before the second arraignment hearing, an Order To Take Into Custody shall be issued for the child.

DONE AND ORDERED this 19th day of April, 2011.

J. PRESTON SILVERNAIL
CHIEF JUDGE

11–14–B (A4). SUPERSEDED BY ADMINISTRATIVE ORDER NO. 16-35-B

11–12–B. SUPERSEDED BY ADMINISTRATIVE ORDER NO. 16–01–B.

11–10–S. [SUPERSEDED BY ORDER 17–17–S, EFFECTIVE MARCH 27, 2017.]

10–33–B. JAIL—DISTRIBUTION OF SUMMARIES OF CRIMINAL HISTORY NCIC/FCIC OF DEFENDANTS APPEARING AT FIRST APPEARANCE AT BREVARD COUNTY JAIL

IN THE CIRCUIT COURT OF THE EIGHTEENTH JUDICIAL CIRCUIT IN AND FOR BREVARD COUNTY, FLORIDA

ADMINISTRATIVE ORDER NO.: 10–33–B

IN RE: JAIL—DISTRIBUTION OF SUMMARIES OF CRIMINAL HISTORY NCIC/FCIC OF DEFENDANTS APPEARING AT FIRST APPEARANCE AT BREVARD COUNTY JAIL

Whereas, Florida Rule of Criminal Procedure 3.130 provides that, except when previously released in a lawful manner, every arrested person shall be taken before a judicial officer within 24 hours of arrest for First Appearance; this rule further provides that the State Attorney or an Assistant State Attorney and Public Defender or Assistant Public Defender shall attend the First Appearance; this rule further provides that the arrested person may be represented at the First Appearance by privately retained counsel, and

Whereas, Florida Rule of Criminal Procedure 3.131(b) provides that the judge at First Appearance may consider, among other delineated factors, the defendant's past and present conduct, including any record of convictions, to determine what form of release is necessary to assure the defendant's appearance, and

Whereas, at the Brevard County Jail, Pretrial Release at First Appearance provides the Court, the State Attorney, the Public Defender, and retained counsel, with a summary of the defendants' criminal history derived from the Florida Crime Information Center (FCIC) and the National Crime Information Center (NCIC), and

Whereas, Pretrial Release in Brevard County now requires an Administrative Order authorizing the continued distribution of the defendants' criminal history at First Appearance at the Brevard County Jail,

IT IS HEREBY ORDERED that;

Pretrial Release is authorized to distribute to the State Attorney and Assistant State Attorneys, the Public Defender and Assistant Public Defenders, and to privately retained counsel, its summary of the criminal histories of defendants appearing at the Brevard County Jail for First Appearance which are derived from the Florida Crime Information Center (FCIC) and the National Crime Information Center (NCIC).

Done and Ordered this 17th day of December, 2010.

J. PRESTON SILVERNAIL
CHIEF JUDGE

10–30–S. JUVENILE—DEPENDENCY MEDIATION—FLORIDA STATUTES CHAPTER 39 MANDATORY REFERRAL OF ALL CONTESTED DEPENDENCY CASES TO MEDIATION

IN THE CIRCUIT COURT OF THE EIGHTEENTH JUDICIAL CIRCUIT, IN AND FOR SEMINOLE COUNTY, FLORIDA

ADMINISTRATIVE ORDER NO.: 10–30–S

IN RE: JUVENILE—DEPENDENCY MEDIATION—FLORIDA STATUTES CHAPTER 39 MANDATORY REFERRAL OF ALL CONTESTED DEPENDENCY CASES TO MEDIATION

WHEREAS, certain Chapter 39 dependency and Termination of Parental Rights matters that include matters of abuse, abandonment and neglect, may, through an informal and non-adversarial mediation process facilitated by a Supreme Court certified dependency mediator, be resolved in an amicable and expeditious manner and

WHEREAS, the parties may be facilitated by a Mediator in the identification of issues, the fostering of joint problem solving, the exploration of settlement alternatives to effect resolution of the dispute between two or more parties and

WHEREAS, the parties may through mediation agree on a means by which the issues may be resolved in order to effect a timely resolution of permanency for children; and

WHEREAS, it has been found that there are numerous benefits to dependency mediation as delineated in the May 30, 2009 Final Report of the Analysis of Dependency Mediation in Florida Courts prepared by The Harrell Center for the Study of Family Violence, including, but not limited to findings that:

- Within counties utilizing mediation, time to permanency was significantly reduced if mediation took place prior to adjudication;
- Children in mediated cases were more likely to be placed with a non-abusive parent or a relative and less likely to be placed in a residential facility;
- Family members reported more satisfaction with mediation compared to court, including more frequent consultation with an attorney before and during the session; that they more frequently thought that all professionals kept an open mind; and that all the participants listened to and understood them.

WHEREAS, the mediation process may result in cost efficiencies to the parties and appears less costly than litigation, and

WHEREAS, mediation is a process whereby a neutral third person acts to encourage the resolution of disputes through a non-adversarial process and assists the parties in reaching a mutually acceptable agreement; and

WHEREAS, the mediation model requires the participation of the parents, parent's attorney(s), guardian ad litem, guardian ad litem attorney, Protective Investigator(s), CBC Seminole Case Manager and Supervisor, and the Children Legal Services attorney, including if possible those parties who may be incarcerated, and other participants and individuals whose participation might be helpful may be invited to attend the mediation, including Foster Parents, custodians and appropriate family members, if agreed upon by the Mediator.

WHEREAS, subject to the Court's ruling, it may be appropriate for children to participate in the mediation process, in consideration of a child's age, developmental stage, and mental health in determining if it is in the best interests of a child to participate in mediation.

WHEREAS, mandatory mediation for dependency increases the availability of judicial resources, and in recognition that Courtroom 3 of the Juvenile Justice Center and related office space may be made available for utilization in Mediation, thereby providing a safe and secure means whereby incarcerated parties may be made available for attendance at Mediation.

WHEREAS, it is necessary for the prompt and efficient administration of justice of this Court.

IT IS HEREBY ORDERED AND ADJUDGED THAT;

1. **Dispute Resolution Services:** This program is conducted under the direction of the Office of the Court Administrator and the Chief Judge of the Eighteenth Judicial Circuit. The Dependency Circuit Court shall promote and, where deemed appropriate, order parties to mediation on Chapter 39 Dependency matters, including any and all issues related to Dependency and Termination of Parental Rights proceeding for parties appearing on matters pending before Dependency Court.

2. **Authority to Refer to Mediation:** Pursuant to Chapter 39.521, Florida Statutes, and Florida Rules of Juvenile Procedure § 8.290, the Court on its own motion may refer all or any part of a Chapter 39 Dependency or Termination of Parental Rights matter to mediation for the purpose of mediating any and/or all Chapter 39 Dependency or Termination of Parental Rights issues.

3. **Notice:** The Court will issue to the parties an Order of Referral to Mediation, the name of the Mediator, and a date and time when Courtroom 3 will be available. It is the responsibility of the parties to notify others who may wish to participate, including the foster parents, custodians, appropriate relatives, and the child.

4. **Procedure: Shelter, Pre and Post Adjudication**: At any time after removal of a child and a finding of shelter care status, or after arraignment, The Court may, on its own motion and/or or upon receipt of a request by a party for Mediation, issue an Order of Referral of the matter to Mediation. The Parties have ten (10) days after filing of the Order of Referral to object to the referral. The matter may be scheduled for Mediation at the Dependency Court, Court Room 3, Juvenile Justice Center, 190 Bush Boulevard, Sanford, Florida 32773, telephone number (407) 665–5344, Fax number (407) 665–5449. The Court will attempt to schedule with both parties. After several unsuccessful attempts to reach the parties the Court may schedule the mediation session. Mediation sessions shall be scheduled and conducted in accordance with F. R. of Juv. P. § 8.290.

5. **Scheduling:** Mediation may be ordered at the shelter hearing, arraignment or at any time the Court believes media-

tion would be beneficial. Mediation shall ideally take place as early as possible, commensurate with the determination of representation by counsel. Once the mediation is ordered, a mediation master calendar shall be maintained wherein mediation dates and times will be coordinated for the use of Courtroom 3, with the cooperation of all the parties. The order containing the mediation information will be copied and distributed to all parties and their attorneys. If mediation cannot be set in Court, all parties will contact the Court within 24 hours of the order of mediation. All questions regarding general information about the mediations will be directed to the appropriate Court liaison at (407) 665–5344. Mediation shall be conducted in Courtroom 3 on Fridays, or at other dates and times as may be available, in accordance with the following time schedule:

a. 08:30am—10:00 am

b. 10:00am—11:30 am

c. 1:00 pm—2:30 pm

d. 3:00pm—4:30 pm

6. Incarcerated Parties: In order to provide appropriate security and participation by an incarcerated party, the attorney representing an incarcerated party incarcerated at the John E. Polk Correctional Facility shall submit to the Court a Motion and Order for Transportation of that party no later than five (5) days before the scheduled mediation date.

7. List of Mediators: A list of contract certified Dependency Mediators shall be maintained by the Court at the Juvenile Justice Center, 190 Bush Boulevard, Sanford Florida 32773 Telephone Number (407) 665–5344, Fax (407) 665–5449 and the Mediation Coordinator, 301 North Park Avenue, Suite N301, Sanford, FL 32771, telephone number (407) 665–4244.

8. Appointment of Mediators: The parties must have a pending Chapter 39 Dependency or Termination of Parental Rights case to be eligible to participate in the mediation program. If one or more of the parties are indigent, the Seminole County Dependency Circuit Judge shall appoint a Florida Supreme Court Certified Dependency Mediator.

9. Referral of Florida Statutes Chapter 39 Dependency and Termination of Parental Rights Matters:

a. Any person who seeks to schedule a final hearing for either pre-adjudication or post adjudication Florida Statutes Chapter 39 Dependency and Termination of Parental Rights matters must first participate in a mediation conference through the Seminole County Dependency Mediation Program herein established, unless waived pursuant to this order.

b. Each person shall have previously filed a financial affidavit with the Court, and there shall have been a determination of civil indigency status and, if so found, appointment of counsel.

c. In order to determine child support, the parent(s) shall bring to the initial mediation conference a current short form financial affidavit, and if the earnings have changed prior to filing; a copy of the most current pay stub voucher or letter from an employer stating current earnings. If self-employed, the person may bring a copy of the most recent 1040 filed with the Internal Revenue Service (IRS).

10. Exception—History of Domestic Violence: Pursuant to Florida Statutes § 44.102(2)(c), upon motion or request of a person, the Court shall not refer any case to mediation it if finds there has been a significant history of domestic violence that would compromise the mediation process.

11. Waivers:

A. *Automatic Waivers:* A person may file a Motion to Vacate the Order of Referral to Mediation and Notice of Trial with a Motion before the Court to dispense with mediation; if it has not been scheduled and if:

1. A mediation was scheduled and the other person failed to appear;

2. A default has been entered; or

3. A person is unavailable for mediation either in person or telephone because he/she:

a. is not subject to the jurisdiction of this Court and refuses to participate; or

b. currently resides in another country; or

c. is imprisoned out of state, or

d. All current issues have been mediated by a certified mediator, and an impasse has been declared.

B. *Waivers on Motion:* If mediation has been scheduled, a person may motion the Court to dispense with mediation based on Paragraph 7 (A). Any person may apply to the Court by written motion for good cause, to waive the mandatory mediation required by this Order prior to filing a notice for trial. The Court may waive such a requirement if it appears (a) that mediation of the issues would not be appropriate under the circumstances of that case or (b) that due to exigent circumstances a hearing before the Court should be expedited. If mediation has already been scheduled, and the mediation is canceled by the Court, both parties shall notify the Seminole County Dependency Mediation Program, in writing, with copy of Order signed by the Judge within five (5) business days prior to the scheduled mediation to cancel the mediation. If the parties do provide appropriate notice, five (5) business days, of cancellation, there shall be no fee. If both parties do not give proper notification of the judicial waiver cancellation, each person may be required to pay a full session fee for the canceled mediation session as the Court may determine, to be paid to the Clerk of the Court.

12. Attendance of Counsel: In the discretion of the mediator and with the agreement of the parties, the mediation session may proceed in the absence of counsel unless otherwise ordered by the Court. If counsel is not present within thirty (30) minutes after the scheduled mediation session time and his /her client does not wish to proceed in the attorney's absence, at the discretion of the mediator, the mediation session may be cancelled. If the mediation is so cancelled, the mediation fees paid by the party who will not proceed without counsel present will not apply to the next mediation. Any fee paid by the other party is applied to the next mediation session. The fee paid by the non cancelling party applied to the rescheduled mediation session because of the cancellation will not be refunded if no future mediation session occurs.

13. Attendance: Each party shall appear at any scheduled mediation session. A party is deemed to appear at a convened mediation session if the named party is physically present at the commencement of the mediation session. Upon the Court's own motion or upon motion of the appearing party, the failure of a party to appear for the mediation session may result in sanctions being imposed by the Court against the non-appearing party including, but not limited to payment of the session fee for both parties plus an additional session fee and attorneys' fees, if any. These fees will not apply to any future mediation sessions. If an indigent party fails to appear, sanctions may include the cost of a session fee.

14. Appearance by Telephone: In the case of an emergency or because of exigent circumstances that preclude personal attendance a person may request an appearance by telephone. In these cases, telephonic appearance is allowed by stipulation of both parties in writing to the Court prior to the mediation session, or by motion and order by the Court. The party appearing by telephone must have access to a fax machine. All mediation session fees from the party appearing by telephone must be received by the specified date on the Order.

15. Cancellations and Continuances by the Parties: Subject to Court approval, a mediation session may be continued or canceled if the parties agree in writing to the continuance or cancellation and the Court and Mediator are properly notified of said continuance or cancellation within five (5) business days of the scheduled mediation. If the parties cannot agree to a continuance, then the party who is requesting the continuance or cancellation shall apply to the Court for a continuance or cancellation. The process for continuation or cancellation must be completed and the Court must receive a signed stipulation by each party allowing the continuance or cancellation at least five (5) business days prior to the scheduled mediation session to avoid a full payment of one session fee. The party requesting the continuance or cancellation is responsible for assuring that the Court receives signed stipulation(s) from the parties.

16. Full Settlement Authority of Parties: Pursuant to F. R. Juv. P. 8.290 the parties appearing for mediation must have full and complete authority to negotiate a Mediated Settlement Agreement, and to bind their respective agency, department or program. Failure to do so may result in sanctions, as ordered by the Court.

17. If an Agreement or Impasse is Reached During the Mediation Session: If an agreement of all the issues is reached, the Mediation Agreement will be drafted by the Mediator while all parties are present at the session, and shall note the full or partial settlement of the issues. The parties and their attorneys shall sign the Agreement, and receive draft copies pending review and action by the Court. The parties may then proceed on the uncontested hearing calendar to request that the Court review it, and, if deemed appropriate, in consideration of the best interests of the child or children, approve and ratify the Mediated Agreement, unless the Court deems other changes are required, or determines that it is not acceptable. The final approved Mediation Agreement shall be distributed to the parties, filed with the Court and made a part of the Court file, and any scheduled Adjudicatory Hearing before the Court may be cancelled. If a partial agreement is reached, the mediation report form shall note that the case has remaining issues and said form shall be filed with the Court. If there is no Agreement, the Mediator shall report to the Court that an impasse has been reached. The Court may then restore the matter to the Trial Calendar.

18. Communications During the Mediation Session: Pursuant to the Mediation Confidentiality and Privilege Act, with the exception of the parties' signed financial affidavits and any other documents which are required to be filed in the public record, all communications, verbal or written, between the parties and from the parties made during the mediation session, including caucus sessions, shall be confidential and inadmissible as evidence if any subsequent legal proceeding, unless both parties agree otherwise, or as otherwise provided in Florida Statutes and Florida Rules of Juvenile Procedure. If an agreement is reached regarding said support, the signed agreement with the Child Support Guidelines Worksheet shall be filed with the Court.

19. Record Keeping: The Court shall keep a record of the case name, number, assigning judge, mediator, the attorney and the outcome of the mediation session in all cases referred to Dependency Mediation. The outcome shall be reported to the Court, who shall cause the entry of the information in the Uniform Reporting Data Index for transmittal to the appropriate governmental agency in Tallahassee without identification of the Parties.

20. Funding: Any funding made available through grants, Federal, State or County funding or by other means shall be administered under the auspices of the Court Administrator, through the Mediation Coordinator.

21. Failure to Mediate in Good Faith: Good cause for objection to an assigned mediator cannot be based solely on the grounds that the assigned mediator had previously handled or is currently handling an unrelated dependency case without a showing of good cause by proper motion accompanying the objection. An expedited hearing will be scheduled before the court to determine any conflicts. Barring a finding of the court as to a conflict, failure to participate in mediation after hearing and order of the court, the court may impose sanctions including, but not limited to, immediate dismissal of the petition for dependency.

22. Effective Date: This Administrative Order shall become effective for cases as described herein which are mediated on or after the date of this order.

Done and Ordered this 13th day of October, 2010.

J. PRESTON SILVERNAIL
CHIEF JUDGE

10–26–B. DOMESTIC RELATIONS—FAMILY DIVISION PARTIES REQUIRED TO READ CERTAIN ADMINISTRATIVE ORDERS

IN THE CIRCUIT COURT OF THE EIGHTEENTH JUDICIAL CIRCUIT IN AND FOR BREVARD COUNTY, FLORIDA

ADMINISTRATIVE ORDER NO.: 10–26–B
SUPERSEDES 09–13–B

IN RE: DOMESTIC RELATIONS—FAMILY DIVISION PARTIES REQUIRED TO READ CERTAIN ADMINISTRATIVE ORDERS

WHEREAS the court sitting and adjudging Domestic Relations cases in the 18th Judicial Circuit in and for Brevard County believes it is appropriate and wise that parties to a dissolution of marriage case read and become familiar with certain relevant Administrative Orders.

NOW THEREFORE pursuant to the authority vested in the Chief Judge by Rule 2.215 of the Florida Rules of Judicial Administration and Section 43.26 of Florida Statutes, it is Ordered that the 18th Judicial Circuit's website shall contain the following Administrative Orders for inspection and reading:

1. **In all cases:**

a. **ADMINISTRATIVE ORDER NO. 06–14 IN RE:** DOMESTIC RELATIONS–FAMILY DIVISION–MODEL FAMILY COURT

b. **ADMINISTRATIVE ORDER NO. 07–19–B IN RE:** MEDIATION–FAMLY[1] MEDIATION MANDATORY REFERRAL OF ALL CONTESTED FAMILY LAW CASES TO MEDIATION

c. **ADMINISTRATIVE ORDER NO. 07–20–B AMENDED IN RE:** DOMESTIC RELATIONS COLLABORATIVE CONFLICT RESOLUTION IN DISSOLUTION OF MARRIAGE CASES

d. **ADMINISTRATIVE ORDER NO. 08–33–B** IN RE: DOMESTIC RELATIONS–FAMILY DIVISION–STANDING TEMPORARY RELATIONS ORDER

2. **The following additional administrative orders must be read if there are minor children of the marriage:**

a. **ADMINISTRATIVE ORDER NO. 95–28–B IN RE:** DOMESTIC RELATIONS ADOPTION OF VISITATION GUIDELINES

b. **ADMINISTRATIVE ORDER NO. 05–28–B IN RE:** DOMESTIC RELATIONS–ATTENDING THE HELPING OUR CHILDREN COPE WITH DIVORCE COURSE BY INTERNET

c. **ADMINISTRATIVE ORDER NO. 05–39 IN RE:** DOMESTIC RELATIONS PARENTING COORDINATORS IN HIGH CONFLICT FAMILY LAW CASES

d. **ADMINISTRATIVE ORDER NO. 06–21–B IN RE:** DOMESTIC RELATIONS REQUIREMENT TO COMPLETE THE PARENT EDUCATION AND FAMILY STABILIZATION COURSE IN DISSOLUTION OF MARRIAGE PROCEEDING WITH MINOR CHILDREN OR A PATERNITY ACTION THAT INVOLVES ISSUES OF PARENTAL RESPONSIBILITY

The petitioner/respondent upon reading the Administrative Orders required shall execute the statement attached hereto (Attachment A) and file said statement with the clerk of court.

DONE AND ORDERED this 5th day of August, 2010.

J. PRESTON SILVERNAIL
CHIEF JUDGE

ATTACHMENT A

IN THE CIRCUIT COURT FOR THE EIGHTEENTH JUDICIAL CIRCUIT IN AND FOR BREVARD COUNTY, FLORIDA

In re: The Marriage of:

______________ CASE NO.: ______________

Petitioner,

And

____

Respondent

ATTESTATION

I, ______________ (petitioner/respondent) have read the administrative orders required to be read by Administrative Order 10–26–B.

Signature: ______________

Printed Name: ______________

Date: ______________

[1] So in original.

10–24–B. [SUPERSEDED BY ORDER 17-40-B, EFFECTIVE OCTOBER 2, 2017.]

10–10–B. SUPPORT—CHILD SUPPORT—REDIRECTION OF PAYMENTS AND ACCOUNT MAINTENANCE IN FORMER TITLE IV–D CHILD SUPPORT ENFORCEMENT CASES

IN THE CIRCUIT COURT OF THE EIGHTEENTH JUDICIAL CIRCUIT IN AND FOR BREVARD COUNTY, FLORIDA

ADMINISTRATIVE ORDER NO.: **10–10–B**

SUPERSEDES 06–16–B

IN RE: SUPPORT—CHILD SUPPORT—REDIRECTION OF PAYMENTS AND ACCOUNT MAINTENANCE IN FORMER TITLE IV–D CHILD SUPPORT ENFORCEMENT CASES

Whereas, pursuant to Title IV–D of the Social Security Act, 42 U.S.C. § 651, et seq., and Florida Statute § 409.2567 and the Department of Revenue is designated as the State Agency responsible for the administration of the Child Support Enforcement Program in the State of Florida;

Whereas, when the following case types ceases to be a Title IV–D case;

- Request to Establish an Account (Interstate case)
- Request to Establish a Registration Account (Interstate case)
- CSE Transmittal (case involving two states)

The Department of Revenue as part of its duties as the State's Title IV–D Agency notifies the Clerk of the Court of Brevard County of that fact and requests the Clerk to redirect payments to the proper person.

Now Therefore, It is Ordered;

1. That upon notification by the Department to the Clerk of the Court of Brevard County, that the following case types have ceased to be a Title IV–D case;

- Request to Establish an Account
- Request to Establish a Registration Account
- CSE Transmittal

and that payments should be redirected, the Clerk of the Court is hereby authorized to proceed as requested by the Department.

2. That the Department's notice to the Clerk shall further state whether the accounts kept by the Clerk relative to the case should be closed and/or zeroed out. The Department's notice shall state the reason for the action requested.

This order will take effect immediately and will be applicable to cases filed on or after February 28, 2001.

DONE and ORDERED the 21st day of April, 2010.

J. PRESTON SILVERNAIL
CHIEF JUDGE

10–07–B. SUPERSEDED BY ADMINISTRATIVE ORDER NO. 16–02–B.

09–26–B. SUPERSEDED BY ADMINISTRATIVE ORDER NO. 16–42–B

09–19–S. DOMESTIC RELATIONS—FAMILY DIVISION—SUPPLEMENTAL PETITIONS FOR MODIFICATION

IN THE CIRCUIT COURT OF THE EIGHTEENTH JUDICIAL CIRCUIT IN AND FOR SEMINOLE COUNTY, FLORIDA

ADMINISTRATIVE ORDER NO.: 09–19–S

IN RE: DOMESTIC RELATIONS—FAMILY DIVISION—SUPPLEMENTAL PETITIONS FOR MODIFICATION

Supplemental Petitions for Modification in Family Division cases must be filed with the clerk along with the appropriate filing fee, if applicable, and served on the opposing party. Such petition shall carry the same case number as the final judgment or order for which modification is sought, and shall remain assigned to the same division where that final judgment or order was obtained.

A party wishing to modify an existing Title IVD Child Support order to address parenting plan issues regarding the children must file a Supplemental Petition for Modification in the Title IVD case and serve the other parent or party. The attorney for the Department of Revenue does not represent the other party in the case and should not be served.

DONE AND ORDERED this 5TH day of March, 2009.

CLAYTON D. SIMMONS
CHIEF JUDGE

09–17–S (A2). CRIMINAL—GPS ELECTRONIC MONITORING—POST–SENTENCING ALTERNATIVES FOR NON–VIOLENT OFFENDERS

IN THE CIRCUIT COURT OF THE EIGHTEENTH JUDICIAL CIRCUIT IN AND FOR SEMINOLE COUNTY, FLORIDA

ADMINISTRATIVE ORDER NO.: 09–17–S 2ND AMENDED

SUPERSEDES 09–17–S AMENDED

IN RE: Criminal—GPS Electronic Monitoring—Post–Sentencing Alternatives For Non–Violent Offenders

The Seminole County Sheriff has requested the Court to allow selected inmates be placed into the GPS Electronic Monitoring Program without further judicial intervention after sentence has been imposed upon meeting certain qualifications. After due consideration of the request,

IT IS ADJUDGED:

1. Offenders who meet the criteria below may be placed in the GPS Electronic Monitoring Program and the limits of their confinement be extended for that purpose without further order of the Court.

2. No offender may qualify for the GPS Electronic Monitoring Program if the sentencing judge places a no-GPS restriction on the sentencing order.

Offense Criteria

Offenders who are incarcerated for non-violent offenses may be considered eligible for GPS Electronic Monitoring Program. However, offenders who are sentenced for violent offenses, to include domestic violence related offenses, offenses involving the abuse of children, offenses involving the use of a deadly weapon, and any violent offense, or whose criminal history indicates a public risk, will not be eligible for this GPS Electronic Monitoring Program.

Offenders are required to first be incarcerated for administrative classification purposes, before extending the limits of confinement to GPS Electronic Monitoring Program. If during the classification process the offender's history indicates that he or she is ineligible, the offender's limits of confinement shall not be extended to GPS.

Offenders must agree to abide by GPS Electronic Monitoring requirements, be responsible for replacement cost of lost or damaged monitoring equipment and to pay cost of monitoring without accruing arrears. Payments will be made to the Seminole County Sheriff's Office per the Offender Fee Schedule Agreement.

Offenders who are acutely psychotic, severely mentally retarded, currently suicidal or otherwise unable to cope with the structured requirements of GPS Monitoring, or unable to understand and comply with the monitoring conditions, will not be eligible for GPS Electronic Monitoring.

Offenders who are placed in the program shall at the discretion of the Sheriff be required to wear, maintain, and comply with all prescribed conditions of GPS–Electronic Monitoring at all times. Equipment value exceeds $300 and malicious damage and/or theft will be criminally prosecuted as a Felony offense. Offenders are required to maintain an approved Seminole County residence with an active residential telephone line and electrical service. Offenders must agree to secure pets for the safety of Law Enforcement personnel.

Offenders must abide by curfew, work schedule, approved routes to and from approved scheduled activities. No recreational activities outside the residence will be permitted. All activity and movement must be approved and scheduled in advance by the Sheriff's Office program staff. Any incident which requires offenders to leave their scheduled location as directed by police, fire, or medical personnel will be reported immediately to the Sheriff's Office program staff. Contact with any Law Enforcement must be reported immediately to program staff.

Offenders must maintain employment/educational/vocational training unless specifically waived. Employment/educational training will be verified by the Sheriff's Office program staff. Employment interviews will be permitted only as needed. Interviews must be approved and scheduled with the Sheriff's Office program staff.

Medical care and expenses will be the offender's responsibility. Offenders are not permitted to possess any drugs or alcohol without a prescription from a duly licensed medical doctor. Medical emergencies must be reported immediately and verifiable. Offenders will be required to submit to random alcohol and urinalysis testing. Offenders must abide by these conditions and any other special conditions as ordered by the Court.

Other Limitations and Provisions

No offender with a "hold" from any other jurisdiction is eligible for GPS Electronic Monitoring but is subject to immediate transport upon resolution of all local charges, if any.

Offenders serving one sentence which may qualify but who are sentenced on other charges that do not meet the requirements of this order are not eligible for GPS Electronic Monitoring.

Offenders who fail to comply with the conditions of the GPS Electronic Monitoring are subject to being returned to the jail to serve the balance of the sentence originally imposed. Upon written motion of the State Attorney's Office the Court may issue a capias to return the defendant to jail if the offender cannot be located

DONE AND ORDERED this 8th day of October, 2009.

J. PRESTON SILVERNAIL
Chief Judge

09–15–B. CRIMINAL—ON SITE VIOLATIONS OF PROBATION AND COMMUNITY CONTROL; FAILURE TO APPEAR, AND VIOLATION OF PROBATION WARRANTS

IN THE CIRCUIT COURT OF THE EIGHTEENTH JUDICIAL CIRCUIT IN AND FOR BREVARD COUNTY, FLORIDA.

ADMINISTRATIVE ORDER NO: 09–15–B

IN RE: CRIMINAL—ON SITE VIOLATIONS OF PROBATION AND COMMUNITY CONTROL; FAILURE TO APPEAR, AND VIOLATION OF PROBATION WARRANTS

Whereas, jail overcrowding has been a long existing problem at the Brevard County Jail; and

Whereas, the Honorable Gregory Presnell, United States District Court Judge, is overseeing an attempt to settle the existing litigation in Federal Court in which Tilman/Lennear is Plaintiff and Brevard County is Defendant, concerning jail overcrowding at the Brevard County Jail; and

Whereas, on August 12, 2008, representatives of the judicial system, law enforcement agencies and county government attended a workshop in Orlando, Florida, to address the issue of jail overcrowding at the Brevard County Jail; and

Whereas, police agencies have the authority by Florida Statute, to make arrests for "on site" violations of probation and community control; and

Whereas, the Clerk of the Court treats an "on site" violation as a new charge and sets "no bond" on all on site violation arrests; and

Whereas, persons may be given reasonable bond on the new law violations but remain incarcerated for a substantial period of time on the on site violation charge without seeing the presiding judge to set bond on the charge; and

Whereas, persons charged with failure to appear warrants remain incarcerated for a substantial period of time on the warrant without seeing the assigned judge; and

Whereas, the foregoing results in inmates being held for substantial periods of time without being brought before the assigned judge for a bond hearing or resolution, thus substantially contributing to jail overcrowding and;

Whereas, it is necessary and essential to reduce the day to day inmate population in an effective way;

Therefore, it is Ordered and Adjudged:

1) To accomplish the reduction of inmates held at the Brevard County Jail, any judge sitting for the initial appearance at the Brevard County Jail has the discretion to authorize reasonable bail for any person held under any "Failure to Appear No Bond", or "Violation of Probation No Bond", or "On-sight Violation of Probation No Bond" warrants. In addition, any judge is authorized to review any bail amount set by any judge on any warrant, with or without the consent of the issuing judge.

2) Any judge sitting at initial appearance must be cognizant of the Jessica Lunsford Act, the offenders of special concern who are on probation or community control who should not be admitted to bail, i.e., those that qualify for violent felony offender, habitual violent felony offender, sexual predator, or other special qualifying offenders by statute. Nothing in this Administrative Order suggests that any County Judge should make rulings on these matters if not properly before that Court.

3) Although any judge sitting at initial appearances has discretion to set bail pursuant to this Order, that judge should give deference to, but not necessarily be controlled by, special instructions noted on the warrant by the issuing judge.

4) In the event that a defendant continues to be held without being admitted to bail following the initial appearance, the assigned circuit or county judge will conduct a bail review hearing within five business days of the initial appearance. The failure of the assigned judge to hold a review within five business days will not be cause for any special relief, other than as specifically provided by the Rules of Criminal Procedure, the Florida Statutes, or the Florida Constitution. It is the responsibility of the assigned or retained defense counsel to set the review hearing.

5) If the assigned judge is unavailable because of illness, vacation, or for any other reason will be out of the office for that period, any other judge may hear the matter, with or without the consent of the assigned judge.

DONE AND ORDERED this 18TH day of FEBRUARY, 2009.

CLAYTON D. SIMMONS
Chief Judge

09–14–B (A2). MEDIATION—MANDATORY MEDIATION CIRCUIT COURT BREVARD COUNTY OWNER OCCUPIED RESIDENTIAL MORTGAGE FORECLOSURE

IN THE CIRCUIT COURT OF THE EIGHTEENTH JUDICIAL CIRCUIT IN AND FOR BREVARD COUNTY, FLORIDA

ADMINISTRATIVE ORDER NO: 09–14–B 2nd AMENDED

SUPERSEDES 09–14–B AMENDED

IN RE: MEDIATION—MANDATORY MEDIATION CIRCUIT COURT BREVARD COUNTY OWNER OCCUPIED RESIDENTIAL MORTGAGE FORECLOSURE

WHEREAS: Residential mortgage foreclosure case filings have substantially increased in Brevard County; and,

WHEREAS: High owner occupied residential foreclosure rates are having a damaging impact on the economy of Brevard County, the State of Florida, and the financial community; and,

WHEREAS: Owner Occupied Residential foreclosures place increased strain on family relationships, leading to higher divorce rates, increased incidents of domestic violence, and adverse impacts on children; and,

WHEREAS: The Judges in the Brevard County Circuit Civil Divisions are routinely advised by litigants that it is difficult, if not outright impossible, to negotiate settlements due to the inability to communicate with appropriate representatives of the lender or the lender's attorneys after the complaint for foreclosure has been filed. In many of these cases, the first opportunity the parties have to discuss the issues and attempt to resolve their differences is at a hearing on the lender's motion for summary judgment, or later at the foreclosure sale. By that time in most cases, all judicial labor has been expended and the costs and attorney's fees have increased significantly. The failure of the parties to communicate in a timely fashion results in unnecessary waste of resources by the court, the court staff, and the clerk's office, and could be obviated by prejudgment mediation; and,

WHEREAS: Florida Rule of Civil Procedure 1.700(a) provides that a presiding judge may enter an order referring all or any part of a contested civil matter to mediation or arbitration; and

WHEREAS: Foreclosure actions are equitable in nature, the law abhors a forfeiture, and the nature of an owner occupied residential foreclosure mandates that the court give full, fair and equitable consideration to all issues in these cases rather than deal with them in a summary fashion; and,

WHEREAS: The seven presiding Brevard Circuit Civil Division judges have determined that greater economy of limited judicial and clerk resources would occur if contested owner occupied residential foreclosure cases in Brevard County were required to undergo mediation before being set for final hearing;

NOW, THEREFORE, IT IS ORDERED:

1. For all owner occupied residential mortgage foreclosure actions filed in Brevard County, Florida, in which responsive pleadings or other filings seeking any form of relief by any owner occupant are filed, this order shall constitute an order of referral to mediation. Counsel for plaintiff shall coordinate and schedule the case for mediation prior to scheduling the matter for final or summary judgment hearing. The plaintiff may schedule mediation with any Supreme Court Certified Civil Mediator or may schedule mediation through the Brevard Civil Mediation Department for discounted mediation services with a member of the courts fixed fee panel. All scheduling information, procedures, forms and orders, using Brevard County's fixed fee panel can be found on the Brevard County website: www.flcourts18.org.

2. The fee for mediations scheduled through the mediation department shall be $250, paid in advance, for a 1 1/2–hour session. All mediation fees shall be borne in advance by the plaintiff. If the matter does not resolve at mediation, the mediation fee may be taxed by the court as a cost of litigation in the final judgment of foreclosure.

3. The plaintiff shall make a reasonable effort to coordinate the mediation with all parties and shall give the defendant homeowner(s) and any undefaulted inferior lien holders reasonable advance notice of the date, time, and place of the mediation. When plaintiff gives notice of the mediation, plaintiff shall also give written notice, using the form attached as Addendum "A" hereto, identifying the lender's representative and attesting to the representative's authority to participate in mediation and settle on behalf of the lender. Mediation may only be waived after hearing on a verified motion filed by the plaintiff asserting that all defendants have been defaulted. Upon filing said motion, Counsel for the plaintiff shall also certify that there has been no communication with any of the defendant(s) or any representative for any of the defendant(s) and that the foreclosure is truly uncontested.

4. A copy of the mediation agenda attached as Addendum "B" to this order shall be served upon the lender representative and homeowner and any undefaulted lien holders along with the notice of the mediation conference.

5. Nothing in this Order is intended to prevent the plaintiff from filing all pleadings necessary to proceed to final or summary judgment; however, hearing on a motion for summary judgment may not be scheduled prior to the conclusion of the scheduled mediation session or waiver of mediation as permitted under paragraph 3 above.

6. A representative of plaintiff with full authority to settle must participate in the mediation. The representative may attend the mediation by telephone, provided notice of such attendance is included in the mediation notice and a toll-free number is provided by plaintiff's counsel. If the representative attends by telephone, his/her attendance must be continuous throughout the mediation session. Plaintiff's counsel, Defendant(s), and defendant's counsel must appear at the mediation in person. Plaintiff's counsel must file with the court a certificate in substantially the same form as that attached hereto as Addendum "A," identifying the lender's representative, describing that representative's position or relationship with the lender, and specifically certifying that the representative has full authority to resolve the foreclosure suit without the need to seek other authorization.

7. If defendant(s) fail to appear at a properly noticed mediation or if the matter impasses after mediation, the matter may be promptly noticed for summary judgment, provided all requirements of F.R.C.P. 1.510 have been met. If plaintiff fails to appear for mediation or no representative with full settlement authority appears, the action shall be dismissed without prejudice.

8. Lenders are encouraged to enter into pre-suit mediation to expedite the process which may result in the filing of fewer foreclosure actions.

DONE AND ORDERED this 21st day of October, 2009.

J. PRESTON SILVERNAIL
CHIEF JUDGE

ADDENDUM "A"

IN THE CIRCUIT COURT FOR THE EIGHTEENTH JUDICIAL CIRCUIT IN AND FOR Brevard COUNTY, FLORIDA

(Name of Lender),

Plaintiff, CASE NO: ____________

vs.

Name of Judge to Whom case is assigned. (essential that this be placed in the style)

(Name of Defendant(s)),

Defendants. ____________/

CERTIFICATION OF SETTLEMENT AUTHORITY

THE UNDERSIGNED COUNSEL, as counsel of record in this cause and as an officer of the court, pursuant to the Administrative Order of the Chief Judge of the Eighteenth Judicial Circuit, does hereby certify as follows:

1. Mediation has been scheduled in this cause as ordered.
2. The plaintiff/lender will be represented by ____________

   ____

   ☐ by personal appearance.

   ☐ by telephone at ____________ (toll free phone #)
3. The plaintiff's representative's relationship to the plaintiff/ lender is: ____________
4. The undersigned has personally spoken with the above designated representative and said representative has confirmed that the person has fully settlement authority.

Signature: ____________
Printed Name: ____________
Bar Number: ____________
Address: ____________

Tel. No. ____________

ADDENDUM "B"

OWNER OCCUPIED RESIDENTIAL MORTGAGE FORECLOSURE MEDIATION AGENDA

The mediation conference shall include for consideration at least one of the following options:

A. Short term financial problems:

1. **Repayment plan:**

Description: This option involves a formal, written agreement between the homeowner, law firm, and lender which is reduced to a stipulation and, in some cases, a consent judgment. The agreement provides for temporary increase in monthly payments until the loan is brought current and may involve a cash down payment on the arrearage.

Benefit: The homeowner is given the opportunity to "make up" missed payments, rather than paying them all at once, and is allowed to remain in the home.

Detriment: Payments are higher than normal for the homeowner and may be unaffordable.

2. **Home Saver Advance:** (Fannie Mae insured loans only.)

Description: The lender agrees to advance funds to allow the homeowner to reinstate the mortgage. The homeowner signs a note at 5% interest payable over 15 years with no payments for the first six months for the amount advanced.

Benefit: The mortgage is brought current. Monthly payments are usually small and spread over a long period of time.

Detriment: Payments are larger than normal after the first six months.

3. **Forbearance:**

Description: A formal, written agreement between the homeowner, law firm, and the lender, often including a written stipulation and consent judgment.

Benefit: Under the agreement, monthly payments are reduced or suspended for a specified period of time. During that time, the homeowner either pays a lower monthly payment or no payment at all. At the end of the period, regular payments resume. The homeowner remains in the home.

Detriment: This option may not be affordable if the lender insists on a large lump sum payment.

B. Longer-term, more severe financial problems:

Modification:

Description: One or more of the terms of the note and mortgage may be changed to bring the loan current; for example, extending the term of the note or reducing the interest rate, temporarily or permanently. Alternatively, delinquent interest, escrow, taxes, and other costs could be added to the principal balance that is owed.

Benefit: The homeowner receives a fresh start and the loan remains a performing asset.

Detriment: Modifications take time to be reviewed by the various investors or mortgage insurance companies and the reductions may not be affordable.

C. Pre-foreclosure sale:

Description: The parties agree to sell the property at current fair market value, even if the proceeds will not cover the debt. The lender and homeowner agree to accept the proceeds of the sale in satisfaction of the debt or the lender agrees to accept a low interest note for the balance.

Benefit: The homeowner is relieved from the debt and avoids the stigma of foreclosure, and the lender is not required to take title to the property.

Detriment: Lender is not satisfied in full for the mortgage and note obligation.

D. Deed in lieu of foreclosure:

Description: The homeowner voluntarily deeds the property to the lender. This is generally a last choice option. The lender receives a consent judgment and waives any deficiency.

This option is not available in some cases where there are junior mortgages or liens. The property must be vacated at the time of the deed transfer.

Benefit: The homeowner is relieved of the debt and the uncertainty of a sheriff's sale. May be beneficial for homeowner's future credit rating.

Detriment: Title issues can arise. Lender gains very little benefit other than taking title to the property.

E. Consent judgment to vacate:

Description: The homeowner agrees to vacate the property on a date certain and stipulates to a judgment of possession in any necessary eviction action.

Benefit: The homeowner retains possession of the property for the agreed period to allow the homeowner to solve school, day care, or commuting concerns.

Detriment: Lender suffers additional cost if homeowner fails to vacate. Lender may not be willing to agree to this option without a significant deposit to cover costs of eviction.

F. Reverse mortgage:

Description: Homeowner must be 62 years of age or older. Amount of reverse mortgage may be up to 60% of the value of the home. Reverse mortgage is used to pay off existing mortgage. There must be substantial equity in the property.

Benefit: Homeowner remains in possession.

Detriment: Homeowner may ultimately lose the property.

G. Other:

The parties may explore any other option or combination of options based upon the circumstances of the situation.

09–07–B (A1). CRIMINAL—PRETRIAL RELEASE PROGRAM—EXPANSION OF THE RELEASE AUTHORITY OF THE PRETRIAL RELEASE PROGRAM

IN THE CIRCUIT COURT OF THE EIGHTEENTH JUDICIAL CIRCUIT IN AND FOR BREVARD COUNTY, FLORIDA

ADMINISTRATIVE ORDER NO:

09–07–B AMENDED

SUPERSEDES 09–07–B

IN RE: CRIMINAL—PRETRIAL RELEASE PROGRAM—EXPANSION OF THE RELEASE AUTHORITY OF THE PRETRIAL RELEASE PROGRAM

Whereas, it is necessary that the undersigned Chief Judge establish, in writing, criteria which the Pretrial Release Program staff must utilize in releasing defendants under their own signature. It has been brought to the Court's attention that Expanded Release Authority is being requested by the Pretrial Release Program to allow for the release of selected non-violent third degree felons and bench warrants with bonds of $2000.00 or less.

Whereas, the purpose of this Expanded Authority is to enhance the current release authority as set forth by the State of Florida Constitution, Section 14, Florida Statute 907.041, Florida Rules of Criminal Procedure 3.125(c)(d), and 3.131(a)(b), and to provide the Pretrial Release Program with an avenue for further reductions in jail over-crowding and increases in jail cost savings.

Whereas, it is necessary to define the role and scope of such an expansion, offenses qualifying for release under this Administrative Order as follows:

1.	212.15	(2)a	Larceny—sale tax fail to remit under 300 dollars 3rd subsq violation
2.	212.15	(2)b	Larceny—sale tax fail to remit 300 dollars under 20,000 dollars
3.	316.193	(3)1	DUI—first offense w/property damage Pretrial Release authorized only if damage is to defendants property or property not associated with an individual or entity such as trees, sign post etc.
4.	322.34	(5)	DWLS—habitual offender
5.	379.101	(23)	Conservation—fish—moleste blue crab trap line buoy
6.	379.3014		Alligator possession, taking of an alligator or skin
7.	403.413	(6)c	Conservation environment—litter over 500 dollars commercial, hazardous any amount
8.	414.39	(2)	Forgery of—alter public assistance stamp ID etc 200 dollars or more
9.	414.39	(1)a	Fraud—impersonate for public aid 200 dollars or more
10.	414.39	(1)a	Fraud—false statement for public aid 200 dollars or more
11.	414.39	(1)a	Fraud—misrepresent fail disclose public aid 200 dollars or more
12.	414.39	(1)b	Fraud—non disclose change status public aid 200 dollars or more
13.	414.39	(3)a	Embezzle—misapprop public assistance funds 200 dollars or more
14.	414.39	(3)b	Embezzle—misapprop food stamp funds 200 dollars or more
15.	414.39	(4)a	False public assistance claim 200 dollars or more
16.	414.39	(4)b	Fraud—fail credit other pay public assistance 200 dollars or more
17.	414.39	(4)c	Fraud—receipt unauthorized public assistance claim 200 dollars or more
18.	414.39		Fraud—unauthorized use etc public assistance 200 dollars or more

19.	440.105	(7)	Fraudulent claims worker's compensation
20.	443.071	(1)	Fraudulent claims unemployment compensation
21.	509.151		Fraud—defraud innkeeper 300 dollars or more
22.	538.04	(4)a	Fraud—false statement—verify ownership 2nd hand dealer under 300 dollars
23.	539.001	(8)b(8)a	Fraud—false ownership info pawn items less than 300 dollars
24.	562.11	(1)	Liquor—sell/give/serve persons under 21 yoa subsq offense
25.	562.11	(2)	Misrepresent age to obtain alcohol
26.	562.451		Liquor—unlawful possess sell trans alcohol beverage container
27.	777.03		Accessory after the fact 3rd degree felony lvl 3 to 10
28.	806.13	(1)b(1)	Damage property—criminal mischief 200 dollars or less subsq offense
29.	806.13	(1)b(2)	Damage property—criminal mischief over 200 dollars under 1000 dollars subsq offense
30.	806.13	(1)b(3)	Damage property—criminal mischief—1000 dollars or more
31.	810.02	(4)b	Burglary—unoccupied conveyance—unarmed
32.	810.09	(2)d	Trespass—posted construction site
33.	810.09	(2)e	Trespass—posted horticultural property
34.	810.115	(1)	Damage property—criminal mischief—break or injure fence 2nd subsq offense
35.	810.115	(2)	Damage property—criminal mischief—break injure fence contain animals
36.	812.014	(2)c(1)	Theft 300 or more but less 5000 dollars
37.	812.014	(2)c(2)	Grand Theft 5000 dollars or more less than 10,000 dollars
38.	812.014	(2)c(3)	Grand Theft 10,000 dollars or more less than 20,000 dollars (However, Pretrial Release is not authorized, without judicial approval, for the theft of firearms or motor vehicles)
39.	812.014	(2)c (7)	Larceny—Grand of farm animals/aqua culture species
40.	812.014		Grand Theft (provided such theft is of $10,000 or less, or property with a value of $10,000 or less.) (However, Pretrial Release is not authorized, without judicial approval, for the theft of firearms or motor vehicles)
41.	812.015	(8)	Retail Theft >300 dollars or more 1st offense
42.	812.015	(8)a & b	Retail Theft alone or coordinates with other
43.	812.015	(8)c & d	Retail Theft
44.	812.155	(3)	Fraud—fail to redeliver hired/leased property 300 dollars or more
45.	812.155	(3)	Failure to Redeliver Leased/Hired personal property
46.	817.02		Fraud—impersonate—obtain property by
47.	817.234	(11)a	Fraud—insurance fraud < 20,000 dollars
48.	817.481	(1)	Fraud—illegal use of credit card—obtain goods 300 dollars or more
49.	817.481	(2)	Fraud—Avoid or attempt to avoid payment phone 300 dollars or more
50.	817.52	(2)	Fraud—swindle—hire vehicle w/I to defraud
51.	817.52	(3)	Fraud—fail to redeliver hired vehicle
52.	817.6	(5)	Fraud—illegal use of credit card—deal in another
53.	826.01		Bigamy
54.	831.01		Forgery—altered public record certificate
55.	831.02		Pass forged—altered instrument
56.	831.02		Pass forged—counterfeited instrument
57.	831.02		Fraud—utter false instrument
58.	831.032	(2)	Vending counterfeit Goods
59.	831.08		Having forged bills
60.	831.09		Uttering forged bills
61.	832.041		Fraud—insufficient funds check—stop pay W/I defraud 150 dollars or more

62.	832.05	(2)	Fraud—insufficient funds check—make utter issue 150 dollars or over
63.	832.05	(4)a	Fraud—insufficient funds check—obtain goods services over 150 dollars
64.	843.15	(1)b	FTA: Misdemeanor First Offense
65.	877.08		Molesting vending machine
66.	893.13	(2)a(2)	Marijuana possess—w/intent to purchase schedule I
67.	893.13	(6)a	Marijuana possession—possess marijuana > 20 grams
68.	893.13	(6)a b	Poss cocaine or cannabis or other controlled substance- First offense third deg fel only
69.	893.13	(7)a(9)	Forgery—obtain controlled substance by
70.	893.13	(7)a(9)	Fraud—obtain controlled substance by
71.	893.13	(7)a(9)	Obtaining controlled substance by false pretenses
72.	893.147	(2)	Possession of Drug Paraphernalia
73.	918.13		Tampering with evidence—drugs only

It is THEREFORE ORDERED that:

The Pretrial Release Program be given expanded authority to release detainees charged with any of the above listed offenses without the prior verbal or written consent of a Judge, provided that the following criteria is met:

1) Detainee demonstrates sufficient ties to the Brevard County community as evidenced by:

a) Detainee owns own home, or has resided in Brevard County for a period of at least twelve (12) consecutive months, or

b) Detainee lives with legal parent(s) or guardian(s) who own their own home in Brevard County, Florida, or

c) Detainee has a source of income and has resided in Brevard County for a period of at least twelve (12) consecutive months, or

d) Detainee is currently registered at an institution of higher learning as a full time student (post high school), with family ties to Brevard County, Florida.

2) Detainee is not currently charged with assault, battery or dangerous crimes listed in section 907.041(4)(a) Florida Statutes, and does not have a previous conviction reflecting same; detainee is not currently charged with an offense greater than a third degree felony; detainee does not have a detainer; detainee does not have a previous failure to appear; detainee does not have a previous violation of probation within the past three years; detainee does not have other pending criminal charges; detainee's prior record does not reflect two or more juvenile delinquency adjudications and/or criminal convictions within the past five (5) years.

3) Detainee does not present a danger to the community because of drug abuse, alcohol abuse, or mental illness;

4) Detainee has not provided any untruthful information in application for pretrial release.

However, in cases where the Sheriff of Brevard County, local Chiefs of Police, the State Attorney of the Eighteenth Judicial Circuit, or any of their deputies, assistants, or designees, objects to a detainee's release by notifying the Pretrial Release Program of said objection; the detainee shall not be released prior to First Appearance. Release decisions for all such detainees shall be made by the Judge presiding at First Appearance.

All those not meeting the above requirements of release shall be evaluated for Pretrial Release consideration by the Judge presiding at First Appearance.

DONE AND ORDERED this 18th day of February, 2009.

CLAYTON D. SIMMONS
CHIEF JUDGE

09–06. COURTROOM DECORUM AND PROCEDURE

IN THE CIRCUIT COURT OF THE EIGHTEENTH JUDICIAL CIRCUIT OF FLORIDA

ADMINISTRATIVE ORDER NO.: 09–06

SUPERSEDES 92–116

IN RE: COURTROOM DECORUM AND PROCEDURE

WHEREAS, some practitioners are unfamiliar with the traditions of the Courts of the Eighteenth Judicial Circuit, and

WHEREAS, certain basic principles of conduct and decorum enhance the dignity of the court, and

WHEREAS, the following provisions will improve the efficiency of court proceedings, it is therefore,

ORDERED:

1. When appearing in any Court of the Eighteenth Judicial Circuit, unless excused by the presiding judge, all counsel (including, where the context applies, all persons at counsel table) shall abide by the following:

a) Stand as Court is opened, recessed, or adjourned, unless directed to remain seated.

b) Stand when the jury enters or retires from the courtroom.

c) Stand when addressing, or being addressed by, the Court.

d) Counsel shall not suggest to the jury that individual voir dire may be requested without first obtaining permission of the court.

e) Stand at the lectern while examining any witness; except that counsel may approach the Clerk's desk or the witness for purposes of handling or tendering exhibits. It is not necessary to request permission to approach a witness unless the witness has been declared adverse or hostile.

f) Stand at the lectern while making opening statements or closing arguments except to show evidence to the jury.

g) Address all remarks to the Court and not to opposing counsel.

h) Avoid disparaging personal remarks or acrimony toward opposing counsel. Do not participate in, or accommodate any ill feeling between the litigants or witnesses, but remain wholly detached therefrom.

i) Refer to all persons, including witnesses, other counsel and the parties by their surnames and not by their first or given names.

j) Only one attorney for each party shall examine, or cross examine each witness. The attorney stating objections, if any, during direct examination, shall be the attorney recognized for cross examination.

k) Counsel should request permission before approaching the bench.

l) Any paper or exhibit should first be handed to opposing counsel and then to the Clerk to be marked for identification before it is tendered to a witness for his or her examination. Any exhibit offered in evidence should, at the time of such offer, be handed to opposing counsel.

m) Counsel should state only the legal grounds when making an objection and should withhold all further comment or argument unless elaboration is requested by the Court.

n) Counsel shall not repeat or echo the answer given by the witness during questioning.

o) Offers of, or requests for, a stipulation should be made privately, not within the hearing of the jury.

p) In opening statements and in arguments to the jury, counsel shall not express personal knowledge or opinion concerning any matter in issue; shall not read or purport to read from deposition or trial transcripts not in evidence, and shall not suggest to the jury, directly or indirectly, that it may or should request transcripts or the reading of any testimony by the reporter.

q) Counsel shall inform all persons at counsel table that gestures, facial expressions, audible comments, or the like, as manifestations of approval or disapproval, during the testimony of witnesses, or at any other time, are absolutely prohibited, and may be the subject of contempt of court or other sanctions.

r) Smoking, eating, and food are prohibited in the courtroom at any time. Counsel may have water available if the Court gives permission.

s) Small children who are unable to behave are not admitted to the courtroom unless absolutely required for the trial or hearing. Children under the age of 12 years are presumed to be too young to sit during court proceedings.

2. In all criminal proceedings unless excused by the presiding judge, all counsel and defendants shall abide by the following in addition to the requirements of Paragraph 1(a-s) above:

a) The prosecuting attorney shall present to the Court at the <u>beginning</u> of each jury trial a full and complete set of jury instructions and verdict forms. The jury instructions may be in electronic format if allowed by the Court. The jury instructions shall include all Category I lesser-included offenses. Defense counsel shall present to the Court at the <u>beginning</u> of each jury trial, any special instructions and Category II lesser-included offenses that will be requested and proposed verdict forms containing all lesser-included offenses.

b) All motions to suppress evidence shall be filed and heard <u>prior</u> to the trial week. Except for good cause shown, the Court will summarily deny any motion that is not timely filed pursuant to Fla. R. Crim. P. 3.060 and 3. 190(h)(4).

c) Motions should contain specific reference to applicable legal authority that is relied upon by the movant in support of the motion. Rule 3.190(a), Fla. R. Crim. P. Copies of applicable statutes or controlling case law may be attached to the motion or a separate memorandum may be submitted. Pertinent portions of authorities may be underlined or highlighted.

d) Cases which will resolve themselves by way of plea should be promptly scheduled for hearing unless the plea is to take place at docket sounding or a pretrial or scheduling conference. It is the primary responsibility of counsel for the defense to see that a specific hearing time is scheduled for the plea.

e) Plea agreements should be used in all negotiated felony pleas. These forms should be fully completed and signed by all parties <u>prior</u> to the plea hearing.

f) Any disputes as to "score sheets" for sentencing shall be resolved <u>prior</u> to the sentencing hearing. Objections to a score sheet should be communicated to the prosecuting attorney prior to the sentencing hearing.

3. The requirements stated in this rule are minimal, not all-inclusive. They are intended to emphasize and supplement, not supplant or limit, the ethical obligations of counsel under the Code of Professional Responsibility or the time honored customs of experienced trial counsel. Individual judges of the Court may, in any case, or generally, announce and enforce additional prohibitions or requirements; or may excuse compliance with any one or more of the provisions of this rule.

DONE and ORDERED this 21st day of January, 2009.

CLAYTON D. SIMMONS
CHIEF JUDGE

08–26–S. [SUPERSEDED BY ORDER 18–13–S, EFFECTIVE MARCH 19, 2018.]

08–24. FEES—COSTS OF DEFENSE; PUBLIC DEFENDER APPLICATION FEE

IN THE CIRCUIT COURT OF THE EIGHTEENTH JUDICIAL CIRCUIT

ADMINISTRATIVE ORDER NO.: <u>08–24</u>

IN RE: FEES—COSTS OF DEFENSE; PUBLIC DEFENDER APPLICATION FEE

WHEREAS, an amendment to Section 938.29, Florida Statutes, effective July 1, 2008, mandates that costs for the public defender shall be set in all criminal cases at no less than $50 per case in misdemeanor or criminal traffic cases and no less than $100 per case when a felony offense is concluded by entry of a guilty or nolo contendere plea or by guilty verdict at trial or hearing, including a proceeding in which the underlying offense is a violation of probation or community control; and

WHEREAS, Section 938.29, Florida Statutes, mandates that the sentencing court order cost of defense without regard to the defendant's present ability to pay; and

WHEREAS, Section 938.29, Florida Statutes, requires the clerk of court to collect and dispense costs of defense in any case; and

WHEREAS, Section 27.52(1)(b) Florida Statutes, mandates that a defendant pay a $50 Public Defender Application Fee within 7 days of the appointment of the Public Defender and mandates that the clerk of court notify the court if the fee has not been paid at time of sentencing; and

WHEREAS, there is a need for direction to the Clerk of Court to properly implement the requirements of Sections 938.29 and 27.52(1)(b) Florida Statutes: IT IS ORDERED THAT:

1. The Clerk of the Court shall include in each criminal judgment, in cases in which the defendant was represented by the Public Defender, costs for the Public Defender in the amount of $50.00 in misdemeanor cases and $100.00 in felony cases, including original actions and violations of probation or community control. A claim for costs higher than $50.00 in misdemeanor cases and $100.00 in felony cases must be submitted by motion and scheduled for hearing before the assigned judge prior to imposition of a sentence or within 60 days after the date a sentence is imposed, if jurisdiction is specifically reserved for that purpose in the judgment and sentence. The motion shall set forth facts justifying the imposition of additional costs with particularity.

2. The Clerk of Court shall, at the time of the appointment of the Public Defender, include in the court minutes and orders that the defendant shall pay to the Clerk of Court within 7 days the $50 Public Defender Application Fee for each application for court-appointed counsel filed. This shall not apply to the appointment of the Public Defender in juvenile delinquency cases.

3. The Clerk of Court at sentencing shall notify the sentencing court if the defendant has not paid the $50 Public Defender Application Fee and the court shall either assess the application fee as part of the sentence or as a condition of probation, of suspension of sentence, or of the withholding the imposition of sentence; or pursuant to s. 938.29, order the defendant pay the application fee in full or in installments, at the time or times specified.

DONE AND ORDERED this 11th day of August, 2008.

CLAYTON D. SIMMONS
CHIEF JUDGE

07–36–B. [SUPERSEDED BY ORDER 17-46-B, EFFECTIVE DECEMBER 4, 2017.]

07–26–S. CRIMINAL—BAIL SCHEDULE FOR SEMINOLE COUNTY

IN THE CIRCUIT COURT OF THE EIGHTEENTH JUDICIAL CIRCUIT IN AND FOR SEMINOLE COUNTY, FLORIDA

ADMINISTRATIVE ORDER NO.: 07–26–S

SUPERSEDES 06–23–S

IN RE: CRIMINAL—BAIL SCHEDULE FOR SEMINOLE COUNTY

Bail is an essential part of the criminal justice system, and the following bail schedule is established so that law enforcement officers and booking officers can set bond on arrests prior to first appearance. This schedule is not binding upon first appearance judges, who have the responsibility to review arrests at first appearance and set conditions of release pursuant to Rule 3.131.

Within this bail schedule, special provisions setting bail for specific offenses control over general provisions that may also be applicable to the specific offense.

Under the provisions of F. S. 903.02(4), a separate and specific bail amount must be set for each offense charged.

IT IS ADJUDGED:

1. Purpose of Bail Schedule

Except in cases where bail has previously been set or denied, the bail schedule set forth in this Order shall govern release from custody of alleged offenders prior to first appearance and thereafter unless modified in accordance with the applicable Rules of Criminal Procedure on a case-by-case basis.

2. Modification of Bail Prior to Arraignment

a. First Appearance

The "first appearance judge" is any judge who presides over daily first appearances. Except as provided in paragraph (c) below, the first appearance judge may decrease or increase the amount of bail or set other conditions of release as authorized by the Rules of Criminal Procedure, including bail set on a capias, from the date of initial first appearance and during any first appearance hearings thereafter until arraignment. First appearance judges may consider motions to release defendants from custody if the State fails to file a formal charge within thirty days as required by Rule 3.134.

b. Violation of Probation/Community Control Warrants (Sexual Predators and Registered Sexual Offenders)

If a person is arrested for violation of probation or community control and is:

1.) A registered sexual predator, or

2.) A registered sexual offender, or

3.) Under supervision for any criminal offense prescribed in Chapter 794 (Sexual Battery); Section 800.04(4) (Lewd or Lascivious Battery); Section 800.04(5) (Lewd or Lascivious Molestation); Section 800.04(6) (Lewd or Lascivious Conduct); Section 827.071 (Sexual Performance by a Child), or Section 847.0145 (Selling or Buying of Minors), or

4.) Under supervision for a criminal offense for which he/she would meet the registration criteria in Section 775.21, Section 943.0435, or Section 944.607 but for the effective date of those sections; such arrestee is to be held without bond pending a "danger to public" hearing regardless of the bond amount set forth in the violation of probation or community control warrant. In all other cases involving a violation of probation or community control warrant, the judge who is assigned to the violation of probation or community control case shall hear any motions to set, reduce, increase, or modify bail on the warrant. The chief judge, or the administrative judge for Seminole County, shall assign a judge to determine bail in those cases in the absence of the judge to whom such case shall be assigned.

c. Assigned Judge

The "assigned judge" is the judge who is assigned to a case pursuant to administrative order. The assigned judge shall consider motions to set, reduce, increase, or modify conditions of bail or other conditions of release after arraignment and may consider those issues at any time. The assigned judge shall set bail or other conditions of release in capital cases and in cases scheduled on this Order to be "No Bail." No judge of a court of equal or inferior jurisdiction shall modify or set a condition of release which has previously been set by the assigned judge except as provided by Rule 3.131(d). The Chief Judge shall assign a judge to determine bail or other conditions of release in the absence of the assigned judge.

3. Extradition Cases

First appearance judges shall not set bail in extradition cases although they shall otherwise act as required by F.S. 941.10(1). The assigned judge shall hear any habeas corpus proceedings in extradition cases and may consider bail when the defendant has been extradited from another state, territory, or country to this state. The first appearance clerk shall identify extradition cases on the first appearance docket.

4. Bail Schedule

Except as otherwise provided herein, the following Schedules shall apply to felony and misdemeanor arrests on probable cause, and on any warrant or capias with no bond set thereon, pursuant to Fla.R.Crim.P. Rule 3.131(j):

5. Procedure to Set Bail by Arresting Officers

Arresting officers shall set bail according to **SCHEDULES I AND II** for persons arrested on probable cause and not on probation or community control. **Bail shall be set on the highest offense for which the person has been arrested. Persons who have been arrested for multiple offenses shall have bail set on the highest offense charged and in the amount of $100.00 for each additional felony offense and $50.00 for each additional misdemeanor offense.**

SCHEDULE I—SPECIFIC CRIMES

Offense	Bail
First Degree Felony Punishable by Life	NO BAIL
Life Felony	NO BAIL
Capital Felony	NO BAIL
Drug Trafficking {F.S. 893.135}	Set at First Appearance
Escape from Department of Corrections or from rehabilitative community reentry program {F.S. 944.405 (1)}	NO BAIL
Rico Act {F.S. 895.03 & 896.101 (2)}	Set at First Appearance
Attempt/ Solicitation/Conspiracy to Commit First Degree Murder {F.S. 777.04 & 782.04}	NO BAIL
Attempt/Solicitation/Conspiracy to Commit Second Degree Murder {F.S. 777.04 & 782.04}	$15,000
Burglary to a Dwelling {F.S. 810.02 (3)}	$4,900
Leaving scene of accident with Death or Personal Injury {F.S. 316.027 (1)}	$4,900
Vehicular Homicide {F.S. 782.071}	$4,900
Manslaughter {including DUI Manslaughter} {F.S. 782.07 & F.S. 316.193 (2)(b)(3)}	$10,000
DUI/Criminal Traffic	$500

SCHEDULE II—OTHER CRIMES

F–3	Non–Violent	Violent	Drug	Sexual Offenses
Local Resident	$1,000	$2,000	$3,000	$3,000
Florida Resident	$1,500	$2,500	$3,500	$3,500
Out of State Resident	$3,000	$4,000	$4,900	$4,900
Out of Country Resident	$4,900	$8,000	Set at first appearance	$7,000

F–2	Non–Violent	Violent	Drug	Sexual Offenses
Local Resident	$2,000	$4,000	$4,900	$10,000
Florida Resident	$3,000	$4,900	$6,000	$10,000
Out of State Resident	$4,000	$6,000	$8,000	$15,000
Out of Country Resident	$4,900	$8,000	Set at First Appearance	$15,000

F–1	Non–Violent	Violent	Drug	Sexual Offenses
Local Resident	$4,900	$7,000	$10,000	$25,000
Florida Resident	$7,000	$9,000	$12,000	$25,000
Out of State Resident	$10,000	$12,000	$14,000	$30,000
Out of Country Resident	$12,000	$14,000	Set at First Appearance	$35,000

M–1		M–2	
All Offenses	$500	All Offenses	$227.50

SCHEDULE III—OFFENDERS ON PROBATION OR COMMUNITY CONTROL FOR FELONY OFFENSES

An individual arrested for a new criminal offense, who is on felony probation or community control, shall be held without bond pending first appearance.

An individual arrested for violation of felony probation or community control shall be held without bond pending first appearance, unless;

i. There is a violation of probation or community control warrant, which, on its face, provides that the arrestee does not meet the qualifications for a "danger to public" hearing as defined in Florida Statute 948.06(4) (as amended by the "Jessica Lunsford Act"), and

ii. The violation of probation or community warrant sets a bond amount.

6. Direct Filed Informations or Indictments

a. Initial Filing of Information or Indictment (F.S. 932.48)

Except as provided in subsection b. the clerk of the circuit court shall endorse on the capias the bail for each offense charged pursuant to the bail schedule herein.

b. Refiled Information after Nolle Prosequi

When an information is refiled after a Nolle Prosequi has been entered and the court has therefore lost jurisdiction over the person of the defendant, only the assigned judge or alternate judge pursuant to 2.c. herein may set the bail or other conditions of release.

7. Special Conditions of Release—Duty of Pretrial Release Officer

a. Persons on Probation—Department of Corrections

Any person who is arrested in Seminole County and who is on probation with supervision by the Department of Corrections, Probation and Parole Services, shall, as an additional condition of release, report to Department of Corrections, Probation and Parole Services, Sanford, Florida, before close of business on the first business day following release.

An offender is considered to be on probation if he is on parole or under any other type of supervision status by the Department of Corrections.

b. Persons on Probation—Seminole County Probation Department

Any person who is arrested in Seminole County and who is on probation with supervision by the Seminole County Probation Department, shall, as an additional condition of release, report to Seminole County Probation Department, Sanford, Florida, before close of business on the first business day following release.

c. Persons arrested for sexual offenses or child abuse

Any person who is arrested for a sexual offense or for child abuse shall, as an additional condition of release, be prohibited from having direct or indirect contact with any victim named in the arrest report. This condition shall include not returning to the defendant's place of residence if any victim resides there.

d. General Conditions for Pretrial Release Applicable to All Cases

1. The defendant shall refrain from criminal activity of any kind.

2. The defendant shall refrain from any contact of any type with the victim(s), except through pretrial discovery pursuant to the Florida Rules of Criminal Procedure.

3. The defendant shall comply with all other conditions of pretrial release.

e. Duty of Pretrial Release Officer

1. Persons arrested who are on probation shall not be released until they have been instructed of the conditions in paragraph 7, subsection b of this Order by a Pretrial Release Officer and have signed a written Notice in the form attached as Exhibit B to this Order.

2. Persons arrested who are alleged to have committed a sexual offense shall not be released until they have been instructed of the conditions in paragraph 7, subsection c of this Order by a Pretrial Release Officer and have signed a written Notice in the form attached as Exhibit C to this Order.

8. Subsequent Offenders

Any alleged offender who is on release status and is subsequently rearrested for a new felony offense shall be released on bail in an amount double that shown on the applicable schedule. Subsequent offenders shall not be released R.O.R. or P.T.R.

9. Domestic Violence Cases

a. Crimes Involving Domestic Violence

Any individual arrested for any crime involving domestic violence, as defined in Section 741.28(1) and (2) Florida Statutes, shall remain incarcerated until First Appearance. At that time the First Appearance Judge shall determine appropriate bail and conditions of release, taking into consideration the factors enumerated in Section 741.2901(3), Florida Statutes, as presented by the State Attorney at First Appearance pursuant to said section. If the State Attorney fails to comply with Section 741.2901(3), the First Appearance Judge may release the individual on recognizance with appropriate conditions of release at the discretion of the Judge.

b. Violation of Injunction for Protection Against Domestic Violence

Any individual arrested for violating Section 741.31, Florida Statutes, for violating an injunction for protection against domestic violence issued pursuant to Section 741.30 shall remain incarcerated until First Appearance. At that time the First Appearance Judge shall determine appropriate conditions of release.

c. Violation of Injunction for Protection Against Repeat Violence

Any individual arrested pursuant to Section 901.15(8), Florida Statutes, for any crime violating an injunction for protection against repeat violence issued pursuant to Section 784.046, Florida Statutes, shall remain incarcerated until First Appearance. At that time the First Appearance Judge shall determine appropriate conditions of release.

10. Temporary Detention

If, in the arresting officer's opinion, further violence, or additional law violations are probable, the duty Assistant State Attorney may contact the duty judge for authority to hold the alleged offender in custody until First Appearance.

11. Guidelines for Arresting Officers and/or Booking Personnel in Considering Release Prior to Judicial Review at First Appearance or Initial Proceeding

Guidelines for arresting officers and/or booking personnel in considering release of alleged offenders prior to judicial review at First Appearance or other initial proceeding are attached as Exhibit A to this Order and reincorporated by reference in this Order.

12. Bail before Conviction; Condition of Undertaking [Rule 3.131(e)(2)]

If a person is admitted to bail for his appearance for a preliminary hearing, or on a charge that a magistrate is empowered to try, the condition of the undertaking shall be that he/she will appear for such hearing, or to answer the charge, and will submit himself/herself to the orders and process of the magistrate trying the same, and will not depart without leave.

If he/she is admitted to bail after having been held to answer by a magistrate, or after an indictment or information on which he/she is to be tried has been filed, the condition of the undertaking shall be that he will appear to answer the charges before the court in which he/she may be prosecuted and submit to the orders and process of the court, and will not depart without leave. The sheriff shall not accept a surety bond which contains conditions of the undertaking which are different from those set forth above. This portion of this order is for the purpose of requiring the provisions of surety bonds to comply with the Rules of Criminal Procedure.

13. Effect of Filing Notice of No Information or Nolle Prosequi

If a person arrested for any offense(s) occurring within Seminole County is admitted to bail and the State Attorney files a notice of No Information or Nolle Prosequi with respect to all charges arising out of a single arrest, the Sheriff shall without further order of the Court release the person from custody as to the charges named.

As to the named charges and person, all bail undertaking, not defaulted, shall be canceled, all sureties shall be exonerated, and all release on recognizance obligations shall be discharged without further order of the court. A bench warrant or capias which may be outstanding and is yet unserved upon a named individual for a specified charge shall also be canceled upon the filing of a No Information or Nolle Prosequi without further order of the court.

14. Effective Date

This bail schedule shall become effective on August 17, 2007.

DONE AND ORDERED this 10th day of August, 2007.

CLAYTON D. SIMMONS
CHIEF JUDGE

EXHIBIT A

Guidelines for Arresting Officers and/or Booking Personnel in Considering Release of Alleged Offender Prior to Judicial Review at First Appearance or Other Initial Proceeding

I. Residence

Community ties required to be considered by the Court pursuant to RCrP 3.131 should properly include factors bearing upon residence of a recently arrested individual.

The following classification of persons by residence is submitted to permit distinctions to be made by the arresting officer and or booking officials in connection with release on cash or surety bail of all persons arrested prior to any first appearance or initial appearance proceedings.

A. Local Resident

Any person taken into custody for an offense which reportedly occurred in Seminole County, who has a verifiable residence address in Seminole, Brevard, Volusia, Orange or Lake Counties is to be considered a "Local Resident".

B. Florida Resident

Any person taken into custody for an offense which reportedly occurred in Seminole County who has a verifiable residence address in the State of Florida but does not reside in a county qualifying him as a Local Resident, as defined above, is considered a "Florida Resident" for purposes of the Bail Schedule but only if the arrest of said person occurred within the State of Florida.

C. Out–Of–State Resident

Any person taken into custody for an offense which reportedly occurred in Seminole County, who has a verifiable residence address within any state in the United States or any of its territories, but outside the State of Florida, is considered an "Out–of–State Resident" for the purposes of the bail schedule.

D. Out–of–Country Resident

Any person taken into custody for an offense which reportedly occurred in Seminole County, who has no verifiable address within the United States, or who has identification which clearly indicates that said person is a resident of a country other than the United States, is to be considered and "Out–of–Country Resident" for the purpose of the bail schedule.

II. Non–Violent vs. Violent Offenses

A. Non–Violent Offense

Any felony offense not involving physical harm or actual threat of physical harm to another person is a "Non–Violent Offense".

B. Violent Offense

Burglary to an occupied dwelling is a "Violent Offense". Also, any felony offense involving physical harm to another person, or having as one of its elements any assault or threat of violence, or involving the use or threatened use of a deadly weapon, or any offense regardless of its character which involves assaultive or combative conduct upon apprehension of the accused, is a "Violent Offense".

EXHIBIT B

IN THE EIGHTEENTH JUDICIAL
CIRCUIT COURT IN AND FOR
SEMINOLE COUNTY, FLORIDA

CASE NO.

STATE OF FLORIDA,

Plaintiff,

–vs–

Defendant.
______________________/

NOTICE OF CONDITIONS OF PRETRIAL RELEASE (DEFENDANT ON PROBATION)

The arrest records in your case show that you are presently on probation.

The Circuit Court Administrative Order setting the bail schedule in Seminole County requires any person arrested who is on probation to accept the following condition of release prior to being released from custody:

If probation is supervised by the Department of Corrections, Probation & Parole Services, you will report to the probation office located at 2684 Orlando Drive, Sanford, Florida, before close of business the first business day following release. You will report to this office regardless of the location of your county of supervision.

If probation is supervised by the Seminole County Probation Department, you will report to the probation office located at 116 N. Hood Avenue, Sanford, Florida, before close of business the first business day following release.

CERTIFICATE OF PRETRIAL RELEASE OFFICER

I hereby certify that I have instructed the defendant about the above special conditions of release and that I have delivered a copy of this Notice to the defendant.

____

Pretrial Release Officer

RECEIPT

I certify that I have received a copy of this notice.

Date: ____________ ____________
Defendant

EXHIBIT C

IN THE EIGHTEENTH JUDICIAL CIRCUIT, IN AND FOR SEMINOLE COUNTY, FLORIDA

CASE NO.

STATE OF FLORIDA,

Plaintiff,

–vs–

Defendant.

____________/

NOTICE OF CONDITIONS OF PRETRIAL RELEASE (ALL ARRESTEES)

The Circuit Court Administrative Order setting the bail schedule in Seminole County requires any person so charged to accept the following special conditions of release prior to being released from custody on bail:

(1) You will have no direct or indirect contact with any victim named in the arrest report.

(2) You shall not go to the residence of any victim named in the arrest report even if that residence is your residence.

(3) You will refrain from criminal activity of any kind.

If you fail to comply with these special conditions, you may be remanded to custody by the Court.

CERTIFICATE OF PRETRIAL RELEASE OFFICER

I hereby certify that I have instructed the defendant about the above special conditions of release and that I have delivered a copy of this Notice to the defendant.

____

Pretrial Release Officer

RECEIPT

I certify that I have received a copy of this notice.

Date: ____________ ____________
Defendant

07–12–S. CRIMINAL—WORK RELEASE PROGRAM SEMINOLE COUNTY

IN THE CIRCUIT COURT OF THE EIGHTEENTH JUDICIAL CIRCUIT IN AND FOR SEMINOLE COUNTY, FLORIDA

ADMINISTRATIVE ORDER NO.: 07–12–S

SUPERSEDES 04–17–S

IN RE: CRIMINAL—WORK RELEASE PROGRAM SEMINOLE COUNTY

The Seminole County Sheriff has requested the court to allow selected inmates to be placed into the Work Release Program without further judicial intervention after sentence has been imposed or upon meeting presentencing qualifications. After due consideration of the request,

IT IS ADJUDGED:

1. Offenders who meet the criteria below may be placed in the Work Release Program and the limits of their confinement is extended for that purpose without further order of court.

2. No offender may qualify for Work Release if the sentencing judge so indicates on the sentencing order or upon the presentencing consideration request.

3. Criteria for Work Release Program:

A. Offense Criteria:

Offenders who are in custody for misdemeanors, traffic offenses, and second and third degree felonies will be considered eligible for participation in the Work Release Program. However, offenders who are in custody for violent offenses (with the exception of battery in domestic cases and the victim agrees to the release), involve the abuse of children or involve the use of a deadly weapon, will not be eligible for the Work Release Program. Specifically, the following crimes will not be accepted into the Program:

1. Homicide
2. Robbery
3. Sexual Battery
4. Child abuse/neglect
5. Lewd act in the presence of a child
6. Trafficking in controlled substances
7. Offenses involving the use of a deadly weapon
8. Arson

B. Prior Record:

The offender must not have been convicted of a felony involving violence, the use of a weapon, or the abuse of children within the past seven years prior to the date of the offense for which the offender has been sentenced.

C. Health Criteria:

1. Physical Condition: Offenders with serious medical conditions requiring frequent care will not be eligible for the Work Release Program.

2. Offenders who are acutely psychotic, severely mentally retarded, current suicidal or otherwise unable to cope with the structured programs in Work Release, or unable to understand and comply with the program conditions, will not be eligible for Work Release.

D. Other Criteria:

No offender with a "hold" from any other jurisdiction is eligible for Work Release. Offenders serving a sentence or that are presentenced on other charges that do not meet the requirements of this order are not eligible for Work Release.

E. Exceptional Cases:

The judge having jurisdiction over the case may allow offenders who do not meet the strict criteria of this order into the Work Release Program upon request of the Sheriff or an authorized representative of the Work Release Program.

4. Revocations:

Offenders who fail to comply with the conditions of the Work Release Program are subject to being returned to the jail for service of the balance of the sentence originally imposed. The court will issue a capias to return the defendant to jail if the offender cannot be located.

DONE AND ORDERED this 21st day of March, 2007.

TONYA RAINWATER
CHIEF JUDGE

07-06-S. CRIMINAL—ADULT CONSEQUENCE PROGRAM

IN THE CIRCUIT COURT OF THE EIGHTEENTH JUDICIAL CIRCUIT OF FLORIDA, SEMINOLE COUNTY

ADMINISTRATIVE ORDER NO.: 07-06-S

IN RE: CRIMINAL—ADULT CONSEQUENCE PROGRAM

Whereas, the number of offenders under community supervision has increase substantially in the past year; and,

Whereas, the number of violations of probation/community control warrants has increased as a result; and,

Whereas, a substantial number of these violations do not involve a new criminal offense or other serious violations; and,

Whereas, arresting and incarcerating certain non-violent offenders for minor violations of probation or community control is both expensive and nonproductive; and,

Whereas, the Department of Corrections and the Sheriff of Seminole County have agreed to sanction certain non-violent offenders who commit minor violations administratively;

NOW, THEREFORE, IT IS ADJUDGED:

1. There is created in Seminole County a program that shall be known as the Adult Consequence Program.

2. **ELIGIBILITY:** To be eligible for the program, offenders must have been placed on probation or community control under the supervision of the Department of Corrections by a judge in Seminole County, have stable community ties, and have a stable residence in Seminole County, Florida. Offenders who are eligible for the program include probation offenders, drug offenders, and community control supervision offenders. The program only applies to offenders who have committed technical violations. The threat an offender poses to public safety is the most important factor in determining eligibility. Offenders with a lengthy or violent criminal history, including sex offenders, are not eligible for the program. Additionally, offenders who have new law violations, are absconders, are in a residential drug treatment program, or have violated a "no contact" condition of supervision are not eligible for the program. No offender is eligible for the program who has two or more previous violations.

3. **QUALIFYING VIOLATIONS:** Offenders who are alleged to have committed one or more of the following violations may qualify for the program:

A. Condition (1): Reporting late but not more than 1 regular business day after the scheduled appointment with probation officer.

B. Condition (2): Failing to pay cost of supervision, or being delinquent, but not less than 90 days prior to termination of sentence.

C. Condition (6): Offenders found to be associating with someone engaging in criminal activity.

D. Condition (7): Testing positive for the presence of marijuana or cocaine in a presumptive office drug screening, or admitting the use of these drugs. (First time positives only)

E. Condition (8): Offenders unable to find or maintain full-time employment, but who are willing to make an effort to do so.

F. Condition (9): Offenders failing to comply with officer's instructions.

G. Condition (H): Offenders failing to make first appointment scheduled for drug/alcohol evaluation.

H. Condition (T): Failing to complete letter of apology within time frame ordered by the Court.

I. Condition (U): Failing to complete monthly requirement of community service hours ordered by the Court.

J. Condition (A): Failing to pay the monthly amount established by the court for court costs and fines.

K. Condition (C): Failing to pay the monthly amount of restitution established by the court.

L. Special Condition (GG): Exclusionary zone violation.

M. Community Control Condition (2): Offenders who commit minor residence violations such as: returning home late from work, school or an absence which was previously approved by the community control officer.

4. **PROCEDURE:**

A. The probation or community control officer shall inform offenders who have committed first or second violations enumerated in paragraph 2 that they may elect to be referred to the Adult Consequence Program for administrative discipline. No offender is required to accept a referral to the Adult Consequence Program and may reject the referral in favor of a formal violation of probation or community control proceeding in Circuit Court. Offenders who do not elect to participate in the Adult Consequences Program will be given an order to appear to answer to the violation after a formal affidavit of violation of probation is filed with the court. A warrant will not be issued by the court unless the offender fails to appear as directed by the order to appear.

B. If the offender agrees to accept the administrative consequence(s) provided by the program, a signed, written waiver of formal violation proceedings and agreement to accept the consequence(s) must be submitted to the Court for filing in the court file along with the Technical Violation Notification letter/form order referring the offender for adult consequences.

If the offender declines to accept administrative consequences, the supervising officer shall submit a violation affidavit, report, and warrant. The report shall plainly state that the offender was offered and declined adult consequences and an order to appear should be issued in lieu of a warrant.

C. The assigned judge shall review the Technical Violation Notification letter/form submitted and, if the offender is to be referred for adult consequences, shall file the Technical Violation Notification letter/form in the court file and issue the order referring the defendant for adult consequences. The officer assigned to supervise the offender and that officer's immediate supervisor shall agree as to the appropriate consequence(s).

D. The assigned probation officer shall provide the Sheriff with a written notice when adult consequences have been satisfied. The assigned probation officer shall notify the Sheriff if an offender fails to complete the consequences as directed and shall submit a violation of probation affidavit, warrant and report to the court. The offender may be taken into custody to answer to the violation.

5. **AVAILABLE CONSEQUENCE:** The following sanction(s) may be imposed upon offenders who elect to accept the Adult Consequence Program in lieu of a formal violation of probation or community control:

A. Up to 24 hours of community service to be completed within 30 days from the date the sanction was imposed.

B. Report on Tuesday and Thursday for drug screens for up to 6 consecutive weeks to begin 14 days after the positive test result is received, or 14 days from the date the offender admitted to last using the substance. The offender must submit to a drug/ alcohol evaluation and successfully complete any treatment as recommended.

C. Place the offender in the EMPACT Monitoring program for up to 15 days and pay the daily cost of the monitor.

D. Require the offender to report every Monday for drug testing for up to 4 consecutive weeks.

E. Require the offender to report every Monday and produce employment sheets for up to 4 consecutive weeks.

F. Require the offender to submit to a drug evaluation through TASC within 30 days and complete any recommended treatment.

G. Require the offender to pay $15.00 per hour for each hour of delinquent community service. The amount must be paid within 60 days to First Step of the Eighteenth Judicial Circuit, Inc. The amount may be in lieu of completion of public service hours or in addition to them.

6. **ADMINISTRATION:** The Adult Consequences Program shall be administered by the Seminole County Sheriff or his designee. The Sheriff or his designee will be responsible for maintaining records of all participants in the program and provide a quarterly report to the Administrative Judge of the Criminal Division.

DONE AND ORDERED this 12th day of January, 2007.

TONYA RAINWATER
CHIEF JUDGE

06–12–B. ARBITRATION—QUALIFICATIONS FOR APPOINTMENT OF ARBITRATORS IN CIVIL CASES

IN THE CIRCUIT COURT OF THE EIGHTEENTH JUDICIAL CIRCUIT IN AND FOR BREVARD COUNTY, FLORIDA

ADMINISTRATIVE ORDER NO.: 06–12–B

IN RE: ARBITRATION—QUALIFICATIONS FOR APPOINTMENT OF ARBITRATORS IN CIVIL CASES

WHEREAS, Chapter 44, Florida Statutes, permits a presiding circuit or county judge to refer civil cases to arbitration without the consent of the parties; and

WHEREAS, Rule 1.810(a), Florida Rules of Civil Procedure requires the Chief Judge or his designee to maintain a list of qualified persons who have agreed to serve within the circuit as arbitrators under Section 44.103, Florida Statutes; and

WHEREAS, Rule 11.130, Florida Rules of Court requires that arbitrators shall serve at the pleasure of the Chief Judge; and

WHEREAS, the Court finds that it is necessary to establish a set for specific qualifications for arbitrators in order for their names to appear on the circuit list of qualified arbitrators maintained in accordance with Administrative Order 05–23–B of this Court.

NOW, THEREFORE pursuant to the authority vested in the Chief Judge by Rule 2.050 of the Florida Rules of Judicial Administration, it is ORDERED that:

1. A person named on the list of persons who are qualified to serve as arbitrators as required by Paragraph 1 of Administrative Order 05–23–B shall have the following qualifications:

(a) A member in good standing of the Florida Bar who has been a member of the Florida Bar for at least five (5) years; and

(b) Has attended four hours of training in an arbitrator training program approved by the Supreme Court of Florida; and

(c) Meets the requirements of one of the following paragraphs:

(1) Has participated as counsel in a minimum of (3) three civil cases in which a jury trial was commenced by the selection of a jury and presentation of testimony; and has served as lead counsel in at least one of those cases; or

(2) Has participated as lead counsel in a minimum of six (6) civil cases in which a jury trial was demanded and were settled prior to trial as the result of formal mediation or arbitration proceedings; or

(3) Is certified as a mediator by the Florida Supreme Court and has mediated or arbitrated to complete settlement at least six (6) civil cases in which a jury trial was demanded by the parties; or

(4) Is a retired justice or retired appellate or circuit judge within the meaning of "retired" as defined in Section 25.073(1), Florida Statutes.

2. The Administrative Judge of Civil Division shall prepare an application form for persons who wish to apply to serve as arbitrators under Chapter 44, Florida Statutes and Administrative Order 05–23–B. The said application form shall require that the applicant demonstrate compliance with the requirements of this order, and shall additionally include a requirement that applicant provide a brief description of the applicant's legal experience.

3. Each trial judge shall have the discretion to appoint an arbitrator to a given type of case (e.g., personal injury, medical

malpractice, commercial litigation, or other civil case) which is consistent with the arbitrator's prior experience.

DONE AND ORDERED this 15TH day of MARCH, 2006.

KERRY I. EVANDER
CHIEF JUDGE

06–06–S (A2). SUPERSEDED BY ADMINISTRATIVE ORDER NO. 16-15-S

05–50. APPEALS TO CIRCUIT COURT

IN THE CIRCUIT COURT OF THE EIGHTEENTH JUDICIAL CIRCUIT

ADMINISTRATIVE ORDER NO: 05–50

SUPERSEDES 04–12 AND 01–25–S

IN RE: **APPEALS TO CIRCUIT COURT**

It appears that the administrative processing of appeals through the use of regularly convened appellate panels has significantly shortened the time from filing to resolution of appeals in this circuit, while retaining the quality of judicial labor devoted to said appeals. Pursuant to Fla. R. Jud–Admin. 2.020(C), it is thereupon,

ORDERED that cases filed with the Clerk of the Circuit Court (hereinafter called Clerk), in Brevard and Seminole Counties pursuant to Fla. R. App. P. 9.030(c) shall be administratively processed as follows:

1. Administrative Judges for appeals (hereinafter called Administrative Judge) shall be appointed annually by the Chief Judge, in Brevard and Seminole Counties of the Eighteenth Judicial Circuit.

2. Appeals of matters encompassed within Fla. R. App. P. 9.030(c)(1)(A)(B)(C), shall be assigned an appropriate appellate (AP. or AC) case number by the Clerk.

3. **IN SEMINOLE COUNTY ONLY**: Criminal appeals from the County Court filed pursuant to Fla.R.App.P. 9.030 (c)(1) (A) and (B) shall be assigned by the Administrative Judge to three (3) judge panels drawn from the panel in the Criminal Division of the Circuit Court and assigned an appellate case number by the clerk. The Administrative Judge shall assign a presiding judge of each panel. If a criminal division judge is unable to serve for any reason the Administrative Judge shall assign a juvenile division judge on a rotating basis.

4. **IN SEMINOLE COUNTY ONLY:** Civil appeals from the County Court filed pursuant to Fla.R.App.P. 9.030 (c)(1) (A) and (B) shall be assigned by the Administrative Judge to a judge on a rotating basis from the judges in the civil division of the Circuit Court and assigned an appellate case number by the clerk.

5. **IN SEMINOLE COUNTY ONLY:** Appeals from administrative action pursuant to Fla.R.App.P. 9.030 (c)(1)(C) shall be assigned by the Administrative Judge to a judge in the same manner as other civil cases to the judges in the civil division of the Circuit Court and assigned an appellate case number by the clerk.

6. Petitions for Writs of Certiorari (both common law and statutory; Petitions for Mandamus, Prohibition, Quo Warranto and Habeas Corpus in civil cases, (Fla. R. App. P. 9.030(c) (2) (3)) which are not combined with other requested forms of relief shall be assigned an appellate (AP or AC) case number by the Clerk and the file immediately forwarded to the Administrative Judge for review. If the Administrative Judge determines:

(a) That the Petition meets the requirements of Fla. R. App. P. 9.100(f), the Administrative Judge shall issue an Order to Show Cause pursuant to said rule.

(b) That the Petition does not meet the requirements of Fla. R. App. P. 9.100(f), the Administrative Judge may enter an order dismissing the Petition or may refer the matter to the next available Appellate Panel for decision on whether the order to Show Cause should be issued.

7. **IN BREVARD COUNTY ONLY:** Petitions for Writs of Certiorari combined in a complaint with other (additional or alternative) requested forms of relief (e.g., injunction, prohibition or mandamus) shall be assigned a regular civil (CA) case number by the Clerk and the file forwarded to the judge to whom the case is assigned, for review and for consideration of the entry of an Order to Show Cause pursuant to Fla. R. App. P. 9.100(f). Such case shall be handled in all other respects as a regular civil case. If, at any stage of the case, the assigned judge determines that Certiorari is the appropriate remedy, the assigned judge shall advise the Administrative Judge and the Clerk of this decision and the Administrative Judge shall then enter an Order to Show Cause, or, if not required, shall set the matter for oral argument before the next available appellate panel.

8. In addition to the above, the Administrative Judge shall have the following duties:

(a) **IN BREVARD COUNTY ONLY**: Prepare (preferably prior to the beginning of the year), for all civil and criminal appeals as well as original proceedings a schedule of monthly Appellate Panels composed of three (3) Circuit Judges, with one judge on each panel designated as Presiding Judge, and shall schedule oral arguments when appropriate pursuant to Fla. R. App. P. 9.320.

(b) **IN BREVARD COUNTY**, periodically review all appellate files and shall prepare orders setting oral arguments.

IN SEMINOLE COUNTY, the presiding judge shall schedule oral arguments when appropriate and notify the Administrative Judge who will then prepare orders setting oral arguments.

(c) Receive the decisions from the appellate panels and disseminate them to the trial judge or administrative agency, counsel, Clerk, unrepresented parties and the law libraries of Brevard and Seminole Counties.

(d) Insure that mandates are issued by the Clerk pursuant to Fla. R. App. P. 9.340 (See paragraph 7 below)

(e) Enter orders concerning matters encompassed within the following Florida Appellate Rules, in order to facilitate expeditious handling of appeals:

(1) 9.040(b) (transfer to appropriate court of proceeding in inappropriate court).

(2) 9.040(d) (motions to amend).

(3) 9.200(e) (motions to enforce preparation and transmittal of record).

(4) 9.200(f) (motions to correct or supplement record).

(5) 9.300 (motions)

(6) 9.320 (motions relating to oral argument)

(7) 9.360 (motions relating to joinder and substitution of parties).

(8) 9.370 (motions relating to Amicus Curiae)

(9) 9.410 (dismissal of proceedings for violation of rules, upon the (10) days notice)

(10) 9.420 (motions relating to service)

(11) 9.440 (motions relating to admission or withdrawal of attorneys)

(12) any other motion filed prior to the assignment of an appellate panel.

9. The Presiding Judge of the Appellate Panel shall insure that decisions are rendered promptly.

10. Sixteen (16) days after the decision of the appellate panel has been filed, the Clerk shall advise the Administrative Judge in writing whether a motion for rehearing or clarification has been filed pursuant to Fla. R. App. P. 9.330.

(a) If no motion for rehearing or clarification has been timely filed, the clerk shall prepare the Mandate pursuant to Fla. R. App. P. 9.340.

(b) If a motion for rehearing or clarification has been timely filed, the Clerk shall forward a copy of same to the presiding judge of the appellate panel and a copy to the Administrative Judge. When the decision is filed on the motion for rehearing or clarification, the Clerk shall prepare the Mandate.

DONE AND ORDERED this 26th day of October 2005.

KERRY I. EVANDER
CHIEF JUDGE

05–46–B. CRIMINAL—RELEASE ON RECOGNIZANCE/SIGNATURE BOND IN VIOLATION OF MISDEMEANOR PROBATION CASES

IN THE CIRCUIT COURT OF THE EIGHTEENTH JUDICIAL CIRCUIT IN AND FOR BREVARD COUNTY, FLORIDA.

ADMINISTRATIVE ORDER NO. 05–46–B

SUPERSEDES 92–3–CR AND 89–89–CR

IN RE: CRIMINAL—RELEASE ON RECOGNIZANCE/SIGNATURE BOND IN VIOLATION OF MISDEMEANOR PROBATION CASES

WHEREAS, judges often recommend that defendants charged with violating probation in misdemeanor cases be released on their own recognizance or by signature bond by writing their recommendations on the face of the warrant for violation of probation; and

WHEREAS, in some of such cases defendants are being held over to initial appearances even though a judge has specified on the face of the warrant that the defendant be released; and

WHEREAS, it would reduce jail population and additional work at the initial appearance hearing if such recommendations for release were promptly followed by pretrial release personnel,

NOW, THEREFORE, IT IS ORDERED:

1) That when a Brevard judge executes a warrant for a violation of misdemeanor probation charge, and indicates on the face of a warrant that the defendant is to be released on his own recognizance or by way of a signature bond, Pretrial Release Personnel at the Brevard County Detention Center shall promptly provide the defendant with the opportunity to execute the Release on Recognizance form or signature bond and upon his/her doing so, release the defendant from custody, unless Pretrial Release Personnel have information indicating the defendant qualifies for a "danger to public" hearing under the Jessica Lunsford Act, in which case the defendant shall be brought before the initial appearance judge.

2) In addition to any special bond conditions appearing on the face of the warrant, Pretrial Release Personnel shall include the following conditions of release in any Release on Recognizance form or signature bond, to wit:

a) The defendant shall keep in close contact with his/her attorney.

b) The defendant shall appear in Court at all subsequent hearings.

c) The defendant shall violate no laws.

d) The defendant shall report in person to his/ her probation officer within 72 hours of release from confinement.

e) The defendant shall provide the Court with his/ her correct residence address and telephone number, if any.

f) The defendant shall comply with the terms and conditions of probation.

g) The date, time, and place of the defendant's next court date shall appear on the face of the Release on Recognizance form or Signature Bond.

4) Provided the conditions of this Order are complied with, the defendant may be released from custody without a judges signature on the signature bond. Pretrial Release Personnel shall present the signature bond to the judge handling the initial appearance hearing on the day following the defendant's release for approval and signature.

DONE AND ORDERED this 21st day of September, 2005.

KERRY I. EVANDER
CHIEF JUDGE

05–45–B. DOMESTIC VIOLENCE—CHILDREN ATTENDING DOMESTIC VIOLENCE INJUNCTION HEARINGS

IN THE CIRCUIT COURT OF THE EIGHTEENTH JUDICIAL CIRCUIT IN AND FOR BREVARD COUNTY, FLORIDA

ADMINISTRATIVE ORDER NO.: 05–45–B

IN RE: DOMESTIC VIOLENCE—CHILDREN ATTENDING DOMESTIC VIOLENCE INJUNCTION HEARINGS

WHEREAS, FS § 741 authorizes the filing of an Injunction on behalf of a minor child; and

WHEREAS, Fla. Fam. L.R.P. 12.407 prohibits the attendance of a minor child at any court hearing, including Domestic Violence Injunction Proceedings, without prior Court approval; and

WHEREAS, that due to mandated time constraints and congested court dockets, there may not be enough time and notice to have a motion for the minor child to testify heard prior to the Final Injunction hearing; and

WHEREAS, the moving party may not be able to prove that violence occurred on behalf of the minor child without the attendance and testimony of the minor child; and

WHEREAS, the adoption of the following provision will provide for the proper administration of hearing Domestic Violence cases on behalf of a minor child within the Eighteenth Circuit, it is

ORDERED:

1. In a Domestic Violence Injunction proceeding which is brought on behalf of a minor child where the allegations are that the child is the victim of direct physical violence and/or direct sexual violence, the minor child may be brought to the hearing to present testimony before the Court without need for a motion, hearing on said motion, and an order for the minor child to attend said court proceeding so long as said minor child is twelve (12) years of age or older.

2. If a Domestic Violence Injunction proceeding is brought on behalf of the minor child and the minor child is less than twelve (12) years of age and/or the allegations are such that the domestic violence involves indirect physical violence; such as the violence occurred in the presence of the minor child; then said Court requires a motion and an order pursuant to Fla. Fam. L.R.P. 12.407.

DONE AND ORDERED this 21st day of September, 2005.

KERRY I. EVANDER
CHIEF JUDGE

05–27. [SUPERSEDED BY ORDER 17-38, EFFECTIVE SEPTEMBER 25, 2017.]

05–23–B. ARBITRATION—CREATION AND MAINTENANCE OF CIRCUIT LIST OF QUALIFIED ARBITRATORS; COURT ORDERED ARBITRATION IN CIRCUIT CIVIL CASES & COUNTY COURT; COMPENSATION AND PROCEDURES

IN THE CIRCUIT COURT OF THE EIGHTEENTH JUDICIAL CIRCUIT IN AND FOR BREVARD COUNTY, FLORIDA.

ADMINISTRATIVE ORDER NO.: 05–23–B

SUPERSEDES 04–19–B

IN RE: ARBITRATION—CREATION AND MAINTENANCE OF CIRCUIT LIST OF QUALIFIED ARBITRATORS; COURT ORDERED ARBITRATION IN CIRCUIT CIVIL CASES & COUNTY COURT; COMPENSATION AND PROCEDURES

Whereas, Florida Statute Chapter 44, permits a presiding Civil Circuit or County Judge to refer civil cases to arbitration without the consent of the parties, in much the same way cases are referred to mediation;

Whereas, Rule 1.810(a), Florida Rules of Civil Procedure, requires the Chief Judge, or his designee, to maintain a list of qualified persons who have agreed to serve within the circuit as arbitrators under § 44.103, Florida Statutes;

Whereas, Rules 11.010 and 11.020, Florida Rules of Court—Appointed Arbitrators, require, with certain exceptions, that arbitrators be members of the Florida Bar and that they complete a training program approved by the Supreme Court of Florida;

Whereas, Rule 1.820(b)(1), Florida Rules of Civil Procedure, requires the Chief Judge to set procedures for determining the time and place of the arbitration hearing;

Whereas, Rule 1.810(b), Florida Rules of Civil Procedure, requires the Chief Judge to establish the compensation for arbitrators in accordance with § 44.013(3), Florida Statutes;

WHEREAS nonbinding arbitration pursuant to Florida Statutes section 44.103 may be effective in the following circumstances, among others:

(a) In personal injury cases where fault is established by summary judgment or is not likely to be seriously contested although not subject to be established by summary judgment, and the remaining issues are proximate cause of loss or injury and the amount of damages.

(b) In probate litigation where the issues are whether the testator or testatrix has testamentary capacity or whether they have been subject to duress or undue influence.

(c) In contract cases where the issue is whether there was a breach of contract and subsequent damages.

Now, therefore, pursuant to the authority vested in the Chief Judge by Rule. 2.050, of the Florida Rules of Judicial Administration,

It is Ordered That:

1. The administrative Judge of the Circuit Civil Division shall create and maintain for Court Administration a list of persons who are qualified to serve as arbitrators.

2. To be qualified as an arbitrator, one must be a member of The Florida Bar for 5 years and comply with the qualifications and training requirements set forth in Florida Rules of Arbitration 11.010, 11.020, and 11.110, unless otherwise agreed by the parties. Attorneys who are interested in being listed as arbitrators should contact Court Administration to obtain an application. Completed applications shall be delivered to the Administrative Judge of the Circuit Civil Division or the Administrative Judge of County Court. The list of qualified arbitrators shall be designated as the 18th Judicial Circuit's List of Qualified Arbitrators.

3. Arbitration shall be conducted in accordance with the rules of practice and procedure adopted by the Supreme Court of Florida, as well as with all orders and directives as may be approved by the Chief Judge. The time and place of the arbitration hearing shall be scheduled by the arbitrator(s), after consulting with the parties and their attorneys. The arbitration hearing shall be conducted within Brevard County Florida.

4. The attached Order of Referral, or a substantially similar order, shall be used by the presiding Judge on all cases referred to arbitration. The Order of Referral will also serve as the Notice of Arbitration, once completed and executed by the arbitrators(s).

5. Arbitrators in this Circuit, conducting court ordered non-binding arbitration, shall be compensated at an hourly rate not to exceed two hundred dollars ($200.00) per hour. In extraordinarily complex cases, the presiding judge may order a fee not in excess of three hundred dollars ($300.00) per hour after a hearing in which good cause is shown for an extraordinary fee. The Arbitrator's fee shall be paid within 15 days of the conclusion of said hearing. Fees shall be equally divided between parties.

Done and Ordered this 7th day of March, 2005.

JAMES E.C. PERRY
CHIEF JUDGE

IN THE CIRCUIT COURT OF THE EIGHTEENTH JUDICIAL CIRCUIT IN AND FOR BREVARD COUNTY, FLORIDA

CASE NO: ______

Petitioner/Plaintiff,

vs

Respondent/Defendant

______/

ORDER REFERRING CASE TO ARBITRATION

Pursuant to Rules 1.700, 1.800 to 1.810, and 1.820, Florida Rules of Civil Procedure; 43.103, Florida Statutes; and Rules 11.010 and 11.020, Florida Rules Court–Appointed Arbitrators; the parties are hereby referred to non-binding arbitration, which shall be conducted according to the aforementioned authorities and rules of practice and procedure adopted by the Supreme Court of Florida.

The Court hereby appoints the following arbitrator(s), that is (are) qualified, pursuant to the Florida Rules for Court Appointed Arbitrators:

CHIEF ARBITRATOR'S NAME: ______

ADDRESS: ______

PHONE NUMBER: ______

If a panel of arbitrators is being appointed;

SECOND ARBITRATOR'S NAME: ______

ADDRESS: ______

PHONE NUMBER: ______

THIRD ARBITRATOR'S NAME: ______

ADDRESS: ______

PHONE NUMBER: ______

The parties may select arbitrator(s) other than those named above. If the parties choose to select the arbitrator(s), they shall do so from the approved arbitrator list maintained by Court Administration. If the parties choose to select a three-member arbitration panel, the plaintiff(s) and the defendant(s) shall each select one arbitrator, and those two arbitrators shall select the third arbitrator who shall serve as the Chief Arbitrator of the panel.

If the parties select an arbitrator(s) other than those named above, notice of such selection shall be given to the court by the parties designating their selected arbitrator(s) on the attached Arbitration Acknowledgement Form, setting forth the name(s), address(es) and telephone number(s) of the selected arbitrator(s). The said form shall be filed by plaintiff's counsel (or by defendant's counsel if the plaintiff is appearing pro–se) no later than 20 days after the date of this order. If the Arbitration Acknowledgement Form is not timely filed, the parties shall be deemed to have waived the option to select the arbitrator(s), and the arbitrator(s) named in this order shall hear and decide the arbitration proceedings.

The first arbitration hearing shall be held within sixty (60) days of this Order.

The arbitrator(s) shall attempt to coordinate the dates and times for arbitration with the parties/attorneys. Within thirty (30) days of this Order, the Chief Arbitrator shall notify the parties of the date, time and place of the arbitration hearing. The actual Notice of Arbitration is attached to, and incorporated into this Order, and shall be completed by the Chief Arbitrator and forwarded to the attorneys for each party and all pro se litigants. If there is a lack of cooperation and/or a failure to meet the time limits imposed by this Order, the arbitrator shall file a Notice of Non–Compliance and shall supply the assigned judge a copy of same.

The parties/attorneys shall follow the arbitration procedures detailed in the Notice of Arbitration.

Done and ordered this ___ day of ______, ______.

______
CIRCUIT JUDGE

Attachments:
Notice of Court Ordered Non–Binding Arbitration
Arbitration Acknowledgement Form
Copies furnished:

IN THE CIRCUIT COURT OF THE EIGHTEENTH JUDICIAL CIRCUIT IN AND FOR BREVARD COUNTY, FLORIDA

CASE NO: ______

Petitioner/Plaintiff,

vs

Respondent/Defendant

______/

NOTICE OF COURT ORDERED ARBITRATION

You are hereby notified that the court-ordered arbitration in this matter shall take place as follows:

NAME OF CHIEF ARBITRATOR: ______

PLACE OF ARBITRATION: ______

DATE OF ARBITRATION: ______

TIME OF ARBITRATION: ______

The non-binding arbitration procedures that were set by the Chief Judge include:

a. Florida Rules of Civil Procedure 1.700, 1.810, and 1.820;

b. Section 44.103, Florida Statutes;

c. Florida Rules of Court–Appointed Arbitrators 11.010, 11.020, and 11.070;

d. And, the following additional provisions;

1. Arbitrators are compensated at an hourly rate not to exceed $200.00 per hour as established by the Arbitrators, unless the Court after hearing determines that an extraordinary fee not in excess of $300.00 per hour may be charged based upon the complexity of the case.

2. The Arbitrator's fee shall be paid within 15 days of the conclusion of said hearing. Fees shall be equally divided between the parties.

3. An arbitrator shall have the power to administer oaths or affirmations; conduct the arbitration proceedings; issue subpoenas for the attendance of witnesses and the production of books, records, documents, and other evidence; and may apply to the court for orders compelling such attendance and production.

4. Subpoenas shall be served and shall be enforceable in the manner provided by law.

5. Individual parties or authorized representatives of corporate parties shall attend the arbitration hearing, unless excused in advance by the arbitrator(s) for good cause shown. If a party, an authorized representative of corporate parties, or an attorney for any party fails to attend an arbitration hearing, the court may apply sanctions including the entry of a final judgment based upon the arbitration award, the striking of pleadings of portions thereof, the awarding of costs and attorney's fees and/or contempt proceedings.

6. Arbitration proceedings are quasi-judicial proceedings and, as such, are to have the same procedural safeguards as judicial proceedings, even though they are not meant to be conducted with formality of court; each party must have a full hearing in the presence of the other party, unless such right is waived by agreement or conduct.

7. When the parties, their attorneys, and their witnesses convene at the hearing, the arbitrator(s) is (are) in charge. The arbitration hearings will follow a logical pattern, with opening statements, introduction of the initiating documents, and final summations. It is customary for the complaining party to be heard first. However, the Chief Arbitrator has authority over the order of the proceedings and has the discretion to vary this procedure when necessary.

8. The hearing shall be conducted informally. Presentation of testimony shall be kept to a minimum; matters shall be presented to the arbitrator(s) primarily through statements and arguments of counsel.

9. Strict conformity to the rules of evidence will not be required. The arbitrators will rule on the admissibility of evidence and will refuse to hear evidence that they deem irrelevant, immaterial, or repetitious. Where two or more arbitrators are serving, rulings will be made by the majority of the panel.

10. The arbitrator(s) may issue such instructions as are necessary for the expeditious and orderly conduct of the hearing.

11. The arbitrator(s) instructions are not appealable. Upon notice to all parties, the arbitrator(s) may apply to the presiding judge for orders directing compliance with such instructions. Instructions enforced by a court order are appealable, as are other orders of the court.

12. When a party fails to appear at a hearing, the arbitrator(s) may proceed with the hearing and shall render a decision, based upon the facts and circumstances, as presented by the parties present.

13. Any party may have a record and transcript made of the arbitration hearing at that party's expense.

14. Arbitration shall be completed within thirty (30) days of the first arbitration hearing, unless extended by order of the court on motion of the arbitrator or of a party. No extension of time shall be for a period exceeding sixty (60) days from the date of the first arbitration hearing.

15. Within ten (10) days of the final adjournment of the arbitration hearing, the arbitrator(s) shall notify the parties, in writing, of the decision. The arbitrator(s) shall indicate in the decision which party prevailed on each claim/counter–claim. The arbitrator's decision and the originals of any transcripts shall be sealed and filed with the Clerk of the Circuit Court at the time the parties are notified of the decision. Any objection that an award was not made within the time required is waived, unless the objecting party notifies the arbitrators in writing of his/her objection prior to the delivery of the award to him/her.

16. An arbitration decision shall be final if a request for a trial de novo is not filed within twenty (20) days of the filing of the sealed decision.

17. If a motion for trial de novo is not made within twenty (20) days of filing of the sealed decision, the decision shall be referred to the presiding judge, who shall enter such orders and judgments as may be required to carry out the terms of the decision, as provided by 44.103(4), Florida Statutes. Such orders shall be enforceable by the contempt powers of the court and execution on such judgments shall issue on request of a party.

18. If the judgment from the trial de novo is not more favorable than the arbitration decision, the party having filed for the trial de novo may be assessed the arbitration costs; additional court costs; and other additional reasonable costs of the other parties, including attorney's fees, investigation expenses, and expenses for expert or other testimony or evidence incurred after the arbitration hearing.

19. The arbitrator shall complete the Arbitrator Statistical Summary Form twenty (20) days after the written decision has been served to all parties and return the form to Court Administration.

____

Date

____

Chief Arbitrator

Certificate of Service

I certify that a copy of this document was ( ) mailed, ( ) faxed and mailed, ( ) hand delivered to the person(s) listed below on (date) ____________

Other party or his/her attorney:

Name: ____________

Address: ____________

City, State, Zip: ____________

Fax Number: ____________

Date: ____________

____
Signature of Party

Original to Clerk for court file

Copies furnished to:

IN THE CIRCUIT COURT OF THE EIGHTEENTH JUDICIAL CIRCUIT IN AND FOR BREVARD COUNTY, FLORIDA

CASE NO.: ____________

ARBITRATION ACKNOWLEDGEMENT FORM

This form shall be filed by counsel for Plaintiff or, if Plaintiff is pro se, by counsel for the Defendant.

In accordance with Order Appointing Arbitrator:

☐ The undersigned hereby acknowledges the appointment of the arbitrator(s) assigned by the judge and the scheduling of the arbitration conference.

☐ The undersigned hereby certifies to the court that the parties have agreed to the use of the arbitrator(s) whose name(s), address(es), and telephone number(s) appear below and who have been selected from the 18th Judicial Circuit list of qualified arbitrators.

Chief Arbitrator's Name: ____________

Address: ____________

Telephone Number: ____________

If a three-member panel has been agreed to:

Second Arbitrator's Name: ____________

Address: ____________

Telephone Number: ____________

Third Arbitrator's Name: ____________

Address: ____________

Telephone Number: ____________

The arbitration conference will be held on ____________.

____
Signature of Party or Party's Attorney Signature

____
Date of

____
Printed Name of Party or Party's Attorney

WITHIN TWENTY DAYS OF THE SIGNED ORDER PLEASE RETURN TO JUDGE ASSIGNED TO CASE:

ARBITRATION STATISTICAL SUMMARY

STYLE OF CASE ____________ **CASE #** ____________

PRESIDING JUDGE ____________ **DIV.** ____________ **CIRCUIT** ____________

COUNTY OF BREVARD DATE OF ARBITRATION ____________ **HRS OF ARB.** ____________

TYPE OF CASE

☐ Personal Injury
☐ Real Property/Mortgage Foreclosure
☐ Property Damage
☐ Malpractice
☐ Products Liability
☐ Other (please indicate)
☐ Contract ____________

☐ Consumer ____________

☐ Employment ____________

☐ Eminent Domain ____________

____________ ____________
Arbitrator (signed) Date

____
Arbitrator (print name)

RETURN TO:
Court Administration
Harry T. & Harriette V. Moore Justice Center
2825 Judge Fran Jamieson Way
Viera, FL 32940

FOR COURT ADMINISTRATION USE ONLY:

A trial de novo was requested within 20 days of the serving of the written decision of the Arbitrator. ☐ **YES** ☐ **NO**

ARBITRATOR APPLICATION

18TH JUDICIAL CIRCUIT

NAME ____________

ADDRESS ____________

TELEPHONE# ____________ **PAGER** ____________ **CELL** ____________ **FAX** ____________

Member of Florida Bar ☐ **YES** ☐ **NO If yes, year and Bar#** ____________

Supreme Court approved Arbitration Training taken: ____________ **Year** ____________ **Trainer** ____________
(PLEASE ATTACH COPY OF TRAINING CERTIFICATE)

Certified Mediator ☐ **YES** ☐ **NO If yes, year and certification #** ____________

Please check all areas of certification.
☐ **Circuit** ☐ County ☐ Family ☐ Dependency

Describe all relevant experience as an Arbitrator:

____
____
____
____
____
____

Please check area of expertise. (Please check up to (3) three)
TYPE OF CASE

☐ **Personal Injury**	☐ **Consumer**	☐ **Malpractice**
☐ **Property Damage**	☐ **Employment**	☐ **Other (please indicate)**
☐ **Products Liability**	☐ **Eminent Domain**	______________
☐ **Contract**	☐ **Real Property/ Mortgage Foreclosure**	______________
		______________

Please include a current resume or curriculum vitae.
Once Application is completed submit to the Administrative Judge of the Circuit Civil Division or the Administrative Judge of County Court.

______________________ ______________________
Signature **Date**

05–02–S. JUDGES—ACTING AS MAGISTRATES/FIRST APPEARANCE DUTIES

IN THE CIRCUIT COURT OF THE EIGHTEENTH JUDICIAL CIRCUIT IN AND FOR SEMINOLE COUNTY, FLORIDA

ADMINISTRATIVE ORDER NO.: 05–02–S

RE: JUDGES—ACTING AS MAGISTRATES/FIRST APPEARANCE DUTIES

1. Duty of Judges to act as Magistrates

All Seminole County Circuit Judges and County Court Judges shall perform the duties of magistrates and shall consider and issue, when appropriate, during regular business hours, upon request by a duly authorized agency or organization, arrest warrants, search warrants and other process. County Court Judges shall perform these duties in felony cases as well as misdemeanor cases.

2. Applications for search warrants and other process

Law enforcement officers requesting these services during the regular work week shall call the main office of Court Administration to arrange an appointment at 407–665–4200. The Court staff will make arrangements with a Judge to entertain these requests. Criminal Judges who are not in trial will be contacted first. The main office of Court Administration is located on the third floor of the Downtown Civil Courthouse at 301 North Park Ave., Sanford, Florida. Absent an emergency, these services should be requested before 9:00 a.m. or at 1:00 p.m.

3. First Appearances Hearings.

A. County Court Judges shall preside over first appearance hearings during the regular work week in both felony an misdemeanor cases. A judge who has issued an arrest warrant in a particular case may designate himself or herself as the first appearance judge and shall preside over the first appearance within the time limits provided by the rules of criminal procedure. Otherwise, the first appearance shall be conducted by the first appearance judge. First appearance judges shall comply with the rules of criminal procedure and shall entertain motions to set or reduce bond in cases where a defendant is entitled to bond as a matter of right from time of arrest until the case is heard on the first arraignment docket. Thereafter, bond motions shall be scheduled before the judge assigned to the case.

B. Persons in custody for violation of probation or community control have already been determined to be guilty of an offense and are presumed not to be entitled to release on conditions other than stated in the warrant. Bond motions in violation of probation or community control cases shall be scheduled before the judge who is permanently assigned to the case unless that judge defers hearing the motion to the first appearance judge or the Chief Judge designates another judge to hear the motion.

C. Persons taken into custody on out of county warrants shall be scheduled for review on the third business day after first appearance. If the sheriff of the county in which the warrant was issued has not made arrangements to transport the defendant by that time, the first appearance judge may release the defendant on recognizance or set such other conditions of release as are deemed appropriate.

D. After first appearance, unless there is an emergency, bonds shall not be increased in felony cases without a written motion made by the State Attorney and duly noticed for hearing.

E. The State Attorney shall make arrangements with the clerk of the court to obtain arrest reports on the first business day following the date of arrest. The arrest report contains the date of arrest and shall constitute notice pursuant to Rule 3.134. Persons held in custody for thirty three days after the date of arrest shall, upon motion made by the defense, be placed on the first appearance docket and be released from custody unless the State Attorney files a charge in the case before first appearance. The release shall be on recognizance without other conditions.

F. The following categories of arrested persons shall not be brought to first appearance:

1. Military deserters.
2. Parolees whose parole has been revoked.
3. Persons turned in by their bondsman.
4. Federal prisoners.
5. Prisoners transferred temporarily to testify.

4. Conditions of Release.

The Seminole County Bond Schedule allows defendants to post bond prior to first appearance and is not a schedule that is presumptively reasonable in individual cases. First appearance judges shall comply with Rule 3.131 and shall presume the defendant is entitled to release unless the offense is not bondable or if the defendant is in custody for violation of probation or community control. With these exceptions, the first appearance judge shall consider release conditions in the following order:

A. Personal recognizance or release into a pretrial release program.

B. Execution of an unsecured (cash) appearance bond, provided that the defendant shall have the option to post a surety bond. If the unsecured bond is less than $500.00 the defendant shall be given the option of posting a $500.00 surety bond.

C. Placement of restrictions on the travel, association, or place of abode of the defendant during the period of release. In considering these restrictions the first appearance judge shall consider (1) whether or not the named victim(s) in the case are in danger or have been provided adequate protection, (2) whether the defendant is truly an immediate danger to the community; (3) whether the defendant has a lawyer who is in control of the defense of the case; (4) whether the victim is residing in a residence that is owned by or jointly owned with the victim; (5) based upon the defendant's prior record or other information the defendant is likely to commit another crime while released from custody or (6) whether the defendant is already on some form of release for another offense and probable cause exists to believe the defendant committed a new offense.

D. Placement of the defendant in the custody of a designated person or organization agreeing to supervise the defendant.

E. Execution of a bail bond with sufficient solvent sureties or the deposit of cash in lieu thereof.

F. Any other condition reasonably necessary to assure appearance as required, including requiring the defendant to comply with day reporting, pretrial release or to return to custody after specified hours.

G. The first appearance judge shall consider all available relevant factors to determine what form of release is necessary to assure the defendant's appearance. If a monetary bail is required, the judge shall determine the amount.

H. In determining whether to release a defendant on bail or other conditions, and what that bail or those conditions may be, the court may consider the nature and circumstances of the offense charged and the penalty provided by law; the weight of the evidence against the defendant; the defendant's family ties, length of residence in the community, employment history, financial resources, and mental condition; the defendant's past and present conduct, including any record of convictions, previous flight to avoid prosecution, or failure to appear at court proceedings; the nature and probability of danger that the defendant's release poses to the community; the source of funds used to post bail; whether the defendant is already on release pending resolution of another criminal proceeding or is on probation, parole, or other release pending completion of sentence; and any other facts the court considers relevant.

I. All information provided by a defendant in connection with any application for or attempt to secure bail, to any court, court personnel, or individual soliciting or recording such information for the purpose of evaluating eligibility for or securing bail for the defendant, under circumstances such that the defendant knew or should have known that the information was to be used in connection with an application for bail, shall be accurate, truthful, and complete, without omissions, to the best knowledge of the defendant. Failure to comply with the provisions of this subdivision may result in the revocation or modification of bail. However, no defendant shall be compelled to provide information regarding his or her criminal record.

J. Information stated in, or offered in connection with setting conditions of release need not strictly conform to the rules of evidence.

5. Appointment of Counsel for Indigent Defendants.

Any prisoner charged with a felony and in custody in the John E. Polk Correctional Facility who does not have a lawyer shall be presumed to be indigent and the Public Defender shall be appointed to represent that prisoner unless the prisoner indicates that private counsel shall be retained immediately. In that event, a counsel review hearing shall be scheduled before the thirty-third day after arrest unless the prisoner is released from custody before that time. The Public Defender shall be appointed to represent any prisoner who does not have private counsel for the purpose of Rule 3.134 motions.

6. Rule 3.134 Motions

(Failure of State to file charges within 33 days.)

This section is for the purpose of establishing procedures to implement the provisions of Rule 3.134 in Seminole County.

A. The Clerk of the Court shall provide the assistant state attorney attending first appearance hearings with a copy of the first appearance docket. Receipt of the docket shall be notice from the court that the defendant is in custody and the date of the first appearance. No further notice shall be required for the defendant or defense counsel to make a motion for release under the provisions of Rule 3.134. The motion may be made ore tenus at first appearance on the 33rd day following arrest.

B. At the hearing on the Rule 3.134 motion, the presiding judge shall presume the defendant is entitled to release from custody unless (1) an information or indictment is filed in the court file or (2) the assistant state attorney attending first appearance presents the original information or indictment or a copy of it with the clerk's filing stamp on it to the presiding judge.

C. Defendants released under the provisions of Rule 3.134 shall be released on their recognizance without further conditions except to appear and answer to the charges.

DONE AND ORDERED this 7TH day of January, 2005.

JAMES E.C. PERRY
CHIEF JUDGE

02–19–S. [SUPERSEDED BY ORDER 18–02–S (A1), EFFECTIVE DECEMBER 18, 2018.]

01–19–S. [SUPERSEDED BY ORDER 18–06–S, EFFECTIVE FEBRUARY 8, 2018.]

97–5. [RESCINDED BY ORDER 17-39, EFFECTIVE SEPTEMBER 25, 2017.]

91–140–CR. [SUPERSEDED BY ORDER 18–42–B, EFFECTIVE SEPTEMBER 13, 2018.]

Twentieth Judicial Circuit (Charlotte, Collier, Glades, Hendry and Lee Counties)

LOCAL RULES

ADMINISTRATIVE ORDERS

CIVIL

JUDICIAL ADMINISTRATION

CRIMINAL

PROBATE

TRAFFIC & MISDEMEANOR

JUVENILE

FAMILY LAW (COLLIER COUNTY).	SUPPORT, ALIMONY, AND VISITATION PROGRAM OF COLLIER COUNTY CLERK OF COURTS.
CRIMINAL COURT (LEE COUNTY).	ORDER ESTABLISHING PROTOCOL FOR THE EMPLOYMENT AND ATTENDANCE OF INTERPRETERS FOR CRIMINAL COURT PROCEEDINGS IN LEE COUNTY [SUPERSEDED BY ADMINISTRATIVE ORDER NO. 2.36].
ORDER ESTABLISHING PROTOCOL FOR THE DETERMINATION OF CREDIT FOR TIME SERVED IN CRIMINAL CASES IN LEE COUNTY.	
PRO SE PROGRAM.	ORDER APPROVING PRO SE LITIGANT PROGRAM AND ORDER AUTHORIZING RETENTION AND COLLECTION OF USER FEES.
JURY DUTY (GLADES COUNTY).	TEMPORARY ORDER WAIVING TIME REQUIREMENT FOR SUMMONING JURORS FOR COURT PROCEEDINGS IN GLADES COUNTY.
DOMESTIC VIOLENCE (HENDRY COUNTY).	ORDER APPROVING DOMESTIC VIOLENCE DIVERSION PROGRAM FOR HENDRY COUNTY AND ORDER AUTHORIZING CLERK TO COLLECT AND MAINTAIN PROGRAM FEES.
DOMESTIC VIOLENCE (COLLIER COUNTY).	ORDER ESTABLISHING DOMESTIC VIOLENCE COURT FOR COLLIER COUNTY.
DOMESTIC VIOLENCE (CHARLOTTE COUNTY.	ORDER APPROVING DOMESTIC VIOLENCE DIVERSION PROGRAM FOR CHARLOTTE COUNTY AND ORDER AUTHORIZING CLERK TO COLLECT AND MAINTAIN PROGRAM FEES.
FAMILY LAW (LEE COUNTY).	ORDER REQUIRING ISSUANCE OF STANDING ORDERS IN DOMESTIC RELATIONS CASES IN LEE COUNTY.
DOMESTIC VIOLENCE (COLLIER COUNTY).	ORDER APPROVING DOMESTIC VIOLENCE DIVERSION PROGRAM FOR COLLIER COUNTY AND ORDER AUTHORIZING CLERK TO COLLECT AND MAINTAIN PROGRAM FEES.
CONFIDENTIALITY WAIVER.	ORDER AUTHORIZING WAIVER OF CONFIDENTIALITY FOR DOMESTIC VIOLENCE/FAMILY LAW INVESTIGATORS AND OTHER COURT PERSONNEL.
DOMESTIC VIOLENCE (LEE COUNTY).	ORDER APPROVING DOMESTIC VIOLENCE DIVERSION PROGRAM FOR LEE COUNTY AND ORDER AUTHORIZING CLERK TO COLLECT AND MAINTAIN PROGRAM FEES.
DOMESTIC VIOLENCE (LEE COUNTY).	ORDER ESTABLISHING DOMESTIC VIOLENCE COURT FOR LEE COUNTY.
APPOINTING CLERK (COLLIER COUNTY).	ORDER APPOINTING CLERK AD INTERIM FOR COLLIER COUNTY.

Local Rules

Rule I. TRAFFIC VIOLATIONS BUREAU

LOCAL RULE I.

IN RE: TRAFFIC VIOLATIONS BUREAU

Pursuant to Florida Traffic Court Rules 6.100 each County within the Twentieth Judicial Circuit shall maintain a Traffic Violations Bureau for the purpose of handling criminal traffic offenses or traffic infractions. The Bureaus shall act under the direction and control of the Chief Judge and the respective County Court Judges. Court costs in traffic infractions shall be assessed as provided in Florida Traffic Court Rules 6.470.

DATE APPROVED: February 26, 1979

Rule II. DRIVER IMPROVEMENT AND DWI COUNTER ATTACK SCHOOLS

LOCAL RULE II

IN RE: DRIVER IMPROVEMENT AND DWI COUNTER ATTACK SCHOOLS

Pursuant to Florida Traffic Court Rules 6.110(a), the following schools are approved as Driver Improvement and DWI Counter Attack Schools for the Twentieth Judicial Circuit of Florida:

Charlotte County Traffic and DWI Counter Attack School under direction of S. W. Florida Safety Council Mrs. Wilma Evers, Coordinator

Naples Traffic School under direction of S. W. Florida Safety Council Mrs. Wilma Evers, Coordinator

Collier County DWI Counter Attack School under direction of Ms Carol Slauson David Lawrence Center, Naples, FL

Hendry, Glades Traffic and DWI Counter Attack School under direction of S. W. Florida Safety Council Mrs. Wilma Evers, Coordinator

Lee County Traffic and DWI Counter Attack School under direction of S. W. Florida Safety Council Mrs. Wilma Evers, Coordinator

DATE APPROVED: February 26, 1979

0706a/A

Rule III. DIVISION OF COURT: APPELLATE DIVISION

IN THE TWENTIETH JUDICIAL CIRCUIT IN AND FORTH STATE OF FLORIDA

LOCAL RULE III

IN RE: DIVISION OF COURT: APPELLATE DIVISION

An Appellate Banc of three Circuit Judges will be established for the purpose of hearing all appeals of orders entered by the County Court in which the jurisdiction of the Circuit Court is invoked pursuant to Fla. R. App. P. 9.030(c)(1)(A) and (B). The judges of the Appellate Banc shall be assigned to the Banc on a rotation basis and shall serve for six months. The Court Administrator shall serve as the ex-officio Clerk of the Appellate Banc.

All other actions which seek to invoke the jurisdiction of the Circuit Court pursuant to any other provision of Rule 9.030(c), including appeals from administrative action pursuant to Rule 9.030(c)(1)(C), certiorari jurisdiction pursuant to Rule 9.030(c)(2) and original jurisdiction pursuant to Rule 9.0303(c)(3), shall be assigned to a single judge on a random basis and in accordance with the assignments established by the Chief Judge pursuant to Administrative Order No: 2.5.

The Chief Judge of the Twentieth Judicial Circuit is hereby authorized to enter such other orders as may be necessary to effectuate the intent and purpose of this rule.

The foregoing rule is hereby adopted and approved as a local rule of procedure for all counties of the Twentieth Judicial Circuit of Florida. **DATE APPROVED: June 27, 1995.**

Rule IV. SELECTION OF JURORS BY COMPUTER IN LEE COUNTY

IN THE TWENTIETH JUDICIAL CIRCUIT IN AND FOR THE STATE OF FLORIDA

LOCAL RULE #IV Amended

IN RE: SELECTION OF JURORS BY COMPUTER IN LEE COUNTY

WHEREAS, the present method of selecting jurors can be expedited without additional expense or loss of the sanctity of random selection by the use of the electronic computer available for use by Lee County, and

WHEREAS, in accordance with Florida Statute § 40.011, the source of such selection is from the database of names from the Department of Highway Safety and Motor Vehicles, restricted to Lee County, which is in computer compatible form and in the custody and control of the Lee County Clerk of the Circuit Court, and

WHEREAS, in accordance with Florida Statute § 40.011, the source of selection is also from the list of those whose names do not appear on the Department database, but who have filed with the Clerk of the Circuit Court an affidavit prescribed in the cited statute, it is therefore,

RESOLVED that the Rules of the Twentieth Judicial Circuit for procedure in all courts of Lee County in which jury trials are held shall be amended to include this additional Rule adopting the following alternative plan for the selection of persons for grand or petit jury service:

1. **EQUIPMENT**: The equipment used in jury selection application will be a Dell PowerEdge 2850 Server with 2 Intel Xeon 3.2Ghz processors, 2 GB of memory and 140G of RAID space running Windows 2003 Server operating system, located in the secured computer room of the Lee County Clerk of the Circuit Court.

2. **ALTERNATIVE METHOD OF SELECTING VENIRE:**

a. The source from which names shall be taken is the same as that which is described above in accordance with Florida Statute § 40.011. On a quarterly basis, the Lee County Clerk of the Circuit Court shall obtain a computerized listing of names from the Department of Highway Safety and Motor Vehicles. The Clerk of the Circuit Court will protect the listing and tapes and keep them securely stored.

b. The Clerk of Circuit Court of Lee County is designated the official custodian of the lists to be used in jury selection and shall ensure they are not accessible to anyone other than those directly involved in selection of venires, as herein provided. Functions of the Clerk of Circuit Court may be performed by his deputies.

c. The entire list of driver's license holders, identification card holders, and those who have filed affidavits pursuant to Florida Statute § 40.011 (hereinafter "eligible jurors") may comprise the master jury list from which venires will be selected according to the provisions of Section 2(d) below. Alternatively, the Chief Judge or his designated representative, with the aid and assistance of the Clerk of Circuit Court, may select the master jury list for the year by lot and at random from the entire list of eligible jurors using the method described in the attachments hereto.

d. The Clerk of Circuit Court shall cause jury venires to be selected from the final jury list programmed into the Lee County computer using the method described in Attachment "A" (Method of Jury Selection For Lee County), Attachment "B" (Jury Selection Algorithm For Lee County), and Attachment "C" (JSI Juror Candidate List Processing Methodology), and in accordance with directions received from the Chief Judge or his designated representative.

e. The initial jury selection programming may exclude persons who have been previously excluded for physical infirmities or inability to comply with other non-correctable statutory qualifications. A detailed description as to how the list of excluded persons is developed and maintained is set forth in the attachments hereto.

f. Attachments "A", "B", and "C" shall be incorporated into this Local Rule as if fully set forth herein.

IN RE: SELECTION OF JURORS BY COMPUTER IN LEE COUNTY

STATE OF FLORIDA

COUNTY OF LEE

CERTIFICATE

I HEREBY certify that, pursuant to Florida Statute § 40.225, a majority of judges authorized to conduct jury trials in Lee County, Florida, have consented to the use of the electronic system which is described in an attachment hereto, and requests the approval of the Supreme Court of Florida for the use of such system in Lee County, Florida.

DATED the 27th day of March 2007.

Hugh D. Hayes
Chief Judge
Twentieth Judicial Circuit

History—Local Rule #IV (March 20, 1998).

Rule V. SELECTION OF JURORS BY COMPUTER IN COLLIER COUNTY

IN THE TWENTIETH JUDICIAL CIRCUIT IN AND FOR THE STATE OF FLORIDA

LOCAL RULE #V Amended

IN RE: SELECTION OF JURORS BY COMPUTER IN COLLIER COUNTY

WHEREAS, the present method of selecting jurors can be expedited without additional expense or loss of the sanctity of random selection by the use of the electronic computer available for use by Collier County, and

WHEREAS, in accordance with Florida Statute § 40.011, the source of such selection is from the database of names from the Department of Highway Safety and Motor Vehicles, restricted to Collier County, which is in computer compatible form and in the custody and control of the Collier County Clerk of the Circuit Court, and

WHEREAS, in accordance with Florida Statute § 40.011, the source of selection is also from the list of those whose names do not appear on the Department database, but who have filed with the Collier County Clerk of the Circuit Court an affidavit prescribed in the cited statute, it is therefore,

RESOLVED that the Rules of the Twentieth Judicial Circuit for procedure in all courts of Collier County in which jury trials are held shall be amended to include this additional Rule adopting the following alternative plan for the selection of persons for grand or petit jury service:

1. **EQUIPMENT**: The equipment used in jury selection will be a Gateway 975 Salaiden Server, 5- 159 gig ScSi HD 1500 rpm, Dual 2.8 ghz intel Xeon processors, 2gig Ram, Redundant power supplies and fans, OS Windows 2003 server Standard Edition, Veritas Backup Software, MS SQL 2000, or a compatible server of an equal or greater efficiency, located in the secured computer room of the Collier County Clerk of the Circuit Court's Data Processing Center.

2. ALTERNATIVE METHOD OF SELECTING VENIRE:

a. The source from which names shall be taken is the same as that which is described above in accordance with Florida Statute § 40.011. On a quarterly basis, the Collier County Clerk of Circuit Court shall obtain a computerized listing of names from the Department of Highway Safety and Motor Vehicles. The Collier County Clerk of the Circuit Court will protect the listing and tapes and keep them securely stored.

b. The Collier Clerk of Circuit Court is designated the official custodian of the computer records of the lists to be used in jury selection and shall ensure they are not accessible to anyone other than those directly involved in selection of venires, as herein provided. Functions of the Collier County Clerk of Circuit Court may be performed by his deputies.

c. The entire list of driver's license holders, identification card holders, and those who have filed affidavits pursuant to Florida Statute § 40.011 (hereinafter "eligible jurors") may comprise the master jury list from which venires will be selected according to the provisions of Section 2(d) below.

d. The Collier County Clerk of Circuit Court shall cause jury venires to be selected from the final jury list programmed into the Collier County computer using the method described in Attachments "A" and "B", and in accordance with directions received from the Chief Judge or his designated representative.

e. The initial jury selection programming may exclude persons who have been previously excluded for physical infirmities or inability to comply with other non-correctable statutory qualifications. A detailed description as to how the list of excluded persons is developed and maintained is set forth in Attachment "A".

f. Attachments "A" and "B" shall be incorporated in to this Local Rules as if fully set forth herein.

IN RE: SELECTION OF JURORS BY COMPUTER IN COLLIER COUNTY

STATE OF FLORIDA

COUNTY OF COLLIER

CERTIFICATE

I HEREBY certify that, pursuant to Florida Statute § 40.225, a majority of judges authorized to conduct jury trials in Collier County, Florida, have consented to the use of the electronic system which is described in an attachment hereto, and requests the approval of the Supreme Court of Florida for the use of such system in Collier County, Florida.

DATED the 27th day of March 2007.

Hugh D. Hayes
Chief Judge
Twentieth Judicial Circuit

History—Local Rule #V (March 20, 1998).

Rule VI. SELECTION OF JURORS BY COMPUTER IN CHARLOTTE COUNTY

IN THE TWENTIETH JUDICIAL CIRCUIT IN AND FOR THE STATE OF FLORIDA

LOCAL RULE VI

IN RE: SELECTION OF JURORS BY COMPUTER IN CHARLOTTE COUNTY

WHEREAS, the present method of selecting jurors can be expedited without additional expense or loss of the sanctity of random selection by the use of the electronic computer available for use by Charlotte County, and

WHEREAS, in accordance with Florida Statute § 40.011, the source of such selection is from the data base of names from the Department of Highway Safety and Motor Vehicles which is in computer compatible form and in the custody and control of the Clerk of the Circuit Court, and

WHEREAS, in accordance with Florida Statute § 40.011, the source of selection is also from the list of those whose names do not appear on the Department data base, but who have filed with the Clerk of the Circuit Court an affidavit prescribed in the cited statute, it is therefore,

RESOLVED, that the Rules of the Twentieth Judicial Circuit for procedure in all courts of Charlotte County in which jury trials are held shall be amended to include this additional Rule adopting the following alternative plan for the selection of persons for grand or petit jury service:

1. EQUIPMENT:

(a) The equipment used in jury selection is a Pentium 300 computer located in the secured computer room of the Clerk of the Circuit Court of Charlotte County.

2. ALTERNATIVE METHOD OF SELECTING VENIRE:

(a) The source from which names shall be taken is the same as that which is described above in accordance with Florida Statutes § 40.011. In every year hereafter, by the first week of January, or as soon thereafter as practicable, the Clerk of the Circuit Court shall obtain a computerized listing of names from the Department of Highway Safety and Motor Vehicles. The Clerk of the Circuit Court will protect the listing and tapes and keep them securely stored.

(b) The Clerk of the Circuit Court of Charlotte County is designated the official custodian of the computer records of the lists to be used in jury selection and shall ensure that they are not accessible to anyone other than those directly involved in selection of venires, as herein provided. Functions of the Clerk of the Circuit Court may be performed by her deputies.

(c) The entire list of driver's license holders, identification card holders, and those who have filed affidavits pursuant to Florida Statute § 40.011 (hereinafter "eligible jurors") may comprise the master jury list from which venires will be selected according to the provisions of Section 2(d) below. Alternatively, the Chief Judge or his designated representative, with the aid and assistance of the Clerk of the Circuit Court, may select the master jury list for the year by lot and at random from the entire list of eligible jurors using the method described in Attachment "A".

(d) The Clerk of the Circuit Court shall cause jury venires to be selected from the final jury list programmed into the Charlotte County computer using the method described in Attachment "A" in accordance with directions received from the Chief Judge or his designated representative.

IN RE: SELECTION OF JURORS BY COMPUTER IN CHARLOTTE COUNTY

STATE OF FLORIDA

COUNTY OF CHARLOTTE

CERTIFICATE

I HEREBY certify that, pursuant to Florida Statute § 40.225, a majority of judges authorized to conduct jury trials in Charlotte County, Florida, have consented to the use of the electronic system which is described in an attachment hereto, and requests the approval of the Supreme Court of Florida for the use of such system in Charlotte County, Florida.

DATED the 23d day of Sept., 1999.

William L. Blackwell
Chief Circuit Judge
Twentieth Judicial Circuit

Rule VII. SELECTION OF JURORS BY COMPUTER IN GLADES COUNTY

IN THE TWENTIETH JUDICIAL CIRCUIT IN AND FOR THE STATE OF FLORIDA

LOCAL RULE #VII

IN RE: SELECTION OF JURORS BY COMPUTER IN GLADES COUNTY

WHEREAS, the present method of selecting jurors can be expedited without additional expense or loss of the sanctity of random selection by the use of an electronic computer available for use by Glades County, and

WHEREAS, in accordance with Florida Statute § 40.011, the source of such selection is from the database of names from the Department of Highway Safety and Motor Vehicles which is in a computer compatible form and in the custody of the Clerk of the Circuit Court, and

WHEREAS, in accordance with Florida Statute § 40.011, the source of selection is also from the list of those whose names do not appear on the Department database, but who have filed with the Clerk of the Circuit Court an affidavit prescribed in the cited statute, it is therefore,

RESOLVED that the Rules of the Twentieth Judicial Circuit for procedure in all courts of Glades County in which jury trials are held shall be amended to include this additional Rule adopting the following alternative plan for the selection of persons for grand or petit jury service:

1. EQUIPMENT:

a. The equipment used in jury selection is Compaq Proliant 370 computer running Unixware 7.1 located in the secured computer room of the Clerk of the Circuit Court for Glades County.

2. ALTERNATIVE METHOD OF SELECTING VENIRE:

a. The source from which names shall be taken is the same as that which is described above in accordance with Florida Statute § 40.011. In every year hereafter, by the first week of January, or as soon thereafter as practicable, the Clerk of the Circuit Court shall obtain a computerized listing of names from the Department of Highway Safety and Motor Vehicles.

The Clerk of the Circuit Court will protect the listing and tapes and keep them securely stored.

b. The Clerk of Circuit Court of Glades County is designated the official custodian of the computer records of the lists to be used in jury selection and shall ensure they are not accessible to anyone other than those directly involved in selection of venires, as herein provided. Functions of the Clerk of the Circuit Court may be performed by his deputies.

c. The entire list of drivers license holders, identification card holders, and those who have filed affidavits pursuant to Florida Statute § 40.011 (hereinafter "eligible jurors") may comprise the master jury list from which venires will be selected according to the provisions of paragraph 2(d) below. Alternatively, the Chief Judge or his designated representative, with the aid and assistance of the Clerk of the Circuit Court, may select the master jury list for the year by lot and at random from the entire list of eligible jurors using the method described in Attachment "A" and its addendum.

d. The Clerk of the Circuit Court shall cause jury venires to be selected from the final jury list programmed into the Glades County computer using the method described in Attachment "A" in accordance with directions received from the Chief Judge or his designated representative.

e. The initial jury selection programming may exclude persons who have been previously excluded for physical infirmities or inability to comply with other non-correctable statutory qualifications.

IN RE: SELECTION OF JURORS BY COMPUTER IN GLADES COUNTY

STATE OF FLORIDA

COUNTY OF GLADES

CERTIFICATE

I HEREBY certify that, pursuant to Florida Statute § 40.225, a majority of judges authorized to conduct jury trials in Glades County, Florida, has consented to the use of the electronic system which is described in an attachment hereto, and requests the approval of the Supreme Court of Florida for the use of such system in Glades County, Florida.

DATED the 16 day of Nov., 2001

William L. Blackwell
Chief Circuit Judge
Twentieth Judicial Circuit

Rule VIII. SELECTION OF JURORS BY COMPUTER IN HENDRY COUNTY

IN THE TWENTIETH JUDICIAL CIRCUIT IN AND FOR THE STATE OF FLORIDA

LOCAL RULE #VIII

IN RE: SELECTION OF JURORS BY COMPUTER IN HENDRY COUNTY

WHEREAS, the present method of selecting jurors can be expedited without additional expense or loss of the sanctity of random selection by the use of the electronic computer available for use by Hendry County, and

WHEREAS, in accordance with Florida Statute § 40.011, the source of such selection is from the data base of names from the Department of Highway Safety and Motor Vehicles which is in computer compatible form and in the custody and control of the Clerk of the Circuit Court, and

WHEREAS, in accordance with Florida Statute § 40.011, the source of selection is also from the list of those whose names do not appear on the Department data base, but who have filed with the Clerk of the Circuit Court an affidavit prescribed in the cited statute, it is therefore,

RESOLVED that the Rules of the Twentieth Judicial Circuit for procedure in all courts of Hendry County in which jury trials are held shall be amended to include this additional Rule adopting the following alternative plan for the selection of persons for grand or petit jury service:

1. EQUIPMENT:

(a) The equipment used in jury selection is an IBM RISC 6000 computer located in the secured computer room of the Clerk of the Circuit Court of Hendry County.

2. ALTERNATIVE METHOD OF SELECTING VENIRE:

(a) The source from which names shall be taken is the same as that which is described above in accordance with Florida Statute § 40.011. In every year hereafter, by the first week of January, or as soon thereafter as practicable, the Clerk of Circuit Court shall obtain a computerized listing of names from the Department of Highway Safety and Motor Vehicles. The Clerk of the Circuit Court will protect the listing and tapes and keep them securely stored.

(b) The Clerk of Circuit Court of Hendry County is designated the official custodian of the computer records of the lists to be used in jury selection and shall ensure they are not accessible to anyone other than those directly involved in selection of venires, as herein provided. Functions of the Clerk of Circuit Court may be performed by his deputies.

(c) The entire list of driver's license holders, identification card holders, and those who have filed affidavits pursuant to Florida Statute § 40.011 (hereinafter "eligible jurors") may comprise the master jury list from which venires will be selected according to the provisions of Section 2(d). Alternatively, the Chief Judge or his designated representative with the aid and assistance of the Clerk of Circuit Court, may select the master jury list for the year by lot and at random from the entire list of eligible jurors using the method described in Attachment A.

(d) The Clerk of Circuit Court shall cause jury venires to be selected from the final jury list programmed into the Hendry County computer using the method described in Attachment A in accordance with directions received from the Chief Judge or his designated representative.

IN RE: SELECTION OF JURORS BY COMPUTER IN HENDRY COUNTY

STATE OF FLORIDA

COUNTY OF HENDRY

CERTIFICATE

I HEREBY certify that, pursuant to Florida Statute § 40.225, a majority of judges authorized to conduct jury trials in Hendry County, Florida, have consented to the use of the electronic system which is described in an attachment hereto, and requests the approval of the Supreme Court of Florida for the use of such system in Hendry County, Florida.

DATED the 20 day of March 1998.

Hugh E. Starnes
Chief Circuit Judge
Twentieth Judicial Circuit

Rule IX. ESTABLISHMENT OF DOMESTIC VIOLENCE COURT

IN THE TWENTIETH JUDICIAL CIRCUIT IN AND FOR THE STATE OF FLORIDA

LOCAL RULE IX

IN RE: ESTABLISHMENT OF DOMESTIC VIOLENCE COURT

Pursuant to Article V, section 7, Florida Constitution and section 43.30, Florida Statutes, there is created within the Twentieth Judicial Circuit a Domestic Violence Court. This court is created to hear all criminal domestic violence cases, as well as all civil injunctions for protection against domestic violence and injunctions for protection against repeat violence. The Court is initially established in Lee County, but may be expanded to other counties in the circuit if caseloads and budgets permit by Order entered by the Chief Judge of the Twentieth Judicial Circuit.

A Domestic Violence Unit is also established under the aegis of the Domestic Violence Court. The Unit shall consist of a domestic violence coordinator, a clerk, and such other personnel as are deemed necessary by the Chief Judge of the Twentieth Judicial Circuit and the Court Administrator. The Unit will assist petitioners in the filing of petitions for injunction for protection against domestic violence and repeat violence, civil motions for contempt, other related motions and applications for orders. The unit will also handle inquiries from the petitioner and the respondent. The domestic violence coordinator will appear at all court proceedings and will assist the court by monitoring all civil court orders.

The Chief Judge of the Twentieth Judicial Circuit is also authorized to enter such other orders as may be necessary to effectuate the intent and purpose of this rule.

This rule shall be effective upon approval by the Supreme Court in accordance with Florida Rules of Judicial Administration 2.050(e)(1).

Approved by the Supreme Court on October 26, 1994.

Administrative Orders

Civil

1.1. JUDICIAL SALES

IN THE TWENTIETH JUDICIAL CIRCUIT IN AND FOR THE STATE OF FLORIDA

ADMINISTRATIVE ORDER NO: 1.1

IN RE: JUDICIAL SALES

The Clerks of the various Courts within the Twentieth Judicial Circuit are hereby directed to conduct Judicial Sales in accordance with Florida Statute § 45.031 unless otherwise ordered by the Judge to whom the case is assigned.

All prior Administrative Orders regarding Judicial Sales are hereby rescinded.

DONE AND ORDERED in Chambers in Fort Myers, Lee County, Florida, this 15 day of Jan, 1991.

Thomas S. Reese
Chief Circuit Judge

History. - Administrative Order 90–4

1.2. PAYMENTS OF CHILD SUPPORT OBLIGATIONS THROUGH THE CLERK OF THE CIRCUIT COURT

IN THE TWENTIETH JUDICIAL CIRCUIT IN AND FOR THE STATE OF FLORIDA

ADMINISTRATIVE ORDER NO. 1.2

IN RE: PAYMENTS OF CHILD SUPPORT OBLIGATIONS THROUGH THE CLERK OF THE CIRCUIT COURT

As provided in Florida Statute § 61.1824, the Court recognizes that the State Disbursement Unit ("SDU") of the Florida Department of Revenue ("DOR") is responsible for the collection and disbursement of payments for all child support cases enforced by DOR pursuant to Title IV–D of the Social Security Act; as well as all child support cases not being enforced by the DOR pursuant to Title IV–D of the Social Security Act in which the initial support order was issued in this state on or after January 1, 1994 and in which the obligor's child support obligation is being paid through an income deduction order.

The Court also recognizes that pursuant to the contract between the Florida Association of Court Clerks, Inc. and Lockheed Martin IMS Corporation ("LMIMS") dated August 17, 1999, LMIMS is responsible for the operation of a Centralized Disbursement Unit for processing private cases in which support payments for child support and alimony cases are not processed through the SDU.

Private cases include cases not being enforced by the Department of Revenue pursuant to Title IV–D of the Social Security Act in which the initial support order was issued in this state prior to January 1, 1994 and in which the obligor's child support obligation is being paid through an income deduction order, and all non–Title IV–D cases not subject to income deduction orders.

With the foregoing in mind, and in accordance with Fla. Fam. L. R. P. 12.750 and Fla. R. Jud. Admin. 2.050, it is ordered and adjudged as follows:

The Clerks of the Circuit Courts for Charlotte, Hendry, and Lee Counties will no longer accept child support payments, with the exception of court-ordered purge and cash payments. Instead, child support payments in those counties are to be sent to the following address:

State of Florida Disbursement Unit
P.O. Box 8500
Tallahassee, FL 32314–8500

A voice response unit ("VRU") is available toll free at 1–877–769–0251. The VRU is available for general payment information about child support collections and payments. In addition, each Clerk of the Circuit Court can provide a payment history.

The Clerks of the Circuit Courts in Collier and Glades Counties will continue to accept child support payments in private cases. However, all other child support payments in those counties are to be sent to the SDU at the address listed above.

DONE AND ORDERED in Chambers at Naples, Collier County, Florida this 13th day of Jan., 2000.

William L. Blackwell
Chief Judge

History. - Administrative Orders 86–7, 85.6; Administrative Order 1.2 (January 28, 1991).

1.3. SUPPORT AND VISITATION ENFORCEMENT

IN THE TWENTIETH JUDICIAL CIRCUIT IN AND FOR THE STATE OF FLORIDA

ADMINISTRATIVE ORDER NO. 1.3

IN RE: SUPPORT AND VISITATION ENFORCEMENT

There is established within the Twentieth Judicial Circuit Court a Support and Visitation Enforcement Program ("S.A.V.E.") which will be operated by the Division of Family Court Services of the Office of the Court Administrator for the Twentieth Judicial Circuit Court.

This Program is hereby established and will be operated under the aegis of this Court and within the guidelines set forth in Fla. Fam. L. R. P. 12.750. The S.A.V.E. Program shall assist pro se litigants in family law actions involving child support and visitation matters so as to achieve a fair and efficient resolution of their family law case.

In addition to those services provided through S.A.V.E., Family Court Services personnel may provide assistance to pro se litigants to establish, modify, and enforce court orders in the following matters:

Dissolution of Marriage
Paternity Petition
Child Support/Custody/Visitation
Child/ Adult Name Change
Adoption by Stepparent

The personnel of Family Court Services/S.A.V.E. may provide pro se litigants with family law forms approved by the Florida Supreme Court, and the judges of the Twentieth Judicial Circuit. The personnel of Family Court Services/S.A.V.E. may provide the following services:

a) Advise litigants that Family Court Services/S.A.V.E. will not represent them in their case, and that legal advice can not be provided;

b) Provide information to direct litigants to the local lawyer referral services;

c) Provide general information on the process, practice, and procedure of the court;

d) Provide docketed case information;

e) Facilitate the setting of hearings by scheduling the hearing.

The main office for Family Court Services/S.A.V.E. is located in Fort Myers and satellite offices are currently staffed on a part-time basis in Punta Gorda and Naples. Family Court Services/S.A.V.E. is authorized to collect fees as prescribed by a schedule of fees maintained in the Office of the Court Administrator. This schedule may be amended by the Court Administrator, at his discretion, with the concurrence of the Court.

DONE AND ORDERED in Chambers at Naples, Collier County, Florida this 13th day of Jan., 2000.

William L. Blackwell
Chief Judge

History. - Administrative Order 86–9, Administrative Order 1.3 (January 28, 1991); Administrative Order 1.3 (December 8, 1992).

1.4. ORDER REPEALING AND RESCINDING ADMINISTRATIVE ORDER 1.4

IN THE TWENTIETH JUDICIAL CIRCUIT IN AND FOR THE STATE OF FLORIDA

ORDER REPEALING AND RESCINDING ADMINISTRATIVE ORDER 1.4

WHEREAS, the Florida Legislature enacted Chapter 96–189, § 10, Laws of Florida, that repealed § 88.121, Florida Statutes,

It is, therefore,

ORDERED that Administrative Order 1.4 is hereby repealed and rescinded.

DONE AND ORDERED in Chambers at Naples, Collier County, Florida, this 13 day of Jan., 2000.

William L. Blackwell
Chief Judge

1.5. INCOME DEDUCTION ORDERS—OVERPAYMENTS

IN THE TWENTIETH JUDICIAL CIRCUIT IN AND FOR THE STATE OF FLORIDA

ADMINISTRATIVE ORDER NO. 1.5

IN RE: INCOME DEDUCTION ORDERS—OVERPAYMENTS

THIS MATTER concerns the overpayment of arrearages pursuant to Income Deduction Orders entered under Florida Statute § 61.1301 and the disposition of such excess amounts held by the Clerk.

It is ORDERED that the Clerks of the Circuit Courts in Collier and Glades Counties shall notify the employer when the Clerk's records indicate the arrearage has been paid and will then request that the employer reduce the amount required or terminate payments, as may be appropriate. It is further,

ORDERED that the Clerks shall forthwith return such excess amounts of support payments to the employer to be paid as wages to the employee.

DONE AND ORDERED in Chambers at Naples, Collier County, Florida, this 13th day of Jan., 2000.

William L. Blackwell
Chief Judge

History.- Administrative Order 89–26; Administrative Order 1.5 (January 28, 1991).

1.6. ADOPTION–HOME STUDIES

IN THE TWENTIETH JUDICIAL CIRCUIT IN AND FOR THE STATE OF FLORIDA

ADMINISTRATIVE ORDER NO. 1.6

IN RE: ADOPTION—HOME STUDIES

WHEREAS, the Department of Health and Rehabilitative Services (HRS), redesignated as the Department of Children and Family Services (DCFS), has advised by the attached letter that it would be unable to perform home studies regarding adoptive placements under Chapter 63, Florida Statutes; it is,

ORDERED, as follows:

1. Pursuant to Florida Statutes § 63.092, an intermediary must report any intended placement of a minor to the court before the minor is placed in the home.

2. Before placing the minor in the intended adoptive home, a preliminary home study must be performed as required by § 63.092.

3. Any licensed child-placing agency, a licensed professional, or agency described in Section 61.20(2), Florida Statutes, are qualified to perform home studies as required by Section 63.092, Florida Statutes.

4. The intermediary may request the home study of the intended placement without further designation by DCFS or order of Court.

5. An intermediary desiring to use any person or entity other than a Florida licensed child placement agency for such a home study must seek court approval before proceeding.

6. The reasonable fees of such home studies shall be paid by the adoptive parents unless waived partially or fully as provided in Section 63.097, Florida Statutes.

DONE AND ORDERED in Chambers, Naples, Collier County, Florida, this 13 day of Jan., 2000.

William L. Blackwell
Chief Judge

History.- Administrative Order 1.6 (April 3, 1992).

1.7. ADMINISTRATIVE REVIEWS BY FLORIDA DEPARTMENT OF CHILDREN AND FAMILIES IN FOSTER CARE CASES

IN THE TWENTIETH JUDICIAL CIRCUIT IN AND FOR THE STATE OF FLORIDA

IN RE: ADMINISTRATIVE REVIEWS BY FLORIDA DEPARTMENT OF CHILDREN AND FAMILIES IN FOSTER CARE CASES

ADMINISTRATIVE ORDER NO. 1.7

Pursuant to Title 42 U.S.C. § 675(5)(b), Federal funding requirements for children in foster care mandate that the status of each child be reviewed at least once every six months either by a court or by administrative review.

The Florida Department of Children and Families ("FDCF") has requested an administrative order allowing administrative reviews in foster care cases if a foster care judicial review cannot be obtained within the required six month time limit. FDCF (through counsel) represents that such action is based upon statewide negotiations with the Department of Health and Human Services and is necessary to preserve funding from the Federal Government.

Although it is the Court's belief that there are no cases within this circuit which cannot be heard within the six month time limit, this Order is entered for the sole purpose of cooperating with the Department so that their obligation to the Federal Government may be fulfilled.

It is therefore ORDERED AND ADJUDGED as follows:

The Department of Children and Families may conduct in-house administrative reviews in dependency cases within the Twentieth Judicial Circuit Court if a hearing cannot be provided by the Court within the six month time limit for foster care judicial reviews. These in-house reviews shall not replace the need for a judicial review and cannot be used in place of the initial judicial review of children pursuant to Florida Statute § 39.453(3)(a).

All foster care cases shall be scheduled by FDCF for judicial review at the first available date on the Court's docket. In the event that the Court is unable to conduct the judicial review within the time frame prescribed by statute, counsel shall notify both the Court and the Chief Judge in each such case. This notice shall include a statement of the reason for the failure of FDCF to bring the matter before the Court within the applicable time frame.

If an administrative review becomes necessary, FDCF shall notify all parties and their attorneys of the date of the review. Such notice shall also be provided to the assigned judge, the assigned case worker and the case worker's supervisor. The FDCF attorney who is assigned to the case must be present at each administrative review. A report following the review shall be furnished to all parties, their attorneys, and to the Court in accordance with Chapter 39.

This Order is expressly intended to be temporary in nature and will expire by operation of law on January 1, 1999, unless extended by the Chief Judge by further order of the Court.

DONE AND ORDERED in Chambers, at Fort Myers, Lee County, Florida this 4th day of March 1998.

Hugh E. Starnes
Chief Judge

History. - New.

1.8. SUBSTITUTION OF DEPARTMENT OF REVENUE FOR DEPARTMENT OF HEALTH AND REHABILITATIVE SERVICES IN TITLE IV–D CASES

IN THE TWENTIETH JUDICIAL CIRCUIT IN AND FOR THE STATE OF FLORIDA

ADMINISTRATIVE ORDER NO: 1.8

IN RE: SUBSTITUTION OF DEPARTMENT OF REVENUE FOR DEPARTMENT OF HEALTH AND REHABILITATIVE SERVICES IN TITLE IV–D CASES

WHEREAS, Chapter 94–124, Laws of Florida, transferred all of the powers, duties and other statutory functions of the Florida Child Support Enforcement Program created pursuant to Title IV–D of the Social Security Act from the Florida Department of Health and Rehabilitative Services to the Florida Department of Revenue effective July 1, 1994; and,

WHEREAS, the Florida Department of Health and Rehabilitative Services is currently listed as a designated party for the Title IV–D client in all Title IV–D paternity and child support cases initiated, enforced, modified or currently being monitored by both the IV–D agency and the local depository for compliance; and

WHEREAS, effective July 1, 1994, pursuant to Chapter 94–124, Laws of Florida, the Department of Revenue shall be substituted and listed as a designated party for the Title IV–D client in all Title IV–D paternity and child support cases initiated, enforced, modified or currently being monitored by both the IV'D agency and the local depository for compliance;

NOW, THEREFORE, to provide for efficient and proper administration of the Title IV–D cases coming before the courts in this circuit, the following procedures shall be implemented:

I. APPLICABILITY

These provisions are intended to implement Chapter 94–124, Laws of Florida, and shall apply to actions in the Family Law

Division of the Circuit Court in and for the Twentieth Judicial Circuit. This order shall be in addition to any other administrative orders applicable to the court generally, and is intended to complement the Rules of Civil Procedure and the Rules of Judicial Administration.

II. SUBSTITUTION OF PARTIES

A. Effective July 1, 1994, the Florida Department of Revenue shall be substituted as a designated party in all Title IV–D paternity and child support cases initiated, enforced, modified or currently being monitored by both the IV–D agency and the local depository for compliance.

B. Effective July 1, 1994, the style of each Title IV–D case shall read Florida Department of Revenue o/b/o (Custodial Parent) v. (Noncustodial Parent). Each pending Title IV–D case shall be stamped as set forth in paragraph II.C. below, or be styled (Custodial Parent) v. (Noncustodial Parent).

C. On or after July 1, 1994, each Title IV–D case brought before the court shall be styled as set forth in paragraph II.B. above, or be stamped or affixed with a sticker with the following language:

CAUTION—PLEASE NOTE: Effective 7/1/94 the Department of Revenue has been substituted for the Department of Health and Rehabilitative Services pursuant to Chapter 94–124, Laws of Florida, and references in this document to the "Department" or the "Department of Health and Rehabilitative Services" shall mean references to the Department of Revenue, unless otherwise indicated by context.

It shall be the responsibility of the Department of Revenue to provide the stamps or stickers as set forth in this order.

Pursuant to this administrative order, there shall be no necessity to file an order substituting parties in each individual Title IV'D matter pending before this court.

DONE AND ORDERED in Chambers at Fort Myers, Lee County, Florida, this 7 day of July, 1994.

Thomas S. Reese
Chief Judge

History. - New. Chapter 94–124, Laws of Florida.

1.9. EXCLUSIONS FROM MEDIATION

IN THE TWENTIETH JUDICIAL CIRCUIT IN AND FOR THE STATE OF FLORIDA

ADMINISTRATIVE ORDER NO. 1.9

EXCLUSIONS FROM MEDIATION

Pursuant to Fla. R. Civ. P. 1.710(b)(5) and Florida Statutes § 51.011, all proceedings subject to summary procedure as set forth in Florida Statutes § 51.011 shall be excluded from mandatory mediation and shall not be referred to mediation except upon petition of all parties to the action.

DONE AND ORDERED in Chambers at Naples, Collier County, Florida, this 13 day of Jan., 2000.

William L. Blackwell
Chief Judge

History. - Administrative Order 1.9 (December 21, 1994).

1.10. TELEPHONIC MOTION HEARINGS SET FOR NOT LONGER THAN FIFTEEN MINUTES IN CIRCUIT AND COUNTY CIVIL CASES

IN THE TWENTIETH JUDICIAL CIRCUIT IN AND FOR THE STATE OF FLORIDA

Administrative Order 1.10

IN RE: TELEPHONIC MOTION HEARINGS SET FOR NOT LONGER THAN FIFTEEN MINUTES IN CIRCUIT AND COUNTY CIVIL CASES

Whereas, Fla. R. Jud. Admin. 2.071(a) (2005) defines "communication equipment" as a conference telephone or other electronic device that permits all those appearing or participating to hear and speak to each other, provided that all conversation of all parties is audible to all persons present; and

Whereas, Fla. R. Jud. Admin. 2.071(c) (2005) provides that a county or circuit judge may, upon the written request of a party upon reasonable notice to all other parties, permit a requesting party to participate through communication equipment in a scheduled motion hearing; and

Whereas, Fla. R. Jud. Admin. 2.071(c) (2005) further provides that any such request (except in criminal, delinquency, and appellate proceedings) must be granted, absent a showing of good cause to deny the same, where the hearing is set for not longer than fifteen (15) minutes; and

Whereas, it is in the interest of the efficient administration of justice to set forth a threshold and uniform set of procedures to be utilized throughout the Twentieth Judicial Circuit;

IT IS HEREBY ORDERED, pursuant to the authority provided by Fla. R. Jud. Admin. 2.050, as follows:

1. In instances where a civil motion hearing is scheduled for not longer than fifteen (15) minutes, a party may file a written request to participate via conference or speaker telephone, or other applicable communication equipment, and shall provide notice to the Court and the parties to the motion.

2. Notice by the requesting party must be provided by mailing a copy of the written request at least five (5) days prior to the day of the hearing, or by delivering a copy of the written request to the other parties or, if represented by counsel, to the other parties' attorney(s) no later than 5:00 p.m. two business days prior to the day of the hearing.

3. The requesting party shall be responsible for contacting the trial judge's Judicial Assistant and ensuring that appropriate arrangements have been made to permit participation through conference or speaker telephone, or other applicable communication equipment, on the scheduled date and time. It shall be at the discretion of the trial judge as to whether the requesting party shall be responsible for initiating the telephone or communication connection or whether the Court shall be responsible for initiating the telephone or communication connection.

4. Absent a showing of good cause, and in accordance with Fla. R. Jud. Admin. 2.071(c) (2005), the trial judge shall grant the request and make reasonable accommodations to permit the requesting party's participation through conference or

speaker telephone, or other applicable communication equipment.

5. Evidentiary hearings are exempted from the application of this Administrative Order.

6. This Administrative Order specifically addresses non-evidentiary civil motion hearings set for not longer than fifteen (15) minutes. It is not intended to limit or address requests for telephonic hearings which are otherwise governed by Fla. R. Jud. Admin. 2.071.

7. To the extent that any provision of this Administrative Order may be construed as being in conflict with any law, statute, or rule, the law, statute, or rule shall prevail.

DONE AND ORDERED in Chambers at Naples, Collier County, Florida this 13th day of April, 2005.

Hugh D. Hayes
Chief Judge

1.11. CERTIFICATION AND REGULATION OF CERTIFIED CIVIL PROCESS SERVERS [Renumbered as 2.30, eff. July 30, 2009]

See now, 2.30, Certified Civil Process Servers.

1.12. CASE MANAGEMENT OF RESIDENTIAL FORECLOSURE CASES AND MANDATORY REFERRAL OF MORTGAGE FORECLOSURE CASES INVOLVING HOMESTEAD RESIDENCES TO MEDIATION [VACATED, EFF. DEC. 20, 2011, *nunc pro tunc*]

ADMINISTRATIVE ORDER NO. 1.12—VACATED—

WHEREAS, local Administrative Order No. 1.12 was entered in accordance with Supreme Court of Florida Administrative Orders AOSC09–54 and AOSC10–57, which established a statewide managed mediation program for residential foreclosure cases, and mandated that each judicial circuit enter a model administrative order for the purpose of implementing the statewide program; and

WHEREAS, on December 19, 2011, the Supreme Court of Florida entered Administrative Order No. AOSC11–44 indicating that it had reviewed the reports on the statewide managed mediation program for residential foreclosure cases and determined that it could not justify continuation of the program, and, therefore, terminated the statewide managed mediation program; and

WHEREAS, Supreme Court of Florida specifically provided in Administrative Order No. AOSC11–44 that cases already referred to and pending in a mediation program on December 19, 2011, will remain in the program through completion of the mediation, but after December 19, 2011, no new cases may be referred to mediation pursuant to the statewide managed mediation program;

IT IS ORDERED that, in strict accordance with the Supreme Court of Florida Administrative Order AOSC11–44 and the intent stated therein, the Twentieth Judicial Circuit's Administrative Order 1.12 locally implementing the statewide managed mediation program is hereby vacated, effective December 20, 2011, *nunc pro tunc.* As provided for by Supreme Court of Florida Administrative Order AOSC11–44, cases already referred to and pending in the managed mediation program for residential foreclosure cases on December 19, 2011, will remain in the program through completion of the mediation, but after December 19, 2011, no new residential foreclosure cases may be referred to the managed mediation program.

As noted by the Florida Supreme Court in Administrative Order No. AOSC11–44, vacating local Administrative Order 1.12 does not prohibit mediation of residential foreclosure cases pursuant to section 44.102, Florida Statutes, and Florida Rule of Civil Procedure 1.700(a), nor does it prohibit the use of any other subsequent measures permitted by statute or court rule to manage pending and new residential mortgage foreclosure cases.

DONE AND ORDERED in Chambers in Fort Myers, Lee County, Florida this 21st day of December, 2011.

Jay B. Rosman
Chief Judge

1.13. ESTABLISHMENT AND IMPLEMENTATION OF CIVIL CASE MANAGEMENT PLAN

IN THE TWENTIETH JUDICIAL CIRCUIT IN AND FOR THE STATE OF FLORIDA

IN RE: ESTABLISHMENT AND IMPLEMENTATION OF CIVIL CASE MANAGEMENT PLAN

ADMINISTRATIVE ORDER NO. 1.13

WHEREAS, it is in the best interest of the citizens of the Twentieth Judicial Circuit for the Court to develop innovative means to further improve the fair, predictable, efficient, and timely disposition of civil cases in the civil division of the Circuit Court;

NOW, THEREFORE, pursuant to the authority prescribed by Fla. R. Jud. Admin. 2.215 and for the purpose of promoting the efficient administration of justice within the Twentieth Judicial Circuit, it is **ORDERED** as follows:

1. There is established within the Twentieth Judicial Circuit a Civil Case Management Plan applicable to circuit civil cases, which will be administered by the Administrative Office of the Courts through direction of the Circuit Administrative Judges in each county for the implementation of enhanced case management procedures and guidelines for the timely and efficient processing of circuit civil cases and reduction in the pending backlog of civil cases.

2. The basis for the Civil Case Management Plan is attached hereto, identified in Attachment A as the "Civil Differentiated Case Management (DCM) Procedures and Backlog Reduction Plan," and is incorporated as if fully set forth herein. The Civil Case Management Plan is to be used as a model for the purpose of establishing time standards, improving the courts ability to provide early and continuous management of civil cases as required by Fla. R. Jud. Admin. 2.545, and to promote uniformity of practice throughout the Twentieth Judicial Circuit.

3. It is intended that the Civil Case Management Plan be implemented uniformly and circuitwide within the Twentieth Judicial Circuit. However, recognizing variations as it relates to staffing and resources among the five counties within the Twentieth Judicial Circuit, the full Civil Case Management Plan and DCM procedures, in the format of the model plan included herein as Attachment A, will be implemented first as a pilot in Lee and Collier counties, effective January 1, 2011, with full implementation to be later expanded, as appropriate, to other counties within the Twentieth Judicial Circuit. Recognizing that Charlotte, Hendry and Glades counties may have differing needs requiring certain deviations from the model plan attached hereto, the Circuit Administrative Judge of each respective county may submit to the Chief Judge a distinct written proposed plan with procedures that, upon approval by the Chief Judge, may be implemented in the respective county. [1]

4. Full implementation of the Civil DCM Case Management Procedures (Attachment A), including all uniform circuit-wide procedures and forms, shall apply to all civil cases filed in Lee and Collier counties, effective January 1, 2011. [2] Even though full implementation may be delayed in Charlotte, Hendry, and Glades counties, all civil time standards and goals, and the use of civil Case Managers and Magistrates to assist trial judges in the process of civil case management and backlog reduction programs, shall be effective circuitwide immediately.

5. It shall be noted that the forms included with Attachment A [3] are intended as models, and any updates or modifications shall be posted and available for viewing on the Court's website at http://www.ca.cjis20.org/web/main/civil.asp. It shall be the responsibility of all parties to check the website for the most recent forms to be used in conjunction with the Civil Case Management Plan and DCM procedures.

6. The procedures and time standards set forth in the model plan, or in any other written plan approved by the Chief Judge, are intended to facilitate the timely, fair and effective resolution of civil cases while ensuring the efficient use of court resources. The procedures and time standards do not supplant any existing rule, statute, or law. Neither this Administrative Order nor the Civil Case Management Plan shall be construed as granting any rights not already provided for by rule, statute, or law.

7. To the extent that any provision of this Administrative Order may be construed as being in conflict with any rule, statute, or law, the rule, statute, or law shall prevail.

DONE AND ORDERED in chambers in Fort Myers, Lee County, Florida, this 11th day of May, 2012.

Jay B. Rosman
Chief Judge

History.—Administrative Order 1.13 (December 10, 2010).

ATTACHMENT A

Twentieth Judicial Circuit

Civil Differentiated Case Management (DCM) Procedures and Backlog Reduction Plan

TABLE OF CONTENTS

Civil Differentiated Case Management (DCM) Procedures and Backlog Reduction Plan

I. Purpose and Goals

This Twentieth Judicial Circuit Civil Caseflow Management and Backlog Reduction Plan seeks to use innovative strategies to address the growing backlog and to implement modern differentiated caseflow management procedures in the circuit civil courts for the future to accomplish the following goals:

• Improve the courts ability as required by Fla. R. Jud. Admin. 2.545, to provide early and continuous control of case processing through use of additional Magistrate and Case Management resources, to ensure fair and prompt resolution of disputes consistent with the nature and complexity of the case.

• Identify immediate strategies for civil and foreclosure case backlog reduction plans to assist in prompt resolution of the current 31% of civil cases pending over 18 months.

• Improve the courts ability to respond to the growing number of commercial, business and other economic based civil filings having a direct impact on economic recovery in the circuit.

• Develop uniform procedures for effective early judicial intervention and management of complex cases consistent with Fla. R. Civ. P. 1.201 for managing complex litigation.

• Reduce public costs of civil litigation through early identification and expedited handling of relatively simple two-party cases to ensure prompt resolution of expedited matters through early referral to mediation or expedited hearing where appropriate.

• Improve the quality and timeliness of Management Information from the Cleric/Court MIS systems to assist judges and the court in management of civil cases and identification of cases pending beyond the Florida Supreme Court time standards set forth in Fla. R. Jud. Admin. 2.250.

II. Circuit-wide Civil and Foreclosure Backlog Reduction Goals

Each Circuit Administrative Judge, in consultation with the civil judges and the local Bar Association, has developed a civil backlog reduction plan to be effective January 1, 2011.

Each county backlog reduction effort may include the following components or other calendar management options as determined by the Circuit Administrative Judge in each county based on nature and volume of civil backlog:

a. Backlog Reduction Goal

1. To reduce the number of economic-related circuit civil cases over 18 months of age by 10 % by June 30, 2011.

b. Civil Backlog Reduction Strategy

• Case Management/Settlement Conferences in Backlogged Circuit Civil Cases–Cases may be scheduled before a Magistrate or Case Manager. Cases not disposed will result in a Case Management Order/Report to the trial judge with firm discovery cut-off dates, pretrial issues to be resolved and date matter to be ready for trial.

III. Civil DCM Case Management Plans—Time Standards & Goals

These time standards/goals are developed consistent with those established by the Florida Supreme Court pursuant to Fla. R. Jud. Admin. 2.250 and are intended to be flexible, presumptive time periods for disposition of civil cases.

Complex case time standard/goal is expanded to 24 months upon designation of a case as complex consistent with Fla. R. Civ. P. 1.201 regarding management of complex civil litigation. The local goal of 80—90% disposition of cases within time standards recognizes, consistent with Fla. R. Jud. Admin. 2.250(a), that there are a portion of cases that present unique pretrial problems that may cause reasonable delay. Time standards established by case track are:

a. Complex cases — 80% disposed within 24 months
b. Standard cases — 80% disposed within 18 months
c. Expedited cases — 90% disposed within 12 months

IV. Case Track Definition and Criteria

a. Complex Case Track—(Goal 24 months)

The complex case track involves those cases with extraordinary complexity as to require or benefit from early intervention and individual judicial management. Complex cases are defined by Fla. R. Civ. P. 1.201. Cases may be designated for management on the complex track in one of the following ways:

1. Complex cases designated by motion or stipulation and approved by the court as cases meeting complex litigation criteria under Fla. R. Civ. P. 1.201(a); OR,

2. Cases identified by the court on its own motion as complex case under Fla. R. Civ. P. 1.201 due to extraordinary procedural complexity, number of parties or other case factors that will require or benefit from individual judicial management;

Presumptive Case Types– Local plans may establish presumptive complex case types for review with the assigned Judge based on local needs and filing trends.

Examples of presumptive complex case types that may be appropriate for early screening and review of case complexity are:

• **Class Action** Cases as noted on Civil Cover Sheet (Form 1.997, section V.)

• **Environmental/Toxic Tort/Mass Tort** Litigation (Form 1.997, section II)

• **Anti–Trust/Securities** Litigation

• **Malpractice**—Medical (or involving Wrongful Death)

• **Nursing home negligence**

• Other complex cases with extraordinary number of parties, experts, pretrial discovery issues

Presumptive complex case types may be designated for early screening and review by Case Managers. Multiple parties are a key factor, as referenced by the rule; however procedures should be developed in cooperation with the Clerk's Office to identify "presumptive" case types from the Civil Case Cover Sheet.

The Case Manager should be notified of presumptive case types upon filing by the clerk so that they may be actively monitored by the Case Manager after all defendants have been served, an appearance has been entered in response to the complaint by each party or a default entered. The Case Manager will review with the assigned Judge each case by evaluating the Civil Cover Sheet, Answer(s) and Complaint to determine the need for assignment to complex track.

b. Standard Case Track—(Goal 18 months)

Standard case track involves the large majority of standard cases that normally will not require a high level of judicial case management to reach timely resolution unless unusual pretrial delay arises. Examples of general case types that would be defined as standard cases, assuming no unusual complexity are:

• Personal injury/tort

• Auto negligence

• Standard contract cases without extraordinary pretrial discovery complexity

1. Case Management Conferences in Standard Cases—a Case Management Conference will be scheduled in standard cases, to be held generally within 190 days from the date of filing the initial complaint. The parties may set the initial case management conference or the Court, in its discretion may set the date for initial case management conference. Parties may also request a case management conference by written request through the Magistrate's office.

The Initial Case Management Conference may be waived/canceled upon submission of the Counsel Stipulated (Agreed) Case Management Plan, signed by all parties, and approved by the Court Forms will be available on the Court's website.

2. Stipulated (Agreed) Case Management Plan—A Stipulated (Agreed) Case Management Plan may be developed jointly by counsel for the parties as well as any parties appearing pro se and filed within 150 days from the filing date of the initial complaint. This will allow counsel and pro se parties to consult early in the case, devise an agreed upon case plan and waive an initial case management conference, if the case plan is approved by the Court.

The use of a Stipulated (Agreed) Case Management Plan early in the case (within 150 days) is intended to allow all parties, pro se or through counsel, to set a reasonable case plan targeting dates for discovery, expert reports and referral to alternative dispute resolution (ADR), without court intervention, provided that the general time parameters are set and adhered to.

c. Expedited Case Track—(Goal 12 months)

Expedited cases are those cases normally requiring little judicial intervention with relatively simple procedural and legal issues that can be resolved promptly by early referral to mediation, ADR or expedited hearing.

Expedited cases may include:

• Contested Residential and Commercial Foreclosure

• Simple, two-party Collection/Indebtedness cases under $50,000.00

• Non Jury cases

Contested cases identified as expedited may be set directly by counsel or pro-se litigant for mediation within 270 days, or as practical, as part of the Stipulated (Agreed) Case Management Plan.

Foreclosure cases will not require a Stipulated (Agreed) Case Management Plan and would continue to be set on a hearing docket, possibly before a Senior Judge.

V. Civil DCM Case Management Procedures

a. Screening and Assignment to Case Tracks

1. Civil Cover Sheet (Fla. R. Civ. P. Form 1.997)

To be filed with the Clerk by the plaintiff along with the initial complaint. After review, data entry clerk will forward Cover Sheet/Complaint/Answer for cases that meet presumptive complex criteria to Case Manager.

2. Case Review and Screening by Case Manager

After responsive pleadings are filed, cases meeting presumptive complex case criteria will be reviewed by a Case Manager for recommended track decision. Potentially complex cases will be reviewed with, and approved by, the assigned trial judge for assignment to the appropriate case track. (Upon complex case designation, case management procedures will follow Section V.b. of this document).

3. Standing Order for Case Management/Stipulated (Agreed) Case Management Plan

Plaintiff will attach the Standing Order for Case Management and Request for Stipulated Case Management Plan with the initial complaint for service on all parties (with the exception of Homesteaded or defaulted Foreclosure actions).

b. Case Management Procedures—Complex Cases

1. Designation to the complex track

Cases may be designated to the complex track as provided under Fla. R. Civ. P. 1.201 by:

• Motion or Stipulation by Parties

Motion or stipulation for designation as a complex case under Fla. R. Civ. P. 1.201 must be filed with the Clerk of Court. The Clerk will provide a copy to the Case Manager in order to assist the judge in case preparation for Initial Case Management Conference or motion hearing;

• On Court's Motion

Case Manager may recommend designation as a complex case to trial judge after receipt of responsive pleadings and review of complaint, answer and civil case cover sheet in presumptive case types.

2. Initial Case Management Conference

Set by the assigned trial judge to occur within 60 days of designation as a complex case with assigned Judge or Magistrate in selected cases;

3. Joint Statement of Parties

At least 20 days prior to the date of the initial case management conference, counsel for the parties as well as any parties appearing pro se shall confer and prepare a joint statement outlining a discovery plan, which shall be filed with the clerk of court no later than 14 days before the conference under Fla. R. Civ. P. 1.201;

4. Case Management Order

To be consistent with the uniform circuit Case Management Order resulting from the conference which provides:

• Pretrial Discovery/Case scheduling plan

• Plan for referral to ADR

• Next Case Management Conference Date

• Date for next Pretrial Conference (not less than 90 days prior to the trial date)

• Estimated date for trial/readiness date within 24 months

5. Interim Case Management Conference or Pretrial Conference

At the trial judge's discretion, an interim case management conference or Pretrial Conference may be set with the Judge or Magistrate to facilitate resolution of pretrial management or discovery matters, resolve outstanding issues and set a firm trial date.

6. Trial

Trial date set by judge at the Final Case Management Conference.

c. Case Management Procedures—Standard/Expedited Cases

1. Standing Order for Case Management/Stipulated (Agreed) Case Management Plan

The Plaintiff will attach the Standing Order for Case Management and Request for Stipulated (Agreed) Case Management Plan with the initial complaint for service on all parties (with exception of Homesteaded and Defaulted Foreclosure actions).

2. Case Management Conference

In standard cases, counsel for the parties as well as any parties appearing pro se may waive the initial case management conference by filing a Stipulated (Agreed) Case Management Plan, approved by the Court, within 150 from the date of filing the initial complaint.

In cases where all of the parties, pro se or through counsel, do not file a Stipulated (Agreed) Case Management Plan within 150 days, or in cases where the plan has been filed but not approved by the Court, all parties will be required to attend an initial Case Management Conference as scheduled by the Court to establish a case management/scheduling plan.

3. Presumptive case scheduling plan/time goals

Stipulated (Agreed) Case Management Plans may be flexible and based upon individual case factors, but should be consistent with reasonable and presumptive pretrial discovery and ADR time goals as follows:

Case Track	Completion Discovery and ADR	Trial/Disposition
Standard	450 days	540 days
Expedited	270 days	365 days

IN THE CIRCUIT COURT FOR THE TWENTIETH JUDICIAL CIRCUIT IN AND FOR ________ COUNTY, FLORIDA CIVIL ACTION

, CASE NO:

Petitioner(s),

vs.

,

Defendant(s).

________________________ /

STANDING ORDER IN CIVIL CASES IN THE TWENTIETH JUDICIAL CIRCUIT

PURSUANT to Florida Rule of Civil Procedure 1.200(a), Florida Rule of Judicial Administration 2.545, and Administrative Order 1.13 entered by the Chief Judge of this Circuit, the parties are ordered to adhere to the following information and procedures applicable to civil lawsuits;

1. **SERVICE OF THIS ORDER.** The Plaintiff is directed to serve a copy of this order with each Summons issued in this case. One copy of this Order is to be filed with the Clerk of the Circuit Court with proof of service. The Plaintiff shall pay the appropriate statutory clerk's fees on copies for each Standing Order issued and attached to the Summons.

2. **CIVIL CASE MANAGEMENT SYSTEM.** The Supreme Court of Florida has established guidelines for the prompt processing and resolution of civil cases. This Court has adopted a case management system to help meet those guidelines. In contested cases (other than foreclosures, involuntary commitment of sexually violent predators and eminent domain cases), the parties are required to participate in the case management system. The case management system requires early consultation and cooperation among the parties for the preparation and submission of an Agreed Case Management Plan, early interaction with a Civil Case Manager and early involvement by the Court. The Agreed Case Management Plan requires the parties to identify a case track, confer in a good faith attempt to narrow the matters in controversy, identify the issues that require direct involvement by the Court, and establish a schedule for addressing those issues.[4] The Agreed Case Management Plan may be accessed at the Court's website at: [http://www.ca.cjis20.org/web/main/civil.asp].

Unless all of the Defendants have been served and have defaulted, an Agreed Case Management Plan will be submitted to the Civil Case Manager, at the *(location by County)* ________________, on or before 150 days from the date of filing of the initial complaint. If the parties are unable to agree on an Agreed Case Management Plan, a case management conference will be scheduled by the Court. If a case management conference is scheduled, attendance by trial counsel and those parties who are not represented by counsel is mandatory.

3. **ALTERNATIVE DISPUTE RESOLUTION (ADR).** ADR provides parties with an out-of-court alternative to settling disagreements. The Court requires the parties to participate in ADR prior to trial. Mediation is mandatory unless the parties agree to another form of ADR. Mediation is a conference at which an independent third party attempts to arrange a settlement between the parties.

4. **RULES OF PROFESSIONALISM.** The Twentieth Judicial Circuit has adopted Administrative Order 2.20, which sets forth standards of professional courtesy and conduct for all counsel or pro-se litigants practicing within the Circuit. The Court requires that all familiarize themselves and comply with Administrative Order 2.20. Administrative Order 2.20 may be viewed on the Court's website at: http://www.ca.cjis20.org/web/main/ao_admin.asp

DONE AND ORDERED in Chambers at ________, ________ County, Florida, on ________.

____
Circuit Judge

IN THE CIRCUIT COURT FOR THE TWENTIETH JUDICIAL CIRCUIT IN AND FOR ________ COUNTY, FLORIDA CIVIL ACTION

, CASE NO:

Plaintiff(s),

vs.

,

Defendant(s).

________________________ /

ORDER SCHEDULING CASE MANAGEMENT CONFERENCE

The Court has scheduled a case management conference in this case, before the Case Manager, ________, pursuant to Florida Rule of Civil Procedure 1.200(a), and Florida Rule of

Judicial Administration 2.545, on *(date)* _________ at *(time)* _________, in Courtroom ___, *(location)* _________.

1. **Prior to Case Management Conference.** Each counsel **must** confer with his or her client(s) prior to the case management conference in order to determine the client's position with respect to settlement, pleading, admissions, and other matters that require the consent of the client. Counsel shall be prepared to make the representation that this conference has taken place. Trial counsel and those parties who are not represented by counsel (hereinafter referred to as "pro se" parties) **must** confer not later than **14 calendar days** prior to the case management conference and discuss agreements on as many of the issues listed below in paragraph 2.A. as possible. Trial counsel and/or the parties shall be prepared to discuss the possibility of settlement of the case. Trial counsel and pro se parties shall work together to agree on the provisions of an agreed Case Management Plan, in the form attached hereto, and shall be prepared to discuss any unresolved issues at the Case Management Conference.

2. **Case Management Conference.** Trial counsel and pro se parties **must** personally appear and attend the case management conference. Those attending shall bring their personal calendars to the case management conference. Those attending **must** have a thorough knowledge of the case, be prepared to discuss it and make stipulations and admissions when appropriate.

A. Those attending **must** be prepared to discuss:

i. Scheduling or rescheduling deadlines for the service of motions, pleadings and other papers. This shall include adding, dropping or amending claims or defenses and adding or dropping parties.

ii. Determining the existence of issues that may be severed and/or resolved pre-trial.

iii. Limiting, scheduling, ordering and expediting discovery. This shall include the desirability of creating document depositories and addressing the handling of privilege and confidentiality claims.

iv. Scheduling hearings and/or deadlines for motions (including motions addressed to the pleadings, motions to declare the case "complex" pursuant to Florida Rule of Civil Procedure 1.201(a) and motions for summary judgment), mediation, alternative dispute resolution and other conferences.

v. Requiring interim status reports, and determining other matters that may aid in the disposition of the action and resolution of pretrial motions, discovery and preparation for mediation, alternative dispute resolution and trial.

vi. Determining whether issues can be narrowed by the filing of preliminary stipulations.

vii. Organizing counsel to include the designation of lead counsel and liaison counsel, the role of other counsel, and responsibility for the preparation and maintenance of a service list.

viii. Establishing procedures for addressing emergencies, including the use of telephone conferences.

ix. Identifying present or potential future related litigation, including the transfer and consolidation of intra-circuit civil cases; civil cases in other circuits; and/or criminal proceedings and investigations.

x. If the case is filed as a class action: establishing a procedure, discovery schedule and deadlines, and a hearing date to determine the issue of class certification, to include a briefing schedule, exchange of witness and exhibit lists, and clarifying disputed issues of fact and law.

xi. Estimating the time needed for trial and setting a tentative trial date.

xii. Any of the issues set forth in Florida Rule of Civil Procedure 1.200(a).

B. At the case management conference, the Case Manager will address the unresolved provisions of the Case Management Plan and submit a proposed plan for the court's consideration and approval.

C. The proceedings at the case management conference shall be informal and will not be reported unless requested by a participant who makes prior arrangements with the court reporter.

3. **Referral of discovery matters to the General Magistrate.** In any civil case before the Court, discovery motions and other appropriate pending matters may be referred to the General Magistrate for hearing pursuant to an Order of Referral to Magistrate. Any party wishing to object to the referral of a matter to the General Magistrate must file an objection no later than the day of the scheduled hearing. The failure to timely object to the referral as set forth herein shall constitute a waiver of any objection to such referral.

4. **Alternative to attending Case Management Conference.** As an alternative to attending a case management conference, counsel and pro se parties may comply with this order by submitting an "Agreed Case Management Plan," in the form attached hereto, to the Civil Case Manager, at the *(location)* _________. The Plan must be signed by all counsel and pro se parties and received by the Civil Case Manager not later than **7 calendar days** prior to the conference. The Plan will also be considered timely if the parties submit a courtesy copy of the signed original to the Civil Case Manager via facsimile *(Fax #)* ___ or e-mail transmission *(email address)* _________ not later than 7 calendar days prior to the conference, **and** if the original is mailed or hand delivered on the same day along with self-addressed and stamped envelopes for all parties. Upon written approval by the Court, the original Plan will be filed with the Clerk of Court, a copy served on all counsel and/or parties of record, and the case management conference shall be cancelled. If the Court does not approve of the Plan, the case management conference will **not** be cancelled. Applicable forms are available on the Court's website at: http://www.ca.cjis20.org/web/services/jacs.asp.

5. **Sanctions.** Counsel and/or parties are hereby cautioned that misconduct, failure to attend the case management conference or noncompliance with the terms of this order may result in sanctions by the Court. Sanctions may include the assessment of special costs, including attorney's fees, the striking of pleadings and/or the dismissal of the action.

DONE AND ORDERED in _________, _________ County on _________.

____

Circuit Judge

Conformed copies provided to Counsel/Parties of Record
(Insert ADA language)

IN THE CIRCUIT COURT OF THE TWENTIETH JUDICIAL CIRCUIT IN AND FOR ________ COUNTY, FLORIDA
CIVIL ACTION

Plaintiff(s),
vs.
Case No.
Defendant(s)

AGREED CASE MANAGEMENT PLAN AND ORDER

The parties hereby submit the following Agreed Case Management Plan to the Court for approval:

Case Track Assignment[1] (check one – *must be completed for cases filed 1/1/10 or thereafter*):

_____ **Expedited Track (Case resolved within 12 months);**
(It is recommended that discovery and an alternative dispute resolution be completed within 270 days after the complaint is filed and a final disposition entered within 365 days after the complaint is filed)

_____ **Standard Track (Case is resolved within 18 months);**
(It is recommended that discovery and an alternative dispute resolution be completed within 450 days after the complaint is filed and a final disposition entered within 540 days after the complaint is filed)

_____ **Complex Track (Case resolved within 2 years)**
(Case will likely be declared complex per Florida Rule of Civil Procedure 1.201)

Case Deadlines and Events

DEADLINE OR EVENT	***AGREED DATE***
Statement of Facts and/or Counterclaim(s) Plaintiff(s):	
Defendant(s):	
Identification of facts the parties believe to be disputed Plaintiff(s):	
Defendant(s):	
Identification of the issues of law to be decided by the Court	
Motions to Add Parties or to Amend Pleadings	
Disclosure of Fact Witnesses Plaintiff(s):	
Defendant(s):	

[1] Case disposition times for all Case Tracks have been established in accordance with Florida Rule of Judicial Administration 2.250(a)(1)(B). Although Standard and Complex Track cases may or may not be resolved with a jury trial, it is expected that Expedited Track cases will be resolved without a Jury trial.

DEADLINE OR EVENT	*AGREED DATE*
Disclosure of Expert Witnesses Plaintiff(s): Defendant(s):	
Filing of Exhibit List Plaintiff(s): Defendant(s):	
Discovery Deadline for Fact Witnesses (All discovery must be commenced in time to be completed before this date) Plaintiff(s): Defendant(s):	
Expert Opinion Available to Opposing Party (It is recommended that the last exchange occur 4 months before trial and 1 – 2 months before discovery deadline to allow time for expert depositions. This does not require a written report unless otherwise required by the rule.) Plaintiff(s): Defendant(s):	
Discovery Deadline for Expert Witnesses Plaintiff(s): Defendant(s):	
Completion of Alternative Dispute Resolution (ADR) (Mediation is mandatory unless the parties agree to another form of ADR. If early ADR is selected and it does not result in settlement or disposition of this entire action, a case management conference will be scheduled within 45 days from the date of ADR.) Deadline: Type of ADR:	
Deadline for Filing Dispositive Motions (Court requires filing not later than 10 days prior to the pretrial management conference)	
Pretrial Conference Date (Unless early ADR is selected, a pretrial conference date will be scheduled within 45 days of the date of ADR not resulting in settlement or disposition of this entire action.)	An Order will be issued by the Court scheduling the Pretrial Conference.
Other Deadlines or Events	

Trial Information

Estimated Date the Case Will Be Prepared To Go To Trial (If counsel and unrepresented parties do not agree on the estimated date on which the case will be prepared to go to trial, the Court may on its own motion set the case for trial)	
Estimated Length of Trial *(specify the number of trial days):*	
Identification of Jury or Non-Jury Trial	

The above-referenced schedule of deadlines will be strictly adhered to by the parties unless a change is otherwise agreed to by the parties and approved by the Court. The Court will consider a request to approve changes to these deadlines upon a showing of good cause by either party based on matters arising from an emergency nature or unavailability. However, once the Agreed Case Management Plan has been approved by the Court, procrastination in completing discovery or the unavailability of counsel will not constitute good cause for a change to these deadlines. The failure to abide by these deadlines may result in sanctions by the Court, including the award of attorney's fees, the striking of pleadings, and/or a dismissal of the action.

Date: ____________________

Signature, address and telephone number of Counsel and Unrepresented Parties. Counsel must state Fl Bar number:

______________________________	______________________________
PLAINTIFF'S COUNSEL Address Telephone # Fax # E-Mail Address Florida Bar #	DEFENDANT'S COUNSEL Address Telephone # Fax # E-Mail Address Florida Bar #
______________________________	______________________________
Or, if pro se, PLAINTIFF Address Telephone #	Or, if pro se, DEFENDANT Address Telephone #

ORDER APPROVING AGREED CASE MANAGEMENT PLAN

THE COURT having reviewed the preceding Agreed Case Management Plan and finding it to be satisfactory, it is

ORDERED AND ADJUDGED that the Agreed Case Management Plan is hereby **APPROVED AND ALL PARTIES SHALL ABIDE BY THE TERMS HEREIN.**

DONE AND ORDERED in __________, ______________County, Florida on __________________.

Conformed Copies To:

____
Circuit Judge

IN THE CIRCUIT COURT OF THE TWENTIETH JUDICIAL CIRCUIT IN AND FOR ________ COUNTY, FLORIDA CIVIL ACTION

CASE NO:

,
Plaintiff(s)

vs

,
Defendant(s).
_______________________________________/

UNIFORM ORDER SETTING JURY TRIAL/NON-JURY TRIAL PRETRIAL CONFERENCE
(Notice for Trial)

THE CAUSE having come before the Court upon the filing of a NOTICE FOR TRIAL, filed by ____________ and it appearing to be otherwise at issue, pursuant to Rule 1.440, Florida Rules of Civil Procedure it is hereby:

ORDERED AND ADJUDGED as follows:

1. **Pretrial Conference**
2.

For Lee County	A Pretrial Conference is scheduled on *(date)*________________ at *(time)*__________ in Courtroom *(#)* ________, ______ Floor, *(location)* Lee County Justice Center, 1700 Monroe St., Ft. Myers, FL 33901, pursuant to Rule 1.200 of the Florida Rules of Civil Procedure, FOR THE PURPOSE OF COMPLETION AND CONFIRMATION OF THE ATTACHED PRETRIAL CONFERENCE ORDER FORM.
For Collier County	__________ *is ordered to schedule a Pretrial Conference through the JACS System (www.ca.cjis20.org/web/services/jacs.asp) before Magistrate ____________, at the Collier County Courthouse, Naples, FL 34112, Hearing Room 3-3* ***within ninety (90) days of the date of this Order. The Pretrial Conference may NOT be set within the first forty-five (45) days of the date of this Order to allow sufficient notice to all parties***

2. **Attendance at Pretrial Conference**

For Lee County	Appearance at the Pretrial Conference by lead counsel trying the case and all pro-se parties is mandatory **UNLESS** an Agreed Pretrial Conference Order (using the attached form) has been submitted to the Civil Case Manager at least 7 calendar days in advance of the scheduled Pretrial Conference and an Order approving the Agreed Pretrial Conference Order has been entered by the Court.
For Collier County	Appearance at the Pretrial Conference by lead counsel trying the case and all pro-se parties is mandatory even if an agreement is

	reached on the form of the Pretrial Conference Order. If the Pretrial Conference is held before the Magistrate, represented parties may appear by telephone. Parties wishing to appear by telephone shall make arrangements with the Court through Court Call no later than ten (10) days prior to the Pretrial Conference. If any objection is made to the Magistrate conducting the Pretrial Conference, the Judge will conduct the Pretrial Conference and lead counsel, all represented parties, and all pro-se parties must attend in person.

3. **Trial Period**

For Lee County	This cause is set for trial during the ***[# of weeks]*** week trial period ***[beginning & ending date of trial period]*** in Courtroom ***[#], [# Floor]***, Lee County Justice Center, 1700 Monroe Street, Fort Myers, Fl 33901, before the undersigned judge. Docket Sounding will be held on ***[date]*** at ***[time]*** in Courtroom ***[#]***. ***[# days]*** have been requested for this trial. The Court will continue this trial if it appears that additional time is required and the other cases set for this trial period are jeopardized. In the event this trial is commenced and it becomes apparent that sufficient time was not requested, a mistrial may be declared and costs assessed against the party causing the over-run.
For Collier County	The Court will confirm a trial period at the Pretrial Conference.

4. **Pre-trial Events**

A. Exchange of Expert & Lay Witnesses. No later than thirty (30) days prior to the Pretrial Conference date, counsel and/or parties shall file and exchange a list of the names and addresses of **all** witnesses they in good faith intend to call at trial and include a concise statement of facts about which the witness will testify or opinion of any expert witness. This is not intended to extend the time frames set forth in the Plan, but rather to identify those witnesses that will in good faith actually be called. No party shall be permitted to call any witness not so disclosed, without prior permission of the Court, or written stipulation executed by all parties, or if represented, their counsel.

B. Fabre Defendants. No later than thirty (30) days prior to the Pretrial Conference date, all Defendants or other persons sought to be placed on the verdict form and against whom some measure of liability may be assessed by the jury, must be disclosed to the court and opposing counsel. No person or entity not so disclosed may be placed on the verdict form without good cause shown.

C. Meeting Before Pretrial Conference. The attorneys for all parties (initiated by counsel for the Plaintiff) and all pro-se parties shall meet no later than ten (10) days before the Pretrial Conference to[1]:

[1] Counsel and/or parties involved in cases to be tried without a jury need not address jury instructions or other pretrial matters that involve a jury, and need not complete these sections of the Pretrial Conference/Trial Order.

1. Identify all exhibits each party in good faith intends to offer into evidence at trial and prepare an exhibit list for use by the Clerk and the Court at trial (actual exhibits and documentary evidence shall be available for inspection at this time). (This is not intended to extend the time frames set forth in the Plan, but rather to identify those exhibits that will in good faith actually be offered into evidence at trial). Any exhibits not so identified will not be admissible absent prior approval of the Court or a written stipulation of all parties.

2. Agree to admit or not admit evidence and list specific objections, if any.

3. Stipulate to any matter of fact or law about which there is no issue in order to avoid unnecessary proof (i.e., chain of custody or records custodian predicates).

4. Review all depositions or any other evidence which will be offered for any purpose other than impeachment to resolve objections to the portions to be offered in evidence.

5. Discuss the possibility of settlement.

6. If applicable, submit an itemized statement of special damages the Plaintiff expects to prove.

7. If a jury trial has been demanded, discuss jury instructions and verdict forms and reach agreement, if possible, on same.

8. Discuss and complete any other matters which may simplify the issues or aid in the speedy disposition of this action, the Pretrial Conference, and trial.

9. Draft one Pretrial Conference Order (using the attached form)[2], signed by all participating counsel and pro-se parties. The Pretrial Conference Order shall be submitted directly to:

For Lee County	The Civil Case Manager at least 7 days prior to the Pretrial Conference. The Agreed Pretrial Conference Order will also be considered timely if the parties submit a courtesy copy of the signed original to the Civil Case Manager via facsimile 239-485-2999 or e-mail transmission to CivilCM@ca.cjis20.org not later than 7 calendar days prior to the Pretrial Conference, **and** if the original is mailed or hand delivered on the same

[2] The Pretrial Conference Order can also be downloaded from the Court's website at http://www.ca.cjis20.org/web.

	day along with self-addressed and stamped envelopes for all parties. Upon written approval by the Court, the original Agreed Pretrial Conference Order will be filed with the Clerk of Court, a copy served on all counsel and/or parties of record, and the Pretrial Conference shall be cancelled. **If the Court does not approve the Agreed Pretrial Conference Plan, the Pretrial Conference will not be cancelled.**
For Collier County	The Magistrate at the Pretrial Conference.

In the event the parties are unable to agree on all matters in the Pretrial Conference Order, they shall leave the unagreed matter(s) blank and same will be resolved at the Pretrial Conference with the Court.[3]

D. Motions. All motions, except Motions in Limine, shall be filed prior to the date of the Pretrial Conference or they are deemed abandoned. All dispositive motions, including Motions for Summary Judgment, **must be filed and scheduled for hearing at least ten (10) days prior** to the Pretrial Conference and **must be heard no later than 30 days prior to the commencement of the trial period**. Motions in Limine **must be filed by the *earlier* of docket sounding *or* 10 days prior to the commencement of the trial period** and **must be** heard **no later than 10 days** prior to the date of the trial. Motions not filed and scheduled in compliance with this Order will be heard only upon a showing of good cause.

E. Discovery. Counsel shall complete all discovery, including examinations and Frye hearings, pursuant to the Plan, if any. The conduct of discovery subsequent to the Pretrial Conference will be allowed only as permitted by the Plan, upon stipulation of the parties or upon Order of the Court for good cause. Any discovery allowed subsequent to the Pretrial Conference shall not be a cause for delay of the trial of this cause.

F. Alternative Dispute Resolution.

For Lee County	All parties are required to participate in mediation or other Alternative Dispute Resolution prior to trial. Unless alternative dispute resolution has already occurred at the time this order is issued and a report has been filed with the Clerk of Court, or the parties file a stipulation agreeing to a mutually acceptable mediator setting forth the name of the mediator, and date and place set for mediation within 10 days after the issuance of this Order, Court Mediation will schedule this cause for mediation. Scheduled mediation may be cancelled only upon Court order.
For Collier County	Alternative Dispute Resolution should have already

[3] Any disputes between the parties regarding the Uniform Pretrial Conference /Trial Order will be resolved at the Pretrial Conference by the Magistrate or Judge. If the Magistrate conducts the Pretrial Conference, the Magistrate shall issue a Report and Recommended Order to the Judge on all such disputed issues. A final Uniform Pretrial Conference /Trial Order will be issued by the Judge once any timely exceptions have been filed and heard to the Report and Recommended Order of the Magistrate.

	occurred at the time this order is issued and a report was filed with the Clerk of Court.

G. Settlement. In the event of settlement at any time prior to trial, Plaintiff's Counsel shall immediately notify the Court and submit a stipulation for an Order of Dismissal and a Final Disposition form.

H. Representation and Authority. In order for the full purpose of the Pretrial Conference procedures to be accomplished, each party shall be represented at all meetings and hearings required herein by the attorney who will participate in the trial of the cause and who is vested with full authority to make admissions and disclosure of facts, and to bind the client by agreement in respect to all matters pertaining to the trial of this cause and the Pretrial Conference Order.

I. Continuances. This Court adheres strictly to Rule of Judicial Administration 2.545(e) and Rule of Civil Procedure 1.460. Accordingly, motions for continuance and stipulations must be in writing and set forth the following:

1. The signature of the party as well as the attorney.

2. A concise statement of the reasons for a continuance. If based on non-availability of a witness, a showing of when it is believed the witness will be available must be stated.

Any stipulation must be approved or motion heard by the Court no later than docket sounding. **No Motion will be heard that is not in compliance with this Order except upon good cause shown.**

5. **Notice**

Plaintiff, or if represented, Counsel for Plaintiff is directed to review this Order to ensure that it was sent to all proper persons at current, proper addresses. The failure to immediately notify the Court may result in this matter not being heard at the scheduled time.

6. **Sanctions**

The failure to comply with the requirements of this Order may subject the party and/or attorney to appropriate sanctions, including the award of attorneys' fees, fines, striking of pleadings, and/or dismissal of the case.

DONE AND ORDERED in Chambers, ______________County, Florida on this _____ day of __________________, 20____.

____
Circuit Judge

Insert ADA language by County here

IN THE CIRCUIT COURT OF THE TWENTIETH JUDICIAL CIRCUIT IN AND FOR _______ COUNTY, FLORIDA CIVIL ACTION

, CASE NO:
Plaintiff(s)

vs

,
Defendant(s).
_______________________/

UNIFORM ORDER SETTING JURY TRIAL/NON-JURY TRIAL PRETRIAL CONFERENCE
(Approved Case Management Plan)

THIS CAUSE comes before the Court on the Approved Case Management Plan of the Parties (the "Plan"). Under the Plan this cause may be set for trial at this time pursuant to Rule 1.440, Florida Rules of Civil Procedure, and it appearing this cause is otherwise at issue, it is hereby:

ORDERED AND ADJUDGED as follows:

1. **Pretrial Conference**

For Lee County	A Pretrial Conference is scheduled on *(date)*_____________ at *(time)*__________ in Courtroom *(#)*_______, ___ Floor, *(location)* Lee County Justice Center, 1700 Monroe St., Ft. Myers, FL 33901, pursuant to Rule 1.200 of the Florida Rules of Civil Procedure, FOR THE PURPOSE OF COMPLETION AND CONFIRMATION OF THE ATTACHED PRETRIAL CONFERENCE ORDER FORM.
For Collier County	Counsel for Plaintiff is ordered to schedule a Pretrial Conference through the JACS System (www.ca.cjis20.org/web/services/jacs.asp) before Magistrate _____________, at the Collier County Courthouse, Naples, FL 34112, Hearing Room 3-3 **within forty-five (45) days of the date of the conclusion of Mediation or Alternative Dispute Resolution not resulting in settlement or disposition of the entire action. Sufficient and reasonable notice shall be given of the date and time of the Pretrial Conference to all parties.**

2. **Attendance at Pretrial Conference**

For Lee County	Appearance at the Pretrial Conference by lead counsel trying the case and all pro-se parties is mandatory **UNLESS** an Agreed Pretrial Conference Order (using the attached form) has been submitted to the Civil Case Manager at least 7 calendar days in

	advance of the scheduled Pretrial Conference <u>and</u> an Order approving the Agreed Pretrial Conference Order has been entered by the Court.
For Collier County	Appearance at the Pretrial Conference by lead counsel trying the case and all pro-se parties is mandatory even if an agreement is reached on the form of the Pretrial Conference Order. If the Pretrial Conference is held before the Magistrate, represented parties may appear by telephone. Parties wishing to appear by telephone shall make arrangements with the Court through Court Call no later than ten (10) days prior to the Pretrial Conference. If any objection is made to the Magistrate conducting the Pretrial Conference, the Judge will conduct the Pretrial Conference and lead counsel, all represented parties, and all pro-se parties must attend in person.

3. **<u>Trial Period</u>**

For Lee County	This cause is set for trial during the ***[# of weeks]*** week trial period ***[beginning & ending date of trial period]*** in Courtroom ***[#]***, ***[# Floor]***, Lee County Justice Center, 1700 Monroe Street, Fort Myers, Fl 33901, before the undersigned judge. Docket Sounding will be held on ***[date]*** at ***[time]*** in Courtroom ***[#]***. ***[# days]*** have been requested for this trial. The Court will continue this trial if it appears that additional time is required and the other cases set for this trial period are jeopardized. In the event this trial is commenced and it becomes apparent that sufficient time was not requested, a mistrial may be declared and costs assessed against the party causing the over-run.
For Collier County	The Court will confirm a trial period at the Pretrial Conference.

4. **<u>Pre-trial Events</u>**

A. <u>Exchange of Expert & Lay Witnesses</u>. No later than thirty (30) days prior to the Pretrial Conference date, counsel and/or parties shall file and exchange a list of the names and addresses of **<u>all</u>** witnesses they in good faith intend to call at trial and include a concise statement of facts about which the witness will testify or opinion of any expert witness. This is not intended to extend the time frames set forth in the Plan, but rather to identify those witnesses that will in good faith actually be called. No party shall be permitted to call any witness not so disclosed, without prior permission of the Court, or written stipulation executed by all parties, or if represented, their counsel.

B. <u>Fabre Defendants</u>. No later than thirty (30) days prior to the Pretrial Conference date, all Defendants or other persons sought to be placed on the verdict form and against whom some measure of liability may be assessed by the jury, must be disclosed to the court and opposing counsel. No person or entity not so disclosed may be placed on the verdict form without good cause shown.

C. <u>Meeting Before Pretrial Conference</u>. The attorneys for all parties (initiated by counsel for the Plaintiff) and all pro-se parties shall meet no later than ten (10) days before the

Pretrial Conference to[1]:

1. Identify all exhibits each party in good faith intends to offer into evidence at trial and prepare an exhibit list for use by the Clerk and the Court at trial (actual exhibits and documentary evidence shall be available for inspection at this time). (This is not intended to extend the time frames set forth in the Plan, but rather to identify those exhibits that will in good faith actually be offered into evidence at trial). Any exhibits not so identified will not be admissible absent prior approval of the Court or a written stipulation of all parties.

2. Agree to admit or not admit evidence and list specific objections, if any.

3. Stipulate to any matter of fact or law about which there is no issue in order to avoid unnecessary proof (i.e., chain of custody or records custodian predicates).

4. Review all depositions or any other evidence which will be offered for any purpose other than impeachment to resolve objections to the portions to be offered in evidence.

5. Discuss the possibility of settlement.

6. If applicable, submit an itemized statement of special damages the Plaintiff expects to prove.

7. If a jury trial has been demanded, discuss jury instructions and verdict forms and reach agreement, if possible, on same.

8. Discuss and complete any other matters which may simplify the issues or aid in the speedy disposition of this action, the Pretrial Conference, and trial.

9. Draft one Pretrial Conference Order (using the attached form)[2], signed by all participating counsel and pro-se parties. The Pretrial Conference Order shall be submitted directly to:

For Lee County	The Civil Case Manager at least 7 days prior to the Pretrial Conference. The Agreed Pretrial Conference Order will also be considered timely if the parties submit a courtesy copy of the signed original to the Civil Case Manager via facsimile

[1] Counsel and/or parties involved in cases to be tried without a jury need not address jury instructions or other pretrial matters that involve a jury, and need not complete these sections of the Pretrial Conference/Trial Order.
[2] The Pretrial Conference Order can also be downloaded from the Court's website at http://www.ca.cjis20.org/web/main/civil.asp.

	239-485-2999 or e-mail transmission to CivilCM@ca.cjis20.org not later than 7 calendar days prior to the Pretrial Conference, **and** if the original is mailed or hand delivered on the same day along with self-addressed and stamped envelopes for all parties. Upon written approval by the Court, the original Agreed Pretrial Conference Order will be filed with the Clerk of Court, a copy served on all counsel and/or parties of record, and the Pretrial Conference shall be cancelled. **If the Court does not approve the Agreed Pretrial Conference Plan, the Pretrial Conference will not be cancelled.**
For Collier County	The Magistrate at the Pretrial Conference.

In the event the parties are unable to agree on all matters in the Pretrial Conference Order, they shall leave the unagreed matter(s) blank and same will be resolved at the Pretrial Conference with the Court.[3]

D. Motions. All motions shall be filed in accordance with the Plan except Motions in Limine. All dispositive motions, including Motions for Summary Judgment, **must be filed and scheduled for hearing at least ten (10) days prior** to the Pretrial Conference and **must be heard no later than 30 days prior to the commencement of the trial period.** Motions in Limine **must be filed by the *earlier* of docket sounding *or* 10 days prior to the commencement of the trial period** and **must be** heard **no later than 10 days** prior to the date of the trial. Motions not filed and scheduled in compliance with this Order will be heard only upon a showing of good cause.

E. Discovery. Counsel shall complete all discovery, including examinations and Frye hearings, pursuant to the Plan. The conduct of discovery subsequent to the Pretrial Conference will be allowed only as permitted by the Plan, upon stipulation of the parties or upon Order of the Court for good cause. Any discovery allowed subsequent to the Pretrial Conference shall not be a cause for delay of the trial of this cause.

F. Alternative Dispute Resolution. All parties are required to participate in mediation or other Alternative Dispute Resolution prior to trial in accordance with the Plan.

G. Settlement. In the event of settlement at any time prior to trial, Plaintiff's Counsel shall immediately notify the Court and submit a stipulation for an Order of Dismissal and a Final Disposition form.

H. Representation and Authority. In order for the full purpose of the Pretrial Conference procedures to be accomplished, each party shall be represented at all meetings and

[3] Any disputes between the parties regarding the Uniform Pretrial Conference /Trial Order will be resolved at the Pretrial Conference by the Magistrate or Judge. If the Magistrate conducts the Pretrial Conference, the Magistrate shall issue a Report and Recommended Order to the Judge on all such disputed issues. A final Uniform Pretrial Conference /Trial Order will be issued by the Judge once any timely exceptions have been filed and heard to the Report and Recommended Order of the Magistrate.

hearings required herein by the attorney who will participate in the trial of the cause and who is vested with full authority to make admissions and disclosure of facts, and to bind the client by agreement in respect to all matters pertaining to the trial of this cause and the Pretrial Conference Order.

I. Continuances. This Court adheres strictly to Florida Rule of Judicial Administration 2.545(e) and Florida Rule of Civil Procedure 1.460. Accordingly, motions for continuance and stipulations must be in writing and set forth the following:

1. The signature of the party as well as the attorney.

2. A concise statement of the reasons for a continuance. If based on non-availability of a witness, a showing of when it is believed the witness will be available must be stated.

Any stipulation must be approved or motion heard by the Court no later than docket sounding. **No Motion will be heard that is not in compliance with this Order except upon good cause shown.**

J. Approved Case Management Plan. Except as modified by this Order, the Approved Case Management Plan shall remain in full force and effect.

5. **Notice**
Plaintiff, or if represented, Counsel for Plaintiff is directed to review this Order to ensure that it was sent to all proper persons at current, proper addresses. The failure to immediately notify the Court may result in this matter not being heard at the scheduled time.

6. **Sanctions**
The failure to comply with the requirements of this Order may subject the party and/or attorney to appropriate sanctions, including the award of attorneys' fees, fines, striking of pleadings, and/or dismissal of the case.

DONE AND ORDERED in Chambers, ______________County, Florida on this _____ day of ____________________, 20_____.

____
Circuit Judge

Insert ADA language by County here

IN THE CIRCUIT COURT OF THE TWENTIETH JUDICIAL CIRCUIT IN AND FOR ________COUNTY, FLORIDA CIVIL ACTION

, CASE NO:

Plaintiff(s)

vs

,

Defendant(s).

_______________________________________/

UNIFORM PRETRIAL CONFERENCE/TRIAL ORDER

Present:

____ for Plaintiff

____ for Defendant

1. Statement of Case:

2. Amendments to pleadings:

3. Issues (agreed to and disputed):

4. Number of peremptory challenges:

5. Admissions to avoid unnecessary proof:

6. Witnesses:
   Counsel and all pro-se parties shall list all witnesses they actually intend to call at trial from the approved Case Management Plan, if any, including a concise statement of the facts about which the witness will testify, by the ____ day of ______________, 2010, and will be limited thereby except for good cause.

   The parties shall assure the availability of their witnesses for the entire trial period or to otherwise preserve their testimony for trial as provided by the Florida Rules of Civil Procedure. If a party expects to call an expert or treating physician to testify at trial, it is strongly suggested that such witness be deposed by video and the testimony transcribed. The Court may not be in a position to allow a witness to testify "out of order," over objection, or to take a recess or adjust its schedule for the convenience of such a witness.

7. **Attached,** if applicable, is a list of itemized statement of special damages claimed by any party.

8. Any problems or special needs for the attendance of witnesses:

9. Stipulations (checked):

______ a) Less than 6 jurors if one becomes incapacitated
______ b) Use of expert testimony any time
______ c) Waive X-ray technicians
______ d) Waive records custodians
______ e) Waive photographers
______ f) Copies of ordinances or foreign laws
______ g) Other: ______________________________
____
____

10. Necessity of taking judicial notice:

11. Length of trial:

12. List Pending Motions:

13. Settlement possibilities:

14. Trial Date:

For Lee County	Parties must be ready to go to trial on day #1 of the trial period, regardless of position on the docket. The docket will proceed numerically in the order established at docket sounding, unless time utilization can be enhanced or scheduling conflicts with other courts occur. In such instances, the sequencing of cases for trial may be adjusted by the Court.[1]
For Collier County	Trial Month – Trial period(4 weeks) beginning:______

[1] Dockets will be posted on each Judge's schedule as soon after Docket Sounding as reasonably feasible. Counsel and parties are responsible for checking the Judge's schedule for updates as to the docket and order in which cases will be tried.

15. List the Fabre, 623 So. 2d 1182 (Fla. 1993), Defendant(s) disclosed in accordance with Paragraph 4B of the Order Setting Jury Trial/Non-Jury Trial, Pretrial Conference that Defendant actually intends to request be placed on the verdict form.

16. If depositions or video depositions of witnesses will be used in accordance with applicable law, are there stipulations as to which portions will be shown to the jury? _____YES
_____NO

If there are disagreements regarding the admissibility of any portion of the depositions, such matters must be resolved by hearing, if necessary prior to the trial.

17. Unless specifically directed by the Court to be filed at an earlier date, jury instructions and verdict forms shall be submitted at the beginning of the trial. Counsel and all pro-se parties shall meet prior to trial to agree upon the verdict form and as many standard instructions as possible. The submitted instructions and verdict forms shall include any of the Florida Standard Jury Instructions and verdict forms with appropriate adaptations for the specifics of the case. On the first day of the trial, the attorney for each party shall submit to the Court both an electronic version in Microsoft Word and a typed copy of the proposed jury instructions and verdict form(s). This paragraph shall not foreclose the right of each party to request modifications of the jury instructions and/or verdict form(s) at the charging conference. Any party who intends to request that the Court provide a set of written jury instructions for the jury's consideration, pursuant to Rule 1.470(b), shall be responsible for providing a clean copy (i.e., without citations to authority) of the jury instructions and verdict form(s) to the Court for this purpose prior to the submission of the case to the jurors.

18. **Attached** is a list of all photographs, documents and exhibits. Counsel shall confer prior to trial and initial those agreed to be admitted in evidence. All exhibits shall be pre-marked using numbers for Plaintiff's Exhibits and Letters for Defendant's Exhibits. Upon request the Clerk will provide Exhibit labels prior to commencement of the trial. To avoid the loss and disintegration of component parts of pages, all composite exhibits shall be satisfactorily marked and/or bound before presentation to the Court. Exhibits to be introduced which are larger than 8 1/2 x 11" may be used at trial, but if practicable, same shall be reduced to 8 1/2 x 11", and the reduced size copy shall be the exhibit retained by the Clerk in the court file. The oversized exhibits, if reduced, shall be returned to counsel at the close of the trial.

19. If a party desires that a proceeding be reported by a court reporter, it is the responsibility of that party to secure such services.

20. Failure to comply with the requirements of this Order may subject the party and/or counsel to appropriate sanctions, including attorneys' fees, fines, striking of pleadings, and/or dismissal of this action.

THE UNDERSIGNED HEREBY AGREE TO AND SUBMIT THE FOREGOING PRETRIAL CONFERENCE/TRIAL ORDER TO THE COURT FOR APPROVAL.

_________________________	_________________________
PLAINTIFF'S COUNSEL Address Telephone # Fax # E-Mail Address Florida Bar #	DEFENDANT'S COUNSEL Address Telephone # Fax # E-Mail Address Florida Bar #
Or, if pro se, PLAINTIFF Address Telephone #	Or, if pro se, DEFENDANT Address Telephone #

THE COURT HEREBY APPROVES AND ADOPTS THE FOREGOING PRETRIAL CONFERENCE/TRIAL ORDER AND THE PARTIES ARE ORDERED TO COMPLY WITH IT.

DONE AND ORDERED in Chambers, ______________ County, Florida on this ______ day of ______________, 20____.

____
Circuit Court Judge

Insert ADA Language by County

ATTACHMENT B

Twentieth Judicial Circuit

Civil Differentiated Case Management (DCM) and Backlog Reduction Plan (Charlotte County)

TABLE OF CONTENTS

c. Agreed Case Management Plan and Order
d. Uniform Order Setting Jury Trial/Non–Jury Trial
e. Uniform Pretrial Conference Order

Civil Differentiated Case Management (DCM) and Backlog Reduction Plan (Charlotte County)

I. Purpose and Goals

This Plan seeks to implement in Charlotte County a program of civil case management and backlog reduction uniform with the procedures and goals established in the Twentieth Judicial Circuit in Administrative Order 1.13. This Plan will establish the strategies and procedures to be used in Charlotte County to accomplish the following goals:

• Improve the Court's ability as required by Fla. R. Jud. Admin. 2.545, to provide early and continuous control of case processing through use of additional case management resources, to ensure fair and prompt resolution of disputes consistent with the nature and complexity of the case.

• Identify immediate strategies for circuit civil case backlog reduction plans to assist in prompt resolution of the current 45% of civil cases pending over 18 months.

• Improve the Court's ability to respond to the growing number of commercial, business and other economic based civil filings having a direct impact on economic recovery in the circuit.

• Develop uniform procedures for effective early judicial intervention and management of complex cases consistent with Fla. R. Civ. P. 1.201 for managing complex litigation.

• Reduce public costs of civil litigation through early identification and expedited handling of relatively simple two-party cases to ensure prompt resolution of expedited matters through early referral to mediation or expedited hearing where appropriate.

• Improve the quality and timeliness of Management Information from the Clerk/Court MIS systems to assist judges and the court in management of civil cases and identification of cases pending beyond the Florida Supreme Court time standards set forth in Fla. R. Jud. Admin. 2.250.

II. Charlotte County Circuit Civil Backlog Reduction Goals

The Administrative Judge, in consultation with the civil judge, magistrate, court administration and the local Bar Association, has developed a civil backlog reduction plan to be effective May 1, 2012.

a. Backlog Reduction Goals

1. To reduce the total number of pending circuit civil cases by 15% by March 31, 2013.

2. To reduce the number of circuit civil cases over 18 months of age by 25% by March 31, 2013.

3. To ensure the filing of a Case Management Plan in all unresolved civil cases within 240 days of the initial filing.

b. Backlog Reduction Strategies

• Expedited Uncontested Judgment Dockets will be scheduled before a Senior Judge to accelerate early disposition of default and summary judgments;

• Civil Motion Dockets will be scheduled before the Magistrate and Senior Judge to provide ample hearing time for all civil motions;

• Additional trial days will be added to the Civil Judge's calendar to allow for the quicker scheduling and resolution of an increased number of trials;

• Case Management Conferences will be scheduled before the Civil Case Manager. A Case Management Plan will be submitted to the trial judge (either by stipulation of the parties or by recommendation of the Civil Case Manager after a Case Management Conference has been held) with firm discovery cut-off dates, pretrial issues to be resolved and date matter to be ready for trial.

III. Civil DCM Case Management Plans—Time Standards & Goals

These time standards/goals are developed consistent with those established by the Florida Supreme Court pursuant to Fla. R. Jud. Admin. 2.250 and are intended to be flexible, presumptive time periods for disposition of civil cases.

Complex case time standard/goal is expanded to 24 months upon designation of a case as complex consistent with Fla. R. Civ. P. 1.201 regarding management of complex civil litigation. The local goal of 80—90% disposition of cases within time standards recognizes, consistent with Fla. R. Jud. Admin. 2.250(a), that there are a portion of cases that present unique pretrial problems that may cause reasonable delay. Time standards established by case track are:

a.	Complex cases	80% disposed within 24 months
b.	Standard cases	80% disposed within 18 months
c.	Expedited cases	90% disposed within 12 months

For all cases filed on or after May 1, 2012, the case track and time goal are established by the date of filing of the case. For all cases filed prior to May 1, 2012, the case track and time goal are established by the date an Agreed Case Management Order is filed or a Case Management Conference is held.

IV. Civil Case Tracks—Definitions & Guidelines

a. Complex Case Track—(Goal 24 months)

The complex case track involves those cases with extraordinary complexity as to require or benefit from early intervention and individual judicial management. Complex cases are defined by Fla. R. Civ. P. 1.201. Cases may be designated for management on the complex track in one of the following ways:

1. Complex cases designated by motion or stipulation and approved by the court as cases meeting complex litigation criteria under Fla. R. Civ. P. 1.201(a); OR,

2. Cases identified by the court on its own motion as complex case under Fla. R. Civ. P. 1.201 due to extraordinary procedural complexity, number of parties or other case factors that will require or benefit from individual judicial management;

Presumptive Case Types—Examples of presumptively complex case types that may be appropriate for early screening and review of case complexity are:

• **Class Action** Cases as noted on Civil Cover Sheet (Form 1.997, section V)

- **Environmental/Toxic Tort/Mass Tort** Litigation (Form 1.997, section II)
- **Anti–Trust/Securities** Litigation
- **Malpractice**—Medical (or involving Wrongful Death)
- **Nursing home negligence**
- Other complex cases with extraordinary number of parties, experts, pretrial discovery issues

Presumptive complex case types may be designated for early screening and review by Case Managers. Multiple parties are a key factor, as referenced by the rule; however procedures should be developed in cooperation with the Clerk's Office to identify "presumptive" case types from the Civil Case Cover Sheet.

The Case Manager should be notified of presumptive case types upon filing by the clerk so that they may be actively monitored by the Case Manager after all defendants have been served, an appearance has been entered in response to the complaint by each party or a default entered. The Case Manager will review with the assigned judge each case by evaluating the Civil Cover Sheet, Answer(s) and Complaint to determine the need for assignment to complex track.

b. Standard Case Track—(Goal 18 months)

Standard case track involves the large majority of standard cases that normally will not require a high level of judicial case management to reach timely resolution unless unusual pretrial delay arises. Examples of general case types that would be defined as standard cases, assuming no unusual complexity are:

- Personal injury/tort
- Auto negligence
- Standard contract cases without extraordinary pretrial discovery complexity

c. Expedited Case Track—(Goal 12 months)

Expedited cases are those cases normally requiring little judicial intervention with relatively simple procedural and legal issues that can be resolved promptly by early referral to mediation, ADR or expedited hearing.

Expedited cases may include:

- Uncontested Residential and Commercial Foreclosure
- Simple, two-party Collection/Indebtedness cases under $50,000.00
- Non–Jury cases

Contested cases identified as expedited may be set directly by counsel or *pro se* litigant for mediation within 270 days of filing, or within the deadline determined as part of the Agreed Case Management Plan.

V. Civil DCM Case Management Procedures

a. Screening and Assignment to Case Tracks

1. <u>Civil Cover Sheet (Fla. R. Civ. P. Form 1.9971)</u>

To be filed with the Clerk by the plaintiff along with the initial complaint. After review, data entry clerk will forward Cover Sheet/Complaint/Answer for cases that meet presumptive complex criteria to Case Manager.

2. <u>Case Review and Screening by Case Manager</u>

After responsive pleadings are filed, cases meeting presumptive complex case criteria will be reviewed by a Case Manager for recommended track decision. Potentially complex cases will be reviewed with, and approved by, the assigned trial judge for assignment to the appropriate case track. (Upon complex case designation, case management procedures will follow Section V.b. of this document).

3. <u>Standing Order in Civil Cases Requiring Case Management</u>

Plaintiff will attach the Standing Order in Civil Cases in Charlotte County with the initial complaint for service on all parties upon the filing of any civil case. **This shall be required for all civil cases filed on or after May 1, 2012.** The Standing Order will be provided by the Clerk at the time of filing.

b. Case Management Procedures—Complex Cases

1. <u>Designation to the complex track</u>

Cases may be designated to the complex track as provided under Fla. R. Civ. P. 1.201 by:

- <u>Motion or Stipulation by Parties</u>

Motion or stipulation for designation as a complex case under Fla. R. Civ. P. 1.201 must be filed with the Clerk of Court. The Clerk will provide a copy to the Case Manager in order to assist the judge in case preparation for Initial Case Management Conference or motion hearing;

- <u>On Court's Motion</u>

Case Manager may recommend designation as a complex case to trial judge after receipt of responsive pleadings and review of complaint, answer and civil case cover sheet in presumptive case types.

2. <u>Initial Case Management Conference</u>

Set by the assigned trial judge to occur within 60 days of designation as a complex case with the assigned judge;

3. <u>Joint Statement of Parties</u>

At least 20 days prior to the date of the initial case management conference, counsel for the parties as well as any parties appearing *pro se* shall confer and prepare a joint statement outlining a discovery plan, which shall be filed with the clerk of court no later than 14 days before the conference under Fla. R. Civ. P. 1.201;

4. <u>Case Management Order</u>

To be consistent with the uniform circuit Case Management Order resulting from the conference which provides:

- Pretrial Discovery/Case scheduling plan
- Plan for referral to ADR
- Next Case Management Conference Date
- Date for next Pretrial Conference (not less than 90 days prior to the trial date)
- Estimated date for trial/readiness date within 24 months

5. <u>Additional Case Management Conference/ Pretrial Conference</u>

At the trial judge's discretion, an additional case management conference or pretrial conference may be set with the judge to facilitate resolution of pretrial management or discovery matters, resolve outstanding issues and set a firm trial date.

6. Trial

Trial date will be set by the judge at the case management or pretrial conference.

c. Case Management Procedures—Standard/Expedited Cases

1. Case Management Conference

A Case Management Conference will be scheduled in standard and expedited cases, to be held generally within 210 days from the date of filing the initial complaint. The parties may request by motion the scheduling of the initial case management conference or the Court, in its discretion may set the date for initial case management conference. ***The Initial Case Management Conference may be waived/canceled upon submission of an Agreed Case Management Plan, signed by all parties, and approved by the Court. Forms will be available on the Court's website.***

In cases where all of the parties, *pro se* or through counsel, do not file an Agreed Case Management Plan within 150 days of filing, or in cases where the plan has been filed but not approved by the Court, all parties will be required to attend an initial Case Management Conference as scheduled by the Court to establish a case management plan.

2. Agreed Case Management Plan —An Agreed Case Management Plan may be developed jointly by counsel for the parties as well as any parties appearing *pro se* and filed within 150 days from the filing date of the initial complaint. This will allow counsel and *pro se* parties to consult early in the case, devise an agreed upon case plan and waive an initial case management conference, if the case plan is approved by the Court.

The use of an Agreed Case Management Plan early in the case is intended to allow all parties, *pro se* or through counsel, to set a reasonable case plan targeting dates for discovery, expert reports and referral to alternative dispute resolution (ADR), without court intervention, provided that the general time parameters are set and adhered to.

3. Presumptive case scheduling plan/time goals

Agreed Case Management Plans may be flexible and based upon individual case factors, but should be consistent with reasonable and presumptive pretrial discovery and ADR time goals as follows:

Case Track	Completion of Discovery and ADR	Trial/ Disposition
Standard	450 days	540 days
Expedited	270 days	365 days

1 This Administrative Order is amended so as to reflect that the Charlotte County Circuit Administrative Judge subsequently submitted a Civil Differentiated Case Management (DCM) and Backlog Reduction Plan tailored to meet the needs of Charlotte County. By letter dated April 9, 2012, this plan was formally approved by the Chief Judge for implementation effective May 1, 2012. A copy of the approved plan for Charlotte County is included herein as Attachment B.

2 Full implementation of the Charlotte County Civil DCM Case Management Procedures (Attachment B) shall apply to all civil cases filed in Charlotte County, effective May 1, 2012.

3 This paragraph applies equally as it relates to the Charlotte County Civil DCM Case Management Procedures (Attachment B).

4 Case Track options include Expedited, Standard or Complex. Case Tracks have been established in order to comply with the case disposition standards set forth in Florida Rule of Judicial Administration 2.250(a)(1)(B).

1.14. HOMESTEAD MEDIATION PROGRAM FOR RESIDENTIAL HOMESTEAD MORTGAGE FORECLOSURE ACTIONS

IN THE TWENTIETH JUDICIAL CIRCUIT IN AND FOR THE STATE OF FLORIDA

ADMINISTRATIVE ORDER NO. 1.14

IN RE: HOMESTEAD MEDIATION PROGRAM FOR RESIDENTIAL HOMESTEAD MORTGAGE FORECLOSURE ACTIONS

WHEREAS, pursuant to Article V, section 2(d) of the Florida Constitution, and section 43.26, Florida Statutes, the Chief Judge of each judicial circuit is charged with the authority and power to do everything necessary to promote the prompt and efficient administration of justice; and

WHEREAS, Rule 2.545 of the Rules of Judicial Administration requires that the trial courts "... take charge of all cases at an early stage in the litigation and ... control the progress of the case thereafter until the case is determined ...," which includes "... identifying cases subject to alternative dispute resolution processes;" and

WHEREAS, Chapter 44, Florida Statutes, and Rules 1.700–1.750, Florida Rules of Civil Procedure, provide a framework for court-ordered mediation of civil actions, except those matters expressly excluded by rule 1.710(b), which does not exclude mortgage foreclosure actions; and

WHEREAS, the number of residential homestead mortgage foreclosure case filings have been substantial in the Twentieth Judicial Circuit, and the high residential homestead mortgage foreclosure rates have been damaging to the economies of the counties in the Twentieth Judicial Circuit; and

WHEREAS, early mediation of contested residential homestead mortgage foreclosure actions could potentially facilitate the laudable goals of communication, facilitation, problem-solving between the parties with the emphasis on self-determination, the parties' needs and interests, procedural flexibility, full disclosure, fairness, and confidentiality. Referring these cases to mediation early in the litigation process will also facilitate and provide a more efficient use of limited judicial and clerk resources in a court system that is already overburdened;

NOW, THEREFORE, IT IS ORDERED:

Definitions

As used in this Administrative Order, the following terms mean:

"Homestead Mediation Program" or "HMP" means the mediation program contemplated by this Administrative Order which makes mediation available to the parties early during the proceedings involving a contested residential homestead mortgage foreclosure action.

"Plaintiff" means the individual or entity filing to obtain a mortgage foreclosure on residential homestead property.

"Plaintiff's representative" means the person who will appear at mediation who has full authority to settle without further consultation and resolve the foreclosure suit. Having full authority to settle includes, but is not limited to, the authority to approve a loan modification, reinstatement, forbearance, repayment plan, short sale, or deed-in-lieu of foreclosure.

"Borrower" means an individual or individuals named as a party/parties in the foreclosure action who is/are a primary obligor(s) on the promissory note which is secured by the mortgage being foreclosed.

"Homestead residence" means a residential property for which a homestead real estate tax exemption was granted according to the certified rolls of the last assessment by the county property appraiser prior to the filing of the suit to foreclose the mortgage.

"Communication equipment" means a conference telephone or other electronic device that permits all those appearing or participating to hear and speak to each other, provided that all conversation of the participants is audible to all persons present.

Scope—*Residential Homestead Mortgage Foreclosures*

This Administrative Order shall apply to all residential homestead mortgage foreclosure actions filed in the Twentieth Judicial Circuit in which the origination of the note and mortgage sued upon was subject to the provisions of the federal Truth in Lending Act, Regulation Z. This Administrative Order does not apply to commercial or residential non-homestead foreclosure actions. Mediation in commercial or residential non-homestead foreclosure actions shall be governed by Chapter 44, Florida Statutes, and Rules 1.700–1.750, Florida Rules of Civil Procedure.

Procedure

1. **Delivery of Notice of HMP with Summons.** After the effective date of this Administrative Order, in all actions to foreclose a mortgage on residential homestead property, the Clerk of Court shall attach to the summons to be served on each defendant a notice regarding mediation in the format of Exhibit 1.

2. **Borrower Opt-in.** Upon receipt of the summons and notice, the Borrower may file a responsive pleading within twenty (20) days, in accordance with the summons and rules of court. If the Borrower elects to contest the action and file a responsive pleading, and if the Borrower would like to participate in early mediation, the Borrower shall, within twenty (20) days of service of the summons and notice:

a. file with the Clerk a written response to the Complaint, with a copy to Plaintiff's attorney.

b. file with the Clerk a completed and signed Homestead Mediation Program Opt–In Form in the format of Exhibit 2, with a copy to Plaintiff's attorney.

c. in addition, the Borrower shall complete and sign the Financial Worksheet attached as Exhibit 3, include all attachments requested, and submit the original to Plaintiff's counsel, with a copy to the Court's Mediation Department. The Financial Worksheet and attachments contain confidential information and should not be filed with the Clerk.

Upon receipt of a completed and signed Homestead Mediation Program Opt–In Form, the Clerk shall forward a copy to the Court's Mediation Department.

3. **Nonparticipation by Borrower.** If the Borrower does not seek to contest the foreclosure action, or if the Borrower files a responsive pleading, but does not want to participate in early mediation, the Borrower need not opt-in and further provisions of this Administrative Order will be inapplicable. This does not preclude a referral to mediation at a later time during the course of proceedings pursuant to Chapter 44, Florida Statutes, and Rules 1.700–1.750, Florida Rules of Civil Procedure.

4. **Multiple Borrowers.** When more than one individual is named as a party in the foreclosure action as the primary obligors on the promissory note secured by the mortgage being foreclosed, those individuals must jointly elect to opt-in to the HMP and each individual must participate in the mediation session. Responsibility for the Borrower's portion of the mediation fee is to be equitably distributed between those individuals.

5. **Proceedings.** An election on the part of the Borrower to opt-in to the HMP does not operate as an automatic stay of the case, but rather, the proceedings, including but not limited to discovery, may continue pending mediation. However, the mediation process must be completed prior to entry of a final judgment.

Participation in the HMP, or lack thereof, does not preclude a referral to mediation at a later time during the course of proceedings pursuant to Chapter 44, Florida Statutes, and Rules 1.700–1.750, Florida Rules of Civil Procedure.

6. **Order of Referral to Mediation.** Upon (1) the filing of a written response to the complaint to foreclosure the mortgage, (2) the filing of a completed and signed Homestead Mediation Program Opt–In Form, and (3) the proper and timely submission of a completed Financial Worksheet, with attachments, the Court's Mediation Department shall submit to the presiding judge a proposed Order of Referral to Mediation in the form of Exhibit 4.

If each of the requirements is not met within twenty (20) days after the summons was served, opt-in to the HMP will be deemed incomplete and ineffective, and the case will proceed accordingly.

7. **Legal Representation.** Borrowers who file a responsive pleading and elect to opt-in to the HMP, but are not represented by an attorney, have a right to consult with an attorney at any time during the mediation process and the right to bring an attorney to the mediation session. The Borrower may contact the Florida Bar, the local bar associations, lawyer referral services, or legal aid services to inquire as to the availability of either a volunteer *pro bono* attorney or a low-cost attorney. If the Borrower applies to one of those agencies and is coupled with an attorney, or if the Borrower otherwise retains an attorney, the attorney shall file a notice of appearance with the Clerk of Court and provide a copy to the attorney for the Plaintiff. The appearance may be limited to representation only to assist the Borrower with mediation, but, if a Borrower secures the services of an attorney, counsel of record must attend the mediation.

8. **Scheduling Mediation.** Unless otherwise ordered by the Court, the Court's Mediation Department shall schedule a mediation session to be held within sixty (60) days of entry of the Order of Referral, in accordance with Rule 1.700(a)(1), Florida Rules of Civil Procedure. The date, time, and location

of the mediation shall be included as part of the Order of Referral, which shall be filed with the Clerk, and copies mailed to all parties as notice. A mediator from the panel of Florida Supreme Court certified circuit civil mediators will be assigned.

If it is necessary for a party to reschedule a mediation session, notice must be filed and submitted to the Court Mediation Department at least three (3) full business days prior to the mediation date (exclusive of the mediation date). When rescheduling a mediation session, a mutually agreeable date and time must be ascertained between the parties and confirmed with the Court Mediation Department at least three (3) full business days prior to the rescheduled mediation session (exclusive of the mediation date).

As per Rule 1.710(a), Florida Rules of Civil Procedure, the mediation process shall be completed within forty-five (45) days of the first scheduled mediation conference, unless extended by order of the Court or by stipulation of the parties.

9. Fee for Mediation. The fee for mediation shall be $300.00 for the first two (2) hours, to be equitably and proportionately divided between the Plaintiff and the Borrower, as provided for by Rule 1.720(g). The Borrower's portion of the mediation fee, $150.00, is due at the beginning of the mediation session, and shall be payable directly to the Mediator. The Plaintiff's portion of the mediation fee, $150.00, is due at the beginning of the mediation session, and shall be payable directly to the Mediator. Any additional fees for mediation in excess of the initial two (2) hours shall be apportioned equally between the Borrower and the Plaintiff and shall be payable directly to the Mediator.

10. Attendance at Mediation. The following persons are required to be physically present at the mediation session: a Plaintiff's representative with full authority to settle; Plaintiff's counsel; the Borrower; and the Borrower's counsel of record, if any.

At the time that the mediation is scheduled to physically commence, a staff member of the Court Mediation Department shall, prior to any discussion of the case, take a written roll. That written roll will consist of a determination of the presence of a Plaintiff's representative with Ml authority to settle; Plaintiff's counsel; the Borrower; and the Borrower's counsel of record, if any. If it is determined that anyone is not present, that party shall be reported as a non-appearance by that party on the written roll. If it is determined that the Plaintiff's representative present does not have full authority to settle, it shall be reported as a non-appearance by the Plaintiff's representative with full settlement authority on the written roll. If it is determined that either party does not have sufficient payment of that party's portion of the mediation fee at the beginning of the mediation session, it shall be reported as a non-appearance by that party. The written roll and any communication associated with taking the written roll, are not mediation communications as defined in Section 13 of this Administrative Order, and, therefore, are not confidential.

Junior lienholders may appear at mediation by a representative with full settlement authority. If a junior lienholder is a governmental entity comprised of an elected body, such junior lienholder may appear at mediation by a representative who has authority to recommend settlement to the governing body. Counsel for any junior lienholder may also attend the mediation.

The participants physically attending mediation may consult on the telephone during the mediation with other persons as long as such consultation does not violate the provisions of sections 44.401–406, Florida Statutes.

Appearance by any party at mediation through the use of communication equipment must be by stipulation of the parties or at the discretion of the Court. Any party appearing through the use of communication equipment shall be responsible for ensuring that the communication equipment functions properly and shall be responsible for all charges incurred. The Mediator cannot be held responsible for the failure of any communication equipment, and failure of the communication equipment shall not constitute good cause for failing to appear at mediation.

11. Failure to Appear at Mediation. If the Plaintiff's representative, Plaintiff's counsel, Borrower, or Borrower's counsel of record, if any, fails to appear at a properly noticed mediation session and the mediation does not occur, the party who failed to appear will be responsible for a "no show" cancellation fee of $300.00.

This is a voluntary program which gives the Borrower the choice to participate. Accordingly, if the Borrower does elect to participate, yet the Borrower or Borrower's counsel of record, if any, fails to appear at mediation, this will be deemed as a waiver of the privilege of further participation in the HMP, mediation will not be rescheduled, the case will proceed accordingly, and the Court Mediation Department shall file a Mediation Coordinator's Report reflecting as such. The Borrower, however, is still responsible for the no show cancellation fee of $300.00 as required above.

If mediation does not take place due to some reason other than the Borrower or Borrower's counsel of record, if any, failing to appear, the Court's Mediation Department will schedule a new mediation session.

12. Mediation Report. If a partial or final agreement is reached, it shall be reduced to writing and signed by the parties and their counsel, if any. Pursuant to Rule 1.730(b), Florida Rules of Civil Procedure, if a partial or full settlement agreement is reached, the Mediator shall report the existence of the signed or transcribed agreement to the Court without comment within ten (10) days after completion of the mediation. If the parties do not reach an agreement as to any matter as a result of mediation, the Mediator shall report the impasse to the Court without comment or recommendation and shall advise the Court who attended the mediation. The Mediator's report to the Court shall be in the format of Exhibit 5.

13. Mediation Communications. All mediation communications occurring as a result of this Administrative Order, including information provided to the Mediator that is not filed with the Court, shall be confidential and inadmissible in any subsequent legal proceeding pursuant to Chapter 44, Florida Statutes, the Florida Rules of Civil Procedure, and the Florida Rules for Certified and Court–Appointed Mediators, unless otherwise provided for by law.

14. Opposition to Mediation. Any party opposing mediation may proceed under Fla. R. Civ. P. 1.700(b).

15. Failure to Comply with Administrative Order. The failure of a party to fully comply with the provisions of this Administrative Order may result in the imposition of any sanctions available to the Court, including dismissal of the cause of action without further notice.

Effective Date

This Administrative Order shall become effective on May 1, 2012, and will remain in full force and effect unless and until otherwise ordered.

Interpretation

This Administrative Order shall be interpreted in a manner so as to be in compliance with all rules of the Florida Supreme Court and laws of the State of Florida. To the extent that this Administrative Order may conflict with any rule, statute, or law, the rule, statute, or law shall prevail.

DONE AND ORDERED in Chambers in Fort Myers, Lee County, Florida this 16 day of April, 2012

Jay B. Rosman
Chief Judge

History.—Administrative Order 1.12 (June 29, 2010); Administrative Order 1.12 (December 6, 2010); Order Vacating Administrative Order 1.12 (December 21, 2011).

—EXHIBIT 1—

IN THE CIRCUIT COURT FOR THE TWENTIETH JUDICIAL CIRCUIT IN AND FOR ________ COUNTY, FLORIDA

A NOTICE FROM THE COURT REGARDING LAWSUITS TO FORECLOSE MORTGAGES ON HOMES

If you are being sued to foreclose the mortgage on your home you may have the opportunity to participate in "mediation." At "mediation," you will meet with a Florida Supreme Court certified mediator appointed by the court and also a representative of the company asking to foreclosure your mortgage to see if you and the company suing you can work out an agreement to stop the foreclosure. **The mediator will not be allowed to give you legal advice or to give you an opinion about the lawsuit.** The mediator's job is to remain neutral and not take sides, but to give both sides a chance to talk to each other to see if an agreement can be reached to stop the foreclosure. If you and the company suing you come to an agreement, a settlement agreement will be written up and signed by you and the company suing you. With some limited exceptions, what each side says at the mediation is confidential and the judge will not know what was said at mediation. The Twentieth Circuit has implemented the **Homestead Mediation Program (HMP)** to provide meaningful mediations early in the foreclosure process for homeowners that meet the criteria listed below. Election into or out of this program does not eliminate the opportunity to mediate at any other time prior to trial as may be allowed by Rule 1.700, Florida Rules of Civil Procedure, and Florida Statute Chapter 44.

Eligibility Criteria for the Homestead Mediation Program:

☐ The home has a homestead exemption; **and**

☐ You are the person who borrowed the money for the mortgage; **and**

☐ The origination of the note and mortgage sued upon was subject to the provisions of the federal Truth in Lending Act, Regulation Z.

To participate in the Homestead Mediation Program, the borrower must provide all the following documents within 20 days after you were served the summons:

- File with the Clerk a written response to the Complaint, with a copy to Plaintiff's attorney.
- File with the Clerk a completed and signed Homestead Mediation Program Opt–In Form, with a copy to Plaintiff's attorney.
- And, the Borrower shall complete and sign the Financial Worksheet, include all attachments requested, and submit the original to Plaintiff's counsel, with a copy to the Court's Mediation Department.

The Homestead Mediation Program Opt–In Form and the Financial Worksheet can be found on the Court's website at http://www.ca.cjis20.org/home/main/foreclosure.asp or by calling the Court Mediation Department at 239–533–3353.

Please note that this program is not to be used as a tactic to delay the foreclosure process and is intended for Borrowers who have the means and ability to effectively mediate their case. An election on the part of the Borrower to opt-in to the HMP does not operate as an automatic stay of the case, but rather, the proceedings, including but not limited to discovery, may continue pending mediation.

The fee for mediation shall be $300.00 for the first two (2) hours, to be equitably and proportionately divided between the Plaintiff and the Borrower, as provided for by Rule 1.720(g). The Borrower's portion of the mediation fee, $150.00, is due at the beginning of the mediation session, and shall be payable directly to the Mediator. Any additional fees for mediation in excess of the initial two (2) hours shall be apportioned equally between the Borrower and the Plaintiff and shall be payable directly to the Mediator.

If it is determined that the Borrower does not have sufficient payment for the Borrower's portion of the mediation fee at the beginning of the mediation session, it shall be reported as a failure to appear by the Borrower. Any party that fails to appear at a properly noticed mediation session and the mediation does not occur; the party who failed to appear will be responsible for a "no show" cancellation fee of $300.00. Due to the voluntary nature of this program by the Borrower, if the Borrower fails to appear, this will be deemed as a waiver of the privilege of further participation in the HMP, mediation will not be rescheduled and the case will proceed accordingly.

If you have questions or for additional information regarding the Homestead Mediation Program, contact the Lee County Mediation office at 239–533–3353 or visit our website at http://www.ca.cjis20.org/home/main/foreclosure.asp.

Resources to Assist in the Foreclosure Process

Collier County Bar Association Lawyer Referral Service 239–252–8138
Lee County Bar Association Lawyer Referral Service 239–334–4491

The Florida Bar Lawyer Referral Service 800–342–8011
(for Charlotte, Hendry, and Glades Counties)
Legal Aid Society of Collier County, Inc.—Naples 239–775–4555
Legal Aid Society of Collier County, Inc.—Immokalee 239–657–7442
Florida Rural Legal Services, Inc.—Fort Myers 239–334–4554
Florida Rural Legal Services, Inc.—Punta Gorda 941–505–9007
HUD of SW Florida, providing credit counseling 239–434–2397

—EXHIBIT 2—

IN THE CIRCUIT COURT OF THE TWENTIETH JUDICIAL CIRCUIT IN AND FOR ________ COUNTY, FLORIDA CIVIL DIVISION

________________ Court Case No ____
Plaintiff

________________ Judge ____
Plaintiff Attorney

PLAINTIFF
Vs

____
Defendant

____
Defendant Attorney

DEFENDANT

____

Homestead Mediation Program Opt–In

I/We hereby certify that I/we voluntarily opt-in to the Homestead Mediation Program (HMP), and meet the eligibility requirements. To ensure a meaningful mediation session I/we also agree to provide all of the following documentation within 20 days of service of the summons and notice.

☐ File with the Clerk a written response to the Complaint, with a copy to Plaintiff's attorney;

☐ File with the Clerk a completed and signed Homestead Mediation Program Opt–In Form, with a copy to Plaintiff's attorney;

☐ And, the Borrower shall complete and sign the Financial Worksheet, include all attachments requested, and submit the original to Plaintiff's counsel, with a copy to the Court's Mediation Department. Do not file the Financial Worksheet and attachments with the Clerk.

I/We also certify that I/we enter into the HMP in good faith. I/We will attend the mediation session, pay the mediation fee at the beginning of the mediation session, and not use this program strictly as a tactic to delay the foreclosure process.

________________ ____ ________________ ____
Signature of Borrower Date Signature of Co–Borrower Date

________________ ________________
Type or Print Name Type or Print Name

- EXHIBIT 3 –
CONFIDENTIAL INFORMATION
DO NOT FILE WITH THE CLERK OF COURTS

HOMESTEAD FORECLOSURE MEDIATION FINANCIAL WORKSHEET

Case No.:

_________________ v. _________________

Plaintiff's Name | First Defendant's Name

SECTION 1: PERSONAL INFORMATION

Borrower's Name		Co-Borrower's Name	
Social Security Number (last 4 digits only) XXX-XX-	Date of Birth (mm/dd/yyyy)	Social Security Number (last 4 digits only) XXX-XX-	Date of Birth (mm/dd/yyyy)
☐ Married	☐ Civil Union/ Domestic Partner	☐ Married	☐ Civil Union/ Domestic Partner
☐ Separated	☐ Unmarried (single, divorced, widowed)	☐ Separated	☐ Unmarried (single, divorced, widowed)
Dependents (Not listed by Co-Borrower)		Dependents (Not listed by Borrower)	
Present Address (Street, City, State, Zip)		Present Address (Street, City, State, Zip)	

SECTION 2: EMPLOYMENT INFORMATION

Employer	☐ Self Employed	Employer	☐ Self Employed
Position/Title	Date of Employment	Position/Title	Date of Employment
Second Employer		Second Employer	
Position/Title	Date of Employment	Position/Title	Date of Employment

	Borrower	Co-Borrower	Total
Gross Salary/Wages			
Net Salary/Wages			
Unemployment Income			
Child Support/Alimony			
Disability Income			
Rental Income			
Other Income			
Total (do not include Gross income)			

SECTION 3: EXPENSE AND LIABILITIES	Monthly Payments	Balance Due
First Mortgage		
Second Mortgage		
Other Liens/Rents		
Homeowners' Association Dues		
Hazard Insurance		
Real Estate Taxes		
Child Care		
Health Insurance		
Medical Charges		
Credit Card/Installment Loan		
Credit Card/Installment Loan		
Credit Card/Installment Loan		
Automobile Loan 1		
Automobile Loan 2		
Auto/Gasoline/Insurance		
Food/Spending Money		
Water/Sewer/Utilities		
Phone/Cell Phone		
Other		
Total		

SECTION 4: ASSETS	Estimated Value
Personal Residence	
Real Property	
Personal Property	
Automobile 1	
Automobile 2	
Checking Accounts	
Saving Accounts	
IRA/401K/Keogh Accounts	
Stock/Bonds/CDs	
Cash Value of Life Insurance	
Other	
Total	

Reason for Delinquency/Inability to Satisfy Mortgage Obligation:

☐ Reduction in income ☐ Medical issues ☐ Death of family member

☐ Poor budget management skills ☐ Increase in expenses ☐ Business venture failed

☐ Loss of Income ☐ Divorce/separation ☐ Increase in loan payment

☐ Other: ____________________

SECTION 4: ASSETS CON'T

Further Explanation:

I / We obtained a mortgage loan(s) secured by the above-described property.

I / We have described my/our present financial condition and reason for default and have attached required documentation.

I / We consent to the release of this financial worksheet and attachments to the mediator and the plaintiff or plaintiff's servicing company by way of the plaintiff's attorney.

By signing below, I / we certify the information provided is true and correct to the best of my / our knowledge.

Signature of Borrower	SSN (last 4 digits only)	Date
Signature of Co-Borrower	SSN (last 4 digits only)	Date

Please attach copies of the following and send to the Plaintiff's Counsel with a copy to the Court's Mediation Department at 1700 Monroe Street, Fort Myers, Florida 33901.

- ✓ Last two (2) federal tax returns filed
- ✓ Proof of income (e.g. pay stubs for the last 30 days)
- ✓ Past two (2) bank statements
- ✓ If self-employed, attach a copy of the past six month's profit and loss statement
- ✓ Copy of current utility bill with the street address of the foreclosed property as the service and billing address
- ✓ Copies of any awards of alimony, child support, social security disability benefits or income from any other source
- ✓ If another person is assisting with the payment of the mortgage, a signed statement of contribution

Do not file this document or attachments with the Clerk of Courts.

This is an attempt to collect a debt and any information obtained will be used for that purpose.

—EXHIBIT 4—

IN THE CIRCUIT COURT OF THE TWENTIETH JUDICIAL CIRCUIT IN AND FOR _________ COUNTY, FLORIDA CIVIL DIVISION

_________________________ Court Case No _____

Plaintiff

_________________________ Mediation No _____

Plaintiff Attorney

Judge _____

PLAINTIFF
Vs

____

Defendant

____

Defendant Attorney

DEFENDANT

____

ORDER OF REFERRAL TO MEDIATION FOR RESIDENTIAL HOMESTEAD MORTGAGE FORECLOSURE ACTIONS

In accordance with local Administrative Order 1.14, and Fla. R. Civ. P. 1.700, IT IS ORDERED that the above-referenced case is hereby referred to mediation, and mediation is hereby scheduled for:

__________ at ________ **at Court Mediation Department**
Day, Date **Time**

____
____
____

The General Provisions attached hereto shall be applicable and are incorporated herein.

DONE AND ORDERED this ___ DAY OF _________, 20 _________, in chambers at _________, _________ County, Florida.

____
Judge Name
Circuit Court Judge

If you are a person with a disability who needs any accommodation in order to participate in this proceeding, you are entitled, at no cost to you, to the provision of certain assistance. Please contact _________ whose office is located in _________, _________, _________, Florida _________, and whose telephone number is (___) ___, at least 7 days before your scheduled appearance, or immediately upon receiving this notification if the time before the scheduled appearance is less than 7 days; if you are hearing or voice impaired, call 711.

GENERAL PROVISIONS

1. For purposes of this Order, ________ is appointed as Coordinator to work with the Mediator and to coordinate the mediation session. The telephone number for questions and inquiries is ________, and the fax number is ___. Any and all correspondence pertaining to mediation should be forwarded to the Court Mediation Department, ________, ________, ________, Florida ________.

2. On the date scheduled for mediation, please report to the Court Mediation Department for assignment of the Mediator and the Mediation conference room.

3. The general rules governing mediation are contained in this Order and in Florida Statute Chapter 44, and Fla. R. Civ. P. 1.700, et seq.

4. A notice seeking to reschedule a mediation session must be filed with the Court Mediation Department at least three (3) full business days prior to the mediation date (exclusive of the mediation date). When rescheduling a mediation session, a mutually agreeable date and time must be ascertained between the parties and confirmed with the Court Mediation Department, at least three (3) full business days prior to the mediation date (exclusive of the mediation date).

5. The parties may submit a brief written summary of the facts and issues with the Court Mediation Department, seven (7) days prior to the mediation. The written summary is not to be filed with the Clerk of Court. However, courtesy copies may be sent to all attorneys of record or opposing parties. The case number, mediation number and date of the conference shall be included in the heading of the mediation summary. In the written summary, counsel for corporate parties shall state the name and general job description of the employee or agent who will attend and represent the corporate party.

6. It is mandatory that the following persons be physically present at the mediation session, unless specifically provided otherwise by the court: a Plaintiff's representative with full authority to settle; Plaintiff's counsel; the Borrower; and the Borrower's counsel of record, if any. When more than one Borrower is named as a party in the foreclosure action who are the primary obligors on the promissory note secured by the mortgage being foreclosed, each individual must participate in the mediation session.

7. The participants shall be prepared to spend as much time as necessary to settle the case and/or be prepared to mediate until an impasse is declared by the Mediator.

8. The Mediator has no power to compel or enforce settlement agreements. If a settlement is reached in this case, it shall be the responsibility of the parties or their attorneys of record to reduce the agreement to writing and to comply with Fla. R. Civ. P. I. 730(b), unless waived.

9. It is the responsibility of the parties or their attorneys of record to advise the Court Mediation Department of any party not identified in this Order, or parties who are added to this case after the issuance of this Order, and to notify those parties of the date, time and location of the mediation session. Additionally, it is the responsibility of the parties or their attorneys to inform the Court Mediation Department of any dispositive matters that would affect the scheduled mediation session.

10. The Mediator shall be compensated at the rate of $150.00 per hour with a two (2) hour minimum. Mediation fees shall be equitably and proportionately divided between the Plaintiff and the Borrower, as provided for by Rule 1.720(g). The Borrower's portion is due at the beginning of the mediation session, and shall be payable directly to the Mediator. The Plaintiff's portion of $150.00 is due at the beginning of the mediation session, and shall be payable directly to the Mediator. Any additional fees for mediation in excess of the initial two (2) hour's shall be apportioned equally between the Borrower and the Plaintiff and payable directly to the Mediator. If it is determined that either party does not have sufficient payment at the beginning of the mediation session, it shall be reported as a non-appearance by that party.

11. If the Plaintiff's representative; Plaintiff's counsel; Borrower; or Borrower's counsel of record, if any, fails to appear at a properly noticed mediation session and the mediation does not occur, the party who failed to appear will be responsible for a no-show cancellation fee of $300.00. Due to the voluntary nature of this program by, if the Borrower or Borrower's counsel of record, if any, fails to appear at mediation, mediation will not be rescheduled, and the case will proceed accordingly. The Borrower, however, is still responsible for the no show cancellation fee of $300.00 as required above. Otherwise, the Court's Mediation Department will schedule a new mediation session.

12. The Court has the power and will impose sanctions against any party failing to attend the mediation session, against any party failing to pay their portion of the mediation fees in a timely fashion, and against any party for misconduct. Sanctions include, but are not limited to, entry of default; costs being assessed, including attorney fees; the striking of pleadings; and removing the case from the trial calendar.

13. All discussions, representations, and statements made at the mediation session shall be privileged as settlement negotiations, and nothing related to the mediation session shall be admitted at trial or subject to discovery.

14. Any party opposing mediation may proceed under Fla. R. Civ. P. 1.700(b).

Certificate of Service

I hereby certify that a true and correct copy of the foregoing has been furnished by regular U.S. mail this ___ day of ________, 20 ___ to the above named parties or their counsel.

By: ________________

—EXHIBIT 5—

IN THE CIRCUIT COURT OF THE TWENTIETH JUDICIAL CIRCUIT IN AND FOR ________ COUNTY, FLORIDA

Case No(s):

Plaintiff(s),

MEDIATOR REPORT

vs.

Defendant(s).

____

Pursuant to the Court's Order, a Mediation Conference was conducted by Florida Supreme Court Certified Circuit Court Mediator ________ on ________, 20 ___.

The following were physically present at the Mediation Conference (please print clearly or type):

____________________	____________________
Plaintiff's Representative	Plaintiff's Attorney
____________________	____________________
Borrower	Borrower's Attorney

Others physically present: ____________________

____

Parties present by electronic equipment: ____________

The result of the Mediation Conference is as follows:

___ The parties reached an agreement. [ ] PARTIAL [ ] FULL

___ The parties reached a total impasse.

___ The mediation has been continued until ________ (Day, Date and Time)

Mediator Signature: ________

[Certificate of Service]

1.15. COURT–ORDERED ARBITRATION IN CIRCUIT AND COUNTY CIVIL CASES

IN THE TWENTIETH JUDICIAL CIRCUIT IN AND FOR THE STATE OF FLORIDA

ADMINISTRATIVE ORDER NO. 1.15

IN RE: COURT–ORDERED ARBITRATION IN CIRCUIT AND COUNTY CIVIL CASES

WHEREAS, Florida Statute § 44.103, permits a presiding Civil Circuit or County Judge to refer civil cases to arbitration without the consent of the parties, in much the same way cases are referred to mediation; and

WHEREAS, Rule 1.810(a), Florida Rules of Civil Procedure, requires the Chief Judge, or the Chief Judge's designee, to maintain a list of qualified persons who have agreed to serve within the circuit as arbitrators; and

WHEREAS, Rules 11.010 and 11.020, Florida Rules for Court–Appointed Arbitrators, require, with certain exceptions, arbitrators to be members of The Florida Bar and to complete a training program approved by the Supreme Court of Florida; and

WHEREAS, Rule 1.820(b)(1), Florida Rules of Civil Procedure, requires the Chief Judge to set procedures for determining the time and place of arbitration hearings and authorizes the Chief Judge to establish any other procedures for the expeditious and orderly operation of arbitration hearings to the extent that such procedures are not in conflict with any rules of court; and

WHEREAS, Rule 1.810(b), Florida Rules of Civil Procedure, requires the Chief Judge to establish the compensation for arbitrators subject to any limitations of Florida Statute § 44.103(3);

Now, therefore, pursuant to the authority vested in the Chief Judge by Rule 2.215 of the Florida Rules of Judicial Administration, and for the purpose of formally memorializing the established procedures utilized within the Twentieth Judicial Circuit,

It is hereby **ORDERED** as follows:

1. The Chief Judge of the Twentieth Judicial Circuit, in conjunction with the Administrative Office of the Courts' Mediation/Arbitration Department shall create a list of persons qualified to serve as arbitrators, which shall be maintained by the Administrative Office of the Courts' Mediation/Arbitration Department.

2. To be qualified as an arbitrator, a person must be a member of the Florida Bar for five (5) years and must comply with the qualification and training requirements set forth in Rules 11.010, 11.020, and 11.110, Florida Rules for Court–Appointed Arbitrators, unless otherwise agreed by the parties. Rule 11.010, Florida Rules for Court–Appointed Arbitrators, provides that persons who are not members of The Florida Bar may serve as arbitrators only on an arbitration panel and then only upon the written agreement of all parties.

3. Written procedures for becoming a court-appointed arbitrator shall be maintained by the Administrative Office of the Courts' Mediation/Arbitration Department. A person interested in being listed as an arbitrator may contact the Administrative Office of the Courts' Mediation/Arbitration Department, to obtain an application and shall deliver a completed application to the Administrative Office of the Courts' Mediation/Arbitration Department. Upon review of the application, the Chief Judge or the Chief Judge's designee, shall determine if the applicant is qualified and, if so, shall add the applicant to the list of qualified arbitrators. The list of qualified arbitrators shall be designated as the Twentieth Judicial Circuit's List of Qualified Arbitrators and shall be made available to all judges of the circuit.

4. Pursuant to Florida Statute § 44.103 and Rules 1.700(a), 1.800, and 1.820(b)(1), Florida Rules of Civil Procedure, the Twentieth Judicial Circuit hereby establishes these procedures to facilitate the use of court-ordered non-binding arbitration in all, or any part, of a contested civil action filed in either Circuit or County Court, except as prohibited by law or by Rule 1.800, Florida Rules of Civil Procedure.[1] The parties to any matter pending before the Court may agree to select their own arbitrator(s); however, in the absence of an agreement by the parties, an arbitrator (or arbitrators) shall be selected by the presiding Judge, or the presiding Judge's designee, from the Twentieth Judicial Circuit's List of Qualified Arbitrators.

5. Upon deciding that a case will be referred to non-binding arbitration, the presiding Judge shall enter an "Order/Referral to Nonbinding Arbitration," which shall (1) establish a deadline for conducting the arbitration, (2) afford the parties ten days to select a mutually acceptable arbitrator(s), (3) establish Plaintiff's counsel as lead attorney for the purpose of coordinating, scheduling and providing notice of the arbitration, (4) provide instructions as to how the parties are to proceed if they do not agree to an arbitrator(s), and (5) provide notice to all parties of the procedures applicable to the arbitration hearing. If the parties do not agree to an arbitrator(s), Plaintiff's counsel shall provide written notification to the Court and to the Administrative Office of the Courts'

Mediation/Arbitration Department within fifteen days of entry of the "Order/Referral to Nonbinding Arbitration." Upon receipt of such written notification, the Court will enter an "Order for Non–Binding Arbitration," which will name an arbitrator(s) selected by the Court from the Twentieth Judicial Circuit's List of Qualified Arbitrators and will schedule the time and location of the arbitration. The Mediation/Arbitration Department will serve as coordinator for the arbitration.

6. The arbitration hearing shall be conducted in the county in which the action is pending, unless otherwise agreed by the parties.

7. Arbitration shall be conducted in accordance with the rules of practice and procedure adopted by the Supreme Court of Florida, in accordance with all laws of the State of Florida, in accordance with all orders and directives as may be approved by the Chief Judge, and in accordance with the written procedures maintained by the Administrative Office of the Courts' Mediation/Arbitration Department and attached hereto.

8. Copies of all written procedures, applications, and sample orders, as well as the Twentieth Judicial Circuit's List of Qualified Arbitrators, shall be on file in the Administrative Office of the Courts' Mediation/Arbitration Department, and shall be posted on the official website for the Twentieth Judicial Circuit.

9. Arbitrators in the Twentieth Judicial Circuit conducting court-ordered non-binding arbitration shall be compensated at a rate which shall not exceed $200.00 per hour, unless otherwise agreed by the parties, and shall be entitled to a minimum fee of $400.00, even if the arbitration hearing does not exceed one hour. The arbitration fee shall not exceed $1,500.00, per day. At a minimum, $200.00 for the first hour of arbitration shall be paid to each arbitrator no later than ten (10) days prior to commencement of the arbitration hearing; the balance, if any, shall be paid at the conclusion of said hearing. Fees shall be equally divided between the parties. However, if any party cancels with less than 48 hours notice or fails to appear, each arbitrator shall be entitled to the $400.00 minimum fee, and the party or parties who cancelled or failed to appear shall be responsible for the cost.

10. In the event that a party is found to be indigent pursuant to Florida Statute § 57.082, the use of state funds is authorized by Florida Statute § 44.103(3) to partially or fully compensate the arbitrator(s) according to the party's present ability to pay. However, prior to approving the use of state funds to reimburse an arbitrator, the Judge must ensure that the party reimburses the portion of the total cost that the party is immediately able to pay and that the party has agreed to a payment plan established by the Clerk of the Court that will fully reimburse the state for the balance of all state costs for both the arbitrator and any costs of administering the payment plan and any collection efforts that may be necessary in the future. Whenever possible, in such instances when a party is found to be indigent, qualified individuals who have volunteered their time to serve as arbitrators shall be appointed.

11. To the extent that any provision of this Administrative Order may be construed as being in conflict with any law, statute, or rule, the law, statute, or rule shall prevail.

DONE AND ORDERED in Chambers at Fort Myers, Lee County, Florida this 12 day of June, 2013.

Jay B. Rosman
Chief Judge

History.—New.

TWENTIETH JUDICIAL CIRCUIT PROCEDURES FOR NON–BINDING ARBITRATION

The following procedures shall apply to non-binding arbitration. See also, Florida Statutes, Section 44.103 and Florida Rule of Civil Procedure 1.820 ("Hearing Procedures for Non–Binding Arbitration"):

(1) Cases referred to arbitration shall be assigned to an arbitrator or to a panel of arbitrators. In the absences of an agreement by the parties as to the designation of the arbitrator(s), the Court shall determine the number of arbitrators and designate the arbitrators. In the case of a panel, one of the arbitrators shall be appointed or designated as the chief arbitrator.

(2) The arbitration fees shall be equally divided and paid by the parties. "At no time may an arbitrator charge more than $1,500.00 per diem, unless all of the parties agree otherwise." Florida Statutes, Section 44.103(3). The arbitrator(s) shall be compensated pursuant to Florida Statutes, Section 44.103(3), or as otherwise agreed to by the arbitrator(s) and the parties.

(3) All parties, including non-counsel representatives of corporate parties with full authority to settle the matter, must attend the arbitration hearing. If insurance is involved, whether or not named as a party, the insurance company shall have a representative present with full authority to resolve the case. Parties may be represented by counsel; however, counsel shall not be considered a representative of the party for purposes of this section. Hearings may continue without the presence of counsel. If a party fails to attend the scheduled hearing, the chief arbitrator may proceed with the hearing, and the arbitrator(s) shall render a decision based upon the facts and circumstances as presented by the parties present. Failure to attend the hearing may also result in the Court applying sanctions including the striking of pleadings or portions thereof, the awarding of fees and costs and/or contempt proceedings.

(4) The parties shall submit case summaries to each arbitrator at least 10 days prior to the hearing.

(5) "[The] arbitrator or, in the case of a panel, the chief arbitrator, shall have such power to administer oaths or affirmations and to conduct the proceedings as the rules of court shall provide. The hearing shall be conducted informally. Presentation of testimony shall be kept to a minimum and facts and issues shall be presented to the arbitrator(s) primarily through documents and the statements and arguments of counsel." Florida Statutes, Section 44.103(4).

(6) Any party may have a record and transcript made of the arbitration hearing at the party's expense.

(7) Arbitration shall be completed within 30 days of the first arbitration hearing unless extended by Order of the Court on motion of the Chief Arbitrator or of a party. No extension of time shall be for a period exceeding 60 days from the date of the first arbitration hearing. Upon the completion of the arbitration process, the arbitrator(s) shall render a decision. In the case of a panel, a decision shall be by a majority vote of the panel.

(8) If the decision establishes or otherwise clearly demonstrates a party to be the prevailing party, the decision should also include a recommendation as to the assessment of costs, and the reasonable amount of those costs. While the issue of attorney's fees, if appropriate, is normally reserved for the trial court, the parties can waive this right and have the arbitrator(s) render a finding on entitlement and/or the reasonable amount of attorney's fees. Such waiver should be in writing and signed by the respective parties or their attorneys. See, generally, Turnberry Associates v. Service Station Aid, Inc., 651 So. 2d 1173 (Fla. 1995).

(9) Within 10 days of the final adjournment of the arbitration hearing, the arbitrator(s) shall provide the parties with a written decision pursuant to Florida Statutes, Section 44.103(5). The arbitration decision may set for the issues in controversy, findings of fact and conclusions of law. The original written decision and the original of any transcripts shall be sealed and filed with the Clerk at the time the parties are notified of the decision.

(10) Any party may file a motion for trial de novo, pursuant of Florida Statutes, Section 44.103(5). "An arbitration decision shall be final if a request for trial de novo is not filed within the time provide by the rules promulgated by the Supreme Court ... If no request for trial de novo is made within the time provided, the decision shall be referred to the presiding judge, who shall enter such orders and judgments as may be required to carry out the terms of the decision." Florida Statutes, Section 44.103(5); Florida Rules of Civil Procedure, Rule 1.820(h).

(11) If a trial de novo is requested and the judgment at trial is not more favorable than the decision of the arbitrator(s), the Court may assess the party requesting the trial, the other party's expenses, costs and fees, including reasonable attorney's fees, if the requirements under Florida Statutes, Section 44.103(6) are met.

[1]In accordance with Rule 1.800, Fla. R. Civ. P., under no circumstances may bond estreatures, bond validations, petitions for habeas corpus or other extraordinary writs, or contempt actions be referred to arbitration.

1.16. COURT–ORDERED MEDIATION IN CIRCUIT CIVIL, FAMILY, DEPENDENCY, AND COUNTY COURT CIVIL CASES

IN THE TWENTIETH JUDICIAL CIRCUIT IN AND FOR THE STATE OF FLORIDA

ADMINISTRATIVE ORDER NO. 1.16

IN RE: COURT–ORDERED MEDIATION IN CIRCUIT CIVIL, FAMILY, NO. 1.16 DEPENDENCY, AND COUNTY COURT CIVIL CASES

WHEREAS, certain contested civil and domestic disputes can be amicably and expeditiously resolved through mediation prior to hearing by the Court; and

WHEREAS, mediation is a process whereby a neutral third person acts to encourage the resolution of disputes through a non-adversarial process and assists the parties in reaching a mutually acceptable agreement; and

WHEREAS, the mediation process can result in cost efficiencies to the parties and the Court; and

WHEREAS, mandatory mediation for certain matters increases the availability of judicial resources; and

WHEREAS, the use of mediation is necessary for the prompt and efficient administration of justice in the Courts of the Twentieth Judicial Circuit;

Now therefore, pursuant to the authority vested in the Chief Judge by Rule 2.215 of the Florida Rules of Judicial Administration, and for the purpose of formally memorializing the established procedures utilized within the Twentieth Judicial Circuit,

It is hereby **ORDERED** as follows;

1. Court Mediation Program: The Court Mediation Program serves the purpose of facilitating mediation of allowed contested matters in Circuit Civil, Family, Dependency, and County Court Civil cases. This program is conducted under the direction of the Administrative Office of the Courts, the Court Administrator, and the Chief Judge of the Twentieth Judicial Circuit. The program is governed by applicable Florida Statutes, Rules of Procedure, and local rules.

2. Program Coverage:

a. *Charlotte County*: This program offers dispute resolution services in Small Claims Court through the use of Florida Supreme Court certified County Court mediators, who serve as volunteers. Florida Supreme Court certified Circuit Civil, Family, Dependency, and County Court mediators, who are compensated, mediate Circuit Civil, Family, Dependency, and County Court Civil cases above Small Claims Court jurisdiction. Circuit Civil mediators do not have contracts with the Court. All other compensated mediators have contracts with the Court and are assigned cases based upon party request, individual competencies, qualifications, or subject matter expertise.

b. *Collier County*: This program offers dispute resolution services in Small Claims Court through the use of Florida Supreme Court certified County Court mediators, who serve as volunteers. This program further offers dispute resolution services through the use of a Florida Supreme Court certified staff mediator who addresses Family, County Court Civil, and Small Claims Court cases. In the event no staff mediator is available, contract mediators certified by the Florida Supreme Court will mediate cases for compensation, and will be assigned cases based upon party request, individual competencies, qualifications, or subject matter expertise.

c. *Lee County*: This program offers dispute resolution services in Small Claims Court through the use of Florida Supreme Court certified County Court mediators, who serve as volunteers. Florida Supreme Court certified Circuit Civil, Family, Dependency, and County Court mediators, who are compensated, mediate Circuit Civil, Family, Dependency, and County Court Civil cases above Small Claims Court jurisdiction. Circuit Civil mediators do not have contracts with the Court. All other compensated mediators have contracts with the Court, and are assigned cases based upon party request, individual competencies, qualifications, or subject matter expertise.

d. *Hendry and Glades Counties*: Dispute resolution services are provided by the Lee County Mediation Program.

3. Contact Information:

a. *Court Mediation Programs*: Mediation services can be obtained by contacting the Court Mediation Program in the appropriate county. Below is the contact information for each county's Court Mediation Program. The addresses listed below shall be used for all notices to be served on the Court Mediation Program:

Charlotte County: Charlotte County Court Mediation Program, Charlotte County Justice Center, 350 East Marion Avenue, Punta Gorda, Florida 33950. Telephone: (941) 637–2281

Collier County: Collier County Court Mediation Program, Collier County Government Complex, 3315 Tamiami Trail E, Suite 504, Naples, Florida 34112. Telephone: (239) 252–8704

Lee County: Lee County Court Mediation Program, Lee County Justice Center, 1700 Monroe Street, Ft Myers, Florida 33901. Telephone: (239) 533–3353

Hendry and Glades Counties: Contact the Lee County Court Mediation Program for mediation of cases in these counties.

b. *Current Contact Information of Parties/Attorneys*: Parties and their attorneys, if represented, are required to provide their current address and telephone number to the Court for inclusion in the court file. If mediation has been court-ordered, the parties and attorneys, if represented, shall provide the Court Mediation Program with their current address and telephone number if there has been a change.

4. Authority to Refer to Mediation: Pursuant to Chapter 44, Florida Statutes, Fla. R. Civ. P. 1.700, et seq., Fla. R. Juv. P. 8.290, and Fla. Fam. L. R. P. 12.740 and 12.741, the Court, on its own motion, may refer all or any part of a filed civil action, including family matters, to mediation for the purpose of resolution of any contested issue. Family matters, including married and unmarried persons before and after judgments involving dissolution of marriage, shared or sole parental responsibility, child residency, child support, payment of alimony, child visitation, or distribution of property, involving emotional or financial considerations may be referred to mediation. Any party may request referral to mediation within the limitations established by statute or rule. However, in accordance with Fla. R. Civ. P. 1.710(b), under no circumstances may bond estreatures, bond validations, petitions for extraordinary writs, or contempt actions be referred to mediation.

All qualified contested Circuit Civil, Family, and County Court Civil cases will be automatically referred to an Alternative Dispute Resolution process within limitations established by statute or rule, unless waived by the presiding judge. Dependency Court cases will be referred to mediation upon order of the presiding judge.

5. Exception: History of Domestic Violence: Pursuant to section 44.102(2)(c), Florida Statutes, upon motion or request of a party, the Court shall not refer any case to mediation if it finds there has been a history of domestic violence that would compromise the mediation process. If such an issue exists, the party shall contact and advise the Court Mediation Program.

6. List of Mediators: A list of Florida Supreme Court certified mediators is maintained by the Florida Supreme Court's Dispute Resolution Center and is available on the Florida State Courts' website (www.flcourts.org). The list identifies individuals by their area of certification and location of where they wish to mediate. Certified mediators participating in the Court Mediation Program who mediate Family, Dependency, and County Court Civil cases above Small Claims Court, shall have a contract with the Court to provide this service. The Administrative Office of the Courts of the Twentieth Judicial Circuit administers all contracts and maintains a record of those individuals who have a contract.

7. Appointment of Mediators: In cases of court-ordered mediation, the parties have ten (10) days from the Mediation Order of Referral to select a mediator and notify the Court Mediation Program of the selection. If the parties have not agreed on a mediator, the Court Mediation Program or presiding judge shall appoint a Florida Supreme Court certified mediator to mediate the case. If the parties choose to use a private mediator, they shall notify the Court as to the date of mediation and the identity of the mediator. In Small Claims Court cases, the mediator will be assigned on the day of the pretrial conference.

In Collier County, the staff mediator will mediate cases referred to the Court Mediation Program. Cases not referred to the Court Mediation Program will be mediated by a mediator selected by the parties or by the presiding judge based on individual mediator competence, qualification or subject matter expertise. In the absence of a staff mediator, cases referred to the Court Mediation Program will have a contract mediator assigned based on a request of the parties or by individual mediator competence, qualification or subject matter expertise. Mediators in Small Claims Court cases shall be assigned randomly.

In Charlotte, Hendry, Glades and Lee Counties, contract mediators will mediate cases referred to the Court Mediation Program. In cases referred to the Court Mediation Program, mediators will be selected based on a request of the parties or by individual mediator competence, qualification or subject matter expertise. Cases not referred to the Court Mediation Program will be mediated by a mediator selected by the parties or by the presiding judge based on individual mediator competence, qualification or subject matter expertise. Mediators in Small Claims Court cases shall be assigned randomly.

8. Notice of Cancellation by Party: In order to cancel court-ordered mediation, the requesting party or parties must do one of the following at least three (3) full business days prior to the scheduled mediation, excluding the date of mediation:

a. File a motion with the Court requesting cancellation of the mediation, with notice being given to the Court Mediation Program;

b. Provide documentation to the Court and the Court Mediation Program that all current issues have been mediated and an impasse has been declared;

c. Provide documentation to the Court and the Court Mediation Program that a private mediation has been scheduled, providing the name of the mediator and the date of the mediation;

d. Provide documentation to the Court Mediation Program that a default has been entered; or

e. Provide documentation to the Court Mediation Program that the presiding judge has cancelled the mediation.

If appropriate notice of cancellation is not provided to the Court Mediation Program at least three (3) full business days prior to the date of the scheduled mediation, excluding the date of mediation, payment of a late cancellation fee may be required. If the late cancellation fee is not paid, an Order to Show Cause may be issued requiring the party to appear before the Court to answer to the nonpayment, and the Court may assess additional sanctions against the party. A fee paid as a late cancellation fee shall not be applied as payment for any subsequently scheduled mediation.

9. Cancellations, Rescheduling, and Continuances by the Parties:

a. *Cancellations*: A mediation session must be cancelled by order of the Court if required by the presiding judge, or by stipulation of the parties if no order is required by the presiding judge. The written order or stipulation of cancellation shall be provided to the Court Mediation Program at least three (3) full business days prior to the mediation date, excluding the date of mediation. Failure to provide timely written notification to the Court Mediation Program may result in the *assessment of a late* cancellation fee.

b. *Late Cancellation Fee*:

(1) Family and County Court Civil: In Family law cases in which the parties have a combined income of less than $100,000.00 per year, and in County Court Civil cases, if mediation is not cancelled at least three (3) full business days prior to the mediation date, excluding the date of mediation, with documentation of cancellation being provided to the Court Mediation Program, a late cancellation fee equal to each parties' session fee may be assessed. This fee shall be paid to the Clerk of Court and shall not be applied to any future mediation. In Family law cases in which the parties have a combined income is $100,000.00 or more per year, if mediation is not cancelled at least three (3) full business days prior to the mediation, exclusive of the date of mediation, with documentation of cancellation being provided to the Court Mediation Program, the parties may be assessed a two (2) hour late cancellation fee. The fee shall be paid directly to the assigned mediator, and shall not be applied to any subsequently scheduled mediation. Additional sanctions may be levied by the Court for a mediator's enforcement of the late cancellation fee.

(2) Circuit Civil: If mediation is not cancelled at least three (3) full business days prior to the mediation date, excluding the date of mediation, with documentation of cancellation being provided to the Court Mediation Program, the parties may be assessed a two (2) hour late cancellation fee. The fee shall be paid directly to the assigned mediator, and shall not be applied to any subsequently scheduled mediation. Additional sanctions may be levied by the Court for a mediator's enforcement of the late cancellation fee.

c. *Cancellation; attorney called to trial*: If an attorney is called to trial less than three (3) business days before a scheduled mediation session, the attorney must immediately notify the other party and the Court Mediation Program. For verification purposes the notification shall include the case number and name of the presiding judge of the conflicting case. If such notice is received by at least 3:30 p.m. on the business day that precedes the mediation date, only one-half the normal late cancellation fee is required. Notice received after 3:30 p.m. on the business day that precedes the mediation date may necessitate payment of the full late cancellation fee.

d. *Rescheduling*: In order to reschedule a Family, Dependency or County Court Civil mediation, the parties are required to provide the Court Mediation Program with a firm rescheduled date agreeable to all parties. The rescheduled date shall be no more than thirty (30) days from the current mediation date. In Family and County Court Civil cases in which there have been more than two (2) rescheduled dates, the parties may be subject to a rescheduling fee equal to the cost of one (1) session of mediation.

e. *Continuances by the Parties*: A continued mediation occurs when the mediator gives an opening statement and the parties agree to begin another mediation session at a subsequent time. Fees paid for the initial session shall not be applied to any subsequent session.

10. Attendance of Parties and Counsel:

a. *Parties*: Each named party shall appear at any scheduled mediation session, unless that party has been dismissed from the case or has been dismissed from attendance by the presiding judge. A party is deemed to appear at mediation if that party is physically present at the commencement of the mediation or has appeared telephonically with written permission of the presiding judge. Upon the Court's own motion, or upon motion of the appearing party or the Court Mediation Program, a party's failure to appear for the mediation session may result in sanctions being imposed by the Court against the non-appearing party, including, but not limited to, payment of session fees and attorney fees, if any. These fees shall not be applied to any subsequently scheduled mediation. If an indigent party fails to appear at mediation, sanctions, including cost of a mediation session for both parties, shall be assessed.

b. *Family Cases; counsel*: In Family law cases, the mediation session may proceed in the absence of counsel, unless otherwise ordered by the Court. Parties in Family law cases are not required to have counsel.

c. *Dependency Cases: Counsel*: In Dependency cases, parties' counsel are required to attend mediation unless dismissed by the presiding judge.

d. *Circuit Civil Cases*: In Circuit Civil cases, it is mandatory that the following persons be physically present at mediation, unless specifically provided otherwise by the Court:

(1) The party or its representative, other than its outside counsel, having full authority to settle without further consideration, shall attend.

(2) The party's counsel of record, if any, shall attend. If another attorney will try the case, the attorney who will try the case shall also attend.

(3) If insurance is involved, a representative of the insurance carrier for any insured party, who is not such carrier's outside counsel and who has full authority to settle without further consultation, shall attend.

(4) If a party to mediation is a public entity required to conduct its business pursuant to Chapter 286, Florida Statutes, that party shall be deemed to appear at a mediation

conference by the physical presence of a representative with full authority to negotiate on behalf of the entity and to recommend settlement to the appropriate decision-making body of the entity. See Fla. R. Civ. P. 1.720.

11. Appearance by Telephone: In case of an emergency, in the event of physical disability, when a party is incarcerated, or when a party resides in excess of one-hundred (100) miles from the Mediation Program location, that party may request an appearance by telephone. Requirements established by the presiding judge will dictate what actions are required when a party wishes to appear by telephone at a mediation conference.

12. Confidentially [1] of Communications During Mediation: In accordance with sections 44.401–44.406, Florida Statutes, known as the Mediation Confidentiality and Privilege Act, with the exception of the parties' signed financial affidavits and any other documents which are required to be filed in the public record, all communications, verbal or written, between the parties and from the parties made during the mediation session, shall be confidential. Confidentiality is to be strictly maintained in accordance with the law. The privileges and exceptions provided for by the Mediation Confidentiality and Privilege Act apply in all cases, and nothing herein shall be construed as limiting or expanding those privileges and exceptions. Civil remedies for violating the Mediation Confidentiality and Privilege Act are provided for by section 44.406, Florida Statutes.

13. Professionalism of Mediators: Mediators shall abide by all standards of professional conduct established by the Florida Supreme Court. Mediators are not authorized to conduct, communicate, nor submit evaluations or recommendations to the Court, nor to otherwise professionally compromise his or her role as mediator with other inapplicable roles such as, investigator, evaluator, therapist, or legal advisor. Mediators shall comply with reporting procedures at the conclusion of mediation and shall report to the Court and the Court Mediation Program designee the fact of attendance or nonattendance at all court-ordered mediation sessions, the existence or non-existence of a mediated agreement or mediated partial agreement, and other information as agreed by all parties.

14. Mediation Session Costs Through the Court Mediation Program:

a. *Fees; General*: The fee for Family and County Court Civil mediations are established by section 44.108, Florida Statutes. The fee for Circuit Civil mediations are provided for by the presiding judge's Mediation Order of Referral. Any portion of an hour will be billed as a full hour. There are no mediation fees for Dependency mediations, nor are there mediation fees for mediation in residential eviction cases, small claims actions, or against parties found to be indigent.

b. *Indigency*: A party with an Application for Determination of Civil Indigent Status and a determination of indigency on file with the Clerk of Court as it relates to the case at issue will not be assessed mediation fees pursuant to section 44.108, Florida Statutes. However, fees assessed as a penalty for failure to abide by a Court Order, or as a late cancellation fee or failure to appear fee, do not constitute mediation fees and are not excused by a prior or subsequent determination of indigency.

c. *Family Cases; Fees*: The fee for Family mediation is paid by the parties and is based on the parties' combined income. The fee is $60.00 per party, per session, if the parties' combined income is less than $50,000.00 per year. The fee is $120.00 per party, per session, if the parties' combined income is greater than $50,000.00 per year and is less than $100,000.00 per year. A session in a Family mediation is identified as a period of time up to three (3) hours in length. Parties will not be required to pay an additional fee until three (3) consecutive hours of mediation have been completed. A continued mediation requires payment of a new fee. If proof of income is not provided, the mediation fee will be assessed at the $120.00 per party, per session rate. Parties having a combined income of $100,000.00 or more per year shall share the cost of mediation equally and, unless a staff mediator is used, shall pay the mediator directly at a rate of $150.00 per hour.

d. *County Court Civil Cases; Fees*: There is no fee to the parties for court-based mediation of Small Claims Court cases when mediated at the pretrial conference. A Small Claims Court session is identified as a period of time one (1) hour in length. There is a fee of $60.00 per party, per session, for those County Court Civil cases filed above the Small Claims Court jurisdictional limit. A County Court Civil mediation session is identified as a block of time of up to ninety (90) minutes in length. Parties will not be required to pay an additional fee until ninety (90) consecutive minutes of mediation have been completed. A continued mediation requires payment of a new fee.

e. *Circuit Civil Cases; Fees*: For Circuit Civil cases, parties shall share the cost of mediation equally and shall pay the mediator directly at a rate of $150.00 per hour. Failure to abide by provisions in the Mediation Order of Referral, or in any other mediation order, may result in penalties.

f. *Dependency Cases; Fees*: Parties will not be assessed a fee for mediation of Dependency cases.

g. *Method of Payment*:

(1) Family and County Court Civil: In Family law cases in which the parties have a combined income of less than $100,000.00 per year, and in County Court Civil cases, prior to the start of the mediation conference, mediation fees shall be paid at the office of the Clerk of Court in the county where the case was filed. The mediation fee may be paid by cash, check, or money order. A Clerk of Court may accept payment by credit card, which may require charging a processing fee. Verification of ability to pay by credit card must be confirmed with the appropriate Clerk of Court, as not all Clerk's offices accept payment in this manner. The Clerk of Court determines if credit card payment over the telephone is acceptable. In Family law cases in which parties have a combined income of $100,000.00 or more per year, mediation fees shall be paid directly to the mediator immediately upon conclusion of the mediation conference.

(2) Circuit Civil: Mediation fees shall be paid directly to the mediator immediately upon conclusion of the mediation conference.

h. *Failure to Pay Mediation Session Fee*:

(1) Family and County Court Civil: In Family law cases in which the parties have a combined income of less than $100,000.00 per year, and in County Court Civil cases, if the party or parties fail to pay the mediation fee in advance and

the mediation session does not go forward, the nonpaying party or parties shall be termed a "no show," which shall be reported to the Court. The "no show" party or parties will be required to pay a fee equal to the assessed session fee for both parties. If the required fee is not paid, an Order to Show Cause may be issued requiring the nonpaying party or parties to appear before a judicial officer to answer for the nonpayment. The Court may assess additional sanctions against the nonpaying party or parties. This "no show" fee shall be paid prior to start of the next or rescheduled mediation session and shall not be credited as payment for the next or rescheduled mediation session. In Family law cases in which the parties have a combined income of $100,000.00 or more per year, if the party or parties fail to pay the mediation fee upon conclusion of the mediation, the party or parties shall be required to pay the fee and for the time that the mediator spends enforcing the Court's order. The nonpaying party or parties may be further sanctioned by the Court.

(2) Circuit Civil: If the party or parties fail to pay the mediation fee upon conclusion of the mediation, the party or parties shall be required to pay the fee and for the time that the mediator spends enforcing the Court's order. The nonpaying party or parties may be further sanctioned by the Court.

i. *Failure to Appear Fee*:

(1) Family and County Court Civil: In Family law cases in which the parties have a combined income of less than $100,000.00 per year, and in County Court Civil cases, if a party or parties fail to appear as ordered by the Mediation Order of Referral and has not cancelled the mediation at least three (3) full business days prior to the mediation date, excluding the date of mediation, and provided cancellation documentation to the Court Mediation Program, the non-appearing party or parties will be required to pay a fee equal to the assessed session fee for both parties. If the required fee is not paid, an Order To Show Cause may be issued requiring the nonpaying party or parties to appear before a judicial officer to answer for the nonpayment. The non-appearing party or parties may be further sanctioned by the Court. A fee paid as a penalty for failure to appear at mediation shall be paid to the Clerk of Court and shall not be applied as payment for any subsequently scheduled mediation. In Family law cases where the parties have a combined income of $100,000.00 or more per year, if the party or parties fail to appear at mediation and have not cancelled the mediation at least three (3) full business days prior to the mediation date, excluding the date of mediation, and provided cancellation documentation to the Court Mediation program, the non-appearing party or parties shall compensate the mediator by paying a two (2) hour mediation fee. This fee shall not be applied as payment for any subsequently scheduled mediation.

(2) Circuit Civil: If a party fails to appear as ordered by the Mediation Order of Referral and has not cancelled the mediation at least three (3) full business days prior to the mediation date, excluding the date of mediation, and provided cancellation documentation to the Court Mediation Program, the non-appearing party or parties shall compensate the assigned mediator by paying a two (2) hour mediation fee. This fee shall not be applied as payment for any subsequently scheduled mediation.

15. Mediator Compensation: Regardless of the mediation fee paid by the parties, contract mediators shall be compensated as follows:

a. Small Claims Court Mediators shall not be compensated for cases addressed at the pretrial conference.

b. County Court Mediators, when mediating cases above the Small Claims Court jurisdiction, will be compensated at a statutorily set rate of $50.00 per hour.

c. Family Law Mediators shall be compensated at a statutorily set rate of $100.00 per hour.

d. Dependency Mediators shall be compensated at a statutorily set rate of $100.00 per hour.

e. Circuit Civil Court Mediators shall be compensated at a rate of $150.00 per hour.

16. General Provisions:

a. This Administrative Order shall remain in effect until amended, modified, or vacated.

b. To the extent that this Administrative Order may conflict with any law or rule, the law or rule shall control.

DONE AND ORDERED in Chambers at Fort Myers, Lee County, Florida, this 12 day of June, 2013.

Jay B. Rosman
Chief Judge

History.—New.

[1] So in original. Probably should be "Confidentiality".

1.17. CASE STATUS REPORTING REQUIREMENTS FOR REAL PROPERTY MORTGAGE FORECLOSURE CASES

IN THE TWENTIETH JUDICIAL CIRCUIT IN AND FOR THE STATE OF FLORIDA

IN RE: CASE STATUS REPORTING REQUIREMENTS FOR REAL PROPERTY MORTGAGE FORECLOSURE CASES

ADMINISTRATIVE ORDER NO. 1.17

WHEREAS, the Supreme Court of Florida has adopted definitions as it relates to the status of foreclosure cases as published in the Foreclosure Initiative Data Plan promulgated by the Office of the State Courts Administrator; and

WHEREAS, on October 16, 2013, the Supreme Court of Florida issued Administrative Order No. AOSC13–51, In Re: Case Status Reporting Requirements for Real Property Mortgage Foreclosure Cases, directing that the chief judge of every circuit issue a local administrative order for the purpose of implementing an effective communication mechanism by which the courts and clerks are notified of case status changes in a timely manner;

It is **ORDERED** as follows:

1. For purposes of data collection and statistical reporting, the Clerks of Court of each county of the Twentieth Judicial Circuit are to be mindful of the Supreme Court of Florida Administrative Order No. AOSC13–51 and the Foreclosure Initiative Data Collection Plan, copies of which are attached and incorporated herein, so as to ensure full compliance.

2. For ease of reference, listed below are the events identified in the Foreclosure Initiative Data Collection Plan as causing the status of a foreclosure case to shift back and forth between being active and inactive, along with the associated reporting codes:

Reason	Codes	
	Active to Inactive	Inactive to Active
A stay of bankruptcy	BKST	BKSTLFT
Resolution of foreclosure case requires resolution of a related case	CPRC	CPCSDISP
On-going settlement negotiations or agreement by both parties	BWAP	BWAPDISP
Foreclosure case is on hold pending appeal	AP	APDISP
A hold is placed on case due to Dept. of Justice or Attorney General Review	DOJAG	DOJAGDISP
When directed by the presiding judge consistent with the definitions of an inactive case	OTH	OTHDISP

3. In instances in which a Clerk may become aware of an event initiating a change in status of a case, based upon a court order or otherwise (i.e. the filing of a suggestion of bankruptcy), the Clerk shall enter said change in status in its Case Management System, using the appropriate code, so that judges, magistrates, case managers, and judicial assistants are timely apprised of the proper status of each case within their purview.

4. In instances in which the Court may become aware of an event initiating a change in status of a case of which the Clerk appears to be unaware, the Court shall issue an order directing the change in status. The Foreclosure Initiative Data Collection Plan provides on Page 24 a form "Order Placing Case on Inactive Status," and on Page 25 a form "Order Renaming Case to Active Status." Attached to this Administrative Order are sample orders that have been tailored specifically for use within the Twentieth Judicial Circuit, and which may be used at the discretion of the Court. Said orders either placing a case on inactive status or returning a case to active status, shall serve to provide notice to the Clerk as to a change in status, and the Clerk shall immediately enter said change in status in its Case Management System, using the appropriate code.

5. It is ultimately the responsibility of the parties to a foreclosure action to ensure that the Court and Clerk are appropriately and timely advised as to events external to the Court which may impact the status of a case as being active or inactive. If a foreclosure case is in an inactive status, it is the responsibility of the parties to file with the Clerk a written motion to return the case to an active status, with notice to all parties, within thirty (30) days of the termination of the grounds for inactive status.

6. To the extent that any provision of this Administrative Order may conflict with any rule, case law, or statute, the rule, case law, or statute will prevail.

DONE AND ORDERED in chambers in Fort Myers, Lee County, Florida, this 27th day of Nov., 2013.

Jay B. Rosman
Chief Judge

History. —New.

Sample Form Order #1

IN THE CIRCUIT COURT OF THE TWENTIETH JUDICIAL CIRCUIT IN AND FOR COUNTY, FLORIDA CIVIL DIVISION

______________,

Plaintiff(s),

vs. **Case No.** ______________

______________,

Defendant(s).

______________/

ORDER PLACING FORECLOSURE CASE ON INACTIVE STATUS

This cause having come before the Court on its own motion or on the motion of the Plaintiff/Defendant to place the case on INACTIVE status due to:

- ☐ Bankruptcy stay, Case No. ______________ **[BKST]**
- ☐ Case pending resolution of another case, Case No. ______________ **[CPRC]**
- ☐ Written agreement of the parties dated ______________ **[BWAP]**
- ☐ Appeal pending, Case No. ______________ **[AP]**
- ☐ Motion to stay or abate due to Department of Justice/Attorney General settlement **[DO JAG]**
- ☐ Other (a reason must be provided in writing by the presiding judge or designee) **[OTH]**

____

____

The Clerk of Court is therefore directed to remove this case from **ACTIVE** status, and designate it as an **INACTIVE** case based on the reason checked above. The parties must return the case to active status by filing a motion seeking an order returning the case to active status, with notice to all parties, within 30 days of the termination of grounds for inactive status.

DONE and **ORDERED** in ______________ County, Florida, this ___ day of ______________ 20___.

____
Presiding Judge

Sample Form Order #2

IN THE CIRCUIT COURT OF THE TWENTIETH JUDICIAL CIRCUIT IN AND FOR COUNTY, FLORIDA CIVIL DIVISION

______________,

Plaintiff(s),

vs. **Case No.** ______

______________,

Defendant(s).

______________/

ORDER RETURNING FORECLOSURE CASE TO ACTIVE STATUS

This cause having come before the Court on its own motion or on the motion of the Plaintiff/Defendant to return the case to ACTIVE status due to:

- ☐ Plaintiff/Defendant stipulate that the bankruptcy stay has been lifted, Case No. ______ **[BKSTLFT]**
- ☐ Plaintiff/Defendant stipulate that the related case has been disposed, Case No. ______ **[CPCSDISP]**
- ☐ By written agreement of the parties dated ______ **[BWAPDISP]**
- ☐ Plaintiff/Defendant stipulate that pending appeal has been disposed, Case No. ______ **[APDISP]**
- ☐ Plaintiff/Defendant stipulates that Department of Justice/Attorney General review is complete **[DOJAGDISP]**
- ☐ Other (a reason must be provided in writing by the presiding judge or designee) **[OTHDISP]**

____

____

The Clerk of Court is therefore directed to remove this case from **INACTIVE** status, and designate it as an **ACTIVE** case based on the reason checked above.

DONE and **ORDERED** in ______ County, Florida, this ___ day of ______ 20 ___.

____

Presiding Judge

Supreme Court of Florida

No. AOSC 13–51

IN RE: CASE STATUS REPORTING REQUIREMENTS FOR REAL PROPERTY MORTGAGE FORECLOSURE CASES

ADMINISTRATIVE ORDER

Consistent with In Re: Final Report and Recommendations of the Foreclosure Initiative Workgroup, No. AOSC13–28 (Fla. June 21, 2013), this Court finds it beneficial to require the chief judge of every circuit court to issue an administrative order establishing a mechanism that enables judges and magistrates to provide explicit direction to each clerk of court's office with regard to designating a change in the status of a mortgage foreclosure case. Likewise, it is also necessary for the clerk of court's office to notify the judge or magistrate when events occur that change the status of a foreclosure case. This Court recognizes that, in many instances, the events initiating a change in the status of a case may become known to either the judge and magistrate or the clerk's office, but not always both. Accordingly, the purpose of the local administrative orders is to implement an effective communications mechanism by which the courts and clerks are notified of case status changes in a timely manner.

The status of a foreclosure case and related definitions have been adopted by this Court and are published in the Foreclosure Initiative Data Collection Plan [1] promulgated by the Office of the State Courts Administrator. Explicit direction for designating the status of cases as active or inactive shall be implemented through an administrative order issued by the circuit chief judge. It is incumbent on each clerk of court to enter the status change of any case so that judges, magistrates, case managers, and judicial assistants are apprised of the proper status of each case within their purview.

For case age reporting purposes, a case on inactive status should not be considered pending until it becomes active by order of the presiding judge or action by the clerk of court.

DONE AND ORDERED at Tallahassee, Florida, on October 16, 2013.

Ricky Polston, Chief Justice

[1] Foreclosure Initiative Data Collection Plan not included. Please see https://www.ca.cjis20.org/pdf/ao/ao_1_17.pdf for published plan.

1.18. STANDING ORDERS AND CIVIL CASE MANAGEMENT PLANS IN RESIDENTIAL MORTGAGE FORECLOSURE CASES IN LEE COUNTY

IN THE TWENTIETH JUDICIAL CIRCUIT IN AND FOR THE STATE OF FLORIDA LEE COUNTY

IN RE: STANDING ORDERS AND CIVIL CASE MANAGEMENT PLANS IN RESIDENTIAL MORTGAGE FORECLOSURE CASES IN LEE COUNTY

ADMINISTRATIVE ORDER NO. 1.18

WHEREAS, it is in the best interest of the citizens of the Twentieth Judicial Circuit for the Court to develop innovative means to further improve the fair, predictable, efficient, and timely disposition of civil cases in the civil division of the Circuit Court; and

WHEREAS, under Rule 2.545(b), Florida Rules of Judicial Administration, the Supreme Court of Florida has established guidelines for the prompt processing and resolution of civil cases, and has expressly mandated that the Court "shall take charge of all cases at an early stage in the litigation and shall control the progress of the case thereafter until the case is determined;" and

WHEREAS, since 2010, the Lee County Circuit Courts have utilized Civil Differentiated Case Management (DCM) Procedures, as approved by local Administrative Order 1.13; and

WHEREAS, the Civil DCM Procedures for the Lee County Circuit Courts exempt residential foreclosure cases from certain procedures, including the initial issuance of a Standing Order and the requirement of case management plans in individual residential foreclosure cases; and

WHEREAS, since 2010, alternative means of case management of residential foreclosure cases have been utilized throughout the State of Florida, and specifically in the Lee County Circuit Courts, to address the special circumstances involving the inordinately large and sudden influx and backlog of residential foreclosure cases; and

WHEREAS, the case management of residential foreclosure cases in Lee County has been successful in addressing the sudden influx of residential foreclosure cases and in reducing the backlog; and

WHEREAS, current caseloads, changing circumstances, and an evaluation of shifting resources have led to a determination that it is in the best interest of the fair, predictable, efficient, and timely disposition of residential foreclosure cases in the Lee County Circuit Court to implement Standing Orders and case management plans for individual residential foreclosure cases; and

WHEREAS, under Rule 2.250(a)(1)(B), Florida Rules of Judicial Administration, the time standard deemed by the Supreme Court of Florida to be presumptively reasonable for the disposition of civil non-jury cases is twelve (12) months from filing to final disposition;

NOW, THEREFORE, pursuant to the authority prescribed by Fla. R. Jud. Admin. 2.215, and for the purpose of promoting the efficient administration of justice within the Twentieth Judicial Circuit, it is **ORDERED** as follows:

1. Included as part of this Administrative Order as "Attachment A" is a form "Standing Order in Residential Mortgage Foreclosure Cases in Lee County," which the Plaintiff shall, in all residential mortgage foreclosure cases filed in Lee County on or after May 1, 2015, serve with each summons issued in the case. The Plaintiff shall be responsible for paying the Clerk the appropriate statutory fee for copies of each Standing Order issued.

2. In addition, in all residential mortgage foreclosure cases filed in Lee County on or after May 1, 2015, and upon the filing of a responsive pleading by any defendant, the Court shall issue a "Residential Foreclosure Case Management Plan and Order" utilizing the Florida Supreme Court's presumptively reasonable time standard of 12 months from filing to final disposition, a form of which is included as part of this Administrative Order as "Attachment B." Prior to issuance of a "Residential Foreclosure Case Management Plan and Order," the established timeframes included as "Attachment B" may only be altered by the Circuit Judge assigned to the case. Once issued by the Circuit Judge assigned to the case, the Case Management Plan may only be amended upon approval by the Circuit Judge assigned to the case.

3. For pending residential mortgage foreclosure cases filed prior to May 1, 2015, and which are not scheduled for trial, the Court will issue the "Standing Order in Residential Mortgage Foreclosure Cases in Lee County" (Attachment A) and will serve copies on all parties. In addition, as it relates to such cases, if a responsive pleading has already been filed, or upon the filing of a responsive pleading, the assigned Circuit Judge will issue a "Residential Foreclosure Case Management Plan and Order" (Attachment B) establishing mandatory timeframes as may be deemed appropriate by that Judge for the purpose of ensuring the fair and timely disposition of the case, based upon the presumptively reasonable time standards established by the Florida Supreme Court. Once issued by the Circuit Judge assigned to the case, the Case Management Plan may only be amended upon approval by the Circuit Judge assigned to the case.

4. Notwithstanding the above paragraph, for pending residential mortgage foreclosure cases filed prior to May 1, 2015, and which are at issue and currently scheduled for a Case Management Conference, and have had at least one prior Case Management Conference, the assigned Circuit Judge may, within his or her discretion, cancel the Case Management Conference and may, alternatively, schedule the case for trial by separate order.

5. It shall be noted that the forms included as part of this Administrative Order, Attachments A and B, are intended as models, and any subsequent updates or modifications shall be posted and available for viewing on the Court's website at http://www.ca.cjis20.org/web/main/civil.asp. It shall be the responsibility of all parties to check the website for the most recent forms to be used in conjunction with this Administrative Order.

6. The procedures and time standards set forth herein are intended to facilitate the timely, fair and effective resolution of residential mortgage foreclosure cases while ensuring the efficient use of court resources. The procedures and time standards do not supplant any existing rule, statute, or law. This Administrative Order shall not be construed as granting any rights not already provided for by rule, statute, or law.

7. To the extent that any provision of this Administrative Order may be construed as being in conflict with any rule, statute, or law, the rule, statute, or law shall prevail.

DONE AND ORDERED in chambers in Fort Myers, Lee County, Florida, this 24th day of April, 2015.

Jay B. Rosman
Chief Judge

History. —New

—ATTACHMENT A—

IN THE CIRCUIT COURT FOR THE TWENTIETH JUDICIAL CIRCUIT IN AND FOR LEE COUNTY, FLORIDA

CIVIL ACTION

CASE NO:

_______________,
Petitioner(s),

vs.

_______________,
Defendant(s).
_______________/

STANDING ORDER IN RESIDENTIAL MORTGAGE FORECLOSURE CASES IN LEE COUNTY

PURSUANT to Rules 2.250 and 2.545, Florida Rules of Judicial Administration, and Rule 1.200(a), Florida Rules of Civil Procedure, the parties are ordered to adhere to the following information and procedures applicable to residential mortgage foreclosure civil lawsuits:

1. **SERVICE OF THIS ORDER**. The Plaintiff is directed to serve a copy of this order with each Summons issued in this case. One copy of this Order is to be filed with the Clerk of the Circuit Court with proof of service. The Plaintiff shall

pay the appropriate statutory clerk's fees on copies for each Standing Order issued and attached to the Summons.

2. **CIVIL CASE MANAGEMENT PLAN**. The Supreme Court of Florida has established guidelines for the prompt processing and resolution of civil cases, and has expressly mandated that the Court "shall take charge of all cases at an early stage in the litigation and shall control the progress of the case thereafter until the case is determined." Fla. R. Jud. Admin. 2.545(b). The time standard deemed by the Supreme Court of Florida to be presumptively reasonable for the disposition of civil non-jury cases is 12 months from filing to final disposition. Fla. R. Jud. Admin, 2.250(a)(1)(B). Accordingly, in Residential Mortgage Foreclosure cases filed on or subsequent to May 1, 2015, and upon the filing of a responsive pleading to the complaint, the Court will issue a Case Management Plan establishing mandatory time-frames with the goal of resolution within 12 months.[1] The parties may request that the plan be amended by submitting a proposed agreed amended plan to the Civil Case Management Department, or if unable to agree on an amended plan, by filing a motion with the Court for a Case Management Conference. Trials will be scheduled before the assigned Circuit Judge, Senior Judge or may be referred to a General Magistrate based on the trial date set forth in the Case Management Plan, or earlier than the trial date set forth in the Case Management Plan upon the filing of a notice of readiness for trial.

3. **ALTERNATIVE DISPUTE RESOLUTION (ADR).** Early mediation shall be available pursuant to local Administrative Order No. 1.14, In re: Homestead Mediation Program for Residential Homestead Mortgage Foreclosure Actions, which can be viewed on the website of the Administrative Office of the Courts: http://www.ca.cjis20.org/pdf/ao/ao_1_14.pdf. In the event that the deadlines for seeking early mediation pursuant to Administrative Order No. 1.14 have expired, and a party subsequently requests that the Court direct mediation, or the Court on its own motion orders mediation, the general provisions of Administrative Order No. 1.14 shall apply to any such mediation ordered.

4. **MOTIONS TO CONTINUE TRIAL.** A Motion to Continue any trial must be filed with the clerk and emailed to the Civil Case Management Department at civilcm@ca.cjis20.org. Motions to Continue can only be heard or granted by the assigned circuit judge or by the senior judge or upon recommendation of a magistrate presiding over the trial.

5. **SERVICE OF PLEADINGS.** A copy of all pleadings or motions filed after the initial complaint shall also be provided to the Civil Case Management Department by email or inclusion in the electronic service list at civilCM@ca.cjis20.org

6. **TELEPHONIC APPEARANCE.** A Motion for Telephonic Appearance at any hearing must be filed with the clerk and emailed to the Civil Case Management Department at civil CM@ca.cjis20.org. Motions for Telephonic Appearance can only be heard or granted by the assigned circuit judge or by the senior judge or upon recommendation of a magistrate presiding at the hearing.

7. **RULES OF PROFESSIONALISM.** The Twentieth Judicial Circuit has adopted local Administrative Order 2.20, which sets forth standards of professional courtesy and conduct for all counsel or pro-se litigants practicing within the Circuit. The Court requires that all parties or counsel for parties familiarize themselves and comply with Administrative Order 2.20. Administrative Order 2.20 may be viewed on the website of the Administrative Office of the Courts: http://www.ca.cjis20.org/web/main/ao_admin.asp

DONE AND ORDERED in Chambers at Fort Myers, Lee County, Florida, on May 1, 2015.

____
Alane Laboda, Circuit Judge
Civil Administrative Judge, Lee County

******* Original on file in the office of the Circuit Clerk of Court, Lee County**

—ATTACHMENT B—

IN THE CIRCUIT COURT OF THE TWENTIETH JUDICIAL CIRCUIT IN AND FOR LEE COUNTY, FLORIDA

CIVIL ACTION

*,

Plaintiff(s),

vs. CASE NO: *–CA–*

*, CASE TYPE: CA *

Defendant(s)

______________________/

RESIDENTIAL FORECLOSURE CASE MANAGEMENT PLAN AND ORDER

Expedited Track (Case resolved within 12 months):

Case Deadlines and Events

DEADLINE OR EVENT	*DATE*
Statement of Facts and/or Counterclaim(s)	180 days prior to trial
Identification of facts the parties believe to be disputed	90 days prior to trial
Identification of the issues of law to be decided by the Court	90 days prior to trial
Motions to Add Parties or to Amend Pleadings	180 days prior to trial
Disclosure of Fact Witnesses	180 days prior to trial
Disclosure of Expert Witnesses	180 days prior to trial
Filing of Exhibit List	60 days prior to trial
Discovery & Deadlines: The requesting party shall file all discovery requests and the responding party shall file a No-	Requests must be filed not later than 45 days from answer. Response must be made within 30 days of filing of request if no

tice of Compliance when completed. If the party fails to timely respond, the requesting party shall file a Notice of Non-compliance and/or Motion to Compel no later than 10 days from the due date.	objection filed. Objections to discovery request must be filed not later than 20 days from the filing of the request.
Expert Opinion Available to Opposing Party	160 days prior to trial
Discovery Deadline for Expert Witnesses	90 days prior to trial
Completion of Alternative Dispute Resolution (ADR) (See Residential Foreclosure Standing Order)	30 days prior to trial.
Deadline for Dispositive Motions	Must be heard not less 30 days prior to trial
Other Deadlines or Events: Motions in Limine	Not less than 30 days prior to trial
Trial Information	
Estimated Date the Case Will Be Scheduled To Go To Trial	**12th month from date of filing of complaint**
Estimated Length of Trial	**All trials will be set for one (1) hour; if you need additional time you must contact the Civil Case Management Dept. at Civilcm@ca.cjis20.org no later than 30 days prior to trial.**
Identification of Jury or Non–Jury Trial	**Non–Jury**

The above-referenced schedule of deadlines will be strictly adhered to by the parties unless a change is otherwise agreed to by the parties and approved by the Court. The Court will consider a request to approve changes to these deadlines upon a showing of good cause by either party based on matters arising from an emergency nature or unavailability. However, procrastination in completing discovery or the unavailability of counsel will not constitute good cause for a change to these deadlines. The failure to abide by these deadlines may result in sanctions by the Court, including the award of attorney's fees, the striking of pleadings, and/or a dismissal of the action.

ALL PARTIES SHALL ABIDE BY THE TERMS HEREIN.

DONE AND ORDERED in Fort Myers, Lee County, Florida on ________.

____

Hon. *, Circuit Judge

1 For pending Residential Mortgage Foreclosure Cases filed prior to May 1, 2015, and which are not scheduled for trial, the Court will issue this Standing Order and will serve copies on all parties, Paragraph 1 above shall not apply. The assigned Circuit Judge shall issue a Case Management Plan establishing mandatory time-frames as may be deemed appropriate by that Judge for the purpose of ensuring the fair and timely disposition of the case, based upon the presumptively reasonable time standards established by the Florida Supreme Court. Paragraph 2 above shall otherwise apply, as shall the remainder of this Standing Order.

1.19. STANDING ORDERS AND CIVIL CASE MANAGEMENT PLANS IN RESIDENTIAL MORTGAGE FORECLOSURE CASES IN CHARLOTTE COUNTY

IN THE TWENTIETH JUDICIAL CIRCUIT IN AND FOR THE STATE OF FLORIDA CHARLOTTE COUNTY

IN RE: STANDING ORDERS AND CIVIL CASE MANAGEMENT PLANS IN RESIDENTIAL MORTGAGE FORECLOSURE CASES IN CHARLOTTE COUNTY

ADMINISTRATIVE ORDER NO. 1.19

WHEREAS, it is in the best interest of the citizens of the Twentieth Judicial Circuit for the Court to develop innovative means to further improve the fair, predictable, efficient, and timely disposition of civil cases in the civil division of the Circuit Court; and

WHEREAS, under Rule 2.545(b), Florida Rules of Judicial Administration, the Supreme Court of Florida has established guidelines for the prompt processing and resolution of civil cases, and has expressly mandated that the Court "shall take charge of all cases at an early stage in the litigation and shall control the progress of the case thereafter until the case is determined;" and

WHEREAS, since 2012, the Charlotte County Circuit Courts have utilized Civil Differentiated Case Management (DCM) Procedures, as approved by local Administrative Order 1.13; and

WHEREAS, the Civil DCM Procedures for the Charlotte County Circuit Courts exempt residential foreclosure cases from certain procedures, including the initial issuance of a Standing Order; and

WHEREAS, since 2012, alternative means of case management of residential foreclosure cases have been utilized throughout the State of Florida, and specifically in the Charlotte County Circuit Courts, to address the special circumstances involving the inordinately large and sudden influx and backlog of residential foreclosure cases; and

WHEREAS, the case management of residential foreclosure cases in Charlotte County has been successful in addressing the sudden influx of residential foreclosure cases and in reducing the backlog; and

WHEREAS, current caseloads, changing circumstances, and an evaluation of shifting resources have led to a determination that it is in the best interest of the fair, predictable, efficient, and timely disposition of residential foreclosure cases in the Charlotte County Circuit Court to implement Standing Orders and case management plans for individual residential foreclosure cases; and

WHEREAS, under Rule 2.250(a)(1)(B), Florida Rules of Judicial Administration, the time standard deemed by the Supreme Court of Florida to be presumptively reasonable for the disposition of civil non-jury cases is twelve (12) months from filing to final disposition;

NOW, THEREFORE, pursuant to the authority prescribed by Fla. R. Jud. Admin. 2.215, and for the purpose of promoting the efficient administration of justice within the Twentieth Judicial Circuit, it is **ORDERED** as follows:

1. Included as part of this Administrative Order as "Attachment A" is a form "Standing Order in Residential Mortgage Foreclosure Cases in Charlotte County," which the Plaintiff shall, in all residential mortgage foreclosure cases filed in Charlotte County on or after August 1, 2015, serve with each summons issued in the case. The Plaintiff shall be responsible for paying the Clerk the appropriate statutory fee for copies of each Standing Order issued.

2. In addition, in all residential mortgage foreclosure cases filed in Charlotte County on or after August 1, 2015, and upon the filing of a responsive pleading by any defendant, the Court shall issue a "Residential Foreclosure Case Management Plan and Order" utilizing the Florida Supreme Court's presumptively reasonable time standard of 12 months from filing to final disposition, a form of which is included as part of this Administrative Order as "Attachment B." Prior to issuance of a "Residential Foreclosure Case Management Plan and Order," the established timeframes included as "Attachment B" may only be altered by the Circuit Judge assigned to the case. Once issued by the Circuit Judge assigned to the case, the Case Management Plan may only be amended upon approval by the Circuit Judge assigned to the case.

3. For pending residential mortgage foreclosure cases filed prior to August 1, 2015, and which are at issue and currently scheduled for a Case Management Conference, and have had at least one prior Case Management Conference, the assigned Circuit Judge may, within his or her discretion, cancel the Case Management Conference and may, alternatively, schedule the case for trial by separate order.

4. It shall be noted that the forms included as part of this Administrative Order, Attachments A and B, are intended as models, and any subsequent updates or modifications shall be posted and available for viewing on the Court's website at http://www.ca.cjis20.org/web/main/civil.asp. It shall be the responsibility of all parties to check the website for the most recent forms to be used in conjunction with this Administrative Order.

5. The procedures and time standards set forth herein are intended to facilitate the timely, fair and effective resolution of residential mortgage foreclosure cases while ensuring the efficient use of court resources. The procedures and time standards do not supplant any existing rule, statute, or law. This Administrative Order shall not be construed as granting any rights not already provided for by rule, statute, or law.

6. To the extent that any provision of this Administrative Order may be construed as being in conflict with any rule, statute, or law, the rule, statute, or law shall prevail.

DONE AND ORDERED this 27th day of July, 2015.

Michael T. McHugh
Chief Judge

History.—New.

—ATTACHMENT A—

IN THE CIRCUIT COURT FOR THE TWENTIETH JUDICIAL CIRCUIT IN AND FOR CHARLOTTE COUNTY, FLORIDA CIVIL ACTION

, CASE NO:

Petitioner(s),

vs.

,

Defendant(s).

/

STANDING ORDER IN RESIDENTIAL MORTGAGE FORECLOSURE CASES IN CHARLOTTE COUNTY

PURSUANT to Rules 2.250 and 2.545, Florida Rules of Judicial Administration, and Rule 1.200(a), Florida Rules of Civil Procedure, the parties are ordered to adhere to the following information and procedures applicable to residential mortgage foreclosure civil lawsuits:

1. **SERVICE OF THIS ORDER.** The Plaintiff is directed to serve a copy of this order with each Summons issued in this case. One copy of this Order is to be filed with the Clerk of the Circuit Court with proof of service. The Plaintiff shall pay the appropriate statutory clerk's fees on copies for each Standing Order issued and attached to the Summons.

2. **CIVIL CASE MANAGEMENT PLAN.** The Supreme Court of Florida has established guidelines for the prompt processing and resolution of civil cases, and has expressly mandated that the Court "shall take charge of all cases at an early stage in the litigation and shall control the progress of the case thereafter until the case is determined." Fla. R. Jud. Admin. 2.545(b). The time standard deemed by the Supreme Court of Florida to be presumptively reasonable for the disposition of civil non-jury cases is 12 months from filing to final disposition. Fla. R. Jud. Admin. 2.250(a)(1)(B). Accordingly, in Residential Mortgage Foreclosure cases filed on or subsequent to August 1, 2015, and upon the filing of a responsive pleading to the complaint, the Court will issue a Case Management Plan establishing mandatory time-frames with the goal of resolution within 12 months. The parties may request that the plan be amended by submitting a proposed agreed amended plan to the Civil Case Management Department, or if unable to agree on an amended plan, by filing a motion with the Court for a Case Management Conference. Trials will be scheduled before the assigned Circuit Judge, Senior Judge or may be referred to a General Magistrate based on the trial date set forth in the Case Management Plan, or earlier than the trial date set forth in the Case Management Plan upon the filing of a notice of readiness for trial.

3. **ALTERNATIVE DISPUTE RESOLUTION (ADR).** Early mediation shall be available pursuant to local Administrative Order No. 1.14, In re: Homestead Mediation Program for Residential Homestead Mortgage Foreclosure Actions, which can be viewed on the website of the Administrative Office of the Courts: http://www.ca.cjis20.org/pdf/ao/ao_1_14.pdf. In the event that the deadlines for seeking early mediation pursuant to Administrative Order No. 1.14 have expired, and a party subsequently requests that the Court direct

mediation, or the Court on its own motion orders mediation, the general provisions of Administrative Order No. 1.14 shall apply to any such mediation ordered.

4. **MOTIONS TO CONTINUE TRIAL**. A Motion to Continue any trial must be filed with the clerk and emailed to the Civil Case Management Office at civilcmcharlotte@ca.cjis20.org. Motions to Continue can only be heard or granted by the assigned circuit judge or by the senior judge or upon recommendation of a magistrate presiding over the trial.

5. **RULES OF PROFESSIONALISM.** The Twentieth Judicial Circuit has adopted local Administrative Order 2.20, which sets forth standards of professional courtesy and conduct for all counsel or pro-se litigants practicing within the Circuit. The Court requires that all parties or counsel for parties familiarize themselves and comply with Administrative Order 2.20. Administrative Order 2.20 may be viewed on the website of the Administrative Office of the Courts: http://www.ca.cjis20.org/web/main/ao_admin.asp

DONE AND ORDERED in Chambers at Punta Gorda, Charlotte County, Florida, on August 1, 2015.

____

Lisa S. Porter, Circuit Judge

*******Original on file in the office of the Circuit Clerk of Court, Charlotte County**

- ATTACHMENT B -

IN THE CIRCUIT COURT OF THE TWENTIETH JUDICIAL CIRCUIT IN AND FOR CHARLOTTE COUNTY, FLORIDA CIVIL ACTION

*,

Plaintiff(s),

vs. CASE NO: *-CA-*

*, CASE TYPE: CA *

Defendant(s)

________________________________/

RESIDENTIAL FORECLOSURE CASE MANAGEMENT PLAN AND ORDER

Expedited Track (Case resolved within 12 months):

Case Deadlines and Events

DEADLINE OR EVENT	***DATE***
Statement of Facts and/or Counterclaim(s)	180 days prior to trial
Identification of facts the parties believe to be disputed	90 days prior to trial
Identification of the issues of law to be decided by the Court	90 days prior to trial
Motions to Add Parties or to Amend Pleadings	180 days prior to trial
Disclosure of Fact Witnesses	180 days prior to trial
Disclosure of Expert Witnesses	180 days prior to trial
Filing of Exhibit List	60 days prior to trial
Discovery & Deadlines: The requesting party shall file all discovery requests and the responding party shall file a Notice of Compliance when completed. If the party fails to timely respond, the requesting party shall file a Notice of Non-compliance and/or Motion to Compel no later than 10 days from the due date.	Requests must be filed not later than 45 days from answer. Response must be made within 30 days of filing of request if no objection filed. Objections to discovery request must be filed not later than 20 days from the filing of the request.

Expert Opinion Available to Opposing Party	160 days prior to trial
Discovery Deadline for Expert Witnesses	90 days prior to trial
Completion of Alternative Dispute Resolution (ADR) (See Residential Foreclosure Standing Order)	30 days prior to trial.
Deadline for Dispositive Motions	Must be heard not less 30 days prior to trial
Other Deadlines or Events: Motions in Limine	Not less than 30 days prior to trial

Trial Information

Estimated Date the Case Will Be Scheduled To Go To Trial	**12th month from date of filing of complaint**
Estimated Length of Trial	**All trials will be set for one (1) hour; if you need additional time you must contact the Civil Case Management Office at civilcmcharlotte@ca.cjis20.org no later than 30 days prior to trial.**
Identification of Jury or Non-Jury Trial	**Non-Jury**

The above-referenced schedule of deadlines will be strictly adhered to by the parties unless a change is otherwise agreed to by the parties and approved by the Court. The Court will consider a request to approve changes to these deadlines upon a showing of good cause by either party based on matters arising from an emergency nature or unavailability. However, procrastination in completing discovery or the unavailability of counsel will not constitute good cause for a change to these deadlines. The failure to abide by these deadlines may result in sanctions by the Court, including the award of attorney's fees, the striking of pleadings, and/or a dismissal of the action.

ALL PARTIES SHALL ABIDE BY THE TERMS HEREIN.

DONE AND ORDERED in Punta Gorda, Charlotte County, Florida on__________________.

____
Hon. Lisa S. Porter, Circuit Judge

Conformed Copies to the Civil Case Manager and to:

*

Judicial Administration

2.1. JURY MANAGEMENT

IN THE TWENTIETH JUDICIAL CIRCUIT IN AND FOR THE STATE OF FLORIDA

Administrative Order No: 2.1

IN RE: JURY MANAGEMENT

In an effort to reduce the expenditure of State funds for juror compensation as well as juror inconvenience and in order to ensure that an adequate number of jurors are provided for each case actually tried in this Circuit, the following rules are hereby adopted throughout this Circuit effective immediately:

I. IN ALL CRIMINAL CASES

No later than 3:00 p.m. on the day before the scheduled trial date, the Defendant (individually or through counsel) and the State Attorney shall notify the presiding judge as to whether the case will go to trial or be the subject of a plea. In the event the Court is advised that the case will be tried and later it is determined that the Defendant wishes to enter a plea, the following procedure may be applied:

1. Negotiated pleas may not be accepted by the Court. In the event the Defendant wishes to plea to the charge(s) the Defendant's sentence will be subject to the discretion of the Court in accordance with the sentencing guidelines.

2. The Court will then conduct an inquiry of Defendant and the State Attorney at the time the plea is taken as to

whether the Defendant was advised of this procedure by his attorney prior to the deadline prescribed above. If the Court determines that the Defendant was not so advised, court costs may be imposed against the defense attorney. Court costs may be imposed against the State Attorney if he or she was not available to consult with the defense attorney about a negotiated plea on or before the deadline.

II. IN ALL CIVIL CASES

No later than 3:00 p.m. on the day before the scheduled trial date, counsel for all parties shall notify the presiding judge as to whether it will be necessary to empanel a jury. In the event the Court is notified that the case will go to trial as scheduled and settlement occurs between that date and the date of trial, the following procedure will be strictly applied:

1. Court costs will be assessed against all parties.

2. The Court will then conduct an inquiry of the parties at the time the case is settled as to whether they were advised by their attorney that court costs would be assessed against them in the event the case settled after the deadline prescribed above. In the event the Court determines that the parties were uninformed by counsel and that this was the cause of non-compliance with this rule, court costs may instead be imposed against counsel.

MAXIMUM NUMBER OF JURORS

Subject to the exceptions set forth below, in standard cases, the maximum number of jurors to be provided are as follows:

1. Capital cases involving only one Defendant — 35 jurors (50 in which the death penalty is sought).

2. Felony trials involving only one Defendant — 18 jurors.

3. Eminent Domain cases involving a single property owner — 22 jurors.

4. Civil jury trial with single Plaintiff and single Defendant — 16 jurors.

5. Misdemeanor trials involving only one Defendant — 14 jurors.

EXCEPTIONS

a) Multi-party civil cases

b) Criminal cases involving co-defendants

c) Criminal cases involving extensive pre-trial publicity.

All such exceptions shall be communicated to the jury clerk by the presiding judge no less than fourteen (14) days prior to trial.

NOTIFICATION TO JURY CLERK

Notwithstanding any prior provision of this Order, the jury clerk is to be notified by the judge or judicial assistant in both civil and criminal cases of the fact that such cases have been resolved prior to trial where the clerk would otherwise be required to provide a jury panel. Said notice shall be provided as soon as it is known.

Due to the fact that a venire is summoned two to three weeks prior to trial, the State Attorney in all criminal cases and the judicial assistant for each presiding judge in all civil cases shall notify the jury clerk of the existence of exceptional cases at the time of summoning for the prospective jurors.

Jury system management reports required by the State on a monthly basis, shall also be provided by the jury clerk to the Administrative Office of the Courts on a weekly basis. Said reports shall contain statistics regarding summoning yield, juror days per trial, people brought in for trial, percent to Voir Dire and average panel size.

DONE AND ORDERED in Chambers in Fort Myers, Lee County, Florida, this 11 day of December, 1990.

Thomas S. Reese
Chief Judge

History. - New.

2.2. COURT REPORTING SERVICES PLAN

IN THE TWENTIETH JUDICIAL CIRCUIT IN AND FOR THE STATE OF FLORIDA

Administrative Order No. 2.2

IN RE: COURT REPORTING SERVICES PLAN

PURSUANT to Fla. R. Jud. Admin. 2.070, and after consultation with the Circuit and County Court Judges of the Twentieth Judicial Circuit, the Court hereby revises, adopts and implements the following Circuit-wide plan for the reporting or recording of all proceedings required to be reported or recorded at public expense.

I. PROVISION OF SERVICES—The Twentieth Judicial Circuit is currently in a period of transition from court reporting services as defined by Fla. R. Jud. Admin. 2.070(a) to electronic court recording and transcription as permitted by Fla. R. Jud. Admin. 2.070(g)(3). During this period of transition, the Twentieth Judicial Circuit hereby implements a hybrid plan which shall incorporate multiple service delivery strategies for the reporting or recording of all proceedings required to be reported or recorded at public expense. The plan utilizes both independent contract court reporters and employee electronic court recorders.

II. APPLICABLE PROCEEDINGS—This Administrative Order and the contracts entered into in accordance with the terms of this Administrative Order and the other authorities cited herein shall apply to all criminal and juvenile proceedings, including depositions, and any other judicial proceedings required by law or the court to be reported or recorded at public expense, as required by Fla. R. Jud. Admin. 2.070(g).

III. METHODS OF REPORTING

A. STENOGRAPHIC REPORTING—In any required proceeding set forth in paragraph II above, stenographic reporting by a court reporter as defined by Fla. R. Jud. Admin. 2.070(a) may be utilized.

B. ELECTRONIC RECORDING

1. Terminology—The term "electronic recording" shall include audio tape recording, videocassette tape recording, or recording by any other electronic means, including, but not limited to, digital or other technology.

2. Applicable Proceedings—Electronic recording as contemplated by Fla. R. Jud. Admin. 2.070(g)(3) may be used in all criminal, juvenile, and mental health proceedings, and any other judicial proceedings required by law or the court to be

reported or recorded at public expense, including, but not limited to, the following:

a. First appearance hearings;

b. Adversary preliminary hearings;

c. Criminal trials and all pre-trial and post-trial proceedings;

d. Criminal contempt proceedings;

e. Criminal depositions;

f. Guardianship proceedings;

g. Baker Act proceedings;

h. Marchman Act proceedings;

i. Juvenile detention and delinquency hearings;

j. Juvenile dependency shelter hearings;

k. Foster care review panel hearings;

l. Dependency and termination of parental rights proceedings;

m. Proceedings for families and children in need of services;

n. Proceedings before General Masters or Magistrates in family law matters;

o. Child support enforcement hearings, including Support and Visitation Enforcement (SAVE) hearings and Department of Revenue (DOR) hearings;

p. Petitions for injunctions against domestic violence hearings;

q. Petitions for Waiver of Parental Notice of Abortion; and

r. Elsewhere as required or so ordered by the court.

IV. INDEPENDENT CONTRACT COURT REPORTERS—Court reporting services as defined by Fla. R. Crim. P. 2.070(a) may be provided by independent contractors subject to contracts entered into between the Administrative Office of the Courts and the court reporters. All contracts executed and in force and effect at any time during the operation and application of this Administrative Order shall be kept on file with the Court Administrator.

A. QUALIFICATIONS—Each independent contract court reporter whose services are utilized pursuant to a contract shall be a proficient Computer-aided Transcription (CAT) court reporter. In addition, independent contract court reporters shall:

1. Be certified by the National Court Reporters Association as a Registered Professional Reporter, Registered Merit Reporter, Registered Diplomate Reporter, or Real-time Reporter; or,

2. Have otherwise demonstrated proficiency in stenographic court reporting.

B. SCOPE OF SERVICES—The scope of services to be provided by independent contract court reporters is specifically limited to that which is covered by the contracts entered into by and between the Administrative Office of the Courts and the court reporters. Should it become necessary to obtain court reporting services in addition to those contemplated by the contracts, the Court Administrator shall coordinate the provision of such court reporting services and shall ensure the proficiency of the court reporters utilized.

C. COURT REPORTERS AS OFFICERS OF THE COURT—Pursuant to Fla. R. Jud. Admin. 2.070(f), an independent contract court reporter is an officer of the court while acting as a reporter in a judicial proceeding or discovery proceeding. As an officer of the court, the court reporter shall comply with all rules and statutes governing the proceeding which are applicable to court reporters, and the failure to do so shall constitute neglect of duty for which sanctions may be imposed in the exercise of the court's inherent authority, or pursuant to Florida Statute § 43.26(4), or as otherwise provided by law.

D. NOTIFICATION PROVISION—In accordance with the duties and obligations of independent contract court reporters as officers of the court pursuant to the authorities cited above, when a request is made for a transcript or portion thereof from a court reporter, such reporter shall forthwith notify, in writing, or orally if written notification is not practicable, all other parties to the action that a request has been received. This provision shall not apply to any transcript ordered by the court.

E. RETENTION OF RECORDS—All independent contract court reporters governed by this Administrative Order shall retain all original notes and electronic records, including dictionaries, of the proceedings or depositions in strict accordance with Fla. R. Jud. Admin. 2.075(f).

V. ELECTRONIC RECORDING AND TRANSCRIPTION—In accordance with Fla. R. Jud. Admin. 2.070(g)(3), the Chief Judge hereby authorizes the electronic recording and subsequent transcription by persons other than court reporters of any judicial proceedings, including depositions, that are otherwise required to be reported by a court reporter.

A. ELECTRONIC COURT RECORDING OFFICE

1. Authorized Proceedings—The Administrative Office of the Courts, Electronic Court Recording Office, is authorized to capture the record for criminal and civil judicial proceedings required by law or by rules of court to be reported or recorded at public expense. This Administrative Order does not authorize the Electronic Court Recording Office to record any proceedings unless those proceedings are required to be recorded at public expense. Parties to civil actions shall arrange for an independent court reporter to record those proceedings that the Court is not required to record or report at public expense.

2. Equipment and Procedures—The Court's electronic recording equipment shall be operated by employees of the Administrative Office of the Courts and/or by such other persons designated by the Court Administrator. The procedures to ensure a reliable and secure record and compliance with applicable statutes and rules of court shall be promulgated by the Court Administrator, shall be on file in the Electronic Court Recording Office, and may be amended from time to time as deemed appropriate by the Chief Judge or the Court Administrator.

3. Employees as Officers of the Court—Employees of the Administrative Office of the Courts who perform electronic court recording and its related functions, as well as any other persons authorized by the Court Administrator to perform these functions, shall be officers of the court and shall not

disclose or discuss any confidential information to which they may be privy.

B. TRANSCRIPTION—Proceedings or depositions electronically recorded at public expense and pursuant to this Administrative Order will be transcribed by court personnel employed by the Administrative Office of the Courts within the Electronic Court Recording Office or by independent contract transcriptionists, at the discretion of the Court Administrator or the Court Administrator's designee.

C. QUALIFICATIONS OF TRANSCRIPTIONISTS—All persons transcribing electronically recorded proceedings or depositions, whether employees of the Administrative Office of the Courts or independent contract transcriptionists, shall meet the qualifications established by the Chief Judge or the Court Administrator to ensure the person's ability to transcribe the proceedings and to certify the correctness of the transcripts.

D. REQUESTS FOR TRANSCRIPT OR ELECTRONIC RECORDING—Requests for either a written transcript or, in instances where independent contract transcriptionists are used, a copy of the original recording of any proceeding or deposition electronically recorded by the Electronic Court Recording Office pursuant to this Administrative Order shall be submitted in writing to the Electronic Court Recording Office. The request shall be on a form available from the Administrative Office of the Courts or the Electronic Court Recording Office, and, if applicable, on any other form approved by the Florida Supreme Court as set forth in the Florida Rules of Appellate Procedure or any other rules of court. If the transcript or copy of the original recording is to be provided at public expense, the party shall attach to the request a conformed copy of the court order authorizing the transcription at public expense. However, if the request is submitted by the Office of the State Attorney, the Office of the Public Defender, or a court-appointed conflict attorney, with the costs and fees to be paid directly from the budgets of each respective office or the Justice Administrative Commission, the requirement that the request be accompanied by a court order authorizing transcription is hereby waived. If the request is for transcripts or copies of original recordings which may include confidential information, the request must be accompanied by an appropriate court order.

1. Notification Provision—When a request is submitted to the Electronic Court Recording Office for a transcript, the Electronic Court Recording Office shall forthwith notify, in writing, or orally if written notification is not practicable, all other parties to the action that a request has been received. In instances where independent contract transcriptionists are used, it shall be the responsibility of the independent contract transcriptionist to notify, in writing, or orally if written notification is not practicable, all other parties to the action that a request has been received. This provision shall not apply to any transcript or copy of an electronic recording ordered by the court.

2. On-Record Events When Court Reporter Present—If a court reporter records a proceeding (trial, hearing, or other court event), the request for a copy of the proceeding shall be submitted to the court reporter. In the event the Electronic Court Recording Office electronically recorded any proceedings covered by a court reporter, the electronic recordings were not made pursuant to any court rule, law, or ordinance, and the proceedings were not recorded in connection with the transaction of official business of the judiciary. As such, the incidental electronic recording of a proceeding that has been covered by a court reporter does not constitute a record of the judicial branch to which the public is entitled access, as defined by Fla. R. Jud. Admin. 2.051. The Electronic Court Recording Office will not provide copies of its electronic recordings of those same proceedings, if any. Exceptions to this policy may be considered and granted by the Chief Judge upon a showing of extraordinary circumstances.

3. Off-Record Events—Electronic recordings by the Electronic Court Recording Office of off-record discussions or conversations were not been made pursuant to any court rule, law or ordinance, and were not recorded in connection with the transaction of official business of the judiciary. As such, the incidental electronic recordings of off-record discussions or conversations, if any, do not constitute a record of the judicial branch to which the public is entitled access, as defined by Fla. R. Jud. Admin. 2.051. In addition, it should be noted that all off-record conversations between attorneys and their clients are protected by the attorney-client privilege and shall remain confidential. The Electronic Court Recording Office will not provide copies of its electronic recordings of off-record discussions or conversations, if any.

E. CERTIFICATION OF TRANSCRIPTS OR ELECTRONIC RECORDINGS—All persons transcribing electronic recordings, whether court personnel or independent contract transcriptionists, shall certify the transcript as a true and accurate text of the electronic recording of the proceeding or deposition. All court personnel providing a copy of the original recording on electronic medium, such as compact diskette, shall certify the copy to be true and accurate.

F. DISPUTES AS TO ACCURACY—If any dispute arises as to whether any transcript truly discloses what occurred, the disputing party shall motion the presiding court for settlement of the dispute, and, upon order of the court, the transcript shall be made to conform accordingly.

G. SAFEKEEPING OF RECORDINGS—All electronic recordings captured by the Electronic Court Recording staff pursuant to this Administrative Order shall be properly identified and securely stored in accordance with procedures promulgated by the Court Administrator and for a period of time as prescribed by the Florida Rules of Judicial Administration.

VI. COURT REPORTING IN CAPITAL CASES—Pursuant to Fla. R. Jud. Admin. 2.070(h), the following requirements are established for all independent contract court reporters who report trials in which the State seeks the death penalty and in all capital postconviction proceedings.

A. PURPOSE—The purpose of this subsection is to require the use of all measures necessary to expedite the preparation of the transcript. Those measures shall include, but are not limited to, the following:

1. The use of a court reporter who has the capacity to provide real-time transcription of the proceedings;

2. If real-time transcription services are not available, the use of a computer-aided transcription qualified court reporter;

3. The use of scopists, text editors, alternating court reporters, or other means to expedite the finalization of the certified transcript; and,

4. The imposition of reasonable restrictions on work assignments by all independent contract court reporters to ensure that transcript production in capital cases is given a high priority.

B. TRANSCRIPTS—In addition to the foregoing requirements, the independent court reporter in cases in which the State seeks the death penalty and all capital postconviction hearings shall be responsible for strict compliance with Fla. R. App. P.9.142(a)(2), and in particular its requirement that the reporter provide to the Clerk clearly labeled computer disks in a format approved by the Florida Supreme Court.

VII. FEES AND RATES

A. ELECTRONIC COURT RECORDING—Fee schedules for transcripts or copies of electronically recorded proceedings or depositions required to be reported at public expense shall be on file in the Electronic Court Recording Office. On and after July 1, 2004, the rates set forth on all fee schedules shall comport with the applicable rates established by the Twentieth Judicial Circuit Article V Indigent Services Committee, if any. If applicable rates have not been established by the Twentieth Judicial Circuit Article V Indigent Services Committee, the rates for electronic court recording and transcription services shall be established by the Chief Judge or the Chief Judge's designee, and may be amended from time to time at the discretion of the Chief Judge or the Chief Judge's designee. On and after July 1, 2004, in circumstances where proceedings are reported and transcribed by the Electronic Court Recording Office or an independent contract transcriptionist at the request of a Justice Administration Commission (JAC) entity (i.e. the Office of the State Attorney, the Office of the Public Defender, court-appointed conflict attorney), the fees for transcripts to be provided at public expense are to be paid directly by the Justice Administration Commission (JAC) entity in accordance with the provisions of Chapter 29, Florida Statutes, as amended by Laws of Florida, Chapter 2003–402 (HB113A) and Chapter 2004–265 (SB2962).

B. COURT REPORTING BY INDEPENDENT CONTRACTORS—Fees and rates for the recording and transcription by independent contract court reporters of court proceedings or depositions required to be reported at public expense shall be as set forth in the court reporting contracts referenced herein. On and after July 1, 2004, those rates shall comport with the applicable rates established by the Twentieth Judicial Circuit Article V Indigent Services Committee, if any. If applicable rates have not been established by the Twentieth Judicial Circuit Article V Indigent Services Committee, the rates for the recording and transcription by independent contract court reporters shall be established by contract, and the Court Administrator may negotiate different rates in circumstances not contemplated by the contracts. Such circumstances may include, but are not limited to, out-of-circuit services, real-time reporting, or such other manner, mode or method of court reporting as circumstances may warrant. If different rates are not agreed to in advance, the rates established in the contracts shall apply. On and after July 1, 2004, in circumstances where proceedings are reported and transcribed by independent contract court reporters at the request of a Justice Administration Commission (JAC) entity (i.e. the Office of the State Attorney, the Office of the Public Defender, conflict counsel), the fees for transcripts to be provided at public expense are to be paid directly to the independent contract court reporter by the Justice Administration Commission (JAC) entity in accordance with the provisions of Chapter 29, Florida Statutes, as amended by Laws of Florida, Chapter 2003–402 (HB113A) and Chapter 2004–265 (SB2962).

VIII. TRANSCRIPTS—All transcripts must comply with the requirements of Fla. R. Jud. Admin. 2.070(e), and any rule or order of the court. A party requesting transcription at public expense must first obtain a court order authorizing transcription at public expense by filing a motion and submitting a proposed order to the presiding judge. In the event that the presiding judge is unavailable and the press of time requires immediate validation of such costs, such motions may be presented to the duty judge on call at the time of the request. Any request submitted to an independent contract court reporter or to the Electronic Court Recording Office for transcription at public expense shall be accompanied by a conformed copy of the court order authorizing the transcription at public expense. However, if the request for transcripts is submitted by the Office of the State Attorney, the Office of the Public Defender, or a court-appointed conflict attorney, with the costs and fees to be paid directly from the budgets of each respective office or the Justice Administrative Commission, the requirement that the request be accompanied by a court order authorizing transcription is hereby waived.

IX. OFFICIAL COURT RECORD—Neither independent contract court reporters nor transcriptionists, nor employees of the Administrative Office of the Courts shall file any written transcript or electronic recording of a court proceeding or deposition with the Clerk of Courts unless directed to do so by the court, or unless otherwise required to do so by the Florida Rules of Appellate Procedure, or by any other rule or statute. The written transcript of any electronic recording shall not become part of the official court record until such time as it is filed with the Clerk of Courts.

X. REMOVAL OF COURT FILES FROM THE COURTHOUSE—No court file shall be removed from any courthouse by any independent contract court reporter or by any independent contract transcriptionist. The Clerk of Court shall provide space for independent contract court reporters and transcriptionists to review court files and shall allow independent contract court reporters and transcriptionists to photocopy a reasonable number of pages in a court file without charge for the purpose of preparing transcripts.

XI. INTERPRETATION AND EFFECTIVE DATE—This Administrative Order shall be read in para materia with Fla. R. Jud. Admin. 2.070, any administrative order promulgated by the Florida Supreme Court, and any other authorities cited herein. To the extent that any provision of this Administrative Order is inconsistent with any statute, rule of court, or administrative order of the Florida Supreme Court, the statute, rule or order shall prevail. This Administrative Order shall be effective September 1, 2003, nunc pro tunc, and shall remain in effect until further order of the Court.

DONE AND ORDERED in Chambers at Naples, Collier County, Florida, this 22nd day of February, 2006.

Hugh D. Hayes
Chief Judge

History. — Administrative Order 2.2 (November 8, 2004); Administrative Order 2.2 (February 10, 2004); Administrative Order 2.2 (March 27, 2001); Administrative Order 2.2 (January 13, 2000); Administrative Order 2.2 (September 28, 1995); Administrative Order 2.2 (January 28, 1991); Administrative Order 88–1; Administrative Order 86–1 and Amendments thereto.

2.3. COURT FILES

IN THE TWENTIETH JUDICIAL CIRCUIT IN AND FOR THE STATE OF FLORIDA

ADMINISTRATIVE ORDER NO: 2.3

IN RE: COURT FILES

No court file shall be removed from any Clerk's Office Court, except that a file may be removed and taken to the Court within the Twentieth Judicial Circuit without an Order from the by officers of the Court for hearings and trials or preparation of transcripts.

No Circuit Court files may be mailed outside of the Circuit, nor may County Court files be mailed outside of the County except upon the request of a Court of equal or greater jurisdiction, and then only to that Court upon its assumption of the responsibility therefor.

DONE AND ORDERED in Chambers in Fort Myers, Florida, Lee County, Florida, this 4 day of Feb, 1991.

Thomas S. Reese
Chief Circuit Judge

History. - Administrative Order #86–2. Supercedes prior Administrative Order No: 2.3.

2.4. ASSIGNMENT OF REFILED CASES

IN THE TWENTIETH JUDICIAL CIRCUIT IN AND FOR THE STATE OF FLORIDA

ADMINISTRATIVE ORDER NO: 2.4

IN RE: ASSIGNMENT OF REFILED CASES

All cases which are refiled after having been previously dismissed for any reason are to be reassigned to the Judge before whom the dismissal was taken.

DONE AND ORDERED in Chambers in Fort Myers, Florida, Lee County, Florida, this 28 day of Jan, 1991.

Thomas S. Reese
Chief Circuit Judge

History. - Administrative Order 86–3.

2.5. JUDICIAL LABOR AND ROTATION POLICY

IN THE TWENTIETH JUDICIAL CIRCUIT IN AND FOR THE STATE OF FLORIDA

IN RE: JUDICIAL LABOR AND ROTATION POLICY

ADMINISTRATIVE ORDER NO. 2.5—Amended

THIS ORDER is designed to set forth a uniform method for the division of judicial labor as well as a voluntary assignment rotation policy within the Twentieth Judicial Circuit. The Order takes into consideration this circuit's geographic, demographic and socio-economic disparity, and to the extent possible, reflects the wishes of the sitting judiciary that judicial assignments be determined primarily on the bases of seniority, ability and desire.

I. DEFINITIONS

A. Seniority—Seniority in all situations contemplated within this Administrative Order will be determined in the following order:

1. Length of service as a full-time Circuit Judge within the Twentieth Judicial Circuit.

2. In the case of simultaneous appointment or election to the Circuit Bench, seniority shall be determined by looking first to the number of years of prior service to the Circuit Bench, and in the case of a tie, then to the length of service to the County Bench, and thereafter, only if there is a tie, to the length of service as any other judicial or quasi-judicial officer, and finally on the basis of the number of years as a member of the Florida Bar.

B. Geographical Divisions—Divisions within the Twentieth Judicial Circuit shall, to the extent possible, be confined to one county. However, due to caseload fluctuations, it may be necessary for divisions to be created which involve judicial responsibilities which are split among more than one county.

C. Case Divisions—To the extent practicable, Circuit Court caseloads shall be broken down into divisions as follows:

1. Civil Law Division.
2. Family Law Division.
3. Criminal Law Division.
4. Juvenile and Dependency Division.

These divisions shall be created and maintained by the Chief Judge and shall be subject to review based upon statistical data provided by the Court Administrator. Assignments within each division shall be as provided herein. However, due to caseload fluctuations, it may be necessary to add other divisions, including split divisions.

D. Judicial Vacancy—As used in this Order, a judicial vacancy is limited to any vacancy in a Circuit Judgeship created by the death, incapacity, removal, retirement, or a vacancy occasioned by any other cause not contemplated herein.

E. Newly Created Judicial Vacancy—As used in this Order, a newly created judicial vacancy is one certified by the Supreme Court of Florida and thereafter funded by the legislature for purposes of appointment or election.

F. Judicial Rotation—As used in this Order, a judicial rotation is defined as a complete cycle of two-year assignments through each of the four case divisions within a county (or any combination of divisions as may be necessitated by the caseload generation in any particular county) as set forth in paragraph I.C. above. Service of at least twelve (12) consecutive months within any division in the county of rotation shall be considered a completed assignment within that particular division.

II. GEOGRAPHICAL DIVISIONS

The Twentieth Judicial Circuit shall be divided into geographical groups with Circuit Judges assigned there as follows:

A. As often as may be necessary, but in no event less than once every two years beginning November 1, 2001, the Chief Judge of the circuit shall direct the Court Administrator to prepare a statistical report of the caseload throughout the circuit for the preceding two years. Based upon this statistical report, the Chief Judge shall divide the circuit into geographical divisions as equitably as possible, and assign each Circuit Judge of the circuit to one geographical division on the basis of seniority.

B. In the event a new Circuit Judgeship is created, the Chief Judge will make a determination as to where judicial labor is most needed and will thereafter provide for creation of geographical and case divisions accordingly. Assignments to these newly created vacancies will be made on the basis of seniority in accordance with this Order.

C. Each Judge of the circuit shall have chambers located in an appropriate county and facility as determined by the Chief Judge; and mileage, per diem, or other travel expenses shall not be chargeable to those chambers from the Judge's residency. Upon the adoption of this Order, no Judge shall be required to change counties during any two-year assignment under the Assignment Rotation Policy as set forth below, unless, in the opinion of the Chief Judge, exigent circumstances exist such that a change is required. After the passage of such circumstances, the Judge shall return to the original county from which the Judge was moved.

III. JUDICIAL VACANCIES AND NEWLY CREATED JUDICIAL VACANCIES

A. Any Judge, elected or appointed, who fills a judicial vacancy or newly created judicial vacancy (as those terms are defined in this Order) shall be entitled to the geographical and case division established for the vacancy unless a Judge of senior tenure should desire the geographical and case division. In that event, the vacancy will be filled on the basis of seniority.

B. For the purpose of determining whether a Judge of senior tenure desires the geographical and case division of that vacancy, the Chief Judge shall issue a written notice to all Circuit Judges announcing the vacancy, and any Judge who desires the vacancy must notify the Chief Judge of such desire no later than ten (10) days following the written notice. All Judges within the circuit may bid on filling the vacancy. The Judge with the most seniority who seeks to fill the vacancy shall receive the assignment.

C. In applying Paragraphs III. A and B, when a Judge moves from one geographical division to another, that Judge's seniority shall be defined as set forth in Paragraph I.A.

D. Beginning July 1, 2012, a Judge who fills a judicial vacancy as set forth in this Administrative Order shall preside in the county of that vacancy for a minimum of twelve (12) months. This is not intended to apply to vacancies filled prior to July 1, 2012.

E. The Chief Judge, upon leaving office, shall be permitted the option of either exchanging dockets with the successor Chief Judge or the divisional assignment of his or her choosing. Any Circuit Judge so displaced by such election shall be assigned to the vacant division.

IV. ASSIGNMENT ROTATION POLICY

A. In accordance with Fla. R. Jud. Admin. 2.215(b)(3), the Twentieth Judicial Circuit hereby adopts a voluntary assignment rotation policy. The purpose of this policy is to develop the capabilities of all Judges within the circuit so that all will be qualified to serve in any case division as provided herein.

B. This Court recognizes that due to population and caseload disparities, it would be impossible to completely divisionalize every county within this circuit. However, Charlotte, Collier and Lee County Circuit Courts are and shall continue to be fully divisionalized. Hendry and Glades Counties do not currently possess the population base or caseloads sufficient to warrant the establishment of any division of judicial labor as does exist in Charlotte, Collier and Lee Counties.

C. Beginning January 1, 2002 and every two years thereafter, or such other time as circumstances may warrant, the Chief Judge shall determine whether any Circuit Judge within the Twentieth Judicial Circuit wishes to participate in an assignment rotation, with rotations effective July 1st of each even numbered year.

D. For the purpose of determining whether any Judges wish to participate in a rotation, the Chief Judge shall issue a written notice to all Circuit Judges within a reasonable time after January 1st of each even numbered year, announcing the two-year rotation period, and any Judge who desires to enter rotation must notify the Chief Judge in writing of such desire no later than ten (10) days following the written notice.

E. Judges electing to rotate may not choose the case division to which they will be assigned. The actual case division of their new assignment will be determined based on seniority as described in paragraph I.A. However, the Chief Judge will request preferences for case divisions and every effort will be made to honor the request after applying the seniority rules.

F. The rotating Judge will displace the Judge with the least seniority in the division into which that Judge rotates. That displaced Judge will thereafter be assigned to the case division of the rotating Judge.

G. A Judge may not return to a case division held immediately before that Judge's election to participate in a judicial rotation until after a complete rotation through the other divisions has been accomplished.

H. To the extent that a Judge is involuntarily displaced by a rotating Judge, that displaced Judge is not prohibited from later entering into rotation, or applying to fill a vacancy, and potentially returning to the division from which he or she was involuntarily displaced.

I. To the extent that a Judge enters into voluntary rotation, that Judge need not further rotate after having completed any two-year assignment, unless another Judge enters into rotation and displaces that Judge based upon seniority.

J. With the approval of the Chief Judge, two Judges may agree to trade geographical or case divisions within a two-year rotation.

V. GENERAL PROVISIONS

A. Nothing in this Order shall be construed so as to affect those judicial rotations which are scheduled to take place on July 1, 2012.

B. This Order becomes effective immediately, and supersedes all prior versions of Administrative Order 2.5.

C. To the extent that this Administrative Order may conflict with any rule, statute, or law, the rule, statute, or law shall prevail.

D. Nothing in this Administrative Order shall be construed as removing any authority afforded to the Chief Judge by Fla. R. Jud. Admin. 2.215(b).

DONE AND ORDERED in Chambers at Fort Myers, Lee County, Florida, this 30th day of May, 2012.

Jay B. Rosman
Chief Judge

History. —Administrative Order 86–4 and Administrative Order 86–5; Administrative Order 2.5 (January 28, 1991) and Administrative Order 2.6 (January 28, 1991); Administrative Order 2.5 (December 17, 1993), which superseded and replaced both Administrative Order 2.5 (January 28, 1991) and Administrative Order 2.6 (January 28, 1991); Administrative Order 2.5 (January 13, 2000); Administrative Order 2.5 (January 4, 2001); Administrative Order 2.5 (May 14, 2010).

2.6. ORDER ESTABLISHING ADMINISTRATIVE CODE

ADMINISTRATIVE ORDER NO: 2.6

IN THE TWENTIETH JUDICIAL CIRCUIT IN AND FOR THE STATE OF FLORIDA

ORDER ESTABLISHING ADMINISTRATIVE CODE

Pursuant to Fla. R. Jud. Admin. 2.050(b)(2) and (e)(3), the Twentieth Judicial Circuit hereby creates the Administrative Code for use within the Twentieth Judicial Circuit in accordance with the authority provided within each Administrative Order.

A complete copy of all currently effective Administrative Orders and Local Rules shall be maintained by the Court Administrator for the Twentieth Judicial Circuit. All Administrative Orders designated as such by the Chief Judge shall be indexed and recorded by the Clerks of the Circuit Court in each county where the Orders are effective as provided in Fla. R. Jud. Admin. 2.050(e)(3).

While all Judges are free to operate their courtrooms as they see fit within the Constitution and laws of the United States and the State of Florida, all previously executed and recorded Orders, no matter how they are designated, are hereby rescinded, revoked and repealed. Only the Administrative Code as designated by the Chief Judge shall govern the practice and procedure within the Twentieth Judicial Circuit as a whole.

DONE AND ORDERED in Chambers at Fort Myers, Lee County, Florida, this 15th day of February, 1994.

Thomas S. Reese
Chief Judge

2.7. DESIGNATION OF BRANCH COURTHOUSES

IN THE TWENTIETH JUDICIAL CIRCUIT IN AND FOR THE STATE OF FLORIDA

IN RE: DESIGNATION OF BRANCH COURTHOUSES

ADMINISTRATIVE ORDER NO. 2.7—AMENDED -

WHEREAS, Article V, Section 7 of the Florida Constitution states that a Circuit or County Court may hold civil and criminal trials and hearings in any place within the territorial jurisdiction of the Court as designated by the Chief Judge; and

WHEREAS, the prompt disposition of cases in the Circuit and County Courts would best be achieved by bringing the courts closer to its officers and residents of the County; and

WHEREAS, the City Council of Cape Coral, Lee County, has petitioned the Chief Judge to hold court in Cape Coral and the caseload in said City warrants such; and

WHEREAS, Clewiston, Hendry County, warrants holding court therein for the convenience of the citizens; and

WHEREAS, Immokalee, Collier County, warrants holding court therein for the convenience of the citizens; and

WHEREAS, Englewood, Charlotte County, warrants holding Court therein for the convenience of the citizens; and

WHEREAS, Murdock, Charlotte County, warrants holding Court therein for the convenience of the citizens; and

WHEREAS, Port Charlotte, Charlotte County, warrants holding Court therein for the convenience of the citizens; and

WHEREAS, the Lee County Justice Center is experiencing severe space limitations due to expanding growth; it is

ORDERED AND ADJUDGED as follows:

(A) The following facility is designated as a branch Courthouse in and for Lee County, Florida:

1. **CAPE CORAL LEE COUNTY GOVERNMENT BUILDING**

(B) The following facility is designated as a branch Courthouse in and for Hendry County, Florida:

1. **HENDRY COUNTY SUB OFFICE FACILITY**

(C) The following facility is designated as a branch Courthouse in and for Collier County, Florida:

1. **IMMOKALEE BRANCH COURTHOUSE**

(D) The following facilities are designated as branch Courthouses in and for Charlotte County, Florida:

1. **CLERK'S FACILITY,** 4318 N. Access Road, in Englewood
2. **PORT CHARLOTTE CULTURAL CENTER**
3. **MURDOCK ADMINISTRATION BUILDING**

(E) The above-listed facilities are acceptable for holding criminal trials and hearings and for the receipt of any instruments deposited incident thereto, when consistent with the administrative procedures established by the Chief Judge.

(F) The following facility adjacent to the Lee County Justice Center is designated as a branch Courthouse in and for Lee County, Florida, for the purpose of holding Grand Jury proceedings:

1. **LEE COUNTY JUSTICE CENTER ANNEX**, 2000 Main Street, in Fort Myers.

(G) In accordance with Fla. R. Crim. P. 3.220(h)(3), the following facility adjacent to the Lee County Justice Center is designated as a branch Courthouse in and for Lee County, Florida, for the purpose of taking discovery depositions:

1. **LEE COUNTY JUSTICE CENTER ANNEX**, 2000 Main Street, in Fort Myers.

DONE AND ORDERED in Chambers in Fort Myers, Lee County, Florida, this 18 day of June, 2010.

G. Keith Cary
Chief Judge

History. Administrative Order 86–6; Administrative Order 2.7 (January 28, 1991); Administrative Order 2.7 (November 3, 1992); Administrative Order 2.7 (March 28, 2003); Administrative Order 2.7 (December 1, 2003).

2.8. STAFF ATTORNEYS AND TRIAL COURT LAW CLERKS

IN THE TWENTIETH JUDICIAL CIRCUIT IN AND FOR THE STATE OF FLORIDA

Administrative Order No. 2.8

IN RE: STAFF ATTORNEYS AND TRIAL COURT LAW CLERKS

WHEREAS, the Chief Judge has employed the services of full-time Staff Attorneys and Trial Court Law Clerks to assist the judges of the Twentieth Judicial Circuit in their day-to-day duties, and

WHEREAS, there is a need to determine scheduling priorities for projects given to the attorneys and clerks by the judges, it is hereby

ORDERED AND ADJUDGED that:

1. Staff Attorneys and Trial Court Law Clerks shall be assigned to assist the Circuit Judges in and for Charlotte, Collier, Glades, Hendry and Lee Counties.

2. Staff Attorneys and Trial Court Law Clerks may provide assistance to the County Judiciary when possible, as determined by the workloads of the Staff Attorneys and Trial Court Law Clerks. Any such projects shall be coordinated through the Staff Attorneys' Offices and the Court Administrator under the supervision of the Chief Judge.

3. In the event a Staff Attorney or Trial Court Law Clerk provides advice to the County Judiciary or performs research for the County Judiciary with respect to a case that is subsequently appealed, the appellate case shall be brought to the attention of the Court Administrator for reassignment to a Staff Attorney or a Trial Court Law Clerk who has had no prior involvement with the case.

4. The duties of the Staff Attorneys and Trial Court Law Clerks shall include, but are not necessarily limited to, legal research, writing and drafting of memoranda, orders and opinions in trial court and appellate matters. The attorneys shall also act as counsel to the judiciary within the ambit of and limitations set forth in Fla. R. Jud. Admin. 2.060(c). The duties are assigned are assigned according to the priorities stated below.

5. The Staff Attorneys and Trial Court Law Clerks work under the supervision of the Chief Judge. The Chief Judge shall establish priorities in the scheduling and use of Staff Attorneys and Trial Court Law Clerks in a manner which will most effectively meet the needs of the Circuit.

6. All judges who seek the assistance of a Staff Attorney or Trial Court Law Clerk shall route their request in the manner prescribed by the Chief Judge, Court Administrator, or Deputy Court Administrator for the requesting judge's county. This process will ensure the expeditious, consistent and efficient disposition of projects, while simultaneously maximizing the expertise and resources available in Staff Attorneys and Trial Court Law Clerks.

7. Assignment priorities shall be established based upon the urgency, complexity, and exigency of each task, with due regard for the time standards established by Fla. R. Jud. Admin. 2.085, the requirements of the Constitutions, the laws of the United States and the State of Florida, the Rules of Court established by the Florida Supreme Court, and with consideration of the resources available for the completion of each task. In general, assignment priorities are established as follows, in descending order of priority:

A. Emergency matters

1. Those matters specifically defined as emergencies By Administrative Order 2.17(b)(2)

2. Petitions, applications or ex parte injunctions involving right-to-die or right-to-life cases

3. Petitions challenging Orders excluding the press or public from access to any proceeding as contemplated by Fla. R. App. P. 9.100(d)

4. Miscellaneous emergency matters

B. Extraordinary writs

1. Habeas Corpus

2. Prohibition

3. Mandamus

4. Certiorari

5. Quo Warranto

C. Appellate issues, including research and memoranda

D. Criminal sentencings

E. Criminal motions

1. 3.851 motions

2. 3.800 motions

3. 3.850 motions

4. Miscellaneous motions

F. Administrative matters

1. Drafting and letting of contracts with the Courts

2. Drafting of Administrative Orders, Local Rules, or Parochial Orders

G. Complex civil litigation matters

H. Family law matters

I. Case management

J. County court matters

K. Contract management

If issues arise as to conflicting priorities, they shall be referred to the Chief Judge for decision as to priority.

The attorneys and clerks shall expend every reasonable effort to complete all projects by the proposed completion dates established by the requesting judge. However, due to unforeseen circumstances and the urgency of concurrent projects, the proposed dates may be delayed.

DONE AND ORDERED in Chambers at Naples, Collier County, Florida, this 6th day of June, 2000.

William L. Blackwell
Chief Judge

History. - Administrative Order 89–22; Administrative Order 2.8 (January 28, 1991); Administrative Order 2.8 (October 30, 1995).

2.9. SIZE OF PAPER

IN THE TWENTIETH JUDICIAL CIRCUIT IN AND FOR THE STATE OF FLORIDA

Administrative Order No: 2.9

IN RE: SIZE OF PAPER

WHEREAS, Rule 2.055 of the Florida Rules of Judicial Administration requires that all pleadings, motions, petitions, briefs, notices, orders, judgments, decrees, opinions, and other papers and official documents filed in any court shall be on paper measuring 8 1/2 by 11 inches; it is therefore

ORDERED that subsequent to January 1, 1991, the Clerks of the Twentieth Judicial Circuit shall comply with Rule 2.055.

When time of filing is critical, the Clerk shall accept pleadings, motions, petitions, briefs, notices, orders, judgments, decrees, opinions, or other papers or official documents on other than 8 1/2 by 11 inch paper but shall then require that the document be resubmitted to comply with the Rule.

Xerographic reduction of legal-size (8 1/2 by 14 inches) documents to letter size (8 1/2 by 11 inches) is prohibited.

Any exhibit or attachment filed with pleadings or papers may be filed in its original size.

DONE AND ORDERED in Chambers in Fort Myers, Lee County, Florida, this 14 day of December, 1990.

Thomas S. Reese
Chief Judge

History. - New.

2.10. INTRACIRCUIT CONFLICT RESOLUTION PROCEDURE

IN AND FOR THE TWENTIETH JUDICIAL CIRCUIT IN THE STATE OF FLORIDA

ADMINISTRATIVE ORDER NO: 2.10

IN RE: INTRACIRCUIT CONFLICT RESOLUTION PROCEDURE

1. Application:

This order shall apply throughout the Twentieth Circuit to resolve intracircuit scheduling conflicts.

2. Procedure:

A. The judges affected by an intracircuit scheduling conflict shall initially confer and determine priorities, giving due consideration to such factors as the age of the case, the number of parties and attorneys involved, the estimated time needed for trial, and the availability of witnesses.

B. The following priorities shall apply in the event that the judges affected cannot resolve an intracircuit scheduling conflict:

(1) Federal trials or other federal proceedings involving a mandatory appearance by counsel.

(2) Appellate proceedings in a District Court of Appeal or the Supreme Court of Florida.

(3) Felony trials set pursuant to motion for discharge [Rule 3.191(i)].

(4) Misdemeanor trials set pursuant to motion for discharge [Rule 3.191(i)].

(5) Capital trials where the death penalty is sought and hearings on Rule 3.850 motions when the death penalty has been imposed.

(6) Non-capital felony jury trials.

(7) Misdemeanor jury trials.

(8) Civil jury trials.

(9) Civil nonjury trials estimated to last four days or more.

(10) Court ordered mediation and arbitration.

(11) Circuit court nonjury trials estimated to last less than four days including violations of probation or community control and Rule 3.850 motions.

(12) County court nonjury trials including violations of probation.

(13) Motions requiring an evidentiary hearing.

(14) Other motions or proceedings not specifically set forth above.

(15) Depositions.

In cases of equal dignity, the oldest case shall have priority. The initial date of filing shall determine the age of the case. Criminal defendants in custody shall have priority over other criminal defendants.

DONE AND ORDERED in Chambers in Fort Myers, Lee County, Florida, this 21 day of Feb, 1991.

Thomas S. Reese
Chief Circuit Judge

History. - New.

2.11. ASSIGNMENT OF FORFEITURE CASES

IN THE TWENTIETH JUDICIAL CIRCUIT IN AND FOR THE STATE OF FLORIDA

ADMINISTRATIVE ORDER NO: 2.11

IN RE: ASSIGNMENT OF FORFEITURE CASES

Pursuant to § 932.704, Fla. Stat. (1995), all civil forfeiture cases filed pursuant to Florida Statutes §§ 893.12, 932.703 and 932.704 for the forfeiture of real or personal property, including vessels, motor vehicles or aircraft, shall be assigned to and heard by a circuit court judge of the civil division. All such assignments shall be made by the Clerk of Court on a random selection basis.

This order supersedes and replaces prior Administrative Order 2.11 (February 5, 1992).

DONE AND ORDERED in Chambers in Fort Myers, Lee County, Florida this 2nd day of August, 1995.

Hugh E. Starnes
Chief Judge

History. - Administrative Order 2.11 (February 5, 1992); Administrative Order 3.3; Amended Administrative Order 86–15; Administrative Order 86–15.

2.12. ESTABLISHMENT OF FAMILY LAW DIVISION

IN THE TWENTIETH JUDICIAL CIRCUIT IN AND FOR THE SATE OF FLORIDA

ADMINISTRATIVE ORDER NO: 2.12

IN RE: ESTABLISHMENT OF FAMILY LAW DIVISION

Pursuant to Rule 2.050, Florida Rules of Judicial Administration, the following Order shall formally provide for the establishment of a Family Law Division within the Twentieth Judicial Circuit and shall apply to certain enumerated family law matters in Lee and Collier Counties. Due to population, caseload and judicial assignments, it is unnecessary that the Order be applied to Charlotte, Hendry and Glades Counties.

This Order is specifically designed to comply with the requirements of Justice Overton's opinion in In re: Report of the Commission on Family Courts, 16 F.L.W. S609 (Fla. Sept. 12, 1991). Additionally, the Order should serve to codify what has been the practice in this circuit since 1985.

Jurisdiction of the Family Law Division shall include dissolution, custody, visitation relief, property, URESA, name change, paternity, adoption, and domestic violence cases. In Lee County, juvenile dependency matters are to be included, but juvenile delinquency proceedings shall not be included. In Collier County, all juvenile matters shall be included within the Family Law Division.

PURPOSE:

The purpose of this Rule is to coordinate family law matters that affect one family by assigning all such cases to one judge.

JUDGE ASSIGNMENT AND ROTATION:

Judges shall be assigned to the Family Law Division by the Chief Judge, who shall give special consideration to the aptitude, demonstrated interest, and experience of each judge, for a term of not less than two years with the opportunity to request rotation after three years. Rotation of judges shall be staggered and shall be accomplished by Administrative Order.

PRACTICE AND PROCEDURE:

In order to ensure that all family law matters which affect one family are assigned to the same judge (with the exception of juvenile delinquency proceedings in Lee County), an Administrative Family Law Judge shall be appointed to serve in the Family Law Divisions of Lee and Collier Counties. The Administrative Family Law Judge shall be responsible for the implementation of this Order within the Family Law Division. The Administrative Family Law Judge shall be designated by Administrative Order for not less than a six month term.

The Administrative Family Law Judge shall also be responsible for ensuring that the division receives proper resources including court connected mediation, domestic violence assistance programs, guardians ad litem, home assessment services, sufficient staff to operate enforcement of support services and case coordination/receptionist staff. Any deficiencies in these resources shall be reported to the Chief Judge by the Administrative Family Law Judge immediately upon discovery or recognition of same.

In order to effectuate the purpose of this order, it shall be incumbent upon every person appearing before any judge within the Family Law Division to advise the judge of all other family law matters which may, in any way, affect the family or families involved in the matter before the judge. If there are other cases pending before any other judge within the division, the presiding judge shall notify the Administrative Judge of the multiple filings and, by appropriate order, the Administrative Judge shall consolidate all such family law matters to be heard before the same circuit judge within the division.

DONE AND ORDERED in Chambers this 23 day of Jan., 1992.

Thomas S. Reese
Chief Judge

History. - New.

2.13. STANDARDS OF COURTROOM DECORUM

IN THE TWENTIETH JUDICIAL CIRCUIT IN AND FOR THE STATE OF FLORIDA

ADMINISTRATIVE ORDER NO: 2.13

IN RE: STANDARDS OF COURTROOM DECORUM

WHEREAS the Judges of the Circuit and County Courts of the Twentieth Judicial Circuit have agreed that certain basic principles of courtroom decorum and behavior should be formally stated for the benefit and guidance of those unfamiliar with local traditions, the following standards of decorum are hereby adopted:

AS TO COUNSEL

When appearing in any court of the Twentieth Judicial Circuit, unless excused by the presiding judge, all counsel shall abide by the following:

(1) Stand as Court is opened, recessed or adjourned.

(2) Stand when the jury enters or retires from the courtroom.

(3) Stand when addressing, or being addressed by, the Court.

(4) Stand at the lectern while examining any witness; except that counsel may approach the Clerk's desk or the witness for purposes of handling or tendering exhibits.

(5) Stand at the lectern while making opening statements or closing arguments.

(6) Address all remarks to the Court, not to opposing counsel.

(7) Avoid disparaging personal remarks or acrimony toward opposing counsel and remain wholly detached from any ill-feeling between the litigants or witnesses.

(8) Refer to all persons, including witnesses, other counsel and the parties by their surnames and not by their first or given names.

(9) Only one attorney for each party shall examine or cross examine each witness. The attorney stating objections (if any) during direct examination shall be the attorney recognized for cross examination.

(10) Request permission before approaching the bench.

(11) Any paper or exhibit not previously marked for identification should first be submitted to the Clerk for marking before it is tendered to a witness; and any exhibit offered into evidence should, at the time of such offer, be handed to opposing counsel.

(12) In making objections, counsel should briefly state only the legal grounds therefore without further elaboration unless such is requested by the Court.

(13) In examining a witness, counsel shall not repeat or echo the answer given by the witness.

(14) Offers or requests for stipulations shall be made out of the presence or hearing of the jury.

(15) In opening statements and in arguments to the jury, counsel shall not express personal knowledge or opinion concerning any matter in issue.

(16) Counsel shall instruct all persons at counsel table that gestures, facial expressions, audible comments, or the like, as manifestations of approval or disapproval during the testimony of witnesses, or at any other time, are absolutely prohibited.

(17) All counsel shall dress in an appropriate manner consistent with the requirements of decorum and dignity appropriate to courtroom proceedings.

The standards set forth above are minimal, not all-inclusive, and are intended to supplement, not supplant or limit, the ethical obligations of counsel under the Rules of Professional Conduct. Individual judges may announce and enforce additional requirements or prohibitions, or may excuse compliance with any one or more of these standards.

AS TO NON–LAWYERS

(1) All persons appearing before the Court shall endeavor to dress in a reasonably conservative manner consistent with the requirements of decorum and dignity appropriate to courtroom proceedings. Generally, shorts, tank-tops and other beach attire are not appropriate as courtroom attire.

(2) All persons attending court proceedings shall refrain from making gestures, facial expressions, audible comments, applause, or the like, as manifestations of approval or disapproval during the testimony of a witness or during the oral presentation of counsel, or at any other time.

(3) In presentations before the Court, unrepresented parties shall observe the same rules of decorum which apply to attorneys.

WHEREFORE these standards are hereby adopted by the judges of the Circuit and County Courts of Lee County, Florida, this 9th day of November, 1992.

Thomas S. Reese
Chief Circuit Judge

History. - New.

ADDENDUM A. STANDARDS OF COURTROOM DECORUM

IN THE TWENTIETH JUDICIAL CIRCUIT IN AND FOR THE STATE OF FLORIDA

IN RE: STANDARDS OF COURTROOM DECORUM

ADMINISTRATIVE ORDER NO: 2.13

(ADDENDUM "A")

THIS CAUSE coming before the Court based upon an inquiry from the Honorable Scott W. Weinstein, Esquire, President of the Lee County Bar Association, and in consultation with the presidents of the Collier, Lee and Charlotte County Bar Associations, as to the advisability of implementing a "Summer Dress Code" for the members of the respective bar associations within the Twentieth Judicial Circuit, the Court finds and it is hereby,

ORDERED AND ADJUDGED:

1. That from Memorial Day through Labor Day (May 26, 2003 through September 1, 2003), the Court finds that it is acceptable and appropriate for all lawyers within the Twentieth Judicial Circuit to wear a coat with no tie or a tie with no coat to those proceedings in which members of the general public do not typically appear, such as motion calendars, docket soundings, and pre trial conferences.

2. That lawyers following the aforestated procedures shall not be deemed in violation of the provisions of Administrative Order 2.13 (17), Re: Standards of Courtroom Decorum.

3. That pursuant to the Rules Regulating the Florida Bar and local Administrative Order 2.20 (Standards of Professional Courtesy and Conduct) lawyers must continue to be guided by the requirements of proper decorum and dignity appropriate for all courtroom proceedings.

4. That notwithstanding anything to the contrary found within this order, individual judges shall continue to be in control of their individual courtrooms/hearing rooms, and the judges may announce or enforce additional dress requirements for their respective facilities.

5. That this Order shall terminate at the conclusion of the Labor Day holiday (01 September 2003), and the Court will assign Administrative Order 2.13 In Re: Standards of Courtroom Decorum to committee review, said committee to be appointed by the Chief Judge of the Twentieth Judicial Circuit.

DONE AND ORDERED in Naples, Collier County, Florida, this the 02 day of July, 2003.

Hugh D. Hayes
Chief Judge

2.14. AMERICANS WITH DISABILITIES ACT—DESIGNATION OF COORDINATOR AND GRIEVANCE PROCEDURE

IN THE TWENTIETH JUDICIAL CIRCUIT IN AND FOR THE STATE OF FLORIDA

ADMINISTRATIVE ORDER NO: 2.14—Amended—

IN RE: AMERICANS WITH DISABILITIES ACT—DESIGNATION OF COORDINATOR AND GRIEVANCE PROCEDURE

I. AUTHORITY

Federal regulations implementing the Americans With Disabilities Act of 1990 (ADA) require public entities with 50 or more employees to designate a responsible employee and adopt grievance procedures which provide for the prompt and equitable resolution of complaints alleging noncompliance with the ADA or complaints alleging any actions that would be prohibited under title II of the ADA (28 C.F.R. 35.107).

II. INTENT AND PURPOSE

It is the intent of the Twentieth Judicial Circuit to fully comply with the ADA and to assure equity, fairness and full participation in the judicial system for persons with disabilities.

The purpose of the procedure set forth in this order is to establish a mechanism for resolving complaints without requiring the complainant to resort to federal complaint procedures. Nonetheless, complainants are not required to exhaust this grievance procedure before filing a complaint at the federal level.

It is the intent of the Twentieth Judicial Circuit that complainants be consulted and advised and that communications be maintained at each step of the grievance process. It is also the intent of the Twentieth Judicial Circuit to utilize alternative dispute resolution techniques whenever required, necessary or mutually agreed upon at any point during the grievance process.

III. DEFINITIONS

A. Americans With Disabilities Act (ADA)—Public Law 101–336, the American With Disabilities Act of 1990, which prohibits discrimination on the basis of disability.

B. ADA Coordinator. Same as "Responsible Employee."

C. Disability or Persons with Disabilities. With respect to an individual, a physical or mental impairment which substantially limits one or more of the major life activities of such individual; a record of such impairment; or being regarded as having such an impairment as defined in Public Law 101–336 and 28 C.F.R. 35.104.

D. Grievance. A formal complaint made by a person, or on behalf of a person, alleging that he or she has been subjected to unlawful discrimination or inaccessibility to facilities, programs, services, benefits or activities on the basis of a disability.

E. Responsible Employee. An employee designated to coordinate a public entity's efforts to comply with and carry out its responsibilities under title II of the ADA. These responsibilities include any investigation and/or follow through of any complaint alleging non-compliance or alleging any actions that would be prohibited by title II of the ADA.

F. State Courts System. All Florida courts at both appellate and trial levels.

G. Title II. The second section of the ADA that prohibits discrimination on the basis of disability in state and local government services.

IV. DESIGNATION OF COORDINATOR

The ADA coordinator (who shall be the "responsible employee" as set forth above) for the Twentieth Judicial Circuit is:

Brooke Dean
Operations Division Manager
Lee County Justice Center
1700 Monroe Street
Fort Myers, Florida 33901
(239) 533–1771

V. GRIEVANCES

A. A formal grievance shall be instituted by filing a complaint.

B. Each complaint shall contain the following minimum information:

1. The name, address and telephone number of the complainant on whose behalf the complaint is being made.

2. The court facility in which the violation is alleged to have occurred.

3. A complete statement of the grievance and the facts upon which it is based.

4. The desired remedy or solution requested.

5. The names of any witnesses who can provide supportive or relevant information.

VI. GRIEVANCE PROCEDURE

A. Filing.

1. Complaints must be filed with the ADA coordinator no later than one hundred eighty (180) days from the date of the alleged violation.

2. The filing deadline may be extended by the coordinator upon a showing of good cause made prior to the expiration of the 180 day period set forth in paragraph A.1.above.

B. Assessment and Determination of Team Members.

1. The ADA coordinator will determine which functions of the court are at issue: facilities, programs, services, benefits and/or activities.

2. The ADA coordinator will notify the Chief Judge and the Court Administrator of the complaint.

3. A team consisting of at least three (3) people, one of whom must be the ADA coordinator (unless the ADA coordinator is the subject of the complaint), shall address the complaint. Individual(s) who are charged in the complaint with alleged discriminatory conduct shall not be a member of the team.

4. The team will involve representatives from county government entities in the resolution of the complaint when the complaint involves a court facility, program, service, benefit or activity that is under the authority of or provided by county government.

C. Fact Finding.

1. The team, or a member of the team, will review the complaint with the complainant.

2. The team, or a member of the team, will interview witnesses who can provide supportive or relative information and complete the fact finding.

D. Test of Legal Sufficiency.

1. The team, or a member of the team, shall determine the legal sufficiency of the complaint.

2. In making any such determination, the team shall consult the General Counsel for the Twentieth Judicial Circuit Court.

E. Action.

1. If a complaint is legally deficient, the complaint shall immediately be brought to closure.

2. If a complaint is legally sufficient, the team will establish a course of action to resolve the complaint.

3. To the extent necessary, the court will make reasonable modifications to its programs, services, benefits and activities to ensure future compliance with the ADA.

4. When appropriate, and to the extent necessary, the court will work with county government to make reasonable modifications to court facilities, programs, services, benefits and activities that are under the authority of or provided by county government to ensure future compliance with the ADA.

5. The court make invoke the course of action described in the regulations implementing the ADA (28 C.F.R. 35.164) when modifications would result in a fundamental alteration in the nature of a service, program or activity or in undue financial and administrative burdens.

F. Closure, Notification and Records Retention.

1. The ADA coordinator shall communicate the results of the investigation and the chosen course of action to the complainant in writing not later than thirty (30) days from the date the complaint was filed.

2. In instances where a grievance against the Twentieth Judicial Circuit is filed with the ADA coordinator of the State Courts System, the ADA coordinator shall also communicate the results of the investigation and the chosen course of action to the ADA coordinator of the State Courts System in writing not later than thirty (30) days from the date the complaint was filed.

3. A record of the grievance shall be maintained for three (3) years and shall be located with the ADA coordinator.

DONE AND ORDERED in Chambers at Fort Myers, Lee County, Florida, this 14th day of April, 2016.

Michael T. McHugh

Chief Judge

History. Administrative Order 2.14 (January 13, 1993); Administrative Order 2.14 (January 19, 1994); Administrative Order 2.14 (October 1, 1997); Administrative Order 2.14 (Nov. 1, 2004); Administrative Order 2.14 (February 5, 2007); Administrative Order 2.14 (May 16, 2011); Administrative Order 2.14 (November 22, 2013).

2.15. AMERICANS WITH DISABILITIES ACT—NOTIFICATION OF COURT PROCEEDINGS

IN THE TWENTIETH JUDICIAL CIRCUIT IN AND FOR THE STATE OF FLORIDA

ADMINISTRATIVE ORDER NO: 2.15—Amended—

IN RE: AMERICANS WITH DISABILITIES ACT—NOTIFICATION OF COURT PROCEEDINGS

Pursuant to the Americans With Disabilities Act of 1990 (ADA), reasonable accommodations are required to be provided to requesting qualified persons with disabilities in order that they might participate fully in court programs, services, activities, and benefits.

It is the intent of the Twentieth Judicial Circuit to facilitate the provision of reasonable accommodations when requested by qualified persons with disabilities. Therefore, in accordance with the ADA and Fla. R. Jud. Admin. 2.540, it is

ORDERED AND ADJUDGED that all notices of court proceedings to be held in public facilities within the Twentieth Judicial Circuit shall include the following statement in bold face, 14 point Times New Roman or Courier font:

IN CHARLOTTE COUNTY

"If you are a person with a disability who needs any accommodation in order to participate in this proceeding, you are entitled, at no cost to you, to the provision of certain assistance. Please contact Jon Embury, Administrative Services Manager, whose office is located at 350 E. Marion Avenue, Punta Gorda, Florida 33950, and whose telephone number is (941) 637–2110, at least 7 days before your scheduled court appearance, or immediately upon receiving this notification if the time before the scheduled appearance is less than 7 days; if you are hearing or voice impaired, call 711."

IN COLLIER COUNTY

"If you are a person with a disability who needs any accommodation in order to participate in this proceeding, you are entitled, at no cost to you, to the provision of certain assistance. Please contact Charles Rice, Administrative Services Manager, whose office is located at 3315 East Tamiami Trail, Suite 501, Naples, Florida 34112, and whose telephone number is (239) 252–8800, at least 7 days before your scheduled court appearance, or immediately upon receiving this notification if the time before the scheduled appearance is less than 7 days; if you are hearing or voice impaired, call 711."

IN GLADES COUNTY

"If you are a person with a disability who needs any accommodation in order to participate in this proceeding, you are entitled, at no cost to you, to the provision of certain assistance. Please contact Dawn Oliver, Administrative Services Manager, whose office is located at the Hendry County Courthouse, 25 E. Hickpochee Avenue, LaBelle, Florida 33935, and whose telephone number is (863) 675–5374, at least 7 days before your scheduled court appearance, or immediately upon receiving this notification if the time before the scheduled appearance is less than 7 days; if you are hearing or voice impaired, call 711."

IN HENDRY COUNTY

"If you are a person with a disability who needs any accommodation in order to participate in this proceeding, you are entitled, at no cost to you, to the provision of certain assistance. Please contact Dawn Oliver, Administrative Services Manager, whose office is located at the Hendry County Courthouse, 25 E. Hickpochee Avenue, LaBelle, Florida 33935, and whose telephone number is (863) 675–5374, at least 7 days before your scheduled court appearance, or immediately upon receiving this notification if the time before the scheduled appearance is less than 7 days; if you are hearing or voice impaired, call 711."

IN LEE COUNTY

"If you are a person with a disability who needs any accommodation in order to participate in this proceeding, you are entitled, at no cost to you, to the provision of certain assistance. Please contact Brooke Dean, Operations Division Manager, whose office is located at Lee County Justice Center, 1700 Monroe Street, Fort Myers, Florida 33901, and whose telephone number is (239) 533–1771, at least 7 days before your scheduled court appearance, or immediately upon receiving this notification if the time before the scheduled appearance is less than 7 days; if you are hearing or voice impaired, call 711."

DONE AND ORDERED at Fort Myers, Lee County, Florida this 14th day of April, 2016.

Michael T. McHugh

Chief Judge

History. Administrative Order 2.15 (Jan. 13, 1993); Amended Administrative Order 2.15 (Feb. 5, 1993); Administrative Order 2.15 (Feb. 1, 1994); Administrative Order 2.15 (October 1, 1997); Administrative Order 2.15 (January 13, 2000); Administrative Order 2.15 (November 1, 2004); Administrative Order 2.15 (Aug. 23, 2005); Administrative Order 2.15 (Feb. 2, 2007); Administrative Order 2.15 (July 21, 2008); Administrative Order 2.15 (July 28, 2008); Administrative Order 2.15 (June 17, 2010); Administrative Order 2.15 (May 16, 2011); Administrative Order 2.15 (April 9, 2012); Administrative Order 2.15 (February 7, 2013); Administrative Order 2.15 (November 22, 2013); Administrative Order 2.15 (February 19, 2014).

2.16. CHANGE OF VENUE PROCEDURES

IN THE TWENTIETH JUDICIAL CIRCUIT IN AND FOR THE STATE OF FLORIDA

ADMINISTRATIVE ORDER NO: 2.16

IN RE: CHANGE OF VENUE PROCEDURES

(A) Purpose and Application. This rule governs change of venue procedure and applies only to criminal cases where venue has been changed pursuant to Fla. R. Crim. P. 3.240.

(B) Preliminary procedures. Prior to the announcement or entry of an order to change venue to a particular circuit, the chief judge or the chief judge's designee should contact the chief judge of the circuit where the case is intended to be moved to determine the receiving county's ability to accommodate the change of venue. It is the intent of this order that the county identified to receive the case should do so unless the physical facilities or other resources in that county are such that moving the case to that county would either create an unsafe situation or would otherwise adversely affect the operations of that court. Any conflict between circuits regarding a potential change of venue should be referred to the Chief Justice of the Florida Supreme Court for resolution.

(C) Presiding Judge. The presiding judge from the originating court shall accompany the case subject to the change of venue, unless both the originating and receiving courts agree otherwise.

(D) Reimbursement of costs. As a general policy, the county where the action originated should reimburse the county receiving the change of venue case for any ordinary expenditure or extraordinary but reasonable and necessary expenditure which would not have been incurred by the receiving county, but for the change of venue. For purposes of this rule, "ordinary expenditure", "extraordinary expenditure" and "nonreimbursable expenditure" shall include but are not necessarily limited to the following:

(1) Ordinary expenditure includes:

(a) Jury costs;

(b) Witness costs;

(c) Attorney travel costs for public counsel;

(d) Judicial travel costs;

(e) Travel costs for all necessary staff of public counsel and the judiciary; and,

(f) Court reporter costs.

(2) Extraordinary expenditure includes:

(a) Security related expenditures;

(b) Facility remodeling or renovation; and,

(c) Leasing or renting of space or equipment;

(3) Nonreimbursable expenditure includes:

(a) Normal operating expenses including the overhead of the receiving county; and,

(b) Equipment purchased and kept by the receiving county which can then be used for other purposes or cases.

(E) Documentation of costs. No expenses should be submitted for reimbursement without supporting documentation, such as a claim, invoice, bill, statement or time sheet. Any required court order or approval of costs should also be sent to the originating court.

(F) Timing of reimbursement. Unless both counties agree to other terms, reimbursement of all expenses which are not questioned by the originating county should be made payable within sixty (60) days of receipt of the claim for reimbursement. Payment of disputed amounts should be made within sixty (60) days of the date of resolution.

(G) Media Relations. Procedures to accommodate the media should be developed by the receiving county in advance when the change of venue trial is expected to generate a high degree of publicity. These procedures must be approved by the chief judge of the receiving circuit and implemented pursuant to administrative order. The presiding judge shall obtain the concurrence of the chief judge of the receiving county before entering any orders which vary from or conflict with existing administrative orders of the receiving circuit.

DONE AND ORDERED at Fort Myers, Lee County, Florida, this 19th day of January, 1994.

Thomas S. Reese
Chief Circuit Judge

History. - New.

2.17. DUTY JUDGE RESPONSIBILITIES

IN THE TWENTIETH JUDICIAL CIRCUIT IN AND FOR THE STATE OF FLORIDA

ADMINISTRATIVE ORDER NO: 2.17

IN RE: DUTY JUDGE RESPONSIBILITIES

(a) Purpose. The prompt and efficient administration of justice requires that a judge be available in chambers during all work hours and on call after work hours to handle specifically enumerated emergency matters.

(b) Definitions. The following definitions apply to this rule:

(1) "Duty Judge" is the judge identified in the annual duty roster who shall be available at all times to handle applications for warrants or other similar matters for law enforcement personnel, petitions for ex parte injunctive relief to prevent domestic and repeat violence, and other emergency matters defined herein.

(2) "Emergency" encompasses the foregoing ex parte applications and other matters of extreme urgency, such as matters of life and death or instances of irreparable harm. Specifically not included in this definition are matters of urgency in cases already assigned to a specific judge which can be scheduled for consideration before that judge within a reasonable period of time.

(c) Availability. The duty judge shall be available from 8:30 a.m. to 5:00 p.m. each work day at the county courthouse where the duty judge is permanently assigned. Coverage on weekends, holidays and after-hours shall be provided by an on-call call system established by the court administrator through which the duty judge can be reached by telephone, beeper, radio, etc. A judge should not have to clear his or her calendar in order to handle the duty judge's responsibilities. During the duty judge assignment, the duty judge is obligated to stop what he or she is doing to accommodate the responsibilities of the duty judge.

(d) Responsibilities. Matters appropriate for consideration by a duty judge include but are not limited to the following:

(1) Applications for search warrants;

(2) Applications for arrest warrants;

(3) Applications for pen registers;

(4) Applications for wiretap orders;

(5) Petitions for ex parte injunctive relief to prevent domestic and repeat violence;

(6) Right-to-die cases;

(7) All other ex parte applications and other matters of extreme urgency which involve matters of life and death or instances of irreparable harm;

(8) First appearances; and,

(9) Shelter Hearings

(10) Detention hearings.

(e) After-hours injunctive relief. To facilitate the acceptance and processing of emergency ex parte applications for injunctive relief to prevent domestic violence pursuant to § 741.30 Fla. Stat. (1991), the clerk of court in each county within the Twentieth Circuit shall make provisions for staff to be available to assist in the disposition of such applications after normal business hours. The sheriffs of each county within the Twentieth Circuit are empowered to accept a certified copy of a faxed signed domestic violence injunction for service of process should the duty judge be equipped with a fax machine.

(f) Disposition of criminal matters. Criminal matters such as bond reduction hearings or modifications of pretrial detention must be scheduled in accordance with Fla. R. Crim. P. 3.131(d)(1). In any case where the assigned criminal court judge is not in a position to "promptly" dispose of any emergency criminal matters, Rule 3.131 controls, and only the judge who set bail, the presiding judge, or the first appearance judge (if authorized by the judge initially setting or denying bail to modify or set conditions of release), may handle the matter.

(g) Limitations. The following matters should not generally be entertained by a duty judge:

(1) Certified questions at depositions;

(2) All regular probate matters;

(3) All cases already assigned to a presiding judge; and,

(4) All motions for protective orders in civil or criminal matters.

DONE AND ORDERED in Chambers at Fort Myers, Lee County, Florida this 15 day of February, 1993.

Thomas S. Reese
Chief Circuit Judge

History. - New.

2.18. COURTHOUSE AND COURTROOM SECURITY

IN THE TWENTIETH JUDICIAL CIRCUIT IN AND FOR THE STATE OF FLORIDA

ADMINISTRATIVE ORDER NO.: 2.18

IN RE: COURTHOUSE AND COURTROOM SECURITY

Pursuant to Rule 2.050, Florida Rules of Judicial Administration, the Twentieth Judicial Circuit hereby adopts the following circuit-wide policy with regard to courthouse and courtroom, security.

1. Each courthouse and courtroom within the Twentieth Judicial Circuit is hereby designated as a secure facility.

2. Any person entering any courthouse (including branch courthouses established by Administrative Order 2.7), may be subject to a search of their person or property anywhere in the building by authorized security personnel through the use of perimeter placed metal detectors, hand held or other specialized electronic equipment or other means available. Exits may be limited in accordance with state and local laws and the intent of this Order.

3. Subject to the exceptions set forth in paragraph 7 of this Order, any person in possession of a weapon, hazardous material or contraband shall be denied access to the courthouse unless the weapon, hazardous material or contraband is surrendered to the proper authorities.

4. Persons who refuse to submit to a search of their person or their possessions shall be denied access to the courthouse or courtroom.

5. If any illegal or unauthorized weapons, hazardous materials or contraband are discovered, the proper law enforcement officials or officers shall be notified immediately for appropriate action, including, prosecution to the fullest extent of the law.

6. The following notice shall be posted at all courthouse entrances and at each security station:

FOR THE PROTECTION OF THE PUBLIC, CERTAIN AREAS WITHIN THIS BUILDING HAVE BEEN DESIGNATED AS SECURE AREAS. ALL PERSONS DESIRING TO ENTER A SECURE AREA MUST PASS THROUGH A METAL DETECTOR OR MAY BE SUBJECT TO INDIVIDUAL SEARCH BY AUTHORIZED SECURITY PERSONNEL. ALL PACKAGES, BRIEFCASES, PURSES, POCKETBOOKS OR OTHER CONTAINERS CARRIED BY ANY PERSON MUST BE OFFERED FOR INSPECTION AT ANY DESIGNATED AREA IF SUCH PERSON WISHES TO ENTER OR REMAIN IN THIS BUILDING. ALL PERSONS ENTERING THIS BUILDING ARE DEEMED TO HAVE GIVEN THEIR CONSENT TO ANY SEARCH CONDUCTED PURSUANT TO ADMINISTRATIVE ORDER 2.18 AND FLORIDA LAW. ALL WEAPONS, INCLUDING LEGALLY AUTHORIZED FIREARMS, MUST BE SURRENDERED PRIOR TO GAINING ENTRY AND ALL LEGAL WEAPONS MAY BE RECLAIMED UPON LEAVING. ILLEGAL WEAPONS OR OTHER CONTRABAND DISCOVERED IN THE COURSE OF ANY SEARCH WILL BE SEIZED AND CONFISCATED AND MAY RESULT IN PROSECUTION TO THE FULLEST EXTENT OF THE LAW.

7. Those individuals who are exempted from this Order include: Bailiffs, Courthouse Security Guards employed by any law enforcement agency or the Office of the Court Administrator, and Judges, both active and retired. However, based upon the local custom and practice in each county, an administrative judge, at his or her discretion, may permit individual exemptions from this Order, in addition to those listed within this provision.

8. Any individual entering any courthouse (including branch courthouses) shall not be permitted to bring any liquid in an open or sealed container into the courthouse. If for the purposes of an evidentiary proceeding, it is necessary to bring a liquid in an open or sealed container into the courthouse, the individual shall be escorted by a bailiff to the designated courtroom. This provision shall not apply to employees of any of the offices located within the courthouse. However, at the discretion of courthouse security personnel, an employee shall allow a container to be inspected.

DONE AND ORDERED in Chambers at Naples, Collier County, Florida, this 20 day of Jan., 2000.

William L. Blackwell
Chief Judge

History. - Administrative Order 2.18 (July 12, 1994).

2.19. HURRICANE PREPAREDNESS

IN THE TWENTIETH JUDICIAL CIRCUIT IN AND FOR THE STATE OF FLORIDA

IN RE: HURRICANE PREPAREDNESS

ADMINISTRATIVE ORDER NO. 2.19—Amended—

Pursuant to Fla. R. Jud. Admin. 2.215(b), Florida Statute § 43.26 and the inherent authority of this Court to regulate the use of courtrooms throughout the Twentieth Judicial Circuit, the Court hereby adopts a policy for hurricane preparedness for all court facilities and judicial proceedings throughout the Circuit.

The Court is aware that The National Weather Service utilizes two salient terms when advising the public on hurricane preparedness. They are "Hurricane Watch" and "Hurricane Warning."

In the event of a hurricane watch, all judicial personnel, with the exception of limited personnel deemed necessary by the Chief Judge and the Trial Court Administrator as determined on a situational or operational basis, should be prepared to cease operations in the event that the hurricane watch is upgraded to a hurricane warning.

In the event that any coastal or inland area within the boundaries of a county of the Twentieth Judicial Circuit is the subject of a hurricane warning (as that term is used by The National Weather Service), all judicial proceedings within that county will be suspended during the period of any such warning.

This Court recognizes that the Twentieth Judicial Circuit is the largest geographic circuit in the State of Florida. Accordingly, the Court affords to the Circuit Administrative Judge for each county within the Twentieth Judicial Circuit the discretion to determine whether a suspension of judicial activities is warranted due to circumstances within that county that may not be present in another part of the circuit, subject to approval of the Chief Judge or the Chief Judge's designee. The ultimate authority for issuing orders to suspend judicial activities and the evacuation of any or all courthouses or court facilities within the circuit rests with the Chief Judge, or the Chief Judge's designee, pursuant to the authorities cited above. Prior to any such request for the suspension of judicial activities or evacuation of courthouse facilities, the Circuit Administrative Judge shall consult with Emergency Management officials in the affected county or counties and the Office of the Trial Court Administrator.

The procedure to be employed in the event of an imminent hurricane landfall is that the Circuit Administrative Judge for any affected county is to report to the Trial Court Administrator the potential need for the suspension of judicial activities or evacuation of courthouse facilities. In such event, the Trial Court Administrator shall advise the public through the Public Information Officer for the Courts. Informational updates will be provided to all local news outlets and will be updated shortly after the 11:00 a.m. and 5:00 p.m. National Weather Service updates.

The purpose of adopting this hurricane preparedness policy is to provide the public with as much advance notice as possible of any closure of court facilities, while at the same time having due regard for the safety and welfare of all court personnel and any others who may be affected by the potential landfall of a hurricane in this area.

In the event of suspension of judicial proceedings or closure of any courthouses within the Twentieth Judicial Circuit pursuant to this Administrative Order, relief from time deadlines imposed by applicable statutes or rules of procedure may only be granted by the Chief Justice of the Florida Supreme Court pursuant to Fla. R. Jud. Admin. 2.205(a)(2)(B)(iv). It shall be the responsibility of the Chief Judge, or the Chief Judge's designee, to apply to the Chief Justice of the Florida Supreme Court for an appropriate tolling order.

DONE AND ORDERED in Chambers at Fort Myers, Lee County, Florida, this 15 day of Sept, 2011.

Jay B. Rosman
Chief Judge

History. Administrative Order 2.19 (March 28, 2000); Administrative Order 2.19 (August 20, 2009).

2.20. STANDARDS OF PROFESSIONAL COURTESY AND CONDUCT AND ESTABLISHMENT OF LOCAL PROFESSIONALISM PANEL

IN THE TWENTIETH JUDICIAL CIRCUIT IN AND FOR THE STATE OF FLORIDA

ADMINISTRATIVE ORDER NO. 2.20—Amended—

IN RE: STANDARDS OF PROFESSIONAL COURTESY AND CONDUCT AND ESTABLISHMENT OF LOCAL PROFESSIONALISM PANEL

In an effort to foster and promote professionalism among lawyers practicing in the Twentieth Judicial Circuit, and in accordance with the Florida Supreme Court's Administrative Order, In re: Commission on Professionalism dated June 11, 1998, and the Florida Supreme Court's opinion, In re Code for Resolving Professionalism Complaints, 116 So. 3d 280 (Fla. 2013), and upon recommendations made by the Twentieth Judicial Circuit Court's Committee on Professionalism, it is

ORDERED AND ADJUDGED as follows:

1. The Standards of Professional Courtesy and Conduct for lawyers practicing in the Twentieth Judicial Circuit were adopted by the original version of this Administrative Order entered May 8, 2000. A modified and updated version of the document entitled "Standards of Professional Courtesy and Conduct for Lawyers Practicing in the Twentieth Judicial Circuit" is attached to this order as Attachment "A" and made a part hereof, and is applicable to all lawyers practicing within the five counties of the Twentieth Judicial Circuit.

2. The Standards of Professional Courtesy and Conduct for Lawyers Practicing in the Twentieth Judicial Circuit are designed to supplement and are not to supplant the Standards of Courtroom Decorum set forth in Administrative Order 2.13. Furthermore, all lawyers practicing in the State of Florida are bound by the existing standards of behavior already codified in the Oath of Admission to The Florida Bar, The Florida Bar Creed of Professionalism, The Florida Bar Ideals and Goals of Professionalism, the Rules Regulating The Florida Bar, and all decisions and opinions of the Florida Supreme Court, including the Code for Resolving Professionalism Complaints adopted by the Florida Supreme Court by opinion issued June 6, 2013.

3. The Peer Review Program of the Twentieth Judicial Circuit and a Peer Review Committee were established by the original version of this Administrative Order entered May 8, 2000. However, the Florida Supreme Court opinion issued June 6, 2013, In re Code for Resolving Professionalism Complaints, 116 So.3d 280 (Fla. 2013), requires modification of the already existing Peer Review Program of the Twentieth Judicial Circuit, which will hereinafter be known as the Local Professionalism Program of the Twentieth Judicial Circuit. Likewise, the Peer Review Committee of the Twentieth Judicial Circuit will hereinafter be known as the Local Professionalism Panel of the Twentieth Judicial Circuit. A modified and updated version of the original document entitled "Peer Review Program of the Twentieth Judicial Circuit" will hereinafter be entitled "Local Professionalism Program of the Twentieth Judicial Circuit," and is attached to this order as Attachment "B" and made a part hereof, and is applicable to all lawyers practicing in the counties of the Twentieth Judicial Circuit.

4. The operation of the Local Professionalism Panel, including referrals to and review by the Panel of allegedly noncompliant behavior, shall be as set forth in Attachment "B."

5. So as to avoid any potential appearance of impropriety or any potential conflicts of interest or issues involving the disqualification of judges from cases over which they may preside, no judge shall serve on the Local Professionalism Panel nor be privy to any referrals to the Local Professionalism Panel nor any documents generated by the Local Professionalism Panel, until such time as, or if, those documents may be made public by the Local Professionalism Panel. The Local Professionalism Panel shall remain independent of the Twentieth Judicial Circuit Professionalism Committee and of the Courts of the Twentieth Judicial Circuit. Neither the Chief Judge nor the Courts of the Twentieth Judicial Circuit shall retain custody of any referrals or documents generated by the Local Professionalism Panel. Referrals and documents generated by the Local Professionalism Panel shall be under the sole control and custody of the President, or Presidents, or designees, of the respective local voluntary bar associations.

6. The Local Professionalism Program is not a disciplinary process and is not intended to deal specifically with alleged violations of the Rules Regulating the Florida Bar. Violations of the Rules Regulating the Florida Bar remain solely within the jurisdiction of the grievance process of the Florida Bar.

7. The amendments to this Administrative Order shall take effect immediately.

8. To the extent that this Administrative Order may conflict with any rule, statute, or law, the rule, statute or law, shall prevail.

DONE AND ORDERED in Chambers at Fort Myers, Lee County, Florida, this 19th day of Feb., 2013.[1]

Jay B. Rosman
Chief Judge

History.—Administrative Order 2.20 (May 8, 2000); Administrative Order 2.20 (July.24, 2012); Administrative Order 2.20 (Feb. 1, 2013).

Attachment A

STANDARDS OF PROFESSIONAL COURTESY AND CONDUCT FOR LAWYERS PRACTICING IN THE TWENTIETH JUDICIAL[2] CIRCUIT

I. FOREWORD

In 1989, the Florida Bar established a task force to study the course of professionalism among lawyers in Florida. The study addressed issues regarding civility among lawyers, public perception of lawyers and lawyers' satisfaction and fulfillment with their profession. The work performed by the task force resulted in the creation of the Florida Bar's Standing Committee on Professionalism. In July, 1996, the Honorable Chief Justice Gerald Kogan signed an administrative order that created the Florida Supreme Court Commission on Professionalism.

In January, 1998, Justice Kogan requested that the Chief Judge of each Judicial Circuit appoint and be involved in a Circuit Committee on Professionalism charged with the overall responsibility of initiating and coordinating professionalism activities within their respective Circuit. Accordingly, in early 1998, the Twentieth Judicial Circuit's Committee on Professionalism was formed. In November, 1999, a subcommittee of the Twentieth Judicial Circuit's Committee was appointed to prepare a practical set of standards of professional courtesy and conduct for lawyers to adhere to in their practice in the Twentieth Judicial Circuit. These Standards of Professional Courtesy and Conduct for Lawyers Practicing in the Twentieth Judicial Circuit ("Standards") were drafted in coordination with the formation of the Peer Review Program of the Twentieth Judicial Circuit. The Peer Review Program is an educational, voluntary, informal and non-punitive enhancement program designed to correct behavioral performance which, although not so serious as to invoke formal disciplinary proceedings or other sanctions, nevertheless fell below the high standard expected of attorneys. In February, 2000, the Standards were adopted and approved by the Twentieth Judicial Circuit's Committee on Professionalism.

In preparing and approving the Standards, the Committee reviewed numerous model guidelines for professional conduct. The Committee utilized the Guidelines for Professional Conduct approved by the Executive Counsel of the Trial Lawyers Section of the Florida Bar, as endorsed by the Florida Conference of Circuit Judges in 1995. The Committee also utilized the standards adopted by the Fourth, Sixth, Eighth and Fifteenth Judicial Circuit's of Florida.

II. PREAMBLE

The practice of law is a privilege, not a right. In exercising this privilege, lawyers must not pursue victory at the expense of justice nor at the risk of the loss of the lawyers' reputation for honesty and professionalism within the legal community. Clients are best represented by attorneys who exhibit professional conduct at all times. The Bar must protect the honor and integrity of the judicial system and improve the public trust and perception of the legal profession. Lawyers must work to enhance communication, respect and courtesy among members of the Bar.

Every attorney practicing law or appearing in judicial proceedings within the Twentieth Judicial Circuit is expected to be entirely familiar with, and practice according to, (a) Standards of Professional Courtesy and Conduct for Lawyers Practicing in the Twentieth Judicial Circuit, (b) The Florida Bar Trial Lawyers Section Guidelines for Professional Conduct, and (c) the Handbook of Discovery Practice published by the Joint Committee of the Trial Lawyers Section of The Florida Bar and Conference of Circuit and County Court Judges.

It shall be the responsibility of attorneys practicing within the Twentieth Judicial Circuit to be aware of Administrative Orders governing practice within the Twentieth Judicial Circuit and to comply with all standards of professionalism. For most lawyers, the Standards will simply reflect their current practice. However, it is hoped that the widespread dissemination and implementation of the Standards will result in an overall increase in the level of professionalism in the practice of law within the Twentieth Judicial Circuit.

III. INTRODUCTION

The effective administration of justice requires the interaction of many professionals and disciplines, but none is more critical than the role of the lawyer. In fulfilling that role, a lawyer performs many tasks, few of which are easy, most of which are exacting. In the final analysis, a lawyer's duty is always to the client. But in striving to fulfill that duty, a lawyer must be ever conscious of his or her broader duty to the judicial system that serves both attorney and client. To the judiciary, a lawyer owes candor, diligence and utmost respect. To the administration of justice, a lawyer unquestionably owes the fundamental duties of personal dignity and professional integrity. Coupled with those duties, however, is a lawyer's duty of courtesy and cooperation with other lawyers for the efficient administration of justice.

The Standards reflect an effort to emphasize decency and courtesy in our professional lives without intruding unreasonably on a lawyer's choice of style or tactic. (Some of the guidelines may not apply in criminal proceedings, or where a specific judge has a different rule.)

The Standards have been codified with the hope that their dissemination will educate attorneys and others who may be unfamiliar with customary local practices. Compliance with the Standards, unlike the "Oath of Admission" and the "rules of Professional Conduct" adopted by the Florida Supreme Court, is intended to be voluntary. The Standards have received the approval of the Twentieth Judicial Circuit Committee on Professionalism as well as the County and Circuit Judges of the Twentieth Judicial Circuit.

IV. STANDARDS

A. CONDUCT TOWARD OTHER ATTORNEYS, THE COURT AND PARTICIPANTS

1. Attorneys should refrain from criticizing or denigrating the court, opposing counsel, parties or witnesses.

2. Attorneys, should be and should impress upon their clients and witnesses to be, courteous and respectful. No one should be rude or disruptive with the court, opposing counsel, parties or witnesses.

3. Attorneys should make an effort to explain to witnesses the purpose of their required attendance at depositions, hearings or trials. They should further attempt to accommodate the schedules of witnesses when setting or resetting their appearance and promptly notify them of any cancellations.

4. Attorneys should respect and abide by the spirit and letter of all rulings of the court.

5. Attorneys should not show marked attention or unusual informality to any judge, except if outside of court and supported by a personal relationship. Attorneys should avoid anything calculated to gain, or having the appearance of gaining, special consideration or favor from a judge.

6. Attorneys should adhere strictly to all express promises and agreements with opposing counsel, whether oral or in writing. Attorneys should adhere in good faith to all agreements implied by the circumstances or by local custom.

7. Attorneys should not knowingly misstate, misrepresent, distort, or exaggerate any fact, opinion, or legal authority to anyone. Attorneys should not mislead by inaction or silence.

B. SCHEDULING

1. Except in emergency situations, attorneys should provide opposing counsel, parties, witnesses, and other affected persons, sufficient notice of depositions, hearings and other proceedings. As a general rule, notice should be provided (not including time for service) no less than five (5) business days for instate depositions, ten (10) business days for out-of-state depositions and five (5) business days for hearings.

2. Except in emergency situations, attorneys should make a good faith effort to communicate with opposing counsel prior to scheduling depositions, hearings and other proceedings, so as to schedule them a time that are mutually convenient for all interested persons. Further a sufficient time should be reserved to permit a complete presentation by counsel for all parties.

3. Attorneys should notify opposing counsel of any hearing time reserved as soon as practicable.

4. When hearing time is obtained, attorneys should promptly prepare and serve all counsel of record with notice of the hearing. Do not delay in providing such notice.

5. The notice of hearing should indicate on its face whether the date and time have been coordinated with opposing counsel. If the attorney has been unable to coordinate the hearing with opposing counsel, the notice should state the specific good faith efforts the attorney undertook to coordinate or why coordination was not obtained.

6. Attorneys should not use the hearing time obtained by opposing counsel for other motion practice.

7. Attorneys should notify opposing counsel, the court, and others affected, of scheduling conflicts as soon as they become apparent. Further, attorneys should cooperate with one another regarding all reasonable rescheduling requests that do not prejudice their clients or unduly delay a proceeding.

8. Attorneys should promptly notify the court or other tribunal of any resolution between the parties that renders a scheduled court appearance unnecessary.

9. Attorneys should grant reasonable requests by opposing counsel for extensions of time within which to respond to pleadings, discovery and other matters when such an extension will not prejudice their client or unduly delay a proceeding.

10. Attorneys should cooperate with opposing counsel during trials and evidentiary hearings by disclosing the identities of all witnesses reasonably expected to be called and the length of time needed to present their entire case, except when a client's material rights would be adversely affected. They should also cooperate with the calling of witnesses out of turn when the circumstances justify it.

11. When scheduling a deposition, attorneys should make a good faith effort to schedule enough time to complete the deposition without adjournment, unless otherwise stipulated with opposing counsel.

12. Attorneys should call potential scheduling problems to the attention of those affected, including the court, as soon as they become apparent and should avoid last minute cancellations.

13. Attorneys should make request for scheduling changes only when necessary and should not request rescheduling, cancellations, extension or postponements solely for the purpose of delay or obtaining unfair advantage.

14. First requests for reasonable extensions of time to respond to litigation deadlines relating to pleadings, discovery, or motions, should be granted as a matter of courtesy unless time is of the essence or other circumstances prohibit same.

15. Attorneys should not attach unfair or extraneous conditions to extensions. However, attorneys may impose conditions required to preserve a client's rights and may seek reciprocal scheduling concessions. When considering an extension request, an attorney should not seek to prohibit an adversary's assertion of substantive rights.

16. Attorneys should advise clients against the strategy of granting no time extensions for the sake of appearing "tough", especially when such extensions will not prejudice their client or unduly delay the proceeding.

17. After a first extension, any additional requests for time should be dealt with by balancing the need for expedition against the deference one should ordinarily give to an adversary, and whether it is likely a court would grant the extension if asked to do so.

C. SERVICE OF PAPERS

1. The timing and manner of service should not be used to the disadvantage of the party receiving the papers.

2. Papers and memoranda of law should not be served at court appearances without advance notice to opposing counsel and should not be served so close to a court appearance so as to inhibit the ability of opposing counsel to prepare for that appearance or to respond to the papers. Should the attorney do so, the court is urged to take appropriate action in response, including continuing the matter to allow opposing counsel to prepare and respond.

3. Papers should not be served in order to take advantage of an opponent's known absence from the office or at a time or in a manner designed to inconvenience an adversary, such as late on Friday afternoon or the day preceding a secular or religious holiday.

4. Service should be made personally or by courtesy copy facsimile transmission when it is likely that service by mail, even when allowed, will prejudice the opposing party or will not provide the opposing party with a reasonable time to respond.

D. COMMUNICATION WITH ADVERSARIES

1. Attorneys should all at all times be civil and courteous in communicating with adversaries, whether in writing or orally.

2. Attorneys should not write letters to ascribe to one's adversary a position he or she has not taken or to create "a record" of events that have not occurred.

3. Letters intended only to make a record should be used sparingly and only when necessary under all the circumstances.

4. Unless specifically permitted or invited by the court, letters between counsel should not be sent to the judge.

5. During the course of representing a client, attorneys should not communicate on the subject of the representation with a party known to be represented by another lawyer in the same matter without having obtained the prior consent of the lawyer representing such other party or unless authorized by law.

E. DISCOVERY

1. Attorneys should pursue discovery requests that are reasonably related to the matter at issue.

2. Attorneys should not use discovery for the purpose of causing undue delay or obtaining unfair advantage.

3. Attorneys should use discovery to ascertain information, to perpetuate testimony, or to obtain documents or things necessary for the prosecution or defense of an action. Attorneys should never use discovery as a means of harassment, intimidation or to impose an inordinate burden or expense.

4. Attorneys should file motions for protective orders as soon as possible and notice them for hearing as soon as practicable.

5. Prior to filing a motion to compel or for protective order, attorneys should confer with opposing counsel in a good faith effort to resolve the issues raised. Attorneys shall file with the motion a statement certifying that the moving counsel so complied and has been unable to resolve the dispute with opposing counsel.

F. DEPOSITIONS

1. In scheduling depositions, reasonable consideration should be given to accommodating schedules of opposing counsel and of the deponent, where it is possible to do so without prejudicing the client's rights.

2. When a deposition is noticed by another party in the reasonably near future, counsel should ordinarily not notice another deposition for an earlier date without the agreement of opposing counsel.

3. Counsel should not attempt to delay a deposition for dilatory purposes. Delays should occur only if necessary to meet real scheduling problems.

4. Counsel should not inquire into a deponent's personal affairs or finances or question a deponent's integrity where such inquiry is irrelevant to the subject matter of deposition.

5. Counsel should not conduct questioning in a manner intended to harass the witness, such as by repeating questions after they have been answered, by raising the questioner's voice, by pointing at or standing over the witness, or by appearing angry at the witness.

6. Counsel should not interrupt the answer of the witness once the question has been asked because the answer is not the one which counsel was seeking or the answer is not responsive to the question. The witness should be allowed to finish his or her answer.

7. Counsel defending a deposition should limit objections to those that are well founded and permitted by the Rules of Civil Procedure or applicable case law. Counsel should bear in mind that most objections are preserved and need to be interposed only when the form of a question is defective or privileged information is sought. When objecting to the form of a question, counsel should simply state "I object to the form of the question." The grounds should not be stated unless asked for by the examining attorney. When the grounds are then stated they should be stated succinctly.

8. While a question is pending, counsel should not, through objections or otherwise, coach the deponent or suggest answers. Should any lawyer do so, the courts are urged to sanction such practices.

9. Counsel for all parties should refrain from self-serving speeches during depositions.

10. Counsel should not engage in any conduct during a deposition that would not be allowed in the presence of a judicial officer.

G. DOCUMENT DEMANDS

1. Demands for document production should not be so broad as to encompass documents clearly not relevant to the subject matter of the case.

2. In responding to document demands, counsel should not strain to interpret the request in an artificially restrictive manner just to avoid disclosure.

3. Documents should be withheld on the grounds of privilege only where appropriate.

4. Counsel should not produce documents in a disorganized or unintelligible fashion, or in a way calculated to hide or obscure the existence of other relevant documents.

5. Document production should not be delayed to prevent opposing counsel from inspecting documents prior to scheduled depositions or for an improper tactical reason.

H. INTERROGATORIES

1. Interrogatories should not be read by lawyers in a strained or an artificial manner designed to assure that answers are not truly responsive.

2. Interrogatories should be answered by the party, and not solely by the party's lawyer.

3. Objections to interrogatories should be based on a good faith belief in their merit and not be made for the purpose of withholding relevant information. If an interrogatory is objectionable only in part, the unobjectionable portion should be-answered.

I. MOTION PRACTICE

1. Before setting a motion for hearing, counsel should make a good faith effort to resolve the issue with opposing counsel.

2. Except in emergency situations, before filing any motion in a civil case, except a motion for injunctive relief, for judgment on the pleadings, for summary judgment, to dismiss or to permit maintenance of a class action, to dismiss for failure to state a cause of action, to dismiss for lack of prosecution, or to otherwise involuntarily dismiss an action, the moving party shall confer with counsel for the opposing party in a good faith effort to resolve the issues raised by the motion, and shall file with the motion a statement certifying that the moving counsel has conferred with opposing counsel and that counsel have been unable to agree on the resolution of the motion.

3. A lawyer should not force his or her adversary to make a motion and then not oppose it.

4. Unless otherwise instructed by the court, or agreed to by counsel, all proposed orders shall be provided to other counsel with a reasonable time for approval or comment prior to submission to the court. Opposing counsel should promptly communicate any objections thereto. Thereafter, the drafting attorney should promptly submit a copy of the proposed order to the court and advise the court as to whether or not it has been approved by opposing counsel.

5. Orders prepared by counsel must fairly and adequately represent the ruling of the court, and counsel shall make a good faith effort to agree upon the form of the order prior to submitting it to the court. Attorneys should not submit controverted orders to the court with a copy to opposing counsel for "objections within ____ days". Courts prefer to know that the order is either agreed upon or opposed.

6. Attorneys should not use post-hearing submissions of proposed orders as a guise to reargue the merits of the matter.

J. EX–PARTE COMMUNICATIONS WITH THE COURT AND OTHERS

1. Attorneys should avoid ex-parte communication about a pending case with the judge, magistrate or arbitrator before whom such case is pending.

2. Even where applicable laws or rules permit an ex-parte application or communication to the court, attorneys should make diligent efforts to notify the opposing party or the lawyer knows to represent the opposing party in order to permit the opposing party to be represented in connection with the application or communication. Attorneys should not make such application or communication unless there is a bona fide emergency and the client will be seriously prejudiced if the application or communication is made on regular notice.

3. Counsel should notify opposing counsel of dates and times obtained from the court for future hearings on the same day that the hearing date is obtained from the court, or as soon as practicable thereafter.

4. Copies of any submissions to the court (such as correspondence, memoranda of law, motions, case law, etc.) should simultaneously be provided to opposing counsel by substantially the same method of delivery by which they are provided to the court. For example, if a memorandum of law is hand-delivered to the court, at substantially the same time a copy should be hand-delivered or faxed to opposing counsel. If asked by the court to prepare an order, counsel should furnish a copy of the order, and any transmitted letter, to opposing counsel at the time the material is submitted to the court.

K. TRIAL CONDUCT AND COURTOORM[3] DECORUM

1. Attorneys should always deal with parties, counsel, witnesses, jurors or prospective jurors, court personnel and the judge with courtesy and civility and avoid undignified or discourteous conduct.

2. Examination of jurors and witnesses should be conducted from a suitable distance. A lawyer should not crowd or lean over the witness or jury and should avoid blocking opposing counsel's view of the witness.

3. Counsel should address all public remarks to the court, not to opposing counsel.

4. Counsel should request permission before approaching the witness or bench. Any documents counsel wish to have the court examine should be handed to the clerk.

5. Any paper or exhibit not previously marked for identification should first be handed to the clerk to be marked before it is tendered to a witness for examination. Any exhibit offered in evidence should, at the time of such offer, be handed to opposing counsel.

6. Generally, in examining a witness, counsel shall not repeat or echo the answer given by the witness.

7. Counsel shall admonish all persons at counsel table that gestures, facial expressions, audible comments, manifestations of approval or disapproval during the testimony of a witness, or at any other time, is prohibited.

8. During trials and evidentiary hearings the lawyers should mutually agree to disclose the identities, and duration of witnesses anticipated to be called that day, including depositions to be read, and should cooperate in sharing with opposing counsel all visual-aid equipment.

9. Counsel should not mark on or alter exhibits, charts, graphs and diagrams without opposing counsel's knowledge or leave of court.

10. A lawyer's word should be his or her bond. The lawyer should not knowingly misstate, distort, or improperly exaggerate any fact or opinion and should not improperly permit the lawyer's silence or inaction to mislead anyone.

11. A charge of impropriety by one lawyer against another should never be made in the course of litigation except when relevant to the issues of the case.

12. A question should not be interrupted by an objection unless the question is patently objectionable or there is reasonable ground to believe that matter is being included which cannot properly be disclosed to the jury.

13. A lawyer should address objections, requests and observations to the court, and not engage in undignified or discourteous conduct which is degrading to court procedure.

14. In civil cases, attorneys should stipulate to all facts and principles of law which are not in dispute.

15. A lawyer should accede to reasonable requests for waivers of procedural formalities when the client's legitimate interests are not adversely affected.

16. In opening statements and in arguments to the jury, counsel should not express personal knowledge or opinion concerning any matter in issue.

17. In appearing in his or her professional capacity before a tribunal, a lawyer should not (a) state or allude to any matter that he or she has no reasonable basis to believe is relevant to the case or that will not be supported by admissible evidence; (b) ask any question that he or she has no reasonable basis to believe is relevant to the case or that is intended to degrade a witness or either person; (c) assert one's personal knowledge of the facts in issue, except when testifying as a witness; (d) assert one's personal opinion as to the justness of a cause, as to the credibility of a witness, as to the culpability of a civil litigant, or as to the guilt or innocence of an accused, but may argue, on the lawyers, analysis of the evidence, for any position or conclusion with respect to matters stated herein.

18. A lawyers should never attempt to place before a tribunal, or jury, evidence known to be clearly inadmissible, nor make any remarks or statements which are intended to improperly influence the outcome of any case.

L. EFFICIENT ADMINISTRATION

1. Attorneys should refrain from actions intended primarily to harass or embarrass and should refrain from actions which cause unnecessary expense or delay.

2. Attorneys should, whenever possible, prior to filing or upon receiving a motion, contact opposing counsel to determine if the matter can be resolved in whole or in part. This may alleviate the need for a hearing on the motion or allow submission of an agreed order in lieu of a hearing.

3. Attorneys should, whenever appropriate, stipulate to all facts and legal authority not reasonably in dispute.

4. Attorneys should encourage principled negotiations and efficient resolution of disputes on their merits.

M. TRANSACTIONAL PRACTICE

1. Attorneys should draft letters of intent, memorializations of oral agreements, and written contracts and documents reflecting agreements in concept so that they fairly reflect the agreement of the parties.

2. Attorneys should point out to opposing counsel that changes have been made from one draft to another draft. If requested to do so, attorneys should identify those changes.

N. SETTLEMENT AND RESOLUTION

1. Unless there are strong and overriding issues of principle, attorneys should raise and explore the issue of settlement as soon as enough is known to make settlement discussions meaningful.

2. Attorneys should not falsely hold out the possibility of settlement to adjourn discovery or delay trial.

3. Attorneys are encouraged to utilize arbitration, mediation or other forms of alternative dispute resolution if economically feasible.

V. STANDARDS FOR THE JUDICIARY

A. DUTIES OF JUDGES TO LAWYERS, PARTIES AND WITNESSES

1. Judges should be courteous, respectful, and civil to lawyers, parties, and witnesses. Judges should maintain control of the proceedings, recognizing that judges have both the obligation and the authority to insure that all litigation, including the actions of the layers [4], parties and the witnesses, is conducted in a civil manner.

2. Judges should not employ hostile, demeaning or humiliating words in opinions or in written or oral communications with lawyers, parties or witnesses.

3. Judges should be punctual in convening all hearing, meetings and conferences.

4. In scheduling hearings, meetings and conferences, judges should be considerate of the time schedules of the lawyers, the parties and the witnesses.

5. Judges should make all reasonable efforts to decide promptly all matters presented to them for decision.

6. Judges should give the issues in controversy deliberate, impartial and studied analysis.

7. Judges should not impugn the integrity or professionalism of a lawyer, based on his or her client or the cause represented by the lawyer.

8. Judges should encourage court personnel to act civilly toward lawyers, parties and witnesses.

9. Judges should not adopt procedures that needlessly increase litigation expense.

B. DUTIES OF JUDGES TO OTHER JUDGES

1. In all written and oral communications, judges should abstain from disparaging personal remarks or criticisms of another judge.

2. Judges should endeavor to work with each together in an effort to foster a spirit of cooperation in the administration of justice.

VI. AMENDMENTS

The Standards may be amended from time to time by an Administrative Order of the Chief Judge of the Twentieth Judicial Circuit.

VII. LOCAL PROFESSIONALISM PROGRAM

Any judge or lawyer who observes conduct by an attorney inconsistent with the Standards, may refer such conduct and the identity of the attorney to any member of the Local Professionalism Panel of the Twentieth Judicial Circuit. The Circuit has formed a Local Professionalism Program to foster and improve professionalism in the Circuit. Every attorney practicing law or appearing in judicial proceedings within the Twentieth Judicial Circuit is expected to be entirely familiar with the Local Professionalism Program of the Twentieth Judicial Circuit.

Revised February 2014

Attachment B

LOCAL PROFESSIONALISM PROGRAM OF THE TWENTIETH JUDICIAL CIRCUIT OF FLORIDA

I. FOREWORD

In 1989, The Florida Bar established a task force to study the course of professionalism among lawyers in Florida. The study addressed issues regarding the lack of civility among lawyers, the public's poor perception of lawyers and the steady decline in lawyers' satisfaction and fulfillment with their profession. The work performed by the task force resulted in the creation of The Florida Bar's Standing Committee on Professionalism. In July, 1996, the Honorable Chief Justice Gerald Kogan signed an administrative order that created the Florida Supreme Court Commission on Professionalism. In January, 1998, Justice Kogan requested that the Chief Judge of each Judicial Circuit appoint a Circuit Committee on Professionalism charged with the overall responsibility of initiating and coordinating professionalism activities within the Circuit. Accordingly, in early 1998, the Twentieth Judicial Circuit Committee on Professionalism was formed.

In November, 1999, a subcommittee of the Twentieth Judicial Circuit Committee on Professionalism was appointed at the direction of the Chief Judge of the Circuit to prepare a practical set of standards of professional courtesy and conduct for lawyers and to explore the formation of a peer review program for lawyers practicing law in the Twentieth Judicial Circuit. The subcommittee, with the guidance, insight and participation of the Circuit Committee on Professionalism, prepared a Peer Review Program as well as the Standards of Professional Courtesy and Conduct for Lawyers Practicing in the Twentieth Judicial Circuit. In February, 2000, The Standards of Professional Courtesy and Conduct for Lawyers Practicing in the Twentieth Judicial Circuit and the Peer Review Program were approved and adopted by the Twentieth Judicial Circuit Committee on Professionalism.

By opinion dated June 6, 2013, the Supreme Court of Florida issued In re: Code for Resolving Professionalism Complaints, 116 So. 3d 280 (Fla. 2013), which subsequently required modification of the program, which is now known as the Local Professionalism Program of the Twentieth Judicial Circuit. The Peer Review Committee is now known as the Local Professionalism Panel of the Twentieth Judicial Circuit.

II. PURPOSE OF THE LOCAL PROFESSIONALISM PANEL

The general purpose of Local Professionalism Panel is to improve the level of professional performance and competence of lawyers who practice in the Twentieth Judicial Circuit. The Local Professionalism Program is not a disciplinary proceeding. Instead, the Local Professionalism Program is intended to be an educational, informal, non-punitive program for the practice of law in the Twentieth Judicial Circuit. The Local Professionalism Program is not intended to deal specifically with violations of ethics or the Rules Regulating The Florida Bar which remain solely within the jurisdiction of the grievance process of The Florida Bar.

III. LOCAL PROFESSIONALISM PANEL

A. MEMBERS OF THE PANEL

The Local Professionalism Panel will consist of the non-judicial members of the Twentieth Judicial Circuit Professionalism Committee as defined by Administrative Order 2.34. The Chairperson of the Local Professionalism Panel shall be a President (or designee) of one of the local bar associations, to be selected by the members of the Local Professionalism Panel. A quorum of the Local Professionalism Panel at any meeting shall consist of a majority of the members of the panel; a vote by the panel shall not occur unless a quorum is obtained.

B. INITIAL REFERRAL TO THE PANEL

Any person may initiate a professionalism complaint against a member of The Florida Bar through The Florida Bar Attorney Consumer Assistance and Intake Program (ACAP), 1–866–352–0707, or through the Local Professionalism Panel.

Names of the members of the Local Professionalism Panel of the Twentieth Judicial Circuit will be posted on the website of the Courts of the Twentieth Judicial Circuit, www.ca.cjis20.org, and will be forwarded periodically to each County Bar Association with in the Twentieth Judicial Circuit with a request for publication so that lawyers practicing within the Circuit and judges will know who they should contact to refer a lawyer to the program. It is recommended that the complainant use the written Referral Form created by the Panel, but using such a form is not mandatory. A copy of the Referral Form which is recommended for use is attached hereto and is available online.

Any judge within the Twentieth Judicial Circuit or any lawyer or any other person who observes conduct by a lawyer inconsistent with the Standards of Professional Courtesy and Conduct for the Twentieth Judicial Circuit ("complainant"), may refer such conduct and the identity of the lawyer to any member of the Local Professionalism Panel. The member shall then promptly forward the referral to the Chairperson of the Local Professionalism Panel ("Panel").

C. REVIEW BY PANEL

At its next meeting, the Panel shall by a majority vote of the quorum, determine how to respond to any referrals or complaints that have been received. The Panel shall first consider whether conduct has been alleged which, if true, does not comply with the Standards of Professional Courtesy and Conduct for the Twentieth Judicial Circuit ("Standards"). If the Panel finds that the conduct alleged, if true, does not comply with the Standards, the Panel may proceed as appropriate, which may include informal discussions, either by telephone or in person, with the lawyer who has been referred to the Panel. The Panel, or a designated member of the Panel, may outline the perceived problem and ask the subject lawyer whether he or she can assist the Panel in finding a solution. The solution may include a referral to a local member of the bar for mentoring purposes. There will be no sanctions or other enforcement mechanism associated with the consultation.

If the lawyer refuses to discuss the matter or otherwise cooperate, the Panel may still discuss the conduct and determine how best to proceed. The Panel has the discretion to direct the referral back to the complainant for clarification or additional information, or to proceed further under paragraph III.D.

Referrals or complaints received by the Local Professionalism Panel may be referred to The Florida Bar Attorney Consumer Assistance and Intake Program (ACAP) at any time depending upon the nature and severity of the complaint.

D. PROCEDURE IF CONDUCT NOT RESOLVED UNDER SECTION III.C.

In the event that a referral to the Panel alleges conduct which, if true, does not comply with the Standards of Professional Courtesy and Conduct for the Twentieth Judicial Circuit ("Standards"), and the matter is not resolved under Section III.C, the Panel may elect to (i) contact the lawyer either by telephone, in person or by letter, (ii) describe the alleged noncompliance or enclose the written referral form, and (iii) request a response from the subject lawyer to be provided within 30 days. The subject lawyer's response shall be provided by the Panel to the complainant. Upon receipt of the response, the Panel shall consider the referral and response. The Panel may thereafter contact the subject lawyer and the complainant to further discuss the referral and response. The Panel thereafter shall determine by majority vote whether conduct has occurred which does not comply with the Standards. The determination of the Panel shall be communicated to the subject lawyer as well as the complainant. A designee of the Panel shall discuss the matter with the lawyer in an attempt to educate the lawyer about the noncompliance and hopefully avoid other or similar conduct in the future which does not comply with the Standards. It is recommended that the entire review process be accomplished within 90 days from the date that the alleged conduct was referred by the complainant to the Panel; however, failure to adhere to this recommended time limit is not fatal to the referral.

In the event that the Panel determines that conduct has occurred which does not comply with the Standards, and depending upon the facts and nature of the conduct, the Panel may, in its discretion, provide a redacted summary to each County Bar Association within the Twentieth Judicial Circuit with a request for it to be published in the newsletters or other regular periodic publications of each bar association. The summary shall briefly and concisely inform the bar of the referral, the alleged facts giving rise to the referral, and the determination of the Committee. The summary shall not identity the complainant, the lawyer, or the members of the Panel who voted. It is the hope that members of the bar will learn from these publications and misunderstandings of the Standards will be reduced.

E. FLORIDA SUPREME COURT REPORTING REQUIREMENTS

The Panel shall comply with all Florida Supreme Court reporting requirements, which at this time include an "Individual Reporting Form for Local Circuit Professionalism Panel" and a "Quarterly Summary Report to the Florida Supreme Court." The forms shall be signed by the Chair of the Local Professionalism Panel of the Twentieth Judicial Circuit, rather than the Chief Judge. The "Quarterly Summary Report to the Florida Supreme Court" shall be filed within the time frames established by the Florida Supreme Court, or if none have been established, by the 15th of the month following the end of the quarter.

Revised February 2014

REFERRAL FORM TO THE LOCAL PROFESSIONALISM PANEL OF THE TWENTIETH JUDICIAL CIRCUIT

1. **Referring Attorney, Judge, or Other Person:**

Your Name: ____________________

Bar Number: [if applicable] ____________________

Your Address: ____________________

Telephone No.: ____________________
e-mail: ____________________

2. **Attorney Being Referred:**

Name of Attorney: ____________________

Bar Number: [if known] ____________________

Address: ____________________

Telephone No.: ____________________
e-mail: ____________________

NOTE THIS IS NOT A DISCIPLINARY PROCEEDING

3. Alleged Noncompliance (check one):

___ Twentieth Judicial Circuit's Standards of Professional Courtesy and Conduct for Lawyers. Standards involved: ____________________

___ The Florida Bar's Ideals and Standards of Professionalism. Ideals or Standards Involved: ____________________

___ Other: ____________________

Briefly describe the facts and circumstances of the alleged conduct which does not, in your opinion, comply with the above Standards. Use the back of this form or attach additional pages if necessary. Please try to be brief and non-judgmental. Please list and attach any papers requiring consideration or needed for clarification of the allegations discussed. Please state the specific provision(s) involved.

Signed: ____________ Date: ____________

Revised February 2014

1 So in original. Probably should read "2014".
2 So in original.
3 So in original.
4 So in original.

2.21. ORDER ESTABLISHING POLICY PROHIBITING COURT EMPLOYEES FROM ACCEPTING GIFTS FROM LAWYERS, VENDORS OR OTHER THIRD PARTIES

IN THE TWENTIETH JUDICIAL CIRCUIT IN AND FOR THE STATE OF FLORIDA

ADMINISTRATIVE ORDER NO. 2.21

IN RE: ORDER ESTABLISHING POLICY PROHIBITING COURT EMPLOYEES FROM ACCEPTING GIFTS FROM LAWYERS, VENDORS OR OTHER THIRD PARTIES

Pursuant to the applicable Canons of the Code of Judicial Conduct and this Court's inherent authority to regulate the courts of the Twentieth Judicial Circuit as provided by Fla. R. Jud. Adm. 2.050(b), the Court hereby establishes the following policy prohibiting the acceptance of gifts by court employees from lawyers, vendors or other third parties.

1. Pursuant to the applicable Canons of the Code of Judicial Conduct, a judicial officer or quasi-judicial officer may not accept gifts, favors, bequests or loans from lawyers or their firms if those lawyers or firms are likely to come before the judicial officer or quasi-judicial officer.

2. In addition, a judicial officer or quasi-judicial officer is prohibited from accepting gifts, favors, bequests or loans from clients of lawyers or their firms when the clients' interests have come or are likely to come before the judicial officer or quasi-judicial officer.

3. Indeed, the receipt of any gifts whatsoever by judicial officers or quasi-judicial officers is specifically regulated and limited by Canon 5 of the Code of Judicial Conduct. In the case of any gift from any other source, if its value exceeds $100, the judge must report its receipt in accordance with the applicable provisions of Canon 6 of the Code of Judicial Conduct.

4. While the Code of Judicial Conduct does not specifically apply to judicial staff, which would include staff attorneys, judicial assistants, bailiffs, and other court personnel, Canon 3C(2) provides that "A judge shall require staff, court officials, and others subject to the judge's direction and control to observe the standards of fidelity and diligence that apply to the judge . . ."

Based upon the foregoing, and in accordance with the authorities cited above and Opinion 2000–08 of the Judicial Ethics Advisory Committee issued March 1, 2000, it is

ORDERED AND ADJUDGED as follows:

1. All court employees, including staff attorneys, judicial assistants, bailiffs, and other court personnel, whether directly or indirectly employed by or subject to the supervision of the judges of the Twentieth Judicial Circuit Court, are hereby directed by this Court not to accept gifts of any kind from lawyers, vendors or other third parties who have or are likely to have any business of any kind before the Court.

The purpose of this order is to ensure that no judicial officer, quasi- judicial officer or court staff of any kind convey or permit others to convey the impression that they are in a special position to influence the court.

DONE AND ORDERED in Chambers at Naples, Collier County, Florida, this 18th day of July, 2000.

William L. Blackwell
Chief Judge

History. - Administrative Order 2.21 (July 13, 2000).

2.22. ASSIGNMENT OF AND PROCEDURES APPLICABLE TO CASES BROUGHT PURSUANT TO THE JIMMY RYCE ACT

IN THE TWENTIETH JUDICIAL CIRCUIT IN AND FOR THE STATE OF FLORIDA

ADMINISTRATIVE ORDER NO. 2.22

IN RE: ASSIGNMENT OF AND PROCEDURES APPLICABLE TO CASES BROUGHT PURSUANT TO THE JIMMY RYCE ACT

This Administrative Order applies to all cases brought pursuant to Part V of Chapter 394 of the Florida Statutes, specifically Florida Statutes §§ 394. 910—394.931, entitled as the "Involuntary Commitment of Sexually Violent Predators Act," and more commonly known as the "Jimmy Ryce Act."

All Jimmy Ryce cases shall be assigned randomly to a judge of the civil division upon filing. Upon the filing by the State Attorney of a Petition for Commitment of any individual pursuant to the Jimmy Ryce Act, the State Attorney shall present to the assigned judge, or in his or her absence, to the Duty Judge on call at the time, an ex parte motion and order for probable cause determination. At that time, the State Attorney will also file proposed motions and orders for detention of the Respondent, transportation of the Respondent, appointment of the Public Defender and a blank order setting a trial date.

The petition, motions and orders shall be presented to the assigned judge, or in his or her absence, to the Duty Judge on call, for his or her review. In the event that the Duty Judge signs the orders, the file will thereafter be transmitted directly to the assigned judge in the civil division for signature of the trial order. The trial order must set a trial date within thirty (30) days of presentation of the file to the Court as provided by Florida Statute § 394.916

All other procedures under the Act shall be as provided in the statutes cited above and any case law interpreting the statutory provisions applicable to these proceedings.

DONE AND ORDERED in Chambers at Naples, Collier County, Florida, this 24 day of Oct., 2000.

William L. Blackwell
Chief Judge

History. - New

2.23. PROCEDURE FOR ELECTION OF CHIEF JUDGE

IN THE TWENTIETH JUDICIAL CIRCUIT IN AND FOR THE STATE OF FLORIDA

ADMINISTRATIVE ORDER No. 2.23

IN RE: PROCEDURE FOR ELECTION OF CHIEF JUDGE

Pursuant to Fla. R. Jud. Admin. 2.215(b) and (c) and the inherent power of the Court to do everything necessary to promote the prompt and efficient administration of justice in the Twentieth Judicial Circuit, the Court hereby adopts the following procedure for the election of the Chief Judge of this circuit.

1. Candidates for Chief Judge shall be nominated or otherwise announce their candidacy for the office of Chief Judge by the filing of a formal notice with the Court Administrator no later than January 5th in every odd-numbered year.

2. The Court Administrator will thereafter prepare a ballot with the names of each candidate for Chief Judge and shall cause that ballot to be distributed to each circuit and county judge within the Twentieth Judicial Circuit within five days thereafter.

3. In the event that more than one candidate for Chief Judge appears on the ballot, the Chief Judge shall schedule and thereafter hold a meeting of all circuit and county judges as soon as is practicable after February 1st of the year during which the Chief Judge's term commences.

4. The date, time and place of this meeting will be published to the judges by the Court Administrator, and each candidate for Chief Judge shall be given equal time at the discretion of the current Chief Judge to address his or her fellow judges. A meeting may also be scheduled by the Chief Judge even if less than two names appear on the ballot.

5. Voting will thereafter commence. The vote for Chief Judge shall be by secret ballot and shall be processed and counted by a committee of three judges in attendance at the meeting who are appointed by the Chief Judge. The committee shall be comprised of two circuit judges and one county judge, and none of the committee members shall be candidates for the position of Chief Judge. The Chief Judge may serve on the committee in the event that he or she is not seeking reelection.

6. Voting by proxy is prohibited by Fla. R. Jud. Admin. 2.215(c).

7. Any judge who will be absent from any meeting called by the Chief Judge may vote in advance by delivering to the Court Administrator by mail or in person a secret ballot prepared in accordance with paragraph 2. Any such ballots tendered in advance of the election shall be retained by the Court Administrator and presented to the committee at the time of the election.

8. In the event that no candidate for Chief Judge obtains a majority on the first ballot, a run-off election will thereafter be held with the first and second place finishers on the first ballot being listed as the only remaining candidates.

9. In the event of a deadlock or tie vote on the second ballot, then pursuant to Fla. R. Jud. Admin. 2.215(c), the Chief Judge shall submit the matter to the Chief Justice for selection of the successor Chief Judge.

10. To the extent that any provision of this Administrative Order may be construed as being in conflict with any law, statute, or rule, the law, statute, or rule shall prevail.

DONE AND ORDERED in Chambers at Fort Myers, Lee County, Florida this 1st day of December, 2008.

G. Keith Cary
Chief Judge

History. - Administrative Order 2.23 (October 30, 2002).

2.24. DELEGATION OF CONTRACT AUTHORITY TO THE COURT ADMINISTRATOR

IN THE TWENTIETH JUDICIAL CIRCUIT IN AND FOR THE STATE OF FLORIDA

ADMINISTRATIVE ORDER NO: 2.24

IN RE: DELEGATION OF CONTRACT AUTHORITY TO THE COURT ADMINISTRATOR

Pursuant to Florida Statute § 43.26(2)(f), as amended by Chapter 2003–402, § 65, Laws of Florida, effective July 1, 2003, it is

ORDERED that the Court Administrator for the Twentieth Judicial Circuit is hereby delegated the authority to bind the Twentieth Judicial Circuit in contract, effective retroactively to July 1, 2003.

DONE AND ORDERED in chambers in Naples, Collier County, Florida, this 22 day of September, 2003.

Hugh D. Hayes
Chief Judge

History. - New.

2.25. SEXUAL HARASSMENT POLICY AND PROCEDURES FOR COMPLAINTS AGAINST TRIAL COURT JUDGES

IN THE TWENTIETH JUDICIAL CIRCUIT IN AND FOR THE STATE OF FLORIDA

ADMINISTRATIVE ORDER NO: 2.25

—AMENDED—

IN RE: SEXUAL HARASSMENT POLICY AND PROCEDURES FOR COMPLAINTS AGAINST TRIAL COURT JUDGES

In accordance with the directive of the Florida Supreme Court's Administrative Order No. AOSC18–6, In re: Sexual Harassment Policy and Procedures for Complaints Against Justices and Judges, the undersigned, as Chief Judge of the Twentieth Judicial Circuit, hereby adopts and implements the Florida Supreme Court's Administrative Order No. AOSC18–6, a copy of which is attached and incorporated herein.

DONE AND ORDERED in chambers in Fort Myers, Lee County, Florida, this 5 day of March, 2018.

Michael T. McHugh

Chief Judge

History - Administrative Order 2.25 (July 23, 2004)

Supreme Court of Florida

No. AOSC18–6

IN RE: SEXUAL HARASSMENT POLICY AND PROCEDURES FOR COMPLAINTS AGAINST JUSTICES AND JUDGES

ADMINISTRATIVE ORDER

The Sexual Harassment Policy and Procedures for Complaints Against Justices and Judges are approved and incorporated into the State Courts System Personnel Regulations. The policy and procedures approved herein replace and supersede the policies and procedures adopted in In re: Sexual Harassment Policy and Procedures for Complaints Against Justices, Fla. Admin. Order No. AOSC04–07 (March 25, 2004), and In re: Sexual Harassment Policy and Procedures for Complaints Against Trial Court Judges, Fla. Admin. Order No. AOSC04–08 (March 25, 2004).

The policy and procedures are attached and incorporated into this administrative order, and are effective immediately. Chief judges of the district courts of appeal and chief judges of the circuit courts are hereby directed to adopt and implement the policy and procedures in their respective courts upon issuance of this administrative order.

DONE AND ORDERED at Tallahassee, Florida, on February 16, 2018.

Chief Justice Jorge Labarga

ATTEST:

AOSC18–6 2/16/18

John A. Tomasino, Clerk of Court

SEXUAL HARASSMENT POLICY AND PROCEDURES FOR SEXUAL HARASSMENT COMPLAINTS AGAINST JUSTICES AND JUDGES

1. Policy

The chief justice's implementation of this policy is under his or her authority as the administrative officer of the judicial branch and of the supreme court pursuant to rule 2.205(a)(2)(B), Florida Rules of Judicial Administration.

It is the policy of the Florida Supreme Court to foster a workplace free of sexual harassment, or sexual misconduct. Sexual harassment occurs if there are unwelcome sexual advances; unwelcome requests for sexual favors; or unwelcome verbal or physical conduct of a sexual nature from or involving an employee's supervisors, peers, subordinates or other persons in contact with an employee during the course of the conduct of the employee's business when:

1. Submission to such conduct is either explicitly or implicitly a term or condition of employment; or

2. Submission to or rejection of such conduct by an individual is used as the basis for employment decisions affecting such individual or as the basis for any official action; or

3. Such conduct has the purpose or effect of interfering with an individual's work performance or creates a persistently intimidating and hostile environment, as that term is defined in state and federal law.

Sexual misconduct is any behavior of a sexual nature that is committed without consent or by force, intimidation, coercion, or manipulation. Sexual misconduct can occur between strangers or acquaintances, including people involved in an intimate or sexual relationship, and is not necessarily actionable sexual harassment.

The Florida Supreme Court and the entire state court system condemn any sexual harassment or sexual misconduct and advance the position that anyone in contact with the state courts system should feel empowered to bring any such inappropriate activity to the attention of all proper authorities, including and especially the Florida Supreme Court. Anyone authorized to investigate or pursue a complaint of sexual harassment or sexual misconduct hereunder must always maintain an open-door policy that fosters the free expression of any complaint. The chief justice or chief justice's designee has the authority to take any administrative action necessary to protect the complainant from further sexual harassment or sexual misconduct and from retaliation related to a complaint hereunder.

It is the policy of the Florida Supreme Court that all complaints of sexual harassment or sexual misconduct against any justice or judge within the state courts system will be treated seriously and acted upon promptly. The following procedures apply to complaints against justices or judges made by employees of the court system, applicants for employment with the court system, and when applicable attorneys, litigants, or other members of the public. Compliance with these procedures by the chief justice, the chief justice's designee, or a chief judge constitutes a presumption of compliance with the disciplinary responsibilities under Canon 3(D)1 of the Code of Judicial Conduct.

2. Notification

The chief justice may designate any court system officer or employee to be responsible for receiving and documenting complaints of sexual harassment or sexual misconduct against justices of the Supreme Court, judges of the district courts of appeal, or judges of any of the trial courts.

Any employee or applicant for employment with the court system who believes that he or she is the subject of sexual harassment by a justice of the Supreme Court, a judge of any of the district courts of appeal, or a judge of any of the trial courts should submit his or her complaint in writing, or if the person prefers he or she may submit the complaint orally. The complaint may be submitted to any of the following: the chief justice or his or her designee; a local administrator, such as a Trial Court Administrator, human resource manager or Marshal; or the Chief of Human Resources at the Office of the State Courts Administrator (OSCA). If the person receiving the complaint is not the chief justice, the chief justice's designee hereunder, or a chief judge, the person receiving the complaint should forward it to the chief justice, the chief justice's designee hereunder, or the chief judge of the court in which the subject judge serves for an investigation pursuant to section 4, below. Student interns working for the state courts system who believe they are the subject of sexual harassment may use these complaint procedures, but in all instances, should submit a complaint to their college or university in accordance with school sexual harassment complaint procedures.

If any person has difficulty writing out the complaint and the person requests assistance in reducing the complaint to writing or if the person prefers to submit the complaint orally, the chief justice, local administrator, or OSCA Chief of Human Resources, as appropriate, shall designate a person, who will not be involved in the investigation or adjudication of the complaint, to aid the person in reducing the complaint to writing.

If the chief justice is the subject of a complaint, the employee or applicant should submit the complaint to the inspector general of the Supreme Court, who will refer the complaint to the most senior justice, excluding the chief justice. The justice to whom such a complaint is referred will assume all complaint investigation and resolution duties for which the chief justice otherwise would be responsible. The justice to whom such a complaint is referred also will be responsible for maintaining records pertaining to the complaint.

If an employee or applicant chooses not to file a formal complaint, and any person designated hereunder to receive complaints has actual knowledge or receives information that a substantial likelihood exists that a justice or judge has engaged in sexual harassment or sexual misconduct, the person may inquire into the matter and take appropriate action.

3. Time for Filing Complaints

In order to ensure that Florida Supreme Court complaint procedures can be utilized without risk of precluding the filing of a charge of discrimination with state or federal entities, an employee or applicant should report an incident of sexual harassment within 90 days of the date of occurrence.

4. Investigations

A complaint of sexual harassment or sexual misconduct against a justice or judge will be investigated promptly and thoroughly. If a complaint has been made, the chief justice, the chief justice's designee hereunder, or the chief judge of the court in which the subject judge serves may designate another person to make an initial inquiry into the complaint.

The chief justice, chief justice's designee, or a chief judge of the court in which the subject judge serves will interview the complainant within five days of the submission of the complaint to ascertain relevant facts and circumstances. If the complainant does not divulge names or details of the incident(s), the chief justice or chief justice's designee, or the chief judge of the court in which the subject judge serves will rely upon any information that is available. If another person has been designated to make an initial inquiry into the complaint, the designee will report details of the complaint, including any relevant facts, circumstances, and information, to the chief justice within ten days of the submission of the complaint.

If the chief justice, chief justice's designee, or the chief judge of the court in which the subject judge serves determines the complaint is unfounded or is insufficient to constitute sexual harassment, he or she may decline to pursue any action on the complaint.

If the chief justices, chief justice's designee, or the chief judge of the court in which the subject judge serves determines the complaint is facially sufficient to constitute sexual harassment, the chief justice, chief justice's designee, or the chief judge of the court in which the subject judge serves may appoint an investigating officer or officers to formally investigate the complaint, or may take any other action appropriate under the circumstances.

If the chief justice or chief justice's designee determines the complaint is insufficient to constitute sexual harassment, but nevertheless indicates potential sexual misconduct, the chief justice or chief justice's designee may take any action appropriate to address the circumstances, including but not limited to appointing an investigating officer or officers to formally investigate the complaint.

The chief justice, chief justice's designee, the chief judge of the court in which the subject judge serves, or investigating officer will interview the complainant, the justice or judge implicated, and witnesses, if any, and will review relevant documents. If any investigating officers have been appointed, they will submit a written report to the chief justice, chief justice's designee, or the chief judge of the court in which the subject judge serves within thirty days of the submission of the complaint for formal investigation.

5. Resolution

The chief justice, or pursuant to rule 2.205(a)(2)(D), Florida Rules of Judicial Administration, the other most senior justice if the chief justice is the subject of a complaint, shall determine the course of action for internal resolution of the complaint, and may appoint another person, other than the subject of the complaint, to recommend the course of action for internal resolution.

If the chief justice or chief justice's designee determines the complaint, including any relevant facts, circumstances, and information, is insufficient to constitute sexual harassment, the chief justice, chief justice's designee, or the chief judge of the court in which the subject judge serves may attempt to resolve the complaint informally through mutual conciliation by meeting with the complainant and the subject justice or judge to discuss a method of resolution, including alternative dispute resolution. In attempting to resolve the complaint, the chief justice, chief justice's designee, or the chief judge of the court in which the subject judge serves may counsel or take other appropriate direct action with the justice or judge involved.

If the complaint and investigation reasonably indicate that the subject justice or judge engaged in activity that constitutes sexual harassment, constitutes sexual misconduct, or otherwise raises a substantial question as to a justice's or judge's fitness for office, the chief justice, chief justice's designee, or the chief judge of the court in which the subject judge serves shall refer the complaint and all written documentation pertaining to the complaint to the Judicial Qualifications Commission.

To the extent not otherwise prohibited by statute or rule, a written summary of the resolution will be provided to the complainant within a reasonable time after a determination is made and any action pursuant thereto is taken.

6. Documentation and Confidentiality

All information pertaining to a complaint of sexual harassment must be documented and maintained by the chief justice, chief justice's designee, or the chief judge of the court in which the subject judge serves whichever officer took final action on the resolution of the complaint.

All records made or received by any person pursuant to these complaint procedures are exempt from public disclosure as provided in rule 2.420(c)(3)(A), Florida Rules of Judicial Administration. Such records are exempt from public disclosure for the duration of an initial inquiry, formal investigation and resolution of the complaint, and at all times thereafter, unless the records are forwarded to the Judicial Qualifications Commission.

If records pertaining to a complaint are forwarded to the Judicial Qualifications Commission, such records will be confidential under rule 2.420(c)(3)(A), and rule 23(a), Rules of the Judicial Qualifications Commission, until any formal charges against the justice or judge are filed by the Investigative Panel of the Commission with the clerk of the Florida Supreme Court.

Records within the possession of any justice, judge, or court staff and pertaining to a complaint that has been forwarded to the Judicial Qualifications Commission will become public upon formal charges being filed with the clerk of the Florida Supreme Court.

7. Referral to the Judicial Qualifications Commission

The Judicial Qualifications Commission is responsible for investigating all reported instances of judicial misconduct. These procedures do not preclude the referral of a complaint against a justice or judge at any time by any person to the Judicial Qualifications Commission. If a complaint has been referred to the Judicial Qualifications Commission, no further action by the chief justice or chief justice's designee is required.

For anyone wishing to file such a complaint, the Commission's mailing address is P.O. Box 141106, Tallahassee, Florida 32317. The Commission's Executive Director, can be contacted by telephone at 850–488–1581 or by email at contact@floridajqc.com.

8. Referral to the Florida Commission on Human Relations or the United State Equal Employment Opportunity Commission

These procedures do not preclude the filing of a charge of employment discrimination with the Florida Commission on Human Relations or the United States Equal Employment Opportunity Commission.

For anyone wishing to file such a complaint, the Florida Commission on Human Relations (FCHR) is located at: 4075 Esplanade Way Room 110 Tallahassee, FL32399. The telephone number for the FCHR is: 850–488–7082 or 1–800–342–8170.

The United States Equal Employment Opportunity Commission (EEOC) office with jurisdiction over complaints arising in Florida is the Miami District Office located at 100 SE 2nd Street, Suite 1500, Miami, FL 33131. The telephone number for the EEOC Miami District office is: 1–800–669–4000.

9. Referral to the Chief of Human Resources, Office of the State Courts Administrator

For anyone wishing to file a complaint under this policy, the Chief of Human Resources, OSCA is located at: 500 South Duval Street Tallahassee, Florida 32399–1925. The telephone number is 850–617–4028.

2.26. CIRCUIT ARTICLE V INDIGENT SERVICES COMMITTEE

IN THE TWENTIETH JUDICIAL CIRCUIT IN AND FOR THE STATE OF FLORIDA

IN RE: CIRCUIT ARTICLE V INDIGENT SERVICES COMMITTEE

ADMINISTRATIVE ORDER NO: 2.26

In accordance with Fla. Stat. § 27.42(1), the undersigned, as Chief Judge of the Twentieth Judicial Circuit, hereby appoints the following members to the Twentieth Judicial Circuit Article V Indigent Services Committee:

Peter D. Ringsmuth, Esquire, an experienced private criminal defense attorney, who is appointed to serve a 2–year term, effective July 1, 2006, *nunc pro tunc*, and who is prohibited from serving as court-appointed counsel during this term; and

Sheldon E. Finman, Esquire, an experienced civil trial attorney, who is appointed to serve a 2–year term, effective July 1, 2006, *nunc pro tunc*, and who is prohibited from serving as court-appointed counsel during this term.

DONE AND ORDERED in chambers in Naples, Collier County, Florida, this 26th day of October, 2006.

Hugh D. Hayes
Chief Judge

History.—Administrative Order 2.26 (July 13, 2004).

2.27. APPOINTMENT AND COMPENSATION OF COURT–APPOINTED ATTORNEYS FOR THE INTERIM PERIOD OF JULY 1, 2004 THROUGH SEPTEMBER 30, 2004

IN THE TWENTIETH JUDICIAL CIRCUIT IN AND FOR THE STATE OF FLORIDA

ADMINISTRATIVE ORDER NO: 2.27

IN RE: APPOINTMENT AND COMPENSATION OF COURT–APPOINTED ATTORNEYS FOR THE INTERIM PERIOD OF JULY 1, 2004 THROUGH SEPTEMBER 30, 2004

WHEREAS, legislation enacted in 2003, effective July 1, 2004, codified as Florida Statute §§ 27.40, 27.42, and 27.5304, significantly revised the procedures for the appointment and compensation of court-appointed attorneys by requiring the establishment in each judicial circuit of a circuit Article V indigent services committee responsible for creating and maintaining a registry of court-appointed attorneys and for developing a schedule of standard fees for compensation of court-appointed attorneys; and

WHEREAS, this same legislation mandated that the Justice Administrative Commission (hereinafter "JAC") shall be responsible for the compensation of court-appointed attorneys for services rendered on and after July 1, 2004; and

WHEREAS, recently enacted legislation under Senate Bill 2962 from the 2004 Legislative Session, codified as Laws of Florida, Ch. 2004–265, addressed the revised procedures for the appointment and compensation of court-appointed attorneys, and extended the deadline for the establishment of registries and schedules of fees by the circuit Article V indigent services committees until October 1, 2004; and

WHEREAS, it is necessary that procedures and approved fees be implemented for the interim period of July 1, 2004 through September 30, 2004, to ensure that attorneys are properly appointed to represent individuals entitled to court-appointed counsel, and to further ensure that those court-appointed attorneys are properly compensated for services rendered on and after July 1, 2004; and

WHEREAS, the Twentieth Judicial Circuit Article V Indigent Services Committee has not yet created a registry of court-appointed attorneys and has not yet approved of rates of compensation for court-appointed attorneys; and

WHEREAS, in circumstances where a circuit Article V indigent services committee has not yet created a registry of court-appointed attorneys or adopted rates of compensation, the JAC has requested that an administrative order be entered to authorize continuing the status quo as it relates to the appointment and compensation of court-appointed attorneys; and

WHEREAS, under such circumstances, the JAC has further advised that it will honor existing arrangements within those judicial circuits under the authority of such an administrative order until such time as the circuit Article V indigent services committee has created a registry of court-appointed attorneys and adopted rates of compensation;

NOW, THEREFORE, pursuant to the authority vested in me as Chief Judge of the Twentieth Judicial Circuit of Florida under Fla. R. Jud. Admin. 2.050, I hereby order as follows:

1. For the interim period of July 1, 2004 through September 30, 2004, or until otherwise ordered, or until otherwise provided for by the Twentieth Judicial Circuit Article V Indigent Services Committee, the attorneys previously approved for court appointment, including both contract attorneys and attorneys who performed services upon appointment without a contract, and who have entered into an Agreement or Interim Agreement with the JAC, are approved for appointment on or after July 1, 2004.

2. As to contract attorneys who have entered into an Agreement or Interim Agreement with the JAC, for the interim period of July 1, 2004 through September 30, 2004, or until otherwise ordered, or until otherwise provided for by the Twentieth Judicial Circuit Article V Indigent Services Committee, the rates provided for by the previous contracts of those court-appointed attorneys in effect through June 30, 2004, shall be the approved rates of compensation for those court-appointed attorneys for services performed on or after July 1, 2004. As to each contract attorney within the Twentieth Judicial Circuit, the JAC has been provided with a copy of each contract in effect through June 30, 2004, for the purpose of referencing the applicable rates of compensation provided for by each contract.

3. As to attorneys who previously performed services upon appointment without a contract and who have entered into an Agreement or Interim Agreement with the JAC, for the interim period of July 1, 2004 through September 30, 2004, or until otherwise ordered, or until otherwise provided for by the Twentieth Judicial Circuit Article V Indigent Services Committee, the rates provided for by Administrative Order 3.5 shall be the approved rates of compensation for those court-appointed attorneys for services performed on or after July 1, 2004. Even though the provisions of Administrative Order 3.5 were to expire on June 30, 2004, the term is hereby extended for the limited purpose stated herein to cover the interim period of July 1, 2004 through September 30, 2004, or until otherwise ordered, or until otherwise provided for by the Twentieth Judicial Circuit Article V Indigent Services Committee. A copy of Administrative Order 3.5 is attached and incorporated herein.

4. To the extent that any provision of this Administrative Order may be construed as being in conflict with any law, statute, or rule, the law, statute, or rule shall prevail.

5. This Administrative Order shall be in effect, nunc pro tune, July 1, 2004 through September 30, 2004, or until otherwise ordered, or until procedures for the appointment and compensation of court-appointed attorneys are otherwise provided for by the Twentieth Judicial Circuit Article V Indigent Services Committee.

DONE AND ORDERED in chambers in Naples, Collier County, Florida, this 16th day of July, 2004.

Hugh D. Hayes
Chief Judge

History. - New.

2.28. JUDICIAL ANNUAL LEAVE

IN THE TWENTIETH JUDICIAL CIRCUIT IN AND FOR THE STATE OF FLORIDA

ADMINISTRATIVE ORDER NO: 2.28

IN RE: JUDICIAL ANNUAL LEAVE

WHEREAS the Judicial Administration Section of the Conference of Circuit Judges has reviewed the leave practices in existence in other judicial branches throughout the United States; and

WHEREAS the American Bar Association's National Conference of Special Court Judges has recommended criteria for sound leave policies to include no less than 21, nor more than 30 working days of vacation leave per year; and

WHEREAS judicial officers, unlike state employees, cannot yet accumulate annual and sick leave for which they are compensated at the termination of service; and

WHEREAS judicial officers are considered to be available for duty twenty-four hours a day and are often required to serve on weekends and after hours without the benefit of defined compensatory time; and

WHEREAS judicial annual leave assures that judges have sufficient time away from the bench to maintain good health and effectiveness and to permit time for rejuvenation and renewal; and

WHEREAS establishment of the following judicial annual leave policy ensures that judges are accountable for the time they are away from the bench while simultaneously emphasizing that some leave time is in the best interest of a properly functioning judiciary; and

WHEREAS judicial annual leave does not encompass sick leave, educational leave, military leave, leave to serve on court committees or other leave in the furtherance of justice; and

WHEREAS all judges are expected to participate - as both faculty and students - in approved continuing judicial education programs; and

WHEREAS judges are also encouraged as part of their regular judicial responsibilities to participate in professional meetings and conferences that advance the administration of justice or the public's understanding of the judicial system, to serve on commissions and committees of state and national organizations that contribute to the improvement of the law or the administration of justice, and to serve on Supreme Court appointed or intra-circuit assignments or committees; and

WHEREAS a judicial office is a constitutionally recognized public office rather than an employment status, and therefore the establishment of a judicial leave policy cannot be required by law and is entirely voluntary on the part of the State Court System; and

WHEREAS this administrative order is entered in accordance with the chief judge's duties and responsibilities as set forth in Article V, Section 2, Florida Constitution; Rule of Judicial Administration 2.050; and section 26.37, Florida Statutes, it is therefore,

Ordered:

1. Circuit court and county court judges are expected to take no more than 30 working days of annual leave. For the purposes of this administrative order, "annual leave" means "time away from judicial duties to provide opportunities for rest, relaxation and personal pursuits." Annual leave does not encompass sick leave, educational leave, military leave, leave to serve on court committees or other leave in the furtherance of justice. The taking of annual leave shall not interfere with the efficient administration of a judicial officer's docket.

2. Because all judges are constitutional officers and professional public servants, each judge shall be self reporting—that is, each judge shall maintain within their office an accurate record of the annual leave time taken and such records shall be available for inspection by the chief judge or his/her designee.

3. Unused judicial annual leave does not accrue from year to year. No judge shall be entitled to be paid for those hours of judicial annual leave not taken within a calendar year.

4. Nothing herein prevents a chief judge, upon good cause shown on a case by case basis, from allowing judicial annual leave in excess of 30 days.

DONE AND ORDERED in chambers in Naples, Collier County, Florida, this 24th day of FEBRUARY, 2006.

Hugh D. Hayes
Chief Judge

History.—New.

2.29. PROCEDURES FOR SEALING COURT FILES AND RECORDS

IN THE TWENTIETH JUDICIAL CIRCUIT IN AND FOR THE STATE OF FLORIDA LEE, COLLIER, CHARLOTTE, HENDRY, AND GLADES COUNTIES

IN RE: PROCEDURES FOR SEALING COURT FILES AND RECORDS

ADMINISTRATIVE ORDER NO. 2.29

- VACATED -

WHEREAS, the Florida Supreme Court issued an opinion on April 5, 2007, In re Amendments to Florida Rule of Judicial Administration 2.420—Sealing of Court Records and Dockets, 954 So. 2d 16 (Fla. 2007); and

WHEREAS, in the opinion, the Florida Supreme Court amended Fla. R. Jud. Admin. 2.420 so as to create a new subdivision setting forth specific procedures governing requests to make circuit and county court records in noncriminal cases confidential; and

WHEREAS, in the opinion, the Florida Supreme Court provided that the amendments would become effective immediately upon issuance of the opinion and would supercede any conflicting procedures established by local administrative orders; and

WHEREAS, local Administrative Order 2.29 is not fully consistent with the amendments to Fla. R. Jud. Admin. 2.420, and, in light of the amendments to Fla. R. Jud. Admin. 2.420, is no longer necessary;

IT IS ORDERED, by the authority vested in the Chief Judge pursuant to Fla. R. Jud. Admin. 2.215, that Administrative Order 2.29 is hereby VACATED.

DONE AND ORDERED in Chambers in Naples, Collier County, Florida, this 07 day of June, 2007.

Hugh D. Hayes
Chief Judge

History. - Administrative Order No. 2.29 (October 5, 2006).

2.30. CERTIFICATION AND REGULATION OF CERTIFIED PROCESS SERVERS

IN THE TWENTIETH JUDICIAL CIRCUIT IN AND FOR THE STATE OF FLORIDA

Administrative Order No. 2.30 (formerly AO 1.11) -AMENDED-

IN RE: CERTIFICATION AND REGULATION OF CERTIFIED PROCESS SERVERS

WHEREAS, section 48.27, Florida Statutes, authorizes the Chief Judge of a judicial circuit to establish an approved list of Certified Process Servers as an alternative means for the service of initial nonenforceable civil process, criminal witness subpoenas, and criminal summonses; and

WHEREAS, the undersigned Chief Judge has previously determined that establishing an approved list of Certified Process Servers for the Twentieth Judicial Circuit would, in fact, serve the interest of justice and judicial economy throughout the Twentieth Judicial Circuit; and

WHEREAS, the undersigned Chief Judge previously established the Twentieth Judicial Circuit Certified Process Server Review Board; and

WHEREAS, the undersigned Chief Judge has since assigned court staff to assist with the ministerial operational aspects of the Certified Process Server Program and has found that the utilization of court staff has been successful; and

WHEREAS, the undersigned Chief Judge has determined that the utilization of court staff furthers the goal of circuit-wide consistency, serves the convenience of the applicants and members of the Certified Process Server List, and allows for improved efficiency in responding to inquires and issues from the public and members of the Certified Process Server List;

It is hereby **ORDERED** that all previous versions of Administrative Order 2.30 are hereby vacated and the approved list of Certified Process Servers for the Twentieth Judicial Circuit shall hereinafter be maintained and regulated in accordance with policies established by the Administrative Office of the Courts.

DONE AND ORDERED in Chambers in Fort Myers, Lee County, Florida, this 26 day of January, 2011.

G. Keith Cary, Chief Judge

History.—Administrative Order 1.11 (October 29, 2007); Administrative Order 1.11 (July 28, 2008); renumbered as Administrative Order 2.30 to account for legislative changes to Fla. Stat. §§ 48.021 and 48.27, Ch. 2009–215, Laws of Florida; Administrative Order 2.30 (July 30, 2009); Administrative Order 2.30 (July 29, 2010).

2.31. PROCEDURES FOR GPS AND ALCOHOL MEASURING DEVICE TECHNOLOGY VENDORS

IN THE TWENTIETH JUDICIAL CIRCUIT IN AND FOR THE STATE OF FLORIDA

ADMINISTRATIVE ORDER NO. 2.31—Amended–

IN RE: PROCEDURES FOR GPS AND ALCOHOL MEASURING DEVICE TECHNOLOGY VENDORS

WHEREAS, pursuant to Article V, Section 2(d) of the Florida Constitution and section 43.26, Florida Statutes, the Chief Judge of each judicial circuit is charged with the authority and the power to do everything necessary to promote the prompt and efficient administration of justice; and

WHEREAS, due to the unique issues accompanying criminal and domestic relation/violence cases; and

WHEREAS, Global Positioning System (GPS) and Continuous Transdermal Alcohol Measuring Device technology serve as an additional tool to monitor compliance with terms and conditions of pretrial supervision and probation; and

WHEREAS, GPS and Continuous Transdermal Alcohol Measuring Device technology is being used with increasing frequency; and

WHEREAS, there is a need for uniform guidelines for vendors providing such technology used in the Twentieth Judicial Circuit;

NOW, THEREFORE, pursuant to the authority vested in me as Chief Judge of the Twentieth Judicial Circuit of Florida under Florida Rule of Judicial Administration 2.215, it is ordered as follows:

1. A vendor may request to be included on the Administrative Office of the Court's (AOC) written list of Electronic Monitoring Service Providers by submitting to the AOC an application. If approved, the vendor must sign a Memorandum of Understanding acknowledging all terms and conditions required for inclusion on the written list. Parties ordered by the Court to submit to electronic monitoring as a condition of pre-trial supervision or county probation may select any vendor from the written list and shall be solely responsible for entering into an agreement with the vendor and for the cost of electronic monitoring services.

2. A party ordered to wear the GPS device and/or the Continuous Transdermal Alcohol Measuring Device shall pay directly to the vendor all costs associated with the wearing of the device.

3. The GPS device and/or the Continuous Transdermal Alcohol Measuring Device must be monitored by the vendor twenty-four (24) hours a day, seven (7) days a week, including weekends and holidays, throughout the United States.

4. The GPS system must be capable of having inclusion and exclusion zones, a violation of which must be reported by the vendor to law enforcement immediately by telephone. A violation of the Continuous Transdermal Alcohol Measuring Device system must be reported by the vendor to the Pre-trial or Probation Officer assigned to the case by telephone as soon as possible during normal business hours, but no later than 11:00 a.m. on the following business day.

5. The vendor must be willing to have the GPS device programmed and monitored such that law enforcement shall be contacted immediately of a violation of an exclusion or inclusion zone.

6. The GPS device must accurately track the wearer of the device and maintain records of his or her actual location,

7. The vendor must have an adequate supply of equipment such that no wearer of the device is ever required to wait for a device to become available, and the vendor must be available to place the device on the wearer of the device seven (7) days a week.

8. This Administrative Order is not intended to apply to any cases in which the offender is supervised by the Florida Department of Corrections,

9. To the extent that any provision of this Administrative Order may conflict with any rule, statute or law, the rule, statute or law shall prevail.

DONE AND ORDERED in Chambers in Fort Myers, Florida, this 16th day of Nov., 2018.

Michael T. McHugh
Chief Judge

Adopted effective August 20, 2009. Amended effective November 16, 2018.

2.32. LEE COUNTY COURT DIVISION FOR THE CITY OF CAPE CORAL

IN THE TWENTIETH JUDICIAL CIRCUIT IN AND FOR LEE COUNTY, FLORIDA

Administrative Order No. 2.32

IN RE: LEE COUNTY COURT DIVISION FOR THE CITY OF CAPE CORAL

Pursuant to this Court's inherent authority to administer and regulate the courts of the Twentieth Judicial Circuit, and that prescribed by Fla. R. Jud. Admin. 2.215 and Florida Statute § 43.26, the Court hereby amends the administrative order previously entered on February 27, 2002 creating a county court division within the City of Cape Coral, a political subdivision of the State of Florida within Lee County, Florida, and it is

ORDERED AND ADJUDGED as follows:

1. There shall be within the Twentieth Judicial Circuit Court in and for Lee County, a County Court Division for the City of Cape Coral. A Lee County Court Judge or Judges shall be assigned to the Lee County Court Division for the City of Cape Coral. The assigned Judge or Judges shall preside over proceedings involving civil citations written by agencies under the jurisdiction of the City of Cape Coral, including but not limited to civil traffic infractions, code enforcement violations, and violations of animal control regulations. The Lee County Court Division for the City of Cape Coral and the Judge or Judges assigned thereto will not conduct proceedings involving other civil or criminal matters, until or unless otherwise directed by subsequent order or amendment hereto. Other civil and criminal matters accruing or arising in the City of Cape Coral, in which venue lies in Lee County, shall be presided over by Lee County Court Judges assigned to the Lee County Justice Center located in Fort Myers, and all proceedings involving such matters shall be conducted at the Lee County Justice Center located in Fort Myers, until or unless otherwise directed by subsequent order or amendment hereto.

2. The Clerk of the Court for Lee County is directed to do the following:

A. Accept for tiling any circuit civil case or pleading which is required to be filed in the courts of Lee County. Florida, and thereafter transfer said case or pleading to the Lee County Justice Center in Fort Myers for processing and assignment before the appropriate judge as designated by this Court.

B. Accept for filing any county civil case or pleading which is required to be filed in the courts of Lee County, Florida, and thereafter transfer said case or pleading to the Lee County Justice Center in Fort Myers for processing and assignment before the appropriate judge as designated by this Court.

C. Accept for filing any case requiring immediate action by a circuit or county judge, such as petitions for extraordinary relief. These include petitions for writs of habeas corpus, mandamus, prohibition, quo warranto and common law certiorari, as well as all actions related to domestic violence and any claim for immediate injunctive relief. In any such case, the Clerk is requested to immediately transmit the case to the Lee County Justice Center in Fort Myers for assignment. Counsel shall take note that although such cases may be filed in Cape Coral, assignments will occur at the time the file is transmitted to the county seat.

3. To the extent that this Administrative Order may conflict with any rule, statute, or law, the rule, statute, or law shall prevail.

DONE AND ORDERED in Chambers in Fort Myers. Lee County, Florida this 21 day of April, 2010.

G. Keith Cary
Chief Judge

History—Order Establishing County Court Division for the City of Cape Coral (Feb. 27, 2002).

2.33. PROCEDURE FOR DETERMINING COMPENSATION OF COURT–APPOINTED COUNSEL IN EXCESS OF FLAT FEE RATES ESTABLISHED BY THE FLORIDA LEGISLATURE

IN THE TWENTIETH JUDICIAL CIRCUIT IN AND FOR THE STATE OF FLORIDA

ADMINISTRATIVE ORDER NO: 2.33

—Amended—

IN RE: PROCEDURE FOR DETERMINING COMPENSATION OF COURT–APPOINTED COUNSEL IN EXCESS OF FLAT FEE RATES ESTABLISHED BY THE FLORIDA LEGISLATURE

WHEREAS, in 1998, the voters of the State of Florida passed Revision 7 to Article V of the Constitution of the State of Florida, requiring that funding for certain essential elements of the state courts system, including funding for court-appointed counsel, be provided from state revenues appropriated by general law; and

WHEREAS, in 2007, the Florida Legislature amended Florida Statute § 27.5304, so as to provide that compensation for court-appointed counsel shall be in accordance with specific flat fee amounts established annually in the General Appropriations Act; and

WHEREAS, the 2007 amendments to Florida Statute § 27.5304 provided a statement indicating that the intent of the Florida Legislature is that the flat fees comprise the full and complete compensation for court-appointed counsel; and

WHEREAS, the Florida Legislature further acknowledged in the 2007 amendments to Florida Statute § 27.5304 that there are rare occasions in which court-appointed counsel may receive a case that requires extraordinary and unusual effort; and

WHEREAS, the 2007 amendments to Florida Statute § 27.5304 provided a specific procedure by which court-appointed counsel may seek compensation in excess of the established flat fee by filing a motion with the Chief Judge of the circuit; and

WHEREAS, the current procedures under the 2012 legislative revisions to Florida Statute § 27.5304 require that an evidentiary hearing be held by the Chief Judge or a single designee, or in multicounty circuits, two designees, and, in granting a motion, that the Chief Judge or designee enter a written order detailing findings and identifying the extraordinary nature of the time and efforts of counsel that warrant exceeding the established flat fee;

NOW, THEREFORE, by the authority vested in the Chief Judge by Fla. R. Jud. Admin. 2.215, and by the authority granted to the Chief Judge by Florida Statute § 27.5304(12) to name two designees to preside over motions filed by court-appointed counsel seeking compensation in excess of the established flat fee, it is **ORDERED** as follows:

1. The original of all motions by court-appointed counsel seeking compensation in excess of the established flat fee shall be filed in the underlying case with the respective Clerk of Court of the county in which the case is pending, and counsel shall be responsible for providing a courtesy copy of the motion, accompanied by a cover letter, to the Chief Judge, to the appropriate designee, as described below, and to the Administrative Office of the Courts, attn. General Counsel 1700 Monroe Street, Fort Myers, FL 33901.

2. The Chief Judge hereby makes the following designations:

a. *Lee County and Charlotte County cases:* As it relates to all Lee County and Charlotte County cases, the Honorable Nicholas R. Thompson, Circuit Judge in Lee County, is designated by the Chief Judge to preside over the motions.

b. *Collier County, Hendry County, and Glades County cases:* As it relates to all Collier County, Hendry County, and Glades County cases, the Circuit Administrative Judge for Collier County is designated by the Chief Judge to preside over the motions.

3. In accordance with Fla. Stat. § 27.5304(12), prior to filing any motion seeking compensation in excess of the established flat fee, counsel must deliver a copy of the intended billing, together with supporting affidavits and all other necessary documentation to the Justice Administrative Commission (JAC). The JAC then has the opportunity to object by written communication to counsel. Counsel may thereafter file the motion, specifying whether the JAC objects to any portion of the billing or the sufficiency of documentation, and shall attach the JAC's letter stating its objection. An evidentiary hearing is only to be held after counsel has complied with this prerequisite.

4. If the designated judge finds that counsel has complied with this prerequisite to filing the motion, the statute then requires that the judge hold an evidentiary hearing. The JAC may participate in the hearing by use of telephonic or other communication equipment, unless otherwise ordered by the designated judge, or may contract with other public or private entities or individuals to appear before the court. The fact that the JAC has not objected to any portion of the billing or to the sufficiency of the documentation is not binding on the judge.

5. Acknowledging that the Twentieth Judicial Circuit is the largest circuit in geographic area and comprised of five counties, and further acknowledging the limitations placed upon the Court by the Legislature's decision to limit multi-county circuits to the use of only two designees, and, finally, acknowledging the expense and inconvenience upon counsel and witnesses who must travel from Charlotte, Hendry, and Glades counties to appear before the designees in Lee County and Collier County, upon motion, the designees in Lee County and Collier County will use discretion in liberally granting telephonic appearances by counsel and witnesses from a county other than Lee or Collier. However, to the extent that evidence or testimony may be presented, counsel shall be responsible for ensuring that it is presented appropriately and in accordance with the rules of evidence, even if that requires an appearance from a remote location in the presence of a person with the authority to administer the proper oath, or a personal appearance in Lee County or Collier County.

6. At the evidentiary hearing, the statute requires that counsel prove by competent and substantial evidence that the case required extraordinary and unusual efforts. The designated judge is to consider criteria such as the number of witnesses, the complexity of the factual and legal issues, and the length of trial, if any. The fact that a trial was conducted in a case does not, by itself, constitute competent substantial evidence of an extraordinary and unusual effort. In a criminal case, as per statute, relief may not be granted if the number of work hours does not exceed seventy-five (75) or the number of the state's witnesses deposed does not exceed twenty (20).

7. After having conducted the evidentiary hearing, if the motion is granted, the statute requires that the designated judge enter a written order detailing the findings and identifying the extraordinary nature of the time and efforts of counsel which warrant exceeding the flat fee set by the Legislature. If the designated judge finds that counsel has proven by competent and substantial evidence that the case required extraordinary and unusual efforts, the judge is to order the compensation to be paid to counsel at a percentage above the flat fee rate, depending upon the extent of the unusual and extraordinary effort required. However, the percentage may be only the rate necessary to ensure that the fees paid are not confiscatory under common law, and may not exceed 200 percent of the established flat fee, absent a specific finding that 200 percent of the flat fee in the case would be confiscatory. If the designated judge determines that 200 percent of the flat fee would be confiscatory, the judge is to order the amount of compensation using an hourly rate not to exceed $75.00 per hour for a noncapital case and $100.00 per hour for a capital case. However, as per statute, the compensation calculated by using the hourly rate may be only that amount necessary to ensure that the total fees paid are not confiscatory.

8. To the extent that any provision of this Administrative Order may be construed as being in conflict with any law, statute, or rule, the law, statute, or rule shall prevail.

9. The amendment to paragraph 2.a of this Administrative Order shall be effective immediately upon execution of this order, even as it relates to motions which may have been filed prior to execution.

DONE AND ORDERED in chambers in Fort Myers, Lee County, Florida, this 23rd day of May, 2018.

Michael T. McHugh
Chief Judge

Adopted effective September 15, 2011. Amended effective May 18, 2012; August 14, 2013; October 4, 2013; May 23, 2018.

2.34. TWENTIETH JUDICIAL CIRCUIT PROFESSIONALISM COMMITTEE

IN THE TWENTIETH JUDICIAL CIRCUIT IN AND FOR THE STATE OF FLORIDA

ADMINISTRATIVE ORDER NO. 2.34 —Amended—

IN RE: TWENTIETH JUDICIAL CIRCUIT PROFESSIONALISM COMMITTEE

In recognition of the fact that the courts of the State of Florida have an inherent interest in promoting and encouraging professionalism within the legal community; and in further recognition of the fact that, in 1998, the Twentieth Judicial Circuit's Professionalism Committee was initially formed as provided for by the Supreme Court of Florida's Administrative Order *In re: Commission on Professionalism* dated June 11, 1998; and in further recognition of the fact that in recent years, the Twentieth Judicial Circuit's Professionalism Committee has been superseded by the professionalism efforts and activities on the part of our local bar associations, it is

ORDERED that, in accordance with the authority vested in the Chief Judge pursuant to Fla. R. Jud. Admin. 2.215, and the Supreme Court of Florida's Administrative Order *In re: Commission on Professionalism* dated June 11, 1998:

1. The Twentieth Judicial Circuit Professionalism Committee is hereby re-established.

2. The Twentieth Judicial Circuit Professionalism Committee shall consist of the following members:

a. The Chief Judge—Chair

b. The Circuit Administrative Judge (or Deputy Chief Judge) for Lee County

c. The Circuit Administrative Judge for Collier County

d. The Circuit Administrative Judge for Charlotte County

e. The Administrative Judge for Hendry County

f. The Administrative Judge for Glades County

g. The President of the Lee County Bar Association, or designee

h. The President of the Collier County Bar Association, or designee

i. The President of the Charlotte County Bar Association, or designee

j. The President of the Hendry/Glades Counties Bar Association, or designee

k. The Twentieth Judicial Circuit State Attorney, or designee

l. The Twentieth Judicial Circuit Public Defender, or designee

m. The Second District Criminal Conflict and Civil Regional Counsel, or designee

n. The President of the Calusa American Inn of Court, or designee

o. The President of the Thomas S. Biggs American Inn of Court, or designee

p. At–large member—a practicing attorney to be appointed by the Chief Judge

3. Each member shall serve during that member's term of office. The at-large member shall serve at the pleasure of the Chief Judge and shall serve during the Chief Judge's term of office, unless otherwise discharged by the Chief Judge.

4. The Twentieth Judicial Circuit Professionalism Committee shall meet quarterly, or on a schedule otherwise established by the Committee.

5. The Twentieth Judicial Circuit Professionalism Committee shall discuss, monitor and/or coordinate professionalism activities within the Twentieth Judicial Circuit, and may take action deemed appropriate by the Committee in furtherance of promoting and encouraging professionalism within the legal community.

6. Each January, the Twentieth Judicial Circuit Professionalism Committee shall submit to the Chair of the Commission on Professionalism an annual report on the status of professionalism and professionalism activities within the Twentieth Judicial Circuit.

7. To the extent that any provision of this Administrative Order may be construed as being in conflict with any law, statute, or rule, the law, statute, or rule shall prevail.

DONE AND ORDERED in chambers in Fort Myers, Lee County, Florida, this 15th day of October, 2014.

Jay B. Rosman
Chief Judge

History. Administrative Order 2.34 (December 21, 2011).

2.35. IDENTIFICATION OF COURT PLEADINGS WITH SPECIFICITY

IN THE TWENTIETH JUDICIAL CIRCUIT IN AND FOR THE STATE OF FLORIDA

ADMINISTRATIVE ORDER NO. 2.35

IN RE: IDENTIFICATION OF COURT PLEADINGS WITH SPECIFICITY

WHEREAS, the Florida State Courts System and Clerks of Court are steadily moving in the direction of increased reliance upon electronic filing, electronic service, electronic scheduling, and electronic case dockets, as provided for by the Florida Supreme Court Standards for Electronic Access to the Courts (adopted June 2009, modifications adopted May 2013);

and

WHEREAS, the ability to accurately and quickly identify or locate court pleadings, orders and other documents serves the interest of minimizing confusion and serves the further purpose of ensuring that judicial proceedings are handled as expeditiously and efficiently as possible;

and

WHEREAS, several provisions within the Florida Rules of Courts already provide that documents filed shall be styled or captioned in such a manner as to indicate clearly the subject matter of the document and the party requesting relief; Fla. R. Civ. P. 1.100; Fla. R. Crim. P. 3.090;

In accordance with the authority vested in the Chief Judge pursuant to Fla. R. Jud. Admin. 2.215, it is **ORDERED** as follows:

1. Title or Caption of Pleadings: When a party to a proceeding before the Courts of the Twentieth Judicial Circuit, or counsel, files a pleading, document or notice of hearing, or submits a proposed order, the party or counsel shall, for ease of further reference, *title or caption with specificity the pleading, document, notice of hearing, or proposed order* so as to facilitate the ability to quickly identify and locate same utilizing only the title or caption.

2. Pleadings Referenced Within Other Pleadings: When a party to a proceeding before the Courts of the Twentieth Judicial Circuit, or counsel, files a pleading, document or notice of hearing, or submits a proposed order, which includes a reference to a previously filed pleading, document or to the motion being scheduled for hearing, the party or counsel shall, for ease of further reference: (1) *identify with specificity the previously filed pleading or document referenced therein, or the motion being scheduled for hearing*; (2) *identify the previously filed pleading or document referenced therein, or the motion being scheduled for hearing, by the date it was filed with the Clerk of Court*; and, (3) *if available, identify the previously filed pleading or document referenced therein, or the motion being scheduled for hearing, by the docket line or docket number*, as may be reflected on the Clerk's online web portal, if accessible by the party or counsel.

3. Hearings Scheduled Through JACS: When a party to a proceeding before the Courts of the Twentieth Judicial Circuit, or counsel, files a notice of a hearing scheduled through the Judicial Automated Calendaring System (JACS), and if the party or counsel receives a JACS confirmation number, the party or counsel shall include the JACS confirmation number within the caption of the written notice of hearing.

4. Failure to comply with the provisions of this Administrative Order or the applicable rules of procedure may, within the discretion of the judge and in accordance with applicable case law, result in the pleading being stricken. However, this Administrative Order is not intended to circumvent any jurisdictional time limitations and shall not be construed or applied as such.

5. To the extent that any provision of this Administrative Order may conflict with any rule, case law, or statute, the rule, case law, or statute will prevail.

DONE AND ORDERED in chambers in Fort Myers, Lee County, Florida, this 30th day of Oct., 2013.

Jay B. Rosman
Chief Judge

History.—New.

2.36. COURT INTERPRETERS FOR COURT OR COURT–ORDERED PROCEEDINGS

IN THE TWENTIETH JUDICIAL CIRCUIT IN AND FOR THE STATE OF FLORIDA

ADMINISTRATIVE ORDER NO. 2.36

IN RE: COURT INTERPRETERS FOR COURT OR COURT–ORDERED PROCEEDINGS

WHEREAS, the entitlement to a Court Interpreter at public expense for court or court-ordered proceedings is governed by applicable laws, statutes, and court rules; and

WHEREAS, the responsibility for determining the entitlement to a Court Interpreter for non-English-speaking or limited-English-proficient persons at public expense for court or court-ordered proceedings rests upon the trial judge; and

WHEREAS, it is in the best interest of justice and due process that a determination as to the need for a Court Interpreter for non-English-speaking or limited-English-proficient defendants or litigants be made at the earliest stages of a case; and

WHEREAS, the Florida Supreme Court has recently enacted more stringent requirements for Court Interpreters providing services for court, court-ordered, and court-related proceedings, resulting in the decreased availability of qualified Court Interpreters; and

WHEREAS, the resources of the Administrative Office of the Courts (AOC) in providing staff Court Interpreters or contract Court Interpreters at public expense are not infinite or unlimited and necessarily require management so as to ensure that all constitutional and due process rights are met;

It is **ORDERED,** pursuant to this Court's inherent authority to administer and regulate the courts of the Twentieth Judicial Circuit and to manage court resources, and by the authority vested in the Chief Judge pursuant to Fla. R. Jud. Admin. 2.215, that policies and procedures for the use of Court Interpreters for court and court-ordered proceedings be delineated and set forth as follows:

A. Entitlement to a Court Interpreter.

1. Pursuant to the rules of the Florida Supreme Court, Fla. R. Jud. Admin. 2.560, spoken language Court Interpreters are to be provided in the state courts of Florida at public expense for court or court-ordered proceedings to the following persons:

- non-English-speaking or limited-English-proficient defendants accused in criminal cases;
- non-English-speaking or limited-English-proficient juveniles accused in delinquency cases; and
- non-English-speaking or limited-English-proficient litigants in all other case types if the trial judge determines (1) that the litigant's inability to comprehend English deprives the litigant of an understanding of the court proceedings, (2) that a fundamental interest is at stake (such as in a civil commitment, termination of parental rights, paternity, or dependency proceeding), and (3) that no alternative to the appointment of an interpreter exists. At this time, in the state courts of Florida, non-English-speaking or limited-English-proficient litigants in ordinary civil or family law cases in which a fundamental interest is not at stake are not automatically entitled to a spoken-language Court Interpreter at public expense.

The Administrative Office of the Courts interprets the due process intent of providing spoken language Court Interpreters at public expense in the above-identified proceedings to defendants, accused juveniles and other litigants to also include providing Court Interpreters at public expense during those same above-identified proceedings, as may be appropriate or ordered by the Court, for necessary witnesses, parents or guardians of juveniles, children in dependency cases, and victims who may be non-English-speaking or limited-English-proficient.

2. Pursuant to the rules of the Florida Supreme Court, Fla. R. Jud. Admin. 2.560, and the Florida Evidence Code, Fla. Stat. § 90.606, Court Interpreters are to be provided in the state courts of Florida at public expense *for a witness* for court or court-ordered proceedings if the trial judge determines that the witness cannot hear or understand the English language, or cannot express himself or herself in English sufficiently to be understood. This is not limited to witnesses who speak a language other than English, but applies also to the language and descriptions of any person, such as a child or a person who is mentally or developmentally disabled, who cannot be reasonably understood, or who cannot understand questioning, without the aid of an interpreter.

3. Pursuant to the Florida Evidence Code, Fla. Stat. § 90.6063, as well as the Americans with Disabilities Act (ADA), Court Interpreters or alternative auxiliary aids, as may be appropriate, are to be provided at public expense for all court or court-ordered proceedings in which a deaf person is a complainant, defendant, witness, or otherwise a party. The Courts of the Twentieth Judicial Circuit fully comply with all provisions of the Americans with Disabilities Act (ADA) so as to ensure full access to the courts and court services to qualified persons with disabilities as defined by the ADA.

B. Determination of Entitlement to a Court Interpreter.

1. Upon the initiation of an action in the Courts of the Twentieth Judicial Circuit, it shall be the responsibility of the party or the party's counsel requesting a Court Interpreter for a non-English-speaking or limited-English-proficient defendant, juvenile (parent or guardian), litigant, child, witness, or victim to bring this matter to a trial judge's attention for the purpose of ensuring that a preliminary inquiry and determination as to the entitlement to a Court Interpreter is made at the earliest practicable court event, for example, at arraignment or the first scheduled Case Management Conference. If a Court Interpreter is being requested for a non-English-speaking or limited-English-proficient child, witness, or victim, it shall be the responsibility of the party or the party's counsel to bring this matter to a trial judge's attention immediately upon learning of the child's, witness', or victim's need for a Court Interpreter and sufficiently in advance of the court proceeding at which the child, witness, or victim will testify or be present.

2. The determination as to whether a person is, in fact, non-English-speaking or limited-English-proficient is within the discretion of a trial judge. The Florida Supreme Court has defined a "limited-English-proficient" person as "[a] person who is unable to communicate effectively in English because the individual's primary language is not English and he or she has not developed fluency in the English language" and who "may have difficulty speaking, reading, writing, or understanding English." Fla. R. Jud. Admin. 2.560. It should be noted that a person is not necessarily non-English-speaking or limited-English-proficient simply because that person may not speak grammatically correct English, or may speak too softly or too swiftly, See Suarez v. United States of America, 309 F. 2d 709 (5th Cir. 1962); See also Pietrzak v. U.S., 188 F.2d 418 (5th Cir. 1951); Bolender v. State, 422 So. 2d 833 (Fla. 1982), *reversed on unrelated grounds*; Larias v. State, 528 So. 2d 944 (Fla. 3d DCA 1988).

3. If a trial judge determines that a non-English-speaking or limited-English-proficient defendant, juvenile (parent or guardian), or litigant is entitled to a spoken language Court Interpreter at public expense for all future court or court-ordered proceedings at which that person is to be present, or for a child, witness or victim at trial or an evidentiary hearing, the trial judge shall make this finding on the record or enter a written order.

4. After having determined that a person is entitled to a spoken language Court Interpreter, a trial judge may re-visit this determination at any time upon motion of any party or on the Court's own motion.

5. If a person is deaf, or has any disability as defined by the ADA, and is in need of a Court Interpreter or other accommodation for the purpose of participating in a court or court-ordered proceeding, the person, or counsel representing the party or person, is to contact the appropriate ADA Coordinator for the AOC at least seven (7) days before the scheduled court appearance, or immediately upon receipt of notice if less than seven (7) days notice of the proceeding was provided, in accordance with Rule 2.540, Fla. R. Jud. Admin., and local Administrative Order 2.15. The appropriate ADA Coordinator for the AOC may be reached as follows:

Lee County: 239–533–1771

Collier County: 239–252–8800

Charlotte County: 941–637–2110

Hendry and Glades Counties: 863–675–5374

If hearing or voice impaired, call 711

6. ADA accommodation requests submitted to the appropriate AOC ADA Coordinator need not be reviewed or approved by a trial judge, unless the AOC ADA Coordinator determines that the requested accommodation impacts court procedures within a specific case, or otherwise determines that deference to a trial judge is appropriate. All ADA accommodation requests will be reviewed and addressed in accordance with Title II of the Americans with Disabilities Act.

C. Procedures for Notification of Need of Court Interpreter.

1. After a determination has been made by a trial judge that a non-English-speaking or limited-English-proficient person is entitled to a Court Interpreter at public expense, the person, or counsel representing the person, shall notify the AOC's Court Interpreter Services of the need for a Court Interpreter for court proceedings, and court-ordered mediations, arbitrations and competency examinations, by submitting written notifications to the AOC's Court Interpreter Services utilizing the AOC's "Notification of Need of Court Interpreter" form. The "Notification of Need of Court Interpreter" form and instructions for submission shall be posted on the AOC's website at www.ca.cjis20.org. Assistance is also available by calling the AOC's Court Interpreter Services for the Twentieth Judicial Circuit at 239–533–1580 or by visiting the AOC's Court Interpreter Services for the Twentieth Judicial Circuit located at the Lee County Justice Center Complex, 1700 Monroe Street, Fort Myers, Florida 33901.

2. For court proceedings held during the initial stages of a case prior to a non-English-speaking or limited-English-proficient defendant, juvenile (parent or guardian), or litigant, or counsel for the defendant, juvenile, or litigant, having had a reasonable opportunity to bring the issue as to the entitlement to a Court Interpreter at public expense before a trial judge for determination (for example, First Appearance, arraignment, or other preliminary hearings), a "Notification of Need of Court Interpreter" form may be submitted to the AOC's Court Interpreter Services in the absence of a trial court order or record finding of entitlement. If said notification is submitted by or on behalf of a non-English-speaking or limited-English-proficient defendant, juvenile (parent or guardian), or litigant who would otherwise be entitled to a Court Interpreter at public expense under Rule 2.560, Fla. R. Jud. Admin., a Court Interpreter will be provided by the AOC's Court Interpreter Services, even in the absence of a trial court order or record finding of entitlement. However, beyond the initial stage of a case (i.e. motion hearing, subsequent or ongoing status or case management conference, plea hearing, trial, sentencing hearing, mediation, arbitration, competency examination), the AOC's Court Interpreter Services will be unable to provide a spoken language Court Interpreter in the absence of a finding by a trial judge of entitlement to a spoken language Court Interpreter at public expense.

3. If a person is deaf, or has any disability as defined by the ADA, and is in need of a Court Interpreter or other accommodation for the purpose of participating in a court proceeding, the person, or counsel representing the party or person, may contact the appropriate ADA Coordinator as identified above and in local Administrative Order 2.15, and may submit an "ADA Title II Accommodation Request Form." The "ADA Title II Accommodation Request Form" and instructions for submission shall be posted on the AOC's website at www.ca.cjis20.org.

4. Advance notification of the need for a Court Interpreter for a court or court-ordered proceeding must be provided to the AOC's Court Interpreter Services, or to the ADA Coordinator as may be appropriate, as follows:

For Spanish language Court Interpreters: At least **2 business days** advance notice (excluding weekends and holidays).

For all other spoken language Court Interpreters: At least **7 business days** advance notice (excluding weekends and holidays).

For American Sign Language or other Court Interpreters or accommodations under the ADA: At least **7 days** advance notice, or immediately upon receipt of notice of less than 7 days notice of the proceeding was provided.

5. An exception to the minimum time for advance notification of the need for a Court Interpreter shall be made for First Appearance and any other court proceeding that, by its nature, involves limited notice, such as proceedings under the Baker Act or the Marchman Act. However, the defendant, juvenile (parent or guardian), litigant or other person, or counsel for the defendant, juvenile, litigant or other person, remains responsible for providing advance notification of the need for a Court Interpreter immediately upon receiving short notice of such proceedings. Under such circumstances, the AOC's Court Interpreter Services, or ADA Coordinators, will make all diligent and reasonable efforts to provide a Court Interpreter requested upon short notice, and if unable to do so will notify the person or counsel who submitted the request, as well as the presiding trial judge or quasi-judicial officer.

6. At this time, neither the AOC's Court Interpreter Services nor ADA Coordinators have the ability or means to accurately predict or automatically receive knowledge as to when a Court Interpreter may be needed without advance notification being submitted by the defendant, juvenile (parent or guardian), litigant or other person, or by counsel for the defendant, juvenile, litigant or other person. Likewise, the AOC may not necessarily have the resources to always and automatically provide "stand-by" Court Interpreters for events such as First Appearance, arraignments, or other court dockets in anticipation of a Court Interpreter potentially being needed. The goal is to utilize technology working in coordination with Case Management Systems in all five (5) counties of the Twentieth Judicial Circuit to facilitate the automatic identification of court proceedings in which a Court Interpreter is needed, so as to minimize or eliminate the need for speculation or manual identification requiring ongoing notification. However, until an automated system is developed, it is incumbent upon the defendant, juvenile (parent or guardian), litigant or other person, or counsel for the defendant, juvenile, litigant or other person, to ensure that advance notification of the need for a Court Interpreter is submitted to the AOC's Court Interpreter Services for any and all court or court-ordered proceeding in accordance with the minimum time frames established herein or, when impossible due to short notice of certain proceedings, with as much advance notice as possible. Automation through the use of technology, in whole or in part, may be available as early as March 1, 2016, and may be utilized as it becomes available and as appropriate to minimize or eliminate the need for ongoing notification upon approval by the Chief Judge.

7. Due process provisions require that the Court provide and incur the budgetary expense of Court Interpreters for court and court-ordered proceedings (including mediation, arbitration, and competency examinations), as may be appropriate, but do not require that the Court incur the budgetary expense or provide interpreter *scheduling* services to other publicly funded agencies (i.e. State Attorney, Public Defender, Regional Counsel), court-appointed counsel (funded by the Justice Administrative Commission), privately-retained attorneys, or self-represented parties, for events occurring *outside* of the context of a court or court-ordered proceeding. Examples of non-court-ordered proceedings or events are depositions, in-custody conferences and visits (jail or holding cells), and office conferences and visits, which may or may not require the retention of an interpreter meeting the more stringent Florida Supreme Court requirements for Court Interpreters.[1] For these types of non-court-ordered events taking place between other publicly funded agencies, court-appointed counsel, privately-retained attorneys, clients, parties, family members, witnesses, or victims, the scheduling and retaining of interpreters shall be the responsibility of those agencies, attorneys, or parties. A list of all interpreters/translators who have entered into contracts with the State of Florida through the Justice Administrative Commission and have agreed to offer services at standard rates established by the legislature is available on the Justice Administrative Com-

mission's website at www.justiceadmin.org under the "Due Process Vendor Search." Upon request, the AOC's Court Interpreter Services will provide names of vendors or a copy of the AOC's list of Court Interpreters with whom the AOC contracts or has contracted. However, it should be noted that the judiciary is not bound by the rates established by the legislature, and the rates of Court Interpreters with whom the AOC contracts or has contracted may exceed those rates by which other agencies, attorneys, or parties are bound. In addition, the AOC cannot guarantee that the rates offered by contract Court Interpreters to the AOC will be the same offered to other agencies, attorneys, or parties.

D. Rules and Procedures Applicable to Court Interpreters.

1. All Court Interpreters providing spoken language interpretation services for court or court-ordered proceedings must be qualified in accordance with the Florida Rules for Certification and Regulation of Spoken Language Court Interpreters, but for the limited exceptions provided by the Florida Supreme Court as memorialized within this Administrative Order. All Court Interpreters providing interpreter services for deaf persons for court or court-ordered proceedings must be qualified and certified by the National Registry of Interpreters for the Deaf or the Florida Registry of Interpreters for the Deaf.

2. All Court Interpreters entering into a contract with the Administrative Office of the Courts (AOC) for the provision of services to the Courts of the Twentieth Judicial Circuit are bound by all contract terms. In addition, for the purpose of providing verification and accountability for the use of public funds, contract Court Interpreters are required to submit with all invoices the "Contract Interpreter Sign-in/Sign-out Sheet" provided by the AOC's Court Interpreter Services. It is the responsibility of the contract Court Interpreter to ensure that the sheet is signed by the trial judge, quasi-judicial officer, or other designee, and that completed sheets are submitted with all invoices.

E. Unavailability of a Certified or Language–Skilled Court Interpreter.

1. Pursuant to Florida Supreme Court rule amendments, Court Interpreters must meet minimum requirements and must be ***registered*** with the Office of State Courts Administrator. Registered Court Interpreters must also be ***designated*** by the State of Florida as *certified* (having passed full oral performance state-certifying examination available for specific language) or *language-skilled* (no full oral performance state-certifying examination currently available for specific language, but having passing an approved oral proficiency interview), or must be actively and diligently pursuing designation as *certified* or *language-skilled* or, alternatively, as *provisionally-approved* (attaining a minimum score on the full oral performance state-certifying examination, but at a level below that required for full certification). The Court is to give preference to certified and language-skilled Court Interpreters, then to Court Interpreters holding a provisionally-approved designation. Fla. R. Jud. Admin. 2.560.

2. If, after a diligent search by the AOC's Court Interpreter Services, a certified, language-skilled, or provisionally-approved Court Interpreter is not available for a court proceeding, the presiding judge, magistrate, or hearing officer, may approve the use of an interpreter for a specific proceeding *who is otherwise registered with the Office of State Courts Administrator* upon making the following findings on the record:

a. good cause exists for appointment of the proposed interpreter; and

b. the proposed interpreter is competent to interpret the proceedings. These findings shall apply only to the specific proceeding and shall not extend to subsequent proceedings without additional findings of good cause and qualification for each subsequent proceeding. Fla. R. Jud. Admin. 2.560.

3. *Exceptional Circumstances.* If, after a diligent search by the AOC's Court Interpreter Services, a certified, language-skilled, provisionally-approved or otherwise registered Court Interpreter is not available for a court proceeding, the presiding judge, magistrate, or hearing officer may approve the use of an interpreter for a specific proceeding *who is not designated and is not otherwise registered with the Office of State Courts Administrator*, upon making the following findings on the record:

a. an interpreter designated or registered with the Office of the State Courts Administrator is unavailable; and

b. good cause exists for appointment of the proposed interpreter, such as the prevention of burdensome delay, the request or consent of the non-English-speaking or limited-English-proficient person, or other unusual or specific exigent circumstances given the demands of the case; and

c. the proposed interpreter is competent to interpret the proceedings and asserts under oath that he or she is able, either in direct or relay/intermediary interpretation, to communicate effectively in the languages in which interpreter services are required.

These findings shall apply only to the specific proceeding and shall not extend to subsequent proceedings without additional findings of good cause and qualification for each subsequent proceeding. Fla. R. Jud. Admin. 2.560

4. In any criminal or juvenile delinquency proceeding in which the interpreter is not certified, language-skilled, or provisionally-approved, the presiding judge, magistrate, or hearing officer shall advise the accused on the record of the fact that the proposed interpreter is not certified, language-skilled, or provisionally-approved, and the accused's objection or waiver of objection shall be on the record. The accused's objection or waiver of objection shall apply only to the specific proceeding and shall not extend to subsequent proceedings without giving the accused the opportunity to object or waive any objection on the record for each subsequent proceeding. Fla. R. Jud. Admin. 2.560.

F. General Provisions.

1. This Administrative Order shall be effective March 1, 2016, and supercedes any prior administrative orders relating to court interpreters, including the "Order Establishing Protocol for the Employment and Attendance of Interpreters for Criminal Court Proceedings in Lee County," entered March 28, 2000.

2. To the extent that any provision of this Administrative Order may conflict with any rule, law, or statute, the rule, law, or statute will prevail.

DONE AND ORDERED in chambers in Fort Myers, Lee County, Florida, this 29th day of Jan., 2016.

Michael T. McHugh

Chief Judge

History.—"Order Establishing Protocol for the Employment and Attendance of Interpreters for Criminal Court Proceedings in Lee County" (March 28, 2000).

[1]Though a deposition is considered a "court-related proceeding" requiring that a Court Interpreter meeting the qualifications of the Florida Supreme Court be utilized (Rule 14.100, Fla. Rules for Certif. & Regul. of Court Interpreters), a deposition does not qualify under the definition of a "proceeding" under Rule 2.560, Fla. R. Jud. Admin., which is limited to "[a]ny hearing or trial, excluding an administrative hearing or trial, presided over by a judge, general magistrate, special magistrate, or hearing officer within the state courts."

2.37. TWENTIETH JUDICIAL CIRCUIT PRO BONO STANDING COMMITTEE

IN THE TWENTIETH JUDICIAL CIRCUIT IN AND FOR THE STATE OF FLORIDA

ADMINISTRATIVE ORDER NO. 2.37

IN RE: TWENTIETH JUDICIAL CIRCUIT PRO BONO STANDING COMMITTEE

WHEREAS, the Supreme Court of Florida has mandated the establishment of a circuit pro bono committee in each judicial circuit, *Amendments to Rules Regulating The Florida Bar–1–3.1(a) and Rules of Judicial Administration 2.065 (Legal Aid),* 630 So. 2d 501 (Fla. 1993); and

WHEREAS, the Twentieth Judicial Circuit has a strong history of providing pro bono legal services to those citizens of the Circuit in need of such services, though not previously memorialized by Administrative Order;

NOW THEREFORE, in accordance with the authority vested in the Chief Judge pursuant to Fla. R. Jud. Admin. 2.215, and the directive of the Supreme Court of Florida, it is ordered as follows:

1. The Twentieth Judicial Circuit Pro Bono Standing Committee shall be charged with the duty to assess pro bono legal services provided within the Twentieth Judicial Circuit, and to plan, develop, prepare and administer a circuit-wide pro bono attorney plan to ensure that the purposes of Rule 4–6.5, Rules Regulating the Florida Bar (See Attachment A) [1], are fully met.

2. The Twentieth Judicial Circuit Pro Bono Standing Committee shall initially consist of the following members:

a. The Chief Judge, or designee

b. The President of the Lee County Bar Association, or designee

c. The President of the Collier County Bar Association, or designee

d. The President of the Charlotte County Bar Association, or designee

e. The President of the Hendry/Glades Counties Bar Association, or designee

f. Representative of Florida Rural Legal Services, Inc.

g. Representative of Lee County Legal Aid Society, Inc.

h. Representative of Legal Aid Society of Collier County, Inc.

i. Representative of the Office of Guardian ad Litem

j. The President of the Southwest Florida Federal Bar Association, or designee

k. Public Members (one or more—as approved and deemed eligible by the Chair)

l. Client Members (one or more—as approved and deemed eligible by the Chair)

3. The Chair is authorized to invite and approve other participants to serve as Members of the Committee at the Chair's discretion, and in accordance with the intent and provisions of Rule 4–6.5, Rules Regulating the Florida Bar.

4. The Committee shall have such duties and responsibilities as set forth in Rule 4–6.5, Rules Regulating the Florida Bar.

5. The Committee shall meet as often as is necessary to fulfill its responsibilities, but not less than twice annually.

6. A copy of any plan developed by the Committee, and a copy of any written report required to be submitted to The Florida Bar Standing Committee on Pro Bono Legal Services shall be provided to the Chief Judge.

7. The Honorable Archie B. Hayward, Jr. is hereby designated as the Chief Judge's designee to serve as Chair of the Twentieth Judicial Circuit Pro Bono Standing Committee until such time as the Committee elects its Chair as provided by Rule 4–6.5(c), Rules Regulating The Florida Bar.

8. To the extent that any provision of this Administrative Order may be construed as being in conflict with any law, statute, or rule, the law, statute, or rule shall prevail.

9. This Administrative Order shall be effective immediately.

DONE AND ORDERED in chambers in Fort Myers, Lee County, Florida, this 15th day of September, 2016.

Michael T. McHugh

Chief Judge

History.—New.

[1] **Publisher's Note:** Attachment A not reproduced here.

2.38. THERAPY/FACILITY DOG PROGRAM

IN THE TWENTIETH JUDICIAL CIRCUIT IN AND FOR THE STATE OF FLORIDA

ADMINISTRATIVE ORDER NO. 2.38 (supersedes AO 12.7)

IN RE: TWENTIETH JUDICIAL CIRCUIT THERAPY/FACILITY DOG PROGRAM

WHEREAS, section 92.55(5), Florida Statutes, authorizes the Court to establish conditions it finds just and appropriate when taking the testimony of a victim or witness under the age of eighteen (18), a person who has an intellectual disability, or a sexual offense victim or witness, including the use of a therapy animal or facility dog in any proceeding involving a sexual offense or child abuse, abandonment, or neglect; and

WHEREAS, a "therapy animal" has been defined by statute to mean "an animal that has been trained, evaluated, and certified as a therapy animal pursuant to industry standards by an organization that certifies animals as appropriate to provide animal therapy," and

WHEREAS, a "facility dog" has been defined by statute to mean "a dog that has been trained, evaluated, and certified as a facility dog pursuant to industry standards and provides unobtrusive emotional support to children and adults in facility settings," and

WHEREAS, for the safety and protection of the public and court staff, as well as for the purpose of ensuring order and decorum within the courthouses of the Twentieth Judicial Circuit, it is necessary to provide specific guidelines for the presence and conduct of therapy/facility dog teams within the courthouses of the Twentieth Judicial Circuit;

NOW, THEREFORE, in accordance with the authority vested in the Chief Judge pursuant to Fla. R. Jud. Admin. 2.215, it is ordered as follows;

1. The use of qualified therapy/facility dog teams consisting of a certified/registered therapy/facility dog and a human handler over the age of eighteen (18), and associated with a court-approved therapy/facility dog provider, is authorized within the Courts of the Twentieth Judicial Circuit for the benefit of victims or witnesses under the age of eighteen (18), persons with an intellectual disability, or sexual offense victims or witnesses, in any proceeding involving a sexual offense or child abuse, abandonment, or neglect, though not mandated. The use of qualified therapy/facility dog teams inside of any courtroom during such proceedings is at the sole discretion and preference of the presiding judge or magistrate, and must be addressed, approved, and/or ordered by the presiding judge or magistrate in advance. The use of qualified therapy/facility dog teams within the courthouse, but outside of the courtroom, prior to such proceedings is permitted without prior approval of the presiding judge or magistrate, but must be in full compliance with any policies and procedures established by the Administrative Office of the Courts, whether written or verbally expressed. Any use of qualified therapy/facility dog teams must be in a manner which does not have any negative impact on any party's right to due process or right to a fair hearing or trial.

2. If the State Attorney's Office, Public Defender's Office, Regional Counsel's Office, Florida Department of Children and Families, Guardian Ad Litem, counsel, or unrepresented party determine that the presence and use of a qualified therapy/facility dog inside of the courtroom (if approved) or outside of the courtroom may aid in the court testimony of a victim or witness under the age of eighteen (18), person with an intellectual disability, or sexual offense victim or witness, in any proceeding involving a sexual offense or child abuse, abandonment, or neglect, that agency or counsel or party may contact a court-approved therapy/facility dog provider to determine the availability of a qualified therapy/facility dog team. Court-approved therapy/facility dog providers shall be posted on the website of the Administrative Office of the Courts of the Twentieth Judicial Circuit ("AOC") at www.ca.cjis20.org.

3. As stated above, the use inside of the courtroom of a qualified therapy/facility dog team associated with a court-approved therapy dog provider is only permitted upon prior approval of the presiding trial judge or magistrate, The presiding judge or magistrate may establish procedures for requesting and utilizing therapy dog teams as may he appropriate and applicable,

4. The agency or counsel or unrepresented party seeking the use of the qualified therapy/facility dog team is responsible for facilitating all communication with the therapy dog provider and handler regarding dates and times and locations of court events, including informing the court-approved therapy/facility dog provider and handler of any changes in dates i or times or locations of scheduled court events.

5. Qualified therapy/facility dog teams provided by a court-approved therapy/facility dog provider are permitted on the grounds and inside the courthouses of the Twentieth Judicial Circuit only if present for a court event. However, under no circumstances shall a qualified therapy/facility dog team, which includes the therapy/facility dog and the handler, be alone in the presence of a victim or witness under the age of eighteen (18), person with an intellectual disability, or sexual offense victim or witness. The qualified therapy/facility dog team shall only be in the presence of the victim or witness under the age of eighteen (18), person with an intellectual disability, or sexual offense victim or witness, if the presiding judge or magistrate is present, or, if in a criminal case, counsel or a non-represented party presenting the victim or witness is present, or, if in a dependency or family law case, if a neutral representative is present such as a Guardian ad Litem or counsel for the Guardian ad litem program. Due to the role of the Court and the role of the qualified therapy/facility dog team as a support mechanism for victims or witnesses under the age of eighteen (18), persons with an intellectual disability, or sexual offense victims or witnesses, the presiding judge, magistrate, and court staff, cannot actively interact with the therapy/facility dog beyond that which may be necessary.

6. Court-approved therapy/facility dog providers shall;

a. Ensure that ah therapy/facility dog teams have completed any and all therapy training and have passed a nationally recognized skills and aptitude test and evaluation by an organization that certifies the team as qualified to provide animal assisted therapy,

b. Ensure that all therapy/facility dog teams adhere to all policies of their individual certifying organizations and remain current on all certifications.

c. Ensure that all therapy/facility dogs have been examined by a Florida veterinarian who is able to attest to the dog's good health within the past year, and ensure that all immunizations, including rabies vaccinations, are current and remain current.

d. Ensure that all therapy/facility dogs are properly registered and licensed in the State of Florida and the applicable county.

e. Carry a minimum of one million dollars ($1,000,000.00) in liability insurance with coverage for all claims for injury, illness, and property damage resulting from therapeutic services offered by the therapeutic dog provider, and a rider naming the Administrative Office of the Courts and applicable county as an insured for coverage purposes.

f. Provide a copy of the liability insurance declaration sheet and rider, and proof of annual renewals, to the Administrative Office of the Courts.

g. Ensure that all handlers are trained and responsible for maintaining dogs on an appropriate leash at all times with the handler in full control of the dog and leash.

h. Ensure that all handlers are trained and responsible for refraining from any and all overt displays of emotion and from any unsupervised interaction with the children.

i. Ensure that all handlers adhere to their certifying organization's policies regarding grooming and zoonotic disease/parasite control.

j. Ensure that all handlers are trained and responsible for inquiring if there are any known allergies or concerns prior to entering an enclosed space, including elevators.

k. Ensure that all handlers are trained and responsible for arriving early enough to exercise the dog to avoid any elimination issues. All dogs must be trained to not eliminate inside of buildings. All handlers must have available appropriate supplies to clean and sanitize, as may be appropriate, any elimination that may occur in the building or outside on the grounds, using proper disposal and odor control methods.

l. Ensure that any incidents are immediately verbally reported to the Presiding Judge or magistrate (if applicable) and the AOC, and that an incident report form is promptly submitted to the AOC as soon as possible, but no later than the next business day. Reportable incidents include, but are not limited to: injuries to a person or animal; situations with a high potential that an injury could have occurred either to a person or animal, even though no one was hurt at the time; situations with a perception of an accident or injury, and damages to property, including elimination by a dog in the courthouse facility, A copy of the incident report form is available on the AOC's website at www.ca.cjis20.org.

m. Ensure that all handlers have signed a release for the purpose of allowing the AOC to conduct a background check. The information contained in any FCIC/NCIC report and specific findings are confidential and are to be used in compliance with all state and federal laws and regulations. The decision as to i whether to allow a handler access to the courthouse facility for the purpose of providing therapy/facility dog services is within the sole discretion of the AOC.

n. Ensure that all handlers immediately report to the court-approved therapy/facility dog provider and the AOC any incident that may change the status of their background check, including but not limited to any arrest, conviction or other incident involving law enforcement.

o. Ensure that all handlers are trained and responsible for maintaining the confidentiality of all information including, but not limited to, information pertaining to the individuals testifying and their families, whether written or verbal, received through the scope of interaction with the individual testifying. All handlers must sign an oath of confidentially, a copy of which is available on the AOC's website at www.ca.cjis20.org.

p. Ensure that all handlers are trained and responsible for reporting and avoiding any potential conflict of interest and for immediately disclosing to the presiding judge ! or magistrate (if applicable) and the AOC any personal knowledge or relationship ! to the parties, children, or other witnesses, or has any independent interest or personal knowledge of facts related to a case.

q. Ensure that all handlers have received, acknowledged and endorsed an Acknowledgment of Terms and Conditions Sheet, a copy of which is available on the AOC's website at www.ca.cjis20.org.

r. Ensure that all handlers carry their certifying organizations identification card or other documentation demonstrating certification/registration, and their identification card or other documentation demonstrating their association with the court-approved therapy/facility dog provider. All handlers shall produce any identification card or other documentation upon request by any court official, including court security officers or bailiffs. In addition, all therapy dogs shall be identified by wearing a dog therapy vest or other identifying garment.

7. All court-approved therapy/facility dog providers and their contact information shall be listed on the AOC's website at www.ca.cjis20.org. Any organization seeking approval to be added to the list of court-approved therapy/facility dog providers may submit to the AOC a written request and proposal. The Chief Judge shall determine, in his or her discretion, whether an organization qualifies and is approved as a therapy/facility dog provider for the Twentieth Judicial Circuit and for which county or counties.

8. To the extent that any provision of this Administrative Order may be construed as being in conflict with any law, statute, or rule, the law, statute, or rule shall prevail.

9. This Administrative Order shall supersede and replace Administrative Order 12.7, and shall be effective August 1, 2018.

DONE AND ORDERED in chambers in Fort Myers, Lee County, Florida, this 30th day of July, 2018.

Michael T. McHugh
Chief Judge

Adopted effective August 1, 2018.

Criminal

3.1. COSTS IN CIRCUIT COURT

IN THE TWENTIETH JUDICIAL CIRCUIT IN AND FOR THE STATE OF FLORIDA

ADMINISTRATIVE ORDER NO. 3.1

IN RE: COSTS IN CIRCUIT COURT

Pursuant to the authorities cited below and the inherent authority of the court as provided in Fla. R. Jud. Admin. 2.215 and Florida Statute § 43.26, the following schedule of fees is applicable in the Circuit Court.

A. Mandatory Court Costs

1. The Circuit Court shall impose the following costs in all felony cases where the defendant pleads guilty or nolo contendere or is otherwise convicted of a felony:

$225 Local Government Criminal Justice Trust Fund

Florida Statute 938.05(1)(a)

$ 65 — County Court Costs
Florida Statute 939.185(1)(a), when assessed by a county ordinance

$ 50 — Crimes Compensation Trust Fund
Florida Statute 938.03(1)

$ 50 — Crime Prevention Fund (only if a fine is ordered)
Florida Statute 775.083(2)

$ 3 — Additional Court Cost Clearing Trust Fund
Florida Statute 938.01(1)

$ 2 — Local Law Enforcement Education and Training
Florida Statute 938.15, when assessed by a county or municipality

2. The Circuit Court shall impose the following surcharges on each felony fine that is assessed against a defendant:

$ 20 — Crime Stoppers Trust Fund
Florida Statute 938.06(1)

5% — 5% surcharge on fine for Crimes Compensation Trust Fund
Florida Statute 938.04

3. The Circuit Court shall impose the following cost in all felony traffic violation cases (violations of F.S. 316) where the defendant pleads guilty or nolo contendere or is otherwise convicted of a felony traffic offense:

$ 15 — Court Facilities
Florida Statute 318.18(13)(a)

$ 3 — State Radio System Surcharge
Florida Statute 318.18(17)

4. The Circuit Court shall impose the following additional court costs for each felony violation of Florida Statute 316.192 (Reckless Driving) where the defendant pleads guilty or nolo contendere or is otherwise convicted:

$ 5 — E.M.S. Trust Fund
Florida Statute 316.192(4)

5. The Circuit Court shall impose the following additional court costs for each felony violation of Florida Statute 316.193 (DUI) where the defendant pleads guilty or nolo contendere or is otherwise convicted:

$135 — E.M.S. Trust Fund
Operating Trust Fund of the Dept. of Law Enforcement
Brain & Spinal Cord Injury Rehab. Trust Fund
Florida Statute 938.07

6. The Circuit Court shall impose the following additional court costs for each felony violation of Florida Statute 327.35 (BUI) where the defendant pleads guilty or nolo contendere or is otherwise convicted:

$135 — E.M.S. Trust Fund
Operating Trust Fund of the Dept. of Law Enforcement
Brain & Spinal Cord Injury Rehab. Trust Fund
Florida Statute 938.07

$ 60 — Brain & Spinal Cord Injury Rehab. Trust Fund
Florida Statute 327.35(9)

7. The Circuit Court shall impose the following additional court costs for each felony violation of Florida Statutes 784.011, 784.021, 784.03, 784.041, 784.045, 784.048, 784.07, 784.08, 784.081, 784.082, 784.083, 784.085, 794.011, or for any offense of domestic violence described in Fla. Stat. 741.28 where the defendant pleads guilty or nolo contendere or is otherwise convicted:

$201 — Domestic Violence Surcharge
Domestic Violence Trust Fund
Florida Statute 938.08

$151 — Rape Crisis Center
Florida Statute 938.085

8. The Circuit Court shall impose the following additional court costs for each felony offense against a minor in violation of Florida Statutes 784.085, chapter 787, chapter 794, 796.03, 800.04, chapter 827, 847.0145, or 985.4045 where the defendant pleads guilty or nolo contendere or is otherwise convicted:

$101 — Child Advocacy Trust Fund
Florida Statute 938.10(1)

9. The Circuit Court shall impose the costs of prosecution, including investigative costs:

$100 unless higher amount ordered by court — Cost of Prosecution & Investigation
Florida Statute 938.27

10. The Circuit Court shall assess attorney's fees and costs to any defendant convicted who has received the assistance of the public defender, regional counsel, or a conflict attorney:

$100 unless higher amount ordered by court — Public Defender Fees
Florida Statute 938.29

B. Discretionary Court Costs

1. The Circuit Court may impose the following additional court costs for each felony violation of Florida Statutes chapter 893, 316.193, 856.011, 856.015, chapter 562, chapter 567, or chapter 568, where the defendant pleads guilty or nolo contendere or is otherwise convicted:

Up to fine amount — Alcohol Drug Abuse Program
Florida Statute 938.21

2. The Circuit Court may impose the following additional court costs for each felony violation of Florida Statutes 893.13, where the defendant pleads guilty or nolo contendere or is otherwise convicted:

$100 Statewide Crime Lab
Florida Statute 938.25

3. The Circuit Court may impose the following fine for each felony violation of Florida Statutes where the defendant pleads guilty or nolo contendere or is otherwise convicted:

Up to $5,000 Fines (3rd Degree Felony)
Florida Statute 775.083

Up to $10,000 Fines (1st or 2nd Degree Felony)
Florida Statute 775.083

Up to $15,000 Fines (Life Felony)
Florida Statute 775.083

All fines, costs, penalties or other assessments against any defendant in accordance with this administrative order shall be collected by the Clerk of the Court and distributed in accordance with the applicable provisions of Florida law and the Distribution Schedule of Court-Related Filing Fees, Service Charges, Costs, and Fines published by the Florida Association of Court Clerks, Inc.

The monetary fines and costs imposed by the court shall be deemed to include only statutory and constitutional costs and fees. Any cost found to be unconstitutional by any court of superior jurisdiction shall be considered as part of the fine imposed and shall be distributed as otherwise provided by law.

To the extent that any provision of this Administrative Order may conflict with any rule, statute or law, the rule, statute or law shall prevail. More specifically, to the extent that the Legislature may make subsequent amendments that increase, decrease, add or delete any cost, fines or fees, those legislative amendments shall prevail.

DONE AND ORDERED in Chambers at Fort Myers, Florida, this 3 day of June, 2009.

G. Keith Cary
Chief Judge

History.—Administrative Order 3.1 (October 1, 1990); Administrative Order 3.1 (August 6, 1992); Administrative Order 3.1 (January 13, 2000); Administrative Order 3.1 (February 8, 2002); Administrative Order 3.1 (February 27, 2002); Administrative Order 3.1 (February 4, 2005).

3.2. ASSIGNMENT OF CRIMINAL CASES INVOLVING CO-DEFENDANTS

IN THE TWENTIETH JUDICIAL CIRCUIT IN AND FOR THE STATE OF FLORIDA

ADMINISTRATIVE ORDER NO: 3.2

IN RE: ASSIGNMENT OF CRIMINAL CASES INVOLVING CO-DEFENDANTS

In the event co-defendants are assigned to different Judges at the booking stage, the Judge assigned the greatest number of defendants will be assigned all companion cases.

If two or more Judges are assigned an equal number of co-defendants, then the Judge assigned the defendant whose name would appear first alphabetically will be assigned all cases.

DONE AND ORDERED in Chambers in Fort Myers, Lee County, Florida, this 28 day of Jan, 1991.

Thomas S. Reese
Chief Circuit Judge

History. - Administrative Order 86-14

3.3. PRACTICE AND PROCEDURE UNDER THE FLORIDA CONTRABAND FORFEITURE ACT

IN THE TWENTIETH JUDICIAL CIRCUIT IN AND FOR THE STATE OF FLORIDA

ADMINISTRATIVE ORDER NO: 3.3

IN RE: PRACTICE AND PROCEDURE UNDER THE FLORIDA CONTRABAND FORFEITURE ACT

This order shall govern practice and procedure within the Twentieth Judicial Circuit in all cases involving the seizure of property pursuant to the Florida Contraband Forfeiture Act, Sections 932.701.–704 of the Florida Statutes (1989)(the Act).

The purpose of this order is to effectuate the intent of the Legislature consistent with the opinion of the Supreme Court in Department of Law Enforcement v. Real Property, 16 F.L.W. S497 (Fla. Aug. 15, 1991). To the extent that this order is in any way inconsistent with that opinion, the opinion shall control and shall be binding upon all parties to forfeiture proceedings.

REAL PROPERTY SEIZURES

In any action for the forfeiture of real property, the state must provide notice and schedule an adversarial hearing for interested parties prior to any initial restraint other than lis pendens.

The action shall be commenced by the state's filing of a petition for rule to show cause in the circuit court where the property is located or where the crime is alleged to have taken place. The state shall simultaneously record a notice of its petition with the appropriate property records clerk of court, which will serve as a lis pendens.

The state must then immediately schedule an adversarial preliminary hearing with the appropriate circuit judge as contemplated by Administrative Order 2.11 (formerly Administrative Order 3.3). This hearing shall take place within ten (10) days of the filing of the petition unless an extension of time is granted by the court upon joint application of the parties.

The purpose of this adversarial preliminary hearing is to determine if probable cause exists to maintain the forfeiture action and to resolve all questions pertaining to the temporary restraints on the property pending final disposition. Notice of the petition and the adversarial preliminary hearing must be served on all interested parties.

If probable cause is found to exist at the hearing, the court may, at its discretion, enter such orders as are necessary to protect the respective interests of the parties.

PERSONAL PROPERTY SEIZURES

In all actions involving the seizure of personal property, the seizure may occur prior to notice or hearing, provided that notice and the opportunity for an adversarial preliminary hearing is made available as soon as possible after seizure.

In those situations where the state has not yet taken possession of the personal property, the state may seek an ex parte preliminary hearing. At that hearing, the court shall authorize seizure of the personal property if it finds probable cause to maintain the forfeiture action.

In those situations where a law enforcement agency has already lawfully taken possession of personal property, as for example, incident to arrest or other lawful police action, an ex parte seizure has effectively been made for the purpose of initiating a forfeiture action.

After the ex parte seizure of personal property, the state must immediately notify all interested parties that they have the right to request a post-seizure adversarial preliminary hearing.

If requested, the preliminary hearing shall be held before the appropriate circuit judge as contemplated by Administrative Order 2.11 within ten (10) days of the request, unless an extension of time is granted by the court upon joint application of the parties.

The purpose of this adversarial preliminary hearing is to make a de novo determination as to whether probable cause exists to maintain the forfeiture action; and to determine whether continued seizure is the least restrictive means warranted by the circumstances to protect against disposal of the property pending final disposition.

NOTICE

In all forfeiture cases, notice shall be served on all persons whom the law enforcement agency knows, or with reasonable investigation should know, have a legal interest in the subject property. Notice shall advise those persons that a forfeiture action is pending against the property or properties which are specifically identified therein.

In real property forfeiture actions, notice must advise interested parties of the time and place of the adversarial preliminary hearing.

In personal property forfeiture actions notice must advise interested parties that they have a right to an adversarial preliminary hearing upon request.

If the state establishes probable cause, the court shall order the property restrained throughout the pendency of the forfeiture action by the least restrictive means necessary under the circumstances.

Under no circumstances may the state continue its restraint on the property pending final disposition unless notice and an opportunity to be heard are provided to all potential claimants.

LITIGATION OF FORFEITURE ACTIONS

All forfeiture actions shall commence by the filing of a petition for issuance of a rule to show cause in the circuit court where the property was restrained or where the alleged offense occurred. The petition shall be assigned as contemplated by Administrative Order 2.11. The petition shall be verified and supported by affidavit.

If the court determines that the petition is facially sufficient to state a cause of action for forfeiture, the court shall sign and issue the rule. A copy of the petition and rule shall be served on all persons who the agency knows, or with reasonable investigation should know, have a legal interest in the property. The rule to show cause shall also require that responsive pleadings and affirmative defenses be filed within twenty (20) days of service of the rule to show cause. The contents of the required notice shall be as set forth previously in this order. The required notices shall be prepared by the state and provided by the state to all interested persons as set forth previously.

The Florida Rules of Civil Procedure shall otherwise control service of process, discovery, and other measures appropriate for the administration of forfeiture proceedings. The burden of proof at trial shall be as set forth in Department of Law Enforcement v. Real Property, supra.

DONE AND ORDERED in Chambers in Fort Myers, Lee County, Florida, this 5th day of Feb, 1992.

Thomas S. Reese
Chief Circuit Judge

History.—New.

3.4. NOTICES TO APPEAR

IN THE TWENTIETH JUDICIAL CIRCUIT IN AND FOR THE STATE OF FLORIDA

ADMINISTRATIVE ORDER NO. 3.4

IN RE: NOTICES TO APPEAR

WHEREAS, Rule 3.125(j) Florida Rules of Criminal Procedure, requires the Chief Judge of each Circuit to establish rules and regulations of procedure governing the exercise of authority to issue Notices to Appear; and

WHEREAS, it has been determined that additional rules and regulations will assist the various Courts, Clerk, law enforcement agencies and the State Attorney's Office within the Twentieth Judicial Circuit with the Notice to Appear system;

IT IS THEREFORE ORDERED that the following additional rules and regulations shall govern the use of Notices to Appear within the Twentieth Judicial Circuit:

1. The form for Notice to Appear shall be as set forth in Rule 3.125(*l*), Florida Rules of Criminal Procedure, unless a satisfactory substitute form is submitted and approved by the Chief Judge of the Twentieth Judicial Circuit.

2. Except in those cases which have been established on the general bond list of the respective counties as requiring a mandatory appearance, the Officer issuing the Notice to Appear shall enter the amount of the bond on the Notice to Appear form in the blank provided for the fine and the said fine shall be equivalent to the bond amount. The issuing Officer shall indicate a mandatory Court appearance date when:

a) It is required by the Court, or

b) The amount of bond and/or fine is unknown. The issuing Officer will enter a Court appearance date which shall be set at least ten days from the date of issuance of the Notice to Appear or the next arraignment date thereafter in the County in which the offense occurred.

3. It will be the obligation of the issuing law enforcement agency to supply the Notice to Appear forms.

4. In all cases where a prosecution on a Notice to Appear form has been continued, it shall be the continuing obligation of the Clerk's Office of the respective counties to re-subpoena necessary witnesses.

DONE AND ORDERED in Chambers in Naples, Collier County, Florida, this 13 day of Jan., 2000.

____
William L. Blackwell
Chief Judge

History. - Administrative Order 3.4 (January 28, 1991); Administrative Order 86–16.

FL ST RCRP Rule 3.125

"I understand the nature of the charge against me; I understand my right to have counsel and waive this right and the right to a continuance. I waive my right to trial before a judge or jury. I plead Guilty [] or Nolo Contendere [] to the charge, being fully aware that my signature to this plea will have the same effect as a judgment of this court."

Total Fine and Cost ______________________

Defendant Signature ______________________

Address ______________________

IN THE COUNTY COURT, IN AND FOR
________ COUNTY, FLORIDA

SCHEDULE OF WITNESSES AND EVIDENCE FOR NOTICE TO APPEAR

____
Agency Case #

____
Last Name First M.I. Aliases

____
Address

______________ Offense(s): (1) ________
Date of Notice to Appear (2) ________

TANGIBLE EVIDENCE: (If none, write "None")

Item: ______________

Obtained from (person and/or place): ________

first received by: ________ given to: ________

WITNESSES: (If none, write "None")

#1 Name: ______________________

Res. Tel. No. ________ Address: ________

Bus. Tel. No. ________ Business: ________

Testimony: ______________________

____

#2 Name: ______________________

Res. Tel. No. ________ Address: ________

[ ] Mandatory appearance in court, ________
Location

________, 19___, at ________ ( ) a.m. ( ) p.m.
Month Day

[ ] You need not appear in court, but must comply with instructions on back.

CO–DEFENDANTS:

1. ______________________ [ ] Cited [ ] Jailed
Name DOB Address

2. ______________________ [ ] Cited [ ] Jailed
Name DOB Address

I AGREE TO APPEAR AT THE TIME AND PLACE DESIGNATED ABOVE TO ANSWER THE OFFENSE CHARGED OR TO PAY THE FINE SUBSCRIBED. I UNDERSTAND THAT SHOULD I WILLFULLY FAIL TO APPEAR BEFORE THE COURT AS REQUIRED BY THIS NOTICE TO APPEAR, I MAY BE HELD IN CONTEMPT OF COURT AND A WARRANT FOR MY ARREST SHALL BE ISSUED.

____
Signature of Defendant

I swear the above and reverse and attached statements are true and correct to the best of my knowledge and belief.

_____ Complainant

_____ Agency or Department

Sworn to and subscribed before me this ___ day of ______, 19___.

________ Notary Public, State of Florida

WAIVER INFORMATION

If you desire to plead guilty or nolo contendere (no contest) and you need not appear in court as indicated on the face of this notice, you may present this notice at the county court named on the reverse of this page.

From ________, ________ to ________, ________
Date Hour Date Hour

and pay a fine of ________ dollars in cash, money order, or certified check.

The waiver below must be completed and attached. Read carefully.

Your failure to answer this summons in the manner subscribed will result in a warrant being issued on a separate and additional charge.

"In consideration of my not appearing in court, I the undersigned, do hereby enter my appearance on the affidavit for the offense charged on the other side of this notice and waive the reading of the affidavit in the above named cause and the right to be present at the trial of said action. I hereby enter my plea of Guilty [ ] or Nolo Contendere [], and waive my right to prosecute appeal or error proceedings.

(1) Form of Notice to Appear and Schedule of Witnesses and Evidence The notice to appear and schedule of witnesses and evidence shall be in substantially the following form:

IN THE COUNTY COURT, IN AND FOR ________
COUNTY, FLORIDA NOTICE TO APPEAR

____
Agency Case #

STATE OF FLORIDA, COUNTY OF ________

In the name of ________ County, Florida: The undersigned certifies that he or she has just and reasonable grounds to believe, and does believe, that:

On the ___ day of __________, 19 ___, at ________ () a.m. () p.m.

Last Name First M.I. Aliases

Street—City and State Date and Place of Birth

Phone Race/Sex Height Weight Hair Eyes Scars/Marks

Occupation Place of Employment Employment Phone

Complexion Driver's License #Yr./St. Social Security #

at (location) __________ in __________ County, Florida, committed the following offense(s):

(1) __________ (2) __________

in violation of section(s): _____: ( ) State Statute ( ) Municipal Ord.

DID (Narrative): ____________________

Name of Officer ID Agency

Bus. Tel. No. __________ Business: __________

Testimony: ____________________

#3 Name: ____________________

Res. Tel. No. __________ Address: __________

Bus. Tel. No. __________ Business: __________

Testimony: ____________________

I certify that the foregoing is a complete list of witnesses and evidence known to me.

__________ Investigating Officer

__________ Agency

3.5. COURT APPOINTED ATTORNEY COMPENSATION

IN THE TWENTIETH JUDICIAL CIRCUIT IN AND FOR THE STATE OF FLORIDA

ADMINISTRATIVE ORDER NO. 3.5

IN RE: COURT APPOINTED ATTORNEY COMPENSATION

Pursuant to Florida Statutes §§ 27.53, 925.035, and 925.036, in all cases requiring court appointed counsel within the Twentieth Judicial Circuit Court where private attorneys are appointed by the Court to represent indigent defendants, the Court hereby establishes a fixed hourly rate of compensation of $75.00 for reasonable billable time, with the exception of representation as it relates to death penalty cases. Taking into consideration the minimum standards for attorneys in capital cases as set forth in Fla. R. Crim. P. 3.112, the Court hereby establishes a fixed hourly rate of compensation of $100.00 for reasonable billable time in death penalty cases.

During trials, compensation shall not exceed $800.00 per day. Fees on appeal of any case are not to exceed half of the fee amount awarded for the trial of the case, unless the Court finds that a larger fee is warranted following a hearing on the matter with notice to all concerned parties.

The Court recognizes that Florida Statute § 925.036(2) provides that compensation for representation shall not exceed the following:

(a)	For misdemeanors and juveniles represented at the trial level:	$1,000
(b)	For noncapital, nonlife felonies represented at the trial level:	$2,500
(c)	For life felonies represented at the trial level:	$3,000
(d)	For capital cases represented at the trial level:	$3,500
(e)	For representation on appeal:	$2,000

Notwithstanding the foregoing, and in accordance with Sheppard & White, P.A. v. City of Jacksonville, 827 So. 2d 925 (Fla. 2002), in capital cases where unusual and extraordinary circumstances exist, court appointed counsel may petition the Court for additional compensation. In any such case, counsel who petitions the Court for such additional compensation shall set the matter for hearing before the Court with notice to the State Attorney's Office and the County Attorney's Office.

This Administrative Order is not applicable to those private attorneys under contract with the Administrative Office of the Courts, Twentieth Judicial Circuit.

In recognition of the legislative changes enacted by Laws 2003, ch. 2003–402, including the amendments to Florida Statute § 27.53, the repeal of Florida Statutes §§ 925.035 and 925.036, and the creation of Florida Statutes §§ 27.40, 27.42, and 27.5304, effective July 1, 2004, it is ordered that this Administrative Order shall expire and shall no longer be effective on or after July 1, 2004.

DONE AND ORDERED in Chambers at Naples, Collier County, Florida, this 03 day of May, 2004.

Hugh D. Hayes
Chief Judge

History. - Administrative Order 3.5 (August 15, 2000); Administrative Order 3.5 (January 13, 2000); Administrative Order 3.5 (January 28, 1991); Administrative Order 88–18.

3.6. USE OF TELEVISION EQUIPMENT IN COURT PROCEEDINGS INVOLVING INCARCERATED DEFENDANTS

IN AND FOR THE TWENTIETH JUDICIAL CIRCUIT IN THE STATE OF FLORIDA

ADMINISTRATIVE ORDER NO. 3.6

IN RE: USE OF TELEVISION EQUIPMENT IN COURT PROCEEDINGS INVOLVING INCARCERATED DEFENDANTS

WHEREAS, it has been determined that it is technically feasible to use television equipment to more efficiently conduct court proceedings for felony and misdemeanor defendants incarcerated in various jails or stockades throughout the Circuit, as well as juveniles being held at the Southwest Florida Regional Juvenile Detention Center, it is therefore ORDERED that:

In accordance with Rules 3.130 and 3.160, Florida Rules of Criminal Procedure; Rules 8.010, 8.015 and 8.070, Florida Rules of Juvenile Procedure; and Rule 2.170, Florida Rules of Judicial Administration, all pretrial court proceedings referenced above involving incarcerated defendants of any jail or stockade within the Circuit and the Southwest Florida Regional Juvenile Detention Center, which do not require the confrontation of witnesses, may be conducted through the use of closed circuit television and microwave equipment to the extent feasible at the election of the presiding judge.

DONE AND ORDERED in Chambers in Naples, Collier County, Florida, this 13 day of Jan., 2000.

William L. Blackwell
Chief Judge

History. - Administrative Order 3.6 (January 27, 1993); Administrative Order 3.6 (June 29, 1992); Administrative Order 3.6 (January 28, 1991); Administrative Order 88–19.

3.7. GUARDIAN AD LITEM FOR MINOR WITNESSES AND VICTIMS IN CRIMINAL PROCEEDINGS

IN THE TWENTIETH JUDICIAL CIRCUIT IN AND FOR THE STATE OF FLORIDA

ADMINISTRATIVE ORDER NO: 3.7

IN RE: GUARDIAN AD LITEM FOR MINOR WITNESSES AND VICTIMS IN CRIMINAL PROCEEDINGS

WHEREAS, Florida Statute § 914.17 gives the court the power to appoint a Guardian Ad Litem or other advocate for the purpose of representing minors who are victims of or witnesses to child abuse or neglect, or if the minor is a victim of a sexual offense or a witness to a sexual offense committed against another minor, and

WHEREAS, the appointment of such a Guardian Ad Litem or other advocate is necessary to ensure the physical and mental well-being of such children; it is hereby

ORDERED AND ADJUDGED that the State Attorney's Office shall, as soon as possible, after determining that a minor is involved in a criminal proceeding as a victim or as a witness, move the appropriate Court to appoint a Guardian Ad Litem or other advocate to represent the minor; and it is further

ORDERED AND ADJUDGED that all Courts of the Twentieth Judicial Circuit, upon being moved by the State Attorney's Office, shall appoint a Guardian Ad Litem or other advocate represent each and every minor involved in any criminal proceeding either as a victim or as a witness.

DONE AND ORDERED in Chambers in Fort Myers, Lee County, Florida, this 28 day of Jan., 1991.

Thomas S. Reese
Chief Circuit Judge

3.8. EXTRADITION INVOLVING INTRASTATE WARRANTS

IN THE TWENTIETH JUDICIAL CIRCUIT IN AND FOR THE STATE OF FLORIDA

IN RE: EXTRADITION INVOLVING INTRASTATE WARRANTS

ADMINISTRATIVE ORDER NO. 3.8

—AMENDED—

In the interest of minimizing jail overcrowding, ensuring speedy trials for all persons incarcerated in the various county jails of the Twentieth Judicial Circuit, limiting the adverse fiscal impact of housing inmates who belong in other jurisdictions, and pursuant to the inherent authority of this Court as prescribed by Fla. R. Jud. Admin. 2.215(b) (formerly Fla. R. Jud. Admin. 2.050(b)) and Florida Statute § 43.26, and in the discharge of this Court's responsibilities as set forth in Fla. R. Jud. Admin. 2.215(b)(8) (formerly Fla. R. Jud. Admin. 2.050(b)(8)), it is

ORDERED AND ADJUDGED as follows:

Any person incarcerated in the county jails of the Twentieth Judicial Circuit solely on a warrant issued in a county other than the arresting county must be extradited to the county issuing the warrant based upon the following deadlines:

1. If the warrant issued from a county bordering the arresting county and both counties are located within the Twentieth Judicial Circuit, the county that issued the warrant shall have forty-eight (48) hours from notification of incarceration to transport the prisoner.

2. If the warrant issued from a county located within a circuit bordering the Twentieth Judicial Circuit, that county shall have seventy-two (72) hours from notification of incarceration to transport the prisoner.

3. If the warrant issued from any other county in the State of Florida, that County shall have five (5) days from notification of incarceration to transport the prisoner.

Upon arrest of any individual on an out-of-county warrant, the arresting agency shall notify the issuing county of the arrest at booking. If the deadlines set forth above are exceeded, then without acknowledgment from the prosecuting or transporting agency, the individual may be released from custody at the discretion and upon the authority of the administrative judge of the county in which the individual is being held.

The time limitations set forth above shall be exclusive of weekends and any holidays that are applicable or otherwise recognized by the Court, and may be extended upon order of the administrative judge of the county in which the individual is being held at the request of the prosecuting or transporting agency.

IN NO EVENT SHALL THIS ORDER APPLY TO FEDERAL WARRANTS OR WARRANTS ISSUED BY ANY OTHER STATE IN THE UNION.

DONE AND ORDERED in Chambers in Naples, Florida, this 02nd day of February, 2007.

Hugh D. Hayes
Chief Judge

History. - Administrative Order 3.8 (February 4, 2002); Administrative Order 3.8 (January 28, 1991); Administrative Order 89–24.

3.9. FCIC/NCIC/THE JESSICA LUNSFORD ACT AND THE ANTI-MURDER ACT

IN THE TWENTIETH JUDICIAL CIRCUIT IN AND FOR THE STATE OF FLORIDA

IN RE: FCIC/ NCIC / THE JESSICA LUNSFORD ACT AND THE ANTI–MURDER ACT

ADMINISTRATIVE ORDER NO: 3.9 -Amended-

WHEREAS, the 2005 Florida Legislature enacted the "Jessica Lunsford Act," Chapter 2005–28, Laws of Florida, relating to high-risk sex offenders; and

WHEREAS, under Section 15 of the Jessica Lunsford Act, the 2005 Florida Legislature created Fla. Stat. § 948.061 to aid in the identification of high-risk sex offenders on probation or community control and to ensure that relevant criminal history information is available to the Court when the person is brought before a judicial officer within twenty-four hours after arrest in accordance with Fla. R. Crim. P. 3.130 (referred to herein as the "First Appearance Hearing"); and

WHEREAS, Fla. Stat. § 948.061(2) specifically requires that the county jail, in the county where an arrested person is booked, provide to the Court at the First Appearance Hearing, the state and national criminal history information and all criminal justice information available in the Florida Crime Information Center (FCIC) and the National Crime Information Center (NCIC), collectively referred to herein as the "FCIC/NCIC records report;" and

WHEREAS, the requirement that the Court be provided with FCIC/NCIC reports also serves the purpose of helping to ensure that the Court has information before it to carry out the intent of the "Anti–Murder Act," Chapter 2007–2, Laws of Florida, as it relates to the detention of certain felony offenders pending probation-violation or community-control-violation hearings;

NOW, THEREFORE, pursuant to the authority prescribed by Fla. R. Jud. Admin. 2.215, it is hereby **ORDERED** as follows:

1. In accordance with Fla. Stat. § 948.061, the Sheriff of each county within the Twentieth Judicial Circuit is responsible for running the FCIC/NCIC records report on each person arrested and booked in each respective county jail.

2. To facilitate the early identification of high-risk sex offenders and violent felony offenders and to ensure that the Court has information available to comply with its duties under Fla. Stat. § 948.06, the Sheriff's staff in the jail shall provide to the Court prior to the First Appearance Hearing the FCIC/NCIC records report for each person arrested and booked.

3. Before releasing prior to First Appearance any probationer or offender in community control who is arrested and jailed, the Sheriff shall certify to the Court that, pursuant to Fla. Stat. § 948.06, the person does not qualify under the Jessica Lunsford Act for a hearing to determine whether the person is a danger to the public and does not qualify under the Anti–Murder Act for detention pending a probation violation or community-control violation hearing. The certification shall comply substantively with the format of "Attachment A." To the extent that the certifications are derived from FCIC/NCIC information, such certifications shall remain confidential in accordance with FDLE/FBI security rules and user agreements. The Sheriff shall file the original of the completed certification form with the Office of the Clerk of Courts for placement in the court file and shall retain a copy for the jail's records. In counties where the Administrative Office of the Courts (AOC) has an established a Pretrial Services Division, the Sheriff shall also provide a copy of the certification to the AOC's Pretrial Services Division, regardless of whether an interlocal agreement exists, as specified in paragraph 4 below.

4. In counties wherein the AOC has an established Pretrial Services Division, the Sheriff of that county may elect to utilize the AOC's pretrial services staff to run the FCIC/NCIC records report required by Fla. Stat. § 948.061. Should the Sheriff so elect, the Court Administrator is hereby authorized to enter into an interlocal agreement for the provision of such services if the AOC has sufficient staff and other resources to accommodate the Sheriff's request. This provision does not mandate that the parties enter into an interlocal agreement, but merely authorizes such. Notwithstanding such an interlocal agreement, it shall remain the Sheriff's responsibility to ensure that the FCIC/NCIC records report is run, that the certification specified herein is provided to the Court, and that a person is not released prior to a First Appearance Hearing if that person qualifies as a high-risk sex offender or qualifies for a hearing to determine whether the person is a danger to the public pursuant to Fla. Stat. § 948.06.

5. Dissemination of FCIC/NCIC records reports, or information contained therein, shall be in strict accordance with federal and state law, and in strict accordance with FDLE and FBI security rules and user agreements. The Sheriff, or the AOC's Pretrial Services Division if the parties have entered into an applicable interlocal agreement, shall maintain a log documenting the dissemination of FCIC/NCIC records reports pursuant to this Administrative Order.

6. To the extent that any provision of this Administrative Order may be construed as being in conflict with any law, statute, or rule, the law, statute, or rule shall prevail.

DONE AND ORDERED in chambers in Fort Myers, Lee County, Florida, this 3rd day of Feb, 2012.

Jay B. Rosman
Chief Judge

History.—Administrative Order 3.9 (January 28, 1991); Administrative Order 3.9 (September 29, 2006); Administrative Order 3.9 (November 7, 2007).

Attachment "A"

CERTIFICATE OF COMPLIANCE
FCIC/NCIC REQUIREMENT
(Jessica Lunsford Act and Anti-Murder Act)

(This form is for use within all counties of the Twentieth Judicial Circuit in and for the State of Florida)

Under penalty of perjury, I, the undersigned, hereby certify that on the ____ day of ________________, 20____, an FCIC/NCIC Criminal History Report was run on the following person:

____

Based upon a review of the FCIC/NCIC Criminal History Report, I further certify that the above-named person:

(Please check applicable boxes)

DOES ☐ DOES NOT ☐ qualify for a "Danger to the Community" hearing under the Jessica Lunsford Act.[1]

- AND -

DOES ☐ DOES NOT ☐ qualify for detention under the Anti-Murder Act.[2]

SHERIFF OF ______________ COUNTY

By: ______________________________ ______________
Employee of the Sheriff Date

- OR -

ADMINISTRATIVE OFFICE OF THE COURTS
TWENTIETH JUDICIAL CIRCUIT

______________________________ ______________
Pretrial Services Officer*, as an agent of the Sheriff Date

Approved by:

______________________________ ______________
Sheriff's Representative/Sgt. on Duty Date

*The Pretrial Officer's signature is valid only if the Sheriff and AOC have entered into an interlocal agreement authorizing the Pretrial Officer to act as the Sheriff's agent.

ORIGINAL: _____Clerk of Courts
COPIES TO: _____Booking Clerk/Jail
_____Pretrial Services

*This form is to be maintained as confidential in accordance with FDLE/FBI rules and policies, as it contains derived state and national criminal history information.

[1] See Fla. Stat. §948.06(4) for the definition of persons who qualify for a "Danger to the Community" hearing under the Jessica Lunsford Act. See also local Administrative Orders 3.9 and 3.23 for further guidance.

[2] See Fla. Stat. §§903.0351(1) and 948.06(4) for the definition of persons who qualify for detention under the Anti-Murder Act. See also local Administrative Orders 3.9 and 3.23 for further guidance.

Rev. 1/2012

3.10. COURT ORDERED RESTITUTION FOR COSTS OF INVESTIGATION/PROSECUTION

IN THE TWENTIETH JUDICIAL CIRCUIT IN AND FOR THE STATE OF FLORIDA

IN RE: COURT ORDERED RESTITUTION FOR COSTS OF INVESTIGATION/PROSECUTION

ADMINISTRATIVE ORDER NO. 3.10

All Clerks of the Circuit Court in and for the Twentieth Judicial Circuit of Florida are hereby ordered to receive and dispense payments as reimbursement for investigative costs, costs of prosecution, or both, as may be ordered in criminal cases.

A service charge for the Clerk of the Circuit Court for handling each payment or installment payment is authorized by Florida law in an amount not to exceed that provided for by Fla. Stat. § 28.24.

Upon receipt of payments or installment payments for reimbursement of investigative or prosecution costs, the Clerk shall, after deducting the service charge, deposit said payments into the Clerk's prosecution/investigative costs account and shall credit the account of each defendant with each payment so received.

The Clerk shall dispense all accumulated payments on a regular basis pursuant to a disbursement schedule established by the Clerk and in accordance with any applicable statutes or procedures established by the Florida Association of Court Clerks, Inc.

To the extent that any provision of this Administrative Order may conflict with any rule, statute or law, the rule, statute or law shall prevail.

DONE AND ORDERED in Chambers at Fort Myers, Lee County, Florida, this 3 day of June, 2009.

G. Keith Cary
Chief Judge

History.—Administrative Order entered May 13, 1986; Administrative Order 3.10 (July 20, 1992).

3.11. CHILD AND SEXUAL ABUSE VICTIMS–LIMITS ON INTERVIEWS

IN THE TWENTIETH JUDICIAL CIRCUIT IN AND FOR THE STATE OF FLORIDA

ADMINISTRATIVE ORDER NO: 3.11

IN RE: CHILD AND SEXUAL ABUSE VICTIMS–LIMITS ON INTERVIEWS

Pursuant to Florida Statute § 914.16, and after consultation with all appropriate persons, this Court finds it necessary to order that reasonable limits be established on the number of interviews that a victim of a violation of Chapters 794, 800, 827, 847 or 39, Florida Statutes, who is under 16 years of age must submit to for law enforcement or discovery purposes.

"Interview" for the purposes of this order means any procedure by which the victim is required to provide a detailed account or demonstration of the nature and circumstances of the child or sexual abuse. "Interview" does not include any of the following:

(1) A history obtained by any health care professional for the purposes of medical or psychological diagnosis or treatment;

(2) initial contact with the victim by law enforcement for the purposes of taking a complaint; or,

(3) initial contact with the victim by the Florida Department of Health and Rehabilitative Services ("HRS") to assess the validity of the complaint or the need to take protective measures on behalf of the victim.

In accord with the foregoing and the need to act in the best interest of victims of child or sexual abuse under the age of 16, it is

ORDERED AND ADJUDGED as follows:

1. No victim of child abuse or sexual abuse who falls within the age guideline of this order shall be required to submit to more than three interviews in the course of the investigation and prosecution of an episode of child abuse or sexual abuse, except upon order of court as provided below.

2. The court directs that the three interviews be allotted to meet the needs of potential parties as follows:

(a) One interview collectively allotted to HRS, law enforcement, and the child protection team;

(b) one interview allotted to the State Attorney; and,

(c) one interview allotted to the representative of the person alleged to be responsible for the abuse.

3. Interested parties or agencies shall make every effort to gain all necessary information in the course of the same interview.

4. Interviews shall be conducted in a setting and in a manner designed to minimize the traumatic effects of the interview on the victim.

5. When more than one party or agency participates in a single interview, the interview shall be conducted by a single person who shall address the concerns of all parties in the course of the interview.

6. A prosecuting attorney who intends to call a victim to testify at trial shall have, with the consent of the Guardian Ad Litem or other advocate appointed by the Court, the right to additional interviews for the purpose of trial preparation.

7. The attorney for HRS in any dependency proceeding who intends to call a victim to testify at trial shall have, with the consent of the Guardian Ad Litem or other advocate appointed by the Court, the right to additional interviews for the purpose of trial preparation.

8. When a child is a witness or victim in both a criminal and a dependency case, the representative(s) of the person(s) alleged to be responsible for the abuse will conduct only one deposition of the victim.

9. Additional interviews shall be allowed only by order of court upon motion for good cause shown. Additional interviews shall be limited in scope to assure the minimum possible impact on the victim.

Pursuant to Florida Statute § 914.17, a guardian ad litem or other advocate appointed by the Court to represent a minor in a criminal proceeding regardless of whether the minor is a witness or a victim of child abuse or neglect, has the right to be present at any interview and shall have access to all evidence and reports as provided in the cited statute. Any interested party or agency may, in the interests of the child and as justice may require, petition the court for a modification of this Order upon motion for good cause shown.

DONE AND ORDERED in Chambers at Fort Myers, Lee County, Florida this 14 day of April, 1993.

Thomas S. Reese
Chief Circuit Judge

History.—New.

3.12. NOTICES OF APPEARANCE IN CRIMINAL CASES

IN THE TWENTIETH JUDICIAL CIRCUIT IN AND FOR THE STATE OF FLORIDA

ADMINISTRATIVE ORDER NO: 3.12

IN RE: NOTICES OF APPEARANCE IN CRIMINAL CASES

WHEREAS, this Court has determined that the Public Defender's Office is routinely appointed at first appearance to represent most criminal Defendants; and,

WHEREAS, Defendants in criminal matters on many occasions retain private counsel at or near the time the Public Defender is appointed; and,

WHEREAS, this sometimes results in private counsel being erroneously appointed by the Court to represent allegedly indigent Defendants; it is, therefore,

ORDERED AND ADJUDGED that all private counsel who are retained to represent criminal Defendants at or after the time of first appearance shall promptly provide the Public Defender with a copy of the initial appearance/notice of appearance as counsel in the case. The certificate of service on this notice should show service to the Honorable Douglas M. Midgley, Public Defender, Post Office Drawer 1980, Fort Myers, Florida, 33902–1980.

DONE AND ORDERED in Chambers at Fort Myers, Lee County, Florida, this 17 day of May, 1993.

Thomas S. Reese
Chief Judge

3.13. GUIDELINES FOR THE ESTABLISHMENT OF BAIL

IN THE TWENTIETH JUDICIAL CIRCUIT IN AND FOR THE STATE OF FLORIDA

ADMINISTRATIVE ORDER NO: 3.13—VACATED—

IN RE: GUIDELINES FOR THE ESTABLISHMENT OF BAIL

WHEREAS, issues involving the conditions or means of satisfying bail are either issues of law to be controlled by applicable Florida Statutes, Florida Rules of Court, and case law, or issues of fact to be determined by the trial court, and, in any event, are not issues of an administrative nature or the appropriate subject of an administrative order; and

WHEREAS, trial court rulings involving pretrial release or bail are subject to review by proper application to the appropriate court;

IT IS ORDERED, by the authority vested in the Chief Judge pursuant to Fla. R. Jud. Admin. 2.050(b), that Administrative Order No. 3.13 is not necessary and is hereby VACATED.

DONE AND ORDERED in chambers in Naples, Collier County, Florida, this 20th day of December, 2005.

Hugh D. Hayes
Chief Judge

History. - Administrative Order No. 3.13 (August 21, 2001); Administrative Order No. 3.13 (December 14, 1993).

3.14. CONFISCATION, SEIZURE, FORFEITURE, DISPOSITION OR DESTRUCTION OF SALTWATER PRODUCTS, ILLEGAL NETS, AND GAME AND FRESHWATER FISH

IN THE TWENTIETH JUDICIAL CIRCUIT IN AND FOR THE STATE OF FLORIDA

ADMINISTRATIVE ORDER NO. 3.14

IN RE: CONFISCATION, SEIZURE, FORFEITURE, DISPOSITION OR DESTRUCTION OF SALTWATER PRODUCTS, ILLEGAL NETS, AND GAME AND FRESHWATER FISH

Pursuant to Florida Statutes §§ 370.061, 372.73 and 43.195; Fla. R. Jud. Admin. 2.075; the authority of this Court conferred by Rule 2.050 and Florida Statute § 43.26; and in order to improve the administration of justice within the Twentieth Judicial Circuit, it is,

ORDERED AND ADJUDGED as follows:

1. When an arrest is made pursuant to Chapter 370 of the Florida Statutes or the applicable provisions of the Florida Administrative Code, and minor amounts of perishable saltwater products illegally taken are seized, the law enforcement agency that seized said products is authorized to destroy them without obtaining individual court orders from the presiding judge at the conclusion of each case.

2. In the event of a conviction, said products shall not be destroyed until the time for taking an appeal has expired. In the event an appeal is taken, said products shall be preserved until the conclusion of the appeal or unless otherwise ordered by the court upon proper application thereto.

3. For the purpose of this order, "minor amounts" of perishable saltwater products shall be defined as amounts having no appreciable commercial value.

4. When an arrest is made pursuant to the provisions of Chapter 370 or the applicable provisions of the Florida Administrative Code, and commercial quantities of illegal, perishable products or perishable products illegally taken or landed are confiscated, the law enforcement agency shall, when feasible, obtain three bids as to the fair market value of the products.

The Defendant may thereafter post a bond equal to the amount specified in the highest bid.

5. The highest bid so obtained shall constitute a determination as to the fair market value of such products, and the Defendant, after posting the requisite bond, shall have twenty-four (24) hours to transport said products outside the borders of Florida for sale or other disposition.

6. Said bond or cash deposit shall be posted within one hour of seizure. If no such bond is posted within one hour, the products shall be sold to the highest of the three bidders, and the funds shall be remitted, held and distributed as provided in Florida Statute § 370.061(2).

7. When it is impractical to seek a judge's approval of fair value, the fair value of seized products shall be determined by the highest of three estimates value from licensed wholesalers, or the higher of two or fewer such estimates if three cannot be found locally. If no such bond or deposit is tendered, the products may be sold by the law enforcement agency making the seizure to the highest of three bidders, or the higher of two or fewer bidders if three cannot be found, without further order of the Court.

8. If no bond or deposit is tendered and no bids for purchase of the products can be found, and the products are still fit for human consumption, the products may be donated to a charitable institution for their use without further order of the Court, so long as a receipt is obtained from that institution for later production in court.

9. If no bond or deposit is tendered and no bids for purchase of said products can be found, and the products are no longer fit for human consumption but are suitable for consumption by fish or wildlife, the products may be donated to a charitable institution for their use without further order of the Court, so long as a receipt is obtained from the institution for later production in court.

10. If no bond or deposit is tendered and no bid for purchase of said products can be found, and the products are spoiled and no longer fit for human or animal consumption, the products may be disposed of in the landfill without further order of the Court, after photographs of the confiscated products are taken and thereafter preserved for production in court.

11. If no bond or deposit is tendered and a bid to purchase said products cannot be found, and the products are enmeshed in a monofilament gill net, are spoiled, and in the judgment of the confiscating officer potentially constitute a health hazard, the net and the products can be disposed of in the landfill without further order of the Court, after the net and product are photographed as evidence and a physical sample of the net is preserved for production in the court.

12. Pursuant to Florida Statute § 372.73, the officers of the Fish and Wildlife Conservation Commission are hereby authorized to donate to a hospital or charitable institution any game or freshwater fish seized as evidence in any action to enforce any provision of Chapter 372 of the Florida Statutes or any enabling rule or regulation codified in the Florida Administrative Code, without further order of the Court, so long as a receipt is obtained from the hospital or institution for later production in court.

13. In the event that any officer of the Fish and Wildlife Conservation Commission or other law enforcement officer encounters upon the navigable waterways of this circuit any illegal and unmarked entangling nets proscribed by Article 10 of the Florida Constitution or other provision of Florida Law, the officers are hereby authorized to gather up, remove from the water and thereafter dispose of or otherwise destroy said entangling nets.

This order shall take effect on the date of its execution and shall thereafter remain in effect until and unless it is otherwise modified or repealed by further order of this Court.

DONE AND ORDERED in Chambers at Naples, Collier County, Florida, this 27 day of Mar., 2001.

William L. Blackwell
Chief Judge

History.—Administrative Order No. 3.14 (February 12, 1998); Administrative Order No. 3.14 (August 22, 1997); Administrative Order No. 3.14 (June 28, 1995).

3.15. ESTABLISHMENT OF DRUG COURTS

IN THE TWENTIETH JUDICIAL CIRCUIT IN AND FOR THE STATE OF FLORIDA

ADMINISTRATIVE ORDER NO. 3.15—AMENDED—

IN RE: ESTABLISHMENT OF DRUG COURTS

Pursuant to Article V, Section 7 of the Florida Constitution and Florida Statute sections 39.001, 39.521, 397.334, 948.01, 948.08, 948.16, and 985.345, the Chief Judge authorizes the establishment and continued maintenance of specialty Drug Courts in any county or counties within the Twentieth Judicial Circuit. Drug Courts shall be within the division of the Criminal Court (felony or misdemeanor), or in some instances within the division of the Family Court (dependency/delinquency), as may be appropriate.

In recognition of the distinct features and resources of the five individual counties of the Twentieth Judicial Circuit, Drug Courts are authorized, though not mandated, and the establishment and continued maintenance of Drug Courts is subject to policies and procedures as may be applicable to individual counties and divisions, and is subject to any Drug Court Program Manuals. Any such policies, procedures, and Drug Court Program Manuals, and the actual establishment and continued maintenance of Drug Courts within any county or division, is subject to the approval of the Chief Judge and/or the Chief Judge's designee.

As established, Drug Courts will preside exclusively over appropriate cases involving arrested persons, either adult or juvenile, or parties in dependency cases, who have substance abuse or addiction problems. Referrals to Drug Courts will be considered on the basis of the facts and circumstances unique to the individual and to that individual's case or cases. All defendants/parties identified for referral to Drug Courts must meet all requirements for participation set forth under applicable Florida Statutes, as well as requirements of any other controlling Drug Court orders and program manuals.

Entry by a qualified defendant/party into a Drug Court program shall be on a voluntary basis. However, once a qualified defendant/party has voluntarily agreed to participate in Drug Court, the defendant/party will be deemed to have accepted the requirements of the program and to have agreed that the Drug Court judge may order (or, if permitted by law, the quasi-judicial officer may recommend) coercive sanctions, which may include (as may be applicable and authorized by law) incarceration, community service, and other coercive measures intended to motivate the defendant/party to overcome substance abuse or addiction.

Upon successful participation and completion of a Drug Court program, a defendant/party may, in certain cases, be permitted to withdraw his or her plea, and the State Attorney's Office may reduce or dismiss the charge or charges.

This Administrative Order supersedes any prior administrative orders relating to the establishment or maintenance of Drug Courts within the Twentieth Judicial Circuit.

To the extent that any provision of this Administrative Order may be construed as being in conflict with any law, statute, or rule, the law, statute, or rule shall prevail.

DONE AND ORDERED in Chambers at Fort Myers, Lee County, Florida, this 5th day of April, 2016.

Michael T. McHugh

Chief Judge

History.—Administrative Order 3.15 (March 27, 2001); Administrative Order 3.15 (November 29, 2006); Administrative Order 3.15 (September 11, 2007).

3.16. JUDICIAL PROCEDURE FOR RETURNS OF SEARCH WARRANTS

IN THE TWENTIETH JUDICIAL CIRCUIT IN AND FOR THE STATE OF FLORIDA

ADMINISTRATIVE ORDER NO. 3.16

IN RE: JUDICIAL PROCEDURE FOR RETURNS OF SEARCH WARRANTS

Pursuant to Florida Statutes §§ 43.26 and 933.14; the authority of this Court conferred by Fla. R. Jud. Admin. 2.050; the provisions of Fla. R. Jud. Admin. 2.051(b)(3) and (c)(e); and the inherent authority of the Court to administer and regulate the courts of the Twentieth Judicial Circuit, the Court finds as follows:

1. Florida Statute 933.14(4) provides in pertinent part the following:

The judge or magistrate to whom said search warrant is returned shall file the same with the inventory and sworn return in the proper office, and if the original affidavit and proofs upon which the warrant was issued are in his or her possession, he or she shall apply to the officer having the same and the officer shall transmit and deliver all of the papers, proofs and certificates to the proper office where the proceedings are lodged.

2. There is no uniform procedure regarding returns of search warrants. In addition, neither the statute cited above nor any applicable case law provides a definition for the term "proper office." Indeed, the Court is aware of at least three different procedures in place throughout the circuit for handling warrant returns depending on the county in question and the issuing judge.

3. It is imperative that a uniform procedure for the processing of search warrants be in place throughout this circuit so as to eliminate any potential confusion among judges, court personnel, law enforcement officers, counsel, their clients, and any other interested persons.

Based upon the foregoing, it is

ORDERED AND ADJUDGED as follows:

1. The Court finds by consent of the various offices that the Clerks of Courts of the five counties of the Twentieth Judicial Circuit are the "proper office" for the handling of search warrant returns as contemplated and referenced by Florida Statute § 933.14(4) and pursuant to Rule 2.051(b)(3).

2. When a return of search warrant, inventory, and related materials are returned to a member of the judiciary after execution, the judge shall review the materials to insure that they are proper. If the materials are in proper order, the judge shall forward these materials to the Office of the Clerk of Courts in that county.

3. Search warrants and their returns may be exempt from public disclosure if they are part of an ongoing criminal investigation. Section 119.07(3)(b), Fla. Stat.; *Florida Publishing Company v. State*, 706 So.2d 54 (Fla. 1st DCA), *review dismissed*, 717 So.2d 531 (Fla. 1998). An applicant for access to search warrant records (applicant) shall apply in writing to the proper office (Clerk) pursuant to the procedure set forth in Rule 2.051(e). The Clerks of Courts shall thereupon disclose these records unless the State Attorney's Office or the law enforcement agency involved in the search warrant contends that it is part of an ongoing criminal investigation.

4. Disagreements between the law enforcement agencies and the applicant shall be resolved before the judge who issued the search warrant upon the filing of a motion by any affected party seeking a determination of the status of the criminal investigation involving the warrant.

5. The Clerk of Courts is a ministerial agency in this proceeding and has no responsibility or authority to resolve disputes regarding search warrants. If the Clerk of Courts is advised that there is a conflict regarding whether an executed search warrant is part of an ongoing criminal investigation, the Clerk shall not disclose the warrant or return until the applicant receives authority from the judge who issued the warrant to release the warrant and presents this authority to the Clerk of Courts.

6. Judges are no longer to retain copies or original records of search warrants in their office files. The Clerks of Courts, as the proper office for handling search warrant returns, is hereby designated to be the proper custodian of all such records pursuant to Chapter 119 of the Florida Statutes and Rule 2.051.

7. This order does not alter the procedure for the issuance of search warrants by a duty judge as set forth in Administrative Order 2.7

This order shall take effect on the date of its execution and shall thereafter remain in effect until and unless it is otherwise modified or repealed by further order of this Court.

DONE AND ORDERED in Chambers this 17th day of December, 2002.

William L. Blackwell
Chief Judge

History. - Administrative Order 3.16 (May 16, 2002); Administrative Order 3.16 (March 13, 2002).

3.17. ORDER VACATING ADMINISTRATIVE ORDER 3.17

IN THE TWENTIETH JUDICIAL CIRCUIT IN AND FOR THE STATE OF FLORIDA

ORDER VACATING ADMINISTRATIVE ORDER 3.17

WHEREAS, the concerns prompting the enactment of Administrative Order 3.17 are being appropriately and adequately addressed by the trial judges throughout the Twentieth Judicial Circuit in and for the State of Florida, and

WHEREAS, the incompetency procedures to be followed in criminal cases are adequately provided for by Fla. R. Crim. P. 3.211, 3.212, 3.213, 3.214, 3.215, and 3.216, and Chapter 916, Florida Statutes (2002),

It is, therefore,

ORDERED AND ADJUDGED that Administrative Order 3.17 is hereby vacated.

DONE AND ORDERED in Chambers at Naples, Collier County, Florida this 21st day of August, 2003.

Hugh D. Hayes
Chief Judge

3.18. ISSUANCE OF ARREST WARRANTS FOR FAILURE TO APPEAR FOR COURT PROCEEDINGS

IN THE TWENTIETH JUDICIAL CIRCUIT IN AND FOR THE STATE OF FLORIDA

ADMINISTRATIVE ORDER NO. 3.18

IN RE: ISSUANCE OF ARREST WARRANTS FOR FAILURE TO APPEAR FOR COURT PROCEEDINGS

Pursuant to Fla. R. Crim. P. 3.121, 3.125 and 3.730; Fla. R. Traf. Ct. 6.165 and 6.190; Florida Statute § 932.48; any other applicable statutes and rules of court and the inherent authority of this Court to regulate and administrate the courts of the Twentieth Judicial Circuit, it is

ORDERED AND ADJUDGED as follows:

1. Any person who has been served with a complaint or information or a notice to appear for violation of the criminal laws of this State or any political subdivision thereof including a criminal traffic violation or a city or county ordinance or other charge, and that person fails to appear before the court in answer to the charge or charges for any proceeding which has been duly noticed and required, a warrant for their arrest shall issue.

2. All such warrants shall be in compliance with Rule 3.121 and shall appropriately reference the court proceeding which resulted in the issuance of the warrant. A form for use throughout this circuit is attached to this order and made a part hereof.

DONE AND ORDERED in Chambers at Punta Gorda, Charlotte County, Florida, this 27 day of Feb., 2002.

William L. Blackwell
Chief Judge

History. - New.

IN THE CIRCUIT COURT OF THE TWENTIETH JUDICIAL CIRCUIT IN AND FOR XX COUNTY, FLORIDA CRIMINAL ACTION

______)
Plaintiff,)
vs.) Case No. ______
______)
Defendant.)
______)

IN THE NAME OF THE STATE OF FLORIDA

TO ALL AND SINGULAR THE SHERIFFS OF THE STATE OF FLORIDA

This is to command you to take the Defendant, ______, into custody if found in your county, and safely keep him/her, so that you have said Defendant before a judge of this Court to answer the charges now pending in said Court, to wit: ______

______

Bail $ ___

Reason: Failure to Appear For ______
on ___ day of ______, 200 ___.

DONE AND ORDERED this ___ day of ______, 200 ___.

Judge of said Court

3.19. COST OF SUPERVISION FOR PROGRAMS ADMINISTERED BY THE FLORIDA DEPARTMENT OF CORRECTIONS, PROBATION AND PAROLE SERVICES

IN THE TWENTIETH JUDICIAL CIRCUIT IN AND FOR THE STATE OF FLORIDA

ADMINISTRATIVE ORDER NO: 3.19

IN RE: COST OF SUPERVISION FOR PROGRAMS ADMINISTERED BY THE FLORIDA DEPARTMENT OF CORRECTIONS, PROBATION AND PAROLE SERVICES

WHEREAS, Fla. Stat. § 948.09 provides that any person ordered by the court to be placed on probation, drug offender probation, or community control must, as a condition of any placement, pay to the Florida Department of Corrections a total sum of money equal to the total month or portion of a month of supervision times the court-ordered amount, but not to exceed the actual per diem cost of supervision, and

WHEREAS, it is desirable to have a uniform rate within the Twentieth Judicial Circuit for equity and enforcement purposes, it is hereby

ORDERED that all offenders within the Twentieth Judicial Circuit placed on probation, drug offender probation, or community control, and under the supervision of the Florida Department of Corrections, shall pay costs of supervision in the amount of $50.00 per month, unless otherwise ordered by the sentencing court. All felony offenders shall also pay a $2.00 per month surcharge pursuant to Fla. Stat. § 948.09(1)(a)2. (2003). This order shall not be construed as limiting the Department's authority to charge any additional surcharges as authorized by statute or rule, and shall not be construed as limiting the Department's authority to exempt any person from payment as authorized by statute or rule.

DONE AND ORDERED in chambers in Naples, Collier County, Florida, this 23 day of March, 2004.

Hugh D. Hayes
Chief Judge

History. - New.

3.20. PRETRIAL SUBSTANCE ABUSE EDUCATION AND TREATMENT INTERVENTION PROGRAMS

IN THE TWENTIETH JUDICIAL CIRCUIT IN AND FOR THE STATE OF FLORIDA

ADMINISTRATIVE ORDER NO: 3.20 –Amended–

IN RE: PRETRIAL SUBSTANCE ABUSE EDUCATION AND TREATMENT INTERVENTION PROGRAMS

WHEREAS, Florida Statute § 948.08(6)(a) provides that a person who is charged with a nonviolent felony and is identified as having a substance abuse problem, or who is charged with a felony of the second or third degree for purchase or possession of a controlled substance under chapter 893, prostitution, tampering with evidence, solicitation for purchase of a controlled substance, or obtaining a prescription by fraud, has not been charged with a crime involving violence, and has not previously been convicted of a felony, may be eligible for voluntary admission into a pretrial substance abuse education and treatment intervention program, including a treatment-based drug court program established pursuant to Florida Statute § 397.334, approved by the chief judge of the circuit, for a period of not less than one year in duration; and

WHEREAS, Florida Statute § 948.08(6)(b) provides that, while enrolled in a pretrial intervention program authorized by subsection (6), the participant is subject to a coordinated strategy developed by a drug court team under Florida Statute § 397.334(4), which may include a protocol of sanctions that may be imposed upon the participant for noncompliance with program rules; and

WHEREAS, local Administrative Order 3.15 authorizes the establishment of drug courts within any county of the Twentieth Judicial Circuit, pursuant to Florida Statute § 397.3334;

NOW, THEREFORE, pursuant to the authority vested in me as Chief Judge of the Twentieth Judicial Circuit of Florida under Florida Statute § 948.08(6) and Fla. R. Jud. Admin. 2.215, the use within the counties of the Twentieth Judicial Circuit of the Substance Abuse and Treatment Pretrial Intervention Program administered by the Florida Department of Corrections is hereby approved to the extent that it provides a coordinated strategy developed by a drug court team under Florida Statute § 397.334(4).

DONE AND ORDERED in chambers in Fort Myers, Lee County, Florida, this 4th day of Oct., 2013.

Jay B. Rosman
Chief Judge

History. Administrative Order 3.20 (July 16, 2004).

3.21. COMPOSITE BONDS

IN THE TWENTIETH JUDICIAL CIRCUIT IN AND FOR THE STATE OF FLORIDA

ADMINISTRATIVE ORDER NO. 3.21

IN RE: COMPOSITE BONDS

WHEREAS, for purposes of this administrative order, a composite bond is defined as a single bond, set for a specific amount, that covers more than one pending case for a single defendant; and

WHEREAS, the administration of a composite bond creates difficulties and uncertainties when the cases covered by the composite bond are not closed or resolved simultaneously;

IT IS HEREBY ORDERED, pursuant to Fla. R. Jud. Admin. 2.050, as follows:

1. The imposition of a composite bond is hereby discouraged. The County and Circuit Judges of the Twentieth Judicial Circuit are encouraged to order a separate bond to be applied to each individual case.

2. However, in instances where a Judge of this circuit orders a composite bond, the composite bond shall be deemed to be divided into equal amounts to be applied as separate bonds to each individual case number. In situations where the composite bond is not equally divisible by the number of separate cases, the composite bond shall be deemed to be divided in a manner in which the separate bonds are rounded up or down to the nearest whole dollar so that the total of the separate bonds equals the composite bond amount, and so that the lowest bond shall apply to the case number which is lowest in sequence and the highest bond shall apply to the case number which is highest in sequence. For example, a $10,000.00 composite bond applied to case numbers 05–001, 05–002, and 05–003 shall be deemed to be divided as follows: $3,333.00 bond in case number 05–001, $3,333.00 bond in case number 05–002, and $3,334.00 in case number 05–003.

3. To the extent that any provision of this Administrative Order may be construed as being in conflict with any law, statute, or rule, the law, statute, or rule shall prevail.

DONE AND ORDERED in chambers in Naples, Collier County, Florida, this 25th day of February, 2005.

Hugh D. Hayes
Chief Judge

History. - New.

3.22. ELECTRONIC SUBPOENAS

IN THE TWENTIETH JUDICIAL CIRCUIT IN AND FOR THE STATE OF FLORIDA

ADMINISTRATIVE ORDER NO. 3.22

IN RE: ELECTRONIC SUBPOENAS

WHEREAS, the State Attorney, the Public Defender and Court Administration, as part of the "CJIS Consortium" of the Twentieth Judicial Circuit, have developed a system by which subpoenas are served on law enforcement officers through the use of electronic means, as an alternative to service by traditional methods; and

WHEREAS, in May of 2008, an application, a copy of which is attached hereto as Attachment A, was submitted to the Florida Supreme Court for approval of the use of the "CJIS Notify Document Portal" for Lee County, which was designed as the means of electronically serving subpoenas on law enforcement officers; and

WHEREAS, the Florida Supreme Court approved the application and use of the "CJISNotify Document Portal" for Lee County by Administrative Order AOSC08–90 entered November 19, 2008, a copy of which is attached hereto as Attachment B; and

WHEREAS, by letter dated June 9, 2010, a copy of which is attached hereto as Attachment C, the Florida Courts Technology Commission advised that it had approved the request to expand and implement the CJISNotify system in Charlotte, Collier, Glades, and Hendry counties, and further advised that no further review or action was required;

IT IS HEREBY ORDERED, pursuant to the authority vested in the Chief Judge by Fla. R. Jud. Admin. 2.215, that when using the "CJISNotify Document Portal" for the purpose of electronically serving subpoenas, as approved by Florida Supreme Court Administrative Order AOSC08–90 and by letter of the Florida Courts Technology Commission dated June 9, 2010, the State Attorney, the Public Defender and the Clerks of Court for Charlotte, Collier, Glades, Hendry, and Lee counties are to use the "CJISNotify Document Portal" subject to the following conditions and consistent with the requirements of Fla. R. Crim. P. 3.361:

1. The issuance and service of subpoenas through the use of electronic means (hereinafter "electronic subpoenas") shall be a matter of record, and evidence of such must appear in the court file.

2. So as to ensure the uniform and proper use of electronic subpoenas, the State Attorney, Public Defender, and Clerks of Court shall comply with the written procedures and policies issued by the "CJIS Consortium," which are attached hereto as part of the application for approval of the use of the "CJISNotify Document Portal" (Attachment A).[1] Such written procedures and policies shall be maintained, kept on file, and available for public viewing in the main offices of the State Attorney, the Public Defender, the Court Administrator, the CJIS Director, and all law enforcement agencies participating in the use of electronic subpoenas.

3. The State Attorney, the Public Defender, and all participating law enforcement agencies shall enter into a written agreement(s) demonstrating each party's intent to participate in the use of electronic subpoenas and assent to all written procedures and policies governing the use of electronic subpoenas. The original of all such written agreements shall be held and maintained by the CJIS Director, with copies to the State Attorney, the Public Defender, the Court Administrator, the applicable law enforcement agency, and the Clerks of Court.

4. This Administrative Order shall not be construed as a mandate requiring that the State Attorney and the Public Defender use electronic subpoenas, and, absent a written agreement between the law enforcement agency, the State Attorney and the Public Defender, this shall not be construed as a mandate requiring that all law enforcement agencies participate in the use of electronic subpoenas. To the extent that the State Attorney and the Public Defender do elect to use electronic subpoenas, the State Attorney and the Public Defender, as attorneys of record defined in Fla. R. Crim. P. 3.361(a), shall be responsible for ensuring compliance with all conditions set forth herein.

5. This Administrative Order does not relieve the State Attorney and the Public Defender of their responsibility to ensure that their respective witnesses appear in Court. It must be acknowledged that in using electronic subpoenas, the State Attorney and the Public Defender are relying upon technology that is subject to disruption or failure. In the event of any technological disruption or failure, regardless of the actual cause, the State Attorney and the Public Defender, as attorneys of record defined in Fla. R. Crim. P. 3.361(a), shall be responsible for ensuring that any necessary subpoenas are served utilizing traditional methods, or to otherwise secure the appearance of any necessary witnesses.

6. To the extent that issues of law or legal procedure may be implicated in any particular case by the use or attempted use of electronic subpoenas, these issues are matters to be raised, addressed, and ruled upon by the trial court judge. This Administrative Order is only administrative in nature and is not intended to address or resolve any issues of law or legal procedure, nor to authorize the use of any procedures that might be in contravention of any law, statute, or rule. To the extent that any provision of this Administrative Order may be construed as being in conflict with any law, statute, or rule, the law, statute, or rule shall prevail.

DONE AND ORDERED in chambers in Fort Myers, Lee County, Florida, this 7TH day of September, 2010.

G. Keith Cary
Chief Judge

History.—News.

[1] Attachments available at http://www.ca.cjis20.org/web/main/ao_admin_criminal.asp

3.23. MONETARY BAIL SCHEDULES AND PROHIBITIONS AGAINST RELEASE PRIOR TO APPEARANCE BEFORE JUDGE (JESSICA LUNSFORD AND ANTI–MURDER ACTS)

IN THE TWENTIETH JUDICIAL CIRCUIT IN AND FOR THE STATE OF FLORIDA

IN RE: MONETARY BAIL SCHEDULES AND PROHIBITIONS AGAINST RELEASE PRIOR TO APPEARANCE BEFORE JUDGE (JESSICA LUNSFORD AND ANTI–MURDER ACTS)

ADMINISTRATIVE ORDER NO: 3.23—Amended—

WHEREAS, Fla. R. Crim. P. 3.130 requires that, except when previously released in a lawful manner, every arrested person shall be taken before a judicial officer within twenty-four hours after arrest (referred to herein as the "First Appearance Hearing"); and

WHEREAS, Fla. R. Crim. P. 3.131 generally provides that conditions of pretrial release, including the amount of any monetary condition of pretrial release, shall be considered at the First Appearance Hearing; and

WHEREAS, the Twentieth Judicial Circuit desires to formalize the use of monetary bail schedules as a means to ensure the timely and efficient processing of court cases, to fix the standard amount of bail for each of the offenses listed on a monetary bail schedule, and to grant to the county sheriffs within the Twentieth Judicial Circuit the authority to release in advance of the First Appearance Hearing any person who has been arrested and jailed for an offense that is listed on the court-approved monetary bail schedule for the sheriff's respective county; and

WHEREAS, the Twentieth Judicial Circuit further desires to ensure compliance with the provisions and requirements of Chapter 2005–28, Laws of Florida, relating to high-risk sex offenders, otherwise known as the "Jessica Lunsford Act;" and

WHEREAS, the Twentieth Judicial Circuit further desires to ensure compliance with the provisions and requirements of Chapter 2007–2, Laws of Florida, relating to violent felony offenders, otherwise known as the "Anti–Murder Act;"

NOW, THEREFORE, pursuant to the authority prescribed by Fla. R. Jud. Admin. 2.215 (formerly Fla. R. Jud. Admin. 2.050) and for the purpose of promoting the efficient administration of justice within the Twentieth Judicial Circuit, it is **ORDERED** as follows:

I. ESTABLISHMENT AND USE OF MONETARY BAIL SCHEDULES

A. The administrative judge for each of the five counties within the Twentieth Judicial Circuit is hereby authorized to create a proposed monetary bail schedule listing those offenses for which monetary bail may be pre-set and prescribing the specific bail amount for each offense listed on the schedule. After consulting with the circuit and county judges who are assigned criminal cases within each respective county, the administrative judge shall submit any proposed monetary bail schedule to the chief judge of the Twentieth Judicial Circuit for approval and adoption. Once approved by the chief judge, the signed original of the monetary bail schedule shall be filed with the respective Office of the Clerk of Courts. A copy shall be forwarded to the court administrator and to the law enforcement agencies within the applicable county.

B. Once a monetary bail schedule has been approved and adopted, changes or amendments may be recommended by the administrative judge after consulting with the circuit and county judges who are assigned criminal cases within each respective county. Such recommendations shall be submitted to the chief judge of the Twentieth Judicial Circuit for approval and adoption. Once the chief judge approves and adopts any amendments, the signed original of the amended monetary bail schedule shall be filed in the respective Office of the Clerk of Courts, and a copy shall be forwarded to the court administrator and to the law enforcement agencies within the applicable county.

C. In making determinations as to reasonable conditions of pretrial release at the time of the First Appearance Hearing, or at any time thereafter, the judges are not bound by the bail amount for any particular offense listed on the monetary bail schedule, but, rather, may use their judicial discretion to determine any reasonable conditions of pretrial release, including any monetary conditions, based upon the facts and circumstances of each individual case.

D. The sheriff of each county is hereby authorized to release prior to the First Appearance Hearing persons who are arrested and jailed within their respective counties for the offenses or violations listed on the monetary bail schedule for their county, however, the person shall first post the applicable bail or bail bond. This provision does not preclude the sheriff or arresting officer from issuing a "notice to appear," in accordance with Fla. R. Crim. P. 3.125, in the case of a misdemeanor of the first or second degree or for a violation of a municipal or county ordinance. Specific procedures for use of the notice to appear must conform to section (1) of Fla. R. Crim. P. 3.125 and to the rules and regulations of procedure governing the exercise of authority to issue notices to appear as may be established by the chief judge pursuant to section (j) of Fla. R. Crim. P. 3.125.

E. In counties where the Administrative Office of the Courts (AOC) has an established pretrial services division, the sheriff shall honor all written requests from a pretrial services officer, as an officer of the court, to hold a person pending the First Appearance Hearing.

F. In counties where the AOC has an established pretrial services division that operates from the county jail twenty-four hours a day, seven days a week, the sheriff shall not release any arrested person prior to that person having been brought before a pretrial officer for screening.

II. COMPLIANCE WITH THE JESSICA LUNSFORD ACT

A. Before releasing any person pursuant to the monetary bail schedule, or any other conditions of release, the sheriff shall run a FCIC/NCIC records report and certify to the court that the person does not qualify as a high-risk sex offender and does not qualify for a hearing to determine whether the person is a danger to the public under the Jessica Lunsford Act, Chapter 2005–28, Laws of Florida. The certification shall comply substantively with the format of "Attachment A." Both the FCIC/NCIC records report and the certification to the court shall also comply with the requirements of local Administrative Order 3.9.

B. The sheriff shall not release prior to the First Appearance Hearing any person who qualifies as a high-risk sex offender and who qualifies for a hearing to determine whether that person is a danger to the public. Such person shall be brought before the First Appearance judge, either in person or by court-approved electronic means. Persons who qualify as high-risk sex offenders and who qualify for a hearing to determine whether they are dangers to the public shall not be released unless or until a determination is made by the court, on the record and in writing, that the person is not a danger to the public, and unless or until the court sets bail or other conditions of release.

C. In accordance with Fla. Stat. § 948.06(4), a person who qualifies as a high-risk sex offender and requires a hearing to determine whether that person is a danger to the public is defined as any felony probationer or offender in community control arrested for violating his or her probation or community control in a material respect, and who:

(1) is under supervision for any criminal offense proscribed in chapter 794, s. 800.04(4), (5), (6), s. 827.071, or s. 847.0145; or

(2) is a registered sexual predator or a registered sexual offender; or

(3) is under supervision for a criminal offense for which he or she would meet the registration criteria in s. 775.21, s. 943.0435, or s. 944.607 but for the effective date of those sections.

III. **COMPLIANCE WITH THE ANTI–MURDER ACT**

A. Before releasing any person prior to a First Appearance Hearing pursuant to the monetary bail schedule, or any other conditions of release, the sheriff shall certify to the court that the person does not qualify for detention under the Anti–Murder Act, Fla. Laws, Ch. 2007–2. The certification shall comply substantively with the format of "Attachment A."

B. The sheriff shall not release prior to the First Appearance Hearing any person who qualifies as a violent felony offender and who qualifies for detention pending a probation-violation or community-control-violation hearing, pursuant to the Anti–Murder Act. Such person shall be brought before the First Appearance judge, either in person or by court-approved electronic means. Persons who qualify as violent felony offenders and who qualify for detention pending a probation-violation or community-control-violation hearing shall under no circumstances be released from custody prior to a recorded violation hearing at which both the State and the offender are represented.

C. In accordance with Fla. Stat. § 903.0351 and Fla. Stat. § 948.06, a person who qualifies for detention pending a probation-violation or community-control-violation hearing is defined as a felony probationer or offender in community control who has been alleged to have committed any violation of felony probation or community control other than a failure to pay costs or fines or make restitution payment if that person is:

(1) A "violent felony offender of special concern," meaning a person who is on:

(a) felony probation or community control related to the commission of a qualifying offense committed on or after March 12, 2007; or

(b) felony probation or community control for any offense committed on or after March 12, 2007, and has previously been convicted of a qualifying offense; or

(c) felony probation or community control for any offense committed on or after March 12, 2007, and is found to have violated that probation or community control by committing a qualifying offense; or

(d) felony probation or community control and has previously been found by a court to be a habitual violent felony offender as defined in § 775.084(1)(b) and has committed a qualifying offense on or after March 12, 2007; or

(e) felony probation or community control and has previously been found by a court to be a three-time violent felony offender as defined in § 775.084(1)(c) and has committed a qualifying offense on or after March 12, 2007; or

(f) felony probation or community control and has previously been found by a court to be a sexual predator under § 775.21 and has committed a qualifying offense on or after March 12, 2007.

(2) a person who is on felony probation or community control for any offense committed on or after March 12, 2007 and who is arrested for a qualifying offense; or

(3) a person who is on felony probation or community control and has previously been found by a court to be a habitual violent felony offender as defined in § 775.084(1)(b), a three-time violent felony offender as defined in § 775.084(1)(c), or a sexual predator under § 775.21, and who is arrested for committing a qualifying offense on or after March 12, 2007.

D. The list of "qualifying offenses" under the Anti–Murder Act are expressly set forth in Fla. Stat. § 948.06(8)(c).

IV. **GENERAL PROVISIONS**

A. This Administrative Order shall not be construed either to mandate that monetary bail schedules be adopted or to mandate that the sheriffs within the Twentieth Judicial Circuit release persons pursuant to the approved and adopted monetary bail schedules.

B. To the extent that any provision of this Administrative Order may be construed as being in conflict with any law, statute, or rule, the law, statute, or rule shall prevail.

DONE AND ORDERED in chambers in Fort Myers, Lee County, Florida, this 30 day of March 2012.

Jay B. Rosman
Chief Judge

History.—Administrative Order 3.23 (September 29, 2006); Administrative Order 3.23 (November 7, 2007).

Attachment "A"

CERTIFICATE OF COMPLIANCE
FCIC/NCIC REQUIREMENT
(Jessica Lunsford Act and Anti-Murder Act)

(This form is for use within all counties of the Twentieth Judicial Circuit in and for the State of Florida)

Under penalty of perjury, I, the undersigned, hereby certify that on the ____ day of ______________, 20____, an FCIC/NCIC Criminal History Report was run on the following person:

____.

Based upon a review of the FCIC/NCIC Criminal History Report, I further certify that the above-named person:

(Please check applicable boxes)

DOES ☐ DOES NOT ☐ qualify for a "Danger to the Community" hearing under the Jessica Lunsford Act.[1]

- AND -

DOES ☐ DOES NOT ☐ qualify for detention under the Anti-Murder Act.[2]

SHERIFF OF ______________ COUNTY

By: ______________________ ______________
Employee of the Sheriff Date

- OR -

ADMINISTRATIVE OFFICE OF THE COURTS
TWENTIETH JUDICIAL CIRCUIT

______________________________________ ______________
Pretrial Services Officer*, as an agent of the Sheriff Date

Approved by:

______________________________________ ______________
Sheriff's Representative/Sgt. on Duty Date

*The Pretrial Officer's signature is valid only if the Sheriff and AOC have entered into an interlocal agreement authorizing the Pretrial Officer to act as the Sheriff's agent.

ORIGINAL: ______ Clerk of Courts
COPIES TO: ______ Booking Clerk/Jail
______ Pretrial Services

*This form is to be maintained as confidential in accordance with FDLE/FBI rules and policies, as it contains derived state and national criminal history information.

[1] See Fla. Stat. §948.06(4) for the definition of persons who qualify for a "Danger to the Community" hearing under the Jessica Lunsford Act. See also local Administrative Orders 3.9 and 3.23 for further guidance.

[2] See Fla. Stat. §§903.0351(1) and 948.06(4) for the definition of persons who qualify for detention under the Anti-Murder Act. See also local Administrative Orders 3.9 and 3.23 for further guidance.

Rev. 1/2012

3.24. AUTHORIZATION FOR USE OF TECHNICAL VIOLATION NOTIFICATION LETTER

IN THE TWENTIETH JUDICIAL CIRCUIT IN AND FOR THE STATE OF FLORIDA

IN RE: AUTHORIZATION FOR USE OF TECHNICAL VIOLATION NOTIFICATION LETTER

ADMINISTRATIVE ORDER NO. 3.24

WHEREAS, in cases in which probation or community control has been imposed, Fla. Stat. § 948.06(1)(e) authorizes the Chief Judge of each circuit to direct the Florida Department of Corrections to use a notification letter of a technical violation in appropriate cases in lieu of a violation report, affidavit, and warrant when the alleged violation is not a new felony or misdemeanor offense;

NOW, THEREFORE, pursuant to the authority prescribed by Fla. R. Jud. Admin. 2.215 (formerly Fla. R. Jud. Admin. 2.050) and for the purpose of promoting the efficient administration of justice within the Twentieth Judicial Circuit, it is **ORDERED** as follows:

1. Within the parameters set forth herein, the Florida Department of Corrections (hereinafter "department") is hereby directed to use a notification letter of a technical violation (hereinafter "notification letter") in appropriate cases in lieu of a violation report, affidavit, and warrant when the alleged violation is not a new felony or misdemeanor offense, and in situations in which the department would not otherwise recommend that probation or community control be revoked or modified.

2. The department is authorized to use a notification letter to report the following violations:

a. Monetary only violations;

b. Failure to report or reporting late;

c. Failure to complete minimum number of Community Service hours ordered;

d. First positive marijuana or cocaine drug test if not in drug court and if no violent past histories;

e. Missing first drug test if not in drug court;

f. First curfew violation if not a sex offender or a violent offender;

g. First out of place for community control cases if not serious after investigation; and

h. Other minor violations.

3. All notification letters must affirmatively state that the probationer or offender does not qualify under the "Jessica Lunsford Act," Laws of Florida, Chapter 2005–28, or the "Anti–Murder Act," Laws of Florida, Chapter 2007–02. The department shall not use a notification letter in lieu of a violation report, affidavit, and warrant if the offender qualifies under the "Jessica Lunsford Act" or the "Anti–Murder Act."

4. This Administrative Order is not intended to mandate that the department use a notification letter in those situations in which the department would otherwise recommend that probation or community control be revoked or modified, regardless of the technical nature of the violation. The department and its supervisory officers are most familiar with the circumstances surrounding each probationer or offender and each specific violation and, accordingly, are in the best position to make a determination as to whether the use of a notification letter may be inappropriate in certain situations. Once the department determines that the use of a notification letter is appropriate and within the parameters of this Administrative Order, the individual trial court judge, as a neutral arbiter, is not authorized to unilaterally override that determination and may reasonably rely upon the determination made by the department. The individual trial court judge need not approve nor sign the notification letter.

5. The department shall file the original notification letter directly with the Clerk of Courts. A copy may be provided to the trial court judge.

6. This Administrative Order shall supercede and replace any and all previous directives as it relates to the use of notification letters of a technical violation.

7. The Administrative Judge of each county within the Twentieth Judicial Circuit, upon consultation with the circuit judges in that county, may elect to not implement the use of "notification letters" in that county. The Administrative Judge may do this by providing written notice to the department's circuit administrator, with a copy to the Chief Judge.

8. To the extent that any provision of this Administrative Order may be construed as being in conflict with any law, statute, or rule, the law, statute, or rule shall prevail.

DONE AND ORDERED in chambers in Fort Myers, Lee County, Florida, this 7 day of Nov, 2007.

G. Keith Cary
Chief Judge

3.25. ESTABLISHMENT AND IMPLEMENTATION OF CRIMINAL CASE MANAGEMENT PLAN

IN THE TWENTIETH JUDICIAL CIRCUIT IN AND FOR THE STATE OF FLORIDA

IN RE: ESTABLISHMENT AND IMPLEMENTATION OF CRIMINAL CASE MANAGEMENT PLAN

ADMINISTRATIVE ORDER NO. 3.25

WHEREAS, it is in the best interest of the citizens of the Twentieth Judicial Circuit for the Court to develop innovative means to further improve the fair, predictable, efficient, and timely disposition of felony criminal cases in the Circuit Criminal Court;

NOW, THEREFORE, pursuant to the authority prescribed by Fla. R. Jud. Admin. 2.215 and for the purpose of promoting the efficient administration of justice within the Twentieth Judicial Circuit, it is **ORDERED** as follows:

1. There is established within the Twentieth Judicial Circuit a Criminal Case Management Plan applicable to felony cases, which will be administered by the Administrative Office of the Courts through the use of case managers, clerical support staff and such personnel as the Court Administrator deems appropriate.

2. The basis for the Criminal Case Management Plan is attached hereto, identified as the "Criminal Case Management Procedures & Time Standards," and is incorporated as if fully set forth herein. The Criminal Case Management Plan is to be used as a model for the purpose of establishing goals and promoting uniformity of practice throughout the Twentieth Judicial Circuit.

3. It is intended that the Criminal Case Management Plan will be initially implemented in Lee County, effective December 31, 2007, with implementation to be later expanded, as appropriate, to other counties within the Twentieth Judicial Circuit.

4. Recognizing that each county may have differing needs requiring certain deviations from the model plan attached hereto, the Circuit Administrative Judge of each respective county may submit to the Chief Judge a distinct written proposed plan with procedures that, upon approval by the Chief Judge, may be implemented in the respective county.

5. The procedures and time standards set forth in the model plan, or in any other written plan approved by the Chief Judge, are intended to facilitate the timely, fair and effective resolution of criminal cases while ensuring the efficient use of court resources. The procedures and time standards do not supplant any existing rule, statute, or law. A defendant's right to a speedy trial is determined by Fla. R. Crim. P. 3.191 and not by reference to this Administrative Order or the Criminal Case Management Plan. Neither this Administrative Order nor the Criminal Case Management Plan shall be construed as granting any rights not already provided for by rule, statute, or law.

6. To the extent that any provision of this Administrative Order may be construed as being in conflict with any rule, statute, or law, the rule, statute, or law shall prevail.

DONE AND ORDERED in chambers in Fort Myers, Lee County, Florida, this 6 day of Dec., 2007.

G. Keith Cary
Chief Judge

History.—New.

20th Judicial Circuit
Criminal Case Management Procedures & Time Standards

I. Purpose

To improve predictability, efficiency and timely disposition of felony criminal cases in the Circuit Criminal Court.

To develop and evaluate Criminal DCM procedures in Lee County with intent to expand the best practices to other counties to promote uniformity in practice throughout the 20th Circuit.

To insure compliance with the provisions and aims of the Florida Rules of Criminal Procedure, specifically, the use of an early, meaningful Pretrial Conference procedure tied to a realistic discovery cut off date, Fla. R. Crim. P. 3.220 (p).

To recognize that a defendant's right to speedy trial, and the public, including victims and witnesses, interest in a timely, fair and just resolution of criminal cases, is best achieved by application of uniform and consistent time standards Fla. R. Crim. P. 2085(f) for the conduct of criminal cases in Circuit Court.

To encourage collaboration between the Court, the State Attorney, the Public Defender and the defense bar with a view towards a just and efficient disposition of criminal cases.

II. Objectives

- To implement an early Case Management Conference event to improve the early court intervention and use of a realistic Case Management Scheduling Order.
- To improve predictability and efficiency in case processing from arraignment to trial.
- To eliminate unproductive events and replace them with meaningful court events in the case process (Arraignment, Case Management Conference, Pretrial Conference and Trial Date).
- To manage cases according to their nature and complexity, to ensure early disposition of appropriate cases, to allow adequate time for trial preparation and individual judge management of more complex cases.
- Establish time goals and initiatives for efficient case processing and backlog reduction which target a 20–30% reduction in cases over 1 year of age and 80% "on-time" case processing of new cases filed as of 1/1/08.

III. Arraignment

At Felony Arraignment, after entry of initial plea, the judge will set a date for a mandatory Case Management Conference to be held within 45 to 60 days. Generally, standard cases will be set within 45 days and complex cases at 60 days.

IV. Case Track Designations and Time Goals

The State Attorney's Office will assign a presumptive track for all cases, at the time that the formal charging document (information) is filed. The presumptive track will be primarily based upon the lead charge in the charging document. Case track designations will establish a time period for completion of all discovery, plea conference, trial or disposition of the case.

Three final case track designations are established by the trial judge based upon: the nature of the charge, procedural complexity and reasonable time needed to prepare for trial and ensure a timely disposition.

- Track "A"—Expedited, 3rd degree or simple, non-violent offenses or cases suitable for diversion. Standard in-custody cases may also be placed on the expedited scheduling track to encourage early disposition.
- Track "B"—Standard, 2nd degree or cases not "A" or "C".
- Track "C"—Complex, 1st degree or 2nd degree with multiple defendants or procedural complexity that require intensive, individual Judge management.

At the Case Management Conference, time to disposition goals is established, consistent with Florida Rules of Court (Fla. R. Jud. Admin. 2.085) as follows:

- 80% of Expedited "A" cases to be disposed within 180 days
- 80% of Standard "B" cases to be disposed within 240 days
- 80% of Complex "C" cases to be disposed within 360 days

The following goals are established for the Felony case management program:

Time Goals	2009 80% Disposed	2010 90% Disposed
A Expedited	120 days	120 days
B Standard	180 days	180 days
C Complex	300 days	240 days

V. Initial Discovery, Score Sheet and Initial Plea Offer

Initial discovery or notice thereof, as defined by Fla. R. Crim. P. 3.220, shall be provided at arraignment or at the earliest time possible, in the exercise of due diligence, in order to permit the State and the Defendant sufficient time, in advance of the case management conference, to evaluate the case and meaningfully participate in the Case Management Conference.

15 Days prior to the Case Management Conference, counsel shall confer and have completed the following:

- Initial discovery exchange
- Score sheet exchange
- Plea offer exchange
- Review of anticipated pretrial activities and dates

Counsel shall be prepared to discuss all aspects of case management and scheduling, to include, without limitation, the following:

- Any discovery issues requiring a motion to compel or an order to show cause

- Any expert witness issues.
- Any pretrial motions pending or contemplated, to include scheduling issues related to motions. This would include suppression motions, child heresay [1] motions, and *Williams* Rule motions.
- Any conflict issues concerning representation.
- Any competency issues.
- Trial date and expected length of trial.
- Pretrial Conference date.
- Plea cut-off date.
- Motions; filing deadline and scheduling.
- Discovery deadline.
- Schedule additional case management conferences if necessary.
- Any other issues affecting a timely resolution of the case.

Counsel shall discuss whether the case can be disposed of by plea or by EID and, if so, a plea may be taken or an immediate plea date will be set in the Case Management Order. Cases identified for EID, Drug Court or Mental Health Court will be set for the next available date on that respective calendar.

The court may use an "ORDER SETTING CASE MANAGEMENT CONFERENCE" (Attachment A) to set any case filed prior to January 1, 2008, for a Case Management Conference.

VI. The Case Management Conference

Counsel and defendant will be present in court at the Case Management Conference, pursuant to Fla. R. Crim. P. 3.180(a)(3) and 3.220(p)(1). At the Case Management Conference, a final case track designation will be set by the Judge, upon consultation with counsel, based upon the nature of the charges and procedural complexity of the case.

In addition, a "CASE MANAGEMENT CONFERENCE ORDER" (Attachment B) will set forth:

- Tentative cut-off dates for pretrial motions, completion of all discovery, depositions and expert evaluations
- A date for any interim pretrial status conferences where deemed necessary by the trial judge
- Estimated time for Trial.

The clerk shall set a mandatory PRETRIAL CONFERENCE date to occur within 120 days of arraignment for an "A" track case and 165 days of arraignment for a "B" track case (120 days on "B" track case without a waiver of speedy trial).

The Scheduling Order shall also state a tentative TRIAL month and year based upon the case track to occur within 180 days of arraignment for "A" track cases (150 days on "A" track cases without a waiver of speedy trial) and 200 days of arraignment for "B" track cases (175 days on "B" track cases without a waiver of speedy trial).

VII. Amendments to the Scheduling Order

The Court recognizes that there are cases, which by their very nature and complexity, require special tracking standards and that unanticipated events may delay the trial of a case or require that a previously determined date be extended or continued. Therefore, a Case Management Order may, for good cause shown, be amended upon Order of the Court.

All requests for an enlargement or limitation of a scheduled event shall be in a filed, written motion to the trial judge or his designee. In the event that the Scheduling Order is amended, the clerk shall enter the amended dates in the court's case management system and shall revise the Case Management Order accordingly.

VIII. Pretrial Conference Date

Counsel and defendant will appear in court for the Pretrial Conference, pursuant to Fla. R. Crim. P. 3.180(a)(3) and 3.220(p)(1). Prior to the Pretrial Conference, counsel will consult and Plea offer will be discussed. At the Pretrial Conference, a "PRETRIAL CONFERENCE ORDER" (Attachment C), will set forth the status of discovery and acceptance/rejection of the Plea offer.

No continuances for lack of time for discovery or depositions will be approved unless received 30 days prior to scheduled date and only granted for extraordinary reasons. All requests for a continuance shall be in submitted in a filed, written motion to the trial judge or his designee.

<u>Cases not reaching a Plea Agreement at the Pretrial Conference will be immediately set for a Trial Call, date to occur within 45 days, with a Trial certain date following within the next 14 days.</u>

In complex cases, or where necessary, a Final Pretrial Conference may be held 14 days prior to the scheduled trial date at the Judge's discretion. This conference is intended for the purpose of planning the trial and to dispose of any remaining trial motions that may be pending. Three (3) days prior to the Final Trial Conference, counsel is to submit a Joint Pretrial Memorandum, with the State being responsible for preparing the first draft to contain:

- **Stipulations of the Parties**
- **List of any trial motions to be heard**
- **Special needs of the case (e.g. interpreter)**
- **Estimated length of the trial**

IX. Trial Date Certainty/Trial Calendaring

Trial dates will only be set on cases ready for trial. Trial dates will be set at the Pretrial Conference to occur within 45 days of the date of the Pretrial Conference.

In order to maintain trial certainty, a reasonable number of cases will be set for trial on every Monday of a trial week. The court will try cases on the day set, or later during the trial week. Cases not reached for trial on or by Thursday of the trial week may be carried over to the following Monday as a priority trial case.

No continuance of the trial date will be granted on basis of discovery or witness unavailability. Requests for continuance to another date within the Trial Cycle will be considered if received within 15 days of the Trial Notice provided at the Pretrial Conference. Requests for continuance made after 15 days from Notice of Trial date will only be considered for extraordinary circumstances.

X. Judicial Discretion

It is understood that specific situations may arise from time to time, which require some variation from the procedures set forth above. In the interest of justice, to address specific concerns in unusual circumstances, and in the promotion of judicial efficiency, the trial Judge, in his or her sound discretion, may extend the time periods and alter procedural requirements herein before mandated.

XI. Circuitwide Application

To promote uniformity in practice throughout the 20th Circuit, it is ultimately intended that these Criminal Case Management procedures and time standards be applied and implemented in each of the five counties within the Twentieth Judicial Circuit. However, recognizing that each county may have differing needs requiring deviations from the plan set forth herein, the Circuit Administrative Judge of each respective county may submit to the Chief Judge a written proposed plan and procedure that, upon approval by the Chief Judge, may be applied in the respective county.

XII. Effect

The procedures set forth herein are intended to facilitate the timely, fair and effective resolution of criminal cases while ensuring the efficient use of court resources. They do not supplant any existing rule of criminal procedure or statute. A defendant's statutory right to a speedy trial is determined by Fla. R. Crim. P. 3.191 and not by reference to these procedures and time standards.

LAST UPDATED DRAFT: November 19, 2007

ATTACHMENT A

IN THE CIRCUIT COURT OF THE TWENTIETH JUDICIAL CIRCUIT

IN AND FOR ________ COUNTY, FLORIDA— CRIMINAL DIVISION

STATE OF FLORIDA

Case No.

v.

________________ /

ORDER SETTING CASE MANAGEMENT CONFERENCE

Pursuant to Rule 2.545, Florida Rules of Judicial Administration, the court, after review of the Court file, hereby **ORDERS**

That Defendant,[2] Defendant's counsel of record, and the Assistant State Attorney assigned to the case, appear for a case management conference on ________, **at ________ p.m./a.m, in ________, Florida.**

It is further ordered that counsel be prepared to discuss all aspects of case management and scheduling, to include, without limitation, the following:

1. Discovery, including initial discovery disclosure, reciprocal discovery, depositions, expert witness issues, any discovery issues requiring a motion to compel or an order to show cause.

2. Any pre-trial motions pending or contemplated, to include scheduling issues related to such motions. This would include suppression motions, child heresay[3] motions, and/or *Williams* Rule motions.

3. Any conflict issues concerning representation.

4. Any competency issues.

5. Trial date and expected length of trial.

6. Pre-trial Conference date.

7. Plea cut-off date.

8. Motions; filing deadline and scheduling.

9. Discovery deadline.

10. Schedule additional case management conferences if necessary.

11. Any other issues affecting a timely resolution of this case.

DONE AND ORDERED at Fort Myers, Lee County, Florida, this ___ day of ________, 20 ___.

____
Circuit Court Judge

If you are a person with a disability in accordance with the Americans with Disabilities Act who needs any accommodation in order to participate in this proceeding, you are entitled, at no cost to you, to the provision of certain assistance. Please contact ________ whose office is located at ________ and whose telephone number is ________, within two working days of your receipt of this notice; if you are hearing or voice impaired, call 1–800–955–8771.

CERTIFICATE OF SERVICE

I HEREBY CERTIFY that a true and correct copy of the above order has been furnished to:
this ___ day of ________, 20 ___.

By: ________________

[1] So in original.

[2] Pursuant to Rules 3.180(a)(3) and 3.220(p)(1), Florida Rules of Criminal Procedure, the Defendant must be present at any pretrial conference.

[3] So in original.

Attachment B

IN THE CIRCUIT COUNTY COURT OF THE TWENTIETH JUDICIAL CIRCUIT
IN AND FOR LEE COUNTY, FLORIDA
CRIMINAL DIVISION

STATE OF FLORIDA CASE NO.:

vs. TRACK:

DATE:

CASE MANAGEMENT CONFERENCE ORDER

A Score Sheet and Plea Offer have been completed and reviewed: ☐ Yes ☐ No
The PLEA has been: ☐ Accepted. PLEA ACCEPTANCE HEARING set for: ________
☐ Rejected.

SPEEDY TRIAL has been: ☐ WAIVED ☐ NOT WAIVED ☐ TOLLED

1. Track Amended to: ☐ A–Expedited ☐ B–Standard ☐ C–Complex

2. All Pretrial Discovery/Depositions/Expert Evaluations TO BE COMPLETED before: ________________

3. All MOTIONS/PRETRIAL HEARINGS, shall be disposed before: ________

4. Estimated length of TRIAL: ________________

5. Projected TRIAL Month and Year: ________________

____

Pre Trial Conference Date and Time: ________________

ALL PARTIES MUST APPEAR

Once approved at this Case Management Conference, this ORDER is your official notice of dates and required court appearance. It may not be modified except by leave of Court upon a showing of good cause; stipulations between counsel shall not be effective to change any deadlines in the order absent Court approval.

If the above named defendant fails to appear at the next or any subsequent court date, a warrant shall be Issued for the defendant's arrest and any bond shall be forfeited.

Defendant

Counsel for Defendant Assistant State Attorney

Signed and approved this ______ day of 2007.

Honorable

CLERK: white STATE ATTORNEY: yellow DEFENSE ATTORNEY: pink BAILIFF: goldenrod

Attachment C

IN THE CIRCUIT COUNTY COURT OF THE TWENTIETH JUDICIAL CIRCUIT IN AND FOR LEE COUNTY, FLORIDA CRIMINAL DIVISION

STATE OF FLORIDA CASE NO.:

vs. TRACK:

DATE:

PRETRIAL CONFERENCE ORDER

A Score Sheet and Plea Offer have been completed and reviewed: ☐ Yes ☐ No

The PLEA has been: ☐ Accepted. PLEA ACCEPTANCE HEARING set for: ______
☐ Rejected.

SPEEDY TRIAL has been: ☐ WAIVED ☐ NOT WAIVED ☐ TOLLED

1. All Pretrial Discovery HAS BEEN COMPLETED: ☐ Yes ☐ No
2. All Depositions HAVE BEEN COMPLETED: ☐ Yes ☐ No
3. All Expert Evaluations HAVE BEEN COMPLETED: ☐ Yes ☐ No
4. All Motions/Pretrial Hearings HAVE BEEN DISPOSED: ☐ Yes ☐ No
IF NOT, MOTION TO BE HEARD:
5. Estimated length of TRIAL:
6. TRIAL on: ______ @ ______

IF ORDERED BY THE COURT: Next Pretrial Conference Date and Time: ______

ALL PARTIES MUST APPEAR

Once approved at this Pretrial Conference, this ORDER is your official notice of dates and required court appearance. It may not be modified except by leave of Court upon a showing of good cause; stipulations between counsel shall not be effective to change any deadlines in the order absent Court approval.

If the above named defendant fails to appear at the next or any subsequent court date, a warrant shall be issued for the defendant's arrest and any bond shall be forfeited.

Defendant

Counsel for Defendant Assistant State Attorney

Signed and approved this ______ day of 2007.

Honorable

CLERK: white STATE ATTORNEY: yellow DEFENSE ATTORNEY: pink BAILIFF: goldenrod

3.26. FELONY CASE MANAGEMENT ADVISORY COMMITTEE FOR LEE COUNTY

IN THE TWENTIETH JUDICIAL CIRCUIT IN AND FOR THE STATE OF FLORIDA

IN RE: FELONY CASE MANAGEMENT ADVISORY COMMITTEE FOR LEE COUNTY

Administrative Order No. 3.26

WHEREAS, it is in the best interest of the citizens of the Twentieth Judicial Circuit for the Court to develop innovative means to further improve the fair, predictable, efficient, and timely disposition of felony criminal cases in the Circuit Criminal Court, and

WHEREAS, in furtherance of this interest, Administrative Order 3.25 was executed on December 6, 2007, for the purpose of formally establishing and implementing a criminal case management plan, and

WHEREAS, this criminal case management plan was initially implemented in Lee County and is currently being used in Lee County, and

WHEREAS, it is recognized that discussions regarding of the implementation and use of the criminal case management plan and recommendations as to how to further the goals of the plan are beneficial to the interests of all parties involved,

It is ORDERED that a standing Felony Case Management Advisory Committee for Lee County is hereby formally created.

The Committee shall be charged with the responsibility of discussing the implementation and use of the criminal case management plan as established by Administrative Order 3.25, and, specifically, with formulating and presenting any recommendations involving:

1. issues concerning felony case management,
2. standardized criminal case management procedures,
3. proposed changes to Administrative Order 3.25, and
4. proposed changes to the current felony case management plan.

The following persons, or successors, are appointed as members of the standing Felony Case Management Advisory Committee for Lee County:

1. all Lee County Circuit Judges serving in the felony division,
2. the Administrative Circuit Court Judge for Lee County,
3. the State Attorney of the Twentieth Judicial Circuit, or designee,
4. the Public Defender of the Twentieth Judicial Circuit, or designee,
5. the Criminal Conflict and Civil Regional Counsel, or designee,
6. the Lee County Clerk of Courts, or designee,
7. the Lee County Sheriff, or designee,
8. a member of the private criminal defense bar to be designated by the Chair of the Committee, and

9. the Criminal Division Director of the Administrative Office of the Courts, or designee.

The Chair of the standing Felony Case Management Advisory Committee for Lee County shall be selected by the Chief Judge. Staff support will be provided by the Administrative Office of the Courts. The Committee shall meet as soon after this Order is entered as is practicable and thereafter under such circumstances and timeframes as the Committee deems appropriate. Any and all recommendations shall be presented to the Chief Judge and the Trial Court Administrator. Travel expenses of Committee members cannot be reimbursed by the Court.

This Administrative Order shall remain in effect until otherwise revoked, amended or modified. To the extent that this order may conflict with any law or rule, the law or rule shall prevail.

DONE AND ORDEREDin chambers in Fort Myers, Lee County, Florida this 16 day of Dec, 2008.

G. Keith Cary
Chief Judge

3.27. ASSIGNMENT OF MULTIPLE FELONY CASES INVOLVING A SINGLE DEFENDANT OR CO–DEFENDANTS IN LEE COUNTY

IN THE TWENTIETH JUDICIAL CIRCUIT IN AND FOR LEE COUNTY, FLORIDA

IN RE: ASSIGNMENT OF MULTIPLE FELONY CASES INVOLVING A SINGLE DEFENDANT OR CO–DEFENDANTS IN LEE COUNTY

Administrative Order 3.27

WHEREAS the assignment and reassignment of specific court cases between or among judges of a multi-judge court is a matter within the internal government of that court and is directed and controlled by policy adopted by the judges of that court, either directly or by and through their chief judge, Kruckenberg v. Powell, 422 So. 2d 994 (Fla. 5th DCA 1982); and

WHEREAS, recognizing the limited nature of judicial resources, it is generally in the interest of judicial economy and efficiency that related cases, companion cases, or cases involving a single defendant or co-defendants be addressed by a single judge;

It is, therefore, by the authority vested in the Chief Judge by Fla. R. Jud. Admin. 2.215(b),

ORDERED as follows as it relates to felony cases in Lee County:

1. In any case in which a single defendant has multiple felony cases arising on the same date of arrest, the Clerk shall assign the first felony case of that defendant to a judge, and shall manually assign to that same judge all additional felony cases of that same defendant arising on that same date of arrest.

2. In any case in which co-defendants are listed on the arrest report, and the arrests occur on the same date, the Clerk shall assign the first case invoking the first defendant to a judge, and shall manually assign to that same judge all additional felony cases of the remaining co-defendants.

3. When a defendant has more than one pending felony case in Lee County involving different dates of arrest, the more recent felony case or cases shall be reassigned to the judge assigned to the pending felony case with the oldest arrest date. Upon becoming aware of the fact that a defendant has more than one pending felony case in Lee County, the Office of the State Attorney shall be responsible for requesting reassignment of the more recent felony case or cases in accordance with this Administrative Order and shall submit a proposed order of reassignment for the signature of the Chief Judge or the Chief Judge's designee.

4. In any case in which the State has filed felony charges against multiple defendants arising from the same set of facts, transactions or occurrences, the judge assigned to the pending felony case with the oldest arrest date, or if the cases have the same arrest date, the judge assigned to the felony case with the lowest case number, shall preside over the related cases against all co-defendants. The related cases shall be reassigned to that judge, and the Clerk shall change the case numbers of the reassigned cases so as to match the case number of the felony case with the oldest arrest date, or lowest case number, and shall assign each co-defendant an alphabetical designator (A, B, C, etc.). The Office of the State Attorney shall be responsible for requesting reassignment of the related case or cases in accordance with this Administrative Order and shall submit a proposed order of reassignment for the signature of the Chief Judge or the Chief Judge's designee.

5. In unique circumstances, in which the Office of the State Attorney is of the opinion that it is not in the best interest of justice that the felony cases of all co-defendants be assigned to a single judge, the Office of the State Attorney shall advise the Lee County Presiding Felony Judge in writing, with copies to opposing counsel, or if unrepresented by counsel, to the defendant or defendants. In such instances, the final decision as to whether a case is to be reassigned shall rest with the Chief Judge, or the Chief Judge's designee, upon consultation with the Lee County Presiding Felony Judge and consideration of the written request submitted by the Office of the State Attorney.

6. All felony cases that are re-filed after having been previously dismissed for any reason, or are reopened after having been previously disposed, are to be assigned or reassigned to the same judge assigned to the case that had been previously dismissed or disposed. In the event that the judge has since retired or is no longer serving in the Lee County Circuit Criminal division for any reason, the re-filed case shall be assigned or reassigned to the judge now presiding over the prior judge's track. If the Clerk does not automatically make the appropriate assignment at the time the case is initially re-filed, the Office of the State Attorney shall be responsible for requesting reassignment of the re-filed case in accordance with this Administrative Order and shall submit a proposed order of reassignment for the signature of the Chief Judge or the Chief Judge's designee.

7. In all situations in which cases are manually assigned or reassigned, the Clerk shall account for these to the extent reasonably practical, and shall assign new felony cases in a

manner so as to allow for the redistribution of caseload to obtain a fair and equal assignment of cases among judges serving in the Lee County Circuit Criminal division.

8. As it relates to capital murder cases, or any other cases involving the death of a victim, the Lee County Presiding Felony Judge is authorized to monitor the caseloads of the judges serving in the Lee County Circuit Criminal division and may, within the discretion of the Lee County Presiding Felony Judge, recommend to the Chief Judge, or the Chief Judge's designee, the reassignment of any such cases so as to allow for the redistribution of caseload to obtain a fair and equal assignment of capital murder cases, or any other cases involving the death of a victim, among judges serving in the Lee County Circuit Criminal division.

9. This Administrative Order shall be effective immediately and shall apply to the assignment and reassignment of cases in the Lee County Circuit Criminal division.

10. To the extent that this Administrative Order may conflict with any prior Administrative Order, this Administrative Order shall prevail.

11. To the extent that this Administrative Order may conflict with any rule, law, or statute, the rule, law, or statute shall prevail.

DONE AND ORDERED in Chambers, in Fort Myers, Lee County, Florida, this 22 day of November, 2010.

G. Keith Cary
Chief Judge

3.28. CONVENING OF GRAND JURY

IN THE TWENTIETH JUDICIAL CIRCUIT IN AND FOR LEE COUNTY, FLORIDA

IN RE: CONVENING OF GRAND JURY

Administrative Order 3.28

WHEREAS, the Florida Legislature during the 2013 session passed House Bill No. 7017, which was entered into law effective January 1, 2014, Laws of Florida, Chapter 2013–25; and

WHEREAS, Chapter 2013–25 amended Florida Statute § 905.01(3) to provide that "The chief judge of each circuit court shall regularly order the convening of the grand jury for a term of 6 months;"

It is, therefore, by the authority vested in the Chief Judge by Fla. R. Jud. Admin. 2.215(b),

ORDERED that effective January 1, 2014, Grand Juries for the counties of the Twentieth Judicial Circuit shall be convened for 6 month terms covering the periods of January 1st through June 30th and July 1st through December 31st. Regardless of the exact date of impanelment, the 6 month term shall terminate as set forth above, unless an extension is requested pursuant to Florida Statute § 905.095.

This Administrative Order shall be effective January 1, 2014, *nunc pro tunc*.

DONE AND ORDERED in Chambers, in Fort Myers, Lee County, Florida, this 21st day of January, 2014.

Jay B. Rosman
Chief Judge

History. —New.

3.29. PROCEDURES FOR ENSURING THE SECURE EXCHANGE OF CIRCUIT COURT SENTENCING MODIFICATION ORDERS AND VERIFICATION FORMS BETWEEN THE COURT AND CLERKS

IN THE TWENTIETH JUDICIAL CIRCUIT IN AND FOR THE STATE OF FLORIDA

ADMINISTRATIVE ORDER NO. 3.29

IN RE: PROCEDURES FOR ENSURING THE SECURE EXCHANGE OF CIRCUIT COURT SENTENCING MODIFICATION ORDERS AND VERIFICATION FORMS BETWEEN THE COURT AND CLERKS

WHEREAS, on March 17, 2014, the Supreme Court of Florida issued Administrative Order No. AOSC14–18, In re: Security of a Circuit Court Order Modifying Sentence of Person in State Correctional Facility or Detention Facility; and

WHEREAS, paragraph 1.C. of Administrative Order No. AOSC14–18 provides that "[t]he chief judge and the clerk of court shall establish a secure process for the exchange of modification orders in paper format and for the exchange of court verification forms or other documents related to modification orders;"

By the authority vested in the Chief Judge pursuant to Fla. R. Jud. Admin. 2.215, it is **ORDERED** that the procedures established by the Court and Clerk of Courts of each of the five counties within the Twentieth Judicial Circuit so as to ensure a secure process for the exchange of paper modification orders, verification forms, and other documents related to modification orders, are hereby memorialized by Attachments A through E included herein.

DONE AND ORDERED in chambers in Fort Myers, Lee County, Florida, this 2nd day of June, 2014.

Jay B. Rosman
Chief Judge

History. –New

Attachment A

–LEE COUNTY—

PROCEDURES FOR SECURE EXCHANGE OF PAPER CIRCUIT COURT SENTENCING MODIFICATION ORDERS AND VERIFICATION FORMS BETWEEN THE COURT AND CLERKS

1. Original signed orders, or other court documents requiring judicial signatures, are transmitted for filing from Judicial Offices to the Lee Clerk's Office by having Judicial staff place those orders, or other court documents, in out-boxes located within Judicial secured areas un-accessible to the public, and are picked up regularly by assigned Clerk staff with approved access to Judicial secured areas.

2. The Lee Clerk will only accept and process orders that are:

a. Signed in open court and received by Clerk staff directly from the Judge;

b. Orders picked up by Clerk staff from the Judicial secured areas as described above in Paragraph 1; or

c. Hand–delivered directly by a known Judicial Assistant to Clerk staff.

3. The Lee Clerk will NOT accept original signed orders, or other court documents requiring judicial signatures, delivered to the Clerk's office or to Clerk staff by an attorney or by any other means outside of the parameters set forth herein, including U.S Mail or inter-office mail.

4. Receipt / Processing of Order:

a. If an Order is received by the Clerk with a Court Verification Form, the documents will be scanned and docketed to the Clerk's Case Management System,

b. If an Order is received without the Clerk Verification Form, the Clerk will create one and send it via email to Court Administration for judicial signature. Once the document has been signed by the appropriate judge, the form will be picked up by assigned Clerk staff from the designated secured judicial area. The documents will then be scanned and docketed to the Clerk's Case Management System.

c. At this time, there is no ability for Judges to submit original signed orders or other court documents through the secure e-filing portal. At such time as the submission of signed orders becomes technologically available, such submissions to the Clerk shall also be deemed an acceptable and secure method of transmission,

5. Distribution of Order

a. A copy of the order, and when applicable, Court Verification Form will be sent to the listed parties within the Certificate of Service, via a secured electronic method or via U.S Mail.

Attachment B

–COLLIER COUNTY—

PROCEDURES FOR SECURE EXCHANGE OF PAPER CIRCUIT COURT SENTENCING MODIFICATION ORDERS AND VERIFICATION FORMS BETWEEN THE COURT AND CLERKS

1. Original signed orders, or other court documents requiring judicial signatures, are transmitted for filing from Judicial Offices to the Collier Clerk's Office by having Judicial staff place those orders, or other court documents, in out-boxes located within Judicial secured areas un-accessible to the public, and are picked up regularly by assigned Clerk staff with approved access to Judicial secured areas.

2. The Collier Clerk will only accept for filing orders that are:

a. Signed in open court and received by Clerk staff directly from the Judge;

b. Orders picked up by Clerk staff from the Judicial secured areas as described above in Paragraph 1; or

c. Hand–delivered directly by a known Judicial Assistant to Clerk staff.

3. The Collier Clerk will NOT accept original signed orders, or other court documents requiring judicial signatures, delivered to the Clerk's office or to Clerk staff by an attorney or by any other means outside of the parameters set forth herein.

4. To the extent that there may be unique situations in which an original signed order, or other court document requiring a judicial signature, must be transmitted by mail, (i.e. a Judge from another county presiding over a Collier case and submitting to the Collier Clerk an original signed order on a matter over with the non–Collier Judge reserved ruling), Judicial staff and Clerk staff shall communicate appropriately so as to ensure the validity of the order and the circumstances requiring transmittal outside of the parameters set forth herein.

5. At this time, there is no ability for Judges to submit original signed orders or other court documents through the secure e-filing portal. At such time as the submission of signed orders and other court documents through the secure e-filing portal becomes technologically available, such submissions to the Clerk shall also be deemed an acceptable and secure method of transmission.

Attachment C

–CHARLOTTE COUNTY—

PROCEDURES FOR SECURE EXCHANGE OF PAPER CIRCUIT COURT SENTENCING MODIFICATION ORDERS AND VERIFICATION FORMS BETWEEN THE COURT AND CLERKS

In response to Florida Supreme Court Administrative Order AOCS14–18, the Charlotte County Clerk of Court has instituted the following procedures.

1. Paper Orders:

A. Sentence modification orders or court minute forms signed by the Judge in court and orders signed in chambers shall be maintained by the court clerk who shall provide a Court Verification Form (CVF) to the Judge for signature. The CVF and order/minutes shall be maintained together and in the control of the clerk until the clerk returns to the secure criminal division offices.

B. The forms will be reviewed by a criminal division supervisor.

C. If the sentence modification is for a Charlotte County Jail inmate, the certified forms are hand delivered to the jail by a clerk courier.

D. If the sentence modification is for a DOC inmate, the certified forms are sent to the DOC at their Tallahassee office. The DOC normally calls the Judge to confirm the authenticity of the forms.

E. Both the DOC and County jail personnel have access to the clerk's case maintenance system.

2. Electronic Transmission:

A. Until an in-court processing system is operational, sentence modification orders will come to the clerk in paper form.

B. When an order is received, the clerk will send a CVF to the Judge for signature.

C. When the CVF is returned, a supervisor will review the forms prior to forwarding to the appropriate party as per paragraph D above.

3. Oral Orders:

A. The Judge signs the court minutes and CVF in court and the process for paper orders above proceeds.

Attachment D

–HENDRY COUNTY—

PROCEDURES FOR SECURE EXCHANGE OF PAPER CIRCUIT COURT SENTENCING MODIFICATION ORDERS AND VERIFICATION FORMS BETWEEN THE COURT AND CLERKS

1. Original signed orders, or other court documents requiring judicial signatures, are transmitted for filing from Judicial Offices to the Hendry Clerk's Office by having them hand-delivered by known Judicial staff directly to known Clerk staff or by having known Clerk staff pick them up directly from known Judicial staff. Original signed orders, or other court documents requiring judicial signatures, are never left in unattended areas that may be accessible to the public.

2. The Hendry Clerk will only accept for filing orders that are:

a. Signed in open court and received by Clerk staff directly from the Judge; or

b. Orders transmitted directly between Judicial staff and Clerk staff as described above in Paragraph 1.

3. The Hendry Clerk will NOT accept original signed orders, or other court documents requiring judicial signatures, delivered to the Clerk's office or to Clerk staff by an attorney or by any other means outside of the parameters set forth herein.

4. To the extent that there may be unique situations in which an original signed order, or other court document requiring a judicial signature, must be transmitted by mail, (i.e. a Judge from another county presiding over a Hendry case and submitting to the Hendry Clerk an original signed order on a matter over with the non–Hendry Judge reserved ruling), Judicial staff and Clerk staff shall communicate appropriately so as to ensure the validity of the order and the circumstances requiring transmittal outside of the parameters set forth herein.

5. At this time, there is no ability for Judges to submit original signed orders or other court documents through the secure e-filing portal. At such time as the submission of signed orders and other court documents through the secure e-filing portal becomes technologically available, such submissions to the Clerk shall also be deemed an acceptable and secure method of transmission.

Attachment E

–GLADES COUNTY—

PROCEDURES FOR SECURE EXCHANGE OF PAPER CIRCUIT COURT SENTENCING MODIFICATION ORDERS AND VERIFICATION FORMS BETWEEN THE COURT AND CLERKS

1. Original signed orders, or other court documents requiring judicial signatures, are transmitted for filing from Judicial Offices to the Glades Clerk's Office by having them hand-delivered by known Judicial staff directly to known Clerk staff or by having known Clerk staff pick them up directly from known Judicial staff. Original signed orders, or other court documents requiring judicial signatures, are never left in unattended areas that may be accessible to the public.

2. The Glades Clerk will only accept for filing orders that are:

a. Signed in open court and received by Clerk staff directly from the Judge; or

b. Orders transmitted directly between Judicial staff and Clerk staff as described above in Paragraph 1.

3. The Glades Clerk will NOT accept original signed orders, or other court documents requiring judicial signatures, delivered to the Clerk's office or to Clerk staff by an attorney, by any member of the public, or by any other means outside of the parameters set forth herein.

4. To the extent that there may be unique situations in which an original signed order, or other court document requiring a judicial signature, must be transmitted by mail, (i.e. a Judge from another county presiding over a Glades case and submitting to the Glades Clerk an original signed order on a matter over with the non–Glades Judge reserved ruling), Judicial staff and Clerk staff shall communicate appropriately so as to ensure the validity of the order and the circumstances requiring transmittal outside of the parameters set forth herein.

5. At this time, there is no ability for Judges to submit original signed orders or other court documents through the secure e-filing portal. At such time as the submission of signed orders and other court documents through the secure e-filing portal becomes technologically available, such submissions to the Clerk shall also be deemed an acceptable and secure method of transmission.

3.30. ESTABLISHMENT OF MENTAL HEALTH COURTS

IN THE TWENTIETH JUDICIAL CIRCUIT IN AND FOR THE STATE OF FLORIDA

ADMINISTRATIVE ORDER NO. 3.30

IN RE: ESTABLISHMENT OF MENTAL HEALTH COURTS

Pursuant to Article V, Section 7 of the Florida Constitution, the Chief Judge authorizes the establishment and continued maintenance of specialty Mental Health Courts in any county or counties within the Twentieth Judicial Circuit. Mental Health Courts shall be within the division of the Criminal Court (felony or misdemeanor), as may be appropriate.

In recognition of the distinct features and resources of the five individual counties of the Twentieth Judicial Circuit, Mental Health Courts are authorized, though not mandated, and the establishment and continued maintenance of Mental Health Courts is subject to policies and procedures as may be applicable to individual counties and divisions, and is subject to any Mental Health Court Program Manuals. Any such policies, procedures, and Mental Health Court Program Manuals, and the actual establishment and continued maintenance of Mental Health Courts within any county or division, is subject to the approval of the Chief Judge and/or the Chief Judge's designee.

As established, Mental Health Courts will preside exclusively over appropriate cases involving arrested persons who suffer from mental health issues. Referrals to Mental Health Courts will be considered on the basis of the facts and circumstances unique to the individual and to that individual's case or cases. All defendants identified for referral to Mental Health Courts must meet all requirements for participation set forth under applicable Florida Statutes, as well as requirements of any other controlling Mental Health Court orders and program manuals.

Entry by a qualified defendant into a Mental Health Court program shall be on a voluntary basis. However, once a qualified defendant has voluntarily agreed to participate in Mental Health Court, the defendant will be deemed to have accepted the requirements of the program and to have agreed that the Mental Health Court judge may order coercive sanctions, which may include (as may be applicable and authorized by law) incarceration, community service, and other coercive measures intended to motivate the defendant to overcome or address his or her mental health problems or issues.

Upon successful participation and completion of a Mental Health Court program, a defendant may, in certain cases, be permitted to withdraw his or her plea, and the State Attorney's Office may reduce or dismiss the charge or charges.

This Administrative Order supersedes any prior administrative orders relating to the establishment or maintenance of Mental Health Courts within the Twentieth Judicial Circuit.

To the extent that any provision of this Administrative Order may be construed as being in conflict with any law, statute, or rule, the law, statute, or rule shall prevail.

DONE AND ORDERED in Chambers at Fort Myers, Lee County, Florida, this 5th day of April, 2016.

Michael T. McHugh

Chief Judge

History.—New.

3.31. ESTABLISHMENT OF MILITARY VETERANS AND SERVICEMEMBERS COURT

IN THE TWENTIETH JUDICIAL CIRCUIT IN AND FOR THE STATE OF FLORIDA

ADMINISTRATIVE ORDER NO. 3.31

IN RE: ESTABLISHMENT OF MILITARY VETERANS AND SERVICEMEMBERS COURT

Pursuant to Article V, Section 7 of the Florida Constitution and Florida Statute sections 394.47891, 948.08, and 948.16 the Chief Judge authorizes the establishment and continued maintenance of specialty Military Veterans and Servicemembers Courts (hereinafter "Veterans Treatment Courts") in any county or counties within the Twentieth Judicial Circuit. Veterans Treatment Courts shall be within the division of the Criminal Court (felony or misdemeanor), as may be appropriate.

In recognition of the distinct features and resources of the five individual counties of the Twentieth Judicial Circuit, Veterans Treatment Courts are authorized, though not mandated, and the establishment and continued maintenance of Veterans Treatment Courts is subject to policies and procedures as may be applicable to individual counties and divisions, and is subject to any Veterans Treatment Court Program Manuals. Any such policies, procedures, and Veterans Treatment Court Program Manuals, and the actual establishment and continued maintenance of Veterans Treatment Courts within any county or division, is subject to the approval of the Chief Judge and/or the Chief Judge's designee.

As established, Veterans Treatment Courts will preside exclusively over appropriate cases involving arrested persons who suffer from a military-related mental illness, traumatic brain injury, substance abuse disorder, or psychological problem. Referrals to Veterans Treatment Courts will be considered on the basis of the facts and circumstances unique to the individual and to that individual's case or cases. All defendants identified for referral to Veterans Treatment Courts must meet all requirements for participation set forth under applicable Florida Statutes, as well as requirements of any other controlling Veterans Treatment Court orders and program manuals.

Entry by a qualified defendant into a Veterans Treatment Court program shall be on a voluntary basis. However, once a qualified defendant has voluntarily agreed to participate in Veterans Treatment Court, the defendant will be deemed to have accepted the requirements of the program and to have agreed that the Veterans Treatment Court judge may order coercive sanctions, which may include (as may be applicable and authorized by law) incarceration, community service, and other coercive measures intended to motivate the defendant to overcome or address his or her military-related problems or issues.

Upon successful participation and completion of a Veterans Treatment Court program, a defendant may, in certain cases, be permitted to withdraw his or her plea, and the State Attorney's Office may reduce or dismiss the charge or charges.

To the extent that any provision of this Administrative Order may be construed as being in conflict with any law, statute, or rule, the law, statute, or rule shall prevail.

DONE AND ORDERED in Chambers at Fort Myers, Lee County, Florida, this 5th day of April, 2016.

Michael T. McHugh

Chief Judge

History.—New.

Probate

5.1. GUARDIANSHIP FINANCIAL RETURNS

IN THE TWENTIETH JUDICIAL CIRCUIT IN AND FOR THE STATE OF FLORIDA

IN RE: GUARDIANSHIP FINANCIAL RETURNS

ADMINISTRATIVE ORDER NO: 5.1

Pursuant to § 744.367 Fla. Stat. (1993), unless the Court requires filing on a calendar-year basis, each Guardian of the person shall file with the Court an annual guardianship plan within 90 days after the last day of the anniversary month the Letters of Guardianship were signed, and the plan must cover the coming fiscal year, ending in such anniversary month. If the Court requires calendar-year filing, the guardianship plan must be filed within 90 days after the end of the calendar year.

Unless the Court requires filing on a calendar-year basis, each Guardian of the property shall file with the Court an annual accounting on or before the first day of the fourth month after the end of the fiscal year. If the Court requires filings on a calendar-year basis, each accounting shall be filed on or before April 1 of each year.

This Order is intended to ameliorate the effects of what would otherwise be a deluge of filings of annual guardianship plans and annual accountings on or before April 1 of each year. Therefore, it is the express intent of this Order that all annual filings required by Florida Statute § 744.367 be accomplished on a fiscal-year basis, unless the Court orders that the filings occur on a calendar-year basis. In that event, the annual plan and/or accounting is required to be filed on or before April 1 of each year.

DONE AND ORDERED in Chambers at Fort Myers, Lee County, Florida, this 14 day of February, 1995.

Thomas S. Reese
Chief Judge

History. - Administrative Order 5.1 (October 1, 1990); Administrative Order 5.1 (January 9, 1994).

5.2. APPOINTMENT OF PUBLIC DEFENDER TO REPRESENT RESPONDENTS IN PROCEEDINGS BROUGHT UNDER "THE FLORIDA MENTAL HEALTH ACT" OR "THE BAKER ACT"

IN THE TWENTIETH JUDICIAL CIRCUIT IN AND FOR THE STATE OF FLORIDA

ADMINISTRATIVE ORDER NO. 5.2

IN RE: APPOINTMENT OF PUBLIC DEFENDER TO REPRESENT RESPONDENTS IN PROCEEDINGS BROUGHT UNDER "THE FLORIDA MENTAL HEALTH ACT" OR "THE BAKER ACT"

Pursuant to Part I of Chapter 394 of the Florida Statutes and this Court's inherent authority to administer and regulate the Courts as provided in Fla. R. Jud. Admin. 2.050, it is **ORDERED AND ADJUDGED** as follows:

1. Each person who is the subject of a petition for involuntary commitment filed in accordance with Florida Statute § 394.451 et seq., also known as "The Florida Mental Health Act" or "The Baker Act," is entitled to legal representation.

2. Each person who is the subject of a petition brought pursuant to the Florida Mental Health Act or the Baker Act is, by operation of this order, initially deemed to be indigent upon the detention of the Respondent or the filing of a petition under the Act, whichever first occurs. All further determinations of indigency following detention shall be governed by Chapter 57 of the Florida Statutes.

3. Pursuant to the spirit and intent of Florida Statute § 394.459 of the Florida Mental Health Act or the Baker Act entitled "Rights of Patients", as well as the express provisions of Florida Statute § 394.467(4), the Public Defender is hereby appointed to represent each person who is the subject of a petition brought pursuant to the Florida Mental Health Act or the Baker

4. In the event that the Respondent is later deemed to be not indigent and not otherwise entitled to the services of an attorney pursuant to Chapter 394, the cost of such representation shall be assessed pursuant to Chapter 27 and any other applicable provision of Florida Law upon proper application to the Court.

The purpose of this order is to ensure that every person who is detained in this circuit pursuant to the provisions of Chapter 394 is represented by counsel in these proceedings.

Nothing in this order shall be construed so as to prevent any person or his or her guardian from hiring private counsel to represent the respondent in any proceeding brought pursuant to the Florida Mental Health Act or the Baker Act.

If private counsel is retained at any stage of the proceedings, the Public Defender shall thereafter withdraw from representation and the appropriate stipulation for substitution of counsel shall be filed with the Court with a concomitant request for substitution of counsel by appropriate order of the Court.

In the event private counsel is retained to represent an allegedly indigent respondent and a wavier [1] of costs is sought, counsel shall file a certificate as required by Florida Statute § 57.081(1).

DONE AND ORDERED in Chambers, at Naples, Collier County, Florida this 19 day of June, 2000.

William L. Blackwell
Chief Judge

History.—New.

[1] So in original.

5.3. APPROVAL OF COMMERCIAL DELIVERY SERVICES PURSUANT TO FLA. PROB. R. 5.040

IN THE TWENTIETH JUDICIAL CIRCUIT IN AND FOR THE STATE OF FLORIDA

ADMINISTRATIVE ORDER NO. 5.3

IN RE: APPROVAL OF COMMERCIAL DELIVERY SERVICES PURSUANT TO FLA. PROB. R. 5.040

WHEREAS, Florida Probate Rule 5.040(a)(3)(A) provides that the Chief Judge may approve the use of any commercial delivery service requiring a signed receipt for the purpose of serving formal notice under the Florida Probate Rules, it is

ORDERED that the following commercial delivery services requiring a signed receipt may be used for providing formal notice pursuant to Florida Probate Rule 5.040 in proceedings pending in the Twentieth Judicial Circuit:

1. Federal Express
2. United Parcel Service
3. Airborne Express
4. DHL Worldwide Express

DONE AND ORDERED in chambers in Naples, Collier County, Florida, this 18th day of December, 2003.

Hugh D. Hayes
Chief Judge

History.—New.

Traffic & Misdemeanor

6.1. COSTS IN COUNTY COURT

IN THE TWENTIETH JUDICIAL CIRCUIT IN AND FOR THE STATE OF FLORIDA

ADMINISTRATIVE ORDER NO: 6.1

IN RE: COSTS IN COUNTY COURT

Pursuant to the authorities cited below and the inherent authority of the court as provided in Fla. R. Jud. Admin. 2.215 and Florida Statute § 43.26, the following schedule of fees is hereby adopted for the County Court.

I. MISDEMEANOR, AND CRIMINAL TRAFFIC

A. Mandatory Court Costs

1. The County Court shall impose the following costs in all misdemeanor, criminal traffic and ordinance violations punishable as misdemeanor cases where the defendant pleads guilty or nolo contendere or is otherwise convicted of a misdemeanor:

$ 60	Local Government Criminal Justice Trust Fund Florida Statute 938.05(1)(a)
$ 65	County Court Costs Florida Statute 939.185(1)(a), when assessed by a county ordinance
$ 50	Crimes Compensation Trust Fund Florida Statute 938.03(1)
$ 20	Crime Prevention Fund Florida Statute 775.083(2)
$ 3	Additional Court Cost Clearing Trust Fund Florida Statute 938.01(1)
$ 2	Local Law Enforcement Education and Training Florida Statute 938.15, when assessed by a county or municipality

2. The County Court shall impose the following surcharges on each misdemeanor fine that is assessed against a defendant:

$ 20	Crime Stoppers Trust Fund Florida Statute 938.06(1)
5%	5% surcharge on fine for Crimes Compensation Trust Fund Florida Statute 938.04

3. The County Court shall impose the following cost in all misdemeanor traffic violation cases (violations of F.S. 316) where the defendant pleads guilty or nolo contendere or is otherwise convicted of a misdemeanor traffic offense:

$ 15	Court Facilities Florida Statute 318.18(13)(a)
$ 3	State Radio System Surcharge Florida Statute 318.18(17)

4. The County Court shall impose the following additional court costs for each misdemeanor case in which the unlawful use of drugs or alcohol is involved, where the defendant pleads guilty or nolo contendere or is otherwise convicted, only if the Board of County Commissioners has adopted an ordinance requiring the collection of these costs:

$ 15	Drug Abuse Trust Fund Florida Statute 938.13(1)(a), when assessed by a county ordinance

5. The County Court shall impose the following additional court costs for each misdemeanor violation of Florida Statute 316.061(1) (Leaving Scene of Accident with Property Damage) or 316.192 (Reckless Driving) where the defendant pleads guilty or nolo contendere or is otherwise convicted:

$ 5	E.M.S. Trust Fund Florida Statute 316.061(1), 316.192(4)

6. The County Court shall impose the following additional court costs for each misdemeanor violation of Florida Statute 316.193 (DUI) where the defendant pleads guilty or nolo contendere or is otherwise convicted:

$135	E.M.S. Trust Fund Operating Trust Fund of the Dept. of Law Enforcement Brain & Spinal Cord Injury Rehab. Trust Fund Florida Statute 938.07

7. The County Court shall impose the following additional court costs for each misdemeanor violation of Florida Statute 327.35 (BUI) where the defendant pleads guilty or nolo contendere or is otherwise convicted:

$135	E.M.S. Trust Fund Operating Trust Fund of the Dept. of Law Enforcement Brain & Spinal Cord Injury Rehab. Trust Fund Florida Statute 938.07
$ 60	Brain & Spinal Cord Injury Rehab. Trust Fund Florida Statute 327.35(9)

8. The County Court shall impose the following additional court costs for each misdemeanor violation of Florida Statutes 784.011, 784.021, 784.03, 784.041, 784.045, 784.048, 784.07, 784.08, 784.081, 784.082, 784.083, 784.085, 794.011, or for any offense of domestic violence described in Fla. Stat. 741.28 where the defendant pleads guilty or nolo contendere or is otherwise convicted:

$201	Domestic Violence Surcharge Domestic Violence Trust Fund Florida Statute 938.08
$151	Rape Crisis Center Florida Statute 938.085

9. The County Court shall impose the following additional court costs for each misdemeanor offense against a minor in violation of Florida Statutes 784.085, chapter 787, chapter 794, 796.03, 800.04, chapter 827, 847. 0145, or 985.4045 where the defendant pleads guilty or nolo contendere or is otherwise convicted:

$101	Child Advocacy Trust Fund Florida Statute 938.10(1)

10. The County Court shall impose the following additional court costs for each municipal or county ordinance violation against the non-prevailing party:

$ 40	Clerk Fee Ordinance Florida Statute 28.2402(1)(b)

11. The County Court shall impose the costs of prosecution, including investigative costs:

$50 unless higher amount ordered by court	Cost of Prosecution & Investigation Florida Statute 938.27

12. The County Court shall assess attorney's fees and costs to any defendant convicted who has received the assistance of the public defender, regional counsel, or a conflict attorney:

$50 unless higher amount ordered by court	Public Defender Fees Florida Statute 938.29

B. Discretionary Court Costs

1. The County Court may impose the following additional court costs for each misdemeanor violation of Florida Statutes chapter 893, 316.193, 856.011, 856.015, chapter 562, chapter 567, or chapter 568, where the defendant pleads guilty or nolo contendere or is otherwise convicted:

Up to fine amount	Alcohol Drug Abuse Program Florida Statute 938.21

2. The County Court may impose the following additional court costs for each misdemeanor violation of Florida Statutes 893.13, where the defendant pleads guilty or nolo contendere or is otherwise convicted:

$100	Statewide Crime Lab Florida Statute 938.25

3. The County Court may impose the following fine for each misdemeanor violation of Florida Statutes where the defendant pleads guilty or nolo contendere or is otherwise convicted:

Up to $1,000	Fines (1st Degree Misdemeanor) Florida Statute 775.083
Up to $500	Fines (2nd Degree or Noncriminal Infraction) Florida Statute 775.083

II. CIVIL TRAFFIC

A. Payable Amounts

1. The following penalties shall be assessed when a person elects to pay the civil penalty by mail or in person:

$15	Pedestrian & Bicycle Violations Florida Statute 318.18(1)—Base Fine
See Appendix Item A	ATV Violations Florida Statutes 318.18(10)
See Appendix Item B	Nonmoving Violations Florida Statutes 318.18(2)
See Appendix Item C	Moving Violations Florida Statutes 318.18 (3)(a)
See Appendix Item D	Failure to stop for school bus Violations Florida Statutes 318.18(5)(a)
See Appendix Item E	Pass school bus on side children enter or exit Florida Statutes 318.18(5)(b)
See Appendix Item F	Illegal handicapped parking Florida Statute 318.18(6)
See Appendix Item G	Toll Violation Florida Statute 318.18(7)
See Appendix Item H	Load on Vehicle Violation Florida Statute 318.18(12)

See Appendix Item I — Speeding/Speeding in school or construction zone
Florida Statute 318.18(3)

2. The following court costs shall be assessed when a person elects to pay the civil penalty by mail or in person: (See Appendix)

$4 Pedestrian Violations
$18 Nonmoving Violations
$35 Moving Violations
Florida Statute 318.18(11)(a)
Up to $5 Driver Education
Florida Statute 318.1215, when assessed by a county ordinance
$2.50 Criminal Justice Education
Florida Statute 318.18(11)(c)
$3 Additional Court Costs Clearing Trust Fund
Florida Statute 938.01(1) & 318.18(11)(d)
$2 Local Law Enforcement Education and Training
Florida Statute 938.15, when assessed by a county or municipality & 318.18(11)(d)
Up to $15 Court Facilities
Florida Statute 318.18(13)(a), when assessed by county ordinance

B. Amounts After Hearing

1. If after a hearing, the official determines that an infraction was committed, the official may impose a civil penalty not to exceed $500, except in cases involving unlawful speed in a school zone, involving unlawful speed in a construction zone, or involving a death, the civil penalty may not exceed $1000.

2. The following court costs shall be assessed when an official determines an infraction has been committed: (See Appendix)

$4 Pedestrian Violations
$18 Nonmoving Violations
$35 Moving Violations
Florida Statute 318.18(11)(a)
Up to $5 Driver Education
Florida Statute 318.1215, when assessed by a county ordinance
$2.50 Criminal Justice Education
Florida Statute 318.18(11)(c)
$3 Additional Court Costs Clearing Trust Fund
Florida Statute 938.01(1) & 318.18(11)(d)
$2 Local Law Enforcement Education and Training
Florida Statute 938.15, when assessed by a county or municipality & 318.18(11)(d)
Up to $15 Court Facilities
Florida Statute 318.18(13)(a), when assessed by county ordinance

All fines, costs, penalties or other assessments against any defendant in accordance with this administrative order shall be collected by the Clerk of the Court and distributed in accordance with the applicable provisions of Florida law and the Distribution Schedule of Court–Related Filing Fees, Service Charges, Costs, and Fines published by the Florida Association of Court Clerks, Inc..

The monetary fines and costs imposed by the court shall be deemed to include only statutory and constitutional costs and fees. Any cost found to be unconstitutional by any court of superior jurisdiction shall be considered as part of the fine imposed and shall be distributed as otherwise provided by law.

To the extent that any provision of this Administrative Order may conflict with any rule, statute or law, the rule, statute or law shall prevail. More specifically, to the extent that the Legislature may make subsequent amendments that increase, decrease, add or delete any cost, fines or fees, those legislative amendments shall prevail.

DONE AND ORDERED in Chambers at Fort Myers, Florida, this 3 day of June, 2009.

G. Keith Cary
Chief Judge

History.—Administrative Order 3.1 (October 1, 1990); Administrative Order 3.1 (August 6, 1992); Administrative Order 3.1 (January 13, 2000); Administrative Order 3.1 (February 8, 2002); Administrative Order 3.1 (February 27, 2002); Administrative Order 3.1 (February 4, 2005).

APPENDIX TO ADMINISTRATIVE ORDER 6.1

A

ATV Violation Penalties

$25.00 Base Fine

Florida Statute 318.18 (10)

$15.00 Court Facilities

Florida Statute 318.18 (13)(a) when assessed by county ordinance

$2.00 Local Law Enforcement Education

Florida Statute 938.15 when assessed by county or municipality (Fort Myers only currently)

$3.00 Additional Court Cost Clearing Trust Fund

Florida Statute 318.18(11)(d)

$2.50 Additional Court Cost—Clerk

Florida Statute 318.18(11)(c)

$18.00 Court Cost

Florida Statute 318.18(11)(a)

$10.00 State Courts Revenue Trust Fund

Florida Statute 318.18(19)(c)

$12.50 Administrative Fee

Florida Statute 318.18(18)

$3.00 Dori Slosberg Driver Education Safety Act (BOCC ordinance states this as $3.00)

Florida Statute 318.1215

B

Nonmoving Violation Penalties

$30.00 Base Fine

Florida Statute 318.18 (10)

$15.00 Court Facilities

Florida Statute 318.18 (13)(a) when assessed by county ordinance

$2.00 Local Law Enforcement Education

Florida Statute 938.15 when assessed by county or municipality (Fort Myers only currently)

$3.00 Additional Court Cost Clearing Trust Fund

Florida Statute 318.18(11)(d)

$2.50 Additional Court Cost—Clerk

Florida Statute 318.18(11)(c)

$18.00 Court Cost

Florida Statute 318.18(11)(a)

$10.00 State Courts Revenue Trust Fund

Florida Statute 318.18(19)(c)

$12.50 Administrative Fee

Florida Statute 318.18(18)

$3.00 Dori Slosberg Driver Education Safety Act (BOCC ordinance states this as $3.00)

Florida Statute 318.1215

C

Moving Violation Penalties

$60.00 Base Fine

Florida Statute 318.18 (10)

$15.00 Court Facilities

Florida Statute 318.18 (13)(a) when assessed by county ordinance

$2.00 Local Law Enforcement Education

Florida Statute 938.15 when assessed by county or municipality (Fort Myers only currently)

$3.00 Additional Court Cost Clearing Trust Fund

Florida Statute 318.18(11)(d)

$2.50 Additional Court Cost—Clerk

Florida Statute 318.18(11)(c)

$35.00 Court Cost

Florida Statute 318.18(11)(a)

$10.00 State Courts Revenue Trust Fund

Florida Statute 318.18(19)(c)

$12.50 Administrative Fee

Florida Statute 318.18(18)

$3.00 Dori Slosberg Driver Education Safety Act (BOCC ordinance states this as $3.00)

Florida Statute 318.1215

$3.00 State Radio System Surcharge

Florida Statute 318.18(3)(a)

D

Failure to Stop for School Bus Violation Penalties

$100.00 Base Fine

Florida Statute 318.18 (10)

$15.00 Court Facilities

Florida Statute 318.18 (13)(a) when assessed by county ordinance

$2.00 Local Law Enforcement Education

Florida Statute 938.15 when assessed by county or municipality (Fort Myers only currently)

$3.00 Additional Court Cost Clearing Trust Fund

Florida Statute 318.18(11)(d)

$2.50 Additional Court Cost—Clerk

Florida Statute 318.18(11)(c)

$35.00 Court Cost

Florida Statute 318.18(11)(a)

$10.00 State Courts Revenue Trust Fund

Florida Statute 318.18(19)(c)

$12.50 Administrative Fee

Florida Statute 318.18(18)

$3.00 Dori Slosberg Driver Education Safety Act (BOCC ordinance states this as $3.00)

Florida Statute 318.1215

$3.00 State Radio System Surcharge

Florida Statute 318.18(3)(a)

E

Pass School Bus on Side Children Enter or Exit

$200.00 Base Fine

Florida Statute 318.18 (10)

$15.00 Court Facilities

Florida Statute 318.18 (13)(a) when assessed by county ordinance

$2.00 Local Law Enforcement Education

Florida Statute 938.15 when assessed by county or municipality (Fort Myers only currently)

$3.00 Additional Court Cost Clearing Trust Fund

Florida Statute 318.18(11)(d)

$2.50 Additional Court Cost—Clerk

Florida Statute 318.18(11)(c)

$35.00 Court Cost

Florida Statute 318.18(11)(a)

$10.00 State Courts Revenue Trust Fund

Florida Statute 318.18(19)(c)

$12.50 Administrative Fee

Florida Statute 318.18(18)

$3.00 Dori Slosberg Driver Education Safety Act (BOCC ordinance states this as $3.00)

Florida Statute 318.1215

$3.00 State Radio System Surcharge

Florida Statute 318.18(3)(a)

F

Illegal Handicapped Parking (316.1956)

$100.00 Base Fine

Florida Statute 318.18 (10)

$15.00 Court Facilities

Florida Statute 318.18 (13)(a) when assessed by county ordinance

$2.00 Local Law Enforcement Education

Florida Statute 938.15 when assessed by county or municipality (Fort Myers only currently)

$2.50 Additional Court Cost—Clerk

Florida Statute 318.18(11)(c)

$18.00 Court Cost

Florida Statute 318.18(11)(a)

$10.00 State Courts Revenue Trust Fund

Florida Statute 318.18(19)(c)

$12.50 Administrative Fee

Florida Statute 318.18(18)

$3.00 Dori Slosberg Driver Education Safety Act (BOCC ordinance states this as $3.00)

Florida Statute 318.1215

G

Toll Violation Penalties

$100.00 Base Fine

Florida Statute 316.18 (7)

$15.00 Court Facilities

Florida Statute 318.18 (13)(a) when assessed by county ordinance

$2.00 Local Law Enforcement Education

Florida Statute 938.15 when assessed by county or municipality (Fort Myers only currently)

$3.00 Additional Court Cost Clearing Trust Fund

Florida Statute 318.18(11)(d)

$2.50 Additional Court Cost—Clerk

Florida Statute 318.18(11)(c)

$35.00 Court Cost

Florida Statute 318.18(11)(a)

$10.00 State Courts Revenue Trust Fund

Florida Statute 318.18(19)(c)

$12.50 Administrative Fee

Florida Statute 318.18(18)

$3.00 Dori Slosberg Driver Education Safety Act (BOCC ordinance states this as $3.00)

Florida Statute 318.1215

$3.00 State Radio System Surcharge

Florida Statute 318.18(3)(a)

Varies Amount of Unpaid Toll

Florida Statute 318.18 (7)

H

Load on Vehicle Violation Penalties

$200.00 Base Fine

Florida Statute 318.18 (7)

$15.00 Court Facilities

Florida Statute 318.18 (13)(a) when assessed by county ordinance

$2.00 Local Law Enforcement Education

Florida Statute 938.15 when assessed by county or municipality (Fort Myers only currently)

$3.00 Additional Court Cost Clearing Trust Fund

Florida Statute 318.18(11)(d)

$2.50 Additional Court Cost—Clerk

Florida Statute 318.18(11)(c)

$18.00 Court Cost

Florida Statute 318.18(11)(a)

$10.00 State Courts Revenue Trust Fund

Florida Statute 318.18(19)(c)

$12.50 Administrative Fee

Florida Statute 318.18(18)

$3.00 Dori Slosberg Driver Education Safety Act (BOCC ordinance states this as $3.00)

Florida Statute 318.1215

I

Speeding Violation Penalties

6–9 MPH

$25.00 Base Fine

Florida Statute 318.18(3)(b)

$15.00 Court Facilities

Florida Statute 318.18 (13)(a) when assessed by county ordinance

$2.00 Local Law Enforcement Education

Florida Statute 938.15 when assessed by county or municipality (Fort Myers only currently)

$3.00 Additional Court Cost Clearing Trust Fund

Florida Statute 318.18(11)(d)

$2.50 Additional Court Cost—Clerk

Florida Statute 318.18(11)(c)

$35.00 Court Cost

Florida Statute 318.18(11)(a)

$10.00 State Courts Revenue Trust Fund

Florida Statute 318.18(19)(c)

$12.50 Administrative Fee

Florida Statute 318.18(18)

$3.00 Dori Slosberg Driver Education Safety Act (BOCC ordinance states this as $3.00)

Florida Statute 318.1215

$3.00 State Radio System Surcharge

Florida Statute 318.18(3)(a)

10–14 MPH

$100.00 Base Fine

Florida Statute 318.18(3)(b)

$15.00 Court Facilities

Florida Statute 318.18 (13)(a) when assessed by county ordinance

$2.00 Local Law Enforcement Education

Florida Statute 938.15 when assessed by county or municipality (Fort Myers only currently)

$3.00 Additional Court Cost Clearing Trust Fund

Florida Statute 318.18(11)(d)

$2.50 Additional Court Cost—Clerk

Florida Statute 318.18(11)(c)

$35.00 Court Cost

Florida Statute 318.18(11)(a)

$10.00 State Courts Revenue Trust Fund

Florida Statute 318.18(19)(c)

$12.50 Administrative Fee

Florida Statute 318.18(18)

$3.00 Dori Slosberg Driver Education Safety Act (BOCC ordinance states this as $3.00)

Florida Statute 318.1215

$3.00 State Radio System Surcharge

Florida Statute 318.18(3)(a)

15–19 MPH

$150.00 Base Fine

Florida Statute 318.18(3)(b)

$15.00 Court Facilities

Florida Statute 318.18 (13)(a) when assessed by county ordinance

$2.00 Local Law Enforcement Education

Florida Statute 938.15 when assessed by county or municipality (Fort Myers only currently)

$3.00 Additional Court Cost Clearing Trust Fund

Florida Statute 318.18(11)(d)

$2.50 Additional Court Cost—Clerk

Florida Statute 318.18(11)(c)

$35.00 Court Cost

Florida Statute 318.18(11)(a)

$10.00 State Courts Revenue Trust Fund

Florida Statute 318.18(19)(c)

$12.50 Administrative Fee

Florida Statute 318.18(18)

$3.00 Dori Slosberg Driver Education Safety Act (BOCC ordinance states this as $3.00)

Florida Statute 318.1215

$3.00 State Radio System Surcharge

Florida Statute 318.18(3)(a)

20–29 MPH

$175.00 Base Fine

Florida Statute 318.18(3)(b)

$15.00 Court Facilities

Florida Statute 318.18 (13)(a) when assessed by county ordinance

$2.00 Local Law Enforcement Education

Florida Statute 938.15 when assessed by county or municipality (Fort Myers only currently)

$3.00 Additional Court Cost Clearing Trust Fund

Florida Statute 318.18(11)(d)

$2.50 Additional Court Cost—Clerk

Florida Statute 318.18(11)(c)

$35.00 Court Cost

Florida Statute 318.18(11)(a)

$10.00 State Courts Revenue Trust Fund

Florida Statute 318.18(19)(c)

$12.50 Administrative Fee

Florida Statute 318.18(18)

$3.00 Dori Slosberg Driver Education Safety Act (BOCC ordinance states this as $3.00)

Florida Statute 318.1215

$3.00 State Radio System Surcharge

Florida Statute 318.18(3)(a)

20–29 MPH

$250.00 Base Fine

Florida Statute 318.18(3)(b)

$15.00 Court Facilities

Florida Statute 318.18(13)(a) when assessed by county ordinance

$2.00 Local Law Enforcement Education

Florida Statute 938.15 when assessed by county or municipality (Fort Myers only currently)

$3.00 Additional Court Cost Clearing Trust Fund

Florida Statute 318.18(11)(d)

$2.50 Additional Court Cost—Clerk

Florida Statute 318.18(11)(c)

$35.00 Court Cost

Florida Statute 318.18(11)(a)

$10.00 State Courts Revenue Trust Fund

Florida Statute 318.18(19)(c)

$12.50 Administrative Fee

Florida Statute 318.18(18)

$3.00 Dori Slosberg Driver Education Safety Act (BOCC ordinance states this as $3.00)

Florida Statute 318.1215

$3.00 State Radio System Surcharge

Florida Statute 318.18(3)(a)

1–9 MPH Construction/School Zone

$50.00 Base Fine

Florida Statute 318.18(3)(b)

$15.00 Court Facilities

Florida Statute 318.18 (13)(a) when assessed by county ordinance

$2.00 Local Law Enforcement Education

Florida Statute 938.15 when assessed by county or municipality (Fort Myers only currently)

$3.00 Additional Court Cost Clearing Trust Fund

Florida Statute 318.18(11)(d)

$2.50 Additional Court Cost—Clerk

Florida Statute 318.18(11)(c)

$35.00 Court Cost

Florida Statute 318.18(11)(a)

$10.00 State Courts Revenue Trust Fund

Florida Statute 318.18(19)(c)

$12.50 Administrative Fee

Florida Statute 318.18(18)

$3.00 Dori Slosberg Driver Education Safety Act (BOCC ordinance states this as $3.00)

Florida Statute 318.1215

$3.00 State Radio System Surcharge

Florida Statute 318.18(3)(a)

10–14 MPH Construction/School Zone

$200.00 Base Fine

Florida Statute 318.18(3)(b)

$15.00 Court Facilities

Florida Statute 318.18 (13)(a) when assessed by county ordinance

$2.00 Local Law Enforcement Education

Florida Statute 938.15 when assessed by county or municipality (Fort Myers only currently)

$3.00 Additional Court Cost Clearing Trust Fund

Florida Statute 318.18(11)(d)

$2.50 Additional Court Cost—Clerk

Florida Statute 318.18(11)(c)

$35.00 Court Cost

Florida Statute 318.18(11)(a)

$10.00 State Courts Revenue Trust Fund

Florida Statute 318.18(19)(c)

$12.50 Administrative Fee

Florida Statute 318.18(18)

$3.00 Dori Slosberg Driver Education Safety Act (BOCC ordinance states this as $3.00)

Florida Statute 318.1215

$3.00 State Radio System Surcharge

Florida Statute 318.18(3)(a)

15–19 MPH Construction/School Zone

$300.00 Base Fine

Florida Statute 318.18(3)(b)

$15.00 Court Facilities

Florida Statute 318.18 (13)(a) when assessed by county ordinance

$2.00 Local Law Enforcement Education

Florida Statute 938.15 when assessed by county or municipality (Fort Myers only currently)

$3.00 Additional Court Cost Clearing Trust Fund

Florida Statute 318.18(11)(d)

$2.50 Additional Court Cost—Clerk

Florida Statute 318.18(11)(c)

$35.00 Court Cost

Florida Statute 318.18(11)(a)

$10.00 State Courts Revenue Trust Fund

Florida Statute 318.18(19)(c)

$12.50 Administrative Fee

Florida Statute 318.18(18)

$3.00 Dori Slosberg Driver Education Safety Act (BOCC ordinance states this as $3.00)

Florida Statute 318.1215

$3.00 State Radio System Surcharge

Florida Statute 318.18(3)(a)

20–29 MPH Construction/School Zone

$350.00 Base Fine

Florida Statute 318.18(3)(b)

$15.00 Court Facilities

Florida Statute 318.18 (13)(a) when assessed by county ordinance

$2.00 Local Law Enforcement Education

Florida Statute 938.15 when assessed by county or municipality (Fort Myers only currently)

$3.00 Additional Court Cost Clearing Trust Fund

Florida Statute 318.18(11)(d)

$2.50 Additional Court Cost—Clerk

Florida Statute 318.18(11)(c)

$35.00 Court Cost

Florida Statute 318.18(11)(a)

$10.00 State Courts Revenue Trust Fund

Florida Statute 318.18(19)(c)

$12.50 Administrative Fee

Florida Statute 318.18(18)

$3.00 Dori Slosberg Driver Education Safety Act (BOCC ordinance states this as $3.00)

Florida Statute 318.1215

$3.00 State Radio System Surcharge

Florida Statute 318.18(3)(a)

>30 MPH Construction/School Zone

$500.00 Base Fine

Florida Statute 318.18(3)(b)

$15.00 Court Facilities

Florida Statute 318.18 (13)(a) when assessed by county ordinance

$2.00 Local Law Enforcement Education

Florida Statute 938.15 when assessed by county or municipality (Fort Myers only currently)

$3.00 Additional Court Cost Clearing Trust Fund

Florida Statute 318.18(11)(d)

$2.50 Additional Court Cost—Clerk

Florida Statute 318.18(11)(c)

$35.00 Court Cost

Florida Statute 318.18(11)(a)

$10.00 State Courts Revenue Trust Fund

Florida Statute 318.18(19)(c)

$12.50 Administrative Fee

Florida Statute 318.18(18)

$3.00 Dori Slosberg Driver Education Safety Act (BOCC ordinance states this as $3.00)

Florida Statute 318.1215

$3.00 State Radio System Surcharge

Florida Statute 318.18(3)(a)

6.2. DISCOVERY IN MISDEMEANOR AND CRIMINAL TRAFFIC CASES

IN AND FOR THE TWENTIETH JUDICIAL CIRCUIT IN THE STATE OF FLORIDA

ADMINISTRATIVE ORDER NO: 6.2

IN RE: DISCOVERY IN MISDEMEANOR AND CRIMINAL TRAFFIC CASES

The Clerk of the Court shall not issue subpoenas for depositions in cases where only misdemeanor or criminal traffic offenses are charged unless authorized by the trial judge.

The trial judge assigned to hear the case will then determine good cause and enter orders directing the clerk to issue subpoenas for discovery depositions.

Each Defendant's written motion showing good cause shall specify facts supporting:

A. The consequences to the Defendant.

B. The complexity of the issues involved.

C. The complexity of the witnesses' testimony (e.g., experts) and,

D. The opportunities available to the Defendant to discover the information sought by deposition.

Upon receipt of the Motion to Show Good Cause to Take Depositions, the trial judge shall initially determine the legal sufficiency thereof. If the Court determines the motion is legally insufficient the Defendant will be so informed. However, if the Court determines the motion to be legally sufficient, then the Court will schedule the matter for an expedited hearing unless both parties waive the same.

The Order Determining the Legal Sufficiency of the Motion Showing Good Cause to Take Depositions shall be substantially as follows:

IN THE COUNTY COURT OF THE TWENTIETH JUDICIAL CIRCUIT IN AND FOR LEE COUNTY CRIMINAL ACTION

STATE OF FLORIDA,)
V.) CASE NO: ___
Defendant.)

ORDER DETERMINING LEGAL SUFFICIENCY OF MOTION SHOWING GOOD CAUSE TO TAKE DEPOSITIONS

THIS MATTER having come on to be heard on the Defendant's Motion to Show Good Cause to Take Depositions and the Court having considered the motion hereby determines that the same is legally:

_______ sufficient

_______ insufficient

DONE AND ORDERED at Fort Myers, Lee County, Florida, this ___ day of _______, 19 ___.

County Judge

DONE AND ORDERED in Chambers, Fort Myers, Lee County, Florida, this 28 day of Jan, 1991.

Thomas S. Reese
Chief Circuit Judge

History. - Administrative Order 89–25.

6.3. PAYMENT OF CIVIL PENALTIES OR COSTS—EXTENSIONS OF TIME BY CLERK

IN THE TWENTIETH JUDICIAL CIRCUIT IN AND FOR THE STATE OF FLORIDA

IN RE: PAYMENT OF CIVIL PENALTIES OR COSTS—EXTENSIONS OF TIME BY CLERK

ADMINISTRATIVE ORDER 6.3—AMENDED—

Pursuant to Fla. R. Traf. Ct. 6.480(b), the Clerks of Court are hereby empowered to allow, at their discretion, a reasonable amount of time before requiring the payment of civil penalties or costs in any case where a traffic violator elects to attend a driver improvement course approved by the Department of Highway Safety and Motor Vehicles in accordance with §§ 318.14 (9) and 318.14 (10), Florida Statutes.

DONE AND ORDERED in Chambers in Fort Myers, Lee County, Florida, this 14 day of April, 2011.

G. Keith Cary
Chief Judge

6.4. CHILD RESTRAINT SAFETY PROGRAM

IN THE TWENTIETH JUDICIAL CIRCUIT IN AND FOR THE STATE OF FLORIDA

ADMINISTRATIVE ORDER NO: 6.4

IN RE: CHILD RESTRAINT SAFETY PROGRAM

Pursuant to Florida Statute § 316.613(5), and this Court's authority to promote the uniform administration of justice throughout the Twentieth Judicial Circuit Court as prescribed by Fla. R. Jud. Admin. 2.050, the Court hereby establishes a Child Restraint Safety Program throughout the Twentieth Judicial Circuit Court.

The following procedures shall be used to implement the Child Restraint Safety Program:

1. The Clerks of the circuit courts throughout the Twentieth Judicial Circuit shall provide an Alternative Sentence Affidavit for persons charged with a child restraint violation.

2. If the offender elects to attend the program, each Clerk of the circuit court shall collect from each offender such fees as are authorized by state and local law.

3. The child restraint safety program classes will be given by the Southwest Florida Safety Council Inc. and a charge of $20.00 is hereby authorized for attendance at the class.

In accordance with the statute cited above, the Court hereby approves of the program which has been established and will be operated by the Southwest Florida Safety Council Inc. The Southwest Florida Safety Council Inc. shall notify the Clerks of the Courts of either the successful completion of the program by each offender or the offender's failure to complete the program.

Upon notification of the successful completion of the program, the penalty specified in Chapter 318 and any associated costs shall be waived and the assessment of points shall also be waived. In the event that the offender fails to complete the program, the Clerks of the Courts are hereby authorized to D–6 the license and levy the original fines, costs and fees on any such offender.

DONE AND ORDERED in Chambers at Fort Myers, Lee County, Florida this 14 day of January, 1998.

Hugh E. Starnes,
Chief Judge

History. - New.

STATE OF FLORIDA

DEPARTMENT OF HEALTH AND REHABILITATIVE SERVICES

January 6, 1992

Mr. Ken Palmer
State Courts Administrator
Supreme Court Building
Tallahassee, FL 32399–1900

Dear Mr. Palmer:

I am writing to request your assistance with an issue that has resulted from the state's large general revenue shortfall. As I'm sure you know, the shortfall has made it necessary for HRS to find ways to reduce expenditures. One of our proposed budget reductions that was selected by the Legislature will have a direct impact on the circuit courts.

As a part of the initial planning for budget cuts, the Children, Youth and Families Program Office recommended elimination of the department's involvement in the intermediary/independent adoption process established in Chapter 63, Florida Statutes. The reasoning behind this recommendation was that private, licensed child placing agencies within the community could provide these services. With the elimination of this function, the department could eliminate the staff positions devoted to those responsibilities.

We ultimately decided not to include this proposal in our recommendations to governor, and the governor did not include this plan as part of his cost cutting measures. As you know, however; the Supreme Court later ruled that budget reductions had to be approved by the Legislature. In making their decision, the Legislature requested and reviewed our original proposals. They subsequently elected to eliminate the staff responsible for this function and thus our involvement in intermediary/independent adoptions.

The effective date of the funding reduction for this function was midnight, December 31. Accordingly, the department is no longer accepting new cases. We will continue to serve and bring to closure all existing cases.

Because of the circuit court's involvement and ultimate responsibility in these adoptions, I wanted to bring this matter to your attention. I would also greatly appreciate your help in letting the appropriate judges know about this change in our involvement with these cases.

If have any questions, please let me know, or feel free to call Ms. Patricia Nichols at 488–8762, or John P. Perry III, at 488–9440.

Sincerely,
Robert B. Williams
Secretary

6.5. ESTABLISHMENT OF MISDEMEANOR PRETRIAL DIVERSION PROGRAM AND AUTHORIZATION FOR FEE COLLECTION

IN THE TWENTIETH JUDICIAL CIRCUIT IN AND FOR THE STATE OF FLORIDA

IN RE: ESTABLISHMENT OF MISDEMEANOR PRETRIAL DIVERSION PROGRAM AND AUTHORIZATION FOR FEE COLLECTION

ADMINISTRATIVE ORDER NO: 6.5

WHEREAS, the Court has a recognized role in promoting the prompt and efficient administration of justice within the Twentieth Judicial Circuit; and

WHEREAS, Fla. R. Jud. Admin. 2.545 (formerly Fla. R. Jud. Admin. 2.085) imposes a duty on the Court to assume early and continuous control of the court calendar and to identify cases subject to alternative dispute resolution processes; and

WHEREAS, there has been an increase in the number of cases being docketed within the Twentieth Judicial Circuit, resulting in an overcrowding of the existing courtroom facilities, thereby hampering the efficient administration of justice; and

WHEREAS, there is a recognized need to reduce overcrowding in the county jails within the Twentieth Judicial Circuit; and

WHEREAS, it is within the interest of justice to provide specific categories of offenders charged with misdemeanor offenses with an alternative to the traditional criminal process of ordinary prosecution;

NOW, THEREFORE, pursuant to the authority vested in me as Chief Judge of the Twentieth Judicial Circuit of Florida under Fla. R. Jud. Admin. 2.215 (formerly Fla. R. Jud. Admin. 2.050), I hereby approve, for use within the Twentieth Judicial Circuit, of the Misdemeanor Pretrial Diversion Program which has been created and is being administered cooperatively by the Office of the State Attorney of the Twentieth Judicial Circuit and the Administrative Office of the Courts of the Twentieth Judicial Circuit, under the supervision of the county probation or pretrial services departments, and which provides for the deferred prosecution of certain qualified persons charged with certain misdemeanor offenses. As to each person placed in the Misdemeanor Pretrial Diversion Program, the Clerk of Court is authorized to collect a supervision fee of up to $50.00 a month, or, in the case of Lee County, a flat fee of $150.00, or in the case of Collier County, a flat fee of $225.00 for each three month period, up to a maximum of $375.00, or, in the case of Charlotte County, a flat fee of $180.00. Upon receipt of payment, the Clerk of Court shall deposit said payments, less an appropriate administrative fee, with the Board of County Commissioners in the county in which it was collected. To the extent that this Administrative Order may conflict with any law, statute, or rule, the law, statute, or rule shall prevail.

The amendments to this Administrative Order shall be effective July 1, 2008, and shall remain in effect until otherwise ordered, amended or rescinded.

The amendment to this Administrative Order of May 30, 2008, was improvidently entered and is rescinded retroactively to May 30, 2008. The version of Administrative Order 6.5 entered on November 7, 2007, is reinstated retroactively and shall remain in effect through June 30, 2008.

DONE AND ORDERED in chambers in Fort Myers, Lee County, Florida, this 4th day of June, 2008.

G. Keith Cary
Chief Judge

History.—Administrative Order 6.5 (July 23, 2004); Administrative Order 6.5 (May 25, 2007); Administrative Order 6.5 (November 7, 2007); Administrative Order 6.5 (May 30, 2008, *rescinded*).

6.6. COST OF SUPERVISION FOR COUNTY PROBATION SERVICES

IN THE TWENTIETH JUDICIAL CIRCUIT IN AND FOR THE STATE OF FLORIDA

IN RE: COST OF SUPERVISION FOR COUNTY PROBATION SERVICES

ADMINISTRATIVE ORDER NO: 6.6

WHEREAS, section 948.09(1)(b), Florida Statutes, requires any person placed on misdemeanor probation to contribute not less than $40 per month to the entity providing misdemeanor supervision; and

WHEREAS, misdemeanor supervision within each county of the Twentieth Judicial Circuit is currently conducted by the county or by the Administrative Office of the Courts through funding by the county; and

WHEREAS, the cost of supervision fees are currently collected in each county in accordance with section 948.09(1)(b), Florida Statutes, by payment through the respective Clerk of Courts; and

WHEREAS, it is in the best interest of the Courts, counties, and citizens of the Twentieth Judicial Circuit to formalize and publicize the standard fees for the cost of supervision when a person is placed on misdemeanor probation;

NOW, THEREFORE, pursuant to the authority vested in me as Chief Judge of the Twentieth Judicial Circuit of Florida under Fla. R. Jud. Admin. 2.215, it is hereby ORDERED as follows:

1. For criminal defendants placed on misdemeanor probation within Lee County and where supervision is conduct by probation officers employed through the Administrative Office of the Courts, the Clerk of Courts in and for Lee County may collect a supervision fee in the amount of fifty dollars ($50.00) per month.

2. For criminal defendants placed on misdemeanor probation within Collier County and where supervision is conduct by probation officers employed through the Administrative Office of the Courts, the Clerk of Courts in and for Collier County may collect a supervision fee in the amount of seventy-five dollars ($75.00) per month.

3. For criminal defendants placed on misdemeanor probation within Charlotte County and where supervision is conduct by probation officers employed through the Administrative Office of the Courts, the Clerk of Courts in and for Charlotte County may collect a supervision fee in the amount of fifty dollars ($50.00) per month.

4. For all criminal defendants placed on misdemeanor probation within Hendry County and where supervision is conduct by probation officers employed through the Administrative Office of the Courts, the Clerk of Courts in and for Hendry County may collect a supervision fee in the amount of fifty dollars ($50.00) per month.

5. For all criminal defendants placed on misdemeanor probation within Glades County, it should be noted that supervision is not currently conducted by probation officers employed through the Administrative Office of the Courts. Accordingly, pursuant to section 948.09(1)(b), Florida Statutes, the Clerk of Courts in and for Glades County may collect a supervision fee in an amount of not less than forty dollars ($40.00), as decided by the sentencing court, or in an amount otherwise established by Glades County.

6. For all criminal defendants placed on misdemeanor home or electronic monitoring, the Clerk of Courts of each

respective county within the Twentieth Judicial Circuit, or the applicable vendor, may collect additional daily fees in amounts to be established by each respective county's probation department, or as decided by the sentencing court. To the extent that these fees are established by a county's probation department, information as to the amount of these fees shall be available at the primary office of the respective county's probation department.

7. Upon receipt of payment of the fees set forth herein for supervision conducted by probation officers employed through the Administrative Office of the Courts, each Clerk of Courts shall remit said fees, less any administrative fee agreed to by the Chief Judge and Clerk of Courts, to each respective Board of County Commissioners on a monthly basis.

8. Nothing in this Administrative Order is intended to infringe upon any authority that an individual sentencing judge may have as it relates to imposing the cost of misdemeanor supervision under section 948.09(1)(b), Florida Statutes, or upon the authority of the Clerk of Courts to collect supervision fees in amounts otherwise ordered by the Court.

9. To the extent that this Administrative Order may conflict with any law, statute, or rule, the law, statute, or rule shall prevail.

10. This Administrative Order is herein amended from its previous version as it relates to paragraph two only, and this amendment to paragraph two shall be effective June 1, 2009.

DONE AND ORDERED in chambers in Fort Myers, Lee County, Florida, this 9 day of April, 2009.

G. Keith Cary
Chief Judge

History. —Administrative Order 6.6 (June 26, 2007); Administrative Order 6.6 (May 4, 2008).

6.7. COURT–ORDERED IMPOUNDMENT OR IMMOBILIZATION AS RELATED TO COUNTY COURT DUI CONVICTIONS

IN THE TWENTIETH JUDICIAL CIRCUIT IN AND FOR THE STATE OF FLORIDA

IN RE: COURT–ORDERED IMPOUNDMENT OR IMMOBILIZATION AS RELATED TO COUNTY COURT DUI CONVICTIONS

ADMINISTRATIVE ORDER NO. 6.7

WHEREAS, subsections (a), (b), (c), and (d) of Florida Statute § 316.193(6) provide that, in conjunction with a conviction for driving under the influence (DUI), the trial court must at the time of sentencing, as a condition of probation, issue an order for the impoundment or immobilization of vehicles in accordance with the terms of subsections (a), (b), and (c); and

WHEREAS, Chapter 2009–206, Laws of Florida, has amended subsection (d) of Florida Statute § 316.193(6) so as to require that the order of impoundment or immobilization include the name and telephone number of all immobilization agencies meeting certain mandatory conditions and restrictions; and

WHEREAS, Chapter 2009–206, Laws of Florida, has created subsection (13) of Fla. Stat. § 316.193, which provides for those mandatory conditions and restrictions that shall apply to all immobilization agencies; and

WHEREAS, Chapter 2009–206, Laws of Florida, has created subsection (14) of Fla. Stat. § 316.193 so as to define the terms "immobilization," "immobilization agencies," and "impoundment;" and

WHEREAS, in creating subsection (14) of Fla. Stat. § 316.193, the legislature defined "immobilization" as including "a governmental agency's act of taking physical possession of the license tag and vehicle registration rendering a vehicle legally inoperable to prevent any person from operating the vehicle pursuant to an order of impoundment or immobilization under subsection (6);" and

WHEREAS, in creating subsection (13) of Florida Statute § 316.193, the legislature exempted personnel of the court or the sheriff who immobilize vehicles from the mandatory conditions and restrictions that apply to immobilization agencies;

NOW, THEREFORE, pursuant to the authority vested in me as Chief Judge of the Twentieth Judicial Circuit of Florida under Fla. R. Jud. Admin. 2.215, it is ordered as follows:

1. Within the Twentieth Judicial Circuit, the County Probation Departments will act as the coordinator for the impoundment or immobilization of vehicles ordered pursuant to Fla. Stat. § 316.193.

2. Recognizing that Glades County is currently the only county within the Twentieth Judicial Circuit that does not use a County Probation Department associated with the Administrative Office of the Courts, it is directed that the Glades County Probation Department shall work in conjunction with Court Administration staff so as to effectuate the intent of this Administrative Order in Glades County.

3. Each County Probation Department shall maintain a list of immobilization agencies that meet the mandatory conditions and restrictions of Fla. Stat. § 316.193(13) and are willing to provide court-ordered immobilization services. This list shall be attached to or referenced in all orders of impoundment or immobilization, and shall otherwise be made available to all offenders subject to the entry of an order of impoundment or immobilization.

4. It shall be within the discretion of each County Probation Department to determine whether it is willing and able to conduct immobilization by making available to offenders the option of taking physical possession of the license tag and vehicle registration, rendering a vehicle legally inoperable to prevent any person from operating the vehicle pursuant to an order of impoundment or immobilization under Fla. Stat. § 3216.193(6).

5. In all orders for impoundment or immobilization, the trial court shall include contact information for the County Probation Department.

6. Subsection (d) of Fla. Stat. § 316.193(6) requires that, within seven (7) business days after the date that the court issues an order of impoundment or immobilization, the Clerk shall send notice by certified mail, return receipt requested, to the registered owner of each vehicle, if the registered owner is a person other than the defendant, and to each person of record claiming a lien against the vehicle.

7. To the extent that the vehicles must be identified in the order of impoundment or immobilization so as to give the County Probation Department or the immobilization agencies notice as to the vehicle subject to impoundment or immobilization, and to the extent that the owners and lien holders must be identified in the order of impoundment or immobilization so as to give the Clerk information necessary for providing notice, it shall be the responsibility of the defendant to provide the trial court with the necessary information identifying the vehicles, owners, and lien holders at the time of sentencing. If the defendant does not have complete information available at the time of sentencing, the defendant shall provide as much information as is available for entry on the face of the order, and shall supplement any missing information by following up thereafter with the County Probation Department.

8. If an exemption may be applicable pursuant to subsections (e), (f), (g), or (h) of Fla. Stat. § 316.193(6), the defendant or any person who owns but was not operating the vehicle when the offense occurred may provide the Court with evidence of the exemption at the time of sentencing and the Court may subsequently dismiss the order of impoundment or immobilization in accordance with subsections (e), (f), (g), or (h) of Fla. Stat. § 316.193(6).

9. After sentencing, the defendant or any person who owns but was not operating the vehicle when the offense occurred may file with the Court a motion to dismiss order of impoundment based upon the grounds set forth under subsections (e), (f), (g), or (h) of Fla. Stat. § 316.193(6), and request an evidentiary hearing.

10. Attached hereto is a sample order of impoundment or immobilization that may be used by the trial court, in its discretion.

11. To the extent that any term or condition of this Administrative Order may be in conflict with any rule, statute, or law, the rule, statute, or law shall prevail.

DONE AND ORDERED in chambers in Fort Myers, Lee County, Florida, this 17 day of Sept, 2009.

____

G. Keith Cary
Chief Judge

ATTACHMENT

IN THE COUNTY COURT OF THE TWENTIETH JUDICIAL CIRCUIT IN AND FOR ________ COUNTY, FLORIDA

State of Florida,
Plaintiff, Case No.________
v.

____________________,
Defendant.
____________________/

ORDER OF IMPOUNDMENT OR IMMOBILIZATION

The Court, having adjudicated Defendant guilty of driving under the influence (DUI) pursuant to Fla. Stat. § 316.193, orders, as a condition of probation, the impoundment or immobilization of the vehicle(s) described below, pursuant to Fla. Stat. § 316.193(6)(d):

Year, make, model, color: ________
VIN No. ________ Vehicle Tag No. ________ State_____
Owner's Name: ________ Address: ________ Ph. No.___
Defendant's Name: ________ Address: ________ Ph. No. ________________
Lien holder: ________ Address: ________ Ph. No._____
The impoundment/immobilization shall be for a consecutive period of: ___ 10 days ___ 30 days ___ 90 days
The impoundment/immobilization must not be concurrent to any term of incarceration, and is a condition of probation. The impoundment/immobilization shall be concurrent with any driver's license revocation imposed under Fla. Stat. § 322.28(2)(a).

All costs and fees for the impoundment or immobilization, including the cost of notification, must be paid by the owner of the vehicle or, if the vehicle is leased or rented, by the person leasing or renting the vehicle, unless the impoundment or immobilization order is dismissed. To the extent that impoundment or immobilization is conducted by an entity other than court personnel, the costs and fees for the impoundment or immobilization must be paid directly to the person impounding or immobilizing the vehicle. Fla. Stat. § 316.193(6)(i).
Dismissal of this order may be sought by motion pursuant to subsections (e), (f), (g), or (h) of Fla. Stat. § 316.193(6).
Within seven (7) business days after the date that the Court issues this order, the Clerk shall send notice by certified mail, return receipt requested, to the registered owner of each vehicle, if the registered owner is a person other than the defendant, and to each person of record claiming a lien against the vehicle. Fla. Stat. § 316.193(6)(d).

Defendant shall immediately, or immediately upon release from incarceration, if any, contact the County Probation Department at ________, phone no. ________ to obtain an up-to-date list of immobilization agencies qualified and available to fulfill the requirements of this order. At its discretion, the County Probation Department may offer, as an alternative, to immobilize the vehicle by taking physical possession of the license tag and vehicle registration.

DONE AND ORDERED this ___ day of ________, 20 ___.

____

County Judge

6.8. DOMESTIC VIOLENCE SUBDIVISION OF COLLIER COUNTY MISDEMEANOR COURT

IN THE TWENTIETH JUDICIAL CIRCUIT IN AND FOR THE STATE OF FLORIDA COLLIER COUNTY

IN RE: DOMESTIC VIOLENCE SUBDIVISION OF COLLIER COUNTY MISDEMEANOR COURT

Administrative Order No. 6.8—Amended—

WHEREAS, the establishment of domestic violence divisions within the Twentieth Judicial Circuit was approved by the Supreme Court of the State of Florida on October 26, 1994, under Local Rule IX; and

WHEREAS, a Domestic Violence Court for Collier County was initially established by administrative order entered October 31, 1996, but has since ceased to operate; and

WHEREAS, the Florida Supreme Court has recognized the extreme importance of having domestic violence issues addressed in an expeditious, efficient, and deliberative manner, In re Report of the Commission on Family Courts, 646 So. 2d 178 (Fla. 1994);

NOW THEREFORE, pursuant to this Court's inherent authority to administer and regulate the courts of the Twentieth Judicial Circuit, as well as the authority prescribed by Fla. R. Jud. Admin. 2.215 and Florida Statute § 43.26, the Court hereby reestablishes the Domestic Violence subdivision of the county misdemeanor court for Collier County, Florida. [1]

It is ORDERED that county court cases in Collier County involving charges of assault under Fla. Stat. § 784.011(2) or battery under Fla. Stat. § 784.03(1)(b) that are based on allegations of domestic violence as identified on either the booking sheet or in the information filed by the State Attorney, and county court cases involving charges of violation of an injunction for protection against domestic violence under Fla. Stat. § 741.31, violation of pretrial release under Fla. Stat. § 741.29(6), violation of any of the prohibitions regarding the possession of firearms and ammunition under Fla. Stat. § 790.233, and violation of an injunction for protection against repeat violence, sexual violence, dating violence, or a foreign protection order under Fla. Stat. § 784.047, shall be assigned to the Misdemeanor Domestic Violence Subdivision. [2]

The previous Order Establishing Domestic Violence Court for Collier County entered October 31, 1996, was vacated by original Administrative Order 6.8 entered October 1, 2009.

Effective May 1, 2010, the County Administrative Judge for Collier County shall make all judicial assignments to the Misdemeanor Domestic Violence Subdivision, and any judicial assignment orders regarding this subdivision entered prior to May 1, 2010 shall thereafter be deemed vacated.

To the extent that this order may conflict with any rule, statute or law, the rule, statute or law shall prevail.

DONE AND ORDERED in Chambers in Fort Myers, Lee County, Florida this 12 day of Sept, 2012.

Jay B. Rosman
Chief Judge

History.—Order Establishing Domestic Violence Court for Collier County (October 31, 1996); Administrative Order 6.8 (October 1, 2009); Administrative Order 6.8 (April 21, 2010); Administrative Order 6.8 (December 3, 2010).

1Effective October 1, 2009, as per original Administrative Order 6.8 entered October 1, 2009.

2Administrative Order 6.8 is herein amended for the substantive purpose of clarifying that violations of any of the prohibitions regarding the possession of firearms and ammunition under Fla. Stat. § 790.233, and violations of an injunction for protection against repeat violence, sexual violence, dating violence, or a foreign protection order under Fla. Stat. § 784.047, shall also be assigned to the Collier Misdemeanor Domestic Violence Subdivision.

Juvenile

8.1. RESCINDED EFFECTIVE JANUARY 13, 2000

8.2. RESCINDED EFFECTIVE JANUARY 13, 2000

8.3. JUVENILES—DEATH WHILE UNDER JURISDICTION

IN THE TWENTIETH JUDICIAL CIRCUIT IN AND FOR THE STATE OF FLORIDA

ADMINISTRATIVE ORDER NO: 8.3

IN RE: JUVENILES—DEATH WHILE UNDER JURISDICTION

When any child dies while under the jurisdiction of the Court, the Department of Health & Rehabilitative Services or any other involved social agency shall, as soon as possible, notify the judge presiding over the case and the Chief Judge of the Twentieth Judicial Circuit of the circumstances surrounding the death and any information regarding the viewing, funeral arrangements, and burial as well as follow-up reports and any other relative information.

DONE AND ORDERED in Chambers, in Fort Myers, Lee County, Florida, this 28 day of Jan, 1991.

Thomas S. Reese
Chief Circuit Judge

History. - Administrative Order 89–21.

8.4. ACCESS TO COMPUTERIZED JUVENILE COURT RECORDS

IN THE TWENTIETH JUDICIAL CIRCUIT IN AND FOR THE STATE OF FLORIDA

Administrative Order NO: 8.4—Amended—

IN RE: ACCESS TO COMPUTERIZED JUVENILE COURT RECORDS

WHEREAS, Florida Statute § 39.0132 grants the right to inspect and copy any official record under Chapter 39 pertaining to a child to the attorney for the child, the attorney for the parents of the child, guardian ad litems, law enforcement agencies, and the Department of Children and Family Services and its designees; and

WHEREAS, Florida Statute § 985.045 grants the right to inspect and copy any official record under Chapter 985 pertaining to a child to the attorney for the child, the attorney for the parents of the child, the attorney for the guardians of the child, the attorney for the legal custodians of the child, law enforcement agencies, the Department of Juvenile Justice and its designees; and

WHEREAS, technology has progressed to the point of providing for the electronic maintenance, transmission, and access of court records; and

WHEREAS, the Clerks within the State of Florida are, in general, moving in the direction of providing paperless electronic systems for the maintenance of court records, thus restricting access to paper court files; and

WHEREAS, the Florida Supreme Court has recognized these advancements in technology and, on September 7, 2007, issued Administrative Order AOSC07–49, In re: Revised Interim Policy on the Electronic Release of Court Records; and

WHEREAS, AOSC07–49 expressly allows the Clerk of Court to make certain records available electronically to attorneys of record in a case, attorneys expressly authorized by a party in a case, and governmental agencies and agents; and

WHEREAS, as expressed above, certain persons and entities are expressly exempt from the confidentiality provisions of Florida Statutes Chapters 39 and 985; and

WHEREAS, AOSC07–49 expressly acknowledges that Article V of the Constitution of the State of Florida charges the chief judges of the circuit courts with the administrative supervision of the courts within their jurisdiction, and directs that any questions that may arise regarding implementation of AOSC07–49 be addressed to the chief judge of the jurisdiction;

By the authority vested in the Chief Judge of the Twentieth Judicial Circuit pursuant to Fla. R. Jud. Admin. 2.215, it is hereby clarified that the Clerks of the Circuit Court for the counties within Twentieth Judicial Circuit may provide access to computerized court records in juvenile cases to persons or entities otherwise entitled to access those records pursuant to Fla. Stat. §§ 39.0132 and 985.045, which may include staff members of the Guardian Ad Litem Program, counsel of record (including Public Defender, Regional Counsel, court-appointed conflict counsel, and State Attorney, as may be applicable), the Department of Children and Family Services and its designees, which may include agents and case managers, and the Department of Juvenile Justice and its designees, which may include agents and case managers. To the extent that these confidential records are, in fact, court records, the Clerks may also provide access to computerized court records in juvenile cases to the judiciary and authorized personnel of the court.

Prior to obtaining access to any computerized court records, persons or entities listed above must comply with all prerequisites and requirements established by the Clerks, which may include, but are not limited to, the execution of confidentiality agreements, the execution of formal authorizations identifying staff members/authorized personnel/designees/agents/case managers, and the payment of fees. This Administrative Order is not to be construed as a mandate directing that the Clerks provide access to computerized juvenile court records to any specific person or entity, but rather is to be construed only as clarification for the Clerks as to whom they may provide access to computerized juvenile court records.

Confidential court records are to be accessed and used by authorized persons and agencies in the exercise of their official duties ONLY and are to otherwise remain confidential or available according to law. This Administrative Order is not intended to grant access to confidential court records to any person or entity not already entitled to access pursuant to statute, law, or Florida Supreme Court rule, but rather is intended to clarify that the Clerks may provide computerized access to confidential court records to those persons or entities otherwise entitled to access. This Administrative Order is not intended to grant computerized access to sealed records absent order of the presiding trial court judge.

To the extent that this Administrative Order may be in conflict with any statute, law, or rule, the statute, law, or rule shall prevail.

DONE AND ORDERED in chambers at Ft. Myers, Lee County, Florida, this 26 day of Sept., 2011.

Jay B. Rosman
Chief Judge

History. Administrative Order 8.4 (August 10, 1993); Administrative Order 8.4 (January 13, 2000); Administrative Order 8.4 (July 28, 2008).

8.5. COMMUNITY ARBITRATORS IN JUVENILE PROCEEDINGS

IN THE TWENTIETH JUDICIAL CIRCUIT IN AND FOR THE STATE OF FLORIDA

ADMINISTRATIVE ORDER NO. 85.

IN RE: COMMUNITY ARBITRATORS IN JUVENILE PROCEEDINGS

Pursuant to § 985.304, Fla. Stat. (1997), and Rule 1.810, Florida Rules of Civil Procedure, the Chief Judge shall maintain a list of qualified persons who have agreed to serve as community arbitrators for the purpose of carrying out the provisions of the Florida Juvenile Justice Continuum.

Toward that end, individuals will be selected as community arbitrators by the Chief Judge, the Senior Circuit Court Judge assigned to juvenile cases in the circuit, and the State Attorney. The community arbitrators shall be trained or experienced in juvenile causes and shall be:

(a) either a graduate of an accredited law school or of an accredited school with a degree in behavioral social work or trained in conflict resolution techniques; and,

(b) a person of the temperament necessary to deal properly with cases involving children and with the family crises likely to be presented to the arbitrator.

The list of community arbitrators shall be updated from time to time as may be appropriate under the circumstances, and will be available in the Administrative Office of the Courts.

DONE AND ORDERED in Chambers at Naples, Collier County, Florida, this 13 day of Jan., 2000.

William L. Blackwell
Chief Judge

History. - Administrative Order 8.5 (January 19, 1994).

8.6. APPOINTMENT OF PUBLIC DEFENDER AS COUNSEL IN JUVENILE DELINQUENCY PROCEEDINGS

IN THE TWENTIETH JUDICIAL CIRCUIT IN AND FOR THE STATE OF FLORIDA

ADMINISTRATIVE ORDER NO. 8.6

IN RE: APPOINTMENT OF PUBLIC DEFENDER AS COUNSEL IN JUVENILE DELINQUENCY PROCEEDINGS

Pursuant to Part II of Chapter 985 of the Florida Statutes, any other applicable provision of Florida Law as it may relate to juvenile delinquency, Part III of Chapter 27 of the Florida Statutes, and this Court's inherent authority to administer and regulate the Courts pursuant to Fla. R. Jud. Admin. 2.050 and Florida Statute § 43.26, it is

ORDERED AND ADJUDGED as follows:

1. Each child who is the subject of a petition for delinquency filed pursuant to Chapter 985 of the Florida Statutes is entitled to be represented by counsel as specifically provided by Florida Statute § 985.203.

2. In accordance with Florida Statute § 27.52(1)(a), all determinations of indigency for the purposes of appointing the Public Defender or a conflict attorney shall be made by the court, and may be made at any stage of the proceedings. Before appointing the Public Defender or a conflict attorney, the court shall consider a completed affidavit that contains the financial information required under Florida Statute § 27.52(1)(f), and shall make a preliminary determination of indigency.

3. The Department of Juvenile Justice, as the agency responsible for implementation of those statutes requiring the imposition of fees for the cost of care, support and maintenance of juveniles in detention or commitment facilities, is hereby ordered to provide the court at the detention hearing with as much additional information as is feasible such that the court may determine whether the accused, or if applicable, a parent or legal guardian of an accused minor, is indigent for the purposes of appointment of the Public Defender as is required by Florida Statute § 27.52(1)(b). The court will provide a form for use in making such determinations.

4. Each person who requests the appointment of the Public Defender or a conflict attorney shall pay to the Clerk of the Court an application fee of $40 at the time the financial affidavit is filed, or within seven (7) days thereafter as set forth in Florida Statute § 27.52(1)(c).

5. In any case where a child is first deemed to be indigent and later deemed to be not indigent, the cost of representation shall be assessed pursuant to Chapter 27 and any other applicable provision of Florida law.

6. In any case where a child is charged with an act of domestic violence or repeat domestic violence, the Public Defender shall be appointed to represent the child at the initial detention hearing. In the event that the child wishes to retain private counsel, either individually or by and through his parents or legal guardian, he or she may do so as set forth below.

Nothing in this order shall be construed as preventing a minor or the parents of the minor from hiring private counsel to represent the child in any juvenile delinquency proceeding. If private counsel is retained at any stage of the proceedings, the Public Defender, if previously appointed, shall thereafter withdraw from representation in accordance with the applicable rules of court.

In the event private counsel is retained to represent an allegedly indigent juvenile and a wavier[1] of costs is sought, counsel shall file a certificate as is required by Florida Statute § 57.081(1).

DONE AND ORDERED in Chambers, at Punta Gorda, Charlotte County, Florida this 27 day of Feb., 2002.

William L. Blackwell
Chief Judge

History. - Administrative Order 8.6 (May 21, 1999); Administrative Order 8.6 (May 10, 1999).

[1] So in original.

8.7. JUDICIAL WAIVER OF PARENTAL NOTICE OF TERMINATION OF PREGNANCY

IN THE TWENTIETH JUDICIAL CIRCUIT IN AND FOR THE STATE OF FLORIDA

IN RE: JUDICIAL WAIVER OF PARENTAL NOTICE OF TERMINATION OF PREGNANCY

ADMINISTRATIVE ORDER NO. 8.7—Amended—

Pursuant to Fla. Stat. § 390.01114, as amended by Chapter 2011–227, Laws of Florida, and Fla. R. Juv. P. 8.800, et seq., and by the authority vested in the Chief Judge by Fla. R. Jud. Admin. 2.215(b), it is

ORDERED AND ADJUDGED as follows:

1. **Filing of the Petition**—Upon request, the Clerk of Court shall provide interested persons with blank copies of Florida Supreme Court approved Form 8.897, Petition for Judicial Waiver of Parental Notice of Termination of Pregnancy. Petitions seeking a judicial waiver of the parental notice requirements of Fla. Stat. § 390.01114 shall be filed with the Clerk of Court of the respective county and shall be file-stamped by the Clerk with the date and time of filing. The Clerk shall assign the petition to the juvenile dependency division of the Court and shall assign a juvenile dependency case number. In accordance with Fla. R. Juv. P. 8.805(d), the Clerk shall immediately provide Petitioner with a copy of Florida Supreme Court approved Form 8.988 (Sworn Statement of True Name and Pseudonym) and Florida Supreme Court approved Form 8.989 (Advisory Notice to Minor).

2. **Assignment of Cases**—The Clerk shall assign petitions filed under section 390.01114, Fla. Stat., to the judge who customarily presides over juvenile dependency cases, or if more than one judge within a county customarily presides over such cases, the Clerk shall assign petitions to those judges on a rotating basis. The Clerk shall immediately contact the assigned judge's judicial assistant for the purpose of advising as to the filing of the petition and determining the assigned judge's availability. If the assigned judge is available, the Clerk shall immediately hand-deliver the file to the assigned judge.

3. **Unavailability of Assigned Judge**—If the Clerk finds that the assigned judge is not available, and if alternative arrangements have not already been made in advance for judicial coverage in that assigned judge's absence, the Clerk shall immediately notify the Circuit Administrative Judge, or in the absence of the Circuit Administrative Judge, the Clerk shall immediately notify the Chief Judge. The Circuit Admin-

istrative Judge or the Chief Judge shall designate a judge who is immediately available to address the petition in the absence of the assigned judge. If the Clerk finds that neither the Circuit Administrative Judge nor the Chief Judge is available, the Clerk shall notify the Duty Judge who shall address the petition. The Clerk shall immediately hand-deliver the file to the judge designated to address the petition by the Circuit Administrative Judge or the Chief Judge, or, if applicable, to the Duty Judge.

4. **Appointment of Counsel**—Upon the filing of the petition, the Clerk shall immediately determine whether Petitioner has requested the appointment of counsel in the petition and, if the Petitioner has not, and is not otherwise represented by counsel, the Clerk shall immediately provide written notice to the Petitioner of her right to counsel at public expense, as provided for by Fla. Stat. § 390.01114(4)(a) and Fla. R. Juv. P. 8.815. This may be accomplished by ensuring that the Petitioner is provided with Florida Supreme Court approved Form 8.989 (Advisory Notice to Minor). If the Petitioner appears before the judge for hearing and has not yet requested the appointment of counsel, the Court at that time shall advise the Petitioner of her right to counsel at public expense. If Petitioner has requested, or requests, the appointment of counsel, the Clerk shall obtain the name of the next attorney in rotation from the Registry of Court–Appointed Attorneys, and shall immediately contact that attorney to determine his or her availability to represent Petitioner. If unavailable, the Clerk shall continue through the rotation to the next available attorney. The Clerk shall advise the assigned judge, or the alternative judge who will address the petition, of the name of the attorney who is available, and the judge shall immediately enter an order appointing that attorney. If the Clerk is unable to locate an available attorney from the Registry of Court–Appointed Attorneys, the Clerk shall so advise the judge, and the judge shall enter an order noting that no private court-appointed attorneys are available, and appointing the Office of Criminal Conflict and Civil Regional Counsel pursuant to Fla. Stat. § 27.511(6)(a). Upon entry of an order appointing either a private court-appointed attorney or the Office of Criminal Conflict and Civil Regional Counsel, the Clerk shall immediately provide a copy of the order of appointment, along with a copy of the petition, to counsel via electronic mail, facsimile transmittal, or any other appropriate method by which counsel is immediately notified in writing of the appointment and the petition.

5. **Hearing and Ruling**—Upon notifying the assigned judge, or the alternative judge who will address the petition, of the filing of the petition, the Clerk shall obtain from that judge's judicial assistant a hearing date, time, and place, which shall be set within three (3) business days of the date the petition was filed, as required by Fla. Stat. § 390.01114(4)(b). The Clerk shall then provide written notice of the hearing to the Petitioner and to counsel, if any. Within the three (3) business day period, the judge shall conduct the hearing, and shall rule and issue written findings of fact and conclusions of law supporting the judge's decision, including factual findings and legal conclusion relating to the maturity of the minor as provided for by Fla. Stat. § 390.01114(4)(c). In accordance with Fla. Stat. § 390.01114(4)(b) and Fla. R. Juv. P. 8.820, the three (3) business day period may be extended at the request of the Petitioner, but the Court is still obligated to rule on the petition as soon as practically possible. In accordance with Fla. Stat. § 390.01114(4)(b), if a hearing is not held within the three (3) business day period, and the Petitioner has not requested an extension, the Petitioner may petition the Chief Judge for a hearing on an emergency basis. The Clerk shall immediately notify the Chief Judge of the filing of any such emergency petition, and the Chief Judge shall thereafter ensure that a hearing is held within forty-eight (48) hours of receipt of the emergency petition, and that an order is entered within twenty-four (24) hours after the hearing.

6. **Record of Proceedings and Transcript**—The judicial assistant for the judge who will conduct a hearing shall notify the Electronic Court Reporting Office so as to ensure that an electronic record is made of the proceeding. On behalf of the Court as required by Fla. Stat. § 390.01114(4)(e), the Electronic Court Reporting Office shall ensure that the electronic record of the proceeding is transcribed and shall ensure that the original transcript is filed with the Clerk. The Court shall be responsible only for costs associated with the production of the original transcript.

7. **Confidentiality**—As provided for by Fla. Stat. §§ 390.01116(4) and 390.01116, and Fla. R. Juv. P. 8.835, any information, including the petition, documents, transcripts, recordings of cases, and any other information that could be used to identify the Petitioner is confidential and exempt from public disclosure, and, likewise, all hearings shall remain confidential and closed to the public. As further provided for by Fla. Stat. § 390.01116(4) and Fla. R. Juv. P. 8.825, the judge's order on the petition shall direct that confidentiality of the record be maintained.

8. To the extent that any provision of this Administrative order conflicts with any rule, statute or law, the rule, statute or law shall prevail.

DONE AND ORDERED in Chambers at Fort Myers, Lee County, Florida this 13 day of Dec., 2011.

Jay B. Rosman
Chief Judge

History.—Administrative Order 8.7 (Aug. 24, 1999).

8.8. TRUANCY PETITIONS

IN THE TWENTIETH JUDICIAL CIRCUIT IN AND FOR THE STATE OF FLORIDA

IN RE: TRUANCY PETITIONS

Administrative Order NO: 8.8

In addressing Truancy Petitions filed pursuant to Florida Statute § 984.151, counties of the Twentieth Judicial Circuit have historically and primarily utilized procedures, policies, and forms, derived and based upon the model policies, procedures and forms originally established in Escambia County. The Escambia County model was acknowledged and promoted by the Florida Department of Education in its Technical Assistance Paper dated December 2000, Paper Number: FY 2001–02, and procedures, policies and forms based upon the Escambia County model were recommended and utilized by School Boards of counties within the Twentieth Judicial Circuit.

By opinion filed December 28, 2012, the Second District Court of Appeal has commented on its belief as to the original legislative intent in creating Florida Statute § 984.151, and the propriety of using some aspects of the policies, procedures, and forms based upon the Escambia County model. Sockwell v. State, 38 Fla. L. Weekly D69 (Fla. 2d DCA, Dec. 28, 2012). The Second District Court of Appeal has opined that, as it relates to truancy proceedings in Florida, "[a] disconnect exists between the goals of the statutes and our normal approaches to due process," and that truancy proceedings are not intended to be criminal or quasi-criminal in nature:

> "Truancy court was intended to be a precursor to a child-in-need-of-services proceeding, It was not a precursor to a juvenile delinquency proceeding or an adult county court criminal proceeding."

Id.

The Twentieth Judicial Circuit acknowledges and respects the direction and guidance offered by the Second District Court of Appeal, and for the purpose of consistency throughout the counties of the Twentieth Judicial Circuit, and by the authority vested in the Chief Judge of the Twentieth Judicial Circuit pursuant to Fla. R. Jud. Admin. 2.215, it is ordered as follows:

1. Truancy Petitions authorized by Florida Statute § 984.151 shall be filed by the Superintendent of Schools with the Juvenile Dependency Division of the Circuit Court of the respective county of the Twentieth Judicial Circuit in which the student is enrolled in school. In accordance with Florida Statute § 984.151(1), the Petition must allege sufficient facts demonstrating that the student is subject to compulsory school attendance and:

(a) has had at least five unexcused absences, or absences for which the reasons are unknown, within a calendar month, or ten unexcused absences, or absences for which the reasons are unknown, within a 90–calendar–day period pursuant to Fla. Stat. § 1003.26(1)(b), or

(b) has had more than fifteen unexcused absences in a 90–calendar–day period.

2. As noted by the Second District Court of Appeal in its Sockwell opinion, Florida Statute § 984.151 provides that the petition is to be filed by "the superintendent of schools." The statute does not give explicit authority for a designee of the Superintendent to file a Truancy Petition or appear on behalf of the Superintendent. Accordingly, the Superintendent, or legal counsel representing the Superintendent, must file the petition and appear at all truancy proceedings.

3. In accordance with Florida Statute § 984.151(5), the Trial Court is required to hear the Petition within thirty (30) days. Accordingly, an initial hearing shall be scheduled to take place within thirty (30) days of the filing of the Petition, and the Clerk shall issue a summons to the parent, guardian, or legal custodian of the student, as identified in the petition, directing that the parent, guardian, or legal custodian and the student appear for the hearing at the time and place specified.

4. At the initial hearing, the allegations of the Petition shall be read to the student and parent, guardian, or legal custodian. If the student and parent, guardian, or legal custodian do not contest the allegations of the Petition, the Trial Court may make findings of fact based upon such admissions and enter a final disposition order as provided for by subsection (7) of Florida Statute § 984.151, and as further described below in paragraph six.

5. If, at the initial hearing, the student and parent, guardian, or legal custodian elect to contest the allegations of the Petition, the matter shall be scheduled for an evidentiary hearing, at which time all parties will have the opportunity to present evidence and testimony as it relates to the allegations of truancy, after which the Trial Court will make a determination as to whether the student qualifies as truant or habitually truant.

6. If, at the initial hearing, based upon admissions of the student and parent, guardian, or legal custodian, or at a subsequent evidentiary hearing, the Trial Court determines that the student did, in fact, miss any of the alleged days, the Trial Court shall, as per Florida Statute § 984.151(7), order the student to attend school and the parent, guardian, or legal custodian to ensure that the student attends school. The Trial Court may further order participation in programs, services, or alternative sanctions, as delineated under subsection (7) of Florida Statute § 984.151, which are as follows:

(a) that the student participate in alternative sanctions to include mandatory attendance at alternative classes to be followed by mandatory community services hours for a period up to six (6) months:

(b) that the student and the student's parent or guardian participate in homemaker or parent aide services;

(c) that the student or the student's parent or guardian participate in intensive crisis counseling;

(d) that the student or the student's parent or guardian participate in community mental health services if available and applicable;

(e) that the student and the student's parent or guardian participate in services provided by voluntary or community agencies as available;

(f) that the student or the student's parent or guardian participate in vocational, job training, or employment services.

7. If the Trial Court finds that Petitioner has failed to meet its burden of demonstrating that the student qualifies as truant, the Trial Court shall enter an order dismissing the petition.

8. The Second District Court of Appeal has opined in its Sockwell opinion that, in granting the Petition, the Trial Court's written order to attend school, as provided for in paragraph six above, is intended to be the final appealable order, and, therefore, the order shall be treated as such. To the extent that the Trial Court's written order to attend school is to be treated as the final appealable order, follow-up review hearings for monitoring purposes shall not be automatically scheduled by the Trial Court. The responsibility for monitoring compliance is that of the Petitioner, as further described below. To the extent that Petitioner finds non-compliance, Petitioner shall resort to the three options set forth below in paragraph 12.

9. Subsection (8) of Florida Statute § 984.151 was included as part of the originally enacted 1999 law, Ch. 99–398, Laws of Florida, and explicitly provides that "[i]f the student does not successfully complete the sanctions ordered in subsection (7), the case ***shall*** be referred to the case staffing committee under s. 984.12 with a recommendation to file a child-in-need-of-services petition under s. 984.15." (emphasis added).

10. Subsection (9) of Florida Statute § 984.151 was added in 2000, Ch. 2000–235, Laws of Florida, and explicitly provides that "[t]he parent, guardian, or legal custodian and the student shall participate, as required by court order, in any sanctions or services required by the court under this section, and the court ***shall*** enforce such participation through its contempt power." (emphasis added).

11. In its Sockwell opinion, the Second District Court of Appeal acknowledges the Trial Court's contempt power both for the purpose of addressing participation in sanctions and services, and for the purpose of enforcing its order to attend school. However, the Second District Court of Appeal further emphasizes that a truancy proceeding is intended to be informal and the precursor to a Child-in-Need-of-Services Petition in the event that the student does not comply with the court-ordered sanctions.

12. Accordingly, it shall be the responsibility of Petitioner to monitor compliance by the student and parent, guardian, or legal custodian, and in the event of non-compliance with any portion of the Trial Court's order, the Petitioner may, if applicable:

(a) refer the matter to the case staffing committee under Florida Statute § 984.12 with a recommendation to file a child-in-need-of-services petition under Florida Statute § 984.15; or

(b) refer the matter to the Office of the State Attorney for consideration of prosecution under Florida Statute § 1003.27(7)(a)1; or

(c) bring the matter before the Trial Court through the filing of an appropriate motion for contempt, alleging sufficient facts which, if true, demonstrate a willful disregard of the Trial Court's order. Any motion for contempt shall be filed by the Superintendent as Petitioner, or by counsel representing the Superintendent as Petitioner. If the motion is legally insufficient in that it fails to allege sufficient facts demonstrating a willful violation, the motion will be dismissed, without the necessity of a hearing. If the motion is legally sufficient, it will be set for hearing. Counsel for Petitioner shall appear at any contempt hearing, shall be responsible for prosecuting the charge of contempt, and shall be responsible for meeting Petitioner's burden of demonstrating, beyond a reasonable doubt, a willful violation of the Trial Court's earlier order.

13. In accordance with the suggestion of the Second District Court of Appeal in its Sockwell opinion, the use of the Trial Court's contempt power as it relates to truancy proceedings is to be used sparingly. If the Trial Court denies a Petitioner's motion for contempt, but still finds non-compliance with the Trial Court's prior order, whether willful or otherwise, the Trial Court may, alternatively and on its own, refer the matter to the case staffing committee under Florida Statute § 984.12 with a recommendation that a child-in-need-of-services petition be filed under Florida Statute § 984.15.

14. Attached hereto are forms which the Trial Court may use, in the Trial Court's discretion, as it relates to truancy proceedings.

15. In light of the entry of this Administrative Order, all prior Administrative Orders entered as it relates to "Truancy Court" within the Twentieth Judicial Circuit are hereby vacated as no longer being necessary. Noting that prior Administrative Orders establishing "Truancy Courts" may include or attach copies of truancy program manuals created and adopted by each counties' respective School Board, it should be noted that vacating these prior Administrative Orders does not serve to necessarily vacate or impact those programs or manuals under the control of each respective School Board. This Court only has authority and jurisdiction over procedures related to the filing of Truancy Petitions as permitted by statute, or other court events. The establishment by the local School Boards of any other policies or procedures designed to ensure school attendance are within the province of the local School Boards pursuant to Florida Statute Chapter 1003, Part II. However, any portions of the local School Boards' current policies or procedures involving the filing of Truancy Petitions or other court events, to the extent that they may be in conflict, are superseded by this Administrative Order.

16. To the extent that this Administrative Order may be in conflict with any statute, law, or rule, the statute, law, or rule shall prevail.

DONE AND ORDERED in chambers at Ft. Myers, Lee County, Florida, this 5th day of April 1, 2013.

____
Jay B. Rosman
Chief Judge

History. Order Establishing Truancy Night Court for Charlotte County (Feb. 27, 2002); Order Establishing Truancy Night Court for Hendry County (Oct. 1, 2003); Order Establishing Truancy Court for Collier County (Jan. 15, 2008).

Attachment 1

IN THE CIRCUIT COURT OF THE TWENTIETH JUDICIAL CIRCUIT IN AND FOR ________ COUNTY, FLORIDA JUVENILE DEPENDENCY DIVISION

In the Interest of:

________________ Case No. ________

a Minor Child, DOB: ________

and ________________
(Parent or Legal Guardian)

________________/

FINAL ADJUDICATION AND DISPOSITION JUDGMENT

(After Admission to Allegations of Truancy)

THIS MATTER comes before the Court on the Truancy Petition filed by the Superintendent of Schools pursuant to Fla. Stat. 984.151.

The petition is legally sufficient in that it alleges either:

__ the minor child has had at least 5 unexcused absences, or absences for which the reasons are unknown, within a calendar month; or

__ the minor child has had at least 10 unexcused absences, or absences for which the reasons are unknown, within a 90–calendar-day period; or

__ the minor child has had more than 15 unexcused absences within a 90–calendar–day period.

A hearing was held on ________, 20 ___, with the following parties present:

___ Parent(s)/Legal Guardian(s)
___ Minor Child
___ Superintendent of Schools
___ Counsel for Superintendent of Schools

The Parent(s)/Legal Guardian(s) and Minor Child having **ADMITTED** at the hearing to the allegations of Truancy as set forth in the Petition, it is **ORDERED AND ADJUDGED** as follows:

1. The Court finds that the above-named minor child did miss the school days as alleged in the Petition.

2. The minor child SHALL attend school each and every day and the Parent(s)/Legal Guardian(s) SHALL ensure that the minor child attends school each and every day. The minor child shall have no unexcused tardies or absences.

3. In addition the Court orders the following, if checked:

___ a. the minor child shall attend alternative classes to be followed by mandatory community services hours for a period of up to 6 months, specifically: ________________
____
____

___ b. the minor child and Parent(s)/Legal Guardian(s) shall participate in homemaker or parent aide services, specifically: ________________
____
____

___ c. the ___ minor child and/or ___ Parent(s)/Legal Guardian (s) shall participate in intensive crisis counseling, specifically: ________________
____
____

___ d. the ___ minor child and/or ___ Parent(s)/Legal Guardian (s) shall participate in community mental health services, specifically: ________________
____
____

___ e. the minor child and Parent(s)/Legal Guardian(s) shall participate in services provided by voluntary or community agencies, specifically: ________________
____
____

___ f. the ___ minor child and/or ___ Parent(s)/Legal Guardian (s) shall participate in vocational, job training, or employment services, specifically: ________________
____
____

4. Failure to comply with all terms of this order may result in a referral to the case staffing committee under Fla. Stat. § 984.12 with a recommendation to file a child-in-need-of-services petition under Fla. Stat. § 984.15.

5. Failure to comply with all terms of this order may also result in the issuance of an order directing that the Parent(s)/Legal Guardian(s) show cause as to why the Parent(s)/Legal Guardian(s) should not be held in contempt of court.

6. This order is a final appealable order.

DONE AND ORDERED at ________, ________ County, Florida, this ___ day of ________, 20 ___.

____
Circuit Judge

Certificate of Service

I HEREBY CERTIFY that a true and correct copy of the above order has been furnished this ___ day of ________, 20 ___, to:

___ Parent(s)/Legal Guardian(s)
___ Minor Child
___ Superintendent of Schools
___ Counsel for Superintendent of Schools
___ Other ________________________.

By: ________________________

Attachment 2

IN THE CIRCUIT COURT OF THE TWENTIETH JUDICIAL CIRCUIT IN AND FOR ________ COUNTY, FLORIDA JUVENILE DEPENDENCY DIVISION

In the Interest of:

________________________ Case No. ________

a Minor Child, DOB: ________

and ________________________
(Parent or Legal Guardian)

________________________/

FINAL ADJUDICATION AND DISPOSITION JUDGMENT

(After Evidentiary Hearing on Allegations of Truancy)

THIS MATTER comes before the Court on the Truancy Petition filed by the Superintendent of Schools pursuant to Fla. Stat. 984.151.

The petition is legally sufficient in that it alleges either:

___ the minor child has had at least 5 unexcused absences, or absences for which the reasons are unknown, within a calendar month; or

___ the minor child has had at least10 unexcused absences, or absences for which the reasons are unknown, within a 90–calendar–day period; or

___ the minor child has had more than 15 unexcused absences within a 90–calendar-day period.

A hearing was originally held on ________, 20 ___ at which time the Parent(s)/Legal Guardian(s) and Minor Child DENIED the allegations of Truancy as set forth in the Petition. Accordingly, an evidentiary hearing was scheduled and held on ________, 20 ___, with the following parties present:

___ Parent(s)/Legal Guardian(s)
___ Minor Child
___ Superintendent of Schools

___ Counsel for Superintendent of Schools

The Court having fully considered the evidence, testimony and argument presented, and upon due consideration, it is **ORDERED AND ADJUDGED** as follows:

1. The Court finds that the above-named minor child did miss the school days as alleged in the Petition.

2. The minor child SHALL attend school each and every day and the Parent(s)/Legal Guardian(s) SHALL ensure that the minor child attends school each and every day. The minor child shall have no unexcused tardies or absences.

3. In addition the Court orders the following, if checked:

___ a. the minor child shall attend alternative classes to be followed by mandatory community services hours for a period of up to 6 months, specifically: ______________________

___ b. the minor child and Parent(s)/Legal Guardian(s) shall participate in homemaker or parent aide services, specifically: ______________________

___ c. the ___ minor child and/or ___ Parent(s)/Legal Guardian (s) shall participate in intensive crisis counseling, specifically: ______________________

___ d. the ___ minor child and/or ___ Parent(s)/Legal Guardian (s) shall participate in community mental health services, specifically: ______________________

___ e. the minor child and Parent(s)/Legal Guardian(s) shall participate in services provided by voluntary or community agencies, specifically: ______________________

___ f. the ___ minor child and/or ___ Parent(s)/Legal Guardian (s) shall participate in vocational, job training, or employment services, specifically: ______________________

4. Failure to comply with all terms of this order may result in a referral to the case staffing committee under Fla. Stat. § 984.12 with a recommendation to file a child-in-need-of-services petition under Fla. Stat. § 984.15.

5. Failure to comply with all terms of this order may also result in the issuance of an order directing that the Parent(s)/Legal Guardian(s) show cause as to why the Parent(s)/Legal Guardian(s) should not be held in contempt of court.

6. This order is a final appealable order.

DONE AND ORDERED at ________, ________ County, Florida, this ___ day of ________, 20 ___.

____
Circuit Judge

Certificate of Service

I HEREBY CERTIFY that a true and correct copy of the above order has been furnished this ___ day of ________, 20 ___, to:

___ Parent(s)/Legal Guardian(s)
___ Minor Child
___ Superintendent of Schools
___ Counsel for Superintendent of Schools
___ Other ______________________

By: ______________________

Attachment 3

IN THE CIRCUIT COURT OF THE TWENTIETH JUDICIAL CIRCUIT IN AND FOR ________ COUNTY, FLORIDA JUVENILE DEPENDENCY DIVISION

In the Interest of:

________________ Case No. ________
a Minor Child, DOB: ________

and ________________
(Parent or Legal Guardian)

________________ /

ORDER DISMISSING TRUANCY PETITION

THIS MATTER comes before the Court on the Truancy Petition filed by the Superintendent of Schools pursuant to Fla. Stat. 984.151. Upon consideration, the Court finds:

___ The petition is legally insufficient.

___ Having conducted an evidentiary hearing on ________, 20 ___, the Court finds that Petitioner, the Superintendent of Schools, has failed to present sufficient evidence or testimony demonstrating that the Minor Child has missed some or all of the school days as alleged in the Petition.

Accordingly, it is **ORDERED AND ADJUDGED** that the Truancy Petition is DISMISSED.

DONE AND ORDERED at ________, ________ County, Florida, this ___ day of ________, 20 ___.

____
Circuit Judge

Certificate of Service

I HEREBY CERTIFY that a true and correct copy of the above order has been furnished this ___ day of ________, 20 ___, to:

___ Parent(s)/Legal Guardian(s)
___ Minor Child
___ Superintendent of Schools
___ Counsel for Superintendent of Schools
___ Other ______________________

By: ______________________

Attachment 4

IN THE CIRCUIT COURT OF THE TWENTIETH JUDICIAL CIRCUIT IN AND FOR ________ COUNTY, FLORIDA JUVENILE DEPENDENCY DIVISION

In the Interest of:

______________________ Case No. ________

a Minor Child, DOB: ________

and ____________________

(Parent or Legal Guardian)

________________________/

ORDER TO SHOW CAUSE

THIS MATTER comes before the Court on the Motion for Contempt filed by Petitioner, the Superintendent of Schools, alleging that the Parent(s)/Legal Guardian(s) have willfully failed to comply with this Court's prior Final Adjudication and Disposition Judgment.

Having reviewed the motion and finding it to be legally sufficient in that it alleges facts that, if proven to be true, would serve to demonstrate a willful disregard of this Court's prior Final Adjudication and Disposition Judgment, it is

ORDERED AND ADJUDGED that the Parent(s)/Legal Guardian(s) shall appear on ________, 20 __, at __: __ a.m./p.m., at ________ for the purpose of showing cause as to why the Parent(s)/Legal Guardian(s) should not be held in contempt of court.

The Parent(s)/Legal Guardian(s) shall be arraigned at the hearing. The Parent(s)/Legal Guardian(s) is advised that he/she is entitled to be represented by counsel, have compulsory process for the attendance of witnesses, testify in his/her own defense, refuse to testify, to have the offense proven beyond a reasonable doubt, and, if found guilty, to present mitigating circumstances.

Punishment, if imposed, may include a fine and incarceration. Should the court determine, based on the evidence presented at the hearing, that the conduct of the Parent(s)/Legal Guardian(s) warrants sanctions for civil contempt in addition to or instead of indirect criminal contempt, the court reserves the right to find the Parent(s)/Legal Guardian(s) guilty of civil contempt and impose appropriate civil sanctions.

The Sheriff of this County shall serve this Order to Show Cause by delivering copies to the Parent(s)/Legal Guardian(s), with proof of Sheriff's service.

DONE AND ORDERED at ________, ________ County, Florida, this __ day of ________, 20 __.

____

Circuit Judge

Copies to:

__ Parent(s)/Legal Guardian(s)

__ Minor Child

__ Superintendent of Schools

__ Counsel for Superintendent of Schools

__ Other ____________________

If you are a person with a disability who needs any accommodation in order to participate in this proceeding, you are entitled, at no cost to you, to the provision of certain assistance. Please contact ________, whose office is located at ________, and whose telephone number is ________, at least 7 days before your scheduled court appearance, or immediately upon receiving this notification if the time before the scheduled appearance is less than 7 days; if you are hearing or voice impaired, call 711.

Attachment 5

IN THE CIRCUIT COURT OF THE TWENTIETH JUDICIAL CIRCUIT IN AND FOR ________ COUNTY, FLORIDA JUVENILE DEPENDENCY DIVISION

In the Interest of:

______________________ Case No. ________

a Minor Child, DOB: ________

and ____________________

(Parent or Legal Guardian)

________________________/

ORDER DISMISSING MOTION FOR CONTEMPT AS LEGALLY INSUFFICIENT

THIS MATTER comes before the Court on the Motion for Contempt filed by Petitioner, the Superintendent of Schools, alleging that the Minor Child and Parent(s)/Legal Guardian(s) have willfully failed to comply with this Court's prior Final Adjudication and Disposition Judgment.

Having reviewed the motion and finding it to be legally insufficient in that it fails to allege facts that, if proven to be true, would serve to demonstrate a willful disregard of this Court's prior Final Adjudication and Disposition Judgment, it is

ORDERED AND ADJUDGED that the Motion for Contempt is DISMISSED.

DONE AND ORDERED at ________, ________ County, Florida, this __ day of ________, 20 __.

____

Circuit Judge

Certificate of Service

I HEREBY CERTIFY that a true and correct copy of the above order has been furnished this __ day of ________, 20 __ to:

__ Parent(s)/Legal Guardian(s)

__ Minor Child

__ Superintendent of Schools

__ Counsel for Superintendent of Schools

__ Other ____________________

By: ____________________

Attachment 6

IN THE CIRCUIT COURT OF THE TWENTIETH JUDICIAL CIRCUIT IN AND FOR ________ COUNTY, FLORIDA JUVENILE DEPENDENCY DIVISION

In the Interest of:

______________________ Case No. ________

a Minor Child, DOB: ______

and ______
(Parent or Legal Guardian)

______/

ORDER DENYING MOTION FOR CONTEMPT AFTER HEARING

THIS MATTER comes before the Court on the Motion for Contempt filed by Petitioner, the Superintendent of Schools, alleging that the Minor Child and Parent(s)/Legal Guardian(s) have willfully failed to comply with this Court's prior Final Adjudication and Disposition Judgment. Having entered an Order to Show Cause and having conducted a hearing, the Court finds and Orders as follows:

___ The Petitioner has failed to meet its burden of demonstrating a willful failure to comply with this Court's prior Final Adjudication and Disposition Judgment, and the Motion is DENIED.

___ The Petitioner has demonstrated a failure to comply with this Court's prior Final Adjudication and Disposition Judgment, though did not demonstrate that such failure was willful. Accordingly, the Motion is DENIED. However, this matter is hereby referred to the case staffing committee under Florida Statute § 984.12 with a recommendation that a Child–In–Need–Of–Services petition be filed under Florida Statute § 984.15.

DONE AND ORDERED at ______, ______ County, Florida, this ___ day of ______, 20 ___.

______
Circuit Judge

Certificate of Service

I HEREBY CERTIFY that a true and correct copy of the above order has been furnished this ___ day of ______, 20 ___, to:

___ Parent(s)/Legal Guardian(s)

___ Minor Child

___ Superintendent of Schools

___ Counsel for Superintendent of Schools

___ Department of Juvenile Justice

___ Department of Children and Family Services

___ Other ______

By: ______

Appellate

9.1. MOTIONS AND ORDERS IN APPELLATE PROCEEDINGS

IN THE TWENTIETH JUDICIAL CIRCUIT IN AND FOR THE STATE OF FLORIDA

IN RE: MOTIONS AND ORDERS IN APPELLATE PROCEEDINGS

ADMINISTRATIVE ORDER NO. 9.1—VACATED—

WHEREAS, the practices authorized by Administrative Order No. 9.1 as it relates to the handling of county-to-circuit appellate motions and the issuance of county-to-circuit appellate orders are out-dated and no longer in use within the Twentieth Judicial Circuit; and

WHEREAS, the appellate practices used within the Twentieth Judicial Circuit are in accordance with procedures of the Florida Rules of Appellate Procedure; and

WHEREAS, Administrative Order 9.1 is obsolete and no longer needed;

NOW THEREFORE, by the power vested in the Chief Judge by Fla. R. Jud. Admin. 2.215, it is **ORDERED** that Administrative Order 9.1. is hereby **VACATED**.

DONE AND ORDERED in Chambers at Fort Myers, Lee County, Florida, this 24th day of April, 2015.

Jay B. Rosman
Chief Judge

History. —Administrative Order 9.1 (August 5, 1994); Administrative Order 9.1 (June 3, 2003); Administrative Order 9.1 (June 20, 2007).

9.2. PROCESSING AND DISTRIBUTION OF OPINIONS IN APPELLATE PROCEEDINGS

IN THE TWENTIETH JUDICIAL CIRCUIT IN AND FOR THE STATE OF FLORIDA

ADMINISTRATIVE ORDER NO: 9.2

IN RE: PROCESSING AND DISTRIBUTION OF OPINIONS IN APPELLATE PROCEEDINGS

Pursuant to Rule 2.050, Florida Rules of Judicial Administration, the Florida Rules of Appellate Procedure, Local Rule III and the inherent power of this Court to promote the administration of justice, it is hereby

ORDERED and ADJUDGED as follows:

1. Whenever an appellate banc of the Twentieth Judicial Circuit generates an opinion pursuant to Local Rule III of the Twentieth Judicial Circuit and the Florida Rules of Appellate Procedure, the Clerks of the Circuit Court for the five counties of the Twentieth Judicial Circuit are hereby ordered to prepare and send to each circuit and county judge of the Twentieth Judicial Circuit a copy of the opinion.

2. This requirement shall not apply to per curiam affirmances of the trial court because said affirmances have no precedential value. In addition, the copies of the opinions shall not be sent until after the opinions become final following issuance of a mandate from the appellate banc.

3. Each Clerk of the Circuit Court is hereby required to generate and send to the Administrative Office of the Courts a status report on each pending appeal from County to Circuit Court on a monthly basis, on or before the tenth of each month. Said status report may take the form of a computer

printout or other internally generated document from the Clerk's office which contains all docket entries for each pending case. The intent of this requirement is to keep the ex-officio Clerk of the Appellate Banc apprised of the status of each pending appeal on a monthly basis.

4. Each Clerk of the Circuit Court shall be required to prepare and send to the Administrative Office of the Courts a list of all appellate cases wherein the Court Reporter's transcript is late or extended beyond the time frame permitted by the appellate rules and a statement of when the transcript is due. Each such report shall also be prepared on a monthly basis on or before the tenth of each month.

DONE AND ORDERED in Chambers at Fort Myers, Lee County, Florida, this 30 day of August, 1995.

Thomas S. Reese
Chief Circuit Judge

History. - New.

9.3. JUDICIAL ASSIGNMENT OF PETITIONS FOR WRIT OF CERTIORARI AND OTHER ACTIONS FILED PURSUANT TO RULE 9.030(c), EXCEPT FOR APPEALS OF FINAL AND NON–FINAL COUNTY COURT ORDERS

IN THE TWENTIETH JUDICIAL CIRCUIT IN AND FOR THE STATE OF FLORIDA

IN RE: JUDICIAL ASSIGNMENT OF PETITIONS FOR WRIT OF CERTIORARI AND OTHER ACTIONS FILED PURSUANT TO RULE 9.030(c), EXCEPT FOR APPEALS OF FINAL AND NON–FINAL COUNTY COURT ORDERS

ADMINISTRATIVE ORDER NO: 9.3

WHEREAS, Local Rule III, In re: Division of Court: Appellate Division, approved by the Florida Supreme Court on June 27, 1995, provides for an Appellate Banc of three (3) Circuit Judges for the purpose of hearing appeals of final and non-final county court orders pursuant to Fla. R. App. P. 9.030(c)(1)(A) & (B); and

WHEREAS, Local Rule III, In re: Division of Court: Appellate Division, approved by the Florida Supreme Court on June 27, 1995, provides that all other actions which seek to invoke the jurisdiction of the Circuit Court pursuant to any other provision of Fla. R. App. P. 9.030(c), including appeals from administrative action pursuant to Rule 9.030(c)(1)(C), certiorari jurisdiction pursuant to Rule 9.030(c)(2), and original jurisdiction pursuant to Rule 9.030(c)(3), shall be assigned to a single judge on a random basis and in accordance with the assignments established by the Chief Judge pursuant to Administrative Order No. 2.5, In re: Judicial Labor and Rotation Policy; and

WHEREAS, Local Rule III, In re: Division of Court: Appellate Division, approved by the Florida Supreme Court on June 27, 1995, expressly authorizes the Chief Judge of the Twentieth Judicial Circuit to enter such other orders as may be necessary to effectuate the intent and purpose of Local Rule III; and

WHEREAS, the intent, purpose and actual historical practice within all counties of the Twentieth Judicial Circuit since the issuance of Local Rule III in 1995, has been that actions other than those under Rule 9.030(c)(1)(A) & (B) seeking to invoke the jurisdiction of the Circuit Court, including appeals from administrative action pursuant to Rule 9.030(c)(1)(C), certiorari jurisdiction pursuant to Rule 9.030(c)(2), and original jurisdiction pursuant to Rule 9.030(c)(3), be assigned on a random basis to a single judge within the Circuit Civil Division of the county in which the action is filed.

NOW, THEREFORE, by the authority vested in the Chief Judge by Fla. R. Jud. Admin. 2.215, and by Local Rule III as approved by the Florida Supreme Court on June 27, 1995, and for the purpose of memorializing the intent, purpose and actual historical practice in applying Local Rule III,

It is **ORDERED** that actions other than those under Rule 9.030(c)(1)(A) & (B) seeking to invoke the jurisdiction of the Circuit Court, including appeals from administrative action pursuant to Rule 9.030(c)(1)(C), certiorari jurisdiction pursuant to Rule 9.030(c)(2), and original jurisdiction pursuant to Rule 9.030(c)(3), shall be assigned by the Clerk of Court on a random basis to a single judge within the Circuit Civil Division of the county in which the action is filed. This Administrative Order shall apply retroactively to any pending actions to the extent necessary to effectuate its intent and the intent of Local Rule III.

DONE AND ORDERED in chambers in Fort Myers, Lee County, Florida, this 24th day of April, 20 15.

Jay B. Rosman
Chief Judge

History. —New.

Family Law

12.1. ESTABLISHMENT OF CITIZEN REVIEW PANELS

IN THE TWENTIETH JUDICIAL CIRCUIT IN AND FOR THE STATE OF FLORIDA

ADMINISTRATIVE ORDER NO. 12.1

IN RE: ESTABLISHMENT OF CITIZEN REVIEW PANELS

Pursuant to Fla. R. Jud. Admin. 2.050(b), § 39.702, Fla. Stat. (Supp. 1998), and the inherent power of this Court to administer and regulate the courts of the Twentieth Judicial Circuit, it is

ORDERED AND ADJUDGED as follows:

1. Citizen Review Panels as contemplated by Florida Statute § 39.702(1) are hereby authorized to be established in each county within the five counties of the Twentieth Judicial Circuit Court.

2. Each Citizen Review Panel shall be administered by an independent not-for-profit agency duly established and maintained as provided by Florida Statute § 39.702(2).

3. Each Citizen Review Panel shall be composed of five volunteer members and shall conform with the requirements of Florida Statute § 39.702. Each panel member shall serve without compensation as provided in § 39.702(3), Fla. Stat. (Supp. 1998).

4. All Citizen Review Panels which are established pursuant to this administrative order shall conduct themselves and their proceedings in accordance with Chapter 39.702.

5. Any Foster Care Review Panel which has been previously established in the Twentieth Judicial Circuit Court by Administrative Order or other order of the Chief Judge pursuant to Chapter 39 or any other applicable provision of Florida law is hereby granted the authority to continue in operation so long as there is substantial compliance with the statutes cited above.

6. The duties, responsibilities and obligations of all citizen review panels duly established pursuant to this administrative order shall be as prescribed in Chapter 39.702.

DONE AND ORDERED in Chambers, at Fort Myers, Lee County, Florida this 29 day of June 1999.

Hugh E. Starnes
Chief Judge

History.—New.

12.2. IMPLEMENTATION OF MODEL FAMILY COURT RECOMMENDATIONS AND ESTABLISHMENT OF UNIFIED FAMILY COURT

IN THE TWENTIETH JUDICIAL CIRCUIT IN AND FOR THE STATE OF FLORIDA

ADMINISTRATIVE ORDER NO. 12.2

IN RE: IMPLEMENTATION OF MODEL FAMILY COURT RECOMMENDATIONS AND ESTABLISHMENT OF UNIFIED FAMILY COURT

Pursuant to the opinion of the Florida Supreme Court in In Re: Report of the Family Court Steering Committee, 794 So. 2d 518 (Fla. 2001), which directs that each circuit court submit a revised local rule or administrative order consistent with the Model Family Court recommendations of the Family Court Steering Committee, including a provision for the establishment of a Unified Family Court in each judicial circuit, and in accordance with what has been the practice within the Twentieth Judicial Circuit as it has evolved over the nearly two decades since the Family Law Division was first established in Lee County, and during that period of time through the adoption of Administrative Order 2.12 and other related administrative and parochial orders, and in accordance with this Court's inherent authority to administer and regulate the courts of the Twentieth Judicial Circuit, it is

ORDERED AND ADJUDGED as follows:

1. *General Provisions.* There shall be a circuit-wide Unified Family Court ("Family Court") in the Twentieth Judicial Circuit based upon the "Coordinated Management" model as approved by the Florida Supreme Court in the opinion referenced above.

In a "Coordinated Management" system, all pending family court cases are coordinated and managed by a staff member or team of staff members to facilitate the delivery of social services as may be appropriate to any particular case through various community organizations, and to maximize judicial resources throughout the circuit, avoid conflicting court orders, and prevent multiple court appearances by litigants on the same or similar issues.

2. *Scope of Cases.* Family Court will preside over family law cases involving family issues germain to a single family or extended family. These family law cases may include but shall not be limited to: dissolution of marriage, division and distribution of property arising out of a dissolution of marriage proceeding, annulment, support unconnected with dissolution of marriage, paternity, child support, URESA/UNIFSA, custodial care of and access to children, adoption, name change, declaratory judgment actions related to premarital, marital, or postmarital agreements, and civil domestic and repeat violence injunctions.

Also included within the defined family law cases are juvenile dependency, termination of parental rights, juvenile delinquency, emancipation of a minor, CINS/FINS, and truancy. All of these cases will be heard within the juvenile division and monitored by a case management team.

The court will also hear modification and enforcement of orders entered in all of the cases mentioned above.

3. *Judicial Assignment.* The assignment of cases and the applicability of this order to the various counties within the Twentieth Judicial Circuit shall be determined and governed by Administrative Orders 2. 5 and 2.12, and such other administrative assignment orders as are necessary to effectuate the purpose of this order.

All family law cases shall be coordinated in a manner that will conserve judicial labor, ensure that no conflicting orders are entered involving the same family, and to the extent possible, either the same judge will hear multiple cases involving the same family, or all relevant admissible evidence or other background information will be provided by case managers, lawyers or litigants to each judge handling a case involving the same family.

4. *Administrative Family Law Judge.* The court hereby formally establishes the office of the Administrative Family Law Division Judge for the Twentieth Circuit Court. In accordance with an administrative assignment order entered by this court on April 25, 2000, that judge is presently Circuit Judge Hugh E. Starnes. Judge Starnes will continue in that capacity until further order of this court. The duties of the Administrative Family Law Division Judge are as prescribed in the administrative assignment order and as further expanded by this administrative order.

5. *General Master and Hearing Officers.* General masters, special masters and hearing officers are approved for use in the Family Law Division. Each general master, special master and hearing officer shall be appointed by separate order of the Chief Judge and shall perform those duties as specified in the order of appointment. All presently appointed general masters, special masters and hearing officers shall continue to perform those functions as specified in their orders of appointment until further order of this court.

6. *Case Management.* A Family Court Services Plan for Lee County was established by parochial order dated October 26, 2001. It is the court's goal that the Model Plan will eventually be implemented in all of the counties within the Twentieth Circuit Court. During the trial phase of this Plan, case management in counties other than Lee County shall remain as currently established until such time as the Model Plan is adopted circuit-wide by order of this court.

7. *Self–Help Program.* The circuit has a Pro Se Litigant Program which is also known as the Family Court Services Program. This was established by order of the court entered September 11, 1997. The Pro Se Litigant Program provides services for self-represented litigants throughout the circuit and shall continue to do so in accordance with the order.

8. *Alternative Dispute Resolution.* It is the general practice within the Twentieth Judicial Circuit that mediation is mandatory prior to trial in all contested family law matters. This will continue to be the case. Mediation may be provided through a private mediator selected by the parties or through the Twentieth Judicial Circuit's Court Mediation Program as the parties may be advised.

9. *Guardian ad Litem.* The circuit has established and will maintain a Guardian ad Litem Program to represent the best interests of children involved in dependency cases and dissolution or custody matters. The program will be made available throughout the circuit with staff members located in each county as the Administrative Family Law Division Judge may deem appropriate.

10. *Supervised Visitation.* Supervised visitation services are available in Lee and Collier counties through various social service organizations. This program will expand to the other counties within the circuit as may be needed or required and as resources become available in the sound discretion of the Administrative Family Law Division Judge.

11. *Parenting Classes.* The requirement of parent education and family stabilization courses for divorcing parents or those involved in custody or dependency actions was established for all dissolution of marriage cases involving minor children in the Twentieth Judicial Circuit. There are presently programs that provide such services for all counties within the circuit.

12. *Drug Court.* Pursuant to Administrative Order 3.15, Drug Court was established throughout the Twentieth Judicial Circuit Court. Juvenile Drug Court shall be operated by separate administrative order and contained within the Administrative Code of the Twentieth Circuit Court.

13. *Domestic Violence Court.* A separate Domestic Violence Court was established throughout the Twentieth Judicial Circuit pursuant to Local Rule IX adopted October 26, 1994. That court shall continue to operate as provided therein and through any orders entered in connection with Local Rule IX.

14. *Citizen Review Panels.* Citizen Review Panels are authorized to operate within the Twentieth Judicial Circuit Court pursuant to Administrative Order 12.1. Such panels may operate within the parameters established by Administrative Order 12.1 and may be expanded as provided therein within the sound discretion of the Administrative Family Law Division Judge.

15. *Disposition.* All cases in Family Court shall have a final hearing date for dispositions established at the earliest possible time, and all cases filed after July 1, 2001 in Lee County shall be reviewed by the Case Management staff for inclusion in the case management process. This requirement may be extended to other counties within the circuit within the sound discretion of the Administrative Family Law Division Judge.

16. *Security.* Security for each courthouse is provided by an amalgam of assistance from the respective Sheriffs' Departments, contract service employees or others hired by the Office of the Court Administrator.

17. *Technology.* The Court Technology Officer for the Twentieth Judicial Circuit shall develop a search mechanism to allow case managers to determine related parties in cases and report this information to the case management staff and to each judge who is assigned any one of the related cases.

The Administrative Family Law Division Judge is hereby authorized to execute whatever additional orders may be necessary to effectuate the intent and purpose of this administrative order. The Model Family Court for Florida recommendations are attached to this administrative order and made a part hereof.

This administrative order shall take effect on January 1, 2002 and shall remain in effect unless or until otherwise modified, revised or supplemented by further order of the court.

DONE AND ORDERED in Chambers, at Punta Gorda, Charlotte County, Florida this 2nd day of Jan., 2001.

William L. Blackwell
Chief Judge

History. - New.

12.3. SUPERVISED VISITATION PROGRAMS

IN THE TWENTIETH JUDICIAL CIRCUIT IN AND FOR THE STATE OF FLORIDA

ADMINISTRATIVE ORDER 12.3

IN RE: SUPERVISED VISITATION PROGRAMS

The Supreme Court of Florida entered an Administrative Order dated November 18, 1999 which adopted minimum standards for supervised visitation centers and the programs associated with such centers. The administrative order signed by then Chief Justice Major Harding is attached to this order and made a part hereof.

Pursuant to the mandate of the Florida Supreme Court, it is incumbent upon this court to enter into agreements with supervised visitation centers that are willing to comply with the minimum standards adopted by the Family Court Steering Committee as referenced in the Supreme Court's administrative order.

In accordance with the Supreme Court's order, and in recognition of the fact that supervised visitations programs are an essential element of the Model Family Court and an important resource to family law judges, it is

ORDERED AND ADJUDGED as follows:

1. Any supervised visitation program operating in the Twentieth Judicial Circuit that wishes to receive cases pursuant to a referral via court order, shall comply with the standards adopted by the Supreme Court through the administrative order referenced above.

2. Prior to accepting cases pursuant to any court order, the visitation programs shall enter into an agreement with the Chief Judge of the Twentieth Judicial Circuit Court as provided by the administrative order from the Supreme Court referenced above.

3. Judges who refer cases to any supervised visitation program shall utilize only the services of those programs that have entered into an agreement pursuant to this order.

4. The Office of the Court Administrator shall maintain a list of supervised visitation programs in the Twentieth Judicial Circuit that comply with the terms of this order. This list shall be updated periodically and circulated to any interested parties.

DONE AND ORDERED in Chambers, at Naples, Collier County, Florida this 26th day of August, 2003.

Hugh D. Hayes
Chief Judge

History. - New.

12.4. UNIFIED FAMILY COURT

IN THE TWENTIETH JUDICIAL CIRCUIT IN AND FOR THE STATE OF FLORIDA LEE, COLLIER, CHARLOTTE, HENDRY, AND GLADES COUNTIES

IN RE: UNIFIED FAMILY COURT

ADMINISTRATIVE ORDER NO. 12.4

WHEREAS, the Florida Supreme Court in Re: Report of the Family Court Steering Committee, 794 So. 2d 518 (Fla. 2001), directed each circuit to submit revised local rules or an administrative order implementing a Unified Family Court consistent with recommendations approved by the Florida Supreme Court in its opinion; and

WHEREAS, the Florida Supreme Court in Re: Report of the Family Court Steering Committee, 794 So. 2d 518 (Fla. 2001), directed each circuit to make every effort to resolve family disputes in a "fair, timely, efficient, and cost effective manner;" and

WHEREAS, the Twentieth Judicial Circuit is desirous of meeting the mandates of the Florida Supreme Court; and

WHEREAS, the Twentieth Judicial Circuit is desirous of assisting litigants with cases involving intra and inter-related family issues to avoid conflicting decisions and minimize inconvenience to the family; and

WHEREAS, the Twentieth Judicial Circuit is desirous of maximizing all resources readily available to assist with resolving familial related case litigation; and

WHEREAS, in an effort to facilitate open and effective communication between court staff, judges, attorneys and social service providers and to better serve the litigants of the court community,

NOW, THEREFORE, pursuant to the authority vested in me as Chief Judge of the Twentieth Judicial Circuit of Florida under Fla. R. Jud. Admin. 2.215, it is hereby ordered that:

Effective January 2, 2008, the unification of family court shall be implemented and shall operate as a pilot program in Lee County, and may later be formally expanded to Collier, Charlotte, Hendry and Glades counties by further order of the Court.[1] Such implementation shall be in accordance with the recommendations of the Florida Supreme Court, the Twentieth Judicial Circuit's FLAG (Family Law Advisory Group), the Twentieth Judicial Circuit's Unified Family Court Implementation Committee, and meetings with community stakeholders. The Unified Family Court shall function as set forth:

I. Unified Family Court Jurisdiction

A. The Unified Family Court shall consist of two components, Unified Family Court/Domestic Relations and Unified Family Court/Juvenile.

B. All related Unified Family Court/Domestic Relations case types will remain in the Unified Family Court/Domestic Relations, except as otherwise provided in section I.D. of this order, and shall be linked upon order of the Court. If a family has a pending dependency case, and subsequently, a member of the family files for a dissolution of marriage (DOM), the Unified Family Court/Juvenile judge handling dependency cases shall decide all issues in the DOM action, including those involving children and financial matters, unless the Unified Family Court/Juvenile judge handling dependency cases files a good cause order as described below in section I.D. If a good cause order is entered, the Unified Family Court/Juvenile judge handling dependency cases may preside over issues in the DOM action involving children, while the Unified Family Court/Domestic Relations judge presides over financial issues, or the Unified Family Court/Juvenile judge handling dependency cases may elect to refer the entire DOM action back to the Unified Family Court/Domestic Relations judge. However, if a family has a juvenile delinquency case(s) and a DOM case, but no other cases pending, the provisions of this Administrative Order shall not be applicable and the cases shall be heard individually in the respective divisions of the Court.

C. All related Unified Family Court/Juvenile case types will remain in the Unified Family Court/Juvenile, except as otherwise provided in section I. D. of this order. If different judges are assigned to related juvenile delinquency and dependency cases, the juvenile delinquency judge shall preside over the adjudicatory hearing portion of the delinquency case. However, the juvenile delinquency case will subsequently be reassigned to the dependency judge for the dispositional hearing portion of the delinquency case.

D. The preferred resolution of related cases is a "one family, one judge" model. However, after receiving a recommendation from a case manager, the courts shall retain discretion to resolve cases in a manner that promotes the best interest of the family and children (if any). If a court determines that following the preferred "one family, one judge" model is not in the best interest of the family and children (if any), the court shall file an order finding good cause for not following the preferred model. The case managers shall maintain the responsibility of sharing information concerning related cases with the various judges presiding over those related cases.

II. Unified Family Court jurisdiction shall consist of and include the following elements:

A. Case Types:
- dissolution of marriage
- division and distribution of property arising out of a dissolution of marriage
- annulment
- support unconnected with dissolution of marriage
- paternity
- child support
- URESA/UIFSA
- custodial care of and access to children
- adoption
- name change
- declaratory judgment actions related to premarital, marital, or post marital agreements
- civil domestic and repeat violence injunctions
- juvenile dependency
- emancipation of a minor
- CINS/FINS
- truancy
- modification and enforcement of orders entered in these cases
- juvenile delinquency
- Marchman and Baker Act

B. Components of Unified Family Court:

1. The Unified Family Court bench shall consist of judges who have received training and have extensive experience in Family, Juvenile, and County Criminal Court.

2. Magistrates to conduct quasi-judicial hearings and maximize judicial resources.

3. Case management to coordinate and assist litigants and the judiciary with various court processes and to link all case types as defined in Section II.A.

4. A social service component to assist litigants and the judiciary by providing prompt linkages to applicable court and community resources.

5. An Alternative Dispute Resolution component to assist families and children with resolving disputes in order to promote long term family stability.

6. A technology component to provide technological services and systems for the purposes of accessing databases essential to case management.

III. General Unified Family Court Operations:

A. At the time of filing any case type delineated in Section II.A., parties should provide the Clerk with a fully executed Unified Family Court Related Case Information Sheet along with the initiating action. The Clerk of Courts shall forward to the UFC case management division of the Administrative Office of the Courts a copy of the filing and the original Unified Family Court Related Case Information Sheet. The Clerk shall not file the Unified Family Court Related Case Information Sheet in the court file. In the event that a Unified Family Court Related Case Information Sheet is not provided with the initiating action, the judge or case manager shall inquire of the attorneys at each court hearing as to whether they are aware of any related cases.

B. In the event parties request assistance with completion of the Unified Family Court Related Case Information Sheet, the Clerk of Courts shall refer parties to the UFC case management division of the Administrative Office of the Courts.

C. The case manager shall review the filing and Unified Family Court Related Case Information Sheet and shall submit an appropriate proposed draft order(s) for Court review.

D. Upon order of the Court, the Clerk of Courts shall enter related case information into the Odyssey or Reflections programs.

E. The Court shall initiate steps to have full access to the databases of all Unified Family Court stakeholders and agencies to ensure open and effective communications. The Clerk of Courts shall notify the presiding judges and the UFC case managers when they identify UFC related cases. The Clerk of Courts shall also designate a case as a UFC case by placing a visible UFC stamp on the outside of the file and by attaching a copy of this Administrative Order and the attached forms to the inside cover of the UFC related case.

F. The Unified Family Court shall be evaluated routinely by the Chief Judge or the Chief Judge's designee to determine its effectiveness in implementing this circuit's goal of addressing family law matters in a comprehensive, coordinated manner.

G. The Twentieth Judicial Circuit's FLAG (Family Law Advisory Group) and the involved stakeholders shall continue to provide input regarding the Twentieth Judicial Circuit's Unified Family Court.

H. The Court shall determine the appropriate schedule/dockets and coordinate with the Clerk of Courts.

IV. Unified Family Court Case Managers' Ability to Access Juvenile Court Records

A. Unified Family Court Case Managers of the Administrative Office of the Courts have a proper interest in juvenile delinquency and dependency official court records in order to implement a Unified Family Court that addresses the multiple legal issues facing families pursuant to Fla. Stat. §§ 985.045(2), 985.04(1), 39.0132(3) and 39.0132(4)(a)1.

B. Accordingly, the Unified Family Court Case Managers shall have access to and may inspect the official juvenile delinquency and juvenile dependency court records in the Twentieth Judicial Circuit.

C. Pursuant to Fla. Stat. § 985.04, all information obtained from juvenile delinquency court records in the discharge of official duty by any judge, any employee of the court, any authorized agent of the Department of Juvenile Justice, the Parole Commission, the Department of Corrections, the juvenile justice circuit boards, any law enforcement agent, or any licensed professional or licensed community agency representative participating in the assessment or treatment of a juvenile may be disclosed to the Unified Family Court Case Managers.

D. Pursuant to Fla. Stat. § 39.0132, all information obtained from juvenile dependency court records in the discharge of official duty by any judge, employee of the court, authorized agent of the Department of Children and Family Services, correctional probation officer, or law enforcement agent may be disclosed to the Unified Family Court Case Managers.

E. Any information the Unified Family Court Case Managers obtain concerning a juvenile delinquency case and/or juvenile dependency case may only be provided to a judge or a magistrate presiding over a unified family court related case and any information in written form must be sealed if it is filed in any unified family court related case file.

V. The following forms are attached hereto and are approved for use in accordance with this Administrative Order:

A. Unified Family Court Related Case Information Sheet

B. Notification of Unified Family Court Related Case

C. Order Identifying Unified Family Court Cases and Transferring/ Assigning them to Unified Family Court

D. Order Setting Unified Family Court First Mandatory Case Conference

E. Order Finding Good Cause for Deviation from Preferred Model

VI. General Provisions

A. This Administrative Order is not intended to grant public access to confidential court records. Court records deemed confidential and exempt from public access pursuant to any law, statute or rule shall remain so, unless otherwise ordered by the Court.

B. To the extent that any provision of this Administrative Order may be construed as being in conflict with any law, statute or rule, the law, statute or rule shall prevail.

DONE AND ORDERED in Chambers in Fort Myers, Lee County, Florida, this 31st day of December, 2007.

G. Keith Cary
Chief Judge

History.—New.

1 Prior to formally expanding the program to Collier, Charlotte, Hendry and Glades counties, no court shall be prohibited or discouraged from informally taking steps to effectuate the intent of this Administrative Order as it relates to resolving intra and inter-related family issues, provided that those steps do not conflict with any provision of this Administrative Order, the Florida Supreme Court's opinion in Re: Report of the Family Court Steering Committee, or any other rule of court or law.

ATTACHMENT A

TWENTIETH JUDICIAL CIRCUIT OF FLORIDA
UNIFIED FAMILY COURT RELATED CASE INFORMATION SHEET

Section I: INSTRUCTIONS FOR USING THIS FORM

The information contained in this form will be utilized to notify the Unified Family Court Division of related cases (i.e. multiple cases in the judicial system involving one family), pursuant to Administrative Order No. 12.4 of the Twentieth Judicial Circuit of Florida.

THIS FORM IS FOR THE INTERNAL USE OF THE UFC CASE MANAGEMENT DIVISION OF THE ADMINISTRATIVE OFFICE OF THE COURTS ONLY. PARTIES SHOULD PROVIDE THE CLERK WITH THIS FULLY EXECUTED FORM ALONG WITH ANY INITIATING ACTION, AND THE CLERK SHALL FORWARD IT TO THE UFC CASE MANAGEMENT DIVISION OF THE ADMINISTRATIVE OFFICE OF THE COURTS. THE CLERK SHALL NOT FILE THIS FORM IN THE CASE FILE. IF THIS FORM CONTAINS INFORMATION THAT IS CONFIDENTIAL PURSUANT TO STATUTE OR RULE, IT SHALL BE EXEMPT FROM PUBLIC DISCLOSURE.

Section II:

Name of Person Completing this Form (please print) ____________
Department: ____________ Date: ____________
Address: ____________ Phone No.: ____________

Section III: COMPLETE ALL INFORMATION BELOW FOR ANY RELATED CASES FILED IN THIS CIRCUIT (including your case)

FAMILY ID#: ____________

( ) DOMESTIC RELATIONS
Case Name: ________ Case No: ________ Judge: ____________ Case Status: ( )Open ( )Closed
Case Type: ( ) Dissolution of Marriage ( ) Paternity ( ) Child Support ( ) Other: ______
Petitioner: ____________ Respondent: ____________
Attorney: ____________ Attorney: ____________
Court ordered services: ____________
Next hearing date (if any): ________ Hearing type: ____________

( ) CIVIL DOMESTIC VIOLENCE INJUNCTION
Case Name: ________ Case No: ________ Judge: ____________ Case Status: ( )Open ( )Closed
Petitioner: ____________ Respondent: ____________

Attorney: ______ Attorney: ______
Injunction Issued: ( ) temporary ( ) permanent Date injunction entered through:
______
Court ordered services: ______
Next hearing date (if any): ______ Hearing type: ______

( ) JUVENILE DEPENDENCY
Case No: ______ Judge: ______ Case Status: ( ) Open ( ) Closed
DCF Atty.: ______ Mother's Atty.: ______
GAL Atty.: ______ Father's Atty.: ______
TPR order in effect: ( ) yes ( ) no ( ) unknown
Parent's (s') court ordered services: ______
Next hearing date (if any): ______ Hearing type: ______

( ) JUVENILE DELINQUENCY
Case No: ______ Judge: ______ Case Status: ( ) Open ( ) Closed
DJJ Caseworker: ______ PD: ______ SAO: ______
Next hearing date (if any): ______ Hearing type: ______

( ) CRIMINAL
Case Name: ______ Case No: ______ Judge: ______ Case Status: ( ) Open ( ) Closed
DOB of defendant: ______
PD/Atty.: ______ SAO: ______
Pre-trial Officer: ______ Probation Officer: ______
Court ordered services: ______
Next hearing date (if any): ______ Hearing type: ______

( ) OTHER CASES PENDING OUTSIDE OF THIS CIRCUIT
Nature of Case: ______ Case Name: ______ Case No: ______ Judge: ______
Plaintiff/Petitioner: ______ Defendant/Respondent: ______
Attorney: ______ Attorney: ______
Court ordered services: ______

ATTACHMENT B

TWENTIETH JUDICIAL CIRCUIT OF FLORIDA
NOTIFICATION OF UNIFIED FAMILY COURT RELATED CASE

If this form contains any information concerning a juvenile delinquency or dependency case, this form and the information contained herein may only be provided to a judge presiding over a unified family court related case and the form must be sealed if it is filed in any unified family court related case file.

To: ______
______

From: ______, UFC Case Manager
Unified Family Court Division, Administrative Office of the Courts, Lee County Justice Center
1700 Monroe St., Ft. Myers, FL 33901
(239) 335–2247 (telephone)

Date: ______

RE: Your Case No(s).: ______
Your Case Name(s): ______

The following case(s) has/have been identified as a related case(s) to that referenced above, which is open and pending in your division:

FAMILY ID#: ______

( ) DOMESTIC RELATIONS
Case Name: ______ Case No: ______ Judge: ______ Case Status: ( ) Open ( ) Closed
Case Type: ( ) Dissolution of Marriage ( ) Paternity ( ) Child Support ( ) Other: ______
Petitioner: ______ Respondent: ______
Attorney: ______ Attorney: ______
Court ordered services: ______
Next hearing date (if any): ______ Hearing type: ______

( ) CIVIL DOMESTIC VIOLENCE INJUNCTION
Case Name: ______ Case No: ______ Judge: ______ Case Status: ( ) Open ( ) Closed
Petitioner: ______ Respondent: ______
Attorney: ______ Attorney: ______
Injunction Issued: ( ) temporary ( ) permanent Date injunction entered through:
______
Court ordered services: ______
Next hearing date (if any): ______ Hearing type: ______

( ) JUVENILE DEPENDENCY

Case No: ______ Judge: ______ Case Status: ( ) Open ( ) Closed
DCF Atty.: ______ Mother's Atty.: ______
GAL Atty.: ______ Father's Atty.: ______
TPR order in effect: ( ) yes ( ) no ( ) unknown
Parent's (s') court ordered services: ______
Next hearing date (if any): ______ Hearing type: ______

( ) **JUVENILE DELINQUENCY**
Case No: ______ udge: ______ Case Status: ( ) Open ( ) Closed
DJJ Caseworker: ______ PD: ______ SAO: ______
Next hearing date (if any): ______ Hearing type: ______

( ) **CRIMINAL**
Case Name: ______ Case No: ______ Judge: ______ Case Status: ( ) Open ( ) Closed
DOB of defendant: ______
PD/Atty.: ______ SAO: ______
Pre-trial Officer: ______ Probation Officer: ______
Court ordered services: ______
Next hearing date (if any): ______ Hearing type: ______

( ) **OTHER CASES PENDING OUTSIDE OF THIS CIRCUIT**
Nature of Case: ______ Case Name: ______ Case No: ______ Judge: ______
Plaintiff/Petitioner: ______ Defendant/Respondent: ______
Attorney: ______ Attorney: ______
Court ordered services: ______

Notes: ______

______

______

ATTACHMENT C

IN THE CIRCUIT COURT OF THE TWENTIETH JUDICIAL CIRCUIT OF FLORIDA,

IN AND FOR ______ COUNTY

IN RE: THE MATTER OF:

______,

Petitioner,

______,

Respondent,

______/

DOMESTIC RELATIONS
CASE NO.:

JUVENILE DIVISION
CASE NO.:

DOMESTIC VIOLENCE DIVISION
CASE NO.:

PROBATE DIVISION
CASE NO.:

OTHER:
CASE NO.:

ORDER IDENTIFYING UNIFIED FAMILY COURT CASES AND TRANSFERRING/ASSIGNING THEM TO UNIFIED FAMILY COURT

THIS CAUSE came for review before the Court pursuant to Administrative Order No. 12.4 as a cross over matter with Unified Family Court Jurisdiction.

A. The Unified Family Court case manager identified cases listed above and they have met the criteria as defined in Administrative Order No. 12.4 to be designated as Unified Family Court cases.

B. Unified Family Court cases shall be coordinated in a manner to avoid conflicting decisions, enhance judicial decision making and minimize inconvenience to the family.

THEREFORE, IT IS HEREBY

ORDERED AND AJUDGED [2] as follows:

☐ 1. The Clerk of Courts is directed to transfer these cases to Unified Family Court division ______, the Honorable ______, presently presiding over all cases, except as otherwise provided for herein:

______

______

☐ 2. If different judges are assigned to related juvenile delinquency and dependency cases, the juvenile delinquency judge shall preside over the adjudicatory hearing portion of the delinquency case. However the juvenile delinquency case will subsequently be reassigned to the dependency judge for the dispositional hearing portion of the delinquency case.

☐ 3. The Clerk of Courts is directed to file this order in each case listed above, as the cases currently lie in the correct Division of the Court.

☐ 4. The Clerk of Courts is directed to link each of the above cases in the "Related Cases" filed in the Odyssey or Reflections System.

☐ 5. The Clerk of Courts is directed to forward all of the above Court files to the Unified Family Court Case Manager in Division ______.

☐ 6. All previous Orders entered in these cases will remain in effect until further Order of the Court.

☐ 7. All previously scheduled hearings will need to be reset (Attorneys contact divisional J.A., self-represented parties will receive an Order Setting Hearing by mail), with the exception of the following hearings:

______

______

☐ 8. Counsel and/or those persons who are self-represented are directed to continue to use the appropriate divisional style and case number when filing pleadings, motions, notices of hearing, etc., in a specific division despite the status of this as a Unified Family Court Case. The Clerk of Courts is directed to forward all UFC related case files to the Judge for hearing or Case Manager for case management purposes, as appropriate.

DONE AND ORDERED in ______ County, Florida this ___ day of ______, 20___.

______
Circuit Judge

Copies Furnished:

ATTACHMENT D

IN THE CIRCUIT COURT OF THE TWENTIETH JUDICIAL CIRCUIT
IN AND FOR ________ COUNTY, FLORIDA
UNIFIED FAMILY COURT DIVISION

CASE NOS.

,

Petitioner,

vs.

,

Respondent.

______________________/

ORDER SETTING UNIFIED FAMILY COURT FIRST MANDATORY CASE CONFERENCE

THIS CAUSE having come before the Court, *sue sponte*, and the Court having duly determined that the above referenced cases meet the criteria for assignment to the newly created Unified Family Court Division, it is hereby,

ORDERED AND ADJUDGED as follows:

1. A Mandatory Case Conference is hereby scheduled before this Court on the ___ day of ________, 20 ___, at ______ am/pm., Courtroom ______, ______. Attendance by all attorneys and parties is mandatory. *Further, attendance is also mandatory for the Unified Family Court Case Manager assigned to these cases.*

2. Prior to the Case Conference, it is suggested and/or recommended that each attorney and/or party review The Twentieth Judicial Circuit's Administrative Order 12.4 and *The Report of Family Court Steering Committee, 794 So. 2d 518 (Florida Supreme Court 2001).*

3. At the Case Conference, the parties shall be prepared to discuss, *inter alia*, the following matters:

a. The status of all pending matters, including but not limited to, all pending and unresolved motions;

b. The possibility or possibilities of mediation and settlement;

c. Discovery related issues;

d. The scheduling of hearings and/or trials;

e. Case management related issues;

f. All issues related to the safety, health and welfare of the minor children involved in these matters.

DONE AND ORDERED in ________ County, Florida, this ___ day of ________, 20 ___.

____
Circuit Judge

Copies Furnished:

ATTACHMENT E

IN THE CIRCUIT COURT OF THE TWENTIETH JUDICIAL CIRCUIT OF FLORIDA,
IN AND FOR ________ COUNTY, FLORIDA

IN RE: THE MATTER OF:

______________________,

Petitioner/Plaintiff, Case Nos.:

______________________,

Respondent/Defendant,

______________________/

ORDER FINDING GOOD CAUSE FOR DEVIATING FROM PREFERRED UFC MODEL

THIS CAUSE came before the Court pursuant to Administrative Order 12.4 as a cross over matter with Unified Family Court jurisdiction. Having reviewed the recommendation of the UFC case manager and having considered the best interest of the family and children (if any), and having been being fully advised in this matter, the Court finds and orders as follows:

1. The Court finds good cause for deviating from the preferred "one family, one judge" model.

2. As an alternative to the "one family, one judge" model, the UFC case manager shall continue to share information concerning related cases with the various judges presiding over those related cases.

DONE AND ORDERED in Chambers in ________, ________ County, Florida, this ___ day of ________, 20 ___.

____
Circuit Judge

[2] So in original.

12.5. LEE COUNTY PAY OR APPEAR PROGRAM FOR ENFORCEMENT OF CHILD SUPPORT ORDERS (RESCINDED)

IN THE TWENTIETH JUDICIAL CIRCUIT IN AND FOR THE STATE OF FLORIDA LEE COUNTY

ADMINISTRATIVE ORDER NO. 12.5—RESCINDED—

IN RE: LEE COUNTY PAY OR APPEAR PROGRAM FOR ENFORCEMENT OF CHILD SUPPORT ORDERS

Pursuant to the authority vested in me as Chief Judge of the Twentieth Judicial Circuit of Florida under Fla. R. Jud. Admin. 2.215, and in light of the opinion of the Florida Supreme Court in Case No. SC10–243, and as a matter of internal housekeeping, it is ordered that Administrative Order No. 12.5 is hereby RESCINDED from the Administrative Code of the Twentieth Judicial Circuit.

DONE AND ORDERED in chambers in Fort Myers, Lee County, Florida, this 15 day of Sept., 2011.

____
Jay B. Rosman
Chief Judge

History. Administrative Order 12.5 (September 24, 2009)

12.6. CIVIL CONTEMPT IN CHILD SUPPORT MATTERS—PROCEDURES UPON ARREST ON WRIT OF BODILY ATTACHMENT

IN THE TWENTIETH JUDICIAL CIRCUIT IN AND FOR THE STATE OF FLORIDA

ADMINISTRATIVE ORDER NO. 12.6

IN RE: CIVIL CONTEMPT IN CHILD SUPPORT MATTERS—PROCEDURES UPON ARREST ON WRIT OF BODILY ATTACHMENT

WHEREAS, the procedures to be used for civil contempt in child support matters are governed by Fla. Fam. L. R. 12.615; and

WHEREAS, Fla. Fam. L. R. 12.615 provides for the issuance of a Writ of Bodily Attachment, with a purge amount, under certain circumstances; and

WHEREAS, Fla. Fam. L. R. 12.615 requires that, upon arrest on a Writ of Bodily Attachment, the alleged contemnor be brought before the court within 48 hours for a determination of the alleged contemnor's present ability to pay the purge amount, but does not specifically identify the judicial officer before whom the alleged contemnor is to be brought; and

WHEREAS, the five counties of the Twentieth Judicial Circuit vary in resources, both judicial and staffing, and require different procedures so as to ensure that alleged contemnors are not detained more than 48 hours after arrest on a Writ of Bodily Attachment before being brought before a judicial officer;

It is therefore, **ORDERED,** by the authority vested in me as Chief Judge of the Twentieth Judicial Circuit of Florida under Fla. R. Jud. Admin. 2.215, that the attached procedures for Lee County, Collier County, Charlotte County, Hendry County and Glades County are approved for implementation.

DONE AND ORDERED in chambers in Fort Myers, Lee County, Florida, this 19th day of Feb., 2014.

Jay B. Rosman
Chief Judge

History.—New.

TWENTIETH JUDICIAL CIRCUIT OF FLORIDA ADMINISTRATIVE OFFICE OF THE COURTS LEE COUNTY JUSTICE CENTER 1700 MONROE STREET FORT MYERS, FLORIDA 33901 TEL. (239) 533–1700 FAX (239) 533–1701

–Civil Contempt in Family Law Child Support Matters–

Procedures to be used after Arrest on Writ of Bodily Attachment

–LEE COUNTY–

The procedures used for civil contempt in child support matters are governed by Fla. Fam. L. R. 12.615, a copy of which is attached hereto. The premise is that when a person is initially ordered by the trial court, in the normal course of proceedings, to pay a specific amount of child support, it is thereafter presumed that the person has the ability to do so. A motion for civil contempt is the mechanism used to address the failure of a party to comply with an order to pay child support. Proper notice of the hearing on the motion for civil contempt must be served on the alleged contemnor.

It is at the hearing on the motion for civil contempt that the person's ability to pay becomes relevant; civil contempt is not intended to serve as punishment, but rather is intended to compel compliance—before a person can be found to be in civil contempt, a finding must be made that the failure to pay the court-ordered child support is willful and that the person has the present ability to pay and, therefore, "holds the keys to the jail cell." The preeminent case explaining the process involving civil contempt in child support matters is Bowen v. Bowen, 471 So. 2d 1274 (Fla. 1985), a copy of which is attached hereto [1].

Motions for civil contempt may be heard by a trial judge or by a DOR Hearing Officer, depending upon the background of the case. If heard by a trial judge and the alleged contemnor appears and is found to be in civil contempt, the judge may remand the contemnor to jail with a purge amount. In such instances, subsection (f) of Rule 12.615 provides that "... at any time after a contemnor is incarcerated, the court on its own motion or motion of any party may review the contemner's present ability to comply with the purge condition and the duration of incarceration and modify any prior orders."

However, if the alleged contemnor fails to appear for the hearing on the motion for civil contempt scheduled before a trial judge, a Writ of Bodily Attachment, with a purge amount, may be issued by the trial judge in accordance with subsection (c)(2)(B) of Rule 12.615. Also, to the extent that the motion for civil contempt is heard by a DOR hearing officer, it is important to remember that a DOR hearing officer does not have the authority to remand persons into custody nor to issue Writs of Bodily Attachment. Rather, if the DOR hearing officer finds that the alleged contemnor has the ability to pay, or if the alleged contemnor fails to appear for the hearing, the DOR hearing officer can only make a recommended finding that the trial judge issue a Writ of Bodily Attachment, with a purge amount.

The below listed procedures are designed to address scenarios in which a Writ of Bodily Attachment has been issued and executed, in accordance with the above-paragraph. Once a Writ of Bodily Attachment has been executed, Rule 12.615 requires that the alleged contemnor be brought before the court within 48 hours for a hearing on whether the alleged contemnor has the present ability to pay support and, if so, whether the failure to pay such support is willful. The rule, however, does not specify the judicial officer before whom the alleged contemnor is to be brought, and, as a matter of practicality, it is not reasonable to presume that the alleged contemnor can be brought before the assigned trial judge within the limited 48 hour period required by the rule. The most logical and practical manner in which to ensure that the 48 hour deadline is met, is to have the alleged contemnor brought before the First Appearance Judge, one of which would be available every day, including weekends and holidays. The issue then is whether the First Appearance Judge is the appropriate judicial officer to be making the actual determination regarding the alleged contemnor's present ability to pay support and, if so, whether the alleged contemner's failure to pay support is willful.

Having reviewed the procedures and methods utilized in other circuits throughout the State of Florida, and upon consultation with the Lee County Family Law Administrative Judge, the following guidelines have been approved by the Chief Judge for use within Lee County:

1. Upon arrest on a Writ of Bodily Attachment issued for failure to pay child support, the alleged contemnor may pay the purge amount stated in the Writ of Bodily Attachment and be released prior to First Appearance.

2. If the alleged contemnor does not pay the purge amount prior to First Appearance, the alleged contemnor shall be brought before the First Appearance Judge within 24 hours of arrest preferably, but in no instance more than 48 hours after arrest. The First Appearance Judge will be provided with a form "Order at First Appearance on Writ of Bodily Attachment for Nonpayment of Support" for the purpose facilitating the proceeding. A copy of the form "Order at First Appearance on Writ of Bodily Attachment for Nonpayment of Support" is attached hereto.

3. At First Appearance, the First Appearance Judge will inquire so as to confirm whether or not the purge amount has been paid and, if the purge amount has, in fact, been paid, the First Appearance Judge will order that the alleged contemnor be released from custody.

4. If the purge amount has NOT been paid, the First Appearance Judge has the following options:

(a) The First Appearance Judge may conduct a legally sufficient inquiry for the purpose of determining whether the alleged contemnor does or does not, in fact, continue to have the present ability to pay the purge amount or any part thereof.

(1) If the First Appearance Judge determines that the alleged contemnor does NOT have the present ability to pay any portion of the purge amount, the First Appearance Judge will order that the alleged contemnor be released from custody.

(2) If the First Appearance Judge determines that the alleged contemnor does, in fact, have the present ability to pay the purge amount, or a portion thereof, the First Appearance Judge will order that the alleged contemnor pay an amount which shall be specified in writing on the Order at First Appearance. The First Appearance Judge will also order that, if the specified amount remains unpaid and the alleged contemnor is not released from custody within 48 hours, the alleged contemnor shall be returned to the next scheduled First Appearance.

<u>OR, ALTERNATIVELY,</u>

(b) If Lee County Pretrial Services advises that the purge amount has, in fact, not been paid, the First Appearance Judge may order that the alleged contemnor be released from custody, AND, will issue a written order with a CONTROL DATE for appearance before a Family Court Judge for the purpose of determining the present ability to pay the purge amount. The Order at First Appearance will be generated and populated by Lee County Pretrial Services and presented to the First Appearance Judge. Prior to release, the alleged contemnor must sign a written acknowledgement at the bottom of the Order at First Appearance of having received a copy of the written order noticing the upcoming date of the appearance. A copy of the Order at First Appearance noticing the upcoming date of appearance shall be provided by the Clerk to the Domestic Violence Docket Specialist

(1) The CONTROL DATE appearance will be scheduled on the rotating two-week "Domestic Violence/Order To Show Cause" docket. The Domestic Violence Unit (Family Division) will provide to the Clerk and to Lee County Pretrial Services a list of pre-scheduled "Order To Show Cause" court dates with a hearing time, the name of the presiding judge, and the assigned courtroom. This list will be used to schedule the CONTROL DATE for the alleged contemnor to appear in court before a Family Court Judge. The court date selected as a CONTROL DATE will be no less than four weeks and no more than six weeks from the First Appearance date.

(2) If an alleged contemnor released with a CONTROL DATE pays the purge amount prior to the scheduled upcoming date of appearance, the hearing may be cancelled and it may be removed from the docket. It shall be the responsibility of the alleged contemnor to ensure that the court file **<u>timely</u>** reflects the filing of proof of payment of the purge, with a copy to all parties and counsel of record, and that a courtesy copy of proof of payment of the purge is provided to the Domestic Violence Unit. The alleged contemnor's obligation to ensure that proof of payment of the purge is **<u>timely</u>** filed, with copies provided as describe above, is critical so as to avoid any confusion or inadvertent issuance of subsequent Writ of Bodily Attachment for failure to appear.

(3) Once released from custody with a CONTROL DATE, Domestic Violence Case Manager will monitor the case file so as to determine whether the file contains evidence of the purge amount having been paid prior to the scheduled upcoming date of appearance. If the file contains timely evidence of the purge amount having been paid, the Domestic Violence Case Manager will prepare a proposed Notice of Cancellation for judicial review, and if approved and the Notice of Cancellation is signed, the Domestic Violence Case Manager will notify all parties. If the alleged contemnor does pay the purge amount prior to the hearing, but does not timely file proof of such and does not timely provide notice, and has not been notified that the hearing has been cancelled, AND fails to appear at the hearing for the purpose of advising and providing proof to the Family Court Judge in person of the payment, it is possible that the Court's lack of knowledge or proof of payment will result in the issuance of a Writ of Bodily Attachment, due to no fault of the Court.

(4) During each rotating two-week "Domestic Violence/Order To Show Cause" docket, if any alleged contemnors are scheduled to appear before the Family Court Judge, a Domestic Violence Case Manager will be prepared to advise the Family Court Judge as to the current status as reflected by the case file.

IN THE CIRCUIT COURT OF THE TWENTIETH JUDICIAL CIRCUIT IN AND FOR LEE COUNTY, FLORIDA

Petitioner

vs. Case No.

Respondent

ORDER AT FIRST APPEARANCE ON WRIT OF BODILY ATTACHMENT FOR NONPAYMENT OF SUPPORT

The Respondent appeared before the Court on the Writ of Bodily Attachment, entered in this case, within 48 hours of arrest as required by Rule 12.615, Fla. Fam. L. R. Upon consideration, it is ordered as follows (Check the Box that Applies):

☐ The purge amount as it appears on the Writ of Bodily Attachment has been paid. The Respondent shall immediately be released from custody.

☐ The purge amount as it appears on the Writ of Bodily Attachment has NOT been paid, but the Court affirmatively finds that the Respondent does NOT have the present ability to pay the purge amount. The Respondent shall immediately be released from custody.

☐ The purge amount as it appears on the Writ of Bodily Attachment has NOT been paid, but the Court affirmatively finds that the Respondent does, in fact, have the present ability to pay $ ___. Upon payment of this amount, the Respondent shall be released from custody. If this amount remains unpaid and the Respondent is not released from custody within 48 hours, the Respondent shall be returned to the next scheduled First Appearance.

☐ The purge amount as it appears on the Writ of Bodily Attachment has NOT been paid. The Respondent shall be immediately released, but is **COMMANDED** to appear before the Honorable ___ at the Lee County Justice Center, 1700 Monroe Street, Fort Myers, Florida 33901, Courtroom ___, on the ___ day of ________, 20 ___, at 1:00 pm, for the purpose of a determination of whether the Respondent continues to have the present ability to pay the purge. If Respondent pays the purge amount prior to the above scheduled hearing, the Respondent must timely file proof of such with the Clerk of Court and shall provide a copy to the Domestic Violence Unit, Court Administration, 1700 Monroe Street, 3rd Floor, Fort Myers, Florida 33901. Upon filing proof of payment and upon timely receipt of the notice from Respondent, the hearing MAY be cancelled at the discretion of the presiding judge. However, unless Respondent receives written notice of cancellation of the hearing, the Respondent must appear even if the purge has been paid, for the express purpose of providing proof of payment.

If Respondent fails to appear at the above scheduled hearing (in the absence of a notice of cancellation), another writ of bodily attachment may issue for the Respondent's arrest. ORDERED in Fort Myers, Lee County, Florida, this ___ day of ______, 20 ___.

____
First Appearance Judge

I, Respondent, hereby acknowledge receipt of notice of the above scheduled hearing.

____
Respondent

AMERICANS WITH DISABILITIES ACT—REQUEST FOR ACCOMMODATION

Please Use the Below Phone Number Only for the Purpose of Requesting an Accommodation under the Americans With Disabilities Act

If you are a person with a disability who needs any accommodation in order to participate in this proceeding, you are entitled, at no cost to you, to the provision of certain assistance. Please contact Dolly Ballard, Operations Division Director, whose office is located at Lee County Justice Center, 1700 Monroe Street, Fort Myers, Florida 33901, and whose telephone number is (239) 533–1771, at least 7 days before your scheduled court appearance, or immediately upon receiving this notification if the time before the scheduled appearance is less than 7 days; if you are hearing or voice impaired, call 711.

TWENTIETH JUDICIAL CIRCUIT OF FLORIDA ADMINISTRATIVE OFFICE OF THE COURTS CHARLOTTE COUNTY JUSTICE CENTER 350 EAST MARION AVE PUNTA GORDA, FLORIDA 33954

–Civil Contempt in Family Law Child Support Matters–

Procedures to be used after Arrest on Writ of Bodily Attachment (Charlotte)

1. Upon arrest on a Writ of Bodily Attachment issued for failure to pay child support, the contemnor may pay the purge amount stated in the Writ of Bodily Attachment and be released prior to First Appearance.

2. If the alleged contemnor does not pay the purge amount prior to First Appearance, the alleged contemnor shall be brought before the First Appearance Judge within 24 hours of arrest.

3. At First Appearance, the judge will inquire as to whether the purge amount has been paid and, if so, the judge will order that the alleged contemnor be released from custody.

4. If at First Appearance, the alleged contemnor advises that the purge amount has not yet been paid, the First Appearance Judge will order that the alleged contemnor be held in custody on the purge amount until posted, AND will be required to be returned to first appearance the following day (if not posted) for the purpose of determining the present ability to pay support and willfulness of the failure to pay support. The alleged contemnor may still pay the purge

amount stated in the Writ of Bodily Attachment and be released prior to the scheduled review.

5. On the next day following the contemnors initial First Appearance, the alleged contemnor will be brought back before the First Appearance Judge, if the alleged contemnor has not yet paid the purge amount, the First Appearance Judge will conduct a hearing and inquire as to the ability of the alleged contemnor to pay the purge amount consistent with rule 12.615 using the attached form order entitled ORDER AT FIRST APPEARANCE ON WRIT OF BODILY ATTACHMENT (see attached order) and make the appropriate determination pursuant to the rule.

6. The order will be completed and filed with the first appearance clerk, with copies provided to the respondent, the jail, Attorney for the Department of Revenue, and the Judge Assigned to the case.

TWENTIETH JUDICIAL CIRCUIT OF FLORIDA ADMINISTRATIVE OFFICE OF THE COURTS COLLIER COUNTY GOVERNMENT COMPLEX 3315 TAMIAMI TRAIL EAST NAPLES, FLORIDA 34112 TEL. (239) 2528800

Operational Plan for Child Support Writs for Collier County

1. Upon arrest on a Writ of Bodily Attachment issued for failure to pay child support, the contemnor may pay the purge amount stated in the Writ and be released prior to first appearance.

2. If the contemnor does not pay the purge amount the case will be brought before a family law circuit court judge within 24 to 48 hours. Excluding weekends and holidays, jail records will immediately notify the judicial assistants for the assigned family law judiciary, the clerk of court supervisor and the criminal division director of all arrests for child support writs within a 24 hour period. The judicial assistant will schedule the hearing date and notify all parties. Both family law Judges have committed to providing hearing time at 8:45 AM each weekday, providing it is not a holiday. Hearings will be conducted in Courtroom 3–4.

3. In the event a Writ of Bodily attachment is served on a Friday, Saturday or the day preceding a holiday and the contemnor does not pay the purge amount, jail records will place the case on the first appearance docket to be addressed by the first appearance judge. The first appearance judge will determine whether the contemnor continues to have the present ability to pay. If the contemnor has the present ability to pay the hearing will be concluded. If the court determines the contemnor no longer has the ability to pay the court has the discretion to order the release of the contemnor with a future court date scheduled before the family law judge or, the court may order the contemnor to remain incarcerated and brought before a family court judge. Any hearings requested following an arrest on Friday or Saturday are to be noticed for the following Tuesday morning at 8:45 AM. These hearings will be heard by the family law judges on their alternating juvenile week. If a contemnor is arrested on a writ the day preceding a court holiday, jail records will place the case on the first appearance docket and any subsequent hearing would be set before the family court judge within 48 hours.

4. Jail records will provide all judiciary assigned to the family law division a weekly printout of all persons arrested on a Writ of Bodily Attachment during that week to assure the statutory requirement has been met and the contemnor has been before the court within 24 hours.

5. The procedure will become effective February 17, 2014. A 60 day review will be held with all the stakeholders to discuss any necessary revisions.

TWENTIETH JUDICIAL CIRCUIT OF FLORIDA ADMINISTRATIVE OFFICE OF THE COURTS HENDRY COUNTY COURTHOUSE 25 E. HICKPOCHEE AVE., LABELLE, FLORIDA 33935

Hendry County Circuit Court Procedure Addressing Arrests on Writs of Bodily Attachment for Failure to Pay Child Support

The procedures used for civil contempt in child support matters are governed by Fla. Fam. L. R. 12.615. The premise is that when a person is initially ordered by the trial court, in the normal course of proceedings, to pay a specific amount of child support, it is thereafter presumed that the person has the ability to do so. A motion for civil contempt is the mechanism used to address the failure of a party to comply with an order to pay child support.

It is at the hearing on the motion for civil contempt that the person's ability to pay becomes relevant; civil contempt is not intended to serve as punishment, but rather is intended to compel compliance—before a person can be found to be in civil contempt, a finding must be made that the failure to pay the court-ordered child support is willful and that the person has the present ability to pay and, therefore, "holds the keys to the jail cell." The preeminent case explaining the process involving civil contempt in child support matters is Bowen v. Bowen, 471 So. 2d 1274 (Fla. 1985).

Motions for civil contempt may be heard by a trial judge or by a DOR Hearing Officer, depending upon the background of the case. If heard by a trial judge and the alleged contemnor appears and is found to be in civil contempt, the judge may remand the contemnor to jail with a purge amount. In such instances, subsection (f) of Rule 12.615 provides that ". . . at any time after a contemnor is incarcerated, the court on its own motion or motion of any party may review the contemnor's present ability to comply with the purge condition and the duration of incarceration and modify any prior orders."

However, if the alleged contemnor fails to appear for the hearing on the motion for civil contempt scheduled before a trial judge, a Writ of Bodily Attachment, with a purge amount, may be issued by the trial judge in accordance with subsection (c)(2)(B) of Rule 12.615. Also, to the extent that the motion for civil contempt is heard by a DOR hearing officer, it is important to remember that a DOR hearing officer does not have the authority to remand persons into custody nor to issue Writs of Bodily Attachment. Rather, if the DOR hearing officer finds that the alleged contemnor has the ability to pay, or if the alleged contemnor fails to appear for the hearing, the DOR hearing officer can only make a recommended finding that the trial judge issue a Writ of Bodily Attachment, with a purge amount.

Once a Writ of Bodily Attachment has been executed, Rule 12.615 requires that the alleged contemnor be brought before the court within 48 hours for a hearing on whether the alleged contemnor has the present ability to pay support and, if so, whether the failure to pay such support is willful. Having reviewed the proposed procedure for the Lee County Family Court, and upon consultation with the Administrative Judge, the following is the procedure that currently in use in Hendry County Court to address Writs of Bodily Attachment issued for failure to pay child support:

1. Upon arrest on a Writ of Bodily Attachment issued for failure to pay child support, the contemnor may pay the purge amount stated in the Writ of Bodily Attachment and be released prior to First Appearance.

2. If the alleged contemnor does not pay the purge amount prior to First Appearance, the alleged contemnor shall be brought before the First Appearance Judge within 24 hours of arrest preferably, but in no instance more than 48 hours after arrest.

3. At First Appearance, the judge will inquire as to whether the purge amount has been paid and, if so, the judge will order that the alleged contemnor be released from custody.

4. If at First Appearance, the alleged contemnor advises that the purge amount has not yet been paid, the First Appearance Judge inquires as to the alleged contemnor's financial circumstances and their present ability to pay the purge amount. If the First Appearance Judge determines that the present financial circumstances of the alleged contemnors is insufficient to pay the purge amount, the alleged contemnor is released from custody and issued a Notice of Appearance for the next DOR Child Support Hearing Date. However, if the First Appearance Judge determines that the alleged contemnor's financial circumstances are sufficient to pay the purge amount, the alleged contemnor remains in custody and the First Appearance Judge issues a Notice of Appearance for the next DOR Child Support Hearing date. A copy of the written order noticing the upcoming date of appearance is sent to the Clerk's Office and the Program Assistant for the DOR Child Support Hearing Officer.

5. If the alleged contemnor pays the purge amount prior to the scheduled upcoming date of appearance, the hearing may be cancelled and it may be removed from the docket. However, it shall be the responsibility of the alleged contemnor to ensure that the court file reflects the filing of proof of payment of the purge. The Clerk's Office advises the Child Support Hearing Officer of the cases which the purge amount has been paid.

Twentieth Judicial Circuit of Florida ADMINISTRATIVE OFFICE OF THE COURTS GLADES COUNTY COURTHOUSE 500 AVENUE J, SW., MOORE HAVEN, FLORIDA 33471

<u>Glades County Circuit Court Procedure Addressing Arrests on Writs of Bodily Attachment for Failure to Pay Child Support</u>

The procedures used for civil contempt in child support matters are governed by Fla. Fam. L. R. 12.615. The premise is that when a person is initially ordered by the trial court, in the normal course of proceedings, to pay a specific amount of child support, it is thereafter presumed that the person has the ability to do so. A motion for civil contempt is the mechanism used to address the failure of a party to comply with an order to pay child support.

It is at the hearing on the motion for civil contempt that the person's ability to pay becomes relevant; civil contempt is not intended to serve as punishment, but rather is intended to compel compliance—before a person can be found to be in civil contempt, a finding must be made that the failure to pay the court-ordered child support is willful and that the person has the present ability to pay and, therefore, "holds the keys to the jail cell." The preeminent case explaining the process involving civil contempt in child support matters is <u>Bowen v. Bowen</u>, 471 So. 2d 1274 (Fla. 1985).

Motions for civil contempt may be heard by a trial judge or by a DOR Hearing Officer, depending upon the background of the case. If heard by a trial judge and the alleged contemnor appears and is found to be in civil contempt, the judge may remand the contemnor to jail with a purge amount In such instances, subsection (f) of Rule 12.615 provides that "... at any time after a contemnor is incarcerated, the court on its own motion or motion of any party may review the contemner's present ability to comply with the purge condition and the duration of incarceration and modify any prior orders."

However, if the alleged contemnor fails to appear for the hearing on the motion for civil contempt scheduled before a trial judge, a Writ of Bodily Attachment, with a purge amount, may be issued by the trial judge in accordance with subsection (c)(2)(B) of Rule 12.615. Also, to the extent that the motion for civil contempt is heard by a DOR hearing officer, it is important to remember that a DOR hearing officer does not have the authority to remand persons into custody nor to issue Writs of Bodily Attachment. Rather, if the DOR hearing officer finds that the alleged contemnor has the ability to pay, or if the alleged contemnor fails to appear for the hearing, the DOR hearing officer can only make a recommended finding that the trial judge issue a Writ of Bodily Attachment, with a purge amount.

Once a Writ of Bodily Attachment has been executed, Rule 12.615 requires that the alleged contemnor be brought before the court within 48 hours for a hearing on whether the alleged contemnor has the present ability to pay support and, if so, whether the failure to pay such support is willful. Having reviewed the proposed procedure for the Lee County Family Court, and upon consultation with the Administrative Judge, the following is the procedure that currently in use in Glades County Court to address Writs of Bodily Attachment issued for failure to pay child support:

1. Upon arrest on a Writ of Bodily Attachment issued for failure to pay child support, the contemnor may pay the purge amount stated in the Writ of Bodily Attachment and be released prior to First Appearance.

2. If the alleged contemnor does not pay the purge amount prior to First Appearance, the alleged contemnor shall be brought before the First Appearance Judge within 24 hours of arrest preferably, but in no instance more than 48 hours after arrest.

3. At First Appearance, the judge will inquire as to whether the purge amount has been paid and, if so, the judge will order that the alleged contemnor be released from custody.

4. If at First Appearance, the alleged contemnor advises that the purge amount has not yet been paid, the First Appearance Judge inquires as to the alleged contemnor's financial circumstances and their present ability to pay the purge amount. If the First Appearance Judge determines that the present financial circumstances of the alleged contemnor are sufficient to pay the purge amount, the alleged contemnor remains in custody. The Judicial Assistant to the First Appearance Judge, who is also the Family Law Judge in Glades County, contacts the Department of Revenue and either facilitates the release of the alleged contemnor or schedules an emergency hearing before the DOR Child Support Hearing or the Family Law Judge depending on the most recent date available. The Judicial Assistant sends a copy of the written order noticing the upcoming date of appearance is sent to the alleged contemnor, the Department of Revenue, and the Clerk's Office.

5. If the alleged contemnor pays the purge amount prior to the scheduled upcoming date of appearance, the hearing may be cancelled and it may be removed from the docket. However, it shall be the responsibility of the alleged contemnor to ensure that the court file reflects the filing of proof of payment of the purge. The Clerk's Office advises the Child Support Hearing Officer or the Family Law Judge if the purge amount has been paid.

Florida Family Law Rules of Procedure

Section I. Family Law Rules of Procedure

Rule 12.615. Civil Contempt in Support Matters

(a) Applicability. This rule governs civil contempt proceedings in support matters related to family law cases. The use of civil contempt sanctions under this rule shall be limited to those used to compel compliance with a court order or to compensate a movant for losses sustained as a result of a contemnor's willful failure to comply with a court order. Contempt sanctions intended to punish an offender or to vindicate the authority of the court are criminal in nature and are governed by Florida Rules of Criminal Procedure 3.830 and 3.840.

(b) Motion and Notice. Civil contempt may be initiated by motion. The motion must recite the essential facts constituting the acts alleged to be contemptuous. No civil contempt may be imposed without notice to the alleged contemnor and without providing the alleged contemnor with an opportunity to be heard. The civil contempt motion and notice of hearing may be served in accordance with Florida Rule of Judicial Administration 2.516 provided notice is reasonably calculated to apprise the alleged contemnor of the pendency of the proceedings. The notice must specify the time and place of the hearing and must contain the following language: "FAILURE TO APPEAR AT THE HEARING MAY RESULT IN THE COURT ISSUING A WRIT OF BODILY ATTACHMENT FOR YOUR ARREST. IF YOU ARE ARRESTED, YOU MAY BE HELD IN JAIL UP TO 48 HOURS BEFORE A HEARING IS HELD." This notice must also state whether electronic recording or a court reporter is provided by the court or whether a court reporter, if desired, must be provided by the party.

(c) Hearing. In any civil contempt hearing, after the court makes an express finding that the alleged contemnor had notice of the motion and hearing:

(1) the court shall determine whether the movant has established that a prior order directing payment of support was entered and that the alleged contemnor has failed to pay all or part of the support set forth in the prior order; and

(2) if the court finds the movant has established all of the requirements in subdivision (c)(1) of this rule, the court shall,

(A) if the alleged contemnor is present, determine whether the alleged contemnor had the present ability to pay support and willfully failed to pay such support.

(B) if the alleged contemnor fails to appear, set a reasonable purge amount based on the individual circumstances of the parties. The court may issue a writ of bodily attachment and direct that, upon execution of the writ of bodily attachment, the alleged contemnor be brought before the court within 48 hours for a hearing on whether the alleged contemnor has the present ability to pay support and, if so, whether the failure to pay such support is willful.

(d) Order and Sanctions. After hearing the testimony and evidence presented, the court shall enter a written order granting or denying the motion for contempt.

(1) An order finding the alleged contemnor to be in contempt shall contain a finding that a prior order of support was entered, that the alleged contemnor has failed to pay part or all of the support ordered, that the alleged contemnor had the present ability to pay support, and that the alleged contemnor willfully failed to comply with the prior court order. The order shall contain a recital of the facts on which these findings are based.

(2) If the court grants the motion for contempt, the court may impose appropriate sanctions to obtain compliance with the order including incarceration, attorneys' fees, suit money and costs, compensatory or coercive fines, and any other coercive sanction or relief permitted by law provided the order includes a purge provision as set forth in subdivision (e) of this rule.

(e) Purge. If the court orders incarceration, a coercive fine, or any other coercive sanction for failure to comply with a prior support order, the court shall set conditions for purge of the contempt, based on the contemnor's present ability to comply. The court shall include in its order a separate affirmative finding that the contemnor has the present ability to comply with the purge and the factual basis for that finding. The court may grant the contemnor a reasonable time to comply with the purge conditions. If the court orders incarceration but defers incarceration for more than 48 hours to allow the contemnor a reasonable time to comply with the purge conditions, and the contemnor fails to comply within the time provided, the movant shall file an affidavit of noncompliance with the court. If payment is being made through the Central Governmental Depository, a certificate from the depository shall be attached to the affidavit. The court then may issue a writ of bodily attachment. Upon incarceration, the contemnor must be brought before the court within 48 hours for a determination of whether the contemnor continues to have the present ability to pay the purge.

(f) Review after Incarceration. Notwithstanding the provisions of this rule, at any time after a contemnor is incarcerated, the court on its own motion or motion of any party may review the contemnor's present ability to comply with the purge condition and the duration of incarceration and modify any prior orders.

(g) Other Relief. Where there is a failure to pay support or to pay support on a timely basis but the failure is not willful, nothing in this rule shall be construed as precluding the court from granting such relief as may be appropriate under the circumstances.

CREDIT(S)

Added Oct. 29, 1998, effective Feb. 1, 1999 (723 So.2d 208). Amended Jan. 28, 1999, effective Feb. 1, 1999 (746 So.2d 1073); July 10, 2003, effective Jan. 1, 2004 (853 So.2d 303); Oct. 18, 2012, effective, nunc pro tunc, Sept. 1, 2012 (102 So.3d 505).

COMMENTARY

1998 Adoption. This rule is limited to civil contempt proceedings. Should a court wish to impose sanctions for criminal contempt, the court must refer to Florida Rules of Criminal Procedure 3.830 and 3.840 and must provide the alleged contemnor with all of the constitutional due process protections afforded to criminal defendants. This rule is created to assist the trial courts in ensuring that the due process rights of alleged contemnors are protected. A court that adjudges an individual to be in civil contempt must always afford the contemnor the opportunity to purge the contempt.

COMMITTEE NOTES

2012 Amendment. Subdivision (b) is amended to provide for service in accordance with Florida Rule of Judicial Administration 2.516.

[1] Referenced case, Bowen v. Bowen, not attached. Case is accessible on Thomson Reuters Westlaw. Case is also available through Florida Weekly at the citation: 10 Fla. L. Weekly 318. .

12.7. [SUPERSEDED BY ORDER 2.38, EFFECTIVE AUGUST 1, 2018]

Parochial Orders

CASE ASSIGNMENTS (COLLIER COUNTY). SUPPLEMENTAL ORDER CASE ASSIGNMENTS

IN THE CIRCUIT COURT OF THE TWENTIETH JUDICIAL CIRCUIT IN AND FOR COLLIER COUNTY, FLORIDA

SUPPLEMENTAL ORDER CASE ASSIGNMENTS

EFFECTIVE January 2, 2009, this Supplemental Order shall apply to the assignments of cases in the Circuit Criminal division in Collier County.

In any case in which the defendant has previously been sentenced to community control or probation, and the defendant is subject to a violation of probation proceeding based upon a new felony charge in Collier County, any proceeding initiated by the State upon the new charge shall be assigned by the Clerk to the judge assigned to the violation of probation proceeding, once the Clerk becomes aware of the relationship between the cases.

In any case in which the defendant has more than one pending felony case in Collier County, the additional felony case(s) shall be assigned by the Clerk to the judge assigned to the pending felony case with the lowest case number, once the Clerk becomes aware of the relationship between the cases.

In cases in which the State has filed felony charges against more than one defendant arising from the same set of facts, transactions or occurrences, upon motion by the State or upon the Court's own motion, those cases shall be assigned by the Clerk to the judge assigned to the pending felony case with the lowest case number.

When the Clerk reassigns a case in accordance with this Supplemental Order, the Clerk shall, so far as is reasonably practical, assign new felony cases in order to obtain an equal assignment of cases in the Circuit Criminal division.

THE CLERK is hereby directed to effectuate assignments in accordance with the above.

DONE AND ORDERED in Chambers, in Fort Myers, Lee County, Florida, this 9TH day of January, 2009.

G. KEITH CARY
CHIEF JUDGE

History—New.

CLERK AD INTERIM (CHARLOTTE COUNTY). ORDER APPOINTING CLERK AD INTERIM FOR CHARLOTTE COUNTY

IN THE TWENTIETH JUDICIAL CIRCUIT IN AND FOR THE STATE OF FLORIDA CHARLOTTE COUNTY

ORDER APPOINTING CLERK AD INTERIM FOR CHARLOTTE COUNTY

WHEREAS, the Clerk of the Circuit Court in and for Charlotte County, Barbara T. Scott, has announced her resignation effective at the end of the day of November 30, 2008, via correspondence from Barbara T. Scott to the Governor of the State of Florida dated November 20, 2008; and

WHEREAS, the current term of office of Barbara T. Scott runs through January 5, 2009; and

WHEREAS, the legislature of the State of Florida enacted Florida Statute § 28.09 as a mechanism to provide for the filling of a vacancy occurring in the office of the clerk of the circuit court until such time as the Governor has the opportunity to fill the vacancy; and

WHEREAS, that mechanism authorizes the judicial appointment of an interim clerk pending the Governor's own appointment of a person to fill the vacancy; and

WHEREAS, to date, the Governor has not appointed a person to fill the vacancy resulting from Barbara T. Scott's resignation, and, in light of the intervening Thanksgiving holiday, it is uncertain as to whether the Governor will have such an opportunity to do so prior to Monday, December 1, 2008; and

WHEREAS, James R. Masch is currently the Chief Deputy of Courts, Records and Administrative Services for the Clerk of the Circuit Court in and for Charlotte County and has served in this capacity since 2003; it is

ORDERED that, pursuant to the authority vested in me by Florida Statute § 28.09, and as Chief Judge of the Twentieth Judicial Circuit, which includes Charlotte County, James R. Masch, is appointed as Clerk Ad Interim for the remaining current term of office, effective December 1, 2008, and until such time as the Governor of the State of Florida makes his own appointment superseding this order, or as otherwise provided by General Law. As Clerk Ad Interim, James R. Masch shall assume and meet all responsibilities, duties, and conditions as provided for by the legislature under Florida Statute § 28.09. This order is effective December 1, 2008, and, in the event that the Governor makes his own appointment to fill the vacancy prior to December 1, 2008, this order is to be deemed null and void in its entirety and shall have no effect. If no appointment is made by the Governor such as to supersede this order prior to January 6, 2009, this order shall automatically expire at the end of the current term of office of the Clerk of the Circuit Court in and for Charlotte County, which runs through January 5, 2009.

DONE AND ORDERED in chambers in Fort Myers, Lee County, Florida this 25 day of November, 2008.

G. Keith Cary
Chief Judge

History.-New.

TRUANCY COURT (COLLIER COUNTY). ORDER ESTABLISHING TRUANCY COURT FOR COLLIER COUNTY

IN THE TWENTIETH JUDICIAL CIRCUIT IN AND FOR THE STATE OF FLORIDA

ORDER ESTABLISHING TRUANCY COURT FOR COLLIER COUNTY

Pursuant to this Court's inherent authority to administer and regulate the courts of the Twentieth Judicial Circuit, as well as the authority prescribed by Fla. R. Jud. Admin. 2.215 and Florida Statute § 43.26, the Court hereby establishes a Truancy Court Program for Collier County, Florida.

Truancy petitions filed with the Clerk of the Court by the Superintendent of Schools are governed by Chapter 1003 of the Florida Statutes. Upon the filing of any such petition with the Clerk of the Court in the Juvenile Division, the Clerk shall assign a case number and a summons shall issue directed to the parent and child for an arraignment hearing the next scheduled truancy court date that is no later than thirty (30) days of the filing of the petition.

Practice and procedures for such petitions are as set forth in Florida Statute § 984.151 and any applicable rules of court. At the initial hearing, the court will arraign both the child and the parent on the petition and if the parent and child admit or consent to the petition, the court shall proceed as prescribed by the Florida Statute § 984.151(7).

If the parent and child deny the allegations in the petition at the initial hearing, the court will set a trial date and notice will be given to the school social worker or other school representative to appear on the trial date to present the school's case. In that instance, the court shall proceed to make findings on the record and issue its ruling pursuant to Florida Statute § 984.151(7).

Copies of the disposition order shall be given to the superintendent, the school social worker or other school representative, the parent or guardian of the child, and the child.

The school district, through its designated representative, is responsible for assisting the parent or guardian and the child with compliance with the order. This representative will be available for review hearings to inform the court of the progress of the case.

The court will set a review hearing, no less than thirty (30) days from the date of disposition, in order to ensure compliance with its order and may set further review hearings as may be necessary within the exercise of its sound discretion. Any order entered by the court is enforceable through its contempt powers pursuant to Florida Statute § 984.151(9).

Truancy Court will be held at the Collier County Courthouse in the courtroom and at such intervals as the court deems necessary in order to carry out the purpose and intent of this order.

Guidelines for the establishment of the Truancy Court Program are as provided in the proposed manual submitted by the District School Board of Collier County and by the Interagency Agreement entered into between the School District of Collier County, the Collier County Sheriff's Office, the State Attorney of the Twentieth Judicial Circuit, Lutheran Social Services, Inc., David Lawrence, the Florida Department of Juvenile Justice, and the Florida Department of Children and Family Services. Copies of the proposed manual and the Interagency Agreement are attached to this order and made a part hereof.

Any incidental costs associated with the operation of this program will be born by the school district. Such costs may include, but are not limited to, costs incident to the provision of security and Clerk's personnel.

This order shall remain in effect until otherwise modified, amended or rescinded by further order of the Court.

DONE AND ORDERED in chambers in Naples, Collier County, Florida this 15 day of January, 2008.

G. Keith Cary
Chief Judge

History.—New.

COLLIER COUNTY TRUANCY COURT MANUAL

Dr. Dennis Thompson

Superintendent of Schools

2007

APPENDIX *

ATTENDANCE LAW—FLORIDA STATUTE

State of Florida Compulsory School Attendance Laws require all children who attained the age of six (6) years, or who will be six (6) years by February 1 of any school year, or who are older than six (6) years of age, but who have not attained the age of sixteen (16) years, to attend school regularly during the entire school term.

Parents failing to properly enroll or require their children to attend school regularly shall be guilty of a misdemeanor of the second degree punishable as provided in the law.

Under the law, children failing to attend school properly will be called to the attention of the School Administrator, and if found to be a habitual truant, may be referred to the juvenile court of the county and dealt with as a dependent child. Parents who do not make a legitimate effort to have their children attend school regularly are also **liable for prosecution in circuit court.**

TRUANCY COURT

Truancy Court is a cooperative effort between The District School Board of Collier County, Collier County Sheriff's Office, and Twentieth Judicial Circuit Court along with the support of the following agencies: The Office of the State Attorney, Lutheran Services Florida, David Lawrence, and the Florida Department of Juvenile Justice—to help reduce truancy in the county.

Truancy Court will begin in August of the 2007–2008 school year.

Students ages 6–16 who are habitually truant (five (5) unexcused absences within a calendar month or fifteen (15) unexcused absences within 90 calendar days), will be referred to Truancy Court when it is determined by the school representative that the student is non-compliant with the Florida Attendance Laws (s. 1003.27(2)(a).

TRUANCY PROCEDURES

Truancy

> Five (5) unexcused absences within a calendar month, or

> Fifteen (15) unexcused absences within a ninety (90) calendar days, with or without the knowledge or consent from parent or legal guardian

>> School sends letter

>> School contacts parent

>> Document all parent contact

> If parent does not respond within five (5) days, skip to attendance investigation

Child and Adolescent Support Team (CAST) Meeting

> School schedules a meeting with parent to discuss concerns

> CAST Meeting held at school with parent and child, if appropriate

> If parent does not attend, CAST may meet with child, if appropriate

> Interventions may include, but are not limited to: monitor attendance, school counselor contact, changes in learning environment, placement in different classroom, attendance contract, referral to outside agencies, review of ESE/504 Plan

If truancy continues:

Attendance Investigation

> Principal or designee makes request to one of the Attendance Assistants

> Executive Director of Student Services reviews results of district Attendance Assistant report

Truancy Referral

> Attendance Assistant prepares school documentation of case

> Executive Director reviews case documentation and refers to Legal Department

> CCPS Legal Department reviews case and determines processing

> CCPS submits truancy petition to filed in truancy court, as needed

Truancy Court

> Judge hears truancy petition

TRUANCY COURT SANCTION LIST BY PROVIDER

Provider—COLLIER COUNTY SHERIFF'S OFFICE

Contact—Sgt. Tom Wedlock (239–793–9125)

> Random Drug screening

> Community Work details (Saturdays 8 a.m.–1p.m.) *10–18 year olds

> JAR Intervention Program (one day consequence awareness program) *10–15 year olds

> Weekly monitoring/mentoring program

> Parent workshops (Gang Awareness, Truancy Awareness, Drug Awareness, Parent Support Group)

> Additional educational opportunities according to needs

> Cool Kids Club—community work in exchange for rewards

Provider—DAVID LAWRENCE CENTER

Contact—Angela Geiger (239–643–6105 ext. 2204)

> Mental Health Assessments

> Drug Screening

> Counseling services

> Youth prevention groups-Substance abuse, Conflict Resolution, S.T.A.R. S.-Students that are Reaching Success, Making Positive Choices, Parent Project, Parenting for Problematic Teens *small fees for some classes

Provider—DISTRICT SCHOOL BOARD OF COLLIER COUNTY

Contact—Angela Valmaña (239–377–0524)

> Attendance Awards/Rewards/Incentives

> Sports Programs and Activities

> School Counseling referral

> Mentor (school staff and volunteer program through school)

> School community service

> J.R.O.T.C.

> Alternative Schools (must qualify)

> Florida Driver License Program (revocation of driving privileges)

> Florida Learnfare Program (reduction or elimination in public assistance)

> Parent volunteer at school (subject to Jessica Lunsford Act clearance)

> Attendance contracts with students

> If student is ESE or 504, reconvene IEP/504 team to review appropriateness of services and determine if changes/additions need to be made

Provider—4H CLUB

Contact—Anne Galdames (239–353–4244)

> Career Development and mentorship program

> Healthy lifestyles and nutrition program

> Program activities—farming, woodworking, fishing, arts and crafts, computers, cooking, performing arts, etc.

> Educational Summer camp

> In process of developing wilderness program

STOPPING TRUANCY BEFORE IT STARTS

REASONS TO STAY IN SCHOOL

> **Finding Work Is Easier**

You are almost twice as likely to be unemployed if you do not finish high school

> **You'll Earn More**

Studies show high school graduates make 50% more money than dropouts

> **What This Means**

High school graduates are:

> Less likely to live at home

> More likely to be able to buy a car and rent an apartment

> Less likely to need welfare or public assistance

> **Less Likely To Be A Prison Inmate**

Seventy–Five (75%) of all inmates are high school dropouts

> **Bottom Line—It's Your Future**

Your choices now will determine how well you live for the rest of your life

TIPS FOR IMPROVING SCHOOL ATTENDANCE

√ Make education a family priority and emphasize the important role education plays throughout life.

√ Meet your child's teachers and other school personnel. They can provide important insights into the child's school performance and suggest ways for improvement.

√ Help your child develop good study and work habits.

√ Schedule daily home study time and help with homework when needed.

√ Get your child tutorial help with subjects that pose learning difficulties.

√ Help your child develop and achieve academic goals.

√ Develop a phone-in policy with the school to check on the child's daily attendance, or have the person in charge of school attendance alert you about non-attendance.

√ Explain how dropouts have more trouble getting and keeping jobs and make half as much money as graduates.

√ Self-confidence is important. Recognize when your child does well in school and other activities.

√ Get to know your child's friends and classmates. They can influence your child's school performance. Lack of friends or problems with classmates can also affect school performance.

CONTACTS

COLLIER COUNTY SHERIFF'S OFFICE

Sgt. Tom Wedlock
239–793–9125

DAVID LAWRENCE CENTER

Angela Geiger
239–643–6105 ext. 2204

DISTRICT SCHOOL BOARD OF COLLIER COUNTY

Angela Valmaña
239–377–0524 (Naples)
Pamela Lee Anderson
239–377–0527 (Naples)
Martha DeLeon–Gonzalez
239–377–4310 (Immokalee)

4H CLUB

Anne Galdames
239–353–4244

INTERAGENCY AGREEMENT

The School District of Collier County, Florida

Collier County Sheriff's Office

State Attorney, 20th Judicial Circuit

Lutheran Social Services, Inc

David Lawrence

Florida Department of Juvenile Justice (DJJ)

The Department of Children and Family Services

I. Purpose: This agreement has been developed between the above-named agencies pursuant to section 1003.27(4), Florida Statutes, to provide consistency in dealing with habitual truancy and related issues.

II. Definition: "Habitual Truant" is a student who has been found to have fifteen (15) unexcused absences from school within ninety (90) calendar days with or without the knowledge or justifiable consent of the student's parent or legal guardian, which student is subject to compulsory school attendance under sections 1003.21(1) and (2)(a), Florida Statues [1], and who is not found to be exempt under sections 1003.21(3) or 1003.24, Florida Statutes, or who otherwise does not satisfy the criteria for an exemption provided by law or by rules of the State Board of Education. Such a student must have been the subject of the activities specified in sections 1003.26 and 1003.27(3), Florida Statutes, without resultant successful remediation of the truancy problem, before being determined to be a child in need of services according to the provisions of Chapter 984, Florida Statutes. See section 1003.01(8), Florida Statutes.

III. All parties agree:

1. To communicate with all other parties to this agreement relative to truancy matters and individual student progress, as necessary. Information shall be shared between parties in order to improve school safety, reduce truancy, in-school and out-of-school suspensions, and to support alternatives to in-school and out-of-school suspensions and expulsions, consistent with the provisions of section 1002.22(3)(d)13, Florida Statutes.

2. To maintain the security and confidentiality of student information received from other parties that is exempt from Chapter 119, Florida Statutes, and to ensure that such information is not re-disclosed to unauthorized persons or agencies.

3. To designate a contact person to facilitate interagency communication under this agreement, and to inform all other parties of the name, address and telephone number of such designee.

4. To cooperate with the other parties to this agreement in current or new truancy programs.

IV. The School District of Collier County, Florida, agrees as follows:

1. The schools shall monitor student attendance daily and promptly contact the parent if truancy develops. The schools shall implement the steps set forth in section 1003.26, Florida Statutes, to enforce regular school attendance.

2. In the event of truancy, the schools shall follow applicable School Board policy.

3. To utilize the court system pursuant to sections 1003.27(1), 1003.27(6), and 984.151, Florida Statutes, for the referral of parents for prosecution and filing of petitions in Truancy Court.

4. To report truancy of children whose academic progress is jeopardized and whose families receive assistance to the Department of Children and Family Services Department through Learnfare and when the children's attendance substantially improves. See section 414.1251, Florida Statutes.

5. To participate in the Child and Adolescent Study Team (CAST) committee with other parties to this agreement, as appropriate. See sections 1003.26(1)(g) and 984.12(2), Florida Statutes.

V. The Collier County Sheriff's Office agrees:

1. To participate in the case staffing committee with other parties to this agreement, as appropriate, consistent with sections 1003.26(1)(g) and 984.12(2), Florida Statutes.

2. To serve notices, pleadings and orders as directed by the Court without cost to the parties to this agreement.

3. To provide a bailiff in proceedings before the Court.

VI. The Office of State Attorney, 20th Judicial Circuit, agrees:

1. To review cases involving parental violation of the compulsory school attendance law and prosecute where appropriate. See section 1003.27(6), Florida Statutes.

VII. Lutheran Social Services agrees:

1. To accept clients into services without regard to race, sex, sexual orientation, handicap, economic status, color, creed, religion or national origin.

2. To facilitate services in partnership with the school district to serve truant youth as well as those at-risk.

3. To use the case staffing committee to assist with Children in Need of Services (CINS) and or Families in Need of Services (FINS) cases when the student has not made satisfactory progress, consistent with section 984.12, Florida Statutes.

4. To assist in filing of CINS petitions for those cases meeting the requirements of section 984.15 (2), Florida Statutes.

VIII. David Lawrence agrees:

1. To accept clients into services without regard to race, sexual orientation, handicap, economic status, color, creed, religion or national origin.

2. To facilitate services in partnership with the school district to serve truant youth as well as those at-risk.

3. To assess clients needing mental health and substance abuse services and make recommendation for services.

4. To provide compliance and noncompliance of counseling recommendation to the court.

IX. The Florida Department of Juvenile Justice (DJJ) agrees:

1. To participate in the case staffing committee with other parties to this agreement, as appropriate, consistent with sections 1003.26(1)(g) and 984.12(2), Florida Statutes.

2. That it will file CINS/FINS petitions and represent the state, when appropriate, consistent with sections 984.15(2) and 984.17(4), Florida Statutes.

3. That when a minor has been placed under DJJ supervision, it will monitor the minor's school attendance and report truancy to the court for review.

X. The Department of Children and Family Services agrees:

1. That a representative of the Department will attend each multi disciplinary staffing.

2. That the Department's representative, in accordance with the law, will provide background information regarding and limited to the truant, if such background information exists.

XI. Timeline: This Interagency Agreement will become effective with the signatures of all the parties, and will remain in effect until June 30, 2011. Any party may terminate its participation at any time upon thirty (30) days written notice to all other parties. Upon agreement by all parties, this Agreement may be amended in writing at any time.

XII. All parties shall assist in the investigation of injury or damages either for or against either party pertaining to their respective areas of responsibility or activities under this agreement and shall contact the other parties regarding the legal actions deemed appropriate to remedy such damage or claims.

This agreement shall be effective upon full execution.

The School District of Collier County, Florida

By: ______________________ 10–18–02
Steven J. Donovan, Chairman Date
Collier County School Board

Attest: ______________________ 10–18–02
Dr. Dennis L. Thompson Date
Superintendent of Schools

Collier County Sheriff's Office

By: ______________________ 26 SEPT. 07
Don Hunter Sheriff Date

____
School Board Attorney Review
9/12/07

____
Collier County Sheriff's Office

State Attorney, 20th Judicial Circuit

By: ______________________ 10/5/07
Assistant State Attorney Date

Lutheran Social Services, Inc.

By ______________________ 10/4/07
District Administrator Date
Lutheran Social Services, Inc.

David Lawrence

By: ______________________ 10/4/07
CEO Date
David Lawrence

Florida Department of Juvenile Justice

By: ______________________
Deputy Secretary Date
Florida Department of Juvenile Justice

Department of Children and Family Services

By: ______________________ 10/5/07
Date

Department of Juvenile Justice (DJJ) Addendum to the Agreement with Various Collier County Agencies to Support Truancy Court

The purpose of this addendum is to replace the section pertaining to The Florida Department of Juvenile Justice (DJJ) with the following:

IX. The Florida Department of Juvenile Justice (DJJ) agrees:

1. To participate in the case staffing committee with other parties to this agreement, as appropriate, consistent with sections 1003.26(1)(g) and 984.12(2), Florida Statutes.

2. That it will file CINS/FINS petitions and represent the state, when appropriate, consistent with sections 984.15(2) and 984.17(4), Florida Statutes.

Signature

____
Perry L. Anderson, Jr.
South Regional Director for Probation & Community Involvement
11/20/07
Date

School Board Attorney Review
11.15.07

* Publisher's Note: Page numbers refer to pages in the original order copy.
[1] So in original.

COURTHOUSE AND COURTROOM SECURITY (LEE COUNTY). COURTHOUSE AND COURTROOM SECURITY FOR LEE COUNTY JUSTICE CENTER COMPLEX

IN THE TWENTIETH JUDICIAL CIRCUIT IN AND FOR LEE COUNTY, FLORIDA

IN RE: COURTHOUSE AND COURTROOM SECURITY FOR LEE COUNTY JUSTICE CENTER COMPLEX

WHEREAS, Administrative Order No. 2.18 sets forth the courthouse and courtroom security policy for the Twentieth Judicial Circuit; and

WHEREAS, paragraph 7 of Administrative Order No. 2.18 allows for special exemptions on a county-by-county basis; and

WHEREAS, upon consultation with the Circuit Administrative Judge for Lee County, it has been determined that a special exemption is appropriate for Lee County;

It is **ORDERED** that, in addition to the exemptions provided for by Administrative Order No. 2.18, an exemption shall also be made for sworn law enforcement officers wearing readily identifiable department issued uniforms who are conducting official law enforcement business within the Lee County Justice Center Complex. All firearms must be in a visible law enforcement approved multiple step retention holster other than friction only. This law enforcement exemption shall be applied in accordance with the attached Exhibit "A", which is hereby adopted and shall be strictly construed and enforced.

DONE AND ORDERED in chambers in Fort Myers, Lee County, Florida this 15th day of January, 2008.

G. Keith Cary
Chief Judge

History.—New

EXHIBIT "A"

The following policy will address the carrying and/or securing of weapons while conducting business in the Lee County Justice Center Complex:

1. Sworn law enforcement officers wearing readily identifiable department issued uniforms may carry their firearms while conducting official law enforcement business within the Lee County Justice Center Complex. These firearms must be in a visible Law Enforcement approved multiple step retention holster other than friction only.

2. Sworn law enforcement officers **NOT** wearing a readily identifiable agency issued uniform may not carry their firearms while conducting official law enforcement business within the Lee County Justice Center Complex. These officers will be required to secure their weapons at the security checkpoint prior to entering the complex. This would include, but not be limited to: undercover officers, detectives in civilian wear and any other civilian attire.

3. At no time will any sworn law enforcement officer, whether in uniform or in plain clothes be permitted to carry their firearm while conducting any type of personal action within the Lee County Justice Center Complex. This would include, but not be limited to the following types of cases: Divorce, Child Custody, Character witness in civil or criminal cases.

****It is recommended that at no time should any law enforcement officer in the above styled cases wear any official department uniform or identifiers while conducting personal business in or out of the courtrooms.****

4. It will be the responsibility of each officer to adhere to their agency's individual regulations regarding personal and official court appearances.

COURTHOUSE AND COURTROOM SECURITY (CHARLOTTE COUNTY). COURTHOUSE AND COURTROOM SECURITY FOR CHARLOTTE COUNTY JUSTICE CENTER COMPLEX

IN THE TWENTIETH JUDICIAL CIRCUIT IN AND FOR CHARLOTTE COUNTY, FLORIDA

IN RE: COURTHOUSE AND COURTROOM SECURITY FOR CHARLOTTE COUNTY JUSTICE CENTER COMPLEX

WHEREAS, Administrative Order No. 2.18 sets forth courthouse and courtroom security policy for the Twentieth Judicial Circuit; and

WHEREAS, paragraph 7 of Administrative Order No. 2.18 allows for special exemptions on a county-by-county basis; and

WHEREAS, upon consultation with the Circuit Administrative Judge for Charlotte County, it has been determined that a special exemption is appropriate for Charlotte County;

It is **ORDERED** that, in addition to the exemptions provided for by Administrative Order No. 2.18, an exemption shall also be made for sworn law enforcement officers wearing readily identifiable department issued uniforms who are conducting official law enforcement business within the Charlotte County Justice Center. All firearms must be in a visible law enforcement approved multiple step retention holster other than friction only. This law enforcement exemption shall be applied in accordance with the attached Exhibit "A", which is hereby adopted and shall be strictly construed and enforced.

DONE AND ORDERED in chambers in Fort Myers, Lee County, Florida this 9th day of June, 2011.

G. Keith Cary
Chief Judge

History. New

EXHIBIT "A"

The following policy will address the carrying of and security of firearms by law enforcement officials in the Charlotte County Justice Center:

1. Sworn law enforcement officers wearing readily identifiable department issued uniforms may carry their firearm(s) while conducting law enforcement business within the Charlotte County Justice Center. Every firearm must be contained and secured in a visible law enforcement approved multiple step retention holster other than friction only.

2. Sworn law enforcement officers not wearing a readily identifiable agency issued uniform may not carry their firearms while conducting official law enforcement business within the Charlotte County Justice Center. A sworn law enforcement officer not wearing such an identifiable department issued uniform along with an approved multiple step retention holster properly securing his/her firearm will be required to secure their firearm(s) at the security checkpoint prior to entering the Justice Center. For example, undercover officers, detectives in civilian wear, and any other civilian attired law enforcement officials would have to check their firearm(s) in at the door; the only exception to this would be in the event of a response to an emergency call within the Charlotte County Justice Center.

3. A law enforcement officer on official business that wishes to enter the courthouse complex with his/her firearm in accordance with the foregoing requirements should be prepared to show appropriate paperwork, as applicable, in regards to his/her business in the building (example given: subpoena, hearing notice, et cetera). Notwithstanding pur-

ported compliance with the foregoing, courthouse security personnel reserve the right to preclude entry with firearm(s) in the event of perceived non-compliance with the foregoing.

4. At no time will any sworn law enforcement officer, whether in uniform or in plain clothes, be permitted or authorized to carry their firearm while conducting any non-law enforcement related business within the Charlotte County Justice Center.

**** It is recommended that at no time whatsoever should any law enforcement officer wear any official department uniform or identifiers while conducting any personal business in the Charlotte County Justice Center.****

5. In addition to the foregoing, it will be the responsibility of each officer to adhere to their agency's individual regulations regarding personal and official court appearances. Each state and local law enforcement agency that wishes to allow its officers authorized to carry firearms to seek entry to the Charlotte County Justice Center with a firearm in conformance with the foregoing must prepare a set of department guidelines, policies, and procedures in regards to the carrying, use, and protection/securing of firearms in the Charlotte County Justice Center, a copy of which must be provided to the Sergeant of the Charlotte County Court Services Section of the Charlotte County Sheriff's Office, Charlotte County Court Administrative Services Manager, Administrative Judge for Charlotte County, and the Chief Judge of the Twentieth Judicial Circuit. Said department guidelines, policies, and procedures should also include the manner in which officers shall be notified and educated with respect to this Order and attachment, as well as said department's enforcement/compliance procedures.

6. Nothing contained in this Order and attachment shall preclude any judge from the issuance of an order barring or otherwise prohibiting the introduction of firearms into their own individual courtroom.

COURTHOUSE AND COURTROOM SECURITY (COLLIER COUNTY). COURTHOUSE AND COURTROOM SECURITY FOR COLLIER COUNTY COURTHOUSE COMPLEX

IN THE TWENTIETH JUDICIAL CIRCUIT IN AND FOR COLLIER COUNTY, FLORIDA

IN RE: COURTHOUSE AND COURTROOM SECURITY FOR THE COLLIER COUNTY COURTHOUSE COMPLEX

WHEREAS, Administrative Order No. 2.18 sets forth courthouse and courtroom security policy for the Twentieth Judicial Circuit, and

WHEREAS, paragraph 7 of Administrative Order No. 2.18 allows for special exemptions on a county-by-county basis, and

WHEREAS, upon consultation with the Circuit Administrative Judge for Collier County, it has been determined that a special exemption is appropriate for Collier County,

NOW THEREFORE it is:

ORDERED that, in addition to the exemptions provided for by Administrative Order No. 2.18, an exemption shall also be made for sworn law enforcement officers from the Collier County Sheriff's Office, Naples Police Department, Marco Island Police Department, and sworn law enforcement officers assigned to Collier County from the Florida Highway Patrol and the Florida Fish and Wildlife Commission, wearing readily identifiable department issued uniforms who are conducting official law enforcement business within the Collier County Courthouse Complex, including the attached Annex.

All firearms must be in a visible law enforcement approved multiple step retention holder (level 2 or 3) other than friction only.

This law enforcement exemption shall be applied in accordance with the attached Exhibit "A," which is hereby adopted and shall be strictly construed and enforced.

And it is further

ORDERED that nothing in this exemption shall preclude a presiding judge from determining who will carry a firearm or concealed weapon in his or her courtroom.

DONE AND ORDERED in Chambers in Fort Myers, Lee County, Florida this 26th day of October, 2016.

Michael T. McHugh
Chief Judge

Exhibit "A"

1. All law enforcement officers that intend to carry a firearm into the courthouse complex shall wear either an agency issued Class A uniform (long sleeve dress uniform) or Class B uniform (short sleeve, standard patrol uniform.)

2. Firearms must be secured in a level 2 or level 3 retention holster (standard road patrol holster.)

3. Law enforcement officers in plain clothes or undercover attire and law enforcement officers conducting any type of personal business shall be required to secure their firearms at the security checkpoint at the main entrance and at the employee entrance.

4. Upon entering the main entrance of the courthouse all law enforcement officers who intend to carry their firearm shall check in at the bailiff station in the front lobby and must present agency issued photo identification and shall sign in on a form that will be at the bailiff station. The bailiff on duty shall record the name and ID number of the law enforcement officer, the assigned agency, the reason for appearing at the courthouse, the attorney or court that issued the subpoena and the time of check in and check out of the courthouse. If the law enforcement officer does not have a subpoena, the officer must notify the bailiff on duty of the reason for being in the courthouse and the bailiff on duty shall verify the legitimate presence of the officer.

5. Upon signing in at the bailiff station the law enforcement officer shall be given a plastic ID card holder that is identifiable to the courthouse to hold his or her agency issued ID and which shall be worn in a visible manner at all times. The ID card holder shall be turned in at the bailiff station when checking out.

6. Each agency to which this exemption applies shall ensure that their respective law enforcement officers are aware of the procedures set forth in this Order.

7. For purposes of this Order, Courthouse Security Guards shall be defined to include those security guards assigned by any law enforcement agency or any other governmental agen-

cy to provide security at the Collier County Courthouse Complex.

MENTAL HEALTH (COLLIER COUNTY). ORDER ESTABLISHING MENTAL HEALTH COURT FOR COLLIER COUNTY

IN THE TWENTIETH JUDICIAL CIRCUIT IN AND FOR THE STATE OF FLORIDA

ORDER ESTABLISHING MENTAL HEALTH COURT FOR COLLIER COUNTY

There is created within the Twentieth Judicial Circuit in and for Collier County, Florida, a Mental Health Court. The court will hear only those criminal court matters that do not impact the public safety or the safety of the victim. The State Attorneys Office shall screen each defendant referred to the Mental Health Court and shall determine which cases will be placed into the Mental Health Court Program. This decision shall be made with input from defense counsel, the court and the Staff of the Mental Health Court.

Beginning October 1, 2007, or as soon thereafter as is practicable, the presiding judge in Mental Health Court will hear those criminal court matters referred to the Mental Health Court Program. The Mental Health Court Program shall be composed of Staff whose services are employed or utilized by or contracted to the Office of the Court Administrator or the Court. The Program Staff shall evaluate defendants who might have or have previously been identified as having a mental illness. The Staff shall also identify treatment options in the community and monitor for the Court an appropriate plan of treatment depending on whether the defendant is on probation, diversion, or pretrial release.

Referrals to the program may be made by any circuit or county judge, a general or special magistrate, the Staff of the Mental Health Court Program, the State Attorney, defense counsel, or staff from the jail or any detention facility. Any family member, guardian or other interested person may request a referral through the State Attorney.

The Mental Health Court shall handle cases under the following two classifications:

I. When the defendant is placed on pretrial release pending trial, has entered into a deferred prosecution agreement, or has been placed on probation and has been diagnosed with a mental illness by a mental health expert.

II. When the defendants attorney, the State Attorney or the Court on its own accord has moved to determine competency to proceed pursuant to Fla. R. Crim. P. 3.210. The mental competency evaluation process, as set forth in the Rules of Criminal Procedure shall be within the purview of the Mental Health Court and shall be applicable to the point of a contested hearing. Any contested hearings will be scheduled before the assigned trial judge as set forth more fully below.

The policies, procedures and conduct of court proceedings in the Mental Health Court shall be as follows:

(1) Pretrial release and bond decisions may be made by the Mental Health Court judge. All such cases referred to the Mental Health Court Program will be monitored by the Mental Health Court Program Staff and the Mental Health Court judge.

(2) Upon screening and recommendation by the State Attorney, and then with the agreement of defense counsel, the Mental Health Court judge may defer prosecution of criminal charges pending compliance by the defendant with an appropriate course of treatment recommended by the Mental Health Court Program Staff.

(3) The appropriate course of treatment may include regular appearances before the Court to report on compliance. Upon completion of the appropriate course of treatment and upon agreement of the parties, the State shall file a notice of nolle prosequi in regard to the pending charges against the defendant. A waiver of speedy trial and an agreement to pay full restitution to any victim will be conditions of any deferred prosecution.

(4) All agreements for deferred prosecution shall be in writing, signed by the defendant, defense counsel and the State Attorney, and shall thereafter be filed in the court file. If the defendant fails to comply with the conditions of the deferred prosecution, the case shall be referred by the Mental Health Court Program Staff or the State Attorney back to the assigned trial judge's docket. The court may retain jurisdiction of the case to monitor compliance for such time as is permitted by law.

(5) Upon agreement of the State Attorney and defense counsel, pleas for sentences of probation based upon mental health treatment may be accepted by the Mental Health Court judge and shall include regular monitoring of probation as that may relate to mental health issues. Violation of probation hearings shall be handled by the assigned trial judge, unless the State Attorney, defense counsel and the Mental Health Court judge agree that the violation of probation hearing should be retained on the Mental Health Court docket.

No decision regarding deferred prosecution or referral to the Mental Health Court will be made without input from the victims and with the opportunity for input from the State Attorney and defense counsel.

The assigned trial judge may have the case removed from the Mental Health Court docket for good cause shown and after notice has been provided by the Court, Staff or counsel for the State or defense to all interested parties and an opportunity to be heard by the litigants has been duly provided.

The public is entitled to access to judicial records pursuant to Fla. R. Jud. Admin. 2.420. However, patient treatment records are deemed confidential by Florida law. In order to be accepted into the Mental Health Court Program, a defendant must sign a waiver of confidentiality to the extent that his treatment may be monitored by Mental Health Court Staff, the State Attorney and defense counsel.

In the event a treatment record or report is placed in the court file of a Mental Health Court case, the court will determine whether such report is confidential under Florida law, and if so, shall order that the document be sealed by the Clerk. Access to such documents will be limited to those authorized by Florida law and only then by court order following a hearing and an opportunity to be heard by the parties.

DONE AND ORDERED in Chambers, at Fort Myers, Lee County, Florida this 18TH day of Oct, 2007.

G. Keith Cary
Chief Judge

History. –New.

LAW LIBRARY (CHARLOTTE COUNTY). ORDER APPOINTING MEMBERS OF THE BOARD OF TRUSTEES OF THE CHARLOTTE COUNTY LAW LIBRARY

IN THE TWENTIETH JUDICIAL CIRCUIT IN AND FOR THE STATE OF FLORIDA CHARLOTTE COUNTY

ORDER APPOINTING MEMBERS OF THE BOARD OF TRUSTEES OF THE CHARLOTTE COUNTY LAW LIBRARY

WHEREAS, Charlotte County Code § 1–6–36(a) provides that three members of the Board of Trustees of the Charlotte County Law Library shall be appointed by the senior circuit judge of the Twentieth Judicial Circuit from nominations submitted by the Charlotte County Bar Association; and

WHEREAS, by letter dated May 29, 2007, a copy of which is attached hereto as Attachment A, the Charlotte County Bar Association has submitted the following three names as nominees to serve on the Board of Trustees of the Charlotte County Law Library:

- Jean Finks, Esquire
- John Charles Heekin, Esquire
- Derek Rooney, Esquire

It is hereby ORDERED that the above listed individuals are appointed to serve on the Board of Trustees of the Charlotte County Law Library. In accordance with Charlotte County Code § 1–6–36(a), each member of the board shall serve at the pleasure of the Charlotte County Bar Association.

DONE AND ORDERED in chambers in Naples, Collier County, Florida this 20th day of June, 2007.

Hugh D. Hayes
Chief Judge

History.- New.

Attachment A

CHARLOTTE COUNTY BAR ASSOCIATION, INC.

PO BOX 510512

Punta Gorda, FL 33950

Honorable Judge Hugh D. Hayes, Chief Judge

The 20th Judicial Circuit of Florida

1700 Monroe Street

Fort Myers, FL 33901

May 29, 2007

Honorable Judge Hayes:

This is to advise you that pursuant to Charlotte County Code § 1–36 et seq., at its March 21, 2007 meeting, the Charlotte County Bar Association nominated the following individuals to serve as the Board of Trustees of the Charlotte County Law Library:

Jean Finks

128 East Olympia Avenue, Suite 408, Punta Gorda, FL 33950

John Charies Heekin

21202 Olean Boulevard, Port Charlotte, FL 33952

Derek Rooney

18500 Murdock Circle, Room #573, Port Charlotte, FL 33948

Charlotte County Code § 1–5–36(a) provides that the Senior Circuit Judge of the Twentieth Judicial District is to appoint these individuals as the Board of Trustees upon their nomination. There are several critical issues that need to be resolved about the Law Library (such as maintenance and location) and we would like the Board of Trustees to meet as soon as possible after your appointment so that they can begin these discussions.

Please advise if you have any questions.

Very Truly Yours,
Janatte S. Knowlton
President
Charlotte County Bar Association

JSK/cas

ORDER ESTABLISHING DUTY JUDGE ASSIGNMENT PROCEDURES FOR LEE COUNTY

IN THE TWENTIETH JUDICIAL CIRCUIT IN AND FOR THE STATE OF FLORIDA

ORDER ESTABLISHING DUTY JUDGE ASSIGNMENT PROCEDURES FOR LEE COUNTY

Pursuant to the authority prescribed by Fla. R. Jud. Admin. 2.215 (formerly Fla. R. Jud. Admin. 2.050), it is hereby ordered that the attached rules and procedures shall henceforth govern the method by which duty judge assignments are made in Lee County, Florida.

DONE AND ORDERED in chambers in Fort Myers, Lee County, Florida, this 14th day of August, 2007.

G. Keith Cary
Chief Judge

History.—Order Establishing Duty Judge Assignment Procedures for Lee County (November 30, 2005).

DUTY JUDGE ASSIGNMENTS For LEE COUNTY, FLORIDA

Duty Week:

Each Duty Week shall commence on Tuesday and end on the following Monday.

Holiday Duty Assignments:

Divide the judges into two lists (as equally as possible—currently there are 24 judges). The judges placed on each list have comparable judicial service based on date of hire and are numbered consecutively (see attached). The two lists are designated as "list 1 and list 2".

Each judge remains on his/her initially designated list throughout the judge's judicial career. Upon a judge's retirement, death or other termination (the replaced judge), every judge on the replaced judge's designated holiday list less senior to the replaced judge moves up by one number on that list and the replaced judge's replacement is then assigned the next (last) number on the replaced judge's list. The next new judge would be assigned to list 2, the next to list 1, the next to list 2 and so on in that rotating order.

The judges on list 1 cover the holiday duty weeks during odd number years and the judges on list 2 cover the holiday duty weeks during even years. Duty weeks containing a major holiday (major holiday duty week) are assigned to the judges on a list in descending numerical order, starting with any new judge on the list either replacing a judge or filling a newly created judgeship and moving up the list skipping any judge who has already served a major holiday duty week prior to a complete cycle through all judges. The judges assigned the major holiday duty weeks in any year choose amongst themselves, based on their date of hire seniority, the major holiday duty week each will serve that year. Major holidays are defined as Thanksgiving Day, Christmas Day and New Year's Day. The judges serving duty on major holiday duty weeks are given credit for 2005. No judge shall be assigned a major holiday duty week twice before all judges have served a major holiday duty week.

The remaining holiday duty weeks for both even and odd years are covered by the remaining judges on the corresponding list. The judges from that list choose which of the remaining holidays (non-major holidays not previously assigned as per the proceeding paragraph) based on seniority. Seniority is determined by the judges' date of hire.

In the event there are more holiday duty weeks than judges for a particular year, the less senior judges on the applicable list shall serve the holidays not assigned under the preceding rules. In the event there are more judges for a particular year than holiday duty weeks, the remaining holidays are covered by the less senior judges on the applicable list.

Non–Holiday Duty Assignments:

A non-holiday duty list shall be maintained, assigning letters alphabetically and consecutively to judges, initially assigning letters A through X, with letter A assigned to the most senior judge, B to the next most senior judge and so on down the list in order of hire (see attached). Upon a judge's retirement, death or other termination, that judge's replacement is assigned that judge's letter on the non-holiday duty list whereas new judges will be assigned the next unassigned letter of the alphabet. After holiday weeks have been assigned, non-holiday duty weeks shall be assigned to judges on the non-holiday list except that in making assignments of non-holiday duty weeks, judges already assigned a holiday duty week for the year shall be passed over on the first rotation through the non-holiday list, and if they have been assigned two holiday duty weeks for the year shall be passed over on the second rotation through the non-holiday list. The assignment for 2006 shall be made in the reverse order of the alphabet, assigning the first non-holiday duty week to Judge S, the next to Judge R, and so on, and in the following year and all subsequent years shall begin where it left off in the preceding year, rotating through the list in the same reverse order and giving credit under the above rule for holiday duty weeks to the judges receiving holiday duty week assignments in that year.

Special Rules:

In the event the assignment of a non-holiday week results in a judge receiving two consecutive duty weeks (i.e., a holiday and non-holiday duty week), the non-holiday week shall be switched with the non-holiday week assigned to the judge determined by dividing the total number of judges by 2 (19/2 = 9.5), rounding down (9) and counting that many judges ahead, but if such switch results in the judge getting a duty week in the following year then by counting that many judges back, and in the event such switch also results in the assignment to either of the switched judges having two consecutive weeks, then by switching with the next judge on the list which does not have such result.

In 2007 and 2008, and in any other two consecutive years, where there are only 2 major holiday duty weeks commencing in one year and 4 major holiday duty weeks commencing in the next year, the three judges who would have received a major holiday duty week assignment in 2007 if 3 major holiday duty weeks had commenced in that year shall serve the two major holiday duty weeks commencing in 2007 and the first duty week commencing in 2008 as if it had commenced in 2007.

If a new judge commences service after duty judge assignments have been made for a calendar year:

a. If the new judge is replacing a judge who has retired, died, or otherwise terminated service (a replacement judge), the new replacement judge shall serve all of the remaining duty week assignments of the replaced judge during that calendar year.

b. For that calendar year, the Lee County Administrative Judge shall have the discretion to equitably make duty judge assignments to a new judge to cover emergency situations or for any other reason; provided a new judge shall not be required to serve a greater number of duty weeks than the maximum number of duty weeks assigned during that calendar year to any other judge.

Application:

Beginning in 2006, the three major holiday duty weeks (the duty weeks within which New Year's Day, Christmas Day, and Thanksgiving Day fall) are assigned to the 3 most junior judges (by date of hire) on List 2. The most senior of the three judges selects a major holiday duty week first, the second most senior judge selects a major holiday duty week and then the junior judge of the three shall serve the remaining major holiday duty week. The non-major holiday duty weeks in 2006 are assigned to the remaining judges on List 2 recognizing that seniority will determine the order of judges selecting non-major holiday duty weeks. For example, the most senior judge not assigned a major holiday duty week shall have the first selection of a non-major holiday duty week, continuing in the same manner until a holiday duty week has been assigned to each judge. In the event there are more holiday duty weeks than judges, the unassigned holiday duty weeks shall be assigned to the least senior judges with those judges selecting in their order of seniority. In the event the number of judges exceeds the number of holiday weeks, the non-major holiday weeks shall be assigned in the same manner except that the selection shall begin with the most senior judge on the applicable list so that judge and every judge less senior on the list will have a holiday duty week. For example, if there are 12 judges on a list and a total of 10 holiday duty weeks for a given year, then after the 3 major holiday duty weeks have been assigned, the remaining 7 holiday duty weeks would be assigned to the 7 most junior judges not already assigned a major holiday duty week with those 7 judges selecting the non-major holiday duty week each will serve in accordance with their date of hire seniority.

Non-holiday duty weeks are then assigned to the judges on the non-holiday list, assigning the first such week in the year to Judge S, the next to Judge R, and so on skipping over any judge already assigned a holiday duty week for that year on the first rotation, and if assigned a second holiday duty week skipping over that judge on the second rotation through the non-holiday list except that if a judge ends up with 2 consecutive weeks, his non-holiday week is switched with the non-holiday week of another judge determined in the manner stated under Special Rules. In year 2007, the holiday assignments would be made only to the judges on List 1 in the same manner (giving credit to judges for major holiday duty weeks served in 2005), and non-holiday assignments would be made to the judges on the non-holiday list picking up where the assignments left off in 2006 in the manner stated above. In year 2008, the holiday assignments would be made only to the judges on List 2, picking up where the assignments left off in 2006 with the exception of the assignment rules above for new or replacement judges.

The above duty week schedule for all major holiday duty weeks, non-major holiday duty weeks and non-holiday duty weeks shall continue for all future years based upon alternating between the two identified lists for holiday duty week assignments and assigning non-holiday duty weeks using the non-holiday duty week list.

HOLIDAY DUTY JUDGE LIST

List 1—Odd Years Lee County Judges	List 2—Even Year Lee County Judges
1. Starnes, Hugh	1. McIver, William
2. Sturgis, Radford	2. Reese, Thomas
3. Rosman, Jay	3. Seals, James
4. Gerald, Lynn	4. Cary, G. Keith
5. Carlin, John	5. Dommerich, John
6. Adams, James	6. Volz, Edward
7. Winesett, Sherra	7. Corbin, R. Thomas
8. Steinbeck, Margaret	8. Hayes, Leigh
9. Gonzalez, Maria	9. Duryea, John
10. Steinbeck, Mark	10. McHugh, Michael
11. Gagliardi, Josephine	11. Simpson, Joseph
12. Fuller, Joseph	12. Paluck, Tara

NON–HOLIDAY DUTY JUDGE LIST

	Lee County Judges	Hire Date
A.	McIver, William	1977 January
B.	Starnes, Hugh	1978 June
C.	Reese, Thomas	1979 October
D.	Sturgis, Radford	1981 September
E.	Seals, James	1985 January
F.	Rosman, Jay	1986 December
G.	Cary, G. Keith	1989 January
H.	Gerald, Lynn	1989 September
I.	Dommerich, John	1989 November
J.	Carlin, John	1991 January
K.	Volz, Edward	1991 January
L.	Adams, James	1993 January
M.	Corbin, R. Thomas	1994 January
N.	Winesett, Sherra	1995 November
O	Hayes, Leigh	1997 January
P.	Steinbeck, Margaret	1998 December
Q.	Duryea, John	2003 September
R.	Gonzalez, Maria	2004 May
S.	Steinbeck, Mark	2006 April
T.	McHugh, Michael	2006 May
U.	Gagliardi, Josephine	2006 September
V.	Simpson, Joseph	2007 January
W.	Fuller, Joseph	2007 January
X.	Paluck, Tara	2007 January

INMATE RELOCATION (COLLIER COUNTY). ORDER DESIGNATING ALTERNATIVE LOCATIONS FOR DEPOSITIONS OF JAIL INMATES AND JUVENILE DETAINEES IN COLLIER COUNTY

IN THE TWENTIETH JUDICIAL CIRCUIT IN AND FOR THE STATE OF FLORIDA

ORDER DESIGNATING ALTERNATIVE LOCATIONS FOR DEPOSITIONS OF JAIL INMATES AND JUVENILE DETAINEES IN COLLIER COUNTY

WHEREAS, there are legitimate security and public safety concerns with transporting jail inmates and juvenile detainees to the Collier County Courthouse for the purpose of taking discovery depositions pursuant to Fla. R. Crim. P. 3.220,

IT IS HEREBY ORDERED, pursuant to the authority provided by Fla. R. Jud. Admin. 2.050 and Fla. R. Crim. P. 3.220(h)(3) as follows:

(1) Discovery depositions of Collier County Jail Inmates or detainees shall be taken at the Collier County Jail, providing that the Collier County Jail has deposition facilities available that can adequately provide for all parties' safety and privacy concerns.

(2) Discovery depositions of juvenile detainees held at the Department of Juvenile Justice Holding Facility in Collier County shall be taken at the Department of Juvenile Justice Holding Facility in Collier County, providing that the Holding Facility has deposition facilities available that can adequately provide for all parties' safety and privacy concerns.

(3) In any particular case, if any party has an objection to a deposition being taken at the Collier County Jail or Department of Juvenile Justice Holding Facility, that party may file an objection or motion with the trial court seeking a determination as to where the deposition shall be taken.

(4) This order is not intended to divest the trial court of its authority under Fla. R. Crim. P. 3.220(h)(3) to designate a location for the taking of a deposition, and is not intended to divest the parties of their right under Fla. R. Crim. P. 3.220(h)(3) to agree upon a location for the taking of a deposition.

(5) To the extent that any provision of this Administrative Order may be construed as being in conflict with any law, statute, or rule, the law, statute, or rule shall prevail.

DONE AND ORDERED in chambers in Naples, Collier County, Florida, this 16 day of November, 2005.

Hugh D. Hayes
Chief Judge

History. - New.

MENTAL HEALTH (CHARLOTTE COUNTY). ORDER ESTABLISHING MENTAL HEALTH COURT FOR CHARLOTTE COUNTY

IN THE TWENTIETH JUDICIAL CIRCUIT IN AND FOR THE STATE OF FLORIDA

ORDER ESTABLISHING MENTAL HEALTH COURT FOR CHARLOTTE COUNTY

There is created within the Twentieth Judicial Circuit in and for Charlotte County, Florida, a Mental Health Court. The court will hear only those criminal court matters that do not impact the public safety or the safety of the victim. The State Attorney's Office shall screen each defendant referred to the Mental Health Court and shall determine which cases will be placed into the Mental Health Court Program. This decision shall be made with input from defense counsel, the court and the Staff of the Mental Health Court.

Beginning January 1, 2005, or as soon thereafter as is practicable, the presiding judge in Mental Health Court will hear those criminal court matters referred to the Mental Health Court Program. The Mental Health Court Program shall be composed of Staff whose services are employed or utilized by or contracted to the Office of the Court Administrator or the Court. The Program Staff shall evaluate defendants who might have or have previously been identified as having a mental illness. The Staff shall also identify treatment options in the community and monitor for the Court an appropriate plan of treatment depending on whether the defendant is on probation, diversion, or pretrial release.

Judge Peter A. Bell will be assigned to handle cases within the Mental Health Court Program. Referrals to the program may be made by any circuit or county judge, a general or special master, the Staff of the Mental Health Court Program, the State Attorney, defense counsel, or staff from the jail or the Southwest Florida Detention Center. Any family member, guardian or other interested person may request a referral through the State Attorney.

The Mental Health Court shall handle cases under the following two classifications:

I. When the defendant is placed on pretrial release pending trial, has entered into a deferred prosecution agreement, or has been placed on probation and has been diagnosed with a mental illness by a mental health expert.

II. When the defendant's attorney, the State Attorney or the court on its own accord has moved to determine competency to proceed pursuant to Fla. R. Crim. P. 3.210. The mental competency evaluation process, as set forth in the Rules of Criminal Procedure shall be within the purview of the Mental Health Court and shall be applicable to the point of a contested hearing. Any contested hearings will be scheduled before the assigned trial judge as set forth more fully below.

The policies, procedures and conduct of court proceedings in the Mental Health Court shall be as follows:

(a) Pretrial release and bond decisions may be made by the Mental Health Court judge. All such cases referred to the Mental Health Court Program will be monitored by the Mental Health Court Program Staff and the Mental Health Court Judge.

(b) Upon screening and recommendation by the State Attorney, and then with the agreement of defense counsel, the Mental Health Court judge may defer prosecution of criminal charges pending compliance by the defendant with an appropriate course of treatment recommended by the Mental Health Court Program Staff.

(c) The appropriate course of treatment may include regular appearances before the court to report on compliance. Upon completion of the appropriate course of treatment and upon agreement of the parties, the State shall file a notice of nolle prosequi in regard to the pending charges against the defendant. A waiver of speedy trial and an agreement to pay full restitution to any victim will be conditions of any deferred prosecution.

(d) All agreements for deferred prosecution shall be in writing, signed by the defendant, defense counsel and the

State Attorney, and shall thereafter be filed in the court file. If the defendant fails to comply with the conditions of the deferred prosecution, the case shall be referred by the Mental Health Court Program Staff or the State Attorney back to the assigned trial judge's docket. The court may retain jurisdiction of the case to monitor compliance for such time as is permitted by law.

(e) Upon agreement of the State Attorney and defense counsel, pleas for sentences of probation based upon mental health treatment may be accepted by the Mental Health Court judge and shall include regular monitoring of probation as that may relate to mental health issues. Violation of probation hearings shall be handled by the assigned trial judge, unless the State Attorney, defense counsel and the Mental Health Court judge agree that the violation of probation hearing should be retained on the Mental Health Court docket. No decision regarding deferred prosecution or referral to the Mental Health Court will be made without input from the victims and with the opportunity for input from the State Attorney and defense counsel.

The assigned trial judge may have the case removed from the Mental Health Court docket for good cause shown and after notice has been provided by the Court, Staff or counsel for the State or defense to all interested parties and on opportunity to be heard by the litigants has been duly provided.

The public is entitled to access to judicial records pursuant to Fla. R. Jud. Admin. 2.071. However, patient treatment records are deemed confidential by Florida law. In order to be accepted into the Mental Health Court Program, a defendant must sign a waiver of confidentiality to the extent that his treatment may be monitored by Mental Health Court Staff, the State Attorney and defense counsel.

In the event a treatment record or report is placed in the court file of a Mental Health Court case, the court will determine whether such report is confidential under Florida law, and if so, shall order that the document be sealed by the Clerk. Access to such documents will be limited to those authorized by Florida law and only then by court order following a hearing and an opportunity to be heard by the parties.

DONE AND ORDERED in Chambers, at Naples, Collier County, Florida this 1st day of December, 2004.

Hugh D. Hayes
Chief Judge

History.—New.

PROBATION (AMENDED). AMENDED ORDER AUTHORIZING CLERK OF COURTS TO COLLECT FEES FOR COUNTY PROBATION SERVICES

IN THE TWENTIETH JUDICIAL CIRCUIT IN AND FOR COLLIER COUNTY, FLORIDA

AMENDED ORDER AUTHORIZING CLERK OF COURTS TO COLLECT FEES FOR COUNTY PROBATION SERVICES

Pursuant to this Court's recognized role in promoting the prompt and efficient administration of justice in the courts of the Twentieth Judicial Circuit, as well as the authority prescribed by Fla. R. Jud. Admin. 2.215 (formerly Fla. R. Jud. Admin. 2.050), the Court hereby establishes a protocol for assessing and collecting fees in connection with Probation services.

IT IS HEREBY ORDERED that for all criminal defendants who are placed on County Probation, the Clerk of Court in and for Collier County is authorized to collect a supervision fee in the amount of Sixty-five Dollars ($65.00) per month effective June 1, 2004.

IT IS FURTHER ORDERED that unless declared indigent by the sentencing court pursuant to Ch. 948.09, F.S., all such persons shall pay to the Clerk of Court the necessary fee. Effective June 1, 2005, the fee will be Seventy Dollars ($70.00) per month.

THE COURT ORDERS that for all persons placed on Home Monitoring, the Clerk of Court in and for Collier County is authorized to collect a supervision fee in the amount of Thirteen Dollars ($13.00) for each day of supervision.

UPON RECEIPT OF PAYMENT, the Clerk of Court shall remit said fees, less an administrative fee, agreed to by the Chief Judge and Clerk of Court, to the Board of County Commissioners on a monthly basis.

DONE AND ORDERED in Naples, Collier County, Florida this 25th day of May, 2007.

Hugh D. Hayes
Chief Judge

History.- Amended Order Authorizing Clerk of Courts to Collect Fees for County Probation Services (Apr. 21, 2004).

CHILD SUPPORT (COLLIER COUNTY). CHILD SUPPORT ENFORCEMENT HEARING OFFICER

IN THE TWENTIETH JUDICIAL CIRCUIT

ORDER

Pursuant to Rule 12.491(c) of the Florida Family Law Rules of Procedure, Jane Lane, Esquire, is hereby appointed as a Child Support Enforcement Hearing Officer for the Twentieth Judicial Circuit and shall expeditiously perform the duties prescribed by the Rule until further Order of this Court.

DONE AND ORDERED in Chambers in Naples, Collier County, Florida this 22nd day of November, 2004.

Hugh D. Hayes
Chief Judge

PROBATION. ORDER AUTHORIZING CLERK OF COURTS TO COLLECT FEES FOR CHARLOTTE COUNTY PROBATION SERVICES

IN THE TWENTIETH JUDICIAL CIRCUIT IN AND FOR CHARLOTTE COUNTY, FLORIDA

ORDER AUTHORIZING CLERK OF COURTS TO COLLECT FEES FOR CHARLOTTE COUNTY PROBATION SERVICES

Pursuant to this Court's recognized role in promoting the prompt and efficient administration of justice in the courts of the Twentieth Judicial Circuit, as well as the authority prescribed by Fla.R.Jud.Admin. 2.050, the Court hereby establishes a protocol for assessing and collecting fees in connection with Probation Services.

IT IS HEREBY ORDERED that for all criminal defendants who are placed on County Probation, the Clerk of Court in and for Charlotte County is authorized to collect a supervision fee in the amount of Forty-five ($45.00) dollars per month effective October 1, 2004.

IT IS HEREBY ORDERED that defendants ordered to do Community Service through the Probation Department shall pay $1.00 per 10 hours of Community Service to cover the costs of Administration and Insurance fee's.

DONE AND ORDERED in chambers, in Naples, Collier County, Florida, this 30th day of September 2004.

____

HONORABLE HUGH D. HAYES
CHIEF JUDGE

DOMESTIC VIOLENCE (COLLIER COUNTY). ORDER APPROVING USE OF FORMS IN DOMESTIC VIOLENCE CASES IN COLLIER COUNTY

IN THE TWENTIETH JUDICIAL CIRCUIT IN AND FOR THE STATE OF FLORIDA

ORDER APPROVING USE OF FORMS IN DOMESTIC VIOLENCE CASES IN COLLIER COUNTY

Pursuant to the authority prescribed by Fla. R. Jud. Admin. 2.050 and Florida Statute § 43.26, and in recognition of the duty to promote the prompt and efficient administration of justice, it is

ORDERED AND ADJUDGED that the following forms, copies of which are attached hereto and incorporated herein, and which are not inconsistent with any Florida Supreme Court standardized forms, are approved for use in all Collier County domestic violence cases:

- Order of Consolidation of Injunction for Protection Against Domestic Violence Issued Pursuant to Section 741.30 Florida Statute
- Order on Motion and Notice of Intent to Dismiss for Lack of Prosecution
- Order on Order to Show Cause
- Order Resetting Hearing on Temporary Injunction
- Order for Surrender of Firearms or Order for Affidavit of No Firearms
- Order on Respondent's Motion for Return of Weapons
- Motion for Return of Weapons
- Bench Warrant
- Writ of Bodily Attachment
- Order of Dismissal Pursuant to Section 741.30 or 784.046 Florida Statutes

DONE AND ORDERED in chambers in Naples, Collier County, Florida, this 18th day of December, 2003.

____

Hugh D. Hayes
Chief Judge

History. - Order Approving Use of Forms in Domestic Violence Cases in Collier County (October 13, 2003).

IN THE CIRCUIT COURT OF THE TWENTIETH JUDICIAL CIRCUIT IN AND FOR COLLIER COUNTY, FLORIDA CIVIL ACTION

____
____________________,
Petitioner,

vs. Case No.: ___ –CA–01

____
____________________,
Respondent.

ORDER OF CONSOLIDATION OF INJUNCTION FOR PROTECTION AGAINST DOMESTIC VIOLENCE ISSUED PURSUANT TO SECTION 741.30 FLORIDA STATUTE

This cause, having come to be heard on _________ and this Court having considered same, it is hereby **ORDERED AND ADJUDGED** as follows:

1. That the Injunction for Protection Against Domestic Violence shall remain in full force and effect:
   _________ until further ordered by this Court.
   _________ and shall expire on the expiration date indicated on the Final Injunction for Protection
   _________ and shall expire on

2. That the Injunction for Protection Against Domestic Violence (and all related pleadings) issued in Case # ___ –CA–01 are herein consolidated with the pending Dissolution of Marriage Action/Paternity Action in Case # ___ –CA–01.

3. Notwithstanding this consolidation, the Injunction for Protection Against Domestic Violence referred to in Paragraph (1) above, together with any modifications to same, shall be construed as being issued pursuant to Section 741.30 Florida Statute for purpose of enforcement and other remedies.

4. Unless otherwise ordered, all future pleadings relating to the Injunction for Protection Against Domestic Violence shall be filed in the above referenced Dissolution of Marriage Action/Paternity Action.

DONE AND ORDERED in Naples, Collier County, Florida on this ___ day of _________, ___.

____

Circuit Court Judge

CERTIFICATE OF SERVICE

I CERTIFY that a copy of this Order was furnished by regular U.S. mail (unless otherwise indicated) this ___ day of ________, ___, to
Petitioner (do not input if Confidential) at ________________
Respondent at ________________
Civil Process (hand delivery)
Civil Department (hand delivery)
Atty ________ at ________________
Atty ________ at ________________
Visitation Agency (DVU in bin) ________

____
Deputy Clerk

IN THE CIRCUIT COURT OF THE TWENTIETH JUDICIAL CIRCUIT IN AND FOR COLLIER COUNTY, FLORIDA CIVIL ACTION

____
________________,

Petitioner,

vs. Case No.: ___ –CA–01

________________,

Respondent.

________________ /

ORDER ON MOTION AND NOTICE OF INTENT TO DISMISS FOR LACK OF PROSECUTION

THIS CAUSE, having come before this Court on its Motion and Notice of Intent to Dismiss for Lack of Prosecution filed pursuant to Florida Rule of Civil Procedure 1.420(e), the Court finds that it does not appear from the Court's file that any pleadings or orders have been entered in this action for a period of one year prior to the date of the Court's Motion and Notice, it is therefore:

ORDERED AND ADJUDGED as follows:

____ That no good cause having been shown by either party pursuant to The Motion and Notice of Intent to Dismiss for Lack of Prosecution, this action is hereby DISMISSED. The Petitioner shall take nothing and the Respondent shall go henceforth without day.

____ That good cause having been shown by the parties as to why this Action should not be dismissed, the Motion and Notice of Intent to Dismiss for Lack of Prosecution is hereby WITHDRAWN.

____ (A) This cause is continued for ___ days.

DONE AND ORDERED in Chambers at Naples, Collier County, Florida, on this ___ day of ________, ___.

____
CIRCUIT COURT JUDGE

Cc: Petitioner at ________________
Respondent at ________________
Civil Process
File (only if action is dismissed)
Visitation Agency ________ (N/A if non–applicable)
Atty ________________
Atty ________________

IN THE CIRCUIT COURT OF THE TWENTIETH JUDICIAL CIRCUIT IN AND FOR COLLIER COUNTY, FLORIDA CIVIL ACTION

____

Petitioner,

vs. Case No.: ___ –CA–01

____

Respondent.

ORDER ON ORDER TO SHOW CAUSE

In reference to the above-styled cause, on the ___ day of ________, 20 ___ a hearing was scheduled in regards to the Order to Show Cause against the ( ) Petitioner ( ) Respondent for ________________

____ The Petitioner/Respondent (is ________) (is not ________) found to be in contempt of Court.

____ The Petitioner/Respondent shall serve ___ days in the Collier County Jail.

____ ___ days shall be suspended upon the following:

A. ___ The Petitioner/Respondent completing an evaluation from a domestic violence facility from the list of providers within ________ and following all recommendations from said evaluation. The Petitioner/Respondent shall provide the Domestic Violence Unit. 3301 Tamiami Trail East, Building L, 5th Floor, Naples, Florida, with written proof of said evaluation within ________________

B. The Petitioner/Respondent not being found in contempt of court for any future violations.

C. ___ Other ________________
____
____

___ The Order to Show Cause against the Petitioner/Respondent shall be quashed.

___ Other: ________________
____

DONE AND ORDERED in Naples, Collier County, Florida this ___ day of ________, 20 ___.

____
CIRCUIT COURT JUDGE

COPIES TO
____ Petitioner ________________
____ Respondent ________________
____ Civil Process
____ File (original to recording if case is not confidential)
____ Case Manager
____ Atty ________________
____ Atty ________________
____ Visitation Agency ________________
____ Other ________________

IN THE CIRCUIT COURT OF THE TWENTIETH JUDICIAL CIRCUIT IN AND FOR COLLIER COUNTY, FLORIDA CIVIL ACTION

____

Petitioner,

vs. Case No.: ___ –CA–01

____
____
____

Respondent.

ORDER RESETTING HEARING ON TEMPORARY INJUNCTION

In reference to the above-styled cause, on the ___ day of ________, 20 ___ a hearing was scheduled/conducted

The Petitioner (was ________) or (was not ________) present

The Petitioner (was ________) advised by DVU not to appear due to the non-service on the Respondent

The Respondent (was ________) or (was not ________) present

The Respondent (was ________) or (was not ________) served with the Temporary Injunction for Protection

Accordingly, after the Court being advised in the premises, it is hereby **ORDERED AND ADJUDGED** as follows

1. The Temporary Injunction previously entered shall remain in full force and effect until further ordered by this court
2. The Petitioner and the Respondent may not agree to violate this injunction and violation of any term of the Temporary Injunction is punishable by Jail. Fine or Both.
3. This case shall be reset for the ___ day of ________, 20 ___, at ___.m., before the Honorable ________ in Courtroom 4C.
4. The purpose of the reset is for the following reason(s):
   ____ Petitioner failed to appear. Injunction may be dismissed if the Petitioner fails to appear at the above hearing
   ____ Respondent was not served.
   ____ Receipt of the final report from the Department of Children & Family Services.
   ____ Criminal case/investigation pending.
   ____ Counsel to be present.
   ____ Other ________
5. The Temporary Injunction for Protection shall be modified as follows: ________

____

________ ________

Petitioner Signature—if present Respondent Signature—if present

DONE AND ORDERED in Naples, Collier County, Florida this ___ day of ________, ___.

____

CIRCUIT COURT JUDGE

"In accordance with the American With Disabilities Act, persons needing a special accommodation to participate in this proceeding should contact the Deputy Court Administrator whose office is located at 3301 Tamiami Trail East, Courthouse Building, Naples, Florida 34112, telephone number (239) 774–8124; telephone 1–800–955–8771 (TDD), or 1–800–955–8770 (V). via Florida Relay Service, not later than (7) days prior to the proceeding."

CERTIFICATE OF SERVICE

I CERTIFY that a copy of this Order Resetting Hearing was furnished to regular U.S. mail (unless otherwise indicated) this ___ day of ________, 20 ________, to

___ Petitioner (do not input if Confidential) at ________
___ Respondent (only if Respondent was previously served) at ________
___ Atty: ________ at ________
___ Atty: ________ at ________
___ Visitation Agency ________
___ Sheriff's Office for Service on Respondent (name of agency) ________
___ DVU Calendar (DVU Office)
___ Civil Process of CCSO (hand delivery)
___ Case Manager
___ Other: ________

I CERTIFY the foregoing is a true copy of the original as it appears on file in the Clerk of the Circuit Court of Collier County. Florida and was forwarded as indicated above.

CLERK OF THE CIRCUIT COURT
By ________
Deputy Clerk

HAND DELIVERY IN OPEN COURT

I, (Petitioner) ________, acknowledge receipt of a certified copy of this order

I, (Respondent) ________, acknowledge receipt of a certified copy of this order

I, (Petitioner's Attorney) ________, acknowledge receipt of a certified copy of this order.

I, (Respondent's Attorney) ________, acknowledge receipt of a certified copy of this order.

IN THE CIRCUIT COURT OF THE TWENTIETH JUDICIAL CIRCUIT IN AND FOR COLLIER COUNTY, FLORIDA CIVIL ACTION

____
Petitioner,

vs. Case No.: ___ –CA–01

____
____
Respondent.

ORDER FOR SURRENDER OF FIREARMS OR ORDER FOR AFFIDAVIT OF NO FIREARMS

THIS CAUSE came before the Court and the Court having reviewed the file and being otherwise fully advised in the premises, it is hereby **ORDERED AND ADJUDGED** as follows:

IF YOU OWN OR ARE IN THE POSSESSION OF ANY FIREARMS YOU SHALL COMPLETE THE FOLLOWING:

1. The Respondent shall deliver to the possession of the law enforcement department with jurisdiction over the Respondent's home any and all firearms in his/her possession.

2. Said firearms shall by delivered by the Respondent within 24 hours to the law enforcement department subject to the following conditions and requirements:

A. You shall call the law enforcement department prior to arriving at the law enforcement department and state the purpose of your visit and the existence of this Order. If Collier County Sheriff's Office is the law enforcement department with jurisdiction, please contact the Duty Officer at (239) 774–4434.

B. You shall arrange to meet with a representative from the law enforcement department outside the main entrance of the Sheriff's Office. **DO NOT BRING FIREARMS INTO ANY COURTHOUSE OR SHERIFF'S OFFICE BUILDING!**

C. Each and every firearm shall be securely encased in a zipped, locked, or wrapped container

D. You shall have prepared a complete inventory of all firearms surrendered to the law enforcement department including type, make, model, serial number, and general condition. A copy of an inventory sheet is attached for your use.

E. All weapons shall be unloaded, with clips removed.

F. No ammunition of any kind shall be contained in any package.

G. Respondent shall deliver to the law enforcement department a copy of this Order

H. The law enforcement representative shall take possession of the firearms from you outside of the Building

I. You shall deliver to the Domestic Violence Unit located at 3301 East Tamiami Trail. Building L. 5th Floor. Naples, Florida 34112 or the Immokalee Clerk of Courts at 106 South First Street. Immokalee, Florida 34142 or the Domestic Violence Unit fax at (239) 732–2718 a copy of the property receipt within forty eight (48) hours from the date said weapons were placed in the possession of the law enforcement department

3. The law enforcement department will keep said firearms in secure storage until the Injunction for Protection is terminated. At said time such firearms shall be returnable to you upon the filing of a motion and a signed order by the assigned judge.

4. The firearms delivered according to the terms of this Order shall remain the total responsibility of the owner or bearer of such firearms, and the law enforcement department shall have no responsibility as bailee or by any other legal status to maintain the value of any such firearm as may be delivered according to the terms of this Order.

5. If you fail to reclaim your firearms within sixty (60) days of the termination date of the injunction, such firearms shall be forfeited to the law enforcement department according to the terms of Chapter 705, Florida Statutes.

6. Failure to complete the above stated process shall result in an Order to Show Cause/Contempt proceeding against the Respondent.

IF YOU DO NOT OWN OR POSSESS ANY FIREARMS YOU SHALL COMPLETE THE FOLLOWING:

1. The Respondent shall complete the attached affidavit stating that he/ she does not own or possess any firearms.

2. The completed affidavit shall be submitted to the Domestic Violence Unit at 3301 East Tamiami Trail, Building L, 5th Floor, Naples, Florida 34112 or the Immokalee Clerk of Courts at 106 South First Street, Immokalee, Florida 34142 or the Domestic Violence Unit fax at (239) 732–2718 within forty eight (48) hours from the date of service of this order. The Respondent shall bring with him/her a picture photo identification or have the affidavit notarized prior to faxing.

3. Failure to complete the above stated process shall result in an Order to Show Cause/Contempt proceeding against the Respondent.

DONE AND ORDERED in Naples, Collier County, Florida on this ___ day of ________, ___

____

CIRCUIT COURT JUDGE

I CERTIFY the foregoing is a true copy of the original as it appears on file in the office of the Clerk of the Circuit Court of Collier County, Florida, and that I have furnished copies of this order as indicated below.

CLERK OF THE CIRCUIT COURT
Dwight E. Brock
By: __________________
Deputy Clerk

cc:
Law enforcement department for service on Respondent
Petitioner
Petitioner service packet

INVENTORY OF FIREARMS

NAME: ____________________________
Last First Middle

CASE #: ____________________________

Type	Make	Model	Serial Number	Ownership

________________ ________________
Date Signature of Respondent

IN THE CIRCUIT COURT OF THE TWENTIETH JUDICIAL CIRCUIT IN AND FOR COLLIER COUNTY FLORIDA CIVIL ACTION

____
________________,
Petitioner,

vs. Case No.: ___ –CA–01

____
________________,
Respondent.

AFFIDAVIT AFFIRMING RESPONDENT DOES NOT OWN/POSSESS ANY FIREARMS

I, {full legal name} ________, being sworn, certify that the following statements are true:

(This section is about you. It must be completed. However, if you are the Petitioner and this is a domestic violence case and you fear that disclosing your address to the respondent would put you in danger, you should complete and file Petitioner's Request for Confidential Filing of Address. Florida Family Law Form 12.980(i), and write "confidential" in the space provided on this form for your address and telephone number.)

1. I am the ( ) Petitioner ( )Respondent ( )Counter Petitioner ( )Counter Respondent.

2. Residence ____________________

Mailing address ____________________

Home telephone number: ____________________

Work telephone number: ____________________

3. Social security number: ____________________

4. Date of birth: ____________________

5. Driver's License number: ____________________

6. I solemnly swear and affirm that I do not own/possess any firearms. I am in compliance with the Weapons Order.

I UNDERSTAND THAT I AM SWEARING OR AFFIRMING UNDER OATH TO THE TRUTHFULNESS OF THE CLAIMS MADE IN THIS AFFIDAVIT AND THAT THE PUNISHMENT FOR KNOWINGLY MAKING A FALSE STATEMENT INCLUDES FINES AND/OR IMPRISONMENT.

____________________ ____________________

DATE SIGNATURE

STATE OF FLORIDA
COUNTY OF COLLIER

Sworn to or affirmed and signed before me on ____ by ____

____

Notary Public or Deputy Clerk

____

[Print, type or stamp commissioned name of notary]

___ Personally Known
___ Produced identification
Type of identification produced ____________________

IN THE CIRCUIT COURT OF THE TWENTIETH JUDICIAL CIRCUIT IN AND FOR COLLIER COUNTY, FLORIDA CIVIL ACTION

xxxx

Petitioner

vs. **Case Number: xxxx–CA–01**

xxxx

Respondent

ORDER ON RESPONDENT'S MOTION FOR RETURN OF WEAPONS

On the respondent's motion for return of weapons, it is ordered:

________ The motion is granted. The Injunction for Protection was dismissed or the Injunction for Protection expired. Therefore, any weapons now in the possession of any law enforcement agency taken from or delivered by the respondent in this case shall be returned to the respondent by such agency or agencies. The Respondent shall contact the Collier County Sheriff's Office Evidence Technician at (239)793–9266 OR (239)793–9291 to schedule an appointment to receive his/her firearms.

________ The motion is denied, without prejudice.

Ordered at Naples, Collier County. Florida ________

____

Circuit Judge

CERTIFICATE OF SERVICE

I CERTIFY a true and correct copy of this Order was furnished by regular U.S. mail this day of ________, ___, to:

(1) respondent at xxxx.
(2) petitioner at (do not indicate if Confidential) xxxx
(3) CCSO Evidence Technician.
(4) atty.: xxxx at xxxx
(5) atty.: xxxx at xxxx

CLERK OF THE CIRCUIT COURT
By: ____________________
Deputy Clerk

IN THE CIRCUIT COURT OF THE TWENTIETH JUDICIAL CIRCUIT IN AND FOR COLLIER COUNTY, FLORIDA CIVIL ACTION

____________________,

Petitioner,

Vs. Case No.: ___ –CA–01

____________________,

Respondent.

MOTION FOR RETURN OF WEAPONS

I, {full legal name} ________, being sworn, certify that the following statement is true:

*MOVING PARTY (This section is about you. It must be completed. However, if you are the Petitioner and this is a domestic violence case and you fear that disclosing your address to the Respondent would put you in danger, you should complete Petitioner's Request for Confidential Filing of Address, ☐Florida Supreme Court Approved Family Law Form 12.980(h). write "confidential" in the space provided on this form for your address and telephone number.)

1. Moving Party is the ( ) Petitioner ( ) Respondent ( ) Counter Petitioner ( ) Counter Respondent in this case.

2. Moving Party receives mail at: {street address} ____

{city, state and zip code} ____________________

Telephone Number: {area code and number} ____________________

3. Moving Party's Social Security Number: ____________________

4. Moving Party's Date of Birth: ____________________

5. Moving Party's Drivers License Number: ____________________

The Moving Party moves for return of any weapons he or she may have delivered to law enforcement or were taken by law enforcement in this action. The Moving Party states he or she is entitled to return of these weapons.

_______________ _______________

Date Signature of Moving Party

STATE OF FLORIDA

COUNTY OF COLLIER

Sworn to or affirmed and signed before me on ________ by

____

CLERK OF CIRCUIT COURT

By: _______________

Deputy Clerk/Notary Public

____

[Print, type or stamp commissioned name of notary]

CERTIFICATE OF SERVICE

I CERTIFY a true and correct copy of this motion was furnished by regular U.S. mail this ___ day of ________, 20 ___, to:

Petitioner at (do not write if confidential): _______________

Respondent at _______________

Other _______________

CLERK OF THE CIRCUIT COURT

By: _______________

Deputy Clerk

IN THE CIRCUIT COURT OF THE TWENTIETH JUDICIAL CIRCUIT IN AND FOR COLLIER COUNTY, FLORIDA CIVIL ACTION

xxxx,

Petitioner,

vs. Case No.: xxxx–CA–01

xxxx

xxxx

Respondent.

DOB:	xxxx	Race:	xxxx
Sex:	xxxx	SS #:	xxxx
Hair:	xxxx	Eyes:	xxxx
D/L. #:	xxxx	MAKE:	xxxx
YEAR:	xxxx	TAG #:	xxxx
STATE:	xxxx		

BENCH WARRANT

IN THE NAME OF THE STATE OF FLORIDA TO ALL AND SINGULAR THE SHERIFFS OF SAID STATE:

You are hereby instructed to arrest xxxx if this person be found in your county, and bring said person before the Honorable Court forthwith to show why the Respondent should not be held in contempt in the following case (s):

The xxxx, xxxx, failed to appear for the scheduled xxxx on the xx day of xx, xx. before the Honorable xx. Notification of the hearing was mailed to the xxxx last known address on the xx day of xxxx. 20xx, as indicated on the Certificate of Service.

Jail personnel shall immediately notify the Domestic Violence Unit, 239–732–2760, upon the arrest of the above-named individual to schedule a court date.

Bond $xxxx

DONE AND ORDERED, this ___ day of ________, 20 ___.

____

CIRCUIT COURT JUDGE /

2

cc:
Warrants

IN THE CIRCUIT COURT OF THE TWENTIETH JUDICIAL CIRCUIT IN AND FOR COLLIER COUNTY, FLORIDA CIVIL ACTION

xxxx,

Petitioner,

vs. Case No.: xxxx–CA–01

xxxx

xxxx

Respondent.

DOB:	xxx	Racc:	xxxx
Sex:	xxxx	SS #:	xxxx
Hair:	xxxx	Eyes:	xxxx
D/L #:	xxxx	MAKE:	xxxx
YEAR:	xxxx	TAG #:	xxxx
STATE:	xxxx		

WRIT OF BODILY ATTACHMENT

THE STATE OF FLORIDA:

To the Sheriffs of the State of Florida:

YOU ARE COMMANDED to take possession of the person of xxxx and deliver same to the Collier County Jail to serve a sentence of xxxx (xx) days for failure to comply with the order signed by the Honorable xxxx on the xxxx day of xxxx. 20xxx. A certified copy of said order is attached hereto.

The xxxx. xxxx. failed to comply with the attached order by failing to xxxx. A certified copy of the Affidavit of Failure to Comply with Contempt Proceedings is attached hereto.

Jail personnel shall immediately contact the Domestic Violence Unit at (239)732–2760 upon the arrest of the above stated individual to schedule a court date.

Dated this ___ day of ________, 20 ___

____

CIRCUIT COURT JUDGE

cc: Warrants

IN THE CIRCUIT COURT OF THE TWENTIETH JUDICIAL CIRCUIT IN AND FOR COLLIER COUNTY, FLORIDA CIVIL DIVISION

Petitioner,

v. CASE NO.:

Respondent.

_______________/

ORDER OF DISMISSAL PURSUANT TO SECTION 741.30 OR 784.046 FLORIDA STATUTES

THIS CAUSE came on to be heard on this ___ day of ________, 20 ___, on [ ] Court's [ ] Petitioner's [ ] Respondent's motion, and it appearing that:

[ ] The order entered on the ___ day of ________, 20 ___, has expired on the ___ day of ________, 20 ___, it is therefore

[ ] NO JUST CAUSE: upon hearing, the evidence presented is insufficient under Florida law (section 741.30 or 784.046, Florida Statutes) to allow the Court to issue an injunction for protection against domestic, repeat or dating violence, it is therefore

[ ] FAILED TO APPEAR: the Petitioner having failed to appear for hearing for a Permanent Injunction on the ___ day of ________, 20 ___, at ________, it is therefore

[ ] FAILED TO APPEAR: both parties having failed to appear for hearing for a Permanent Injunction on the ___ day of ___, 20 ___, at ________, it is therefore

[ ] FAILED TO COMPLETE: Petitioner failed or declined to complete application process, it is therefore

[ ] FAILURE TO EFFECT SERVICE: Respondent has not been served, and 120 days have passed since the filing of the petition.

ORDERED AND ADJUDGED that this cause is hereby DISMISSED with ________ without ________ prejudice

Court Costs.

[ ] Pursuant to section 741.30(2)(a) and 784.046(3)(b), Florida Statutes, no filing fees to the Clerk of the Circuit Court or service fees to the sheriff are assessed for a protection for protection against domestic, repeat, dating, or sexual violence, due to the statutory prohibition.

DONE AND ORDERED at Naples, Collier County, Florida, this the ___ day of ________, 20___

____
Judge, Circuit Court

Respondent's Date of Birth:

Petitioner's Address:

Respondent's Address:

CLERK'S CERTIFICATE OF SERVICE

I hereby certify that a certified copy of this Order was delivered to:

[ ] Petitioner, ________, by [ ] hand [ ] mail [ ] certified mail [ ] certified mail at ___ AM/PM

[ ] Petitioner's counsel, ________, by [ ] hand [ ] mail [ ] certified mail at ___ AM/PM

[ ] Respondent, ________, by [ ] hand [ ] mail [ ] certified mail [ ] sending it to sheriff for personal service at ___ AM/PM

[ ] Respondent's counsel, ________, by [ ] hand [ ] mail [ ] certified mail at ___ AM/PM

[ ] Law Enforcement Agency

[ ] Warrants Department

this the ___ day of ________, 20 ___.

CLERK OF THE CIRCUIT COURT
By ________________
Deputy Clerk

TRUANCY NIGHT COURT (HENDRY COUNTY). ORDER ESTABLISHING TRUANCY NIGHT COURT FOR HENDRY COUNTY

IN THE TWENTIETH JUDICIAL CIRCUIT IN AND FOR THE STATE OF FLORIDA

ORDER ESTABLISHING TRUANCY NIGHT COURT FOR HENDRY COUNTY

Pursuant to this Court's inherent authority to administer and regulate the courts of the Twentieth Judicial Circuit, as well as the authority prescribed by Fla. R. Jud. Admin. 2.050 and Florida Statute § 43.26, the Court hereby establishes a Truancy Night Court Program for Hendry County, Florida.

Truancy petitions filed with the Clerk of the Court by the Superintendent of Schools are governed by Chapter 1003 of the Florida Statutes. Upon the filing of any such petition with the Clerk of the Court in the Juvenile Division, the Clerk shall assign a case number and a summons shall issue directed to the parent and child for an arraignment hearing the next scheduled truancy court date that is no later than thirty (30) days of the filing of the petition.

Practice and procedures for such petitions are as set forth in Florida Statute § 984.151 and any applicable rules of court. At the initial hearing, the court will arraign both the child and the parent on the petition and if the parent and child admit or consent to the petition, the court shall proceed as prescribed by the Florida Statute § 984.151(7).

If the parent and child deny the allegations in the petition at the initial hearing, the court will set a trial date and notice will be given to the school social worker or other school representative to appear on the trial date to present the school's case. In that instance, the court shall proceed to make findings on the record and issue its ruling pursuant to Florida Statute § 984.151(7).

Copies of the disposition order shall be given to the superintendent, the school social worker or other school representative, the parent or guardian of the child, and the child.

The school district, through its designated representative, is responsible for assisting the parent or guardian and the child with compliance with the order. This representative will be available for review hearings to inform the court of the progress of the case.

The court will set a review hearing, no less than thirty (30) days from the date of disposition, in order to ensure compliance with its order and may set further review hearings as may be necessary within the exercise of its sound discretion.

Any order entered by the court is enforceable through its contempt powers pursuant to Florida Statute § 984.151(9).

Truancy Night Court will be held at the Hendry County Courthouse located at the corner of Rt. 80 and Rt. 29, LaBelle, Florida in the courtroom and at such intervals as the court deems necessary in order to carry out the purpose and intent of this order.

Guidelines for the establishment of the Truancy Night Court Program are as provided in the proposed manual submitted by the Hendry County School Board's Truancy Intervention Program. A copy of the proposed manual is attached to this order and made a part hereof.

Any incidental costs associated with the operation of this program will be born by the school district. Such costs may include, but are not limited to, costs incident to the provision of security and Clerk's personnel.

This order shall remain in effect until otherwise modified, amended or rescinded by further order of the Court.

DONE AND ORDERED in chambers in Naples, Collier County, Florida this 1st day of October, 2003.

ATTEST:

L. Caron Jeffreys
Court Administrator

Hush D. Hayes
Chief Judge

MENTAL HEALTH (LEE COUNTY). ORDER ESTABLISHING MENTAL HEALTH COURT FOR LEE COUNTY

IN THE TWENTIETH JUDICIAL CIRCUIT IN AND FOR THE STATE OF FLORIDA

ORDER ESTABLISHING MENTAL HEALTH COURT FOR LEE COUNTY

There is created within the Twentieth Judicial Circuit in and for Lee County, Florida, a Mental Health Court. The court will hear only those criminal court matters that do not impact the public safety or the safety of the victim. The State Attorney's Office shall screen each defendant referred to the Mental Health Court and shall determine which cases will be placed into the Mental Health Court Program. This decision shall be made with input from defense counsel, the court and the Staff of the Mental Health Court.

Beginning May 1, 2002, or as soon thereafter as is practicable, and through separate Administrative Assignment Order, the presiding judge in Mental Health Court will hear those criminal court matters referred to the Mental Health Court Program. The Mental Health Court Program shall be composed of Staff whose services are employed or utilized by or contracted to the Office of the Court Administrator or the Court. The Program Staff shall evaluate defendants who might have or have previously been identified as having a mental illness. The Staff shall also identify treatment options in the community and monitor for the Court an appropriate plan of treatment depending on whether the defendant is on probation, diversion, or pretrial release.

The judge who conducts weekday first appearance hearings will be assigned to handle cases within the Mental Health Court Program. Referrals to the program may be made by any circuit or county judge, a general or special master, the Staff of the Mental Health Court Program, the State Attorney, defense counsel, or staff from the jail or the Southwest Florida Detention Center. Any family member, guardian or other interested person may request a referral through the State Attorney.

The Mental Health Court shall handle cases under the following two classifications:

I. When the defendant is placed on pretrial release pending trial, has entered into a deferred prosecution agreement, or has been placed on probation and has been diagnosed with a mental illness by a mental health expert.

II. When the defendant's attorney, the State Attorney or the court on its own accord has moved to determine competency to proceed pursuant to Fla. R. Crim. P. 3.210. The mental competency evaluation process, as set forth in the Rules of Criminal Procedure shall be within the purview of the Mental Health Court and shall be applicable to the point of a contested hearing. Any contested hearings will be scheduled before the assigned trial judge as set forth more fully below.

The policies, procedures and conduct of court proceedings in the Mental Health Court shall he as follows:

(a) Pretrial release and bond decisions may be made by the Mental Health Court judge. All such cases referred to the Mental Health Court Program will be monitored by the Mental Health Court Program Staff and the Mental Health Court judge.

(b) Upon screening and recommendation by the State Attorney, and then with the agreement of defense counsel, the Mental Health Court judge may defer prosecution of criminal charges pending compliance by the defendant with an appropriate course of treatment recommended by the Mental Health Court Program Staff.

(c) The appropriate course of treatment may include regular appearances before the court to report on compliance. Upon completion of the appropriate course of treatment and upon agreement of the parties, the State shall file a notice of nolle prosequi in regard to the pending charges against the defendant. A waiver of speedy trial and an agreement to pay full restitution to any victim will be conditions of any deferred prosecution.

(d) All agreements for deferred prosecution shall be in writing, signed by the defendant, defense counsel and the State Attorney, and shall thereafter be filed in the court file. If the defendant fails to comply with the conditions of the deferred prosecution, the case shall be referred by the Mental Health Court Program Staff or the State Attorney back to the assigned trial judge's docket. The court may retain jurisdiction of the case to monitor compliance for such time as is permitted by law.

(e) Upon agreement of the State Attorney and defense counsel, pleas for sentences of probation based upon mental health treatment may be accepted by the Mental Health Court judge and shall include regular monitoring of probation as that may relate to mental health issues. Violation of probation hearings shall be handled by the assigned trial judge, unless the State Attorney, defense counsel and the Mental Health Court judge agree that the violation of probation hearing should be retained on the Mental Health Court docket. No decision regarding deferred prosecution or referral to the Mental Health Court will be made without input from the victims and with the opportunity for input from the State Attorney and defense counsel.

The assigned trial judge may have the case removed from the Mental Health Court docket for good cause shown and after notice has been provided by the Court, Staff or counsel for the State or defense to all interested parties and an opportunity to be heard by the litigants has been duly provided.

The public is entitled to access to judicial records pursuant to Fla. R. Jud. Admin. 2.071. However, patient treatment records are deemed confidential by Florida law. In order to be accepted into the Mental Health Court Program, a defendant must sign a waiver of confidentiality to the extent that his treatment may be monitored by Mental Health Court Staff, the State Attorney and defense counsel.

In the event a treatment record or report is placed in the court file of a Mental Health Court case, the court will determine whether such report is confidential under Florida law, and if so, shall order that the document be sealed by the Clerk. Access to such documents will be limited to those authorized by Florida law and only then by court order following a hearing and an opportunity to be heard by the parties.

This order supercedes the prior Order Establishing Mental Health Court entered May 13, 2002.

DONE AND ORDERED in Chambers, at Naples, Collier County, Florida this 8 day of August, 2003.

Hugh D. Hayes
Chief Judge

History.—Order Establishing Mental Health Court for Lee County (May 13, 2002).

COUNTY COURT (CHARLOTTE COUNTY). ORDER IMPLEMENTING A RECORDING SYSTEM FOR THE COUNTY COURTS OF CHARLOTTE COUNTY

IN THE CIRCUIT COURT OF THE TWENTIETH JUDICIAL CIRCUIT IN AND FOR CHARLOTTE COUNTY, FLORIDA COUNTY COURT

In Re: Recordings of County Court Proceedings

ORDER IMPLEMENTING A RECORDING SYSTEM FOR THE COUNTY COURTS OF CHARLOTTE COUNTY

WHEREAS It has become necessary to implement a sound recording system for the two County Courts in Charlotte County, Florida in order to establish records of proceedings in these courts, it is therefore **ORDERED AND DECREED** that:

1. All County Court Criminal proceedings and Juvenile proceedings being conducted by County Court Judges as acting Circuit Judges shall be recorded on tape.

2. These tapes are to be maintained, filed, and stored as necessary by the Clerk of Court, who is custodian of court records and proceedings as a matter of law.

3. In the event that transcripts are required by parties or counsel, it will be required that such parties requesting transcripts hire court reporters or other acceptable transcriptionists to come to the courthouse where space will be provided with the subject tape recordings so that the transcriptionist may make a written record of that portion of the proceedings desired.

DONE AND ORDERED in Chambers at Punta Gorda, Charlotte County, Florida, this 23d day of April, 2002.

WILLIAM L. BLACKWELL, Chief
Circuit Judge

COUNTY COURT (CAPE CORAL). ORDER ESTABLISHING COUNTY COURT DIVISION FOR THE CITY OF CAPE CORAL

IN THE TWENTIETH JUDICIAL CIRCUIT IN AND FOR THE STATE OF FLORIDA

ORDER ESTABLISHING COUNTY COURT DIVISION FOR THE CITY OF CAPE CORAL

Pursuant to this Court's inherent authority to administer and regulate the courts of the Twentieth Judicial Circuit, and that prescribed by Fla. R. Jud. Admin. 2.050 and Florida Statute § 43.26, the Court hereby creates a county court division within the City of Cape Coral, a political subdivision of the State of Florida within Lee County, Florida.

Based upon the authorities cited above, it is **ORDERED AND ADJUDGED** as follows:

1. There shall be created within the Twentieth Judicial Circuit Court a County Court Division for the City of Cape Coral. Where venue is proper in Lee County, this division will preside over cases that accrue or arise within the boundaries of the City of Cape Coral, Lee County, Florida or where the plaintiff or law firms representing the plaintiff reflect a residential or business address within the jurisdictional boundaries of the City of Cape Coral, Florida.

2. A county court judge shall be assigned to conduct all non-criminal proceedings assigned to the county court division within the City of Cape Coral, Florida. The judge so assigned shall preside over all civil citations written by agencies under the jurisdiction of the City of Cape Coral, including but not limited to civil traffic infractions, code enforcement violations, or violations of animal control regulations.

3. The county court judge shall also preside over those civil cases within the statutory jurisdiction of the county court where the plaintiff or law firms representing the plaintiff reflect residential or business addresses within the boundaries of the City of Cape Coral, Florida.

4. Additional cases may be assigned to this division from time to time where the parties or their attorneys do not reflect a business or residential address within the boundaries of the

City of Cape Coral, Florida, at the discretion of the Chief Judge of the Twentieth Judicial Circuit Court.

5. Beginning on the effective date of this order, the Clerk of the Court for Lee County is directed to do the following:

A. Assign to the Cape Coral Division all small claims and county civil cases in which the plaintiff or the law firm representing the plaintiff reflect a residential or business address within the jurisdictional boundaries of the City of Cape Coral, regardless of whether the case was initially filed in the county seat.

B. Accept for filing any circuit civil case which is required to be filed in the courts of Lee County, Florida, and thereafter transfer those circuit civil cases to the Fort Myers courthouse for assignment before the appropriate judge as may be appropriate or otherwise designated by this Court.

C. Accept for filing any civil case which is required to be filed in the county court for Lee County, Florida and thereafter transfer to the Fort Myers courthouse for assignment before the appropriate county court judge those cases where the address of the plaintiff or the law firm representing the plaintiff does not reflect a residential or business address within the jurisdictional boundaries of the City of Cape Coral, Florida.

6. The Clerk shall accept for filing any cases requiring immediate action by a circuit or county judge, such as petitions for extraordinary relief. These include petitions for writs of habeas corpus, mandamus, prohibition, quo warranto and common law certiorari, as well as all actions related to domestic violence and any claim for immediate injunctive relief.

7. In any such case, the Clerk is requested to immediately transmit the case to the county seat for assignment. Counsel shall take note that although such cases may be filed in Cape Coral, assignments will occur at the time the file is transmitted to the county seat.

This order shall not apply to criminal trials, jury or non-jury. The order will take effect on March 1, 2002 and shall remain in effect until further order of this Court.

DONE AND ORDERED in Chambers in Punta Gorda, Charlotte County, Florida this 27 day of Feb., 2002.

ATTEST:

____

William D. Wilkinson, Sr.

Court Administrator

____

William L. Blackwell

Chief Judge

TRUANCY NIGHT COURT (CHARLOTTE COUNTY). ORDER ESTABLISHING TRUANCY NIGHT COURT FOR CHARLOTTE COUNTY

IN THE TWENTIETH JUDICIAL CIRCUIT IN AND FOR THE STATE OF FLORIDA

ORDER ESTABLISHING TRUANCY NIGHT COURT FOR CHARLOTTE COUNTY

Pursuant to this Court's inherent authority to administer and regulate the courts of the Twentieth Judicial Circuit, as well as the authority prescribed by Fla. R. Jud. Admin. 2.050 and Florida Statute § 43.26, the Court hereby establishes a Truancy Night Court Program for Charlotte County Florida.

Truancy petitions filed with the Clerk of the Court by the Superintendent of Schools are governed by Chapter 232 of the Florida Statutes. Upon the filing of any such petition with the Clerk of the Court in the Juvenile Division, the Clerk shall assign a case number and a summons shall issue directed to the parent and child for an arraignment hearing at the next scheduled truancy court date that is no later than thirty (30) days of the filing of the petition.

Practice and procedures for such petitions are as set forth in Florida Statute § 984.151 and any applicable rules of court. At the initial hearing, the court will arraign both the child and the parent on the petition and if the parent and child admit or consent to the petition, the court shall proceed as prescribed by Florida Statute § 984.151(7).

If the parent and child deny the allegations in the petition at the initial hearing, the court will set a trial date and notice will be given to the school social worker or other school representative to appear on the trial date to present the school's case. In that instance, the court shall proceed to make findings on the record and issue its ruling pursuant to Florida Statute § 984.151(7).

Copies of the disposition order shall be given to the superintendent, the school social worker or other school representative, the parent or guardian of the child, and the child.

The school district, through its designated representative, is responsible for assisting the parent or guardian and the child with compliance with the court order. This representative will be available for review hearings to inform the court of the progress of the case.

The court will set a review hearing, no less than thirty (30) days from the date of disposition, in order to ensure compliance with its order and may set further review hearings as may be necessary within the exercise of its sound discretion. Any order entered by the court is enforceable through its contempt powers pursuant to Florida Statute § 984.151(9).

Truancy Night Court will be held at the Charlotte County School Board Office located at 1445 Education Way, Port Charlotte, Florida in the school board meeting room and at such intervals as the court deems necessary in order to carry out the purposes and intent of this order.

Guidelines for the establishment of the Truancy Night Court Program are as provided in the proposal submitted by the Supervisor of Social Work Services for the Charlotte County Public Schools. A copy of the proposal is attached to this order and made a part hereof.

Any incidental costs associated with the operation of this program shall be born by the school district as provided in the proposal. Such costs may include, but are not limited to, costs incident to the provision of security and clerk's personnel.

This order shall remain in effect until otherwise modified, amended or rescinded by further order of the Court.

DONE AND ORDERED in Chambers in Punta Gorda, Charlotte County, Florida this 27 day of Feb., 2002.

ATTEST:

____

William D. Wilkinson, Sr.
Court Administrator

William L. Blackwell
Chief Judge

FAMILY LAW. ORDER ESTABLISHING AND IMPLEMENTING FAMILY COURT SERVICES PLAN FOR LEE COUNTY

IN THE TWENTIETH JUDICIAL CIRCUIT IN AND FOR LEE COUNTY, FLORIDA

–VACATED–

IN RE: ORDER ESTABLISHING AND IMPLEMENTING FAMILY COURT SERVICES PLAN FOR LEE COUNTY

WHEREAS, an "Order Establishing and Implementing Family Court Services Plan for Lee County," was entered October 26, 2001, by the Administrative Family Law Judge expressly for the purpose of establishing and implementing an intake, screening and referral process for family law cases in Lee County, Florida; and

WHEREAS, the 2001 Order expressly identified itself as a "pilot project;" and

WHEREAS, local Administrative Order 12.2, entered January 2, 2001, by the Chief Judge in accordance with direction from the Florida Supreme Court, expressly set forth the groundwork for the establishment and implementation within the Twentieth Judicial Circuit of Family Law Court plans and Unified Family Courts based upon recommendations for Model Family Courts of the Florida Supreme Court's Family Court Steering Committee; and

WHEREAS, local Administrative Order 12.2, provides for implementation of the Model Court Plan, which includes the use of Self–Help Programs and Case Management, which are among the primary functions performed by the Lee County Family Court Services division; and

WHEREAS, since 2001 and prior, the Administrative Office of the Courts has continuously maintained, funded, and operated the Family Court Services division within Lee County staffed by employees of the Administrative Office of the Courts, which is a permanent division, and has long ceased to be considered a "pilot project;" and

WHEREAS, the reference in the 2001 Order to the "Family Court Resource Center" as a division of the Administrative Office of the Courts charged with administering the "pilot project," is an out-dated reference which could lead to confusion; and

WHEREAS, the Family Court Services division of the Administrative Office of the Courts is charged with administering the permanent self-help program as it relates to family law cases, not the "Family Court Resource Center;" and

WHEREAS, the Family Court Services division provides resources and services at no additional cost to the parties; and

WHEREAS, information as to various community resources and services have continuously been made available and will continue to be made available by the Family Court Services division, but care must be taken so as to ensure the avoidance of any appearance of impropriety on the part of the Administrative Office of the Courts, such as the endorsement or promotion of any private or personal interests, or any conflict of interest, and, therefore, discretion necessarily must be retained by the Administrative Office of the Courts as to the method and format of making such information available so as to ensure that the integrity of the Court is maintained; and

WHEREAS, the reference in the 2001 Order to the "High Conflict Custody Case Team" is an out-dated reference in that it is no longer utilized, and, therefore, could lead to confusion; and

WHEREAS, the supplemental coversheet attached as Exhibit "A" to the 2001 Order is out-dated and no longer utilized; and

WHEREAS, the 2001 Order is not required as continuing authority for the purpose of operating the Family Court Services division, providing information related to community resources and services to pro se litigants, and providing services such as intake and case management;

It is **ORDERED** that the "Order Establishing and Implementing Family Court Services Plan for Lee County" is hereby **VACATED.** This order should not be construed as having any impact or limiting the authority of the Administrative Office of the Courts to continue to operate the Family Court Services division, nor should it be construed as having any impact or limiting the authority of the Family Court Services division to provide services.

DONE AND ORDERED in chambers in Fort Myers, Lee County, Florida, this 16th day of July, 2014.

Jay B. Rosman
Chief Judge

History.–Order Establishing and Implementing Family Court Services Plan for Lee County (October 26, 2001).

JUVENILE DETENTION (LEE COUNTY). ORDER ESTABLISHING PROCEDURE FOR HOLDING JUVENILE DETENTION HEARINGS ON WEEKENDS AND HOLIDAYS IN LEE COUNTY

IN THE TWENTIETH JUDICIAL CIRCUIT IN AND FOR THE STATE OF FLORIDA

ORDER ESTABLISHING PROCEDURE FOR HOLDING JUVENILE DETENTION HEARINGS ON WEEKENDS AND HOLIDAYS IN LEE COUNTY

—Amended—[1]

Pursuant to this Court's inherent authority to administer and regulate the Courts of the Twentieth Judicial Circuit, as well as the authority prescribed by Fla. R. Jud. Admin. 2.215 and Florida Statute § 43.26, the Court hereby establishes the following procedure for holding juvenile detention hearings on weekends and holidays in Lee County Florida.

1. Juvenile detention hearings will be held by the assigned duty judge on weekends and holidays **beginning at 8:30 a.m.** However, in the event that any duty judge who will be presiding over juvenile detention hearings on weekends or holiday wishes to hold such proceedings at a time other than

8:30 a.m., it shall be the responsibility of that judge to notify the Clerk's Office, the Department of Juvenile Justice, the Bailiff's Division, Court Administration Security, Court Administration (i.e., Electronic Court Reporting Department, Pretrial Services Office), the State Attorney, and the Public Defender, no later than 48 hours beforehand.

2. The Department of Juvenile Justice will be responsible for transporting juveniles from the Southwest Florida Juvenile Detention Center to the courthouse for these hearings as provided in Fla. R. Juv. P. 8.100.

3. The Sheriff of Lee County is hereby directed to provide appropriate levels of security in the form of uniformed bailiffs on duty to handle these proceedings on weekends and holidays. Court Administration Security shall assist the Sheriff in providing security for these proceedings.

4. In the event that any duty judge who will be presiding over juvenile detention hearings on weekends or holidays wishes to hold such proceedings at the Juvenile Detention Center instead of the Courthouse, it shall be the responsibility of that judge to notify the Clerk's Office, the Department of Juvenile Justice, the Bailiffs' Division, Court Administration Security, Court Administration (i.e., Electronic Court Reporting Department, Pretrial Services Office), the State Attorney, and the Public Defender, no later than 48 hours beforehand. The purpose of such notice is to permit the affected agencies to make appropriate adjustments to their duties accordingly.

DONE AND ORDERED in Chambers at Fort Myers, Lee County, Florida, this 8th day of January, 2013.

Jay B. Rosman
Chief Judge

History—Order Establishing Procedure for Holding Juvenile Detention Hearings on Weekends and Holidays in Lee County (July 20, 2001).

1Amended primarily for the purpose of updating paragraph 1 and adding clarification as to those who should be notified of changes.

TRANSPORTATION (COLLIER COUNTY). ORDER ESTABLISHING THE "REINSTATE DRIVING EASILY" (RIDE) PROGRAM FOR COLLIER COUNTY

IN THE TWENTIETH JUDICIAL CIRCUIT IN AND FOR THE STATE OF FLORIDA

ORDER ESTABLISHING THE "REINSTATE DRIVING EASILY" (RIDE) PROGRAM FOR COLLIER COUNTY

The Court hereby establishes a program to facilitate the reinstatement of driver license privileges for those individuals who have outstanding criminal or civil traffic fines in Collier County only and who would otherwise be eligible for driver licenses in the State of Florida. The program will be known as the "RIDE" program, an acronym for "ReInstate Driving Easily."

The program is established pursuant to Article V, Section 20(c)(8) of the Florida Constitution; Fla. R. Jud. Admin. 2.050; Fla. R. Traf. Ct. 6.480; Florida Statutes §§ 34.191, 318.14, 322.245(4), 322.42, 775.083, and 938.30; and the inherent authority of this Court as presiding judge of this circuit to administer and regulate the courts as provided by Florida Statute § 43.26.

The RIDE program shall be administered by the Clerk of the Circuit Court for Collier County. Entering into the RIDE program shall be completely voluntary. As a condition of participation in the program, the defendant must agree and acknowledge that he or she will abide by the terms and conditions of the program in a signed application and will also pay any additional fees or costs related to the program as authorized herein.

The fees and costs associated with the RIDE program will be paid to the Clerk of the Circuit Court and may be modified as reasonably necessary in order to support the administration of the program.

At its inception, the program may charge the following fees:

a) The defendant will pay an additional application fee of Five Dollars ($5.00) to be used to investigate the defendant's driving record and other pertinent matters. This fee shall not be refunded should eligibility be denied;

b) Upon acceptance into the RIDE program, the defendant will pay a nonrefundable set-up and processing fee of Twenty–Five Dollars ($25.00);

c) A state-imposed nonfundable [1]e license reinstatement fee of Twenty–Five Dollars ($25.00) will be paid at the time of enrollment; and,

d) The defendant will pay a Two Dollar ($2.00) administrative fee per payment.

Upon payment of the additional fees and the mandatory reinstatement fee, the defendant's driver license privilege will be reinstated immediately. Driving privileges will continue as long as the defendant makes the timely and proper payments as set forth in the executed RIDE agreement.

Should the defendant fail to make proper payments in accordance with any RIDE agreement, driving privileges will be immediately suspended and a delinquency fee will be assessed as set forth in the agreement.

An overview of the program and a copy of the brochure setting forth the details of the program is attached to this order and made a part hereof.

DONE AND ORDERED in Naples, Collier County, Florida, this 23rd day of Feb., 2001.

William L. Blackwell
Chief Judge

History. - New.

1 So in original. Probably should read "nonrefundable".

FAMILY LAW (COLLIER COUNTY). SUPPORT, ALIMONY, AND VISITATION PROGRAM OF COLLIER COUNTY CLERK OF COURTS

IN THE TWENTIETH JUDICIAL CIRCUIT IN AND FOR THE STATE OF FLORIDA

SUPPORT, ALIMONY, AND VISITATION PROGRAM OF COLLIER COUNTY CLERK OF COURTS

There is established within the Twentieth Judicial Circuit Court for Collier County a Support, Alimony, and Visitation Enforcement Program (S.A.V.E.). The Collier County S.A.V.E Program will be operated by the Office of the Clerk of the Circuit Court.

This Program is hereby established and will function under the aegis of this Court and within the guidelines set forth in Fla. Fam. L. R. P. 12.750. Consistent with the intent of this rule, that the Circuit Court should fulfill its responsibility to make available to the citizens within its jurisdiction an organized system for full-service support and visitation cases, the S.A.V.E. Program shall assist in non Title IV–D family law actions involving child support, alimony, and visitation matters so as to achieve a fair and efficient resolution of these issues. It shall have the power to enforce existing support judgments and orders and to resolve collateral matters reasonably related to support or visitation issues.

The Clerk of the Circuit Court as the Support, Alimony, and Visitation Administrator may charge reasonable fees and costs may be assessed against any party in an action or hearing handled by the S.A.V.E. administrator.

DONE AND ORDERED in Chambers at Naples, Collier County, Florida, this 25th day of May, 2000.

William L. Blackwell
Chief Judge

History.—New

CRIMINAL COURT (LEE COUNTY). ORDER ESTABLISHING PROTOCOL FOR THE EMPLOYMENT AND ATTENDANCE OF INTERPRETERS FOR CRIMINAL COURT PROCEEDINGS IN LEE COUNTY [SUPERSEDED BY ADMINISTRATIVE ORDER NO. 2.36]

ORDER ESTABLISHING PROTOCOL FOR THE DETERMINATION OF CREDIT FOR TIME SERVED IN CRIMINAL CASES IN LEE COUNTY

IN THE TWENTIETH JUDICIAL CIRCUIT IN AND FOR THE STATE OF FLORIDA

ORDER ESTABLISHING PROTOCOL FOR THE DETERMINATION OF CREDIT FOR TIME SERVED IN CRIMINAL CASES IN LEE COUNTY

Pursuant to this Court's inherent authority to administer and regulate the Courts of the Twentieth Judicial Circuit, as well as the authority prescribed by Fla. R. Jud. Admin. 2.050, the Court hereby establishes a protocol for the determination of credit for time served by persons under a sentence of the Court for crimes committed in Lee County, Florida.

For the purposes of this order, the Court hereby recognizes that the correct determination of credit for time served is reliant upon the cooperation of the Lee County Sheriff, the State Attorney, the criminal defense attorney and the Clerk of the Circuit Court. The purpose of this order is to limit, to the extent possible, the number of cases where incorrect determinations of credit for time served have resulted in various forms of postconviction motions.

Based upon the foregoing, it is **ORDERED AND ADJUDGED** as follows:

1. The primary responsibility for the correct determination of credit for time served rests with the trial judge assigned to the case; however, this Court recognizes that any such determination is largely dependent upon information supplied by the attorneys for the State and the defense. Accordingly, the primary duty for providing correct information to the Court rests with counsel.

2. The Sheriff of Lee County, as the constitutional officer charged with the responsibility of housing pretrial detainees, perhaps is in the best position to provide the most accurate information to counsel and to the Court regarding the number of days any inmate has served in the Lee County Jail. The Court hereby requests that the Sheriff devote the resources necessary to ensure that a correct and proper determination of credit for time served is supplied to the Court at the time of each sentencing.

3. The Court hereby requests that the Clerk of the Circuit Court through his deputies assist in calculating the amount of credit for time served which is applicable to each criminal case by making a notation on the file jacket of each such case. Counsel should be prepared to provide such information at every critical stage of the proceeding in each criminal case throughout Lee County.

DONE and ORDERED in Chambers in Fort Myers, Lee County, Florida, this 29th day of April, 1999.

Hugh E. Starnes
Chief Judge

ATTEST:

William D. Wilkinson, Sr.
Court Administrator

PRO SE PROGRAM. ORDER APPROVING PRO SE LITIGANT PROGRAM AND ORDER AUTHORIZING RETENTION AND COLLECTION OF USER FEES

IN THE TWENTIETH JUDICIAL CIRCUIT IN AND FOR THE STATE OF FLORIDA LEE, COLLIER, CHARLOTTE, HENDRY, AND GLADES COUNTIES

–VACATED–

IN RE: ORDER APPROVING PRO SE LITIGANT PROGRAM AND ORDER AUTHORIZING RETENTION AND COLLECTION OF USER FEES

WHEREAS, an "Order Approving Pro Se Litigant Program and Order Authorizing Retention and Collection of User Fees," was entered September 11,1997; and

WHEREAS, this order is out-dated in that user fees have long ceased being collected for utilizing any Pro Se Litigant Program within the Twentieth Judicial Circuit; and

WHEREAS, local Administrative Order 12.2, entered January 2, 2001, in accordance with direction from the Florida Supreme Court, provides for implementation within the Twentieth Judicial Circuit of Family Law Court plans and Unified Family Courts based upon recommendations for Model Family Courts of the Florida Supreme Court's Family Court Steering Committee, which include the use of Self–Help Programs; and

WHEREAS, the 1997 Order is not required as continuing authority for the purpose of operating any Self–Help or Pro Se Litigant Program;

It is **ORDERED** that the "Order Approving Pro Se Litigant Program and Order Authorizing Retention and Collection of User Fees" is hereby **VACATED.** This order should not be construed as having any impact or limiting the authority for the on-going use or future implementation of any Pro Se Litigant or Self–Help Program within the Twentieth Judicial Circuit.

DONE AND ORDERED in chambers in Fort Myers, Lee County, Florida, this 16th of July, 2014.

Jay B. Rosman
Chief Judge

History.–Order Approving Pro Se Litigant Program and Order Authorizing Retention and Collection or User Fees (September 11, 1997).

JURY DUTY (GLADES COUNTY). TEMPORARY ORDER WAIVING TIME REQUIREMENT FOR SUMMONING JURORS FOR COURT PROCEEDINGS IN GLADES COUNTY

IN THE TWENTIETH JUDICIAL CIRCUIT IN AND FOR THE STATE OF FLORIDA

TEMPORARY ORDER WAIVING TIME REQUIREMENT FOR SUMMONING JURORS FOR COURT PROCEEDINGS IN GLADES COUNTY

Due to circumstances beyond the control of the Glades County Clerk of the Court (specifically an equipment failure), it appears that the selection of jurors by computer in Glades County pursuant to Local Rule VII of the Twentieth Judicial Circuit Court may or will be impossible until after repairs are properly effected.

Accordingly, pursuant to Florida Statute § 40.23(1), and this Court's inherent authority to administer and regulate the courts of the Twentieth Judicial Circuit pursuant to Fla. R. Jud. Admin. 2.050(b), it is

ORDERED AND ADJUDGED that jurors may be summoned for circuit and county court proceedings in Glades County by the Clerk of the Court on less than fourteen (14) days' notice.

This order shall remain in effect until further order of the Court. The Court will periodically revisit the necessity of this order at least once each week and thereafter until the express provisions of Local Rule VII can be reinstituted.

DONE AND ORDERED in Chambers at Fort Myers, Lee County, Florida, this 25 day of June, 1997.

Hugh E. Starnes
Chief Judge

History.–New.

DOMESTIC VIOLENCE (HENDRY COUNTY). ORDER APPROVING DOMESTIC VIOLENCE DIVERSION PROGRAM FOR HENDRY COUNTY AND ORDER AUTHORIZING CLERK TO COLLECT AND MAINTAIN PROGRAM FEES

IN THE TWENTIETH JUDICIAL CIRCUIT IN AND FOR THE STATE OF FLORIDA

ORDER APPROVING DOMESTIC VIOLENCE DIVERSION PROGRAM FOR HENDRY COUNTY AND ORDER AUTHORIZING CLERK TO COLLECT AND MAINTAIN PROGRAM FEES

The Court having been fully advised and informed of the State Attorney's Office Domestic Violence Diversion Program, the Court hereby approves this Program and allows the State Attorney to enter into deferred prosecution agreements at the State Attorney's discretion and under such terms and conditions as are provided in the attached sample agreement.

It is hereby ordered that the Clerk of Court in and for Hendry County is authorized to collect a diversion fee in the amount of Thirty-Five Dollars ($ 35.00) and maintain it in a fund for use by the State Attorney. It is further ordered that each qualified participant in the Domestic Violence Diversion Program shall, subject to the limitations set forth below, pay to the Clerk of the Court the diversion fee upon entering into the diversion agreement.

A service charge for the Clerk of the Circuit Court for handling each payment or installment payment is hereby established in the amount of Three Dollars ($3.00) per payment. Upon receipt of payment or any installment payments for the Domestic Violence Diversion Program, the Clerk shall, after deducting the service charge of $3.00, deposit said payments into the Clerk's Domestic Violence Diversion Account and shall thereafter credit the account of each Defendant with each payment so received.

The Clerk shall dispense all accumulated payments at the end of each calendar month to the State Attorney's Office. Monthly disbursements to the State Attorney by the Clerk shall be made not later than the tenth day of each month.

No Respondent in a domestic violence case shall be precluded from participating in the Domestic Violence Diversion Program because of indigency or a current inability to pay.

In the event a Respondent demonstrates indigency or a current inability to pay the diversionary program fee, the Respondent may be ordered to reimburse the Clerk of Court at a later date for any outstanding fees based upon Chapter 741, as well as any pre-existing fees, fines or costs accrued prior to entering into the Diversion Program. Reimbursement of any outstanding fees, fines or other costs may be made a special condition of any deferred prosecution agreement, depending upon the circumstances presented by each case.

This Order applies only in Hendry County and supersedes any prior orders regarding the Domestic Violence Diversion Program in Hendry County and the authority of the Clerk to collect and maintain the State Attorney's Diversion Program fee.

DONE AND ORDERED in Chambers at Fort Myers, Lee County, Florida, this 14th day of April, 1997.

Hugh E. Starnes
Chief Judge

History. - New.

STATE ATTORNEY'S OFFICE DOMESTIC VIOLENCE PROGRAM

DEFERRED PROSECUTION AGREEMENT

STATE OF FLORIDA

VS CASE NO. (CASE NO)

(NAME)

The State of Florida, by and through the undersigned Assistant State Attorney, and the defendant in this cause hereby agree that the interests of both parties will best be served by entering into this pre-trial intervention deferred prosecution agreement.

The defendant understands that he/she is waiving any rights to a speedy trial under the constitution and laws of the State of Florida and the United States of America and further understands that no criminal charges will be filed if all conditions and terms of this agreement are met.

The State Attorney's Office, in and for the Twentieth Judicial Circuit, Hendry County, Florida agrees that prosecution in this cause will be deferred for a period of nine months from this date, provided the undersigned defendant meets the following conditions:

1. The defendant will refrain from any violation of the law. Any subsequent incidents or arrests may result in a capias being issued for the defendant's arrest. The defendant may be held without bond pending arraignment.

2. The defendant will successfully complete the 29 session Safeguard Program. This includes complying with the Safeguard attendance policy and program rules.

3. The defendant will not change his/her residence or employment or leave the State of Florida without first obtaining the consent of the pre-trial intervention coordinator.

4. The defendant will pay all costs of the Safeguard program as described in the Safeguard service contract.

5. The defendant will pay $35.00 Diversion Fee within 5 working days from signing this contract, payable to the Clerk of Court.

6. The defendant will register for the Safeguard program within 5 working days of signing this contract; if the defendant fails to register within five working days a Capias may be issued for his or her arrest.

7. The defendant shall have no direct contact with the victim(s) until the SAO approves it upon the written recommendations of a Safeguard counselor and the written consent of the victim(s).

8. The defendant will make restitution to the victim for damage or loss caused directly or indirectly by the defendant's offense and damage or loss related to the defendant's criminal episode.

9. After entering into this agreement any cash bond will be released, deducting the $35.00 Diversion Fee.

10. Special Conditions: (a) ____________
(b) ____________
(c) ____________

Should the defendant not comply with any of these conditions the State Attorney's Office may void this agreement and prosecute for the offense in this cause. Further, the State Attorney's Office may void this agreement if it is determined the defendant has as a prior adult criminal record or criminal charges being prosecuted in another jurisdiction.

If the defendant satisfactorily meets all of the conditions of this agreement the State Attorney's Office will not pursue a criminal prosecution regarding this cause.

____________ ____________
Assistant State Attorney Date

The undersigned acknowledges that the above has been read by him/her with full understanding or in the alternative has been read to him/her and explained. Also, the undersigned agrees to all of the conditions as set forth in this Agreement and will comply with them. Further, the undersigned acknowledges receipt of the Safeguard program rules, policies and procedures and understands them.

____________ ____________
Defendant Date

____________ ____________
Pre-trial Coordinator Date

DOMESTIC VIOLENCE (COLLIER COUNTY). ORDER ESTABLISHING DOMESTIC VIOLENCE COURT FOR COLLIER COUNTY

IN THE TWENTIETH JUDICIAL CIRCUIT IN AND FOR THE STATE OF FLORIDA

ORDER ESTABLISHING DOMESTIC VIOLENCE COURT FOR COLLIER COUNTY

There is created within the Twentieth Judicial Circuit in and for Collier County Florida a Domestic Violence Court. Beginning December 1, 1995, Collier County Judge Brenda C. Wilson will hear all criminal misdemeanor domestic violence cases, as well as all civil injunctions for protection against domestic violence and injunctions for protection against repeat violence. The Chief Judge may reassign or substitute other judges to preside over these matters as he deems appropriate or necessary under the circumstances without further order of the court. It is anticipated that the domestic violence court will handle a large number of cases. Therefore, a domestic violence unit has also been created to assist and provide support to the Domestic Violence Court.

DOMESTIC VIOLENCE UNIT:

The domestic violence until currently consists of a domestic violence coordinator, two clerks and a domestic violence investigator, all of whom work under the direction of the Deputy Court Administrator for the Family Law Division. The character and composition of the domestic violence unit may change without further order of the court as the Chief Judge or his designee may prescribe.

The unit will assist petitioners in the filing of petitions for injunctions for protection against domestic violence and repeat violence, civil motions for contempt, and other related motions and applications for orders. The unit will also handle inquiries from the petitioner and the respondent.

The domestic violence coordinator may appear at court proceedings as the court deems appropriate and will assist the court by monitoring all civil and criminal court orders. The coordinator will also act as liaison with the service providers in the community and keep the court apprised of the availability of and changes in such services.

In addition, in criminal cases the Domestic Violence Investigator will act as liaison with the State Attorney, Public Defender, Clerk's Office, Probation Department, Court Investigations, and private attorneys. The coordinator or Domestic Violence Investigator or both will track both civil and criminal cases and inform the court of any other matters which may have a bearing upon the court's decision. This practice is designed to decrease the likelihood of duplicate sentences and allow the court to dispose of all matters in a timely fashion.

DOMESTIC VIOLENCE COURT ARRAIGNMENTS:

All misdemeanor domestic violence arrests occurring after 12:00 a.m., December 1, 1995, shall be given a Domestic Violence Court arraignment date. This shall include all arrests for failure to appear in an existing domestic violence case. In addition, all misdemeanor domestic violence arrest capiases, non-arrest capiases, and summons served after 12:00 a.m., December 1, 1995, shall also be given a Domestic Violence Court arraignment date.

DONE AND ORDERED in Chambers at Fort Myers, Lee County, Florida, this 31st day of October, 1996, nunc pro tunc to December 1, 1995.

Hugh E. Starnes
Chief Judge

History. –New.

DOMESTIC VIOLENCE (CHARLOTTE COUNTY). ORDER APPROVING DOMESTIC VIOLENCE DIVERSION PROGRAM FOR CHARLOTTE COUNTY AND ORDER AUTHORIZING CLERK TO COLLECT AND MAINTAIN PROGRAM FEES

IN THE TWENTIETH JUDICIAL CIRCUIT IN AND FOR THE STATE OF FLORIDA

ORDER APPROVING DOMESTIC VIOLENCE DIVERSION PROGRAM FOR CHARLOTTE COUNTY AND ORDER AUTHORIZING CLERK TO COLLECT AND MAINTAIN PROGRAM FEES

The County having been fully advised and informed of the State Attorney's Office Domestic Violence Diversion Program, the Court hereby approves this Program and allows the State Attorney to enter into deferred prosecution agreements at the State Attorney's discretion and under such terms and conditions as are provided in the attached sample agreement.

It is hereby ordered that the Clerk of the Court in and for Charlotte County is authorized to collect a diversion fee in the amount of Thirty Five Dollars ($35.00) and maintained it in a fund for use by the State Attorney. It is further ordered that each qualified participant in the Domestic Violence Diversion Program shall, subject to the limitation set forth below, pay to the Clerk of the Court the diversion fee upon entering into the diversion agreement.

A service charge for the Clerk of the Circuit Court for handling each payment or installment payment is hereby established in the amount of Three Dollars ($3.00) per payment. Upon receipt of payment or any installment payments for the Domestic Violence Diversion Program, the Clerk shall, after deduction the service charge of $3.00, deposit said payments into the Clerk's Domestic Violence Diversion Account and shall thereafter credit the account of each Defendant with each payment so received.

The Clerk shall dispense all accumulated payments at the end of each calendar month to the State Attorney's Office. Monthly disbursements to the State Attorney by the Clerk shall be made not later than the tenth day of each month.

No Respondent in a domestic violence case shall be precluded from participating in the Domestic Violence Diversion Program because of indigency or a current inability to pay.

In the event a Respondent demonstrates indigency or a current inability to pay the diversionary program fee, the Respondent may be ordered to reimburse the Clerk of Court at a later date for any outstanding fees based upon Chapter 741, as well as any pre-existing fees, fines or costs accrued prior to entering into the Diversion Program. Reimbursement of any outstanding fees, fines or other costs may be made a special condition of any deferred prosecution agreement, depending upon the circumstances presented by each case.

This Order supersedes all prior orders regarding the Domestic Violence Diversion Program and the authority of the Clerk to collect and maintain the State Attorney's Diversion Program fee.

DONE AND ORDERED in Chambers at Fort Myers, Lee County, Florida, this 30 day of Nov., 1995.

Hugh E. Starnes
Chief Judge

CERTIFICATE BY CLERK

I HEREBY CERTIFY that a true and correct copy of the above and foregoing has been furnished to the Honorable Joseph P. D'Alessandro, State Attorney, Fort Myers, Florida, and William D. Wilkinson, Sr., Court Administrator, Fort Myers, Florida, this ___ day of __________, 1995.

BARBARA SCOTT, CLERK OF THE COURT
BY: ____________________
Deputy Clerk

STATE ATTORNEY'S OFFICE DOMESTIC VIOLENCE PROGRAM

DEFERRED PROSECUTION AGREEMENT

STATE OF FLORIDA

VS CASE NO.

The State of Florida, by and through the undersigned Assistant State Attorney, and the defendant in this cause hereby agree that the interests of both parties will best be served by entering into this pre-trial intervention deferred prosecution agreement.

The defendant understands that he/she is waiving any rights to a speedy trial under the constitution and laws of the State of Florida and the United States of America and further understand that no criminal charges will be filed if all conditions and terms of this agreement are met.

The State Attorney's Office, in and for the Twentieth Judicial Circuit, Charlotte County, Florida agrees that prosecution in this cause will be deferred for a period of nine months from this date, provided the undersigned defendant meets the following conditions:

1. The defendant will refrain from any violation of the law. Any subsequent incidents or arrests may result in a capias being issued for the defendant's arrest. The defendant may be held without bond pending arraignment.

2. The defendant will successfully complete the prescribed counseling sessions at Charlotte Mental Health Services. This includes complying with the attendance policy and program rules.

3. The defendant will not change his/her residence or employment or leave the State of Florida without first obtaining the consent of the pre-trial intervention coordinator, 637–2104.

4. The defendant will pay all costs of the counseling program as described by Charlotte Mental Health Services.

5. The defendant will pay $35.00 Diversion Fee within 5 working days from signing this contract, payable to the Clerk of Court, for Charlotte County.

6. The defendant will register for the counseling program within 5 working days of signing this contract; if the defendant fails to register within five working days a Capias may be issued for his or her arrest.

7. The defendant will have no further contact with the victim unless the victim so states in writing to a representative of the Domestic Violence Unit that he or she desires to have contact with the defendant. If there is an existing order by the Court prohibiting contact then the defendant shall abide by the Court Order.

8. The defendant will pay for all amounts of restitution associated to injury caused to the victim by the defendant within a reasonable period of time.

9. After entering into this agreement any cash bond will be released, deducting the $35.00 Diversion Fee.

10. Special Conditions: (a) ____________________
(b) ____________________
(c) ____________________

Should the defendant not comply with any of these conditions the State Attorney's Office may void this agreement and prosecute for the offense in this cause. Further, the State Attorney's Office may void this agreement if it is determined the defendant has as a prior adult criminal record or criminal charges being prosecuted in another jurisdiction.

If the defendant satisfactorily meets all of the conditions of this agreement the State Attorney's Office will not pursue a criminal prosecution regarding this cause.

____________________ __________
Assistant State Attorney Date

The undersigned acknowledges that the above has been read by him/her with full understanding or in the alternative has been read to him/her and explained. Also, the undersigned agrees to all of the conditions as set forth in this Agreement and will comply with them.

____________________ __________
Defendant Date

____________________ __________
Pre-trial Coordinator Date

FAMILY LAW (LEE COUNTY). ORDER REQUIRING ISSUANCE OF STANDING ORDERS IN DOMESTIC RELATIONS CASES IN LEE COUNTY

IN THE TWENTIETH JUDICIAL CIRCUIT IN AND FOR THE STATE OF FLORIDA

ORDER REQUIRING ISSUANCE OF STANDING ORDERS IN DOMESTIC RELATIONS CASES IN LEE COUNTY

Pursuant to Administrative Order 2.12 and the responsibilities delegated by the Chief Judge to the Administrative Family Law Judge of the Family Law Division, and in an effort to more expeditiously process domestic relations cases filed in the circuit court of the Twentieth Judicial Circuit in and for Lee County, Florida, the Clerk of the Court is hereby authorized and directed to issue and serve the following documents as set forth below on all parties to all domestic relations matters filed in Lee County:

1. STANDING TEMPORARY DOMESTIC RELATIONS ORDER

This order shall be issued and served upon all parties to every dissolution of marriage proceeding where minor children are involved and no marital settlement agreement has been attached to or referenced in the Petition.

2. STANDING ORDER FOR PARENTAL–EDUCATION CLASSES

This order shall be issued and served upon all parties to all dissolution of marriage cases where minor children are involved.

3. STANDING TEMPORARY DOMESTIC RELATIONS ORDER (NO CHILDREN INVOLVED)

This order shall be issued and served upon all parties to dissolution of marriage proceedings in which no minor children are involved and no marital settlement agreement has been attached to or referenced in the Petition.

4. NOTICE TO ALL PARTIES IN THE FAMILY COURTS

This "notice" regarding the policies of the Family Law Division of the Lee County Circuit Court shall be issued and served upon all parties to all dissolution of marriage proceedings without exception.

The Clerk of Court is hereby authorized and directed to issue and serve these orders, where applicable, on the Petitioner upon filing of the action and on the Respondent by attaching a copy to the summons to be served on Respondent. This directive shall not apply to those proceedings governed by the simplified dissolution procedures prescribed by Rule 1.611(c), Florida Rules of Civil Procedure.

DONE AND ORDERED in Chambers at Fort Myers, Lee County, Florida, this 29th day of Sept., 1995.

JAMES H. SEALS
Administrative Circuit Judge
Family Law Division—Lee County

History. - New.

DOMESTIC VIOLENCE (COLLIER COUNTY). ORDER APPROVING DOMESTIC VIOLENCE DIVERSION PROGRAM FOR COLLIER COUNTY AND ORDER AUTHORIZING CLERK TO COLLECT AND MAINTAIN PROGRAM FEES

IN THE TWENTIETH JUDICIAL CIRCUIT IN AND FOR THE STATE OF FLORIDA

ORDER APPROVING DOMESTIC VIOLENCE DIVERSION PROGRAM FOR COLLIER COUNTY AND ORDER AUTHORIZING CLERK TO COLLECT AND MAINTAIN PROGRAM FEES

The County having been fully advised and informed of the State Attorney's Office Domestic Violence Diversion Program, the Court hereby approves this Program and allows the State Attorney to enter into deferred prosecution agreements at the State Attorney's discretion and under such terms and conditions as are provided in the attached sample agreement.

It is hereby ordered that the Clerk of the Court in and for Collier County is authorized to collect a diversion fee in the amount of Thirty Five Dollars ($35.00) and maintain it in a fund for use by the State Attorney. It is further ordered that each qualified participant in the Domestic Violence Diversion Program shall, subject to the limitations set forth below, pay to the Clerk of the Court the diversion fee upon entering into the diversion agreement.

A service charge for the Clerk of the Circuit Court for handling each payment or installment payment is hereby established in the amount of Three Dollars ($3.00) per payment. Upon receipt of payment or any installment payments for the Domestic Violence Diversion Program, the Clerk shall, after deducting the service charge of $3.00, deposit said payments into the Clerk's Domestic Violence Diversion Account and shall thereafter credit the account of each Defendant with each payment so received.

The Clerk shall dispense all accumulated payments at the end of each calendar month to the State Attorney's Office. Monthly disbursements to the State Attorney by the Clerk shall be made not later than the tenth day of each month.

No Respondent in a domestic violence case shall be precluded from participating in the Domestic Violence Diversion Program because of indigency or a current inability to pay.

In the event a Respondent demonstrates indigency or a current inability to pay the diversionary program fee, the Respondent may be ordered to reimburse the Clerk of Court at a later date for any outstanding fees based upon Chapter 741, as well as any pre-existing fees, fines or costs accrued prior to entering into the Diversion Program. Reimbursement of any outstanding fees, fines or other costs may be made a special condition of any deferred prosecution agreement, depending upon the circumstances presented by each case.

This Order supersedes all prior orders regarding the Domestic Violence Diversion Program and the authority of the Clerk to collect and maintain the State Attorney's Diversion Program fee.

DONE AND ORDERED in Chambers at Fort Myers, Lee County, Florida, this 4 day of April, 1995.

Thomas S. Reese
Chief Judge

STATE ATTORNEY'S OFFICE DOMESTIC VIOLENCE PROGRAM

DEFERRED PROSECUTION AGREEMENT

STATE OF FLORIDA

VS CASE NO. (CASE NO.)

‹NAME›

The State of Florida, by and through the undersigned Assistant State Attorney, and the defendant in this cause hereby agree that the interests of both parties will best be served by entering into this pre-trial intervention deferred prosecution agreement.

The defendant understands that he/she is waiving any rights to a speedy trial under the constitution and laws of the State of Florida and the United States of America and further understand that no criminal charges will be filed if all conditions and terms of this agreement are met.

The State Attorney's Office, in and for the Twentieth Judicial Circuit, Lee County, Florida agrees that prosecution in this cause will be deferred for a period of nine months from this date, provided the undersigned defendant meets the following conditions:

1. The defendant will refrain from any violation of the law. Any subsequent incidents or arrests may result in a capias being issued for the defendant's arrest. The defendant may be held without bond pending arraignment.

2. The defendant will successfully complete the 26 session BAN Program. This includes complying with the BAN attendance policy and program rules.

3. The defendant will not change his/her residence or employment or leave the State of Florida without first obtaining the consent of the pre-trial intervention coordinator.

4. The defendant will pay all costs of the BAN program as described in the BAN service contract.

5. The defendant will pay the State Attorney diversion fee of $35.00 to the Clerk of the Court for Lee County.

6. Special Conditions:

(a) ______________________________

(b) ______________________________

(c) ______________________________

Should the defendant not comply with any of these conditions the State Attorney's Office may void this agreement and Prosecute for the offense in this cause. Further, the State Attorney's Office may void this agreement if it is determined the defendant has as a prior adult criminal record or criminal charges being prosecuted in another jurisdiction.

By entering into this agreement the defendant understands and agrees that successful completion of this program is a condition of his/her release from custody. Should the defendant violate any terms of this agreement a capias may be issued for his/her arrest.

If the defendant satisfactorily meets all of the conditions of this agreement the State Attorney's Office will not pursue a criminal prosecution regarding this cause.

______________________ __________

Assistant State Attorney Date

The undersigned acknowledges that the above has been read by him/her with full understanding or in the alternative has been read to him/her and explained. Also, the undersigned agrees to all of the conditions as set forth in this Agreement and will comply with them. Further, the undersigned acknowledges receipt of the BAN program rules, policies and procedures and understands them.

______________________ __________

Defendant Date

______________________ __________

Pre-trial Coordinator Date

CONFIDENTIALITY WAIVER. ORDER AUTHORIZING WAIVER OF CONFIDENTIALITY FOR DOMESTIC VIOLENCE/FAMILY LAW INVESTIGATORS AND OTHER COURT PERSONNEL

IN THE TWENTIETH JUDICIAL CIRCUIT IN AND FOR THE STATE OF FLORIDA

ORDER AUTHORIZING WAIVER OF CONFIDENTIALITY FOR DOMESTIC VIOLENCE/ FAMILY LAW INVESTIGATORS AND OTHER COURT PERSONNEL

In accordance with Local Rule IX of the Twentieth Judicial Circuit, the Administrative Judge of the Family Law Division is empowered to enter such orders as may be necessary to authorize the Domestic Violence/Family Law Investigator or such other personnel employed by the Court to be persons for whom confidentiality under Florida Statutes §§ 39.045 and 39.443 is waived. Such orders shall be executed by the Administrative Judge and kept on file with the Chief Judge and the Court Administrator of the Twentieth Circuit. Any orders entered pursuant to this order are to remain in effect for only so long as the employee(s) are employed by the Court in the capacity for which the order was entered.

DONE AND ORDERED in Chambers at Fort Myers, Lee County, Florida, this 18 day of January, 1995.

____

Thomas S. Reese
Chief Judge

History. - New.

DOMESTIC VIOLENCE (LEE COUNTY). ORDER APPROVING DOMESTIC VIOLENCE DIVERSION PROGRAM FOR LEE COUNTY AND ORDER AUTHORIZING CLERK TO COLLECT AND MAINTAIN PROGRAM FEES

IN THE TWENTIETH JUDICIAL CIRCUIT IN AND FOR THE STATE OF FLORIDA

ORDER APPROVING DOMESTIC VIOLENCE DIVERSION PROGRAM FOR LEE COUNTY AND ORDER AUTHORIZING CLERK TO COLLECT AND MAINTAIN PROGRAM FEES

The Court having been fully advised and informed of the State Attorney's Office Domestic Violence Diversion Program, the Court hereby approves this Program and allows the State Attorney to enter into deferred prosecution agreements at the State Attorney's discretion and under such terms and conditions as are provided in the attached sample agreement.

It is hereby ordered that the Clerk of the Court in and for Lee County is authorized to collect a diversion fee in the amount of Thirty Five Dollars ($35.00) and maintain it in a fund for use by the State Attorney. It is further ordered that each qualified participant in the Domestic Violence Diversion Program shall, subject to the limitations set forth below, pay to the Clerk of the Court the diversion fee upon entering into the diversion agreement.

A service charge for the Clerk of the Circuit Court for handling each payment or installment payment is hereby established in the amount of Three Dollars ($3.00) per payment. Upon receipt of payment or any installment payments for the Domestic Violence Diversion Program, the Clerk shall, after deducting the service charge of $3.00, deposit said payments into the Clerk's Domestic Violence Diversion Account and shall thereafter credit the account of each Defendant with each payment so received.

The Clerk shall dispense all accumulated payments at the end of each calendar month to the State Attorney's Office. Monthly disbursements to the State Attorney by the Clerk shall be made not later than the tenth day of each month.

No Respondent in a domestic violence case shall be precluded from participating in the Domestic Violence Diversion Program because of indigency or a current inability to pay.

In the event a Respondent demonstrates indigency or a current inability to pay the diversionary program fee, the Respondent may be ordered to reimburse the Clerk of Court at a later date for any outstanding fees based upon Chapter 741, as well as any pre-existing fees, fines or costs accrued prior to entering into the Diversion Program. Reimbursement of any outstanding fees, fines or other costs may be made a special condition of any deferred prosecution agreement, depending upon the circumstances presented by each case.

This Order supersedes all prior orders regarding the Domestic Violence Diversion Program and the authority of the Clerk to collect and maintain the State Attorney's Diversion Program fee.

DONE AND ORDERED in Chambers at Fort Myers, Lee County, Florida, this 7th day of April, 1994.

____
Thomas S. Reese
Chief Judge

History. - Order Authorizing the Clerk to Collect and Maintain the State Attorney's Diversion Program fee (March 8, 1994).

STATE ATTORNEY'S OFFICE DOMESTIC VIOLENCE PROGRAM

DEFERRED PROSECUTION AGREEMENT

STATE OF FLORIDA :
:
VS : CASE NO.
:
:

The State of Florida, by and through the undersigned Assistant State Attorney, and the defendant in this cause hereby agree that the interests of both parties will best be served by entering into this pre-trial intervention deferred prosecution agreement.

The defendant understands that he/she is waiving any rights to a speedy trial under the constitution and laws of the State of Florida and the United States of America and further understand that no criminal charges will be filed if all conditions and terms of this agreement are met.

The State Attorney's Office, in and for the Twentieth Judicial Circuit, Lee County, Florida agrees that prosecution in this cause will be deferred for a period of nine months from this date, provided the undersigned defendant meets the following conditions:

1. The defendant will refrain from any violation of the law.

2. The defendant will successfully complete the 26 session BAN Program. This includes complying with the BAN attendance policy and program rules.

3. The defendant will not change his/her residence or employment or leave the State of Florida without first obtaining the consent of the pre-trial intervention coordinator.

4. The defendant will pay all costs of the BAN program as described in the BAN service contract.

5. The defendant will pay the State Attorney diversion fee of $35.00 to the Clerk of the Court for Lee County.

6. Special Conditions: (a) ____________________

(b) ____________________

(c) ____________________

Should the defendant not comply with any of these conditions the State Attorney's Office may void this agreement and prosecute for the offense in this cause. Further, the State Attorney's Office may void this agreement if it is determined the defendant has a prior adult criminal record or criminal charges being prosecuted in another jurisdiction.

If the defendant satisfactorily meets all of the conditions of this agreement the State Attorney's Office will not pursue a criminal prosecution regarding this cause.

____________________ __________
Assistant State Attorney Date

The undersigned acknowledges that the above has been read by him/her with full understanding or in the alternative has been read to him/her and explained. Also, the undersigned agrees to all of the conditions as set forth in this Agreement and will comply with them. Further, the undersigned acknowledges receipt of the BAN program rules, policies and procedures and understands them.

____________________ __________
Defendant Date

____________________ __________
Pre-trial Coordinator Date

DOMESTIC VIOLENCE (LEE COUNTY). ORDER ESTABLISHING DOMESTIC VIOLENCE COURT FOR LEE COUNTY

IN THE TWENTIETH JUDICIAL CIRCUIT IN AND FOR THE STATE OF FLORIDA

ORDER ESTABLISHING DOMESTIC VIOLENCE COURT FOR LEE COUNTY

There is created within the Twentieth Judicial Circuit in and for Lee County, Florida a Domestic Violence Court. Beginning April 11, 1994, Circuit Judge Hugh E. Starnes will hear all criminal misdemeanor domestic violence cases, as well as all civil injunctions for protection against domestic violence and injunctions for protection against repeat violence. County Judge G. Keith Cary will also handle the Domestic Violence Court docket during his ancillary weeks, approximately once every six weeks. It is anticipated that the Domestic Violence Court will handle a large number of cases. Therefore, a domestic violence unit has also been created to assist and provide support to the Domestic Violence Court.

DOMESTIC VIOLENCE UNIT:

The domestic violence unit currently consists of a domestic violence coordinator and a clerk, both of whom work under the direction of the Deputy Court Administrator for the Family Law Division. The unit will assist petitioners in the filing of petitions for injunction for protection against domestic violence and repeat violence, civil motions for contempt, other related motions and applications for orders. The unit will also handle inquiries from the petitioner and the respondent.

The domestic violence coordinator will appear at all court proceedings and will assist the court by monitoring all civil court orders. The coordinator will also act as liaison with the service providers in the community and keep the court apprised of the availability of and changes in such services.

In addition, in criminal cases the coordinator will act as liaison with the State Attorney, Public Defender, Clerk's Office, Probation Department, Court Investigations, and private attorneys. The coordinator will track both civil and criminal cases and inform the court of any other pending matters. This practice is designed to decrease the likelihood of duplicate sentences and allow the court to dispose of all matters in a timely fashion.

DOMESTIC VIOLENCE COURT ARRAIGNMENTS

All misdemeanor domestic violence arrests occurring after 12:00 A.M., March 21, 1994, shall be given a Domestic Violence Court arraignment date. This shall include all arrests for failure to appear in an existing domestic violence case. In addition, all misdemeanor domestic violence arrest capiases, non-arrest capiases, and summonses served after 12:00 A.M., Monday, March 21, 1994, shall also be given a Domestic Violence Court arraignment date.

DONE AND ORDERED in Chambers, this 18 day of March, 1994.

Thomas S. Reese
Chief Judge

History. –New.

APPOINTING CLERK AD INTERIM FOR COLLIER COUNTY

IN THE TWENTIETH JUDICIAL CIRCUIT IN AND FOR THE STATE OF FLORIDA COLLIER COUNTY

ORDER APPOINTING CLERK AD INTERIM FOR COLLIER COUNTY

WHEREAS, the Clerk of the Circuit Court in and for Collier County, The Honorable Dwight E. Brock, passed away on June 12, 2018; and

WHEREAS, the current term of office for The Honorable Dwight E. Brock was to run through Monday, January 4, 2021; and

WHEREAS, the legislature of the State of Florida has enacted Florida Statute § 28.09 as a mechanism to provide for the filling of a vacancy occurring in the office of the Clerk of the Circuit Court until such time as the Governor has the opportunity to fill the vacancy; and

WHEREAS, that mechanism authorizes the judicial appointment of an interim clerk pending the Governor's own appointment of a person to fill the vacancy; and

WHEREAS, to date, and to the undersigned's knowledge, the Governor has not appointed a person to fill the vacancy; it is

ORDERED that, pursuant to the authority vested in me by Florida Statute § 28.09, and as Chief Judge of the Twentieth Judicial Circuit, which includes Collier County, **Laird A. Lile,** is appointed as Clerk Ad Interim for the remaining current term of office of the Clerk of the Circuit Court, effective immediately, and until such time as the Governor of the State of Florida makes his own appointment superseding this order, or as otherwise provided by General Law. As Clerk Ad Interim, **Laird A. Lile** shall assume and meet all responsibilities, duties, and conditions as provided for by the legislature under Florida Statute § 28.09. This order is effective immediately, and, until such time as the Governor makes his own appointment. If no appointment is made by the Governor such as to supersede this order, this order shall automatically expire at the end of the current term of office of the Clerk of the Circuit Court in and for Collier County, which runs through Monday, January 4, 2021.

DONE AND ORDERED in chambers in Fort Myers, Lee County, Florida this 15th day of June, 2018.

Michael T. McHugh
Chief Judge

Adopted effective June 15, 2018.

COMBINED INDEX TO FLORIDA RULES OF COURT — LOCAL